The New
Cambridge Bibliography
of English Literature

in five volumes

Volume 2

The New Cambridge Bibliography of English Literature

Edited by
GEORGE WATSON

Volume 2
1660–1800

CAMBRIDGE
AT THE UNIVERSITY PRESS
1971

Published by the Syndics of the Cambridge University Press
Bentley House, 200 Euston Road, London N.W.1
American Branch: 32 East 57th Street, New York, N.Y.10022

© Cambridge University Press 1971

Library of Congress Catalogue Card Number: 69–10199

ISBN: 0 521 07934 9

Printed in Great Britain
at the University Printing House, Cambridge
(Brooke Crutchley, University Printer)

CONTENTS

v

CONTENTS

V. Book production and distribution

2. POETRY

I. Histories and surveys

II. Miscellanies, anthologies and collections of poetry

CONTENTS

III. Restoration poetry

IV. Minor poetry 1660–1700

V. Early eighteenth-century poetry

VI. Minor poetry 1700–50

VII. Later eighteenth-century poetry

CONTENTS

VIII. Minor poetry 1750–1800

3. DRAMA

I. General introduction

II. Theatres and actors

III. Restoration drama

IV. Minor Restoration drama 1660–1700

CONTENTS

IV. Children's books

5. PROSE

I. Essayists and pamphleteers

II. Periodical publications

CONTENTS

CONTENTS

xii

CONTENTS

CONTENTS

X. Classical and oriental studies

XI. Philosophy

XII. Science

XIII. Law

XIV. Education

EDITOR'S PREFACE

This is the second volume of the *New Cambridge Bibliography of English Literature* to appear; and like its forerunner, volume 3 (1800–1900), it is firmly based upon a volume of *CBEL* (1940), edited by F. W. Bateson, and its *Supplement* of 1957. In this case it represents a total revision of the old volume 2 together with appropriate sections of the 1957 volume. Once again the original order of the Bibliography has proved, with rare exceptions, too familiar and informative to be abandoned; and as I hopefully predicted in the preface to volume 3, the period of the Restoration and eighteenth century has proved less problematical than the romantic and Victorian ages, and has called for fewer alterations of design and scope. Apart from the historical aids which appeared in 1940 under Social and Political Background, no section has had to be dropped from this revision, and it has been possible to preserve the order of the rest of the volume almost unchanged, including the characteristic arrangement of major and minor authors under the great literary kinds such as Poetry, Drama and the Novel.

Each volume of *New CBEL* has been designed, if necessary, to be used in isolation from the rest; and it is natural that much of this preface should repeat with minor variations of detail the information already provided in the preface to volume 3. As before, the task of the fifty contributors and more who have compiled this volume has been to revise and integrate the existing lists of 1940 and 1957, to add materials of the past ten years and more, to correct and refine the bibliographical details already available, and to reshape the whole according to the new conventions which have been designed to give the Bibliography a clearer and more consistent air.

Inevitably, however, one at least of the ambitions which seemed realistic in the more limited scholarly world of the 1930s has had to be abandoned. *CBEL* is a bibliography of literature, not of publications in the wider sense; and difficult of definition as the distinction is, it has not been thought practical to preserve in their entirety such non-literary sections as Political and Social Background. Such sections, as in volume 3, would have had to be vastly inflated in order to represent modern historical scholarship, and could in that event only have presumed to rival the bibliographies of historical studies themselves. The new index in the present volume will show which individuals of literary note have been retained from these sections in some other section of the book. As before, *New CBEL* is confined to literary authors native to or mainly resident in the British Isles—a definition less troublesome here than in the case of the nineteenth century. But, as in the *Concise CBEL* (1958), no restriction of nationality or language has been imposed on the choice of secondary materials, mainly biography and criticism, concerning the British and Irish authors included here. The concept of period remains unchanged: an author who was in some sense established after 1660 and before 1800 qualifies, if of sufficient literary interest, for inclusion in this volume. The remaining four periods of *CBEL* remain:

the Old English period (600–1100); the Middle English (1100–1500); the Renaissance to the Restoration (1500–1660); and the Nineteenth Century (1800–1900). A sixth period, the Earlier Twentieth Century (1900–50), is now in preparation as a separate volume. It is hoped that the index to this and to successive volumes of *New CBEL*, which will include the names of primary authors and certain headings, will answer at a glance any questions concerning which authors are included in any individual volume.

The scope of the Bibliography in detail remains largely unchanged: it aims to represent the whole of English studies, so far as these concern the literature of the British Isles, both in primary and in secondary materials, 'works by' and 'works about'. The symbols §1 and §2 have again been imposed upon author-sections to mark this distinction in an unmistakable way. The canon of an author's works, or the primary section, has usually been merged into a single chronological list, with the object of demonstrating more clearly the shape of his literary career; though exceptions of convenience have been encouraged, and certain special categories such as letters, diaries and private papers, or contributions to periodicals, have often been allowed subsections of their own. Author-sections ordinarily begin with bibliographies, where they exist, and collections, followed by the primary section and its subsections, followed in turn by a chronological list of secondary material with works by individual scholars and critics grouped together. In a few instances, for the sake of greater clarity, secondary works have been grouped under the titles of individual primary works, especially in cases of doubtful attribution.

The Bibliography continues to aim at completeness, but as before this must be understood as completeness in its own terms. Certain categories of material have normally been excluded, notably unpublished dissertations and their published abstracts, ephemeral journalism, encyclopaedia articles, reviews of secondary works, brief notes of less than crucial interest to scholarship, and sections in general works such as literary histories which are listed in their own sections at the head of each major division of the volume. In addition, contributors have been encouraged to drop certain antiquated articles which are now either superseded or absorbed into later studies and editions. But the history of an author's reputation remains an object of study, and articles which represent it memorably have been retained, even where they may have been discredited by later scholarship. Details of format are not normally included except to distinguish between early editions of major primary works.

The location of copies, as before, remains essentially outside the scope of the Bibliography, which cannot undertake to rival the *Short-Title Catalogue* in its listing of library holdings. But brief headnotes on manuscripts have sometimes been included; and where a unique copy of a work is known to exist outside the British Museum, such information has at times been admitted into the Bibliography, though in neither case has any attempt at consistency been made.

The page, already familiar in the new volume 3, has been designed to accommodate about one quarter more than the old *CBEL* page while still presenting a clear and simple aspect to the reader. A radical attempt has been made to simplify and standardize the existing conventions of the Bibliography. Punctuation has been enormously reduced: colons regularly precede subtitles, semicolons divide titles; and commas rather than semicolons now ordinarily separate the dates of reprints. Capitalization has been reduced to the level of ordinary prose, which has enabled titles within titles to be distinguished by a capital letter, and contractions expanded. Roman numerals have been greatly reduced in favour of arabic. Abbreviations, apart from certain indispensable initials to represent some periodicals, have been moderately used, and it is hoped that they are largely self-explanatory. The use of brackets has been much reduced, and headnotes and endnotes which serve as editorial explanations have been allowed to define themselves simply by their position. Titles, as in *CBEL*, are 'short', and omissions are not marked; and, as before, the number of volumes is entered unless it is one, and the place of publication unless it is London; for this purpose, books published in England by the Oxford University Press have been entered as 'Oxford'. Such details continue to apply in any given entry until contradicted, and '1 vol' and 'London' may then be used to contradict. In citing periodical articles, monthlies are normally quoted by the month and quarterlies by volume-number. Translations of primary works have been admitted in summary form only, and commonly without details of translator or place of publication, e.g. 'tr French, 1738'. In the case of secondary works, only translations into English have normally been cited.

The provision of bibliographical detail in the primary section, which is perhaps the chief function of the Bibliography, is a matter which eludes definition and which necessarily varies according to the state of knowledge of the subject, and even according to the preoccupations of the contributor. It hardly needs to be emphasized again that the Bibliography practises the degressive principle to the full. The detail of an entry tends to be most intense in the early years of the life of a book; late editions are usually cited only when revised or enlarged by the author; and modern reprints may not be included at all unless they justify themselves by reason of an introduction or editorial apparatus. Major authors tend to be more minutely treated than minor, and headnotes to individual sections often define the limits that have been placed. As in volume 3, the proper demands of consistency have not been interpreted as signifying that every author should be treated in the same way. On the contrary, it is recognized that in a bibliography of literature certain authors and subjects are central and others peripheral, and that many intermediate cases exist and demand to be treated as such.

ACKNOWLEDGEMENTS

My deepest acknowledgements are due to the fifty and more contributors in Europe and North America who have sacrificed time and patience to make this volume; many of them have advised on the period 1660–1800 far beyond the scope of their own sections. The Advisory Committee of H. S. Bennett

(Chairman), R. W. David, P. G. Burbidge, A. N. L. Munby and Ian Willison, who initiated the project of a total revision of *CBEL*, have again watched benignly over the progress of the volume for nearly three years. Early advice of great benefit to the undertaking was received from members of the staff of the British Museum and of the Bodleian Library; and on various individual sections from Mr Giles Barber, Mr T. H. Bowyer, Professor James Clifford, Dr A. G. Cross, Dr Peter Marshall, Professor Earl Miner, Dr V. G. Mylne, Dr J. M. Osborn, Dr Philip Gaskell, Mr A. J. Stead and Professor James Sutherland. Once again, the Cambridge University Library has generously allowed us the use of an office in which Mrs Phyllis Parsons has typed by far the greater part of the volume.

GEORGE WATSON

St John's College, Cambridge
December 1969

LIST OF CONTRIBUTORS
TO VOLUME 2

E.L.A.	Emmett L. Avery	R.H.L.	Roger H. Lonsdale
J.B.	John Barnard	D.A.L.	Donald A. Low
M.C.B.	Martin C. Battestin	J.H.M.	John H. Middendorf
T.B.	Terry Belanger	A.M.	Arnold Muirhead
G.E.B.	G. E. Bentley jr	M.E.N.	Maximillian E. Novak
D.F.B.	Donald F. Bond	J.C.T.O.	J. C. T. Oates
W.W.S.B.	W. W. S. Breem	P. and I.O.	Peter and Iona Opie
R.L.B.	R. L. Brett	G.B.P.	George B. Parks
A.B.	Anthony Burton	A.P.	André Parreaux
J.C.	John Carroll	H.P.	Henry Pettit
J.A.V.C.	John A. V. Chapple	H.G.P.	H. G. Pollard
R.A.D.	Robert A. Day	F.A.P.	Frederick A. Pottle
V.A.D.	Vinton A. Dearing	P.R.	Patrick Rogers
O.W.F.	Oliver W. Ferguson	G.R.R.	G. Ross Roy
A.F.	Arthur Friedman	N.H.R.	Norma H. Russell
J.F.	John Fuller	R.S.	Roger Sharrock
R.H.	Robert Halsband	A.S.	Arthur Sherbo
J.H.	John Harrison	I.S.	Irène Simon
A.T.H.	Allen T. Hazen	A.H.S.	Albert H. Smith
P.H.	Peter Heyworth	D.S.T.	Donald S. Taylor
A.J.	Arthur Johnston	S.S.B.T.	Samuel S. B. Taylor
H.W.J.	H. W. Jones	W.B.T.	W. B. Todd
E.J.K.	E. J. Kenney	J.T.	James Trainer
L.M.K.	Lewis M. Knapp	J.W.	John Wilders
G.J.K.	Gwin J. Kolb	R.M.W.	R. M. Wiles
R.L.	Robert Latham	C.A.Z.	Curt A. Zimansky

ABBREVIATIONS

Acad	Academy	illustr	illustrated by
addn	addition	Inst	Institute
Amer	American	introd	introduction
anon	anonymous	JEGP	Journal of English and Germanic Philology
Archiv	Archiv für das Studium der neueren Sprachen	JHI	Journal of the History of Ideas
AS	Anglo-Saxon	Jnl	Journal
Assoc	Association	Lang	Language
b.	born	Lib	Library
Bibl	Bibliographical	Lit	Literature
bk	book	MÆ	Medium Ævum
BM	British Museum	Mag	Magazine
Br	British	ME	Middle English
Bull	Bulletin	ML	Muses' Library
BNYPL	Bulletin of New York Public Library	MLN	Modern Language Notes
		MLQ	Modern Language Quarterly
		MLR	Modern Language Review
c.	circa	MP	Modern Philology
ch	chapter	ms	manuscript
CHEL	Cambridge History of English Literature	Nat	National
col	column	nd	no date
CQ	Critical Quarterly	no	number
d.	died	N & Q	Notes and Queries
DNB	Dictionary of National Biography	OE	Old English
		OHEL	Oxford History of English Literature
ed	edited by		
edn	edition	OSA	Oxford Standard Authors
E & S	Essays and Studies	p.	page
et al	and others	pbd	published
EC	Essays in Criticism	pbn	publication
EETS	Early English Text Society	PBSA	Publications of the Bibliographical Society of America
EHR	English Historical Review		
EL	Everyman's Library	PMLA	Publications of the Modern Language Association of America
ELH	Journal of English Literary History		
EML	English Men of Letters	PQ	Philological Quarterly
Eng	English	priv	privately
E Studien	Englische Studien	Proc	Proceedings
E Studies	English Studies	prop	proprietor
facs	facsimile	pt	part
fl.	floruit	ptd	printed
GM	Gentleman's Magazine	Quart	Quarterly
HLQ	Huntington Library Quarterly	REL	Review of English Literature

rev	revised by	STS	Scottish Text Society
Rev	Review	Stud	Studies
RES	Review of English Studies	suppl	supplement
rptd	reprinted	TLS	Times Literary Supplement
SB	Studies in Bibliography (University of Virginia)	tr	translated by
		trn	translation
SE	Studies in English (University of Texas)	Univ	University
		unpbd	unpublished
ser	series	UTQ	University of Toronto Quarterly
Sh Jb	Shakespeare Jahrbuch	vol	volume
Soc	Society	WC	World's Classics
SP	Studies in Philology		

1. INTRODUCTION

I. GENERAL WORKS

A. BIBLIOGRAPHIES

Catalogues of books pbd in Scotland, Ireland, Wales and the English provinces will be found in vol 1, where bibliographies of the principal religious bodies are also listed. Other specialized lists are included under Book Production and Distribution, below, and the Literature of Sport, below.

Walpole, Horace. A catalogue of the royal and noble authors of England, with lists of their works. 2 vols Strawberry Hill 1758; rev T. Park 5 vols 1806 ('continued to the present time').

A general catalogue of books in all languages, arts and sciences that have been printed in Great Britain, and published in London, since the year MDCC to the present time. 1779. With Appendix for 1779, 1781, and Supplement to July 1783.

Nichols, J. Literary anecdotes of the eighteenth century. 9 vols 1812–16.

—— Illustrations of the literary history of the eighteenth century. 8 vols 1817–58.

Watt, R. Bibliotheca britannica: or a general index to British and foreign literature. 4 vols Edinburgh 1824.

Arber, E. The term catalogues 1668–1709, with a number for Easter term 1711. 3 vols 1903–6. *See* C. Blagden, The missing term catalogue, SB 7 1955.

Johnston, G. P. A catalogue of English pamphlets printed between 1618 and 1700. Edinburgh 1906 (priv ptd).

Straus, R. Chronological list of all the books published by Robert Dodsley 1735–64. In his Robert Dodsley, 1910.

—— Handlist [of Curll's pbns] 1706–46. In his Unspeakable Curll, 1927.

Cowan, R. E. and W. A. Clark jr. The library of William Andrews Clark jr. 19 vols San Francisco 1920–31.

Wrenn, H. B. and T. J. Wise. A catalogue of the library of John Henry Wrenn. 5 vols Austin 1920.

Wise, T. J. The Ashley library. 10 vols 1922–30.

The Britwell handlist: or short-title catalogue of the principal volumes to the year 1800 formerly in the library of Britwell Court. 2 vols 1933.

Morgan, W. T. and C. S. A bibliography of British history 1700–15, with special reference to the reign of Queen Anne. 5 vols Bloomington 1934–42.

Tobin, J. E. Eighteenth-century English literature and its cultural background. New York 1939. Addns by D. F. Bond, Lib Quart 10 1940.

The Carl H. Pforzheimer library: English literature 1475–1700. [Ed W. A. Jackson] 3 vols New York 1940.

Hazen, A. T. A bibliography of the Strawberry Hill Press. New Haven 1942.

Williams, H. The eighteenth century. In The Bibliographical Society 1892–1942: studies in retrospect, ed F. C. Francis 1945.

Wing, D. G. Short-title catalogue of books printed in England, Scotland, Ireland, Wales and British America, and of English books printed in other countries 1641–1700. 3 vols New York 1945–51 (Index Soc). *See also* Wing, The making of the short-title catalogue, PBSA 45 1951, and A gallery of ghosts: books published 1641–1700 not found in the Short-Title Catalogue, New York 1967; M. I. Fry and G. Davies, Supplement, HLQ 16 1953; P. G. Morrison, Index of printers, publishers and booksellers, Charlottesville 1955; J. E. Tucker, Wing's short-title catalogue and translations from the French, PBSA 49 1955; J. Alden, Bibliographia hibernica, Charlottesville 1956, and Wing addenda and corrigenda, Charlottesville 1958; W. G. Hiscock, Christ Church

holdings in Wing's short-title catalogue, Oxford 1956, and Christ Church supplement to Wing's short-title catalogue, Oxford 1956; E. Wolf 2nd, Check-list of books in the Library Company of Philadelphia in and supplementary to Wing, Philadelphia 1959.

Rochedieu, C. A. Bibliography of French translations of English works 1700–1800. Chicago 1948.

Kunitz, S. J. and H. Haycraft. British authors before 1800: a biographical dictionary. New York 1952.

Gordan, J. D. A doctor's benefaction: the Berg collection at the New York Public Library. PBSA 48 1954.

The Rothschild library: a catalogue of the collection of eighteenth-century printed books and manuscripts formed by Lord Rothschild. 2 vols Cambridge 1954 (priv ptd).

The Sterling library: a catalogue of the printed books and manuscripts collected by Sir Louis Sterling and presented by him to the University of London. 1954.

Wikelund, P. Restoration literature: an annotated bibliography. Folio (Indiana Univ) 19 1954.

Wiles, R. M. Serial publication in England before 1750. Cambridge 1957. Appendix B: Short-title catalogue of books published in fascicules before 1750.

Todd, W. B. New adventures among old books: an essay in eighteenth-century bibliography. Lawrence Kansas 1958.

Gaskell, P. John Baskerville: a bibliography. Cambridge 1959.

—— A bibliography of the Foulis Press. 1964.

Deed, S. G. and J. Francis. Catalogue of the Plume Library at Maldon, Essex. Maldon 1959. On library of Archdeacon Thomas Plume 1630–1704.

Metzdorf, R. F. The Tinker library: a bibliographical catalogue of the books and manuscripts collected by Chauncey Brewster Tinker. New Haven 1959.

Witten, L. Contemporary collectors XXIII: James Marshall Osborn. Book Collector 8 1959.

Rosebery, E. Unfamiliar libraries VII: Barnbougle Castle. Book Collector 11 1962.

Foxon, D. F. Libertine literature in England 1660–1745. Book Collector 12 1963; New Hyde Park NY 1965 (rev).

—— (ed). English bibliographical sources: ser 1. 1964–6 (facs of 18th-century lists of books and pamphlets); Bibliotheca annua [J. Nutt], 1700–3/4; Catalogue of all books, sermons and pamphlets [B. Lintott], 1714–17; The monthly catalogue [J. Wilford], 1723–30; Register of books 1728–32, extracted from the Monthly Chronicle; List of books [from GM], collected with annual indexes and the index to the first twenty years compiled by Edward Kimber 1731–51; Monthly catalogues from the London Magazine 1732–66, with the index for 1732–58 compiled by Edward Kimber; The annual catalogue 1736–7; List of books from the British Magazine 1746–50.

Neuburg, V. Chapbooks: a bibliography of references to English and American chapbook literature of the eighteenth and nineteenth centuries. 1964.

McKenzie, D. F. The Cambridge university press 1696–1712: a bibliographical study. 2 vols Cambridge 1966.

Spence, J. Observations, anecdotes and characters of books and men. Ed J. M. Osborn 2 vols Oxford 1966.

Amory, H. A selected bibliography of eighteenth-century English documents and autograph manuscripts. Manuscripts 20 1968.

Schulz, H. C. English literary manuscripts in the Huntington Library. HLQ 31 1968.

Current Bibliographies and Surveys

Crane, R. S. et al. English literature of the Restoration and eighteenth century: a current bibliography. PQ 5 1926-. Continued annually. The first 25 lists 1926–50 rptd (with index by L. A. Landa) 2 vols Princeton 1950–2; the next 10 lists 1951–60 rptd (with index by G. J. Kolb and C. A. Zimansky) 2 vols Princeton 1962.

Thomson, M. A. The age of Johnson. History 20 1935.

Graham, W. et al. The romantic movement: a current selective and critical bibliography. ELH 4–16 1937–49;

PQ 29–43 1950–64; Eng Lang Notes 1 1965-. Continued annually.

Wellek, R. Studies in eighteenth-century English literature 1938–45. Erasmus 1 1947.

Stamm, R. Englische Literatur. Berne 1957.

Clifford, J. L. The eighteenth century. In Contemporary literary scholarship: a critical review, ed L. Leary, New York 1958.

— The eighteenth century. MLQ 26 1965.

Fabian, B. Neuere Arbeiten zur Geschichte der englischen und amerikanischen Literatur: eine Übersicht. Germanisch-romanische Monatsschrift 40 1959.

Greene, D. J. et al. Recent studies in the Restoration and eighteenth century. Stud in Eng Lit 1500–1900 1 1961-. Continued annually.

Wolff, E. Englische Literatur im 18 Jahrhundert: ein Forschungsbericht 1950–60. Deutsche Vierteljahrsschrift für Literaturwissenschaft und Geistesgeschichte 35 1961.

B. LITERARY HISTORIES

Histories of Scottish literature are listed col 1955 below.

Hettner, H. Literaturgeschichte des achtzehnten Jahrhunderts: die englische Literatur von 1660–1770. Brunswick 1856, 1912 (7th rev edn).

Beljame, A. Le public et les hommes de lettres en Angleterre 1660–1744. Paris 1881, 1897; tr E. O. Lorimer, ed B. Dobrée 1948.

Oliphant, M. O. The literary history of England in the end of the eighteenth and beginning of the nineteenth century. 3 vols 1882.

Perry, T. S. English literature in the eighteenth century. New York 1883.

Gosse, E. From Shakespeare to Pope: an inquiry into the causes and phenomena of the rise of classical poetry in England. Cambridge 1885.

— A history of eighteenth-century literature 1660–1780. 1889.

Dennis, J. The age of Pope 1700–44. 1894.

Minto, W. The literature of the Georgian era. Ed W. Knight, Edinburgh 1894.

Garnett, R. The age of Dryden. 1895.

Saintsbury, G. A history of nineteenth-century literature 1780–1895. 1896.

— The peace of the Augustans. 1916, Oxford 1946 (WC).

Elton, O. The Augustan ages. Edinburgh 1899.

— A survey of English literature 1780–1830. 2 vols 1912.

— A survey of English literature 1730–80. 2 vols 1928.

Seccombe, T. The age of Johnson 1748–98. 1899, 1907 (rev).

Millar, J. H. The mid-eighteenth century. Edinburgh 1902.

Stephen, L. English literature and society in the eighteenth century. 1904, 1940.

Cambridge history of English literature. Ed A. W. Ward and A. R. Waller 15 vols Cambridge 1907–16. Vol 8: The age of Dryden 1911; vol 9: From Steele and Addison to Pope and Swift, 1912; vol 10: The age of Johnson, 1913; vol 11: The period of the French Revolution, 1914.

Bailey, J. C. Dr Johnson and his circle. 1913.

Cazamian, L. L'évolution psychologique et la littérature en Angleterre 1660–1914. Paris 1920.

— Epoques moderne et contemporaine 1660–1914. Pt II of E. Legouis and L. Cazamian, Histoire de la littérature anglaise, Paris 1924; tr 1927.

Schück, H. Allmän litteraturhistoria vol 5: upplysningen och förromantiken. Stockholm 1924.

Van Tieghem, P. Précis d'histoire littéraire de l'Europe depuis la Renaissance. Paris 1925; tr New York 1930.

Vines, S. The course of English classicism. 1930.

Fehr, B. Die englische Literatur des 17 und 18 Jahrhunderts. Potsdam 1931.

Dyson, H. V. D. and J. Butt. Augustans and Romantics 1689–1830. 1940, 1950 (rev), 1961 (rev).

Evans, B. I. The eighteenth century. In his Tradition and romanticism, 1940.

McKillop, A. D. English literature from Dryden to Burns. New York 1948.

Sherburn, G. The Restoration and eighteenth century 1660–1789. Bk 3 of A literary history of England, ed A. C. Baugh, New York 1948; rev D. F. Bond, New York 1967.

Bredvold, L. I. The literature of the Restoration and the eighteenth century 1660–1798. Bk 3 of A history of English literature, ed H. Craig, New York 1950.

Butt, J. The Augustan age. 1950.

McCutcheon, R. P. Eighteenth-century English literature. Oxford 1950 (Home Univ Lib).

Wedgwood, C. V. Seventeenth-century English literature. Oxford 1950 (Home Univ Lib).

Churchill, R. C. English literature of the eighteenth century. 1953.

Humphreys, A. R. The Augustan world. 1954, 1964.

Ward, A. C. Illustrated history of English literature. 1953–5. Vol 2: Ben Jonson to Samuel Johnson. 1954; vol 3: Blake to Bernard Shaw, 1955.

Ford, B. (ed). Pelican guide to English literature vols 4–5: From Dryden to Johnson; From Blake to Byron. 1957.

Burton, K. M. P. Restoration literature. Oxford 1958 (Home Univ Lib).

Dobrée, B. English literature in the early eighteenth century 1700–40. Oxford 1959 (OHEL vol 7).

Hamilton, K. G. The two harmonies: poetry and prose in the seventeenth century. Oxford 1963.

Renwick, W. L. English literature 1789–1815. Oxford 1963 (OHEL vol 9).

Korninger, S. English literature and its background: the Restoration period and the eighteenth century 1660–1780. Vienna 1964.

Sutherland, J. English literature of the late seventeenth century. Oxford 1969 (OHEL vol 6).

Definitions

Van Tieghem, P. Classique. Revue de Synthèse 1 1931.

Peyre, H. Qu'est-ce que le classicisme? Paris 1933.

— Le classicisme français. New York 1942.

Burgum, E. B. The neo-classical period in English literature: a psychological definition. Sewanee Rev 52 1944.

Zeydel, E. H. The concepts 'classic' and 'romantic'. Germanic Rev 19 1944.

Wellek, R. The concept of baroque in literary scholarship. Jnl of Aesthetics 5 1946.

—— The term and concept of 'classicism' in literary history. In Aspects of the eighteenth century, ed E. R. Wasserman, Baltimore 1965.

Willoughby, L. A. Classic and romantic: a re-examination. German Life & Letters 6 1952.

Hatzfeld, H. The baroque from the viewpoint of the literary historian. Jnl of Aesthetics 14 1955.

—— Use and misuse of 'baroque' as a critical term in literary history. UTQ 31 1962.

Stechow, W. The baroque: a critical summary of the essays by Bukofzer, Hatzfeld and Martin. Jnl of Aesthetics 14 1955.

Wolff, E. Zur Methodik der literarhistorischen Erschliessung des 18 Jahrhunderts. Anglia 72 1955.

Frye, N. Towards defining an age of sensibility. ELH 23 1956.

Luck, G. Scriptor classicus. CL 10 1958.

Stanley, E. G. The use in English of the word Aufklärung. N & Q Sept 1959.

Maxwell, J. C. Classic. N & Q June 1963.

Boas, G. In search of the age of reason. In Aspects of the eighteenth century, ed E. R. Wasserman, Baltimore 1965.

Bronson, B. H. When was neoclassicism? In Studies in criticism and aesthetics 1660–1800: essays in honor of S. H. Monk, Minneapolis 1967.

Cohen, R. The Augustan mode in English poetry. Eighteenth-Century Stud 1 1967.

Cruttwell, P. The eighteenth century: a classical age? Arion 7 1967.

Erskine-Hill, H. H. Augustans on Augustanism: England 1655–1759. Renaissance & Modern Stud 11 1967.

Greene, D. Augustinianism and empiricism: a note on eighteenth-century English intellectual history. Eighteenth-Century Stud 1 1967. See V. de Sola Pinto and Greene 2 1969.

Watt, I. Three aspects of the Augustan tradition. Listener 6–13, 27 April 1967.

Ford, F. L. The Enlightenment: towards a useful redefinition. In Studies in the eighteenth century, ed R. F. Brissenden, Canberra 1968.

Surveys of the Literary Kinds

Restricted to the more specialized types. Surveys of the criticism, poetry, drama and fiction of the period, and their subdivisions, are listed under the appropriate sections below.

Allegory

Greene, H. E. The allegory as employed by Spenser, Bunyan and Swift. PMLA 4 1889.

Bloom, E. A. The allegorical principle. ELH 18 1951.

Honig, E. Dark conceit: the making of allegory. Evanston 1959.

Biography and Autobiography

Stauffer, D. A. English biography before 1700. Cambridge Mass 1930.

—— The art of biography in eighteenth-century England. 2 vols Princeton 1941.

Longaker, M. English biography in the eighteenth century. Philadelphia 1931.

Lewis, W. S. The difficult art of biography. Yale Rev 44 1954.

Shumaker, W. English autobiography: its emergence, materials and form. Berkeley 1954.

Matthews, W. British autobiographies: an annotated bibliography of British autobiographies published or written before 1951. Berkeley 1955.

Pinto, V. de S. Seventeenth-century biographies. 1955.

Bottrall, M. Every man a phoenix: studies in seventeenth-century autobiography. 1958.

Pascal, R. Design and truth in autobiography. 1960.

Clifford, J. L. (ed). Biography as an art: selected criticism 1560–1960. Oxford 1962.

—— Roger North and the art of biography. In Restoration and eighteenth-century literature: essays in honor of A. D. McKillop, Chicago 1963.

Butt, J. Biography in the hands of Walton, Johnson and Boswell. Los Angeles 1966.

Morris, J. N. Versions of the self: studies in English autobiography from John Bunyan to John Stuart Mill. New York 1966.

Daghlian, P. B. (ed). Essays in eighteenth-century biography. Bloomington 1968.

Delany, P. British autobiography in the seventeenth century. 1969.

Dialogue

Merrill, E. The dialogue in English literature. New York 1911.

Egilsrud, J. S. Le dialogue des morts dans les littératures française, allemande et anglaise 1644–1789. Paris 1934.

Purpus, E. R. The 'plain, easy and familiar way': the dialogue in English literature 1660–1725. ELH 17 1950.

Smallman, B. Endor revisited: English biblical dialogues of the seventeenth century. Music & Letters 46 1965.

Essay

Bryan, W. F. and R. S. Crane. The English familiar essay: representative texts. Boston 1916. Introd.

Thompson, E. N. S. The seventeenth-century English essay. Iowa City 1926.

Watson, M. R. The Spectator tradition and the development of the familiar essay. ELH 13 1946.

—— Magazine serials and the essay tradition 1746–1820. Baton Rouge 1956.

Dobrée, B. English essayists. 1947.

History

Liddell, M. F. Der Stil der englischen Geschichtsschreibung im 18 Jahrhundert. In Anglica: Untersuchungen zur englischen Philologie, Alois Brandl zum siebzigsten Geburtstage überreicht, vol 2, Leipzig 1925.

Black, J. B. The art of history: a study of four great historians of the eighteenth century. 1926. On Robertson, Voltaire, Gibbon, Hume.

Peardon, T. P. The transition in English historical writing 1760–1830. New York 1933.

Barnes, H. E. A history of historical writing. Norman Oklahoma 1937.

Douglas, D. C. English scholars 1660–1730. 1939, 1951 (rev).

Wellek, R. The rise of English literary history: the origins and development of literary historiography from Bacon to Thomas Warton. Chapel Hill 1941, New York 1966.

Thompson, J. W. and B. J. Holm. A history of historical writing. 2 vols New York 1942.

Neff, E. E. The poetry of history: the contribution of literature and literary scholarship to the writing of history since Voltaire. New York 1947.

Butterfield, H. Man on his past: the study of the history of historical scholarship. Cambridge 1954.

Thomson, M. A. Some developments in English historiography during the eighteenth century. 1957.

Davis, H. The Augustan concept of history. In Reason and the imagination: studies in the history of ideas 1600–1800, essays in honor of M. H. Nicolson, New York 1962.

Trevor-Roper, H. The historical philosophy of the Enlightenment. In T. Besterman (ed), Transactions of the first international congress on the Enlightenment, Geneva 1963.

Hale, J. R. (ed). The evolution of British historiography from Bacon to Namier. 1967.

Humour

Hazlitt, W. Lectures on the English comic writers. 1819.

Thackeray, W. M. The English humourists of the eighteenth century. 1853.

Clarke, C. C. On the comic writers of England. GM April–Dec 1871.

Draper, J. W. The theory of the comic in eighteenth-century England. JEGP 37 1938.

Snuggs, H. L. The comic humours: a new interpretation. PMLA 62 1947.

Hooker, E. N. Humour in the age of Pope. HLQ 11 1948.

Cazamian, L. The development of English humor. 2 pts Durham NC 1952, Cambridge 1953.

Ramondt, M. Between laughter and humour in the eighteenth century. Neophilologus 40 1956.

Tave, S. M. The amiable humorist: a study in the comic theory and criticism of the eighteenth and early nineteenth centuries. Chicago 1960.

Letters

Hornbeak, K. G. The complete letter-writer in English 1568–1800. Northampton Mass 1934.

Bond, R. P. Eighteenth-century correspondence: a survey. SP 33 1936.

Robertson, J. The art of letter-writing: an essay on the handbooks published in England during the sixteenth and seventeenth centuries. Liverpool 1942.

Humiliata, Sr M. Standards of taste advocated for feminine letter-writing 1640–1797. HLQ 13 1950.

Firth, J. R. Modes of meaning. E & S new ser 4 1951.

Hobman, D. L. Letters as literature. Quart Rev 292 1954.

Irving, W. H. The providence of wit in the English letter writers. Durham NC 1955.

Davis, H. The correspondence of the Augustans. In Essays in English literature from the Renaissance to the Victorian age, presented to A. S. P. Woodhouse, Toronto 1964.

Anderson, H., P. B. Daghlian and I. Ehrenpreis (ed). The familiar letter in the eighteenth century. Lawrence Kansas 1966.

Rhetoric and Oratory

McGrew, J. F. A bibliography of the works on speech composition in England during the 16th and 17th centuries. Quart Jnl of Speech 15 1929.

Sandford, W. P. English theories of public address 1530–1828. Columbus Ohio 1929.

Fritz, C. A. Sheridan to Rush: the beginnings of English elocution. Quart Jnl of Speech 16 1930.

Harding, H. F. The listener on eloquence 1750–1800. In Studies in speech and drama in honor of A. M. Drummond, Ithaca 1944. On reception of speeches by Burke, Sheridan et al.

Gauger, H. Die Kunst der politischen Rede in England. Tübingen 1952.

Howell, W. S. Logic and rhetoric in England 1500–1700. Princeton 1956. See V. Harris, The arts of discourse in England 1500–1700, PQ 27 1958.

—— Sources of the elocutionary movement in England 1700–48. Quart Jnl of Speech 45 1959.

After Goodrich: new resources in British public address, a symposium. Quart Jnl of Speech 48 1962.

Ragsdale, J. D. Invention in English 'stylistic' rhetoric 1600–1800. Quart Jnl of Speech 51 1965.

Burwick, F. Associational rhetoric and Scottish prose style. Speech Monographs 34 1967.

Bevilacqua, V. M. Philosophical influences in the development of English rhetorical theory 1748 to 1783. Proc Leeds Philosophical & Literary Soc (Literary & Historical Section) 12 1968.

Satire

Previté-Orton, C. W. Political satire in English poetry. Cambridge 1910.

Leavitt, S. E. Paul Scarron and English travesty. SP 16 1919.

Burchardt, C. Engelsk humor og vidd under Dronning Annas regjering. Edda 22 1924.

Walker, H. English satire and satirists. 1925.

Fornelli, G. La satira in Inghilterra durante la guerra di successione di Spagna. Rivista d'Italia June 1928.

Kitchin, G. A survey of burlesque and parody in English. 1931.

West, A. H. L'influence française dans la poésie burlesque en Angleterre entre 1660 et 1700. Paris 1931.

Bond, R. P. English burlesque poetry 1700–50. Cambridge Mass 1932.

Vines, S. (ed). Georgian satirists. 1934.

Richards, E. A. Hudibras in the burlesque tradition. New York 1937.

Bredvold, L. I. A note in defence of satire. ELH 7 1940.

—— The gloom of the Tory satirists. In Pope and his contemporaries: essays presented to George Sherburn, Oxford 1949.

Worcester, D. The art of satire. Cambridge Mass 1940.

Randolph, M. C. 'Hide and seek' satires of the Restoration and xviii-century. N & Q 10 Oct 1942.

—— The structural design of the formal verse satire. PQ 21 1942.

—— Diamond-satires in the eighteenth century. N & Q 31 July 1943.

—— 'Candour' in xviiith-century satire. RES 20 1944.

—— 'The sinful suburbs of cookery': satirical recipes of the xviii century. N & Q 15 Jan 1944.

Bishop, C. R. 'Peace is my dear delight'. West Virginia Univ Bull Philological Stud 4 1943.

Boyce, B. News from Hell: satiric communications with the nether world in English writing of the seventeenth and eighteenth centuries. PMLA 58 1943.

Brown, W. C. Dramatic tension in neo-classic satire. College Eng Feb 1945.

Clark, A. M. Studies in literary modes. Edinburgh 1946. On the art of satire.

Brooks, H. F. The 'imitation' in English poetry, especially in formal satire, before the age of Pope. RES 25 1949.

Jack, I. Augustan satire: intention and idiom in English poetry 1660–1750. Oxford 1952.

Wilkinson, A. M. The decline of English verse satire in the middle years of the eighteenth century. RES new ser 3 1952.

—— The rise of English verse satire in the eighteenth century. E Studies 34 1953.

Elliott, R. C. The satirist and society. ELH 21 1954.

—— The power of satire: magic, ritual, art. Princeton 1960.

Lawlor, J. Radical satire and the realistic novel. E & S new ser 8 1955.

Leyburn, E. D. Satiric allegory: mirror of man. New Haven 1956.

Sutherland, J. English satire. Cambridge 1958.

Limentani, U. La satira nel seicento. Milan 1961.

Highet, G. The anatomy of satire. Princeton 1962.

Youngren, W. Generality in Augustan satire. In R. A. Brower and R. Poirier (ed), In defense of reading, New York 1962.

Jones, C. E. Satire and certain English satirists of the Enlightenment. In T. Besterman (ed), Transactions of the First International Congress on the Enlightenment, Geneva 1963.

Pinkus, P. Satire and St George. Queen's Quart 70 1963.

McDonald, C. O. Restoration comedy as drama of satire: an investigation into seventeenth-century aesthetics. SP 61 1964.

Chernaik, W. L. The heroic occasional poem: panegyric and satire in the Restoration. MLQ 26 1965.

Goldgar, B. A. Satires on man and 'the dignity of human nature'. PMLA 80 1965.

Hempel, W. Parodie, Travestie und Pastiche: zur Geschichte von Wort und Sache. Germanisch-romanische Monatsschrift new ser 15 1965.

Kernan, A. B. The plot of satire. New Haven 1965.

Sutherland, W. O. S., jr. The art of the satirist: essays on the satire of Augustan England. Austin 1965.

Symposium: the concept of the persona in satire. Satire Newsletter 3 1966.

Fabian, B. Notizen zu didaktischen Burlesken des achtzehnten Jahrhunderts. In Symposion für Rudolf Sühnel, Berlin 1967.

Paulson, R. The fictions of satire. Baltimore 1967.

— Satire and the novel in eighteenth-century England. New Haven 1967.

Bloom, E. A. and L. D. The satiric mode of feeling: a theory of intention. Criticism 11 1969.

Weinbrot, H. D. The formal strain: studies in Augustan imitation and satire. Chicago 1969.

Sermons

Richardson, C. F. English preachers and preaching 1640–70. 1928.

Pützer, F. Prediger des englischen Barock, stilistisch untersucht. Bonn 1929.

Jones, R. F. The attack on pulpit eloquence in the Restoration: an episode in the development of the neo-classical standard for prose. JEGP 30 1931; rptd in his Seventeenth century, Stanford 1951.

Mitchell, W. F. English pulpit oratory from Andrewes to Tillotson: a study of its literary aspects. 1932.

Pollard, A. English sermons. 1962.

Miscellaneous

Crawford, B. V. Questions and objections. PMLA 41 1926.

MacDonald, H. Banter in English controversial prose after the Restoration. E & S 32 1947.

Miller, H. K. The paradoxical encomium with special reference to its vogue in England 1600–1800. MP 53 1956.

Wyman, L. A. The tradition of the formal meditation in Rowe's The fair penitent. PQ 42 1963.

Starr, G. A. Escape from Barbary: a seventeenth-century genre. HLQ 29 1965.

The Intellectual Background

Stephen, L. History of English thought in the eighteenth century. 2 vols 1876.

Schöffler, H. Protestantismus und Literatur: neue Wege zur englischen Literatur des 18 Jahrhunderts. Leipzig 1922.

Elton, O. Reason and enthusiasm in the eighteenth century. E & S 10 1924.

Burtt, E. A. The metaphysical foundations of modern physical science. 1925.

Randall, J. H., jr. The making of the modern mind. Boston 1926.

Perdeck, A. A. Theology in Augustan literature: being an inquiry into the extent of orthodox Protestant thought in the literature of Pope's time. Groningen 1928.

Grierson, H. J. C. Cross currents in English literature of the seventeenth century. 1929.

Smith, P. A history of modern culture. Vol 1: The great renewal 1543–1687; vol 2: The Enlightenment 1687–1776, New York 1930–4.

Wilde, H. O. Der Gottesgedanke in der englischen Literatur: das Problem der Entwicklung von puritanischer zu romantischer Literatur. Breslau 1930.

Meissner, P. Die rationalistische Grundlage der englischen Kultur des 17 Jahrhunderts. Anglia 55 1931.

— Die Stellung des Menschen im englischen Geistesleben des 17 Jahrhunderts. E Studien 67 1932.

— Die geistesgeschichtlichen Grundlagen des englischen Literaturbarocks. Munich 1934.

Schirmer, W. F. Die geistesgeschichtlichen Grundlagen der englischen Barockliteratur. Germanisch-romanische Monatsschrift 19 1931.

Becker, C. L. The heavenly city of the eighteenth-century philosophers. New Haven 1932. See also Carl Becker's Heavenly City revisited, ed R. O. Rockwood, Ithaca 1958; and R. Emerson, JHI 28 1967.

Cassirer, E. Die Philosophie der Aufklärung. Tübingen 1932; tr Princeton 1951. See also H. Dieckmann, An interpretation of the eighteenth century, MLQ 15 1954.

Pensa, H. Sorcellerie et religion: du désordre dans les esprits et dans les moeurs aux xviie et xviiie siècles. Paris 1933.

Crane, R. S. Anglican apologetics and the idea of progress 1699–1745. MP 31 1934; rptd in his Idea of the humanities and other essays vol 1, Chicago 1967.

Willey, B. The seventeenth-century background: studies in the thought of the age in relation to poetry and religion. 1934.

— The eighteenth-century background: studies on the idea of nature. 1940.

— The touch of cold philosophy. In R. F. Jones et al, The seventeenth century, Stanford 1951.

Bredvold, L. I. The intellectual milieu of John Dryden: studies in some aspects of seventeenth-century thought. Ann Arbor 1935.

— The brave new world of the Enlightenment. Ann Arbor 1961.

Hazard, P. La crise de la conscience européenne 1680–1715. 3 vols Paris 1935; tr 1953.

— La pensée européenne au xviiième siècle de Montesquieu à Lessing. Paris 1946; tr 1954.

Lovejoy, A. O. The great chain of being: a study of the history of an idea. Cambridge Mass 1936.

Bryson, G. Man and society: the Scottish inquiry of the eighteenth century. Princeton 1945.

Fink, Z. S. The classical republicans. Evanston 1945.

Humphreys, A. R. The eternal fitness of things: an aspect of eighteenth-century thought. MLR 42 1947.

— Literature and religion in eighteenth-century England. Jnl of Ecclesiastical History 3 1952.

Bethell, S. L. The cultural revolution of the seventeenth century. 1951.

Kliger, S. The Goths in England: a study in seventeenth and eighteenth century thought. Cambridge Mass 1952.

Wiley, M. L. The subtle knot: creative scepticism in seventeenth-century England. Cambridge Mass 1952.

Wasserman, E. R. Nature moralized: the divine analogy in the eighteenth century. ELH 20 1953.

Colie, R. L. Light and enlightenment: a study of the Cambridge Platonists and the Dutch Arminians. Cambridge 1957.

— Some paradoxes in the language of things. In Reason and the imagination, studies in the history of ideas 1600–1800: essays in honor of M. H. Nicolson, New York 1962.

Macklem, M. The anatomy of the world: relations between natural and moral law from Donne to Pope. Minneapolis 1958.

Manuel, F. E. The eighteenth century confronts the gods. Cambridge Mass 1959.

Simon, I. 'Pride of reason' in the Restoration. Revue des Langues Vivantes 25 1959.

Røstvig, M.-S. The background of English neo-classicism, with some comments on Swift and Pope. Oslo 1961.

Bullough, G. Mirror of minds: changing psychological beliefs in English literature. 1962.

Jones, R. F. The humanistic defence of learning in the mid-seventeenth century. In Reason and the imagination, studies in the history of ideas 1600–1800: essays in honor of M. H. Nicolson, New York 1962.

Pettit, H. The limits of reason as literary theme in the English Enlightenment. In T. Besterman (ed), Trans of the First International Congress on the Enlightenment, Geneva 1963.

Voitle, R. The reason of the English Enlightenment. Ibid.

Cragg, G. R. Reason and authority in the eighteenth century. Cambridge 1964.

Mollenauer, R. (ed). Introduction to modernity: a symposium on eighteenth-century thought. Austin 1965.

Gay, P. The Enlightenment: an interpretation. New York 1966.

Vereker, C. H. Eighteenth-century optimism: a study of the interpretations of moral and social theory in English and French thought between 1689 and 1789. Liverpool 1967.

Clifford, J. L. (ed). Man versus society in eighteenth-century Britain: six points of view. Cambridge 1968.

Watt, I. (ed). The Augustan age: approaches to its literature, life and thought. Greenwich Conn 1968.

C. SPECIAL STUDIES

(1) ROMANTICISM

Phelps, W. L. The beginnings of the English romantic movement. Boston 1893.

Beers, H. A. A history of English romanticism in the eighteenth century. New York 1898.

Vaughan, C. E. The romantic revolt. Edinburgh 1900.

Farley, F. E. Scandinavian influences in the English romantic movement. Boston 1903.

MacClintock, W. D. Some paradoxes of the English romantic movement of the eighteenth century. Chicago 1903.

Richter, H. Geschichte der englischen Romantik. 2 vols Halle 1911–16.

Havens, R. D. Romantic aspects of the age of Pope. PMLA 27 1912.

—— Discontinuity in literary development: the case of English romanticism. SP 47 1950.

Babbitt, I. Rousseau and romanticism. Boston 1919.

Ker, W. P. Romantic fallacies. In his Art of poetry, Oxford 1923.

Longueil, A. E. The word 'Gothic' in eighteenth-century criticism. MLN 38 1923.

Robertson, J. G. Studies in the genesis of romantic theory in the eighteenth century. Cambridge 1923.

Snyder, E. D. The Celtic revival in English literature 1760–1800. Cambridge Mass 1923.

De Maar, H. G. A history of modern English romanticism vol 1: Elizabethan and modern romanticism in the eighteenth century. 1924.

Lovejoy, A. O. On the discrimination of romanticisms. PMLA 39 1924; rptd in his Essays on the history of ideas, Baltimore 1948.

—— Optimism and romanticism. PMLA 42 1927.

—— The first Gothic revival and the return to nature. MLN 47 1932; rptd with above.

—— The Chinese origin of a romanticism. JEGP 32 1933; rptd with above, 1948.

—— Monboddo and Rousseau. MP 30 1933; rptd with above.

—— The meaning of romanticism for the historian of ideas. JHI 2 1941.

Smith, L. P. Four words: romantic, originality, creative, genius. 1924 (Soc for Pure Eng); rptd in his Words and idioms, 1925.

Van Tieghem, P. La préromantisme: études d'histoire littéraire européenne. 3 sers Paris 1924–47.

Kaufman, P. Defining romanticism: a survey and a program. MLN 40 1925.

Reynaud, L. Le romantisme: ses origines anglo-germaniques. Paris 1926.

Railo, E. The haunted castle: a study of the elements of English romanticism. 1927.

Draper, J. W. The funeral elegy and the rise of English romanticism. New York 1929.

Bernbaum, E. Guide through the romantic movement. New York 1930.

Yvon, P. Le gothique et la renaissance gothique en Angleterre 1750–1880. Caen 1931.

Erhardt-Siebold, E. von. Some inventions of the pre-romantic period and their influence upon literature. E Studien 66 1932.

Ustick, W. L. Romantic. TLS 2 Dec 1933.

Aubin, R. A. Grottoes, geology and the gothic revival. SP 31 1934.

—— Some Augustan gothicists. Harvard Stud 17 1935.

Stevenson, S. W. Romantic tendencies in the works of Dryden, Addison and Pope. Baltimore 1934.

Meinecke, F. Die englische Präromantik des 18 Jahrhunderts als Vorstufe des Historismus. Historische Zeitschrift 152 1935.

Weber, C. A. Bristols Bedeutung für die englische Romantik und die deutsch-englischen Beziehungen. Halle 1935.

Baldensperger, F. 'Romantique': ses analogues et ses équivalents: tableau synoptique de 1650 à 1810. Harvard Stud 19 1937.

—— 1793–4: climacteric times for 'romantic' tendencies in English ideology. JHI 5 1944.

Gill, F. C. The romantic movement and Methodism. 1937.

Piggott, S. Prehistory and the romantic movement. Antiquity 11 1937.

Addison, A. Romanticism and the gothic revival. New York 1938.

Johnstone, P. H. Turnips and romanticism. Agricultural History 12 1938.

Stunz, A. N. Romantic. TLS 8 April 1939.

Whitney, E. A. Humanitarianism and romanticism. HLQ 2 1939.

Stern, B. H. The rise of romantic Hellenism in English literature 1732–86. Menasha 1940.

Holbrook, W. C. The adjective 'gothique' in the xviiith century. MLN 56 1941.

Barzun, J. Romanticism and the modern ego. Boston 1943. See N. Suckling, A further contribution to the classic-romantic debate, Durham Univ Jnl 39 1946.

Liljegren, S. B. Essence and attitude in English romanticism. Upsala 1945.

Wellek, R. The concept of 'romanticism' in literary history. Comparative Lit 1 1949; rptd in his Concepts of criticism, New Haven 1963.

Tuveson, E. L. Space, Deity and the 'natural sublime'. MLQ 12 1951.

—— The imagination as a means of grace: Locke and the aesthetics of romanticism. Berkeley 1960.

Abrams, M. H. The mirror and the lamp: romantic theory and the critical tradition. New York 1953.

Bronson, B. H. The pre-romantic or post-Augustan mode (in English poetry). ELH 20 1953.

Poulet, G. Timelessness and romanticism. JHI 15 1954.

Kuhn, A. J. English deism and the development of romantic mythological syncretism. PMLA 62 1956.

Frankl, P. The gothic: literary sources and interpretations through eight centuries. Princeton 1960.

Immerwahr, R. The first romantic aesthetics. MLQ 21 1960.

Mahoney, J. L. Akenside and Shaftesbury: the influence of philosophy on English romantic theory. Discourse 4 1961.

—— Addison and Akenside: the impact of psychological criticism on early English romantic poetry. Br Jnl of Aesthetics 6 1966.

Haslag, J. 'Gothic' in 17 und 18 Jahrhundert: eine wort- und ideengeschichtliche Untersuchung. Cologne 1963.

Parks, G. B. The turn to the romantic in the travel literature of the eighteenth century. MLQ 25 1964.

Simches, S. O. Le romantisme et le goût esthétique du xviiie siècle. Paris 1964.

Roston, M. Prophet and poet: the Bible and the growth of romanticism. Evanston 1965.

Scoggins, J. The preface to Lyrical Ballads: a revolution in dispute. In Studies in criticism and aesthetics 1660–1800: essays in honor of S. H. Monk, Minneapolis 1967.

Trawick, L. M. (ed). Backgrounds of romanticism: English philosophical prose of the eighteenth century. Bloomington 1967.

Furst, L. R. 'Romanticism' in perspective. 1969.

(2) PRIMITIVISM

Crane, R. S. An early eighteenth-century enthusiast for primitive poetry: John Husbands. MLN 37 1922.

Tinker, C. B. Nature's simple plan. Princeton 1922.

Bissell, B. The American Indian in English literature of the eighteenth century. New Haven 1925.

Fairchild, H. N. The noble savage: a study in romantic naturalism. New York 1928.

— The romantic quest. New York 1931.

Murray, E. The 'noble savage'. Scientific Monthly March 1933.

Frantz, R. W. The English traveller and the movement of ideas 1660–1732. Lincoln Nebraska 1934.

Whitney, L. Primitivism and the idea of progress in English popular literature of the eighteenth century. Baltimore 1934.

Lovejoy, A. O. and G. Boas. Primitivism and related ideas in antiquity. Baltimore 1935.

Huse, W. A. A noble savage on the stage. MP 33 1936.

Pearce, R. H. The eighteenth-century Scottish primitivists: some reconsiderations. ELH 12 1945.

Fitzgerald, M. M. First follow nature: primitivism in English poetry 1725–50. New York 1947.

Foerster, D. M. Scottish primitivism and the historical approach. PQ 29 1950.

Foster, J. R. A forgotten noble savage, Tsonnonthouan. MLQ 14 1953.

Chalker, J. Thomson's Seasons and Virgil's Georgics: the problem of primitivism and progress. Studia Neophilologica 35 1963.

(3) SENTIMENTALISM

Whittuck, C. The 'good man' of the xviiith century. 1901.

Whitford, R. C. Satire's views of sentimentalism in the days of George the Third. JEGP 18 1919.

Reed, A. L. The background of Gray's Elegy: a study in the taste for melancholy poetry 1700–51. New York 1924.

Fehr, B. Ein Wort zur englischen Empfindsamkeitsliteratur. In Anglica: Untersuchungen zur englischen Philologie, Alois Brandl zum siebzigsten Geburtstage überreicht vol 2, Leipzig 1925.

Moore, C. A. Whig panegyric verse 1700–60: a phase of sentimentalism. PMLA 41 1926; rptd in his Backgrounds of English literature, 1953.

Van Tieghem, P. Quelques aspects de la sensibilité préromantique dans le roman européen au xviiie siècle. Edda 26 1927.

Burra, P. Baroque and gothic sentimentalism. 1931.

Sickells, E. M. The gloomy egoist: moods and themes of melancholy from Gray to Keats. New York 1932.

Allen, B. S. The dates of 'sentimental' and its derivatives. PMLA 48 1933.

Harder, J. H. Observations on some tendencies of sentiment and ethics chiefly in minor poetry and essay in the eighteenth century. Amsterdam 1933.

Crane, R. S. Suggestions toward a genealogy of the 'Man of Feeling'. ELH 1 1934; rptd in his Idea of the humanities and other essays vol 1, Chicago 1967.

Williamson, G. Mutability, decay and seventeenth-century melancholy. ELH 2 1935.

Babb, L. The cave of spleen. RES 12 1936.

Herbert, T. W. et al. 'Sentimental'. TLS 16–23 May 1936.

Hazard, P. Les origines philosophiques de l'homme de sentiment. Romanic Rev 28 1937.

Wright, W. F. Sensibility in English prose fiction 1760–1814: a re-interpretation. Urbana 1937.

Davis, J. L. Mystical versus enthusiastic sensibility. JHI 4 1943.

Warner, J. H. 'Education of the heart': observations on the eighteenth-century English sentimental movement. Papers of Michigan Acad 29 1943.

Babcock, R. W. Benevolence, sensibility and sentiment in some eighteenth-century periodicals. MLN 62 1947.

Humphreys, A. R. 'The friend of mankind' 1700–60: an aspect of eighteenth-century sensibility. RES 24 1948.

Aldridge, A. O. The pleasures of pity. ELH 16 1949.

Erämetsä, E. A study of the word 'sentimental' and of other linguistic characteristics of eighteenth-century sentimentalism in England. Helsinki 1951.

Frye, N. Towards defining an age of sensibility. ELH 23 1956.

Jones, W. P. The captive linnet: a footnote on eighteenth-century sentiment. PQ 33 1954.

Lévy, M. Le premier renouveau gothique et la sensibilité anglaise au milieu du dix-huitième siècle. Etudes Anglaises 14 1961.

Bredvold, L. I. The natural history of sensibility. Detroit 1962.

Parnell, P. E. The sentimental mask. PMLA 78 1963.

Smith, I. H. The concept 'sensibilité' and the Enlightenment. AUMLA 27 1967.

(4) FEELING FOR EXTERNAL NATURE

Veitch, J. The feeling for nature in Scottish poetry. 2 vols 1887.

Biese, A. Die Entwicklung des Naturgefühls im Mittelalter und in der Neuzeit. Leipzig 1888; tr 1905.

— Zur Litteratur der Geschichte des Naturgefühls. Zeitschrift für Vergleichende Litteraturgeschichte new ser 7 1894, 11 1897.

Reynolds, M. The treatment of nature in English poetry between Pope and Wordsworth. Chicago 1896, 1909 (rev).

Klenze, C. von. Literature on the nature-sense: part I. Jnl of Germanic Philology 2 1898.

Havens, R. D. Nature in the early eighteenth century. Nation (New York) 26 March 1914.

Moore, C. A. The return to nature in English poetry of the eighteenth century. SP 14 1917; rptd in his Backgrounds of English literature, 1953.

Beatty, J. M. jr. The English lake district before Wordsworth. South Atlantic Quart 22 1923.

Moesch, V. Naturschau und Naturgefühl in den Romanen

der Mrs Radcliffe und in der zeitgenössischen englischen Reiseliteratur. Zürich 1924.

Manwaring, E. W. Italian landscape in eighteenth-century England. New York 1925.

Crump, P. E. Nature in the age of Louis XIV. 1928.

Das, P. K. Evidences of a growing taste for nature in the age of Pope. Calcutta 1928.

Haas, C. E. de. Nature and the country in English poetry of the first half of the eighteenth century. Amsterdam 1928.

Blunden, E. Nature in literature. 1929.

Huscher, H. Über Eigenart und Ursprung des englischen Naturgefühls. Leipzig 1929.

—— Die englische Naturdichtung im Lichte der vergleichenden Literaturbetrachtung und der jüngsten Kritik. Anglia 62 1938.

Schirmer, G. Die Schweiz im Spiegel englischer und amerikanischer Literatur bis 1848. Zürich 1929.

Engel, C.-E. La littérature alpestre en France et en Angleterre au xviiie et xixe siècles. Chambéry 1930.

Williams, G. G. The beginnings of nature poetry in the eighteenth century. SP 27 1930.

de Beer, G. R. Early travellers in the Alps. 1931.

Bryan, J. I. The interpretation of nature in English poetry. Tokyo 1932.

Spindler, R. Die Alpen in der englischen Literatur. Leipzig 1932.

Katow, M. The Englishman's love of nature in the eighteenth century. Stud in Eng Lit (Tokyo) 14 1934.

Deane, C. V. Aspects of eighteenth-century nature poetry. Oxford 1935.

Thorpe, C. D. Two Augustans cross the Alps: Dennis and Addison on mountain scenery. SP 32 1935.

Aubin, R. A. Topographical poetry in xviiith-century England. New York 1936.

Chicoteau, M. Note sur la Suisse alémanique et les pélerins anglais de Joseph Addison à William Wordsworth. Comparative Lit Stud 2 1941.

Stuart, A. M. Landscape in Augustan verse. E & S 26 1941.

Johnstone, P. H. The rural Socrates. JHI 5 1944.

Litz, F. E. Richard Bentley on beauty, irregularity and mountains. ELH 12 1945.

Nicolson, M. H. Newton demands the Muse. Princeton 1946.

—— Mountain gloom and mountain glory: the development of the aesthetics of the infinite. Ithaca 1959.

Ogden, H. V. S. Thomas Burnet's Telluris theoria sacra and mountain scenery. ELH 14 1947.

Priestley, F. E. L. Newton and the romantic concept of nature. UTQ 17 1948.

Arthos, J. The language of natural description in eighteenth-century poetry. Ann Arbor 1949.

Kirchner, W. Mind, mountain and history. JHI 11 1950.

Staver, F. 'Sublime' as applied to nature. MLN 70 1955.

Korninger, S. Die Naturauffassung in der englischen Dichtung des 17 Jahrhunderts. Vienna 1956.

Zucker, P. Ruins: an aesthetic hybrid. Jnl of Aesthetics 20 1961.

Stanzel, F. K. Das Bild der Alpen in der englischen Literatur des 17 und 18 Jahrhunderts. Germanisch-romanische Monatsschrift new ser 14 1964.

Dobrée, B. Nature poetry in the early eighteenth century. E & S new ser 18 1965.

Scoular, K. W. Natural magic: studies in the presentation of nature in English poetry from Spenser to Marvell. Oxford 1965.

Malins, E. English landscaping and literature 1660–1840. Oxford 1966.

Frodsham, J. D. Landscape poetry in China and Europe. Comparative Lit 19 1967.

(5) PROSE STYLE

Croll, M. W. Juste Lipse et le mouvement anticicéronien. Revue du Seizième Siècle 2 1914.

—— The cadence of English oratorical prose. SP 16 1919.

—— Attic prose in the seventeenth century. SP 18 1921.

—— Attic prose: Lipsius, Montaigne, Bacon. In F. E. Schelling anniversary papers, New York 1923.

—— Muret and the history of 'Attic' prose. PMLA 39 1924.

—— The baroque style in prose. In Studies in English philology: a miscellany in honor of F. Klaeber, Minneapolis 1929; rptd in Literary English since Shakespeare, ed G. Watson, New York 1970.

All rptd in his Style, rhetoric and rhythm: essays, ed J. M. Patrick et al, Princeton 1966.

Jones, R. F. Science and English prose style in the third quarter of the seventeenth century. PMLA 45 1930; rptd in Literary English since Shakespeare, ed G. Watson, New York 1970.

—— The attack on pulpit eloquence in the Restoration: an episode in the development of the neo-classical standard for prose. JEGP 30 1931.

—— Science and language in England of the mid-seventeenth century. JEGP 31 1932.

All rptd in Jones et al, The seventeenth century: studies in the history of English thought and literature from Bacon to Pope, Stanford 1951.

—— The triumph of the English language: a survey of opinions concerning the vernacular from the introduction of printing to the Restoration. Stanford 1953.

Tietze, H. Le style baroque. Revue de Synthèse 9 1935.

Sutherland, J. Some aspects of eighteenth-century prose. In Essays on the eighteenth century presented to D. N. Smith, Oxford 1945.

—— On English prose. Toronto 1957.

—— and I. Watt. Restoration and Augustan prose. Los Angeles 1957.

Christensen, F. John Wilkins and the Royal Society's reform of prose style. MLQ 7 1946.

Howell, A. C. Res et verba: words and things. ELH 13 1946.

Williamson, G. The Senecan amble: a study in prose form from Bacon to Collier. 1951.

Fisch, H. The Puritans and the reform of prose style. ELH 19 1952.

Freimarck, V. The Bible and neo-classical views of style. JEGP 51 1952.

Cope, J. I. Seventeenth-century Quaker style. PMLA 62 1956.

Kenney, W. Addison, Johnson and the 'energetick' style. Studia Neophilologica 33 1961.

Beum, R. The scientific affinities of English baroque prose. Eng Miscellany (Rome) 13 1962.

Brady, F. Prose style and the 'Whig' tradition. BNYPL Sept 1962.

Greene, D. J. Is there a 'Tory' prose style? Ibid.

Wackwitz, B. Die Theorie des Prosastils im England des 18 Jahrhunderts. Hamburg 1962.

Boulton, J. T. The language of politics in the age of Wilkes and Burke. 1963.

Gordon, I. A. The movement of English prose. 1966.

Adolph, R. The rise of modern prose style. Cambridge Mass 1968.

Bailey, R. W. and D. M. Burton. English stylistics: a bibliography. Cambridge Mass 1968. Separate lists for 1660–1800.

(6) LITERATURE AND SCIENCE

Duncan, C. S. The new science and English literature in the classical period. Menasha 1913.

Greenlaw, E. The new science and English literature in the seventeenth century. Johns Hopkins Alumni Mag 13 1925.

Ornstein, M. The rôle of scientific societies in the seventeenth century. Chicago 1928.

Jones, R. F. Science and English prose style in the third quarter of the seventeenth century. PMLA 45 1930; rptd in Literary English since Shakespeare, ed G. Watson, New York 1970.

—— Science and language in England of the mid-seventeenth century. JEGP 31 1932.

—— Science and criticism in the neo-classical age of English literature. JHI 1 1940.

All rptd in Jones et al, The seventeenth century, Stanford 1951.

—— The background of the attack on science in the age of Pope. In Pope and his contemporaries: essays presented to George Sherburn, Oxford 1949.

—— The rhetoric of science in England of the mid-seventeenth century. In Restoration and eighteenth-century literature: essays in honor of A. D. McKillop, Chicago 1963.

Crum, R. B. Scientific thought in poetry. New York 1931.

Simpson, H. C. The vogue of science in English literature 1600–1800. UTQ 2 1933.

Nicolson, M. H. The microscope and English imagination. Northampton Mass 1935.

—— Milton and the telescope. ELH 2 1935.

—— The 'new astronomy' and English literary imagination. SP 32 1935.

—— The telescope and imagination. MP 32 1935.

All rptd in her Science and imagination, Ithaca 1956.

—— A world in the moon: a study of the changing attitude toward the moon in the seventeenth and eighteenth centuries. Northampton Mass 1936.

—— English almanacs and the 'new astronomy'. Annals of Science 4 1939.

—— Newton demands the Muse: Newton's Opticks and the eighteenth-century poets. Princeton 1946. *See also* W. P. Jones, Newton further demands the Muse, Stud in Eng Lit 1500–1900 3 1963.

—— Voyages to the moon. New York 1948.

—— The breaking of the circle: studies in the effect of the 'new science' upon seventeenth-century poetry. Evanston 1950, New York 1960 (rev).

Stimson, D. Puritanism and the new philosophy in seventeenth-century England. Bull Inst History of Medicine 3 1935.

Coffin, C. M. John Donne and the new philosophy. New York 1937.

Willey, B. The touch of cold philosophy. In R. F. Jones et al, The seventeenth century, Stanford 1951.

Literature and science: proceedings of the sixth triennial conference, Oxford 1954. Ed S. C. Aston et al, Oxford 1955.

Meyer, G. D. The scientific lady in England 1650–1760: an account of her rise, with emphasis on the major roles of the telescope and microscope. Berkeley 1955.

De Mott, B. Science versus mnemonics: note son John Ray and on John Wilkins' Essay toward a real character and a philosophical language. Isis 48 1957.

Jeffares, A. Norman. Language, literature and science: an inaugural lecture. Leeds 1959.

O'Malley, C. D. and A. R. Hall. Scientific literature in sixteenth- and seventeenth-century England. Los Angeles 1961.

Davie, D. The language of science and the language of literature 1700–40. 1963.

Jones, W. P. The rhetoric of science: a study of scientific ideas and imagery in eighteenth-century English poetry. 1966.

Shapiro, B. J. Latitudinarianism and science in seventeenth-century England. Past & Present 40 1968.

(7) THEMES AND SPECIAL TOPICS

Wirl, J. Orpheus in der englischen Literatur. Vienna 1913.

Duncan, C. S. The scientist as a comic type. MP 14 1916.

Kalkühler, F. Die Natur des Spleens bei den englischen Schriftstellern in der ersten Hälfte des 18 Jahrhunderts. Leipzig 1920.

Reynolds, M. The learned lady in England 1650–1760. Boston 1920.

Havemann, E. Kaufmann und Handel in der englischen schönen Literatur im Zeitalter der Königin Anna und George I. Freiburg 1921.

Kluckhohn, P. Die Auffassung der Liebe in der Literatur des 18 Jahrhunderts und in der deutschen Romantik. Halle 1922.

Hughes, W. J. Wales and the Welsh in English literature from Shakespeare to Scott. Wrexham 1924.

Bissell, B. The American Indian in English literature of the eighteenth century. New Haven 1925.

Janney, F. L. Childhood in English non-dramatic literature from 1557 to 1798. Greifswald 1925.

Brie, F. Imperialistische Strömungen in der englischen Literatur. Halle 1928 (2nd edn).

Schneider, Rudolf. Der Mönch in der englischen Dichtung bis auf Lewis's Monk 1795. Leipzig 1928.

Mezger, F. Der Ire in der englischen Literatur bis zum Anfang des 19 Jahrhunderts. Leipzig 1929.

Saupe, G. Die Sophonisbetragödien in der englischen Literatur des 17 und 18 Jahrhunderts. Halle-Wittenberg 1929.

Thomas, P. K. Die literarische Verkörperung des philan-thropischen Zuges in der englischen Aufklärung. Münsterberg 1929.

Marcus, H. Friedrich der Grosse in der englischen Literatur. Leipzig 1930.

Maxfield, E. K. The Quakers in English stage plays before 1800. PMLA 45 1930.

Pfitzner, K. Die Ausländertypen im englischen Drama der Restorationszeit. Breslau 1931.

Watson, H. F. The sailor in English fiction and drama 1550–1800. New York 1931.

Brinkley, R. F. Arthurian legend in the seventeenth century. Baltimore 1932.

Hecht, J. Der heroische Frauentyp im Restaurations-drama. Leipzig 1932.

Wind, E. Humanitätsidee und heroisiertes Porträt in der englischen Kultur des 18 Jahrhunderts. In England und die Antike: Vorträge der Bibliothek Warburg, Leipzig 1932.

Bamberger, B. Die Figur des Propheten in der englischen Literatur bis zum Ausgang des 18 Jahrhunderts. Würzburg 1934.

Frantz, R. W. The English traveller and the movement of ideas 1660–1732. Lincoln Nebraska 1934.

Marshall, R. Italy in English literature 1755–1814. New York 1934.

Leisering, W. Das Motiv des Einsiedlers in der englischen Literatur des 18 Jahrhunderts und der Hochromantik. Halle 1935.

Veen, H. R. S. van der. Jewish characters in eighteenth-century English fiction and drama. Groningen 1935.

Kain, R. M. The problem of civilization in English abolition literature 1772–1808. PQ 15 1936.

Mau, H. Das 'junge Mädchen', ein Beitrag zu dem Thema: die Frau in der Komödie der Restauration. Britannica 13 1936.

Slagle, K. C. The English country squire in English prose fiction from 1740 to 1800. Philadelphia 1938.

Modder, M. S. The Jew in the literature of England to the end of the 19th century. Philadelphia 1939.

Sypher, W. The West-Indian as a 'character' in the eighteenth century. SP 36 1939.

Stern, B. H. The rise of romantic Hellenism in English literature 1732–86. Menasha 1940.

Valency, M. J. The tragedies of Herod and Mariamne. New York 1940.

Boas, F. S. The soldier in Elizabethan and later English drama. Essays by Divers Hands new ser 19 1942.

Houghton, W. E., jr. The English virtuoso in the seventeenth century. JHI 3 1942.

Heilman, R. B. America in English fiction 1760–1800. Baton Rouge 1943.

Le Comte, E. S. Endymion in England. New York 1944.

Richmond, H. The naval officer in fiction. E & S 30 1945.

Mignon, E. Crabbed age and youth: the old men and women in the Restoration comedy of manners. Durham NC 1946.

Tarr, Sr Mary M. Catholicism in Gothic fiction 1762–1820. Washington 1946.

Brown, W. C. The Near East in English drama 1775–1825. JEGP 46 1947.

Heltzel, V. B. Fair Rosamund: a study of the development of a literary theme. Evanston 1947.

Anderson, G. K. The neo-classical chronicle of the Wandering Jew. PMLA 63 1948.

— The legend of the Wandering Jew. Providence 1965.

Smith, J. H. The gay couple in Restoration comedy. Cambridge Mass 1948.

Dobrée, B. The theme of patriotism in the poetry of the early eighteenth century. 1949.

Galbraith, L. H. The established clergy as depicted in English prose fiction from 1740 to 1800. Philadelphia 1950.

Berkeley, D. S. The penitent rake in Restoration comedy. MP 49 1952.

— The 'précieuse' or distressed heroine in Restoration comedy. Stillwater Oklahoma 1959.

Noyes, R. G. The Thespian mirror: Shakespeare in the eighteenth-century novel. Providence 1953.

— The neglected muse: Restoration and eighteenth-century tragedy in the novel 1740–80. Providence 1958.

Bartley, J. O. Teague, Shenkin and Sawney: being an historical study of the earliest Irish, Welsh and Scottish characters in English plays. Cork 1954.

Røstvig, M.-S. The happy man: studies in the metamorphoses of a classical ideal 1600–1700. Oslo 1954, 1962 (rev).

— The happy man, vol 2: 1700–60. Oslo 1958.

Dédéyan, C. Le thème de Faust dans la littérature européenne. 2 vols Paris 1954–5.

Mish, C. C. Reynard the fox in the seventeenth century. HLQ 17 1954.

Morton, R. and W. M. Peterson. Peter the Great and Russia in Restoration and eighteenth-century drama. N & Q Oct 1954.

Spencer, T. J. B. Fair Greece sad relic: literary philhellenism from Shakespeare to Byron. 1954.

Stanford, W. B. The Ulysses theme: a study in the adaptability of a traditional hero. Oxford 1954.

Wright, H. G. The theme of solitude and retirement in seventeenth-century literature. Etudes Anglaises 7 1954.

Bodmer, D. Die granadischen Romanzen in der europäischen Literatur: Untersuchung und Texte. Zürich 1955.

Meyer, G. D. The scientific lady in England 1650–1760. Berkeley 1955.

Axelrod, A. J. Le thème de Sophonisbe dans les principales tragédies de la littérature occidentale (France, Angleterre, Allemagne). Lille 1956.

Lindenberger, Ö. The transformations of Amphitryon. Stockholm 1956.

Ure, P. The widow of Ephesus: some reflections on an international comic theme. Durham Univ Jnl 49 1956.

Coveney, P. Poor monkey: the child in literature. 1957, 1967 (rev).

Kluth, K. Die Negerfrage in der englischen Literatur des 18 Jahrhunderts. Zeitschrift für Anglistik und Amerikanistik 5 1957.

Rodger, G. Hero and Leander in Scottish balladry. Comparative Lit 9 1957.

Taylor, G. R. The angel-makers: a study in the psychological origins of historical change 1750–1850. 1958. On heroines of fiction.

Fisch, H. The dual image: a study of the figure of the Jew in English literature. 1959.

Weinstein, Leo. The metamorphoses of Don Juan. Stanford 1959.

Rosenberg, E. From Shylock to Svengali: Jewish stereotypes in English fiction. Stanford 1960.

Mönch, W. Don Juan: ein Drama der europäischen Bühne. Revue de Littérature Comparée 35 1961.

Owen, A. L. The famous Druids: a survey of three centuries of English literature on the Druids. Oxford 1962.

Mandel, O. The theatre of Don Juan: a collection of plays and views 1630–1963, edited with a commentary. Lincoln Nebraska 1963.

Nichols, J. W. Shakespeare as a character in drama 1679–1899. Educational Theatre Jnl 15 1963.

Osborn, J. M. Travel literature and the rise of neohellenism in England. BNYPL May 1963.

Stanzel, F. K. Das Bild der Alpen in der englischen Literatur des 17 und 18 Jahrhunderts. Germanisch-romanische Monatsschrift new ser 14 1964.

Kallich, M. Oedipus: from man to archetype. Comparative Lit Stud 3 1966.

Traugott, J. The rake's progress from Court to comedy: a study in comic form. Stud in Eng Lit 1500–1900 6 1966.

Broich, U. Libertin und heroischer Held: das Drama der englischen Restaurationszeit und seine Leitbilder. Anglia 85 1967.

Silvette, H. The doctor on the stage: medicine and medical men in seventeenth-century England. Nashville 1967.

Vinge, L. The Narcissus theme in western European literature up to the early 19th century. Lund 1967.

Wolff, C. G. Literary reflections of the Puritan character. JHI 29 1968.

D. COLLECTIONS OF ESSAYS

Collections of miscellaneous unconnected studies, often rptd from periodicals and wholly or largely devoted to English literature 1660–1800.

D'Israeli, I. Calamities of authors. 2 vols 1812.

— Quarrels of authors. 3 vols 1814.

Macaulay, T. B. Critical and historical essays. 3 vols 1843.

Forster, J. Historical and biographical essays. Vol 2, 1858, 1860 (rev).

Stephen, L. Hours in a library. 3 sers 1874–9, 4 vols 1907 (rev).

— Studies of a biographer. 4 vols 1898–1902.

Dilke, C. W. The papers of a critic. 2 vols 1875.

Dennis, J. Studies in English literature. 1876.

Bagehot, W. Literary studies. 2 vols 1879.
Hitchman, F. Eighteenth-century studies. 1881.
Dobson, A. Eighteenth-century vignettes. 3 sers 1892–6, Oxford 1923 (WC).
— Miscellanies. 2 sers New York 1898–1901.
— Side-walk studies. 1902.
— Old Kensington Palace and other papers. 1910.
— At Prior Park and other papers. 1912.
— Rosalba's Journal and other papers. 1915.
— Later essays. 1921.
Collins, J. C. Essays and studies. 1895.
Dowden, E. Puritan and Anglican. 1900.
'Paston, George' (E. M. Symonds). Little memoirs of the eighteenth century. 1901.
— Sidelights on the Georgian period. 1902.
Elwin, W. Some eighteenth-century men of letters. 2 vols 1902.
More, P. E. The Shelburne essays. 11 sers New York 1904–Boston 1921. Especially ser 10, With the wits, 1919.
Birrell, A. In the name of the Bodleian and other essays. 1905.
Fyvie, J. Wits, beaux and beauties of the Georgian era. 1909.
— Noble dames and notable men of the Georgian era. 1910.
Eighteenth-century literature: an Oxford miscellany. Oxford 1910.
Strachey, L. Books and characters. 1922.
— Portraits in miniature. 1931.
Raleigh, W. Some authors. 1923.
Wilson, M. These were Muses. 1924.
Bracey, R. Eighteenth-century studies. Oxford 1925.
Ker, W. P. Collected essays. Ed C. Whibley 2 vols 1925. Includes The eighteenth century, 1916 (Eng Assoc lecture).
— On modern literature: lectures and addresses. Oxford 1955.
Grierson, H. J. C. Cross-currents in English literature of the xviith century. 1929.
Wallas, A. Before the Bluestockings. 1929.
Beresford, J. D. Mr Du Quesne and other essays. Oxford 1932.
Dobrée, B. Variety of ways. 1932.
— (ed). From Anne to Victoria. 1937.
Shafer, R. (ed). Seventeenth-century studies by members of the graduate school, University of Cincinnati. 2 vols Princeton 1933–7.
Praz, M. Studi e svaghi inglesi. Florence 1937.
Roberts, M. The modern mind. 1937.
Firth, C. H. Essays historical and literary. Oxford 1938.
Seventeenth-century essays presented to Sir Herbert Grierson. Oxford 1938.
Mackail, J. W. Studies in humanism. 1938.
Tompkins, J. M. S. The polite marriage: eighteenth-century essays. Cambridge 1938.
Tillotson, G. Essays in criticism and research. Cambridge 1942.
— Augustan studies. 1961.
Rowse, A. L. The English spirit: essays in history and literature. 1944.
Essays on the eighteenth century presented to David Nichol Smith. Oxford 1945.

Lovejoy, A. O. Essays in the history of ideas. Baltimore 1948.
— The thirteen pragmatisms and other essays. Baltimore 1963.
Pope and his contemporaries: essays presented to George Sherburn. Oxford 1949.
The age of Johnson: essays presented to C. B. Tinker. New Haven 1949.
The seventeenth century: studies in the history of English thought and literature from Bacon to Pope, by Richard Foster Jones and others writing in his honor. Stanford 1951.
Studies in the literature of the Augustan age: essays in honor of A. E. Case. Ann Arbor 1952.
Moore, C. A. Backgrounds of English literature 1700–60. Minneapolis 1953.
Studies in intellectual history, by the History of Ideas Club. Baltimore 1953.
Wimsatt, W. K., jr. The verbal icon: studies in the meaning of poetry. Lexington Kentucky 1954.
The rhetorical idiom: essays in rhetoric, oratory, language and drama presented to H. A. Wichelns, with a reprinting of his Literary criticism of oratory 1925. Ithaca 1958.
Roberts, S. C. Dr Johnson and others. Cambridge 1958.
Clifford, J. L. (ed). Eighteenth-century English literature: modern essays in criticism. New York 1959.
Schilling, B. N. (ed). Essential articles for the study of English Augustan backgrounds. Hamden Conn 1961.
Reason and the imagination, studies in the history of ideas 1600–1800: essays in honor of M. H. Nicolson. New York 1962.
Garrod, H. W. The study of good letters. Oxford 1963.
Plumb, J. H. Men and places. 1963.
Restoration and eighteenth-century literature: essays in honor of Alan Dugald McKillop. Chicago 1963.
Of books and humankind: essays and poems persented to Bonamy Dobrée. 1964.
Dyson, A. E. The crazy fabric: essays in irony. 1965.
From sensibility to romanticism: essays presented to Frederick A. Pottle. New York 1965.
Johnson, Boswell and their circle: essays presented to Lawrence Fitzroy Powell in honour of his eighty-fourth birthday. Oxford 1965.
Wasserman, E. R. (ed). Aspects of the eighteenth century. Baltimore 1965.
Renaissance and modern essays, presented to Vivian de Sola Pinto in celebration of his seventieth birthday. 1966.
Crane, R. S. The idea of the humanities and other essays critical and historical. 2 vols Chicago 1967.
Essays in English literature of the classical period presented to Dougald MacMillan. Chapel Hill 1967.
Studies in criticism and aesthetics 1660–1800: essays in honor of Samuel Holt Monk. Minneapolis 1967.
Brissenden, R. F. (ed). Studies in the eighteenth century: papers presented at the David Nichol Smith memorial seminar in Canberra 1966. Canberra 1968.
Bronson, B. H. Facets of the Enlightenment: studies in English literature and its contexts. Berkeley 1968.
Mack, M. and I. Gregor (ed). Imagined worlds: essays on some English novels and novelists in honour of John Butt. 1968.

II. LITERARY THEORY

The following omissions are to be noted: (1) Shakespearian criticism, for which see under Shakespeare, vol 1; (2) dramatic criticism, col 706, below; (3) periodical criticism (see Periodical Publications, col 1255, below); (4) prosody (see vol 1); (5) the theory of translation, col 1485, below.

(1) BIBLIOGRAPHIES

Spingarn, J. E. Critical essays of the seventeenth century. 3 vols Oxford 1908–9. Vol 3.

Durham, W. H. Critical essays of the eighteenth century 1700–25. New Haven 1915.

Krutch, J. W. Comedy and conscience after the Restoration. New York 1924. Pp. 259–64: Some critical works published between 1660 and 1700.

Draper, J. W. Eighteenth-century English aesthetics: a bibliography. Heidelberg 1931. Pt 1: General works on aesthetics; pt 2: Architecture and gardening; pt 3: Pictorial and plastic arts; pt 4: Literature and drama; pt 5: Music, including opera. Appendix: Some recent comment on eighteenth-century aesthetics. Includes some extracts from contemporary reviews and brief descriptions and references. Addns by R. D. Havens, MLN 47 1932; W. D. Templeman, MP 30 1933.

Maurocordato, A. La critique classique en Angleterre de la Restauration à la mort de Joseph Addison. Paris 1964. Pp. 619–731: Bibliographie raisonnée.

(2) MODERN STUDIES

General Surveys

Gayley, C. M. and F. N. Scott. A guide to the literature of aesthetics. Berkeley 1890.

— An introduction to the methods and materials of literary criticism. Boston 1899.

Wylie, L. J. Studies in the evolution of English criticism. Boston 1894.

Hamelius, P. Die Kritik in der englischen Literatur des 17 und 18 Jahrhunderts. Leipzig 1897.

Bray, J. W. History of English critical terms. Boston 1898.

Saintsbury, G. History of criticism and literary taste in Europe. 3 vols Edinburgh 1900–4.

— A history of English criticism. Edinburgh 1911. Excerpted from preceding.

Spingarn, J. E. Critical essays of the seventeenth century. 3 vols Oxford 1908–9. Introd.

Mainzer, P. Die schöne Literatur Englands und die literarische Kritik in einigen der kleineren englischen Zeitschriften des 18 Jahrhunderts. Leipzig 1911.

Petsch, R. Zur Geschichte der literarischen Kritik in England. Germanisch-romanische Monatsschrift 3 1911.

Miller, G. M. The historical point of view in English criticism from 1570–1770. Heidelberg 1913, Amsterdam 1967.

Durham, W. H. Critical essays of the eighteenth century 1700–25. New Haven 1915. Introd.

Routh, J. The rise of classical English criticism to the death of Dryden. New Orleans 1915.

Gayley, C. M. and B. P. Kurtz. Methods and materials of literary criticism: lyric, epic and allied forms. Boston 1920.

Omond, T. S. English metrists from Elizabethan times to the present day. Oxford 1921.

Folkierski, W. Entre le classicisme et le romantisme: étude sur l'esthétique et les esthéticiens du xviiie siècle. Paris 1925.

Wood, P. S. Native elements in English neo-classicism. MP 24 1926.

— The opposition to neo-classicism in England between 1660 and 1700. PMLA 43 1928.

Mirabent y Vilaplana, F. La estética inglesa del siglo xviii. Barcelona 1927.

Bredsdorff, M. Engelsk literaer kritik in det 18 aarhundert. Edda 29 1929.

Havens, R. D. Changing taste in the eighteenth century: a study of Dryden's and Dodsley's Miscellanies. PMLA 44 1929.

Bosker, A. Literary criticism in the age of Johnson. Groningen 1930; Groningen and New York 1953 (rev).

Vines, S. The course of English classicism. 1930.

Thomas, P. G. Aspects of literary theory and practice 1550–1870. 1931.

Draper, J. W. The rise of English neo-classicism. Revue Anglo-américaine 10 1933.

Williamson, G. The Restoration revolt against enthusiasm. SP 30 1933; rptd in his Seventeenth-century contexts, 1960.

Croce, B. Iniziazione all' estetica del settecento. In his Ultimi saggi, Bari 1934.

Green, F. C. Minuet: a critical survey of French and English literary ideas in the eighteenth century. 1935.

Steegman, J. The rule of taste: from George I to George IV. 1936, 1967.

Meinecke, F. Klassizismus, Romantizismus und historisches Denken im 18 Jahrhundert. In Authority and the individual: Harvard Tercentenary Conference of Arts and Sciences, Cambridge Mass 1937.

Gallaway, F. Reason, rule and revolt in English classicism. New York 1940.

Jonas, L. The divine science: the aesthetic of some representative seventeenth-century English poets. New York 1940. On Davenant, Cowley, Marvell, Denham.

Sharp, R. L. From Donne to Dryden: the revolt against metaphysical poetry. Chapel Hill 1940.

Crane, R. S. Neo-classical criticism. In Dictionary of world literature, ed J. T. Shipley, New York 1943; rptd in Critics and criticism ancient and modern, ed Crane, Chicago 1952.

— The languages of criticism and the structure of poetry. Toronto 1953.

— On writing the history of English criticism 1650–1800. UTQ 22 1953; rptd in his Idea of the humanities vol 2, Chicago 1967.

— Literature, philosophy and the history of ideas. MP 52 1954; rptd in his Idea of the humanities vol 1, Chicago 1967.

Bate, W. J. From classic to romantic: premises of taste in eighteenth-century England. Cambridge Mass 1946.

Bredvold, L. I. The rise of English classicism. Comparative Lit 2 1950.

Atkins, J. W. H. English literary criticism: seventeenth and eighteenth centuries. 1951.

Baine, R. M. The first anthologies of English literary criticism, Warton to Haslewood. SB 3 1951.

Kristeller, P. O. The modern system of the arts: a study in the history of aesthetics (II). JHI 13 1952.

Abrams, M. H. The mirror and the lamp: romantic theory and the critical tradition. New York 1953.

Marks, E. R. Relativist and absolutist: the early neo-classical debate in England. New Brunswick 1955.

—— The poetics of reason: English neoclassical criticism. New York 1966.

Walton, G. Metaphysical to Augustan: studies in tone and sensibility in the seventeenth century. 1955.

Wellek, R. A history of modern criticism 1750–1950. Vol 1: The later eighteenth century, New Haven 1955.

McCutcheon, R. P. Eighteenth-century aesthetics: a search for surviving values. Harvard Lib Bull 10 1956.

Frye, N. Anatomy of criticism: four essays. Princeton 1957.

Wimsatt, W. K., jr. and C. Brooks. Literary criticism: a short history. New York 1957. *See also* M. Krieger, Critical dogma and the new critical historians, Sewanee Rev 66 1958; and R. Marsh, The 'fallacy' of universal intention, MP 55 1958.

Hanzo, T. A. Latitude and Restoration criticism. Copenhagen 1961.

Allison, A. W. Toward an Augustan poetic: Edmund Waller's 'reform' of English poetry. Lexington Kentucky 1962.

Sackett, S. J. English literary criticism 1726–50. Fort Hays Stud (Literature ser) no 1 1962.

Watson, G. The literary critics: a study of English descriptive criticism. 1962 (Pelican), 1964 (rev).

Maurocordato, A. La critique classique en Angleterre de la Restauration à la mort de Joseph Addison: essai de définition. Paris 1964.

Marsh, R. Four dialectical theories of poetry: an aspect of English neoclassical criticism. Chicago 1965. On Shaftesbury, Akenside, Hartley, James Harris.

Melchionda, M. Davenant, Hobbes, Sprat: introduzione alla critica litteraria della Restaurazione. Filologia e Letteratura 11 1965.

Sen, S. K. English literary criticism in the second half of the eighteenth century: a reconsideration. Calcutta 1965.

Stone, P. W. K. The art of poetry 1750–1820: theories of poetic composition and style. 1967.

Thorpe, P. Some fallacies in the study of Augustan poetry. Criticism 9 1967.

Korshin, P. J. The evolution of neoclassical poetics: Cleveland, Denham and Waller as poetic theorists. Eighteenth-Century Stud 2 1968.

Critical Terms and Theories

The Ancients and Moderns Controversy

See C. Perrault, Parallèle des anciens et des modernes en ce qui concerne les arts et les sciences, ed H. R. Jauss and M. Imdahl, Munich 1964.

Rigault, H. Histoire de la querelle des anciens et des modernes. Paris 1856.

Diede, O. Der Streit der Alten und der Modernen in der englischen Literaturgeschichte des 16 und 17 Jahrhunderts. Greifswald 1912.

Gillot, H. La querelle des anciens et des modernes en France. Paris 1914.

Burlingame, A. E. The battle of the books in its historical setting. New York 1920.

Bury, J. B. The idea of progress. 1920, 1932.

Seeger, O. Die Auseinandersetzung zwischen Antike und Moderne in England bis zum Tode Dr Samuel Johnsons. Leipzig 1927.

Tilley, A. The decline of the age of Louis XIV. Cambridge 1929.

Jones, R. F. Ancients and moderns: a study of the background of the battle of the books. St Louis 1936, 1961 (rev with index and new preface).

Montgomery, G. Dryden and the battle of the books. Berkeley 1943.

Tuveson, E. L. Millennium and Utopia: a study in the background of the idea of progress. Berkeley 1949.

Maxwell, J. C. Charles Gildon and the quarrel of the ancients and moderns. RES new ser 1 1950.

Ginsberg, M. The idea of progress: a revaluation. 1953.

Baron, H. The querelle of the ancients and the moderns as a problem for Renaissance scholarship. JHI 20 1959.

Schueller, H. M. The quarrel of the ancients and the moderns. Music & Letters 41 1960.

Crane, R. S. The quarrel of the ancients and moderns and its consequences. In his Idea of the humanities vol 1, Chicago 1967.

Wager, W. W. Modern views of the origins of the idea of progress. JHI 28 1967.

Special Doctrines

Howard, W. G. Good taste and conscience. PMLA 25 1910.

Draper, J. W. Aristotelian mimesis in eighteenth-century England. PMLA 36 1921.

Nethercot, A. H. The term 'metaphysical poets' before Johnson. MLN 37 1922.

Wolf, H. Versuch einer Geschichte des Geniebegriffs in der deutschen Aesthetick des 18 Jahrhunderts: I, Von Gottsched bis auf Lessing. Heidelberg 1923.

Smith, L. P. Four words: romantic, originality, creative, genius. 1924 (Soc for Pure Eng); rptd in his Words and idioms, 1925.

Kaufman, P. Heralds of original genius. In Essays in memory of Barrett Wendell, Cambridge Mass 1926.

Zilsel, E. Die Entstehung des Geniebegriffs. Tübingen 1926.

Lovejoy, A. O. 'Nature' as aesthetic norm. MLN 42 1927.

—— The parallel of deism and classicism. MP 29 1932. *See also* R. N. Stromberg, Lovejoy's 'Parallel' reconsidered, Eighteenth-Century Stud 1 1968.

—— Reflections on human nature. Baltimore 1961.

Thüme, H. Beiträge zur Geschichte des Geniebegriffs in England. Halle 1927.

Bouillier, V. Silvain et Kant: ou les antécédents français de la théorie du sublime. Revue de Littérature Comparée 8 1928.

Granger, F. 'Magnificence' as a term of art. TLS 14 Aug 1930.

Tumarkin, A. Die Überwindung der Mimesislehre in der Kunsttheorie des xviii Jahrhunderts. In Festgabe Samuel Singer, ed H. Mayne et al, Tübingen 1930.

Lempicki, Z. Les idées directrices dans l'art et les catégories esthétiques au déclin du xviiie et au commencement du xixe siècle. Bulletin Internationale de l'Académie Polonaise des Sciences et des Lettres 1931.

Woodhouse, A. S. P. Collins and the creative imagination. In Studies in English by members of University College, Toronto 1931.

Bredvold, L. I. The tendency toward Platonism in neoclassical esthetics. ELH 1 1934.

Goodman, P. Neo-classicism, Platonism and romanticism. Jnl of Philosophy 31 1934.

Hooker, E. N. The discussion of taste, from 1750 to 1770, and the new trends in literary criticism. PMLA 49 1934.

—— The reviewers and the new criticism 1754–70. PQ 13 1934.

—— The reviewers and the new trends in poetry 1754–70. MLN 51 1936.

Sharp, R. L. The pejorative use of 'metaphysical'. MLN 49 1934.

Babcock, R. W. The idea of taste in the eighteenth century. PMLA 50 1935.

Bond, D. F. 'Distrust' of imagination in English neoclassicism. PQ 14 1935.

—— The neo-classical psychology of the imagination. ELH 4 1937.

Monk, S. H. The sublime: a study of critical theories in xviiith-century England. New York 1935, Ann Arbor 1960.

—— 'A grace beyond the reach of art.' JHI 5 1944.

Williamson, G. The rhetorical pattern of neo-classical wit.

MP 33 1935; rptd in his Seventeenth-century contexts, 1960.
—— 'Strong lines.' E Studies 18 1936; rptd in his Seventeenth-century contexts, 1960.
—— The proper wit of poetry. 1961.
Ustick, W. L. and H. H. Hudson. Wit, 'mixt wit' and the bee in amber. Huntington Lib Bull Oct 1935.
Scheffer, J. D. The idea of decline in literature and the fine arts in eighteenth-century England. MP 33 1936.
Wiley, M. L. 'Genius': a problem in definition. SE no 16 1936.
Fehr, B. The antagonism of forms in the eighteenth century. E Studies 18–19 1936–7; Frauenfeld 1944.
Carritt, E. F. Addison, Kant and Wordsworth. E & S 22 1937. On 'sublime', 'beauty' etc.
Thorpe, C. D. Addison and some of his predecessors on 'novelty'. PMLA 52 1937.
—— Some notices of 'empathy' before Lipps. Papers of Michigan Acad 23 1938.
Vietor, K. De sublimitate. Harvard Stud in Philology 19 1937.
Willey, B. The turn of the century. In Studies on the seventeenth century presented to Sir Herbert Grierson, Oxford 1938. On 'Nature'.
Mann, E. L. The problem of originality in English literary criticism 1750–1800. PQ 18 1939.
Larrabee, S. A. Il poco più and the school of taste. ELH 8 1941.
Emery, C. Optics and beauty. MLQ 3 1942.
Jones, R. F. The moral sense of simplicity. In Studies in honor of F. W. Shipley, St Louis 1942.
Brett, R. L. The aesthetic sense and taste in the literary criticism of the early eighteenth century. RES 20 1944.
Clough, W. O. Reason and genius: an eighteenth-century dilemma (Hogarth, Hume, Burke, Reynolds). PQ 23 1944.
Bate, W. J. The sympathetic imagination in eighteenth-century English criticism. ELH 12 1945.
Bullitt, J. M. and W. J. Bate. Distinctions between fancy and imagination in eighteenth-century English criticism. MLN 60 1945. See also E. R. Wasserman, Another eighteenth-century distinction, MLN 64 1949.
Taylor, H. W. 'Particular character': an early phase of a literary evolution. PMLA 60 1945.
Elledge, S. The background and development in English criticism of the theories of generality and particularity. PMLA 62 1947.
—— Cowley's ode Of wit and Longinus on the sublime: a study of one definition of the word 'wit'. MLQ 9 1948.
Faussett, H. I'A. The Augustan citadel. In his Poets and pundits, 1947.
Kennedy, W. L. The English heritage of Coleridge of Bristol 1798: the basis in eighteenth-century English thought for his distinction between imagination and fancy. New Haven 1947.
Abrams, M. H. Archetypal analogies in the language of criticism. UTQ 18 1949.
McKenzie, G. Critical responsiveness: a study of the psychological current in later eighteenth-century criticism. Berkeley 1949.
Ogden, H. V. S. The principles of variety and contrast in seventeenth-century aesthetics, and Milton's poetry. JHI 10 1949.
Ong, W. J. Psyche and the geometers: aspects of the associationist critical theory. MP 48 1951.
Smith, H. W. 'Reason' and the Restoration ethos. Scrutiny 18 1951.
Havens, R. D. Simplicity: a changing concept. JHI 14 1953.
Watson, G. 'Imagination' and 'fancy'. EC 3 1953.
Kallich, M. The argument against the association of ideas in eighteenth-century aesthetics. MLQ 15 1954.
Hipple, W. J., jr. The beautiful, the sublime and the picturesque in eighteenth-century British aesthetic theory. Carbondale 1957.

—— Philosophical language and the theory of beauty in the eighteenth century. In Studies in criticism and aesthetics 1660–1800: essays in honor of Samuel Holt Monk, Minneapolis 1967.
Goldberg, M. A. Wit and the imagination in eighteenth-century aesthetics. Jnl of Aesthetics 16 1958.
Borinski, L. Ideale der Restaurationszeit. In Festschrift für Walther Fischer, Heidelberg 1959.
Danzinger, M. K. Heroic villains in eighteenth-century criticism. Comparative Lit 11 1959.
Simon, I. 'Pride of reason' in the Restoration. Revue des Langues Vivantes 25 1959.
—— Critical terms in Restoration translations from the French. Revue Belge de Philologie et d'Histoire 42–3 1964–5.
Fraser, R. The origin of the term 'image'. ELH 27 1960.
Dulck, J. La définition de 'wit': position du problème. Etudes Anglaises 14 1961.
Knox, N. The word 'irony' and its context 1500–1755. Durham NC 1961.
Stolnitz, J. 'Beauty': some stages in the history of an idea. JHI 22 1961.
—— On the origins of 'aesthetic disinterestedness'. Jnl of Aesthetics 20 1961. See also M. Allentuck, A note on eighteenth-century 'disinterestedness', Jnl of Aesthetics 21 1962; R. G. Saisselin, A second note on eighteenth-century 'disinterestedness', ibid.
—— A third note on eighteenth-century 'disinterestedness'. Jnl of Aesthetics 22 1963.
Ramsey, Paul. The lively and the just: an argument for propriety. University Alabama 1962.
Kinghorn, A. M. Literary aesthetics and the sympathetic emotions: a main trend in eighteenth-century Scottish criticism. Stud in Scottish Lit 1 1963.
Edgley, R. The object of literary criticism. EC 14 1964.
Mattingly, A. S. Follow nature: a synthesis of eighteenth-century views. Speech Monographs 31 1964.
Papajewski, H. Chimäre und Metapher: ein Beitrag zum kritischen Problem von Phantasie und Rationalität im englischen Neoklassizismus. Anglia 82 1964.
Praz, M. Baroque in England. MP 61 1964.
Price, M. To the palace of wisdom: studies in order and energy from Dryden to Blake. Garden City NY 1964.
Schiller, J. An alternative to 'aesthetic disinterestedness'. Jnl of Aesthetics 22 1964.
Fussell, P. The rhetorical world of Augustan humanism: ethics and imagery from Swift to Burke. Oxford 1965.
Jackson, W. Affective values in later eighteenth-century aesthetics. Jnl of Aesthetics 24 1965.
—— Affective values in early eighteenth-century aesthetics. Jnl of Aesthetics 27 1968.
Wittkower, R. Imitation, eclecticism and genius. In Aspects of the eighteenth century, ed E. R. Wasserman, Baltimore 1965.
Johnson, J. W. The formation of neo-classical thought. Princeton 1967.
Klein, H. There is no disputing about taste: Untersuchung zum englischer Geschmacksbegriff im 18 Jahrhundert. Münster 1967.
Boyd, J. S. The function of mimesis and its decline. Cambridge Mass 1968.
Sanders, C. 'First follow nature': an annotation. E Studies 49 1968.
Youngren, W. H. Generality, science and poetic language in the Restoration. ELH 35 1968.

Particular Forms

For drama see col 701, below.

Poetry

Hustvedt, S. B. Ballad criticism in Scandinavia and Great Britain during the eighteenth century. New York 1916.
Smith, M. E. The fable as poetry in English criticism. MLN 32 1917.

Whitney, L. English primitivistic theories of epic origins. MP 21 1924.

Partridge, E. The 1762 efflorescence of poetics. SP 25 1928.

Lange, V. Die Lyrik und ihr Publikum im England des 18 Jahrhunderts: eine geschmacks-geschichtliche Untersuchung über die englischen Anthologien von 1670–1780. Weimar 1935.

Behrens, I. Die Lehre von der Einteilung der Dichtkunst vornehmlich vom 16 bis 19 Jahrhundert. Halle 1940.

Swedenberg, H. T. The theory of the epic in England 1650–1800. Berkeley 1944.

Perkinson, R. H. The epic in five acts. SP 43 1946.

Myers, R. M. Neo-classical criticism of the ode for music. PMLA 62 1947.

Herrick, M. T. The place of rhetoric in poetic theory. Quart Jnl of Speech 34 1948.

Jones, C. E. Poetry and the Critical Review 1756–85. MLQ 9 1948.

Miles, J. The primary language of poetry in the 1740's and 1840's. Berkeley 1950.

Millar, B. P. Eighteenth-century views of the ballad. Western Folklore 9 1950.

Wallerstein, R. Studies in seventeenth-century poetic. Madison 1950.

Wasserman, E. R. The inherent values of eighteenth-century personification. PMLA 65 1950.

Mace, D. T. The doctrine of sound and sense in Augustan poetic theory. RES new ser 2 1951.

Congleton, J. E. Theories of pastoral poetry in England 1684–1798. Gainesville 1952.

Greene, D. J. 'Logical structure' in eighteenth-century poetry. PQ 31 1952.

Maclean, N. From action to image: theories of the lyric in the eighteenth century. In Critics and Criticism ancient and modern, ed R. S. Crane, Chicago 1952.

Cohen, R. Association of ideas and poetic unity. PQ 36 1957.

Stewart, K. The ballad and the genres in the eighteenth century. ELH 24 1957.

Fabian, B. Die didaktische Dichtung in der englischen Literaturtheorie des achtzehnten Jahrhunderts. In Festschrift für Walther Fischer, Heidelberg 1959.

Friedman, A. B. The ballad revival. Chicago 1961.

Leach, M. and T. P. Coffin (ed). The critics and the ballad. Carbondale 1961.

Pagrot, L. Den klassiska Verssatirens teori: debatten kring genren från Horatius t.o.m. 1700–talet. Stockholm 1961.

Foerster, D. M. The fortunes of epic poetry: a study in English and American criticism 1750–1950. Washington 1962.

Levine, J. A. The status of the verse epistle before Pope. SP 59 1962.

Marks, E. R. Pragmatic poetics: Dryden to Valéry. Bucknell Rev 10 1962.

Suzuki, Z. The background of the pastoral controversy in the eighteenth century. Stud in Eng Lit (Tokyo) 40 1964. In Japanese, with English synopsis.

Lessenich, R. P. Dichtungsgeschmack und althebräische Bibelpoesie im 18 Jahrhundert: zur Geschichte der englischen Literaturkritik. Cologne 1967.

Broich, U. Studien zum komischen Epos. Tübingen 1968.

Fowler, D. C. A literary history of the popular ballad. Durham NC 1968.

References to the theory of poetry will also be found under Poetry, col 313, below.

Prose Fiction

Tieje, A. J. The expressed aim of long prose fiction from 1579 to 1740. JEGP 11 1912.
—— The theory of characterization in prose fiction prior to 1740. Minneapolis 1916.

Heidler, J. B. The history from 1700–1800 of English criticism of prose fiction. Urbana 1928.

Gove, P. B. The imaginary voyage in prose fiction: a history of its criticism and a guide to its study. New York 1941.

Taylor, J. T. Early opposition to the English novel: the popular reaction from 1760 to 1830. New York 1943.

Cooke, A. L. Some sidelights on the theory of the Gothic romance. MLQ 12 1951.

Dooley, D. J. Some uses and mutations of the picaresque. Dalhousie Rev 37 1958.

Jones, C. E. The English novel: a Critical view 1756–85. MLQ 19 1958.

Corstius, J. C. B. Prelude to the historical novel: new eighteenth-century views on history and novel. In Comparative Literature: Proceedings of the Second Congress, Chapel Hill 1959.

Mylne, V. G. Changing attitudes towards truth in fiction. Renaissance & Modern Stud 7 1963.

Baker, S. The idea of romance in the eighteenth-century novel. Papers of Michigan Acad 49 1964.

Goldberg, H. Comic prose epic or comic romance: the argument of the preface to Joseph Andrews. PQ 43 1964.

Frohock, W. M. The idea of the picaresque. Yearbook of Comparative & General Lit 16 1967.

Park, W. Change in the criticism of the novel after 1760. PQ 46 1967.

Barnett, G. L. (ed). Eighteenth-century British novelists on the novel. New York 1968.

Simon, I. Early theories of prose fiction: Congreve and Fielding. In Imagined worlds: essays on some English novels and novelists in honour of John Butt. 1968.

Stewart, K. History, poetry and the terms of fiction in the eighteenth century. MP 66 1968.

Earlier Literature
in order of subject

McKillop, A. D. A critic of 1741 on early poetry. SP 30 1933.

Kliger, S. The neo-classical view of Old English poetry. JEGP 49 1950.

Stewart, K. Ancient poetry as history in the eighteenth century. JHI 19 1958.

Birrell, T. A. The Society of Antiquaries and the taste for Old English 1705–1840. Neophilologus 50 1966.

Brinkley, R. F. Arthurian legend in the seventeenth century. Baltimore 1932.

Weisinger, H. The Middle Ages and the late eighteenth-century historians. PQ 27 1948.

Johnston, A. K. Enchanted ground: the study of medieval romance in the eighteenth century. 1964.

Weisinger, H. The study of the revival of learning in England from Bacon to Hallam. PQ 25 1946.
—— The English origins of the sociological interpretation of the renaissance. JHI 11 1950.

Williams, R. D. Antiquarian interest in Elizabethan drama before Lamb. PMLA 53 1938.

Hunt, C. The Elizabethan background of neoclassic polite verse. ELH 8 1941.

Weisinger, H. The seventeenth-century reputation of the Elizabethans. MLQ 6 1945.

Wasserman, E. R. Elizabethan poetry in the eighteenth century. Urbana 1947.

Rulfs, D. J. Reception of the Elizabethan playwrights on the London stage 1776–1833. SP 46 1949.

Nethercot, A. H. The reputation of the 'Metaphysical' poets during the seventeenth century. JEGP 23 1924.
—— The reputation of the 'Metaphysical' poets during the age of Pope. PQ 4 1925.
—— The reputation of the 'Metaphysical' poets during the age of Johnson and the romantic revival. SP 22 1925.

—— The reputation of native versus foreign Metaphysical poets in England. MLR 25 1930.

Sharp, R. L. From Donne to Dryden: the revolt against Metaphysical poetry. Chapel Hill 1940.

Sorelius, G. 'The giant race before the flood': Pre-Restoration drama on the stage and in the criticism of the Restoration. Upsala 1966.

Particular Authors

excluding Shakespeare (see vol 1) and writers between 1660 and 1800.

Bacon
Cochrane, R. C. Francis Bacon in early eighteenth-century English literature. PQ 37 1958.
Bevilacqua, V. M. Baconian influences in the development of Scottish rhetorical theory. Proc Amer Philosophical Soc 3 1967.

Beaumont and Fletcher
Sprague, A. C. Beaumont and Fletcher on the Restoration stage. Cambridge Mass 1926.
Wilson, J. H. The influence of Beaumont and Fletcher on Restoration drama. Columbus 1928.
Appleton, W. W. Beaumont and Fletcher: a critical study. 1956.

Chaucer
Five hundred years of Chaucer criticism and allusion. Ed C. F. E. Spurgeon 3 vols Cambridge 1925.
Bond, R. P. Some eighteenth-century Chaucer allusions. SP 25 1928.
—— et al. A collection of Chaucer allusions. SP 28 1931.
Boys, R. C. Some Chaucer allusions 1705–99. PQ 17 1938.
Oliver, A. M. Chaucer allusions in xviii-century minor poetry. N & Q 5 Feb 1938.
Harris, B. Some seventeenth-century Chaucer allusions. PQ 18 1939.
Zimansky, C. A. Chaucer and the School of Provence: a problem in eighteenth-century literary history. PQ 25 1946.
Dandridge, E. P., jr. An eighteenth-century theft of Chaucer's 'purse'. MLN 68 1953.
Dobbins, A. C. More seventeenth-century Chaucer allusions. MLN 68 1953.
—— Chaucer allusions 1619–1732. MLQ 18 1957.

Cleveland
Kimmey, J. L. John Cleveland and the satiric couplet in the Restoration. PQ 37 1958.

Cowley
Nethercot, A. H. The reputation of Abraham Cowley 1660–1800. PMLA 38 1923.
Loiseau, J. Abraham Cowley's reputation in England. Paris 1931.
Rawlinson, D. Cowley and the current status of Metaphysical poetry. EC 13 1963.
Spencer, L. M. G. Johnson and Cowley. New Rambler 3 1967.

Crashaw
Warren, A. The reputation of Crashaw in the seventeenth and eighteenth centuries. SP 31 1934.

Denham
Aubin, R. A. Materials for a study of the influence of Cooper's Hill. ELH 1 1934.

Donne
Nethercot, A. H. The reputation of John Donne as a metrist. Sewanee Rev 30 1922.
Potter, G. R. Donne's Paradoxes in 1707. MLN 55 1940.
Stein, A. Donne and the couplet. PMLA 57 1942.
Milgate, W. References to John Donne. N & Q Oct 1953.
Alvarez, A. The school of Donne. 1961.

Sparrow, J. George Herbert and John Donne among the Moravians. BNYPL Dec 1964.

Drayton
Noyes, R. Drayton's literary vogue since 1631. Indiana Univ Stud 22 1935.

Fairfax
Bell, C. C. A history of Fairfax criticism. PMLA 62 1947.

Fletcher
Wasserman, E. R. Moses Browne and the 1783 edition of Giles and Phineas Fletcher. MLN 56 1941.

Geoffrey of Monmouth
Jones, E. Geoffrey of Monmouth 1640–1800. Berkeley 1944.

Herbert
Select hymns taken out of Mr Herbert's Temple 1697. Ed W. E. Stephenson, Los Angeles 1962 (Augustan Reprint Soc).
Sloane, W. George Herbert's reputation 1650–1710: good reading for the young. N & Q June 1962.
Williamson, K. Herbert's reputation in the eighteenth century. PQ 41 1962.
Sparrow, J. George Herbert and John Donne among the Moravians. BNYPL Dec 1964.

Herrick
Roeckerath, N. Der Nachruhm Herricks und Wallers. Leipzig 1931.
Hooker, E. N. Herrick and song-books. TLS 2 March 1933. *See also* 20 April, 1, 22 June 1933.

Heywood
Wright, L. B. Notes on Thomas Heywood's later reputation. RES 4 1928.

Jonson
Schelling, F. E. Ben Jonson and the classical school. PMLA 13 1898; rptd in his Shakespeare and 'Demi-science', Philadelphia 1927.
Noyes, R. G. Ben Jonson on the English stage 1660–1776. Cambridge Mass 1935.
—— Ben Jonson's masques in the eighteenth century. SP 33 1936.
Graham, C. B. Jonson allusions in Restoration comedy. RES 15 1939.
Bentley, G. E. Shakespeare and Jonson: their reputations in the seventeenth century compared. 2 vols Chicago 1945.
Tiedje, E. Die Tradition Ben Jonsons in der Restaurationskömodie. Hamburg 1963.

Layamon
Willard, R. Layamon in the seventeenth and eighteenth centuries. SE 27 1948.

Massinger
McManaway, J. G. Philip Massinger and the Restoration drama. ELH 1 1934.
Kermode, J. F. A note on the history of Massinger's The fatal dowry in the eighteenth century. N & Q 3 May 1947.

Milton
Dowden, E. Milton in the eighteenth century 1701–50. Proc Br Acad 3 1908.
Good, J. W. Studies in the Milton tradition. Urbana 1915.
Havens, R. D. The influence of Milton on English poetry. Cambridge Mass 1922.
Gertsch, A. Der steigende Ruhm Miltons: die Geschichte einer Heteronomie der literarischen Urteilsbildung. Leipzig 1927.
Moore, C. A. Miltoniana 1679–1741. MP 24 1927.
Oras, A. Milton's editors and commentators. Dorpat 1931.
—— Milton's editors and commentators from Patrick Hume to H. J. Todd 1695–1801: a study in critical views and methods. 1931.
Parker, W. R. Milton's contemporary reputation. Columbus 1940. With list of Milton references 1641–74.

Alspach, R. K. A Dublin Milton enthusiast. MLN 61 1941. On Samuel Whyte.

Aubin, R. A. Nathanael Salmon on Milton 1728. MLN 56 1941.

Shudofsky, M. M. An early eighteenth-century rhymed paraphrase of Paradise Lost II 1–225. MLN 56 1941.

Barker, A. '. . . And on his crest sat horror': eighteenth-century interpretations of Milton's sublimity and his Satan. UTQ 11 1942.

Wasserman, E. R. Early evidences of Milton's influence. MLN 58 1943. On poems of 1712, 1728.

Sensabaugh, G. F. Milton in the revolution settlement. HLQ 9 1946.

— Milton and the doctrine of passive obedience. HLQ 13 1950.

— Adaptations of Areopagitica. Ibid.

— Milton bejesuited. SP 47 1950.

— Milton and the attempted Whig revolution. In The seventeenth century: studies in the history of English thought and literature from Bacon to Pope, by R. F. Jones and others writing in his honor, Stanford 1951.

— That grand Whig Milton. Stanford 1952.

Anderson, P. B. Anonymous critic of Milton: Richard Leigh? or Samuel Butler? SP 44 1947.

Moore, J. R. Milton among the Augustans: the infernal council. SP 48 1951.

Schick, G. B. Appreciation of Milton as a criterion of eighteenth-century taste. N & Q March 1957.

Browne, R. B. Dryden and Milton in nineteenth-century 'popular' song-books. Bull of Bibliography 22 1958.

Gossman, A. and G. W. Whiting. Comus, once more, 1761. RES new ser 11 1960.

Riffe, N. L. Eighteenth-century translation of Milton into Latin. N & Q April 1965.

— Milton in the eighteenth-century periodicals: 'Hail, wedded love!' N & Q Jan 1965. On lines frequently quoted 1709–75.

— Milton's minor poetry in British periodicals before 1740. N & Q Dec 1965.

Williamson, G. Dryden's view of Milton. In his Milton and others, 1965.

Fogle, R. H. Johnson and Coleridge on Milton. Bucknell Rev 14 1966.

Sir Thomas More
Hudson, H. T. Current English translations of the Praise of folly. PQ 20 1941.

Quarles
Nethercot, A. H. The literary legend of Francis Quarles. MP 20 1923.

Spenser
Cory, H. E. The critics of Edmund Spenser. Berkeley 1911.

Wurtsbaugh, J. Two centuries of Spenserian scholarship 1609–1805. Baltimore 1936.

Hook, J. N. Three imitations of Spenser. MLN 55 1940.

Baker, C. Spenser, the eighteenth century and Shelley's Queen Mab. MLQ 2 1941.

Judson, A. C. The seventeenth-century lives of Edmund Spenser. HLQ 10 1946.

— The eighteenth-century lives of Edmund Spenser. HLQ 16 1953.

Mueller, W. R. Spenser's critics: changing currents in literary taste. Syracuse 1959.

St Thomas Aquinas
Ryan, J. K. The reputation of St Thomas Aquinas among English Protestant thinkers of the seventeenth century. New Scholasticism 22 1948.

Waller
Roeckerath, N. Der Nachruhm Herricks und Wallers. Leipzig 1931.

Foreign Sources and Influences

See also Literary Relations with the Continent, below.

Harrison, C. T. The ancient atomists and English literature of the seventeenth century. Harvard Stud 45 1934.

Humphreys, A. R. A classical education and eighteenth-century poetry. Scrutiny 8 1939.

Thomson, J. A. K. The classical background of English literature. 1948.

— Classical influences on English poetry. 1951.

— Classical influences on English prose. 1956.

Highet, G. The classical tradition: Greek and Roman influences on western literature. New York 1949.

Bolgar, R. R. The classical heritage and its beneficiaries. Cambridge 1954.

Clarke, M. L. Classical education in Britain 1500–1900. Cambridge 1959.

Fisch, H. Jerusalem and Albion: the Hebraic factor in seventeenth-century literature. New York 1964.

Ogilvie, R. M. Latin and Greek: a history of the influence of the classics on English life from 1600 to 1918. 1964.

Meller, H. and H.-J. Zimmermann (ed). Lebende Antike: Symposion für Rudolf Sühnel. Berlin 1967.

Greek

Clarke, M. L. Greek studies in England 1700–1830. Cambridge 1945.

Aesop
Smith, M. E. Aesop, a decayed personality: changing conception as to Aesop's personality in English writers before Gay. PMLA 46 1931.

Aristotle
Cooper, L. and A. Gudeman. A bibliography of the Poetics of Aristotle. New Haven 1928; suppl by M. T. Herrick, Amer Jnl of Philology 52 1931.

Herrick, M. T. The Poetics of Aristotle in England. New Haven 1930.

Cooper, L. The Poetics of Aristotle: its meaning and influence. Ithaca 1956.

Riley, L. W. Aristotle texts and commentaries to 1700 in the University of Pennsylvania library: a catalogue. Philadelphia 1961.

Olson, E. (ed). Aristotle's Poetics and English literature. Chicago 1965.

Epicurus
Mayo, T. F. Epicurus in England 1650–1725. Dallas 1934.

Homer
Wild, F. Die Batrachomyomachia in England. Vienna 1918.

Foerster, D. M. Homer in English criticism: the historical approach in the eighteenth century. New Haven 1947.

Myres, J. L. Homer and his critics. Ed D. Gray 1958.

Broich, U. Batrachomyomachia und Margites als literarische Vorbilder: einige Bemerkungen zu einem literarkritischen Topos. In Symposion für Rudolf Sühnel, Berlin 1967.

Longinus
Rosenberg, A. Longinus in England bis zum Ende des 18 Jahrhunderts. Berlin 1917.

Henn, T. R. Longinus and English criticism. Cambridge 1934.

Monk, S. H. The sublime: a study of critical theories in xviii-century England. New York 1935.

Nitchie, E. Longinus and the theory of poetic imitation in seventeenth- and eighteenth-century England. SP 32 1935.

Plato
Shorey, P. Platonism ancient and modern. Berkeley 1938.

Evans, F. B. Platonic scholarship in eighteenth-century England. MP 41 1943.

Theocritus

Kerlin, R. T. Theocritus in English literature. Lynchburg Virginia 1910.

Latin

Catullus

Duckett, E. S. Catullus in English poetry. Menasha 1925.

McPeek, J. A. S. Catullus in strange and distant Britain. Cambridge Mass 1939.

Cicero

Rolfe, J. C. Cicero and his influence. 1923.

Horace

Goad, C. Horace in the English literature of the xviiith century. New Haven 1918.

Showerman, G. Horace and his influence. Boston 1922.

Saintonge, P. F., L. G. Burgevin and H. Griffith. Horace: three phases of his influence. Chicago 1936.

Papajewski, H. Die Bedeutung der Ars poetica für den englischen Neoklassizismus. Anglia 79 1962.

Juvenal

Whitford, R. C. Juvenal in England 1750-1802. PQ 7 1928.

Lucretius

Hadzsits, G. D. Lucretius and his influence. New York 1935.

Shapiro, L. Lucretian 'domestic melancholy' and the tradition of Vergilian 'frustration'. PMLA 53 1938.

Hathaway, B. The Lucretian 'return upon ourselves' in eighteenth-century theories of tragedy. PMLA 62 1947.

Fleischmann, W. B. Lucretius and English literature 1680-1740. Paris 1964.

Martial

Nixon, P. Martial and the modern epigram. New York 1927.

Ovid

Papajewski, H. Die literarische Wertung Ovids am Ausgang des 17 und zu Beginn des 18 Jahrhunderts. Anglia 78 1960.

Dörrie, H. L'épître héroique dans les littératures modernes: recherches sur la postérité des Epistulae Heroidum d'Ovide. Revue de Littérature Comparée 40 1966.

Persius

Frost, W. English Persius: the golden age. Eighteenth-Century Stud 2 1968.

Silius Italicus

Bassett, E. L. Silius Italicus in England. Classical Philology 48 1953.

Virgil

Mustard, W. P. Virgil's Georgics and the British poets. Baltimore 1908.

Nitchie, E. Vergil and the English poets. New York 1919.

Mackail, J. W. Virgil and his meaning to the world of today. Boston 1922.

Olivero, F. Virgil in xvii- and xviii-century English literature. Poetry Rev 21 1930.

— Allusions to Vergil in the 17th and 18th centuries. In Studi britannici, Turin 1931.

Gordon, G. Virgil in English poetry. 1931.

Boddy, M. P. The 1692 fourth book of Virgil. RES new ser 15 1964.

French

Dowden, E. The French Revolution and English literature. 1897.

Vreeland, W. V. Etude sur les rapports littéraires entre Genève et l'Angleterre jusqu'à la publication de la Nouvelle Héloïse. Geneva 1901.

Charlanne, L. L'influence française en Angleterre au xviie siècle. Paris 1906.

Macintire, E. J. French influence on the beginnings of English classicism. PMLA 26 1911.

Wollstein, R. H. English opinions of French poetry 1660-1750. New York 1923.

Wray, E. English adaptations of French drama between 1780 and 1815. MLN 43 1928.

Kinne, A. W. Revivals and importations of French comedies in England 1749-1800. New York 1939.

Dechamps, J. La révolution française et les lettres anglaises. Comparative Lit Stud 2 1941.

— Les Îles britanniques et la Révolution française 1789-1803. Brussels 1949.

Adams, M. R. Studies in the background of English radicalism, with special reference to the French Revolution. Lancaster Pa 1947.

Tucker, J. E. John Davies of Kidwelly 1627?-93, translator from the French, with an annotated bibliography of his translations. PBSA 44 1950.

Quaintance, R. E. French sources of the Restoration Imperfect enjoyment poem. PQ 42 1963.

Boileau

Clark, A. F. B. Boileau and the French classical critics in England 1660-1830. Paris 1925.

Bouhours

Hamm, V. M. Father Dominic Bouhours and neo-classical criticism. In Jesuit thinkers of the Renaissance: essays presented to John F. McCormick SJ, Milwaukee 1939.

Corneille

Voisine, J. Corneille et Racine en Angleterre au xviiie siècle. Revue de Littérature Comparée 22 1948.

Hartnoll, P. Corneille in England. Theatre Research 7 1958.

Descartes

Nicolson, M. H. The early stage of Cartesianism in England. SP 26 1929.

Lamprecht, S. P. The role of Descartes in seventeenth-century England. Stud in History of Ideas 3 1935.

Garai, P. Le cartésianisme et le classicisme anglais. Revue de Littérature Comparée 31 1957.

Saveson, J. E. Differing reactions to Descartes among the Cambridge Platonists. JHI 21 1960.

Du Bos

Lombard, A. L'Abbé du Bos, un initiateur de la pensée moderne 1670-1742. Paris 1913.

Du Fresnoy

Folkierski, W. Ut pictura poesis: ou l'étrange fortune du De arte graphica de Du Fresnoy en Angleterre. Revue de Littérature Comparée 27 1953.

Lipking, L. The shifting nature of authority in versions of De arte graphica. Jnl of Aesthetics 23 1965.

Encyclopédie

Lough, J. The Encyclopédie in eighteenth-century Scotland. MLR 38 1943.

Genlis, Mme de

Wahba, M. Madame de Genlis in England. Comparative Lit 13 1961. On the epistolary courtesy-book.

La Rochefoucauld

Tucker, J. E. The earliest English translation of La Rochefoucauld's Maximes. MLN 64 1949.

Pagliaro, H. E. Paradox in the aphorisms of La Rochefoucauld and some representative English followers. PMLA 79 1964.

Malebranche

Hankins, T. L. The influence of Malebranche on the science of mechanics during the eighteenth century. JHI 28 1967.

Molière

Gillet, J. E. Molière en Angleterre 1660-70. Brussels and Paris 1913.

Wilcox, J. The relation of Molière to Restoration comedy. New York 1938.

Tucker, J. E. The eighteenth-century English translations of Molière. MLQ 3 1942.

Mandach, A. de. The first translation of Molière in the world. Comparative Lit Stud 21-2 1946.

— Molière et la comédie des moeurs en Angleterre 1660-8. Neuchâtel 1946.

Jones, C. E. Molière in England to 1775: a checklist. N & Q Sept 1957.

Copley, J. On translating Molière into English. Durham Univ Jnl 52 1960.

Montaigne

Dédéyan, C. Montaigne chez ses amis anglo-saxons. 2 vols Paris 1946.

Montesquieu

Fletcher, F. T. H. Montesquieu and English politics 1750-1800. 1939.

— Montesquieu and British education in the eighteenth century. MLR 38 1943.

Lough, J. L'esprit des lois in a Scottish university in the eighteenth century. Comparative Lit Stud 13 1944.

Pascal

Jansen, P. De Blaise Pascal à Henry Hammond: les Provinciales en Angleterre. Paris 1954.

Rabelais

Brown, H. Rabelais in English literature. Cambridge Mass 1933.

Racine. See also Corneille, above.

Wheatley, K. E. Racine and English classicism. Austin 1956.

Ramus

Howell, W. S. Ramus and English rhetoric 1574-1681. Quart Jnl of Speech 37 1951.

Rapin

Dubois-Pichler, E. T. Influence exercée en Angleterre par les Hortorum libris IV du P. Rapin. XVII Siècle: Bulletin de la Société d'Étude du XVIIᵉ Siècle 20 1953.

Rousseau, J.-B.

Grubbs, H. A. The vogue of Jean-Baptiste Rousseau. PMLA 55 1940.

Rousseau, J. J.

Texte, J. Rousseau et les origines du cosmopolitisme littéraire au xviiiᵉ siècle. Paris 1895; tr 1899.

Warner, J. H. The reaction in eighteenth-century England to Rousseau's two Discours. PMLA 48 1933.

— Eighteenth-century English reactions to the Nouvelle Héloïse. PMLA 52 1937.

— The basis of Rousseau's contemporary reputation in England. MLN 55 1940.

— Emile in eighteenth-century England. PMLA 59 1944.

Sewall, R. B. Rousseau's First discourse in England. PMLA 52 1937.

— Rousseau's Second discourse in England from 1755 to 1762. PQ 17 1938.

— Rousseau's Second discourse in England and Scotland from 1762 to 1772. PQ 18 1939.

— An early manuscript translation of Rousseau's second Discours. MLN 57 1942.

Roddier, H. Rousseau en Angleterre au xviiiᵉ siècle: l'oeuvre et l'homme. Paris 1950.

Voisine, J. Rousseau en Angleterre à l'époque romantique: les écrits autobiographiques et la légende. Paris 1956.

Barber, G. G. Two English editions of La nouvelle Héloïse. MLR 56 1961.

Saint-Pierre

Wallas, M. Sur la fortune de l'abbé de Saint-Pierre en Angleterre au xviiiᵉ Siècle. Revue de Littérature Comparée 20 1940.

Voltaire

Oake, R. B. Political elements in criticism of Voltaire in England 1732-47. MLN 57 1942.

Hennig, J. Voltaire in Ireland. Dublin Mag 19 1944.

Evans, H. B. A bibliography of eighteenth-century translations of Voltaire. In Studies presented to R. L. Graeme Ritchie, Cambridge 1949.

Schilling, B. N. Conservative England and the case against Voltaire. New York 1950.

Italian

Quigley, H. Italy and the rise of a new school of criticism in the eighteenth century. Perth 1921.

Robertson, J. G. Studies in the genesis of romantic theory in the eighteenth century. Cambridge 1923. On Italy and Germany.

Babcock, R. W. English interest in Italy and Italian romantic criticism in the eighteenth century. PQ 26 1947.

Baretti

Gallup, D. C. Baretti's reputation in England. In The age of Johnson: essays presented to C. B. Tinker. New Haven 1949.

Boccaccio

Wright, H. G. Boccaccio in England from Chaucer to Tennyson. 1957.

Boccalini

Brotanek, R. Trajano Boccalinis Einfluss auf die englische Literatur. Archiv 111 1903.

Thomas, R. Trajano Boccalini's influence upon English literature. Aberystwyth Univ Stud 3 1922.

Conti

Hamm, V. M. Antonio Conti and English aesthetics. Comparative Lit 8 1956.

Machiavelli

Raab, F. The English face of Machiavelli: a changing interpretation 1500-1700. Toronto 1964.

Vico

Vico, G. Autobiography. Tr Ithaca 1944. Introd.

German

Stokoe, F. W. German influences in the English romantic period 1788-1818. Cambridge 1926.

Stockley, V. German literature as known in England 1750-1830. 1929.

Allen, D. C. Early eighteenth-century literary relations between England and Germany. MLN 49 1934.

Price, L. M. Holland as a mediator of English-German literary influences in the seventeenth and eighteenth centuries. MLQ 2 1941.

Roloff, W., M. Mix and M. Nicolai. German literature in British magazines 1750-1860. Ed B. Q. Morgan and A. R. Hohlfeld, Madison 1949.

Forster, L. John Disney and the study of German in early eighteenth-century England. German Life & Letters new ser 16 1963.

Grieder, T. The German drama in England 1790-1800. Restoration & 18th Century Theatre Research 3 1964.

Böhme

Closs, K. Jakob Böhmes Aufnahme in England. Archiv 148 1925.

Struck, W. Der Einfluss Jakob Boehmes auf die englische Literatur des 17 Jahrhunderts. Berlin 1936.

Goethe

Alford, R. G. Goethe's earliest critics in England. Pbns of Eng Goethe Soc 7 1893.

Kant

Wellek, R. Immanuel Kant in England 1793-1838. Princeton 1931.

Kotzebue

Gosch, M. 'Translators' of Kotzebue in England. Monatshefte für Deutschen Unterricht 31 1939.

Lessing

Todt, W. Lessing in England 1767-1850. Heidelberg 1912.

Kenwood, S. H. Lessing in England. MLR 9 1914.

Dvoretzky, E. The eighteenth-century English translations of Emilia Galotti. Rice Univ Stud 52 1966.

Schiller

Waterhouse, G. Schiller's Räuber in England before
1800. MLR 30 1935.

Schiller in England 1787–1960: a bibliography compiled
under the direction of R. Pick. 1961.

Trainer, J. The first English translation of Kabale und
Liebe. MLR 59 1964.

Milburn, D., jr. The first English translation of Die
Räuber: French bards and Scottish translators.
Monatshefte 59 1967.

Spinoza

Colie, R. L. Spinoza and the early English Deists.
JHI 20 1959.

Wieland

Colwell, W. A. The first English translation of Wieland's
Oberon. PMLA 57 1942.

Spanish

Becker, G. Die Aufnahme des Don Quijote in der
englischen Literatur 1608–c. 1770. Berlin 1906.

Randall, D. B. J. The golden tapestry: a critical survey of
non-chivalric Spanish fiction in English translation
1543–1657. Durham NC 1963.

Starkie, W. F. Miguel de Cervantes and the English
novel. Essays by Divers Hands new ser 34 1966.

Others

Brown, W. C. Prose fiction and English interest in the
Near East 1775–1825. PMLA 53 1938.

Clark, T. B. Oriental England: a study of Oriental
influences in eighteenth-century England as reflected in
the drama. Shanghai 1939.

Yohannan, J. D. The Persian poetry fad in England 1770–
1825. Comparative Lit 4 1952.

Sellin, P. R. Daniel Heinsius and Stuart England. 1968.

Influence of Other Arts

Cust, L. History of the Society of Dilettanti. Ed S.
Colvin 1898.

Howard, W. G. Ut pictoria poesis. PMLA 24 1909.

Cecil, E. A history of gardening in England. 1910 (rev).
With list of English books on gardening to 1837.

Gotheim, M. L. Geschichte der Gartenkunst. Jena 1914;
tr 1928.

Binyon, L. English poetry in its relation to painting and
the other arts. Proc Br Acad 8 1921.

— Landscape in English art and poetry. Tokyo 1930.

Hussey, C. The picturesque. 1927.

Clark, K. The Gothic revival. 1928. On architecture.

Evans, J. Pattern: a study of ornament in western Europe
from 1180 to 1900. 2 vols Oxford 1931.

Yvon, P. Le Gothique et la Renaissance Gothique en
Angleterre 1750–1880. Caen 1931.

Draper, J. W. Poetry and music in eighteenth-century
aesthetics. E Studien 67 1932.

Erhardt-Siebold, E. von. Harmony of the senses in
English, German and French romanticism. PMLA 47
1932.

— Some inventions of the pre-romantic period and their
influence upon literature. E Studien 66 1932.

Weisbach, W. Die klassische Ideologie: ihre Entstehung
und ihre Ausbreitung in den künstlerischen Vorstellungen der Neuzeit. Deutsche Vierteljahrsschrift für
Literaturwissenschaft und Geistesgeschichte 11 1933.

Davies, C. Ut pictura poesis. MLR 30 1935.

Thielke, K. L. F. Literatur- und Kunstkritik in ihren
Wechselbeziehungen: ein Beitrag zur englischen
Ästhetik des 18 Jahrhunderts. Halle 1935.

Allen, B. S. Tides in English taste 1619–1800. 2 vols
Cambridge Mass 1937.

Tinker, C. B. Painter and poet: studies in the literary
relations of English painting. Cambridge Mass 1938.

Lee, R. W. Ut pictura poesis: the humanistic theory of
painting. Art Bull 22 1940.

Wellek, R. The parallelism between literature and the arts.
Eng Inst Annual 1941.

Larrabee, S. A. English bards and Grecian marbles: the
relationship between sculpture and poetry, especially in
the romantic period. New York 1943.

Sypher, W. Baroque afterpiece: the picturesque. Gazette
des Beaux-Arts 27 1945.

Ogden, H. V. S. and M. A bibliography of seventeenth-
century writings on the pictorial arts in English. Art
Bull 29 1947.

— English taste in landscape in the seventeenth century.
Ann Arbor 1955.

Schueller, H. M. Literature and music as sister arts: an
aspect of aesthetic theory in eighteenth-century Britain.
PQ 26 1947.

— The pleasures of music: speculation in British music
criticism 1750–1800. Jnl of Aesthetics 8 1950.

— The use and decorum of music as described in British
literature 1700 to 1780. JHI 13 1952.

— Correspondences between music and the sister arts,
according to eighteenth-century aesthetic theory. Jnl of
Aesthetics 11 1953.

de Beer, E. S. Gothic: origin and diffusion of the term—
the idea of style in architecture. Jnl of Warburg &
Courtauld Inst 11 1948.

Giovannini, G. Method in the study of literature in its
relation to the other fine arts. Jnl of Aesthetics 8 1950.

Sirén, O. China and the gardens of Europe in the eighteenth century. New York 1950.

Salerno, L. Seventeenth-century English literature on
painting. Jnl of Warburg & Courtauld Inst 14 1951.

Gilbert, K. Aesthetic studies: architecture and poetry.
Durham NC 1952.

Folkierski, W. Ut pictura poesis: ou l'étrange fortune du
De arte graphica de Du Fresnoy en Angleterre. Revue
de Littérature Comparée 27 1953.

Rogerson, B. The art of painting the passions. JHI 14
1953.

Music and literature in England in the seventeenth and
eighteenth centuries: papers delivered by J. E. Phillips
and B. H. Bronson at the Second Clark Library Seminar
24 Oct 1953. Los Angeles [1954].

Sypher, W. Four stages of renaissance style: transformations in art and literature 1400–1700. Garden City NY
1955.

Hagstrum, J. H. The sister arts: the tradition of literary
pictorialism and English poetry from Dryden to Gray.
Chicago 1958.

Darenberg, K. H. Studien zur englischen Musikästhetik
des 18 Jahrhunderts. Hamburg 1960.

Nivelle, A. Kunst- und Dichtungstheorien zwischen
Aufklärung und Klassik. Berlin 1960.

Hollander, J. The untuning of the sky: ideas of music in
English poetry 1500–1700. Princeton 1961.

Saisselin, R. G. Ut pictura poesis: Du Bos to Diderot.
Jnl of Aesthetics 20 1961.

Artz, F. B. From the Renaissance to romanticism:
trends in style in art, literature and music 1300–1830.
Chicago 1962.

Cohen, R. Literary criticism and artistic interpretation:
eighteenth-century English illustrations of the Seasons.
In Reason and the imagination, studies in the history of
ideas 1600–1800: essays in honor of M. H. Nicolson,
New York 1962.

Topazio, V. W. Art criticism in the Enlightenment.
In T. Besterman (ed), Transactions of the First
International Congress on the Enlightenment, Geneva
1963.

Kinsley, J. The music of the heart. Renaissance & Mod
Stud 8 1964. On poetry and music from Dryden to
Burns.

Lipking, L. The shifting nature of authority in versions of De arte graphica. Jnl of Aesthetics 23 1965.

Mellers, W. Harmonious meeting: a study of the relationship between English music, poetry and theatre c. 1600–1900. 1965.

Price, M. The picturesque moment. In From sensibility to romanticism: essays presented to Frederick A. Pottle, New York 1965.

Duckles, V. and F. B. Zimmerman. Words to music: papers on English seventeenth-century song read at a Clark Library Seminar, Dec 11 1965. Ed W. H. Rubsamen, Los Angeles 1967.

Halewood, W. H. 'The reach of art' in Augustan poetic theory. In Studies in criticism and aesthetics 1660–1800: essays in honor of Samuel Holt Monk, Minneapolis 1967. On poetry and painting.

Burke, J. The Grand Tour and the rules of taste. In Studies in the eighteenth century, ed R. F. Brissenden, Canberra 1968.

Studies of Particular Critics
in alphabetical order

Addison
Thorpe, C. D. Addison's contribution to criticism. In The seventeenth century: studies by R. F. Jones et al, Stanford 1951.
Wilkinson, J. Some aspects of Addison's philosophy of art. HLQ 28 1964.
Hansen, D. A. Addison on ornament and poetic style. In Studies in criticism and aesthetics 1660–1800: essays in honor of Samuel Holt Monk, Minneapolis 1967.

Akenside
Marsh, R. Four dialectical theories of poetry: an aspect of English neo-classical criticism. Chicago 1965.

Alison
Kallich, M. The meaning of Archibald Alison's Essays on taste. PQ 27 1948.

Beattie
Bevilacqua, V. M. James Beattie's theory of rhetoric. Speech Monographs 34 1967.

Bentley
Jolliffe, H. R. The critical methods and influence of Bentley's Horace. Chicago 1939.
Litz, F. E. Richard Bentley on beauty, irregularity and mountains. ELH 12 1945.

Berkeley
Brunet, O. Le sentiment esthétique chez Berkeley. Deuxième Congrès International d'Esthétique et de Science de l'Art, Paris 1937.

Blackwell
Whitney, L. Thomas Blackwell: a disciple of Shaftesbury. PQ 5 1926.
Costa, G. La critica Omerica di Thomas Blackwell 1701–57. Florence [1959].

Blair
Schmitz, R. M. Hugh Blair. New York 1948.
Bevilacqua, V. Philosophical assumptions underlying Hugh Blair's Lectures on rhetoric and belles lettres. Western Speech 31 1967.

Blake
Lipa, C. B. The critical theory of William Blake. Ithaca 1941.
Adams, H. The Blakean aesthetic. Jnl of Aesthetics 13 1954.

Boswell
Lustig, I. S. Boswell's literary criticism in the Life of Samuel Johnson. Stud in Eng Lit 1500–1900 6 1966.

John Brown
Flasdieck, H. M. John Brown 1715–66 und seine Dissertation on poetry and music. Halle 1924. See also J. G. Robertson, MLR 21 1926.

Burke
A philosophical enquiry into the origin of our ideas of the sublime and beautiful. Ed J. T. Boulton 1958.

Wecter, D. Burke's theory of words, images and emotion. PMLA 55 1940.
Boulton, J. T. The language of politics in the age of Wilkes and Burke. 1963.

Charles Burney
Nangle, B. C. Charles Burney, critic. New Haven 1949.
Lonsdale, R. Dr Burney: a literary biography. Oxford 1965.

Campbell
McDermott, D. George Campbell and the classical tradition. Quart Jnl of Speech 49 1963.

Collins
Page, F. An essay by Collins. TLS 11 July 1935. On Of the essential excellencies in poetry.

Erasmus Darwin
Logan, J. V. The poetry and aesthetics of Erasmus Darwin. Princeton 1936.

Dennis
Critical works. Ed E. N. Hooker 2 vols Baltimore 1939–43.

Dryden
Of dramatic poesy and other critical essays. Ed G. Watson 2 vols 1962 (EL).
Aden, J. M. Dryden and the imagination: the first phase. PMLA 74 1959.
— The critical opinions of John Dryden: a dictionary. Nashville 1963.
Nänny, M. John Drydens rhetorische Poetik: Versuch eines Aufbaus aus seinem kritischen Schaffen. Berne 1959.

Fielding
Thornbury, E. M. Henry Fielding's theory of the comic prose epic. Madison 1931.
Bissell, F. O. Fielding's theory of the novel. Ithaca 1933.

Garrick
MacMillan, D. David Garrick as critic. SP 31 1934.

Gerard
Grene, M. Gerard's Essay on taste. MP 41 1943.

Gildon
Anderson, G. L. Charles Gildon's total academy. JHI 16 1955.

Gilpin
Templeman, W. D. The life and work of William Gilpin 1724–1804, master of the picturesque and Vicar of Boldre. Urbana 1939.
Barbier, C. P. William Gilpin: his drawings, teaching, theory of the picturesque. Oxford 1963.

Goldsmith
Crane, R. S. A neglected mid-eighteenth-century plea for originality and its author. PQ 13 1934. On Goldsmith's review of Critical dissertations upon the Iliad of Homer, Critical Rev 1760.
Reynolds, W. V. Goldsmith's critical outlook. RES 14 1938.

Gray
Starr, H. W. Gray as a literary critic. Philadelphia 1941.

Harris
Marsh, R. Four dialectical theories of poetry: an aspect of English neo-classical criticism. Chicago 1965.

Hartley
Marsh, R. Four dialectical theories of poetry: an aspect of English neo-classical criticism. Chicago 1965.

Hobbes
Thorpe, C. D. The aesthetic theory of Thomas Hobbes. Ann Arbor 1940.

Hogarth
The analysis of beauty, with the rejected passages from the manuscript drafts and autobiographical notes. Ed J. Burke, Oxford 1955.
Moore, R. E. Hogarth's literary relationships. Minneapolis 1948.

Hume. See also Hutcheson, below.
Brunius, T. David Hume on criticism. Stockholm [1952].

Brunet, O. Philosophie et esthétique chez David Hume. Paris 1965.

Mossner, E. C. Hume's Of criticism. In Studies in criticism and aesthetics 1660–1800: essays in honor of Samuel Holt Monk, Minneapolis 1967.

Hurd

Trowbridge, H. Bishop Hurd: a reinterpretation. PMLA 58 1943.

Curry, S. J. Richard Hurd's genre criticism. Texas Stud in Lit & Lang 8 1966.

Hutcheson

Kallich, M. The associationist criticism of Francis Hutcheson and David Hume. SP 43 1946.

Johnson

Watkins, W. B. C. Johnson and English poetry before 1660. Princeton 1936.

Leavis, F. R. Johnson as critic. Scrutiny 12 1944.

Hagstrum, J. H. Samuel Johnson's literary criticism. Minneapolis 1952, Chicago 1967 (with new preface).

Keast, W. R. The theoretical foundations of Johnson's criticism. In Critics and criticism ancient and modern, ed R. S. Crane, Chicago 1952.

Kames

Randall, H. W. The critical theory of Lord Kames. Northampton Mass 1944.

Locke

Tuveson, E. L. The imagination as a means of grace: Locke and the aesthetics of romanticism. Berkeley 1960.

Stolnitz, J. Locke and the categories of value in eighteenth-century British aesthetic theory. Philosophy 38 1963.

Percy

Dennis, L. Percy's essay On the ancient metrical romances. PMLA 49 1934.

Hecht, H. Th. Percy als Bearbeiter spanischer Romanzen. Anglia 58 1934.

Pope

Warren, A. Alexander Pope as critic and humanist. Princeton 1929.

Feder, L. Sermon or satire: Pope's definition of his art. In Studies in criticism and aesthetics 1660–1800: essays in honor of Samuel Holt Monk, Minneapolis 1967.

Reid

Robbins, D. O. The aesthetics of Thomas Reid. Jnl of Aesthetics 5 1942.

Reynolds

Hilles, F. W. The literary career of Sir Joshua Reynolds. Cambridge Mass 1936.

Burke, J. Hogarth and Reynolds: a contrast in English art theory. Oxford 1943.

Rymer

Critical works. Ed C. A. Zimansky, New Haven 1956.

Saint Evremond

Hope, Q. M. Saint Evremond: the honnête homme as critic. Bloomington 1962.

Shaftesbury

Marsh, R. Four dialectical theories of poetry: an aspect of English neo-classical criticism. Chicago 1965.

Tuveson, E. L. Shaftesbury and the age of sensibility. In Studies in criticism and aesthetics 1660–1800: essays in honor of Samuel Holt Monk, Minneapolis 1967.

Adam Smith

Bevilacqua, V. M. Adam Smith and some philosophical origins of eighteenth-century rhetorical theory. MLR 63 1968.

Golden, J. L. The rhetorical theory of Adam Smith. Southern Speech Jnl 33 1968.

Dugald Stewart

Hipple, W. J., jr. The aesthetics of Dugald Stewart: culmination of a tradition. Jnl of Aesthetics 14 1955.

Warburton

Curry, S. J. The literary criticism of William Warburton. E Studies 48 1967.

Ryley, R. M. William Warburton as 'new critic'. In Studies in criticism and aesthetics 1660–1800: essays in honor of Samuel Holt Monk, Minneapolis 1967.

Joseph Warton

Trowbridge, H. Joseph Warton on the imagination. MP 35 1937.

Schick, G. B. Joseph Warton's conceptions of the qualities of a true poet. Boston Univ Stud in Eng 3 1957.

Thomas Warton

Rinaker, C. Thomas Warton: a biographical and critical study. Urbana 1916.

Havens, R. D. Thomas Warton and the eighteenth-century dilemma. SP 25 1928.

Webb

Hecht, H. Daniel Webb: ein Beitrag zur englischen Ästhetik des achtzehnten Jahrhunderts mit einem Abdruck der Remarks on the beauties of poetry 1762. Hamburg 1920.

Young

McKillop, A. D. Richardson, Young and the Conjectures. MP 22 1925.

(3) COLLECTIONS AND ANTHOLOGIES

The artist: a collection of essays on painting, poetry, sculpture, architecture, the drama. Ed P. Hoare 1810.

The gleaner. Ed N. Drake 1811. A selection from the periodical essays of the 18th century, including many critical essays.

English literary criticism. Ed C. E. Vaughan 1896.

Critical essays and literary fragments. Ed J. C. Collins 1903 (Arber's English Garner).

Eighteenth-century essays on Shakespeare. Ed D. N. Smith, Glasgow 1903, Oxford 1963.

Loci critici. Ed G. Saintsbury, Boston 1903.

Critical essays of the seventeenth century. Ed J. E. Spingarn 3 vols Oxford 1908–9. Vols 2–3.

Critical essays of the eighteenth century 1700–25. Ed W. H. Durham, New Haven 1915.

English critical essays (sixteenth, seventeenth and eigh-

teenth centuries). Ed E. D. Jones, Oxford 1922 (WC).

Caritt, E. F. A calendar of British taste from 1600–1800: a museum of specimens and landmarks. 1949.

Taste and criticism in the eighteenth century: a selection of texts illustrating the evolution of taste and the development of critical theory. Ed H. A. Needham 1952.

Periodical essays of the eighteenth century. Ed J. A. Stone 1954.

The continental model: selected French critical essays of the seventeenth century, in English translation. Ed S. Elledge and D. Schier 1960.

Eighteenth-century critical essays. Ed S. Elledge 2 vols Ithaca 1961.

Literary criticism in England 1660–1800. Ed G. W. Chapman, New York 1966.

(4) AESTHETIC THEORY

Casaubon, Meric. A treatise of enthusiasm. 1655.

More, Henry. Enthusiasmus triumphatus. 1662; ed M. V. De Porte, Los Angeles 1966 (Augustan Reprint Soc).

Mackenzie, Sir George. Religio stoici. Edinburgh 1663, 1693 (as The religious stoic).

— Reason: an essay. 1690.

Cavendish, Margaret (Duchess of Newcastle). CCXI sociable letters. 1664.

Parker, Samuel. A free and impartial censure of the Platonick philosophie. Oxford 1666.

Sprat, Thomas. The history of the Royal-Society of London for the improving of natural knowledge. 1667, 1702 ('corrected'), 1722, 1734; tr French, 1669. *Excerpt in Spingarn vol 2, above.*

[Charleton, Walter]. A brief discourse concerning the different wits of men. 1669.

— Natural history of the passions. 1674.

[Rymer, Thomas]. The preface of the translator. In his Reflections on Aristotle's treatise of poesie by R. Rapin, 1674.

LeGrand, Antoine. Man without passion: or the wise stoick, englished by G.R. 1675.

— The divine Epicurus. Tr Edward Cooke 1676.

— An entire body of philosophy, according to the famous Renate Des Cartes. Tr Richard Blome 1694. First Latin edn 1671.

Hyde, Edward (Earl of Clarendon). A brief view and survey of the Leviathan. Oxford 1676.

Burnet, Thomas. Telluris theoria sacra. 2 vols 1681–9; tr 1684 (as The theory of the earth).

Burnet, Gilbert. Utopia, written in Latin by Sir Thomas More, translated into English. 1684. Preface.

Abercromby, David. A discourse of wit. 1685.

[Wolseley, Robert]. Valentinian: a tragedy, as 'tis alter'd by the late Earl of Rochester; together with a preface concerning the author and his writings. 1685. *Spingarn vol 3, above.*

Norris, John. A collection of miscellanies. 1687.

Behn, Aphra. Essay on translated prose. Prefixed to her trn of Fontenelle, A discovery of new worlds, 1688.

A moral essay upon the soul of man. 1690.

Temple, Sir William. Miscellanea, the second part, in four essays: I, Upon ancient and modern learning; II, Upon the gardens of Epicurus; III, Upon heroick virtue; IV, Upon poetry. 1690, 1692 ('corrected and augmented').

— Miscellanea: the third part. 1701. Includes Defence of the essay upon antient and modern learning.

— Essays on ancient and modern learning and on poetry. Ed J. E. Spingarn, Oxford 1909.

Blount, Sir Thomas Pope. Essays on several subjects. 1691, 1692, 1697 (with addns). Essay IV, Of the ancients, and the respect that is due unto them.

Lowde, James. A discourse concerning the nature of man. 1694.

— Moral essays. 1699.

Wotton, William. Reflections upon ancient and modern learning. 1694, 1697 (with Bentley's Dissertation), 1705 (with A defense of the Reflections, with observations upon the Tale of a tub).

[Wright, James]. Country conversations: being an account of some discourses that happen'd in a visit to the country last summer on divers subjects, chiefly of the modern comedies, of drinking, of translated verse, of painting and painters, of poets and poetry. 1694.

B[oyle], C[harles] (Earl of Orrery). Phalaridis epistolae, ex mss recensuit C.B. Oxford 1695. Preface.

— Dr Bentley's Dissertations on the Epistles of Phalaris examin'd. 1698. Mainly by Atterbury.

Dryden, John. A parallel betwixt painting and poetry. In De arte graphica: the art of painting, by C. A. Du Fresnoy, 1695.

Nourse, Timothy. A discourse upon the nature and faculties of man. 1697.

Collier, Jeremy. Essays upon several moral subjects. 3 pts 1698–1705. Pt 2 includes Of the entertainment of books; pt 3, Of authors.

R., T. An essay, concerning critical and curious learning; in which are contained some reflections on the controversie betwixt Sir W. Temple and Mr Wotton. 1698. This provoked An answer, which was met by A vindication, both pbd in 1698. Hearne attributes Essay to Rymer.

— An essay concerning critical and curious learning. 1698; ed C. A. Zimansky, Los Angeles 1965 (Augustan Reprint Soc).

Bentley, Richard. A dissertation upon the Epistles of Phalaris. 1699. First ptd, in a shorter form, with William Wotton, Reflections, 1697 (2nd edn). The 1699 edn adds Answer to the objections of the Hon C. Boyle.

[Barker, Henry]. The polite gentleman: or reflections upon the several kinds of wit, done out of French. 1700.

[Boyer, Abel]. The English Theophrastus. 1702. Selections on contemporary ideas of authors and critics; ed W. E. Britton, Los Angeles 1947 (Augustan Reprint Soc).

Examen miscellaneum. 1702. Preface. By Gildon?

Broughton, John. Psychologia: or an account of the nature of the rational soul. 1703. *See* Henry Layton, Observations upon a treatise intitled Psychologia, 1703.

W., G. Magazine: or animadversions on the English spelling. 1703; ed D. Abercrombie, Los Angeles 1958 (Augustan Reprint Soc).

Swift, Jonathan. An account of a battel between the antient and modern books in St James's library. Appended to A tale of a tub, 1704.

— A discourse concerning the mechanical operation of the spirit. 1704.

— A proposal for correcting, improving and ascertaining the English tongue. 1712.

Wanley, Humfrey. How to judge of the age of manuscripts, the style of learned authors, printers etc. Philosophical Trans of Royal Soc 24 1705.

The letters of Monsieur L'Abbé de Bellegarde, done in English; with a preface by the translator of the French manner of writing, compar'd with the English. 1705.

Cobb, Samuel. Poems on several occasions, to which is prefix'd a discourse on criticism and the liberty of writing. 1707, 1710 (3rd edn). The prefatory discourse and Of poetry: a poem ed L. I. Bredvold, Los Angeles 1946 (Augustan Reprint Soc).

Oldfield, Joshua. An essay towards the improvement of reason. 1707.

[Cooper, A. A. (Earl of Shaftesbury)]. Sensus communis: an essay on the freedom of wit and humour, in a letter to a friend. 1709.

— Characteristics of men, manners, opinions, times. 3 vols 1711, 1711, 1714 (rev), 1723, 1727, 1732, 1733, 1737 etc; ed J. M. Robertson 2 vols 1900.

— Second characteristicks: or the language of forms. Ed B. Rand, Cambridge 1914.

Fowler, Edward. Reflections upon a letter concerning enthusiasm. 1709.

[Brightland, John]. A grammar of the English tongue, with the arts of rhetorick, logick, poetry etc. 1711, 1714, 1721. Often attributed to Steele. *See* H. M. Flasdieck, Zur Verfasserschaft der Grammatik von John Brightland, Anglia 39 1928.

[Gay, John]. The present state of wit. 1711; ed D. F. Bond, Los Angeles 1947 (Augustan Reprint Soc).

Pope, Alexander. An essay on criticism. 1711.

Wagstaffe, William. A comment upon the history of Tom

Thumb. 1711; ed W. K. Wimsatt jr, Los Angeles 1957 (with the Knave of hearts, 1787, by George Canning) (Augustan Reprint Soc).

[Mainwaring, Arthur, et al]. The British academy: being a new-erected society for the advancement of wit and learning, with some few observations upon it. 1712; ed L. A. Landa, Los Angeles 1948 (Augustan Reprint Soc).

[Oldmixon, John]. Reflections on Dr Swift's letter to the Earl of Oxford about the English tongue. [1712]; ed L. A. Landa, Los Angeles 1948 (Augustan Reprint Soc).

—— An essay on criticism. 1728; ed R. J. Madden, Los Angeles 1964 (Augustan Reprint Soc).

Welsted, Leonard. Dionysius Longinus on the sublime, with some remarks on the English poets. 1712.

—— Epistles, odes etc, written on several subjects; to which is prefix'd a dissertation concerning the perfection of the English language, the state of poetry etc. 1724.

Felton, Henry. A dissertation on reading the classics and forming a just style. 1713, 1715 (with addns), 1718, 1730, 1753. See R. S. Crane, Imitation of Spenser and Milton in the early eighteenth century, SP 15 1918.

Elstob, Elizabeth. The rudiments of grammar for the English-Saxon tongue. 1715. Preface, ed C. Peake, Los Angeles 1956 (Augustan Reprint Soc).

Blackmore, Sir Richard. Essays upon several subjects. 1716. An essay upon wit, with Addison's Freeholder no 45 1716, ed R. C. Boys, Los Angeles 1946 (Augustan Reprint Soc).

Of genius. 1719. Occasional papers 3 no 10; ed G. G. Pahl, Los Angeles 1949 (Augustan Reprint Soc).

[Gordon, Thomas]. The humourist: being essays upon several subjects. 1720. Especially On criticism.

Reresby, Tamworth. A miscellany of ingenious thoughts and reflections. 1721.

Crousaz, Jean Pierre de. A new treatise of the art of thinking, done into English. 2 vols 1724.

Fiddes, Richard. A general treatise of morality. 1724. Ch on imagination.

Pearce, Zachary. Longinus: De sublimitate commentarius. 1724.

The many advantages of a good language to any nation; with an examination of the present state of our own. 1724.

Bragge, Robert. A brief essay concerning the soul of man. 1725.

Hutcheson, Francis. An inquiry into the original of our ideas of beauty and virtue. 1725, 1726 (rev), 1729, Glasgow 1738, 1753; tr French, 1749.

—— An essay on the nature and conduct of the passions and affections. 1728, 1742, 1756.

—— Reflections upon laughter and remarks upon the Fable of the bees. Glasgow 1750.

—— A system of moral philosophy. 2 vols 1755.

Watts, Isaac. Logick. 1725.

—— The improvement of the mind. 1741.

Campbell, Archibald. A theory or rationale of ideas. 1727.

—— ΑΡΕΤΗ-ΛΟΓΙΑ: or an enquiry into the original of moral virtue. Westminster 1728.

[Browne, Peter]. The procedure, extent and limits of human understanding. 1728.

Mayne, Zachary. Two dissertations concerning sense and the imagination. 1728.

Arbuckle, James. A collection of letters and essays. 1729. Usually known as Hibernicus's letters.

Collins, Anthony. A discourse concerning ridicule and irony in writing. 1729.

Lamotte, Charles. An essay upon poetry and painting, with an appendix concerning obscenity in writing and painting. 1730, Dublin 1742.

Constable, John. Reflections upon accuracy of style. 1731, 1734, 1738.

Henley, John. A course of academical lectures on various subjects. 5 pts 1731. University learning; English history and historians; belles lettres, and forming a fine taste; languages; on the English tongue.

Stubbes, George. A dialogue on beauty. 1731.

Morrice, [B]. The amour of Venus. 1732. Preface on painting and poetry.

Clarke, John. A new grammar of the Latin tongue comprising all in the art necessary for grammar schools; to which is annex'd a dissertation on language. 1733.

—— An essay upon study. 1731, 1737.

[Forbes, A., Baron Pitsligo]. Essays moral and philosophical. 1734.

Hughes, John. Poems on several occasions, with some select essays in prose. 2 vols 1735. On style.

Jacob, Hildebrand. Of the sister arts: an essay. 1734; rptd in his Works, 1735.

[Coventry, Henry]. Philemon to Hydaspes, relating a second conversation with Hortensius. 1737.

Bancks, John. Miscellaneous works. 2 vols 1738. Preface; vol 2, A discourse concerning language, especially the English.

An essay on design and beauty. Edinburgh 1739. With prose advertisement.

Turnbull, G. Principles of moral philosophy. 1740.

[Campbell, John?]. The polite correspondence: or rational amusement. 1741, 1754. See A. D. McKillop, SP 30 1933.

Melmoth, William. Letters of Sir Thomas Fitzosborne on several subjects. 2 vols 1742-9. Especially xiv (oratory), xxiv (metaphors), xxix (grace in writing), xxxix (taste), lxi (style).

Whitehead, William. An essay on ridicule. 1743. Verse.

An essay on the soul of man. 1744. Verse.

H[arris], J[ames]. Three treatises: the first concerning art; the second concerning music, painting and poetry; the third concerning happiness. 1744, 1765 (rev), 1772, 1783, 1792.

—— Hermes: or a philosophical inquiry concerning universal grammar. 1751, 1765, 1771, 1794; tr French, [1796].

—— Upon the rise and progress of criticism. 1752.

—— Philosophical arrangements. 1775.

—— Philological inquiries. 2 vols 1780-1, 1802; tr French, 1789. See O. Funke, Studien zur Geschichte der Sprachphilosophie 1: zur Sprachphilosophie des 18 Jahrhunderts: Harris' Hermes, Berne 1927.

[Morris, Corbyn]. An essay towards fixing the true standards of wit, humour, raillery, satire and ridicule. 1744; ed J. L. Clifford, Los Angeles 1947 (Augustan Reprint Soc).

Skelton, Philip. The candid reader. 1744.

Fordyce, David. Dialogues concerning education. 1745.

Baillie, [John]. An essay on the sublime. 1747; ed S. H. Monk, Los Angeles 1953 (Augustan Reprint Soc).

Spence, Joseph. Polymetis: or an enquiry concerning the agreement between the works of the Roman poets and the remains of the ancient artists. 1747, 1755, 1777; tr German, 1773-6.

An essay on wit. 1748; ed E. N. Hooker, Los Angeles 1946 (with two essays by R. Flecknoe (1665), Adventurer, nos 127, 133 1754, and Of wit from Weekly Register no 119 1732 (Augustan Reprint Soc).

Whalley, Peter. An enquiry into the learning of Shakespeare. 1748.

[Cooke, Thomas]. Some observations on taste, and on the present state of poetry in England. Prefixed to An ode on beauty, 1749; An ode to martial virtue, 1750; An ode on the powers of poetry, 1751.

[Fortescue, James]. A view of life in its several passions, with a preliminary discourse on moral writing. 1749.

Free, John. An essay towards a history of the English tongue. 1749, 1773 (3rd edn), 1788.

Gwin, J. Essay on design. 1749.

Hartley, D. Observations on man. 1749.

Hurd, Richard. Q. Horatii Flacci Ars poetica, with an English commentary and notes. 1749.

—— Q. Horatii Flacci epistola ad Augustum, with an English commentary and notes; to which is added a discourse concerning poetical imitation. 1751. Both epistles rptd, with additional critical appendices, 1753, 1766, 1776; tr German, 1772.

—— A letter to Mr Mason, on the marks of imitation. Cambridge 1757.

—— Letters on chivalry and romance. 1762, 1762, Dublin 1762; ed E. J. Morley 1911; ed H. Trowbridge, Los Angeles 1963 (Augustan Reprint Soc). Also appended to Moral and political dialogues, 3 vols 1765, 1771, 1776, 1788.

The polite arts: or a dissertation on poetry, painting, music etc. 1749.

Allen, G. Some occasional thoughts on genius. 1750.

Dove, John. A creed founded on truth and common sense. 1750.

Berington, Joseph. Miscellaneous dissertations on the origin of plays, poetry etc. 1751.

Brown, John. Essays on the characteristics [of Shaftesbury]. 1751, 1751, 1752, Dublin 1752, 1752, London 1755, 1764 etc. On ridicule etc.

—— A dissertation on the rise, union and power, the progressions, separations and corruptions of poetry and music. 1763, Dublin 1764; tr German, 1769; Italian, 1772.

—— The history of the rise and progress of poetry, through its several species. Newcastle 1764. A recast of the dissertation 'for the sake of such classical readers as are not particularly conversant with music'.

See H. M. Flasdieck, John Brown und seine Dissertation on poetry and music, Halle 1924.

[Harris, George]. Observations upon the English language, in a letter to a friend. [1752].

Spence, Joseph. Crito: or a dialogue on beauty, by Sir Harry Beaumont. 1752, 1752.

Weekes, N. The abuse of poetry: a satire. 1752, 1754. Preface, on critics.

An essay on ridicule. 1753. On oratory and poetry.

Francklin, Thomas. Translation: a poem. 1753, 1754.

Hogarth, William. The analysis of beauty, written with a view of fixing the fluctuating ideas of taste. 1753; ed J. Burke, Oxford 1955.

St John, Henry (Viscount Bolingbroke). Works. 5 vols 1754. Vol 3: Essay the first, concerning the nature, extent and reality of human knowledge.

[Cooper, J. G.]. Letters concerning taste. 1755, 1755, 1757 (with additional essays). Selections ed R. Cohen, Los Angeles 1951 (Augustan Reprint Soc).

Richardson, J. Thoughts upon thinking, or a new theory of the human mind. 1755, 1773 ('enlarged').

Sharpe, William. A dissertation upon genius. 1755.

Green, John. Beauty: a poem. [1756].

[Greville, Fulke]. Maxims, characters and reflections: critical, satyrical and moral. 1756, 1757. Preface.

Sheridan, Thomas. British education: or the source of the disorders of Great Britain. 1756. Especially pt 3.

[Burke, Edmund]. A philosophical enquiry into the origin of our ideas of the sublime and beautiful. 1757, 1759 (with introductory discourse concerning taste) etc; ed J. T. Boulton 1958; tr German, 1773; French, 1803; Spanish, 1807.

Hume, David. Four dissertations. 1757. Includes Of the standard of taste.

—— Essays moral, political and literary. Ed T. H. Green and T. H. Grose 2 vols 1875.

—— Letters. Ed J. Y. T. Greig 2 vols Oxford 1932.

[Armstrong, John]. Sketches: or essays on various subjects. 1758; rptd in Miscellanies vol 2, 1770. Selections ed R. Cohen, Los Angeles 1951 (Augustan Reprint Soc).

Bayly, Anselm. Introduction to the study of languages. 1758.

—— The alliance of musick, poetry and oratory. 1789. Anon.

Kirby, Thomas. An essay on criticism. 1758.

An essay on the sublime in writing. Universal Mag Jan 1759.

Gerard, Alexander. An essay on taste. 1759, Edinburgh 1764 ('with additions and corrections'); ed W. J. Hipple, Gainesville 1963 (facs of 3rd edn of 1780); tr French, 1766, with 3 dissertations on the same subject by Voltaire, D'Alembert, Montesquieu.

—— An essay on genius. 1774; ed B. Fabian, Munich 1966.

Moor, James. Essays read to a literary society within the College at Glasgow. Glasgow 1759.

Smith, Adam. The theory of moral sentiments; to which is added a dissertation on the origin of languages. 1759.

—— Lectures on rhetoric and belles lettres reported by a student in 1762–3. Ed J. M. Lothian 1963.

—— Essays on philosophical subjects. Ed D. Stewart 1795. Includes Imitation in the imitative arts; Music, dancing and poetry; English and Italian verses.

Young, Edward. Conjectures on original composition. 1759, 1759; ed E. J. Morley, Manchester 1918. See M. W. Steinke, Edward Young's Conjectures on original composition in England and Germany, New York 1917; A. D. McKillop, Richardson, Young and the Conjectures, MP 22 1925.

[Lyttelton, George, Baron]. Dialogues of the dead. 1760 etc.

Gibbon, Edward. Essai sur l'étude de la littérature. 1761; tr 1764; rptd in his Miscellaneous works vol 4, 1814.

—— Miscellaneous works. Vol 2, 1796. Contains several critical essays.

Lancaster, Nathaniel. Plan of an Essay on delicacy. In his Fugitive pieces vol 1, 1761.

Priestley, Joseph. The rudiments of English grammar, with observations on style. 1761, 1768, 1772, 1789 (rev), 1798 etc.

—— A course of lectures on the theory of language. 1762.

—— A course of lectures on oratory and criticism. 1777; ed V. M. Bevilacqua and R. Murphy, Carbondale 1965.

Home, Henry (Lord Kames). Elements of criticism. 3 vols Edinburgh 1762, 1763 (with addns), 2 vols Edinburgh 1769, 1785 ('with the author's last corrections and additions'), 1788, 1796 etc; tr German, 1763–6.

[Langhorne, John]. Letters on religious retirement. 1762.

—— The effusions of friendship and fancy. 1763.

Letters to a young nobleman. 1762. Contains On taste; On taste and liberty.

[Ramsay, Allan (the younger)]. The investigator: containing the following tracts: I, On ridicule; II, On Elizabeth Canning; III, On naturalization; IV, On taste. 1762.

Warburton, William. The doctrine of grace. 2 vols 1762. On the sublime.

Webb, Daniel. Remarks on the beauties of poetry. 1762. See H. Hecht, Daniel Webb: ein Beitrag zur englischen Ästhetik des achtzehnten Jahrhunderts, mit einem Abdruck der Remarks on the beauties of poetry, Hamburg 1920.

—— Observations on the correspondence between poetry and music. 1769.

—— Literary amusements. 1787.

An introduction to the polite arts and sciences, including the principles of literature and the belles lettres. 1763.

Shenstone, William. Works in verse and prose. 2 vols 1764. Especially vol 1, Essay on elegy; vol 2, On writing and books, On taste.

Some observations on Dr Brown's Dissertation. 1764. This was followed by Remarks on some observations, 1764.

Gregory, John. A comparative view of the state and faculties of man, with those of the animal world. 1765.

Buchanan, James. An essay towards establishing a standard for an elegant and a uniform pronunciation of the English language. 1766. See B. Emsley, PMLA 48 1933.

[Bowle, John]. Reflections on originality in authors: being remarks on a letter to Mr Mason on the marks of imitation. 1766.

H[ighmore], J[oseph]. Essays, moral, religious and miscellaneous. 1766.

Pye, H. J. Beauty: a poetical essay. 1766.

— Sketches on various subjects. 1797. Anon. Includes On grammar and languages, ancients and moderns.

[Duff, William]. An essay on original genius in philosophy and the fine arts, particularly in poetry. 1767; ed J. L. Mahoney, Gainesville 1964 (facs).

— Critical observations on the writings of the most celebrated writers and geniuses in original poetry. 1770.

Ferguson, Adam. Essay on the history of civil society. Edinburgh 1767, London 1768, 1769, 1773, 1782 etc; ed D. Forbes, Edinburgh 1966.

Jennings, J. An ode to genius. 1767.

U[sher], J[ames]. Clio: or a discourse on taste. 1767, 1770.

— An introduction to the theory of the human mind. 1771.

Browne, Isaac Hawkins. On design and beauty: an epistle. In his Poems upon various subjects, 1768.

A letter to his Excellency Count [Caylus?] on poetry, painting and sculpture. 1768.

[Newburgh, B.]. Essays, political, moral and critical. Dublin 1769.

Ogilvie, John. Poems. 2 vols 1769. Preface on literary criticism; Introd [to Providence] on allegory.

— Philosophical and critical observations on the nature, character and various species of composition. 2 vols 1774.

Walcot, D. Observations on the correspondence between poetry and music. 1769.

[Bethune, John]. A short view of the human faculties and passions. Edinburgh 1770 (2nd edn).

— Essays and dissertations. 2 vols 1771.

Of the effects of genius on the temper and character. Universal Museum & Complete Mag June 1770.

An essay on the use and advantages of the fine arts. New Haven [1770?].

[Greene, Edward Burnaby]. Critical essays. 1770.

An essay on genius. Universal Mag May 1771.

Jones, Sir William. Poems consisting chiefly of translations from the Asiatic languages; to which are added two essays: I, On the poetry of the Eastern nations; II, On the arts commonly called imitative. Oxford 1772.

[Plumer, F.?]. A letter from a gentleman to his nephew at Oxford. 1772. Against Burke's sublime.

Burnett, James, Lord Monboddo. Of the origin and progress of language. 6 vols 1773-9.

Marat, J. P. A philosophical essay on man. 2 vols 1773.

Prescot, K. Letters and classic amusements. 1773.

Stockdale, Percival. The poet. 1773, 1773. Verse.

Encyclopaedia britannica: or a dictionary of arts and sciences. 3 vols 1773, 10 vols Edinburgh 1778-83, 22 vols Edinburgh 1797-1801.

Lloyd, Robert. Poetical works. 1774.

Barry, James. Real and imaginary obstruction to the acquisition of the arts in England. 1775. Contains general aesthetic dicta.

Beattie, James. Essays. Edinburgh 1776, 1776, 2 vols Dublin 1778, 1 vol 1779. Especially On poetry and music; On laughter and ludicrous composition; On the utility of classical learning.

— Dissertations moral and critical. 1783, 2 vols Dublin 1783. Especially On memory and imagination; On dreaming; On the theory of language; On fable and romance; Illustrations on sublimity.

— The theory of language. 1788. Rptd from Dissertations, 'corrected'.

— Dialogues of the dead. Appended to his Minstrel, 2 vols 1799.

— A letter to the Rev Hugh Blair on the improvement of psalmody in Scotland. 1839. On translation. Written

1778. See W. H. G. Flood, An eighteenth-century essayist on poetry and music, Musical Quart 2 1916.

Campbell, George. The philosophy of rhetoric. 2 vols 1776, Edinburgh 1808 ('with the author's last additions'), 1816. See W. F. Bryan, A late eighteenth-century purist, SP 23 1926.

Howes, T. Critical observations on books antient and modern. 1776.

Serle, Ambrose. The art of writing. 1776. Preface.

Knox, Vicesimus. Essays, moral and literary. 1778, 2 vols 1779, 1782, 1785, 3 vols 1787, 2 vols 1791 etc. See E. Partridge, A critical medley, Paris 1926.

— Liberal education: or a poetical treatise on useful and polite learning. 1781, 1782, 1784, 1788 etc.

— Winter evenings: or lucubrations on life and letters. 1788, 2 vols 1790 (enlarged), 3 vols 1795 (enlarged).

— Personal nobility: or letters to a young nobleman on the conduct of his studies. 1793.

Sherlock, Martin. Lettres d'un voyageur anglais. Geneva 1779; tr 1780.

— Consiglio ad un giovane poeta. Naples 1779.

— Letters on several subjects. 1781.

Donaldson, John. The elements of beauty; also reflections on the harmony of sensibility and reason. Edinburgh 1780.

Lectures on belles lettres and logic. 1780.

[Macaulay, Aulay]. Essays on various subjects of taste and criticism. 1780.

[Nichols, John]. Select collection of poems. 1780. See vol 3, note on allegory.

Pownall, Thomas. A treatise on the study of antiquities. 1782.

Purshouse, A. An essay on genius. Canterbury 1782.

[Stedman, John]. Laelius and Hortensia: or thoughts on the nature and objects of taste and genius. 1782.

Blair, Hugh. Lectures on rhetoric and belles lettres. 2 vols 1783, Dublin 1783, Edinburgh 1783, Philadelphia 1784, 3 vols 1785 (rev), 1787, 1790, 1793, 1796 etc; ed H. F. Harding, Carbondale 1965; tr French, 1797; Italian, 1801; Spanish, 1816-7.

[Jackson, William]. Thirty letters on various subjects. 2 vols 1783.

— The four ages, together with essays on various subjects. 1798. See H. B. Wright, MLR 31 1936.

Potter, Robert. An inquiry into some passages in Dr Johnson's Lives of the poets, particularly his observations on lyric poetry. 1783.

— The art of criticism as exemplified in Dr Johnson's Lives of the poets. 1789. See H. G. Wright, Potter as a critic of Dr Johnson, RES 12 1936.

Percival, Thomas. Moral and literary dissertations. 1784, 1789 ('enlarged').

Robertson, Thomas. An inquiry into the fine arts. 1784.

Barnes, Thomas. On the nature and essential characters of poetry as distinguished from prose. Memoirs of Manchester Literary & Philosophical Soc 1 1785; Dublin 1791.

Hall, Samuel. An attempt to show that a taste for the beauties of nature and the fine arts has no influence favorable to morals. Memoirs of Manchester Literary & Philosophical Soc 1 1785; Dublin 1791.

Kershaw, Thomas. On the comparative merit of the ancients and moderns, with respect to the imitative arts. Memoirs of Manchester Literary & Philosophical Soc 1 1785; Dublin 1791.

Reid, Thomas. Essays on the intellectual powers of man. Edinburgh 1785.

[Reynolds, Frances]. An enquiry concerning the principles of taste, and of the origin of our ideas of beauty etc. 1785; ed J. L. Clifford, Los Angeles 1951 (Augustan Reprint Soc).

Enquiry into the causes of the extraordinary excellence of ancient Greece in the arts. 1786.

Stack, Richard. An essay on sublimity of writing. Trans Royal Irish Acad 1 1787.

Preston, William. Essay on ridicule, wit and humour. Trans Royal Irish Acad 2 1788.

Seally, J. The lady's encyclopaedia: or a concise analysis of the belles lettres, the fine arts and the sciences. 1788.

Belsham, William. Essays, philosophical, historical and literary. 2 vols 1789, 1799 (enlarged). Includes On style.

Darwin, Erasmus. The botanic garden: pt II, The loves of the plants. 1789 etc. Interludes.

Twining, Thomas. Aristotle's treatise on poetry, translated with notes, and two dissertations on poetical and musical imitation. 2 vols 1789, 1812.

—— Recreations and studies of a country gentleman of the eighteenth century. 1882.

Alison, Archibald. Essays on the nature and principles of taste. Edinburgh 1790, 2 vols Edinburgh 1812, 1815.

D'Israeli, Isaac. A defence of poetry. Appended to specimens of a new version of Telemachus, 1790.

—— Curiosities of literature. 1791–4, 1793, 1798–1817 (with addns), 1827 etc.

—— A dissertation on anecdotes. 1793.

—— An essay on the manners and genius of the literary character. 1795.

—— Miscellanies: or literary recreations. 1796. Style; On the character of Dennis; On reading; On literary genius; On French and English poetry etc.

Parsons, J. W. Hints on producing genius. 1790.

Sharp, Richard. On the nature and utility of eloquence. Memoirs of Manchester Literary & Philosophical Soc 3 1790.

Henry, Thomas. Twenty essays on the advantages of literature and philosophy in general, and specially on the consistency of literary and philosophical with commercial pursuits. Dublin 1791; rptd in part from Memoirs of the Manchester Literary & Philosophical Soc 1 1785.

Polier, Charles de. An essay on the pleasure which the mind receives from the exercise of its faculties, and that of taste in particular, in twenty essays. Dublin 1791. Also in Memoirs of Manchester Literary & Philosophical Soc 5.

Tytler, A. F. (Lord Woodhouselee). Essay on the principles of translation. 1791, 1797 ('corrected'); rptd [1907] (EL).

[Withers, P.]. Aristarchus: or the principles of composition. [1791], [1792?], 1822.

Rylands, John. Select essays on moral virtue, genius, science and taste. 1792.

Stewart, Dugald. Elements of the philosophy of the human mind. 1792.

Sayers, Frank. Disquisitions, metaphysical and literary. 1793, Norwich 1808. Includes Of beauty.

Miller, George. An essay on the origin and nature of our idea of the sublime. Trans Royal Irish Acad 5 1794.

[Whiter, Walter]. A specimen of a commentary on Shakespeare: containing an attempt to explain and illustrate various passages in a new principle of criticism, derived from Mr Locke's Doctrine of the association of ideas. 1794; ed A. Over and M. Bell 1967 (enlarged).

Burrowes, Robert. Essay on style in writing considered with respect to thoughts and sentiments as well as words. Trans Royal Irish Acad 5 1795.

Murray, Lindley. English grammar. 1795 etc.

Thomson, Alexander. The paradise of taste. 1796. Verse.

—— Pictures of poetry. 1799. Verse.

On benevolence and friendship, as opposed to principle. In Essays by a Society of Gentlemen at Exeter, Exeter [1796]. On sentimentalism.

Godwin, William. The enquirer: reflections on education, manners and literature. 1797.

Hurdis, James. Lectures shewing the several sources of that pleasure which the human mind receives from poetry. Bishopstone 1797.

Reynolds, Sir Joshua. Works. Ed E. Malone 2 vols 1797. See E. N. S. Thompson, The discourses of Reynolds, PMLA 32 1917.

Drake, Nathan. Literary hours: or sketches critical, narrative and poetical. Sudbury 1798, 2 vols 1800 (enlarged), 3 vols 1804, 1820.

MacLaurin, John. Works. Vol 2, Edinburgh 1798.

Scott, John Robert. Dissertation on the progress of the fine arts. 1800; ed R. H. Pearce, Los Angeles 1954 (Augustan Reprint Soc).

—— Dissertations, essays and parallels. 1804. Includes Essay on the influence of taste on morals, and reprints A dissertation on the progress of the fine arts, 1800.

Thomson, William. An enquiry into the elementary principles of beauty in the works of nature and art, to which is prefixed an introductory discourse on taste. [1800].

Belsham, Thomas. Elements of the philosophy of the mind. 1801.

Berdmore, Samuel. Specimens of literary resemblances in the works of Pope, Gray and other celebrated writers. 1801.

Price, Sir Uvedale. A dialogue on the distinct characters of the picturesque and the beautiful in answer to the objections of Mr Knight, prefaced by an introductory essay on beauty with remarks on the ideas of Sir Joshua Reynolds and Mr Burke upon that subject. Hereford 1801.

Knight, [R. P.]. An analytical inquiry into the principles of taste. 1805, 1805, 1808.

[Mangin, Edward?]. Essay on the sources of the pleasures received from literary compositions. 1809.

Walker, George. Essays on various subjects. 1809.

Harpur, Joseph. An essay on the principles of philosophical criticism applied to poetry. 1810.

Barrett, B. Pretensions to a final analysis of the nature and origin of sublimity, style, beauty, genius and taste; with an appendix explaining the causes of the pleasure which is derived from tragedy. 1812.

Duncan, John. An essay on genius: or the philosophy of literature. 1814.

(5) THE LITERARY FORMS

Lyric and Epic Poetry

Poole, Joshua. The English Parnassus: proeme. 1657.

Dryden, John. Essays. Ed W. P. Ker 2 vols Oxford 1900; Of dramatic poesy and other critical essays, ed G. Watson 2 vols 1962 (EL).

—— An account of the ensuing poem. Prefixed to his Annus mirabilis, 1667.

—— The author's apology for heroique poetry and poetique license. Prefixed to his State of innocence, 1677.

—— The works of Virgil. 1697. Dedication to Aeneis.

Hobbes, Thomas. To the Honourable Edward Howard esq on his intended impression of his poem of the British Princes. 1669. Prefixed to Howard's British Princes.

—— To the reader concerning the vertues of an heroique poem. 1675. Prefixed to Hobbes's trn of Odyssey; Spingarn vol 2.

Woodforde, S. A paraphrase upon the psalms of David. 1670. Preface.

Phillips, Edward. Theatrum poetarum: or a compleat collection of the poets of all ages, particularly those of our own nation; together with a prefatory discourse of the poets and poetry in generall. 2 pts 1675; ed S. E.

Brydges 1800, Geneva 1824; Spingarn vol 2. *See* W. Albrecht, Über das Theatrum poetarum von Miltons Neffen Edward Phillips, Berlin 1928.

Wilmot, John (Earl of Rochester). An allusion to the tenth satyr of the first book of Horace. 1677-9? Verse; Spingarn vol 2.

Sheffield, John (Earl of Mulgrave). An essay upon poetry. 1682, 1691, 1697, 1701 (with Death), 1713, 1716 etc; Spingarn vol 2; tr French, 1764.

Dillon, Wentworth (Earl of Roscommon). An essay on translated verse. 1684, 1685 (adds Miltonic imitation); Spingarn vol 2.

Waller, E. Of this translation and of the use of poetry. Prefixed to Roscommon's trn of Horace's Art of poetry, 1684.

Winstanley, William. The lives of the most famous English poets. 1687.

[Atterbury, Francis]. The second part of Mr Waller's poems. 1690. Preface.

Blount, Sir Thomas Pope. Censura celebriorum authorum; sive tractatus in quo varia virorum doctorum de clarissimis scriptoribus judicia traduntur. 1690, 1694, Geneva 1700 (corrected).

— De re poetica; or remarks upon poetry, with characters and censures of the most considerable poets, whether ancient or modern, extracted out of the best criticks. 2 pts 1694 (with 1690, above).

Walsh, William. Collection of letters and poems. 1692. Preface on love poetry.

Wesley, Samuel. The life of our blessed Lord and Saviour. 1693. Preface: being an essay on heroick poetry.

— Epistle to a Friend concerning poetry. 1700. Verse. Both ed E. N. Hooker, Los Angeles 1947 (Augustan Reprint Soc).

Miscellaneous letters and essays on several subjects. Ed Charles Gildon 1694, 1696. Includes: To Mr T. S. in vindication of Mr Milton's Paradise lost; An essay at a vindication of the love-verses of Cowley and Waller; To my honoured and ingenious friend Mr Harrington, for the modern poets against the ancients.

Blackmore, Sir Richard. Prince Arthur: an heroick poem. 1695. Preface; Spingarn vol 3.

— A paraphrase of the Book of Job. 1700. Preface.

— A satyr against wit. 1700; Spingarn vol 3.

— The creation. 1712. Preface.

— Essays upon several subjects. 1716. Includes An essay upon epic poetry.

— Alfred. 1723. Preface.

[Phillips, John?]. A reflection on our modern poesy: an essay. 1695. Verse.

Dennis, John. Remarks on a book entitul'd Prince Arthur, with some general critical observations. 1696; ed E. N. Hooker, Baltimore 1939-43 (in Critical works).

— The advancement and reformation of modern poetry. 1701; ed Hooker (with above).

— The grounds of criticism in poetry. 1704; ed Hooker (with above).

Granville, George (Baron Lansdowne). An essay upon unnatural flights in poetry. In A new miscellany of original poems, ed C. Gildon 1701; Spingarn vol 3.

Bysshe, Edward. The art of English poetry: containing I, Rules for making verses; II, A dictionary of rhymes; III, A collection of the most natural, agreeable and noble thoughts, viz allusions, similes, descriptions and characters of persons and things that are to be found in the best English poets. 1702, 1705, 1708, 1710, 1714, 1718, 1724, 1725, 1737, 1762. Altered and expanded in the later edns; Pt I ed A. D. Culler, Los Angeles 1953 (Augustan Reprint Soc) (from 1708).

Oldmixon, John. A pastoral poem on the victories of Schellenburgh and Blenheim, with a large preface, shewing the antiquity and dignity of pastoral poetry. 1704.

Congreve, William. A discourse on the Pindarique ode.

Prefixed to A Pindarique ode, on the victorious progress of her Majesty's arms, 1706.

Prior, M. An ode humbly inscribed to the Queen. 1706. Preface.

— Poems on several occasions. 1718. Preface to Solomon.

Tate, Nahum. The Muses memorial with an account of the present state of poetry. 1707.

Coward, William. Licentia poetica discuss'd: or the true test of poetry. 1709. Verse, with prose notes.

Philips, Ambrose. Pastorals. 1709. Preface.

Watts, Isaac. Horae lyricae. 1709 (2nd edn). Preface.

— Miscellaneous thoughts. 1734.

Chetwood, Knightly. Preface [on pastorals] to eclogues in Dryden's Virgil, 1710.

Fenton, Elijah. An epistle to Mr Southerne. 1711. Verse.

Tickell, Thomas. De poesi didactica. Lecture delivered in Oxford 1711; tr in R. E. Tickell, Thomas Tickell, 1931.

Trapp, Joseph. Praelectiones poeticae. 2 vols Oxford 1711-15, 1722, 1736; tr 1742 (as Lectures on poetry).

[Parnell, Thomas]. An essay on the different stiles of poetry. 1713. Verse.

— Posthumous works. 1758. Includes The gift of poetry.

Cobb, Samuel. Clavis Virgiliana: new observations on the works of Virgil with rules for writing pastorals. 1714.

Hughes, John. The works of Mr Edmund Spenser. 6 vols 1715, 1750. Includes Remarks on the Fairy Queen, and allegorical poetry.

— Of style. In his Poems vol 1, 1735.

— On descriptions in poetry. In his Poems vol 2, 1735.

Pope, Alexander. The Iliad of Homer. Vol 1, 1715. Preface.

— A discourse on pastoral poetry. In his Poems, 1717.

— The Odyssey of Homer. Vol 5, 1726. Postscript.

Purney, Thomas. A full enquiry into the true nature of pastoral. 1717; ed E. R. Wasserman, Los Angeles 1948 (Augustan Reprint Soc).

— Pastorals: viz The bashful Swain; and Beauty and simplicity. 1717. Advertisement. *See* H. O. White, E & S 15 1929.

Gildon, Charles. The complete art of poetry. 2 vols 1718.

— The laws of poetry as laid down by the Duke of Buckinghamshire, by the Earl of Roscommon and by the Lord Landsdowne, explain'd and illustrated. 1721. Anon.

Dart, John. The works of Tibullus, with some observations on elegiack verse; with characters of the most celebrated Greek, Latin and English elegiack poets. 1720.

Hill, Aaron. The creation: a Pindaric. 1720. With Preface to Mr Pope concerning the sublimity of the ancient Hebrew poetry, and a material and obvious defect in the English; Preface ed G. G. Pahl, Los Angeles 1949 (Augustan Reprint Soc).

Porter, John. A critical essay upon epistolary and elegiac poetry. 1720, [1728?], 1729, 1732.

Morrice, Bezaleel. An essay on the poets. 1721. Preface.

[Philips, Ambrose?]. A collection of old ballads, with introductions historical and critical. 3 vols 1723-5. Vol 2, preface on Chevy-Chase; vol 3, preface on old songs.

Baker, Henry. Original poems. 1725. Preface.

Thomson, James. Winter. 1726 (2nd edn). Preface.

Broome, William. Poems on several occasions. 1727,1739, 1750. Preface.

[Oldys, William?]. A collection of epigrams, to which is prefix'd a critical dissertation on this species of poetry. 1727, 2 vols 1735-7.

Young, Edward. On lyric poetry. Prefixed to his Ocean: an ode, 1728.

Husbands, John. A miscellany of poems. Oxford 1731. Preface; *see* R. S. Crane, An early 18th-century enthusiast for primitive poetry, MLN 37 1922.

[Madan, Judith]. The progress of poetry. In The flower-piece, ed [M. Concanen?] 1731. Verse.

Bowden, Samuel. Poetical essays on several occasions. 2 vols 1733–5. Preface.

Cooper, E. The Muses library: or a series of English poetry from the Saxons to the reign of King Charles II, containing the lives and characters of all the known writers in that interval. Vol 1 (all pbd), 1737, 1738 (as The historical and poetical medley), 1741.

Hayward, Thomas. The British Muse: or a collection of thoughts, moral, natural and sublime, of our English poets who flourished in the sixteenth and seventeenth centuries, with an historical and critical review. 3 vols 1738, 1740 (as The quintessence of English poetry).

Pemberton, Henry. Observations on poetry, especially the lyric, occasioned by the late poem upon Leonidas. 1738.

Martyn, John. Pub. Virgilii Maronis georgicorum libri quatuor. 1741, 1746, 1755 etc. Preface on didactic poetry.

— Pub. Virgilii Maronis bucolicorum eclogae decem. 1749. Preface on pastoral poetry.

[Akenside, Mark]. The pleasures of the imagination. 1744 etc. Advertisement.

— The balance of poets. In Dodsley's Museum, 1746, and Bucke's Life of Akenside, 1832.

Manwaring, Edward. Of harmony and numbers in Latin and English prose, and in English poetry. 1744.

Say, Samuel. Poems on several occasions and two critical essays: viz the first on the harmony, variety and power of numbers, whether in prose or verse; the second on the numbers of Paradise lost. 1745. The first essay ed P. Fussell jr, Los Angeles 1956 (Augustan Reprint Soc).

An essay on Pindaric poetry. Prefixed to An hymn to God, 1746.

Newbery, John. The art of poetry made easy. 1746, 1748 (as Poetry made familiar), 1769.

Warton, Joseph. Odes. 1746. Advertisement.

— The works of Virgil in English verse by Christopher Pitt and Joseph Warton. 4 vols 1753. Vol 1, Reflections on didactic poetry; vol 4, Postscript.

Mason, J. Three essays: viz on elocution, on the principles of harmony in poetic composition and the power of harmony in prosaic numbers. 1749.

West, Gilbert. The odes of Pindar. 1749. Preface.

Beauties of poetry displayed: containing observations on the different species of poetry and the rules of English versification. 1750.

Kirkpatrick, J. The sea-piece: a poem. 1750. Preface.

Warburton, William. Discourse on pastoral poetry. In Pope's Works vol 1, 1751. See also his notes to Pope.

Lowth, Robert. De sacra poesi hebraeorum praelectiones academicae. Oxford 1753; tr 1787.

Browne, Isaac Hawkins. The immortality of the soul: a poem, translated from the Latin by William Hay. 1754. Preface on poetic style.

Comberbach, Roger. A dispute consisting of a preface in favour of blank verse; with an experiment of it in an ode, an epistle from Dr Byrom in defence of rhyme and Mr Comberbach's reply. [1755].

Drummond, T. Poems sacred to religion and virtue. 1756. Preface.

[Andrews, Robert]. Eidyllice: or miscellaneous poems. Edinburgh 1757. Hint to the British poets prefixed.

Free, John. Poems on several occasions. 1757 (2nd edn). Includes Historical and critical account of the origin and peculiar nature of English poetry.

Thompson, William. An hymn to May. 1757. Preface.

Wilkie, William. Epigoniad. 1757, 1769. Preface; 2nd edn adds critical apologia in verse, A dream in the manner of Spenser.

Reason: a poem, to which is prefixed a Notion of poetry: an essay. 1758.

Macpherson, James. Fragments of ancient poetry.

Edinburgh 1760; ed J. J. Dunn, Los Angeles 1966 (Augustan Reprint Soc).

The art of poetry on a new plan. 2 vols 1762. Usually ascribed to the publisher J. Newbery. Rev Goldsmith? Largely based upon The art of poetry made easy.

Ogden, James. Epistle on poetic composition. [1762?]. Verse.

— The revolution. 1790. Includes An essay upon poetry, and particularly upon the epic.

Ogilvie, John. An essay on the lyric poetry of the ancients. In his Poems 1762, 1764, 1769.

— Rona: a poem. 1777. Introd.

— A critical dissertation on epic machinery. Prefixed to his Britannia: a national epic poem, Aberdeen 1801.

Percy, Thomas. Reliques of ancient English poetry. 3 vols 1765, 1767, 1775, 1794 etc. Includes essays on Ancient minstrels in England; Metre of Pierce Plowman's visions; ancient metrical romances.

Hurd, Richard. A dissertation on the idea of universal poetry. 1766.

Goldsmith, Oliver. The beauties of English poesy. 1767, Dublin 1771.

G[reene], E. B. An essay on pastoral poetry. In The idylliums of Theocritus, tr Francis Fawkes 1767.

Poetry made familiar and easy to young gentlemen and ladies. 1769.

[Downman, Hugh]. An elegy wrote under a gallows, with a preface concerning the nature of elegy. [1770].

Aikin, John. Essays on song-writing, with a collection of such English songs as are most eminent for poetical merit. 1772, 1774 (rev), Dublin 1777; rev R. H. Evans 1810.

— An essay on the application of natural history to poetry. Warrington 1777.

— Letters from a father to his son, on various topics, relative to literature and the conduct of life. 2 vols 1793–1800.

— Essays literary and miscellaneous. 1811. On similes in poetry, On poetical personification etc.

— Memoir of John Aikin by Lucy Aikin, with a selection of his miscellaneous pieces. 2 vols 1823.

Jones, Sir William. On the poetry of the eastern nations. In his Poems, Oxford 1772.

Aikin, John and Anna Laetitia. Miscellaneous pieces in prose. 1773, 1775, 1792.

Byrom, John. Miscellaneous poems. 2 vols Manchester 1773. Vol 1, An epistle to a friend on the art of English poetry; vol 2, Enthusiasm: a poetical essay.

[Aikin, Anna Laetitia]. The origin of song-writing. In her Poems, 1774 (4th edn).

Mercer, Thomas. Poems. Edinburgh 1774. Includes Of poetry: an epistolary essay.

Bath and its environs. Bath 1775. The author to the reader.

Essay on English versification. In Sentimental fables by a country curate, Brentford 1775.

Yonde, John. Essay on rhyme. Prefixed to his Adventures of Telemachus, 1775.

Mickle, W. J. The Lusiad. Oxford 1776 etc. Introd on epic poetry.

More, John. Strictures, critical and sentimental, on Thomson's Seasons, with hints and observations on collateral subjects. 1777.

Schomberg, A. C. Bagley: a poem. Oxford 1777. Prolegomena on the poetry of the present age.

— Ode on the present state of English poetry. Oxford 1779. Anon.

Stockdale, Percival. An enquiry into the nature and genuine laws of poetry. 1778.

Tickell, Richard. The wreath of fashion or the art of sentimental poetry. 1778.

Hayley, William. An essay on epic poetry in five epistles. 1782, Dublin 1782. Verse.

Pinkerton, John. Letters of literature, 1785. Pbd under pseudonym 'Robert Heron'.

— Literary correspondence. 2 vols 1830.

[Polwhele, Richard]. The art of eloquence: a didactic poem. 1785. Advertisement.

Preston, William. Thoughts on lyric poetry. Trans Royal Irish Acad 1 1787.

Belsham, William. Essays philosophical, historical and literary. 2 vols 1789, 1799 (enlarged). Includes On English versification.

Richards, George. An essay on the characteristic differences between ancient and modern poetry. [Oxford 1789].

Weston, Joseph. An essay on the superiority of Dryden's versification over that of Pope and the moderns. In John Morfitt, Philotoxi ardenae, Birmingham [1788]. For Anna Seward's comments see GM April–June 1789.

Webb, F. Poems. Salisbury 1790. Preface and Ode to genius.

Gifford, William. The Baviad. 1791.

— The Maeviad. 1795. See J. Longaker, The Della Cruscans and William Gifford, Philadelphia 1924.

Pye, H. J. A commentary illustrating the Poetics of Aristotle by examples taken chiefly from the modern poets. 1792.

Coleridge, S. T. Poems on various subjects. 1796. Preface.

Campbell, Alexander. An introduction to the history of poetry in Scotland. Edinburgh 1798. Especially the Conversation on Scotish song prefixed.

[Fawcett, Joseph]. Poems; to which [is] added the art of poetry according to the latest improvements. 1798.

Penn, John. Art of English poetry. In his Critical, poetical and dramatic works vol 2, 1798. Verse, with prose notes.

[Wordsworth, William]. Lyrical ballads. Bristol 1798. Advertisement.

[Manners, Lady Catharine Rebecca]. Review of poetry, ancient and modern: a poem. 1799.

Inquiry into the propriety of the rules prescribed for pastoral poetry. Appended to Allan Ramsay, The gentle shepherd, Edinburgh 1808.

Dyer, George. Poetics: or a series of poems and disquisitions on poetry. 1812.

Radcliffe, Ann. On the supernatural in poetry. New Monthly Mag 1826. Written 1802. See A. D. McKillop, JEGP 31 1932.

Satire and Burlesque

For additional titles see R. P. Bond, English burlesque poetry, Cambridge Mass 1932.

Dennis, John. Miscellanies in verse and prose. 1693. Preface on burlesque.

Dryden, John. A discourse concerning the original and progress of satire. In Satires of Juvenalis, 1693.

Pendragon. 1698. An advertisement on burlesque verse is prefixed.

Brown, Tom. A short essay on English satire. In his Works vol 1, 1707.

Ozell, John. Boileau's Lutrin rendered into English verse. 1708. Dedication.

Parodies of ballad criticism 1711–87: William Wagstaffe, A comment upon the history of Tom Thumb 1711; George Canning, The knave of hearts 1787. Ed W. K. Wimsatt jr, Los Angeles 1957 (Augustan Reprint Soc).

Harte, Walter. An essay on satire particularly on the Dunciad. 1730. Verse; ed T. B. Gilmore, Los Angeles 1968 (Augustan Reprint Soc).

Cooke, Thomas. Some observations on satire. In his Mournful nuptials, 1739.

— A prologue on comic poetry. 1753. Anon.

Brown, John. An essay on satire. 1745, 1749. Verse.

Cambridge, Richard Owen. The Scribleriad. 1751. Preface.

Bacon, Montague. A dissertation upon burlesque poetry. Appended to Zachary Grey, Critical notes upon Hudibras, 1752.

Erskine, Andrew. Town-eclogues: 1, The hangmen; 2, The harlequins; 3, The street-walkers; 4, The undertakers. [1773]. Preface.

Combe, William. The justification: a poem. 1777. Preface.

Hayley, William. The triumphs of temper: a poem. 1781. Preface.

Abbott, Charles (Baron Tenterden). An essay on the use and abuse of satire. [Oxford 1786?].

Stevens, G. A. Lecture on heads. Dublin 1788. Contains An essay on satire.

[Boscawen, W.] The progress of satire: an essay in verse. 1798. Preface.

Novel

Boyle, Roger, Lord Broghill. Parthenissa. 1655. Preface; ed C. Davies, Los Angeles 1953 (Augustan Reprint Soc).

I[ngelo], N[athaniel]. Bentivolio and Urania. 1660. Preface; ed C. Davies, with above.

Mackenzie, Sir George. Apologie for romances, prefixed to Aretina. 1660; ed C. Davies, with above.

Head, Richard. The English rogue described, in the Life of Meriton Latroon. 1665. Preface.

Scudéry, Georges de. Ibrahim. Tr Henry Cogan 1674. Preface; ed B. Boyce, Los Angeles 1952 (Augustan Reprint Soc).

Boyle, Robert. Theodora and Didymus. 1687. Preface; ed C. Davies, Los Angeles 1953 (Augustan Reprint Soc).

Manley, Mary de la Riviere. The secret history of Queen Zarah. 1705. Preface; ed B. Boyce, Los Angeles 1952 (Augustan Reprint Soc).

Prefaces to three eighteenth-century novels 1708–51–97: Mateo Aleman, Dedication and preface of the Life of Guzman d'Alfarache (tr 1708); Francis Coventry, Chapter 1 of Book 1 and Chapter 2 of the History of Pompey the Little 1751; Dedication of third edition 1752; Royal Tyler, Dedication and preface of the Algerine captive (1797). Ed C. E. Jones, Los Angeles 1957 (Augustan Reprint Soc).

Croxall, Samuel. A select collection of novels. Vol 1, 1720. Preface.

Richardson, Samuel. Pamela, introduction to 1741 (2nd edn). Ed S. W. Baker, Los Angeles 1954 (Augustan Reprint Soc).

— Clarissa: preface, hints of prefaces and postscript. 1751 (3rd edn). Ed R. F. Brissenden, Los Angeles 1964 (Augustan Reprint Soc).

Warburton, William. Dissertation on the origin of the books of chivalry. Prefixed to C. Jervas's trn of Don Quixote, 2 vols 1742.

— Preface to Richardson's Clarissa vols 3–4. Ed B. Boyce, Los Angeles 1952 (Augustan Reprint Soc). See R. S. Crane, MP 16 1919; MLR 17 1922.

Remarks on Clarissa. 1749.

An essay on the new species of writing founded by Mr Fielding; with a word or two upon the modern state of criticism. 1751; ed A. D. McKillop, Los Angeles 1962 (Augustan Reprint Soc).

Fielding, Sarah. The cry. 3 vols 1754. Preface.

— The Countess of Dellwyn. 1759. Preface.

Hurd, Richard. Letters on chivalry and romance. 1762; ed H. Trowbridge, Los Angeles 1963 (Augustan Reprint Soc).

Beattie, James. Dissertations moral and critical. 1783, 2 vols Dublin 1783. Includes On fable and romance.

Reeve, Clara. The progress of romance. Colchester 1785, New York 1930 (facs).

Moore, John. A view of the commencement and progress of romance. Prefixed to Smollett's Works, 1797.

Sermon

See also W. F. Mitchell, English pulpit oratory, 1932.

Wright, Abraham. Five sermons, in five several styles. 1656. Preface.

Eachard, John. The grounds and occasions of the contempt of the clergy. 1670, 1685 (9th edn), 1696; ed E. Arber 1877 (English Garner vol 7).

A[rderne], J. Directions concerning the matter and stile of sermons. 1671; ed J. Mackay, Oxford 1952 (Luttrell Soc).

Ferguson, Robert. The interest of reason in religion. 1675.

Glanvill, Joseph. An essay concerning preaching, written for the direction of a young divine. 1678. Excerpt in Spingarn vol 2.

—— A seasonable defence of preaching and the plain way of it. 1678. *See* F. Greenslet, Joseph Glanvill, New York 1900.

Edwards, John. The preacher. 3 vols 1705–9.

[Dodsley, Robert]. The art of preaching, in imitation of Horace's Art of poetry. 1738.

Fordyce, David. Theodorus: a dialogue concerning the art of preaching. 1752, 1755 (3rd edn).

An essay on the action proper for the pulpit. 1753.

Sanderman, Robert. An essay on preaching. Edinburgh 1763.

[Langhorne, John]. Letters on the eloquence of the pulpit. 1765.

Mainwaring, John. Sermons on several occasions; to which is prefixed a dissertation on that species of composition. Cambridge 1780.

Miscellaneous Types

Selections from seventeenth-century songbooks. Ed J. W. Angel, Los Angeles 1954 (Augustan Reprint Soc).

Five miscellaneous essays by Sir William Temple. Ed S. H. Monk, Ann Arbor 1963.

Ballads and songs loyal to the Hanoverian succession 1703–61. Ed J. J. McAleer, Los Angeles 1962 (Augustan Reprint Soc).

[Defoe, Daniel]. A vindication of the press: or an essay on the usefulness of writing, on criticism and the qualifica-

tion of authors. 1718; ed O. C. Williams, Los Angeles 1951 (Augustan Reprint Soc).

Gally, Henry. A critical essay on characteristic-writings. Prefixed to his trn of Theophrastus, 1725. Selections ed A. H. Chorney, Los Angeles 1952 (Augustan Reprint Soc).

An historical view of the political writers in Great Britain. 1740; ed R. Haig, Los Angeles 1958 (Augustan Reprint Soc).

[Whalley, Peter]. An essay on the manner of writing history. 1746; ed K. Stewart, Los Angeles 1960 (Augustan Reprint Soc).

Twenty moral fables, with a dissertation on fables. 1747.

St John, Henry (Viscount Bolingbroke). Letters on the study and use of history. 1752.

[Newbery, John]. Letters by writers of distinguished merit; with a dissertation on epistolary style. 1758 (4th edn), 1760, 1787.

Dodsley, Robert. Select fables of Aesop and other fabulists. 1761. Preface: An essay on fable; ed J. K. Welcher and R. Dircks, Los Angeles 1965 (Augustan Reprint Soc).

Lectures on rhetoric and belles lettres delivered in the University of Glasgow by Adam Smith, reported by a student in 1762–3. Ed J. M. Lothian 1963.

Campbell, George. The philosophy of rhetoric. 2 vols 1776; ed L. F. Bitzer, Carbondale 1963.

[Graves, Richard]. Euphrosyne: or amusements on the road of life. 2 vols 1776–80. Vol 2, Essay on the nature of the epigram.

Hayley, William. An essay on history, in three epistles. 1780, 1781. Verse.

Hill, John. An essay upon the principles of historical composition, with an application of those principles to Tacitus. Trans Royal Soc of Edinburgh 2 1788.

Richardson, William. On the dramatic or ancient form of historical composition. Ibid.

Young, Sir William. [Proposals for] Contemplatio philosophica: a posthumous work of the late Brook Taylor. 1793. Introd to Taylor's life, on biography.

Wallace, Thomas. Essay on the variations of English prose from the Revolution to the present time. Trans Royal Irish Acad 6 1797.

(6) CRITICISM OF PARTICULAR WRITERS

B[rathwait], R[ichard]. A comment upon two tales of our ancient poet Sr Jeffray Chaucer. 1665; ed C. F. E. Spurgeon, 1901 (Chaucer Soc).

Sprat, Thomas. An account of the life and writings of Mr Abraham Cowley. Prefixed to Works of Cowley, ed Sprat 1668.

[Howard, Edward?]. Spencer redivivus. 1687. Preface.

Echard, Lawrence. Prefaces to Terence's comedies and Plautus's comedies. 1694; ed J. Barnard, Los Angeles 1968 (Augustan Reprint Soc).

Select hymns taken out of Mr Herbert's Temple. 1697; ed W. E. Stephenson, Los Angeles 1962 (Augustan Reprint Soc).

Milbourne, [Luke]. Notes on Dryden's Virgil, in a letter to a friend, with an essay on the same poet. 1698.

Dryden, John. Fables ancient and modern. 1700. Preface: On Homer, Ovid and Chaucer.

Rowe, Nicholas. Some account of the life of Mr William Shakespear. 1709; ed S. H. Monk, Los Angeles 1948 (Augustan Reprint Soc).

On the death of Mr Edmund Smith, a poem in Miltonick verse, with a preface containing some remarks upon Milton. 1712.

Parnell, Thomas. An essay on the life, writings and learning of Homer. In Pope's trn vol 1, 1715 etc.

Blackwall, Anthony. An introduction to the classics. 1718.

—— The sacred classics defended and illustrated. 1725, 1737.

Addison, Joseph. A dissertation upon the Roman poets. Appended to his Poems on several occasions, 1719.

—— Notes upon the twelve books of Paradise lost, collected from the Spectator. 1719, 1731, 1738 etc; tr French, 1721 etc; German, 1740.

Tickell, Thomas. Life of Addison. Prefixed to his edn of Addison vol 1, 1721, 1730, 1741 etc.

[Spence, Joseph]. An essay on Mr Pope's Odyssey. 2 pts 1726–7.

Fenton, Elijah. Observations on the works of Edmund Waller. 1730. Also included in his edn of Waller, 1729.

Jortin, John. Miscellaneous observations upon authors. 2 vols 1731–2. A periodical, ed Jortin.

—— Remarks on Spenser's poems. 1734. Includes Remarks on Milton.

—— The life of Erasmus. 2 vols 1758–60, 1805.

—— Tracts, philological, critical and miscellaneous. Ed R. Jortin 2 vols 1790.

[Routh, B.]. Lettres critiques sur le Paradis perdu et reconquis de Milton. 1731.

King, William. Miscellaneous reflections and various readings upon classical authors and other modern writers. In his Remains, 1732.

Meadowcourt, R. A critique on Milton's Paradise regained. 1732.

—— A critical dissertation with notes on Paradise regained. 1748.

Crusius, Lewis. Lives of the Roman poets, with an introduction concerning the origin and progress of poetry. 2 vols 1733, 1753.

Richardson, Jonathan, and Jonathan the younger. Explanatory notes and remarks on Milton's Paradise lost. 1734.

Theobald, Lewis. Preface to the works of Shakespeare. 1734; ed H. G. Dick, Los Angeles 1949 (Augustan Reprint Soc).

Blackwell, Thomas. An enquiry into the life and writings of Homer. 1735. *See* L. Whitney, Thomas Blackwell: a disciple of Shaftesbury, PQ 5 1926.

Some remarks on the tragedy of Hamlet. 1736; ed C. D. Thorpe, Los Angeles 1947 (Augustan Reprint Soc).

Manwaring, Edward. An historical and critical account of the most eminent classic authors. 1737.

[Benson, William]. Letters concerning poetical translations and Virgil's and Milton's arts of verse. 1739.

Geddes, James. Essay on the composition and manner of writing of the antients, particularly Plato. Glasgow 1748; tr German, 1759.

Critical remarks on Sir Charles Grandison, Clarissa and Pamela. 1754; ed A. D. McKillop, Los Angeles 1950 (Augustan Reprint Soc).

Warton, Thomas. Observations on the Faerie Queene of Spenser. 1754.

— The history of English poetry. 4 vols 1774–89. *See* also An unpublished continuation, ed R. M. Baine, Los Angeles 1953 (Augustan Reprint Soc).

— Poems upon several occasions by John Milton. 1785. Preface and notes.

Warton, Joseph. An essay on the writings and genius of Pope. 2 vols 1756–82.

— Works of Alexander Pope. 9 vols 1797. Memoir and notes. *See* E. J. Morley, Joseph Warton: a comparison of the Essay on the genius of Pope with his edition of Pope's works, E & S 9 1924.

[Gordon, John]. Occasional thoughts on the study and character of classical authors, with some incidental comparisons between Homer and Ossian. 1762.

Ogilvie, John. Poems on several subjects; to which is prefix'd An essay on the lyric poetry of the Ancients. 1762.

[Blair, Hugh]. A critical dissertation on the poems of Ossian. 1763, 1765; Dublin 1765 etc.

[Wood, Robert]. An essay on the original genius and writings of Homer. 1769, 1775.

G[reene], E. B. Critical essays. 1770. On Longinus, the Aeneid etc.

Murphy, Arthur. An essay on the life and genius of Henry Fielding esq. In Works of Fielding vol 1, 1771.

— An essay on the life and genius of Samuel Johnson. 1792.

Hurd, Richard. Select works of Cowley, with a preface and notes. 1772.

— Remarks on the plan and conduct of the Faerie Queene. In Spenser's Works vol 2, 1805.

Stockdale, Percival. The life of Edmund Waller. 1772.

— An inquiry into the nature and genuine laws of poetry, including a particular defence of the writings and genius of Mr Pope. 1778.

— Lectures on the truly eminent English poets. 2 vols 1807. On Spenser, Shakespeare, Milton, Dryden, Pope, Young, Thomson, Chatterton, Gray.

Roberts, W. H. A poetical epistle to Christopher Anstey esq on the English poets, chiefly those who have written in blank verse. 1773.

Mason, William. The poems of Mr Gray; to which are prefixed memoirs of his life. 1775.

Tyrwhitt, Thomas. The Canterbury tales of Chaucer, [with] an essay on his language and versification. 5 vols 1775–8.

— Poems supposed to have been written at Bristol by Thomas Rowley and others. 1777.

'Melmoth, Courtney' (S. J. Pratt). Observations on the Night thoughts of Dr Young; with occasional remarks on the beauties of poetical composition. 1776.

More, J. Strictures, critical and sentimental, on Thomson's Seasons; with hints and observations on collateral subjects. 1777.

Aikin, John. An essay on the plan and character of Thomson's Seasons. 1778.

Johnson, Samuel. Prefaces, biographical and critical, to the works of the English poets. 10 vols 1779–81, 4 vols 1781 (as Lives).

[Young, John]. A criticism on the Elegy written in a country church yard: being a continuation of Dr J—n's criticism on the poems of Gray. 1783, Edinburgh 1810.

Scott, John, of Amwell. Critical essays on some of the poems of several English poets. 1785.

Headley, H. Select beauties of English poetry. 1787, 1810 (with memoir by H. Kett). Notes.

Rutherford, William. A view of antient history, including the progress of literature and the fine arts. 2 vols 1788–91.

Neve, Philip. Cursory remarks on some of the ancient English poets, particularly Milton. 1789.

Keir, James. An account of the life and writings of Thomas Day esq. 1791.

Sayers, Frank. Of the poetical character of Horace. In his Disquisitions, metaphysical and literary, 1793 etc.

Hayley, William. The life of Milton. In Poetical works of Milton vol 1, 1794; rptd separately with Conjectures on Paradise lost, 1796.

— The life and posthumous writings of William Cowper. 3 vols Chichester 1803–4 etc.

[Pye, H. J.]. Sketches on various subjects. 1797. Includes Gray and Shenstone, Voltaire, Richardson etc.

Ferriar, John. Illustrations of Sterne. Manchester 1798, 2 vols 1812.

Barbauld, Anna Laetitia (née Aikin). Life of Richardson. Prefixed to edn of Richardson's correspondence, 1804.

(7) LITERARY SURVEYS, HANDBOOKS AND SATIRES

Pack, Richardson. Essays on study and conversation, in two letters to D[avid] C[ampbell]. 1719. Appended to Miscellanies in verse and prose, 1719, 1719, Dublin 1726 (with 'some account of the author').

[Ralph, James]. The touch-stone. 1728, 1731 (as The taste of the town).

Savage, Richard. An author to be lett. 1729; ed J. Sutherland, Los Angeles 1960 (Augustan Reprint Soc).

The present state of letters in an epistle to a friend. 1761.

[Campbell, Archibald]. The sale of authors: a dialogue in imitation of Lucian's Sale of philosophers. 1767. Satire.

Gifford, William. The Baviad. 1791. Satire on the Della Cruscans.

— The Maeviad. 1795. Satire on corruptions of drama.

Mathias, Thomas James. The pursuits of literature. 1794; enlarged in later edns. Satire on J. Warton, Parr, Godwin, Payne Knight and Monk Lewis.

(8) TRANSLATIONS OF FOREIGN LITERARY CRITICISM

The Greek Critics

Aristotle

See L. W. Riley, Aristotle texts and commentaries to 1700 in the University of Pennsylvania Library: a catalogue, Philadelphia 1961.

Hobbes, Thomas. The art of rhetoric. 1681. An abridgment; first pbd 1636.

C., H. Aristotle's Rhetoric. 1686, 1693.

Aristotle's Art of poetry. 1705, 1709, 1713. From Dacier.

Aristotle's Poetics. 1775.
Pye, H. J. The poetics. 1788, 1792 (with commentary).
Twining, Thomas. Aristotle's Treatise on poetry. Oxford 1789, 2 vols 1812.

Longinus
P[ulteney], J. A treatise of the loftiness or elegancy of speech, written originally in Greek by Longin and now translated out of French. 1680. From Boileau.
An essay upon sublime style, translated from the Greek of Longinus, compared with the French of Boileau. Oxford 1698.
A treatise of the sublime. In Boileau, Complete works vol 2, 1711 etc.
Welsted, Leonard. The works of Dionysius Longinus on the sublime: or a treatise concerning the sovereign perfection of writing, translated from the Greek, with some remarks on the English poets. 1712. Based on Boileau.
Holmes, J. The art of rhetoric made easy: or the elements of oratory. 1738, 1755, 1766, 1786 etc. Bk 2, Being the substance of Dionysius Longinus's celebrated treatise of the sublime.
Smith, William. Dionysius Longinus on the sublime, translated. 1739, 1741, 1743, 1751, 1752, 1756, 1757, 1770, Dublin 1777.

Plato
Works abridg'd. 1701, 1720, 1749, 1772 etc.
The idea of beauty. Edinburgh 1756. An epitome of Phaedrus.
Sydenham, Floyer. A synopsis or general view of the works of Plato. 1759.
Taylor, Thomas. Phaedrus: a dialogue concerning beauty and love. 1792.
— The Cratylus, Phaedo, Parmenides and Timaeus. 1793.

Plotinus
Taylor, Thomas. Concerning the beautiful: or a paraphrase translation from the Greek of Plotinus. 1787.

The Latin Critics

Horace
Dillon, Wentworth (Earl of Roscommon). Horace's Art of poetry. 1680 etc.
Colman, George. The art of poetry. 1783. *For other trns see col 1497, below.*

Quintilian
Guthrie, William. M. Fabius Quinctilianus his institutes of eloquence. 2 vols 1756.
Patsall, J. Quintilian's Institutes of the orator. 2 vols 1774.

Vida
Pitt, Christopher. Vida's Art of poetry. 1725.
Hampson, John. The poetics of Vida. 1793.

The French Critics

d'Alembert, Jean Lerond
Miscellaneous pieces. 1764. Translation, Style etc.

Batteux, Charles
Principles of translation. Edinburgh 1760.
Miller, —. A course of the belles lettres: or the principles of literature, translated from the French. 4 vols 1761. Adds examples from the English poets.

Bielfeld, J. F. Baron de
Hooper, W. The elements of universal erudition. 1770.

Blondel
Sherburne, Sir Edward. The comparison of Pindar and Horace english'd. 1696.

Boileau
Soame, Sir William and John Dryden. The art of poetry made English. 1683, 1708, 1710, 1715.
Works, made English by several hands. 3 vols 1711-13, 1736, 1752.

Bouhours
The art of criticism: or the method of making a right judgment upon subjects of wit and learning. 1705.
Oldmixon, John. The arts of logick and rhetorick; to which are added parallel quotations out of the most eminent English authors. 1728.

Callières, F. de
Bladen, [Martin]. Characters and criticisms upon the ancient and modern authors. 1705.

Charron
Stanhope, George. Of wisdom: three books. 3 vols 1697, 2 vols 1707.

Condillac
Nugent, T. Essay on the origin of human knowledge. 1756.

Dacier
Essay upon satyr. In Miscellany poems, ed C. Gildon 1692; rptd with Monsieur Bossu's Treatise of the epick poem, 1695 etc.
Aristotle's art of poetry with Mr D'Acier's notes translated from the French. 1705, 1709, 1713. Preface ed S. H. Monk, Los Angeles 1959 (Augustan Reprint Soc).

Du Bos
Nugent, Thomas. Critical reflections on poetry, painting and music. 1748.

Fénelon
Reflections upon the art of writing with propriety, elegance and accuracy, with a discourse upon poetry in general. 1717.
Stevenson, W. Dialogues concerning eloquence in general, with his letter to the French Academy, concerning rhetoric, poetry, history and a comparison betwixt the antients and the moderns. 1722, 1750, 1760, 1806.

Fleury
The history, choice and method of studies. 1695.

Fontenelle
D., J. New dialogues of the dead, made English. 1692.
Motteux, P. A. Of pastorals, englished. With Monsieur Bossu's Treatise of the epick poem, 1695 etc.
Hughes, John. Fontenelle's dialogues of the dead, translated from the French. 1708, 1730, Glasgow 1754.

Formey, J. H. S.
Forman, Sloper. Elementary principles of belles lettres. 1766, Glasgow 1767.

Hardouin, J.
An apology for Homer. 1716.

Helvétius
De l'esprit: or essays on the mind. 1759.

Huet
A treatise of romances and their original. 1672.
Lewis, Stephen. The history of romances. 1715.
Letter to Segrais upon the original of novels. In A select collection of novels, ed S. Croxall vol 1, 1720.
Memoirs. Tr John Aikin 2 vols 1810.

La Bruyère
The characters: or the manners of the age, made English by several hands. 2 pts 1698-9, 1700 (corrected).

Le Blanc, J. B.
Letters on the English and French nations. 1747.

Le Bossu
J., W. Monsieur Bossu's Treatise of the epick poem, done into English, with a new original preface upon the same subject. 1695, 2 vols 1719. Includes Dacier's Essay upon satyr and Fontenelle's Treatise upon pastorals.

Le Clerc
Parrhasiana: or thoughts upon several subjects, as criticism, history, morality and politics, done into English. 1700.

Maury, Abbé
Lake, J. N. The principles of eloquence. 1793.

Montesquieu
Gerard, A. An essay on taste. In Gerard's essay, Edinburgh 1764, and Montesquieu's Works vol 4, 1777.
Of the pleasures of the soul. In his Works vol 4, 1777.
Muralt
Letters describing the character and customs of the English and French nations. 1726, 1726 (enlarged).
Pellisson
S[ome], H[enry]. The history of the French Academy. 1657.
A preface to the works of M. Sarasin. In A collection of select discourses out of the most eminent wits of France and Italy, 1678.
Pouilly, L. J. L. de
Theory of agreeable sensations. 1749.
Rapin
Davies, John. Observations on the poems of Homer and Vergil. 1672.
Dancer, John. Judgment on Alexander and Caesar, and also on Seneca, Plutarch and Petronius. 1672.
— The comparison of Plato and Aristotle. 1673.
Reflections upon the use of the eloquence of these times. Oxford 1672.
[Rymer, Thomas]. Reflections on Aristotle's Treatise of poesie: containing the necessary, rational and universal rules for epick, dramatick and the other sorts of poetry. 1674.
Creech, Thomas. The idylliums of Theocritus, with Rapin's Discourse of pastorals. Oxford 1684. Rapin's De carmine pastorali rptd in trn, ed J. E. Congleton, Los Angeles 1947 (Augustan Reprint Soc).
The modest critick: or remarks upon the most eminent historians, antient and modern. 1689.
Kennett, Basil, et al. Whole critical works. 2 vols 1706, 1716, 1731.
Rollin, Charles
[Usher, James]. Taste: an essay. 1732.
The method of teaching and studying the belles lettres. 4 vols 1734, 1742 (3rd edn), 4 vols 1749, 1758, Edinburgh 1768, 3 vols 1769, 4 vols 1770 etc.
Saint Evremond
Reflections upon tragedies, comedies and operas. 1684.
Mixt essays, written originally in French. 1685.
Spence, Ferrand. Miscellanea: or various discourses made English. 1686.
Miscellaneous essays, translated by various hands. 2 vols 1692–4.
Works, made English, with the author's life, by Mr des Maizeaux. 2 vols 1700, 3 vols 1714, 1728.
Letters. Ed J. Hayward 1930.

Sainte-Palaye
[Dobson, Susanna]. The literary history of the troubadours. 1779.
Memoirs of ancient chivalry. 1784.
Scudéry, Madeleine de
Spence, Ferrand. Conversations upon several subjects. 2 vols 1683.
Terrasson, Jean
A discourse of ancient and modern learning. 1716.
Brerewood, F. A critical dissertation upon Homer's Iliad. 1722.
Trublet, abbé
Essays moral and critical. 1744.
Voltaire
An essay upon the civil wars of France, as also upon the epick poetry of the European nations, from Homer down to Milton. 1727, 1728, 1731.
[Lockman, John]. Letters concerning the English nation. 1733, 1741.
Essay on taste. In A. Gerard's Essay, Edinburgh 1764 (2nd edn).

The Italian Critics

Baretti, Giuseppe
A dissertation on the Italian poetry. 1753.
Denina, Carlo
Murdock, John. An essay on the revolutions of literature. [1771].

The German Critics

Adelung, J. C.
Willich, A. F. M. Three philological essays. 1798. Also appended to Willich's study of Kant.
Schiller
Pick, R. Schiller in England 1787–1960: a bibliography. 1961.
Sulzer, J. G.
Brusasque, Elizabeth. Illustrations of the theory and principles of taste, considered as they are applicable to the fine arts in general and the various species of literary composition. 1806.

The Spanish Critics

Feijoó y Montenegro, B.
Brett, John. Essays: or discourses. 1780.

(9) THE OTHER ARTS

Music, Painting, Architecture and Landscape Gardening

A brief selection. For other titles see J. W. Draper, Eighteenth-century English aesthetics, 1931. Aesthetic theory, above, should be consulted for comparisons of music and poetry etc.

Playford, John. An introduction to the skill of musick. 1658, 1660, 1662 etc.
[North, Francis, Baron Guilford?]. A philosophical essay of musick. 1677.
Bedford, A. The great abuse of music. 1711.
Richardson, [Jonathan]. Essays on the theory of painting. 1715, 1725, tr French, 1728.
— Two discourses. 1719. Especially An essay on criticism as it relates to painting.
Langley, Batty. New principles of gardening: or the laying out and planting of pastures, groves, wildernesses, labyrinths, avenues, parks etc. 1728, 1739, 1756.
Gilpin, William. A dialogue upon the gardens of Viscount Cobham, at Stowe. 1748. Anon.

— An essay upon prints. 1768, 1768 (both anon), 1781, 1792, 1802.
— Observations on the river Wye relative chiefly to picturesque beauty. 1782.
— Observations on the mountains and lakes of Cumberland and Westmoreland. 2 vols 1786.
— Observations on several parts of Great Britain, particularly the Highlands of Scotland. 2 vols 1789.
— Remarks on forest scenery and other woodland views. 2 vols 1791.
— Three essays: on picturesque beauty; on picturesque travel; and on sketching landscape. 1792.
— Observations on the western parts of England. 1798.
Wren, Sir Christopher. Parentalia: or memoirs of the family of the Wrens. 1750. For Wren's notes.
Hogarth, William. The analysis of beauty, written with a view of fixing the fluctuating ideas of taste. 1753; ed J. Burke, Oxford 1955.
Chambers, Sir William. Designs of Chinese buildings. 1757.

—— A treatise on civil architecture. 1759.
—— A dissertation on Oriental gardening. 1772, 1773 ('with additions'); tr French, 1772.
Webb, Daniel. An inquiry into the beauties of painting. 1760, 1761, 1769, 1777; tr Italian, 1791.
[Newbery, John]. Essay on perfecting the fine arts in Great Britain and Ireland. 1767.
Mason, William. The English garden. 4 pts 1772–81.
Hawkins, Sir John. A general history of the science and practice of music. 1776.
Burney, Charles. General history of music. 4 vols 1776–89.
Heely, Joseph. Letters on the beauties of Hagley, Envil and the Leasowes with critical remarks and observations on the modern taste in gardening. 1777.
Hayley, William. A poetical epistle to an eminent painter. 1778, 1779 ('corrected').
—— An essay on painting. 1781. Verse.
—— An essay on sculpture. 1800. Verse.
Walpole, Horace. Essay on modern gardening. Strawberry Hill 1785.
Bromley, R. A. A philosophical and critical history of the fine arts. 2 pts 1793–5.
[West, Benjamin]. A discourse delivered to the students of the Royal Academy. 1793.
Knight, R. P. The landscape: a didactic poem. 1794, 1795.
Repton, Humphrey. Letter to Uvedale Price esq. 1794.
—— Sketches of hints on landscape gardening. 1795.

—— Observations on the theory and practice of landscape gardening. 1803.
—— An enquiry into changes of taste in landscape gardening. 1806.
Price, Sir Uvedale. An essay on the picturesque as compared with the sublime and the beautiful. 2 vols 1794–8.
—— Letter to H. Repton esq on the application of the principles of landscape painting to landscape architecture. 1795, Hereford 1798.
—— Dialogue on the picturesque. 1801.
Reynolds, Sir Joshua. Works. Ed E. Malone 2 vols 1797.
Barry, James. A letter to the dilettante society respecting the improvement of public taste. 1798.
—— Remarks on the present state of the art of painting. In M. Pilkington, The gentleman's dictionary of painters, 1798.
—— Lectures in painting delivered at the Royal Academy. In his Works vol 1, 1809.
Essays on Gothic architecture by the Rev T. Warton, Rev J. Bentham, Captain Grose and the Rev J. Milner. 1800.
Fuseli, Henry. Lectures on painting delivered at the Royal Academy. 2 pts 1801–20.
Opie, John. Lectures on painting delivered at the Royal Academy. 1809.

D. F. B. and G. J. K.

III. LITERARY RELATIONS WITH THE CONTINENT

This section, which is selective, is divided according to languages or groups of languages : French ; German ; Italian ; Spanish and Portuguese ; Dutch and Flemish; Scandinavian ; Russian etc ; and others. Individual authors, British and foreign, are entered in separate alphabetical lists under each language. Trns into English and from English are within the scope of the section. A more comprehensive list of trns into English will be found col 1484, below. Secondary works are confined to comparative studies and to works on the impact of an author in a foreign country. Extra-European relations are not considered.

No distinction is drawn between translators and editors using hack-translators, unless positively known ; the distinction between trn, adaptation and mere imitation, where given, is offered merely as a guide.

The use of 'London' as bibliographical address was widespread, especially for surreptitious works, and has been qualified only in flagrant cases, where known. Elsewhere the spurious address is followed.

Annual lists may be found in Yearbook of comparative and general literature, Bloomington 1952–; English literature 1660–1800: a bibliography compiled for Philological Quarterly (1926–60), 4 vols Princeton 1950 *and subsequently in* PQ; *and* PMLA: yearbook of work in the modern languages.

(1) GENERAL

See also the corresponding sections for 1500–1660 and 1800–1900, and the special section Shakespeare on the Continent in vol 1, above ; also further sections, below, on relations with individual countries.

Howell, J. Lexicon tetraglotton: or an English-French-Spanish-Italian dictionary. 1659–60.
Chappuzeau, S. L'Europe vivante. Geneva 1669.
Rochefort, J. de. Le voyageur d'Europe. 3 vols Paris 1672.
P[atin], C. Quatre relations historiques [de voyages en Allemagne, Angleterre, Hollande, Bohème, Suisse etc]. Rouen 1673.
Acta eruditorum. Leipzig 1682–1731; Nova acta eruditorum, Leipzig 1732–55; Supplementa, 1692–1757; Indices, 1685–1745.
Burnet, G. Some letters containing an account of Switzerland, Italy etc. Rotterdam 1686.

Morhof, D. G. Polyhistor: sive de notitia auctorum et rerum commentarii. Lübeck 1688–92.
Voyage remarquable fait dans les années 1697–98 en Angleterre, Ecosse et Irlande. Utrecht 1699.
Reisbeschryving door Vrankyk, Spanien, England etc. Leyden 1700.
[Jordan, C. E.] Histoire d'un voyage littéraire fait en 1733, en France en Angleterre et en Hollande. Hague 1735.
Riccoboni, L. Réflexions historiques et critiques sur les différens théâtres de l'Europe. Paris 1738; tr 1741.
Georgi, G. Allgemeines europäisches Bücher-Lexicon. 8 vols Leipzig 1742–53 (and 3 vols suppl).
Keysler, J. G. Neueste Reise. Hanover 1740; Travels through Germany, Bohemia, Hungary, Switzerland, Italy and Lorrain, 4 vols 1756.

Goldsmith, O. An enquiry into the present state of polite learning in Europe. 1759.

Denina C. G. M. Discorso sopra le vicende della letteratura. Glasgow 1763 (2nd edn); tr J. Murdoch [1771].

Montagu, Lady M. W. Letters written during her travels in Europe, Asia and Africa. 1763.

Smollett, T. G. Travels through France and Italy. 1766. No French trn known.

Sterne, L. A sentimental journey through France and Italy. 1768.

Marshall, J. Travels through Holland, Flanders, Germany, Denmark, Sweden etc. 4 vols 1768–71, 1772–6.

Wraxall, N. W. Cursory remarks made in a tour through some of the northern parts of Europe. 1775.

Moore, J. View of society and manners in France, Switzerland and Germany. 1779; View of society and manners in Italy, 1781; A journal during a residence in France, 2 vols 1793.

De l'influence de la littérature française sur l'anglaise, et de l'anglaise sur l'allemande. Berlin 1790.

Dutens, L. Le guide moral des étrangers qui voyagent en Angleterre. 1792.

[Tooke, W.]. Varieties of literature from foreign literary journals and original mss now published. 1795.

Petzhold, J. Bibliotheca bibliographica: kritisches Verzeichnis der das Gesammtgebiet der Bibliographie betreffenden Literatur des In- und Auslandes. Leipzig 1866.

Betz, L. P. La littérature comparée: essai bibliographique. Strasbourg 1900, 1904 (2nd edn).

Texte, J. J. J. Rousseau et les origines du cosmopolitisme littéraire. Paris 1895; tr J. W. Matthews 1899.

Lewis, C. M. The foreign sources of modern English versification. New Haven 1898.

Texte, J. Etudes de littérature européenne. Paris 1898.

Thomson, C. L. Samuel Richardson. 1900. Influence on foreign drama and novel in bibliography.

Tucker, T. G. The foreign debt of English literature. 1907.

Harris, W. J. The first printed translations into English of the great foreign classics. 1909.

Van Tieghem, P. Histoire littéraire générale et comparée. Revue de Synthèse Historique 23 1911–.

—— La littérature comparée. Paris 1931.

—— Histoire littéraire de l'Europe. Paris 1946.

Brüggemann, F. Utopie und Robinsonaden. Weimar 1914.

Finzi, G. Lira italica e lira nordica: saggio sopra le due grande correnti della letteratura europea. Turin 1914.

Magnus, L. English literature in its foreign relations. 1927.

—— A history of European literature. New York 1934.

Wais, K. Zeitgeist und Volksgeist in der vergleichenden Literaturgeschichte. Germanish-romanische Monatsschrift 22 1934.

Allen, B. S. Tides in English taste. 2 vols Cambridge Mass 1937.

Peyre, H. English literature seen through foreign eyes. French Stud 6 1950.

Babits, M. Geschichte der europäischen Literatur. Vienna 1948.

Ségur, N. Histoire de la littérature européenne. 5 vols Paris 1949–52.

Ballam, H. and R. Lewis. The visitors' book: England and the English as others have seen them. 1950.

Spemann, A. Vergleichende Zeittafel der Weltliteratur vom Mittelalter bis zur Neuzeit. Stuttgart 1951.

Baldensperger, F. and W. P. Friederich. Bibliography of comparative literature. Chapel Hill 1950. Annual suppl: Yearbook of comparative and general literature, Chapel Hill (later Bloomington) [1952–].

Bibliographie générale de littérature comparée. Paris 1951–9. From Revue de Littérature Comparée.

Friederich, W. P. Outline of comparative literature from Dante to Eugene O'Neill. Chapel Hill 1954.

Collison, R. L. Dictionaries of foreign languages. 1955.

Zaumüller, W. Bibliographisches Handbuch der Sprachwörterbücher. Stuttgart 1958.

Klapp, O. Bibliographie der französischen Literaturwissenschaft. Frankfurt 1960–.

Block, A. The English novel, including translations of foreign fiction. 1961 (rev).

Rancoeur, R. Bibliographie de la littérature française du Moyen-Age à nos jours. Paris 1962–.

Zeitschrift für vergleichende Literaturgeschichte. Ed M. Koch, Berlin 1887–1910.

Studien zur vergleichenden Literaturgeschichte. Ed M. Koch, Berlin 1901–9.

Revue de littérature comparee. Ed F. Baldensperger, P. Hazard et al, Paris 1921–.

Comparative literature. Ed C. B. Beall and W. P. Friederich, Eugene Oregon 1949–.

Comparative literature studies. Ed A. O. Aldridge and M. J. Friedman, Maryland (later Urbana) 1964–.

Literary Themes
in alphabetical order according to subject

Ullmann, S. de. *Anglicism* and Anglophobia in continental literature. Modern Languages 27 1946.

Hatzfeld, H. A critical survey of the recent *baroque* theories. Colombia Instituto Caro y Cuervo Boletin 4 1948.

—— The baroque from the point of view of the literary historian. Jnl of Aesthetics 14 1955.

Praz, M. Baroque in England. MP 61 1964.

Wellek, R. The concept of baroque in literary scholarship. Jnl of Aesthetics 5 1946.

Mercier, R. L'*enfant* dans la société du xviiie siècle avant l'Emile. Dakar 1961. *Child*.

Brown, H. A bibliography of *classical influence* on English literature. Cambridge Mass 1935.

Burlingams, A. E. The battle of the books in its historical setting. New York 1920.

Eliosoff, L. A. The cultural milieu of Addison's literary criticism. Houston 1963.

Highet, G. The battle of the books. In his Classical tradition, Oxford 1949.

Johnson, J. W. The formation of English neo-classical thought. Princeton 1967.

Maurocordato, A. La critique classique en Angleterre de la restauration à la mort de J. Addison. Paris 1964.

Ogilvie, R. M. Latin and Greek: a history of the influence of the classics. 1964.

Robertson, J. G. The beginnings of a new aesthetics in England: Addison. In his Studies in the genesis of romantic theory, New York 1962.

Thomson, J. A. K. The classical background of English literature. 1948.

—— Classical influences on English poetry. 1951.

—— Classical influences on English prose. 1956.

Wellek, R. A history of modern criticism 1750–1950 vol i. New Haven 1954.

Weinstein, L. The metamorphosis of *Don Juan*. Stanford 1959.

Becker, C. L. The heavenly city of the eighteenth-century philosophers. New Haven 1932. *Enlightenment*.

Brunschvicg, L. Les progrès de la conscience dans la philosophie occidentale. Paris 1953.

Cassirer, E. Die Philosophie der Aufklärung. Tübingen 1932; tr Princeton 1951. *See* H. Dieckmann, MLQ 15 1954; K. B. Price, JHI 18 1957.

Dieckmann, H. An interpretation of the 18th century. MLQ 15 1954.

—— Themes and structures of the Enlightenment. In H. Dieckmann, H. Levin et al, Essays in comparative literature, St Louis 1961.

Gay, P. The Enlightenment: an interpretation. Vol I, The rise of modern paganism, New York 1966.

Hazard, P. La crise de la conscience européenne 1680–1715. 3 vols Paris 1935.

— La pensée européenne au xviiie siècle. 3 vols Paris 1946.

Niklaus, R. The age of the Enlightenment. In The age of the Enlightenment: studies presented to T. Besterman, Edinburgh 1967.

Talmon, G. The origins of totalitarian democracy. 1952.

Spence, L. The fairy tradition in Britain. 1948.

Storer, M. La mode des contes de fées. Paris 1928.

Dédéyan, C. Le thème de Faust dans la littérature européenne. 6 vols Paris 1954–67.

Fay, B. La franc-maçonnerie et la révolution intellectuelle du xviiie siècle. Paris 1935.

Knoop, D. and G. P. Jones. The genesis of freemasonry. Manchester 1947.

Birkhead, E. The tale of terror: a study of the Gothic romance. 1921.

Evans, B. Gothic drama from Walpole to Shelley. Berkeley 1947.

Garte, H. Kunstform Schauerroman. Leipzig 1935.

Haslag, J. Gothic im 17 und 18 Jahrhundert. Cologne 1963.

Holbrook, W. C. The adjective 'Gothic' in the 18th century. MLN 56 1941.

Killen, A. M. Le roman terrifiant ou le roman noir. Paris 1923.

Longueil, A. E. The word 'Gothic' in 18th-century criticism. MLN 38 1923.

Summers, M. The Gothic quest: a history of the Gothic novel. New York 1938.

— A Gothic bibliography. [1941].

Varma, D. P. The Gothic flame. 1957.

Ehrard, J. L'idée de nature en France. 2 vols Paris 1963.

Fairchild, H. N. The noble savage: a study in romantic naturalism. New York 1928.

Van Tieghem, P. Le sentiment de la nature dans le préromantisme européen. Paris 1959.

Aldridge, A. O. International influences upon biography as a literary genre. Proc 4th Congress International Comparative Lit Assoc, ed F. Jost, Hague 1966. Novel.

Alter, R. Rogue's progress: studies in the picaresque novel. Cambridge Mass 1964.

Block, A. The English novel 1740–1850: a catalogue. 1961 (rev).

Foxon, D. Libertine literature in England 1660–1745. 1963.

Kany, C. E. The beginnings of the epistolary novel. Berkeley 1937.

Mayo, R. D. The English novel in the magazines 1740–1815. Oxford 1962.

Parker, A. A. Literature and the delinquent: the picaresque novel in Spain and Europe. Edinburgh 1967.

Tompkins, J. M. S. The popular novel in England 1770–1800. 1932.

Van Tieghem, P. La sensibilité et la passion dans le roman européen au xviiie siècle. Revue de Littérature Comparée 6 1926.

— Le roman sentimental en Europe 1740–61. Revue de Littérature Comparée 20 1940.

— Ossian et l'ossianisme dans la littérature européenne au XVIIIe siècle. Groningen 1920.

Bury, J. B. The idea of progress: its origin and growth. 1920.

Hexter, J. H. More's Utopia: the biography of an idea. Princeton 1952.

Tuveson, E. L. Millennium and Utopia: the idea of progress. Berkeley 1949.

Herrick, M. T. Tragicomedy: its origin and development in Italy, France and England. Urbana 1955. Theatre.

Nolte, F. O. The early middle-class drama 1696–1774. Lancaster Pa 1935. See also F. Gaiffe, Le drame en France au XVIIIe siècle, Paris 1910.

Prinsen, J. Het drama in de 18e eeuw in W-Europa. Zutphen 1931.

Walmsley, D. M. The influence of foreign opera on English operatic plays of the Restoration period. Anglia 52 1928.

Béguin, A. L'âme romantique et le rêve. 2 vols Marseilles 1937. Romanticism.

Erhardt-Siebold, E. von. Harmony of the senses in English, German and French romanticism. PMLA 47 1942.

Friederich, W. P. English contributions to preromanticism. In his Outline of comparative literature, Chapel Hill 1954.

Hazard, P. Les origines philosophiques de l'homme de sentiment. Romanic Rev 28 1937.

Praz, M. La carne, la morte e il diavolo nella letteratura romantica. Milan 1930; tr as The romantic agony, Oxford 1933.

Robertson, J. G. Studies in the genesis of romantic theory in the 18th century. Cambridge 1923, New York 1962.

Schenk, H. G. The mind of the European romantics. 1966.

Van Tieghem, P. La place du romantisme anglais dans le romantisme européen. Lettres 5–6 1946.

— Le préromantisme: études d'histoire littéraire européenne. 3 vols Paris 1924–48.

— Le romantisme dans la littérature européenne. Paris 1948.

Wellek, R. The concept of romanticism in literary history. Comparative Lit 1 1949; rptd in his Concepts of criticism, New Haven 1963.

Trousson, R. Le thème de Prométhée dans la littérature européenne. 2 vols Geneva 1964.

Roe, F. C. La découverte de l'Écosse 1760–1830. Revue de Littérature Comparée 27 1953. Scotland.

Michéa, R. Le tombeau dans la pensée du xviiie siècle. Annales de l'Université de Grenoble 14 1937. Tombs.

— Le plaisir des tombeaux. Revue de Littérature Comparée 18 1938.

Van Tieghem, P. La poésie de la nuit et des tombeaux en Europe au XVIIIe siècle. Paris 1921.

Aldridge, A. O. Le problème de la traduction au xviiie siècle. Revue Belge 39 1961. Translation.

Amos, F. R. Early theories of translation. New York 1920.

Frost, W. Dryden and the art of translation. New Haven 1955.

Praz, M. Stanley, Sherburne and Ayres as translators and imitators of Italian, Spanish and French poets. MLR 20 1925.

Adams, P. G. Travels and travel-liars 1660–1800. Berkeley 1962.

Atkinson, G. Les relations de voyage du xviie siècle et l'évolution des idées. Paris 1924.

Cawley, R. R. Milton and the literature of travel. Princeton 1951.

Coe, C. N. Wordsworth and the literature of travel. New York 1953.

Cox, E. G. A reference guide to the literature of travel. 3 vols Seattle 1935–8.

Frantz, R. W. The English traveller and the movement of ideas 1660–1732. Lincoln Nebraska 1935, 1967.

Gove, P. B. The imaginary voyage in prose fiction 1700–1800. New York 1941.

Horn, D. B. The British diplomatic service 1689–1789. 1961.

Laubriet, P. Les guides de voyage au début du xviiie siècle et la propagande philosophique. Stud on Voltaire & Eighteenth Century 32 1965.

Levin, H. Literature and exile. In H. Dieckmann et al, Essays in comparative literature, St Louis 1961.

McKillop, A. D. Local attachment and cosmopolitanism: the 18th-century pattern. In From sensibility to romanticism: essays presented to F. A. Pottle, New York 1965.

Mead, W. E. The Grand Tour in the 18th century. New York 1914.

Parks, G. B. The turn to the romantic in the travel literature of the 18th century. MLQ 25 1964.

Pomeau, R L'Europe des lumières, cosmopolitisme et unité européenne. Paris 1966.

Stout, G. D. (ed). Sterne, A sentimental journey, Berkeley 1967. Includes account of travel literature.

Stoye, J. W. English travellers abroad 1604–67. 1952.

Thomas, G. R. The Enlightenment and *Wales* in the 18th century. Stud on Voltaire & Eighteenth Century 27 1963.

Authors

in alphabetical order

Campbell, H. H. The sale catalogue of Addison's library. Eng Lang Notes 4 1967.

Hegnauer, A. G. Der Einfluss von Addisons Cato. Zürich 1912.

Cone, C. B. Edmund Burke's library. PBSA 44 1950.

Isaacs, J. Congreve's library. Library 3rd ser 20 1939.

Guckel, W. and E. Günther. Defoes und Swifts Belesenheit. Berlin 1925.

Scholte, J. H. Robinsonades. Neophilologus 35 1951.

Ullrich, H. Defoes Robinson Crusoe: die Geschichte eines Weltbuches. Leipzig 1924.

— Robinson und Robinsonaden: Bibliographie. Weimar 1898; Nachträge und Ergänzungen, Zeitschrift für Bücherfreunde 11 1907.

Bredvold, L. I. The intellectual milieu of Dryden. Ann Arbor 1934.

Blanchard, F. T. Fielding the novelist. New Haven 1926. On his reputation abroad.

Giarrizzo, G. Gibbon e la cultura europea del settecento. Naples 1956.

Trevor-Roper, H. R. The idea of the Decline and fall. In The age of the Enlightenment: studies presented to T. Besterman, ed W. H. Barber et al, Edinburgh 1967.

Mossner, E. C. The continental reception of Hume's Treatise 1739–41. Mind 56 1947.

Shackleton, R. Johnson and the Enlightenment. In Johnson, Boswell and their circle: essays presented to L. F. Powell, Oxford 1965.

Price, L. M. George Barnwell abroad. Comparative Lit 2 1950. On Lillo.

Harrison, J. and P. Laslett. The library of J. Locke. Oxford 1965.

Thompson, H. W. A Scottish man of feeling: Henry Mackenzie. Oxford 1927.

Parker, W. R. Milton's contemporary reputation. Columbus 1940.

— Milton: a biography. 2 vols Oxford 1968.

Robertson, J. G. Milton's fame on the Continent. Proc Br Acad 3 1908.

Taylor, I. E. Milton's views on the teaching of foreign languages. Modern Lang Jnl 33 1949.

Boas, F. S. Richardson's novels and their influence. E & S 1911.

Canby, H. S. Pamela abroad. MLN 18 1903.

Dottin, P. L'accueil fait à Pamela. Revue Anglo-américaine 7 1930.

McKillop, A. D. Richardson: printer and novelist. 1936.

Poetzsche, E. Richardsons Belesenheit. Kiel 1907.

Purdie, E. Some adventures of Pamela on the continental stage. In German studies presented to H. G. Fiedler, Oxford 1938.

Thomson, C. L. Samuel Richardson. 1900.

Schudt, E. Das Ausland in Smolletts Romanen. Giessen 1923.

Gückel, W. and E. Günther. Defoes und Swifts Belesenheit. Berlin 1925.

Williams, H. Dean Swift's library. Cambridge 1932.

Coe, C. N. Wordsworth acknowledges his debt to foreign languages. N & Q 28 May 1949.

S.S.B.T.

(2) INTERNATIONAL LATIN LITERATURE

This section excludes neo–Latin verse and other original works in Latin of the period, except in so far as they were translated into the vernacular in Britain or on the Continent. For influence of Latin writings themselves, see sections on individual authors; and below, under separate countries, for the impact of Latin writings abroad. See also the corresponding section for the period 1500–1660, vol 1, above.

Barclay, John. Argenis. Paris 1621; Argienida, tr W. Potocki, Lipsku 1728; The adventures of Poliarchus and Argenis, tr J. Jacob, Dublin 1734 (abridged); Argenis, 2 vols Augsburg 1770; The Phoenix, translated by a lady [Clara Reeve], 1772; Argenisse, tr 2 vols Egerben 1792.

Bacon, Francis, Baron Verulam and Viscount St Albans. Omnia opera quae extant. Frankfurt 1665; Oeuvres, tr A. Lasalle, Dijon [1800]; *see also* J. A. de Luc (elder), Bacon tel qu'il est; ou dénonciation d'une traduction par A. Lasalle, Berlin 1800; Précis de la philosophie de Bacon, Paris 1802.

d'Alembert, J. le Rond. Discours préliminaire. In Encyclopédie vol 1, Paris 1751.

Diderot, D. Pensées sur l'interprétation de la nature. [Paris] 1754.

Deleyre, A. Analyse de la philosophie du chancelier Bacon. Leyden 1756. Tr Pouillot from D. Mallet, The life of Francis Bacon, 1740.

— Novum organum. 1620; Nuovo organo delle scienze, tr A. P. Bassano 1788; Bacons von Verulam neues Organon, tr G. W. Bartholdy, Berlin 1793.

Fischer K. Bacon und seine Schule. Heidelberg 1904.

White, H. B. The influence of Bacon on the philosophes. Stud on Voltaire & Eighteenth Century 27 1963.

Dedekind, Friedrich. Grobianus. Frankfurt 1549; Grobianus: or the complete booby, tr R. Bull 1739.

Du Fresnoy, Charles Alphonse. De arte graphica. Paris 1668; De arte graphica: the art of painting, tr J. Dryden 1695; tr J. Wills 1754; tr W. Mason 1783.

Erasmus, Desiderius. Colloquiorum formulae. Basle 1516; The colloquies or familiar discourses, tr H. M. [Henry More? Henry Munday?] 1671; tr R. L'Estrange 1680, 1689; tr T. Brown [1699?]; tr N. Bailey 1725.

— Moriae encomium. Paris 1509; Moriae encomium: or the praise of folly, tr J. Wilson 1668; Wit against wisdom, tr W. Kennett 1683; Samuel Butler, Hudibras, 3 pts 1663–78 (an imitation).

Knight, S. The life of Erasmus. Cambridge 1726.

Burigny, J. L. de. Vie d'Erasme. 2 vols Paris 1757.

Grotius [Groot], Hugo. De jure belli ac pacis. Paris 1625; Of the rights of war and peace, tr W. Evats 1682; tr 1715.

More, Henry. Enchiridion metaphysicum. 1668; Von unkörperlichen Dingen in der Welt, wider Cartesium, tr C. Rautner, Frankfurt 1680 (with his trn of Sir Thomas Browne, Pseudodoxia epidemica).

More, Thomas. Utopia. 1516; L'Utopie de Morus, tr Gueudeville, Leyden 1715 (earlier trns 1550, 1643); tr T. Rousseau, Paris 1780.

Newton, Sir Isaac. Philosophiae naturalis principia mathematica. 1687.

Clarke, Samuel. A collection of papers which passed between the late learned Mr Leibniz and Dr Clarke. 1717.

Pemberton, Henry. A view of Newton's philosophy. 1728; Eléments de la philosophie newtonienne, tr E. de Joncourt, Amsterdam 1755.

Voltaire. Eléments de la philosophie de Newton. Paris 1738.

Owen, John. Epigrammata. 1606–12; Teutsch redender
Owenus, tr V. Löbern, Jena 1661; Owen's Latin epi-
grams, tr T. Harvey 1677; Agudezas, tr F. de la Torre,
vol 2 Madrid 1674–82; Épigrammes d'Owen, tr A. L.
Le Brun, Paris 1709.
Feinler, G. Poetische Lust-gärtgen. Zeitz 1677.
Pufendorf, Samuel. De jure naturae et gentium libri viii.
Lund 1672; Of the law of nature and nations, tr B.
Kennett 1710.
— De officio hominis et civis juxta legem naturalem libri
duo. Lund 1673 (abstract of De jure); tr 1698.
— De habitu religionis christianae ad vitam civilem liber
singularis. Bremen 1687; Of the relation between
Church and State, tr 1719.
— Jus feciale divinum. Lübeck 1695; The divine feudal
law, tr 1703.
Spinoza, Benedictus de. Tractatus theologico-politicus.
Hamburg [Amsterdam] 1670; A treatise partly theologi-
cal and partly political, tr 1689; Miracles no violation of
the law of nature [from bk 6], tr 1683.
Clarke, S. A demonstration of the being and attributes
of God, more particularly in answer to Spinoza. 1705.
Tindal, M. Spinoza revived: or the rights of the
Christian church. 1709.
An account of the life and writings of Spinosa; to which
is added an abstract of his Theological political
treatise. 1720.
Innes, A. Ἀρετη-Λογια: or an enquiry into the original
of moral virtue, wherein the false notions of Spinoza
are examined and confuted. 1729.
Swedenborg, Emanuel. Arcana coelestia. 1749–56;
Arcana coelestia: or heavenly mysteries, tr J. Clowes
1782–1806.
— De coelo et de inferno. 1758 (extracts from Arcana
coelestia); Treatise concerning heaven and hell, tr W.
Cookworthy 1778.
— De telluribus in mundo nostro solari. 1758; Concerning the earths in our solar system, tr J. Clowes 1787.

— Doctrina vitae pro nova hierosolyma. Amsterdam
1763; the doctrine of life for the New Jerusalem, tr 1786
(2nd edn).
— De commercio animae et corporis. 1769; A theosophic
lucubration on the nature of influx, tr T. Hartley 1770.
— Vera christiana religio. Amsterdam 1771; True
Christian religion, tr J. Clowes 1781.
Other translations
Sketch of the delights of conjugal love, tr 1789.
Delights of wisdom concerning conjugal love, tr 1790.
The apocalypse revealed, tr 1791.
Continuation of the last judgement and the spiritual
world, tr 1791.
Clowes, John. A letter to a Member of Parliament on
the character and writings of Baron Swedenborg.
1799.
Lamm, M. Swedenborg en Angleterre. Revue Bleue
74 1936.
Erdman, D. V. Blake's early Swedenborgianism: a 20th-
century legend. Comparative Lit 5 1953.

Thou, Jacques Auguste de (Thuanus). Historiae suae
temporis. Paris 1604–20.
Burnet, Gilbert. History of my own time. 2 vols 1724–
34.
Vida, Hieronymus. De arte poetica. Rome 1527; Vida's
Art of poetry, tr C. Pitt 1725.
— Bombycum libri II. Rome 1527; Silkworms: a poem,
tr 1723; Bombyx the silkworm: a poem, tr S. Pullein,
Dublin 1750.
— M. H. Vicae christiados libri sex. Cremona 1535; The
Christiad: a poem, tr J. Cranwell 1678; tr E. Granan
1771.
Highet, G. The classical tradition. Oxford 1949.
Myers, W. T. The relations of Latin and English as living
languages in England during the age of Milton. Dayton
1913.

S.S.B.T.

(3) FRENCH

*For studies and bibliographies of other aspects of Franco-
British relations, see* G. Ascoli, La Grande-Bretagne devant
l'opinion française au xviie siècle, 2 vols Paris 1930; G.
Bonno, La culture et la civilisation britanniques devant
l'opinion française 1713–34, Philadelphia 1948. *Aside from*
I. Charlanne, L'influence française en Angleterre au xviie
siècle, 2 vols Paris 1906, *no comprehensive work exists on
the French impact on British society and letters 1660–1800.*

Dictionaries and Grammars

Cotgrave, R. A dictionarie of the French and English
tongues. 1611; ed W. S. Woods, Chapel Hill 1950; rev
J. Howell as A French and English dictionary, 1650.
See V. E. Smalley, The sources of Cotgrave, Baltimore
1948.
Festeau, P. Nouvelle grammaire anglaise. 1672.
— Nouvelle double grammaire française-anglaise et
anglaise-française. Hague 1693. With Mauger.
Miège, G. A new dictionary French and English, with
another English and French. 1677; A dictionary of
barbarous French, 1679; Nouvelle nomenclature
française et anglaise, 1685; Short French dictionary,
1684; Great French dictionary, 2 vols 1688.
— Nouvelle facile méthode pour apprendre l'anglais.
1685.
Villiers, J. Vocabularium analogicum. 1680.
Maugier, C. Grammaire anglaise. Bordeaux 1685.
Bérault, P. A new plain, short and compleat French and
English grammar. 1688.
A., E. Grammaire anglaise et française. Rouen 1695.
Boyer, Abel. Royal dictionary in two parts. 2 vols 1699;
abridged 1700; tr as Le dictionnaire royal, 2 vols Hague
1702.

— The compleat French master for ladies and gentlemen.
1748.
Dyche, Thomas. A new general English dictionary. 1740;
Nouveau dictionnaire universel des arts et des sciences,
tr père Esprit Pézenas and J. F. Férand, 2 vols Avignon
1753–4; also as Encyclopédie françoise latine et angloise,
2 vols 1761.
Johnson, Samuel. A dictionary of the English language.
1755; tr as Dictionnaire anglois de Johnson, 2 vols 1773.
Nugent, T. A new pocket dictionary for the French and
English languages. 1767.

Studies

Du Verdier. Abrégé de l'histoire d'Angleterre [by
Duchesne 1614]. 3 vols Paris 1661. Further abridged
by Vanel, Paris 1689.
Hermannides, R. Britannia magne. Amsterdam 1661.
Menteith de Salmonet, Robert. Histoire des troubles de la
Grande-Bretagne 1633–50. 2 vols Paris 1661.
Camden, W. Britannia 1586; Description générale de
l'Angleterre, tr S. J. Sorbière, Amsterdam 1662.
Payen. Les voyages de M. Payen. Paris 1663.
Le Pays, René. Amitiez, amours et amourettes. Paris
1664. Includes Relation d'un voyage d'Angleterre.
Sorbière, S. J. Relation d'un voyage en Angleterre. Paris
1664; tr 1709. On Hobbes et al.
Monconys, B. de. Journal des voyages de M. de Monconys.
3 vols Lyons 1665–6.
Duchesne, André. Histoire d'Angleterre, d'Ecosse et
d'Irlande. 2 vols Paris 1666 (new edn).
Childrey, J. Britannia Baconica. 1661; Histoire des
singularités naturelles d'Angleterre, tr [Briot], Paris
1667.

Chamberlayne, E. Angliae notitia. 1669; L'esprit présent de l'Angleterre, tr [Neuville] 2 vols Amsterdam 1669.

L'Estrange, Sir R. The dissenter's sayings. 1681; Le non-conformiste anglois dans ses écris, tr 1683.

Leti, G. Il teatro britanico. 2 vols 1683.

Gilbert, John. An answer to the bishop of Condom, now of Meaux [Bossuet], his exposition of the Catholic faith. 1686.

d'Orléans, prince. Histoire des révolutions d'Angleterre. Paris 1689.

Langbaine, Gerard. Account of the English dramatick poets. Oxford 1691. Notes French sources and influences.

D.C. [de Callières]. Des mots à la mode. Paris 1693.

Temple, W. An introduction to the history of England. 1695; Introduction à l'histoire d'Angleterre, Amsterdam 1695; Abrégé, Hague 1695.

Larrey, I. de. Histoire d'Angleterre, d'Ecosse et d'Irlande. 4 vols Rotterdam 1697–1713.

Misson de Valberg, H. Mémoires et observations faites par un voyageur en Angleterre. Hague 1698.

Howard, E. Remarks on the new philosophy of Descartes. 1700.

Perrault, C. Des hommes illustres qui ont paru en France. Paris 1700; tr J. Ozell 1704–5.

Defoe, D. A review of the affairs of France and of all Europe. 1705–12.

Beeverell, J. Les délices de la Grande-Bretagne. 7 vols Leyden 1707.

Miège, G. New state of England. 1691; L'état présent de la Grande-Bretagne, tr G.M. 2 vols Amsterdam 1708.

Collier, Jeremy. A short view of the immorality and profaneness of the English stage. 1698; La critique du théâtre anglois, tr [J. de Courbeville], Paris 1715.

Lesage, G. L. Remarques sur l'Angleterre. Amsterdam 1715.

Dissertation sur la poésie angloise. Journal Littéraire 9 1717.

de Cize. Histoire du whigisme et du torisme. Leipzig 1717. Locke in France.

Rapin de Thoyras, P. Dissertation sur les Whigs et les Torys. Hague 1717.

—— Histoire d'Angleterre. Hague 1724–7; tr Tindal 1726–32.

Jacob, Giles. Poetical register: or the lives and characters of the English dramatick poets. 2 vols 1719–20.

Baillet, Adrien. Jugemens des sçavans sur les principaux ouvrages des auteurs. 4 vols Paris 1685–6; rev La Monnoye, Amsterdam 1722.

Muralt, Béat Louis de. Lettres sur les Anglois et les François et sur les voiages. [Cologne] 1725; tr 1726. [Desfontaines, P. F. Guyot]. Apologie du caractère des Anglois et Français: ou observations sur le livre intitulé Lettre sur les Anglais et les Français. Paris 1726.

Boissy, L. de. Le Français à Londres. Paris 1727. A play.

Voltaire. Essay upon the epic poetry. 1727; Essay sur la poesie épique, tr [P. F. G. Desfontaines], Paris 1728. Voltaire later replaced this unauthorized trn with his own.

Prévost d'Exiles, Antoine François. Mémoires et aventures d'un homme de qualité. Paris 1728–32; ed M. E. I. Robertson, Paris 1927 (vol 5); tr 1738.

Voltaire. Discours sur la tragédie. 1731. Préface to Brutus.

—— Lettres philosophiques. 1734. Appeared variously as Lettres écrites de Londres sur les Anglois et autres sujets par M.D.V***, Basle [London] 1734, and as Lettres philosophiques par M.D.V***; Letters concerning the English nation by Mr de Voltaire, tr [J. Lockman], 1733. The English trn appeared before the French original.

Lenglet-Dufresnoy, N. A. De l'usage des romans. 2 vols Amsterdam 1734.

Bibliothèque française. Ed C. P. Goujet, Paris 1740–56. Vol 8 contains trns of English poets.

Burnet, Gilbert. Histoire de ce qui s'est passé en Angleterre pendant la vie de Gilbert Burnet, évêque de Salisbury. Hague 1735.

Riccoboni, L. Réflexions historiques et critiques sur les différents théâtres de l'Europe. Paris 1738.

Aubert de La Chesnaye des Bois, F. A. de. Lettres amusantes et critiques sur les romans en général, anglais et français, tant anciens que modernes. Paris 1743.

Macky, J. A journey through England. 1714; Le guide de l'Angleterre, tr Moreau de Brasey, Amsterdam 1744.

Dissertation sur les poèmes de Mrs Boileau, Addison et Voltaire. Mercure de France Sept 1745.

Laplace, P. A. de (editor and translator). Le théâtre anglois. 4 vols 1745–6, 8 vols 1746–9 (includes Discours sur le théâtre anglois).

Le Blanc, Jean Bernard. Lettres d'un François sur les Anglais. Hague 1745; Letters on the English, tr 1747.

Green, John. Collection of voyages and travels. 1745–7; Histoire générale des voyages, tr [A. R. Prévost d'Exiles] 7 vols Paris 1746–9; 20 vols 1746–[1802.]

Trochereau de La Berlière, Jean Arnold. Choix de différents morceaux de poésie traduits de l'anglois. Paris 1749.

Yart (ed). Idée de la poésie angloise ou traduction des meilleurs poètes anglois qui n'ont point encore paru dans notre langue. 8 vols Paris 1749–56.

Encyclopédie: ou dictionnaire raisonné des sciences, des arts et des métiers. 17 vols (with 11 vols of illustrations). Paris 1751–65. At least in early stages the Encyclopédie was trn of Chambers' Cyclopoedia, 1728.

d'Alembert, Jean le Rond. Discours préliminaire. In Encyclopédie vol 1, Paris 1751.

Mélanges de différentes pièces traduites de l'anglois. Tr [Mme du Bocage] 3 vols Berlin 1751.

Du Bocage, A. M. Fiquet. Lettre sur le théâtre anglais. 2 vols Paris 1752.

Foote, Samuel. The Englishman in Paris. 1753; Anglois à Paris, tr 1767.

Rouquet, J. A. L'état des arts en Angleterre. Paris 1755.

Formey, Jean Henri Samuel. Conseils pour former une bibliothèque peu nombreuse mais choisie. 1755; rev Berlin 1756.

Choix de petites pièces du théatre anglois, tr [P. Patu] 2 vols 1756.

Brown, John. An estimate of the manners and principles of the times, 1757; Les mœurs anglaises, tr [C. Chais], Hague 1758.

Fougeret de Monbron, Louis Charles. Préservatif contre l'Anglomanie. Minorca 1757.

Moore, Edward. The world. 1753–6; Le monde par Adam Fitz-Adam et autres sur les moeurs du temps, tr G. J. Monod [or G. Joël?] 2 vols Leyden 1757; also as Tableau critique des moeurs anglaises, Hague 1761.

Legion. The humble remonstrances of the mob of Great Britain against the importation of French words. Annual Register 1758.

Favart, C. S. L'Anglais à Bordeaux. Paris 1763. A play.

Montagu, Lady Mary Wortley. Letters written during her travels in Europe etc 1763–7; Lettres de milady Wortlay Montagute écrites pendant ses voyages en diverses parties du monde, tr 1764.

Le nouveau théâtre anglois. [Tr Mme Riccoboni] 2 vols 1767, 2 further vols Paris 1769.

Young, Arthur. Letters concerning the present state of the French nation. 1769.

[Andrews, John]. An account of the character and manners of the French, with occasional observations on the English. 2 vols 1770; rev 1785; Essai sur le caractère et les mœurs des François comparés à ceux des Anglais, tr [J. J. Rutledge] 1776.

—— A comparative view of the French and English nations. 1785.

Talbot, Robert. Letters on the French nation. 1771.

Batteux, C. Principes de la littérature. 5 vols Paris 1774 (5th edn).

Caraccioli. L'Europe française. Turin 1776.

Rutledge, Jean-Jacques. La quinzaine angloise à Paris. 1776; The Englishman's fortnight, tr 'an Observer' 1777.

—— The adventures of Monsieur Provence, gentleman to Lord R. 2 vols 1788.

Dorat, C. J. Le chevalier français à Londres. Paris 1779.

Gibbon, Edward. Exposition of the conduct of the King of France towards England. 1780; Mémoire justificatif pour servir de réponse à l'exposé de la cour de France, 1779.

La Rochefoucauld, François duc de. Mélanges sur l'Angleterre. 1784–5; tr Cambridge 1933.

Traduction du théâtre anglois. [Tr Mme de Vasse] 12 vols Paris 1784.

La Coste, de. Voyage philosophique d'Angleterre fait en 1783 et 1784. 2 vols 1786.

Burke, Edmund. Reflections on the Revolution in France. 1790.

—— Thoughts on the prospect of a peace with the regicide directory. 1796.

Young, Arthur. Travels [in France] through the years 1787, 1788 and 1789. 2 vols 1792.

Moore, John. A journal during a residence in France. 1793–4.

Berry, W. Cabinet littéraire: or a catalogue of a circulating library consisting of French books only at W. Berry bookseller and stationer. Edinburgh 1796.

Wollstonecraft, Mary. An historical and moral view of the origin and progress of the French Revolution. 1794.

Laharpe, J. F. De l'état des lettres en Europe jusqu'au règne de Louis XIV. Paris 1797.

Sayous, A. Le xviiie siècle à l'étranger: histoire de la littérature française en Angleterre. Paris 1861.

Taine, H. Histoire de la littérature anglaise. 4 vols Paris 1863–5.

Morley, J. Voltaire. 1872, 1885 etc. See F. Brunetière, Voltaire, in Etudes critiques, who qualifies Morley's claims for the influence of England on Voltaire.

Griswold, W. M. A descriptive list of novels and tales dealing with life in France. Cambridge 1894.

Texte, J. B. L. de Muralt e vles origines du cosmopolitisme littéraire. Revue d'Histoire Littéraire de la France 1 1894.

—— J.-J. Rousseau et les origines du cosmopolitisme littéraire: études sur les relations de la France et de l'Angleterre au xviiie siècle. Paris 1895; tr J. W. Matthews 1899.

Saroléa, C. Influence de la culture française sur la culture anglaise. Revue Française d'Edimbourg 1 1897.

—— Le caractère anglais et le caractère français: influences réciproques. In his Essais de littérature et de politique, Brussels 1906.

Baldensperger, F. L'Angleterre et les Anglais vus à travers la littérature française. Bibliothèque Universelle 38 1905.

—— Quelques-uns des nos préférés anglo-français. Annual Bull Modern Humanities Research Assoc 1931.

Caussy, F. Propos sur l'influence mutuelle de la France et de l'Angleterre. Ermitage Dec 1905.

Charlanne, L. L'influence française en Angleterre au xviie siècle. 2 vols Paris 1906.

Collins, J. C. Bolingbroke: historical study, and Voltaire in England. 1886.

—— Voltaire, Montesquieu and Rousseau in England. 1908.

Upham, A. H. The French influence in English literature. New York 1908.

Lanson, G. (ed). Voltaire, Lettres philosophiques. 2 vols Paris 1909.

—— Manuel bibliographique de la littérature française. Paris 1921 (rev); suppl by J. Giraud, Manuel de bibliographie littéraire, Paris 1939.

Lee, S. The French Renaissance in England. Oxford 1910.

Mornet, D. Les enseignements des bibliothèques privées 1750–80. Revue d'Histoire de la Littérature Française 21 1914.

White, N. J. D. A catalogue of books in the French language in Archbishop Marsh's library. Dublin 1918.

Cazamian, L. Le romantisme en France et en Angleterre: quelques differences 1660–1914. Paris 1920.

Lockitt, C. H. The relations between French and English society 1763–93. New York 1920.

Haustein, M. Die französische Literatur im Urteil der englischen Romantiker Wordsworth, Coleridge, Southey. Leipzig 1921.

Held, M. A. Ludwig XIV und sein Hof in der englischen Prosadichtung. Zürich 1922.

Partridge, E. The French Romantics' knowledge of English literature. Paris 1924.

Van Tieghem, P. Le préromantisme: études d'histoire européenne. 3 vols Paris 1924–47.

—— Les influences étrangères sur la littérature française 1550–1880. Paris 1961.

Dubosq, Y. Z. Le livre français en Hollande de 1750 à 1780. Amsterdam 1925. Includes influences elsewhere.

Offor, R. A collection of books in the University Library Leeds. Proc Leeds Philosophical Soc 1–6 1925–48. Also TLS 15 Feb 1936.

Robertson, M. E. I. (ed). Prévost, Mémoires d'un homme de qualité vol 5. Paris 1927.

Ascoli, G. La Grande-Bretagne devant l'opinion française au xviie siècle. 2 vols Paris 1930. With meticulous bibliography of primary materials covering all aspects of English impact on France.

Trahard, P. Les maîtres de la sensibilité française au xviiie. 4 vols Paris 1931–3.

Blassneck, M. Frankreich als Vermittler englisch-deutscher Einflüsse im xviiten und xviiten Jahrhundert. Leipzig 1934.

Green, F. C. Minuet: a critical survey of French and English literary ideas in the 18th century. 1935.

Streeter, H. W. The 18th-century English novel in French translation. New York [1936].

Bond, D. F. American scholarship in the field of 18th-century Anglo-French studies. Romanic Rev 29 1938. With bibliography.

Reimeringer, A. L'opinion anglaise sur les institutions françaises au xviiie siècle. Paris 1938.

Gausin, L. F. Les lettres anglaises dans l'Encyclopédie. New York 1942.

Tucker, J. E. English translations from the French 1650–1700: corrections and additions to the CBEL. PQ 21 1942.

Bonno, G. La culture et la civilisation britanniques devant l'opinion française de la paix d'Utrecht aux Lettres philosophiques 1713–34. Philadelphia 1948.

Rochedieu, C. A. Bibliography of French translations of English works 1700–1800. Chicago 1948. See also M. M. Barr, PBSA 43 1949. Excludes early trns in periodicals.

Mackenzie, F. An Anglo-French collection of books in the Royal Malta library. In Studies presented to G. Ritchie, Cambridge 1949.

Dubois-Pichler, E. T. Au sujet de quelques ouvrages consacrés en Angleterre à la littérature du xviie siècle français. XVIIe Siècle 6 1950.

Cabeen, D. C. (ed). A critical bibliography of French literature: vol 3, The seventeenth century, ed N. Edelman, Syracuse NY 1961; vol 4, The eighteenth century, ed G. R. Havens and D. F. Bond, Syracuse NY 1951; Supplement, ed R. A. Brooks, Syracuse NY 1968.

Carrière, J. M. Anglo-French and Franco-American studies: a current bibliography. French-Amer Rev 4 1952.

Pottinger, D. T. The French book-trade in the Ancien Régime. Cambridge Mass 1958.

Evans, H. B. Provisional bibliography of English editions and translations of Voltaire. Stud on Voltaire & Eighteenth Century 8 1959.

Bibliothèque de Voltaire: catalogue des livres. Moscow and Leningrad 1961. Ed in Russian, cataloguing one of largest 18th-century book collections.

Barber, G. The Cramers of Geneva and their trade in Europe 1755–66. Stud on Voltaire & Eighteenth Century 30 1964. On Voltaire's Genevan publishers.

Wais, K. Le cosmopolitisme littéraire à travers les âges. Proc 4th Congress of International Comparative Lit Assoc (Hague) 1966.

Campos, C. The view of France. Oxford 1965.

Dédéyan, C. Rousseau et la sensibilité littéraire à la fin du xviiie siècle. Paris 1967.

Themes
Anglophobia and Anglomania

Acomb, F. Anglophobia in France 1763–89. Durham 1950.

Baldensperger, F. Voltaire anglophile avant son séjour d'Angleterre. Revue de Littérature Comparée 9 1929.

Bastide, C. Anglo-French entente in the 17th century. 1914.

Bruch, J. Die Anglomanie in Frankreich. Stuttgart 1941.

Dargan, E. P. The question of Voltaire's primacy in establishing the English vogue. In Mélanges d'histoire littéraire générale et comparée offerts à F. D. Baldensperger, Paris 1930.

Green, F. C. Anglomaniacs and Francophiles. In his 18th-century France, 1929.

Havens, G. R. The abbé Le Blanc and English literature. MP 18 1921.

Ternois, R. Les débuts de l'Anglophilie en France. Revue de Littérature Comparée 13 1933.

Chivalry

La Curne de Sainte-Palaye, J. B. de. Mémoires sur l'ancienne chevalerie. Paris 1759–81; Memoirs of ancient chivalry, tr S. Dobson 1784.

— Histoire littéraire des troubadours. Paris 1774; The literary history of the troubadours, tr S. Dobson 1779.

Jacoubet, H. Le genre troubadour et les origines françaises du romantisme. Paris 1928.

Johnston, A. Enchanted ground: the study of medieval romance in the 18th century. 1964.

Language

Baldensperger, F. Le classicisme française et les langues étrangères. Revue de Littérature Comparée 13 1933.

Bonnafé, A. Dictionnaire étymologique et historique des anglicismes. Paris 1920.

Boulan, H. P. Les mots d'origine étrangère en France 1650–1700. Amsterdam 1934.

Brunot, F. Histoire de la langue française. Vol 5, Le français en France et hors de France au xviie siècle, Paris 1927; vol 8, Le français hors de France au xviiie siècle, Paris 1934–5.

Cobb, L. P. A. de Laplace. Paris 1928.

Cushing, M. G. P. Le Tourneur. New York 1908.

Frost, W. Dryden and the art of translation. New Haven 1955.

Horsman, E. A. Dryden's French borrowings. RES new ser 1 1950. On vocabulary.

Lambley, K. R. The teaching and cultivation of the French in England during Tudor and Stuart times. Manchester 1920.

Las Vergnas, R. Le chevalier Rutledge. Paris 1932.

Mackenzie, F. Les relations de l'Angleterre et de la France d'après le vocabulaire. 2 vols Paris 1939.

Morris, T. L'abbé Desfontaines. Stud on Voltaire & Eighteenth Century 19 1961. Includes a study of 18th-century trn.

Plattard, J. Où et comment les étrangers séjournant en France au xviie siècle apprenaient le français. Revue des Cours et des Conférences Feb 1937.

Streeter, H. W. French theories of translation in the 18th century. In his The 18th-century English novel in French translation, New York [1936].

West, C. B. La théorie de la traduction au xviiie siècle. Revue de Littérature Comparée 12 1932.

Nature

Dubois-Pichler, E. T. L'influence exercée en Angleterre du P. Rapin. xviie Siècle 20 1953.

Ehrard, J. L'idée de Nature en France dans la première moitié du xviiie siècle. 2 vols Paris 1963.

Engel, C. E. La littérature alpestre en France et en Angleterre. Chambéry 1930.

Scotland: see also Beattie, Boswell, Ferguson, Hume, Adam Smith and Ossian, below.

d'Alembert, J. le Rond. Eloge de milord maréchal [George Keith]. Paris 1779.

Bain, M. Les voyageurs français en Ecosse 1770–1830. Paris 1932.

Boutroux, E. De l'influence de la philosophie écossaise sur la philosophie française. In his Etudes d'histoire de la philosophie, Paris 1897.

Brumfitt, J. H. Scotland and the French Enlightenment. In The age of the Enlightenment: studies presented to T. Besterman, ed W. H. Barber et al, Edinburgh 1967.

De Beer, G. and A. M. Rousseau. Voltaire's British visitors. Stud on Voltaire & Eighteenth Century 49 1967.

Du Bosq, G. de Beaumont and M. Bernos. La cour des Stuarts à St Germain-en-Laye 1689–1718. Paris 1912.

Duncan, D. T. Ruddiman: Scottish scholarship of the 18th century. Edinburgh 1966.

Howard, A. K. Montesquieu, Voltaire and Rousseau in the 18th-century Scotland: a checklist of editions, translations etc. Bibliothek (Glasgow) 2 1959–62.

McLean, H. R. Urie printer in Glasgow. Records of Glasgow Bibl Soc 3 1914.

Marchand, J. La Rochefoucauld voyageur en Ecosse. Correspondant March 1932.

Meixle, H. W. Voltaire and Scotland. Etudes Anglaises 2 1958.

Michel, F. Les Ecossais en France et les Français en Ecosse. 2 vols Paris 1962.

Trevor-Roper, H. R. The Scottish Enlightenment. Stud on Voltaire & Eighteenth Century 55 1967.

Travel

Atkinson, G. The extraordinary voyage in French literature before 1700. New York 1920.

— The extraordinary voyage 1700–20. Paris 1922.

Babeau, A. Les voyageurs en France. Tours 1928.

Bain, M. Les voyageurs français en Ecosse 1770–1830. Paris 1931.

Baldensperger, F. Chateaubriand et l'émigration française à Londres. Revue d'Histoire Littéraire de la France 1907. Also Etudes d'Histoire Littéraire 2nd ser 1910.

— Intellectuels français hors de France. Revue des Cours et des Conférences 35–6 1933–4.

— Le mouvement des idées dans l'émigration française. 2 vols Paris 1924.

Carré, A. L'influence des huguenots français en Irlande. Paris 1937.

Clark, R. Strangers at Port-Royal. Cambridge 1932.

Daumet, G. Notice sur les établissements religieux anglais à Paris. Mémoires de la Société d'Histoire de Paris 37, 39 1912.

de Beer, G. and A. M. Rousseau. Voltaire's British visitors. Stud on Voltaire & Eighteenth Century 49 1967.

Engels, C. E. English visitors at the Court of France in the 18th century. History Today 11 1961.

Horn, D. B. British diplomatic representatives 1689–1789. Camden Soc 3rd ser 46 1932.

Laubriet, P. Les guides de voyage et la propagande philosophique. Stud on Voltaire & Eighteenth Century 32 1965.

Maxwell, C. The English traveller in France 1698–1715. 1932.

Palmer, R. E. French travellers in England 1600–1900. 1960.

Roe, F. C. French travellers in Britain. 1928.

Schickler, F. de. Les églises du Refuge en Angleterre 1550–1685. 3 vols Paris 1892.

Smiles, S. The Huguenots: their settlements in England and Ireland. 1889.

Ternois, R. Les Français en Angleterre 1660–76. Revue de Littérature Comparée 34 1960.

Thompson, J. M. English witnesses of the French Revolution. Oxford 1938.

Tinker, C. B. The salons and English letters. New York 1915.

Voisine, J. Les Anglais en Provence au xviiie siècle. Revue de Littérature Comparée 30 1956.

Voyages imaginaires, romanesques, allégoriques. 39 vols Amsterdam and Paris 1787–9. Source of utopian and travel literature.

Authors and Individual Travellers

Boswell, James. *For Journals and his descriptions of Holland, Corsica, the Grand Tour etc, see cols 1216–17, below.*
—— An account of Corsica. 1768; Relations de l'Ile de Corse, tr [J.P.I. Dubois], Hague 1769; Etat de la Corse, tr M.S[eigneux] D[e] C[orrevon] 2 vols 1769.
—— The Journal of a tour to the Hebrides. 1786; Détail authentique des malheurs et de la fuite du prince Charles-Édouard dans les Hébrides, Paris 1786.

Leigh, R. A. Boswell and Rousseau. MLR 47 1952.

Pottle, F. A. Boswell: the earlier years 1740–69. New York 1966.

Roth, G. Boswell and J.-J. Rousseau. Mercury 8 1923.

Tinker, C. B. The young Boswell. Boston 1922.

Burney, Frances and Dr Charles Burney
Delachaux, E. Fanny Burney: intermédiaire manquée entre l'Angleterre et la France. Revue de Littérature Comparée 15 1935.

Glover, C. H. Dr Burney's continental travels 1770–2. 1927.

Horsley, P. M. Dr Burney and Rousseau. Comparative Lit Stud 23–4 1946.

Leigh, R. A. Les amitiés françaises du Dr Burney. Revue de Littérature Comparée 25 1951.

Chastellux, François Jean de
Bonno, G. Lettres inédites de Chastellux à Wilkes. Revue de Littérature Comparée 12 1932.

Varnum, F. Un philosophe cosmopolite du xviiie siècle. Paris 1936.

Chesterfield, Philip Dormer Stanhope, 4th Earl of
Dobrée, B. Chesterfield in France. In English miscellany, ed M. Praz, Oxford 1951 (2nd edn).

Gulick, S. L. A Chesterfield bibliography to 1800. Chicago 1935.

Desmaizeaux, Pierre
Daniels, W. M. Des Maizeaux en Angleterre. Revue Germanique 4 1908.

Destouches, Phillipe Néricault
Wade, I. O. Destouches in England. MP 29 1931.

Fénelon, François de Salignac de La Mothe
Warren, A. Fénelon among the Anglo-Saxons. In his New England saints, Ann Arbor 1956.

Garrick, David
The private correspondence. 2 vols 1831–2.

Hedgecock, F. A. Garrick et ses amis français. Paris 1911; tr 1912.

Stone, G. W. The journal of Garrick [France and Italy 1763]. New York 1939.

Genlis, Stéphanie Félicité Ducrest de Saint-Aubin, marquise de Sillery, comtesse de
Ward, P. J. Mme de Genlis in England. Revue de Littérature Comparée 16 1936.

Wahba, M. Mme de Genlis in England. Comparaitve Lit 13 1961.

Geoffrin, Marie Thérèse
Brown, H. Mme Geoffrin and M. Ffolkes. MLQ 1 1940.

Johnson, Samuel
Tyson, M. and H. Guppy. The French journals of Mrs Thrale and Dr Johnson. Manchester 1932.

Justel, Henri
Brown, H. Un cosmopolite du grand siècle: Justel. Bulletin de la Société d'Histoire du Protestantisme Français 82 1933.

La Rochefoucauld, François de
Marchand, J. (ed). A Frenchman in England, tr S. C. Roberts, Cambridge 1933.

Le Blanc, Jean Bernard
Havens, G. R. The abbé Le Blanc and English literature. MP 18 1920.

Monod-Cassidy, H. Un voyageur-philosophe: l'abbé Le Blanc. Cambridge Mass 1941.

Mulhöfer, L. Abbé J. B. Le Blanc. Würzburg 1936.

Montagu, Lady Mary Wortley
Collected letters. Ed R. Halsband 3 vols Oxford 1965–7.

Halsband, R. Algarotti: his influence on Lady Montagu. In Friendship's garland: essays presented to Mario Praz, 2 vols Rome 1966.

Montesquieu, Charles de Secondat, baron de La Brède et de
Voyages. Ed A. de Montesquieu 2 vols Bordeaux 1894–6.

Doumic, R. Les voyages de Montesquieu. Revue des Deux Mondes 15 1897.

Muralt, Béat Louis de
Texte, J. De Muralt et les origines du cosmopolitisme littéraire au xviiie siècle. Revue d'Histoire de la Littérature Française I 1894.

Roland, Mme.
May, Gita. 18th-century England as seen by [Mme Roland]. French Stud 19 1965.

Smollett, Tobias George
Travels through France and Italy. 2 vols 1766.

Suard, Jean Baptiste
Lettres inédites à Wilkes. Ed G. Bonno, Berkeley 1932.

Legouis, P. Suard et Wilkes. Bulletin de l'Académie de Mâcon 1934.

Walpole, Horace
Correspondence. Ed W. S. Lewis et al, New Haven 1939– ; in particular Correspondence with Mme du Deffand and Wiart, ed Lewis and W. H. Smith 6 vols 1939 (including Walpole's Paris journal).

Finch, M. B. and A. E. Peers. Walpole's relations with Voltaire. MP 18 1921.

Koven, A. de. Walpole and Mme du Deffand. New York 1929.

Yvon, P. La vie d'un dilettante: Walpole. Paris 1924.

Periodicals

See L. E. Hatin, Bibliographie de la presse périodique française, Paris 1866. *The order in this selection is alphabetical by name of the principal editor, or by title for minor periodicals and those under multiple editorship.*

Addison, Joseph and Sir Richard Steele. The tatler. 1709–11; Le babillard ou le nouvelliste philosophe, tr A.D.L.C. [Armand de La Chapelle], Amsterdam 2 vols 1719–35; excerpts in Variétés morales et amusantes, tr Blanchet, ed Dusaulx, Paris 1784.

The spectator. 1711–12, 1714; Le spectateur ou le Socrate moderne, tr D. Mortier, Amsterdam, Rouen, Paris (variously) 1714–18; P. C. de C. de Marivaux, Le spectateur françois [imitation], Paris 1722–3; Réduction de Spectateur anglois à ce qu'il renferme de meilleur, Amsterdam 1753.

The guardian. 1713; Le mentor moderne, tr J. van Effen, Hague 1723, Rouen 1725.

The freeholder. 1715–16; Le freeholder ou l'Anglois jaloux de sa liberté, Amsterdam 1727.

The beauties of the Spectators, Tatlers and Guardians. 1763; L'esprit d'Addison, tr M.J.P.A. Yverdon 1777.

Imitations

Van Effen, J. Le misanthrope. 1711–12.
—— Le nouveau spectateur françois. 1725.
La Chapelle, A. de. Le philosophe nouvelliste: ou le babillard. 1719.
Marivaux, P. C. de C. de. Le spectateur françois. 1722–3.
Diderot, D. and J.-J. Rousseau. Le persifleur. 1781.
L'avantcoureur. Ed Jonval and J. Lacombe, Paris 1759–74.
Bayle, Pierre. Nouvelles de la république des lettres. Amsterdam 1684–9, 1699–1718. From 1687 ed Bernard.
Bibliothèque britannique: ou histoire des ouvrages des savants de la Grande-Bretagne. Ed Desmaizeaux and J. Bernard, Hague 1733–47.
Bibliothèque raisonnée des ouvrages des savans de l'Europe. Ed A. de La Chapelle, Barbeyrac and Desmaizeaux, Amsterdam 1728–53.
Bibliothèque universelle des romans. [Ed Paulmy], Paris 1775–89; Nouvelle bibliothèque des romans, Paris 1798–1805.
Clément, Pierre. Les cinq années littéraires 1748–52. Hague 1754.
Courrier de l'Europe: gazette franco-anglaise. 1776–92.
The daily courant. Ed S. Buckley 1702–35.
Desfontaines, Pierre François Guyot. Le nouvelliste du Parnasse. Paris 1731–2.
—— Observations sur les écrits modernes. Paris 1735–43.
—— Jugemens sur quelques ouvrages nouveaux. Avignon 1744–6.
Ephémérides [Nouvelles éphémérides] du citoyen. Paris 1765–76.
L'Esprit des journaux français et étrangers. Ed abbé Coste, de Lignac, abbé Outin and Millon. Liège 1772–1818.
Europe savante. Hague 1718–20.
Fréron, Elie Catherine. Observations sur les écrits modernes. Paris 1735–43. With Desfontaines.
—— Jugemens sur quelques ouvrages nouveaux. Avignon 1744–6.
—— Lettres de Mme la Ctesse de *** sur quelques écrits modernes. Geneva [Paris] Sept 1745–Jan 1746; rptd 1752.
—— Lettres sur quelques écrits de ce temps. Geneva [Paris] 1749–54. With La Porte.
—— L'année littéraire. Amsterdam etc 1754–91. With Baculard d'Arnaud, Dorat, Palissot; after Fréron's death ed his son L. M. Stanislas Fréron, Clément, Geoffroy, Grosier, Royou.
Gazette de France. Paris 1631–1792; Table 3 vols Paris 1766–8; also A. Granges de Surgères, marquis de, Répertoire historique de la Gazette de France 1631–1790, Paris 1902–6.
Gazette littéraire de l'Europe. *See Suard, col 88 below.*
Gentleman's journal. Ed P. A. Motteux 1692–4.
The gentleman's magazine. Ed Cave et al 1731–1914.
Grimm, Friedrich Melchior, Baron (with Diderot, Raynal and Meister). Correspondance littéraire, philosophique et critique: a literary journal with limited but choice clientèle. Ed M. Tourneux 16 vols Paris 1877–82.
Histoire littéraire de l'Europe. Hague 1726–7.
Journal anglais. Paris 1775–8.

Journal britannique. Ed M. Maty, Hague 1750–5.
Journal des scavans. Paris 1665–1858; A. de Claustre, Table générale 1665–1750, 10 vols Paris 1753–64. The Amsterdam 1665–1792 edn is an eclectic counterfeit, forbidden in France but with wide circulation elsewhere; T. B. Robinet, Table pour l'édition de Hollande, 2 vols Amsterdam 1765.
Le Journal de Trévoux. *See* Mémoires pour l'histoire des sciences.
Journal encyclopédique. Ed P. Rousseau, Liège 1756–93.
Le journal étranger. Paris 1754–9, 1760–2. Ed Grimm, Toussaint, Prévost (1754–5); Fréron (1755–6); Deleyre (1756–8); Suard, Arnaud (1760–2); a monthly devoted mainly to English literature.
Le journal littéraire. Hague 1713–23, 1729–37. *See* Dissertation sur la poésie anglaise, vol 9 1717.
La Porte, Joseph de. Observations sur la littérature moderne. Hague 1749–52.
—— La France littéraire. Paris 1755.
—— L'observateur littéraire. Amsterdam 1758–61.
La Roche, Michel de. Bibliothèque anglaise: ou histoire littéraire de la Grande-Bretagne [from 1719 ed A. Boislebeau de La Chapelle]. Amsterdam 1717–28.
—— Mémoires littéraires de la Grande-Bretagne. Hague 1720–4. From 1767–9, ed Edward Gibbon and G. Deyverdun.
Leclerc, Jean. Bibliothèque universelle et historique. Amsterdam 1686–93.
—— Bibliothèque choisie. Amsterdam 1703–13.
—— Bibliothèque ancienne et moderne. Amsterdam (later Hague) 1714–30.
Linguet, Simon Nicolas Henri. Journal de politique et de littérature. Brussels 1774–83.
—— (with Mallet Dupan and Durey de Morsan). Annales politiques, civiles et littéraires du xviiiᵉ siècle. 1777–92.
Marivaux, Pierre de Chamblain de, and Delacroix. Le spectateur françois. 1722–3.
Mémoires pour servir à l'histoire des sciences et des beaux-arts [known as Journal de Trévoux]. Trévoux (Paris from 1734) 1701–67; P. C. Sommervogel, Table, 3 vols Paris 1864–5.
Mercure galant. Paris 1672–4; Nouveau Mercure galant, 1677; Mercure galant, Paris 1677–1714; Nouveau Mercure galant, 1714–16; Nouveau Mercure, 1717–21; Mercure de France, 1721–91.
Nouvelles littéraires. Hague 1715–20.
Nouvelles ordinaires de Londres. Ed Du Gard 1650–61.
Prévost d'Exiles, Antoine François. Le pour et contre. Paris 1733–40. Also Hague counterfeit edn 1733–8, circulating widely abroad, but heavily diluted with material from other periodicals.
Steele. *See Addison, col 86 above.*
Suard, Jean Baptiste. Etat politique de l'Angleterre. Paris 1757–.
—— (with Palissot). Gazettes et papiers anglais. Paris 1760–2.
—— (with abbé Arnaud). Journal étranger. 1760–2.
—— (with Arnaud). Gazette littéraire de l'Europe. Paris 1764–6.
—— (with Arnaud). Variétés littéraires. Paris 1768–70. Compiled from earlier gazettes.

Secondary Sources

Hatin, L. E. Les gazettes de Hollande et la presse clandestine. Paris 1865.
—— Bibliographie de la presse périodique française. Paris 1866.
Sander, C. Die Franzosen und ihre Literatur im Urteil der moralischen Zeitschriften Steeles und Addisons. Strasbourg 1903.
Sichel, J. Die englische Literatur im Journal étranger. Darmstadt 1907.
Cushing, M. G. Pierre Le Tourneur. New York 1908.

Clapp, J. M. An 18th-century attempt at a critical review of the novel. PMLA 25 1910. On Bibliothèque universelle des romans.

Charlanne, L. P. M. Motteux. Revue Bleue 26 1911. On editor of Gentleman's Jnl.

Staab, J. Das Journal étranger. Strasbourg 1912.

Hemprich, P. Le Journal littéraire de La Haye. Berlin 1915.

Cornou, F. Elie Fréron 1718–76. Paris 1922.

Hendrix, W. S. Quevedo, Guevara, Lesage and the Tatler. MP 19 1922.

McCutcheon, R. P. The Journal des sçavans and the Philosophical Transactions of the Royal Society. SP 21 1924.

Hunter, A. C. Suard. Paris 1925.

—Les opinions du baron Grimm sur le roman anglais. Revue de Littérature Comparée 12 1932.

Morgan, B. T. Histoire du Journal des sçavans. Paris 1928.

Pienaar, W. J. B. In his English influences in Dutch literature and Justus van Effen as intermediary, Cambridge 1929.

Bédarida, H. Voltaire collaborateur de la Gazette littéraire de l'Europe 1764. In Mélanges d'histoire littéraire, générale et comparée offerts à F. Baldensperger, 2 vols Paris 1930.

Lovering, S. L'activité intellectuelle de l'Angleterre d'après l'ancien Mercure de France. Paris 1930.

Papenheim, W. Die Charakterschilderungen im Tatler, Spectator und Guardian. Munich 1930.

Reesink, H. J. L'Angleterre dans les trois plus anciens périodiques français de la Hollande. Paris 1931.

Beckwith, F. The Bibliothèque britannique, 1733–47. Library 4th ser 12 1932.

Helming, V. P. Gibbon and Deyverdun: collaborateurs in the Mémoires littéraires de la Grande-Bretagne. PMLA 47 1932.

Cunningham, R. N. Motteux. Oxford 1933.

La Harpe, J. de. Le Journal des savants et la renommée de Pope en France. Berkeley 1933.

— Le Journal des savants et l'Angleterre 1702–89. Univ of California Pbns in Modern Philology 20 1941.

Carrière, J. M. Berquin's adaptations from English periodical literature. PQ 13 1934.

King, G. C. La Roche et ses Mémoires. Revue de littérature Comparée 15 1935.

Robertson, M. E. I. La contrefaçon hollandaise du Pour et contre. Revue de Littérature Comparée 15 1935.

Gelobter, H. Le Spectateur von Marivaux und die englischen moralischen Wochenschriften. Limburg 1936.

Davray, H. D. L'activité intellectuelle de l'Angleterre d'après l'ancien Mercure de France 1672–78. Mercure de France April 1937.

Ewen, F. Criticism of English literature in Grimm's Correspondance littéraire. SP 33 1937.

Miller, M. M. The English as portrayed in certain French journals 1700–60. MP 34 1937.

Barnes, A. Leclerc et la république des lettres. Paris 1938.

Bonno, G. Liste chronologique des périodiques de langue française du xviiie siècle. MLQ 5 1944.

Wieder, R. Motteux et les débuts du journalisme en Angleterre. Paris 1944.

Turner, M. The influence of La Bruyère on the Tatler and the Spectator. MLR 48 1958.

Labrousse, E. Bayle: le philosophe de Rotterdam. Amsterdam 1959.

Morris, T. L'abbé Desfontaines. Stud on Voltaire & Eighteenth Century 19 1961.

Labriolle, M. R. de. Le Pour et contre et son temps. Stud on Voltaire & Eighteenth Century 34–5 1965.

— Les sources anglaises du Pour et contre. In L'abbé Prévost: actes du Colloque d'Aix 1963, Annales de la Faculté des Lettres Aix-en-Provence 50 1965.

— Le Journal étranger dans l'histoire du cosmopolitisme littéraire. Stud on Voltaire & Eighteenth Century 56 1967.

Van Tieghem, P. L'année littéraire comme intermédiaire en France des littératures étrangères. Paris 1917, Geneva 1966.

Philosophy, Politics, Deism, Enlightenment

This section includes works of literary and cultural relevance and those significant in the history of ideas. It excludes scientific, historical and travel works without such impact, even when other works by the same author are quoted. It also excludes Latin originals or trns which frequently achieved wide impact abroad.

French Authors

d'Alembert, Jean Le Rond. Reflections on the use and abuse of philosophy in matters that are properly relative to taste. In A. Gerard, An Essay on taste, 1757.

— Miscellaneous pieces in literature, history and philosophy. Tr C. Henderson 1764.

— Sur la destruction des Jésuites en France. [Geneva] 1765; An account of the destruction of the Jesuits in France, 1766.

— Eloge de Fénelon; Eulogy of Fénelon, 1770.

— Lettres au roi [Frederick II]. In Frederick II: oeuvres posthumes, Berlin 1788; Letters between d'Alembert and Frederick II, 1789.

— Eloge de Massillon; Life of Massillon. In Massillon's Sermons, 1797.

— Select eulogies of members of the French Academy. Ed. J. Aikin 2 vols 1799.

For the Hume-Rousseau quarrel see Hume, col 107 below.

d'Argens, Jean Baptiste de Boyer, marquis. Lettres juives: ou correspondance philosophique, historique et critique. Hague 1736; The Jewish spy, tr 5 vols 1739.

— La philosophie du bon sens. London [Hague] 1737; The impartial philosopher: or the philosophy of common sense, 2 vols 1749.

— Lettres chinoises. Hague 1739–40; The Chinese spy, 1752 (2nd edn).

Goldsmith, O. The citizen of the world. 1762.

Crane, R. S. and H. J. Smith. A French influence on Goldsmith's Citizen of the world. MP 19 1921. *See also Goldsmith, col 106 below.*

Balzac, Jean Louis Guez de. Aristippe: ou de la cour. Leyden 1658; Aristippus, tr R. W. 1659; A survey of princes and their favourites, in T. Sheridan, Aristippus abridg'd, 1703; Politics in select discourses which he call's his Aristippus, tr B. Kennett 1709; The French favourites, tr B. Kennett 1709.

Bayle, Pierre. Pensées diverses à l'occasion de la comète. Rotterdam 1683; Miscellaneous reflections occasion'd by the comet [of] December 1680, 2 vols 1708.

— Commentaire philosophique. 4 vols Canterbury 1686–8; A philosophical commentary on these words of the Gospel, Luke XIV. 23: Compel them to come in, 2 vols 1708.

— Dictionnaire historique et critique. Rotterdam 1697; Dictionary, tr De La Roche et al 4 vols 1709; An historical and critical dictionary, tr P. Desmaizeaux 4 vols 1710; tr J.P. Bernard, T. Birch et al, A general dictionary, historical and critical, 10 vols 1734–41; The life of Persius (extract from Dictionary), in T. Brewster, Satires of Persius, 1751.

Chandler, S. A critical history of the life of David in which the chief ideas of Mr Bayle are examined. 1766.

Martin, S. A dissertation, [with] a review of the reasonings in Mr Bayle on the entrance of sin and misery into the world. 1766.

Courtines, L. P. Bayle's relations with England. New York 1938.

Labrousse, E. Pierre Bayle. 2 vols Hague 1964.

— Inventaire critique de la correspondance de Bayle. Paris 1961.

Osborn, J. M. T. Birch and the General dictionary 1734–41. MP 36 1938.

Thijssen-Schouten, C. L. La diffusion européenne des idees de Bayle. In his P. Bayle, Amsterdam 1959.

Whitmore, P. J. S. English learning and thought in Bayle. French Stud 8 1954.

Bernardin de Saint-Pierre, Jacques Henri. Etudes de la nature. Paris 1784; Studies of nature, tr H. Hunter 5 vols 1796; tr L. T. Rede 1798.

Bonnet, Charles. La contemplation de la nature. Amsterdam 1764; The contemplation of nature, 2 vols 1766.

— Recherches philosophiques sur les preuves du christianisme. Geneva 1769; Philosophical and critical inquiries concerning Christianity, tr J. L. Boissier 1787; Interesting views of Christianity, 1787 (extracts).

— Palingénésie philosophique. Geneva 1769; Conjectures concerning the nature of future happiness, tr J. Wesley 1790.

Bossuet, Jacques Bénigne. Exposition de la doctrine de l'Eglise catholique. Paris 1671; An exposition of the doctrine of the catholique church, tr W. M. [W. A. Montagu], Paris 1672; tr J. Johnston, Paris 1685; tr [J. Delusseux?], Paris 1729.

— Discours sur l'histoire universelle. Paris 1681; A discourse on the history of the whole world, tr 1686; tr R. Spencer 1730 (abridged); A view of universal history, tr J. Elphinston 2 vols 1778.

— Conférence avec M. Claude. 1682. A conference with M. Claude, concerning the authority of the Church, tr 1684.

— Traité de la communion sous les deux espèces. Paris 1682; A treatise of communion under both species, tr 1685.

— Histoire des variations des églises protestantes. Paris 1688; The history of the variations of the Protestant churches, 2 vols Antwerp 1728.

— Maximes et réflexions sur la comédie. Paris 1694; Maxims and reflections upon plays, tr 1699.

— Relation sur le quiétisme. Paris 1698; Quakerism-à-la-mode: or a history of quietism, tr 1698.

Boyer, Jean Baptiste de, marquis d'Argens. See Argens.

Buffon, Georges Louis Leclerc, comte de. Histoire naturelle générale et particulière. Paris 1749–67; The natural history of animals, tr W. Kendrick and J. Murdoch 6 vols 1775–6; Natural history, general and particular, tr W. Smellie 9 vols 1781; Natural history abridged, Dublin 1791; Barr's Buffon: Natural history, tr Barr 10 vols 1792.

— Histoire naturelle des oiseaux [with P. Guéneau de Montbellard and abbé Bexon]. Paris 1770–86; The natural history of birds, 9 vols 1793 (in abridged versions from 1791).

Brown, H. Buffon and the Royal Society of London. In Studies offered to G. Sarton, New York [1948].

Burlamaqui, Jean Jacques. Principes du droit naturel. Geneva 1748; The principles of natural and political law, tr T. Nugent 2 vols 1748–52.

Condillac, Etienne Bonnot de. No trns of Condillac into English have been traced prior to 1800.

Brockdorff, L. G. C. Wahrheit und Wahrscheinlichkeit bei Hobbes und Condillac. Kiel 1937.

Kaye, F. B. Mandeville on the origin of language. MLN 39 1924.

Leroy, G. La psychologie de Condillac. Paris 1937.

Condorcet, Marie Jean Antoine Nicolas de Caritat, marquis de. Vie de M. Turgot. 1786; The life of Turgot, 1787.

— Vie de Voltaire. 1789; The life of Voltaire, to which are added Memoirs of Voltaire written by himself, 2 vols 1790.

— Réflexions sur la Révolution de 1688 et sur celle du 10 août 1792. [1792]; Reflections on the English Revolution 1688 and that of 10th of August 1792. In J. B.

d'Aumont, Narrative of the proceedings relating to the suspension of the King of the French, 1792.

— Convention nationale: Discours le 13 mai 1793. [Paris 1793]; Plan of the French constitution and declaration of rights, 1793.

— Esquisse d'un tableau historique des progrès de l'esprit humain. [Paris?] 1795; Outlines of an historical view of the progress of the human mind, 1795.

Lough, J. Condorcet et R. Price. Revue de Littérature Comparée 24 1950.

Descartes, René. Discours de la méthode pour bien conduire sa raison. Leyden 1637; A discourse of a method, 1649.

— Meditationes de prima philosophia. Paris 1641; Méditations, Paris 1647; W. Molyneux, Six metaphysical meditations, 1680.

— Les passions de l'âme. Paris 1649; The passions of the soule, 1650.

— Traité de la méchanique. Paris 1668; Discourses of the mechanicks (in T. Salusbury, Mathematical collections vol 2, 1665); The use of geometrical playing cards, as also a discourse of the mechanick powers, 1697.

Adam, C. Descartes: ses contemporains anglais. Revue de Littérature Comparée 17 1937.

Anderson, P. R. Descartes' influence in 17th-century England. Etudes Cartésiennes 3 1937.

Frondizi, R. Descartes y la filosofia inglesa del siglo xvii. In Escritos en honor de Descartes, La Plata 1938.

Garai, P. Le cartésianisme et le classicisme anglais. Revue de Littérature Comparée 31 1957.

Gilson, E. Descartes et Harvey. Revue Philosophique 90–1 1920.

Kantonen, T. A. The influence of Descartes on Berkeley. Philosophical Rev 43 1934.

Lamprecht, S. P. The role of Descartes in 17th-century England. New York 1935.

Nicolson, M. H. The early stages of Cartesianism in England. SP 26 1929.

Ware, C. S. The influence of Descartes on Locke: a bibliographical study. Revue Internationale de Philosophie 4 1950.

Diderot, Denis. Lettre sur les aveugles. 1749; An essay on blindness, [1750?] (3rd edn).

— Encyclopédie. Paris and Neuchâtel 1751–72; A plan of the French encyclopaedia, 1752 (with d'Alembert); Select essays from the encyclopedy, 1772 (with d'Alembert et al).

— Tooke, W. On sculpture. In E. M. Falconet, Pieces written by Falconet and Diderot, 1777.

— Jacques le fataliste; James the fatalist and his master, 3 vols 1797.

— La religieuse; The nun, 2 vols 1797.

See also Shaftesbury, Hobbes, cols 111, 107 below.

Casini, P. Diderot e Shaftesbury. Giornale Critico della Filosofia Italiana 39 1960.

Crocker, L. G. Toland et le matérialisme de Diderot. Revue d'Histoire Littéraire de la France 53 1953.

Dédéyan, C. L'Angleterre dans la pensée de Diderot. Paris 1958.

Dieckmann, H. Diderot: membre honoraire de la société d'antiquaires d'Ecosse. Cahiers Haut-Marnais 24 1951.

— The influence of F. Bacon on Diderot's Interprétation de la nature. Romanic Rev 34 1943.

Doolittle, J. R. James, Diderot and the Encyclopédie. MLN 71 1956.

Fellows, O. Diderot's debt to Prior. Stud on Voltaire & Eighteenth Century 56 1967.

Folkierski, W. Comment Shaftesbury a-t-il conquis Diderot? In Studi Carlo Pellegrini, Turin 1964.

— L'anglais de Diderot. Revue de Littérature Comparée 34 1960.

Legros, R. P. Diderot et Shaftesbury. MLR 19 1924.

Luxembourg, L. K. Bacon and Diderot. Copenhagen 1967.

Meyer, P. (ed). Diderot: Lettre sur les sourds et muets. Diderot Stud 7 1965. On English influence.

Schlegel, D. Diderot: transmitter of Shaftesbury's romanticism. Stud on Voltaire & Eighteenth Century 27 1963.

See also the standard authorities on Diderot's formative years, notably J. Pommier, Diderot avant Vincennes, Paris 1939; F. Venturi, La jeunesse de Diderot, Paris 1939; J. Proust, Diderot et L'Encyclopédie, Paris 1962; A. M. Wilson, Diderot: the testing years, New York 1957.

Duclos, Charles Pinot
Duthil, A. and C. Dédéyan. Duclos et la Société Royale de Londres. Revue de Littérature Comparée 24 1950.

Encylopédie: ou dictionnaire raisonné des sciences, des arts et des métiers publié par M. Diderot et M. d'Alembert. 17 vols Paris 1751–7, Neuchâtel 1765–72.

See also Diderot, above, and bibliographies of sources and influence pbd by J. Proust *in* Diderot et l'Encyclopédie, Paris 1962 *and in* L'Encyclopédie, Paris 1965. *See also Hobbes, col 107 below.*

Gaudin, L. S. Les lettres anglaises dans l'Encyclopédie. 1942.

Lough, J. Le rayonnement de l'Encyclopédie en Grande-Bretagne. Cahiers de l'Association Internationale des Etudes Françaises (Paris) 1952. *See also,* for Britain, French Stud 6 1952, and for Scotland MLR 38 1943.

— Essays on the Encyclopédie. Oxford 1968.

Venturi, F. Le origini dell' Enciclopedia. Florence 1946.

Schalk, F. Zur Vorgeschichte der Diderotschen Enzyklopädie. Romanische Forschungen 70 1959.

Trenard, L. Le rayonnement de l'Encyclopédie. Jnl of World History 9 1966.

Fénelon, François de Salignac de La Mothe. *For devotional writings, see col 1510 below.*

— L'éducation des filles. Paris 1687; Instructions for the education of a daughter, tr G. Hickes 1707.

— Dialogues des morts. Paris 1712; Fables and dialogues of the dead, tr [J. Ozell] 1723 (2nd edn); Dialogues of the dead, tr G. Lyttelton 1760; tr 1765; tr 2 vols 1776.

Fontenelle, Bernard Le Bouyer de. Dialogues des morts. Paris 1683; New dialogues of the dead, tr J. D[ryden?] 1683; Dialogues of the dead, tr J. Hughes 1708.

— Entretiens sur la pluralité des mondes. Paris 1686; A discovery of new worlds, tr Aphra Behn 1688 (later as The theory or system of several new inhabited worlds); A plurality of worlds, tr J. Glanvill 1688; Conversations on the plurality of worlds, tr W. Gardiner 1715; tr 1760.

— Histoire des oracles. Paris 1686; The history of oracles, tr A. Behn 1688; tr [S. Whatley] 1750.

— Eloge de Neuton. nd; The eulogium of Sir Isaac Newton, 1728, 1728.

Formey, Jean Henri Samuel. Mélanges philosophiques. Leyden 1754; Philosophical miscellanies, 1759; The logic of probabilities, [1760?].

— Histoire abrégée de la philosophie. Amsterdam 1760; A concise history of philosophy and philosophers, 1766.

— A discourse on the death of Marshall [George] Keith. Edinburgh 1764.

— Abrégé de l'histoire ecclésiastique. Amsterdam 1763; An ecclesiastical history, 2 vols 1766.

— Principes élémentaires des belles-lettres. Amsterdam 1763; Elementary principles of the belles lettres, tr S. Foreman 1766.

Genlis, Stéphanie Félicité Ducrest de Saint-Aubin, marquise de Sillery, comtesse de. Adèle et Théodore: ou lettres sur l'éducation. Paris 1782; Adelaide and Theodore: or letters on education, 3 vols 1783.

— Le théâtre à l'usage des jeunes personnes. Paris 1779–80; The theatre of education, 4 vols 1781 (2nd edn), 3 vols 1787.

Helvétius, Claude Adrien. De l'esprit. Paris 1758; De l'esprit: or essays on the mind, tr [W. Mudford] 1759; J. Bentham, A fragment on government, 1776.

— De l'homme. 1773; A treatise on man, tr W. Hooper 2 vols 1777.

Cumming, I. Helvétius in England. Etudes Anglaises 16 1963.

d'Holbach, Paul Henri Dietrich, baron. *For d'Holbach's primary role as translator of English freethinkers, see below under Annet, Collins, Gordon, Tindal, Toland, Woolston*

— Le christianisme dévoilé par feu M. Boulanger [d'Holbach]. 1756, [1767]; Christianity unveiled, tr N. A. Boulanger [W. M. Johnson], New York 1795.

For the complex bibliography of d'Holbach and of his trns see J. Lough, Revue d'Histoire Littéraire de la France 43 1936, 46 1939, 47 1947; D. Mornet, Revue de l'Histoire Littéraire de la France 40 1933. *See also* Catalogue des livres de la bibliothèque de feu M. le baron d'Holbach, Paris 1789.

Naville, P. D'Holbach et la philosophie scientifique. Paris [1943].

Topazio, V. W. D'Holbach's moral philosophy. Geneva 1956.

Huber, Marie
— The world unmask'd: or the philosopher the greatest cheat. 1736. Trn attributed to Defoe and also to Mandeville.

— Lettres sur la religion essentielle à l'homme. Amsterdam 1738; Letters concerning the religion essential to man, 1738; Natural and revealed religion explaining each other, Harleian Miscellany 6 1744.

— The divine instinct recommended to men. 1781.

Huet, Pierre Daniel. Traité de la faiblesse de l'esprit humain. Amsterdam 1723; An essay concerning the weakness of the human understanding, tr E. Combe 1725 (2nd edn); A philosophical treatise etc, 1725.

La Bruyère, Jean de. Les caractères de Théophraste, traduits du grec, avec les caractères ou les moeurs de ce siècle. Paris 1688; The characters or manners of the age, 1698–9; The moral characters of Theophrastus, tr E. Budgell 1713; tr N. Rowe 2 vols York 1776.

— Works. 2 vols 1776.

Anderson, P. B. La Bruyère and Mrs Crackenthorpe's Female Tatler. PMLA 52 1937.

La Rochefoucauld, François de. Sentences et maximes de morale. Hague 1664 (unauthorized edn, disavowed by La Rochefoucauld); Réflexions ou sentences et maximes morales, Paris 1665 (first authorized edn), 1666 (2nd edn), 1671 (3rd edn); Epictetus junior: or maximes of modern morality, tr J[ohn] D[avies] 1670 (from 1664 pre-original text); Reflections on morality or Seneca unmasqued, tr A. Behn in Miscellany: being a collection of poems by several hands, 1685 (attributed to 'Duke of Rushfaucave'); Moral maxims and reflections, tr M. de Sablé in Maxims and mixed thoughts, 1694 (claiming to be first complete trn), 1706 (2nd edn); Discourses on the deceitfulness of humane virtues, tr W. Beauvoir 1706; Curious amusements, tr 'A gentleman of Pembroke Hall in Cambridge' nd; Moral maxims, 1749; Maxims and moral reflections, 1775; The Duke de La Rochefoucault's celebrated maxims, 1799 (verse).

— A Frenchman in England, Tr S. C. Roberts, ed J. Marchand, Cambridge 1933 (as La Rochefoucauld's English diary).

Granges de Surgères, marquis de. Traductions des Réflexions de La Rochefoucauld: essai bibliographique. Paris 1883.

Hutt, A. G. La Rochefoucauld and his English translators. Bibliographer 2 1882.

Pagliaro, H. E. Paradox in La Rochefoucauld and some English followers. PMLA 79 1964.

Le Bouyer (also Le Bovier) de Fontenelle, Bernard. *See Fontenelle, above.*

Leclerc de Buffon, Georges Louis. *See Buffon, above.*

Malebranche, Nicolas. De la recherche de la vérité. Paris 1674-5 (suppl 1786); Treatise concerning the search after truth; to which is added the author's Treatise of nature and grace, tr T. Taylor 2 vols Oxford 1694; Search after truth, tr R. Sault 2 vols 1694-5.
— Conversations chrétiennes. Mons 1677; Christian conferences, tr [P. A. Motteux] 1695.
— Traité de la nature et de la grâce. Amsterdam 1680; Treatise of nature and grace, tr T. Taylor, in Treatise concerning the search after truth [above], Oxford 1694; tr 1695.
— Traitté de morale. Cologne 1683; A treatise of morality, tr J. Shipton 1699.
Massillon, Jean Baptiste. Sermons. 1705 etc; Sermons 'On the duties of the great', tr W. Dodd 1769; Discourses tr H. Crabb in Sermons on practical subjects, 1796; tr W. Dickson 3 vols Edinburgh 1797 (with d'Alembert's life of Massillon).
— An episcopal charge addressed to the Catholic clergy of Great Britain and Ireland. 1784 (from Latin).
Montaigne, Michel Eyquem de. Essais. Bordeaux 1580, Paris 1588; tr J. Florio 1603; Essays, tr C. Cotton 3 vols 1685-6.
— An abstract of the most curious and excellent thoughts. 1701.
See also A. Cowley, Several discourses, 1668; Sir W. Temple, Miscellanea, 1680-1701; J. Locke, Some thoughts concerning education, 1693; J. Dryden, Fables ancient and modern, 1700 (preface).
Dédéyan, C. Montaigne chez ses amis anglo-saxons. 2 vols Paris 1946.
Hall, M. L. Montaigne and his translators. Madison 1940.
Willey, P. L'influence de Montaigne sur les idées pédagogiques de Locke et de Rousseau. Paris 1911.
Montesquieu, Charles de Secondat, baron de La Brède et de
— Lettres persanes. Amsterdam 1721; Persian letters, tr J. Ozell 1722; Letters from a Persian in England, tr G. Lyttleton 1735 (retranslated into French as Nouvelles lettres persanes, 1736; Lettres d'un Persan en Angleterre, 1770); Letters from an Armenian in Ireland to his friends at Trebisond, Dublin 1756; freely adapted by O. Goldsmith in The citizen of the world, 1762; The true history of the Troglodites, Chelmsford 1766.
— Considérations sur les causes de la grandeur des Romains et de leur décadence. Amsterdam 1734; Reflections on the causes of the grandeur and declension of the Romans, 1734; Reflections on the rise and fall of the Roman Empire, 1751.
— De l'esprit des loix. Geneva 1748; The spirit of the laws, tr T. Nugent 2 vols 1750; A view of the English constitution: 6th book of L'esprit des loix, tr F. Maseres 1781.
— Essai sur le goût. In Encyclopédie vol 7, 1757; An essay on taste, tr A. Gerard 1759.
— Miscellaneous pieces. 1759.
— Complete works. 4 vols 1777.
— A sketch of an historical panegyric of the marshall of Berwick. 1779.
See also Hume, col 107 below; E. P. Dargan, MLN 30 1915; and D. C. Cabeen, Montesquieu: a bibliography, New York 1947.
Dedieu, J. Montesquieu et la tradition politique anglaise en France. Paris 1909. But see E. Carcassone, Montesquieu et la constitution française, Paris [1927].
Fletcher, F. T. H. Montesquieu and English politics 1750-1800. [1939]. See also UTQ 6 1937; MLR 38 1943; Economic History 1934; Revue de Littérature Comparée 13-14 1933-4 for detailed aspects.
Crane, R. S. Montesquieu and British thought. Jnl of Political Economy 49 1941.
Lough, J. L'esprit des lois in a Scottish university. Comparative Lit Stud 13 1945.
Shackleton, R. Montesquieu, Bolingbroke and the separation of powers. French Stud 3 1949.

— Montesquieu: a critical biography. Oxford 1961.
Desgraves, L. Catalogue de la bibliothèque de Montesquieu. Geneva 1954. See also F. Weil, Les lectures de Montesquieu, Revue d'Histoire Littéraire de la France 57 1957.
Dédéyan, C. Montesquieu et l'Angleterre. Paris [1958].
Ludwig, M. Montesquieu und die Engländer. Archiv für Kulturgeschichte 46 1964.
Trevor-Roper, H. R. The idea of the decline and fall of the Roman Empire. In The age of the Enlightenment: studies presented to T. Besterman, ed W. H. Barber et al, Edinburgh 1967.
Pascal, Blaise. Les provinciales. Cologne 1656-7; Les provinciales: or the mysterie of Jesuitisme, tr [Henry] H[ammand] 1657; Letters relating to the Jesuits, tr W. A[ndrews] 1744.
— Pensées. Paris 1669 (for 1670?); Monsieur Pascall's thoughts, meditations and prayers, tr J. Walker 1688; Thoughts upon religion, tr B. Kennet 1704.
Pons, E. Swift et Pascal. Langues Modernes 45 1951.
Jansen, P. De Pascal à H. Hammond: les Provinciales en Angleterre. Paris 1954
'Pluche, Antoine' (Noël Pluche). Histoire du ciel. Paris 1739; The history of the heavens, tr J. B. de Freval 2 vols 1740.
— Le spectacle de la nature. Paris 1732-51; Spectacle de la nature: or nature display'd, tr J. Humphreys 1733; Spectacle de la nature: or nature delineated, tr J. Kelly et al 4 vols 1743-4 (3rd edn).
— The truth of the gospel demonstrated. 2 vols 1751.
Poullain de La Barre, François. De l'égalité des deux sexes. Paris 1673; The woman as good as the man: or the equality of both sexes, tr A.L. 1677.
Quesnay, François (anon). Tableau économique. Versailles 1758; Adam Smith, An inquiry into the nature and causes of the wealth of nations, 2 vols 1776.
Rapin de Thoyras, Paul. Histoire d'Angleterre. Hague 1724-7; The history of England, tr N. Tindal 15 vols 1725-31; 5 vols 1732-51 with continuation by Tindal; tr J. Kelly 3 vols 1732-7, 3 vols 1747 (abridged).
Raynal, Guillaume Thomas François. Histoire du Stadhouderat. Hague 1747; The history of the Stadtholdership, 1749.
— Histoire philosophique et politique des établissements et du commerce des Européens dans les deux Indes. Amsterdam 1770; The sentiments of a foreigner on the disputes of Britain and France (extract from Histoire des établissements), Philadelphia 1775; A philosophical and political history of the settlements in the East and West Indies, tr J. O. Justamond 5 vols 1776.
— Révolution de l'Amérique. 1781; The revolution of America, 1781.
— Lettre de Raynal à l'Assemblée nationale. Paris [1791?]; A letter to the National Assembly on the subject of the Revolution, 1791.
Irvine, D. D. Raynal and British humanitarianism. Jnl of Modern History 3 1931.
Rousseau, Jean-Jacques. Discours sur cette question: si le rétablissement des sciences et des arts a contribué à épurer les moeurs. Geneva [Paris] 1750; The discourse whether the reestablishment of arts and sciences has contributed to the refining of manners, tr [W. Bowyer] 1751; tr R. Wynne 1752; tr 1760; A dissertation on the effects of cultivating the arts and sciences, tr W. Kenrick in Miscellaneous Works vol 1, 1767; tr W. Waring [1770?]; tr [1779?].
— Discours sur l'origine et les fondemens de l'inégalité parmi les hommes. Amsterdam 1755; A discourse upon the origin and foundation of the inequality among mankind, tr [John Farrington? author of ms trn dated 1756] 1762 (or 1761? see London Chron 11 1762); A dissertation, tr W. Kenrick in Miscellaneous Works vol 1, 1767; [1791?].
— Jean-Jacques Rousseau à M. d'Alembert, sur son article Genève [Lettre à d'Alembert]. Amsterdam 1758;

A letter from M. Rousseau to M. d'Alembert concerning theatrical entertainments, 1759 (only separate edn in 18th century).

—— Extrait du projet de paix perpétuelle de l'abbé de Sainte-Pierre. Amsterdam 1761; A project of perpetual peace, 1761; A project for perpetual peace, 1767 (2nd edn).

—— Julie: ou la nouvelle Héloïse. *See Prose fiction, below.*

—— Emile: ou de l'éducation. Amsterdam 1762; Emilius and Sophia: or a new system of education, tr [W. Kenrick] 4 vols 1762; Emilius: or an essay on education, tr M. Nugent 2 vols 1763; Emilius: or a treatise of education, 3 vols Edinburgh 1763; (the spurious Emilius and Sophia, or the solitaires: being a sequel to Emilius, 1783, is added to some edns). T. Day, The history of Sandford and Merton, 1783–9 is an imitation. The Profession de foi du vicaire savoyard also appeared separately as The gospel of reason, [1795?].

—— Du contract social. Amsterdam 1762; A treatise on the social compact, tr [W. Kenrick] 1764 (Murray's 1791 re-edition was composed of unsold copies with fresh title-page); tr 1791 (ptd Robinson).

—— J.-J. Rousseau à Christophe de Beaumont. Amsterdam 1763; An expostulatory letter from J.-J. Rousseau to Christophe de Beaumont, 1763.

—— Lettres écrites de la montagne. Amsterdam 1764; Letters written from the mountains, in Miscellaneous works vol 4, 1767, and in later edns of Works.

—— Dictionnaire de musique. Paris 1768; first pbd in sections, possibly in New Musical & Universal Mag, ed J. French c. 1769–70; ?A complete dictionary of music, tr W. Waring 1770. Only 1779 edn known, but *see* Grove's Dictionary of music.

—— Les lettres sur la botanique. In Œuvres, 1782; Letters on the elements of botany, tr T. Martyn 1785; various separate edns of plates.

—— Miscellaneous works. Tr [W. Kenrick] 5 vols 1767.

—— Thoughts on different subjects. Tr [H. Colebrooke] 2 vols 1768.

—— The works of J.-J. Rousseau. 10 vols Edinburgh 1773–4, 1774.

—— The beauties of Rousseau selected by a lady [Eliza Roberts]. 2 vols 1788.

—— [Correspondence]. Various letters appeared in magazines, notably Scots Mag 1763–, and in A new collection of letters in Confessions vol 3, 1790, and in Original letters of J.-J. Rousseau, 1799.

The Bibliographie générale des œuvres de Rousseau, Paris 1950, *by* J. Sénelier *must be checked with* Th. Dufour, Recherches bibliographiques, 2 vols Paris 1925, *and with the standard edns of the works* (Œuvres complètes, ed B. Gagnebin and M. Raymond, Paris 1959–) *and of the correspondence :* Correspondance complète de Rousseau, ed R. A. Leigh, Geneva 1965–.

Contemporary reactions

Smith, Adam, A letter to the editors of the Edinburgh Review. Edinburgh 1755; Theory of moral sentiments, 1757.

Bordes, Ch. Prédiction tirée d'un vieux manuscrit. 1761; A prophecy, by M. de Voltaire, 1761.

Kenrick, W. (translator of Rousseau). Observations on M. Rousseau's new system of education, with some remarks on the different translations of that celebrated work. 1763. *See also articles in* Monthly Rev.

Hume, D. A concise and genuine account of the dispute between Mr Hume and Mr Rousseau. 1766; Exposé succinct de la contestation qui s'est élevée entre M. Hume et M. Rousseau, tr [J. B. A. Suard and J. L. d'Alembert] 1766.

Greene, B. A defence of M. Rousseau against the aspersions of Mr Hume, Mr Voltaire and their associates. 1766.

Heathcote, R. A letter to the Hon Mr Walpole. 1767.

[Fuseli, Henri]. Remarks on the writings and conduct of Rousseau. 1767.

Burke, E. Reflections on the French Revolution. 1790.

Guinguenné. Letters on the Confessions of Rousseau. 1793.

Corancez. Anecdotes of the last twelve years of Rousseau. 1798.

Herder, J. C. Humes und Rousseaus Abhandlungen über den Urvertrag. Nachrichten von gelehrten Sachen 1797.

For list of minor writings occasioned by Rousseau see J. H. Warner, A bibliography of 18th-century English editions of Rousseau, PQ 13 1934. *See also under Godwin and Hume, cols 106, 107 below.*

Secondary sources. See especially H. Roddier, Rousseau en Angleterre au xviiie siècle. Paris [1950], completed by J. Voisine in Rousseau en Angleterre à l'époque romantique [1778–1830], Paris 1956.

Courtois, L. J. Le séjour de Rousseau en Angleterre. Annales de la Société J.-J. Rousseau 6 1910.

Pons, J. L'éducation en Angleterre 1750–1800: aperçu sur l'influence pédagogique de Rousseau. Paris 1919.

Reichenburg, M. Essai sur les lectures de Rousseau. Geneva 1934. *See also* C. Bouvier, La bibliothèque des Charmettes, Chambéry 1914, and Annales de la Société J.-J. Rousseau 21 1932.

Warner, J. H. A bibliography of 18th-century English editions of Rousseau. PQ 13 1934. *See also* 19 1940.

—— The basis of Rousseau's contemporaneous reputation in England. MLN 55 1940. Also articles on reaction to two Discourses, PMLA 48 1933; Nouvelle Héloïse, PMLA 52 1937; Emile, PMLA 59 1944.

Sewall, R. B. Rousseau's First discourse in England. PMLA 52 1937.

Bandy, W. T. Rousseau's flight from England. Romanic Rev 39 1948.

Derathé, R. Rousseau et la science politique de son temps. Paris 1950.

Pire, G. Rousseau et Crusoe. Revue de Littérature Comparée 30 1956.

Leigh, R. A. Rousseau et ses amis anglais. Ibid.

Cranston, M. Rousseau's visit to England. Essays by Divers Hands 31 1962.

Taylor, E. G. Rousseau's debt to Hobbes. In Currents of thought: essays G. T. Clapton, ed T. V. Benn, Oxford 1965.

Saint Evremond, Charles de Marguetel de Saint-Denis, seigneur de

Barnwell, H. T. Saint Evremond: a French political exile. Proc Huguenot Soc of London 1947–52.

Petit, L. La Fontaine et Saint Evremond: ou la tentation de l'Angleterre. Toulouse 1953.

Saint-Pierre, Charles Castel, abbé de

Wallas, M. Sur la fortune de l'abbé de Saint-Pierre en Angleterre. Revue de Littérature Comparée 20 1940.

Perkins, M. L. The Leviathan and Saint-Pierre's Projet de paix perpétuelle. Proc Amer Philosophical Soc 99 1955.

Turgot, Anne Robert Jacques. *See under Adam Smith, col 111 below.*

Réflexions sur la formation et la distribution des richesses. 1776; Reflections on the formation and distribution of wealth, tr [Adam Smith?] 1793.

Voltaire, François Marie Arouet de

See indexes to Œuvres complètes, ed L. Moland 52 vols Paris 1877–85; Voltaire's Correspondence, ed T. Besterman 107 vols Geneva 1953–65; R. Pomeau, La religion de Voltaire, Paris 1969 (2nd edn); Complete works, ed T. Besterman, W. H. Barber, O. R. Taylor et al, Geneva and Toronto 1968–.

A number of works by Voltaire were written under the influence of his contact with England. These include Essay on epick poetry; Brutus [*first act composed in English*]; Lettres philosophiques [*sections probably composed in English*]; Œdipe (preface); Discours sur la tragédie à milord Bolingbroke; La mort de César *and* 1736 preface;

Lettre aux auteurs du Nouvelliste du Parnasse (June 1731); Eriphyle (discours); Zaïre (*and* Epître dédicatoire à M. Falkener); Les originaux; Adélaïde du Guesclin; Lettre à un premier commis 1746 (written 1733); Le temple du goût; Alzire (Discours préliminaire); L'enfant prodigue (preface); Conseils à un journaliste 1744; La vie de Molière; Mérope (preface); Lettre à M. de Lindelle; Réponse à M. de Lindelle.

For dramatic works the date given is that of pbn. No distinction is drawn between trns and adaptations.

La Ligue. Geneva 1723. *See La Henriade, below.*

L'indiscret. Paris 1725; No one's enemy but his own, 1764.

An essay upon the civil wars of France also upon the epick poetry of the European nations. 1727; Essai sur les guerres civiles de France, tr Granet, Hague 1729.

Essay on epick poetry. 1727; Essai sur la poésie épique tr [P. F. G. Desfontaines], Paris 1728; tr Voltaire 1732–3.

La Henriade [10 cantos]. 1728; The Henriade (1st canto only), tr J. Ozell 1729; 10 cantos, tr J. Lockman 1732; tr [C. M. Bury] 2 vols 1797.

Brutus. Paris 1731; Junius Brutus, tr W. Duncombe 1735. 1st act written in English during Voltaire's English exile.

Discours sur la tragédie à mylord Bolingbroke. In Brutus, Paris 1731, above; Dissertation sur la tragédie ancienne et moderne, in Semiramis, Paris 1749 (2 distinct essays); Critical essays on dramatic poetry, Glasgow 1761.

Histoire de Charles XII. Basle (for Rouen) 1731; The history of Charles XII, King of Sweden, Dublin 1732; tr [A. Henderson?] 1734; tr W. A. Dilworth 1760.

Lettres philosophiques. Amsterdam (for Rouen, Jore) 1734; Lettres écrites de Londres sur les Anglois, Basle (for London) 1734; Letters concerning the English nation, tr [J. Lockman] 1733. The English trn was pbd before the first French edn. Parts of the Lettres appear to have been originally composed in English; *see* H. Brown, The composition of the Letters, in The age of the Enlightenment: studies presented to T. Besterman, ed W. H. Barber et al, Edinburgh 1967.

Le Temple du goût. Rouen 1733; The temple of taste, 1734.

Zaïre. Rouen 1733; The tragedy of Zara, tr A. Hill 1736.

Alzire. Paris 1736; Alzira, tr A. Hill 1736.

La mort de César. 1736; The Roman revenge, tr A. Hill 1754.

Eléments de la philosophie de Newton. Amsterdam 1738; The elements of Sir Isaac Newton's philosophy, tr J. Hanna 1738; The metaphysics of Sir Isaac Newton, tr D. E. Baker 1747; The Newtonian philosophy, Glasgow 1764.

Discours en vers sur l'homme [6 poems]. In Recueil de pièces fugitives, 1740; first pbd as Epîtres sur le bonheur [2 poems], Paris 1738, and Epîtres sur le bonheur, la liberté et l'envie [3 poems], Amsterdam 1738; Epistles: on happiness, liberty and envy, tr W. Gordon 1738; Three epistles in the ethic way, 1738.

L'enfant prodigue. Paris 1738; The prodigal son, tr [D. Williams?] in Works of the late M. de Voltaire, ed W. Kenrick 14 vols 1779–81; also separate edn 1738?.

Essai sur le siècle de Louis XIV. 1739; An essay on the age of Louis XIV, tr J. Lockman 1739. Voltaire's Essay was precursor of the Siècle de Louis XIV, 1751.

Préface to Examen du prince de Machiavel. Hague 1740. The Examen itself is by Frederick, Crown Prince of Prussia; Anti-Machiavel, 1741.

Mahomet. Brussels 1742; Mahomet the imposter, tr [J. Miller and J. Hoadley] 1744.

Mérope. Paris 1744; Merope, tr J. Theobald 1744; tr A. Hill 1749.

Memnon, histoire orientale. London (for Paris) 1747; Zadig: ou la destinée, 1748 (Memnon 1749 is a

distinct work); Zadig: or the book of fate, 1749; tr [J. Collyer?] in Select pieces of M. de Voltaire, 1754; tr F. Ashmore 1780; [c. 1775]. One ch was pbd separately as The hermit: an oriental tale, 1779.

Le monde comme il va: vision de Babouc. In Œuvres vol 8, Dresden 1748; Babouc: or the world as it goes, 1754.

Sémiramis. Paris 1749; Semiramis, 1760; tr G. E. Ayscough 1776. Cyrus, tr J. Hoole 1768; Alzuma, tr J. Murphy are distant relations only.

Nanine. Paris 1749; The man of the world, tr C. Macklin, Dublin 1785.

Dissertations sur la tragédie ancienne et moderne. 1749. *See* Discours sur la tragédie, 1731, above.

Oreste. Paris 1750; Orestes, tr T. Francklin 1776, 1786 (adapted as Electra).

Le siècle de Louis XIV. Berlin 1751 (under name of de Francheville); The age of Lewis XIV, 2 vols 1752.

Défense de milord Bolingbroke 1752; A defence of the late Lord Bolingbroke's letters on the study and use of history, 1753.

Micromégas. 1752; Micromégas, 1753.

Rome sauvée. Berlin 1752; Rome preserv'd, 1760.

Abrégé de l'histoire universelle, Hague 1753. *See* Essai sur les moeurs, *below.*

Annales de l'Empire. Basle 1753; Annals of the Empire, 2 vols 1755; tr D. Williams [?] in Works, 1781.

Epître de Mr de V*** en arrivant dans sa terre. [1755]; Epître etc, An epistle of Mr de Voltaire upon his arrival at his estate near the lake of Geneva, 1755 (parallel texts).

Histoire de la guerre de 1741. Amsterdam (for Paris) 1755 (sections later incorporated into Précis du siècle de Louis XV, 1769); The history of the war of 1741, 1756.

L'orphelin de la Chine. Paris 1755; The orphan of China, 1755; tr A. Murphy 1756.

La pucelle d'Orléans. Paris 1755; The maid of Orleans, 2 vols 1758 (prose); Canto 1, 1780; La pucelle: or the maid of Orleans [5 cantos], 2 vols 1785–6; 21 cantos tr [C. M. Bury Countess of Charleville] 2 vols [Dublin] 1796–7 (priv ptd).

Epître au prince royal de Prusse. In Mélanges de poésies, [Geneva] 1756; An epistle to the King of Prussia, 1757.

[Essai sur les moeurs]. Essay sur l'histoire générale et sur les moeurs. [Geneva] 7 vols 1756. This work evolved over 1745–56 and was variously entitled Nouveau plan d'une histoire de l'esprit humain, 1745; Histoire des croisades, 1750–1; Abrégé de l'histoire universelle, 1753; Essai sur l'histoire universelle, 1754; Essay sur l'histoire générale. The Philosophie de l'histoire, 1765 was later added as preface to 4° Œuvres edn. English trns follow this growth in part: The general history and state of Europe, 6 pts 1754; The universal history and state of all nations, 3 vols Edinburgh 1758; An essay on universal history, tr T. Nugent 4 vols 1759, 4 vols Dublin 1759 ('3rd edn'); A supplement, 2 vols 1764.

Histoire des voyages de Scarmentado. In Suite des mélanges vol 5, Geneva 1756; The history of the voyages of Scarmentado, 1757.

Encyclopédie vol 7. 1757. Goût; An essay on taste by Alexander Gerard with three dissertations by Voltaire, d'Alembert, Montesquieu, 1759 (supposedly checked through press by David Hume). Gerard's book was tr into French as Essai sur le goût, tr E[idous], Paris 1766 and Voltaire's article tr from English without reference to original French.

Encyclopédie vol 7. 1757. Guerre; Thoughts on the pernicious consequences of war, [1790?].

Candide ou l'optimisme. [Geneva?] 1759; Candid: or all the best, 1759; Candidus, tr W. Rider 1759; Edinburgh 1759 (new trn with spurious 2nd pt).

Histoire de l'empire de Russie sous Pierre le grand. [Geneva] 1759; History of the empire of Russia (vol 1 only pbd), Dublin 1761; The history of the Russian empire, tr [J. Johnson] 2 vols 1761–3; 2 vols Glasgow 1764.

Socrate. Amsterdam (for Paris) 1759; Socrates, 1760.

Le caffé ou l'Ecossaise: comédie par M. Hume traduit en français. London (for Geneva) [1760]; The coffee-house: or fair fugitive, 1760; see also G. Coleman, The English merchant, 1767 (imitation).

Conversation de Mr l'intendant des menus avec M. l'abbé [Grizel]. [Paris 1761?]; The dispute between Mlle Clairon and the Fathers of the Church, 1768.

Tancrède. Paris 1761; Almida, tr [D. Celesia] 1771.

Pièces originales concernant la mort des sieurs Calas. [Geneva 1762]; Original pieces relative to the trial of J. Calas, 1762 (parallel French and English texts).

Traité sur la tolérance. [Geneva] 1763; A treatise on religious toleration, tr [W. Kenrick] 1764, Glasgow 1765.

Dictionnaire philosophique portatif. London (for Geneva) 1764; The philosophical dictionary for the pocket, written in French by a society of men of letters [with notes refuting irreligious passages], 1765 (the publisher 'Thomas Brown' being fictitious), Glasgow 1766.

La philosophie de l'histoire. Amsterdam (for Geneva) 1765; The philosophy of history, 1766.

Adélaïde du Guesclin. Paris 1765; Matilda: a tragedy, tr [T. Francklin] 1775.

Commentaire sur le livre des délits et des peines [by Beccaria]. [Geneva] 1766; An essay on crimes and punishments, 1767.

Lettre de M. de Voltaire à M. Hume. Ferney (for Geneva) 1766; A letter from Mons de Voltaire to Mr Hume on his dispute with M. Rousseau, 1766.

[Lettre de M. de Voltaire au docteur J.-J. Pansophe [Rousseau]]; A letter from M. Voltaire to M. J.-J. Rousseau, 1766 (French and English texts).

Le philosophe ignorant. [Geneva] 1766; The ignorant philosopher, with an address upon the parricides imputed to the families of Calas and Sirven, 1767.

Avis au public sur les parricides imputés aux Calas et aux Sirven. [Geneva] 1766; An address upon the parricides etc, in Ignorant philosopher, 1767 (above).

La défense de mon oncle. [Geneva] 1767; A defence of my uncle, 1768.

L'ingénu. Utrecht (for Geneva) 1767; L'ingénu: or the sincere Huron, Glasgow 1768 (also as The pupil of nature, 1771); The sincere Huron, tr F. Ashmore 1786.

Lettres à son altesse monseigneur le prince de *** [Brunswick] sur Rabelais etc. Amsterdam 1767; Letters addressed to his Highness the Prince of ***, 1768.

Les Scythes. Geneva 1767; Zobeide, tr J. Cradock 1771.

La guerre civile de Genève: poème héroïque. Besançon (for Geneva) 1678; The civil war of Geneva, tr T. Teres 1769.

L'homme aux quarante écus. [Geneva] 1768; The man of 40 crowns, 1768.

La princesse de Babylone. [Geneva] 1768; The Princess of Babylon, 1768.

Lettre de Mr l'évêque etc; Lettres de Mr l'évêque de Genève [d'Annecy] à M. de Voltaire, [1769]; Genuine letters between the Archbishop of Anneci and M. de Voltaire, 1770.

Précis du siècle de Louis XV. Geneva 1769; The age of Louis XV, 2 vols 1770; see also Histoire de la guerre de 1741, above.

Fragments sur l'Inde. [Geneva] 1773; Fragments relating to the late revolutions in India, 1774.

Le taureau blanc. Memphis (for Geneva) 1774; The white bull, tr [J. Bentham?] 1774; Le taureau blanc: or the white bull, 1774.

Histoire de Jenni. London (for Geneva) 1775; Young James: or the sage and the atheist, 1776.

Les oreilles du comte de Chesterfield. In Nouveaux mélanges pt 17, 1775; The ears of Lord Chesterfield, tr J. Knight, Berne 1786.

Commentaire historique sur les œuvres de l'auteur de la Henriade. Basle (for Geneva) 1776; Historical memoirs of the author of the Henriade, 1777.

Lettre de M. de Voltaire à l'académie française. [Geneva 1776]; A letter from M. Voltaire to the French Academy on the merits of Shakespeare, 1777.

Mémoires de M. de Voltaire écrits par lui-même, Geneva 1784; Memoirs of the life of Voltaire, 1784; La vie privée du roi de Prusse, Amsterdam 1785.

[Voltaire's correspondence with Frederick II]. Œuvres posthumes de Frédéric II. Berlin 1788; Correspondence: letters between Frederic II and M. de Voltaire, tr T. Holcroft 1789 (vols 6–8 of Posthumous works of Frederick II, King of Prussia).

The history of the misfortunes of John Calas, written by M. de Voltaire, 1772, 1775, Edinburgh 1776 *has not been identified, but could possibly be* Edouard Thomas Simon, Histoire des malheurs de la famille Calas, 1766.

English collections

Select pieces. Tr J. Collyer 1754.

Works. Tr T. Smollett, T. Francklin et al 25 vols 1761–5.

Dialogues and essays, literary and philosophical. Glasgow 1764.

Letters to several friends. Tr T. Francklin 1770.

Works, 20? vols Edinburgh 1769 (reprint of Smollett, above?).

Works. ? vols [c. 1770–] ('3rd edn').

Works. Tr Smollett and Francklin 38 vols 1778–81.

Works. Ed W. Kenrick, tr D. Williams et al 14? vols 1779–81.

Miscellanies. Tr Smollett and Francklin 3 vols 1778.

Miscellanies philosophical, literary, historical. Tr J. Perry [Parry?] 1779.

These Miscellanies are possibly part of, or supplements to, an edn of complete works.

A collection of the tales and smaller pieces of M. de Voltaire. Edinburgh 1792.

Romances tales and smaller pieces of M. de Voltaire. 2 vols 1794.

This list of trns omits magazines and reviews, which offered a constant flow of extracts and summaries. The bibliography of trns of Voltaire is incomplete and inexact, given the confusion that reigns between fresh trns, counterfeit edns and barely modified versions of existing trns.

Voltaire. Notebooks. Ed T. Besterman in Complete works vols 81–2, Geneva and Toronto 1968. A unique source for Voltaire's impressions of England, edited 'in large part for the first time'.

Desnoiresterres, G. Voltaire et la société au xviiie siècle. Paris 1869–76 (2nd edn). Vol 1, Stay in England.

Foulet, L. Le voyage de Voltaire en Angleterre. Revue d'Histoire Littéraire de la France 13 1906, 15 1908.

Morize, A. L'apologie du luxe au 18e siècle. Paris 1909. On Voltaire and Mandeville. *See also* G. Ascoli (ed), Voltaire, Poèmes philosophiques, Paris 1936.

Crane, R. S. The diffusion of Voltaire's writings in England 1750–1800. MP 20 1923. 213 library catalogues show small role played in diffusion by trns.

Torrey, N. L. Voltaire and the English Deists. New Haven 1930.

Havens, G. R. Voltaire's marginal comments upon Pope's Essay on man. MLN 43 1928.

Barr, M. M. A century of Voltaire study. New York 1929; suppl MLN 48 1933, 56 1941; suppl Paris 1969.

—— Voltaire in America 1744–1800. Baltimore 1941.

Dargan, E. P. The question of Voltaire's primacy in establishing the English vogue. Paris 1930.

Libby, M. The attitude of Voltaire to magic and the sciences. New York 1935. Includes Newtonian physics.

Wade, I. O. Voltaire and Mme de Châtelet. Princeton 1941. On English scientific influence.

— Studies on Voltaire. Princeton 1947. On Mandeville.

— (ed). Voltaire's Micromégas. Princeton 1950.

Oake, R. B. Political elements in criticism of Voltaire in England. MLN 57 1942.

Brown, H. Voltaire and the Royal Society of London. UTQ 13 1944.

— The composition of the Letters concerning the English nation. In The age of the Enlightenment: studies presented to T. Besterman, ed W. H. Barber et al, Edinburgh 1967.

Hennig, J. Voltaire in Ireland. Dublin Mag 19 1944.

Schiller, B. N. Conservative England and the case against Voltaire. New York 1950. See also JHI 4 1943.

de Beer, G. Voltaire FRS. Notes & Records of Royal Soc 8 1951.

— Voltaire et les sciences naturelles. In The age of the Enlightenment, above.

— [with A. M. Rousseau]. Voltaire's British visitors. Stud on Voltaire & Eighteenth Century 49 1967.

Dédéyan, C. Voltaire et la pensée anglaise. Paris 1956.

Meixle, H. W. Voltaire and Scotland. Etudes Anglaises 2 1958.

Gay, P. Voltaire's politics. Princeton 1959.

Conlon, P. M. Voltaire's literary career 1728–30. Stud on Voltaire & Eighteenth Century 14 1961.

Seguin, J. A. R. Voltaire and the Gentleman's Magazine. New York 1962.

— Voltaire and the Monthly Review. Jersey City 1963.

Barber, W. H. L'Angleterre dans Candide. Revue de Littérature Comparée 37 1963.

— Voltaire and Quakerism. Stud on Voltaire & Eighteenth Century 24 1963. See also E. Philips, Revue de Littérature Comparée 39 1932.

Lanson, G. (ed). Voltaire, Lettres philosophiques, revised by A. M. Rousseau. 2 vols Paris 1964.

Winton, C. Voltaire and Walpole. PQ 46 1967.

Besterman, T. Voltaire. 1969.

Pomeau, R. La religion de Voltaire. Paris 1969 (2nd edn).

English Authors

For a summary bibliography of deistic literature see G. Gawlick, Vorwort *to* G. V. Lechler, Geschichte des englischen Deismus, Hildesheim 1965.

Addison, Joseph. See Periodicals, above.
The evidence of the Christian religion. 1731; De la religion chrétienne, tr G. Seigneux de Correvon 2 vols Lausanne 1757.

Annet, Peter. History and character of St Paul examined. 1749; Examen critique de la vie et des ouvrages de St Paul, tr [d'Holbach], Amsterdam 1766.

— The life of David. 1761 (anon, attributed to A. Campbell); David: ou l'histoire de l'homme selon le coeur de Dieu, tr [d'Holbach], London (for Amsterdam) 1768.

Bacon, Francis. Essays. 1597; Essais, tr C. P. Goujet, Paris 1734. First tr 1619.

— History of the reign of Henry VII. 1622; Histoire du règne de Henry VII, tr Latour Hotman, Brussels [1673].

— The New Atlantis. 1627; La nouvelle Atlantide [first tr P. Amboise 1631], tr G. B. R[auguet], Paris 1702; La politique de chevalier Bacon, ed C. P. Goujet 2 vols 1740; tr M. Du Moulin (from Shaw edn),

Amsterdam 1765; Le christianisme de Bacon, tr J. A. Emery, Paris 1799.
See also Diderot, above.

Dieckmann, H. The influence of Bacon on Diderot. Romanic Rev 34 1944.

White, H. B. The influence of Bacon on the philosophes. Stud on Voltaire & Eighteenth Century 27 1963.

Beattie, James
Mossner, E. C. Beattie on Voltaire: an unpublished parody. Romanic Rev 41 1950.

Bentham, Jeremy. View of the hard labour bill. 1778; Lois pénales, tr [C. de Saint-Aubin] in Beccaria, Traité des délits et des peines, ed Morellet, Paris 1797.

—Defence of usury. 1787; Apologie de l'usure, Paris 1790 (also as Lettres sur la liberté des taux d'intérêt).

Burns, J. H. Bentham and the French Revolution. Trans of Royal Historical Soc 5th ser 16 1966.

Bentley, Richard. Remarks upon Collins' Discourse on free-thinking. 1713; La friponnerie laïque des prétendus esprits-forts de l'Angleterre, tr [A. de La Chappelle], Amsterdam 1738.

Berkeley, George. Three dialogues. 1713; Dialogues entre Hylas et Philonoüs contre les sceptiques et les athées, tr J. P. Gua de Malves (original editor of Encyclopédie before Diderot), Amsterdam 1750.

— An essay towards preventing the ruin of Great-Britain. 1721; Caractéristiques de l'état politique de la Grande-Bretagne, Hague 1759.

— Alciphron. 1732; tr E. de Joncourt 2 vols Paris 1734.

Luce, A. A. Berkeley and Malbranche. Oxford 1934. See also Fritz, JHI 15 1954; T. E. Jessop, Revue Internationale de Philosophie 1 1938.

Gueroult, M. Berkeley. Paris [1956].

Blake, William
Bruce, H. L. Blake, Carlyle and the French Revolution. In C. M. Gayley anniversary papers, Berkeley 1922.

Bolingbroke, Henry St John. A dissertation upon parties. 1733–4; La politique des deux partis, Hague 1734; tr [E. de Silhouette] 1739.

— Letters on the spirit of patriotism. 1749; Lettres sur l'esprit de patriotisme, tr [C. de Thyard de Bissy] 1750.

— Some reflections on the present state of the nation. 1749; Testament politique de milord Bolingbroke, 1754; tr Le Blanc 1754.

— Letters on the study and uses of history. 1752; Lettres sur l'histoire, tr [J. Barbeu de Bourg] 2 vols 1752; see also Voltaire, Défense de milord Bolingbroke, Geneva 1767; also Examen important de milord Bolingbroke.

— Reflections on exile. 1752; tr J. Barbeu du Bourg 1752.

— A letter to Sir W. Windham. 1753; Mémoires secrets de mylord Bolingbroke, tr J. L. Favier 1754; Le siècle politique, tr [J. Barbeu du Bourg], Sièclopolie [1753].

— Introductory letter to Pope. 1753; Lettre de Mylord Bolingbroke servant d'introduction à ses lettres philosophiques à M. Pope, 1754.
See also Voltaire, above.

Fletcher, D. J. The fortunes of Bolingbroke in France. Stud on Voltaire & Eighteenth Century 47 1966.

— Bolingbroke and the diffusion of Newtonianism in France. Stud on Voltaire & Eighteenth Century 53 1967.

Bourne, Samuel. Popery a craft. 1735; Sermon sur les fourberies du clergé romain, tr [d'Holbach] 1767.

Browne, Sir Thomas. Religio medici. 1642, 1643; tr Latin, 1644; La religion du médecin, tr [N. Lefèvre?] (probably from English text) 1668.

— Pseudodoxia epidemica. 1646; Essai sur les erreurs populaires, tr [J. B. Souchay] 2 vols Paris 1733. Latin trn by J. Merryweather rendered trn into other languages largely superfluous. The many imitations include: J. B. Thiers, Traité des superstitions, 4 vols Avignon 1774; P. Lebrun, Histoire critique des pratiques super-

stitieuses, 2 vols Rouen 1702; J. L. Castillon, Essai sur les erreurs, Amsterdam 1765; C. Buffier, Examen des préjugez vulgaires, Paris 1704; J. D. T. Bienville, Traité des erreurs populaires, Hague 1775; D'Iharce, Erreurs populaires, Paris 1783.
Leroy, O. A French bibliography of Browne. 1931.

Burke, Edmund. A vindication of natural society. 1756; Apologie de la société naturelle, 1776.
—— Reflections on the Revolution in France. 1790; Réflexions sur la révolution en France, tr [Dupont] 1790. For Sur la révolution arrivée en France, tr le B. de B., 1790, see Speech etc, below.
—— Speech on the army estimates, Feb 9th 1790; Discours de M. Burke, [Paris 1790]; Extrait du discours, Paris 1790 (with Sur la révolution arrivée en France).
—— A letter to a member of the National Assembly. 1791; Lettre de M. Burke à un membre de l'Assemblée nationale, Paris 1791; Suite des Réflexions sur la Révolution de France, Paris 1792.
—— An appeal from the New to the Old Whigs. 1791; Appel des Whigs modernes aux Whigs anciens, tr L. Mater-Flint 1791.
—— Speech in the House of Commons on the French Revolution. 1791; Discours improvisés par MM Burke et Fox le 6 mai 1791, Paris 1791.
—— A letter to a noble lord on the attacks made upon him and his pension. 1796; Lettre du très-honorable Edmund Burke à un noble lord, [Paris 1796].
—— Thoughts on the prospect of a peace with the regicide Directory. 1796; Lettre sur les négociations de paix, tr [J. C. Peltier], Paris 1796.
—— Three memorials on French affairs. 1797; Trois mémoires sur les affaires de France, 1797.
Cobban, A. Burke and the revolt against the 18th century. 1929.
Osborn, A. M. Rousseau and Burke. Oxford 1940.
Godechot, J. La contre-Révolution. Paris 1961.
Stanlis, P. J. Burke and the sensibility of Rousseau. Thought 36 1961.
Courtney, C. P. Montesquieu and Burke. Oxford 1963.

Burnet, Gilbert. History of my own time. 1723–35; Histoire des dernières révolutions d'Angleterre, tr F. de La Pillonnière 4 vols Hague 1725–35.

Chambers, Ephraim. Cyclopaedia. 1728; Diderot and d'Alembert, Encyclopédie: ou dictionnaire raisonné des sciences, des arts et des métiers, 17 vols Paris/Neuchâtel (for Paris), 1751–72 (with later supplements, reprints, imitations etc). For bibliography see J. Lough, Essays on the Encyclopédie of Diderot and d'Alembert, Oxford 1968.

Clarke, Samuel. Demonstration of the being and attributes of God. 1706; De l'existence et des attributs de Dieu, tr Ricotier, Amsterdam 1717. See P. M. Masson, La profession de foi du vicaire savoyard de J-J. Rousseau, Fribourg 1914, and La religion de J.-J. Rousseau, Paris 1916, for fullest account of his influence on Rousseau's Emile.
—— Exposition of the church catechism. 1729; Explication du catéchisme, Amsterdam 1737.

Clarkson, Thomas. An essay on the slavery of the human species. 1787; De la traité du commerce des nègres, tr Maubert 1788.
—— Essay on the impolicy of the African slave-trade. 1788; Essai sur les désaventures de la traite des nègres, Neuf-châtel 1789.

Collins, Anthony. Vindication of the divine attributes. 1710; Essai sur la nature et la destination de l'œuvre humaine, London (for Amsterdam) 1769.
—— Discourse of freethinking. 1713 (anon); Discours sur la liberté de penser, tr [H. Scheurleer and J. Rousset de Missy] 1714.
—— Philosophical inquiry concerning human liberty. 1715; Recherches philosophiques sur la liberté de l'homme, tr De Pons, in Recueil de diverses pièces sur la philosophie, [ed P. Desmaizeaux] 2 vols 1720; Paradoxes

métaphysiques sur le principe des actions humaines, [tr P. Lefèvre de Beauvray], Eleuthéropolis 1754.
—— A discourse of the grounds and reasons of Christian religion. 1724; L'esprit du judaïsme, [tr D'Holbach], London (for Amsterdam) 1770; Examen des prophéties [tr, or adapted and abridged by d'Holbach], London (for Amsterdam) 1768 (for 1769?). Latter includes abridged version of A scheme of literal prophecy examined 1726, below, and d'Holbach's Essai de critique sur les prophètes.
—— Scheme of literal prophecy considered. 1726; Examen du système de ceux qui prétendent que les prophéties se sont accomplies, in Examen des prophéties, [tr d'Holbach], London (for Amsterdam) 1768 [1769?] as above.
Torrey, N. L. Voltaire and the English Deists. New Haven 1930.
Gawlick, G. (ed). Collins, A discourse on freethinking. Stuttgart 1965.

Ferguson, Adam. Essay on the history of civil society. 1767; tr Bergier and Meunier 2 vols Paris 1783.
—— Institutes of moral philosophy. 1769; Institutions de philosophie morale, tr [E. S. P. Reverdil], Geneva 1775.
—— History of the Roman republic. 1783; Histoire du progrès et de la chute de la république romaine, tr [J. N. Dumeunier and J. Gibelin] 3 vols Paris 1784.

Gibbon, Edward. History of the decline and fall of the Roman Empire. 6 vols 1776–88; Histoire de la décadence et de la chute de l'empire romain, [tr Leclerc de Sept-Chênes, also attributed in part to Louis XVI], vol 1 Paris 1776, 2 vols 1777 (with collaborators), 11 vols 1788–92; vols 4–16 tr J. N. Démeunier, A. S. M. Cantwell and Boulard; vols 17–18 tr Boulard, 18 vols Paris 1788–95.
—— Miscellaneous works, with memoirs of his life and writings. 1796; Mémoires de Gibbon, 2 vols Paris 1797. See also Mémoires littéraires de la Grande-Bretagne, col 88, above.
Keynes, G. L. (ed). The library of Gibbon. 1940.
Bonnard, G. A. (ed). Le journal de Gibbon à Lausanne. 1945; tr 1961.
Giarrizzo, G. Gibbon e la cultura europea del settecento. Naples 1954.

Godwin, William. Things as they are: or adventures of Caleb Williams. 1794; Les aventures de Caleb Williams, tr G. Garnier 2 vols Paris 1794; tr J. Constant 3 vols Paris 1795; 3 vols Paris 1796; Les choses comme elles sont, 3 vols Lausanne 1796.
Palacio, J. de. La fortune de Godwin en France. Revue de Littérature Comparée 41 1967.

Goldsmith, Oliver. History of England in a series of letters. 1764; Précis philosophique, tr [J. B. Laboreau] 2 vols 1776; tr Hérissant de Carrières 2 vols 1777; Lettres philosophiques et politiques, tr [Brissot de Warville] 2 vols Paris 1786.
—— History of England. 1771; Nouveau précis de l'histoire d'Angleterre, tr D[u] P[ont] [Brissot de Warville]. Paris 1783; tr Le Bas de St Amand 1788.

Gordon, Thomas. An apology for the dangers of the Church. 1719; Des dangers de l'église, in d'Holbach, De l'imposture sacerdotale, 1767.
—— The independent Whig. 1721 (ch 45–7, 51–4); L'esprit du clergé [from pts 1–2], [tr d'Holbach and J. A. Naigeon] 2 vols London (for Amsterdam) 1767; L'intolérance convaincue de crime et de folie [from pt 3],[tr d'Holbach] in Crellius (J. Crell), De la tolérance dans la religion, [tr C. Le Cène], London (for Amsterdam) 1769.
—— Trenchard's Tracts. 1751 (with Giannone and 'Davisson'), 1763; De l'imposture sacerdotale, [tr d'Holbach], London (for Amsterdam) 1767.

Henry, Robert. History of Great Britain. 6 vols 1771–85; Histoire d'Angleterre, [tr A. M. H. Boulard] 2 vols Paris 1788–9; 6 vols [vols 3, 6 tr A. S. M. Cantwell], Paris 1789–96.

Hobbes, Thomas. De corpore politico: or the elements of law, moral and politick. 1650; Le corps politique, tr S. de Sorbière, Amsterdam 1653; Les éléments de la politique de Mr Hobbes, tr Du Verdun, Paris 1660; *see also* J. B. Bossuet, Politique tirée de l'Ecriture sainte, Paris 1709.

—— Human nature. 1650; De la nature humaine, [tr d'Holbach], London (for Amsterdam) 1772.

—— Moral and political works. 1750; Œuvres philosophiques et politiques, tr d'Holbach 2 vols Neufchâtel 1787.

Lacour-Gayet, G. Les traductions françaises de Hobbes sous le règne de Louis XIV. Archiv für Geschichte der Philologie 12 1889.

Souilhé, H. La pensée et l'influence de Hobbes. Blanchesne 1936.

Derathé, R. Rousseau et la science politique de son temps. Paris 1950.

Thielmann, L. Hobbes dans l'Encyclopédie. Revue d'Histoire Littéraire de la France 51 1951.

—— Diderot and Hobbes. Diderot Stud 2 1953.

—— Voltaire and Hobbism. Stud on Voltaire & Eighteenth Century 10 1960.

Taylor, E. G. Rousseau's debt to Hobbes. In Currents of thought in French literature: essays in memory of G. T. Clapton, ed T. V. Benn et al, Oxford 1965.

Hume, David. Treatise of human nature. 3 vols 1739–40 (anon). No trns listed, but early reviews in Bibliothèque Britannique (ed Desmaizeaux) 40–1 1739–40; Bibliothèque Raisonnée des Ouvrages des Savans de l'Europe (ed Desmaizeaux, Barbeyrac et al) 22 1739, 24 1740, 25 1741; Nouvelle Bibliothèque (ed Barbeyrac et al, Hague) 6 1740.

—— Essays moral and political, 1741 (5th essay); Considérations sur l'état présent de la littérature en Europe, tr [J. B. A. Robinet] 1762.

—— Essays. Vol 2, 1742 (nos 6–9); Le temple du bonheur, in Recueil des plus excellents traités sur le bonheur vol 1, [ed J. B. Mérian], Bouillon 1769.

—— Philosophical essays concerning human understanding. 1748; Essais philosophiques sur l'entendement humain, in Œuvres vol 1, Amsterdam 1758.

—— An inquiry concerning the principle of morals. 1751; Essais sur la morale, tr J. B. A. Robinet, in Œuvres vol 5, Amsterdam 1760.

—— Political discourses. 1752; Essais sur le commerce etc, tr [Mlle de La Chaux?], Amsterdam 1752; Discours politiques de M. David Hume, tr [de Mauvillan] 5 vols Amsterdam 1754–7; tr J. B. Le Blanc, Amsterdam 1754; tr P. A. O'Heguerty [de Magnières], Amsterdam nd; Essai sur la population [no 10], tr Le Michadière 1778.

—— The history of Great Britain. 6 vols 1754–62; Histoire de la maison de Stuart, tr A. F. Prévost d'Exiles 3 vols 1760; Histoire d'Angleterre, tr Mme Belot (later Mme Durey de Meynières), Amsterdam and Paris 1670–9. For bibliography *see* Rochedieu pp. 160–1. Turgot is believed to have played important role in trn.

—— Oeuvres philosophiques. Tr [J. B. Mérian, J. B. R. Robinet et al] 5 vols Amsterdam 1758–60, 1759–64 (2nd edn), 6 vols 1764 (new edn), 3 vols 1788 (new edn).

—— A concise and genuine account of the dispute between Mr Hume and Mr Rousseau. 1766; Exposé succinct de la contestation qui s'est élevée entre M. Hume et M. J.-J. Rousseau, Londres (tor Paris) 1766 (tr J. B. A. Suard, ed Suard and J. le Rond d'Alembert). Suard worked from English ms; the English edn appeared after French trn. For d'Alembert's role *see* Boiteux, Le rôle de d'Alembert, Annales de la Société J.-J. Rousseau 32 1952.

—— Pensées philosophiques. Tr Desboulmiers [J. A. Julien] 1767; Le génie de M. Hume, Paris 1770.

—— The life of David Hume esq written by himself. 1777; La vie de David Hume, tr [Suard], Paris 1777.

—— Two essays [suicide and immortality]. 1777; Dissertation sur le suicide, [tr d'Holbach], in Recueil philosophique, ed J. A. Naigeon 2 vols 1770.

—— Dialogues concerning natural religion. 1779; Dialogues sur la religion naturelle, Edinburgh 1779.

For relations of Hume and Continent see E. C. Mossner, The life of Hume, Edinburgh 1954; Letters of Hume, ed J. Y. T. Greig 2 vols Oxford 1932 (appendix B on early trns of Hume into French), and New letters, ed Mossner and R. Klibansky, Oxford 1954.

Peoples, M. H. La querelle Rousseau-Hume. Annales de la Société J.-J. Rousseau 18 1928; *see also* P. H. Mayer, Comparative Lit 4 1952.

Mossner, E. C. The continental reception of Hume's Treatise. Mind 56 1947.

—— Hume and the French men of letters. Revue Internationale de Philosophie 6 1952.

Meyer, P. H. Voltaire and Hume as historians. PMLA 73 1958. *See* MLN 66 1951.

Bongie, L. Hume and the official censorship of the Ancien Régime. French Stud 12 1958.

—— Hume 'philosophe' and philosopher in France. French Stud 15 1961.

—— Hume: prophet of the counter-revolution. Oxford 1965.

Grimsley, R. D'Alembert and Hume. Revue de Littérature Comparée 35 1961.

Courtney, C. P. Hume et l'abbé Raynal. Revue de Littérature Comparée 36 1962.

Benn, T. V. Les Political discourses de Hume et Diderot. In Currents of thought in French literature: essays in memory of G. T. Clapton, ed T. V. Benn et al, Oxford 1965.

Kuypers, M. S. The background of Hume's empiricism. New York 1966.

Pottle, F. A. The part played by Walpole in the quarrel between Rousseau and Hume. In Horace Walpole: essays dedicated to W. S. Lewis, ed W. H. Smith, New Haven 1967.

Hutcheson, Francis. An inquiry into the original of our ideas of beauty and virtue. 1725; Recherches sur l'origine des idees que nous avons de la beauté et de la vertu, [tr M. A. Eidous], Amsterdam 1749.

—— An essay on the nature and conduct of the passions and affections. 1728; Traité des passions, tr [M. A. Eidous], Amsterdam 1749.

—— A system of moral philosophy. 1755; Système de philosophie morale, [tr Eidous] 2 vols Lyons 1770 (also as La philosophie naturelle).

James, Robert. A medicinal dictionary. 3 vols 1743–5; Dictionnaire universel de médecine, tr Diderot, Eidous and Toussaint 6 vols Paris 1746–8.

Johnson, Samuel. Parliamentary debates GM. These were tr 1742–. *See* E. A. Bloom, Johnson in Grub St, Providence 1957.

'Layman, A'. The ax laid to the root of Christian priestcraft. 1742; Les prêtres démasqués, [tr d'Holbach], London (for Amsterdam) 1768 (for 1767).

Locke, John. An essay concerning humane understanding. 1690; Extrait d'un livre anglais qui n'est pas encore publié intitulé Essai philosophique concernant l'entendement, tr Le Clerc in Bibliothèque Universelle 8 1688 (extract preceded pbn of first English edn, and was based on extract supplied by Locke, who was thus first known as author on Continent); Essai philosophique concernant l'entendement humain, tr P. Coste, Amsterdam 1700, 1729 (augmented); Abrégé, tr J. P. Bosset 1720; tr Walther Dresden 1788.

—— Two treatises of government. 1690. Review with extracts tr Le Clerc in Bibliothèque Universelle 19 1690; Traité du gouvernement civil, tr D. Mazel, Amsterdam 1691, 1695 (2nd edn based on 1694); tr P. Coste, Amsterdam 1700 (4th edn).

—— Thoughts concerning education. 1693; De l'éducation des enfants, tr P. Coste, Amsterdam 1695.

—— The reasonableness of Christianity. 1695; Que la religion chrétienne est très raisonnable, tr [P. Coste], Amsterdam 1696; Le christianisme raisonnable, [tr Coste, not Le Clerc] 2 vols Amsterdam 1715.

—— Works. 1706; Œuvres diverses, tr [Le Clerc], Amsterdam 1710 (with Eloge historique de feu M. Locke par M. J. Leclerc), 2 vols Amsterdam 1732 (new edn).

Coste, P. Eloge. Nouvelles de la République des Lettres Feb 1705.

Le Clerc, J. Eloge historique de M. Locke. In Bibliothèque choisie vol 6, 1705.

Erdbrügger, G. Die Bedeutung Lockes für die Pädagogik Rousseaus. Würzburg 1912.

Bonno, G. The diffusion and influence of Locke's Essay concerning human understanding in France before Voltaire's Lettres philosophiques. Proc Amer Philosophical Soc 1947.

—— Les relations intellectuelles de Locke avec la France. Berkeley 1955. See also Revue de Littérature Comparée 33 1959, and P. Bastid, Sieyès et les philosophes, Revue de Synthèse 17 1939; also P. Hazard, Revue de Littérature Comparée 17 1937.

James, D. G. Locke and Pascal. In his Life of reason, 1949. See also L. Obertello, Locke e Port-Royal, Trieste 1964.

Derathé, R. J.-J. Rousseau et la science politique de son temps. Paris 1950.

Lough, J. Locke's travels in France 1657–79. Cambridge 1953.

Hampton, J. Les traductions françaises de Locke. Revue de Littérature Comparée 29 1955.

Harrison, J. and P. Laslett. The library of Locke. 1965.

Mandeville, Bernard. The fable of the bees. 1705, 1715, 1723; La fable des abeilles, [tr J. Bertrand] 4 vols 1740.

M[elon, J. F.]. Essai politique sur le commerce. 1734.

Voltaire. Le mondain. 1736 (in ms); Défense du Mondain, 1737 (in ms).

[Mandeville]. Free thoughts on religion. 1720; Pensées libres sur la religion, tr J. van Effen 2 vols Hague 1722.

Kaye, F. B. The influence of Mandeville. SP 19 1922.

Wade, I. O. Studies on Voltaire. Princeton 1947.

Labriolle-Rutherford, M. R. de. L'évolution de la notion du luxe depuis Mandeville jusqu'à la Révolution. Stud on Voltaire & Eighteenth Century 26 1963.

Milton, John. Areopagitica. 1644; Areopagitica: sur la liberté de presse, Paris 1788 (adapted by Mirabeau l'aîné).

—— Tractate of education. 1644; Lettre de Milton, [tr J. B. Leblanc] in C. de Nonnay de Fontenai, Lettres sur l'éducation des princes, Edinburgh 1746.

—— Eikonoklastes. 1649; tr J. Drury 1652.

—— Pro populo anglicano defensio. 1651; tr 1789.

Wolfe, D. M. Milton and Mirabeau. PMLA 49 1934.

Briet, S. L'Areopagitica de Milton: histoire d'une traduction. Revue de Littérature Comparée 26 1952. See also O. Lutaud, Stud on Voltaire & Eighteenth Century 26 1963.

More, Hannah. Thoughts on the importance of the manners of the great. 1788; Pensées sur les moeurs des grands, tr Mme de la Fite, Hague 1790.

More, Thomas. Utopia. 1516 (Latin); tr 1551; L'Utopie, tr de Gueudeville, Leyden 1715, Amsterdam 1730 (as Idée d'une république heureuse).

Le Flamane, A. Les utopies pré-révolutionnaires. Paris 1934.

Needham, John Turberville. Observations upon the generation, composition and decomposition of animal and vegetable substances. 1749; Nouvelles observations microscopiques, [tr L. A. Lavirotte], Paris 1750.

Needham, Marchamont. Discovery of the excellence of the State. 1649; De la souveraineté du peuple, [tr d'Eon de Beaumont] et enrichie de notes de Rousseau, Mably etc, Paris 1790.

Newton, Isaac. See also International Latin Literature, above; this section restricted to English versions of Newton.

—— On the number of colours. 1672; Essai sur le mélange des couleurs, [tr Rivoire], Amsterdam 1759.

—— Optics. 1704; Traité d'optique, tr P. Coste 2 vols Amsterdam 1720; [tr Marat] 2 vols Paris 1787.

—— The chronology of ancient kingdoms amended. 1728. First pbd from English ms in French abridgement as Abrégé de la chronologie, [tr N. Fréret], Paris 1725, an unauthorized pbn with critical commentary that Newton replied to in Philosophical Trans 23 1725; tr Réponse aux Observations sur la chronologie de M. Newton, Paris 1726; La chronologie des anciens royaumes corrigée, [tr F. Granet and Marthan], Paris 1728 (trn of first authorized English edn); Abrégé de la chronologie, [tr J. A. Butini], Geneva 1743.

—— Mathematical principles of natural philosophy. 1729 (trn of Principia, 1687); Principes de philosophie de Newton, 2 vols 1729; Principes de mathématiques de la philosophie naturelle, tr G. E. Le Tonnelier de Breteuil du Châtelet-Lomont (preface by Cotes and Voltaire), 2 vols Paris 1759.

—— Universal arithmetic. 1729; Arithmétique universelle, tr G. F. Castilhon 2 vols 1761.

—— The method of fluxions. 1736; La méthode des fluxions, tr [Buffon], Paris 1740.

Fontenelle, B. Eloge de Newton. 1717. In Œuvres diverses vol 3, Hague 1729.

Brunet, P. L'introduction des théories de Newton en France au xviiie siècle avant 1738. Paris 1931.

Bonno, G. La culture et la civilisation britanniques devant l'opinion française. Trans Amer Philosophical Soc 38 1948.

Hahn, R. Laplace as a Newtonian scientist. Los Angeles 1967.

Pepys, Samuel
Holmes, U. T. Pepys in Paris and other essays. Chapel Hill 1954.

Pope, Alexander. Essay on man. 1733; Essai sur l'homme, [tr E. de Silhouette], [Paris] 1736 (prose); tr J. F. Du Resnel du Bellay, Paris 1737 (verse); Maximes et réflexions morales, [tr J. de Séré de Rieux] 1739; [tr J. C. de Schleinitz], Helmstedt 1749; [tr C. F. X. Millot], Lyons 1761; tr Saint-Simon, Haarlem 1771, in Essai de traduction littérale et énergique; tr de Fontanes, Paris 1783; [tr Nivernois] 1796.

Voltaire. Discours en vers sur l'homme. 1738–9; Candide, 1759.

Gaultier, Le poème de Pope intitulé Essay sur l'homme convaincue d'impiété. Hague 1746.

Rousseau, J.-J. Lettre de Rousseau à Monsieur de Voltaire, le 18 août 1756. 1759 (1758 edn also?). See Rousseau, Correspondance complète, ed R. A. Leigh, Geneva 1965 (vol 4, letter 424).

—— Universal prayer. 1738; La prière universelle, [tr J. J. Lefranc de Pompignan] Londres (for Paris?) 1740; tr Saint-Simon in Essai de traduction littérale et énergique, Haarlem 1771.

—— Mélanges de littérature et de philosophie. [Tr E. de Silhouette] 2 vols 1742.

—— Les pensées de Pope. Ed Lacombe de Prézel, Paris 1766.

Van Tieghem, P. La prière universelle et le déisme française. Revue de Littérature Comparée 3 1923.

Audra, E. L'influence française dans l'œuvre de Pope. Paris 1931.

—— Les traductions françaises de Pope. Paris 1931. Addns by F. Beckwith, MLR 29 1934.

La Harpe, J. de. Le Journal des savants et la renommée de Pope en France. Berkeley 1933.

Rogers, R. W. Critiques of the Essay on man in France and Germany. ELH 15 1948.

Leigh, R. A. From the Inégalité to Candide: notes on a desultory dialogue between Rousseau and Voltaire.

In The age of Enlightenment: studies presented to T. Besterman, ed W. H. Barber et al, Edinburgh 1967.

Reid, Thomas. An inquiry into the human mind. 1763; Recherches sur l'entendement humain, 2 vols Amsterdam 1768.

Robertson, William. The history of Scotland during the reigns of Queen Mary and King James VI. 2 vols 1758–9; Histoire d'Ecosse, tr N. P. Besset de la Chapelle 3 vols 1764.

—— The history of the reign of the Emperor Charles V. 1769; L'histoire du règne de l'empereur Charles-Quint, tr J. B. A. Suard, Roger et Letourneur 6 vols Amsterdam 1771.

—— The history of America. 1777; Histoire de l'Amérique, tr E[idous] 4 vols Maestricht 1777; tr J. B. A. Suard and A. Morellet, Paris 1778.

—— An historical disquisition concerning the knowledge which the Ancients had of India. 1791; Recherches historiques sur la connoissance que les anciens avaient de l'Inde, tr Paris 1792.

Shaftesbury, Anthony Ashley Cooper, 3rd Earl of. Inquiry concerning virtue. 1699; Principes de la philosophie morale, tr Paillet 1744; Essai sur le mérite et la vertu, tr D. Diderot 2 vols 1745 (adaptation).

—— Letter concerning enthusiasm. 1708; Lettre sur l'enthousiasme, [tr P. A. Samson], Hague 1709; Lettres, tr Lacombe 1761. See also Journal des sçavans, 1708; Leclerc's article in Bibliothèque choisie 1711.

—— Sensus communis. 1709; Essai sur l'usage de la raillerie, tr J. van Effen, Hague 1710.

—— Characteristicks. 1711; Les caractéristiques de Shaftesbury, tr J. van Effen and Samson 3 vols Geneva 1769.

Diderot, D. Pensées philosophiques. Hague (for Paris) 1746.

See also Diderot, above. For early impact through periodicals see Bonno, La culture et la civilisation britanniques devant l'opinion française, Trans Amer Philosophical Soc 38 1948.

Whitaker, S. F. P. Coste et Shaftesbury. Revue de Littérature Comparée 25 1951.

Schlegel, D. Diderot as the transmitter of Shaftesbury's romanticism. Stud on Voltaire & Eighteenth Century 27 1963.

—— Shaftesbury and the French Deists. Chapel Hill 1965.

Sidney, Algernon. Sydney redivivus. 1689; Discours sur le gouvernement civil, tr P. A. Samson 3 vols Hague 1702.

Smith, Adam. The theory of moral sentiments. 1759; Métaphysique de l'âme: ou théorie des sentiments moraux, [tr Eidous] 2 vols Paris 1764; tr Blavet, Paris 1774–5; tr Mme Grouchy 2 vols Paris 1798.

—— A dissertation on the origin of languages. 1761; Dissertation sur l'origine des langues, [tr A. M. H. Boulard], Paris 1796 (also as Considérations sur la première formation des langues).

—— An inquiry into the nature and causes of the wealth of nations. 1776; Recherches sur la nature et les causes de la richesse des nations, tr Blavet 4 vols 1778–9; [tr J. A. Roucher] 4 vols Paris 1790–1, 1795 (with notes by Condorcet); tr G. Garnier, Paris 1800.

—— Essays on philosophical subjects. 1795; Essais philosophiques, tr P. Prévost 2 vols Paris 1797.

Feilbogen, S. Smith und Turgot. Vienna 1892. Turgot's Réflexions sur la formation et la distribution des richesses first pbd in Ephémérides 1769–70, then separately 1776. The trn, by Adam Smith?, appeared 1788 as Reflections on the formation and distribution of wealth. See also S. Lundberg, Turgot's unknown translator [Adam Smith?], Hague 1964.

Laufer, S. Smith and Helvétius. Berne 1902.

Mizuta, H. Adam Smith's library. Cambridge 1967.

Steele, Sir Richard. The importance of Dunkirk. 1713; Réflexions sur l'importance de Dunkerque, 1715.

—— The crisis [in royal succession]. 1714; La crise et quelques remarques nécessaires sur le danger d'une succession papiste, Amsterdam 1714.

—— Ladies library. 1714. Bibliothèque des dames, [tr F. M. Janiçon], Amsterdam 1716.

—— Political writings. 1715; Recueil de quelques pièces de M. Steele, Amsterdam 1714; Oeuvres diverses, 1715. See also Addison, above, and Select list of journals.

Sterne, Laurence. Fifteen sermons. 1768; Sermons choisis, Lausanne 1770; tr G. de la Baume 1786.

—— Letters. 1775; Lettres de Sterne à ses amis, [tr G. de La Baume] 1788; tr D. de Saint-Georges, Hague 1789.

Swift, Jonathan. Predictions for the year 1708 by Isaac Bickerstaff. 1708; Renversement des prédictions frivoles d'Isaac Bickerstaff, Lunéville 1708.

—— The conduct of the allies. [1711]; Lettres et mémoires sur la conduite de la présente guerre, Hague 1712, 1712 (as La conduite des alliez; Manifeste pour le ministère; Traduction d'un écrit anglois; Recueil de quelques piéces nouvelles), Brussels 1769 (as Apologie de la reine Anne [from Good Queen Anne vindicated, later adaptation], tr L.B.C.D.G. [Lebeau], Brussels 1769).

—— Some remarks on the Barrier Treaty. 1712; Remarques sur le traité de La Barrière, Luxembourg 1712.

—— The public spirit of the Whigs. 1714; L'esprit des Whigs, Amsterdam 1714.

—— An argument to prove that the abolishing of Christianity may be attended with some inconvenience 1717; tr in Histoire de Martinus Scriblerus, 1755.

—— The history of the four last years of the Queen. 1758; Histoire du règne de la reine Anne, [tr Eidous and d'Holbach], Amsterdam 1765. See also Prose fiction, below.

Temple, Sir William. Miscellanea. 1680–1701; Œuvres mêlées tr Utrecht 1693; Œuvres diverses, Amsterdam 1708.

Tindal, Matthew. Christianity as old as the creation. 1730; Le christianisme aussi ancien que le monde, [tr d'Holbach] in Recueil philosophique, 2 vols Londres (for Amsterdam) 1770.

Toland, John. Letters to Serena. 1704 (anon); Lettres philosophiques sur l'origine des préjugés, [tr d'Holbach], Londres (for Amsterdam) 1768.

—— Nazarenus. 1718; Le Nazaréen, [tr d'Holbach?], Londres (for Amsterdam) 1777.

Walpole, Horace. See Hume, above, and Prose fiction, below.

Warburton, William. The alliance between Church and State. 1736; Dissertations sur l'union de la religion, de la morale et de la politique, tr Silhouette 2 vols Hague 1742.

Cherpack, C. Warburton and the Encyclopédistes. Comparative Lit 7 1955.

—— Warburton and some aspects of the primitive in 18th-century France. PQ 36 1957.

Brumfitt, J. H. Voltaire and Warburton. Stud on Voltaire & Eighteenth Century 16 1961.

Wollaston, William. Religion of nature delineated. 1722; Ebauche de la religion naturelle, tr [Garrigue?], Hague 1726.

Wollstonecraft, Mary. Thoughts on the education of daughters. 1787; Marie et Caroline, [tr A. J. N. Lallemant], Paris 1799.

—— A vindication of the rights of woman. 1792; Défense des droits des femmes, tr Paris 1792.

—— The wrongs of woman; or Maria. 1798; Maria, adapted B. Ducos, Paris 1798.

Bouten, J. Mary Wollstonecraft and the beginnings of female emancipation in France and England. Amsterdam 1922. See also R. Blanchard, MLN V4 1929.

Woolston, Thomas. A discourse [–A sixth discourse] on the miracles of our Saviour. 1727–9; Discours sur les miracles, [tr d'Holbach?] 2 vols [1769].

Hancock, A. C. The French Revolution and the English poets. New York 1899.

Belin, J. P. Le commerce des livres prohibés à Paris de 1750–89. Paris 1913.

—— Le mouvement philosophique de 1748–89: étude sur la diffusion des idées des philosophes à Paris. Paris 1913.

Dechamps, J. Napoléon en Angleterre. French Quart 10 1928.

—— La Révolution française et les lettres anglaises. Comparative Lit Stud 2 1941.

Martin, G. Manuel d'histoire de la franc-maçonnerie française. Paris 1929.

Miller, M. M. Science and philosophy as precursors of the English influence in France. PMLA 45 1930.

Torrey, N. L. Voltaire and the English Deists. New Haven 1930.

Lovejoy, A. O. The parallel of Deism and classicism. MP 29 1931.

Bonno, G. La constitution britannique devant l'opinion française de Montesquieu à Bonaparte. Paris 1932.

—— La culture et la civilisation britanniques devant l'opinion française de la Paix d'Utrecht aux Lettres philosophiques 1713–34. Trans Amer Philosophical Soc 38 1948. The sole authoritative work in this field, tracing impact through periodicals and trns.

Mornet, D. Les origines intellectuelles de la Révolution française. Paris 1933. See also L. Cahen, A propos des origines intellectuelles, Revue de Synthèse 17 1939; H. Peyre, JHI 10 1949.

Briggs, E. R. L'incrédulité et la pensée anglaise en France au début du xviiie siècle. Revue d'Histoire de la Littérature Française 41 1934.

Brown, H. Scientific organisation in 17th-century France 1620–80. Baltimore 1934.

Pintard, R. Le libertinage érudit dans la première moitié du xviie siècle. Paris 1943. For 1680–1715 see P. Hazard, La crise de la conscience européenne, Paris 1935.

Carré, A. L'influence des Huguenots français en Irlande. Paris 1938.

Laski, H. The English constitution and French public opinion 1789–94. Politica 3 1938.

Wade, I. O. The clandestine organisation and diffusion of philosophical ideas in France 1700–50. Princeton 1938.

Hudson, A. P. and V. M. The coast of France: French invasion and English literature. South Atlantic Quart 40 1941.

Leighton, R. M. The tradition of the English constitution in France on the eve of the Revolution. Ithaca 1941.

Luhn, K. Angelsächsische Berichterstattung über die Ereignisse der französische Revolution bei Burke, Paine, Mackintosh und Young. Frankfurt 1941.

Courtines, L. P. Bayle, Hume and Berkeley. Revue de Littérature Comparée 21 1947.

Dodge, G. H. The political theories of the Huguenots of the dispersion. New York 1947.

Index librorum prohibitorum. SSMI D.N PII.PP XII IUSSI EDITUS, Vatican 1948.

Gillespie, C. C. The edge of objectivity: an essay in the history of scientific ideas. Princeton 1960.

Gossman, L. Berkeley, Hume and Maupertuis. French Stud 14 1960.

Spink, J. S. French free-thought from Gassendi to Voltaire. 1960.

Roger, J. Les sciences de la vie dans la pensée française du xviiie siècle. Paris 1963. See also] D. Mornet, Les sciences de la nature en France au xviiie siècle, Paris 1911.

Hill, C. Intellectual origins of the English Revolution. Oxford 1965.

Gay, P. The Enlightenment: an interpretation. 2 vols New York 1966–. Includes critical bibliography.

Pomeau, R. L'Europe des lumières: cosmopolitisme et unité europeenne au xviiie siècle. Paris 1966.

Theology

Only literary aspects are dealt with here. Deistic works are included under Philosophy, above. The massive exchange of works of devotion, theological controversy, commentaries, sermons etc has been partially explored by G. Ascoli, La Grande-Bretagne devant l'opinion française, 2 vols Paris 1920 (pp. 312–34), *and by* G. Bonno, La culture et la civilisation britanniques devant l'opinion française 1713–34, Trans Amer Philosophical Soc 38 1948.

French Authors

Bossuet, Jacques Bénigne. *See Philosophy, above for trns.*
Lambin, G. Les rapports de Bossuet avec l'Angleterre. Bulletin du Bibliophile et du Bibliothécaire 1909–10.
Rébelliau, A. Bossuet et sa renommée en Angleterre. Revue Anglo-américaine 1 1924.

Fénelon, François de Salignac de La Mothe. Explication des maximes des saints sur la vie intérieure. Paris 1697 (defence of quietism); The maxims of the saints explained concerning the interior life, 1698.

—— Démonstration de l'existence de Dieu. Paris 1713; A demonstration of the existence, wisdom and omnipotence of God, tr [A. Boyer] 1713; tr S. Boyse 1749.
Chérel, A. Ramsay et la tolérance de Fénelon. Revue du xviiie Siècle 1918.
Orcibal, J. L'influence spirituelle de Fénelon dans les pays anglo-saxons au xviiie siècle. Bulletin del a Société d'Etudes du xviie siècle 1953.

Guyon, Jeanne Marie Bouvier de La Mothe. Vie écrite par elle-même. 1720; The life of Lady Guion now abridged, 2 vols Bristol 1772; An extract of the life of Madam Guion, ed John Wesley 1776.

—— Moyen court et très facile pour l'oraison. Grenoble 1685; A short and easy method of prayer, tr T. D. Brooke 1775; The worship of God in spirit and in truth: or a short and easy method of prayer, Bristol 1775; The exemplary life of the pious Lady Guion, [and] a new translation of her method of prayer, Dublin 1775.
Bossuet. Relation sur le quiétisme. Paris 1698 etc; Quakerism à la-mode particularly that of the Lord Archbishop of Cambrai and Madam Guyone, 1698.

Malebranche, Nicolas. De la recherche de la vérité. Paris 1674–5; Treatise concerning the search after truth, tr T. Taylor 2 vols Oxford 1694; Search after truth: or a treatise of the humane mind, tr R. Sault 2 vols 1694–5.

—— Conversations chrétiennes. Paris 1676; Christian conferences, tr [P. A. Motteux] 1695.

—— Traité de la nature et de la grâce. Amsterdam 1680; A treatise of nature and grace, tr T. Taylor, in Treatise concerning truth 2 vols Oxford 1694; tr 1695.

—— Traité de morale. Cologne 1683; A treatise of morality, tr J. Shipton 1699.

English Authors

Barclay, Robert. An apology for the true Christian divinity. 1678; Apologie de la véritable divinité chrétienne, tr 1702; tr E. P. Bridel 1797.

Burnet, Gilbert. A defence of natural and revealed religion. 1737; Défense de la religion tant naturelle que révélée, tr [A. Boislebeau de La Chappelle] 6 vols Hague 1738–44.

Bunyan, John. The pilgrim's progress. 1678, 1684; Voyage d'un chrétien vers l'éternité, Amsterdam 1685; Voyage du chrétien, Neuchâtel 1716; Le pélerinage d'un nommé Chrétien, tr R. Estienne, Paris 1772.

Penn, William. No cross, no crown. 1682; Point de croix, point de couronne, tr [C. Gray], Bristol 1741; tr E. P. Bridel 1793.

—— A key opening the way. 1693; La clef pour ouvrir la voye à quiconque a le sens commun, tr 1701.

—— Some fruits of solitude. 1693; Fruits de la solitude, tr [E. P. Bridel] 1790.

— A brief account of the rise of the Quakers. 1694;
Exposition succincte de l'origine et des progrès du
peuple qu'on appelle les Quakers, tr C. Gay 1764; tr
E. P. Bridel 1790.

Pope, Alexander. *See Philosophy, above.*

Wesley, John
Gounelle, E. Wesley et ses rapports avec les Français.
Nyon 1890.
Léger, A. La jeunesse de Wesley. Paris 1910. On
Pascal's impact.
Moore, S. H. Wesley and Fénelon. London Quart 169
1944.

Henderson, A. D. Foreign religious influences in 17th-
century Scotland. Edinburgh Rev 249 1929.
Clark, R. Great Britain, Port Royal and Jansenism. Cam-
bridge 1932.
Préclin, E. L'influence du Jansénisme français à l'étranger.
Revue Historique 182 1938.
— Introduction à l'étude des rapports religieux entre la
France et la Grande-Bretagne 1763–1848. Revue
d'Histoire Moderne et Contemporaine 13 1938. Biblio-
graphical survey.
Cooper, B. The relation of Le Philosophe anglais by
Prévost to religious controversies in France and
England. Trans Wisconsin Acad Arts & Letters 32
1940.
Simonetti, M. Possibili influenze di Hobbes sul pensiero
Pascaliano. Humanitas 10 1955.

Literary Theory and Criticism
French Authors

d'Aubignac, François Hédelin. Pratique du théâtre. Paris
1657; The whole art of the stage, tr 1684.
Boileau-Despréaux, Nicolas. L'art poétique. Paris 1674;
The art of poetry, tr W. Soames 1683; 'rev J. Dryden'
1710; *see also* John Sheffield, Earl of Mulgrave, Essay
upon poetry, 1682.
— Traité du sublime ou du merveilleux dans le discours.
Paris 1674; An essay upon sublime, Oxford 1698.
Boileau's Traité was tr from Longinus inaccurately,
through intermediaries.
— Œuvres diverses. Paris 1674; Works, tr J. Ozell 3
vols 1712–13.
A discourse on satires. In W. Harte, An essay on satire,
1730.
A new abridgement of the rules of French prosody
[with 4th Satire]. Tr T. Ryley 1758 (2nd edn).
Walter, V. Boileaus Wirkung auf seine englische Zeit-
genossen. Strasbourg 1911.
Lemonnier, C. Pope traducteur de Boileau. Revue de
Littérature Comparée 14 1934.
Clark, A. F. B. Boileau and the French classical critics
in England 1660–1830. Paris 1925, New York 1965.
Bouhours, Dominique. La manière de bien penser dans
les ouvrages d'esprit. Paris 1687; The art of criticism:
or the method of making a right judgement upon sub-
jects of wit and learning, tr 'a person of quality' 1705;
The arts of logic and rhetoric, tr J. Oldmixon 1728.
Corneille, Pierre. Discours. Paris 1660; Examens, Paris
1660 (critical commentaries to plays), 1682 (rev);
Writings on the theatre, ed H. T. Barnwell, Oxford
1965.
Dryden, J. Of dramatick poesie: an essay. 1668.
— Of heroick plays. In his Conquest of Granada, 1672.
Diderot, Denis
Beau. In Encyclopédie vol 2, 1752. Later entitled
Recherches philosophiques sur l'origine et la nature
du beau.
Génie. In Encyclopédie vol 7, 1757. *See* H. Dieck-
mann, JHI 2 1941.
Entretiens avec Dorval [sur Le fils naturel]. In Le fils
naturel, Amsterdam 1757.

De la poésie dramatique. In Le père de famille,
Amsterdam 1758.
Eloge de Richardson. Journal Etranger Jan 1762.
Paradoxe sur le comédien [written 1769–78]. In Corre-
spondance Littéraire [ms periodical] Oct–Nov 1770
(fragment); rev 1773, 1777, 1830, 1875, 1902.
Salons [of painting 1759–1781]. Paris 1795, 1798, 1813,
1857; ed J. Seznec 4 vols Oxford 1957–.
Œuvres esthétiques. Ed P. Vernière, Paris 1959.

Belaval, Y. L'esthétique sans paradoxe de Diderot.
Paris 1950.
Dubos, Jean Baptiste. Réflexions critiques sur la poésie et
la peinture. Paris 1719; Critical reflections on poetry,
painting and music, tr T. Nugent 3 vols 1748. *See* A. P.
Bertocci, Du Bos and English literature, New York
1949.
Fénelon, François de Salignac de La Mothe. Dialogues sur
l'éloquence. Paris 1718; Dialogues concerning eloquence, tr W. Stevenson 1722.
Fontenelle, Bernard Le Bovier de. Digression sur les
anciens et les modernes. Paris 1688. *See Perrault, below.*
Huet, Pierre Daniel. Traité sur l'origine des romans.
Paris 1670; A treatise of romances and their original,
1672; tr S. Lewis 1715.
Le Bossu, René. Traité du poème épique. Paris 1675;
Monsieur Bossu's Treatise of the epick poem, tr W. J.
1695; A general view of the epic poem and of the Iliad
and Odyssey, extracted from Bossu, tr A. Pope 1725
(with Pope's Odyssey). *See* J. Addison's essays on
Paradise lost, Spectator 1711–12.
Perrault, Charles. Parallèle des anciens et modernes. 4
vols Paris 1688–97.
Temple, Sir William. Upon ancient and modern learning. 1690.
Wotton, William. Reflections upon ancient and modern
learning. 1694.
Swift, Jonathan. An account of the battel between the
antient and modern books in St James's Library.
1704.
Rapin, René. Réflections sur la poétique d'Aristote. Paris
1674; Reflections on Aristotle's Treatise of poesie, tr T.
Rymer 1674; Whole critical works, tr B. Kennett et al
1706.
Saint Evremond, Charles de Marguetel de Saint-Denis,
seigneur de
Œuvres meslées. 5 pts Paris 1668–78; Miscellanea, tr
F. Spence 1686.
— Œuvres. 1668 etc; Works tr 2 vols 1700. *See Philo-
sophy, above.*
Staël-Holstein, Anne Louise Germaine Necker, baronne de
Lettres sur les ouvrages et le caractère de J.-J. Rousseau.
[Paris] 1788; Lettres on the works and character of
Rousseau, tr 1789.
De la littérature. Paris 1800; De l'Allemagne, 1814.
Escarpit, R. L'Angleterre dans l'œuvre de Mme de
Staël. Paris 1954.
Voltaire, François Marie Arouet de
See Philosophy, above, for Essay upon epick poetry,
1727; Préface to Oedipe, 1729; Discours sur la
tragédie à milord Bolingbroke, 1730 (with Brutus);
Lettres philosophiques, 1734 (first pbd as Letters
concerning the English nation, 1733); Préface to Mort
de César, 1736; Dissertation sur la tragédie ancienne
et moderne, 1749 (with Sémiramis); Le siècle de
Louis XIV, 1751; Goût, in Encyclopédie vol 7, 1757.
Merian-Genast, E. W. Voltaires Essai sur la poésie
épique und die Entwicklung der Idee der Weltliteratur. Leipzig 1920. *See also* Romanische Forschungen
40 1927.
Naves, R. Le goût de Voltaire. Paris [1938].
Williams, D. Voltaire: literary critic. Stud on Voltaire &
Eighteenth Century 48 1966.

English Authors

Addison, Joseph. *See* G. Bonno, La culture et la civilisation britanniques, Trans Amer Philosophical Soc 38 1948 pp. 63–6, who notes periodical references from 1709 in France; Criticism on Milton's Paradise lost, Spectator 1711–12; Remarques sur le Paradis perdu, tr Dupré and Barret 3 vols Paris 1729; tr E. de Joncourt, Paris 1754; tr L. Racine, Paris 1755.
  Voltaire. Lettres philosophiques. Amsterdam (for Rouen) 1734.
— Art dramatique. In Questions sur l'Encyclopédie pt 2, [Geneva] 1770.
  Baldwin, E. C. La Bruyère's influence upon Addison. PMLA 19 1904.

Blair, Hugh. Lectures on rhetoric. 1783; Leçons de rhétorique et de belles lettres, tr Cantwel 4 vols Paris 1797.
— A critical dissertation on the poems of Ossian. 1763; Observations sur l'ancienne poésie, particulièrement la runique et la celtique, in Recueil anglois, 2 vols Amsterdam 1763.

Burke, Edmund. A philosophical enquiry into the origin of our ideas of the sublime and beautiful. 1757; Recherches philosophiques sur l'origine des idees du beau et du sublime, précédées d'une dissertation sur le goût, tr D[es] F[rançois] 2 vols 1765.
  May, G. Diderot and Burke: a study in aesthetic affinity. PMLA 75 1960.

Coleridge, Samuel Taylor
  Lindsay, J. Coleridge's marginalia in a volume of Descartes. PMLA 49 1934.

Dryden, John. Of dramatick poesie: an essay. 1668. *See* also Drama, below.
  Legouis, P. Corneille and Dryden as dramatic critics. In Seventeenth-century studies presented to Sir Herbert Grierson, Oxford 1938.
  Aden, J. M. Dryden and Boileau. Storico Philosofico 50 1953.
— Dryden and Corneille. RES new ser 6 1955. Also MLN 71 1956.
— Dryden and Saint Evremond. Comparative Lit 6 1954.

Garrick, David
  Garrick ou les acteurs anglais: ouvrage contenant des réflexions sur l'art dramatique, sur l'art de la représentation et le jeu des acteurs. Tr A. Sticote, Paris 1769.
  Diderot, D. Paradoxe sur le comédien. Paris 1830, 1875, 1902.

Gibbon, Edward. Essai sur l'étude de la littérature. 1761 (written in French); An essay on the study of literature, tr (not by Gibbon) 1764.
— Mémoires littéraires de la Grande-Bretagne. 1768. With Deyverdun.

Hume, David
  Mossner, E. C. Hume and the Ancient-Modern controversy. SE 28 1949.

Hutcheson, Francis. *See Philosophy, above, for trns of aesthetic works.*
  Aldridge, A. O. A French critic of Hutcheson's aesthetics. MP 45 1948.

Johnson, Samuel. [Lives of the poets]. 1779–81; Vie de Milton, tr [A. M. H. Boulard], Paris 1797.
  Abbott, J. L. Johnson's translations from the French. UTQ 36 1967.
  Klenker, R. Johnsons Verhältnis zur französischen Literatur. Strasbourg 1907.
  Tyson, M. and H. Guppy. The French journals of Mrs Thrale and Dr Johnson. Manchester 1932.
  Schinz, A. Johnson et Rousseau. MLN 57 1942.
  Springer-Miller, F. Johnson and Boileau. N & Q 10 Nov 1951.

Pope, Alexander. Essay on criticism. 1711; Essai sur la critique, tr [Robethon], Amsterdam 1717 (imitation);

tr (G. Delage or La Pillonière), Paris 1717 (abridged); tr [J. F. Du Resnel Du Bellay], Paris 1730 (in verse); tr [P. F. G. Desfontaines], Paris 1738; tr de Crousaz, Paris 1766; tr M. de S[ilhouette], Paris 1736.
— An essay on Homer [by Thomas Parnell, prefixed to Pope's Iliad 1715]; Traduction de la première partie de la préface de l'Homère anglois de M. Pope, tr A. Pérelle, in Nouveau Mercure 1718, [1719]; Remarques sur Homère [also as Essai], tr P. F. G. Desfontaines (from Pérelle?), Paris 1728; Eloge historique d'Homère, tr [Keating], Paris 1749.
— (with Arbuthnot). Memoirs of Martin Scriblerus. 1741; Histoire de Martin Scriblerus, tr [Larcher?] 1755.
  Audra, E. L'influence française dans l'œuvre de Pope. Paris 1931.
  Hamm, V. M. Pope and Malebranche: a note on the Essay on criticism. PQ 24 1945.
  Fairclough, G. T. Pope and Boileau. Neuphilologische Mitteilungen 64 1963.

MacIntyre, E. J. French influence on the beginnings of English classicism. PMLA 26 1911.
Delattre, F. La querelle des anciens et des modernes en France et en Angleterre. Revue des Pyrénées 1913.
Bray, R. La formation de la doctrine classique en France. Paris 1927.
Atkins, J. W. H. In his English literary criticism: 17th and 18th century, 1951.
Garai, P. Le cartésianisme et le classicisme anglais. Revue de Littérature Comparée 31 1957.
Maurocardato, A. La critique classique en Angleterre de la Restauration à la mort d'Addison. Paris 1964.
Simon, I. Critical terms in Restoration translation from the French. Revue Belge 42 1964.
Saisselin, R. G. In his Taste in 18th-century France, Syracuse NY 1965.
Dieckmann, H. Zur Theorie der Lyrik im 18 Jahrhundert. In Immanente Ästhetik, ed W. Iser, Munich 1966.

Drama

Where known, the date of first performance is given in brackets before the date of pbn. Adaptations are listed after trns. Scenes and incidents were borrowed without scruple or attribution and the distinction between trn, adaptation and imitation was blurred, especially in the minor drama of the time.

French Authors

Beaumarchais, Pierre Augustin Caron de
  Eugénie (1767). Paris 1767; The school for rakes, tr and adapted E. Griffith 1769.
  Les deux amis. Paris 1770; The two friends, or the Liverpool merchant, tr C.H. 1800.
  Le barbier de Séville (1775). Paris 1775; The barber of Seville: or the useless precaution, tr E. Griffith 1776.
  La folle journée: ou le mariage de Figaro (Gennevilliers 1783, Paris 1784). Paris 1785; The follies of a day: or the marriage of Figaro, tr T. Holcroft 1785.
  James, C. Tarare: an opera. 1787.
  Rees, G. O. Beaumarchais in translation: the two friends. N & Q 30 Aug 1952.
  Proschwitz, G. von. Beaumarchais et l'Angleterre. Revue d'Histoire Littéraire de la France 68 1968.

Corneille, Pierre
  Mélite (1630). Paris 1633; Melite, tr 1776.
  Le Cid (1637). Paris 1637; The Cid, tr J. Rutter 1638; tr J. Ozell 1714; Colley Cibber, Ximena: or the heroick daughter, 1719.
  Horace (1640). Paris 1641; Horatius: a Roman tragedy, tr Sir W. Lowther 1656; Horace, tr K. Philips 1667 (in part), completed by Sir J. Denham 1669; tr C. Cotton 1671; W. Whitehead, The Roman father 1750.
  Cinna (1640–1). Paris 1643; Cinna's conspiracy, tr C. Cibber, 1713.

Polyeucte (1641–2). Paris 1643; Polyeuctes: or the martyr, tr Sir W. Lowther 1655.

La mort de Pompée (1642–3). Paris 1644; Pompey, tr K. Philips 1663; Pompeius the Great, tr 'by certain persons of honour' [Waller, Sedley, Sidney Godolphin, Lord Buckhurst] 1664; Colley Cibber, Caesar in Egypt, 1725.

Le menteur (1643). Rouen 1644; The mistaken beauty: or the lyar, tr [1671]; Richard Steele, The lying lover, 1704; Samuel Foote, The lyar, 1776.

Rodogune (1664–5). Paris 1647; Rodogune or the rival brothers, tr S. Aspinwall 1765.

Heraclius (1646–7). Rouen 1647; Heraclius, Emperour of the East, tr L. Carlell (c. 1655), 1664; Honorius: opera, 1734.

Don Sanche d'Aragon (1649–50). Rouen 1650; The conflict, tr H. Brand, in Plays and poems, 1798.

Nicomède (1650–1). Rouen 1651; tr J. Dancer 1671.

Kleinschmidt, J. R. The date of Le Cid in English. MLN 55 1940.

Voisine, J. Corneille et Racine en Angleterre au xviiie siècle. Revue de Synthèse 22 1948.

Lebègue, R. Corneille et le théâtre anglais? Revue d'Histoire du Théâtre 2 1950.

Aden, J. M. Dryden and Corneille. RES new ser 6 1955.

Padgett, L. E. Dryden's edition of Corneille. MLN 71 1956.

Hartnoll, P. Corneille in England Theatre Research 1 1958.

Corneille, Thomas

Le feint astrologue (1648). Rouen 1651; The feign'd astrologer, tr [1668?]; John Dryden, An evening's love: or the mock astrologer, 1671.

L'amour à la mode (1651). Rouen 1653; The amorous Orontus: or the love in fashion, tr [J. Bulteel?] 1665.

Le berger extravagant (1652). Rouen 1653; The extravagant shepherd, tr T.R. 1653.

Le galand doublé (1660). Amsterdam 1690; Susanna Centlivre, Love at a venture, 1706.

Maximian (1662). Rouen 1662; Maximian, tr Lady S. Burrell 1800; Philip Francis, Constantine, 1754.

Persée et Démétrius (1664). Amsterdam 1690; Edward Young, The brothers, 1753.

Ariane (1672). Paris 1672; The labyrinth: or fatal embarrassment, tr A. Stratford 1795; Arthur Murphy, The rival sisters, 1786.

La mort d'Achille (1673). Paris 1690; The rival father: or the death of Achilles, tr W. Hatchett 1730.

La devineresse (1679). Paris 1680; E. Ravenscroft, Dame Dobson: or the cunning woman, 1684.

Smith, J. H. T. Corneille to Betterton to Congreve. JEGP 45 1946.

Crébillon, Prosper Jolyot de (Crébillon père)

Rhadamiste et Zénobie (1711). Paris 1711; Zénobia, tr A. Murphy 1768.

Dancourt, Florent Carton

La maison de campagne. Paris 1691; The country house: a farce, tr Sir John Vanbrugh 1715 (later as La maison rustique).

Les bourgeoises à la mode. Paris 1692; The confederacy, tr Sir J. Vanbrugh 1705; R. Estcourt, The fair example, 1706.

Les curieux de Compiègne. Paris 1698; Charles Shadwell, The humours of the army, 1713.

Deschamps, François Michel Chrétien

Caton d'Utique (1715). Paris 1715; Cato of Utica: a tragedy; to which is appended a paralel betwixt this piece and the tragedy of Cato written by Mr Addison, tr 1716; Cato, tr J. Ozell 1716.

Destouches, Philippe Néricault

L'irrésolu (1713). Paris 1713; Arthur Murphy, Know your own mind, 1777.

La fausse Agnès (1759). Paris 1736; Arthur Murphy, The citizen, 1763.

Le dissipateur (1753). Paris 1736; O'Beirne, Generous imposter, 1780.

Le glorieux (1732). Paris 1732; Thomas Holcroft, School for arrogance (1791).

Le philosophe marié (1727). Paris 1727; The married philosopher, 1732; Elizabeth Inchbald, The married man (1789).

L'amour usé (1741). Paris 1742; Cross partners, 1792; Elizabeth Inchbald?, Next-door neighbours (1791).

Oeuvres de théâtre. Paris 1745; Samuel Foote, The comic theatre. 1762 (vol 1: The young hypocrite, The spendthrift, The triple marriage; vol 2: The imaginary obstacle; The sisters; The libertine; vol 3: The legacy, The generous artifice, The whimsical lovers).

Wade, I. O. Destouches in England 1717–18. MP 29 1932.

Diderot, Denis

Le père de famille (1761). Amsterdam 1758; The family picture, tr 'by a Lady' 1781; J. Burgoyne, The heiress, 1786; Thomas Holcroft, Deserted daughter, 1795.

Le fils naturel (1771). Amsterdam 1757 (anon); Dorval: or the test of virtue, tr 1767; The natural son, 2 vols 1799 (novel).

Favart, Charles Simon

Iacuzzi, A. The European vogue of Favart. New York 1932.

Genlis, Stéphanie Félicité Ducrest de Saint-Aubin, marquise de Sillery, comtesse de.

Zélie. In Théâtre à l'usage des jeunes personnes, Paris 1779–80; The child of nature, tr Elizabeth Inchbald 1788.

Le souterrain; Albert and Adelaide, 1798; Captive of Spilburg; tr Hoare 1798.

Théâtre à l'usage des jeunes personnes [Théâtre d'éducation]. Paris 1779–80; The theatre of education, 4 vols 1781 (2nd edn), 3 vols Dublin 1787 (new trn).

La Harpe, Jean François de

Le comte de Warwick. Paris 1764; The Earl of Warwick, tr P. Hiffernan 1764; tr T. Francklin 1766.

Lesage, Alain René

Crispin rival de son maître. Paris 1707; David Garrick, Neck or nothing: a farce, 1766.

Marivaux, Pierre Carlet de Chamblain de

La surprise de l'amour. Paris 1728; The agreeable surprise, 1766.

Marmontel, Jean François

Sylvain [music by Grétry]. Paris 1770; John Burgoyne, Lord of the manor, 1781 (opera).

Les Incas. Paris 1771; T. Morton, Columbus, 1792.

Mercier, Louis Sébastien

Le déserteur. Paris 1770; Point of honour, tr Kemble 1800.

L'indigent. Paris 1772; The distressed family, 1787.

Inchbald, Elizabeth. Next door neighbours. 1791 (with Destouches, Le dissipateur).

Molière, Jean Baptiste Poquelin

No trn of Molière's collected works appeared in English before 1714, despite an apparently abortive project of 1693 recorded in the Stationers' Register. *Piracy of earlier trns was normal and extensive in all edns of the* Works; *see J. E. Tucker, The 18th-century English translations of Molière, MLQ 32 1942. Trns of Molière's plays are relatively rare, the vast majority of texts being adaptations, deforming the original and often amalgamating elements from several plays. No definite line may be drawn between trns and the habitual plundering of scenes by 'original' writers. Trns of separate works listed below ignore texts in the 1714 and later edns of* Works.

The works of Monsieur de Molière. Tr J. Ozell 6 vols 1714 (all 31 plays); Select comedies of Mr de Molière, French and English, tr B[aker], H[enry], [James Miller], [J. M.] Clare et al 8 vols 1732 (17 plays), 10 vols 1739 (31 plays), 1748, Glasgow 1751, 1753, 1755; Works, 6 vols Berwick 1771 (31 plays).

L'étourdi (1653). Paris 1663; Etourdi: or the blunderer, [nd]; Sir George Etherege, The comical revenge (1664), 1664 (with other sources); John Dryden, Sir Martin Mar-All: or the feign'd innocent (1667), 1668 (with Quinault, Amant discret, 1654); Susanna Centlivre, The busy-body, 1709, and her Marplot in Lisbon, 1710; Arthur Murphy, All in the wrong, 1761 (with Ecole des femmes and Sganarelle).

Le dépit amoureux (1656-7). Paris 1663; Sir George Etherege, The comical revenge: or love in a tub (1664), 1664 (with L'étourdi, Le dépit amoureux etc); John Dryden, An evening's love: or the Mock astrologer (1668), 1671 (with Thomas Corneille, Le feint astrologue and Les précieuses ridicules); E. Ravenscroft, Wrangling lovers (1676), 1677; rev Susanna Centlivre as Wonder, a woman keeps a secret, 1714; Sir John Vanbrugh, The mistake (1705), 1706, rev W. Lyon as The wrangling lovers, 1745; J. Hewitt, A tutor for the beaus, 1737; The amorous quarrel, 1762 (anon).

Les précieuses ridicules (1659). Paris 1660; Richard Flecknoe, The damoiselles à la mode (1666), 1667 (with Ecole des femmes, Ecole des maris etc); Aphra Behn, False count: or a new way to play an old game, 1682; J. Crowne, Sir Courtly Nice: or it cannot be, 1685; Thomas Shadwell, Bury Fair (1689), 1701; James Miller, The man of taste, 1735, 1752 (rev and abridged anon), (with Ecole des maris, Comtesse d'Escarbagnas, Femmes savantes); The conceited ladies, 1762 (anon).

Sganarelle: ou le cocu imaginaire (1660), Paris 1660; H. Howard, The playhouse to be let (1663-4), 1673 (see A. Mandach, MLN 66 1951); T. Rawlins, Tom Essence: or the modish wife, 1677; Thomas Otway, Soldier's fortune, 1681, 1748 (rev and abridged, with Ecole des maris); Sir John Vanbrugh, The cuckold in conceit, 1706; [C. Molloy], The perplex'd couple: or mistake upon mistake, 1715; John Arbuthnot, John Gay and Alexander Pope, Three hours after marriage, 1717; J. Miller, The picture, 1745.

Dom Garcie de Navarre (1661). Paris 1684; C. Johnson, Masquerade, 1719.

L'école des maris (1661). Paris 1661; Sir Charles Sedley, The mulberry garden, 1668; William Wycherley, The gentleman dancing master (1671-2), 1673; and his The country wife, 1673, rev J. Lee 1765; rev David Garrick as The country girl, 1766 (with Ecole des femmes); Thomas Otway, The soldier's fortune, 1681 (with Sganarelle); The blunderer, 1762 (or from L'étourdi?).

Les fâcheux (1661). Paris 1662; tr 1732 (separate from 1732 Works); Thomas Shadwell, The sullen lovers (1668), 1668 (with Le misanthrope and Le mariage forcé).

L'école des femmes (1662). Paris 1663; J. Caryll, Sir Salomon: or the cautious coxcomb (1669-70), 1671; William Wycherley, The country wife, 1673; rev J. Lee as The country wife, 1765; rev David Garrick as The country girl, 1766 (with L'école des maris); E. Ravenscroft, The London cuckolds, 1682; Female innocence: or a school for a wife, [1737?] (anon); Isaac Bickerstaffe, Love in the city, 1767; [Arthur Murphy], The school for guardians, 1767 (with L'école des maris and L'étourdi); Mrs Cowley, More ways than one, 1783; Hoadley, Tatlers, 1797.

La critique de l'Ecole des femmes (1663). Paris 1663 (see Misanthrope, below); T. Brown, Stage beaux toss'd in a blanket: or hypocrisy à la mode, 1704.

Le mariage forcé (1664). Paris 1668; Love without interest: or the man too hard for the master. 1699; The forced marriage, tr 1762; An hour before marriage, tr 1772; David Garrick, The Irish widow, 1772.

La princesse d'Elide (1664). Paris 1664; J. Miller, The universal passion, 1737.

Tartuffe: ou l'imposteur (1664). Paris 1669; Tartuffe: or the French puritan, tr M. Medburne 1670; tr J. M. Clare 1732 (separate from 1732 Works); Sir George Etherege, She wou'd if she cou'd (1668), 1668 (with other plays); J. Crowne, The English frier, 1690; Colley Cibber, The non-juror (1717), [1718?]; Henry Fielding, The old debauchees, 1732, 1745 (2 versions); Isaac Bickerstaffe, The hypocrite, 1768.

Le festin de Pierre [Dom Juan] (1665). Paris 1683; Thomas Shadwell, The libertine, 1676; William Congreve, Love for love, 1695 (with Misanthrope).

L'amour médecin (1665). Paris 1666; The quacks: or love's the physician, tr O. MacSwinney 1705, 1745 (rev); Love is the doctor (1734); J. Miller, Art and nature, 1738.

Le misanthrope (1666). Paris 1667; The misanthrope, tr J. Hughes 1709 (adapted by J. Ozell in 1714 Works); The man-hater, tr 1762; William Wycherley, The plain dealer (1674?), 1677 (with Critique de l'école des femmes); rev I. Bickerstaffe (1765), 1766; William Congreve, Love for love, 1695 (with Dom Juan); and his Way of the world, 1700; Henry Fielding, Love in several masques, 1728; J. Kelly, Timon in love, 1733.

Le médecin malgré lui (1666). Paris 1667; J. Lacy, The dumb lady: or the farrier made physician (c. 1669), 1672 (with L'amour médecin); Susanna Centlivre, Love's contrivance, 1703, 1705 (rev), 1761 (with Le mariage forcé and Sganarelle); [Henry Fielding], The mock doctor: or the dumb lady cur'd, 1732; The faggot binder: or the mock doctor, 1762 (anon).

Le Sicilien: ou l'amour peintre (1667). Paris 1668 (see Georges Dandin, below); J. Crowne, The country wit, 1675; Richard Steele, The tender husband: or the accomplished fools, 1705; R. B. Sheridan, The duenna (1715), 1794.

Amphitryon (1668). Paris 1668; John Dryden, Amphitryon: or the two Sosies, 1690; rev J. Hawkesworth 1756.

Georges Dandin (1668). Paris 1669; Georges Dandin, tr [Miller, Baker et al] from 1732 Works; Georges Dantin [sic], tr (1747); No wit like a woman's, tr (1769); Thomas Betterton, The amorous widow (c. 1670?, 1677); Barnaby Brittle, (1781) (a farce much abridged); Charles Dibdin, The metamorphosis (1775), 1776 (with Le Sicilien).

L'avare (1668). Paris 1669; The miser, tr T. Shadwell (1671), 1672; tr J. Ozell 1732 (separate edn, not acted); J. Corey, The metamorphosis: or the old lover outwitted, 1704 (with Le médecin malgré lui); J. Hughes, The miser, in Monthly Amusement 1709 (periodical ed J. Ozell, who adopted this text for 1714 Works); trn later reworked by Hughes for act i, pbd posthumously 1735 (in Poems on several occasions); Henry Fielding, The miser (1734), 1733; M. de Boissy, The miser, 1752.

Monsieur de Pourceaugnac (1669). Paris 1670; Monsieur de Pourceaugnac: or Squire Trelooby, tr [J. Ozell] 1704 (possibly ptd as pirated version of Congreve's unpbd version of 1704); E. Ravenscroft, The careless lovers, 1673; rev as Canterbury guests: or a bargain broken (1694), 1695; Sir John Vanbrugh, William Congreve and William Walsh, Squire Trelooby (1704), rev (1706) (not pbd, but see Ozell's trn, above); Charles Shadwell, The plotting lovers, 1720; J. Ralph, The Cornish squire, 1734; Thomas Sheridan, Captain O'Blunder: or the brave Irishman, 1754; E. Parsons, Intrigues of the morning (1792).

Le bourgeois gentilhomme (1670). Paris 1671; E. Ravenscroft, Mamamouchi: or the citizen turned gentleman. 1671 (or 1672?) (with M. de Pourceaugnac); George Farquhar, Love and a bottle, 1699; The gentleman cit, 1762 (anon); Samuel Foote, The commissary, 1765; R. B. Sheridan, The rivals, 1775.

Psyché (1671). Paris 1671; Thomas Shadwell, Psyche: a tragedy, 1675 (pt adapted from Molière); P. Motteux, Loves of Mars and Venus, 1697.

Les fourberies de Scapin (1671). Paris 1671; The cheats of Scapin, tr T. Otway 1677; tr J. Ozell [1730?] (never acted); The cure for covetousness (1733); E. Ravenscroft, Scaramouch a philosopher, Harlequin schoolboy, 1677 (with Le mariage forcé, Dom Juan and Bourgeois gentilhomme).

La comtesse d'Escarbagnas (1672). Paris 1684. See Précieuses ridicules, above.

Les femmes savantes (1672). Paris 1672; T. Wright, The female virtuoso's, 1693; rev J. Gray as No fools like wits, 1721; Colley Cibber, The refusal, 1721.

Le malade imaginaire (1673). Paris 1674; The hypo-chondriac, tr [T. Otway] 1701; Aphra Behn, Sir Patient Fancy, 1678 (with L'amour médecin, M. de Pourceaugnac); Richard Steele, Funeral: or grief à la mode (1701), 1702; J. Miller, Mother in law: or the Doctor the disease, 1734, 1734; Isaac Bickerstaffe, Doctor Last in his chariot, 1769 (with L'amour médecin); R. B. Sheridan, St Patrick's Day: or the scheming Lieutenant (1775), 1788 (pirated).

Estime des Anglais pour Molière. In Le pour et contre vol 1, 1733.

Van Laun, H. Les plagiaires de Molière en Angleterre. Le Moliériste 2–3 1880–2.

Currier, T. F. and E. L. Gay. Catalogue of the Molière collection in Harvard College Library. Cambridge Mass 1906.

Besing, M. Molières Einfluss auf das englischen Lust-spiel bis 1700. Münster 1913.

Gillet, J. E. Molière en Angleterre 1660–70. Brussels 1913.

Stoll, E. E. Molière and Shakespeare. Romanic Rev 35 1944. See G. Greenwood, Anglo-French Rev 1 1919.

Tucker, J. E. Molière in England 1700–50. Madison 1937.

—— The 18th-century English translations of Molière. MLQ 3 1942. On collections.

Wilcox, J. The relation of Molière to Restoration comedy. New York 1938.

Schmidt, K. E. Molière in der angelsächsischen Kritik. Hamburg 1940.

Mandach, A. de. Molière et la comédie de moeurs en Angleterre. Neuchatel 1946.

—— The first translator of Molière: Sir W. Davenant or Colonel Henry Howard. MLN 66 1951.

Goggin, L. P. Fielding and the Select comedies of Mr de Molière. PQ 21 1952.

Loiselet, J. L. L'apport de Molière au théâtre anglais. La Révolution Française 6 1954.

Shelton, F. V. Molière et les écrivains comiques de la Restauration anglaise 1664–1707. Annales de l'Uni-versité de Paris 34 1964.

Neri, N. Molière e il teatro inglese della restaurazione. Turin 1966.

Racine, Jean

La Thébaïde (1664). Paris 1664; J. Robe, The fatal legacy, 1723.

Alexandre (1665). Paris 1666; Alexandre the Great, tr J. Ozell 1714.

Andromaque (1667). Paris 1668; [J. Crowne?], Andro-mache, 1675; Ambrose Philips, The distrest mother, 1712.

Les plaideurs (1668). Paris 1669; The litigants, tr J. Ozell 1715.

Britannicus (1669). Paris 1670; Britannicus, tr J. Ozell 1714; Thomas Gray, Agrippina [written c. 1747].

Bérénice (1670). Paris 1671; Thomas Otway, Titus and Bérénice, 1677. See L. Villard, Les traductions anglaises de la Bérénice de Racine, Revue de l'Univer-sité de Lyon 1928; A. Lefèvre, Revue de Littérature Comparée 34 1960.

Bajazet (1672). Paris 1672; The sultaness, tr C. Johnson 1717; William Congreve, The mourning bride, 1697.

Mithridate (1673). Paris 1673; John Dryden, Aureng–Zebe: or the Great Mogul, 1676.

Iphigénie (1674). Paris 1675; tr A. Boyer 1700; C. Johnson, The victim, 1714.

Phèdre (1677). Paris 1677; E. Smith, Phaedra and Hippolytus, 1706; Phedra, 1776 (anon).

Esther (1689). Paris 1689; Esther: or faith triumphant, tr T. Brereton 1715.

Athalie (1691). Paris 1691; Athaliah, tr W. Duncombe 1722.

Canfield, D. F. Corneille and Racine in England. New York 1904, 1966.

Lefèvre, A. Racine en Angleterre au xviie siècle. Revue de Littérature Comparée 34 1960.

Lerner, L. Racine and the Elizabethans. EC 12 1962.

Regnard, Jean François Renard

Le joueur (1695). Paris 1697; Susanna Centlivre, The gamester, 1705. See also E. Moore, The gamester, 1753.

Le retour imprévu (1700). Paris 1700; Henry Fielding, The intriguing chambermaid, 1734.

Le légataire universel. Paris 1714; T. King, Wit's last stake: a farce, 1769. See G. Roth, Une adaptation anglaise du Légataire universel, Revue d'Histoire Littéraire de la France 21 1914.

Rousseau, Jean-Jacques

Le devin du village (1752). Paris 1753; The cunning man, tr C. Burney 1766. Pastoral with music by Rousseau.

Narcisse: ou l'amant de lui-même (1752). [Paris?] 1753; tr 1767.

Pygmalion. Mercure de France 1771; Pygmalion: a poem (1777), 1779. 'Scène lyrique' music by Rousseau and H. Coignet; better score was added by Viennese Aspelmayer in 1772.

Scarron, Paul

Jodelet: ou le maître valet. Paris 1645; Sir William Davenant, The man's the master, 1669.

Scudéry, Georges de

Ibrahim: ou l'illustre Bassa (1642). Paris 1643; Robert Boyle, Earl of Orrery, Mustapha 1665.

Sedaine, Michel Jean

Le philosophe sans le savoir (1765). Paris 1766; W. O'Brien, The duel, 1772.

Cœur de lion; MacNally, Richard cœur de lion, 1786; J. Burgoyne, Richard coeur de lion, 1786.

Voltaire, François Marie Arouet de. See also under Philo-sophy, col 98, above.

Bruce, H. L. Voltaire on the English stage. Berkeley 1918. See also MLN 33 1918.

Oliver, T. E. The Mérope of George Jeffreys as a source of Voltaire's Mérope. Urbana 1927. See also MLN 43 1928.

Trahard, P. La sensibilité dans le théâtre de Voltaire. In his Les maîtres de la sensibilité française, 4 vols Paris 1931–3.

Horsley, P. M. Aaron Hill: an English translator of Mérope. Comparative Lit Stud 12 1944.

Russell, T. W. Voltaire, Dryden and heroic tragedy. New York 1946. On Dryden to Shakespeare as influence on Voltaire.

—— Dryden inspirateur de Voltaire. Revue de Littéra-ture Comparée 22 1948.

Fenger, H. Voltaire et le théâtre anglais. Copenhagen 1949. See also Orbis Litterarum 7 1949.

Perkins, M. Dryden and Voltaire's Alzire. Comparative Lit 9 1957.

For the influence of Shakespeare on Voltaire see Shakes-peare on the Continent, col 223, below.

English Authors

The main sources for this field are G. Ascoli, La Grande-Bretagne devant l'opinion française, 2 vols Paris 1930, for the period up to 1700, and C. A. Rochedieu, Bibliography of French translations of English works 1700–1800, Chicago 1948, *supplemented by* M. Horn-Monval, Répertoire bibliographique des traductions et adaptations françaises du théâtre étranger vol 5: English plays, Paris 1963, *for the later period. See also* C. D. Brenner, A bibliographical list of plays in the French language 1700–89, Berkeley 1947. *Rochedieu lists (appendix 3) collections of English works in trn that appeared in France; only the more important are listed below. For Shakespeare in France see col 223, below.*

Le théâtre anglois: ou choix de plusieurs tragédies angloises. Tr de La Place 8 vols 1745–9.

Mélanges de différentes pièces de vers et de prose, traduites d'après l'anglois, d'après Mmes Elize Haywood et Suzanne Centlivre, et Mrs Pope, Southern et autres par Fiquet Duboccage. 3 vols Berlin 1751.

Nouveau théâtre anglois: ou choix des meilleures pièces de théâtre représentées à Londres. Tr Mme Riccoboni 2 vols 1767.

Choix de petites pièces du théâtre anglois [Dodsley and Gay]. Tr [C. P. Patu] 2 vols 1756; Nouvelles pièces dramatiques du théâtre anglois, tr Patu, Paris 1775.

Traduction du théâtre anglois. Tr [baronne de Vasse] 12 vols Paris 1784–7.

Addison, Joseph
Cato: a tragedy. 1713; Caton, tr A. Boyer 1713; Caton d'Utique, tr M. Deschamps, Paris 1715 (*see* Mercure Galant March 1715); tr [A. de Laplace], Utrecht 1738; tr J. B. Du Bos, Hague 1745 (3 scenes in Nouvelles Littéraires de La Haye Oct 1716); tr G. Guillemard, Paris 1767; tr Dampmartin [1786? or 1789?]; tr Chéron de La Bruère 1789. *See also* Journal des Savants and Journal Littéraire 1714.

The drummer: or the haunted house. 1716; Le tambour nocturne: ou le mari devin, tr P. N. Destouches, Paris 1733; La prétendue veuve ou l'époux magicien, tr Desgranges-Descazeaux, Paris 1737.

Campbell, H. H. Addison's 'Cartesian' passages and Malebranche. PQ 46 1967.

Brooke, Henry
Gustavus Vasa. 1739; Gustave Vasa, tr [A. Maillet-Duclairon] 1766.

La Harpe, Jean Françoise de. Gustave Wasa (1766). Paris 1806 (in Œuvres choisies et posthumes). The play, an imitation of Brooke, was a failure.

Centlivre, Susanna Freeman
The wonder, a woman keeps a secret. 1714; Le prodige, in Traduction du théâtre anglois, tr baronne de Vasse, Paris 1784.

A bold stroke for a wife. 1718; tr 1751; L'orpheline, in Mélange de différentes pièces, tr Dubocage, Berlin 1851.

Palissot, de Montenoy, Charles de. Les tuteurs. 1754.

Parnasse des dames vol 7. Ed Billardon de Sauvigny, Paris 1773. Contains Marplot à Lisbonne; Aurélie ou l'époux parjure [Perjur'd husband]; Le prince de Milan [Prince of Milan].

For Centlivre's adaptations of Molière, see above.

Hohrmann, F. Das Verhältnis Susanna Centlivres zu Molière und Regnard. Zeitschrift für Vergleichende Literaturgeschichte 14 1901.

Cibber, Colley
She would and she would not. 1703; Le déguisement, tr milady Craven, Anspach 1791.

The provok's husband. 1728 (from Vanbrugh's Journey to London); Le mari poussé à bout, tr [P. Clément] 1761; tr baronne de Vasse, in Traduction du théâtre anglois vol 3, Paris 1784–7.

Congreve, William
The double-dealer. 1694; Le fourbe, tr [J. F. Peyron], Paris 1776.

Love for love. 1695; Amour pour amour, tr Laplace, in Le théâtre anglois vol 7, 1749.

The mourning bride. 1697; L'épouse en détail, tr Laplace, in Le théâtre anglois vol 6, 1748.

The way of the world. 1700; Le train du monde, tr [Laplace?] 1759; Ainsi va le monde, tr de Gérès de Camarsac, Amsterdam 1782.

Crawford, J. P. W. Congreve's Mourning bride and Racine's Bajazet. MLN 9 1904.

Dryden, John. *See also Voltaire, above.*
The Indian emperour. 1667; Montesuma: ou la conquête du Mexique, 1743; Montesuma: ou Fernand Cortez, tr [D. B. Du Bourg], Paris 1743.

All for love: or the world well lost. 1678; Tout pour l'amour, tr [Prévost], Paris 1735.

Aureng-Zebe. 1676; Aureng-Zeb: ou le Grand Mogol, tr Laplace in Théâtre anglois vol 6, 1748.

The Duke of Guise. 1683; Le duc de Guise, Pièces intéressantes, Paris 1790.

Alexander's feast. 1697; La fête d'Alexandre: ou le pouvoir de la musique, cantate, in Trochereau, Choix de morceaux de poésie, Paris 1749; tr [Bruté de Loirelle], in Pastorales et poèmes de M. Gessner, Paris 1766.

[C. J. Dorat]. Pouvoir de l'harmonie: poème lyrique imité de Dryden. Paris 1774.

Hartmann, K. Einfluss Molières auf Drydens komisch-dramatische Dichtungen. Leipzig 1885.

Horsman, E. A. Dryden's French borrowings. RES new ser 1 1950.

Kirsch, A. C. Dryden, Corneille and the heroic play. MP 59 1962.

—— Dryden's heroic drama. Princeton 1965.

Fielding, Henry. *For dramatized versions of Tom Jones see col 146, below.*
Waldschmidt, C. Die Dramatisierungen von Fieldings Tom Jones. Wetzlar 1906. On English, French and German versions.

Parfitt, G. E. L'influence française dans les œuvres de Fielding. Paris 1928.

Goggin, L. P. Fielding and the Select comedies of Mr de Molière. PQ 31 1952.

Garrick, David
Dramatic works. 1774; Œuvres, tr baronne de Vasse 2 vols Paris 1784.

The clandestine marriage [with Richard Colman]. 1766; Le mariage clandestin, tr [Mme Riccoboni], Paris 1768; tr [Le Monnier] (1775) (not pbd); tr baronne de Vasse in Traduction du théâtre anglois vols 6–7, Paris 1784–7.

Hedgecock, F. A. Garrick and his French friends. 1911.

Gay, John
What d'ye call it? 1713; Comment l'appelez-vous? in C. P. Patu, Choix du théâtre anglois vol 2, Paris 1756.

The beggar's opera. 1728; L'opéra de quat' sous, [1735]; L'opéra du gueux, tr A. Hallam 1750; tr [C. P. Patu] in Choix de petites pièces du théâtre anglois vol. 2, 1756; tr Mme d'Arcanville in Nouveau théâtre anglois vol 1, ed Mme Riccoboni, Paris 1767.

Goulding, S. Eighteenth-century French taste and the Beggar's opera. MLR 24 1929.

Goldsmith, Oliver
The earliest known trn of She stoops to conquer, 1773, *is Paris 1832.*

Sells, A. L. Goldsmith's influence on the French stage. Durham Univ Jnl 33 1941.

Grossman, B. French sources of Goldsmith's The good-natur'd man. PQ 39 1960.

Lillo, George
George Barnwell: or the London merchant. 1731; tr [Prévost?], Le Pour et Contre 3–4, 1734 (5 scenes). Le marchand de Londres, tr [P. Clément], [Hamburg?] 1748 (incomplete); tr 1751 (with 2 new scenes); tr [Pillement?] 1751 (same as previous item?); tr in Théâtre bourgeois: ou recueil des meilleures pièces de differens auteurs, Paris 1755; tr Bruté de Loirelle, Paris 1762; tr Paris 1767, in Le nouveau théâtre anglois vol 1, ed Mme Riccoboni, Paris 1767.

Diderot, D. Le fils naturel. Paris 1757; Le père de famille, Paris 1768. Imitations.

Dorat, C. J. Lettre de Barnevelt dans sa prison à Truman son ami. Paris 1763. *See* Almanach des Muses 1764. A prose monologue.

Anseaume, L. L'école de jeunesse: ou le Barnevelt françois. Paris 1765. A comic opera, score by Duni, few traces of Lillo.

[Mercier, L. S.] Jenneval: ou le Barnevelt français. Paris 1769 etc. At least 8 edns of this version.

Fenouillot de Falbaire de Quingey, C. G. Le fabricant de Londres. 1771.

Blin de Sainmore, A. M. H. Orphanis. Paris 1773.

La Harpe, J. F. de. Barnevel: drame imité de l'anglais. In Théâtre de M. de La Harpe vol 1, Paris 1778.

André, J. F. Barnwell, traduit de l'anglais. Paris 1800. Tr from Thomas Skinner's novel, 1798, itself inspired by Lillo.

Saurin's Beverley was inspired not by Lillo but by Moore's Gamester, 1753.

Price, L. M. George Barnwell abroad. Comparative Lit 2 1950.

Hallowell, R. E. C. J. Dorat, opponent of the drame bourgeois and critic of the English theatre. French Rev 25 1952.

Hamard, J. (ed). Le marchand de Londres. Paris 1962.

— Le drame bourgeois, l'influence de Lillo. Revue de Littérature Comparée 39 1965.

Milton, John

Comus. 1637; Comus, tr Yart in Idée de la poésie angloise vol 8, Paris 1756.

Paradise lost. *See col 133, below, for dramatic adaptation.*

Samson agonistes. 1671; Samson, tr Yart as oratorio, score by Heindel, in Idée de la poésie angloise vol 7, Paris 1756.

Moore, Edward

The foundling. 1748; The foundling: ou l'enfant trouvé, tr Mme Riccoboni, in Le nouveau théâtre anglois vol 1, Paris 1767.

The gamester. 1754; Le joueur, tr D. Diderot, Paris 1760 (abridged); tr [Bruté de Loirelle] 1762.

Saurin, B. Béverlei: tragédie bourgeoise. Paris 1768. First entitled Le joueur anglais. It used Diderot's trn.

Otway, Thomas

Venice preserv'd. 1682; Venise sauvée, tr [P. A. de La Place] (1746), Paris 1747 (9 edns by 1782).

La Fosse, A. de. Manlius Capitolinus. Paris 1698.

Johnson, A. Etude sur la littérature comparée de la France et de l'Angleterre: Lafosse, Otway, Saint-Réal [Venice preserv'd]. Paris 1901. *See also* F. Winther, Venice preserved: Otway, Lafosse and Hofmannsthal, Trans Amer Philosophical Assoc 40 1909.

Lefèvre, A. Racine en Angleterre au xviie siècle: Titus et Bérénice de T. Otway. Revue de Littérature Comparée 34 1960.

Pope, Alexander

Three hours after marriage. 1717 (with Gay and Arbuthnot, from Molière's Sganarelle: ou le cocu imaginaire; *see Molière, above*); Trois heures après le mariage, in Pope, Œuvres diverses vol 2, Amsterdam 1767; tr J. de La Porte 1779.

Rowe, Nicholas

The ambitious stepmother (1700). 1701; La marâtre ambitieuse, tr baronne de Vasse in Traduction du théâtre anglois vol 2, Paris 1784.

Tamerlane (1702). 1701; tr P. A. de La Place, in Théâtre anglois vol 5, 1747.

The fair penitent. 1703; La belle pénitente, tr P. A. de La Place in Théâtre anglois vol 5, Paris 1746; Caliste, tr de Mauprié, Paris 1750; tr Colardeau 1761 (verse); tr L.D.C.V.G.D.N. 1797 (verse).

The tragedy of Jane Shore. 1714; tr in Œuvres, Paris 1784; tr L.D.C.V.G.D.N. 1797.

The tragedy of Lady Jane Grey. 1715; Jeanne Grey, tr P. A. de La Place, Paris 1781.

Shadwell, Thomas

The miser. 1672 (from Molière, L'avare); L'avare, tr A. M. L. Fiquet Dubocage in Lettres sur le théâtre anglois vol 1, 1751.

Sheridan, Richard Brinsley

The rivals. 1775; Les rivaux, in Œuvres de R. B. Sheridan, 1784; tr baronne de Vasse in Traduction du théâtre anglois vol 7, Paris 1784.

Bunel. L'épreuve des deux neveux. Lille 1791 (or tr Bunel de Lille 1791?).

The school for scandal. Dublin 1777; L'école de la médisance, tr baronne de Vasse in Traduction du théâtre anglois vol 1 [?], Paris 1784; Gabiot, Les deux neveux, Paris 1788; Bunel Delille, L'école du scandale, 1789; L. S. Mercier, Le nouveau doyen de Killerine, [Paris] 1790; T. P. Bertin, Le faux usurier, Paris 1797; L. C. Chéron de la Bruyère, L'homme à sentiments (1789), Paris 1800–1.

Pizarro. 1799; tr Paris 1799.

Milne, J. M. Molière and Sheridan. Glasgow 1912.

Southerne, Thomas

The fatal marriage. 1694; L'adultère innocente, in Théâtre anglois vol 8, tr P. A. de La Place 1749.

Oroonoko. 1696 (from Aphra Behn's novel, c. 1678); tr A. M. L. Fiquet Dubocage, in Mélanges de différentes pièces de vers et de prose, 3 vols Berlin 1751; tr L. de Laus de Boissy 1769.

Steele, Sir Richard

The funeral: or grief à la mode. 1701; Les funérailles: ou le deuil à la mode, tr P. A. de La Place, Paris 1749; tr [Rochon de Chabannes], Paris 1757.

The conscious lovers. 1721; L'amour confident de lui-même, tr Prévost, in Le pour et contre vol 8, 1736; Les amans réservés, tr [A. F. Quétant] 1778; Les amans généreux, tr baronne de Vasse, Paris 1784.

Voltaire. Zaïre. Rouen 1733.

Bonno, G. La culture et la civilisation britanniques devant l'opinion française. Trans Amer Philosophical Soc 38 1948.

Thomson, James

Agamemnon. 1738; tr [C. J. Panckoucke] 1780.

Edward and Eleanore. 1739; B. Saurin, Blanche et Guiscard (1763), Paris 1764.

Tancred and Sigismunda. 1745; Mercure de France 1761–2 (extracts); tr P. A. de La Place, Paris 1772.

Voltaire used Thomson's name for his Socrate, traduit de l'anglais de feu M. Tompson, Amsterdam 1759. See R. M. Davis, Thomson and Voltaire's Socrate, PMLA 49 1934.

Vanbrugh, Sir John

The provok'd wife. 1697; La femme poussée à bout, tr C. de Saint-Evremond, Amsterdam 1700.

The relapse. 1697; Voltaire, L'échange: ou quand est-ce qu'on se marie [or Le petit boursoufle] (1736, privately performed, 1761 at Théâtre italien, pirated?). Also Les originaux, or Le grand boursoufle (first performed 1862). *See* E. Böttcher, Der englische Ursprung des Comte de Boursoufle, Rostock 1906.

The provok'd husband [completed by C. Cibber from Vanbrugh, Journey to London]. 1728; Le mari poussé à bout, tr C. Clément 1761; [P. A. de La Place], L'épouse à la mode, Paris 1760.

Wycherley, William. *See also Molière, above.*

The country wife (1672–3). 1675; La femme de campagne, tr A. M. L. Fiquet Dubocage in Lettre sur le théâtre anglois, 2 vols Paris 1752.

The plain dealer [from Molière, Le misanthrope] (1664?). 1677.

Voltaire. La prude [or La dévote] (written 1740, privately performed 1747). 1748.

Williams, E. Furetière and Wycherley: Le roman bourgeois in Restoration comedy. MLN 53 1938.

Humbert, B. Die Lustspiele Wycherleys und Shadwells

in ihrer Beziehungen zu den Komödien Molières. Hamburg 1950.

Friedson, A. M. Wycherley and Molière. MP 64 1967. On Plain dealer.

Young, Edward

Busiris, King of Egypt. 1719; Busiris, tr P. A. de La Place in Le théâtre anglois vol 7, 1746; tr Le Tourneur in Œuvres diverses d'Edward Young vol 2, Paris 1770; [Mouslier de Moissy], Le vertueux mourant, Paris 1770.

The revenge. 1721; 'Dumaniant' (A. J. Bourlin), La vengeance, Paris 1792.

Rapin, R. Réflexions sur la poétique d'Aristote. Paris 1674; tr T. Rymer 1674. Produced loss of favour for French theatre in England.

Collier, J. A short view of the profaneness and immorality of the English stage. 1698; tr J. de Courbeville, Paris 1715.

— The ancient and modern stages surveyed. 1699; La critique du théâtre anglois comparé au théâtre d'Athènes, de Rome et de France, tr J. de Courbeville, Paris 1715.

Relations between French and English Stages

Translations, adaptations etc

Horn-Monval, M. Répertoire bibliographique des traductions et adaptations françaises du théâtre étranger du xvᵉ siècle à nos jours. Vol 5, English and American plays, Paris 1963. Standard source. *See also for details of trns from authors not included above, notably Aphra Behn, George Colman, Mrs Harriet Cowley, Richard Cumberland, Robert Dodsley, George Farquhar, Samuel Foote, Richard Glover, John Hughes, Hugh Kelly, Nathaniel Lee, Hannah More, Arthur Murphy, William Whitehead, Lady Winchilsea.*

Wray, E. English adaptations of French dramas 1780–1815. MLN 43 1928.

Kinne, W. A. Revivals and importations of French comedies in England 1749–1800. New York 1939.

Rochedieu, C. A. Bibliography of French translations of English works 1700–1800. Chicago 1948.

Messner, C. The French theatre in England: a bibliography. French Stud 6 1950.

General

Charlanne, L. L'influence française en Angleterre au xviiᵉ siècle. 2 vols Paris 1906.

Gaiffe, D. Le drame en France au xviiiᵉ siècle. Paris 1910.

Gerothwohl, M. A. and J. W. Eaton. The Englishman in 18th-century French comedy. Fortnightly Rev May 1911. *See also* H. Kurz, European characters in French drama of the 18th century, New York 1916; J. Lux, Les Anglais dans les comédies françaises du xviiᵉ siècle, Revue Bleue May-June 1911.

Lancaster, H. C. A history of French dramatic literature in the 17th century. 9 vols Baltimore 1929–42, 1952; Sunset: a history of Parisian drama 1701–15, Baltimore 1945; French tragedy in the time of Louis XV 1715–74, 2 vols Baltimore 1950 (no suppl for comedy in last period); French tragedy in the reign of Louis XVI etc 1771–92, Baltimore 1953. The standard history.

Hill, L. A. The Tudors in French drama. Baltimore 1932.

Ellenhauge, M. English Restoration drama: its relation to past English and past and contemporary French drama. Copenhagen 1933.

Macaulay, T. C. French and English drama in the 17th century: some contrasts. E & S 20 1935.

Saer, H. A. Themes from the Spectator in 18th-century French plays. Modern Languages 21 1939.

Brenner, C. D. A bibliographical list of plays in the French language 1700–89. Berkeley 1947.

Smith, J. H. French sources for six English comedies 1600–1750. JEGP 47 1948.

Voisine, J. Corneille et Racine en Angleterre au xviiiᵉ siècle. Revue de Synthèse 22 1948.

Berkeley, D. S. Préciosité and the Restoration comedy of manners. HLQ 18 1955.

Rutherford, M. R. Prévost and the English theatre 1730–40. Theatre Notebook 9 1956. *See* P. B. Anderson, MLN 49 1934.

Engel, C. E. Connaissait-on le théâtre anglais en France au xviiᵉ siècle. XVIIᵉ Siècle 48 1960.

— Echos de la Révocation [of Edict of Nantes] dans le théâtre anglais. Bulletin de la Société d'Histoire du Protestantisme Français 1932.

Daniel, G. B. 18th-century British travellers and the French theatre. Kentucky Foreign Lang Quart 8 1961. *See also* K. L. Woods, The French theatre in the 18th century according to some English travellers, Revue de Littérature Comparée 12 1932; M. and P. Fuchs, Comédiens français à Londres 1738–55 13 1933.

Cioranescu, A. Bibliographie de la littérature française du xviiᵉ siècle. 3 vols Paris 1965–6. Standard authority.

Suckling, N. Molière and English Restoration comedy. In Restoration comedy, ed J. R. Brown and B. Harris 1965.

Satirical and Allegorical Poetry

Boileau-Despréaux, Nicolas. Satires. Paris 1666; tr J. Dennis in his Miscellany poems, 1697.

Rochester, 2nd Earl of. A satyr against mankind. [1679].

Oldham, J. A satire touching nobility. In his Poems and translations, 1683.

Butler, S. Satires. In his Genuine remains in verse and prose, 1759.

Mulgrave, Earl of. Essay on satire. In his Works, 1721.

Epîtres. Paris 1669–77; tr J. Dennis in his Miscellany poems, 1697.

Le lutrin. Paris 1674; Lutrin, tr N.O. 1682; tr J. Ozell 1708; tr N. Rowe 1708 (with A letter giving some account of Boileau and his works).

Garth, Sir Samuel. The dispensary. 1699.

Pope, Alexander. The rape of the lock. 1712.

Audra, D. L'influence française dans l'œuvre de Pope. Paris 1931.

Moore, F. The originality of Rochester's Satire against mankind. PMLA 58 1943.

Butler, Samuel. Hudibras. 3 pts 1663–78; Hudibras, tr French by J. Towneley 3 vols 1757. Canto i only in Année Littéraire 3 1755.

Bentley, N. E. Hudibras' Butler abroad. MLN 60 1945.

Gresset, Jean Baptiste Louis. Ver-Vert. Paris 1734; Ver-Vert, or the nunnery parrot: an heroic poem, tr 1790.

La Fontaine, Jean de. Contes et nouvelles en vers. Paris 1665.

Tales and novels in verse from the French by several hands. 2 vols 1735. By Congreve, S. Humphreys et al.

Lockman, J. The loves of Cupid and Psyche, in verse and prose. 1744.

The spectacles: a tale. 1753.

Fables choisies. Paris 1668; Some fables after the easie and familiar method of La Fontaine, tr [Bernard de Mandeville] 1703.

Fables and tales in French and English, tr 1734.

Gay, J. Fables. 1727.

Dryden, J. Fables ancient and modern. 1700.

Uhlemeyer, B. Der Einfluss Lafontaines auf die englische Fabeldichtung des 18 Jahrhunderts. Nuremberg 1900.

Petit, L. La Fontaine et Saint Evremond: ou la tentation de l'Angleterre. Toulouse 1953.

Mandeville, Bernard. *See Philosophy, above.*

Scarron, Paul

Typhon. Paris 1644; Typhon: or the gyants' war with the gods, tr [J. Phillips] 1665; tr [B. Mandeville] 1704.

Virgile travesty. Paris 1648–53; Scarronides: or Virgile travestie, tr C. Cotton 1664; tr R. M[onsey] 1665; tr [C. Cotton] 1667; tr J. Phillips 1672; Ovid travestie, tr A. Radcliffe 1680; tr [J. Smyth] 1692; tr T. Brown, J. Savage et al in Whole comical works of M. Scarron, 1700.

Scudamore, J. Homer à la mode. 1664.

Butler, Samuel. Hudibras. 3 pts 1663–78.

'Nasco Scarronomimus'. Ovidius exalans: or Ovid travestie. 1673.

The Irish Hudibras: or Fingallian prince. 1689.

Burnet, Sir T. and G. Duckett. Homerides. 1716.

Bridges, T. Homer travestie. 1762.

Voltaire, François Marie Arouet de
For Pucelle d'Orleans, see Philosophy, col 100, above.
Morse, J. M. La Pucelle and Paradise lost. Comparative Lit 9 1957.

Young, Edward. Love of fame: the universal passion. 1728; Satyres de Young: ou l'amour de la renommée, tr T. P. Bertin 1787.

Verse

Mainly epic, descriptive or didactic. Only selective use is made in this section of the periodical press as an important source for early trns of poetry.

French Authors

Boileau-Despréaux, Nicolas. Ode sur la prise de Namur. Paris 1693.
Prior, M. An English ballad in answer to Mr Despréaux's Pindarique ode on the Taking of Namur. 1695.

Chénier, André
Legros, R. P. Chénier en Angleterre. MLR 19 1924.

Delille, Jacques. Les Géorgiques. Paris 1769; The rural philosopher: or French Georgics, tr J. Maund 1801.
Les jardins. Paris 1780; The gardens: or the art of laying out grounds, tr 1789.

Rousseau, Jean-Jacques. L'allée de Sylvie. Mercure de France July 1750; Sylvia's walk: a poem, tr in Miscellaneous works vol 2, 1767.

Saint-Amant, Marc Antoine de Gérard, de
Kastner, L. E. Saint-Amant and the English poets. MLR 26 1931.
Aubin, R. A. Saint-Amant. MLN 50 1935.

Voiture, Vincent. Oeuvres. Paris 1650; Works, tr John Dryden, John Dennis and J. Drake 1736 (3rd edn); tr J. Ozell 1753 (4th edn); Select poems, tr Webster 1735.

Voltaire, François Marie Arouet de. *For Henriade, see Philosophy, col 99, above.*

English Authors

Burns, Robert
There were no 18th-century trns of Burns. The earliest recorded versions are:
Vie du poète Burns. Bibliothèque Britannique 14 1801.
Le miroir. 9, 16, 21 March 1821. 3 poems.
Morceaux choisis de Burns, poète écossais. Tr J. Aytoun and J. B. Mesnard, Paris 1826 (prose trn).
See Burns in French, Scotsman 25 Jan 1930.
Lehmann, E. Die französischen Lehn- und Fremdwörter in den Werken von Burns. Breslau 1933.

Chaucer, Geoffrey. The knight's tale. In his Canterbury tales, 1478; Palemon et Arcite, in Idée de la poésie anglaise vol 7, ed Yart, Paris 1756.
Pardoner's tale. Journal Etranger 1755.
Wife of Bath's tale. Tr [Deleyre?], Journal Etranger June 1757. First trn of a complete tale, drawn from Dryden's version.
Voltaire. Ce qui plaît aux dames. Partout (for Geneva) 1764 (for 1763). *See also* Année Littéraire Jan 1764.
[Favart, C. S. and C. H. Fusée de Voisenon]. La fée Urgèle: ou ce qui plaît aux dames. Paris 1765.
Hunter, A. C. Le conte de la femme de Bath en français

au xviii⁰ siècle. Revue de Littérature Comparée 9 1929. On preference of French for Dryden's modernized version.

Spurgeon, C. F. E. Chaucer devant la critique en Angleterre et en France depuis son temps jusqu'à nos jours. Paris 1911. No evidence of knowledge of Chaucer in the original before 1803.
—— 500 years of Chaucer criticism and allusion. Cambridge 1925.

Dryden, John
Various minor poems included in Idée de la poésie angloise, ed Yart 8 vols Paris 1749–56. See also Chaucer, above.
Proudfoot, L. Dryden's Aeneid and its 17th-century predecessors. Manchester 1960.

Gay, John. The fan. 1714; L'éventail, in Fables de Gay, tr Mme de Kéralio 1759; tr Constant de Massi, Paphos 1768.
Fables. 1728, 1738; Fables, tr Mme de Kéralio 1759; 1764; tr [de Mauroy], Philadelphia 1784.
See also Idée de la poésie angloise vols 4, 6, 8, ed Yart 1753–6, for minor poems.

Goldsmith, Oliver. The traveller. 1764; Le voyageur, tr A. de Laborde, Paris 1785.
The deserted village. 1770; Le retour du philosophe: ou le village abandonné, tr chevalier R[utlidge], Brussels 1772; Le village abandonné, tr A. de Laborde, Paris 1785; tr C. V[ictorine] d[e] C[hastenay], Paris 1797. *See* E. D. Seeber, MLR 41 1946.

Gray, Thomas. An elegy wrote in a country church yard. 1751; Elégie écrite sur un cimetière de campagne, tr [S. Curchod, Mme Necker], Gazette Littéraire 1765; also in Suard, Variétés littéraires vol 4, Paris 1769; Elégie sur un cimetière de campagne, in Edward Young, Les nuits, tr P. P. F. Le Tourneur 2 vols Paris 1769; tr [de Villevielle, J. F. Dufour de], *see* Gray to Nicholls, 22 May 1770; tr L. P. C. de Villeneuve, Mercure de France 1770; tr Merlin de Douai, Année Littéraire 1788; tr M.P.G.D.B. [P. Guédon de Berchère], Croydon and Paris 1788; tr 'F.N.', Le Magasin Encyclopédique 1795; tr J. F. N. Dusaulchoy, Les Soirées Littéraires 1796; tr [Mme de Luynes née Montmorency], Paris 1797; tr P. J. G. Cabanis, in Mélanges de littérature allemande, Paris 1797; Les tombeaux champêtres, tr F. de Chateaubriand, Journal de Peltier, 11 Dec 1797; tr N. Le Deist de Kérivalent in Almanach des Muses, Paris 1797; tr D. B. [Dubois?] in Poetical works of Gray, 1797.
Poetical works. (Bilingual edn) tr D. B. [Dubois?] 1797; Poésies de Gray, Paris 1798 (most major poems, including Eton College and Elegy).

Peers, E. A. The influence of Young and Gray in Spain. MLR 21 1926. Also in France.
Rovillain, E. L. S. Mercier et l'Elegy de Gray. MLN 43 1928. On L'homme sauvage, 1767.
Fothergill, R. An early influence on the poetry of Gray. Revue de Littérature Comparée 9 1929. On Gresset.
Briggs, E. R. Gray's Elegy: a French source [Racan?]. Revue de Littérature Comparée 19 1939.

Hervey, James. Meditations among the tombs. 1746. *See Prose fiction, below.*

Keate, George
For the influence of Voltaire and of the Swiss scene, see The Alps, 1763 *and* Ferney: an epistle to Monsr de Voltaire, 1768; *also* De Beer and A. M. Rousseau, Voltaire's British visitors, Stud on Voltaire & Eighteenth Century 49 1967.

Macpherson, James ('Ossian')
Fragments of ancient poetry. Edinburgh 1760; Fingal, 1762; Temora, 1763; Works of Ossian, 1765. Macpherson received immediate notice in France.
Fragments d'ancienne poésie. Tr [Turgot, Suard, Diderot], Journal Etranger 1760–2; Grimm et al, Correspondance littéraire [ms periodical], Dec 1761 (*see* Correspondance littéraire, ed Tourneux, Paris 1877–

82, vol 4 p. 494); Carthon: poème traduit de l'anglois, tr [duchesse d'Aiguillon and F. L. C. Marin?], 1762; Gazette Littéraire de l'Europe 1764–5; Variétés littéraires, tr [Turgot], Paris 1768–9; Choix de contes et de poésies erses, 2 vols Amsterdam 1772; Témora: poème épique en VIII chants, tr marquis de Saint-Simon, Amsterdam 1774; Journal Anglois, 2 vols Paris 1776; Ossian fils de Fingal: poésies galliques, tr P. Le Tourneur, 2 vols Paris 1776 (first major trn); [S. E. de Bridel], Poésies helvétiennes, Lausanne 1782; Léonard: idylles et poèmes champêtres, Paris 1782; [Prévost], Trésor de littérature étrangère, 2 vols Paris 1784; [Restif de la Bretonne], Les veillées du marais, tr Nichols-Doneraill 2 vols Waterford 1785; 1er chant de Fingal, tr S. M. A. de Clermont Tonnerre, Paris 1786; Essai d'une traduction d'Ossian, tr Lombard, Berlin 1789; Bridel, Calthon et Clessamor, Paris 1791; Poèmes d'Ossian pour servir de suite à l'Ossian de Letourneur, 3 vols Paris 1795; Les poèmes d'Ossian, tr Hill [Griffet de La Baume, D. de Saint-Georges] 3 vols Paris 1796.

Blair, H. Critical dissertation on the poems of Ossian. 1763; Observations sur l'ancienne poésie, in Recueil anglois, 2 vols Amsterdam 1763.

Van Tieghem, P. Ossian en France. 2 vols Paris 1917 (with lists of trns and study). See also his Ossian et l'ossianisme dans la littérature européenne au xviiie siècle, Groningen 1920.

Hazard, P. Ossian chez les Français. Nouvelle Revue d'Italie (Rome) 15 April 1920.

Garlington, A. S. Lesueur [Ossian ou les bardes 1799], Ossian and A synthesis of the arts. Symposium 18 1964.

Milton, John
L'Allegro, Il Penseroso. In his Poems, 1645; with Lycidas, Hymne sur la nativité, in Le paradis reconquis, tr de Mareuil, Paris 1730; L'Allegro et le Penseroso, tr Ribbonville 1766; tr marquis de Saint-Simon, in Essai de traduction littérale et énergique, 2 vols Haarlem 1771; tr Brimontier, Rouen 1797.
Paradise lost. 1667; Le paradis perdu, tr [Dupré de Saint-Maur with C. J. de Boismorand], 3 vols Amsterdam 1729 (in prose, with Addison's 18 Spectator essays on Milton of Jan–May 1712; these essays not ptd in 1718 French trn of Spectator); tr de Mareuil 3 vols Paris 1736; tr Chéron de Boismorand 3 vols Paris 1729; Le paradis terrestre, tr Fiquet D[u] b[ocage] 1748; tr [Durand] 3 vols Hague 1730; tr [L. Racine] 3 vols Paris 1754–5; Les larmes de Milton [opening of bk 3] in Héroïde, 1764; tr Duduit de Maizières, Paris 1771–4 (2 cantos); tr Le Roy, 2 vols Rouen 1772; tr Beaulaton 2 vols Paris 1778; tr P. J. F. Luneau de Boisgermain 1784; tr [J. de Mosneron] 3 vols Paris 1786; tr Nivernois, Paris 1796.

Tanevot, A. Adam et Eve: tragédie. Paris 1735. A verse drama.

Josse. L'origine du monde. Paris 1763. A play.

Paradise regained. 1671; Le paradis reconquis, tr [P. de Mareuil], Paris 1730; tr R[outh], Paris 1736; Le triomphe de Jésus-Christ dans le désert, tr Lancelin, Paris 1755.

Works, 1695, 1698; Oeuvres traduites de l'anglois, tr N. F. Dupré de Saint-Maur [with C. J. Chéron de Moismorand, E. Fenton, B. Routh] 4 vols Amsterdam 1753.

Bayle, P. Dictionnaire historique et critique. Rotterdam 1697. Biographical account of Milton.

Dissertation. Journal Littéraire 1717.

Voltaire. Essay on epick poetry. 1727; Essai sur la poésie épique, tr [P. E. G. Desfontaines], Paris 1728; tr Voltaire in La Henriade, 1732–3. See Candide [Pococurante] in Oeuvres, ed L. Moland, Paris 1877–85. Addison's articles in French appear to have affected Voltaire's opinion.

Nicéron, J. P. Mémoires vol 2. Paris 1729.

Constantin de Magny, C. F. Dissertation critique sur le Paradis perdu. Paris 1729.

Journal des Sçavans Nov 1729; Journal littéraire de La Haye 13 1729, 15 1730; Journal de Trévoux 114 1730; Bibliothèque Française 15 1730.

R[outh, B.] Lettres critiques sur la Paradis perdu et reconquis de Milton. Paris 1731.

Racine, L. Le Paradis perdu avec la vie de l'Auteur. 3 vols Paris 1754–5.

Addison, J. Criticism of Milton's Paradise lost. Spectator 1711–2; Remarques sur le paradis perdu, tr Dupré and Barret 3 vols Paris 1729.

Telleen, J. M. Milton dans la littérature française. Paris 1904.

Robertson, J. G. Milton's fame on the Continent. Proc Br Acad 3 1908.

Baker, A. T. Milton and Chateaubriand. French Quart 1 1919.

John, K. (ed). Louis Racine's life of Milton. 1930.

Bonno, G. La culture et la civilisation française. Trans Amer Philosophical Soc 38 1948. On early reception.

Blondel, J. (ed). Milton: le Paradis reconquis, étude critique, traduction. Paris 1955. French opinion of this poem.

Lutaud, O. D'Areopagitica à la Lettre à un premier commis. Stud on Voltaire & Eighteenth Century 26 1963.

Saillens, E. Coups d'oeil sur les débuts de Milton en France. Etudes Anglaises 20 1967. On Eikonoklastes.

Percy, Thomas
No 18th-century trn of the Reliques, 1765 has been found. On Percy's debt to continental and Scandinavian sources see P. Van Tieghem, Ossian et l'ossianisme, Groningen 1920.

Carrière, J. M. Notes on Berquin's adaptations from English poetry. Romanic Rev 26 1933.

Campion, C. M. Oeuvres. Ed E. D. Seeber and H. H. H. Remak, Bloomington 1945.

Pope, Alexander. See also Philosophy, Literary Theory and Criticism, above.
Pastorals. 1709; Eglogues, tr Mme de Montegut in Receuil de plusieurs pièces d'éloquence et de poésie, Toulouse [1748]; Les pastorales, avec son discours sur la poésie pastorale, tr [de Lustrac], Paris 1753; L'automne, La solitude, tr Maistral, Mercure de France 1769; tr de Balami, Mercure de France 1771–2; Traduction des églogues, tr R. de B. [de Racquigny de Bulonde], Paris 1789; [L'automne, tr L. de Lancival, Paris 1795]. See also Discourse on pastoral poetry, first tr Pérelle, Nouveau Mercure Feb 1717.

Rape of the lock. 1712, 1714; La boucle de cheveux enlevée, tr [P. F. G. Desfontaines, despite attributions to Mme de Caylus and prince de Conti], Paris 1728 (prose); tr D[espréaux], Paris 1742 (verse adaptation of Desfontaines); tr [Costard des Ifs], Caen 1744 (verse); tr [Marmontel], Paris 1746; tr Du Resnel in Les principes de la morale et du goût, Paris 1748; tr L. S. Mercier, Amsterdam 1764. 5 different trns before 1750, 41 edns by 8 translators 1728–1825; Desfontaines version alone saw 19 reprints in this period.

Windsor Forest. 1713; Poème sur la forêt de Windsor, tr de Lustrac in Les pastorales, Paris 1753; tr Vieihl de Boisjolin, Almanach des Muses 1798.

The Temple of Fame. 1715; Le temple de la Renommé, tr [A. M. L. Fiquet Dubocage], 1749; tr Mme G. C. Thiroux d'Arcanville] in Mélange de poésie angloise, 1764 (with other poems by Pope).

Works. 1717 etc; Principes de la morale et du goût, tr Du Resnel, Paris 1737; Mélanges de littérature et de philosophie, tr [E. de Silhouette] 2 vols 1742; Oeuvres diverses, 2 vols Amsterdam 1749; ed Joncourt, Amsterdam 1753, 6 vols Amsterdam 1754 (7th vol 1758), 7 vols Vienna 1761; Essai de traduction littérale et énergique, tr Saint-Simon 2 vols Haarlem 1771.

Works. 1751 (complete); Oeuvres complettes, ed Laporte 8 vols Paris 1779.

Epistle of Eloise to Abelard. 1720; Epître d'Héloïse à Abailard, [tr Fiquet Dubocage] in Mélanges de différentes pièces de vers et de prose, Berlin 1751; tr Feutry [1751]; tr C[olardeau], Au Paraclet 1758; tr [duchesse d'Aiguillon], Geneva 1758; tr [L. S. Mercier] 1763; tr Saurin, Gazette Littéraire de l'Europe 8 1765 (imitation); tr Saint-Simon in Essai de traduction littérale et énergique, 2 vols Haarlem 1771.

Dunciad. 1728; La Dunciade: ou l'Angleterre démasquée, Hague 1744; tr P[alissot] 1781.

See also Idée de la poésie angloise vols 2–7, ed Yart, Paris 1753–6 (mostly minor poems).

Pope was the most translated of all English authors before 1750 and the sole contemporary English poet well known on the Continent.

Béclard, L. Sébastien Mercier. Paris 1903. On Pope's translator.

Hoffman, A. Voltaires Stellung zu Pope. Königsberg 1913.

Audra, E. L'influence française dans l'œuvre de Pope. Paris 1931.

— Les traductions françaises de Pope 1717–1825. Paris 1931.

Morris, T. L'abbé Desfontaines. Stud on Voltaire & Eighteenth Century 19 1961.

Thomson, James. The seasons. 1730; Les saisons, in Idée de la poésie anglaise, ed Yart 8 vols Paris 1749–56 (vol 4); tr [M. J. de Châtillon] as Bontems, Paris 1759; Le printems, l'été, tr W. d'Abancourt, Mercure de France 1770–3; Les mois, tr J. A. Roucher, Paris 1779.

Saint-Lambert, J. F. Les saisons. 2 vols Amsterdam (for Paris) 1769.

Cameron, M. M. L'influence des Saisons de Thomson sur la poésie descriptive en France 1759–1810. Paris 1927.

Châlons, Y. Les saisons de Thomson: autour de leur dédicace française. Revue de Littérature Comparée 32 1958. On Physiocrats' interest in trn.

Seeber, E. D. Anti-slavery opinion in the poems of some early French followers of Thomson. MLN 50 1935.

Young, Edward. The complaint: or night thoughts. 9 pts 1742–5; [first night], tr count C. Thiard de Bissy, Journal Etranger Feb 1762; [second night], tr de Bissy, Gazette Littéraire de l'Europe July 1764; les nuits, tr P. Le Tourneur 2 vols Paris 1769; tr Collardeau, Amsterdam 1770 (first night); tr Sabatier de Castres, nd. Also various extracts, *see* C. A. Rochedieu, Bibliography of French translations of English works, Chicago 1948.

Oeuvres diverses. Tr P. P. F. Le Tourneur 2 vols Paris 1770.

Oeuvres complètes. Tr P. P. F. Le Tourneur 6 vols Berne 1796.

Baldensperger, F. Young et ses nuits en France. In Etudes d'histoire littéraire vol 1, Paris 1907.

Van Tieghem, P. La poésie de la nuit et des tombeaux en Europe au xviiie siècle. Paris 1921.

The main source of transmission of verse was the periodical press and ephemeral almanachs, 'magasins', 'soirées' etc. Such sources antedate separate pbn by many years and reached wider audiences. They have been shown above only in selected cases. A further important source was the anthologies, for which see F. Lachèvre, Bibliographie des recueils collectifs de poésie publiés de 1577 à 1700, 4 vols Paris 1901–6; and C. A. Rochedieu, Bibliography of French translations of English works, Chicago 1948, appendix 3.

Dissertation sur la poésie anglaise. Journal Littéraire 9 1717.

Blake, W. The French Revolution. 1791.

Cestre, C. La Révolution française et les poètes anglais. Paris 1906. *See also* A. E. Hancock, The French Revolution and the English poets, New York 1899.

Wallstein, R. H. English opinions of French poetry 1660–1750. New York 1923.

West, A. H. L'influence française dans la poésie burlesque en Angleterre entre 1660 et 1700. Paris 1930.

Woledge, G. Saint-Amand, Fairfax and Marvell. MLR 25 1930.

McCourt, E. A. The invasion theme in English poetry. Dalhousie Rev 22 1942.

Congleton, J. E. Theories of pastoral poetry in England 1684–1717. SP 41 1944.

Boase, A. M. Poètes anglais et français de l'époque baroque. Revue des Sciences Humaines 55–6 1949.

de Mourgues, O. Metaphysical, baroque and précieux poetry. Oxford 1953.

Quaintance, R. F. French sources of the Restoration 'imperfect enjoyment' poem. PQ 42 1963.

Letters, Memoirs etc

Letters of Abelard and Heloise, extracted from Monsieur Bayle. Tr J. Hughes 1722.

Chesterfield, Philip Dormer, 4th Earl of Stanhope. Letters written to his son. 1774; Lettres écrites à son fils, 5 vols Paris 1775; Lettres du Lord Chesterfield à son fils, 4 vols Amsterdam 1776; Choix de lettres, tr Peyron 1776.

Du Deffand, Marie de Vichy de Chamrond, marquise. Correspondence. In Yale edition of Horace Walpole's correspondence, ed W. S. Lewis et al, New Haven 1937–.

Hamilton, Antoine. Mémoires de la vie du comte de Grammont. Cologne 1713; Memoirs of the life of count de Grammont, tr A. Boyer 1714.

Rousseau, Jean-Jacques. Correspondance complète. Ed R. A. Leigh, Geneva 1965–.

Les confessions [bks 1–6] suivies des Rêveries du promeneur solitaire. Geneva 1782; Second supplément à la collection des œuvres de Rousseau [bks 7–12 of Confessions], Geneva 1789; Confessions, [1–6] with the Rêveries of the solitary walker, tr [W. Combe?]; *see* C. Barbier, Revue de Littérature Comparée 28 1954] 2 vols 1783, 1790, 10 vols 1786–90 (vols 1–6); Confessions: part the second [bks 7–12]; to which is added a new collection of letters, 3 vols 1790.

Jephson, R. The confessions of Jean Baptiste Couteau, citizen of France. 2 vols 1794. A burlesque.

The Dialogues, and Rousseau juge de Jean-Jacques, were not tr in 18th century, though the latter was first pbd at Lichfield for Rousseau by Sir Brooke-Boothby, 1780 (in French).

Saint-Simon, Louis de Rouvroy, duc de. Mémoirs: nouvelle édition. Ed A. de Boislisle et al 43 vols Paris [1879–] 1881–1928.

Sévigné, Marie de Rabutin-Chantal, marquise de. Lettres. 1725; Letters to the Countess de Grignan, 2 vols 1727; Court secrets: or the lady's chronicle extracted from the letters, tr E. Curll 1727; Letters, tr 10 vols 1764.

Voiture, Vincent. Lettres. Paris 1650; Select letters of Voiture, tr J. Dryden in John Dennis, Letters upon several occasions, 1696.

Voltaire, François Marie Arouet de. Correspondence. Ed T. Besterman 107 vols Geneva 1953–65 (with 5 vols of index; List of works cited [by Voltaire], vol 101); Correspondence and related documents: definitive edition, ed Besterman, in Complete works of Voltaire, ed Besterman, W. H. Barber, O. R. Taylor et al, Geneva and Toronto 1968–.

Walpole, Horace. The Yale edition of Walpole's correspondence. Ed W. S. Lewis, New Haven 1937–.

Prose Fiction

Bibliographies

Esdaile, A. List of English tales and prose romances printed before 1740. 1912; rev C. C. Mish, English prose fiction 1600–1700, Charlottesville 1952.

Mornet, D. (ed). J.-J. Rousseau, La nouvelle Héloïse. Paris 1925. Lists c. 2,000 titles 1740–80.

Williams, R. C. Bibliography of the 17th-century novel in France. New York 1931. *See also F. P. Rolfe, below.*

Rolfe, F. P. On the bibliography of 17th-century prose fiction. PMLA 49 1934. Corrections and addns to R. C. Williams, above.

Streeter, H. W. The 18th-century English novel in French translation: a bibliographical study. New York [1936]. Includes survey of impact of English novel in France.

Jones, S. P. A list of French prose fiction 1700–50. New York 1939.

Tucker, J. E. English translations from the French 1650–1700: corrections and addns to CBEL. PQ 21 1942.

Rochedieu, C. A. Bibliography of French translations of English works 1700–1800. Chicago 1948.

Monglond, A. La France révolutionnaire et impériale. Grenoble 1930–8, 1949, Paris 1953.

McBurney, W. H. A checklist of English prose fiction 1700–39. Cambridge Mass 1960. *See* corrections by D. F. Bond, MP 59 1962.

Block, A. The English novel 1740–1850: a catalogue. 1961 (2nd edn).

Cioranescu, A. Bibliographie de la littérature française du xviie siècle. 3 vols Paris 1965–6.

Martin, A. Towards a checklist of French prose fiction 1751–8. Australian Jnl of French Stud 3 1966. Includes A first listing of French prose fiction 1780–3.

Baldner, R. Bibliography of 17th-century French prose fiction. New York 1967. Revision of R. C. Williams, above.

Anthologies, Collections etc

See select list of journals, col 86 above, for various Bibliothèques offering digests of foreign fiction.

Lenglet Du Fresnoy, N. A. De l'usage des romans. 2 vols Amsterdam 1734.

Mélanges de différentes pièces de vers et de prose. Tr A. M. L. Fiquet Dubocage 3 vols Berlin 1751.

Formey, H. S. Conseils pour former une bibliothèque peu nombreuse mais choisie. Berlin 1756.

Mélanges de littérature angloise. Tr Mme Belot [Durey de Meynières by marriage] 2 vols Hague 1759.

Romans traduits de l'anglois. Tr Mme Thiroux d'Arcanville. Amsterdam (for Paris) 1761.

Bibliothèque universelle des romans. Ed [A. R. de Voyer d'Argenson, marquis de Paulmy] 112 vols Paris 1775–89.

Chaudon, L. M. Bibliothèque d'un homme de goût. Avignon 1772, 1773, Paris 1777.

Paulmy, A. R. de Voyer d'Argenson, marquis de, and A. G. Contant d'Orville. Mélanges tirés d'une grande bibliothèque. 70 vols Paris 1779–88. Vol 2 of 2nd edn, Paris 1785 as Bibliothèque littéraire à l'usage des dames.

Collection choisie des plus célèbres auteurs anglois, italiens etc. Paris 1780.

Le Décaméron anglois: ou recueil des plus jolis contes. Tr [M. Wouters, baronne de Vasse] 1783.

Le cabinet des fées. Ed C. G. T. Garnier 41 vols Geneva 1785–9.

Bibliothèque anglaise: ou recueil d'histoires, contes moraux, romans etc tirés des meilleurs auteurs anglois. Tr B. C. Gourney 4 vols Paris 1787.

Les voyages imaginaires, romanesques etc. Ed C. G. T. Garnier 39 vols Amsterdam 1787–9.

Collection de romans et contes imitées de l'anglais. Tr P. A. de La Place 8 vols Paris 1788.

Nouvelle bibliothèque des romans. 56 vols Paris 1789–1805. Continuation of Bibliothèque des romans.

Recueil de fables, de contes etc, traduits des ouvrages anglais. 1796.

Recueil de contes et historiettes traduits librement de l'anglais et de l'italien. 2 vols Cologne 1798.

Contes moraux à l'usage des enfants, traduits de l'anglais. Berlin 1799.

French Authors

[Arabian nights]. Les mille et une nuits: contes arabes traduits en françois par M. G. [Antoine Galland]. 12 vols Paris 1704–17; Arabian nights entertainments, translated into French by M. Galland and now done into English, 3 vols 1707.

Argens, Jean Baptiste de Boyer, marquis de. Lettres juives. 6 vols 1736–8; The Jewish spy, 5 vols 1739 [–40?].

Lettres chinoises. Hague 1739–40; The Chinese spy, 1752 (2nd edn).

d'Arnaud, François Thomas Marie de Baculard. *See also Richardson, below.*

Nancy: ou la nouvelle Paméla. Paris 1762; rev as Fanny: ou l'heureux repentir, Paris 1764; rev as Fanny: ou la nouvelle Paméla, in Les épreuves du sentiment, 5 vols Paris 1767; Fanny: or the happy repentance, tr 1766 (from 1764 text). *See* D. F. Bond, The 18th-century English novel in translation, MP 35 1938.

Les épreuves du sentiment. 5 vols Paris 1767; The tears of sensibility, tr J. Murdock 2 vols 1773, 1783 (with 2 new pieces).

Sidney et Volsan. Paris 1770; The history of Sidney and Volsan, Dublin 1772.

Varbeck. Paris 1774; Warbeck: a pathetic tale, tr S. Lee 1785.

Le comte de Gleichen. [?]; The history of Count Gleichen, 1786.

Inklaar, D. Baculard d'Arnaud: ses imitateurs en Hollande et dans d'autres pays. Hague 1925.

d'Aulnoy, Marie Catherine Le Jumel de Barneville, baronne. Nouvelles d'Elizabeth, reyne d'Angleterre. Paris 1674; The novels of Elizabeth, tr 1680–1.

Histoire de Jean de Bourbon. Paris 1691; The Prince of Carency: a novel, tr 1719.

Les illustres fées. Paris 1689; Tales of the fairies, 1699; also tr in The diverting works of the countess d'Anois, 1707; T. Southerne, Money the mistress, 1726.

Les avantures d'Hippolyte, comte de Douglas. Paris 1690; Hypolitus, Earl of Douglas, tr 1708.

Mémoires de la cour d'Espagne. Paris 1690; The present Court of Spain, tr J. P. 1693.

Relation du voyage d'Espagne. Paris 1691; The ingenious and diverting letters of the lady —'s travels into Spain, 1691–2.

Mémoires des avantures singulières de la cour de France. Hague 1692; Memoirs of the Court of France, tr [P.B.] 1692.

Beckford, William. *See English Authors, below.*

Challes, Robert. Les illustres Françoises. Hague 1713; The illustrious French lovers, tr P. Aubin 2 vols 1727; The unnatural mother [Mlle de L'Epine episode], tr 1734.

Roddier, H. Challes inspirateur de Richardson et de Prévost. Revue de Littérature Comparée 21 1947.

Crébillon, Claude Prosper Jolyot de (Crébillon fils)

Lettres de la marquise de M*** au comte de R***. 1732; Letters from the Marchioness de M*** to the Count of R***, tr S. Humphreys 1742. Crébillon the first French author to exploit letter-novel.

Tanzaï et Néadarné: histoire japonaise. 'Pekin' (for Paris) 1734 (for 1733?), 1735 (as L'écumoire); The skimmer, 2 vols 1735.

Les égarements du coeur et de l'esprit. 3 vols Paris

1736–8; The wanderings of the heart and mind: or the memoirs of Mr de Meilcour, tr M. Clancy 1751.

Le Sopha: conte moral. 'Gaznah' (for Paris?) [1742 or 1740?]; The sopha: a moral tale, 2 vols 1742.

Les amours de Zéokinizul. Amsterdam 1746 (for 1740?); The secret history of Zeolsinesul, King of the Kofingns; being an authentic account of the amours of Lewis XV, 1761.

Les heureux orphelins. Paris 1754 (from E. Haywood, The fortunate foundlings, 1744); The happy orphans, 1758 (see H. S. Hughes, Notes on 18th-century translations, MP 17 1920).

Day, D. A. Crébillon fils et l'Angleterre. Revue de Littérature Comparée 33 1959.

Cyrano de Bergerac, Savinien de. Oeuvres diverses. Paris 1654; Satyrical characters and handsome descriptions in letters, tr 'a person of honour' 1658.

Histoire comique par M. Cyrano Bergerac: contenant les estats et empires de la lune. Paris 1657 (earlier ptd version of this posthumous pbn: Histoire comique ou voyage dans la lune, [c. 1650?]; [Selenarchia]: or the government of the world in the moon, tr Sir T. StSerf [or Sydserf] 1659 (attributed to Sir R. Stapleton by G. Langbaine); tr A. Lowell 1687 (with 'Sun').

Histoire comique des estats et empires de la lune et du soleil. Paris 1662; Comical history of the states and empires of the world of the moon and sun, tr A. Lovell 1687; Voyage to the moon with some account of the solar world, tr S. Derrick 1753.

Swift, Jonathan. Travels into several remote nations of the world, by Lemuel Gulliver. 1726.

Toldo, P. Les voyages merveilleux de Cyrano et de Swift, et leurs rapports avec l'œuvre de Rabelais. Revue des Etudes Rabelaisiennes 4–5 1906–7.

Henriot, E. Cyrano plagiaire et plagié. In Livres et portraits vol 1, Paris 1923.

Bennett, R. E. Cyrano–Swift criticism. MLN 43 1928.

Diderot, Denis. See also Sterne, below.

Les bijoux indiscrets. [1748]; Les bijoux indiscrets: or the indiscreet toys, tr 1749.

La religieuse [written c. 1760–]. Paris 1796 (first pbd 1780); The nun, 2 vols 1797.

Jacques le fataliste [written 1771–]. In Opuscules, Paris 1796 (first pbd in Correspondance littéraire c. 1780); James the fatalist and his master, 3 vols 1797. First pbd in Schiller's trn of an extract, 1785, and in Mylius German trn of 1792.

Taupin, R. Richardson, Diderot et l'art de conter. French Rev 12 1939.

Warning, R. Illusion und Wirklichkeit in Tristram Shandy und Jacques le fataliste. Munich 1965. See also his Fiktion und Wirklichkeit in Sterne und Diderot, in Nachahmungen und Illusion, ed H. R. Jausz, Munich 1964.

Fénelon, François de Salignac de La Mothe

Les avantures d'Aristonoüs. Hague 1696; The adventures of Aristonous, tr J. Ozell, in Adventures of Telemachus, 2 vols 1715; tr M. A. Meilan 1774 (verse); tr J. Falla 1799 (verse).

Les avantures de Télémaque. Paris 1699; The adventures of Telemachus pt 1, tr I. Littlebury 1699; 5 pts 1703; tr Littlebury with A. Boyer and A. Oldes 2 vols [1721]; bk 1, tr 1712 (verse); tr J. Ozell 2 vols 1715; bks 1–2 (blank verse) tr 1729; rev Desmaizeaux 2 vols 1742; tr J. Kelly 2 vols 1743; A new translation of Telemachus in English verse, tr G. Bagnall 2 vols 1756; tr J. Hawkesworth 1768, rev G. Gregory 2 vols 1795; tr W. H. Melmoth [1770?]; tr P. Proctor 2 vols 1774; tr M. A. Meilan 1774 (verse, with Aristonoüs); tr 2 vols Aberdeen 1776; tr T. G. Smollett 2 vols 1776 (see PQ 44 1965); bks 1–2, tr S. Leacroft 1785 (verse); bk 1, tr G. Canton 1788 (blank verse); Specimen of a new version [in verse], tr I.

d'Israeli 1791 (2nd edn); tr 'F. Fitzgerald' [C. Taylor] 1792; tr J. Youde 1793 (blank verse)

Furetière, Antoine. Le roman bourgeois. Paris 1666; The city romance, 1671 (attributed to Scarron by translator).

Williams, E. Furetière and Wycherley: Le roman bourgeois in Restoration comedy. MLN 53 1938.

Genlis, Stéphanie Félicité Ducrest de Saint-Aubin, marquise de Sillery, comtesse de

Adèle et Théodore: ou lettres sur l'éduction. Paris 1782; tr as Adelaide and Theodore, 3 vols 1783.

Les veillées du château. Paris 1782; Tales of the castle, tr T. Holcroft 5 vols 1785.

Les chevaliers du cygne. Paris 1795; The knights of the swan: or the Court of Charlemagne: a historical tale, tr J. Beresford 3 vols 1796; abridged by C. Butler as The age of chivalry, 1799.

Les petits émigrés. Paris 1798; The young exiles: or correspondence of some juvenile emigrants, 3 vols 1799.

Les vœux téméraires: ou l'enthousiasme. Altona 1799; Rash vows: a novel, 3 vols 1799.

Les mères rivales: ou la calomnie. Paris 1800; The rival mothers, 4 vols 1800.

The beauties of Genlis: being a collection of tales. [Perth 1787].

Wahba, M. Mme de Genlis in England. Comparative Lit 13 1961.

Guilleragues, Lavergne de. Lettres portugaises. 1669. Also as Lettres d'une religieuse portugaise, and Lettres d'Héloïse et d'Abelard: Letters de la religieuse portugaise. Five love letters from a nun to a cavalier, tr Sir R. L'Estrange 1678; Letters from Portugal, tr [J. Blankett or P. Stevens] 1777; [tr W. Bowles, as M. Alcoforado, Letters from a Portuguese nun, 1808].

Deloffre, F. (ed). Guilleragues, Lettres portugaises. Paris 1962. See his Etat présent des études sur Guilleragues, Information Littéraire 19 1967.

Hamilton, Antoine. Mémoires de la vie du comte de Grammont. Cologne 1713; Memoirs of the life of the count de Grammont, tr A. Boyer 1714.

Histoire de Fleur d'Epine: conte. Paris 1730; History of May Flower, Salisbury 1796 (2nd edn).

Huet, Pierre Daniel. Diane de Castro: ou les faux Incas. Paris 1729 (posthumous); Diane de Castro: a novel, tr (c. 1730?] (ms date of 1724 incorrect).

Traité de l'origine des romans. In Mme de La Fayette, Zayde, Paris 1670; also as Lettre à M. de Segrais; A treatise of romances and their original, tr 1672; tr S. Lewis 1715; tr S. Croxall in Select collection of novels vol 1, 1720.

La Calprenède, Gautier de Costes de. Cassandre. 10 vols Paris 1642–5; Cassandra: the fam'd romance, tr Sir C. Cotterell 1652; The rival kings: or the loves of Oroondates and Statira, tr J. Banks 1677; The rival queens: or the death of Alexander the Great, tr N. Lee 1677.

La Cléopâtre. 10 vols Paris 1646–57; Cleopatra; Hymen's Praeludia [pt 1], tr R. Loveday 1652–5; Gloriana: or the Court of Augustus Caesar, tr N. Lee 1676.

Faramond [Pharamond]. 12 vols Paris 1661–70 (vols 8–12 by P. d'Ortigue de Vaumorière); Pharamond, tr J. Davies 1662; tr J. Phillips 1677.

Hill, H. W. La Calprenède's Romances and the Restoration drama. Chicago 1910.

Laclos, Choderlos de. Les liaisons dangereuses. Paris 1782; Dangerous connections: or letters collected in a society by M. C*** de L***, 4 vols 1784; Thomas Holcroft, Seduction, [1787] (play).

Lison, L. Un précurseur de Talleyrand, Laclos et l'alliance anglaise. Annales de Sciences Politiques 19 1904.

Thelander, D. R. Laclos and the epistolary novel. Geneva 1963.

La Fayette, Marie Madeleine Pioche de la Vergne comtesse de. Zayde: histoire espagnole par M. de Segrais. Paris 1670–1; Zayde: a Spanish history, tr P. Porter 2 vols 1678; tr S. Croxall, in Select collection of novels vol 1, 1720; also in E. Griffith, A collection of novels vol 1, 1777.

La Princesse de Clèves. Paris 1678; The Princess of Cleves, tr 'a person of quality' 1679. Also in Croxall and Griffith, as above.

Histoire de Madame, Henriette d'Angleterre. Amsterdam 1720; Fatal gallantry: or the secret history of Henrietta, Princess of England, tr A. Floyd 1722.

Ashton, H. Mme de La Fayette. Cambridge 1922 (with bibliography).

Stroup, T. B. The Princesse de Clèves and sentimental comedy. RES 11 1935.

Lesage, Alain René. Nouvelles avantures de l'admirable Don Quichotte de la Manche, par A. F. de Avellaneda. Paris 1704 (free and partly original trn); Avellaneda, A continuation of the comical history of Don Quixote, tr J. Stevens 1784 (from Lesage's Nouvelles avantures, themselves based on La segunda parte del ingenioso Hidalgo D. Quijote de la Mancha, 1614).

Le diable boiteux. Paris 1707, 2 vols 1726 (full text); Le diable boiteux: or the Devil upon two sticks [incomplete], tr 1708; 2 vols tr 1729 (6th edn) (full text); The Devil upon crutches, 2 vols tr [T. G. Smollett?] [1748?], 1750 (see L. M. Knapp, MLN 47 1932); tr 2 vols Berwick 1773; W. Combe, The Devil upon two sticks in England, 6 vols 1790–1.

Histoire de Gil Blas de Santillane. Paris 1715–35; The history and adventures of Gil Blas de Santillane, 2 vols 1716–37; tr T. G. Smollett 4 vols 1749; tr P. Proctor 2 vols 1774.

The history and adventures of Don Alfonso de Lirias, son of Gil Blas, 'translated from Spanish original'. 1741. See Revue d'Histoire Littéraire de la France 44 1937; Tobias Smollett, The adventures of Roderick Random, 1748; E. Moore, Gil Blas, 1751; Le Maire; the French Gil Blas or the adventures of H. Lanson, 4 vols tr 1793 (trn of a French adaptation).

Les avantures de Monsieur Robert Chevalier, dit Beauchêne. Paris 1732; The adventures of Robert Chevalier, 2 vols 1745.

Histoire d'Estevanille Gonzales, tirée de l'espagnol. Paris 1734 (free adaptation of Vida y hechos de E. Gonzalez, 1646; tr J. Stevens in The Spanish libertines, 1707); The comical history of Estevanille Gonzalez, tr 1735; The history of Vanillo Gonzales, 2 vols tr 1797.

Le Bachelier de Salamanque. Paris and Hague 1736–8; The bachelor of Salamanca, tr [J.] Lockman 2 vols 1737–9.

See also Smollett and Swift, below.

Lawrence, A. L'influence de Lesage sur Smollett. Revue de Littérature Comparée 12 1932.

Willers, H. Le diable boiteux. Romanische Forschungen 49 1935. On European vogue.

Marguerite d'Angoulême, reine de Navarre. L'Heptaméron des nouvelles de la reine de Navarre. Paris 1559 (first tr R. Codrington 1654); Novels tales and stories, tr 1750.

Marivaux, Pierre Carlet de Chamblain de. Vie de Marianne. 11 pts Paris 1731–41 (12th pt of 1745 spurious, by Mme Riccoboni); The life of Marianne, tr 1736–42 (see GM); The virtuous orphan: or the life of Marianne, tr [M. Collyer c. 1737–43] (later in Novelists's Mag); also as Memoirs of the Countess of Bressol, 2 vols tr M. Collyer 1743?; rptd as The life and adventures of Indiana, the virtuous orphan, 1746 (see H. S. Hughes, MP 15 1917).

Le paysan parvenu. 5 pts Paris 1734–6 (some edns with apocryphal pts 6–8); Le paysan parvenu: or the fortunate peasant, tr 1735; The fortunate villager: or memoirs of Sir Andrew Thompson [freely adapted] (see H. S. Hughes, MP 17 1919).

Pharsamon[d]: ou les nouvelles folies romanesques [written 1712]. Hague (or Paris?) 1737; Pharsamond: or the new knight errant, 2 vols tr J. Lockman 1750. *See also Richardson, below.*

Hughes, H. S. Translations of the Vie de Marianne and contemporary English fiction. MP 15 1917.

Swaen, A. E. H. Marianne and Pamela. Neophilologus 23 1938.

Dédéyan, C. Marivaux à l'école d'Addison et de Steele. Annales de l'Université de Paris 1955.

Marmontel, Jean François. Contes moraux. Paris 1758; Select moral tales, tr [R. Roberts] 1763; Moral tales, tr C. Dennis and R. Lloyd 3 vols 1764–6; New moral tales, tr 1792; The tales of an evening, 4 vols tr 1792–4; tr M. Pilkington, Tales selected and abridged, 1799; Marmontel's Tales, tr 1799; also E. Trapaud, Aglaura, 1774.

L'amitié à l'épreuve. Paris 1765; H. Kelly, The romance of an hour, 1774.

Bélisaire. Paris 1767; Belisarius, tr 1767; tr 1768; tr F. Ashmore 1789.

Les Incas: roman poétique. Paris 1777; T. Morton, Columbus, 1792.

Montesquieu, Charles de Secondat, baron de La Brède et de. *See Philosophy, above, for Lettres persanes.*

Perrault, Charles. Histoires ou contes du temps passé [Contes de ma mère Loye]. Paris 1697; Tales of Mother Goose, tr R. Samber 1729.

Halsband, R. An imitation of Perrault: Lady Mary Wortley Montagu's Carabosse. Comparative Lit 3 1951.

Prévost, Antoine François, called Prévost d'Exiles. Mémoires et avantures d'un homme de qualité qui s'est retiré du monde. Paris etc 1728–31; Memoirs of a man of quality, tr 1738 (incomplete?); Memoirs of a man of honour, tr 1747; tr 2 vols 1770.

Histoire du chevalier Des Grieux et de Manon Lescaut. Amsterdam 1731 (vol 7 of: Mémoires d'un homme de qualité); The memoirs and adventures of the marquis de Bretagne and duc d'Harcourt, to which is added the history of the chevalier des Grieu and Moll Lescaut, tr Erskine 3 vols 1743; The history of the chevalier Des Grieux, 2 vols 1767; Manon L'Escaut, tr C. T. Smith 2 vols 1786; see F. C. Green, Minuet, 1935 (appendix 4); Henry Mackenzie, Julie de Roubigné, 1777.

Le philosophe anglois: ou histoire de Monsieur Cleveland, fils naturel de Cromwell, traduite de l'anglois par [Prévost]. 8 vols [Utrecht or Paris?] 1731–9; The life of Mr Cleveland, 4 vols 1731, 5 vols 1734–5.

Le doyen de Killerine. 3 vols Paris 1735–9, 6 vols Paris 1739–40; The dean of Coleraine: a moral history, 3 vols 1742–3.

Havens, G. R. Prévost and English literature. Princeton 1921.

Foster, J. R. The abbé Prévost and the English novel. PMLA 42 1927.

Robertson, M. E. J. (ed), Prévost, Mémoires d'un homme de qualité vol 5 [Séjour en Angleterre]. Paris 1927.

Wilcox, F. H. Prévost's translations of Richardson's novels. Berkeley 1927. On role of Aubert de La Chesnaye des Bois.

Hazard, P. Etudes critiques sur Manon Lescaut. Chicago 1929.

Engel, C. E. Autour de voyage de l'abbé Prévost en Angleterre. Revue de Littérature Comparée 18 1938. *See also his Voyages et découvertes, Paris 1939, and*

Le véritable abbé Prévost, Monaco 1958 (English sources in detail).

Swaen, A. E. H. Marianne-Pamela. Neophilologus 23 1938.

Waïs, K. Abbé Prévost in seiner Wirkung auf den europäischen Roman. Arcadia 1 1966.

Rabelais, François. Pantagruel. Lyons [1532]; Gargantua, Lyons 1534; Tiers livre, 1546; Quart livre, Lyons 1549, Paris 1552; Cinquième livre [authorship in doubt], Lyons 1562; The first book of the works of Mr Francis Rabelais: containing five books of the lives etc of Gargantua and his sonne Pantagruel, tr Sir T. Urquhart 1653 (bks 1–2); The third book, tr 1693; bks 4–5 tr P. A. Le Motteux 1693–4.

The whole works of Rabelais. Tr Sir T. Urquhart, P. A. Le Motteux et al 2 vols 1708; Remarques de Pierre Le Motteux sur Rabelais, tr C.D.M. [César de Missy] 1740 (or earlier?); rev J. Ozell 5 vols 1737.

Butler, Samuel. Hudibras. 3 pts 1663–78.

Swift, Jonathan. Gulliver's travels. 1726. *See also Cyrano de Bergerac, above.*

A faithful and full account of the surprising life and adventures of Dr Sartorius Sinegradibus. 1749. *See also Swift, below.*

Sainéan, L. Les interprètes de Rabelais en Angleterre et en Allemagne; II, Urquhardt. Revue des Etudes Rabelaisiennes 7 1909. *See also his* Les interprètes de Rabelais en Angleterre 7 1910.

McKillop, A. D. Some early traces of Rabelais in English literature. MLN 36 1921.

Brown, H. Rabelais in English literature. Cambridge Mass 1933, 1968.

Pons, E. Rabelais et Swift. In Mélanges Lefranc, Paris 1936.

Riccoboni, Marie Jeanne Laboras de Mézières. Histoire de M. le Mis de Cressy, traduite de l'anglois. Amsterdam 1758; The history of the marquis de Cressy, tr 1765.

Lettres de Mylady Juliette Catesby. Paris 1759; Letters from Juliet Lady Catesby, tr [F. Brooke] 1760.

Histoire d'Ernestine. In Recueil de pièces détachées, Paris 1765; The continuation of the life of Marianne, to which is added the history of Ernestina, tr 1766 (*see Marivaux, above*).

Lettres d'Adelaïde de Dammartin Csse de Sancerre. Paris 1767; Letters from the Countess de Sancerre, 2 vols 1767.

Lettres d'Elisabeth-Sophie de Vallière à Louise Hortense de Canteleu. Paris 1772; Letters etc, tr Maceuen 2 vols 1772.

Lettres de Mylord Rivers à Sir Charles Cardigan. Paris 1777; Letters from Lord Rivers to Sir Charles Cardigan, tr P. Stockdale 2 vols 1778.

Collection complète des œuvres. 7 vols Neuchâtel 1780; Select novels, tr 1781.

Histoire de Christine, reine de Suabe. Paris 1783; The history of Christina, 2 vols 1784.

Crosby, E. A. Une romancière oubliée: Mme Riccoboni, sa place dans la littérature anglaise du xviiie siècle. Paris 1927.

Rousseau, Jean-Jacques. *See also Philosophy etc, above.*

Julie ou la Nouvelle Héloïse: lettres de deux amans. Amsterdam 1761; Eloisa or a series of original letters, tr [W. Kenrick] 4 vols 1761.

Letters of an Italian nun and an English gentleman, translated from the French of Rousseau. 1781 (imitation). By [William Combe?]. *See* C. P. Barbier, MLR 56 1961; *See also Combe, below, and* Revue de Littérature Comparée 28 1954.

Reynolds. Eloisa. 1786. A play.

Parallèle entre la Clarice de Richardson et la Nouvelle Héloïse de Rousseau. Journal Etranger Dec 1761.

Mornet, D. (ed). Rousseau, La nouvelle Héloïse. 4 vols

Paris 1925–6. *See his* L'influence de Rousseau au xviiie siècle, Annales Rousseau 8 1912.

Nourrisson, P. Rousseau et Robinson Crusoe. Paris 1931.

Roddier, H. Rousseau en Angleterre au xviiie siècle. Paris [1950].

Voisine, J. J. Rousseau en Angleterre à l'époque romantique [1778–1830]. Paris 1956.

Sainte-Palaye, J. B. Lacurne de. Histoire littéraire des troubadours. Paris 1774; The litterary history of the troubadours, tr S. Dobson 1779.

Mémoires sur l'ancienne chevalerie. Paris 1759–81; Memoirs of ancient chivalry, tr S. Dobson 1784.

These writings, with Les amours du bon vieux temps, 1760 (including Aucassin et Nicolette) were partially responsible for the birth of the romantic cult of the Middle Ages; see L. Gossmann, Medievalism and the ideologies of the Enlightenment: La Curne de Sainte-Palaye, Baltimore 1968.

Saint-Pierre, Jacques Henri Bernardin de. Paul et Virginie. Paris 1787; Paul and Virginie, tr 1788; Paul and Virginia, tr 1789; Paul and Mary tr [D. Malthus] 2 vols 1789; Paul and Virginia, tr H. M. Williams, [Paris?] 1795; tr C. Barett in Old tales and romances, 1795.

La chaumière indienne. Paris 1790; The Indian cottage, tr [E. A. Kendall] 1791; tr 1797.

Scarron, Paul. Le romant comique. Paris 2 pts 1651–7; Scarron's comical romance, tr J. B. [J. Bulteel?] 1665; The comic romance of Monsieur Scarron, tr O. Goldsmith [and another] 1775 (Goldsmith's section an adaptation of Brown's text from Works).

Les nouvelles tragi-comiques. Paris 1655; Dernières œuvres, Paris 1663; Scarron's novels, tr J. Davies [c. 1660] (includes The fruitless precaution; The hypocrites; The innocent adultery), 1665 (suppl including The judge in his own cause: The rival brothers; The invisible mistress: The chastisement of avarice), 1665 (all 7 novels). The unexpected choice, tr J. Davies 1670 is a trn of Plus d'effets que de parolles from Les nouvelles tragi-comiques, 1655.

Oeuvres. Paris 1659; The whole comical works, tr T. Brown, J. Savage etc 3 vols 1700 (vol 2, Avarice chastis'd: or the miser punished, The useless precaution, The hypocrites, The innocent adultery, The generous lover).

Stein, H. Goldsmith's translation of the Roman comique. MLN 49 1934.

Scudéry, Georges de. *See* G. Montgrédien, Bibliographie des œuvres de G. et M. Scudéry, Revue d'Histoire Littéraire de la France 40 1933, 42 1935; *and* A. Cioranescu, Bibliographie de la littérature française du xvii siècle vol 3, Paris 1966.

Les femmes illustres. Paris 1642; tr J. Innes, Edinburgh 1681; The female orators, tr 1714.

Scudéry, Madeleine de. Ibrahim: ou l'illustre Bassa. Paris 1641; Ibrahim: or the illustrious Bassa, tr H. Cogan 1652. Also tragicomedy by Georges de Scudéry (1643) under same title; E. Settle, Ibrahim: the illustrious Bassa, 1677 (play).

Artamène: ou le grand Cyrus. 10 vols Paris 1649–53; The history of Philoxypes and Polyorite, tr 1652 (extrait); Artamenes: or the Grand Cyrus, tr F.G. 5 vols 1653–5; Thomas Killigrew, Cecilia and Clorinda, 1664 (play); John Dryden, Secret love, 1668 (play); J. Banks, Cyrus the Great: or the tragedy of love, 1696 (play).

Clélie. 10 vols Paris 1654–60; Clelia, tr [J. Davies and G. Havers] 5 vols 1656–61.

Almahide: ou l'esclave reine. 8 vols Paris 1660–3; Almahide: or the captive Queen, tr J. Phillips (or J. P. Gent?; *see* Montgrédien, Revue d'Histoire Littéraire de la France 42 1935) 1677; John Dryden, The conquest of Granada, 1672.

Amaryllis to Tityrus: a witty and pleasant novel. Tr 1681.
Boyle, Robert. Partenissa. 1654.
Mackenzie, Sir G. Aretina. 1661.
Crown, J. Pandion and Amphiegia. 1665.

Aragonnes, C. M. de Scudéry, reine du tendre. Paris 1934. On her English reputation.
Schweitzer, J. W. Dryden's use of George [Madeleine] de Scudéry's Almahide. MLN 54 1939, 62 1947.
d'Urfé, Honoré. L'Astrée. Paris 1607–27; tr J. D[avies] 1657–8. First trn 1620.
Voltaire, François Marie Arouet de
For Voltaire's prose works, see under Philosophy, col 99, above. See also Swift, below.
Jovicevich, A. A propos d'une Paméla de Voltaire. French Rev 36 1963. The Lettres d'Amabed.
Croxall, Samuel (ed). A select collection of novels in 6 volumes translated from the originals, by several eminent hands. 6 vols 1720–2. *See* W. H. McBurney, A checklist of English prose fiction 1700–3, Cambridge Mass 1960 pp. 42–3 for contents.

English Authors

Beckford, William. Vathek: conte arabe. Lausanne 1787; Vathek, tr S. Henley 1786. Henley's English trn pbd before French original without authorization.
Hunter, A. O. Le Vathek de Beckford: historique des éditions françaises. Revue de Littérature Comparée 15 1935.
Behn, Mrs Aphra. Oroonoko: or the slave. 1688; Oroonoko, tr P. A. de Laplace, Amsterdam 1745 (widely read in France). *See T. Southern under Drama, above, for French trns and imitations of his dramatized version of Behn's novel;* V. Pinot, Les sources de l'Orphelin de Chine [Voltaire], Revue d'Histoire Littéraire de la France 14 1907.
The fatal beauty of Agnes de Castro. In Aphra Behn, Two new novels, 1688; tr Mme Thiroux d'Arconville, in Romans traduits de l'anglois, 1761. Mrs Behn's novels itself a trn of J. B. de Brilhac, Agnès de Castro, Amsterdam 1688.
Lover's watch: or the art of love. 1696. Not the same as The art of making love, 1688, which is trn of D. L. C. Middlebourg, Le langage muet, 1688; this is an abridgement of Du Vignau des Joannots, Le secrétaire turc, Paris 1688; L'art de faire l'amour: ou la pendule de l'amant, tr B. Bonnecourse, Paris nd.

Rolfe, F. P. 17th-century prose fiction. PMLA 49 1934.
Seeber, E. D. Oroonoko in France. PMLA 51 1936. On place in negrophile literature.
[Bickerstaffe, Isaac]. The life and strange adventures of Ambrose Gwinett. 1770; Le mendiant boiteux ou les aventures d'Ambrose Gwinett, tr [M. L. Castilhon?], Bouillon 1770.
Le Candide anglois. Frankfurt 1781.
Burney, Frances, Mme d'Arblay. Evelina. 1778; Evelina, tr H. Renfer 3 vols Paris 1779; tr G. de La Baume 3 vols 1784.
Cecilia. 1782; Cécilia, tr [H. Rieu], Neuchâtel 1782.
Camilla. 1796; Camilla, tr J. B. Denis Després and J. M. Deschamps 5 vols Paris 1797.
Oeuvres. Tr H. Rieu and H. Renfer 10 vols Geneva 1784 (with Evelina and Cecilia).
Cleland, John. Memoirs of a woman of pleasure. 1748; La fille de joye, tr Lambert [or L. C. Fougeret de Monbron], Lampsaque 1751; tr 2 vols 1776.
[Combe, William? but attributed to J.-J. Rousseau, E. Blower, Marianna Alcoforado]. Letters of an Italian nun and an English gentleman, translated from the French of J.-J. Rousseau. 1781; Maria ou Lettres d'un gentilhomme anglais à une religieuse, tr Paris 1787; Lettres d'un jeune lord à une religieuse italienne, tr [Mme Suard ?], Paris 1788.

Barbier, C. P. Letters of an Italian nun and an English gentleman 1781. Revue de Littérature Comparée 28 1954.
Day, Thomas. The history of Sandford and Merton. 3 pts 1783–9; Sandford et Merton, tr [A. Berquin] 2 pts in 7 instalments Paris 1786–7. Important in development of juvenile literature in France.
Carrière, J. M. A French adaptation of Sandford and Merton. MLN 50 1935.
Defoe, Daniel. The life and strange surprizing adventures of Robinson Crusoe. 3 vols 1719–20; La vie et les avantures surprenantes de Robinson Crusoe, tr Thémiseul de Saint-Hyacinthe and Justus van Effen 3 vols Amsterdam 1720–1, 2 vols 1720 (as Les avantures surprenantes de Robinson Crusoe); L'Isle de Robinson Crusoe, tr de Montreille [abbé Savin] 1758 (also as Robinson dans son île); tr G.E.J.M.L. [G. E. J. de Montmorency-Laval] 2 vols Paris 1797 (bilingual edn). Rochedieu alone lists 26 edns for 18th century.
[Imitations of Robinson Crusoe]. *See* C. A. Rochedieu, Bibliography of French translations of English works, Chicago 1948, p. 80; *also* Zeitschrift für Vergleichende Litteratur-Geschichte, 4, 6, 9 1891–6; P. Dottin, Defoe et la France, É & S 13 1931; W. E. Mann, Robinson Crusoe en France, Paris 1916; G. Bonno, La culture et la civilisation britanniques, Trans Amer Philosophical Soc 38 1948 pp. 67–9 etc. The clearest and best known example is Prévost, Le philosophe anglois: ou histoire de Monsieur Cleveland, 8 vols Paris 1731–9.
The fortunes and misfortunes of the famous Moll Flanders. 1722; Mémoires et aventures de Mlle Moll Flanders, tr 1761. Prévost's Manon Lescaut not now regarded as influenced by Moll Flanders.
Prévost d'Exiles, A. F. Possible echoes in Doyen de Killerine, 1735–40; possible use of Defoe, A tour through the whole island of Great Britain, 1721–6 for the Mémoires d'un homme de qualité, 1728–31. Bonno claims that 'Prévost est à cette époque le seul auteur français pour qui Defoe soit autre chose que l'auteur de Robinson Crusoe'.
A narrative of all the robberies of Jack Shepherd. 1724; La vie et les vols du fameux Jean Sheppard, tr Amsterdam 1725.
The political history of the Devil. 1726; Histoire du diable, 2 vols Amsterdam 1729.

Mann, W. E. Robinson Crusoe en France. Paris 1916.
Dottin, P. Defoe et la France. É & S 13 1931.
—— Defoe et ses romans. 3 vols Paris 1924.
Pire, G. Rousseau et Robinson Crusoe. Revue de Littérature Comparée 30 1956.
Fielding, Henry. History of Joseph Andrews. 2 vols 1742; Les aventures de Joseph Andrews, tr [P. F. G. Desfontaines] 2 vols 1743.
The life of Mr Jonathan Wild the Great. 1743; Histoire de Jonathan Wild le Grand, tr C. Picquet 2 vols 1763.
Journey from this world to the next. 1743; Julien l'apostat: ou voyage dans l'autre monde, tr [Kaufmann] 1765 (for 1754?).
Adventures of Roderick Random. *See* Smollett, *below;* at first attributed to Fielding by French translator.
History of Tom Jones, a foundling. 6 vols 1749; Histoire de Tom Jones: ou l'enfant trouvé, tr M.D.L.P. [Laplace] 2 vols Amsterdam 1750, 4 vols 'Londres' (for Paris) 1750; tr P. A. de Laplace and Davaux 4 vols Paris 1796. Laplace's abridged trn suppressed on pbn; suppression not enforced, however. Cuts restored by Davaux in 1796 edn; Poinsinet, Tom Jones: comédie lyrique, [1765], Paris 1766; Desforges, Tom Jones à Londres, Paris 1782 (play); Desforges, Fellamar et Tom Jones, 1787 (play).
Amelia. 4 vols 1752; Amélie, tr M. J. Riccoboni 3 vols Paris 1743; tr [P. F. or Mme de Puisieux] 2 vols 1762.

Works. 4 vols 1762; Oeuvres, 14 vols Geneva 1781–2; tr P. A. de Laplace, P. F. G. Desfontaines, Picquet et al 23 vols Paris 1797.

Wells, J. E. Henry Fielding and the History of Charles XII. JEGP 11 1912.
Digeon, A. Les romans de Fielding. Paris 1923.
Eaves, T. C. The publication of the first translations of Tom Jones. Library 3rd ser 26 1945.
Jones, B. P. Was there a temporary suppression of Tom Jones in France? MLN 76 1961.
Powers, L. H. Tom Jones and J. de La Vallée [Marivaux]. Papers of Michigan Acad 47 1962.
Fielding, Sarah. The adventures of David Simple in search of a faithful friend. 1744; Le véritable ami: ou la vie de David Simple, tr Skunk [P. A. de Laplace], Amsterdam 1749.
History of Charlotte Summers, the fortunate parish girl. 1749; L'orpheline angloise: ou histoire de Charlotte Summers, tr [P. A. de Laplace] 4 vols 1751.
History of Betty Barnes. 1753; Betsy Barnes, tr [Eidous] 2 vols nd.
History of Ophelia. 1760; Ophélie tr [Mme Belot, later Mme Durey de Meynières] 2 vols Amsterdam 1763.
Goldsmith, Oliver. The citizen of the world. 1760–1; collected 1762; Le citoyen du monde, tr [P.] P[oivre] 3 vols Amsterdam 1763. Goldsmith's novel based on d'Argens' Lettres chinoises, Hague 1739; hence original title of Chinese letters.
Asem: an eastern tale. 1765; Asême: conte philosophique, tr B. A. Golitzyn [1787?].
The vicar of Wakefield. 1766; Le vicaire de Wakefield, tr Mme de Montesson 2 vols 1767; Le ministre de Wakefield, tr Rose 2 vols 1767; tr E. Aignan 2 vols Paris 1796; tr P. L. C. Gin, Paris 1797; Le curé de Wakefield, tr J. Bizet, Dublin 1797; Le curé anglois, tr E. de Flinville 2 vols Paris 1799.
The history of Francis Wills. nd; Histoire de François Wills, tr 1773; tr Neuchâtel 1774. By Goldsmith? See A. L. Sells, RES 11 1935.

Sells, A. L. Les sources françaises de Goldsmith. Paris 1924.
Smith, H. J. Goldsmith's The citizen of the world. New Haven 1926. See also MP 19 1921.
Barbier, C. P. Goldsmith en France au xviiie siècle. Revue de Littérature Comparée 25 1951.
Haywood, Eliza. The British recluse. 1722; La recluse angloise; tr Amsterdam 1770.
Idalia. 1723; Idalie, tr Amsterdam 1770.
Cleomelia. 1727; Histoire de Cléomélie, tr 1777.
The fortunate foundlings. 1744: C. P. J. de Crébillon, Les heureux orphelins, Paris 1754; The happy orphans, tr 1758. See H. S. Hughes, MP 17 1920.
A letter from H . . . G . . . g esquire. 1750; Lettre de H . . . G . . . g [Henry Goring], écuyer, tr 1757.
History of Miss Betsy Thoughtless. 1751; L'étourdie, tr de Fleuriau 4 vols Paris 1754.

Whicher, G. F. Life and romances of Mrs E. Haywood. New York 1915. With bibliography.
Hervey, James. Meditations among the tombs, Contemplations on the night. 1746–7; Méditations sur les tombeaux, [tr M. Peyron, rev Le Tourneur] in Les nuits de Young, Paris 1770; also as Les méditations et contemplations, Paris 1770; and as Méditations d'Hervey, Paris 1771; Méditations sur les tombeaux, tr Mme Thiroux d'Arcanville, Paris 1771.
Bridel, J. P. L. Les tombeaux. Lausanne 1779.
Holcroft, Thomas. The adventures of Hugh Trevor. 6 vols 1794–7; Aventures de Hugues Trévor ou le Gil Blas anglais, tr A. S. M. Cantwell 4 vols Paris 1798.
Baine, R. M. Holcroft and the revolutionary novel. Athens Georgia 1965.

Johnson, Samuel. An account of the life of Mr Richard Savage. 1744; Histoires de Richard Savage, tr P. P. F. Le Tourneur, Paris 1771.
The rambler. 1750–2; Morceaux choisis du Rambler ou du Rôdeur, tr Boulard, Paris 1785.
The idler. 1758–60; Le paresseux, tr Varney 2 vols Paris 1790.
Journey to the Western Islands of Scotland. 1775; tr in Nouveau recueil de voyages au nord de l'Europe et de L'Asie, tr Geneva 1785–6. Boswell's Journal of a tour to the Hebrides with Samuel Johnson, 1785, was tr as Détail authentique des malheurs et de la fuite du prince Charles Edouard dans les Hébrides, Paris 1786.
The Prince of Abissinia: a tale [Rasselas]. 1759; Histoire de Rasselas, prince d'Abissinie, tr Mme B[elot] 2 vols Amsterdam 1760; tr de Fouchecour, Paris 1789.

Clifford, J. L. For Candide and Rasselas. New York Times Book Rev 19 April 1959.
Clifford, J. L. and D. J. Greene. Bibliography of Johnsonian studies [section B.XVII]. In Johnsonian studies, ed M. Wahba, Cairo 1962.
Lewis, Matthew Gregory. The monk: a romance. 1796; Le moine, tr J. M. Deschamps et al 4 vols 1796; tr Paris 1797; also as Le Jacobin espagnol, 4 vols Paris 1798.
Camille St Aubin and Ribié. Le moine. Paris 1798. A play; also as 3-act melodrama.
Baldensperger, F. Le moine de Lewis dans la littérature française. Jnl of Comparative Lit 1 1903.
Mackenzie, Henry. The man of feeling. 1771; L'homme sensible, traduit de l'anglais de Brook, tr F. de Saint-Ange, Amsterdam 1775; tr Peyron 1775; Harley: ou l'homme sensible, tr J. M. Plane, Paris 1797.
The man of the world. 1773; L'homme du monde, tr [F. de Saint-Ange] 4 vols Amsterdam 1775.
Julia de Roubigné. 1777; Histoire de Julie de Roubigné, Rotterdam 1779; Lettres de Julie Roubigné à Pauline Clermont, tr [J. J. A. David de Saint-Georges] 1789.

Cameron, M. M. L'essai sur Mackenzie de Chateaubriand. Canada Français 28 1941.
Macpherson, James. See Verse, above.
Manley, Mary de La Rivière. The secret history of Queen Zarah and the Zarazians. Albigeon (for London) 1705; Histoire secrète de la reine Zarah et des Zarasiens ou de la duchesse de Marlborough, 2 vols Albigion (for Paris?) 1708. 1712 edn gives key to names.
Secret memoirs and manners of several persons of quality from the New Atlantis. 1709; L'Atlantis, tr [H. Scheurléer and J. Rousset] 2 vols Hague 1713.
Moore, John. Seluco. 1786; Zelucco, tr S. de Cantwell 4 vols Paris 1796.
Edward. 1796; Edouard, tr [A. S. M. Cantwell] 3 vols Paris 1797.
Mordaunt: being sketches of life in various countries. 1800; L'histoire de Miss Mordaunt, 2 vols 1798 (first pbd in French).
Radcliffe, Ann. The castles of Athlin and Dunbayne. 1789; Le château d'Athlin et de Dunbayne, tr [Soulès] 2 vols Paris 1798.
Sicilian romance. 1790; Julia: ou les souterrains du château de Mazzini, tr [M. Fleury] 2 vols Paris 1798.
Romance of the forest. 1791; La forêt, tr [F. Soulès] 3 vols Paris 1794.
Mysteries of Udolpho. 1794; Les mystères d'Udolphe, tr V. de Chastenay et al 4 vols Paris 1797: G. Duval, Montoni: ou le château d'Udolphe, Paris 1798 (play); Loisel-Fréogate, Le château du diable, Paris 1798 (play); J.H.F.L. [J. H. Ferdinand La Martelière], Le testament, Paris 1798 (play); [R. C. Guilbert de Pixérécourt], Le château des Apennins: ou le fantôme vivant, Paris 1799 (play).

The Italian. 1797; L'Italien, tr [A. M. Morellet] 3 vols Paris 1796; Éléonore de Rosalba, tr [M. Gay-Allard] 7 vols Paris 1797.

Lévy, M. Une source d'Ann Radcliffe: Les mémoires du comte de Comminge [Baculard d'Arnaud]. Caliban 1 1964.

Mayo, O. A. Radcliffe and Ducray-Duminil. MLR 36 1941.

Reeve, Clara. The champion of virtue. 1777, 1778 (as the old English baron); Le vieux baron anglais, tr M.D.L.P. [de Laplace], Amsterdam 1787; also as Le champion de la vertu, and as Edouard ou le spectre du château, 1800. A novel of terror.

The two mentors. 1783; Les deux mentors, tr [de Laplace], Amsterdam 1784.

Richardson, Samuel. *See also Diderot, Prévost, Rousseau above.*

Pamela. 2 vols 1740; Paméla ou la vertu récompensée, tr [A. F. Prévost and Aubert de La Chesnaye des Bois] 2 vols 1742; Lettres sur Paméla, tr and adapted 1742; L. de Boissy, Paméla en France (1743), Paris 1745 (play); P. C. Nivelle de La Chaussée, Paméla (1743), Paris 1762 (play); Voltaire, Nanine (1743), Paris 1749 (play); F. T. M. de Baculard d'Arnaud, Nancy: ou la nouvelle Paméla, Paris 1762; 1764 (as Fanny ou l'heureux repentir: histoire angloise); tr 1766 (as Fanny or the happy repentance), 1767 (as Fanny ou la nouvelle Paméla); M. J. Riccoboni, Paméla françoise: ou la vertu en célibat et en mariage, Amsterdam 1768; Histoire de Paméla dans le temps de sa liberté jusqu'à son mariage, 2 vols Frankfurt 1771 (anon); F. de Neufchâteau, Paméla (1793), Paris 1795 (play).

Marianne : ou la nouvelle Paméla, 2 vols Rotterdam 1765 is trn of E. Kimber, Maria, 1764.

Clarissa. 7 vols 1747–8; Lettres angloises: ou histoire de Miss Clarisse Harlowe, tr A. F. Prévost 6 vols 1751–2 (incomplete); Supplément aux lettres angloises tr [J. B. A. Suard], Lyons 1762 (with Lettres posthumes etc); Clarisse Harlow, tr P. P. F. Le Tourneur 12 vols Geneva 1785–6 (fuller text); Mme M. Leprince de Beaumont, La nouvelle Clarice, 2 vols Lyons 1767 (title is sole link with Richardson); J. F. Née de La Rochelle, Clarisse Harlowe, Paris 1786 (play); [N. Lemercier], Clarisse Harlow, Paris 1792 (play).

The history of Sir Charles Grandison. 7 vols 1753–4; Nouvelles lettres angloises: ou histoire du chevalier Grandison, tr A. F. Prévost 4 vols Amsterdam 1755–6[8]; Histoire de Sir Charles Grandisson, tr [G. J. Monod] 7 vols Göttingen 1756; Suite des nouvelles lettres angloises, tr A. F. Prévost 4 vols Paris 1758; Bastide, Gésancourt à Clémentine: tragédie bourgeoise (1766), Paris 1766; Alphonse d'Inange: ou le nouveau Grandisson, 4 vols Paris 1788 (anon).

Canby, H. S. Pamela abroad. MLN 18 1903.

Macaulay, G. C. Richardson and his French predecessors. MLR 8 1913.

Crane, R. S. Richardson's relation to French fiction. MP 16 1919; also MLR 17 1922. On Marivaux's Vie de Marianne; *see also Marivaux, above.*

Facteau, B. A. Les romans de Richardson sur la scène française. Paris 1927.

Roddier, H. R. Challes, inspirateur de Richardson et de l'abbé Prévost. Revue de Littérature Comparée 21 1947.

Pons, C. Richardson et la Nouvelle Héloïse. Etudes Anglaises 14 1961.

Jovicevich, A. A propos d'une Pamela de Voltaire. French Rev 36 1963.

Sheridan, Frances, Mrs Thomas. Memoirs of Miss Sidney Bidulph. 1761; Mémoires de Miss Sidney Bidulph, tr [J. B. R. Robinet] 3 vols Amsterdam 1762; Mémoires

pour servir à l'histoire de la vertu, [tr A. F. Prévost], Cologne (for Paris) 1762. *See* S. C. Chew, Prévost's Mémoires, MLN 54 1939; S. Mercier, L'habitant de Guadeloupe, tr 1762.

Nourjahad. 1767; Nourjahad: histoire orientale, tr [Mme de Sérionne], Frankfurt 1769.

Smollett, Tobias. The adventures of Roderick Random. 2 vols 1748; Aventures de Roderick Random, traduites de l'anglois de Fielding, tr [P. Hernandez, P. F. de Puisieux] 3 vols 1761. Random continued to be attributed to Fielding and entered his works.

The adventures of Peregrine Pickle. 4 vols 1751; Histoire et avantures de Sir Williams Pickle, tr [F. V. Toussaint] 4 vols Amsterdam 1753 (anon).

The adventures of Ferdinand, Count Fathom. 2 vols 1753; Fathom et Melville: roman traduit de Smollet [first novel over Smollett's name in France], tr D. de Saint-George 4 vols Paris 1796; tr [T. P. Bertin] 4 vols Paris 1798; also as Les aventures de Ferdinand count Fathom, and as Falhemel et Melvil.

A complete history of England. 4 vols 1757–8 11 vols 1758–9; Histoire d'Angleterre, tr Targe 19 vols Orléans 1759–64.

Travels through France and Italy. 1766. Smollett was long known as the historian and author of the Travels in France, his novels appearing anon or attributed to Fielding until Count Fathom. Despite their reputation, the Travels were apparently not translated.

Works. 1783; Oeuvres complètes, tr Frenais 6 vols 1787; [with La Baume] 3 vols Paris 1797.

See also Lesage, above. On Smollett as translator and editor, *see* F. Cordasco, N & Q 24 Dec 1948; L. M. Knapp, PQ 44 1965 (Fénelon); Cordasco, MLQ 10 1949; Knapp, MLN 47 1932; A. Lawrence, Revue de Littérature Comparée 12 1932 (Lesage); E. Joliat, MLN 54 1939 (Voltaire).

Joliat, E. Smollett et la France. Paris 1935.

Streeter, H. W. Smollett's novels in France. Romanic Rev 26 1935.

Sterne, Laurence. *See also Diderot, above.*

The life and opinions of Tristram Shandy. 9 vols York (later London) 1760–7; La vie et les opinions de Tristram Shandy, tr J. P. Frenais 1760 (pt i); 2 vols York and Paris 1776 (pts 1–2); tr [J. P. Frenais and Griffet de La Baume), Paris 1784–5 (full text); tr [C. F. de Bonnay] 2 vols York and Paris 1785; at least 12 edns before 1800; Gorgy, Ann' Quin Bredouille: ou le petit cousin de Tristram Shandy, 6 vols Paris 1791–2; Denis Diderot, Jacques le fataliste, Paris 1796 (written c. 1773–4).

A sentimental journey. 2 vols 1768; Le voyage sentimental, tr J. F. Frenais 2 vols Amsterdam 1769; Voyage sentimental en France, tr [F. Michel], Paris 1787; rev [P. Crassous] 3 vols Paris 1799; at least 23 edns before 1800; Gorgy, Nouveau voyage sentimental, 1784; [G. de La Baume], Nouveau voyage en France de Sterne, tr M.D.L.B., Geneva and Paris 1785 (largely Tristram Shandy); F. Vernes, Voyageur sentimental, Neuchâtel 1786; X. de Maistre, Voyage autour de ma chambre, Turin 1794.

Letters from Yorick to Eliza. 1773; Lettres d'Yorick à Eliza, tr [J. P. Frenais], Paris 1776; tr M. Peyron 1776; tr G. T. F. Raynal 1784.

Baldwin, C. S. The literary influence of Sterne in France. PMLA 17 1902.

Barton, F. B. Étude sur l'influence de Laurence Sterne en France. Paris 1911.

Fredman, A. G. Diderot and Sterne. New York 1955.

Dédéyan, C. L'Angleterre dans la pensée de Diderot. Paris 1958.

Fluchère, H. Laurence Sterne. Paris 1961.

Mayoux, J.-J. Sterne parmi nous. Revue de Littérature Comparée 36 1962.

Stout, G. D. Borrowings in Sterne from Rabelais and Cervantes. Eng Lang Notes 3 1965.

Swift, Jonathan. A tale of a tub. 1704; Le conte du tonneau, tr [J. van Effen] 2 vols Hague 1721; vol 3, Traité des dissensions entre les nobles et le peuple, 'Alethobathopseudopolis' (for Amsterdam) 1733; Productions de l'esprit, tr [Saunier de Beaumont, after J. van Effen] 2 vols Paris 1736.

[Macé, R.]. Les trois just-au-corps: conte bleu. Dublin (for Hague?) 1721.

Travels into several remote nations of the world by Lemuel Gulliver. 1726; Voyages du capitaine Lemuel Gulliver en divers pays éloignez, 2 vols Hague 1726 (virtually complete text, unidentified translator); vol 3, Hague 1730, is spurious, being d'Alais, Voyages de Sévarambes, 1677, and Corolini di Marco's Key, 1726, in trn; Voyages de Gulliver, tr [P. F. G. Desfontaines] 2 vols Paris 1727 (abridged, gallicized, adapted, omitting vol 3 of original). Goulding records 14 edns before 1797 of Desfontaines' trn and over 180 since 1813. T. Morris has disposed of claims that Markan ghosted Desfontaines' trn; see Stud on Voltaire & Eighteenth Century 19 1961.

[Desfontaines, P. F. G.] Le nouveau Gulliver: ou voyage de Jean Gulliver fils du capitaine Gulliver [forming 2 vols of Voyages de Gulliver]. 4 vols Paris 1730; tr English as The travels of Mr John Gulliver, tr J. Lockman 2 vols 1731.

Marivaux, P. C. de C. de. Les voyages de Glantzby. 1729. A comedy.

Béthune. Relation du monde de Mercure. 1750.

Voltaire. Micromégas. [1752].

Villeneuve, de. Le voyageur philosophe. 1761.

Robert. Les voyages de milord Céton. Paris 1765.

Gloor, G. Swift und die Franzosen. Zürich 1922.

Goulding, S. Swift en France. Paris 1924. See also C. M. Webster, Omissions from Swift en France, MLN 47 1932.

Digeon, A. Gulliver et La Bruyère. Revue Anglo-américaine 3 1926.

Williams, H. Dean Swift's library. Cambridge 1932. French books one-fifth of total.

Pons, E. Rabelais and Swift. In Mélanges Lefranc, Paris 1936.

— Swift et Pascal. Etudes Anglaises 4 1952.

Pagliaro, H. E. Paradox in La Rochefoucauld and some English followers. PMLA 79 1964.

Irwin, A. B. Swift as translator of the French of Sir W. Temple. Stud in Eng Lit 1500–1900 6 1966.

Thacker, C. Swift and Voltaire. Hermathena 1968.

Walpole, Horace. The castle of Otranto. 1765; Le château d'Otrante, tr M.E. [M. A. Eidous] 2 vols Amsterdam 1767; Isabelle et Théodore, tr 2 vols Leipzig 1797.

Loaisel-Tréogate. Le château du diable. 1792.

Secondary Sources

See sections on the Gothic novel, or novel of terror, and on Prose fiction, in General Literary Relations, above.

MacFarlan, J. English romance in French translation. Library 4 1892.

Texte, J. J.-J. Rousseau et les origines du cosmopolitisme littéraire. Paris 1895, 1899.

Clapp, J. M. An 18th-century attempt at a critical view of the novel: the Bibliothèque Universelle des Romans. PMLA 25 1910.

Mornet, D. Les enseignements des bibliothèques privées 1750–80. Revue d'Histoire Littéraire de la France 17 1910. 440 English novels (for 369 French) in 392 18th-century library lists.

— Rousseau, La nouvelle Héloïse. 4 vols Paris 1925–6. Introd on 18th-century novel in England and France.

Gregory, A. The French Revolution and the English novel. Paris 1915.

Hughes, H. S. Notes on 18th-century fictional translations. MP 17 1920.

Gill-Mark, G. A. M. de Boccage. Paris 1927.

Green, F. C. French novelists, manners and ideas. 1928.

— Minuet: a critical survey of French and English literary ideas in the 18th century. 1935.

Storer, M. E. La mode des contes de fées 1685–1700. Paris 1928. On Mme d'Aulnoy, Mlle Bernard, Mlle de La Force, Mme Murat, Perrault et al.

Hunter, A. C. Les opinions du baron Grimm sur le roman anglais. Revue de Littérature Comparée 12 1932.

Tompkins, J. M. S. The popular novel in England 1770–1800. 1932.

Roberts, W. Spurious 'English' novels. TLS 26 Jan 1933.

Streeter, H. W. The 18th-century English novel in French translation: a bibliographical study. New York 1936.

Baldensperger, F. English artistic prose and its debt to French writers. Modern Languages Forum 29 1944.

Castex, P. G. Le conte fantastique en France. Paris 1951.

Bundy, J. Fréron and the English novel. Revue de Littérature Comparée 36 1962.

Barchilon, J. The uses of the fairy-tale in the 18th century. Stud on Voltaire & Eighteenth Century 24 1963.

May, G. Le dilemme du roman au xviiie siècle. Paris 1963.

— The influence of English fiction on the French mid-18th-century novel. In Aspects of the 18th century, ed E. R. Wasserman, Baltimore 1965.

Alter, R. The rogue's progress: studies in the picaresque novel. Cambridge Mass 1964.

Jost, F. Le roman épistolaire au xviiie siècle. Comparative Lit Stud 3 1966.

Weitzman, A. J. The oriental tale in the 18th century. Stud on Voltaire & Eighteenth Century 58 1967.

Lévy, M. Le roman gothique anglais 1764–1824. Toulouse 1968. With chronological bibliography.

S. S. B. T.

(4) GERMAN

See also Translations from German, col 1537, below.

General Studies

The High Dutch Minerva à la mode. 1680. A German grammar frequently attributed to Martin Aedler.

Offelen, Heinrich. Zweyfache gründliche Sprach-Lehr, für Hochteutsche englisch, und für Engländer hochteutsch zu lernen. 1687.

King, John (Johann Koenig). A compleat English guide for High Germans. 1706. A German edn appeared Leipzig 1716.

— A royal compleat grammar, English and High German: das ist, eine königliche vollkommene Grammatica in Englisch und Hochteutscher Sprach, mit einem

Wegweiser aller Curiositäten so in und umb London herumb und sonsten in Engelland zu sehen und zu finden sind. 1715. An English grammar with examples tr into German.

Ludwig, C. Englisch-teutsch-französisches Lexikon. Leipzig 1706.

Bachmair, John James. A complete German grammar. 1751.

Johnson, Samuel. A dictionary of the English language. 1755.

Adelung, J. C. Neues grammatisch-kritisches Wörterbuch der englischen Sprache für die Deutschen aus dem grösseren englischen Werke des Hrn Samuel Johnson gezogen. Leipzig 1783–96.

The true guide to the German language. 1758.

Wendeborn, G. F. A. The elements of German grammar. 1774.
— An introduction to German grammar. 1790.
Hesse, E. A vocabulary of the German tongue. 1793.
Crabb, G. A complete introduction to the knowledge of the German language: or a translation from Adelung, arranged and adapted to the English learner [i.e. J. C. Adelung's Deutsche Sprachlehre für Schulen, Berlin 1781]. 1799, 1800.
— Elements of German and English conversation. 1800.
— Selections of German prose and poetry, with a dictionary. 1800.
Render, W. A practical grammar of the German tongue. 1799.
Noehden, G. H. A grammar of the German language. 1800.
Carr, C. T. German grammars in England in the nineteenth century. MLR 30 1935.
— Early German grammars in England. JEGP 36 1937.
Aehle, W. Die Anfänge des Unterrichts in der englischen Sprache besonders auf den Ritterakademien. Hamburg 1938.
Erämetsä, E. Englische Lehnprägungen in der deutschen Empfindsamkeit des 18 Jahrhunderts. 1955.
— Über den englischen Einfluss auf den deutschen Wortschatz des 18 Jahrhunderts. Neuphilologische Mitteilungen 59 1958.
Ganz, P. F. Der Einfluss des Englischen auf den deutschen Wortschatz 1640–1815. 1957.
Acta eruditorum. Leipzig 1682–1739; Nova acta eruditorum (Leipzig) 1732–55. Reviews of works of Locke, Milton, Dryden etc.
Morhof, D. G. Unterricht von der deutschen Sprache. Lübeck and Frankfurt 1682. Contains earliest connected account of English literature in German. First German writer to mention Shakespeare.
Meibom, Heinrich. Programma publicis in notitiam regnorum et rerumpublicarum Europae praelectionibus praemissum in qua simul de anglicanae historiae periodis et praecipuis scriptoribus disseretur. Helmstadt 1702.
Toland, John. An account of the Courts of Prussia and Hanover. 1705.
Lessing, G. E. et al. Briefe, die neueste Litteratur betreffend. 23 pts Berlin 1759–65.
Mackenzie, H. An account of the German theatre. Trans of Royal Soc of Edinburgh 1790.
A concise review of original German books. Pt I, Edinburgh 1796.
Thompson, Alexander. The German miscellany. Perth 1796.
The German Museum: or Monthly Repository of the Literature of Germany, the North and the Continent in General. 1800–1. Founded C. Geisweiler. Ed P. Will and A. F. M. Willich.
Joret, Charles. La littérature allemande au xviiie siècle dans ses rapports avec la littérature française et avec la littérature anglaise. Paris 1876.
Weddigen, O. Vermittler des deutschen Geistes in England und Nord-Amerika. Archiv 59 1878.
Haller, A. von. Tagebücher seiner Reise nach Deutschland, Holland und England 1723–7. Ed L. Hirzel, Leipzig 1883.
Koch, Max. Über die Beziehungen der englischen Literatur zur deutschen im 18 Jahrhundert. Leipzig 1883.
— Zur Geschichte der englischen Einwirkungen auf die deutsche Literatur im xviii Jahrhundert. Zeitschrift für Vergleichende Literaturgeschichte 4 1891.
Schaible, K. H. Geschichte der Deutschen in England. Strasbourg 1885.
Cook, A. S. Germans in England in the 18th century. MLN 4 1889.
Seidensticker, O. The relation of English to German literature in the 18th century. Philadelphia 1890.
Vetter, T. Zürich als Vermittlerin englischer Literatur im xviii Jahrhundert. Zürich 1891.

— Bodmer und die englische Literatur. In Bodmer Denkschrift, Zürich 1899.
Süpfle, T. Beiträge zur Geschichte der deutschen Literatur in England im letzten Drittel des 18 Jahrhunderts. Zeitschrift für Vergleichende Literaturgeschichte 6 1893.
Flindt, E. Über den Einfluss der englischen Literatur auf die deutsche des xviii Jahrhunderts. Charlottenburg 1897.
Markgraf, E. Einfluss der deutschen Literatur auf die englische am Ende des achtzehnten und im ersten Drittel des neunzehnten Jahrhunderts. Leipzig 1901.
Walz, A. The American Revolution and German literature. MLN 16 1901.
Zeiger, T. Beiträge zur Geschichte des Einflusses der neueren deutschen Literatur auf die englische. Leipzig 1901.
Haney, J. L. German literature in England before 1790. Americana Germanica 4 1902.
Herzfeld, G. Zur Geschichte der deutschen Literatur in England. Archiv 110 1903.
Koeppel, E. Deutsche Strömungen in der englischen Literatur. Strasbourg 1910.
Waterhouse, G. The literary relations of England and Germany in the seventeenth century. Cambridge 1914.
Simmons, L. V. T. Goethe's lyric poems in English translation prior to 1860. Madison 1919.
Kelly, J. A. England and the Englishman in German literature of the eighteenth century. New York 1921.
Morgan, B. Q. A critical bibliography of German literature in English translation 1481–1927. Madison 1922, New York 1965 (rev and enlarged); Supplement 1928–55, New York 1965.
— German literature in British magazines 1750–1860. Madison 1949.
Stokoe, F. W. German influence in the English romantic period 1788–1818. Cambridge 1926.
Orrick, J. B. Matthew Arnold and Goethe. Pbns of Eng Goethe Soc 4 1928.
Stockley, V. German literature in England 1750–1830. 1929.
Schirmer, G. Die Schweiz im Spiegel englischer und amerikanischer Literatur bis 1848. Zürich 1929.
Blömker, F. Das Verhältnis von Bürgers lyrischer und epischlyrischer Dichtung zur englischen Literatur. Münster 1930.
Matheson, P. E. German visitors to England 1770–95. In Studies in European literature: Taylorian lectures, Oxford 1930.
Schort, L. Herders Beziehungen zur englischen Literatur. Breslau 1930.
Jantzen, H. Zeugnisse für das Eindringen der englischen Literatur des 18 Jahrhunderts in Deutschland. E Studien 116 1931.
Marcus, H. Friedrich der Grosse in der englischen Literatur. Leipzig 1931.
Price, L. M. The reception of English literature in Germany. Berkeley 1932.
— Holland as a mediator of English-German literary influences in the seventeenth and eighteenth centuries. MLQ 2 1941.
— C. H. Schmid and his translations of English drama 1767–89. Berkeley 1942.
— English literature in Germany. Berkeley 1953.
— The English domestic novel in Germany 1740–99. In Libris et litteris, 1959.
Hunter, A. C. Les opinions du Baron Grimm sur le roman anglais. Revue de Littérature Comparée 12 1932.
Ewen, F. The prestige of Schiller in England 1788–1859. New York 1932.
Boyd, J. Goethe's knowledge of English literature. Oxford 1933.
Radczun, W. Das englische Urteil über die Deutschen bis zur Mitte des 17 Jahrhunderts. Berlin 1933.
Blassneck, M. Frankreich als Vermittler englisch-

deutscher Einflüsse im 17 und 18 Jahrhundert. Leipzig 1934.

Allen, D. C. Early eighteenth-century literary relations between England and Germany. MLN 49 1934.

Price, M. B. and L. M. Price. The publication of English literature in Germany in the eighteenth century. Berkeley 1934.

—— The publication of English Humaniora in Germany in the 18th century. Berkeley 1955.

Weber, C. A. Bristols Bedeutung für die englische Romantik und die deutsch-englischen Beziehungen. Halle 1935.

Gillies, A. A Scottish correspondent of Wieland's and the importation of German into Scotland. MLR 30 1935.

Willoughby, L. A. Schiller in England and Germany. Pbns of Eng Goethe Soc 11 1935.

—— Coleridge und Deutschland. Germanisch-romanische Monatsschrift 24 1936.

—— Goethe looks at the English. MLR 50 1955.

—— Goethe and the English language. German Life & Letters 10 1957.

—— Oscar Wilde and Goethe. Pbns of Eng Goethe Soc 35 1965.

Vail, C. C. D. Lessing's relation to the English language and literature. New York 1936.

Carritt, E. F. Addison, Kant and Wordsworth. E & S 22 1937.

Frehn, P. Der Einfluss der englischen Literatur auf Deutschlands Musiker und Musik. Düsseldorf 1937.

Klein, K. K. Literaturgeschichte des Deutschtums im Ausland. Leipzig 1939.

Morley, E. J. Coleridge in Germany, 1799. In her Wordsworth and Coleridge, Princeton 1939.

Metz, R. England und die deutsche Philosophie. Stuttgart 1941.

Loomis, C. G. English writers in Gottsched's Handlexikon. JEGP 42 1943.

Walz, J. A. English influence on the German vocabulary of the eighteenth century. Monatshefte 35 1943.

Hegemann, D. V. Boswell's interviews with Gottsched and Gellert. JEGP 46 1947.

Weydt, G. Die Einwirkung Englands auf die deutsche Literatur des 18 Jahrhunderts. Minden 1948.

Federmann, A. Der junge Goethe und England. Berlin 1949.

Purdie, E. Some problems of translation in the 18th century in Germany. E Studies 30 1949.

—— Observations on some eighteenth-century German versions of the witches' scenes in Macbeth. Shakespeare Jahrbuch 92 1956.

Scott, D. F. S. Some English correspondents of Goethe. 1949.

Baldensperger, F. and W. P. Friederich. Bibliography of comparative literature. Chapel Hill 1950.

Todd, F. M. Wordsworth in Germany. MLR 47 1952.

Robson-Scott, W. D. German travellers in England 1400–1800. Oxford 1953.

Metzdorf, R. F. Samuel Johnson in Brunswick. MLN 68 1953.

Rehder, H. J. N. Meinhard und seine Übersetzungen. Urbana 1953.

Oppel, H. Der Einfluss der englischen Literatur auf die deutsche. Berlin 1954.

Wais, K. Schillers Wirkungsgeschichte im Ausland. Deutsche Vierteljahrsschrift für Literaturwissenschaft 29 1955.

Wilkie, J. R. Goethe's English friend Lupton. German Life & Letters 9 1955.

Guthke, K. S. Englische Vorromantik und deutscher Sturm und Drang: M. G. Lewis' Stellung in der Geschichte der deutsch-englischen Literaturbeziehungen. Göttingen 1958.

Frey, J. R. American Schiller literature: a bibliography. JEGP 57 1958.

Witte, W. Schiller and Burns and other essays. Oxford 1959.

Mason, E. C. Deutsche und englische Romantik: eine Gegenüberstellung. Göttingen 1959.

Vulpius, W. Schiller-Bibliographie 1893–1958. Weimar 1959; vol 2 1959–63, Weimar 1967.

Thiergard, U. Schiller und Walpole: ein Beitrag zu Schillers Verhältnis zur Schauerliteratur. Jahrbuch der Deutschen Schillergesellschaft 3 1959.

Pick, R. Schiller in England 1787–1960: a bibliography. 1961.

Ritchie, J. M. German books in Glasgow and Edinburgh 1500–1750. MLR 57 1962.

Brown, F. A. Shakespeare in Germany: Dryden, Langbain and the Acta eruditorum. Germanic Rev 40 1965.

Hennig, J. Goethe und die englisch sprechende Welt. Jahrbuch der Goethe Gesellschaft 28 1966.

Blumenthal, L. Geisweiler und Weimar: zur Rezeption deutscher Dichter in England um 1800. Jahrbuch der Deutschen Schillergesellschaft 11 1967.

The tatler. 1709–11.

The spectator. 1711–12.

Der Zuschauer. Tr Luise A. V. Gottsched 1739–43.

The guardian. 1713.

Der Aufseher oder Vormund. Tr Luise A. V. Gottsched 1745.

Der Engelländische Guardian oder Aufseher. Tr 1749.

The English 'Moral Weeklies' produced scores of imitations in German, e.g.

Der Vernünfftler. Hamburg 1713.

Discourse der Mahlern. Zürich 1721–3.

Der Patriot. Hamburg 1724–6.

Der getreue Hofmeister, sorgfältige Vormund und neue Mentor. Frankfurt and Leipzig 1725.

Der nordische Aufseher. Copenhagen and Leipzig 1758–61.

Der Hypochrondist. Schleswig 1763.

Jacoby, K. Die ersten moralischen Wochenschriften Hamburgs am Anfange des xviii Jahrhunderts. Hamburg 1880.

Kawcynski, M. Studien zur Literaturgeschichte des xviii Jahrhunderts: moralische Zeitschriften, I: Einleitung und Verzeichnis; ii: Über den Tatler. Leipzig 1880.

Milberg, E. Die deutschen moralischen Wochenschriften des xviii Jahrhunderts. Leipzig 1880.

Vetter, T. Der Spectator als Quelle der Diskurse der Maler. Frauenfeld 1887.

Keller, L. Die deutschen Gesellschaften des xviii Jahrhunderts und die moralischen Wochenschriften. Monatshefte der Comenius-Gesellschaft 9 1900.

Brown, F. A. Addison's 'imagination' and the 'Gesellschaft der Mahlern'. MLQ 15 1954.

Philosophy, Politics etc

German Authors

Herder, Johann Gottfried von (1744–1803). Denkmal Ulrichs von Hutten. 1766; A tribute to the memory of Ulric of Hutten, tr A. Aufrère 1789. Wrongly ascribed by translator to Goethe.

—— Ideen zu einer Philosophie der Geschichte der Menschheit. Riga and Leipzig 1784–91; Outlines of a philosophy of the history of man, tr T. O. Churchill 1800.

Heydet, X. La fortune de Herder dans les pays de langue anglaise. Revue de L'Enseignement des Langues Vivantes 55 1938.

Kant, Immanuel (1724–1804). Kritik der reinen Vernunft. Riga 1781; Kritik der praktischen Vernunft, Riga 1788; Kritik der Urteilskraft, Berlin 1790.

The principles of critical philosophy selected from the

works of Emanuel Kant and expounded by J. S. Beck, translated by an auditor of the latter [A. F. M. Willich], London and Hamburg 1797.

Elements of the critical philosophy: essays and treatises on moral, political and various philosophical subjects. Tr A. F. M. Willich 1798–9.

— Grundlegung zur Metaphysik der Sitten. Riga 1785; The metaphysics of morals, tr J. Richardson 1799.

— Zum ewigen Frieden. 1795; Project for perpetual peace, tr 1796.

Nitsch, F. A. A general and introductory view of Professor Kant's philosophy. 1796.

Wellek, R. Immanuel Kant in England 1793–1838. Princeton 1931.

Wentscher, E. Englische Wege zu Kant. Leipzig 1931.

Lavater, Johann Kaspar (1741–1801). Geheimes Tagebuch von einem Beobachter seiner selbst. Leipzig 1771–3; Secret journal of a self-observer, tr P. Will 1795.

— Physiognomische Fragmente zur Beförderung der Menschenkenntnis und Menschenliebe. Leipzig 1775–8; Essays on physiognomy, tr H. Hunter 1789–98 (from a French version); Essays on physiognomy, tr T. Holcroft [1789?]; Physiognomy, tr Samuel Shaw [1791?]; Essays on physiognomy, tr C. Moore 1797 (from a French version).

—Vermischte unphysiognomische Regeln zur Selbst- und Menschenkenntnis; Aphorisms on man, tr J. H. Fuessli 1788 (from the original ms).

Leibniz, Gottfried Wilhelm von (1646–1716)

A collection of papers which passed between the late Mr Leibnitz and Dr Clarke relating to the principles of natural philosophy and religion. 1717.

Leroy, G. von. Die philosophischen Probleme in dem Briefwechsel zwischen Leibniz und Clarke. Giessen 1893.

Klibansky, R. Leibniz' unknown correspondence with English scholars and men of letters. Mediaeval & Renaissance Stud 1 1941.

The Leibniz-Clarke correspondence. Ed H. G. Alexander, Manchester 1956.

Luther, Martin (1483–1546). Der kleine Catechismus Lutheri, durch ettliche kurtze Fragstück erkleret. Nuremberg 1559; The shorter catechism of Dr Martin Luther, translated from the Latin into English and now published together with the German by G. A. Wachsel, 1770.

Tischreden: oder Colloquia. Eisleben 1566. Set down by Anton Lauterbach and pbd by J. Aurifaber.

Dris Martini Lutheri Colloquia mensalia: or Dr Martin Luther's divine discourses at his table. Tr Henrie Bell (with introd by T. Thorowgood) 1652, 1791 (with preface, Life and character of Luther, by J. G. Burckhardt).

Milward, Richard. Table talk: being the discourses of John Selden esq. 1689.

Dr Martin Luther's prophecies of the destruction of Rome and the downfall of the Romish religion. Edinburgh 1679.

Hare, J. C. Vindications of Luther against his recent English assailants. 1855 (2nd edn).

Jaeger, O. John Wycliffe und seine Bedeutung für die Reformation. Halle 1854.

Maturin, B. The English Reformation in connection with the work of Luther. 1884.

Tjernagel, N. S. Henry VIII and the Lutherans. 1965.

Mendelssohn, Moses (1729–1786). Phädon. Berlin 1767; Phaedon: or the death of Socrates, tr C. Cullen 1789.

Winckelmann, Johann Joachim (1717–1795). Gedanken über die Nachahmung der griechischen Werke in der Malerei und Bildhauerkunst. 1755; Reflections on the painting and sculpture of the Greeks, tr H. Fusseli 1765; Reflections concerning the imitation of the Grecian artists in painting and sculpture, tr Glasgow 1766.

Zimmermann, Johann Georg (1728–1795). Über die Einsamkeit. Zürich 1756; Solitude considered with respect to its influence on the mind and heart, tr from the French version by Mercier 1791; Solitude: or the effects of occasional retirement on the mind, tr 1797.

— Von dem Nationalstolze. Zürich 1758; An essay on national pride, tr 1771; Strictures on national pride, tr Philadelphia 1778; An essay on national pride, tr S. H. Wilcocke 1797.

— Zerstreute Blätter vermischten Inhalts; Reflections on the perfectibility of man etc, tr 1799.

English Authors

Berkeley, George. Three dialogues between Hylas and Philonus. 1713; Unterredung zwischen Hylas and Philonus, tr Rostock 1756.

— Alciphron: or the minute philosopher. 1732; Alciphron, tr Lemgo 1737.

Browne, Sir Thomas. Religio medici. 1642; Religion eines Arztes, tr Halberstadt 1741; tr G. Venzky, Prenzlau 1746. John Merryweather's Latin trn, Libellus de religione medici, 1644, was pbd Strasbourg 1692 with notes by Levinus Nicolaus Moltkenius.

— Pseudodoxia epidemica: or enquiries into very many received tenents and commonly presumed truths. 1646; Des vortrefflichen Engelländers Thomas Brown, der Artzney Dr, Pseudodoxia epidemica, tr Christian Rautner (Peganius), Frankfurt and Leipzig 1680.

— Christian morals. 1716; Christliche Sittenlehre, tr Halle 1724; tr Nördlingen 1787.

Burke, Edmund. A philosophical enquiry into the origin of our ideas of the sublime and beautiful. 1757; Burkes philosophische Untersuchungen über den Ursprung unsrer Begriffe vom Erhabnen und Schönen, tr C. Garve, Riga 1773.

— Reflections on the revolution in France. 1790; Betrachtungen über die französische Revolution, tr Vienna 1791; tr F. Gentz, Berlin 1793.

Ferguson, Adam. Institutes of moral philosophy. 1769; Grundsätze der Moralphilosophie, tr C. Garve, Leipzig 1772.

— Principles of moral and political science. 1792; Darstellung der Gründe der Moral und Politik, tr K. G. Schreiter, Zürich 1796.

Bresky, D. Schiller's debt to Montesquieu and Adam Ferguson. Comparative Lit 13 1961.

Fordyce, David. Elements of moral philosophy. 1754; Anfangsgründe der philosophischen Sittenlehre, tr J. G. Müchler, Berlin 1757.

Gibbon, Edward. The decline and fall of the Roman Empire. 6 vols 1776–88; Geschichte des Verfalls und Untergangs des römischen Reichs, tr F. A. W. Wenck et al 19 pts Leipzig 1779–1806; Geschichte der Abnahme und des Falls der römischen Republik, tr C. W. von Rienburg, Magdeburg 1788–92.

Home, Henry (Lord Kames). Essays on the principles of morality and natural religion. 1751; Versuche über die ersten Gründe der Sittlichkeit und der natürlichen Religion, tr C. G. Rautenberg, Brunswick 1768.

— Elements of criticism. 1762; Grundsätze der Critik, tr J. N. Meinhard 3 vols Leipzig 1763–6.

Hume, David. Treatise of human nature. 1739; Über die menschliche Natur, tr L. H. Jacob 3 vols Halle 1790–2.

— Essays moral and political. 1741; tr J. A. Pistorius, Hamburg 1754 (vol 4 of Hume, Vermischte Schriften).

— Enquiry concerning human understanding. 1748; Über die menschliche Erkenntnis, tr J. G. Sulzer, Hamburg 1755; Untersuchung über den menschlichen Verstand, tr W. G. Tennemann, Jena 1793.

— Political discourses. 1752; Politische Aufsätze, tr Zürich 1791; tr C. A. Fischer, Leipzig 1795; tr Königsberg 1800.

Erdmann, B. Kant und Hume um 1762. Archiv für Geschichte der Philosophie 1888.

Metz, R. Englandhass, Frankophilie und Deutschland-bild bei Hume. Neuphilologische Monatsschrift 14 1943.

Mossner, E. C. The continental reception of Hume's Treatise 1739–41. Mind 56 1947.

Locke, John. Letter concerning toleration. 1689; Sendschreiben von der Toleranz, tr 1711, 1724; Über Duldung: ein Epistel, tr Leipzig 1796.

— An essay concerning human understanding. 1690; Herrn J. Lockens Versuch vom menschlichen Verstande, tr H. E. Poleyen, Altenburg 1757; Lockes Versuch über den menschlichen Verstand, tr W. G. Tennemann, Jena and Leipzig 1795–7.

— Two treatises of government. 1690; Le gouvernement civil: oder die Kunst, wohl zu regieren, tr G., Frankfurt 1718.

— Some thoughts concerning education. 1693; Gedanken von Erziehung junger Edelleute, tr S. G. Starck, Greifswald 1708; Unterricht von Erziehung der Kinder, tr Hamburg 1708; Gedanken von Erziehung der Kinder, tr Leipzig 1761; tr Coste, Vienna 1762; Abhandlung über die Erziehung der Jugend unter den höheren Volksclassen, tr C. S. Ouvrier, Leipzig 1787; Abhandlung über die Erziehung der Jugend in den gesitteten Ständen, tr L. E. G. Rudolphi, Brunswick 1787.

Brown, F. A. Locke's Essay and Bodmer and Breitinger. MLQ 10 1949.

— German interest in Locke's Essay 1688–1800. JEGP 50 1951.

— Some thoughts on the conduct of the understanding in the search of truth. 1706; Anleitung des menschlichen Verstandes zur Erkenntnis der Wahrheit, tr G. D. Kypke, Königsberg 1755.

Paine, Thomas. Commonsense. 1776; Die gesunde Vernunft, tr Philadelphia 1776.

— The rights of man. 2 pts 1791–2; Die Rechte des Menschen, tr D. M. Liebeskind, Berlin 1792–3.

— The age of reason. 1794; Zeitalter der Vernunft, tr H. C. Albrecht 2 vols Hamburg 1794–5.

— Dissertation on the first principles of government. 1795; Über die Regierungen und die Ur-grundsätze einer jeden derselben, tr Paris 1795.

Paley, William. Principles of moral and political philosophy. 1785; Grundsätze der Moral und Politik, tr C. A. Garve, Leipzig 1787.

Shaftesbury, Anthony Ashley Cooper, 3rd Earl of. Characteristicks of men, manners, opinions, times. 1711; Charakteristik: oder Schilderungen von Menschen, Sitten Meynungen und Zeiten, nebst einem Schreiben des Uebersetzers, welches die Anmerkungen des Freyherrn von Leibnitz enthält, tr C. A. Wichmann, Leipzig 1768.

Rehorn, F. Über das Verhältnis Shaftesburys zu Lessings Laokoon. Berichte des Freien Deutschen Hochstifts zu Frankfurt am Main 1886–7.

Hatch, J. C. Der Einfluss Shaftesburys auf Herder. Studien zur Vergleichenden Literaturgeschichte 1 1901.

Walzel, O. Shaftesbury und das deutsche Geistesleben des 18 Jahrhunderts. Germanisch-romanische Monatsschrift 1 1909.

Elson, C. Wieland and Shaftesbury. New York 1913.

Grudzinski, H. Shaftesburys Einfluss auf Chr. M. Wieland, mit einer Einleitung über den Einfluss Shaftesburys auf die deutsche Literatur bis 1760. Breslauer Beiträge zur Literaturgeschichte 34 1913.

Weiser, C. F. Shaftesbury und das deutsche Geistesleben. Leipzig 1916.

Stellner, L. Das philosophische System Shaftesburys und Wielands Agathon. Bausteine zur Geschichte der Deutschen Literatur 28 1929.

Portmann, P. F. Die deutschen Übersetzungen von Shaftesburys Soliloquy. Willisau 1942.

Smith, Adam. Theory of moral sentiments. 1759; Theorie der moralischen Empfindungen, tr C. G. Rautenberg, Brunswick 1770.

— Wealth of nations. 1776; Untersuchung der Natur und Ursachen von Nationalreichthümern, tr J. F. Schiller 2 vols Leipzig 1776–8; Untersuchung über die Natur und die Ursachen des Nationalreichthums, tr C. Garve 3 vols Breslau 1794–6.

Oncken. A. Adam Smith und Immanuel Kant. Leipzig 1877.

Hasbach, W. Untersuchungen über Adam Smith. Leipzig 1891.

Hasek, C. W. The introduction of Adam Smith's doctrines into Germany. New York 1925.

Erämetsä, E. Adam Smith als Mittler englisch-deutscher Spracheinflüsse. Helsinki 1961.

Wood, Robert. Essay on the original genius of Homer. 1769; Essay über den Originalgenius Homers, tr C. F. Michaelis, Frankfurt 1773.

Young, Edward. Conjectures on original composition. 1759; Gedanken über die Original-Werke, tr H. E. von Teubern, Leipzig 1760.

Zart, G. Der Einfluss der englischen Philosophie seit Bacon auf die deutsche Philosophie des 18 Jahrhunderts. Berlin 1881.

Theology, Hymns etc

German Authors

Boehme, Jakob (1575–1624). Des gottseeligen hoch erleuchteten Jacob Böhmens Teutonici Philosophi alle theosophische Werke. Amsterdam 1682.

— Theosophische Schrifften. 15 pts Amsterdam und Frankfurt 1698.

— Theosophia revelata: das ist, alle göttliche Schriften J. Böhmens. 2 pts Amsterdam 1730–1.

The works of Jacob Behmen the Teutonic theosopher. Ed George Ward and Thomas Langcake 4 vols 1764–81. 'Law's edition'. Trns basically those of J. Sparrow, J. Ellistone and H. Blunden.

Several treatises of Jacob Behmen. Tr J. Sparrow 1661. The remainder of books written by Jacob Behmen. Tr J. Sparrow 7 pts 1661–2. For trns of other single works by John Sparrow et al, see col 1658, below.

Mercurius teutonicus: or Christian information concerning the last times. Tr 1649.

Hotham, D. The life of Jacob Behmen. 1654.

Anderdon, J. One blow at Babel in those of the people call Behmenites. 1662.

A looking glass for George Fox. 1667.

Pordage, John. A treatise of eternal nature. 1681.

Taylor, E. Jacob Behmen's theosophick philosophy unfolded. 1691.

Propositions extracted from the reasons for the foundation of a Philadelphian Society. 1697.

Law, William. An appeal to all that doubt. 1740.

— The way to divine knowledge. 1752.

Lee, Francis. ΑΠ ΟΛ ΕΙΠΟΜΕΝΑ, or dissertations. 1752. In Works of Jacob Behmen vol 4; attributed to William Law.

Brooke, Henry. The fool of quality. 4 vols 1766–70.

Theological and practical divinity; with extracts of several treatises written by Jacob Behmen. 1769.

A compendious view of the grounds of Teutonick philosophy. 1770.

Okely, Francis. Memoirs of the life, death, burial and wonderful writings of Jacob Behmen. Northampton 1780. A trn of the life by A. von Frankenberg with the narrative by C. Weissner.

Walton, Christopher. Notes and materials for an adequate biography of Law. 1854. On influence of Boehme on Law.

Jones, R. M. Studies in mystical religion. 1909.

Closs, K. Böhmes Aufnahme in England. Archiv 148 1925.

Struck, W. Der Einfluss Jakob Boehmes auf die englische Literatur des 17 Jahrhunderts. Berlin 1936.

Francke, August Hermann (1663–1727). Segensvolle Fusstapfen des noch lebenden Gottes. Halle 1701; Pietas hallensis: or a publick demonstration of the footsteps of a Divine Being in an historical narration of the orphan house at Glaucha together with a short history of pietism, tr 1705.

— Nicodemus: ein Tractat über die Menschenfurcht. Halle nd; Nicodemus: or a treatise against the fear of man, tr A. W. Boehme [?] 1706.

Jacobi, Johann Christian. A collection of divine hymns. Tr 1720.

— Psalmodia germanica; or a specimen of divine hymns. Tr 1722.

Zinzendorf, Nikolaus Ludwig, Graf von (1700–60). Sixteen discourses on the redemption of man, preached at Berlin. Tr 1740.

— Seven sermons on the Godhead of the Lamb. Tr 1742.

Wesley, J. Extract of Count Zinzendorf's Discourses on the redemption of man. Newcastle 1744.

Maxims, theological ideas and sentences out of the present Ordinary of the Brethren's Churches, his dissertations and discourses from 1738–47, extracted by J. Gambold. 1751.

Queries humbly proposed to Count Zinzendorf. 1755. Ascribed to John Wesley.

Julian, J. Dictionary of hymnology. 1892. *See under German Hymnology.*

Hatfield, J. T. John Wesley's translations of German hymns. PMLA 11 1896.

Nuelsen, J. L. John Wesley und das deutsche Kirchenlied. Bremen 1938.

Bett, H. John Wesley's translations of German hymns in reference to metre and rhyme. London Quart 165 1940.

English Authors

Abernethy, John. Discourses concerning the Being and natural perfections of God. 1740–3; Von dem Daseyn und der Vollkommenheit Gottes, tr Grynäus, Basle 1781.

Addison, Joseph. Evidences of the Christian religion. 1730; Zeugnisse der alten Heiden und Juden von der Wahrheit der Geschichte unsers Heilandes, tr Zürich 1745; Überzeugende und unumstössliche Beweisgründe der christlichen Religion, tr T. Arnold, Lemgo 1749; Von der Wahrheit der christlichen Religion, tr H. J. von Hahn, Frankfurt 1782–4 (from French).

Alleine, Joseph. An alarm to unconverted sinners. 1672; Grundlegung zum thätigen Christenthum, tr M. T. C. Mittelstedt 1754; tr F. E. Rambach, Leipzig 1775.

Amner, Richard. Account of the occasion and design of the positive institutions of Christianity. 1774; Über Abendmahl, Sonntagfeier und Taufe, tr J. C. F. Schulz, Leipzig 1775.

— Essays towards the interpretation of the prophecies of Daniel. 1776; Versuch über die sämmtlichen Weissagungen Daniels, tr Halle 1779.

Appleton, Nathaniel. Gospel ministers must be fit for the Master's use. 1735; Predigt bey der Ordination des Herrn Joh Sargent, tr Halle 1741.

Archer, James. Sermons. 1789; Predigten, tr I. Schwarz 2 vols Bamberg 1795–6.

Asgill, John, Argument proving that man can be translated into eternal life. 1700; Die Unsterblichkeit der Menschen auf Erden an Leib und Seele, tr J. B. Pritio, Leipzig 1702.

Atterbury, Francis. Sermons. 1740; Heilige Reden, tr Leipzig 1764.

Balguy, Thomas. Divine benevolence asserted. 1782; Die göttliche Güte gegen Zweifel gerechtfertigt, tr J. A. Eberhard, Leipzig 1782.

Barclay, Robert. Catechism and confession of faith. 1673; Catechismus und Glaubensbekenntniss, tr Amsterdam 1679.

— Apology for the true Christian divinity. 1678; Apologie der christlichen Gottesgelehrtheit unter den Quäkern, tr Leipzig 1740.

Barrington, John Shute. Essay on the several dispensations of God to mankind. 1728; Versuch über das Christenthum und den Deismus, tr Halle 1783.

Barrow, Isaac. 'But Godliness is profitable for all things.' In his Sermons preached upon several occasions, 1678; Nutz der Gottesfurcht, tr D. R. Erythropel, Hanover 1678.

— Practical discourses upon our latter end. 1694; Vier Predigten über die Sterblichkeit, tr J. Tobler, Zürich 1765.

Bate, Julius. The blessing of Judah by Jacob considered. 1753; Abhandlungen von dem Segen Jacobs, tr Bremen 1754.

Bates, William. The four last things. 1691; Abhandlungen von den vier letzten Dingen, tr C. F. Uhrlandt 2 vols Gera 1775–6.

— Harmony of the divine attributes. 1697; Übereinstimmung der göttlichen Eigenschaften, tr Panzer, Nuremberg 1766.

Baxter, Richard. The Quaker's catechism or the Quakers questioned. 1655; Der Quacker Catechismus, tr Danzig 1663.

— True Christianity. 1655; Die wahre Kirche, tr Frankfurt and Leipzig 1721; Lehre von dem wahren Christenthum, tr 2 vols Jena 1746.

— Treatise on conversion. 1659; tr Cassel 1673.

— A treatise on self denyall. 1660; Die nothwendige Lehr von der Verläugnung unser Selbst, tr J.F.L., Hamburg 1665.

— Treatise on death. 1660; tr Hamburg 1665.

— True Catholick and Catholick church. 1660; Die wahre Kirche in allen Secten, tr J. Pritio, Frankfurt 1721.

— Call to the unconverted. 1660 (6th edn); Die Stimme Gottes an die Sünder, tr J. H. Germler, Basle 1712.

— Saint or a brute. 1662; Ein Heiliger oder ein Vieh, tr J. Deusing, Frankfurt 1716.

— Christian's converse with God. 1664; Eines Christen Umgang mit Gott, tr Solingen 1757.

Bayly, William. Call and visitation from the Lord. 1673; Eyferiges Christenthum, tr J.N.J.S., Altdorf 1704.

Benn, William. Sermons on the soul's prosperity. 1683; Von der Glückseligkeit und Gesundheit der Seele, tr Magdeburg 1732.

Benson, George. The end and design of prayer. 1731; Vernunftmässige Vertheidigung des Gebeths, tr M. C. Kortholt, Leipzig 1736.

— Reasonableness of the Christian religion. 1746; Vernunftmässigkeit der christlichen Religion, tr J. P. Bamberger, Halle 1763.

Beveridge, William. Private thoughts upon religion. 1709; Private-Gedancken von der Religion, tr Frankfurt 1714; Sonderbare Gedancken von der christlichen Religion, tr 1722.

Bowyear, William. Conjectures on the New Testament. 1772; Konjekturen über das Neue Testament, tr J. C. F. Schulz, Leipzig 1774.

Bunyan, John. Grace abounding. 1666; tr Hamburg 1698.

— The pilgrim's progress. 1678; Eines Christen Reise nach der seligen Ewigkeit, tr J. Lange, Hamburg 1685.

— The holy war. 1682; Der heilige Krieg, tr J. Lange, Hamburg 1693.

Burkitt, William. Expository notes with practical observations on the New Testament. 1700; Praktische Erklärung des Neuen Testaments, tr F. E. Rambach 7 vols Halle 1763–8.

Burnet, Gilbert. The abridgement of the history of the Reformation of the Church of England. 1682; tr

Frankfurt 1691; Reformationsgeschichte der Kirche von England, tr M. T. C. Mittelstedt, Brunswick 1760–70.

Butler, Joseph. Analogy of religion, natural and revealed. 1736; Bestätigung der natürlichen und geoffenbarten Religion, tr J. J. Spalding, Leipzig 1756.

Chandler, Samuel. Plain reasons for being a Christian. 1703; Deutliche Gründe, warum man ein Christ seyn müsse, tr J. D. Schumann, Leipzig 1747.

— Discourse on the nature and use of miracles. 1728; Von der Beschaffenheit der Wunderwerke, tr M. C. Wollen, Leipzig 1729.

— Critical history of the life of David. 1766; Kritische Lebensgeschichte Davids, tr J. C. W. Diederichs 2 vols Bremen 1777–80.

Charnock, Stephen. Treatise of divine providence. 1680; Unterricht von der göttlichen Fürsehung, tr Berlin 1716.

— Vindication of the Christian religion. 1725; Fester Grund der christlichen Religion, tr F. E. Rambach, Rostock 1756.

Clarke, Samuel. A demonstration of the being of God. 1705; Abhandlung von dem Dasein und den Eigenschaften Gottes, tr Brunswick 1756.

— Paraphrase of the four Evangelists. 1706; Paraphrase der vier Evangelisten, tr 3 vols Marburg 1762–3.

— Scripture doctrine of the Trinity. 1712; Die Schrift-Lehre von der Dreyeinigkeit, tr J. S. S. Semlers, Frankfurt 1774.

Clayton, Robert. Impartial inquiry into the time of the coming of the Messiah. 1751; Unparteiische Untersuchung, welche die Person, das Amt und die Zeit des Messias betrifft, tr Leipzig 1754.

Cougal, S. The life of God in the soul of man. 1671; Das göttliche Leben in der Seele des Menschen, tr F. W. Berchtelmann, Frankfurt 1730; Das Leben Gottes in der Seele des Menschen, Germantown 1755.

Craig, William. Essay on the life of Jesus Christ. 1769; Versuch über das Leben Jesu Christi, tr Winterthur 1773.

Derham, William. Astrotheology. 1714; Astrotheologie oder himmlisches Vergnügen in Gott, tr J. A. Fabricio, Hamburg 1728.

— Physico-theology: or a demonstration of the being of God. 1713; Physicotheologie oder Natur-Leitung zu Gott, tr J. A. Fabricio, Hamburg 1730.

Ditton, Humphrey. A discourse concerning the resurrection of Jesus Christ. 1712; Die Wahrheit der christlichen Religion aus der Auferstehung Jesu Christi, tr G. W. Goetten, Brunswick 1732.

Doddridge, Philip. Ten sermons on the power and grace of Christ. 1736; Betrachtungen über die Macht und Gnade Jesu, tr F. E. Rambach, Magdeburg 1749.

— Family expositor or a paraphrase and version of the New Testament. 6 vols 1739–56; Paraphrastische Erklärung der sämtlichen Schriften Neuen Testaments, tr F. E. Rambach, Magdeburg 1750.

— Practical sermons on regeneration. 1742; Reden von der Wiedergeburt, tr F. E. Rambach, Rostock 1754.

— Rise and progress of religion in the soul. 1745; Anfang und Fortgang wahrer Gottseligkeit, tr G. L. Münter, Hanover 1750.

Doolittle, Thomas. A treatise concerning the Lord's supper. 1672; Von würdigem Gebrauch des Heiligen Abendmahls, tr J. Alssners, Berlin 1735.

Farmer, Hugh. Dissertation on miracles. 1771; Abhandlung über die Wunderwerke, tr von Collin, Berlin 1776.

— Essay on the demoniacs of the New Testament. 1775; Versuch über die dämonischen Leute im Neuen Testament, tr von Collin, Berlin 1776.

Goodwin, Thomas. Discourse of the true nature of the Gospel. 1695; Die Herrlichkeit des Evangelii, tr Königsberg 1747.

— Discourse of the three several ages which Christians do run through. 1704; Betrachtungen über die drey Alter der Christen, tr Züllichau 1736.

Hall, Joseph. The balme of Gilead: or comforts for the distressed both morall and divine. 1646; Balsaam aus Gilead. Tr H. Schmettau, Breslau 1663; tr J. J. Schädler, Zürich 1663.

Jortin, John. Discourses on the truth of the Christian religion. 1746; Abhandlungen über die Wahrheit der christlichen Religion, tr J. A. Ebert, Hamburg 1769.

— Remarks on ecclesiastical history. 1751; Anmerkungen über die Kirchenhistorie, tr J. P. Cassel, Bremen 1755.

— Sermons on different subjects. 7 vols 1771–5; Predigten über verschiedene Gegenstände, tr 6 vols Hanover 1775–82.

Lardner, Nathaniel. The credibility of the Gospel history. 2 pts 1727–33; Die Glaubwürdigkeit der evangelischen Geschichte, tr Berlin 1749.

— A vindication of three of our Blessed Saviour's miracles. 1729; Vertheidigung der Wunderwerke Jesu, tr Dresden 1732; Vertheidigung der Wahrheit und Göttlichkeit dreier Wunder unsers hochgelobten Erlösers, tr J. H. Meyenberg, Zelle 1751.

— An argument for the truth of Christianity. 1743; Beweis von der Wahrheit der christlichen Religion, tr J. G. Pfeil, Halle 1754.

— The case of the demoniacs. 1758; Von den Besessenen, tr J.P.C.P., Bremen 1760.

Locke, John. The reasonableness of Christianity as delivered in the Scriptures. 1695; Johann Locks gründlicher Beweis, dass die christliche Religion vernünftig und raisonable sey; tr J. C. Meinigen, Brunswick 1733; Vernunftmässiges Christenthum, tr 2 vols Berlin, Leipzig und Glogau 1758–9.

Lucas, Richard. Enquiry after happiness. 1685; Sicherer Weg zur wahren Glückseligkeit, tr Karlsruhe 1756.

— Practical Christianity. 1690; Die evangelische Tugend-Lehre, tr Hamburg 1705; Moral des Evangelii, tr Karlsruhe 1775.

— Twelve sermons preached on several occasions. 2 vols 1702–9; Predigten bey verschiedenen Gelegenheiten, tr 2 vols Schwerin 1760–76.

— Duty of servants. 1710; Die Pflicht des Gesindes, tr Berlin 1724.

Paley, William. Horae Paulinae: or the truth of the Scripture history of St Paul. 1790; Horae Paulinae: oder Beweis der Glaubwürdigkeit der Geschichte und Aechtheit der Schriften des Apostels Paulus, tr H. P. C. Henke, Helmstedt 1797.

— A view of the evidences of Christianity. 1794; Übersicht und Prüfung der Beweise und Zeugnisse für das Christenthum, tr Leipzig 1797.

Sherlock, William. Practical discourse concerning a future judgement. 1692; Geistreicher und höchst nützlicher Tractat vom jüngsten Gericht, tr Lübeck and Leipzig 1717.

— Discourse concerning divine providence. 1694; Buch von der Vorsehung Gottes, tr J. L. Mosheim, Hamburg 1726.

— Discourse concerning the happiness of good men. 1704; Betrachtung über die Glückseligkeit der Frommen, tr A. W. Franzen, Lübeck 1755.

Stackhouse, Thomas. Complete body of divinity. 1729; Lehrbegriff der ganzen christlichen Religion, tr F. E. Rambach 7 vols Rostock 1755–64.

— Defence of the Christian religion. 1731; Vertheidigung der christlichen Religion, tr H. C. Lemker 2 vols Hanover und Göttingen 1750.

— History of the Holy Bible. 1742; Vertheidigung der biblischen Geschichte, tr F. E. Rambach 8 vols Rostock 1752–9.

— New and practical exposition of the Apostle's creed. 1747; Betrachtungen über das apostolische Glaubensbekenntniss, tr F. E. Rambach, Rostock 1765–71.

Taylor, John. Scripture doctrine of original sin. 1740; Schriftmässige Lehre von der Erbsünde, tr Frankfurt 1769.

— Key to the apostolic writings. 1745; Schlüssel zu den apostolischen Schriften, tr Zürich 1774.

— Scheme of scripture divinity. 1762; Entwurf der Schrift-Theologie, tr J. J. Hess, Leipzig 1777.

Tillotson, John. Advantages of an early piety. 1662; Vortheile einer früh-zeitigen Gottseligkeit, tr H. Lindenberg, Berlin 1709.

— Rule of faith. 1666; Glaubensregeln, Streitschrift wider das Pabstthum, tr J. G. Lessing, 2 vols Dresden 1730–1.

— Evidence of the truth of the Christian religion. 1728; Grundlegung der vornehmsten Wahrheiten zur Erkenntnis und Ausübung eines thätigen Christenthums, tr J. G. Lessing, Dresden 1728.

Tindal, Matthew. Christianity as old as the creation. 1730; Beweis, dass das Christenthum so alt als die Welt sey, tr L. Schmidt, Frankfurt 1741.

Toland, John. Christianity not mysterious. 1696; Christenthum ohne Geheimnis, tr W. Lunde, ed L. Zscharnack, Giessen 1908 (with Leibniz, Annotatiunculae, 1701).

Tomkin, C. Credibility of the Gospel. 1761; Vertheidigung der apostolischen Lehre von Jesu Christo, tr F. E. Rambach, Halle 1765.

Townson, Thomas. Discourses on the four gospels. 1778; Abhandlungen über die vier Evangelisten, tr J. S. Semler 2 vols Leipzig 1783–4.

Turnbull, George. A philosophical enquiry concerning the connexion betwixt the doctrines and miracles of Jesus Christ. 1731; Philosophische Untersuchung der Connexion, die sich zwischen der Lehre und den Wunder-Wercken Jesu findet, tr Leipzig 1732.

Warburton, William. Divine legation of Moses. 2 vols 1737–8; Göttliche Sendung Mosis, tr J. C. Schmidt 3 vols Frankfurt 1751–3.

— Principles of natural and revealed religion. 1753; Grundlehren der natürlichen und geoffenbarten Religion, tr J. C. Schmidt, Leipzig 1760.

Watson, Richard. An apology for Christianity. 1776; Anrede an die heutigen Freunde des Christenthums, tr Bamberger, Berlin 1779.

— Apology for the Bible. 1796; Apologie der Bibel, tr J. F. Lehzen, Hanover 1798.

Watts, Isaac. Guide to prayer. 1715; Anweisung zum Gebet, tr E. C. Reichard, Ludwigsburg 1746.

— Discourse on the love of God and its influence on all the passions. 1729; Reden von der Liebe Gottes und ihrem Einfluss in alle menschliche Leidenschaften, tr S. J. Baumgarten, Frankfurt 1740.

— Holiness of times, places and peoples. 1738; Die Heiligkeit gewisser Zeiten, Orte und Menschen, tr Pfeil, Halle 1741.

— Useful and important questions concerning Jesus the Son of God. 1746; Wichtige und vernünftige Fragen, welche Jesum, den Sohn Gottes, betreffen, tr G. L. Zollikofer, Frankfurt 1753.

— Evangelical discourses on several subjects. 1747; Reden über allerhand Glaubenslehren und Lebenspflichten, tr Pfeil, Gotha 1761.

Wilkins, John. Discourse concerning the beauty of providence. 1651; Discours von der Gabe zu beten, tr G. Dewerdeck, Frankfurt 1701.

— Principles and duties of natural religion. 1675; Zwey Bücher von den Grundsätzen und Pflichten der natürlichen Religion, tr J. H. Tiling, Bremen 1750.

Williams, David. Liturgy on the universal principles of religion. 1776; Liturgie nach den allgemeinen Grundsätzen der Religion und Sittenlehre, tr F. L. Schönemann, Leipzig 1785.

— Lectures on the principles and duties of religion and morality. 2 vols 1776–9; Vorlesungen über die allgemeinen Grundsätze und Pflichten der Religion und Sittenlehre, tr J. A. Eberhard, Halle 1785.

Price, L. M. Albrecht von Haller and English theology. PMLA 41 1926. For a full list of German trns of the works of Baxter, Hall and other English divines, see M. B. and L. M. Price, The publication of English Humaniora in Germany in the eighteenth century, 1955.

Biography, Letters etc

Kotzebue, August Freiherr von (1761–1819). Mein literärischer Lebenslauf; Sketch of the life and literary career, with the journal of his tour to Paris, 1790; tr Anne Plumptre 1800.

Lichtenau, Wilhelmine Rietz, Gräfin von (1752–1820). Geheime Papiere der Gräfin von Lichtenau, vulgo Minchen Encken; Confessions of the celebrated Countess of Lichtenau, tr R. B-t-n 1799.

Lichtenberg, G. C. (1742–99). Briefe aus England. In Deutsches Museum, Leipzig 1776, 1778.

Hecht, H. Briefe aus Lichtenbergs englischem Freundeskreis. Göttingen 1925.

Lichtenberg's visits to England as described in his letters and diaries. Tr M. L. Mare and W. H. Quarrell, Oxford 1938.

Moritz, Karl Philipp (1756–93). Reisen eines Deutschen in England im Jahre 1782.

Travels, chiefly through several parts of England in 1782, described in letters to a friend, translated by a lady. 1795.

Trenck, Friedrich von der (1726–94). Merkwürdige Lebensgeschichte. 4 pts Berlin 1786–7; The life of Baron Trenck, tr T. Holcroft 1788; Memoirs of Baron Trenck, by an officer in the RA, 1788.

Hennig, J. Trenck and Britain. MLR 41 1946.

Boswell, James. The journal of a tour to the Hebrides with Samuel Johnson LlD. 1785; Tagebuch einer Reise nach den Hebrideschen Inseln mit Dr S. Johnson, tr A. Wittenberg, Lübeck 1787.

Nugent, T. Travels through Germany. 1678. Die unterhaltsame Reise des Herrn Dr Nugent durch Mecklenburg: Reisebrief aus dem Jahre 1766. Wismar 1936.

Plumptre, Anne. Letters from various parts of the Continent between the years 1785 and 1794 containing a variety of anecdotes relative to the present state of literature in Germany. 1797; tr Halle 1797.

Sterne, Laurence. Letters to his most intimate friends. 1775; Briefe an sein vertrautesten Freunde, tr C. F. Weisse, Leipzig 1776.

Lyric Poetry

German Authors

Bürger, Gottfried August (1747–94). Lenore. Göttingen 1773; Ellenore: a ballad, tr W. Taylor 1790; Monthly Mag March 1796; Leonora: a tale, tr J. T. Stanley 1796; tr H. J. Pye 1796; tr W. R. Spencer 1796; William and Helen, tr Walter Scott 1796; Leonora, tr B. Beresford 1798; Miss Kitty: a parody on Lenore, translated from the German by several hands, 1797.

— Der wilde Jäger. Göttingen 1786; The chase, and William and Helen [i.e. Lenore]: two ballads from the German of Bürger, tr Walter Scott, Edinburgh 1796; The wild hunter, tr W. Taylor 1796; Scots Mag 59 1797.

Brandl, A. Lenore in England. In E. Schmidt, Charakteristiken, Berlin 1886.

Greg, W. W. English translations of Bürger's Lenore. Modern Quart of Lang & Lit 2 1899.

Herzfeld, G. Zur Geschichte von Bürgers Lenore in England. Archiv 106 1901.

Blömker, F. Das Verhältnis von Bürgers lyrischer und epischlyrischer Dichtung zur englischen Literatur. Münster 1930.

Parsons, C. O. Scott's translation of Bürger's Das Lied von der Treue. JEGP 33 1934.

Gessner, Salomon (1730–88). Idyllen. Zürich 1756; Pastorals, Monthly Rev 1762; Rural poems from Gessner, tr 1762; Select idylls from Mr Gessner's Pastorals, tr Anne Penny 1762; New idylls, tr W. Hooper 1776; Idyls: or pastoral poems, tr Edinburgh 1798.

Goethe, Johann Wolfgang von (1749–1832). Der Erlkönig. Weimar 1782; The Erl-King, tr Walter Scott 1797.
— Klaggesang von der edlen Frauen des Asan Aga. Leipzig 1778; Morlachian Ballad, tr Walter Scott [c. 1798].
Hohlfeld, A. R. Scott als Übersetzer. Studien zur Vergleichenden Literaturgeschichte 3 1903.
Simmons, L. T. V. Goethe's lyric poems in English translation prior to 1860. Madison 1919.
Ruff, W. Walter Scott and the Erl-King. E Studien 69 1935.
Stolbert, Friedrich Leopold Graf zu (1750–1819). Hymne an die Erde. [1779?]; Hymn to the earth, tr S. T. Coleridge 1799; tr John Whitehouse 1800.
Beresford, B. The German Erato: or a collection of favourite songs. Berlin 1798.
— The German songster: or a collection of favourite airs. 1798.

English Authors

Dryden, John. Alexander's feast. 1697; tr C. F. Weisse 1752; tr Ramler 1766.
Percy, Thomas. Reliques of ancient English poetry. 3 vols 1765; Altenglische Balladen, tr 2 vols Zürich 1780–1.
Herder, J. F. Von Ähnlichkeit der mittleren englischen und deutschen Dichtkunst. Leipzig 1777.
Volkslieder. Leipzig 1778–9.
Bürger, G. A. Gedichte. Göttingen 1778.
Bodmer, J. J. Altenglische Balladen. 1780.
— Altenglische und altschwäbische Balladen. 1781.
Bothe, F. H. Volkslieder, nebst untermischten anderen Stücken. 1795.
Bonet-Maury, G. Bürger et les origines anglaises de la ballade littéraire en Allemagne. Paris 1889.
Waag, A. Über Herders Übertragungen englischer Gedichte. Heidelberg 1892.
Wagener, H. F. Das Eindringen von Percys Reliques in Deutschland. Heidelberg 1897.
Lohre, H. Von Percy zum Wunderhorn. Berlin 1902.
Boyd, E. I. M. The influence of Percy's Reliques of ancient English poetry on German literature. MLQ 7 1904.
Guthke, K. S. Some unidentified early English translations from Herder's Volkslieder. MLN 73 1958.
Clark, R. T. Herder, Percy and the Song of Songs. PMLA 61 1946.
Pope, Alexander. Ode on St Cecilia's Day. 1713; Ode auf die Musik, tr C. F. Weisse, Leipzig 1752; Ode am Tag der Heil. Cäcilia, tr D.M. 1796.
Kosegarten, L. T. Preis der Tonkunst nach Pope. 3 vols Leipzig 1790–1801.
Frick, A. Über Popes Einfluss auf Hagedorn. Vienna 1900.
Prior, Matthew. Poems on several occasions. 1707; A second collection, 1716; Gedichte bey verschiedenen Gelegenheiten, Leipzig 1783; F. von Hagedorn, Poetische Werke, Hamburg 1757.
Wukadinovič, S. Prior in Deutschland. Graz 1895.
Quarles, Francis. Enchiridion. 1640; D. G. Morhof, Teutsche Gedichte, Kiel 1682.
Rochester, John Wilmot, 2nd Earl of. Poems on several occasions. 1680; J. B. Menke, Philanders von der Linde Galante Gedichte, Leipzig 1706; Nicolaus von Bostel, Poetische Neben-Werke, Hamburg 1708.
Sherburne, Sir Edward. Salamacis with several other poems. 1651; J. B. Menke, Galante Gedichte, Leipzig 1706.

Epic, Descriptive and Didactic Poetry
German Authors

Bodmer, Johann Jakob (1698–1783). Noah. 12 pts Frankfurt and Zürich 1750–2; Noah, tr Joseph Collyer 1767.

Gessner, Salomon (1730–88). Der Tod Abels. Zürich 1758; The death of Abel, tr Mary Collyer 1761 (20 edns to 1800); The thanksgiving song of Adam, on his recovery from sickness, tr S. Boyce, Br Mag 3 1762; The death of Abel, tr Thomas Newcomb 1763.
McGowan, J. Death: a vision. 1776.
Hall, W. H. The death of Cain. 1789.
Coleridge, S. T. The wanderings of Cain. Written 1798.

Reed, B. The influence of Gessner on English literature. Philadelphia 1905.
Haller, Albrecht von (1708–77). Versuch schweizerischer Gedichte. Berne 1732; Die Alpen, Berne 1734; Poems of Baron Haller, tr Mrs J. Howorth 1794; The Alps: a moral and descriptive poem of the great Haller, tr Henry Barrett 1796.
Wyplel, L. Englands Einfluss auf die Lehrdichtung Hallers. Vienna 1888.
Klopstock, Friedrich Gottlieb (1724–1803). Messias. 4 vols Leipzig and Halle 1748–73; The Messiah, tr Joseph and Mary Collyer 2 vols 1763–71.
Schönaich, Christof Otto (1725–1807). Hermann: oder das befreite Deutschland. 1751; Arminius: or Germania freed, tr 1764 (from 3rd edn).
Wieland, Christoph Martin (1733–1813). Der gepryfte Abraham. Zürich 1753; The trial of Abraham, tr 1764.
— Oberon. Weimar 1780; tr W. Sotheby 1798.
Beyer, W. W. Coleridge, Wieland's Oberon and the Ancient Mariner. RES 15 1939.
— Coleridge, Wieland's Oberon and the Wanderings of Cain. RES 16 1940; both rptd in his Enchanted forest, 1963.
Colwell, W. A. The first English translation of Wieland's Oberon. PMLA 57 1942.

English Authors

Akenside, Mark. The pleasures of imagination: a poem in three books. 1744; Die Ergötzungen der Einbildungskraft, tr 1757 (in part); Die Vergnügungen der Einbildungskraft, tr Greifswald 1757 (prose); Die Freuden der Einbildungskraft, tr J. J. Eschenburg 1797.
ten Hoor, G. J. Akenside's The pleasures of imagination in Germany. JEGP 38 1939.
Glover, Richard. Leonidas: a poem. 1737: Glovers Leonidas: ein Heldengedicht, tr J. A. Ebert, Leipzig 1748; tr Grynäus, Basle 1757.
Kleist, E. von. Cissides und Paches. Berlin 1759.
Wieland, C. M. Cyrus. Zürich 1759.
Briggs, F. Glover's influence on Klopstock. PQ 1 1922.
Macpherson, James. Fragments of ancient poetry collected in the Highlands of Scotland and translated from the Gallic or Erse language. Edinburgh 1760.
— Fingal: an ancient epic poem in six books. 1762.
— Temora: an epic poem. 1763.
— The works of Ossian, translated by James Macpherson. 2 vols 1765.
Fragmente der alten hochschottländischen Dichtkunst. Tr J. A. Engelbrecht, Hamburg 1764.
Fragmente der alten Dichtkunst in den Hochländern von Schottland. Tr Bremen 1766.
Die Gedichte Ossians. Tr Michael Denis 3 vols Vienna 1768–9.
Gerstenberg, H. W. von. Gedicht eines Skalden. Copenhagen and Leipzig 1766.
Kretschmann, K. F. Gesang Rhingulfs des Barden. Leipzig 1768.
Denis, M. Lieder Sinods des Barden. Vienna 1772.
Herder, J. F. Ossian und die Lieder alter Völker. In Blätter von deutscher Art und Kunst, Hamburg 1773.
Goethe, J. W. von. Die Leiden des jungen Werther. Leipzig 1774. Contains trns.
Die Gedichte Ossians. Tr E. von Harold, Düsseldorf 1775.

Die Werke der Caledonischen Barden. Tr Leipzig 1779.

Gallische Alterthümer: oder eine Sammlung alter Gedichte aus dem Gallischen. Tr C. F. Weisse, Leipzig 1781.

Die Gedichte Ossians. Tr J. W. Petersen, Tübingen 1782.

Denis, M. Ossians und Sinods Lieder. Vienna 1784.

Neu entdeckte Gedichte Ossians. Tr E. von Harold, Düsseldorf 1787.

Pfaff, C. H. Neu aufgefundene Gedichte Ossians. Frankfurt and Leipzig 1792.

Balbach, J. Tales of Ossian for use and entertainment: ein Lesebuch fur Anfänger im Englischen. Nuremberg 1794 (2nd edn).

Ossians Gedichte. Tr J. G. Rhode, Berlin 1800.

Stern, L. C. Die ossianischen Heldenlieder. Zeitschrift für Vergleichende Literaturgeschichte 8 1895.

Tombo, R. Ossian in Germany: bibliography. General survey; Ossian's influence on Klopstock and the bards. New York 1902.

Heuer, O. Eine unbekannte Ossianübersetzung Goethes. Jahrbuch des Freien Deutschen Hochstifts 1908.

Merker, Erna. Ossianische Dichtung. In Reallexikon vol 2, 1926–8.

Horstmeyer, R. Die deutschen Ossianübersetzungen des 18 Jahrhunderts. Greifswald 1926.

Gillies, A. Herder und Ossian. Berlin 1933.

Betteridge, H. F. The Ossianic poems in Herders Volkslieder. MLR 30 1935.

Hennig, J. Goethe's translations of Ossian's Songs of Selma. JEGP 45 1946.

—— Goethe's translation from Macpherson's Berrathon. MLR 42 1947.

Milton, John. Paradise lost. 1667.

Das ver-lustigte Paradeiss aus und nach dem Englischen I M's durch T.H. zu übersetzen angefangen—voluisse sat. Ms trn of bks 1–3 by Theodore Haak. Preserved in the Landesbibliothek, Cassel, c. 1680. See P. R. Barnett, below.

Das verlustigte Paradeis in unser gemein Teutsch übertragen und verlegt durch E.G.V.B. [Ernst Gottlieb von Berge]. Zerbst 1682.

Johann Miltons Verlust des Paradieses. Tr J. J. Bodmer, Zürich 1732 (prose).

Miltons Verlorenes Paradies. Tr J. F. W. Zachariä, Altona 1760.

Verlorenes Paradies. Tr Bürde, Berlin 1792.

—— Paradise regained. 1671.

Wiedererobertes Paradies. Tr Grynäus, Basle 1752. With trns of L'Allegro, Il Penseroso and Samson Agonistes.

Wiedererobertes Paradies. Tr Dessau 1782. With trns of L'Allegro and Lycidas.

Bodmer, J. J. Critische Abhandlung von dem Wunderbaren in der Poesie und dessen Verbindung mit dem Wahrscheinlichen, in einer Verteidigung des Gedichtes Joh Miltons von dem Verlohrnen Paradiese, der beygefüget ist Joseph Addisons Abhandlung von den Schönheiten in demselben Gedichte. Leipzig 1740.

Klopstock, F. G. Der Messias. 4 vols Halle 1748–73.

Zachariä, J. F. W. Die Schöpfung der Hölle. Altenburg 1760.

Brandl, A. Zur ersten Verdeutschung von Miltons Verlorenem Paradies. Anglia 1 1878.

Bolte, J. Die beiden ältesten Verdeutschungen von Miltons Verlorenem Paradies. Zeitschrift für Vergleichende Literaturgeschichte 1 1888.

Muncker, F. Miltons Einwirken auf die deutsche Literatur. In his Klopstock, Stuttgart 1888.

Jenny, G. K. Miltons Verlorenes Paradies in der deutschen Literatur des 18 Jahrhunderts. Leipzig 1890.

Häbler, F. Milton und Klopstock. Reichenberg 1896.

Byse, F. Milton on the Continent. MLQ 3 1901.

Robertson, J. G. Milton's fame on the Continent. Proc Br Acad 3 1908.

Münch, W. Versuche der Verdeutschung von Miltons Paradise lost. Deutsche Literatur-Zeitung 31 1910.

Ibershoff, C. H. Bodmer as a literary borrower. PQ 1 1922.

—— Bodmer and Milton once more. PMLA 43 1928.

Schulze, H. G. Miltons Verlorenes Paradies in deutschem Gewand. Bonn 1928.

Ulrich, H. Deutsche Milton-Übersetzungen vom 18 Jahrhundert bis zur Gegenwart. Euphorion 29 1928.

Magon, L. Die ersten drei Versuche einer Übersetzung von Miltons Paradise lost. Weimar 1956.

Barnett, P. R. Theodore Haak FRS, the first German translator of Paradise lost. Hague 1962.

Bender, W. J. J. Bodmer und Miltons Verlohrnes Paradies. Jahrbuch der Deutschen Schillergesellschaft 11 1967.

Tisch, J. H. Milton and the German mind in the eighteenth century. In Studies in the eighteenth century, ed R. F. Brissinden, Canberra 1968.

Pope, Alexander. Pastorals. 1709; tr B. H. Brockes, Hamburg 1740; tr Grynäus, Basle 1759.

—— Essay on criticism. 1711; Versuch von den Eigenschaften eines Kunstrichters, tr K. F. Drollinger, Zürich 1741; Versuch über die Critik, tr G. E. Müller, Dresden 1745.

Graner, K. Die Übersetzungen von Popes Essay on criticism und ihr Verhältnis zum Original. Aschaffenburg 1910.

—— Windsor-Forest. 1713; tr B. H. Brockes, Hamburg 1740.

Brockes, B. H. Das irdische Vergnügen in Gott. Hamburg 1721.

—— The temple of fame. 1715.

Pyra, J. I. Der Tempel der wahren Dichtkunst. Halle 1937.

—— Essay on man. 4 pts 1733–4; Versuch vom Menschen, tr B. H. Brockes, Hamburg 1740; tr Mylius, 4 pts Halle 1745–7; Philosophisches Lehrgedicht vom Menschen, J. G. E. Schmidt, Leipzig 1756; Der Mensch: ein philosophisches Gedicht, tr Jena 1759; tr F. K. von Creutz, Frankfurt 1769; Versuch am Menschen in vier Briefen an Bolingbroke, tr J. J. Harder, Halle 1772.

Schweinsteiger, H. Das Echo von Popes Essay on man im Ausland. Munich 1913.

Rogers, R. W. Critiques on the Essay on man in France and Germany. ELH 15 1948.

Dusch, J. J. Moralische Briefe. Leipzig 1759.

Lessing, G. E. and M. Mendelssohn. Pope ein Metaphysiker. Danzig 1755.

Lichtwer, M. G. Das Recht der Vernunft. Leipzig 1758.

Neue Sammlung auserlesener Stücke aus Popens, Eachards, Newtons und anderer Schriften. Tr Luise A. V. Gottsched, Leipzig 1749.

Wyplel, L. Englands Einfluss auf die Lehrdichtung Hallers. Vienna 1888.

Maack, R. Über Popes Einfluss auf die Idylle und das Lehrgedicht im Deutschen. Hamburg 1895.

Heinzelmann, J. H. A bibliography of German translations of Pope in the 18th century. Bull of Bibl Soc of America 4 1912.

—— Pope in Germany in the 18th century. MP 10 1913.

Krumpelmann, J. T. Schiller's Hoffnung and Pope's Essay on man. Germanic Rev 3 1928.

Prior, Matthew. Alma. 1718.

Wieland, C. M. Musarion: oder die Philosophie der Grazien. Leipzig 1768.

Wukadinović S. Prior in Deutschland. Graz 1895.

Rowe, Elizabeth. Letters moral and entertaining. 1736. Moralische und unterhaltende Briefe. Tr E. Klausing, Frankfurt 1771.

Vermischte poetische Werke. Tr J. J. Ebert, Frankfurt 1772.

Wieland, C. M. Erzählungen. Tübingen 1752.

Klopstock, Meta. Hinterlassene Schriften. Hamburg 1759.

Thomson, James. The seasons. 4 pts 1726–30; Jahreszeiten des Herrn Thomson, tr B. H. Brockes, Hamburg 1745; Frühling, Sommer, Herbst, Winter, tr J. Tobler, Zürich 1757–64; Die Jahreszeiten, tr J. F. von Palthen, Rostock 1758; tr Basle 1768–9; Die Jahreszeiten, tr L. Schubart, Berlin 1789; Die vier Jahreszeiten in deutschen Iamben, tr H. Harries, Altona 1796; Thomsons Jahreszeiten mit Anmerkungen von G. F. Hermann, Weissenfels 1798.

Kleist, Ewald von. Der Frühling. Berlin 1749.

Haydn, Joseph. Die Jahreszeiten. Vienna 1799.

Gjerset, K. Der Einfluss von Thomsons Jahreszeiten auf die deutsche Literatur des 18 Jahrhunderts. Heidelberg 1898.

Stewart, M. C. B. H. Brockes' rendering of Thomson's Seasons (and the later German translations). JEGP 10 1911.

Williams, C. A. Thomson's Seasons and three of Goethe's poems. JEGP 47 1948.

Young, Edward. The complaint: or night thoughts. 9 pts 1742–5; Klagen oder Nachtgedanken, tr J. A. Ebert, Brunswick 1751; Die Nacht, tr C. B. Kayser, Göttingen 1752.

Geusau, H. von. Der Christensieg als das einzige Mittel wider die Furcht des Todes, aus den Nachtgedanken. Jena 1752.

Cronegk, J. P. von. Einsamkeiten. Zürich 1758.

Basedowische Chrestomathie von Youngs Lehren der natürlichen Religion und Tugend aus seinen Nachtgedanken. Leipzig and Dessau 1778.

Barnstorff, J. Youngs Nachtgedanken und ihr Einfluss auf die deutsche Literatur. Bamberg 1895.

Kind, J. L. Young in Germany. New York 1906.

Diener, G. Die Nacht in der deutschen Dichtung von Herder bis zur Romantik. Würzburg 1931.

Ebert, J. A. Übersetzungen einiger poetischen und prosaischen Werke der besten englischen Schriftsteller. 2 vols Brunswick 1754–6.

Satire

German Authors

Lessing, Gotthold Ephraim (1729–81). Fabeln. Berlin 1759; Fables from the German, tr J. Richardson, York 1773.

Rabener, Gottlieb Wilhelm (1714–71). Sammlung satirischer Schriften. 4 vols Leipzig 1751–5; Satirical letters, tr 2 vols 1757.

Wieland, Christoph Martin (1733–1813). Σωκρατης μαινομενος: oder die Dialogen des Diogenes von Sinope. Leipzig 1770; Socrates out of his senses: or Dialogues of Diogenes of Sinope, tr Wintersted 1771.

— Göttergespräche. Leipzig 1791; Dialogues of the gods, tr W. Taylor 1795; tr W. Tooke 1795; tr T. Holcroft 1795.

Holcroft, T. Dialogues of the Gods: an imitation of Wieland. Monthly Mag 1796, 1798.

Zachariä, Just Friedrich Wilhelm (1726–77). Murner in der Hölle: ein scherzhaftes Heldengedicht. Rostock 1757; Tabby in Elysium, tr R. E. Raspe 1781.

English Authors

Butler, Samuel. Hudibras. 3 pts 1663–78.

Bodmer, J. J. Versuch einer deutschen Übersetzung von Samuel Butlers Hudibras. Frankfurt and Leipzig 1737; completed by J. H. Waser 1765; tr D. W. Soltau 1787.

Dryden, John. Mac Flecknoe: or a satire on the true blue protestant poet T.S. 1682.

Wernicke, Christian. Ein Heldengedicht, Hans Sachs genannt, aus dem englischen übersetzt. Hamburg 1702.

Eichler, A. Wernickes Hans Sachs und sein Drydensches Vorbild. Zeitschrift für Vergleichende Literaturgeschichte 17 1909.

Mandeville, Bernard. The fable of the bees: or private vices, public benefits. 1714.

Sakmann, P. Mandeville und die Bienenfabel-Controverse. Freiburg 1897.

Pope, Alexander. The rape of the lock. 1712, 1714 (enlarged); Popes Lockenraub, tr Luise A. V. Gottsched, Leipzig 1744.

Zachariä, J. F. W. Der Renommist. Leipzig 1744.

Uz, J. P. Der Sieg des Liebesgottes. Leipzig 1753.

Dusch, J. J. Der Schosshund. 1756.

Petzet, E. Die deutschen Nachahmungen des Popeschen Lockenraubes. Zeitschrift für Vergleichende Literaturgeschichte 4 1891.

— The Dunciad. 1728, 1742 (with bk 4).

Bodmer, J. J. Popens Duncias. Zürich 1747.

Wieland, C. M. Ankündigung einer Dunciade für die Deutschen. Frankfurt 1755.

Maack, R. Über Popes Einfluss auf die Idylle und das Lehrgedicht in Deutschland. Hamburg 1895.

Lenz, W. Wielands Verhältnis zu Spenser, Pope und Swift. Hersfeld 1903.

Swift, Jonathan. Works. 1755.

Satyrische und ernsthafte Schriften. Tr J. H. Waser 8 vols Hamburg 1756–66.

Rabener, G. W. Sammlung satirischer Schriften. 4 vols Leipzig 1751–5.

Caro, J. Lessing und Swift. Jena 1869.

Meyer, R. M. Swift und Lichtenberg. Berlin 1886.

Philippoviç, Vera. Swift in Deutschland. Zürich 1903.

Roch, H. Richter ihrer Zeit: Grimmelshausen, Swift, Gogol. Berlin 1957.

Adams, R. M. Swift and Kafka. Ithaca 1958.

Thomas, L. H. C. Swift in German literature. Hermathena 104 1967.

Stathis, J. A bibliography of Swift studies 1945–65. Nashville 1967.

— The tale of a tub. 1704; Des berühmten Herrn D.: Schwifts Mährgen von der Tonne, tr Altona 1729.

— Gulliver's travels. 1726; Des Capitän Lemuel Gullivers Reisen, tr J. H. Riebers, Leipzig and Hamburg 1728 (from French); Gullivers Reisen, tr Hamburg 1731; tr J. H. Waser, Frankfurt and Leipzig 1761; Gullivers Reisen nach Lilliput, tr C. H. Kröger 2 vols Copenhagen 1786–7; Gullivers sämmtliche Reisen, tr J. K. Risbeck, Zürich 1788.

Rossi, M. M. Notes on the 18th-century German translations of Swift's Gulliver's Travels. Lib Chron 25 1959.

Drama

German Authors

Babo, Josef Marius von (1756–1822). Otto von Wittelsbach. Munich 1782; Otto von Wittelsbach, tr Walter Scott in ms c. 1796 from stage edn by Ritter v. Steinsberg, unpbd.

Die Strelitzen. 1790; The Strelitzes, tr [1800?].

Goethe, Johann Wolfgang von (1749–1832). Götz von Berlichingen. Frankfurt 1773; Goetz von Berlichingen with the iron hand, tr Walter Scott 1799; Gortz of Berlingen, tr Rose d'Aguilar, Liverpool 1799.

— Clavigo. Leipzig 1774; Clavidjo: a tragedy, tr B. Thompson 1798; Clavido, tr C. Leftley 1798.

— Stella. Berlin 1776; tr 1798.

— Die Geschwister. Leipzig 1787; The sister, tr W. Taylor 1792; tr H. Mackenzie, Edinburgh 1792.

— Iphigenie auf Tauris. Leipzig 1787; Iphigenia in Tauris, tr W. Taylor 1793.

Brandl, A. Die Aufnahme von Goethes Jugendwerken in England. Goethe-Jahrbuch 1882.

Heinemann, W. Goethe on the English stage. Pbns of Eng Goethe Soc 4 1888.

Alford, R. G. Goethe's earliest critics in England. Pbns of Eng Goethe Soc 7 1893.

Oswald, E. Goethe in England and America. Pbns of Eng Goethe Soc 8 1899.

Carré, J. M. Goethe en Angleterre. Paris 1920.

Boyd, J. Goethe's knowledge of English literature. Oxford 1932.

Federmann, A. Der junge Goethe und England. Berlin 1949.

Rose, W. Goethe's reputation in England during his lifetime. In Essays on Goethe, ed W. Rose 1949.

Bruford, W. H. Goethe's reputation in England since 1832. Ibid.

Dickson, A. J. Goethe in England 1909–49. Pbns of Eng Goethe Soc new ser 19 1951.

Wonderley, Wayne. An English Goethe parody. Monatshefte 48 1956.

Iffland, August Wilhelm (1759–1814). Verbrechen aus Ehrsucht. Mannheim 1784; Crime from ambition, tr M. Geisweiler 1800.

— Die Mündel. Berlin 1785; tr Walter Scott in ms c. 1796, unpbd; The nephews, tr Hannibal E. Lloyd 1799.

— Die Jäger. Berlin 1785; The foresters, tr Bell Plumptre 1799.

— Die Hagestolzen. Leipzig 1793; The bachelors, tr 1799.

— Die Advokaten. Leipzig 1796; The lawyers, tr C. Ludger 1799.

— Das Gewissen. Leipzig 1799; Conscience, tr B. Thompson 1800.

Klinger, Friedrich Maximilian von (1752–1831). Die neue Arria. Berlin 1776; The modern Arria, tr 1795.

Klopstock, Friedrich Gottlieb (1724–1803). Der Tod Adams. Copenhagen 1757; The death of Adam, tr Robert Lloyd 1763.

Kotzebue, August Friedrich Ferdinand von (1761–1819). On trns and adaptations see Stockley, and Stokoe, above.

— Menschenhass und Reue. Berlin 1789; The stranger, tr G. Papendick 1798; tr A. Schink 1798; Misanthropy and repentance, tr J. Hemet, Monthly Mirror 8 1799; The stranger, tr B. Thompson 1800.

— Adelheid von Wulfingen. Leipzig 1789; Adelaide of Wulfingen, tr B. Thompson 1798.

— Die Indianer in England. Leipzig 1790; The Indians in England, tr A. Thompson 1796; The Indian exiles, tr B. Thompson 1800.

— Das Kind der Liebe. Leipzig 1791; Lovers' vows: or the child of love, tr S. Porter 1798; Lovers' vows, tr E. Inchbald 1798; The natural son, tr Anne Plumptre 1798; Lovers' vows: or the natural son, tr B. Thompson 1800.

— Die Sonnen-Jungfrau. Leipzig 1791; The virgin of the sun, tr Anne Plumptre 1799; Rolla: or the virgin of the sun, tr B. Thompson 1799; The virgin of the sun, tr W. Dunlap 1799; The virgin of the sun, tr J. Lawrence, New York 1800.

— Graf Benjowsky: oder die Verschwörung auf Kamtschatka. Leipzig 1795; Count Benyowsky, tr W. Render 1798; Count Bergowsky; tr B. Thompson 1800.

— Armuth und Edelsinn. Leipzig 1795; Poverty and nobleness of mind, tr M. Geisweiler 1799; Sighs: or the daughter, adapted by P. Hoare 1799.

— Die Spanier in Peru: oder Rollas Tod. Leipzig 1796; Rolla, or the Peruvian hero, tr M. G. Lewis (1797?]; Pizarro in Peru: or the death of Rolla, tr T. Dutton 1799; Pizarro, tr 'a North Briton' 1799; Pizarro in Peru, tr R. Heron 1799; The Spaniards in Peru: or the death of Rolla, tr Anne Plumptre 1799; Pizarro, adapted for the English stage by R. B. Sheridan 1799.
Probably based on Lewis' trn, there were 26 edns by 1800; the 26th edn contained a re-trn into German by C. Geisweiler. Pizarro: or the Spaniards in Peru, tr New York 1800; Pizarro in Peru: or the death of Rolla, tr W.

Dunlap, New York 1800; Pizarro: or the death of Rolla, tr B. Thompson 1800.

Matlaw, M. English versions of Die Spanier in Peru. MLQ 16 1955.

— Die Wittwe und das Reitpferd. Leipzig 1796; The widow and the riding-horse, tr Anne Plumptre 1799; The horse and the widow, adapted by T. Dibdin 1799.

— Der Wildfang. Leipzig 1798; The wild goose chace, tr W. Dunlap 1798; The wild youth, tr C. Smith, New York 1800.

— Der Graf von Burgund. Leipzig 1798; The Count of Burgundy, tr Anne Plumptre 1798; The Count of Burgundy, tr C. Smith, New York 1800.

— Der Opfertod. Leipzig 1799; Self-immolation: or the sacrifice of love, tr H. Neumann 1799.

— Die Versöhnung. Leipzig 1798; The reconciliation, or the birth-day, tr C. Ludger 1799; The birth-day, adapted by T. Dibdin 1800.

— Falsche Schaam. Leipzig 1798; False shame, tr 1799; False delicacy, tr B. Thompson 1800; False shame: or the American orphan in Germany, tr Charleston 1800.

— Die Corsen. Leipzig 1799; The Corsicans, tr 1799; tr 'Eleanor', Lady's Mag 31 1800.

— Die silberne Hochzeit. Leipzig 1799; The happy family, tr B. Thompson 1799.

Britton, John. Sheridan and Kotzebue. 1799.

Oulton, W. C. The beauties of Kotzebue. 1800.

Plumptre, Anne. The life and literary career of Kotzebue. 1800.

Bahlsen, L. Kotzebue and Sheridan. Berlin 1899.

Sellier, W. Kotzebue in England. Leipzig 1901.

Thompson, L. F. Kotzebue: a survey of his progress in France and England. Paris 1928.

Gosch, M. 'Translators' of Kotzebue in England. Monatshefte für den Deutschen Unterricht 31 1939.

Sinko, G. Sheridan and Kotzebue. Wroclaw 1949.

Lindsay, D. W. Kotzebue in Scotland 1792–1813. Pbns of Eng Goethe Soc 33 1963.

Kratter, Franz (1758–1830). Die Verschwörung wider Peter den Grossen. Vienna 1794; Natalia und Menzikof: or the conspiracy against Peter the Great, tr 1798.

— Das Mädchen von Marienburg. Frankfurt 1795; The maid of Marienburg, tr 1798.

Leisewitz, Johann Anton (1752–1806). Julius von Tarent. Leipzig 1776; Julius of Tarentum, tr P. Will 1800.

Lessing, Gotthold Ephraim (1729–81). Miss Sara Sampson. Berlin 1755; Lucy Sampson: or the unhappy heyress, tr D. Rittenhouse, Philadelphia 1789; The fatal elopement, tr Eleanore H., Lady's Mag 30 1799.

— Minna von Barnhelm. Berlin 1767; The disbanded officer: or the Baroness of Bruchsal, tr J. Johnstone 1786; The school for honour: or the chance of war, tr probably R. Harvey 1799.

— Emilia Galotti. Berlin 1772. Extracts tr H. Maty, New Rev 9 1786; tr Berrington 1794; tr B. Thompson 1801.

— Nathan der Weise. Berlin 1779; Nathan the Wise, tr R. E. Raspe 1781; tr W. Taylor 1791.

Caro, J. Lessing und die Engländer. Euphorion 6 1899.

Todt, W. Lessing in England 1767–1850. Heidelberg 1912.

Kenwood, S. H. Lessing in England. MLR 9 1914.

Kies, P. P. The sources and basic model of Lessing's Miss Sara Sampson. MP 24 1926.

— Lessing's early study of English drama. JEGP 28 1929.

— Lessing's relation to early English sentimental comedy. PMLA 47 1932.

Vail, C. C. D. Lessing's relation to the English language and literature. Columbia Univ Germanic Stud 3 1936.

— Pastor Lessing's knowledge of English. Germanic Rev 20 1945.

Schneider, H. Lessing's Miss Sara Sampson: die erste englische Übersetzung. PMLA 54 1939.

Roedder, E. Lessing's Nathan der Weise auf der englischen Bühne. Monatshefte 34 1942.

Garland, H. B. Lessing, the founder of modern German literature. Cambridge 1949.

Price, L. M. English theological works in Pastor Lessing's library. JEGP 3 1954.

Guthke, K. S. Lessing-Forschung 1932 bis 1962. Deutsche Vierteljahrsschrift für Literatur 38 1964.

Dvoretzky, E. The 18th-century English translations of Emilia Galotti. Rice Univ Stud 52 1966.

Maier, Jakob (1739–84). Fust von Stromberg. Mannheim 1782; tr Walter Scott in ms c. 1796, unpbd.

Schiller, Johann Friedrich von (1759–1805). Die Räuber. Frankfurt 1781; The robbers, tr A. F. Tytler (Lord Woodhouselee) 1792 (largely from the French trn of Bonneville-Friedel); tr and altered from the German by the Margravine of Anspach (i.e. Lady Craven) 1799; tr W. Render 1799 (from Tytler's trn).

Holman, J. G. The Red Cross knights, founded on the Robbers. 1799.

The robbers. Tr B. Thompson 1800–1 (from the stage edn); tr Perth 1800.

Cooke, Margaret W. Schiller's Robbers in England. MLR 11 1916.

Willoughby, L. A. English translations and adaptations of Schiller's Robbers. MLR 16 1921.

Waterhouse, G. Schiller's Räuber in England before 1800. MLR 30 1935.

Milburn, D. The first English translation of Die Räuber: French bards and Scottish translators. Monatshefte 59 1967.

— Die Verschwörung des Fiesko zu Genua. Mannheim 1783; Fiesco: or the Genoese conspiracy, tr G. H. Noehden and J. Stoddart 1796.

— Kabale und Liebe. Mannheim 1784; Cabal and love, tr P. Colombine (with J. J. C. Timäus?) 1795; The minister, tr M. G. Lewis 1797.

Willoughby, L. A. Schiller's Kabale und Liebe in English translation. Pbns of Eng Goethe Soc new ser 1 1924.

Trainer, J. The first English translation of Kabale und Liebe. MLR 59 1964.

— Don Carlos. Leipzig 1787; tr 1795; tr G. H. Noehden and J. Stoddart 1798; tr [Symonds?] 1798; Don Carlos, adapted by W. Dunlap, New York 1799; Don Carlos, Infant of Spain, tr B. Thompson 1801.

— Wallenstein. Tübingen 1800; tr S. T. Coleridge 1800 (Piccolomini and Death of Wallenstein).

— Maria Stuart. Tübingen 1801; tr J. C. Mellish 1801.

Rea, T. Schiller's dramas and poems in England. 1906.

Kelly, J. A. Schiller's attitude toward England. PMLA 39 1924.

Ewen, F. The prestige of Schiller in England 1788-1859. New York 1932.

Garland, H. B. Schiller. 1949.

Witte, W. Schiller. 1949.

Mainland, W. F. Schiller and the changing past. 1957.

Witte, W. Schiller and Burns and other essays. Oxford 1959.

Pick, R. Schiller in England: a bibliography 1787–1960. Pbns of Eng Goethe Soc 30 1961.

Törring-Cronsfeld, Joseph August (1753–1836). Agnes Bernauerinn. Munich 1780; The tournament, tr M. Starke 1800.

Unzer, Johann Christoph (1747–1809). Diego und Leonore. Hamburg 1775; The inquisitor, tr and adapted by J. P. Andrews and H. J. Pye 1798, tr T. Holcroft, Monthly Rev 1798.

Vulpius, Christian August (1762–1827). Das Geheimnis. Leipzig 1800; The mystery, tr M. Geisweiler [c. 1800].

Mackenzie, Henry. Account of the German theatre. Trans Royal Soc of Edinburgh 1790.

English Authors

Addison, Joseph. Cato: a tragedy. 1713; tr Luise A. V. Gottsched, Leipzig 1735 (prose); tr Grynäus?, Basle and Frankfurt 1758 (verse); tr J. H. Merck, Leipzig and Frankfurt 1763 (prose); tr Berlin and Leipzig 1770.

Gottsched, J. C. Der sterbende Cato. Leipzig 1732.

Banks, John. The unhappy favourite: or the Earl of Essex. 1687; Die Gunst der Fürsten, tr Danzig and Leipzig 1773; Der Graf von Essex, ed J. D. Dyk, Leipzig 1777.

Brooke, Henry. Gustavus Vasa. 1739; tr Danzig 1776; tr Kotzebue 1796.

Brown, John. Athelstan 1756; tr Leonhardi, Hamburg 1778.

Burgoyne, John. The heiress. 1786; Die Erbin, tr W. Schenk, Hanover 1788.

Cibber, Colley. Love makes a man: or the fop's fortune. 1701; Liebe macht den Mann, tr C. F. Huber, Berlin 1784.

— She would and she would not: or the kind impostor. 1703; Die Wankelmütige: oder der weibliche Betrüger, tr Vienna 1782.

— The careless husband. 1705; Der sorglose Ehemann, tr J. D. Michaelis, Göttingen 1750; Der leichtsinnige Ehemann, tr Leipzig 1771; Der blinde Ehemann, tr Berlin 1784.

— The double gallant: or the sick lady's cure. 1707; Der doppelte Liebhaber, adapted J. F. Jünger, Leipzig 1786.

Colman, George. The jealous wife. 1761; Die eifersüchtige Ehefrau, tr J. J. C. Bode, Hamburg 1762.

— The clandestine marriage. 1766; Die heimliche Heirath, tr Schmid?, Frankfurt and Leipzig 1769.

— The man of business. 1774; Der Negotiant, tr Kepner, Vienna 1775; Der Mann von Geschäften, tr Danzig 1776.

— Bon ton. 1775; Der Ton der grossen Welt, adapted C. G. von Harold, Alternburg 1776.

Congreve, William. The double dealer. 1694; Der Arglistige, tr J. H. Schlegel?, Copenhagen 1763.

— The old bachelor. 1694; Der Hagestolz, tr Frankfurt and Leipzig 1770.

— Love for love. 1695; Der unversöhnliche Vater, tr H. E. von Spilcker, Leipzig and Rostock 1754; Liebe für Liebe, tr E.T.A., Copenhagen 1766.

— The mourning bride. 1697; Allmeria: oder die trauernde Braut, tr Grynäus?, Basle and Frankfurt 1759; Die Braut in Trauer, tr J. E. Schlegel 2 vols Copenhagen and Leipzig 1761-70.

— The way of the world. 1698; Der Lauf der Welt, tr Rostock 1757.

Cowley, Hannah. The runaway. 1776.

Helmolt, C. G. Der schöne Flüchtling. Augsburg 1776.

— Who's the dupe? 1779.

Leonardi, J. Wer ist angeführt? Hamburg 1785.

— The belle's stratagem. 1780; So muss man die Männer fangen, tr 1781.

— The school for eloquence. 1780.

Kurzböck, J. E. von. Der Schulgelehrte. Vienna 1782.

— A day in Turkey: or the Russian slaves. 1792; Alexina: oder ein Tag in der Türkei, tr Berlin 1792.

Crisp, Samuel. Virginia. 1754.

Lessing, G. E. Emilia Galotti. Berlin 1772.

Crowne, John. Sir Courtly Nice: or it cannot be. 1685; Sir Phantast oder es kann nicht sein, tr C. H. Schmid, Bremen 1762; Die unmögliche Sache, tr F. R. Schröder, Vienna 1773.

Cumberland, Richard. The brothers. 1768; Die Brüder, tr Klausing, Leipzig 1770; Die ungleichen Brüder, tr E. L. M. Rathlef, Jena 1779; Die Brüder, tr W. H. von Dalberg, Mannheim 1786.

— The West Indian. 1771; Der Westindier, tr J. J. C. Bode, Hamburg 1772.

— The fashionable lover. 1772; Miss Obre: oder die gerettete Unschuld, tr K. C. H. Rost, Leipzig 1774.

— The choleric man. 1775; Der Kolerische, tr W. H. von Dalberg 2 vols Mannheim 1785-6.

—— Arundel. 1780; Arundel: oder der Sieg des Edelmuths, 2 vols Leipzig 1790–1.

—— The Carmelite. 1785; Der Mönch von Carmel, adapted Dalberg, Mannheim 1786.

—— The natural son. 1785; Der natürliche Sohn, tr C. G. Küttner, Leipzig 1785.

—— The Jew. 1794 (2nd edn); Der Jude, tr J. F. H. Brockmann, Vienna 1795; tr Dengel, Königsberg 1798.

Dodsley, Robert. Cleone. 1758; Cleone und Elvire: zwei Trauerspiele, tr C. A. Herzog, Leipzig 1764.

Dryden, John. The tempest: or the enchanted island. 1670; Der Sturm: oder die bezauberte Insel, tr Leipzig 1780.

—— The state of innocence and fall of man. 1677; Der Stand der Unschuld und Fall des Menschen, tr Grynäus?, Frankfurt and Leipzig 1754.

—— All for love: or the world well lost. 1678; Cleopatra, tr C. H. Schmid, Leipzig 1769; Alles für Liebe, tr Mannheim 1781.

—— Oedipus. 1679 (with Nathaniel Lee); tr Grynäus, Basle and Frankfurt 1759.

Farquhar, George. The constant couple. 1700.

Schröder, F. L. Der Ring. Berlin 1786. *For Schröder's other adaptations from English plays, see* B. Litzmann, Friedrich Ludwig Schröder, Hamburg 1890.

—— Inconstant: or the way to win him. 1702.

Lessing, K. G. Der Wildfang. Berlin 1769.

—— The recruiting officer. 1706; Der Werbeoffizier, tr Frankfurt and Leipzig 1769.

Stephanie, G. Die Werber. Vienna 1769.

—— The beaux' stratagem. 1707; Die Stutzerlist, tr Leonhardi, Berlin 1782.

Schlosser, J. F. Die Glücksritter. Vienna 1783.

Robertson, J. G. Farquhar and Lessing. MLR 2 1907.

Fielding, Henry. Love in several masques. 1728; Die Liebe unter verschiedenen Larven, tr Copenhagen 1759; tr Mannheim 1781.

—— The temple beau. 1730; Der akademische Stutzer, tr Mannheim 1782.

—— The modern husband. 1732; Der Ehemann nach der Mode, tr Strasbourg 1781.

—— The intriguing chambermaid. 1734; Das verschlagene Kammermädchen, tr Mannheim 1781.

—— The wedding day. 1743; Der Hochzeitstag, tr Copenhagen 1759; tr Vienna 1764.

Clarke, C. H. Fielding und der deutsche Sturm und Drang. Freiburg 1897.

Price, L. M. The works of Fielding on the German stage 1762–1801. JEGP 41 1942.

Glover, Richard. Leonidas. 1737; tr J. A. Ebert, Leipzig 1748; tr Grynäus, Basle 1757.

—— Boadicea. 1753; tr Hamburg and Leipzig 1756.

—— Medea. 1761; tr C. G. von Murr, Nuremberg 1763.

Goldsmith, Oliver. The good natured man. 1768; tr F. Schröder as Der Gutherzige, Danzig 1777; tr Schmidt as Zu gut ist nicht gut, Gotha 1778; tr A. G. F. Rebmann as Der Universalfreund: oder Gutherzigkeit und Windbeuteley, Gera 1796.

—— She stoops to conquer. 1773; Sie lässt sich herab, um zu siegen, tr A. Wittenburg, Hamburg 1773; Irrthümer in einer Nacht, tr Hamburg 1774.

Hennig, J. The Auerbachs Keller scene and She stoops to conquer. Comparative Lit 7 1955.

Price, L. M. The works of Goldsmith on the German stage 1776–95. MLQ 5 1944.

Greatheed, Bertie. The Regent. 1788; tr Mannheim 1789.

Hoadly, Benjamin. The suspicious husband. 1747; Der argwöhnische Ehemann, tr J. J. C. Bode, Hamburg 1754.

Holcroft, Thomas. The seduction. 1787; Die Verführung, tr Stendal 1789.

—— The road to ruin. 1792; Güte rettet, tr L. F. Huber, Leipzig 1793; Leichtsinn und kindliche Liebe: oder der Weg zum Verderben, tr Berlin 1794.

Kelly, Hugh. False delicacy. 1768; Die zu zärtliche Zurückhaltung, adapted Beck, Königsberg [1769?]; Die ungegründete Bedenklichkeit, tr Leipzig 1770.

—— Clementina. 1771; Clementine, tr A. Wittenberg, Hamburg 1774.

—— The school for wives. 1774; Die Schule der Weiber, tr 1774.

Bock, J. C. Wie man eine Hand umkehrt. Hamburg 1776.

Lee, Sophia. A chapter of accidents. 1780; Glück bessert Thorheit, tr Vienna 1783; Die Zufälle, tr Berlin 1782.

Lillo, George. The London merchant: or the history of George Barnwell. 1731; Der Kaufmann von London: oder die Begebenheit Georg Barnwells, tr H. A. Bassewitz, Hamburg 1752.

Lessing, G. E. Miss Sara Sampson. Berlin 1755.

—— The Christian hero. 1735; Der christliche Held, tr Leipzig 1777.

—— Fatal curiosity. 1737; Die unglückliche Neubegierde, tr Hamburg 1761.

W. H. Brömel. Wilmot und Agnes: oder Stolz und Verzweiflung. Leipzig 1784.

—— Elmerich: or Justice triumphant. 1740; Elmerich, tr Schwerin 1790.

—— Collected works. 1775; Sämmtliche theatralische Werke, tr J. G. Gellius 2 vols Leipzig 1777–8.

Weilen, A. von. Der Kaufmann von London auf deutschen und französischen Bühnen. Beiträge zur Neueren Philologie 1902.

Walz, J. A. Goethe's Götz von Berlichingen and Lillo's History of George Barnwell. MP 30 1906.

Kunze, A. Lillos Einfluss auf die englische und die deutsche Literatur. Magdeburg 1911.

Price, L. M. George Barnwell on the German stage. Monatshefte 35 1943.

—— George Barnwell abroad. Comparative Lit 2 1950.

Mallet, David. Elvira. 1763; Cleone und Elvire: zwei Trauerspiele, tr C. A. Herzog, Leipzig and Zittau 1764.

Miller, James. The man of taste. 1735; Der Mann von Geschmack, tr Danzig 1777.

Moore, Edward. The foundling. 1747; Die Unbekannte, tr J. F. Kepner, Vienna 1774; Der Fündling, tr Frankfurt and Leipzig 1778; Wer ist sie?, tr Hamburg 1786.

—— The gamester. 1753; Der Spieler, tr J. J. C. Bode, Hamburg 1754; Beverley: oder der Spieler, tr J. H. Steffens, Celle 1755; Beverley, tr J. J. C. Timäus, Hanover 1798.

More, Hannah. Percy. 1778; freely tr Hamburg 1779.

—— Sacred dramas, chiefly intended for young persons. 1782; Dramen zur Belehrung junger Frauenzimmer, tr C. F. Weisse, Leipzig 1787; Geistliche Dramen und biblische Geschichten, tr Erlangen 1792.

Murphy, Arthur. All in the wrong. 1761; Die Eifersüchtigen: oder Keiner hat Recht, tr Schwerin 1770; tr J. Bergobzoomer as Alle irren sich, Vienna 1777.

—— The old maid. 1761; Die Übereilung, tr F. L. W. Meyer, Schwerin 1790.

Otway, Thomas. Don Carlos, Prince of Spain. 1676; Don Carlos, Prinz von Spanien, tr Frankfurt and Leipzig 1757.

Löwenberg, J. Über Otways und Schillers Don Carlos. Lippstadt 1886.

Müller, Ernst. Otways, Schillers und St Reals Don Carlos. Tübingen 1888.

—— Friendship in fashion. 1678: Freundschaft nach der Mode, tr E.T.A., Copenhagen and Leipzig 1767.

—— The orphan. 1680; Die Waise, tr Grynäus?, Basle and Frankfurt 1759; Die Wayse und das gerettete Venedig, tr C. H. Böttger, Langensalza 1767.

—— Venice preserv'd. 1682; Die Verschwörung wider Venedig, tr Vienna 1749 (partly from Otway, partly from La Place); tr J. F. Lauson as Gafforio, Leipzig 1755.

Sulzer-Gebing, E. Schiller und das gerettete Venedig. Studien zur Vergleichenden Literaturgeschichte 5 1905.

Klieneberger, H. R. Otways' Venice preserved and Hofmannsthal's Das gerettete Venedig. MLR 62 1967.

Pilon, Frederick. The deaf lover. 1780; tr F. L. Schröder as Der taube Liebhaber, Vienna 1788.

— He would a soldier be. 1786; Er wird Soldat werden, tr 1790.

Ravenscroft, Edward. The anatomist: or the sham doctor. 1696; Der Anatomist oder Parforce-Doctor, tr Frankfurt and Leipzig 1748.

Reynolds, Frederick. Rage. 1795; Modethorheiten, tr Leipzig 1797; C. H. Schale, Die Ränke, Leipzig 1798.

Rowe, Nicholas. The ambitious stepmother. 1698; Die eifersüchtige Stiefmutter, tr F. T. Hase, Frankfurt and Leipzig 1773.

— The fair penitent. 1703; Kallista, die schöne Reuerin, tr Grynäus, ? Basle and Frankfurt 1759; Die büssende Schöne, tr Mannheim 1782.

— Jane Shore. 1714; tr S. Reval, Hamburg 1771.

— Tragedy of the Lady Jane Grey. 1715. Wieland, C. M. Lady Johanna Grey. Zürich 1758.

St John, John. Mary Queen of Scots. 1789; Maria Königin von Schottland, tr K. Kramer 1790.

Sheridan, Richard Brinsley. The rivals. 1775; Die Nebenbuhler, tr J. A. Engelbrecht, Hamburg 1775; Die zwey Nebenbuhler, tr Vienna 1787; Die beyden Nebenbuhler, tr Hanover 1795.

— The school for scandal. 1777; Die Lästerschule, tr J. Leonhardi, Berlin 1782.

Steuber, F. Sheridans Rivals: Entstehungsgeschichte und Beiträge zu einer deutschen Theatergeschichte des Stücks. Marburg 1913.

Southerne, Thomas. The fatal marriage. 1694; Die unglückliche Heirath, tr F. L. Schröder, Hamburg 1784.

—Oronooko. 1696; tr W. H. von Dalberg, Mannheim 1786.

Steele, Sir Richard. The conscious lovers. 1722; Die sich mit einander verstehenden Liebhaber, tr Dresden 1752.

— Steelens Lustspiele. Tr C. H. Schmid, Leipzig 1767. Contains Der zärtliche Ehemann, Die heimlich Lieben-den, Das Leichenbegängnis, Der lügenhafte Liebhaber.

Thomson, James. Sophonisba. 1730; Sophonisbe, tr J. G. Bernhold 1750; Sophonisba, tr J. H. Schlegel, Leipzig 1758.

— Agamemnon. 1738; tr J. D. Michaelis, Göttingen 1750; tr Frankfurt 1751; tr J. H. Schlegel, Leipzig 1760; tr Karlsruhe 1771.

— Edward and Eleanora. 1739; Eduard und Eleanora, tr J. H. Schlegel, Leipzig 1764.

— Tancred and Sigismunda. 1745; Tankred und Sigismunda, tr J. H. Schlegel, Leipzig 1764; tr Karlsruhe 1771.

— Coriolanus. 1749; tr J.F.C., Frankfurt and Leipzig 1756; tr J. H. Schlegel, Leipzig 1760.

Sämtliche Trauerspiele, mit einer Vorrede von G. E. Lessing. Leipzig 1756.

Vanbrugh, Sir John. The relapse: or virtue in danger. 1697; Der Rückfall: oder die Tugend in Gefahr, tr Göttingen 1750.

— The provoked wife. 1697; Wie man's treibt, so geht's: oder die aufgebrachte Ehefrau, tr Frankfurt and Leipzig 1769; Die Weiberverschwörung, tr C. H. Schmid 1788.

— The false friend. 1702; Der verdächtige Freund, tr J. Leonhardi, Hamburg 1785.

— The country house. 1715; Das Landhaus, tr K. C. H. Rost, Leipzig 1770.

— The mistake. 1706; Die Verwechslung, tr Lauder, Vienna 1764 (from the French version of Sticcoti); Das Missverständnis, tr Frankfurt and Leipzig 1770.

— The provoked husband: or a journey to London. 1728; Der aufgebrachte Ehemann, tr Frankfurt 1748.

Whitehead, William. The school for lovers. 1762; tr C. G. Klemm as Die Schule der Liebhaber, Vienna 1765; tr J. J. C. Bode, Hamburg 1771.

Wycherley, William. The country wife. 1675; Das Land-

mädchen, tr Danzig 1776; tr B. C. d'Arien as Das Landmädchen, Schwerin 1794.

Young, Edward. Busiris, King of Egypt. 1719; Busiris, Grynäus, ? Basle and Frankfurt 1759.

— The revenge. 1721; Die Rache, tr Grynäus, ? Basle and Frankfurt 1759; Zanga oder die Rache, tr J. C. Huber, Vienna 1761.

Blümner, H. Die Rache. Leipzig 1794.

— The brothers. 1753; Die Brüder, tr Frankfurt and Leipzig 1756; tr J. H. Schlegel, Copenhagen and Leipzig 1764.

Youngs Trauerspiele nebst der Boadicea von Glover. Tr Hamburg and Leipzig 1756.

King, J. L. Young in Germany. New York 1906.

Neue Probestücke der englischen Schaubühne übersetzt von einem Liebhaber des guten Geschmacks. Basle 1758. Contains trns of 8 plays by Young, Addison, Dryden and Lee, Otway, Shakespeare, Congreve, Rowe.

Englisches Theater. Ed C. H. Schmid 7 pts Frankfurt, Leipzig and Danzig 1769–78. Trns of 21 English plays.

Theater der Britten. Berlin and Leipzig 1770. Trns of plays by Thomson, Otway, Lillo, Addison, Dodsley, Moore, Young.

Hamburgisches Theater I–IV. Ed F. L. Schröder 3 vols Hamburg 1776–81. Contains trns of 8 English plays.

Sammlung von Schauspielen fürs Hamburgische Theater I–IV. 4 vols Schwerin and Hamburg 1792–4. Contains trns of a further 8 English plays.

Clarke, C. H. Lenz Übersetzungen aus dem Englischen. Zeitschrift für Vergleichende Literaturgeschichte 10 1897.

Beam, J. N. Die ersten deutschen Übersetzungen englischer Lustspiele. Hamburg 1906.

Wihan, J. Johann Joachim Christoph Bode als Vermittler englischer Geisteswerke in Deutschland. Prager Deutsche Studien 1906.

Betz, L. Lichtenberg as a critic of the English stage. JEGP 23 1924.

Price, L. M. Christian Heinrich Schmid and his translations of English dramas 1767–89. Berkeley 1942.

Prose Fiction

German Authors

Gellert, Christian Fürchtegott (1715–69). Das Leben der schwedischen Gräfinn von G. 2 vols Leipzig 1747–8; The history of the Swedish Countess of Guildenstern, tr 1752; The life of the Countes of G., tr 'by a lady' 1776; The life of the Swedish Countess de G., tr Rev Mr N. 1776.

Goethe, Johann Wolfgang von (1749–1832). Die Leiden des jungen Werther. Leipzig 1774; The sorrows of Werter, tr R. Graves 1779 (from the French of Aubry); The sorrows and sympathetic attachments of Werter, tr Philadelphia 1784; Werther and Charlotte, tr 1786.

The sorrows of Werter, tr J. Gifford 1789 (from the French of Aubry); tr Philadelphia 1794, New York 1795, Ludlow 1799.

Reynolds, F. Werter: a tragedy. Acted 1785, ptd 1802.

Pickering, Amelia. The sorrows of Werter: a poem. 1789.

Farrel, Sarah. Charlotte: or a sequel to the sorrows of Werter. 1792.

Brandl, A. Die Aufnahme von Goethes Jugendwerken in England, I: Werther 1779–98. Goethe-Jahrbuch 3 1882.

Long, O. W. English translations of Goethe's Werther. JEGP 14 1915.

Hill, C. J. The first English translator of Werther 1779. MLN 47 1932.

Erämetsä, E. Der sprachliche Einfluss Richardsons auf Goethes Werther. Neuphilologische Mitteilungen 57 1956.

Grosse, Karl ('Graf von Vargas') (1761–1800). Der Genius, aus den Papieren des Marquis C. von G. 2 vols Halle 1791–4; The genius: or the mysterious adventures of Don Carlos de Grandez, tr Joseph Trapp 2 vols 1796; Horrid mysteries, tr P. Will 1796.
— Der Dolch. Berlin 1794–5; The dagger, tr 1794.

Haller, Albrecht von (1708–77). Usong. Berne 1771; Usong: an Eastern narrative, tr 1772.

Heinse, Johann Jacob Wilhelm (1746–1803). Ardinghello. Lemgo 1785.

Lewis, M. G. The monk. 1796.

Klinger, Friedrich Maximilian (1752–1831). Reisen vor der Sündfluth. Riga 1795; Travels before the flood, tr 1796.

Knigge, Adolf Franz Friedrich von (1752–96). Geschichte Peter Clausens. Riga 1783–5; The German Gil Blas: or the adventures of Peter Claus, tr 3 vols 1793.
— Geschichte des Amtrats Gutmann. Hanover 1794; The history of the Amtsrath Gutmann, tr 1799.

Kotzebue, August Friedrich Ferdinand von (1761–1819). Ildegerte, Königin von Norwegen. Reval and Leipzig 1788; Ildegerte, Queen of Norway, tr B. Thompson 1798.
— Die Leiden der Ortenbergischen Familie. St Petersburg 1785–92; The sufferings of the family of Ortenberg, tr P. Will 3 vols 1799.
— Die Geschichte meines Vaters. Reval 1788; The history of my father: a romance, tr 1798.
— Die Flucht; The escape, tr B. Thompson 1799.
— Geprüfte Liebe; The constant lover, tr 1799.

Lafontaine, August Heinrich (1758–1831). Saint Julien. Berlin 1798; tr 1798, 1799.
— Die Familie von Halden; The family of Halden, tr 1799.
— Romulus. Tr P. Will 1799.

Laroche, Sophie von (1731–1807). Geschichte des Fräuleins von Sternheim. 1771; The history of Lady Sophia Sternheim, tr J. Collyer 1776; The adventures of Miss Sophia Sternheim, tr E. Harwood 1776.

Miller, Johann Martin (1750–1814). Siegwart: eine Klostergeschichte. Leipzig 1776; Sigevart: a tale, tr H.L. 1799.

Musäus, Johann Karl August (1735–87). Physiognomische Reisen. Altenburg 1778; Physiognomical travels, tr Anne Plumptre 1800.
— Volksmärchen der Deutschen. 5 vols Gotha 1782–6; Popular tales of the Germans, tr W. Beckford 1791.

Naubert, Christiane Benedikte (1756–1819). Hermann von Unna. Leipzig 1788; tr 1794.

Boaden, James. The secret tribunal: a play. 1795.
— Alfons von Dülmen. Leipzig 1790; Alf von Deulmen: or the history of the Emperor Philip and his daughters, tr A. E. Booth 1790.

Nicolai, Friedrich (1733–1811). Leben und Meinungen des Herrn M. Sebaldus Nothanker. 3 vols Berlin 1773–6; The life and opinions of Sebaldus Nothanker, tr Thomas Dutton 3 vols 1796–8.

Schiller, Johann Friedrich von (1759–1805). Der Geisterseher. Leipzig 1789; The ghost-seer: or apparitionist, tr D. Boileau 1795; The Armenian: or the ghost-seer, tr W. Render 1800.

Schulz, Johann Christoph Friedrich. Moritz. Leipzig 1785; Maurice: a German tale, tr 1796 from a French version.

Spiess, Christian Heinrich (1755–99). Das Petermännchen; The mountain cottager, tr Anne Plumptre 1798.

Tschinck, Cajetan (d. 1809). Geschichte eines Geistersehers. Vienna 1791; The victim of magical delusion, tr P. Will, Dublin 1795.

Vulpius, Christian August (1762–1827). Rinaldo Rinaldini, der Räuberhauptmann. Leipzig 1798; The history of Rinaldo Rinaldini, tr J. Hinckley 1800.

Wächter, Leonhard ('Veit Weber') (1762–1837). Der Müller des Schwarztals; The black valley and the Sorcerer, tr J. Powell 1796.

— Die Teufelsbeschwörung; The sorcerer, tr R. Huish ? 1795.

Wieland, Christoph Martin (1733–1813). Die Abenteuer des Don Sylvio de Rosalva. Ulm 1764; Reason triumphant over fancy, exemplified in the adventure of Don Sylvio de Rosalva, tr 1773.
Geschichte des Agathon. Frankfurt 2 vols 1766–7, 1773 (rev); History of Agathon, tr J. Richardson 4 vols 1773.
— Der goldene Spiegel. 1772; The golden mirror, tr 1798.
— Geheime Geschichte des Philosophen Peregrinus Proteus. Leipzig 1791; Private history of Peregrinus Proteus, the philosopher, tr W. Tooke 1796; Confessions in Elysium: or the adventures of a Platonic philosopher, tr J. B. Elrington 1804.

Zschokke, Johann Heinrich Daniel (1771–1848). Abällino, der grosse Bandit. 1794; Aballino, the great bandit, tr and adapted for stage by W. Dunlap, New York 1792.

Lewis, M. G. Tales of terror. Kelso 1799. Adaptations from the German.

Raspe, R. E. Baron Munchausen's Narrative of his marvellous travels and campaigns in Russia. 1785. Pbd in English and tr German by G. A. Bürger as Des Freiherrn von Münchhausen wunderbare Reisen und Abenteuer, 1786.

English Authors

Beckford, William. Vathek. 1786; Der Thurm von Samarah, tr G. Schatz, Leipzig 1788; Vathek, tr G. C. Römer, Mannheim 1788.

Bunyan, John. The pilgrim's progress. 1678; Eines Christen Reise nach der seligen Ewigkeit, tr J. Lange, Hamburg 1685.
— Pilgrim's progress: part 2. 1684; Reise der Christin, tr C. M. Seidel, Hamburg 1708.
— The heavenly footman. 1698; Der himmlische Läufer, tr C. M. Seidel, Berlin 1718.
Sann, Auguste. Bunyan in Deutschland. Giessen 1951.

Cleland, John. Fanny Hill: or memoirs of a woman of pleasure. 1748; Das Fräulein von Vergnügen, tr 1778; Abenteuer eines Frauenzimmers von Vergnügen, tr London 1782.

Defoe, Daniel. Robinson Crusoe. 1719; Das Leben und die gantz ungemeinen Begebenheiten des Robinson Crusoe, tr L. F. Vischer, Frankfurt 1720; Leben und die ausserordentlichen Begebenheiten des Robinson Crusoe von York, tr Nuremberg 1782.

Campe, J. H. Robinson der Jüngere, für Kinder. Hamburg 1779.
There were c. 50 imitations in German, including J. G. Schnabel, Die wunderlichen Fata einiger Seefahrer absonderlich Alberti Julii und seiner auf der Insel Felsenburg zu Stande gebrachten Kolonien, 4 vols Nordhausen 1731–43. *See* K. Goedeke, Grundriss zur Geschichte der deutschen Dichtung vol 3, 1887.
Hettner, H. Robinson und die Robinsonaden. Berlin 1854.
Kippenberg, A. Robinson in Deutschland bis zur Insel Felsenburg. Archiv 90 1893.
Rötteken, H. Weltflucht und Idylle in Deutschland von 1720 bis zur Insel Felsenburg, 1: Robinsonaden. Zeitschrift für Vergleichende Literaturgeschichte 9 1896.
Ulrich, H. Robinson und Robinsonaden, i: Bibliographie. Weimar 1898.
Zobeltitz, F. von. Eine Bibliographie der Robinsonaden. Zeitschrift für Bücherfreunde 8–9 1898.
Deneke, O. Robinson Crusoe in Deutschland: die Frühdrucke 1720–80. Göttingen 1934.
— Moll Flanders. 1722; Moll Flanders: das ist einer also genannten Engländerinn erstaunenswerthe Glücks- und Unglücksfälle, tr Matteson, Hamburg 1723.

Hatfield, T. M. Moll Flanders in Germany. JEGP 32 1933.
—— The history and remarkable life of the truly honourable Col Jacque. 1722; Leben und Begebenheiten des Obristen Jacque, tr Frankfurt and Leipzig 1740.
—— Fortunate mistress: or a history of Roxana. 1724; Die glückliche Maitresse, tr Cologne 1736.
Fielding, Henry. Joseph Andrews. 1742; Begebenheiten des Joseph Andrews, tr Danzig 1745; tr Berlin 1761; Abenteuer Joseph Andrews, tr F. von Oertel, Berlin 1775.
—— The life of Mr Jonathan Wild the Great. 1743; Geschichte Herrn Jonathan Wilde des Grossen, tr Copenhagen 1754; Fieldings Jonathan Wilde, Rinaldo Rinaldinis Antipode, tr Ronneburg and Leipzig 1800.
—— The history of Tom Jones, a foundling. 6 vols 1749; Historie des menschlichen Herzens in den sonderbaren Begebenheiten Thomas Jones, eines Findlings, tr M. A. Wodarch 6 vols Hamburg 1749–51; Geschichte des Tom Jones, eines Findlings, tr F. Schmid, Nuremberg 1780; Geschichte des Tom Jones, eines Fündlings, tr J. J. C. Bode 6 vols Leipzig 1786–8.
—— Amelia. 1752; Amelia: oder das Muster ehelicher Liebe, tr Frankfurt and Leipzig 1752; Emelia Booth: ein Muster ehelicher Liebe, tr Leipzig 1780; Aemilie, tr from French of Maria Riccoboni by C. L. Heyne 2 vols Leipzig 1781–2.
Wood, A. Der Einfluss Fieldings auf die deutsche Literatur. Heidelberg 1895.
Clarke, C. H. Fielding und der deutsche Sturm und Drang. Freiburg 1897.
Krieg, H. J. J. C. Bode als Übersetzer des Tom Jones von Fielding. Greifswald 1909.
Stern, G. Fielding and the sub-literary German novel: a study of Opitz' Wilhelm von Hohenberg. Monatshefte 48 1956.
—— A German imitation of Fielding: Musäus' Grandison der Zweite. Comparative Lit 10 1958.
Godwin, Mary Wollstonecraft. Mary: a fiction. 1788; Maria oder das Unglück, Weib zu sein, tr Leipzig 1800.
—— Original stories from real life. 1788; Erzählungen für Kinder, tr 1795.
Godwin, William. Adventures of Caleb Williams. 3 vols 1794; Caleb Williams: ein philosophischer Roman, tr D. M. Liebeskind, Riga 1795; Begebenheiten Caleb Williams, adapted A. Wilhelmi 2 vols Leipzig 1797–8.
—— Saint Leon. 1799; tr Ahlwardt, Hamburg 1800.
Goldsmith, Oliver. The Vicar of Wakefield. 1766; Der Landpriester von Wakefield, tr J. G. Gellius, Leipzig 1767; Der Dorfprediger von Wakefield, tr J. J. C. Bode, Leipzig 1776.
Jester, F. E. Der Dorfprediger: ein Schauspiel. Augsburg 1788.
Voss, J. H. Luise. Königsberg 1795.
Levy, S. Goethe and Goldsmith. Goethe-Jahrbuch 6 1885.
Ziegert, M. Goldsmiths Landprediger in Deutschland. Berichte des Freien Hochstifts (Frankfurt) 10 1894.
Brandl, A. Goethe und Goldsmith. Chronik des Wiener Goethevereins 12 1898.
Sollas, H. Goldsmiths Einfluss in Deutschland im 18 Jahrhundert. Heidelberg 1903.
Walz, J. A. Goldsmith und Goethes Werther. MLN 18 1903.
Hammer, C. Goethe's estimate of Goldsmith. JEGP 44 1945.
Holcroft, Thomas. Anna St Ives. 1792; tr K. P. Moritz 5 vols Berlin 1792–4.
Johnson, Samuel. Rasselas. 1759; Der Prinz von Abyssinien, tr Küster, Frankfurt 1762; Prinz Rasselas, tr Knigge, Meissen 1787.
Lathom, Francis. Midnight bell. 1798; Die Mitternachtsglocke, tr Erfurt 1800.
Lee, Harriet. Errors of innocence. 1786; Die Irrthümer aus Unschuld, tr Leipzig 1787.

Leland, Thomas. Longsword, Earl of Salisbury. 1762; Longsword, Graf von Salisbury, tr Leipzig 1775.
Lewis, Matthew Gregory. The monk. 1796; Der Mönch, tr F. von Oertel, Leipzig 1797.
Koziol, H. E. T. A. Hoffmans Die Elixiere des Teufels und M. G. Lewis' The monk. Germanisch-romanische Monatsschrift 26 1938.
Peck, L. F. The monk and Musäus' Die Entführung. PQ 32 1953.
Mackenzie, Henry. The man of feeling. 1771; Der Mann von Gefühl, tr C. G. Lessing, Danzig 1774; tr Mylius, Berlin 1778.
—— The man of the world. 1773; Sir Thomas Sindal: oder der Mann nach der Welt, tr Leipzig 1773.
Pye, Henry James. The democrat. 1795; Der Demokrat, tr W. H. Wackenroder (but frequently ascribed to Tieck), Berlin 1796.
Radcliffe, Ann. A Sicilian romance. 1790; Die nächtliche Erscheinung im Schlosse Mazzini, tr Mme Forkel, Hanover 1791.
—— The romance of the forest. 1791; Adeline: oder das Abenteuer im Walde, tr D. M. Liebeskind, Leipzig 1793.
—— The mysteries of Udolpho. 1794; Udolphos Geheimnisse, tr D. M. Liebeskind 4 pts Riga 1795–7.
—— The Italian. 1797; Die Italienerin, tr D. M. Liebeskind 3 vols Königsberg 1797–9.
Reeve, Clara. The old English Baron. 1778 (formerly The champion of virtue); Der alte englische Baron, tr F. Schmit, Nuremberg 1789.
—— The two mentors. 1783; Die zween Mentor: eine Geschichte jetzigen Zeitalters, tr Leipzig 1784.
—— The memoirs of Sir Roger de Clarendon. 1793; Roger Clarendons Leben und Denkwürdigkeiten, tr Leipzig 1795.
Richardson, Samuel. Pamela. 2 vols 1740; tr J. Mattheson, Leipzig 1742; tr F. Schmit, Liegnitz 1772.
Ehrenburg, F. (G. K. Claudius). Leonore Schmidt, nach Richardsons Pamela. 2 vols Leipzig 1789–91. A dramatization.
Gellert, C. F. Das Leben der schwedischen Gräfinn von G. 2 vols Leipzig 1747–8.
Hermes, J. T. Geschichte der Miss Fanny Wilkes. Leipzig 1766.
—— Sophiens Reise von Memel nach Sachsen. 2 vols Leipzig 1769–73.
Laroche, Sophie von. Geschichte des Fräuleins von Sternheim. Leipzig 1771.
Knigge, A. von. Der Roman meines Lebens. 2 vols Riga 1781–2.
Ridderhoff, K. Sofie la Roche: die Schülerin Richardsons und Rousseaus. Göttingen 1895.
Purdie, E. Some adventures of Pamela on the continental stage. In German studies presented to H. G. Fielder, Oxford 1938.
—— Clarissa Harlowe. 7 vols 1748; tr J. D. Michaelis 8 vols Göttingen 1748–53 (in part); Klarissa, tr Vienna and Mannheim 1790; tr L. T. Kosegarten 8 vols Leipzig 1790–3.
Lessing, G. E. Miss Sara Sampson. Berlin 1755.
Steffens, J. H. Clarissa: eine Tragödie. Celle 1765.
Schulz, J. C. F. Albertine. Berlin 1788.
Kettner, G. Lessings Emilia Galotti und Richardsons Clarissa. Zeitschrift für Deutschen Unterricht 11 1897.
—— The history of Sir Charles Grandison. 7 vols 1754; Geschichte des Herrn Carl Grandison, tr Leipzig 7 vols 1754–5; tr Dresden 2 pts 1780–90.
Musäus, J. K. A. Grandison der Zweite: oder Geschichte des Herrn von N. 3 vols Eisenach 1760–2. A parody.
Wieland, C. M. Clementina della Porretta. Zürich 1760. A dramatization.
Schmidt, E. Richardson, Rousseau und Goethe. Jena 1875.
Donner, J. O. E. Richardson in der deutschen Romantik. Weimar 1896.

Price, L. M. Richardson in the moral weeklies of Germany. In Studies in German literature in honor of A. R. Hohlfeld, Madison 1926.
—— On the reception of Richardson in Germany. JEGP 25 1926.
—— Richardson, Wetzlar and Goethe. In Mélanges F. Baldensperger, Paris 1939.
Smollett, Tobias George. Roderick Random. 2 vols 1748; tr J. G. Büsch, Hamburg 1755; tr W. C. S. Mylius, Berlin 1791.
—— Peregrine Pickle. 4 vols 1751; tr Leipzig 1753; tr W. C. S. Mylius, Berlin 1785.
—— Ferdinand Count Fathom. 2 vols 1753; Begebenheiten Ferdinands, Grafen von Fathom, tr F. von Oertel 2 vols Copenhagen 1770–1.
—— Launcelot Greaves. 2 vols 1762; Abenteuer des Ritters Launcelot Greaves, tr Copenhagen 1772; freely tr Vienna 1791.
—— Humphry Clinker. 3 vols 1771; Reise des Humphrey Klinker, tr J. J. C. Bode, Leipzig 1772.
Stephanie der Jüngere. Bekanntschaften im Bade. Vienna 1775. A dramatization.
Price, L. M. Smollett, Jünger und Stephanie der Jüngere. Monatshefte 30 1938.
Sterne, Laurence. The life and opinions of Tristram Shandy. 9 vols York (later London) 1760–7; Das Leben und die Meynungen des Herrn Tristram Shandy, tr Zückert 9 vols Berlin 1763–7; tr J. J. C. Bode, Hamburg 1774.
Stephanie der Jüngere. Der Eigensinnige. Leipzig 1774. A dramatization.
—— A sentimental journey. 2 vols 1768; Yoricks empfindsame Reise, tr J. J. C. Bode, Hamburg 1768; Versuch über die menschliche Natur in Yoricks Reisen, tr Mittelstedt, Brunswick 1769; tr Eckert, Mannheim 1780.
Schummel, J. G. Empfindsame Reisen durch Teutschland. Wittenberg 1770.
Wieland, C. M. Sokrates Mainomenes: oder die Dialogen des Diogenes von Sinope. Leipzig 1770.

Thümmel, M. A. von. Reise in die mittäglichen Provinzen von Frankreich. 10 vols Leipzig 1791–1805.

Mager, A. Wielands Nachlass des Diogenes von Sinope und das englische Vorbild. Marburg 1890.
Düntzer, H. Goethe und Tristram Shandy. Archiv 9 1880.
Bauer, F. Über den Einfluss Sternes auf Chr. Wieland. 2 vols Karlsbad 1898–9.
Lonzo, J. Sterne und Joh. G. Jacobi. Vienna 1898.
Behmer, C. A. Sterne und C. M. Wieland. Munich 1899.
Baker, T. S. The influences of Sterne upon German literature. Americana Germanica 2 1900.
Czerny, J. Sterne, Hippel und Jean Paul. Berlin 1904.
Thayer, H. W. Sterne in Germany. New York 1905.
Pinger, W. R. R. Sterne and Goethe. Berkeley 1920.
Hallamore, G. J. Das Bild Sternes in Deutschland von der Aufklärung bis zur Romantik. Berlin 1936.
Doernenburg, E. W. Raabe und Sterne. Mitteilungen für die Gesellschaft der Freunde W. Raabes 29 1939.
Michelsen, P. Sterne und der deutsche Roman des 18 Jahrhunderts. Göttingen 1962.
Brandi-Dohrn, B. Der Einfluss Sternes auf Jean Paul. Munich 1964.
Walpole, Horace. The Castle of Otranto. 1765; Seltsame Begebenheiten im Schlosse Otranto, tr Leipzig 1768; Die Burg von Otranto, tr F. L. W. Meyer, Berlin 1794.
—— Works. 1798; Historische, literarische und unterhaltende Schriften, tr A. W. Schlegel, Leipzig 1800.

Heine, C. Der Roman in Deutschland 1774–8. Halle 1892.
Kost, E. Die Technik des deutschen Romans von Musäus bis Goethe in ihren Beziehungen zu Fielding und Smollett. Tübingen 1922.
Price, L. M. The English domestic novel in Germany 1740–99. In his Libris et litteris, Hamburg 1959.

J. T.

(5) ITALIAN

General Studies

Vasari, G. Della vite de' piu eccellenti pittori, scultori ed architettori. Florence 1550; Choice observations upon painting, together with Vasari's Lives of the most eminent painters, tr W. Aglionby 1719.
Torriano. An Italian-English and English-Italian dictionary. 1659.
Magalotti, L. Relazione d'Inghilterra dell' anno 1668 [unpbd]. See W. Moretti, Un' opera inedita di Lorenzo Magalotti, Giornale Storico della Letteratura Italiana 1964.
Lassels, R. The voyage of Italy. 1670.
Leti, G. Il teatro brittanico. 2 vols 1683, Amsterdam 1684.
Addison, J. Remarks on several parts of Italy in the years 1701, 1702, 1703. 1705, 1718 (rev).
Baretti, G. M. A. The Italian library: an account of the lives and works of the most valuable authors of Italy. 1757.
—— A dictionary of the English and Italian languages. 1760.
—— Lettere familiari vol 1. Milan 1762; vol 2, Venice 1763; tr 1770. See G. Rossi, Gentes y paisajes de la España de 1760 en las cartas de G. Baretti, in Actas del primer Congreso Internacional de Hispanistas, Oxford 1964.
—— An account of the manners and customs of Italy. 1768.
—— A journey from London to Genoa. 1770.
—— An introduction to the most useful European languages: consisting of select passages from the most

celebrated English, French, Italian and Spanish authors. 1772. Includes passages from Fray Gerundio de Campazas, by J. Francisco de Isla antedating first separate edn.
—— Easy phraseology for the use of young ladies who intend to learn the colloquial part of the Italian language. 1773.
Collison-Morley, L. Baretti: his literary friendships and relationships. 1909.
Gallup, D. C. Baretti's reputation in England. In The age of Johnson: essays presented to C. B. Tinker, New Haven 1949.
Lubbers van der Brugge, C. J. Johnson and Baretti. Groningen 1951.
Jonard, N. Baretti: l'homme et l'œuvre. Clermont-Ferrand 1963.
Andrés, P. J. Dell' origine, progresso et stato attuale d'ogni letteratura. 7 vols Parma 1782–99.
Swinburne, H. Travels in the Two Sicilies in the years 1777–80. 4 vols 1785.
Lettere sopra l'Inghilterra, Scoozia e Olanda. 2 vols Florence 1790.
Fränkel, L. Romanische, insbesondere italienische Wechselbeziehungen zur englischen Literatur. Erlangen 1900.
Hazard, P. L'invasion des littératures du nord dans l'Italie du xviiie siècle. Revue de Littérature Comparée 1 1921.
Farinelli, A. Divagazioni erudite: Inghilterra e Italia. Turin 1925.
Meozzi, A. Azione et diffusione della letteratura italiana in Europa. Pisa 1932.

Marshall, R. Italy in English literature 1755–1815. New York 1934.

Rebora, P. Civiltà italiana e civiltà inglese. Florence 1936.

Caraccio, A. Ugo Foscolo 'comparatiste'. Revue de Littérature Comparée 17 1937.

Praz, M. Ricerche anglo-italiane. Rome 1944.
— Rapporti tra la letteratura italiana e la letteratura inglese. In Letteratura comparate, ed A. Momigliano, Milan 1948.
— The flaming heart: essays in the relationship between Italian and English literature. New York 1958.

Babcock, R. W. English interest in Italy. PQ 26 1947.

Pellegrini, C. Tradizione italiana e cultura europea. Messina 1947.

Viglione, F. L'Italia nel pensiero degli scrittori inglesi. Milan 1947.

Prezzolini, G. The legacy of Italy. New York 1948.

Baldensperger, F. and W. P. Friederich. Bibliography of comparative literature. Chapel Hill 1950. Annual supplements in Yearbook of comparative and general literature, Chapel Hill (later Bloomington) [1952–].

Brand, C. P. Italy and the English Romantics. Cambridge 1957.
— and K. Foster et al. Italian studies presented to E. R. Vincent. Cambridge 1962.

Venturi, F. Illuminismo Italiana ed illuminismo europeo. In La cultura illuministica in Italia, ed M. Fubini, Turin 1957.

Robertson, J. G. Studies in the genesis of Romantic theory in the 18th century. Cambridge 1923, New York 1962.

Sells, A. L. The Italian influence on Englishmen in the 17th century. Bloomington 1964.

Hargreaves-Mawdsley, W. N. The English Della Cruscans and their time 1783–1828. Hague 1967.

Themes (in alphabetical order)

Graf, A. Gallomani, Gallofobia, Anglomania etc. In Nuova antologia di scienze, lettere ed arti, Rome 1910. Anglomania.
— L'Anglomania e l'influsso inglese in Italia nel secolo xviii°. Turin 1911.

Rhodes, D. Libri inglesi recensiti a Roma 1681–8. Studi Secenteschi 6 1965. Booktrade; survey of English book reviews in periodicals.
— Notes on the import of books from Italy 1628–50. Studi Secenteschi 7 1966.

Bouvy, E. L'Italianisme en Angleterre. In A travers cinq siècles de littérature italienne, Paris 1928. Language.

Foligno, C. and M. Praz. Italia e paesi di lingua inglese. In Un cinquantennio di studi, dedicati a V. Rossi vol 2, Florence 1937.

King, R. W. Italian influence on English scholarship and literature during the Romantic revival. MLR 20–1 1925–6.

Pellegrini, C. Gli studi di letteratura straniera in Italia. Rome 1938.

Praz, M. Fortuna della lingua e della cultura italiana in Inghilterra. Romana 3 1939.

Thorne, E. H. Italian teachers and teaching in 18th-century England. Eng Miscellany (Rome) 9 1958.

Crane, T. F. Italian social customs of the 16th century and their influences on the literature of Europe. New Haven 1920. Travel.

Collison-Morley, L. 17th-century Englishmen in Italy. Edinburgh Rev 242 1925.

Manwaring, E. W. Italian landscape in 18th-century England. New York 1925.

Marshall, R. Italy in English literature 1755–1815. New York 1934.

Babcock, R. W. English interest in Italy. PQ 26 1947.

Sells, A. L. Englishmen in Padua from Chaucer to Shelley. Durham Univ Jnl 30 1947.

— The paradise of travellers. The Italian influence on Englishmen in the 17th century. Bloomington 1964.

Kirby, P. F. The Grand Tour in Italy 1700–1800. New York 1952.

Roe, F. C. Venise dans la littérature anglaise depuis le xvi° siècle. Proc of International Comparative Lit Assoc Sept 1955.

Voisine, J. Voyageurs anglais à Venise au xviii° siècle. Proc of International Comparative Lit Assoc Sept 1955.

Thorne, E. H. V. Martinelli in England 1748–74. Italian Stud 11 1956.

Schudt, L. Italienreisen im 17 und 18 Jahrhundert. Vienna and Munich 1960.

Dorris, G. E. Paolo Rolli and the Italian circle in London 1715–44. Princeton 1966.

Philosophy, Politics, Enlightenment

Italian Authors

Algarotti, Francesco. Il newtonianismo per le dame. Naples 1737; Sir Isaac Newton's philosophy explain'd for the use of ladies, tr [E. Carter] 2 vols 1739.
Viglione, F. L'Algarotti e l'Inghilterra. Naples 1919.

Beccaria, Cesare Bonesana. Dei delitti e delle pene. [Monaco] 1764; An essay on crimes and punishments; with a commentary attributed to Mons de Voltaire, tr 1767 (from French Commentaire sur le livre des délits et des peines, pbd by Voltaire [Geneva] 1766.)
Elementi di economia pubblica; A discourse of public œconomy and commerce, tr 1769.

Galileo. Dialogo sopra i due massimi sistemi del mondo Tolemaico e Copernicano. Florence 1632; The systeme of the world in four dialogues, tr T. Salusbury 1661.
Discorsi e dimostrazioni matematichè intorno a due nuove scienze. Leyden 1638; Mathematical collections and translations, tr T. Salusbury 5 vols 1661–2; Mathematical discourses concerning two new sciences, tr T. Weston 1730.

Giannone, Pietro. Dell' istoria civile del regno di Napoli. Naples 1723; The civil history of the kingdom of Naples, tr 2 vols 1729–31.

Giarrizzo. Edward Gibbon e la cultura europea del settecento. Naples 1954. On direct influence upon Gibbon. See Gibbon's Autobiography.
See also Gibbon, below.

Machiavelli, Niccolò di Bernardo dei. Discorsi sopra la prima Deca di T. Livio. Florence 1531; Il principe, Rome 1532; Discourses upon the first decade of T. Livius, to which is added the Prince, tr E. Dacres (Discourses from 1636 trn, Prince from 1640 trn, both by Dacres).
Praz, M. Machiavelli in Inghilterra. Rome 1943.
Villani, F. Il Machiavelli e il 'mito' del Machiavelli in Inghilterra. Cultura e Società 1 1959.
Raab, F. The English face of Machiavelli: a changing interpretation 1500–1700. 1964.
Procacci, G. Studi sulla fortuna di Machiavelli. Rome 1965.

Vico, Giambattista
De Mas, E. Bacone e Vico. Turin 1959. On debt of Vico to Bacon. See also Libri et Riviste d'Italia 122 1960.
Berlin, I. The philosophical ideas of Vico. In Art and ideas in 18th-century Italy, Rome 1960.

English Authors

Addison, Joseph
Anderson, P. B. Addison's Letter from Italy. MLN 47 1932.
Segré, C. Il viaggio dell' Addison in Italia. Nuovo Antologia di Scienze, Lettere ed Arti (Rome) 1, 16 March 1930.

Bolingbroke, Henry St John

Ribner, I. Bolingbroke: a true Machiavellian. MLQ 9 1948.

Browne, Sir Thomas. Pseudodoxia epidemica. 1646; Saggia sopra gli errori popolareschi, tr S. Canturani, Venice 1737 (from French).

Burke, Edmund. Letter to a member of the National Assembly. 1791; Lettera del signor Burke a un membro dell' Assemblea Nazionale, Ferrara 1793.

Gibbon, Edward. *See also Vico, above.*
    The decline and fall of the Roman Empire. 6 vols 1776–88; Istoria della decadenza e rovina dell' Impero Romano, tr A. Fabbroni and Foggi 9 vols Pisa 1779–86; tr C. Ginesi 3 vols Lausanne (for Florence) 1779; tr Ginesi, Grazioli, Raffaelli 10 vols Pisa 1779–92; tr Gatti 10 vols 1789–94.
    Bonnard, G. A. (ed). Gibbon's journey from Geneva to Rome: his journal from 20 April–2 October 1764. 1961.
    Baridon, M. Gibbon en Italie. Etudes Anglaises 15 1962.
    Saunders, J. J. Gibbon in Rome 1764. History Today 14 1964.

Hume, David. Essays moral and political. 1758; Saggi politici, tr [D. I. Bianchi?], Venice 1774.

Locke, John. Some thoughts concerning education. 1693; Educazione dei fanciulli del Signor Locke, tr [1763?]; tr 1782 (5th edn). From French version by P. Coste.
    Doria, P. M. Difesa della metafisica degli antichi filosofi contro G. Locke. Venice 1732–3.

Milton, John. *See Epic, descriptive and didactic poetry, below.*

Pope, Alexander. Essay on man. 1733; Il principi della morale: o sia saggio sopra l'uomo, tr A. F. Adami, Venice 1758; Saggio sull' uomo, tr G. Castiglione, Berna 1760; tr G. and S. Ippolito 1783; tr G. M. Pagnini, Reggio 1802.
    Clark, D. B. The Italian fame of Pope. MLQ 22 1961.

Shaftesbury, Anthony Ashley Cooper, 3rd Earl of
    Croce, B. Shaftesbury in Italy. Cambridge 1924.

Literary Theory and Criticism
alphabetically by name of author

Devalle, A. La critica letteraria nel '700: Gius, Baretti, suoi rapporti con Voltaire, Johnson e Parini. Milan 1932. *Baretti; see also in General Studies, above.*

MacHamm, V. Antonio *Conti* and English aesthetics [Addison, Hutcheson]. Comparative Lit 8 1965.

Sherwood, J. C. *Dryden* and the critical theories of Tasso. Comparative Lit 18 1966.

Longaker, J. The Della Cruscans and *William Gifford*. Philadelphia 1924.

Müller, M. 16th-century Italian criticism and Milton's theory of Catharsis. Stud in Eng Lit 1500–1900 6 1966.

Quigley, H. Italy and the rise of a new school of criticism in the 18th century. Perth 1921.

Robertson, J. G. Studies in the genesis of Romantic theory in the 18th century. Cambridge 1923, New York 1962.

Baretti, Giuseppe. Dissertation upon the Italian poetry. 1753; The Italian library, 1757.
    Wellek, R. Italian criticism. In A history of modern criticism vol 1: the later 18th century, 1955.

Pope, Alexander. Essay on criticism. 1711; Il principi de buon gusto: overro saggio di critica, tr G. Gozzi 1758; Saggio sopra la critica, tr A. Pillori, Florence 1759.

Drama
Italian Authors

This section excludes the Commedia dell' arte in its traditional, popular form, of which details may be found in A. Nicoll, The world of Harlequin, Cambridge 1963; T. Niklaus,

Harlequin, New York 1956; W. Smith, The Commedia dell' arte, New York 1964. The scenarios of the Commedia dell' arte; *and* Flaminio Scala's Il Teatro delle favole rappresentative, tr H. F. Salerno 1967, *give 50 plots tr from 1611. See also* C. D. Brenner, The Théâtre italien: its reputation 1716–93, Berkeley 1961.

Alfieri, Vittorio
    Branca, V. Alfieri anglomane e due inedite traduzioni dal Pope. Humanitas 1947.
    — Alfieri e la ricerca della stile. Florence 1949.

Goldoni, Carlo. *No arbitrary distinction is drawn here between comic operas, plays with musical accompaniments and straight plays, the preference in England being for musical or operatic settings. Many of the plays are in bilingual setting.*
    Il padre di famiglia. Venice 1751; The father of a family, tr 1757.
    Pamela nubile. 1751; Pamela: a comedy, tr 1756. *Richardson was a source, but see* K. M. Lynch, Pamela nubile, l'Ecossaise (Voltaire) and the English merchant, MLN 47 1932.
    Bertoldo. Tr 1755.
    Il filosofo di campagna. Tr 1761; The wedding ring, tr C. Dibdin 1773.
    La buona figliuola. Lucca 1762; The accomplish'd maid, tr E. Toms 1767; The maid of the vale, tr G. G. Bottarelli 1775.
    La cascina; The dairy house, tr G. G. Bottarelli 1763.
    La calamita dei cuori; The magnet of hearts, tr 1763.
    Il signor dottore. Tr 1767.
    La buona figliuola maritata. Tr 1767.
    La cameriera spiritosa; The coquet: a musical entertainment, tr S. Storace 1771.
    Germondo; Germondo: a new serious opera, tr F. Bottarelli 1776.
    Vittorina; Vittorina: a new comic opera, tr 1777.
    L'Amor artigiano. Tr 1778.
    La bottega del caffè; The coffee house, tr H. B. Fuller [?].
    Maddalena, E. Goldoni in Inghilterra e in America. Rivista d'Italia 15 Sept 1923.
    — Goldoni in inglese. Marzocco 7 Jan 1923.

Guarini, Giovanni Battiste. Il pastor fido. Venice 1590; tr Sir R. Fanshawe 1647; Pastor Fido, tr E. Settle 1677 adapted from Fanshawe); tr W. Grove 1782.
    Staton, W. F. and W. E. Simeone (ed). Sir Richard Fanshawe, Il pastor Fido. Oxford 1964 (critical edn from 1647).

Maffei, Scipione. Merope. Modena 1713; tr W. Ayre 1740.

Metastasio, Pietro Trapassi. Endimione. Naples 1721; tr 1758.
    Didone abbandonata. Rome 1722; tr 1754.
    Ciro riconosciuto. Rome 1724; J. Hoole, Cyrus, 1768.
    Artaserse. Rome 1729; Artaxerxes: an opera, 1734; Artaxerxes: an English opera, adapted by T. Arne [1761].
    Adriano in Siria. Vienna 1730; adapted 1735.
    Issipile. Paris 1735; tr 1735; also as Hypsipile: an opera, 1735.
    La morte d'Abele. Paris 1755; The death of Abel: an oratorio, tr 1768.
    L'isola disabitata. Paris 1755; The desert island: a dramatic poem, tr A. Murphy 1760; The uninhabited island, tr A. Williams in Miscellanies in verse, 1766.
    Demofoönte. Paris 1755; J. Hoole, Timanthes, 1770.
    La clemenza di Tito. Paris 1755; Titus Vespasian: a tragedy, tr 1755; Conspiracy: a tragedy, tr 1796.
    Il re pastore. Paris 1755; tr 1757; The royal shepherd, tr R. Rolt, Dublin 1764.
    Themistocles; The patriot, tr C. Hamilton (1784), 1785.
    Works. Tr J. Hoole 1767 (Artaxerxes, Olympiad, Hypsipile, Titus, Demetrius, Demophoon).

Dramas and other poems. Tr J. Hoole 3 vols 1800. Contains works of 1767 edn and also The dream of Scipio, Achilles in Scyros, Adrian in Syria, Dido, Aetius, The uninhabited isle, The triumph of Glory, Zenobia, Themistocles, Siroes, Regulas, Romulus and Hersilia, Discovery of Joseph and several cantatas. Translations chiefly from the Italian of Petrarch and Metastasio. Tr [T. Le Mesurier], Oxford 1795. Three dramatic pieces. Tr T. Olivari [Dream of Scipio, Birth of Jupiter, Astrea appeased]. Dublin 1797.

Burney, C. Memoirs of the life and writing of the Abate Metastasio. 3 vols 1796.

Scarlatti, Alessandro [and Adriano Morselli]. Pirro e Demetrio. Naples 1694; Pyrrhus and Demetrius, tr O. MacSwinny 1709.

Vanneschi, Francesco. Fetonte. 1747; tr J. Lockman 1747. With discourse on opera.

Motteux, P. The novelty: every act a play, being a short pastoral, comedy, masque, tragedy and farce after the Italian manner. 1697.

Dennis, J. An essay on the opera after the Italian manner, which are about to be established on the English stage; with some reflection on the damage which they may bring to the public. 1706.

Carey, H. Amelia: a new English opera after the Italian manner. 1732.

Bickerstaff, I. The Ephesian matron: a comic serenata, after the manner of the Italian. 1769.

Burney, C. A general history of music vol 4. 1789. Translations chiefly from the Italian of Petrarch and Metastasio. 1795.

Nicoll, A. Italian opera in England 1705–10. Anglia 46 1922.

Welsford, E. Italian influence on the English Court masque. MLR 18 1923.

Kaufman, H. The influence of Italian drama on pre-Restoration English comedy. Italica 31 1954.

English Authors

Addison, Joseph. Cato: a tragedy. 1713; Il Catone: tragedia, tr A. M. Salvini, Venice 1715; Il Catone in Utica, tr E. Corinteo [G. Golt], Rome [1776].
—— The drummer: or the haunted house. 1716; Il tamburo, tr Florence 1750.

Sheridan, Richard Brinsley. The school for scandal. Dublin 1777, London 1783; La scuola della maldicenza, tr D.T., Venice 1796.

Steele, Sir Richard. The funeral: or grief à la mode. 1701; Il funerale, tr 1742.
—— The conscious lovers. 1722; Gli amanti interni, tr P. Rolli 1724.

Epic, Descriptive and Didactic Poetry

Ariosto, Lodovico. Orlando furioso. Ferrara 1516, 1532 (first tr J. Harington 1591); Orlando furioso, tr [W. Huggins] 2 vols 1755, (trn wrongly ascribed to Temple Henry Croker, to whom trn is dedicated); Orlando furioso, tr J. Hoole 5 vols 1783 (in decasyllabic couplets). Hoole pbd A translation of part of the 23rd Canto of the Orlando furioso, 1774 (decasyllabic quatrains) before main work. Hoole's version is abridged.

Boyd, H. A specimen of a new translation of the Orlando furioso [from cantos 24, 29]. In A translation of Dante's Inferno vol 2, 1785 (in Spenserian stanzas).

Benedetti, A. L'Orlando furioso nella vita intellettuale del popolo inglese. Florence 1914.

Croce, B. Ariosto, Shakespeare e Corneille. Bari 1920.

Olivero, F. La fortuna dell' Ariosto in Inghilterra. Rome 1933.

Bottazzi, B. Ariosto e l'Inghilterra. Reggio Emilia 1941.

Dante Alighieri. See also Milton, vol 1, above.
La divina commedia; The Inferno, tr [C. Rogers] 1782 (blank verse); The Inferno, tr H. Boyd 2 vols Dublin 1785 (paraphrase in 6-line stanzas); The Inferno, tr H. F. Cary 1805–6 (blank verse), 1814 (complete, as The vision).

Toynbee, P. English translation from Dante 14th–17th century. Jnl of Comparative Lit 1 1903.
—— Dante in English literature. 2 vols 1909. See also F. P. Wilson, A supplement, Italian Stud 3 1948.
—— Britain's tribute to Dante in literature and art (c. 1380–1920). [1921].
—— Chronological list of English translations from Dante, from Chaucer to the present day. In Dante studies, Oxford 1921.
—— English translations of Dante in the 18th century. Ibid.

King, R. W. The translator of Dante: H. F. Cary 1772–1844. 1925.

Friederich, W. P. Dante's fame abroad 1350–1850: the influence of Dante Alighieri upon the poets and scholars of Spain, France, England etc. Chapel Hill 1950.

Roe, A. S. Blake's illustrations to the Divine Comedy. Princeton 1953.

Roe, A. S. Blake's illustrations to the Divine Comedy. Princeton 1953.

Dédéyan, C. Dante en Angleterre. Les Lettres Romanes 12–15 1958–61; Revue d'Etudes Italiennes 8 1961, 10 1964, 12 1966.

Cattaui, G. Le rayonnement de Dante dans les pays anglo-saxons. Bulletin de la Société d'Etudes Dantesques 11 1962.

Spoerri, T. Dante in der europäischen Literatur. Stuttgart 1963.

De Sua, W. J. Dante into English. Chapel Hill 1964.

Brand, C. P. Dante and the English poets. In The mind of Dante, ed W. Limentani, Cambridge 1965.

Cunningham, G. F. The Divine comedy in English: a critical bibliography 1782–1900. Edinburgh 1965.

Guidobaldi, E. Dante Europeo. 2 vols Florence 1965–6.

Praz, M. Dante in England. Forum for Modern Lang Stud 1 1965.

Reynolds, B. English fashions in translating Dante. Ibid.

Marino, Giovanni Battista. La strage degli innocenti. Venice [1610]; A poem on the slaughter of the innocents, tr T.R. 1675.

Petrarch, Francesco. Rime sparse; Sonnets and odes with the original texts and some account of his life, tr [J. Nott?] 1777.

Tytler, A. F. Essay on the life and character of Petrarch; to which are added seven of his sonnets. 1784.

Borhesi, P. Petrarch and his influence on English literature. Bologna 1906.

Fucilla, J. G. Petrarchan translations in British periodicals. Bull of Bibliography 18 1943.
See also G. Watson, The English Petrarchans: a critical bibliography, 1967 (Warburg Inst).

Tasso, Torquato. Gerusalemme liberata. Parma 1581 (first trns: R. Carew 1594, E. Fairfax 1600 as Godfrey of Buloigne; The third book of Jerusalem delivered, tr W. Bond 1718; Tasso's Jerusalem bks 1–3, tr H. Brooke 1738; The Jerusalem bk 1, tr T. Hooke 1738; Tasso's xv book of Jerusalem deliver'd (xvi book of recovery of Jerusalem, tr H. Layng in Several pieces in prose and verse, 1748); The delivery of Jerusalem, tr P. Doyne 2 vols 1761; Jerusalem delivered, tr J. Hoole 2 vols 1763 (decasyllabic couplets, the best known 18th-century trn).

Baretti, G. M. A. A dissertation upon the Italian poetry, in which are interspersed some remarks on Mr Voltaire's Essay on the epic poets. 1753.

Praz, M. Tasso in Inghilterra. In Tasso: celebrazioni ferraresi 1954, Milan 1957.

Chandler, S. La fortuna del Tasso epico in Inghilterra 1650–1800. Studi Tassiani 5 1955.

Brand, C. P. Tasso: a study of the poet and of his contribution to English literature. Cambridge 1965.

English Authors

Akenside, Mark. The pleasures of imagination. 1744; I piaceri dell' imaginazione, tr A. Massa, Paris (for Venice?) 1764.

Gay, John. Fables. 1727; Le nuove favoli di G. Gaye, tr G. F. Giorgetti 1767.

Gray, Thomas. Elegy written in a country churchyard. 1751; Elegia inglese sopra un cimitero di campagna, tr G. Gennari, Padua 1772; tr M. Cesarotti, Padua 1772; tr A. Crocchi in Sleator's edn, Dublin 1775; tr G. Torelli, Verona 1776; tr J. Giannini 1782; tr A. Isola in Elegia, Cambridge 1782.
Poesie liriche di Gray. Tr D. M. Lastri, Florence 1784.
Poesie inglese. 1791.
Il bardo e I progressi della poesia. Tr A. Dalmistro, Venice 1792.
Micale, O. Gray e la sua influenza sulla letteratura italiana. Catania 1934.
Mackerness, E. D. The progress of an Italophile: Gray and music. Italian Stud 12 1957.

Keate, George. Ancient and modern Rome: a poem. 1760.
Ettlinger, L. D. With all convenient speed to Rome. Eng Miscellany (Rome) 4 1953.

Macpherson, James ('Ossian')
Fragments of ancient poetry. Edinburgh 1760; Fingal, 1762; Temora, 1763; The works of Ossian, 2 vols 1765; Poesie di Ossian antico poeta celtico, tr M. Cesarotti, Padua 1763; Oinamora: poemetto d'Ossian, tr M. Cesarotti, Turin 1797.
Weitnauer, K. Ossian in der italienischen Literatur bis etwa 1832. Zeitschrift für Vergleichende Literaturgeschichte 16 1906.
Van Tieghem, P. Ossian et l'ossianisme dans la littérature européenne au xviiie siècle. Groningen 1920.
Fabrizzi, A. Studi inediti di V. Alfieri sull' 'Ossian' del Cesarotti. Asti 1964.

Marvell, Andrew
Margoliouth, H. M. Marvell in Rome. TLS 5 June 1924.

Milton, John. See also vol 1, above.
Paradise lost. 1667; Il paradiso perduto, tr P. Rolli 1729 (in part), 1730 (complete), 1735.

Addison, J. Notes upon the twelve books of Paradise lost. 1719; Nota sopra i dodici libri del Paradiso perduto, tr P. Rolli 1742; Critiche di Mr Addison al Paradiso perduto, tr M. Mariottini 1794.

Sherburne, Sir Edward
The poems and translations of Sir Edward Sherburne 1616–1702. Ed F. J. van Beech, Assen 1961.

Sherburne, Stanley
Praz, M. Sherburne and Ayres as translators and imitators of Italian, Spanish and French poets. MLR 20 1925.

Stanley, Thomas
Wilson, E. M. and E. R. Stanley's translations and borrowings from Spanish and Italian poems. Revue de Littérature Comparée 32 1958

Thomson, James. The seasons. 1730; [A hymn]; Inno al Creatore, tr A. Mazza, Parma 1771; Inno al Creatore, in Saggio di libere versioni poetiche, tr G. Fossati, Padua 1781.
A poem sacred to the memory of Sir Isaac Newton. 1727; Le lodi di Newton, tr A. Bonducci, Naples 1760.

Young, Edward. The force of religion: or vanquished love. 1714; Giovanna Gray, o l' Amor vinto: poemetto di Young, tr G. A. Soave, Turin 1797.

The complaint: or Night thoughts. 9 pts 1742–5; Le quattro prime notti, tr G. Bottini, Pisa 1770 (form Le Tourneur's French trn); [first 6 Nights], tr Siena 1771; tr Alberti 2 vols Paris 1771; Le lamentazioni, ossieno le notti d'Odoardo Young, tr L. A. Loschi 3 vols Venice 1774–6; Della notti di Young, tr G. Bottini, Siena 1775 (3rd edn).
Thomas, W. Le poète Young. Paris 1901. Ch 8.
Massarini, T. Poeti inglesi nelle versione italiane. In his Studi di Lettere e d'Arte, Florence 1899.
Gardner, E. The Arthurian Legend in Italian literature. 1930.
Sells, A. L. The Italian influence in English poetry from Chaucer to Southwell. Bloomington 1955.
Pellegrini, G. La poesia didascalia inglese nel Settecento italiano. Milan 1958.

Lyrical Poetry

Achillini, Claudio. Rime e prose. Venice 1651.

Ayres, Philip. Lyric poems made in imitation of the Italians. 1687. Also from Marino, Preti et al.

Wordsworth, William
These notes refer solely to earlier Italian influences on the poet; see also vol 3.
Shackford, M. H. Wordsworth's Italy. PMLA 38 1923.
Rossi, S. Wordsworth e l'Italia. Letteratura Moderne (Milan) 4 1953.
Smith, H. R. Wordsworth and his Italian studies. N & Q June 1953.

Satire and Allegory

Boccalini, Trajano. Ragguagli di Parnaso. Milan 1613; Advertisements from Parnassus, tr Henry Earl of Monmouth 1756; Advices from Parnassus, revised and corrected by Mr Hughes, 1706; Characters of all the great men of the age after the manner of Boccalini, 1708.

Tassoni, Alessandro. La secchia rapita: poema eroicomico. Paris 1622; Alexander Pope, The rape of the lock, 1712.

Pope, Alexander. See also Philosophy, Literary theory etc, above.
Pastorals. 1709; Le quattro stagioni egloghe di Pope, tr E. Pilenejo [G. M. Pagnini], Parma 1780.
Rape of the lock. 1712, 1714; Il riccio rapito, tr [A. Bonducci], Florence 1739; tr A. Conti 1751.
The temple of Fame. 1715; Il tempio delle Fama, in Saggio sopra l'uomo, Naples 1768.
Eloisa to Abelard. 1717; Letterara di Elise ad Abelardo, tr A. Bonducci, Naples 1760 (with Il Riccio rapito).

Prose, Fiction, Biography etc

Italian Authors

Boccaccio, Giovanni. Il Decameron [written 1344–50]. First partial pbd trn 1532, first full trn 1620; see H. G. Wright, The first English translation of the Decameron, MLR 31 1936.
Dryden, John. Fables ancient and modern. 1700.
Centlivre, Susanna. The cruel gift: or the royal resentment. 1716.

Raith, J. Boccaccio in der englischen Litteratur. Leipzig 1936.
Wright, H. G. Boccaccio in England from Chaucer to Tennyson. 1957.
Pruvost, R. Boccace en Angleterre. Etudes Anglaises 12 1959.

Casanova de Seingalt, Giacomo
Bleackley, H. Casanova in England 1763–4. 1923.

Marana, Giovanni Paolo. Esploratore turco. 1684; tr as Letters written by a Turkish spy, 8 vols 1694, 1730 (21st edn). Vols separately tr [W. Bradshawe?] [c. 1690–].

English Authors

Beckford, William
Parreaux, A. Beckford en Italie. Revue de Littérature Comparée 33 1959.
Boswell, James
Lalou, R. Boswell en Italie et en Corse, Revue de Paris Sept 1956.
Warnock, R. Boswell and Wilkes in Italy. ELH 3 1936.
— Boswell and some Italian literati. Interchange 1 1940.
Bunyan, John
Smyth, M. W. Puritan Bunyan and Catholic Dante. Nineteenth Century Aug 1928.
Defoe, Daniel. Robinson Crusoe. 3 vols 1719–20; La vita e le avventure di Robinsone Crusoe: storia galante, 2 vols Venice 1731; tr 2 vols Venice 1799.
Praz, M. Defoe and Cellini. E Studies 13 1931.
Fielding, Henry. History of Joseph Andrews. 1742; Avventure di Gioseffe Andrewes, tr N. Scamandrio 2 vols Venice 1752 (from Desfontaines' French trn).
History of Tom Jones, a foundling. 1749; La storia di Tom Jones, tr 2 vols 1756–7 (from Laplace's French trn).

Shea, B. Machiavelli and Fielding's Jonathan Wild. PMLA 62 1957.
Johnson, Samuel. The Prince of Abissinia: a tale [Rasselas]. 1759; Il principe d'Italia, tr M. Ceo [C. Mei], Padua 1764. Baretti's unpbd trn was into French, not Italian.

Blakiston, N. Dr Johnson and Italy. In Art and ideas in 18th-century Italy, Rome 1960.
De Beer, E. S. Johnson's Italian tour. In Johnson, Boswell and their circle: essays presented to L. F. Powell, Oxford 1965.
Richardson, Samuel. Pamela. 1740; Carlo Goldoni, Pamela fanciulla, Venice 1750; Pamela maritata, Venice 1750.

Clarissa. 7 vols 1748; Istoria di Miss Clarissa Harlowe, tr 5 vols Venice 1783–6.
The history of Sir Charles Grandison. 7 vols 1754; Nuove lettere inglesi: ovvero storia del cavalier Grandisson, tr 4 vols Venice 1784–9.

Holmes, W. C. Pamela transformed. Music Quart 38 1952. On Goldoni, La buona figliuola, 1762.
Smollett, Tobias George. The adventures of Ferdinand Count Fathom. 2 vols 1753; Aventure di Ferdinando conte Fathom, tr 2 vols Venice 1791.
Ferrando, G. Le impressioni italiane di Smollett. Marzocco 15 May 1921.
Sterne, Laurence. A sentimental journey. 1768; Viaggio sentimentale di Yorick, lungo la Francia e l'Italia, tr D. Chierico [Ugo Foscolo], Pisa 1813.
Rabbizziani, G. Sterne in Italia. Rome 1920.
Varese, V. Linguaggio sterniano e linguaggio foscoliano. Florence 1947.
Fasano, P. L'amicizia Foscolo-Sterne et la traduzione didemea del Sentimental journey. Eng Miscellany (Rome) 30 1963.
Swift, Jonathan. Travels into several remote nations of the world by Lemuel Gulliver. 1726; Viaggi del capitano Lemuel Gulliver in diversi paesi lontani, tr Z. Marsecco, Venice 1749 (from French).
Eddy, W. A. Gulliver's travels and le théâtre italien. MLN 44 1929.
Gamba, B. Delle novelle italiane in prosa: bibliografia. Florence 1835 (2nd edn).
Papanti, G. Catalogo dei novellieri italiani in prosa. Leghorn 1871.
Passano, G. Inovelieri italiani in prosa. Turin 1878 (2nd edn).
Savage, H. J. The beginning of Italian influence in English prose fiction. PMLA 25 1917.
Colombo, R. M. Lo Spectator e i giornali veneziani del settecento. Bari 1966.

S. S. B. T.

(6) SPANISH AND PORTUGUESE

Bibliographies

Hills, E. C. A catalogue of English translations of Spanish plays. Romanic Rev 10 1919.
Bell, A. F. G. Portuguese bibliography. New York 1922 (Hispanic Soc of America).
Alpern, H. English translations of Spanish classics. Hispania (Stanford) 7 1924.
Flores, A. Spanish literature in English translation: a bibliographical syllabus. New York 1926.
Thomas, H. English translations of Portuguese books before 1660. Library 3rd ser 7 1926.
Ford, J. D. M. and R. Lansing. Cervantes: a tentative bibliography of his works and material concerning him. Cambridge Mass 1931.
Bourne, J. A. Some English translations of xviith-century Spanish novels. MLR 31 1936.
Catálogo da exposição de livros portugueses traduzidos do inglês. Lisbon 1944 (Instituto Británico em Portugal).
Pane, R. U. English translations from the Spanish 1484–1943: a bibliography. New Brunswick 1944.
Mathews, E. G. English translations from Spanish: a review and a contribution. JEGP 44 1945. Suppl to R. U. Pane, above.
Seris, H. Manual de bigliografía de la literatura española. Syracuse 1948. Includes relations abroad.
Baldensperger, F. and W. P. Friederich. Bibliography of comparative literature. Chapel Hill 1950; Annual suppls in Yearbook of Comparative & General Lit (Chapel Hill, later Bloomington) [1952–].
Estorninho, C. Portuguese literature in English transla-

tion. In Portugal and Brazil, ed H. V. Livermore and W. J. Entwistle, Oxford 1953.
Montesinos, J. F. Introducción a una historia de la novela en España, en el siglo xix. Castalia 1955. With bibliography of Spanish trns of foreign novels, some of 18th century.
Sacks, N. P. Hispanic literature in English translation. Hispania (Stanford) 42 1959.
Díaz, J. S. Bibliografía de la literatura hispánica. Madrid 1960–. The standard authority, in progress.
— Manual de bibliografía de la literatura española. Barcelona 1963. Complete, abridged reference-work.

General Studies

Casas, Bartolomé de las. Brevissima relacion de la destrucion de las Indias. Seville 1552; The tears of the Indians: being an historical and true account of the cruel massacres and slaughters of above twenty millions of innocent people, tr J. Phillips 1656.
Mariana, Juan de. Historia general de España. Toledo 1601 (first pbd in Latin, Toledo 1593); The general history of Spain, tr J. Stevens 1699.
Lasso de Vega, Garcia. Commentarios reales que tratan del Origen de los Incas. Lisbon 1609– Cordova 1616; Royal commentaries of Peru, tr Sir P. Rycaut 1688.
Faria y Sousa, Manuel de. Asia Portuguesa. Lisbon 1666–75; The Portuguese Asia, tr J. Stevens 1695.
— Historia del reino de Portugal. Lisbon 1675; The history of Portugal, tr Sir J. Stevens 1698.
Minscheu, John. The Portugal history. 1667–8, 1677.

Colbatch, J. An account of the Court of Portugal. 1700.

Fanshawe, Sir R. Original letters during his embassies in Spain and Portugal. 1702.

Brockwell, Charles. The natural and political history of Portugal from its first creation into a Kingdom. 1726.

Mayáns y Sicar, Gregorio. Vida de Miguel de Cervantes Saavedra. Briga-Real 1737; Life of Cervantes, in Don Quixote, tr J. Ozell and R. Tonson 1738.

Southwell, R. The history of the revolutions of Portugal to the year 1667. 1740.

Iberian tales and novels, as they were publickly rehearsed for the entertainment of the Spanish nobility, by that celebrated Lady Donna Isabella. 1745.

Clarke, Edward. Letters concerning the Spanish nation. 1763.

Percy, Thomas. Ancient songs upon Moorish subjects. 1775.

Twiss, Richard. Travels through Portugal and Spain in 1772–3. 1775.

Dalrymple, William. Travels through Spain and Portugal in 1774. 1777.

Swinburne, Henry. Travels through Spain in the years 1775–6. 1779.

Cumberland, Richard. Anecdotes of eminent painters in Spain. 2 vols 1782.

The history of Spain, by the author of the history of France. 2 vols Dublin 1793.

Murphy, James Cavanagh. Travels in Portugal. 1795.

Laborde, A de. A view of Spain. Tr 1809.

Beckford, William. Recollections of an excursion to the monasteries of Alcobaca and Batalha. 1835. Travels of 1794 in Portugal.

Fitzmaurice-Kelly, J. The relations between Spanish and English literature. Liverpool 1910.

Walter, F. La littérature portugaise en Angleterre à l'époque romantique. Paris 1927.

Madariaga, S. de. Genius of Spain. Oxford 1928.

Poyatos y Atance, V. Historica de la literatura española comparada con las extranjeras. Valencia 1930 (9th edn).

Figaniere, F. F. de la. Catálogo dos manuscriptos portuguêses existentes no Museu Británico. Lisbon 1853; C. de Tovar, Catálogo dos manuscritos portuguêses ou relativos a Portugal existentes no Museu Británico, Lisbon 1932.

Figueiredo, F. de Pirene. Ponto de vista para uma introdução a história comparada das literaturas portuguesa e espanhola. Lisbon 1935.

Prestage, E. Chapters in Anglo-Portuguese relations. Watford 1935.

Zaluar Nunes, M. Algunas influencias anglo-germanicas nas Viagens na minha terra. Boletim de Filologia 3 1935.

Paxeco, F. The literary relations between Portugal and Great Britain. Modern Languages 18 1936.

Mathews, E. G. Studies in Spanish-English cultural and literary relations. New York 1938.

Ley, C. D. A Inglaterra e os escritores portugêses. Lisbon 1939.

Hatzfeld, H. A. El predominio del espiritu español en la literatura europea del siglo xvii. Revista de Filología Hispánica 3 1941.

Barker, J. W. Influencia de la literatura española en la literatura inglesa. Universidad (Saragossa) 23 1946.

Pastor, A. Breve historia del hispanismo inglés. Arbor (Madrid) 9 1948.

Salazar, Chapela E. Clásicos españoles en Inglaterra Cuadernos Americanos (Mexico) 61 1952.

Russell, P. E. English seventeenth-century interpretations of Spanish literature. Atlante 1 1953.

Green, O. Spain and the Western tradition: the Castilian mind in literature from El Cid to Calderon. 4 vols Madison 1936–6.

Reckert, S. The matter of Britain and the praise of Spain. Cardiff 1967.

Themes (in alphabetical order)

Hendrix, W. S. Quevedo, Guevara, Lesage and the Tatler. MP 19 1922. Journals.

Peterson, H. Notes on the influence of Addison's Spectator and Marivaux's Spectateur français upon El Pensador. Hispanic Rev 4 1936.

Percevall, R. Dictionary Spanish and English. 1599. Language, grammar.

Wadsworth, J. (tr César Oudin). A grammar, Spanish and English. 1622.

Stevens, J. A new general Spanish and English dictionary. 1706. See R. H. Williams, Revue de Littérature Comparée 16 1936.

— A new Spanish grammar 1725.

Giral del Pino, H. S. J. A dictionary Spanish and English, and English and Spanish. 1763.

Vieyra, Antonio. A dictionary of the Portuguese and English languages. 1773.

Connelly, T. and T. Higgins. Dictionary of the Spanish and English languages. 4 vols Madrid 1797–8.

Gonçalves, Rodrigues A. A lingua portuguesa em Inglaterra nos seculos xvii e xviii. Coimbra 1951. List of Portuguese grammars of 17th-18th centuries; see also Biblos 27 1951.

Gaselee, S. The Spanish books in the library of Samuel Pepys. Trans of Bibl Soc, London (suppl) 1926. Scholarship.

Matthews, W. Samuel Pepys and Spain. Neophilologus 20 1935.

Russell, P. E. A Stuart hispanist: James Mabbe. Bull of Hispanic Stud 30 1953.

West, S. G. The work of W. J. Mickle, the first Anglo-Portuguese scholar. RES 10 1934. See also Camões, below.

Wiener, L. Spanish studies in England in the 16th and 17th centuries. MLQ 2 1899.

Alexander, B. (ed). The journal of William Beckford in Portugal and Spain 1787–8. New York 1954. Travel, trade etc.

Cox, E. G. A reference guide to the literature of travel. 2 vols. Univ of Washington Pbns in Lang & Lit 9–10 1935–9.

Fisher, H. E. S. Anglo-Portuguese trade 1700–70. Economic History Rev 16 1963.

Foulché-Delbosq, R. Bibliographie des voyages en Espagne et au Portugal. Revue Hispanique 3 1896.

Garcia Mercadal, J. Viajes de extrangeros por España y Portugal vol 3 [18th century]. Madrid 1962.

Linnhoff, L. Spanische Protestanten und England. Emsdetten 1935.

Livermore, H. V. The 'privilege of an Englishman in the kingdoms and dominions of Portugal'. Atlante 2 1954.

Macaulay, R. They went to Portugal. 1946. Beckford, Byron, shippers etc.

Pfandl, L. Zur Bibliographie der Voyages en Espagne. Archiv 133 1915.

Shillington, V. M. and W. Chapman. The commercial relations of England and Portugal. 1907.

Varey, J. E. Notes on English theatrical performances in Spain 1767–1817. Theatre Notebook 1954. Theatre.

Philosophy, Theology, History etc

Spanish Authors

Feijóo y Montenegro, Benito Jerónimo. Theatro crítico universal: discursos varios en todo género de materias, para desengaño de errores communes. 9 vols Madrid 1726–40; The honour and advantage of agriculture, tr Tilson, Dublin 1764; An essay on the learning, genius and abilities of the fair sex, tr 1774; Essays or discourses, tr J. Brett 1777 (all from Theatro crítico).

Delpy, G. L'Espagne et l'esprit européen. L'œuvre de Feijóo. Paris 1936.

Otero Pedrayo, R. Lord Bacon y el P. Feijóo. In Ensayos hispanoingleses: homenaje a W. Starkie, Barcelona 1948.

Gatti, J. F. Referencias a Feijoo en Inglaterra. Filologia (Buenos Aires) 1949.

Gracián, Baltasar. El héroe. Huesca 1637; The hero, tr J. Skeffington 1652; A gentleman of Oxford, tr G. Risk, Dublin 1726.
El discreto. Huesca 1646; The compleat gentleman, tr T. Saldkeld 1730.
Oráculo manual y arte de prudencia. Huesca 1647; The courtier's manual oracle, tr [Flesher?] 1685; The art of prudence, tr Savage 1702.
El criticón. 3 pts Saragossa 1651–7; The critic, tr P. Rycaut 1681.

English Authors

Bunyan, John. The pilgrim's progress. 1678, 1684 (9th edn); Peregrinação de hum Christão: ou viagem para a cidade celeste, tr Lisbon 1782.

Milton, John
Hesselberg, A. K. A comparative study of the political ideas of Ludovicus Molina and Milton. Washington 1952.

More, Thomas. Utopia. 1516 (book 2 only); tr G. A. de Medinilla i Porres, Cordova 1637 (with note by F. de Quevedo Villagas), Madrid 1790.

Pope, Alexander. Essay on man. 1733; Ensayo sobre el hombre, tr D.B.L. [Diego Balcarcel Lara], in El Correo Literario de Murcia 7 1794. *See Niess, below.*
Niess, R. J. A little-known translation of Pope's Essay on man. Hispanic Rev 7 1939.
Forcione, A. M. Valdes and the Essay on man. Hispanic Rev 34 1966.

Robertson, William. The history of the discovery and colonisation of America. 1777; Reflexiones imparciales sobre la humanidad des los Españoles en las Indias para ilustrar las histórias de Robertson, tr G. Nuix, Madrid 1782 (from Italian).

Swift, Jonathan. The conduct of the allies. 1712 (for 1711); Conducta de los aliados, tr Madrid 1712.
Some remarks on the barrier treaty. 1712; Breves reflexiones sobre el tratado de la Barrera, tr 1712.

Robertson, J. G. Studies in the genesis of the romantic theory. Cambridge 1923.

Moser, G. M. 18th-century Enlightenment in Portugal: aims and achievements of the Outlandish [os Estrange-irados]. In Proceedings of the International Colloquium on Luso-Brazillian studies, Washington 1950, Nash-ville 1953.

Sarrailh, J. L'Espagne éclairée de la seconde moitié du xviiiᵉ siècle. Paris 1954.

Rodriguez, Aranda, L. El desarrollo de la razón en la cultura española. Madrid 1962.

Defourneaux, M. L'inquisition espagnole et les livres français au xviiiᵉ siècle. Paris 1963. On insularism and penetration of foreign ideas.

Herr, R. España y la Revolución del siglo xviii. Aguilar 1964; tr Princeton 1958.

Epic and Didactic Poetry

Portuguese Authors

Camões, Luis de. Os Lusíados. Lisbon 1572; The Lusiad: or Portugal's historical poem, tr R. Fanshawe 1655; The Lusiad, tr W. J. Mickle, Oxford 1776.

Wolcot, John ('Peter Pindar'). The Lousiad: an heroi-comic poem. 1785–95 (5 cantos).

Cardim, L. Projecção de Camões nas letras inglesas. Lisbon 1940.

Estorninho, C. O culto de Camões em Inglaterra. Arquivo de Bibliografia Portuguesa (Coimbra) 6 1960.

On trn and criticism of Camões in England since Fanshawe.

Bullough, G. (ed). Camões: the Lusiads in Sir Richard Fanshawe's translation. 1963.

Letzring, M. Revista Camoniana (Assis) 1–2 1964–5. Rejects Camões' influence on Waller, Denham and Milton, but notes minor interest by Dryden and Philip Ayres.

Mello, Francisco Manuel de. Carta de Guia de Casados. Lisbon 1651; The government of a wife, tr J. Stevens 1697.

English Authors

Gray, Thomas. Elegy first tr 1805; *see* Young, below.
The progress of poesy. 1759 (written 1754); Ode de Gray sobre o progreço da poezia, tr Lisbon c. 1792 (priv ptd), Hamburg 1799.

Peers, E. A. The influence of Young and Gray in Spain. MLR 21 1926.

Starr, H. W. Spanish translations of Gray's Elegy. N & Q 12 May 1951.

MacPherson, James. Fingal y Temora. Tr P. Montengon, Madrid 1800 (vol 1 only pbd).

Van Tieghem, P. Ossian et l'ossianisme dans la littéra-ture européenne au xviiiᵉ siècle. Groningen 1920.

Peers, A. The influence of Ossian in Spain. PQ 4 1925.

Catena, E. Ossian en España. Cuadernos de Literatura (Madrid) 1948.

Montel, I. Dos traductores de Ossian en España: Alonso Ortiz y el Exjesuita Montengón (Pedro). Romance Notes 9 1967.

Milton, John. Paradise lost. 1667; [Fragments tr [c. 1740], 1754, 1778; see Peers, below]; tr J. Amara de Silva 1789.

Peers, E. A. Milton in Spain. SP 23 1926.

Howell, A. C. Anibal Galinda's Spanish translations of Milton's Paradise lost. Revue de Littérature Comparée 36 1962.

Partrides, C. A. As relações de Milton com Portugal. Revista da Faculdade de Letras da Universidade de Lisboa 6 1962.

Cobb, C. W. Milton and blank verse in Spain. PQ 42 1963.

Pope, Alexander
Effross, S. H. The influence of Pope in 18th-century Spain. SP 63 1966.

Stanley, Thomas
Wilson, E. M. and E. R. T. Stanley's translation and borrowings from Spanish and Italian poems. Revue de Littérature Comparée 32 1958. *See also* Jnl of Ecclesiastical History 9 1958 (on religious poetry).

Wordsworth, William
Coe, C. N. Wordsworth's debt to Laborde's view of Spain. MLN 64 1949.

Young, Edward. *See also Gray, above.*
The complaint: or night thoughts. 9 pts 1742–5; Noites de Young, tr J. M. Ribeiro Pereira 2 vols Lisbon 1787–94 (3rd edn) (first edn c. 1780? probably from French trn, though it claims to follow English original); Obras selectas, tr Juan de Escóiquiz 3 vols Madrid 1789–97 The last day; Paraphrase of Job; The Centaur; Night thoughts; in verse and in prose).

Thomas, W. Le poète Young. Paris 1901. Ch 8.

Van Tieghem, P. La poésie de la nuit et des tombeaux en Europe au xviiiᵉ siècle. Paris 1921.

Peers, E. A. The influence of Young and Gray in Spain. MLR 21 1926. On influence on Morõna, Cadalso, Cienfuegos and Meléndez Valdés.

Entwistle, W. J. The Arthurian legend in the literature of the Spanish peninsula. 1925.

Fucilla, J. G. Spanish poetry in English till 1850. Hispania (Stanford) special no 1 1934.

Wilson, E. M. Spanish and English religious poetry of the 17th century. Jnl of Ecclesiastical History 9 1958.

Bryant, S. M. English translations of Spanish ballads. Hispania (Stanford) 46 1963.

Drama

Spanish and Portuguese Authors

Calderón de la Barca, Pedro. Primera parte [quarta parte] de las comedias. 4 pts 1636–72. For chronology, see W. H. Hilborn, A chronology of plays of Calderon, Toronto 1938. Plays are listed below in order of trn.

Mejor está que estaba; Better 'tis than it was, tr G. Digby Earl of Bristol (1662–5).

Peor está que estaba; Worse and worse, tr G. Digby (1662–5).

Dama duende; The parson's wedding, tr T. Killigrew 1664.

No siempre lo peor es cierto; Elvira: or the worst not always true, tr G. Digby 1667.

Maestro de danzar; Gentleman dancing master, tr W. Wycherley 1673.

El astrólogo fingido; An evening's love, tr J. Dryden 1691.

El escondido y la tapada; 'Tis well its no worse, tr I. Bickerstaffe 1770.

Murphy, E. English translations of Calderon. Catholic Univ Bull 5 1899.

Armas, J. de. Calderón en Inglaterra. In Essayos criticos de literatura inglesa y española, Madrid 1910.

—— Calderon en la literatura inglesa. Madrid 1916.

Lancaster, H. C. Still more about Calderon and Ravenscroft. MLN 62 1947.

Oppenheimer, M. French and English adaptations of El Astrologo fingido. Revue de Littérature Comparée 22 1948.

Shergold, N. D. and P. Ure. Dryden and Calderon: a new Spanish source for the Indian Emperor. MLR 61 1966.

Ferreira, António. I. de Castro; Agnes de Castro: a tragedy, tr 1696; see also Mrs Aphra Behn, col 145 above.

Hurtado de Mendoza, Antonio. Fiestas de Aranjuez. Madrid 1623; tr Sir R. Fanshawe 1670.

Querer por solo querer. Madrid 1623; tr Sir R. Fanshawe 1670.

Moreto y Cabana, Agustín. No puede ser el guardar una mujer. Madrid 1661. T. St Serfe, Tarugo's wiles: or the coffee house, 1668; J. Crowne, Sir Courtly Nice: or it cannot be. 1685. See also Molière, Les précieuses ridicules, col 121, above.

Rojas Zorrilla, Francisco de. La traición busca el castigo. Madrid 1640.

Vanbrugh, Sir J. The false friend. 1702. Through Lesage, Le traître puni.

Salas Barbadillo, Alonso Jerónimo de. El necio bien afortunado. Madrid 1621; The fortunate fool, tr P. Ayres 1670; also as The lucky idiot, 1712.

Vega Carpio, Felix Lope de [Lope de Vega]. Los Castelvinis y Monteses. Saragossa. 1647; Romeo and Juliet, tr 1770 (abridged).

For further influence, see Lope de Vega studies 1937–62: a critical survey and annotated bibliography, ed J. H. Parker and A. M. Fox, Toronto 1964; also J. Simón Díaz and J. de Juan Prades, Ensayo de una bibliografía de la obras y artículos sobre Lope de Vega, Merkur 1955.

English Authors

Dryden, John
Loftis, J. The Hispanic element in Dryden. Emory Univ Quart 20 1964.

Wycherley, William
Rundle, J. U. Wycherley and Calderón: a source for Love in a wood. PMLA 64 1949.

Young, Edward. Busiris. 1719; The revenge, 1721; Nova tragedia intitulada A vingança do Doutor Young, tr V. C. de Oliveira, Lisbon 1788.

Hills, E. J. A catalogue of English translations of Spanish plays. Romantic Rev 10 1919.

Johnson, D. H. Don Juan in England. ELH 11 1944.

Cordasco, F. Spanish influence on Restoration drama: G. Digby's Elvira. Revue de Littérature Comparée 27 1953.

Loftis, J. Spanish drama in neo-classical England. Comparative Lit 11 1959.

O'Brien, R. Spanish plays in English translation. New York 1963.

Singer, A. E. The Don Juan theme: a bibliography. Morgantown 1965.

Hogan, F. T. Notes on 31 English plays and their Spanish sources. Restoration & 18th Century Research 6 1967.

Prose Fiction

Bibliographies include C. B. Bourland, Short story in Spain in the 17th century, Northampton Mass 1927; F. W. Chandler, A bibliography of Spanish romances of roguery 1554–68 and their translations, in his Romances of roguery, 1961; Menéndez y Pelayo, Orígenes de la novela, 4 vols Madrid 1905–15; D. B. J. Randall, The golden tapestry: a critical survey of non-chivalric Spanish fiction in English trn 1543–1657, Durham NC 1963; C. Sturgis, The Spanish world in English fiction: a bibliography, Boston 1927. *Works listed as trns include many free adaptations and plagiarizations.*

Spanish and Portuguese Authors

La vida de Lazarillo de Tormes. 1554 (pt 2, Paris 1620, by Juan de Luna, pt i possibly by Diego Hurtado de Mendoza) (first trn 1568–9); The pleasant history of Lazarillo de Tormes, tr D. Rowland 1576; The most pleasant and delectable historie, tr W. Phiston 1596. Segunda parte [by Juan de Luna]. Paris 1620; tr T. W. Calkey 1622 (also as The witty Spaniard).

Alcoforado, Marianna. See Guilleragues, col 140, above. The Cartas de uma religiosa Portugueza, 1819, was tr Filinto Elysio from the French.

Aleman, Mateo. Guzman de Alfarache. Lisbon 1599, 1604; The rogue: or the life of Guzman de Alfarache, tr Don Diego Puede [James Mabbe] 2 vols 1622; The life of Guzman d'Alfarache or the Spanish rogue, tr F. W. Chandler 1707; The amour of Count Palviano and Eleanora, in a select collection of novels 6 vols 1720–9 vol 5; The loves of Osmin and Daraxa vol 6.

La picara Justina [spurious 2nd pt by Mateo Lujan de Sayavedra]. 1605; The Spanish libertine, tr J. Stevens 1707.

Castillo Solórzano, Alonso. La garduña de Sevilla, y anzuelo de las bolsas. Madrid 1642; La picara: or the triumphs of female subtility, tr J. Davies of Kidwelly 1665 (from French trn); The life of donna Rosina, tr E.W. [Edward Ward?] [c. 1700]; The Spanish polecat: or the adventures of Señiora Rufina, tr Sir R. L'Estrange and J. Ozell 1717.

Cervantes Saavedra, Miguel de. El ingenioso Hidalgo Don Quixote de la Mancha. 2 pts Madrid 1605–15; The history of the valorous and wittie knight errant Don Quixote of the Mancha, tr T. Shelton 1612; The history of the most renowned Don Quixote of la Mancha, tr J. Phillips 1687; The history of the most ingenious knight

Don Quixote de la Mancha, tr T. Shelton, rev J. Stevens 2 vols 1700; The history of the renown'd Don Quixote de la Mancha, tr P. Motteux 4 vols 1700–3; The life and notable adventures of that renown'd knight Don Quixote de la Mancha, translated into Hudibrastic verse, tr E. Ward 2 vols 1711–12; tr P. Motteux, rev J. Ozell, R. Knaplock et al 4 vols 1719; The life and exploits, tr C. Jarvis 1742; The history and adventures of the renowned Don Quixote, tr T. Smollett 1755; The history of the renowned Don Quixote, tr [G. Kelley?] 4 vols 1769; tr C. H. Wilmot 2 vols 1774.
Many abridged forms appeared in trn, together with individual episodes, apocryphal sequels etc. Imitations proliferated, a few of them indicated below.
El curioso impertinente [from Don Quixote]; T. Southerne, The disappointment: or the mother in fashion, 1684 (play); J. Crowne, The married Beau: or the curious impertinent, 1694 (play); J. Ozell, The captive and the curious impertinent, 1709.
La Galatea. Alcala 1585; Galatea: a pastoral romance, tr Dublin 1791.
Novelas exemplares. Madrid 1613. 8 novels appeared in trn in A select collection of novels in six volumes, written by the most celebrated authors in several languages, all new translated by several eminent hands, 6 vols 1720–2:
El amante liberal; The liberal lover (vol 3).
El celoso extremeño: The jealous estramaduras, tr J. Ozell in The monthly amusement, 1709; The generous husband, tr C. Johnson 1713; The jealous estramaduran in A select collection (vol 1).
Coloquio que pasó entre los perros Cipión y Berganza; A dialogue between Scipio and Bergansa, two dogs belonging to Toledo, tr 1767.
Las dos doncellas; J. Fletcher, Love's pilgrimage, rev J. Shirley nd; The rival ladies, in A select collection (vol 4).
La Española inglesa: The Spanish lady of England (vol 6).
La fuerza de la sangre; The prevalence of blood (vol 3); The force of blood, tr E. Haywood 1724–6; tr 1800.
La gitanilla; The little gypsie, tr 1709; tr [C. Middleton?], A select collection (vol 5).
La illustra fregona; The fair maid of the inn (vol 2).
La señora Cornelia; The lady Cornelia (vol 6).
Los trabajos de Persiles y Sigismunda. Madrid 1617; Persiles and Sigismunda, tr 1741.

Imitations etc (selected)

Butler, Samuel. Hudibras. 3 pts 1663–78.
Cervantes [Juan Perez de Montalban]. The diverting works of the famous Miguel de Cervantes, now first translated from the Spanish. 1709, 1710 (as A week's entertainment at a wedding). From Para todos, exemplos morales, La semaine de Montalban, tr J. Vanel 1684.
Fielding, Henry. Don Quixote in England. 1734 (play).
— The history of the adventures of Joseph Andrews. 1742.
Smollett, T. G. Remarks on proposals lately published for a new translation of Don Quixote. 1755.
Sterne, Laurence. The life and opinions of Tristram Shandy. 9 pts 1760–7.
Fernandez de Avellaneda. A continuation of the history and adventures of the renowned Don Quixote de la Mancha. Tr W. A. Yardley 1784. From: Fernandez's Segundo tomo del ingenioso hidalgo Don Quixote, Tarragona 1614.

Secondary sources

Espinas, V. Las realizaciones musicales del 'Quijote' [Purcell's Comic history]. Revista de la biblioteca, Archivo y Museo del Ayuntamiento de Madrid 10 1933.

Hazard, P. La fortuna de Don Quixote en la literatura europea. Boletín del Instituto de las Españas 1934.
Buck, G. Written in imitation of Cervantes. Germanische-romanische Monatsschrift 29 1941.
Pons, E. Fielding, Swift et Cervantes. Studia Neophilologica 15 1942.
Peers, E. A. Cervantes in England. Bull of Spanish Stud 24 1947.
Bruton, J. G. Cervantes en Inglaterra. In his Cervantes, Montevideo 1948.
Fitzgerald, T. A. Cervantes' popularity abroad. Modern Lang Jnl 32 1948.
Wilson, E. M. Cervantes and the English literature of the 17th century. Bulletin Hispanique 50 1948.
Groult, P. Cervantes et les écrivains anglais du xvii⁰ siècle. Lettres Romanes 5 1951.
Booth, W. C. The self-conscious narrative in comic fiction before Tristram Shandy. PMLA 67 1952.
Cordasco, F. Smollett and the translation of Don Quixote. MLQ 13 1952. See PQ 31–2 1952–3.
Linsalata, C. R. Smollett's hoax. Stanford 1956. On Smollett's probable ignorance of Spanish and use of collaborators; see Symposium 5 1950.
Knowles, E. B. Four articles on Don Quixote in England. New York 1941; MLQ 16 1955 (Smollett's trn).
— Cervantes and English literature. In Cervantes across the centuries, ed Flores and Bernadette, New York 1947.
Parker, A. A. Fielding and the structure of Don Quixote. Bull of Hispanic Stud 33 1956.
Auburn, C. Smollett et Cervantes. Études Anglaises 15 1962.
Stout, G. D. Some borrowings in Sterne from Rabelais and Cervantes. Eng Lang Notes 3 1965.
Starkie, W. Cervantes y la novela inglesa. In Homenaje a Cervantes, Valencia 1950. See also Cervantes and the English novel, Essays by Divers Hands 34 1966.
Penner, A. R. Fielding's adaptation of Cervantes' Knight and Squire. Revue de Littérature Comparée 41 1967.
Burton, A. P. Cervantes the man through English eyes in the 17th and 18th centuries. Bull of Hispanic Stud 45 1968.
Isla y Rojo, José Francisco de. Aventuras de Gil Blas de Santillana. 4 vols Madrid 1787–8. Like the English versions, this text derives from Lesage's work and not from a Spanish original, which is purely fictitious.
Jovellanos, Gaspar Melchor de
Pott, J. H. R. Jovellanos and his English sources. Trans of Amer Philosophical Soc 54 1964.
Quevedo Villegas, Francisco de. Sueños. Barcelona 1627. [First trn 1640]; The visions of Don Francisco de Quevedo Villegas, tr Sir R. L'Estrange 1667; Novels, with the marriage of Belphegor, tr 1671; Quevedo's Fortune in her wits; tr J. Stevens 1697; The visions burlesqued: a person of quality, 1702.
Historia de la vida del Buscón (llamado Don Pablos). Saragossa 1626; The life and adventures of Buscon, tr J.D. [John Davies] 1657; The pleasant story of Paul of Segovia, tr W.B. 1683; The life of Paul the Spanish sharper, tr J. Stevens, in Comical works of Quevedo, 1707.
Quevedo's comical works. Tr J. Stevens 1707; rev P. Pineda? [1743].
Works. Tr Edinburgh 1798.
Various poems of Quevedo are in Lyric poems made in imitations of the Italians, 1687. The novels of Quevedo, 1671, is entirely spurious.

Thomas, H. The English translations of Quevedo's La vida del Buscón. Revue Hispanique 81 1933.
Quintana, Francisco de. Historia de Hipólito y Aminta. Madrid 1627; History of Hippolyto and Aminta, tr J. Stevens 1718.

Salas Barbadillo, Alonso Jerónimo de. Don Diego de noche. Madrid 1623; The night adventurer, in Novels of Quevedo, 1671.

Collections of Spanish Novels in Translation
The Spanish Decameron: or ten novels made English. Tr Sir R. L'Estrange, 1687.
The Spanish libertines. Tr J. Stevens 1707. Includes Lives of Justina, Celestina, E. Gonzales, and a play: An evening's adventures, by J. de Avila.
A select collection of novels. 6 vols 1720–2.

English Authors

Defoe, Daniel. The life and strange surprizing adventures of Robinson Crusoe. 3 pts 1719–20; Aventuras de Robinsón Crusoe, tr D. T. de Iriarte 1789.
Fielding, Henry. The history of Tom Jones, a foundling. 6 vols 1749; Tom Jones, ó el expósito, tr I. de Ordejón, 4 vols Madrid 1796 (from Laplace's French trn).
Amelia. 4 vols 1752; Historia de Amelia Booth, tr D.R.A.D.Q. 5 vols Madrid 1795–6.
Pagliaro, H. E. (ed). Fielding: Journal of a voyage to Lisbon. New York 1963.
Johnson, Samuel. The Prince of Abissinia: a tale [Rasselas]. 1759; El príncipe de Abisinia, tr I. Joyes y Blake, Madrid 1798.
Percy, Thomas
Hecht, H. Percy als Bearbeiter spanischer Romanzen. Anglia 58 1934.
Richardson, Samuel. Pamela. 2 vols 1741; Pamela Andrews ó la virtud recompensada, 8 vols tr Madrid 1794–5; [tr 1799?].
Clarissa. 7 vols 1747–8; Clara Harlowe, tr J. Marcos Gutiérrez 11 vols Madrid 1794–5 (from Le Tourneur's French trn).
The history of Sir Charles Grandison. 7 vols 1753–4;

Historia del Caballero Carlos Grandisson, tr E.T.D.T. 6 vols Madrid 1798.

Coe, A. M. Richardson in Spain. Hispanic Rev 3 1935.
Sterne, Laurence
Sentimental journey first tr as Viaje sentimental, Madrid 1821; Tristram Shandy not tr before 2nd half of 19th century.
Swift, Jonathan. Travels into several remote nations of the world, by Lemuel Gulliver. 4 pts 1726; Viagens de Gulliver a varios paizes remotos, tr J. B. G. 2 vols Coimbra 1793; Viajes del capitán Lemuel Gulliver, tr R. M. Espartel 3 vols Madrid 1793 (from French).

Secondary sources
Thomas, H. Spanish and Portuguese romances of chivalry: extension and influence abroad. Cambridge 1920. On 16th and early 17th centuries.
Parreaux, A. Le Portugal dans l'œuvre de William Beckford. Paris 1935.
Montesinos, J. F. Introducción a una historia de la novela en España, en el siglo xix. Castalia 1955. Includes valuable bibliography of trns of foreign novels into Spanish, some from 18th century.
Walton, L. B. Bunyan's Pilgrim's progress and Gracian's El criticon. Bulletin of Hispanic Soc 36 1959.
Demerson, G. Don Juan Meléndez Valdés et son temps. Paris 1961. Includes handlist of famous library of foreign works.
Randall, D. B. J. The Golden tapestry: a critical survey of non-chivalric Spanish fiction in English. Durham NC 1963.
Alter, R. Rogue's progress, studies in the picaresque novel. Cambridge Mass 1964.
Parker, A. A. Literature and the delinquent: the picaresque novel in Spain and Europe 1599–1753. Edinburgh 1967.

S. S. B. T.

(7) DUTCH AND FLEMISH

French trns were a principal medium for the circulation of English influence in the Netherlands, especially novels, as well as French-language periodicals ptd in Holland.

General Studies

Hexham, H. A large Netherdutch and English dictionarie. Rotterdam 1658.
Sewel, W. A large dictionary, English and Dutch. Amsterdam 1691, 1754.
Vries, J. D. de. Holland's influence on English language and literature. Chicago 1916.
Pienaar, W. J. B. English influences in Dutch literature and Justus van Effen as intermediary. Cambridge 1929.
Reesink, H. J. L'Angleterre et la littérature anglaise dans les trois plus anciens périodiques français de Hollande de 1684 à 1709. Paris 1931.
Scherpbier, H. Milton in Holland: a study in the literary relations of England and Holland before 1730. Amsterdam 1933.
Downs, B. W. Anglo-Dutch literary relations 1867–1900. MLR 31 1936. Introd.
Gielen, J. J. Comparativistisch uitzicht in onze Nederlandse Literaturgeschiedschrijving. De Nieuwe Taalgids 31 1936.
Llewellyn, E. C. The influence of Low Dutch on the English vocabulary. Oxford 1936.
Roberts, W. English books in Holland 1744. TLS 29 Jan 1938.
Bense, J. F. Dictionary of the Low Dutch element in the English vocabulary. Hague 1939.
Price, L. M. Holland as mediator of English-German literary influences in the 17th and 18th centuries. MLQ 2 1941.

Lefèvre, J. L'Angleterre et la Belgique à travers les cinq derniers siècles. Paris 1946.
Arents, P. De vlaamse schrijvers in het Engels vertaald 1481–1949. Ghent 1950.
Vooys, C. Engelse invloed op het Nederlands. De Nieuwe Taalgids 49 1956.
Bachrach, A. G. H. A note on Huygens: visitor to mid-17th century England and Wales. E Studies 40 1959.
— Sir C. Huygens and Britain 1596–1687. Oxford 1962–. *See also* UTQ 25 1956.
De Graaf, D. A. La littérature néerlandaise dans ses rapports internationaux. Revue de Littérature Comparée 33 1959.
Riewald, J. G. New light on the English actors in the Netherlands c. 1590–1660. E Studies 41 1960.
Begemann, N. De engelse komedianten in de Nederlanden. De Gids 127 1964.
Zandvoort, R. W. English in the Netherlands: a study in linguistic infiltration. Groningen 1964.
Davies, D. W. Dutch influences on English culture 1558–1625. Ithaca 1965.
Hans, N. Holland in the 18th century Enlightenment. Paedagogica Historica 5 1965.
Borgen, J. J. Justus van Effen: een publicist uit de 18e eeuw. Gorinchem 1967.
Bromley, J. S. and E. Kossman (ed). Britain and the Netherlands. Groningen 1968. Includes J. R. Jones, English attitudes to Europe in the 17th century; J. W. Smith, The Netherlands and Europe in the 17th-18th centuries.

The tatler. 1709–11; De snapper of de britsche tuchtmeester tr P. Leclerc 1733–52.

The spectator. 1711–12, 1714; De hollandsche spectator, ed Justus van Effen 1731–5.

The guardian. 1713; De guardiaen of de britsche zedenmeester, tr J. van Effen, Amsterdam 1723.

Philosophy, Theology etc

Browne, Sir Thomas. Religio Medici. 1642, 1643; tr Latin, 1644; Religio medici in de nederlantsche tale overgeset, tr J. R., Leyden 1665.

Bunyan, John. Grace abounding to the chief of sinners. 1666; De tedere ingewanden van Christi liefde, aan den Zondaar open gelegt, tr Groningen 1721.

The strait gate. 1676; De enge poorte, tr Amsterdam 1725.

The pilgrim's progress. 1678, 1684; Eens Christens reyse naa de euwigheid, tr Amsterdam 1682 etc.

The holy war. 1682; Den heyligen oorlogh, tr Amsterdam 1685.

Locke, John
Muller, F. Locke in Nederland. Nederlandsche Spectator 1871.

[Mandeville]. Free thoughts on religion. 1720; tr Van Offen 1722.

Milton, John. Defensio [pro populo anglicano defensio]. 1651; tr 1651.

Nieuwentÿdt, Bernard. Het regt gebruik der werelt beschouwingen. Amsterdam 1717 (2nd edn); The religious philosopher: or the right use of contemplating the works of the creator, tr J. Chamberlayne 3 vols 1718–19.

Smith, Adam
Erämetsä, E. Adam Smith als Mittler englischniederländischer Spracheinflüsse. Neuphilologische Mitteilungen 64 1963.

Smollett, Tobias George. A complete history of England. 11 vols 1758–9; Historie van Engeland, Utrecht 1791.

Spinoza, Benedictus de. See International Latin Literature, above.
Thayer, V. T. A comparison of the ethical philosophies of Spinoza and Hobbes. Monist 32 1922.
Vernière, P. Spinoza et la pensée française avant la Révolution. Paris 1954.

Poetry and Theory of Poetry

Macpherson, James ('Ossian')
Daas, Q. W. Z. De gezangen van Ossian in Nederland. Nijmegen 1963.

Milton, John. Paradise lost. 1667; Paradys verlooren, tr J. van Zanten, Haarlem 1728; tr L. van der Broek ('Paludanus') 1730, 1735; tr J. H. Reisig et al, 4 vols Zutphen 1791–1811.

Scherbpier, H. Milton in Holland: literary relations of England and Holland before 1730. Amsterdam 1933.
See also Vondel under Drama, below.

Sidney, Sir Philip. The defence of poesie. 1595; Verdediging der poëzy, tr J. de Haes, Rotterdam 1712. Arcadia was tr as D'Engelsche Arcadia, Delft 1642–1 by F. van Sambix.

Thomson, James
Halberstadt, B. G. De nederlandsche vertalingen en navolgingen van Thomsons Seasons. Leipzig 1923.

Young, Edward. The complaint: or night thoughts. 9 pts 1742–5; Nachtgedanken van den heer Edward Young, 4 vols Amsterdam 1785.

Russell, J. A. Dutch poetry and English: a study of the romantic revival. Amsterdam 1939.

Van Veen, P. A. F. De soeticheydt des buyten-levens vergheselschapt met de boucken: het hofdicht als tak van een georgische litteratur. Hague 1960. Includes survey of European georgic poetry as foil to Dutch and classical originals.

Weevers, T. Poetry of the Netherlands in its European context. 1170–1930. 1960.

Drama

Dryden, John
Welle, J. A. van der. Dryden and Holland. Groningen 1962.

Holcroft, Thomas. The road to ruin. 1792; Dornton, of de jeugdige losheid en uitspoorige kinderliefde, in Spectatoriaale Schouwburg (Amsterdam) 23 1775–1801.

Lillo, George. The London merchant: or the history of George Barnwell. 1731; De koopman van Londen, tr in Spectatoriaale Schouwburg 8.

Moore, Edward. The gamester. 1753; De dobbelaar: burgerlyk treuerspel, tr in Spectatoriaale Schouwburg, deel 4.

Otway, Thomas. Venice preserv'd. 1682; Het gered Venetie, tr [G. Muyser], Utrecht 1755 (from French version).

Vondel, Joost van den
Grierson, H. J. C. A note upon Samson agonistes of Milton and Samson by Vondel. In Mélanges Baldensperger, Paris 1930.

Mody, J. R. P. Vondel and Milton. Bombay 1942.

Smit, W. A. P. Van Pascha tot Noah. 3 vols Zwolle 1956–62.

— with P. Brachin. Vondel: contribution à l'histoire de la tragédie au xviie siècle. Paris 1964.

Bekker, H. Vondel's Lucifer, Milton's Paradise lost and Grotius' Adamus. Neophilologus 44 1960.

Voisine, J. Un grand tragique du xviie siècle: Vondel. Revue de Litterature Comparée 39 1965.

Prinsen, J. Het drama in de 18e eeuw in West-Europa. Zutphen 1931.

Prose Fiction (including Satirical Fiction)

Defoe, Daniel. The life and strange surprizing adventures of Robinson Crusoe. 3 pts 1719–20; Het leven en de wonderbaare gevallen van Robinson Crusoe: eerste deel, tr Amsterdam 1720 (anon); Tweede deel, Amsterdam 1721; Derde deel, Amsterdam 1722.

The fortunes and misfortunes of the famous Moll Flanders. 1722; De levensgevallen en bedryven van Vlaamsche Mie, tr Amsterdam 1752 anon, from T. Read's abridgement 1723.

Colonel Jacque. 1722; Zeldzame levensbeschryving van Kolonel Jack, tr 2 vols Hague 1729 (anon).

Hubbard, L. L. A Dutch source for Robinson Crusoe [Hendrik Smeers 1708]. Ann Arbor 1921.

Staverman, W. H. Robinson Crusoe in Nederland. 1907.

Fielding, Henry. History of Joseph Andrews. 1742; De historie of gevallen van Joseph Andriessen, 2 vols Amsterdam 1744.

The history of Jonathan Wild the Great. 1743; Leevensbeschryving van wylen den heere Jonathan Wild den grooten, tr Amsterdam 1757.

History of Tom Jones, a foundling, 1749; Historie van den vondeling Tomas Jones, tr P. Le Clercq, 3 vols Amsterdam 1749–50.

Goldsmith, Oliver
Barnouw, A. J. Goldsmith's indebtedness to Justus van Effen. MLR 8 1913.

Brown, J. E. Goldsmith's indebtedness to Voltaire and J. van Effen. MP 23 1926.

Richardson, Samuel. Clarissa. 7 vols 1747–8; tr J. Stinstra, Harlingen 1752–3.

Wolff, Betje and A. Deken. Historie van Mejuffrouw Sara Burgerhart. Hague 1782.

The history of Sir Charles Grandison. 7 vols 1753–4; Historie van den Ridderbaronet Karel Grandison, tr 7 vols Amsterdam 1756–7.

Slattery, W. C. Richardson and the Netherlands. Papers on Eng Lang & Lit 1 1965.

Smollett, Tobias. The adventures of Ferdinand, Count

Fathom. 1753; Fathom en Melvil; door Smollett, tr J. C. van Leeuwestijn 2 vols Hague 1798.

Humphry Clinker. 1771; Reizen van Humphry Klinker, tr 3 vols Hague 1780.

Worp, J. A. Smollett over ons Tooneel. Nederlandsche Spectator 1881.

Sterne, Laurence. The life and opinions of Tristram Shandy. 9 vols 1760–7; A sentimental journey, 1768; Het leven en de gevoelens van Tristram Shandy, bevattendende de Sentimenteele reis van den Heere Yorick, tr B. Brunius 5 vols Amsterdam [1776–9].

Swift, Jonathan. A tale of a tub. 1704; Vertelsel van de ton, tr P. Le Clercq, Amsterdam 1735; vol 2 [Bathos, Art of political lying etc], Utrecht 1743.

Predictions for the year 1708 by Isaac Bickerstaff. 1708; Wonderlijke prognosticatie, tr Hague 1708.

Some remarks on the Barrier Treaty. 1712; Tractaat tusschen hare Brittannische Majesteit en de hoog Mog Heeren Staten General, tr Amsterdam 1712.

The public spirit of the Whigs. 1714; De publijke geest der Whigs, tr Amsterdam nd.

Travels into several remote nations of the world by Lemuel Gulliver. 1726; Reisbeschryving na verscheyde afgelegene natien in de wereld, tr 3 vols Hague 1727–8.

Leyburn, E. D. Swift's view of the Dutch. PMLA 66 1951.

Clark, J. K. Swift and the Dutch. HLQ 17 1954.

Prinsen, J. De roman in de 18e eeuw in West-Europa. Groningen and Hague 1925.

Russell, J. A. English translations of Dutch novels. Gazette de Hollande 28 Oct 1927. See also English books in Holland, TLS 29 Jan 1938.

S. S. B. T.

(8) SCANDINAVIAN

General works are given together, irrespective of country. Trns and works on individual authors follow under separate countries.

General Studies

Wormii, Olai. Antiquitates danicae; literatura runica; lexicon runicum; monumenta runica; additamenta; fasta danici. Copenhagen 1643–51. Reissue of separate works under general title.

Temple, Sir W. On the death song of Ragnar Lodbroke etc. In his Miscellanea pt 2, 1690.

Hickes, George. Institutiones grammaticae anglo-saxonicae moeso-gothicae. Oxford 1688–9.

Linguarum veterum septentrionalium thesaurus. 2 vols Oxford 1703–5.

Molesworth, Robert. An account of Denmark as it was in the year 1692. 1694 (3rd edn).

Robinson, John. Account of Sweden. 1695.

Novum dictionarium latino-sueco-germanicum, sueco-latinum et germanico-latinum. 3 vols Hamburg 1700.

Somerville, William. Occasional poems, translations, fables, tales. 1727.

Then Swänska Argus. 1732–4. An imitation of Spectator.

Serenius, Jakob. Dictionarium suethico-anglo-latinum. Stockholm 1741.

Pontoppidan, E. Glossarium norvegicum. Bergen 1749.

Urbain, Roger (ed) Le traducteur: ou traduction de diverses feuilles choisies. 4 vols Copenhagen 1753–6.

Mallet, Paul Henri. Introduction à l'histoire de Dannemarc, où l'on traite de la religion, des loix, des moeurs et des usages des anciens Danois. 2 vols Copenhagen 1755–6.

Northern antiquities. Tr T. Percy 2 vols 1770. Includes trn of Edda etc.

Percy, Thomas. Five pieces of Runic poetry from the Islandic language. Tr 1763.

Gray, Thomas. The descent of Odin. 1768.

— The fatal sisters. 1768.

Sahlstedt, Abraham. Dictionarium suecicum cum interpretione latinae. Stockholm 1773.

Sheridan, Charles Francis. History of the late revolution in Sweden. 1778.

Johnstone, James. Anecdotes of Olave the Black with xviii eulogies on Haco, King of Norway, by Snorro Sturlson. Tr 1780.

— Lodbrokar-Quida: or the death-song of Lodbroc. Tr [Copenhagen] 1782.

Mathias, Thomas James. Runic odes imitated from the Norse tongues in the manner of Mr Gray. 1781.

Coxe, William. Travels in Poland, Russia, Sweden and Denmark. 1784.

Jerningham, Edward. The rise and progress of the Scandinavian poetry. 1784.

The robbing of the nunnery: a Danish ballad. Tr J. Johnston, Copenhagen 1786.

Consett, M. A tour through Sweden etc. 1789.

Sterling, Joseph. Poems. 1789.

[Drevon]. Voyage en Suède. Hague 1789; A journey through Sweden, tr W. Radcliffe 1790.

Sayers, Frank. Dramatic sketches of Northern mythology. 1790.

[Thomson, W.] Letters from Scandinavia. 1796.

Wollstonecraft, Mary Godwin. Letters written during a short residence in Sweden, Norway and Denmark. 1796.

Icelandic poetry: or the Edda of Saemund translated into English verse. Bristol 1797.

Knox, [Vicesimus]. Moralske og literanske forsog, oversatte af det Engelske efter 6 udg med Hensyn paa danske Loesere. 2 vols Copenhagen 1797.

Bruun, C. V. Bibliotheca Danica. Copenhagen 1877–1902. Suppl by L. M. Nielsen, Copenhagen 1914, 1931, and Ehrencron-Muller, 1948.

Solberg, T. A bibliography of the important books in English relating to the Scandinavian countries. In F. W. Horn, History of the literature of the Scandinavian north, Chicago 1884.

Nordby, C. H. The influence of Old Norse literature upon English literature. New York 1901.

— Scandinavian influence on English literature. New York 1903.

Farley, F. E. Scandinavian influences in the English Romantic movement. Harvard Stud 9 1903. A bibliography.

Hustvedt, S. B. Ballad criticism in Scandinavia and Great Britain during the 18th century. New York 1916.

Herford, C. H. Norse myth in English poetry. 1919.

Wright, H. G. Studies in Anglo-Scandinavian literary relations. Bangor 1919.

— Swedish literature: its influence in England. TLS 29 May 1923.

Primus-Nyman, E. Engelsk literature om Finland. Finsk Tidskrift 102 1927.

Afzelius, N. Sverige i utländsk och utlandet i svensk Litteratur: en bibliografisk oversikt. Biblioteksbladet 15 1930.

— A bibliographical list of books in English on Sweden and literary works translated into English from Swedish. Stockholm 1936.

— Books in English on Sweden: a bibliographical list. Stockholm 1951.

Gustafson, W. W. The influence of the Tatler and Spectator in Sweden. Scandinavian Stud & Notes 12 1932.

Beck, R. Milton in Iceland. JEGP 32 1933.

— Alexander Pope and Iceland. Reykjavik 1936.

Allen, R. Old Icelandic sources in the English novel. Philadelphia 1933.

Craigie, W. A. The northern element in English literature. Toronto 1933.

Seaton, E. Literary relations of England and Scandinavia in the 17th century. Oxford 1935.

Stangerup, C. H. Romanen i Danmark i det attende aarhundrede. Copenhagen 1936.

Dietz, H. Nordischer Mythus in der englischen Literatur. Neuphilologische Monatsschrift 10 1939.

Sylwan, N. Svensk realistik roman 1795–1830. Stockholm 1942.

Christopherson, P. Early Anglo-Danish relations. Norseman 3 1945.

Lindsay, J. The Norse hero in the English 18th century. Norseman 4 1946.

Bredsdorff, E. English influence on Danish literature. Denmark 1947.

— Danish literature in English translation: a bibliography. Copenhagen 1950.

Oksnevad, R. Det britiske samvelde og eire i norsk litteratur. Oslo 1949.

Mitchell, P. M. A bibliographical guide to Danish literature. Copenhagen 1951.

— A history of Danish literature. Copenhagen 1957. With list of trns into English.

— A bibliography of English imprints of Denmark through 1900. Univ of Kansas Libraries 1960.

Platen, M., I. Holm et al. La littérature suédoise. Forum 1957. On foreign influences.

Grönland, E. Norway in English 1936–59. Oslo 1961. With survey of trns from 1742.

Arvet fran Newton och Linné. Stockholm (Museum of Nat Antiquities 1962); abridged trn as The heritage from Newton and Linnaeus: scientific links between England and Sweden (with bibliography).

Gustafson, A. A list of translations of Swedish literature into English. Stockholm 1962.

Wasberg, G. C. The influence of the 'enlightened' philosophy of history on Scandinavian political thought. Stud on Voltaire & 18th Century 27 1963.

Karnell, K. A., L. Vinge and B. Isaksson (ed). Svensk litteraturlexikon. Lund 1964.

Aaltonen, H. Books in English on Finland: a bibliographical list, including Finnish literature in English translation. Turku 1964.

Lindner, N. C. and E. Lunch-Petersen. Verdens litteratur pa Dansk. Copenhagen 1965.

Durand, F. Histoire de la littérature danoise. Paris 1967. Includes foreign influence.

Denmark

Addison, Joseph. Cato: a tragedy. 1713; Cato overset ved Niels Qvistgaard, Copenhagen 1792.

Centlivre, Susanna Freeman. The busie body. 1709; Han har sin naese allevegne, tr D. Staal 1794.

Cumberland, Richardson. The West Indian. 1771; Verstindianeran, tr B. J. Lodde, Copenhagen 1779.

The natural son. 1785; Den naturlige søn, tr F. Schwartz, Copenhagen 1791.

The Jew. 1794; Jøden, tr F. Schwartz, Copenhagen 1796.

The wheel of fortune. 1795; Lykkens hiul, tr F. C. Schneider, Copenhagen 1797.

Defoe, Daniel. The life and strange surprizing adventures of Robinson Crusoe. 3 pts 1719–20; Den navnkundige Engellaenders Robinson Crusoe levnet og meget selsomme Skiebne, tr 2 vols Copenhagen 1744–5.

Fielding, Henry. History of Joseph Andrews. 2 vols 1742; Historie om Joseph Andrews, tr S. C. Stanley, 2 vols Copenhagen 1749.

Journey from this world to the next. 1743; Reyse til den andere Verden, tr P. T. Wandal, Copenhagen 1769.

History of Tom Jones, a foundling. 6 vols 1749; Tom Jones historie eller hittebarnet, tr 4 vols Copenhagen 1781–1813.

Amelia. 4 vols 1752; Amalia: eller den retskafne kone, tr 4 vols Copenhagen 1782–3.

Fielding's Danish translator [S. Stanley]. TLS 3 April 1937.

Goldsmith, Oliver. The vicar of Wakefield. 1766; Landsbypraesten af Wakefield, tr P. D. Bast, Copenhagen 1779.

Heiberg, P. A. Heckingborn; Poverty and wealth, tr C. H. Wilson 1799.

Holberg, Ludwig. Nicolai Klimii iter subterraneum novam telluris theoriam [Niels Klims Reise under Jordan]. 1741; A journey to the world underground by N. Klimius, tr [from Latin] 1742.

Synopsis historiae universalis. 1733; An introduction to universal history, tr G. Sharpe 1755.

Mascarade; The masquerades, tr F. T. Kühne, Helmstadt 1782.

Campbell, O. J. The comedies of Holberg. Cambridge Mass 1914.

Olsvig, V. Holberg og England. Kristiana 1913; Holberg and England. Amer Scandinavian Rev 1 1920.

Harthan, J. P. Holberg and Oxford. Norseman 8 1950.

Holcroft, Thomas. The road to ruin. 1792; Vejen til ødelaeggelse, tr F. Schwarz, Copenhagen 1794.

Lewis, Matthew Gregory. The monk: a romance. 1796; Ambrosio eller munken, tr N. T. Bruun, 3 vols Copenhagen 1800.

Lillo, George. George Barnwell: or the London merchant. 1731; Kiøbmanden i London eller Jørgen Barnvels historie, tr F. D. Bøeg, Copenhagen [1759].

Macpherson, James ('Ossian'). Fragments of ancient poetry. Edinburgh 1760; Fingal, 1762; Temora, 1763; The works of Ossian, 1865; Ossians digte oversatte af det engelske ved Andr. Chr. Alstrup, 2 vols Copenhagen 1790–1.

Milton, John. Paradise lost. 1667; Det tabte paradiis, tr J. H. Schønheyder, Copenhagen 1790.

Paradise regained. 1671; tr J. H. Schønheyder, Copenhagen 1792.

Pope, Alexander. Moral essays. 4 pts 1731–5; Pope's tredie moralske brev om rigdoms brug til Allen, Lord Bathurst, tr B. W. Luxdorph [Copenhagen 1767].

Essay on man. 1733; Forsøg om mennsket i iv breve til Lord Bolingbroke, tr C. C. Lous, Sorøe 1759.

Oversat poesie for Poeter og Kunst-Dommeri, tr H. Schjermann, Copenhagen 1762. With works by other poets in trn.

Richardson, Samuel. Pamela. 2 vols 1740; tr B. J. Lodde 4 pts Copenhagen 1743–6.

Clarissa. 7 vols 1747–8; Miss Clarissa Harlowes historie, tr H. C. Amberg, Copenhagen 1783–8.

The history of Sir Charles Grandison. 7 vols 1753–4; Sir Carl Grandison's historie, tr H. C. Amberg 7 vols Copenhagen 1780–2.

Sheridan, Richard Brinsley. The rivals. 1775; Medbejlerne, tr N. T. Brunn, Copenhagen 1798.

School for scandal. Dublin 1777; Bagtalelsens skole, tr A. G. Thoroup, Copenhagen 1788.

Smollett, Tobias. The adventures of Roderick Random. 2 vols 1748; Roderick Random, tr J. C. Tode 2 vols Copenhagen 1802–3.

The adventures of Peregrine Pickle. 4 vols 1751; Peregrine Pickles tildragelser, tr [J. C. Tode] 4 vols Copenhagen 1787–95.

Sir Lancelot Greaves. 2 vols 1762; Ridderen Sir Lancelot Greaves, tr [J. C. Tode], Copenhagen 1790.

Humphry Clinker. 3 vols 1771; Humphry Clinckers reise; ved forfatteren til Peregrine Pickle, tr [J. C. Tode] 2 vols Copenhagen 1796–8.

Sterne, Laurence. The life and opinions of Tristram Shandy. 9 vols York (later London) 1760–7; Tristram Shandy, tr C. M. Zetlitz, Copenhagen 1794.

A sentimental journey. 2 vols 1768; Yorick's følsomme reise igiennem Frankerig og Italien, tr H. J. Birch, Copenhagen 1775.

Swift, Jonathan. Travels into several remote nations of the world by Lemuel Gulliver. 4 pts 1726; Kapitain Lemuel Gullivers reise til Lilliput, tr [S. Olrog], Copenhagen 1768; tr C. H. K. Krögen, Copenhagen 1786; Capitain Lemuel Gullivers reise til Brobdingnag, tr [C. Hamming], Copenhagen 1775.

Kruuse, J. Swift og Holberg. In his Fem danske studier, Copenhagen 1935.

Wessel, Johannes Hermann
Skalberg, J. H. B. Wessels Koerlighed uden strømper og en tragedie parodi hos Fielding. Edda 53 1953. On Wessel, Fielding and Lillo.

Young, Edward. Force of religion. 1714; Religions magt eller den seiervundne kierlighed i 2 sange, tr Copenhagen 1758; Forsøg til en oversaettelse af Dr Youngs yppertige afhandlinger om den yderste Dag, tilligerned religionens magt, tr E. Balling, Helsinki 1770.
The complaint: or night thoughts. 9 pts 1742–5; Forsøg til en oversaettelse af Dr Edward Youngs klager eller nattetanker, tr E. Balling, Helsinki 1767; tr B. J. Lodde, Copenhagen 1783.

Iceland

Beck, R. Milton in Iceland. JEGP 32 1933.
— Pope and Icelandic literature. Scandinavian Stud 25 1953.

Norway

Milton, John. Paradise lost. 1667; Adam og Evas morgensang, tr 1787.
Young, Edward. The complaint: or night thoughts. 9 pts 1742–5; Youngs Klager eller nat-tanker. Oslo 1764.

Sweden

Bacon, Francis. Essays. 1597; Lord Verulam's uprightiga utlatelser, Stockholm 1726.

Christina, Queen of Sweden. Works. 1753 (from French).

Defoe, Daniel
Wright, H. G. Defoe's writings on Sweden. RES 16 1940.

Smollett, Tobias. Travels through France and Italy. 2 vols 1766; Fransoserne äro ej hvad de utopas för, tr [Stolpe], Stockholm 1784.

Swedenborg, Emanual
Lamm, M. Swedenborg en Angleterre. Revue Bleue 1936.
Erdman, D. V. Blake's early Swedenborgianism: a 20th-century legend. Camparative Lit 5 1953.

Swift, Jonathan. Travels into several remote nations of the world by Lemuel Gulliver. 1726; Capitain Lemuel Gullivers resor til åtskillige långt bort belägne land, tr O.B.R. 2 vols Wästeras 1772 (from French).

Tessin, Carl Gustaf. Letters from an old man to a young Prince. Tr [J. Berkenhout] 3 vols 1756–9.

Thomson, James
Johnson, W. G. A Swedish imitator of Thomson [Dalin]. Scandinavian Stud 12 1933.
— Thomson's influence on Swedish literature in the 18th century. Univ of Illinois Bull 19 1936.
Persson, T. Á. E. Johan Olof Wollin och James Thomson. Samlaven 1951.

Thorild, Thomas
Cassirer, E. Thorilds Stellung in der Geistesgeschichte des achtsehnten Jahrhunderts. Stockholm 1941.

Young, Edward. The complaint: or night thoughts. 9 pts 1742–5; Sömnlösa nätter, Stockholm 1770; Doctor Youngs nätter, tr A. von Landtingshausen, Stockholm 1787–90 (9 in prose); tr 2 vols Stockholm 1798–9.

S. S. B. T.

(9) RUSSIAN etc

Bibliographies

Neustroyev, A. N. Istoricheskoye razyskaniye o russkikh povremennykh izdaniyakh i sbornikakh za 1703–1802 gg. St Petersburg 1874.
— Ukazatel' k russkim povremennym izdaniyam i sbornikam za 1703-1802 gg. i k Istoricheskomu razyskaniyu o nikh. St Petersburg 1898.

Sipovsky, V. V. Iz istorii russkogo romana i povesti (materialy po bibliografii, istorii i teorii russkogo romana). St Petersburg 1903.

Sopikov, V. Opyt rossiyskoy bibliografii, ili polnyy slovar' sochineniy i perevodov, napechatannykh na slavyanskom i rossiyskom yazykakh ot nachala zavedeniya tipografii do 1813 goda. Ed V. N. Rogozhin, St Petersburg 1904–6 (2nd edn).

Semennikov, V. P. Sobraniye starayushcheyesya o perevode inostrannykh knig, uchrezhdyonnoye Yekaterinoy II. St Petersburg 1913.

Kerner, R. J. Slavic Europe: a selected bibliography. Cambridge Mass 1918.

Line, M. B. A bibliography of Russian literature in English translation to 1900. 1963.

Svodnyy katalog russkoy knigi xviii veka 1725–1800. 5 vols Moscow 1963–7. Lists trns from English authors pbd in book form.

Mel'nikova, N. N. Izdaniya napechatannyye v tipografii moskovskogo universiteta xviii veka. Moscow 1966.

Levin, Y. D. Materialy k bibliografii angliyskoy zhurnalistiki v russkikh perevodakh xviii veka. In Epokha Prosveshcheniya: iz istorii mezhdunarodnykh svyazey russkoy literatury, Leningrad 1967.

Stepanov, V. P. and Yu. V. Stennik. Istoriya russkoy literatury xviii veka: bibliograficheskiy ukazatel'. Leningrad 1968.

General Studies

Storch, H. The picture of Petersburg. 1801. Contains first English verse trn of poems by A. P. Sumarokov and G. R. Derzhavin, tr W. Tooke.

Sreznevsky, I. I. Angliyskiye ocherki russkoy literatury. Zapiski Imperatorskoy Akademii Nauk, ii, bk 2 1867.

Belozerskaya, N. A. Vliyaniye perevodnogo romana i zapadnoy tsivilizatsii na russkoye obshchestvo xviii v. Russkaya Starina 22 1895.

Aleksandrenko, V. N. Russkiye diplomaticheskiye agenty v Londone v XVIII veke. 2 vols Warsaw 1897.

Rezanov, V. I. Iz razyskaniy o sochineniyakh V. I. Zhukovskogo. 2 vols St Petersburg 1906–16.

Sipovsky, V. V. Ocherki iz istorii russkogo romana. 2 vols St Petersburg 1909–10. Ch 6, vol 2: Influence of English novel.

Lazursky, V. F. Le Spectateur i Vsyakaya vsyachina. Russkiy Bibliofil 8 1914.

Veselovsky, A. N. Zapadnoye vliyaniye v novoy russkoy literature. Moscow 1916 (5th edn).

Trubnikov, A. A. Gravyor Skorodumov, pensioner Akademii. Russkiy Bibliofil 3 1916.

Mathesius, V. English literature and the Czecho-Slovaks. 1921.

Meyendorff, A. Anglichane xvii i xviii stoletiya o russkikh i o Rossii. In Sbornik statey posvyashchonnykh P. V. Struve, Prague 1925.

Chayanova, O. Teatr Maddoxa v Moskve 1776–1805. Moscow 1927.

Helsztyński, S. English literature in 18th-century Poland. Slavonic Rev 6 1927.

Berkov, P. N. Izucheniye russkoy literatury inostrantsami v xviii v. Yazyk i Literatura 5 1930.

—— English plays in St Petersburg in the 1760's and 70's. Oxford Slavonic Papers 8 1958.

—— Thomas Consett, kapellan angliyskoy faktorii v Rossii (k istorii russko-angliyskikh literaturnykh svyazey v 1720—ye gody). In Problemy mezhdunarodnykh literaturnykh svyazey, Leningrad 1962.

Osborne, E. A. Early translations from the Russian: (i) Before Pushkin. Bookman (London) July 1932.

Simmons, E. J. English literature and culture in Russia 1553–1840. Cambridge Mass 1935, New York 1964.

Alekseyev, M. P. Adam Smith and his Russian admirers of the 18th century. In his Adam Smith as student and professor, Glasgow 1937.

—— O svyazyakh russkogo teatra s angliyskim v kontse xvii– nachala xviii vv. Uchonyye Zapiski Leningradskogo Universiteta, (Seriya Gumanitarnykh Nauk) 87 1943.

—— Angliyskiy yazyk v Rossii i russkiy yazyk v Anglii. Uchonyye Zapiski Leningradskogo Universiteta (Seriya Filologicheskikh Nauk) 72 vypusk 9 1944.

—— Iz istorii angliyskoy literatury. Moscow and Leningrad 1960.

—— Putevyye zapiski anglichanina i russkiy fol'klor. Russkaya Literatura 4 1962.

—— Slovari inostrannykh yazykov v russkom azbukovnike xvii veka. Leningrad 1968.

Kovalenskaya, N. Svyazi Rossii i Anglii v oblasti iskusstva. International'naya Literatura 11–12 1941.

Sache, G. Der Einfluss Englands auf die politische Ideologie der russischen Gesellschaft in der zweiten Hälfte des 18 Jhs. Archiv für Kultur-geschichte 30 1941.

Yelistratova, A. Angliyskaya klassicheskaya literatura v Rossii. International'naya Literatura 9–10 1941.

Kleiner, K. Sedm set lat angloceských vztahu. 1942.

Kamenetsky, B. Materialy o politicheskikh i kul'turnykh otnosheniyakh Rossii i Anglii v xvi-xix vv. v russkikh izdaniyakh. Istoricheskiy Zhurnal 11 1942.

Lesnorski, B. Le siècle des lumières en Pologne. Acta Poloniae Historica 1961.

Grabowski, T. Les relations entre la Pologne et l'Angleterre à l'époque de la réforme et au xviiie siècle. Comptes Rendus de la Société des Amis des Sciences (Poznan) 1948.

Fabre, J. Stanlislas-Auguste Poniatowski et l'Europe des lumières. [Paris] 1952.

Putnam, P. (ed). Seven Britons in Imperial Russia 1698-1812. Princeton 1952.

Malnick, B. David Garrick and the Russian theatre. MLR 50 1955.

Loewenson, L. Lady Rondeau's letters from Russia (1728–39). Slavonic & East European Rev 35 1957.

Anderson, M. S. Britain's discovery of Russia 1553–1815. 1958.

—— Some British influences on Russian intellectual life in the 18th century. Slavonic & East European Rev 39 1960. See V. M. Vazhinsky, Anglo-russkiye kul'turnyye svyazi v xviii v. v predstavlenii burzhuaznogo istorika, Voprosy Istorii no 12 1961.

Dzhincharadze, V. Z. Iz istorii russko-angliyskikh kul'turnykh otnosheniy v xviii veke. Vestnik Istorii Mirovoy Kul'tury no 5 1960.

Haier, E. William Robertson and L. H. Nicolay, his German translator at the Court of Catherine II. Scottish Historical Rev 41 1962.

Luźny, R. Z badán nad rosyjskim czasopiśmiennictwem satyrycznym okresu Oświecenia. Warsaw and Cracow 1962.

Zaborov, P. R. Literatura-posrednik v istorii russko-zapadnykh literaturnykh svyazey xviii-xix vv. In Mezhdunarodnyye svyazi russkoy literatury, Moscow and Leningrad 1963.

Zapadov, A. V. Angliyskiye avtory v izdaniyakh N. I. Novikova. In Russko-yevropeyskiye literaturnyye svyazi, Moscow and Leningrad 1966.

Levin, Yu. D. Angliyskaya prosvetitel'skaya zhurnalistika

v russkoy literature xviii veka. In Epokha Prosveshcheniya: iz istorii mezhdunarodnykh svyazey russkoy literatury, Leningrad 1967.

Pampmehl, K. A. Samuel Bentham and the Sobesednik, 1783. Slavonic & East European Rev 46 1968.

Russian Authors

Catherine the Great. Skazka o tsareciche Khlore. 1781; Ivan Czarowitz: or the rose without prickles that stings not, tr 1793 (first English trn of a Russian literary work).

Kantemir, Antiokh Dmitriyevich
Stoyunin, V. Ya. Kantemir v Londone. Vestnik Yevropy no 3 (section 1) 1867, no 6 (section 1) 1867.
Grasshoff, H. Antioch Dmitrievič Kantemir und West-Europa. Berlin 1965.

Karamzin, Nikolay Mikhaylovich. Pis'ma russkogo puteshestvennika (1791–1801). Tr A. A. Feldborg 1803. Russian tales. Tr A. A. Feldborg 1803.

Galakhov, A. D. Karamzin kak optimist. Otechestvennyye Zapiski 116 1858. On Karamzin and Pope.
Sipovsky, V. V. N. M. Karamkin, avtor Pisem russkogo puteshestvennika. St Petersburg 1899.
Maslov, V. I. Ossianizm Karamzina. Priluki 1928.
Cross, A. G. Karamzin and England. Slavonic & East European Rev 43 1964.

Kniaźnin, Franciszek Dionizy
Pietrikiewicz, J. Collins and Kniaźnin: a parallel and its background. Slavonic & East European Rev 28 1950.

Lukin, Vladimir Ignat'yevich
McLean, H. The adventures of an English comedy in 18th-century Russia: Dodsley's toy shop and Lukin's Shchepetil'nik. In American contributions to the 5th International Congress of Slavists, Sofia 1693 vol 2 (literary contributions), Hague 1963.

Murav'yov-Apostol, Ivan Matveyevich
Kubasov, I. A. Dramaticheskiye opyty I. M. Murav'yova-Apostola. Izvestiya Otdelehiya Russkogo Yazyka i Slovesnotsi 8 1903. On Sheridan in trn.

Radishchev, Aleksandr Nikolayevich
Lang, D. M. Sterne and Radishchev: an episode in Russian sentimentalism. Revue de Littérature Comparée 21 1947.
Thaler, R. P. Radiščev, Britain and America. Harvard Slavic Stud 4 1957.

Trediakovsky, Vasily Kirillovich
Serman, I. Z. Neizdannaya filosofskaya poema V. Trediakovskogo (Feoptiya). Russkaya Literatura 1 1961.

English Authors

Many trns derive not from the English text, but from French versions.

Defoe, Daniel, The life and strange surprizing adventures of Robinson Crusoe. 3 pts 1719–20; tr Ya. Trusov, 2 vols St Petersburg 1762-4.

Alekseyev, M. P. Sibir' v romane Defoe. Sibirskiy Literaturno-krayevedcheskiy Sbornik (Irkutsk) 1 1928.
—— Robinson Crusoe v russkikh perevodakh. Mezhdunarodnyye Svyazi Russkoy Literatury (Moscow and Leningrad) 1963.
Privalova, Ye. P. Robinson Crusoe v detskoy i pedagogicheskoy literature. Kniga Detyam 2–3 1929.
Smith, I. H. An English view of Russia in the early 18th century. Canadian Slavic Papers 1 1967.

Fielding, Henry. Joseph Andrews. 1742; tr I. Sytensky 2 vols St Petersburg 1772–3.
The life of Mr Jonathan Wild the Great. 1743; tr I. Sytensky 2 vols St Petersburg 1772–3.
The history of Tom Jones. 1749; tr 4 vols Ye. Kharlamov, St Petersburg 1770-1; Podrzutok czyli historya Tom Džona, tr Warsaw 1783.

Amelia. 4 vols 1752; tr P. von Berg 2 vols St Petersburg 1772–3.

Alekseyev, M. P. Fielding in the Russian language. Voks Bulletin 87 1954.

Levidova, I. M. (ed.) Fielding bio-bibliograficheskiy ukazatel'. Moscow 1957 (2nd edn).

Johnson, Samuel
Simmons, J. S. G. Samuel Johnson 'On the banks of the Wolga'. Oxford Slavonic Papers 11 1964.

Levin, Yu. D. Kto byl avtor 'vostochnoy' povesti Obidag. Izvestiya Akademii Nauk SSSR 25 (seriya literatury i yazyka no 5) 1966.

Macpherson, James ('Ossian'). Fragments of ancient poetry. Edinburgh 1760; Fingal, 1762; Temora, 1763; The works of Ossian, 1765; tr Ye. Kostrov, Moscow 1792.

Balavanova, Ye. Pushkin i Ossian. In Sochineniya Pushkina vol 1, St Petersburg 1907.

Piksanov, N. K. Etyud o vliyanii ossianovskoy poezii v russkoy literature. Ibid.

Szyjkowski, S. Ossian en Pologne. Comptes Rendus de l'Académie (Crakow) 17 1912.

Vvedensky, D. N. Etyudy o vliyanii ossianovskoy poezii v russkoy literature. Nezhin 1918.

Maslov, V. I. K voprosu o pervykh russkikh perevodakh poem Ossiana-Makfersona. Sbornik Otdeleniya Russkogo Yazyka i Slovesnosti Akademii Nauk SSSR 101 1928.

—— Ossian v Rossii (bibliografiya). Leningrad 1929.

Iyezuitova, R. Poeziya russkogo ossianizma. Russkaya Literatura 3 1965.

Milton, John. A ms trn of Paradise lost by A. G. Stroganov dates from c. 1745.

Paradise lost. 1667; tr V. P. Petrov, St Petersburg 1777; tr A. Podobedov 1780; tr A. Amvrosii [A. Serebrennikov], Moscow 1785 (from French).

Paradise regained. 1670; tr I. Greshishchev, Moscow 1778 (from French).

Miltona Ray utracony, tr J. I. Przybylski, Cracow 1791–2 (both poems).

Starinnyy russkiy perevod Miltonova Poteryannogo raya. Moskovskiye Vedomosti 14 May 1838. A. G. Stroganov's trn of Paradise lost, 1745.

Heltsztyński, S. Milton in Poland. SP 26 1929.

Tihany, L. C. Milton's brief history of Muscovia. PQ 13 1934.

Cawley, R. R. Milton's literary craftsmanship: a study of a brief history of Moscovia. Princeton 1941 (with text).

Löwenson, L. E. G. von Berge, translator of Milton and Russian interpreter 1649–1722. Slavonic & East European Rev 34 1956

Gleason, J. B. The nature of Milton's Moscovia. SP 61 1964.

Sentsi, I. Milton o Rossii. In Russko-yevropeyskiye literaturnyye svyazi, Moscow and Leningrad 1966.

More, Sir Thomas. Utopia. 1551; tr St Petersburg 1790.

Chechulin, N. O russkom perevode Utopii Mora, sdelannom v xviii veke. Zhurnal Ministerstva Narodnogo Prosveshcheniya 5 1905.

Otway, Thomas. Venice preserved. 1682; tr St Petersburg 1764.

Pope, Alexander. The rape of the lock. 1712, 1714 (enlarged); tr Moscow 1761.

The temple of fame. 1715; tr M. M. Kheraskov, Moscow 1761.

An essay on man. 4 pts 1733–4; tr N. N. Popovsky, Moscow 1757.

Tikhonravov, N. S. Istoriya izdaniya opyta o cheloveke v perevode Popovskogo. In his Sochineniya vol 3 1898.

Helsztynski, S. Pope und der polnische Pseudo-Klassizismus. Anglia Beiblatt 40 1929.

Richardson, Samuel. Pamela. 2 vols 1740; tr P. P. Chertkov 4 vols St Petersburg 1787.

Clarissa. 7 vols 1748; tr N. P. Osipov and P. Kil'dyushevsky, 6 vols St Petersburg 1791–2.

Sir Charles Grandison. 7 vols 1754; tr A. Kondratovich 8 vols St Petersburg 1793–4.

Batyushkov, F. Richardson, Pushkin i L. Tolstoy. Zhurnal Ministerstva Narodnogo Prosveshcheniya 19 1917. On Clarissa and Anna Karenina.

Smollett, Tobias. The adventures of Roderick Random. 2 vols 1748; tr Moscow 1788.

The adventures of Peregrine Pickle. 4 vols 1751; tr St Petersburg 1788.

The expedition of Humphry Clinker. 3 vols 1771; tr I. Zakharov, St Petersburg 1789.

As in France, Smollett's anonymity led to Fielding being named as author of Roderick Random and Humphry Clinker.

Sterne, Laurence. A sentimental journey. 2 vols 1768; tr A. Kolmakov, St Petersburg 1793.

Maslov, V. I. Interes k Sternu v russkoy literature kontsa xviii i nachala xix vv. In Istoriko-literaturnyy sbornik, posvyashchonnyy V. I. Sreznevskomu, Leningrad 1924.

Modzalevsky, B. L. Pushkin i Sterne. Russkiy Sovremennik 2 1924.

Azadovsky, M. K. Sterne v vospriyatiyakh dekabristov. In Bunt dekabristov, Leningrad 1926.

Vertsman, I. Sterne. Literaturnyy Kritik 7 1938.

Grebenícková, R. Sternianství v ruské próze. Ceskoslovenská Rusiatika 10 1965.

Swift, Jonathan. Travels into several remote nations of the world by Lemuel Gulliver. 1726; Puteshestviy Gulliverovykh kniga pervaya-[chetvertaya], tr Ye. E. Korzhavin 4 vols St Petersburg 1772–3 (from French).

Thomson, James. The seasons. 1730; tr D. I. Dmitrevsky, Moscow 1798.

Zaborov, P. R. Neizdannaya poema M. V. Khrapovitskogo Chetyre vremeni goda, xviii vek vol 5. Moscow and Leningrad 1962. Imitation of Seasons.

Young, Edward. The complaint: or night-thoughts 9 pts 1742–5; tr A. M. Kutuzov, Moscow 1785.

Smŏv, A. V. Yungovy nochi. Antikvar 9 1920. S. N. Glinka's 1806 trn.

Zaborov, P. R. Nochnyye razmyshleniya Younga v rannikh russkikh perevodakh. In Russkaya literatura xviii veka: epokha klassitsizma vol 6, Moscow and Leningrad 1964.

S. S. B. T.

(10) OTHER COUNTRIES

Belgium

Singleton, R. H. Milton's Comus and the Comus of Erycius Puleanus. PMLA 58 1943.

Lefèvre, J. L'Angleterre et la Belgique à travers les cinq derniers siècles. Paris 1946.

Hoppe, H. R. English actors at Ghent in the 17th century. RES 25 1949.

Greece

Robertson, William. The history of the discovery and colonization of America. 1777; Ἱστορια της Ἀμερικης Μεταφρασθεισα Παρα Γ. Βεντοτη, Vienna 1792–3.

Legrand, E. Bibliographie hellénique du xviiie siècle. 2 vols Paris 1918, 1928.

Dimaras, C. T. D. Catargi: 'philosophe' grec. Stud on Voltaire & 18th Century 25 1963.
— Rapports sur le développement des littératures du sud-est européen en relation avec les autres littératures, du xviie siècle à nos jours. Sofia 1966.

Hungary

Vambéry. Milton in Hungary. In Milton memorial lectures, Oxford 1909. S. Bessenyei's trn of Paradise lost, 1796; see also H. von Wlislocki, Zeitschrift für Vergleichende Litteraturgeschichte 4 1891.
Fest, S. Pope és a magyar költök. Egyetemes philologia Közlöny 40 1916. From late 18th century.
— Angol irodalmi hatások hazánkban szechenyi István fellépéséig. Budapest 1917. On British influence from 16th century.
Tronchon, H. En guise d'introduction à une bibliographie critique de l'influence anglaise en Hongrie. Revue des Etudes Hongroises 1928.
Elek, O. Ossian-kultusz Magyarországon. Egyetemes Philologiai Közlöny 57 1933. On late 18th century Ossian cult in Hungary.
Szentkirályi, J. és A. Lásló. Hungaro-Britannica bibliographia. Angol Filológiai, Tanulmányok 1–6, 1936–8, 1944.
Gal, I. Early travellers from Upper-Hungary in England. Danubian Rev 7 1939.
— Magyarország, Anglia és Amerika. Budapest 1945.
— Hungary and the Anglo-Saxon world. Budapest 1947.
Maller, S. Ossian Magyarországon 1788–1849. In Debrecen, debreceni Magyar Királyi Tisza István-Tudomanyegetem 1940 (with English summary).
Hankiss, J. The culmination of the Hungarian Ossian-cult. In Festschrift E. Ekwall, Upsala 1942.
Berg, P. Angol hatások tizenhetedik századi irodalmunkban. Budapest 1946.
Laslo, Cs. Szabo. Ossian Magyarhonban. Magyarok 2 1946. Survey of trns.
Tezla, A. An introductory bibliography to the study of Hungarian literature. Cambridge Mass 1964. With bibliography of foreign influences and trns.

Rumania

It was through Serbian, Greek and above all French intermediaries that the work of Pope, Addison, Defoe, Chesterfield, Swift and Young (and later Byron and Dickens) entered Rumania from 1790 onwards. The first original trns from English were pbd from 1840.

Early Manuscript Translations

Beveridge. Synedicon. Tr S. M. Clain. 1789 (in Cluj library).
Pope, Alexander. Essay on man. Tr J. Cantacuzino 1794 (in Library of Rumanian Academy, ms 6002).

Authorities

Grimm, P. Traduceri şi imitaţii din literatura engleză. Cluj 1924. With trns from English.
Iorga, N. La pénétration des idées de l'occident dans le sud-est de l'Europe au xviie et au xviiie siècles. Revue Historique du Sud-est Européen Jan-Sept 1924.
— A history of Anglo-Rumanian relations. Bucharest 1931.
Cartojan, N. Les premiers éléments occidentaux dans la littérature roumaine. Revue de Littérature Comparée 14 1934.
Popovici, D. Pope si conachi. In Studii literari, Sibiu 1942.
— La littérature roumaine à l'époque des lumières. Sibiu 1945.
Cioranescu, A. La Roumanie vue par les étrangers. Bucharest 1944.

Guillermou, A. La littérature roumaine et l'Europe. Revue de Littérature Comparée 23 1949.
Muntéano, B. La littérature comparée chez les Roumains. Yearbook of Comparative Lit 2 1953.
Dutu, A. National and European consciousness in the Romanian Enlightenment. Stud on Voltaire & 18th Century 55 1967.
— Prolegomene la studiul comparat al literaturii române primele contacte cu literatura engleză. Studii de Literatură Universală (Bucharest) 9 1967. Comprehensive bibliographical survey of early English influence.
— Coordonate ale culturii românesti in secolul xviii (1700–1821.) Bucharest 1968. On foreign influences on Rumanian cultural life : French synopsis given.
— Primele contacte literare anglo-române. In his Explorari in istoria literaturii române, Bucharest 1969 (with French synopsis).

Switzerland

See also sections on French and German, above, for works of Bodmer, Breitinger, Gessner, Haller, Rousseau and Mme de Staël. The canton de Genève was not at this time a member of the Swiss confederation.

Stanyan, T. An account of Switzerland. 1714.
Bodmer, J. J. Ablehnung des Verdachtes dass die schweizerische Nation sich habe überreden lassen, an Miltons Verloren Paradiese einen Geschmack zu finden. Zürich 1741.
Keate, George. A short account of the ancient history, present government and laws of Geneva. 1761; Abrégé de l'histoire de Genève, tr A. Lorovich 1774.
The alps. 1763. Albrecht von Haller, Die Alpen, Berne 1734, tr 1794.
Ferney: an epistle to Monsr de Voltaire. 1768. See Voltaire's correspondence, ed T. Besterman, Geneva 1953–65 for his extensive correspondence with Voltaire.
Engel, C. E. G. Keate et la Suisse. Zeitschrift für Schweizerische Geschichte 1948.
Coxe, William. Sketches on the natural, civil and political state of Switzerland. 1779.
Travels in Switzerland. 1789.
Bodemann, E. Julie von Bondeli und ihr Freundeskreis. Hanover 1874.
Vetter, T. Zürich als Vermittlerin englischer Literatur im 18 Jahrhundert. Zürich 1891.
— Bodmer und die englische Literatur. In Denkschrift zum Geburtstag, Zürich 1900.
Vreeland, W. U. Etude sur les rapports littéraires entre Genève et l'Angleterre jusqu'à la publication de la Nouvelle Héloïse. Geneva 1901.
Saussure, César de. Lettres et voyages de César de Saussure en Allemagne, en Hollande et en Angleterre 1725–9. Ed B. van Muyden, Paris 1903. See G. Lanson, Deux voyages en Angleterre, Revue d'Histoire Littéraire de la France 13 1906 for Saussure's borrowings from Voltaire's Lettres philosophiques.
Viles, G. B. Comparison of Bodmer's translation of Paradise lost with the original. Leipzig 1904.
Reed, B. The influence of Gessner upon English literature. Philadelphia 1906.
Schirmer, G. Edward Gibbon und die Schweiz. In Festschrift zum 14 Neophilogentage, Zürich 1910.
— Die Schweiz im Spiegel englischer und amerikanischer Literatur bis 1848. Zürich 1929.
Wirz, E. Die literarische Tätigkeit des Malers J. H. Fuessli. Basle 1912.
Beck, C. La Suisse vue par les grands écrivains et les voyageurs célèbres. Paris 1914.
Ibershoff, C. H. Bodmer und Milton. JEGP 17 1918–19; also PMLA 43 1928.
— Bodmer and Young. JEGP 24 1925.

—— Bodmer and Newton. MLR 21 1926.
—— Bodmer and Thomson's Seasons. MLN 41 1926.
Baldensperger, F. L'helvétisme littéraire et ses relations avec les grands courants de la pensée occidentale. In La Suisse et ses Français, ed A. Castell, Paris 1920.
Lätt, A. Les relations intellectuelles entre la Grande-Bretagne et la Suisse. Bibliothèque Universelle et Revue Suisse 1919.
Stadler, H. Paul Henri Mallet. Lausanne 1924.
Jones, H. M. Albrecht von Haller and English philosophy. PMLA 40 1925.
Ziehen, E. Philhelvetism. Die Neueren Sprachen 4 1925.
Ernst, F. La tradition médiatrice de la Suisse au xviii⁰ et au xix⁰ siècle. Revue de Littérature Comparée 6 1926.
—— Die Schweiz als geistige Mittlerin von Muralt bis Burckhardt. Zürich 1932.
Price, L. M. Albrecht von Haller and English theology. PMLA 41 1926.
Bonjour, E. Die Schweiz und England: ein geschichtlicher Rückblick. Berne 1934.
Funke, O. Die Schweiz und die englische Literatur. Berne 1937.
Chicoteau, M. Note sur la Suisse alémanique et les pélerins anglais de J. Addison à Wordsworth. Comparative Lit Stud 2 1941.
Eaton, J. W. Bodmer and Breitinger and European literary theory. Monatshefte für Deutschen Unterricht 33 1941.
Fuessli, Heinrich. Briefe. Ed B. Muschg, Basle 1942.
Thomas, J. La Suisse et le cosmopolitisme littéraire. Confluences 2 1942.
Engel, C. E. English novels in Switzerland in the 18th century. Comparative Lit Stud 14–15 1944–5.
—— Genève et l'Angleterre: les De Luc 1727–1817. Revue d'Histoire Suisse 4 1946.
Wildi, M. Der angelsächsische Roman und der Schweizer Leser. Zürich 1944.
Lunn, A. Switzerland in English prose and poetry. 1947.

Bon, P. B. English words in Swiss-German usage. Amer Speech 23 1949.
Brown, A. Locke's Essay and Bodmer and Breitinger. MLQ 10 1949.
de Beer, G. R. English visitors in Switzerland: Edward Gibbon's friends. N & Q 14–28 May 1949.
—— Travellers in Switzerland. Oxford 1949.
—— Anglais au pays de Vaud. Revue d'Histcire Vaudoise 1951.
—— With G. A. Bonnard. Miscellanea Gibboniana: Journal de mon voyage dans la Suisse 1755. Lausanne 1952.
—— With A. M. Rousseau. Voltaire's British visitors. Stud on Voltaire & 18th Century 49 1967.
Schindler, J. Das Bild des Engländers in der Kunst- und Volksliteratur der deutschen Schweiz von 1798–1898. Berne 1950.
Grubenmann, Y. de A. Un cosmopolite suisse: J. H. Meister 1744–1820. Geneva 1954.
Boswell, James. Boswell on the Grand Tour: Germany and Switzerland 1763. Ed F. A. Pottle 1954.
Stanzel, F. K. Das Bild der Alpen in der englischen Literatur des 17 und 18 Jahrhunderts. Germanisch-romanische Monatsschrift 45 1964.
Perrochon, H. Cosmopolitisme et littérature au xviii⁰ siècle en Suisse française. In Proceedings of 4th Congress of International Comparative Literature Association, ed F. Jost 2 vols Hague 1966.
Fischer, B. de. Swiss in Great Britain in the 18th century. In The age of the Enlightenment: studies presented to T. Besterman, Edinburgh 1967.

Yugoslavia

Fiedler, H. G. The first link between English and Serbo-Croat literature. Slavonic Rev 6 1927.
Stojanovic, D. Anglo-Yugoslav cultural relations. Contemporary Rev Feb 1940.

S. S. B. T.

(11) SHAKESPEARE ON THE CONTINENT

A select list, excluding occasional borrowings from Shakespeare. For additional information see bibliographies listed below, as well as the Shakespeare section in vol 1.

General Studies

Horn, F. Shakespeare und das herrschende ästhetische Prinzip des 17 und des 18 Jahrhunderts. Blätter für Literarische Unterhaltung 25–7 Jan, 20 March 1831.
Thimm, F. Shakespeariana from 1564–1864: an account of the Shakespearian literature of England, Germany, France and other European countries. 1865.
Riedel, W. Über Shakespeares Würdigung in England, Frankreich und Deutschland. Archiv 48 1882.
Wetz, W. Shakespeare vom Standpunkt der vergleichenden Literaturgeschichte. Worms 1890.
Schiavello, G. La fama dello Shakespeare nel secolo xviii. Camerino 1904.
Adler, J. Shakespeare Kritik des xviii Jahrhunderts. Königsberg 1906.
Robertson, J. G. The knowledge of Shakespeare on the Continent at the beginning of the 18th century. MLR 1 1906.
Croce, B. Ariosto, Shakespeare e Corneille. Bari 1920.
Herford, C. H. A sketch of the history of Shakespeare's influence on the continent. Bull John Rylands Lib 9 1925.
Stoll, E. E. Shakespeare studies, historical and comparative in method. New York 1927.

Smith, D. N. Shakespeare in the 18th century. Oxford 1928.
Babcock, R. W. The genesis of Shakespeare idolatry 1766–99. Chapel Hill 1931.
Ebisch, W. and L. L. Schücking. A Shakespeare bibliography. Oxford 1931; Supplement 1930–5, Oxford 1937. See G. R. Smith, below.
Ralli, A. A history of Shakespeare criticism. 2 vols Oxford 1932.
Pillai, V. K. A. Shakespeare criticism from the beginnings to 1765. 1933.
Ford, H. L. Shakespeare 1700–40. Oxford 1935.
Praz, M. La fortuna del dramma elisabettiano. Florence 1937.
Naranyana-Menon, C. Shakespeare criticism: an essay in synthesis. Oxford 1938.
Van Teighem, P. Shakespeare devant la critique continentale au xviii⁰ siècle. Essais et Etudes Universitaires 1 1945–6.
—— Adaptations scéniques de Shakespeare sur le continent. Rivista di Letterature Moderne 1 1946.
—— La découverte de Shakespeare sur le continent. In his Le Préromantisme, Paris 1947.
Chambrun, C. L. Shakespeare across the Channel. In J. Q .Adams memorial studies, Washington 1948.
Lancaster, H. C. The alleged first foreign estimate [1684] of Shakespeare. MLN 63 1948.
Wagner, B. M. (ed). The appreciation of Shakespeare: a collection of criticism. Washington 1949.
Price, L. M. Shakespeare as pictured by Voltaire, Goethe and Öser. Germanic Rev 25 1950.

Shimada, K. Shakespeare on the European continent. In Introduction to comparative literature, ed Nakajima and Nakano, Tokyo 1951.

Calgari, G. Fortuna di Shakespeare in Italia e in Francia. Hesperia (Zürich) 3 1953.

Lewinter, O. (ed). Shakespeare in Europe. Cleveland 1963.

Smith, G. R. A classified Shakespeare bibliography 1936–58. Philadelphia 1963.

Baldini, G. (ed). La fortuna di Shakespeare 1593–1964. 2 vols Milan 1965. A critical anthology of English, German, French, Russian and Italian references.

Solt, A. The formation of the Shakespeare image in the Enlightenment and the Romantic era. Shakespeare Stud 3 1965.

Velz, J. W. Shakespeare and the classical tradition 1660–1960. Minneapolis 1968.

Shakespeare in France

Bibliographies

Traduction française de Shakespeare. Intermédiaire des Chercheurs et des Curieux 10 Dec 1882.

Dubeux, A. Les traductions françaises de Shakespeare. Paris [1928].

Horn-Monval, M. Les traductions françaises de Shakespeare. In his Répertoire bibliographique des traductions et adaptations du théâtre étranger vol 5, Paris 1963.

Translations and Adaptations

This list excludes individual texts pbd after Le Tourneur's collected edn.

Brécourt. Les flatteurs trompez: ou l'ennemy des faux amis. Caen 1699. Timon.

D[elisle de La Drevetière]. Thimon le misanthrope. Paris 1722.

Voltaire. La mort de César. Amsterdam 1735. From Julius Ceasar; *See also his* literal version of 1764 (written 1762), ed A. M. Rousseau, Paris 1964.

[Robert-Boistel, J. B.]. Antoine et Cléopâtre. Paris 1743.

Destouches, P. N. Scènes tirées de la Tempête. In his Œuvres de théâtre, Paris 1745. From Davenant's play.

Laplace, P. A. de (tr). Le théâtre anglois. 4 vols 1745–6, 8 vols 1746–9. 10 plays in first edn, 27 plays in 2nd, which also included Analyses and sommaires of plays omitted. For contents of Laplace's anthology, *see Horn-Monval, above, nos 345–7.* Free adaptations.

Portelance, M. A trompeur trompeuses et demi. Mannheim 1759. Merry Wives.

Bret, A. Les deux amies: ou le vieux coquet. Performed 1761. Comic opera from Merry Wives.

Barthe. Les fausses infidélités. Amsterdam 1768. Merry Wives.

Rochon de Chabannes. Hylas et Sylvie. Paris 1769. Pastoral based on Tempest.

Ducis, J. F. Hamlet. Paris 1770. Performed 1769.
—— Roméo et Juliette. Paris 1772.
—— Le roi Léar. Paris 1783.
—— Macbeth. Paris 1790. Performed 1784.
—— Jean-sans-Terre: ou la Mort d'Arthur. Paris 1792. Performed 1791.
——Othello. Paris 1792.
Ducis gallicized, purified and transformed the originals.

[Ozicourt]. Roméo et Juliette. Paris 1771.

Douin. Le more de Venise. Paris 1773.

R[adet], R. [or Carrière-Doisin (Rosirocci)]. Roméo et Paquette: parodie en 5 actes. Verona 1773.

Shakespeare traduit de l'anglois. Tr P. P. F. Le Tourneur with de Catuelan and J. Fontaine-Malherbe. 20 vols Paris 1776–82. The first complete trn, and the first to follow text with only minor modifications. In prose. Remained standard.

Early Criticism

Clément, N. Bibliotheca telleriana: sive catalogus librorum bibliothecae. Paris 1675–84, 1693. A mere catalogue entry. *See* H. C. Lancaster, The alleged first foreign estimate of Shakespeare, MLN 63 1948, who restores 1717 as the first significant mention.

Dissertation sur la poésie angloise. Journal Littéraire de La Haye 9 1717.

Prévost, A. F. Mémoires et avantures d'un homme de qualité. 7 vols Paris etc 1728–31. *See* M. E. J. Robertson (ed), Mémoires vol 5: Séjour en Angleterre, Paris 1927.

—— Le pour et contre. Paris 1733–40. Especially vol 14, 1738.

Voltaire, F. M. A. de. Œdipe. Préface to 1730 edn.
—— Discours sur la tragédie. In his Brutus, Paris 1731.
—— Essai sur la poésie épique. Paris 1733. Tr Voltaire.
—— Lettres philosophiques. Amsterdam (for Rouen) 1734. Lettre 18: Sur la tragédie.
—— Lettre de M. de Voltaire à l'Académie française. [Geneva 1776].
See T. Besterman, Voltaire on Shakespeare, Stud on Voltaire & Eighteenth Century 54 1967 (an anthology).

Shakespeare et Corneille. Journal Encyclopédique 15 Oct 1760. *See* also Voltaire's reply, Jérome Carré [Voltaire], Appel à toutes les nations d'Europe.

Baretti, G. Discours sur Shakespeare et sur M. de Voltaire. 1771. *See* F. Biondolillo's edn, Lanciano 1911.

Montagu, E. An essay on the writings and genius of Shakespeare, with some remarks upon the misrepresentations of Mons de Voltaire. 1769; Apologie de Shakespeart, en réponse à la critique de M. de Voltaire, tr Paris 1777.

Rutledge, J. Observations à l'Académie française au sujet d'une lettre de M. de Voltaire. Paris 1777.

Modern Studies

'Stendhal' (Henri Beyle). Racine et Shakespeare. Paris 1823.

Lacroix, A. Histoire de l'influence de Shakespeare sur le théâtre français jusqu'à nos jours. Brussels 1856.

Elze, K. Shakespeare in Frankreich. Sh Jb 1 1865.

Kühn, C. Über Ducis in seiner Beziehung zu Shakespeare. Jena 1875.

Harrisson, J. A. The Shakespeare cult in France. Shakespeariana May 1884.

Stapfer, P. Molière et Shakespeare. Paris 1887 (4th edn).

Legouve, E. Corneille et Shakespeare. Revue Universitaire 15 1894.

Engel, J. Shakespeare in Frankreich. Sh Jb 34 1898.

Jusserand, J. J. Shakespeare en France sous l'ancien régime. Paris 1898; tr 1899. *See also* Une légende de Cyrano, Revue d'Histoire Littéraire de la France 6 1899. Reply by H. C. Lancaster, MLN 63 1948.

Dejob, C. La tragédie historique chez Voltaire et Shakespeare. Revue des Cours et des Conférences 7 1899.

Fierlinger, E. Shakespeare in Frankreich. Olmütz 1900.

Larroumet, G. Voltaire: l'influence de Shakespeare sur son théâtre. Revue des Cours et des Conférences 8 1900.

Liéby, A. Etude sur le théâtre de M. J. Chénier. Paris 1901.

Redard, E. Shakespeare dans les pays de la langue française. Paris 1901.

Lounsbury, T. R. Shakespeare and Voltaire. 1902. *See* Nation 6 Nov 1902; E. J. Dubedout, MP 3 1906.

Zollinger, O. Ein französischer Shakespeare-Bearbeiter des xviii Jahrhunderts [L. S. Mercier]. Sh Jb 1902. *See also* L. Béclard, S. Mercier, Paris 1903.

Baldensperger, F. Esquisse d'une histoire de Shakespeare en France. In his Etudes d'histoire littéraire, Paris 1910 (2nd ser).

Hedgcock, F. A. Garrick et ses amis français. Paris 1911; tr 1911.

Cushing, M. G. Pierre Le Tourneur. New York 1908.

Dargan, E. P. Shakespeare and Ducis. MP 10 1913.

Havens, G. R. The abbé Prévost and Shakespeare. MP 17 1920. *See also* J. C. Carpenter, MLR 10 1915.

— Voltaire and English critics of Shakespeare. Franco-American Pamphlets (New York) 1944.

Lanson, G. Esquisse d'une histoire de la tragédie française. New York 1920.

— (ed), rev A. M. Rousseau. Voltaire: Lettres philosophiques. 2 vols Paris 1964.

Serrurier, C. Voltaire et Shakespeare. Neophilologus 5 1920.

Haak, P. Die ersten französischen Übersetzungen von La Place und Le Tourneur. Steinau 1922.

Roosebroeck, G. L. van. Hamlet in France in 1663. PMLA 37 1922.

Gilman, M. Othello in French. Paris 1925.

— Le dissipateur and Timon of Athens. MLN 42 1927. Destouches' play, based on Shadwell's adaptation.

Haines, C. M. Shakespeare in France: criticism. 1925.

Looten, C. La première controverse internationale sur Shakespeare entre l'abbé Leblanc et W. Guthrie 1745–58. Lille 1927.

Cobb, L. La Place: sa vie, son oeuvre. Paris 1928.

Moraud, M. The conflict between the French classical and the Shakespearian conception of the drama. Rice Institute Pamphlets 15 1928.

Babcock, R. W. The English reaction against Voltaire's criticism of Shakespeare. SP 27 1930.

Keys, A. C. Les adaptations musicales de Shakespeare en France. Paris 1933.

Green, F. C. Minuet. 1935.

Lebègue, R. La tragédie 'shakespearienne' en France au temps de Shakespeare [1580–1640]. Revue des Cours et des Conférences 38 1937.

Smith, F. P. Shakespeare in France. Revue de Littérature Comparée 17 1937.

Lefranc, A. La question shakespearienne au xviiie siècle. Revue Bleue 76 1938.

Naves, R. Le goût de Voltaire. Paris [1938].

Adams, P. G. How much of Shakespeare did Voltaire know? Shakespeare Assoc Bull 16 1941.

Shackleton, R. Shakespeare in French translation. Modern Languages 23 1941.

Stoll, E. E. Molière and Shakespeare. Romanic Rev 35 1944.

Horsley, P. M. G. Keate and the Voltaire-Shakespeare controversy. Comparative Lit Stud 16 1945.

Russell, T. W. Voltaire, Dryden and heroic tragedy. New York 1946.

Fenger, H. Voltaire et le théâtre anglais. Orbis Litterarum (Copenhagen) 1959.

Benchettrit, R. Hamlet at the Comédie française 1769–1896. Shakespeare Stud 9 1956.

England, M. W. Garrick's Stratford Jubilee: reaction in France and Germany. Shakespeare Stud 9 1956.

Keys, A. Shakespeare en France: La Mégère apprivoisée en 1767. Revue de Littérature Comparée 31 1957.

Pichois, C. Préromantiques, Rousseauistes et Shakespeare 1770–8. Revue de Littérature Comparée 33 1959.

— Voltaire et Shakespeare: un plaidoyer. Jahrbuch der Deutschen Shakespeare-Gesellschaft 98 1962.

Shakespeare en France. Etudes Anglaises 13 1960 (special course).

Grivelet, M. La critique dramatique française devant Shakespeare. Ibid.

Jeune, S. Hamlet d'Otway, Macbeth de Dryden: ou Shakespeare en France en 1714. Revue de Littérature Comparée 36 1962.

Mattauch, H. A propos du premier jugement sur Shakespeare en France. MLN 78 1963. On J. de Courbeville.

Bailey, H. P. Hamlet in France. Geneva 1964.

Jacquot, J. Shakespeare en France: mises en scène d'hier et d'aujourd'hui. Paris 1964.

Lawrenson, T. E. Voltaire and Shakespeare: ordeal by translation. In Papers, ed G. I. Duthie, Edinburgh 1964.

Rousseau, A. M. Voltaire, La mort de César. Paris 1964. With Voltaire's trn of Julius Caesar acts 1–3.

Suckling, N. Shakespeare in French. Durham Univ Jnl 25 1964.

Bochner, J. Shakespeare in France: a survey of dominant opinion 1733–1800. Revue de Littérature Comparée 39 1965.

Desvignes, L. Molière et Cyrano ont-ils connu Shakespeare? Revue de Littérature Comparée 40 1966.

Besterman, T. (ed). Voltaire on Shakespeare. Stud on Voltaire & 18th Century 54 1967. A critical anthology. *See also his* Voltaire, 1969, pp. 125–52.

Desné, R. Diderot et Shakespeare. Revue de Littérature Comparée 41 1967.

S. S. B. T.

Shakespeare in Germany

See also the comprehensive bibliographies pbd by the Shakespeare-Gesellschaft etc. Current bibliographies are pbd in the Shakespeare-Jahrbuch series.

Bibliographies

Die Shakespeare-Literatur in Deutschland 1762–1851. Cassel 1852. Lists trns.

Unflad, L. Die Shakespeare-Literatur in Deutschland. Munich 1880. On trns of individual plays.

Beam, J. Die ersten deutschen Übersetzungen englischer Lustspiele im 18 Jahrhundert. Jena 1904.

Translations and Adaptations

This excludes individual texts pbd after collected edn. For full bibliography of works on German Shakespeare trn, see Sh Jb 92 1956.

Borck, C. W. von. Versuch einer gebundenen Übersetzung des Trauerspiels vom Tode des Julius Cäsar. Berlin 1741. *See* W. Pätow, Die erste metrische deutsche Shakespeare-Übersetzung, Rostock 1892.

Wieland, C. M. Shakespear, Theatralische Werke aus dem Englischen übersetzt. 8 vols Zürich 1762–6. Prose. *See* F. W. Meisnest, Wieland's translation of Shakespeare, MLR 9 1914; H. Pongs, Wieland und Shakespeare, in Festschrift zum 200 Geburtstag des Dichters Wieland, Biberach 1933.

Eschenburg, J. J. William Shakespears Schauspiele. 13 vols Zürich 1775–82, 22 vols Strasbourg-Mannheim 1778–83. Prose. *See* H. Uhde-Bernays, Der Mannheimer Shakespeare, Berlin 1902; H. Schrader, Eschenburg und Shakespeare, Marburg 1911.

Schlegel, A. W. Shakespeares dramatische Werke übersetzt. 8 vols Berlin 1797–1801; vol 9, 1810. Completed by Graf W. Baudissin and Dorothea Tieck under supervision of Ludwig Tieck: 17 plays in verse. *See* B. Seuffert, Wielands, Eschenburgs und Schlegels Shakespeare Übersetzungen, Archiv für Literatur-Geschichte 13 1884; M. Atkinson, August Wilhelm Schlegel as a translator of Shakespeare, Oxford 1958 and Wolf Baudissin translator, German Life & Letters 16 1963.

Early Criticism

Schlegel, J. E. Vergleichung Shakspears und Andreas Gryphs. 1741.

Lessing, G. E. Briefe, die neueste Litteratur betreffend [no 17]. Berlin 1759.

—Hamburgische Dramaturgie. Hamburg 1767–9.

Gerstenberg, H. W. Briefe über Merkwürdigkeiten der Litteratur. Schleswig 1766-7.

Goethe, J. W. von. Zum Schäkespears Tag. 1771.

Herder, J. G. Shakespear. In Von deutscher Art und Kunst, Hamburg 1773.

Eschenburg, J. J. Über Wilhelm Shakespeare. Zürich 1787.

Modern Studies

Cohn, A. Shakespeare in Germany in the 16th and 17th centuries: an account of English actors in Germany and the Netherlands. 1865.

Vincke, G. von. F. L. Schröder der deutsche Shakespeare-Begründer. Sh Jb 11 1876.

Böhtlingk, A. Shakespeare und unsere Klassiker: i, Lessing und Shakespeare; ii, Goethe und Shakespeare; iii, Schiller und Shakespeare. 3 vols Leipzig 1909–10.

Gundolf, F. Shakespeare und der deutsche Geist. Berlin 1911.

Richter, K. A. Beiträge zum Bekanntwerden Shakespeares in Deutschland. 3 vols Breslau 1909–12, Oppeln 1912.

— Shakespeare in Deutschland in den Jahren 1739–70. Oppeln 1912.

Lüdeke, H. (ed). Das Buch über Shakespeare: handschriftliche Aufzeichnungen von Ludwig Tieck. Halle 1920.

Price, L. M. English-German literary influences: bibliography and survey. Berkeley 1920.

— The publication of English literature in Germany in the 18th century. Berkeley 1934.

— English literature in Germany. Berkeley 1953. Pt 3: Shakespeare in Germany.

Walzel, O. Der Kritiker Lessing und Shakespeare. Sh Jb 65 1929.

Isaacson, H. Der junge Herder und Shakespeare. Berlin 1930.

Bruder, E. Die erste deutsche Shakespeare-Aufführung unter Wieland 1761. Biberach 1931.

Würtenberg, G. (ed). Shakespeare in Deutschland. Bielefeld 1931. Reprint of source material.

Würtenberg, G. Shakespeare in Deutschland. Bielefeld 1939.

Deetjen, W. Shakespeare Aufführungen unter Goethes Leitung. Sh Jb 68 1932.

Drews, W. König Lear auf der deutschen Bühne bis zur Gegenwart. Berlin 1932.

Kelly, J. A. German visitors to English theatres in the 18th century. Princeton 1936.

Brüggemann, F. (ed). Die Aufnahme Shakespeares auf der Bühne der Aufklärung in den sechziger und siebziger Jahren. Leipzig 1937.

Pascal, R. Shakespeare in Germany 1740–1815. Cambridge 1937.

— Goethe und das Tragische: die Wandlung von Goethes Shakespeare-Bild. Goethe Gesellschaft 26 1964.

Fechter, P. Deutsche Shakespeare-Darsteller. Sh Jb 77 1941.

Kies, P. P. Shakespeare in Germany. MLN 56 1941.

Kane, R. J. Tolstoy, Goethe and King Lear. Shakespeare Assoc Bull 21 1946.

Stahl, E. L. Shakespeare und das deutsche Theater. Stuttgart 1947.

Raeck, K. Shakespeare in the German open-air theatre. Shakespeare Survey 3 1950.

Lüthi, H. J. Das deutsche Hamletbild seit Goethe. Berne 1951.

Lüthi, M. Kleist und Shakespeare. Sh Gessellschaft 95 1959.

Oppel, H. Stand und Aufgabe der deutschen Shakespeare-Forschung 1952–7. Stuttgart 1958.

Heun, H. G. Shakespeare in deutschen Übersetzungen. Berlin 1959.

— Probleme der deutschen Shakespeare-Übersetzungen. Sh Jb 102 1966.

Hultberg, H. B. Brecht und Shakespeare. Orbis Litterarum (Copenhagen) 14 1959.

Guthke, K. S. Gerstenberg und die Shakespeare-Deutung der deutschen Klassik und Romantik. JEGP 58 1959.

— Richtungskonstanten in der deutschen Shakespeare-Deutung des 18 Jahrhunderts. Sh Jb 98 1962.

Wolffheim, H. Die Entdeckung Shakespeares: deutsche Zeugnisse des 18 Jahrhunderts. Hamburg 1959.

Himmel, H. Shakespeare und die deutsche Klassik. Chronik Wiener Goetheverein 66 1960.

Steck, P. Der Einfluss Shakespeares auf die Technik der Meisterdramen Schillers. Shakespeare Gesellschaft 96 1960.

Jost, W. Stilkrise der deutschen Shakespeare-Übersetzungen. Deutsche Vierteljahrsschrift für Literaturgeschichte 35 1961.

McNamee, L. F. The secret of Shakespeare's power in Germany. Educational Theatre Jnl 14 1962.

Brennecke, E. and H. Shakespeare in Germany 1590–1700. Chicago 1964.

Kindermann, H. Shakespeare und das Burgtheater. Vienna 1964.

Musiol, M. Shakespeare in German: the modern period. Durham Univ Jnl 25 1964.

Stamm, R. Rudolf Alexander Schröder als Shakespeare-Übersetzer. Shakespeare Gesellschaft 100 1964.

Stellmacher, W. Grundfragen der Shakespeare-Rezeption in der Frühphase des Sturm und Drang. Weimarer Beiträge 10 1964.

Brown, F. A. Shakespeare and English drama in German popular journals 1717–59. Kentucky Foreign Lang Quart 12 1965.

Grimm, R., W. Jäggi and H. Oesch (ed). Der deutsche Shakespeare: kritische Beiträge zu aktuellen Theaterfragen. Basle, Hamburg and Vienna 1965.

Girnus, W. Deutsche Klassik und Shakespeare. Sinn und Form 18 1966.

Schanze, H. Shakespeare-Kritik bei Friedrich Schlegel. Germanisch-romanische Monatsschrift 46 1966.

J. T.

Shakespeare in Greece

Wagner, W. Shakespeare in Griechenland. Sh Jb 12 1877.

Sideris, M. J. Shakespeare in Greece. Theatre Research 6 1964.

Shakespeare in Italy

Translations

See A. M. Crino, Le traduzioni di Shakespeare in Italia nel Settecento, Rome 1950; M. Praz, Shakespeare translations in Italy, Sh Jb 92 1956.

Conti, A. Il Cesare. Faenza 1726.

Quadrio, F. Della storia e della regione d'ogni poesia. 5 vols Bologna 1739–52.

Valentini, D. Il Giulio Cesare. Siena 1756.

Opere drammatiche di Shakespeare vol 1: vita di Shakespeare; Othello. Venice 1797. Prose.

Falstaff, osia le tre burle. Dresden 1799.

Modern Studies

Battaglia, G. Nota sui traduttori italiani di Shakespeare. In his Mosaico saggi diversi di critica drammatica, Milan 1845.

Birch, W. J. Shakespeare and his Italian critics. N & Q 29 May, 3–17 July 1886.

Rosa, L. de. Shakespeare, Voltaire e Alfieri e la tragedia de Cesare. Camerino 1900.

Graf, A. Il teatro inglese in Italia: Shakespeare. In his L'Anglomania e l'influsso inglese in Italia nel secolo xviii, Turin 1911.

Angeli, D. La fortuna di Shakespeare in Italia. Marzocco 21 1916.

Collison-Morley, L. Shakespeare in Italy. Stratford 1916.

Nulli, S. A. Shakespeare in Italia. Milan 1918.

Pascot, G. Shakespeare e Alfieri. Città del Pieve 1922.

Ferrando, G. Shakespeare in Italy. Shakespeare Assoc Bull 5 1930.

Praz, M. Come Shakespeare è letto in Italia. Rivista Italiana del Dramma 2 1938.

— Shakespeare translations in Italy. Sh Jb 92 1956.

Ortolani, G. Goldoni e Shakespeare. Rivista Italiana del Dramma 4 1940.

Fucilla, J. G. Shakespeare in Italian criticism. PQ 20 1941.

Rebora, P. Comprensione e fortuna di Shakespeare in Italia. Comparative Lit 1 1949.

Orsini, N. Shakespeare in Italy. Comparative Lit 3 1951.

Obertello, A. Shakespeare e l'Italia. Lettere Italiane 16 1964.

Baldini, G. (ed). La fortuna di Shakespeare 1593–1964. Milan 1965.

Dorris, G. E. The first Italian criticism of Chaucer and Shakespeare. Romance Notes 6 1965.

Lombardo, A. La fortuna di Shakespeare in Italia. Terzo Programma (Rome) 1 1965.

Shakespeare in the Netherlands

Translations

The first trn of all the works was to be : Shakespeare's dramatische Werken vertaald en toegelicht door A. S. Kok, 50 pts Amsterdam 1872–9, 1 vol Amsterdam 1880.

Vos, J. Aran en Titus, 1641. Titus Andronicus.

Gramsbergen. Kluchtige tragoedie of den Haartog van Pierlepon. 1650. Midsummer Night's Dream.

Sybant. Dolle Bruiloft. Tr 1654. Taming of the Shrew.

Tooneelspelen. Met de bronwellen en aanteekeningen van verscheide beroemde schrijveren uit het Engelsch vertaald. 5 vols Amsterdam 1778–82. With 14 of Shakespeare's plays, 6 tr by B. Brunius. Prose trn.

Works in the Shakespearian Manner

Starter, J. J. Timbre de Cardone ende Fenecie van Messina. Leeuwarden 1618. Much ado.

Struys, J. Romeo en Juliette. Amsterdam 1634.

Brandt (Geeraert the elder). De Veinzende Torquatus. Amsterdam 1645. From Hamlet.

Modern Studies

Moltzer, H. E. Shakespeare's invloed op het nederlandsch tooneel der zeventiende eeuw. Groningen 1874.

Arnold, T. J. I. Shakespeare in de nederlandsche letterkunde en op het nederlandsch tooneel. Bibliographische Adversaria (Hague) 4 1879.

Worp, J. A. Engelsche tooneelspelers op het vasteland in de 16de en 17de eeuw. Nederlandsch Museum 1886; *see also* Nederlandsch Spectator 1880.

Fränkel, L. Zur Geschichte von Shakespears Bekanntwerden in den Niederlanden. E Studien 15 1891.

Schneider, L. Shakespeare in den Niederlanden. Sh Jb 26 1891.

Downs, B. A. Anglo-Dutch literary relations 1867–1900. MLR 31 1936.

Peenink, R. Nederland en Shakespeare. Hague 1936. On early versions.

Albach, B. Shakespeare on the Dutch stage. Delta 7 1964.

Swart, J. Shakespeare in Dutch translation. Ibid.

Shakespeare in Rumania

Iorga, N. Shakespeare in romăneste. Ramuri 1922.

Beza. M. Shakespeare in Rumania. 1931. First play introduced 1844.

Radulescu, I. H. Les intermédiaires français de Shakespeare en Roumanie. Revue de Littérature Comparée 18 1938.

Dutu, A. Shakespeare in Rumania: a bibliographical essay. Bucharest 1964.

— Etapele receptării operei Shakespeariene. In his Explorări în istoria literaturii române, Bucharest 1969. With synopsis in French.

Shakespeare in Russia etc

Translations

Julius Caesar. Tr N. M. Karamzin, Moscow 1787. First Russian trn of a play by Shakespeare.

Merry wives of Windsor. 1787. Adapted; *see Lirondelle, below.*

Hamlet. Tr Hungarian, 1790; *see Z. Haraszti, below.*

Modern Studies

Bayer, J. Shakespeare drámái hazánkban. 2 vols Budapest 1909. First Hungarian performance 1777; lists trns.

Lirondelle, A. Shakespeare en Russie 1748–1840. Paris 1912.

Riedl, F. Shakespeare és a magyar irodalom. Budapest 1916. Influence on Hungarian literature.

Császar, E. Shakespeare és a magyar költeszet. Budapest 1917. Influence on Hungarian poetry.

Elek, O. Shakespeare a magyar irodalmi közludalban. Magyar Shakespeare-Tár 11 1919.

Calina, J. (Mrs A. Nicoll). Shakespeare in Poland. Oxford 1923.

Popović, V. Shakespeare in Serbia. 1928.

Haraszti, Z. Shakespeare in Hungary. Boston 1929.

Simmons, E. J. English literature and culture in Russia 1553–1840. Cambridge Mass 1935. *See* PMLA 47 1932.

Yolland, A. Shakespeare in Hungary. Hungarian Quart 5 1938.

Bryner, C. Shakespeare among the Slavs. ELH 8 1941.

Zanco, A. Shakespeare in Russia e altri saggi. Turin 1945.

Pokorný, J. Shakespeare in Czechoslovakia. Prague 1955.

Bida, C. Shakespeare in Polish and Russian classicism and romanticism. Etudes Slaves et Est-européennes 6 1962.

Levidova, I. M. Shakespeare: bibliografiya russkikh perevodov i kriticheskoy literatury na russkom yazyke 1748–1962. Moscow 1964. Comprehensive listing of all Russian trns and criticisms of Shakespeare.

Alekseev, M. P. (ed). Shakespeare i russkaya kul'tura. Moscow and Leningrad 1965.

Solt, A. Shakespeare in Hungarian criticism during the Enlightenment and Romanticism. Acta Litteraria 7 1965.

Levin, Yu. D. O pervom upominanii p'yes Shakespeara v russkoy pechati. Russkaya Literatura 1 1965. First ptd reference to Shakespeare 1731.

Vočadlo, O. Shakespeare and the Slavs. Slavonic & East European Rev 44 1966.

Shakespeare in Scandinavia

Translations

[Boye, J.]. Hamlet Prinz af Dannemark. Copenhagen 1777.

Rosenfeldt, N. Shakespeare: skuespil. 2 vols Copenhagen 1790–2.

Riber, H. W. Kong Lear. Copenhagen 1794.

Modern Studies

V[incke, G. von]. Shakespeare in Schweden. Sh Jb 12 1877.

Bolin, Hamlet in Schweden. Sh Jb 14 1879.

— Zur Shakespeare-Literatur Schwedens. Sh Jb 15 1880.

Gering, H. Shakesper in Island. Sh Jb 14 1879.

Bolte, J. Englische Komödianten in Dänemark und Schweden. Sh Jb 23 1888.

Hirn, Y. Shakespeare in Finland. Finsk Tidskrift April 1916.

Rund, M. B. Towards a history of Shakespeare in Denmark. Minneapolis 1920.

Rubow, P. V. Shakespeare paa Dansk. Copenhagen 1932.

Seaton, E. Literary relations of England and Scandinavia in the 17th century. Oxford 1935.

Henriques, A. Shakespeare i Danmark og i Sverige. Nordisk Tidskrift 16 1940.

— Shakespeare og Danmark indtil 1840. Copenhagen 1941.

— Shakespeare and Denmark. Shakespeare Survey 3 1950.

Konow, S. Holberg of Shakespeare. Edda 46 1946.

Molin, N. Shakespeare translated into Swedish. Sh Jb 92 1956.

Jensen, N. L. Shakespeare in Denmark. Durham Univ Jnl 25 1964.

Hansen, G. Den første Shakespeare offøvelse i Odense [Hamlet 1792]. Fynske Aarbøger 8 1967.

Shakespeare in Spain and Portugal

Ramón de la Cruz's trn from the French of Ducis was performed Madrid 1772, but failed. The unpbd ms is in Biblioteca Municipal de Madrid.

Moratín, F. F. de. Hamlet: tragedia de Guillermo Shakespeare. Madrid 1798.

Cladera. Examen de la tragedia Hamlet. Madrid [c. 1798]. An attack on Moratín.

Marchena. Lecciones de filosofía moral. Bordeaux 1820. Written earlier, attacking Shakespeare as 'filthy dunghill of barbarity'.

Muntadas, J. F. Discurso sobre Shakespeare y Calderon. Madrid 1849.

Carrière, M. Shakespeare und die spanischen Dramatiker. Sh Jb 6 1870–1.

Vasconcellos, C. M. de. Shakespeare in Portugal. Sh Jb 15 1880.

Martínez, E. J. Shakespeare en España. Revista de Archivos 1918.

Ujaravi, R. R. Y. Shakespeare in España: traducciones, imitaciones e influencia de las obras. Madrid 1920.

Schütt, M. Hat Calderon Shakespeare gekannt? Sh Jb 61 1925.

Fey, E. Calderón und Shakespeare. Neuphilologische Monatsschrift 1 1930.

Par, A. Contribución a la bibliographia española de Shakespeare. Barcelona 1930.

— Shakespeare en la literatura española. 2 vols Madrid 1935.

— Representaciones shakespearianas en España. 2 vols Madrid 1936–.

Thomas, H. Shakespeare in Spain. Oxford 1950.

Fitzgerald, T. A. Shakespeare in Spain and Spanish America. Modern Lang Jnl 35 1951.

Ley, C. D. Shakespeare para los Españoles. Madrid 1951.

Estorninho, C. Shakespeare na literatura portuguesa. Ocidente (Lisbon) 67 1964. Includes trns, performances from 1761.

Jorge, M. As primeiras referências a Shakespeare na literatura portuguesa. Ocidente 66 1964.

Shakespeare in Switzerland

Vetter, T. Shakespeare und die deutsche Schweiz. Sh Jb 48 1912.

Ibershoff, C. H. Bodmer and Shakespeare. MP 15 1917.

Engel, C. E. Shakespeare in Switzerland in the 18th century. Comparative Lit Stud 17–18 1945.

Benz-Burger, L. Shakespeare auf den Schweizer Bühnen. Sh Jb 97–9 1961–3.

Shakespeare und die Schweiz. Schweizer Theater: Jahrbuch der Schweizerischen Gesellschaft für Theaterkultur 1964.

S. S. B. T.

IV. MEDIEVAL INFLUENCES

See also Literary Historians and Antiquaries, col 1741, below. For studies of the Gothic novel, see under Novel, col 870, below.

(1) MODERN STUDIES

Metcalfe, F. The Englishman and the Scandinavian. 1880.

Hales, J. W. The revival of English ballad poetry in the 18th century. In his Folia litteraria, 1893.

Phelps, W. L. The beginnings of the English romantic movement. Boston 1893.

Herzfeld, G. Bemerkung über die nordischen Stoffe in der englischen Poesie des vorigen Jahrhunderts. Appendix to his William Taylor von Norwich, Halle 1897.

Beers, H. A. History of English romanticism in the eighteenth century. New York 1899, 1910 (rev), 1968.

Nordby, C. H. The influence of old Norse literature upon English literature. New York 1901.

Farley, F. E. Scandinavian influences on the English romantic movement. Boston 1903.

Toynbee, P. Dante in English literature from Chaucer to Cary. 2 vols 1909.

Reuning, K. Das Altertümliche im Wortschatz der Spenser-Nachahmungen des 18 Jahrhunderts. Strasbourg 1912.

Brooke, C. F. T. The renascence of Germanic studies in England 1559–1689. PMLA 29 1914.

Crane, R. S. The vogue of Guy of Warwick from the close of the Middle Ages to the romantic revival. PMLA 30 1915.

Hustved, S. B. Ballad criticism in Scandinavia and Great Britain during the 18th century. New York 1916.

Adams, E. N. Old English scholarship in England from 1566–1800. New Haven 1917.

Longueil, A. E. The word 'Gothic' in 18th-century criticism. MLN 38 1923.

Snyder, E. D. The Celtic revival in English literature 1760–1800. Cambridge Mass 1923.

Haferkorn, R. Gotik und Ruine in der englischen Dichtung des 18 Jahrhunderts. Leipzig 1924.

Hughes, W. J. Wales and the Welsh in English literature to Scott. Wrexham 1924.

Partridge, E. Eighteenth-century English romantic poetry. Paris 1924.

Spurgeon, C. F. E. Five hundred years of Chaucer criticism and allusion. 3 vols Cambridge 1925. Addns by R. P. Bond et al, SP 35 1928, 38 1931; R. C. Boys, PQ 17 1938; A. M. Oliver, N & Q 5 Feb 1938; and B. Harris, PQ 18 1939.

Railo, E. The haunted castle: a study of the elements of English romanticism. 1927.

Clark, K. The Gothic revival. 1928, 1964 (Pelican).

Havens, R. D. Changing taste in the 18th century. PLMA 44 1929.

Bosker, A. Literary criticism in the age of Johnson. Groningen 1930, 1953 (rev).

Jones, W. P. The contemporary reception of Gray's Odes. MP 28 1930.

Yvon, P. Le gothique et la renaissance gothique en Angleterre. Caen and Paris 1931.

Brinkley, R. F. Arthurian legend in the 18th century. Baltimore 1932.

Lovejoy, A. O. The first Gothic revival and the return to nature. MLN 47 1932; rptd in his Essays in the history of ideas, Baltimore 1948, New York 1960.

Craigie, W. The Northern element in English literature. Toronto 1933.

Hooker, E. N. Johnson's understanding of Chaucer's metrics. MLN 48 1933.

McKillop, A. D. A critic of 1741 on early poetry. SP 30 1933.

Aubin, R. A. Grottoes, geology and the Gothic revival. SP 31 1934.

—— Some Augustan Gothicists. Harvard Stud 17 1935.

—— Three notes on 'graveyard' poetry. SP 32 1935.

Seaton, E. Literary relations of England and Scandinavia in the seventeenth century. Oxford 1935.

Weber, C. A. Bristols Bedeutung für die englische Romantik. Halle 1935.

Bennett, J. A. W. The beginnings of Norse studies in England. Saga-Book 12 1937.

Addison, A. Romanticism and the Gothic revival. New York 1938.

Reid, M. J. C. The Arthurian legend: comparison of treatment in modern and medieval literature. Edinburgh [1938]. Ch 3.

Douglas, D. C. English scholars 1660–1730. 1939, 1951 (rev).

Wellek, R. The rise of English literary history. Chapel Hill 1941, New York 1966.

Kliger, S. The 'Goths' in England: the Gothic vogue in eighteenth-century aesthetic discussion. MP 43 1945.

—— The Gothic revival and the German 'translatio'. MP 45 1947.

—— The neo-classical view of Old English poetry. JEGP 49 1950.

—— The Goths in England: a study in seventeenth- and eighteenth-century thought. Cambridge Mass 1952.

Zimansky, C. A. Chaucer and the school of Provence: a problem in eighteenth-century literary history. PQ 25 1946.

Evans, B. Gothic drama from Walpole to Shelley. Berkeley 1947.

de Beer, E. S. Gothic: origin and diffusion of the term. Jnl of Warburg & Courtauld Inst 11 1948.

Weisinger, H. The Middle Ages and the late eighteenth-century historians. PQ 27 1948.

Willard, R. Layamon in the seventeenth and eighteenth centuries. SE 27 1948.

Millar, B. P. Eighteenth-century views of the ballad. Western Folklore 9 1950.

Osborn, J. M. The first history of English poetry. In Pope and his contemporaries: essays presented to George Sherburn, Oxford 1949. Ms history by Joseph Spence transcribed.

Pocock, J. G. A. The ancient constitution and the feudal law: a study of English historical thought in the seventeenth century. Cambridge 1957.

Stewart, K. Ancient poetry as history in the eighteenth century. JHI 19 1958.

Frankl, P. The Gothic: literary sources and interpretations through eight centuries. Princeton 1960. Pp. 370–414.

Sloane, W. Chaucer, Milton and the Rev William Stukeley. N & Q June 1960.

Friedman, A. B. The ballad revival. Chicago 1961.

Hasley, J. 'Gothic' im 17 und 18 Jahrhundert. Anglistische Studien 1 1963.

Johnston, A. Enchanted ground: the study of medieval romance in the eighteenth century. 1964.

Holloway, J. Widening horizons in English verse. 1966. Ch 1.

MacKenzie, M. L. Ballad collectors in the eighteenth century. Humanities Assoc Bull 17 1966.

(2) CONTEMPORARY CRITICISM

SIR THOMAS BROWNE

1605–82

Of languages and particularly of the Saxon tongue. In Certain miscellany tracts, 1684.

SIR WILLIAM TEMPLE

1628–99

Of heroick virtue; Of poetry. In Miscellanea pt 2, 1690; Of poetry, ed J. E. Spingarn, Oxford 1909.

JONATHAN SWIFT

1667–1745

The battel of the books. 1704.

A proposal for correcting, improving and ascertaining the English tongue. 1712.

JOSEPH ADDISON

1672–1719

The spectator. Nos 70, 74, 21, 25 May 1711. On Chevy Chase.

The spectator. No 85, 7 June 1711. On the ballad of The two children in the wood.

Broadus, E. K. Addison's influence on the development of interest in folk poetry in the eighteenth century. MP 8 1910.

McCutcheon, R. P. Two 18th-century emendations to Chevy Chase. MLN 37 1922.

—— Addison and the Muses Mercury. SP 20 1923.

—— Another burlesque of Addison's ballad criticism. SP 23 1926.

Parodies of ballad criticism 1711. Ed W. K. Wimsatt, Los Angeles 1957 (Augustan Reprint Soc).

Friedman, A. B. Addison's ballad papers and the reaction to metaphysical wit. Comparative Lit 12 1960.

ELIZABETH ELSTOB

1683–1756

The rudiments of grammar for the English Saxon tongue, first given in England; with an apology for the study of northern antiquities. 1715.

An apology for the study of northern antiquities. Ed C. Peake, Los Angeles 1956 (Augustan Reprint Soc).

LEWIS THEOBALD

1688–1744

Memoirs of Sir Walter Raleigh. 1719.

A succinct account of Stone-henge and Merlin. Prefixed

to The vocal parts of an entertainment call'd Merlin: or the devil of Stone Henge, 1734.
>   Jones, R. F. Theobald: his contribution to English scholarship. New York 1919.

JOHN TOLAND
1670–1722

A critical history of the Celtic religion. In his Collection of several pieces, 2 vols, 1726.

JOHN HUSBANDS
1706–32

A miscellany of poems by several hands. Oxford 1731. Ed with preface by Husbands.
>   Crane, R. S. An early 18th-century enthusiast for primitive poetry. MLN 37 1922.

WILLIAM WARBURTON
1697–1779

Dissertation on the origin of books of chivalry. Prefixed to Don Quixote, tr Charles Jervas 2 vols 1742.
>   Cherpack, C. Warburton and some aspects of the search for the primitive in eighteenth-century France. PQ 36 1957.

RICHARD HURD
1720–1808

Moral and political dialogues. 1759.
Letters on chivalry and romance. 1762; ed E. J. Morley 1911; ed H. Trowbridge, Los Angeles 1963 (Augustan Reprint Soc.)
>   Nankivell, J. Extracts from the destroyed letters of Hurd to William Mason. MLR 45 1950.
>   Curry, S. J. Hurd's genre criticism. Texas Stud in Lit & Lang 8 1966.

PAUL HENRI MALLET
1730–1807

Introduction à l'histoire de Dannemarc. 2 vols Copenhagen 1755–6.
>   Goldsmith, Oliver. Review of vol 2 of Introduction in Monthly Rev April 1757. See MLN 45 1930.
>   Percy, Thomas. Northern antiquities, with a translation of the Edda and other pieces from the ancient Icelandic tongue, translated from Mons Mallet's Introduction. 2 vols 1770.
>   Gibbon, Edward. An examination of Mallet's Introduction. In Miscellaneous works vol 2, 1796.

HUGH BLAIR
1718–1800

A critical dissertation on the poems of Ossian. 1763.
>   Schmitz, R. M. Blair. New York 1948.
>   Golden, J. L. Blair, Minister of St Giles. Quart Jnl of Speech 38 1952.
>   Corbett, E. P. J. Blair's three (?) critical dissertations. N & Q Nov 1954.
>   —— Blair as an analyzer of English prose style. College Composition & Communication 9 1958.
>   Edney, C. W. Blair's theory of dispositio. Speech Monographs 23 1956.
>   Cohen, H. Blair's theory of taste. Quart Jnl of Speech 44 1958.

>   Bowers, J. W. A comparative criticism of Blair's Essay on taste. Quart Jnl of Speech 47 1961.
>   Grimsley, R. J.-J. Rousseau jugé par un pasteur écossais. Revue de Littérature Comparée 36 1962.

JAMES BOSWELL
1740–95

Critical strictures on the new tragedy of Elvira [by David Mallet]. 1763; ed F. A. Pottle, Los Angeles 1952 (Augustan Reprint Soc). With Andrew Erskine and George Dempster.

THOMAS PERCY
1729–1811

Four essays, as improved and enlarged in the second edition of the Reliques of ancient English poetry. 1767.
>   Dennis, L. Percy's essay On the ancient metrical romances. PMLA 49 1934.

JOHN WALTERS
1721–97

A dissertation on the Welsh language, pointing out it's antiquity, copiousness, grammatical perfection, with remarks on it's poetry and other articles not foreign to the subject. Cowbridge 1771.

THOMAS TYRWHITT
1730–86

On the language and versification of Chaucer. Prefixed to The Canterbury tales of Chaucer, 5 vols 1775–8.

JEAN BAPTISTE LA CURNE DE SAINTE-PALAYE
1697–1781

The literary history of the troubadours: containing their lives, extracts from their works, and many particulars relative to the 12th, 13th and 14th centuries; collected and abridged from the French of Sainte-Palaye by the author of the Life of Petrarch [Mrs Susannah Dobson]. 1779.
Memoirs of ancient chivalry; to which are added the anecdotes of the times from the romance writers and historians of those ages; translated [from the French of Sainte-Palaye] by the translator of the Life of Petrarch [Mrs Dobson]. 1784.
>   Gossman, L. Medievalism and the ideologies of the Enlightenment. Baltimore 1968.

JOHN SMITH
1747–1807

Galic antiquities: consisting of a history of the druids, particularly those of Caledonia; a dissertation on the authenticity of the poems of Ossian; and a collection of ancient poems, translated from the Galic of Ullin, Ossian, Orran etc. Edinburgh 1780.

JOSEPH STERLING
The history of the Chevalier Bayard. 1781.

JOSEPH RITSON
1752–1803

Observations on the first three volumes of [Warton's] History of English poetry. 1782.

EDWARD JERNINGHAM
1727–1812

The rise and progress of the Scandinavian poetry. 1784.
  Bettany, L. Jerningham and his friends. New York [1919].

JOHN PINKERTON
1758–1826

Two dissertations. Prefixed to Select Scottish ballads, 2 vols 1783. For Ritson's exposure of forgeries in this, see GM Nov 1784.
An essay on the origin of Scotish poetry. Prefixed to Ancient Scotish poems never before in print, 1786.
A dissertation on the origin and progress of the Scythians or Goths. 1787.
A critique upon Ritson's Scotish songs. Added to Letters from Joseph Ritson esq to Mr George Paton, Edinburgh 1829.

JOSEPH COOPER WALKER
1762–1810?

Historical memoirs of the Irish bards. 1786.

PHILIP NEVE

Cursory remarks on some of the ancient English poets, particularly Milton. 1789.

GEORGE ELLIS
1753–1815

Specimens of the early English poets. 1790, 3 vols 1801 (rev).
Specimens of early English metrical romances chiefly written during the early part of the 14th century; to which is prefixed an historical introduction. 3 vols 1805, 1811.
See A. Johnston, Enchanted ground, 1964.

WILLIAM OWEN PUGHE, WILLIAM OWEN
1759–1835

An essay on bardism. Prefixed to Heroic elegies and other pieces of Llywarc Hen, 1792.

SHARON TURNER
1768–1847

The history of the Anglo-Saxons, to the death of Egbert. Vol 4: The history of manners, landed property, religion, government, laws, poetry, literature and language. 4 vols 1799–1805.
Vindication of the genuineness of the ancient British poems of Aneurin, Taliesin, Llynwarch Hen and Merdhin, with specimens. 1803.
The history of England during the Middle Ages, and also the history of the literature, poetry, religion and language during that period. 5 vols 1825 (2nd edn). Revision of first edn, The history of England from the Norman conquest to the accession of Edward I, 4 vols 1814–23.

(3) IMITATIONS AND WORKS REFLECTING THE REVIVAL

SIR RICHARD BLACKMORE
1653–1729

Prince Arthur: an heroick poem in X books. 1695.
King Arthur: an heroick poem in XII books. 1697.
Alfred: an epic poem in XII books. 1723.
  Dennis, John. Remarks on a book entitul'd Prince Arthur. 1696.
  Brown, Thomas et al. Commendatory verses on the author of the two Arthurs. 1700.
  Liss, O. Die Arthurepen des Sir Richard Blackmore. Strasbourg 1911.
  Boys, R. C. Blackmore and the Wits. Ann Arbor 1949.
  Rosenberg, A. Sir Richard Blackmore. Lincoln Nebraska 1953.

JOHN DRYDEN
1631–1700

Fables ancient and modern: translated into verse from Homer, Ovid, Boccace and Chaucer. 1700.
  Rzesnitzek, F. Das Verhältnis der Fables von Dryden zu den entsprechenden mittelenglischen Vorlagen. Rabitor 1903.

MATTHEW PRIOR
1664–1721

See under Poetry, col 489 below.

SAMUEL COBB
1675–1713

The carpenter of Oxford: or the Miller's tale of Chaucer attempted in modern English; to which are added two imitations of Chaucer by Matthew Prior. 1712.

DAVID MALLET
1705?–65

William and Margaret: an old ballad. [1725?].
  Sleigh, G. F. The authorship of William and Margaret. Library 5th ser 8 1953.

GEORGE OGLE
1704–46

Gualtherus and Griselda: or the clerk of Oxford's tale, from Boccace, Petrarch and Chaucer; to which are added a letter to a friend with the clerk of Oxford's character. [1739].
The Canterbury tales of Chaucer, modernized by several hands, published by Mr Ogle. 3 vols 1741, 1742, 1785.

WILLIAM COLLINS
1721–59

See under Poetry, col 585 below.

JOSEPH WARTON
1722–1800

See under Poetry, col 689 below.

THOMAS GRAY
1716–71
See under Poetry, col 577 below.

THOMAS WARTON
1728–90
See under Poetry, col 690 below.

JAMES MACPHERSON
1736–96
See under Poetry, col 603 below.

WILLIAM MASON
1725–97
Musaeus: a monody. 1747.
An archaeological epistle to the reverend and worshipful Jeremiah Milles DD. 1782.
 Draper, J. W. Mason: a study in 18th-century culture. New York 1924.

MICHAEL BRUCE
1746–67
Poems on several occasions [including 2 Danish odes]. Edinburgh 1770.

JAMES BEATTIE
1735–1803
The minstrel: or the progress of genius. 2 pts 1771–4.
 Honour, H. Two letters from Joseph Wright of Derby. Connoisseur 138 1956. To Beattie on Minstrel.

RICHARD HOLE
1746–1803
Fingal. 1772.
Arthur, or the northern enchantment: a poetical romance in seven books. 1789.
 Dredge, J. I. Bibliography of Hole. Trans Devonshire Assoc 31 1899.

WILLIAM BAGSHAW STEVENS
1756–1800
Poems: consisting of Indian odes and miscellaneous pieces. Oxford 1775. Including Hervor and Argantyr: an ode imitated from an antient scald.
The journal of Rev William Bagshaw Stevens. Ed G. Galbraith, Oxford 1965.
 Tucker, S. I. Stevens and late eighteenth-century English. N & Q Dec 1966.

THOMAS CHATTERTON
1752–70
See under Poetry, col 605 below.

JOHN OGILVIE
1733–1813
Rona: a poem in seven books. 1777.
Fane of the Druids. 1784.

Fane of the Druids: book the second. 1789.
Britannia. Aberdeen 1801.

RICHARD POLWHELE
1760–1838
The fate of Lewellyn: or the Druid's sacrifice; to which is added the genius of Carnbre. Bath 1777. Anon.
Poems chiefly by gentlemen of Devon and Cornwall. Ed R. Polwhele, 2 vols Bath 1792.
Sketches in verse. 1796.
The Cambrian bards. In poems vol. 2, Truro 1810.

WILLIAM TASKER
1740–1800
Ode to the warlike genius of Great Britain. 1778; rptd in Poems, 1779; and GM Dec 1798-Aug 1799.

THOMAS JAMES MATHIAS
1754?–1835
Runic odes imitated from the Norse tongue in the manner of Mr Gray. 1781; rptd in Odes English and Latin, 1790, 1798; rptd in The garden of flowers, New York 1806.
For Mathias's works relating to Chatterton, see col 671 below.

JOSEPH STERLING
Poems. Dublin 1782, 1789. Including odes from the Icelandic.
Cambuscan: or the Squire's tale of Chaucer, modernized by Mr Boyle, continued from Spenser's Fairy Queen by Mr Ogle, and concluded by Mr Sterling. Dublin 1785.

JAMES MYLNE
d. 1788
Poems: consisting of miscellaneous pieces and two tragedies. Edinburgh 1790.

WILLIAM SOTHEBY
1757–1833
Poems: consisting of a tour through parts of north and south Wales, sonnets, odes and other poems. Bath 1790, 1794.
Oberon. 1798. Tr from German of C. M. Wieland.
The Cambrian hero: or Llywelyn the great. Egham [1800?].
Tragedies. 1814.

GEORGE RICHARDS
1767–1837
Aboriginal Britons: a prize poem. Oxford 1791.
Songs of the aboriginal bards of Britain. Oxford 1792.
Odin: a drama. 1804.
Llangollen Vale and other poems. 1796.
Poetical works. Ed W. Scott, vol 3, 1810. Contains Crugal's ghost; The ghost of Cuchullin; Harold's complaint.

(4) TRANSLATIONS, EDITIONS AND COLLECTIONS

CHRISTOPHER WASE
1625?–90

Aelfredi magni invictissimi vita tribus libris comprehensa a Johanne Spelman. Oxford 1678. To this Obadiah Walker added as appendix Alfred's OE version of the Preface to Gregory's Pastoral care, and the Voyages of Ohthere and Wulstan.

EDMUND GIBSON
1669–1748

Polemo-Middinia. Carmen macaronicum [by Drummond of Hawthornden?], accedit cantilena rustica, vulgo inscripta Crists Kirk on the Green, recensuit notisque illustravit E. G. Oxford 1691.

CHRISTOPHER RAWLINSON
1679–1733

A. S. M. Boethii consolationis philosophiae libri v, Anglo-Saxonice redditi ab Alfredo. Oxford 1698.

GEORGE HICKES
1642–1715

Linguarum vett. septentrionalium thesaurus grammatico-criticus et archaeologicus. 2 vols Oxford 1703–5.
Hervor at Argantyr's grave, reprinted from Hickes' Thesaurus. In Dryden's Miscellany poems pt 6, 1716.
For conspectus and trn of the Thesaurus, see under Old English Scholarship, col 1791 below.

ELIZABETH ELSTOB
1683–1756

See under Old English Scholarship, col 1793 below.

THOMAS HEARNE
1678–1735

The life of Aelfred the Great [by Sir John Spelman] from the original ms in the Bodleian library, with considerable additions. Oxford 1709.
Joannis Glastoniensis chronica. 2 vols Oxford 1726. Including fragments from the Battle of Maldon.

JOHN DAVIES, O FALLWYD

Flores poetarum britannicorum. Shrewsbury 1710, Swansea 1814, 1864.

SIR RICHARD STEELE
1672–1729

The spectator. Nos 366, 406, 30 April, 16 June 1712. Trns of 2 Lapland love poems from Scheffer.

ALLAN RAMSAY
1686–1758

Chryste-Kirke on the greene. Edinburgh 1716.
Scots songs. Edinburgh 1718.
Fables and tales. Edinburgh 1722.

The ever green. 2 vols Edinburgh 1724–7.
The tea table miscellany. 4 vols Edinburgh 1724–40.
A Scots ode to the British antiquarians. Edinburgh 1726.
Hardyknute: a fragment of an antient Scots poem by Lady Wardlaw, with additions by Ramsay. [Edinburgh?] 1740, 1745, 1748, 1754, 1783.
Works. Ed B. Martin and J. W. Oliver 2 vols Edinburgh 1951–3.
    Martin, B. The life and works of Ramsay, with some hundred unpublished poems edited from manuscripts and a bibliography of his writings. Cambridge Mass 1931.
See also under Scottish Literature, col 1965 below.

LADY ELIZABETH WARDLAW
1667–1727

Hardyknute: a fragment. Edinburgh 1719; rptd with 8 additional stanzas by Ramsay in his Ever green, 1724, and Tea table miscellany vol 2, 1725, and separately 1740. *See Ramsay, above.*

THOMAS MORELL
1703–84

The Canterbury tales of Chaucer, in the original, from the most authentic manuscripts; and as they are turn'd into modern language by Mr Dryden, Mr Pope and other eminent hands, with explanatory notes. 1737. Some of the notes signed T.M.

THOMAS TYRWHITT
1730–86

An epistle to Florio at Oxford. 1749; rptd GM Dec 1835.
Translations in verse. Oxford 1752.
Proceedings and debates of the House of Commons 1620–1, from an original ms at Queen's College, Oxford. 2 vols 1766.
The manner of holding Parliaments in England, by Henry Elsynge, corrected and enlarged by T. Tyrwhitt. 1768.
The Canterbury tales of Chaucer, with an essay on his language and versification and an introductory discourse, together with notes and a glossary. 5 vols 1775–8, Oxford 1798.
For works relating to the Rowley controversy, see under Chatterton, col 605 below.

THOMAS PERCY
1729–1811

Bibliographies

Powell, L. F. Percy's Reliques. Library 3rd ser 9 1928.

§ I

O Nancy will you go with me. In Dodsley's Collection of poems vol 6, 1758.
Hau Kiou Choaan, or the pleasing history: a translation from the Chinese; to which are added the argument or story of a Chinese poetry, with notes. 4 vols 1761.
Miscellaneous pieces relating to the Chinese. 2 vols 1762.
The matrons: six short histories. 1772 (for 1762?). Ed and in part tr Percy.
Five pieces of Runic poetry translated from the Islandic language. 1763.
The Song of Solomon newly translated from the original Hebrew; with a commentary and annotations. 1764.

Reliques of ancient English poetry. 3 vols 1765, 1767, 1775; [nominally] ed his nephew T. Percy (really by Percy himself) 1794, 1812; ed G. Gilfillan 3 vols Edinburgh 1855; ed H. B. Wheatley 3 vols 1876–7, 1891; ed M. M. A. Schröer 2 vols Berlin 1893.

A letter describing the ride to Hulme Abbey. 1765.

A key to the New Testament. 1766 etc.

The household books of the Earl of Northumberland in 1512. 1768, 1770, 1827. Ed Percy.

A sermon. [1769]. On John xiii. 35.

Northern antiquities: or a description of the manners, customs, religion and laws of the ancient Danes, with a translation of the Edda and other pieces from the ancient Islandic tongue. 2 vols 1770, Edinburgh 1809. Tr from Mallet's Introduction à l'histoire de Dannemarc, with additional notes, and Goranson's Latin version of the Edda.

The hermit of Warkworth: a Northumberland ballad. 1771, 1771, 1772, 1775 etc.

On some large fossil horns. Archaeology 7 1785.

A sermon. Dublin 1790. On Proverbs xxvii. 6.

An essay on the origin of the English stage, particularly on the historical plays of Shakespeare. 1793.

Memoir of Goldsmith. In Goldsmith's Miscellaneous works vol 1, 1801.

Bishop Percy's folio ms. Ed J. W. Hales and F. J. Furnivall 3 vols 1867, 1868; ed I. Gollancz 4 vols 1905. Life of Percy by John Pinkerton prefixed to vol 1.

Ancient songs, chiefly on Moorish subjects, translated from the Spanish by Thomas Percy, with a preface by D. Nichol Smith. Oxford 1932.

Letters

Letters from Thomas Percy, John Callander, David Herd and others to George Paton. Edinburgh 1830.

Correspondence. In J. Nichols, Illustrations of the literary history of the eighteenth century vols 6–8, 1817–58.

Lewis, S. A school of Welsh Augustans. 1924. Contains Percy letters.

The R. B. Adam library. Oxford 1929. Vol 3 contains Percy letters.

The Percy letters. Ed D. Nichol Smith and C. Brooks. Baton Rouge and New Haven 1944–.
  The correspondence of Percy and Edmond Malone. Ed A. Tillotson, Baton Rouge 1944.
  The correspondence of Percy and Richard Farmer. Ed C. Brooks, Baton Rouge 1946.
  The correspondence of Percy and Thomas Warton. Ed M. G. Robinson and L. Dennis, Baton Rouge 1951.
  The correspondence of Percy and David Dalrymple, Lord Hailes. Ed A. F. Falconer, Baton Rouge 1954.
  The correspondence of Percy and Evan Evans. Ed A. Lewis, Baton Rouge 1957.
  The correspondence of Percy and George Paton. Ed A. F. Falconer, New Haven 1961.

§ 2

Schlegel, A. W. Bürger. 1800.

Blackley, W. S. Percy's changes in folio mss. Contemporary Rev Nov 1867.

Waag, A. Über Herders Übertragungen englischer Gedichte. Heidelberg 1892.

Wagener, H. F. Das Eindringen von Percys Reliques in Deutschland. Heidelberg 1897.

Gaussen, A. C. C. Percy, prelate and poet. 1908.

Hecht, H. Percy und William Shenstone. Strasbourg 1909.

— Percy, R. Wood und J. D. Michaelis. Stuttgart 1934.

— Percy als Bearbeiter spanischer Romanzen. Anglia 58 1934.

Dobson, A. Percy and Goldsmith. In his Old Kensington Palace and other papers, 1910.

Rinaker, C. Percy as a sonneteer. MLN 35 1920.

Kittredge, G. L. Percy and his Nancy. In J. M. Manly anniversary studies, Chicago 1923.

Balderston, K. C. The history and source of Percy's memoir of Goldsmith. Cambridge 1926.

Milner-Barry, A. A note on the early literary relations of Oliver Goldsmith and Percy. RES 2 1926. See also 3 1927.

— and L. F. Powell. A further note on Hau Kiou Choaan. RES 3 1927.

Powell, L. F. Hau Kiou Choaan. RES 2 1926.

Dennis, L. The text of the Percy-Warton letters. PMLA 46 1931.

— Blandamour in the Percy-Ritson controversy. MP 29 1931.

— Percy's essay On the ancient metrical romances. PMLA 49 1934.

— Percy: antiquarian versus man of taste. PMLA 57 1942.

Watkin-Jones, A. While Dr Johnson toured Scotland. Cornhill Mag Aug 1932.

— Percy and the Scottish ballads. E & S 18 1933.

— Percy, Thomas Warton and Chatterton's Rowley poems. PMLA 50 1935.

— Percy mss. TLS 8 March 1934.

— A pioneer Hispanist: Percy. Bull Spanish Stud 14 1937.

Willinsky, M. Bischof Percys Bearbeitung der Volksballaden und Kunstgedichte seines Foliomanuskriptes. Leipzig 1932.

Churchill, I. L. The Percy-Warton letters: additions and corrections. PMLA 48 1933.

— Editions of Percy's memoir of Goldsmith. MLN 50 1935.

— Shenstone's share in the preparation of the Reliques. PMLA 51 1936.

— Shenstone's billets. PMLA 52 1937.

— Percy: scholar. In The age of Johnson: essays presented to C. B. Tinker, New Haven 1949.

Ogburn, V. H. The Wilkinson mss and Percy's Chinese books. RES 9 1933.

— Further notes on Percy. PMLA 51 1936.

— A forgotten chapter in the life of Percy. RES 12 1936.

— Percy's unfinished collection, Ancient English and Scottish poems. ELH 3 1936.

Marwell, H. Percy und die Ossian-Kontroverse. Anglia 58 1934.

— Percy: Studien zur Entstehungsgeschichte seiner Werke. Göttingen 1934.

Shearer, T. and A. Tillotson. Percy's relations with Cadell and Davies. Library 3rd ser 15 1934.

Leslie, C. The Percy library. Book-Collector's Quart 14 1934.

Brooks, C. Percy's History of the wolf in Great Britain. JEGP 34 1935.

— The country parson as research scholar: Percy 1760–70. PBSA 53 1959.

Metzdorf, R. F. An unpublished Johnson letter concerning Percy's Reliques. MLN 50 1935.

Munby, A. N. L. Cancels in Percy's Reliques. TLS 31 Oct 1936. Reply by L. F. Powell 7 Nov 1936.

Tuttle, D. R. Christabel sources in Percy's Reliques and the Gothic romance. PMLA 53 1938.

Chapman, R. W. Johnson's letters to Percy. TLS 22 Jan 1938.

Bronson, B. H. Edward, Edward: a Scottish ballad. Southern Folklore Quart 4 1940.

Bate, W. J. Percy's use of his folio-manuscript. JEGP 43 1944.

Fan, T. C. Percy and du Halde. RES 21 1945.

— Hau Kiou Choaan. RES 22 1946.

Mackenzie, E. K. A. Percy and ballad correctness. RES 21 1945.

—— Percy's great schemes. MLR 43 1948.

Clark, R. T. Herder, Percy and the Song of songs. PMLA 61 1946.

Randall, D. A. Percy's Reliques and its cancel leaves. New Colophon 1 1948.

Campbell, J. J. Sir David Dalrymple's ballad work. PQ 29 1950.

Baine, R. M. Percy's own copies of the Reliques. Harvard Lib Bull 5 1951.

Friedman, A. B. The first draft of Percy's Reliques. PMLA 69 1954.

—— Percy's folio manuscript revalued. JEGP 53 1954.

Smith, D. Nichol. The Constance Meade collection and the University Press museum. Bodleian Lib Record 6 1958.

Mason, J. F. A. Percy's account of his own education. N & Q Nov 1959.

Schwarz, A. Percy at the Duke of York's private theatre. BNYPL Aug 1959.

Mahoney, J. L. Some antiquarian and literary influences of Percy's Reliques. College Lang Assoc Jnl 7 1964.

DAVID JONES

Blodeugerdd Cymry. Shrewsbury 1759, 1779, Holywell 1823.

Y Cydymaith Dyddan. Chester 1766.

HUGH JONES, BARDD LLANGWM

Dewisol Ganiadau yr Oes Hon. Shrewsbury 1759, Merthyr 1827.

Diddanwch Teuluaidd. 1763. Introductory essay by Lewis Morris.

EVAN EVANS
1731–89

Some specimens of the poetry of the antient Welsh bards, translated into English. 1764, Llanidloes 1862.

Crane, R. S. Johnson and Evans. MLN 45 1930.

The correspondence of Thomas Percy and Evans. Ed A. Lewis, Baton Rouge 1957.

DAVID HERD
1732–1810

Ancient and modern Scottish poems. 1769, 2 vols Edinburgh 1776 (with addns).

SIR DAVID DALRYMPLE, Lord HAILES
1726–92

Ancient Scottish poems published from the ms of George Bannatyne. Edinburgh 1770.

For Dalrymple's historical and biographic works, see col 1733, below.

Campbell, J. J. Dalrymple's ballad work. PQ 29 1950.

Carnie, R. H. Lord Hailes' notes on Johnson's Lives of the poets. N & Q Jan-Nov 1956.

—— Lord Hailes's contributions to contemporary magazines. SB 9 1957.

—— A letter from Lord Hailes to James Boswell in Holland. N & Q Feb 1954.

Horace Walpole's correspondence with Dalrymple [et al]. Ed W. S. Lewis, C. H. Bennett and A. G. Hoover, New Haven 1951.

DAINES BARRINGTON
1727–1800

The Anglo-Saxon version from the historian Orosius, by Alfred the Great, together with an English translation from the Anglo-Saxon. 1773.

Gorchestion Beirdd Cymru. Shrewsbury 1773.

Parry, J. J. Dr Johnson's interest in Welsh. MLN 36 1921.

HUGH DOWNMAN
1740–1809

The death-song of Ragnar Lodbrach, translated from the Latin of Olaus Wormius. 1781.

Poems: second edition, altered and corrected, with several additions. Exeter 1790, 1791.

JOHN PINKERTON
1758–1826

Rimes. 1781, 1782.

Scottish tragic ballads. 1781.

Select Scottish ballads: Hardy Knute, an heroic ballad now first published complete, with other nine approved Scotish ballads and some hitherto not made public; to which are prefixed two dissertations 1783. For attack by Joseph Ritson, *see* GM Nov 1784.

Ancient Scotish poems never before in print. Prefixed by an essay on the origin of Scotish poetry, 1786.

The Bruce. 1789.

Scotish poems reprinted from scarce editions, with three pieces before unpublished. 1792.

The literary correspondence of John Pinkerton esq, now first printed from the originals in the possession of Dawson Turner. 2 vols 1830.

Horace Walpole's correspondence with Chatterton, Lort, Pinkerton [et al]. Ed W. S. Lewis, A. D. Wallace and R. M. Williams, New Haven 1951.

JAMES JOHNSTONE
d. 1798

Lodbrokar-Quida: or the death-song of Lodbroc, with a free English translation. [Copenhagen] 1782, Copenhagen 1813.

The robbing of the nunnery, or the abbess outwitted: a Danish ballad translated into English in the style of the 16th century. [Copenhagen] 1786.

JOHN WALTERS the younger
1759–89

Translated specimens of Welsh poetry in English verse, with some original pieces and notes. 1782.

JOSEPH RITSON
1752–1803

Bibliographies

Burd, H. A. In his Ritson, Urbana 1916.

Bronson, B. H. In his Ritson vol 2, Berkeley 1938.

§ 1

A select collection of English songs. 3 vols 1783; ed T. Park 3 vols 1813.

The Yorkshire garland: being a curious collection of old and new songs concerning that famous county. Pt 1 (all pbd), York 1788.

Ancient songs from the time of King Henry III to the revolution. 1790, 2 vols 1829; ed W. C. Hazlitt 1877.

Pieces of ancient popular poetry. 1791, 1833.

The English anthology. 3 vols 1793-4.

Scotish songs. 2 vols 1794, 1866, Glasgow 1869.

Robin Hood: a collection of all the ancient poems, songs and ballads, now extant relative to that celebrated English outlaw. 2 vols 1795, 1832, 1885, etc.

Poems on interesting events in the reign of King Edward III written in the year MCCCLII by Laurence Minot. 1795, 1825.

Ancient English metrical romances. 3 vols 1802; ed E. Goldsmid 1884-5.

Bibliographica poetica: a catalogue of English poets of the 12th, 13th, 14th, 15th and 16th centurys, with an account of their works. 1802.

Northern garlands. 1810. 4 pts Edinburgh 1887-8.

The Caledonian muse: a chronological selection of Scotish poetry from the earliest times. 1821. Ptd in 1785 but not pbd.

The life of King Arthur from ancient historians and authentic documents. 1825.

Memoirs of the Celts or Gauls. 1827.

Annals of the Caledonians, Picts and Scots. 2 vols 1828.

Fairy tales, now first collected; to which are prefixed two dissertations: I, On pigmies; II, On fairies. 1831, 1875.

Ritson also wrote works on legal and constitutional history; see Bronson, below.

Letters

Letters from Joseph Ritson esq to Mr George Paton; to which is added a critique by John Pinkerton esq upon Ritson's Scotish songs. Edinburgh 1829.

Frank, J. The letters of Ritson; to which is prefixed a memoir of the author by Sir H. Nicholas. 2 vols 1833.

§ 2

MacCunn, F. A. In his Sir Walter Scott's friends, Edinburgh 1909.

Burd, H. A. Ritson: a critical biography. Urbana 1916, New York 1968.

Ker, W. P. Ritson. Cambridge 1922; rptd in his Collected essays vol 1, 1925.

Hopkins, A. B. Ritson's Life of King Arthur. PMLA 43 1928.

Bronson, B. H. The Caledonian Muse. PMLA 46 1931.

—— Ritson's Bibliographia scotica. PMLA 52 1937.

—— Ritson: scholar-at-arms. 2 vols Berkeley 1938.

Moreland, C. C. Ritson's Life of Robin Hood. PMLA 50 1935.

Pearsall, R. B. Scott and Ritson on Allan Ramsay. MLN 66 1951.

Todd, W. B. Ritson, Observations on the history of English poetry 1782. Book Collector 6 1957.

THOMAS FORD HILL
d. 1795

Ancient Erse songs. 1784.

EDWARD JONES
1752-1824

Musical and poetical relicks of the Welsh bards. 2 pts 1784, 1794 (with addns), 1812.

The bardic museum of primitive British poetry. 1802.

Cambro-British melodies: third volume of the musical and poetical relicks of the Welsh bards. [1824].

JAMES JOHNSON
d. 1811

The Scot's musical museum. 6 vols Edinburgh 1787-1803, 1839, 1853. Several of the prefaces by Robert Burns.

Schwebsch, E. Schottische Volkslyrik in Johnsons The Scot's musical museum. Berlin 1920.

MATTHEW YOUNG
1750-1800

Antient Gallic poems. Dublin 1787.

CHARLOTTE BROOKE
d. 1793

Reliques of Irish poetry. Dublin 1789.

OWEN JONES, OWAIN MYVYR
1741-1814

Barddoniaeth Dafydd ab Gwilym. Ed Jones and William Owen Pughe 1789, Liverpool 1873.

The Myvyrian archaiology of Wales. Ed Jones, William Owen Pughe and Edward Williams 3 vols 1801-7, Denbigh 1870.

WILLIAM OWEN PUGHE, WILLIAM OWEN
1759-1835

Heroic elegies and other pieces of Lylwarc Hen. 1792. Contains prefatory sketch on bardism.

Cambrian register. 3 vols 1796-1818. Ed Pughe.

For works edited jointly with Owen Jones see under Jones, above.

AMOS SIMON COTTLE
1768?-1800

Icelandic poetry: or the Edda of Saemund translated into English verse. Bristol 1797. Includes long prefatory poem on Northern themes by Robert Southey.

EDWARD WILLIAMS, IOLO MORGANWY
1746-1826

Iolo manuscripts: a selection of ancient Welsh mss in prose and verse, from the collection made by the late Edward Williams, for the purpose of forming a continuation of the Myfyrian archaiology, with English translations and notes by his son, the late Taliesin Williams (Ab Iolo). Llandovery 1848, Liverpool 1888.

See also under Owen Jones, above.

Wright, H. G. The relations of the Welsh bard Iolo Morganwy with Dr Johnson, Cowper and Southey. RES 8 1932.

(5) SOME DRAMATIC TREATMENTS OF ANCIENT AND MEDIEVAL THEMES

Rymer, T. Edgar, or the English monarch: an heroick tragedy. 1678, 1691, 1693.

Dryden, J. King Arthur: or the British worthy. 1691.

Bancroft, J.? King Edward the third, with the fall of Mortimer, Earl of March: an historicall play. 1691. Anon.

—— Henry the second, King of England, with the death of Rosamond. 1693. Both these plays are also attributed to William Mountford.

Hopkins, C. Boadicea, Queen of Britain. 1697.

Gildon, C. Love's victim. 1701.

Addison, J. Rosamond. 1707.

Rowe, N. The royal convert. 1708.

Hill, A. Elfrid: or the fair inconstant. 1710, 1731 (rev as Athelwold).

Manley, Mrs Mary. Lucius, the first Christian King of Britain. 1717.

Philips, A. The Briton. 1722.

Jeffreys, G. Edwin. 1724.

Fielding, H. The life and death of Tom Thumb. 1730; rev as The tragedy of tragedies, 1731 etc.

Theobald, L. Merlin: or the devil of Stone-henge. 1734.

Dodsley, R. The King and the miller of Mansfield. 1737.

—— The blind beggar of Bethnal Green. 1741.

Carey, H. The dragon of Wantley. 1738.

Thomson, J. Edward and Eleonora. 1739.

—— and D. Mallet. Alfred. 1740.

Mason, W. Elfrida. 1752.

—— Caractacus. 1759.

—— Argentile and Curran. In Poems, 3 vols York 1796–7. Written c. 1766.

Glover, R. Boadicia. 1753.

Mallet, D. Britannia. 1755.

—— Elvira. 1763.

Brown, J. Barbarossa. 1755.

—— Athelstan. 1756.

Francklin, T. The Earl of Warwick. 1766.

Home, J. The fatal discovery. 1769.

—— Alfred. 1778.

Garrick, D. The institution of the garter. 1771.

Howard, George Edmund. The siege of Tamor. 1773.

Fisher, John Abraham. Masque of the Druids. 1774.

Brooke, H. Cymbeline. In A collection of the pieces formerly published by Henry Brooke esq, to which are added several plays and poems now first printed, 1778.

More, Hannah. Percy. 1778.

Downman, Hugh. Editha: a tragedy. Exeter 1784.

Sayers, Frank. Moina. In Dramatic sketches of Northern mythology, 1790.

—— Starno. With above.

Mylne, James. Darthula. In Poems, consisting of miscellaneous pieces and two tragedies, Edinburgh 1790.

Tasker, William. Arviragus. Exeter 1796.

Bowden, J. Cambro-Britons. 1798.

Sotheby, W. The Cambrian hero: or Llewelyn the great. [c. 1800].

P. R.

V. BOOK PRODUCTION AND DISTRIBUTION

A. GENERAL BIBLIOGRAPHY

B. BIBLIOGRAPHICAL EVIDENCE

C. PAPERMAKING AND THE IMPORTATION OF PAPER

D. WRITING–MASTERS AND PENMANSHIP

E. TYPEFOUNDING AND TYPOGRAPHY: (1) *Typefounding*; (2) *Layout*.

F. STEREOTYPING

G. THE HISTORY AND PRACTICE OF PRINTING: (1) *Bibliographies*; (2) *Dictionaries, lists and accounts of printers and booksellers*; (3) *General history*; (4) *Manuals and practice of printing*; (5) *Labour relations*; (6) *The Stationers' Company*; (7) *Patentees*; (8) *Private presses and printing societies*; (9) *Individual printers and houses : London*.

H. PRINTING AND BOOKSELLING IN THE PROVINCES

I. SCOTTISH PRINTING AND BOOKSELLING

J. IRISH PRINTING AND BOOKSELLING

K. REGULATION OF THE PRESS

L. BOOKSELLING: (1) *Bibliographies*; (2) *General history*; (3) *Individual London booksellers*; (4) *Special forms of publication*.

M. AUTHORSHIP AND COPYRIGHT: (1) *The author and the publisher*; (2) *Legislation*.

N. BOOKBINDING: (1) *Bibliographies and dictionaries*; (2) *History and practice*; (3) *Exhibitions, individual collections and catalogues*.

O. BOOK ILLUSTRATION: (1) *Catalogues and dictionaries*; (2) *History and practice*.

P. TRADE CATALOGUES: GENERAL

Q. OTHER LISTS: (1) *General*; (2) *Divinity*; (3) *Plays*; (4) *Lawbooks*; (5) *Miscellaneous*.

R. CATALOGUES OF INDIVIDUAL PUBLISHERS AND AUCTIONEERS: (1) *Trade sales*; (2) *Advertisement lists*.

S. LIBRARIES: (1) *Circulating and proprietary libraries*; (2) *Public libraries and those of corporate bodies*; (3) *London*; (4) *Oxford*; (5) *Cambridge*; (6) *Edinburgh*; (7) *Other towns*.

T. BOOK COLLECTORS AND COLLECTING: (1) *The choice of books and the arrangement of libraries*; (2) *Book collectors*; (3) *Book plates*; (4) *Individual collectors*; (5) *Catalogues of private collections before 1801*.

A. GENERAL BIBLIOGRAPHY

See also bibliographies at the beginning of G : Printing, and L : Bookselling, below.

Dibdin, T. F. Bibliographical decameron: or ten days pleasant discourse upon illuminated mss and subjects connected with early engraving, typography, and bibliography. 3 vols 1817.

Lowndes, W. T. The bibliographer's manual of English literature. 4 vols 1834; rev H. G. Bohn. 1857–64.

Bohn, H. G. Appendix to the Bibliographer's manual of English literature: containing an account of books issued by literary and scientific societies and printing clubs; books printed at private presses; privately printed series; and the principal literary and scientific serials. 1864 (as vol 6 of Bibliographer's manual; thereafter ptd with it).

Cole, G. W. Do you know your Lowndes? a bibliographical essay on William Thomas Lowndes and incidentally on Robert Watt and Henry G. Bohn. PBSA 33 1939.

Catalogue of an exhibition of books etc illustrative of the history and progress of printing and bookselling in England 1477–1800 held at Stationers' Hall 1912. 1912.

Catalogus der bibliotheek van de vereeniging ter bevordering van de belangen des boekhandels te Amsterdam. 4 vols Hague 1920–34. Supplements: 1927–39, 1940; 1940–49, 1949; 1949–64, 1965.

Handbuch der Bibliothekswissenschaft. Ed F. Milkau and G. Leyh 3 vols Leipzig 1931–40; rev G. Leyh, 3 vols Wiesbaden 1950–61; index, 1965.

Cole, G. W. Index to bibliographical papers 1877–1932. 1933.

Morgan, W. T. and C. S. Bibliography of British history 1700–15. 5 vols Bloomington 1934–42.

Higgs, H. Bibliography of economics 1751–75. Cambridge 1935.

Wroth, L. C. (ed). A history of the printed book. Dolphin 3 NY 1938 (priv ptd).

Ulrich, C. F. and K. Küp. Books and printing: a selected list of periodicals 1800–1942. New York 1943. For a list of more recent periodicals, *see* Bibliography in Britain, *below*.

Selective check list of bibliographical scholarship for 1949: pt 2, later Renaissance to the present. SB 3 1951– (annually). 1949 list by L. Clark and F. T. Bowers, lists since 1950 by H. J. Heaney. Lists for 1949–55 with single index pbd separately SB 10 1957. Lists (ser B) 1956–62, 1968 (Bibl Soc of Univ of Virginia).

Carter, J. The ABC of book collecting. 1952, 1967 (4th rev edn).

Binns, N. Introduction to historical bibliography. 1953, 1962 (enlarged).

Glaister, G. A. Glossary of the book. 1960.

Bibliography in Britain: a classified list of books and articles published in the United Kingdom 1962. Ed J. S. G. Simmons, Oxford 1963–(annually).

Hanson, L. W. Contemporary printed sources for British and Irish economic history 1701–50. Cambridge 1963.

Harvard University Library. Widener Library shelflist no 7, bibliography and bibliographical periodicals: classified listing by call numbers, alphabetical listing by author or title, chronological listing. Cambridge Mass 1966.

Taubert, S. Bibliopola: pictures and texts about the book trade. 2 vols [1966]. Primarily pictures.

Mullins, E. L. C. A guide to the historical and archaeological publications of societies in England and Wales 1901–33. 1968.

B. BIBLIOGRAPHICAL EVIDENCE

Foxon, D. F. The technique of bibliography. Book 6 1955 (Nat Book League).

Neill, D. G. Printed books 1640–1800. Lib Trends 7 1959.

McKerrow, R. B. An introduction to bibliography for literary students. Oxford 1927, 1928 (corrected).

Esdaile, A. A student's manual of bibliography. 1931; ed R. Stokes 1967 (4th edn). Primarily for students of librarianship.

Greg, W. W. A formulary of collation. Library 4th ser 14 1934.

— The rationale of copy-text. SB 3 1951. Both rptd in his Collected papers, ed J. C. Maxwell, Oxford 1966.

Bowers, F. T. Principles of bibliographical description. Princeton 1949.

— Textual and literary criticism. Cambridge 1959.

— Bibliography and textual criticism. Oxford 1964.

— Bibliography revisited. Library 5th ser 24 1969.

Bald, R. C. Editorial problems: a preliminary survey. SB 3 1951.

Todd, W. B. Bibliography and the editorial problem in the 18th century. SB 4 1952.

— New adventures among old books: an essay in 18th-century bibliography. Univ of Kansas Pbns Lib Ser 4 1958.

Dearing, V. A. A manual of textual analysis. Berkeley 1959.

Bateson, F. W. Modern bibliography and the literary artifact. English Studies Today: 2nd series, Berne 1961.

Tanselle, G. T. Tolerances in bibliographical description. Library 5th ser 23 1968.

McKenzie, D. F. Printers of the mind: some notes on bibliographical theories and printing-house practices. SB 22 1969.

C. PAPERMAKING AND THE IMPORTATION OF PAPER

The case of the paper-traders. [c. 1697].

Reasons for laying a further duty on all foreign paper, by which means the making of writing and printing papers in England will be preserved and encouraged. [1698].

Reasons against further additional duties upon paper. [1698].

Reasons against laying a further duty upon stock in hand of paper. [1698?].

Reasons against laying a farther duty upon paper. [c. 1699].

The case of the merchants importing Genoa paper in relation to the intended duty on cards. [1711].

Considerations in relation to the imposition on cards. [1711].

Considerations relating to the intended duties on paper. [1712]. 2 slightly different broadsides with this title.

Considerations relating to the duties on paper, intended upon stock in hand. [1712].

The case of the manufacturers of paper relating to several duties on paper and printing now voted in the House. [1712].

The case of the book-binders of Great Britain relating to the excessive duty resolved to be laid on mill-boards. [1712].

The case of the paper-makers of Great Britain. [1712].

The case of the poor paper-makers and printers, farther stated. [1712].

Proposals for raising £40,000 or upwards per annum by laying additional duties on foreign papers and past-boards imported, and all sorts of papers and pastboards, call'd mill'd-boards, made in Great-Britain. [1712].

Reasons for further additional duties on paper, shewing that such a tax will raise the public revenue. [1712].

The case of the past-board-makers of the city of London. [1712].

Reasons for amending the clause for a drawback to be allow'd to the universities. [c. 1712].

Observations on the intended duties on paper. [c. 1713].

The case of the papermakers. 1737.

Report from the Committee [of the House] on the book-sellers' and printers' petition relating to the high duties on paper. [1802]. Evidence and appendix.

See A collection of the statutes now in force relating to the stamp duties, 2 vols 1716–22; index by P. Pinckney, 1722. Largely on paper duties.

MacFarlane, J. The paper duties of 1696–1712. Library 2nd ser 1 1900.

Goldsmith's Library of Economic Literature, London. Catalogue of the collection of broadsides in the University Library. 1930.

Churchill, W. A. Watermarks in paper in Holland, England, France etc in the 17th and 18th centuries, and their interconnection. Amsterdam 1935.

Labarre, E. J. A dictionary of paper and paper-making terms. Amsterdam 1937, Oxford 1952 (rev); suppl, Amsterdam 1969.

Heawood, E. Watermarks mainly of the 17th and 18th centuries. Hilversum 1950. See A. H. Stevenson, below.

Shorter, A. H. Paper mills and paper makers in England 1495–1800. Hilversum 1957 (Papers Pbns Soc).

Phillips, J. W. A trial list of Irish papermakers 1690–1800. Library 5th ser 13 1958.

[Baxter, J.] The sister arts: or a concise view of the nature and history of paper-making, printing and bookbinding. Lewes 1809.

Cyclopedia of useful arts. 1853.

Patent Office. Abridgement of specifications relating to the manufacture of paper, pasteboard and papier mâché. 1858.

— Abridgements of specifications relating to cutting, folding and ornamenting paper: pt 2, 1636–1866, 1879 (2nd edn).

Garnett, R. The manufacture of fine paper in England in the 18th century. In his Essays in librarianship and bibliography, 1899.

Jenkins, R. Paper-making in England 1588–1788. Lib Assoc Record 2–4 1900–02; rptd in his Collected papers, 1936 (Newcomen Soc).

Scott, W. R. The constitution and finance of English, Scottish and Irish joint-stock companies to 1720. 3 vols Cambridge 1910–12.

Chapman, R. W. An inventory of paper 1674. Library 4th ser 7 1927.

Hunter, D. Papermaking through 18 centuries. New York 1930, 1957 (rev and enlarged).

— Papermaking: the history and technique of an ancient craft. 1943, 1947 (enlarged).

George, R. H. A mercantilist episode. Jnl of Economic & Business History 3 1931. The French Ambassador's economic warfare 1680–90.

Hazen, A. T. Eighteenth-century quartos with vertical chain-lines. Library 4th ser 16 1936.

— Eustace Burnaby's manufacture of white paper in England [c. 1675]. PBSA 48 1954.

Wardrop, J. Mr Whatman, paper-maker. Signature 9 1938.

Lloyd, L. C. Paper-making in Shropshire 1656–1912. Trans of Shropshire Archaeological Soc 49 1938; suppl 53 1950.

Beloff, M. A London apprentice's notebook 1703–05. History 27 1942. John Coggs, apprentice to John Stevens, paper-merchant.

Pollard, H. G. Notes on the size of the sheet. Library 4th ser 22 1942.

Oldman, C. B. Watermark dates in English paper. Library 4th ser 25 1945.

Waterston, R. Early paper making near Edinburgh. Book of Old Edinburgh Club 25 1945. Further notes 27 1949.

Heawood, E. Further notes on paper used in England after 1600. Library 5th ser 2 1948.

Labarre, E. J. The sizes of paper: their names, origin and history. In Buch und Papier, Leipzig 1949.

— The study of watermarks in Great Britain. In Briquet album, Hilversum 1952.

Stevenson, A. H. New uses of watermarks as bibliographical evidence. SB 1 1949.

— A critical study of Heawood's Watermarks. PBSA 45 1951.

— Watermarks are twins. SB 4 1952.

— Chain-indentations in paper as evidence. SB 6 1954.

— Observations on paper as evidence. Univ of Kansas Pbns Lib Ser 11 1961.

Povey, K. and I. J. C. Foster. Turned chain-lines. Library 5th ser 5 1951.

Davis, H. Bowyer's paper stock ledger. Library 5th ser 6 1951.

Smith, W. C. New evidence concerning John Walsh and the duties on paper 1726. Harvard Lib Bull 6 1952.

Balston, T. William Balston, paper maker 1759–1849. 1954.

— James Whatman, father and son. 1957.

Coleman, D. C. Combinations of capital and labor in the English paper industry 1789–1825. Economics 21 1954.

— The early British paper industry and the Huguenots. Proc of Huguenot Soc of London 19 1958.

— The British paper industry 1495–1860: a study in industrial growth. Oxford 1958.

Carter, H. Wolvercote mill: a study in paper-making at Oxford. Oxford 1957 (Oxford Bibl Soc).

Finerty, E. T. History of paper mills in Hertfordshire. Paper-Maker & British Paper Trade Jnl April–June 1957.

Gaskell, P. Notes on 18th-century British paper. Library 5th ser 12 1957.

Jarvis, R. C. The paper-makers and the excise in the 18th century. Library 5th ser 14 1959.

Davies, A. E. Paper-mills and paper-makers in Wales 1700–1900. National Lib of Wales Jnl 15 1968.

Thomas, J. H. Paper-making and local history: a guide to sources. Local Historian 8 1968.

Papermaking: art and craft. Washington 1968 (Lib of Congress).

D. WRITING MASTERS AND PENMANSHIP

Bickham, G. The universal penman. Issued in pts 1733–41; partially rptd several times without date; ed P. Hofer 1941 (complete). An anthology of the work of 24 contemporary writing masters *See* P. H. Muir, Library 4th ser 25 1945.

Massey, W. The origin and progress of letters. 1763. The

2nd pt contains an alphabetical list of English writing masters to date, with biographies and descriptions of their works.

Heal, A. A biographical dictionary of the old English writing masters and bibliography of English copy books 1550–1800. Cambridge 1931.

E. TYPEFOUNDING AND TYPOGRAPHY

Howe, E. Bibliotheca typographica: printing-types and typography. Signature new ser 10 1950.

(1) TYPEFOUNDING

Moxon, J. Mechanick exercises. 1677–84; pt 2, ed T. L. De Vinne 2 vols New York 1896; ed H. Davis and H. G. Carter, Oxford 1958, 1962 (rev). The section on printing and typefounding occupies pt 2.

B., A. The art of cutting, casting and preparing of letter for printing, with a neat representation of a letter-founder's warehouse. Universal Mag 6 1750.

Mores, E. R. A dissertation upon English typographical founders and founderies. 1778 (priv ptd); 1779 (with appendix by John Nichols); ed D. B. Updike New York 1924 (Grolier Club); ed H. G. Carter and C. B. Ricks, Oxford 1961 (Oxford Bibl Soc).

Hansard, T. C. Treatises on printing and type-founding: from the 7th edn of the Encyclopaedia britannica. Edinburgh 1841.

Reed, T. B. A history of the old English letter foundries. 1887; rev A. F. Johnson, Oxford 1952 (enlarged).

Hart, H. Notes on a century of typography at the University Press, Oxford 1693–1794. Oxford 1900 (priv ptd).

Updike, D. B. Printing types: their history, forms and use. 2 vols Cambridge Mass 1922, 1937 (rev), 1962 (rev).

Berry, W. T. and A. F. Johnson. Catalogue of specimens of printing types by English and Scottish printers and founders 1665–1830. Oxford 1935.

— A note on the literature of British type specimens, with a supplement to the Catalogue of specimens 1665–1830. Signature new ser 16 1952.

Johnson, A. F. Type designs: their history and development. 1934, 1966 (rev). With bibliography.

Gaskell, P. Type sizes in the 18th century. SB 5–6 1953–4.

Musson, A. E. The Typographical Association: origins and history up to 1949. Oxford 1954.

— The London Society of Master Letter-Founders 1793–1820. Library 5th ser 10 1955.

Berry, W. T. and A. M. Fern. Typographical specimen books: a checklist of the Broxbourne collection, with an introduction. Book Collector 5 1956.

Mosley, J. The type foundry of Vincent Figgins 1792–1836. Motif 1 1958.

Simmons, J. S. G. Specimens of printing types before 1850 in the typographical library at the University Press, Oxford. Book Collector 8 1959.

Abercrombie, D. Augmenting the Roman alphabet: some orthographic experiments of the last four centuries. Monotype Recorder 42 1962.

Dowding, G. An introduction to the history of printing types: an illustrated summary of the main stages in the development of type design from 1440 up to the present time. [1962].

Dreyfus, J. (ed). Type specimen facsimiles; reproductions of 15 type specimen sheets issued between the 16th and 18th centuries. 1963.

Tanselle, G. T. The identification of type faces in bibliographical description. PBSA 60 1966; Jnl of Typographic Research 1 1967.

Morison, S. and H. G. Carter. John Fell the University Press and the 'Fell' types bequeathed in 1686 to Oxford by Fell. Oxford 1967.

Wolpe, B. (ed). Vincent Figgins' type specimens 1801 and 1815. 1967 (Printing Historical Soc).

(2) LAYOUT

Updike, D. B. Printing types: their history, forms and use. 2 vols Cambridge Mass 1922, 1962 (rev).

Morison, S. Four centuries of fine printing: 600 examples 1500–1914. 1924, 1949 (abridged), 1960 (rev).

— The typographic book 1450–1935: a study of fine typography in 350 title and text pages, with supplementary material by Kenneth Day. 1963.

Hazen, A. T. New styles in typography. In The age of Johnson: essays presented to C. B. Tinker, New Haven 1949.

Bronson, B. H. Printing as an index of taste in 18th-century England. BNYPL 1958; New York 1958, 1963 (rev).

Lewis, J. N. C. Printed ephemera: the changing uses of types and letterforms in English and American printing. Ipswich 1962.

John Baskerville

See under Baskerville in H : Provincial Printers, Birmingham, below.

William Caslon

[McRae, J. F.] Caslon foundry, two centuries of typefounding: annals of the letter foundry established by Caslon in London in 1720. 1920 (priv ptd).

Wolpe, B. On the origin and design of the letters cut and cast by William Caslon II: Caslon architectural. Alphabet 1 1964.

Webb, W. The punch-cutter's hand: a history of Caslon's typefaces. Print in Britain Dec 1966.

Mosley, J. The early career of William Caslon. Jnl of Printing Historical Soc 3 1967.

F. STEREOTYPING

[Nichols, J.] Biographical memoirs of William Ged: including a particular account of his progress in the art of block-printing. 1781, 1819 (with addns).

Hodgson, T. Essay on the origin and progress of stereotype printing. Newcastle 1820.

Hansard, T. C. Typographia: an historical sketch of the

origin and progress of printing, with a description of stereotype lithography. 1825.

Gibb, J. S. Notes on William Ged and the invention of stereotyping. Edinburgh Bibl Soc Pbns 1 1895; suppl 1896.

Hart, H. Charles Earl Stanhope and the Oxford University Press. Collectanea 3 1896 (Oxford Historical Soc); ed J. Mosley 1966 (Printing Historical Soc).

Kubler, G. A. Historical treatises, abstracts and papers on stereotyping. New York 1936.

— The era of Charles Mahon, 3rd Earl of Stanhope, stereotyper: 1750–1825. New York 1938. A collection of contemporary documents relating to stereotyping.

Carter, J. William Ged and the invention of stereotype. Library 5th ser 15–16 1960–1, 18 1963. See R. Donaldson, William Ged: a 2nd postscript 22 1967.

G. THE HISTORY AND PRACTICE OF PRINTING

See also A : General Bibliography, cols 251–2 above.

(1) BIBLIOGRAPHIES

Bullen, G. (ed). Caxton celebration 1877: catalogue of the loan collection of antiquities, curiosities and appliances concerned with the art of printing. [1877].

Bigmore, E. C. and C. W. H. Wyman. A bibliography of printing. 3 vols 1880–6.

Peddie, R. A. St Bride Foundation: catalogue of the technical reference library of works on printing and the allied arts. 1919.

Hart, H. Bibliotheca typographica. Rochester NY 1933.

Catalogue of the periodicals relating to printing and allied subjects in the technical library of the St Bride Institute, with an introduction by Ellic Howe. [1952].

Newberry Library, Chicago. Dictionary catalogue of the history of printing from the John M. Wing Foundation. 6 vols Boston 1961.

(2) DICTIONARIES, LISTS AND ACCOUNTS OF PRINTERS AND BOOKSELLERS

Contemporary Lists

Smyth, R. The obituary of Richard Smyth: being a catalogue of all such persons as he knew in their life [1627–74]. Ed Henry Ellis 1849 (Camden Soc).

Dunton, J. The life and errors of John Dunton, late citizen of London: written by himself. 1705; ed John Nichols 1818 (with memoir and some omissions). Contains a long list of the more important booksellers and printers of his time, with characters of each.

[Negus, S.] A compleat and private list of all the printing-houses in and about the cities of London and Westminster, together with the printers' names, what newspapers they print, and where they are to be found. [1724]; rptd by J. Nichols in Literary Anecdotes vol 1, 1812. See L. W. Hanson, Government and the Press, Oxford 1936; and for commentary, E. Howe, London compositor, 1947. Introd.

[Dell, H.] The booksellers: a poem. 1766. 'A wretched [but informative] rhyming list of booksellers in London and Westminster': John Nichols.

Pendred, J. London and country printers, booksellers and stationers vade mecum. 1785. Directory of the London trade, ed H. G. Pollard 1955 (Bibl Soc) (with discussion of earlier and later directories).

Later Compilations

Nichols, J. Biographical and literary anecdotes of W. Bowyer. 1782. Largely incorporated in Literary anecdotes, below.

— Literary anecdotes of the 18th century. 9 vols 1812–16. Indexed in 2 pts, vols 1–6, 8–9.

— Illustrations of the literary history of the 18th century. 8 vols 1817–58.

Beloe, W. Anecdotes of literature and scarce books. 6 vols 1807–12.

Spence, J. Observations, anecdotes, and characters of books and men. 1820 (abridged); ed J. M. Osborn 2 vols Oxford 1966 (complete).

Timperley, C. H. A dictionary of printers. 1839, 1842 (as An encyclopedia of literary and typographical anecdote).

Rees, T. Reminiscences of literary London 1779–1853, with anecdotes of publishers, authors and book auctioneers of that period; with extensive additions by John Britton. 1853 (priv ptd), 1896.

Gerring, C. Notes on printers and booksellers, with a chapter on chap books. 1900.

Marston, E. Sketches of booksellers of other days. 1901. On Tonson, Thomas and Alice Guy, Dunton, Richardson, Gent, Hutton, Lackington.

— Sketches of some booksellers of the time of Dr Johnson. 1902. On Millar, Thomas Davies, T. Osborne jr, the Lintots, Thomas Evans etc.

Plomer, H. R. A dictionary of the booksellers and printers who were at work in England, Scotland and Ireland 1641–67. 1907 (Bibl Soc).

— A dictionary of printers and booksellers 1668–1725. 1922 (Bibl Soc).

— G. H. Bushnell and E. R. McC. Dix. A dictionary of printers and booksellers 1726–75. 1932 (Bibl Soc).

For addns and corrections to these dictionaries, the following may be consulted:

Heal, A., F. T. Wood et al. Notes on booksellers 1700–50. N & Q 18 July 1931–13 Feb 1932.

Aspinall, A. Statistical accounts of the London newspapers in the 18th century. EHR 63 1948. Lists many printers.

Durham Philobiblion. Durham 1949–69.

Sale, W. Samuel Richardson, master printer. Ithaca 1950. See index of booksellers and printers.

Morrison, P. G. Index of printers, publishers, and booksellers in Wing's Short-title catalogue of books 1641–1700. Charlottesville 1955 (Bibl Soc of Univ of Virginia).

Hodgson, N. and C. Blagden. The notebook of Thomas Bennet and Henry Clements. Oxford 1956 (Oxford Bibl Soc).

Wiles, R. M. Serial publication in England before 1750. Cambridge 1957. See index of booksellers and printers.

St John, J. The Osborne Collection of early children's books 1566–1910. Toronto 1958. See list of publishers, booksellers and printers.

Neuberg, V. E. Chapbooks: a bibliography of references to English and American chapbook literature of the 18th and 19th centuries. 1964. With lists of printers and publishers both London and provincial.

Snyder, H. L. The reports of a press spy for Robert Harley: new bibliographical data for the reign of Queen Anne. Library 5th ser 22 1967. With lists of printers.

For suppl on Scotland see Carnie and Doig, col 271, below.

Heal, A. London tradesmen's cards of the 18th century. 1925.

Mortimer, R. S. The first century of Quaker printers. Jnl of Friends Historical Soc 40 1948.

— Quaker printers 1750–1850. Jnl of Friends Historical Soc 50 1963.

Norton, J. E. Guide to the national and provincial direc-

tories of England and Wales, excluding London, published before 1856. 1950 (Royal Historical Soc).

Humphries, C. W. and W. C. Smith. Music publishing in the British Isles: a dictionary of engravers, printers, publishers and music sellers. 1954.

Hamill, F. Some unconventional women before 1800: printers, booksellers and collectors. PBSA 49 1955.

Smyth, A. L. Trades, professional, and official directories as historical source material. Manchester Rev 11 1969.

(3) GENERAL HISTORY

A brief discourse concerning printing and printers. 1663. *See* C. Blagden, The 'Company' of printers, SB 13 1960.

Burges, F. Some observations on the use and original of the noble art and mystery of printing. Norwich 1701; rptd in Harleian miscellany vol 3, 1745, 1809.

Watson, J. The history of the art of printing. Edinburgh 1713; preface ed W. J. Couper 1913; ed J. Munro 1963.

— A contemplation upon the mystery of man's regeneration, in allusion to the mystery of printing (originally issued with the above) 1713; ed L. C. Wroth, Portland Maine 1939 (priv ptd).

An essay on the original use and excellency of the noble art and mystery of printing. 1752.

Hansard, T. C. Typographia: an historical sketch of the origin and progress of the art of printing. 1825.

Patent Office. Abridgments of specifications relating to printing 1617–1857. 1859, 1969 (Printing Historical Soc).

Plomer, H. R. A short history of English printing 1476–1898. 1899, 1915 (rev).

Burch, R. M. Colour printing and colour printers, with a chapter on modern processes by W. Gamble. 1910 (2nd edn).

Peddie, R. A. An outline of the history of printing; to

which is added the history of printing in colours. 1917 (2nd edn enlarged).

Wroth, L. C. The colonial printer. New York 1931 (priv ptd), Portland Maine 1938 (2nd edn, rev and enlarged). Illuminates London practice.

Plant, M. The English book trade: an economic history of the making and sale of books. 1939, 1965 (rev).

Howe, E. The trade: passages from the literature of the printing craft 1550–1935. 1943 (priv ptd).

Steinberg, S. H. Five hundred years of printing. 1955 (Pelican), 1962 (rev).

Philip, I. G. William Blackstone and the reform of the Oxford University Press in the 18th century. 1957 (Oxford Bibl Soc).

Handover, P. Printing in London from 1476 to modern times: competitive practice and technical invention. 1960.

Printing and the mind of man: catalogue of an exhibition at Earl's Court. 1963; ed J. Carter and P. H. Muir 1967 (enlarged).

Clair, C. A history of printing in Britain. 1965.

Berry, W. T. and H. E. Poole. Annals of printing: a chronological encyclopedia. Oxford 1966.

Todd, W. B. London printers' imprints 1800–40; with an addendum on English provincial imprints 1799–1869 by P. C. Morgan. Library 5th ser 21 1966.

(4) MANUALS AND PRACTICE OF PRINTING

There are many articles on Restoration and 18th-century printing practices in SB 1949– and in Library c. 1950–. Though important, some are brief, and only a few can be given here. See P. Gaskell, G. Barber and G. Warrilow, An annotated list of printers' manuals to 1850, Jnl of Printing Historical Soc 4 1968.

Moxon, J. Mechanick exercises. 1677–84; pt 2 ed T. L. De Vinne 2 vols New York 1896; ed H. Davis and H. G. Carter, Oxford 1958, 1962 (rev). The section on printing and typefounding occupies pt 2.

Smith, J. The printer's grammar. 1755; rev C. Stower 1787.

[Luckombe, P.] A concise history of the origin and progress of printing; with practical instructions to the trade in general. 1770, 1771 (with the author's name).

Chambers, E. Cyclopaedia or general dictionary of arts and sciences. vol 3, 1785 (8th edn). *See* under Method of printing.

Magrath, W. The printer's assistant; containing typographical tables and a few select schemes of difficult impositions; with scales of prices for compositors and pressmen. 1804.

Stower, C. The printer's grammar. 1808. Re-writing of 1787 edn of Smith's Printer's grammar.

[Mason, W.]. The printer's assistant. 1810, 1812, 1814, 1821, 1823.

Johnson, J. Typographia: or the printers' instructor. 2 vols 1824.

Hansard, T. C. Typographia: an historical sketch of the origin and progress of the art of printing; with practical

directions for conducting every department in an office; with a description of stereotype and lithography. 1825.

Savage, W. On the preparation of printing ink. 1832.

— Dictionary of the art of printing. 1841, 1967.

Knight, C. The old printer and the modern press. 1854.

Wiborg, F. B. Printing ink: a history with a treatise on modern methods of manufacture and use. New York 1926.

Chapman, R. W. Cancels. 1930.

Pottle, F. A. Printer's copy in the 18th century. PBSA 27 1933.

Simpson, P. Proof-reading in the 16th, 17th and 18th centuries. Oxford 1935.

Gaskell, P. Eighteenth-century press numbers: their use and usefulness. Library 5th ser 4 1950.

Bowers, F. T. Bibliographical evidence from the printer's measure. SB 2 1950.

Todd, W. B. Observations on the incidence and interpretation of press figures. SB 3 1951.

— Concurrent printing: an analysis of Dodsley's Collection of poems by several hands. PBSA 46 1952.

— Recurrent printing. SB 12 1959.

Davis, H. Bowyer's paper stock ledger. Library 5th ser 6 1952.

Dunkin, P. S. The ghost of the turned sheet. PBSA 45 1951.

Miller, C. W. Thomas Newcomb: a Restoration printer's ornament stock. SB 3 1951.

— A London ornament stock 1598–1683. SB 7 1955.

Povey, K. On the diagnosis of half-sheet impositions. Library 5th ser 11 1956.
—— A century of press-figures. Library 5th ser 14 1959.
—— Working to rule 1600–1800: a study of pressmen's practice. Library 5th ser 20 1965.
Manzalaoui, M. A. Typographical justification and grammatical change in the 18th century. PBSA 56 1962.
Fleeman, J. D. Eighteenth-century printing ledgers. TLS 19 Dec 1963. On Bowyer-Nichols records 1710–1829.
McKenzie, D. F. Press-figures: a case-history of 1701–3. Trans of Cambridge Bibl Soc 3 1963.

—— The Cambridge University Press 1696–1712. 2 vols Cambridge 1966.
—— Printers of the mind: some notes on bibliographical theories and printing-house practices. SB 22 1969.
—— and J. C. Ross. A ledger of Charles Ackers. 1968 (Oxford Bibl Soc).
Sayce, R. A. Compositorial practices and the localization of printed books 1530–1800. Library 5th ser 21 1966.
Tanselle, G. T. The recording of press figures. Ibid. On earlier scholarship.
Bloy, C. H. A history of printing ink 1440–1850. 1967.
Twyman, M. The lithographic hand press 1796–1850. Jnl of Printing Historical Soc 3 1967.

(5) LABOUR RELATIONS

An account of the rise and progress of the dispute between the masters and journeymen printers. 1799.
Plant, M. The English book trade: an economic history of the making and sale of books. 1939, 1965 (rev).
Howe, E. (ed). The trade: passages from the literature of the printing craft 1550–1935. 1943 (priv ptd).
—— The London compositor: documents relating to wages, working conditions and customs of the London printing trade 1785–1900. 1947. Introd has information about earlier period.
Musson, A. E. The Typographical Association: origins and history up to 1949. Oxford 1954.
Cannon, I. C. The roots of organization among journeymen printers. Jnl of Printing Historical Soc 4 1968.

(6) THE STATIONERS' COMPANY

The orders, rules and ordinances made by the Mystery of Stationers of London. 1678; suppls 1681, 1683; 1692; [c. 1860] (facs of 1692 edn).
The charters and grants of the Company now in force. 1741, 1825.
Nichols, J. Literary anecdotes of the 18th century vol 3. 1812.
Abstract of the charitable donations in the disposal of the Court of Assistants of the Worshipful Company of Stationers. 1844.
Nichols, J. G. Historical notices of the Worshipful Company of Stationers of London. Trans of London & Middlesex Archaeological Soc 2 1861; 1861 (priv ptd).
Arber, E. (ed). Transcript of the registers of the Company of Stationers of London 1554–1640. 5 vols 1875–94. Also on later period.
Rivington, C. R. The records of the Worshipful Company of Stationers of London. 1883; rev in E. Arber, Transcript of the registers vol 5, 1894.
A concise account of the origin and present position of the English Stock of the Stationers' Company; also the charter of the Company, and the grants of the English Stock, and the byelaws regulating the Stock. 1893 (priv ptd).

Index of titles and proprietors of books entered in the book of the Stationers' Company 1710–73. [1910] (priv ptd).
Eyre, G. E. B. (ed). Transcript of the registers of the Worshipful Company of Stationers 1640–1708 [1709]. 3 vols 1913–14 (Roxburghe Club).
[Plomer, H. R.] Catalogue of records at Stationers' Hall, with an introductory note by A. W. Pollard. Library 4th ser 6 1926.
Hodgson, S. Papers and documents recently found at Stationers' Hall. Library 4th ser 25 1945.
Howe, E. The London compositor. 1947; A list of London bookbinders 1648–1815, 1950 (Bibl Soc). See introds for the operation of the Company.
Blagden, C. The Stationers' Company: a history 1403–1959. 1960. Lists principal records of the Company both printed and ms; contains a bibliography of other Blagden writings on the Company.
Kahl, W. F. A checklist of books, pamphlets, and broadsides on the London Livery companies. Guildhall Miscellany 2 1962.
Bond, R. P. John Partridge and the Company of Stationers. SB 16 1963.

(7) PATENTEES

Steele, R. Bibliography of royal proclamations 1485–1714. 1910. Introd on the various patents.
The King's Printer
Baskett, J. et al, appellants; James Watson, respondent. The appellants' case; The respondent's case. [1717].
[Watson, J.] A previous view of the case between John Baskett, one of his Majesty's printers, plaintiff, and Henry Parson, stationer, defendant. Edinburgh 1720.
Information for R. Freebairn, his Majesty's printer for Scotland, and J. Baskett, his Majesty's printer for England, his partner, v. the representatives and assignies of J. Watson, printer in Edinburgh, deceast. [Edinburgh 1740].
Lee, J. Memorial for the Bible societies in Scotland. Edinburgh 1824. For associated pieces see under I: Scottish printing, col 271 below.
Brooke, S. An appeal to the Legislature on the subject of the office of King's Printer in England. 1830; A second appeal, 1832.
House of Commons. Report from the Select Committee on King's Printer's patents, with minutes of evidence and appendix. 1831–2.
Plomer, H. R. The King's printing house under the Stuarts. Library 2nd ser 2 1901.
Johnson, A. F. The King's printers 1660–1742. Library 5th ser 3 1949.
Lydenberg, H. M. The problem of the pre-1776 American Bible. PBSA 48 1954. On the Basketts.
Haig, R. New light on the King's printing office 1680–1730. SB 8 1956.
The English Stock of the Stationers' Company
The charters and grants of the Company now in force. 1741, 1825.
A concise account of the origin and present position of the English Stock of the Stationers' Company; also the charter of the Company, and the grants of the

English Stock, and the byelaws regulating the Stock. 1893 (priv ptd).

Blagden, C. The Stationers' Company: a history 1403–1959. 1960.

—— Thomas Carnan and the almanack monopoly. SB 14 1961.

The Law Patent

Atkins, R. The original and growth of printing, collected out of history and the records of this kingdome, wherein is also demonstrated that printing apperteineth to the prerogative royal; and is a flower of the crown of England. 1664.

The case of the booksellers and printers stated; with answers to the objections of the patentee (Colonel Atkins). [1666].

The case of the booksellers and printers, relating to the patentees for the sole printing all books of the common-law. [1669?].

The King's grant of privilege for the sole printing common-law-books defended and the legality thereof asserted. 1669.

Gibson, S. and W. Holdsworth. Charles Viner's Abridgment of law and equity. Proc of Oxford Bibl Soc 4 1930.

Miller, C. W. In the Savoy: post-Restoration imprints. SB 1 1949.

The Contest with the Universities

Johnson, J. and S. Gibson. Print and privilege at Oxford to 1700. 1946.

McKenzie, D. F. The Cambridge University Press 1696–1712. 2 vols Cambridge 1966.

Government Printing

House of Commons. Ninth report from the Committee on Public Expenditure on books and stationery. 1810.

Bellot, H. H. Parliamentary printing 1660–1837. Bull of Inst of Historical Research 11 1934.

Lambert, S. Guides to parliamentary printing 1696–1834. Bull of Inst of Historical Research 38 1965.

—— Printing for the House in the 18th century. Library 5th ser 23 1968.

(8) PRIVATE PRESSES AND PRINTING SOCIETIES

Martin, J. Bibliographical catalogue of privately printed books. 2 vols 1834, 1854.

Hume, A. The learned societies and printing clubs of the United Kingdom. 1847, 1853 (with addns by A. I. Evans).

Bohn, H. G. Appendix [vol 6] to the Bibliographer's manual of English literature: containing an account of books issued by literary and scientific societies and printing clubs; books printed at private presses; privately printed series; and the principal literary and scientific serials. 1864.

Terry, C. S. A catalogue of the publications of Scottish historical and kindred clubs and societies 1780–1908. Glasgow 1909.

Walpole, H. Journal of the printing office at Strawberry Hill. Ed P. Toynbee 1923, Boston 1923 (with facs).

Williams, H. H. Book clubs and printing societies of Great Britain and Ireland. 1929 (First Edns Club).

Hazen, A. T. A bibliography of the Strawberry Hill Press. New Haven 1942.

Cave, R. and T. Rae. English private presses 1757–1961. 1961.

(9) INDIVIDUAL PRINTERS AND HOUSES: LONDON

Charles Ackers

McKenzie, D. F. and J. C. Ross (ed). A ledger of Charles Ackers. Oxford 1968 (Oxford Bibl Soc).

John Barber

An impartial history of the life of John Barber, City-printer and Lord Mayor of London. 1741.

The life and character of John Barber esq, late Lord-Mayor of London, deceased. 1741, 1741.

John Bell

Morison, S. John Bell 1745–1831: bookseller, printer, publisher, typefounder, journalist. Cambridge 1930 (priv ptd).

Byrne, M. StC. Bell's Shakespeare. TLS 31 Jan 1948.

The Bowyers

Nichols, J. Biographical and literary anecdotes of W. Bowyer. 1782. Largely incorporated in his Literary anecdotes, 1812.

Fleeman, J. D. Eighteenth-century printing ledgers. TLS 19 Dec 1963.

Samuel Buckley

[Buckley, S.] A letter to Dr Mead, concerning a new edition of Thuanus's history. 1728; A second letter, 1728; A third letter, 1730. See M(2), below, Copyright legislation, under 1735.

Handover, P. M. A history of the London Gazette 1665–1965. 1965. Buckley was concerned with the Gazette 1714–17.

William Bulmer

Marrot, H. V. William Bulmer, Thomas Bensley: a study in transition. 1930.

Croft, W. The achievement of Bulmer and Bensley. Signature new ser 16–17 1952–3.

Isaac, P. C. G. William Bulmer 1757–1830: an introductory essay. Library 5th ser 13 1958.

—— Checklist of books and periodicals printed by William Bulmer. Wylam Northumberland 1961; suppl 1962.

Croft, W. William Bulmer. Bulmer Papers vol 1 1962.

Edward Cave

[Johnson, S.] The life of Edward Cave. GM Feb 1754.

Carlson, C. L. The first magazine: a history of the GM. Providence RI 1938.

Clifford, J. L. In his Young Samuel Johnson, Oxford 1955.

Ichabod Dawks

Carter, H. G. Ichabod Dawks and his script type. Book Collector's Quart 6 1932.

Morison, S. The Dawks family of booksellers, stationers and printers 1635–1750, with particular reference to Ichabod Dawks and his newspapers and newsletters 1685–1716. Cambridge 1932 (priv ptd).

William Ged

See under F: Stereotyping, col 255 above.

Thomas Gent

See also under H: Printing and Bookselling in the Provinces, York, col 270 below.

Gent, T. The life of Thomas Gent, printer, of York; written by himself [in 1746]. 1832; ed A. A. Barr and B. Wolpe 1969 (Printing Historical Soc). On the London pamphlet trade c. 1720.

The Hansards

[Rickman, J.] Biographical memoir of Luke Hansard. 1829 (priv ptd).

Howe, E. The Hansard family. Signature new ser 6 1948.

Ford, P. and G. (ed). Luke Graves Hansard: his diary 1814–41. Oxford 1962.

Henry Hills sr and jr
  A view of the many traitorous actions of H. H. Senior.
  1684.
  [Hills, H.] The life of H. H. 1688.
  Primrose, J. B. A London printer's visit to India [1674–
  79]. Library 4th ser 20 1940.
  Cameron, W. J. Henry Hills—pirate. Turnbull Lib
  Record (Wellington) 14 1960.
  Bond, R. P. The pirate [Hills] and the Tatler. Library
  5th ser 18 1963.
John McCreery
  Barker, J. R. John McCreery: a radical printer 1768–
  1832. Library 5th ser 16 1961.
John Martyn
  Rostenberg, L. John Martyn, 'printer to the Royal
  Society'. PBSA 46 1952; rptd in her Literary etc
  publishing, printing and bookselling 1551–1700 vol 2,
  New York 1965.
John Nichols
  Nichols, J. G. A memoir of John Nichols. 1858 (priv
  ptd); rptd in his Literary illustrations vol 8, 1858.
  Smith, A. H. John Nichols, printer and publisher.
  Library 5th ser 18 1963.
The Nutt-Meres family
  Deacon, E. The family of Meres, and some early English
  newspapers. Bridgeport Conn 1891 (priv ptd).

Samuel Richardson
  Sale, W. M. Samuel Richardson: master printer.
  Ithaca 1950.
William Strahan
  Hill, G. B. (ed) Letters of David Hume to William
  Strahan. Oxford 1888.
  Austen Leigh, R. A. The story of a printing house:
  being a short account of the Strahans and Spottis-
  woodes. 1911, 1912 (2nd edn).
  —— William Strahan and his ledgers. Library 4th ser 3
  1923.
  Cochrane, J. A. Dr Johnson's printer: the life of
  William Strahan. 1964.
  Hernlund, P. William Strahan's ledgers: charges
  for printing and paper 1738–85. SB 20, 22 1967–9.
Strawberry Hill Press
  See Private Presses, col 263 above.
The Woodfalls
  P., P. T. Pope and Woodfall; The Woodfall ledgers.
  N & Q 19 May, 15–22 Sept 1855.
  Dilke, C. W. In his Papers of a critic, 1875.
John Walter
  [Morison, S.] The history of the Times vol 1. 1935.
  Chs 1–3.

H. PRINTING AND BOOKSELLING IN THE PROVINCES

Pendred, J. The London and country printers, booksellers
  and stationers vade mecum. 1785; ed H. G. Pollard
  1955 (Bibl Soc)
Cotton, H. Typographical gazetteer attempted. Oxford
  1825, 1831 (2nd edn); ser 2, Oxford 1866.
Alnutt, W. H. Notes on printers and printing in the provincial towns of England and Wales. 1879. Contains an
  alphabetical list of towns, giving date, printer, book and
  reference.
—— English provincial presses [to 1750]. Bibliographica
  2 1896.
—— Notes on the introduction of printing-presses into the
  smaller towns of England and Wales 1750–1800.
  Library 2nd ser 2 1901.
Humphreys, A. L. A handbook to county bibliography.
  1917.
Cole, G. W. Index to bibliographical papers. 1933.
Morgan, P. English provincial printing. Birmingham
  1959 (priv ptd).
Historical Manuscripts Commission. Record repositories
  in Great Britain. 1964.
Isaac, P. C. G. The history of the book trade in the North:
  a preliminary report on a group research project.
  Library 5th ser 23 1968.

Alnwick
  Burman, C. C. An account of the art of typography
  as practiced in Alnwick 1781–1815. Alnwick
  1896.
  —— An account 1748–1900. History of Berwickshire
  Naturalists Club 23 1918.
  Isaac, P. C. G. William Davison of Alnwick, pharmacist
  and printer. Library 5th ser 24 1969.
Banbury
  [Cheney, C. R., J. and W. G.] John Cheney and his
  descendants, printers in Banbury since 1767. Ban-
  bury 1936 (priv ptd).
Birmingham
  Hutton, W. An history of Birmingham to the end of the
  year 1780. Birmingham 1781, 1835 (6th edn, with
  addns).
  —— The life of William Hutton, written by himself and
  published by his daughter C. Hutton. 1816; ed L.
  Jewitt 1841.

Hill, J. The book makers of Old Birmingham: authors,
  printers and book sellers. Birmingham 1907.
John Baskerville
  Straus, R. and R. K. Dent. Baskerville: a memoir.
  1907.
  Pollard, H. G. Baskerville's jobbing work. Fleuron 7
  1930.
  Bennett, W. Baskerville: his press, relations and
  friends. 2 vols Birmingham 1937–9.
  Dreyfus, J. The survival of Baskerville's punches.
  Cambridge 1949 (priv ptd); rev as The Baskerville
  punches 1750–1950, Library 5th ser 5 1951.
  —— Baskerville's methods of printing. Signature new
  ser 12 1951.
  —— Baskerville's ornaments. Trans Cambridge Bibl Soc
  1 1953.
  —— Baskerville's books. Book Collector 8 1959.
  Hazen, A. T. Baskerville and James Whatman. SB 5
  1953.
  Gaskell, P. Baskerville: a bibliography. Cambridge
  1959. See L. W. Hanson, Library 5th ser 15 1960.
Bolton
  Scholes, J. C. Bolton bibliography, with notes on local
  authors and printers. Manchester 1886.
Bristol
  Hyett, F. A. Notes on the first Bristol and Gloucester-
  shire printers. Trans of Bristol & Gloucestershire
  Archaeological Soc 20 1896.
Cambridge
  Bowes, R. Biographical notes on the University printers.
  Cambridge Antiquarian Soc Communications 5
  1886; Cambridge 1886 (separately).
  —— A catalogue of books printed at or relating to
  Cambridge 1521–1893. Cambridge 1894. Index by
  E. J. Worman, Cambridge 1894.
  Bartholomew, A. T. Catalogue of books bequeathed to
  the University by John Willis Clark. 1912.
  Gray, G. J. and W. M. Palmer. Abstracts from the
  wills and testamentary documents of printers, binders
  and stationers of Cambridge 1504–1699. 1915.
  Roberts, S. C. A history of the Cambridge University
  Press 1521–1921. Cambridge 1921.
  —— The Bentley revival. In his Evolution of Cambridge
  publishing, Cambridge 1956.

Barnes, G. R. A list of books printed in Cambridge at the University Press 1521–1800. Cambridge 1935.

Blagden, C. Early Cambridge printers and the Stationers' Company. Trans of Cambridge Bibl Soc 2 1958.

McKenzie, D. F. The Cambridge University Press 1696–1712. 2 vols Cambridge 1966.

Canterbury

Plomer, H. R. James Abree: printer and bookseller of Canterbury. 1913.

Cheshire

Cooke, J. H. Bibliotheca cestriensis. Warrington 1904.

Chester

Plomer, H. R. A Chester bookseller [John Minshull] 1667–1700, some of his customers and the books he sold them. Library 2nd ser 4 1903.

Brown, R. S. The stationers, booksellers and printers of Chester. Trans of Lancashire & Cheshire Historical Soc 83 1932.

Cirencester

Norris, H. E. The booksellers and printers of Cirencester. Cirencester 1912. See N & Q 20 Feb 1915.

Kaufman, P. A bookseller's record of 18th-century book clubs. Library 5th ser 15 1960. The ledgers of Timothy Stevens.

Cornwall

Potts, R. A. J. Early Cornish printers 1740–1850. Jnl of Royal Inst of Cornwall 2nd ser 4 1963. See also Devonshire, below.

Cumberland

Hodgson, H. W. A bibliography of the history and typography of Cumberland and Westmorland. 1968.

Derbyshire

Wallis, A. A sketch of the early history of the printing press in Derbyshire. Derby 1881. Rptd from Jnl of Derbyshire Archaeological & Natural History Soc 3 1881.

Taylor, N. Derbyshire printing and printers before 1800. Jnl of Derbyshire Archaeological Soc 70 1950.

Devonshire

Dredge, J. I. Devon booksellers and printers in the 17th and 18th centuries, with three supplements. Plymouth 1885–91 (priv ptd).

Attwood, J. S. Booksellers and printers in Devon and Cornwall in the 17th and 18th centuries. Plymouth 1917 (priv ptd). Suppl to Dredge, above.

Dorset

Mayo, C. H. Bibliotheca dorsetiensis. 1885.

Durham

Hunt, C. J. Directory of the book trade in Northumberland and Durham. Newcastle 1969.

Essex

Peddie, R. A. Notes on provincial printers and booksellers: Essex. Lib World Sept 1904.

Eton

Austen-Leigh, R. A. Joseph Pote of Eton and Bartlett's Farriery. Library 4th ser 17 1937.

—— Pote's day-book. Etoniana 109 1950.

Exeter

Dickinson, M. G. Early Exeter printers and booksellers 1669–1741. Devon & Cornwall N & Q 29 1963.

Gloucester

Gregory, A. Robert Raikes: journalist and philanthropist. 1877.

Gloucestershire

Hyett, F. A. and W. Bazeley. The bibliographer's manual of Gloucestershire literature. 3 vols Gloucester 1895–7.

—— and R. Austen. Biographical supplement [to the preceding]. 2 vols Gloucester 1915–16.

Austen, R. Catalogue of the Gloucester Collection in the Gloucester Public Library. Gloucester 1928.

Halifax

Turner, J. H. Halifax books and authors, with notices of the local printers. Brighouse 1906 (priv ptd).

Hampshire

Gilbert, H. M. and G. N. Godwin. Bibliotheca hantoniensis: a list of books relating to Hampshire. Southampton 1891 (2nd edn). See suppl below.

Edwards, F. A. Early Hampshire printers. Southampton 1891. Rptd from Papers & Proc of Hampshire Field Club 2, 1891. Suppl by S. Wilson 3 1898, also issued separately. See also N & Q 26 May, 23 June, 14 July 1906.

Hawick

Sinton, J. Bibliography of works relating to or published in Hawick; with an appendix containing a list of Hawick newspapers, local maps and music. Hawick 1908.

Herefordshire

Allen, J. Bibliotheca herefordiensis. Hereford 1821.

Morgan, F. C. Herefordshire printers and booksellers. Trans Woolhope Naturalists' Field Club 3 1941. Supplementary notes in later issues. Rptd 1944.

—— (ed). A Hereford bookseller's catalogue of 1695 [priced, annotated bankruptcy list of Roger Williams]. Hereford 1942.

Hull

Page, W. G. B. Notes on early Hull authors, booksellers, printers and stationers. Hull 1930 (priv ptd).

Ipswich

Watson, S. F. Some materials for a history of printing and publishing in Ipswich. Proc of Suffolk Inst of Archaeology 24 1949.

Isle of Man

Harrison, W. Bibliotheca monensis. Douglas 1861, 1876 (Manx Soc).

Wroth, L. C. William Parks, printer and journalist of England and colonial America. Richmond Va 1926 (priv ptd).

Cubbon, W. A bibliographical account of works relating to the Isle of Man. 2 vols Oxford 1933. With index of papermakers, printers, periodicals and societies.

Lancashire

Hawkes, A. J. Lancashire printed books: a bibliography to 1800. Wigan 1925.

Lichfield

Reade, A. L. Early career of Dr Johnson's father. TLS 24 June 1949.

Clifford, J. L. In his Young Samuel Johnson, Oxford 1955.

Liverpool

Mott, A. J. Catalogue of books published in Liverpool. Trans of Lancashire & Cheshire Historical Soc 1 1861.

Catalogue of books, mss etc in the Reference Library relating to Liverpool. Liverpool 1908. Lists books pbd at Liverpool before 1800.

Barker, J. R. Cadell and Davies and the Liverpool booksellers. Library 5th ser 14 1959.

Manchester

Earwaker, J. P. and W. H. Allnutt. Bibliographical notes on Manchester books, with a list of Manchester printers of the 18th century. In Local gleanings related to Lancashire and Cheshire vol 1, 1875.

Earwaker, J. P. Notes on the booksellers and stationers of Manchester prior to 1700. Trans of Lancashire & Cheshire Antiquarian Soc 6 1888; rptd 1889.

Axon, G. R. The Manchester press before 1801. Manchester 1931. Lists books ptd in Manchester primarily at the Manchester Reference Library.

Monmouthshire

See under Wales, below.

Newark

B[lagg], T. L. Newark as a publishing town. Newark 1898 (priv ptd).

Newcastle
Welford, R. Early Newcastle typography 1639–1800. Newcastle 1907. Rptd from Archeologia Aeliana 3rd ser 3 Newcastle 1907.

Newcastle upon Tyne Public Libraries Committee. Local catalogue of material concerning Newcastle and Northumberland. Newcastle 1932. With index of printers 1639–1850.

Norfolk
Woodward, S. The Norfolk topographer's manual, revised and augmented by W. C. Ewing. 1842.

Fawcett, T. Some aspects of the Norfolk book-trade 1800–24. Trans of Cambridge Bibl Soc 4 1968.

Northampton
[Eastman, P. M.] Robert Raikes and Northamptonshire Sunday Schools, with an appendix of books printed by the Raikes family at Northampton. Taylor's Tracts on History of Northampton 3rd ser 39–40 1880.

Bibliographical list of Northampton poll books and election pamphlets 1628–1883. Taylor's Tracts 3rd ser 49 1884.

Brown, R. W. Northamptonshire printing, printers and booksellers. Jnl of Northants Natural History Soc & Field Club 19–20 1919–21.

Northumberland
Hunt, C. J. Directory of the book trade in Northumberland and Durham. Newcastle 1969.

Nottinghamshire
Creswell, S. F. Collections towards the history of printing in Nottinghamshire. 1863.

Clarke, W. J. Early Nottingham printers and printing. Nottingham 1942, 1953 (priv ptd).

Oxford
Madan, F. A chart of Oxford printing '1468'–1900. 1904 (Bibl Soc).

—— The Oxford Press: the struggle for a place in the sun 1650–75. Library 4th ser 6 1926.

—— Oxford books: vol 3 1650–1800. Oxford 1931. Suppl 1681–1713, 1954 (typescript). Copy in Bodley.

Gibson, S. and J. Johnson. The first Minute Book of the delegates of the Oxford University Press 1668–1756. Oxford 1943 (Oxford Bibl Soc).

—— Print and privilege at Oxford to the year 1700. Oxford 1946.

Philip, I. G. William Blackstone and the reform of the Oxford University Press in the 18th century. Oxford 1957 (Oxford Bibl Soc).

Morison, S. and H. G. Carter. John Fell, the University Press and the 'Fell' types bequeathed in 1686 to Oxford by Fell. Oxford 1967.

Batey, C. The Oxford partners: some notes on the administration of the University Press 1780–1881. Jnl of Printing Historical Soc 3 1967.

Cordeaux, E. H. and D. H. Merry. A bibliography of printed works relating to the University of Oxford. Oxford 1968.

Richmond
Piper, A. C. The booksellers and printers of Richmond, Surrey. Library 4th ser 13 1933.

St Neot's
Norris, H. E. Notes on St Neot's printers. St Neot's 1901.

Sheffield
Hester, G. Nevill Simmons, bookseller and publisher. 1893.

Freemantle, W. T. A bibliography of Sheffield and vicinity. Sheffield 1911. Section 1, to 1700.

Shropshire
Lloyd, L. C. The book trade in Shropshire: some account of the stationers, booksellers and printers at work in the county to about 1800. Trans of Shropshire Archaeological & Natural History Soc 48 1936.

Somerset
Green, E. Bibliotheca somersetiensis. 3 vols Taunton 1902.

Staffordshire
Simms, R. Bibliotheca staffordiensis. Lichfield 1894.

Stratford-upon-Avon
Morgan, P. Early booksellers, printers and publishers in Stratford. Trans of Birmingham Archaeological Soc 67 1948.

Strawberry Hill
See under G(8) : Private Presses, above.

Sussex
Piper, A. C. Notes on the introduction of printing into Sussex to 1850. Library 3rd ser 5 1914.

Ulverston
Twyman, M. John Soulby, printer, Ulverston: a study of the work printed by Soulby father and son 1796–1827. Pbn of Reading Univ Museum of Eng Rural Life 1966.

Warrington
Kendrick, J. Eyres' Warrington press. Warrington Guardian Jan–May 1881.

Rylands, W. H. Booksellers and stationers in Warrington 1639–57. Liverpool 1888.

Warwickshire
Bates, W. Catalogue raisonné of books, pamphlets etc printed at or relating to Birmingham, Coventry, Lichfield and the County of Warwick, on sale by J. H. W. Cadby. Birmingham 1870.

Westmorland
Hodgson, H. W. A bibliography of the history and topography of Cumberland and Westmorland. 1968.

Whitby
Smales, G. Whitby authors and books printed in Whitby. Whitby 1867.

Winchester
Piper, A. C. The early printers and booksellers of Winchester. Library 3rd ser 5 1914.

—— The book trade in Winchester 1549–1789. Library 2nd ser 7 1916.

—— The early printers and booksellers of Winchester. Library 4th ser 1 1921.

Wolverhampton
Lawley, G. T. The bibliography of Wolverhampton. Bilton 1890 (priv ptd).

Worcestershire
Burton, J. R. Early Worcestershire printers and books. Associated Architectural Socs Reports (Lincoln) 24 1897.

Yarmouth
Farrell, F. J. Yarmouth printing and printers. Gt Yarmouth 1912.

York
Gent, T. The life of Thomas Gent, printer, of York, written by himself [in 1746]. 1832.

Davies, R. A memoir of the York Press in the 16th, 17th and 18th centuries. Westminster 1868.

Pressly, I. P. A York printer: Thomas Gent. In her York miscellany, 1938.

Wales
Williams, M. Cofrestr o'r holl lyfrau printjedig gan mwyaf a gyfansoddwyd yn y jaith Gymraeg, neu a gyfjeithwyd iddi hyd y Flwyddyn. 1717, 1912 (Welsh Bibl Soc).

Rowlands, W. Cambrian bibliography [1546–1800]. Llanidloes 1869.

Davies, W. Ll. Welsh books entered in the Stationers' Registers 1554–17–8. Jnl of Welsh Bibl Soc 2 1921.

—— Short-title list of Welsh books 1546–1700. Ibid.

Jones, I. A history of printing and printers in Wales to 1810, and of successive and related printers to 1923; also a history of printing and printers in Monmouthshire to 1923. Cardiff 1925.

Rees, E. Developments in the book trade in 18th-century Wales. Library 5th ser 24 1969.

Trevecca
Ballinger, J. The Trevecca press. Library 2nd ser 6
1905.

Kaufman, P. Bunyan's popularity in 18th-century
Wales. Bedfordshire Mag 10 1966. Welsh trns ptd
by J. Ross of Carmarthen 1767–90.

I. SCOTTISH PRINTING AND BOOKSELLING

Reid, J. Bibliotheca Scoto-Celtica. Glasgow 1832.

MacKay, A. J. G. A short note on the local presses of
Scotland. Edinburgh Bibl Soc Pbns 3 1898.

Aldis, H. G. A list of books printed in Scotland before
1700, with brief notes on the printers and stationers.
1904 (Edinburgh Bibl Soc).

MacLean, D. Typographica Scoto-Gadelica: or books
printed in the Gaelic of Scotland 1567–1914. Edinburgh
1915.

Keir, D. The house of Collins: the story of a Scottish
family of publishers from 1789 to the present day.
1953.

Carnie, R. H., and R. P. Doig. Scottish printers and booksellers 1668–1775: a supplement. SB 12 1959. 2 suppls
by Carnie, SB 14–15 1961–2. Suppl to *H. R. Plomer*,
col 258, above.

Hancock, P. D. Books and printing. In Bibliography of
works relating to Scotland 1916–50 vol 2, Edinburgh 1960.

Carnie, R. H. Scottish printers and booksellers 1668–
1775: a study of source-material. Bibliotheck 4 1966.

Aberdeen
Edmond, J. P. The Aberdeen printers 1620–1736. 4 vols
Aberdeen 1884–6.
— Last notes on the Aberdeen printers. Aberdeen 1888.

Aberdeenshire etc
Robertson, A. W. Hand-list of bibliography of the shires
of Aberdeen, Banff and Kincardine. Aberdeen 1893
(New Spalding Club).
— and J. F. K. Johnstone. Bibliographia aberdonensis: being an account of books relating to or printed in
the shires of Aberdeen, Banff, Kincardine, or written
by natives or residents or by officers, graduates or
alumni of the University of Aberdeen. Vol 2, 1641–
1700. Aberdeen 1930 (Third Spalding Club).
Keith, A. Aberdeen University Press. Aberdeen 1963.

Ayrshire
Thomson, F. M. John Wilson: an Ayrshire printer,
publisher and bookseller. Bibliotheck 5 1967.

Berwick
Hilson, J. L. Berwick upon Tweed typography 1753–
1900. [1902] (priv ptd).

Dumfries
Stewart, W. The Rae Press at Kirkbride and Dumfries
1711–20. Edinburgh Bibl Soc Papers 6 1906.
Shirley, G. W. Mr. Peter Rae. Records of Glasgow Bibl
Soc 1 1914.

Dunbar
[Miller, George]. Later struggles in the journey of life.
Edinburgh 1833.

Edinburgh
To the Right Hon the Lords of his Majesty's most Hon
Privy Council, the petition of the book-sellers of
Edinburgh, for themselves, and the rest of the book
sellers of the Kingdom (for the free exercise of the
trade of printing). [Edinburgh 1696?]
Chalmers, G. The life of Thomas Ruddiman. 1794.
Kerr, R. Memoirs of the life, writings and correspon-
dence of William Smellie, late printer in Edinburgh.
2 vols Edinburgh 1811.
Lee, J. Memorial for the Bible Societies in Scotland.
Edinburgh 1824.
— Remarks on the answers to the petition of G. Buchan
and others. Edinburgh 1826.
Couper, W. J. An index to Principal Lee's Memorial
for the Bible Societies of Scotland. Glasgow 1918.
A short memoir of Gavin Hamilton, bookseller in
Edinburgh in the 18th century. Edinburgh 1840
(priv ptd).

Constable, T. Archibald Constable and his literary correspondents. 3 vols Edinburgh 1873. See Appendix
to vol 1.

Gibb, J. S. James Watson, printer: notes of his life and
work, with a hand-list of books and pamphlets printed
by him 1697–1722. Edinburgh Bibl Soc Pbns 1 1896.

Carrick, J. C. William Creech: Robert Burns's best
friend. Dalkeith 1903.

Cowan, W. The Holyrood Press 1686–8. Edinburgh
Bibl Soc Pbns 6 1904.

Couper, W. J. James Watson, King's Printer. Scottish
Historical Rev 7 1910; 1910 (priv ptd).
— Watson's History of printing. Library 3rd ser 1 1910.

Fairley, J. A. Agnes Campbell, Lady Roseburn.
Scottish 'King's Printer', 1676–1716. Edinburgh
1925 (priv ptd).

Martin, B. Allan Ramsay. Cambridge Mass 1931.

Law, A. William Perry: his academy and printing press
in Edinburgh and his publications. Trans Edinburgh
Bibl Soc 4 1963.

Parks, S. Justice to Wm Creech [Burns's bookseller].
PBSA 60 1966.

Glasgow
[Duncan, W. J.] Notices and documents illustrative of
the literary history of Glasgow during the greater
part of the last century. Glasgow 1831 (Maitland
Club), 1886 (rev).
Couper, W. J. The origins of Glasgow printing. Edin-
burgh 1911 (priv ptd).
— Robert Sanders the Elder 1661–94. Records of
Glasgow Bibl Soc 3 1914.
Printing in Glasgow 1638–1742. Records of Glasgow
Bibl Soc 2 1913.
Murray, D. Robert and Andrew Foulis and the Glasgow
press, with some account of the Glasgow Academy
of Fine Arts. Glasgow 1913.
M'Lean, H. A. Robert Urie, printer in Glasgow. Records
of Glasgow Bibl Soc 3 1914.
A century of books printed in Glasgow 1638–1868,
shown in the Kelvingrove Galleries, Glasgow, June
1918. Records of Glasgow Bibl Soc 5 1920.
Maclehose, J. The Glasgow University Press 1638–1931.
Glasgow 1931.
Gaskell, P. The early work of the Foulis Press and the
Wilson foundry. Library 5th ser 7 1952.
A bibliography of the Foulis Press. 1964.

Haddington etc
Couper, W. J. The Millers of Haddington, Dunbar and
Dunfermline: a record of Scottish bookselling. 1914.

Kelso
Hilson, J. L. Kelso typography. Proc Berwickshire
Naturalists' Club 22 1915.

Perth
Minto, J. A notable publishing house: the Morisons of
Perth. Library 2nd ser 1 1900.
Couper, W. J. The Pretender's printer. Glasgow 1918
(priv ptd).
— The 'King's Press' at Perth 1715–6 (of Robert
Freebairn). Perth 1919 (priv ptd).
Carnie, R. H. Perth booksellers and bookbinders in
the records of the Wright calling 1538–1864. Biblio-
theck 1 1958.
— Publishing in Perth before 1807. Dundee 1960
(Abertay Historical Soc).

St Andrews
Carnie, R. H. Stationers and bookbinders in the
records of the Hammermen of St Andrews. Bibliotheck 3 1962.

J. IRISH PRINTING AND BOOKSELLING

Catalogue of books printed in Ireland, and published in Dublin, from 1700: alphabetically and classically arranged. Dublin 1791. Copy at Trinity College Dublin.

Dix, E. R. McC. Irish bibliography [lists of books ptd before 1800 at Strabane, Armagh, Drogheda, Monaghan, Limerick, Londonderry and Ennis Co Clare]. Irish Bibl Pamphlets nos 1–8 1901–12.

— List of books, pamphlets etc printed wholly or partly in Irish. Dublin 1905.

— Early printing in the south east of Ireland: reprint of six articles which appeared during 1906–9. Waterford 1910. Carlow, Clonmel, Carrick-on-Suir, Cashel, Roscrea, Thurles, Wexford.

— A list of Irish towns and the dates of the earliest printing in each. Dublin 1909 (2nd edn).

— [Numerous articles in Irish Book Lover 1–6 1910–15: Trim, Cavan, Sligo, Galway, Athlone, Tuam, Mullingar, Loughrea, Enniskillen, Birr, Youghal etc.]

Maffett, R. S. [Articles in Irish Book Lover; The Roundhead Press 1 1909, 3 1912; Achill Press 2 1910. Printing in Newry 6 1914].

Dottin, G. Les livres irlandais imprimés de 1571 à 1820. Paris 1910.

Casaide, S. U. Bibliography of local printing in Ireland. Irish Book Lover 2 1911.

Lynam, E. W. The Irish character in print 1571–1923. Library 4th ser 4 1924.

Alden, J. E. Deception in Dublin: problems in 17th-century Irish printing. SB 6 1954.

— Deception compounded: further problems in 17th-century Irish printing. SB 11 1958.

Walsh, M. O'N. Irish books printed abroad 1475–1700: an interim checklist. Irish Book 2 1963.

Eager, A. R. A guide to Irish bibliographical material: being a bibliography of Irish bibliographies and some sources of information. 1964.

Belfast
Anderson, J. Catalogue of early Belfast printed books 1694–1830. Belfast 1887, 1890 (enlarged); suppls 1894, 1902.

Dix, E. R. McC. List of books and tracts printed in Belfast in the 17th century. Proc of Royal Irish Acad 33 1917.

Belfast Municipal Museum and Art Gallery. Quarterly Notes 52 1934. Lists early Belfast printers and books.

Cork
Dix, E. R. McC. List of books etc printed in the city of Cork in the 17th and 18th centuries. 13 pts Cork 1904–12. Rptd from Jnl Cork Historical & Archaeological Soc. See Proc of Royal Irish Acad 30 1913.

Dublin
Dunton, J. The Dublin scuffle. 1699; ed J. Nichols 1818. Contains notices of book auctions and of some of the booksellers of Dublin at the end of the 17th century.

Dix, E. R. McC. Catalogue of early Dublin-printed books 1601–1700. 5 pts Dublin 1898–1912.

Wall, T. The sign of Dr Hay's head: some account of the hazards and fortunes of Catholic printers and publishers in Dublin from the later penal times to the present. Dublin 1958.

Kilkenny
Dix, E. R. McC. Printing in the city of Kilkenny in the 17th century. Proc of Royal Irish Acad 32 1916.

— Kilkenny printing in the 18th century. Irish Book Lover 16 1928.

Limerick
Buckley, J. Some account of the earliest Limerick printing. Cork Historical & Archaeological Soc Jnl 2nd ser 8 1902.

Herbert, R. Limerick printers and printing: pt 1 of Catalogue of the local collection in the Limerick Public Library. Limerick 1942.

Strabane
Campbell, A. A. Notes on the literary history of Strabane. Omagh 1902.

K. REGULATION OF THE PRESS

No bills or acts of Parliament are included in this list; the Licensing Act of 1662 (13 & 14 Car II, c 33), which restricted printing to London, Oxford, Cambridge and York, was originally enacted for two years, and renewed up to May 1679. It was again brought into force in June 1685, and so remained until it was finally allowed to lapse in May 1695. For the various Stamps Acts and other laws affecting printing, see Siebert, below.

Cobbett's complete collection of state trials [continued by T. B. and T. J. Howell]. 34 vols 1809–28.

Public Record Office. Calendar of state papers. Domestic series: Charles II [1660–85]. Ed M. A. E. Green, F. H. B. Daniell and F. Bickley 28 vols 1860–1938.

— Calendar of state papers. Domestic series: James II. Vols 1–2, 1960–4.

— Calendar of state papers. Domestic series: William III [1689–1702]. Ed W. J. Hardy and E. Bateson 11 vols 1895–1937.

— Calendar of state papers. Domestic series: Queen Anne [1702–04]. Ed R. P. Mahaffy 2 vols 1916–24.

— Calendar of Treasury papers 1557–1745. Ed W. A. Shaw 11 vols 1868–1903.

— Calendar of Treasury books 1660–1718. Ed W. A. Shaw 22 vols in 63 1904–57.

— Calendar of state papers. Home Office papers [1760–75]. Ed J. Redington and R. A. Roberts 4 vols 1878–99.

Steele, R. Bibliography of royal proclamations 1485–1714, with an historical essay. 2 vols 1910. Forms vols 5–6 of the Bibliotheca Lindesiana.

— Handlist of proclamations issued by royal and other constitutional authorities 1714–1910. 1913 (priv ptd).

L'Estrange, R. Truth and loyalty vindicated from the clamours of Ed Bagshawe 1662.

— Considerations and proposals in order to the regulation of the press. 1663.

— A seasonable memorial in some historical notes upon the liberties of the press and the pulpit. 1680 (anon), Edinburgh 1680.

A brief discourse on printing and printers. 1663.

An exact narrative of the tryal and condemnation of John Twyne, for printing and dispersing of a treasonable book, with the tryals of Thos Brewster, bookseller, Simon Dove, printer and Nathan Brooks, bookbinder for printing and publishing pamphlets. 1664.

Atkins, R. The original and growth of printing, collected out of history and the records of this Kingdome. 1664. A plea for printing under the Royal Prerogative rather than the Licensing Act.

— The King's grant of privilege for sole printing of common law books defended. 1669. Anon.

[Blount, C.] A just vindication of learning: or an humble address to Parliament in behalf of the liberty of the press; by Philopatris. 1679.

— Reasons humbly offered for the liberty of unlicens'd printing; to which is subjoin'd the just and true character of Edmund Bohun, the licenser of the press. 1693.

[Smith, F.] An account of the injurious proceedings of Sir George Jeffries against Francis Smith, bookseller. [1680?]. Summarized in State trials vol 7.

—— An impartiall account of the trial of Francis Smith, as also of the trial of Jane Curtis. 1680.

—— The case of Francis Smith [apparently first ptd as an appendix to The speech of a noble peer (Shaftesbury)]. 1698 (3rd edn). A copy is in the Guildhall Lib; perhaps issued separately.

[Tindal, M.] Four discourses: On the laws of nations, the liberty of the press etc. 1694, 1709.

—— Reasons against restraining the press. 1704; rptd with the author's name in R. Barron, Pillars of priest-craft vol 4, 1768.

Reasons humbly offered to be considered before the Act for Printing be renewed (unless with alterations): viz for freedom of trade in lawful books, and setting severe penalties on scandalous and seditious books against the Government. [1694?]; suppl [1694?].

A letter to a Member of Parliament: shewing that a restraint of the press is inconsistent with the Protestant religion and dangerous to the liberties of the nation. 1698, 1700. Ascribed to Matthew Tindal.

Gregory, F. A modest plea for the due regulation of the press. 1698.

A letter to a member of Parliament: shewing the necessity of regulating the press. Oxford 1699.

An essay on the regulation of the press. 1704. Ascribed to Daniel Defoe.

James, Eleanor. Mrs James's reasons that printing may not be a free-trade; because it is not for the peace of the Kingdom, nor for the good of the people. 1704. Broadside.

A method for the regulation of the press, in order to hinder and deter the daily insolence of libels, by an easy discovery of their authors, printers and publishers. [c. 1712].

Arguments relating to a restraint upon the press, fully and fairly handled in a letter to a Bencher, from a gentleman of the Temple. 1712.

The printers proposal for a regulation of the press. [c. 1712].

Thoughts of a Tory author concerning the press. 1712.

[Asgill, J.] An essay for the press. 1712.

An attempt towards a coalition of English Protestants; to which is added Reasons for restraining the licentiousness of the pulpit and the press. 1715.

State law; or The doctrine of libels, discussed and examined. [1729] (2nd edn).

A letter to a great man concerning the liberty of the press. 1729.

The doctrine of innuendo's discuss'd: or The liberty of the press maintain'd. 1731.

The Craftsman's doctrine and practice of the liberty of the press, explained to the meanest capacity. 1732.

A faithful report of a genuine debate concerning the liberty of the press, addressed to a candidate at the ensuing election wherein a sure method is proposed of restraining the abuse of that liberty, without the least encroachment upon the rights and liberties of the subject. 1740, 1763.

A serious remonstrance to the publick; with a hint on the use and abuse of the press; by a friend to liberty. 1740.

Oldmixon, J. Memoirs of the press, historical and political 1710-40. 1742.

[Hayter, T.] An essay on the liberty of the press. [c. 1752], 1755.

Detraction: an essay in two parts; wherein is described the precipice on which every man stands, with some just remarks on the liberty of the press. 1755.

The liberty of the press. 1762.

Webb, P. C. (ed). Copies taken from the records of the King's Bench at Westminster of warrants issued by Secretaries of State for seizing persons suspected of

being the authors, printers and publishers of libels, from the Restoration to the present time. 1763.

A digest of the law concerning libels; by a gentleman of the Inner Temple. 1765. By J. Rayner.

Considerations on proceedings by information and attachment; by a barrister at law. 1768.

The advantages arising from the liberty of the press. 1768.

Copy of an information filed ex officio by his Majesty's Attorney General against John Almon, bookseller, for publishing a libel. [1770].

A letter to the jurors of Great Britain occasioned by an opinion of the Court of King's Bench read by Lord Chief Justice Mansfield in the case of King and Woodfall; and said to have been left by his Lordship with the Clerk of the Parliament. 1771.

[Woodfall, H. S.] A summary of the law of libel; in four letters signed Phileleutherus Anglicanus, printed in the Public Advertiser. 1771.

The freedom of the press and the privileges of the Commons considered: in a letter to a country friend. 1771.

The case of William Bingley, bookseller, who was two years imprisoned without trial: containing a genuine narrative of the proceedings of the Court against him; compiled by a barrister of the Middle-Temple. 1773.

Reasons against the intended bill for laying some restrictions upon the liberty of the press. 1773.

The liberty of the press considered; addressed to Lord Quicksand by Magna Charta in weeds. 1774.

[Lofft, C.] An essay on the law of libel. 1785.

Pigot, R. Liberty of the press. Paris 1790.

Letters on the subject of the liberty of the press; by an Englishman. 1790.

The whole proceedings on the trial of an information exhibited ex officio against John Stockdale; for a libel on the House of Commons. 1790.

Four letters on the subject of Mr Stockdale's trial for a supposed libel on the House of Commons; by a Briton. 1790.

Areopagitica. An essay on the liberty of the press. 1791.

Spence, T. The case of Thomas Spence, bookseller, who was committed to Clerkenwell Prison for selling the second part of Thomas Paine's Rights of man. 1792. *See also* a letter from Spence in Morning Chron 3 Jan 1795.

—— Dh'e 'imp'ort'ant tri'al öv To'mis Sp'ens. 1803 (priv ptd).

The whole proceedings on the trial against Thomas Paine for a libel upon the Revolution and settlement of the Crown and regal government as by law established. 1792, 1793.

Erskine, T. Speech at a meeting of the Friends to the Liberty of the Press, at Free-Mason's Tavern, 22 Dec 1792, with the resolutions of that truly patriotic society. 1793.

—— Declaration of the Friends of the Liberty of the Press; assembled at the Crown and Anchor Tavern, 19 Jan 1793; to which is added the other proceedings of the day. 1793, 1793 (rev).

—— The speeches on subjects connected with the freedom of the press, and against constructive treasons; collected by James Ridgway. 4 vols 1810.

Boyne, J. A letter to Richard Brinsley Sheridan esq MP on his late proceedings as a member of the Society for the Freedom of the Press. 1793.

Bernard, T. Observations on the proceedings of the Friends of the Liberty of the Press. 1793.

Bowles, J. A short answer to the declaration of the persons calling themselves Friends of the Liberty of the Press. 1793, 1794.

The legal and constitutional principles of the Declaration of the Friends of the Liberty of the Press, examined; and the Association vindicated. 1793.

Hall, R. An apology for the freedom of the press, and for general liberty. 1793, 1822 (7th edn).

Frend, W. An account of the proceedings in the University of Cambridge, against William Frend. Cambridge 1793.

Eaton, D. I. The pernicious effects of the art of printing upon society. 1793.

— The trial of, for publishing a supposed libel, intituled Politics for the people; or Hog's wash. 1794.

Stockdale, P. A letter to a gentleman of the Philanthropick Society on the liberty of the press. 1794.

Erskine, Thomas and S. Kyd. The speeches at the Court of King's Bench on the trial of T. Williams for publishing Paine's Age of reason. 1797, [1797].

George, J. A treatise on the offence of libel, with a disquisition on the right benefits and proper boundaries of political discussion. 1812.

Holt, F. L. The law of libel. 1812, 1816 (enlarged).

Bentham, J. On the liberty of the press and public discussion. 1821.

Bohun, E. The diary and autobiography. Ed S. W. Rix, Beccles 1853.

Masson, D. The life of John Milton. 7 vols 1859–94.

Hart, W. H. Index expurgatorius anglicanus. 5 pts (all pbd) 1872–8.

Routledge, J. Chapters in the history of popular progress

chiefly in relation to the freedom of the press and trial by jury 1660–1820. 1876.

Fisher, J. R. and J. A. Strahan. The law of the press. 1891, 1898 (enlarged).

Grassi, C. La legislazione inglese sulla stampa. Bologna 1895.

Kitchin, G. Sir Roger L'Estrange: a contribution to the history of the press in the 17th century. 1913.

Muddiman, J. G. The King's journalist. 1923.

Gillett, C. R. Burned books: neglected chapters in British history and literature. 2 vols New York 1932.

Hanson, L. W. Government and the press 1695–1763. Oxford 1936. With bibliography.

Walker, J. The censorship of the press during the reign of Charles II. History new ser 35 1950.

Siebert, F. S. Freedom of the press in England 1476–1776. Urbana 1952.

Ingles, B. The freedom of the press in Ireland 1784–1841. 1954.

Moore, J. R. 'Robin Hog' Stephens: messenger of the press. PBSA 50 1956.

Snyder, H. L. The reports of a press spy for Robert Harley: new bibliographical data for the reign of Queen Anne. Library 5th ser 22 1967.

Thomas, D. Long time burning: a history of literary censorship in England. 1969.

L. BOOKSELLING
(1) BIBLIOGRAPHIES

See also Section A, General Bibliography, above.

Katalog der Bibliothek des Börsenvereins der deutschen Buchhändler. 2 vols in 3 Leipzig 1885–1902.

Growell, A. Three centuries of English booktrade bibliography. 1903.

Peet, W. H. Bibliography. In F. A. Mumby, The

romance of bookselling, 1910, 1956 (rewritten as Publishing and bookselling) (4th edn).

London School of Economics. Classified catalogue of a collection of works on publishing and bookselling in the British Library of Political and Economic Science. 1936, 1962.

(2) GENERAL HISTORY

There is no single detailed history of the 18th-century booktrade. The following should be supplemented by the accounts of individual booksellers in part 3, below; by the dictionaries, lists and accounts of booksellers and printers in part 2 of G: Printing, above; by the 18th-century pamphlets in the copyright controversies listed in M, below; and by biographies of Dryden, Swift, Pope, Johnson etc.

Knight, C. Shadows of the old booksellers. 1865; ed S. Unwin 1927.

Curwen, H. A history of booksellers. [1873].

Roberts, W. The early history of English bookselling. 1889, 1892.

Wheatley, H. B. Prices of books: an inquiry into the changes in the prices of books which have occurred in England at different periods. 1898.

Plomer, H. R. The booksellers of London Bridge. Library 2nd ser 4 1903.

— Westminster Hall and its booksellers. Library 2nd ser 6 1905.

— The Church of St Magnus and the booksellers of London Bridge. Library 3rd ser 2 1911.

Mumby, F. A. The romance of bookselling: a history from the earliest times to the 20th century. 1910, 1930 (rewritten as Publishing and bookselling: a history), 1956 (4th edn rev). With bibliography by W. H. Peet.

Shaylor, J. The fascination of books. 1912.

Longman, W. Tokens of the 18th century connected with booksellers and bookmakers. 1916.

Chapman, R. W. Eighteenth-century imprints. Library 4th ser 11 1931.

Plant, M. The English book trade: an economic history of the making and sale of books. 1939, 1965 (rev).

Sutherland, J. 'Polly' among the pirates. MLR 37 1942.

Baxter, W. T. The house of Hancock: business in Boston 1724–75. Cambridge Mass 1945. On dealings with London booksellers.

Mossner, E. C. and H. Ransom. Hume and the 'conspiracy of the booksellers': the publication and early fortunes of the History of England. SE 29 1950.

Hazen, A. T. One meaning of the imprint. Library 5th ser 6 1951.

Alden, J. Pills and publishing: some notes on the English book trade 1660–1715. Library 5th ser 7 1952.

Munby, A. N. L. The distribution of the first edition of Newton's Principia. Notes & Records of Royal Soc 10 1953.

Blagden, C. Notes on the ballad market in the second half of the 17th century. SB 6 1954.

— The distribution of almanacks in the second half of the 17th century. SB 11 1958.

Phillips, H. Mid-Georgian London. 1964. A topographical survey.

Harlan, R. D. Some additional figures of distribution of 18th-century English books. PBSA 59 1965.

Redlich, F. Some English stationers of the 17th and 18th centuries in the light of their autobiographies. Business History 8 1966.

Rostenberg, L. Literary, political, scientific, religious and legal publishing, printing, and bookselling in England 1551–1700: 12 studies. 2 vols New York 1965. On Robert Scott, Nathaniel Thompson, John Martyn, Richard and Anne Baldwin. *See* J. Horden, Library 5th ser 21 1966.

(3) INDIVIDUAL LONDON BOOKSELLERS

John Almon
Almon, J. Memoirs of John Almon, bookseller, of Piccadilly. 1790.
Rea, R. R. John Almon, bookseller to John Wilkes. Indiana Quart for Bookmen 4 1948.
— Bookseller as historian. Indiana Quart for Bookmen 5 1949.

John Bell
See under G (9): Printers, above

Thomas Bennet
Hodgson, N. and C. Blagden. The notebook of Bennet and Henry Clements. Oxford 1956 (Oxford Bibl Soc).

William Bingley
A sketch of William Bingley, bookseller. 1793.

John Brindley
Smith, G. and F. Benger. The oldest London bookshop 1728–1928. 1928. On Brindley-Robson-Ellis.

John Boydell
Balston, T. John Boydell, publisher, 'the commercial Maecenas'. Signature new ser 8 1949.

Cadell & Davies
Besterman, T. (ed). The publishing firm of Cadell & Davies 1793–1836. Oxford 1938.
Barker, J. R. Cadell and Davies and the Liverpool booksellers. Library 5th ser 14 1959.

Thomas Carnan
Blagden, C. Thomas Carnan and the almanack monopoly. SB 14 1961.

Edward Cave
See under G (9): Printers, above.

Alexander Cruden
Chalmers, A. The life of Cruden. Prefixed to the 1805 edn of the Concordance, and frequently rptd with it.
Olivier, E. The eccentric life of Cruden. 1934.

Edmund Curll
[Thoms, W. J.] Curll papers: stray notes on the life and publications of Edmund Curll. 1859. Rptd from N & Q.
Straus, R. The unspeakable Curll. 1927.
Gallaway, R. J. Bibliographical evidence of a piracy by Edmund Curll. SE 28 1949.
Hill, P. M. Two Augustan booksellers: Dunton and Curll. Univ of Kansas Pbns Lib Ser 3 1958.

E. and C. Dilly
Butterfield, L. H. The American interests of the firm of E. and C. Dilly, with their letters to Benjamin Rush. PBSA 45 1951.

Robert Dodsley
Straus, R. Dodsley: poet, publisher and playwright. 1910.

John Dunton
Religio bibliopolae, by Benj. Bridgewater [John Dunton]. 1691, 1694, [1702], 1728, 1742.
Dunton, J. The life and errors of John Dunton, written by himself. 1705; ed John Nichols 1818 (with memoir and some omissions), 1818.
Parks, S. John Dunton and the Works of the learned. Library 5th ser 23 1968.

Thomas Edlin
See under 1732 in M: Authorship and Copyright, below.

W. N. Gardiner
Gardiner, W. N. A brief memoir of himself. GM June 1814.

Ralph Griffiths
Knapp, L. M. Ralph Griffiths, author and publisher 1746–50. Library 4th ser 20 1940.

Thomas Guy
A true copy of the last will and testament of Thomas Guy esq, late of Lombard St, bookseller. 1725 (3 edns).

Dunton, J. An essay on death-bed charity, exemplify'd in Mr Thomas Guy, bookseller. 1728.
Wilks, S. and G. T. Bettany. A biographical history of Guy's Hospital. 1892.

Henry Herringman
Miller, C. W. Herringman: Restoration bookseller-publisher. PBSA 42 1948.
— Herringman imprints: a preliminary checklist. 1949 (Bibl Soc of Univ of Virginia).

John How
How, J. Some thoughts on the present state of printing and bookselling. 1709.

Francis Kirkman
Head, R. and F. Kirkman. The English rogue. 1665, 1672, 1680; 1679, [1700?], 1723, 1759, 1786 etc (abridged). Pt 2, Chs 22–4. Fiction, but illuminating.
Bald, R. C. Kirkman: bookseller and author. MP 41 1944.
Gibson, S. A bibliography of Kirkman. Pbns Oxford Bibl Soc new ser 1 1949.
Gerritsen, J. The dramatic piracies of 1661: a comparative analysis. SB 11 1958.

James Lackington
Lackington, J. Memoirs of the first 45 years of the life of Lackington, bookseller, written by himself. [1791], 1792 (enlarged), 1794 (further enlarged), [1810] (13th edn).
— The confessions of Lackington. 1804.
'Paston, George' (E. M. Symonds). In her Little memoirs of the 18th century, 1901.
Brown, A. Lackington: bookseller 1746–1815. New Rambler ser B 17 1965.
Honour, F. M. Lackington: proprietor, Temple of the Muses. Jnl of Lib History 2 1967.

Bernard Lintot
Nichols, J. Literary anecdotes of the 18th century. 1814. Vol 8 gives extracts from Lintot's copyright-acquisition notebook.

The Longmans
Cox, H. and J. E. Chandler. The house of Longman 1724–1924. 1925 (priv ptd).
Longman, C. J. The house of Longman 1724–1800: a bibliographical history. 1936 (priv ptd).
Blagden, C. Fire more than water: notes for the story of a ship. 1949 (priv ptd).

Humphrey Moseley
Reed, J. C. Humphrey Moseley, publisher. Proc & Papers of Oxford Bibl Soc 2 1930. Addns and corrections, Papers of Oxford Bibl Soc 1 1947.

John Murray
Smiles, S. A publisher and his friends: memoir and correspondence of the late John Murray, with an account of the origin and progress of the house 1768–1843. 2 vols 1891.

John Newbery
Welsh, C. A bookseller of the last century: being some account of the life of Newbery and of the books he published, with a notice of the later Newberys. 1885.
Weedon, M. J. P. Richard Johnson and the successors to Newbery. Library 5th ser 4 1950.
Roscoe, S. Newbery-Carnan-Power: a provisional check-list of books for the entertainment, instruction and education of children and young people, issued under the imprints of John Newbery and his family 1742–1802. 1966.
Thwaite, M. F. John Newbery. Private Lib 8 1967.

John Payne
[Payne, J.] A case. 1756 (priv ptd).

Moses Pitt
Pitt, M. The cry of the oppressed, together with the case of the publisher. 1691. See J. Johnson and S. Gibson, Print and Privilege at Oxford to 1700, 1946 (ch 5).

Henry Rhodes
  Blagden, C. The memorandum book of Rhodes 1695–1720. Book Collector 3 1954.
  —— Rhodes and the Monthly Mercury 1702–20. Book Collector 5 1956.
The Rivingtons
  Rivington, S. The publishing house of Rivington. 1894, 1919 (enlarged as The publishing family of Rivington).
Richard Sare
  Stanhope, G. Sermon preach'd at the funeral of Richard Sare. 1724.
Francis Smith
  See under 1680 in K: Regulation of the Press, above.
Samuel Smith
  Hodgson, N. and C. Blagden. The notebook of Thomas Bennet and Henry Clements. 1956 (Oxford Bibl Soc). With index of Smith's foreign correspondence 1683–92.
Jacob Tonson
  Clapp, S. L. C. (ed). Tonson in ten letters by and about him. Austin 1948.
  —— Jacob Tonson, eminent hand. Texas Univ Lib Chron 3 1949.
  Papali, G. F. Jacob Tonson, publisher. Wellington 1968.
William West
  [West, W.] Fifty years' recollections of an old bookseller. Cork 1835. Till 1785; for later recollections see his articles in the Aldine Mag 1838–9.

(4) SPECIAL FORMS OF PUBLICATION

Subscription and Number Books

[Edlin, T.] The case of Thomas Edlin. 1732. Broadside; copy in Chetham Library, Manchester.
Stackhouse, T. The book-binder, book-printer and bookseller confuted: or the author's vindication of himself from the calumnies of a paper by one Edlin, with observations on the History of the Bible as it is at present publish'd by said Edlin. 1732. Copy in Library of Congress, Washington. Portions rptd in J. Nichols, Literary anecdotes vol 2.
Pote, J. A letter to A. B. esq concerning subscriptions and the compleat edition of Dr Cave's Historia literaria. 1737.
Malton, T. Essay concerning the publication of works, on science and literature, by subscription; to which is added a true case, between the author, his printer and paper-merchant. [1777].
Clapp, S. L. C. Subscription publishers prior to Jacob Tonson. Library 4th ser 13 1933.
—— Subscription enterprises of John Ogilby and Richard Blome. MP 30 1933.
Philip, I. G. Thomas Hearne as a publisher. Bodleian Lib Record 3 1951.
Wiles, R. M. Serial publication in England before 1750. Cambridge 1957.
John Johnson Collection, Bodley. Index to proposals for English books up to 1800. Oxford 1960; suppl 1961. Typescript reproduction.
Barnard, J. Dryden, Tonson, and subscriptions for the 1697 Virgil. PBSA 57 1963.
Pollard, H. G. and A. Ehrman. The distribution of books by catalogue to 1800. 1965 (Roxburghe Club). Ch 9.

Chapbooks

Neuberg, V. E. Chapbooks: a bibliography of references to English and American chapbook literature of the 18th and 19th centuries. 1964. With lists of printers and publishers both London and provincial.
Halliwell [-Phillipps], J. O. Notices of fugitive tracts and chap-books printed at Aldermary Churchyard, Bow Churchyard etc. 1849.
—— Some account of a collection of early penny merriments and histories printed at Glasgow 1695–98 in the possession of J. O. Halliwell. 1864.
Harvard College Library. Catalogue of English and American chap-books and broadside ballads. Cambridge Mass 1905.
New York Public Library. Catalogue of the chapbooks, compiled by H. B. Weiss. New York 1936.
Harris Public Library. A catalogue of the Spencer Collection of early children's books and chapbooks presented to the Harris Public Library; by D. Good. Preston 1967.

Fraser, J. The humorous chap books of Scotland. 2 pts Glasgow 1873–4.
Ashton, J. Chap-books of the 18th century. 1882.
Graham, D. Collected writings, with a bibliographical introduction and a sketch of the chap book literature of Scotland by G. MacGregor. 2 vols Glasgow 1883.
Federer, C. A. Yorkshire chap-books: Thomas Gent's tracts with a memoir of the author. 1889.
Pearson, E. Banbury chap-books and nursery toy book literature. 1890.
Cropper, P. J. The Nottinghamshire printed chap-books, with notices of their printers and vendors. Nottingham 1892.
Ferguson, R. S. On some local chap-books. Trans Cumberland & Westmorland Antiquarian & Archaeological Soc 14 1896; suppl 16 1900.
Gerring, C. Notes on printers and booksellers, with a chapter on chap-books. 1900.
Harvey, W. Scottish chap book literature. Paisley 1903.
Fairley, J. A. Dougal Graham and the chap-books attributed to him. Glasgow 1914.
[Cheney, C. R., J. and W. G.] John Cheney and his descendants, printers in Banbury since 1767. Banbury 1936 (priv ptd).
Weiss, H. B. A book about chapbooks. Trenton NJ 1942 (priv ptd).
Bland, D. S. Chapbooks and garlands in the Robert White Collection in the library of King's College, Newcastle upon Tyne. Newcastle 1956.
Altick, R. D. The English common reader. Chicago 1957.

Children's Books

Welsh, C. A bookseller of the last century; being some account of the life of John Newbery and of the books he published, with a notice of the later Newberys. 1885.
Field, L. F. The child and his book: some account of children's literature in England. [1891], [1895].
Tuer, A. W. History of the horn-book. 2 vols 1896–7.
—— Pages and pictures from forgotten children's books. 1898–9.
Barry, F. V. A century of children's books. 1922. Chiefly on 18th century.
Darton, F. J. H. Children's books in England. Cambridge 1932; ed K. Lines 1958. With bibliography.
Mahony, B. E., L. P. Latimer and B. Folmsbee. Illustrators of children's books 1744–1945. Boston 1947.
Meigs, C. L. (ed). A critical history of children's literature in English from earliest times to the present. New York 1953, 1969 (rev).
Muir, P. H. English children's books 1600–1900. 1954.
Sloane, W. Children's books in England and America in the 17th century, a history and checklist. New York 1955.

Targ, W. (ed). Bibliophile in the nursery. Cleveland 1957.

St John, J. The Osborne Collection of early children's books 1566–1910. Toronto 1958. With list of publishers, booksellers and printers.

Thwaite, M. F. From primer to pleasure: an introduction to the history of children's books in England from the invention of printing to 1900. 1963. With annotated bibliography.

Good, D. A catalogue of the Spencer Collection of early children's books and chapbooks presented to the Harris Public Library. Preston 1967.

Music

Kidson, F. British music publishers, printers and engravers, with bibliographical lists of musical works published. [1900].

Humphries, C. W. and W. C. Smith. Music publishing in the British Isles from the earliest times to the middle of the 19th century: a dictionary. 1954.

Walker, A. D. Music printing and publishing: a bibliography. Lib Assoc Record 65 1963.

Catalogue of English song books: part of the library of Sir John Stainer. 1891 (priv ptd). Sold at Hodgson's, June 1932. See W. N. H. Harding, Book Collector 11 1962.

Squire, W. B. Catalogue of the printed music published between 1487 and 1800 now in the British Museum. 2 vols 1912; suppls 1912; ed W. C. Smith 1940.

Day, C. L. and E. B. Murrie. English song-books 1651–1702. 1940 (Bibl Soc). With index of printers.

Schnapper, E. B. (ed). The British Union-Catalogue of early music printed before 1801. 2 vols 1957.

Flower, D. On music printing 1473–1701. Book Collector's Quart 4 1931.

Deutsch, O. E. Music bibliography and catalogues. Library 4th ser 23 1943.

King, A. H. Recent work in music bibliography. Library 4th ser 26 1946.

— Some British collectors of music c. 1600–1960. Cambridge 1963.

— Four hundred years of music printing. 1964, 1968 (rev).

Smith, W. C. John Walsh, music publisher: the first 25 years. Library 5th ser 1 1947. See 3 1949.

— A bibliography of the musical works published by John Walsh 1695–1720. 1948 (Bibl Soc), 1968 (rev).

— and C. Humphries. Walsh bibliography 1721–66. 1968 (Bibl Soc).

Poole, H. E. New music types: invention in the 18th century. 2 pts Jnl of Printing Historical Soc 1–2 1965–6.

Hebrew Books

Roth, C. Magna bibliotheca anglo-judaica. 1937.

— Hebrew printing in London [in Hebrew]. Kirjath Sepher (Jerusalem) 14 1937.

— The origins of Hebrew typography in England. Jnl of Jewish Bibliography (New York) 1 1939.

Maps

British Museum. Catalogue of printed maps, charts, and plans. 2 vols 1885, 15 vols 1967 (to 1964). The London entry is available separately.

Phillips, P. L. A list of geographical atlases in the Library of Congress. 4 vols 1909–20; vols 5–6 by C. E. Le Gear, 1958–63.

Fordham, H. G. John Cary: engraver, map, chart and print-seller and globe-maker 1754–1835. Cambridge 1925.

— Hand-list of catalogues and works of reference relating to carto-bibliography 1720–1927. Cambridge 1928.

Chubb, T. The printed maps in the atlases of Great Britain and Ireland 1579–1870. 1927.

Cox, E. G. A reference guide to the literature of travel, including voyages, geographical descriptions, adventures, shipwrecks and expeditions. 3 vols Seattle 1935–49.

Crone, G. R. and R. A. Skelton. English collections of voyages and travels 1625–1846. In Richard Hakluyt and his successors, ed E. Lynam 1946.

Varley, J. John Rocque: engraver, surveyor, cartographer and map-seller. Imago Mundi 5 1948.

Tolley, R. V. Maps and map-makers. 1949, 1952.

— A dictionary of mapmakers: including cartographers, geographers, publishers, engravers etc from the earliest times to 1900. Map Collectors' Ser 28 1966 (Map Collectors' Circle).

Crone, G. R. Maps and their makers. 1953, 1968 (3rd edn).

Robinson, A. H. W. Marine cartography in Britain: history of the sea chart to 1855. Leicester 1962.

Darlington, I. and J. L. Howgego. Printed maps of London c. 1553–1850. 1964. See Jnl of Soc of Archivists 3 1966.

Skelton, R. A. County atlases of the British Isles 1646–1850. 1964 (priv ptd).

— The early map printer and his problems. Penrose Annual 57 1964.

Lister, R. How to identify old maps and globes; with a list of cartographers, engravers, publishers and printers concerned with printed maps and globes from c. 1500 to c. 1850. 1965.

M. AUTHORSHIP AND COPYRIGHT

(1) THE AUTHOR AND THE PUBLISHER

Baxter, R. Reliquiae Baxterianae. 1696. Appendix 7, 117–8: Baxter and his bookseller.

[Gordon, T.] A dedication to a great man, concerning dedications. 1718 (3rd edn).

Pope, A. The Dunciad. 1728, 1729 (enlarged), 1742 (further enlarged); ed J. Sutherland 1963 (3rd rev edn).

[Savage, R.] The author to be lett. 1729; ed J. Sutherland, Los Angles 1960 (Augustan Reprint Soc).

Fielding, H. The author's farce. 1730.

[Edlin, T.] The case of Thomas Edlin. 1732. Copy in Chetham Library, Manchester.

Stackhouse, T. The book-binder, book-printer and book-seller confuted: or the author's vindication of himself

from the calumnies of a paper by one Edlin. 1732. Copy in Library of Congress, Washington. Portions rptd by J. Nichols in his Literary anecdotes vol 2.

A letter to the society of booksellers on the method of forming a true judgment of the mss of authors, and on the leaving them in their hands, or those of others, for the determination of their merit; also of the knowledge of new books and of the method of distributing them for sale. 1738.

[Bramston, J.] The crooked six-pence, with a learned preface. 1743.

Johnson, S. Life of Savage. 1744.

An essay on the antiquity, dignity, and advantages of living in a garret. 1751.

Foote, S. The author: a comedy in two acts. 1757.

[Ralph, J.] The case of authors by profession or trade stated, with regard to booksellers, the stage and the public. 1758 (anon), 1762 (signed).

Kenny, R. James Ralph: an 18th-century Philadelphian in Grub Street. Penn Mag of History & Biography 64 1940.

Churchill, C. The author: a poem. 1763.

[Campbell, A.] The sale of authors: a dialogue in imitation of Lucian's Sale of philosophers. 1767.

Appendix to the Patriot: containing the author's conversation with his bookseller. Cambridge 1768.

Hayes, D. The authors. In his Works in verse, 1769.

D'Israeli, I. The calamities of authors. 2 vols 1812–13.

— The quarrels of authors. 3 vols 1814.

Beljame, A. Le public et les hommes de lettres en Angleterre 1660–1744. Paris 1881, 1897; tr 1948.

Collins, A. S. Authorship in the days of Johnson: being a study of the relation between author, patron, publisher and public 1726–80. 1927.

— The profession of letters: a study of the relation of author to patron, publisher and public 1780–1832. 1928.

Chapman, R. W. Authors and booksellers. In Johnson's England vol 2, ed A. S. Turberville 1933, 1952 (corrected).

Kent, E. E. Goldsmith and his booksellers. 1933.

Ransom, H. The rewards of authorship in the 18th century. SE 1938.

Atto, C. The Society for the Encouragement of Learning. Library 4th ser 19 1939.

Bush, D. Seventeenth-century authorship. Mint 2 1948.

Weedon, M. J. P. Richard Johnson and the successors to John Newbery. Library 5th ser 4 1950.

Watt, I. Publishers and sinners: the Augustan view. SB 12 1959.

Saunders, J. W. The profession of English letters. 1964.

Hepburn, J. The author's empty purse and the rise of the literary agent. Oxford 1968. Contains an extensive bibliography on the author-publisher relationship.

(2) LEGISLATION

No bills have been included in this list. The copyright acts are 8 Anne c. 19; 15 George III, c. 53; 41 George III, c. 107, for the text of which see the Statutes of the Realm. For the abortive petitions of 1703 and 1706, the Act of 1709, and the proceedings on the bills of 1735, 1737 and 1774 see the Journals of the House of Commons. The text of these bills may be found in the Library of the House of Lords. There are also a considerable number of broadsides, 2 pp. folio Cases etc ptd for gratuitous circulation to Members of Parliament et al both in 1709 and 1735, not generally included below.

For the period before 1712, see also K: Regulation of the Press, above.

How, J. Some thoughts on the present state of printing and bookselling. 1709.

More reasons humbly offer'd to the Honourable House of Commons, for the Bill for encouraging learning, and for securing property of copies [i.e. copyrights] of books to the rightful owners thereof. [1709?].

A short state of the publick encouragement given to printing and bookselling in France, Holland, Germany and at London, with reasons humbly offered to Parliament for granting to S. Buckley such privilege for Thuanus in Latin, as is already granted to every British subject who is possessed of the copy of any book in English. [c. 1735]. See Buckley, col 263 above.

A letter from an author to a member of Parliament occasioned by a late letter. 1735; A second letter, 1735.

The case of authors and proprietors of books. [c. 1735]. On importation of books.

[Carte, T. H.] Farther reasons humbly offered to the consideration of the House of Commons for making more effectual an Act [8 Anne c. 19]. [c. 1737]. See J. Nichols, Literary anecdotes vol 2 pp. 60, 476, 508.

A memorial for the booksellers of Edinburgh and Glasgow, relating to the process against them by some of the London booksellers. [Edinburgh 1747]. Millar vs Kincaid.

[Warburton, W.] A letter from an author to a Member of Parliament concerning literary property. 1747, 1762. In favour of perpetual copyright.

— An enquiry into the nature and origin of literary property. 1762. Against perpetual copyright and his own pamphlet of 1747.

Grant, W. Petition for Daniel Midwinter, William Innys, Aaron Ward and others, all of London booksellers, unto the Lords of Council and Session. 1747.

Andrew Millar and others, appellants, against Alexander Kincaid and others: the case of the appellants [The case of the respondents]. [1750]. The ptd statement of the case in the appeal to the House of Lords.

Richardson, S. The case of Samuel Richardson of London, printer; with regard to the invasion of his property in the History of Sir Charles Grandison before publication by certain booksellers in Dublin. [1753]. See also his Address to the public at the end of Grandison vol 7, 1754.

A vindication of the exclusive right of authors to their own works: a subject now under consideration before the twelve judges of England. 1762. A reply to Warburton's pamphlet of 1762.

Some thoughts on the state of literary property, humbly submitted to the consideration of the public. 1764. Pbd by Donaldson. Exposes the London booksellers' monopolistic practices.

Remarkable decisions of the Court of Sessions 1730–52. Edinburgh 1766. Pp. 154–61, the Court of Equity decision in Daniel Midwinter v. Gavin Hamilton.

[MacLaurin, J., Lord Dreghorn]. Considerations on the nature and origin of literary property: wherein that species of property is clearly proved to subsist no longer than for the terms fixed by [8 Anne c. 19]. Edinburgh 1767. Pbd by Donaldson.

A letter from a gentleman in Edinburgh, to his friend in London, concerning literary property. [Edinburgh] 1769.

Ransom, H. H. From a gentleman in Edinburgh 1769: an early sidelight on literary property. Sewanee Rev 44 1936.

Donaldson, A. [Advertisement, c. 1770]. Gives a statement of his case for underselling, a list of 88 books rptd and a comparative table of his own and London prices. Copy in Bodley.

[Law, E.] Observations occasioned by the contest about literary property. [half-title: Observations concerning literary property]. Cambridge 1770. Anti-monopolistic.

Information for John Robertson, printer in Edinburgh, against John Mackenzie of Delvin and other trustees appointed by the widow of Thomas Ruddiman. [Edinburgh] 1771.

Speeches or arguments of the judges of the Court of King's Bench in April 1769; in the cause of Millar against Taylor for printing Thomson's Seasons; to which are added explanatory notes and an appendix containing a short state of literary property; by the editor. Leith 1771. Copy in Bodley.

Burrow, J. The question concerning literary property, determined by the Court of King's Bench on 20th April 1769 in the cause between Andrew Millar and Robert Taylor. 1773.

Campbell, I. Information for Alex. Donaldson [et al],

defenders against John Hinton, bookseller in London. 1773.

Boswell, J. The decision of the Court of Session upon the question of literary property; in the cause of John Hinton of London, bookseller, against Alexander Donaldson [and others] published by James Boswell esq, advocate, one of the counsel. Edinburgh 1774.

The pleadings of the counsel before the House of Lords in the great cause concerning literary property. [1774].

The cases of the appellants and respondents in the cause of literary property before the House of Lords: wherein the decree of Lord Chancellor Apsley was reversed 26 Feb 1774, by a gentleman of the Inner Temple. 1774.

Alexander Donaldson and John Donaldson, booksellers, appellants; Thomas Becket [et al], printers and booksellers, respondents: the appellants' case [the respondents' case]. [1774]. The ptd statements of case in the appeal to the House of Lords.

Enfield, W. Observations on literary property. 1774.

Hargrave, F. An argument in defence of literary property. 1774, 1774 (with postscript).

Kenrick, W. An address to the artists and manufacturers of Great Britain: respecting an application to Parliament for the further encouragement of new discoveries and inventions in the useful arts; to the facilitating useful improvements in the produce, manufactures and commerce of these kingdoms; to which is added, an appendix containing some strictures on some singular consequences, attending the late decision on literary property. 1774.

Macaulay, C. A modest plea for the property of copyright. Bath 1774, London 1774. Pro-bookseller.

Modest exceptions from the court of Parnassus to Mrs Macaulay's Modest plea; signed 'Stella'. 1774.

The case of the booksellers of London and Westminster. [1774]. Asking for a 'farther limited term for the sole reprinting of such books as are not protected by [8 Anne c. 19]'.

The petition of the booksellers of London and Westminster to the House of Commons. 1774.

The report of the committee of the House of Commons on the petition of the booksellers of London and Westminster. 1774.

A list of books, printed by the booksellers of London and Westminster, in different sizes; by which it will appear that cheap editions of all useful books that are capable of being reduced into a small size have been published by the said booksellers, with the number of years an impression of each is selling. [1774]. This and the next items were pbd as propaganda for a new Copyright Act, after the decision of the House of Lords in Becket v. Donaldson.

Books, printed by the booksellers of London and Westminster, in different sizes and prices; of which there remains a large stock on hand: with the number of years an impression of each is in selling. [1774].

An account of the expence of correcting and improving sundry books. [1774]. A list of payments to authors for revising their own works or making new edns of old authors.

General observations on the expediency of granting relief in literary property. [1774]. Pro-bookseller.

Observations on the case of the booksellers of London and Westminster. 1774. Attack on the booksellers' new bill.

Petitions and papers relating to the bill of the booksellers, now before the House of Commons. [1774]. In 8 pts, giving: the petition of the London booksellers for leave to bring in the bill; the petition of other London booksellers against the bill; the petitions of the booksellers of Edinburgh, of Glasgow and of Donaldson against the bill; observations on the evidence given before the Parliamentary committee; observations of Oliver Goldsmith on the bill, against perpetual copyright; a description (with documents) of the attempts of Whiston

and other London booksellers to circumvent copyright legislation by monopolistic distribution policies.

Further remarks and papers on the booksellers bill. [1774]. An appendix to the preceding item, though not always now found with it. An analysis of the petitions and papers, strongly anti-monopolistic.

Remarks on the petitions of Mr Alexander Donaldson and others, against the petition now depending in Parliament for affording relief to the booksellers of London and Westminster in literary property. [1774].

Petition and complaint of James Dodsley bookseller unto the Lords of Council and Session. 1775. Dodsley v. Macfarquhar et al.

Answers for Colin MacFarquhar, printer in Edinburgh and others; to the petition of James Dodsley bookseller in London. 1774.

Anhang zur Abhandlung von Verlagseigenthum. Goettingen Magazin 1780.

The laws concerning property in literary productions, in engravings, designings and etchings. [c. 1780].

Argument in defence of literary property. [c. 1798]. Beckford v. Hood.

Montefiore, J. The law of copyright: being a compendium of Acts of Parliament and adjudged cases, relative to authors, publishers, printers, artists, musical composers and printsellers. 1802.

Acts relating to copyright in books. 1812.

Maugham, R. A treatise on the laws of literary property, comprising the statutes and cases relating to books, mss, lectures etc. 1828.

Copinger, W. A. The law of copyright in works of literature and art. 1870; ed F. E. and E. P. Skone James 1965 (10th edn rev).

Scrutton, T. E. The laws of copyright. 1883, 1903 (4th edn).

Bowker, R. R. Copyright: its law and its literature. 1886. With bibliography by T. Solberg.

— Copyright: its history and its law. New York 1912.

Birrell, A. Seven lectures on the law and history of copyright in books. 1899.

Brown, W. F. W. The origin and grown of copyright. Law Mag & Rev Nov 1908.

Pollard, A. W. Some notes on the history of copyright in England 1662–1774. Library 4th ser 3 1923.

Collins, A. S. Some aspects of copyright from 1700 to 1780. Library 4th ser 7 1927.

Holdsworth, W. and S. Gibson. Charles Viner's General abridgment of law and equity. Proc Oxford Bibl Soc 2 1930.

Couper, W. J. Copyright in Scotland before 1709. Records of Glasgow Bibl Soc 9 1931.

Stockwell, L. T. The Dublin pirates and the English laws of copyright 1710–1801. Dublin Mag new ser 12 1937.

Partridge, R. C. B. The history of the legal deposit of books throughout the British Empire. 1938.

Pforzheimer, W. Copyright and scholarship. English Inst Annual 1940.

Bald, R. C. Early copyright litigation and its bibliographical interest. PBSA 36 1942.

Dawson, G. E. The copyright of Shakespeare's dramatic works. Missouri Univ Stud 21 1946.

Bloom, E. A. Samuel Johnson on copyright. JEGP 47 1948.

McNair, A. Dr Johnson and the law. Cambridge 1948. Brings together Johnson's views on copyright.

Horne, C. J. Boswell and literary property. N & Q 8 July 1950.

Walker, J. The censorship of the press during the reign of Charles II. History new ser 35 1950.

Ransom, H. H. The personal letter as literary property. SE 30 1951.

— The first copyright statute: an essay on An act for the encouragement of learning. Austin 1956.

Ardagh, P. St Andrew's Univ Library and the Copyright Acts. Trans Edinburgh Bibl Soc 3 1957.

Oates, J. C. T. The deposit of books at Cambridge under the licensing acts 1662–95. Trans Cambridge Bibl Soc 2 1958.

Bond, R. P. The pirate [Henry Hills] and the Tatler. Library 5th ser 18 1963. On background of the 1710 Act.

Rudd, B. W. and F. J. Kase (ed). A selected list of materials on the philosophy of copyright. Washington 1964 (priv ptd) (US Copyright Office).

Tanselle, G. T. Copyright records and the bibliographer. SB 22 1969. With survey of scholarship.

N. BOOKBINDING

(1) BIBLIOGRAPHIES AND DICTIONARIES

Prideaux, S. T. Bibliography of works on bookbinding. 1892 (priv ptd); rptd in her Historical sketch of bookbinding, 1893.

Mejer, W. Bibliographie der Buckbinderei-Literatur. Leipzig 1925; suppl 1924–32 by H. Herbst, 1933.

Hobson, G. D. Books on bookbinding. Book Collector's Quart 7 1932.

Howe, E. A list of London bookbinders 1648–1815. 1950 (Bibl Soc).

Hobson, A. R. A. The literature of bookbinding. Cambridge 1954.

Ramsden, C. Bookbinders of the United Kingdom (outside London) 1780–1840. 1954 (priv ptd).

— London bookbinders 1780–1840. 1956.

(2) HISTORY AND PRACTICE

A general note of the prices of binding all sorts of books. 1669; ed W. A. Jackson, Cambridge Mass 1951.

The bookbinders case unfolded [c. 1690]. Ed B. C. Middleton, Library 5th ser 17 1962. With glossary of 17th-century binders' terms.

A general note of the prices of binding all sorts of books in calves-leather; agreed on by the book-binders, Freemen of the City of London. 1695. Broadside; copy in BM Harleian mss 5910 pt 1, fol 115.

Bagford, J. [Notes on bookbinding]. [c. 1700]; ed J. Davenport, Trans Bibl Soc 7 1904.

The case of the bookbinders of Great Britain. [1711?]. 2 broadsides.

Address to the bookbinders of London and Westminster. 1781. Broadside; copy in John Johnson Collection, Bodley.

The corrected list of prices as agreed on by the booksellers and bookbinders of London and Westminster. 1808.

The bookbinders' price-book calculated for the different modes of binding as agreed upon at a general meeting of the trade. 1813; suppl 1824.

Chambers, E. In his Cyclopedia: or universal dictionary of arts and sciences, 1728. See under Bookbinding.

Hüttner, J. C. Über einige bequeme Vortheile und Handgritte in der Buchbinderei in England. Englische Miscellen (Tübingen) 6 1802.

[Baxter, J.] The sister arts: or a concise view of the nature and history of paper-making, printing and bookbinding. Lewes 1809.

[Minshull, N.] The whole art of bookbinding. Oswestry 1811, Richmond Va 1824.

Martin, T. The circle of the mechanical arts pp. 72–84. 1813, 1820 (4th edn); rptd separately as by 'G. Martin', Petershead 1823.

Dibdin, T. F. Of bookbinding, ancient and modern. In his Bibliographical Decameron vol 2, 1817.

Parry, H. The art of bookbinding: containing a description of the tools, forwarding, gilding and finishing, stationery binding, edge-colouring, marbling, sprinkling etc. 1817 or 1818. The author's name and the earlier date appear on the printed boards; the later date appears on the title-page, which lacks author's name.

[Hannett, J.] Bibliopegia: or the art of bookbinding in all its branches, by J. A. Arnett. 1835, 1865 (6th edn) as part 1 of An inquiry into the nature and form of the books of the ancients, with a history of the art of bookbinding by J. A. Arnett, 1837, 1843, 2 pts 1865.

Woolnough, C. W. The art of marbling as applied to book-edges and paper. 1853, 1881.

Patent Office. Abridgements of specifications [for patents] relating to books, port-folios, card-cases etc 1768–1866. 1871.

— Abridgements of specifications relating to skins, hides and leather 1627–1866. 1872.

— Abridgements of specifications relating to cutting, folding and ornamenting paper etc 1636–1866. 1879.

Prideaux, S. T. An historical sketch of bookbinding, with a chapter on early stamped bindings by E. G. Duff. 1893.

Horne, H. P. The binding of books: an essay in the history of gold-tooled bindings. 1894, 1915 (rev).

Davenport, C. J. Royal English bookbindings. 1896.

— English embroidered bookbindings. 1899.

— English heraldic book-stamps. 1909. A copy with much necessary annotation by W. A. Jackson is in the Houghton Lib, Harvard.

Sullivan, E. Ornamental bookbinding in England in the 18th century. Studio 36 1905.

Duff, E. G. Scottish bookbinding, armorial and artistic. Trans Bibl Soc 15 1919.

Hobson, G. D. Bindings in Cambridge libraries. 1929.

Sadleir, M. The evolution of publishers' binding styles 1770–1900. 1930.

Loring, R. B. Decorated book papers. Cambridge Mass 1942; ed P. Hofer 1952.

Diehl, E. Bookbinding: its background and technique. 2 vols New York 1946.

Howe, E. London bookbinders: masters and men 1780–1840. Library 5th ser 1 1947.

— London bookbinders 1780–1806. 1950.

— and J. Child. The Society of London Bookbinders 1780–1951. 1952.

Jackson, W. A. English title-labels to the end of the 17th century. Harvard Lib Bull 2 1948.

— Printed wrappers of the 15th to 18th centuries. Harvard Lib Bull 6 1952.

Weber, C. J. One thousand and one fore-edge paintings. Waterville Maine 1949; Irvington-on-Hudson NY 1966 (rev as Fore-edge painting; a historical survey of a curious art in book decoration).

Munby, A. N. L. Collecting English signed bindings. Book Collector 2 1953.

Nixon, H. M. Twelve books in fine bindings in the library of J. W. Hely-Hutchinson. 1953 (priv ptd). With essay on Restoration bindings.

— Baumgarten's will. In Festschrift Ernst Kyriss, Stuttgart 1961. German craftsmen in London in 2nd half of the 18th century.

Craig, M. J. Irish bookbindings 1660–1880. 1954.

Mitchell, W. S. A history of Scottish bookbinding 1432–1650. Aberdeen 1955. With bibliography which covers later period.
— Bookbinders of Northumberland and Durham. Pbns of Soc of Antiquaries of Newcastle-upon-Tyne 4th ser 33 1955.
Pollard, H. G. Changes in the style of bookbinding 1550–1830. Library 5th ser 11 1956. On development of non-splendid bindings throughout the period.

Ramsden, C. Bookbinders to George III and his immediate descendants and collaterals. Library 5th ser 13 1958.
— John Holl of Worcester: binder to George III. Private Lib Assoc Quart 1 1958.
Hobson, A. R. A. William Beckford's binders. In Festschrift Ernst Kyriss, Stuttgart 1961.
Middleton, B. C. A history of English craft bookbinding technique. 1963.

(3) EXHIBITIONS, INDIVIDUAL COLLECTIONS AND CATALOGUES

Burlington Fine Arts Club. Catalogue of the exhibition of bookbindings. 1891.
Holmes, R. R. Specimens of royal fine and historical bookbinding selected from the Royal Library, Windsor Castle. 1893.
Fletcher, W. Y. English bookbindings in the British Museum. 1895.
Quaritch, B. A catalogue of English and foreign bookbindings offered for sale. 1921.
Hobson, G. D. Thirty bindings described by G. D. Hobson. 1926 (First Edns Club).
— Bindings in Cambridge libraries. Cambridge. 1929.
— (ed). English bindings 1490–1940 in the library of J. R. Abbey. 1940 (priv ptd).
De Ricci, S. British and miscellaneous signed bindings in the Mortimer L. Schiff Collection. New York 1935.
Oldham, J. B. Shrewsbury School Library bindings. 1943 (priv ptd). Includes Christopher Chapman, Thomas Elliott.
Nixon, H. M. [Quarterly ser of illustrated descriptions of English bindings]. Book Collector 1952–.
— (ed). Broxbourne library: styles and designs of bookbindings from the 12th to the 20th century. 1956.
Abbey, J. R. British signed bindings in my library. Trans Cambridge Bibl Soc 1 1953.
Mitchell, W. S. British signed bindings in the library of King's College, Newcastle-upon-Tyne. 1953 (typescript reproduction).
Miner, D. (ed). The history of bookbinding 525–1950. An exhibition at the Baltimore Museum of Art. Baltimore 1957.
Sommerlad, M. J. Scottish 'wheel' and 'herring-bone' bindings in the Bodleian Library: an illustrated handlist. Oxford 1967 (Oxford Bibl Soc).
Samuel Mearne
  Davenport, C. J. Samuel Mearne and his bindings. 1905.
  — Samuel Mearne, binder to King Charles II. Chicago 1906 (Caxton Club).
  Duff, E. G. The great Mearne myth. Trans Edinburgh Bibl Soc 11 1921.

Roger Bartlett
  Philip, I. G. Roger Bartlett, bookbinder. Library 5th ser 10 1955.
Richard Mountague
  Phillips, J. W. Richard Mountague, bookbinder. Library 5th ser 8 1953.
John Brindley
  Smith, G. and N. Benger. The oldest London bookshop. 1928.
Sylvanus Chirm
  Munby, A. N. L. Chirm's banded bindings. Trans Cambridge Bibl Soc 1 1953.
Roger Payne
  Andrews, W. L. Roger Payne and his art. New York 1892.
  Dobson, A. The two Paynes. In his Eighteenth-century vignettes 2nd ser, 1894.
  Davenport, C. J. Roger Payne: English bookbinder of the 18th century. Chicago 1929 (Caxton Club). But see E. Howe, List of bookbinders, 1950.
  Two bindings by Roger Payne in the library of Lord Rothschild. 1947 (priv ptd).
  Birley, R. Roger and Thomas Payne; with some account of their earlier bindings. Library 5th ser 15 1960.
Edwards of Halifax
  Hanson, T. W. Edwards of Halifax. Bookbinding Trades Jnl 2 1911.
  — Edwards of Halifax, bookbinders. Book Handbook 1 1950.
Auguste-Marie de Caumont
  Hammelman, H. A. The Comte de Caumont. TLS 1 Nov 1963.
John Bowtell
  Gray, A. B. John Bowtell, bookbinder, of Cambridge 1753–1813. Cambridge 1907. Rptd from Proc Cambridge Antiquarian Soc 11.
The Kitcats
  Adams, J. The house of Kitcat: a story of bookbinding 1798–1948. 1948 (priv ptd).

O. BOOK ILLUSTRATION

Hind, A. M. A short history of engraving and etching. 1908, 1923 (3rd edn rev). With large bibliography.

Bland, D. A bibliography of book illustration. 1951, 1954 (rev).

(1) CATALOGUES AND DICTIONARIES

Walpole, H. A catalogue of engravers who have been born or resided in England. Strawberry Hill 1763; ed J. Dallaway 1828; ed R. P. Wornum 1849.
'Bromley, Henry' (A. Wilson). A catalogue of engraved British portraits. 1793.
Stephens, F. G. Catalogue of political and personal satires in the British Museum 1320–1770. 4 vols 1870–83; Catalogue 1771–1832 by M. D. George, vols 5–11, 1935–54.

O'Donoghue, F. M. and H. M. Hake. Catalogue of engraved British portraits in the British Museum. 6 vols 1908–25. Includes suppl.
Johnson, A. F. A catalogue of engraved and etched English title-pages to 1691. 1934 (Bibl Soc).
Tooley, R. V. English books with coloured plates 1790–1860: a bibliographical account of the most important books illustrated by English artists in colour, aquatint and colour lithography. 1935, 1954 (rev).

Bushnell, G. E. Scottish engravers: a biographical dictionary of Scottish engravers and of engravers who worked in Scotland to the beginning of the 19th century. Oxford 1949.

Scenery of Great Britain and Ireland in aquatint and lithography 1770–1860; from the library of J. R. Abbey: a bibliographical catalogue. 1952 (priv ptd).

Life in England. 1953.

Travel: vol 1, World, Europe, Africa; vol 2, Asia, Oceania, Antarctica, America. 1956–7. *See* Book Collector 10 1961.

(2) HISTORY AND PRACTICE

Evelyn, J. Sculptura: or the history and art of chalcography and engraving in copper; with an ample enumeration of the most renowned masters and their works; to which is annexed a new manner of engraving or mezzo tinto. 1662, 1755; ed F. C. Bell 1906 (with unpbd pt 2).

Edwards, E. Anecdotes of painters. 1808.

Chatto, W. A. A treatise on wood engraving, historical and practical; with illustrations engraved by J. Jackson. 1839; ed H. G. Bohn 1861.

Wright, T. A history of caricature and grotesque in literature and art, with illustrations by F. W. Fairholt. 1865.

Colvin, S. Early engravings and engravers in England 1545–1695. 1905.

'Paston, George' (E. M. Symonds). Old coloured books. 1905.

— Social caricature in the 18th century. 1905.

Hardie, M. English coloured books. 1906.

Salaman, M. C. The old engravers of England 1540–1800. 1906.

Austin, S. E. History of engraving to the time of Bewick. [1908].

Hind, A. M. A short history of engraving and etching. 1908, 1923 (rev).

— Introduction to a history of woodcuts. 1936.

Prideaux, S. T. Aquatint engravings. 1909.

Burch, R. M. Colour printing and colour printers. 1910.

Williams, I. A. English book illustration 1700–75. Library 4th ser 17 1937.

Gray, B. The English print. 1937.

[Morison, S.] Richard Austin, engraver. Cambridge 1937 (priv ptd).

Weitenkampf, F. The illustrated book. Cambridge Mass 1938.

Benesch, O. Artistic and intellectual trends from Rubens to Daumier as shown in book illustration. Cambridge Mass 1943.

Wolf, E. C. J. Rowlandson and his illustrations of 18th-century English literature. Copenhagen 1945.

Boase, T. S. R. Illustrations of Shakespeare's plays in the 17th and 18th centuries. Jnl Warburg & Courtauld Inst 10 1947.

Mahony, B. E., L. P. Latimer and B. Folmsbee. Illustrators of children's books 1744–1945. Boston 1947.

Baker, C. H. C. Some illustrators of Milton's Paradise lost 1688–1850. Library 5th ser 3 1949.

Hammelman, H. A. Gravelot in England. Book Handbook 2 1952.

— English 18th-century book illustrators. Book Collector: Isaac Taylor the Elder 1 1952; Samuel Wale ibid; Francis Hayman 2 1953; Anthony Walker 3 1954; Henry Fuseli 6 1957; John Vanderbank 17 1968. All with handlists of illustr books.

Bland, D. The illustration of books. 1951, 1962 (3rd edn enlarged).

— A history of book illustration. 1958.

Hofer, P. Baroque book illustration: a short survey from the collection in the Department of Graphic Arts, Harvard College Library. Cambridge Mass 1951.

— Eighteenth-century book illustrations. Los Angeles 1956 (Augustan Reprint Soc).

Gardner, H. Milton's first illustrator [J. B. Medina]. Essays & Studies new ser 9 1956.

J., C. Hogarth as illustrator: a checklist. N & Q Dec 1957.

Cleaver, J. A history of graphic art. 1963.

Rostenberg, L. English publishers in the graphic arts 1599–1700: a study of the printsellers and publishers of engravings, art and architectural manuals, maps and copy books. New York 1963. *See* J. Horden, Library 5th ser 19 1964.

British Museum. English book illustration 966–1846. 1965.

Paulson, R. (ed). Hogarth's graphic works, compiled and with a commentary by R. Paulson. 2 vols New Haven 1965.

Eichholz, J. P. William Kent's career as literary illustrator. BNYPL Dec 1966.

George, M. D. Hogarth to Cruikshank: social change in graphic satire. 1967.

Thomas Bewick

Bewick, T. A memoir of Thomas Bewick, written by himself. Ed J. Bewick 1862 (abridged); ed A. Dobson 5 vols Newcastle 1887; ed M. Weekley 1961 (abridged).

Robinson, R. Bewick: his life and times. Newcastle 1887.

Roscoe, S. Bewick: a bibliography raisonné. Oxford 1953.

Weekley, M. Thomas Bewick. Oxford 1953.

P. TRADE CATALOGUES: GENERAL

Growell, A. Three centuries of English booktrade bibliography. New York 1903. With bibliography of general book-trade catalogues by W. Eames.

Pollard, H. G. General lists of books printed in England. Bull of Inst of Historical Research 12 1935.

— and A. Ehrman. The distribution of books by catalogue from the invention of printing to 1800, based on materials in the Broxbourne Library. Cambridge 1965 (priv ptd) (Roxburghe Club).

Blagden, C. The genesis of the Term Catalogues. Library 5th ser 8 1953.

— The missing Term Catalogue. SB 7 1955. A reconstruction; the real catalogue has since been found at Christ Church, Oxford.

Taylor, A. Book catalogues: their varieties and uses. Chicago 1957.

Foxon, D. F. Monthly catalogues of books published. Library 5th ser 18 1963.

OKelley, F. Irish book-sale catalogues before 1801. Papers of Bibl Soc of Ireland 6 1953.

T[okefield], G. A catalogue of such books as have been entered in the register of the Company of Stationers and printed from 25 Dec 1662 to 25 Dec 1663. 1664. Copy in Bodley.

[Rookes, T.] The late conflagration consumed my own, together with the stock of books (as it were) of the Company of Stationers, London: wherefore to let all men know, notwithstanding the late dreadful calamity, that there are books yet to be had; and for the convenience of the ingenious buyers, I publish the ensuing Catalogue. [1667]. Copy in Bodley.

Mercurius librarius: or a catalogue of books printed and published in Michaelmas term 1668. Nos 1–8 to Trinity Term 1670. Continued as A catalogue of books continued, printed and published at London in Easter term 1670, nos 1–18 to Trinity term 1674; ser 2 nos 1–24, Michaelmas 1674 to Trinity 1680; ser 3 nos 1–57 (for 58), Michaelmas 1680 to Trinity 1695; ser 4, nos 1–52, Hilary 1696 to Easter and Trinity terms, 1709. There is also a single number extant for Easter term, 1711.

Arber, E. The Term Catalogues 1668–1709, with a number for Easter Term 1711. 3 vols 1903 (priv ptd).

Clavel, R. A catalogue of all the books printed in England since the dreadful fire of London in 1666 to the end of Michaelmas Term 1672. 1673.

—— The general catalogue to the end of Trinity Term 1674. 1675.

—— The General Catalogue to the end of Trinity Term 1680. 1680.

—— A catalogue to the end of Michaelmas Term 1695. 1696, 1965.

Mercurius librarius: or a faithful account of all books and pamphlets. No 1, 16 April—no 3, 29 April 1680.

Weekly advertisement of books. No 1, 7 Oct—no 6, 11 Nov 1680. Suppl issued weekly with City Mercury.

Bibliotheca novissima: or a catalogue of books on divers subjects. [1693]. Copy in Bodley.

Bibliotheca annua: or the annual catalogue for the year 1699. 1700. Vols 2–3 cover the years 1700, 1701; vol 4, which is the latest extant, covers both 1702 and 1703.

Lintot, Bernard. The Monthly Catalogue. No 1, May 1714—no 28, April 1717–[?].

[Wilford, J.] The monthly catalogue: or a general register of books, sermons, plays and pamphlets. 4 vols 1723–9. Nos 1–80, March 1723–Dec 1729 reissued with 4 general titles. For a continuation see below under Monthly Chronicle.

Warner, Thomas. The monthly catalogue. Jan–Mar 1732.

Wilford, John. The monthly catalogue. Mar 1732.

Worrall, John. The annual catalogue. 1737, 1738.

Catalogue of the most esteemed modern books. 1751.

A catalogue of the most esteemed modern books that have been published for fifty years past, to the present time; with prices affixed. 1760.

A catalogue of all the English books that have been published for these sixty years, to the present time. 1764. Copy at St Bride's Institute, London.

A complete catalogue of modern books published from the beginning of this century to the present time, with the prices affixed. 1766.

A new and correct catalogue of all the English books which have been printed from the year 1700 to the present time. 1767.

[Bell, J.] The universal catalogue Jan 1772–[5]. [1772–5]. Copy at Yale.

[Bent, W.] The London catalogue of books in all languages, arts and sciences, that have been printed since the year 1700, properly classed under the several branches of literature and alphabetically disposed under each head, with their size and prices. 1773. The 2nd title reads An appendix to the London catalogue, including the first appendix, containing the books that have been published since Nov 1772 and many articles published before that time, with alterations and corrections to be made in the catalogue.

—— A general catalogue of books in all languages. 1779; appendix, 1781.

—— A general catalogue of books in all languages. 1785, 1786.

—— A modern catalogue of books printed in Great Britain and published in London, since the year 1785 to the present time. 1788.

—— The London catalogue of books selected from the General catalogue published in 1786, and including additions and alterations to Sept 1791. 1791. Appendix, 1792.

—— The London catalogue of books, with their sizes and prices, corrected to Sept 1799. 1799. Appendix, 1800.

—— The modern catalogue of books, with their sizes and prices, and the names of the publishers: containing the books which have been published in London since the year 1792, and such as have been altered in size or price since the London catalogue of 1800. 1803.

1797–1800. Monthly Epitome and Catalogue of New Publications. 4 vols.

The gaps and deficiencies in the catalogues listed above may be partly remedied from the following reviews and magazines, which contain lists or notices of books.

Jan 1682–Jan 1683. Weekly Memorials for the Ingenious.

Jan–March 1687. Universal Historical Bibliothèque, [ed J. de la Croze].

May 1692–April 1694. Compleat Library 3 vols [ed R. Wooley].

Jan 1699–March 1712. History of the Works of the Learned 14 vols.

March 1710–April 1717. Memoirs of Literature, rptd 8 vols 1722. [Ed M. de la Roche].

1717–28. Bibliothèque angloise. 15 vols Amsterdam. [Ed M. de la Roche—Armand de la Chapelle.]

1720–24. Mémoires littéraires de la Grande Bretagne. 16 vols Hague. Ed M. de la Roche.

Jan 1728–March 1732. The Monthly Chronicle. *See* note by D. F. Cook, Book Collector 16 1967. A monthly Register of books, which is an avowed continuation of Wilford's Monthly catalogue; also separate annual indexes.

1730–3. Historia literaria. 4 vols. Ed A. Bower.

1731 onwards. Gentleman's Magazine. Ed E. Cave.

1732–85. London Magazine; with index for 1732–58 compiled by E. Kimber, 1760. Lists, index rptd 1964.

1733–47. Bibliothèque britannique: ou histoire des ouvrages des savans de la Grande Bretagne. 25 vols Hague. Ed P. Desmaizeaux. *See* F. Beckwith, Library 4th ser 12 1932.

Jan–Jun 1735. The Literary Magazine. Ed J. Wilford.

1746–50. British Magazine.

1749 onwards. The Monthly Review. Ed R. Griffiths. *See* A compleat catalogue of all books and pamphlets published for ten years past, with their prices; and references to their characters in The Monthly Review, the whole forming a general index to all the articles in the first twenty volumes of the said Review, 1760.

1750–57. Journal britannique. 24 vols Hague. Ed M. Maty and — de Mauve.

1756 onwards. Critical Review. [Ed T. Smollett.]

1756–7. Nouvelle bibliothèque angloise. 3 vols Hague. Ed E. de Joncourt.

Q. OTHER LISTS

(1) GENERAL

[Stationers' Company]. Transcript of the registers of the Worshipful Company of Stationers 1640–1708 [1709]. Ed G. E. Briscoe Eyre 3 vols 1913–14 (Roxburghe Club).

A compleat catalogue of all the stich't books and single sheets printed since the first discovery of the Popish Plot [Sept 1678] to Jan 1680. 1680. 2 suppl, both 1680. Re-issued together as A general catalogue of all the stich't books, 1680.

[Marshall]. A catalogue of 500 celebrated authors of Great Britain, now living: including a complete list of their publications. 1788.

Reuss, J. D. An alphabetical register of all authors living in Great Britain, Ireland and the United States 1770–90. Berlin and Stettin 1791. The same work continued to 1803, 2 pts Berlin and Stettin 1804.

Library memoirs of living authors of Great Britain. 2 vols 1798.

Clarke, A. A bibliographical dictionary: containing a chronological account, alphabetically arranged, of the most curious, scarce, useful and important books, which have been published from the infancy of printing to the beginning of the 19th century, with biographical anecdotes of authors, printers and publishers. 6 vols (with suppl 2 vols) 1802–6.

Watt, R. Bibliotheca Britannica: or a general index to British and foreign literature. 4 vols Edinburgh 1824. 2 vols under Authors and 2 under Subjects.

Lowndes, W. T. The bibliographer's manual of English literature. 4 vols 1834; rev H. G. Bohn 6 vols 1857–64.

Hazlitt, W. C. Handbook to the popular, poetical and dramatic literature of Great Britain from the invention of printing to the Restoration. 1876.

— Collections and notes, 1867–76. 1876; ser 2, 1882; ser 3 [final], 1887; suppl to ser 3, 1889; 2nd suppl to ser 3, 1892; ser 4, 1902.

Gray, G. J. General index to Hazlitt's Handbook and Collections 1867–89. 1893.

Wing, D. G. Short-title catalogue of books printed in England, Scotland, Ireland, Wales and British America, and of English books printed in other countries 1641–1700. 3 vols New York 1945–51.

Fry, M. I. and G. Davies. Supplements to the STC 1641–1700. HLQ 16 1953.

Alden, J. Bibliographica hibernica: additions and corrections to Wing. Charlottesville 1955 (Bibl Soc of Univ of Virginia).

Morrison, P. G. Index of printers, publishers and booksellers in Donald Wing's STC 1641–1700. Charlottesville 1955 (Bibl Soc of Univ of Virginia).

Tucker, J. E. Wing's STC and translations from the French 1641–1700. PBSA 49 1955.

Hiscock, W. G. The Christ Church supplement to Wing's STC 1641–1700. Oxford 1956.

Wolf, E. Check-list of the books in the Library Company of Philadelphia in and supplantary to Wing's STC 1641–1700. Philadelphia 1959.

(2) DIVINITY

Smith, W. M. A list of bibliographies of theological and biblical literature published in Great Britain and America 1595–1931. Coatesville 1931.

[Crowe, W.] An exact collection or catalogue of our English writers on the Old and New Testament. 1663, 1668 (rev).

— Elenchus scriptorum in sacram scripturam. 1672.

[Claget, W.] The present state of the controversie between the Church of England and the Church of Rome: or an account of the books written on both sides. 1687.

[Wake, W.] A continuation of the present state of the controversy between the Church of England and the Church of Rome: being a full account of the books that have been of late written on both sides. 1688, 1688.

[Gee, E.] A catalogue of all the discourses published against popery in the reign of James II. 1689.

A letter giving an account of all the treatises published with relation to the present persecution against the Church of Scotland. 1692.

[Whiting, J.] A catalogue of Friends' books. 1708. Incorporated in Joseph Smith, Descriptive catalogue of Friends' books, 2 vols 1867; suppl 1893. *See also* his Bibliotheca anti Quakeriana, 1873.

Hawes, W. A compleat collection of all the sermons that are printed and sold for one penny, two-pence or three-pence to the end of July 1709. 1709.

'Dodd, Charles' (H. Tootell). Certamen utriusque ecclesiae: or a list of all the eminent writers of controversy, Catholicks and Protestants, since the Reformation. 1724; rptd in Thomas Jones, Catalogue of the collection of tracts pt 2, Manchester 1865 (Chetham Soc).

Johnson, A. An historical account of the several English translations of the Bible. 1730; rptd in Edward Watson, Collection of theological tracts vol 3, 1791.

Letsome, S. Index to the sermons published since the Reformation. 1734, 1751.

— The preacher's assistant, in two parts: part 1, A series of the texts of all the sermons and discourses preached upon, and published since the Restoration to the present time; Part 2, An historical register of all the authors in the series. 1753.

Peck, F. A complete catalogue of all the discourses written both for and against popery in the time of James II, with an alphabetical list of the writers on each side. 1735; ed with addns by Thomas Jones as A catalogue of the collection of tracts for and against popery in Manchester Library, 2 pts Manchester 1859–65 (Chetham Soc).

[Ducarel, A. C.] A list of the various editions of the Bible and parts thereof in English from 1526 to 1776. 1776, 1778; rptd as an appendix to W. Newsome, An historical view of the English Biblical translations, Dublin 1792.

Cooke, J. The preacher's assistant (after the manner of Mr Letsome). 2 vols Oxford 1783.

Watson, E. A catalogue of books in divinity. In Collection of theological tracts vol 6, 1791 (2nd edn).

(3) PLAYS

Baker, D. E., I. Reed and S. Jones. Biographia dramatica. 3 vols in 4 1812–13. Introd.
See also under Drama, *col 701, below.*

Kirkman, F. (bookseller). Catalogue of all [690] the English stage playes. At the end of Tom Tyler and his wife: a comedy, 1661. Another edn with 806 plays at the end of Corneille, Nicomède, tr John Dancer 1671.

Langbaine, G. Momus triumphans. 1688, 1688 (re-issued as A new catalogue of English plays).
— An account of the English dramatic poets. Oxford 1691.
— The lives and characters of the English dramatic poets. [1698]. This shorter edn has addns by Charles Gildon et al.
[Mears, W. (bookseller)]. A compleat catalogue of all the plays that were ever yet printed in the English language. 1714, 1719, 1726.
Jacob, G. The poetical register: or the lives and characters of all the English poets, with an account of their writings. 2 vols 1723.
[Feales, W. (bookseller)]. A true and exact catalogue of all the plays and other dramatick pieces that were ever yet printed in the English tongue. 1713, 1715, 1732.
[Mottley, J.] A compleat list of all the English dramatic poets, and of all the plays ever printed in the English language to the present year 1747. At the end of T. Whincop, Scanderbeg, 1747.
[Chetwood, W. R.] The British theatre: containing the lives of the English dramatic poets; with an account of all their plays. Dublin 1750, 1751.
[Cave, E. (bookseller)]. A complete catalogue of all the dramatic pieces in the English language, ranged under the names of their authors, with the dates of the first appearances, and an enumeration of their several editions. 1751.
[Dodsley, R. (bookseller)]. Theatrical records: or an account of English dramatic authors and their works. 1756.
Baker, D. E. The companion to the playhouse: or an historical account of all the dramatic writers (and their works) that have appeared in Great Britain and Ireland from the commencement of our theatrical exhibitions to the present year 1764. 2 vols 1764; ed I. Reed 2 vols 1782 (as Biographia dramatica); ed S. Jones 3 vols in 4 1812–13 (as Biographia dramatica).
[Potter, J.] The theatrical review: or new companion to the playhouse, by a society of gentlemen independent of managerial influence. 2 vols 1772.
The playhouse pocket companion. 1779.
Egerton, J. The theatrical remembrancer; containing a complete list of all the dramatic performances in the English language, their several editions, dates and sizes. 1788; Continuation 1787 to 1801 by Barker, 1801; Appendix, 1803.
[Lowndes, W. (bookseller)]. Catalogue of comedies, farces, interludes, musical pieces etc. [c. 1790]. Broadside.
[Barker and Son (booksellers)]. List of plays. Feb 1803. Broadside.

(4) LAW BOOKS

See also under Law, col 1911 below.
[Bassett, T. (bookseller)]. A catalogue of the common and statute law books of this realm. 1671, 1682, 1684, 1699.
[Walthoe, J. (bookseller)]. A catalogue of the common and statute law books of this realm. 1714 etc.

Worrall, J. (bookseller). Bibliotheca legum: or a new and compleat list of all the common and statute law books from their first publication. 1731; ed E. Brooke 2 vols 1788 (as Bibliotheca legum Angliae).

(5) MISCELLANEOUS

Gore, T. Catalogus plerumque omnium authorum, qui de re heraldica scripserunt. Oxford 1668, 1674 (enlarged).
[Cooper, W. (bookseller)]. A catalogue of chymical books. At the end of The philosophical epitaph of W. C. esq, 1673.

[Tooker, C. (bookseller)]. The famous collection of papers and pamphlets of all sorts from the year 1600 down to this day, commonly known by the name of William Miller's Collection. [c. 1695], [c. 1696], [c. 1705].
Worrall, J. (bookseller). Bibliotheca topographica anglicana. 1736.

R. CATALOGUES OF INDIVIDUAL PUBLISHERS AND AUCTIONEERS

Cooper, W. [A list of 74 auctions 1676–86.] In Catalogus librorum bibliothecae viri cujusdam literati, 14 Feb 1687, on the verso of the last leaf of 2nd sheet; rptd in Hartshorne, Book rarities of the University of Cambridge, 1829. The first 30 of these had been previously listed by Cooper in his auction catalogue of the library of Walter Rea, sold 19 June 1682.
Gough, R. Progress of selling books by catalogues [1788]. In J. Nichol, Literary anecdotes vol 3. Rptd from GM.
[Sotheby]. A list of the original catalogues of the principal libraries which have been sold by auction by Mr Samuel Baker [and his successors] 1744–1818. 1818, 1828 (with addns to date).
Lawler, J. Book auctions in England 1676–1700. 1898, 1906.
British Museum. List of catalogues of English book sales 1676–1900 now in the British Museum, compiled H. Mattingly, I. A. K. Burnett and A. W. Pollard. 1915.

Interleaved xerox copies of this book, extensively annotated under the supervision of A. N. L. Munby, are on deposit in major research libraries in England and US.
Hodgson, J. E. Romance and humour of the auction room. Connoisseur June 1939.
O'Kelley, F. Irish book-sale catalogues before 1801. Papers of Bibl Soc of Ireland 6 1953.
Ash, P. Fathers of auctioneering [W. Cooper, E. Millington etc]. Estates Gazette 22–9 Dec 1962, 5–12 Jan 1963.
Pollard, H. G. and A. Ehrman. The distribution of books by catalogue from the invention of printing to 1800. Cambridge 1965 (Roxburghe Club).
Christopher Cock
Fielding, H. The historical register, 1736. Cock is satirized as Christopher Hen.
Baker, C. H. C. and M. I. The life and circumstances of James Brydges, first Duke of Chandros. Oxford 1949.

(1) TRADE SALES

On the death, retirement or bankruptcy of a bookseller it was the custom to sell his copyrights, his shares in joint pbns, and his unbound stock in quires at an auction to which only members of the trade were invited. Early examples in the BM are those in the List of English book sales under the dates 24 Feb 1679 (Moses Pitt and Oxford Univ Press), 7, 28 Sept 1691, 4 Jan 1692, 17 Feb 1692. Other early catalogues, formerly owned by J. F. Fulton, are now in the Yale Medical School Library. Longmans Green & Co have a collection from 1718–68, a xerox of which is in the BM. Another collec-

tion, formerly owned by the Rivingtons but annotated by Aaron Ward and his son, is now in the John Johnson Collection in Bodley. Information about the trade sales may be found in the copyright controversy pamphlets listed in M, above, especially those of 1774.

Shaylor, J. The fascination of books. 1912. Prints the only surviving text of rules for trade sales.

Blagden, C. Booksellers' trade sales 1718–68. Library 5th ser 5 1951.

(2) ADVERTISEMENT LISTS

The practice of printing lists of books for sale by a publisher at the end of a book, either on the unused remnant of a sheet, or on separate leaves inserted, appears to have originated about 1649; from then it became a common practice. They are numerous, and no attempt can be made to list them here. There is a large collection of these advertisement lists in the John Johnson Collection in Bodley.

S. LIBRARIES

Cannons, H. G. T. Bibliography of library economy: a classified index to the professional periodical literature relating to library economy, printing, methods of publishing, copyright, bibliography etc 1876–1920. Chicago 1927; Library literature 1921–32, 1934 [supple-

ment to preceding]. Suppls 1933–5, 1936–9, 1940–2 and triennially.

Burton, M. and M. E. Vosburgh. A bibliography of librarianship: classified and annotated guide to the library literature of the world. 1934.

(1) CIRCULATING AND PROPRIETARY LIBRARIES

Kaufman, P. Checklists of English circulating and sub-scription libraries to 1800, in his The community library. Trans Amer Philosophical Soc new ser 57 1967; *see below.*

[Shillito, C.] The country book club: a poem. 1788.
The use of circulating libraries considered; with instructions for opening and conducting a library, either upon a large or small plan. 1797. Copy in Bodley.
Hints of a plan for a book-club. Oeconomist 1798.
Mangin, E. An essay on light reading, as it may be supposed to influence moral conduct and literary taste. 1808.
Country book-clubs 50 years ago. GM June 1852.
Clarke, A. The reputed first circulating library in London. Library 2nd ser 1 1900. *See* W. E. A. Axon, ibid.
Martin, B. Allan Ramsay. Cambridge Mass 1931.
Minto, J. A history of the public library movement in Great Britain and Ireland. 1932. Discusses precursors of the public library.
McKillop, A. D. English circulating libraries 1725–50. Library 4th ser 14 1934.

Blakey, D. The Minerva Press 1790–1820. 1939 (Bibl Soc).
Hamlyn, H. M. Eighteenth-century circulating libraries in England. Library 5th ser 1 1947.
Beckwith, F. The 18th-century proprietary library in England. Jnl of Documentation 3 1948.
Kaufman, P. A bookseller's record of 18th-century book clubs. Library 5th ser 15 1960.
— Community lending libraries in 18th-century Ireland and Wales. Lib Quart 33 1963.
— English book clubs and their role in social history. Libri 14 1964.
— The community library: a chapter in English social history. Trans Amer Philosophical Soc new ser 57 1967.
Kelly, T. Early public libraries: a history of public libraries in Great Britain before 1850. 1966. Primarily on precursors of the public library.
McDonald, W. R. Circulating libraries in the north-east of Scotland in the 18th century. Bibliotheck 5 1968.

(2) PUBLIC LIBRARIES AND THOSE OF CORPORATE BODIES

Central Council for the Care of Churches. The parochial libraries of the Church of England; with an historical introduction [by N. R. Ker], notes on early printed books and their care and an alphabetical list of parochial libraries past and present. 1959.
Tallon, M. Church of Ireland diocesan libraries. Dublin 1959.
— Church in Wales diocesan libraries. 1962.
Kelly, T. Checklist of early endowed libraries. In his Early public libraries, 1966. *See below.*

Bray, T. Bibliotheca parochialis. 1697, 1707 (rev).
— Bibliotheca catechetica: or the country curate's library. 1702.
[Smith, S.?] Public spirit illustrated in the life and designs of Dr Bray. 1746; rev J. H. Todd 1808.
An account of the designs of the associates of the late Dr Bray, with an abstract of their proceedings. 1762.

Steiner, B. C. Rev Thomas Bray: his life and selected works. 1901 (Maryland Historical Soc).
Smith, G. Dr Thomas Bray. Lib Assoc Record 12 1910.
Thompson, H. P. Thomas Bray. 1954.
Kelly, T. Early public libraries. 1966. With list of Bray libraries to 1850.
[Kirkwood, J.] An overture for founding and maintaining bibliotheques in every paroch throughout the Kingdom. [Edinburgh] 1699. Copy in Wigan Public Library; ed W. Blades 1889 (priv ptd).
— A copy of a letter anent a project for erecting a library in every presbytery, or at least in every county in the Highlands, from a Rev Minister of the Scots nation now in England. [c. 1703].
Maclean, D. Highland libraries in the 18th century. Records of Glasgow Bibl Soc 7 1923.
Minto, J. In his History of the public library movement in Great Britain and Ireland, 1932.

[Bagford, J.] An account of London libraries. Monthly Miscellany or Memoirs for the Curious 2 1708.

Oldys, W. Memoir of William Oldys together with his diary, choice notes from his adversaria, and an account of the London libraries. [Ed J. Yeowell] 1862 (priv ptd). Rptd from N & Q.

Uffenbach, Z. C. von. Merkwürdige Reisen. Ulm and Memmingen 1753–4; [excerpts] tr and ed W. H. Quarrell and M. Mare 1934 (as Oxford in 1710: from the travels of Uffenbach).

Thomas, E. C. London libraries in 1710. Library Chron 2 1885.

Kelly, W. A. A scourge of English libraries. Literary Rev 21 1968.

Struve, B. G. Introductio in notitiam rei litterariae et usum bibliothecarum. Ed J. C. Fischer, Leipzig 1754.

[Clarke, W. and W. Beckford]. Repertorium bibliographicum: or some account of the most celebrated British libraries. 1819.

Botfield, B. Notes on English cathedral libraries. 1849.

Edwards, E. Memoirs of libraries including a handbook of library economy. 2 vols 1859.

— Free town libraries. 1869.

Clark, J. W. The care of books: an essay on the development of libraries and their fittings to the end of the 18th century. Cambridge 1901, 1902.

Savage, E. A. The story of libraries and book collecting. [1909].

Streeter, B. H. The chained library: four centuries of the evolution of the English library. 1931.

Minto, J. A history of the public library movement in Great Britain and Ireland. 1932.

Hands, M. S. G. and M. S. Smith. The cathedral libraries catalogue. Library 5th ser 2 1948. With appendix listing ptd catalogues of books and mss in cathedral libraries in England and Wales.

Thornton, J. L. A mirror for librarians: selected readings in the history of librarianship. 1948; Classics of librarianship, 1957. Combined as Selected readings in the history of librarianship, 1966.

Irwin, R. The origins of the English library. 1958, 1966 (rev as The English library: sources and history).

— The heritage of the English library. 1964.

Durkan, J. and A. Ross. Early Scottish libraries. Glasgow 1961.

Kaufman, P. Reading vogues at English cathedral libraries of the 18th century. BNYPL Dec 1964, Jan–March 1965.

Kelly, T. Early public libraries: a history of public libraries in Great Britain before 1850. 1966. Primarily on the precursors of the public library. With list of early endowed libraries.

Ker, N. R. Cathedral libraries. Lib History 1 1969.

(3) LONDON

Rye, R. A. Students' guide to the libraries of London. 1908, 1910, 1927 (rev and enlarged).

Irwin, R. (ed). The libraries of London. 1949; ed R. Irwin and R. Staveley 1961 (rev).

British Museum
Catalogues:
    Cottonian mss. Ed T. Smith, Oxford 1696.
    Mss in the King's library. Ed D. Casley 1734.
    Harleian mss. 2 vols 1759.
    Cottonian mss. Ed S. Hooper 1777.
    Mss hitherto undescribed. Ed S. Ayscough 2 vols 1782.
    Printed books. 2 vols 1787.
    Sir Joseph Banks collections. Ed J. Dryander 5 vols 1798–1800.
    Francis, F. C. The catalogues of the printed books. 1948.
Report from the Committee [of the House] appointed to view the Cottonian library. 1732; rptd in Parliamentary reports vol 1, 1715–1801.
The general contents of the British Museum; with remarks serving as a directory in viewing that noble cabinet. 1761.
Edwards, E. The lives of the founders of the British Museum 1570–1870. 1870.
Cowtan, R. Memories of the British Museum. 1872.
Barwick, G. F. The Reading Room of the British Museum. 1929.
Esdaile, A. The British Museum library: a short history and survey. 1946.
King, A. H. The Royal music library. TLS 25 April 1958; Book Collector 7 1958.

The Inns of Court and Chancery
The Middle Temple. Catalogue. Ed B. Shower 1700; Catalogue, [ed C. Worsley?] 1754.
Bland, D. S. A bibliography of the Inns of Court and Chancery. 1965 (Seldom Soc, suppl ser 3). Section L on libraries.

Lambeth Palace
Cox-Johnson, A. Lambeth Palace Library 1610–64. Trans Cambridge Bibl Soc 2 1958.
James, M. R. The history of Lambeth Palace Library. Trans Cambridge Bibl Soc 3 1963.
Bill, G. Lambeth Palace Library. Library 5th ser 21 1966.

Merchant Taylor's School
Sayle, R. T. D. Annals of Merchant Taylors' School Library. Library 4th ser 15 1935.

Royal College of Physicians
Museum Harveianum. Ed C. Merrett 1660.
Bibliothecae collegii regalis medicorum londiniensis catalogus. 1757.

Royal College of Surgeons
LeFanu, W. R. The history of the library of the college. Annals of Royal College of Surgeons 9 1951.

Royal Society
Bibliotheca Norfolciana. 1681.

St Paul's School
A catalogue of all the books in the library of St Paul's School, with the names of the benefactors. 1743.

Sion College
Catalogues:
    Printed books. Ed J. Spencer 1650.
    Printed books. Ed W. Reading 1724.
Reading, W. The history of the ancient and present state of Sion College and of the London clergy's library there. 1724.
Milman, W. H. Some account of Sion College in the City of London, and its library. [1880].
Pearce, E. H. Sion College and library. Cambridge 1913.
Edmonston, E. Sion College. Book Collector 14 1965.

Westminster Library
Kaufman, P. The Westminster Library: history and mystery. Library 5th ser 21 1966. See R. J. Roberts, Lib History 1 1969.

Dr Williams's Library
Bibliothecae quam vir doctus, et admodum reverendus Daniel Williams, S.T.P. bono publico legavit, catalogus. [Ed I. Bates] 1727.
Catalogue. 1801. Appendixes 1808, 1814.
Herford, R. T. and S. K. Jones. A short account of the charity and library established under the will of the late Daniel Williams. 1917 (priv ptd).
Jones, S. K. Dr Williams and his library. 1948.

Society for the Propagation of the Gospel in Foreign Parts
Bibliothecae americanae primordia: an attempt towards laying the foundation of an American library. [Ed W. Kennett] 1713; rev H. Homer 1789.

(4) OXFORD

Myres, J. N. L. Oxford libraries in the 17th and 18th centuries. In The English library before 1700: studies in its history, ed F. Wormald and C. E. Wright 1958.

Bodleian Library
Catalogues:
[Printed books, alphabetical]. Ed T. Hyde 1674.
[Printed books, alphabetical]. Ed R. Fysher 2 vols 1738.
[Oriental mss, pt 1]. Ed J. Uri 1787.
[Incunabula and Aldines]. Ed J. Randolph and W. Jackson 1795.
Macray, W. D. The annals of the Bodleian Library. 1868, 1890 (with addns).

The Bodleian in the 17th century: guide to an exhibition 1951. Oxford 1951.
Philip, I. G. Reconstruction in the Bodleian and Convocation House in the 18th century. Bodleian Lib Record 6 1961.

Magdalen Hall (now Hertford College)
Catalogus librorum in bibliotheca aulae magdalensis. Ed H. Wilkinson, Oxford 1661.

Jesus College
Knox, T. M. and C. J. Fordyce. The library of Jesus College, Oxford, with an appendix on the books bequeathed thereto by Lord Herbert of Cherbury. Papers of Oxford Bibl Soc 5 1939.

(5) CAMBRIDGE

Hartshorne, C. H. Book rarities of the University of Cambridge. 1829.
Oates, J. C. T. The libraries of Cambridge 1570–1700. In English libraries before 1700, ed F. Wormald and C. E. Wright 1958.
Munby, A. N. L. Cambridge college libraries: aids for research students. Cambridge 1960, 1962 (rev).

University Library
Sayle, C. E. The annals of Cambridge University Library: part 3, 1641–1800. Library 3rd ser 6 1915.
Corpus Christi College
[Matthew Parker Collection]. [Ed. W. Stanley], Cambridge 1722; ed J. Nasmyth 1777.
St Catharine's College
Catalogus librorum. Cambridge 1771.

(6) EDINBURGH

Edinburgh University Library
[James Narne Bequest]. Edinburgh 1678.
[Catalogue of the medical books]. Edinburgh 1773.
Catalogue of the books in the Divinity Hall Library. Edinburgh 1787.
Finlayson, C. P. and S. M. Simpson. The library of the University of Edinburgh: the early period 1580–1710. Lib History 1 1969.
Advocates' Library
Catalogues:
Catalogus librorum bibliothecae juris utriusque. Edinburgh 1692.

[General catalogue pt 1, ed T. Ruddiman and W. Goodall]. Edinburgh 1742.
[General catalogue pt 2, ed A. Brown]. Edinburgh 1776.
[General catalogue pt 3]. Edinburgh 1807.
Dickson, W. K. The printed catalogues of the Advocates' Library. Edinburgh Bibl Soc Pbns 9 1913.
Rae, T. I. and W. Beattie. Boswell and the Advocate's Library. In Johnson, Boswell and their circle: essays presented to L. F. Powell, Oxford 1965.

(7) OTHER TOWNS

Aberdeen
Ogilvie, W. Proposal for a public library at Aberdeen. Aberdeen 1764; rptd in Scottish N & Q 3 1890.
Catalogue of books belonging to the theological library of Marischal College. Aberdeen 1790, 1811.
Lough, J. and M. Aberdeen circulating libraries in the 18th century. Aberdeen Univ Rev 31 1946.
Bamburgh Castle
The books are now at Durham.
[Bell, T.] Catalogue of the library at Bamburgh Castle. Durham [1794]. Catalogue, ed J. Stevenson 2 vols 1859.
Doyle, A. I. The Bamburgh Library. Book Collector 8 1959.
Birmingham
Parish, C. History of the Birmingham Library: an 18th-century proprietary library 1779–99, with a chapter on the later history to 1955. 1966.
Bradford
Scruton, W. The Bradford Library and Literary Society. Lib Assoc Record 8 1906.
Bristol
Tovey, C. A free library for Bristol; with a history of the City Library, its founders and its benefactors. Bristol 1855.
Matthews, E. R. N. History of the Public Library in Bristol. Bristol 1906.

Kaufman, P. Borrowings from the Bristol Library 1773–84: a unique record of reading vogues. Charlottesville 1960 (Bibl Soc of Univ of Virginia).
Booth, S. M. Three hundred years of public libraries in Bristol. Bristol 1964.
Bury St Edmunds
Bartholomew, A. T. and C. Gordon. On the library at King Edward VI School, Bury St Edmunds. Library 3rd ser 1 1910.
Canterbury Cathedral
[Eyre and Norris]. Catalogus librorum bibliothecae ecclesiae Christi Cantuariensis. Canterbury 1743; Catalogue of the mss, Canterbury 1793; Catalogue of books, both ms and printed, 1802. See M. Beazeley, Trans Bibl Soc 8 1907.
Carlisle
Holtby, R. T. Carlisle Cathedral Library and records. Trans Cumberland & Westmorland Antiquarian Soc new ser 66 1966.
Cashel Cathedral, Tipperary
Alderson, F. Cashel Cathedral [library]. Book Collector 17 1968.
Church Langton, Leicestershire
Hanbury, W. A plan for a public library at Church Langton. 1760.
Russell, A. W. A plan for a public library at Church Langton 1760. Lib History 1 1969.

Dublin
Abbott, T. K. The book of Trinity College, Dublin 1591–1891. Dublin 1892. Ch 7.
White, N. J. D. An account of Archbishop Marsh's Library, Dublin. Dublin 1926.
The library of Trinity College, Dublin. TLS 16 March 1956.

Dunblane
Catalogues. Edinburgh 1793, 1843.
Couper, W. J. Bibliotheca Leightoniana Dunblane. Glasgow 1917 (priv ptd).

Durham
Hughes, H. D. A history of Durham Cathedral Library. Durham 1925.

Eton College
Birley, R. The history of Eton College Library. Library 5th ser 11 1956.
— The Storer Collection in Eton College Library. Book Collector 5 1956.

Exeter
Lloyd, L. J. The library of Exeter Cathedral. 1956.

Fife
Anderson, A. The old libraries of Fife. Fife 1953.

Glasgow
[Taylor, W.] A catalogue of Stirling's Library. Glasgow 1792; suppl 1795.
Patterson, W. J. S. Stirling's and Glasgow Public Library. Glasgow 1907.

Glasgow University Library
Arthur, A. Catalogus librorum impressorum in bibliotheca. 2 vols Glasgow 1791; suppls 1825, 1835.
Dickson, W. P. Notes on the history of Glasgow University Library. Glasgow 1888.
Black, H. M. and P. Gaskell. Special collections in Glasgow University Library. Book Collector 16 1967.

Halton, Cheshire
Reprint of the Rules and orders 1732, and Catalogue of books 1733 at Halton Library in the Parish of Runcorn, made by Sir John Chesshyre, with a preface by the Rev G. D. Wray. 1898.

Hereford Cathedral
Morgan, F. C. Hereford Cathedral Library: its history and contents. Hereford 1963 (3rd edn rev).

Holt, Norfolk
Lee, P. J. A catalogue of the Foundation Library [at Gresham's School]. Holt Norfolk 1965 (priv ptd).

Innerpeffray
Dickie, W. M. Innerpeffray Library. Lib Assoc Record new ser 6 1928.
Kaufman, P. A unique record of a people's reading. Libri 14 1964.

Ipswich
An account of the gifts to charitable uses in Ipswich. Ipswich 1747. See also H. Ogle, Library Assistant Aug 1904.
A catalogue of the books in the Town Library under the Public Grammar School. Ipswich 1799.

King's Norton
Brassington, W. S. Thomas Hall and the old library founded by him at King's Norton. Lib Chron 5 1888.

Lancashire
Christie, R. C. The old church and school libraries of Lancashire. Manchester 1885 (Chetham Soc).

Leeds
Beckwith, F. The beginnings of the Leeds Subscription Library. Thoresby Soc Pbns 37 1945.

Leicester
Deedes, C. and J. E. and J. L. Stocks. The Old Town Hall Library of Leicester. Oxford 1919 (priv ptd).

Lewes
Button, J. The Lewes Library Society. 1804. A poem.

Manchester, Chetham's Library
Radcliffe, J. Bibliotheca Chethamensis: sive bibliothecae publicae mancuniensis catalogus. 2 vols Manchester 1791; vol 3 ed W. P. Greswell, Manchester 1826; vol 4 ed T. Jones, Manchester 1862; index by T. Jones, Manchester 1863.
Raines, F. R. and C. Sutton. Life of Humphrey Chetham. 2 vols Manchester 1903 (Chetham Soc).
Lofthouse, H. Chetham's Library. Book Collector 5 1956.
Smith, H. S. A. Readers and books in a 17th-century library. Lib Assoc Record 65 1963.

Newark
Morley, J. Newark Book Society 1777–1872. Lib History 1 1969.

Norton, Worcestershire
The parochial library of Norton and Lenchwick, Worcestershire, left by the Rev P. Cassy. [c. 1780]. See also W. C. Boulter, N & Q 30 March 1895.

Norwich
Bret. A catalogue of the books in the Library of the City of Norwich. Norwich 1706.
Mackerell, B. A new catalogue of the books in the Publick Library of the City of Norwich. Norwich 1732; ed F. G. Kitton, Norwich 1883 (3rd edn).
Stephen, G. A. Three centuries of a city library: an historical and descriptive account of the Norwich Public Library, established 1608. Norwich 1917.
Hepworth, P. and M. Alexander. City of Norwich Libraries: history and treasures. Norwich 1957, 1965 (rev as Norwich Public Libraries).
Keeling, D. F. Norwich Public Library: a select bibliography. 1966.

Pembroke
Walters, G. The 18th-century 'Pembroke Society'. Welsh History Rev 3 1967.

St Andrews
Bushnell, G. H. St Andrew's University Library. Book Collector 7 1958.

Sheffield
Ward, T. A. A short account of the Sheffield Library. Sheffield 1825.

Shrewsbury
Oldham, J. B. Shrewsbury School Library: its earlier history and organization. Library 4th ser 16 1936.
— Shrewsbury School Library. Trans of Shropshire Archaeological Soc 51 1943.
— Shrewsbury School Library. Library 5th ser 14 1959.
Kaufman, P. The loan records of Shrewsbury School Library. Library 5th ser 22 1967.

Suffolk
Fitch, J. A. Some ancient Suffolk parochial libraries. Proc Suffolk Inst of Archaeology 30 1966.

Winchester College Library
Oakeshott, W. Winchester College Library before 1750. Library 5th ser 9 1954.
Blakiston, J. M. G. Winchester College Library in the 18th and early 19th centuries. Library 5th ser 17 1962.
— Winchester College. Book Collector 16 1967.

Worcester Cathedral
Floyer, J. K. A thousand years of a cathedral library. Reliquary Jan 1901.

T. BOOK COLLECTORS AND COLLECTING

Vail, R. W. G. The literature of book collecting. New York 1936 (2nd edn).

(1) THE CHOICE OF BOOKS AND THE ARRANGEMENT OF LIBRARIES

Naudé, G. Instructions concerning erecting of a library now interpreted by Jo Evelyn. 1661. First pbd in French, Paris 1628.
Crawford and Balcarres, Earl of. Gabriel Naudé and John Evelyn. Library 4th ser 12 1932.
Barlow, T. Directions for the choice of books in the study of divinity; published by W. Offley. Oxford 1699. First pbd by Sir Peter Pett in Barlow's genuine remains, 1693.
Davies, M. Icon libellorum: or a critical history of pamphlets. 1715.
Middleton, C. Bibliothecae cantabrigiensis ordinandae methodus. Cambridge 1723.
Boswell, J. A method of study: or an useful library in two parts: part 1, containing short directions and a catalogue of books for the study of several valuable parts of learning, viz geography, chronology, history etc; part 2, for divinity. 2 pts 1738–[43].
N., N. Directions for a proper choice of authors to form a library, intended for those readers who are only acquain-

ted with the English language, with a correct list of proper books. 1766.
Kaufman, P. Two 18th-century guides to the choice of books. Lib History 1 1969. Boswell's and N. N.'s.
[Crabbe, G.] The library: a poem. 1781, 1783.
[Sanden, Dr]. On the use of books: a discourse delivered at the anniversary meeting of the Library Society at Chichester. 1800.
Mangin, E. A view of the pleasures arising from the love of books. 1814.
Collins, J. An address to instructors and parents on the right choice and use of books. [1802], 1805 (4th edn); rev S. Catlow 1818.
Dibdin, T. F. The library companion: or the young man's guide and the old man's comfort in the choice of a library. 2 vols 1824.
Dana, J. C. and H. W. Kent (ed). The literature of libraries in the 17th and 18th centuries. 6 vols Chicago 1906–7, Methuen NJ 1967. Reprint of Naudé, Durie etc.

(2) BOOK COLLECTORS

[Oldys, W.] The British librarian. 1738.
Beloe, W. Anecdotes of literature and scarce books. 6 vols 1807–12.
Dibdin, T. F. Bibliomania. 1809, 1811 (enlarged), 1842 (further enlarged).
— The bibliographical Decameron. 3 vols 1817.
[Beresford, J.] Bibliosophia, or book-wisdom: containing some account of the pride, pleasure and privileges of that glorious vocation book-collecting. 1810.
Burton, J. H. The book-hunter. 1860, Edinburgh 1882 (enlarged).
Edwards, E. Libraries and founders of libraries. 1865.
— Free town libraries in Britain, France, Germany and America; together with brief notices of book-collectors, and of the respective places of deposit of their surviving collections. 1869.
— Lives of the founders of the British Museum 1570–1870. 1870.
Quaritch, B. (ed). Contributions towards a dictionary of English book collectors. 14 pts 1892–1921.

Elton, C. I. and M. A. The great book-collectors. 1893.
Roberts, W. The book-hunter in London. 1895.
Fletcher, W. Y. English book collectors. 1902.
Hazlitt, W. C. The book-collector. 1904.
Davenport, C. English heraldic book-stamps. 1909. A copy with much necessary annotation by W. A. Jackson is in Houghton Library, Harvard.
De Ricci, S. English collectors of books and mss 1530–1930 and their marks of ownership. Cambridge 1930.
Carter, J. Taste and technique in book-collecting. Cambridge 1948.
King, A. H. Some British collectors of music, c. 1600–1960. Cambridge 1963.
Morgan, F. C. Dr William Brewster of Hereford, c. 1665–1715: a benefactor to libraries. Medical History 8 1964.
Munby, A. N. L. The libraries of English men of letters. 1964.
Harrison, J. and P. Laslett. The library of John Locke. Oxford 1965 (Oxford Bibl Soc).

(3) BOOK PLATES

Fineham, H. W. and J. R. Brown. The bibliography of book plates. Plymouth 1892 (priv ptd).
Castle, E. English book-plates. 1892.
Hamilton, W. Dated book-plates, with a treatise on their origin. 1895.
Almack, E. Bookplates. 1904.

Evans, C. T. and C. S. Baer. A census of bookplate collections in public, college and university libraries in the United States. Washington 1938.
Viner, G. H. The origin and evolution of the bookplate. Library 5th ser 1 1947.

(4) INDIVIDUAL COLLECTORS

Richard Smith
[Sale catalogue of his library, with preface, priced]. 1682.
Duff, E. G. The library of Richard Smith. Library 2nd ser 8 1907.
George Thomason
Spencer, L. The professional and literary connexions of George Thomason. Library 5th ser 13 1958.
John Evelyn
Keynes, G. L. Evelyn: a study in bibliophily and a

bibliography of his writings. Cambridge 1937, Oxford 1968 (rev).
Samuel Pepys
Bibliotheca Pepysiana: a descriptive catalogue of the library of Pepys. 4 vols 1914–40.
Gaselee, S. Pepys's Spanish books. Library 4th ser 2 1922. See Suppl to Bibl Soc Trans 2 1921.
Jackson, W. A. Tunc et nunc: or the Pepys and Taylor collections of early English books on navigation. In Essays honoring L. C. Wroth, Portland Maine 1951.

Emslie, MacD. Pepys's songs and songbooks in the diary period. Library 5th ser 12 1957.

Goldstein, L. M. The Pepys ballads. Library 5th ser 21 1966.

John Gray

Gray, W. F. A 17th-century Scottish library [of the Rev John Gray, at Haddington, E. Lothian].TLS 5 June 1948.

Richard Coffin

The Portledge papers 1687–97. Ed R. J. Kerr and I. C. Duncan 1928.

John Bagford

Fletcher, W. Y. Bagford and his collections. Bibl Soc Trans 4 1898.

Humfrey Wanley

Gillam, S. G. and R. W. Hunt. The curators of the [Bodleian] Library and Wanley. Bodleian Lib Record 5 1956.

Wright, C. E. A 'lost' account-book [of N. Noel] and the Harleian Library. BM Quart 31 1967.

— and R. C. Wright (ed). The diary of Wanley 1715–26. 2 vols 1966 (Bibl Soc). Introd pbd separately.

Thomas Hearne

Remarks and collections of Hearne [Collectanea 1705–33]. Ed C. E. Doble et al 11 vols 1885–1921 (Oxford Historical Soc).

Thomas and Richard Rawlinson

[Sale] catalogue of the library of Thomas Rawlinson FRS. 16 pts 1721–33.

Bibliotheca Rawlinsonia [sale catalogue]. 1756; Catalogue of the remaining part of the books of R. Rawlinson, 1757.

Fletcher, W. Y. Thomas and Richard Rawlinson and their collections. Bibl Soc Trans 5 1899.

Enright, B. J. Rawlinson and the chandlers. Bodleian Lib Record 4 1953.

— The later auction sales of Thomas Rawlinson's library, 1727–34. Library 5th ser 11 1956.

Edward Harley, Earl of Oxford

[Johnson, S. and W. Oldys]. Catalogus bibliothecae Harleianae [printed books]. 5 vols 1743–5; Catalogue of the Harleian mss in the British Museum, 2 vols 1759–63, 4 vols 1808–12.

Turberville, A. S. A history of Welbeck Abbey and its owners vol 1. 1938.

Wright, C. E. Edward Harley, 2nd Earl of Oxford

1689–1741. Book Collector 11 1962. *See also under Humfrey Wanley, above.*

James West

Lucas, R. C. Book-collecting in the 18th century: the library of James West. Library 5th ser 3 1949.

Joseph Massie

Bibliography of the collection of books and tracts on commerce, currency and poor law 1557–1763 formed by Joseph Massie. Ed W. A. Shaw 1937.

Horace Walpole

Lewis, W. S. Horace Walpole's library. Cambridge 1958.

Hazen, A. T. The earlier owners of Walpole's books. In Horace Walpole: writer, politician and connoisseur, ed W. H. Smith, New Haven 1967.

— A catalogue of Horace Walpole's library. 3 vols New Haven 1969.

Thomas Hollis

Blackburne, F. Memoirs of Thomas Hollis. 1780.

Thomas Percy

Leslie, S. The Percy library. Book Collector's Quart 14 1934.

Shearer, T. and A. Tillotson. Percy's relations with Cadell and Davies. Library 4th ser 15 1935.

Brooks, C. The country parson as research scholar: Percy 1760–70. PBSA 53 1959.

Edward Gibbon

Keynes, G. L. The library of Gibbon: a catalogue of his books. 1940, 1969.

George III

[Bernard, F. A.] Bibliothecae regiae catalogus. 5 vols 1820–9.

Holmes, R. R. George III as a collector. Proc Royal Institution 16 1901.

Edmond Malone

A [sale] catalogue of the greater portion of the library of Edmond Malone esq. 1818.

Osborn, J. M. Edmond Malone: scholar-collector. Library 5th ser 19 1964.

John Byng, Viscount Torrington

Andrews, C. B. A book-collector of the 18th century. Book Collector's Quart 13 1934.

Anthony Storer

Birley, R. The Storer Collection in Eton College Library. Book Collector 5 1956.

Charles Burney

Forshall, J. Catalogue of the mss in the British Museum. New ser 1 pt 2, 1840.

(5) CATALOGUES OF PRIVATE COLLECTIONS BEFORE 1801

[Gibson, E.] Librorum manuscriptorum in duabus insignibus bibliothecis; altera Tenisoniana; altera Dugdaliana Oxonii; catalogus. Oxford 1692.

Bridges, J. Catalogus librorum. 1725. Sold by auction 7 Feb 1726 and following days.

Pierrepont, E., Duke of Kingston. Catalogus bibliothecae Kingstonianae. [1726].

Sydenham, P. Catalogue of the library of. 1727.

Bruce, Viscount, C. Catalogue of the books of Charles Viscount Bruce, son of the Earl of Ailesbury, in his library at Totenham, Wilts. 1733.

Douglas, J. Catalogus editionum Quinti Horatii Flacci 1476–1739 quae in bibliotheca Jacobi Douglas adservantur. 1739.

Ruddiman, T. Bibliotheca classica. Edinburgh 1757. A catalogue of the best edns of the classics, collected by Ruddiman; sold by auction in Edinburgh, Feb 1757.

Campbell, A., Duke of Argyll. [Catalogue by A. McBean]. Glasgow 1758.

Hoblyn, R. Bibliotheca Hoblyniana: sive catalogus librorum. 2 vols 1768, 1769.

Catalogus librorum in bibliotheca Osterleiensi. 1771. This catalogue was compiled by Thomas Morell; the books had been collected by Brian Fairfax, and on his death

in 1759 passed into the possession of the Earls of Jersey. Sold on 6 May 1885 and following days.

Martin, T. A catalogue of the library of Thomas Martin of Palsgrave in Suffolk, deceased. Lynn 1772. Sold by auction 28 April 1773 and following days.

Willett, R. A description of the library at Merly. 1776 (8°); 1785 (folio with plates); A catalogue of the books in the library at Merly, 1790. Sold by auction 6 Dec 1813 and following days.

Capell, E. Catalogue of Mr Capell's Shakespeariana. Presented by him to Trinity Coll Cambridge. 1779 (priv ptd); rptd in C. H. Hartshorne, Book rarities in the University of Cambridge, 1829.

Important English collections dispersed by auction before 1801 include: Richard Smith, 1682; Francis Bernard, 1698; Thomas Britton, 1715, Nov 1694; Thomas Rawlinson, 1721–34; Thomas Hearne, 1736; Michael Maittaire, 1748; Richard Mead, 1754–5, 1783; Richard Rawlinson, 1756–7; Joseph Ames, 1760; James West, 1773; Anthony Askew, 1775, 1785; John Ratcliffe, 1776; Thomas Crofts, 1783; Edward Wynne [including Narcissus Luttrell's library], 1786; Thomas Pearson, 1788; George Steevens, 1800.

T. B. and H. G. P.

2. POETRY

I. HISTORIES AND SURVEYS

(1) LITERARY HISTORIES

Johnson, S. Prefaces biographical and critical to the works of the English poets. 10 vols 1779–81; ed G. B. Hill as Lives of the English poets, 3 vols Oxford 1905.

Hazlitt, W. Lectures on the English poets. 1818; ed F. W. Baxter, Oxford 1929.

Gosse, E. From Shakespeare to Pope: an inquiry into the causes and phenomena of the rise of classical poetry in England. Cambridge 1885.

Phelps, W. L. The beginnings of the English romantic movement. Boston 1893.

Beers, H. A. A history of English romanticism in the eighteenth century. New York 1898, 1899, 1910 (rev).

Courthope, W. J. History of English poetry. Vols 3–6, 1903–10.

Symons, A. The romantic movement in English poetry. 1909.

Brooke, S. A. Naturalism in English poetry. 1920, 1922 (abbreviated).

de Maar, H. G. A history of modern English romanticism. Vol 1, Elizabethan and modern romanticism in the eighteenth century, Oxford 1924, New York 1964.

Partridge, E. H. Eighteenth-century English romantic poetry. Paris 1924.

Berger, P. Les poètes préromantiques anglais. Paris [1925].

Williamson, G. The Donne tradition: a study in English poetry from Donne to the death of Cowley [1677]. Cambridge Mass 1930.

Elton, O. The English Muse. 1933.

Sharp, R. L. From Donne to Dryden: the revolt against metaphysical poetry. Chapel Hill 1940, Hamden 1965.

Grierson, H. J. C. and J. C. Smith. A critical history of English poetry. 1947 (2nd edn).

Lemonnier, L. Les poètes anglais du dix-huitième siècle. Paris 1947.

Sherburn, G. The Restoration and eighteenth century 1660–1789. In A literary history of England, ed A. C. Baugh, New York 1948, 1967 (with suppl by D. F. Bond).

Sutherland, J. R. A preface to eighteenth-century poetry. Oxford 1948, 1962 (with additional notes).

— English literature of the late seventeenth century. Oxford 1969 (OHEL vol 6).

Bredvold, L. I. The literature of the Restoration and eighteenth century. In A history of English literature, ed H. Craig, New York 1950.

Walton, G. Metaphysical to Augustan: studies in tone and sensibility in the seventeenth century. 1955.

Bald, R. C. Seventeenth-century English poetry. New York 1959.

Dobrée, B. English literature in the early eighteenth century 1700–40. Oxford 1959 (OHEL vol 7).

Hopkins, K. English poetry: a short history. 1962.

Renwick, W. L. English literature 1789–1815. Oxford 1963 (OHEL vol 9).

Price, M. To the palace of wisdom: studies in order and energy from Dryden to Blake. New York 1964.

Trickett, R. The honest Muse: a study in Augustan verse [1660–1760]. Oxford 1967.

(2) CRITICAL SURVEYS

[Palgrave, F. T.] English poetry from Dryden to Cowper. Quart Rev 112 1862.

Shairp, J. C. English poetry in the eighteenth century. Princeton Rev 14 1881.

Dixon, W. M. English poetry from Blake to Browning. 1894. Ch 2, An era of transition.

Seccombe, T. and G. Saintsbury. Lesser verse writers [1700–50]. CHEL 9 1912.

Whibley, C. The Court poets. CHEL 8 1912; rptd in his Literary studies, 1919.

Saintsbury, G. Young, Collins and lesser poets of the age of Johnson. CHEL 10 1913.

— Lesser poets of the later eighteenth century. CHEL 11 1914.

Thompson, A. H. Thomson and natural description in poetry. CHEL 10 1913.

Murry, J. M. English poetry of the eighteenth century. In his Discoveries, 1924.

Williams, I. A. Seven eighteenth-century bibliographies. 1924. Contains essays on Armstrong, Shenstone, Akenside, Goldsmith, Collins, Churchill, Sheridan.

Buxton, C. R. Eighteenth-century poetry and the classical and the romantic in poetry. In his A politician plays truant, 1929.

Bernbaum, E. The pre-romantic movement. In his Guide through the romantic movement, New York 1930, 1949 (rev and enlarged).

Leavis, F. R. English poetry in the seventeenth [and eighteenth] century. Scrutiny 4–5 1935–6.

— Revaluation: tradition and development in English poetry. 1936. Chs 1–4.

Smith, D. N. Some observations on eighteenth-century poetry. Oxford 1937.

Evans, B. I. The eighteenth century. In his Tradition and romanticism, 1940.

Miles, J. The naming of emotions: its place in the theory and poetry of the eighteenth century. In her Wordsworth and the vocabulary of emotion, Berkeley 1942.

Renwick, W. L. Notes on some lesser poets of the eighteenth century. In Essays in the eighteenth century presented to D. N. Smith, Oxford 1945.

Doughty, W. L. Studies in religious poetry of the seventeenth century. 1946.

Wilson, J. H. The Court wits of the Restoration: an introduction. Princeton 1948.

The age of Johnson: essays presented to C. B. Tinker, New Haven 1949.

Wallerstein, R. C. Studies in seventeenth-century poetic. Madison 1950.

Bronson, B. The pre-romantic or post-Augustan mode. ELH 20 1953.

Wimsatt, W. K. The Augustan mode in English poetry. ELH 20 1953; rptd in his Hateful contraries, Lexington Kentucky 1965.

— The verbal icon: studies in the meaning of poetry. Lexington 1954.

Cruttwell, P. The Shakespearean moment and its place in the poetry of the seventeenth century. 1954. Chs 8–9.

Unwin, R. The rural Muse: studies in the peasant poetry of England. 1954.

Ker, W. P. On modern literature. Oxford 1955. Essays on Butler, Milton, Dryden, Burns, Crabbe.

Callan, N. Augustan reflective poetry. In From Dryden to Johnson, ed. B. Ford, 1957 (Pelican).

Miles, J. Eras and modes in English poetry [1500–1900]. Berkeley 1957, 1964 (rev).

— Towards a theory of style and change. Jnl of Aesthetics 22 1964.

Nikoljukin, A. N. Die Massenpoesie in England am Ende des 18 und zum Beginn des 19 Jahrhunderts. Zeitschrift für Anglistik und Amerikanistik 5 1957.

Ernst, F. Die Entdeckung der Volkspoesie in 18 Jahrhundert in Forschungsprobleme der vergleichenden Literaturgeschichte. Tübingen 1958.

Wasserman, E. R. The subtler language: critical readings of neoclassic and romantic poems. Baltimore 1959. On Windsor forest etc.

Friedman, A. B. The ballad revival: studies in the influence of popular on sophisticated poetry. Chicago 1961.

Allison, A. W. Towards an Augustan poetic: Edmund Waller's reform of English poetry. Lexington Kentucky 1962.

Praz, M. Baroque in England. MP 61 1964.

Pinto, V. de S. The Restoration Court poets. 1965. On Rochester, Dorset, Sedley, Etherege.

Buxton, J. A tradition of poetry. 1967. On Waller, Cotton, Lady Winchelsea.

Cohen, R. The Augustan mode in English poetry. Eighteenth-century Stud 1 1967; rptd in Studies in the eighteenth century, ed R. F. Brissenden, Canberra 1968.

Spacks, P. M. The poetry of vision: five eighteenth-century poets. Cambridge Mass 1967. Cowper, Gray, Smart, Collins, Thomson.

Stone, P. W. K. The art of poetry 1750–1820: theories of poetic composition and style. 1967.

Thorpe, P. Some fallacies in the study of Augustan poetry. Criticism 9 1967.

(3) THE POETIC KINDS

Fehr, B. The antagonism of forms in the eighteenth century. E Studies 19 1937.

Epic

Clark, J. A history of epic poetry. Edinburgh 1900.

Dixon, W. M. English epic and heroic poetry. 1912.

Abercrombie, L. The epic. 1914.

Nitchie, E. Vergil and the English poets. New York 1919.

Swedenberg, H. T. The theory of the epic in England 1650–1800. Berkeley 1944.

— Rules and English criticism of epic. In Essential articles for the study of English Augustan backgrounds, ed B. N. Schilling, Hamden Conn 1961.

Perkinson, R. H. The epic in five acts. SP 43 1946.

Tillyard, E. M. W. The English epic and its background. Oxford 1954.

Proudfoot, L. Dryden's Aeneid and its seventeenth-century predecessors. Manchester 1960.

Broich, U. Das Lehrgedicht als Teil der epischen Tradition des englischen Klassizismus. Germanische-romanische Monatsschrift 44 1963.

Hägin, P. The epic hero and the decline of heroic poetry. Berne 1964.

Eade, C. Some English Iliads: Chapman to Dryden. Arion 6 1967.

Hayley, W. An essay on epic poetry 1782. Ed M. C. Williamson, Gainesville 1968.

Lyric

Dennis, J. English lyrical poetry. In his Studies in English literature, 1876. Rev from Cornhill Mag 1874.

Reed, E. B. English lyrical poetry from its origins to the present time. New Haven 1912.

Saintsbury, G. The historical character of the English lyric. Proc Br Acad 5 1912.

Rhys, E. Lyric poetry. 1913.

Schelling, F. E. The English lyric. Boston 1913.

Schafer, R. The English ode and 1660: an essay in literary history. Princeton 1920.

Doughty, O. English lyric in the Age of Reason. 1922.

— Eighteenth-century song. E Studies 7 1925.

Lieser, P. Die englische Ode im Zeitalter des Klassizismus. Bonn 1932.

Noyes, R. G. Songs from Restoration drama in contemporary and eighteenth-century poetical miscellanies. ELH 3 1936.

— and R. Lamson. Broadside ballad versions of the songs in Restoration drama. Harvard Stud 19 1937.

Lamson, R. Henry Purcell's dramatic songs and the English broadside ballad. PMLA 53 1938.

Sands, M. English song-writers of the eighteenth century. Monthly Musical Record 1939.

Shuster, G. N. The English ode from Milton to Keats. New York 1940.

Sampson, G. The century of divine songs. Proc Br Acad 29 1943.

Peltz, C. W. The neo-classic lyric 1660–1725. ELH 11 1944.

Myers, R. M. Neo-classical criticism of the ode for music. PMLA 62 1947.

Maclean, N. From action to image: theories of lyric in the eighteenth century. In Critics and criticism, ancient and modern, ed R. S. Crane, Chicago 1952.

Hart, E. F. The Restoration catch. Music & Letters 34 1953.

— Caroline lyrics and contemporary song-books. Library 5th ser 8 1953.

Røstvig, M.-S. Casimire Sarbiewski and the English ode. SP 51 1954.

Maclean, N. Personification but not poetry. ELH 23 1956. On lyric.

Cohen, J. M. The baroque lyric. 1963.

Richmond, H. M. The school of love: the evolution of the Stuart love lyric. Princeton 1964.

Schlüter, K. Die englische Ode. Bonn 1964.

Sonnet

Attenborough, G. M. The sonnet from Milton to Wordsworth. GM April 1902.

Rinaker, C. Thomas Edwards and the sonnet revival. MLN 34 1919.

Havens, R. D. A history of the sonnet in the eighteenth and early nineteenth centuries. Ch 19 of his Influence of Milton on English poetry, Cambridge Mass 1922, New York 1961. With bibliographies; suppl by R. P. McCutcheon, MLN 40 1925.

— More eighteenth-century sonnets. MLN 45 1930.

Eclogue

Mantz, H. E. Non-dramatic pastoral in Europe in the eighteenth century. PMLA 31 1916.

Jones, R. F. Eclogue types in English poetry of the eighteenth century. JEGP 24 1925.

Bragg, M. K. The formal eclogue in eighteenth-century England. Maine Univ Stud ser 2 no 6 1926.

Empson, W. Some versions of pastoral. 1935.

Lang, V. Crabbe and the eighteenth century. ELH 5 1938.

Wasserman, E. R. Introd to T. Purney, Full enquiry into the true nature of pastoral (1717), Los Angeles 1948 (Augustan Reprint Soc).

Congleton, J. E. Theories of pastoral poetry in England 1684–1798. Gainesville 1952.

Suzuki, Z. The background of the pastoral controversy

in the eighteenth century. Stud in Eng Lit (Tokyo) 40 1964. English synopsis given.

Fowler, J. Decay in the corporate mind: some perversions of pastoral words. Wellington 1965.

McCoy, D. S. Tradition and convention: a study of periphrasis in English pastoral poetry from 1557–1715. Hague 1965.

Georgic

Lilly, M. L. The georgic: a contribution to the study of the Vergilian type of didactic poetry. Baltimore 1919.

Durling, D. L. Georgic tradition in English poetry. New York 1935.

Hooker, E. M. Dryden's Georgics and English predecessors. HLQ 9 1946.

Boddy, M. P. The 1692 fourth book of Virgil. RES new ser 15 1964. On verse trns.

Burlesque and Mock-Heroic

Imitations of Hudibras 1663–1755. Retrospective Rev 3 1821.

Whibley, C. Writers of burlesques and translators. CHEL 9 1912.

Whitford, R. C. On the origin of 'Probationary odes for the Laureateship'. MLN 35 1920.

Brie, F. Englische Rokoko-epik 1710–30. Munich 1927.

West, A. H. L'influence française dans la poésie burlesque en Angleterre entre 1660 et 1700. Paris 1931.

Kitchin, G. A survey of burlesque and parody in English. 1931. Chs 3–7.

Bond, R. P. English burlesque poetry 1700–50. Cambridge Mass 1932.

Bush, D. Mythology and the Renaissance tradition in English poetry. Minneapolis 1932. Ch 15.

Richards, E. A. Hudibras in the burlesque tradition. New York 1937. With list of Hudibrastic poems 1662–1830.

Broich, U. Studien zum komischen Epos: ein Beitrag zur Deutung, Typologie und Geschichte des komischen Epos im englischen Klassizismus 1680–1800. Tübingen 1968.

Satire

Hannay, J. Satire and satirists: six lectures. 1854.

— English political satires. In his Essays, 1861.

Previté-Orton, C. W. Political satire in English poetry. Cambridge 1910.

Whitford, R. C. Satire's view of sentimentalism in the days of George III. JEGP 18 1919.

— Juvenal in England 1750–1802. PQ 7 1928.

Walker, H. English satire and satirists. 1925.

Bond, R. P. —iad: a progeny of the Dunciad. PMLA 44 1929. Suppl by M. Kelley 46 1931.

Wells, H. W. The seven against London: a study in the satirical tradition of Augustan poetry. Sewanee Rev 47 1939. In verse.

Randolph, M. C. 'Hide-and-seek' satires of the Restoration and eighteenth century. N & Q 10 Oct 1942.

— The structural design of the formal verse satire. PQ 21 1942.

— Diamond-satires in the eighteenth century. N & Q 31 July 1943.

— 'Candour' in eighteenth-century satire. RES 20 1944.

— Satirical recipes of the eighteenth century. N & Q 15 Jan 1944.

Boyce, B. News from Hell: satiric communications with the nether world in English writing of the seventeenth and eighteenth centuries. PMLA 58 1943.

Bishop, C. R. Peace is my dear delight. West Virginia Univ Bull, Philosophical Stud 4 1943. On conventions of satire.

Brown, W. C. Dramatic tension in neo-classic satire. College Eng Feb 1945.

Bredvold, L. I. The gloom of the Tory satirists. In Pope and his contemporaries: essays presented to George Sherburn, Oxford 1949; rptd in Eighteenth-century English literature, ed J. L. Clifford, New York 1959.

Brooks, H. F. The 'imitation' in English poetry, especially in formal satire, before Pope. RES 25 1949.

Jack, I. Augustan satire: intention and idiom in English poetry 1660–1750. Oxford 1952.

Mack, M. The Muse of satire. Yale Rev 41 1951; rptd in Studies in the literature of the Augustan age: essays in honor of A. E. Case, Ann Arbor 1952.

Wilkinson, A. M. The decline of English verse satire in the middle years of the eighteenth century. RES new ser 3 1952.

— The rise of English verse satire in the eighteenth century. E Studies 34 1953.

Leyburn, E. D. Satiric allegory: mirror of man. New Haven 1956.

Hopkins, K. Portraits in satire. 1958. Churchill to 'Peter Pindar'.

Sutherland, J. R. English satire. Cambridge 1958.

Pagrot, L. Den klassiska verssatirens teori, debatten kring genren från Horatius t.o.m. 1700-talet. Stockholm 1961. On theory of formal verse satire.

Youngren, W. Generality in Augustan satire. In In defense of reading, ed R. A. Brower and R. Poirier, New York 1962.

Goldgar, B. A. Satires on man and 'the dignity of human nature'. PMLA 80 1965. On prose and poetry.

Sutherland, W. O. S. The art of the satirist: essays on the satire of Augustan England. Austin 1965. On prose and poetry.

Weinbrot, H. D. The pattern of formal verse satire in the Restoration and eighteenth century. PMLA 80 1965.

— The formal strain: studies in Augustan imitation and satire. Chicago 1969.

Hayman, J. Raillery in Restoration satire. HLQ 31 1968.

Frost, W. English Persius: the Golden Age. Eighteenth-Century Stud 2 1969.

Pinkus, P. The new satire of Augustan England. UTQ 38 1969.

Other Types

Holland, J. The psalmists of Britain. 2 vols 1843.

Plessow, M. Geschichte der Fabeldichtung in England bis zu John Gay 1726. Berlin 1906.

Müller, C. Robert Blair's Grave und die Grabes-und nachtdichtung. Weimar 1909.

Bett, H. The hymns of Methodism in their literary relations. 1913, 1920, 1945 (rev and enlarged).

Thomson, C. L. English history in contemporary poetry: the eighteenth century. 1914.

Hustvedt, S. B. Ballad criticism in Scandinavia and Great Britain during the eighteenth century. New York 1916.

Smith, M. E. Notes on the rimed fable in England. MLN 31 1916.

Griffith, R. H. The progress pieces of the eighteenth century. Texas Rev 5 1920. Suppl by R. A. Aubin, MLN 49 1934.

Hittmair, R. England im Spiegel der State-poems, Ende des 17, Aufgang des 18 Jahrhunderts. In Festschrift der Nationalbibliothek in Wien, Vienna 1926.

Moore, C. A. Whig panegyric verse 1700–60: a phase of sentimentalism. PMLA 41 1926; rptd in his Backgrounds of English literature 1700–60, Minneapolis 1953.

Nichols, C. L. The Holy Bible in verse 1699–1754. Proc Amer Antiquarian Soc 36 1927.

Draper, J. W. The funeral elegy and the rise of English romanticism. New York 1929.

Wright, L. S. Eighteenth-century replies to Pope's Eloisa. SP 31 1934.

Aubin, R. A. Topographical poetry in eighteenth-century England. New York 1936.

Gaertner, A. Die englische Epithalamienliteratur im siebzehnten Jahrhundert und ihre Vorbilder. Coburg 1936.

Schirmer, W. F. Das Problem des religiösen Epos im 17 Jahrhundert in England. Deutsche Vierteljahrschrift für Literaturwissenschaft 14 1936.

Swayne, M. The progress piece in the seventeenth century. SE 16 1936.

Draper, J. W. The metrical tale in eighteenth-century England. PMLA 52 1937.

Wallis, N. H. 'Fugitive poetry': an eighteenth-century collection. Trans of Royal Soc of Lit 18 1940.

Osborne, M. T. Advice-to-a-painter poems 1633–1856: an annotated finding list. Austin 1949.

Miles, J. The sublime poem. Univ of Calif Pbns, English Stud 11 1955.

Hibbard, G. R. The country house poem of the seventeenth century. Jnl of Warburg & Courtauld Inst 19 1956.

Miller, H. K. The paradoxical encomium with special reference to its vogue in England 1600–1800. MP 53 1956.

Goldberg, M. A. The language of art and reality: a study of eighteenth-century hill poems. Boston Univ Stud in Eng 3 1957.

Stewart, K. The ballad and the genres in the eighteenth century. ELH 24 1957.

Levine, J. A. The status of the verse epistle before Pope. SP 59 1962.

Nevo, R. The dial of virtue: a study of poems on affairs of state in the seventeenth century. Princeton 1963.

Quaintance, R. E. French sources of the Restoration 'imperfect enjoyment' poem. PQ 42 1963.

Chernaik, W. L. The heroic occasional poem: panegyric and satire in the Restoration. MLQ 26 1965.

England, M. W. and J. Sparrow. Hymns unbidden: Donne, Herbert, Blake, Emily Dickinson and the hymnographers. New York 1966.

Weinbrot, H. D. Translation and parody: towards the genealogy of the Augustan imitation. ELH 33 1966.

Bernhardt-Kabitsch, E. The epitaph and the romantic poets: a survey. HLQ 30 1967. The 18th-century tradition considered.

Moskovit, L. A. Pope and the tradition of neoclassical imitation. Stud in Eng Lit 1500–1900 8 1968.

Price, M. The sublime poem: pictures and powers. Yale Rev 58 1968.

(4) INFLUENCE OF EARLIER ENGLISH POETS

Milton

Pancoast, H. S. Some paraphrases of Milton. Andover Rev 15 1891.

Dowden, E. Milton in the eighteenth century 1701–50. Proc Br Acad 3 1908.

Havens, R. D. Seventeenth-century notices of Milton. E Studien 40 1909.

— The influence of Milton on English poetry [1660–1837]. Cambridge Mass 1922, New York 1961; suppl by E. R. Wasserman, MLN 58 1943.

Good, J. W. Studies in the Milton tradition. Urbana 1915.

Sherburn, G. The early popularity of Milton's minor poems. MP 19 1920.

Moore, C. A. Miltoniana 1679–1741. MP 24 1927.

Moore, J. R. Milton among the Augustans: the infernal council. SP 48 1951. On prose and verse.

Other Poets

Schelling, F. E. Ben Jonson and the classical school. PMLA 13 1898; rptd in his Shakespeare and 'demi-science', Philadelphia 1927.

Reuning, K. Das Altertümliche im Wortschatz der Spensernachahmungen des 18 Jahrhunderts. Strasbourg 1912.

Cory, H. E. Edmund Spenser: a critical study. Berkeley 1917.

Crane, R. S. Imitation of Spenser and Milton in the early eighteenth century: a new document. SP 15 1918.

Nethercot, A. H. The reputation of the 'metaphysical poets' during the seventeenth century. JEGP 23 1924.

— The reputation of the 'metaphysical poets' during the Age of Pope. PQ 4 1925.

— The reputation of the 'metaphysical poets' during the age of Johnson and the 'romantic revival'. SP 22 1925.

McPeek, J. A. S. Catullus in strange and distant Britain. Cambridge Mass 1939.

Hunt, C. The Elizabethan background of neo-classic polite verse. ELH 8 1941.

Wasserman, E. R. Elizabethan poetry in the eighteenth century. Urbana 1947.

Kliger, S. The neo-classical view of Old English poetry. JEGP 49 1950.

Kimney, J. L. John Cleveland and the satiric couplet in the Restoration. PQ 37 1958.

(5) THEORIES, MOVEMENTS AND IDEAS

Nature and Natural Description

Reynolds, M. The treatment of nature in English poetry between Pope and Wordsworth. Chicago 1896, 1909 (rev), New York 1966.

Palgrave, F. T. Landscape in poetry, from Homer to Tennyson. 1897. Ch 13.

Heide, A. von der. Das Naturgefühl in der englischen Dichtung im Zeitalter Miltons. Heidelberg 1915.

Moore, C. A. The return to nature in English poetry of the eighteenth century. SP 14 1917; rptd in his Backgrounds of English literature, Minneapolis 1953.

Manwaring, E. W. Italian landscape in English poetry of the eighteenth century. In her Italian landscape in eighteenth-century England, Oxford 1926.

Hussey, C. The picturesque. 1927.

Vines, S. Nature and the Augustan poets. Stud in Eng Lit (Tokyo) 1927.

Das, P. K. Evidences of a growing taste for nature in the age of Pope. Calcutta 1928.

de Haas, C. E. Nature and the country in English poetry of the first half of the eighteenth century. Amsterdam 1928.

Van Tieghem, P. L'automne dans la poésie ouest-européenne 1720–1820. In Mélanges F. Baldensperger vol 2, Paris 1930.

— Les divers aspects du sentiment de la nature dans la littérature ouest-européenne du dix-huitième siècle. Rptd from Omagui lui Ramiro Ortiz, Bucharest 1930.

Williams, G. G. The beginnings of nature poetry in the eighteenth century. SP 27 1930.

Wilson, M. The twilight of the Augustans. E & S 20 1934.

Deane, C. V. Aspects of eighteenth-century nature poetry. Oxford 1935.

Willey, B. The turn of the century [1700]. In Seventeenth-century studies presented to Sir Herbert Grierson, Oxford 1938.

— The eighteenth-century background. 1940.

Neff, E. A revolution in European poetry 1660–1900. New York 1940.

Stuart, D. M. Landscape in Augustan verse. E & S 26 1940.

Bush, M. D. Rational proof of a Deity from the order of nature. ELH 9 1942.

Emery, C. M. Optics and beauty. MLQ 3 1942.

— The poet and the plough. Agricultural History 16 1942.

Fitzgerald, M. M. First follow nature: primitivism in English poetry 1725–50. New York 1947.

Priestley, F. E. L. Newton and the romantic concept of nature. Univ of Texas Quart 17 1948.

Arthos, J. The language of natural description in eighteenth-century poetry. Ann Arbor 1949.

Hunter, W. B. The seventeenth-century doctrine of plastic nature. Harvard Theological Rev 43 1950.

Wasserman, E. R. Nature moralized: the divine analogy in the eighteenth century. ELH 20 1953.

Nicolson, M. H. Mountain gloom and mountain glory: the development of the aesthetics of the infinite. Ithaca 1959.

Elioseff, L. A. Pastorals, politics and the idea of nature in the reign of Queen Anne. Jnl of Aesthetics 21 1963.

Dobrée, B. Nature poetry in the early eighteenth century. E & S new ser 18 1965.

Malins, E. G. English landscaping and literature 1660–1840. Oxford 1966.

Stewart, S. The enclosed garden: the tradition and the image in seventeenth-century poetry. Madison 1966.

Frodsham, J. D. Landscape poetry in China and Europe. Comparative Lit 19 1967.

Williams, R. 'Nature's threads'. Eighteenth-Century Stud 2 1968. On Thomson, Goldsmith, Gray, Cowper, Shenstone.

Other Themes

Brooke, S. A. The development of theology as illustrated in English poetry from 1780–1830. 1893.

Harrison, J. S. Platonism in English poetry of the sixteenth and seventeenth centuries. New York 1903.

Farley, F. E. Scandinavian influences in the English romantic movement. Boston 1903.

— Three 'Lapland songs'. PMLA 21 1906.

— The dying Indian. In G. L. Kittredge anniversary papers, Boston 1913.

Havens, R. D. Literature of melancholy. MLN 24 1909.

— Changing taste in the eighteenth century: a study of Dryden's and Dodsley's Miscellanies. PMLA 44 1929.

Cory, H. E. Spenser, Thomson and romanticism. PMLA 26 1911.

Cazamian, L. L'intuition panthéiste chez les romantiques anglais. In his Études de psychologie littéraire, Paris 1913.

Burd, H. A. The Golden Age idea in eighteenth-century poetry. Sewanee Rev 23 1915.

Moore, C. A. Shaftesbury and the ethical poets in England 1700–60. PMLA 31 1916.

Osborne, E. Oriental diction and theme in English verse 1740–1840. Kansas Univ Bull 2 1916.

Crane, R. S. An early eighteenth-century enthusiast for primitive poetry: John Husbands. MLN 37 1922.

Snyder, E. D. The Celtic revival in English literature 1760–1800. Cambridge Mass 1923.

Haferkorn, R. Gotik und Ruine in der englischen Dichtung des achzehnten Jahrhunderts. Leipzig 1924.

Reed, A. L. The background of Gray's Elegy: a study in the taste for melancholy poetry 1700–51. New York 1924.

Van Tieghem, P. La notion de vraie poésie dans le préromantisme européen. In his Le préromantisme ser 1, Paris 1924.

— La poésie de la nuit et des tombeaux au dix-huitième siècle [rev]; Les idylles de Gessner et le rêve pastoral. In his Le préromantisme ser 2, Paris 1930.

Draper, J. W. The funeral elegy and the rise of English romanticism. New York 1929; rptd 1967.

Martin, A. C. The love of solitude in eighteenth-century poetry. South Atlantic Quart 29 1930.

Crum, R. B. Scientific thought in poetry. New York 1931. Chs 3–6.

Horning, M. E. Evidences of romantic treatment of religious elements in late eighteenth-century minor poetry 1771–1800. Washington 1932.

Sickels, E. M. The gloomy egoist: moods and themes of melancholy from Gray to Keats. New York 1932.

Harder, J. H. Observations on some tendencies of sentiment in some minor poetry and essay in the eighteenth century. Amsterdam 1933.

Rose, R. O. Poetic hero-worship in the late eighteenth century. PMLA 48 1933.

Sherwood, M. Undercurrents of influence in English romantic poetry. Cambridge Mass 1934.

Whelan, M. K. Enthusiasm in English poetry of the eighteenth century 1700–74. Washington 1935.

Hooker, E. N. The reviewers and the new trends in poetry 1754–1770. MLN 51 1936.

Bush, D. Mythology and the romantic tradition in English poetry. Cambridge Mass 1937.

Jones, J. The 'distress'd' negro in English magazine verse [1749–1832]. SE 17 1937. With bibliography.

Fairchild, H. N. Religious trends in English poetry [1700–1830]. Vols 1–3, New York 1939–49. Protestantism and the cult of sentiment; Religious sentimentalism; Romantic faith.

Stern, B. H. The rise of Romantic Hellenism in English literature 1732–86. Madison 1940.

McKillop, A. D. The poet as patriot: Shakespeare to Wordsworth. Houston 1942 (Rice Inst pamphlet).

Nicolson, M. H. Newton demands the Muse: Newton's Optics and the eighteenth-century poets. Princeton 1946. Suppl by W. P. Jones, Newton further demands the Muse, Stud in Eng Lit 1500–1900 3 1963.

— The breaking of the circle: the effect of the 'new science' upon seventeenth-century poetry. Urbana 1950, New York 1960 (rev).

— Science and imagination. Ithaca 1956. Includes rev version of her Microscope and imagination.

Butt, J. Science and man in eighteenth-century poetry. Durham Univ Jnl 39 1947.

Clarke, G. H. Christ and the English poets. Queen's Quart 55 1948.

Dobrée, B. The theme of patriotism in the poetry of the early eighteenth century. Proc Br Acad 35 1949.

Jones, R. F. The background of the attack on science in the age of Pope. In Pope and his contemporaries: essays presented to George Sherburn, Oxford 1949.

Hoskins, H. H. Science on Parnassus: some eighteenth-century instructive poets. Groningen 1949.

Bush, D. Science and English poetry 1590–1950. New York 1950.

Reaver, J. R. The retirement theme: a study of the ways of a romanticism in eighteenth-century English poetry. Florida State Univ Stud 3 1951.

Yohannan, J. D. The Persian poetry fad in England 1770–1825. Comparative Lit 4 1952.

Havens, R. D. Assumed personality, insanity and poetry. RES new ser 4 1953.

— Solitude and the neoclassicists. ELH 21 1954.

Guerlac, H. The poets' nitre. Isis 45 1954. On John Mayow's theory of atmosphere and eighteenth-century poetry.

Røstvig, M.-S. The happy man: studies in the metamorphoses of a classical ideal. Vol 1 (1600–1700) Oslo 1954, 1962 (rev); vol 2 (1700–60) Oslo 1958.

Bullough, G. Changing views of the mind in English poetry. Proc Br Acad 41 1955.

— Reason, the passions and associations from Dryden to Wordsworth. Ch 3 in his Mirror of minds: changing psychological beliefs in English poetry, Toronto 1962.

Hagstrum, J. H. The sister arts: the tradition of literary pictorialism and English poetry from Dryden to Gray. Chicago 1958.

Macklem, M. The anatomy of the world: relations between natural and moral law from Donne to Pope. Minneapolis 1958.

Priestley, F. E. L. Science and the poet. Dalhousie Rev 38 1958.

Richmond, W. K. The English disease: a study in despondency. 1958.

George, M. D. English political caricature to 1792. Oxford 1959.

Jones, W. P. Science in biblical paraphrases in eighteenth-century England. PMLA 74 1959.

— Imitations of Gray's Elegy 1751–1800. Bull of Bibliography 23 1963. Includes list.

— The rhetoric of science: a study of scientific ideas and imagery in eighteenth-century English poetry. Berkeley 1966.

Simon, I. Shaftesbury and eighteenth-century poetry. Revue de Langues Vivantes 3 1961.

Spacks, P. M. The insistence of horror: aspects of the supernatural in eighteenth-century poetry. Cambridge Mass 1962.

Bate, W. J. The English poet and the burden of the past 1660–1820. In Aspects of the eighteenth century, ed E. R. Wasserman, Oxford 1965.

Kovacevich, I. The mechanical Muse: the impact of technical inventions on eighteenth-century neo-classical poetry. HLQ 28 1965.

McKillop, A. D. Local attachment and cosmopolitanism: the eighteenth-century pattern. In From Sensibility to romanticism: essays presented to F. A. Pottle, ed F. W. Hilles and H. Bloom, New York 1965.

Roston, M. Prophet and poet: the Bible and the growth of romanticism. 1965.

Lessenich, R. P. Dichtungsgeschmack und althebräische Bibelpoesie im 18 Jahrhundert: zur Geschichte der englischen Literaturkritik. Cologne 1967.

(6) STYLE AND DICTION

Havens, R. D. Poetic diction of the English classicists. In G. L. Kittredge anniversary papers, Boston 1913.

Barstow, M. L. Wordsworth's theory of poetic diction. New Haven 1917. Ch 2.

Cruickshank, A. H. Thomas Parnell: or what was wrong with the eighteenth century. E & S 7 1921.

Quayle, T. Poetic diction: a study of eighteenth-century verse. 1924.

Redin, M. Word-order in English verse from Pope to Sassoon. Upsala 1925.

Bredvold, L. I. The element of art in eighteenth-century poetry. In Selected poems of Alexander Pope, New York 1926.

Eliot, T. S. Johnson's London and the Vanity of human wishes. Introd to 1930 edn; rptd in English critical essays: twentieth century, ed P. M. Jones, Oxford 1933 (WC) and in From Dryden to Johnson, ed B. Ford, 1957 (Pelican).

Bateson, F. W. English poetry and the English language. Oxford 1934.

— English poetry: a critical introduction. 1950, 1966 (rev).

Wasserman, E. R. The return of the enjambed couplet. ELH 7 1940.

— The inherent values of eighteenth-century personification. PMLA 65 1950.

Tillotson, G. Eighteenth-century poetic diction. In his Essays in criticism and research, Cambridge 1942; rev for his Augustan studies, 1961.

— The manner of proceeding in certain eighteenth-century poems. In his Augustan studies, 1961. Chs 1–4 rptd as Augustan poetic diction, 1964.

— The methods of description in eighteenth-century poetry. In Restoration and eighteenth-century essays in honor of A. D. McKillop, Chicago 1963.

Monk, S. H. A 'grace beyond the reach of art'. JHI 5 1944.

Miles, J. Major adjectives in English poetry from Wyatt to Auden. Berkeley 1946.

— The primary language of poetry in the 1740s and 1840s. Berkeley 1950.

Bronson, B. H. Personification reconsidered. ELH 14 1947.

Brown, W. C. The triumph of form: a study of the later masters of the heroic couplet. Durham NC 1948.

Arthos, J. Poetic diction and scientific language. Isis 32 1950.

Mack, M. Wit and poetry and Pope. In Pope and his contemporaries: essays presented to George Sherburn, Oxford 1949, and in Eighteenth-century English literature: modern essays in criticism, ed J. Clifford, New York 1959.

Atkinson, A. D. A prospect of words. N & Q 11–25 Oct 1952. Landscape gardening and poetic vocabulary.

Davie, D. Purity of diction in English verse. 1952, 1967 (with postscript).

— Articulate energy: an inquiry into the syntax of English poetry. 1955.

Greene, D. J. 'Logical structure' in eighteenth-century poetry. PQ 31 1952.

Trickett, R. The Augustan pantheon: mythology and personification in eighteenth-century poetry. E & S new ser 6 1953.

— The idiom of Augustan poetry. In Discussions of poetry: form and structure, ed F. Murphy, Boston 1964.

Awad, L. Poetic diction in the eighteenth century. In his Studies in literature, Cairo 1954.

Chapin, C. F. Personification in eighteenth-century English poetry. New York 1955.

Sypher, W. Four stages of Renaissance style: transformations in art and literature 1400–1700. Garden City NY 1955.

Muraoka, I. Imagery of English poems of the seventeenth century. Tokyo 1958.

Miles, J. Renaissance, eighteenth-century and modern language in English poetry: a tabular view. Berkeley 1960.

— Towards a theory of style and change. Jnl of Aesthetics 22 1963.

Williamson, G. The proper wit of poetry. Chicago 1961. Supersedes his Rhetorical pattern of neoclassic wit, MP 33 1935.

Spacks, P. M. Horror-personification in late eighteenth-century poetry. SP 59 1962.

Bannerji, C. Modes of coarseness: a footnote to eighteenth-century poetic diction. English Miscellany (St Stephens College Delhi) 2 1963.

Brown, C. S. Monosyllables in English verse. Stud in Eng Lit 1500–1900 3 1963.

Göller, K. H. Die poetic Diction des 18 Jahrhunderts in England. Deutsche Vierteljahrsschrift für Literaturwissenschaft und Geistesgeschichte 38 1964.

Prince, F. T. The study of form and the renewal of poetry. Proc Br Acad 50 1964.

Balliet, C. A. The history and rhetoric of the triplet. PMLA 80 1965. Ends with Johnson.

Fussell, P. The rhetorical world of Augustan humanism: ethics and imagery from Swift to Burke. Oxford 1965.

Rodway, A. E. By algebra to Augustanism. In Essays on

style and language: linguistic and critical approaches to literary style, ed R. Fowler 1966.

Halewood, W. H. The 'reach of art' in Augustan poetic theory. In Studies in criticism and aesthetics: essays in honor of S. H. Monk, Minneapolis 1967.

Brower, R. Form and defect of form in eighteenth-century poetry: a memorandum. College Eng March 1968.

Youngren, W. H. Generality, science and poetic language in the Restoration. ELH 35 1968.

Miner, E. From narrative to 'description' and 'sense' in eighteenth-century poetry. Stud in Eng Lit 1500–1900 9 1969.

Stevick, P. Miniaturization in eighteenth-century English literature. UTQ 38 1969. On prose and poetry.

(7) MISCELLANEOUS STUDIES

Mustard, W. P. Virgil's Georgics and the British poets. Amer Jnl of Philology 29 1908.

Broadus, E. K. Addison's influence on the development of interest in folk-poetry in the eighteenth century. MP 8 1910.

Courtney, W. P. Dodsley's collection of poetry: its contents and contributors. 1910.

Kerlin, R. T. Theocritus in English literature. Lynchburg Va 1910.

Cox, E. M. Sappho and the Sapphic metre in English. 1916.

Goad, C. M. Horace in the English literature of the eighteenth century. New Haven 1918.

Nitchie, E. Virgil and the English poets. New York 1919.

Patton, J. The English village: a literary study 1750–1850. New York 1919.

Babenroth, A. C. English childhood: Wordsworth's treatment of childhood in the light of English poetry from Prior to Crabbe. New York 1922.

Longaker, J. M. The Della Cruscans and William Gifford. Philadelphia 1924.

Duckett, E. S. Catullus in English poetry. Northampton Mass 1925.

Hesselgrave, R. A. Lady Miller and the Batheaston Literary Circle. New Haven 1927.

Murray, G. The classical tradition in poetry. 1927.

Bush, D. Musaeus in English verse. MLN 43 1928.

Matthes, H. Die Verschleierung der Verfasserschaft bei englischer Dichtung des 18 Jahrhunderts. Beiträge Englands und Nordamerikas 4 1928.

Schneider, Rudolf. Der Mönch in der englischen Dichtung bis auf Lewis's Monk 1795. Leipzig 1928.

Whitford, R. C. Juvenal in England 1750–1802. PQ 7 1928.

Williams, I. A. Some poetical Miscellanies of the early eighteenth century. Library 3rd ser 10 1930.

— Points in eighteenth-century verse: a bibliographer's and collector's scrapbook. 1934.

Nicoll, A. Mr T. S. Eliot and the revival of classicism. English Jnl April 1934.

Lange, V. Die Lyrik und ihr Publikum im England des 18 Jahrhunderts. Weimar 1935.

Yost, C. D. The poetry of the Gentleman's Magazine: a study in eighteenth-century literary taste. Philadelphia 1936.

Brown, W. C. English travel books and minor poetry about the Near East 1775–1825. PQ 16 1937.

Reid, M. J. C. The Arthurian legend: comparison of treatment in modern and medieval literature. [1938]. Ch 3.

Tinker, C. B. Painter and poet: studies in the literary relations of English painting. Cambridge Mass 1938.

Flower, D. The pursuit of poetry: letters about poetry written by English poets 1550–1930. 1939.

Humphreys, A. R. A classical education and eighteenth-century poetry. Scrutiny 8 1939.

Macdonald, H. Some poetical Miscellanies 1672–1716. E & S 26 1940.

Stern, B. H. The rise of Romantic Hellenism in English literature 1732–86. Menasha 1940.

Wells, H. W. New poets from old. New York 1940. The influence of Augustans on twentieth-century poets.

Davies, H. S. The poets and their critics: Chaucer to Collins. 1943, 1960 (rev).

Larrabee, S. A. English bards and Grecian marbles: the relationship between sculpture and poetry. New York 1943. Chs 3–4.

Boys, R. C. The beginnings of American poetical miscellany 1714–1800. Amer Lit 17 1945. On American reading of English poetry.

Humphrey, G. W. Spanish ballads in English: part 1, historical survey. MLQ 6 1945. Starts with Percy.

Tillotson, G. Matthew Arnold and eighteenth-century poetry. In Essays presented to D. Nichol Smith, Oxford 1945.

Jones, C. E. Poetry and the Critical review 1756–85. MLQ 9 1948.

Highet, G. The classical tradition: Greek and Roman influence on Western literature. Oxford 1949.

Hoskins, H. H. Science on Parnassus: some eighteenth-century instructive poets. Groningen 1949.

Limouze, A. S. Burlesque criticism of the ballad in Mist's Weekly Journal. SP 47 1950.

Millar, B. P. Eighteenth-century views of the ballad. Western Folklore 9 1950.

Short, H. L. From Watts to Martineau: a century of Unitarian hymn-books in England. Trans Unitarian Historical Soc 10 1951.

Thomson, J. A. K. Classical influences on English poetry. 1951.

Cruttwell, P. The war's and fortune's son. EC 2 1952. On the conqueror in English poetry.

Hilton-Young, W. Translations of the Pervigilium Veneris into English verse. Cambridge Jnl 5 1952.

Smith, C. C. The seventeenth-century drolleries. Harvard Lib Bull 6 1952.

Abrams, M. H. The mirror and the lamp. New York 1953.

Phillips, J. E. and B. H. Bronson. Music and literature in the seventeenth and eighteenth centuries. Los Angeles 1953.

Blagden, C. Notes on the ballad market in the second half of the seventeenth century. SB 6 1954.

Stuart, D. M. The Prince Regent and the poets. Trans Royal Soc of Lit. 27 1955.

Ehrenpreis, I. A survey of eighteenth-century anthologies. College Eng Dec 1958.

Bevan, A. R. Poetry and politics in Restoration England. Dalhousie Rev 39 1959.

Emden, C. S. Poets in their letters. Oxford 1959. Sections on Pope, Gray and Cowper.

García Blanco, M. Poetas ingleses en la obra de Unamuno. Bull Hispanic Stud 36 1959.

Kinsley, J. The rustic inmates of the hamlet. REL 1 1960.

Papajewski, H. Die literarische Wertung Ovids am Ausgang des 17. und zu Beginn des 18 Jahrhunderts. Anglia 78 1960.

— Chimäre und Metapher: ein Beitrag zum kritischen Problem von Phantasie und Rationalität in englischen Neoklassizismus. Anglia 82 1964.

Wedgwood, C. V. Poetry and politics under the Stuarts. Cambridge 1960.

Congleton, J. E. The effect of the Restoration on poetry. Tennessee Stud in Lit 6 1961.

Hollander, J. The untuning of the sky: ideas of music in English poetry 1500–1700. Princeton 1961.

Swardson, H. R. Poetry and the fountain of light: observations on the conflict between Christian and classical traditions in seventeenth-century poetry. 1962.

Hamilton, K. G. The two harmonies: poetry and prose in the seventeenth century. Oxford 1963.

Vieth, D. Attribution in Restoration poetry: a study of Rochester's Poems of 1680. New Haven 1963.

Cohen, R. The art of discrimination: Thomson's The seasons and the language of criticism. 1964.

Fleischman, W. B. Lucretius and English literature 1680–1740. Paris 1964.

Kinsley, J. The music of the heart. Renaissance & Modern Stud 8 1964.

Mellers, W. Harmonious meeting: a study of the relation-ship between English music, poetry and theatre c. 1600–1900. 1965.

Moloney, B. The Della Cruscan poets, the Florence Miscellany and the Leopoldine reforms. MLR 60 1965.

Simpson, C. M. The British broadside ballad and its music. New Brunswick NJ 1966.

Menon, K. P. K. Woman in English poetry from Milton to Wordsworth. Trivandrum [196–].

Spate, O. H. K. The Muse of mercantilism: Jago, Grainger and Dyer. In Studies in the eighteenth century, ed R. F. Brissenden, Canberra 1968.

II. MISCELLANIES, ANTHOLOGIES AND COLLECTIONS OF POETRY

(1) POETICAL MISCELLANIES, SONG BOOKS AND VERSE COLLECTIONS OF MULTIPLE AUTHORSHIP

This bibliography purposely excludes—with a few important exceptions—periodicals, chap-books, garlands, almanacs and calendars, books of riddles etc in rime, jest books containing only stray epigrams, 18th-century song-books in folio by single composers, programmes, hymn-books, academical collections with fewer than 3 poems in English, laudatory poems prefixed to an author's works, and books purporting to have been written by one man. Otherwise it contains all that it has been possible to locate of the extant collections of verse (or verse and prose) containing the work of 3 or more hands. Most are in BM or Bodley; when a book has not been found in either place and is not recorded in one of 3 standard works, below, a location or an owner is usually mentioned.

Wing, D. G. Short-title catalogue of books printed in England, Scotland 1641–1700. 3 vols New York 1945–51. *Wing.*

Case, A. E. Bibliography of English poetical miscellanies 1521–1750. 1935. *Case.*

Day, C. L. and E. B. Murrie. English song-books 1621–1700: a bibliography. 1940. *D & M.*

The original compiler of the CBEL list had access to the annotated catalogues of the Stainer Collection and his references have been retained below. Now, however, this collection forms part of what is probably the largest private library of 18th-century song-books in existence, owned by Mr W. N. H. Harding of Chicago. Many of the books in this library must be unique. Other references are to booksellers' catalogues, a class it has not been possible to eliminate entirely, and to the following works:

Griffith, R. H. Alexander Pope: a bibliography. 2 pts Austin 1922–7. *Griffith.*

Schnapper, E. B. The British union-catalogue of early music printed before the year 1801. 2 vols 1957. *Schnapper.*

Teerink, H. A bibliography of the writings of Jonathan Swift. Ed A. H. Scouten, Philadelphia 1963 (rev). *Teerink.*

1660

A brief introduction to the skill of musick. Ed J. Playford 1660 (3rd edn). First pbd 1654; from 6th to 19th edn, 1672–1730, as An introduction to. . . Edns with words dated 1655, 1660, 1662, 1664, 1666, 1667, 1670, 1672, 1674, 1679, 1683, 1687, 1700, 1703, 1713, 1718, 1724, 1730.

Britannia rediviva. Oxford 1660.

Cheerfull ayres or ballads. Ed J. Wilson, Oxford 1660. Copy dated 1659: Sotheby, 24 May 1917.

Dregs of drollery: or old poetry in its ragges. 1660.

Epicedia academiae oxoniensis, in obitum Mariae principis Arausionensis. Oxford 1660. See 1661, *below.*

J. Cleaveland revived, with some other exquisite remains of his contemporaries. 1660 (2nd edn). First edn 1659. See 1662, 1668, *and* The works, 1687, 1699, 1742, *below.*

Poems written by the earl of Pembroke; answered by Sr Benjamin Ruddier. 1660. Slight differences between issues; ed S. E. Brydges 1817.

Le prince d'amour: or the prince of love; with a collection of several ingenious poems and songs by the wits of the age. 1660. See 1669, *below.*

Ratts rhimed to death: or the Rump-Parliament hang'd up in the shambles. 1660; rptd with addns as The rump: or a collection of songs and ballads made upon those who would be a Parliament, 1660. See 1661, 1662; *also* A collection of loyal songs, 1731, *below.*

Votivum Carolo: or a welcome to his sacred Majesty Charles the II from the Master and scholars of Woodstock-School, Oxford. 1660.

1661

An antidote against melancholy made up in pills. Ed N. D. 1661; ed J. P. Collier, c. 1870; ed J. W. Ebsworth, Boston 1876. See 1669, *and* Wit and mirth, 1682, 1684, *below.*

Choyce poems: being songs, sonnets, satyrs and elegies by the wits of both universities. 1661. This is Poems consisting of epistles and epigrams, 1658, with addns.

Epicedia academiae oxoniensis, in obitum Mariae principis Arausionensis. Oxford 1661. See 1660, *above.*

Merry drollery: the first part, collected by W. N., C. B., R. S., J. G. [1661]. Also The second part of Merry drollery, [1661]. See 1670, 1691, *below.*

New carolls for this merry time of Christmas. 1661. See 1670, 1681, 1725, *below.*

Rump: or an exact collection of the choycest poems and songs, by the most eminent wits, from 1640 to 1660. 2 pts 1661. Sotheby, 1 June 1911. See 1660, *above.*

Scholae edinensis in Caroli II reditum. Gideon Lithgo, Edinburgh 1661. Dobell, 1937; imperfect copy only.

Wit and drollery: joviall poems; with additions by Sir J. M., Ja. S., Sir W. D., J. D. and the most refined wits of the age. 1661. First pbd 1656; see 1682, *below.*

1662

The art of courtship, whereunto are annexed odes, epigrams, songs, sonnets. Ed B. D. 1662.

Cantus: songs and fancies. [Ed J. Forbes], Aberdeen 1662. See 1666, 1682, *below.*

C[ardonnel], P. D[e]. Complementum fortunatarum insularum, p. II: sive Galathea Vaticinans. 1662, 1662.

The crown garland of golden roses. Ed R. Johnson [1662]. First known edn, 1612; *see* 1680, 1683, 1692, *below*.

Domiduca oxoniensis: sive musae academicae gratulatio ob principis Catherinae Lusitanae in Angliam appulsum. Oxford 1662.

The entertainment of his most excellent Majestie Charles II. Ed J. Ogilby 1662. *See* Wing O171–2.

J. Cleaveland revived; with some other exquisite remains of his contemporaries. 1662 (3rd edn). *See* 1660, *above*.

Ovid: De arte amandi; as also the Loves of Hero and Leander, together with choice poems and rare pieces of drollery. 1662. *See* Case 103(d) and (e). Earlier edns of Hero and Leander, 1651, 1653; *see also* 1672, 1677, 1682, 1684, 1689, 1705, *below*.

Rump: or an exact collection of the choycest poems and songs, by the most eminent wits, from 1639 to 1661. 2 pts 1662; rptd 1874; *see* 1660, *above*.

Wits interpreter: the English Parnassus. Ed J. C[otgrave] 1662 (2nd edn, with addns). First pbd 1655; *see* 1671, *below*.

The wits: or sport upon sport; in select pieces of drollery digested into scenes. Pt 1, ed H. Marsh 1662; ed J. J. Elson, 1932; *see* 1672, 1673, *below*.

1663

The academy of complements. 1663. A title often used for quite different collections; *see* 1664, 1670, 1684, 1685, 1705, 1750, 1760, 1790, 1795, *below*.

Catch that catch can: or a new collection of catches, rounds and canons. Ed J. Hilton and J. Playford 1663. Earlier edns in 1652 and 1658; *see also* D & M 19.

[Rowlands, S.] A crew of kind London gossips; to which is added ingenious poems. 1663. *See* 1684, *below*.

A help to discourse: or more merriment mixt with serious matters. 1663 (15th edn). First known edn dated 1619; *see* 1667, 1682, *below*.

Robin Hoods garland: or delightful songs, with new editions and emendations. 1663. The many undated edns, e.g. Wing R1640, cannot be noticed here; for dated edns, often varying in title and contents, *see* 1670, 1689, 1704, 1737, 1746, 1769, 1778, 1779, 1786, 1789, 1792, 1794, 1796, 1797, 1799, *below*. *See also* J. Ritson, Robin Hood, 1795.

Witt's recreations refined. 1663. Type-set title reads Recreations for ingenious head-peeces [Grolier copy, nd]; ed T. Park 1817; ed J. C. Hotten 1874. First edn 1640; *see* 1667, 1683, *below*.

1664

The academy of complements: the last edition. 1664. Harding copy. *See* 1663, *above*.

Sir Thomas Overbury his wife; with additions of new characters. 1664 (17th impression). *See* The wife, 1709, *below*.

1666

Cantus: songs and fancies. Aberdeen 1666 (2nd edn, enlarged). Also found with Edinburgh imprint added. *See* 1662, *above*.

Musick's delight on the cithren; to which is added several new songs and ayres. Ed J. Playford 1666.

The poems of Horace, rendred in English verse by several persons. Ed A. Brome 1666. *See* Case 138(a) and (b). *See* 1671, 1680, *below*.

1667

Catch that catch can: or the musical companion; to which is now added a second book. [Ed. J. Playford] 1667. 2 issues; *see* D & M 26. *See also* 1672, 1673, 1685, 1686,

1687, 1701, 1702, 1707, 1709, 1720, 1724, 1726, 1740, 1790, *below*.

A help to discourse: or more merriment mixt with serious matters. 1667 (16th edn). Sotheby, 1931. *See* 1663, *above*.

Musical companion, containing catches and rounds; with a second book. 1667. Sotheby, 23 May 1917. Probably the same as Catch, 1667, *above*.

Several copies of verses on the death of Cowley. 1667.

A treasury of divine raptures, alphabetically rank'd and fil'd by a private chaplain to the lady Urania. [Ed N. Billingsley] 1667. By several hands?

Witt's recreations refined. 1663. Type-set title, 1667. 2 issues; *see* Case 95(g) and (h). *See also* 1663, *above*.

1668

J. Cleaveland revived; with some other exquisite remains of his contemporaries. 1668 (4th edn). *See* 1660, *above*.

Poems of Cowley and others, composed into songs and ayres by William King. Oxford 1668.

1669

An antidote against melancholy made up in pills, compounded of witty ballads, jovial songs and merry catches. 1669. *See* 1661, *above*.

The new academy of complements. 1669. Earliest known appearance of this title. *See* 1681, 1694, 1719, *below*; for other series, *see* 1671, 1715, 1748, *below*.

The new help to discourse. Ed W. W[instanley] 1669. *See* 1672, 1680, 1684, 1696, 1702, 1716, 1721, 1733, *below*.

Le prince d'amour. 1669. Harvard copy. *See* 1660, *above*.

Select ayres and dialogues, composed by Henry Lawes. Bks 2–3, 1669. Bk 1 pbd 1659; *see* The treasury, *below*.

Threni cantabrigienses in exequiis Henriettae Mariae Caroli secundi matris. Cambridge 1669.

The treasury of musick: containing ayres and dialogues composed by Henry Lawes and other masters. 3 bks 1669. Bks 1 and 3, and perhaps 2, are reissues of earlier pbns. *See* Select ayres, *above*.

1670

The academy of complements newly refin'd. 1670. Sotheby, 15 June 1931. *See* 1663, *above*.

[A jovial garland]. Ed R. S. [1670?] BM copy lacks a title-page, but has above as head-title.

Merry drollery, complete. Pts 1–2, 1670. *See* 1661, *above*.

Musarum cantabrigiensium threnodia in obitum Georgii ducis Albaemarlae. Cambridge 1670.

New Christmas carrols: being fit also to be sung at Easter, Whitsontide and other festival days in the year. [c. 1670?] *See* 1661, *above*.

Robin Hoods garland: containing his merry exploits, some of them never before printed. 1670. *See* 1663, *above*.

1671

Epicedia cantabrigiensia in obitum principis Annae ducissae eboracensis. Cambridge 1671.

The loyal garland: containing choice songs and sonnets. Ed S. N. 1671. *See* 1678, 1685, 1686, *below*.

The new academy of complements, compiled by L[ord] B[uckhurst?] and others. 1671. 2nd edn: Sotheby, 29 May 1911. *See* 1669, *above*; 1698, 1713, *below*.

Oxford drollery: being new poems and songs. Ed W. H[ickes], Oxford 1671. *See* 1674, 1679, *below*.

The poems of Horace, rendred in English and paraphrased by several persons. 1671 (2nd edn, with alterations). *See* 1666, *above*.

Westminster-Drollery: or a choice collection of the newest songs and poems both at court and theaters by a person of quality, never before publish'd. 1671. Grolier, 1905. *See* 1672, 1674, *below*.

Westminster-Drollery: or a choice collection, with additions. 1671. *See* Case 150(1)(a)–(1)(c). Apostrophe 's erased from imprint of Malone copy in Bodley.

Windsor drollery: an exact collection of the newest songs, poems and catches in use at Court; collected by a person of quality. 1671. Worcester College Oxford copy; begins with 15 songs, the body of the book being pt of The academy of complements, paged 171–328. *See below, and* 1672, *below*.

Windsor drollery: an exact collection of the newest songs, poems and catches now in use both in city and countrey. 1671. Begins with 19 songs; the rest as above. *See* Academy, 1684, *below*.

Wits interpreter: the English Parnassus. Ed J. Cotgrave 1671 (3rd edn, with addns). *See* 1662, *above*.

1672

A collection of poems written upon several occasions by several persons. 2 pts 1672. *See* 1673, 1693, 1695, 1701, 1702, 1716, *below*.

Covent Garden drolery: or a colection of all the choice songs, poems, prologues and epilogues; collected by R. B. 1672; collected by A. B., 1672. Copies show partial resetting, cancellation, etc; *see* Case 152. Ed M. Summers 1927.

Covent Garden drolery, collected by A. B.: the second impression, with additions. 1672. C. H. Wilkinson copy; ed G. T. Drury 1928. Wing C6624B?

The musical companion, in two books. Ed J. Playford. [1672]. Title-pages mutilated; bk 2, dated 1672. *See* 1673, *below, and* Catch, 1667, *above*.

New court-songs and poems. Ed R. V[eal] 1672.

The new help to discourse. 1672 (2nd edn). *See* 1669, *above*.

Ovid: De arte amandi. 1672. *See* 1662, *above*.

The poems of Ben Johnson junior: being a miscelanie of seriousness, wit, mirth and mysterie; composed by W. S., gent. 1672. By several hands?

Poor Robins collection of antient prophecyes. 1672.

Reliquiae Wottonianae. 1672 (3rd edn, with addns). First pbd 1651; *see* 1685, *below*.

Westminster-Drollery: or a choice collection of the newest songs and poems. 1672. *See* 1671, *above*.

Westminster drollery, the second part: being a compleat collection of songs and poems. 1672. *See* Case 150(2)(a) and (2)(b). Both pts ed J. W. Ensworth, Boston 1875–6.

The last, and now only compleat collection of the newest and choisest songs and poems; with above forty new songs, which are now added to this second part of Westminster drollery. 1672.

Westminster quibbles in verse: or a miscellany of quibling catches, joques and merriments. 1672. By several hands?

Windsor-Drollery: being a more exact collection of the newest songs, poems and catches now in use; with additions; collected by a person of quality. 1672. *See* Case 154; Wing W2980. Huth copy, extra leaves.

The wits: or sport upon sport in selected pieces of drollery. Pt 1, 1672. *See* 1662, *above*; F. Kirkman's name now takes the place of Marsh's in the imprint and signature of the preface.

The wits: or sport upon sport in selected pieces of drollery. Pt 1 [really 2 pts], ed F. Kirkman 1672. A new Black man group becomes pt 1; old pt 1, the Bouncing knight group, becomes pt 2. *See* 1662, *above, and* 1673, *below*.

1673

The canting academy: or the devils cabinet opened; with several new catches and songs compos'd by the choisest wits of the age. Ed R. Head 1673. *See* 1674, *below*.

Choice songs and ayres: being most of the newest songs sung at Court; the first book. Ed J. Playford; address signed N. D. 1673. *See* 1675, 1676, 1679, 1681, 1683, 1684, *below*.

A collection of poems written upon several occasions by several persons; with many additions. 1673. *See* 1672, *above*.

Holborn-Drollery: or the beautiful Chloret surprized in the sheets. 1673.

London drollery: or the wits academy; by W. H[ickes]. 1673. At least 6 hands in this.

Methinks the poor town has been troubled too long: or a collection of all the new songs that are generally sung. 1673.

Methinks the poor town: the several songs now in mode. 1673 (2nd edn, with addns).

The musical companion, in two books. Ed J. Playford 1673. For issues with extra leaves, *see* D & M 36. *See also* Catch, 1667, *above*.

The wits or sport upon sport: being drols and farces newly collected by Francis Kirkman. 1673. Black man group only. Also a new issue of the 1672 edn containing both groups; ed J. J. Elson 1932. *See* 1662, *above*.

1674

The canting academy: or villanies discovered. 1674 (2nd edn). *See* 1673, *above*.

Cupids garland set round about with gilded roses: containing many pleasant songs and sonnets. 1674. Another edn, nd; Pepysian copy.

Cupids posies, for bracelets, handkercers and rings. 1674. Ed E. Arber, in An English garner vol 8, 1877.

Joanereidos; with several copies of verses by a club of gentlemen. Ed J. Strong 1674. Rptd from 1645 edn, with addns.

Loves garland. 1674; ed J. R. Brown 1883; ed A. L. Humphreys 1894. Earlier edns in 1624, 1648.

Loves school: or a new merry book of complements, made up of dialogues and discourses, letters, songs and sonnets. 1674.

A new collection of poems and songs written by several persons. Ed J. Bulteel 1674. *See* Case 157(a) and (b); *also* Melpomene, 1678, *below*.

A new collection of new songs and poems, none of them ever printed before. 1674. Another issue of the above, lacking index: Harding copy.

Oxford drollery. 1674. *See* 1671, *above*.

Remains concerning Britain [by Camden]: 7th impression, much amended by John Philipot. 1674. First pbd 1605; rptd in Library of old authors, 1870.

The royal garland of love and delight; with other love songs and sonnets full of delight. Ed T. D[eloney] 1674.

Westminster-Drollery: or a choice collection of the newest songs and poems. Pt 1 1674 (3rd edn); rptd J. W. Ebsworth, Boston 1876. *See* 1671, *above*.

Wit at a venture: or Clio's privy-garden, containing songs and poems. Ed C. F. 1674. At least 3 hands in this.

1675

The amours of the English gallantry in several historical poems. 1675. By several hands?

Choice ayres, songs and dialogues. Bk 1 1675 (2nd edn). *See* D & M 40; *also* 1673, *above*.

The circle: or conversations; with several new songs. Ed N. Noel 1675. *See* 1676, *below*.

Mock songs and joking poems, all novel; by the author of Westminster drollery. 1675.

A perfect collection of the several songs now in mode either at the Court or theatres. 1675.

A perfect collection of all the songs now in mode; with new additions. 1675.

1676

Choice ayres, songs and dialogues; newly re-printed with large additions. Bk 1, 1676. *See* 1673, *above*.

The circle: or conversations on love and gallantry; with several new songs. 1676. The 1675 edn with new title-page and errata.

Letters and poems in honour of Margaret, Dutchess of Newcastle. 1676. *See* A collection, 1678, *below*.

A new collection of the choicest songs now in esteem in town or Court. 1676.

1677

The English Parnassus: or a help to English poesie. Ed J. Poole 1677. First edn 1657; *see* 1678, *below*.

Epithalamium in desideratissimis nuptiis principum Guilielmi-Henrici Arausii & Mariae Britanniarum ab academia cantabrigiensi decantatum. Cambridge 1677.

The last and best edition of new songs such as are of the most general esteem. 1677.

Ovid, De arte amandi. 1677. *See* 1662, *above*.

Songs for 1, 2 and 3 voyces, composed by Henry Bowman. [Oxford 1677]. *See* 1678, 1679, *below*.

The wits academy: or the Muses delight. Ed W. P. 1677. *See* 1696, 1701, 1704, *below*.

1678

A collection of letters and poems written by several persons to the late Duke and Dutchess of Newcastle. 1678. *See* Letters, 1676, *above*.

The English Parnassus. 1678. *See* 1677, *above*.

The last and most exact edition of new songs such as are now in most general esteem either in town or Court. 1678.

The loyal garland: containing choice songs and sonnets of our late unhappy revolutions. Ed S. N. 167[8?] (4th edn, with addns). Copy in Bodley. *See* 1671, *above*.

Melpomene: or the Muses delight, written by I. D., T. F., S. W., T. S., C. O., I. B. 1678. Another issue of A new collection, 1674.

New ayres and dialogues composed for voices and viols. Ed J. Banister and T. Low 1678.

Songs for one, two and three voyces; collected out of Cowley and others, and composed by Bowman. Oxford 1678. D & M 47 has slightly variant title. *See* 1677, *above*.

1679

Choice ayres and songs: the second book. Ed J. Playford 1679. *See* 1673, *above*.

Oxford drollery. Oxford 1679. *See* 1671, *above*.

Songs for one, two and three voyces. Oxford 1679 (2nd edn). A re-issue of 1677 edn with corrected plates.

Versatile ingenium, the wittie companion: or jests of all sorts by Democritus junior. Amsterdam 1679. Book prices current, 1902; by several hands? London imprint: Wing V257.

1680

The crown garland of golden roses. 1680. *See* 1662, *above*.

Cupid's soliciter of love; with sundry complements; with certain verses and sonnets. Ed R. Grimsal 1680.

The new help to discourse. 1680 (2nd edn). *See* 1669, *above*.

Ovid's epistles, translated by several hands. 1680. *See* 1681, 1683, 1688, 1693, 1701, 1705, 1712, 1716, 1720; *see also* 1725, *below*.

The poems of Horace. 1680 (3rd edn, with alterations). *See* 1666, *above*.

R[ochester], E[arl] of. Poems on several occasions. 'Antwerp' (for London) 1680, [c. 1680]. At least 10 edns, containing many spurious poems. *See* D. M.

Vieth, Attribution in Restoration poetry, New Haven 1963. *See also* 1685, 1701, 1713, *below*.

Songs set by signior Pietro Reggio. 2 pts [1680]. *See* 1692, *below*.

Synopsis of vocal musick. Ed A. B. 1680. For 1690 edn, *see* A. Deakin, A musical bibliography, 1892.

1681

Choice ayres and songs: the third book. Ed J. Playford 1681. *See* 1673, *above*.

A choice compendium: or an exact collection of the newest and most delightful songs. Ed J. H. 1681.

The new academy of complements. 1681. *See* 1671, *above*.

New Christmas carrols: being fit also to be sung at Easter, Whitsontide and other festival days in the year. 1681. *See* New carolls, 1661, *above*.

Ovid's epistles, translated by several hands. 1681 (2nd edn). *See* 1680, *above*.

1682

Cantus: songs and fancies. Aberdeen 1682 (3rd edn, enlarged); rptd Paisley 1879. *See* 1662, *above*.

Female poems on several occasions; written by Ephelia. 1682 (2nd edn). Poems on pp. 112–169 by various authors, not in 1679 edn.

Grammatical drollery: consisting of poems and songs. Ed W. H[ickes] 1682.

A help to discourse. 1682 (17th edn). *See* 1663, *above*.

The key of knowledg. Ed T. W. 1682. Also an edn, nd.

Monumenta Westmonasteriensia; with all the epitaphs. Ed H. K[eepe] 1682. *See* 1683, *below*.

A new collection of the choicest songs, as they are sung at Court, both the theaters, the musick-schools and academies. 1682.

Ovid, De arte amandi. 1682. *See* 1662, *above*.

Dryden, Sprat and Waller. Three poems upon the death of the late usurper Oliver Cromwel. 1682. First edn 1659; *see also* A panegyrick, 1709.

Wit and drollery: jovial poems, with new additions. 1682. *See* 1661, *above*.

Cowley, Butler et al. Wit and loyalty reviv'd in a collection of some smart satyrs in verse and prose. 1682; ed W. Scott, in Somers tracts vol 5, 1811.

Wit and mirth: an antidote against melancholy compounded of ballads, songs and catches. Ed H. P[layford] 1682 (3rd edn, enlarged). *See* An antidote, 1661, *above*.

1683

Anacreon done into English out of the original Greek. Ed S. B. Oxford 1683; rptd 1923. *See* 1713, *below*.

Choice ayres and songs: the fourth book. Ed J. Playford 1683. *See* 1673, *above*.

The compleat courtier: or Cupid's academy, containing songs, poems, epigrams. Ed J. Shirley 1683.

The crown garland of golden roses. 1683. *See* 1662, *above*.

Hymenaeus cantabrigiensis, Cambridge 1683. With variant settings.

Monumenta Westmonasteriensia. 1683. With addns; *see* 1682, *above*.

The newest collection of the choicest songs, as they are sung at Court. 1683.

Ovid's epistles, translated by several hands. 1683 (3rd edn). *See* Case 165(c) and (d); *also* 1680, *above*.

Rochester, Wild et al. Rome rhym'd to death. 2 pts 1683.

Triumphs of female wit, in some Pindarick odes. 1683.

Witt's recreations refined. 1683. *See* 1663, *above*.

1684

The academy of complements; with many new additions of songs and catches a-la-mode by the most refined wits of this age. 1684. The section of songs reprints much of Windsor-Drollery, 1671. *See* 1663, *above*.

Choice ayres and songs: the fifth book. Ed J. Playford 1684. *See* 1673, *above*.

A choice collection of 120 loyal songs written since the two late plots. Ed N. T[hompson] 1684. *See* 1685, 1694, *below*.

Choice ayres, songs and dialogues. 1684. *See* 1673, *above*.

A crew of kind London gossips. 1684. *See* 1663, *above*.

Delights for the ingenious, in above fifty choice emblems. Ed R. B. [N. Crouch] 1684. *See* Choice emblems, 1721, 1732, *below*.

Miscellany poems, by the most eminent hands. Ed Dryden 1684. *See* 1685, 1688, 1692, 1693, 1694, 1702, 1704, 1706, 1708, 1709, 1716, 1727, *below*.

The new help to discourse. 1684 (3rd edn). *See* 1669, *above*.

Ovid, De arte amandi. 1684. *See* 1662, *above*.

Verses by the university of Oxford on the death of Sir Bevill Grenvill. 1684. First pbd 1643.

Wit and mirth: an antidote against melancholy. 1684 (3rd edn). *See* Case 130 (c) and An antidote, 1661, *above*.

Wits cabinet: or a companion for young men and ladies. 1684. Harding copy. *See* 1698, 1703, 1711, 1731, 1737, 1740, 1745, *below*.

1685

The academy of complements: or a new way of wooing. 1685. *See* 1663, *above*.

Catch that catch can: or the second part of the musical companion. Ed J. Playford 1685. *See* 1667, *above*.

A choice collection of 180 loyal songs. 1685 (3rd edn). *See* 1684, *above*.

A collection of 86 loyal poems written upon the two late plots; with several poems on their Majesties coronation. Ed N. T[hompson] 1685.

A collection of twenty four songs, written by several hands and set by several masters of musick. 1685. *See also* D & M 75: unlocated collection of 31 songs.

Cupid's masterpiece. 1685. First edn 1656. *See* 1670, *above*.

Latine songs, with their English; and poems. H. Bold. Ed W. Bold 1685.

Loyal garland of mirth and pastime, set forth in sundry pleasant new songs. 1685. Sotheby, 22 July 1864. *See* 1671, *above*.

Loyal poems and satyrs upon the times, since the beginning of the Salamanca Plot; written by several hands. Ed M. T[aubman] 1685.

The marrow of complements. 1685; ed J. S. Farmer, in National ballad and song vol 1, 1897. Not in Wing; *see* Case 109 for 1655 edn.

Miscellany: being a collection of poems by several hands. Ed A. Behn 1685.

Miscellany poems, by the most eminent hands. 1685. Wise copy. A reissue of 1684 edn, not in Wing.

Miscellany poems and translations by Oxford hands. Ed A. Stephens 1685.

Moestissimae ac laetissimae academiae cantabrigiensis affectus, decedente Carolo II, succedente Jacobo II. Cambridge 1685.

The mysteries of love and eloquence: or the arts of wooing and complementing. Ed E. P[hillips] 1685 (3rd edn, with addns). First edn 1658. *See* The beau's academy, 1699, *below*.

Poems by several hands and on several occasions. Ed N. Tate 1685.

Poems on several occasions, written by a late person of honour. 1685. *See* 1680, *above*.

Reliquae Wottonianae. 1685 (4th edn, with addns). *See* 1672, *above*.

Sylvae: or the second part of poetical miscellanies. Ed Dryden 1685. *See* Miscellany poems, 1684, *above*.

The theater of music: the first book. Ed H. P[layford] and R. C. 1685. Also The second book, 1685. *See* 1686, 1687, *below*.

1686

The art of courtship: or the school of delight. 1686. *See* 1688, *below*.

The illustrious history of women; the whole work enrich'd and intermix'd with curious poetry and delicate fancie. Ed J. Shirley 1686.

The loyal garland: or a choice collection of songs highly in request, made by divers ingenious persons. 1686 (5th edn, with addns). Ed J. O. Halliwell-Phillipps 1850. *See* 1671, *above*.

The second book of the pleasant musical companion. Ed J. Playford 1686 (2nd edn, enlarged). *See* D & M 85; *also* Catch, 1667, *above*, and 1687, *below*.

The theater of music: the third book. 1686. Title varies.

1687

A collection of the choyest and newest songs, sett by severall masters: the second book. 1687. *See* D & M 88.

Comes amoris or the companion of love: being a choice collection of the newest songs. Ed S. Scott 1687. *See* 1688, 1689, 1693, 1694, *below*.

The lives of the most famous English poets. Ed W. Winstanley 1687.

The new London drollery: or a poesy made up of choice songs [1687]. Pepysian copy, Magdalene College Cambridge.

Quadratum musicum: or a collection of xvi new songs made upon the greatest and best subjects. 1687.

The second book of the pleasant musical companion. Ed J. Playford [1687?] (2nd edn, enlarged). *See* Catch, 1667, and 1686, *above*.

The theater of music: the fourth and last book. 1687. *See* 1685, *above*.

Vinculum societatis: or the tie of good company. Ed J. Carr and R. C. 1687. *See* 1688, 1691, *below*.

The works of Cleveland. 1687. *See* 1699, 1742, *below*; *also* J. Cleaveland revived, 1660, *above*.

1688

The art of courtship: or the school of delight. 1688. *See* 1686, *above*.

The banquet of musick: the words by the ingenious wits of this age. Ed H. Playford 2 bks 1688. *See* 1689, 1690, 1691, 1692, *below*.

A cabinet of choice jewels: or the Christians joy and gladness set forth in sundry pleasant new Christmas-Carrols. 1688.

Comes amoris: the second book. 1688. *See* 1687, *above*.

Flora's fair garland deckt and adorned with the most delightful new songs. 1688. Sotheby, 22 July 1864.

Harmonia sacra: or divine hymns and dialogues. Ed H. Playford 1688. A. Deakin in A musical bibliography, 1892, cites a 1686 edn. *See* 1693, 1700, 1703, 1714, 1726, *below*.

The idea of Christian love; with a large paraphrase on Waller's poem of divine love [with] some copies of verses from Mrs Wharton [et al]. 1688.

Illustrissimi principis ducis Cornubiae et comitis Palatini, Genethliacon. Cambridge 1688. Case 183; *see also* Case 258.

Behn, A. Lycidus: or the lover in fashion; together with a miscellany of new poems by several hands. 1688. *See* Poems upon several occasions, 1697, *below*.

Miscellany poems. 1688. *See* 1684, *above*.

Ovid's epistles, translated by several hands. 1688 (4th edn, enlarged). *See* 1680, *above*.

Poems to the memory of that incomparable poet Edmond Waller, by several hands. 1688.

Barker, J. Poetical recreations: part i; part ii: by several gentlemen of the universities and others. 1688.

Strenae natalitiae academiae oxoniensis in celsissimum principem. Oxford 1688. Case 187; *see also* Case 258.

The triumph of wit: or ingenuity display'd in its perfection. Ed J. Shirley 1688. C. H. Wilkinson copy. *See* 1692, 1702, 1707, 1712, 1724, 1735; *also* 1760, *below.*

Vinculum societatis: the second book. 1688. *See* 1687, *above.*

Youth's treasury; with a collection of songs. 1688.

1689

The banquet of musick: the third book. 1689. *See* 1688, *above.*

A collection of the newest and most ingenious poems against Popery. 1689. *See* Case 189(1)(a) and (1)(b).

A second collection of poems against Popery and tyranny. 1689. *See* Case 189(2). Some pages reset etc.

A third collection of poems against Popery and tyranny. 1689. *See* Case 189(3). Minor variants.

The fourth (and last) collection of poems, satyrs, songs etc. 1689. *See* Case 189(4). This vol may conclude the series above or below; it is found with both.

A collection of poems on affairs of state, by A– M–l esq and other eminent wits. 1689. *See* Case 188(1)(a) and (1)(b); *also* Augustan satirical verse, ed G. deF. Lord et al, New Haven 1963–.

The second part of the collection of poems on affairs of state. 1689; *see* Case 188(2); The third part, 1689; *see* Case 188(3).

The fourth (and last) collection of the newest and most ingenious poems. 1689.

Comes amoris: the third book. 1689. *See* 1687, *above.*

The court of curiosities, and the cabinet of rarities. [1689?].

C., P. An exact collection of many wonderful prophesies relating to the government of England. 1689. *See* 1691, 1714, *below.*

The Irish garland, composed of new songs; with a second part of Court songs. [c. 1689] Harding copy.

The loves of Hero and Leander. 1689. Harvard copy. *See* Ovid, 1662, *above.*

Musae cantabrigiensis, principibus Wilhelmo et Mariae publicae salutis ac libertatis vindicibus, haec officii & pietatis ergò D. D. Cambridge 1689.

The Muses farewel to Popery and slavery: or a collection of miscellany poems, satyrs, songs made by the most eminent wits of the nation. 1689. *See* 1690, *below.*

A supplement to the collection of miscellany poems against Popery and slavery. 1689. *See* Case 191(2)(a) and (2)(b).

The new crown garland of princely pastime and mirth, adorn'd with many sweet and melodious new songs. 1689. Sotheby, 22 July 1864.

The Protestant garland of joy and delight, compos'd of nine pleasant new songs upon this late and prosperous change. 1689.

The Protestant orange garland: new songs, upon the joyful arrival of William and Mary. [c. 1689]. Harding copy.

The Quakers art of courtship: or the yea-and-nay academy of complements. 1689. *See* 1710, 1737, *below.*

Robin Hood's garland. 1689. *See* 1663, *above.*

The theatre of compliments: or new academy. 1689. *See* J. Ritson, Ancient songs, 1790, p. 235.

The third part of the works of Cowley: being his six books of plants, made English by several hands. 1689. *See* 1700, *below.*

Vota oxoniensa pro Guilhelmo rege et Maria regina nuncupata. Oxford 1689.

1690

The banquet of musick: the fourth and last book. 1690. *See* 1688, *above.*

The golden garland of princely delight: being most pleasant songs and sonnets. 2 pts 1690 (13th edn, with addns).

The Muses farewel to Popery and slavery. 1690 (2nd edn, enlarged). *See* 1689, above; also Poems on affairs of state pt 2, 1697, *below.*

A supplement to the Muses farewel to Popery and slavery. 1690. Reprints songs from 1689 Farewel and Supplement which were omitted in the collected Farewel of 1690.

Remedium melancholiae, or the remedy of melancholy: being a choice collection of new songs. Ed J. W. Franck, bk 1, 1690. No more pbd.

1691

Apollo's banquet: the second book. 1691. No words in bk 1.

The banquet of musick: the fifth book. 1691. *See* 1688, *above.*

A collection of many wonderful prophesies relating to the English nation. 1691. *See* 1689, *above.*

The history of Adolphus, Prince of Russia; with a collection of songs and love-verses by several hands. 1691.

Merry drollery compleat. Pts 1–2, 1691. Ed J. W. Ebsworth, Boston 1875–6. *See* 1661, *above.*

Rochester, Earl of. Poems on several occasions; with Valentinian. 1691. *See* 1696, 1705, 1710, 1714, 1718, 1732, *below.*

Vinculum societatis: the third book. 1691. *See* 1687, *above.*

1692

The banquet of musick: the sixth and last book. 1692. *See* 1688, *above.*

The crown garland of golden roses. 1692. *See* 1662, *above.*

Miscellany poems: in two parts; published by Dryden. 1692 (2nd edn). *See* Case 172(1)(b) and (1)(c); issued with Sylvae, 1685 etc as pt 2. *See* 1684, *above.*

Miscellany poems upon several occasions. Ed C. Gildon. 1692.

Ovid's Art of love; with Hero and Leander of Musaeus; translated by several hands. 1692. Halkett and Laing; really Thos Hoy, Two essays, 1682.

Songs for one, two and three voices, composed by R. King. [1692?]. *See* A second booke, 1695, *below.*

Songs by Pietro Reggio. 1692. *See* 1680, *above.*

Sylvae: or the second part of poetical miscellanies. 1692 (2nd edn). *See* Miscellany poems, 1684, *above.*

The triumph of wit. 1692 (2nd edn). *See* 1688, *above.*

1693

A collection of poems by several hands, most of them written by persons of eminent quality. 1693. Expansion of 1672 edn, now pbd F. Saunders. *See* 1695, *below.*

Comes amoris: the fourth book. 1693. *See* 1687, *above.*

England's merry jester: or Court, city and country jests; to which are added bulls, banters and poems. Ed J. S. 1693. *See* 1694, *below.*

Examen poeticum: being the third part of miscellany poems. 1693. *See* Case 172(3)(a) and (3)(b); *also* 1684, *above.*

Harmonia sacra: the second book. 1693. *See* 1688, *above.*

Ovid: Epistles translated by several hands and the Epistles of Aulus Sabinus made English by Mr Salusbury. 1693 (5th edn). *See* 1680, *above.*

The satires of Decimus Junius Juvenalis; together with the satires of Persius. Tr Dryden et al 1693. *See* 1697, 1702, 1711, 1713, 1726, 1732, 1735, 1754, *below.*

Sylvae: or the second part of poetical miscellanies. 1693 (2nd edn). *See* Miscellany poems, 1684, *above.*

Synopsis musicae or the musical inventory: being ayres, jiggs; to which are added songs and catches. 1693.

Thesaurus musicus: being a collection of the newest songs. Ed J. Hudgebut, bk 1 1693. *See* 1694, 1695, 1696, *below.*

1694

The annual miscellany: for the year 1694 [Miscellany poems, pt 4]. 1694. *See* 1684, *above*.

Chorus poetarum: or poems on several occasions. Ed C. Gildon MDCLXIXIV [1694]. *See* Poems on several occasions, 1696, and Poetical remains, 1698, *below*.

A collection of one hundred and eighty loyal songs. 1694 (4th edn). *See* 1684, *above*.

Comes amoris: the fifth book. 1694. *See* 1687, *above*.

The compleat French-Master. Ed A. Boyer 1694. *See* 1699, 1710, 1717, 1721, 1729, *below*.

England's merry jester. 1694. *See* 1693, *above*.

Innocui sales: a collection of new epigrams. Vol 1, 1694. Apparently no more pbd.

The ladies dictionary: being a general entertainment for the fair-sex. Ed N. H. 1694.

Miscellanea: or a choice collection of sayings by G. M[iège]. 1694. *See* Delight, 1697, *below*.

Miscellaneous letters and essays in prose and verse, by several gentlemen and ladies. Ed C. Gildon 1694. *See* 1696, *below*.

New academy of compliments, with an exact collection of the newest and choicest songs à la mode. 1694. Puttick and Simpson, 1907. *See* 1669, *above*.

[Song book, possibly 3rd edn of the Pleasant musical companion, bk 2 1694.] *See* 1667, *above* and BM catalogue.

Poems on several occasions: originals and translations. 1694. Possibly by one hand.

Thesaurus musicus: the second book. 1694. 2 imprints noted: D & M 129. *See* 1693, *above*.

1695

Deliciae musicae: being a collection of the newest and best songs. Ed H. Playford, bks 1–2 1695. *See* 1696, *below*.

Joyful cuckoldom: a collection of new songs. [1695?]. Ms title-page. *See* D & M 133.

Lacrymae cantabrigienses in obitum reginae Mariae. Cambridge 1695.

The new treasury of musick: or a collection of the choicest and best song-books. Ed H. Playford 1695. Includes The theater, bks 1–2, 4, 1685–7; also Choice ayres, bks 4–5, 1683–4, *above*.

A second booke of songs; with a pastorall elegy on Queen Mary, composed by R. King. [1695?]. *See* Songs, 1692, *above*.

The temple of death: a poem written by the Marquess of Normanby; together with several other excellent poems by Rochester [et al]. 1695 (2nd edn). A reissue of A collection, 1693, above.

Thesaurus musicus. Bks 3–4, 1695. Some copies lack imprint. *See* 1693, *above*.

1696

A collection of new songs: the first book. Ed N. Matteis 1696. *See* 1699, *below*.

A collection of songs set to musick by Henry Purcell and John Eccles. [1696?].

Deliciae musicae. Bks 3–4, 1696. *See* 1695, *above*.

Deliciae musicae: the first volume compleat. 1696. Bks 1–4 with general title; some copies also include Three elegies (D & M 141). *See* 1695, *above*.

Deliciae musicae: the first [second] book of the second volume. 1696. *See* 1695, *above*.

Miscellanea sacra: or poems on divine and moral subjects. Ed N. Tate, vol 1 1696. No more pbd; *see* 1698, *below*.

Miscellaneous letters and essays. Ed C. Gildon 1696.

The new help to discourse. 1696 (4th edn). *See* 1669, *above*.

Buckingham, Duke of. Poems on several occasions. 1696. *See* Chorus poetarum, 1694, *above*.

Rochester, Earl of. Poems on several occasions; with Valentinian. 1696. *See* 1691, *above*.

Thesaurus musicus: the fifth book. 1696. *See* 1693, *above*.

Wit's academy, or the Muses delight: being the newest academy of complements. 1696 (6th edn) (Stainer copy). *See* 1677, *above*.

1697

A collection of new songs compos'd by Morgan. 1697.

Delight and pastime: or pleasant diversion for both sexes. Ed G. M[iège] 1697. Reprint of Miscellanea, 1694, above.

An essay on poetry written by the Marquis of Normanby; with several other poems. Ed N. Tate 1697.

Familiar letters written by John, late Earl of Rochester, and several other persons. 2 vols 1697, 1697. *See* 1699, 1705, *below*.

Miscellanies over claret: being a collection of poems, translations. Nos 1–2, 1697. In Forster Collection. *See* 1698, *below*.

Miscellany poems; with the cure of love. 1697. Ptd for Will Rogers and Francis Hicks.

[A new book of songs]. Ed R. Leveridge [1697]. Lacks title-page. *See* 1699; *also* 1726, *below*.

Ovid's Metamorphosis, translated by several hands. Ed N. Tate, vol 1 1697.

Poems on affairs of state; from the time of Oliver Cromwell to the abdication of James the Second. 1697. *See* Case 211(1)(a), (1)(b) and (1)(c). *See also* 1698–9, 1702–5, 1707, 1710, 1716, *below*.

Poems on affairs of state: the second part, written during the reign of James the II. 1697. The Muses farewel and Supplement of 1690 with cancel title.

State-Poems; continued from the time of O. Cromwel to this present year 1697. 1697. Usually accompanies Poems on affairs of state, 1697, and later edns.

Poems upon several occasions; also Lycidus by Mrs A. Behn [and] a miscellany of new poems and songs by several hands. 1697 (2nd edn). Case 184(b): a made-up miscellany. *See* Lycidus, 1688, *above*.

The satires of Decimus Junius Juvenalis. Tr Dryden et al 1697 (2nd edn). Case 200(b) and (c): two issues. *See* 1693, *above*.

1698

Aesop in select fables: at Tunbridge, at Bathe, at Epsom, at Whitehall, from Tunbridge, at Amsterdam; with a dialogue. 1698.

The alamode musician: being a new collection of songs, compos'd by some of the most eminent masters. 1698.

A collection of new songs, sett to musick by Gillier. 1698.

Miscellanea sacra. Ed N. Tate 1698 (2nd edn, with addns). *See* 1696, *above*.

Miscellanies over claret. Nos 3–4 1698. In Forster Collection. *See* 1697, *above*.

Musica oxoniensis: a collection of songs. 1698. D & M 164; 2 issues.

The new academy of complements. 1698. *See* 1671.

Orpheus britannicus, compos'd by Henry Purcell. Bk 1, 1698. *See* 1702, 1706, 1711, 1712, 1721, 1745, *below*.

Pecuniae obediunt omnia: money masters all things, or satyrical poems [with 4 other titles]. 1698. First edn, 1696, not a miscellany.

Poems on affairs of state; from Oliver Cromwell to this present time: Pt III; with other miscellany poems. 1698. Not pt of the 1697–1716 ser.

Buckingham, Etherege, Milton et al. Poetical remains. Ed C. Gildon 1698. *See* Chorus poetarum, 1694, *above*.

Wits cabinet: or a companion for young men and ladies. 1698 (8th edn). Harding copy. *See* 1684, *above*.

1699

The beau's academy. 1699. The mysteries of love, 1685, with a cancel title.

Brown, Thomas. A collection of miscellany poems, letters. 1699. Case 216(a) and (b); 2 imprints. *See* 1700, *below*.

A collection of new songs, set by Nicola [Matteis]: the second book. [1699]. *See* 1696, *above*.

The compleat French-master. 1699 (2nd edn). *See* 1694, *above*.

Familiar letters. 2 vols 1699 (3rd edn). *See* 1697, *above*.

A new academy: or the accomplish'd secretary. 1699 (2nd edn).

Poems on affairs of state; from the time of Oliver Cromwell to the abdication of James the Second. 1699 (3rd edn).

State-Poems; continued from the time of O. Cromwel to the year 1697. 1699. *See* 1697, *above*.

A second book of songs. Ed R. Leveridge [1699]. D & M 176; 2 imprints. *See* 1697, *above*.

Twelve new songs, compos'd by [11 names]; with two new dialogues. 1699.

The whole volume of Mercurius musicus for the year 1699. Ed H. Playford 1699. *See* 1700–2, *below*.

Wit and mirth: or pills to purge melancholy. Ed H. P[layford] 1699. *See* 1700, 1705, 1706–7, 1709, 1712, 1714, 1719, 1720, *below*.

Cleveland, J. The works, collected into one volume. 1699. The 1687 edn with cancel title.

1700

Amphion Anglicus: a work of many compositions for voices, by John Blow. 1700.

Brown, Thomas. A collection of miscellany poems, letters. 1700 (2nd edn, with addns). *See* 1699, *above*.

Commendatory verses on the author of the two Arthurs, by some of his particular friends. Ed O. S. [Thomas Brown?]. Some copies end at p. 28. *See* 1702, *below*.

Discommendatory verses on those which are truly commendatory, on the author of the two Arthurs. 1700.

Luctus britannici: or the tears of the British Muses for the death of Dryden, by the most eminent hands. 1700.

Mercurius musicus for the year 1700. 1700. Pbd in 7 pts. *See* 1699, *above*.

The nine Muses: or poems written by nine several ladies upon the death of Dryden. 1700.

Cowley, A. The third part of the works: being his six books of plants made English by several hands. 1700 (2nd edn). Later included in vol 3 of Works, 1708, 1711, 1721 etc. *See* 1689, *above*.

Two divine hymns: being a supplement to the second book of Harmonia sacra. 1700. Also edn, nd, at Royal College of Music. *See* 1693, *above*.

Venus looking-glass: or a rich store-house of choice drollery. Ed J. O. [1700?].

Wit and mirth: or pills to purge melancholy. Ed H. Playford, pt 2 1700. *See* 1699, *above*.

Wits secretary: or the lovers magazine. [1700?] Book-auction records, 1920–1.

1701

Chaucer's whims: being some select fables and tales in verse. 1701.

A collection of poems, viz: the temple of death. 1701. A further expansion of 1672 edn; leaves 13 and 16 sometimes cancelled. *See* 1702, 1716, *below*.

Letters of wit, politicks and morality; also select letters of gallantry, original letters of love and friendship. Ed A. Boyer 1701.

Mercurius musicus. 1701. Pbd in 5 pts. *See* 1699, *above*.

A new collection of poems on several occasions. Ed C. Gildon 1701. *See* A new miscellany; also A new collection, 1715, *below*.

A new miscellany of original poems on several occasions. 1701. A reissue of above; various cancels.

Ovid's Epistles, translated by several hands. 1701 (6th edn). *See* 1680, *above*.

A pacquet from Will's: or a new collection of original

letters; with several satyrical characters in prose and verse, written and collected by several hands. 1701. McLeish, 1931. *See* 1705, *below*.

Poems on several occasions, by the E. of R[ochester]. 1701. *See* 1680, *above*.

The second book of the pleasant musical companion. 1701 (4th edn, enlarged). *See* Catch, 1667, *above*.

Wits academy, or the Muses delight: being the newest academy of complements. 1701 (8th edn). *See* 1677, *above*.

1702

The art of English poetry. Ed E. Bysshe 1702. *See* 1705, 1708, 1710, 1714, 1718, 1724, 1725, 1737, 1739, 1762, *below*.

A collection of poems, viz: the temple of death. 1702 (2nd edn). *See* 1701, *above*.

Commendatory verses: or a step towards a poetical war, by several hands. 1702 (2nd edn). *See* 1700, *above*.

Examen miscellaneum, consisting of verse and prose. [Ed C. Gildon?] 1702. Variant imprints.

Letters from the living to the living. 1702. Sotheby, 23 Nov 1931. *See* 1703, *below*.

Mercurius musicus [for 1702]. 1702. D & M 199; no complete copy known. *See* 1699, *above*.

Miscellany poems: the first part. 1702 (3rd edn). *See* 1684, *above*.

The monthly mask of vocal music [1702–27]. Issued annually in monthly pts; BM and Royal College of Music have incomplete sets.

The new help to discourse. 1702 (5th edn). *See* 1669, *above*.

Orpheus britannicus: the second book. 1702. *See* 1698, *above*.

A pacquet from Parnassus: or a collection of papers. Vol 1, nos 1–2; ed H. D. 1702.

Poems on affairs of state. 1702 (4th edn). *See* 1697, *above*.

State-Poems; continued from the time of O. Cromwel to the year 1697. 1702. *See* 1697, *above*.

The satires of Decimus Junius Juvenalis. Tr Dryden et al 1702 (3rd edn). *See* 1693, *above*.

Supplement to the second book of the pleasant musical companion. 1702. *See* 1701, *above*.

Sylvae: or the second part of poetical miscellanies. 1702 (3rd edn). *See* Miscellany poems, 1684, *above*.

The triumph of wit: or ingenuity display'd in its perfection. 1702 (4th edn). Harding copy. *See* 1688, *above*.

1703

Apollo's feast: or wits entertainment. Ed 'Dr Merryman' 1703. *See* 1718, *below*.

The Athenian oracle. Ed J. Dunton, vols 1–2 1703. *See* 1704, 1706, 1710, 1728, *below*.

Harmonia sacra: the first book. 1703 (2nd edn, enlarged). *See* 1688, *above*.

Laugh and be fat: or the fireside companion. 1703. Harvard copy.

Letters from the living to the living, written by several hands. 1703. *See* 1702, *above*.

London lampoon'd formerly in the Jacobite's songs. 1703.

Man's treachery to woman. [1703?] (4th edn).

Poems on affairs of state; from the time of Cromwell. 1703 (5th edn). *See* 1697, *above*.

State-Poems: continued from the time of Cromwel to the year 1697. 1703. *See* 1697, *above*.

Poems on affairs of state; from the reign of James the first to this present year 1703. Vol 2, 1703. Analysis of 3 edns: *see* W. J. Cameron, Princeton Univ Lib Chron 24 1963.

Wits cabinet. 1703 (11th edn, much enlarged). *See* 1684, *above*.

1704

The arraignment of lewd, idle, froward and unconstant women; to which is added a second part containing merry dialogues, witty poems and jovial songs. 1704.

Athenae redivivae: or the new Athenian oracle. Vol 1, pts 1–6 1704.

The Athenian oracle. Ed J. Dunton, vols 1–2 1704 (2nd edn); Vol 3 and last, 1704. *See* 1703, *above*.

A collection of songs, compos'd by John Eccles. [1704?]

A collection of the choicest songs and dialogues composd by the most eminent masters of the age. [1704]. Harding copy. Other collections of single-sheet songs were issued from time to time under this title; *see* 1710 and 1715 for 2 more of them.

Divine hymns and poems. 1704. *See* A collection, 1709, 1719, *below*.

Miscellaneous works written by George, late Duke of Buckingham; also State poems on the late times by Dryden, Etherege [et al]. 1704. P. M. Hill Catalogue, 1967, notes slightly variant copy; 2nd edn at Queen's College, Oxford. *See* 1705, 1707, 1715, *below*.

Poems on affairs of state; from 1640 to this present year, 1704. Vol 3, 1704. *See* 1697, *above*.

Poetical miscellanies: the fifth part. Ed N. Rowe 1704. *See* Miscellany poems, 1684, *above*.

Robin Hood's garland: being a compleat history of all his merry exploits. 1704. *See* 1663, *above*.

The theatre of ingenuity, containing poems, odes, elegies, pastorals. Ed N. D[ancer] 1704.

An theater of mortality: or the illustrious inscriptions extant. Ed R. Monteith, Edinburgh 1704. *See* 1713, *below*.

Wits academy, or the Muses delight: being the newest academy of complements. 1704 (9th edn). Book-auction records, 1918–19. *See* 1677, *above*.

1705

The academy of complements; to which is added the newest songs. 1705. *See* 1663, *above*.

The art of English poetry. 1705 (2nd edn). *See* 1702, *above*.

The catch club or merry companions: being a collection of most diverting catches. 1705. Puttick and Simpson, 1907. *See* 1720, 1733, 1740, 1762, *below*.

A collection of the most celebrated songs and dialogues, composed by ye late famous Henry Purcell. [1705?]

The compleat academy of complements; with a collection of the newest songs. 1705. *See* 1729, *below*.

The diverting post, for the entertainment of Court, city and country. Ed H. P[layford], vol 1 1705. D. Nichol Smith copy. *See* 1706, *below*.

Familiar letters, written by Rochester [et al]. 2 vols 1705 (4th edn). Manchester Central Lib. *See* 1697, *above*.

Miscellanea sacra: or a curious collection of original poems upon divine and moral subjects, collected from the works of several pious persons. Ed S. Phillips 1705. *See* 1707–8, 1732, *below*.

Miscellaneous poetical novels or tales of wit and gallantry in both sexes. 1705. In Forster Collection; also Miscellaneous poetical novels: the second collection, 1705. Possibly by one hand.

A new collection of poems relating to state affairs, from Cromwel to this present time. 1705. Pirated edn, repudiated in vol 4 of 1707 edn. *See* 1697, *above*.

Ovid, De arte amandi. 1705. *See* 1662, *above*.

Ovid's Epistles, translated by several hands. 1705 (7th edn). *See* 1680, *above*.

A pacquet from Will's. 1705. In Voiture's works, vol 2. *See* 1701, *above*.

Rochester, Earl of. Poems on several occasions; with Valentinian. 1705. Princeton Univ copy. *See* 1691, *above*.

The second volume of miscellaneous works written by George, late Duke of Buckingham; with a collection of poems. Ed Thomas Brown 1705. *See* 1704, *above*.

Wit and mirth: or pills to purge melancholy. 1705 (2nd edn). *See* 1699, *above*.

1706

The Athenian oracle. Vols 1 and 3, 1706. McLeish, 1931. *See* 1703, *above*.

A choice collection of comic and serious Scots poems, both ancient and modern, by several hands. Pt 1 Edinburgh 1706. Watson's collection. *See* 1709, 1711, 1713, 1717, 1719, *below*.

Deliciae poeticae: or Parnassus display'd in a choice collection of poems and songs. 1706. *See* Mirth diverts, 1708–9, 1715, *below*.

The diverting-post for the year 1705. Vol 1, 1706. The 1705 vol, *above*, with a new title-page.

Dunton's whipping-post. Vol 1, 1706.

Examen poeticum: being the third part of miscellany poems. 1706 (2nd edn). *See* 1684, *above*.

Orpheus britannicus. Bk 1, 1706 (2nd edn, with addns). D & M 210; 2 issues. *See* 1698, *above*.

The poetical courant. Vol 1, 1706. Ed S. Philips?

The primer: or office of the B. Virgin Mary, revis'd. 1706. Hymns by Dryden et al; rptd Berkeley 1937.

Wit and mirth: or pills to purge melancholy. Vol 4, 1706. *See* 1699, *above*.

1707

The adventures of Catullus, intermixt with translations of his choicest poems by several hands. 1707.

Athenian sport: or two thousand paradoxes; with improvements from Boyle, Lock, Norris and other illustrious wits. [Ed J. Dunton] 1707.

The diverting muse: or the universal medley, written by a society of merry gentlemen. Pt 1, 1707. Case 241. Also pts 1–6, 1707. Sotheby, 24 April 1891. *See* E. Ward's Writings, vol 4, 1709; but other hands seem to be present.

Essays serious and comical; to which are added miscellaneous poems by a person of quality. 1707. Harding copy. By several hands? *See* 1710, *below*.

Miscellanea sacra. Ed S. Phillips, vols 1–2 1707 (3rd edn). *See* Case 236(1)(c) and (2).

The miscellaneous works of George, late Duke of Buckingham. Vol 1, 1707. *See* 1704, *above*.

The miscellaneous works of the late Earls of Rochester and Roscommon; to which is added a curious collection of original poems by the Earl of Dorset [et al]. 1707. *See* 1709, 1714, 1718, 1721, 1731, 1735, 1739, 1752, 1756–8, 1767, 1771, 1774, 1777, 1800, *below*.

The works of Rochester and Roscommon; with a collection of original poems by the most eminent hands. 1707 (2nd edn). Mostly sheets of above edn; Princeton Univ copy.

The Muses mercury. Ed J. O[ldmixon] 1707. *See* 1708, *below*.

A new-years gift for batchelors: containing the Scratching match, two satyrs against women. 1707. Dobell, 1927.

Poems on affairs of state; from 1620 to this present year, 1707. Vol 4, 1707. *See* 1697, *above*.

Sedley, C. The poetical works; with a new miscellany of poems by several of the most eminent hands. 1707. *See* 1710, *below*.

Satyrical reflections on the vices and follies of the age: part the first. 1707. *See* 1708, *below*.

Reflections, moral, comical, satyrical: part the second [-fourth], by several good hands. 1707.

The second book of the pleasant musical companion. 1707 (5th edn). D & M 212; 2 issues. *See* Catch, 1667, *above*.

The triumph of wit. 1707 (5th edn). *See* 1688, *above*.

Wit and mirth: or pills to purge melancholy. Vol 1, 1707 (3rd edn). 2 edns: sold by John Cullen; sold by John Young. *See* D & M and 1699, *above*.

Wit and mirth: or pills to purge melancholy. Vols 2–3, 1707 (2nd edn). *See* 1699, *above.*

Wit and mirth: or pills to purge melancholy. Vol 4, 1707. *See* 1699, *above.*

1708

The annual miscellany for the year, 1694. 1708 (2nd edn). *See* Miscellany poems, 1684, *above.*

The art of English poetry. 1708 (3rd edn). *See* 1702, *above.*

A collection of poems upon the victories of Blenheim and Ramilies, by the most eminent hands. 1708. Sotheby, 23 Nov 1931.

Cyder: a poem; with the Splendid shilling, Paradise lost and two songs. 1708. *See* 1709, *below.*

Divine hymns and poems on several occasions, by several eminent hands. 1708. D. Nichol Smith copy.

The Flanders new garland. [c. 1708].

Mirth diverts all care: being songs by the most celebrated wits of the age. 1708 (Folger Lib copy); Deliciae poeticae, 1706, with a new title-page.

Miscellanea sacra. Vol 2, ed S. Phillips 1708. BM copy; vol 2 erased to read vol 1. *See* 1705, *above.*

The Muses mercury. 1708. *See* 1707, *above.*

Oxford and Cambridge miscellany poems. Ed E. Fenton [1708]. *See* Case 248.

Reflections, moral, comical, satyrical: part the seventh. 1708. *See* 1707, *above.*

Poetical reflexions, moral, comical, satyrical: part the ninth. 1708.

Poetical reflexions, moral, comical, satyrical: part the tenth. [1708?] Possibly an imitative collection by a different printer, J. Read.

Poetical reflexions, moral, comical, satyrical; to be continu'd occasionally by several good hands. 1708. Also by J. Read.

The satyrical works of Titus Petronius Arbiter, made English by Wilson [et al; also] The charms of liberty. 1708. *See* 1710, 1713–14.

1709

The bottle companions, or Bacchanalian club: being merry drinking songs by the most ingenious masters. [c. 1709].

The charms of liberty, by the late Duke of D—; to which is added epigrams, poems and satyrs, written by several hands. 1709. Case 250(a) and (b). Re-setting of type.

A choice collection of comic and serious Scots poems. Pt 2 Edinburgh 1709. *See* 1706, *above.*

Roscommon, Dryden et al. A collection of divine hymns and poems on several occasions. 1709. *See* Divine hymns, 1704, *above.*

Cyder; with the Splendid shilling, Paradise lost and two songs. 1709. Included in J. Philips, Works, 1714; also in A collection of the best English poetry vol 1, 1717. *See* 1708, *above.*

Daphnis: or a pastoral elegy upon the unfortunate death of Thomas Creech; with the Despairing lover and the Despairing shepherd. 1709. Included in A collection of the best English poetry vol 1, 1717.

Addison, Congreve et al. A letter from Italy 1701; together with the Mourning Muse of Alexis, 1695; to which is added the Despairing lover. 1709. *See* Case 251(a) and (b).

Mirth diverts all care. 1709. Harding copy. Deliciae poeticae, 1706, reissued by a different bookseller. *See* 1708, *above.*

Ovid's Art of love; together with his Remedy of love, translated by several eminent hands. 1709. *See* 1712, 1719, 1735, 1747, 1750, 1757, 1764, 1776–7, 1782, 1791, 1793, 1795, 1799, *below.*

Waller, E. A panegyrick on Oliver Cromwell and his victories; with three poems on his death. 1709. *See* Three poems, 1682, *above.*

The pleasant musical companion. 1709 (5th edn). *See* Catch, 1667, *above.*

Poetical miscellanies: the sixth part. Ed N. Rowe 1709. *See* Case 172(6)(a). *See also* Miscellany poems, 1684, *above.*

Overbury, T. The wife: a poem; with an elegy on the untimely death of the author, poyson'd in the Tower etc. 1709 (17th edn). *See* Sir Thomas Overbury his wife, 1664, *above.*

Wit and mirth: or pills to purge melancholy. Vol 4, 1709 (2nd edn). *See* 1699, *above.*

The works of Rochester and Roscommon; to which is added a collection of miscellany poems. 2 pts 1709 (3rd edn), pt 1 1709 (3rd edn). *See* 1707, *above.*

1710

The art of English poetry. 1710 (4th edn). *See* 1702, *above.*

Athenianism, or the new projects of J. D[unton]: being six hundred distinct treatises in prose and verse. 1710.

Beaumont, J. Bosworth-Field; with several verses in praise of the author and elegies on his death, by the greatest wits then living. 1710.

Callipaedia: or the art of getting pretty children, translated by several hands. 1710, Philadelphia 1872 (facs). Differs from 1712 trn. *See* 1719, 1729, 1776, *below.*

A collection of new songs set to musick by Wm. Morley and John Isum. [1710?]. Sometimes lacks imprint.

A collection of poems for and against Dr Sacheverell. 1710. *See* Case 254(1)(a) and (b). *See* 1711; *also* Whig and Tory, 1712, 1713, *and* A Tory pill, 1715, *below.*

A collection of poems, for and against Dr Sacheverell. Pts 2–3, 1710.

A collection of poems, for and against Dr Sacheverell. Pt 4, 1710. A spurious continuation. *See* 1711, *below.*

A collection of the choicest songs and dialogues composd by the most eminent masters of the age. [1710?]. Harding copy; differs in part from 1704, *above.*

The compleat French-Master. 1710 (5th edn). *See* 1694, *above.*

The jovial companions, or merry club: being a choice collection of catches. [c. 1710]. Leaves of some copies not numbered.

Poems and epistles on several occasions; with the Stage vindicated, the Murmurers, Nugae canorae. 1710. *See* Lowndes; by several hands?

Poems on affairs of state; from the time of Oliver Cromwell to the abdication of James Second. 1710 (6th edn). With this edn the Continuation loses its bibliographical entity. *See* 1697, *above.*

Rochester, Earl of. Poems on several occasions; with Valentinian. 1710. Yale Univ copy. *See* 1791, *above.*

Poems on the death of her late Majesty Queen Mary, of blessed memory. 1710.

Sedley, C. Poetical works; with a new miscelany of poems by several of the most eminent hands. 1710 (2nd edn). *See* Case 243 (b) and 1707, *above.*

The Quakers art of courtship. 1710. *See* 1689, *above.*

Serious and comical essays; with ingenious letters, occasional thoughts and reflections; also the English epigrammatist and the Instructive library. 1710. Several hands in this? *See* 1707, *above.*

The state bell-man's collection of verses for the year 1711. 1710. By several hands?

A supplement to the Athenian oracle. 1710. *See* 1703, *above.*

The works of T. Petronius Arbiter, made English by Wilson and several others; to which is prefix'd the Charms of liberty. 1710 (2nd edn). *See* 1708, *above.*

1711

The antiquities of St Peters, or the abbey church of Westminster: containing all the inscriptions, epitaphs.

Ed J. C[rull] 1711. *See* 1713, 1715, 1722, 1741, 1742, *below.*

The British Apollo. Vol 1, 1711 (2nd edn). Original nos pbd 1708–11. *See* 1726, 1740, *below.*

A choice collection of comic and serious Scots poems. Pt 3, Edinburgh 1711. Pts 1–3 rptd Glasgow 1869. *See* 1706, *above.*

A collection of hymns and poems for the use of the October club. 1711.

A collection of poems for and against Dr Sacheverell: the fourth part. 1711. *See* 1710, *above.*

Delights for the ingenious: or a monthly entertainment for the curious of both sexes. Ed J. Tipper [1711].

Orpheus britannicus: the second book. 1711 (2nd edn). *See* 1698, *above.*

The satires of Decimus Junius Juvenalis. Tr Dryden et al 1711 (4th edn). *See* 1693, *above.*

State-Amusements, serious and hypocritical; with some select copies of amusing verses. 1711.

Wit's cabinet: a companion for gentlemen and ladies; to which is added a choice collection of the best songs. [c. 1711?] Apparently a rival of the ser beginning in 1684, *above.*

The works of Monsr Boileau Despreaux. Vol 2, 1711. *See* 1712–14, 1736, *below.*

1712

Callipaedia, in four books; with some other pieces, made English by Rowe [et al]. 1712; rptd in Rowe's Poetical works, 1715 etc. A different work from the 1710 vol. *See* 1733, 1761, 1771, *below.*

A collection of new songs adapted to the times. [1712].

A collection of poems on state-affairs, several never before printed. Pt 1, 1712.

Miscellaneous poems and translations by several hands. [Ed Pope] 1712. *See* 1714, 1720, 1722; *also* Miscellany poems, 1726–7, 1732, *below.*

Occasional poems on the late Dutch war. 1712. Harding copy.

Orpheus britannicus: the second book. 1712 (2nd edn). *See* 1711, *above.*

Ovid's Art of love. Tr Dryden, Congreve et al 1712. *See* 1709, *above.*

Ovid's Epistles, translated by several hands. 1712 (8th edn). *See* 1680, *above.*

The poetical entertainer. Ed E. Ward 1712. Includes nos 1–3. *See* 1713, *below.*

Sentences and maxims divine, moral and historical, in prose and verse. Ed G. Shelley 1712.

The triumph of wit. 1712 (6th edn). *See* 1688, *above.*

The Tunbridge-Miscellany: consisting of poems written at Tunbridge-Wells this summer by several hands. 1712. *See* 1713–14, 1719, 1722, 1730, 1733, 1740, *below.*

Whig and Tory, or wit on both sides: being a collection of poems. 1712. Pts 1–4, 1710–11, of the Sacheverell collection reissued. *See* 1713; *also* A Tory pill, 1715, *below.*

Wit and mirth: or pills to purge melancholy. Vols 2–4, 1712 (3rd edn). Vol 4: Dobell, 1932. *See* 1699, *above.*

The works of Boileau, made English by several hands. Vol 1 1712. *See* 1711, *above.*

1713

The antiquities of St Peter's, Westminster. 1713. *See* 1711, *above.*

A choise collection of comic and serious Scots poems. Pt 1, Edinburgh 1713 (2nd edn). *See* 1706, *above.*

English gratitude: or the Whig miscellany. 1713.

Tate, N. et al. An entire set of the monitors: containing forty one poems on several subjects. 1713. *See* 1715, *below.*

Heraclitus ridens. Vols 1–2, 1713. Reprint of the 1681–2 nos.

The new academy of complements, compiled by L. B., Sir C. S., Sir W. D. and others. 1713. *See* 1671, *above.*

Poems on several occasions. 1713. *See* 1680, *above.* Victoria and Albert Museum copy.

The poetical entertainer. Nos 4–5, 1713. Nos 1–5, though by several hands, rptd in E. Ward, Miscellanies, 1717, and perhaps edited by him. *See* 1712, *above.*

Posthumous works of Boileau, made English by several hands. 1713. *See* 1711, *above.*

Sacred miscellanies: or divine poems upon several subjects. 1713. 6 titles and authors cited.

The satires of Decimus Junius Juvenalis. Tr Dryden et al 1713 (5th edn). *See* 1693, *above.*

A select collection of modern poems by several hands. Dublin 1713. *See* 1731, *below.*

A supplement to the antiquities of St Peter's, Westminster. 1713. *See* 1711, *above.*

An theater of mortality: or a further collection of funeral inscriptions. Ed R. Monteith, Edinburgh 1713. *See* 1704, *above.*

The Tunbridge miscellany. 1713. *See* 1712, *above.*

The second part of the Tunbridge miscellany for 1713. 1713.

The university miscellany: or more burning work for the Ox—f—d Convocation. 1713. 4 titles cited.

The university miscellany. 1713 (2nd edn, corrected).

Verses on the peace by the scholars of Croyden school, Surry. 1713. D. Cleverdon, 1936.

Whig and Tory: or wit on both sides. 1713 (2nd edn). Some copies lack last quire. *See* 1712, *above.*

The works of Anacreon and Sappho, done from the Greek by several hands. Ed G. S[ewell] 1713. *See* 1683, *above.*

The works of Petronius Arbiter, translated by several hands; to which is added some other of the Roman poets. 1713 (4th edn). *See* 1708, *above.*

1714

The art of English poetry. 2 vols 1714 (5th edn). *See* 1702, *above.*

The British Parnassus: or a compleat common-place-book of English poetry. Ed E. Bysshe 2 vols 1714. *See* The art, vols 3–4, 1718.

A collection of original poems, translations and imitations, by Prior, Rowe, Swift and other hands. 1714.

The compleat English secretary and newest academy of complements. 1714.

The Court of Atalantis, intermixt with fables and epistles in verse and prose by several hands. Ed J. Oldmixon 1714. Dobell, 1932. *See* Court tales, 1717, 1720, 1732, *below.*

An exact collection of many wonderful prophesies. 1714. *See* 1689, *above.*

A farther hue and cry after Dr Sw—t. [1714]. *See* Case 273(a) and (b). 1714 (2nd edn).

Harmonia sacra: the first book. 1714 (3rd edn). *See* 1688, *above.*

Harmonia sacra: book ii. 1714 (2nd edn, enlarged). *See above.*

Miscellaneous poems and translations by several hands, particularly Pope. 1714 (2nd edn). *See* Case 260(1)(b); *also* 1712, *above.*

Hill, A., L. Eusden, W. Broome et al. Original poems and translations. Case 275; later inclusions noted.

Poems and translations by several hands; to which is added the Hospital of fools, by William Walsh. 1714. *See* Case 277 for cancels; *also* Original poems, and 1719, *below.*

Original poems and translations by several hands; to which is added Æsculapius, or the hospital of fools, by William Walsh. 1714 (2nd edn) *See* Case 277 (b).

The Oxford packet [3 titles]. 1714. P. M. Hill, 1949.

Poems on several occasions by the Earls of Roscommon and Dorset. 1714. *See* 1707, *above.*

Poetical miscellanies: consisting of original poems and translations by the best hands, publish'd by Steele. 1714. *See* Case 279(a) and (b); *also* 1726–7, *below*.

Political merriment: or truths told to some tune. 2 pts 1714. *See* 1715, *below*.

The Tunbridge and Bath miscellany for the year 1714. 1714. *See* 1712, 1713, *above*.

Wit and mirth: or pills to purge melancholy. Vol 1, 1714 (4th edn); vol 5, 1714. *See* 1699, *above*.

The works of John, Earl of Rochester; with Valentinian. 1714. Yale Univ copy. *See* 1691, *above*.

The works of John Philips; to which are added Pastorals by Ambrose Philips. 1714. Includes a reissue of Cyder, 1709, *above*.

The works of Monsieur Boileau. 3 vols 1714. A reissue of the 1711–13 vols.

The works of Petronius Arbiter, translated by several hands. 1714 (4th edn). *See* 1708, *above*.

The works of the Earls of Rochester, Roscommon, Dorset. 1714 (4th edn). *See* 1707, *above*.

1715

The antiquities of St Peter's, Westminster. 1715 (2nd edn). *See* 1711, *above*.

The bee: a collection of choice poems. 3 pts 1715. Pt 3 entitled The bee: select poems.

A collection of new songs, compos'd by several masters. [1715?].

A collection of the choicest songs and dialogues, composd by the most eminent masters of the age. [1715?]. *See* 1704, *above*.

The Elzivir miscellany: consisting of original poems, translations and imitations, by [8 names]. 1715 (2nd edn). A made-up miscellany. *See* Miscellanea: the second volume, 1727, *below*.

England's witty and ingenious jester: jests; a curious collection of the newest songs. Ed W. W[instanley?] [c. 1715?] (15th edn). *See* 1718, *below*.

An entire set of the monitors; in several poems on divine subjects by M. Smith [et al] [1715?]. *See* 1713, *above*.

Mirth diverts all care. 1715. N & Q, 10 March 1860. Half-title: Deliciae poeticae. *See* 1708, *above*.

A new academy of complements: or the lover's secretary. 1715 (4th edn). *See* 1721, 1727, 1741, 1743, 1750, 1754, 1766, 1784, 1788, *below*; *also* 1669, *above*.

A new collection of miscellany poems for the year 1715. [1715]. Harding copy.

A new collection of original poems on several occasions [1715?]. *See* I. A. Williams, Library 4th ser 10 1930. A reissue of A new miscellany, 1701.

The new year's miscellany. 1715. Book-prices current, 1900.

The odes and satyrs of Horace, done into English by the most eminent hands. Tr Rochester et al 1715. J. Tonson's edn; *see* 1717, 1721, 1730, *below*.

The odes and satires of Horace, done into English by the most eminent hands. Tr Rochester et al 1715. A piracy of the above, ptd for A. Bell and 4 others.

A pill to purge state-melancholy: or a collection of excellent new ballads. 1715. *See* 1716, 1718, *below*.

The pleasant musical companion: or a choice collection of new and old catches by the best masters. [1715?]. Pickering and Chatto, 1929. Not the Playford ser.

Political merriment: or truths told to some tune. Pts 3–4, 1715. *See* 1714, *above*.

Butler, S. Posthumous works in prose and verse. 1715, 1715 (2nd edn), 2 vols 1715 (3rd edn); vol 2, 1715; vol 2, 1715 (3rd edn). Mostly by other hands. *See* 1716–17, 1719–20, 1730, 1732, 1754, *below*.

A Tory pill to purge Whig melancholy: or a collection of above one hundred new loyal ballads, poems. 1715. *See* Case 254 (e)

Tory pills to purge Whig melancholy: being a collection of the best poems, songs. 1715 (2nd edn).

The works of George Villiers, late Duke of Buckingham. 2 vols 1715 (3rd edn). *See* 1704, *above*.

1716

Ballads and some other occasional poems. Ed W. T[unstall] 1716. *See* Poems of love, 1716, and A collection of ballads, 1727, *below*.

A collection of poems; viz The temple of death. 1716 (3rd edn). 1702 edn, with addns, still retaining much of 1672 edn.

A collection of state songs, poems, publish'd since the Rebellion. 1716. *See* Pills, 1718, *below*.

Court poems: The basset-table, The drawing-room, The toilet. MDCCVI [1716]. Possibly by 3 hands; rptd in Pope's miscellany, 1717, and Mr Pope's literary correspondence vol 4, 1736, *below*. *See* 1717, 1719, 1726, *below*.

Court poems. Dublin 1716. With 2 additional poems.

The first [-sixth] part of miscellany poems, publish'd by Dryden. 6 vols 1716 (4th edn). Re-setting in pt 1. *See* 1684, *above*.

Honest amusemenst: being a collection of political songs. 1716. Harding copy.

The loyal mourner for the best of princes: being a collection of poems to the memory of Queen Anne, by a society of gentlemen. Ed C. Oldisworth 1716.

The loyal mourner for the best of princes, reprinted in Dublin. 1716. Dobell, 1926.

The merry musician: or a cure for the spleen. Pt 1, 1716. Type-set music. *See* 1728, 1730; for another ser, *see* 1729, 1730, *below*.

The new help to discourse. Ed W. W. 1716. Myers, 1935. *See* 1669, *above*.

New miscellaneous poems; with five love-letters from a nun to a cavalier; with the cavalier's answer. 2 pts 1716 (4th edn). Harding copy. *See* 1718, 1725, *below*.

New miscellaneous poems; with the cavalier's answers to the nun's five love-letters. 1716. Harding copy.

Ovid's Epistles, translated by several hands. 1716. *See* 1680, *above*.

A pill to purge state-melancholy. 1716 (3rd edn, with addns). *See* 1715, *above*.

Poems of love and gallantry, written in the Marshalsea and Newgate by several prisoners. 1716. Partly a reprint of Ballads, 1716, *above*.

Poems on affairs of state. Vol 1, 1716 (6th edn), vols 2–4 (2nd edn). *See* 1697, *above*.

Butler, S. Posthumous works in prose and verse. 2 vols 1716 (4th edn, with addns); vol 1, 1716. *See* 1715, *above*.

[A race at Sheriff-Muir]. [1716?]. Title missing; *see* I. A. Williams, Library 4th ser 10 1930.

Rowe, N., Pope et al. State poems, viz: Verses upon the sickness and recovery of Walpole. 1716. *See* Court poems pt 2, 1717, *below*.

1717

The agreeable variety, in two parts. 1717. *See* 1724, 1742, *below*.

The art of dress: a poem. Ed J. D. Breval 1717. Includes major pt of Court poems, pt 2, 1717, etc. Possibly The ladies miscellany, 1718, without general title.

A choise collection of comic and serious Scots poems. Pt 1, Edinburgh 1717 (2nd edn). Sotheby, 21 March 1907. *See* 1706, *above*.

A collection of songs set to musick by James Graves. [1717]. Harding copy.

A collection of the best English poetry, by several hands; in two vol's octavo. 1717. A made-up miscellany. Contents differ widely: *see* W. J. Cameron, N & Q July 1958.

The compleat French-Master. 1717 (7th edn). *See* 1694, *above.*

Court poems. Pt 2, 1717. A made-up miscellany, incorporating State-Poems, 1716, *above*; later included in The ladies miscellany, 1718, *below.*

Court tales: or a history of the amours of the present nobility. 1717. The Court of Atalantis, 1714, with a new title-page.

The inscriptions upon the tombs, gravestones, in the Dissenters burial place near Bunhill-Fields. 1717.

Miscellaneous poems on state-affairs, written by the greatest wits of the age. Pts 1–2, Stamford 1717. Dobell, 1932.

Monumenta anglicana: being inscriptions on the monuments of several eminent persons deceased, 1700–1715. Ed J. Le Neve 1717. *See* 1718, 1719, *below.*

Mughouse-Diversion: or a collection of loyal prologues and songs. 1717 (3 edns). *See* 1719, *below.*

The odes and satyrs of Horace, done into English by the most eminent hands. 1717. *See* 1715, *above.*

Ovid's Metamorphoses in fifteen books, translated by the most eminent hands. Ed S. Garth 1717. *See* 1720, 1727, 1732, 1736, 1751, 1773, 1794, *below.*

Ovid's Metamorphoses in fifteen books: a new translation by several hands. Ed G. Sewell 2 vols 1717. *See* 1724, 1733, *below.*

The parson's daughter: a tale; to which are added epigrams and the Court ballad, by Pope. 1717. Pope's share uncertain; rptd in Pope's miscellany, pt 2, 1717, with addns, and in Court poems, 1719, *below.*

Poems by the Earl of Roscomon; to which is added an essay on poetry, by the Earl of Mulgrave; Poems by Duke. 1717.

Poems of Henry Howard, Earl of Surrey; with the poems of Sir Thomas Wiat and others his famous contemporaries. 1717. Reprint of Tottel's miscellany, 1557.

Poems on several occasions by the Duke of Buckingham, Wycherly and other eminent hands. 1717. Compiled by Pope; ed N. Ault, as Pope's own miscellany, 1935.

Poems on several occasions: viz Waller's anniversary on the government of the Lord Protector, anno 1655; A pastoral courtship. 1717.

Pope's miscellany. 1717. Book-Prices current, 1891.

Pope's miscellany: viz The basset-table. 1717 (2nd edn). Caption-title is Court poems, of which book, 1716, this is a reprint with addns. *See* Court poems, 1719, *below.*

Pope's miscellany: the second part. 1717. Only one poem in common with Court poems, pt 2, 1717.

The rape of the smock. 1717. Included in The ladies miscellany, 1718, *below. See* 1727, 1736, *below.*

Butler, S. The third and last volume of posthumous works. 1717 (2 edns).

Twenty new songs of humour compos'd by Wm Turner. [1717?].

The virgin Muse: being a collection of poems from English poets. Ed J. Greenwood 1717. *See* 1722, 1731, *below.*

1718

Apollo's feast: or wit's entertainment. 1718. Book-Auction records 1916–17. *See* 1703, *above.*

The art of English poetry. Vols 1–2, 1718 (6th edn). *See* 1702, *above.*

The art of English poetry, vol the iiid and ivth. 1718. Bysshe's British Parnassus vol 1, 1714, with cancel title.

The complete art of poetry. Ed C. Gildon, vols 1–2 1718.

England's witty and ingenious jester, in two parts. 1718 (17th edn). Harding copy, nd and different imprint. *See* 1715, *above.*

Familiar letters of love, gallantry and several occasions, by the wits of the last and present age. 2 vols 1718. *See* 1724, *below.*

The ladies miscellany: consisting of original poems by the most eminent hands, viz [6 titles; with] Court-poems. 1718. A made-up miscellany. *See* 1720, 1730–2.

Letters, poems and tales; amorous, satyrical and gallant: originals found in the cabinet of Mrs Anne Long, since her decease. 1718. A made-up miscellany, later included in A second collection, 1720, and in Miscellanies by Swift, 1722, *below.*

Memoirs of the life of Theophilus Keene; to which is added elegies, pastorals, odes and poems, by several hands. 1718.

Monumenta anglicana 1650–79. Ed J. le Neve 1718; 1680–99, 1718. *See* 1717, *above.*

New miscellaneous poems; with five love-letters from a nun to a cavalier. 1718 (5th edn). Worcester College Oxford copy. *See* 1716, *above.*

New miscellaneous poems; with the cavalier's answers to the nun's five love-letters. 1718. Dobell, 1932.

Pills to purge state-melancholy, part the second: being a collection of excellent new ballads. 1718. *See* 1715, *above.*

A pill to purge state-melancholy. Vol 2, 1718 (2nd edn, with addns). Stainer copy. *See* 1715, *above.*

Remains of John, Earl of Rochester: being satyrs, songs and poems. 1718. *See* 1761, *below.*

The whole prophecies of Scotland, England, France, Ireland and Denmark. Edinburgh 1718. Ellis, 1932. *See* 1745, 1781, *below.*

The works of John, Earl of Rochester, consisting of satires, songs, translations and other occasional poems. 1718. *See* 1691, *above.*

The works of the Earls of Rochester, Roscomon, Dorset, in two volumes. 1718. *See* 1707, *above.*

Poems on several occasions by the Earl of Roscomon. Vol 2, 1718.

1719

An abstract of a sermon preached at Brenchley in Kent, by H. C., with several divine hymns. 1719. Dobell, 1937.

Callipaedia: or the art of getting pretty children. Tr W. Oldisworth 4 bks 1719 (2nd edn). In spite of title, preface refers to the translators. *See* 1710, *above.*

A choise collection of comic and serious Scots poems. Pt 2, Edinburgh 1719 (2nd edn). Book-Prices current, 1906. *See* 1706, *above.*

A collection of divine hymns and poems. 1719 (3rd edn). *See* Divine hymns, 1704, *above.*

The Court miscellany, in prose and verse. Nos 1–2 1719. Pt 2, nd.

Court poems in two parts, compleat; to which are added [2 titles] by Pope. 1719 (2 issues, one with 2 pp. book-list and pt title-pages). *See* 1716, *above.*

A guide for malt-worms: the second part, done by several hands. [1719?]. Pt 1 not known.

Monumenta Anglicana 1600–49. 1719; 1650–1718, 1719. *See* 1717, *above.*

Mug-House diversion. 1719 (5th edn, with addns). *See* 1717, *above.*

Musapaedia: or miscellany poems never before printed, by several members of the Oxford poetical club. 1719 (3 issues).

Musarum lachrymae: or poems to the memory of Nicholas Rowe, by several hands. Ed C. Beckingham 1719.

New academy of compliments. 1719. Puttick & Simpson, 1907. A reissue of 1694 edn?

Original poems and translations by the most eminent hands; to which is added Aesculapius, by Walsh. 1719 (2nd edn). In Forster Collection. *See* 1714, *above.*

Ovid's Art of love, translated by several eminent hands. 1719. *See* 1709, *above.*

Addison. Poems on several occasions. 1719. Includes trns of the Latin poems by several hands. *See* Miscellanies, 1725, *below.*

Poems upon divine and moral subjects by Dr Patrick and other eminent hands. 1719. *See* A collection, 1734, *below.*

Tunbrigalia: or Tunbridge miscellanies for the year 1719. 1719; pt 1, 1719 (2nd edn). *See* 1712, *above.*

Songs compleat, pleasant and divertive. Ed T. D'Urfey 5 vols 1719. D & M 231–5. A much expanded and re-arranged edn of Wit and mirth, 1699–1714, vols 1 and 2 devoted almost exclusively to D'Urfey's own songs; vol 3 also bears his name, wrongly. *See below.*

Wit and mirth: or pills to purge melancholy. 5 vols 1719 (4th edn). Another issue of Songs compleat, above; a reprint, partly of this issue and the 1720 vol, and partly of Songs compleat, pbd c. 1870; 6 vols New York 1959. *See* 1720, 1791, *below.*

1720

The catch club: or merry companions. Bks 1–2, [1720?]. *See* 1705, *above.*

A collection of songs on various subjects, fitted to all capacities. 1720.

Court-Tales: or a history of the amours of the present nobility. 1720. Sotheby, 29 April 1891. *See* 1717, *above.*

The Edinburgh miscellany: consisting of original poems, translations, by various hands. Ed W. C., Edinburgh 1720. Vol 1 only; a 2nd edn (reissue) in 1720.

Eloisa to Abelard; written by Pope. 1720 (2nd edn). Verses by 5 others included.

The ladies miscellany: consisting of original poems. 1720. Sotheby, 24 July 1866. *See* 1718, *above.*

Love's last shift: or the Mason disappointed; to which is annex'd a song. [1720?].

Miscellanea aurea: or the golden medley. 1720. Chiefly by T. Killigrew the younger.

Miscellaneous poems and translations, by several hands. 2 vols 1720 (3rd edn). Lintot's miscellany; *see* 1712, *above.*

The new merry companion. [1720]. Sotheby, 30 July 1884.

The new miscellany, consisting of poems and translations, with a song. 1720.

A new miscellany of original poems, translations and imitations by the most eminent hands. Ed A. H[ammond] 1720. *See* 1740, *below.*

Ovid's epistles, translated by several hands. 1720. *See* 1680, *above.*

Ovid's Metamorphoses. Ed S. Garth 2 vols 1720 (2nd edn). *See* 1717, *above.*

The pleasant musical companion. 1720 (6th edn, enlarged). *See* Catch, 1667, *above.*

Butler, S. Posthumous works in prose and verse. 3 vols 1720 (6th edn); vol 2, 1720 (6th edn). *See* 1715, *above.*

A second collection of miscellanies, written by Swift. 1720. A made-up miscellany, which includes Letters, 1718, *above.*

Strephon's revenge: a satire on the Oxford toasts. 1720 (3rd edn). First edn to contain An appendix: being a collection of verses. *See* 1724, *below.*

Three poems, viz. [Reason, by Pomfret; The female Phaeton, by Harcourt (or Prior); The judgment of Venus, by Harcourt]. 1720.

Twenty new songs compos'd by James Graves. [c. 1720]. Harding copy.

Wit and mirth, or pills to purge melancholy: the sixth and last vol. 1720. *See* 1719, *above.*

The yearly subscription, or the harmonious entertainment: being a miscellany of new songs for the year 1720. Bk 1, [1720]. Stainer copy; no more pbd?

1721

The Basia of Bonefonius. 1721. Sotheby, 31 May 1911. Possibly another issue of Pancharis, 1721, both pbd E. Curll.

Choice emblems, divine and moral. 1721. H. Start and Sons, 1932. *See* Delights, 1684, *above.*

The compleat French-Master. 1721 (8th edn). *See* 1694, *above.*

Cupid's bee-hive: or the sting of love, translated by several hands; with some original poems. 1721.

The grove: or a collection of original poems, translations, by [9 names] and other eminent hands. 1721. *See* A miscellany, 1732, *below.*

The laws of poetry, explain'd and illustrated. 1721. By C. Gildon?

A miscellaneous collection of poems, songs and epigrams by several hands, publish'd by T. M[osse?] 2 vols Dublin 1721.

Miscellanies in prose and verse: the fourth edition, with the following additions [5 items]. Dublin 2721 [i.e. 1721].

A miscellany of ingenious thoughts and reflections in verse and prose. Ed T. Reresby 1721.

A new academy of complements: or the lover's secretary. 1721 (7th edn). Harding copy. *See* 1715, *above.*

A new collection of poems. Vol 1, Dublin 1721. R. H. Lonsdale copy.

The new help to discourse. 1721 (8th edn). *See* 1669, *above.*

The odes and satyrs of Horace, done into English. Tonson's edn; *see* 1715, *above.*

Orpheus britannicus. Bks 1–2 1721 (3rd edn). *See* 1698, *above.*

Pancharis, queen of love, or woman unveil'd: being the Basia of Bonefonius translated by several hands. 1721. *See* 1722–3, *below.*

Penkethman's jests: or wit refin'd. Pt 1, 1721 (2nd edn); pt 2, 1721. *See* 1735, *below.*

The pleasures of coition; with some other love-pieces. 1721 (Dobell, 1932), 1721 (2nd edn).

South-Sea pills to purge Court melancholy: being a collection of poems, satires, by Stanhope, Arundel, Cowper and Foxton. 1721. No known copy.

Three new poems, viz: Family duty, from Chaucer, moderniz'd; The curious wife, by Fenton; Buckingham-House, by the late Duke of Buckinghamshire. 1721. Pickering & Chatto, 1937.

Chaucer, G. Works. Ed J. Urry 1721. Contains pieces by Lydgate, Gower et al.

The works of the Earls of Rochester, Roscommon, Dorset, Devonshire. 1721, 1721. *See below and* 1707, *above.*

Poems on several occasions, by Roscommon, Dorset, Devonshire, Buckinghamshire. Vol 2, 1721. Some copies are dated 1720; *see* TLS 10 Oct 1935.

1722

The antiquities of St Peter's, Westminster. 2 vols 1722 (3rd edn). *See* 1711, *above.*

Miscellaneous poems and translations, by several hands. 2 vols 1722 (4th edn). Lintot's miscellany; *see* 1712, *above.*

Miscellanies, written by Jonathan Swift; viz The art of punning. 1722 (4th edn).

Pancharis, queen of love, by several hands. 1722 (2nd edn). *See* 1721, *above.*

Tunbrigialia: or the Tunbridge miscellany for the year 1722. [1722]. *See* 1712, *above.*

The virgin muse. 1722 (2nd edn). 1717 reissued.

1723

A collection of old ballads, corrected from the best and most ancient copies extant; with introductions. 2 vols 1723; vol 1, 1723 (2nd edn); ed A. Philips? *See* 1725–7, 1738, *below.*

The constitutions of the Free-Masons: containing the history, charges, regulations. 1723. Ed J. T. Desaguliers. *See* 1731, 1738, 1746, 1751, 1756, 1762, 1765, 1767, 1769, 1784, 1792, *below*; ed L. Vibert 1923 (facs).

Cythereia: or new poems upon love and intrigue. 1723. Later included in The altar, 1727, *below.*

Ebrietatis encomium: or the praise of drunkenness, by

Boniface Oinophilus. 1723, 1723. Ed J. Pearce, 1873. *See* 1743, *below*.

Pancharis, queen of love, by several hands. [Dublin] 1723. *See* 1721, *above*.

Pleasure for a minute: or the amorous adventure; The Grecian dame and other love-poems. 1723.

The second part of pleasure for a minute: containing [7 titles], with other love-poems. 1723. Harding copy. *See* The town mistress, 1726, *below*.

1724

The agreeable variety: in two parts. 1724 (2nd edn). Dedication signed J. M. 1717 reissued.

The art of English poetry. 2 vols 1724 (7th edn). *See* 1702, *above*.

A collection of original poems: viz [7 titles]. 1724 (2nd edn). A made-up miscellany.

The ever green: being a collection of Scots poems, wrote before 1600. Ed A. Ramsay 2 vols Edinburgh 1724; rptd Glasgow, 1824, 1874–6. *See* 1761, *below*.

Familiar letters of love, gallantry and several other occasions. 2 vols 1724 (6th edn). *See* 1718, *above*.

The hive: a collection of the most celebrated songs of our best English poets. Vol 1 1724, 1724 (2nd edn). Harding copy. *See* 1725–7, 1729, 1732–3, *below*.

The hive: volume the second. 1724, 1724 (2nd edn). Dobell, 1929.

Miscellaneous poems, original and translated, by several hands. Ed M. Concanen 1724.

Ovid's Metamorphoses, made English by several hands. Ed G. Sewell 2 vols 1724 (2nd edn). *See* 1717, *above*.

The pleasant musical companion. 1724 (8th edn). *See* Catch, 1667, *above*.

A pocket companion for gentlemen and ladies. Ed R. Neale [1724]. *See* 1725, *below*.

Strephon's revenge. 1724 (4th edn). *See* 1720, *above*.

The tea-table miscellany. Ed A. Ramsay, Edinburgh 1724. Vol 1 only; no copies known of vols 2–4. *See* B. Martin, Bibliography of Ramsay, Glasgow 1931. *See also* 1729–30, 1733–4, 1740, 1750, 1753, 1760, 1762–3, 1765, 1768–9, 1775, 1782–3, 1788, 1793–4, *below*; also A new miscellany, 1727, and The charms, 1791, *below*.

Thesaurus dramaticus: containing all the celebrated passages and other poetical beauties in the English plays. 2 vols 1724. *See* 1737, 1756; *also* Beauties of the English drama, 1777, *below*.

The triumph of wit. 1724 (8th edn). *See* 1688, *above*.

1725

The art of English poetry. 2 vols 1725 (7th edn). *See* 1702, *above*.

A collection of old ballads. Vol 3 1725. *See* 1723, *above*. Vols 1–3 rptd c. 1871.

A collection of sea songs on several occasions. [c. 1725].

A collection of songs, compos'd by John Sheeles. [c. 1725]. Harding copy.

Fraud detected: or the Hibernian patriot; Prometheus, a poem; Also a new poem to the Drapier and the songs sung at the Drapier's club. Dublin 1725. *See* The Hibernian patriot, 1730, *below*.

The hive: volume the third. 1725. *See* 1724, *above*.

Addison, J. Miscellanies in verse and prose. 1725. Contains trns of Latin poems by Newcomb, Sewell and Amherst. *See* Poems, 1719, *above*.

Mr Henr[y] Purcell's favourite songs out of Orpheus britannicus and the rest of his works. [1725?].

A new canting dictionary; to which is added a complete collection of songs in the canting dialect. 1725.

New Christmas carrols; fit also to be sung at Easter and other festivals. 1725. A reprint of pt of 1681 edn.

A new collection of poems on several occasions by Prior and others. 1725. *See* Case 334(a) and (b).

New miscellaneous poems; with the cavalier's answers to the nun's five love-letters. 1725. Worcester College Oxford copy. *See* 1716, *above*.

Original and genuine letters sent to the Tatler and Spectator. Ed C. Lillie 2 vols 1725.

Ovid's epistles with his Amours, translated into English verse by the most eminent hands. 1725. *See* 1680, *above; also* 1727, 1729, 1736, 1748, 1761, 1768, 1775, 1795, *below*.

A pocket companion for gentlemen and ladies. Ed R. Neale 2 vols [1725?]. This contains a 2nd issue of vol 1. *See* 1724, *above*.

Thesaurus aenigmaticus: or a collection of aenigma's or riddles. Pt 1, 1725. *See* 1726–7, *below*.

1726

The British Apollo. 3 vols 1726 (3rd edn). *See* 1711, *above*.

A collection of old ballads. Vol 2, 1726 (2nd edn). *See* 1723, *above*.

A collection of songs by Richard Leveridge. [c. 1726]. Stainer copy. *See* 1727, *below; also* 1697, *above*.

Court poems in two parts, by Pope [et al]. 1726. Included in most variants of Miscellanea vol 2, 1727, and in Mr Pope's literary correspondence vol 4, 1736 (2nd edn). *See* 1716, *above*.

Harmonia sacra. Bks 1–2 1726 (3rd edn). *See* 1688, *above*.

The hive. Vol 1 1726 (3rd edn). *See* 1724, *above*.

Honey-Moon; to which are added Melting Caelia and other love-poems. 1726. Harding copy.

Miscellaneous poems and translations by several hands. Ed R. Savage 1726. Case 336(a) and (b): 2 issues with different preliminaries.

Miscellaneous poems by several hands. Ed D. Lewis 1726. Leaves T2 and T4 may be cancels in some copies. *See* 1730, *below*.

Miscellany poems by Pope. Vol 1, 1726 (5th edn). Lintot's miscellany; 2 vols pbd, but only first located. *See* Miscellaneous poems, 1712, *above*.

The monthly collection of songs. 3 pts [c. 1726]. For Aug–Oct; Harding copy.

A new miscellany: being pieces of poetry, from Bath, Tunbridge, in the year 1725; written chiefly by persons of quality. [1726?].

The new year's gift: or advice to a nephew about his choice in marriage. [c. 1726]. Harding copy.

Orpheus caledonius: or a collection of the best Scotch songs set to musick by W. Thomson. [1726]. *See* 1733, *below*.

The pleasant musical companion. 1726 (9th edn). *See* Catch, 1667, *above*.

Poems in English and Latin on the archers, by several hands. Edinburgh 1726.

Poetical miscellanies, consisting of original poems and translations by the best hands. Ed R. Steele, Dublin 1726 (pirated). *See* 1714, *above*.

The satyrs of Decimus Junius Juvenalis. Tr Dryden et al 1726 (5th edn). *See* 1693, *above*.

The sixpenny miscellany. 1726.

Thesaurus aenigmaticus. Pts 2–4, 1726. *See* 1725, *above*.

The town mistress: or street-walker; [7 titles]; with other love-poems. 1726. Harding copy. Pleasure, pt 2, 1723, with a new title-page and 3 leaves prefixed.

1727

The altar of love, consisting of poems and other miscellanies by the most eminent hands. 1727, 1727. A made-up miscellany. *See* 1731, *below*.

Atterburyana: being miscellanies by the late Bishop of Rochester [et al]. 1727.

A collection of ballads, and some other occasional poems. Ed W. Tunstall 1727. *See* Ballads, 1716, *above*.

A collection of epigrams. 1727. *See* 1735, 1737, *below*.

A collection of old ballads. Vol 1, 1727 (3rd edn). *See* 1723, *above*.

A collection of songs, with the musick by Leveridge. 2 vols 1727. Also 1726 edn (Sotheby, 19 April 1898). *See* 1726, *above*.

A collection of the most celebrated prologues. 1727 (2nd edn).

The Dublin quarterly maske: being a choice collection of English songs sett with basses. Dublin [1727?]. Stainer copy.

The first [-sixth] part of miscellany poems. 6 vols 1727 (5th edn). *See* 1684, *above*.

The hive. Vol 2, 1727 (3rd edn). *See* 1724, *above*.

Miscellanea in two volumes, never before published. Vol 1, 1727.

Miscellanea: the second volume. 1727. A made-up miscellany, usually including Court poems, 1726, and The Elzivir miscellany, 1715, *above*. *See* R. H. Griffith, Pope bibliography, Austin 1922.

Miscellanies: the last volume. 1727. Pbd in 1728; *see* Teerink 25(3a–d) and the bibliographical notes in E. L. Steeves, The art of sinking in poetry: a critical edition, New York 1952 (facs). *See also* 1728, 1731–3, 1735–6, 1738, 1742, 1745, 1747, 1749, 1751, *below*.

Miscellany poems by Pope. 2 vols 1727 (5th edn). Lintot's miscellany, a reprint of 1726 edn. *See also* Miscellaneous poems, 1712, *above*.

A new academy of complements: or the lover's secretary. 1727 (9th edn, with addns). *See* 1715, *above*.

A new miscellany of Scot's sangs. 1727. Abridged (pirated?) edn of Ramsay's Tea-table miscellany, bks 1–2, 1724, *above*.

Ovid's Epistles with his Amours, translated by the most eminent hands. Dublin 1727. *See* 1725, *above*.

Ovid's Metamorphoses. Ed S. Garth 2 vols 1727 (3rd edn). *See* 1717, *above*.

Pietas universitatis oxoniensis in obitum Georgii I et gratulatio in Georgii II inaugurationem. Oxford 1727.

Prior, M. et al. Poems on several occasions. Vol 3, 1727 (2nd edn).

Poetical miscellanies by the best hands. Ed R. Steele 1727 (2nd edn, augmented). *See* 1714, *above*.

The rape of the smock. 1727 (2nd edn). Later included in The altar of love, 1727, *above*. *See also* 1717, *above*.

Sepulchrorum inscriptiones: or a curious collection of above 900 epitaphs, antient and modern. Ed James Jones 2 vols Westminster 1727.

Thesaurus aenigmaticus. 4 pts, Dublin 1727. Sotheby, 9 July 1919. *See* 1725, *above*.

Twelve new songs compos'd by several eminent masters. Pt 1, [1727?]. Harding copy. Pt 2 is entitled Eight new songs.

Whartoniana: or miscellanies in verse and prose, by the Wharton family and several other persons. 2 vols 1727. Vol 2 title: Letters to the Lady Wharton; in vol 1, D3 is sometimes a cancel. *See* 1731, 1740, *below*.

The works of Pope; to which are added Cooper's-Hill [and 6 other titles]. Dublin 1727.

1728

The Athenian oracle. Vols 1–4, 1728 (3rd edn). *See* 1703, *above*. Selection ed J. Underhill, [c. 1892].

The Christian poet: a miscellany of divine poems, all written by the late Mr Secretary Addison. 1728. *See* Case 348; a made-up miscellany with variable contents.

Comitia Westmonasteriensium. 1728. Case 349(a) and (b), 2 issues; Editio secunda, 1728.

A compleat collection of all the verses, essays, letters, occasioned by the three volumes of Miscellanies, by Pope and company. 1728. Ed M. Concanen or J. Dennis?

Cupid's Metamorphoses, or love in all shapes: being [vol 2 of W. Pattison's] Poetical works. 1728. Several hands in this.

Gulliveriana: or a fourth volume of miscellanies; Alexanderiana and many things in verse and prose. 1728.

Letters in prose and verse to the celebrated Polly Peachum. 1728 (P. M. Hill, 1949), 1728 (2nd edn).

The merry musician: or a cure for the spleen. Vol 2, [1728?]. *See* 1716, *above*.

Miscellanies: the last volume [vol 3]. 1728. Teerink 25(3e). *See* 1727, *above*.

Miscellanies in prose and verse, in two volumes, by Swift and Pope. Dublin 1728 (2nd edn). Teerink 33(1a). Reprint of the 3 vol London edn, 1727, with addns. *See* Miscellanies in prose and verse, Dublin 1732–3.

Poems on several occasions: containing [18 titles], by a lady. 1728. Harding copy. Includes poems by 3 named authors.

1729

Callipaedia: or the art of getting pretty children. Tr W. Oldisworth. 1729 (3rd edn). Preface still refers to the translators. *See* 1710, *above*.

The choice: being a collection of two hundred and fifty celebrated songs. 1729. *See* 1732–3, 1737, *below*.

A collection of Bacchanalian songs. 1729. A reprint of The triumphs, 1729, with addns.

A collection of letters and essays publish'd in the Dublin Journal. Ed J. Arbuckle 2 vols 1729. *See* Hibernicus's letters, 1734, *below*.

The comedian's tales: or jests, songs. 1729. Book-Auction records, 1902–3.

The compleat academy of complements: or lover's magazine. 1729.

The compleat French-Master. 1729 (10th edn). *See* 1694, *above*.

The hive. Vol 3, 1729 (3rd edn). *See* 1724, *above*.

The merry musician: or a cure for the spleen. [1729?]. Harvard copy. Not in ser beginning 1716.

Miscellaneous poems by several hands, particularly the D— of W—n [et al]; publish'd by Ralph. 1729. *See* A present, 1743, *below*.

The musical miscellany: being a collection of choice songs. Vols 1–2, 1729. *See* 1730, 1731, *below*.

Ovid's epistles; with his Amours. 1729. *See* 1725, *above*.

Poetical miscellanies: consisting of original poems and translations, by the best hands. Ed J. Gay, Dublin 1729.

Robin's panegyrick: or the Norfolk miscellany. [1729]. *See* 1731–2, *below*.

The St James's miscellany: or the citizens amusement. Ed 'Tim Merriman' [1729?].

The tea-table miscellany: or a complete collection of Scots sangs. Vols 1–3, Dublin 1729. *See below, and* 1724, *above*.

The tea-table miscellany. Dublin 1729. Harding copy; ptd by S. Powell for George Risk; called 5th edn in preface.

The triumphs of Bacchus: or the delights of the bottle. 1729. *See* A collection of Bacchanalian songs, 1729, *above*.

1730

An entire set of the monitors, undertaken by M. Smith with assistance. [c. 1730]. P. M. Hill, 1949.

The gentleman's miscellany in verse and prose: [28 titles]. Ed 'Sir Butterfly Maggot, Kt.' 1730, 1730 (2nd edn, with addns). *See* 1731, *below*.

Graffanio-Mastix: or a collection of curious poems on the censor. Dublin 1730.

The harp, or musical miscellany: being a collection of choice songs and lyrick poems set to musick. 1730. Mitchell Lib, Glasgow, copy; probably vol 3 of Musical miscellany, 1730, *below*.

The Hibernian patriot; to which are added poems and songs. 1730. *See* Fraud detected, 1725, *above*.

The ladies miscellany: or a curious collection of amorous poems and merry tales. 1730. Harding copy. No connection with edns of 1718 and 1720, *above*.

The London miscellany: being a collection of several scarce and valuable pieces. 1730.

Lusus Westmonasterienses: sive epigrammatum et poematum minorum delectus. Westminster 1730. Some dedications signed R. Prior, other variations between copies. *See* 1734, 1740, 1750, *below*.

The merry musician: or a cure for the spleen. 4 vols 1730–3 (2nd edn). A reprint of 1716 edn, above; Euing Musical Lib Glasgow copy.

The merry musician: or pills to purge melancholy reviv'd, a choice collection of 100 diverting songs of diff'rent humer. Vol 1, [1730?]. Not in above ser; no more pbd.

Miscellaneous poems by several hands, published by D. Lewis. Vol 2, 1730. *See* 1726, *above*.

The modern musick-master: or the universal musician. 1730. *See* Schnapper; also 1731, 1738, 1742, *below*. This work includes Prelleur's Introduction to singing, for which *see* 1745, 1752, 1770, 1785, *below*.

The Muses holiday: or the polite songster. [1730?]. Harvard copy. *See* 1757, *below*.

The musical miscellany. Vols 3–4, 1730. *See* 1729, *above*; also The harp, 1730, 1750, *and* The spinnet, 1750, *below*.

A new collection of original Scotch songs. 2 bks [1730?]. Harding copy.

A new miscellany: containing [31 titles]. 1730.

Farmer, P. A new model for the rebuilding Masonry; to which is added several songs by Masons of the old order and some new ones. 1730. Texts in Early Masonic pamphlets, ed D. Knoop et al, Manchester 1945.

The new vocal miscellany: containing near 200 songs. [1730?]. Stainer copy.

The odes and satyrs of Horace. 1730, Dublin 1730. Yale Univ copy. Tonson's edn; *see* 1715, *above*.

The opera miscellany: being a pocket collection of songs transpos'd for the flute by Bolton. [1730?].

The plain dealer, publish'd originally in 1724. 2 vols 1730. *See* 1734, *below*.

The polite correspondence, or rational amusement: being letters in prose and verse. [1730?]. BM catalogue: 1740?

The posthumous works of Butler, compleat in one volume. 1730 (3rd edn). *See* 1715, *above*.

Select poems from Ireland, printed at Dublin: London, reprinted. 2 pts 1730.

The session of the critics, to which is added a dialogue, with the following miscellanies [16 items]. [1730?]. Pickering & Chatto, 1934.

The skylark: a collection of all the divine odes and hymns taken out of the Spectators, set to musick by Sheeles. [1730?].

The tea-table miscellany: or Ramsay's collection of Scots sangs. 1730. Vols 1–2 only; 5th edn. *See* 1724, *above*.

Tunbrigialia: or Tunbridge miscellanies for 1730. 1730. *See* 1712, *above*.

1731

The altar of love: or the whole art of kissing, consisting of poems and other miscellanies by the most eminent hands. 1731 (3rd edn). A made-up miscellany; contents unlike 1727 edn, *above*.

The antient constitutions of the Free and Accepted Masons; to which is added a curious collection of songs. Ed B. Cole 1731 (2nd edn). *See* 1723, *above*.

Basia Joannis Secundi Nicolai Hagensis: or the kisses in verse. Tr J. Ward, E. Fenton and another 1731.

The beau's miscellany, by several hands. Pt 2, [1731]; Pt 1, 1731 (no known copy). *See* 1736, *below*.

A collection of loyal songs written against the Rump Parliament, between 1639 and 1661. 2 vols 1731. *See* Rump, 1662, *above*.

A collection of poems on several occasions; publish'd in the Craftsman. Ed C. D'Anvers 1731. Apparently 3 hands in this.

The Court miscellany: being a curious collection of amorous poems [19 items]. 1731. Harding copy.

The Court parrot: a new miscellany in prose and verse. 1731. Harding copy. *See* 1733, *below*.

A curious collection of songs in honour of Masonry 1731. Usually with B. Cole, A book of the antient constitutions, 1731. *See* Early Masonic pamphlets, ed D. Knoop et al, Manchester 1945; *also* A second collection, 1735, *below*.

The doctor's miscellany: or a curious collection of wondrous cures, amorous poems, sonnets and translations. 1731. Edinburgh Univ copy; possibly by one hand.

Fables and other short poems. Ed J. Bickham 3 vols 1731. *See* 1737, *below*.

The flower-piece: a collection of miscellany poems by several hands Ed M Concanen 1731.

The gentleman's miscellany in verse and prose. Dublin 1731. Pickering & Chatto, 1929. *See* 1730, *above*.

The Grub-Street miscellany, in prose and verse, containing [25 pieces] by Mr Bavius jun, FGS. 1731. Possibly by one hand.

The honeysuckle: a curious collection of poems. 1731. P. M. Hill, 1949.

The ladies miscellany: containing [7 titles] and twenty nine other poems. [1731]. Wilkinson copy has slightly different title.

The London medley: containing the exercises spoken at the annual meeting of the Westminster scholars. [1731].

The merry-thought: or the glass-window and bog-house miscellany, published by Hurlo Thrumbo. [1731] (Harding copy), [1731] (2nd–3rd edns). *See* 1732, *below*.

The merry-thought. Pt 2, [1731] (Harding copy), [1731] (2nd edn).

Miscellanies: the last volume [vol 3]. 1731. *See* 1727, *above*.

A miscellany of poems by several hands. Ed J. Husbands, Oxford 1731.

The modern musick-master. 1731. *See* 1730, *above*.

The musical miscellany. Vols 5–6, 1731. *See* 1729, *above*.

Poems on several occasions. 1731. Folger Lib copy. *See* 1680, *above*.

Poetical works of Philip, late Duke of Wharton, and others of the Wharton family and acquaintance. 2 vols [1731?]. A reissue, with addns, of Whartoniana, 1727, *above*. *See also* 1740, *below*.

Robin's panegyrick: or the Norfolk miscellany. Pt 2, 1731. *See* 1729, *above*.

A select collection of modern poems by the most eminent hands. Dublin 1731. *See* 1713, *above*.

The venture: being a collection of poems on several occasions. 1731. H. F. B. Brett-Smith copy. By several hands?

A view of the beau monde: or memoirs of the celebrated coquetilla; with several original songs. 1731. Harding copy.

A view of the town: or memoirs of London. 1731 (Sotheby, 1 May 1891), 1731 (2nd edn).

The virgin muse. 1731 (3rd edn). Pickering & Chatto, 1933. *See* 1717, *above*.

The Windsor medley: being a choice collection of pieces in prose and verse [15 titles]. 1731. Harding copy; 17 titles.

The Windsor medley [20 titles]. 1731, 1731 (3rd edn, with addns). *See* Case 371 (b) and (c).

Wit musically embellish'd: being a collection of forty new English ballads; the words by divers eminent hands; set to musick by Lampe. [1731]. Issued in pts.

Wit's cabinet. 1731 (15th edn). *See* 1684, *above*.

The works of Rochester, Roscomon [et al]. 1731. *See* below, and 1707, *above*.

Poems by Roscomon and Dorset [et al]. Vol 2, 1731.

1732

The Charing-Cross medley. 1732.

Chloe surpriz'd: or the second part of the lady's dressing-room; to which are added Thoughts upon reading the lady's dressing-room, and The gentleman's study; the former wrote by D[ea]n S[wif]t, the latter by Miss W—. Dublin 1732. By three hands?

The choice. 1732 (2nd edn). *See* 1729, *above*.

Choice emblems, divine and moral, antient and modern. Ed R. B. 1732 (6th edn). *See* Delights, 1684, *above*.

Clio and Strephon, [with] a collection of miscellanies. 1732. A made-up miscellany.

A collection of new state songs, in old popular tunes, by Jeremiah van Jews-Trump esq. 1732. Possibly by one hand.

A collection of original Scotch songs. 4 bks [1732?].

A collection of pieces in verse and prose, which have been publish'd on occasion of the Dunciad. Ed R. Savage 1732. A made-up miscellany.

Certain epigrams in laud and praise of the gentlemen of the Dunciad. [1732]. In above collection, but perhaps issued separately.

A collection of poems. Ed J. Whaley 1732.

Count Piper's packet: being a choice and curious collection of manuscript papers in prose and verse, containing [14 titles]. 1732.

Court tales. 1732 (2nd edn). *See* 1717, *above*.

D[ea]n Sw[if]t's medley. [c. 1732]. P. M. Hill, 1949.

Desiderata curiosa: memoirs, letters, wills and epitaphs. Ed F. Peck, vol 1, 1732. *See* 1735, 1779, *below*.

Dirty dogs for dirty puddings. 1732.

Female inconstancy display'd in three diverting histories; to which is added tales and merry jokes, viz. [14 titles]. 1732.

Female inconstancy display'd: the second edition; to which is prefix'd [3 titles]. 1732.

Grubiana: or a compleat collection of all the poems and material letters from the Grubstreet journals. 1732. No known copy of an issue entitled The Grub-Street miscellany, for which *see* Griffith, Pope bibliography. *See also* Memoirs, 1737, *below*.

Faithful memoirs of the Grubstreet society, now first published by Mr Bavius. 1732. This is Grubiana with a cancel title-page.

The hive. Vol 1, 1732 (4th edn); vol 4, 1732. *See* 1724, *above*.

The ladies delight: containing [4 items]. 1732. Possibly by one hand.

The ladies miscellany: being a collection of original poems, novels and other curious tracts by the most eminent hands. 1732 (3rd edn). A made-up miscellany, differing widely from earlier edns. *See* 1718, *above*.

The London medley: or the humours of the present age. 1732. Harding copy.

The luscious poet: or Venus's miscellany. 1732. 64 pp., but Harding copy has 57 pp.

The merry mountebank, or the humourous quack-doctor: old and new songs compiled by Timothy Tulip. Vol 1, 1732.

The merry-thought. Pt 3, [1732] (Harding copy), [1732] (2nd edn); pt 4, [1732?]. *See* 1731, *above*.

Miscellanea sacra: or a curious collection of original poems. 1732. A reprint of 1705 edn with 4 extra poems, called a 2nd edn; but *see* 1707, *above*.

Miscellanies: the last volume [vol 3]. 1732. With minor variants. *See* 1727, *above*.

Miscellanies: the third volume [vol 3]. 1732. Teerink 27(3a).

Miscellanies: the third volume [vol 4]. 1732. In some copies the verse precedes the prose.

Miscellanies in prose and verse, by Swift and Pope; to which are added several poems not in any former impression. Dublin 1732 (3rd edn). Teerink 33(2a). *See* vols 1-2, Dublin 1728, *above*.

A miscellany of original poems, translations, collected by Theobald. 1732. The grove, 1721, with a cancel title-page.

Miscellany poems by Pope. 2 vols 1732 (6th edn). *See* 1727, and Miscellaneous poems, 1712, *above*.

Ovid's Metamorphoses in Latin and English, translated by the most eminent hands. 2 vols Amsterdam 1732. Garth's edn; *see* 1717, *above*.

The Pall-Mall miscellany: containing many curious pieces in prose and verse. [1732], [1732?] (2nd-3rd edns), Dublin 1732. *See* Case 378 (a)-(d) and 1735, *below*.

The posthumous works of Butler compleat in one volume. 1732 (4th edn). *See* 1715, *above*.

Robin's panegyrick: or the Norfolk miscellany. Pt 3, [1732]. *See* 1729, *above*.

St James's miscellany. 1732. P. M. Hill, 1949.

The satyrs of Decimus Junius Juvenalis. Tr Dryden et al, Dublin 1732 (6th edn). *See* 1693, *above*.

The Scarborough miscellany: an original collection of poems, odes, by several hands. 1732. *See* 1734, *below*.

The unhappy lovers: or the history of John Welston; to which is added several curious pieces. 1732.

The works of John, Earl of Rochester; with Valentinian. 1732. Princeton Univ copy. *See* 1691, *above*.

1733

Callipaedia, made English by Rowe [et al]. 1733 (3rd edn). *See* 1712, *above*.

The catch club: or merry companions. 2 pts [1733]. *See* 1705, *above*.

The choice: being two hundred and fifty songs. Vol 1, 1733 (Harding copy); vols 2-3, 1733. *See* 1729, *above*.

A collection of poems, by the author of a poem on the Cambridge ladies. Cambridge 1733.

The Court parrot: a new miscellany in prose and verse. 1733. *See* 1731, *above*.

The Cyprian cabinet: containing portraits of love. 1733. Book-prices current, 1906. Verse by several hands?

The Dublin magazine: or the gentleman's new miscellany. Dublin 1733.

Gartulatio academiae cantabrigiensis Gulielmi principis Auriaci et Annae Georgii II filiae nuptias celebrantis. Cambridge 1733.

The hive. Vol 2, 1733 (4th edn); vol 3, [1733?] (4th edn). *See* 1724, *above*.

Laugh and be fat: or an antidote against melancholy. 1733 (11th edn). *See* 1741, 1753, 1761, *below*.

The lovers pacquet: or the marriage-miscellany; together with letters, poems and songs. 1733. A made-up miscellany.

Miscellanies: the last volume [vol 3]. 1733. Teerink 27(3b and c).

Miscellanies: the third volume [vol 3]. 1733. Teerink 27(3c).

Miscellanies: the last volume [vol 4]. 1733. Teerink 27(4a).

Miscellanies: the third volume [vol 4]. 1733. Teerink 27(4b and c). *See* 1727, *above*.

Miscellanies in prose and verse: the third volume, to which are added several poems not in the English edition. Dublin 1733 (2nd edn). Teerink 33(3). An expanded edn of The third volume [vol 4], London 1732. *See* vols 1-2, Dublin 1728, *above*.

The new help to discourse. 1733 (9th edn). *See* 1669, *above*.

Orpheus caledonius. 2 vols 1733, 1733 (2nd edn). Vol 1 reprints the 1726 collection; vol 2 is new.

Ovid's Metamorphoses, made English by several hands. 2 vols 1733 (3rd edn). Sewell's edn; *see* 1717, *above*.

The palace miscellany: containing among many other curious pieces [5 titles]. 1733.

Poems on affairs of state, collected from the daily, evening and weekly papers. 1733. Anti-Jacobite.

The tea-table miscellany in three volumes. 1733 (9th edn). *See* 1724, *above.*

Tunbrigialia: or Tunbridge miscellanies for the year 1733. 1733. *See* 1712, *above.*

The vocal miscellany. 1733. *See* 1734, 1738, *below.*

The young clerk's assistant. [1733]. Contains The virgin Muse: or select poems for the fair sex.

1734

The British musical miscellany. Vols 1–2, [1734]. Issued in pts. *See* 1735–6, *below.*

A collection of select original poems and translations, chiefly on divine subjects, by Dr Patrick and other eminent hands. 1734. Dobell, 1934. *See* Poems, 1719, *above.*

The contest: being poetical essays on the Queen's grotto. 1734.

The Court oracle: a new miscellany. 1734.

England's genius, or wit triumphant: being a collection of jests and witticisms, [and] merry poems. 1734.

Epithalamia oxoniensa. Oxford 1734.

A general dictionary, historical and critical. Ed P. Bayle vol 1, 1734. This includes numerous poems and poetical excerpts. *See* 1735–9, 1741, *below.*

Hibernicus's letters, interspersed with poems and translations. 2 vols 1734 (2nd edn). *See* A collection of letters, 1729, *above.*

The honey-suckle: consisting of original poems, epigrams, songs, tales, odes, by a society of gentlemen. Vol 1, 1734. No more pbd.

The humours of a country election; to which are added songs. 1734. *See* 1741, *below.*

The humours of new Tunbridge Wells at Islington; with songs, epigrams. 1734.

The je-ne-scai-quoy: containing poems on various subjects. 1734. Harding copy.

Lashley's York miscellany. York 1734.

Lusus westmonasterienses. 1734. *See* 1730, *above.*

Miscellanea curiosa [Miscellaneae curiosae in first no]: or entertainments for the ingenious. 3 nos York 1734. *See* 1735, *below.*

A new miscellany for the year 1734. Pts 1–2, 1734. *See* 1737–9, *below.*

The plain dealer. 1734 (2nd edn). *See* 1730, *above.*

Poematia, latinè partim reddita, partim scripta. Ed V. Bourne 1734. *See* 1735, 1743, 1750, 1764, *below.*

Barber, M. et al. Poems on several occasions. 1734. *See* 1735–6, *below.*

A prologue and an epilogue, and songs, spoken and sung to the Society of Freemasons. Dublin 1734.

The St James's tatler: or the Court of Request miscellany, containing [20 titles]. 1734.

The Scarborough miscellany for the year 1732. 1734 (2nd edn); For the year 1733, 1734; For the year 1734, 1734. *See* 1732, *above.*

The tea-table miscellany. Dublin 1734 (10th edn). *See* 1724, *above.*

The toasts of the Rump-Steak Club. 1734.

The toasts of the Patriots Club at London. 1734. Apparently another edn of the above.

The vocal miscellany: a collection of above four hundred celebrated songs. Vol 1, 1734 (2nd edn); Vol 2, 1734. *See* 1733, *above.*

1735

The Bath, Bristol, Tunbridge and Epsom miscellany: containing poems, tales, songs. 1735.

The British musical miscellany. Vols 3–4, [1735]. Issued in pts. *See* 1734, *above.*

Pomfret, J., Roscommon et al. The Christian poet: or divine poems on the four last things. 1735.

A collection of epigrams. Vol 1, 1735 (2nd edn, with addns). *See* 1727, *above.*

A collection of merry poems: consisting of facetious tales, epigrams. 1735. P. M. Hill, 1948. *See* 1736, *below.*

A complete collection of old and new English and Scotch songs. Vols 1–2, 1735. 2 nos in vol 2. *See* 1736, *below.*

The cuckold's miscellany. 1735. Sotheby, 26 June 1903; Case 401 (copy now lost).

Desiderata curiosa. Vol 2, 1735. *See* 1732, *above.*

A general dictionary. Vols 2–3, 1735. *See* 1734, *above.*

The Gentleman's Magazine extraordinary, following July, 1735: containing several poems upon life, death, judgment, heaven and hell. [1735].

Miscellanea curiosa. York 1735. 3 nos; *see* 1734, *above.*

Miscellaneous poems on several occasions, by Dawson; to which are added a letter and verses. 1735.

Miscellanies in prose and verse: volume the fifth, which compleats this author's works. 1735. Teerink 25(5a and b); 2 issues. *See* 1727, *above.*

Mr Pope's literary correspondence. Vols 2–3, 1735. Vol 1 contains very little verse; vols 2–3, 1735 (2nd edn). *See* 1736–7, 1741, *below.*

The mottoes of the Spectators, Tatlers and Guardians, translated into English. 1735, Dublin 1735. Pickering & Chatto, 1933. *See* 1737, *below.*

Nayland miscellany, containing Virgin unmask'd: a dramatick satire; Secret history of six stately bucks and does. 1735. Sotheby, 28 April 1890.

Ovid's Art of love. Tr Dryden, Congreve et al 1735. *See* 1709, *above.*

The Pall-Mall miscellany. [1735?] (4th edn). *See* 1732, *above.*

Pinkethman's jests: or wit refin'd. 1735 (4th edn). *See* 1721, *above.*

A pocket companion for Free-Masons. Ed W. Smith 1735. See The Free Mason's pocket companion, 1736. For different collections under either title, *see* 1752, 1754, 1761, 1763, 1765, 1771, 1792, 1798, *below.*

Poematia: iterum edita. 1735. *See* 1734, *above.*

Barber, M. et al. Poems on several occasions. 1735. *See* 1734, *above.*

The satyrs of Decimus Junius Juvenalis. Tr Dryden et al 1735 (6th edn). *See* 1693, *above.*

[A second collection of songs. c. 1735]. Usually with late issues of B. Cole, Constitutions, 1731. *See* A curious collection, 1731, *above.* Pts 3–4: Sotheby, 25 April 1891.

The Syren: containing a collection of four hundred and twenty of the most celebrated English songs. 1735. Harding copy. *See* 1737–9, 1750 *below.*

Tales and novels in verse from La Fontaine, by several hands. Ed S. Humphreys, vol 1, 1735. No more vols issued. *See* 1762, *below.*

The triumph of wit. 1735 (9th edn). *See* 1688, *above.*

Twelve arietts or ballads and two cantatas, composed by Hayes. Oxford 1735.

The works of Rochester, Roscomon, and Dorset; the cabinet of love and several other poems. 1735. *See* 1707, *above.*

1736

The beau's miscellany: a new and curious collection of amorous tales, diverting songs and entertaining poems, by several hands. 2 pts 1736. Sotheby, 24 April 1901. *See* 1731, *above.*

The British musical miscellany. Vols 5–6, [1736]. Issued in pts. *See* 1734, *above.*

A collection of merry poems: consisting of facetious tales, epigrams, from Oldham, Brown, Prior, Swift and other eminent poets. 1736 (2nd edn). *See* 1735, *above.*

A complete collection of old and new English and Scotch songs. Vols 3–4 (each of 2 nos), 1736. *See* 1735, *above.*

The Cupid: a collection of love songs, in twelve parts. 1736; rptd Derby, 1891. *See* 1737, 1739, *below.*

The flowers of Parnassus: or the ladies miscellany for the year [1735]. Ed T. G. 1736. *See* 1737, *below.*

The Free Mason's pocket companion: containing a collection of Free Masons songs; prologues and epilogues.

Ed W. Smith 1736. A Pocket companion, 1735, re-issued.

A general dictionary. Vol 4, 1736. *See* 1734, *above.*

Gratulatio academiae cantabrigiensis Frederici Walliae principis et Augustae principissae Saxo-Gothae nuptias celebrantis. Cambridge 1736.

Gratulatio academiae oxoniensis in nuptias Frederici et Augustae. Oxford 1736.

Miscellanies: the last volume [vol 3]. 1736. Teerink 28(3).

Miscellanies: the last volume [vol 4]. 1736. Griffith 439.

Miscellanies: the third volume [vol 4]. 1736. Teerink 29(4a–d).

Miscellanies in prose and verse: the fifth and sixth volumes. Vol 5, 1736. Teerink 28(5). Vol 6 is entirely prose. *See* 1727, *above.*

A miscellany of new poems on several occasions. Ed R. Luck 1736.

Mr Pope's literary correspondence. Vol 4, 1736. Includes Court poems, 1716, *above*; Vol 4, 1736 (2nd edn), includes Court poems, 1726, *above.*

Ovid's Epistles with his Amours, translated by the most eminent hands. 1736. Yale Univ copy. *See* 1725, *above.*

Ovid's Metamorphoses. Ed S. Garth 2 vols 1736. McLeish, 1929. *See* 1717, *above.*

Poems: a chosen collection: viz [12 titles]. Edinburgh [1736?]. Griffith 441.

Barber, M. et al. Poems on several occasions. 1736. 1735 edn, with new title-page. *See* 1734, *above.*

Post-Office intelligence, or universal gallantry: being a collection of love letters. 1736.

The prologue and epilogue and songs spoke and sung for the benefit of sick and decay'd Masons. Dublin 1736; facs in J. M. Lepper and P. Crossle, History of the Masons in Ireland, Dublin 1925.

The rape of the smock, by Jacob: the third edition; with other miscellanies. 1736. *See* 1717, *above.*

The rarities of Richmond: being exact descriptions of the royal hermitage and Merlin's cave; with his life and prophesies. 5 pts 1736, 1736 (2nd edn), 1736 (pirated edn?). Ptd for E. Curll; includes only the contents of pt 1 and a portion of pt 2.

Sacrae scripturae locorum quorundam versio metrica, adolescentibus C. C. C. Ed J. Burton, Oxford 1736.

The St James's register: or taste a-la-mode. 1736.

The temple of love, no 1: the monthly mask, consisting of songs. [1736]. Stainer copy. 15 nos in all.

The works of Boileau. 2 vols 1736 (2nd edn). Vol 1, entitled Life, has also pt of Works; both vols reissues of the 1712–11 edn with new preliminary pages.

1737

The art of English poetry. 2 vols 1737 (8th edn). *See* 1702, *above.*

Bacchus and Venus: or a select collection of near 200 songs and catches; to which is added songs in the canting dialect. 1737.

The beauties of the English stage. 2 vols 1737. A reprint Thesaurus dramaticus, 1724.

The Canterbury tales of Chaucer turn'd into modern language by Dryden, Pope and other eminent hands. Ed T. Morell 1737. *See* 1740, *below.*

The choice: being two hundred and fifty songs. Vol 1, 1737 (2nd edn). Also 2nd edn, nd, with different imprint. Harding copy. *See* 1733, *above.*

A collection of epigrams. Vol 2, 1737. *See* 1735, *above.*

A collection of miscellany poems, never before publish'd. 1737. *See* The delights, 1738, *below.*

The Cupid. Dublin 1737. Harding copy. *See* 1736, *above.*

English miscellanies: consisting of various pieces collected out of the most approved authors. Ed J. T[ompson], Göttingen 1737.

The exercises performed at a visitation of the grammar-school of Bristol. Ed A. S. Catcott, Bristol [1737].

Fables and other short poems. 3 vols 1737. *See* 1731, *above.*

The flowers of Parnassus: or the ladies miscellany for the year [1737]. Dublin 1737. Differs from 1736 collection, *above.*

A general dictionary. Vol 5, 1737. *See* 1734, *above.*

Medulla poetarum romanorum: or passages of the Roman poets; with translations by the most eminent hands. Ed H. Baker, 2 vols 1737. Some copies have no names in the imprint.

Memoirs of the society of Grub-street. 2 vols 1737. *See* 1732, *above.*

Mr Pope's literary correspondence: volume the fifth. 1737. Bodley copy has an extra title: New letters of Pope. *See* 1735, *above.*

The mottoes of the Spectators, Tatlers and Guardians, translated. 1737 (2nd edn). *See* 1735, *above.*

The Muses library: or a series of English poetry, from the Saxons to Charles II. Ed. E. Cooper and W. Oldys, vol 1 1737, vol 1 [1737?] (2nd edn). The same book, with a cancel title-page. *See* The historical and poetical medley, 1738, and 1741, *below.*

The musical entertainer, engrav'd by George Bickham junr. Vol 1, [1737]. *See* 1738, 1740, *below.*

A new miscellany for the year 1737. 1737. *See* 1734, *above.*

The Quaker's art of courtship. 1737. With differing collations of 2 issues. *See* 1689, *above.*

The Syren: containing a collection of four hundred and thirty English songs. 1737 (2nd edn). Stainer copy. *See* 1735, *above.*

The universal musician: or songster's delight. [1737?]. No frontispiece; 127 leaves. *See* 1738, 1750, *below.*

The whole life and merry exploits of bold Robin Hood; to which is added several songs. 1737. *See* 1663, *above.*

Wits cabinet. 1737 (16th edn). *See* 1684, *above.*

1738

Bickham's musical entertainer. Vol 2, [1738]. *See* 1737, *above.*

The British Muse: or a collection of thoughts of our English poets. Ed T. Hayward and W. Oldys 3 vols 1738. *See* Quintessence, 1740, *below.*

The chaplet: being a collection of twelve English songs. 1738.

A choice collection of poetry, by the most ingenious men of the age. Ed J. Yarrow 2 vols York 1738.

[A collection of diverting songs, epigrams]. [c. 1738]. C. H. Wilkinson copy. Known copies lack title-page; collection of about 1,350 songs.

A collection of old ballads. Vol 3, 1738 (2nd edn). *See* 1725, *above.*

The curiosity: or the gentleman and lady's general library. York 1738. *See* 1739, *below.*

The delights of the Muses. 1738. A collection of miscellany poems, 1737, with a cancel title-page.

Ein kurzer Versuch, den Character Carolinä, Königin von Gross-Britannien, zu entwerfen übersetzt. Ed G. L. Meyer, Altona 1738. Partly reprints contents of Pietas cantab and oxon, *below.*

A general dictionary. Vols 6–7, 1738. *See* 1734, *above.*

The historical and poetical medley: or Muses library. 1738. The Muses library, 1737, with a cancel title-page.

Miscellanies: the last volume [vol 3]. 1738. Teerink 30(1). *See* 1727, *above.*

Miscellanies in prose and verse: the fifth and sixth volumes. Vol 5, 1738. In Forster Collection. Teerink 30(2). *See* 1727, *above.*

The modern music master. 1738 (4th edn). Stainer copy. *See* 1730, *above.*

The new book of constitutions of the Free and Accepted Masons. Ed J. Anderson 1738. *See* 1723, *above.*

A new miscellany for the year 1738. 1738. *See* 1734, *above*.

The nightingale: containing a collection of four hundred and twenty two English songs. 1738. *See* 1742, *below*. For other collections with this title, *see* 1760, 1770, 1776, 1785, 1798, *below*.

Pietas academiae cantabrigiensis in funere principis Wilhelminae Carolinae et luctu Georgii II. [Cambridge] 1738. *See* Ein kurzer Versuch, *above*.

Pietas academiae oxoniensis in obitum reginae Carolinae. Oxford 1738. *See* Ein kurzer Versuch, *above*.

The Syren: a collection of English songs. 1738. Book-auction records, 1907–8. *See* 1735, *above*.

The universal musician: or songster's delight. Vol 1, 1738. Ptd for Wm Rayner, 145 leaves; ptd for Wm Lloyd, 123 leaves. *See* 1737, *above*.

Verses on the death of Queen Caroline. 1738. 3 poems, by different hands?

The vocal miscellany. Vol 1, 1738 (3rd edn); vol 2, 1738 (2nd edn); Dublin 1738 (3rd edn). *See* 1734, *above*.

1739

The art of English poetry. 2 vols 1739. Dobell, 1932. *See* 1702, *above*.

British melody: or the musical magazine, consisting of English and Scotch songs. Ed J. F. Lampe 1739.

Calliope, or English harmony: a collection of English and Scots songs. 2 vols 1739. *See* 1746, 1770, 1780; *also* The new Calliope, 1743, *below*.

The Cupid. 1739 (2nd edn, with addns). *See* 1736, *above*.

The curiosity: or gentleman and lady's library. 1739 (2nd edn). *See* 1738, *above*.

A general dictionary. Vols 8–9, 1739. *See* 1734, *above*.

The merry companion: or universal songster. 1739. Above 450 songs. *See* 1742, 1745, 1750, *below*.

Prior, M. Miscellaneous works. Ed J. Bancks, Dublin 1739. Contains verses sent to Prior. *See* 1740, *below*.

A new miscellany for the year 1739. 1739. *See* 1734, *above*.

The poetical works of Rochester, Roscomon, Dorset, Devonshire, Buckinghamshire. 1739. *See* 1707; *also* The works of Rochester, *below*.

Poems by Roscomon and Dorset and other eminent hands. Vol 2, 1739.

The school of Venus: or the lady's miscellany, being a collection of original poems and novels. 1739 (2nd edn).

A supplement to Swift's and Pope's works. Dublin 1739. Contains material from 1727 and 1732 Miscellanies, *above*.

The Syren: a collection of four-hundred-and-thirty-two English songs. 1739. Harding copy. Case 423(c): 3rd edn, 1739, with slightly different title. *See* 1735, *above*.

The works of Rochester, Roscomon, Dorset, Devonshire, Buckinghamshire. 1739. *See* 1707; *also above*.

Poems by Roscomon and Dorset, Devonshire, Buckingham. Vol 2, 1739.

1740

The British Apollo: in three volumes. 1740 (4th edn). Selections, ed G. W. Niven, Paisley 1903. *See* 1711, *above*.

The Caledonian miscellany, consisting of pastorals by Ramsay and other bards; to which is added the adventures of a farthing. [1740?]. *See* 1762, 1770, *below*.

The Canterbury tales of Chaucer turn'd into modern language by several eminent hands. 1740 (2nd edn). *See* 1737, *above*.

The catch club: or merry companions. [c. 1740]. *See* 1705, *above*.

The lark: containing a collection of above four hundred and seventy English and Scotch songs. 1740. *See* 1742, *below*.

The lover's magazine, or Cupid's decoy: being a collection of love-songs and cetches. [1740?].

Lusus westmonasterienses. 1740. *See* 1730, *above*.

Memoirs of the life and actions of Cromwell; to all which is added a collection of historical pieces relating to Cromwell and other remarkable persons. Ed F. Peck 1740.

Prior, M. Miscellaneous works: volume the second, containing a new collection of poems. 1740, 1740 (2nd edn). *See* 1739, *above*.

A miscellany of lyric poems performed in the Academy of Music. 1740.

The musical entertainer. Vol 1, [1740]. *See* 1737, *above*.

Bickham's musical entertainer. Vol 2, [1740].

A new miscellany of original poems, translations and imitations. 1740 (2nd edn). I. A. Williams copy 1720 edn, with cancel title-page.

The nimble heave: or the sporting ladies miscellany. 1740.

The pleasant musical companion. [1740?] (10th edn). Many alterations in this edn; *see* Catch, 1667, *above*.

The quintessence of English poetry. 3 vols 1740. The British Muse, 1738, with cancel title-pages; Vol 1, collected by Thomas Hayward (Yale copy); by several eminent hands (Pickering & Chatto, 1933).

State [garland] of antient and m[odern] loy[al] songs. Pt 1, Dublin [174–]. *See* Case 477 (mutilated copy).

The tea-table miscellany: or a collection of choice songs, Scots and English. 4 vols in 1740 (10th edn). *See* 1724, *above*.

The tea-table miscellany: or a collection of Scots sangs. Dublin 1740 (12th edn, with addns). Falkner Greirson, 1966. *See* 1724, *above*.

Tunbrigalia: or the Tunbridge miscellany for the years 1737, 1738, 1739, by a society of gentlemen and ladies. 1740. *See* 1712, *above*.

Vernon's glory: containing fourteen new songs occasion'd by the taking of Porto-Bello and Fort Chagre. 1740; Containing fifteen new songs, 1740; Containing several new songs pt 2, 1740. C. H. Wilkinson copy.

Wit's cabinet. [1740?] (17th edn). Harding copy. *See* 1684, *above*.

The works of Philip, late Duke of Wharton; with a few pieces by the Duke's intimate acquaintance. 2 vols 1740 (3rd edn). *See* Poetical works, 1731, *above*.

1741

The antiquities of St Peter's, Westminster. 2 vols 1741 (4th edn). *See* 1711, *above*.

The Bath miscellany for the year 1740, wrote by the gentlemen and ladies at that place. Bath 1741, 1741 (2nd edn?).

The British Orpheus: a collection of favourite English songs. Bks 1–3, [1741–3].

The Canterbury tales of Chaucer, modernis'd by several hands. Ed G. Ogle 3 vols 1741. *See* 1742, *below*.

Caribbeana: containing letters and dissertations, together with poetical essays wrote by several hands in the West-Indies. Ed S. Keimer 2 vols 1741.

The city-hermit: or the life of Henry Welby; with epitaphs and elegies. 1741.

A general dictionary. Vol 10, 1741. *See* 1734, *above*.

The humours of a country election; to which are added songs. 1741. Harding copy: 2nd edn on title page. *See* 1734, *above*.

An impartial history of the life of John Barber, written by several hands. 1741.

The ladies delight: or the merry songster, containing a collection of one hundred new songs. 1741. Sotheby, 27 July 1864. 1741 (3rd edn). Book-prices current, 1914.

Laugh and be fat. 1741 (12th edn). *See* 1733, *above*.

The Muses library: or a series of English poetry. 1741. *See* 1737, *above*.

The musical companion, or lady's magazine: a collection of English and Scotch songs. 1741.

A new academy of complements: or the lover's secretary. 1741 (12th edn). Harding copy. See 1715, *above*.

Poems on several occasions collected from the Spectators and other authors. 1741.

Poems on several subjects, by a land-waiter. 1741. Harding copy. By several hands.

The potent ally: or succours from Merryland. Paris 1741 (2nd edn). Ptd London, for E. Curll. First edn, 1741, not relevant.

1742

An agreeable companion: being a choice collection of curious remarks. 1742.

The agreeable variety. 2 pts 1742 (3rd edn). 1724 edn, with cancel title-page. See 1717, *above*.

The antiquities of St Peter's, Westminster. 2 vols 1742 (5th edn). See 1711, *above*.

The Canterbury tales of Chaucer, modernis'd by [9 names]. 2 vols Dublin 1742. See 1741, *above*.

The compleat works of the late John Cleveland in prose and verse. 1742. London Lib copy. The 1687 edn reissued with a new title-page.

Cupid and Hymen: a voyage to the isles of love and matrimony by John Single esq. 1742. Pickering & Chatto, 1935. By H. Carey et al? See 1745, 1748, 1772, *below*.

The Englishman's miscellany. 1742. Prose and verse.

Joe Miller's jests: or the wit's vade-mecum; to which is added a collection of epigrams. 1742 (5th edn). The first edn with epigrams. See 1743–7, 1751, 1754, 1757, 1762, 1768–9, 1772, 1780, 1790, *below*.

The lark: containing four hundred and seventy four songs. 1742. Ptd for John Osborn. Harding copy; ptd for J. Osborn, C. Hitch and J. Hodges. See 1740, *above*.

Love at first sight: or the wit of a woman. Ed J. Yarrow, York 1742. Includes a collection of poems.

The merry companion: or universal songster, consisting of above 500 songs. 1742 (2nd edn). See 1739, *above*.

Miscellanies: the third volume, by Arbuthnot, Pope and Gay. 1742. Lefferts copy. See 1727, *above*.

Miscellanies: the fourth volume, by Swift, Arbuthnot, Pope and Gay. 1742. Teerink 66. The 4th vol of Miscellanies in four volumes (4th edn), containing the verse of the former vols 3–4, with addns. See 1727, *above*.

Miscellanies, the fifth and sixth volumes by Swift and others. Vol 5 1742 (3rd edn). Teerink 66. See 1727, *above*.

The modern musick-master. 7 bks [1742?]. See 1730, *above*.

The new ministry: containing a collection of all the satyrical poems, songs. 1742. See Case 435(1)(a) and (1)(b); Part 2, 1742. See 1743, *below*.

A new miscellany in prose and verse by Swift, Holles St John and other eminent hands. 1742. In Forster Collection.

The nightingale: containing a collection of four hundred and ninety two songs. 1742. Stainer copy. Imprint: J. Osborn. 1742 (2nd edn). Harding copy. Ptd for J. Osborn, C. Hitch and J. Hodges. See 1738, *above*.

Prior, M. Poems on several occasions. Vol 2, 1742 (4th edn). Includes Original poems and translations by several hands.

Winstanley, J. Poems written occasionally, interspers'd with many others, by several ingenious hands. Dublin 1742. See 1751, *below*.

Politicks in miniature; to which is added the political rehearsal; taken from the Westminster Journal 1742. [1742?].

The summer miscellany: or a present for the country. 1742. 2 issues; with 14 and with 22 titles on title-page.

The vocal musical mask: a collection of English songs. [c. 1742]. Set by J. F. Lampe et al.

1743

Cibber and Sheridan: or the Dublin miscellany. Dublin 1743.

Court whispers, or a magazine of wit: a satyr for the country, containing [18 titles]. 1743.

Ebrietatis encomium. 1743 (2nd edn). See 1723, *above*.

[English Orpheus]. [1743?]. BM copy lacks title-page. See Universal harmony, 1743, *below*.

The foundling hospital for wit. No 1, ed 'Samuel Silence' 1743. Case 440(1)(a) and (b); 2 edns. No 2, ed 'Timothy Silence' 1743. See 1744, 1746–9, 1763, *below*.

Joe Miller's jests. 1743 (6th edn). Harding copy. See 1742, *above*.

Thomas, E. The metamorphoses of the town; to which are added the Female metamorphosis [and 3 other titles]. 1743 (4th edn).

A new academy of complements: or the lover's secretary. Dublin 1743 (12th edn). See 1715, *above*.

The new Calliope: or English harmony in taste. Vol 1, 1743. Harding copy. See Calliope, 1739, *above*; *and* 1746, *below*.

The new ministry. Pt 3, 1743. See 1742, *above*.

Poematia: tertio edita. 1743. See 1734, *above*.

A present for a young lady. 1743. Miscellaneous poems, 1729, with cancel title-page.

Thesaurus musicus: a collection of two, three and four part songs set to musick by the most eminent masters. Vol 1, [c. 1743]. See 1745, 1763, 1765, *below*.

Universal harmony: or the gentleman and lady's social companion. [1743]; The English Orpheus, 1743 (with addns). See 1745–6, *below*.

1744

The aviary, or magazine of British melody: one thousand three hundred and forty four songs. [1744]. Imprint of BM copy has 12 names; Harding copy, 10. See 1750, 1756, 1763, *below*.

The charmer, or entertaining companion: being a choice collection of favourite songs (both old and new). Coventry 1744. Stainer copy.

Collection of loyal songs. Edinburgh 1744. No known copy.

A collection of moral and sacred poems from English authors. Ed John Wesley 3 vols Bristol 1744.

A collection of poems by several hands. Boston 1744.

The foundling hospital for wit. No 2, ed 'Timothy Silence' 1744. See 1743, *above*.

The Harleian miscellany. Ed W. Oldys 2 vols 1744. See 1745–6, 1753, *below*.

Jemmy Carson's collections; with pieces upon different subjects by several hands. Dublin 1744. See 1787, *below*.

Joe Miller's jests. 1744 (7th edn). See 1742, *above*.

The merry medley: or a Christmas box for gay gallants and good companions. Vol 1, 1744. Book-prices current, 1899. See 1745, 1748–50, *below*.

The modern miscellany. 3 pts 1744.

The Muse in good humour: or a collection of comic tales from Chaucer, Prior, Swift; together with some originals. 1744. Myers, 1931. Noble's collection. See 1745–6, 1751, 1757, 1766, 1770, 1785, *below*.

The Norfolk poetical miscellany. Ed A. Cowper 2 vols 1744. See Poetical miscellany, 1754, *below*.

Philomel: being a small collection of only the best English songs. 1744.

A select collection of modern poems by the most eminent hands. Glasgow 1744. See 1750, 1757, 1763, *below*.

The toper's delight: or a pipe of the best, extracted from the magazines. 1744. Differences in Harding copy.

1745

The agreeable companion: or an universal medley of wit and good-humour. 1745.

The canary bird: being a collection of songs such as are chiefly in vogue. 1745. Britwell Court Lib. *See* 1760, *below*.

A collection of original poems and translations. Ed J. Whaley. 1745.

A collection of songs for two or three voices by Handel, Blow, Leveridge, Greene [et al]. [1745?]. Harding copy.

Cupid and Hymen: a voyage to the isles of love and matrimony by Simon Single. 1745 (2nd edn). Pickering & Chatto, 1933; By the facetious Harry Carey, 1745. Book-auction Records, 1922–3. *See* 1742, *above*.

A full collection of all poems upon Charles, Prince of Wales. 1745.

The Harleian miscellany. Vols 3–6, 1745. *See* 1744, *above*.

An introduction to singing; to which is added a choice collection of songs. Ed P. Prelleur [1745?]. Perhaps 1747; imprint: J. Simpson. *See* 1752, 1770, 1785, *below*; *also* Modern musick-master, 1730, *above*.

Joe Miller's jests. 1745 (8th edn). *See* 1742, *above*.

Memoirs of the life and writings of Pope. Ed W. Ayre 2 vols 1745.

The merry companion, or universal songster: a new collection of 500 songs. 1745. Sotheby, 12 Nov 1858. *See* 1739, *above*.

The merry medley: or a Christmas-Box for gay gallants. Vol 1, 1745 (Book-prices current, 1912); vol 2, 1745 (Harding copy). *See* 1744, *above*.

Miscellanies: the fifth and sixth volumes by Swift and others. Vol 5, 1745 (3rd edn). *See* 1727, *above*.

Miscellanies: the tenth volume, by Swift. 1745. Teerink 66. A few poems by other hands. *See* 1727, *above*.

The Muse in good humour: or a collection of comic tales. Pt 1, 1745 (4th edn); pt 2, 1745 (2nd edn). Noble's collection; *see* 1744, *above*.

The Muse in good humour: or a collection of the best poems, comic tales, fables, enigmas, from the most eminent poets; in two parts. Vol 2, 1745. Cooper's collection, in imitation of Noble's. Pts are found separately and variations in make-up exist.

The Muse in masquerade: or a collection of riddles, serious and comic. 1745.

The Muse's vagaries: or the merry mortal's companion, by Sir Solomon Gundy Knt and Margery Merrypin, spinster. Pts 1–2, 1745. Harding copy.

The musical companion: songs set to musick by Saml Howard. [1745?].

The publisher: containing miscellanies in prose and verse. Ed J. Crokatt 1745.

Thesaurus musicus: a collection of two, three and four part songs. 2 vols [1745]. *See* 1743, *above*.

Universal harmony: or the gentleman and ladies' social companion. 1745. *See* 1743, *above*.

The whole prophecies of Scotland, England, France, Ireland and Denmark. 1745. *See* 1718, *above*.

Wit's cabinet. [1745?] (18th edn). *See* 1684, *above*.

1746

Amaryllis: being a collection of such songs as are most in vogue. 1746. Stainer copy. *See* 1747, 1750, 1760, 1778, *below*.

Amaryllis: consisting of songs sung at the publick theatres and gardens. Vols 1–2, 1746.

The art of poetry made easy, and embellish'd with epigrams, epitaphs, songs, odes, pastorals, from the best authors: being the seventh volume of the Circle of the sciences. 1746. Pbd J. Newbery. *See* Poetry, 1748, 1762, 1769, 1770, 1776, *below*.

A banquet of the Muses: or the miscellany of miscellanies,

by the most eminent authors. 1746. The theatre of wit, 1746, with addns.

The buck's delight, or the merry companion: a collection of 200 songs, sung at Vauxhall, Ranelagh, Marylebone, Sadler's Wells. 1746. Sotheby, 7 Aug 1877.

Calliope: or English harmony. 2 vols [1746?]. A reissue of New Calliope, 1743, much enlarged. *See* 1739, *above*.

The entertainer: consisting of pieces in prose and verse. Vol 1, 1746. No more pbd.

The foundling hospital for wit. No 3, ed 'Timothy Silence' 1746. With different settings and ornaments. *See* 1743, *above*.

The Harleian miscellany. Vols 7–8, 1746. *See* 1744, *above*. The whole rptd 12 vols 1808–11, 10 vols 1808–13.

The history and constitutions of the Free and Accepted Masons. Ed J. Anderson [1746]. *See* 1723, *above*.

Joe Miller's jests: or the wit's vade-mecum. 1746. Sotheby, 16 March 1906. *See* 1742, *above*.

The lyre: consisting of a great variety of English and Scotch songs. 1746. Stainer copy; contains nos 1–2.

Miscellanies by Swift: the eleventh volume. 1746. Teerink 66. Contains a few poems by other hands. *See* 1727, *above*.

Motets, madrigals and other pieces performed by the Academy of Ancient Music. 1746.

The Muse in good humour: or a collection of comic tales. 2 pts 1746. Sotheby, 12 Nov 1887. *See* 1744, *above*.

Poems divine, moral and philosophical; to which is annex'd an appendix of divine and philosophical subjects, collected from the best authors. Ed M. C. Gloucester 1746.

Robin Hood's garland: being a compleat history of all the exploits. 1746, Coventry 1746. Both Harding copies; different edns. *See* 1663, *above*.

The theatre of wit: or a banquet of the Muses selected from the most eminent authors. 1746. *See* A banquet, 1746, *above*.

Universal harmony. 1746. Number of leaves varies. *See* 1743, *above*.

1747

Amaryllis: consisting of such songs as are most esteemed. Vols 1–2, [c. 1747]. Pbd by T. J. and sold by Cooper, J. Wood and I. Tyther. *See* 1746, *above*.

A collection of poems on several occasions written in the last century. Ed R. Cross 1747.

Cupid triumphant: containing several amorous poems, love letters; with several other poems. [1747]. Harding copy.

The foundling hospital for wit. No 4, ed 'Timothy Silence' 1747. *See* 1743, *above*.

Joe Miller's jests: or the wit's vade-mecum. 1747 (9th edn). Harding copy. *See* 1742, *above*.

Miscellanies: the fourth volume, consisting of verses by Swift [et al]. 1747. *See* 1742, *above*.

The New-Year's miscellany: containing [16 titles]. 1747.

Ovid's Art of love translated by several eminent hands. 1747. Pickering & Chatto, 1930. *See* 1709, *above*.

The temple of Apollo for the month of April 1747, by a society of gentlemen. [1747]. Harding copy.

1748

The agreeable medley: or universal entertainer. Malton 1748.

The bull-finch: being a choice collection of English songs. [1748?]. Stainer copy. Pp. vii + 184; 253 songs; all later edns vary. *See* 1750, 1753, 1757, 1760–61, 1763–4, 1769, 1772, 1775, 1780–1, 1788, *below*.

A collection of poems by several hands, in three volumes. 1748. Dodsley's miscellany. *See* below, and 1749, 1751, 1755, 1758, 1760, 1763, 1765, 1766, 1770, 1775, 1782, *below*.

A collection of poems in three volumes, by several hands. 1748. Dodsley's miscellany, with many alterations and addns.

A collection of political and humorous letters, poems and articles of news, publish'd in the National Journal. 1748.

Cupid and Hymen: a voyage to the isles of love and matrimony in prose and verse, by the facetious Harry Carey and other persons. 1748, 1748 (5th edn). Harding copy. *See* 1742, *above*.

The foundling hospital for wit. No 5, ed 'Timothy Silence' 1748. *See* 1743, *above*.

The goldfinch: being a select collection of the most celebrated English songs. 1748. Several different collections have this title. *See* 1750, 1753, 1762, 1777, 1782–3, 1785, 1788, 1800, *below*.

Gratulatio academiae cantabrigiensis de reditu Georgii II, post pacem & libertatem Europae feliciter restitutam. Cambridge 1748.

Ladies amusement: being a new collection of songs, ballads. Dublin [1748?]. Music by F. Lampe.

The merry medley for gay gallants, by C. F., president of the comical club. Dublin 1748. Book-auction records, 1902–3. *See* 1744, *above*.

A new academy of compliments: or the compleat English secretary. 1748. *See* 1772, 1789, *below*; *also* 1669, *above*.

Ovid's Epistles; with his Amours. 1748. *See* 1725, *above*.

Poems in the Scottish dialect by several celebrated poets. Glasgow 1748.

Poems on several occasions. Dublin 1748.

Poetry made familiar and easy: being the fourth volume of the Circle of the sciences. 1748 (2nd edn). *See* The art of poetry, 1746, *above* and Case 452 (b).

1749

An antidote against melancholy: being a collection of fourscore merry songs. 1749.

The charmer: a choice collection of songs, English and Scots. Edinburgh 1749. C. H. Wilkinson copy. *See* 1751–2, 1765, 1782, *below*.

A collection of loyal songs for the use of the Revolution Club. Edinburgh 1749. Also another edn, nd, in Edinburgh Univ Lib. *See* 1761, 1770, *below*.

A collection of poems by several hands, in four volumes. Vol 4, 1749. Dodsley's collection. Bodley copy seems unique, and includes in one vol the poems added to the 3 vols of 2nd edn. *See* 1748, *above*.

The foundling hospital for wit. Nos 2, 6, ed 'Timothy Silence' 1749. *See* 1743, *above*.

A general history of the stage with pieces of poetry never before published. Ed W. R. Chetwood 1749.

The Irish miscellany, or Teagueland jests: being a compleat collection of amorous letters, sublime poetry. 1749 (3rd edn). *See* 1750, *below*.

The linnet. 1749. *See* Orpheus, *below*.

The merry medley: or a Christmas-Box for gay gallants. Vol 1, 1749. Harding copy. *See* 1744, *above*.

Miscellanea nova et curiosa: the new and curious miscellany; to which is added a collection of poems. Ed H. C., Dublin 1749.

Miscellanies: the fifth and sixth volumes. Vol 5, 1749 (4th edn). Dobell, 1932. Teerink 67A(3a). *See* 1727, *above*.

A new and choice collection of loyal songs. 1749.

A new miscellany published for the benefit of John Maxwell, being blind. York 1749. T. C. Godfrey, 1932.

Orpheus: a collection of one thousand nine hundred seventy four English and Scotch songs: vol 1, The linnet; vol 2, The thrush; vol 3, The robin. 1749. *See* Vocal melody, 1751, *below*.

Poems on several occasions, from genuine manuscripts of Dean Swift [et al]. 1749.

The polite companion: containing essays illustrated with passages from the poets, orators. 2 vols Birmingham 1749.

The robin. 1749. *See* Orpheus, *above*.

T[ren]t[ha]m and V[an]d[epu]t: a collection of the advertisements and hand-bills published during the election for Westminster, 1749. [1749], Dublin 1749. Trinity College Dublin copy.

The thrush. 1749. *See* Orpheus, *above*.

A true and impartial collection of pieces in prose and verse published during the Westminster election. 1749.

The two candidates, or charge and discharge: being letters, songs, acrosticks, published on both sides during [the Westminster election]. [1749].

The vocal medley, or universal songster: a choice collection of two hundred and thirty one songs. York [1749?]. Harding copy. *See* 1755, *below*.

The warbling Muses: or treasure of lyric poetry, containing seven hundred and thirty-one songs. Ed B. Wakefield. 1749.

The works of the most celebrated minor poets. 2 vols 1749. *See* A supplement, 1750, *below*.

1750

The academy of complements. [1750?]. *See* 1663, *above*.

Amaryllis. Vols 1–2, [1750?] (2nd edn, improved). Stainer copy; imprint, J. Tyther. *See* 1746, *above*.

Ars amandi: or Ovid's Art of love, translated. Dublin 1750. *See* 1709, *above*.

The aviary: containing new songs. [1750?] (2nd edn). *See* 1744, *above*.

The best and compleatest academy of compliments yet extant; with a choice collection of new playhouse songs. [1750?].

The bull-finch. [1750?] (2nd edn). Pp. vii + 184; 255 songs. *See* 1748, *above*.

The Chester miscellany: being a collection of prose and verse [from Chester Courant]. Chester 1750.

A collection of loyal songs, poems, printed in the year 1750. [1750].

A collection revival and refining (from the more gross and obscene songs) by Abraham Milner. [1750?].

Pennecuik, A. A compleat collection of all the poems; to which is annexed some curious poems by other worthy hands. Pts 1–2, Edinburgh [1750?]. *See* A collection of Scots poems, 1756, *below*.

The Edinburgh entertainer: containing historical and poetical collections. Edinburgh 1750.

An entire new collection of humourous songs. 1750. Harding copy.

The goldfinch, or Comus's court: being a collection of two hundred and thirty one English and Scotch songs. [1750?]. Stainer copy. *See* 1748, *above*.

The harp, or musical miscellany: being a collection of choice songs. 1750. Harding copy. Musical miscellany, vol 3, 1730, with a new title-page.

Arbuthnot, Swift et al. The history of John Bull, and poems on several occasions, with several miscellaneous pieces. [1750?].

The Irish miscellany. 1750 (4th edn). Dobell, 1938. *See* 1749, *above*.

The Kapélion: or poetical ordinary. Nos 1–6, ed W. Kenrick [1750].

Love at first sight, or the gay in a flutter: being a collection of advertisements, chiefly comic. 1750. *See* 1751, *below*.

Lusus westmonasterienses. 1750. *See* 1730, *above*.

The merry companion, or universal songster: consisting of a new collection of celebrated songs. 1750 (4th edn). Stainer copy. *See* 1739, *above*.

The merry man's companion and evening's agreeable entertainer: containing near six hundred songs, catches, airs. 1750. Stainer copy.

The merry medley: or a Christmass-Box. Ed C. F., vol 1 [1750?]. *See* 1744, *above*.

A new academy of compliments: or the lover's secretary. [1750?] (16th edn). *See* 1715, *above*.

A new tea-table miscellany: or bagatelles for the amusement of the fair sex. 1750, 1750 (2nd edn). Harding copy; much augmented.

Poematia: quartò edita. 1750. *See* 1734, *above*.

The rhapsody: being a display of the wit and humour of past times. 1750.

A select collection of modern poems. Glasgow 1750 (2nd edn). Yale copy. *See* 1744, *above*.

The spinnet, or musical miscellany: being a collection of choice songs and lyrick poems. 1750. Musical miscellany, vol 4, 1730, with a new title-page.

Splenetick pills, or mirth alamode: being a collection of humorous songs; the words by John Rumfish esqr; set to music by Dr Merriwagg. [1750].

The student: or the Oxford and Cambridge monthly miscellany. Ed C. Smart, vol 1, Oxford 1750. Subtitle of nos 1–5: the Oxford monthly miscellany. *See* 1751, *below*.

A supplement to the works of the most celebrated minor poets. 1750. *See* 1749, *above*.

The Syren: a choice collection of songs. [1750?].

The tea-table miscellany, in four volumes. 1750 (11th edn). *See* 1724, *above*.

Three songs in English and Latin. [1750?].

The universal musician: or songster's delight. [1750?]. Stainer copy; sold by the Booksellers; frontispiece + 129 leaves. *See* 1737, *above*.

The works of celebrated authors. 2 vols 1750.

1751

Academiae cantabrigiensis luctus in obitum Frederici Walliae principis. Cambridge 1751.

Ben Johnson's jests: or the wit's pocket companion. 1751. Harding copy; Harding also has copy dated Dublin 175–. *See* 1757, 1761, *below*.

Ben Johnson's jests. 1751 (2nd edn). Harding copy. 3rd edn, nd: Sotheby, 23 July 1864.

The cabinet for wit. Ed T. Sharpe 1751.

The charmer: a choice collection of songs, Scots and English. Ed J. G. 2 vols Edinburgh 1751. *See* 1749, *above*.

A collection of poems in three volumes, by several hands. 1751 (3rd edn). *See* 1748, *above*.

A collection of poems in two volumes. Dublin 1751 (3rd edn). The Dodsley collection with much substitution and rearrangement. *See* 1748, *above*.

Constitutions and charges of Freemasons; [with] a complete collection of songs. 1751. Sotheby, 25 April 1891. *See* 1723, *above*.

The English poems collected from the Oxford and Cambridge verses on the death of Frederick Prince of Wales. Edinburgh 1751.

Epicedia oxoniensa in obitum Frederici principis Walliae. Oxford 1751.

Joe Miller's jests. [1751?] (10th edn). Sotheby, 3 March 1891. *See* 1742, *above*.

Love at first sight: or the gay in a flutter. 1751 (2nd edn, with addns). Dobell, 1932. *See* 1750, *above*.

The minor poets: or the works of the most celebrated authors. 2 vols Dublin 1751. Reprint, with much rearrangement, of most of the 1749–50 vols.

Swift, Arbuthnot, Pope and Gay. Miscellanies, in four volumes. 1751. *See* H. Teerink, Bibliography of Swift, rev A. H. Scouten, Philadelphia 1963, nos 68–9. *See* 1727, *above*.

The morning walk; with a prologue and appendix from the best poets on similar subjects. [Ed W. H. Draper] 1751.

The Muse in good humour: or a collection of comic tales. 1751 (6th edn). *See* 1744, *above*.

The nut-cracker: containing jests, epigrams, epitaphs. Ed 'Ferdinando Foot' [C. Smart] 1751. *See* 1760, 1769, *below*.

Ovid's Metamorphoses, translated by [10 names] and other eminent hands. 2 vols 1751 (5th edn). *See* 1717, *above*.

Pills to expel spleen: or a cure for the vapours, containing a collection of miscellaneous poems. [1751?]. Possibly by one hand.

Winstanley, J. Poems, interspers'd with many others by several ingenious hands. Vol 2, Dublin 1751. *See* 1742, *above*.

Spenser, Jonson et al. Poems on moral and divine subjects, by several celebrated English poets. Glasgow 1751. Hunterian Lib Glasgow copy.

Sacred poems: or a collection of translations and paraphrases by various authors. Ed Sir David Dalrymple, Edinburgh 1751. Dyce Lib copy.

The student: or the Oxford and Cambridge monthly miscellany. Vol 2, Oxford 1751. *See* 1750, *above*.

Vocal melody or the songster's magazine: being a collection of 2,000 of the most celebrated English and Scotch songs. 3 vols 1751. Stainer copy. This is Orpheus, 1749, with addns.

1752

The charmer. Ed J. G. vol 1 Edinburgh 1752 (2nd edn). *See* 1749, *above*.

A collection from the Spectator, Tatler, Guardian, Pope, Dryden; for the benefit of English schools. Newcastle 1752. Webster, 1931. *See* 1761, 1765, *below*.

The Free-Mason's pocket companion. Edinburgh 1752. Dobell, 1930. *See* A pocket companion, 1735, *above*.

An introduction to singing; to which is added a collection of the newest songs. Ed P. Prelleur [1752?] Ellis, 1912. *See* 1745, *above*.

The merry companion: or humourous miscellany. Dublin 1752. Harding copy.

Miscellaneous pieces: consisting of select poetry and prose, and methods of improvement in husbandry. Sherborne 1752. Webster, 1934.

Miscellaneous pieces: consisting of select poetry and methods of improvement in husbandry. Sherborne 1752 (3rd edn).

The Muses banquet, or a present from Parnassus: being a collection of English and Scots songs. 2 vols Reading 1752.

Poetical pieces by several hands. Ed J. Stevens 1752.

The repository: containing original letters, speeches; likewise epigrams, elegies, epitaphs. 1752.

The sports of the Muses: containing a select collection of English and Scotch songs by [21 names]. 2 vols 1752.

The works of Rochester, Roscomon, Dorset, Devonshire, Buckinghamshire. 1752. *See* 1707, *above*.

Poems by Roscomon, Dorset, Devonshire, Buckingham. Vol 2, 1752.

The wreath: a collection of two hundred [songs] sung at Vauxhall, Ranelagh, Marybone, Cuper's Gardens. 1752. Sotheby, 27 July 1864. *See* 1753, 1755, 1757, *below*.

1753

The bull-finch. Dublin 1753 (4th edn). Harding copy. *See* 1748, *above*; *also* Sappho, *below*.

The chanter or the merry companion, in two parts: being a choice collection of songs lately sung. 1753. With suppl. Stainer copy.

The election magazine or the Oxfordshire register: being a compleat collection of all the pieces in prose and verse lately published. Oxford 1753.

The Essex harmony: being a choice collection of songs and catches. Ed J. Arnold 1753. Harding copy. *See* 1767, 1769, 1774, 1777, 1786, 1791, 1793, *below*.

The goldfinch: or new modern songster. Glasgow [1753]. Book-auction records, 1913–14. *See* 1782, 1783, *below*; *also* 1748, *above*.

The Harleian miscellany. Vol 1, 1753 (2nd edn). *See* 1744, *above*.

Laugh and be fat. 1753 (12th edn). *See* 1733, *above*.

The lover's manual: being a choice collection of poems from modern authors. Ed E. W. 1753. *See* Muses library, 1760, *below.*

Melpomene: or the songster's merry companion. Waltham [1753?]. Harding copy.

The merry lad: a choice collection of songs sung by Warner Bennett. Sheffield 1753. Stainer copy.

Miscellaneous tracts: or select passages from eminent authors. Ed A. Simm, Edinburgh 1753.

A miscellany: consisting of the following particulars. 1753.

The old and new interest or a sequel to the Oxfordshire contest: being a complete collection of all the pieces in prose and verse. 1753.

The Oxfordshire contest: or the whole controversy between the old and new interest, containing letters, songs. 1753. 2 issues, one with A true blue song ptd on blue paper, the other on white.

Oxfordshire in an uproar: or the election magazine, containing songs, poems. Oxford [1753]. Muirhead, 1960.

Sappho: a new collection of songs; being a proper supplement to the Bullfinch. Dublin 1753. Harding copy. *See* Bull-finch, 1753, *above.*

Songs sung in the several lodges of the order of bucks. 1753. Sotheby, 29 April 1891.

The tea table miscellany. 4 vols Glasgow 1753. Book-auction records, 1911–12. *See* 1724, *above.*

The Ulster miscellany: containing [prose and verse]. [Belfast?] 1753.

The Union: or select Scots and English poems. Ed T. Warton, Edinburgh 1753. A complete resetting of type in same year. *See* 1759, 1761, 1766, 1796, *below.*

The wreath: a curious collection of above two hundred new songs. 1753 (2nd edn). Stainer copy; Harvard has a copy of the 3rd edn, 1753. *See* 1752, *above.*

1754

The Free-Mason's pocket companion. Edinburgh 1754. Dobell, 1930. *See* 1752, *above.*

Joe Miller's jests: or the wit's vade-mecum. 1754. Sotheby, 27 April 1891. *See* 1742, *above.*

The merry fellow: a collection of the best modern jests, poems, epigrams, epitaphs. 1754. *See* 1757, *below.*

The Muses' choice or the merry fellow: being a collection of wit and humour. 1754. Harding copy. *See* 1759, 1770, *below.*

The Muses delight: an accurate collection of English and Italian songs. 1754, Liverpool 1754. *See* Apollo's cabinet, 1756, 1757, 1758; Apollo's delight, 1757, *and* The compleat tutor, 1760, *below.*

A new academy of compliments: or the lover's secretary. 1754 (14th edn, with addns). *See* 1715, *above.*

The pocket companion and history of Free-Masons. 1754. *See* 1759, 1764, *below.*

A pocket companion for Free-Masons: containing a collection of the songs of Masons, prologues and epilogues. Glasgow 1754. Dobell, 1930. *See* 1735, *above.*

A pocket companion for Freemasons, containing songs, prologues and epilogues. Edinburgh 1754. Dobell, 1935.

Poems, divine and moral, many of them originals. Ed J. Hawes, Norwich 1754.

The poetical miscellany. 1754. Yale copy. A reprint of Norfolk poetical miscellany, 1744.

Butler, S. Posthumous works, compleat in one volume. 1754 (6th edn). *See* 1715, *above.*

The rational amusement: comprehending a collection of letters. 1754.

The satyrs of Decimus Junius Juvenalis and of Aulus Persius Flaccus. Tr Dryden et al 1754. *See* 1693, *above.*

The scoundrel's dictionary; to which is prefixed the art of wheedling and a collection of their flash songs. 1754.

The universal jester: or a pocket companion for the wits. 1754. Harding copy.

1755

Carmina ad nobilissimum Thomam Holles. Cambridge 1755.

A collection of poems in four volumes, by several hands. 1755 (4th edn). 4th edn of vols 1–3; first of vol 4. *See* 1748, *above.*

A compleat tutor for the guittar; to which is added eighteen favourite songs. Bk 1, [c. 1755]. *See below.*

The pocket companion for the guittar: containing Italian, French, English and Scots songs. Bks 2–6, [c. 1755]. Harding copy complete. *See above.*

The fairies: an opera taken from A midsummer night's dream; the songs from Shakespear, Milton, Waller, Dryden [et al]. 1755, 1755 (2nd edn, with prologue by Garrick added).

The jovial companion: or the alive and merry fellow. [1755?]. Harding copy.

The lover's cabinet: a collection of poems. 2 pts Dublin 1755. *See* 1756, *below.*

Martialis epigrammata selecta. Tr W. Hay, A. Cowley et al. 1755. With Latin and English texts. Dyce copy with English text only: Select epigrams of Martial, with an appendix, 1755. *See* Works of Hay, 1794, *below.*

The myrtle: being a collection of above two hundred English and Scotch songs. 1755.

Poems by eminent ladies. Ed G. Colman and B. Thornton vols 1–2 1755. *See* 1757, 1773, 1780, *below.*

A select collection of original love letters, to which are sub-join'd poems by eminent ladies. Ed G. Gaylove 1755.

Select epitaphs. Ed W. Toldervy vols 1–2 1755.

The vocal medley, part the second: being a collection of two hundred and forty one songs. York [1755?]. BM Catalogue dates [1760?]. *See* 1749, *above.*

The wreath: a curious collection of new songs. 1755 (4th edn). Harding copy. *See* 1752, *above.*

1756

Ahiman rezon: or a help to a brother. Ed L. Dermott 1756. *See* 1760, 1764, 1778, 1780, 1782, 1787, 1790, 1795, 1800; *also* Charges and regulations, 1786, *below*; *also* C. Adams, Ahiman rezon, 1933.

Apollo's cabinet: or the Muses delight. Vols 1–2, Liverpool 1756. This is Muses delight, 1754, with alterations.

The aviary. [1756?] (3rd edn). Dobell, 1917. *See* 1744, *above.*

The beauties of the English stage. 3 vols 1756 (3rd edn). *See* 1737, *above.*

Ben Johnson's last legacy to the sons of wit, mirth and jollytry. 1756 (2nd edn). Harding copy.

British songs sacred to love and virtue. Ed Sir David Dalrymple, Edinburgh 1756. Lowndes.

Bungiana: or an assemblage of what-d'ye-call-em's in prose and verse relative to a certain naval commander [Byng]. Dublin 1756.

A choice collection of Masons songs, with several prologues and epilogues. 1756.

Pennecuik, A. et al. A collection of Scots poems on several occasions. Edinburgh 1756. *See* 1769, 1787, *below*; also A compleat collection, 1750, *above.*

A collection of several pamphlets, letters and sundry detached pieces relative to the case of Admiral Byng. 1756.

The comic miscellany. 2 vols 1756. Book-prices current, 1908. Verse and prose by several hands?

Anderson, J. The constitutions of the Free and Accepted Masons. Rev J. Entick 1756. *See* 1723, *above.*

The lovers cabinet: a collection of poems. Dublin 1756. Blackwell, 1932. *See* 1755, *above.*

Original prologues, epilogues and other pieces never before printed. 1756.

Swift et al. Poems on various subjects: The legion club;

The gymnasiad; The causidicade; An epistle to Dr Thompson. Glasgow 1756.

The repository or general review: a select collection of literary compositions extracted from periodical productions now publishing. 1756.

A select collection of the psalms of David, as imitated by the most eminent English poets. Ed H. Dell 1756. Hill, 1967.

The works of Rochester, Roscommon and Dorset. 1756. Book-auction records, 1912–13. See 1707, above.

1757

Apollo's cabinet: or the Muses delight. Vols 1–2, Liverpool 1757. The 1756 edn with new title-pages; vol 2 misprinted vol 1.

Apollo's delight: songs with music; also several hundred English and Irish songs without the music. 2 vols Liverpool 1757. Sotheby, 30 April 1890.

The Bacchanalian: or choice spirits feast, containing all the most celebrated new songs. [1757?] (2nd edn). Harding copy. See 1759, above.

The beauties of poetry display'd. 2 vols 1757.

The beauties of the Spectators, Tatlers and Guardians. 2 vols Dublin 1757. Dobell, 1937. See 1763, 1787, below.

Ben Johnson's jests: or the wit's pocket companion. [1757?] (5th edn). Harding copy. See 1751, above.

The bull-finch. Pts 1–2, [1757?]. Stainer copy. Pt 1, pp. viii + 184; pt 2, pp. viii + 192. See 1748, above.

A collection of comic songs, by H— R—. 1757. Hodgson, 26 June 1925. By several hands?

A collection of pretty poems for the amusement of children six foot high. 1757. Book-auction records, 1916–17. See 1760, 1770, 1775, 1779, below.

A collection of select epigrams by the most eminent hands. Ed J. Hackett 1757.

Joe Miller's jests. [1757?] (12th edn). See 1742, above.

'Lively, Luke'. The merry fellow: or jovial companion. Dublin 1757. Harding copy. See 1754, above.

The merry fellow: or entertaining magazine. Vol 2, Dublin 1757. Harding copy.

The monthly masque: or an entertainment of musick. Dublin [c. 1757]. Stainer copy: nos 73–92.

The Muse in a moral humour: being a collection of tales, fables, pastorals, by several hands. 1757. See 1758, below.

The Muse in good humour: or a collection of comic tales. Vol 2, 1757. See 1744, above.

The Muses holiday: or the polite songster. [1757].

Ned Ward's jests: or repository of wit and humour. 1757. Harding copy.

The nonpareil: or the quintessence of wit and humour. 1757.

Ovid's Art of love; with his Remedy of love. 1757. See 1709, above.

Poems by eminent ladies. 2 vols Dublin 1757. Dyce copy. See 1755, above.

Poems by several gentlemen of Oxford. 1757.

The poetical works of Rochester, Roscomon, Dorset, Devonshire, Buckinghamshire. 1757. Grolier, 1905. See 1707, above.

Poems by Roscomon, Dorset, Devonshire, Buckinghamshire and other eminent hands. Vol 2, 1757. Grolier, 1905.

Selected poetical works of the Earls of Rochester, Roscomon and Dorset. 1757. No known copy; rptd c. 1885.

Select and remarkable epitaphs. Ed J. Hackett 2 vols 1757.

A select collection of modern poems. 1757 (3rd edn). See 1744, above; also Case p. 325.

Tales to kill time, by the Society of the Court of Comus. 1757.

Ramsay, A. et al. Thirty Scots songs adapted from the most genuine sets extant. Edinburgh [1757]. Nat Lib of Scotland copy. R. Bremner also issued a 2nd set c. 1759. See 1770, 1780, 1790, 1795, below.

Tom Brown's complete jester: or the wit's merry companion. [1757?] (4th edn). Harding copy. First pbd 1755.

The vocal companion: or the delightful and merry songster. [1757?]. Harding copy. Apparently 2nd of a ser pbd by M. Cooper, of which Jovial companion, [1759?], is 3rd.

The works of Horace in English verse, by several hands. Ed W. Duncombe, vol 1, 1757. See 1759, 1767, below.

The wreath: a curious collection of new songs. 1757 (5th edn). See 1752, above.

1758

Apollo's cabinet: or the Muses delight. 2 vols Liverpool 1758. Edinburgh Univ Lib copy. See 1756, above.

Clio and Euterpe: or British harmony, in two volumes. Vol 1, 1758. See 1759, 1762, 1768, 1778, below.

A collection of all the new songs sung this season at Vauxhall, Ranelagh. 1758. Harding copy.

A collection of poems in six volumes, by several hands. 1758 (5th edn). 5th edn of vols 1–3; 2nd of vol 4; first of vols 5–6. Some change of contents in vols 1–4. See 1748, above.

The moral miscellany: or a collection of select pieces in prose and verse. 1758. See 1764, 1768, 1778, 1787, below.

The Muse in a moral humour. Vol 2, 1758. Myers, 1929. See 1757, above.

The polite songster: a collection of three hundred English and Scots songs. 1758. See 1760, below.

Thoughts moral and divine. Ed W. Calcott, Birmingham 1758 (2nd edn). See 1759, 1761, and A collection of thoughts, 1764, below.

The works of the Earls of Rochester, Roscommon and Dorset. 1758. Book-auction records, 1914–15. See 1707, above.

1759

The Apollo or the Muses choice: being a collection of new songs. 1759.

The Bacchanalian: or choice spirits feast. [1759?] (5th edn). Stainer copy. See 1757, above.

The book of fun, collected from all the jolliest authors. 1759.

Clio and Euterpe, in two volumes. Vol 1, 1759 (Mitchell Lib Glasgow copy); vol 2, 1759. See 1758, above.

A collection of songs set to musick by Mr Pixell. Birmingham [1759].

The jovial companion: or the new sentimental merry songster. [1759?]. Vol 3 ptd at foot of p. 1; see Vocal companion, 1757, above.

Killigrew's jests: or a pocket companion for the wits. 1759. Harding copy.

Mrs Pilkington's jests: or the cabinet of wit and humour in prose and verse. 1759. See 1764, below.

The Muses choice: or the merry fellow. 1759 (3rd edn). Harding copy. See 1754, above.

The musical companion. 1759. Harding copy.

The pocket companion and history of Free-Masons. 1759 (2nd edn). See 1754, above.

The secrets of the Free-Masons revealed; to which is added songs. 1759 (2nd edn).

A select collection of epitaphs from the tombstones of England, Scotland and Ireland. 1759.

Thoughts moral and divine. Coventry 1759 (3rd edn). See 1758, above.

The Union. 1759 (2nd edn). See 1753, above.

The Union song book. 1759. No known copy.

The vocal companion or songster's delight: being a choice collection of all the celebrated new songs. 1759. Stainer copy.

The whole life and merry exploits of Robin Hood; to which are added several songs. 1759. See 1663, above.

Winter-Evenings companion: being a new collection of diverting essays, merry stories, songs. 1759. Harding copy. *See* 1760, 1780, *below*.

The works of Horace in English verse, by several hands. Vol 2, 1759. *See* 1757, *above*.

1760

Academiae cantabrigiensis luctus in obitum Georgii II. Cambridge 1760.

The academy of compliments, with a choice collection of songs. [1760?]. *See* 1663, *above*.

Ahiman rezon. Dublin 1760. *See* 1756, *above*.

Amaryllis. Vols 1–2, [1760?] (2nd edn). Sotheby, 3 July 1905. Imprint: J. Lewer. *See* 1746, *above*.

The American mock bird: containing a new collection of the most favourite songs now in vogue. New York 1760. Harding copy.

The bull-finch. Pts 1–2, [1760]. Harding copy. Pt 1, pp. viii + 194; pt 2, pp. viii + 192. *See* 1748, *above*.

The canary bird: or gentlemen and lady's polite amusement. Pts 1–2, [1760?]. The 2 pts also issued as separate vols: Stainer copy. *See* 1745, *above*.

Chloe or the musical magazine: a collection of celebrated songs. [1760?].

Blacklock, T. et al. A collection of original poems by Scotch gentlemen. Vol 1, Edinburgh 1760. *See* 1762, *below*.

A collection of poems. 1760 (5th edn). Copy noted by R. Straus, Robert Dodsley, 1910. *See* 1748, *above*.

A collection of pretty poems for the amusement of children six foot high. [1760?]. *See* 1757, *above*.

A collection of songs for two and three voices by Handel, Blow [et al]. [c. 1760]. Nat Lib of Scotland copy.

The compleat tutor. [Liverpool c. 1760]. Includes The Muses delight. King's College Cambridge copy. *See* 1754, *above*.

'Funny, Ferdinando'. The droll miscellany: or book of fun. Dublin 1760. Harding copy.

The Free Masons songs. Edinburgh [1760?].

Harmonia anglicana: a collection of two, three and four part songs. [1760?]. 4 bks? [c. 1745–64].

The Muse's banquet or compleat songster: being a collection of all the new songs. Dublin 1760. Stainer copy.

The Muse's delight: or the songster's jovial companion. 2 pts 1760. Harding copy.

The Muses library, and young gentleman and ladies polite instructor. [1760?]. D. Nichol Smith copy. This is Lover's manual, 1753, *above*.

The musical miscellany or songster's pocket companion: an intire new collection of all the favourite English songs. 1760.

The nightingale: being a choice collection of English songs sung at the public theatres and gardens. Southwark [1760?]. *See* 1738, *above*.

The nut-cracker: containing jests, epigrams, epitaphs. 1760. Sotheby, 26 April 1901. *See* 1751, *above*.

Orpheus britannicus: or the gentleman and lady's musical musaeum; engraved by B. Cole 1760.

Poems, moral and divine: collected from the best authors. [1760?].

The polite companion: or wit a-la-mode; including jests, epigrams, rildles [*sic*], monumental inscriptions. 1760. Harding copy.

The polite songster: a collection of above three hundred English and Scots songs. 1760 (2nd edn). Stainer copy. *See* 1758, *above*.

Prolusions: or select pieces of antient poetry. Ed E. Capell 1760.

The reveller: a curious collection of favourite new songs, containing upwards of two hundred. [1760?]. Harding copy. [1760?] (2nd edn). Pickering & Chatto, 1925.

Pope, J. Dillon et al. A small but choice collection of curious pieces. 2 pts [1760?]. A made-up miscellany; includes Unfortunate lovers, 1756.

The tea-table miscellany, in four volumes. Edinburgh 1760 (12th edn). Nat Lib of Scotland copy. *See* 1724, *above*.

Tom Gaylove's compleat jester: or the wit's joyous companion. [1760?]. Harding copy.

The town and country jester; together with the Complete English songster. [1760?]. Harding copy.

The triumph of wit: or the new canting dictionary; illustrated with poems, songs and various intrigues. Dublin [c. 1760?]. Tregaskis, 1934. *See* 1767, 1780, *below*; *also* 1688, *above*.

The winter evening's companion: being a new collection of diverting essays; to which are added a choice collection of songs. [1760?]. *See* 1759, *above*.

Fawkes, F., W. Broome et al. The works of Anacreon translated into English by a gentleman of Cambridge. 1760. Hill, 1967.

1761

Apollo or the songster's universal library: first part of vol 1. Dublin [1761?] N. Ault 1760. *See* 1772; *also* The wreath, 1761; The chaplet, 1763; Wit, women and wine, 1763; The oaten pipe, 1785, *below*.

Ben Johnson's jests: or the wit's pocket companion. 1761 (7th edn). Harding copy. 7th edn, nd: Dobell, 1937. *See* 1751, *above*.

The bull-finch. Pts 1–2 [1761]. Stainer copy. Pt 1, pp. xiv + 190; pt 2, pp. 194. *See* 1748, *above*.

Callipaedia, in four books. Tr Rowe et al. 1761. *See* 1712, *above*.

A collection from the Spectator, Tatler, Guardian, Pope, Dryden; for schools. Ed J. Warden, Newcastle 1761. *See* 1752, *above*.

A collection of loyal songs for the use of the Revolution Club. Edinburgh 1761. Harding copy. *See* 1749, *above*.

Colley Cibber's jests: or the diverting witty companion. Newcastle 1761.

Divine, moral and historical miscellanies in prose and verse. Ed A. Dutton, vol 1, 1761. *See* 1762, 1763, *below*.

Epithalamia oxoniensa sive gratulationes in Georgii III et Sophiae Charlottae nuptias. Oxford 1761.

The ever green: being a collection of Scots poems, wrote before 1600. Vols 1–2, Edinburgh 1761. *See* 1724, *above*.

The Free Masons pocket companion; to which is added a complete collection of Free-Mason songs, prologues, epilogues. Ed W. Auld, Edinburgh 1761. *See* 1763 *below*; *also* A pocket companion, 1735, *above*.

Gratulatio academiae cantabrigiensis Georgii III et Charlottae nuptias celebrantis. Cambridge 1761.

Gratulationes juventutis academiae dubliniensis: a collection of poems on the late royal nuptials. Ed W. H. Burgh, Dublin 1761.

Laugh and be fat. 1761 (10th edn). *See* 1733, *above*.

The musical magazine, by Mr Oswald and other celebrated masters. [1761?].

New boghouse miscellany: or companion for the close-stool. 1761. Book-auction records, 1907–8. By several hands?

Ovid's Epistles, with his Amours. Tr Dryden, Pope et al 1761. *See* 1725, *above*.

Pietas et gratulatio collegii cantabrigiensis apud Novanglos. Boston (Mass) 1761.

Pietas universitatis oxoniensis in obitum Georgii II et gratulatio in Georgii III inaugurationem. Oxford 1761.

A poetical dictionary: or the beauties of the English poets alphabetically displayed. Ed S. Derrick 4 vols 1761.

Wilmot, John. The poetical works of that witty lord, never before printed. 1761. Only one genuine poem? Harvard copy. *See* 1718, *above*.

Thoughts, moral and divine. Manchester 1761 (4th edn). *See* 1758, *above*.

The Union. Dublin 1761. With addns not ptd in the London or Scotch edns. *See* 1753, *above*.

Verses on the coronation of George II and Caroline, October 11 1727: spoken by the scholars of Westminster School. 1761.

The words of such pieces as are performed by the Academy of Ancient Music. 1761. *See* 1768, *below*.

The wreath: being the second part of the first volume of Apollo. Dublin [1761?]. N. Ault copy. *See* 1772, *below*; *and* Apollo, 1761, *above*.

1762

Ancient constitutions and charges of Masons, with their songs and odes. 1762. Book-auction records, 1902–3. *See* 1723, *above*.

The art of English poetry. 2 vols 1762 (9th edn, enlarged). *See* 1702, *above*.

The art of poetry on a new plan. Ed J. Newbery and O. Goldsmith 2 vols 1762.

The British antidote to Caledonian poison. [1762]. Book-auction records, 1919–20. *See* 1763, 1764; *also* Scots scourge, 1763, 1765, *below*.

The British miscellany: a selected collection of songs perform'd at theatres. Pt 1, [1762]. *See* 1764, *below*.

The British phoenix: or the gentleman and lady's polite literary entertainer. 1762.

The Caledonian miscellany. Newcastle 1762. Omits last 3 items in 1740 edn, *above*.

The catch club: or merry companions. Bks 1–2, [1762]. Settings by Purcell, Blow et al; with numerous addns. *See* 1705, *above*.

Rollos, G. et al. The chaplet or gentleman and lady's musical companion: consisting of songs. [c. 1762].

Clio and Euterpe, in 3 volumes. 1762. *See* 1758, *above*.

A collection of modern poems, by several hands. 1762.

A collection of original poems, by Scotch gentlemen. Vol 2, Edinburgh 1762. *See* 1760, *above*.

A collection of songs. Edinburgh 1762. *See* A collection of Bacchanalian songs, 1763, *and* Buck's bottle companion, 1775, *below*.

A collection of the best old Scotch and English songs. Ed J. Oswald [1762?].

The complete English songster. [1762?]. Sotheby, 8 July 1918. *See* Lark, 1770, *below*.

Divine, moral and historical miscellanies in prose and verse. Vol 2, 1762. *See* 1761, *above*.

England's glory: a collection of loyal songs sung at the theatres. 1762. Book-prices current, 1913.

The goldfinch: a collection of choice songs. Gainsborough 1762. Sotheby, 24 July 1866. *See* 1748, *above*; *also* another Gainsborough edn, 1788, *below*.

Gratulatio academiae cantabrigiensis natales Georgii Walliae principis Georgii III et Charlottae filii celebrantis. Cambridge 1762.

Gratulatio solennis universitatis oxoniensis ob Georgium Walliae principem Georgio III et Charlottae natum. Oxford 1762.

The harangues or speeches of quack-doctors; with mountebank songs by various hands. 1762. Harding copy; Harding also has copy with more pages, [1762?].

Joe Miller's jests. 1762 (13th edn). Sotheby, 3 March 1891. 13th edn, nd: Chicago Public Lib. *See* 1742, *above*.

The Parnassium: or beauties of English poetry. 1762 (new edn).

Dryden, Milton et al. The poetical miscellany, consisting of select pieces for the use of schools. 1762. *See* 1769, 1778, 1789, *below*.

Poetry made familiar and easy: being the fourth volume of the Circle of the sciences. 1762. Case notes an edn. *See* Art of poetry, 1746, *above*.

The select poems of Akenside, Gray, Mason, Shenstone, Mess Wartons, Lyttleton, Dyer, Beattie, Blacklock, Scott. Edinburgh 1762. D. Nichol Smith copy.

Tales and novels in verse from the French of La Fontaine, by several hands. Ed S. Humphreys, Edinburgh 1762. *See* 1735, *above*.

The tea-table miscellany, in four volumes. Edinburgh 1762 (13th edn). Bodley copy has 12th edn's engraved title also. *See* 1724, *above*.

The yearly chronicle for MDCCLXI. Ed H. Baldwin 1762. From St James's Chron.

The young gentleman's complete jester; to which is added several poems, songs and epitaphs. Nottingham 1762. Sotheby, 24 June 1903.

1763

The aviary, [with] an appendix containing new songs. [c. 1763] (4th edn). *See* 1744, *above*.

The beauties of the Spectators, Tatlers and Guardians. 2 vols 1763. *See* 1757, *above*.

The British antidote to Caledonian poison for the year 1762. [1763] (5th edn); for 1762 and 1763, 2 vols [1763?]. Sotheby, 23 April 1891. *See* 1762, *above*.

The bull-finch. [1763?]. Stainer copy. Pp. xiii + 368; songs, 381. *See* 1748, *above*.

'Euphrosyne'. The chaplet of chearfulness: first part of the second vol of Apollo. Dublin 1763 (Harding copy), Dublin 1763 (2nd edn) (N. Ault copy). *See* Apollo, 1761, *above*; *and* The coal-hole of Cupid, 1768, *below*.

A collection of Bacchanalian songs. Edinburgh 1763. This is A collection of songs, 1762, reissued.

A collection of catches, canons and glees. Ed T. Warren, 2 bks 1763, 32 bks [1763–94]. Also an expurgated edn in 25 pts, nd: Royal College of Music copy. *See* 1765, 1785, *below*.

A collection of poems in six volumes. 1763. *See* 1748, *above*.

A collection of the most celebrated songs set by several authors, adapted for the guittar. Ed F. Schuman [1763]; A second set, [c. 1770] (Mitchell Lib Glasgow copy).

The complete Free Mason: or multa paucis for lovers of secrets. [1763]; abridged in J. Thorpe, Masonic Reprints (Leicester) no 7 1924. *See* 1769, *below*.

The Court of Comus: a new collection of three hundred songs, medleys and cantatas. Dublin 1763. Harding copy.

Divine, moral and historical miscellanies in prose and verse. Vol 3, 1763. *See* 1761 above.

The foundling hospital for wit. Nos 1–6, 1763. With different sets. *See* 1743, *above*.

The Free-Mason's pocket-companion; with a collection of songs. Edinburgh 1763 (2nd edn). *See* 1761, *above*.

Gratulatio academiae cantabrigiensis in pacem Georgii III. Cambridge 1763.

The honest fellow or reveller's memorandum-book: the humours of Dublin in a collection of jocular songs by Bumper Allnight. 1763. Sotheby, 30 April 1901. *See* 1767, *below*.

The London and Edinburgh polite songster: a curious collection of celebrated English and Scotch new songs. 1763. No known copy.

The London polite songster: being a new and choice collection of the most approved English and Scotch songs, in two volumes. 1763.

Gay, Prior et al. A museum for young gentlemen and ladies. 1763 (4th edn). *See* 1790, *below*.

The poetical calendar: intended as a supplement to Dodsley's collection. Ed F. Fawkes and W. Woty 12 vols 1763.

Scots scourge: being a compleat supplement to the British antidote to Caledonian poison. 2 vols [1763?]. Sotheby, 23 April 1891. *See* British antidote, 1762, *above*.

A select collection of modern poems, by the most eminent hands. Edinburgh 1763. *See* 1744, *above*.

Social harmony: consisting of a collection of songs and catches; to which are added several choice songs on

Masonry, by Thomas Hale. 4 pts and suppl 1763, [Liverpool?] 1763. *See* 1770, 1775, 1780, *below.*

The songster's delight: being a choice collection of English songs. Coventry 1763. Stainer copy. *See* 1765, *below.*

The tea-table miscellany, in four volumes. 1763 (12th edn). *See* 1724, *above.*

Thesaurus musicus: a collection of two, three and four part songs. 2 vols [c. 1763]. *See* 1743, *above.*

Wit, women and wine. Dublin 1763 (Harding copy); vol 2, pt 2, of Apollo, 1761. *See* Chaplet of chearfulness, 1763, *above.*

1764

Ahiman rezon: or a help to all that are (or would be) Free and Accepted Masons. 1764 (2nd edn). *See* 1756, *above.*

The blackbird: a choice collection of the most celebrated songs. Ed W. Hunter, Edinburgh 1764. Stainer copy. *See* 1771, 1783, *below.*

The British miscellany: a selected collection of songs. Pt 4, [1764]. *See* 1762, *above.*

The bucks delight: being a collection of humourous songs. [1764?] (2nd edn). *See* 1780, *below.*

The buck's merry companion: an entire new and choice collection of songs, catches and cantatas. [1764?]. Harding copy.

The bull-finch. [1764?]. Harding copy. Pp. xvi + 368; songs, 426. *See* 1748, *above.*

The celebrated Mrs Pilkington's jests: or the cabinet of wit and humour. 1764 (2nd edn). *See* 1759, *above.*

The charmer: or the lady's garland, containing two hundred and thirty-five songs. [1764?]. A different collection from the Edinburgh ser, 1749, *above.*

A choice collection of Scotch and English songs. Glasgow 1764.

A collection of catches by Arne [et al], printed by Welcker. [1764?]. *See* A second collection, 1766, *below.*

A collection of poems from the best authors. Ed J. Elphinston 1764.

A collection of thoughts, moral and divine, in prose and verse. Exeter 1764 (5th edn). *See* Thoughts, 1758, *above.*

The complete London jester or wit's companion: jests, epigrams, merry tales, choice songs. 1764. Myers & Co., 1936. *See* 1765, 1766, 1768, 1771, 1779, 1780, 1781, 1784, 1785, *below.*

The Court and city medley: or political shaver in prose and verse. Ed 'Sir Daniel Downright' 1764. Possibly by one hand.

The macaroni jester and pantheon of wit; with epigrams and epitaphs. [1764?]. Sotheby, 24 June 1903.

The moral miscellany. Leipzig and Züllichau 1764. *See* 1758, *above.*

Ovid's Art of love. Tr Dryden et al 1764. Dyce copy. *See* 1709, *above.*

The Oxford sausage: or select poetical pieces written by the most celebrated wits of the University of Oxford. Ed T. Warton 1764. *See* 1766, 1772, 1777, *below.*

The pocket companion and history of Free-Masons, containing a selection of songs. 1764 (3rd edn). *See* 1754, *above.*

Poematia: quintò edita. 1764. *See* 1734, *above.*

The poetical magazine: or the Muses monthly companion. Vol 1, 1764.

Prior, Pope et al. The poetical tell-tale: or Muses in merry story. 1764.

The polite miscellany: an elegant collection of essays both in prose and verse. Manchester 1764.

[Reliques of ancient English poetry. Ed T. Percy, vols 1–2, 1764.] First unpbd state, containing poems not in pbd edns. Bodley copy. *See* 1765, *below.*

The second volume of the British antidote to Californian poison, for the years 1762 and 1763. [1764]. *See* 1762, *above.*

The temple of Comus or every gentleman and lady's Beard, Brent and Lowe: being songs for the year 1764. [1764]. Stainer copy.

1765

The Brent: or English syren. 1765. Stainer copy.

The British miscellany: a selected collection of the most favourite songs. [1765?]. Stainer copy.

The charmer. Vol 1, Edinburgh 1765 (3rd edn). *See* 1749, *above.*

A collection of canons, catches and glees. 32 bks [c. 1765–c. 1795]. *See* 1763, *above.*

A collection of poems in six volumes. 1765. A large-paper and large-letter edn. *See* 1748, *above.*

A collection of select pieces from the Spectator, Tatler, Guardian, Dryden and Pope, for schools. Edinburgh 1765. *See* 1752, *above.*

The complete London jester: or wit's companion. 1765 (2nd edn). *See* 1764, *above.*

Constitutions of the Free-Masons. Ed J. Entick 1765 (3rd edn). Book-auction records, 1916–17. *See* 1723, *above.*

The delightful new academy of compliments; to which is added a choice collection of the newest songs. Newcastle [1765?].

The entertainer: being the third volume of the Merryfellow, containing select pieces in prose and verse. Dublin 1765. Harding copy.

The Free Masons pocket companion. Glasgow 1765. London Lib copy. *See* 1752, *above.*

Freemasonry stripped naked. Ed C. Warren [1765?] Hodgson, 26 June 1925.

Harmonia anglicana: or English harmony reviv'd. [1765?]. Bks 1–3, pbd separately; bks 1–4 also pbd as 1 vol, with title-page still imprinted Book 1.

[Harmonia sacra: or divine and moral songs]. [c. 1765]. BM copy lacks title-page. *See* 1770, 1790, *below.*

The lark: being a select collection of songs, Scots and English. Vol 1, Edinburgh 1765. Stainer copy. No more pbd.

Howard, L. Miscellaneous pieces in prose and verse; to which are added tracts, poems, of some eminent personages of wit and humour. 1765; vol 2, 1765. Harding copy.

Miscellaneous pieces of poetry, selected from various eminent authors. Edinburgh 1765.

The musical companion: being a collection of all the new songs sung at the play houses. [1765?] (3rd edn). Harding copy.

Reliques of ancient English poetry. Ed T. Percy 3 vols 1765. *See* 1764, *above*; 1766, 1767, 1775, 1790, 1791, 1794, *below.*

The Scots scourge: or Pridden's supplement to the British antidote to Californian poison. 2 vols [1765]. *See* The British antidote, 1762, *above.*

Select lessons in prose and verse, from various authors. Ed J. N., Bristol 1765. *See* 1774, 1778, 1783, 1785, 1797, 1798, *below.*

A selection of Masonic songs. Dublin [c. 1765]. Maggs Bros, 1935. *See* 1798, *below.*

The songster's delight: being a choice collection of English songs. Coventry 1765. *See* 1763, *above.*

A specimen of a book, intituled, Ane compendious booke of godly and spiritual sangs. Edinburgh 1765.

The syren: a choice collection of songs performed at the theatres and other public places. [1765?]. Stainer copy. Pp. xiv + 360. *See* 1770, *below.*

The tea-table miscellany, formerly in four volumes, now in one. Glasgow 1765 (14th edn). Harvard copy. *See* 1724, *above.*

Thesaurus musicus: a collection of two, three and four part songs. Vol 1, [c. 1765]. King's College Cambridge copy. *See* 1743, *above.*

1766

The chearful companion: a collection of songs. Edinburgh 1766. Harding copy.

A choice collection of Scots poems, antient and modern, selected from the writers in this Kingdom during the two last centuries. Edinburgh 1766.

A collection of poems in six volumes. 1766. *See* 1748 *above*; *also* W. P. Courtney, Dodsley's collection: its contents and contributors, 1910.

The complete London jester: or wits companion. 1766 (3rd edn). Harding copy. *See* 1765, *above*.

The entertainer: collected by Charles Telltruth. 2 vols 1766.

The entertaining companion: or merry songster's delight. [1766].

Feriae poeticae. Ed S. Bishop 1766.

The festoon: a collection of epigrams, ancient and modern. Ed R. Graves 1766. *See* 1767; *also* Christmas treat, 1767, *below*.

A genuine collection of all the new songs, ballads, now singing at Vaux-Hall Garden. 1766.

A genuine collection of the several pieces of political intelligence extraordinary, epigrams, poetry, that have appeared before the public. 1766.

The Muse in good humour: or a collection of comic tales. Vols 1–2, 1766 (7th edn). *See* 1744, *above*.

The Muses' delight: the London polite songster for the year 1766. 1766. Stainer copy.

A new academy of compliments: or the lover's secretary. Dublin 1766 (18th edn). Harding copy. *See* 1715, *above*.

The new buck's delight or the merry companion: being a choice collection of two hundred songs. 1766. Stainer copy.

Original prologues, epilogues and other theatrical pieces [never before ptd]. Ed H. Dell 1766. A different collection from 1756, *above*.

The Oxford sausage. Dublin 1766. *See* 1764, *above*.

Poetical blossoms: or the sports of genius, by the young gentlemen of Rule's Academy at Islington. Ed J. Rule 1766.

Quin's jests: or the facetious man's pocket-companion; with a compleat collection of epigrams. 1766.

A rattle for grown children, containing odes, songs and catches. Ed 'Young D'Urfey' [F. Forrest] 1766. A. Deakin, A music bibliography, 1892, cites a 1765 edn.

Reliques of ancient English poetry. 3 vols Dublin 1766. *See* 1765, *above*.

A second collection of catches, by Arne [et al]. [1766?]. *See* A collection, 1764, *above*.

The Union. 1766 (3rd edn). *See* 1753, *above*.

The universal melody: or songster's magazine, by Lyrick Chaunter. Vol 1, 1766. Stainer copy.

1767

Antient funeral monuments. Ed W. Tooke 1767. First pbd by J. Weever, 1631.

The beauties of English poesy. Ed O. Goldsmith 2 vols 1767.

A choice collection of songs compos'd by Purcell, Blow, Handell. [1767]. Sotheby, 22 May 1917. *See* 1775, *below*.

The Christmas treat or gay companion: being a collection of epigrams, ancient and modern. Dublin 1767. Another edn of Festoon, 1766, above, differently arranged.

Mendez, M. et al. A collection of the most esteemed pieces of poetry. 1767. Intended as suppl to Dodsley's collection. *See* 1770, *below*.

The constitutions of the Free and Accepted Masons. 1767 (new edn). Issue lacking appendix: Dobell, 1930. *See* 1723, *above*.

A curious collection of Scots poems. [Edinburgh 1767]. Containing Ajax his speech, etc.

The delicate songster: or entertaining companion. 1767.

The entertaining medley. 1767, 1767 (2nd edn).

The Essex harmony. 1767 (3rd edn, with addns). *See* 1753, *above*.

The festoon: a collection of epigrams. 1767 (2nd edn, augmented). *See* 1766, *above*.

The festoon: a select collection of epigrams. [1767?] (4th edn). *See above*.

The honest fellow or reveller's memorandum book: the humours of the world in jocular songs. 1767. Lowndes. *See* 1763, *above*.

Jachin and Boaz: or an authentic key to Free-Masonry. 1767 (6th edn). Dobell, 1930. *See* 1776, 1780, 1785, 1790, 1793, 1797, *below*.

The London songster: or polite musical companion, containing four hundred and fifty-four songs. 1767. *See* 1768, 1773, 1774, 1783, 1784, 1788, *below*.

The masque: a new and select collection of the best English, Scotch and Irish songs. 1767. Harding copy. *See* 1768–70, 1777, 1790, *below*.

The musical magazine: or compleat pocket companion for the year 1767. Vol 1, [1767]. *See* 1768–72, *below*.

Poems for young ladies. Ed O. Goldsmith 1767. *See* 1770, 1785, 1792, *below*.

Reliques of ancient English poetry. 3 vols 1767 (2nd edn). *See* 1765, *above*.

The triumph of wit and compleat cant-book, illustrated with poems, songs. Dublin 1767. *See* 1760, *above*.

The warbler's delight: or English harmony. [1767?].

The works of Horace in English verse. Tr W. Duncombe et al 4 vols 1767 (2nd edn). *See* 1757–9, *above*.

The works of the earls of Rochester, Roscomon, Dorset, Devonshire, Buckinghamshire; with memoirs. 1767. Pickering & Chatto, 1929. *See* 1707, *above*.

1768

The battle of the quills or Wilkes attacked and defended: an impartial selection of pieces in prose and verse. 1768.

The cheerful companion: or songster's pocket-book. 1768.

Clio and Euterpe. Vols 1–3, 1768. Book-auction records, 1921–2. *See* 1758, *above*.

The coal-hole of Cupid: a collection of songs. 1768. Stainer copy. A reprint of Chaplet of chearfulness, 1763, *above*.

A collection of one hundred and fifty Scots songs. Vol 1, 1768. No more pbd.

A collection of poems in two volumes, by several hands. Ed G. Pearch 1768. A suppl to Dodsley's collection. *See* 1770, 1775, 1783, *below*.

The complete London jester: or wit's companion. 1768. Sotheby, 16 March 1906. *See* 1765, *above*.

The contest: or a collection of papers in prose and verse publish'd [during the Norfolk election] in 1768. 1768.

The Dunniad: being a collection of pieces in prose and verse [pbd during Pontefract election]. [1768?].

The essence of theatrical wit: being a select collection of prologues and epilogues. 1768.

Joe Miller's jests; to which are added epigrams. [1768?]. Ptd for John Lever; probably pirated. *See* 1742, *above*.

The lark: a collection of choice Scots songs; together with a few songs for the bottle. Edinburgh 1768. Harding copy.

The London songster: or polite musical companion. 1768. Sotheby, 26 June 1903. *See* 1767, *above*.

The masque. 1768 (2nd edn). *See* 1767, *above*.

Mirth's magazine or Momus's fund: a collection of humourous songs. Ed R. Pickersgill [1768?]. Harding copy.

The moral miscellany. 1768 (3rd edn, enlarged). *See* 1758, *above*.

The musical companion or songster's magazine: near one hundred songs lately sung at the theatres. 1768.

The musical magazine for 1768. Vol 2, [1768]. *See* 1767, *above*.

The new foundling hospital for wit: being a collection of pieces in verse and prose. Pts 1–2, 1768. *See* 1769, 1771, 1772, 1773, 1784, 1786, *below*.

The new foundling hospital for wit. Pt 1, 1768 (2nd edn).

Ovid's Epistles. Dublin 1768. Dobell, 1918. *See* 1725, *above*.

A select collection of poems from the most approved authors. 2 vols Edinburgh 1768. *See* 1772, *below*.

The tea-table miscellany in four volumes. Edinburgh 1768 (14th edn). Harvard copy. *See* 1724, *above*.

The tea-table miscellany; formerly in four volumes, now comprised in two. Glasgow 1768. Mitchell Lib Glasgow copy. *See* 1724, *above*.

Witticisms and strokes of humour. Ed R. Baker [1768?]. Harding copy.

The words of such pieces as are performed by the Academy of Ancient Music. 1768 (2nd edn). *See* 1761, *above*.

1769

The ancient and modern Scots songs, heroic ballads; now first collected from the various miscellanies. Ed D. Herd, Edinburgh 1769. *See* 1776, 1791, *below*.

The Bath contest: being a collection of all the papers, advertisements, published by the candidates. Bath [1769]. *See* Conciliade, 1769, *below*.

The bull-finch. [1769]. Harding copy. Pp. xvi + 404; songs, 456. *See* 1748, *above*.

Calcott, W. A candid disquisition of the principles and practices of the Society of Free and Accepted Masons. 1769. *See* 1772, *below*.

Pennecuik, A. et al. A collection of Scots poems on several occasions. Edinburgh 1769. C. H. Wilkinson copy. *See* 1756, *above*.

A companion for a leisure hour: being fugitive pieces in prose and verse by several gentlemen. 1769.

The compleat universal jester: or pocket companion for the wits. 1769.

The complete Free Mason. 1769. Dobell, 1930. *See* 1763, *above*.

The conciliade: being a supplement to the Bath contest, containing the several poetical and other pieces. Bath [1769]. Maggs Brothers, 1934. *See* Bath contest, 1769, *above*.

Constitutions of the Free-Masons. 1769. *See* 1723, *above*.

The Court of Thespis: being a collection of the most admired prologues and epilogues. 1769.

The cure for the spleen or kill care and laugh: a collection of songs, odes. Ed S. Massey, Newcastle 1769. Harding copy.

Derrick's jests: or the wits chronicle; also a collection of poetical pieces by Derrick and others. 1769.

The dramatic Muse: or jubilee songster, containing 390 songs. [1769?]. Stainer copy.

Elegiac and other poems by several hands. Bristol 1769. To the memory of A. R. Hawksworth; rptd Dublin. *See* Poems, 1775, *below*.

The English Roscius: Garrick's jests or genius in high glee. [1769?]. Harding copy. *See* Garrick's jests, 1790, *below*.

The Essex harmony. Vol 2, 1769. *See* 1753, *above*.

The exploits of the renowned Robin Hood, interspers'd with variety of songs. 1769. *See* 1663, *above*.

Joe Miller's jests. [1769?] (14th edn). *See* 1742, *above*.

The ladies polite songster: or harmony for the fair-sex. [1769?]. Imprint: T. Shepherd and Stephen Smith. *See* 1770, *below*.

Love and beauty: a collection of poems, written by the best authors. 1769.

The masque: a new edition, carefully corrected. [1769?]. Pp. xiv + 335; songs 331. *See* 1767, *above*.

The merry droll: or pleasing companion; including also some poetical recreations. 1769.

The musical magazine for 1769. Vol 3, [1769]. *See* 1767, *above*.

The new foundling hospital for wit. Pt 2, 1769 (2nd edn); pt 3, 1769. *See* 1768, *above*.

Harington, Sir John, et al. Nugae antiquae: being a miscellaneous collection of original papers in prose and verse. 1769. *See* 1775, 1779, 1792, *below*.

The nut-cracker. 1769. Sotheby, 16 March 1906. *See* 1751, *above*.

The patriotic miscellany: being a collection of papers, epigrams, in the case of John Wilkes. 1769.

The poetical miscellany: consisting of select pieces for the use of schools. 1769 (2nd edn). D. Nichol Smith copy. *See* 1762, *above*.

Poetry made familiar and easy: being the fourth volume of the Circle of the sciences. 1769 (3rd edn). *See* Art of poetry, 1746, *above*.

Polyhymnia or the complete song book: being a genuine collection of English songs. 1769. Stainer copy.

Shakespear's garland, or the Warwickshire jubilee: being a collection of ballads as perform'd in the great booth at Stratford upon Avon; composed by Mr Dibdin. 2 bks [1769]. 2 settings of title-page have been noted: Harding copy and Myers, 1932. Also, As perform'd at the Theatre Royal, Drury Lane, 2 bks [1769]. *See* Essays and poems, 1770; *and* Songs, 1669, *and* 1776, *below*.

2d part Shakespear's garland or the Warwickshire jubilee. [1769]. Harding copy.

Shakespeare's garland: being a collection of new songs, ballads, performed at the jubilee at S[t]ratford upon Avon. 1769, Dublin [1769]. Sotheby, 24 May 1917.

Songs, chorusses, which are introduced in the new entertainment of the jubilee at the Theatre-Royal in Drury-Lane. 1769. Pickering & Chatto, 1937. *See* 1776, *below*.

The tea-table miscellany. Dublin 1769 (14th edn, with addns). *See* 1724, *above*.

1770

Ancient Scottish poems, published from the ms of George Bannatyne. Ed Sir David Dalrymple, Edinburgh 1770; rptd 1815, for Longman, etc.

Bacchus and Venus: or the harmony of love and wine, containing a curious collection of songs. [1770?]. Stainer copy.

Ramsay, A. et al. The Caledonian miscellany: consisting of pastorals, choice fables and tales, with other occasional poems. [1770?]. Pickering & Chatto, 1935.

Calliope: or English harmony. 2 vols 1770. Book-auction records, 1919–20. *See* 1739, *above*.

Candid inquiry into the principles and practises of the most ancient and honourable society of bucks. 1770. Poems and songs at end; no known copy.

The chearful companion: or songster's delight. Cork 1770. Harding copy. *See* 1772, *below*.

A choice collection of favorite hunting songs, composed by Handel, Boyce. Bks 1–2, [1770?].

A collection of loyal songs for the use of the Revolution Club. Edinburgh 1770. Harding has 2 issues with differently set title-pages. *See* 1749, *above*.

A collection of original miscellaneous poems. Ed J. Coates 1770.

A collection of poems in four volumes, by several hands. 1770. Pearch's collection; 2nd edn of vols 1–2. *See* 1768, *above*.

A collection of poems in six volumes. 1770. *See* 1748, *above*.

A collection of pretty poems for children six foot high. [1770?] (6th edn). *See* 1757, *above*.

A collection of the most esteemed pieces of poetry. 1770 (2nd edn). *See* 1767, *above*.

The company keeper's assistant: being a collection of toasts and songs. Dublin 1770. Stainer copy.

Johnson, C. The complete art of writing letters; with the addition of some elegant poetical epistles. 1770 (5th edn).

Cupid and Bacchus: or love and the bottle, containing near six hundred songs. 1770. Stainer copy.

Elegant Extracts: or useful and entertaining pieces of poetry, selected for the improvement of youth. [Ed V. Knox, c. 1770]. See 1789, 1791, 1796; also Poetical epitome, 1792, below. Many nineteenth-century edns, dated and undated.

Dodd, J. S. Essays and poems. Cork 1770. Contains A collection of all the airs, catches, glees, cantatas and roundelays performed at Stratford upon Avon on occasion of the jubilee in honour of Shakespeare, 1769. See Shakespear's garland, 1769, above.

The frisky songster: or songs of jollity, high taste and humour. 1770. Hodgson, 26 June 1925. See 1776, below.

Harmonia sacra: or divine and moral songs by several eminent masters, adapted to the German flute. [c. 1770]. See 1765, above.

The humours of London: a choice collection of songs. [1770].

An introduction to singing; to which is added a choice collection of songs. [1770?]. Harding copy; imprint, C. & S. Thompson. See 1745, above.

Jemmy Twitcher's jests: or wit with the gravy in it. Ed D. Gunston 1770. See 1776, 1798, below.

Johnson's lottery song book: or vocal adventurer, containing a choice collection of songs. [1770?]. Contains frontispiece and pp. iv + 60. See 1777, below.

The ladies polite songster: or harmony for the fair-sex. [1770?]. Harding copy; imprint, R. Mariner and Stephen Smith; contents differ from 1769 edn, above.

[The lark: or English songster. 1770?]. Stainer copy; lacks title-page. This is an expanded edn of Complete English songster, [1762?], above.

The lover's best instructor: or the whole art of courtship. Wolverhampton [1770?]. By several hands? See 1777, below.

The masque: a new edition, with great additions. [1770?]. Stainer copy. Pp. xiv + 356; songs, 342. See 1767, above.

Miss Catley and Miss Weiwitzer's new London and Dublin songbook. Dublin [1770?]. Harding copy.

The modern catch-club: being a choice collection of catches. Langtoft [1770?].

The Muse in good humour: a collection of comic tales. Dublin 1770 (8th edn). Sotheby, 18 April 1898. See 1744, above.

The Muses choice: or the merry-fellow. Dublin 1770 (4th edn). See 1754, above.

The musical magazine for 1770. Vol 4, [1770]. See 1767, above.

The new entertaining humorist: miscellanies in prose and verse. Berwick 1770. See 1778, below.

The nightingale: being a choice collection of love songs, as well as other songs. 1770. Stainer copy. See 1738, above.

The nightingale: a choice collection of new songs. [1770?]. See 1738, above.

Poems for young ladies: a collection by Goldsmith. 1770 (new edn). See 1767, above.

Bruce, M. Poems on several occasions. Edinburgh 1770. Preface states they were by different authors.

Poetry made familiar and easy: being the fourth volume of the Circle of the sciences. Dublin [1770] (4th edn). See Art of poetry, 1746, above.

A select collection of vocal music, serious and comic. [1770]. Ptd by John Johnson, pp. 126; ptd for the Editor, pp. 88; for the Editor, pp. 126 + 12. Harding copies and BM copy.

The sentimental connoisseur: or the beauty and folly of virtue and vice displayed, in prose and verse. [c. 1770]. Muirhead, 1959.

Social harmony. [c. 1770] (2nd edn). Royal Academy of Music copy. See 1763, above.

The songster's pocket book: or jubilee concert. 1770. Harding copy.

The spouter's companion: or theatrical remembrancer, containing prologues and epilogues. [1770?].

The sprightly Muse: being a choice collection of humorous tales by the most celebrated poets. 1770. Sotheby, 27 April 1901.

The syren: a choice collection of songs performed at the theatres and other public places. [1770?] Pp. xiv + 430. See 1765, above.

Ramsay, A. et al. Thirty Scots songs adapted for a voice and harpsichord. Bk 1, [c. 1770]. A second set, [c. 1770]. Schnapper also notes another edn of bk 1, [c. 1770], another issue of bk 2, [c. 1770], and a different collection with the same title, 2 bks [c. 1770]. See 1757, above.

Vocal music: or the songster's companion. Vol 1, [1770?]. See 1771-2, 1775, 1778, below.

The warbling Philomell: a new and select collection of the best songs sung this year. [1770?] (2nd edn). Harding copy.

Wilkes's jest book or the merry patriot: being a collection of epigrams, drolleries, songs, respecting John Wilkes. 1770.

Yorick's jests: being a new collection of jokes; to which are added poems, fables, tales, epigrams. 1770. See 1774, 1783, below.

Yorick turned trimmer: or the gentleman's jester, and newest collection of songs. [1770?]. See 1797, below.

1771

The blackbird: containing one hundred and twenty-four songs, Scots and English. Edinburgh 1771 (3rd edn). See 1764, above.

Callipaedia, in four books; to which are added a few select tales. Tr Rowe et al Dublin 1771. See 1712, above.

The Catley: containing all the songs and airs in the Beggar's opera. Dublin 1771. Stainer copy.

The chearful linnet: a choice collection of songs taken from the operas and polite miscellanies. 1771 (Stainer copy); The second part: containing hunting and Bacchanalian songs, 1771 (Stainer copy).

The choice spirit's chaplet: or a posy from Parnassus, from the most approved authors. Ed G. A. Stevens, Whitehaven 1771. Stainer copy adds Dublin booksellers to imprint.

Choice spirits delight: a collection of pleasing poems by several hands. 1771. Book-auction records, 1903-4.

A collection of catches, glees. Edinburgh 1771. Cleverdon, 1936. 2 vols dedicated to Catch Club at Edinburgh.

A collection of modern fables. 1771.

A collection of poems, essays and epistles. Dublin 1771 (2nd edn). R. H. Lonsdale copy.

A collection of the best modern poems. 1771.

A compleat collection of prologues and epilogues. 1771.

Complete London jester: or wit's companion. 1771. Book-auction records, 1919-20. See 1765, above.

The Court jester: or museum of entertainment; to which is added a collection of songs. [1771]. See 1787, 1790, below.

Democritus or the laughing philosopher: a collection of merry stories, jests, epigrams. Berwick 1771. Harding copy, nd. See 1784, below.

The Free Masons pocket companion, [with] a complete collection of Free Mason songs, prologues, epilogues. Glasgow 1771. See A pocket companion, 1735, below.

Stanhope, P. D. et al. The humours of the times: being a collection of pieces in verse and prose, by the most celebrated geniusses. 1771.

The musical magazine for 1771. Vol 5, [1771]. See 1767, above.

The new foundling hospital for wit. Pt 1, 1771 (3rd edn); pt 4, 1771. *See* 1768, *above.*

The new polite instructor: or universal moralist, selected from the most eminent authors. 1771.

Sir John Fielding's jests: or new fun for the parlour and kitchen. [1771 ?]. BM copy, [1781].

Vocal music: or the songsters companion. Vol 2, 1771. With different imprints. BM copy, nd. *See* 1770, *above.*

The works of the Earls of Rochester, Roscommon and Dorset. 1771. Book-auction records, 1912–13. *See* 1707, *above.*

1772

The Apollo: being the first part of the first volume of the Masque. Dublin 1772. Harding copy. *See* 1761, *above*; *and* Wreath, 1772, *below.*

The bull-finch. [1772?]. Stainer copy. Pp. xvi + 416; songs, 469. *See* 1748, *above.*

A candid disquisition of the principles and practices of the Society of Free and Accepted Masons. Boston 1772. *See* 1769, *above.*

The chearful companion: or songster's delight. Cork 1772. Harding copy. *See* 1770, *above.*

The choice spirit's pocket companion or the buck's treasury: being a complete collection of songs. 1772. Lowndes.

A collection of original Scots songs, poems, by various hands. 1772.

The comic Muse: a choice collection of humourous tales, witty epigrams, epitaphs. 1772. Harding copy.

A companion for the fire-side: or winter evening's amusement. 1772.

Cupid and Hymen. 1772. *See* 1742, *above.*

Essays on song-writing; with a collection of songs. Ed J. Aikin [1772]. *See* 1774, 1777, *below.*

The history of Masonry; to which is added a large collection of songs, prologues, epilogues. Edinburgh 1772 (3rd edn).

Illustrations of Masonry. Ed W. Preston 1772. *See* 1775, 1781, 1788, 1792, 1796, *below.*

Joe Miller's jests. [1772?] (15th edn). *See* 1742, *above.*

The merry companion: being a collection of English and Scotch songs, ancient and modern. Newcastle 1772.

Miscellaneous poems, consisting of originals and translations. Ed V. Bourne 1772.

Musae seatonianae: a complete collection of the Cambridge prize poems. 1772; rptd as vol 1 of Musae seatonianae, Cambridge 1808. *See* 1773, 1787, *below.*

The musical magazine for 1772. Vol 6, [1772]. *See* 1767, *above.*

A new academy of compliments: or compleat English secretary. 1772. C. H. Wilkinson copy. *See* 1748, *above.*

The new foundling hospital for wit. Pt 5, 1722 [1772]. *See* 1768, *above.*

The new merry companion: or complete modern songster. [c. 1772]. *See* 1778, *below.*

The Oxford sausage: a new edition. Oxford 1772. *See* 1764, *above.*

The rival beauties: a poetical contest. [1772]. By several hands?

A select collection of poems. Vols 1–2, Edinburgh 1772 (2nd edn). *See* 1768, *above.*

Select essays from the Batchelor. Dublin 1772. *See* 1773, *below.*

The shamrock or Hibernian cresses: a collection of poems, songs, epigrams, the original production of Ireland. Ed S. Whyte, Dublin 1772. *See* A collection of poems, 1773, 1774, *below.*

The sky-lark: containing a new collection of well chosen English songs. 1772. Harding copy.

Vocal music: or the songster's companion. Vol 2, 1772 (2nd edn, improved). *See* 1770, *above.*

The warbler: or sweets of harmony selected. 1772.

The wreath: being the second part of the first volume of the Masque. Dublin [1772]. Harding copy. *See* 1761, *and* Apollo, 1772, *above.*

1773

Baratariana: a select collection of fugitive political pieces published during the administration of Townshend in Ireland. Ed Simpson, Dublin 1773 (2nd edn). The first edn includes only 2 poems. *See* 1777, *and* Essays historical, 1780, *below.*

The beauties of the poets. Ed T. Janes, Bristol 1773. R. H. Lonsdale copy. *See* 1777, 1788, 1790, 1792, 1799, 1800, *below.*

The British spouter: or stage assistant, containing prologues and epilogues. 1773.

A collection of poems, the productions of Ireland, selected from the Shamrock. 1773. *See* 1774, *below*; *and* Shamrock, 1772, *above.*

A collection of scarce, curious and valuable pieces, both in verse and prose, from the fugitive productions of the present age. Ed W. Ruddiman, Edinburgh 1773. *See* 1785, *below.*

A companion in a post-chaise: containing pieces in verse and prose. Salisbury 1773.

Essays from the Batchelor, in prose and verse. 2 vols Dublin 1773 (2nd edn). 2 issues of vol 2, 226 pp. and 228 pp. *See* 1772, *above.*

Goldsmith et al. Four poems: Armine and Elvira; The hermit of Warkworth; The deserted village; The traveller. Altenburgh [1773].

The London songster: or polite musical companion, containing five hundred and sixty-four songs. 1773 (new edn, enlarged). *See* 1767, *above.*

Lord Chesterfield's witticisms; to these is added a curious poetical desert. [1773].

Johnson, S. et al. Miscellaneous and fugitive pieces. Ed T. Davies, vols 1–2, [1773]. *See* 1774, *below.*

Musae seatonianae; to which are added two poems. 1773. *See* 1772, *above.*

The new foundling hospital for wit. Pt 6, 1773. *See* 1768, *above.*

Ovid's Metamorphoses. 1773. No known copy; Case. *See* 1717, *above.*

Poems by the most eminent ladies of Great-Britain and Ireland: a new edition. Vols 1–2, 1773. *See* 1755, *above.*

1774

A collection of poems: the productions of Ireland. 1774 (2nd edn). *See* 1773, *above.*

A complete collection of all the papers in the present contest for members for Northumberland. Newcastle 1774.

Essays on song-writing; with a collection of songs. Warrington 1774 (2nd edn). *See* 1772, *above.*

The Essex harmony. Vol 1, 1774 (4th edn). *See* 1753, *above.*

The fugitive miscellany: a collection of fugitive pieces in prose and verse. Ed J. Almon 1774. *See* 1775, *below.*

The London songster: containing 564 songs. 1774 (new edn). *See* 1767, *above.*

Miscellaneous and fugitive pieces. Vols 1–2, 1774 (2nd edn); vol 3, 1774. *See* 1773, *above.*

The polite preceptor: or improving moralist, selected from the most eminent English authors. 1774.

The robin: or the ladies polite songster, containing a new and choice collection of songs. [1774?]. Stainer copy. Pp. xii + 276. *See* 1775, *below.*

Select lessons in prose and verse. Bristol 1774 (2nd edn, with addns). *See* 1765, *above.*

The sentimental spouter: or young actor's companion. 1774.

The speaker: or miscellaneous pieces selected from the best English writers. Ed W. Enfield. 1774. *See* 1782, 1785, 1789, 1790, 1792, 1799, *below.*

The winter medley. 1774. No known copy.

The wit's miscellany: or a companion for the choice spirits. 1774.

The works of the Earls of Rochester, Roscommon and Dorset. 1774. Book-auction records, 1909–10. *See* 1707, *above.*

Yorick's jests. 1774. Sotheby, 16 March 1906. Undated edn, Sotheby, 23 July 1864. *See* 1770, *above.*

1775

The accomplish'd courtier: or a new school of love; to which is added a choice collection of songs. Newcastle [1775?].

The antiquarian repertory: a miscellany of old times. Vol 1, 1775. *See* 1779, 1780, 1784, *below.*

The British Muse: a collection of the most esteemed songs, sung by John Vint. Newcastle 1775. Stainer copy. *See* 1784, *below.*

The buck's bottle companion: being a complete collection of humourous, bottle and hunting songs. 1775. A reprint of A collection of songs, 1762, *above.*

The bull-finch. [1775]. Pp. xvi + 392; songs, 453. *See* 1748, *above.*

The Caledoniad: a collection of poems written chiefly by Scottish authors. 3 vols 1775.

A choice collection of songs compos'd by Purcell, Blow, Handell and other masters. Bk 2, [1775?]. *See* 1767, *above.*

A collection of poems in four volumes, by several hands. 1775. *See* 1768, *above.*

A collection of poems in six volumes. 1775. *See* 1748, *above.*

A collection of poems on divine and moral subjects, selected from various authors. Ed W. Giles 1775.

A collection of pretty poems for children six foot high. [1775?] (7th edn). *See* 1757, *above.*

A collection of vocal harmony, consisting of catches, canons and glees, motetts and madrigals. Ed T. Warren 2 vols [c. 1775]. *See* 1780, *below.*

The delightful vocal companion: or polite songster. [1775?].

The Diarian miscellany in five volumes. Ed C. Hutton 1775.

The Dublin songster: or polite musical companion, containing several hundreds of songs. Dublin 1775. Stainer copy.

[Ethic tales and fables. 1775?]. Title-page missing.

The fugitive miscellany: part the second. 1775. *See* 1774, *above*; *also* Flower-piece, 1780, *below.*

Illustrations of Masonry. 1775 (2nd edn). *See* 1772, *above.*

The Kentish songster: or the ladies and gentlemen's miscellany. Canterbury [1775?]. Stainer copy. *See* 1778, 1784, 1792; *also* Humming bird, 1776, *below.*

Love tales and elegies; with pastorals and other curious poems, selected from the best authors. 1775.

The modern Freemason's pocket book. [1775?]. Sotheby, 10 December 1904.

Moral instructions of a father to his son; to which is added some pieces from Milton, Thompson and other authors. Newcastle 1775 (Dobell, 1930), Newcastle 1775 (3rd edn).

The Muses and Graces on a visit to Grosvenor Square: being a collection of original songs sung at Mrs Crewe's elegant ball. 1775.

The musical Mason or Free Mason's pocket companion: being a collection of songs used in all Lodges. [1775?]. Stainer copy.

The new entertaining frisky songster: or Muses holiday. [1775?]. Harding copy.

The new musical and universal magazine: consisting of the most favourite songs. Vol 1, [1775?]. Schnapper records as 4 vols [1774–5]. *See* 1776, 1777, *below.*

A new select collection of epitaphs, in two volumes. Ed T. Webb 1775. 2 vols nd: Sotheby, 17 March 1906.

Nugae antiquae. Vol 2, 1775. *See* 1769, *above.*

Odes, cantatas, songs; divine, moral, entertaining; set to music by Pixell; opera seconda. Birmingham 1775.

Ovid's Epistles; with his Amours, translated by the most eminent hands. 1775. *See* 1725, *above.*

Poems inscribed to the memory of Hawksworth. Dublin [1775?]. *See* 1769, *above.*

Poetical amusements at a villa near Bath. Ed Lady A. Miller, Bath 1775. *See* 1776, 1777, 1781, *below.*

Pranceriana: a select collection of fugitive pieces published since the appointment of the present Provost of the university of Dublin. Dublin 1775. *See* 1776, 1779, 1784, *below.*

The Ranelaugh concert: a choice collection of the newest songs. [1775?].

Reliques of ancient English poetry. 3 vols 1775 (3rd edn). *See* 1765, *above.*

The robin: or the ladies polite songster. [1775?]. Stainer copy; same frontispiece and title-page as the 1774 edn, but having pp. xiv + 294.

Select poems from a larger collection. Glasgow 1775.

The sky lark: being a choice collection of new songs. [1775?]. Stainer copy.

Social harmony. Ed T. Hale [1775] (3rd edn). Imprint: Longman, Lukey & Co. *See* 1763, *above.*

Solitary walks; to which are added the consolations of religion. Ed G. Wright 1775 (3rd edn). *See* 1787, *below.*

The songster's polite tutor; to which is added a collection of the most celebrated songs. [1775?]. Harding copy. Imprint: Longman, Lukey and Co. *See* 1790, *below.*

The tea-table miscellany. Edinburgh 1775. 4 issues; *see* B. Martin, A bibliography of Allan Ramsay, 1931. *See* 1724, *above.*

Vocal music: or the songster's companion. Vol 3, 1775. *See* 1770, *above.*

Walking amusements for chearful Christians: various pieces in prose and verse. Ed G. Wright 1775.

Water poetry: a collection of verses written at several public places. [1775?].

Wit à-la-mode; to which is added the agreeable medley. 1775. Sotheby, 23 June 1920. Verse and prose by several hands?

1776

Additions to the works of Pope, together with many original poems and letters of contemporary writers, never before published. 2 vols 1776.

Ancient and modern Scottish songs in two volumes. Edinburgh 1776 (2nd edn); rptd Glasgow 1869; ed S. Gilpin, Edinburgh 1870. *See* 1769, *above.*

Appendix Pranceriana, which completes the select collection of fugitive pieces. Dublin 1776. *See* Pranceriana, 1775, *above.*

An asylum for fugitives; published occasionally. Vol 1, no 3 1776. *See* 1779, *below.*

The beauties of poetry: or a portable repository of English verse in three books. Ed W. Le Tans'ur, Cambridge 1776.

The cabinet of curiosities. Norwich [1776?].

Callipaedia, in four books, translated by several hands. 1776. Oldisworth's name is omitted again; *see* 1710, *above.*

The charms of melody: being a select collection of humourous, drinking and loyal songs. Dublin 1776. Harding copy.

The charms of melody: being a select collection of love and sentimental songs. Dublin 1776. Harding copy; contents differ from the above.

The frisky songster: being songs distinguished for their jollity, high taste and humour. 1776 (new edn). Harding copy. *See* 1770, *above.*

The humming bird: a new and choice collection of English and Scots songs, cantatas. 1776. Stainer copy. A reprint of Kentish songster, 1775, *above*; *see also* 1785, *below*.

Jachin and Boaz: or an authentic key to Free-Masonry, containing anthems, odes, songs. 1776 (new edn). *See* 1767, *above*.

Jemmy Twitcher's jests. Paisley 1776 (2nd edn). Harding copy. *See* 1770, *above*.

Modern poems, selected chiefly from miscellanies published lately. Glasgow 1776.

The new musical and universal magazine. Vol 2, [1776?]. *See* 1775, *above*.

The nightingale: a collection of ancient and modern songs, Scots and English. Edinburgh 1776. Ptd for J. Murray, Stainer copy; by W. Darling, Harding copy. *See* 1738, *above*.

Ovid's Art of love. Tr Dryden, Congreve et al 1776. *See* 1709, *above*.

Poems on various subjects, by different hands. 1776. Pickering & Chatto, 1933.

Poetical amusements at a villa near Bath. Vol 1, 1776 (2nd–3rd edns) (3rd, Dyce copy); vol 2, 1776.

Poetry made familiar and easy: being the fourth volume of the Circle of the sciences. 1776 (4th edn). *See* Art of poetry, 1746, *above*.

Grammar and rhetorick: being the first and third volumes of the Circle of the sciences, considerably enlarged. 1776.

Logic, ontology and the art of poetry: being the fourth and fifth volumes of the Circle of the sciences, considerably enlarged. 1776.

Songs, chorusses, which are introduced in the new entertainment of the jubilee. 1776. Forster copy. *See* 1769, *above*; *also* Shakespear's garland, 1769, *above*.

Swift, Sheridan et al. A supplement to Swift's works: being a collection of miscellanies in prose and verse by the Dean and others. Ed J. Nichols 1776. Trinity College, Dublin, copy. *See* 1779, *below*.

The theatrical museum or fugitive repository: being a collection of interludes, prologues and epilogues, songs, tales. 1776.

1777

Baratariana. Dublin 1777 (3rd edn). *See* 1773, *above*.

The beauties of the English drama. 4 vols 1777. Amplified edn of Beauties of the English stage, 1756, *above*.

The beauties of the poets: or a collection of moral and sacred poetry from the most eminent authors. 1777. *See* 1773, *above*.

The blackbird: an elegant collection of well chosen songs. Doncaster 1777. Stainer copy.

Calliope: or the agreeable songster. 1777. Harding copy.

Pope, Congreve, Young et al. A collection of poems: containing [15 titles]. Dublin 1777 (4th edn, with addns). Pickering & Chatto, 1930.

A collection of pretty poems for the amusement of children three feet high. Ed T. Tagg 1777.

Essays on song-writing; with a collection of songs. Dublin 1777 (3rd edn). Ed R. H. Evans 1810; *see also* Vocal poetry, to which is prefixed an essay on song-writing, 1810. *See* 1772, *above*.

The Essex harmony. Vol 2, 1777 (2nd edn). *See* 1753, *above*.

Evans's edition: old ballads, historical and narrative, with some of modern date. Vols 1–2, 1777. *See* Old ballads, 1784.

Exercises for improvement in elocution: being select extracts from the best authors. Ed J. Walker 1777.

The gold-finch: a choice collection of songs, Scots and English. Edinburgh 1777. *See* 1748, *above*.

Johnson's lottery song-book: or the vocal adventurer for the year 1777, containing four hundred songs. [1777]. Has frontispiece and pp. xii + 240. *See* 1770, *above*.

Johnson's lottery song-book: containing a great variety of the newest songs. [1777?]. Stainer copy; similar to the above, but with a different title-page.

The linnets: or songster's companion. Wolverhampton 1777. Harding copy.

The lover's instructor: or the whole art of courtship. 1777. Also an edn, nd; both, Harding copies. By several hands? *See* 1794, *below*.

The masque: a new edition, with great additions. [1777?]. Pp. xviii + 366; songs, 354. *See* 1767, *above*.

The musical companion: or songster's magazine for the year 1777. [1777].

The new musical and universal magazine. Vol 3, [1777?]. *See* 1775, *above*.

Moore, Sir J. H. The new paradise of dainty devices: consisting of original poems by different hands. 1777. Mostly, if not entirely, by Moore.

The new universal story-teller: or a modern picture of human life in prose and verse. Ed W. H. Melmoth [1777?].

Ovid's Art of love. Tr Dryden, Congreve et al. 1777. Book-auction records, 1915–16. *See* 1709, *above*.

The Oxford sausage: a new edition. Oxford 1777. At least 3 more undated edns before 1800, and others in 1804, 1814, 1815, 1821. *See* 1764, *above*.

Poems for ladies, selected under the inspection of a lady. 1777.

Poetical amusements at a villa near Bath. Vol 3, 1777. *See* 1775, *above*.

The poetical preceptor: or a collection of select pieces from English poets. 1777. *See* 1780, 1785, *below*.

The principles of Free-Masonry delineated. Exeter 1777. Dobell, 1930.

The repository: a select collection of fugitive pieces in prose and verse. Ed I. Reed, vols 1–2, 1777. *See* 1783, 1790, *below*.

A select collection of Scots poems, chiefly in the Buchan dialect. Edinburgh 1777. Harding copy. *See* 1785, *below*.

Select poems and ballads, from miscellanies printed since the publication of Dodsley's collection. Glasgow 1777. Harding copy.

Six odes, presented to that historian Mrs Catherine Macaulay. Bath [1777].

Songs and chorusses in the Tempest. 1777. Huntington Lib copy. At least 4 hands in this.

Wit for the ton! the convivial jester: or Samuel Foote's last budget opened. [1777?]. *See* 1779, *below*.

The works of the Earls of Rochester, Roscommon and Dorset. 1777. Book-auction records, 1904–5. *See* 1707, *above*.

1778

Ahiman rezon: or a help to Free and Accepted Masons. 1778 (3rd edn). *See* 1756, *above*.

Amaryllis, in two volumes. [1778?] (2nd edn). Imprint: Longman, Lukey & Broderip; without Broderip, cited by Kidson, in British music publishers. *See* 1746, *above*.

Aristophanes: being a classic collection of true Attic wit. 1778.

The charms of chearfulness: a collection of comic songs. Carlisle 1778.

Clio and Euterpe, in IIII volumes. [1778?]. Imprint: John Welcker; odd vols in various libraries. *See* 1758, *above*.

A collection of favourite English, Scotch, Irish and French songs. Ed E. Jones [1778].

A collection of the most favourite Scots songs. [1778?]. Stainer copy.

A favourite collection of the most admir'd glees and catches, selected from celebrated composers. Dublin [1778?] Ellis, 1905.

The female jester: or wit for the ladies, compiled by a lady. [1778].

The Kentish songster: or the ladies and gentlemen's miscellany. Canterbury [1778?] (2nd edn). Harding copy. *See* 1775, *above*.

The ladies most elegant lottery pocket book for the year 1778: containing the new songs. [1778]. Harding copy.

The merry quack doctor: or the fun box broke open. Ed 'Tom Killigrew, junior' [c. 1778].

The moral miscellany. 1778 (5th edn). See 1758, above.

The Muse's mirrour: being a collection of poems by [39 names]. 2 vols 1778. See 1783, below.

The new entertaining humorist: miscellanies in prose and verse. 1778. Harding copy. See 1770, above.

The new merry companion: or vocal remembrancer. [c. 1778] (2nd edn, with addns). See 1772, above.

The new theatre of fun, concluding with merry songs. 1778.

Pieces selected from the Italian poets by Agostino Isola, and translated into English verse by some gentlemen of the university, Cambridge. 1778. See 1784, below.

A pocket book for the German flute or violin: containing airs, duets and songs. Bks 1–4, Dublin [1778?–82]. See 1784, 1790, below.

Pocket book for the guitar; to which is added an entertaining collection of songs. [1778?] (2nd edn). Stainer copy.

The poetical miscellany: select pieces. 1778. See 1762, above.

The Scots nightingale: or Edinburgh vocal miscellany. Ed J. Murray, Edinburgh 1778. Harding copy. See 1779, above.

Select lessons in prose and verse. Bristol 1778 (3rd edn). See 1765, above.

Select letters between the late Duchess of Somerset, Shenstone and others, and some poetical pieces. Ed T. Hull, vols 1–2, 1778.

The songs of Robin Hood. 1778. See 1663, above.

Thompson's pocket companion for the German-flute. 4 vols [c. 1778].

Tom Gay's comical jester: or the wit's merry medley. [1778?]. Harding copy.

The vocal magazine: or British songster's miscellany. 1778. Yale copy. See 1779, 1781, 1784, below.

Vocal music: or the songster's companion. [1778?]. Selected from vol 1, 1770, and vol 2, 1771, with addns.

Wit a-la-mode: or Lord Chesterfield's witticisms; to which is added epigrams, epitaphs, songs. 1778.

1779

The antiquarian repertory. Vol 2, 1779. See 1775, above.

Asylum for fugitives. 2 vols 1776–9. Sotheby, 7 Nov 1887. See 1776, above.

A collection and selection of English prologues and epilogues [from Shakespeare to Garrick] in four volumes. 1779.

A collection of more than eight hundred prologues and epilogues. Ed R. Griffith 4 vols 1779. Queen's College, Oxford, copy; apparently another issue of the above.

A collection of poems by several hands. Paris 1779.

Beattie, Langhorne, Pope et al. A collection of poems: containing [10 titles]. 1779. C. H. Wilkinson copy.

A collection of pretty poems for the amusement of children six feet high. 1779. Book-auction records, 1917–18. See 1757, above.

The complete London jester: or wit's companion. 1779. Sotheby, 16 March 1906. See 1765, above.

Desiderata curiosa: or a collection of pieces relating chiefly to English history. Ed F. Peck 2 vols 1779 (new edn). See 1732, above.

The English archer: or Robert, Earl of Huntington, vulgarly called Robin Hood. Falkirk 1779. See 1663, above.

Nugae antiquae: a new and enlarged edition in 3 vols. 1779. See 1769, above.

Pranceriana poetica or Prancer's garland: being a collection of fugitive poems written since the publication of Pranceriana and the appendix. Dublin 1779. See 1775, above.

St Cecilia: or the lady's and gentleman's harmonious com-

panion. Edinburgh 1779. Stainer copy; this also has an engraved title: Wilson's musical miscellany, 1779. See 1782, below.

The Scot's nightingale: or Edinburgh vocal miscellany. Edinburgh 1779 (2nd edn). Stainer copy; 100 modern songs added. See 1778, above. Also another edn, differently set, lacking title-page. Harding copy.

A select collection of the most admired songs, duetts, in three books. Ed D. Corri, Edinburgh [1779?]. See 1795, below.

The shepherd's pastime or pastoral companion: being a selection of elegant pastorals. 1779. Mitchell Lib Glasgow copy. See 1789, below..

The strains of the British Muses, collected from the works of [18 poets]. Ed P. Pepin, Göttingen 1779.

Swift et al. A supplement to Dr Swift's works: containing miscellanies in prose and verse. 3 vols 1779. See below.

Swift et al. A supplement to Dr Swift's works: being the fourteenth in the collection, containing miscellanies in prose and verse. 1779. This edn is in 1 vol 4°. See above, and 1776, above.

The true loyalist or chevalier's favourite: being a collection of elegant songs. 1779 (priv ptd).

The vocal magazine: or British songster's miscellany. 1779. Sotheby, 7 Aug 1877. See 1778, above.

Wilson's musical miscellany. 1779. See St Cecilia, 1779, above.

Wit for the ton! the convivial jester: or Samuel Foote's last budget opened. 1779 (2nd edn, with addns). See 1777, above.

1780

Ahiman rezon. Dublin 1780 (4th edn, with addns). Also a reissue with alternative title-pages, and a Drogheda edn, c. 1780. See 1756, above.

Amphion: or the chorister's delight. New York [1780?].

Amusement for the ladies: being a selection of favorite catches, glees and madrigals. Vols 1–3, [1780?]. See 1791, 1792, 1793, 1800 below.

The antiquarian repertory. Vol 3, 1780. See 1775, above.

Beauties of fables in verse, selected to form the judgment of youth. [1780?].

The bird: containing a choice collection of love, hunting and Bacchanalian songs. 1780. Harding copy. See 1781, below.

The buck's delight: being a collection of humorous songs. [1780?] (2nd edn, with addns). See 1764, above.

The buck's delight: or feast for the sons of Comus, containing humorous, entertaining songs. Dublin [1780?]. Harding copy.

The bull-finch. [1780]. Harding copy. Pp. xvi + 392; songs, 440. See 1748, above.

Calliope: or English harmony. Vols 1–2, [1780?] (2nd edn). Sotheby, 5 June 1912; Leeds Public Lib has vol 2. See 1770, above.

The chearful companion: a collection of favourite Scots and English songs, catches. Ed J. Gillies, Perth 1780. See 1783, below.

The chearful companion: or complete modern songster. [1780?]. Stainer copy. A different collection from the above.

A collection of catches, canons, glees, duettos of the most eminent composers. Vols 1–4, Edinburgh [1780].

A collection of vocal harmony. Ed T. Warren [1780?]. See 1775, above.

The complete fabulist: or a choice collection of fables in prose and verse from the best authors. Ed G. Grey, Newcastle. 1780. See 1782, below.

The complete London jester. 1780. Sotheby, 3 March 1891. See 1765, above.

Concerts of antient music, as performed at the New Rooms, Tottenham-Street. 1780. Later titles differ slightly; see 1781–1800, below.

The court of Apollo, containing comic, social, naval and love songs sung at Ranelagh, Vauxhall [1780?].

The delicate jester: or wit and humour divested of ribaldry. [1780?]. *See* Revived 1800, *below.*

Essays historical, political and moral: being a proper supplement to Baratariana. 2 vols Dublin [1780?]. BM catalogue dates [1774?]. *See* Baratariana, 1773, *above.*

Exercises in elocution selected from various authors, intended as a sequel to the Speaker. Ed W. Enfield, Warrington 1780. *See* 1791, *below*; *also* 1774, *above.*

The flower-piece: a collection of modern poems. 1780. A reprint of Fugitive miscellany pt 2, 1775, *above.*

The gentleman and ladies polite songster. 1780. Sotheby, 29 April 1891. Another edn, nd [c. 1780]: Stainer copy.

Jachin and Boaz: or an authentic key to Free-Masonry. 1780. Dobell, 1930. *See* 1767, *above.*

Joe Miller's jests, as originally edited by John Mottley, with epigrams and epitaphs: a new edition. [1780?]. *See* 1742, *above.*

The lark: being a choice collection of [15] songs. Stockport [1780?].

The masque [c. 1780]. *See* 1790, *below.*

The merry miscellany: being the second part of Daniel Gunston's jests. 1780. *See* 1770, *above.*

The minstrell: being a new and select collection of English songs, with some Scotch songs. [1780?]. *See* 1793, *below.*

Narrative of the proceedings at the contested election, Norwich. Norwich 1780 (3rd edn).

The new London and country songster: or a banquet of vocal music. Ed J. Vernon [1780?].

The offspring of wit and harmony: a new collection of songs, to which is prefixed laws and rules for playing whist. Dublin [c. 1780]. Harding copy.

Pills to purge melancholy: containing all the songs sung by Mr Edwin. [1780?]. Book-prices current, 1888–9. *See* Edwin's pills, 1788, 1789, *below.*

Poems by the most eminent ladies of Great Britain and Ireland. Vols 1–2, [1780?]; rptd with addns. *See* 1755, *above.*

The poetical preceptor: or a collection of select pieces. 1780. Hill, 1948. *See* 1777, *above.*

Prologues and epilogues, celebrated for their poetical merit. Oxford [1780?]. BM catalogue dates [1810?].

The Scots vocal miscellany: a choice collection of songs. Edinburgh 1780. Stainer copy.

[A select collection of new songs. 1780?]. Stainer copy; no title-page. Pp. vi + 112; numbered songs, 120.

A select collection of poems. Ed J. Nichols vols 1–4, 6, 1780. *See* 1781, 1782, 1784, *below.*

Social harmony. [c. 1780] (3rd edn). Edinburgh Univ copy; imprint: Longman and Broderip. *See* 1763, *above.*

The songster's favourite: containing the best new English, Scotch and Irish songs. 1780. Stainer copy.

The theatre of mirth: or fun a-la-mode. [c. 1780]. Maggs Bros, 1934.

The theatrical bouquet: containing prologues and epilogues from Colley Cibber to the present year. 1780.

Ramsay, A. et al. Thirty Scots songs. Bks 1–2, Edinburgh [1780?]. N. Stewart's collection; *see* 1757, *above*, for Bremner's collection. *See also* Schnapper for London edns, [c. 1780] and [c. 1789], of bk 1.

The triumph of wit: or the canting dictionary, with poems, songs. Dublin [1780?]. *See* 1760, *above.*

The winter evenings companion. [1780?] (2nd edn). Stainer copy. *See* 1759, *above.*

Wits museum: or the new London jester. [1780?]. *See* 1794; *also* a new edn, nd, Harding copy.

Woman's wit: or amusement for the fair sex; to which are annexed select songs. [1780?] (new edn).

1781

The bird: containing a choice collection of love, hunting and Bacchanalian songs. 1781. *See* 1780, *above.*

The bull-finch. [1781?]. Harding copy. Pp. 322 + (14); songs not numbered. *See* 1748, *above.*

A choice collection of hymns and moral songs; to which is added specimens of divine poetry by several authors. Newcastle 1781.

A collection of English prose and verse for schools, selected from different authors. Ed A. Barrie, Edinburgh 1781 (2nd edn).

The complete London jester: or wit's companion. 1781 (10th edn). Harding copy. *See* 1765, *above.*

Concerts of antient music. 1781. *See* 1780, *above.*

Illustrations of Masonry. Ed W. Preston 1781 (new edn). *See* 1772, *above.*

The ladies' complete pocket-book for the year 1781: containing the favourite new songs. Newcastle [1781]. Harding copy.

The lady's poetical magazine: or beauties of British poetry. Vols 1–2, 1781. *See* 1782, 1791, *below.*

Hughes, J. Letters of Abelard and Heloise, to which are added four poems by Pope and other hands. 1781. *See* 1787, 1788, *below.*

The London mercury: containing the history, politics and literature of England for the year 1780. 1781 (new edn).

The modern syren: or enchanting songstress. Sunderland 1781. N. Ault copy. *See* 1790, *below.*

Poetical amusements at a villa near Bath. Vol 4, Bath 1781. *See* 1775, *above.*

The polite singer: a collection of choice songs. North Shields. 1781. Harding copy.

Roundelay or the new syren: a collection of choice songs, including the modern. [1781?]. Harding copy. Pp. xii + 244. *See* 1782, 1783, 1790, 1794, 1795, *below.*

Scottish tragic ballads. Ed J. Pinkerton 1781. *See* 1783, *below.*

A select collection of poems. Vol 7, 1781. *See* 1780, *above.*

The Union song-book or vocal miscellany: Scots and English songs. Berwick 1781. See Vocal miscellany, 1797, *below.*

The universal Scots songster. Edinburgh 1781. Harding copy.

The vocal magazine: or compleat British songster. 1781. *See* 1778, *above.*

The whole prophecies of Scotland, England, Ireland, France and Denmark. Edinburgh 1781. *See* 1718, *above.*

The wood-lark: containing a collection of English and Scotch songs, airs, ballads, cantatas. 1781. *See* 1784, *below.*

The world as it goes, exemplified in the characters of nations, states, princes; selected from the English poets, from Chaucer to Churchill. Ed W. Combe 1781.

1782

Ahiman rezon: or a help to a brother. Belfast 1782 (5th edn). 2 different imprints found. *See* 1756, *above.*

The beauties of music and poetry. Vol 1, [1782?]. *See* 1790, *below.* Stainer copy.

The charmer. 2 vols Edinburgh 1782. Vol 1, 4th edn; vol 2, a new collection. *See* 1749, *above.*

A collection of poems in six volumes. 1782. A new edn of Dodsley, by I. Reed. *See* 1748, *above.*

A collection of Scots songs. Edinburgh [1782]. Pbd by N. Stewart.

A collection of songs, chiefly such as are eminent for poetical merit. 1782. Harvard copy.

The complete fabulist. Newcastle MDCCXXXII [1782] (2nd edn). *See* 1780, *above.*

Concerts of antient music. 1782. *See* 1780, *above.*

The convivial songster. [1782]. 2 issues, with different toasts at end: last page blank, BM copy; or having advertisements, Harding copy. *See* 1783, 1788, 1790, *below.*

Dear variety, suited to all ages and conditions in life. Ed G. Wright 1782.

The festival of wit. 1782. Sotheby, 5 March 1891. *See* 1783, 1789, 1791, 1793, 1795, 1800, *below*.

The gold finch: or new modern songster. Edinburgh [1782] (2nd edn), Glasgow [1782?]. Edns differ slightly. *See* 1753; *also* 1748, *above*.

The lady's poetical magazine: or beauties of British poetry. Vols 3–4, 1782. *See* 1781, *above*.

The Liverpool songster: presenting an elegant selection of hunting, sea, love and miscellaneous songs. Liverpool [1782?]. Stainer copy. *See* 1784, *below*.

Mirth and glee: or the songster's favourite. 1782.

The most agreeable companion: a choice collection of detached pieces in prose and verse. Ed J. Moxon 2 vols Leeds 1782.

The Muse's pocket companion: a collection of poems by [20 names]. 1782. *See* 1785, 1787, 1800, each having some variation of contents.

The new story-teller: or historical medley. Newcastle 1782 (2nd edn). Harding copy.

Ovid's Art of love. Tr Dryden, Congreve et al 1782. *See* 1709, *above*.

Poems on various subjects, selected to comprise in one volume the beauties of English poetry. Ed T. Tomkins 1782 (2nd edn). *See* 1793, 1800, *below*.

Roundelay or the new syren: a new edition. [1782?]. Preface says 2nd edn; pp. xii + 266. Harding copy. Also pp. xii + 274 + 2 (toasts). *See* 1781, *above*.

St Cecilia: or the British songster. Edinburgh 1782. 2 edns: 372 pp., ptd for W. Coke; 324 pp., ptd for P. Anderson. *See* 1779, *above*.

A select collection of poems. Ed J. Nichols, vols 5, 8, 1782. *See* 1780, *above*.

The speaker: or miscellaneous pieces. 1782. *See* 1774, *above*.

The tea-table miscellany. Glasgow 1782 (18th edn). Nat Lib of Scotland copy. *See* 1724, *above*.

The universal songster: or harmony and innocence. [1782?]. Pp. xvi + 412; BM catalogue dates [1800?]. *See* 1787, 1792, 1795, *below*.

The vocal magazine: or compleat songster. Vol 1, Cork 1782. No more pbd.

1783

The agreeable companion: a collection of polite tales and fables. Berwick 1783.

The Bacchanalian songster: or a select collection of droll, satyrical, humourous and Bacchanalian songs. Winchester 1783. Stainer copy.

Beauties in prose and verse, selected from the most celebrated authors, antient and modern. Stockton 1783.

The blackbird: containing one hundred and thirty songs, Scots and English. Berwick 1783 (new edn, with addns). *See* 1764, *above*.

The buck's delight: or merry companion; by the sons of Comus. 1783. *See* 1786, *below*.

The charms of chearfulness: or merry songster's companion. [1783?] (new edn). Harding copy. Pp. viii + 244. *See* 1789, 1792, *below*.

The chearful companion: containing a select collection of Scots and English songs. Perth 1783 (2nd edn) (Stainer copy), 1783 (3rd edn). *See* 1780, *above*.

Choice of the best poetical pieces of the most eminent English poets. Ed J. Retzer, vol 1, Vienna 1783. *See* 1785, 1786, *below*.

A collection of poems in four volumes, by several hands. 1783. Queen's College Oxford copy. New edn of Pearch's collection, with notes by I. Reed. *See* 1768, *above*.

Concerts of antient music. 1783. *See* 1780, *above*.

The convivial songster: being a select collection of the best songs. 1783. Sotheby, 18 May 1917. *See* 1782, *above*.

The festival of wit: or the small talker, selected from a voluminous work in the possession of G***** K***, at Windsor. Dublin 1783. Also London 1783 (new edn, with addns). *See* 1782, *above*.

The gold finch or new modern songster: being a select collection of Scots and English songs. Glasgow [1783?]. *See* 1753; *also* 1748, *above*.

Hal's looking glass, with tales, epigrams, songs, by the eldest son of G[eorge] K[ing]. 1783. Harding copy.

Hal's looking-glass: or the 1***l exhibition; with tales, epigrams, songs, composed and compiled by the eldest son of G***** K***. [1783?] (6th edn).

The linnet or chearful companion: being a select collection of Scots and English songs. Glasgow 1783. Stainer copy.

The London songster, containing 544 songs. 1783 (new edn). *See* 1767, *above*.

The Muse's mirrour. 2 vols 1783 (2nd edn). *See* 1778, *above*.

The repository. Vols 1–2, 1783 (2nd edn) (McLeish, 1931); vols 3–4, 1783. *See* 1777, *above*.

Roundelay or the new syren: a new edition. [1783?]. Stainer copy. Pp. xi + 273 + 3 (toasts). Also edn of 1783, not seen. *See* 1781, *above*.

A select collection of English songs, in three volumes. Ed Ritson 1783; ed T. Park 1813 (2nd edn).

Select lessons in prose and verse. Bristol 1783 (4th edn). *See* 1765, *above*.

Select poems: Hammond's love elegies; Stillingfleet's essay on conversation; Akenside's odes, and Philips' pastorals. 3 pts Glasgow 1783.

Select Scotish ballads. 2 vols 1783. 2nd edn of vol 1; *see* 1781, *above*.

Songs, hymns and psalms, adapted to moral and instructive amusement. Ed J. H[anway] 1783.

The tea-table miscellany in four volumes. Vols 3–4, Aberdeen 1783 (16th edn). D. Cook copy. Vols 1–2 not known; *see* B. Martin, Bibliography of Allan Ramsay, 1931. *See* 1724, *above*.

The use and abuse of Free-Masonry. Ed G. Smith 1783.

The vocal enchantress: presenting an elegant selection of songs. [1783].

Yorick's jests: or wit's common-place book. 1783. Also another edn, nd: Sotheby, 26 April 1901. *See* 1770, *above*.

1784

An alphabetical list of the freemen of Chester at the general election, 1784, with the papers and songs of each party. Chester [1784].

The antiquarian repertory. Vol 4, 1784. *See* 1775, *above*.

Merry, R., B. Greatheed et al. The Arno miscellany, by the members of the Oziosi at Florence. Florence 1784.

The bishopric garland: or Durham minstrel. Ed Ritson, Stockton 1784. *See* 1792, *below*.

The boquet or cluster of sweets: being a collection of epigrams. Dublin 1784. Harding copy.

The British Muse. Ed J. Vint, Newcastle 1784 (2nd edn). Sotheby, 17 March 1906. *See* 1775, *above*.

A collection of choice pieces composed on different persons. Kilmarnock 1784.

The complete London jester. 1784. Sotheby, 26 April 1890. *See* 1765, *above*.

Concerts of antient music. 1784. *See* 1780, *above*.

Constitutions of the Free and Accepted Masons. Rev J. Noorthouck 1784. *See* 1723, *above*.

Richardson, J., R. Tickell et al. Criticisms on the Rolliad. 1784. *See* 1785, 1787, 1788, 1790, 1791; *also* Rolliad, 1795, 1796, *below*.

The dairymaid: or vocal miscellany. Edinburgh 1784. No known copy.

Democritus: or the laughing philosopher. 1784. Sotheby, 3 March 1891. *See* 1771, *above*.

Dramatic miscellanies, in three volumes. Ed T. Davies 1784, 3 vols Dublin 1784. Dobell, 1935. *See* 1785, *below*.

The election magazine: being an impartial collection of the essays, songs, epigrams, distributed during the [Norwich election]. Norwich [1784].

History of the Westminster election: containing every material occurrence. 1784. See 1785, below.

The jovial songster: or sailor's delight. 1784. Harding copy. See 1785, 1789, below.

The Kentish songster: or ladies and gentlemen's miscellany. Canterbury 1784 (3rd edn). See 1775, above.

The Liverpool songster. Liverpool [1784?] (2nd edn). Stainer copy. See 1782, above.

The London songster: containing 544 songs. 1784 (new edn). Reprint of 1783 edn. See 1767, above.

Musical and poetical relicks of the Welsh bards. Ed E. Jones 1784. See 1794, 1800, below.

Musical miscellanies. Vol 1, 1784.

A new academy of compliments: or the lover's secretary. 1784 (17th edn). See 1715, above.

The new foundling hospital for wit, in six vols. 1784 (new edn). See 1768, above.

Old ballads, historical and narrative, with some of modern date, with notes. Ed T. Evans 4 vols 1784. Vols 1–2, 2nd edn. Rptd in 4 vols 1810, ed R. H. Evans. See Evans's edn, 1777, above.

Pieces selected from the Italian poets and translated into English verse by some gentlemen of the university. Cambridge 1784 (2nd edn). See 1778, above.

A pocket book for the German flute or violin. Vols 5–8, Dublin [1784–7]. Stainer copy. See 1778, above.

Poemata partim reddita, partim scripta. Ed M. Madan, [Epsom?] 1784.

Poems by a literary society: comprehending original pieces in the several walks of poetry. 1784.

The poetical museum: containing songs and poems on almost every subject. Hawick 1784. Pbd by G. Caw.

Pranceriana, with several additions and cuts. 2 vols 1784 (2nd edn). See 1775, above.

A select collection of poems. Vol 8, ed J. Nichols 1784. See 1780, above.

Select fables, in three parts. Newcastle 1784 (new edn). 2 issues, with many variations in signatures L–O.

The temple of mirth: a collection of the songs from collections, and operas, now performing. Dublin [1784?].

The vocal magazine: or compleat British songster. 1784. Harding copy. See 1778, above.

The vocal miscellany: a collection of above 400 songs. 1784. Yale copy.

The wit of the day: or the humours of Westminster. 1784.

The woodlark: containing a collection of English and Scotch songs. 1784. Stainer copy. See 1781, above.

The young Freemason's assistant: being a choice collection of Masons' songs. Dumfries 1784. Sotheby, 17 March 1906.

1785

Anacreontic songs, composed and selected by Doctr Arnold. 1785.

The Asiatick miscellany: consisting of original productions, translations, fugitive pieces. Vol 1, Calcutta 1785. See 1786, 1787, below.

An asylum for fugitive pieces in prose and verse, not in any other collection. [Ed J. Almon] vol 1, 1785; A new edn, 1785. See 1786, 1793, 1795, 1798, below.

A supplement to the asylum for fugitive pieces, containing probationary odes. 1785.

The burlettas, duets, interludes, as performed in the Spa-gardens, Bermondsey. [1785?]. Harding copy. See A favourite collection, 1787, below.

The Caledonian Muse: a chronological selection of Scotish poetry, printed 1785, and now first published. Ed Ritson 1821. The introductory portion was destroyed by fire on the eve of pbn in 1785.

Cambuscan: or the Squire's tale of Chaucer; modernized by Boyse, continued from Spenser's Fairy Queen by Ogle, and concluded by Sterling. Dublin 1785.

Caps well fit: or select epigrams by Titus in Sandgate, and Titus everywhere. Newcastle 1785. By several hands?

A choice collection of new songs. Nos 1–21, Tewkesbury [1785?]. Also nos 22, 25, 28. Stainer copy.

A choice collection of songs. Dublin 1785. Hodgson, 26 June 1925. Freemasonry item.

Choice of the best poetical pieces. Ed J. Retzer, vols 2–3, Vienna 1785. See 1783, above.

A collection of catches and glees, humbly dedicated to Uvedale Price, compos'd by Gaetano Quilici. [c. 1785?]. Dobell, 1936.

A collection of canons, catches and glees. 27 bks [c. 1785–c. 1795]. See 1763, above.

A collection of scarce, curious and valuable pieces, both in verse and prose. Edinburgh 1785. Dobell, 1931. See 1773, above.

The complete London jester: or wit's companion. 1785 (12th edn). Edinburgh Univ Lib copy. See 1765, above.

Concerts of antient music. 1785. See 1780, above.

Criticisms on the Rolliad, with corrections and additions. 1785. Part the first, corrected and enlarged, 1785; Part the first (2nd edn), corrected and enlarged, 1785; Part the first (3rd edn), 1785. See 1784, above.

Criticisms on the Rolliad. Dublin 1785.

Criticisms on the Rolliad, part the second; to which are added, political eclogue, no 1, and an epithalamium. 1785.

Dramatic miscellanies, in three volumes. Ed T. Davies 1785 (new edn). See 1784, above.

The Florence miscellany. Florence 1785.

The general songster: or every man's social companion. [c. 1785]. Harding copy. See 1787, 1793, below.

The goldfinch or vocal miscellany: being an elegant collection of choice modern songs. 1785. Stainer copy. See 1788, below; also 1748, above.

The goldfinch: a choice collection of songs, Scots and English. Glasgow 1785. Stainer copy. See 1748, above.

History of the Westminster election. 1785 (2nd edn). See 1784, below.

The humming bird: containing above fourteen hundred songs. Canterbury 1785 (3rd edn). See 1776, above.

An introduction to singing; to which is added a choice collection of songs. [1785?]. Imprint: S. A. & P. Thompson. See 1745, above.

Jachin and Boaz: or an authentic key to Free-Masonry, containing anthems, odes, songs. 1785 (new edn). See 1767, above.

The jovial songster or sailor's delight: a collection of chearful and humourous songs. [1785?] (new edn). Stainer copy. See 1784, above.

The ladies' own memorandum-book for the year 1785, containing new songs. [1785]. Harding copy.

Miscellanies in prose and verse intended as a specimen of the types at the logographic printing office. Ed J. Walter 1785.

The Muse in good humour: a collection of comic tales. Vols 1–2, 1785 (8th edn). Pickering & Chatto, 1932. See 1744, above.

The Muse in good humour or Momus's banquet: a collection of choice songs. [1785?]. Stainer copy.

The Muse's pocket companion: a collection of poems. Carlisle 1785. See 1782, above.

The new British songster. 1785. No known copy; Lowndes cites Falkirk edn. See 1798, below.

The new Rolliad. No 1, 1785. By one hand? See Criticisms, 1785, above.

The nightingale: or vocal songster. Edinburgh [1785?]. Stainer copy. See 1738, above.

The oaten pipe, being the seventh volume of the Masque: or Hoey's collection of songs. Dublin 1785. Stainer copy. This belongs to the ser beginning with Apollo, 1761, above.

The Paphian doves: a new book of kisses; the songs and music by different ingenious masters. [1785?] (new edn).

Poems for young ladies. Ed Goldsmith 1785. With many addns; *see* 1767, *above*.

The poetical preceptor: or a collection of select pieces of poetry. 1785. Ingpen, 1931. *See* 1777, *above*.

Probationary odes by the various candidates for the office of poet laureat to his Majesty, in the room of William Whitehead, deceased. 1785. *See* 1787, 1791; *also* Rolliad, 1795, *below*.

Probationary odes for the laureateship, with a preliminary discourse by Sir John Hawkins. 1785 (3 edns).

A select collection of Scots poems, chiefly in the broad Buchan dialect. Edinburgh 1785. *See* 1777, *above*.

Select lessons in prose and verse. Tamworth 1785 (4th edn, with addns). *See* 1765, *above*.

The songster's favourite: containing forty songs. Ed L. Ding, Edinburgh [1785?].

The speaker. Ed W. Enfield 1785 (new edn). *See* 1774, *above*.

1786

Ancient Scotish poems from the ms collections of Sir Richard Maitland. Ed J. Pinkerton 2 vols 1786.

The Asiatick miscellany. Vol 2, Calcutta 1786. *See* 1785, *above*.

An asylum for fugitive pieces. Vol 2, 1786. *See* 1785, *above*.

Boletarium: or a collection of papers, squibs, songs, written on the contest at Carlisle. Carlisle 1786. *See* Supplement, 1787.

The buck's delight: or merry companion; by the sons of Comus. 1786 (3rd edn). Harding copy. *See* 1783, *above*.

The cabinet of Momus and Caledonian humorist: being a collection of stories in prose and verse. [1786].

Charges and regulations of the Free and Accepted Masons, extracted from Ahiman rezon. Halifax Nova Scotia 1786. *See* Ahiman rezon, 1756, *above*.

The chearful companion: being a select collection of favourite Scots and English songs, catches. Glasgow 1786. Stainer copy.

Choice of the best poetical pieces. Ed J. Retzer, vols 4–6, Vienna 1786. *See* 1783, *above*.

Concerts of antient music. 1786. *See* 1780, *above*.

The English archer: or Robert, Earl of Huntington, vulgarly called Robin Hood. Paisley 1786. *See* 1663, *above*.

The Essex harmony. 2 vols 1786 (3rd edn with addns). Vol 2: Birmingham Public Lib copy. Edn, nd: Hill, 1967. *See* 1753, *above*.

The festival of Momus: a collection of comic songs. [1786?]. Pp. viii + 292. *See* 1787, 1792, 1796, 1800, *below*.

The merry companion: or feast for the sons of Comus. 1786 (3rd edn). Also another edn, nd: Sotheby, 29 April 1891.

The musical miscellany: a select collection of the most approved Scots, English & Irish songs, set to music. Ed Alexander Smith, Perth 1786.

The new election budget. Nos 1–25, Norwich 1786.

The new foundling hospital for wit, in six vols. 1786 (new edn). *See* 1768, *above*.

The new school of love; to which is added a choice collection of love songs. Glasgow 1786. *See* 1793, 1800, *below*.

The new school of love; to which is added several love-letters and songs. Falkirk 1786. A different collection from above.

Poems on various subjects; with poems from other authors. Ed Miss [Jane] Cave. Bristol 1786. *See* 1789, *below*.

1787

Ahiman rezon. 1787 (4th edn). *See* 1756, *above*.

The Anacreontic song, as sung by Mr Bannister, with the catches and glees. 1787.

Chambers, W., Sir W. Jones et al. The Asiatic miscellany: consisting of translations, fugitive pieces. Calcutta ptd; London, rptd 1787. *See* 1785–6, *above*.

The beauties of the Spectators, Tatlers, Guardians. 2 vols 1787 (new edn). *See* 1757, *above*.

The cabinet of genius. 2 vols 1787. Irregularly pbd from 1 May 1786 to 1 Jan 1790, but both title-pages dated 1787. *See* 1792, 1787, *below*.

The catch club: a collection of all the songs, catches, glees. [1787?] (3rd edn, with addns).

Pennecuik, A. et al. A collection of Scots poems on several occasions. Glasgow 1787. *See* 1756, *above*.

The complete London and Dublin jester: or wit's companion. Dublin 1787. Maggs Bros, 1934.

Concerts of antient music. 1787. *See* 1780, *above*.

The Court jester: or museum of entertainment; to which is added a collection of songs. [1787?]. Harding copy. *See* 1771, *above*.

Criticisms on the Rolliad. Pt 1, 1787 (4th edn, enlarged). *See* 1785, *above*.

The English Lyceum: or choice of pieces in prose and in verse, selected from the best periodical papers. Vols 1–2, Hamburg 1787. Pbd by J. W. v. Archenholtz. *See* 1788, *below*.

A favourite collection of songs sung at the Spa Gardens, Bermondsey. [1787?]. Harding copy. *See* Burlettas, 1785, *above*.

The festival of Momus: a collection of comic songs. [1787?] (new edn). Harding copy. Pp. viii + 292. Different contents from 1786, *above*.

The festival of Momus: or polite musical companion. Dublin 1787 (new edn).

The general songster: or every man's social companion. 1787 (6th edn). Stainer copy. Also another edn, nd: Sotheby, 29 April 1891. *See* 1785, *above*.

The gentleman's collection of catches, selected from the most eminent composers. Ed J. Bland 1787.

Jemmy Carson's collections, with pieces by several hands. Dublin 1787. Maggs Brothers, 1934. *See* 1744, *above*.

The juvenile speaker: or dialogues and miscellaneous pieces in prose and verse. 1787.

The ladies collection of catches, glees, canons. Ed J. Bland 12 pts [1787?] etc.

Hughes, J. Letters of Abelard and Eloisa; to which are added several poems by Pope and other authors. 1787. *See* 1781, *above*.

The lyric repository: a selection of original, ancient and modern songs. Vol 1, 1787. Harding copy. *See* 1788, *below*.

The melodious songster or the soaring lark's invitation: being select collection of the newest songs. Richmond 1787. Stainer copy.

Miscellaneous pieces, original and collected, by a clergyman of Northamptonshire. 1787.

Miscellanies, moral and instructive, in prose and verse; collected from various authors for the use of schools. Philadelphia, London 1787. *See* 1789, 1800, *below*.

The moral miscellany. 1787 (6th edn, enlarged). *See* 1758, *above*.

Musae seatonianae. 1787. *See* 1772, *above*.

The Muse's pocket companion: a collection of poems. Dublin 1787. *See* 1782, *above*.

New vocal miscellany: or a fountain of pure harmony, containing sixty new songs. 1787. By several hands; ed W. Collins?

Parsley's fashionable lyric companion: a collection of songs sung during the present season. 1787. *See below*, and Parsley's lyric repository, 1788, *below*.

Parsley's lyric companion: second edition with great additions, for 1787. [1787]. Harding copy.

Pleasing reflections on life and manners, with essays, characters and poems from fugitive publications. Ed G. Wright [1787]. *See* 1788, *below*.

The pleasing songster: or festive companion. 1787.

Political miscellanies, part the first, by the authors of the

Rolliad and Probationary odes. 1787. *See* 1790, *and* Rolliad, 1795, *below*.

Probationary odes, with a discourse by Sir John Hawkins. 1787 (8th edn). *See* 1785, *above*.

Retired pleasures, in prose and verse. Ed G. Wright 1787. *See* 1791, *below*.

Robin Hood's garland or Sherwood songster: a collection of pastoral and elegant songs. 1787 (4th edn). Harding copy.

The Scots musical museum. Ed J. Johnson, vol 1, Edinburgh [1787]. 2 issues, one dedicated to Catch Club, the other to Soc of Antiquaries (Stainer copy). *See* 1788, 1790, 1792, 1797, *below*.

Select beauties of ancient English poetry. Ed H. Headley 2 vols 1787, 1810, 1830.

Solitary walks. 1787 (4th edn, enlarged). *See* 1775, *above*.

The songster's companion. Coventry [c. 1787]. Harding copy. Later edns vary much in contents. *See* 1788, 1789, 1790, 1792–3, 1795–6, 1798–1800, *below*.

Supplement to Boletarium. 1787. Carlisle election. *See* Boletarium, 1786, *above*.

The town and country songster: or vocal companion. 1787 (4th edn).

The universal songster: or harmony and innocence. [1787?] (new edn). Stainer copy: pp. iv + xii + 378 + 2. Called 2nd edn in preface. *See* 1782, *above*.

1788

The album of Streatham: or ministerial amusements. 1788 (2nd edn). *See* 1789; *also* Extracts, 1788, *below*.

The American songster: being a select collection of American, English, Scotch and Irish songs. New York 1788. Lowndes cites a London edn, 1788.

The banquet of Thalia: or the fashionable songsters pocket memorial. [1788?]. *See* 1790, 1791, 1792, 1798, *below*.

The beauties of the poets. 1788. *See* 1773, *above*.

The British songster: being a select collection of three hundred and fourteen favourite English and Scotch songs. 1788. Stainer copy.

The bull-finch. [1788?]. Stainer copy; pp. xv + 320. *See* 1748, *above*.

Calliope, or the musical miscellany: a collection of English, Scots and Irish songs. 1788. A different collection from 1739, *above*; *see* 1789, *below*.

Calliope or the vocal enchantress: a collection of English, Scots and Irish songs. Edinburgh 1788. J. Grant, 1921.

Concerts of antient music. 1788. *See* 1780, *above*.

The convivial songster: being a select collection of the best songs. 1788. Stainer. *See* 1782, *above*.

Criticisms on the Rolliad, part the first. 1788 (8th edn, enlarged). *See* 1785, *above*.

Edwin's pills to purge melancholy. 1788 (2nd edn). *See* Pills to purge, 1776, *above*.

The English Lyceum: or choice of pieces in prose and in verse. Vol 3, Hamburg 1788. *See* 1787, *above*.

Extracts from the album at Streatham: or ministerial amusements. 1788, 1788 (2nd edn, enlarged). *See* Album, 1788, *above*.

The feast of Apollo: containing eleven lessons and twenty two favourite songs. [1788].

The festival of Anacreon: containing a collection of modern songs. Pt 2, [1788?]. First pt pbd 1788. *See* 1789, 1792, *below*.

The gentleman's musical magazine: or monthly convivial companion, by the principal composers in Europe. Vol 1, 1788. Stainer copy.

The goldfinch: or vocal miscellany. Gainsborough 1788. Harding copy. *See* 1785; *also* 1748, *above*.

Illustrations of Masonry. 1788 (new edn). Dobell, 1930. *See* 1772, *above*.

The institutes of Freemasonry; to which are added a choice collection of epilogues, songs. Ed J. Turnough, Liverpool 1788.

Letters of Abelard and Eloisa. 1788. *See* 1781, *above*.

The London songster: containing 544 songs. 1788 (new edn). Another reprint of the 1783 edn. *See* 1767, *above*.

The lyric miscellany: or the essence of harmony and humour. 1788. Stainer copy. *See* 1789, *below*.

The lyric repository: a selection of original, ancient and modern songs. 2 vols 1788. Stainer copy. *See* 1787, *above*.

The man of pleasure's song book: a high-season'd collection. [1788?]. Sotheby, 19 April 1898.

A new academy of compliments: or the lover's secretary; with a choice collection of above an hundred love songs. Dublin [1788?]. Stainer copy. *See* 1715, *above*.

A new and complete collection of Scots songs. Ed D. Corri, bks 1–2, Edinburgh [1788]. *See* 1790, *below*.

The new vocal enchantress: containing an elegant selection of all the newest songs lately sung at the Theatres Royal, Vauxhall. [1788]. *See* 1789, 1791, *below*.

Nimrod's songs of the chace: the best collection of hunting songs. 1788.

No 1 [–6] of Macklin's British poets. 1788–1799.

The Oriental asylum for fugitive pieces. Ed J. O'Reilly, Calcutta 1788. Hill, 1953.

Parsley's lyric repository for 1788. [1788]. Harding copy. *See* 1789, 1790, *and* New lyric repository, 1792, 1793, *below*; *also* Parsley's lyric companion, 1787, *above*.

Pleasing reflections on life and manners, with essays, characters and poems from fugitive publications. 1788 (new edn, enlarged). *See* 1787, *above*.

The poetry of the world. Ed E. Topham 2 vols 1788. *See* 1791; *also* British album, 1790, *below*.

The progresses and public processions of Queen Elizabeth. Ed J. Nichols, vols 1–2, 1788. Vol 3, 1805; 3 vols 1823 (2nd edn), 4 vols 1828 (3rd edn).

Prolusiones poeticae: or a selection of poetical exercises in Greek, Latin and English. Chester 1788.

The royalty songster and convivial companion: a collection of songs from the works of [9 names] and other writers. [1788].

The Scots musical museum. Vol 2, Edinburgh [1788]. 2 issues as in 1787.

The sky lark: or the lady's and gentleman's harmonious companion. Edinburgh [1788?].

The songster's companion: a select collection of more than two hundred songs. Coventry [1788?] (2nd edn). Stainer copy. *See* 1787, *above*.

The tea-table miscellany, in two volumes. Kilmarnock 1788 (17th edn). *See* 1724, *above*.

The treasury of wit. Sunderland 1788.

The Yorkshire garland: being a curious collection of old and new songs concerning that famous county. Ed Ritson, pt 1, York 1788; rptd in Northern garlands, 1810.

1789

The album of Streatham: or ministerial amusements. 1789 (4th edn, enlarged). *See* 1788, *above*.

The annual harmony: or the convivial companion, by a company of gentlemen. Southwark 1789. Harding copy. *See* Kemmish's annual harmonist, 1793, *below*.

The Attic miscellany. Vol 1, 1789. *See* 1790, 1791, *below*.

Bell's classical arrangement of fugitive poetry. Vols 1–10, 1789. Queen's College Oxford copy. *See* 1790–4, 1796, 1797, *below*.

Both sides of the gutter: or all parties laughing at each other. Dublin 1789; Pt 2, Dublin 1789.

Both sides of the gutter: or the humours of the Regency. Dublin [1789] (3rd edn, with addns). Includes The songs of love in a village, the nettle, and the political mirror: being parodies on the songs of the poor soldier. *See below*.

Caliope: or the musical miscellany. Edinburgh 1789. Lowndes. *See* 1788, *above*.

The charms of chearfulness: or merry songster's companion 1789. Book-prices current, 1898. *See* 1783, *above*.

A collection of poems, mostly original, by several hands. Ed J. Edkins, vol 1, Dublin 1789. *See* 1790, *below*.

The comic songster: or laughing companion. 1789 (4th edn). *See* 1794, *below*.

Concerts of antient music. 1789. *See* 1780, *above*.

A diary of the royal tour in 1789, interspersed with anecdotes, poetry and descriptions. 1789.

Each side of the gutter: or fugitive pieces. Dublin 1789.

Edwin's pills to purge melancholy. [1789] (3rd edn). *See* Pills to purge, 1780, *above*.

Elegant extracts: or useful and entertaining pieces of poetry. Dublin 1789 (3rd edn). *See* 1770, *above*.

The entertaining history of William Watling, and sweet Poll of Plymouth; to which are added a variety of sea songs. 1789. Harding copy.

The female reader: or miscellaneous pieces in prose and verse, selected from the best writers. Ed Cresswick 1789. *See* 1791, *below*.

The festival of Anacreon. [1789] (6th edn). Book-prices current, 1911. [1789] (7th–8th edns) (Harding copies); Second part, [1789?] (7th edn) (Harding copy).

The festival of love: or a collection of Cytherean poems procured and selected by G—e P—e. 1789. Book-prices current, 1913. Also edn, nd: Book-auction records, 1907–8. *See* 1793, 1796, *below*.

The festival of wit, procured and selected by G— K—, summer resident at Windsor. 1789 (15th edn, with addns). *See* 1782, *above*.

Jack Sprit-Sail's frolic; to which is added a new collection of choice songs. 1789. *See* 1791, 1793, *below*.

The jolly companion or a cure for care: being a curious collection of songs, cantatas. 1789. Stainer copy.

Jordan's elixir of life and cure for the spleen: or a collection of songs sung by Mrs Jordan. 1789.

The jovial songster: or sailor's delight. 1789 (4th edn). Harding copy. *See* 1784, *above*.

The lyric miscellany: or the essence of harmony and humour. [1789?] (2nd edn). Harding copy. *See* 1788, *above*.

Miscellanies, moral and instructive, in prose and verse; collected from various authors for the use of schools. Dublin 1789. *See* 1787, *above*.

Mrs Crouch's favourite pocket companion. 1789. Sotheby, 29 April 1891. *See* 1790, *below*.

The musical miscellany: or songster's companion. North-Shields 1789. The North-Shield's engraved frontispiece is dated 1788; it is also found with a London issue of 1789.

The nettle, an Irish bouquet, to tickle the nose of an English viceroy: being a collection of political songs and parodies. Ed 'Scriblerus Murtough O'Pindar' [W. P. Carey], Dublin 1789. *See* Both sides, *above*.

A new academy of compliments: or the complete English secretary. Glasgow 1789. *See* 1748, *above*.

The new Liverpool songster: or musical companion. Liverpool 1789. Stainer copy.

The new vocal enchantress for 1789. [1789] (new edn). Stainer copy. *See* 1788, *above*.

Parsley's lyric repository for 1789. [1789], [1789] (2nd edn improved). *See* 1788, *above*.

Poems on various subjects, with poems from other authors. Shrewsbury 1789 (2nd edn). *See* 1786, *above*.

The poetical miscellany. 1789 (4th edn). *See* 1762, *above*.

The Preston songster: or the new roundelay. Preston 1789. Harding copy. *See* Modern songster, 1790, *below*.

Robin Hood's garland: being a complete history of all the notable and merry exploits. [1789]. *See* 1663, *above*.

The shepherd's pastime: or pastoral songster. 1789 (2nd edn). Stainer copy. *See* 1779, *above*.

The songs of love in a village, with additional songs, as performed at the fancy ball in the Castle of Dublin on St Patrick's night. Dublin 1789. Trinity College Dublin copy. *See* Both sides, *above*.

The songster's companion. Coventry [1789?] (3rd edn). Harding copy. *See* 1788, *above*.

The speaker. 1789 (new edn). *See* 1774, *above*.

The syren or musical bouquet: being a new selection of modern songs. Edinburgh [1789?]. Stainer copy ptd for J. Elder and T. Brown; Harding copies ptd for T. Brown and J. Elder, also for W. Millar, London; otherwise identical.

1790

Ahiman rezon. [c. 1790]. *See* 1756, *above*.

The academy of complements. [1790?]. *See* 1663, *above*.

All the favourite oratorios set by Handel; with Acis and Galatea; Alexander's feast; The choice of Hercules; Milton's L'allegro, Il penseroso. Pts 1–2 [1790?]. Words only.

Ancient songs, from the time of Henry the third to the Revolution. Ed Ritson MDCCXC. For ascribed date of pbn, *see* 1792, *below*.

The art of story-telling: or merry jester. Ed C. F. Newry 1790. Harding copy.

The Attic miscellany. Vol 1, 1790 (Dobell, 1932); vol 2, 1790. *See* 1789, *above*.

The banquet of Thalia. Ed F. Atkinson [1790]. Harvard copy. *See* 1788, *above*.

The beauties of music and poetry. Vol 1 [1790?]. Much enlarged; BM catalogue dates [1784?]. *See* 1782, *above*.

The beauties of the poets. 1790, 1790. *See* 1773, *above*.

Bell's classical arrangement of fugitive poetry. Vols 11–12, 1790. Also reprint of vol 1. *See* 1789, *above*.

The Billington: or town and country songster, containing upwards of seven hundred songs. 1790.

The Billington: or vocal enchantress; and town and country songster. Dublin 1790. Stainer copy. A different edn from above.

The blackbird: being a collection of favourite Scotch, English and Irish songs. Falkirk 1790. Harding copy.

'Broadgrin, Sir Toby'. The book of oddities: or agreeable variety for town and country. Dublin 1790. *See* 1791, *below*.

The British album: containing the poems of Della Crusca, Anna Matilda. 2 vols 1790 (2nd edn) (first pbd as Poetry of the world, 1788), 1790 (3rd edn), Dublin 1790 (3rd edn). *See* 1792, 1793, *below*.

The busy bee: or vocal repository. Vols 1–3, [1790].

The charmer: being a select collection of English, Scots and American songs. Philadelphia 1790. Harding copy.

The children's miscellany. Ed T. Day 1790 (new edn). No verse in 1788 edn. *See* 1797, *below*.

The choir of Anacreon: or captain Morris's lyric repository, containing songs composed and sung by the most celebrated bon vivans. 1790. Harding copy. By several hands.

A collection of odes, songs and epigrams against the Whigs, in which are included Hewerdine's political songs. 1790, Dublin 1790. Harding copy.

A collection of poems, mostly original, by several hands. Vol 2, Dublin 1790. *See* 1789, *above*.

The companion: being a choice collection from the best authors, in prose and verse, by a society of gentlemen. Vols 1–2, Edinburgh 1790. *See* 1791, *below*.

Concerts of antient music. 1790. *See* 1780, *above*.

The convivial jester: or bane of melancholy. Ed 'Godfrey Broadgrin' [1790?], Anderson USA 19 April 1912. *See* 1800, *below*.

The convivial songster. 1790. No known copy. *See* 1782, *above*.

The Court jester: or museum of entertainment. [1790?]. No other words in title; *see* 1771, *above*.

Criticisms on the Rolliad. Pt 2, 1790 (2nd edn). Also 3rd–4th edns 1790. *See* 1785, *above*.

The filberd: or the compleatest medley of wit. [1790?].

Frobisher's new select collection of epitaphs. [1790?].

Gallery of poets: catalogue of the third exhibition of pictures painted for Macklin by the artists of Britain, illustrative of the British poets and the Bible. 1790. *See* 1791, *and* Poets' gallery, 1792–3, *below*.

Garrick's jests: or genius in high glee; to which are added a new selection of epigrams, poems. [1790?]. *See* English Roscius, 1769, *above*.

Harmonia sacra: or divine and moral songs by several eminent masters. [c. 1790] (3rd edn). *See* 1765, *above*.

Jachin and Boaz. 1790. Book-auction records, 1915–16. *See* 1767, *above*.

Joe Miller's jests: or the wits vade-mecum. [1790?], Anderson USA 28 April 1911. *See* 1742, *above*.

The ladies and gentlemen's musical memorandum: or Norfolk songster. Norwich [1790?]. Stainer copy.

The London complete songster: or musical bouquet. [1790?]. Stainer copy.

The masque. [1790?] (new edn). Harvard copy; pp. 366; songs, 354 + 1. Date more probably c. 1780. *See* 1777, *above*.

A miscellaneous collection of the best English and Irish songs. Glasgow [1790?].

Miscellaneous poems. Manchester [c. 1790?]. Harding copy.

The modern songster: or the new roundelay. Preston [1790?]. Stainer copy. This is Preston songster, 1789, *above*.

The modern syren: a collection of the most celebrated new songs. Newcastle 1790. Stainer copy. *See* 1781, *above*.

Mrs Crouch's favourite pocket companion: being a select assemblage of songs. [1790?]. Stainer copy. *See* 1789, *above*.

A new edition: Mrs Crouch's favourite companion. [1790?]. Harding copy.

The Muses banquet: or vocal repository. 1790. Stainer copy. *See* 1791, 1792, *below*.

A museum for young gentlemen and ladies. Dublin 1790. Pickering & Chatto, 1932. *See* 1763, *above*.

Musicae vocalis deliciae: being a collection of madrigals, glees, catches, canzonets, rounds and canons. [1790?].

The musical companion: containing a collection of the newest songs, as sung at theatres and public gardens in England and Ireland. Dublin 1790. Nat Lib of Ireland copy. *See* 1667, *above*.

The musical miscellany: or songster's companion. Newcastle MDCXC [1790]. Differs from 1789 collections, *above*.

Naval glory: an entire collection of sea songs, with toasts and sentiments. [1790?]. Stainer copy.

A new and complete collection of Scots songs. Bk 1, Edinburgh [1790?]. A reprint of bk 1, 1788, *above*.

The new whim of the day: or musical olio. 1790 (2nd edn). Stainer copy; ptd by J. Barker.

A new whim of the day: or musical olio. 1790 (new edn). Harding copy. Ptd by T. Axtell; a different collection from the above. Edn, nd: Sotheby, 24 April 1891.

Parsley's lyric repository for 1790. [1790]; The second part for 1790, [1790]. Stainer copy. *See* 1788, *above*.

A pocket book for the German flute or violin. Vols 1–3, Dublin [1790–3?]. Stainer copy. *See* 1778, *above*.

Political miscellanies, by the authors of the Rolliad and Probationary odes. 1790. *See* 1787, *above*.

The professional collection of glees composed by the following authors: Callcott, Cooke [and 4 others]. [1790?].

Reliques of ancient English poetry. Vols 1–2, London and Frankfurt 1790. *See* 1791, *below*, *and* 1765, *above*.

The repository. 4 vols 1790. Vols 1–2 (3rd edn, with addns); vols 3–4 (2nd edn). *See* 1777, *above*.

The road to Hymen made plain in a new collection of familiar letters, pleasing dialogues and verses. [1790?].

Roundelay: or the new syren. [1790?] (new edn). N. Ault copy. Preface headed 9th edn; pp. xii + 290 + 2 (Toasts). *See* 1781, *above*.

The Scots musical museum. Vol 3, Edinburgh [1790]. 2 issues as in 1787, *above*.

A select collection of favourite Scotish ballads. Ed R. Morison, vols 1–4 Perth 1790.

Select collection of favourite Scots songs. Ed D. Corri, Edinburgh [1790?] J. Grant, 1921.

A select collection of poems from admired authors and scarce miscellanies; with many pieces never before published. North Shields 1790.

A selection of the most favourite Scots-songs Ed W. Napier, vol 1, [1790]. *See* 1792, *below*.

The songster's companion. Coventry [1790?] 4th edn). Harding copy. Issued with 6 names in imprint, and with one. *See* 1788, *above*.

The songster's miscellany: or vocal companion, containing upwards of two hundred songs, duets. Kidderminster [1790?]. Stainer copy. *See* 1800, *below*.

The songster's polite tutor: containing plain directions and a collection of the most celebrated songs. [1790?]. Stainer copy; imprint, Longman and Broderip. *See* 1775, *above*.

The speaker. 1790 (new edn). *See* 1774, *above*.

Specimens of the early English poets. Ed G. Ellis 1790. 3 vols 1801 (2nd edn); other edns in 1803, 1805, 1811, 1845; ed J. O. Halliwell-Phillipps 1848.

Ramsay, A. et al. Thirty Scots songs adapted by Robert Bremner. Bk 1, [c. 1790] (Harvard copy; ptd and sold by Preston and Son); A second set, [c. 1790] (Harvard copy; same imprint). *See* 1757, *above*.

The town and country song-book: containing a choice collection of new hunting, love, songs. [1790?].

The whim of the day for 1790. [1790] (Sotheby, 31 July 1884); containing the choicest and most approved songs now singing, [1790] (2nd edn). *See* yearly to 1800, *below*.

1791

Amusement for the ladies. Vol 1, [1791]. A reprint of 1780 edn, renaming former vols 1–3 as bks 1–3.

Antient and modern Scotish songs, heroic ballads, in two volumes. Edinburgh 1791. *See* 1769, *above*.

The Apollo: being an elegant selection of approved modern songs. Bath 1791. Stainer copy. Another issue, with frontispiece in red, 1791. Harding copy. *See* 1794, *below*.

The Attic miscellany. Vol 1, 1791. Thorp, 1931. Vol 3, 1791. *See* 1789, *above*.

Attick wit: or a medley of humour in prose and verse. 1791. Harding copy.

The banquet of Thalia: or the fashionable songsters pocket memorial. [1791?]. *See* 1788, *above*.

Beauties of literature, selected from various authors by Henry Waylett. 2 vols Lewes 1791.

Bell's classical arrangement of fugitive poetry. Vols 13–14, 1791. Also reprint of vol 2. *See* 1789, *above*.

The book of oddities: or agreeable variety. Dublin 1791 (3rd edn). *See* 1790, *above*.

The British songster: or pocket companion. [1791?]. Harding copy. *See* 1794, 1798–1800, *below*.

Cabinet of fancy: or bon ton of the day. [1791?]. Contains songs; no known copy.

The charms of chearfulness: an elegant and polite selection of English and Scotch songs. 2 vols 1791. Stainer copy. Reprint of Tea-table miscellany, 12th edn, with new preliminary pages.

A collection of favourite songs sung at the Beef Steak Club and the Anacreontic Society. [1791?]. Harding copy.

A collection of spiritual songs. 1791. Stainer copy.

The companion. Vol 3, Edinburgh 1791. *See* 1790, *above*.

Concerts of antient music. 1791. *See* 1780, *above*.

Criticisms on the Rolliad. Pt 1, 1791 (9th edn, enlarged). *See* 1785, *above*.

Edinburgh fugitive pieces. [Ed W. Creech], Edinburgh 1791.

The Essex harmony. Vol 2, 1791 (3rd edn). Stainer copy. *See* 1753, *above*.

Exercises in elocution, selected from various authors. 1791 (new edn). *See* 1780, *above*.

Extracts, elegant, instructive and entertaining, in poetry; from the most approved authors. 1791. *See* 1770, *above*.

The female reader: or miscellaneous pieces in prose and verse, selected from the best writers. Dublin 1791. N. Ault copy. *See* 1789, *above*.

The festival of wit, procured and selected by G— K—, summer resident at Windsor. Dublin 1791 (16th edn). Trinity College Dublin copy. *See* 1782, *above*.

Volume the second: the festival of wit, collected from the manuscript of George K—, summer resident at Windsor. 1791.

Free Masonry for the ladies; to which are added anthems and odes. Dublin [1791].

Gallery of poets: catalogue of the fourth exhibition of pictures, painted for T. Macklin. *See* 1790, *above*.

Jack Sprit-sail's frolic. 1791 (2nd edn). Stainer copy. *See* 1789, *above*.

The lady's poetical magazine: or beauties of British poetry. Vols 1–2, 1791. Harding copy. *See* 1781, *above*.

Miscellanies in prose and verse. Edinburgh 1791.

The Muses banquet: or vocal repository for the year 1791. [1791]. Harding copy. *See* 1790, *above*.

Music and dancing: new songs by the most eminent composers. 1791. Harding copy.

The musical companion: or songster's ever new miscellany. Portsea [c. 1791]. Stainer copy.

The new Thespian oracle: containing a select collection of all the modern prologues and epilogues. 1791. No known copy; *see* R. W. Lowe, A bibliographical account of English theatrical literature, 1888.

The new vocal enchantress: a new edition for 1791. [1791]. Stainer copy. *See* 1788, *above*.

The Oriental Masonic Muse: containing a collection of songs, odes, anthems. Calcutta 1791.

Ovid's Art of love, translated by several eminent hands. 1791. *See* 1709, *above*.

Paddy Whack's bottle companion: a collection of convivial songs in high estimation. 1791.

Pieces of ancient popular poetry. Ed Ritson 1791, 1833 (2nd edn).

The poetry of the world. Vols 1–2, 1791 (3rd edn); vols 3–4, 1791. *See* 1788, *above*.

Probationary odes, with a discourse by Sir John Hawkins. 1791 (9th edn). *See* 1785, *above*.

Reliques of ancient English poetry. Vol 3, London and Frankfurt 1791. *See* 1790, *above*.

Retired pleasures in prose and verse. 1791. *See* 1787, *above*.

The royal toastmaster; also the seaman's bottle companion: being a selection of sea songs. [1791?]. Stainer copy. Another Stainer copy has the same title but different contents. *See* 1793, *below*.

The skylark: being an elegant collection of the best and newest songs in the English language. [1791]. Harding copy. *See* 1800, *below*.

The sportsman's evening brush: consisting of songs of the chace, ancient and modern. [1791]. *See* 1795, *below*.

The vocal enchanter. 1791. No known copy.

The whim of the day for 1791. [1791], [1791] (2nd–3rd edns) (Harding copies), [1791] (4th edn). *See* 1790, *above*.

Wit and mirth: or Tom D'Urfey's pills to purge melancholy. 1791. Harding copy. By several hands. *See* 1719, *above*.

1792

Amusement for the ladies. Vol 2, [1792]. A new collection; *see* 1780, *above*.

Anacreontic magazine: or songster's musical companion, containing songs, glees. Vol 1, 1792. *See* 1793, 1794, *below*.

Ancient songs, from the time of Henry the third to the Revolution. [Ed Ritson] MDCCXC[II]. Most copies have 2 strokes added with a pen to the date. Rptd 2 vols 1829, with Ritson's name; ed W. C. Hazlitt 1877. *See* 1790, *above*.

The banquet of Thalia. [Ed F. Atkinson], York 1792. *See* 1788, *above*.

The beauties of the poets. 1792 (4th edn). D. Nichol Smith copy. *See* 1773, *above*.

Bell's classical arrangement of fugitive poetry. Vol 15, 1792. Also a reprint of vol 3. *See* 1789, *above*.

The bishopric garland: or Durham minstrel. Ed Ritson, Newcastle 1792 (new edn); rptd in Northern garlands, 1810, 1887. *See* 1784, *above*.

The bouquet: a selection of poems from the most celebrated authors. Vols 1–2, 1792.

The British album. 2 vols 1792 (4th edn, with addns). *See* 1790, *above*.

The British Apollo: or songster's magazine, containing a choice selection of English, Irish and Scotch songs. 1792. Stainer copy.

The buck's delight: or vocal companion. Gainsborough 1792 (new edn). *See* 1793, *below*.

The cabinet of genius. 2 vols 1792. Book-auction records, 1918–19. *See* 1787, *above*.

The cabinet of love. 1792. Sotheby, 23 April 1891.

The charms of chearfulness: or merry songster's companion. [1792?]. Stainer copy; pp. 172 + index; different from 1783, *above*.

The chearful companion: or Suffolk, Norfolk and Essex song-book for the year 1792. Bury [1792]. Harding copy.

A collection of poems on various subjects. Ed. S. Whyte, Dublin 1792 (2nd edn). *See* Poems, 1795, *below*.

Concerts of antient music. 1792. *See* 1780, *above*.

The constitutions of the Free and Accepted Masons, together with a large collection of songs. Worcester Mass 1792. Ed T. M. Harris.

The Edinburgh musical miscellany. Ed D. Sime, vol 1, Edinburgh 1792. *See* 1793, *below*.

The Edinburgh syren. 1792. *See* Syren, 1792.

The favorite new glees composed by Cooke, Callcott, Danby and Webbe. 1792. Harding copy.

The festival of Anacreon. Pt 3, [1792?]. Dobell, 1937. *See* 1788, *above*.

The festival of Momus: a collection of comic songs. [1792?] (new edn). Harding copy. Pp. xii + 284 + 4. *See* 1786, *above*.

The Free Mason's pocket companion; to which is now added a collection of English, Scotch and Irish songs. Ayr 1792. Dobell, 1930. *See* A pocket companion, 1735, *above*.

Ramsay, Burns, Dibdin et al. The Glasgow miscellany: a select collection of Scots and English songs. Glasgow [1792?].

Illustrations of Masonry. 1792 (8th edn). Dobell, 1930. *See* 1772, *above*.

The Kentish songster. Canterbury 1792 (4th edn). Harding copy. Including Songs, 1784–92, not in previous edns: Hill, 1967. *See* 1775, *above*.

The lady's preceptor: consisting of a selection of moral essays and poetical compositions. Ed Cresswick 1792.

The linnet: a collection of an hundred and thirty choice songs. Glasgow 1792. Stainer copy.

The literary museum: or ancient and modern repository. Ed F. G. Waldron 1792.

The Manchester songster: being a collection of the most favorite songs. Manchester 1792.

Miscellaneous extracts, chiefly poetical, selected from various authors. Ed R. Osborne, Northampton 1792. Harding copy.

Miscellanies by Swift, Arbuthnot, Pope and Gay. 9 vols 1792. Myers & Co, 1934.

The Muses banquet: or vocal repository for the year 1792. [1792]. *See* 1790, *above*.

The musical charmer: or warbler in the woods. Edinburgh [1792?]. Harding copy.

The new lyric repository for 1792, collected by W. Dale, successor to R. Parsley. [1792]. Stainer copy. *See* 1793, *below*; *also* Parsley's lyric repository, 1788, *above*.

Nugae antiquae. 3 vols 1792 (new edn); ed T. Park, 2 vols 1804. *See* 1769, *above*.

The olio: being a collection by the late Francis Grose. 1792. *See* 1793, 1796, *below*.

The pleasing jester: or merry companion. 1792. Harding copy.

Poems, chiefly by gentlemen of Devonshire and Cornwall. Ed R. Polwhele 2 vols Bath 1792.

Poems for young ladies. Perth 1792. Hill, 1967. *See* 1767, *above*.

Poems on miscellaneous subjects. Ed C. Beverley, Hull 1792.

Poems selected and printed by a small party of English. Strasbourg 1792.

The poetical epitome: or extracts, elegant, instructive and entertaining, abridged from the larger volume. 1792. Harding copy. *See* Extracts, 1791, *above*.

The poets' gallery: catalogue of the fifth exhibition of pictures painted for T. Macklin. 1792. *See* 1790, *above*.

Robin Hood's garland: being a complete history of all the notable and merry exploits. Nottingham 1792. *See* 1663, *above*.

The royal jester: or prince's cabinet of wit. 1792.

The science of love: or the whole art of courtship. 1792.

Scotish poems reprinted from scarce editions. Ed J. Pinkerton 3 vols 1792.

The Scots musical museum. Vol 4, Edinburgh [1792]. 2 issues as in 1787.

Scrapeana: fugitive miscellany. Ed J. Croft 1792; Or a medley of choice bon mots, repartees, York 1792 (2nd edn).

A selection of original Scot's songs; the harmony by Haydn. Vol 2, [1792]. *See* 1790, *above*.

The songster's companion. Coventry [1792?] (5th edn). Harding copy. *See* 1788, *above*.

The speaker: or miscellaneous pieces. 1792. *See* 1774, *above*.

The syren: or musical bouquet. Edinburgh [1792]. A 2nd title-page: The Edinburgh syren, 1792. Harding copy has Thomas Brown in its imprints; Stainer has John Elder in first and Thomas Hill in second. *See* 1789, *above*.

The universal songster: or harmony and innocence. [1792?] (new edn). Harding copy. Pp. xii + 284 + 4. *See* 1782, *above*.

The whim of the day for 1792. [1792] (Stainer copy), [1792] (2nd edn) (Harding copy).

1793

American poems, selected and original. Vol 1, Litchfield Conn [1793].

Amusement for the ladies. Vol 3, [1793]. A new collection; *see* 1780, *above*.

Amusement for the ladies. Bk 8, vol 3, [1793]. A different collection from 1791–3, *above*.

Anacreontic magazine: or songster's musical companion. Vol 2, 1793. Stainer copy. *See* 1792, *above*.

Anthologia hibernica: or monthly collections of science, belles-lettres and history. Vols 1–2, Dublin 1793. *See* 1794, *below*.

The antigallican songster. Nos 1[–2], 1793.

The anti-levelling songster. Nos 1[–2], 1793.

The anti-gallican and anti-levelling songster: being a selection of curious political songs. 4 pts [c. 1793].

Apollo's lyre: being a selection of songs in the year 1793. [1793]. *See* 1797, 1798, *below*.

An asylum for fugitive pieces. Vol 4, 1793. Harding copy. *See* 1785, *above*.

The beauties of thought in prose and verse, selected from the best authors. Bridlington 1793.

The bee: a selection of poetry. 1793. R. H. Lonsdale copy. *See* 1795–7, *below*.

Bell's classical arrangement of fugitive poetry. Vol 4, 1793. *See* 1789, *above*.

Blackguardiana: or a dictionary of rogues, bawds; interspersed with flash songs. Ed J. Caulfield [c. 1793].

The British album. Vol 2, 1793 (4th edn, with addns). This is vol 2, 1792, with new preliminaries.

The British album: first American edition, from the fourth London. Boston 1793. *See* 1790, *above*.

The British lyre: or Muses' repository for the year 1793. [Ed W. Collins 1793].

The British songster: or Dibdin's delight. 1793. Harding copy.

The buck's delight: or vocal companion. Gainsborough 1793 (new edn). Stainer copy. *See* 1792, *above*.

A collection of interesting anecdotes, memoirs, allegories, essays and poetical fragments. Ed 'Mr. Addison' 1793. Marks, 1931. *See* Interesting anecdotes, 1794, *below*.

Concerts of antient music. 1793. *See* 1780, *above*.

The Edinburgh musical miscellany. Vol 2, Edinburgh 1793. *See* 1792, *above*.

The English anthology. [Ed Ritson], vol 1, 1793. *See* 1794, *below*.

Essex harmony. [1793?]. Vol 1 imprint: Bland & Wellers. Harding copy. Vol 2 a reprint of 1769 edn. Also 2 vols, Dublin nd. Book-auction records, 1904–5. *See* 1753, *above*.

The festival of love: or a collection of Cytherean poems. [1793?] (4th edn). Harding copy. *See* 1789, *above*.

The festival of wit. 1793 (16th edn). *See* 1782, *above*.

The general songster: or every man's social companion. Gainsborough 1793. Grant, 1932. *See* 1785, *above*.

Jachin and Boaz: or an authentic key to Free-Masonry. 1793. Book-auction records, 1916–17. *See* 1767, *above*.

Jack Sprit-sail's frolic. 1793 (new edn). Stainer copy. *See* 1789, *above*.

Kemmish's annual-harmonist: or the British Apollo. Southwark [1793] (Stainer copy), [1793?] (2nd edn) (Harding copy). *See* 1795–6, *below*; *also* Annual harmony, 1789, *above*.

The lady's miscellany: or pleasing essays, poems, stories and examples. Ed G. Wright 1793. *See* 1797, *below*.

The minstrel: being a new and select collection of English songs. 1793. No known copy; *see* 1780, *above*.

Modern beauties in prose and verse, selected from the most eminent authors. Darlington 1793.

Monstrous good songs, toasts and sentiments for 1793. [1793]. *See* 1794–6, 1798–9, *below*.

The new lyric repository for 1793. [1793]. Stainer copy. *See* 1792, *above*.

The new school of love. Glasgow 1793. *See* 1786, *above*.

The Northumberland garland: or Newcastle nightingale. [Ed Ritson], Newcastle 1793; rptd in Northern garlands, ed Ritson 1810.

The olio. 1793. *See* 1792, *above*.

Ovid's Art of love, translated by several eminent hands. 1793. McLeish, 1930. *See* 1709, *above*. Later edns in 1804, 1808, 1815, 1824 etc.

The patriot's calendar for the year 1794, with a collection of the best odes and fugitive pieces written in favour of liberty. [1793]. *See* 1794, 1795, *below*.

Pleasing melancholy: or a walk among the tombs; to which are added epitaphs, elegies and inscriptions in prose and verse. Ed G. Wright 1793.

Poems on various subjects. 1793 (7th edn). Harding copy. *See* 1782, *above*.

Poetical blossoms: being a selection of short poems intended for young people. Ed Rev Cooper 1793.

The poets' gallery: catalogue of the sixth exhibition of pictures painted for T. Macklin. 1793. *See* 1790, *above*.

The polite songster: or vocal melody, containing songs sung at the theatres. [1793?]. Harding copy. *See* 1794, *below*.

The royal toastmaster. 1793. Harding copy. *See* 1791, *above*.

A select collection of original Scottish airs. Ed G. Thomson, sets 1–4, [1793–7].

The songs, duets, choruses, now singing at Vauxhall. 1793.

Songs, trios, choruses as performed at Sadler's Wells from 1793 to 1796. 1793–6. Sotheby, 30 April 1890.

The songster's companion. Coventry [1793?] (6th edn). Harding copy. *See* 1788, *above.*

The songster's repository: or convivial companion for the year 1793. [1793]. Harding copy.

The tea-table miscellany, in two volumes. Edinburgh 1793 (18th edn). Aberdeen Univ Lib copy. 4 vols Berwick 1793 (new edn). Mitchell Lib Glasgow copy. *See* 1724, *above.*

A tribute to liberty: or a new collection of patriotic songs, entirely original. 1793. Stainer copy. By one hand? *See* 1800, *below.*

The universal songster: being a collection of ancient and modern songs. Banbury [1793?]

The whim of the day for 1793. [1793] (2nd edn). Stainer copy. *See* 1790, *above.*

The young gentleman's agreeable companion: containing an excellent and genteel collection of songs. 1793. Harding copy.

1794

Anacreontic magazine. [c. 1794?]. Harding copy. Vol 2, 1793, with addns. *See* 1792, *above.*

Anthologia hibernica. Vols 3–4, Dublin 1794. *See* 1793, *above.*

The Apollo: being an elegant selection of approved modern songs. Bath 1794. Two Harding copies have different imprints. *See* 1791, *above.*

The beauties of ancient poetry: a companion to the beauties of English poetry. 1794.

Bell's classical arrangement of fugitive poetry. Vol 16, 1794. Queen's College Oxford copy. *See* 1789, *above.*

The British songster: or pocket companion. [1794?] (new edn). BM dates its edn [1800?]. *See* 1791, *above.*

The Columbian Muse: a selection of American poetry, from various authors of established reputation. New York 1794.

The comic songster: or laughing companion. [1794?]. Stainer copy. *See* 1789, *above.*

Concerts of antient music. 1794. *See* 1780, *above.*

Crosby's modern songster. [1794?]. Harding copy.

Dale's collection of sixty favourite Scotch songs. Bks 1, 3, 1794. Quaritch, Dec 1887. *See* 1795, *below.*

The English anthology. Vols 2–3, 1794. *See* 1793, *above.*

Every lady's own Valentine writer in prose and verse for the year 1794. [1794]. Harding copy. *See* 1798, *below.*

The honest fellow or buck's necessary companion: a collection of jocular songs. Dublin 1794. Harding copy.

Interesting anecdotes, memoirs, allegories, essays and poetical fragments. Ed 'Mr Addison', vols 1–5, 1794 (priv ptd). *See* 1795–7, *below; also* A collection, 1793, *above.*

The lover's instructor. 1794. Harding copy. By several hands? *See* 1777, *above.*

Monstrous good songs for the year 1794. [1794]. Stainer copy. *See* 1793, *above.*

Musae Berkhamstedienses: or poetical prolusions by some young gentlemen of Berkhamsted School. Berkhamsted 1794. *See* Poetical prolusions, 1799, *below.*

Musical and poetical relicks of the Welsh bards. Ed E. Jones 1794 (new edn, augmented). *See* 1784, *above.*

The new Edinburgh musical miscellany. 1794. No known copy.

New frisky songster. 1794. Sotheby, 22 July 1864.

The new vocal companion: a selection of the most favourite modern songs. 1794. Stainer copy.

The offspring of fancy: or Suffolk, Norfolk and Essex song-book for the year 1794. Bury [1794]. Harding copy.

Ovid's Metamorphoses. Tr Dryden et al 4 vols 1794; rptd 1807, 1807, 1810, 1812, 1813, 1815 etc. *See* 1717, *above.*

The patriot's calendar for the year 1795, with a collection of odes and fugitive pieces. [1794]. *See* 1793, *above.*

Pleasing variety: or literary amusements in prose and verse. Edinburgh 1794.

The poetical farrago: being epigrams and other jeux d'esprit, selected from the most approved writers. Vols 1–2, 1794.

The polite songster: or vocal melody. 1794 (new edn). *See* 1793, *above.*

Reliques of ancient English poetry. 3 vols 1794 (4th edn); ed H. B. Wheatley 3 vols 1876–7, 1891. Many other edns. *See* 1765, *above.*

Roach's beauties of the poets of Great Britain, in six volumes. 1794. Some plates, frontispieces etc, dated 1795.

Robin Hood's garland. Nottingham 1794. Sotheby, 29 April 1891. *See* 1663, *above.*

Roundelay or the new syren: a collection of choice songs. [1794?] (new edn). Hill, 1965. *See* 1781, *above.*

Scotish songs, in two volumes. Ed Ritson 1794. Vol 1, sometimes found with title-page reading Scotish song, MDCCXIV. Rptd 1866, 1869.

A selection of Scots songs harmonized by P. Urbani. Bks 1–4, Edinburgh [1794–5?].

Songs, political, satyrical and convivial, dedicated to the goddess Vestina by John Devonshire. [1794].

Sudbury's new royal whim of the night: or songster's banquet for 1794. 1794. Stainer copy.

Sweet Robin or the children in the wood: a select collection of the choicest songs, ancient and modern. 1794. Stainer copy.

The tea-table miscellany. Dublin 1794 (19th edn). Mitchell Lib Glasgow copy. *See* 1724, *above.*

Pope, Denham and Gray. Three select poems: Windsor Forest; Cooper's Hill; A distant prospect of Eton College. Windsor 1794. Also bound with The beauties of the royal palaces, Windsor [1796], [1798].

Twopence worth of hog's bristles, to sweep away the cob-webs of despotism and ignorance. Edinburgh [1794?]. Ellis, 1906.

The whim of the day for 1794. [1794]. Stainer copy. *See* 1790, *above.*

The wits museum: or the new London jester. Dublin 1794 (new edn). This has little in common with the 1780 edn.

The words of the favourite pieces, as performed at the glee club. Ed J. P. Hobler 1794. Harding copy has an extra 30-page appendix.

Hay, W. Works. 2 vols 1794. Vol 2 reprints Select epigrams of Martial, some by Cowley and other hands, 1755.

1795

Academical collections of original and translated poetry. Cambridge 1795.

The academy of compliments. Dublin [1795?] Sotheby, 24 April 1890. *See* 1663, *above.*

Ahiman rezon: or a help to a brother. Belfast 1795 (6th edn). *See* 1756, *above.*

Amusement for the ladies. Bk 7, [c. 1795]. *See* 1780, *above.*

Apollonian harmony: a collection of glees. 6 vols [1795?–8?]. Ptd for S. A. & P. Thompson; *see* 1799, 1800, *below.*

An asylum for fugitive pieces. Vol 3, 1795 (2nd edn). *See* 1785, *above.*

The bee: a selection of poetry from the best authors. 1795 (new edn). *See* 1793, *above.*

The cabinet, by a society of gentlemen. 3 vols Norwich 1795.

The Caledonian bee: or a select collection of interesting extracts from modern publications. Perth 1795.

A choice collection of ancient and modern Scots songs. [1795?]. Stainer copy.

Collection of Masonic songs. Ed Brother R. Gaudry 1795. Book-prices current, 1909.

A collection of the most favorite new songs, taken from all the operas and the theatres. Bath [1795?]. Stainer copy.

Concerts of antient music. 1795. *See* 1780, *above.*

Cowley's history of plants, translated from the Latin by Tate and others. 1795.

Dale's collection of sixty favorite Scotch songs. Bks 1–3, [1795?]. *See* 1794, *above.*

The delicate songster: or ladies vocal repository. [1795?].

The Dibdin or Irish nosegay: being a complete collection of the best songs of every species. Dublin 1795 (2nd edn). With Incledon's and other new songs; Stainer copy.

The eclipses: or luminaries involved in darkness. Vol 1 for the year 1795, Newmarket [1795].

Entertaining extracts: being a select collection from new books of merit. Perth 1795.

The festival of wit: being a collection of bon-mots, anecdotes. Dresden 1795. Harding copy. *See* 1782, *above.*

The gentleman's miscellany: consisting of essays, characters and poems. Ed G. Wright 1795. Myers, 1929. *See* 1797, *below.*

The green room songster. 1795. Dobell, 1918.

[The hive. c. 1795?]. No title-page, but Hive, 1796, probably rptd from this.

Interesting anecdotes and poetical fragments. Ed 'Mr Addison', vols 6–9, 1795. *See* 1794, *above.*

Kemmish's annual harmonist and whim of the night for 1795. Southwark [1795]. Harding copy. *See* 1793, *above.*

Laugh and be fat: or the merry companion. [1795?] 2 issues with differently set title-pages.

Monstrous good songs for the year 1795. [1795]. Harding copy. *See* 1793, *above.*

The moral instructor: consisting of miscellaneous essays, poems, anecdotes, maxims. Ed J. Fallowfield, Penrith 1795.

The new London jester, together with the complete English songster. 1795.

The new olio: or a collection of choice whims, containing songs, catches, glees. [1795?].

Ovid's Art of love. 1795. *See* 1709, *above.*

Ovid's Epistles, translated by eminent persons, in two volumes. 1795. *See* 1725, *above.*

Patriot's calendar for the year 1796, with prose and poetry on patriotic subjects. [1795]. *See* 1793, *above.*

Poems on various subjects. [Ed E. A. Whyte], Dublin 1795 (3rd edn). *See* A collection, 1792, *above.*

Popular ballads preserved in memory. Belfast 1795. No known copy.

Robin Hood: a collection of all the ancient poems, songs and ballads now extant, in two volumes. Ed Ritson 1795. 1832 (2nd edn); other edns, 1820, 1853, 1854, 1862, 1884, 1885, 1887.

Richardson, J. et al. The Rolliad, in two parts: probationary odes and political miscellanies [and political eclogues] 1795. *See* 1796, 1799, *below*; *also* Criticisms, 1784, 1785, 1787, *above.*

Roundelay: or the new syren. [1795?] (new edn). Harding copy. Pp. 288 + 8 + 2 (toasts). *See* 1781, *above.*

Satyrical, humourous and familiar pieces: poetry. [Ed G. Nicholson], Manchester 1795.

Select collection of the most admired songs, duetts, in four books. 4 vols Edinburgh [1795?]. *See* 1779, *above.*

Select pieces of poetry intended to promote piety and virtue in young people. Ed R. Barclay 1795. *See* Poems 1797, *below.*

Select poems. 1795. By different authors.

The skylark or gentlemen and ladies complete songster: American, English and Scotch songs. Worcester Mass 1795. Sotheby, 19 April 1898.

The songster's companion. Coventry [1795?] (8th edn). Harding copy. *See* 1788, *above.*

The sportsman's evening brush: consisting of songs of the chace. 1795. Sotheby, 30 April 1890. *See* 1791, *above.*

Ramsay, A. [et al]. Thirty Scots songs. 2 bks Edinburgh [c. 1795]. Not the same collection as Stewart's [c. 1780] edn. *See also* 1757, *above.*

The universal songster: or harmony and innocence. [1795?] (new edn). Harding copy. Pp. xii + 285 + 3. *See* 1782, *above.*

The Vauxhall songs for the year 1795. [1795].

The whim of the day for 1795. [1795]. Harding copy. *See* 1790, *above.*

1796

Ancient ballads, songs and poems. Ed G. Nicholson, Manchester 1796. *See* 1799, *below.*

The bee: a selection of poetry from the best authors. Dublin 1796. Cambridge Univ Lib copy. *See* 1793, *above.*

The bouquet: or blossoms of fancy. Vols 1–2, [1796]. Originally issued in nos, 1795–6.

The charms of melody or siren medley: being the most extensive collection of songs. Dublin [1796?]. Harding copy.

A classical arrangement of fugitive poetry. Vol 17, 1796. G. Cawthorn's continuation of Bell's ser, 1789–94, *above.*

A collection of English songs, with an appendix of original pieces. Ed A. Dalrymple 1796.

The comick magazine: or compleat library, by the greatest wits. Vol 1, 1796. Harding copy.

Concerts of antient music. 1796. *See* 1780, *above.*

Elegant extracts: poetry. 1796 (new edn). *See* 1770, *above.*

Essays, by a society of gentlemen at Exeter. Exeter [1796].

The famous English archer: or Robert, Earl of Huntingdon, commonly called Robin Hood. Monaghan 1796. *See* 1663, *above.*

The festival of love: or a collection of Cytherean poems. [1796?] (7th edn). Harding copy. *See* 1789, *above.*

The festival of Momus: a collection of comic songs. [1796?] (new edn). Harding copy. Pp. xii + 282 + 6. *See* 1786, *above.*

Ross, A., F. Douglas, C. Keith and [H. Macneil]. The fortunate shepherdess; Rural love; The farmer's ha'; Will and Jean. Aberdeen 1796.

The gallimaufry: or budget of Momus. [1796?] (2nd edn, with addns).

The hive: a selection from modern writers, in prose and verse. Edinburgh 1796.

The hive: or a collection of thoughts selected from the best and most approved authors in verse and prose. Philadelphia 1796. *See* 1795, *above.*

Illustrations of Masonry. 1796 (9th edn). *See* 1772, *above.*

Interesting anecdotes and poetical fragments. Ed 'Mr Addison', vols 1–4, 1796. The 1794 edn with cancel titles?

Kemmish and Co's annual harmonist: or British Apollo, containing the newest songs. Southwark [1796]. Stainer copy. *See* 1793, *above.*

The mermaid or nautical songster: being a new collection of favourite sea-songs. New York 1796 (5th edn). Harding copy.

A miscellaneous collection of songs, ballads and elegies, in two vols. Ed F. A. Hyde, vol 1, [1796?]. *See* 1798, *below.*

Monstrous droll songs. 1796. Harding copy. *See* 1798–9, *below.*

Monstrous good songs 1796. [1796]. Harding copy. *See* 1793, *above.*

The monthly banquet of Apollo: containing songs all composed by [J.] Hook. 1796.

Mother Goose's melody: or sonnets for the cradle. 2 pts [1796?]. Also Mother Goose's melody, [2 pts] [Canterbury 1796].

The new whim of the night: or the town and country songster for 1797. [1796]. Stainer copy. *See* 1797, 1799, *below.*

The odd fellow's song book and merry medley, written, compiled and selected by Brother Funny Whimsy. 1796. Stainer copy.

The olio. 1796 (2nd edn). See 1792, above.

Pope, H. M. Williams, et al. Poems, moral, elegant and pathetic: Essay on man, Original sonnets. 1796.

The poetical monitor: consisting of pieces select and original. 1796. See 1798, below.

The polite jester: or theatre for wit, interspersed with a great variety of comic poetry. 1796. Sotheby, 26 April 1901.

The Rolliad, in two parts; probationary odes. Dublin 1796. McLeish, 1935. See 1795, above.

Scotish ballads and songs. Manchester 1796. Harding copy. See Ballads and songs, 1799, below.

A select collection of epigrams. Ed T. C. Rickman 1796.

A select collection of new, favourite and popular songs, by the most celebrated composers. [1796?]. Stainer copy.

Sheridan's and Henderson's practical method of reading English poetry, elucidated by examples. 1796.

Songs, descriptive, moral and pastoral: humourous. [Ed G. Nicholson], Manchester 1796. See 1799, above.

Songs: elegiac, sea. [Ed G. Nicholson], Manchester 1796. Harding copy. See 1799, below.

The songster's companion. Coventry [1796?] (9th edn). Stainer copy. See 1788, above.

The spouter's new guide: containing all the modern prologues and epilogues. Ed W. Henderson 1796. No known copy; see R. W. Lowe, A bibliographical account of English theatrical literature, 1888.

Thoughts on a future state, occasioned by the death of Mrs H. A. Rogers. Bristol 1796. Hill, 1967.

The Union. Oxford 1796 (new edn). See 1753, above.

The whim of the day for 1796. [1796]. Harding copy. See 1790, above.

The whole of the chapters, songs, circulated during the late election for Hull. Hull 1796.

1797

Apollo's lyre: being a selection of songs. Huddersfield [1797?]. Harding copy. Pp. 120, in 3 pts. See 1798, below, and 1793, above.

The bee: a selection of poetry from the best authors. 1797 (new edn). See 1793, above.

The Berkshire repository for original, fugitive, selected and miscellaneous pieces: poetry. Vol 1, Maidenhead 1797.

The buck's pocket companion or the merry fellow: a choice collection of songs. [1797?] (new edn). Harding copy.

The cabinet of genius. 1797. Book-auction records, 1915–16. See 1787, above.

The cabinet of wit: containing droll and merry stories in prose and verse. 1797.

The cheerful companion in his hours of leisure, containing upwards of two hundred songs. Ed G. Cunningham, Bath 1797.

The children's miscellany. 1797 (new edn). Pickering & Chatto, 1932. See 1790, above.

A choice selection of favourite new songs. 1797. Sotheby, 29 April 1891. See 1798, below.

A classical arrangement of fugitive poetry. Vol 17, 1797. Also reprint of vol 16; see 1796, above.

A collection of poems on religious and moral subjects, extracted from the most celebrated authors. Elizabeth-Town USA 1797.

Comic conviviality: or Dighton's drops to drown dullness, containing favorite songs. [1797]. Harding copy.

Concerts of antient music. 1797. See 1780, above.

The convivial companion: or the delights of harmony. [1797?] (new edn). Stainer copy.

Dibdin's charms of melody: a new collection of songs. Dublin 1797. Harding copy.

English lyricks. Liverpool 1797.

The famous English archer: or Robert, Earl of Huntingdon, commonly called Robin Hood. Monaghan 1797. Harding copy. See 1663, above.

The flowers of harmony. Ed G. Walker 4 vols [1797?].

Fugitive pieces: a collection of original poems by the most eminent writers. Edinburgh 1797. McLeish, 1929.

The gentleman's miscellany: consisting of essays, characters, poems: first American edition. Exeter 1797. See 1795, above.

The hive: or the songster's miscellany. Southampton [1797?] (4th edn). Harding copy.

Interesting anecdotes and poetical fragments. Ed 'Mr Addison', vols 5–16, 1797. Vols 5–9 are rptd from 1794–5 edns.

Jachin and Boaz: or an authentic key to Free-Masonry, containing anthems, odes, songs. 1767 (new edn). See 1767, above.

The lady's miscellany. Boston 1797. See 1793, above.

Laugh and grow fat: or a cure for melancholy. 1797. Harvard copy.

Masonic miscellanies in poetry and prose. Ed S. Jones 1797.

Mental amusement, consisting of moral essays, with poetical pieces by different writers. 1797. Pickering & Chatto, 1933. See 1798, below.

The musical banquet of choice songs. Glasgow [1797?]. Harding copy.

The new whim of the night: or songster for 1798. [1797]. No known copy. See 1796, above.

The Parnassian garland, forming the poetry of the monthly visitor. Vols 1–2, 1797.

Pieces on the subjects of love and marriage: verse. [Ed G. Nicholson], Manchester 1797.

Coleridge, S. T. Poems, second edition; to which are now added poems by Charles Lamb and Charles Lloyd. 1797.

Poems intended to promote piety and virtue. Ed R. Barclay 1797 (2nd edn). See 1795, above.

Preceptive, moral and sentimental pieces. [Ed G. Nicholson], Manchester 1797.

The Scots musical museum. Vol 5, Edinburgh [1797]. 2 issues as in 1787. Vol 6, 1803. Set rptd, with notes by W. Stenhouse, 6 vols Edinburgh 1839; ed D. Laing 4 vols Edinburgh 1853.

Select epigrams, in two volumes. 1797.

Select lessons in prose and verse. Bath 1797. See 1765, above.

A selection of favourite catches, glees, as sung at the Harmonic Society, Bath. Bath 1797. See 1799, below.

The selector: being a collection of visions, tales and allegories. 1797.

The songs, trios, glees, as sung this season at Vauxhall. 1797.

The syren. 5 pts Wilmington [1797?]. Harvard copy.

The vocal magazine, containing a selection of English, Scots and Irish songs. Vol 1, Edinburgh 1797 See 1798, 1799, below.

The vocal miscellany of Great Britain and Ireland: or Union song book. Berwick 1797. Harding copy. A reissue of Union song-book, 1781, above.

The well-bred scholar: or practical essays. Ed W. Milns, New York 1797. Vol 1 of Columbian Library, 1797–8.

The whim of the day for 1797. [1797]. Harding copy. See 1790, above.

Yorick turned trimmer: or the gentleman's jester. [1797?]. Sotheby, 26 April 1901. See 1770, above.

1798

The American musical miscellany: a collection of the newest songs. Northampton Mass 1798.

Apollo's lyre: being a selection of songs. Huddersfield [1798?]. Harding copy. Pp. 144; not in pts. See 1797, above.

An asylum for fugitive pieces. Vol 4, 1798 (new edn). *See* 1785, *above*.

Banquet of Thalia. 1798. Whitehead, 13 May 1890. *See* 1788, *above*.

The British songster: or pocket companion. 1798. Harding copy. *See* 1791, *above*.

The buck's delight: or pills to purge melancholy for 1798. [1798]. Stainer copy. *See* 1799, *below*.

The cherub: or vocal miscellany. [1798]. Harding copy.

A choice selection of favourite new songs. [1798?]. Stainer copy. *See* 1797, *above*.

A collection of loyal songs, as sung at all the Orange Lodges in Ireland. Dublin 1798. Harding copy.

Concerts of antient music. 1798. *See* 1780, *above*.

Dramatic dialogues for the use of schools. Ed C. Stearns, Leominster Mass 1798.

Elegies. [Ed G. Nicholson], Manchester 1798.

Every lady's own Valentine writer, in prose and verse, for 1798. [1798]. *See* 1794, *above*.

Extracts from the works of the most celebrated Italian poets, with translations by admired English authors. 1798.

The Free Mason's pocket companion: being a choice collection of Masonic songs. Glasgow 1798. Harding copy. *See* A pocket companion, 1735, *above*.

Hilaria: the festive board. 1798. At least 3 hands in this.

Campbell, A. An introduction to the history of poetry in Scotland; to which are subjoined sangs of the Lowlands of Scotland. 2 pts Edinburgh 1798–9.

The Irish harp attun'd to freedom: a collection of patriotic songs selected for Paddy's amusement. Dublin 1798. Stainer copy.

Jemmy Twitcher's jests. Ed D. Gunston, Glasgow 1798. Book-prices current, 1910. *See* 1770, *above*.

The melodist or chearful songster: a select collection. 1798. Stainer copy.

Mental amusement: or the juvenile moralist, interspersed with poetical pieces. [1798] (2nd edn), 1798 (3rd edn). *See* 1797, *above*.

A miscellaneous collection of songs, ballads and elegies, in two vols. [1798]. Ellis, 1909. *See* 1796, *above*.

Monstrous droll songs, including those sung at Drury-Lane. [1798]. Stainer copy. *See* 1796, *above*.

Monstrous good songs, 1798. [1798]. Harding copy. *See* 1793, *above*.

The new British songster: or a complete vocal pocket companion. Manchester [1798?]. Harding copy. *See* 1785, *above*.

The new spouters companion: or a selection of prologues and epilogues. [1798?].

The new syren: or the Suffolk, Norfolk, Cambridge and Essex song-book for the year 1799. Bury [1798]. Dobell, 1918.

The nightingale: a choice collection of favourite songs. Bath [1798?]. Stainer copy. *See* 1738, *above*.

Paddy's resource: or the harp of Erin attuned to freedom. Dublin 1798. Harding copy.

The pleasing companion: or guide to fame. 1798.

Poetical beauties of modern writers. 1798 (Hill, 1950), 1803 (2nd edn). Verses by Coleridge, Burns.

The poetical monitor. 1798 (2nd edn). *See* 1796, *above*.

The poetry of various glees, songs, as performed at the Harmonists. Ed. G. Fryer 1798.

Select lessons in prose and verse. Tamworth 1798 (5th edn), Bristol 1798 (6th edn), Bristol 1798 (7th edn). *See* 1765, *above*.

A selection of fables from the best English writers. New York 1798. Vol 2 of Columbian library, 1797–8.

A selection of Masonic songs, arranged and dedicated to the Brethren. Ed S. Holden, Dublin [1798?]. Stainer copy. *See* 1765, *above*.

Song book for 1798: the Winchester syren. Winchester [1798]. Harding copy.

The songster's companion. Coventry [1798] (10th edn). Harding copy. *See* 1788, *above*.

The town and country songster's companion: containing the newest songs. [1798?]. Harding copy.

The vocal magazine. Vol 2, Edinburgh 1798. *See* 1797, *above*.

The whim of the day for 1798. [1798]. Harding copy. *See* 1790, *above*.

1799

Amatory pieces. [Ed G. Nicholson], Ludlow 1799.

Ancient ballads, songs and poems. [Ed G. Nicholson], Ludlow 1799. *See* 1796, *above*.

The annual anthology. Ed R. Southey, vol 1, Bristol 1799. *See* 1800, *below*.

Apollonian harmony. Vols 1–6. [1799?]. Harding copy. Ptd at Henry Thompson's warehouse. *See* 1790, *above*.

An asylum for fugitive pieces. Vol 3, 1799. Hill, 1949. *See* 1785, *above*.

Ballads and songs: Scotish. [Ed G. Nicholson] Ludlow 1799. *See* Scotish ballads, 1796, *above*.

The beauties of the Anti-Jacobin: or weekly examiner. 1799.

The beauties of the poets. 1799 (6th edn). *See* 1773, *above*.

The British songster: or pocket companion. 1799. Harding copy. *See* 1791, *above*.

Buck's delight: or merry fellow's companion. 1799. Sotheby, 26 April 1901.

Buck's delight: or pills to purge melancholy for 1799. [1799]. Harding copy. *See* 1798, *above*.

A collection of constitutional songs. Cork 1799. Harding copy. *See* 1800, *below*.

A collection of songs, selected from the works of Dibdin; to which is added American patriotic songs. Philadelphia 1799. Harding copy.

The Columbian songster: being a large collection of fashionable songs. 1799.

Concerts of antient music. 1799. *See* 1780, *above*.

Constitutional songs. [Dublin 1799]. Harding copy.

The hive of modern literature: a collection of essays, narratives, allegories. Newcastle 1799. *See* 1800, *below*.

The laughing philosopher's legacy to dull mortals. [c. 1799]. Harding copy.

The literary miscellany: or selections and extracts in prose and verse. [Ed G. Nicholson], Ludlow 1799. A title-page, varying in date and place, affixed to varying collections of small books of different dates by the same publisher, Nicholson. For these, *see* 1795–1800.

The London musical museum: a select collection of Scots, English and Irish songs. Glasgow 1799. Harding copy.

The London songster: or vocal companion. 1799. Harding copy.

Monstrous droll songs for the year 1799. [1799]. Sotheby, 26 June 1903. *See* 1796, *above*.

Monstrous good songs, toasts and sentiments, 1799. [1799] (Harding copy); Second edition of songs, toasts and sentiments, 1799. [1799] (Harding copy). *See* 1793, *above*.

The musical bouquét: or popular songs and ballads composed by Edward Jones. [1799].

The musical repository: a collection of Scotch, English and Irish songs. Glasgow 1799. Nat Lib of Ireland has 2 issues, one possibly unique.

The new whim of the night for 1800. [1799]. R. H. Lonsdale copy. *See* 1796, *above*.

Ovid's Art of love; Court of love; and History of love. 1799. Book-auction records, 1902–3. *See* 1709, *above*.

The patriotic songster or loyalist's vocal companion: being constitutional and loyal songs. Kidderminster [1799] (new edn). Stainer copy.

The pleasing companion. Congleton [c. 1799]. Harding copy. No connection with 1798 vol of same title.

Poetical prolusions in the English and Latin languages. Berkhamsted 1799 (2nd edn, enlarged). *See* Musae, 1794, *above*.

Poetry of the Anti-Jacobin. 1799. *See* 1800, *below*.

The polyhymnia: poetry, original and selected, by a society of gentlemen. Glasgow [1799]. Mitchell Lib, Glasgow, copy.

The president's guide: or the club room companion, containing a collection of songs. Ed M. Winston [1799?] (2nd edn). Harding copy.

Prologues and epilogues, written for the L.D.T. on various occasions. 1797–8–9. Oxford [1799?].

Robin Hood's garland: being a complete history of all the notable exploits. Whitchurch 1799. See 1663, above.

Richardson, J. et al. The Rolliad: probationary odes and political eclogues. 1799 (21st edn). See 1795, above.

The sacred oratorios, as set by Handel. Pts 1–2, 1799; Pt 2: The miscellaneous pieces. Words only.

Sangs of the Lowlands of Scotland. Edinburgh 1799. Harding copy.

Selection of favourite catches, glees, as sung at the Bath Harmonic Society. 1799. Harding copy. See 1797, above.

Songs, descriptive, moral and pastoral: humourous. Ludlow 1799. See 1796, above.

Songs: elegiac, sea. Ludlow 1799. See 1796, above.

The songster's companion. Coventry [1799?] (12th edn). Harding copy. See 1788, above.

The speaker: or miscellaneous pieces. 1799. See 1774, above.

The vocal magazine: containing a selection of English, Scots and Irish songs. Vols 1–2, Edinburgh 1799.

The vocal magazine. Vols 3–4, Edinburgh 1799. Harding copy. See 1797, above.

The whim of the day for 1799. [1799]. Harding copy. See 1790, above.

The whimsical songster or food for all palates: being an entire new selection of songs now singing. Manchester [1799?]. Stainer copy.

Pope, A. Windsor forest, with the French translation by Viel de Boisjolin. 1799.

1800

Ahiman rezon. 1800. See 1756, above.

Amatory poems, selected from many literary characters. 1800. Sotheby, 23 April 1891.

Amusement for the ladies: being a selection of the most favourite catches, canons, glees and madrigals. 3 vols [c. 1800]. Ptd by Broderip and Wilkinson. See 1780, above.

The annual anthology. Vol 2, Bristol 1800. See 1799, above.

Apollonian harmony. 2 vols [1800?]. Pbd at Thompson's Music Warehouse. See 1795, above.

Bath Harmonic Society: glees, catches, duets, to be performed at the Lower Assembly Rooms. 1800. Harding copy.

The beauties of the poets. [1800?]. Later edns in 1806, 1810. See 1773, above.

Britannia's delight: a collection of patriotic, loyal and entertaining songs. Oswestry [1800?]. Harding copy.

The British Muse: a choice collection of English, Scotch and Irish songs. Morpeth [1800?]. Harding copy.

The British poetical miscellany. Pts 1–30, Huddersfield [1800?]. Issues with one name in imprint, and with 8.

The British songster: or the pocket companion. 1800. Harding copy. Contents differ from previous edns; see 1791, above.

Chalmeriana: or a collection of papers reprinted from the Morning Chronicle. Ed 'Owen Junior' and 'Jasper Hargrave' 1800. Some copies have Collection the first on title-page.

A collection of constitutional songs. Vol 2, Cork 1800. Harding copy. See 1799, above.

A collection of favorite glees, catches and rounds, presented by the candidates for the premiums, 1800. Harding copy.

A collection of papers, all the favourite songs and satirical

poems, published [during Durham election] in March, 1800. Durham [1800].

Concerts of antient music. 1800. See 1780, above. BM ser continues to 1848.

The contest: being a collection of the papers, including poems and songs, published [during Durham election] in March, 1800. Durham [1800].

Convivial harmony: or wit and humour blended with sentiment and honour. Edinburgh [1800?]. Stainer copy.

The convivial jester: or bane of melancholy. Ed 'Godfrey Broadgrin' [1800] (2nd edn). Harding copy. See 1790, above.

Wilmot, J. The dictionary of love. [1800?].

The dramatic budget or olio of fancy: being a choice collection of scenes; to which are added prologues, epilogues. 1800. Anderson, 19 May 1912.

Essays in prose and verse, partly collected and partly original. [1800?].

The festival of humour: or banquet of wit. 1800.

The festival of mirth, consisting of stories and anecdotes. 1800.

The festival of Momus: a collection of comic songs. [1800] (new edn). Stainer copy. Pp. 282 + index and toasts. See 1786, above.

The festival of wit. 1800 (17th edn, with addns). See 1782, above.

The frisky songster: or merry fellows companion. Glasgow [1800?] (Harding copy), [1800?]. Caption title: Or Caledonian chanter; a different collection from above. Harding copy.

Gammer Gurton's garland: or the nursery Parnassus. Ed Ritson, Stockton [1800?]; rptd with addns, 1810.

Burns, R., G. A. Stevens, J. Wilmot et al. The giblet pie: being the heads, tails and wings of Anacreontic songs. Shamborough [1800?]. Harding copy.

The Glasgow miscellany: or amusing companion. Vol 2, Glasgow 1800. No known copy of vol 1.

The goldfinch: being a collection of the most esteemed modern songs. 1800 (Stainer copy), 1803. See 1748, above.

The hive of modern literature: a collection of essays, narratives, allegories. Newcastle [1800?]. See 1799, above.

Joke upon joke: or the last packet from the land of festivity and mirth. 1800. Harding copy.

The jovial companion: being an entire new collection of songs. [1800?].

Jovial sailor's chearful companion for the year 1800: containing an elegant selection of sea songs. [1800]. Stainer copy.

The leisure hour improved: consisting of a variety of interesting subjects, in prose and verse. Newbury [1800?].

The lively jester or complete museum of fun: being a collection of jests, epigrams, epitaphs. [1800?].

Love's repository: or a new collection of Valentines, selected from the best British poets. 1800.

The meteors. Vols 1–2, 1800. Six nos to each vol pbd in book form; nos 1–3 are dated 1799.

Miscellanies, moral and instructive, in prose and verse; for the use of schools. Philadelphia [1800?] (new edn, with addns.) See 1787, above.

Momus's cabinet of amusement: the new encyclopaedia or world of wit. [1800?].

The Muses pocket companion: a collection of poems by the most eminent modern authors. Dublin [1800?]. See 1782, above.

Museum of wit: being a choice collection of poetical pieces. 1800. Book-prices current, 1914.

The musical banquet: or buck's delight. Glasgow [1800?]. Harding copy.

The musical olio: or songster's companion. Penrith [1800?] (Stainer copy), [1800?] (2nd edn) (Harding copy).

Musical relicks of the Welsh bards. Ed E. Jones. Dublin [1800?] (new edn); Part the second, 1800 (2nd edn). *See* 1784, *above*.

The musical repository. Edinburgh [c. 1800]. Mitchell Lib Glasgow copy. *See* 1799, *above*.

The myrtle and vine: or complete vocal library: containing several thousands of songs. Ed C. H. Wilson, vols 1–2, 1800; vols 3–4, 1801.

The naval songster: or Jack Tar's chest of conviviality for 1800. [1800]. Sotheby, 30 April 1890.

The new general songster: or social companion. North Shields [1800?].

Johnston, W. A new introduction to Enfield's Speaker. 1800.

The new London and country jester. Ed P. Cunningham [1800?]. Harding copy.

The new school of love. Glasgow [1800?]. *See* 1786, *above*.

The new spouter's companion: or a choice collection of prologues and epilogues. [1800?] (new edn). Rev Mr Palmer.

The new theatrical songster, containing comic songs. [1800?]. Harding copy.

Odes. [Ed G. Nicholson], Ludlow 1800.

Pocock's everlasting songster. Gravesend 1800. Harding copy.

Poems on various subjects. Ed E. Tomkins, Oxford 1800 (new edn). *See* 1782. Later edns in 1804, 1806.

Poetry of the Anti-Jacobin. 1800 (2nd edn), 1801 (4th edn), ed C. Edmonds 1852, 1854, 1890; another edn, 1890; ed L. Rice-Oxley 1924. *See* 1799, *above*.

Poetry, original and selected. Glasgow [1800?].

The polite songster for the year 1800. Bury [1800]. Dobell, 1918.

Revived: the delicate jester, or wit and humour without ribaldry. [1800?]. *See* 1780, *above*.

The rural songster: a collection of popular English songs. Edinburgh [1800?]. Stainer copy.

The shamrock: or the Hibernian songster. Edinburgh [1800?]. Harding copy.

The skylark: being an elegant collection of the best and newest songs in the English language. [1800]. *See* 1791, *above*.

Social harmony: being a choice collection of catches, glees, songs. Ed R. Willoughby 2 vols [1800?].

The social magazine or cabinet of wit: being a complete repository of epigrams. [1800]. Anderson, 19 May 1912.

The songster for the year 1800. Chippenham [1800]. Stainer copy.

The songster's companion. Coventry [1800?] (13th edn). Harding copy. *See* 1788, *above*.

The songster's companion: being a collection of the most favourite songs sung this season. [1800?]. No connection with the above.

The songster's favourite companion: a collection of new and much-esteemed songs. Glasgow [1800?]. Also a London edn, c. 1800; both, Harding copies.

The songster's miscellany: or vocal companion. Kidderminster [1800?] (7th edn). *See* 1790, *above*.

A tribute to liberty: or a collection of select songs. [c. 1800]. Pickering & Chatto, 1937. *See* 1793, *above*.

Tom Smart's new comical jester, the first part. Worcester [1800?].

The whim of the day for 1800. [1800]. Harding copy. *See* 1790, *above*.

The works of Rochester, Roscommon, Dorset, Devonshire, Buckinghamshire, in two volumes. [c. 1800]. Also a late eighteenth-century edn, nd, with spelling Roscomon. *See* 1707, *above*.

The Yorkshire musical miscellany: comprising an elegant selection of the most admired songs. Halifax 1800.

(2) LATER ANTHOLOGIES AND SELECTIONS

This list is limited to anthologies pbd since 1800 which either are specifically concerned with poetry written between 1660 and 1800 or mainly devoted to it. The arrangement below is chronological, except that it has sometimes seemed more useful to group an author's works under the date of his first pbn.

Mavor, W. and S. J. Pratt. Classical English poetry. 1801 etc.

[Riddell, M.] The metrical miscellany: consisting chiefly of poems hitherto unpublished. 1802.

Scotish descriptive poems. Ed J. Leyden, Edinburgh 1803.

The British Martial: or an anthology of English epigrams. 2 vols 1806.

The Caledonian musical repository. 1806. *See below*, 1811.

Jamieson, R. Popular ballads and songs. 2 vols Edinburgh 1806.

A select collection of songs. Newcastle 1806.

Southey, R. Specimens of the later English poets. 3 vols 1807.

Pratt, S. J. The cabinet of poetry: containing the best entire pieces of the British poets. 6 vols 1808.

The Muses' bower, embellished with the beauties of English poetry. 3 vols 1809.

Specimens of the British poets from Lord Surrey to Cowper. 2 vols 1809.

Select British poets: containing the entire works of Milton, Young, Thomson, Gray and Pope's Iliad and Odyssey [with Johnson's Lives]. 8 pts 1810 [1808–10].

Cromek, R. H. Select Scottish songs, ancient and modern. 2 vols 1810.

English minstrelsy: being a selection from the best English authors. 2 vols Edinburgh 1810.

The English musical repository. Edinburgh [1810?].

The Caledonian musical repository. Edinburgh 1811. Not the same as the 1806 collection, above.

Poetical selections: consisting of the most approved pieces of our best modern British poets. Birmingham 1812 (new edn).

Clifford, A. Tixall poetry. Edinburgh 1813.

Lofft, C. Laura: or an anthology of sonnets. 5 vols 1813–14.

Pieces of ancient poetry, from unpublished manuscripts and scarce books. Ed John Fry, Bristol 1814.

Gilchrist, J. A collection of ancient and modern Scottish ballads, tales and songs. 2 vols Edinburgh 1815.

The wreath, containing the Minstrel and other favourite poems. 1806 etc.

The Suffolk garland: or a collection of poems, songs, tales relative to that county. Ipswich 1818.

Campbell, T. Specimens of the British poets. Vols 3–7, 1819, 1 vol 1841.

Hogg, James. The Jacobite relics of Scotland. 2 vols Edinburgh 1819–21, Paisley 1874.

Aikin, J. Select works of the British poets; with biographical and critical prefaces. 1820; ed L. Aikin 1845.

Ritson, J. The Caledonian muse. 1821. Ptd 1785, but not pbd till 1821.

Bullar, J. Selections from the British poets. 1822.

Davenport, R. A. New elegant extracts from the most eminent British poets. 6 vols Chiswick 1823–7.

Campbell, F. Beauties of the British poets. 2 vols 1824.

Hazlitt, W. Select British poets, Chaucer to the present time. 1824 (suppressed).

— Select poets of Great Britain. 1825.

Maidment, J. A north countrie garland. Edinburgh 1824 (anon); ed T. G. Stevenson, Edinburgh 1868; ed E. Goldsmid, Edinburgh 1884.

—— A book of Scotish pasquils [A 2nd, a 3rd]. Edinburgh 1827–8, 1868 (enlarged).
—— Scotish elegiac verses. 1629–1729. Edinburgh 1842. Anon.
—— A new book of old ballads. Edinburgh 1844 (anon); ed T. G. Stevenson, Edinburgh 1868; ed E. Goldsmid, Edinburgh 1885.
—— Scotish ballads and songs. Edinburgh 1859.
—— A packet of pestilent pasquils. Edinburgh [1868].
Buchan, P. Gleanings of Scotch, English and Irish, scarce old ballads. Peterhead 1825.
—— Ancient ballads and songs of the North of Scotland. 2 vols Edinburgh 1828, Edinburgh 1875.
Cunningham, A. The songs of Scotland, ancient and modern. 4 vols 1825.
Dyce, A. Specimens of British poetesses. 1825, 1827.
Plumptre, J. One hundred fables in verse by various authors. 1825.
Chambers, R. The Scottish songs. 2 vols Edinburgh 1829.
—— The songs of Scotland prior to Burns. Edinburgh 1862, 1873, 1880, 1890.
Jacobite minstrelsy from 1640 to 1784. Ed R. Malcolm, Glasgow 1829.
[Sharp, C.] The bishoprick garland: or a collection of legends, songs, ballads, belonging to the county of Durham. 1834, Sunderland 1906.
Selections from the English poets, from Spenser to Beattie. 1835.
The songs of England and Scotland. 2 vols 1835.
Chappell, W. A collection of national English airs. 2 vols 1838–40.
—— Popular music of the olden time. 2 vols [1855–9]. Also issued as The ballad literature and popular music of the olden time (a rev and enlarged edn of National English airs).
—— The Roxburghe ballads. Vols 1–3, 1869–80 (Ballad Soc).
—— Old English popular music. Ed and rev H. E. Wooldridge 2 vols 1893.
The contemporaries of Burns, and the more recent poets of Ayrshire, with selections. Ed J. Paterson, Edinburgh 1840.
Croker, T. C. The historical songs of Ireland. 1841 (Percy Soc vol 1).
—— Popular songs, illustrative of the French invasions of Ireland. 1845–7 (Percy Soc vol 21).
Halliwell[-Phillipps], J. O. The early naval ballads of England. 1841 (Percy Soc vol 2).
Rimbault, E. F. Old ballads illustrating the Great Frost of 1683–4. 1844 (Percy Soc vol 9).
Whitelaw, A. The book of Scottish song. Glasgow 1844, 1857, [1867], 1875.
Fairholt, F. W. The civic garland: a collection of songs from London pageants. 1845 (Percy Soc vol 19).
—— Satirical songs and poems on costume. 1849 (Percy Soc vol 27).
Dixon, J. H. Ancient poems, ballads and songs of the peasantry of England. 1846 (Percy Soc vol 17); ed R. Bell 1857 (rev and enlarged) as Ballads and songs of the peasantry of England.
Sandys, W. Festive songs, principally of the sixteenth and seventeenth centuries. 1848 (Percy Soc vol 23).
Bell, R. Songs from the dramatists. 1854, 1855.
Wilkins, W. W. Political ballads of the seventeenth and eighteenth centuries. 2 vols 1860.
Mackay, C. The Jacobite songs and ballads of Scotland from 1688 to 1746. 1861.
—— The Cavalier songs and ballads of England from 1642 to 1684. 1863.
Harland, J. Ballads and songs of Lancashire chiefly older than the 19th century. Edinburgh 1865; ed T. T. Wilkinson 1875 (rev and enlarged).
Poetic voices of the eighteenth century: comprising the poems of Gray, Beattie, Blair, Collins, Thomson, Kirke White, complete. 1866.

Stevenson, T. G. Four books of choice old Scottish ballads 1823–44. Edinburgh 1868.
Jacobite songs of Scotland, chronologically arranged, with notes. Glasgow 1871.
Ebsworth, J. W. The Bagford ballads, illustrating the last years of the Stuarts. 4 pts 1876–8 (Ballad Soc).
—— The Amanda group of Bagford poems [c. 1688]. 1880 (Ballad Soc).
—— The Roxburghe ballads, illustrating the last years of the Stuarts. Vols 4–8, 1883–95 (Ballad Soc).
Ward, T. H. The English poets: selections. Vols 2–3, 1880, 1883–4 (2nd edn). Ben Jonson to Blake.
English lyrics [Wyatt to Beddoes]. 1883.
Goldsmid, E. Bibliotheca curiosa: some political satires of the seventeenth century. 2 vols Edinburgh 1885.
Macquoid, G. S. Jacobite songs and ballads. 1887, 1888.
Bullen, A. H. Musa proterva: love-poems of the Restoration. 1889 (priv ptd), 1895, 1902, [1922].
—— Speculum amantis: love poems of the seventeenth century. 1889 (priv ptd), 1895, 1902, [1922].
Dircks, W. H. Cavalier and courtier lyrists: an anthology of seventeenth-century minor verse. [1891].
Douglas, G. Poems of the Scottish minor poets [Ramsay to David Gray]. [1891].
Saintsbury, G. Political verse. 1891.
—— Seventeenth-century lyrics. 1892, 1893, [1900].
Caine, R. H. Love songs of English poets 1500–1800. 1892.
Greig, J. Scots minstrelsie: a national monument of Scottish song. 6 vols Edinburgh [1892–5].
The songs of Scotland chronologically arranged. 1893 (3rd edn).
Baring-Gould S. English minstrelsie. 8 vols Edinburgh 1895–7.
Eyre-Todd, G. Scottish poetry of the eighteenth century. 2 vols Glasgow 1896.
Farmer, J. S. Musa pedestris: three centuries of canting songs [1536–1896] 1896.
—— National ballad and song; Merry songs and ballads prior to the year 1800. 5 vols 1897 (priv ptd).
Schelling, F. E. A book of 17th century lyrics. Boston 1899.
Arber, E. The Dryden anthology [1675–1700]. 1899; The Pope anthology [1701–44], 1899; The Goldsmith anthology [1745–74], 1900; The Cowper anthology [1775–1800], 1901. General title: British anthologies; reissued 1901, with plates, as Selections from the English poets.
Austin, A. An eighteenth-century anthology. [1904], [1924].
Hecht, Hans. Songs from David Herd's manuscripts. Edinburgh 1904.
Meynell, A. A seventeenth-century anthology. [1904].
Masefield, J. and C. Lyrists of the Restoration. 1905, 1908.
Songs and Lyrics from the dramatists 1533–1777. 1905.
Bronson, W. C. The Restoration and eighteenth century. Vol 3 of his English poems, Chicago 1908 etc.
Braithwaite, W. S. The book of Restoration verse. 1909, [1925].
—— The book of Georgian verse. 1909.
Firth, C. H. An American garland: ballads relating to America 1563–1759. Oxford 1915.
Roth, H. L. and J. T. Jolley. War ballads and broadsides of previous wars 1779–95. Bankfield Museum Notes (Halifax) 1915.
Percival, M. Political ballads illustrating the administration of Sir Robert Walpole. Oxford 1916.
Bernbaum, E. English poets of the eighteenth century. New York [c. 1918].
Loane, G. G. Longer narrative poems: eighteenth century. 1921.
Saintsbury, G. Minor poets of the Caroline period vol 3. Oxford 1921. Cleveland, King, Stanley, Flatman and Whiting.

Thorn–Drury, G. A little ark containing sundry pieces of seventeenth-century verse. 1921.

Williams, I. A. By-ways round Helicon. 1922.

—— The shorter poems of the eighteenth century. 1923.

Ingpen, R. A choice of the best English lyrics: eighteenth century. [1923].

Austen, J. Rogues in porcelain: a miscellany of eighteenth-century poems. 1924.

Doughty, O. Forgotten lyrics of the eighteenth century. 1924.

Prescott, F. C. and J. H. Nelson. Prose and poetry of the Revolution. New York 1925.

Barnes, A. G. A book of English verse satire. 1926.

Brotanek, K. Beschreibung der HS. 14090 (Suppl 1776) der Nationalbibliothek in Wien. Festschrift der Nationalbibliothek in Wien, Vienna 1926. On c. 1670–90.

Campbell, K. W. Poems on several occasions: eighteenth century. Oxford 1926.

—— An anthology of English poetry: Dryden to Blake. [1930], New York 1930.

Old English love songs and madrigals [before 1699]. 1926.

Scott, H. English song book. New York 1926. Words and music of eighteenth and nineteenth-century popular songs.

Smith, D. N. The Oxford book of eighteenth-century verse. Oxford 1926 etc.

Duncan, E. Lyrics from the old song books. 1927.

Judson, A. C. Seventeenth-century lyrics. Chicago 1927.

Rollins, H. E. The pack of Autolycus 1624–93. Cambridge Mass 1927.

—— The Pepys ballads vols 3–7. Cambridge Mass 1930–1. Ballads of 1666–1702.

Ault, N. Seventeenth-century lyrics from the original texts. 1928, New York 1950.

—— A treasury of unfamiliar lyrics. 1938.

Draper, J. W. A century of broadside elegies. 1928.

Bernbaum, E. Selections from the pre-romantic movement. Vol 2 of his Anthology of romanticism, New York 1929.

Blickensderfer, J. P. The eighteenth century. New York 1929.

Clark, E. M. The seventeenth century. New York 1929.

Irving, W. H. John Gay's London illustrated from the poetry of the time [1685–1732]. Cambridge Mass 1929.

Jones, R. F. Seventeenth-century literature. New York 1929.

—— Eighteenth-century literature. New York 1929.

Fausset, H. I'A. Minor poets of the eighteenth century [Winchilsea, Parnell, Green, Dyer and Collins]. [1930] (EL).

Fawcett, F. B. Broadside ballads of the Restoration period. 1930.

Kerr, W. Restoration verse 1660–1715. 1930.

Masefield, J. and C. Lyrists of the Restoration: Sherbourne to Congreve. 1930.

Peacock, W. English verse vol 3. 1930. Dryden to Wordsworth.

Sitwell, E. The pleasures of poetry. Ser 1, 1930. Milton and the Augustan age.

Winslow, O. E. American broadside verse from imprints of the 17th and 18th centuries. New Haven 1930.

Turner, W. J. Eighteenth-century poetry: an anthology. [1931].

Wood, F. T. An anthology of Augustan poetry 1700–51. 1931.

Crane, R. S. A collection of English poems 1660–1800. New York 1932. Notes for, by Crane and H. W. Taylor, New York 1937.

Boulton, H. Prince Charlie in song. [1933].

Quennell, P. C. Aspects of seventeenth-century verse. [1933], 1947 (rev).

Tupper, J. W. English poems from Dryden to Blake. New York 1933.

Grierson, H. J. C. and G. Bullough. The Oxford book of seventeenth-century verse. Oxford 1934 etc.

Moore, C. A. Restoration literature: poetry and prose 1660–1700. New York 1934.

—— English poetry of the eighteenth century. New York 1935.

Needham, F. A collection of poems by several hands never before published. 1934. Contains Newcastle, Strode, Whitehall, Dryden, Shadwell, Rochester, Thornhill and S. Wesley jr.

Shepard, O. and P. S. Wood. English prose and poetry 1660–1800. Boston 1934.

Thorpe, W. Songs from the Restoration theatre. Princeton 1934.

Vines, S. Georgian satirists. 1934.

Ault, N. Pope's own miscellany: being a reprint of Poems on several occasions. 1935.

Brinkley, R. F. English poetry of the seventeenth century. New York 1936.

Kronenberger, L. An eighteenth-century miscellany. New York 1936.

Marshall, L. B. Rare poems of the seventeenth century. Cambridge 1936.

Martin, R. Les préromantiques anglais: choix traduit. Paris 1939.

Bredvold, L. I., A. D. McKillop and L. Whitney. Eighteenth-century poetry and prose. New York 1939, 1956 (rev).

Mendenhall, J. C. English literature 1650–1800. Philadelphia 1940.

Aubin, R. A. London in flames: London in glory: poems on the Fire and rebuilding of London 1666–1709. New Brunswick NJ 1943.

Betjeman, J. and G. Taylor. English, Scottish and Welsh landscape 1700–c. 1860. 1944.

Grigson, G. Before the Romantics: an anthology of the Enlightenment. 1946.

Witherspoon, A. M. and F. J. Warnke. Seventeenth-century prose and poetry. New York 1946, 1965 (rev).

Quennell, P. C. Aspects of seventeenth-century verse. 1947.

Sypher, W. Enlightened England: an anthology of eighteenth-century literature. New York 1947.

Hayward, J. Seventeenth-century poetry. 1948.

Stead, P. J. Songs of the Restoration theatre. 1948.

Auden, W. H. and N. H. Pearson. Poets of the English language. Vols 3–4, New York 1950, London 1952. Milton to Poe.

Hadfield, J. Georgian love songs. 1950.

—— Restoration love songs. 1950.

Gordon, I. A. Shenstone's Miscellany 1759–63. Oxford 1952. From ms.

White, H. C., R. C. Wallerstein and R. Quintana. Seventeenth-century verse and prose vol 2. New York 1952. Verse 1660–1700.

Angel, J. W. Selections from seventeenth-century songbooks. Los Angeles 1954. Byrd to Vanbrughe.

Hanford, J. H. A Restoration reader. Indianapolis 1954.

Pinto, V. de S. Restoration carnival: a biography-anthology of the Courtier Poets [Rochester, Dorset, Sedley, —— and A. E. Rodway. The common Muse. 1957. Etherege and Sheffield]. 1954.

Burrows, L. and D. Bradley. Charitable malice: a choice of Augustan satirical poetry. Nedlands 1955.

Brinton, C. The portable Age of Reason reader. New York 1956.

Cutts, J. P. and F. Kermode. Seventeenth-century songs. Reading 1956.

Davie, D. The late Augustans: longer poems of the later eighteenth century. 1958 etc.

Cutts, J. P. Seventeenth-century songs and lyrics. Columbia Missouri 1959. From music mss.

Brady, F. and M. Price. English prose and poetry 1660–1800. New York 1961.

Highet, G. Metamorphoses: translated into English verse under the direction of Sir Samuel Garth by John Dryden and others. New York 1961.

Mack, M. The Augustans. Englewood Cliffs NJ 1961.

McAleer, J. J. Ballads and songs loyal to the Hanoverian succession 1703–61. Los Angeles 1962.

Blunden, E. and B. Mellor. Wayside poems of the seventeenth century. Hong Kong 1963.

— Wayside poems of the early eighteenth century. Hong Kong 1964.

Lord, G. de F. et al. Poems on affairs of state: Augustan satirical verse 1660–1714. New Haven 1963–8: 1660–78, ed Lord; 1678–81, ed E. Mengel; 1682–85, ed H. H. Schless; 1685–88, ed G. M. Crump. 4 vols, in progress.

Martz, L. L. The meditative poem: an anthology of seventeenth-century verse. Garden City NY 1963.

Quintana, R. and A. Whitley. English poetry of the mid and late eighteenth century: an historical anthology. New York 1963.

Spacks, P. M. Eighteenth-century poetry. Englewood Cliffs NJ 1964.

Sutherland, J. Early eighteenth-century poetry. 1965.

Ehrenpreis, A. H. The literary ballad. 1966.

Kinsley, J. and J. T. Boulton. English satiric poetry: Dryden to Byron. 1966.

Pinto, V. de Sola. Poetry of the Restoration 1653–1700. New York 1966.

Danielsson, B. and D. M. Vieth. The Gyldenstolpe manuscript miscellany of poems by John Wilmot, Earl of Rochester, and other Restoration authors. Stockholm 1967.

French, D. P. Minor English poets 1660–1780: a selection from Chalmers. New York 1967.

Peake, C. Poetry of the landscape and the night: two eighteenth-century traditions. 1967.

Starkman, M. K. Seventeenth-century English poetry. 2 vols New York 1967.

Jarrell, M. L. and W. Meredith. Eighteenth-century English minor poets. 1969.

Love, H. The Penguin book of Restoration verse. 1969.

Wardroper, J. Love and drollery. 1969.

(3) COLLECTIONS IN SERIES

This section is limited to those sers which contain the more or less complete works of the poets from 1660 to 1800, and were ostensibly produced under one editor. Series of multiple authorship (e.g. Aldine Poets) are noticed elsewhere under the names of the poets included.

The British poets. 44 vols Edinburgh 1773–6.

Bell's edition: the poets of Great Britain complete from Chaucer to Churchill. 109 vols Edinburgh 1776–83. Includes biographical and critical prefaces; Bell's 2nd edn began to be issued in 1783. See Bagster, below.

A collection of the English poets: containing the poetical works of Pope, Dryden, Swift, Prior, Gay, Shenston, Pomfret, Gray and Littleton, Thomson, Young. 20 vols Aberdeen 1776–7.

Johnson, S. The works of the English poets; with prefaces biographical and critical. 68 vols 1779–81, 75 vols 1790.

Anderson, Robert. The works of the British poets, with prefaces biographical and critical. Vols 1–13, Edinburgh

1792–5. Engraved title: A complete edition of the poets of Great Britain. Vol 14, 1807.

Cooke's pocket edition of select British poets. 48 [possibly more?] vols 1794–1805.

Park, T. The works of the British poets. 70 vols 1805–12. Sometimes called Sharpe's edition; rptd 36 vols 1828.

Bagster, S. The poets of Great Britain. 124 vols 1807. An enlarged rpt of Bell's edn.

Chalmers, A. The works of the English poets, from Chaucer to Cowper; the additional lives by Alexander Chalmers. 21 vols 1810. Includes ser ed Samuel Johnson 1779–81.

Sanford, E. and R. Walsh. The works of the British poets, with lives of the authors. 50 vols Philadelphia 1819–23.

The British poets. 100 vols Chiswick 1822. Lives by Johnson, S. W. Singer, R. A. Davenport et al.

Bell, Robert. The annotated edition of the English poets. 29 vols 1854–7. With memoirs.

J. A. V. C.

III. RESTORATION POETRY

SAMUEL BUTLER
1613–80

Bibliographies

Johnson, R. B. Bibliographical notes. In Poetical works vol 1, 1893, below.

Lamar, R. In Complete works vol 3, Cambridge 1928, below.

Thorson, J. D. The publication of Hudibras. PBSA 60 1966.

Wilders, J. In Hudibras, Oxford 1967, below.

Collections

Poetical works. Ed R. B. Johnson 2 vols 1893.

Complete works. 3 vols Cambridge 1905–28. Vol 1, Hudibras, ed A. R. Waller; vol 2, Characters and passages from notebooks, ed Waller; vol 3, Satires and miscellaneous poetry and prose, ed R. Lamar.

§ 1

Mola asinaria by William Prynne. 1659; rptd in Posthumous works, below.

The Lord Roos his answer to the Marquesse of Dorchester's letter. [1660]. See C. J. Hindle, TLS 21 March 1936.

Hudibras: the first part. 1663 (9 edns).

Hudibras: the second part. 1664, 1664.

To the memory of the most renowned Du-Vall. 1671; rptd in Posthumous works and Genuine remains, below.

Two letters, one from John Audland to William Prynne; the other, William Prynnes answer. 1672; rptd in Posthumous works and Genuine remains, below.

Hudibras: the first and second parts, corrected and amended with several additions and annotations. 1674, 1678.

Hudibras: the third and last part. 1678 (3 edns), 1679, 1680.

Cydippe her answer to Acontius. In Ovid's epistles, 1680; rptd in Poetical works, ed R. B. Johnson, above.

Mercurius Menippeus: the loyal satirist. 1682; rptd in Posthumous works, below, and Somers tracts vol 7, 1810.

Hudibras in three parts. 1684, 1704 (includes biography), 1710 (illustr), 1726 (illustr Hogarth); ed Z. Grey 2 vols Cambridge 1744; ed T. R. Nash 3 vols 1793; ed J. Wilders, Oxford 1967.

The plagiary exposed. 1691; rptd in The secret history of the Calves Head Club, 1705 (5th edn), Posthumous works, Genuine remains, below, and Somers tracts vol 4, 1748. Variously entitled A vindication of the royal martyr, The case of King Charles I truly stated and The character of King Charles I.

Posthumous works in prose and verse. 3 vols 1715-17, 1732, 1754. Spurious apart from works listed above, admitted to the canon by Lamar.

Genuine remains. Ed R. Thyer 2 vols 1759; vol 1 (enlarged), 1822, 1827.

§ 2

Pepys, S. In his Diary, ed H. B. Wheatley 10 vols 1893-9.
Aubrey, J. In his Brief lives, ed A. Clark 2 vols Oxford 1898.
à Wood, A. In his Athenae oxonienses, ed P. Bliss 4 vols 1813-20.
Dryden, J. Discourse concerning satire. In his Satires of Juvenalis translated, 1693.
Dennis, J. Preface. In Miscellanies in verse and prose, 1693.
[Astry, J.?] Life. Appended to Hudibras, 1704.
Johnson, S. In his Lives of the poets, 1779-81.
Hazlitt, W. In his English comic writers, 1819.
Craig, H. Hudibras part I and the politics of 1647. In J. M. Manly anniversary studies, Chicago 1923.
Lamar, R. Du nouveau sur l'auteur d'Hudibras. Revue Anglo-américaine 1 1924.
de Beer, E. S. The later life of Butler. RES 4 1928.
Curtiss, J. T. Butler's Sidrophel. PMLA 44 1929.
Bond, R. P. In his English burlesque poetry, Cambridge Mass 1932.
Gibson, D. In Seventeenth-century studies, ed R. Shafer, Princeton 1933.
Quintana, R. The Butler-Oxenden correspondence. MLN 48 1933.
—— Butler: a Restoration figure in a modern light. ELH 18 1951.
Hindle, C. J. A broadside by Butler. TLS 21 March 1936.
Richards, E. A. Hudibras in the burlesque tradition. New York 1937.
Brooks, H. F. Gift to Butler. TLS 6 July 1940.
Bentley, N. E. Butler abroad. MLN 60 1945.
—— Another Butler manuscript. MP 46 1948.
Allen, D. C. Donne, Butler and ? MLN 61 1946. Reply by N. E. Bentley, ibid.
Anderson, P. B. Anonymous critic of Milton: Richard Leigh? or Butler? SP 44 1947.
Bauer, J. Verse fragments and prose characters not included in complete works. MP 45 1948.
Jack, I. In his Augustan satire, Oxford 1952.
Leyburn, E. D. Hudibras considered as satiric allegory. HLQ 16 1953.
Ker, W. P. In his On modern literature, Oxford 1955.
Granger, B. I. Hudibras in the American revolution. Amer Lit 27 1956.
Wilding, M. Butler at Barbourne. N & Q Jan 1966.
J. W.

CHARLES COTTON
1630-87

Bibliographies

Westwood, T. A list of the works of Cotton. N & Q 6 Jan 1866. See W. C. Hazlitt, N & Q 10 Oct 1868.

Collections

The genuine works: containing Scarronides, Lucian burlesqued, The wonders of the Peake, The planters manual. 1715, 1725 (as The genuine poetical works; omits Planters manual), 1734, 1741, 1765, Dublin 1770, London 1771.
Poems. Ed J. Beresford 1923.
Poems. Ed J. Buxton 1958 (ML).

§ I

A panegyrick to the King's most excellent Majesty. 1660.
The morall philosophy of the Stoicks, written originally in French by Monsieur du Vair. 1664, 1667, 1671.
Scarronides, or Virgile travestie: being the first book of Virgil's Æneis in English burlesque. 1664, 1664.
Scarronides: or Virgile travestie, in imitation of the fourth book of Virgil's Æneis in English burlesque. 1665.
Scarronides, or Virgile travestie: a mock-poem on the first and fourth books of Virgil's Æneis. 1667, 1670, 1672, 1678, 1682, 1691, 1692, 1692, 1700, 1709 etc.
The nicker nicked: or the cheats of gaming discovered. 1669. An abbreviated version of the chapter Of gaming in general in Compleat gamester, below.
The history of the life of the Duke of Espernon, englished. 1670.
Horace: a French tragedy of Monsieur Corneille, englished. 1671, 1677.
The fair one of Tunis, out of French. 1674.
The commentaries of Messire Blaize de Montluc. 1674, 1688.
The compleat gamester. 1674, 1676, 1680, 1687 (as How to play at billiards, trucks, bowls and chess), 1696, 1709 (adds The game at basset), 1710, 1721, 1725, 1726; ed C. H. Hartmann 1930 (in Games and gamesters of the Restoration).
Burlesque upon burlesque, or the scoffer scoft: being some of Lucians dialogues newly put into English fustian. 1675, [1686].
The planters manual. 1675.
The compleat angler: part 2. 1676; ed M. Browne 1750; ed J. Hawkins 1760; ed N. H. Nicolas 2 vols 1836; ed R. B. Marston 2 vols 1888.
The wonders of the Peake. 1681, 1683, 1694, 1699, Nottingham 1725; rptd in Poems, ed Buxton, above.
Essays of Michael Seigneur de Montaigne and an account of the author's life, newly rendered into English. 3 vols 1685 (vol 2 1686), 1693, 1700, 1711, 1738, 1743 etc; ed W. C. Hazlitt 3 vols 1877, 1892, 4 vols 1902, 1923.
Poems on several occasions. 1689.
Memoirs of the Sieur de Pontis, faithfully englished. 1694.
The valiant knight: or the legend of St Peregrine. 1888. Perhaps spurious.

§ 2

Langbaine, G. In his An account of the English dramatick poets, Oxford 1691.
Oldys, W. Life of Cotton. In Compleat angler, ed J. Hawkins, above.
Wordsworth, W. Preface to his Poems, 1815.
Coleridge, S. T. In his Biographia literaria ch 19, 1817.
Lamb, C. New Year's Eve. In his Essays of Elia, 1823.
Nicolas, N. H. Preface to Compleat angler, above.
Sembower, C. J. The life and poetry of Cotton. New York 1911.
Beresford, J. The poetry of Cotton. London Mercury Nov 1921.
Heywood, G. G. P. Cotton and his river. Manchester 1928.
Turner, E. M. Cotton's poems. TLS 22 Jan 1938. Reply by J. Beresford 29 Jan 1938.
Evans, W. M. Henry Lawes and Cotton. PMLA 53 1938.

Hussey, R. The text of Cotton's poems. N & Q 12 Feb 1944.

Duncan-Jones, E. E. Cotton's 'sister'. N & Q July–Aug 1959.

J. W.

JOHN DRYDEN
1631–1700

Bibliographies etc

Catalogue of first and other editions of the works of Dryden. New York 1900 (Grolier Club).

Dobell, P. J. Dryden: bibliographical memoranda. 1922.

Wise, T. J. A Dryden library: a catalogue of printed books, manuscripts and autograph letters collected by T. J. Wise. 1930.

Haraszti, Z. Dryden's adaptations and operas: a list of Dryden's plays in the Boston Public Library. More Books 8 1933.

Macdonald, H. Dryden: a bibliography of early editions and of Drydeniana. Oxford 1939, 1967. For addns etc, see J. M. Osborn, Macdonald's bibliography of Dryden: an annotated check list of selected American libraries, MP 39 1941.

Monk, S. H. Dryden: a list of critical studies 1895–1950. Minneapolis 1950. Addns by W. R. Keast, MP 48 1951.

Montgomery, G. et al. Concordance to the poetical works of Dryden. Berkeley 1957.

Cameron, W. J. Dryden in New Zealand: an account of early editions in New Zealand. Wellington 1960.

Gatto, L. C. An annotated bibliography of critical thought concerning Dryden's Essay of dramatic poesy. Restoration & Eighteenth-Century Theatre Research 5 1965.

Collections
Works

Complete sets of Dryden's works, made by binding together 4°s of different dates and adding general title-pages dated 1691, 1693, 1694 and 1695, were advertised by Tonson. See Macdonald, above, p. 146.

The works of Mr John Dryden. 1695. 4°s bound together. The make-up of sets varies. *See* Macdonald no 106.

The works of the late famous Mr John Dryden. 4 vols 1701. This folio edn was made up from existing edns of the poems, plays and trns: vols 1–2 from the 2-vol Comedies, tragedies and operas, 1701, with a general title-page added; vol 3 from Poems on various occasions, 1701 and Fables ancient and modern, 1701 (with general title-page added); vol 4 from the 2nd edn of Works of Virgil, 1698 with a substituted title-page.

The works of John Dryden now first collected, illustrated with notes historical, critical and explanatory and a life of the author by Walter Scott. 18 vols 1808, Edinburgh 1821, 1882–92 (rev G. Saintsbury). Life, ed B. Kreissman, Lincoln Nebraska 1963.

Poetry and prose. Ed D. Nichol Smith, Oxford 1925.

The best of Dryden. Ed L. I. Bredvold, New York 1933.

Poetry, prose and plays. Ed D. Grant 1952 (Reynard Lib).

Selected works. Ed W. Frost, New York 1953.

Poems and prose. Ed D. Grant 1955 (Penguin).

Works. Ed E. N. Hooker, H. T. Swedenberg et al, Los Angeles 1956–.

Poems

Annus mirabilis; also a poem on the happy restoration and return of his late sacred Majesty Charles the Second; likewise a panegyrick on his coronation; together with a poem to my Lord Chancellor presented on New-Years-Day 1662. 1688.

MacFlecknoe, Absalom and Achitopel. 1692; The medal, 1692. Often included in Works, 1694 etc.

Fables ancient and modern, translated into verse from Homer, Ovid, Boccace and Chaucer; with original poems. 1700, 1713, 1721, 1734, 1745.

Poems on various occasions and translations from several authors by Mr John Dryden, now first publish'd together in one volume. 1701. Pbd in vol 3 of Works, 1701.

Original poems and translations, now first collected and publish'd together. [Ed Thomas Broughton] 2 vols 1743.

Poems and fables. Dublin 1753.

Original poems. 2 vols Glasgow 1756, 1770, 1775.

Miscellaneous works: containing all his original poems, tales and translations. [Ed Samuel Derrick] 4 vols 1760, 1767 (life and many notes omitted).

Poetical works, collated with the best editions. Ed T. Park 3 vols 1806.

Poetical works, with notes by Joseph Warton DD, John Warton MA and others. [Ed H. J. Todd] 4 vols 1811, 1851.

Poetical works. Ed J. Mitford 5 vols 1832–3, 1852, 1865 (with new life by R. Hooper), 1866, 1891.

Poetical works. Ed R. Bell 3 vols 1854.

Poetical works. Ed G. Gilfillan 2 vols 1855.

Poetical works. Ed W. D. Christie 1870 etc (Globe).

Select poems. Ed W. D. Christie, Oxford 1871, 1873, 1911 (5th edn, rev C. H. Firth).

Satires. Ed J. C. Collins 1905.

Poetical works. Ed G. R. Noyes, Boston 1908, 1909 etc, 1950 (rev).

Poems. Ed J. Sargeaunt, Oxford 1910, 1935.

Songs. Ed C. L. Day, Cambridge Mass 1932.

Poems [selected]. Ed B. Dobrée 1934 (EL).

Poèmes choisis. Ed P. Legouis, Paris 1946. With French trn.

Selected poems. Ed G. Grigson 1950.

Prologues and epilogues. Ed W. B. Gardner, New York 1951.

Poems. Ed J. Kinsley 4 vols Oxford 1958, 1 vol 1962 (OSA).

Also Johnson vols 13–19; Anderson vols 6, 12 (includes Aeneid, Persius, Juvenal), Chalmers 8, 19 (includes Æneid and Juvenal) etc.

Dramatic Works

Dryden's plays, along with his other works, first appeared in collected edns 1691–5 made up from sets of 4° vols bound together. See Macdonald no 106.

The comedies, tragedies and operas written by John Dryden esq. 2 vols 1701 (2 issues; the 2nd issue of vol 2 adds Secular masque). Pbd as vols 1–2 of Works, 1701.

Dramatick works. Ed William Congreve 6 vols 1717, 1725, 1735, 1762.

Selected plays. Ed G. Saintsbury 2 vols 1904 (Mermaid).

Selected dramas. Ed G. R. Noyes, Chicago 1910.

All for love and the Spanish friar. Ed W. Strunk, Boston 1911.

Dramatic works. Ed M. Summers 6 vols 1931–2.

Four comedies; Four tragedies. Ed F. T. Bowers and L. Beaurline 2 vols Chicago 1967.

Prose

Select essays on the belles lettres. Glasgow 1750.

The critical and miscellaneous prose works of John Dryden, now first collected, with notes and illustrations. Ed Edmond Malone 3 vols in 4 1800. Malone's annotated copy for a 2nd edn in Bodley.

An English garner vol 3. Ed E. Arber 1877.

Essays. Ed C. D. Yonge 1882.

Essays on the drama. Ed W. Strunk, New York 1898.

Essays. Ed W. P. Ker 2 vols Oxford 1900, 1926.

An English garner: critical essays and literary fragments. Ed J. C. Collins 1903.

Dramatic essays. Ed W. H. Hudson 1912 (EL).

Dryden and Howard 1664–8. Ed D. D. Arundell, Cambridge 1929.

Of dramatic poesy and other critical essays. Ed G. Watson 2 vols 1962 (EL).

The critical opinions of Dryden. Ed J. Aden, Nashville 1963.

An essay of dramatic poesy; A defence of an essay of dramatic poesy; Preface to the Fables. Ed J. L. Mahoney, Indianapolis 1965.

Literary criticism. Ed A. Kirsch, Lincoln Nebraska 1966.

§ 1

The songs originally contributed to his own and other plays and to various miscellanies have been excluded; reference should be made to C. L. Day's edn, above, which however omits the 2 songs in John Dryden the younger, The husband his own cuckold, 1696, *attributed to Dryden by C. E. Ward,* RES 13 1937 pp. 303–4.

Dryden's poems appeared frequently in contemporary and later collections, such as Westminster drolery, 1671–2; New court-songs and poems by R. V. Gent, 1672; Covent Garden drolery, 1672 (3 edns); A new collection of poems and songs collected by John Bulteel, 1674; Poetical recreations 1–2, 1688; Poems of affairs of state, 1689 etc; The history of Adolphus by a person of quality, 1691; A new collection of poems on several occasions written by Mr Dryden, 1701 (*generally known as* Gildon's Miscellany); Miscellaneous poems and translations by several hands, 1712 (*generally known as* Lintott's Miscellany); Tixall poetry, *with notes and illustrations by Arthur Clifford,* Edinburgh 1813 (*attributed poems to Dryden from mss: see Macdonald p. 83*).

Dryden's dramatic works, including prologues and epilogues, are arranged by date of production. The following abbreviations are used: C = comedy; T = tragedy; TC = tragi-comedy; DO = dramatic opera; O = opera. A number of Dryden's pieces are rptd in Rare prologues and epilogues 1642–1700, ed A. N. Wiley 1940; *see also* W. B. Gardner's *edn of* Prologues and epilogues, New York 1951. *Unless otherwise stated, the prologues and epilogues appeared with the first edn of the play.*

Verse trns are restricted to works pbd separately and to the more important of the other pieces. The trns in The primer: or office of the B. Virgin Mary, revis'd (*rptd* Orby Shipley in Annus sanctus, 1884, *and in* Hymns attributed to Dryden, ed G. R. Noyes and G. R. Potter, Berkeley 1937) *have now been shown by Noyes and Potter to have been incorrectly ascribed.*

Upon the death of the Lord Hastings. Signed Johannes Dryden Scholae Westm, alumnus. In Lachrymae musarum: the tears of the Muses upon the death of Henry Lord Hastings, collected and set forth by R[ichard] B[rome?]. 1649, 1650; rptd in Miscellany poems 1st pt, 1702 (3rd edn).

To his friend the author on his divine epigrams. Signed J. Dryden of Trin C. In John Hoddesdon, Sion and Parnassus: or epigrams on severall texts of the Old and New Testament, 1650.

Three poems upon the death of his late Highnesse Oliver, Lord Protector of England, Scotland and Ireland, written by Mr Edm Waller, Mr Jo Dryden, Mr Sprat of Oxford. 1659, 1682 (as Three poems upon the death of the late usurper Oliver Cromwel). 1682. Dryden's poem was separately ptd 3 times: 1, An elegy on the usurper O. C. by the author of Absalom and Achitophel, published to shew the loyalty and integrity of the poet, 1681, 1682; 2, A poem upon the death of the late usurper, Oliver Cromwel, by the author of the H—d and the P—r, 1687; 3, A poem upon the death of his late Highness Oliver, Lord Protector of England, Scotland and Ireland, written by Mr Dryden, 1659 (Tonson's reprint c. 1691, for inclusion in his made-up sets of Dryden's poems).

To my honored friend Sr Robert Howard on his excellent poems. In Howard, Poems, 1660.

Astraea redux: a poem on the happy restoration and return of his sacred Majesty Charles the Second. 1660, 1660, 1688.

To his sacred Majesty: a panegyrick on his coronation. 1661, 1661, 1688; rptd in Complementum fortunatarum insularum, written originally in French by P. D. C[ardonnel], 1662, 1662.

To my Lord Chancellor, presented on New-years-day. 1662, 1688.

To my honour'd friend Dr Charleton, on his learned and useful works; and more particularly this of Stone-Heng, by him restored to the true founders. In W. Charleton, Chorea gigantum: or the most famous antiquity of Great Britain, vulgarly called Stone-heng, standing on Salisbury Plain, restored to the Danes, 1663 (Dryden's poem in several states); rptd in Poetical miscellanies 5th pt, 1704.

The wild gallant. C (theatre in Vere St, 5 Feb 1663). 1669, 1669, 1684, 1694. 2 prologues and 2 epilogues; preface.

The Indian-queen. T (Theatre Royal, 25 Jan 1664). 1665 (in Four new plays), 1692 (in Five new plays), 1700 (ibid), 1722 (in Dramatick works of Sir Robert Howard). With Howard. Prologue and epilogue by Dryden?

The rival ladies. TC (Theatre Royal, June 1664). 1664, 1669, 1675, 1693. Prologue. Epilogue (not certainly Dryden's) ed R. G. Ham, RES 13 1937. Dedication.

The Indian Emperour: being the sequel of the Indian queen. T (Theatre Royal, April 1665). 1667, 1668, 1670, 1681, 1686, 1692, 1694, 1696, 1696, 1703, 1709. Prologue and epilogue. Dedication: Connexion of Indian emperour to the Indian Queen.

Annus mirabilis, the year of wonders 1666: an historical poem. 1667 (4 issues), 1668 (pirated edn preserving original stanzas 67 and 105), 1688; ed W. D. Christie, Oxford 1893; Oxford 1927 (facs of 1667). Dedication: An account of the ensuing poem.

Secret-love: or the maiden Queen. TC (Theatre Royal, late Feb 1667). 1668, 1669, 1669, 1679, 1691, 1698. 2 prologues. Preface. Prologue and epilogue spoken by the women only (ptd in Covent Garden drolery, 1672).

Sr Martin Mar-all. C (Lincoln's Inn Fields, 15 Aug 1667). 1668, 1668 (some copies of 2nd edn dated 1669), 1678, 1691, 1697. Prologue and epilogue.

The tempest: or the enchanted island. C (Lincoln's Inn Fields, 7 Nov 1667). 1670 (2 issues?), 1701 (in Comedies, tragedies and operas written by John Dryden esq); ed M. Summers 1922 (in Shakespearean adaptations). By Davenant and Dryden. Prologue and epilogue.

Of dramatick poesie: an essay. 1668, 1684 (rev), 1693; ed T. Arnold, Oxford 1889, rev W. T. Arnold 1903; ed D. Nichol Smith 1900; rptd 1928 (with A dialogue on poetic drama by T. S. Eliot).

Prologue to Albumazar, by Thomas Tomkis. (22 Feb 1668). In Covent Garden drolery, 1672, and Miscellany poems, 1684.

An evening's love: or the mock-astrologer. C (Theatre Royal, 12 June 1668). 1671, 1671, 1675, 1691. Prologue and epilogue. Dedication. Preface.

A defence of An essay of dramatique poesie: being an answer to the Preface of the Great favorite: or the Duke of Lerma. 1668; ed A. Mawer 1901. In early copies of Indian Emperour, 2nd edn. Not rptd by Dryden, but in Congreve's edn, 1717.

Tyrannick love: or the royal martyr. T (Theatre Royal, 24 June 1669). 1670, 1672, 1677, 1686, 1695, 1702. Prologue and epilogue. Dedication (with extra paragraph added in 1672 edn). Preface.

The conquest of Granada by the Spaniards, in two parts. T (Theatre Royal, pt 1 c. Dec 1670; pt 2 Jan 1671). 1672, 1673, 1678, 1687, 1695, 1704. Pt 1: Prologue and epilogue (for variants *see* G. Thorn-Drury, RES 1 1925). Dedication; Of heroique plays: an essay; Pt 2:

Prologue and epilogue (for variants see G. Thorn-Drury, ibid). Defence of the epilogue: or an essay on the dramatique poetry of the last age (some passages omitted in 1678 edn, and whole Defence not rptd in later 4° edns). For texts of later edns of pt 1 see G. H. Nettleton, MLN 50 1935.

Prologue to Julius Caesar by William Shakespeare. (1672?). Ptd in Covent-garden drolery, 1672; accepted as Dryden's by J. Kinsley, Poems, Oxford 1958.

Prologue [to Beaumont and Fletcher, Wit without money], spoken the first day of the King's house acting after the fire. (Lincoln's Inn Fields, 26 Feb 1672). In Westminster-drollery, pt 2, 1672, Covent Garden drolery, 1672, Miscellany poems, 1684.

Marriage-a-la-mode. C (Lincoln's Inn Fields, April 1672). 1673, 1684, 1691, 1698; ed J. R. Sutherland 1934. Prologue and epilogue (also ptd in Covent Garden drolery, 1672). Dedication.

Prologue for the women when they acted at the old theatre in Lincoln's Inn Fields. (c. June 1672). In Miscellany poems, 1684.

The assignation: or love in a nunnery. C (Lincoln's Inn Fields, Nov 1672). 1673, 1678, 1692. Prologue and epilogue. Dedication.

Prologue to Arviragus and Philicia, by Lodowick Carlell. (At revival, 1673). In Miscellany poems, 1684.

Amboyna. T (Lincoln's Inn Fields, May 1673). 1673, 1691. Prologue and epilogue (for variants see G. Thorn-Drury, RES 1 1925). Dedication.

Prologue and epilogue to the University of Oxford, spoken by Mr Hart at the acting of the Silent woman. (July 1673). In Miscellany poems, 1684.

The mistaken husband. C (Lincoln's Inn Fields, March 1674). 1675. Anon. Dryden possibly wrote one scene and the prologue and epilogue.

Prologue and epilogue spoken at the opening of the new house, March 26 1674. (Drury Lane). In Miscellany poems, 1684.

The tempest: or the enchanted island [rev Thomas Shadwell]. DO (Dorset Garden, 30 April 1674). 1674, 1676, 1690, 1676 (for c. 1692), 1695, 1701. The 1674 edn has the same title-page as the 1670 edn of Dryden's comedy, but the text differs.

To the Lady Castlemain. In A new collection of poems and songs, ed J. Bulteel 1674.

Notes and observations on the Empress of Morocco [by Elkanah Settle]: or some few erratas to be printed instead of the sculptures with the second edition of that play. 1674. Preface and Postscript probably by Dryden, and possibly further parts. See G. McFadden, PQ 43 1964, H. H. R. Love, N & Q Jan 1966, and A. Doyle, Stud in Eng Lit 1500–1900 6 1966. Dryden was helped by Crowne and Shadwell.

Prologue and epilogue to the University of Oxford. (July 1674). In Miscellany poems, 1684.

Epilogue to Calisto or the chaste nymph, by John Crowne ['intended to have been spoken by the Lady Henrietta Maria Wentworth, who took the character of Jupiter when Calisto was acted at Court']. (15 Feb 1675). Not certainly Dryden's: in Miscellany poems, 1684.

Aureng-zebe. T (Drury Lane, 17 Nov 1675), 1676, 1685, 1690, 1692, 1694, 1699, 1704. Prologue and epilogue. Dedication.

Epilogue to the Man of mode: or Sir Fopling Flutter, by Sir George Etherege. (11 March 1676). 1676. For ms variants see RES 1 1925, 9 1933 pp. 198–9.

Prologue to the University of Oxford ['Tho' actors cannot much of learning boast']. (1676?). In Miscellany poems, 1684; for Bodleian ms see R. G. Ham, London Mercury March 1930.

The state of innocence and fall of man. O (unacted). 1677, 1678, 1684, 1684, '1684' (pirated edn c. 1695?), 1690, 1692, 1695, 1695, 1703. Written c. 1674. Dedication: The author's apology for heroique poetry and poetique licence.

Prologue to Circe, by Charles Davenant. (12 May 1677). 1677. Shorter version entitled An epilogue in Miscellany poems, 1684.

To Mr Lee, on his Alexander. In The rival Queens: or the death of Alexander the Great, 1677.

All for love: or the world well lost. T (Drury Lane, 12 Dec 1677). 1678, 1692, 1696, 1703, 1709, San Francisco 1929 (facs of 1678); ed J. Encks, New York 1966. Prologue and epilogue. Dedication. Preface.

Epilogue to Mithridates, King of Pontus, by Nathaniel Lee. (c. Feb 1678). 1678. For Dryden's prologue and epilogue, written for a revival mid-Oct 1681, see below.

The kind keeper: or Mr Limberham. C (Dorset Garden, 11 March 1678). 1680, 1690, 1701. Prologue and epilogue. Dedication.

Prologue to A true widow, by Thomas Shadwell. (21 March 1678). Rptd with Aphra Behn, The widdow Ranter, 1690.

Oedipus. T (Dorset Garden, c. Sept 1678). 1679, 1682, 1687, 1692, [1696?], 1701, 1711. With N. Lee. Prologue and epilogue. Preface.

Troilus and Cressida: or truth found too late. T (Dorset Garden, c. April 1679). 1679, '1679' (for c. 1692), 1695. Prologue and epilogue. Dedication. A preface containing the grounds of criticism in tragedy.

Prologue to Caesar Borgia, by Nathaniel Lee. (May 1679). 1680.

Prologue to the University of Oxford, for Settle (1679?), altered for Sophonisba by Nathaniel Lee. (1680?). 1681 (2nd edn of Lee); rptd in Miscellany poems, 1684.

Prologue to the Loyal general, by Nahum Tate. (Dec 1679). 1680.

Ovid's epistles, translated by several hands. 1680, 1681. Canace to Macareus, Helen to Paris (with J. Sheffield, Earl of Mulgrave), Dido to Aneas, and Preface, are by Dryden.

Prologue to the University of Oxford ['Discord and plots which have undone our age']. (Nov 1680–March 1682). In Miscellany poems, 1684.

The Spanish fryar: or the double discovery. C (Dorset Garden, 1 Nov 1680). 1681, 1681, 1686, 1690, 1695, 1704 ('second edition'), 1717. Prologue. Dedication.

Prologue and epilogue to the Princess of Cleves, by Nathaniel Lee. (Late 1680–early 1682). In Miscellany poems, 1684.

Prologue to the University of Oxford. [1681]. In Examen poeticum, 1693.

Prologue to the University of Oxford ['The fam'd Italian Muse, whose rhymes advance']. (1681). In Examen poeticum, 1693.

Epilogue to Tamerlane the great, by Charles Saunders. (Mid–March 1681). 1681.

Epilogue [to above] spoke before his Majesty at Oxford, March 19 1680 [i.e. 1681] ['As from a darkened room some optick glass']. Single sheet, 1681; 1681; Oxford 1932 (facs). See R. G. Ham, TLS 27 Dec 1928, London Mercury March 1930, and W. G. Hiscock, TLS 5 March 1931.

Prologue to the King and Queen, at their coming to the house: epilogue for the Unhappy favourite: or the Earl of Essex, by John Banks. (May 1681). 1681.

His Majesties declaration defended. 1681; ed G. Davies, Los Angeles 1950 (Augustan Reprint Soc).

A prologue [and epilogue] spoken at Mithridates King of Pontus [by Nathaniel Lee], the first play acted at the Theatre Royal this year 1681. (Mid-Oct 1681). [1682]. Single sheet: Scott first ascribed the epilogue to Dryden, and R. G. Ham, TLS 27 Dec 1928, the prologue. See also J. H. Smith, PMLA 68 1953.

Absalom and Achitophel: a poem. 1681 (4 issues, 4°), [Dublin 1681?], London 1681 (2nd edn, but not so-called on title-page, folio), 1681 ('the second edition', 4°, containing addn of ll. 180–91, 957–60; 2 issues), [Dublin 1681?], 1682 (3rd–5th edns) etc; ed J. and H. Kinsley, Oxford 1961. For Second part, see below.

Prologue and epilogue to the Loyal brother: or the Persian prince, by Thomas Southerne. (4 Feb 1682). 1682. The prologue also ptd on a single sheet [1682].

The medall: a satyre against sedition, by the author of Absalom and Achitophel. 1682, 1682, Edinburgh 1682, Dublin 1682, London 1692. Prefaced by Epistle to the Whigs.

Prologue to his Royal Highness upon his first appearance at the Duke's Theatre since his return from Scotland, written by Mr Dryden, spoken by Mr Smith. (21 April 1682). Single sheet [1682], [1682]; rptd in Sylvae, 1702 (3rd edn).

Prologue to the Dutchess on her return from Scotland. (31 May 1682). 1682. Single sheet; rptd in Examen poeticum, 1693.

Mac Flecknoe: or a satyr upon the true-blew-Protestant poet T.S., by the author of Absalom and Achitophel. 1682, 1692 (with Absalom and Achitophel and Medall), 1924 (facs). Written 1678?

The second part of Absalom and Achitophel: a poem. 1682 (2 issues), 1682, Dublin 1682, London 1709, 1716 (with Key in 4th edn of first pt of Miscellany poems). By Nahum Tate, with addns by Dryden.

Prologue to the King and Queen, at the opening of their theatre, spoken by Mr Batterton, written by Mr Dryden, with epilogue; spoken by Mr Smith, written by the same author. (16 Nov 1682). 1683. 2 leaves.

The Duke of Guise. T (Drury Lane, 28 Nov 1682). 1683, 1687, 1699, 1699. With N. Lee. Prologue and epilogues (also ptd as Prologue, epilogue and second epilogue. 2 leaves). Dedication.

Religio laici, or a layman's faith: a poem. 1682 (3 issues), 1682 (perhaps pirated), 1683. Preface.

The vindication: or the parallel of the French Holy-League, and the English League and Covenant, turn'd into a seditious libell by Thomas Hunt. 1683. Running-title: The vindication of the Duke of Guise.

Plutarch's Lives, translated from the Greek by several hands. 5 vols 1683-6, 1693, 1700, 1703. Life of Plutarch as well as a Dedication and Advertisement of the publisher attributed by Malone.

Epilogue to Constantine the great, by Nathaniel Lee. (12 Nov 1683). 1684. Single sheet, 2 edns, one pirated; rptd in Miscellany poems, 1702 (3rd edn).

Soames, Sir William. The art of poetry, written in French by Boileau. 1683. Dryden revised and contributed some lines; rptd in The annual miscellany, 1708 (2nd edn); rptd separately, 1710, 1715, Glasgow 1755.

Miscellany poems. 1684. Contains trns: Ovid, Amours II xix; Theocritus, Idyll 3; Virgil, Eclogues 4, 9.

Prologue to Disappointment: or the mother in fashion, by Thomas Southerne. (April 1684). 1684. Single sheet; rptd in Miscellany poems, 1702 (3rd edn).

The history of the League written in French by M. Maimbourg. 1684. Dedication and Postscript.

To the Earl of Roscommon on his excellent Essay on translated verse. In An essay on translated verse, by the Earl of Roscommon, 1684, 1685.

To the memory of Mr Oldham. In Remains of Mr John Oldham in verse and prose, 1684.

Sylvae: or the second part of poetical miscellanies. 1685. [Contains trns: Horace Odes, I iii, I ix, III xxix, 2nd Epode; Lucretius, portions of bks 1-5; Theocritus, Idylls 18, 23, 27 (rptd Poems, 1701); passages from Virgil etc.

Threnodia Augustalis: a funeral-pindarique poem sacred to the happy memory of King Charles II. 1685 (3 edns; 'the second edition' in fact a re-issue of first edn), Dublin 1685.

Albion and Albanius. DO (Dorset Garden, 3 June 1685). 1685, 1685, 1687, 1691. Prologue and epilogue (also ptd as single sheet). Preface.

To my friend Mr J. Northleigh. In The triumph of our monarchy over the plots and principles of our rebels and republicans, 1685.

To the pious memory of the accomplisht young lady Mrs Anne Killigrew, excellent in the two sister-arts of poesie and painting. In Poems by Mrs Anne Killigrew, 1686 (for 1685?); rptd with alterations in Examen poeticum, 1693.

A defence of the papers written by the late King of blessed memory, and Duchess of York, against the answer made to them [by Stillingfleet], by command. 1686. C. E. Ward, Life, 1960, p. 219, attributed all 3 defences to Dryden; earlier writers the 3rd only.

To my ingenious friend, Mr Henry Higden esq, on his translation of the tenth satyr of Juvenal. In Henry Higden, A modern essay on the tenth satyr of Juvenal, 1687.

The hind and the panther: a poem in three parts. 1687 (7 states of last leaf), 1687 (2nd-3rd edns), Edinburgh 1687, Dublin 1687; ed W. H. Williams 1900. To the reader.

A song for St Cecilia's Day 1687, written by John Dryden esq, and compos'd by Mr John Baptist Draghi. 1687 (single sheet), 1693 (in Examen poeticum).

Britannia rediviva: a poem on the birth of the Prince. 1688, Edinburgh 1688, London 1688 (for c. 1691).

Dedication to the life of St Francis Xavier, trnd from D. Bouhours. 1688.

An epitaph on Sir Palmes Fairborne's tomb. In Poetical recreations: part 1 by Mrs Jane Barker, part 2 by several gentlemen, 1688; rptd in Examen poeticum, 1693.

Prologue ['Gallants, a bashful poet bids me say']. 1689? (but see E. de S. Beer, N & Q 21 Dec 1940). In Examen poeticum, 1693.

Prologue and epilogue to the Widdow ranter: or the history of Bacon in Virginia, by Aphra Behn. (c. Nov 1689). 1689 (separately ptd). J. Knapton ptd the play in 1690, but replaced these pieces with Dryden's prologue to Shadwell, A true widow, 1679 and, as epilogue, the Prologue to the Double marriage, ptd in Covent-Garden drolery, 1672. See R. G. Ham, London Mercury March 1930 and A. N. Wiley, Rare prologues and epilogues, 1940.

Don Sebastian, King of Portugal. T (Drury Lane, 4 Dec 1689). 1690, 1692. Prologue and epilogue. Dedication. Preface.

Prologue to the Prophetess: or the history of Dioclesian [by Fletcher turned into an opera by Betterton]. (June 1690). 1690. In Poems of affairs of state pt 3, 1698, Muses Mercury Jan 1707, Annual Miscellany 1708 (2nd edn). Prohibited after first night on account of political allusions. See R. P. McCutcheon, MLN 39 1924.

Amphitryon: or the two Socia's. C (Drury Lane, early Oct? 1690). 1690, 1691, 1694, 1706. Prologue and epilogue. Dedication.

Prologue to the Mistakes: or the false report, by Joseph Harris. (Mid-Dec 1690). 1691.

King Arthur: or the British worthy. DO (Dorset Garden, c. May 1691). 1691 (re-issued twice in same year with prologue and epilogue added). 1695; rptd (with alterations adopted by H. Purcell) Cambridge 1928.

Dedication to the vocal and instrumental musick of the Prophetess: or the history of Dioclesian, by Henry Purcell. 1691. See R. G. Ham, PMLA 50 1935 on BM mss of these pieces; also Macdonald p. 172.

Preface to A dialogue concerning women: being a defence of the sex, by William Walsh. 1691. Walsh was assisted by Dryden's comments on the Dialogue.

A letter to Sir George Etheridge. In The history of Adolphus Prince of Russia, to which is added two letters in verse from Sir G.E. to the E. of M. with Mr D's answer to them, 1691; rptd in Familiar letters vol 2, 1697, and Sylvae, 1702 (3rd edn). Written c. 1686.

To Mr Southern on his comedy, called the Wives excuse. In The wives excuse, or cuckolds make themselves: a comedy, by Tho Southern[e], 1692.

Eleonora: a panegyrical poem dedicated to the memory of the late Countess of Abingdon. 1692. Dedication.

Cleomenes, the Spartan heroe. T (Drury Lane, mid–April 1692). 1692. Prologue and epilogue. Dedication. Preface.

Miscellaneous essays by Monsieur St Evremont, translated out of French, with a character by a person of honour here in England [Knightly Chetwood]; continued by Mr Dryden. 1692. A 2nd vol trn by Tom Brown was pbd in 1694.

Epilogue to Henry II, King of England [by John Bancroft]. (8 Nov 1692). 1693.

The character of Polybius and his writings. In The history of Polybus the megalopolitan, translated by Sir H[enry] S[heeres], 2 vols 1693 etc.

Homer, The last parting of Hector and Andromache. In Examen poeticum, 1693.

Ovid, Metamorphoses bk 1 and episodes from bks 9 and 13. Ibid.

Veni, creator spiritus, translated in paraphrase. Ibid.

The satires of Juvenalis, translated into English verse by Mr Dryden and several other eminent hands; together with the Satires of Persius, made English by Mr Dryden. 1693, 1697, 1697. Juvenal, Satires 1, 3, 6, 10, 16 and all Persius by Dryden; also A discourse concerning the original and progress of satire.

To my dear friend Mr Congreve on his comedy called the Double-dealer. In Congreve, The double-dealer: a comedy, 1694.

Love triumphant: or nature will prevail. TC (Drury Lane, mid–Jan 1694). 1694. Prologue and epilogue.

A parallel betwixt painting and poetry. In De arte graphica: the art of painting, by C. A. Du Fresnoy, 1695, 1716, 1750. Dryden's Parallel, ed E. Malone in Works of Sir Joshua Reynolds, 1797, 1801 (3rd edn).

Preface and epilogue to the Husband his own cuckold, by John Dryden jr. (Feb 1696). 1696.

An ode on the death of Mr Henry Purcell, late servant to his Majesty and organist of the Chapel Royal, and of St Peter's Westminster: the words by Mr Dryden, and sett to musick by Dr Blow. 1696; rptd in Orpheus britannicus, 1698.

The works of Virgil: containing his Pastorals, Georgics and Æneis; translated into English verse. 1697, 1698, 1709, 1716, 1721, 1730; ed J. Kinsley, Oxford 1961. The 4th and 9th Eclogues first pbd in Miscellany poems, 1684. 3 episodes from the Æneid in Sylvae, 1685, and bk 3 of the Georgics in Annual Miscellany 1694. Dryden wrote the Dedications for Pastorals, Georgics, Æneis; Discourse on epick poetry; Postscript.

Alexander's feast: or the power of musique; an ode in honour of St Cecilia's Day. 1697, 1700 (in Fables); Oxford 1925 (facs); tr Latin by John Hughes, Oxford 1751.

To Mr Granville on his excellent tragedy call'd Heroick love. In Heroick love: a tragedy, by George Granville afterwards Baron Lansdowne, 1698.

To my friend the author [Peter Anthony Motteux]. In Motteux, Beauty in distress: a tragedy, 1698.

Fables ancient and modern. 1700, 1713. Dedication and preface To her Grace the Dutchess of Ormond, 7 trns from Chaucer, 8 trns from Ovid's Metamorphoses, 3 trns from Boccaccio, trn of Homer's Iliad bk 1, To my honoured kinsman John Driden, lines on The monument of a fair maiden lady: ed A. Mawer 1901; Oxford 1910; ed W. H. W. Williams, Cambridge 1912; ed M. G. L. Thomas, Oxford 1928.

The secular masque etc. In The pilgrim as it is acted at the Theatre Royal, written originally by Mr Fletcher, and now very much alter'd with several additions [by Sir John Vanbrugh]; likewise a prologue, epilogue, dialogue and masque, written by the late great poet Mr Dryden, just before his death, being the last of his works, 1700. There are 2 issues of 1st edn. In one Dryden's contributions have a separate pagination, in the other they are paginated on from the play. These pages are ptd in a considerably larger type than the rest of the play.

Ovid, Amours I [iv]. In Poetical miscellanies, 5th pt, 1704.

[Epigram on Tonson]. In William Shippen, Faction display'd, 1704, and in a letter from R. Powys to Prior, 1698, Historical mss Commission Bath 3 238.

Ovid's art of love, in three books. 1709. Bk 1 'translated some years since by Mr Dryden'.

Life of Lucian. In The works of Lucian, translated by several eminent hands, 4 vols 1711 etc.

[Heads of an answer to Rymer's remarks on the tragedies of the last age]. In Works of Mr Francis Beaumont and Mr John Fletcher vol 1, 1711, pp. xii–xxvi; another text in Johnson's Life, 1781. See also G. Watson, RES new ser 14 1963.

Epitaph on the Marquis of Winchester. In Miscellaneous poems and translations by Mr Pope, 1712.

Ovid, Metamorphoses bk 11 (56 lines). In Ovid's Metamorphoses in fifteen books, 1717.

Lines to Honor Dryden. In GM May 1785; rptd in Critical and miscellaneous prose works of Dryden, ed E. Malone 1800 I. i. 341–2. Probably written in 1653; see Works vol 1, ed E. N. Hooker and H. T. Swedenberg, Berkeley 1955.

Lines to Mrs Creed. In Critical and miscellaneous prose works of John Dryden, ed E. Malone 1800 I. i. 341–2.

Ode on the marriage of Mrs A. Stafford. In Tixall poetry, ed A. Clifford, Edinburgh 1813. Written c. 1687. Rptd in Aldine edn.

Epitaph on the poet's nephew, Erasmus Lawton. In J. Prior, Life of Malone, 1860.

Miscellanies

The successive edns of each vol vary greatly in content. See R. D. Havens, PMLA 44 1929; A. E. Case, Bibliography of English poetical miscellanies 1521–1750, 1935 (Bibl Soc); *and* Macdonald pp. 67–83.

Miscellany poems: containing a new translation of Virgills Eclogues, Ovid's Love elegies, Odes of Horace and other authors, with several original poems; by the most eminent hands. 1684, 1688, 1692, 1692, 1702, 1716, 1727.

Sylvae: or the second part of poetical miscellanies. 1685, 1685, 1692, 1693, 1702, 1716, 1727. Preface.

Examen poeticum, being the third part of miscellany poems: containing variety of new translations of the ancient poets; together with many original copies by the most eminent hands. 1693, 1693, 1706, 1716, 1727. Dedication.

The annual miscellany for the year 1694, being the fourth part of miscellany poems: containing great variety of new translations and original copies by the most eminent hands. 1694, 1708, 1716, 1727.

Poetical miscellanies: the fifth part. 1704, 1716, 1727. This and the 6th pt, below, were ed J. Tonson assisted by N. Rowe.

Poetical miscellanies: the sixth part. 1709, 1716, 1727.

Prose translations

The history of the League, written in French by Monsieur [L.] Maimbourg. 1684.

The life of St Francis Xavier by Dominick Bo[u]hours. 1688.

De arte graphica: the art of painting by C. A. De Fresnoy; with remarks; translated into English together with an original preface containing a Parallel betwixt painting and poetry; by Mr Dryden. 1695, 1716 (rev and abridged Charles Jervas assisted by Pope?), 1750.

Letters upon several occasions; with a new translation of select letters of Monsieur Voiture. Ed J. Dennis 1696. Dryden translated Voiture's letter 'To my Lord Cardinal de la Valette', p. 136.

The annals and history of Cornelius Tacitus, made English by several hands. 3 vols 1698. Bk 1 by Dryden.

Letters

Letters. Ed C. E. Ward, Durham NC 1942.

Some letters from Dryden were ptd in Poems and letters upon several occasions, 1685; Charles Gildon, Miscellaneous letters and essays, 1694; John Dennis, Letters upon several occasions, 1696; Elizabeth Thomas, Poems on several occasions, 1699 (2nd edn); A paquet from Will's [2nd vol of Familiar and courtly letters of Voiture], 1701; Miscellanea in two volumes, 1727. *First attempts to collect were in the edns of Malone, Scott and Scott-Saintsbury.*

§ 2

For Drydeniana see Macdonald, for critical studies 1895–1948 see S. H. Monk, both under Bibliographies, above.

[Villiers, George, Duke of Buckingham, Thomas Sprat, and Martin Clifford.] The rehearsal. 1672, 1672, 1675, 1683 etc, ed M. Summers Stratford 1914.

[Settle, Elkanah]. Notes and observations on the Empress of Morocco revised; with some few erratas to be printed instead of the Postscript with the next edition of the Conquest of Granada. 1674, 1687 (as Reflections on several of Mr Dryden's plays, particularly the first and second part of the Conquest of Granada, by E. Settle gent).

— Absalom senior, or Achitophel transpos'd: a poem. 1682, 1682 (with addns); rptd in Anti-Achitophel 1682: three verse replies, ed H. W. Jones, Gainesville 1961.

— A prologue by Mr Settle to his new play called the Emperor of Morocco, with the life of Gayland. 1682. Single sheet; the play was first ptd as The heir of Morocco.

[An essay upon satyr: or a poem on the times; to which is added the Satyr against the separatists]. Recorded in the Term catalogues for 1680, but no copy known: this, the 'Rose Alley satire', first appears in Poems of affairs of state: the fourth collection, 1689. It has been ascribed to Rochester.

Poetical reflections on a late poem entituled Absalom and Achitophel, by a person of honour. 1681, 1682; rptd in Anti-Achitophel, 1682: three verse replies, ed H. W. Jones, Gainesville 1961. Ascribed, apparently erroneously, by Anthony à Wood to George Villiers, Duke of Buckingham.

Azaria and Hushai. 1682, 1682. Attributed to Samuel Pordage and also to Elkanah Settle.

[Shadwell, Thomas]. The medal of John Bayes: a satyr against folly and knavery. 1682; rptd with most of the Drydeniana attributed to Shadwell in Works of Shadwell, ed M. Summers 5 vols 1927.

— The tenth satyr of Juvenal: English and Latin. 1687.

The Tory-poets: a satyr. 1682; rptd in Anti-Achitophel 1682: three verse replies, ed H. W. Jones, Gainesville 1961. Sometimes attributed to Shadwell.

The true history of the Duke of Guise published for the undeceiving such as may perhaps be imposed upon by Mr Dryden's late tragedy of the Duke of Guise. 1683.

[Prior, Matthew and Charles Montagu]. The hind and the panther transvers'd to the story of the country-mouse and the city-mouse. 1687, Dublin 1687.

Clifford, Martin. Notes upon Mr Dryden's poems in four letters; to which are annexed some reflections upon the Hind and the panther, by another hand [Tom Brown]. 1687, 1687. Clifford died in 1677 and the 4th letter is dated 1 July 1672, but the letters do not appear to have been ptd before 1687.

A collection of poems on affairs of state. 7 pts 1689; rptd much enlarged 1697 etc. Many attacks on Dryden and on poems falsely attributed to him. Index of first lines, N & Q 18 Nov–30 Dec 1876–8.

The address of John Dryden, Laureat, to his Highness the Duke of Orange. 1689; rptd in State poems pt 3, 1689,

and attributed to Shadwell. Full title and preliminary discourse ptd by G. Thorn-Drury, RES 1 1925.

Langbaine, Gerard. An account of the English dramatick poets. Oxford 1691. Essay on Dryden rptd in Critical essays of the 17th century vol 3, ed J. E. Spingarn, Oxford 1909.

Dennis, John. The impartial critick. 1693; rptd in Spingarn, above, and in his Critical works vol 1, ed E. N. Hooker Baltimore 1939.

— Letters upon several occasions. 1696.

— Remarks upon Mr Pope's translation of Homer. 1717; rptd in his Critical works vol 2, above.

Miscellaneous letters and essays on several subjects directed to John Dryden and others. Ed Charles Gildon 1694.

Collier, Jeremy. A short view of the immorality and profaneness of the English stage. 1698 etc. Dryden mentioned in this book, and throughout the Collier controversy; *see col 721, below.*

Milbourne, [Luke]. Notes on Dryden's Virgil in a letter to a friend, with an essay on the same poet. 1698.

A comparison between the two stages. 1702; ed S. B. Wells, Princeton 1942. Wells argues against the attribution to Gildon.

Downes, John. Roscius anglicanus: or an historical review of the stage. 1708; ed M. Summers [1928].

Hughes, Jabez. Verses occasion'd by reading Mr Dryden's Fables. 1721.

Swift, Jonathan. On poetry: a rapsody. 1733.

G., W. On the poets and actors in Charles II's reign. GM Feb 1745. A concoction of previously ptd matter? But *see* C. Leech, N & Q 10 June 1933, who attributes it to Southerne.

Johnson, Samuel. In his Lives of the poets vol 1, 1781.

Weston, Joseph. An essay on the superiority of Dryden's versification over that of Pope and the moderns. In John Morfitt, Philotoxi Ardenae, Birmingham [1789].

Stockdale, Percival. In his Lectures on the truly eminent English poets, 2 vols 1807.

Hallam, H. Edinburgh Rev 13 1808. Review of Scott's edn.

Hazlitt, William. In his Lectures on the English poets, 1818.

[Southern, H.] Dryden's dramatic works. Retrospective Rev 1 1820.

[Barker, C.] Dryden's prose works. Retrospective Rev 4 1821.

Macaulay, T. B. Dryden. Edinburgh Rev 47 1828.

[Genest, J.] In his Some account of the English stage from 1660 vol 1, Bath 1832.

Wilson, J. North's Specimens of the British critics. Blackwood's Mag Feb 1845.

Masson, D. Dryden and the literature of the Restoration. Br Quart Rev 20 1854.

[Wilkins, J. W.] The genius of Dryden. Edinburgh Rev 102 1855.

Corneille and Dryden. Fraser's Mag Sept 1862.

'Shirley' (J. Skelton). Dryden: a vindication. Fraser's Mag Aug 1865; rptd in his Essays in history and biography, Edinburgh 1883.

Lowell, J. R. In his Among my books ser 1, 1870; rptd in his Writings vol 3, Boston 1890.

[Collins, J. C.] John Dryden. Quart Rev 146 1878; rptd in his Essays and studies, 1895.

Schöpke, O. Drydens bearbeitung Chaucerscher Gedichte. Anglia 2–3 1879–80.

Beljame, A. Quae e gallicis verbis in anglicam linguam Dryden introduxerit. Paris 1881.

— In his Le public et les hommes de lettres en Angleterre 1660–1744, Paris 1881.

Bobertag, F. Drydens Theorie des Dramas. E Studien 4 1881.

Saintsbury, G. Dryden. 1881 (EML).

Dennis, J. John Dryden. Fraser's Mag Feb 1882.

B[owen], G. S. A study of the prologue and epilogue in English literature from Shakespeare to Dryden. 1884.

Shipley, O. Annus sanctus. 1884.

— Dryden as hymnologist. Dublin Rev 12 1884.

Hartmann, C. Der Einfluss Molières auf Drydens komisch-dramatische Dichtungen. Leipzig 1885.

Tüchert, A. Dryden als Dramatiker in seine Beziehungen zu M. de Scudérys Romandichtung. Zweibrücken 1885.

Collins, G. S. Dryden's dramatic theory and praxis. Leipzig 1892.

Weselmann, F. Dryden als Kritiker. Mülheim 1893.

Dierberger, J. Drydens Reime. Freiburg 1895.

Garnett, R. The age of Dryden. 1895.

Tupper, F. Dryden and Speght's Chaucer. MLN 12 1897.

Sherwood, M. Dryden's dramatic theory and practice. Boston 1898.

Bridges, R. Dryden on Milton. Speaker 24 Oct 1903; rptd in Collected essays pt 10, 1932.

Chase, L. N. In his English heroic play, New York 1903.

Lawrence, W. J. Did Thomas Shadwell write an opera on the Tempest? Anglia 27 1904, rptd in The Elizabethan playhouse ser 1, Stratford 1912.

— Oxford Restoration prologues. TLS 16 Jan 1930.

— Dryden's abortive opera. TLS 6 Aug 1931. With subsequent correspondence.

Parsons, E. S. A note upon Dryden's heroic stanzas on the death of Cromwell. MLN 19 1904.

Churchill, G. B. The relation of Dryden's State of innocence to Milton's Paradise lost and Wycherley's Plain dealer. MP 4 1906.

Frye, P. H. Dryden and the critical canons of the eighteenth century. Nebraska Univ Stud 7 1907.

Root, R. K. Dryden's conversion to the Roman Catholic faith. PMLA 22 1907.

Macpherson, C. Ueber die Vergil-Übersetzung des Dryden. Berlin 1910.

Heigl, F. Die dramatischen Einheiten bei Dryden. Munich 1912.

Steeves, H. R. The Athenian virtuosi and the Athenian Society. MLR 7 1912.

Baumgartner, M. D. On Dryden's relation to Germany in the 18th century. Lincoln Nebraska 1914.

Verrall, A. W. Lectures on Dryden. Cambridge 1914.

Williams, W. A. Palamon and Arcite and the Knight's tale. MLR 9 1914.

Gaw, A. Sir Samuel Tuke's Adventures of five hours in relation to the Spanish plot and to Dryden. Baltimore 1917.

Babington, P. L. Dryden not the author of MacFlecknoe. MLR 13 1918.

Thorn-Drury, G. Dryden's MacFlecknoe: a vindication. Ibid.

— Some notes on Dryden. RES 1 1925.

— Shadwell and the operatic Tempest. RES 3 1927.

— Dryden's verses To the Lady Castlemain upon her incouraging his first play. RES 6 1930.

Huxley, A. Forgotten satirists. London Mercury March 1920.

Van Doren, M. The poetry of Dryden. New York 1920, 1931 (rev), 1946 (as Dryden: a study of his poetry).

Broadus, E. K. In his Laureateship, Oxford 1921.

Emerson, O. F. Dryden and a British academy. Proc Br Acad 10 1921.

Nicoll, A. Dryden, Howard and Rochester. TLS 13 Jan 1921.

— Dryden as an adapter of Shakespeare. 1922 (Shakespeare Assoc).

— Dryden and his poetry. 1923.

Jameson, R. D. Notes on Dryden's lost prosodia. MP 20 1922.

Noyes, G. R. Crites in Dryden's Essay of dramatic poesy. MLN 38 1923.

— and G. R. Potter. Hymns attributed to Dryden. Berkeley 1937.

Pendlebury, B. J. Dryden's heroic plays: a study of the origins. 1923.

Raleigh, W. Dryden and political satire. In his Some authors, Oxford 1923.

Eliot, T. S. Homage to John Dryden. 1924.

— Dryden: the poet, the dramatist, the critic. New York 1932.

— In his Use of poetry and the use of criticism, 1933.

Freeman, E. A proposal for an English Academy in 1660. MLR 19 1924. See O. F. Emerson 20 1925 pp. 189-90.

Mark, J. Dryden and the beginnings of opera in English. Music & Letters 5 1924.

Bondurant, A. L. The Amphitrus of Plautus, Molière's Amphitryon and the Amphitryon of Dryden. Sewanee Rev 33 1925.

Ellis, A. M. Horace's influence on Dryden. PQ 4 1925.

Lubbock, A. The character of Dryden. 1925.

Lynch, K. M. D'Urfé's L'Astrée and the 'proviso' scenes in Dryden's comedy. PQ 4 1925. See also her Social mode of Restoration comedy, New York 1926.

Payne, F. W. The question of precedence between Dryden and the Earl of Orrery with regard to the English heroic play. RES 1 1925.

Ham, R. G. Otway's duels with Churchill and Settle. MLN 41 1926.

— Dryden versus Settle. MP 25 1928.

— Some uncollected verse of Dryden. London Mercury March 1930.

— The date of Dryden's birth. TLS 20 Aug 1931. With subsequent correspondence.

— Dryden and the colleges. MLN 49 1934.

— Dryden as Historiographer-Royal: the authorship of His Majesties declaration defended. RES 11 1935.

— Dryden's dedication for the music of the Prophetesse 1691. PMLA 50 1935.

— Epilogue to the Rival ladies. RES 13 1937.

Diffenbaugh, G. L. The rise and development of the mock heroic poem from 1660 to Dryden's MacFlecknoe. Urbana 1926.

Walmsley, D. M. Shadwell and the operatic Tempest. RES 2-3 1926-7.

Clark, W. S. Dryden's relations with Howard and Orrery. MLN 42 1927.

— Correspondence on C. E. Ward's notes on Dryden. RES 14 1938.

Harrison, T. P. Othello as a model for Dryden's All for love. SE 7 1927.

Bredvold, L. I. Dryden, Hobbes and the Royal Society. MP 25 1928.

— Dryden and the University of Oxford. MLN 46 1931.

— Political aspects of Dryden's Amboyna and the Spanish fryar. In Essays and studies by the English Department of the University of Michigan, Ann Arbor 1932.

— Notes on Dryden's pension. MP 30 1933.

— The intellectual milieu of Dryden. Ann Arbor 1934.

Starnes, D. T. More about Dryden as an adaptor of Shakespeare. SE 8 1928.

Havens, R. D. Changing taste in the eighteenth century: a study of Dryden's and Dodsley's miscellanies. PMLA 44 1929.

Lloyd, C. Dryden and the Royal Society. PMLA 45 1930. See 46 1931.

Newdigate, B. H. An overlooked ode by Dryden. London Mercury 1930.

Allen, R. J. The Kit-Cat Club and the theatre. RES 7 1931.

Boswell, E. Chaucer, Dryden and the Laureateship: a seventeenth-century tradition. Ibid.

D., S. N. Dryden's Ode on St Lucy's Day. Month Dec 1931.

Deane, C. V. In his Dramatic theory and the rhymed heroic play, 1931.

Glazier, G. E. Dryden's associations with Northamptonshire. Bedford 1931.

Granville-Barker, H. Wycherley and Dryden. In his On dramatic method, 1931.

Jones, R. F. The originality of Absalom and Achitopel. MLN 46 1931.

Jordan, A. The conversion of Dryden. Month July 1931.

Legouis, P. Quinault et Dryden: une source de the Spanish friar. Revue de Littérature Comparée 11 1931.

— La religion dans l'œuvre de Dryden avant 1682. Revue Anglo-américaine 9 1932.

— Dryden and Eton. MLN 52 1937.

— Corneille and Dryden as dramatic critics. In Seventeenth-century studies presented to Sir Herbert Grierson, Oxford 1938.

— Dryden's letter to Ormond. MLN 66 1951.

— Ouvrages récents sur Dryden. Etudes Anglaises 17 1964.

— Dryden plus miltonien que Milton. Etudes Anglaises 20 1967.

MacDonald, W. L. Dryden 1631–1931. Bookman (New York) Jan 1931.

Riske, E. T., L. I. Bredvold and T. B. Stroup. Dryden and Waller as members of the Royal Society. PMLA 46 1931. Comment on C. Lloyd, above.

Fornelli, G. La restaurazione inglese nell' opera di Dryden. Florence 1932.

Jünemann, W. Drydens Fabeln und ihre Quellen. Hamburg 1932.

McKeithan, D. M. The occasion of MacFlecknoe. PMLA 47 1932.

Ward, C. E. A biographical note on Dryden. MLR 27 1932.

— Was Dryden Collector of Customs? MLN 47 1932.

— The dates of two Dryden plays. PMLA 51 1936.

— Some notes on Dryden. RES 13 1937.

— Massinger and Dryden. ELH 2 1935.

— The publication and profits of Dryden's Virgil. PMLA 53 1938.

— An unpublished Dryden letter. TLS 29 Oct 1938.

— The Spanish Fryar and a provincial touring company. N & Q 11 Feb 1939.

— Religio laici and Father Simon's History. MLN 61 1946.

— The tempest: a Restoration opera problem. ELH 13 1946.

— The life of Dryden. Chapel Hill 1961.

— Challenges to Dryden's biographer. In Dryden: papers read at a Clark Library seminar, Feb 27 1967, Los Angeles 1967.

Hollis, C. Dryden. 1933.

Mundy, P. D. Portraits of Dryden. N & Q 17 June 1933 (with subsequent correspondence); 2 May 1936.

— Dryden's heritage. N & Q 5 Feb 1938.

— The Cumberland ancestry of Dryden. N & Q 26 April, 7 June 1941.

— Recent work on Dryden. N & Q 6 Sept 1941.

— The baptism of Dryden. N & Q 8 May, 5 June 1943.

— The brothers and sisters of Dryden. N & Q 20 March 1948.

— Dryden's Dominican son. N & Q 27 Oct 1951.

— Dryden baronetcy: additions to GEC. N & Q Oct 1953.

Brennecke, E. Dryden's Odes and Draghi's music. PMLA 49 1934.

Hooker, E. N. The Dryden almanac story. PQ 13 1934.

— Dryden's allusion to the poet of excessive wit. N & Q 15 June 1935.

— The purpose of Dryden's Annus mirabilis. HLQ 10 1946.

— Dryden and the atoms of Epicurus. ELH 24 1957.

Niemeyer, C. The Earl of Roscommon's academy. MLN 49 1934.

Allen, N. B. The sources of Dryden's comedies. Ann Arbor 1935.

— The sources of the Mock astrologer. PQ 36 1957.

Brooks, H. F. Notes on Dryden, Cowley and Shadwell. N & Q 9 Feb 1935.

— When did Dryden write Mac Flecknoe? RES 11 1935.

— Dryden and Cowley. TLS 19 April 1957. Reply by A. Arber 7 June 1957.

Fletcher, E. G. A Dryden anecdote. MLN 50 1935.

Havens, P. S. Dryden's 'tagged' version of Paradise lost. In T. M. Parrott presentation volume, Princeton 1935.

Nettleton, G. H. Author's changes in the Conquest of Granada part 1. MLN 50 1935.

Parsons, C. O. Dryden's letter of attorney. MLN 50 1935.

Turnell, G. M. Dryden and the religious elements in the classical tradition. E Studien 70 1935.

Dobrée, B. Milton and Dryden. ELH 3 1936.

— John Dryden. 1956 (Br Council pamphlet).

Edison, J. O. Dryden's criticism of Shakespeare. SP 33 1936.

Leavis, F. R. Antony and Cleopatra and All for Love: a critical exercise. Scrutiny 5 1936.

Macdonald, H. The attacks on Dryden. E & S 21 1936.

Walcott, F. G. Dryden's answer to Rymer's The tragedies of the last age. PQ 15 1936.

Bennett, J. A. W. Dryden and All Souls. MLN 52 1937.

Dryden's conversion. TLS 17 April 1937.

Irvine, M. Identification of characters in Mulgrave's Essay upon satyr. SP 34 1937.

Kevin, N. The argument from poetry. Irish Ecclesiastical Record 50 1937.

Osborn, J. M. Edmond Malone and the Dryden Almanac story. PQ 16–17 1937–8. See H. G. Dick 18 1939.

— Dryden: some biographical facts and problems. New York 1940, Gainesville 1965 (rev).

Stroup, T. B. Scenery for the Indian queen. MLN 52 1937.

Wasserman, E. R. Pre-Restoration poetry in Dryden's Miscellany. MLN 52 1937.

— The return of the enjambed couplet. ELH 7 1940.

— Dryden's Epistle to Charleton. JEGP 55 1956; rptd in his Subtler language, Baltimore 1959.

— The meaning of Poland in the Medal. MLN 73 1958.

Hartsock, M. E. Dryden's plays: a study in ideas. In Seventeenth-century studies, ed R. Shafer, ser 2, Princeton 1938.

Maillet, A. Dryden et Voltaire. Revue de Littérature Comparée 18 1938.

Barron, M. Dryden the Catholic. Dominicana 24 1939.

Bronowski, J. In his Poet's defence, Cambridge 1939.

Brower, R. A. Dryden's poetic diction and Virgil. PQ 18 1939.

— Dryden's epic manner and Virgil. PMLA 55 1940.

— An allusion to Europe: Dryden and tradition. ELH 19 1952.

— Dryden and the 'invention' of Pope. In Restoration and eighteenth-century literature, ed C. Camden, Chicago 1963.

Gordon, R. K. Dryden and the Waverley novels. MLR 34 1939.

Huntley, F. L. Dryden, Rochester and the eighth satire of Juvenal. PQ 18 1939.

— Dryden's discovery of Boileau. MP 45 1947.

— The persons in An essay of dramatic poesy. MLN 63 1948.

— On Dryden's Essay of dramatic poesy. Univ Michigan Contributions in Modern Philology 16 1951.

L., G. G. 'Ever fair and ever young'. N & Q 1 April 1939.

Lewis, C. S. Shelley, Dryden and Mr Eliot. In his Rehabilitations, Oxford 1939.

Schweitzer, J. W. Dryden's use of Scudéry's Almahide. MLN 54 1939, 62 1947.

Wilson, J. H. Rochester, Dryden and the Rose-Street affair. RES 15 1939.

Boys, R. C. Some problems of Dryden's Miscellany. ELH 7 1940.

de Beer, E. S. Dryden: The kind keeper, the poet of scandalous memory. N & Q 24 Aug 1940.
—— Dryden's anti-clericalism. N & Q 12 Oct 1940.
—— Dryden: date of a prologue, 'Gallants a bashful poet'. N & Q 21 Dec 1940.
—— Absalom and Achitophel: literary and historical notes. RES 17 1941.
Evans, B. I. Dryden and Pope. In his Tradition and romanticism, 1940.
Harbage, A. Elizabethan-Restoration palimpsest. MLR 35 1940.
Jefferson, D. W. The significance of Dryden's heroic plays. Proc Leeds Philosophical & Literary Soc (Historical & Literary section) 5 1940.
—— Aspects of Dryden's imagery. EC 4 1954.
—— 'All, all of a piece throughout': thoughts on Dryden's dramatic poetry. In Restoration theatre, ed J. R. Brown and B. Harris 1965.
Muir, K. The imagery of All for love. Proc Leeds Philosophical & Literary Soc (Historical & Literary section) 5 1940.
Pinto, V. de S. Rochester, Dryden and the Duchess of Portsmouth. RES 16 1940.
—— Dryden and Thomas Shipman. N & Q 6 Sept 1947.
—— Rochester and Dryden. Renaissance & Modern Stud 5 1961.
Rösecke, I. Drydens Prologe und Epiloge. Hamburg 1940.
Hooker, H. M. Charles Montagu's reply to the Hind and the panther. ELH 8 1941.
—— Dryden's and Shadwell's Tempest. HLQ 6 1943.
—— Dryden's Georgics and English predecessors. HLQ 9 1946.
Long, R. B. Dryden's importance as a spokesman of the Tories. SE 1941.
Dunne, J. W. Dryden: Catholic apologist. Clergy Rev 21 1942.
Evans, G. B. Dryden's State of innocence. TLS 21 March 1942.
—— A seventeenth-century reader of Shakespeare. RES 21 1945.
—— The text of MacFlecknoe. Harvard Lib Bull 7 1953.
—— Dryden's MacFlecknoe and Dekker's Satiromastic. MLN 76 1961.
Richards, I. A. The interaction of words. In A. Tate, The language of poetry, Princeton 1942.
Smith, R. J. The date of MacFlecknoe. RES 18 1942.
—— Shadwell's impact upon Dryden. RES 20 1944.
Bottkol, J. M. Dryden's Latin scholarship. MP 40 1943.
Hathaway, B. Dryden and the function of tragedy. PMLA 58 1943. See E. N. Hooker, PQ 23 1944.
Loane, G. G. Notes on the Globe Dryden. N & Q 6 Nov 1943.
McManaway, J. G. Notes on A key to Absalom and Achitophel. N & Q 19 June 1943.
Montgomery, G. Dryden and the battle of the books. Univ of California Pbns in Eng 14 1943.
Trowbridge, H. Essay on the dramatic poetry of the last age. PQ 22 1943.
—— The place of the rules in Dryden's criticism. MP 44 1946.
Wallerstein, R. Dryden and the analysis of Shakespeare's techniques. RES 19 1943.
—— To madness near allied: Shaftesbury in Absalom and Achitophel. HLQ 6 1943.
—— On the death of Mrs Killigrew: the perfecting of a genre. SP 44 1947.
—— Studies in seventeenth-century poetic. Madison 1950.
Scott, F. R. Lady Honoria Howard [and the Honoria of Rival ladies]. RES 20 1944.
Wright, H. G. The reputation and influence of Dryden's Fables. RES 21 1945.
Davies, G. The conclusion of Absalom and Achitophel. HLQ 10 1946.

Hoefling, Sr M. C. A study in the structure of meaning in the satiric verse 'characters' of Dryden. Washington 1946.
Milton, W. M. Tempest in a teapot. ELH 14 1946.
Monk, S. H. Dryden the craftsman. Sewanee Rev 54 1946.
—— Dryden studies: a survey 1920–45. ELH 14 1947.
—— Dryden's 'eminent French critic' in A parallel of poetry and painting. N & Q Oct 1955.
—— Shadwell 'flail of sense'. N & Q Feb 1960.
Ribner, I. Dryden's Shakespearian criticism and the neo-classical paradox. Shakespeare Assoc Bull 21 1946.
Russell, T. W. Voltaire, Dryden and heroic tragedy. New York 1946.
—— Dryden, inspirateur de Voltaire. Revue de Littérature Comparée 22 1948.
Williamson, G. The occasion of An essay of dramatic poesy. MP 44 1946.
Prior, M. E. Tragedy and the heroic play: Aureng-zebe and All for love. In his Language of tragedy, New York 1947.
Rundle, J. U. The source of Dryden's comic plot in the Assignation. MP 45 1947.
Tyler, H. Milton and Dryden. TLS 12 April 1947.
Gardner, W. B. Dryden and the authorship of the Epilogue to Crowne's Calisto. SE 27 1948.
—— Dryden's interest in judicial astronomy. SP 47 1950.
Tillyard, E. M. W. Ode on Anne Killigrew. In his Five poems 1470–1870, 1948.
—— A note on Dryden's criticism. In The seventeenth century, by R. F. Jones et al, Stanford 1951.
Dunkin, P. S. The Dryden Troilus and Cressida imprint: another theory. SB 2 1949.
Perkinson, R. H. A note on Religio laici. PQ 27 1949.
Bowers, F. T. The first edition of Dryden's Wild gallant 1669. Library 5th ser 5 1950.
—— The 1665 manuscript of Dryden's Indian emperour. SP 48 1951.
—— Dryden as Laureate: the cancel leaf in King Arthur. TLS 10 April 1953. See also K. Young 8 May 1953.
—— The pirated quarto of Dryden's State of innocence. SB 5 1953.
Horsman, E. A. Dryden's French borrowings. RES new ser 1 1950.
MacMillan, D. The sources of the Indian emperour. HLQ 13 1950.
Nichol Smith, D. Dryden. Cambridge 1950 (Clark Lectures 1948–9).
Purpus, E. R. A deistical essay attributed to Dryden. PQ 29 1950.
Sherwood, J. C. Dryden and the rules: the Preface to Troilus and Cressida. Comparative Lit 2 1950.
—— Dryden and the rules: the Preface to the Fables. JEGP 52 1953.
—— Dryden and the critical theories of Tasso. Comparative Lit 18 1966.
Steck, J. S. The Indian emperour: the text. SB 2 1950.
Swedenberg, H. T. One diting Dryden's early poems. In Essays dedicated to L. B. Campbell, Berkeley 1950.
—— England's joy: Astraea redux in its setting. SP 50 1953.
—— (ed). Essential articles for the study of Dryden. Hamden Conn 1966.
—— Challenges to Dryden's editor. In Dryden: papers read at a Clark Library seminar, Feb 27 1967, Los Angeles 1967.
—— Dryden's obsessive concern with the heroic. SP extra ser 4 1967.
Johnson, M. Dryden's notes on depilation. N & Q 27 Oct 1951.
Korn, A. L. Mac Flecknoe and Cowley's Davideis. HLQ 14 1951.
Martin, R. H. A note on Dryden's Aeneid. PQ 30 1951.
Söderlind, J. Verb syntax in Dryden's prose. 2 vols Upsala 1951–8.

Adams, H. H. A prompt copy of Tyrannick love. SB 4 1952.

Calder-Marshall, A. Dryden and the rise of modern publishing. History Today Sept 1952.

Davie, D. Dramatic poetry: Dryden's conversation piece. Cambridge Jnl June 1952.

Kinsley, J. Dryden's Character of a good parson and Bishop Ken. RES new ser 3 1952.

—— Dryden and the art of praise. E Studies 34 1953.

—— Dryden and the 'encomium musicæ'. RES new ser 4 1953. On Alexander's feast.

—— Dryden's bestiary. RES new ser 4 1953. On Hind and panther.

—— A Dryden play at Edinburgh. Scottish Historical Rev 33 1954.

—— Historical allusions in Absalom and Achitophel. RES new ser 6 1955. Reply by E. S. de Beer 7 1956, with Kinsley's reply, ibid.

—— The 'three glorious victories' in Annus mirabilis. RES new ser 7 1956.

Suckling, N. Dryden in Egypt: reflexions on All for love. Durham Univ Jnl 14 1952.

Aden, J. M. Dryden and Boileau: critical influence. SP 50 1953.

—— Dryden and St Evrémond. Comparative Lit 6 1954.

—— Dryden and Swift. N & Q June 1955.

—— Dryden, Corneille and the Essay of dramatic poesy. RES new ser 6 1955.

—— Shakespeare in Dryden's first published poem. N & Q Jan 1955.

—— Dryden and the imagination: the first phase. PMLA 74 1959.

Cameron, W. J. An overlooked Dryden printing. N & Q Aug 1953.

—— Dryden and Henry Herringman. N & Q May 1957.

Hamilton, M. H. The early editions of Dryden's State of innocence. SB 5 1953.

—— The manuscripts of the State of innocence. SB 6 1954.

Morgan, E. Dryden's drudging. Cambridge Jnl April 1953.

Smith, J. H. Dryden's prologue and epilogue to Mithridates revived. PMLA 68 1953.

—— Dryden and Buckingham: the beginnings of the feud. MLN 69 1954.

—— Dryden and Flecknoe: a conjecture. PQ 33 1954.

—— The Dryden-Howard collaboration. SP 51 1954.

—— Some sources of Dryden's Toryism 1682-4. HLQ 20 1957.

Winterbottom, J. The development of the hero in Dryden's tragedies. JEGP 52 1953.

—— The place of Hobbesian ideas in Dryden's tragedies. JEGP 57 1958.

—— Stoicism in Dryden's tragedies. JEGP 61 1962.

Cooke, A. L. Two parallels [Wild gallant and Congreve's Love for love]. N & Q Jan 1954.

Feder, L. Dryden's use of classical rhetoric. PMLA 69 1954.

Freedman, M. A note on Milton and Dryden as satirists. N & Q Jan 1954.

—— Dryden's 'memorable visit' to Milton. HLQ 18 1955.

—— All for love and Samson Agonistes. N & Q Dec 1956.

—— Dryden's miniature epic. JEGP 57 1958.

—— Dryden's reported reaction to Paradise lost. N & Q Jan 1958.

—— Milton and Dryden on rhyme. HLQ 24 1961.

Hammond, H. One immortal song [Absalom and Achitophel]. RES new ser 5 1954.

Moore, F. H. Heroic comedy: a new interpretation of Dryden's Assignation. SP 51 1954.

—— Dr Pelling, Dr Pell and Dryden's Lord Nonsuch. MLR 49 1954.

—— The nobler pleasure: Dryden's comedy in theory and practice. Chapel Hill 1963.

—— The composition of Sir Martin Mar-all. SP extra ser 4 1967.

Young, K. Dryden: a critical biography. 1954.

Dearing, V. A. Mac Flecknoe: the case for authorial revision. SB 7 1955.

Emerson, E. H., H. E. Davis and I. Johnson. Intention and achievement in All for love. College Eng Nov 1955.

Frost, W. Dryden and the art of translation. New Haven 1955.

Merzbach, M. K. The third source of Dryden's Amphitryon. Anglia 73 1955.

Whitlock, B. W. Elijah and Elisha in Dryden's Mac Flecknoe. MLN 70 1955.

Biggins, D. Source notes for Dryden, Wycherley and Otway. N & Q July 1956.

Brossman, S. W. Dryden's Cassandra and Congreve's Zara. N & Q March 1956.

—— Dryden's Cleomenes and Fletcher's Bonduca. N & Q Feb 1957.

Cameron, L. W. The cold prose fits of Dryden. Revue de Littérature Comparée 30 1956.

Cope, J. I. Science, Christ and Cromwell in Dryden's Heroic stanzas. MLN 71 1956.

Deering, B. Some views of a beast. MLN 71 1956.

Dobbins, A. C. Dryden's Character of a good parson: background and interpretation. SP 53 1956.

Manley, F. Ambivalent allusions in Dryden's fable of the swallows. MLN 71 1956.

Miner, E. R. Dryden's MacFlecknoe. N & Q Aug 1956.

—— Dryden's Messianic eclogue. RES new ser 9 1960.

—— Dryden and the issue of human progress. PQ 40 1961.

—— Some characteristics of Dryden's use of metaphor. Stud in Eng Lit 1500-1900 2 1962.

—— The wolf's progress in the Hind and the panther. BNYPL Oct 1963.

—— Dryden as prose controversialist: his role in A defence of the Royal papers. PQ 43 1964.

—— The significance of plot in the Hind and the panther. BNYPL Sept 1965.

—— Dryden's Annus mirabilis 653-6. Explicator 24 1966.

—— Chaucer in Dryden's Fables. In Studies in Criticism and aesthetics 1660-1800, ed H. Anderson and J. S. Shea, Minneapolis 1967.

—— Dryden's ode on Mrs Anastasia Stafford. HLQ 30 1967.

—— Dryden's poetry. Bloomington 1967.

Myers, R. M. Handel, Dryden and Milton: observations on the poems of Milton and Dryden. 1956.

Padgett, L. E. Dryden's edition of Corneille. MLN 71 1956.

Spector, R. D. Dryden's translation of Chaucer: a problem in neo-classical diction. N & Q Jan 1956.

Sutherland, W. O. S. Dryden's use of popular imagery in the Medal. SE 35 1956.

Bowers, R. H. Dryden's influence on Cuthbert Constable. N & Q Jan 1957.

Coshow, B. G. Dryden's zambra dance. Explicator 16 1957.

Crinò, A. M. John Dryden. Florence 1957.

—— Dryden: poeta satirico. Florence 1958.

—— Dryden ms. TLS 22 Sept 1966.

—— Uno sconosciuto autografo drydeniana al British Museum. Eng Miscellany (Rome) 17 1966.

Falle, G. G. Dryden: professional man of letters. UTQ 26 1957.

—— Sir Walter Scott as editor of Dryden and Swift. UTQ 36 1966.

Hemphill, G. Dryden's heroic line. PMLA 72 1957.

Hitchman, P. J. King Arthur at Nottingham. Theatre Notebook 9 1957.

Kermode, F. Dryden: a 'Poet's poet'. Listener 30 May 1957.

Maurer, A. E. W. Dryden and Pyrrhonism. N & Q June 1957.

—— N & Q May, July, Aug 1958. 3 notes.

—— Dryden's Balaam well hung? RES new ser 10 1959.

—— Dryden's knowledge of historians, ancient and modern. N & Q July-Aug 1959.

—— Dryden's Absalom and Achitophel 745-6. Explicator 20 1961.

—— Who prompted Dryden to write Absalom and Achitophel? PQ 40 1961.

—— The design of Dryden's The medall. Papers on Language & Lit 2 1966.

—— The structure of Dryden's Astraea redux. Ibid.

—— Dryden's memory vindicated: proceed with bibliographical caution. N & Q Sept 1967.

Nathanson, L. The context of Dryden's criticism of Donne and Cowley's love poetry. N & Q Feb 1957.

—— Dryden, Donne and Cowley. N & Q May 1957.

Perkins, M. L. The Indian emperour and Voltaire's Alzire. Comparative Lit 9 1957.

Bleuler, W. Das heroische Drama Drydens als Experiment dekorativer Formkunst. Berne 1958.

Browne, R. B. Dryden and Milton in nineteenth-century 'popular' songbooks. Bull of Bibliography 22 1958.

Cable, C. H. Absalom and Achitophel as epic satire. In Studies in honor of John Wilcox, ed A. D. Wallace and W. O. Ross, Detroit 1958.

Howarth, R. G. Dryden's letters. Eng Stud in Africa 1 1958.

Le Comte, E. S. Samson Agonistes and Aureng-zebe. Etudes Anglaises 9 1958.

Morton, R. 'By no strong passion swayed': a note on Aureng-zebe. Eng Stud in Africa 1 1958.

Moore, J. R. Alexander's feast: a possible chronology of development. PQ 37 1958.

—— Political allusions in Dryden's later plays. PMLA 73 1958.

Osborn, S. C. Heroical love in Dryden's heroic drama. PMLA 73 1958.

Chambers, A. B. Absalom and Achitophel: Christ and Satan. MLN 74 1959.

Hoffman, A. W. Note on a Dryden ode. TLS 19 June 1959. Reply by P. Legouis 3 July 1959.

—— Dryden's To Mr Congreve. MLN 75 1960.

—— Dryden's imagery. Gainesville 1962.

Joost, N. Dryden's Medal and the baroque in politics and the arts. Modern Age 3 1959.

Lowens, I. St Evremond, Dryden and the theory of opera. Criticism 1 1959.

Nänny, M. Drydens rhetorische Poetik. Berne 1959.

Strang, B. M. H. Dryden's innovations in critical vocabulary. Durham Univ Jnl 51 1959.

Emslie, M. Dryden's couplets: imagery vowed to poverty. CQ 2 1960.

—— Dryden's couplets: wit and conversation. EC 11 1961.

Fujimura, T. H. The appeal of Dryden's heroic plays. PMLA 75 1960.

—— Dryden's Religio laici: an Anglican poem. PMLA 76 1961.

Prince, F. T. The birth of modern England: Dryden's political satires. Listener 28 July 1960.

—— Dryden redivivus. REL 1 1960.

Proudfoot, L. Dryden's Aeneid and its seventeenth-century predecessors. Manchester 1960.

Steadman, J. M. Timotheus in Dryden, E.K. and Gafori. TLS 16 Dec 1960.

Ball, A. Charles II: Dryden's Christian hero. MP 59 1961.

Birrell, T. A. Dryden's purchases at two book auctions 1680 and 1682. E Studies 42 1961. See J. M. Osborn, PQ 41 1962 p. 580.

Brown, D. D. Dryden's Religio laici and the 'judicious and learned friend'. MLR 56 1961.

—— John Tillotson's revisions and Dryden's 'talent for English prose'. RES new ser 12 1961.

Chiasson, E. J. Dryden's apparent scepticism in Religio laici. Harvard Theological Rev 54 1961.

Hughes, R. E. Dryden's greatest compromise. Texas Stud in Lit & Lang 2 1961.

Johnson, J. W. Dryden's Epistle to Robert Howard. Ball State Teacher's College Forum 2 1961.

McFadden, G. Dryden's 'most barren period'—and Milton. HLQ 24 1961.

—— Dryden and the numbers of his native tongue. In Essays and studies in language and literature, ed H. H. Petit, Duquesne 1964.

—— Dryden, Boileau and Longinian imitation. Proc of 4th Congress of the International Comparative Lit Assoc, ed F. Jost, Fribourg 1964, Hague 1966.

—— Elkanah Settle and the genesis of Mac Flecknoe. PQ 43 1964.

Ricks, C. Dryden's Absalom. EC 11 1961.

Schilling, B. N. Dryden and the conservative myth: a reading of Absalom and Achitophel. New Haven 1961.

—— (ed). Dryden: a collection of critical essays. Englewood Cliffs NJ 1963.

Schless, H. H. Dryden's Absalom and Achitophel and A dialogue between Nathan and Absolome. PQ 40 1961.

Singh, S. Dryden and the unities. Indian Jnl of Eng Stud 2 1961.

Tanner, J. E. The Messianic image in MacFlecknoe. MLN 76 1961.

Alssid, M. W. The perfect conquest: a study of the theme, structure and characters in Dryden's The Indian Emperor. SP 59 1962.

—— The design of Dryden's Aureng-zebe. JEGP 64 1965.

—— Shadwell's Macflecnoe. Stud in Eng Lit 1500–1900 7 1967.

Amarasinghe, U. Dryden and Pope in the early nineteenth century. Cambridge 1962.

Baumgartner, A. M. Dryden's Caleb and Agag. RES new ser 13 1962.

Forrest, J. E. Dryden, Hobbes, Thomas Goodwin and the nimble spaniel. N & Q Oct 1962. Reply by G. Watson, June 1963.

Golden, S. A. A numismatic view of Dryden's Medal. N & Q Oct 1962.

—— Dryden's To my honored friend Dr Charleton 37–44. Explicator 24 1965.

—— Dryden's praise of Dr Charleton. Hermathena 103 1966.

Irie, K. The auxiliary 'do' in Dryden's plays. Anglica (Osaka) 5 1962.

Jeune, S. Hamlet d'Otway, Macbeth de Dryden: ou Shakespeare en France en 1714. Revue de Littérature Comparée 36 1962.

King, B. Don Sebastian: Dryden's moral fable. Sewanee Rev 70 1962.

—— Absalom and Achitophel: Machiavelli and the false Messiah. Etudes Anglaises 16 1963.

—— Dryden's Absalom and Achitophel 150–66. Explicator 21 1963.

—— Dryden's intent in All for love. College Eng Jan 1963.

—— The significance of Dryden's State of innocence. Stud in Eng Lit 1500–1900 4 1964.

—— Absalom and Dryden's earlier praise of Monmouth. E Studies 46 1965.

—— Anti-Whig satire in the Duke of Guise. Eng Lang Notes 2 1965.

—— Dryden, Tillotson and Tyrannick love. RES new ser 16 1965.

—— Dryden's Marriage-a-la-mode. Drama Survey 4 1965.

—— Lycidas and Oldham. Etudes Anglaises 19 1966.

—— Dryden's major plays. Edinburgh 1966.

—— Dryden's ark: the influence of Filmer. Stud in Eng Lit 1500–1900 7 1967.

—— (ed). Twentieth-century interpretations of All for love. Englewood Cliffs NJ 1968.

Kirsch, A. C. Dryden, Corneille and the heroic play. MP 59 1962.

—— The significance of Dryden's Aureng-zebe. ELH 29 1962.

—— Dryden's heroic drama. Princeton 1965.

Mace, D. T. Dryden's dialogue on drama. Jnl of Warburg & Courtauld Inst 25 1962.

— Musical humanism, the doctrine of rhythms and the St Cecilia Odes of Dryden. Jnl of Warburg & Courtauld Inst 27 1964.

Marks, E. R. Pragmatic poetics: Dryden to Valéry. Bucknell Rev 10 1962.

Miller, C. H. The styles of the Hind and the panther. JEGP 61 1962.

Roper, A. H. Dryden's Medal and the divine analogy. ELH 29 1962.

— Dryden's Secular masque. MLQ 23 1962.

— Dryden's poetic kingdoms. 1965.

Waith, E. M. The Herculean hero in Marlowe, Chapman, Shakespeare and Dryden. New York 1962.

— The voice of Mr Bayes. Stud in Eng Lit 1500–1900 3 1963.

Welle, J. A. van der. Dryden and Holland. Groningen 1962.

Barnard, J. Dryden, Tonson and subscriptions for the 1697 Virgil. PBSA 57 1963.

— The dates of six Dryden letters. PQ 42 1963.

Boddy, M. Dryden-Lauderdale relationships: some bibliographical notes and a suggestion. PQ 42 1963. Reply J. Barnard, ibid.

— The manuscripts and printed editions of Lauderdale's Virgil and Dryden. N & Q April 1965.

Hope, A. D. Anne Killigrew or the art of modulating. Southern Rev (Adelaide) 1 1963.

Klima, S. Some unrecorded borrowings from Shakespeare in All for love. N & Q Nov 1963.

Murakami, S. Reverence for human nature: the poetry of Dryden and Pope. Jnl of Faculty of Letters (Osaka) 10 1963.

Nazareth, P. All for love: Dryden's hybrid play. Eng Stud in Africa 6 1963.

Ringler, R. N. Two sources for Dryden's Indian Emperour. PQ 42 1963.

— Two Dryden notes. Eng Lang Notes 1 1964.

— Dryden at the House of Busirane. E Studies 49 1968.

Rudd, N. Dryden on Horace and Juvenal. UTQ 32 1963.

Schultz, M. F. Coleridge's 'debt' to Dryden and Johnson. N & Q May 1963.

Simon, I. Dryden's revision of the Essay of dramatic poesy. RES new ser 14 1963.

— Dryden's prose style. Revue des Langues Vivantes 31 1965.

Stratman, C. J. All for love: unrecorded editions. PBSA 57 1963.

Sutherland, J. Dryden: the poet as orator. Glasgow 1963 (W. P. Ker Memorial Lecture).

Towers, T. H. The lineage of Shadwell: an approach to MacFlecknoe. Stud in Eng Lit 1500–1900 3 1963.

Watson, G. Dryden's first answer to Rymer. RES new ser 14 1963. On the Heads. Reply by R. D. Hume, below.

Bately, J. M. Dryden's revisions in the Essay of dramatic poesy. RES new ser 15 1964.

— Dryden and branded words. N & Q April 1965.

Benson, D. R. Theology and politics in Dryden's conversion. Stud in Eng Lit 1500–1900 4 1964.

— Who 'bred' Religio laici? JEGP 65 1966.

Caracciolo, P. Some unrecorded variants in the first edition of All for love. Book Collector 13 1964.

Cooke, M. G. The Restoration ethos of Byron's classical plays. PMLA 79 1964. On All for love and Byron's Sardanapalus.

Eleanor, Mother M. Anne Killigrew and Mac Flecknoe. PQ 43 1964.

Gallagher, M. Dryden's translation of Lucretius. HLQ 28 1964.

Goggin, L. P. This bow of Ulysses. In Essays and studies in literature, ed H. H. Petit, Duquesne 1964.

Greany, H. T. On the opening lines of Absalom and Achitophel. Satire News Letter 2 1964.

Hart, J. Dryden: the politics of style. Modern Age 8 1964.

Hughes, R. Upon the death of Lord Hastings: Royalist polemic. Siena Stud in Lit 7 1964.

Lewalski, B. K. 'David's troubles remembered': an analogue to Absalom and Achitophel. N & Q Sept 1964.

— The scope and function of biblical allusion in Absalom and Achitophel. Eng Lang Notes 2 1965.

Levine, J. A. Dryden's Epistle to John Driden. JEGP 63 1964.

— Dryden's Song for St Cecilia's Day 1687. PQ 44 1965.

Loftis, J. The Hispanic element in Dryden. Emory Univ Quart 20 1964.

— Exploration and enlightenment: Dryden's The Indian Emperour and its background. PQ 45 1966.

Masson, D. I. Dryden's phonetic rhetoric: some passages from his original poems. Proc Leeds Philosophical & Literary Soc (Historical & Literary section) 11 1964.

Rosenberg, B. A. Annus mirabilis distilled. PMLA 79 1964.

Russ, J. R. RES new ser 15 1964. On Dryden's use of Topsell.

Starnes, D. T. Imitation of Shakespeare in Dryden's All for love. Texas Stud in Lang & Lit 6 1964.

Crider, J. R. Dryden's Absalom and Achitophel 169–72. Explicator 23 1965.

Davies, H. N. Dryden's All for love and Thomas Mays's The tragedie of Cleopatra. N & Q April 1965.

— Dryden and Vossius: a reconsideration. Jnl of Warburg & Courtauld Inst 29 1966. Replies by D. Mace and Davies, ibid.

— Dryden's All for love and Sedley's Antony and Cleopatra. N & Q June 1967.

Hamm, V. M. Dryden's Religio laici and Roman Catholic apologetics. PMLA 80 1965.

— Dryden's The hind and the panther and Roman Catholic apologetics. PMLA 83 1968.

Jackson, W. Dryden's Emperor and Lillo's Merchant: the relevant bases of action. MLQ 26 1965.

Kiehl, J. M. Dryden's Zimri and Chaucer's pardoner: a comparative study in verse portraiture. Thoth 6 1965.

Murphree, A. A. Wit and Dryden. In All these to teach: essays in honor of C. A. Robertson, ed R. A. Bryan etc, Gainesville 1965.

Vieth, D. M. Irony in Dryden's Ode to Anne Killigrew. SP 62 1965.

Wasserman, G. R. The domestic metaphor in Astraea redux. Eng Lang Notes 3 1965.

— John Dryden. New York 1965.

— Dryden's The hind and the panther III. 1–21. Explicator 24 1966.

— A note on Dryden's panther. N & Q Oct 1966.

Zebouni, S. A. Dryden: a study in heroic characterization. Baton Rouge 1965.

Anselment, R. A. Martin Marprelate: a new source for Dryden's fable of the martins and swallows. RES new ser 17 1966.

Archer, S. Benaiah in Absalom and Achitophel 2. Eng Lang Notes 3 1966.

— The persons in An essay of dramatic poesy. Papers on Lang & Lit 2 1966.

Doyle, A. Dryden's authorship of Notes and observations on the Emperor of Morocco 1674. Stud in Eng Lit 1500–1900 6 1966.

Kinneavy, G. B. Judgment in extremes: a study of Dryden's Absalom and Achitophel. Univ of Dayton Rev 3 1966.

Leed, J. A difficult passage in Astraea redux. E Studies 47 1966.

Novak, M. E. The demonology of Dryden's Tyrannick love and 'Anti-Scott'. Eng Lang Notes 4 1966.

— Dryden's 'Ape of the French eloquence' and Richard Flecknoe. BNYPL Oct 1968.

Shergold, N. D. and P. Ure. Dryden and Calderón: a new Spanish source for the Indian Emperour. MLR 61 1966.

Thale, M. Dryden's critical vocabulary: the imitation of nature. Papers on Lang & Lit 2 1966.

—— Dryden's dramatic criticism: polestar of the ancients. Comparative Lit 18 1966.

Wellington, J. E. Conflicting concepts of man in Dryden's Absalom and Achitophel. Satire News Letter 4 1966.

Adams, P. G. 'Harmony of numbers': Dryden's alliteration, consonance, assonance. Texas Stud in Lang & Lit 9 1967.

Angel, M. D. Five translations of the Aeneid. Classical Jnl April 1967.

Archer, S. Dryden's Mac Flecknoe 47–48. Explicator 26 1967.

—— On Dryden's History of the League 1684. Papers on Lang & Lit 4 1968.

Cerevini, S. Dryden e Teocrito: barocco e neoclassismo nella Restaurazione inglese. Milan 1967.

Corder, J. W. Rhetoric and meaning in Religio laici. PMLA 82 1967.

Fowler, A. and D. Brooks. The structure of Dryden's Song for St Cecilia's Day 1687. EC 17 1967.

Hamilton, K. J. Dryden and the poetry of statement. Brisbane 1967.

Peterson, R. G. Large manners and events: Sallust and Virgil in Absalom and Achitophel. PMLA 82 1967.

Taylor, A. M. Dryden's 'enchanted isle' and Shadwell's 'dominion'. SP extra ser 4 1967.

Weinbrot, H. D. Alexas in All for love: his genealogy and function. SP 64 1967.

Burnett, A. D. An early verse reply to Dryden's Hind and the panther. N & Q Oct 1968. By William Darrell.

Freehafer, J. Dryden's Indian Emperour. Explicator 27 1968.

French, A. L. Dryden, Marvell and political poetry. Stud in Eng Lit 1500–1900 8 1968.

Gamble, G. Y. Dryden's Mac Flecknoe 25–28. Explicator 26 1968.

Harth, P. Contexts of Dryden's thought. Chicago 1968.

Hinnant, C. H. Dryden's Gallic rooster. SP 65 1968.

Hume, R. D. Dryden's Heads of an answer: notes towards a hypothetical revolution. RES new ser 19 1968.

Levine, G. R. Dryden's 'inarticulate poesy': music and the Davidic King in Absalom and Achitophel. Eighteenth-Century Stud 1 1968.

Welcher, J. K. The opening of Religio laici and its Virgilian associations. Stud in Eng Lit 1500–1900 8 1968.

Zwicker, S. N. Dryden's borrowing from Ben Jonson's Panegyre. N & Q March 1968.

J. B.

SIR CHARLES SEDLEY
1639?–1701

Bibliographies

Pinto, V. de S. Poetical and dramatic works. 2 vols 1928. Bibliography in vol 2 lists poems by or attributed to Sedley and the miscellanies in which many are ptd.

Collections

The miscellaneous works, to which is added the death of Marc Antony, a tragedy never before printed, published from the original manuscripts by Capt [W.] Ayloffe. 1702.

The poetical works, and his speeches in Parliament, with large additions never before made publick, published by Capt Ayloffe. 1707, 1710. With many spurious addns.

The works, with memoirs of the author's life by an eminent hand [Defoe?]. 2 vols 1722, 1776, 1778. Contains much that is certainly not Sedley's.

§ 1

Pompey the Great: a tragedy translated out of French [of Corneille] by certain persons of honour [Waller, Sedley, Godolphin, Filmer, Dorset]. 1664.

The mulberry garden: a comedy. (Theatre Royal 1668). 1668, 1675, 1688.

Antony and Cleopatra: a tragedy. (Drury Lane 1677). 1677, 1696.

Bellamira, or the mistress: a comedy. (Drury Lane 1687). 1687.

The oration of Cicero for M. Marcellus. 1689. Anon, attributed to Sedley in Works, 1722.

Reflections upon our late and present proceedings in England. 1689 (anon), Edinburgh 1689; rptd in Somers tracts, ed W. Scott vol 10, 1813.

The speech of Sir Charles Sidley in the House of Commons. 1691; rptd in Somers tracts, ed W. Scott vol 10, 1813. See Remarques upon a late printed speech under the name of Sir Charles Sidley, 1691.

The happy pair: or a poem on matrimony. 1702, 1705 (corrected).

The grumbler. In Works, 1722 with own title-page 1719. Tr from de Brueys and de Palaprat, adapted by Garrick 1754 (Larpent ms 112) and Goldsmith 1773 (ed A. I. P. Wood, Cambridge Mass 1931).

§ 2

Pinto, V. de S. Sir Charles Sedley. 1927.

—— In his Restoration carnival, 1954. Selections with introd and notes.

—— In his Restoration Court poets, 1966.

Wilson, J. J. In his Court wits of the Restoration, Princeton 1948.

Boddy, M. P. The 1692 fourth book of Virgil. RES new ser 15 1964.

C. A. Z.

JOHN WILMOT,
2nd EARL OF ROCHESTER
1647–80

Bibliographies

Prinz, J. In his Rochester, Leipzig 1927.

Vieth, D. M. In his Attribution in Restoration poetry, New Haven 1927. See Complete poems, below.

Collections

The early edns are classified as in Vieth, above.

Series A. Poems on several occasions by the Right Honourable the E. of R—. 1680 (at least 10 edns, with Antwerp or Antwerpen on title-page), 1685, 1690 (no known copy), 1701, 171[3], 1731; ed J. Thorpe, Princeton 1950 (facs).

Series B. Poems etc on several occasions; with Valentinian: a tragedy. 1691 (preface by T. Rymer), 1696, 1705, 1710, 1714, 1718, 1732 (4th edn).

Series C. Miscellaneous works of the Right Honourable the late Earls of Rochester and Roscommon. 1707, 1707, 1709 (2 3rd edns), 1711, 2 vols 1714 (with works of Dorset etc), 1718, 1721, 1721, 1731, 1 vol 1735, 2 vols 1739 (3 edns), 1752, 1756, 1756, 1757, 1758, 1767, 1771, 1774, 1777.

Series D. Remains from a manuscript found in a gentleman's lodging. 1718, 1761 (as Poetical works). This ser contains only one or two genuine poems.

Johnson 10 ; Anderson 6 ; Chalmers 8.

Collected works. Ed J. Hayward 1926.

Poetical works. Ed Q.Johns, Manchester 1933.

Satire against mankind and other poems. Ed H. Levin, Norfolk Conn 1943.

Selected lyrics and satires. Ed R. Duncan 1948.

Poems by John Wilmot, Earl of Rochester. Ed V. de S. Pinto, 1953, 1964 (ML).

The Gyldenstolpe manuscript miscellany of poems by John Wilmot, Earl of Rochester and other Restoration authors. Ed B. Danielsson and D. M. Vieth, Stockholm 1967.

Complete poems. Ed D. M. Vieth, New Haven 1968. With bibliography of Rochester studies 1925–67.

§ 1

Corydon and Cloris: or the wanton shepherdess. [1676?]. Anon.

A satyr against mankind, by a person of honour. [1679].

A letter from Artemiza in the town to Chloe in the country, by a person of honour. [1679] (2 edns with varying titles).

Upon nothing: a poem. [1679], [1679], 1711.

A very heroical epistle from My Lord All-Pride to Dol-Common. 1679. Anon.

Sodom: or the quintessence of debauchery. 1684 (lost, perhaps never existent); ed L. S. A. M. von Römer, Paris 1904; Paris 1957, North Hollywood Cal 1966; tr German, 1909. In dramatic form, almost certainly not by Rochester.

Valentinian: a tragedy, as 'tis altered by the late Earl of Rochester. 1685. Preface by R. Wolseley, rptd in J. E. Spingarn, Critical essays of the seventeenth century vol 3, Oxford 1909. Ms of play, BM add 28692, as Lucina's rape.

The famous pathologist: or the noble mountebank, by Thomas Alcock and John Earl of Rochester. Ed V. de S. Pinto, Nottingham 1961. Rochester's mountebank bill, first rptd in Poems 1691, above, ed from transcript by Alcock.

Single poems pbd after 1680 and selections are not listed. An allusion to Horace, ed J. E. Spingarn in Critical essays of the seventeenth century vol 2, Oxford 1909. 7 poems ed G. de F. Lord in Poems on affairs of state vol 1, New Haven 1963.

Letters

A letter to Dr Burnet from the Earl of Rochester. 1680.

Familiar letters written by John late Earl of Rochester and several other persons of honour and quality. 2 vols 1697, 1697, 1699, 1705, 1705. Vol 1 ed T. Brown, vol 2 ed C. Gildon.

Some original letters of the Earl of Rochester to his lady and son. Museum 31 1747.

The Rochester-Savile letters 1671–80. Ed J. H. Wilson, Columbus Ohio 1941.

§2

For articles on single poems and textual problems see Complete poems, ed D. M. Vieth, *above.*

Parsons, R. A sermon preached at the funeral of the Right Honourable John Earl of Rochester. 1680.

Burnet, G. Some passages of the life and death of John Earl of Rochester. 1680.

Johnson, S. In his Lives of the poets vol 1, 1781.

Longueville, T. Rochester and other literary rakes. 1902.

Nicoll, A. Dryden, Howard and Rochester. TLS 13 Jan 1921. Ms of Valentinian and of A scene of Sir Robert Howard's play.

Prinz, J. Rochesteriana: being some anecdotes concerning John Earl of Rochester. Leipzig 1926.

— John Wilmot Earl of Rochester: his life and writings. Leipzig 1927.

Dobrée, B. Rochester: a conversation. 1926.

Williamson, G. The Restoration Petronius. Univ of Cal Chron 29 1927.

Pinto, V. de S. The poetry of John Wilmot. Trans Royal Soc of Lit 13 1934.

— Rochester: portrait of a Restoration poet. 1935, 1962 (as Enthusiast in wit).

— John Wilmot and the right veine of satire. E & S new ser 6 1953.

— In his Restoration carnival, 1954. Selections with introd and notes.

— Rochester and Dryden. Renaissance & Modern Stud 5 1961.

— In his Restoration Court poets, 1966.

Williams, C. Rochester. 1935.

Whitfield, F. Beast in view: a study of Rochester's poetry. Cambridge Mass 1936.

Wilson, J. H. Rochester's Valentinian and heroic sentiment. ELH 4 1937.

— Satiric elements in Rochester's Valentinian. PQ 16 1937.

— Rochester, Dryden and the Rose-street affair. RES 15 1939. *See also* V. de S. Pinto, Rochester, Dryden and the Duchess of Portsmouth, RES 16 1940.

— Rochester's A session of the poets. RES 22 1946.

— In his Court wits of the Restoration, 1948.

Crocker, S. F. Rochester's Satire against mankind. West Virginia Univ Stud 3rd ser 2 1937.

Legouis, P. Rochester et sa réputation. Etudes Anglaises 1 1937.

— Three notes on Rochester's poems. MLN 69 1954.

Murdock, K. A very profane wit. In his Sun at noon, New York 1939.

Huntley, F. L. Dryden, Rochester and the eighth satire of Juvenal. PQ 18 1939.

Moore, J. F. The originality of Rochester's Satyr against mankind. PMLA 58 1943.

Baine, R. M. Rochester or Fishbourne: a question of authorship. RES 22 1946. Sodom probably by Fishbourne.

Bruser, F. Disproportion: a study in the works of Rochester. UTQ 15 1946.

Lane, J. Court rake. In her Puritan, rake and squire, 1950.

Norman, C. Rake Rochester. 1954.

Vieth, D. M. The text of Rochester and the editions of 1680. PBSA 50 1956.

— Poems by 'My Lord R.' PMLA 72 1957. On poems by Edward Radclyffe, Earl of Derwentwater.

— Order of contents as evidence of authorship: Rochester's Poems of 1680. PBSA 53 1959.

— Attribution in Restoration poetry: a study of Rochester's Poems of 1680. New Haven 1963.

Duclos, P.-C. John Wilmot, 2ᵉ Comte de Rochester. Revue des Langues Vivantes 22 1956.

Kellow, K. Rochester—the mad Earl. 1957. Fiction.

Fujimura, T. H. Rochester's Satyr against mankind: an analysis. SP 55 1958.

Auffret, J. Rochester's Farewell. Etudes Anglaises 12 1959.

Hook, L. Something more about Rochester. MLN 75 1960. *See also* V. de S. Pinto, Godfrey Thacker and Sir Charles Sedley, N & Q March 1964.

Main, C. F. The right vein of Rochester's Satyr. In Essays presented to J. M. French, ed R. Kirk and C. F. Main, New Brunswick 1960.

Quaintance, R. E. French sources of the Restoration 'imperfect enjoyment' poem. PQ 42 1963.

Berman, R. Rochester and the defeat of the senses. Kenyon Rev 26 1964.

Giddey, E. Rochester: poète baroque. Etudes de Lettres 2nd ser 7 1964.

Ellis, F. H. John Freke and the History of the insipids. PQ 44 1965. Freke, not Rochester, author of the poem.

Erskine-Hill, H. H. Rochester: Augustan or explorer? In Renaissance and modern essays presented to V. de S. Pinto, 1966.

Righter, A. John Wilmot, Earl of Rochester. Proc Br Acad 53 1968.

Davies, P. C. Rochester and Boileau: a reconsideration. Comparative Lit 21 1969.

— Rochester: Augustan and explorer. Durham Univ Jnl new ser 30 1969.

C. A. Z.

IV. MINOR POETRY 1660–1700

This section excludes poets whose works appeared only in Miscellanies, for which see col 327, above ; and Scottish poets, col 1959, below.

References
Johnson, Anderson, Chalmers: *see col 435–6, above.*
POAS Poems on affairs of State, ed G. deF. Lord 6 vols New Haven 1963–71.

RICHARD AMES
d. 1693

Sylvia's revenge: or a satyr against man, in answer to the Satyr against woman [by Robert Gould]. 1688, 1692, 1697 (2nd edn), 1707 (11th edn), 1709 (with Gould's poem), 1710, 1720 (separately). Anon.

The folly of love: or an essay upon satyr against woman. 1691, 1693 (corrected, adds The bachelors lettany), 1700 (4th edn), 1701. Anon.

A letter from Leghorn, March 24 1690/1. 1691. Anon; prose.

An elegy on the death of Dr Thomas Saffold. 1691. Anon.

The pleasures of love and marriage: a poem in praise of the fair sex in requital for the Folly of love. 1691. Anon.

The siege and surrender of Mons: a tragicomedy. 1691. Anon.

Islington-wells: or the three-penny-academy. 1691 (anon); ed J. O. Halliwell[-Phillipps] 1861 (30 copies).

The search after claret: or a visitation of the vintners. 1691, 1691 (anon); ed A. L. Simon 1912 (with Farther search and Last search) (50 copies).

A search after wit: or a visitation of the authors. 1691. Anon.

A farther search after claret. 1691. Anon.

The last search after claret in Southwark. 1691, 1691. Signed Satyrical Dick.

An auction of whores. 1691. Anon; prose.

Lawyerus bootatus and spurratus: or the long vacation. 1691. By a student of Lincoln's-inn.

The female fire-ships: a satyr against whoring. 1691. Anon.

The character of a bigotted prince. 1691, 1692 (as Chuse which you will, liberty or slavery). Anon.

An elegy upon the death of that learned, pious and laborious minister of Jesus Christ, Mr Richard Baxter. 1691. Anon.

A dialogue between claret and Derby-ale. 1692. Anon.

The Jacobite conventicle. 1692. Anon.

Sylvia's complaint of her sexes unhappiness: being the second part of Sylvia's revenge. 1692 (includes The emulation: a Pindarique ode), 1697, 1698. Anon.

An elegy on the death of that brave sea-commander, Rear-admiral Carter. 1692. Anon.

Britannia victrix, or the triumphs of the royal navy: a Pindarick poem. 1692. Anon.

The double descent. 1692, 1692. Anon.

The present state of England: a vision. 1692. Anon.

Fatal friendship: or the drunkard's misery. 1693. By the author of The search after claret.

The rake: or the libertine's religion. 1693. Anon.

The bacchanalian sessions, with A farewell to wine. 1693. Anon, but contains a poem To the memory of Mr Richard Ames.

All the above pieces except the Sylvia poems, A search after wit, and perhaps The pleasures of love and marriage, are attributed 'to the same author' in the 1693 edn of Folly of love, together with the following now lost : The auction of ladies; The circulation of money, or the travels of half a crown; Elegy on the French fleet; The lent keepers.

EDMUND ARWAKER
c. 1655–1730

An elegy on her Grace Elizabeth Duchess of Ormond. 1684. Signed E.A.

The vision: a Pindarick ode occasion'd by the death of our late gracious sovereign King Charles II. 1685, 1685.

The second part of the vision: a Pindarick ode occasioned by their Majesties happy coronation. 1685.

Pia desideria: or divine addresses, written in Latine by Herm Hugo. 1686, 1690 (with alterations and addns), 1702 (corrected), [1727 ?] (as Divine entertainments).

Fons perennis: a poem on the excellent and useful invention of making sea-water fresh. 1686.

The ministration of publick baptism of infants to be used in the church. 1687. Prose.

A poem humbly dedicated to the Queen on the occasion of her Majesty's happy conception. 1688.

A votive table consecrated to the church's deliverers, the present King and Queen. 1689.

The apparition: or the genius of Ireland complaining of her present misery. 1689.

An epistle to Monsieur Boileau inviting his Muse to forsake the French interest and celebrate the King of England. 1694.

An elegy on his Excellency Lieutenant-General Tolmach. 1694.

A Pindaric ode upon our late soveraign lady of blessed memory Queen Mary. 1695.

Thoughts well employ'd: or the duty of self-observation. 1695, 1697 (with Pythagoras's golden verses).

God's King the people's blessing: a sermon. Dublin 1698.

Truth in fiction, or morality in masquerade: a collection of two hundred and twenty five select fables of Æsop and other authors, done into English verse. 1708.

The following are by a younger Edmund Arwaker : An embassy from heav'n: or the ghost of Queen Mary, 1705 (by Mr Edmund Arwaker jun); The birth-night: a pastoral. 1705.

JOHN AYLOFFE
d. 1685

Ayloffe's work was anon, circulated in ms and ptd later in miscellanies. Some pieces ed in POAS 1–2.
Lord, G. deF. Satire and sedition: the life and work of Ayloffe. HLQ 29 1966.

PHILIP AYRES
1638–1712

§ 1

Emblemata amatoria, emblems of love, emblemi d'amore, emblemes d'amour. 1683, [1687?–1700?] (3 edns entitled Emblems of love), 1714 (with first title), [1725?], [1750?]. Text engraved, same in all edns. English poems ed G. Saintsbury in Minor poets of the Caroline period vol 2, Oxford 1906.

Lyric poems made in imitation of the Italians, of which many are translations from other languages. 1687; ed G. Saintsbury, above.

Ayres also expanded Edward Chamberlayne, Angliae notitia, 1682, *edited* Voyages of B. Sharp and others, *and translated from French, Spanish and Italian.*

§ 2

Thomas, H. The Emblemata amatoria of Ayres. Library 3rd ser 1 1910.

—— Three translators of Gongora. Revue Hispanique 48 1920.

Praz, M. Stanley, Sherburne and Ayres as translators and imitators of Italian, Spanish and French poets. MLR 20 1925.

DANIEL BAKER
c. 1654–1723

Poems upon several occasions. 1697.
The history of Job: a sacred poem. 1706.

JANE BARKER

Poetical recreations: consisting of original poems, songs, odes etc, with several new translations. 1688.
For the novels, *see col 987, below.*

NICHOLAS BILLINGSLEY
1633–1709

Brachy-martyrologia: or a breviary of all the greatest persecutions. 1657, 1657.
Κοσμοβρεφια: or the infancy of the world, by N.B. 1658.
A treasury of divine raptures: the first part. 1667. Also issued as Thesauro-phulakion. No pt 2.

SIR RICHARD BLACKMORE
1654–1729

Bibliographies

Rosenberg, A. Sir Richard Blackmore. Lincoln Nebraska 1953.

§ 1

Prince Arthur: an heroick poem. 1695, 1695 (corrected), 1696, 1697, 1714; tr Latin by W. Hogg 1700. Preface rptd in J. E. Spingarn, Critical essays of the seventeenth century vol 3, Oxford 1909.

King Arthur: an heroick poem. 1697.

A short history of the last Parliament. 1699. Anon, rptd Somers tracts vol 11, ed W. Scott 1813 as by —— Drake MD. Prose.

A satyr against wit. 1700 (3 edns), Dublin 1700; ed F. H. Ellis, POAS 6.

A paraphrase on the book of Job, as likewise on the songs of Moses, Deborah, David, on four select psalms, some chapters of Isaiah, and the third chapter of Habakkuk. 1700, 1716.

A hymn to the light of the world, with a short description of the cartoons of Raphael Urbin. 1703.

Eliza: an epick poem. 1705.

Advice to the poets: a poem occasion'd by the wonderful success of her Majesty's arms in Flanders. 1706, 1706 (corrected). Anon.

The Kit-cats: a poem. 1708 (3 edns), 1709, 1718. Anon.

Instructions to Vander Bank, a sequel to the Advice to the poets: a poem occasion'd by the glorious success of her Majesty's arms. 1709 (3 edns). Anon.

The nature of man: a poem in three books. 1711, 1720. Anon.

Creation: a philosophical poem in seven books. 1712, 1712, 1715, 1718, Dublin 1727 etc; rptd Johnson 24, Anderson 6, Chalmers 10.

The lay-monastery: consisting of essays, discourses etc, publish'd singly under the title of the Lay-monk. 1714. The lay-monk, a tri-weekly periodical by Blackmore and John Hughes, ran from 16 Nov 1713 to 15 Feb 1714.

Essays upon several subjects. 1716, 2 vols 1717; vol 1 Dublin 1716. An essay upon wit, ed R. C. Boys, Los Angeles 1946 (Augustan Reprint Soc).

A collection of poems on various subjects. 1718.

Just prejudices against the Arian hypothesis. 1721. Prose.

Modern Arians unmask'd. 1721. Prose.

A new version of the psalms of David. 1721.

Redemption: a divine poem. 1722.

A true and impartial history of the conspiracy against the person and government of King William in 1695. 1723. Prose.

Alfred: an epick poem. 1723.

Natural theology: or moral duties consider'd apart from positive. 1728. Prose.

The accomplished preacher: or an essay on divine eloquence. Ed J. White 1731. Prose.

Blackmore also published medical works.

§ 2

Dennis, J. Remarks on a book entitul'd Prince Arthur. 1696; ed E. N. Hooker in Critical works of Dennis vol 1, Baltimore 1939.

[Brown, T. et al]. Commendatory verses on the author of the two Arthurs and the Satyr against wit. 1700, 1700; ed R. C. Boys, Blackmore and the Wits, Ann Arbor 1949.

Discommendatory verses on those which are truly commendatory 1700; ed Boys, with above.

Johnson, S. In his Lives of the poets vol 3, 1781.

Brinkley, R. F. In her Arthurian legend in the seventeenth century, Baltimore 1932.

Newton, T. F. M. Blackmore's Eliza. Harvard Stud 18 1935.

Hodges, J. C. Pope's debt to one of his dunces. MLN 51 1936. On The Kit-cats.

Douglas, L. A severe animadversion on Bossu. PMLA 62 1947. Pope's Receipt to make an epic poem attacks Blackmore, not Bossu.

Boys, R. C. Blackmore and the Wits. Ann Arbor 1949.

—— The authorship of poems in Commendatory verses. PQ 30 1951.

Rosenberg, A. Sir Richard Blackmore. Lincoln Nebraska 1953.

Cameron, W. J. The authorship of Commendatory verses 1700. N & Q Feb 1963.

HENRY BOLD
1627–83

Wit a sporting in a pleasant grove of new fancies. 1657. Signed H.B.

A poem to Charles II by H. Beeston with another by Hen. Bold. 1660.

Elegy on the death of her Highness Mary of Aurange. 1660.

Anniversary to the King's most excellent Majesty on his birth- and restauration-day. 1661.

St George's day sacred to the coronation of his most excellent Majesty Charles the II. 1661.

On the thunder happening after the solemnity of the coronation. 1661; rptd in Somers tracts vol 7, ed W. Scott 1812.

Satyr on the adulterate coin inscribed the Commonwealth. 1661.

Poems lyrique macaronique heroique etc. 1664.

Latine songs with their English and poems. Ed William Bold 1685.

SIR JAMES CHAMBERLAYNE
1640–99

A sacred poem, wherein the birth, miracles, death, resurrection and ascension of Jesus are delineated; also eighteen of David's Psalms with the book of Lamentations paraphrased, together with poems on several occasions. 1680, 1699.

Manuductio ad coelum. 1681. Tr from Latin of G. Bona.

MARY, LADY CHUDLEIGH
1656–1710
Selections

Poems by eminent ladies vol 1. 1755.

§ 1

The ladies defence: a poem, in a dialogue between Sir John Brute, Sir William Loveall, Melissa and a parson. 1701. Signed M—y C. Included in Poems on several occasions 1709.

Poems on several occasions, together with the song of the three children paraphras'd. 1703, 1709, 1713, 1722.

Essays upon several subjects in prose and verse. 1710.

Lady Chudleigh's letters to Mrs E. Thomas ('Marissa' to 'Corinna') are in Poetical works of Philip late Duke of Wharton vol 2, nd *and in* R. Swinnett's Pylades and Corinna vol 2, 1732.

MATTHEW COPPINGER

Poems, songs and love verses upon several subjects. 1682.

JOHN CUTTS, 1st BARON CUTTS
1661–1707

La muse de cavalier. 1685. Anon. Rptd in his Poetical exercises, below.

Poetical exercises written upon several occasions. 1687; ed S. S. Swartley in his Life and poetry of Cutts, Philadelphia 1917.

On the death of the Queen. 1685. Anon.

Cutts' letters to Colonel Dudley were printed Proc Mass Historical Soc 1886, *rptd* Cambridge 1886.

CHARLES DARBY
c. 1635–1709

Bacchanalia: or a description of a drunken club. 1680, 1680, 1683, 1698, 1746 (with The drunkard's looking-glass). Anon.

An elegy on the death of the Queen, by C.D., Rector of K[edington] in S[uffolk]. 1695.

The psalms in English metre. 1704.

JOHN DEAN

§ 1

The Dutch miller. [1680]. Anon.

The badger in the fox-trap. [1681]. Anon.

The wine-coopers delight. 1681, 1681. Anon.

The hunting of the fox: a new song. 1682. Anon.

Iter boreale: or Tyburn in mourning for the loss of a saint, by J.D. 1682; ed H. H. Schless, POAS 3.

The Lord Russels last farewel to the world. 1683. Anon.

The loyal conquest: or destruction of treason. 1683. Anon.

Oates's bug-bug-boarding-school at Camberwell. 1684.

§ 2

Levy, R. H. The date of the Badger in the fox-trap. Eng Lang Notes 1 1964.

CHARLES SACKVILLE,
BARON BUCKHURST,
6th EARL OF DORSET AND
4th EARL OF MIDDLESEX
1643–1706
Bibliographies

Bagley, H. A. A checklist of the poems of Dorset. MLN 47 1932. Addns by R. G. Howarth 50 1935.

Collections

The works of the Earls of Rochester, Roscommon, Dorset etc. 2 vols 1714, 1718, 1721, 1731, 1735. At least 12 further edns before 1800.

The works of the most celebrated minor poets vol 1. 1749; Supplement, 1750.

The works of celebrated authors vol 1. 1750.

Johnson 11, Anderson 6, Chalmers 8, POAS 1–2, 4–5.

§ 1

Pompey the great: a tragedy translated out of French [of Corneille] by certain persons of honour [Waller, Sedley, Godolphin, Filmer, Dorset]. (Acted at Court, Duke's Company, Jan 1664). 1664.

Dorset's name appears on the title page of 15 miscellanies between 1697 and 1718.

§ 2

Prior, M. Dedication to his Poems on several occasions. 1718 etc.

Johnson, S. In his Lives of the poets vol 1, 1781.

Sackville-West, V. In her Knole and the Sackvilles, New York 1922.

Phillips, C. J. In his History of the Sackville family, 1930.

Harris, B. Charles Sackville, patron and poet. Urbana 1940.

Wilson, J. H. In his Court wits of the Restoration, Princeton 1948.

Legouis, P. The original of Dorset's lampoon on Madame de Maintenon. MLR 54 1949.

Pinto, V. de S. In his Restoration carnival, 1954. Selections with introd and notes.

—— In his Restoration Court poets, 1966.

RICHARD DUKE
1658–1711

Poems upon several occasions. 1717 (appended to Poems by the Earl of Roscom[m]on).

Johnson 11, Anderson 6, Chalmers 9.

§ 1

A panegyrick upon Oates. [1679?] (anon); ed with next 2 items by E. F. Mengel jr, POAS 2.

An epithalamium upon the marriage of Capt William Bedloe. [1679]. Anon.

Funeral tears upon the death of Captain William Bedloe. 1681. Anon.

Floriana: a pastoral upon the death of the Duchess of Southampton. 1681. Anon.

Duke also contributed to Dryden's trns of Juvenal and Plutarch and to the 1683 version of Ovid's Heroides, and pbd several sermons.

§ 2

Johnson, S. In his Lives of the poets vol 2, 1781.

SARAH EGERTON, née FYGE
b. c. 1672

The female advocate: or an answer to a late satyr against the pride, lust and inconstancy of woman [by Robert Gould]. 1686, 1687. Preface signed S.F.

Poems on several occasions, together with a pastoral, by Mrs S.F. [1706]. Dedication signed S.F.E.

THOMAS ELLWOOD
1639–1713

Bibliographies
Graveson, S. In his edn of Life of Ellwood, 1906.

§ 1

Rogero-mastix: a rod for William Rogers in return for his riming scourge. 1685.

A collection of poems on various subjects. [c. 1710–30, 2 edns].

Davideis: the life of David King of Israel, a sacred poem in five books. 1712, Dublin 1722 (2nd edn with addns), London 1727 (2nd edn), 1749 (3rd edn), Philadelphia 1751 (4th edn corrected), 1753 (4th edn), 1754 (5th edn), 1762, London 1763 (4th edn) etc; ed W. Fischer, Heidelberg 1936.

The history of the life of Thomas Ellwood written by his own hand. Ed J[oseph] W[yeth] 1714, 1714, 1765, 1791 etc; ed W. D. Howells, Boston 1877; ed C. G. Crump 1900; ed S. Graveson 1906. Includes hymns and religious verse.

Poems by Ellwood will also be found in M. Webb, The Penns and Peningtons, 1867. *Ellwood also wrote much controversial religious prose see col 1649, below.*

§ 2

Snell, B. S. Ellwood: friend of Milton. 1934, 1949.

Patrick, J. M. Influence of Ellwood upon Milton's epics. In Essays in history and literature presented to Stanley Pargellis, Chicago 1965.

'EPHELIA'

Female poems on several occasions. 1679, 1682 (with large addns). Written by Ephelia, ascribed to Mrs Joan Philips; 1682 addns are from Rochester's works.

Advice to his Grace. [1682?]. Signed Ephelia. Perhaps by a different hand.

THOMAS FLATMAN
1637–88
§ 1

On the death of George, Duke of Albemarle: a Pindariqu' ode. 1670, Dublin [1670]; rptd in Poems and songs.

Poems and songs. 1674, 1676 (with addns), 1682, 1686 (4th edn with many addns); rptd in G. Saintsbury, Minor poets of the Caroline period vol 3, Oxford 1921; ed J. R. Tutin, Cottingham near Hull 1906 (selection).

On the death of Thomas Earl of Ossory: a Pindarique ode. Dublin 1680, 1681, London 1681; rptd in Poems and songs, 1681. Title varies.

On the death of Prince Rupert: a Pindarique ode. 1683; rptd in Poems and songs, 1686.

On the death of our lord King Charles II: a Pindarique ode. 1685, Edinburgh 1685; rptd in Poems and songs, 1686.

A song for St Caecelia's day. 1686.

On the death of the Duke of Ormond: a Pindarique ode. 1688.

To Flatman are ascribed Naps upon Parnassus, 1658, *signed by Adoniram Bonstittle alias Tinderbox (Flatman made slight contributions to this), and* A panegyrick to Charles the Second, 1660, signed T.F. (*perhaps Thomas Forde). In prose, Flatman may be concerned in* Montelion: or the propheticall almanack 1661 (*sometimes ascribed to J. Phillips*); Don Juan Lamberto: or comical history of the late times, 2 pts 1661, 1 vol 1664 (both pts, 3rd edn) by Montelion, Knight of the Oracle; *and* Heraclitus ridens, nos 1–82, 1 Feb 1681–Aug 22 1682, rptd 2 vols 1713.

§ 2
Child, F. A. The life and uncollected poems of Flatman. Philadelphia 1921.

Murry, J. M. In his Countries of the mind ser 2, 1931.

Newton, T. F. M. The mask of Heraclitus. Harvard Stud 16 1934.

Simpson, P. Poems of Flatman in the ms Rawlinson Poet 84. Bodleian Quart Record 8 1937.

THOMAS FLETCHER
1666–1713

Poems on several occasions and translations, wherein the first and second books of Virgil's Aeneis are attempted in English. 1692.

SIR SAMUEL GARTH
c. 1660–1718

Collections
Works of the most celebrated minor poets vol 1. 1749.

Works of celebrated authors vol 1. 1750.

Works. Dublin 1769.

Poetical works. Glasgow 1771.

Johnson 20, Anderson 7, Chalmers 9.

§ 1

The dispensary: a poem. 1699 (anon), 1699 (corrected), 1699, 1700 (with addns), 1703, 1706 (6th edn with several descriptions and episodes never before ptd), 1709 (2 unauthorized edns), 1714 (7th edn), 1718, Dublin 1725 (9th edn), London 1726 (9th edn), Dublin 1730 (10th and 12th edns), London 1741 (10th edn), 1768 (11th edn); ed W. J. Leicht, Weimar 1905; F. H. Ellis, POAS 6.

A prologue to Tamerlane. London [i.e. Dublin] 1704.

Prologue spoken at the first opening of the Queen's new theatre in the Hay-market. [1705]. Anon.

A poem to the Earl of Godolphin, by Dr G—h. 1710.

A prologue for the 4th of November 1711. 1711.

Claremont. 1715, [1715?] (with corrections and annotations variorum). Anon.

Ovid's metamorphoses, translated by the most eminent hands. 1717. Garth signed dedication and translated bk 14.

§ 2

A compleat key to the Dispensary. 1706, 1709, 1714, 1718, 1726 (adds A continuation of the key), 1734 (3rd edn), 1746 (4th edn), 1768 (5th edn). Ptd separately to be bound with edns of Dispensary; Key is integral in Dublin edns.

Johnson, S. In his Lives of the poets vol 2, 1781.

Schenk, T. Garth und seine Stellung zum komischen Epos. Heidelberg 1900.

Boyce, B. The dispensary, Sir Richard Blackmore and the captain of the Wits. RES 14 1938.

Cornog, W. H. Garth: a court physician of the eighteenth century. Isis 29 1938.

Rosenberg, A. The authorship of the verses on Marlborough's exile. N & Q Oct 1956. By Sewell, not Garth.

—— The London dispensary for the sick poor. Jnl History of Medicine 14 1959.

—— The last days of Garth. N & Q July–Aug 1959.

Cook, R. I. Garth's Dispensary and Pope's Rape of the lock. CLA Jnl 6 1962.

Ellis, F. H. Garth's Harveian oration. Jnl History of Medicine 18 1963.

—— The background of the London dispensary. Jnl History of Medicine 20 1965.

JOHN GLANVILL
1664?–1735

Some odes of Horace imitated with relation to his Majesty and the times. 1690; rptd in Poems, below.

A poem dedicated to the memory and lamenting the death of her sacred Majesty. 1695; rptd in Poems, below.

Damon: a pastoral lamenting the death of Mr Henry Purcell, by J.G. 1696. Authorship doubtful.

The happy pair. [1702?]. Anon. Several edns with music, nd, with titles Ianthe or The loyal swain or The happy pair; rptd in Poems, below, as Iphis and Ianthe.

A panegyrick to the King. 1967 (for 1697); rptd in Poems, below.

Poems consisting of originals and translations. 1725, 1725.

Glanvill also translated Fontenelle, A plurality of worlds, *1688.*

CHARLES GOODALL
1671–89

Poems and translations, by a late scholar of Eton. 1689.

ROBERT GOULD
d. 1709

Bibliographies

Sloane, E. H. Gould: seventeenth-century satirist. Philadelphia 1940.

Collections

Poems, chiefly consisting of satyrs and satyrical epistles. 1689, 1697.

Works. 2 vols 1709. Dedication signed Martha Gould.

§ 1

Love given o're: or a satyr against the pride, lust and inconstancy of woman. 1683 (with paste-over imprint 1682), 1683, 1686 (amended), 1690, 1709 (with R. Ames, Sylvia's revenge), 1710. Anon.

Presbytery rough-drawn: a satyr. 1683. Anon.

A funeral eclogue to the pious memory of the incomparable Mrs Wharton. 1685. Anon.

The laureat. [1687], [1687]. Anon.

To the society of the beaux esprits: a Pindarick poem. 1687. Anon.

A satyrical epistle to the female author of a poem call'd Silvia's revenge [R. Ames], by the author of the Satyr against woman. 1691.

Mirana: a funeral eclogue to the memory of the Countess of Abingdon. 1691. Anon.

The corruption of the times by money: a satyr. 1693.

A poem most humbly offered to the memory of Queen Mary. 1695, 1695.

The rival sisters, or the violence of love: a tragedy. (Drury Lane 1696). 1696.

A satyr against wooing, by the author of the Satyr against woman. 1698.

The mourning swain: a funeral eclogue to the memory of James, Earl of Abingdon. 1700.

Innocence distress'd, or the royal penitents: a tragedy. 1737.

§ 2

Sloane, E. H. Gould: seventeenth-century satirist. Philadelphia 1940.

Weinbrot, H. D. Gould: some borrowing from Dryden. Eng Lang Notes 3 1965.

CHARLES MONTAGU, 1st EARL OF HALIFAX
1661–1715

Collections

Works and life. 2 pts 1715, 1716.

The works of the most celebrated minor poets vol 1. 1749.

The works of celebrated authors vol 1. 1750.

Johnson 12, Anderson 6, Chalmers 9.

§ 1

Ode on the marriage of the Princess Anne and Prince George. 1683. Anon.

On the death of his most sacred Majesty King Charles II. 1685. Anon.

The hind and the panther transvers'd to the story of the country-mouse and the city-mouse. 1687, Dublin 1687 (anon); ed G. M. Crump, POAS 4. Prose and verse, with M. Prior.

The man of honour, occasion'd by the postscript of Pen's letter. [1689?]; ed G. M. Crump, with above.

An epistle to the Earl of Dorset occasion'd by his Majesty's victory in Ireland. 1690, 1690, 1702, 1716.

§ 2

Johnson, S. In his Lives of the poets vol 2, 1781.

Kern, J. D. An unpublished ms of Montagu. JEGP 32 1933.

Hooker, H. M. Montagu's reply to the Hind and the panther. ELH 8 1941.

Anderson, G. L. Lord Halifax in Gildon's New rehearsal. PQ 33 1954.

POAS 4.

JOHN HARINGTON
1627–1700

The history of Polindor and Flostella, with other poems. 1651. 1657 (3rd edn).

The Grecian story: being an historicall poem in five books; to which is annexed the Grove, consisting of divers shorter poems, by J.H. esq. 1684.

The odes and epodes of Horace translated into English, by J. H. esq. 1684.

A pindarick ode on the death of his late sacred Majesty King Charles II, by J.H. esq. 1685.

BENJAMIN HAWKSHAW
c. 1672–1738

Poems upon several occasions. 1693.

The reasonableness of constant communion with the Church of England represented to the dissenters. 1709. Prose.

Hawkshaw also pbd sermons Dublin 1704, 1706.

THOMAS HEYRICK
1650?–94

The new Atlantis: a poem in three books, with some reflections upon the Hind and the panther. 1687 (anon), 1690 (as A true character of Popery and Jesuitism, by Thomas Heyrick) (2nd edn).

Miscellany poems. Cambridge 1691. Includes with separate title-page, The submarine voyage: a Pindarick poem in four parts.

Heyrick also pbd 2 sermons preached at Market Harborow, both 1685.

HENRY HIGDEN

A modern essay on the thirteenth satyr of Juvenal. 1686.

A modern essay on the tenth satyr of Juvenal. 1687.

The wary widdow, or Sir Noisy Parrat: a comedy. (Drury Lane, Feb 1693). 1693.

JOHN HOPKINS
b. 1675

The triumphs of peace, or the glories of Nassaw: a Pindarick poem. 1698.

The victory of death, or the fall of beauty: a visionary Pindarick poem occasion'd by the death of Lady Cutts. 1698.

Milton's Paradise lost, imitated in rhyme, in the fourth, sixth and ninth books. 1699.

Gloria: a poem in honor of pious Majesty occasioned by the return of King William, by Mr Hopkins. 1700.

Amasia, or the works of the Muses: a collection of poems. 3 vols in 1 1700.

BENJAMIN KEACH
1640–1704
Bibliographies

Wilson, W. In his History and antiquities of dissenting churches vol 4, 1814.

Angus, J. In his Baptist authors no 4, 1889.

§ 1

War with the Devil, by B.K. 1673, 1674, 1675, 1676, 1684 (8th edn), 1700 (10th edn) etc.

The grand impostor discovered: or the Quakers doctrine weighed in the ballance, a poem by way of dialogue. 1675. Signed B.K.

An elegy on the death of John Norcot. 1676. Signed B.K.

The glorious lover: a divine poem. 1679, 1685, 1685, 1696 (4th edn), 1764 (3rd edn with addns).

Zion in distress. [1679?]. Anon; rev in following.

Sion in distress: or the groans of the Protestant church. 1681, 1681, 1682, Boston 1683 (3rd edn), London 1691, 1692, 1692.

Distressed Sion relieved. 1689.

Spiritual melody; containing near three hundred sacred hymns. 1691.

The banquetting-house: or a feast of fat things. 1692, 1696 (as A feast of fat things), 1700 (as Spiritual songs).

The everlasting covenant: a sermon, to which is added an elegy on the death of the said Minister [Henry Forty]. 1693.

Keach also wrote much controversial religious prose.

§ 2

Reid, A. A. Keach. Baptist Quart 10 1940.

PETER [or PATRICK] KER

Flosculum poeticum: poems divine and humane, panegyrical, satyrical, ironical, by P.K. 1684.

A mournful elegy on the death of Charles the II. 1685. Signed P.K.

An elegy on the deplorable death of Charles the II. 1685. Signed P.K. Facs in J. W. Draper, A century of broadside elegies, 1928.

The mournful mite: or the true subject's sigh, on the death of Charles II. [1685].

Scotland's loyalty: or sorrowful sighs on the death of our late soveraign Charles II. 1685. Anon.

A panegyrick poem on the coronation of James II. [1685]. Double broadside with Latin text: Composuit P.K., English: by Peter Ker.

A poem on the coronation of James the II. 1685. Signed P.K.

The map of man's misery: being a perpetual almanack of spiritual meditations1690,. Boston 1732. Signed P.K.

Λογμαχια: or the conquest of eloquence, by P.K. 1690.

Πολιτικος μεγας: the grand politician, written originally in Latin by Conradus Reinking. 1691. Signed Pat. Ker.

ANNE KILLIGREW
1660–85
Selections

Poems by eminent ladies vol 2. 1755.

§ 1

Poems. 1686, Gainesville 1967 (facs).

RICHARD LEIGH
c. 1649–1728
§ 1

The censure of the rota on Mr Driden's Conquest of Granada. Oxford 1673. Anon; prose.

The transproser rehears'd: or the fifth act of Mr Bayes's play. Oxford 1673. Anon; prose, on Marvell-Parker controversy. By Butler? *See* Anderson, *below.*

Poems upon several occasions, by the author of the Censure of the rota. 1675; ed H. Macdonald, Oxford 1947.

§ 2

Anderson, P. B. Anonymous critic of Milton: Leigh or Samuel Butler. SP 44 1947.

JOHN MASON
c. 1646–94

Spiritual songs: or songs of praise. 1683, 1685 (including Dives and Lazarus), 1692, 1696, 1701, 1704, 1718, 1742 (15th edn) etc.

Mason also pbd a millennial sermon, The midnight cry, 1691, *and other religious works. Contemporary writing about Mason was concerned with his religious views.*

MARY MOLLINEUX,
née SOUTHWORTH
1651–95

Fruits of retirement, or miscellaneous poems moral and divine: being some contemplations, letters etc; to which is prefixed some account of the author. 1702, 1720, 1739 etc.

JOHN SHEFFIELD,
3rd EARL OF MULGRAVE,
MARQUIS OF NORMANBY,
DUKE OF BUCKINGHAM
AND NORMANBY
1648–1721
Collections

The works of the most noble John Sheffield, late Duke of Buckingham, published by his Grace in his lifetime. 1721. Unauthorized edn, suppressed.

The works of John Sheffield, Earl of Mulgrave, Marquis of Normanby, Duke of Buckingham. Ed A. Pope 2 vols 1723, [Hague] 1726, London 1729 (2nd edn corrected), 1740 (3rd edn), 1752, 1753 (4th edn) etc. Some account of the revolution and A feast of the gods were deleted from most copies of 1723 edn, were rptd probably at the Hague in several edns, sometimes with half-title The castrations, also with title page Buckingham restor'd, Hague 1727; 1740 is the first authorized edn to include these pieces.

Poems on several occasions. Glasgow 1752.

Miscellanea from the works. Halifax 1933 (250 copies).

Johnson 25, Anderson 7, Chalmers 10.

§ 1

A collection of poems written on several occasions by several hands. 1672, 1673, 1693, 1695 (as The temple of death by the Marquess of Normanby), 1701 (A collection of poems: viz The temple of death), 1702, 1716. Tr from French of P. Habert.

The character of a Tory. 1681. Anon. Prose.

An essay upon poetry. 1682 (anon), Dublin 1683 (anon), London 1691 (with Latin version by J. N[orris]), 1697 (with poems by others), 1709, Dublin 1731; ed J. E. Spingarn in Critical Essays of the seventeenth century vol 2, Oxford 1908.

A letter from the Earl of Mulgrave to Dr Tillotson. 1689, 1689 (as A true copy of the letter), 1689 (as To Dr Tillotson). Prose.

The character of Charles II. 1696 (anon), 1725 (7th edn), 1729. Prose.

The Earl of Mulgrave's speech. [1693?], 1712.

The Duke of Buck—g—m's speech relating to the sentence against Dr Henry Sacheverell. 1710.

The Duke of Buckingham's speech spoken in the House of Lords, Feb the 15th. 1715.

An unpbd account of the Revolution of 1688, Humanum est errare: or false steps on both sides, is in BM MS Add 27382.

§2

Gildon, C. The laws of poetry, as laid down by the Duke of Buckinghamshire in his Essay on poetry. 1721.

A character of John Sheffield, to which is annex'd his Grace's last will and testament. 1729.

Johnson, S. In his Lives of the poets vol 2, 1781.

Irvine, M. Identification of characters in Mulgrave's Essay upon satyr, SP 34 1937.

Noyes, G. R. and H. R. Mead. An essay upon satyr 1680. Berkeley 1948. Distinguishes this book from Mulgrave's poem.

Pinto, V. de S. In his Restoration carnival, 1954. Selections with introd and notes.

POAS 1.

JOHN NORRIS
1657–1711
Collections

Poems. Ed A. B. Grosart 1871.

§1

An idea of happiness. 1683; rptd in Poems and discourses, and in A collection of miscellanies, below. Prose.

Poems and discourses occasionally written. 1684; largely rptd in A collection of miscellanies, below.

A collection of miscellanies: consisting of poems, essays, discourses and letters. Oxford 1687, 1692 (corrected), London 1699, 1706, 1710, 1730 (9th edn).

For Norris's philosophical works, see col 1848, below.

§2

Drennon, H. James Thomson and Norris. PMLA 53 1939.

Walton, G. In his Metaphysical to Augustan, 1955.

JOHN OLDHAM
1653–83
Bibliographies

Brooks, H. F. Bibliography of Oldham. Oxford Bibl Soc Proc 5 1940.

Collections

The works of Mr John Oldham, together with his remains. 1684, 1684, 1686 (3 issues), 1692, 1694, 1695, 1698, 1703, 1704, 1710 (7th edn), 2 vols 1722 (with memoirs and notes). Collections through 1704 consist of separate works with general title-page.

Compositions in prose and verse. Ed E. Thompson 3 vols 1770.

Poetical works. Ed R. Bell 1854, [1870]; ed B. Dobrée 1960 (facs of 1854). A selection.

§1

Upon the marriage of the Prince of Orange. 1677. Anon.

Garnet's ghost. [1679]. Anon, pirated. Included in Satyrs upon the Jesuits.

A satyr against vertue. 1679. Anon.

The clarret drinker's song. 1680, [1680?] (anon); rptd in Poems and translations, below, as The careless good fellow; ed E. F. Mengel jr, POAS 2.

Satyrs upon the Jesuits, together with the satyr against vertue and some other pieces. 1681, 1682 (anon); rptd in Works, above. Satyrs upon the Jesuits ed E. F. Mengel jr, POAS 2.

Some new pieces never before publisht. 1681, 1684. By the author of Satyrs upon the Jesuits.

Poems and translations. 1683, 1684.

Remains of Mr Oldham in verse and prose. 1684.

A second musical entertainment perform'd on St Cecilia's day. 1685.

§2

Bryant, W. C. Oldham's poems. Old & New 6 1872.

Rosenfeld, S. The family of Oldham. N & Q 18 Feb 1933. *See also* H. F. Brooks 14 July 1934.

Williams, W. M. The genesis of Oldham's Satyrs upon the Jesuits. PMLA 58 1943.

—— The influence of Ben Jonson's Catiline upon Oldham's Satyrs upon the Jesuits. ELH 11 1944.

Cable, C. H. Oldham's borrowing from Buchanan. MLN 66 1951.

Vieth, D. M. Oldham, the Wits and A satyr against vertue. PQ 32 1953.

Mackin, C. R. The satiric technique of Oldham's Satyrs upon the Jesuits. SP 62 1965.

KATHERINE PHILIPS
1632–64
Selections

Poems by eminent ladies vol 2. 1755.

Selected poems. Ed L. I. Guiney, 2 vols Cottingham near Hull 1904–5.

§1

Pompey: a tragedy. (Smock Alley 1663). Dublin 1663, London 1663.

Poems by the incomparable, Mrs K.P. 1664. Pirated, suppressed.

Poems by Mrs Katherine Philips, the matchless Orinda; to which is added Corneille's Pompey and Horace. 1667, 1669, 1678, 1710; rptd except for plays in G. Saintsbury, Minor poets of the Caroline period vol 1, Oxford 1905.

Familiar letters written by the late Earl of Rochester, with letters written by Mr Thomas Otway and Mrs K. Philips. Ed T. Brown 1697.

Letters from Orinda to Poliarchus. 1705, 1729 (with new letter).

§2

Souers, P. W. The matchless Orinda. Cambridge Mass 1931.

Elmen, P. Some manuscript poems by the matchless Orinda. PQ 30 1951.

Roberts, W. Saint-Amant, Orinda and Dryden's miscellany. Eng Lang Notes 1 1964.

—— The dating of Orinda's French translations. PQ 49 1970.

JOHN PHILLIPS
1631–1706

For a bibliography see W. R. Parker, Milton: a biography, 2 vols Oxford 1968.

§ 1

Johannis Philippi Angli responsio ad apologiam anonymi cujusdam tenebrionis pro rege & populo anglicano infantissimam. 1652 (4 edns). Rptd in most edns of Milton's works, tr in Works of Milton vol 4, New Haven 1966. Probably with Milton's assistance.

A satyr against hypocrites. 1655 (3 edns), 1661, 1661 (as The religion of hypocritical presbyterians), 1671 (with first title), 1674, 1677, 1680, 1689, 1710 (as Mr John Milton's satyre); ed L. Howard, Los Angeles 1953 (Augustan Reprint Soc).

Montelion 1660: or the prophetical almanack. [1659]. Anon. Prose. Montelion 1661 is probably also by Phillips, though it and other works by 'Montelion' have been ascribed to T. Flatman.

An introduction to astrology. 1661. Anon. Prose.

Don Juan Lamberto: or comical history of the late times. Part 1, 1661, 1661; Part 2, 1661; 1664 (both pts). By Montelion knight of the oracle.

Typhon, or the gyants war with the gods: a mock poem. 1665. From Scarron.

Montelions predictions. 1672. Anon. Prose.

Maronides, or Virgil travestie: being a new paraphrase upon the fifth book of Virgil's Aeneids. 1672, 1672; Sixth book, 1673, 1678 (with 5th book). From Scarron.

Mercurius verax: or the prisoners prognostication for the year 1675, by the author of the first Mentelion and Satyr against hypocrites. 1675. Prose.

Duellum musicum. 1673 (added to M. Locke, The present practice of musick vindicated). Prose.

A brief account of the most memorable transactions in England, Scotland and Ireland, and foreign parts, from the year 1662 to the year 1675. 1676 (added to J. Heath, a chronicle of the late intestine war, 2nd edn). Prose.

Jockey's downfall: a poem on the defeat given to the Scotish covenanters. 1679. Anon.

Dr Oates's narrative of the Popish plot vindicated, by J. P. Gent. 1680. Prose.

Speculum crape-gownorum: or a looking-glass for the young academicks, with reflections on some of the late high-flown sermons, by a guide to the inferiour clergie. 1682, 1682 (enlarged); pt 2, 1682, 1732 (both pts). Prose.

The character of a Popish successor: part the second. 1681, 1681. Anon. Prose. Pt 1 by Elkanah Settle.

Horse-flesh for the Observator, by T.D. B.D. chaplain to the inferiour clergies guide. 1682. Prose.

An anniversary poem on the sixth of May. 1683. Anon.

An humble offering to the sacred memory of Charles II. 1685.

A poem on the coronation of King James II and his royal consort Queen Mary. [1685].

Modern history: or a monethly account of all considerable occurrences, civil, ecclesiastical and military. 1687-9. Prose.

Sam Ld Bp of Oxon his celebrated reasons for abrogating the test. [1688] (3 edns). Anon. Prose.

Advice to a painter. 1688. Anon.

In memory of our late most gracious Lady Mary, Queen of Great-Britain, France and Ireland. 1695.

A reflection on our modern poesy: an essay. 1695. Anon.

Augustus britannicus: a poem upon the conclusion of the peace. 1697.

The vision of Mons Chamillard concerning the battle of Ramillies, by a nephew of the late Mr John Milton. 1706.

Phillips edited Sportive wit 1656, signed J.P. *and* Wit and drollery, 1656, signed J.P. *He translated extensively from French, Spanish and Latin, including a trn of* Le Mercure histoire et politique 1690-1706. *Other attacks on* L'Estrange's Observator *may be is. A life of Milton ascribed to Phillips,* ed H. Darbishire in her Early lives of Milton, 1932 *is probably by Cyriack Skinner.*

§ 2

Godwin, W. The lives of Edward and John Phillips. 1815, 1911.

Beaty, F. L. Three versions of John Phillips' Satyr against hypocrites. Harvard Lib Bull 6 1952.

Hone, R. E. New light on the Milton-Phillips family relationship. HLQ 22 1958.

Ayers, R. W. The date [dec 1651] of the John Phillips-John Milton responsio. PQ 38 1959.

—— The John Phillips-John Milton Angli responsio: editions and relations. PBSA 56 1962.

WALTER POPE
c. 1629-1714

Memoirs of Monsieur Du Vall. 1670 (anon); rptd Harleian Miscellany vol 3, 1809. Prose.

The Catholick ballad: or an invitation to Popery. 1674 (broadside with two pts), 1675, 1678, 1679, 1689; tr Latin, 1675. Anon.

The Salsbury-ballad, with the learned commentaries of a friend. 1676.

The old man's wish. 1684. 1685 (anon), 1693 (as Doctor Pope's wish), 1697 (as The wish), 1710, 1719 etc (many undated edns with music); rptd in Pope's Life of Seth, ed J. B. Bamborough, Oxford 1961; tr Latin, 1728.

The miser, by the author of the Old man's wish. 1685.

Select novels by Cervantes and Petrarch, translated. 1694.

The life of Seth, Lord Bishop of Salisbury. 1697; ed J. B. Bamborough, Oxford 1961 (facs).

Moral and political fables done into measured prose intermixed with ryme. 1698.

SAMUEL PORDAGE
1633-91?

Troades Englished, by S.P. 1660. Tr from Seneca.

Poems upon several occasions, by S.P. gent. 1660.

Heroick stanzas on his Majesties coronation. 1661.

Mundorum explicatio, or an explanation of an hieroglyphical figure: a sacred poem by S.P. armig. 1663.

Herod and Marianne: a tragedy. (Lincoln's Inn Fields, Sept 1671?). 1673, 1674. Dedication signed by E. Settle, who had been given the play by the unknown author.

The siege of Babylon: a tragi-comedy. (Dorset Garden, c. Sept 1677). 1678.

Azaria and Hushai: a poem. 1682, 1682 (rev). Anon, sometimes attributed to E. Settle, perhaps by neither. Facs in H. W. Jones, Anti-Achitophel, Gainesville 1961.

The medal revers'd: a satyre against persecution, by the author of Azaria and Hushai. 1682; ed POAS 3.

The loyal incendiary, or the generous bontefieu: a poem occasioned by the setting fire to the Rye House. 1684. Signed S.P.

Pordage was translator of medical works by Thomas Willis, 1679, 1681, 1683, *and editor of 6th edn of* J. Reynolds, The triumphs of God's revenge against murder, 1679.

ALEXANDER RADCLIFFE

Ovid travestie: a burlesque upon Ovid's epistles. 1680, 1681 (enlarged with ten epistles never before printed), 1696, 1705, 1889 (priv ptd).

Bacchinalia coelestia. 1680 (anon); rptd in Ramble, below.

The ramble: an anti-heroic poem, together with some terrestrial hymns and carnal ejaculations. 1682, 1696 (in edn of Ovid travestie as The works of Capt Alexander Radcliffe, the third edition augmented).

JOHN RAWLET
1642–86

A treatise of sacramental covenanting. 1667, 1710 (6th edn). Prose.
A dialogue betwixt two Protestants. 1685, 1686, 1686, 1691. Prose.
The Christian monitor. 1686, 1686 (7th edn), 1699 (25th edn). Anon. Prose.
Poetick miscellanies. 1687, 1691, 1721.

WENTWORTH DILLON, 4th EARL OF ROSCOMMON
1637–85

Collections

The miscellaneous works of the late Earls of Rochester and Roscommon. 1707, 1709, 1709, 1711, 2 vols 1714 etc.
Poems by the Earl of Roscom[m]on, to which is added An essay on poetry by the Earl of Mulgrave, together with poems by Mr Richard Duke. 1717.
Works. Glasgow 1749.
The works of the most celebrated minor poets vol 1. 1749; Supplement, 1750.
The works of celebrated authors vol 1. 1750.
Works. Glasgow 1753.
Johnson 10, Anderson 6, Chalmers 8.

§ 1

Horace's art of poetry made English. 1680, 1684, 1695, 1709 etc.
An essay on translated verse. 1684, 1685 (enlarged); ed J. E. Spingarn in Critical essays of the seventeenth century vol 2, Oxford 1908.

§ 2

Gildon, C. The laws of poetry, as laid down by the Duke of Buckinghamshire, by the Earl of Roscommon in his Essay on translated verse, and by the Lord Lansdowne. 1721.
Fenton, E. Observations on the works of Edmund Waller. 1730. Contains brief biography of Roscommon.
Johnson, S. In his Lives of the poets vol 1, 1781.
Niemeyer, C. The birth date of the Earl of Roscommon. RES 9 1933.
—— The Earl of Roscommon's academy. MLN 49 1934.
—— A Roscommon canon. SP 36 1939.
Stuart, D. M. Roscommon of the 'unspotted bays'. English 1 1936.
POAS 2.

THOMAS ROSS
d. 1675

§ 1

The second Punick war, englished from the Latine of Silius Italicus, with a continuation. 1661, 1672.
Cicero's prince, by T.R. esq. 1668. Prose tr from W. Bellenden formerly ascribed to T. Rymer.
An essay upon the third Punique war, to which are added Theodosius's advice to his son, and the Phenix out of Claudian, by T.R. esq. 1671.

§ 2

Zimansky, C. A. The literary career of Ross. PQ 21 1942.
POAS 2.

SIR EDWARD SHERBURNE
1618–1702

Collections

Miscellaneous poems. Ed S. Fleming 1819.
Poems and translations excluding Seneca and Manilius. Ed F. J. van Beeck, Assen 1961.

§ 1

Medea: a tragedy, written in Latine by Seneca, englished with annotations. 1648; rptd in Tragedies of Seneca, below.
Seneca's answer to Lucilius, translated into English verse. 1648.
Salmacis with other poems and translations. 1651, 1651 (reissued as Poems and translations amorous, lusory, morall, divine); rptd Chalmers 6.
The sphere of Manilius made an English poem. 1675.
Troades: or the royal captives. 1679; rptd in Tragedies of Seneca, below.
The comparison of Pindar and Horace written in French by Monsieur Blondel, englished. 1696. Prose.
The tragedies of Seneca translated. 1701. Medea, Hippolytus, Troades; also Rape of Helen out of the Greek of Coluthus.
Sherburne also edited the poems of W. Cartwright, 1651, *and* Thomas Stanley's trn of Aelian, 1665.

§ 2

Praz, M. Stanley, Sherburne and Ayres as translators and imitators of Italian, Spanish and French poets. MLR 20 1925.
Crump, G. M. Sherburne's acquaintances. TLS 14 March 1958.

THOMAS SHIPMAN
1632–80

§ 1

Henry the third of France, stabb'd by a fryer, with the fall of the Guise: a tragedy. 1678.
Carolina: or loyal poems. Ed Thomas Flatman 1683.

§ 2

Pinto, V. de S. Shipman: a forgotten Nottinghamshire poet. Trans Thoroton Soc of Notts 53 1950.

SAMUEL SLATER
c. 1629–1704

Epithalamium: or Solomon's song digested into meter. 1653.
A rhetorical rapture at the mournful moving of his highnes stately effigies. 1658; facs in J. W. Draper, A century of broadside elegies, 1928.
Poems in two parts. 1679; tr German, 1706.
Slater also pbd sermons and other religious works.

SAMUEL SPEED
d. 1681

The prisoner's complaint to the King's most excellent Majestie, by S.S. 1673.
Fragmenta carceris: or the King's bench scuffle. 1674, 1675.
Prison-pietie: or meditations divine and moral. 1677.
Romae antiquae descriptio: a view of the religion rendred into English. 1678. Prose, from Valerius Maximus, anon.

THOMAS SPRAT
1635–1713

See mimeographed bibliography by H. W. Jones and T. A. Whitworth, Sprat: a check list, 1952.

Collections

A supplement to the works of the most celebrated minor poets. 1750.
The works of celebrated authors vol 2. 1750.
Johnson 9, Anderson 6, Chalmers 9.

§ 1

Three poems upon the death of his late Highness Oliver Lord Protector, written by Mr Edm Waller, Mr Jo Dryden, Mr Sprat. 1659, 1682, 1709.
The plage of Athens, first describ'd in Greek by Thucydides, then in Latin by Lucretius, now attempted in English after incomparable Dr Cowley's Pindarick way. 1659, 1665, 1667, 1676, 1683, 1688, 1703, 1709.
Observations on Monsieur de Sorbier's voyage into England. 1665, 1668, 1709. Prose.
The history of the Royal-Society of London. 1667, 1702, 1722, 1734; tr French, 1669; ed J. I. Cope and H. W. Jones, St Louis 1958. Prose.
Sprat also pbd sermons, pastoral letters and controversial pamphlets. He wrote the Life *prefixed to Cowley's* Works, 1668, *and probably assisted Buckingham in the* Rehearsal.

§ 2

Johnson, S. In his Lives of the poets vol 2, 1781.
Fisch, H. and H. W. Jones. Bacon's influence on Sprat's History of the Royal Society. MLQ 12 1951.
Jones, H. W. Thomas Sprat. N & Q 5 Jan, 15 March 1952.
Rosenberg, A. Bishop Sprat on science and imagery. Isis 43 1952.
Melchionda, M. Davenant, Hobbes, Sprat: introduzione alla critica litteraria della Restaurazione. Filologia e Letteratura 11 1965.

GEORGE STEPNEY
1663–1707

Collections

The works of the most celebrated minor poets vol 2. 1749.
The works of celebrated authors vol 2. 1750.
Johnson 12, Anderson 6, Chalmers 8.

§ 1

An epistle to Charles Montagu on his Majesty's voyage to Holland. 1691.
A poem dedicated to the blessed memory of her late gracious Majesty Queen Mary. 1695, Dublin 1695.
Poems. 1701.
An essay upon the present interest of England. 1701, 1701; rptd in Somers tracts vol 11, ed W. Scott 1814. Prose.
Stepney's translation of the eighth satire of Juvenal. Ed T. and E. Swedenberg, Berkeley 1948.
Stepney's name appears on title-page of 5 miscellanies between 1697 and 1721.

§ 2

Johnson, S. In his Lives of the poets vol 1, 1781.
Halbeisen, E. K. Stepney: a calendar. N & Q 9–16 Aug 1930.
Swedenberg, H. T. Stepney, my Lord Dorset's Boy. HLQ 10 1946.
POAS 4.

JOHN TUTCHIN
1661–1707

Selections

Selected poems. Ed S. Peterson, Los Angeles 1964 (Augustan Reprint Soc).

§ 1

Poems on several occasions with a pastoral; to which is added A discourse of life. 1685.
An heroick poem upon the late expedition of his Majesty. 1689.
Civis militaris: or a poem on the city royal regiment of horse. 1690.
Reflections upon the French Kings declaration for the restauration of the late King James. 1690. Prose.
A poem upon their Majesties speeches to the nonconformist Ministers. [1690].
The tribe of Levi. 1691 (3 edns) (anon); ed W. J. Cameron, POAS 5.
A congratulatory poem to the reverend Dr John Tillotson. 1691.
A funeral poem on the death of Mr Richard Baxter. 1692.
The earthquake of Jamaica, describ'd in a Pindarick poem. 1692.
An epistle to Mr Benjamin Bridgwater, occasion'd by the death of Queen Mary. 1694.
A Pindarick ode in the praise of folly and knavery. 1696, 1704.
A search after honesty. 1697.
White-hall in flames: a Pindarick poem. 1698.
The foreigners: part 1 [all pbd]. 1700. Anon; ed F. H. Ellis, POAS 6.
The apostles, by the author of the Foreigners. 1701.
A poem to the memory of William III. 1701.
The British Muse, or tyranny expos'd: a satyr. [1701]. Anon.
The tackers. [1705]. Anon.
Tutchin wrote controversial pamphlets, particularly in connection with his editorship of the Observator *1702–7. He added autobiographical material, often false, to the 5th edn of* Western martyrology, 1705 *and may have contributed to other accounts of the bloody assizes.*

WILLIAM WALSH
1662–1708

Collections

The works in prose and verse. 1736. Composite, binding together pp. 113–241 of Mr Pope's literary correspondence vol 3, 1735 and a new printing of Letters and poems amorous and gallant.
The works of the most celebrated minor poets vol 2. 1749.
The works of celebrated authors, vol 2. 1750.
Johnson 12, Anderson 6, Chalmers 8.

§ 1

A dialogue concerning women: being a defence of the sex. 1691. Anon. Preface signed John Dryden. Prose.
Letters and poems, amorous and gallant. 1692 (anon); rptd in Annual miscellany for the year 1694, 1708 (with separate title-page dated 1709), 1716.
A funeral elegy upon the death of the Queen. 1695, 1695.
Ode for the thanksgiving day. 1706. Anon.
Aesculapius: or the hospital of fools. In J. Oldmixon, Poems and translations by several hands, 1714. Prose dialogue.
Walsh also translated Squire Trelooby *with Congreve and Vanbrugh. See col 751, below.*

§ 2

Johnson, S. In his Lives of the poets vol 1, 1781.
Freeman, P. William Walsh's letters and poems in Ms
  Malone 9. Bodleian Quart Record 7 1934.
— Who was Sir Roger de Coverley? Quart Rev 285
  1947.
— Walsh and Dryden: recently discovered letters. RES
  24 1948.
Vetter, D. B. Walsh's In defence of painting. MLN 66
  1951.
Sambrook, A. J. Walsh and the Golden age from Virgil
  1703. MP 64 1967. Distinguishes 2 poems with that
  title from Walsh's.
POAS 6.

NATHANIEL WANLEY
1634–80
Collections

Poems. Ed L. C. Martin, Oxford 1928 (from mss).

§ 1

An ingenious contention between Mr Wanley and Dr
  Wild. 1668, 1668 (as The fair quarrel).
The wonders of the little world: or a general history of
  man. 1678, 1704 (as The history of man, anon, a
  plagiarized rearrangement), 1750 (as A view of human
  nature, anon, abridgement), 1756 (reissue as Every
  man entertained), 1774 (original title and work, with
  alterations and additions), 1788, 1791, 2 vols 1806–7
  (with additions). Prose.
Wanley also pbd religious works and a trn from Lipsius.

§ 2

Martin, L. C. A forgotten poet of the seventeenth century.
  E & S 11 1925.

SAMUEL WESLEY the elder
1662–1735

§ 1

Maggots: or poems on several occasions, never before
  handled, by a schollar. 1685, 1685.
The life of our blessed lord and saviour Jesus Christ: an
  heroic poem; also a prefatory discourse concerning
  heroic poetry. 1693, 1694, 1697, 1809 (abridged);
  Essay on heroic poetry, ed E. N. Hooker, Los Angeles
  1947 (Augustan Reprint Soc) (facs of 1697).
Elegies on the Queen and Archbishop. 1695, 1695.
An epistle to a friend concerning poetry. 1700; ed E. N.
  Hooker, Los Angeles 1947 (Augustan Reprint Soc).
History of the new testament attempted in verse. 1701,
  1715, 1717.
History of the Old Testament in verse. 2 vols 1704, 1715.
  With preceding item as History of the Old and New
  Testaments, 3 vols 1716.
Marlborough, or the fate of Europe: a poem. 1705.
A hymn on peace. 1713.
*Wesley was also connected with Athenian Gazette, 1691–7,
  and pbd religious works.*

§ 2

Clarke, A. Memoirs of the Wesley family. 1823.
Tyermann, L. The life and times of the Rev Samuel
  Wesley. 1866.
Stevenson, G. J. Memorials of the Wesley family. 1876.
Beecham, H. A. Samuel Wesley Senior: new biographical
  evidence. Renaissance & Modern Stud 7 1963.

JOHN WHITEHALL

Miscellaneous poems. 1685, 1690 (as Miscellany poems).
Whitehall also wrote attacks on Hobbes.

ROBERT WHITEHALL
1625–85

Τέχνηπολιμογαμία: or the marriage of armes and arts,
  July 12 1651, being an accompt of the act at Oxon, by
  R.W. 1651.
Viro honoratissimo Edvardo Hide carmen gratulatorium.
  [Oxford? 1660?]. Latin and English.
The coronation: a poem. [1661].
Urania: or a description of the painting of the top of the
  theater at Oxon. 1669.
Ἐξαστιχον ἱερον, sive iconum quarundam extranearum,
  numero 258, explicatio breviuscula: being an epi-
  grammatical explanation of the most remarkable stories
  throughout the Old and New Testament. Oxford 1677
  (12 copies).
Gratulamini mecum: or a congratulatory essay upon his
  Majesties most happy recovery. 1679.
The English rechabite: or a defyance to Bacchus and all
  his works, a poem in lxvii hexastichs, by R.W. Oxford
  [1681].
A sermon concerning edification in faith and discipline.
  Oxford 1694.

ROBERT WILD
1609–79
Collections

Iter boreale. 1668. Contains Wild's earlier works.
Poems. Ed J. Hunt 1870.

§ 1

Alas poore scholler, whither wilt thou goe. [1642?].
  Anon.
The tragedy of Christopher Love at Tower-hill. [1651],
  [1651] (both anon), 1660; facs in J. W. Draper, A
  century of broadside elegies, 1928.
The arraignment of a sinner at the bar of divine justice.
  1656. Sermon.
A horrible, terrible and troublesome historical narrative:
  or the relation of a cock fight fought at Wisbech. 1660.
  Anon.
Iter boreale: attempting something upon the successful
  march of General Monck, by a rural pen. 1660 (several
  issues), 1661 (adds 20 poems, some signed R.W.), 1605
  (for 1665), 1668, 1668 (both enlarged by R. Wild),
  1670 (reissued 1674), 1671; ed G. de F. Lord, POAS 1.
A poem upon the imprisonment of Mr Calamy. [1663],
  [1663]; ed G. de F. Lord, POAS 1.
The recantation of a penitent Proteus. [1663] (3 edns).
  Anon.
The grateful non-conformist. [1665]. Anon.
An essay upon the late victory obtained against the Dutch,
  by the author of Iter boreale. 1665, 1665 (as A gratu-
  latory verse upon our late glorious victory), Edinburgh
  1665.
The loyal non-conformist. 1666, Dublin 1666; ed G. de
  F. Lord, POAS 1.
An ingenious contention between Mr Wanley and Dr
  Wild. 1668, 1668 (as The fair quarrel).
Upon the rebuilding the city. 1669. Anon; authorship
  doubtful.
Dr Wild's humble thanks for his Majesties gracious
  declaration for liberty of conscience. 1672.
A letter from Dr Wild to his friend Mr J.J. upon occasion
  of his Majesty's declaration, together with his Poetica
  licentia and A friendly debate between a conformist
  and a nonconformist. 1672.

A panegyrique addrest to the King's most excellent Majesty on meeting his two Houses of Parliament, by R.W. 1673.

An exclamation against Popery: or, a broadside against Rome, by R.W. DD. 1678.

Oliver Cromwell's ghost: or Old Noll newly revived. [1678?]. Signed R.W. DD.

Dr Wild's poem, In nova fert animus, upon the hopeful new Parliament. [1679], [1679].

Dr Wild's last legacie; or a poem sent with a guinney to Mr B.D. for a new-year's gift. [1679].

The benefice: a comedy, by R.W. DD, author of Iter boreale. 1689.

§ 2

Dunton, J. In his Life and errors, 1705.

Pirie, R. Two editions of Iter boreale 1668. Book Collector 12 1963.

POAS 1–2.

SAMUEL WOODFORD
1636–1700

§ 1

A paraphrase upon the psalms of David. 1667, 1678, 2 vols 1713.

A paraphrase upon the Canticles and some select hymns of the New and Old Testament, with other occasional compositions in English verse. 1679.

§ 2

Hooker, E. N. The early poetical career of Woodforde. In Essays critical and historical dedicated to Lily B. Campbell, Berkeley 1950.

MINOR BURLESQUES AND TRAVESTIES

See S. E. Leavitt, Paul Scarron and English travesty, SP 16 1919; A. H. West, L'influence française dans la poésie burlesque en Angleterre entre 1660 et 1700, Paris 1930;

G. Kitchin, A survey of burlesque and parody in English, Edinburgh 1931. E. A. Richards, Hudibras in the burlesque tradition, New York 1937.

[Scudamore, James?]. Homer a la mode: a mock poem upon the first and second book of Homer's Iliads. Oxford 1664, 1665.

[Monsey], R. Scarronides, or Virgil travestie: a mock-poem, being the second [and seventh] book of Virgil's Aeneis translated into English burlesq. 1665.

Lanii triumphantes: or the butcher-prize. 1665.

A[tkins], M[aurice]. Cataplus: or Aeneas his descent into hell. 1672.

Chaucer's ghoast: or a piece of antiquity containing twelve pleasant fables of Ovid, penn'd after the ancient manner of writing. 1672.

Ovidius exulans. 1673. By Nazo Scarronnomimus.

Hogan-Moganides: or the Dutch Hudibras. 1674.

The wits paraphras'd. 1680. Parodies Ovid's epistles translated by several hands, 1680.

Homer a la mode, the second part in English burlesque: or a mock-poem upon the ninth book of the Iliads. 1681.

C[olvil], S[amuel]. Mock poem: or Whiggs supplication. 2 pts 1681, Edinburgh 1687 (as Whiggs supplication), London 1692 (as The Scotch Hudibras), Edinburgh 1695 etc.

Γιγαντομαχια: or a full and true relation of the great and bloody fight between three pagan knights and a Christian giant. 1682.

D[ixon], R[obert]. Canidia, or the witches: a rhapsody in five parts. 1683.

Part of Lucian's dialogues (not) from the original Greek, done into rhyme. 9 nos 1684.

Lucian's dialogues (not) from the Greek, done into English burlesque: the second part. 1684.

[Farewell, James]. The Irish Hudibras: or Fingallian prince, taken from the sixth book of Virgil's Aenaeids and adapted to the present times. 1689.

[Smith, James]. Scarronides. 1692. Burlesques Aeneid bk 2.

Pendragon: or the carpet knight his kalendar. 1698.

Other burlesques or Hudibrastic pieces will be found under Butler, Cotton, Ames, Duke, J. Phillips and Radcliffe above, and under Prior, col 489, Wycherley, col 742, Crowne, col 759, D'Urfey, col 761, Flecknoe, col 764, Dennis, col 1041, and Cleland, col 996.

C. A. Z.

V. EARLY EIGHTEENTH-CENTURY POETRY

MATTHEW PRIOR
1664–1721

Collections

Poems on several occasions. 1707. Unauthorized.

Poems on several occasions. 1709, 1709, 1711, 1713, 1717. For variants in the first edn see R. W. Chapman, RES 3 1927.

A second collection of poems on several occasions. 1716. Unauthorized.

Poems on several occasions. 1718, Dublin 1719, London 1720, 1721, 1725, 1733, 1734, 1741, Glasgow 1751, London 1754, Aberdeen 1754, Glasgow 1759, London 1766, Berwick 1766, Glasgow 1771, Edinburgh 1773.

A supplement to Mr Prior's poems. 1722, 1722 (with Curll's Memoirs), Dublin 1723, 1728 (with Poems on several occasions, above).

A new collection of poems on several occasions. 1725.

For this and next 3 items see D. Foxon, Book Collector 8 1959.

Poems on several occasions, vol III: the second edition. 1727.

Poems on several occasions, volume the third and last: the third edition. 1733, 1734 (as 3rd vol of Poems on several occasions 1733, above).

Poems on several occasions, volume the second: the fourth edition. 1742, 1754, 1767.

Miscellaneous works. 1740. Pbd by J. Bancks from Adrian Drift's mss.

Lyric poems. 1741.

Poems on several occasions. Dublin 1768.

Poetical works. Edinburgh 1777, 1784 (Bell's edn).

Poetical works. Ed T. Evans 2 vols 1779.

Poetical works. Ed J. Mitford, 2 vols 1835, Boston 1853, London 1866; rev R. B. Johnson, 1892, 1907 (Aldine edn).

Poetical works. Ed G. Gilfillan, Edinburgh 1858.

Selected poems. Ed A. Dobson 1889.

Writings. Ed A. R. Waller 2 vols Cambridge 1905–7.

Shorter poems. Ed F. Bickley [1923].

Occasional verses 1702–19. Oxford 1927. Facs of To a young gentleman in love, An English padlock, Upon Lady Katharine H-de's first appearing, Verses to Lady Henrietta Harley.

Literary works. Ed H. B. Wright and M. K. Spears 2 vols Oxford 1959.

Johnson 30–1; Anderson 7; Chalmers 10.

§ 1

On the coronation. 1685. Anon.

The hind and the panther transvers'd to the story of the country mouse and the city mouse. 1687 (anon), Dublin 1687, London 1709. With Charles Montagu, later Earl of Halifax.

The orange. 1688. Anon. A broadside.

An ode in imitation of the second ode of the third book of Horace. 1692.

For the New Year: to the sun. [1694].

To the King: an ode on his Majesty's arrival in Holland. 1695.

An English ballad in answer to Mr Despreaux's Pindarique ode on the taking of Namure. 1695.

Verses humbly presented to the King at his arrival in Holland. 1696.

A new answer to an argument against a standing army. 1697.

Carmen saeculare for the year 1700. 1700, 1701 (with Latin trn by T. Dibben).

To a young gentleman in love. 1702.

Prologue spoken at Court before the Queen on her Majesty's birth-day 1703/4. 1704.

A letter to Monsieur Boileau Depreaux occasion'd by the victory at Blenheim. 1704. Anon.

An English padlock. 1705.

Pallas and Venus: an epigram. 1706.

An ode humbly inscrib'd to the Queen. 1706.

Phaedra and Hippolitus, by Mr Edmund Smith. [1707]. Epilogue by Prior.

Horace lib I epist ix imitated. [1711].

To the Right Honorable Mr Harley, wounded by Guiscard. 1711.

Archibaldi Pitcarnii Scoti carmen imitated. [1712].

Walter Danniston ad amicos imitated. [1712?].

Earl Robert's mice. 1712 (H. Baldwin, unauthorized), 1712 (J. Morphew, authorized).

Two imitations of Chaucer. 1712. Susannah and the two elders, Erle Robert's mice.

A fable of the widow and her cat. 1712, 1712. Anon; see C. H. Firth, RES 1 1925.

Thos Britton small-coal-man. [c. 1714]. A print.

A memorial against the fortifying of the ports of Dunkirk and Mardike. 1715.

The dove. 1717.

Lucius, by Mrs Manley. 1717. Epilogue by Prior.

Upon Lady Katharine H-de's first appearing at the play-house. 1718. Later called The female Phaeton. Probably by Simon Harcourt.

Chit-chat, by Mr Killigrew. [1719]. Prologue by Prior.

Verses spoke to the Lady Henrietta Cavendish Holles Harley in the library of St John's College Cambridge November the 9th 1719. Cambridge [1719], 1720.

Engraved on three sides. [1720?]. Engraving.

Prologue to the Orphan. 1720.

The conversation. 1720.

The lame and the blind. [1720?]. A broadside engraving.

Colin's mistakes. 1721.

The turtle and the sparrow. 1723 (3 edns).

Down-hall. 1723, 1727.

On Fleet Shepheards takeing. Oxford Bibl Soc Proc 1 1927.

Letters

Original letters from Prior [et al]. Ed R. Warner 1817.

Historical Mss Commission: calendar of the mss of the Marquis of Bath. Vol 2 (Prior papers), 1908.

Meyerstein, E. H. W. A letter of Prior. TLS 20 June 1952.

§ 2

Some memoirs of the life of Prior, with a copy of his will. 1722.

Johnson, S. In his Lives of the English poets, 4 vols 1779–81.

Thackeray, W. M. In his English humourists of the eighteenth century, 1853.

Dennis, J. In his Studies in English literature, 1876.

Dobson, A. Matthew Prior. New Princeton Rev 6 1888; rptd in his Eighteenth-century vignettes ser 2, 1894.

Aitken, G. A. Matthew Prior. Contemporary Rev May 1890.

Roberts, W. Prior as a book collector. Athenaeum 19 June 1897.

Bickley, F. Life of Prior. 1914.

Frey, E. Der Einfluss der englischen, französischen, italienischen und lateinischen Literatur auf die Dichtungen Priors. Strasbourg 1915.

Legg, L. G. W. Matthew Prior. 1921.

Basride, C. Un secrétaire d'ambassade anglais à Paris sous Louis XIV. Revue des Sciences Politiques 48 1923.

Doughty, O. The poet of the 'familiar style'. E Studies 7 1925.

Barrett, W. P. Prior's Alma. MLR 27 1932.

Carroll, E. L. A memoir of Prior. Union College Bull 26 1932.

Chandler, W. K. Prior's Poems 1718: a duplicate printing. MP 32 1935.

Hills, A. Prior in Essex. Essex Rev 44 1935.

Wright, H. B. William Jackson on Prior's use of Montaigne. MLR 31 1936.

—— Prior's 'wellbeloved and dear cossen'. RES 15 1939.

—— The birthplace of Prior. TLS 29 April 1939.

—— Prior's funeral. MLN 57 1942.

—— Prior and Elizabeth Singer. PQ 24 1945.

—— and H. C. Montgomery. The art collection of a virtuoso. Art Bull 27 1945.

—— Ideal copy and authoritative text: the problem of Prior's Poems on several occasions 1718. MP 49 1952.

Shepherd, T. B. John Wesley and Prior. London Quart Rev 162 1937.

Eves, C. K. Prior: poet and diplomatist. New York 1939.

Ewing, M. Musical settings of Prior's lyrics in the eighteenth century. ELH 10 1943.

Spears, M. K. The meaning of Prior's Alma. ELH 13 1946.

—— Prior's attitude toward natural science. PMLA 63 1948.

—— Prior's religion. PQ 27 1948.

—— Ethical aspects of Prior's poetry. SP 45 1948.

Jack, I. The 'choice of life' in Johnson and Prior. JEGP 49 1950.

Rosenberg, A. Prior's feud with the Duchess of Marlborough. JEGP 52 1953. Reply by H. B. Wright, ibid.

Anderson, G. L. Gildon vs Prior. N & Q Feb 1954. On Harley and the Patriot. Reply by H. B. Wright, Jan 1956.

Griffith, R. H. Not by Prior. RES new ser 6 1955.

Ketton-Cremer, R. W. Matthew Prior. Cambridge 1957.

Ellis, F. H. and D. Foxon. Prior's simile. PBSA 57 1963.

Kline, R. B. Prior and Dennis. N & Q June 1966.

—— Prior and 'dear Will Nuttley': an addition to the canon. PQ 47 1968.

Goldschalk, W. L. Prior's copy of Spenser's Works 1679. PBSA 61 1967.

Morton, R. Prior's Dialogues of the dead. Ball State Univ Forum 8 1967.

J. F.

EDWARD YOUNG
1683–1765
Bibliographies

Thomas, W. In his Le poète Young, Paris 1901.

Kind, J. L. Bibliography of German translations, editions, reviews and notices. In his Young in Germany, New York 1906.

Pettit, H. Preface to a bibliography of Young's Nightthoughts. In Elizabethan studies in honor of G. F. Reynolds, Boulder 1945.

—— A check-list of Night-thoughts in America. PBSA 42 1948; W. D. Templeman, Additions to the check-list 43 1949; Pettit, Further additions 44 1950.

—— A bibliography of Young's Night-thoughts. Univ of Colorado Stud in Lang & Lit 5 1954.

Cordasco, F. Young: a handlist of critical notices and studies. New York 1950.

Collections

Poetic works. Dublin 1726.

Poetical works. Ed E. Curll 2 vols 1741, 1752.

The works of the author of the Night-thoughts. 4 vols 1757, 1762, Dublin 1764, 5 vols 1767, 4 vols Edinburgh 1770, 5 vols 1773, 1774, 6 vols 1778–9, 3 vols 1792, 1798, 1802 etc, 4 vols Philadelphia 1805, 3 vols Charlestown Mass 1811 etc.

Poems on several occasions. Glasgow 1711.

Dramatic works. 1778.

Poetical works. 2 vols 1830 (Aldine). With life by J. Mitford.

The poetical works of Milton, Thomson and Young. Ed E. F. Cary 1841.

Complete works. Ed J. Nichols with life by J. Doran 2 vols 1854, Hildesheim 1968.

Johnson 50–3; Anderson 10; Chalmers 13.

§ 1

An epistle [in verse] to Lord Lansdown. 1713.

A poem on the last day. Oxford 1713, 1713, London 1714, 1715, 1725, Dublin 1725, 1730, London 1741, Elizabeth NJ 1797 etc; tr German, 1754, 1757; French, 1772; Italian, 1775; Portuguese, 1804. Frequently rptd in edns of Night-thoughts, below.

An epistle [in verse] to the Lord Viscount Bolingbroke, sent with A poem on the last day. 1714; rptd by C. K. Firman, An unrecorded poem by Edward Young, N & Q June 1963.

The force of religion, or vanquish'd love: a poem. 1714, 1715, Dublin 1725, 1735, London 1762; tr German, 1754; French, 1770; Italian, 1770; Portuguese, 1804.

On the late Queen's death, and His Majesty's accession to the throne. 1714, 1716 (in The loyal mourner for the best of princes: being a collection of poems, sacred to the immortal memory of Queen Anne).

Orationes duae Codringtone sacrae. Oxford 1716. One oration by Young.

Busiris, King of Egypt: a tragedy. 1719, 1719, [Hague?] 1719, London 1722, Dublin 1730, London 1733, 1735, Dublin 1761, London 1781; tr French, 1746; German, 1756, 1758, 1761; rptd in Bell's British theatre vol 16, 1776, vol 29 1797 etc. Produced at Drury Lane 7 March 1719.

A paraphrase on part of the Book of Job. 1719, 1719, Dublin 1719, London 1726; tr German, 1754. Frequently rptd in edns of the Night-thoughts, below.

A letter to Mr Tickell occasioned by the death of Joseph Addison. 1719, 1719.

The revenge: a tragedy. 1721, Dublin 1726, 1733, London 1735, Dublin 1749, London 1752, Glasgow 1755, Cork [1760], London 1764, 1769, 1775; rptd in New English theatre vol 2, 1776; Bell's British theatre vol 12, 1776 etc; tr German, 1756, 1767. Produced at Drury Lane 18 April 1721.

The universal passion: satire i. 1725; satire ii, 1725;

satire iii, 1725; satire iv, 1725; satire the last, 1726, Dublin 1726; satire v, 1727, Dublin 1727; satire vi, 1728. Collected as Love of fame, below.

Cynthio. 1727, [1872] (in Poetical works of Milton and Young), Paris 1901 (in W. Thomas, Le poète Young).

A vindication of providence, or a true estimate of human life, in which the passions are consider'd in a new light: a sermon preach'd soon after the late King's death; discourse I. 1728, Dublin 1728, London 1729, Dublin 1729, London 1737, 1747, 1765, 1802; tr German, 1755. All pbd.

Love of fame, the universal passion, in seven characteristical satires: the second edition [the 7 pts of Universal passion, above, 'satire the last' becoming 'satire VII', the whole 'corrected and alter'd']. 1728, Dublin 1728, London 1730 ('third edition'), 1731, Dublin 1731, London 1741 ('fourth edition'), 1741 (in Collected works of Young, ed E. Curll, with 'key' to the satires), 1752 ('fifth edition'), 1762 (in Parnassium), 1763 ('sixth edition'); tr German prose, 1755, verse 1771; French prose, 1787, 1788, verse 1802, 1818.

Ocean: an ode occasion'd by his Majesty's late royal encouragement of the sea-service; to which is prefix'd An ode to the King and A discourse on ode. 1728, Dublin 1728.

An apology for princes, or the reverence due to government: a sermon before the House of Commons, January 30 1728 [i.e. 1729]. 1729.

Imperium pelagi: a naval lyrick written in imitation of Pindar's spirit, occasion'd by his Majesty's return September 1729 and the succeeding peace. 1730, Dublin 1730 (as The merchant), London 1771 (as The merchant).

Two epistles [in verse] to Mr Pope concerning the authors of the age. 1730, Dublin 1730, London 1732 (in R. Savage, A collection of pieces in verse); tr German, 1756.

The foreign address [in verse]: or the best argument for peace; occasioned by the British fleet, and the posture of affairs, when the Parliament met 1734. 1735.

The complaint, or night-thoughts on life, death and immortality: night the first. 1742 (4 edns), 1743 (3 edns), 1744; tr German, 1755; Latin, 1786.

The complaint [etc]: night the second. 1742, 1742, 1743, 1744. Nights 1–2 rptd, illustr W. Blake, ed A. M. Butterworth 1911; tr Swedish, 1770.

The complaint [etc]: night the third. 1742 (3 edns), 1743, 1744.

The complaint [etc]: night the fourth. 1743, 1743, 1744.

The complaint [etc] [nights 1–4]. 1743, 1743, Dublin 1744; ed R. Edwards, illustr W. Blake 1797; tr German, 1752, 1756, 1760; Italian, 1770; Russian, 1803; Swedish, 1850.

The complaint [etc]: night the fifth. 1743; tr German, 1754.

The complaint [etc]: night the sixth. 1744.

The complaint [etc] [nights 1–6]. 1743 (for 1744), 1747, 1749.

The complaint [etc]: night the seventh. 1744; tr German prose, 1751. Nights 1, 2, 4–7 pirated by J. Wesley, Bristol 1744.

The complaint [etc]: night the eighth. 1745; tr German prose, 1752.

The consolation [night the ninth and last] and Some thoughts occasioned by the present juncture. 1745 (for 1746); tr German prose, 1752.

The complaint [etc]: volume II [nights 7–9]. 1748, 1749.

The complaint [etc] [nights 1–9]. 1750, 1750, 1751, 1751, 1755, 1756, 1758, 1760, 1767, 1769, Bristol 1770 (ed J. Wesley, without Night 3), London 1771, 1771, 1773, 1773 (with life by G. Wright), 1777 (with life by W. Waring), Philadelphia 1777, Berwick [1780], London 1783, Philadelphia 1787, Newburyport Mass [1790], Philadelphia 1791, 1791, London [1793] (with life by C. E. de Coetlogon), 1796, New York 1796: rptd in scores of edns into the 1880's; noteworthy edns: ed J. R. Boyd, New York 1851 (with life); ed C. C. Clarke, Edinburgh 1853 (with life by G. Gilfillan); ed J. Nichols 1853 (with life by J. Doran); tr German 1753, 1756, 1760–71; French, 1763, 1769, 1770, 1787; Norwegian, 1764; Danish, 1767, 1783; Italian, 1770, 1774–6, 1775, 1783, 1789; Russian, 1780, 1785, 1799, 1812; Dutch, 1785; Portuguese, 1787, 1804; Swedish, 1787, 1798–9; Spanish, 1797, 1798–9, 1799; Polish, 1803; Hungarian, 1815. Usually pbd as Night-thoughts.

The brothers: a tragedy. 1753, Dublin 1753, London 1763, Dublin 1764, London 1776 (in New English theatre vol 12), 1776 (in Bell's British theatre vol 14), 1777, 1778; tr German, 1756, 1764, 1767, 1768, 1769. Produced at Drury Lane 3 March 1753.

The centaur not fabulous, in five [6 in 3rd and later edns] letters to a friend on the life in vogue. 1755 (3 edns), 1765, 1783, 1786, Newburyport Mass 1806; tr German, 1755.

A sea piece containing the British sailor's exultation and his prayer before engagement, occasioned by the rumour of war. 1755; tr German, 1783, 1784.

An argument drawn from the circumstances of Christ's death for the truth of his religion: a sermon preached before His Majesty at Kensington June 1758. 1758.

Conjectures on original composition in a letter to the author [S. Richardson] of Sir Charles Grandison. 1759, 1759: ed A. Brandl, Berlin 1903 (in Jahrbuch der deutschen Shakespeare-Gesellschaft vol 39); ed M. W. Steinke, New York 1917; ed E. J. Morley, Manchester 1918; photocopy of 1st edn, Leeds 1966; tr German 1760, 1761, 1787.

Resignation [in 5 pts with A funeral epithalamium]. 1761 (priv ptd), 1762 (in 2 pts and a Postscript to Mrs B[oscawen]), 1762, 1764, 1767, Philadelphia 1791 etc; tr German prose, 1763.

The beauties of Dr Young's Night thoughts. 1769; tr French, 1804; Russian 1806.

Letters

The correspondence of Samuel Richardson. Ed A. L. Barbauld 6 vols 1804. 21 from Young; *but see* H. Pettit, The text of Young's letters to Samuel Richardson, MLN 57 1942.

One hundred and fifty original letters between Young and Richardson. Monthly Mag 1813–18. 110 from Young.

Correspondence of Dr Young. In Complete works, ed J. Nichols vol 1, 1854. 27 from Young.

Thomas, W. Le poète Young. Paris 1901. 23 to various correspondents and 18 to G. Keate.

Historical Manuscripts Commission. In Calendar of the mss of the Marquis of Bath vol 1, 1904. 107 to the 2nd Duchess of Portland.

Tickell, R. E. In his Thomas Tickell and the eighteenth-century poets, 1931. 19 from Young to Tickell.

Letters [20] of Young to Mrs Judith Reynolds. Ed H. T. Swedenberg, HLQ 2 1938.

Correspondence. Ed H. Pettit, Oxford 1970.

§ 2

'Melmoth, Courtney' (S. J. Pratt). Observations on the Night thoughts. 1776.

Johnson, S. In his Lives of the poets vol 4, 1781. Life by H. Croft, rev Johnson.

'Eliot, George' (M. A. Evans). Worldliness and other-worldliness: the poet Young. Westminster Rev 67 1857.

Thiel, R. A critical analysis of Young's Night thoughts. Berent 1890.

Clages, H. Der Blankvers in Thomsons Seasons and Youngs Night thoughts. Halle 1892.

Barnstorff, J. Youngs Nachtgedanken und ihr Einfluss auf die deutsche Literatur. Bamberg 1895.

Lange, R. Youngs Natursinn. Leipzig 1901.

Thomas, W. Le poète Young. Paris 1901.

Krebs, C. A. A. Young als Dramatiker. Königsberg 1905.

Kind, J. L. Young in Germany. New York 1906.

Baldensperger, F. Young et ses Nuits en France. In his Etudes d'histoire littéraire, Paris 1907.

Shelley, H. C. The life and letters of Young. 1914.

Mackail, J. W. Young's Night thoughts. Trans Royal Soc of Lit 36 1918.

O'Connor, H. W. Narcissa episode in Young's Night thoughts. PMLA 34 1919.

Van Tieghem, P. La poésie de la nuit et des tombeaux. Paris 1921.

Mutschmann, H. Zur Psychologie des Verfassers der Nachtgedanken. Anglia Beiblatt 32 1922.

—— Das Schlüssel zu Youngs Nachtgedanken. Leipzig 1936.

—— The origin and meaning of Young's Night thoughts. Acta et Commentationes (Tartu) 43 1939.

Clark, H. H. A study of melancholy in Young. MLN 39 1924.

—— The romanticism of Young. Trans of Wisconsin Acad 24 1929.

Ibershoff, C. H. Bodmer and Young. JEGP 24 1925.

McKillop, A. D. Richardson, Young and the Conjectures. MP 22 1925.

Peers, E. A. The influence of Young and Gray in Spain. MLR 21 1926.

Kaufman, P. Heralds of original genius. In Essays in memory of Barrett Wendell, Cambridge Mass 1926.

Keynes, G. L. Illustrations [30] to Young's Night thoughts by William Blake. Cambridge Mass 1927.

—— Blake's illustrations to Young's Night thoughts. In his Blake studies, 1949.

Boas, F. S. A manuscript copy of Young's Busiris. TLS 22 May 1930.

Hughes, W. R. Dr Young and his curates. Blackwood's Mag May 1932.

Bliss, I. St J. Young's Night thoughts in relation to contemporary Christian apologetics. PMLA 49 1934.

Laux, K. Das Pseudoklassizistische und Romantische in Youngs Night thoughts. Munich 1938.

Wicker, C. V. The romantic melancholy of Young: its cause and influence. Pittsburgh Univ Bull 16 1940.

—— Young and the fear of death. Albuquerque 1952.

Crawford, C. E. Young and the Wycombe election. MLN 60 1945.

—— What was Pope's debt to Young? ELH 13 1946.

Eaves, T. C. D. Joseph Highmore's portrait of Young. SP 43 1946.

Brown, W. C. Young and Cowper. In his Triumph of form, Chapel Hill 1948.

Lindsay, J. Young and the concept of space. Life & Letters Feb 1947.

Bailey, M. In The age of Johnson: essays presented to C. B. Tinker, New Haven 1949.

Potts, A. F. The Recluse-Prelude-Excursion and Night thoughts. In her Wordsworth's Prelude, Ithaca 1953.

König, E. Young: Versuch einer gedanklichen Interpretation auf Grund der Frühwerke. Berne 1954.

Kemper, W. Die deutschen Übersetzungen der Youngschen Nachtgedanken. Berlin 1956.

Margoliouth, H. M. Blake's drawings for Young's Night thoughts. In K. Raine et al, The divine vision, ed V. de S. Pinto 1957.

Pettit, H. The English rejection of Young's Night-thoughts. Univ of Colorado Stud in Lang & Lit 6 1957.

—— Young and the case of Lee vs D'Aranda. Proc Amer Philosophical Soc 107 1963.

—— and E. Collins. The genealogy of Young. Univ of Colorado Stud in Lang & Lit 10 1966.

Pettit, H. The occasion of Young's Night thoughts. E Studies (suppl) 1969.

—— Lost Young letters. Johnsonian News Letter 29 1969.

Ferrara, F. Fra classicismo e romanticismo: la genesi della poetica di Young. Convivium 26 1958.

Birley, R. In his Sunk without trace, 1962.

Forster, H. B. The ordination of Young. Eng Lang Notes 1 1963.

de-Jong, M. J. G. Geen overspel in de hemel. Gids 128 1965.

Kelly, R. M. Imitation of nature: Young's attack upon Alexander Pope. Xavier Univ Stud 4 1965.

Tolley, M. J. The Book of Thel and Night thoughts. BNYPL June 1965.

Odell, D. W. Locke, Cudworth and Young's Night thoughts. Eng Lang Notes 4 1967.

Leek, H. An illegible word in a letter from Young to Pope. N & Q June 1968.

—— The Edward Young-Edmund Curll quarrel. PBSA 62 1968.

H. P.

JOHN GAY
1685–1732

Bibliographies

Faber, G. C. In his edn of Poetical works, Oxford 1926.

Collections

Poems on several occasions. 2 vols 1720, Dublin 1730, London 1731, 1737, 1745, Glasgow 1751, 1757, London 1767, Glasgow 1770, Edinburgh 1773, London 1775.

Plays; to which is added an account of the life and writings of the author. 1760, 1772. Omits The mohocks, The wife of Bath, The what d'ye call it, Three hours after marriage, Dione, Acis and Galatea.

Works. 4 vols Dublin 1770, 1772, 1773.

Poems and fables. 2 vols Aberdeen 1772.

Poetical works. 3 vols Edinburgh 1777, 1784, London [1804?], 1811.

Poetical dramatic and miscellaneous works, [with] Dr Johnson's biographical and critical preface. 6 vols 1795. The fullest collection.

Poetical works. 2 vols Boston 1854.

Poetical works. Ed J. Underhill 2 vols 1893.

Poems. Ed F. Bickley [1923].

Plays. 2 vols [1923]. Omits The wife of Bath, Three hours after marriage, Dione, Acis and Galatea.

Poetical works: including Polly, The beggar's opera and selections from the other dramatic work. Ed G. C. Faber, Oxford 1926 (OSA).

Selected poems. Ed A. Ross 1950.

Johnson 39–40; Anderson 8; Chalmers 10.

§ 1

Wine. 1708, 1708 (both anon), 1708 (with Old England's new triumph, not by Gay), 1709; 1926 (facs).

The present state of wit. 1711 (anon); ed J. C. Collins 1903 (in Critical essays: Arber's English garner); ed D. F. Bond, Ann Arbor 1947 (Augustan Reprint Soc).

The mohocks. 1712. Dedication signed W.B. Unacted.

An argument proving that the present mohocks and hawkubites are the Gog and Magog mention'd in the Revelations. 1712. Anon.

The wife of Bath. 1713, 1730 (rev), Vienna 1788. Drury Lane 12 May 1713.

Rural sports. 1713, 1713; ed O. Culbertson, New York 1930.

The fan. 1714, 1714.

The shepherd's week. 1714 (3 edns), 1721, 1728, Dublin 1729, London 1742; ed H. F. B. Brett-Smith, Oxford 1924.

A letter to a lady. 1714, 1714, Dublin 1714.

The what d'ye call it. 1715, 1715, Dublin 1715, London 1716, 1725, 1736, Dublin 1752; ed C. P. Patu, Paris 1756 (in Choix de petites pièces du théâtre anglais); London 1763, [1778?]. Drury Lane 23 Feb 1715.

Two epistles, one to the Earl of Burlington, the other to a lady. [1715?].

Trivia. [1716], Dublin [1716?], London [1720?], Dublin 1727, London 1730, 1740, 1807; ed J. P. Briscoe 1899; ed W. H. Williams 1922.

Three hours after marriage. 1717, 1757 (in A supplement to the works of Pope), Dublin 1758, 1761 (with key); ed R. Morton and W. M. Peterson, Painesville Ohio 1961; ed J. H. Smith, Los Angeles 1961 (Augustan Reprint Soc). With Pope and Arbuthnot.

Horace epod iv, imitated by Sir James Baker Kt. [1717?]. Anon.

The poor shepherd. [1720?], [1730?].

Dione. In Poems, 1720, Glasgow 1752, London 1763. Unacted.

A panegyrical epistle to Mr Thomas Snow. 1721, 1721. Anon.

An epistle to her Grace Henrietta Dutchess of Marlborough. 1722.

A poem address'd to the Quidnunc's. 1724. Anon.

The captives. 1724, 1724. Drury Lane 15 Jan 1724.

Blueskin's ballad. 1725 (anon), [1725?].

To a lady on her passion for old china. 1725 (anon), 1925 (facs). See H. Williams, RES 7 1931.

Daphnis and Cloe. [1725?].

Molly Mogg. [1726], [1727?], [1730].

Fables. 1727, 1728, 1729, Dublin 1730, London 1733, Amsterdam 1734, London 1737, 1746, 1753.

The beggar's opera. 1728, 1728, 1729, Dublin 1732, London 1733, 1735, 1737, 1742, 1749, 1754, Glasgow 1758, Edinburgh 1760, London 1763, Belfast 1764, London 1765; ed G. Sarrazin, Weimar 1898; ed G. H. MacLeod 1905, Leipzig 1906; ed O. Doughty 1922; ed F. W. Bateson 1934; ed H. Höhne, Halle 1959 (with Polly etc); Larchmont NY 1961 (facs of 1729). Lincoln's Inn Fields 29 Jan 1728.

Polly. 1729, [1729], 1729, Dublin 1729, London 1755; ed G. Sarrazin, Weimar 1898; ed O. Doughty 1922. Unacted.

Acis and Galatea. [1732] (anon), 1732, 1740, 1742, 1747, Oxford [1760?]. Lincoln's Inn Fields 26 March 1731.

Achilles. 1733. Lincoln's Inn Fields 10 Feb 1733.

Fables: volume the second. 1738, 1742, nd, 1747.

The distress'd wife. 1743, Dublin 1743, 1750. Covent Garden 5 March 1734.

Fables. 2 vols 1750 (numerous edns before 1800); ed A. Dobson 1884; ed W. H. K. Wright 1889 (with bibliography); ed V. A. Dearing, Los Angeles 1967 (Augustan Reprint Soc).

The rehearsal at Goatham. 1754. Unacted.

Gay's chair, poems never before printed. 1820. Probably spurious.

Some unpublished translations from Ariosto. Ed J. D. Bruce, Brunswick 1910.

Letters

Letters. Ed C. F. Burgess, Oxford 1966.

§ 2

C[urll], E. The life of Mr John Gay. 1733.

Johnson, S. In his Lives of the English poets, 4 vols 1779–81.

Coxe, W. The life of Gay. Salisbury 1797. From his edn of Fables, 1796.

Hazlitt, W. In his Lectures on the English poets, 1818.

Thackeray, W. M. In his English humourists of the eighteenth century, 1853.

Swaen, A. E. H. The airs and tunes of Gay's Beggar's opera. Anglia 43 1919.

—— The airs and tunes of Gay's Polly. Anglia 60 1936.

Melville, L. Life and letters of Gay. 1921.

Kidson, F. The beggar's opera: its predecessors and successors. Cambridge 1922.

Schultz, W. E. Gay's Beggar's opera: its content, history and influence. New Haven 1923.

Sherburn, G. The fortunes and misfortunes of Three hours after marriage. MP 24 1926.

— The Duchess replies to the King. Harvard Lib Bull 6 1952.

Bateson, F. W. In his English comic drama 1700–50, Oxford 1929.

Goulding, S. Eighteenth-century French taste and the Beggar's opera. MLR 24 1929.

Williams, H. To a lady on her passion for old china. RES 7 1931.

Loiseau, J. Gay et le Beggar's opera. Revue Anglo-américaine 1934.

Empson, W. In his Some versions of pastoral, 1935. On Beggar's opera.

Berger, A. V. The beggar's opera, the burlesque and Italian opera. Music & Letters 17 1936.

Gegey, E. M. Ballad opera. New York 1937.

Kern, J. B. A note on the Beggar's opera. PQ 17 1938.

Gaye, P. F. John Gay. 1938.

Irving, W. H. Gay: favorite of the wits. Durham NC 1940.

Bronson, B. H. The beggar's opera. California Univ Pbns in Eng 8 1941.

Sutherland, J. R. Polly among the pirates. MLR 37 1942.

— In Pope and his contemporaries: essays presented to George Sherburn, Oxford 1949.

Barnett, G. L. Gay, Swift and Tristram Shandy. N & Q Dec 1943.

Trowbridge, H. Pope, Gay and the Shepherd's week. MLQ 5 1944.

Loewenberg, A. The beggar's opera. N & Q June 1945.

Brown, W. C. Gay's mastery of the heroic couplet. PMLA 61 1946.

Mack, M. Gay Augustan. Yale Univ Lib Gazette 21 1946. On the Tinker collection at Yale.

Stroup, T. B. Gay's Mohocks and Milton. JEGP 46 1947.

Knotts, W. E. Press numbers as a bibliographical tool: the Beggar's opera 1728. Harvard Lib Bull 3 1949. Reply by W. B. Todd, PQ 29 1950.

Ault, N. In his New light on Pope, 1949.

Bogorad, S. N. Paradise lost and Gay's Trivia: a borrowing. N & Q March 1950.

Moore, J. R. Gay's burlesque of Sir Richard Blackmore's poetry. JEGP 50 1951.

Rosenberg, A. The date of Gay's An epistle to Burlington. PQ 30 1951.

Boas, F. S. In his Introduction to eighteenth-century drama, Oxford 1953.

McLeod, A. L. Pope and Gay: two overlooked manuscripts. N & Q Aug 1953. Reply by J. Butt, Jan 1955. Fortescue material in Pierpont Morgan Library.

Ruhe, E. L. Pope's hand in Thomas Birch's account of Gay. RES new ser 5 1954.

Armens, S. M. Gay: social critic. New York 1954.

Aden, J. M. The 1720 version of Rural sports and the Georgic tradition. MLQ 20 1959.

Sherwin, J. J. The world is mean and man uncouth. Virginia Quart Rev 35 1959. On Beggar's opera and Brecht's Dreigroschenoper.

Ellis, W. D., jr. Thomas D'Urfey, the Pope-Philips quarrel and the Shepherd's week. PMLA 74 1959.

Smith, R. A. The 'great man' motif in Jonathan Wild and the Beggar's opera. College Lang Assoc Jnl 2 1959.

Burgess, C. F. Gay's Twas when the seas were roaring and Chaucer's Franklin's tale: a borrowing. N & Q Dec 1962.

— The genesis of the Beggar's opera. Cithara 2 1962.

— Scriblerian influence in the Shepherd's week. N & Q June 1963.

— The ambivalent point of view in Gay's Trivia. Cithara 4 1964.

— Political satire in Gay's The beggar's opera. Midwest Quart 6 1965.

— Gay and Polly and a letter to the King. PQ 47 1968.

Osborn, J. M. 'That on Whiston' by Gay. PBSA 56 1962.

Fuller, J. Cibber, the Rehearsal at Goatham and the suppression of Polly. RES new ser 13 1963.

Forsgren, A. Gay: poet 'of a lower order'. Stockholm 1964.

— Some complimentary epistles by Gay. Studia Neophilologica 36 1964.

— Gay among the defenders of the faith. Studia Neophilologica 38 1966.

— Lofty genii and low ghosts: vision poems and Gay's True story of an apparition. Studia Neophilologica 40 1968.

Spacks, P. M. Gay: a satirist's progress. EC 14 1964. Reply by C. J. Rawson, ibid.

— John Gay. New York 1965.

Warner, O. John Gay. 1964 (Br Council pamphlet).

Bronson, B. H. The true proportion of Gay's Acis and Galatea. PMLA 80 1965.

Höhne, H. Gays Beggar's opera und Polly. Zeitschrift für Anglistik und Amerikanistik 13 1965.

Teske, C. B. Gay's Twas when the seas were roaring and the rise of pathetic balladry. Anglia 83 1965.

Preston, J. The ironic mode: a comparison of Jonathan Wild and the Beggar's opera. EC 16 1966.

Battestin, M. C. Menalcas' song: the meaning of art and artifice in Gay's poetry. JEGP 65 1966.

Rees, J. O., jr. A great man in distress: Macheath as Hercules. Colorado Stud 12 1966.

Lewis, P. E. Gay's burlesque method in the What d'ye call it. Durham Univ Jnl 29 1967.

J. F.

ALEXANDER POPE
1688–1744

For mss see Butt, below.

Bibliographies etc

Pope, A. A list of books, papers and verses in which our author was abused; a list of our author's genuine works. In The Dunciad, 1729 etc, Appendixes 2, 7.

Abbott, E. A concordance to the works of Pope. 1875.

Heintzelman, J. H. A bibliography of German translations of Pope in the 18th century. Bull Bibl Soc of America 4 1912.

Griffith, R. H. Pope: a bibliography. Vol 1, 2 pts Austin 1922–7, London 1962 (no more pbd). The standard descriptive bibliography of Pope's writings 1709–51. Addns and corrections to pt 1 in pt 2. See also Todd, Maslen, below.

Wise, T. J. In his A catalogue of the Ashley Library vol 4, 1923.

— A Pope library: a catalogue of plays, poems and prose writings by Pope. 1931. Both with facs of many title-pages.

Audra, E. Les traductions françaises de Pope 1717–1825. Paris 1931. For Italian trns of Pope see § 2, G. Lenta, 1931, and D. B. Clark, 1961, below. For other trns see the BM Catalogue.

Tobin, J. E. Pope: a list of critical studies 1895–1944. New York 1945.

Butt, J. [List of autograph manuscripts]. Proc Br Acad 40 1954. See also his Twickenham edn of Poems, below.

Rogers, R. W. Pamphlet campaigns concerning Pope 1728–44. In The major satires of Pope, 1955, appendix E.

Todd, W. B. Concealed Pope editions. Book Collector 5 1956. See D. F. Foxon, ibid.

Peavy, C. D. The Pope-Cibber controversy: a bibliography. Restoration & 18th-Century Theatre Research 3 1964.

Maslen, K. I. D. New editions of Pope's Essay on man 1745–8. PBSA 62 1968.

Pope commemoration 1888, Loan Museum. Catalogue of the books, autographs, paintings, drawings, engravings and personal relics exhibited in the Town Hall, Twickenham. Richmond Surrey 1888.

Collections

The works of Mr Alexander Pope. 1717 (3 edns); 8° reprints: Dublin 1718, London 1718 and 1720 (T. Johnson's piracies), Dublin 1727; vol 2, 1735; 8° reprint: Ethic epistles, satires etc, 1735 (T. Johnson's piracy). Dunciad, 1735, Poems and imitations of Horace, 1738 etc were sometimes arranged with the contents of Vol 2 to make 2 vols in 4°. The title-page of vol 2 might then be moved to 3 (the 'II' altered in ink to 'III') and replaced by a separate leaf, The works of Mr Alexander Pope: containing his epistles and satires; with some never before printed, 1737.

Epistles of Horace imitated. 1738. See above; reissued in following.

Poems and imitations of Horace. 1738.

The works of Mr Alexander Pope, in prose. 1737 (3 edns); (Letters of Mr Alexander Pope and several of his friends); 8° reprint: 1737 (as Letters, T. Johnson's piracy; suppressed); vol 2, 1741 (rptd from a copy of 8° Works vol 7, 1741, not pbd until later); 8° and 12° reprints: Dublin 1741, 1741 (as Letters), London 1741 (in Dean Swift's literary correspondence).

The works of Alexander Pope. Vols 1–4, 1736 (8°), 1736 (except vol 2, 1736, 1739); 12° reprint: 3 vols Dublin 1736; vols 5–6, 1737, 1737, 1739, 1739; vol 7, 1741; 4 vols in 9: 1, pt 1, 1740, 1743; 1, pt 2, 1741, 1745; 2, pt 1, 1740, 1743; 2, pt 2, 1738, 1738, 1740, 1743; 3, pt 1, 1742, 1743; 3, pt 2, 1741, 1742 (3 edns); 4, pts 1–3, 1742.

Dunciad, 1743, Essay on man, 1743, Essay on criticism, [1743], and Four ethic epistles, 1748 (ptd 1744) were parts of a projected edn by Pope and Warburton.

Warburton, William. The works, with his last corrections, additions and improvements, together with commentaries. 9 vols 1751, 1751, 1752, 1753, 1754, 1756, 10 vols 1757, 9 vols 1757, 1760, 10 vols Berlin 1762–4, 6 vols 1764, 4 vols Edinburgh 1764, 9 vols 1766, 6 vols Edinburgh 1767, 4 vols Glasgow 1768, 9 vols Dublin 1769, 5 vols 1769 (with Ruffhead's Life; a supplementary vol 1807), 9 vols 1770, 6 vols 1770, 9 vols 1776, 4 vols 1778 (rev anon), 6 vols 1787, 1788, 1789. A royal licence gave Warburton sole right for 14 years from 24 July 1759 to print, publish and vend the Works which he had annotated.

A supplement to the works: containing such poems, letters etc as are omitted in the edition by Dr Warburton; to which is added a key to the letters. 1757. Culled from Literary correspondence, except Fourth epistle of the first book of Horace (not by Pope), Lord Paget's Essay on human life, and John Gay's Three hours after marriage.

The British poets. Vols 19–22, Edinburgh 1773.

The poetical works. 4 vols Edinburgh 1776 (Bell's Poets).

Additions to the works, together with many original poems and letters of contemporary writers never before published. 2 vols 1776, Dublin 1776. Ed W. ('Conversation') Cooke or George Steevens?

Johnson, Samuel. Prefaces biographical and critical to the works of the English poets. Vol 7, 1781 etc.

Poetical works. 3 vols Glasgow 1785 (Foulis Press).

Wakefield, Gilbert. The works, with remarks and illustrations. Vol 1 (all pbd), 1794.

Poetical works. 1796 (Cook's Poets).

Warton, Joseph. The works, with notes and illustrations. 9 vols 1797, Basle 1803, London 1822. Warton's memoir is a blend of his Essay and Johnson's Life.

Du Roveray, F. J. Poetical works, adorned with plates. 6 vols 1804.

Park, T. Poetical Works. 4 vols 1808 (Works of the British poets).

Bowles, W. L. The works, with additional observations, and memoirs. 10 vols 1806, 8 vols 1812 (Johnson's Life substituted and notes drastically reduced [by Nichols?]).

Poems. 3 vols 1822 (Chiswick Poets). With Johnson's Life.

Roscoe, William. The works, to which are added a new life of the author, an estimate of his poetical character and writings, and occasional remarks. 10 vols 1824, 8 vols 1847.

Supplemental volume to the works: containing a considerable addition to his private correspondence. 1825.

Dyce, A. Poetical works. 3 vols 1831 etc; rev G. R. Dennis 1891 (Aldine Poets).

Valpy, A. J. Works. 4 vols 1835, 1835, 1839. With Life by G. Croly.

Cary, H. F. Poetical works. 1839, 1853, 1859, 1880. With life.

Poetical works. 1847 (Bohn's Poets).

Carruthers, R. Poetical works. 4 vols 1853, 2 vols 1858 (rev).

Elwin, W. and W. J. Courthope. The works, including several hundred unpublished letters and other new materials. 10 vols 1871–89. Planned by John Murray c. 1850 in 1 vol, but many unpbd mss were discovered and the plan grew. J. W. Croker (d. 1857) and Peter Cunningham began the editing; in 1860 Elwin took over and issued vols 1–2, 6–8, 1871–2; Courthope continued, completing the edn with the Life vol 5, in 1889.

Ward, A. W. Poetical works. 1869 etc (Globe edn). With life.

— Poetical works. New York 1877 etc (Astor Poets). Reprint of Globe edn, with addns.

Pattison, M. Satires and epistles. Oxford [1872].

Rossetti, W. M. Poetical works. 1873.

Boynton, H. W. Complete poetical works. Boston 1903, 1967 (Cambridge Poets). Poems arranged chronologically in groups.

Parrott, T. M. The rape of the lock and other poems. Boston 1906.

Dobrée, B. Collected poems. 1924 (EL), 1956 (rev).

Bredvold, L. I. Selected poems. New York 1926.

Sherburn, G. The best of Pope. New York 1929, 1940 (rev).

Poetry and prose. Ed H. V. Dyson, Oxford 1933.

Ault, N. Prose works. Vol 1, [1711–20], Oxford 1936. Some attributions doubtful. To be continued by M. Mack. Meanwhile vol 10 of Elwin and Courthope's edn of Works, above, is the most convenient collection of the rest of the prose, though superseded in individual instances.

The Twickenham edition of the poems. Ed J. Butt et al. Vol 1, Pastoral poetry and An essay on criticism, ed E. Audra and A. Williams 1961; vol 2, The rape of the lock and other poems, ed G. Tillotson 1940, 1954 (rev), 1962 (3rd edn, reset); vol 3. i, An essay on man, ed M. Mack 1950; vol 3. ii, Epistles to several persons (Moral essays), ed F. W. Bateson 1951; vol 4, Imitations of Horace etc, ed Butt 1939, 1953 (rev); vcl 5, The Dunciad, ed J. R. Sutherland 1943, 1953 (rev); vol 6, Minor poems, ed N. Ault and J. Butt 1954; vols 7–10, Translations of Homer, ed M. Mack et al 1967. The standard edn of the poems. One vol edn, ed Butt 1963.

Poems. Ed D. Grant 1950 (Penguin).

Selected poetry and prose. Ed W. K. Wimsatt, New York 1951, 1958.

Epistles to several persons (Moral essays). Ed J. E. Wellington, Miami 1963.

Horation satires and epistles. Ed H. H. Erskine-Hill, Oxford 1964.

Literary criticism. Ed B. A. Goldgar, Lincoln Nebraska 1965.

Poetical works. Ed H. Davis, Oxford 1966 (OSA).

§ I

The numerous reprints of the minor poems are listed in vol 6 of Twickenham edn of the poems.

January and May; The episode of Sarpedon; Pastorals. In Tonson's Poetical Miscellanies: sixth part, 1709 etc. Pastorals also in Miscellany pastorals, Dublin [1714]. Sarpedon rptd in the Iliad, 1717, 1718.

An essay on criticism. 1711, 1711, 1713 (3 edns), Dublin [1713], 1713 (in A select collection of modern poems), London 1714 (in Lintott's Miscellany, 2nd edn), 1716 (T. Johnson piracy), 1716, 1719, 1722, 1744 (in An essay on man, below, with Warburton's notes); ed A. S. West, Cambridge 1896; ed J. C. Collins 1896; ed F. Ryland 1900; ed R. M. Schmitz, St Louis 1962 (with facs of ms).

The critical specimen. 1711.

Sapho to Phaon. In Tonson's Ovid's epistles, 1712 (8th edn) etc.

Messiah. Spectator no 378; in A collection of divine hymns and poems, 1719 (3rd edn); Lintott's Miscellany, 1720 (3rd edn); Windsor Forest, 1720 (4th edn); tr Latin by S. Johnson in J. Husband, A miscellany of poems, Oxford 1731.

Miscellaneous poems and translations by several hands. 1712, 1714, 2 vols 1720, 1722; Miscellany poems, 1727 (vol 1 sometimes 1726), 1732. Lintott's Miscellany, ed Pope. Edns vary in contents; first printings in each are separately noted.

The first book of Statius his Thebais; Vertumnus and Pomona; To a young lady with the works of Voiture; On silence; To the author of a poem entitled Successio; Verses design'd to be prefix'd to Mr Lintott's Miscellany; The rape of the locke [in two-canto form]. In Lintott's Miscellany, 1712 (1st edn). The Rape rptd in Windsor Forest, Dublin 1713.

[Contributions to] Spectator nos 406, 452, 457, 532, 16 June–10 Nov 1712. Other attributions in Prose works, above.

[On a fan]. Spectator no 527, 4 Nov 1712.

Windsor-Forest, to the Right Honourable George Lord Lansdown. 1713, 1713, Dublin 1713, London 1714 (in Lintott's Miscellany, 2nd edn), 1716 (in pirated Essay on criticism), 1720; ed R. M. Schmitz, St Louis 1952 (with facs of holograph).

[Contributions to] Guardian nos 4, 11, 40, 61, 78, 91, 92, 132, 173, 16 March–29 Sept 1713. Other attributions in Prose works, above.

Prologue to Cato. Guardian no 33, 18 April 1713; in Cato, 1713 etc.

Ode for Musick [on St Cecilia's Day]. 1713, 1719 (3rd edn), 1722; tr Latin by C. Smart, 1743, 1746.

Proposals for a translation of Homer's Ilias. [1713 or 1714]. No original or reprint known to be extant; *see* J. Nichols, Literary anecdotes vol 1, p. 76.

The narrative of Dr Robert Norris, concerning the strange and deplorable frenzy of Mr John Denn—. 1713.

Upon a Tory lady who happen'd to open her floodgates at the tragedy of Cato. Poetical Entertainer no 5 1713.

The Wife of Bath her prologue; Prologue, designed for Mr D—'s last play; The arrival of Ulysses in Ithaca. In Steele's Poetical Miscellanies, 1714, 1714 etc. Wife of Bath her prologue rptd in Ogle, Canterbury tales of Chaucer moderniz'd, 1741. Arrival of Ulysses rptd in Odyssey, 1725.

The rape of the lock, in five canto's. 1714 (3 edns), Dublin 1714 (in Windsor Forest, 1713), 1715, 1716 (T. Johnson piracy), 1718, 1720 (in Lintott's Miscellany, 3rd edn), 1723, Dublin 1732 (in Swift-Pope Miscellanies), 1896 (9 drawings by A. Beardsley); ed A. S. West, Cambridge 1896; ed G. Tillotson 1941; ed E. G. Fletcher, SE 1944, Austin 1944; ed J. S. Cunningham 1966.

Epigram upon two or three; Upon a girl of seven years old. In some copies of Lintott's Miscellany, 1714 (2nd edn).

The temple of fame: a vision. 1715, 1715, 1716 (in pirated Essay on criticism), 1727 (in Lintott's Miscellany, 5th edn).

A key to the lock: or a treatise proving beyond all contradiction the dangerous tendency of a late poem entitled the Rape of the lock to government and religion, by Esdras Barnivelt, apoth. 1715, 1715 (with commendatory verses added), 1718, 1723.

The dignity, use and abuse of glass-bottles. 1715, 1752 (as An ingenious and learned discourse, 5th edn).

The Iliad of Homer. Folio and 4°: Vol 1, 1715; vol 2, 1716; vol 3, 1717; vol 4, 1718; vols 5–6, 1720. 12° reprints: 1718–21 (T. Johnson piracy), 1720, 1720–1 (2nd edn), 1732 (3rd edn), 1736 (4th edn), 1743; ed G. Wakefield 5 vols 1806; ed R. A. Brower and W. H. Bond, New York 1965.

To Mr Jervas. In The art of painting, by C. A. Du Fresnoy, 1716 (2nd edn).

A full and true account of a horrid and barbarous revenge by poison on the body of Mr Edmund Curll, bookseller. [1716].

To the ingenious Mr Moore, author of the celebrated worm-powder. 1716 (3 edns).

A further account of the most deplorable condition of Mr Edmund Curll, bookseller, since his being poison'd on the 28th of March. 1716.

A Roman Catholick version of the first Psalm. 1716.

God's revenge against punning. 1716.

Prologue. In Three hours after marriage, 1717 etc. Pope and Arbuthnot collaborated with Gay in the play.

The Court ballad. [1717], [1717].

Epigrams, occasioned by an invitation to Court. In The parson's daughter, 1717.

The preface; A discourse on pastoral poetry; The fable of Dryope; Two chorus's to the tragedy of Brutus; Verses to the memory of an unfortunate lady; To the same [a young lady] on her leaving the town after the Coronation; Epitaph [on Trumbull]; Epilogue to Jane Shore; Occasion'd by some verses of his Grace the Duke of Buckingham; Eloisa to Abelard. In Works [vol 1], 1717 etc. Eloisa to Abelard rptd (with Verses to the memory of an unfortunate lady and 6 poems by others), 1720 (2nd edn), in Lintott's Miscellany, 1720 (3rd edn); Eloisa, ed J. E. Wellington, Gainesville 1965.

Ode on solitude; Of a lady singing to her lute; Verses in imitation of Waller (5); Weeping; Verses in imitation of Cowley (2); On the statue of Cleopatra; Psalm xci; Stanzas from the French of Malherbe; From Boetius De cons philos; To Belinda on the Rape of the lock; Imitation of Martial; Written over a study. In Poems on several occasions, 1717, 1735 (Pope's Own Miscellany, ed N. Ault). Ed Pope.

The plot discover'd: or a clue to the comedy of the Nonjuror. 1718 (3 edns).

Epitaph on John Hewett and Sarah Drew. White-hall Evening Post no 3, 20–3 Sept 1718.

What is prudery. Weekly Packet 11–18 Oct 1718.

The prayer of Brutus. In A. Thompson, The British history, 1718.

Mr Alexander Pope. In Giles Jacob, Historical account, 1720 etc.

Duke upon Duke. 1720, [1720] (as An excellent old ballad, called Pride will have a fall), [1720], 1723.

Epitaph design'd for Mr Rowe. In Lintott's Miscellany, 1720 (3rd edn).

Verses occasioned by Mr Addison's treatise of medals. In Works [vol 1], 1720.

Verses sent to Mrs T.B. with his Works; In behalf of Mr Southerne. In The grove, 1721.

To the Right Honourable Robert Earl of Oxford. In T. Parnell, Poems, 1722. Ed Pope.

If meaner Gil—n draws' [the Atticus satire upon Addison]. St James's Jnl no 34, 15 Dec 1722.

The works of John Sheffield, Duke of Buckingham. 2 vols 1723, 1724, 1726, 1729, 1740 etc. Ed Pope.

[On Simon Harcourt]. London Jnl 17 Oct 1724.

[To Mrs M. B. on her birthday]. Br Jnl 14 Nov 1724.

[Proposals for the Odyssey; Proposals for the Shakespear. No known copies].

The works of Shakespear in six volumes collated and corrected by Mr Pope. 1725 (separate title-leaves to vols are dated 1723), 1728, 1747 (re-edited by Warburton).

The Odyssey of Homer. [Folio, 4°, 12°]. Vols 1–3, 1725; vols 4–5, 1726; G. Wakefield 4 vols 1806.

Rondeau. Mist's Weekly Jnl 26 Feb 1726.

Letters to Henry Cromwell; Argus; Verses occasioned by Mr Durfy's adding an etc at the end of his name; An epistle to Henry Cromwell; The translator [epigram occasioned by Ozell's translation of Boileau's Lutrin]; Three gentle shepherds; Epigram in a maid of honor's prayerbook. In Curll's Miscellanea, 2 vols 1727.

Epitaph designed for Mr Dryden's monument. In Lintott's Miscellany, 1727 (5th edn).

The discovery. 1727, 1727, 1727 (as The 'Squire turn'd ferret).

A receipt to make a soop. [1727].

Epitaph on James Craggs. In Some memoirs of the life of Lewis Maximilian Mahomet, 1727.

''Tis thus that vanity'. 6 lines in J. M. Smyth, Rival modes, 1727, next ptd in the version of To Mrs M. B. on her birthday in the Swift-Pope miscellanies, 1727 ('last' vol).

Miscellanies in prose and verse. Vols 1–2, 1727; vol 'the last', 1727; vol 3, 1732. The Swift-Pope miscellanies, pbd by Motte. Apparently Pope edited only 4 vols, but the ser was often rptd and was ultimately extended to 11 vols. See under Swift, col 1056, below. First pbns in the various vols are separately noted.

Preface; Memoirs of P.P. clerk of this parish; Stradling versus Stiles; Thoughts on various subjects. In the Swift-Pope miscellanies vols 1–2, 1727.

To Quinbus Flestrin; The lamentation of Glumdalclitch; To Mr Lemuel Gulliver; Mary Gulliver to Captain Gulliver; The words of the King of Brobdingnag. In Swift, Travels by Lemuel Gulliver vol 1, 1727 (2nd edn).

To Kneller on his painting statues of Apollo. In Steele's miscellanies, 1727 (2nd edn).

Peri bathous: or the art of sinking in poetry; fragments of Alcander; The happy life of a country parson; A tale of Chaucer; The alley; Sandys's ghost; Umbra; Macer; Sylvia; Artimesia; Phryne; The capon's tale; The balance of Europe. In the Swift-Pope miscellanies, 1727 ('last' vol); Peri bathous, ed E. L. Steeves, New York 1952 (as The art of sinking in poetry) (facs).

Rapin of Gardens in four books, translated by James Gardiner. 1728 (3rd edn). Bks 1–2 corrected by Pope for this edn.

The Dunciad: an heroic poem in three books. 'Dublin' (actually London), 1728, 1728, 1728 ('Gold chains' edn, pirated), 1728 (2nd edn), 1728 (2nd edn), 1728 (3rd edn), 1728 (3rd edn), Dublin 1728, Oxford 1928 (type facs of larger London 8°). A key, pbd by Curll, ran through 3 edns in 1728; another 4 pp. 12° Key, with a dropped heading but no title-page, may have been prepared by Pope himself.

The Dunciad variorum. 1729 (3 edns), 1729 (8° as A Dob; a Curll piracy), 1729 (2nd edn), Dublin 1729, 1729, London [1735], (sheets of the large paper folio Works, vol 2, issued separately with a half-title leaf but without a title-page leaf), [1735], 1736; Princeton, 1929 (facs of 1729 4°). The document for the sale of the copyright from the noble lords to Gilliver, dated 16 Oct 1729, is preserved in BM as Egerton ms 1951, fol 6.

The new Dundiad. 1742 (3 edns; the 8° may be a piracy), 1742, 1742 (Hubbard piracies); Dublin 1742, 1742, London 1742 (The Dunciad, book the fourth, 2nd edn).

The Dunciad in four books. 1743, Dublin 1743, London 1749.

The bookseller to the reader; Table of contents; Letters to Wycherley; additions to Wycherley's poems. In Post-

humous works of William Wycherley esq in prose and verse vol 2, 1729. Ed Pope. Suppressed?; unsold sheets used in Letters, 1735.

Prologue. In James Thomson, The tragedy of Sophonisba, 1730 etc. In part attributed to Pope by Johnson.

Kneller, by heaven. St James's Evening Post 21 April 1730. An epitaph.

When other ladies [epigram]; Adriani morientis ad animam translated [and] imitated; Epitaph on Mrs Corbet; Epitaph on Digby. In D. Lewis, Miscellaneous poems, 1730.

[Epigrams] On Mr M—re's going to law; A gold watch [on J.M.S. gent]; Here lyes what had [epitaph on James Moore Smyth]; On the candidates for the laurel; An epigram [on the same]; Epigram [on Dennis]; Occasion'd by seeing some sheets of Dr B—tl—y's edition of Milton's Paradise lost. Grub-street Jnl nos 25–6, 29, 45–6, 78, 100, 25 June 1730–2 Dec 1731.

Epitaph intended for Sir Isaac Newton. Present State of the Republick of Letters June 1730.

Epitaph on Mr Elijah Fenton. Daily Post-boy 22 Oct 1730.

Canticle. Grub-street Jnl no 46, 19 Nov 1730. Pope may be the author of the whole article.

Epitaph on General Henry Withers. Grub-street Jnl no 50, 17 Dec 1730.

To prove himself [on J.M.S. gent.] Evening Post 26–8 Aug 1731.

An epistle to the Right Honourable Richard Earl of Burlington. 1731, 1731, 1732 (as Of taste), 1731 (2nd edn), 1732 (in A miscellany on taste), 1732 (as Of false taste, 3rd edn) (3 edns), Dublin 1732, 1732, 1733 (in Stowe, The gardens of Viscount Cobham).

To J. Gay esq. Daily Post-boy 22 Dec 1731. A letter; see Correspondence 3, p. 254.

Horace, Satyr 4, lib 1, paraphrased. London Evening Post 22–5 Jan 1732.

To the Earl of Middlesex [dedication]; Postscript. In Richard Savage, A collection of pieces on occasion of the Dunciad, 1732.

A strange but true relation how Edmund Curll; An essay of the origine of sciences; Here Francis Ch—s lies; You beat your pate; Well then, poor, G—; On the toasts of the Kit-Cat Club; To a lady with the Temple of Fame; On the Countess of B—; On a certain lady at Court; Epitaph [Of by-words]; Epigram from the French; Epigram [Peter complains]; Verses to be placed under the picture of England's arch-poet. In the Swift-Pope Miscellanies vol 3, 1732.

Of the use of riches, An epistle to Bathurst. 1732, 1733, 1733 (2nd edn), 1733 (2nd edn), Dublin 1733, 1733; ed E. R. Wasserman, Baltimore 1960.

The first satire of the second book of Horace, imitated. 1733, 1733, Dublin 1733, London 1734 (with Second satire) (3 or 4 edns).

An essay on man: part i. [1733] (5, 6 or 7 edns; Griffith's books 294–5 may be the same; also 303 and 305), [1733] (Epistle I, corrected by the author), [1733], Dublin [1733], 1734, London 1735.

An essay on man: epistle ii. [1733] (4 edns), Dublin [1733], [1733].

An essay on man: epistle iii. [1733] (4 edns), Dublin [1733] (3 edns).

An essay on man: epistle iv. [1734], [1734], Dublin 1734, 1734.

An essay on man: being the first book of ethic epistles [4 epistles as one book]. 1734, 1734, Dublin 1734, [1735], London 1736 (for Witford; 2 7th edns, piracies), 1744 (with Warburton's notes); ed M. Pattison 1869; Oxford [1871], 1932; ed M. Mack 1962 (with facs of ms). The 18th- and 19th-century American edns furnish a history of culture in the USA.

Epitaph on Mr Gay. GM June 1733.

The impertinent [Donne, Satire 4]. 1733, 1737, 1737, Dublin 1737.

An epistle to the Right Honourable Richard Lord Visct Cobham [Of the knowledge and characters of men]. 1733, 1734, Dublin 1734.

The second satire. In The first satire of the second book of Horace, imitated, to which is added the second satire of the same book, 1734 (5 edns), 1735.

Sober advice from Horace. [1734], 1735, 1735, Dublin 1737, London [1738] (reissue of 1735 folio sheets as A sermon against adultery).

An epistle to Dr Arbuthnot. 1734, 1734, Dublin 1735, Oxford 1926 (facs); ed J. Butt 1954. Title later changed to Prologue to the satires.

An essay on reason, by Walter Harte. 1735. Pope contributed lines to this poem.

Of the characters of women. 1735, 1735, Dublin 1735, Oxford 1924 (facs). Title changed in Works to Epistle ii: to a lady.

The author to the reader; Advertisement; The second satire of Dr John Donne; On the Earl of Dorset; On Mr Fenton; By the author a declaration. In Works vol 2, 1735. The original version of Second satire of Dr John Donne was first ptd from the ms in vol 4 of the Twickenham edn of the Poems, 1939. The Epitaph for Atterbury was cancelled before pbn and first ptd by Warburton in 1751.

Wrote by Mr P. in a volume of Evelyn on Coins. GM May 1735.

Letters of Mr Pope and several eminent persons. 1735 (21 or more edns, issues or varieties, often in 2-vol sets; rptd as Mr Pope's literary correspondence, annotated and continued by E. Curll; vols 1–3, 1735; vol 4, 1736; vol 5, 1737 (5 includes New letters of Mr Pope, also issued separately and rptd Dublin 1737 as Letters from Alexander Pope, and additional letters from Pope's authorized edn 1737); see Works in prose vol i.

A narrative of the method by which the private letters of Mr Pope have been procured and published by Edmund Curll. [1735], 1735 (in all 12° edns of Letters).

Epistle ii: to James Craggs. In 8° edn of Works vol 2, 1735.

Advertisement; The garden. In 8° edn of Works vol 3, 1736.

O fairest pattern [epitaph on John Knight]. Daily Gazetteer 17 July 1736.

To the Earl of Burlington. Grub-Street Jnl no 352, Sept 1736.

Bounce to Fop. 1736, Dublin 1736.

[Conclusion to A fit of the spleen]. White-hall Evening Post 19–22 March 1737. Later used as last 8 lines of To Mr Gay, first pbd in Dallaway's edn of Lady Mary Wortley Montagu's Works, 1803.

Horace his Ode to Venus lib iv, Ode i, Imitated, 1737, 1737.

The second epistle of the second book of Horace imitated. 1737 (3 edns), Dublin 1737, 1737.

The first epistle of the second book of Horace imitated. 1737 (3 edns), Dublin 1737.

The second book of the epistles of Horace, imitated. 1737. Reissues of the first edn of First epistle and 2nd edn of Second epistle.

The sixth epistle of the first book of Horace imitated. 1738, 1738, Dublin 1738.

An imitation of the sixth satire of the second book of Horace. 1738. By Swift and Pope; Swift's part rptd from Swift-Pope Miscellanies, 1727 ('last' vol).

The first epistle of the first book of Horace imitated. 1738, 1738, Dublin 1738.

One thousand seven hundred and thirty eight [Epilogue to the Satires, Dialogue i]. [1738], 1738, 1738, Dublin 1738.

The universal prayer. 1738, 1738.

One thousand seven hundred and thirty eight. Dialogue ii [Epilogue to the Satires]. 1738, 1738, Dublin 1738.

The seventh epistle of the first book imitated; On Edmund Duke of Buckingham; For one who would not be buried in Westminster ['Heroes and Kings']; Epigram on one who made long epitaphs; Engraved on the collar of a dog; Cloe; a character. In Works vol 2 pt 2, 1738.

Fair Mirror of foul times. In John Milton, Works vol 1, 1738.

May these put money in your purse. In J. Bancks, Miscellaneous works vol 2, 1738.

On lying in the Earl of Rochester's bed. London Mag Aug 1739.

On the benefactions in the late frost. GM March 1740.

Selecta poemata Italorum qui latine scripserunt. 2 vols 1740.

Epigram by Mr Pope, who had cut down three walnut trees. Publick Register no 1, 3 Jan 1741.

Under this marble [epitaph]; Verbatim from Boileau. Publick Register no 2, 10 Jan 1741.

A prologue by Mr Pope to a play for Mr Dennis's benefit. Publick Register no 3, 17 Jan 1741.

On the grotto at Twick'nham. GM Jan 1741. Latin and Greek trns by R. Dodsley and W.H., 1743.

The booksellers to the reader; Letters; Memoirs of Scriblerus. In Works in prose vol 2 1741; Dublin 1741 (Memoirs of Scriblerus alone). Memoirs of Scriblerus also in Aitken's edn of Arbuthnot's Works, 1892; in Eddy's edn of Swift's Satires and personal writings, Oxford 1932; and alone, ed C. Kerby-Miller, New Haven 1950.

To Lady Winchilsea. In A general dictionary vol 10, p. 180, 1741. Pope also revised the article on Gay in the Dictionary.

[Epigram on Shakespeare's monument]. In frontispiece to Shakespeare, Poems on several occasions, sold by Murden, Newton et al [1741?].

The idea of a patriot King. [1741?]. Pope edited and had Bolingbroke's pamphlet ptd, but never pbd it. The edn was burned after Pope's death. One copy is in BM, another in the Univ of Texas Lib.

Tom Southerne's birth-day dinner. GM Feb 1742.

Epigram [on Bishop Hough]. In the Swift-Pope miscellanies vol 4, 1742 (4th edn).

Epigram: on Cibber's declaration that he will have the last word with Mr Pope. In The summer miscellany, 1742.

A blast upon bays; or a new lick at the Laureate. 1742.

Epitaph on Mr Rowe. Common Sense 25 June 1743.

Posthumously pbd letters, some of which contain scraps of verse, are not noted.

The last will and testament. 1744.

Verses upon the late D—ss of M—. 1746, 1746. First pbn of lines added to Of the character of women in Four ethic epistles, 1738 (ptd 1744).

The character of Katharine, late Duchess of Buckinghamshire and Normanby, 1746.

Polyphemus and Acis. London Mag Dec 1749.

On seeing the ladies at Crux-Euston; Inscription on a grotto. In The student, Oxford 1750.

On receiving a Standish and two pens; Part of the ninth ode of the fourth book; On Dr Francis Atterbury; A letter to a noble lord. In Warburton's edn of Works, 1751, vol 4, p. 339; vol 6, pp. 37, 99; vol 8, p. 253.

[Plan of an epic poem]. In Ruffhead's Life, 1769, pp. 316 f.

To Mr C. Edinburgh Mag July 1774.

A farewell to London. St James's Chron 14–16 Sept 1775.

Lines suppressed at the end of the Epistle [to a young lady] on leaving the town. St James's Chron 10–12 Aug 1775.

A dialogue [Since my old friend]; Lord Coningsby's epitaph. St James's Chron 21–23 Sept 1775.

Couplets on wit. In Additions to the works, 1776.

A prayer of St Francis Xavier. GM Oct 1791.

On Queen Caroline's death-bed; On a picture of Queen Caroline; 1740: a poem. In Warton's edn of Works, 1797.

Lady M. W. Montagu's portrait. In Dallaway's edn of Lady Mary's Works, 1803.

Lines on Swift's ancestors. In Scott's edn of Swift's Works vol 1, 1814.

To the Right Honourable the Earl of Oxford upon a piece of news. GM July 1809.

Let Clarke make half his life. In Singer's edn of Spence's Anecdotes, 1820.

Inscription on a punch-bowl. In Supplemental volume, 1825.

A hymn written in Windsor Forest. In A. Dyce's Aldine edn of Poetical works, 1831.

Epitaph on Lady Kneller. In T. Hanmer's Correspondence, 1838.

Lines to Lord Bathurst. In J. Mitford's edn of Gray's Correspondence with Rev Norton Nicholls, 1843.

A paraphrase on Thomas à Kempis; Epitaph on John Lord Caryll. Athenaeum 15 July 1854.

Mss notes on Tickell's Homer. Fraser's Mag Aug 1860.

[Epigram on Shakespeare's monument]. In The autobiography of Mary Granville, Mrs Delaney vol 2, 1861.

A memorial list of departed relations and friends; [A character of Marlborough]; O all-accomplished Caesar. In Elwin and Courthope's edn of Works vol 1, 1871, 3, 1881 (facs), 8 p. 320, n. 2, 1872.

Epigrams occasioned by Cibber's verses in praise of Nash. In F. D. Senior, Life and times of Colley Cibber, 1928.

In the character of a legislator [fragment of Brutus]. In F. Brie, Pope's Brutus, Anglia 63 1939. Better transcript in H.-J. Zimmerman, Bemerkungen zum Manuscript und Text von Popes Brutus, Archiv 199 1963.

Presentation verses to Nathaniel Pigott. In G. Sherburn, An accident in 1726, Harvard Lib Bull 2 1948.

A master key to Popery. Ed J. Butt in Pope and his contemporaries: essays presented to George Sherburn, Oxford 1949.

Inscription, Martha Blount—A: P:; The six maidens. In N. Ault, New light on Pope, 1949.

[Lines on the monument to John Oliver and his wife]. In G. C. F. Mead, A Pope inscription, TLS 7 Oct 1949.

To Ld Hervey and Lady Mary Wortley. In Earl of Ilchester, Lord Hervey and his friends, 1950.

To Eustace Budgell esq; Lines on Ministers. In the Twickenham edn of Poems vol 6, 1954, which includes also a list of rejected attributions.

Letters

For the history of the pbn of Pope's letters, see Sherburn's introd and notes.

Correspondence. Ed G. Sherburn 5 vols Oxford 1956.

Sherburn, G. Letters of Pope, chiefly to Sir William Trumbull. RES new ser 9 1958.

Rawson, C. J. Some unpublished letters of Pope and Gay. RES new ser 10 1959.

Letters. Ed J. Butt, Oxford 1960 (WC).

Arlidge, E. A new Pope letter. RES new ser 12 1961.

Link, F. M. A new Pope letter. RES new ser 15 1964.

Rousseau, G. S. A new Pope letter. PQ 45 1966.

Eddy, D. D. A new note from Pope. Cornell Lib Jnl 3 1967.

§ 2

The number of ptd pieces relating to Pope within his lifetime, friendly, inimical and neutral, mounted into the hundreds; in 1733 no fewer than 80 were pbd. For Pope's own list of attacks on himself, and fuller lists than the following, see Bibliographies, above. Pope's list being available in any one of numerous edns of the Poetical works, the titles are generally not repeated here; the principal name entirely omitted is John Dennis.

There are lives of Pope in the edns of works by Warton, Bowles, Roscoe and Courthope, and in the edns of poetical works by Dyce, Croly and Ward.

Addison, Joseph. Spectator no 253, 20 Dec 1711 (on the Essay on criticism); no 523, 30 Oct 1712.

Guardian nos 22–3, 28, 30, 32, 6 April etc 1713. Praise of Philips's Pastorals.

Fiddes, Richard. A prefatory epistle concerning some remarks to be published on Homer's Iliad. 1714.

Burnet, Sir Thomas. A second tale of a tub. 1715.

'Ninnyhammer, Nickydemus'. Homer in a nut-shell. 1715.

Curll, Edmund. Flying Post March–April 1716. Advertisements.

— Cythereia: or new poems upon love and intrigue. 1723. Ed Curll.

Theobald, Lewis. The Odyssey of Homer. Bk I, 1716.

— Censor no 33, 5 Jan 1717.

— Shakespeare restored. 1726.

— The posthumous works of William Wycherley. 1728.

— Proposals for printing by subscription notes and remarks on Shakespeare. Mist's Weekly Jnl 22 June 1728.

— The works of Shakespeare. 1733, 1740.

Jacob, Giles. An historical account of the lives and writings of our most considerable English poets. 1720, 2 vols 1723 (as Poetical register), 1724. Jacob's Lives; the account of Pope was probably prepared by Pope himself.

Gildon, Charles. Memoirs of the life of William Wycherley. 1718. *See* G. Sherburn, TLS 11 May 1922.

Macky, Spring. The adventures of Pomponius. Pt 2, 1726.

Spence, Joseph. An essay on Pope's Odyssey. 2 pts Oxford 1726–7, 1 vol 1737, 1747.

— Anecdotes, observations and characters of books and men collected from the conversations of Mr Pope and other eminent persons of his time. Ed S. W. Singer 1820; ed E. Malone 1820; ed J. M. Osborn 2 vols Oxford 1966 (the standard edn).

Madan, J. C. To Mr Pope. Composed 1720; ptd in 5th edn of Lintott's Miscellany vol 1, 1727; rptd in Johnson's Lives, 1779.

Amhurst, Nicholas. The Twickenham hotch-potch. 1728.

Cooke, Thomas. Penelope: a dramatick opera. 1728.

— The Comedian. No 2, May 1732.

A pope upon Pope. 1728; rptd in The Popiad, 1728.

Duckett, George. Dean Jonathan's parody on the 4th Chap of Genesis. 1729, 1742 (as Blast upon blast, and lick for lick); ed W. P. Jones, Los Angeles 1960 (Augustan Reprint Soc).

Savage, Richard. An author to be lett. 1729; rptd in A collection of pieces publish'd on occasion of the Dunciad, ed Savage 1732.

Ward, Edward. Durgen: or a plain satyr upon a pompous satyrist. 1729, 1742 (as The cudgell: or a crab-tree lecture, by Hercules Vinegar).

Concanen, Matthew. The speculatist. 1730, 1732.

— A miscellany on taste. 1732. Frontispiece by Hogarth. Ed Concanen.

Harte, Walter. An essay on satire. 1730; ed T. B. Gilmore, Los Angeles 1968 (Augustan Reprint Soc) (facs).

— An epistle to Mr Pope on reading his translations of Homer. 1731.

— An essay on reason. 1735 (3 edns).

Hill, Aaron. The progress of wit: a caveat. 1732.

Lyttelton, George, Baron. An epistle to Mr Pope from Rome. 1730; rptd in John Whaley, A collection of poems, 1732.

Russel, Alexander, John Martin et al. The Grub-street Jnl nos 1–418 weekly, 8 Jan 1730 to 29 Dec 1737. Selections rptd 1737 in Memoirs of the society of Grub-street, 2 vols.

Welsted, Leonard. One epistle to Mr A. Pope. 1730; ed J. V. Guerinot, Los Angeles 1965 (Augustan Reprint Soc) (facs).

Young, Edward. Two epistles to Mr Pope. 1730, Dublin 1730.

Burnet, Alexander. Achilles dissected. 1733, 1734 (as The case of Alexander Pope).

Mallet, David. Of verbal criticism. 1733.

Voltaire, F. A. de. In his Letters concerning the English nation, 1733, 1741. Letter no 22 on Pope.

Advice to a nobleman [Lord Hervey]. Grub-street Jnl 6 Dec 1733.

An epistle to the little satyrist of Twickenham. 1733.

Mr Taste's tour from the island of politeness to that of dulness and scandal. 1733.

Dodsley, Robert. The modern reasoners. 1734.

— An epistle to Mr Pope, occasion'd by his Essay on man. 1734, 1745. Both pieces in Trifles.

Gerard, —. An epistle to the egregious Mr Pope. 1734, 1734 ('with a new preface').

A letter on the Essay on man. In The present state of the republick of letters vol 14, Oct 1734, pp. 254 f.

A most proper reply to the nobleman's epistle. 1734.

A tryal of skill between a Court lord, and a Twickenham 'squire. 1734.

An epistle from a gentleman at Twickenham to a nobleman. [1734].

Tit for tat: or an answer to the epistle to a nobleman. 1734, 1734 (with addns); ed W. P. Jones, Los Angeles 1960 (Augustan Reprint Soc) (facs). Pt 2 advertised 1735.

Budgell, Eustace. The bee. Nos 1–118, 3 Feb 1733–14 June 1735 (weekly).

Bentley, Thomas. A letter to Mr Pope occasioned by sober advice. 1735.

An epistle to the author of the Essay on reason. 1735.

The rake of taste, dedicated to Alexander Pope esq. [1735].

Crousaz, J. P. de. Examen de l'Essai de M. Pope sur l'homme. Lausanne 1737, Paris 1748, 1766; tr Elizabeth Carter 1739.

— Commentaire sur la traduction en verse de M. l'Abbé du Resnel de l'Essai sur l'homme. Paris 1738; tr Charles Forman 1738, 1740 (in Miscellanies by Lady Margaret Pennyman); Samuel Johnson 1739, 1742.

[Dale, Thomas?] An epistle to Alexander Pope esq from South Carolina. 1737.

'Bickerstaff the younger'. August the second, one thousand seven hundred and thirty eight. 1738.

Paget, T. C., Baron. An epistle to Mr P— in anti-heroicks. 1738.

Warburton, William. Letters. In The works of the learned vol 4, Dec 1738 pp. 425 f.; vol 5, Jan–April 1739, pp. 56, 89, 159, 330; rptd in A vindication of Mr Pope's Essay on man from the misrepresentations of Mr de Crousaz in six letters, 1740, 1740; also in A critical and philosophical commentary on Mr Pope's Essay on man, 1742.

— A seventh letter, which finishes the Vindication. 1740.

A dialogue on one thousand seven hundred and thirty-eight. 1738.

Ayre (or Eyre), W. Truth: a counterpart to the Essay on man. 1739; Epistle 2, 1739.

— Memoirs of the life and writings of Pope. 2 vols 1745.

— Four ethic epistles, opposing some of Mr Pope's opinions. 1753.

Dudgeon, William. A view of the necessitarian or test scheme. 1739.

Johnson, Samuel. An essay on epitaphs. GM Dec 1740; rptd in Universal Visiter & Memorialist 1756, [1757]; Idler, 1767 (3rd edn); Life of Pope, 1781.

— Letter to Mr Urban on controversy between Crousaz and Warburton. GM March, Nov 1743.

— In his Prefaces biographical and critical to the works of the English poets vol 7, 1781; ed G. B. Hill vol 2, Oxford 1905.

Cibber, Colley. An apology for the life of Mr Colley Cibber, comedian. 1740, 1740, 2 vols 1750, 1756; ed R. W. Lowe 2 vols 1888.

— A letter from Mr Cibber to Mr Pope. 1742, 1742, 1742 (a pirated edn), Dublin 1742, Glasgow [1743?], London 1768, 1777. 3 (perhaps 4) different copperplate illustrations were made of the incident of Pope's misadventure.

— A second letter from Mr Cibber to Mr Pope. 1743.

— The egotist: or Colley upon Cibber. 1743, Dublin 1743.

— Another occasional letter from Mr Cibber to Mr Pope. 1744, Glasgow [1744], London 1777.

Fielding, Henry. An apology for the life of Mr T— C— 1740, Dublin 1741.

Johnson, T. The tryal of Colley Cibber for writing a book intitled An apology; together with an indictment exhibited against Pope for not exerting his talents at this juncture. 1740.

Lorleach, —. A satirical epistle to Mr Pope. 1740.

The Laureat: or the right side of Colley Cibber. 1740.

Hervey, J., Baron. A letter to Mr C—b—r, on his letter to Mr P—. 1742.

— The difference between verbal and practical virtue. 1742; ed A. J. Sambrook, Los Angeles 1967 (Augustan Reprint Soc) (facs).

A blast upon bays: or a new lick at the Laureat. 1742, 1742; rptd in Lick upon lick, 1744.

The blatant beast. 1742; ed J. V. Guerinot, Los Angeles 1965 (Augustan Reprint Soc) (facs).

Sawney and Colley: a poetical dialogue. 1742; ed W. P. Jones, Los Angeles 1960 (Augustan Reprint Soc) (facs).

The Scribleriad: being an epistle to the Dunces. 1742; ed A. J. Sambrook, Los Angeles 1967 (Augustan Reprint Soc) (facs).

Henley, John. Why how now, gossip Pope? or the sweet singing-bird of Parnassus taken out of its pretty cage to be roasted. 1743. Henley carried on his controversies with Pope principally by sermons at his Oratory and by advertizements in newspapers 1728–44 rather than by poems or pamphlets.

Mr Pope's picture in miniature, but as like as it can stare: a poem. 1743.

Lick upon lick, occasion'd by another occasional letter. 1744.

The Norfolk miscellany. Ed A. Cowper 2 vols 1744.

Brown, John. An essay on satire. 1745, 1748 (in Dodsley's collection vol 3), 1749, 1751 (in Warburton's edn of Works).

Serle, John. A plan of Mr Pope's garden. 1745.

Mason, William. Musaeus: a monody to the memory of Mr Pope. 1747, 1748 (3rd edn), 1748 (in Dodsley's collection vol 3).

Melmoth, W. In his Letters of Sir Thomas Fitzosborne, 1747–8 etc. Letters of 10 Oct 1719, 2 July, 20 Aug 1722, ed G. Cronin jr and P. A. Doyle, Washington 1960 (as Pope's Iliad: an examination).

Saint-John, H. (Viscount Bolingbroke) and D. Mallet. Letters on the spirit of patriotism: on the idea of a patriot King. 1749, 1750 etc.

Warburton, William. A letter to the editor of the letters. 1749, 1769 (in Ruffhead's edn of Pope).

A familiar epistle to the most impudent man living. 1749.

A letter to the Lord Viscount B—ke. [1749].

An apology for the late Mr Pope. 1749.

The impostor detected and convicted. 1749.

To the author of a libel entitled A letter to the editor. 1749.

A new book of the Dunciad. 1750.

The Horatian cannons of friendship. 1750.

'Almondes'. Common sense a common delusion. 1761.

B., A. Vindication of Mr Pope. GM Dec 1751.

Cooper, J. G. Cursory remarks on Mr Warburton's new edition of Mr Pope's works. 1751.

'Midnight, Mary'. The old woman's Dunciad. 1751. See MLN 30 1915.

Lessing, G. E. Pope ein Metaphysiker? Dantzig 1755; rptd in his Sämmtliche Schriften, ed K. Lachmann, 3rd edn rev F. Muncker, vol 6, Leipzig 1890.

Warton, Joseph. An essay on the writings and genius of Mr Pope. 1756, 1762, Dublin 1764, London 1772, 1782, 1806; vol 2, 1782, 1806. See W. D. MacClintock, Joseph Warton's Essay on Pope, Chapel Hill 1933.

Ruffhead, Owen. The life of Alexander Pope from

original manuscripts, with a critical essay. 1769. Ruffhead had the help of Warburton.

Gay, John. Mr Pope's welcome from Greece. Written in 1720; first pbd in Additions, 1776.

Richardson, Jonathan. Richardsoniana: or occasional reflections with several anecdotes interspersed. 1776.

Blackstone, Sir William. The Pope-Addison quarrel: a long note in Biographia britannica vol 1, 1778, pp. 45–63, under Addison.

Stockdale, Percival. An enquiry into the nature and genuine laws of poetry, including a particular defence of the writings and genius of Mr Pope. 1778.

Nichols, John. In his Biographical and literary anecdotes of William Bowyer, 1782.

—— In his Literary anecdotes [illustrations] of the eighteenth century, 17 vols 1812–58.

Tyers, Thomas. An historical rhapsody on Mr Pope. 1782, 1782.

Mathias, T. J. In his Pursuits of literature: 4 dialogues, 4 pts in 1 vol 1794–7, 1797 (4th edn), 1798 (4 edns), Dublin 1798, London 1812 (16th edn).

—— The shade of Pope on the banks of the Thames. 1799.

Wakefield, Gilbert. Observations on Pope. 1796.

Wordsworth, William. Preface. In Lyrical ballads, 1800 (2nd edn) etc.

Swiftiana. 2 vols 1804.

Bowles, W. L. Memoir. In his edn of Works, 1806.

—— The invariable principles of poetry, in a letter addressed to Thomas Campbell. Bath 1819, London 1822 (in 3rd edn of Letters to Lord Byron).

—— A reply to the charges brought by the reviewer of Spence's Anecdotes. Pamphleteer 17 1820.

—— Observations on the poetical character of Mr Pope. Pamphleteer 17–18 1821.

—— Two letters to the Right Hon Lord Byron. 1821.

—— A final appeal to the literary public relative to Pope. 1825.

—— Lessons in criticism to W. Roscoe. 1826. See also T. E. Casson, Bowles on 18th-century literature, in An Oxford miscellany, Oxford 1909.

Byron, George Gordon, Baron. English bards and Scotch reviewers. 1809.

—— Letter to [John Murray] on the Rev W. L. Bowles's strictures on the life and writings of Pope. 1821.

—— A second letter; first pbd in 1835. See R. E. Prothero's edn of Byron's Letters and journals vol 5, Appendix III.

D'Israeli, I. In his Quarrels of authors, 1814.

Hazlitt, William. In his Lectures on the English poets, 1818.

—— Pope, Lord Byron and Mr Bowles. London Mag June 1821.

Campbell, Thomas. Specimens of the British poets, with biographical and critical notices and an essay on English Poetry. Vol 1, 1819.

C., L. S. Mr Bowles—as editor of Pope. London Mag July 1820.

Gilchrist, O. G. The character of Pope. London Mag Aug 1820.

—— Letter to the Rev William Lisle Bowles. Stamford 1820.

Lloyd, Charles. Poetical essays on the character of Pope. 1821.

Roscoe, W. A letter in reply to [Bowles's] final appeal. 1825.

De Quincey, Thomas. Pope. In Encyclopaedia britannica (7th edn); The poetry of Pope; Lord Carlisle on Pope. All in Collected works vols 4, 11, ed D. Masson 1888–90.

Bell, W. C. Analysis of Pope's Essay on man. Lexington Kentucky 1836.

Sainte-Beuve, C.-A. Qu'est ce qu'un classique? In his Causeries du lundi vol 3, Paris 1850.

Carruthers, R. The life of Pope. 2 vols 1857.

Hunter, J. Pope: his descent and family connections. 1857. No 5, Hunter's critical and historical tracts.

Davies, R. Pope: additional facts concerning his maternal ancestry. 1858.

Conington, J. The poetry of Pope. In Oxford essays, 1858; rptd in his Miscellaneous works vol 1, 1872.

Arnold, M. On translating Homer. 1861. Especially Lecture 1.

—— General introduction to T. H. Ward's edn of English poets, 1880; rptd as The study of poetry in his Essays in criticism 2nd ser, 1888.

Taine, H. A. In his Histoire de la littérature anglaise vol 4, Paris 1864 etc.

Lowell, J. R. In his My study windows, 1871.

Stephen, L. Pope as a moralist. Cornhill Mag Nov 1873; rptd in his Hours in a library vol 1, 1874.

—— Alexander Pope. 1880 (EML).

Dilke, C. W. In his Papers of a critic vol 1, 1875.

Deetz, A. Pope: ein Beitrag zur Literaturgeschichte des 18 Jahrhunderts, nebst Proben Pope'scher Dichtungen. Leipzig 1876.

Dennis, J. In his Studies in English literature, 1876.

Bobertag, F. Zu Popes Rape of the Lock; zu Popes Essay on criticism; Popes Verhältnis zur Aufklärung des 18 Jahrhunderts. E Studien 1–3, 29 1877–1901.

Beljame, A. In his Le public et les hommes de lettres en Angleterre 1660–1744. Paris 1881; tr, ed B. Dobrée 1948.

Gosse, E. In his From Shakespeare to Pope, 1885.

Montégut, E. Heures de lecture d'un critique. Revue des Deux Mondes 15 March 1888.

Mead, W. E. The versification of Pope in its relation to the 17th century. Leipzig 1889.

McLean, L. M. The riming system of Pope. PMLA 6 1891.

Petzet, E. Die deutschen Nachahmungen des Popeschen Lockenraubes. Zeitschrift für Vergleichende Litteraturgeschichte 4 1891.

Maack, R. Ueber Popes Einfluss auf die Idylle und das Lehrgedicht in Deutschland. Hamburg 1895.

Leather, M. S. Pope as a student of Milton. E Studien 25 1898.

Schade, A. Ueber das Verhältnis von Popes January and May und The Wife of Bath her prologue zu den entsprechenden Abschnitten von Chaucers Canterbury Tales. E Studien 25–6 1898–9.

Tupper, J. W. Pope's Imitations of Horace. PMLA 25 1900.

Lounsbury, J. R. In his Text of Shakespeare, New York 1906, London 1906 (as The first editors of Shakespeare).

Chesterton, G. K. Pope and the art of satire. In his Varied types, 1908.

Saintsbury, G. In his A history of English prosody vol 2, 1908.

'Paston, George' (E. M. Symonds). Mr Pope his life and times. 2 vols 1909. Contains newly pbd materials from Mapledurham and elsewhere.

Lochner, L. Popes literarische Beziehungen zu seinen Zeitgenossen. Leipzig 1910.

Moore, P. E. In his With the Wits, 1918.

Mackail, J. W. Pope. Cambridge 1919 (Stephen lecture).

Cobb, M. E. Pope's lines on Atticus. MLN 36 1921.

Morley, E. J. Joseph Warton's criticism of Pope. Ibid.

—— Joseph Warton: a comparison of his Essay on Pope with his edition of Pope's Works. E & S 9 1923.

Bickley, F. Pope and the lyrical cry. Sewanee Rev 31 1923.

Ker, W. P. In his Art of poetry, Oxford 1923; rptd in English critical essays, ed P. M. Jones, Oxford 1933.

Sherburn, G. Notes on the canon of Pope's works 1714–20. In J. M. Manly anniversary studies, Chicago 1923.

—— The early career of Pope 1688–1727. Oxford 1934.

—— Timon's villa and Cannons. Huntington Lib Bull 8 1935.

—— Walpole's marginalia in additions to Pope 1776. HLQ 1 1938.

—— Pope's letters and the Harleian Library. ELH 7 1940.

—— The Dunciad bk IV. SE 1944; rptd in Essential articles for the study of Pope, ed M. Mack, Hamden Conn 1964, 1968 (enlarged).

—— Pope at work. In Essays on the eighteenth century presented to David Nichol Smith, Oxford 1945.

—— An accident in 1726. Harvard Lib Bull 2 1948.

—— Pope and 'the great shew of nature'. In The seventeenth century: studies by R. F. Jones et al, Stanford 1951.

—— The Swift-Pope miscellanies of 1732. Harvard Lib Bull 6 1952. Correction 7 1953.

—— New anecdotes about Pope. N & Q Aug 1958.

—— Pope on the threshold of his career. Harvard Lib Bull 13 1959.

—— The 'copies of verses' about Gulliver. Texas Stud in Lit & Lang 3 1961.

Case, A. E. Some new poems by Pope? London Mercury Oct 1924. Corrections, Feb 1925.

—— Pope, Addison and the Atticus lines. MP 33 1935.

—— New attributions to Pope. MP 34 1937. Reply by N. Ault 35 1937. Rptd in Studies in literature of the Augustan age: essays collected in honor of A. E. Case, Ann Arbor 1952, New York 1966.

—— The game of ombre in the Rape of the lock. SE 1944.

Lemonnier, L. Pope traducteur de Boileau. Revue de Littérature Comparée 4 1924.

Fitzgerald, L. Pope's Catholic neighbors. Month April 1925.

Hillhouse, J. T. Teresa Blount and Alexis. MLN 40 1925.

—— The Grub-street Journal. Durham NC 1928.

Strachey, L. Pope. Cambridge 1925 (Stephen lecture); rptd in Essays, formal and informal, ed F. W. Scott and J. Zeitlin, New York 1930; in his Characters and commentaries, 1933.

—— Pope, Addison, Steele and Swift. In his Characters and commentaries, 1933.

Ratchford, F. E. Pope and the Patriot King. SE 6 1926.

Tate, A. Pope and other poems. New York 1928.

Bond, R. P. -iad: a progeny of the Dunciad. PMLA 44 1929. Further notes by M. Kelley 46 1931.

Heinsius, W. Pope. Der Kreis 6 1929.

Helsztynski, S. Pope und der polnische Pseudo-Klassizismus. Anglia 40 1929.

Hughes, H. S. More Popeiana. PMLA 44 1929.

—— Pope and his grotto. MP 28 1930.

Warren, A. Pope as critic and humanist. Princeton 1929, Gloucester Mass 1963.

—— Pope and Ben Jonson. MLN 45 1930.

—— Pope's index to Beaumont and Fletcher. MLN 46 1931.

—— Henry Layng, assistant in Pope's Odyssey. RES 8 1932.

—— To Mr Pope: epistles from America. PMLA 48 1933.

—— The mask of Pope. Sewanee Rev 54 1946; rptd in Essential articles for the study of Pope, ed M. Mack, Hamden Conn 1964, 1968 (enlarged).

Beck, R. Pope's Essay on man in Icelandic. Scandinavian Notes & Stud 11 1930.

—— Jón Þorláksson: Icelandic translator of Pope and Milton. JEGP 32 1933, 34 1935.

—— Pope and Icelandic literature. Scandinavian Stud 25 1953.

Roberts, M. Pope and English classicism. Poetry Rev 21 1930.

Sitwell, E. Alexander Pope. 1930.

Wyld, H. C. Observations on Pope's versification. MLR 25 1930.

Audra, E. L'influence française dans l'œuvre de Pope. Paris 1931.

Blunden, E. C. Pope and Theobald. In his Votive tablets, 1931.

Chandler, W. K. The first edition of the Dunciad. MP 29 1931.

—— Pope's self-plagiarism. MP 30 1932.

Griffith, R. H. A piracy of Pope's Iliad. SP 28 1931.

—— The Dunciad duodecimo. Colophon 3 1938.

—— Early Warburton or late Warburton? SE 1940. On text of Essay on criticism.

—— Pope editing Pope. SE 1944.

—— The Dunciad. PQ 24 1945; rptd in Essential articles for the study of Pope, ed M. Mack, Hamden Conn 1964, 1968 (enlarged).

—— Pope's reading. N & Q 19 Aug 1950.

—— Pope on the art of gardening. SE 31 1952.

Lenta, G. Pope in Italia. Florence 1931.

Sale, W. M. Pope and Lord Dysart. MLN 46 1931.

Willard, R. Notes on the poems of Pope. New Haven 1931.

McColley, G. Locke's Essay concerning human understanding as a partial source of Pope's Essay on man. Open Court 46 1932.

Ryan, J. K. Philosophy and Pope. Catholic World Sept 1932.

Segar, M. Some notes on Pope's religion. Dublin Rev April 1932.

Babcock, R. W. The text of Pope's To Mrs M.B. on her birth-day. MLN 48 1933.

—— Pope's grotto today. South Atlantic Quart 42 1943.

The Essay on man. TLS 10 Aug 1933.

La Harpe, J. de. Le Journal des Savants et la renommée de Pope en France au XVIIIᵉ siècle. Berkeley 1933.

Leavis, F. R. Pope. Scrutiny 2 1934; rptd in his Revaluation, 1935; in Essential articles for the study of Pope, ed M. Mack, Hamden Conn 1964, 1968 (enlarged).

—— The Dunciad. In his Common pursuit, 1952.

Williams, C. Reasoning but to err: the Essay on man. In his Reason and beauty in the poetic mind, Oxford 1934.

Davies, C. The Rape of the Lock and Evelyn's Mundus muliebris: a parallel. RES 10 1934.

Durham, W. H. Pope as poet. In Essays in Criticism by members of the Dept of English, University of California, 2nd ser, Berkeley 1934.

Stevenson, S. W. 'Romantic' tendencies in Pope. ELH 1 1934; Baltimore 1934 (separately).

Wright, L. S. Eighteenth-century replies to Pope's Eloisa. SP 31 1934.

Ault, N. Pope's lost sermon on glass-bottles. TLS 6 June 1935. Replies by G. Sherburn 20 June 1935; J. R. Sutherland 27 June 1935.

—— New light on Pope. 1949. Pope and Addison rptd in Essential articles for the study of Pope, ed M. Mack, Hamden Conn 1964, 1968 (enlarged).

Fletcher, E. G. Belinda's game of ombre. SE 1935.

Sutherland, J. R. Pope or Arbuthnot? TLS 22 Nov 1935. On authorship of Annus mirabilis.

—— The Dunciad of 1729. MLR 31 1936.

—— Wordsworth and Pope. Proc Br Acad 30 1944.

—— The dull duty of an editor. RES 21 1945; rptd in Essential articles for the study of Pope, ed M. Mack, Hamden Conn 1964, 1968 (enlarged).

Bishop, C. R. Pope and the battle of the poets. West Virginia Univ Stud 1 1936.

Butt, J. Pope's taste in Shakespeare. 1936 (Shakespeare Assoc Lecture).

—— The inspiration of Pope's poetry. In Essays on the eighteenth century presented to David Nichol Smith, Oxford 1945.

—— Pope's poetical manuscripts. Proc Br Acad 40 1954; rptd in Essential articles for the study of Pope, ed M. Mack, Hamden Conn 1964, 1968 (enlarged).

Potter, G. R. and J. Butt. Editing Donne and Pope. Los Angeles 1954.

Butt, J. Pope: a new view of his character. Listener 20 June 1957; rptd as Pope seen through his letters in Eighteenth-century English literature, ed J. L. Clifford, New York 1959.

—— Pope's letters: some notes and corrections. N & Q Nov 1957.

—— Pope: the man and the poet. In Of books and humankind: essays and poems presented to Bonamy Dobrée, 1964.

Hodges, J. C. Pope's debt to one of his dunces. MLN 51 1936.

Tillotson, G. Lady Mary Wortley Montagu and Pope's Elegy to the memory of an unfortunate lady. RES 12 1936.

— On the poetry of Pope. Oxford 1938, 1950 (rev).

— In his Essays in criticism and research, Cambridge 1942.

— The moral poetry of Pope. Newcastle 1946.

— Pope's epistle to Harley. In Pope and his contemporaries: essays presented to George Sherburn, Oxford 1949; rptd in his Augustan studies, 1961.

— Poet of plenitude. Listener 3 Aug 1950.

— Pope and the common reader. Sewanee Rev 66 1958.

— Pope and human nature. Oxford 1958.

Auden, W. H. In Anne to Victoria, ed B. Dobrée 1937; rptd EC 1 1951 and in Essential articles for the study of Pope, ed M. Mack, Hamden Conn 1964, 1968 (enlarged).

Baker, H. K. Pope and Bacon. Baconiana 22 1937; 1937 (separately).

Jensen, H. de Wet. Die menschliche und dichterische Entwicklung Popes. Anglia 62 1938.

Meyerstein, E. H. W. Concealed verse in Pope's prose. TLS 17 July 1937.

Mizener, A. Pope on the Duke of Buckingham. MLN 53 1938.

Ransom, H. Riddle of the world: a note on Pope and Pascal. Sewanee Rev 46 1938.

— The personal letter as literary property. SE 30 1951.

Root, R. K. The poetical career of Pope. Princeton 1938.

— Pope's contributions to the Lintott miscellanies of 1712 and 1714. ELH 7 1940.

Winslow, A. Re-evaluation of Pope's treatment of nature. Univ of Wyoming Pbns 4 1938.

Wright, A. Joseph Spence as defender of Pope's reputation. MP 36 1938.

— The beginning of Pope's friendship with Spence. MLN 54 1939.

Aldridge, A. O. Milton and Pope's conception of God and man. Bibliotheca Sacra 96 1939.

Brie, F. Pope's 'Brutus'. Anglia 63 1939.

Dobrée, B. Pope's Horace. TLS 12 Aug 1939.

— Alexander Pope. 1951.

— Critics who have influenced taste, II: Pope. Times 13 June 1963.

Wilson Knight, G. The vital flame: an essay on Pope. In his Burning oracle, 1939.

— Laureate of peace. 1955, 1965 (as The poetry of Pope).

Mack, M. The first printing of the letters of Pope and Swift. Library 4th ser 19 1939.

— Pope's Horatian poems: problems of bibliography and text. MP 41 1943.

— Letters of Pope to Atterbury. RES 21 1945.

— A manuscript of Pope's imitation of the first ode of the fourth book of Horace. MLN 60 1945.

— On reading Pope. College Eng Feb 1946, Nov 1960.

— Wit and poetry and Pope: his imagery. In Pope and his contemporaries: essays presented to George Sherburn, Oxford 1949; rptd in Eighteenth-century English literature, ed J. L. Clifford, New York 1959 and in The modern critical spectrum, ed G. J. and N. M. Goldberg, Englewood Cliffs NJ 1962.

— The Muse of satire. Yale Rev 41 1951; rptd in Studies in literature of the Augustan age: essays collected in honor of A. E. Case, Ann Arbor 1952.

— Some annotations in the second Earl of Oxford's copies of Pope's epistle to Dr Arbuthnot and Sober advice from Horace. RES new ser 8 1957.

— Two variant copies of Pope's works vol II. Library 5th ser 12 1957. On authorship, bibliography, text.

— 'The shadowy cave': some speculations on a Twicken-

ham grotto. In Restoration and eighteenth-century literature: essays in honor of A. D. McKillop, Chicago 1963.

— (ed). Essential articles for the study of Pope. Hamden Conn 1964, 1968 (enlarged).

— A poet in his landscape: Pope at Twickenham. In From sensibility to romanticism: essays presented to F. A. Pottle, New York 1965.

— Secretum iter: some uses of retirement literature in the poetry of Pope. In Aspects of the eighteenth century, ed E. R. Wasserman, Baltimore 1965.

Quennell, P. C. Pope: an Augustan portrait. Cornhill Mag March 1939.

— Pope: the education of a genius. 1968.

Vincent, H. P. Some Dunciad litigation. PQ 18 1939.

Olson, E. Rhetoric and the appreciation of Pope. MP 37 1940.

Russev, R. Pope i literaturata. Godišnik na Sofiiskiya Universitet Istoriko-filologičeski Facultet 36 1940.

Bateson, F. W. The game of ombre in the Rape of the lock. TLS 1 March 1941. Replies by D. Morrah 8 March; G. Tillotson 22 March; and Morrah 29 March 1941.

Hooker, E. N. Pope and Dennis. ELH 7 1940.

— Pope on wit: the Essay on criticism. Hudson Rev 2 1950; rptd in The seventeenth century: studies by R. F. Jones et al, Stanford 1951; in Eighteenth-century English literature, ed J. L. Clifford, New York 1959; and in Essential articles for the study of Pope, ed M. Mack, Hamden Conn 1964, 1968 (enlarged).

Blanchard, R. Pope's Ode for St Cecilia's Day. ELH 8 1941.

Highet, G. The Dunciad. MLR 36 1941.

— Pope: the lady and the poet. In his Powers of poetry, New York 1960.

Stamm, R. Der umstrittene Ruhm Popes. Schweizer Anglistische Arbeiten 12 1941. A history of Pope criticism.

Altick, R. D. Mr Pope expands his grotto. PQ 21 1942.

Strachan, L. R. M. Pope's rhymes. N & Q 24 Jan 1942.

Brooks, C. The case of Miss Arabella Fermor. Sewanee Rev 51 1943; rptd in his Well wrought urn, New York [1947], and in Essential articles for the study of Pope, ed M. Mack, Hamden Conn 1964, 1968 (enlarged).

Dearing, V. A. New light on the first printing of the letters of Pope and Swift. Library 4th ser 24 1943.

— The 1737 editions of Pope's letters. In Essays dedicated to L. B. Campbell, Berkeley 1950.

— The Prince of Wales's set of Pope's works. Harvard Lib Bull 4 1950. Extract in Essential articles for the study of Pope, ed M. Mack, Hamden Conn 1964, 1968 (enlarged).

— Pope, Theobald and Wycherley's Posthumous works. PMLA 58 1953.

— Two notes on the copy for Pope's letters. PBSA 51 1957.

Tobin, J. E. Pope and the classical tradition. Bull of Polish Acad of Arts & Sciences in America 3 1943.

— Pope 1744–1944. Thought 19 1944. A defence of his character.

— Pope and Homer. Classical Bull 21 1944.

Pope: the voice of Augustan England. TLS 3 June 1944.

Bond, D. F. Pope's contributions to the Spectator. MLQ 5 1944.

— The importance of Pope's letters. MP 56 1958; rptd in Essential articles for the study of Pope, ed M. Mack, Hamden Conn 1964, 1968 (enlarged).

Churchill, R. C. The enduring element in Pope. Dublin Rev 218 1944.

Laird, J. Essay on man. RES 20 1944; rptd in his Philosophical incursions into English literature, Cambridge 1946.

Martin, L. C. Lucretius and the Rape of the lock. RES 20 1944.

Maurer, O. Pope and the Victorians. SE 1944.

Monk, S. H. A grace beyond the reach of art. JHI 5 1944; rptd in Essential articles for the study of Pope, ed M. Mack, Hamden Conn 1964, 1968 (enlarged).

— Die of a rose. HLQ 21 1958.

Stenberg, T. Quotations from Pope in Johnson's Dictionary. SE 1944.

Trowbridge, H. Pope, Gay and the Shepherd's week. MLQ 5 1944.

Wimsatt, W. K. One relation of rhyme to reason. MLQ 5 1944; rptd in Studies in the literature of the Augustan age: essays collected in honor of A. E. Case, Ann Arbor 1952, and in Essential articles for the study of Pope, ed M. Mack, Hamden Conn 1964, 1968 (enlarged).

— Rhetoric and poems: the example of Pope. Eng Inst Essays 1949.

— The game of ombre in the Rape of the lock. RES new ser 2 1950.

— 'Amicitiae causa': a birthday present from Curll to Pope. In Restoration and 18th-century literature: essays in honor of A. D. McKillop, Chicago 1963.

— An image of Pope. In From sensibility to romanticism: essays presented to F. A. Pottle, New York 1965.

— The portraits of Pope. New Haven 1965.

Ames, A. C. Early criticism of Pope's Nightpiece. MLN 60 1945.

Bickersteth, H. L. Pope and his friends. In his Three lectures, 1945.

Hamm, V. M. Pope and Malebranche: a note on the Essay on criticism pt II. PQ 24 1945.

Sypher, W. Arabesque in verse. Kenyon Rev 7 1945; rptd in his Rococo to Cubism, New York 1960.

Gress, E. The culmination of formalism in English literature: Pope as a literary critic. Orbis Litterarum 2 1945.

Crawford, C. E. Pope's debt to Edward Young. ELH 13 1946.

MacDonald, W. L. A French life of Pope [1763]. UTQ 15 1946.

— Pope and his critics. Seattle 1951.

Shaver, C. L. A Wordsworth-Pope parallel. MLN 61 1946.

Weatherley, E. H. Churchill's literary indebtedness to Pope. SP 43 1946.

Douglas, L. A severe animadversion on Bossu. PMLA 62 1947.

Frost, W. The Rape of the lock and Pope's Homer. MLQ 8 1947; rptd in Essential articles for the study of Pope, ed M. Mack, Hamden Conn 1964, 1968 (enlarged).

— Ulysses, Diomed and Dolon: Pope and his predecessors. In Lebende Antike: Symposium für Rudolf Sühnel, Berlin 1967.

Rogers, R. W. Pope's collaboration with Warburton in the Essay on Man. PQ 26 1947.

— Critiques of the Essay on man in France and Germany 1736–55. ELH 15 1948.

— Pope's Universal prayer. JEGP 54 1955; rptd in Essential articles for the study of Pope, ed M. Mack, Hamden Conn 1964, 1968 (enlarged).

— The major satires of Pope. Urbana 1955.

Bagnani, G. The classical technique: Virgil, Dante and Pope. Phoenix (Jnl of Classical Assoc of Canada) 2 1947.

Bloom, L. D. Pope as textual critic: a bibliographical study of his Horatian text. JEGP 47 1948; rptd in Essential articles for the study of Pope, ed M. Mack, Hamden Conn 1964, 1968 (enlarged).

Oliver, L. M. New sources for Pope's Eclogues? Research Stud of State College Washington 15 1947.

Johnson, E. Freedom in restraint. In If by your art: testament to Percival Hunt, Pittsburgh 1948.

Surtz, E. L. Epithets in Pope's Messiah. PQ 27 1948.

Allen, R. J. Pope and the sister arts. In Pope and his contemporaries: essays presented to George Sherburn, Oxford 1949.

Bishop, C. R. General themes in Pope's satires. West Virginia Univ Bull Philological Papers 6 1949.

Bracher, F. Pope's grotto: the maze of fancy. HLQ 12 1949; rev in Essential articles for the study of Pope, ed M. Mack, Hamden Conn 1964, 1968 (enlarged).

Friedman, A. Pope and Deism (Dunciad IV 459–92). In Pope and his contemporaries: essays presented to George Sherburn, Oxford 1949.

Krutch, J. W. Pope and our contemporaries. Ibid.

Parkin, R. P. Pope's use of the implied dramatic speaker. College Eng Dec 1949.

— The quality of Pope's humor. College Eng Jan 1953.

— Tension in Pope's poetry. Univ of Kansas City Rev 19 1953; rptd in Essential articles for the study of Pope, ed M. Mack, Hamden Conn 1964, 1968 (enlarged).

— Mythopoeic activity in the Rape of the lock. ELH 21 1954.

— The poetic workmanship of Pope. Minneapolis 1955.

— The role of time in Pope's Epistle to a lady. ELH 32 1965; rptd in Essential articles for the study of Pope, ed M. Mack, Hamden Conn 1964, 1968 (enlarged).

— Pope's use of biblical and supernatural allusions. Stud on Voltaire 57 1967.

Sibley, A. M. Pope's prestige in America 1725–1835. New York 1949.

Empson, W. Wit in the Essay on criticism. Hudson Rev 2 1950; rptd in his Structure of complex words, 1951, and in Essential articles for the study of Pope, ed M. Mack, Hamden Conn 1964, 1968 (enlarged).

Jackson, J. L. The Rape of the lock as a five-act epic. PMLA 65 1950.

Koppang, O. En sammenlikning mellom Anthony Ashley Cooper, Earl of Shaftesbury, og Pope. Edda 50 1950.

Cameron, J. M. Doctrinal to an age: notes towards a revaluation of Pope's Essay on man. Dublin Rev 225 1951; rptd in his Night battle, 1962; rev in Essential articles for the study of Pope, ed M. Mack, Hamden Conn 1964, 1968 (enlarged).

Fineman, D. A. The case of the lady 'killed' by Pope. MLQ 12 1951.

— The motivation of Pope's Guardian 40. MLN 67 1952.

Gregory, H. Double vision in Pope's poetry. Poetry 77 1951.

Jack, I. Pope and the weighty bullion of Dr Donne's satires. PMLA 66 1951; rptd in Essential articles for the study of Pope, ed M. Mack, Hamden Conn 1964, 1968 (enlarged).

— A complex mock-heroic: the Rape of the lock; Studies on the moral essays; Imitations of Horace; The Dunciad. In his Augustan satire: intention and idiom, Oxford 1952.

— Pope. 1954 (Br Council pamphlet), 1962 (rev).

— 'The true raillery'. Cairo Stud in Eng 1960.

Knight, D. C. Pope and the heroic tradition: a critical study of his Iliad. New Haven 1951.

— Pope as a student of Homer. Comparative Lit 4 1952.

— The development of Pope's Iliad preface: a study of the manuscript. MLQ 16 1955; rptd in Essential articles for the study of Pope, ed M. Mack, Hamden Conn 1964, 1968 (enlarged).

— Translation: the Augustan mode. In On translation, ed R. A. Brower, Cambridge Mass 1959.

Koziol, H. Popes Sylphen und William Congreves Incognita. Anglia 70 1951.

Moore, J. R. Windsor Forest and William III. MLN 66 1951; rptd in Essential articles for the study of Pope, ed M. Mack, Hamden Conn 1964, 1968 (enlarged).

Shudofsky, M. M. A dunce objects to Pope's dictatorship. HLQ 14 1951.

Brower, R. A. An allusion to Europe: Dryden and poetic tradition. ELH 19 1952; rptd in Essential articles for the study of Pope, ed M. Mack, Hamden Conn 1964, 1968 (enlarged).

— Pope: the poetry of allusion. Oxford 1959.

— Dryden and the 'invention' of Pope. In Restoration

and 18th-century literature: essays in honor of A. D. McKillop, Chicago 1963.

Howard, L. The American revolt against Pope. SP 49 1952.

Reichard, H. M. Pope's social satire: belles-lettres and business. PMLA 67 1952; rptd in Essential articles for the study of Pope, ed M. Mack, Hamden Conn 1964, 1968 (enlarged).
— The love affair in Pope's Rape of the lock. PMLA 69 1954.
— The independence of Pope as political satirist. JEGP 54 1955.
— The drift of Pope's first epilogue. Boston Univ Stud in Eng 4 1960.

Thornton, F. B. Pope: Catholic poet. New York 1952.

Callan, N. Pope's Iliad: a new document. RES new ser 4 1953; rptd in Essential articles for the study of Pope, ed M. Mack, Hamden Conn 1964, 1968 (enlarged).

Halsband, R. Pope, Lady Mary and the Court poems 1716. PMLA 68 1953.

McKillop, A. D. The geographical chapter in Scriblerus. MLN 68 1953.

Petit, H. Pope's Eloisa to Abelard: an interpretation. Univ of Colorado Stud no 4 1953; rptd in Essential articles for the study of Pope, ed M. Mack, Hamden Conn 1964, 1968 (enlarged).
— Apposite metaphor in Pope's Essay on criticism. Books abroad 35 1961; rptd in Langue et littérature: actes du VIIIe Congrès de la Fédération Internationale des Langues et Littératures Modernes, Paris 1961.

Simon, I. Echoes of the Rape of the lock in the Waste land. E Studies 34 1953.
— Pope and the fragility of beauty. Revue des Langues Vivantes 24 1958.

Speaight, G. Pope in the toy theatre. Theatre Notebook 7 1953.

Williams, A. L. Pope's Duchesses and Lady Mary's. RES new ser 4 1953. See N. W. Bawcutt, N & Q 1 July 1961. On Dunciad II 123–32.
— Literary background to book four of the Dunciad. PMLA 68 1953.
— Pope's Dunciad: a study of its meaning. Baton Rouge 1955.
— Submerged metaphor in Pope. EC 9 1959.
— The 'fall' of China and the Rape of the lock. PQ 41 1962; rptd in Essential articles for the study of Pope, ed M. Mack, Hamden Conn 1964, 1968 (enlarged).
— Pope and Horace: the second epistle of the second book. In Restoration and 18th-century literature: essays in honor of A. D. McKillop, Chicago 1963.
— Pope's 'knack' at versifying. In All these to teach: essays in honor of C. A. Robertson, Gainesville 1967.

Boyce, B. Samuel Johnson's criticism of Pope in the Life of Pope. RES new ser 5 1954.
— An annotated volume from Pope's library. N & Q Feb 1958. Replies by W. J. Cameron, July 1958; J. A. V. Chapple, July 1958; G. Tillotson, Oct 1958.
— Baroque into satire: Pope's frontispiece for the Essay on man. Criticism 4 1962.
— The character-sketches in Pope's poems. Durham NC 1962.
— Mr Pope, in Bath, improves the design of his grotto. In Restoration and 18th-century literature: essays in honor of A. D. McKillop, Chicago 1963.
— The poet and the postmaster: the friendship of Pope and Ralph Allen. PQ 45 1966.

Clifford, F. B. Horace in the Imitations of Pope. Lexington Kentucky 1954.

Mengel, E. Patterns of imagery in Pope's Arbuthnot. PMLA 59 1954; rptd in Essential articles for the study of Pope, ed M. Mack, Hamden Conn 1964, 1968 (enlarged).

Provost, F. Pope's pastorals: an exercise in poetical technique. In Contributions to the humanities, Baton Rouge [1954].

Ruhe, E. L. Pope's hand in Thomas Birch's account of Gay. RES new ser 5 1954.

Sparrow, J. Pope's Anthologia again. PQ 33 1954.

Urner, U. Pope und die klassischlateinische Literatur. Schweizer Anglistische Arbeiten 36 1954.

Altenbernd, L. On Pope's horticultural romanticism. JEGP 54 1955; rptd in Essential articles for the study of Pope, ed M. Mack, Hamden Conn 1964, 1968 (enlarged).

Bland, D. S. Pope's colour-sense. Durhan Univ Jnl 47 1955.

Gillie, C. Pope: Elegy to the memory of an unfortunate lady. In Interpretations, ed J. Wain 1955.

Hughes, R. E. Pope's Essay on man: the rhetorical structure of Epistle i. MLN 60 1955; rptd in Essential articles for the study of Pope, ed M. Mack, Hamden Conn 1964, 1968 (enlarged).
— Pope's Imitations of Horace and the ethical focus. MLN 71 1956.

Kronenberger, L. In his Republic of letters, New York 1955.

Osborn, J. M. Pope, the Byzantine Empress and Walpole's whore. RES new ser 6 1955; rptd in Essential articles for the study of Pope, ed M. Mack, Hamden Conn 1964, 1968 (enlarged).
— 'That on Whiston' by John Gay. PBSA 56 1962.
— Addison's tavern companion and Pope's Umbra. PQ 42 1963.
— Spence, natural genius and Pope. PQ 45 1966.

Peterson, W. M. Pope and Cibber's The non-juror. MLN 60 1955.

Aden, J. M. First follow nature: strategy and stratification in An essay on criticism. JEGP 55 1956.
— The doctrinal design of An essay on criticism. College Eng Feb 1961.
— Pope and the satiric adversary. Stud in Eng Lit 1500–1900 2 1962; rptd in Essential articles for the study of Pope, ed M. Mack, Hamden Conn 1964, 1968 (enlarged).
— Pope and the receipt to make a satire. Satire Newsletter 5 1967.
— That impudent satire: Pope's sober advice. In Essays in English literature presented to D. MacMillan, Chapel Hill 1967.
— Swift, Pope and 'the sin of wit'. PBSA 62 1968.

de Selincourt, A. In his Six great poets, 1956.

Goldstein, M. Pope, Sheffield and Shakespeare's Julius Caesar. MLN 71 1956.
— Pope and the Augustan stage. Stanford 1958.

Hibbard, G. R. The country house poem of the seventeenth century. Jnl of Warburg & Courtauld Inst 19 1956; rptd in Essential articles for the study of Pope, ed M. Mack, Hamden Conn 1964, 1968 (enlarged).

Litz, F. E. Pope and [Jeremiah Seed]. MLQ 17 1956.
— Pope's use of Derham. JEGP 60 1961.

Cope, J. I. Shakerly Marmion and Pope's Rape of the lock. MLN 72 1957.

Eastman, A. M. The quality of mercy: a reply to Pope's apologists. Papers of Michigan Acad of Science, Arts & Letters 43 1957.

Ehrenpreis, I. Orwell, Huxley, Pope. Revue des Langues Vivantes 23 1957.
— The cistern and the fountain: art and reality in Pope and Gray. In Studies in criticism and aesthetics in honor of S. H. Monk, Minneapolis 1967.

Fabian, B. Rückkehr zu Pope. Die Neueren Sprachen July 1957.
— Zur Morallehr in Popes Essay on man. Germanisch-romanische Monatsschrift 38 1957.
— German echoes of a famous Popean line. N & Q Jan 1958. On Essay on man II, 1–2 in Lessing, Goethe, Moritz.
— Pope's Konzeption der 'ruling passion'. Archiv 195 1959.
— Pope und die goldene Kette Homers. Anglia 82 1964.

Maud, R. N. Pope and Miss Betty Marriot. MLN 72 1957.
— Some lines from Pope. RES new ser 9 1958.
Pyle, F. Six notes on the Rape of the lock. N & Q June 1957.
Schmitz, R. M. Two new holographs of Pope's Birthday lines to Martha Blount. RES new ser 8 1957.
— The 'arsenal' proof sheets of Pope's Iliad: a third report. MLN 74 1959; rptd in Essential articles for the study of Pope, ed M. Mack, Hamden Conn 1964, 1968 (enlarged).
Alpers, P. J. Pope's To Bathurst and the Mandevillian State. ELH 25 1958; rptd in Essential articles for the study of Pope, ed M. Mack, Hamden Conn 1964, 1968 (enlarged).
Bluestone, M. Suppressed metaphor in Pope. EC 8–9 1958–9. Reply by F. W. Bateson 9 1959.
Crittenden, W. M. The letters of Pope. Personalist 39 1958.
Edwards, T. R., jr. The colors of fancy: an image cluster in Pope. MLN 73 1958.
— Light and nature: a reading of the Dunciad. PQ 39 1960; rptd in Essential articles for the study of Pope, ed M. Mack, Hamden Conn 1964, 1968 (enlarged).
— 'Reconcil'd extremes': Pope's Epistle to Bathurst. EC 11 1961.
— Heroic folly: Pope's satiric identity. In In defense of reading, ed R. A. Brower and R. Poirier, New York 1962.
— This dark estate: a reading of Pope. Berkeley 1963.
Felps, J. I. Pope's common sense. Boston 1958.
Foxon, D. Two cruces in Pope bibliography. TLS 24 Jan 1958.
Hagstrum, J. H. In his Sister arts, Chicago 1958.
Macklin, M. The anatomy of the world: relations between natural and moral law from Donne to Pope. Minneapolis 1958.
Sühnel, R. Homer und die englische Humanität: Chapmans und Popes Übersetzungskunst. Tübingen 1958.
Zoellner, R. H. Poetic cosmology in Pope's Essay on man. College Eng Jan 1958. Reply by J. M. Aden, May 1958.
Ellis, W. D., jr. Thomas D'Urfy, the Pope-Philips quarrel and the Shepherd's week. PMLA 74 1959.
Golliet, J. La correspondence d'Alexander Pope. Etudes Anglaises 12 1959.
Tinling, M. Pope in Congress. Manuscripts 11 1959.
Tuveson, E. An Essay on man and the way of ideas. ELH 26 1959. Some further remarks, PQ 40 1961.
Wasserman, E. R. Pope: Windsor Forest. In his Subtler language, Baltimore 1959.
— Pope's Epistle to Bathurst: a critical reading with an edition of the mss. Baltimore 1960.
— Pope's Ode for musick. ELH 28 1961; rptd in Essential articles for the study of Pope, ed M. Mack, Hamden Conn 1964, 1968 (enlarged).
— The limits of allusion in the Rape of the lock. JEGP 65 1966.
Brett, R. L. Pope's Essay on man. In his Reason and imagination, 1960.
Cruttwell, P. Pope and his Church. Hudson Rev 13 1960.
— Pope in the Augustan world. Centennial Rev 10 1966.
Fenner, A., jr. The unity of Pope's Essay on criticism. PQ 39 1960; rev in Essential articles for the study of Pope, ed M. Mack, Hamden Conn 1964, 1968 (enlarged).
Fleischmann, W. B. Pope and Lucretian 'anonymity'. Neophilologus 44 1960.
Fraser, R. A. Pope and Shakespeare. South Atlantic Quart 59 1960.
Hunter, G. K. The 'romanticism' of Pope's Horace. EC 10 1960; rptd in Essential articles for the study of Pope, ed M. Mack, Hamden Conn 1964, 1968 (enlarged).
Hyman, S. E. The rape of the lock. Hudson Rev 13 1960.

James, G. I. and F. W. Bateson. Prose and poetry and Mack. EC 10 1960.
Lombardo, A. Osservazioni sulla poesia di Pope. Letteratura Moderne 10 1960.
O Hehir, B. P. Virtue and passion: the dialectic of Eloisa to Abelard. Texas Stud in Lit & Lang 2 1960; rptd in Essential articles for the study of Pope, ed M. Mack, Hamden Conn 1964, 1968 (enlarged).
Schafer, R. G. Cannons no canon: Pope's Epistle to Burlington. Papers of Michigan Acad of Science, Arts & Letters 45 1960.
Troy, F. S. Pope's images of man. Mass Rev 1 1960.
Adler, J. H. Pope and the rules of prosody. PMLA 76 1961.
— Balance in Pope's Essays. E Studies 43 1962.
— The reach of art: a study in the prosody of Pope. Gainesville 1964.
Clark, D. B. The Italian fame of Pope. MLQ 22 1961.
— Pope. New York 1967.
Cunningham, J. S. Pope: the Rape of the lock. 1961.
Hauser, D. F. Medea's strain and Hermes' wand: Pope's use of mythology. MLN 76 1961.
Hutchens, E. N. Gray's cat and Pope's Belinda. Tennessee Stud in Lit 6 1961.
Jones, E. Verse, prose and Pope. Melbourne Critical Rev 4 1961.
Krieger, M. The 'frail china jar' and the rude hand of chaos. Centennial Rev 5 1961; rptd in his Play and place of criticism, Baltimore 1967; in Essential articles for the study of Pope, ed M. Mack, Conn 1968 (enlarged).
Perella, N. J. Pope's judgment of the Pastor Fido and a case of plagiarism. PQ 40 1961.
Røstvig, M. S. The background of English neo-classicism, with some observations on Swift and Pope. Oslo 1961.
Schlütter, K. Pope's Windsor Forest: ein Ortsgedicht in pastoraler Gestaltung. Anglia 79 1962.
Sen, S. K. Joseph Warton and the romantic heresy that Pope was not a poet. Bull of Dept of Eng, Univ of Calcutta 2 1961.
— Shakespeare and Pope on man's middle state. Bull of Dept of Eng, Univ of Calcutta 4 1963.
Serman, I. An unpublished philosophical poem by V. Trediakovsky. Russian Lit 1 1961.
Amarasinghe, U. Dryden and Pope in the early nineteenth century: a study of changing literary taste 1800–30. Cambridge 1962.
Cawley, A. C. Chaucer, Pope and fame. REL 3 1962.
Cook, R. I. Garth's dispensary and Pope's Rape of the lock. Classical Jnl 6 1963.
Erskine-Hill, H. H. The 'new world' of Pope's Dunciad. Renaissance & Modern Stud 6 1962; rptd in Essential articles for the study of Pope, ed M. Mack, Hamden Conn 1964, 1968 (enlarged).
— The metal against time: Pope's Epistle to Addison. Jnl of Warburg & Courtauld Inst 28 1965.
— Pope at fifteen: a new manuscript. RES new ser 17 1966. A suggested addn to the canon.
Goldgar, B. A. Pope's theories of the passions. PQ 41 1962.
Honoré, J. Charles Gildon, rédacteur du British Mercury 1711–12: les attaques contre Pope, Swift et les Wits. Etudes Anglaises 15 1962.
Kernan, A. B. The Dunciad and the plot of satire. Stud in Eng Lit 1500–1900 2 1962; rptd in Essential articles for the study of Pope, ed M. Mack, Hamden Conn 1964, 1968 (enlarged).
Levine, J. A. The status of the verse epistle before Pope. SP 59 1962.
Praz, M. La poesia di Pope e le sue origini. Rome 1962.
Ryskamp, C. The receipts for Pope's Iliad. Princeton Univ Lib Chron 24 1962.
Torchiana, D. T. Brutus: Pope's last hero. JEGP 61 1962; rptd in Essential articles for the study of Pope, ed M. Mack, Hamden Conn 1968 (enlarged).

Zimmerman, H.-J. '. . . as Brault translated it'. Archiv 199 1963.
—— Ein Autograph-fragment von Popes The second satire of Dr John Donne, versifyed. Ibid.
—— Bemerkungen zum Manuskript und Text von Popes Brutus. Ibid.
—— Popes Noten zu Homer. Heidelberg 1966.
—— Pope und die Homerischen Fliegen. In Lebende Antike: Symposium für Rudolf Sühnel, Berlin 1967.
Carroll, J. Richardson on Pope and Swift. UTQ 33 1963.
Clark, D. R. Landscape painting effects in Pope's Homer. Jnl of Aesthetics 22 1963; rptd in Essential articles for the study of Pope, ed M. Mack, Hamden Conn 1968 (enlarged).
De Lisle, H. F. Structure in Part 1 of Pope's Essay on criticism. Eng Lang Notes 1 1963.
Dixon, P. The theme of friendship in the Epistle to Dr Arbuthnot. E Studies 44 1963.
—— Pope's Shakespeare. JEGP 43 1964.
—— Talking upon paper: Pope and 18th-century conversation. E Studies 46 1965.
Fairclough, G. T. Pope and Boileau: a supplementary note. Neuphilologische Mitteilungen 64 1963.
Fogle, R. H. Metaphors of organic unity in Pope's Essay on criticism. Tulane Stud in Eng 13 1963.
Goggin, L. P. La caverne aux vapeurs. PQ 42 1963.
Johnston, A. The purple year in Pope and Gray. RES new ser 14 1963.
Julow, V. The first Hungarian translation of the Rape of the lock. Hungarian Stud in Eng 1 1963.
Loomis, E. R. The turning point in Pope's reputation: a dispute which preceded the Bowles-Byron controversy. PQ 42 1963.
Melchiori, G. Pope in Arcady: the theme of 'et in Arcadia ego' in his pastorals. Eng Miscellany (Rome) 14 1963; rptd in Essential articles for the study of Pope, ed M. Mack, Hamden Conn 1968 (enlarged).
Nierenberg, E. H. Pope and God at Twickenham. Personalist 44 1963.
Wain, J. An introduction to Pope. In his Essays on literature and ideas, 1963.
Barber, G. Bolingbroke, Pope and the Patriot King. Library 5th ser 19 1964.
Chambers, J. R. The episode of Annius and Mummius: Dunciad 4 347–96. PQ 43 1964.
Crowther, J. W., jr. Pope's defense of theology, philosophy and the arts in Dunciad iv. In Essays and studies in language and literature, ed H. H. Petit, Pittsburgh 1964.
Curtis, P. Pope the good Augustan. Melbourne Critical Rev 7 1964.
Goldberg, S. L. Pope. Ibid.
Huseboe, A. R. Pope's critical views of the London stage. Restoration & 18th-century Theatre Research 3 1964.
Maresca, T. E. Pope's defense of satire: the first satire of the Second book of Horace, imitated. ELH 31 1964.
—— Pope's Horatian poems. Columbus 1966.
Priestley, F. E. L. Pope and the great chain of being. In Essays in English literature presented to A. S. P. Woodhouse, Toronto 1964.
Dorris, G. E. Scippione Mafei amid the Dunces. RES new ser 16 1965.
Farcione, A. Melendez Veldez and the Essay on man. Hispanic Rev 34 1965.
Green, D. J. Dramatic texture in Pope. In From sensibility to romanticism: essays presented to F. A. Pottle, New York 1965.
Johnson, C. Pope's Dunciad: requisitions of verity. Southern Rev 1 1965.
Kallich, M. Thomas Gray's annotations to Pope's Essay on man. N & Q Dec 1965.
—— Heav'n's first law: rhetoric and order in Pope's Essay on man. De Kalb Illinois 1967.
—— Image and theme in Pope's Essay on criticism. Ball State Univ Forum 8 1967.

—— Pegasus on the seesaw: balance and antithesis in Pope's Essay on criticism. Tennessee Stud in Lit 12 1967.
Kelley, R. M. Imitation of nature: Edward Young's attack on Pope. Xavier Univ Stud 4 1965.
Moscovit, L. Pope's purposes in sober advice. PQ 45 1965.
—— Pope and the tradition of neoclassical imitation. Stud in Eng Lit 1500–1900 8 1968.
Ridley, M. R. In his Second thoughts, 1965.
Robb, B. Beardsley's illustrations to the Rape of the lock. Listener 23 Sept 1965.
Stein, W. B. Pope's An essay on criticism: the play of Sophia. Bucknell Rev 13 1965.
Sutherland, W. O. S., jr. In his Art of the satirist: essays on the satire of Augustan England, Austin 1965.
Tanner, T. Reason and the grotesque: Pope's Dunciad. CQ 7 1965; rptd in Essential articles for the study of Pope, ed M. Mack, Hamden Conn 1968 (enlarged).
Bross, A. C. Pope's revisions of Donne's satires. Xavier Univ Stud 5 1966.
Cowler, R. Shadow and substance: a discussion of Pope's correspondence. In The familiar letter in the 18th century, ed H. Anderson et al, Lawrence Kansas 1966.
De Stasio, C. Pope, Berkeley e il Guardian. Acme 19 1966.
Fuller, J. New epilogue by Pope? RES new ser 17 1966. To Gay's Wife of Bath.
Hauser, D. R. Pope's Lodona and the uses of mythology. Stud in Eng Lit 1500–1900 6 1966.
Kiehl, J. M. Windsor Forest as epical counterpart. Thoth 7 1966.
Milburn, D. J. The grace of wit. In his Age of wit, New York 1966.
Peavey, C. D. Pope, Cibber and the crown of dulness. South Central Bull 26 1966.
Preston, J. The' informing soul: creative irony in the Rape of the lock. Durham Univ Jnl 58 1966.
Quintana, R. The Rape of the lock as a comedy of continuity. REL 7 1966.
Robb, P. The nature of The rape of the lock. In Words 2, ed P. T. Hoffmann et al, Wellington 1966.
Rogal, S. J. Pope's treatment of Colley Cibber. Lock Haven Rev no 8 1966.
Battestin, M. C. Pope's Magus in Fielding's Vernoniad: the satire of Walpole. PQ 46 1967.
Beaumont, C. A. The rising and falling metaphor in Pope's An essay on man. Style 1 1967.
Donaghey, B. S. Pope's and Sir William Trumbull's translations of Boethius. Leeds Stud in Eng 1 1967.
Effross, S. H. The influence of Pope in 18th-century Spain. SP 63 1967.
Fedder, L. Sermon or satire: Pope's definition of his art. In Studies in criticism and aesthetics in honor of S. H. Monk, Minneapolis 1967.
Hardy, J. Stockdale's defence of Pope. RES new ser 18 1967.
Jurgens, H. Windsor Forest and Augustan stability. Unisa Eng Stud 2 1967.
Lawlor, N. K. Pope's Essay on man: oblique light for a false mirror. MLQ 28 1967.
Levine, J. A. Pope's Epistle to Augustus, lines 1–30. Stud in Eng Lit 1500–1900 7 1967.
Mahaffey, K. Timon's villa: Walpole's Houghton. Texas Stud in Lit & Lang 9 1967.
Mandell, B. J. Pope's Eloisa to Abelard. Ibid.
Miller, J. H. Pope and the principle of reconciliation. Ibid.
Pittock, J. Joseph Warton and his second volume of the Essay on Pope. RES new ser 18 1967.
Ramsey, P. The watch of judgment: relativism and An essay on criticism. In Studies in criticism and aesthetics in honor of S. H. Monk, Minneapolis 1967.
Rawlinson, D. H. Pope and Addison on classical greatness. Wascana Rev 2 1967.

Ryley, R. M. A note on the authenticity of some lines from Pope. PQ 46 1967. On Lines suppressed at the end of the Epistle, 1775.

— Warburton, Warton and Ruffhead's Life of Pope. Papers on Lang & Lit 4 1968.

Wellington, J. E. Pope's 'Alas! how chang'd': some variations on a Vergilian theme. Carrell 7 1967.

— Pope and charity. PQ 46 1967.

Adams, P. G. Pope's concern with assonance. Texas Stud in Lit & Lang 9 1968.

Choudhuri, A. D. Prévost on the Essay on man. E Studies 49 1968.

Curry, H. W. Two neglected philosophical poems. Expository Times June 1968.

Dixon, P. The world of Pope's satires: an introduction to the Epistles and Imitations of Horace. 1968.

Ferns, J. Neoclassical structure: the Rape of the lock and Pride and prejudice. Queen's Quart 75 1968.

Foster, E. E. Rhetorical control in Pope's Eloisa to Abelard. Tennessee Stud in Lit 13 1968.

French, D. P. Pope, Milton and the Essay on man. Bucknell Rev 16 1968.

Haber, G. S. Pope—imployed in grottofying. Texas Stud in Lit & Lang 10 1968.

Hassett, M. E. Pope, Byron and satiric technique. Satire Newsletter 6 1968.

Howard, W. J. The mystery of the Cibberian Dunciad. Stud in Eng Lit 1500–1900 8 1968.

Hunt, J. D. (ed). Pope, the Rape of the lock: a casebook. 1968.

Kallen, H. M. In Liberty, laughter and tears: reflections on the relations of comedy and tragedy to human freedom. De Kalb Illinois 1968.

Kalmey, R. P. Pope's Eloisa to Abelard and 'those celebrated letters'. PQ 47 1968.

— 'The struggles of grace and nature' in the poems of Pope. Shippensburg (Pa) State Coll Rev Oct 1968.

Mell, D. C., jr. Pope's idea of the imagination and the design of Elegy to the memory of an unfortunate lady. MLQ 29 1968.

Newton, J. M. Alive or dead? Pope on Shakespeare's best passages. Cambridge Quart 3 1968.

Nichols, J. W. Nathanael West, Sinclair Lewis, Pope and satiric contrasts. Satire Newsletter 5 1968.

Nicolson, M. H. and G. S. Rousseau. 'This long disease my life': Pope and the sciences. Princeton 1968.

O'Neill, J. (ed). Critics on Pope. 1968.

Sanders, C. 'First follow nature': an annotation. E Studies 49 1968.

Schonhorn, M. The arduous contemporaneity of Pope's Epistle to Augustus. Stud in Eng Lit 1500–1900 8 1968.

Thomas, W. K. Sataric catharsis. Univ of Windsor Rev 3 1968.

Tolliver, H. The Augustan balance of nature and art in the Rape of the lock. Concerning Poetry 1 1968.

Warfel, H. R. Image vs abstraction: Coleridge vs Pope and the tests of poetry. In Essays in American and English literature presented to B. R. McElderry jr, ed M. F. Schulz, Athens Ohio 1968.

V. A. D.

JAMES THOMSON

1700–48

Bibliographies

Cohen, R. In his Art of discrimination, 1964. Contains bibliography of Seasons.

Collections

Works. 1736 (2nd vol of Seasons, 1730, 4°), 2 vols 1738, 1744 (rev), 3 vols 1749.

Works. [Ed Lyttelton] 4 vols 1750, 1752, 1756, 1757, 2 vols 1762 (with Murdoch's life and Collins's ode), 1763, 1766, 1768, 4 vols Edinburgh 1772, London 1773, 2 vols Glasgow 1784 (Foulis), 3 vols 1788, 2 vols 1788, 3 vols 1802, 1803.

Poetical works. Ed H. Nicholas 2 vols 1830; rev P. Cunningham 1860, 1862, 1866; rev D. C. Tovey 1897 (Aldine edn).

Poetical works of Milton, Thomson and Young. Ed H. F. Cary 1841.

Poetical works. Ed G. Gilfillan, Edinburgh 1853; ed C. Cowden Clarke, Edinburgh 1868; ed W. M. Rossetti [1873].

The seasons, The castle of indolence and other poems. Ed H. D. Roberts and E. Gosse 2 vols [1906].

Complete poetical works. Ed J. L. Robertson, Oxford 1908, 1951.

Johnson 48, 49; Anderson 9; Chalmers 12.

§ I

The Edinburgh miscellany. Edinburgh 1720. Contains 3 poems by Thomson.

Winter. 1726 (March, 405 lines), 1726 (June, rev, adding 58 lines), 1726, 1726, Dublin 1726, London 1728, 1730 (787 lines), Dublin 1730, London 1734; ed W. Willis 1900; Oxford 1929 (type facs of 1st edn). In Seasons 1746, below, Winter is 1069 lines.

Summer. 1727 (1146 lines), Dublin 1727, London 1728, 1730 (1206 lines), Dublin 1730, London 1735, Dublin 1740. In Seasons 1746, below, Summer is 1805 lines.

A poem sacred to the memory of Sir Isaac Newton. 1727 (3 edns), Dublin 1727, London 1730; tr Italian, 1760.

Spring. 1728 (1082 lines), Dublin 1728, London 1729, 1731 ('second edn', 1087 lines), 1734, Dublin 1740. In Seasons 1746, below, Spring is 1176 lines.

Britannia. 1729, 1730 ('corrected'), 1730, 1925 (facs). Also rptd with the 1738 trn (by Thomson?) of Milton, Scriptum domini protectoris contra Hispanos, 1655.

A poem to the memory of Mr Congreve. 1729 (2 issues, anon); ed P. Cunningham 1843 (Percy Soc). Ascribed to Thomson by H. F. Cary. See G. G. Williams, PMLA 45 1930.

Miscellaneous poems by several hands. Ed J. Ralph 1729. Contains 4 poems by Thomson.

The tragedy of Sophonisba. 1730 (3 issues), Dublin 1730. Performed Drury Lane 28 Feb 1730.

The seasons. 1730 (4°, 4464 lines), 1730 (8, adding 6 lines to Winter), 1744 (5531 lines, Summer and Winter especially rev), 1744, 1746 (rev, adding 10 lines), 1752, 1758, Dublin 1758, London 1761, Edinburgh 1761, London 1762, 1764, 1766, 1767, 1768, Glasgow 1769; ed G. Wright [1770]; 1773, Dublin 1773, London 1774 (with Murdoch's life from Works 1762), Edinburgh 1774, London 1776, 1779 (with J. Aikin's Essay), Paris 1780; ed J. J. C. Timaeus, Hamburg 1791; ed R. Heron, Perth 1793; ed P. Stockdale 1793 (with glossary); ed J. Evans 1802; ed A. Cunningham 1841 (with Castle of indolence); ed J. L. Robertson, Oxford 1891 (with Castle of indolence); ed O. Zippel, Berlin 1908 (variorum edn); ed J. Beresford 1927; tr German, 1745, 1757, 1765, 1758, 1766, 1796, 1796, 1798; French, 1759, 1760, 1761, 1763, 1763; Italian, 1791.

Winter, A hymn on the seasons, A poem to the memory of Sir Isaac Newton and Britannia. 1730, 1734.

Autumn. 1730 (2nd edn, 1269 lines). 1st edn in Seasons 1730, below.

The seasons, A hymn, A poem to the memory of Sir Isaac Newton and Britannia. 4 pts 1730, 1735. Some 1730 edns in 5 pts.

The four seasons and other poems. 4 pts 1735.

Antient and modern Italy compared: being the first part of Liberty. 1735.

Greece: being the second part of Liberty. 1735.

Rome: being the third part of Liberty. 1735.

Britain: being the fourth part of Liberty. 1736.

The prospect: being the fifth part of Liberty. 1736.

A poem to the memory of the right honourable the Lord Talbot, late Chancellor of Great Britain. 1737.

Liberty. 1738, Glasgow 1776 (Foulis).

Areopagitica. 1738. By Milton. Preface by Thomson.

Agamemnon. 1738, Dublin 1738. Performed Drury Lane 6 April 1738.

Edward and Eleonora. 1739, Dublin 1739, 1751, London 1758; tr German, 1764.

Alfred. 1740, 1745, 1751, 1753 (rev as Alfred the Great), 1754, 1773, 1781. Performed Cliefdon 1 Aug 1740. Written with David Mallet.

Tancred and Sigismunda. 1745, Dublin 1745, 1748, London 1752, 1755, Edinburgh 1755, London 1758, Glasgow 1759, London 1761, Edinburgh 1764, London 1766, Dublin 1767, 1768, Edinburgh 1768, London 1775, 1776, 1777, 1784 etc; tr German, 1764. Performed Drury Lane 18 March 1745.

The castle of indolence. 1748, 1748, 1779, [c. 1780], 1787; ed A. Cunningham 1841 (with Seasons); ed J. L. Robertson, Oxford 1891 (with Seasons); ed A. M. Hardie, Hong Kong 1956; ed A. D. McKillop, Lawrence Kansas 1961.

Coriolanus. 1749, Dublin 1749, 1767. Performed Covent Garden 13 Jan 1749.

Poems on several occasions. 1750.

Poems: Britannia, The castle of indolence and lesser poems, with Alfred. Glasgow 1776 (Foulis).

Letters

A collection of letters written to Aaron Hill esq. 1751. Includes 14 from Thomson.

Goodhugh, W. The English gentleman's library manual. 1827. Contains uncollected poems and letters by Thomson.

Unpublished letters from Thomson to Mallet. Ed F. Cunningham, Philobiblon Soc Miscellany 4 1854.

Letters and documents. Ed A. D. McKillop, Lawrence Kansas 1958.

McKillop, A. D. Two more Thomson letters. MP 60 1962.

§2

More, J. Strictures critical and sentimental on Thomson's Seasons. 1777.

Aikin, J. An essay on the plan and character of Thomson's Seasons. 1778.

Johnson, S. In his Lives of the poets, 4 vols 1779–81.

Scott, J. In his Critical essays on some of the poems of several English poets, 1785.

Erskine, D. S. Essays on the lives and writings of Fletcher of Saltoun and the poet Thomson, with some pieces of Thomson's never before published. 1792.

Stockdale, P. In his Lectures on the truly eminent English poets, 2 vols 1807.

Shairp, J. C. In his On poetic interpretation of nature, Edinburgh 1877.

Schmeding, G. A. Jacob Thomson: ein vergessener Dichter des achtzehnten Jahrhunderts. Brunswick 1889.

'Haliburton, H.' (J. L. Robertson). Of the poet of the Seasons. In his Furth in field, 1894.

Morel, L. Thomson: sa vie et ses oeuvres. Paris 1895.

Bayne, W. James Thomson. Edinburgh 1898.

Gjerset, K. Der Einfluss von Thomsons Jahreszeiten auf die deutsche Literatur des achtzehnten Jahrhunderts. Heidelberg 1898.

Zippel, O. Entstehungs- und Entwicklungsgeschichte von Thomsons Winter. Berlin 1907.

Macaulay, G. C. James Thomson. 1908 (EML).

Wells, J. E. Thomson and Milton. MLN 24 1909.

—— The manuscripts of Thomson's poems to Amanda and elegy on Ackman. PQ 15 1936.

—— Variants in the 1746 edition of Thomson's Seasons. Library 4th ser 16 1936.

—— The castle of indolence: an alternative stanza. N & Q 10 Dec 1938.

—— The seasons 1744: an unnoticed edition. E Studien 72 1938.

—— Thomson's poem On the death of his mother. MLR 33 1938.

—— Thomson's subscription Seasons. N & Q May 1941.

—— Thomson's Agamemnon and Edward and Eleanora: first printings. RES 18 1942.

—— Thomson's Britannia. MP 40 1943.

—— Thomson's minor poems: more manuscripts. PQ 22 1943.

—— The seasons 'corrected and amended'. JEGP 42 1943.

Blau, A. Thomsons Seasons. Berlin 1910.

Ibershoff, C. H. A German translation of passages in Thomson's Seasons. MLN 26 1911.

—— Bodmer and Thomson's Seasons. MLN 41 1926.

Halberstadt, B. G. De nederlandsche vertalingen en navolgingen van Thomson's Seasons. Leipzig 1923.

Mackail, J. W. In his Studies of English poets, 1926.

Potter, G. R. Thomson and the evolution of spirits. E Studien 61 1926.

Cameron, M. M. L'influence des Saisons de Thomson sur la poésie descriptive en France 1759–1810. Paris 1927.

Hughes, H. S. Thomson and the Countess of Hertford. MP 25 1928.

—— Thomson and Lady Hertford again. MP 28 1931.

Das, P. K. Thomson's appreciation of mountain scenery. E Studien 64 1929.

Anwander, E. Pseudoklassistisches und Romantisches in Thomsons Seasons. Leipzig 1930.

Cronk, G. G. Lucretius and Thomson's autumnal fogs. Amer Jnl of Philology 51 1930.

Havens, R. D. Primitivism and the idea of progress in Thomson. SP 29 1932.

Drennon, H. PMLA 49 1934, SP 31 1934, MP 32 1934, PQ 14 1935, E Studien 70 1936. On Newtonianism.

—— Thomson and John Norris. PMLA 53 1938.

Johnson, W. G. Thomson's influence on Swedish literature in the eighteenth century. Urbana 1936.

Kern, J. B. The fate of Edward and Eleanora. MLN 52 1937.

Davenport, W. H. An uncollected poem by Thomson. N & Q Oct 1939.

Dibdin, E. R. The bi-centenary of Rule Britannia. Music & Letters 21 1940.

Holthausen, F. Die Quellen von Thomsons Edward and Eleanora. Beiblatt zur Anglia 51 1940.

Noyes, A. In his A pageant of letters, New York 1940.

McKillop, A. D. The background of Thomson's Seasons. Minneapolis 1942.

—— Thomson's visit to Shenstone. PQ 23 1944.

—— Ethics and political history in Thomson's Liberty. In Pope and his contemporaries: essays presented to George Sherburn, Oxford 1949.

—— The early history of Thomson's Liberty. MLQ 11 1950.

—— Thomson and the jail committee. SP 47 1950.

—— The background of Thomson's Liberty. Rice Inst Pamphlet 38 1951.

—— Peter the Great in Thomson's Winter. MLN 67 1952.

—— Thomson's juvenile poems. Newberry Lib Bull 4 1955.

—— Armstrong's anecdotes of Thomson. N & Q Sept 1958.

—— Some heroic couplets by Thomson. MLN 73 1958.

—— Thomson and the licensers of the stage. PQ 27 1958.

—— The early history of Alfred. PQ 41 1962.

A hitherto unpublished portrait. TLS 29 Aug 1942. Discussed 26 Sept, 7, 28 Nov 1942.

[Taylor, E. S.] Thomson's library. TLS 20 June 1942.

Hamilton, H. E. Thomson recollects Hagley Park. MLN 62 1947.

—— A note on Thomson's sources. MLN 63 1948.

—— The seasons: shifts in the treatment of popular subject matter. ELH 15 1948.

Nature's volume broad displayed. TLS 28 Aug 1948.
Williams, C. A. Thomson's Summer and three of Goethe's poems. JEGP 47 1948.
Gray, W. F. The poet of the Seasons. Quart Rev 287 1949.
Rashbrook, R. F. Keats and Thomson. N & Q Nov 1949.
Doughty, W. L. The place of Thomson in the poetry of nature. London Quart 174 1949.
Grant, D. Thomson: poet of the Seasons. 1951.
Todd, W. B. Unauthorized readings in the first edition of Thomscn's Coriolanus. PBSA 46 1952.
— The text of the Castle of indolence. E Studies 34 1953.
Boas, F. S. In his Introduction to eighteenth-century drama, Oxford 1953.
Williams, R. M. Thomson's Ode on the winter solstice. MLN 70 1955.
Aden, J. M. Scriptural parody in canto 1 of the Castle of indolence. MLN 71 1956.
Francis, T. R. The quarto edition of Thomson's Works 1762. N & Q May 1956.
— Some Dublin editions of Thomson's Tancred and Sigismunda. Book Collector 7 1958.
— The ghost in James Thomson's poem Summer. N & Q Sept 1958.
— Thomson's Tancred and Sigismunda. Book Collector 8 1959.
Châlon, Y. Les saisons de Thomson: autour de leur dédicace française. Revue de Littérature Comparée 32 1958.
Cooke, A. L. Thomson and William Hinchliffe. JEGP 57 1958.
Foxon, D. F. Oh! Sophonisba! Sophonisba! Oh! SB 12 1959. On the printing of the tragedy.
Spacks, P. M. The varied god: a critical study of Thomson's The seasons. Berkeley 1959.
— Vision and meaning in Thomson. Stud in Romanticism 4 1965.
— The poetry of vision. Boston 1967.
Stratman, C. J. Tancred and Sigismunda. Book Collector 9 1960. Unrecorded edns.
Griffin, R. J. Thomson's The castle of indolence. Explicator 20-1 1962-3.
Reaves, R. B., jr. Borrowings from Pope in Thomson. N & Q Dec 1962.
Chalker, J. Thomson's Seasons and Virgil's Georgics: the problem of primitivism and progress. Studia Neophilologica 35 1963.
Cohen, R. The art of discrimination: Thomson's The seasons and the language of criticism. Los Angeles 1964.
— Thomson's poetry of space and time. In Studies in criticism and aesthetics 1660-1800: essays in honor of S. H. Monk, Minneapolis 1967.
— An introduction to the Seasons. Southern Rev (Adelaide) 3 1968.
Werkmeister, L. Thomson and the London daily press 1789-97. MP 62 1965.
Kern, J. B. Thomson's revisions of Agamemnon. PQ 45 1966.
Corder, J. W. A new nature in revisions of the Seasons. N & Q Dec 1966.
Marsh, R. The seasons of discrimination. MP 64 1967.
J. F.

WILLIAM SHENSTONE
1714-63

Bibliographies
Williams, I. A. In his Seven eighteenth-century bibliographies, 1924.

Collections
Poems upon various occasions. Oxford 1737 (anon), 1737. Includes The school-mistress in 12 stanzas.

Works in verse and prose. Ed Robert Dodsley 2 vols 1764, 3 vols 1765, 2 vols 1768, Edinburgh 1768.
Works. 3 vols 1773, 2 vols 1776, 3 vols 1777, 1791, 1796, 1798. Adds 1769 letters.
Poetical works. Edinburgh 1771, 1778, 2 vols 1798, 1812; ed G. Gilfillan, Edinburgh 1854.
Twenty songs. Shaftesbury 1926.
Songs. 1930.
Johnson 54; Anderson 9; Chalmers 13.

§1
The judgment of Hercules. 1741.
The school-mistress. 1742 (anon), Oxford 1924 (facs). 28 stanzas; 35-stanza version in Dodsley's Collection vol 1, 1748 (2nd edn).
Cleone. 1758. By Dodsley; prologue by Shenstone.
Miscellaneous poems, revised and corrected by the late Mr William Shenstone. 1771. By Joseph Giles.
Shenstone's miscellany 1759-63. Ed I. A. Gordon, Oxford 1952. Verses by the Leasowes circle, ballads etc collected by Shenstone.
Shenstone also contributed a large number of poems to Dodsley's Collection vols 1, 3-5, 1748-58.

Letters
The works in verse and prose, vol 3: containing letters to particular friends. 1769.
Select letters between the late Duchess of Somerset, Lady Luxborough, Mr Whistler, Miss Dolman, Mr R. Dodsley, William Shenstone esq and others. Ed T. Hull 2 vols 1778.
Thomas Percy und Shenstone. Ed H. Hecht, Strasbourg 1909.
Letters. Ed M. Williams, Oxford 1939. 300 letters.
Letters. Ed D. Mallam, Minneapolis 1939. 270 letters, including some new.
Hughes, H. S. Shenstone's letters. PQ 21 1942. 2 letters, one previously unpbd.
Lewis, R. Shenstone and Edward Knight: some new letters. MLR 42 1947.
Haden, H. J. A Shenstone draft letter. N & Q July 1961.

§2
Woodhouse, J. Poems on several occasions. 1766. Almost entirely on Shenstone.
[Nicholls, T.] Shenstone: or the force of benevolence. 1776.
Heely, J. Letters on the beauties of Hagley, Envil and the Leasowes. 2 vols 1777.
Graves, R. Columella. 1779. A novel based on Shenstone's life.
— Recollections of some particulars in the life of the late William Shenstone esq. 1788. Anon.
Johnson, S. In his Lives of the poets, 4 vols 1779-81.
Grazebrook, H. S. The family of Shenstone the poet. 1890.
Hutton, W. H. In his Burford papers, 1905.
Daniel, E. R. O. Shenstones Schoolmistress und das Aufkommen des Kleinepos in der neuenglischen Litteratur. Weimar [1908].
Müller, M. Shenstone: ein Vorläufer der englischen Romantik. Zürich 1909.
Wells, J. E. The dating of Shenstone's letters. Anglia 35 1912. See Fullington, below.
Hazeltine, A. I. A study of Shenstone and of his critics. Menasha 1918. Contains 15 unpbd poems and 5 unpbd Latin inscriptions.
Ellis, H. William Shenstone. Dial 82 1927; rptd with selection from Shenstone's Men and manners, Waltham St Lawrence 1927.

Williams, M. Shenstone: a chapter in eighteenth-century taste. Birmingham 1935.
— A portrait of Shenstone. TLS 22 Jan 1944.
Gammans, H. W. Shenstone's appreciation of Vergil. Classical Weekly 14 Jan 1929.
Bond, R. P. Shenstone's heroi-comical poem. SP 28 1931.
Churchill, I. L. Shenstone's copy of Macpherson's poems. Yale Univ Lib Gazette 6 1931.
— Shenstone's share in the preparation of Percy's Reliques. PMLA 51 1936.
— Shenstone's billets. PMLA 52 1937.
Fullington, J. F. The dating of Shenstone's letters. PMLA 46 1931. Supplements Wells, above.
— Some early versions of Shenstone's letters. MP 29 1932.
Hughes, H. S. Shenstone and the Countess of Hertford. PMLA 46 1931.
Purkis, E. M. Shenstone: poet and landscape gardener. Wolverhampton 1931.
Hecht, H. Shenstone's Mitarbeit an den Reliques of ancient English poetry. Anglia 58 1934.
Humphreys, A. R. William Shenstone. Cambridge 1937.
Ward, M. M. Shenstone's birthplace. MLN 51 1936.

Fisher, J. Shenstone, Gray and the moral elegy. MP 34 1937.
Mallam, D. The dating of Lady Luxborough's letters to Shenstone. PQ 19 1940.
— Inter-relationships of Shenstone's essays, letters and poems. PQ 28 1949.
Nichol Smith, D. The early version of Shenstone's Pastoral ballad. RES 17 1941.
Tillotson, G. In his Essays in criticism and research, Cambridge 1942.
McKillop, A. D. Thomson's visit to Shenstone. PQ 23 1944.
Street, J. The poets and the English garden. Listener 19 Sept, 3 Oct 1963. On Shenstone's Unconnected thoughts on gardening.
Pagliaro, H. E. Paradox in the aphorisms of La Rochefoucauld and some representative English followers. PMLA 79 1964. On Halifax, Swift, Chesterfield and Shenstone.
Gregg, R. A. Pushkin and Shenstone: the case reopened. Comparative Lit 17 1965.
Sambrook, A. J. Another early version of Shenstone's Pastoral ballad. RES new ser 18 1967.

J. F.

VI. MINOR POETRY 1700–1750

This section is restricted to writers born between 1665 and 1715. See also Religion, col 1599, below; and Scottish Literature col 1959, below.

References

Johnson   The works of the English poets, ed S. Johnson 68 vols 1779–81, 75 vols 1790.
Anderson   The works of the British poets, ed R. Anderson 13 vols Edinburgh 1792–5; vol 14, 1807.
Chalmers   The works of the English poets, ed A. Chalmers 21 vols 1810.

See generally W. L. Renwick, Notes on some lesser poets of the eighteenth century, *in* Essays on the eighteenth century presented to David Nichol Smith, Oxford 1945; *and* Minor poets of the eighteenth century, ed H. I'A. Fausset 1930 (EL).

NICHOLAS AMHURST, 'CALEB D'ANVERS'

1697–1742

An epistle from a student at Oxford to the Chevalier, occasioned by his removal over the Alps. 1717, 1718, 1719.
Protestant popery: or the convocation, in five cantos. 1718.
A congratulatory epistle from his Holiness the Pope to the reverend Dr Snape. 1718; rptd with both the above as Political poems, 1719.
The resurrection: a poem [in Latin], written by Mr Addison [with trn by Amhurst]. 1718, 1718, 1728 (in T. Burnet, A re-survey of the Mosaic system), 1735, 1808.
Strephon's revenge: a satire on the Oxford toasts. 1718, 1718, 1720, 1724.
The Protestant session, by a member of the Constitution Club at Oxford. 1719. Attributed to Amhurst by Giles Jacob.
An epistle [in verse] with a petition in it to Sir John Blount Bart, one of the directors of the South-Sea Company. 1720, 1720.
Poems on several occasions. 1720, 1723 (with A test of love).
A familiar epistle from Tunbridge-Wells to a gentleman at Oxford. 1720.
Terrae filius. 52 nos 11 Jan–12 July 1721, 2 vols 1726.
The British General: a poem sacred to the memory of John Duke of Marlborough. 1722, 1722.

Pasquin. 119 nos 28 Nov 1722–26 March 1724. With G. Duckett and R. Steele.
Oculus Britanniae: an heroi-panegyrical poem on the university of Oxford. 1724.
Essays on the vices and follies of the time. 1726. From Pasquin and London Jnl.
Terrae-filius: or the secret history of the University of Oxford, in several essays; to which are added remarks upon a late book entitled University education, by R. Newton. 2 vols 1726, 1754.
The Twickenham hotch-potch: being a sequel to the Beggars opera, written by Caleb D'Anvers. 1728.
A collection of poems on several occasions, published in the Craftsman, by Caleb D'Anvers. 1731.

JOHN ARMSTRONG

1709–79

Bibliographies

Williams, I. A. In his Seven eighteenth-century bibliographies, 1924.

Collections

Miscellanies. 2 vols 1770; ed R. Cohen, Los Angeles 1951 (Augustan Reprint Soc).
Medical essays. 1773.

§ 1

Dissertatio medica inauguralis de tabe purulenta. Edinburgh 1732.

An essay for abridging the study of physick; to which is added A dialogue relating to the practice of physick, as also An epistle from Usbek the Persian to J[oshua] W[ar]d. 1735.

The oeconomy of love: a poetical essay. 1736, 1737, 1745, 1749, 1753, 1763, 1768 (expurgated by Armstrong), 1777, 1781 etc; tr Italian, 1755.

A synopsis of the history and cure of venereal diseases. 1737.

The art of preserving health: a poem. 1744, Dublin 1744, London 1745, 1748, 1754, 1757, Dublin 1765, London 1765, 1768, 1768, 1795 (with critical essay by J. Aikin) etc; tr Italian, 1824.

The muncher's and guzzler's diary: in a word, the universal pocket almanach, by Noureddin Alrasxhin. 1749.

Of benevolence: an epistle to Eumenes. 1751.

Taste: an epistle to a young critic. 1753.

Sketches: or essays on various subjects, by Launcelot Temple. 1758.

A short ramble through some parts of France and Italy, by Launcelot Temple. 1771.

A day: an epistle to John Wilkes. 1661 (for 1761). With numerous omissions by Wilkes without Armstrong's permission.

Armstrong also contributed 4 stanzas to J. Thomson, The castle of indolence, 1748.

Letters

Anglo-Jewish letters 1158–1917. Ed C. Roth 1938.

§ 2

Johnson, S. In his Lives of the poets, 1779–81.

Knapp, L. M. Armstrong: littérateur and associate of Smollett, Thomson, Wilkes and other celebrities. PMLA 59 1944.

— Armstrong's Of benevolence. N & Q June 1959.

Smith, H. R. Medicine and poetry. N & Q Sept 1952.

McKillop, A. D. Armstrong's anecdotes of Thomson. N & Q Sept 1958.

CORNELIUS ARNOLD
1711–57
Collections

Poems on several occasions. 1757.

§ 1

Distress: a poetical essay. [1750], 1751 (corrected and enlarged).

Commerce. 1751, 1751.

The mirror: a poetical essay in the manner of Spenser. 1755.

PHANUEL BACON
1700–83
Bibliographies

Solly, E. Bibliographer 4 1883.

§ 1

The kite: an heroi-comical poem in three cantos. Oxford 1722, 1729.

The taxes: a dramatic entertainment. 1757.

The tryal of the time-killers: a comedy in five acts. 1757.

The insignificants: a comedy. 1757.

The moral quack: a dramatic satire. 1757.

The oculist: a dramatic entertainment. 1757.

HENRY BAKER
1698–1774

§ 1

An invocation of health: a poem. 1723.

Original poems, serious and humorous. 1725; The second part of original poems, 1726.

The universe: a poem intended to restrain the pride of man. [1727], [1734], [1750], [1760], 1808 (with Life).

Medulla poetarum romanorum: or the most beautiful and instructive passages of the Roman-poets, with translations in English verse. 2 vols 1737.

The works of Molière. 8 vols 1739, 1 vol 1929 (selection). Tr Baker and J. Miller.

The universal spectator, by Henry Stonecastle. 907 nos 12 Oct 1728–22 Feb 1746, 4 vols 1747, 1756. Baker's contributions ended 19 May 1733.

The microscope made easy. 1743 etc.

Employment for the microscope. 1753.

Baker also pbd other scientific works.

§ 2

Potter, G. R. Henry Baker FRS. MP 29 1932.

MARY BARBER
1690?–1757
Bibliographies

Williams, I. A. Bibliographical notes. London Mercury March 1922.

Selections

Poems by eminent ladies. 1755.

§ 1

Poems on several occasions. 1734, 1735, 1736.

§ 2

Jackson, R. W. In his Swift and his circle: a book of essays, Dublin 1945.

DANIEL BELLAMY the elder
b. 1687
Selections

Miscellanies in prose and verse: consisting of dramatic pieces, poems, humorous tales and fables. 2 vols 1739–40. Includes 'several select essays, never before published, by D. Bellamy jun'.

Ethic amusements by Mr Bellamy revised by his son D. Bellamy. 1768.

Ethic amusements by Mr Bellamy, revised and published by D. Bellamy [tales and fables from Fénelon, supplementing the preceding]. [1770].

§ 1

Thoughts on the Trinity. 1721. By Lord Morny du Plessis-Marly; tr Bellamy.

The Cambro-Britannic engineer, or the original mouse-trapp-maker: a mock heroic poem, by a gentleman of Oxford. 1722.

Love triumphant, or the rival goddesses: a pastoral opera [with] other original poems and translations. 1722. Mrs Bellamy's School 26 March 1722.

The young ladies miscellany: or youth's innocent and rational amusement, written for the young ladies of Mrs Bellamy's school. 1723.

Twenty-seven moral tales and fables [tr from Fénelon]. 1729.

Back-gammon, or the battle of the friars: a tragi-comic tale. 1734.

Phaedri fabulae selectae. 1734. Ed Bellamy.

The rival priests: a farce. 1739, 1741.

Nature delineated: being a translation of those universally admir'd philosophical conversations entitled Spectacle de la nature. 4 vols 1739. Vols 1–3 tr Bellamy.

The perjur'd devotee, or the force of love: a comedy. 1741.

The languishing lover. 1746. A musical interlude.

ROBERT BLAIR
1700–46

Collections

Works. Stourport 1814.

Poetical works of Beattie, Blair and Falconer. Ed G. Gilfillan, Edinburgh 1854.

Anderson 8; Chalmers 15.

§ 1

A poem dedicated to the memory of William Law. Edinburgh 1728.

The grave: a poem. 1743, Edinburgh 1747 (adds An ode: translated from Florentus Volusenus Scotus), London 1749, 1753, 1756, Edinburgh 1761, 1767, London 1769, [1770], 1782, 1783, Glasgow 1786, London 1786, 1787, Glasgow 1790, London [1790], 1796 (with Life by W. Anderson), 1797, Glasgow 1798, London 1800, 1804, 1808 (illustr W. Blake) etc; tr Dutch, 1764, 1773; Italian, 1840.

Poems signed 'B' in Edinburgh Miscellany vol 1, 1720, are attributed to Blair.

§ 2

Drake, W. A. A note on Blair. Freeman 6 Feb 1924.

Rogers, T. The birth date of Blair. N & Q Sept 1951.

—— The testament dative of Blair. N & Q Dec 1955.

—— A letter of Blair. N & Q Nov 1959.

Hennig, R. A note on Goethe and Blair. MLR 50 1955.

BARTON BOOTH
1681–1733

§ 1

The death of Dido: a masque. 1716. Produced at Drury Lane 17 April 1716.

§ 2

[Victor, B.] Memoirs of the life of Booth with his character; to which are added several poetical pieces written by himself. 1733.

Cibber, T. Life and character of Booth. In his Lives and characters of the most eminent actors and actresses, 1753.

SAMUEL BOYSE
1708–49

Collections

Anderson 10; Chalmers 14.

§ 1

Translations and poems written on several subjects. Edinburgh 1731, 1734, 1738.

Verses occasioned by seeing the palace and park of Dalkeith. Edinburgh 1732, 1732.

Verses sacred to the memory of the Right Honourable Charles Earl of Peterborough and Monmouth. Edinburgh 1735.

The tears of the Muses: a poem sacred to the memory of the Right Honourable Anne late Viscountess of Stromont. Edinburgh 1736.

The olive: an ode occasion'd by the auspicious success of his Majesty's counsels, in the stanza of Spenser. 1737.

The deity: a poem. 1739, 1740, 1749, 1763, 1808, 1823.

The Canterbury tales modernis'd [by Boyse et al] 1741, 1742, 1785.

The praise of peace: a poem in three cantos from the Dutch of Mr Van Haren. 1742.

Albion's triumph. 1743.

An historical review of the transactions of Europe from the commencement of the war with Spain in 1739 to the insurrection in Scotland in 1745. 2 vols Reading 1747.

Impartial history of the late rebellion in 1745, from authentic memoirs particularly the journal of a general officer. Reading 1748.

A demonstration of the existence of God from the French [of Fénelon]. 1749, 1821.

The tablature of Cebes. 1750. Tr Boyse.

The new pantheon: or fabulous history of the heathen gods. 1753, Salisbury [1760], Waterford 1772, Salisbury 1777.

Boyse contributed verses to GM over the signatures 'Y' and 'Alceus'.

§ 2

Shiels, R. In C. Cibber, Lives of the poets vol 5, 1753.

Kippis, A. In Biographia britannica vol 2, 1780.

Nichols, J. In A select collection of poems, 1780–2.

Griffith, R. H. Boyse's Albion's triumph. SE 13 1933.

Hart, E. Portrait of a grub: Boyse. Stud in Eng Lit 1500–1900 7 1967.

JAMES BRAMSTON
1694?–1744

The art of politicks, in imitation of Horace's Art of poetry. 1729 (3 edns), Dublin 1729, London 1731, 1773.

The man of taste, occasion'd by an epistle of Mr Pope's on that subject. 1733, 1733, Dublin 1733, London 1773.

Ignorami lamentatio super legis communis translationem. 1736.

The crooked sixpence. 1743.

THOMAS BREREWOOD
d. 1748

Galfred and Juetta, or the road of nature: a tale, in three cantos. 1772.

The seasons, in four pastorals. In Poetry original and selected vol 3, [1796–9].

Brerewood also contributed verses to GM.

JOHN DURANT BREVAL
1680?–1738

The art of dress. 1717, 1739 (in The school of Venus).

The confederates: a farce, by Mr Gay. 1717.

Mac-Dermot, or the Irish fortune-hunter: a poem in six cantos. 1717.

Calpe: or Gibraltar. 1708 (for 1718), 1720, 1727.

The play is the plot: a comedy. 1718. Produced at Drury Lane 19 Feb 1718.

A compleat key to the Non-juror [of Cibber], by Mr Joseph Gay. 1718 (4 edns).

Ovid in masquerade: being a burlesque upon the xiiith book of his Metamorphoses, by Mr Joseph Gay. 1719, 1721.

The church-scuffle, or news from St Andrew's: a ballad written by Mr Joseph Gay. 1719.

The strolers. 1727, 1729, 1761, 1767. A farce adapted from The play is the plot, produced at Drury Lane 16 July 1723.

Remarks on several parts of Europe. 4 vols 1726-38.

The lure of Venus, or a harlot's progress: an heroi-comical poem in six cantos by Mr Joseph Gay, founded upon Mr Hogarth's six paintings. 1733.

The history of the house of Nassau. 1734, Dublin 1734.

The rake's progress: or the humours of Drury Lane, with a compleat key to the eight prints by Mr Hogarth. 1735, 1769, 1784.

The rape of Helen: a mock-opera. 1737. Produced at Covent Garden 19 May 1733.

HENRY BROOKE
1703?-83

See col 785, below.

WILLIAM BROOME
1689-1745
Collections

Johnson 43; Anderson 7; Chalmers 12.

§ I

The Iliad of Homer done from the French by Mr Ozell. 1712. With Broome and Oldisworth.

The Iliad of Homer, translated from the Greek into blank verse, by Mr Ozell, Mr Broome and Mr Oldisworth. 1714, 1734.

The Iliad of Homer, translated by Mr Pope. 6 vols 1715-20. With notes partly by Broome.

The duty of publick intercession and thanksgiving for princes: a sermon preach'd on the 20th of October 1722, being the anniversary of the coronation of his Majesty. 1723.

The Odyssey of Homer. 5 vols 1725-6. Tr into verse by Pope, Broome (bks 2, 6, 8, 11-12, 16, 18, 23) and Fenton.

Poems on several occasions. 1727, 1739 (enlarged), 1750.

The oak and the dunghill. 1727. Attributed to Broome.

A sermon preach'd at the assizes of Norwich, August 8th 1737. 1737.

Odes d'Anacréon, traduites de français en vers anglais par Fawkes, Broome, Greene. Paris 1835. Broome's trns first pbd in GM over the pseudonym 'Chester'.

§ 2

Johnson, S. In his Lives of the poets, 1779 81.

Barlow, T. W. Memoir of Broome with selections from his works. 1855.

ISAAC HAWKINS BROWNE the elder
1705-60
Collections

Poems upon various subjects, Latin and English, published by his son. 1768.

Fragmentum Isacci Hawkins Browne completum, Anti-Bolinbrokius, liber secundus, Religio medici altera, adjecta versione Anglica, auctore D. Gulielmo Browne. 1768, 1769.

§ I

On design and beauty: an epistle. 1734.

The fire-side: a pastoral soliloquy. [1735]. *See* I. A. Williams, Bibliographical notes, London Mercury Feb 1922.

Of smoking: four poems in praise of tobacco. 1736. Pirated edn of 4 of the 6 pieces in the next item; the other 2 pbd separately 1736 without a title-page.

A pipe of tobacco, in imitation of six several authors [Cibber, A. Philips, Thomson, Young, Pope, Swift]. 1736, 1736 (with trns of Latin quotations), 1744; ed H. F. B. Brett-Smith, Oxford 1923.

De animi immortalitate: poema. 1754; tr W. Hay 1754; R. Grey 1754; J. Byrom 1754 (bk 1); J. Cranwell, Cambridge 1765; J. Highmore 1766 (prose, in Essays vol 2); J. Lettice 1795; S. Henyns 1796.

§ 2

Kippis, A. In Biographia britannica vol 2, 1780.

MOSES BROWNE
1704-87

§ I

The throne of justice: a Pindaric ode. 1721.

The Richmond beauties. 1722. Includes 3 other poems, 2 by Browne.

Polidus or distress'd love: a tragedy; with a farce call'd All bedevil'd or the house in a hurry. 1723.

Piscatory eclogues: an essay to introduce new rules and new characters into pastoral. 1729, 1773 (as Angling sports).

The compleat angler, in two parts, by Charles Cotton esq and published by Mr Walton. 1750, 1759, 1772. Ed Browne.

The works and rest of the creation containing I: an essay on the universe; II: Sunday thoughts. 1752, 1753, 1764, 1781 (enlarged), 1806.

Percy-lodge: a poem. 1755.

The excellency of the knowledge of Jesus Christ. 1772, 1773 etc. Tr Browne from Zimmerman.

Browne also pbd a number of sermons.

§ 2

Biographical account. GM April 1787.

Wasserman, E. R. Browne and the 1783 edition of Giles and Phineas Fletcher. MLN 56 1941.

JOHN BYROM
1692-1763

See col 1655, below.

HENRY CAREY
1687?-1743

See col 782, below.

MARY CHANDLER
1687-1745

§ I

Ralph, J. Miscellaneous poems by several hands, particularly the D— of W—n [and] Mrs C[handle]r. 1729.

A description of Bath: a poem in a letter to a friend. [1733], 1734, 1736 (enlarged), 1738, 1741, [1744] (adds A true tale), 1755, 1767.

§ 2

Doughty, O. A Bath poetess of the eighteenth century. RES 1 1925.

SAMUEL COBB
1675–1713

A Pindarique ode humbly offer'd to the ever-blessed memory of our late Queen Mary. 1694 (signed J.D.), 1694.

Bersaba, or the love of David: a poem. 1695. Imitated from Beza.

Pax redux: a Pindarick ode on the return of his Majesty, and the happy conclusion of the peace. 1697.

Poetae britannici: a poem, satyrical and panegyrical, upon our English poets. [1700].

The Portugal expedition. 1704.

Honour retriev'd: a poem occasion'd by the late victories. 1705.

A psalm of thanksgiving to be sung by the children of Christ's-Hospital. 1706.

Poems on several occasions, with imitations of Horace, Ovid [etc]. 1707, 1709 (enlarged), 1710.

The female reign: an ode attempted in the style of Pindar. 1709, 1709, 1717 (in A collection of English poetry), 1748 (in Dodsley's Collection of poems), 1755 (in GM pp. 282–5), 1782 (with other poems by Cobb in Nichols's Select collection of miscellaneous poems vol 7).

A synopsis of algebra, done from the Latin [of J. Alexander]. 1709.

The mouse-trap, written in Latin by Edward Holdsworth, made English. 1712, 1714, 1731, [1741], 1749, 1771.

A panegyrical elegy on the death of Gassendus. 1712. Tr from C. Quillet.

The carpenter of Oxford: or the miller's tale attempted in modern English. 1712, 1714 (in A collection of original poems), 1725, 1741 (in The Canterbury tales modernis'd, ed G. Ogle).

News from both universities, containing I: Mr Cobb's Tripos speech at Cambridge, with a complete key inserted; II: The brawny priest, or the captivity of the nose: a poem. 1714.

Clavis Virgiliana: or new observations upon the works of Virgil. 1714.

Discourse on criticism and Of poetry. Ed L. I. Bredvold, Ann Arbor 1946 (Augustan Reprint Soc).

MATTHEW CONCANEN the elder
1701–49

A match at foot-ball: a poem in three cantos. Dublin 1720, London 1721 (as A match at football: or the Irish champions).

Wexford Wells: a comedy. 1721. Produced in Dublin.

Miscellaneous poems, original and translated, by several hands. 1724.

A compleat collection of all the verses, essays, letters by Pope and company, with a large dedication by M. Concanen. 1728.

A supplement to the profund: containing several examples very proper to illustrate the rules laid down in a late treatise called the Art of sinking in poetry, written by Pope. 1728.

The specialist: a collection of letters and essays. 1730, 1732. Rptd from London Jnl and Br Jnl 3 July 1725–6, Oct 1728.

The flowerpiece. 1731. A miscellany, perhaps ed Concanen.

The jovial crew: a comic opera. 1731, 1732, 1760, 1761, 1766, 1767. Produced at Drury Lane 2 Feb 1731. Adapted from Broome by E. Roome, Concanen and Sir W. Yonge.

A miscellany on taste. 1732. Perhaps ed Concanen.

WILLIAM CONGREVE
1670–1729

See col 750, below.

THOMAS COOKE
1703–56

Collections

Mr Cooke's original poems, with imitations and translations of several select passages of the antients. 1742.

§ I

Marlborough: a poem in three cantos occasion'd by the death of the late Duke of Marlborough. 1722.

Albion, or the Court of Neptune: a masque. 1724.

The idylliums of Moschus and Bion, translated from the Greek with annotations. 1724.

The battle of the poets: an heroick poem in two cantos. 1725, 1731. A stage version, attributed to Cooke, was produced at the Haymarket Theatre 30 Nov 1730.

The bath: a tale. 1726, Dublin 1726.

The works of Andrew Marvell; to which is prefixed an account of the life and writings of the author. 2 vols 1726, 1772.

Philander and Cydippe. 1726. In verse.

The works of Hesiod, translated from the Greek. 2 vols 1728, 1740 etc. Rptd Anderson 13, Chalmers 20.

Penelope: an English opera. 1728. With J. Mottley. Produced at Haymarket 8 May 1728.

Tales, epistles, odes, fables etc, with translations from Homer and other antient authors. 1729.

The candidates for the bays: a poem written by Scriblerus Tertius. 1730.

The bays miscellany: or Colley triumphant, by Scriblerus Quartus. 1730.

The triumphs of love and honour: a play; to which are added Considerations on the stage and on the advantages which arise to a nation from the encouragement of arts. 1731. Produced at Drury Lane 18 Aug 1731.

The letters of Atticus, as printed in the London Journal. 1731.

The comedian: or philosophical enquirer. April 1732–April 1733. A monthly periodical.

Liberty, the support of truth and the natural property of mankind. 1732.

The life of King Edward III of England. 1733, 1734.

P. Terentii Afri comoediæ. 3 vols 1734, 2 vols 1748–9. Latin text with prose trn.

The eunuch, or the Darby captain: a farce. 1737. Produced at Drury Lane 17 May 1737.

The battle of the sexes. 1738, 1739. By S. Wesley the younger with a preface by Cooke.

A rhapsody on virtue and pleasure. 1738.

The mournful nuptials, or love the cure of all woes: a tragedy to which are prefixed Some observations on the present state of our public entertainments. 1739.

Petworth: a poem. 1739.

P. Virgilii Maronis Bucolica, Georgica et Aeneis nunc primum edita. 1741. With notes and Latin prose paraphrase.

The country journal: or the craftsman. 1741–. Ed Cooke from 1741.

A letter concerning persecution for religion and freedom of debate. 1742.

An epistle to the Right Honourable the Countess of Salisbury with a prologue and epilogue on Shakespeare and his writings. 1743.

Love the cause and cure of grief, or the innocent murderer: a tragedy. 1744. Produced at Drury Lane 19 Dec 1743. Rev from The mournful nuptials, above.

Immortality reveal'd: a poem in four epistles. 1745.

Mr Cooke's edition and translation of the comedies of Plautus. 1746. Latin text with prose trn of Amphytrio only.

An hymn to liberty. 1746.

An ode on beauty: to which are prefixed some observations on taste and on the present state of poetry in England. 1749.

An ode on martial virtue; to which are prefixed some observations [extending those to An ode on beauty, above]. 1750.

An ode on the powers of poetry; to which are prefixed observations. 1751.

The tryal of Hercules: an ode on glory, virtue and pleasure. 1752.

Pythagoras: an ode; to which are prefixed observations on taste and on education. 1752.

An ode on benevolence; to which are prefixed observations on education, taste and poetry. 1753.

A prologue on comic poetry and an epilogue on the comic characters of women; with a pastoral dialogue, to which is prefixed an ode to John Rich esq. 1753.

An ode on poetry, painting and sculpture. 1754.

An ode to pleasure. 1754.

An hymn to May. 1754.

An ode to the power of eloquence. 1755.

Ancient letters. [Ed L. Howard] vol 2 1756. Includes unpbd poems and letters by Cooke.

§ 2

Mawbey, J. GM Dec and suppl 1791, Jan–April 1792, July 1797.

Bishop, C. R. Pope and the Battle of the poets. West Virginia Univ Stud 1 1936.

NATHANIEL COTTON the elder
1705–88
Collections

Various pieces in verse and prose, many of which were never before published. Ed N. Cotton the younger 2 vols 1791.

Poems, with the author's life. Ludlow 1800.

Anderson 11; Chalmers 18.

§ 1

Observations on a particular kind of scarlet fever. 1749.

Visions in verse for the entertainment and instruction of younger minds. 1751 (3 edns), 1752 (enlarged), Dublin 1752, London 1753, 1755, 1760, 1767, 1771, 1776, 1781; Lady's Poetical Mag 2 1781; 1782, 1790, 1798, Wellington 1807, London 1808.

§ 2

GM June 1807.

SAMUEL CROXALL
c. 1690–1752
§ 1

An original canto of Spencer design'd as part of his Fairy Queen but never printed: now made publick, by Nestor Ironside esq. 1713, 1714, 1714.

The Examiner examin'd in a letter to the Englishman, occasion'd by the Examiner of Friday Dec 18 1713 upon the canto of Spencer, by Nestor Ironside. 1713, 1713.

Another original canto of Spencer, by Nestor Ironside. 1714.

An ode humbly inscrib'd to the King. 1714.

The vision: a poem by Mr Croxall, author of the two original cantos of Spencer. 1715.

Incendiaries no Christians: a sermon preached October the 9th 1715. 1715.

Ovid's Metamorphoses in fifteen books translated by the most eminent hands. Ed S. Garth 1717. Croxall tr bks 6 and parts of 8, 10–11, 13.

The fair Circassian: a dramatic performance done from the original [Song of Solomon] by a gentleman-commoner of Oxford. 1720, 1721 (includes Several occasional poems by the same author), 1723, 1729, 1732, 1751, 1755, 1756, 1759, 1765 (with The royal manual), 1770.

A select collection of novels in six volumes all new translated from the originals by several eminent hands. 6 vols 1720–2, 1729; rptd in The novelist: or tea table miscellany, 2 vols 1765. Ed Croxall.

The secret history of Pythagoras, part I, translated from the original lately found at Otranto by J.W., MD. 1721, 1722, 1751. Attributed to Croxall.

Fables of Aesop and others newly done into English with an application to each fable. 1722, 1724, 1728, 1731, 1747 etc.

A sermon preach'd before the honourable House of Commons at St Margaret's Westminster. 1730.

Scripture politics. 1735.

The antiquity, dignity and advantages of music: a sermon. 1741.

Croxall also pbd other sermons.

§ 2

Kippis, A. In Biographia britannica vol 4, 1780.

de Maar, H. The life and works of Croxall DD. In his A history of modern English romanticism vol 1, Oxford 1924.

JOHN DART
d. 1730

The complaint of the black knight from Chaucer: a verse paraphrase. 1718.

The works of Tibullus; also some observations on the original design of elegiac verse; with characters of the most celebrated Greek, Latin and English elegiac poets. 1720.

Westminster Abbey: a poem. 1721.

Life of Chaucer. In Works of Geoffrey Chaucer, ed J. Urry 1721.

A poem on Chaucer and his writings. 1722.

Westmonasterium: or the history and antiquities of the abbey church of St Peter's Westminster. 2 vols [1723], 1742.

The history and antiquities of the cathedral church of Canterbury. 1726, 1727.

SNEYD DAVIES
1709–69

See under John Whaley, below.

WILLIAM DIAPER
1686?–1717
Collections

Complete works. Ed D. Broughton 1951 (ML).

§ 1

Nereides: or sea-eclogues. 1712.

Dryades, or the nymphs prophecy: a poem. 1713.

An imitation of the seventeenth epistle of the first book of Horace, address'd to Dr S[wi]ft. 1714.

Oppian's Haliuticks of the nature of fishes and fishing of the ancients. Oxford 1722. Pt i tr Diaper.

Diaper also contributed to Rowe's version of Quillet's Callipaedia, 1712.

ROBERT DODSLEY
1703–64
See col 788, below.

STEPHEN DUCK
1705–56
Collections

Poems on several subjects. 1730 (10 edns), 1731, 1733, 1736.
Poems on several occasions [with life by J. Spence]. 1736, 1737, 1738, 1753 (as The beautiful works of Duck), 1753, 1764.
Curious poems on several occasions, viz I: On poverty; II: The thresher's labour; III: The Shunamite; all newly corrected and much amended by the author. 1738.

§ 1

Royal benevolence: a poem; to which is annexed A poem on Providence. 1730.
To the Duke of Cumberland, on his birthday April the 15th 1732. 1732. Verse.
A poem on the marriage of the Prince of Orange: to which are added Verses to the author, by a divine, with the author's answer and his poem on truth and falsehood. 1734.
Truth and falsehood: a fable. 1734. Verse.
The vision: a poem on the death of Queen Caroline. 1737, 1737.
The year of wonders. 1737.
Alrick and Isabel, or the unhappy marriage: a poem. 1740.
Hints to a school-master, address'd to Dr Turnbull. 1741.
Every man in his own way: an epistle to a friend. 1741.
An ode on the battle of Dettingen. 1743.
Caesar's camp, or St George's Hill: a poem. 1755.
The Shunamite: a poem. Canterbury 1830.
The thresher's labour. 1930.

§ 2

Spence, J. A full and authentick account of Duck. 1731.
Southey, R. Lives of uneducated poets. 1836; ed J. S. Childers, Oxford 1925.
Davis, R. M. Duck: the thresher-poet. Orono Maine 1926.
Blunden, E. In his Nature in literature, 1929.
Wiley, M. L. A Spence letter [to Pope on Duck]. In Studies in honor of J. S. Wilson, Richmond Va 1951.
Furnival, R. G. Duck: the Wiltshire phenomenon. Cambridge Jnl May 1953.
Nevinson, J. L. Duck at Kew. Surrey Archaeological Collections 58 1961.
Peel, J. H. B. From farm labourer to Court poet. Listener 18 Oct 1962. *See* A. Warner 1 Oct 1962.
Osborn, J. M. Spence, natural genius and Pope. PQ 45 1966.
Warner, A. Duck: the thresher poet. REL 8 1967.

JOHN DYER
1700?–58
Collections

Miscellaneous poems and translations. Ed R. Savage 1726. Includes Pindaric version of Grongar Hill and other poems by Dyer.
A collection of poems by several hands. Ed R. Dodsley vol 1 1748. Includes Grongar Hill and Ruins of Rome.
Poems: viz Grongar Hill, The ruins of Rome, The fleece. 1761, 1765 (as Poetical works of Dyer), 1770 (as Poems).
Poetical works of Mark Akenside and Dyer. Ed R. A. Willmott 1855.
Poems. Ed E. Thomas 1903.

Minor poets of the eighteenth century. Ed H. I'A. Fausset 1930 (EL).
Johnson 53; Anderson 9; Chalmers 13.

§ 1

A new miscellany: being a collection of pieces of poetry from Bath, Tunbridge, Oxford, Epsom and other places in 1725. 1726 with Grongar Hill, 1st version, 174 lines in octosyllabics).
Miscellaneous poems by several hands. Ed D. Lewis 1726. With final version of Grongar Hill, 157 lines in octosyllabics.
The ruins of Rome: a poem. 1740.
The fleece: a poem in four books. 1757.
Grongar Hill. Ed R. C. Boys, Baltimore 1941.

Letters

Letters to several eminent persons, including the correspondence of John Hughes. Ed W. Duncombe vol 3 1771 (2nd edn).

§ 2

Johnson, S. In his Lives of the poets, 1779–81.
Gilpin, W. In his Observations on the river Wye, 1782.
Scott, J. In his Critical essays on some of the poems of several English poets, 1785.
Greever, G. The two versions of Grongar Hill. JEGP 16 1917.
Hughes, H. S. Dyer and the Countess of Hertford. MP 27 1930.
Kohlsaat, K. Die vorromantischen Züge in den Dichtungen von Dyer. Britannica 13 1936.
Parker, E. Dyer. TLS 22 July 1939.
—— and R. M. Williams. Dyer: the poet as farmer. Agricultural History 22 1948.
Williams, R. M. Coleridge's parody of Grongar Hill. MLR 41 1946.
—— Dyer's degree from Cambridge. MLN 61 1946.
—— The publication of Dyer's Ruins of Rome. MP 44 1946.
—— Thomson and Dyer: poet and painter. In The age of Johnson: essays presented to C. B. Tinker, New Haven 1949.
—— Poet, painter and parson: the life of Dyer. New York 1956.
Johnston, A. Dr Johnson, Dyer and the Ruins of Rome. New Rambler 14 1964.

THOMAS EDWARDS
1699–1757
Collections

Edwards's sonnets, originally contributed to the collections of Dodsley and Pearch, were rptd in the 6th (1758) and later edns of The canons of criticism.

§ 1

A letter to the author of a late epistolary dissertation addressed to Mr Warburton. 1744.
A supplement to Mr Warburton's edition of Shakespear: being the Canons of criticism, and glossary, collected from the notes in that celebrated work. 1747, 1748 (as The canons of criticism), 1750, 1750, 1758 (with An account of the trial of the letter y, and sonnets), 1765.
An account of the trial of the letter y alias Y. 1753.
Free and candid thoughts on the doctrine of predestination. 1761.

Letters

The correspondence of Samuel Richardson. Ed A. L. Barbauld vol 3 1804.

§ 2

Rinaker, C. Edwards and the sonnet revival. MLN 34 1919.
Gilbert, V. M. The altercation of Edwards with Samuel Johnson. JEGP 51 1952.
—— Edwards as the wooden Inigo. N & Q Dec 1955.

LAURENCE EUSDEN
1688–1730
Collections

Original poems and translations by Mr Hill, Mr Eusden etc. 1714.
Select collection of miscellaneous poems. Ed J. Nichols vol 4 (pp. 128–63, 226–49) 1780.

§ 1

Hero and Leander translated [from Musaeus]. In Tonson's Poetical miscellanies: the sixth part, 1709 etc; Glasgow 1750 (separately).
A letter to Mr Addison on the King's accession to the throne. 1714, 1714 (as The royal family: a letter).
Translations from Claudian and Statius: poem to Lord Halifax on reading the critique in the Spectator on Milton etc. In R. Steele, Poetical miscellanies, 1714.
Verses at the last publick commencement at Cambridge. 1714, 1714.
A poem on the marriage of his Grace the Duke of Newcastle. 1717.
Poems by the Earl of Roscommon [with Eusden's Latin version of his Essay on translated verse]. 1717.
Ovid's Metamorphoses in fifteen books, translated [into English verse] by the most eminent hands [J. Dryden, J. Addison, L. Eusden, A. Mainwaring, S. Croxall, N. Tate, J. Gay, W. Congreve, and the editor Sir S. Garth]. 1717.
A poem to the Royal Highness on the birth of the Prince. 1718.
An ode for the New Year. 1720.
An ode for the birthday. 1720.
An ode for the New Year. 1721.
An ode for the birthday. 1721.
Three poems, I: To the Lord High Chancellor; II: To Lord Parker, on his return from his travels; III: To Lord Parker, on his marriage. 1722.
An ode for the birthday, in English and Latin. Cambridge 1723.
The origin of the Knights of the Bath: a poem. 1725.
Three poems: the first, Sacred to the immortal memory of the last king; the second, On the happy succession and coronation of his present Majesty; and a third humbly inscrib'd to the Queen. 1727, 1727.
A poem humbly inscribed to his Royal Highness Prince Frederic. 1729.
Eusden also contributed to Spectator *and* Guardian.

§ 2

Austin, W. S. and J. Ralph. In their Lives of the laureates, 1853.
Broadus, E. K. In his Laureateship, Oxford 1921.
Nicholson, G. Eusden. TLS 18 May 1946.

ABEL EVANS
1679–1737

§ 1

The apparition; a dialogue [in verse] betwixt the devil and a doctor concerning the rights of the Christian church. 1710 (3 edns); The second part, 1710.

Vertumnus: an epistle to Mr Jacob Bobart. Oxford 1713, 1782 (in J. Nichols, Select collection of poems vol 5).
Prae-existence: a poem in imitation of Milton. 1740.

ELIJAH FENTON
1683–1730
Collections

Miscellaneous poems and translations by several hands [including Fenton's]. 1712, 1714, 1720, 1722.
Poems on several occasions. 1717.
Poetical works of Fenton with the life of the author. 1802.
Johnson 29, Anderson 7, Chalmers 10.

§ 1

An ode to the sun, for the New-Year. 1707.
Oxford and Cambridge miscellany poems. 1708. Ed Fenton.
To the Queen, on her Majesty's birthday. [1710?].
An ode addressed to the Savoir Vivre Club. [1710?].
An epistle to Mr Southerne, from Mr El. Fenton, from Kent, Jan 28 1710/11. 1711.
Florelio: a pastoral lamenting the death of the Marquis of Blandford. In A. Pope, Eloisa to Abelard, 1720 (2nd edn).
Mariamne: a tragedy. 1723, Dublin 1723, London [1723], 1726, 1735, 1745, Dublin 1759, London 1760. Produced at Lincoln's Inn Fields 22 Feb 1723.
Life of John Milton. Prefixed to Paradise lost, 1725 etc.
The Odyssey of Homer, translated into English verse by Pope, Broome and Fenton. 1725–6 etc. Bks 1, 4, 19–20.
The works of Edmund Waller. 1729, 1730, 1744, 1752, 1772, 1796. Ed Fenton.
Observations on the works of Edmund Waller. 1730. Originally prefixed to his edn of Waller, above.
Fenton also contributed to D. Lewis, Miscellanies, 1726, 1730; *and to* G. Ogle's *trn of* Secundus, 1731.

§ 2

Johnson, S. In his Lives of the poets, 1779–81.
Lloyd, W. W. Fenton: his poetry and friends. Ed G. L. Fenton, preceded by a new Life by R. Fenton. 1894.
Valency, M. J. The tragedies of Herod and Mariamne. New York 1940.
Tasch, P. A. The death of Sir Cloudesly Shovell in Fenton's Mariamne. N & Q July 1962.

THOMAS FITZGERALD
1695?–1752

§ 1

Poems on several occasions. 1733, 1736; ed T. Wintour, Oxford 1781 (with addns).
Georgia, a poem; Tomo Chachi, an ode: a copy of verses on Mr Oglethorpe's second voyage to Georgia. 1736. Tomo Chachi at least by Fitzgerald.
Publii Terentii comoediae sex etc. 1736. Ed Fitzgerald.
M. V. Martialis epigrammata etc. 1790. Ed Fitzgerald.

§ 2

Williams, I. A. Another by-way round Helicon. Bookman (London) Aug 1923.

PHILIP FRANCIS
1708?–73
Collections

Chalmers 19.

§ 1

The odes, epodes and Carmen seculare of Horace, in Latin and English. 2 vols 1742, Dublin 1742, London 1743, 1746.

The satires of Horace. Vol 3, 1746.

The epistles and Art of poetry. Vol 4, 1746.

A poetical translation of the works of Horace, with the original text. 4 vols 1747, 1749, 1750, 1753, 1756, 1760, 2 vols 1760, 1765, 1791 etc.

Eugenia: a tragedy. 1752. Produced at Drury Lane 17 Feb 1752.

Constantine: a tragedy. 1754. Produced at Drury Lane 23 Feb 1754.

The orations of Demosthenes. 2 vols 1757–8.

A letter from a Right Honourable person, and the answer to it, translated into verse. 1761. This and a further Letter, 1761, are also attributed to A. Murphy.

THOMAS GILBERT
d. 1747
Collections

Poems on several occasions by Thomas Gilbert esq, late Fellow of Peter-house in Cambridge. 1747.

§ 1

A view of the town: a satire. 1735.

A satire. 1738.

The first satire of Juvenal imitated. 1739.

The second epistle of the first book of Horace imitated. 1741.

RICHARD GLOVER
1712–85
Collections

Anderson 11, Chalmers 17.

§ 1

A poem on Sir I. Newton. In H. Pemberton, A view of Newton's philosophy, 1728.

The spleen, by M. Green. 1737. Ed Glover.

Leonidas: a poem. 1737 (9 bks), Dublin 1737, London 1738, 1739, Leipzig 1766, Glasgow 1769, 2 vols 1770 (12 bks) etc; tr French, 1738 (prose); German, 1766.

London, or the progress of commerce: a poem. 1739, 1739, Dublin 1739.

Admiral Hosier's ghost. 1740.

Boadicea: a tragedy. 1753, 1753, Dublin 1753. Produced at Drury Lane 1 Dec 1753.

Medea: a tragedy. 1761, Dublin 1761, London 1762 (3 edns), 1777. Produced at Drury Lane 4 March 1767.

The Athenaid: a poem. Ed Mrs Halsey 1787, Dublin 1788.

Jason: a tragedy. 1799.

Memoirs of a celebrated and literary and political character, written by himself. Ed R. Duppa 1813.

§ 2

[Duppa, R.] An inquiry concerning the author of the Letters of Junius. 1814. Suggests Glover.

Schaaf, J. G. Glover: Leben und Werke. Leipzig 1900.

GEORGE GRANVILLE,
BARON LANSDOWNE
1667–1735

See col 790, below.

MATTHEW GREEN
1696–1737
Collections

The spleen and other poems, with a prefatory essay by J. Aikin. 1796.

The poems of Gray, Parnell, Collins, Green and Warton. Ed R. A. Willmott 1853.

The spleen and other poems. Ed R. K. Wood 1925.

Minor poets of the eighteenth century. Ed H. I'A. Fausset 1930 (EL).

Johnson 69, Anderson 10, Chalmers 15.

§ 1

The grotto: a poem written by Peter Drake, fisherman of Brentford. 1733, 1758 (in Dodsley's collection vol 5, with some omissions).

The spleen: an epistle [in verse] inscrib'd to his particular friend Mr C. J[ackson]. Ed R. Glover 1737 (3 edns), Dublin 1737, London 1738 (with Some other pieces by the same hand), 1748, 1758; ed W. H. Williams 1936.

§ 2

Smith, H. R. Matthew Green. N & Q June–July 1954.

CONSTANTIA GRIERSON
1706–33
Collections

Poems on several occasions. Ed M. Barber 1734. Includes verses by Mrs Grierson with account of her life.

Poems by eminent ladies. Vol 1, 1755.

§ 1

The art of printing: a poem. Dublin 1764. Single sheet.

Mrs Grierson also edited Latin classics pbd by her husband: Virgil, 1724; Terence, Dublin 1727; Tacitus, Dublin 1727.

§ 2

Ballard, G. In his Memoirs of ladies, Oxford 1752, London 1755.

Cibber, T. In his Lives of the poets vol 5, 1753.

JAMES HAMMOND
1710–42
Collections

Love elegies, written in the year 1732. 1743, 1743, 1745, 1752, 1754, 1757, Dublin 1762, London 1768, 1770, 1771, 1773, 1777, Glasgow 1787 etc; ed T. Park 1805 (with preface by Chesterfield); ed G. Dyer 1808.

Johnson 39, Anderson 8, Chalmers 11.

§ 1

An elegy to a young lady, in the manner of Ovid with an answer by a lady [M. W. Montagu]. 1733.

§ 2

Johnson, S. In his Lives of the poets, 1779–81.

Radice, S. Not all sleep. 1938.

Gove, P. B. Johnson's copy of Hammond's Elegies. MLQ 5 1944.

WILLIAM HARRISON
1685–1713

§ 1

Woodstock Park: a poem. 1706, 1706 (rev), 1758 (in Dodsley's collection vol 5).
On his Grace the Duke of Marlborough going for Holland, in imitation of the third ode of the first book of Horace. 1707.
Harrison also edited and wrote most of the continuation of Tatler *Jan–May* 1711.

§ 2

Elliott, R. C. Swift's 'little' Harrison: poet and continuator of the Tatler. SP 46 1949.

WALTER HARTE
1709–74
Bibliographies

A catalogue of the entire library of Harte. 1785 (Leigh and Sotheby).

§ 1

Poems on several occasions. 1727, 1739.
An essay [in verse] on satire, particularly on the Dunciad. 1730; ed T. B. Gilmore, Los Angeles 1968 (Augustan Reprint Soc).
Part of Pindar's first Pythian ode, paraphrased. [1730], 1749.
An epistle [in verse] to Mr Pope on reading his Iliad. 1731.
Verses presented to the Prince of Orange, on his visiting Oxford. 1734. With D. Mallet.
An essay [in verse] on reason. 1735 (3 edns), 1736.
The union and harmony of reason, morality and revealed religion: a sermon. Oxford 1737, London 1737, 1737, 1738.
The reasonableness and advantage of national humiliations upon the approach of war: a sermon. Oxford 1740.
The history of the life of Gustavus Adolphus, King of Sweden. 2 vols 1759; tr German, 1760.
Essays on husbandry. 1764, 1770 (rev and enlarged).
The amaranth: or religious poems. 1767.

§ 2

Russell, G. E. A parson on farming 1764. Estate Mag 37 1937.

BEVIL HIGGONS
1670–1735
Collections

Historical works. 2 vols 1736.

§ 1

To the Queen on the birth of the Prince. In Illustrissimi principis ducis Cornubiae genethliacon, Oxford 1688.
The generous conqueror, or the timely discovery: a tragedy. 1702. Produced at Drury Lane c. Dec 1701.
A short view of the English history; with reflections on the reigns of the kings to the Revolution 1688. 1723, Hague 1727, London 1734 (enlarged), 1748; tr French, 1729.
Historical and critical remarks on Bishop Burnet's History of his own time. 1725, 1727 (enlarged).
A poem on the glorious peace of Utrecht, inscribed in the year 1713 to the late Earl of Oxford. 1731.
A poem on nature, in imitation of Lucretius. 1736.
Higgons also contributed to Dryden's Examen poeticum, 1693 (pp. 250–66) *and to Fenton's* Poems on several occasions, 1717.

AARON HILL
1685–1750

See col 791, below.

JABEZ HUGHES
1685?–1731
Collections

Miscellanies in verse and prose. Ed W. Duncombe 1737.

§ 1

On November 4 1712, the anniversary of the birth of King William III. [1712], 1715.
The rape of Proserpine, from Claudian; with the story of Sextus and Erichtho, from Lucan's Pharsalia. 1714, 1723.
The lives of the xii Caesars [by Suetonius], translated into English with notes [by Hughes]. 1717.
Verses occasion'd by reading Mr Dryden's Fables. 1721.
Hughes also pbd trns of Cervantes in S. Croxall, Select collection of novels and histories, 6 vols 1729 (2nd edn).

JOHN HUGHES
1677–1720
Collections

Poems on several occasions, with some select essays in prose. Ed W. Duncombe 2 vols 1735.
Johnson 22, Anderson 7, and Chalmers 10.

§ 1

The triumph of peace. 1698.
The court of Neptune. 1699.
The house of Nassau: a Pindarick ode. 1702.
An ode in praise of music. 1703.
A review of the case of Ephraim and Judah. 1705.
A complete history of England [by W. Kennett]. 3 vols 1706. With Hughes' trn of a life of Queen Mary from the Latin of F. Godwin.
Advices from Parnassus, all translated from the Italian by several hands, revis'd and corrected by Mr Hughes. 1706.
Fontenelle's Dialogues of the dead, translated from the French; and two original dialogues. 1708, 1730, Glasgow 1754.
Calypso and Telemachus: an opera. 1712, 1717, 1735 etc. Produced at Haymarket 17 May 1712.
The history of the revolution in Portugal by the Abbot de Vertot. 1712. Tr Hughes from French.
An ode to the creator of the world, occasion'd by the fragments of Orpheus. 1713, 1713.
The lay-monastery: consisting of essays, discourses etc publish'd singly under the title of the Lay-monk. 1714.
The works of Mr Edmund Spenser, with a glossary explaining the old and obscure words. 6 vols 1715, 1750 etc. The remarks on the Fairy Queen and allegorical poetry rptd in Critical essays of the eighteenth century, ed W. H. Durham, New Haven 1915.
Apollo and Daphne: a masque set to musick. 1716 etc. Produced at Drury Lane 12 Jan 1716.
An ode for the birthday of her Royal Highness the Princess of Wales. 1716.
Orestes: a tragedy. 1717. Unacted.
A layman's thoughts on the late treatment of the Bishop of Bangor. 1717.
Charon, or the ferry-boat: a vision. 1719. Prose.
Conversations with a lady on the plurality of worlds: to which is added A discourse concerning the antients and moderns, translated [from Fontenelle]. 1719. Discourse tr Hughes.

The ecstacy: an ode. 1720.

The siege of Damascus: a tragedy. 1720, 1721, 1744 etc; tr French, 1749 (in Le théâtre anglois vol 7). Produced at Drury Lane 17 Feb 1720.

Letters of Abelard and Heloise, extracted chiefly from Monsieur Bayle, translated from the French [by Hughes]. 1722, 1743, 1765 etc, 1904 (Temple Classics).

The complicated guilt of the late Rebellion. 1745. Written 1716.

Letters

Letters by several eminent persons deceased. Ed J. Duncombe 1772, 1773, 2 vols 1773. Includes Hughes' correspondence, some new pieces and the original plan of Siege of Damascus.

§ 2

Johnson, S. In his Lives of the poets, 1779–81.

Bisset, R. In his Biographical sketch of the authors of the Spectator, 1793.

McKillop, A. D. Some Newtonian verses in Poor Richard. New England Quart 21 1948.

HILDEBRAND JACOB
1693–1739
Collections

Works: containing poems on various subjects, and occasions; with the Fatal constancy: a tragedy; and several pieces in prose, the greatest part never before publish'd. 1735.

§ 1

Bedlam. 1723.

The fatal constancy: a tragedy. 1723. Produced at Drury Lane 22 April 1723.

Chiron to Achilles. 1732.

Hymn to the goddess of silence. 1734.

Of the sister arts: an essay. 1734.

Brutus the Trojan founder of the British Empire: an epic poem. 1735.

The progress of religion. 1737.

Donna Clara to her daughter Teresa: an epistle [in verse]. 1737.

The nest of plays, consisting of three comedies: The prodigal reform'd, The happy constancy, and The tryal of conjugal love. 1738. Produced at Covent Garden 25 Jan 1738.

The curious maid, The peeper, The members to their soveraign, *and* The unequal match, *possibly by Jacob.*

GEORGE JEFFREYS
1678–1755
Collections

Miscellanies in verse and prose. 1754. Includes an unacted opera, 'The triumph of truth.

§ 1

Edwin: a tragedy. 1724. Produced at Lincoln's Inn Fields 24 Feb 1724.

Merope: a tragedy [tr from Italian of Maffei]. 1731. Produced at Lincoln's Inn Fields 27 Feb 1731.

Father Francis and sister Constance: a poem from a story in the Spectator; and Chess: a poem translated into English from Vida. 1736.

§ 2

Oliver, T. E. The Merope of Jeffreys as a source of Voltaire's Mérope. Urbana 1927. With text.

SOAME JENYNS
1704–87
Collections

Poems. 1752.

Miscellaneous pieces in verse and prose. 2 vols 1761, 1770.

Miscellanies. 1770.

Works. Ed C. N. Cole 4 vols 1790, 1793. With memoir.

Johnson 73; Anderson 11; Chalmers 17.

§ 1

The art of dancing: a poem in three cantos. 1729.

Versus inopes rerum, nugaeque canorae: commonly call'd poems on several occasions. [1730].

An epistle [in verse] to Lord Lovelace. 1735.

The modern fine gentleman. 1746.

An ode to the Hon Philip Y—ke, imitated from Horace, lib ii, ode xvi; to which is added the same ode imitated and inscribed to the Earl of B—on on his creation. 1747.

The 'squire and the parson: an eclogue. [1749].

The modern fine lady. 1751 (3 edns).

A free enquiry into the nature and origin of evil. 1757; tr French, 1791.

The objections to the taxation of our American colonies considered. 1765.

Thoughts on the causes and consequences of the present high price of provisions. 1767.

A scheme for the coalition of parties. 1772.

A view of the internal evidence of the Christian religion. 1776 (5 edns), Dublin 1776, London 1790, Edinburgh 1798, London 1799; tr Polish, 1782; French, 1797; Greek, 1804.

An ode. 1780.

Disquisitions on several subjects. 1782, Dublin 1782.

Thoughts on parliamentary reform. 1784.

On the immortality of the soul, translated [by Jenyns] from the Latin of I. H. Browne. 1796, 1808.

§ 2

Goodson, L. Samuel Johnson's review of Soame Jenyns' A free enquiry into the nature and origin of evil: a re-examination. New Rambler 1968.

WILLIAM KING
1662–1712
See col 1046, below.

WILLIAM KING,
Principal of St Mary Hall, Oxford
1685–1763
Collections

Opera Gul. King LlD, Aulae BMV apud oxonienses olim princip. [1760]. Hydra and monitor first pbd here.

§ 1

An ode to Mira. [Dublin] 1730 (half sheet), London 1730 (with Myra's answer, not by King).

The toast: an epic poem in four books, written in Latin by Frederick Scheffer, done into English by Peregrine Odonald esq. Vol 1, Dublin 1732, 1732, 1736 (rev and enlarged), 1747 (enlarged), 1772–3 (in New foundling hospital for wit, pts 5–6).

A letter from Mr Lewis O Neil, to Peregrine O Donald esq, with Mr O Donald's answer. Dublin 1734.

Common sense: or the Englishman's journal. 1737, 2 vols 1739. With contributions by King.

Miltonis epistola ad Pollionem [Lord Polwarth]. 1738, 1738; tr 1740.

Sermo pedestris. 1739, 1739.

Scamnum: ecloga. 1740; tr 1741 (as The bench).

Templum libertatis. 2 pts 1742-3. Verse.

Tres oratiunculae, habitae in domo convocationis oxon. Oxford 1744, London 1744.

Epistola objurgatoria ad Gulielmum King LlD, cui accessit epistola canonici reverendi admodum ad archidiaconum reverendum admodum. 1744, 1744.

A letter to a friend occasioned by Epistola objurgatoria etc. 1744.

Antonietti, ducis Corsorum, epistola ad Corsos de rege eligendo. 1744.

Five additional volumes of sermons preached upon several occasions. Vols 7-11, 1744. By R. South, ed King.

A proposal for publishing a poetical translation, both in Latin and English, of the reverend Mr Tutor Bentham's Letter to a young gentleman of Oxford. 1748, 1749.

A poetical abridgment, both in Latin and English, of the reverend Mr Tutor Bentham's Letter etc, to which are added Some remarks on the letter. 1749, 1749.

Oratio in theatro Sheldoniano habita idibus Aprilibus MDCCXLIX, die dedicationis bibliothecae Radclivianae. Oxford 1749, London 1749, Oxford 1750, London 1750; tr 1750 (not by King).

An answer to Dr King's speech: by the Rev Mr John Burton, Batchelor in Divinity, and Fellow of Eton College. Oxford 1750 (broadside, 3 edns). By King.

Elogium famae inserviens Jacci Etonensis, sive gigantis: or the praises of Jack of Eton, commonly called Jack the giant. Oxford 1750.

A key to the fragment, by Amias Riddings BD, with a preface by Peregrine Smyth [King?]. 1751.

The dreamer. 1754. Copies with and without A translation of the Latin epistle in The dreamer.

Doctor King's apology: or vindication of himself from the several matters charged on him by the society of informers. Oxford 1755 (3 edns).

The last blow: or an unanswerable vindication of the society of Exeter College. 1755.

Oratiuncula habita in domo convocationis oxon, die Oct 27 1756. Oxford 1757, 1757.

Aviti epistola ad Perillam, virginem Scotam. 1760.

Elogium [on John Taylor, oculist]. [1761].

H. S. E. Richardus Nash. [1761].

Political and literary anecdotes of his own times. [Ed P. B. Duncan] 1818, 1819.

§ 2

[Rowan, A. B.] The history of an unreadable book [The toast]. Bentley's Miscellany 41 1857.

Williams, H. The old trumpeter of liberty hall. Book-Collector's Quart 1-4 1931.

—— The toast. Opuscula of the sette of odd volumes no 94 1932.

—— Swift to Dr William King. In his Correspondence, ed H. Williams vol 5, Oxford 1965.

GEORGE LYTTLETON,
1st BARON LYTTLETON
1709-73
Bibliographies

Todd, W. B. Variant editions of To the memory of a lady lately deceased. PBSA 44 1950.

Collections

A collection of poems by several hands [including Lyttleton's]. Vol 2, 1748.

The new foundling hospital for wit: a collection of pieces in verse and prose [including Lyttleton's]. 1771.

Poems. Glasgow 1773, 1777.

The works of George Lord Lyttleton, now first collected together; with some other pieces never before printed. Ed G. E. Ayscough 1774, 2 vols Dublin 1774, London 1785, Dublin 1785, 3 vols 1776 etc; tr German, 1791.

Poetical works. 1785, Glasgow 1787 etc.

Johnson 56; Anderson 10; Chalmers 14.

§ 1

Blenheim. 1728. Verse.

An epistle [in verse] to Mr Pope, from a young gentleman at Rome. 1730.

The progress of love, in four eclogues. 1732, 1732.

Advice to a lady. 1733. Verse.

Letters from a Persian in England to his friend at Ispahan. 1735 (4 edns, vol 2 not by Lyttleton); tr French, 2 vols 1735.

Considerations upon the present state of our affairs at home and abroad. 1739, 1739.

Farther considerations on the present state of affairs, containing a true state of the South Sea Company's affairs in 1718. 1739, 1739.

Observations on the life of Cicero. 1741.

The Court secret: a melancholy truth. 1742, 1746 (as The new Court secret).

To the memory of a lady [Lyttleton's first wife] lately deceased: a monody. 1747, Dublin 1747, London 1748, 1748.

Observations on the conversion and apostleship of St Paul in a letter to Gilbert West. 1747, Dublin 1747, London 1748, 1749, 1754, 1799 etc; tr French, 1754, 1758.

A modesty apology for my own conduct. 1748.

The fourth ode of the fourth book of Horace. 1749. Tr Lyttleton.

Dialogues of the dead [nos 26-8 by E. Montagu]. 1760 (3 edns), 1765, 1768, Worcester Mass 1797; tr French, 1767.

An additional dialogue of the dead between Pericles and Aristides: being a sequel to the dialogue between Pericles and Cosmo. 1760.

Four new dialogues of the dead. 1765.

The history of the life of King Henry the second and of the age in which he lived. 4 vols 1767-71, 1767-71, 6 vols 1769-73, 1790.

A gentleman's tour through Monmouthshire. 1781.

Lyttleton also contributed to Common sense 5 Feb 1737-Aug 1743.

§ 2

Johnson, S. In his Lives of the poets, 1779-81.

Dobson, A. Lyttleton as a man of letters. In his Old Kensington Palace and other papers, 1910.

Johnson, F. P. Lyttleton. PQ 7 1928.

Roberts, S. C. An eighteenth-century gentleman. Cambridge 1930.

Rao, A. V. A minor Augustan: being the life and works of George Lord Lyttleton. Calcutta 1934.

Davis, R. M. The correspondents. PMLA 51 1936.

—— The good Lord Lyttleton. Bethlehem Pa 1939.

DAVID MALLET, originally MALLOCH
1705?-65
Collections

Works. 4 pts 1743, 3 vols 1759.

Johnson 53; Anderson 9; Chalmers 14.

§ 1

William and Margaret: an old ballad. [1723].

A poem in imitation of Donaides. [1725].

The excursion: a poem in two books. 1728.

Eurydice: a tragedy. 1731, 1731, 1735, 1759, 1780. Produced at Drury Lane 22 Feb 1731.

Of verbal criticism: an epistle to Mr Pope, occasioned by
Theobald's Shakespear and Bentley's Milton. 1733.
Verses presented to the Prince of Orange on his visiting
Oxford. 1734. With W. Harte.
Mustapha: a tragedy. 1739, 1760. Produced at Drury
Lane 13 Feb 1739.
Alfred: a masque. 1740, 1745. With J. Thomson. Pro-
duced at Cliefden, 1 Aug 1740. *See* Alfred, *below.*
The life of Francis Bacon. 1740, 1740, 1753, 1760, 1768;
tr French, 1742, 1755; Italian, 1768; German, 1780.
Poems on several occasions. 1743.
Amyntor and Theodora, or the hermit: a poem in three
cantos. 1747, 1747, Dublin 1747, 1748, 1748 (corrected).
A congratulatory letter to Selim on the three letters to the
Whigs. 1748.
Letters on the spirit of patriotism: on the idea of a patriot
king. 1749. By Bolingbroke, ed Mallet.
Alfred: a masque. 1751, 1753, 1754. Rev Mallet. Pro-
duced at Drury Lane 23 Feb 1751.
Works of Lord Bolingbroke. 5 vols 1754. Ed Mallet.
Britannia: a masque. 1755. Produced at Drury Lane 9
May 1755.
Observations on the twelfth article of war. 1757. On the
case of Admiral Byng.
Edwin and Emma. Birmingham 1760, London 1777; ed
F. T. Dinsdale 1849.
Verses on the death of Lady Anson. 1760.
Poems on several occasions. 1762. Different from 1743
edn, above.
Elvira: a tragedy. 1763, Edinburgh 1763, Dublin 1763,
London 1778. Produced at Drury Lane 19 Jan 1763.
Ballads and songs. Ed F. T. Dinsdale 1857.

§ 2

Boswell, J., A. Erskine and G. Dempster. Critical stric-
tures on the new tragedy of Elvira written by Mr David
Malloch. 1763; ed F. A. Pottle, Los Angeles 1952
(Augustan Reprint Soc).
Johnson, S. In his Lives of the poets, 1779–81.
D'Israeli, I. Bolingbroke and Mallet's posthumous
quarrel with Pope. In his Quarrels of authors, 1814.
Swaen, A. E. H. Fair Margaret and sweet William.
Archiv 136 1917.
Boys, R. C. Malloch and the Edinburgh Miscellany.
MLN 54 1939.
McKillop, A. D. The authorship of A poem to the memory
of Mr Congreve. MLN 54 1939.
—— The early history of Alfred. PQ 41 1962.
Starr, H. W. Notes on Mallet. N & Q 20 April 1940.
—— Sources of Mustapha: a tragedy. N & Q 22 Nov 1941.

BERNARD MANDEVILLE
1670?–1731

See col 1095, below.

MARY MASTERS
1694?–1771

Poems on several occasions. 1733.
Familiar letters and poems on several occasions. 1755.
Also in Colman and Thornton's Poems by eminent ladies,
1755.

JAMES MILLER
1706–44

See col 795, below.

JOSEPH MITCHELL
1684–1738

Lugubres cantus. 2 pts 1719. Pt 1 by Mitchell.
The doleful swains: a pastoral poem written originally in
the Scotch dialect, with an English version. 1720.
Jonah. 1720, 1724.
An ode to the power of musick. 1721.
An epistle to John, Earl of Stairs, on the death of Sir D.
Dalrymple. 1722.
Two poetical petitions to Robert Walpole. 1725.
The sine-cure: a poetical petition. 1725. One of
above.
The promotion and the alternative: two poetical petitions.
1726.
The shoe-heel: a rhapsody. 1727.
The judgment of Hercules. 1727.
The totness address versified. 1727 (8 edns).
A tale and two fables in verse. 1727.
Poems on several occasions. 2 vols 1729, 1732.
The monument: or the Muse's motion, upon the death of
Sir Richard Steele. 1729.
The Highland fair, or union of the clans: an opera. 1731.
Produced at Drury Lane 20 March 1731.
Three poetical epistles: to Mr Hogarth, Mr Dandridge and
Mr Lambert, masters of the art of painting. 1731.
The royal hermitage, or temple of honour: a poem.
1732.
A familiar epistle to Sir R. Walpole. 1735.
A sick-bed soliloquy to an empty purse, in Latin and
English verse. [1735].
Mitchell also pbd as his The fatal extravagance: a tragedy,
*acted at Lincoln's Inn Fields 21 April 1721 but later
admitted it had been given him by Aaron Hill. See* P. S.
Dunkin, The authorship of the Fatal extravagance,
MLN 60 1945.

MARY MONK
d. 1715

Marinda: poems and translations upon several occasions.
Ed her father, Robert (later Viscount) Molesworth.
1716.
Also in Colman and Thornton's Poems by eminent ladies,
1755.

LADY MARY WORTLEY MONTAGU
1689–1762

See col 1584, below.

EDWARD MOORE
1712–57

Collections

Poems fables and plays. 1756.
Dramatic works; to which is prefixed a short account of
the author's life. 1788.
Johnson 65; Anderson 10; Chalmers 14.

§ 1

Fables for the female sex. 1744, 1746 1749 Dublin 1749,
London 1755, 1766, 1768, 1770, 1771, 1777, 1783, 1786,
1795, 1799 etc; tr German, 1772. Last 3 by H. Brooke.
The trial of Selim the Persian for divers high crimes and
misdemeanours. 1748. On George Lord Lyttleton.
The foundling: a comedy. 1748, 1780, 1792, 1797 etc;
tr French, 1818. Produced at Drury Lane 13 Feb 1748.
An ode to David Garrick upon the talk of the town. 1749.
Solomon: a serenata. 1750.
Gil Blas: a comedy. 1751, Dublin 1751. Produced at
Drury Lane 2 Feb 1751.

The world. 209 nos 11 Jan 1753–30 Dec 1756, 6 vols 1755–7, 4 vols 1761, 1767, 1772, 1782, Edinburgh 1793, London 1794. Ed Moore as Adam FitzAdam; Moore also contributed 61 of the papers.

The gamester: a tragedy. 1753, 1753, Dublin 1763, London 1771, 1779, Dublin 1783, London 1784, 1792, 1797 etc; ed C. H. Peake and P. R. Wikelund, Ann Arbor 1948 (Augustan Reprint Soc); tr German, 1765; French, 1767, 1785; Dutch, 1775.

§ 2

Caskey, J. H. The life and works of Moore. New Haven 1927.

Collins, R. L. The foundling: an intermediary. PQ 17 1938.

Winship, G. P., jr. The printing history of the World. In Studies in the early English periodical, ed R. P. Bond, Chapel Hill 1957.

HENRY NEEDLER
1690–1718

§ 1

Works. 1728; ed M. Allentuck, Los Angeles 1961 (Augustan Reprint Soc).

§ 2

Williams, E. K. New lights on Needler. Princeton Univ Lib Chron 24 1958.

ROBERT NUGENT or CRAGGS, EARL NUGENT
1702–88

Collections

Works of the British poets. Ed E. Sanford vol 37, Philadelphia 1819.

§ 1

An ode to his Royal Highness [Frederick Prince of Wales] on his birth-day. 1739.

An ode to Mr Pulteney; to which is added a new epitaph. 1739.

Odes and epistles. 1739, 1739.

Faith: a poem. 1774.

Verses addressed to the Queen with a New Year's gift of Irish manufacture. 1775, 1775.

Nugent also contributed to Dodsley's Collection vol 1, 1748, and pbd some political tracts.

§ 2

Nugent, C. Memoir of Nugent with letters, poems. 1898.

GEORGE OGLE
1704–46

§ 1

Basia, or the kisses [Secundus], in Latin and English verse. 1731. Partly by E. Fenton and E. Ward.

Epistles [of bk 1, 1 and 4] of Horace imitated. 1735.

The second epistle of Horace imitated. 1735, 1738.

Antiquities explained: being a collection of figured gems illustrated by descriptions taken from the classics. 1737.

The legacy hunter: the fifth satire of the second book of Horace imitated. 1737.

The miser's feast: the eighth satire of the second book of Horace imitated. 1737.

The third epistle of the first book of Horace imitated. 1738.

The fifth epistle of the first book of Horace imitated. 1738.

The eleventh epistle of the first book of Horace imitated. 1738.

The twelfth epistle of the first book of Horace imitated. [1738].

Gualtherus and Griselda: or the clerk of Oxford's tale. 1739, Dublin 1741. With 4 other Chaucerian pieces.

The Canterbury tales of Chaucer, modernis'd by several hands. 3 vols 1741, 2 vols Dublin 1742. Largely by Ogle.

Trns by Ogle are also appended to J. Sterling, The loves of Hero and Leander, 1728.

§ 2

Dixon, P. Pope, Ogle and Horace. N & Q Nov 1959.

WILLIAM OLDISWORTH
1680–1734

The cupid. 1698.

A dialogue between Timothy and Philatheus, written by a layman. 3 vols 1709–11.

Annotations on the Tatler, written in French by Monsieur Bournelle and translated into English by Walter Wagstaff. 1710.

Callipaedia: or the art of getting pretty children, translated from the original Latin of Claudius Quilletus by several hands. 1710 (anon), 1719 (as 'by Mr Will. Oldisworth').

A Pindarick ode to the memory of Dr William King. [1712].

The odes, epodes and Carmen seculare of Horace, in Latin and English. 24 pts 1712–13, 2 vols 1713 ('by several hands'), 1719.

State and miscellany poems, by the author of the Examiner. 1715.

Oldisworth edited Examiner vols 2–6. *See* R. J. Allen, Oldisworth: the author of the Examiner, PQ 17 1938.

JOHN OLDMIXON
1673–1742

See col 1708, below.

RICHARDSON PACK
1682–1742

§ 1

Miscellanies in verse and prose. 1719, 1719, Dublin 1726 (with an account of Pack).

The life of T. P. Atticus [by C. Nepos], translated with remarks by R.P. 1719.

Religion and philosophy: a tale; with five other pieces. 1720.

Dissertation upon the Roman elegiac poets. 1721, 1725.

Select translations from Catullus, Tibullus and Ovid. 1725.

The force of love: or the nun's complaint. 1725.

A congratulatory poem to his Majesty George the II upon his accession. Cambridge 1727.

The posthumous works of William Wycherley; to which are prefixed some memoirs by Major Pack. 1728.

The whole works, in prose and verse. 1729.

The lives of T. P. Atticus, Miltiades and Cimon, translated from Cornelius Nepos by Pack. 1735.

Poetical remains. 1738.

§ 2

Cain, R. D. N & Q 16 May 1936. Suppl to DNB article.

THOMAS CATESBY PAGET, BARON PAGET
1689–1742

An essay [in verse] on human life. 1734, 1735, 1736 ('corrected and much enlarged by the author'), 1736, Stafford 1739.
An epistle to Mr P—, in anti-heroicks. 1738.
Reflections upon the administration of government. 1740.
Miscellanies in prose and verse. 1741.

THOMAS PARNELL
1679–1718
Collections

Works in verse and prose, enlarged with variations and [7] poems not before publish'd. Glasgow 1755.
Poetical works. Glasgow 1786.
Poetical works. Ed J. Mitford 1833, 1852 (Aldine edn).
Poetical works [with Gray, Collins, Green and Warton]. Ed R. A. Willmott 1854.
Poetical works. Ed G. A. Aitken 1894.
Poems. Ed L. Robinson, Dublin 1927.
Minor poets of the eighteenth century. Ed H. I'A. Fausset 1930 (EL).
Johnson 44; Anderson 7; Chalmers 9.

§ 1

An essay [in verse] on the different stiles of poetry. 1713.
An essay on the life, writings and learning of Homer. Prefixed to Pope's Iliad vol 1, 1715.
Homer's battle of the frogs and mice, with the remarks of Zoilus, to which is prefix'd the life of the said Zoilus. 1717. Later appended to Pope's Iliad and Odyssey.
Poems on several occasions, published by Mr Pope. 1722, 1726, Dublin 1735, London 1737, Dublin 1744, Glasgow 1752, 1770 (with Goldsmith's Life), Dublin 1771.
Posthumous works. 1758, Dublin 1758.

§ 2

Goldsmith, O. The life of Parnell. 1770.
Johnson, S. In his Lives of the poets, 1779–81.
Cruickshank, A. H. Parnell: or what was wrong with the eighteenth century. E & S 11 1925.
Wasserman, E. R. Coleridge's Metrical experiments. MLN 55 1940.
Starr, H. W. Gray's opinion of Parnell. MLN 57 1942.
Green, R. L. Notes on Parnell and his Chester relations. N & Q 20 Nov 1943.
Havens, R. D. Hymn to contentment. MLN 59 1944.
Jackson, R. W. Parnell the poet. Dublin Mag Jan 1945.
Dircks, R. J. Parnell's Batrachomoumachia and the Homer translation controversy. N & Q Aug 1956.
Rawson, C. J. Parnell's Night-piece on death. N & Q Feb 1961.
—— Swift's certificate to Parnell's posthumous works. MLR 57 1962.
—— Parnell on Whiston. PBSA 57 1963.

WILLIAM PATTISON
1706–27
Collections

Poetical works, with memoirs of the author's life. 2 vols 1728.
Anderson 8.

§ 1

An epistle to his Majesty on his accession to the throne. 1727.

AMBROSE PHILIPS
1674–1749
Collections

Three tragedies. 1725.
Pastorals, epistles, odes and other original poems, with translations from Pindar, Anacreon and Sappho. 1748, 1765.
A variorum text of four pastorals. Ed R. H. Griffith, Texas Univ Stud 12 1932.
Poems. Ed M. G. Segar, Oxford 1937 (with biography).
Ten new poems 1674–1749. Ed W. J. Cameron, N & Q Nov 1957.
Johnson 44, Anderson 9, Chalmers 13.

§ 1

Life of John Williams. 1700. Abridgement of J. Hacket, Scrinia reserata.
Persian tales. 1709. Tr from French of Pétis de la Croix. See R. H. Griffith, TLS 16 Nov 1935.
Pastorals. 1710. First 4 pieces originally ptd in Fenton's Oxford and Cambridge miscellany [1706]; rptd with 2 more in Tonson's Poetical miscellanies: the sixth part, 1709.
The distrest mother: a tragedy. 1712, 1712, 1718, Hague [1723], 1726, London 1731, 1734, 1735, 1748, 1749, 1751, Dublin 1754, 1756 etc. Produced at Drury Lane 17 March 1712. Tr from Racine, Andromaque.
An epistle to the Right Honourable Charles Lord Halifax. 1714.
An epistle to the Honourable James Craggs esq. 1717.
The freethinker. 24 March 1718–28 July 1721, 3 vols 1722, 1733, 1739.
The Briton: a tragedy. 1722, 1725. Produced at Drury Lane 19 Feb 1722.
Humfrey, Duke of Gloucester: a tragedy. 1723, 1723, Dublin 1723, London 1725. Produced at Drury Lane 15 Feb 1723.
A collection of old ballads. 3 vols 1723–5, 1723–38, [1872]. Ed Philips? See S. B. Hustvedt, TLS 6–13 Dec 1923; M. G. Segar, TLS 3 March 1932; L. de la Torre Bueno, Anglia 59 1935.
An ode in the manner of Pindar on the death of the Right Honourable William, Earl Cowper. 1723.
To the Honourable Miss Carteret. 1725, Dublin 1725.
To Miss Georgiana, youngest daughter of Lord Carteret. Dublin 1725.
Supplication for Miss Carteret in the smallpox. Dublin 1726.
To Miss Margaret Pulteney, daughter of Daniel Pulteney esq. Dublin 1727.
Philips was a principal contributor to Grumbler, 1715.

§ 2

Pope, A. Guardian no 40 1713.
Johnson, S. In his Lives of the poets, 1779–81.
Bueno, L. de la T. Ambrose Philips. TLS 17 Dec 1938.
—— The canon of Philips: some observations of criteria. PQ 19 1940.
Reade, A. L. The date of Philips's death. TLS 12 Feb 1938.
Fogle, S. F. MLN 54 1939.
Bryan, A. J. Humphrey, Duke of Gloucester. In Studies for W. A. Read, Baton Rouge 1940.
Mander, G. P. Philips's English background. TLS 10 Oct 1942. Reply by M. G. Segar 26 Dec 1942.
Joost, N. T. Burnet's Grumbler and Philips. N & Q 7 Aug 1948.

—— The Fables of Fénelon and Philips's Freethinker. SP 47 1950.
—— Gulliver and the Free-thinker. MLN 65 1950.
—— The authorship of the Free-thinker. In Studies in the early English periodicals, ed R. P. Bond, Chapel Hill 1957.
Wheatley, K. E. Andromaque as the Distrest mother. Romanic Rev 39 1948.
Ellis, W. D., jr. Thomas D'Urfey, the Pope-Philips quarrel and the Shepherd's week. PMLA 74 1959.
Parnell, P. E. The distrest mother, Philips' morality play. Comparative Lit 11 1959.
Winton, C. Some manuscripts by and concerning Philips. Eng Lang Notes 5 1967.

JOHN PHILIPS
1676-1709

Collections

Poems, to which is prefixed his life [by G. Sewell]. 1712, 1715, 1720, 1728, Dublin 1730, London 1744, 1762, Glasgow 1763, London 1776. Variously titled.
Poems. Ed M. G. L. Thomas, Oxford 1927. With bibliography.
Johnson 21; Anderson 6; Chalmers 8.

§ 1

The sylvan dream: or the mourning Muse. 1701.
The splendid shilling: an imitation of Milton. 1705. First ptd as In imitation of Milton in A collection of poems, viz The temple of death [etc], 1701, and in A new miscellany of original poems, ed C. Gildon 1701; pirated edn by B. Bragg, 1705.
Blenheim: a poem. 1705 (3 edns), 1709.
Cerealia: an imitation of Milton. 1706, 1706 (enlarged).
Honoratissimo viro Henrico Saint John, armigero: ode. 1707.
Ode gratulatoria Willielmo Cowper. 1707.
Cyder: a poem in two books. 1708, 1708, 1709, 1727; tr Italian, 1749, 1752.

§ 2

Johnson, S. In his Lives of the poets, 1779-81.
Harrach, L. A. Philips: Beiträge zur englischen Literatur-geschichte. Kreuznach 1906.
de Maar, H. In his A history of modern English romanticism vol 1, Oxford 1924.

MATTHEW PILKINGTON
fl. 1733

Poems on several occasions. Dublin 1730, London 1731 (rev J. Swift, with addns).
An ode to be performed at the castle of Dublin. Dublin 1734.

CHRISTOPHER PITT
1699-1748

§ 1

A poem on the death of the late Earl Stanhope. 1721.
Vida's Art of poetry, translated into English verse. 1725, 1726, 1742; rptd Chalmers 19.
Poems and translations. 1727.
An essay on Virgil's Æneid: being a translation of the first book. 1728.
The Æneid of Virgil, translated. 2 vols 1740, 1743; rptd Anderson 12, Chalmers 19.

Poems by the celebrated translator of Virgil's Aeneid. 1756.
Johnson 43; Anderson 8; Chalmers 12.

§ 2

Johnson, S. In his Lives of the poets, 1779-81.

JOHN POMFRET
1667-1702

Collections

Poems. 1699, 1702, 1707, 1710, 1710, 1716, 1724, 1727, 1735, 1736, 1740, 1751, 1773, 1790 (with remains).
Johnson 21; Anderson 6; Chalmers 8.

§ 1

An epistle to Charles, Earl of Dorset. 1690.
The sceptical Muse. 1699.
A prospect of death. [1700], 1709 (with Lady Winchilsea, Spleen).
Reason: a poem. 1700.
The choice or wish. 1700, 1700, 1701.
Two love poems. 1701.
Quae rara, chara: a poem on Panthea's confinement. 1707.

§ 2

Johnson, S. In his Lives of the poets, 1779-81.
Kellett, E. E. Pomfret's Choice. In his Reconsiderations, Cambridge 1928.

THOMAS PURNEY
1695-1728?

Collections
Works. Ed H. O. White, Oxford 1933.

§ 1

Pastorals, after the simple manner of Theocritus. 1717.
Pastorals, viz The bashful swain and Beauty and simplicity. 1717.
A full enquiry into the true nature of pastoral. 1717; ed E. R. Wasserman, Ann Arbor 1948 (Augustan Reprint Soc).
The Chevalier de St George: an heroi-comick poem in six cantos. 1718.
The last day: a poem in xii books by the late J. Bulkeley esq. 1720. Ed Purney, with critical preface.
The ordinary of Newgate's account of the behaviour, confession and last dying speech of Matthias Brinsden. 1722.
The ordinary of Newgate's account [etc] of the male-factors that were executed the 9th of November 1722. 1722.
A true account of Capt J. Massey. 1723.
The behaviour [etc] of the four malefactors that was executed May the 24th 1725. 1725.

§ 2

Whibley, C. Purney: prisoner ordinary. New Rev 12 1895.
White, H. O. Purney: a forgotten poet and critic of the eighteenth century. E & S 15 1929.

JOSIAH RELPH
1712-43

A miscellany of poems consisting of original poems, translations, pastorals in the Cumberland dialect, familiar epistles, fables, songs and epigrams, by the late Rev Josiah Relph of Sebergham, Cumberland. Glasgow 1747, London 1797 (with woodcuts by Bewick and life by T. Sanderson), Carlisle 1798, London 1805 (as Poems, humorous and sentimental).

ELIZABETH ROWE
1674–1737
Collections

Miscellaneous works, in prose and verse, the greater part now first published. 2 vols 1739, 1749, 1750, 1756, 1772, 4 vols 1796 (enlarged). With life by Theophilus Rowe and poems by Thomas Rowe.

§ 1

Poems on several occasions by Philomela. 1696, 1737 (as Philomela: or poems by Mrs E. Singer [Rowe]).
Friendship in death, in twenty letters from the dead to the living. 1728, 1733, 1736 (enlarged), 1738; tr French, 1740, 1753; German, 1745.
Letters moral and entertaining. 3 pts 1729–33.
The history of Joseph: a poem in eight books. 1736, 1738 (in 10 bks), 1744 etc, Boston 1807.
Devout exercises of the heart. Rev and ed I. Watts 1737, 1738 etc, Newry 1762, Edinburgh 1766, 1781, Dublin 1771.

§ 2

Vetter, T. Die göttliche Rowe. Zürich 1894.
Hughes, H. S. Elizabeth Rowe and the Countess of Hertford. PMLA 59 1944.
Richetti, J. J. Mrs Elizabeth Rowe: the novel as polemic. PMLA 82 1967.

RICHARD SAVAGE
1697?–1742
Bibliographies

Tracy, C. Some uncollected authors 36: Savage. Book Collector 12 1963.
Hinton, P. F. Savage's Various poems 1761. Book Collector 13 1964.

Collections

Various poems: The wanderer, The triumph of mirth and health and The bastard. 1761.
Works, with an account of the life and writings by Samuel Johnson. 2 vols 1775, 1777, Dublin 1777.
Poetical works. Ed C. Tracy, Cambridge 1962.
Johnson 45; Anderson 8; Chalmers 11.

§ 1

The convocation, or a battle of pamphlets: a poem. 1717.
Love in a veil: a comedy. 1719. Produced at Drury Lane 17 June 1718. Tr from Calderón.
The tragedy of Sir Thomas Overbury. 1724, 1777 (altered by W. Woodfall). Produced at Drury Lane 12 June 1723.
Miscellaneous poems and translations by several hands, publish'd by Savage. 1726, 1728 (with Savage's account of his early life).
A poem sacred to the glorious memory of our late King George. 1727, Dublin 1727.
Nature in perfections: or the mother unveil'd. 1728.
An author to be lett, by Iscariot Hackney. 1729; ed J. Sutherland, Los Angeles 1960 (Augustan Reprint Soc). With Pope.
The wanderer: a poem in five cantos. 1729.

Verses occasion'd by the Viscountess Tyrconnel's recovery at Bath. 1730.
A poem to the memory of Mrs Oldfield. 1730. Perhaps by Savage.
An epistle to the Right Honourable Sir Robert Walpole. 1732.
A collection of pieces in verse and prose, on the occasion of the Dunciad. 1732.
The volunteer laureat: a poem to her Majesty on her birthday. 1732. Similar verses yearly to 1738.
On the departure of the Prince and Princess of Orange: a poem. 1734.
The progress of a divine: a satire. 1735. Verse.
A poem on the birth-day of the Prince of Wales. 1735.
Of public spirit in regard to public works: an epistle. 1737, 1739. Verse.
A poem sacred to the memory of her Majesty. 1738.
London and Bristol compar'd: a satire. 1744.

§ 2

The life of Mr Richard Savage. 1727, 1728, 1728.
Johnson, S. An account of the life of Mr Richard Savage. 1744 etc; rev in his Lives of the poets vol 3, 1781.
Sutherland, J. R. TLS 1 Jan 1938.
Carrigan, E. Savage. TLS 25 Sept 1943.
Poet and interloper: Savage. TLS 31 July 1943.
Bergler, E. Samuel Johnson's life of the poet Savage: a paradigm for a type. Amer Imago 4 1947.
Tracy, C. The artificial bastard: a biography of Savage. Cambridge Mass 1953.
—— More poems by Savage. N & Q Dec 1965.
McKillop, A. D. Letters from Aaron Hill to Savage. N & Q Sept 1954.
Boyce, B. Johnson's life of Savage and its literary background. SP 53 1956.
Shugrue, M. Savage in the columns of Applebee's original Weekly Journal. N & Q Feb 1961.

GEORGE SEWELL
1690?–1726
Collections

Posthumous works; to which are added Poems on several occasions publish'd in his lifetime. Ed Gregory Sewell 1728.

§ 1

The patriot: a poem. 1712.
The life and character of Mr John Philips. 1712, 1715, 1720 etc.
Observations upon [Addison's] Cato. 1713.
An epistle from Sempronia to Cethegus. 1713.
A true account of the life and writings of Thomas Burnet. 1715, 1715.
A vindication of the English stage, exemplified in Cato. 1716.
The whole works of Dr Archibald Pitcairne, done from the Latin by Sewell and J. T. Desaguliers. 1717.
Poems of Henry Howard Earl of Surrey. 1717. Ed Sewell.
The proclamation of Cupid or a defence of women: a poem from Chaucer. 1718.
The tragedy of Sir Walter Raleigh. 1719, 1719, Dublin 1719, 1722 (with a new scene), 1745. Produced at Lincoln's Inn Fields 16 Jan 1719.
Poems on several occasions. 1719.
A new collection of original poems. 1720.
Verses to the Right Honble the Lord Carteret. 1721.
Ovid's Metamorphoses: the second edition, with great improvements by Mr Sewell. 1724.
Venus and Adonis and miscellany poems, revised and collected by Mr Sewell. Vol 7 of Works of Shakespeare by Mr Pope, 1725 etc.
The tragedy of Richard the I King of England; to which

are annexed some other papers. 1728. An unfinished play ed Gregory Sewell.

Sewell also wrote a large number of controversial squibs and pamphlets and contributed to periodical essay pbns of Steele and Addison.

THOMAS SHERIDAN
1687-1738
Collections

Poems by the celebrated translator of Virgil's Aeneid. 1756.
Johnson 43; Anderson 8; Chalmers 12.

§ I

An easy introduction of grammar in English for the understanding of the Latin tongue. Dublin 1714.
Ars pun-ica, sive flos linguarum: the art of punning, or the flower of languages. Dublin 1719, London 1720 (3 edns). Ascribed to Swift, but mainly attributed to Sheridan.
Prologue spoke at the Theatre-Royal in behalf of the poor weavers of Dublin. Dublin 1721.
Mr Sheridan's prologue to the Greek play of Phaedra and Hypolitus. Dublin 1721.
The wonderful wonder of wonders. Dublin 1721.
The blunderful blunder of blunders: being an answer to the Wonderful wonder of wonders. Dublin 1721. Both pieces attributed to Sheridan.
To the Honourable Mr D[ick] T[igh,] great pattern of piety. Dublin 1725. Attributed to Sheridan.
Philoctetes. Dublin 1725. Tr from Sophocles.
A true and faithful inventory of the goods belonging to Dr Sw—t, Vicar of Lara Cor, upon lending his house to the Bishop of M[eath] till his own was built. Dublin 1726.
Tom Punsibi's letter to Dean Swift. Dublin 1727.
To the Right Honourable the Lord Viscount Mont-Cassell this fable is humbly dedicated by a person who had some share in his education. 1727.
The satyrs of Persius, translated into English. Dublin 1728, London 1728, 1739.
The intelligencer. Dublin 1728, London 1729. A periodical written with Swift.
An answer to the Christmas box, in defence of Doctor D[ela]n—y, by R[uper]t B[arbe]r. Dublin 1729. Attributed to Sheridan.
A new simile for the ladies with useful annotations. Dublin 1732.
The satires of Juvenal translated [into prose]. 1739, 1745, Dublin 1769, Cambridge 1777.
Verses by Sheridan are also to be found in the Pope-Swift Miscellanies; early edns of Swift's works; John Barrett, Essay on the early part of the life of Swift, 1808; and Poems of Swift, ed H. Williams 1937.

Letters

Correspondence of Jonathan Swift. Ed H. Williams vols 4-5, Oxford 1965.

JOHN SMALLWOOD
fl. 1705

§ I

A congratulatory poem to his Grace the Duke of Marlborough on his glorious success and victories over the French and Bavarians. 1704; rptd in Horn, below.

§ 2

Horn, R. D. The authorship of the first Blenheim panegyric. HLQ 24 1961.

JONATHAN SMEDLEY
1671-1729?

An hue and cry after Dr S[wif]t, occasion'd by a true and exact copy of part of his own diary found in his pocket-book wherein he has set down a faithful account of himself and of all that happen'd to him for the last week of his life. 1714 (3 edns), 1748.
Rational and historical account of the principles [of] the late rebellion and the present controversies of the English clergy. 1718.
A familiar epistle to his Excellency Charles Earl of Sunderland. 1720.
Poems on several occasions. 1721, 1730. Not all by Smedley.
Dean Smedley's petition to the Duke of Grafton. 1724.
A satyr: canit ante victoriam triumphum. 1725.
A Christmas invitation to the Lord Carteret. Dublin 1725.
The metamorphoses: demonstrated in the persons of P[o]pe and Sw[if]t. 1728.
Gulliveriana, or a fourth volume of miscellanies: being a sequel of the three volumes published by Pope and Swift. 1728.
Smedley also pbd sermons and contributed to Miscellaneous poems, ed M. Concanen 1724.

EDMUND SMITH
1672-1710

See col 800, below.

JOHN SMITH
fl. 1713

Poems upon several occasions. 1713.

WILLIAM SOMERVILE
1675-1742
Bibliographies

Fleeman, J. D. Somervile's The chace 1735. PBSA 58 1964.

Collections

Poetical works. 2 vols Glasgow 1766.
Johnson 47; Anderson 8; Chalmers 11.

§ I

The two springs: a fable. 1725.
Occasional poems translations, fables, tales etc. 1727.
The chace: a poem. 1735 (3 edns), Dublin 1735, London 1749 ('in heroick verse, written originally in blank verse'), 1757, 1767, Birmingham 1767 (with Hobbinol), London 1773, 1786 etc, 1796 (with essay by J. Aikin), 1802 (with engravings by T. Bewick from designs by J. Bewick); ed R. F. Sharp 1896; ed A. H. Higginson, New York 1929.
Hobbinol, or the rural games: a burlesque poem in blank verse. 1740 (3 edns), Dublin 1740, Glasgow 1755, London 1757, 1768 etc.
Field sports: a poem. 1742, Dublin 1742.
A collection of miscellaneous poetry. Ed F. G. Waldron 1802 (includes The wicker chair, a first version of Hobbinol).

§ 2

Johnson, S. In his Lives of the poets, 1779-81.
Havens, R. D. Somervile's earliest poem. MLN 41 1926.
Guide to the hunt: Somervile. TLS 18 July 1942.

GEORGE ALEXANDER STEVENS
1710–84

Collections

The cabinet of fancy. 1780.
Works. 1807, 1823 (with life by W. H. Badham).

§ 1

Religion, or the libertine repentant: a rhapsody. 1751.
Distress upon distress or tragedy in true taste: a heroi-comi-parodo-tragedi-farcical burlesque in two acts. 1752, Dublin 1752.
The choice spirit's feast: a comic ode. 1754.
The birthday of folly: an heroi-comical poem by Peter. 1755, Whitehaven 1771 (pirated as The choice spirit's chaplet, or a poesy from Parnassus: being a select collection of songs from the most approved authors many of them written and the whole compiled by G.A.S. esq).
Albion restored, or time turned occulist: a masque. 1758.
The history of Tom Fool. 2 vols 1760. A novel.
The beauties of the magazines selected. 3 vols 1762–4. Ed Stevens.
The dramatic history of Master Edward, Miss Anne and others the extraordinaries of these times. 1763, 1785, 1786.
The celebrated lecture on heads which has been exhibited upwards of one hundred successive nights and met with the most universal applause. 1765, 1765, 1770, 1772 (with An essay on satirical entertainments), 1784.
The French flogged or the British sailors in America: a farce in two acts. 1767.
The court of Alexander: an opera in two acts. 1770, 1770, Dublin 1770. Produced at Covent Garden 5 Jan 1770.
The storm: or dangers of the sea. 1770.
The fair orphan: a comic opera of three acts. 1771.
Songs, comic and satyrical. Oxford 1772, Dublin 1778, Oxford 1782, London 1788, 1801.
The trip to Portsmouth: a comic sketch of one act with songs. 1773. Produced at Haymarket 11 Oct 1773.
Songs in the Trip to Portsmouth. 1773.
The Vicar and Moses: a new song. 1780.
The songs [etc] in the Cabinet of fancy: or evening exhibition. 1780.
A lecture on heads written by Stevens with additions by Mr Pilon. 1785, 1787, Dublin 1788, London 1799, 1800, 1802, 1806, 1808 (illustr Rowlandson), 1821, 1823.
The adventures of a speculist: or a journey through London. 2 vols 1788. Compiled from the papers of Stevens, with a life.
Management: a dramatic satire by Humphrey Hum esq, dedicated without permission to a mighty lessee from the unpublished ms of the late G. A. Stevens. [1820?].

§ 2

Jones, S. In his Biographia dramatica vol 1, 1812.

WILLIAM THOMPSON
1712–67

Collections

Anderson 10; Chalmers 15.

§ 1

An hymn to May. 1740.
Sickness: a poem in three books. 3 pts 1745.
Poems on several occasions; to which is added Gondibert and Birtha: a tragedy. 2 vols Oxford 1751–7.
Hall's Virgidemiarum. Oxford 1753. Ed Thompson.

Gratitude: a poem on the Countess of Pomfret's benefactions. Oxford 1756, London 1756.
The works of William Browne. 3 vols 1772. Ed Thompson.

ISAAC THOMSON
fl. 1731

A collection of poems occasionally writ on several subjects. Newcastle-upon-Tyne 1731.

JOSEPH THURSTON
fl. 1730

Poems on several occasions. 1729.
The toilette, in three books. 1730, 1730.
The fall, in four books. 1732.

THOMAS TICKELL
1685–1740

Bibliographies

Butt, J. E. Notes for a bibliography of Tickell. Bodleian Quart Record 5 1928.
—— A first edition of Tickell's Colin and Lucy. Bodleian Quart Record 6 1931.
Tickell, R. E. In his Tickell and the eighteenth-century poets, 1931.

Collections

The works of the most celebrated minor poets. Vol 2, 1749.
The works of celebrated authors, of whose writings there are but small remains. Vol 2, 1750.
Poetical works. 1796, Boston 1854.
Johnson 26; Anderson 8; Chalmers 11.

§ 1

Oxford: a poem. 1707.
A poem to his Excellency the Lord Privy-Seal on the prospect of peace. 1713 (5 edns), 1714.
The prologue to the University of Oxford. 1713, 1714 (in R. Steele, Poetical miscellanies).
An imitation of the prophecy of Nereus, from Horace, book I, ode XV. 1715, 1715, 1716.
The first book of Homer's Iliad. 1715.
An epistle from a lady in England to a gentleman at Avignon. 1717 (5 edns), 1721 (in A miscellaneous collection of poems).
An ode occasioned by his Excellency the Earl Stanhope's voyage to France. 1718.
An ode inscribed to the Right Honourable the Earl of Sunderland at Windsor. 1720.
The works of the Right Honourable Joseph Addison esq. 4 vols 1721 etc. Ed with preface by Tickell.
Kensington Garden. 1722.
To Sir Godfrey Kneller, at his country seat. 1722.
Lucy and Colin: a song written in imitation of William and Margaret. Dublin 1725, 1729 (in The musical miscellany vol 1), 1730 (in The merry musician).
A poem in praise of the horn-book. 1726 (in D. Lewis, Miscellaneous poems), Dublin 1728, London 1732.
On her Majesty's re-building the lodgings of the Black Prince and Henry V at Queen's-College, Oxford. 1733.
Tickell also contributed to Tonson's Poetical miscellanies, 6th pt 1709; Spectator; Guardian; Steele, Poetical miscellanies, 1714; Poems on several occasions, 1717; Cytheria: or new poems, 1723 etc; minor pieces ptd from mss in R. E. Tickell, Life, 1931, below.

§ 2

Johnson, S. In his Lives of the poets, 1779–81.
Tickell, R. E. Tickell and the eighteenth-century poets. 1931.

ELIZABETH TOLLET
1694–1754

Poems on several occasions, with Anne Boleyn to King Henry VIII: an epistle. 1755.

JOSEPH TRAPP
1679–1747

§ 1

Aedes badmintonianae: a poem. 1701.
A prologue to the University of Oxford. 1703.
The tragedy of King Saul, written by a deceased person of honour. 1703. Attributed to Trapp.
Abra-mule, or love and empire: a tragedy. 1704, 1708, Hague 1711, London 1720, Dublin 1725, London 1727, 1728, 1735, 1743 etc. Produced at Lincoln's Inn Fields 18 Jan 1704.
Praelectiones poeticae. 2 vols 1711–15; tr W. Clarke and W. Bowyer 1742.
Peace: a poem. 1713, 1713, Dublin 1713.
The Aeneis of Virgil translated. 2 vols 1718–20, 3 vols 1731 (complete works).
Thoughts upon the four last things: death, heaven, judgment, hell. 4 pts 1734–5, 1 vol 1749.
Paradisus amissus latine redditus. 2 vols 1741–2.
Anacreontis carmina accurate edita. 1742.
Trapp also pbd many sermons and controversial pamphlets.

§ 2

Freimarck, V. Trapp's conception of metaphor. PQ 29 1950.
Moran, B. The source of Trapp's Abramule. MLR 53 1958.

H. TRAVERS
fl. 1730

Miscellaneous poems and translations. 1731, York 1740.

EDWARD ('NED') WARD
1667–1731

See col 1091, below.

THOMAS WARTON the elder
1688?–1745

Bibliographies

Willoughby, E. E. The chronology of the poems of Thomas Warton the elder. JEGP 30 1931.

Collections

Poems on several occasions. 1748, New York 1930 (facs).
The three Wartons: a choice of their verse. Ed E. Partridge 1927.

§ 2

Bishop, D. H. The father of the Wartons. South Atlantic Quart 16 1917.
Kirschbaum, L. The imitations of Thomas Warton the elder. PQ 22 1943. *See* 24 1945.

ISAAC WATTS
1674–1748

Collections

Works. Ed D. Jennings and P. Doddridge 6 vols 1753; rev G. Burder 6 vols 1810–11, 9 vols Leeds 1812–13.
A guide to prayer. Ed H. Escott 1948.
Johnson 46; Anderson 9; Chalmers 13.

§ 1

Horae lyricae, poems chiefly of the lyric kind. 1706, 1709 (enlarged), 1715, 1722, 1727, 1731, 1737, 1743, Boston 1748 etc; ed R. Southey 1834, 1837.
Hymns and spiritual songs. 1707, 1709 (enlarged), 1716, 1720, 1723, 1725, 1728, 1734, 1740, 1744, 1748 etc; ed S. L. Bishop 1962.
Divine songs attempted in easy language for the use of children. 1715, 1716, 1719, Boston 1719, London 1720, 1727, 1728, 1729 etc. For later edns see W. M. Stone, Divine and moral songs of Watts, New York 1918.
The psalms of David imitated. 1719 etc.
Sermons on various subjects. 3 vols 1721–7. Includes hymns.
Logic. 1725.
The knowledge of the heavens and earth. 1726.
Reliquiae juveniles: miscellaneous thoughts in prose and verse. 1734, 1737, 1742, 1766 etc.
The improvement of the mind. 1741.
Watts also pbd many sermons and theological works; see col 1668, below.

§ 2

Johnson, S. In his Lives of the poets, 1779–81.
Milner, T. Life, times and correspondence of Watts. 1834.
Hood, E. P. Watts: his life and writings. 1875.
Wright, T. In his Lives of the British hymn writers vol 3, 1914.
Pinto, V. de S. Watts and the adventurous Muse. E & S 20 1935.
—— Watts and his poetry. Wessex 3 1935.
—— Watts and Blake. RES 20 1944.
—— William Blake, Watts and Mrs Barbauld. In his Divine vision, 1957.
—— Libertines and puritans: a note on some lyrics of the late seventeenth and early eighteenth centuries. N & Q June 1960.
Pratt, A. S. Watts and his gift of books to Yale College. New Haven 1938.
Manning, B. L. The hymns of Wesley and Watts: five informal papers. 1942.
Davis, A. P. Watts: his life and works. New York 1943.
Cairns, W. T. The constituents of a good hymn. In his Religion of Dr Johnson and other essays, Oxford 1946.
Laird, J. Concerning Watts. In his Philosophical incursions into English literature, Cambridge 1946.
P., A. S. A letter from Watts. Yale Lib Gazette 22 1947.
Parry, K. L. Watts: hymn-writer and divine. Listener 2 Dec 1948.
Stevenson, R. Watts in America: bicentenary reflections on the growth of Watts's reputation in America. Harvard Theological Rev 41 1948.
—— Dr Watts' 'flights of fancy'. Harvard Theological Rev 42 1949.
Davidson, J. Emily Dickinson and Watts. Boston Public Lib Quart 6 1954.
Birell, T. A. Sarbiewski, Watts and the later metaphysical tradition. E Studies 37 1956.
Rupp, E. G. Six makers of English religion 1500–1700. New York 1957.
Tucker, S. I. Dr Watts looks at the language. N & Q July–Aug 1959.

Escott, H. Watts, hymnographer: a study of the beginnings, development and philosophy of the English hymns. 1962.

Arens, J. C. Sarbiewski's Ode against tears imitated by Lovelace, Yalden and Watts. Neophilologus 47 1963.

Steese, P. B. Dennis's influence on Watts's preface to Horae lyricae. PQ 42 1963.

Leicester, J. H. Dr Johnson and Watts. New Rambler 15 1964.

England, M. W. Emily Dickinson and Watts: Puritan hymnodists. BNYPL Feb 1965.

Stephenson, W. E. Watts and Bishop Wilkins's Ecclesiastes. N & Q Dec 1966.

LEONARD WELSTED
1688–1747
Collections

Works in verse and prose. Ed J. Nichols 1787.

§ 1

A poem occasioned by the late famous victory of Audenard. 1709.

The Duke of Marlborough's arrival: a poem. 1709.

A poem to the memory of the incomparable Mr [John] Philips. 1710.

Dionysius Longinus on the sublime; with some remarks on the English poets. 1712.

An epistle to Mr Steele on the King's accession. 1714. Verse.

An ode on the birth-day of the Prince of Wales [etc]. 1716.

Palaemon to Caelia, at Bath: or the triumvirate. 1717. Verse.

An epistle to his Grace the Duke of Chandos. 1720. Verse.

A prologue to the town, as it was spoken at the theatre in little Lincoln's-Inn fields. 1721. Verse.

An epistle to the late Dr Garth. 1722. Verse.

Epistles, odes etc written on several subjects. 1724, 1725. Preliminary essay rptd in Critical essays of the eighteenth century, ed W. H. Durham, New Haven 1915.

Oikographia: a poem. 1725.

An ode to Major General Wade. 1726.

A hymn to the creator, by a gentleman on the death of his only daughter. 1726.

The dissembled wanton, or my son get money: a comedy. 1727, 1728, 1787. Produced at Lincoln's Inn Fields 14 Dec 1726.

A discourse to Sir Robert Walpole; to which is annex'd Proposals for translating the whole works of Horace, with a specimen. 1727.

One epistle to Mr A. Pope [with James Moore Smythe]. 1730; ed J. V. Guerinot in Two poems against Pope, Los Angeles 1965 (Augustan Reprint Soc).

Of false-fame: an epistle to the Earl of Pembroke. 1732. Verse.

Of dulness and scandal, occasion'd by the character of Lord Timon, in Mr Pope's Epistle to the Earl of Burlington. 1732, 1732. Verse.

The scheme and conduct of providence from the creation to the coming of the Messiah. 1736.

The summum bonum: or wisest philosophy. 1741. Verse.

§ 2

Horne, C. J. Welsted's Apple-pye. N & Q 17 Nov 1945.

Fineman, D. A. Welsted: gentleman poet of the Augustan age. Philadelphia 1950.

Williams, A. Welsted's lines to the Duke of Buckingham. N & Q Nov 1955.

CHARLES WESLEY
1707–88
See col 1637, below.

JOHN WESLEY
1703–91
See col 1630, below.

SAMUEL WESLEY the younger
1691–1739
Collections

Poems on several occasions. 1736, Cambridge 1743 (with addns pbd separately in Some account of the life of Samuel Wesley, with a few short poems never before published, 1743); ed J. Nichols 1862 (with unpbd pieces and a life by W. Nichols).

§ 1

Neck or nothing, a consolatory letter from Mr D[u]nt[o]n to Mr C[ur]ll. 1716.

The battle of the sexes: a poem [with preface by T. Cooke]. 1723, 1724, Dublin 1724, London 1738, 1740.

The story of the three children. 1724. Verse.

The pig and the mastiff: two tales. 1725, 1727, 1735. Verse.

The Iliad in a nutshell: or Homer's Battle of the frogs and mice. 1726. Trn of Batrachomyomachia.

The prisons open'd: a poem. 1729.

The parish priest: a poem upon a clergyman lately deceas'd. 1732, 1732.

The Christian poet. 1735.

Four tales after the manner of the ingenious Matt Prior, viz The pig, Mastif, Grocer, Cobler. [1735?]. Verse.

Wesley also contributed to D. Lewis, Miscellanies, 1726 *and* 1730.

GILBERT WEST
1703–56
Collections

Johnson 56; Anderson 9; Chalmers 13.

§ 1

Stowe, the gardens of the Right Honourable Richard Lord Viscount Cobham. 1732, 1732.

A canto of the Faery Queen [imitated]. 1739.

The institution of the Order of the Garter: a dramatick poem. 1742; altered by D. Garrick 1771.

Observations on the resurrection of Jesus Christ. 1747, Dublin 1747, London 1749, 1754, 1767 etc; tr German, 1748.

The odes of Pindar, with several other pieces translated. 1749, 1751; rptd Anderson vol 12.

Education: a poem in two cantos, written in imitation of the style and manner of Spenser's Faery Queen, canto the first. 1751. All pbd.

Two orations [by Thucydides] in praise of Athenians slain in battle. 1759, 1768. Plato's tr West.

§ 2

Johnson, S. In his Lives of the poets, 1779–81.

JOHN WHALEY
1710–45

Blenheim: a poem. 1728.

A collection of poems. 1732.

A collection of original poems and translations. 1745.

Both collections contain many poems by Sneyd Davies 1709–69.

PAUL WHITEHEAD
1710–74
Bibliographies

Todd, W. B. Whitehead's State dunces 1733. Book
Collector 9 1960.

Collections

The poems and miscellaneous compositions of Whitehead,
with notes on his writings and his life written by Captain
Edward Thompson. 1777.
Johnson 70; Anderson 10; Chalmers 16.

§ 1

The state dunces: a satire. 1733, 1733; pt 2, 1733, 1733.
Verse.
The state dunces inscribed to Mr Pope, in two parts.
1733 (3 edns).
Manners: a satire. 1739 (4 edns). Verse.
Satires written by Mr Whitehead, viz I: Manners, written
in 1738; II: The state dunces, written in 1733. 1739,
1748.
The state of Rome under Nero and Domitian. 1739. Tr
from Juvenal and Persius.
The gymnasiad: or boxing match. 1744.
An apology for the conduct of Mrs Theresia Constantia
Phillips. 3 vols 1748. Ed Whitehead.
The case of the Hon Alexander Murray esq. 1751.
The history of an old lady and her family. 1754, 1754.
An epistle to Doctor Thompson. 1755, Dublin 1755,
London 1756. Verse.
Satires, I: Manners; II: The state dunces; III: Honour;
IV: The gymnasiad; V: An epistle to Dr Thompson.
1760.
The rehearsal with the new occasional prologue by Paul
Whitehead. 1768.
Conduct of the four managers of Covent Garden Theatre
stated. 1768.

§ 2

A friendly epistle to the author of the State dunces. 1733.

ANNA WILLIAMS
1706–83

Miscellanies in prose and verse. 1766. Includes an advertisement and some pieces by Dr Johnson.

SIR CHARLES HANBURY WILLIAMS
1708–59
Collections

A collection of poems principally consisting of the most
celebrated pieces of Sir Charles Hanbury Williams,
Knight of the Bath. 1763, 1775 (enlarged as Odes),
1780, 1784, 1785, 1786.
The works of the Right Honourable Sir Chas Hanbury
Williams KB from the originals in the possession of his
grandson with notes by Horace Walpole, Earl of
Orford. Ed E. Jeffrey 3 vols 1822.

§ 1

An ode to the Duke of Argyll, to which is added one to the
Earl of Marchmont. 1740.
A dialogue between G[ile]s E[arl]e and B[ub]b D[oding-
to]n. 1741. Verse.
The country girl: an ode. 1742, 1742.

A new ode to a great number of great men newly made.
[1742].
An ode humbly inscribed to the Right Honourable
W[illiam Pulteney] E[arl] of B[ath]. [1742].
An epistle to the Right Honourable William Pultney esq
upon his late conduct in public affairs. 1742.
The old coachman: a new ballad to which is added
Labour in vain. 1742, 1742.
Letter to Mr Dodsley, bookseller in Pall Mall. 1743.
The wife and the nurse: a new ballad. 1743.
S[andy]s and J[ekyl]l: a new ballad. 1743 (3 edns).
Eog S–y's budget open'd. 1743.
Plain thoughts in plain language: a new ballad. 1743.
Solomon's porch S—s and W—r. 1743.
Peter and my Lord Quidam. 1743.
An ode from the E[arl] of B[ath] to ambition. nd.
Old England's Te deum. nd.
Place book for the year seventeen-hundred forty-five: a
new ballad. 1744–5.
An ode to the Right Honourable Lord Viscount Lonsdale.
1745.
The heroes: a new ballad. 1745.
An ode imitated from ode xi, book 2d of Horace. 1745.
Sir C.H.W. to E[dwar]d H[usse]y esq. 1746.
A new ballad on Lord D[o]n[erai]l[e]'s altering his chapel
at Gr[ov]e into a kitchen. 1746.
An ode to the Honourable H[enry] F[o]x on the marriage
of the Du[ches]s of M[ancheste]r to H[us]s[e]y esq.
1746, 1746.
An ode addressed to the author of the Conquered Duchess.
1746.
H[usse]y to Sir C. H. W—s: or the rural reflections of a
Welch poet. 1746.
An ode to the Right Honourable Stephen Poyntz esq.
1746.
The unembarrassed countenance: a new ballad. 1746.
Tar water: a ballad inscribed to the Rt Hon Philip Earl of
Chesterfield. 1747 (3 edns).
Williams also contributed to The summer miscellany, 1742;
The new ministry 1742; The foundling hospital for wit
nos 1–6 1743–8; Dodsley's Collection vols 4–5, 1758;
and The new foundling hospital for wit vols 1, 3–4, 6
1768.

Letters

Correspondence de Catharine II et de Sir C. Hanbury
Williams 1756–7. Moscow 1909. In Russian and
French.
Correspondence of Catherine the Great, when Grand-
Duchess, with Sir Charles Hanbury Williams. 1928.

§ 2

Coxe, W. In his Historical tour in Monmouthshire, 1801.
Hutchinson, J. In his Herefordshire biographies, 1890.

ANNE FINCH,
COUNTESS OF WINCHILSEA
1666–1720
Collections

Miscellany poems on several occasions written by a lady.
1713, 1714 (as Poems on several occasions).
Poems. Ed M. Reynolds, Chicago 1903.
Poems and extracts, chosen by William Wordsworth [in
1819] for an album. 1905.
Poems. Ed J. M. Murry 1928. A selection.
Minor poets of the eighteenth century. Ed H. I'A.
Fausset 1930 (EL).

§ 1

The spleen: a Pindarique ode by a lady; together with A
prospect of death: a Pindarique essay [by J. Pomfret].

1709. Spleen first ptd in C. Gildon, New miscellany, 1701.

Free-thinkers: a poem in dialogue. 1711.

Lady Winchilsea also contributed to Steele's Miscellany, 1714.

§2

Reynolds, M. In her Treatment of nature in English poetry between Pope and Wordsworth, Chicago 1896.

Anderson, P. B. Mrs Manley's texts of three of Lady Winchilsea's poems. MLN 45 1930.

Brower, R. A. Lady Winchilsea and the poetic tradition of the seventeenth century. SP 42 1945.

Buxton, J. The poems of the Countess of Winchilsea. Life & Letters 65 1950.

—— In his A tradition of poetry, 1967.

GEORGE WOODWARD
fl. 1717–27
Collections

Poems on several occasions. Oxford 1730.

§1

Merton walks: or the Oxford beauties. 1717.

Poem to the glorious memory of his Sacred Majesty King George I. 1727.

THOMAS YALDEN
1670–1736
Collections

Johnson 45; Anderson 7; Chalmers 11.

§1

On the conquest of Namur: a Pindarique ode. 1695.

Aesop at court: or state fables. 1702. Verse.

An essay on the character of Sir Willoughby Aston. 1704.

The education of poor children: a sermon. 1728.

§2

Johnson, S. In his Lives of the poets, 1779–81.

H. P.

VII. LATER EIGHTEENTH-CENTURY POETRY

THOMAS GRAY
1716–71
Bibliographies etc

Cook, A. S. A concordance to the English poems of Gray. Boston 1908.

Northup, C. S. A bibliography of Gray. New Haven 1917. Lists all printings of Gray's writings and writings about him. *See* Starr, below.

Fukuhara, R. Bibliographical study of Gray. Tokyo 1933.

Starr, H. W. A bibliography of Gray 1917–51. Philadelphia 1953. A continuation of Northup, above.

Collections

The poems of Mr Gray, with memoirs prefixed. Ed W. Mason, York 1775, 1775, 2 vols Dublin 1775, 4 vols 1778, 2 vols 1807 etc. Contains posthumous poems and fragments; Mason's memoirs are largely composed from Gray's letters, many in a garbled form.

The poems of Mr Gray, with notes [and life]. Ed G. Wakefield 1786.

Poetical works. [Ed S. Jones, with life and notes] 1799, 1800 (enlarged). Contains previously uncollected poems.

Poems, with critical notes, a life of the author and an essay on his poetry. Ed J. Mitford 1814.

Works, with memoirs by William Mason, to which are subjoined extracts philosophical, political and critical. Ed T. J. Mathias 2 vols 1814. Vol 1 adds letters from Gray to Walpole to Mason's edn and life; vol 2 contains extracts from Gray's commonplace book and postscript by Mathias on Gray.

Works. Ed J. Mitford 2 vols 1816. Vol 1, poems; vol 2, letters.

Works. Ed J. Mitford 4 vols 1835–7, 1857–8. Vol 1, poems; vols 2–4, letters, many pbd for first time. Aldine edn. Gray's Correspondence with Nichols, 1843 (Letters, below) was also issued as vol 5 of this edn.

Poetical works. Ed J. Moultrie, Eton 1845, 1847 (adds An original life of Gray by J. Mitford).

Poetical works. Ed R. A. Wilmott 1854, 1883. With Parnell, Collins, Green and T. Warton.

The life and poems. Ed G. Gilfillan, Edinburgh 1855. With Johnson, Parnell and Smollett.

Works in prose and verse. Ed E. Gosse 4 vols 1884, 1902–6.

Poetical works, with introduction, life, notes and bibliography. Ed J. Bradshaw 1891.

Selections from the poetry and prose. Ed W. L. Phelps, Boston 1894.

Gray's English poems. Ed D. C. Tovey, Cambridge 1898, 1922.

Essays and criticisms. Ed C. S. Northup, Boston 1911.

The poetical works of Gray and Collins. Ed A. L. Poole, Oxford 1917, 1937 (rev L. Whibley).

Gray, Collins and their circle. Ed W. T. Williams and G. H. Vallins [1937].

Poems. Ed L. Whibley, Oxford 1939 (WC).

Poems in Latin. Ed J. Sparrow, Oxford 1941.

Complete poems, English, Latin and Greek. Ed H. W. Starr and J. R. Hendrickson, Oxford 1966.

Selected poems of Gray and William Collins. Ed A. Johnston 1967.

Poems. Ed R. H. Lonsdale 1969. With Collins and Goldsmith.

Also Johnson vol 56; Anderson vol 10; Chalmers vol 14.

Letters

See Collections, above.

The works of Lord Orford. Vol 5, 1798. Gray's letters to Walpole.

The correspondence of Gray and the Rev Norton Nicholls. 1843. Includes Nicholls's reminiscences of Gray.

The correspondence of Gray and William Mason, with letters to James Brown. Ed J. Mitford 1853, 1855 (with additional notes).

Letters. Ed D. C. Tovey 3 vols 1900–12.

The correspondence of Gray, Walpole, West and Ashton 1734–71. Ed P. Toynbee 2 vols Oxford 1915.

Correspondence. Ed P. Toynbee and L. Whibley 3 vols Oxford 1935.

Walpole's correspondence with Gray, West and Ashton. Ed W. S. Lewis, G. L. Lam and C. H. Bennett, New Haven 1948. Vols 13–14 of Yale edn of Walpole's correspondence.

Selected letters. Ed J. W. Krutch, New York 1952.

Whibley, L. A new letter by Gray. TLS 23 Oct 1937. Gray's letter to West 22 May 1737.

Starr, H. W. Pot pourri: a missing Gray letter. TLS 30 March 1951. Part of his letter to Cole 7 July 1764.

§ 1

Ode on a distant prospect of Eton College. 1747 (anon), Oxford 1924 (facs).

Ode [on the spring]; Ode on the death of a favourite cat. In Dodsley's Collection of poems, vol 2 1748 etc. Anon, with Eton ode, above.

An elegy wrote in a country church yard. 1751 (anon). 5 edns in 1751 and 8 more pbd by Dodsley 1752–71. 3rd and 8th edns rev Gray. 3rd and later edns entitled An elegy written in a country churchyard. For a full account of the mss and all printings to 1771, see edns by F. G. Stokes, Oxford 1929, and R. Fukuhara and H. Bergen, 1933. Rptd Oxford 1927 (facs); facs of 1st edn and Eton ms in edn by G. Sherburn, Los Angeles 1951 (Augustan Reprint Soc); ed H. Walpole 1938; ed D. Flower and A. N. L. Munby 1938 (in their English poetical autographs, with facs of Wharton ms); ed R. P. T. Coffin, New York 1940.

Designs by Mr R. Bentley for six poems by Mr T. Gray. 1753. Adds to the above A long story and Hymn to adversity. Rptd with Odes, 1757, 1765, 1766, 1775, 1789. Poems by Mr T. Gray. Dublin 1756. Reprints 6 poems in Bentley edn.

Odes, by Mr Gray. Strawberry Hill 1757. The Progress of poesy and The bard. See A. T. Hazen, A bibliography of the Strawberry Hill press, New Haven 1942.

Epitaph on Mrs Clerke. GM Oct 1759.

The union. Dublin 1761. Contains poems in the Bentley edn and adds the Odes, 1757.

Poems by Mr Gray. 1768, 1768, Glasgow 1768, Dublin 1768, Cork 1768, 1770, Dublin 1771, Edinburgh 1773 (British poets, vol 42), 1774 (with life), Dublin 1775, 1776, Glasgow 1777, 1778, Dublin 1779, 1779, 1786, 1790, Parma 1793. Adds The fatal sisters, The descent of Odin, and The triumphs of Owen, but omits A long story.

Ode performed in the Senate-House at Cambridge July 1 1769, at the installation of his Grace Augustus Henry Fitzroy, Duke of Grafton, Chancellor of the University. Cambridge 1769, 1769. Anon.

On Lord Holland's seat near Margate, Kent. Anon and unauthorized, as Inscription for a villa of a decayed statesman on the sea coast, in The new foundling hospital for wit pt 3, 1769.

The candidate. Apparently first pbd, without title, in London Evening Post Feb 1777. The flysheet containing the poem and once thought to have been circulated in Cambridge in 1764, when the poem was written, was printed after Gray's death, perhaps as late as 1787.

Ode on the pleasure arising from vicissitude. Ed L. Whibley 2 vols San Francisco 1933. Facs of Mason's trial printing of the text (with his own ending) ptd in his Memoirs of Gray in 1775.

§ 2

[Hill, J.] The inspector. Vol 1, 1753. First ptd in Daily Advertiser March 1751.

[Goldsmith, O.] Monthly Rev 17 Sept 1757. Review of Odes.

Stockdale, P. An enquiry into the nature and genuine laws of poetry 1778.

Johnson, S. In his Lives of the poets, 1779–81.

[Fitzthomas, ?] A cursory examination of Dr Johnson's strictures on the lyric performances of Gray. 1781.

[Tindal, W.] Remarks on Dr Johnson's life, and critical observations on the works of Gray. 1782.

Potter, R. An inquiry into some passages in Dr Johnson's Lives of the poets, particularly on the odes of Gray. 1783.

—— The art of criticism as exemplified in Dr Johnson's Lives of the poets. 1789.

[Young, J.] A criticism on the Elegy written in a country churchyard: being a continuation of Dr J—n's criticism on the poems of Gray. 1783, Edinburgh 1810.

[Scott, J.] Critical essays on some of the poems, of several English poets. 1785. On the Elegy.

Berdmore, S. Specimens of literary resemblances in the works of Pope, Gray and other celebrated writers. 1801.

Mathias, T. J. Observations on the writings and character of Mr Gray. 1815. Rptd from his edn of the Works.

Hazlitt, W. In his Lectures on the English poets, 1818.

[Bowles, W. L.] A letter to the Rt Hon Lord Byron, protesting against the immolation of Gray, Cowper and Campbell at the shrine of Pope. 1821. See Byron's Letter in reply, 1821.

Bonstetten, C. V. de. In his Souvenirs, Paris 1832.

Howitt, W. In his Homes and haunts of the British poets, 1847.

[Elwin, W.] Life and works of Gray. Quart Rev 94 1853; rptd in his Some xviii-century men of letters vol 2, 1902.

Brooke, S. A. In his Theology of the English poets, 1874.

[Courthope, W. J.] Wordsworth and Gray. Quart Rev 141 1876.

Stephen, L. Gray and his school. Cornhill Mag July 1879.

Gosse, E. Gray. 1882 (EML).

—— Gray's notes on Churchill. Trans Royal Soc of Lit 36 1918.

Arnold, M. In T. H. Ward's English poets vol 3, 1884; rptd in his Essays in criticism ser 2, 1888.

Lowell, J. R. Gray. New Princeton Rev 1 1886; rptd in Latest literary essays, Boston 1891.

Tovey, D. C. Gray and his friends. Cambridge 1890.

Kittredge, G. L. Gray's knowledge of old Norse. In Selections from Gray's poetry and prose, ed W. L. Phelps, Boston 1894.

Warren, T. H. Gray and Dante. Monthly Rev 1901; rptd in his Essays of poets and poetry, 1909.

Norton, C. E. The poet Gray as a naturalist. Boston 1903.

Farley, F. E. In his Scandinavian influences in the English romantic movement, Boston 1903.

Northup, C. S. Addison and Gray as travellers. In J. M. Hart studies, New York 1910.

—— On some editions of Gray's poems. E Studien 43 1911.

—— Gray and Chatterton. Mark Twain Quart 5 1943.

Vebel, O. Grays Einfluss auf die deutsche Lyrik im achtzehnten Jahrhundert. Heidelberg 1914.

Snyder, E. D. Gray's interest in Celtic. MP 11 1914.

—— In his Celtic revival in English literature, Cambridge Mass 1923.

Shepard, O. A youth to fortune and to fame unknown. MP 20 1923.

Reed, A. L. The background of Gray's Elegy. New York 1924.

Carlton, W. N. C. Gray's Elegy: a bibliographical and descriptive note. New York 1925 (priv ptd).

Fothergill, R. An early influence on the poetry of Gray. Revue de Littérature Comparée 9 1929.

Draper, J. W. In his Funeral elegy and the rise of English romanticism, New York 1929.

Whibley, L. Gray at Eton. Blackwood's Mag May 1929.

—— Gray, undergraduate. Blackwood's Mag Feb 1930.

—— The foreign tour of Gray and Walpole. Blackwood's Mag June 1930.

—— The candidate, by Mr Gray. TLS 21 Aug 1930.

—— Gray's satirical poems. TLS 9 Oct 1930.

—— A satirical ode by Mason. TLS 24 Sept 1931.

—— Notes on two manuscripts by Gray. E & S 23 1937. Mss of A long story.

—— Garrick's verses to Gray. TLS 12 Feb 1938.

—— Gray: Odes 1757. Bibl N & Q 2 1938.

Jones, W. P. The contemporary reception of Gray's Odes. MP 28 1930.
—— Books owned by Gray. TLS 1 June 1933.
—— The vogue of natural history in England 1750–70. Annals of Science 2 1937.
—— Gray, scholar. Cambridge Mass 1937.
—— Gray's library. MP 35 1938.
—— Mute inglorious Gray. Emory Univ Quart 11 1955.
—— Johnson and Gray: a study in literary antagonism. MP 56 1959.
—— Imitations of Gray's Elegy 1751–1800. Bull of Bibliography 23 1963.
Toynbee, P. A newly discovered draft of Gray's lines, William Shakespeare to Mrs Anne. MLR 25 1930.
—— Gray and Lady Bath in 1769. TLS 17 July 1930.
—— A Gray query. TLS 18 Sept 1930. Reply by E. Bensly 25 Sept 1930.
—— Portraits of Gray. Times 30 Oct 1930.
—— Mrs E. in Gray's letters. TLS 12 Feb 1931. Replies by E. G. Box 19 Feb, Toynbee 26 Feb 1931.
—— Gray on the origin and date of Amadis de Gaul. MLR 27 1932.
—— Walpole's memoir of Gray. MLR 27 1932.
McDermott, F. William Penn, Gray and an account of Stoke Poges. [1930].
Rylands, G. English poets and the abstract word. E & S 16 1930.
Martin, R. Chronologie de la vie et de l'oeuvre de Gray. Toulouse 1931.
—— Essai sur Gray. Paris 1934.
Ghosh, P. C. Gray and Catullus. Beiblatt zur Anglia 42 1931.
Hazard, P. Foscolo et Gray au Nouveau-Monde. Revue de Littérature Comparée 11 1931.
Brown, H. H. Gray and Shenstone. TLS 14 Jan 1932. Replies by L. Whibley 21 Jan, M. Williams 28 Jan 1932.
Correspondence of Hurd and Mason and letters of Hurd to Gray. Ed E. H. Pearce and L. Whibley, Cambridge 1932.
Kellett, E. E. Gray's Thyrsis. TLS 11 Feb 1932.
Leiser, P. Die englische Ode im Zeitalter des Klassizismus. Grossenhain 1932.
Chesterton, G. K. On Gray. In his All I survey, 1933.
Gray's Elegy. TLS 27 July 1933. See E. E. Kellett 10 Aug 1933.
Hall, E. B. The temple of tragedy. TLS 18 May 1933.
R., V. Gray's Elegy: classical reminiscence. N & Q 25 Nov 1933.
—— Gray's Elegy: a restored reading. N & Q 13 Feb 1943. Reply by Hibernicus 27 March 1943.
Strachey, L. Gray and Cowper. In his Characters and commentaries, 1933.
Micale, O. Gray e la sua influenza sulla letteratura italiana. Catania 1934.
Crick, W. Gray's Elegy. Times 20 April 1934. Reply by W. A. S. Archbold 24 April 1934.
Fisher, J. James Hammond and the quatrain of Gray's Elegy. MP 32 1935.
—— Shenstone, Gray and the moral elegy. MP 34 1937.
Ketton-Cremer, R. W. Thomas Gray. 1935.
—— In his Horace Walpole, 1940, 1946 (rev).
—— In his Norfolk portraits, 1944.
—— Advice for Richard West. TLS 29 March 1947.
—— A portrait of Gray. TLS 28 Oct 1949.
—— Gray: a biography. Cambridge 1955.
—— Thomas Gray. 1958 (Nat Book League).
—— The poet who spoke out: the letters of Gray. In Familiar letter in the eighteenth century, ed H. Anderson, P. B. Daghlian and I. Ehrenpreis, Lawrence Kansas 1966.
Empson, W. In his Some versions of pastoral, 1935.
Gray's letters. TLS 24 Oct 1935.
Van Hook, La R. New light on the classical scholarship of Gray. Amer Jnl of Philology 57 1936.

G., W. H. Gray: Odes 1757. Bibl N & Q 2 1936. Replies by J. Carter, S. N. Smith and N. van Patten, ibid.
Wright, H. G. Robert Potter as a critic of Johnson. RES 12 1936.
Yost, C. D. Poetry of the Gentleman's Magazine. Philadelphia 1936.
Leavis, F. R. The Augustan tradition and the eighteenth century. In his Revaluation, 1936.
—— Johnson and Augustanism. In his Common pursuit, 1952.
Hibernicus. Gray's Elegy: 'await' or 'awaits'? N & Q 1 May 1937.
Stokes, F. G. Gray's Elegy. TLS 6 Feb 1937.
Wolf, E. Wolfe's copy of Gray's Elegy. Colophon 2 1937.
Churchill, R. C. Gray and Matthew Arnold. Criterion 17 1938.
Eastman, J. A. Gray: in and out of the library. BNYPL Oct 1938.
Martineau, H. Gray, Baudelaire et P.-J. Toulet. Yggdrasill 25 Feb 1938.
Rothkrug, M. An apparently unrecorded appearance of Gray's Elegy 1751. In Papers in honor of A. Keogh, New Haven 1938.
Winterich, J. T. Gray's Elegy. In his Twenty-three books, Berkeley 1938.
Briggs, E. R. Gray's Elegy: a French source? Revue de Littérature Comparée 19 1939.
Rhedecynian. Imitations of Gray's Elegy. N & Q 5 Aug 1939. Replies by W. Jaggard 19 Aug; L. Thompson 16 Sept; J. W. McCain 23 Sept; F. C. White 14 Oct 1939.
Watson, H. D. Punctuation of Gray's Elegy. TLS 11 Feb 1939. See G. G. Loane 18 Feb 1939.
Evans, B. I. Gray and Blake. In his Tradition and romanticism, 1940.
Swedenberg, H. T. Gray's Journal for 1754. HLQ 3 1940.
Tillotson, G. Warton on the Rowley papers. MLR 25 1940.
—— On Gray's letters; Gray the scholar poet. In his Essays in criticism and research, Cambridge 1942.
—— Gray's Ode on the spring; Gray's Ode on a favourite cat. In his Augustan studies, 1961.
Bradner, L. In his Musae anglicanae, New York 1940.
Shuster, G. N. Collins, Gray and the return of the imagination. In his English ode from Milton to Keats, New York 1940.
Griffin, M. H. Gray, classical Augustan. Classical Jnl 36 1941.
A., C. Gray's The fatal sisters. N & Q 16 Aug 1941. See L. R. M. Strachan 6 Sept 1941.
Glasheen, F. J. Shelley's use of Gray's poetry. MLN 56 1941.
Starr, H. W. Gray as a literary critic. Philadelphia 1941.
—— An echo of L'Allegro in Gray's Bard. MLN 57 1942.
—— Gray's opinion of Parnell. MLN 57 1942.
—— Gray's revisions of his friends' poetry. JEGP 44 1945.
—— Gray's craftsmanship. JEGP 45 1946.
—— Gray and Trumbull. N & Q 14 June 1947.
—— Trumbull and Gray's Bard. MLN 62 1947.
—— A youth to fortune and to fame unknown. JEGP 48 1949.
—— John Gardiner's imitations of Gray's odes. N & Q 25 Nov, 9 Dec 1950, 6 Jan 1951.
—— Spanish translations of Gray's Elegy. N & Q 12 May 1951
—— A central-American translation of Gray's Elegy. N & Q 10 May 1952.
—— A paraphrase of Martial by Thomas Gray? N & Q Oct 1954.
—— Dickens's parody of Gray's Elegy. Dickensian 51 1955.
—— and J. R. Hendrickson. The final couplet of Gray's Candidate. N & Q Feb 1961.
—— A mistaken reading in Gray's Vah, tenero. N & Q Feb 1961.

—— Two poems attributed to Gray. N & Q Feb 1961.

—— Supplementary note on Gray's Gratia magna. N & Q Nov 1967.

Botting, R. B. Gray and Smart. MLN 57 1942.

Lauritis, J. A. Stanza by Gray. Saturday Rev of Lit 26 Dec 1942.

Vivante, L. A creative principle in Collins and Gray. Comparative Lit Stud 8 1942.

Osgood, C. G. Lady Knight and her Boswell. Princeton Univ Lib Chron 4 1943.

Brodribb, C. W. Gray's so-called prophecy of aerial warfare. N & Q 13 Feb 1943.

Halsband, I. R. A parody of Gray. PQ 22 1943. Two odes, 1760, by Robert Lloyd and George Colman the elder.

Bell, C. F. Gray and the fine arts. E & S 30 1944.

Gudger, E. W. Two fishing cats that made history. Natural History 53 1944. On Bentley's illustrations 1753.

B., D. G. Byron, Gray and Dante. N & Q 16 June 1945.

Cecil, D. The poetry of Gray. Proc Br Acad 31 1945; rptd in Yale Rev 36 1947; and in his Poets and story-tellers, 1949.

—— School-days of Gray. Life & Letters Dec 1947; rptd in his Two quiet lives, 1948.

—— Gray at Cambridge. Life & Letters Jan 1948; rptd in his Two quiet lives, 1948.

Eastwood, S. K. Horace Walpole. N & Q 28 July 1945.

Garrod, H. W. Notes on the composition of Gray's Elegy. In Essays on the eighteenth century presented to David Nichol Smith, Oxford 1945.

Gunn, D. General Wolfe and Gray's Elegy. N & Q 20 Oct 1945.

Hazen, A. T. Bentley's Gray. TLS 3 Feb 1945.

—— New steps in typography. In The age of Johnson: essays presented to C. B. Tinker, New Haven 1949.

Russell, J. Gray. Cornhill Mag 161 1945.

Steuert, Dom H. Two Augustan studies. Dublin Rev 216 1945. On Gray and Peacock.

Newman, W. M. When curfew tolled the knell. Nat Rev 127 1946.

Brooks, C. Gray's storied urn. In his Well wrought urn, New York 1947.

Gray's cookery notes in holograph. In W. Verral, The cook's paradise, ed R. L. Mégroz 1948.

Mackerness, E. D. Gray. Contemporary Rev Sept 1948.

—— The progress of an Italophile: Gray and music. Italian Stud 12 1957.

Capetanakis, D. Gray and Walpole. In his Shores of darkness, New York 1949.

Bland, D. S. Gray and the spirit of romanticism. Cambridge Jnl Dec 1949.

Eaves, T. C. D. The second edition of Gray's Ode on the death of a favourite cat. PQ 28 1949.

—— Further pursuit of Selima. PQ 30 1951.

Foerster, D. M. Gray. In The age of Johnson: essays presented to C. B. Tinker, New Haven 1949.

Senhouse, R. Occasional memorandums being extracts from a journal for the year 1767. Stanford Dingley 1950.

P., H. Gray's Elegy. Explicator 8 1950. Replies by T. C. Hoepfner, ibid; R. Rapin 9 1951.

Baldi, S. L'unità sentimentale dell' Elegia di Gray. Rivista di Letterature Moderne new ser 1 1950.

Bateson, F. W. Gray's Elegy reconsidered. In his English poetry, 1950.

H., R. V. Gray's The progress of poesy. Explicator 9 1951. Reply by A. Dickson, ibid.

Thompson, K. F. Gray's Eton Ode. Explicator 9 1951.

Ellis, F. H. Gray's Elegy: the biographical problem in literary criticism. PMLA 66 1951.

Gaskell, P. The first editions of William Mason. Cambridge 1951 (Cambridge Bibl Soc monograph).

Hussey, M. Gray's Favourite cat: additional publication. N & Q 10 Nov 1951.

Jones, H. W. A new allusion in Gray's Elegy? N & Q 28 April 1951. Reply by J. C. Maxwell 9 June 1951.

Brown, T. J. English literary autographs vii: Gray. Book Collector 2 1953.

Roberts, S. C. Gray of Pembroke. Glasgow 1953; rptd in his Dr Johnson and others, Cambridge 1958.

Glazier, L. Gray's Elegy. Univ Kansas City Rev 19 1953.

Smith, H. R. Gray and his Italian teacher. N & Q March 1953.

Brooks, E. L. Gray's 'civil young farmer' of Grange. N & Q Oct 1954.

Maxwell, J. C. Gray's cat as Helen of Troy. N & Q July 1954. See G. Tillotson, Oct 1954.

Esdaile, A. Thomas Gray. Quart Rev 293 1955.

John, L. C. Wordsworth and Gray. N & Q May 1955.

Howarth, R. G. Gray and Green. N & Q Jan 1956. Reply by W. S. Lewis, May 1956.

Peckham, M. Gray's Epitaph revisited. MLN 71 1956.

Dyson, A. E. The ambivalence of Gray's Elegy. MP 55 1957.

Sutherland, J. H. The stonecutter in Gray's Elegy. MP 55 1957.

Roberts, M. A note on Gray's Elegy. E Studies 39 1958.

Hagstrum, J. H. In his Sister arts, Chicago 1958.

Emden, C. S. In his Poets in their letters, Oxford 1959.

Foladare, J. Gray's 'frail memorial to West'. PMLA 75 1960.

Johnston, A. Gray's The triumph of Owen. RES new ser 11 1960.

—— Gray's use of the Gorchest y beirdd in the Bard. MLR 59 1964.

—— 'The purple year' in Pope and Gray. RES new ser 14 1963.

—— Gray and the Bard. Cardiff 1966.

Fukuhara, R. Essays on Gray. Tokyo 1960.

Ryskamp, C. Gray's Christmas piece 1727. Princeton Univ Lib Chron 22 1960.

Hutchens, E. N. Gray's cat and Pope's Belinda. Tennessee Stud in Lit 6 1961.

Basden, E. B. Gray in Buckinghamshire. N & Q July-Sept 1962, June 1966.

Berry, F. The sound of personification in Gray's Elegy. EC 12 1962.

Combecher, H. Von der spät klassizistischen zur romantischen Ode. Die Neueren Sprachen 11 1962.

Dale, J. Pope's 'wayward queen' and a letter from Gray. N & Q Dec 1962.

Hertz, N. H. Poetry in an age of prose. In In defence of reading, ed R. A. Brower and R. Poirier, New York 1962.

Macdonald, A. The poet Gray in Scotland. RES new ser 13 1962.

Doherty, F. The two voices of Gray. EC 13 1963.

Sparrow, J. Gray's 'spring of tears'. RES new ser 14 1963. See C. B. Ricks, TLS 21 June 1963.

Golden, M. Thomas Gray. New York 1964.

Lyles, A. M. Historical perspective in Gray's Eton College ode. Tennessee Stud in Lit 9 1964.

Anderson, A. Gray's Elegy in Miscellaneous pieces 1752. Library 5th ser 20 1965.

Brady, F. Structure and meaning in Gray's Elegy. In From sensibility to romanticism, ed F. W. Hilles and H. Bloom, New York 1965.

Bronson, B. H. On a special decorum in Gray's Elegy. Ibid.

Jack, I. Gray's Elegy reconsidered. Ibid.

Kallich, M. Gray's annotations to Pope's Essay on Man. N & Q Dec 1965.

Short, J. D. Gray's Elegy: a possible source. N & Q Dec 1965.

Spacks, P. M. Statement and artifice in Gray. Stud in Eng Lit 1500–1900 5 1965.

—— Artful strife: conflict in Gray's poetry. PMLA 81 1966.

— Gray: action and image. In her Poetry of vision, Cambridge Mass 1967.

Vernon, P. F. The structure of Gray's early poems. EC 15 1965.

McCarthy, F. I. The Bard of Gray: its composition and its use by painters. Nat Lib of Wales Jnl 14 1965.

Kenney, E. J. An imitation of Martial attributed to Gray. N & Q Dec 1966.

Greene, R. L. Gray's Elegy. Explicator 24 1966.

Ehrenpreis, I. The cistern and the fountain: art and reality in Pope and Gray. In Studies in criticism and aesthetics 1660–1800: essays in honor of S. H. Monk, Minneapolis 1967.

Wilkins, F. C. Gray's Ode on a distant prospect of Eton College. Explicator 25 1967.

Dilworth, E. Landor on Gray's sonnet. N & Q June 1968.

Mell, D. C. Form as meaning in Augustan elegy. Papers in Lang & Lit 4 1968.

Wilding, M. The epitaph to Gray's Elegy. N & Q June 1968.

R. H. L.

WILLIAM COLLINS
1721–59

Bibliographies etc

Bronson, W. C. In his Poems of Collins, Boston 1898.

Williams, I. A. In his Seven eighteenth-century bibliographies, 1924.

Booth, B. A. and C. E. Jones. A concordance of the poetical works of Collins. Berkeley 1939.

Collections

The poetical calendar. Ed F. Fawkes and W. Woty, vols 11–12 1763. With a Life by John Hampton? and a Character by Johnson. Contains all the verse pbd in Collins lifetime and, erroneously, To Miss Aurelia C—R from GM Jan 1739.

The poetical works of Mr William Collins, with memoirs of the author; and observations on his genius and writings by J. Langhorne. 1765, 1765 (pirated?; see I. A. Williams, Points in eighteenth-century verse, 1934), 1771 (introd rev), 1776, 1781. Contents as in Poetical calendar, above, omitting To Miss Aurelia C—R.

A collection of poems by several hands. [Ed G. Pearch] Vol 2, 1768, 1770, 1775, 1783. Contains poems omitted in Dodsley's Collection; adds Verses written on a paper from GM May 1765.

Poetical works. Glasgow 1770, 1771, 1775, 1777. With Hammond's Elegies.

British poets. Vol 43, Edinburgh 1773.

The works of the English poets. Ed S. Johnson, vol 49 1779; vol 58 1790 (adding Ode on popular superstitions and Song: The sentiments borrow'd from Shakespear, by H. Headley?, from GM Feb 1788).

Bell's poets of Great Britain. Vol 87, Edinburgh 1781, 1787, 1807 (S. Bagster's edn).

Poetical works, with preface and notes. Glasgow 1787.

Poetical works. Philadelphia 1788. Adds Ode on popular superstitions.

Poetical works. 1796.

Eclogues and miscellaneous pieces. [Ed B. Strutt], Colchester 1796. Incomplete.

Poetical works. Manchester 1796. Incomplete.

Poetical works. 1797, 1800, 1802. With essay by Mrs Barbauld. Other edns with this title in 1798, 1800, 1804, 1811, 1815, 1823 (with Beattie), 1824 (with engraving of Flaxman's monument), 1825 etc.

Poems. Ludlow 1799, 1801. Incomplete; as vol 2 of The literary miscellany, ed G. Nicholson.

Works of the British poets. Ed T. Park, vol 30 1805, 1808.

Poems by Collins and Gay. Paris 1806 (Parson's and Galignani's British Library vol 39).

The laurel. 1808. With Johnson, Pomfret and Hammond.

The bouquet. New York 1815. Incomplete.

British poets. Ed R. Walsh, vol 23, Philadelphia 1819.

Select works of the British poets. Ed J. Aikin 1820. Incomplete.

British poets, vol 44. Chiswick 1822.

Poetical works. Ed A. Dyce 1827. Includes notes by J. Mitford; and adds Sonnet from GM Oct 1739.

Poetical works. Ed W. Crowe, Bath 1828. Includes G. B. Martelli's Italian trn of The dirge.

Poetical works. Ed S. E. Brydges 1830, 1853 (Aldine edn). With essay by Brydges and memoir by Sir Harris Nicolas. Adds Our late taste in music from GM Oct 1740, erroneously attributed to Collins.

Poetical works. Ed S. E. Brydges, Geneva 1832.

Poetical works. Ed T. Miller 1846, 1856 (with Beattie), [1881] (with Beattie and Gray).

Poetical works. Ed G. Gilfillan, Edinburgh 1854, [1874]. With Goldsmith and Thomas Warton jr.

Poetical works. Ed R. A. Wilmott 1854, 1883. With Gray, Parnell, Green and Warton.

Poetical works. Ed W. M. Thomas 1858, 1866, 1894 (Aldine edn).

Poems. Ed W. C. Bronson, Boston 1898; ed T. M. Ward 1905 (ML); ed C. Stone 1907.

Poetical works. Ed C. Stone and A. L. Poole, Oxford 1917 (OSA); rev F. Page 1937. With Gray.

Poems. Ed E. Blunden 1929.

The minor poets of the eighteenth century. Ed H. I'A. Fausset 1929 (EL).

Gray, Collins and their circle. Ed W. T. Williams and G. H. Vallins [1937].

Selected poems. Ed A. Johnston 1967. With Gray.

Poems. Ed R. H. Lonsdale 1969. With Gray and Goldsmith.

Also Anderson vol 9; Chalmers vol 13.

§ 1

Persian eclogues, written originally for the entertainment of the ladies of Tauris and now first translated. 1742 (anon), 1757 (as Oriental eclogues), 1760; Oxford 1925 (facs of 1742 edn); tr German, 1767, 1770.

Verses humbly address'd to Sir Thomas Hanmer on his edition of Shakespear's works, by a gentleman of Oxford. 1743 (anon), 1744 (rev as An epistle address to Sir Thomas Hanmer on his edition of Shakespear's works: the second edition, to which is added a song from Cymbeline of the same author), 1755 (in Dodsley's Collection, vol 4).

Ode to a lady on the death of Colonel Ross in the action of Fontenoy. In Museum, ed M. Akenside no 6, 7 June 1746.

Odes on several descriptive and allegorical subjects. 1747 (pbd 20 Dec 1746), 1926 (facs), New York 1934; tr Italian, 1814. Rev texts of Ode to a lady, Ode to evening and Ode written in the beginning of the year 1746, in Dodsley's Collection, 2nd edn, vol 2 1748 etc.

Ode occasion'd by the death of Mr Thomson. 1749; in Union, ed T. Warton, 'Edinburgh' (for Oxford) 1753 (with Ode to evening); Oxford 1927 (facs); tr German, 1769 (in H. Schmid, Biographie der Dichter).

The passions: an ode. Oxford [1750], Winchester [1750], Gloucester 1760. These separate edns have an altered conclusion by the Earl of Litchfield.

An ode on the popular superstitions of the Highlands of Scotland, considered as the subject of poetry. Trans Royal Soc of Edinburgh 1 1788 (missing stanzas supplied by Henry Mackenzie), 1788 (Bell's spurious edn), 1789.

Drafts and fragments of verse, edited from the manuscripts. Ed J. S. Cunningham, Oxford 1956.

§ 2

Cooper, J. G. In his Letters concerning taste, 1755; rptd in Universal Mag 1758.

[Grainger, J.) Monthly Rev June 1757. A review of Oriental eclogues.

[Goldsmith, O.] In his An enquiry into the present state of polite learning in Europe, 1759.

[Hampton, J.?] Account of the life of Collins. In Poetical calendar, ed F. Fawkes and W. Woty vol 12, 1763; rptd GM Jan 1764. Includes a Character by Johnson, rptd in Lives of the poets vol 4, 1781.

[Langhorne, J.] Monthly Rev Jan 1764. A review of Poetical calendar.

—— Monthly Rev Feb 1764. A review of Hampton's Life of Collins.

[Griffiths, R.] Monthly Rev April 1765. A review of Langhorne's edn of Poetical works, 1765.

Supplement to A new and general biographical dictionary, 1767.

Noorthouck, J. An historical and classical dictionary, 1776.

Encyclopaedia britannica. 1778 (2nd edn).

Johnson, S. In his Lives of the poets, 1779–81.

White, Gilbert. GM Jan 1781.

GM Jan 1782. Notes by Philo-lyristes and H.

Scott, J. In his Critical essays on some of the poems of several English poets, 1785. On Oriental eclogues.

European Mag Aug 1785. Letters from X.

Biographia britannica. Ed A. Kippis vol 4, 1789.

GM Dec 1789. Letter from W.G. concerning monument to Collins. GM Sept, Nov 1795 gives account of Flaxman's monument.

A new biographical dictionary, ed S. Jones 1794.

Seward, W. Supplement to Anecdotes of some distinguished persons, 1797. Collins's letter to William Hayes 1750.

[Maude, T.] The reaper no 26. York Chron 16 Feb 1797; rptd in N. Drake, The gleaner vol 4, 1811. Contains letters on Collins by Thomas Warton jr and J. Ragsdale; a slightly fuller text of Ragsdale's letter in Monthly Mag July 1806.

Hay, A. In his History of Chichester, Chichester 1804.

Wooll, J. In his Memoirs of Joseph Warton, 1806.

Hazlitt, W. In his Lectures on the English poets, 1818.

Campbell, T. In his Specimens of the British poets vol 5, 1819.

Swinburne, A. C. In The English poets, ed T. H. Ward, vol 3, 1880.

Montégut, E. In his Heures de lecture d'un critique, Paris 1891.

Stone, C. The story of a poem. Academy 8 Dec 1906. On Ode on the popular superstitions.

—— Variations in the Ode to evening. Academy 12 June 1909.

Holt-White, R. In Letters to Gilbert White of Selborne from John Mulso, [1909].

Coffman, G. R. Collins and Thomson. MLN 31 1916.

Mackail, J. W. Collins and the English lyric. Trans Royal Soc of Lit 1921; rptd in his Studies of English poets, 1926.

[Murry, J. M.] William Collins. TLS 29 Dec 1921; rptd in his Countries of the mind, 1922.

White, H. O. Collins and his contemporary critics. TLS 5–12 Jan 1922.

—— The dirge in Cymbeline. TLS 16 Feb 1922.

—— The letters of Collins. RES 3 1927.

—— William Collins. TLS 14 Feb 1929.

—— Collins and Miss Bundy. RES 6 1930.

Havens, R. D. In his Influence of Milton on English poetry, Cambridge Mass 1922.

McKillop, A. D. A poem in the Collins canon. MLN 37 1922.

—— The romanticism of Collins. SP 20 1923.

—— A bibliographical note on Collins. MLN 38 1923.

—— A lost poem by Collins. TLS 6 Dec 1928.

—— Collins's Ode to the passions. TLS 7 March 1936.

—— Collins's Ode to evening. Tennessee Stud in Lit 5 1960.

Himmler, G. Collins Gedichte. Giessener Beiträge 2 (pt 1) 1924.

Meyerstein, E. H. W. Collins's letter to Cooper. London Mercury Dec 1924.

—— Collins's Ode on Col Ross. TLS 4 July 1935.

Garrod, H. W. The poetry of Collins. Proc Br Acad 14 1928.

—— Errors in the text of Collins. TLS 15 March 1928. Replies by J. R. Macphail 22 March, M. Bourke 29 March, H. O. White 5 April; J. Sparrow 12 April 1928.

—— Collins. Oxford 1928.

—— William Collins. TLS 14 Feb 1929. Anon reply 21 Feb 1929.

Woodhouse, A. S. P. Collins and Martin Martin. TLS 20 Dec 1928. Reply by W. C. Mackenzie 10 Jan 1929.

—— Thomas Warton and the Ode to horror. TLS 24 Jan 1929.

—— Imitations of the Ode to evening. TLS 30 May 1929. Reply by D. Cook 6 June 1929.

—— Collins in the eighteenth century. TLS 16 Oct 1930. Lists eighteenth-century references to Collins.

—— Collins and the creative imagination. In Studies in English, ed M. W. Walker, Toronto 1931.

—— The poetry of Collins reconsidered. In From sensibility to romanticism, ed F. W. Hilles and H. Bloom, New York 1965.

Bailey, R. William Collins. TLS 11 April 1929. On imitations of Ode to evening. Reply by H. O. White 18 April 1929.

Blunden, E. William Collins. TLS 25 July 1929. Replies by H. W. Garrod 8 Aug; E. Blunden and H. W. Garrod 29 Aug 1929.

—— Collins and Dodsley's Museum. TLS 8 Aug 1935.

Legouis, P. Les amours de Dieu chez Collins et Milton. Revue Anglo-américaine 8 1930.

Saito, T. Collins and Keats. TLS 20 Nov 1930.

Delamare, M. L'originalité de Collins. Revue Anglo-américaine 9 1931.

Wilmshurst, W. L. Signatures of Collins. TLS 9 Feb 1933.

Page, F. An essay by Collins. TLS 11 July 1935. Attributes an essay in Dodsley's Museum to Collins. Reply by E. H. W. Meyerstein 25 July 1935.

Ainsworth, E. G. Poor Collins: his life, his art and his influence. Ithaca 1937.

Carver, P. L. Collins and Alexander Carlyle. RES 15 1939.

—— Notes on the life of Collins. N & Q 19–26 Aug, 2–30 Sept, 7–14 Oct 1939.

—— The life of a poet: a biographical sketch of Collins. 1967.

Wasserman, E. R. A doubtful poem in the Collins canon. MLN 54 1939.

—— Collins's Young Damon of the vale is dead. N & Q 16 March 1940. Reply by P. L. Carver 7 June 1941.

Shuster, G. N. Collins, Gray and the return of the imagination. In his English ode from Milton to Keats, New York 1940.

Tillotson, G. Notes on Collins. In his Essays in criticism and research, Cambridge 1942.

Vivante, L. A creative principle in Collins and Gray. Comparative Lit Stud 8 1942.

Musgrove, S. The theme of Collins's odes. N & Q 9, 23 Oct 1943.

Sypher, W. The morceau de fantaisie in verse: a new approach to Collins. UTQ 15 1945.

Tompkins, J. M. S. In yonder grave a druid lies. RES 22 1946.

Cunningham, J. S. Thomas Warton and Collins. Durham Univ Jnl 46 1953.

Rota, D. F. Collins. Padua 1953.

Jennings, A. Collins's house in Chichester. N & Q Feb 1954.

Brooks, E. L. Collins's Ode on the poetical character. College Eng April 1956.

Wright, B. A. Note on Collins's use of the word 'springs'. N & Q May 1958.

Hagstrum, J. H. In his Sister arts, Chicago 1958.

Collins at Winchester. TLS 3 July 1959.

Tillyard, E. M. W. Collins's Ode on the death of Thomson. REL 1 1960; rptd in his Essays literary and educational, 1962. Reply by A. Henderson, REL 1 1960.

Brown, M. E. On William Collins's Ode to evening. EC 11 1961.

Lynskey, W. Collins's Ode on the poetical character. Explicator 19 1961.

Crider, J. R. Structure and effect in Collins's progress poems. SP 60 1963.

Quintana, R. The scheme of Collins's odes. In Restoration and eighteenth-century literature, ed C. Camden, Chicago 1963.

Doughty, O. William Collins. 1964.

Pettit, H. Collins's Ode to evening and the critics. Stud in Eng Lit 1500–1900 4 1964.

Braekman, W. The influence of Collins on poems written by Coleridge in 1793. Revue des Langues Vivantes 21 1965.

Sigworth, O. F. William Collins. New York 1965.

Spacks, P. M. Collins's imagery. SP 62 1965.

— Collins: the controlling image. In her Poetry of vision, Cambridge Mass 1967.

Werkmeister, L. Collins and the London daily press 1788–98. N & Q June 1965.

Kallich, M. Plain in thy neatness: Horace's Pyrrha and Collins's Evening. Eng Lang Notes 3 1966.

Stewart, M. M. Collins's letter to Cooper. N & Q Nov 1967.

— Mr Clarke of Collins's letter. N & Q June 1968.

— Collins and Cackham manor. RES new ser 20 1969.

— Collins and Thomas Barrow. PQ 48 1969.

Wasserman, E. R. Collins's Ode on the poetical character. ELH 34 1967.

Lamont, C. Collins's Ode on the popular superstitions of the Highlands of Scotland: a newly recovered manuscript. RES new ser 19 1968.

R. H. L.

CHRISTOPHER SMART

1722–71

Bibliographies

Gray, G. J. A bibliography of the writings of Smart, with biographical references. Trans Bibl Soc 6 1903. Also rptd separately.

Collections

Poems: consisting of his prize poems, odes, sonnets and fables, Latin and English translations, together with many original compositions not included in the quarto edition; to which is prefixed an account of his life and writings. 2 vols Reading 1791. Omits A song to David and much else.

Collected poems. Ed N. Callan 2 vols 1949 (ML). Excludes trns, libretti and Latin poems.

Poems. Ed R. E. Brittain, Princeton 1950. Selection, including some trns.

Anderson vol 11 (adds one poem); Chalmers vol 16 (omits one poem).

§ I

Carmen Cl. Alexandri Pope in S Caeciliam, Latine redditum. Cambridge 1743, 1746 (adds Ode for musick on St Cecilia's Day).

Gratulatio Academiae Cantabrigiensis de reditu Georgii II. 1748. Contains poem by Smart.

The Horatian canons of friendship: being the third satire of the first book of Horace imitated. 1750.

On the eternity of the Supreme Being. Cambridge 1750, 1752, 1756. Seatonian Prize poem for 1750.

The student: or Oxford and Cambridge monthly miscellany 1750–1. 50 or more contributions; ed Smart.

An occasional prologue and epilogue to Othello. [1751], [1751].

A solemn dirge, sacred to the memory of Frederic, Prince of Wales. 1751.

The nut-cracker. 1751.

On the immensity of the Supreme Being. Cambridge 1751, 1753, 1757, 1761. Seatonian Prize poem for 1751.

An index to mankind: or maxims selected from the wits of all nations. 1751, 1754.

Poems on several occasions. 1752.

The Muses banquet: or a present from Parnassus. 2 vols Reading 1752. For Smart as probable editor see A. Sherbo, BNYPL March 1960.

On the omniscience of the Supreme Being. Cambridge 1752, 1756, 1761. Seatonian Prize poem for 1762.

Be merry and be wise: or the cream of the jests, and the marrow of maxims, for the conduct of life. 1753, 1756, 1761 (5th edn). For Smart as probable editor see A. Sherbo, BNYPL March 1960.

The Hilliad: an epic poem bk 1. 1753, 1753. All pbd.

Mother Midnight's comical pocket-book. 1753. Probably by Smart; see A. Sherbo, BNYPL Aug 1957.

On the power of the Supreme Being. Cambridge 1754, 1758, 1761. Seatonian Prize poem for 1753.

On the goodness of the Supreme Being. Cambridge 1756, 1756, 1761. Seatonian Prize poem for 1755.

A collection of poems for the amusement of children six foot high. 1756. For Smart as probable editor see A. Sherbo, BNYPL March 1960.

A collection of pretty poems for the amusement of children three feet high. 1756. For Smart as probable editor see A. Sherbo, BNYPL March 1960.

Hymn to the Supreme Being on recovery from a dangerous fit of illness. 1756.

The universal visiter and memorialist for the year 1756. 1756. Ed Smart and Richard Rolt.

The apprentice, by Mr Murphy. 1756. Epilogue by Smart.

To Miss Harriot's squirrel. Literary Mag May 1758. Attributed to Smart; see A. Sherbo, MLR 62 1967.

The works of Horace, translated literally into English prose. 2 vols 1756, 1762, 1770, Dublin 1772, 1780, 1790 etc; rptd 1911.

The nonpareil, or the quintessence of wit and humour: being a choice selection of those pieces that were most admired in the ever-to-be-remember'd Midwife: or Old Woman's Magazine. 1757.

To the editor of the Christian's Magazine. Christian's Mag Sept 1762. Attributed to Smart; see A. Sherbo, MLR 62 1967.

Mrs Midnight's orations and other select pieces as they were spoken at the Oratory in the Hay-market, London. 1763.

A song to David. 1763, 1819, 1827, 1895; ed J. R. Tutin 1898; ed R. A. Streatfeild, 1901; ed E. Blunden 1924; ed P. Searle 1924; rptd Oxford 1926 (facs); ed A. Hillyer, Los Angeles 1934; ed R. Todd 1947; ed J. B. Broadbent, Cambridge 1960.

Poems, viz Reason and imagination: a fable [and 3 other pieces]. [1763].

Poems on several occasions, viz Munificence and modesty [and 8 other pieces]. [1763].

Hannah: an oratorio, as perform'd at the King's Theatre in the Hay-market. [1764].

Ode to the Right Honourable the Earl of Northumberland on his being appointed Lord Lieutenant of Ireland, with some other pieces. 1764.

A poetical translation of the fables of Phaedrus. 1765, 1831, 1853 (Bohn's Lib).

A translation of the Psalms of David [including A song to David]. 1765. Selections in miscellaneous poems by Mrs Le Noir, 1825, and in a Song to David, ed E. Blunden 1924.

The works of Horace translated into verse. 4 vols 1767.

Abimelech: an oratorio as it is performed at the Theatre-Royal in Covent-Garden. [1768].

The parables of Our Lord and Saviour Jesus Christ, done into familiar verse, for the use of younger minds. 1768.

Hymns for the amusement of children. [?], Dublin 1772, London 1775 (3rd edn), Oxford 1947 (Luttrell Soc) (facs of 3rd edn).

Providence: an oratorio. 1777. Recitatives selected from Seatonian Prize poems.

Rejoice in the Lamb. Ed W. F. Stead 1939; ed W. H. Bond, Cambridge Mass 1954.

§ 2

[Griffiths, R.] On the immensity of the Supreme Being. Monthly Rev May 1751.

[Hill, J.] Poems on several occasions. Monthly Rev Aug 1752.

The Hilliad. Monthly Rev Feb 1753.

[Derrick, S.] The universal visiter. Critical Rev Jan 1756.

[Grainger, J.] On the goodness of the Supreme Being. Monthly Rev June 1756.

The works of Horace, translated literally into English prose. Monthly Rev Jan 1757.

[Langhorne, J.] A song to David. Monthly Rev April 1763.

A song to David. Critical Rev April 1763.

Poems, viz Reason and imagination. Critical Rev July 1763; Monthly Rev Sept 1763.

Poems on several occasions, viz Munificence and modesty. Monthly Rev Nov 1763; Critical Rev Nov 1763.

Ode to the Right Honourable the Earl of Northumberland. Critical Rev July 1764; [J. Langhorne], Monthly Rev Sept 1764.

A poetical translation of the fables of Phaedrus. Critical Rev Sept 1764; [J. Langhorne], Monthly Rev Jan 1765.

A translation of the Psalms of David. Critical Rev Sept 1765; Monthly Rev Sept 1765 (by Langhorne?).

The works of Horace translated into verse. Critical Rev Aug 1765.

Parables of our Lord and Saviour Jesus Christ. Critical Rev April 1768; Monthly Rev May 1768.

Gosse, E. In his Gossip in a library, 1891.

—— In his Leaves and fruit, 1927.

Falls, C. In his Critic's armoury, 1924.

Murry, J. M. In his Discoveries, 1924.

McKenzie, K. A. Smart: sa vie et ses oeuvres. Paris 1925.

Whibley, L. The jubilee at Pembroke Hall in 1743. Blackwood's Mag Jan 1927.

Piggott, S. New light on Smart. TLS 13 June 1929.

Abbott, C. D. Smart's madness. PLMA 45 1930.

Olivero, F. In his Studi britannici, Turin 1931.

Binyon, L. The case of Smart. 1934 (Eng Assoc lecture).

Brittain, R. E. Smart and Dr Delany. TLS 7 March 1936.

—— An early model for A song to David. PMLA 56 1941. Replies by P. R. Wikelund, ELH 9 1942; A. D. McKillop, PMLA 58 1943.

—— Hymns for the amusement of children. PBSA 35 1941.

—— Smart in the magazines. Library 4th ser 21 1941.

Wood, F. T. Christopher Smart. E Studien 71 1936.

Jones, C. Smart, Richard Rolt and the Universal Visiter. Library 4th ser 18 1937.

Ainsworth, E. G. An unrecorded work by Smart. TLS 15 Oct 1938.

—— and C. E. Noyes. Smart: a biographical and critical study. Columbia Missouri 1943.

Havens, R. D. The structure of Smart's Song to David. RES 14 1938.

Stead, W. F. A Smart manuscript. TLS 5 March 1938.

—— Smart's cat. Criterion 17 1938.

—— Smart's metrical psalms. TLS 22 Oct 1938.

Botting, R. B. Johnson, Smart and the Universal Visiter. MP 37 1939.

—— Smart in London. Washington State College Research Stud 7 1939.

—— Gray and Smart. MLN 57 1942.

—— Smart and the Lilliputian Magazine. ELH 9 1942.

—— Smart's association with Arthur Murphy. JEGP 43 1944.

Wilson, M. My poor friend Smart. English 2 1939.

Emery, J. P. Murphy's authorship of the notes of Smart's Hilliad. MLN 61 1946.

Bond, W. H. Smart's Jubilate agno. Harvard Lib Bull 4 1950.

—— Smart's last years. TLS 10 April 1953.

Greene, D. J. Smart, Berkeley, the scientists and the poets. JHI 14 1953.

Side, K. Smart's heresy. MLN 69 1954.

Sherbo, A. Smart and the Universal Visiter. Library 5th ser 10 1955.

—— Smart, free and accepted mason. JEGP 54 1955.

—— The probable date of composition of Smart's Song to David, Psalms and Hymns and spiritual songs. JEGP 55 1956.

—— The dating and order of the fragments of Smart's Jubilate agno. Harvard Lib Bull 10 1956.

—— Smart, reader of obituaries. MLN 71 1956.

—— Smart's knowledge of occult literature. JHI 18 1957.

—— Mother Midnight's comical pocket-book. BNYPL Aug 1957.

—— Survival in Grub Street: another essay in attribution. BNYPL March 1960.

—— Smart and the problem of ordination in the eighteenth century. Church Quart Rev 167 1966.

—— Two pieces newly attributed to Smart. MLR 62 1967.

—— Smart's three translations of Horace. JEGP 66 1967.

—— Smart: scholar of the University. East Lansing 1967.

Williamson, K. Another edition of Smart's Hymns for the amusement of children. Library 5th ser 10 1955.

—— Smart's Hymns and spiritual songs. PQ 38 1959.

Devlin, C. Smart and the seven pillars. Month Aug 1960.

—— Poor Kit Smart. 1961.

Merchant, W. M. Patterns of reference in Smart's Jubilate agno. Harvard Lib Bull 14 1960.

Grigson, G. Christopher Smart. 1961 (Br Council pamphlet).

Lonsdale, R. Smart's first publication in English. RES new ser 12 1961.

Parish, C. Smart's knowledge of Hebrew. SP 58 1961.

—— Smart's pillars of the Lord. MLQ 24 1963.

Rogers, K. M. The pillars of the Lord: some sources of A song to David. PQ 40 1961.

Kuhn, A. J. Smart: the poet as patriot of the Lord. ELH 30 1963.

Sutton, M. K. Smart's 'compleat cat'. College Eng Jan 1963.

Adams, F. D. The seven pillars of Smart. Papers in Eng Lang & Lit 1 1965.

Blaydes, S. Smart as a poet of his times: a reappraisal. Hague 1966.

Spacks, P. M. In her Poetry of vision: five eighteenth-century poets, Cambridge Mass 1967.

Friedman, J. B. The cosmology of praise: Smart's Jubilate agno. PMLA 82 1967.

Dearnley, M. The poetry of Smart. 1968.

A. S.

CHARLES CHURCHILL
1731–64

Bibliographies

Lowe, R. W. In his A bibliographical account of English theatrical literature, 1888.

Williams, I. A. In his Seven xviiith-century bibliographies, 1924.

Collections

Poems. 1763, 1765. The Rosciad, The apology, Night, The prophecy of famine, An epistle to William Hogarth, The ghost; various edns with general title-page.

Poems. Vol II, 1765. The conference, The author, The duellist, Gotham, The candidate, The farewell, The times, Independence, The journey.

Poems. 2 vols Dublin 1764, 3 vols Dublin 1764, 4 vols Dublin 1765 (as Works), 3 vols Dublin 1766, 2 vols 1766, 3 vols 1767 (with life from Annual Register for 1764), 3 vols Dublin 1768, 2 vols 1768, 1769, Hague 1769, 3 vols 1772, 4 vols 1774 (as Works), 3 vols 1776 etc.

The poetical works of Churchill, with an authentic account of his life by W. Tooke. 2 vols 1804, 3 vols 1830 etc; rev J. L. Hannay 2 vols 1866, 1892 (rev) (Aldine edn).

Poetical works. Ed G. Gilfillan, Edinburgh 1855, [1880].

Poems. Ed J. Laver 2 vols 1933.

Poetical works. Ed D. Grant, Oxford 1956.

Johnson 66, 67; Anderson 10; Chalmers 14.

§ I

The Rosciad. 1761 (5 edns), 1762, 1763 (61 lines not in previous edns), 1763, 1765, Dublin 1765, London 1772; ed R. W. Lowe 1891 (with Apology).

The apology. 1761 (5 edns), 1763; ed R. W. Lowe 1891 (with Rosciad).

Night: an epistle to Robert Lloyd. 1761, 1760 (for 1762) (2nd-3rd edns), 1763.

The ghost, books I and II. 1762, 1762, 1763.

The ghost, book III. 1762, 1763.

The ghost, book IV. 1763.

The North Briton. 1762–3, 3 vols 1763. Churchill is said to have written 'quite half', including a verse-satire, The poetry professor, in nos 22 and 26.

The conference. 1763, 1764.

The author. 1763, 1764.

An epistle to William Hogarth. 1763 (3 edns), Dublin 1763.

The prophecy of famine: a Scots pastoral. 1763 (5 edns).

The duellist. 1764, 1764.

The candidate. 1764.

Gotham, bk I. 1764.

Gotham, bk II. 1764.

Gotham, bk III. 1764.

Independence. 1764.

The times. 1764.

The farewell. 1764.

The journey: a fragment. 1765.

Sermons. 1765, Dublin 1765, London 1774, Dublin 1774. Contains satirical dedicatory verses to Warburton. The sermons may be by the poet's father.

Letters of John Wilkes. Vol 1, 1769. Includes letters from Churchill.

The correspondence of John Wilkes, vol 3. Ed J. Almon 1805.

Correspondence of Wilkes and Churchill. Ed E. H. Weatherley, New York 1954.

§ 2

The Rosciad. Critical Rev 11 1761. By Smollett?

[Lloyd, R.] The apology. Monthly Rev May 1761.

[Kirkpatrick, J.] The ghost. Monthly Rev April 1762.

[Griffiths, R.] The prophecy of famine. Monthly Rev Jan 1763.

[Langhorne, J.] An epistle to William Hogarth. Monthly Rev Aug 1763.

— The conference. Monthly Rev Nov 1763.

— The duellist. Monthly Rev appendix 1763.

— The author. Monthly Rev Jan 1764.

— Gotham. Monthly Rev Feb, April, Aug 1764.

— The times. Monthly Rev Sept 1764.

[— and O. Ruffhead]. Independence. Monthly Rev Oct 1764.

[Rose, W.] Churchill's sermons. Monthly Rev Feb 1765.

The genuine memoirs of Churchill, with an account of and observations on his writings; together with some original letters between him and the author. 1765. A fabrication.

A short essay on Churchill. Monthly Rev 1775. Also separately 1775.

Kippis, A. Biographia Britannica vol 3, 1784 (2nd edn).

Southey, R. Churchill's poems. Annual Rev 3 1804.

— The life of Cowper. In Works of Cowper vol 1, 1836.

— A review of Churchill's poems. 1852 (priv ptd).

Forster, J. Poetical works of Churchill. Edinburgh Rev 81 1845. Review of Tooke edn of 1884; rptd Traveller's Lib 16 1855–6; Historical and biographical essays vol 2, 1858 etc.

Hannay, J. In his Satire and satirists, 1854.

Hitchman, S. F. Churchill: parson and poet. St James's Mag June 1865; rptd in his Eighteenth-century studies, 1881.

Churchill the satirist. Temple Bar Aug 1876.

Devey, J. Churchill. Nat Rev Oct 1885.

Putschi, F. Churchill: sein Leben und seine Werke. Vienna 1909.

Brockhurst, T. F. Parson, poet and beau. Sewanee Rev 25 1917.

Gosse, E. Gray's notes on Churchill. Trans Royal Soc of Lit 36 1918.

Beatty, J. M. The battle of players and poets. MLN 35 1919.

— Churchill's treatment of the couplet. PMLA 34 1919.

— Political satires of Churchill. SP 16 1919; rptd in Bones of Ben Jonson, 1919.

— An essay in critical biography. PMLA 35 1920.

— Mrs Montagu, Churchill and Miss Chere. MLN 41 1926.

— Churchill's influence on minor eighteenth-century satirists. PMLA 42 1927.

— Churchill and Freneau. Amer Lit 2 1930.

Whitford, R. C. Gleanings of Churchill bibliography. MLN 43 1928.

Blunden, E. Charles Churchill. TLS 5 Feb 1931; rptd in his Votive tablets, 1931.

Butterfield, L. H. Churchill and A fragment of an epic poem. Harvard Stud 15 1933.

Churchill. TLS 5 Feb 1931.

Nobbe, G. The North Briton. New York 1939.

Brown, W. C. Churchill: a revaluation. SP 40 1943.
— Churchill and criticism in transition. JEGP 43 1944.
— In his Triumph of form, Chapel Hill 1948.
— Churchill: poet, rake and rebel. Lawrence Kansas 1953.
Weatherley, E. H. Possible additions to the Churchill canon. MLN 40 1945.
— Foote's revenge on Churchill and Lloyd. HLQ 9 1946.
— Churchill's literary indebtedness to Pope. SP 43 1946.
— The personal and literary relations of Churchill and Garrick. In Studies in honor of A. H. R. Fairchild, Columbia Missouri 1946.
— Churchill: neo-classic master. Univ of Kansas Rev 20 1954.
Waldhorn, A. Churchill and Statira. MLN 63 1948.
Hopkins, K. In his Portraits in satire, 1958.
Golden, M. Lines attributed to Churchill. N & Q Oct 1958.
— Churchill's literary influence on Cowper. JEGP 58 1959.
— Sterility and eminence in the poetry of Churchill. JEGP 66 1967.
Lindsay, J. A Churchill poem? TLS 25 April 1958. See Golden, N & Q Oct 1958, above.
Simon, I. An eighteenth-century satirist: Churchill. Revue Belge 37 1959.
Winters, Y. The poetry of Churchill. Poetry 98 1961; rptd in his Forms of discovery, Denver 1967.
Cunningham, W. F. In Essays and studies in language and literature, ed H. H. Petit, Duquesne 1964.

A. S.

WILLIAM COWPER
1731–1800

Bibliographies etc

Neve, J. Concordance to the poetical works of Cowper. 1887.
Hartley, L. C. Cowper, the continuing revaluation: bibliography of Cowperian studies from 1895–1960. Chapel Hill 1960. A much enlarged version of his List of critical and biographical studies of Cowper 1895–1949, Chapel Hill 1950.
Russell, N. H. Bibliography of Cowper to 1837. Oxford 1963.
Povey, K. Handlist of mss in the Cowper and Newton Museum, Olney. Trans Cambridge Bibl Soc 4 1965.

Collections

Works. Ed John Johnson 10 vols (poems 3 vols, letters 3 vols, Iliad and Odyssey 4 vols) 1817. Some copies of Iliad and Odyssey dated 1816.
Miscellaneous works; with a life and notes by J. S. Memes. 3 vols Edinburgh 1834, 1835.
Works: life and letters by W. Hayley, completed by Cowper's private correspondence. Ed T. S. Grimshawe 8 vols 1835, 1836, 1 vol 1847.
Works: comprising his poems, correspondence and translations. Ed with life by R. Southey 15 vols 1835–7, 8 vols 1853–5 (Bohn's Lib).

§ I

Connoisseur no 111 11 March 1756. Billy Suckling (anon); no 115 8 April 1756, Complaints of an old bachelor [signed Christopher Ironside]; no 119 6 May 1756, On keeping a secret (anon); no 134 19 Aug 1756, Letter from Mr Village [signed T]; no 138 16 Sept 1756, On conversation [signed W]; rptd 1757, 1761, 1767, 1774, 1793 etc.
GM Sept 1758. Letter to Mr Urban on chanting in choirs. Signed W.C., probably by Cowper.

St James's Mag April 1763. A dissertation on the modern ode, anon. Rptd Public Advertiser 16 Aug 1763.
Olney hymns [66 by Cowper, 9 already pbd (see Russell, above), the rest by J. Newton]. 1779, 1781, 1783, 1787, 1788, 1792, 1797, 1797, 1806, 1807, 1810, 1812, 1815, 1815, 1816, 1817, 1818, 1819, 1820, 1821, 1822, 1824, 1825, 1829, 1830, 1831, 1831, Edinburgh 1797, 1821 etc. Also provincial and Scottish edns, and in edns of Newton's Works, 1808, Edinburgh 1809 etc; ed W. Willis 1911.
Anti-Thelyphthora: a tale in verse. 1781. Anon.
Poems. 1 vol 1782 (a few copies have preface by J. Newton); The task, 1785 (vol 2); 2 vols 1786 (2 issues of Task), 1787, 1788, 1793 (with preface by Newton), 1794–5 (adding 9 poems), St Andrews 1797, London 1798 (adding 2 poems; 4 edns, one being the St Andrews edn with cancel titles and the new poems), 1799, 1800 (3 edns, with appendixes of new poems), 1801, 1802 (incorporating appendixes), 1803, 1805, 1806 (3 edns), 1806 (1 vol 4° incorporating trns from Mme Guyon and Olney hymns), 1808 (adding 3 poems, 3 edns), 1810, 1810 (Chalmers vol 18), 1811, 1812, 1813–14, 1814, Dublin 1787, 1790, 1792, 1803, 1805. Edns 1786–1814 in 2 vols except 4° 1806.
The history of John Gilpin. Public Advertiser 14 Nov 1782. Anon. Separately pbd J. Fielding [1785], [c. 1785] (3rd edn); with Life of John Gilpin, London and Dublin 1785; with 6 illustrations by G. Cruikshank 1828; illustr R. Searle 1953; ed N. H. Russell 1968. At least 50 London, provincial and Scottish chapbook edns up to 1836 (see Russell, above). Many later edns, some illustr (see H. T. Kirby, John Gilpin in picture, Bookman (London) Dec 1931; A. M. Coleman, Illustrated editions of John Gilpin, N & Q 29 Dec 1934, 12 Jan, 2 Feb 1935; Print Collector's Quart 23 1936.
For the first pbn of other single poems and hymns in newspapers, periodicals and books, see OSA, rev N. H. Russell, Oxford 1967.
GM June 1784, letter on his hares, signed W.C.; Aug 1785, letter on the defects of Pope's Homer, signed Alethes; Sept 1790, letter parodying discussions in GM, signed Indagator. For pbn of 17 poems in GM see Russell, Bibliography, above.
Stanzas subjoined to the bills of mortality for the parish of All-Saints Northampton, for the years 1787, 1788, 1789, 1790, 1792, 1793. Northampton 1787–93. Anon.
Analytical Review. Review in March, April (2), May, Sept, Oct, Nov, Dec (2) 1789, Feb, April 1790, March 1793. Signed G.G. or P.P.
A good song ('Here's a health to honest John Bull'). [c. 1792–3]. Anon; probably by Cowper. Also found with variant titles 'John Bull: a song' etc.
Poems, 1: On the receipt of my mother's picture; 11: The dog and the water-lily. 1798, Oxford 1926 (facs).
Adelphi. Ed J. Newton 1802, 1816. Extracts pbd during Cowper's lifetime by the Rev David Simpson; abridged in Religious Tract Soc no 161 [c. 1819]; ed H. P. Stokes, Olney 1904 (in Cowper memorials); tr French, 1819, 1832. Written before 8 Aug 1772.
Many new poems were first pbd in W. Hayley, Life of Cowper, 1803–6; see §2, below.
Posthumous poetry [=Poems vol 3]. Ed John Johnson 1815. Contains nearly all the poems and trns pbd by Hayley, with a few unpbd ones.
Memoir of the early life of William Cowper esq written by himself. 1816, 1816, 1817, 1818, Birmingham 1817 (as Narrative of the life) (all pbd Edwards), 1816 (pbd Cox, as Memoirs of the most remarkable and interesting parts of the life), 1822 (with Olney hymns by Cowper), 1835 (as Autobiography of Cowper); ed M. J. Quinlan, Proc Amer Philosophical Soc 97 1953 (see C. Ryskamp, N. H. Hodgson (Russell) and M. J. Quinlan, MP 53 1956; C. Ryskamp 54 1957). See J. Sparrow and J. E. Wells, Bibl N & Q 2 1936. Written c. 1766–7.
Poems, the early productions of Cowper, now first

published; with anecdotes of the poet. Ed J. Croft 1825.
About 60 London and Scottish edns were pbd 1815–30, incorporating from 1817 many of the poems pbd by Hayley. Among those pbd from 1830, including vol 3, Posthumous poetry, are :
Poems, with memoir [by N. H. Nicolas]. 3 vols 1830–1 (Aldine); ed H. F. Cary 1839 (including trn of Homer); rev T. S. Grimshawe 1845; ed G. Gilfillan 2 vols Edinburgh 1854; ed R. Bell 3 vols 1854; ed J. Bruce 3 vols 1865 (Aldine) (with memoir); ed W. Benham 1870 (Globe); ed W. M. Rossetti [1872]; ed H. T. Griffith 2 vols Oxford 1874 (vol 2, Task etc, rptd Oxford 1896); Shorter poems, ed W. T. Webb 1896; Task, ed A. J. Grieve 1900.
Unpublished and uncollected poems. Ed T. Wright 1900.
Poems. Ed A. Meynell 1904. Selections.
Poems. Ed J. C. Bailey 1905.
Poetical works. Ed H. S. Milford, Oxford 1905 (OSA), 1913 (with addns), 1926 (enlarged), 1934 (with appendix of new poems); rev N. H. Russell, Oxford 1967.
Poems chosen by A. T. Quiller-Couch. Oxford [1908].
Through the loopholes of retreat: selections from the letters and poems. Ed H. Watt [1909].
Cowper. Ed E. Storer [1912]. Selected letters and poems.
Selections from Cowper: poetry and prose; with essays by Hazlitt and Bagehot. Ed H. S. Milford, Oxford 1921.
Selected poems. Ed J. C. Bailey [1925].
Poems. Ed H. I'A. Fausset 1931 (EL). Selections.
New poems. Ed F. Madan 1931.
Selections: poetry and prose. Ed D. Cecil 1933.
Poems selected by N. Nicholson. 1951.
Selected poems and letters. Ed A. N. Jeffares, Oxford 1963.
Poetry and prose. Ed B. Spiller 1968 (Reynard Lib). Selections.

Translations

Horace, Works in English verse by several hands, collected by Mr Duncombe. 2 vols 1757–9, 4 vols 1767. Cowper's trns of bk 1, satires 5 and 9 are in vol 2 of first edn and vol 3 of 1767 edn.
Voltaire, The Henriade, translated by T. Smollett, T. Francklin and others. 1762, 1772, 1781, Paris etc 1901, New York 1927. Cantos 5–8 tr Cowper, anon.
Homer, The Iliad and Odyssey, translated into blank verse by Cowper. 2 vols 1791, Dublin 1792, 4 vols 1802, 1809, 1810 (with 50 plates), 1817 (vols 7–10 of Works), 2 vols 1820; in Poems, ed H. F. Cary 1839; Odyssey, 1910 (EL).
[Van Lier, H. R.] The power of grace illustrated in six letters from a minister of the Reformed Church to John Newton, translated from the Latin by Cowper. London and Edinburgh 1792. Signed Christodulus.
Guyon, J. M. B. de la Motte. Poems translated from the French by the late William Cowper. Ed W. Bull 1801 (adding a few uncollected poems), 1802, 1803, 1811.
Latin and Italian poems of Milton translated into English verse, and a fragment of a commentary on Paradise lost by the late William Cowper. Ed W. Hayley 1808. Extracts from Cowper's trns first pbd in Hayley's Life of Milton, 1796, with excerpts from their joint trn of the Adamo of Andreini. Rptd by Southey and Grimshawe, and in Poetical works of Milton, ed C. G. Osgood, New York 1935. *See* next entry.
Cowper's Milton. Ed W. Hayley 4 vols 1810, 1811, 1835. Includes the trns of the Latin and Italian poems, the commentary on Paradise lost and the joint trn of Adamo, above.

Works Revised by Cowper

Scott, T. The force of truth. 1779. This edn, or 2nd edn of 1789, rev Cowper.

Hill, Rowland. Divine hymns for children. 1790. Includes 2 unpbd hymns by Cowper, later rptd.
[Cowper, M. F. C.] Original poems by a lady, revised by William Cowper. 1792, 1807, 1810, [c. 1818].
[Hurdis, J.] Sir Thomas More: a tragedy. 1792, 1793.

Letters

The letters in Hayley's Life of Cowper *(see §2, below), were rptd as vols 4–6 of* Works, 1817, *and in 1 vol* 1820, 1827.
Private correspondence. Ed J. Johnson 2 vols 1824 (3 edns).
Letters. Ed W. Benham 1884.
Selections. Ed W. T. Webb 1895.
Correspondence. Ed T. Wright 4 vols 1904.
The best letters of Cowper. Ed A. MacMahon 1905.
Selection. Ed E. V. Lucas, Oxford 1908 (WC); rptd with notes by M. L. Milford, Oxford 1911.
Letters. Ed J. G. Frazer 2 vols 1912.
Unpublished and uncollected letters. Ed T. Wright 1925.
Selected letters. Ed W. Hadley 1926 (EL); ed M. Van Doren, New York 1951.
See also selections from poems and letters, above.
Single letters were pbd in Monthly Mirror Jan 1801, May–Nov 1803 *(all to T. Park)*; Posthumous letters to Francis and George Colman, 1820; J. E. B. Mayor, N & Q 2 July–24 Sept 1904; R. Thornton, N & Q 18 Nov 1922; Antiquarian Quart 1 1926; R. A. Pratt, TLS 19 Nov 1931; G. H. Parks, TLS 22 Feb 1952; by A. H. Driver, TLS 10 July 1953; M. J. O'Neill, N & Q Jan 1954; by D. B. Green, N & Q Dec 1956; F. M. Link, MP 62 1964; M. C. Bates, Harvard Lib Bull 11 1957. *See* L. Hartley, K. Povey and C. Ryskamp under §2, below.

§2

[Knox, A.] Flapper 14, 28 May, 11 June 1796. Signed 'L'. On Cowper's poetry.
Public Characters 1799–1800. 1800.
Hayley, W. Life and posthumous writings of Cowper. Vols 1–2, 1803, 1803; vol 3, 1804; Supplementary pages, 1806; 4 vols 1806, 1809 (as Life and letters), 1812, 3 vols 1824, 1 vol 1835. Contains letters and many unpbd poems.
—— How Cowper got his pension: from a manuscript by Hayley. Ed H. R. S. Caldicott, Cornhill Mag April 1913.
Corry, J. Life of Cowper. 1803, 1803.
Greatheed, S. A practical improvement of the divine counsel. Newport Pagnell 1800, 1801 (rev). A sermon on Cowper's death.
—— Memoirs of Cowper. Evangelical Mag April–May 1803.
—— Memoirs of Cowper. 1803, 1814 (rev). Based on preceding.
Brayley, E. W. Cowper illustrated. 1803, 1804, 1810.
Johnson, J. Memoir of Cowper. In Poems vol 3 (Posthumous poetry), 1815.
Rural walks of Cowper. 1822, [1826] (rev), [c. 1835] (with Appendix). Rev text of Brayley, above.
Hazlitt, W. In his Lectures on the English poets, 1818. Lecture 5 on Thomson and Cowper.
P[otter, J. P.] Essays on the lives of Cowper, Newton and Heber. 1830. Rptd from Quart Rev 30 1823.
Hayley, W. In his Memoirs, ed J. Johnson 1823.
Taylor, T. Life of Cowper. 1833 (3 edns), 1835.
Memes, J. S. Life of Cowper. 1837. First pbd as vol 1 of his edn of the Works, 1834.
[Seeley, R. B.] Life of Cowper, with selections from his correspondence. 1855.
Bagehot, W. Cowper. Nat Rev 1 1855; rptd in his Estimations in criticism, 1908.
Sainte-Beuve, C. A. Cowper: ou de la poésie domestique. In his Causeries du lundi vol 11, Paris 1856.

The insanity of Cowper. Amer Jnl of Insanity 14 1858.

Pollock, J. M. The life, genius and poetry of Cowper. 1860.

Elwin, W. Cowper. Quart Rev 107 1860; rptd in his Some eighteenth-century men of letters vol 1, 1902.

D[onne], W. B. Cowper's poems. Fraser's Mag Dec 1861.

Bull, J. In his John Newton, [1868].

Brooke, S. A. In his Theology in the English poets, 1874.

Boucher, A. Cowper: sa correspondance et ses poésies. Paris 1874.

Stephen, L. Cowper and Rousseau. In his Hours in a library ser 3, 1879.

Smith, G. Cowper. 1880 (EML).

Wright, T. The town of Cowper. 1886.

—— The life of Cowper. 1892, 1921 (rev).

—— The loved haunts of Cowper. 1894.

—— The life of Cowper. Edenvale biographical ser no 4 1895.

—— The diary of Samuel Teedon. 1902.

Collyer, A. Some unpublished mss of Cowper. Universal Rev June 1890. Unpbd letters and poems.

Birrell, A. In his Res judicatae, 1892; rptd in his Collected essays, 1899.

Historical Mss Commisison. 15th report vol 3, appendix pt 1 1896. On Dartmouth mss.

Hartmann, H. Über Cowpers Tirocinium. In Festschrift zum siebzigsten Geburtstage Oskar Schades, Königsberg 1896.

Holmes, E. D. Cowper's indebtedness to Churchill. MLN 13 1898.

Bolton, W. Cowper and his surroundings. Trans Royal Soc of Lit ser 2, 1900.

Francis, J. C. The Cowper centenary. N & Q 21 April 1900. Summarizes previous contributions on Cowper.

Roberts, W. Romney's portrait of Cowper. Athenaeum 17 Feb 1900.

Hesketh, H. Letters of Lady Hesketh to the Rev John Johnson concerning Cowper. Ed C. Barham Johnson 1901.

Symington, A. J. The poet of home life. 1901.

Bayne, T. Isaac Watts and Cowper. N & Q 22 Oct 1904.

Stokes, H. P. Cowper memorials. Olney 1904.

Ainger, A. In his Lectures and essays vol 1, 1905.

More, P. E. The correspondence of Cowper. In his Shelburne essays ser 3, 1905.

Smith, B. Some features of Cowper's obsessions. Medical Times 27 May 1905.

Cowper in London: papers read before the Cowper Society. 1907.

Dowden, E. Cowper and Hayley. Atlantic Monthly July 1907; rptd in his Essays modern and Elizabethan, 1910.

Hoffman, C. W. Cowper's Belesenheit und literarische Kritik. Berlin 1908.

Cowper's pronunciation of his name. N & Q 2, 23 Oct, 6, 27 Nov, 25 Dec 1909, 5, 26 Feb, 19 March, 9, 23 April, 7 May 1921.

Willis, W. Cowper and his connection with the law. Norwich [1910] (Cowper Soc).

Lynn, W. T. et al. God moves in a mysterious way. N & Q 21 Jan, 25 Feb 1911.

Boutin, J. Etude médico-psychologique sur Cowper. Lyons 1913.

Norman, H. J. Cowper and Blake. Olney 1914 (Cowper Soc).

Roy, J. A. Cowper and his poetry. 1914.

Charnwood, D. Letters by ten literary men. Cornhill Mag Dec 1918.

Olivero, F. Un precursore del romanticismo inglese. Nuova Antologia 16 Jan 1923.

Madan, F. A newly recovered poem of Cowper. TLS 3 Jan 1924.

Harting, J. E. et al. Cowper's nightingale. N & Q 4, 18 April 1925.

Whiting, M. B. 'A burning bush': a new light on the relations between Cowper and Newton. Hibbert Jnl 24 1926.

—— Cowper and Newton. Nation (London) 11 Oct 1930.

Hurdis, J. Letters to Cowper 1791–4. Ed J. F. Tattersall, Bishopstone 1927. Rptd from Sussex County Mag April 1927. Another letter pbd W. Clarke, Theology June 1954.

Martin, L. C. Vaughan and Cowper. MLR 22 1927.

Povey, K. Cowper's spiritual diary. London Mercury March 1927.

—— The text of Cowper's letters. MLR 22 1927.

—— Some notes on Cowper's letters and poems. RES 5 1929.

—— New Cowper letters. Times 25, 28 April 1930.

—— Lawrence and Cowper. Times 6 May 1930.

—— Notes for a bibliography of Cowper's letters. RES 7–8 1931–2, 10 1934, 12 1936.

—— Cowper and Lady Austen. RES 10 1934.

The banishment of Lady Austen. RES 15 1939.

—— Two letters from Cowper to Greatheed. N & Q 8 July 1939.

—— Dean Spencer Cowper's poetical miscellany. Trans Architectural & Archaeological Soc of Durham & Northumberland 11 1958.

Spiller, R. E. Cowper, a new biographical source: the Rev J. Johnson's holograph memorandum book 1795–1800. PMLA 42 1927. Addns by H. N. Fairchild 43 1928. See Cowper's last years, TLS 5–12 Oct 1951.

Taffe, V. Le sentiment de la nature chez Cowper. Revue Anglo-américaine 4 1927.

Fausset, H. I'A. William Cowper. 1928.

Cecil, D. The stricken deer: or the life of Cowper. 1929.

—— William Cowper. Listener 17 June 1931.

—— William Cowper. 1932 (Eng Assoc pamphlet).

Förster, M. Cowpers Ballade John Gilpin. E Studien 64 1929, 65 1931.

Manning, B. L. History, politics and religion in certain poems of Cowper. Congregational Quart 7 1929.

Lloyd, J. H. The case of Cowper. Archives of Neurology & Psychiatry 24 1930.

Owlett, F. C. On the alleged effeminacy of Cowper. In his Chatterton's apology, 1930.

Probert, G. C. The stricken deer. N & Q 31 May 1930.

Blunden, E. Cowper: harmonist of the countryside. Times 13 Nov 1931.

Brash, W. B. Cowper 1731–1931. London Quart Rev 156 1931.

Carmichael, M. Cowper's Selkirk. TLS 30 July 1931.

—— Cowper and the Throckmortons. Dublin Rev April 1932.

—— Cowper 1731–1931. Catholic World Nov 1931.

—— Cowper's friends. Catholic World Jan 1932.

Hannay, N. C. The tragedy of Cowper. Saturday Rev of Lit 28 Nov 1931.

Power and gentleness. TLS 19 Nov 1931.

Shafer, R. William Cowper. Bookman (New York) Nov 1931.

Sturge, J. The Cowper centenary. Listener 1 July 1931.

Thomas, G. Cowper. Contemporary Rev Nov 1931.

—— Cowper and the eighteenth century. 1935, 1948 (rev).

Waugh, A. William Cowper. Fortnightly Rev Nov 1931.

Carver, P. L. A continuation of John Gilpin [by J. Oakman]. RES 8 1932.

Forster, E. M. Cowper, an Englishman. Spectator 16 Jan 1932.

Grew, S. and E. M. Cowper: his acceptance and rejection of music. Music & Letters 13 1932.

Howes, R. F. Cowper on conversation. Quart Jnl of Speech 18 1932.

Irvine, L. L. In his Ten letter writers, 1932.

Monti, G. Nel secondo centenario della nascita di Cowper. Emporium 76 1932.

Woolf, V. Cowper and Lady Austen. In her Common reader ser 2, 1932. Rptd from Nation 21 Sept 1929.

Wright, H. G. Relations of Iolo Morganwy with Johnson, Cowper and Southey. RES 8 1932.

— Cowper's Retirement and Balzac's Entretiens. MLR 40 1945.

Batterham, E. N. An epigram. TLS 1 June 1933.

Strachey, G. L. Gray and Cowper. In his Characters and commentaries, 1933.

Wells, J. E. John Gilpin and Charles Lamb. E Studien 67 1933.

Schmidt, T. F. K. Das Verhalten der Romantiker zur Public School (Cowper, Shelley, Byron). Bonn 1935.

Blyton, W. J. A Puritan's Catholic friends: Cowper and the Throckmortons. Month March 1937.

Mabbott, T. O. The Miltonic epitaph on Mazarin: Cowper's opinion. N & Q 13 March 1937. See 17 Nov 1934, 22 June 1935.

Weiss, H. B. Cowper's frolic in rhyme: John Gilpin. BNYPL Sept 1937.

Flower, D. and A. N. L. Munby. In their English poetical autographs, 1938.

Hartley, L. C. Cowper, humanitarian. Chapel Hill 1938.

— The stricken deer and his contemporary reputation. SP 36 1939.

— Cowper and Mme Guyon. PMLA 56 1941.

— Cowper's The castaway. Explicator Dec 1946.

— The worm and the thorn: Cowper's Olney Hymns. Jnl of Religion 29 1949.

— Cowper and the evangelicals: notes on early biographical interpretations. PMLA 65 1950.

— Cowper and the polygamous parson. MLQ 16 1955.

— An uncollected Cowper letter. RES new ser 17 1966.

Arrieta, R. A. Un poet rural inglés del siglo xviii. In his Estudios en tres literaturas, Buenos Aires [1939]. Rptd from Humanidades 22 1934.

Gilbert, D. L. and Pope, R. The Cowper translation of Mme Guyon's poems. PMLA 54 1939. Addns by L. C. Hartley 56 1941.

Barnard, E. A. B. Cowper's Mr Gregson. N & Q 2 Aug 1941.

Hunt, R. N. C. Newton and Cowper. Nineteenth Century Aug 1941.

M[acPike], E. F. Cowper and John Johnson. N & Q 5 Dec 1942, 18 Dec 1943.

Thein, A. E. The religion of John Newton. PQ 21 1942.

Wake, J. John Gilpin. TLS 14 Feb, 11 April 1942.

Barham Johnson sale. Sotheby's catalogue 21 April 1943. Described TLS 22 May 1943.

Quinlan, M. J. Cowper and the unpardonable sin. Jnl of Religion 23 1943.

— An intermediary between Cowper and Johnson. RES 24 1948.

— Cowper's [biblical] imagery. JEGP 47 1948.

— Cowper and the French Revolution. JEGP 50 1951.

— Cowper: a critical life. Minneapolis 1953.

C[hapman], R. W. A book from Cowper's library. N & Q 17 June 1944.

[Starkey, J.] Cowper and Newton. In his Essays and recollections by 'Seumas O'Sullivan', Dublin 1944.

Myers, R. M. Newton. Fifty sermons [by J. Newton] on Handel's Messiah. Harvard Theological Rev 39 1946.

Gray, W. F. Cowper and flying machines. Fortnightly Rev Jan 1947.

Wormhoudt, A. Cowper's The task iv 36–41. Explicator Oct 1948.

MacLean, K. In The age of Johnson: essays presented to C. B. Tinker, New Haven 1949.

Zanco, A. Vita e poesia di Cowper. Milan 1949.

Hudson, W. M. The Homer of the North translates Homer. Texas Univ Lib Chron 4 1950.

Knight, G. L. Cowper as a hymn writer. Hymn 1 1950.

Martin, B. New light on Cowper. English 8 1950; rptd MLQ 13 1952.

— In his John Newton, 1950.

'Bishop, Morchard' (O. Stonor). In his Blake's Hayley, 1951.

Cowper's last years. TLS 5–12 Oct 1951. Extracts from John Johnson's diary, ed G. L. Keynes.

Nicholson, N. Cowper. 1951.

— Cowper. 1960 (Br Council pamphlet).

Wright, G. W. Cowper and the Quakers. N & Q 18 Aug 1951.

Davie, D. A. The critical principles of Cowper. Cambridge Jnl Dec 1953.

Pollard, A. Cowper's Olney hymns. Churchman 69 1955.

— Five poets on religion, ii: Cowper and Blake. Church Quart Rev 160 1959.

Sherbo, A. Cowper's Connoisseur essays. MLN 70 1955.

Bentley, G. E., jr. William Blake and 'Johnny of Norfolk'. SP 53 1956.

— Blake, Hayley and Lady Hesketh. RES new ser 7 1956.

Brooks, E. L. Cowper's periodical contributions. TLS 17 Aug 1956.

Gregory, H. K. The prisoner and his crimes: comments on a longer study of the mind of Cowper. Lit & Psychology 6 1956.

Johansen, J. H. The Olney hymns. Papers of Hymn Soc of America 20 1956.

Letters of Dean Spencer Cowper. Ed E. Hughes, Surtees Soc 165 1956.

Huang, R. Cowper: nature poet. Oxford 1957.

Ryskamp, C. Cowper and Darwin's Economy of vegetation. Harvard Lib Bull 11 1957.

— Cowper and Thomas Wright. Durham Univ Jnl 49 1957. Correcting attribution of letter to Cowper by E. Hughes 46 1954.

— Blake's Cowperian sketches. RES new ser 9 1958.

— William Cowper of the Inner Temple esq. Cambridge 1959.

— Lawrence's portrait of Cowper. Princeton Lib Chron 20 1959.

— Cowper's ambition: two documents. Yale Lib Gazette 34 1960.

— Cowper on the King's sea-bathing. Library 5th ser 15 1960.

— Cowper and his circle: a study of the Hannay collection; Blake's drawing of Cowper's monument. Princeton Lib Chron 24 1962.

— The cast-away: text of original ms and first printing of Cowper's Latin translation. Princeton 1963.

— Johnson and Cowper. Princeton 1965.

— Richardson and Cowper. Library 5th ser 19 1968.

Todd, W. B. Cowper's commentary on the Life of Johnson. TLS 15 March 1957.

Legouis, P. Donne and Cowper. Anglia 76 1958. On Task iii 712–24.

Keynes, G. L. The library of Cowper. Trans Cambridge Bibl Soc 3 pt 1 1959. Addns by Keynes, pt 2 1960; by N. H. Russell, pt 3 1961.

Emden, C. S. In his Poets in their letters, Oxford 1959.

Golden, M. Churchill's literary influence on Cowper. JEGP 58 1959.

— In search of stability: the poetry of Cowper. New York 1960.

Kroitor, H. P. Cowper, Deism and the divinization of nature. JHI 31 1960.

—— The influence of popular science on Cowper. MP 61 1964.

Zall, P. M. Landor's marginalia on a volume of Cowper's poems. BNYPL Jan 1960.

—— A variant version of the Rose. HLQ 25 1962.

Aldridge, A. O. Cowper and La Rochefoucauld. N & Q July 1962. Addn, Oct 1962.

Brown, T. J. English literary autographs 43: Cowper. Book Collector 11 1962.

Tompkins, A. D. R. A nursery version of John Gilpin. N & Q Dec 1962.

Werkmeister, L. Two early version of the Negro's complaint. N & Q Jan 1962.

Price, C. Books owned by Smart and Cowper. N & Q June 1963.

Fargeix, P. Cowper: la vie et l'oeuvre. Draguignan 1964 (priv ptd).

Danchin, P. Cowper's poetic purpose as seen in his letters. E Studies 46 1965.

Morris, J. N. The uses of madness: Cowper's Memoir. Amer Scholar 34 1965.

Cagle, W. R. Cowper's letters: mirror to the man. In The familiar letter in the eighteenth century, ed H. Anderson, P. B. Daghlian and I. Ehrenpreis, Lawrence Kansas 1966.

Chalon, Y. Cowper's Against interested love. N & Q Dec 1966.

Eaves, T. C. D. and B. D. Kimpel. Cowper's An ode on reading Mr Richardson's History of Sir Charles Grandison. Papers on Lang & Lit 2 1966.

Standley, F. L. Cowper: an unpublished note. N & Q Dec 1966.

Westcott, I. M. A full set of Cowper's poems in parts. Ibid.

Gregory, H. K. Cowper's love of subhuman nature: a psychoanalytic approach. PQ 46 1967.

Ringler, R. N. The genesis of Cowper's Yardley Oak. Eng Lang Notes 5 1967.

Desai, R. W. Cowper and the visual arts. BNYPL June 1968.

Paley, M. D. Cowper as Blake's spectre. Eighteenth-Century Stud 1 1968.

N. H. R.

JAMES MACPHERSON
1736–96

Bibliographies

Black, G. F. Macpherson's Ossian and the Ossianic controversy. BNYPL June–July 1926.

Collections

Fragments of ancient poetry collected in the highlands of Scotland. Edinburgh 1760, 1760 (rev with one addn), 1881; ed L. Jiriczek, Heidelberg 1915; Edinburgh 1917; ed J. J. Dunn, Los Angeles 1966 (Augustan Reprint Soc).

Fingal: an ancient epic poem, with several other poems translated from the Galic language. 1762, 1762.

Temora: an ancient epic poem, with several other poems translated from the Galic language. 1763.

The works of Ossian, translated by James Macpherson. 2 vols 1765 (with Hugh Blair, Critical dissertation), Dublin 1765, London 1773, Darmstadt 1773–5, 4 vols Frankfurt 1773–7, Frankfurt and Leipzig 1783, Paris 1783, 2 vols 1784–5, 1790, Dublin 1790, Philadelphia 1790, Edinburgh 1792, 1792, Berwick 1795, Perth 1795, London 1796, London and Glasgow [1796–7]. Black, above, notes 80 English edns of Works 1765–1902, pbd throughout the British Isles, in America and on the Continent. He also notes trns of Works into Gaelic 1818, Czech 1827, Danish 1790, Dutch 1793,

French 1777, German 1768–9, Hungarian 1833, Italian 1763, Polish 1840, Russian 1792, Spanish 1788, Swedish 1794 (first trns only); as well as 64 trns of individual poems into various languages and 34 selected edns in various languages.

The poems of Ossian. 2 vols Dublin 1802.

The poems of Ossian: containing the poetical works of Macpherson. Ed M. Laing 2 vols Edinburgh 1805.

Poems of Ossian. 2 vols 1807 (illustr), 1807.

Ossian: Faksimile-neudruck der Erstausgabe von 1762–3 mit Begleitband: die Varianten. Ed O. L. Jiriczek 3 vols Heidelberg 1940.

§ 1

The Highlander: an heroic poem in six cantos. 1758.

An introduction to the history of Great Britain and Ireland. 1771.

The Iliad translated into prose. 2 vols 1773.

The history of Great Britain from the Restoration to the accession of the House of Hanover. 2 vols 1775.

Original papers: containing the secret history of Great Britain from the Restoration to the accession of the House of Hanover. 2 vols 1775.

The rights of Great Britain asserted against the claims of America. 1776.

A short history of the opposition during the last session of Parliament. 1779.

§ 2

Blair, H. A critical dissertation on the poems of Ossian. 1763.

Hill, T. F. Interesting particulars of Ossian. GM Dec 1782–Feb 1783, May–June 1783.

Nutt, A. Ossian and the Ossianic literature. 1899.

Report of the committee of the Highland Society of Scotland, appointed to enquire into the nature and authenticity of the poems of Ossian. 3 vols Edinburgh 1805.

Scott, W. Edinburgh Rev 6 1805. Review of Laing's 1805 edn, above.

'Talvj' (T. A. L. von Jacob). Die Unächtheit der Lieder Ossians und des Macphersonschen Ossians insbesordere. Leipzig 1840.

Macbain, A. Macpherson's Ossian. Celtic Mag Feb–April 1887.

Saunders, T. B. The life and letters of Macpherson. 1894.

Stern, L. C. Die ossianischen Heldenlieder. Zeitschrift für Vergleichende Litteraturgeschichte 3 1895; tr J. L. Robertson, Trans Gallic Soc of Inverness 25 1898.

Nutt, A. Ossian and the Ossianic literature. 1899. Also lists genuine texts.

Tombo, R. Ossian in Germany. New York 1901.

Smart, J. S. James Macpherson. 1905.

Weitenauer, K. Ossian in der italienischen Litteratur. Munich 1905.

Heuer, O. Eine unbekannte Ossianübersetzung Goethes. Jahrbuch des Freien Deutschen Hochstifts 1908.

Tedeschi, A. Ossian en France. Milan 1911.

Wetterwald, F. Die literarischen Anfänge Macphersons. Basle 1918.

Malmstedt, A. Ossian studier i modern språkvetenskap. Nyfilofiska Sällskapet, Stockholm 1920.

van Tieghem, F. Ossian et l'ossianisme dans la littérature européenne au XVIIIe siècle. Groningen [1920].

Hamel, A. G. van and K. R. Gallas. Over Ossian. Neophilologus 6 1921.

Snyder, E. D. The Celtic revival in English literature. Cambridge Mass 1923.

Fraser, G. M. The truth about Macpherson's Ossian. Quart Rev 245 1925.

Moore, J. R. Wordsworth's unacknowledged debt to Ossian. PMLA 40 1925.

Peers, E. The influence of Ossian in Spain. PQ 4 1925.

Christiansen, R. T. Ossian og folkedigtningen. Edda 25 1926.

Carpenter, F. I. The vogue of Ossian in America. Amer Lit 2 1931.

Chapman, R. W. Blair on Ossian. RES 7 1931.

Gillies, A. Herder und Ossian. Berlin 1933.

Marwell, H. Percy und die Ossian-kontroverse. Anglia 58 1934.

Betteridge, G. T. The Ossianic poems in Herder's Volkslieder. MLR 30 1935.

Jiriczek, O. L. Loda in Macphersons Ossian. Anglia 59 1935.

—— Zur Bibliographie und Textgeschichte von Blairs Critical dissertation on Ossian. E Studien 70 1935.

—— Brumo in Ossian. Beiblatt zur Anglia 48 1937.

Clayton, V. In his Prose poem in French literature of the eighteenth century, New York 1936.

Hanson, W. G. Macpherson. London Quart 161 1936.

Büscher, E. Ossian in der Sprache des 18 Jahrhunderts. Köslin 1937.

Gantz, K. F. Charlotte Brooke's Reliques of Irish poetry and the Ossianic controversy. SE 20 1940.

Beutler, E. Bilder zu Ossian. Goethe-kalendar auf das Jahr 1941.

Schöffler, H. Ossian. Ibid.

Leary, L. Ossian in America. Amer Lit 14 1943.

Hennig, J. Goethe's translation of Ossian's Songs of Selma. JEGP 45 1946.

Meyerstein, E. H. W. The influence of Macpherson. English 7 1948.

Fridén, G. James Fenimore Cooper and Ossian. Upsala 1949.

Hudson, W. M. The Homer of the north translates Homer. Texas Univ Lib Chron 4 1950.

—— Ossian in English before Macpherson. SE 29 1950.

Sheehan, C. A. Notes on the Ossianic controversy. N & Q 8 July 1950.

Thomson, D. S. The Gaelic sources of Ossian. Edinburgh 1952.

—— Ossian Macpherson and the Gaelic world of the eighteenth century. Aberdeen Univ Rev 40 1963.

Chapman, A. Heredia's Ossian translations. Hispanic Rev 23 1955.

Thomas, R. G. Lord Bute, John Home and Ossian: two letters. MLR 51 1956.

Todd, W. B. Macpherson's Fingal and Temora. Book Collector 8 1959.

Carnie, R. H. Macpherson's Fragments of ancient poetry and Lord Hailes. E Studies 41 1960.

Chancellor, P. British bards and continental composers. Musical Quart 44 1958.

Roddier, H. Littérature populaire, littérature savante: le cas de Macpherson. AUMLA no 20 1963.

Mackechnie, J. The Gaelic manuscripts in Scotland. Stud in Scottish Lit 1 1964.

Sasse, H. C. Michael Denis as translator of Ossian. MLR 60 1965.

Weisweiler, J. Hintergrund und Herkunft der Ossianischen Dichtung. Literaturwissenschaftliches Jahrbuch der Görresgesellschaft 4 1963.

Fitzgerald, R. P. The style of Ossian. Stud in Romanticism 6 1966.

Okun, H. Ossian in painting. Jnl Warburg & Courtauld Inst 30 1967.

D. S. T.

THOMAS CHATTERTON
1752–70

The major ms collections are in BM and Central Library, Bristol.

Bibliographies

Hyett, F. A. and W. Bazeley. Chattertoniana. Gloucester 1914. Rptd from The bibliographer's manual of Gloucestershire literature.

Mathews, E. R. N. Chatterton: a bibliography. In his Bristol bibliography, Bristol 1916.

Collections

Poems, supposed to have been written at Bristol, by Thomas Rowley, and others, in the fifteenth century. [Ed T. Tyrwhitt] 1777, 1777, 1778 (with Tyrwhitt's An appendix tending to prove that they were written by Chatterton); ed J. Milles 1782 (with addns); ed L. Sharpe, Cambridge 1794; ed M. E. Hare, Oxford 1911 (from 1778).

Miscellanies in prose and verse. [Ed J. Broughton] 1778. A supplement to the miscellanies. 1784.

Barrett, W. The history and antiquities of Bristol. Bristol [1789]. 23 pieces and many extracts.

Poetical works. Edinburgh 1795 (Anderson's Works of the British poets vol 11).

Original poems of Chatterton. In E. Gardner, Miscellanies in prose and verse, Bristol 1798.

Works. Ed R. Southey [and J. Cottle] 3 vols 1803. With G. Gregory's life.

Select poems. Philadelphia 1822 (Walsh's Works of the British poets vol 29).

Dix, J. The life of Chatterton. 1837. 9 pieces.

Chatterton's Ella and other pieces. Ed J. Glassford, Edinburgh 1837. First modernized Rowleyan collection.

Poetical works. [Ed Willcox] 2 vols Cambridge 1842, Boston 1857 etc.

Poems. Ed F. Martin [1865].

Poetical works. Ed W. W. Skeat 2 vols 1871 (Aldine).

Poetical works. Ed J. Richmond 1885.

The Rowley poems. Ed R. Steele 2 vols 1898 (decorated by C. Ricketts).

Poems. Ed S. Lee 2 vols [1905], 1906–9.

Complete poetical works. Ed H. D. Roberts 2 vols 1906. Tr French, 1839.

Many pieces ptd in E. H. W. Meyerstein, A life of Chatterton, 1930, below.

§1

The execution of Sir Charles Bawdin. 1772.

Song to Ælle. Westminster Mag 1775.

A short account of William Cannings. Town & Country Mag 7 1775.

Fragment of a sermon by the celebrated Rowlie. GM Sept 1777.

Chatterton on heraldry. GM Nov 1787. Letter to R. Bigland, Somerset Herald.

The romaunte of a knyghte. [no place] 1788 (single sheet).

European Mag 20–1 1791–2. 6 pieces.

The revenge: a burletta, with additional songs. 1795.

Impromptu on the immortality of the soul. In J. Evans, Chronological outline of the history of Bristol, Bristol 1824.

Another Chatterton relic. Bristol Times & Mirror 27 June 1904.

Meyerstein, E. H. W. Chatterton's infidelity. TLS 2 March 1922. Includes a poem.

Mabbott, T. O. A new poem by Chatterton. MLN 39 1924.

Ellinger, E. P. Chatterton: the marvelous boy. Philadelphia 1930. Includes The exhibition: a personal satire.

The letter paraphras'd. Ed 'M. O. Hunter' [New York 1933]. Girl's letter to Chatterton and his obscene paraphrase.

Meyerstein, E. H. W. A satirical eclogue by Chatterton. TLS 12 July 1934.

Supplement to Chatterton's miscellanies: Kew gardens. Probably published between 1778 and 1800.

During Chatterton's lifetime he pbd anon or pseudonymously in Felix Farley's Bristol Jnl 1768–9 (*2 pieces*), Bristol Jnl 1769 (*one piece*), Town & Country Mag 1769–70 (*29 pieces*), Universal Mag 1769 (*one piece*), Middlesex Jnl 1770 (*13 pieces*), Freeholder's Mag 1770 (*2 pieces*), Boddeley's Bath Jnl 1770 (*one piece*), Court & City Mag 1770 (*3 pieces*), London Mag 1770 (*2 pieces*). *After his death, pieces he had submitted were pbd in* Town & Country Mag 1770 (*one piece*), 1771 (*2 pieces*), 1783 (*one piece*). *For these periodicals, see index to* E. H. W. Meyerstein, A life of Chatterton, 1930, *below.*

Letters

[Croft, H.] Love and madness: a story too true in a series of letters. 1780 etc. Letter 49, a sketch of Chatterton, first prints 3 of his poems and 8 of his letters.

Walpole, H. Works. 1798. Vol 4 first prints 3 Chatterton letters.

Britton, J. An historical essay relating to Redcliffe church. 1813. First prints 2 letters to Dodsley.

Mabbott, T. O. Two letters of Chatterton in America. N & Q 7 March 1931.

—— Notes on Chatterton: letter to William Smith. N & Q 2 April 1932.

—— Notes on Chatterton. N & Q 6 Jan 1940. Reply by E. H. W. Meyerstein 20 April 1940.

Walpole's correspondence with Chatterton. Ed W. S. Lewis et al, New Haven 1951 (vol 16 of Yale Walpole).

§2

Interest in Chatterton and the Rowley controversy can be traced in GM, where articles appear annually 1777–92, thereafter frequently till 1840.

Warton, T. In his History of English poetry, 3 vols 1774–81 (vol 2 and addenda).

—— An enquiry into the authenticity of the poems attributed to Rowley. 1782, 1782.

[Dampier, H. or F. Woodward]. Remarks upon the eighth section of the second volume of Warton's History. [1779 or 1780].

Walpole, H. A letter to the editor of the Miscellanies of Chatterton. Strawberry Hill 1779; rptd GM 1782.

Bryant, J. Observations upon the poems of Rowley. 1781.

An examination of the poems attributed to Rowley and Canynge. Sherborne [1782].

[Mason, W.] An archaeological epistle to the Rev J. Milles. 1782.

[Greene, E. B.] Strictures upon a pamphlet intitled Cursory observations on the poems attributed to Rowley. 1782.

[Hardinge, G.] Rowley and Chatterton in the shades. 1782.

[Hickford, R.] Observations on the poems attributed to Rowley; with remarks on the appendix of the editor of Rowley's poems [by J. Fell]. [1782].

[Malone, E.] Cursory observations on the poems attributed to Rowley. 1782; ed J. M. Kuist, Los Angeles 1966 (Augustan Reprint Soc).

[Mickle, W. J.] The prophecy of Queen Emma. 1782.

Tyrwhitt, T. A vindication of the appendix to the poems called Rowley's. 1782.

Mathias, T. J. An essay on the evidence relating to the poems attributed to Rowley. 1783.

Gregory, G. The life of Chatterton. 1789; rptd in Biographia britannica, 1789; Works, 1803.

Davis, J. The life of Chatterton. [1806].

Sherwen, J. Introduction to an examination of some part of the evidence respecting certain publications said to have been found at Bristol. Bath 1809.

Cottle, J. Malvern hills. 2 vols 1829.

—— Early recollections. 2 vols 1837.

Vigny, A. de. Chatterton. [Paris?] 1835. A play.

Dix, J. The life of Chatterton. 1837.

Püttmann, H. Chatterton. Barman 1840.

Browning, R. Foreign Quart Rev 29 1842; ed D. A. Smalley, Cambridge Mass 1948 (as Browning's essay on Chatterton). A review of R. H. Wilde, Tasso.

Masson, D. Chatterton: a story of the year 1770. Dublin Univ Mag 38 1851; rev and ptd separately 1874.

—— Chatterton: a biography. 1899.

Pryce, G. Memorials of the Canynges family. Bristol 1854.

—— Fact versus fiction. Bristol 1858.

Maitland, S. R. Chatterton: an essay. 1857.

Thomas W. M. The inquest on Chatterton. Athenaeum 5 Dec 1857, 23 Jan 1858.

Wilson, D. Chatterton. 1869.

Thornbury, W. John Dix, the biographer of Chatterton. N & Q 13 April 1872.

Forman, H. B. Chatterton and his latest editor. 1874. On Skeat's edn.

Watts-Dunton, T. Chatterton. In Ward's English poets vol 3, 1880.

Noel, R. In his Essays on poetry and poets, 1886.

Richter, H. Thomas Chatterton. Vienna and Leipzig 1900.

—— Chatterton's Rowley-sprache: Bausteine. Zeitschrift für Neuenglische Wortforschung 1 1905.

Russell, C. E. Thomas Chatterton. New York 1908.

Ingram, J. H. The true Chatterton. 1910.

—— Chatterton and his poetry. 1916.

Clarke, E. New lights on Chatterton. Trans Bibl Soc 13 1916.

Meyerstein, E. H. W. Lydgate and Chatterton. TLS 16 April 1925.

—— Chatterton: a correction. TLS 16 July 1925.

—— Wordsworth and Chatterton. TLS 21 Oct 1926.

—— De Quincey's copy of Chatterton's Miscellanies. TLS 8 May 1930.

—— A life of Chatterton. 1930.

—— Chatterton's spelling of Ælla. TLS 4 Feb 1932.

—— An elegy on Chatterton. TLS 8 Feb 1934.

—— Chatterton's Birtha. TLS 18 July 1936.

—— Chatterton, Coleridge and Bristol. TLS 21 Aug 1937. Reply by W. Sypher 28 Aug 1937.

—— Chatterton: his significance today. Essays by Divers Hands 16 1937.

—— Chatterton and Kilburn priory. TLS 30 July 1938.

—— Chatterton and the angel. TLS 21 Jan 1939.

—— Chatterton's Bristowe tragedy. TLS 5 Aug 1939.

—— The forged letter from Peel to Marlowe. TLS 29 June 1940. Reply by E. St J. Brooks 20 July 1940.

—— Chatterton's last days. TLS 28 June 1941.

—— John Baker's letters to Chatterton. TLS 26 April 1947.

—— A Chatterton manuscript. TLS 27 December 1947.

—— Chatterton and Sir William Jones. N & Q 1 May 1948.

—— The influence of Macpherson. English 7 1949.

—— Chattertoniana. TLS 6 Jan 1950.

—— A Bristol friendship: Chatterton and John Baker. Essays by Divers Hands 25 1950.

Dixon, W. M. Chatterton. Proc Br Acad 16 1930.

Ellinger, E. P. Chatterton: the marvelous boy. Philadelphia 1930.

The problem of Chatterton. TLS 31 July 1930.

Powell, L. F. Thomas Tyrwhitt and the Rowley poems. RES 7 1931.

Mabbott, T. O. Chatterton's Execution of Sir Charles Bawdin. Bibl N & Q 1 1935. Reply by R. W. Chapman, ibid.

—— Chatterton: an uncollected poem. N & Q 15 Jan 1938.

—— Chatterton: a poem attributed to him. N & Q 19 Feb 1938.

—— Chatterton and Milton: a question of forgery. N & Q 28 Oct 1939.

Staubert, P. Chatterton und seine Rowley-dichtung: untersucht auf Grund der Psychologie der Reifezeit. Bonn 1935.

Watkin-Jones, A. Bishop Percy, Thomas Warton and Chatterton's Rowley poems. PMLA 50 1935.

Hermann, H. Dichter oder Fälscher. Germania no 108 1937.

Walpole, H. The Yale edition of Walpole's correspondence. Ed W. S. Lewis et al, New Haven 1937–.

Sypher, W. Chatterton's African eclogues and the deluge. PMLA 54 1939.

Wasserman, E. R. The Walpole-Chatterton controversy. MLN 54 1939.

Muir, P. H. A Chatterton edition. TLS 5 April 1941.

Miller, F. S. The historic sense of Chatterton. ELH 11 1944.

Nevill, J. C. Chatterton. 1948.

Bronson, B. H. Chatterton. In The age of Johnson, New Haven 1949.

— Chattertoniana. MLQ 11 1950.

Scudder, H. H. Chatterton on money. N & Q 22 July 1950.

Grigson, G. In his Essays from the air, 1951.

Waldhorn, A. Chatterton, De Burgham and John Dix. N & Q 17 March 1951.

Taylor, D. S. Chatterton's suicide. PQ 31 1952.

— The authenticity of Chatterton's Miscellanies. PBSA 55 1961.

— Chatterton: the problem of Rowley chronology. PQ 46 1967.

Miles, J. The language of ballads. Romance Philology 7 1953.

Gittings, R. Keats and Chatterton. Keats-Shelley Jnl 4 1955.

Ting, N-T. The influence of Chatterton on Keats. Keats-Shelley Jnl 5 1956.

Guthke, K. S. The Rowley myth in 18th-century Germany. PBSA 51 1957.

Greenacre, P. The imposter. Psychoanalytic Quart 27 1958.

— The family romance of the artist. Psychoanalytic Study of the Child 13 1958.

White, E. W. Chatterton and the English burletta. RES new ser 9 1958.

Cottle, B. Thomas Chatterton. Bristol 1963 (Bristol Historical Assoc pamphlet).

Rodway, A. E. In his Romantic conflict, 1963.

Wolpe, H. Chatterton: the marvelous boy. Revue de Littérature Comparée 37 1963.

Schulze, F. W. An excelente balade of charitie. In Versdichtung der englischen Romantik: Interpretationen, ed T. A. Riese and D. Riesner, Berlin 1968.

D. S. T.

GEORGE CRABBE
1754–1832

Bibliographies

Memoir of the Crabbe celebration and catalogue of the exhibits at Aldeburgh. Ed C. Ganz, Lowestoft [1905].

Huchon, R. Brief appreciation of the Crabbe collection formed by A. M. Broadley. Bath 1905.

East Suffolk County Library. Catalogue of the bicentenary exhibition of books and mss. Aldeburgh 1954; rptd in Proc Suffolk Institute of Archaeology & Natural History 26 1954. See Crabbe in Aldeburgh, TLS 2 July 1954.

Bibliographies are included in R. Huchon, Un poète réaliste anglais: Crabbe, Paris 1906, tr 1907; in Poems, ed A. W. Ward 3 vols Cambridge 1905–7; in R. Chamberlain, Crabbe, New York 1965; in O. Sigworth, Nature's sternest painter, Tucson 1965; in Poems, ed N. H. Russell and A. Pollard, Oxford 1973, by K. Povey.

Collections

Poetical works (Poems, Borough, Tales). 4 vols 1816, 1816, 3 vols 1816?; Poems, Borough, Tales, Tales of the hall, 7 vols 1820, 5 vols 1820?; 5 vols 1823, 8 vols 1823; with letters and journals, and life by his son, 8 vols 1834 etc (includes Posthumous tales). Rptd in 1 vol 1847,

1851, 1854, 1866, 1901. Illustrations by Heath after Westall pbd separately 1822; by Finden after Stanfield advertised 1834. See Pocket Mag under §2, below. Reviewed Br Critic 16 1834 (by Hartley Coleridge); Edinburgh Rev 60 1835 (by W. Empson); London Rev 1 1835; Monthly Rev Sept 1834; Quart Rev 50, 52 1834 (by J. G. Lockhart).

Poetical works: with memoir by C.T. [C. Taylor?]. Paris 1829, [1835?].

Beauties of Crabbe, with a biographical sketch. 1832.

Cullings from Crabbe: with memoir [by T. Taylor]. Bath 1832.

Tales and miscellaneous poems. 1847.

Other selections pbd 1828, Paris 1828, Frankfurt 1828 (in British Poets of the Nineteenth Century), 1854, 1858, [1873], 1888 (ed E. Lamplough), Edinburgh [1855], [1881], Glasgow [1878], Miles 1 (1); tr Russian in various Russian journals, 1856–69.

Poems: a selection by B. Holland. 1899, 1909.

Selections. Ed A. Deane 1903, 1932.

Poems. Ed A. W. Ward 3 vols Cambridge 1905–7.

Selections. Ed A. T. Quiller-Couch, Oxford [1908], [1912].

Poetical works. Ed A. J. and R. M. Carlyle, Oxford 1908 (OSA), 1914.

Crabbe: an anthology. Ed F. L. Lucas, Cambridge 1933.

Poems, selected by P. Henderson. 1946.

Poems, selected by G. Grigson. 1950.

Selections. Ed F. Whitehead 1955.

A selection. Ed G. Newbold 1967.

Tales and miscellaneous poems. Ed H. Mills, Cambridge 1967.

A selection. Ed J. Lucas 1967.

§1
Poems

Poetical essay on hope, To Mira, The bee, An allegorical fable, On melancholy. Lady's Mag (ptd for J. Wheble) Sept–Dec 1772. Signed C. or G.C.

Solitude, A song, To Emma, Despair, Cupid, Song. Lady's Mag (ptd for G. Robinson) Sept–Nov 1772. Signed 'G. Ebbare' or 'G. Ebbaac'.

Inebriety: a poem in three parts. Ipswich 1775. Anon.

The candidate: a poetical epistle to the authors of the Monthly Review. 1780. Anon. Reviewed Monthly Rev Sept 1780 (by Edmund Cartwright); Critical Rev Sept 1780.

The library. 1781 (anon), 1783 (signed); rptd in Poems, 1807; A miscellany, ed H. Morley 1888; illustr E. J. G. Ardizzone 1930; Boston 1966 (facs of 1781). Reviewed Critical Rev Aug 1781; GM Oct 1781; Monthly Rev Dec 1781 (by Edmund Cartwright).

The village: a poem in two books. 1783. Trial issue ptd by J. Nichols c. 1781? (see A. H. Smith, John Nichols printer and publisher, Library 5th ser 18 1963), New York 1790, Boston 1791. Extracts pbd in Annual Register 26 1783, Elegant extracts in poetry, 1789, 1796. Rptd in Poems, 1807, 1833 (separately), 1879; ed A. Sale 1950.

The news-paper. 1785; rptd in Poems, 1807; tr German, 1856.

Poems. 1807 (first pbn of The parish register), Philadelphia [1807], London 1808, 1808, New York 1808, Philadelphia 1808, 2 vols 1809, 1810, 1812, 1 vol 1812, 1813, 1816, 1817, 1820, 1835, 1837, 1840, [1850?], 1863 etc; ed H. Morley 1886. Parish register tr Dutch, 1858; to Russian, 1875 (extracts).

A poem for the anniversary of the Literary Fund, April 20 1809. GM April 1809. Lines 188–336 of Borough iii, with variants.

The borough: a poem in twenty-four letters. 1810 (3 edns, one in 2 vols), Philadelphia 1810, 2 vols 1812, 1 vol 1813, 1816, 1820; ed H. Williams 1903. Letter 22 (Peter

Grimes) tr French, 1831, 1833; tr Russian, 1875 (extracts). Reviewed Edinburgh Rev 16 1810 (by F. Jeffrey); Quart Rev 4 1810 (by Robert Grant?), Monthly Rev April 1810 (by T. Denman); Eclectic Rev June 1810.

Tales. 1812, 2 vols 1812, 1 vol 1813, 2 vols 1813, New York 1813, 1 vol 1814, 2 vols 1814, 1815, 1 vol 1816, 2 vols 1820, 1 vol 1854; ed H. Morley 1891 (selected); tr Russian, 1902, nd (tales 17 and 20). Reviewed Edinburgh Rev 20 1812 (by F. Jeffrey); Eclectic Rev Nov 1812; Monthly Rev Dec 1812 (by T. Denman).

Verses by the Rev G. Crabbe, written on the night of the 15th of April 17** [1782?]. Literary Gazette 16 Aug 1817. See W. H. Davenport, N & Q 31 Dec 1938.

Tales of the hall. 2 vols 1819, 1819, Boston 1819, 3 vols 1820. Reviewed Edinburgh Rev 32 1819 (by F. Jeffrey); Blackwood's Mag July 1819 (by J. Wilson); Br Critic Sept 1819; Monthly Rev Nov 1819; Eclectic Rev Feb 1820. See E. FitzGerald, §2 below.

Lines by the Rev George Crabbe LlB. [Edinburgh 1822]; rptd in Occasional verses on the King's visit to Scotland [Edinburgh 1822]; GM Sept 1822; in Royal Scottish minstrelsy, Leith 1824.

A collection of poems from living authors. Ed J. Baillie 1823. Includes Hope and memory.

The casket: a miscellany. [Ed P. Blencowe] 1829. Includes Lines to the Dowager Duchess of Rutland.

Green, R. The history, topography and antiquities of Framlingham and Saxsted. 1834. Includes epitaph on W. S. Levett.

Posthumous tales. First pbd in Poetical works vol 8, 1834.

Blackwood's Mag April 1837. The world we live in, no 6. Includes Parham revisited and A new version of the parable (from Woman).

The sacred casket. 1839 (2nd edn). Includes Sir Eustace Grey, lines 348–71 as a hymn (The Christian pilgrim).

Dowden, E. Relics of Crabbe. Illustr London News 20 June 1891. Unpbd extracts from Midnight and The deserted wife.

Literary anecdotes of the nineteenth century. Ed W. R. Nicoll and T. J. Wise 1896. Vol 2 includes Two poetical epistles.

Huchon, R. Two unpublished poems of Crabbe [The Squire and O give me the hour that I love to spend]. Monthly Rev March 1904.

Jourdain, M. Treasure trove: some unpublished verse by Crabbe. Book Monthly May 1906. Includes unpbd stanza of The friend in love.

London Mercury Sept 1922. To Miss E.V. in her 10th year.

New poems by Crabbe. Ed A. Pollard, Liverpool 1960. Hester, Joseph and Jesse, Poins, David Morris and 10 other unpbd poems.

See A. M. Broadley and W. Jerrold under §2, below.

Sermons and Prose Writings

The atheist reclaimed: a prose anecdote. Lady's Mag (ptd for J. Wheble) Nov 1772.

Character of Lord Robert Manners. Annual Register 26 1783. Anon.

A discourse on 2 Corinthians 1.9 read in the chapel at Belvoir Castle after the funeral of the Duke of Rutland. 1788.

The natural history of the Vale of Belvoir. In J. Nichols, The history and antiquities of the county of Leicester vol 1 pt 1, 1795.

A catalogue of plants growing in and near Framlingham. In R. Hawes, History of Framlingham ed R. Loder, Woodbridge 1798. Crabbe also contributed notes to D. Turner and L. Dillwyn, The botanist's guide to England and Wales, 1805.

Memoirs of eminent persons: biographical account of the Rev G. Crabbe [written by himself]. New Monthly Mag Jan 1816; rptd in Annual biography and obituary for

1833; Catalogue of the bicentenary exhibition, Aldeburgh 1954.

The variation of public opinion and feelings considered as it respects religion: a sermon preached before the Lord Bishop of Sarum, 15 August 1817. 1817.

Posthumous sermons. Ed J. D. Hastings 1850.

Brumbaugh, T. B. Crabbe: an unpublished sermon. N & Q Jan 1961.

Letters

Jackson, W. Old-fashioned wit and humour; with a prefatory letter from Crabbe. 1860.

Correspondence with Mary Leadbeater. In Leadbeater papers vol 2 pt 3, 1862.

Bullough, G. A letter of Crabbe to Scott. TLS 22 Sept 1932. See 29 Sept 1932.

Forster, E. M. Crabbe on smugglers. Spectator 20 Feb 1932. A letter to Hatchard.

Wecter, D. Four letters from Crabbe to Burke. RES 14 1938.

TLS 20 Sept 1941. Tenbury discoveries. Includes letter by Crabbe; rptd in Tenbury letters, ed E. H. Fellowes and E. Pine 1942.

Pollard, A. Two new letters of Crabbe. RES new ser 2 1951.

Link, F. M. Three Crabbe letters. Eng Lang Notes 2 1965.

For other letters, see catalogues of Crabbe exhibitions at Aldeburgh [1905] and 1954 above,; and J. H. Bransby, A. M. Broadley and W. Jerrold under §2, below.

§2

For reviews by Jeffrey, Lockhart et al see §1, above.

[Smith, J. and H.] Rejected addresses: or the new theatrum poetarum. 1812 (no 20, The theatre, 'By the Rev G.C.'), 1812 (with addns), 1833 (with notes).

Talfourd, T. N. An attempt to estimate the poetical talent of the present age: Crabbe. Pamphleteer 5 1815.

For Crabbe's autobiographical memoir, 1816, see §1, Sermons and prose writings, above.

Memoir of Crabbe. European Mag Sept 1819. Anon.

Pocket Mag of Classic & Polite Literature; with engravings [by Corbould] illustrative of Crabbe 6 1820. Later pbd separately.

Hazlitt, W. Mr Crabbe. London Mag May 1821; rptd in part in his Spirit of the age, 1825 (in Mr Campbell and Mr Crabbe).

Balfour, A. Characters omitted in the Parish register. Edinburgh Mag 10–12 1822–3; rptd with other tales by the author, 1825. Imitations of Crabbe.

Pichot, A. In his Voyage historique et littéraire en Angleterre et en Ecosse vol 2, Paris 1825. Letter 63.

Bransby, J. H. Brief notices of the late Rev G. Crabbe. Carnarvon 1832. Contains a letter from Crabbe to the author.

Crabbe, George, jr. The life of the Rev George Crabbe by his son. In Poetical works vol 1, 1834; rptd in edns of the Works; Cambridge Mass 1834; ed E. M. Forster, Oxford 1932 (WC); ed E. Blunden 1947.

Gilfillan, G. In his Second gallery of literary portraits, Edinburgh 1850.

Druzhinin, A. V. Krabb i ego proizvedenia [Crabbe and his works]. In Sovremennik, St Petersburg 1855–6; rptd in Druzhinin, Collected works, 1865.

Clodd, E. Crabbe: a biography. Aldeburgh 1865.

[FitzGerald, E.] In his Sea words and phrases used along the Suffolk coast, [1869]. Appendix I: Crabbe's Suffolk. Signed E.F.G. From East Anglian N & Q Jan 1869; rptd in Works of FitzGerald, 2 vols New York 1887; and in W. Prideaux, Notes for a bibliography of FitzGerald, 1901.

—— Readings in Crabbe's Tales of the hall. [Guildford 1879]; rptd 1882 (with introd), 1883 (with rev introd). Original introd rptd in Works of FitzGerald, 2 vols New

York 1887. Rev introd rptd in vol 3 of his Letters and literary remains, ed W. A. Wright 3 vols 1889.

Stephen, L. Hours in a library no 9: Crabbe's poetry. Cornhill Mag Oct 1874; rptd in his Hours in a library ser 2, 1876.

Woodberry, G. E. A neglected poet. Atlantic Monthly May 1880; rptd in his Studies in letters and life, Boston 1890.

Kebbel, T. E. Life of Crabbe. 1888.

Patmore, C. Crabbe and Shelley. In his Principle in art, 1889.

Saintsbury, G. Crabbe. Macmillan's Mag June 1889; rptd in his Essays in English literature 1780–1860, 1890.

Holgate, C. W. The skull of Crabbe. Wiltshire Archaeological & Natural History Mag 29 1896.

Hillier, A. C. Jane Austen's husband. Temple Bar Nov 1897.

Pesta, H. Crabbe: eine Würdigung seiner Werke. Vienna 1899.

Hutton, W. H. Some memories of Crabbe. Cornhill Mag June 1901; rptd in his Burford papers, 1905.

More, P. E. A plea for Crabbe. Atlantic Monthly Dec 1901; rptd in his Shelburne essays ser 2, New York 1905.

[Statham, H.] Crabbe. Quart Rev 193 1901.

Ainger, A. C. Crabbe. 1903 (EML).

Groves, J. Crabbe as a botanist. Proc Suffolk Institute of Archaeology & Natural History 12 pt 2 1905.

Boynton, H. W. Life and work of Crabbe. Bookman (New York) March 1906.

Huchon, R. Un poète réaliste anglais: Crabbe. Paris 1906; tr 1907.

Collins, J. C. The poetry of Crabbe. Fortnightly Rev Oct 1907.

Shorter, C. To the immortal memory of Crabbe. In his Immortal memories, 1907.

Elton, O. The poetry of Crabbe. Blackwood's Mag Jan 1909.

Wohlgemüth, J. Der Stil in Crabbes Dichtungen. Würzburg 1910.

Bailey, J. The commemoration of Crabbe. TLS 15 Sept 1905; rptd in his Poets and poetry, Oxford 1911.

Holme, J. W. The treatment of nature in Crabbe. In Primitiae: essays by students of the University of Liverpool, 1912.

Broadley, A. M. and W. Jerrold. The romance of an elderly poet. 1913. Contains letters to Elizabeth Charter and 3 unpbd poems.

Broadley, A. M. In Crabbe centennial commemoration booklet, Trowbridge 1914.

Non-couplet poetry of Crabbe. Spectator 14 March 1914.

Strang, W. Crabbe. [1914].

Wylie, L. J. The England of Crabbe. In Social studies in English literature, New York 1916.

Pound, E. The Rev G. Crabbe Llb. In The Future, 1917; rptd in his Literary essays, 1954.

Thomas, E. In his A literary pilgrim in England, 1917.

Olivero, F. Crabbe. Nuova Antologia 1 Nov 1923.

Bär, H. Crabbe als Epiker: eine Studie zur Technik seiner Verserzählungen. Leipzig 1929.

Boyden, A. R. Masefield and Crabbe. Bookman (London) Dec 1930.

Looker, S. J. In praise of Crabbe. Nineteenth Century Oct 1931.

Lucas, F. L. The poet of prose. Life & Letters Feb 1931.

Waugh, A. Crabbe. Bookman (London) Feb 1932.

Crabbe. TLS 4 Feb 1932.

Forster, E. M. Crabbe. Spectator 20 Feb 1932.

—— Crabbe: the poet and the man. Listener 29 May 1941; rptd with alterations in Peter Grimes: an opera, 1945. See M. Slater, below.

—— Crabbe and Peter Grimes. In his Two cheers for democracy, [1951].

Grierson, H. J. C. Scott, Shelley and Crabbe. TLS 15 Sept 1932.

Masefield, J. In his Recent prose, 1932.

Ottley, M. Crabbe. London Mercury June 1932.

Evans, J. H. The poems of Crabbe: a literary and historical study. 1933.

Richards, F. Crabbe. London Quart 158 1933.

Abrams, M. H. In his Milk of paradise: the effects of opium visions on the works of De Quincey, Crabbe, Francis Thompson and Coleridge, Cambridge Mass 1934.

Heinlein, H. Die sozialen Anschauungen Crabbes. Kallmünz 1935.

Kellner, K. Crabbe und seine Stellung zu den sozialen Ergebnissen der Industrie-Revolution. Göttingen 1935.

Lang, V. Crabbe and Tess of the D'Urbervilles. MLN May 1938.

—— Crabbe and the eighteenth century. ELH 5 1938.

Clarke, M. The attitude of the early nineteenth-century reviewers towards the poetry of Crabbe. Eugene Oregon 1939.

Hering, G. F. Crabbe und Shakespeare. Shakespeare Jahrbuch 77 1941.

Shepherd, T. B. Crabbe and Methodism. London Quart 166 1941.

Slater, M. Peter Grimes: an opera derived from the poem [The borough] by Crabbe; words by M. Slater, music by B. Britten, [1945] (Sadlers Wells Opera Books 3); rptd with alterations in M. Slater, Peter Grimes and other poems, 1946.

Van den Bergh, G. Der Pessimismus bei Hardy, Crabbe und Swift. Menziken 1945.

Mercier, V. The poet as sociologist: Crabbe. Dublin Mag 22 1947.

Sale, A. Chaucer in cancer. English 6 1947.

—— The development of Crabbe's narrative art. Cambridge Jnl May 1952.

Brown, W. C. Crabbe: neo-classic narrative. In his Triumph of form, Chapel Hill 1948.

Batdorf, F. P. An unrecorded edition of Crabbe. PBSA 43 1949.

—— The background of Crabbe's Village. N & Q 29 Oct 1949.

—— Three editions of Crabbe's Tales. PBSA 44 1950.

—— An unrecorded early anthology of Crabbe. SB 3 1951.

—— The Murray reprints of Crabbe: a publisher's record. SB 4 1952.

—— John Bonnycastle, friend of Crabbe. N & Q Sept 1957.

Lawson, S. Crabbe thanks Jeffrey. N & Q 9 Dec 1950.

Spingarn, L. P. Crabbe as realist. Univ of Kansas City Rev 17 1950.

Woolf, V. In her Captain's death bed, 1950.

Graham, W. H. Crabbe: poet of penury. Contemporary Rev Feb 1951.

Todd, W. B. Two issues of Crabbe's Works 1823. PBSA 45 1951.

Broman, W. E. Factors in Crabbe's eminence in the early nineteenth century. MP 51 1954.

Duncan-Jones, E. E. Jane Austen and Crabbe. RES new ser 5 1954.

Mabbott, T. An intentional parody of Pope by Crabbe. N & Q Dec 1954.

Prichard, M. F. L. Crabbe's first appearance in print? N & Q June 1954.

Cruttwell, P. The last Augustan. Hudson Rev 7 1955.

Gregor, I. The last Augustan: some observations on the poetry of Crabbe. Dublin Rev 229 1955.

Haddakin, L. The poetry of Crabbe. 1955.

Ker, W. P. In his On modern literature, 1955.

Levin, Y. D. Krest'yanskaya tema v angliyskoy poezii xviii-nachala xix veka i derevenskie poemy Krabba [The peasant theme in English poetry of the 18th–early 19th century and Crabbe's village poems]. In Iz istorii demokraticheskoy literatury v Anglii xviii-xix vekov: sbornik statey [History of democratic literature in England in the 18th–early 19th centuries: a symposium], Leningrad 1955.

—— Kyukhel'beker and Crabbe. Oxford Slavonic Papers 12 1964.

Pollard, H. G. The early poems of Crabbe and the Lady's Magazine. Bodleian Lib Record 5 1955.

Brett, R. L. Crabbe. 1956 (Br Council pamphlet).

Pollard, A. Crabbe's theology. Church Quart Rev 157 1956.

Thale, R. M. Crabbe's Village and topographical poetry. JEGP 55 1956.

Thomas, W. K. The flavour of Crabbe. Dalhousie Rev 40 1961.

—— Crabbe's view of the poor. Revue de l'Université d'Ottawa 36 1966.

—— Crabbe's Borough: the process of montage. UTQ 36 1967.

—— Crabbe: not quite the sternest. Stud in Romanticism 7 1968.

Chamberlain, R. L. Crabbe and Darwin's amorous plants. JEGP 61 1962.

—— Crabbe. New York 1965.

Brady, M. B. Crabbe, 'Clutterbuck and Co'. Brigham Young Univ Stud 5 1964.

Hodgart, P. and T. Redpath. Romantic perspectives: the work of Crabbe, Blake, Wordsworth and Coleridge as seen by their contemporaries and by themselves. 1964.

Sigworth, O. F. Nature's sternest painter: five essays on the poetry of Crabbe. Tucson 1965.

Gallon, D. N. Silford Hall or the happy day. MLR 61 1966.

Hibbard, G. R. Crabbe and Shakespeare. In his Renaissance and modern essays, 1966.

Speirs, J. Crabbe as master of the verse tale. Oxford Rev 1 1966.

Hayter, A. In her Opium and the romantic imagination, 1968.

Diffey, C. T. Journey to experience: Crabbe's Silford Hall. Durham Univ Jnl 30 1969.

N. H. R.

WILLIAM BLAKE
1757–1827
Manuscripts

'then she bore pale desire...' and 'Woe cried the Muse...' [c. 1783] (Berg Collection, New York Public Library).

[An island in the moon]. [c. 1784] (Fitzwilliam Museum Cambridge).

Tiriel. [c. 1789] (BM). Facs and transcript, reproduction of drawings and commentary by G. E. Bentley jr, Oxford 1967.

Notebook (also known as Rossetti ms). A sketch-book and commonplace book used by Blake from 1793 to 1818 containing chiefly (1) miscellaneous poems, including drafts of many Songs of experience, c. 1793; (2) miscellaneous poems, c. 1800–4; (3) miscellaneous verses and fragments, c. 1807–11; (4) the Public address and the Vision of the Last Judgment, c. 1809–10; (5) The Everlasting Gospel, c. 1818, part written on a separate ms (in Rosenbach Foundation). The Notebook is in BM, reproduced in facs, ed G. L. Keynes 1935.

The four Zoas: the torments of love and jealousy in the death and judgement of Albion the ancient man. c. 1795–1807. The first form of title was: Vala or the death and judgement of the eternal man: a dream of nine nights. 1797. 144 illustr pages (BM).

　　Facsimile of the manuscript, a transcript of the poem and a study of its growth and significance by G. E. Bentley jr, Oxford 1963.

Pickering (or Ballads) ms. [c. 1807]. Miscellaneous poems, including Auguries of innocence, privately owned.

Blake's memorandum in refutation of the information and complaint of John Scholfield. Aug 1803. (Trinity College, Hartford, Connecticut).

Marginalia: Swedenborg's Heaven and Hell (1784), c. 1788 (Harvard); Lavater's Aphorisms (1788), c. 1788 (Huntington Library); Swedenborg's Divine love and divine wisdom (1788), c. 1789 (BM); Swedenborg's Divine providence (1790), c. 1790 (priv owned); Watson's Apology for the Bible (1798), c. 1798 (Huntington Library); Bacon's Essays (1798), c. 1798 (priv owned); Dante's Inferno (1785), c. 1800 (priv owned); Reynold's Works (1798), c. 1801–9 (BM); Spurzheim's Observations on insanity (1817), c. 1818 (untraced); Berkeley's Siris (1744), c. 1820 (priv owned); Ceninni's Trattato della pittura (1821), c. 1822 (untraced); Wordsworth's Poems (1815), c. 1826 (Cornell); Wordsworth's Excursion (1814), c. 1826 (Dr Williams' Library, London); Thornton's trn of the Lord's Prayer (1827), 1827 (Huntington Library).

Letters. 92 letters are known, including several important poems. One ptd in Monthly Mag July 1806; Letters from Blake to Thomas Butts 1800–3 printed in facsimile, ed G. L. Keynes, Oxford 1926.

Bibliographies etc

Russell, A. G. B. The engravings of Blake. 1912.

—— The Graham Robertson collection. Burlington Mag 37 1920.

Keynes, G. L. A bibliography of Blake. New York 1921; expanded in Japanese by B. Jugaku, Tokyo 1929.

—— and E. Wolf. Blake's illuminated books: a census. New York 1953.

Keynes, G. L. Engravings by Blake: the separate plates, a catalogue raisonné. Dublin 1956.

—— Blake's illustrations to the Bible. 1957.

Binyon, L. The engraved designs of Blake. 1926.

Blake: the description of a small collection of his works in the library of a New York collector [G. C. Smith]. New York 1927.

Lowery, M. R. A census of copies of Blake's Poetical sketches 1783. Library 4th ser 17 1936.

Baker, C. H. C. Catalogue of Blake's drawings and paintings in the Huntington Library. San Marino 1938, 1957 (enlarged and rev R. R. Wark).

Robertson, W. Graham. The Blake collection of W. Graham Robertson. Ed K. Preston 1952.

Butlin, M. [R. F.] Blake: a catalogue of the works of Blake in the Tate Gallery. Ed A. Blunt 1957.

Frye, N. In The English romantic poets and essayists: a review of research and criticism, ed C. W. and L. H. Houtchens, New York 1957.

Preston, K. Notes for a catalogue of the Blake library at the Georgian House, Merstham. Cambridge 1960, 1962 (rev). The collection is now in Westminster Public Library.

Bentley, G. E., jr and M. K. Nurmi. A Blake bibliography: annotated lists of works, studies and Blakeana. Minneapolis 1964.

Erdman, D. V. et al. A concordance to the writings of Blake. 2 vols Ithaca 1967.

Exhibitions

Burlington Fine Arts Club exhibition of the works of Blake. 1876.

[Boston] Museum of Fine Arts exhibition of drawings, water colors and engravings by Blake. Boston 1880, 1880.

[Boston] Museum of Fine Arts Print Department exhibition of books, water colors, engravings etc by Blake. Boston 1891.

Philadelphia Academy of the Fine Arts. Examples of the English pre-Raphaelite school of painters, including Rossetti, Burne-Jones, Madox-Brown and others, together with a collection of the works of Blake. Philadelphia 1892.

Carfax & Co. Exhibition of works by Blake. 1904.

Grolier Club catalogue of books, engravings, water-colors and sketches by Blake. New York 1905.

Carfax exhibition of works by Blake. 1906.

Russell, A. G. B. Catalogue of loan exhibition of works by Blake [in] the National Gallery of British art. 1913, 1913.

—— Burlington Fine Arts Club catalogue: Blake centenary exhibition. 1927.

Manchester Whitworth Institute Catalogue of a loan collection of works by Blake. 1914.

City of Nottingham Art Museum, Nottingham Castle catalogue of a loan exhibition of works by Blake. Nottingham 1914.

National Gallery of Scotland Catalogue of loan exhibition of works by Blake and David Scott. Edinburgh [1914].

Yanagi, M. Annotated catalogue of an exhibition of the reproductions from the works of Blake at the Russian Gallery, Tokyo, and the Imperial University YMCA Hall, Kyoto. Tokyo 1919. In Japanese.

Grolier Club. Blake: an exhibition. New York 1919.

Catalogue of an exhibition of original water-colour drawings by Blake to illustrate Dante. Ed M. Birnbaum, New York 1921.

Works by Blake lent to the Fogg Art Museum. Cambridge Mass 1924.

Victoria and Albert Museum. Catalogue of an exhibition of drawings, etchings and woodcuts by Samuel Palmer and other disciples of Blake. Ed A. H. Palmer 1926.

Print Club of Philadelphia. Illustrated books and original drawings of Blake loaned by Lessing J. Rosenwald. [Philadelphia 1930].

Fogg Art Museum Loan exhibition of works of Blake. Cambridge Mass 1930.

Millard, Mrs G. M. A descriptive hand-list of a loan exhibition of books and works of art by Blake, chiefly from the collection of Mr Lessing J. Rosenwald, at the Little Museum of La Miniatura. [Pasadena 1936].

Baker, C. H. C. An exhibition of Blake's water-colour drawings of Milton's Paradise lost, Henry E. Huntington Library and Art Gallery. San Marino 1936.

Dodgson, C. Acquarelles de Turner, oeuvres de Blake: Association Franco-Britannique Art et Tourisme, Bibliothèque Nationale. [Paris 1937].

—— Ausstellung von englischen Graphiken und Aquarellen: Blake und J. M. W. Turner. Vienna 1937 (Sammlung Albertina Verein der Museumsfreunde in Wien).

[Wolf, E. and E. Mongan]. Blake: a descriptive catalogue of an exhibition of the works of Blake selected from collections in the United States. Philadelphia 1939 (Philadelphia Museum of Art).

Water colors of Blake for Bunyan's The pilgrim's progress, at the galleries of M. Knoedler and Company. New York 1941.

Fogg Museum Exhibition of water colors and drawings by Blake. [Cambridge Mass 1947].

Tate Gallery. Blake: [exhibition] organized by the British Council. 1947.

Galérie René Drouin. Blake: catalogue de l'exposition organisée par la Galerie René Drouin et The British Council. Paris 1947.

Musée Royal des Beaux-Arts, Antwerp. Blake: exposition organisée par The British Council. Brussels [1947].

Kunsthaus, Zürich. Ausstellung der Werke von Blake [organized by] the British Council. Zürich 1947.

Bournemouth Arts Club Exhibition of original works by Blake from the Graham Robertson Collection. Bournemouth 1949.

Lady Lever Art Gallery, Port Sunlight, Cheshire exhibition of works by Blake. Port Sunlight [1950].

Arts Council of Great Britain. The tempera paintings of Blake: a critical catalogue. 1951.

Winnipeg Art Gallery. Blake exhibition. [Winnipeg 1957?].

[Rienaecker, V.] Blake bicentenary celebrations: paintings, drawings and facsimiles [in the] Whitworth Art Gallery. Manchester [1957].

Fogg Museum exhibition of water colors and drawings by Blake. [Cambridge Mass 1957].

[Mongan, E.] The art of Blake: bicentennial exhibition [in the] National Gallery of Art, Smithsonian Institution. Washington [1957].

City and County of Kingston upon Hull. Ferens Art Gallery Bicentenary exhibition of works by Blake. Hull [1957].

British Museum. Blake and his circle: bicentenary exhibition. [1957].

Buvelot and Childers Galleries. Blake exhibition. [Melbourne 1957].

Hosei University, Tokyo. Catalogue of an exhibition of Blakeana held in commemoration of the bicentenary of Blake's birth. [Tokyo] 1958.

Blake Trust Exhibition of the illuminated books of Blake, poet, printer, prophet: a commemorative handbook, with a study by Geoffrey Keynes. Clairvaux 1964. The study rptd as G. L. Keynes, A study of the illuminated books of Blake, poet, printer, prophet, 1965.

[Roe, A. S.] Blake: an annotated catalogue [of an exhibition at the] Andrew Dickson White Museum of Art, Cornell University. [Ithaca 1965].

[Wark, R. R.] Blake and his circle: two exhibitions at the Henry E. Huntington Library and Art Gallery. [Pasadena 1965].

Ryskamp, C. Songs of innocence and of experience and Miss Caroline Newton's Blake collection. Princeton Univ Lib Chron 29 1968. Catalogue of an exhibition.

[Johnston, E.] 'For friendship's sake': Blake and William Hayley. Manchester 1969 (City Art Gallery).

Blake: a loan exhibition. Edinburgh 1969 (Nat Lib of Scotland).

§ I

Works in Illuminated Printing
The works are etched in relief unless otherwise stated.

There is no natural religion, series a and b. [c. 1788]. 19 plates. 13 very imperfect copies known.

All religions are one. [c. 1788]. 10 plates. The one known copy is in Huntington Library.

The book of Thel. 1789. 8 plates. 16 copies.

Songs of innocence. 1789. 31 plates. 22 copies.

The marriage of Heaven and Hell [including A song of liberty]. [c. 1793]. 27 plates. 10 copies.

Prospectus: to the public. 1793. One plate. Untraced.

For children: the gates of Paradise. 1793. 18 plates. 5 copies. Reissued, with additional text as For the sexes: the gates of Paradise, [c. 1818].

Visions of the daughters of Albion. 1793. 11 plates. 16 copies.

America: a prophecy. 1793. 18 plates. 17 copies.

Songs of innocence and of experience, shewing the two contrary states of the human soul. 1794. 54 plates. 27 contemporary copies, 5 incomplete.

Europe: a prophecy. 1794. 18 plates. 12 copies.

The first book of Urizen. 1794. 28 plates. 7 copies.

The book of Ahania. 1795. 6 plates in ordinary etching. The one known copy is in Library of Congress.

The book of Los. 1795. 5 plates in ordinary etching. The one known copy is in BM.

The song of Los. 1795. 8 plates. 5 copies.

Milton: a poem in 2 books. 1804 (completed c. 1808). 50 plates. 4 copies.

Jerusalem: the emanation of the giant Albion. 1804 (completed c. 1820). 100 plates. 8 copies traced, 3 posthumous.

For the sexes: the gates of Paradise. [c. 1818]. 21 engraved plates. 7 copies. A rev issue of For children: the gates of Paradise, 1793, with additional text.

[The Laocoon]. [c. 1818]. 2 copies. A line engraving of the Laocoon group with detached sentences inscribed in all directions around it.

On Homer's poetry [and] On Virgil. [c. 1820]. One plate. 6 copies.

The ghost of Abel: a revelation in the visions of Jehovah seen by William Blake. 1822. 2 plates. 4 copies.

Works Printed in Ordinary Type

Poetical sketches. 1783. 20 copies.

The French Revolution, a poem, in seven books: book the first. 1791. The one known copy is in Huntington Library.

Exhibitions of paintings in fresco, poetical and historical inventions. [May 1809]. A broadside leaflet. 2 copies.

Blake's Chaucer: the Canterbury pilgrims. [May 1809]. A broadside leaflet. The one known copy is in BM.

A descriptive catalogue of pictures, poetical and historical inventions. 1809. 18 copies.

Blake's Chaucer: an original engraving. [c. 1810]. A broadside leaflet. 2 copies.

Engravings by or after Blake

Enfield, W. The speaker. 1774 (for 1780), 1781, 1785, 1795, 1797, 1799, 1801, 1805, 1820. One plate.

Olivier, [J]. Fencing familiarized. 1780. One plate.

The Protestants family Bible. [1781?]. 5 plates.

Kimpton, E. A new and complete universal history of the Holy Bible. [1781?]. 3 plates. The same plates are rptd in Genuine and complete works of Flavius Josephus, ed G. H. Maynard [1786?], [1790?], [1800?].

The royal universal family Bible. Ed J. Herries 2 vols 1780 (for 1782). 5 plates.

Bonnycastle, J. An introduction to mensuration and practical geometry. 1782, 1787, 1791, 1798. One plate.

The poetical works of Geoff Chaucer. 14 vols 1782 (Bell's edn). One plate.

The lady's pocket book. 1782. 2 plates; proofs of the prints, no known copy of the book.

Novelist's Mag 8–11 1782–3, 1784–5, 1792–2. 7 plates.

Scott, John. Poetical works. 1782, 1786, 1795. 4 plates.

Ariosto. Orlando furioso. Tr J. Hoole 5 vols 1783, 1785, 2 vols 1791, 5 vols 1799. One plate.

Henry, T. Memoirs of Albert de Haller MD. 1783. One plate.

[Ritson, J.] A select collection of English songs. 3 vols 1783. 9 plates.

Seally, J. and I. Lyons. A complete geographical dictionary. [1784?], 1787. 3 plates.

Wit's Mag 1 1784. 5 plates.

Fenning, D. and J. Collyer. A new system of geography. 1785, 1787. 2 plates.

Commins, T. An elegy, set to music. 1786. One plate.

[Gough, R.] Sepulchral monuments in Great Britain. 2 vols 1786, 1796. 8 plates.

Lavater, J. C. Aphorisms on man. [Tr J. H. Fuseli] 1788, 1789, 1794. One plate.

— Essays on physiognomy. Tr H. Hunter 3 vols 1789, 1792, 1798. 3 plates.

Hogarth, William. Works. 1790, [1795?], 1822, 1822 (for 1826?), [1830?], [1835?], [1838?]; Die Werke von William Hogarth, Brunn and Vienna 1878. One plate.

Darwin, E. The botanic garden. 2 vols 1791, 1791, 1795, 1799. 7 plates.

Hartley, D. Observations on man. 2 vols 1791, 1791. One plate.

Salzmann, C. G. Elements of morality for the use of children. [Tr Mary Wollstonecraft] 3 vols 1791, 1792, 1799. 17 plates.

Wollstonecraft, Mary. Original stories from real life. 1791, 1796. 6 plates.

Bellamy's picturesque Mag 1 1793. One plate.

Gay, John. Fables. 1793, [1811]. 12 plates.

Hunter, J. An historical journal of the transactions at Port Jackson and Norfolk Island. 1793, 1793. One plate.

Stuart, J. and N. Revett. The antiquities of Athens. Vol 3, 1794. 4 plates.

Brown, John. The elements of medicine. Tr from Latin 2 vols 1795. One plate.

Catullus, C. V. Poems. [Tr J. Nott] 2 vols 1795. 2 plates.

Bürger, G. A. Leonora: a tale. Tr J. T. Stanley 1796. 3 plates.

Cumberland, G. Thoughts on outline. 1796. 8 plates, 4 rptd in his Outlines from the antients, 1829.

Stedman, Capt J. G. Narrative of a five years' expedition against the revolted negroes of Surinam in Guiana. 2 vols 1796, 1806, 1813. 16 plates.

Euler, L. Elements of Algebra. Tr from French 2 vols 1797. One plate.

Monthly Mag Oct 1797. One plate.

Young, Edward. The complaint and the consolation: or night thoughts. 1797. 43 plates.

Allen, Charles. A new and improved history of England. 1798. 4 plates.

— A new and improved Roman history. 1798. 4 plates.

Flaxman, John. A letter to the committee for raising the naval pillar. 1800. 3 plates.

Hayley, William. An essay on sculpture. 1800. 3 plates.

[Hayley, W.] Little Tom the sailor. Folkstone 1800. The etched broadsheet is reproduced in Century Guild Hobby Horse 1 1886, [Edmonton 1886?], 1917.

Salzmann, C. G. Gymnastics for youth. 1800. 17 plates.

Fuseli, John Henry. Lectures on painting. 1801. One plate.

Hayley, W. Designs to a series of ballads. 1802. 14 plates.

[John and Josiah] Boydell's graphic illustrations of the dramatic works of Shakespeare. [1803?]. One plate. The plates are the same as those in Dramatic works of Shakspeare, ed G. Steevens 9 vols 1802 (for 1803), 1832.

Hayley, W. The life and posthumous writings of William Cowper. 3 vols 1803, 1804. 6 plates.

Hayley, W. The triumphs of temper: the twelfth edition. 1803; Thirteenth edition, 1807. 6 plates.

Hoare, Prince. Academic correspondence. 1804. One plate.

Hayley, W. Ballads. 1805. 5 plates.

Shakspeare, W. Plays. Ed G. Steevens and A. Chalmers 10 vols 1805, 9 vols 1805, 1811, 1805 (for 1812). 2 plates.

Flaxman, J. The Iliad of Homer. 1805, 1870, 1879, [1890?]. 3 plates.

Hoare, P. An inquiry into the requisite cultivation and present state of the arts of design in England. 1806. One plate.

Malkin, B. H. A father's memoirs of his child. 1806. One plate.

Blair, Robert. The grave: a poem. 1808, 1808, 1813, 1813. 12 plates, rptd in J. J. de Mora, Meditaciones poeticas, 1826; 1926 (for G. C. Smith jr without text). Reduced copies appeared in New York 1847, 1858, 1903 (Illustr Lib of Plain and Coloured Books), 1906 (Photogravure ser).

Hayley, W. The life of George Romney. 1809. One plate.

Chaucer, G. The prologue and characters of Chaucer's pilgrims. 1812. One plate.

[Wedgwood's Catalogue of earthenware and porcelain]. [1816?]. 18 plates.

Flaxman, J. Compositions from the works, days and Theogony of Hesiod. 1817, 1870, 1881. 37 plates.

Whitaker, J. The seraph: a collection of sacred music. 2 vols [1818–28?]. One plate.

Rees, A. The cyclopaedia. 39 vols 1820. 7 plates.

Virgil. Pastorals. Ed R. J. Thornton 2 vols 1821 (3rd edn). 27 plates, reproduced in Century Guild Hobby Horse 3 1888; Blake: XVII designs to Thornton's Virgil, Portland Maine 1899; Blake: being all his woodcuts photographically reproduced, ed L. Binyon 1902 (Little Engravings Classical & Contemporary); Blake's illustrations to Thornton's Pastorals of Virgil, enlarged fac-similes in platinotype by Frederick Evans, 1912; Bibelot 20 1914; Blake's illustrations to the Pastorals of

Virgil: platinotype enlargements by Frederick H. Evans, 1919; The illustrations of Blake for Thornton's Virgil, ed G. L. Keynes 1937.

Seaman's recorder. 3 vols 1824–7. 6 plates.

Remember me! 1825, 1826. One plate.

Illustrations of the Book of Job. 1825 (for 1826), 1874. 22 plates, reproduced in Blake's Illustrations of the Book of Job, ed C. E. Norton, Boston 1875; Illustrations of the Book of Job, 1902; Illustrations of the Book of Job, New York 1903; Illustrations of the Book of Job, 1903 (Illustrated Pocket Lib of Plain & Coloured Books); Blake, volume 1: illustrations of the Book of Job, ed L. Binyon 1906; F. Coutts, The heresy of Job, 1907; Illustrations of the Book of Job, 1912; Illustrations of the Book of Job: enlarged facsimiles in platinotype by Frederic H. Evans, 1914; Illustrations of the Book of Job, 1923; The Book of Job, 1927; Job, invented and engraved by Blake, ed K. Patchen, New York 1947.

Varley, John. A treatise on zodiacal physiognomy. 1828. 2 plates.

Dante. Blake's illustrations to Dante. 1838, [1892?], 1955, 1968. 7 plates, reproduced in Inferno, tr H. F. Cary, New York 1931.

Keynes, G. L. (ed). Blake's engravings. 1950.

Facsimiles

The marriage of Heaven and Hell. 1868.

Works by Blake. Songs of innocence [a], 1789; Songs of experience [a], 1794; Book of Thel [D?], 1789; Vision[s] of the daughters of Albion [B], 1793; America: a prophecy [F?], 1793; Europe: a prophecy, [D?], 1794; The first book of Urizen [D], 1794; The song of Los [A or D], 1794 (for 1795), reproduced in facsimile from the original editions, one hundred copies printed for private circulation, 1876.

Jerusalem [D]. [1877].

The edition of the works of Wm Blake produced by William Muir at the Blake Press at Edmonton consisted of separately issued editions of Thel [D]. 1884; Visions of the daughters of Albion [A], 1884; Songs of innocence [D], 1884; Songs of experience [U], 1885; The marriage of Heaven and Hell [A], 1885; Milton [A], 1886; There is no natural religion, 1886; America, 1887; For the sexes: the gates of Paradise, 1888; Urizen [B], 1888; Europe, 1888; The Song of Los [A], 1890.

Poetical sketches. 1890. Lithographed by W. Griggs.

The book of Ahania. 1892. Copy A lithographed by W. Griggs.

Songs of innocence and of experience [U]. 1893.

For the sexes: the gates of Paradise. New York 1913.

The book of Thel [J]. 1920. A Muir facs.

Songs of innocence. 1923.

Songs of innocence and of experience. Liverpool 1923.

The book of Thel. 1924.

For the sexes: the gates of Paradise [E]. 1925.

All religions are one [A]. 1926.

Poetical sketches [A]. 1926, 1927 (Noel Douglas Replicas).

Letters from Blake to Thomas Butts 1800–3. Ed G. L. Keynes, Oxford 1926.

Songs of innocence [A]. 1926.

The marriage of Heaven and Hell [I]. Ed M. Plowman 1927.

Songs of innocence [A]. 1927. Facs by Muir.

Songs of experience [A]. 1927. A Muir facs.

Songs of experience. [New York? 1927?].

The book of Thel [D]. 1928.

The first book of Urizen [A]. Ed D. Plowman 1929.

Muzen no uta [Songs of innocence]. Tr Japanese B. Jugaku, Kyoto 1932.

Visions of the daughters of Albion [A]. Ed J. M. Murry 1932.

Yurizen no sho [Book of Urizen]. Tr Japanese B. Jugaku, Kyoto 1932.

Poetical sketches. New York 1934.

The book of Thel. Tr Japanese B. Jugaku, Kyoto 1933.

Notebook. Ed G. L. Keynes 1935.

Songs of experience: facsimile. Tr Japanese B. Jugaku, Kyoto 1935.

Songs of innocence and of experience. 1941. 20 copies ptd for R. Todd and G. L. Keynes from electrotypes of the original plates of 1789 and 1794.

Songs of experience [b]. [New York? 1947].

America. New York 1947.

Songs of innocence [b?]. New York [1947?].

Songs of innocence and of experience [b]. London and New York 1947.

There is no natural religion [D]. Cambridge Mass 1948.

Jerusalem [E]. 1951 (Blake Trust).

Jerusalem [C]. 1952, 1955 (Blake Trust).

Songs of innocence [b]. 1954 (Blake Trust).

Songs of innocence and of experience [Z]. 1955 (Blake Trust).

The book of Urizen [G]. 1958 (Blake Trust).

Visions of the daughters of Albion. 1959 (Blake Trust).

The marriage of Heaven and Hell [D]. 1960 (Blake Trust).

Vala, or the Four Zoas: facsimile, transcript and study by G. E. Bentley jr. Oxford 1963.

America [M]. 1963 (Blake Trust).

The marriage of Heaven and Hell. Ed C. Emery, Coral Gables 1963.

The book of Urizen [G]. Ed C. Emery, Miami 1966.

Milton [D]. 1967 (Blake Trust).

Songs of innocence and experience [Z]. 1967.

The gates of Paradise: for children [D]; for the sexes [F]. Introductory vol by G. L. Keynes 1968 (Blake Trust).

Europe [B, G]. 1969 (Blake Trust).

Tiriel: facsimile and transcript of the manuscript, and reproduction of the drawings, and a commentary on the poem by G. E. Bentley jr. Oxford 1967.

Typographical Reprints

For isolated poems by Blake ptd before 1863 in books by others, see Bentley and Nurmi, Blake bibliography, 1964, *especially nos 209, 211, 218, 220–1, 223, 226–7, 229, 259, 276–8, 280.*

Songs of innocence and of experience. [Ed J. J. Garth Wilkinson] 1839, 1925.

Songs of innocence and of experience. [1843?].

Songs of innocence and experience, with other poems. [Ed R. H. Shepherd] 1866, 1868.

Selections from his poems and other writings. [Ed D. G. Rossetti]. In vol 2 of A. Gilchrist, Life of Blake, 1863, 1880.

Poetical sketches. Ed R. H. Shepherd 1868.

Poems. [Ed R. H. Shepherd] 1874, 1887.

Poetical works. Ed W. M. Rossetti 1874, 1875, 1890, 1911, 1914.

The poems, with specimens of the prose writings. Ed J. Skipsey 1885, [1904?] (Canterbury Poets).

Songs. Oxford 1885.

The lamb. Oxford 1889.

Blake, his songs of innocence. Oxford 1893.

Works. Ed E. J. Ellis and W. B. Yeats, with a memoir and interpretation 3 vols 1893. Most of the illuminated works reproduced from lithographs; the text not very reliable.

Poems. Ed W. B. Yeats 1893 (ML), 1905, 1910 (Books that Marked Epochs), New York 1920 (Modern Lib).

Selections. Ed L. Housman 1899.

Poetical sketches, decorated by C. Ricketts. 1899

Songs of innocence; designs by Celia Levetus. 1899.

Selections. Ed M. Perugini 1901 (Little Lib).

Songs of experience; designs by Celia Levetus. [1902].

Songs of innocence; illustrations by Geraldine Morris. 1902.

Letters of Blake to George Cumberland. Ed R. Garnett, Hampstead Annual 1903.

The Passions [then she bore Pale desire . . .]: an unpublished poem by Blake. Ed W. M. Rossetti, Monthly Rev Aug 1903.

Songs of innocence. Portland Maine 1904.

Songs of innocence. [1905] (Broadway Booklets).

Auguries of innocence. [Ed E. V. Lucas] 1905.

Prophetic books. Ed E. R. D. Maclagan and A. G. B. Russell 1904 (Jerusalem); 1907 (Milton).

Songs of innocence, illustrated by Olive Allen. [1906].

Poetical works. Ed J. Sampson, Oxford 1905, 1947. The first bibliographically reliable edn.

Lyrical poems. Ed J. Sampson, introd by W. Raleigh, Oxford 1905.

The marriage of Heaven and Hell. 1906.

Songs of innocence and of experience. [Ed R. F. Seymour], Chicago 1906.

Poetical works. Ed E. J. Ellis 2 vols 1906.

The letters, together with a life by Frederick Tatham. Ed A. G. B. Russell 1906.

Poems. Ed A. T. Quiller-Couch, Oxford [1908] (Select English Classics).

The marriage of Heaven and Hell. Ed F. G. Stokes 1911.

Poems. Ed A. Meynell 1911 (Red Letter Lib); [1927].

Songs of innocence. Preface by T. Seccombe, illustrations by Honor C. Appleton [1911].

Songs of experience. [1911]; Songs of innocence, [1911] (Langham Booklets).

Songs of innocence. 1911.

Songs of innocence [and of experience]. 1911.

Songs of innocence and Songs of experience. 1911.

Songs of innocence and other poems. [1911], [1912].

Songs of innocence, decorated by Charles and Mary H. Robinson. [1912].

Songs of experience. [1912]; Songs of innocence, [1912] (Arden Books).

The Blake calendar: a quotation for every day in the year. Ed T. Wright 1913.

Poetical works. Ed J. Sampson, Oxford 1913 etc. The text of 1905, above, with the first pbn of French Revolution and with the shorter symbolic works, and a selection from the longer ones.

Auguries of innocence, written out by Lillian Frost. Flansham 1914.

Selections from the symbolical poems. Ed F. E. Pierce, New Haven 1915.

The book of Thel. Illustr R. N. Kean [1917?].

Songs and poems. Ed M. Kingsdowne [1920] (Stead's Poets).

Selections. [1923].

Songs of innocence. San Francisco 1924.

Writings. Ed G. L. Keynes 3 vols 1925, 1 vol 1957 (as Complete writings), 1966. The first comprehensive edn.

William Blake. [Ed F. Thompson] [1925?] (Augustan Books of Poetry).

Poems and prose. Ed F. Dell, Girard Kansas 1925 (Little Blue Books no 677).

Songs of innocence and of experience. Ed G. H. Cowling 1925 (Methuen's Eng Classics).

Songs of innocence and of experience. Ed A. D. Innes 1926.

Prophetic writings. Ed D. J. Sloss and J. P. R. Wallis 2 vols Oxford 1926, 1957, 1964. A fresh text with an index of symbols.

Songs of innocence. New York 1926.

Eight songs. New York 1926.

Eight songs of innocence for treble voices, unison and two part; music by D. W. Stewart. 1926 (Year Book Press Series of Unison & Part-Songs no 264).

Songs of innocence. Illustr Jacynth Parsons, preface by W. B. Yeats 1927.

Poems and prophecies. Ed M. Plowman [1927], 1934, 1950, 1954, 1959 (rev G. L. Keynes) (EL).

Poetry and prose. Ed G. L. Keynes 1927, 1932, 1939, 1943 (reset), 1948, 1956. A popular revision of the text of 1925, above, omitting most variants, notes etc.

Poetical sketches. [Ed E. Partridge], with an essay on Blake's metric by J. Lindsay 1927.

Ideas of good and evil. Yellow Springs Ohio 1927.

Selected poems. Ed B. de Selincourt, Oxford 1927 (WC).

Selected poems. Ed G. D. H. and M. I. Cole 1927.

The marriage of Heaven and Hell. Maastricht 1928.

The land of dreams: twenty poems illustrated by Pamela Bianco. New York 1928.

Auguries of innocence. Birmingham 1930.

The book of Thel; decoration by Julian A. Links. San Francisco 1930.

Poems. Ed L. Binyon 1931.

Exoteric writings. Ed B. Jugaku, Kyoto 1933.

Songs of innocence and experience. New Rochelle NY 1935.

Poems. Ed M. Redlich 1937. Introd by E. de Selincourt, rptd from his Oxford lectures on poetry, Oxford 1934.

Songs of innocence and experience. Mount Vernon NY [1937].

Songs of innocence and experience. 1938.

Songs of innocence. Flansham 1939. Written out by Helen Hinkley, decorated by James Guthrie.

The complete poetry and selected prose of John Donne and the complete poetry of Blake. Ed R. S. Hillyer, New York 1941 (Modern Lib). The text is that of Keynes.

Songs of innocence and experience. 1941 (Zodiac Books).

The portable Blake. Ed A. Kazin, New York 1946.

Selections from Songs of innocence and experience, pen written by Reynard Biemiller. New York 1946.

Selected poems. Ed D. Saurat 1947.

Select poems. Ed M. Sangu, Tokyo 1948.

The book of Thel. Pawlet Vermont [1949].

Poems. Ed R. Todd 1949.

A cradle song, The divine image, A dream, Night, illuminated by Valenti Angelo. New York 1949.

Genesis: verses from a ms of Blake. Cummington Mass 1952. K. Povey, TLS 3 Oct 1952, has shown that this work in Blake's hand, now at Princeton, is a trn probably by Hayley of part of Tasso, Le sette giornate del mondo creato.

Selected poetry and prose. Ed N. Fyre, New York 1953 (Modern Lib).

Vala: Blake's numbered text. Ed H. M. Margoliouth, Oxford 1956.

Selected poems. Ed F. W. Bateson 1957.

Visions of the daughters of Albion. Pawlet Vermont 1957.

A selection of poems and letters. Ed J. Bronowski 1958 (Penguin).

Songs of innocence and of experience. Ed A. M. Wilkinson 1958.

Songs of innocence and experience. Mount Vernon NY [1958].

A Blake manuscript in the Berg Collection: Then she bore pale desire and Woe cried the Muse. Ed D. V. Erdman, BNYPL 1958.

Songs of innocence; decorations by Harold Jones. 1958.

Auguries of innocence; wood engravings by Leonard Baskin. Northampton Mass 1959.

Selected poetry. Ed R. Todd [New York 1960] (Laurel Poetry ser).

Selected poems. Ed S. Gardner 1962.

Jerusalem: a simplified version. Ed W. R. Hughes 1964.

Poems. Ed A. H. Munson, New York 1964.

Selections. Berkeley 1964.

A memorable fancy; lithographs by Rosemary Killen. [Northampton Mass] 1965.

Poetry and prose. Ed D. V. Erdman, commentary by H. Bloom, Garden City NY 1965. A fresh text with Blake's punctuation.

A grain of sand: poems for young readers. Ed R. Manning 1967.

William Blake. Ed V. de S. Pinto 1965.

Selected writings. Ed R. F. Gleckner, New York 1967 (Crofts Classics).

Blake: an introduction. Ed A. Malcolmson 1967.

A divine image: four poems by Blake; lino-cuts by Duine Campbell. Leicester 1968.

Translations

The marriage of Heaven and Hell. Tr C. Grolleau, Paris 1900.

Ausgewählte Dichtungen. Tr A. Knoblauch 2 vols Berlin 1907.

Die Ethick der Fruchtbarkeit. Tr Otto von Taube, Jena 1907.

Bu-re-i-ku ko-to-ba [Selections from Blake's letters and prose]. Tr M. Yanagi, Tokyo 1921.

The marriage of Heaven and Hell. Tr A. Gide, Nouvelle Revue Française 19 1922; Paris 1922 etc.

Il matrimonio del Cielo e dell' Inferno, Canti dell'innocenza e altri poemi. Tr E. Dodsworth, Lanciano [1923?].

Chants d'innocence et d'expérience. Tr M. L. et P. Soupault, Paris 1927.

Premiers livres prophétiques. Tr P. Berger, Paris 1927.

Tiriel. [Tr O. F. Babler], Olomouc Czechoslavakia 1927.

The marriage of Heaven and Hell. Tr F. Gonzalez-Blanco, Madrid 1928.

Seconds livres prophétiques: contenant Milton; Poèmes et fragments divers; L'évangile éternel. Tr P. Berger, Paris 1930.

Bu-re-i-ku Shi-shu [Blake's poems]. Tr B. Jugaku, Tokyo 1931, 1950.

Chansons d'innocence. Tr P. Messiaen, Paris 1934.

Kniha Thel [The book of Thel]. [Tr O. F. Babler, illustr Jan Konupek], Suaty Kopecek 1935.

Ein no fukuin [The everlasting gospel]. Tr B. Jugaku, [Kyoto?] 1938.

The marriage of Heaven and Hell. Tr X. Vallaurrutio, prefatory note by G. K. Chesterton. [Mexico City?] 1942.

Poèmes choisis. Tr M. L. Cazamian, Paris [1943], 1950.

Bu-re-i-ku shi-shu [Blake's poems]. Tr N. Irie, Tokyo 1943. With Yeats's preface to ML edn (1905).

El fantasma de Abel: prefatory note by P. Berger. La Plata 1943. Anon trn.

Jerusalem. Milan 1943. Anon trn.

Bu-re-i-ku shi-sen [Select poems]. Tr K. Doi, Tokyo 1946.

The marriage of Heaven and Hell. Tr Daniel-Rops [J. C. H. Petiot], [Paris] 1946.

The marriage of Heaven and Hell. Tr M. Doi, Tokyo 1946.

Poèmes choisis. Tr V. and E. Vauthier, Paris and Brussels [1943], Paris 1950.

Les chants d'innocence et de l'expérience. Tr P-L. Matthey, Lausanne 1947.

Road to Jerusalem. Tr B. Jugaku 1947.

Aegteskabet mellem himmel og helvede [Marriage of Heaven and Hell] og andre skrifter. Tr N. Alkjaer, Copenhagen 1952.

Dikter och Profetior. Tr F. Isaksson [et al], Stockholm 1957.

Poemes y profecias. Tr E. Caracciolo, Cordoba Argentina, 1957.

Gedichte. Tr A. von Bernus and W. Schmiele, Heidelberg 1958.

Gedichte. Tr G. von der Vring, Wiesbaden 1958.

Werke. [Ed G. Klotz, tr W. Wilhelm], Berlin 1958.

Söngvar sakleysisins og ljod lifsreynslunnar [Songs of innocence and experience]. Tr T. Gudmunsson, Reykjavik 1959.

Taivaan ja helvetin avioliitto ja muuta proosaa. [Tr T. Anhava], Hämeenlinna [1959].

Versek és próféciák. [Ed K. László, notes by S. Miklós], Budapest 1959.

Pu-lai-k'o shih-hsüan [Selected poems]. Tr Y. K'o-chia, Hong Kong 1960.

Primeros libros profeticos, poemas. Tr A. Bartra, Mexico City 1961.

Blake. Tr Jean and A-M. Rousselot, Paris 1964.

Visioni di Blake. Tr G. Ungaretti, [Rome?] 1965.

Reproductions of Drawings and Paintings

Scott, W. B. Etchings from his works. 1878.

Illustrations to Milton's Comus. 1890; ed D. Figgis 1926.

Milton, John. Paradise lost. Liverpool 1906. Prefaces by P. Hofer and J. T. Winterich, New York 1941 (Heritage Club); New York 1947.

Illustrations to the Divine comedy of Dante. 1922; ed G. L. Keynes 1927; tr M. B. Anderson, ed A. Livingston, New York [1944] (Heritage Book Club); Blake's illustrations for Dante: selections from the originals in the National Gallery of Victoria, Melbourne, Australia and the Fogg Art Museum, Cambridge Massachusetts, Cambridge Mass 1953; The Melbourne Dante illustrations, ed V. Hoff, Melbourne 1961.

Designs for Gray's poems. Ed H. J. C. Grierson 1922.

The drawings and engravings of Blake. Ed L. Binyon 1922.

Milton, John. On the morning of Christ's nativity. Ed G. L. Keynes, Cambridge 1923.

The heads of the poets. Ed T. Wright, Olney 1925; ed W. Wells, [Manchester 1969].

Figgis, D. The paintings of Blake. 1925.

Twenty-seven drawings by Blake. McPherson Kansas 1925.

Milton, John. Poems in English. Ed G. L. Keynes 2 vols 1926.

Illustrations to Young's Night thoughts. Ed G. L. Keynes 1927.

Pencil drawings by Blake. Ed G. L. Keynes, 2 sers 1927, 1956.

Illustrations of the Book of Job by Blake: being all the water-colour designs, pencil drawings and engravings. Ed L. Binyon and G. L. Keynes, New York 1935; Illustrations of the Book of Job, reproduced in facsimile from the original New Zealand set, ed P. Hofer 1937.

Bunyan, John. The pilgrim's progress. Ed G. L. Keynes, New York 1941 (Limited Edns Club); New York 1942.

Blake. Ed G. L. Keynes 1945 (Faber Gallery).

Bertram, A. William Blake. 1948.

The Bible for my grandchildren. Ed R. H. Greenough, [New York?] 1950.

The home Bible, arranged for family reading. Ed R. H. Greenough, New York 1950.

Milton, John. L'allegro. Ed W. P. Trent, New York 1954; Il penseroso, ed C. B. Tinker, New York 1954.

Blake's water-colour drawings. [Ed P. A. Wick and H. D. Willard], Boston 1957.

Yanagi, M. Bu-re-i-ku se-i-sho ga-shu [Blake's biblical illustrations]. Tokyo 1958. In Japanese.

Blake. Ed G. L. Keynes 1965.

Butlin, M. William Blake. 1966 (Tate Gallery).

Letters

Letters of Blake and George Cumberland. Ed R. Garnett, Hampstead Annual 1903.

Letters to Thomas Butts 1800–3. Ed G. L. Keynes, Oxford 1926 (facs).

Letters. Ed G. L. Keynes 1956, 1968 (rev).

§ 2

For incidental references to Blake before 1863, see Bentley and Nurmi, Blake bibliography, 1964.

Farington, J. Diary. Ed J. Greig 8 vols 1922–8.

Malkin, B. H. A father's memoirs of his child. 1806. Introductory biography of Blake.

The grave: a poem illustrated by Blake. Antijacobin Rev & Mag 31 1808. Anon review.

Hunt, Robert. Blake's edition of Blair's grave. Examiner 7 Aug 1808. Review.

—— Mr Blake's exhibition. Examiner 17 Sept 1809. Review.

[Robinson, Henry Crabb]. Blake: Künstler, Dichter und

religiöser Schwärmer. [Tr Dr N. H. Julius], Vater-landisches Museum 1 1811.
— Diary, reminiscences and correspondence. Ed T. Sadler 3 vols 1869 etc.
— On books and their writers. Ed E. J. Morley 3 vols 1938.
— Blake, Coleridge, Wordsworth, Lamb etc: being selections from the remains. Ed E. J. Morley, Manchester 1922, 1932.
Nativity of Mr Blake, the mystical artist. Urania 1 1825. Anon.
[Anon obituary]. Blake: the illustrator of the grave etc. Literary Gazette 18 Aug 1827; rptd in A. Symons, William Blake, 1907, and with minor alterations in Monthly Mag Oct 1827, GM Oct 1827, New Monthly Mag Dec 1827, Annual Register 69 1828, and Annual Biography & Obituary 12 1828.
Hayley, William. Memoirs. 2 vols 1823.
Smith, J. T. Nollekens and his times. 2 vols 1828, 1829, 1920.
— A book for a rainy day. 1845, 1845, 1861; ed W. Whitten 1905.
Cunningham, A. In his Lives of the most eminent British painters, sculptors and architects vol 2, 1830. The first edn of the life of Blake was rptd New York 1831, 1837, 1839, 1842, 1844, 1846. The expanded version of the life in the second edn (1830) was rptd 1879 (ed Mrs C. Heaton), 1886 (Great English Painters, ed W. Sharp, Camelot Classics), 1893.
The inventions of Blake, painter and poet. London Univ Mag March 1830.
The last of the supernaturalists. Fraser's Mag March 1830.
Tatham, Frederick. The life of Blake. [c. 1832]. First ptd with Letters, ed A. G. B. Russell 1906.
Gilchrist, Alexander. Life of Blake. 2 vols 1863, 1880 (rev); ed W. Graham Robertson 1906 etc; ed R. Todd 1942 (EL), 1945.
M., P. William Blake. Light Blue 2 1867.
Milsand, J. Un précurseur du xixe siècle: Blake le peintre, le poëte et le visionnaire. Revue Moderne 44 1868; rptd in his Littérature anglaise et philosophie, Dijon 1893.
Swinburne, A. C. Blake: a critical essay. 1868.
Scott, W. B. A Varley-and-Blake sketch-book. Portfolio 2 1871.
[Crawford, O.] Blake: artist, poet and mystic. New Quart Mag 2 1874.
Palmer, Samuel. Fictions concerning Blake. Athenaeum 11 Sept 1875.
C[arr], J. C. William Blake. Cornhill Mag June 1875.
Carr, J. C. William Blake. Belgravia 29 1876.
Hewlett, H. E. Imperfect genius: Blake. Contemporary Rev Oct 1876.
Gilchrist, A. Anne Gilchrist: her life and writings. Ed H. H. Gilchrist 1887.
Palmer, A. H. In his Life and letters of Samuel Palmer, 1892.
Story, A. T. In his Life of John Linnell, 2 vols 1892.
— Blake: his life, character and genius. 1893.
[Calvert, S.] In his Memoir of Edward Calvert, 1893.
Garnett, R. Blake: painter and poet. 1895.
— John Linnell and Blake at Hampstead. Hampstead Annual 1902.
— Gleanings from the Cumberland papers: Blake and Poole. Hampstead Annual 1904–5.
Nicoll, W. R. and T. J. Wise. The trial of Blake for sedition. In their Literary anecdotes of the nineteenth century vol 1, 1895.
Guthrie, J. Blake: poet and artist. Sewanee Rev 5 1897; rptd in his Vital study of literature, Chicago 1912.
Kassner, R. In his Die Mystik, der Künstler und das Leben, Leipzig 1900; rev and rptd in his Englische Dichter, Leipzig 1920.
Nutt, T. Lord Crewe's Blake collection. Critic 42 1903.
Yeats, W. B. In his Ideas of good and evil, 1903.

Boyle, C. S. Blake, Rossetti and Walt Whitman. Trivandrum 1904.
Langridge, I. Blake: a study of his life and art work. 1904.
Benoit, F. Un maître de l'art: Blake le visionnaire. Lille 1906.
Binyon, L. Blake's work as a painter. Putnam's Monthly 3 1907.
— The engravings of Blake and Edward Calvert. Print Collector's Quart 7 1917.
— Blake's woodcuts. Burlington Mag 37 1920.
— The followers of Blake. 1925.
— The engraved designs. 1926.
B., W. Blake's Tyger. N & Q 22 Sept 1906.
Richter, H. William Blake. Strasbourg 1906.
Berger, P. Blake: mysticisme et poésie. Paris 1907; tr D. Conner 1914.
Briggs, A. F. Mr Butts, the friend and patron of Blake. Connoisseur Oct 1907.
Brooke, S. A. In his Studies in poetry, 1907.
Cary, E. L. The art of Blake. New York 1907.
Ellis, E. J. The real Blake: a portrait biography. 1907.
Symons, A. William Blake. 1907. Includes Robinson, Malkin, Smith, Cunningham, above, and other early authorities.
MacDonald, G. The sanity of Blake. Saint George 11 1908.
Perugini, M. E. An eighteenth-century occult magazine and a query as to Blake. Bibliophile 2 1908.
Swainson, W. P. Blake: seer, poet and artist. [1908].
de Selincourt, B. William Blake. 1909.
Chesterton, G. K. William Blake. 1910, 1920.
Keynes, G. L. Blake's Laughing song: a new version. N & Q 24 Sept 1910.
— and G. Raverat. Job: a masque for dancing founded on Blake's Illustrations to the Book of Job. [1931?].
Keynes, G. L. Blake, Tulk and Garth Wilkinson. Library 4th ser 26 1945.
— Blake studies. 1949. Reprints 17 essays.
— Blake's Vision of the circle of the life of man. In Studies in art and literature for Belle Da Costa Greene, ed D. Miner, Princeton 1954.
— Blake's copy of Dante's Inferno. TLS 3 May 1957.
— Blake's trial at Chichester. N & Q Nov 1957.
— Blake and Sir Francis Bacon. TLS 8 March 1957.
— Blake and John Linnell. TLS 13 June 1958.
— John Linnell and Mrs Blake. TLS 20 June 1958.
— Blake's library. TLS 6 Nov 1959.
— Blake's miniatures. TLS 29 Jan 1960.
— A Blake engraving in Bonnycastle's Mensuration 1782. Book Collector 12 1963.
— On editing Blake. In English studies today: 3rd series, ed G. I. Duthie 1964.
— Blake and John Gabriel Stedman. TLS 20 May 1965.
— Blake's Little Tom the sailor. Book Collector 17 1968.
Wicksteed, J. H. Blake's Vision of the Book of Job. 1910, 1924 (rev).
— The so-called 'madness' of Blake. Quest 3 1911.
— Blake's Innocence and experience. 1928.
— Blake's Songs of innocence. TLS 18 Feb 1932.
— Blake's river of life: its poetic undertones. Bournemouth [1951?].
— Blake's Jerusalem. [1954].
Vries, J. C. F. Bassalik-de. Blake in his relation to Dante Gabriel Rossetti. Basle 1911.
Butterworth, A. M. Blake, mystic. Liverpool and London 1911.
Beeching, H. C. Blake's religious lyrics. E & S 3 1912.
Dickinson, K. L. Blake's anticipation of the individualistic revolution. New York 1915.
Morris, H. N. Flaxman, Blake, Coleridge and other men of genius influenced by Swedenborg. 1915.
Olivero, F. Sulla tecnica poetica di Blake. In his Studi sul romanticisma inglese, Bari 1914.
Norman, H. J. Cowper and Blake. Olney [1913].
— William Blake. Jnl of Mental Science 61 1915.

Higham, C. Blake and the 'Swedenborgians'. New Church Weekly Jan 1915; rptd N & Q 10 April 1915.
—— Swedenborg annotated by Blake. New Church Weekly 23 Feb 1918.
Gardner, C. Vision and vesture: Blake in modern thought. 1916, 1929.
—— Blake the man. 1919.
Blake's designs for Gray: light on their history. Times 5 Nov 1919.
Eliot, T. S. In his Sacred wood, 1920; rptd in his Selected essays, 1932, and in his Points of view, 1941.
Fehr, B. Blake und die Kabbala. E Studien 54 1920.
Saurat, D. Blake and Milton. Bordeaux 1920, New York 1924, 1935, New York 1965.
—— Blake et les Celtomanes. MP 23 1925.
—— Blake and modern thought. 1929, New York 1964.
—— Blake, la pensée moderne et les Gnostiques. Yggdrasil nos 5–6 1936.
—— William Blake. Paris 1954.
Babenroth, A. C. In his English childhood, New York 1922.
Wright, T. Blake for babes: a popular illustrated introduction to the works of Blake. Olney 1923.
—— The life of Blake. Olney 1929.
Ba-Han, M. Blake: his mysticism. Bordeaux 1924.
—— The evolution of Blakean philosophy. Rangoon 1926.
Havens, R. D. In his Influence of Milton on English poetry, Cambridge Mass 1922.
—— 'Hand' in Blake's Sons of Albion. N & Q 12 Nov 1949.
Damon, S. F. Blake: his philosophy and symbolism. Boston 1924, New York 1947.
—— A Blake dictionary. Providence 1965.
Pierce, F. E. Blake and seventeenth-century authors. MLN 39 1924.
—— The genesis and general meaning of Blake's Milton. MP 25 1927.
—— Blake and Klopstock. SP 25 1928.
—— Blake and Thomas Taylor. PMLA 48 1928.
—— Taylor, Aristotle and Blake. PQ 9 1930.
—— Etymology as explanation in Blake. PQ 10 1931.
Bruce, H. L. Blake in this world. 1925.
—— Blake and Gilchrist's 'remarkable coterie of advanced thinkers'. MP 23 1926.
Jenkins, H. William Blake. 1925. 5 essays first ptd elsewhere.
Short, E. H. Blake. 1925.
Walter, J. Blakes Nachleben in der englischen Literatur des neunzehnten und zwanzigsten Jahrhunderts. Schaffhausen 1925, 1927.
Burdett, O. William Blake. 1926 (EML).
Blake, Cromek and Hoppner. TLS 7 Oct 1926.
Bertram, A. Blake: an aesthetic approach. Nineteenth Century March 1926.
Povey, K. Blake's 'heads of the poets'. 24 July 1926.
—— The case of Rex v. Blake. Nation (London) 21 July 1928.
—— Blake's Genesis. TLS 3 Oct 1952.
Hataya, M. William Blake. Tokyo 1927. In Japanese.
Lindsay, J. Blake: creative will and the poetic image. 1927, 1929 (rev).
Orchard, M. A commentary and questionnaire on Songs of innocence and Songs of experience. 1927.
Plowman, M. An introduction to the study of Blake. 1927, 1952; ed R. H. Ward 1967.
Clarke, J. H. Blake on the Lord's Prayer. 1927.
—— From Copernicus to Blake. [1928].
—— The God of Shelley and Blake. 1930.
Allen, L. H. Blake: a centenary address. Sydney 1927.
White, H. C. The mysticism of Blake. Madison 1927, New York 1964.
Wilson, M. The life of Blake. 1927, 1932 (without notes), 1948 (rev).
Barrett, J. A. S. Carlyle on Blake and Vitalis. TLS 26 April 1928.

Fairchild, H. N. Unpublished references to Blake by Hayley and Lady Hesketh. SP 25 1928.
—— In his Religious trends in English poetry vol 3, New York 1949.
Pryke, J. S. Blake and the imagination. New Church Life 48 1928.
Soupault, P. William Blake. Tr J.L. May 1928.
Wright, H. G. Blake and Sir Joshua Reynolds: a contrast in theories of art. Nineteenth Century March 1927.
Hamblen, E. S. On the minor prophecies of Blake. 1930.
—— The Book of Job interpreted. New York 1939.
—— Interpretation of Blake's Job. New York [1939].
Jugaku, B and M. Yanagi (ed). Bu-re-i-ku ko Ho-i-tsu-to-ma-n. Vols 1–2, 1931–2. This Japanese journal on Blake and Whitman includes trns by Jugaku: Poetical sketches, Island in the moon, then she bore pale desire, and Woe cried the Muse, the Songs inscribed in a copy of Poetical sketches, marginalia to Lavater's Aphorisms and Swedenborg's Divine love and divine wisdom, There is no natural religion, All religions are one, and Tiriel; and essays on Blake by M. Umegaki, On Blake's Canterbury pilgrims; Blake's earliest illuminated printings; the technique in Blake's engravings; The calligraphy of Blake's illuminated printings; S. Ojima, Blake's imagination on nature; Blake and Celtism, Jugaku, Introduction to the study of Blake; Blake of the Poetical sketches; Pedigree of Blake; Blake's childhood; Blake in apprenticeship; M. Hashizume, Orientalism in the development of Blake's idea of line; and trns of articles by Herford, T. S. Eliot, Strachey and J. M. Murry.
Pitfield, R. L. Blake and his tree full of angels. Medical Life 38 1931.
Partington, W. A Blake discovery and its lesson. Bookman (London) March 1932.
—— Some marginalia. TLS 28 Jan 1939.
Clutton-Brock, A. Blake. 1933.
Birss, J. H. Herman Melville and Blake. N & Q 5 May 1934.
Murry, J. M. William Blake. 1933, 1936, 1964.
Bagdasarianz, W. Blake: Versuch einer Entwicklungsgeschichte des Mystikers, erster Teil, bis 1795. Zürich and Leipzig 1935. No more pbd.
Grønbach, V. Blake: kunster, digter, mystiker. Copenhagen 1933.
Baker, C. H. C. Blake, painter. Huntington Lib Bull 10 1936.
—— The sources of Blake's pictorial expression. HLQ 4 1941.
Quinn, K. Blake and the new age. Virginia Quart Rev 13 1937.
Wackrill, H. R. The inscription over the gate. 1937. On the Blakes in the Tate Gallery.
Alper, B. S. The mysticism of Blake. Poet Lore 44 1938; rptd in Poetry Rev 29 1938.
Blunt, A. Blake's Ancient of Days: the symbolism of the compasses. Jnl of Warburg & Courtauld Inst 2 1938.
—— Blake's Glad day. Ibid.
—— Blake's Brazen serpent. Jnl of Warburg & Courtauld Inst 6 1943.
—— Blake's pictorial imagination. Ibid.
—— The art of Blake. New York 1959.
Jameson, G. Irish poets of today and Blake. PMLA 53 1938.
Lelj, C. Blake. Milan 1938.
Percival, M. O. Blake's circle of destiny. New York 1938, 1964.
Jugaku, B. A study of Blake. Tokyo 1939. In Japanese.
—— A bibliographical study of Blake's Note-book. Tokyo 1953.
Brown, A. R. Blake's drawings for the Book of Enoch. Burlington Mag 77 1940.
Lowery, M. R. Windows of the morning: a critical study of Blake's poetical sketches. New Haven 1940.
—— Blake and the Flaxmans. In The age of Johnson: essays presented to C. B. Tinker, New Haven 1949.

—— Blake and the Divine imagination. Northwest Missouri State College Stud 14 1950.

Shepherd, T. B. In his Methodism and the literature of the eighteenth century, 1940.

Hungerford, E. B. Blake's Albion. In his Shores of darkness, New York 1941.

Williams, C. Blake and Wordsworth. Dublin Rev 208 1941.

Ortiz Bahety, L. Blake: o la transfiguration. Buenos Aires 1942.

Larrabee, S. A. In his English bards and Grecian marbles, New York 1943.

Wolf, E. The Blake-Linnell accounts in the library of Yale University. PBSA 37 1943.

Bronowski, J. Blake: a man without a mask. 1943, 1965 (rev as Blake and the age of revolution).

Preston, K. Blake and Rossetti. 1944.

—— Notes on Blake's large painting in tempera: the spiritual condition of man. 1949.

—— Fragments from Blake's Jerusalem. Apollo 67 1958.

—— A note on Blake sources. Apollo 84 1964.

Duncan-Johnstone, L. A. A psychological study of Blake. 1945, 1958.

Schorer, M. Blake: the politics of vision. New York 1946, 1959.

Meyerstein, E. H. W. A true maid and the sick rose. TLS 22 June 1946.

Oppenheimer, J. M. A note on Blake and John Hunter. Jnl of History of Medicine 1 1946.

Bolt, S. F. Blake: the Songs of innocence. Politics & Letters 1 1947.

Frye, N. Fearful symmetry: a study of Blake. Princeton 1947.

—— Blake's treatment of the archetype. Eng Inst Essays 1950.

—— Poetry and design in Blake. Jnl of Aesthetics 10 1951.

—— Blake after two centuries. UTQ 27 1957; rptd in English romantic poets: modern essays in criticism, ed M. H. Abrams, New York 1960, and in Frye, Fables of identity, New York 1963.

—— Blake's introduction to experience. HLQ 21 1957.

—— (ed). Blake: a collection of critical essays. Englewood Cliffs NJ 1965. Essays by W. J. Keith, Frye, I. H. Chayes, R. F. Gleckner, J. E. Grant, J. H. Hagstrum, M. K. Nurmi, H. Adams, H. Bloom, A. Blunt and D. V. Erdman.

—— The keys to the gates. In Some British Romantics: a collection of essays, ed J. V. Logan, J. E. Jordan and N. Frye, [Columbus Ohio] 1966.

Grigson, G. Palmer and Blake. In his Samuel Palmer: the visionary years, 1947.

Mankowitz, W. Blake: the songs of experience. Politics & Letters 1 1947.

Nanavutty, P. A title page in Blake's illustrated Genesis manuscript. Jnl of Warburg & Courtauld Inst 10 1947.

—— Blake and emblem literature. Jnl of Warburg & Courtauld Inst 15 1952.

O'Malley, F. The wasteland of Blake. Rev of Politics 9 1947.

Todd, R. Blake and the eighteenth-century mythologists. In his Tracks in the snow, 1947.

—— The techniques of Blake's illuminated printing. Print Collector's Quart 29 1948.

—— Blake's Dante plates. TLS 29 Aug, 26 Sept 1968; rcv in Book Collecting & Lib Monthly 1968.

Margoliouth, H. M. The marriage of Blake's parents. N & Q 6 Sept 1947.

—— Notes on Blake. RES 24 1948. On biblical references and human sacrifice.

—— Blake's family. N & Q 10 July 1948.

—— Blake's Sons of Albion. N & Q 5 March 1949.

—— Blake's Mr Mathew. N & Q 14 April 1951.

—— William Blake. Oxford 1951 (Home Univ Lib).

Davies, J. G. The theology of Blake. Oxford 1948, Hamden Conn 1965.

Breton, G. le and E. Souffrin. Lettres et entretiens de Blake. Paris 1948.

Erdman, D. V. Blake, Flaxman and the £100. PQ 27 1948.

—— Blake's debt to James Gillray. Art Quart 12 1949.

—— Blake's exactness in dates. PQ 28 1949.

—— Lambeth and Bethlehem in Blake's Jerusalem. MP 48 1951.

—— Blake's vision of slavery. Jnl of Warburg & Courtauld Inst 15 1952.

—— The dating of Blake's engravings. PQ 31 1952.

—— Blake's early Swedenborgianism: a twentieth-century legend. Comparative Lit 5 1953.

—— Blake's Nest of villains. Keats-Shelley Jnl 2 1953.

—— Blake entries in Godwin's diary. N & Q Aug 1953.

—— Blake and Godwin. N & Q Feb 1954.

—— Blake: prophet against empire. Princeton 1954.

—— Blake's debt to Joel Barlow. Amer Lit 26 1954.

—— Reliques of the contemporaries of William Upcott, 'Emperor of autographs'. BNYPL Nov 1960. Blake's comments in Upcott's album.

—— The suppressed and altered passages in Blake's Jerusalem. SB 17 1964.

—— Blake's Jerusalem: plate 3 fully restored. SB 18 1965.

—— 'Terrible Blake in his pride': an essay on the Everlasting Gospel. In From sensibility to romanticism: essays presented to F. A. Pottle, ed F. W. Hilles and H. Bloom, New York 1965.

Hood, T. L. Browning and Blake. Trinity Rev new ser 2 1948.

James, D. G. The gospel of Hell. In his Romantic comedy, Oxford 1948, 1963.

Wasser, H. H. Notes on the Visions of the daughters of Albion. MLQ 9 1948.

Blackstone, B. English Blake. Cambridge 1949, Hamden Conn 1966.

—— Poetical sketches and Hyperion. Cambridge Jnl Dec 1952.

—— The traveller unknown. In his Lost travellers, 1962.

Hamilton, K. M. Blake and the religion of art. Dalhousie Rev 29 1949.

Nathan, N. Prince William B: the philosophical conceptions of Blake. New York 1949.

Van Sinderen, A. Blake: the mystic genius. Syracuse NY 1949.

Witcutt, W. P. Blake: a psychological study. 1946.

Bottrall, M. F. The divine image: a study of Blake's interpretation of Christianity. Rome 1950.

Bullett, G. In his English mystics, 1950.

Peckham, M. Blake, Milton and Edward Burney. Princeton Univ Lib Chron 11 1950.

Baldi, W. La figure e l'arte di Blake. Salerno 1951.

Hirst, D. Problem of a Blake painting [Spiritual condition of man]. Country Life 17 Feb 1950.

—— Hidden riches: traditional symbolism from the Renaissance to Blake. 1964.

'Bishop, M.' (Oliver Stoner). Blake's Hayley. 1951.

—— Blake and Buckingham. TLS 2 April 1964.

Bowman, M. B. Blake: a study of his doctrine of art. Jnl of Aesthetics 10 1951.

Brown, J. E. Neo-Platonism in the poetry of Blake. Ibid.

Fiske, I. Bernard Shaw's debt to Blake. 1951 (Shavian Tract no 2).

Mason, E. C. (ed). The mind of Henry Fuseli: selections from his writings, with an introductory study. 1951.

Miles, J. The language of Blake. Eng Inst Essays 1950; rptd as The sublimity of Blake in her Eras and modes in English poetry, Berkeley 1957.

Raine, K. William Blake. 1951 (Br Council pamphlet), 1965 (rev); tr Japanese, 1956.

—— Who made the tyger? Encounter June 1954.

—— The sea of time and space. Jnl of Warburg & Courtauld Inst 20 1957.

—— Some sources of Tiriel. HLQ 21 1957.

—— Blake and England. Cambridge 1960.

—— Yeats's debt to Blake. Dublin Mag 5 1966; rptd in her Defending ancient springs, 1967.

—— Blake and tradition, 2 vols Princeton [1969].

Roos, J. Aspects littéraires du mysticisme philosophique et l'influence de Boehme et de Swedenborg au début du romanticisme: Blake, Novalis, Ballanche. Strasbourg 1951.

White, H. S. A primer of Blake. Ames Iowa 1951.

Harper, G. M. The source of Blake's Ah! sunflower! MLR 48 1953.

—— Blake's Nebuchadnezzar in the City of Dreadful Night. SP 50 1953.

—— The Neo-Platonic concept of time in Blake's prophetic books. PMLA 69 1954.

—— Blake's Neo-Platonic interpretation of Plato's Atlantis myth. JEGP 54 1955.

—— Thomas Taylor and Blake's Drama of Persephone. PQ 34 1955.

—— Symbolic meaning in Blake's Nine years. MLN 72 1957.

—— The Neoplatonism of Blake. Chapel Hill 1961.

—— Blake's lost letter to Hayley 4 December 1804. SP 61 1964.

—— Apocalyptic vision and pastoral dream in Blake's Four Zoas. South Atlantic Quart 64 1965.

Hofer, P. An illustration by Blake for the Circle of the Traitors, Dante's Inferno canto xxxii. Meriden Conn 1953.

Roe, A. S. Blake's illustrations to the Divine comedy. Princeton 1953.

—— A drawing of the Last Judgment. HLQ 21 1957.

Rudd, M. Divided image: a study of Blake and W. B. Yeats. 1953.

—— Organiz'd innocence: the story of Blake's prophetic books. 1956.

Adams, H. The Blakean aesthetic. Jnl of Aesthetics 13 1954.

—— Blake and Yeats: the contrary vision. Ithaca 1955.

—— Blake and Gulley Jimson: English symbolists. Critique 3 1959.

—— Reading Blake's lyrics: the Tyger. Texas Stud in Lit & Lang 2 1960.

—— Blake: a reading of the shorter poems. Seattle 1963.

Bentley, G. E., jr. Blake and Swedenborg. N & Q June 1954.

—— Thomas Butts, White Collar Maecenas. PMLA 71 1956.

—— A. S. Mathew: patron of Blake and Flaxman. N & Q April 1958.

—— An unknown early biography of Blake [by Thomas Dodd]. TLS 16 March 1962.

—— Blake's Hesiod. Library 5th ser 20 1965.

—— Blake's annotations to Swedenborg's Heaven and Hell. UTQ 34 1965.

—— A collection of prosaic William Blakes. N & Q May 1965.

—— The date of Blake's Pickering manuscript: or the way of a poet with paper. SB 19 1966.

—— The printing of Blake's America. Stud in Romanticism 6 1966.

—— Blake records. Oxford 1969.

Gardner, S. Infinity on the anvil: a critical study of Blake's poetry. Oxford 1954.

—— Blake. 1968.

Boase, T. S. R. An extra-illustrated second folio of Shakespeare. BM Quart 20 1955.

Balakian, A. The literary fortune of Blake in France. MLQ 17 1956.

Gaunt, W. Arrows of desire: a study of Blake and his romantic world. 1956.

Gleckner, R. F. Blake's religion of the imagination. Jnl of Aesthetics 14 1956.

—— Irony in Blake's Holy Thursday I. MLN 71 1956.

—— Blake's Tiriel and the state of experience. PQ 36 1957.

—— The piper and the bard: a study of Blake. Detroit 1959.

—— Blake's Thel and the Bible. BNYPL Nov 1960.

—— Blake and the human abstract. PMLA 76 1961.

—— Joyce and Blake: notes toward defining a literary relationship. In A James Joyce miscellany, ed M. Magalaner, Carbondale 1962.

—— Blake and the senses. Stud in Romanticism 5 1965.

—— Blake's Seasons. Stud in Eng Lit 1500–1900 5 1965.

Goddard, H. C. Blake's Fourfold vision. Wallingford Pa 1956.

James, L. D. Blake: the finger on the furnace. New York 1956.

Kiralis, K. The theme and structure of Blake's Jerusalem. ELH 23 1956.

—— Joyce and Blake: a basic source for Finnegans Wake. Modern Fiction Stud 4 1959.

—— A guide to the intellectual symbolism of Blake's later prophetic writings. Criticism 1 1959.

Nurmi, M. K. Blake's revisions of the Tyger. PMLA 71 1956.

—— Blake's Marriage of Heaven and Hell: a critical study. Kent Ohio 1957.

—— Fact and symbol in the Chimney sweeper of Blake's Songs of innocence. BNYPL April 1964.

—— Joy, love and innocence in Blake's Mental traveller. Stud in Romanticism 3 1964.

Adler, J. H. Symbol and meaning in the Little black boy. MLN 72 1957.

Digby, G. F. Symbol and image in Blake. Oxford 1957.

Kuhn, A. J. Blake on the nature and origins of pagan gods and myths. MLN 72 1957.

Petter, H. Enitharmon: Stellung und Aufgabe eines Symbols im dichterischen Gesamtwerk Blakes. Berne 1957.

Pinto, V. de S. (ed). The divine vision: studies in the poetry and art of Blake. 1957. Reprints essays by Frye, Damon, Raine, Pinto, Kiralis, Nanavutty, Margoliouth, Nurmi.

Rienacker, V. Blake: a natural visionary. 1957.

Will, F. Blake's quarrel with Reynolds. Jnl of Aesthetics 15 1957.

Miner, P. Blake's London residences. BNYPL Nov 1958.

—— Blake's Divine analogy. Criticism 3 1961.

—— The Tyger: genesis and evolution in the poetry of Blake. Criticism 4 1962.

—— The apprentice of Great Queen Street. BNYPL Dec 1963.

Morton, A. L. The Everlasting Gospel: a study in the sources of Blake. 1958.

Ryskamp, C. A. Blake's Cowperian sketches. RES new ser 9 1958.

—— Lawrence's portrait of Cowper. Princeton Univ Lib Chron 20 1959.

—— A Blake collection for Princeton. Princeton Univ Lib Chron 21 1960.

—— The Blake collection of Mrs Gerald B. Lambert presented to Library. Princeton Alumni Weekly 12 Feb 1960.

—— Blake's drawing of Cowper's monument. Princeton Univ Lib Chron 24 1962.

Beaumont, E. de. William Blake. 1959 (Curiosa Typografica).

Fisher, P. F. Blake and the Druids. JEGP 58 1959.

—— Blake's attacks on the classical tradition. PQ 40 1961.

—— The valley of vision: Blake as prophet and revolutionary. Ed N. Frye, Toronto 1961.

Joyce, James. William Blake. Ed E. Mason, Criticism 1 1959.

Merchant, W. M. In his Shakespeare and the artist, Oxford 1959.

—— Blake's Shakespeare. Apollo 79 1964.

Stevenson, W. H. Blake's Jerusalem. EC 9 1959.

—— The shaping of Blake's America. MLR 55 1960.

— Blake's From Cratetos: a source and a correction. N & Q 213 1968.

Daugherty, J. William Blake. New York 1960. For children.

Grant, J. E. The art and argument of the Tyger. Texas Stud in Lit and Lang 2 1960.

— Misreadings of the Fly. EC 11 1961.

— (ed). Discussions of Blake. Boston 1961. Reprints essays by Adams, Erdman, Fisher, Frye [2], Grant, Keynes, Kiralis, Nurmi, Sutherland, M. Van Doren, and letters by Coleridge and Lamb.

— Interpreting Blake's The fly. BNYPL Nov 1963.

— and F. C. Robinson. Tense and the sense of Blake's The tyger. PMLA 81 1966.

Hutin, S. Blake et Boehme. In his Les disciples anglais de Jacob Boehme aux xviiᵉ and xviiiᵉ siècles, Paris 1960.

Kemper, F. C. The interlinear drawings in Blake's Jerusalem. BNYPL Nov 1960.

Bloom, H. In his Visionary company, New York 1961.

— Blake's Apocalypse: a study in poetic argument. Garden City NY 1963.

Chayes, I. H. Plato's statesman myth in Shelley and Blake. Comparative Lit 13 1961.

Takeshima, Y. Wi-ri-a-mu Bu-re-i-ku no Ken-kyu [A study of Blake]. Tokyo 1961. In Japanese.

Lister, R. In his Edward Calvert, 1962.

— Beulah to Byzantium: a study of parallels in the works of W. B. Yeats, Blake, Samuel Palmer and Edward Calvert. [Dublin] 1965.

— Blake: an introduction to the man and to his work. 1968.

Owen, A. L. All things begin and end in Albion's ancient Druid rocky shore. In his Famous Druids, Oxford 1962.

Paley, M. D. Blake in Nighttown. In a James Joyce miscellany, ed M. Magalaner, Carbondale 1962.

— Tyger of wrath. PLMA 81 1966.

— (ed). Blake newsletter. 1967–. A mimeographed quarterly.

— Cowper as Blake's spectre. Eighteenth-century Stud 1 1968.

Maillet, A. Blake et Nietzsche. Revue des Lettres Modernes 76–7, 1962–3.

Nekrasova, E. A. Tvorchestvio Vil'iama Bleika. Moscow 1962.

Tolley, M. J. Blake's use of the Bible in a section of the Everlasting Gospel. N & Q May 1962; addn, Jan 1968.

— The Book of Thel and Night thoughts. BNYPL June 1965.

— The Auckland Blakes [America and Europe]. Biblionews & Australian Notes & Queries 2nd ser 2 1967.

Hagstrum, J. H. Blake's Blake. In Essays in history and literature presented by Fellows of the Newberry Library to Stanley Pargellis, ed H. Bluhm, Chicago 1963.

— Blake's The clod and the pebble. In Restoration and eighteenth-century literature, essays in honor of A. D. McKillop, ed C. Camden, Chicago 1963.

— Blake rejects the Enlightenment. Stud on Voltaire & Eighteenth Century 25 1963.

— Blake, poet and painter: an introduction to the illuminated verse. Chicago 1964.

Moore, C. H. Amédée Pichot's discovery of Blake. Etudes Anglaises 16 1963.

Rodway, A. E. In his Romantic conflict, 1863.

Rose, E. J. The structure of Blake's Jerusalem. Bucknell Rev 11 1963.

— Mental forms creating: fourfold vision and the poet as prophet in Blake's designs and verse. Jnl of Aesthetics 23 1964.

— Blake's hand: symbol and design in Jerusalem. Texas Stud in Lit & Lang 6 1964.

— Visionary forms dramatic: grammatical and iconographical movement in Blake's verse and designs. Criticism 8 1966.

Hirsch, E. D., jr. Innocence and experience: an introduction to Blake. New Haven 1964.

Robinson, F. C. Verb tense in Blake's The tyger. PMLA 79 1964.

Wolf-Gumpold, K. Blake: Versuch einer Einführung in sein Leben und Werk. Stuttgart 1964.

Ansari, A. A. Arrows of intellect: a study in Blake's Gospel of the imagination. Aligarh 1965.

Boldereff, F. M. A Blakean translation of Joyces Circe. Woodward Pa 1965.

Butlin, M. Blake's God judging Adam rediscovered. Burlington Mag 107 1965.

Kreiter, C. S. Evolution and Blake. Stud in Romanticism 4 1965.

Ostriker, A. Vision and verse in Blake. Madison 1965.

Price, M. Blake: vision and satire. In his To the palace of wisdom, Garden City NY 1965.

Rawson, C. J. Ida's shady brow: parallels to Blake. N & Q May 1965.

Roston, M. In his Prophet and poet: the Bible and the growth of romanticism, 1965.

Bogen, N. An early listing of Blake's Poetical sketches. Eng Lang Notes 3 1966.

England, M. W. Blake and the Hymns of Charles Wesley. BNYPL Jan–April 1966; rptd in M. W. England and J. Sparrow, Hymns unbidden: Donne, Herbert, Blake, Emily Dickinson and the hymnographers, New York 1966.

Gillham, D. G. Blake's contrary states: the Songs of innocence and of experience as dramatic poems. Cambridge 1966.

Schulz, M. F. Point of view in Blake's The clod and the pebble. Papers on Lang & Lit 2 1966.

Altizer, T. J. J. The New Apocalypse: the radical Christian vision of Blake. East Lansing 1967.

Connolly, T. E. and G. R. Levine. Pictorial and poetic design in two songs of innocence. PMLA 82 1967.

Dorfman, D. Blake in 1863 and 1880: the Gilchrist life. BNYPL April 1967.

— Blake in the nineteenth century: his reputation as a poet from Gilchrist to Yeats. New Haven 1969.

Ehrstine, J. W. Blake's Poetical sketches. [Pullman Washington] 1967.

Beer, J. Blake's humanism. Manchester 1968.

Holloway, J. Blake: the lyric poetry. 1968.

Wells, W. Blake's heads of the poets for Turret House, the residence of William Hayley, Felpham. [Manchester 1969].

G. E. B.

VIII. MINOR POETRY 1750–1800

References

Anderson   The works of the British poets, ed R. Anderson 13 vols Edinburgh 1792–5.
Chalmers   The works of the English poets, ed A. Chalmers 21 vols 1810.
Johnson   The works of the English poets, ed S. Johnson 68 vols 1779–81.

Numerals following these names refer to vol-nos in these collections.

MARK AKENSIDE
1720–71

Bibliographies

Williams, I. A. In his Seven xviiith-century bibliographies, 1924.
See also C. T. Houpt under §2, below.

Collections

Poems. [Ed J. Dyson] 1772, 1772, Edinburgh 1773.
Works. Ed J. Garnett, New Brunswick 1808.
Poems. Ed A. Dyce 1835 etc (Aldine).
The poetical works of Akenside and John Dyer. Ed R. A. Willmott 1855.
Poetical works. Ed G. Gilfillan, Edinburgh and London 1857.
Anderson 9, Chalmers 14, Johnson 55.
Many 18th- and 19th-century edns.

§ 1

A British philippic. GM Aug 1738; 1738, 1738 (as The voice of liberty: a British philippic).
The pleasures of imagination. 1744 (for various issues *see* Chapman and Foxon, §2 below), Dublin 1748, London 1754 (5th edn), Edinburgh 1758 (with Odes on several subjects), London 1763, 1765, Edinburgh 1768, London 1769, Glasgow 1771, 1775, 1777, 1780, London 1786, 1788, 1794 (with essay by Mrs Barbauld), 1795, New York 1795, Portland Maine 1807 etc; tr French, 1759, 1806; German, 1757; Italian, 1764. Final revision and fragment of bk iv first ptd in 1772 collected edn.
An epistle to Warburton. 1744. Often attributed to J. Dyson.
An epistle to Curio. 1744.
Dissertatio medica inauguralis, de ortu et encremento foetus humani. Leyden 1744.
Odes on several subjects. 1745, 1745, 1760 (rev).
Friendship and love: a dialog; to which is added A song. 1745.
An ode to the Earl of Huntingdon. 1748, 1748.
An ode to the country gentlemen of England. 1758, 1758.
Notes on the postscript to a pamphlet by Alexander Monro. 1758.
Oratio anniversaria in theatro Collegii Regalis. 1760.
De dysenteria commentarius. 1764.
An ode to the late Thomas Edwards. 1766.
The works of William Harvey. 1766. Ed Akenside.
Williams, R. M. Two unpublished poems by Akenside. MLN 57 1942.
Akenside contributed to Dodsley's Collection vol 6, 1758 (5 *poems*) *and to* The new foundling hospital for wit vol 6, 1773. *He edited* The museum: or the literary and historical register 29 March 1746-12 Sept 1747. *He contributed medical papers to* Philosophical Trans of Royal Soc 1757, 1763 *and to* Medical Trans 1772.

§ 2

Johnson, S. In his Lives of the poets, 1779–81.
Bucke, C. On the life, writings and genius of Akenside. 1832.
Dowden, E. Akenside. In Ward's English poets vol 3, 1880.
Bundt, O. Akensides Leben und Werke. Leipzig 1897. Continued in Anglia 20–1 1898–9.
Gosse, E. Akenside: poet and physician. Living Age 311 1921.
Chapman, R. W. A note on the first edition of the Pleasures of imagination. RES 1 1925.
Potter, G. R. Akenside, prophet of evolution. MP 24 1926.
Buck, H. Smollett and Akenside. JEGP 31 1932.

ten Hoor, G. J. The pleasures of imagination in Germany. JEGP 38 1939.
Renwick, W. L. Akenside and others. Durham Univ Jnl new ser 3 1942.
—— Notes on some lesser poets of the eighteenth century. In Essays on the eighteenth century presented to David Nichol Smith, Oxford 1945.
Aldridge, A. O. The eclecticism of the Pleasures of imagination. JHI 5 1944.
—— Akenside and imagination. SP 42 1945.
—— Akenside and the hierarchy of beauty. MLQ 8 1947.
—— Akenside, Anna Seward and colour. N & Q 24 Dec 1948.
Houpt, C. T. Akenside: a biographical and critical study. Philadelphia 1944. With bibliography.
Kallich, M. Association of ideas and Akenside's Pleasures of imagination. MLN 62 1947.
Foxon, D. F. Akenside's The pleasures of imagination. Book Collector 5 1956.
Pollard, A. Keats and Akenside: a borrowing in the Ode to a nightingale. MLR 51 1956.
Hart, J. Akenside's revision of the Pleasures of imagination. PMLA 74 1959.
Mahoney, J. L. Akenside and Shaftesbury. Discourse 4 1961.
—— Addison and Akenside: the impact of psychological criticism on early English romantic poetry. Br Jnl of Aesthetics 6 1966.
Marsh, R. Akenside and Addison. MP 59 1961.
—— Four dialectical theories of poetry. Chicago 1965.

CHRISTOPHER ANSTEY
1724–1805

Bibliographies

Williams, I. A. Bibliographical notes and news. London Mercury Jan–July 1925. On first edns of Anstey.
See also Powell under §2, below.

Collections

The poetical works, with some account of the life and writings by his son John Anstey. 1808.

§ 1

Elegia scripta in coemeterio rustico latine reditta. Cambridge 1762, 1778. With W. H. Roberts.
On the death of the Marquis of Tavistock. 1767 (4 edns).
The new Bath guide: or memoirs of the B[lunde]R[hea]D family in a series of poetical epistles. 1766 (3 edns), Dublin 1766, London 1767, 1768 (6th edn), Dublin 1768, London 1772 (8th edn), 1773, 1776, 1784 (12th edn), 1788, 1797, 1804, 1830, 1832 etc; ed P. Sainsbury 1927.
The patriot: a pindaric address to Lord Buckhorse. Cambridge 1767, 1768 (with appendix), 1779.
Appendix to the Patriot. 1768.
Ode on an evening view of the Crescent at Bath. 1773.
The priest dissected: a poem addressed to the Rev Mr ——, author of Regulus, Toby, Caesar and other satirical pieces, canto 1. Bath 1774, 1774, nd.
An election ball in poetical letters in the Zomersetshire dialect from Mr Inkle of Bath to his wife at Glocester; with a poetical address to John Miller. 1776 (several edns), Dublin 1776, 1776, Bath 1776 ('the second edition with considerable additions'), 1779, 1787.
Fabulae selectae auctore Johanne Gay latine redditae. [1777], 1798.
Ad C. W. Bampfylde, arm: epistola poetica familiaris. Bath, London, Cambridge, Oxford 1776, 1776, Bath 1777. Tr anon as A familiar epistle from C. Anstey to C. W. Bampfylde, 1777, Dublin 1777.
Envy: a poem, addressed to Mrs Miller. [1778].

Winter amusements: an ode. [1778].

A paraphrase of the thirteenth chapter of first Corinthians. 1779.

Speculation, or a defence of mankind: a poem. 1780.

Liberality, or the decayed macaroni: a sentimental piece. 1788, [1790?].

The farmer's daughter: a poetical tale. Bath 1795, 1795.

The monopolist: a poetical tale. 1795.

Britain's genius: a song occasioned by the late mutiny at the Nore. Bath 1797.

Contentment: a poetical epistle. 1800.

Ad Edvardum Jenner: carmen alcaicum. Bath 1803. Tr J. Ring as A translation of Anstey's Ode to Jenner, 1804 (2nd edn).

Anstey contributed to Lady Miller's Poetical amusements at a villa near Bath, Bath 1781, *and to* Cambridge Chron 1769, GM1 768–87, Annual Register 1786; *see Powell under §2, below.*

§ 2

Madge's addresses to Christopher Twist-wit. 1777.

Cary, H. F. In his Lives of English poets, 1846.

Maier, W. Anstey und der New Bath guide. Heidelberg 1914.

Hesselgrave, R. A. Lady Miller and the Batheaston literary circle. New Haven 1927.

Munby, A. N. L. Anstey's Election ball and the Epistle to Bampfylde. Book-Collector's Quart 16 1934.

Powell, W. C. Anstey: Bath laureate. Philadelphia 1944. With bibliography.

Day, M. S. Anstey and anapestic satire in the late 18th century. ELH 15 1948.

Hopkins, K. In his Portraits in satire, 1958.

JOHN CODRINGTON BAMPFYLDE
1754–96

Sixteen sonnets. 1778; rptd in Southey's Specimens of the later English poets vol 3, 1807; Park's Works of the British poets vol 41, 1808; The British poets vol 73, Chiswick 1822; Sanford's Works of the British poets vol 37, Philadelphia 1822; Routledge's British poets (Thomson vol), 1853.

ANNA LAETITIA AIKIN,
later BARBAULD
1743–1825
Collections

Miscellaneous pieces in prose. 1773, 1775, 1792. With J. Aikin.

Poems. 1773 (3 edns), 1774, 1777, 1792 (with Epistle to Wilberforce).

Evenings at home. 6 vols 1792–5, 1798 (4th edn of 1–3, 2nd edn of 4–6, with J. Aikin.

Works. 2 vols 1825, New York 1826. With memoir by L. Aikin.

Things by their right names. Ed S. J. Hale, Boston 1840. Selection.

Tales, poems and essays. Boston 1884. Biographical sketch by G. A. Oliver.

See also Ellis under §2, below.

Mrs Barbauld edited Collins, 1794, 1797; Akenside's Pleasures of imagination, 1794; Selections from the Spectator, Tatler etc, 3 vols 1804; Correspondence of Samuel Richardson, 6 vols 1804; The British novelists, 50 vols 1810; The female speaker, 1811.

§ 1

Corsica: an ode. 1768.

Lessons for children. 1778, 1779, 1787, 1788, 1808, 1812, 1821; tr French, 1821. Many subsequent edns, variously titled.

Hymns in prose for children. 1781, 1814 (16th edn), 1836 (28th edn), 1845 (30th edn) etc; tr French, 1818; German, 1849; Hungarian, 1864; Italian, 1819; Spanish, 1827.

Address to the opposers of the repeal of the corporation and test acts. 1790 (4 edns).

Epistle to Wilberforce. 1791, 1791.

Civic sermons to the people. 1792.

Remarks on Wakefield's Enquiry. 1792 (3 edns).

Sins of the government, sins of the nation, by a volunteer. 1793.

Eighteen hundred and eleven. 1812, Philadelphia 1812.

A discourse on being born again. Boston 1830 (2nd edn). A tract.

Letters

Whiting, M. B. A century-old friendship: unpublished letters from Mrs Barbauld. London Mercury Sept 1932.

§ 2

Ellis, G. A. A memoir, letters and a selection from the writings of Anna Barbauld. 2 vols Boston 1874.

Le Breton, A. L. A memoir of Mrs Barbauld, including letters. 1874.

Murch, J. Mrs Barbauld and her contemporaries. 1877.

Ritchie, A. T. In her A book of sibyls, 1883

Brodribb, C. W. Mrs Barbauld's school. Contemporary Rev 1935.

'Life, I know not': Mrs Barbauld. TLS 19 June 1943.

Rodgers, B. Georgian chronicle: Mrs Barbauld and her family. 1958.

JAMES BEATTIE
1735–1803
Collections

Original poems and translations. 1760, Aberdeen 1761.

Poems on several subjects. 1766.

Essays. Edinburgh 1776, 1776, 2 vols Dublin 1778, Edinburgh 1778, 1779; tr French, 1798.

Poems on several occasions Edinburgh 1776, 1780 (4th edn).

Dissertations moral and critical. 1783, 2 vols Dublin 1783, London 1786.

Poetical works. Ed A. Dyce 1831, Boston 1854, 1866, 1891 (Aldine).

Chalmers 18.

Many 19th-century edns, frequently in combination with such other late 18th-century poets as Collins, Thomson, Goldsmith, Blair, Falconer, Campbell.

§ 1

The judgment of Paris: a poem. 1765.

Verses occasioned by the death of Churchill. 1765.

An essay on the nature and immutability of truth. 1770, Edinburgh 1771, London 1772, 1773, 1774, Edinburgh 1774, 1777, London 1778, 1807, 1810 etc.

The minstrel, or the progress of genius: a poem, book the first. 1771, 1771, 1772, 1774, 1775; Book the second, 1774 (3 edns); In two books, with some other poems, 1775, Dublin 1775, London 1777, 1779, 1784, 1795, 1797, 2 vols 1799 (with life and miscellaneous poems), Edinburgh 1803, 1805, 1806, Alnwick 1807, 1807, Edinburgh 1807, London 1807, 1821, 1858 etc; tr French, 1823; Italian, 1824.

A letter to the Rev H. Blair on the improvement of psalmody. 1778, Edinburgh 1829.

Scoticisms, arranged in alphabetical order. 1779, 1787, Edinburgh 1811.

Evidences of the Christian religion briefly stated. 2 vols Edinburgh 1786, Philadelphia 1787, London 1795, 1814 etc.

The theory of language. 1788.
Elements of moral science. 2 vols Edinburgh 1790–3, 1807, 1817.
Essays and fragments in prose and verse, by James Hay Beattie. 1794, 1799. Ed elder Beattie, with biographical sketch.
Mossner, E. C. Beattie's The castle of scepticism: an unpublished allegory against Hume, Voltaire and Hobbes. SE 27 1948.
—— Beattie on Voltaire: an unpublished parody. Romanic Rev 41 1950.
See also Tave under §2, below.

Letters and Diaries

Letters of Beattie. In British prose writers vol 5, 1819–21.
Mackie, A. Beattie, the Minstrel: some unpublished letters. Aberdeen 1908.
Beattie's London diary 1773. Ed R. S. Walker, Aberdeen 1946.
Day-book 1773–98. Ed R. S. Walker, Aberdeen 1948.
Honour, H. Two letters from Joseph Wright of Derby. Connoisseur 138 1956.

§ 2

Bower, A. An account of the life of Beattie. 1804.
Forbes, W. An account of the life and writings of Beattie, including many letters. 2 vols Edinburgh 1806, 3 vols 1807, 2 vols 1824.
Mallet, C. A. Mémoire sur Beattie. Paris 1863.
Saintsbury, G. In The English poets, ed T. H. Ward vol 3, 1880.
Pueschel, C. Beattie's Minstrel. 1904.
Gray, J. Beattie and the Johnson circle. Queen's Quart 58 1952.
Tave, S. M. Some essays by Beattie in the London Magazine 1771. N & Q 6 Dec 1952.
Bevilacqua, V. M. The authorship of Gerard's lectures. Eng Lang Notes 5 1967. Notes taken from Beattie's lectures.
—— Beattie's theory of rhetoric. Speech Monographs 34 1967.

JOHN BENNET

Collections

Poems on several occasions by John Bennet, a journeyman shoemaker. 1774.

§ 1

Redemption: a poem in two books. Oxford [1796].

§ 2

Southey, R. In his Lives of uneducated poets, 1836; ed J. S. Childers, Oxford 1925.

SAMUEL BISHOP
1731–95
Collections

The poetical works, to which are prefixed memoirs by Thomas Clare. 2 vols 1796, 1800, 1802.
Sermons chiefly upon practical subjects. 1798.
Select poems. In Works of the British poets, ed E. Sanford vol 37, Philadelphia 1822.

§ 1

Ode ad S. Poyntz. [1750]. With English text by C. H. Williams.
Epicedia oxoniensia in obitum Frederici Principis Walliae. Oxford 1751. Bishop contributed an English ode.

An ode to the Earl of Lincoln on the Duke of Newcastle's retirement. 1762.
Feriae poeticae: sive carmina anglicana elegiaci plerumque argumenti latine reditta. 1766.
Also verse in Publick Ledger 1763–4.

§ 2

GM 1795. Obituary, addn, letter from T[homas] C[lare], eulogy.

SUSANNA BLAMIRE
1747–94
§ 1

Poetical works, for the first time collected by H. Lonsdale, with a preface, memoir and notes by P. Maxwell. Edinburgh 1842.
The songs and ballads of Cumberland. Ed S. Gilpin 1866. Includes unpbd poems.

§ 2

Lonsdale, H. In his Worthies of Cumberland vol 4, 1873.

SAMUEL BOWDEN
fl. 1733–61
§ 1

Poetical essays on several occasions. 2 vols 1733–5.
Poems on various subjects with essays, letters and a treatise on health. Bath 1754.

§ 2

Rosenberg, C. Bowden of Frome, Somersetshire. N & Q 13 Nov 1937.

WILLIAM LISLE BOWLES
1762–1850
Bibliographies

Woolf, C. Some uncollected authors XVIII: Bowles. Book Collector 7 1958.

Collections

Fourteen sonnets, elegiac and descriptive, written during a tour. Bath and London 1789, 1789 (rev, 21 sonnets, as Sonnets written chiefly on picturesque spots), London 1794 (27 sonnets, 13 other poems, as Sonnets, with other poems), Bath 1796 (as Sonnets, and other poems), 1796, London and Bath 1798, Bath 1800 (with Poems, 1801, issued as suppl), 2 vols Bath and London 1801–2, London 1803, 2 vols 1805, Zürich 1950 (16 sonnets with trns).
The poetical works of Milman, Bowles, Wilson and Cornwall. Paris 1829.
Poetical works. Ed G. Gilfillan 2 vols Edinburgh 1855.
Poetical works. 2 vols [1879].
The poetical works of Bowles, Lamb and Hartley Coleridge. Ed W. Tirebuck 1887.

§ 1

Verses to John Howard FRS. Bath, London and Oxford 1789.
The grave of Howard: a poem. Salisbury and London 1790.

Verses on the benevolent institution of the philanthropic society. Bath and London 1790.
A poetical address to Edmund Burke. 1791.
Elegy written at the Hot-wells, Bristol. Bath and London 1791.
Monody, written at Matlock. Salisbury, London and Bath 1791.
Elegiac stanzas, written during sickness at Bath. Bath and London 1796.
Hope: an allegorical sketch. London and Bath 1796.
St Michael's Mount: a poem. Salisbury, Shaftesbury and London 1798.
Coombe Ellen: a poem. Bath and London 1798.
Song of the battle of the Nile. 1799.
The sorrows of Switzerland: a poem. London and Bath 1801.
The picture: verses suggested by a landscape of Rubens. 1803.
The spirit of discovery, or the conquest of ocean: a poem in five books. Bath and London 1804, 1809. Issued as suppl to Poems, 1801 (see Fourteen sonnets, above).
Bowden Hill: the banks of the Wye. Southampton [1806].
The works of Pope. 10 vols 1806. Ed Bowles.
Poems, written chiefly at Bremhill. London and Bath 1809. Issued as vol 4, suppl to Spirit of discovery, above.
The missionary: a poem. 1813, 1815 (enlarged), 1816, 1835 (5th edn as The ancient missionary of Chili).
The invariable principles of poetry. Bath and London 1819.
A reply to the reviewer. Bath and London 1820.
A vindication of the editor of Pope's Works. 1821. Ptd as 2nd edn, first pbd in Pamphleteer.
Two letters to Lord Byron. 1821.
The grave of the last Saxon: a poem. London and Edinburgh 1822.
Ellen Gray: a poem. Edinburgh and London 1823.
Charity: a poem. Bath and London 1823.
The ark: a dramatic oratorio. Bath [1824?].
A final appeal relative to Pope. 1825.
Lessons in criticism. 1826.
Days departed: or Banwell Hill. London and Bath 1828, 1829 (with revision of Ellen Gray, above).
The parochial history of Bremhill. 1828.
The life of Thomas Ken. 2 vols 1830.
St John in Patmos: a poem. London and Bath 1832 (anon), 1835.
The grave of Anna. [Bath 1833]. From Spirit of discovery, above.
Annals and antiquities of Lacock Abbey. 1835.
Scenes and shadows of days departed. London and Bath 1835, 1837. Incomplete memoir.
The little villager's verse book. 1837. Pbd under various titles, perhaps as early as 1815: see Woolf bibliography, above.
Bowles also pbd many sermons and antiquarian and theological works: see Woolf bibliography, above. Certain of the Pope-controversy essays were first pbd in Pamphleteer 17–20 1820–2.

Letters

Greeve, G. A Wiltshire parson and his friends: the correspondence of Bowles. 1926.

§ 2

Quart Rev 23 1820, 32 1825. Reviews of Pope controversy.
Byron. Letter to **** ****** on Bowles' strictures on Pope. 1821.
—— Observations upon Observations: a second letter to Murray. [1832].
Hazlitt, W., jr. Pope, Byron and Bowles. Appendix to W. Hazlitt, Lectures on the English poets, 1841.
Casson, T. E. In his Eighteenth-century literature: an Oxford miscellany, Oxford 1909.

van Rennes, J. J. Bowles, Byron and the Pope-controversy. Amsterdam 1927.
Waldock, A. J. A. Bowles: a lecture. Sydney 1928.
Rietmann, O. William Lisle Bowles. Basle 1940.
Fayen, G. S. The pencil and the harp of Bowles. MLQ 21 1960.
Werkmeister, L. Coleridge, Bowles and feelings of the heart. Anglia 78 1960.
Doughty, O. Coleridge and Bowles. Eng Miscellany (Rome) 14 1963.
Kaiser, R. Vier Sonette. Die Neueren Sprachen 6 1963.

SAMUEL BOYCE
d. 1775
Collections
Poems on several occasions. 1757.

§ I

The friend of liberty: an ode. 1751.
The rover, or happiness at last: a pastoral drama. 1752.
An ode to the Marquis of Hartington. 1755.
Paris, or the force of beauty: a poem. 1755.

§ 2

Williams, I. A. In his Points in eighteenth-century verse, 1934. Contains bibliographical essay on Boyce.
—— Boyce's Poems on several occasions. Book-Collector's Quart 1934.

JOHN FREDERICK BRYANT
1753–91
§ I

Verses by Bryant, late tobacco-pipe maker at Bristol. 1787, 1787. With autobiographical sketch.

§ 2

Southey, R. In his Lives of uneducated poets, 1836.

SIR JAMES BLAND BURGES,
after 1821 Sir James Lamb
1752–1824
Collections
Dramas. 2 vols 1817.

§ I

Heroic epistle from Serjeant Bradshaw to John Dunning. 1780.
Considerations on the law of insolvency. 1783.
A letter to the Earl of Effingham. 1783.
Address to the country gentlemen of England. 1789.
Letters on the Spanish aggression at Nootka. 1790. Signed Verus.
Narrative of the negociation between France and Spain in 1790. [1790?].
Alfred's letters: a review of the political state of Europe. [1792].
The birth and triumph of love. 1796, 1822, 1823.
Richard the first: a poem in eighteen books. 2 vols 1801.
The exodiad. 2 pts 1807–8. With R. Cumberland.
Riches, or the wife and brother: a play. 1810, 1810, 1814 (4th edn); ed 'D. G.' (George Daniel) 1826 (Cumberland's Br Theatre).
Songs in Tricks upon travellers. 1810 (2nd edn).
The dragon knight: a poem in twelve cantos. 1818.

Reasons in favour of a new translation of the holy scriptures. 1819.
M. A. Burges. The progress of the pilgrim good-intent. Ed Burges 1814 (9th edn), 1822 (10th edn).
An inquiry into the procrastination attributed to the House of Lords. 1824.
Burges was a founder and contributor to the London newspaper Sun 1792–.

Letters

Selections from the letters. Ed J. Hutton 1885. With biography.

RICHARD OWEN CAMBRIDGE
1717–1802
Collections

Works. Ed G. O. Cambridge 1803. With biography. Chalmers 18.

§ 1

Verses. In Gratulatio in nuptias principium. Oxford 1736; rptd GM 1738.
The scribleriad: an heroic poem in six books. 1751, 1751, 1752. Books first pbd separately, Jan–March 1751.
A dialogue between a Member of Parliament and his servant, in imitation of Horace. 1752.
The intruder: in imitation of Horace book 1 satire 9. 1754.
The fable of Jotham: to the borough-hunters. 1754; Lady's Poetical Mag 1 1781.
An elegy written in an empty assembly room. 1756 (3 edns). Parody of Eloisa to Abelard.
The fakeer: a tale. 1756.
The genius of Britain: an iambic ode addressed to William Pitt. 1756.
An account of the war in India on the coast of Coromandel. 1761, 1761, 1762; tr French, 1766.
Altick, R. D. Cambridge serenades the Berry sisters. N & Q 12 Sept 1942. Prints several poems.
Cambridge contributed to Dodsley's collection vol 6, 1758, *to* World 1753–6 (21 essays), *to* Monthly Review 1783–6 *and to* Times 1789; *see Altick under* §2, *below.*

§ 2

Cary, H. F. In his Lives of English poets, 1846.
Dobson, A. Eighteenth-century vignettes: series 3. 1896.
Hodgson, F. C. In his Thames-side in the past, 1913.
Baddeley, St C. Richard Owen Cambridge. N & Q 17 Nov 1923.
Altick, R. D. Cambridge: belated Augustan. Philadelphia 1941. With bibliography.
Emery, C. M. The Scribleriad's electrifying climax. PQ 21 1942.
Fox, R. C. The imaginary submarines of Dr Johnson and Cambridge. PQ 40 1961.

GEORGE CANNING
1770–1827
See also under Anti-Jacobin, col 698, below.
Collections

Poetical works. [1823] (with biography), Glasgow 1825, 1827, Paris 1828.
The beauties of Canning. [1827].
A biographical memoir of Canning; to which is added the whole of his poems. [Ed T. Forster], Brussels 1827.
Speeches; with a memoir by R. Therry. 6 vols 1828; tr French, 1832.
Poetical works. In Cabinet edition of the British poets vol 4, 1851.
Selections from the Anti-Jacobin, together with some later poems. 1904.

§ 1

Ulm and Trafalgar. 1806, 1806.
A letter to Earl Camden connected with the late duel. 1809, 1809.
Two letters to Earl Camden. 1809.
The doctor: a parody. In The man in the moon, 1820 (24 edns).
New morality. In The British satirist, Glasgow 1826.
The pilgrimage to Mecca. Warwick 1829; rptd in Translations of the Oxford prize poems, 1831.
An anglo-sapphic ode to Robert Beverley. 1833.
The knave of hearts. In Parodies of ballad criticism, ed W. K. Wimsatt, Los Angeles 1957 (Augustan Reprint Soc).
Canning, with J. Smith, R. Smith and J. H. Frere, edited the Microcosm: a periodical work, by 'Gregory Griffin', in 40 nos, Eton 6 Nov 1786–30 July 1787, Windsor 1788, 2 vols Windsor 1790, London 1825, *also in* British essayists vol 28, 1827. *He contributed to* Quart Rev. *For his pbd despatches and speeches, see* BM General Catalogue.

§ 2

Bell, R. The life of Canning. 1846.
Stapleton, A. G. Canning and his times. 1859.
Hill, F. H. George Canning. 1887 (vol 8 in A. Lang's English worthies).
Marriott, J. A. R. Canning and his times. 1903.
Phillips, W. A. George Canning. 1903.
Temperley, H. W. V. Life of Canning. 1905.
Bagot, J. Canning and his friends. 2 vols 1909.
Gale, F. R. Some unpublished letters of Canning. N & Q 20–7 Aug 1927.
—— Peter Pindar and Canning. N & Q 9 Oct 1937.
—— Canning's alleged blasphemy. N & Q 27 March 1943.
Petrie, C. A. George Canning. 1930, 1946.
Hanson, L. W. Canning's copy of the Anti-Jacobin. BM Quart 11 1937.
Marshall, D. The rise of Canning. 1938.
George, M. D. Pictorial propaganda 1793–1815: Gillray and Canning. History 31 1946.
Wonderley, W. An English Goethe parody. Monatshefte 48 1956. By Canning.
Rolo, P. J. V. Canning: three biographical studies. 1965.
This list does not include most studies of Canning's political career.

JAMES CAWTHORN
1719–61
Collections

Poems. 1771.
Select poems. In Park's Works of the British poets vol 4, 1808.
Select poems. In Sanford's Works of the British poets vol 24, Philadelphia 1819.
Poems. In The British poets vol 60, Chiswick 1822.
Anderson 10, Chalmers 14, Johnson (1790) 65.

§ 1

The perjured lovers. Sheffield 1736
A sermon before the burgesses of Westminster. 1745.
Abelard to Heloise. 1747; also rptd in The poetical calendar vol 4, 1763; Pearch's collection of poems vol 1, 1768; Letters of Abelard and Heloise, 1805, 1818; and with two other poems in Pratt's Cabinet of poetry vol 5, 1808.
Benevolence: a sermon. [1748].

§ 2

GM Dec 1791.

JOHN COLLINS
1742–1808

Collections

Scripscrapologia: or Collins's doggerel dish of all sorts. Birmingham 1804.

§ 1

The brush. [Newcastle 1800?]. Performed and ptd under various titles, e.g. with W. Oxberry, The theatrical banquet or the actor's budget, 2 vols 1809, as Collins' Evening brush.
The golden days of good Queen Bess. In [G. A. Steven], Lectures on heads, [1787].
The chapter of Kings. 1818.
Collins owned and contributed to Birmingham Chronicle.

§ 2

Hitchcock, R. In his An historical view of the Irish stage vol 2, Dublin 1794.
Pinkerton, W. Collins, author of To-morrow. N & Q 5 Dec 1863.
— The prototype of Collins's Tomorrow. N & Q 4 June 1864.
— N & Q 3 Nov 1866. Letter giving biographical details.
Collins, M. John Collins. Belgravia 16 1872.
Dent, R. K. The making of Birmingham. 1894.

WILLIAM COMBE
1742–1823

Bibliographies

Hamilton, H. W. In his Doctor Syntax, Kent Ohio 1969.

§ 1

Nearly all of the following were issued anonymously or pseudonymously.
Clifton: a poem in imitation of Spenser. Bristol 1775, Bristol and London 1776, 1803.
The philosopher in Bristol. Bristol 1775; Part the second, Bristol 1775; 2 vols Bristol and London 1776.
The diaboliad: a poem, dedicated to the worst man in his Majesty's dominions. 1677, 1677 (both for 1777), Dublin 1777; Additions to the Diaboliad, 1677 (for 1777); The diaboliad: a new edition, 1677 (for 1777), 1778; The diaboliad, a poem: part the second, 1778 (3 edns).
A dialogue in the shades, between an unfortunate divine and a Welch member of Parliament. [1777].
The first of April, or the triumphs of folly: a poem. 1777 (3 edns).
An heroice pistle to the noble author of the Duchess of Devonshire's cow. 1777.
The justification: a poem. 1777, 1778.
A letter to the Duchess of Devonshire. 1777.
A poetical epistle to Sir Joshua Reynolds. 1777.
A second letter to the Duchess of Devonshire. 1777.
The auction: a town eclogue. 1778 (3 edns), 1780.
An interesting letter to the Duchess of Devonshire. 1778, 1779.
The r[oya]l register. 9 vols 1778–84.
An heroic epistle to Sir James Wright. 1779.
Letters supposed to have been written by Yotick and Eliza. 2 vols 1779, 1780; ed M. R. B. Shaw 1929 (as Sterne's Second journal to Eliza). See H. W. Hamilton, Doctor Syntax, Kent Ohio 1969, ch 4.
The world as it goes: a poem. 1779, 1779, 1781.
The fast-day: a Lambeth eclogue. 1780.
Letters of the late Lord Lyttelton. 1780 (3 edns), 2 vols 1782, 1806, Troy NY 1807.

Letters between two lovers. 1781.
Letters of an Italian nun and an English gentleman. 1781.
The traitor: a poetical rhapsody. 1781.
Original love letters, between a lady of quality and a person of inferior rank. 2 vols 1784, Dublin 1784, 1 vol Dublin 1811.
The royal dream, or the P[rince] in a panic: an eclogue. 1785, 1791.
Original letters of Sterne. 1788.
An history of the late important period. 1789.
A letter from a country gentleman to a Member of Parliament. 1789 (7 edns).
The royal interview. 1789 (3 edns).
Considerations on the approaching dissolution of Parliament. 1790.
The devil upon two sticks in England. 4 vols 1790, 6 vols 1791, 1811. See H. W. Hamilton, Doctor Syntax, Kent Ohio 1969.
Observations on the Royal Academy. 1790.
A word in season to the traders and manufacturers of Great Britain. 1792 (6 edns), 1793, 1793.
An history of the principal rivers of Great Britain. 2 vols 1794, 1796.
Two words of counsel and one of comfort. 1795.
Letter to a retired officer. 1796.
Plain thoughts of a plain man. 1797.
Brief observations on a letter to Pitt by W. Boyd. 1801.
The letters of Valerius. 1804. First pbd separately in Times.
The tour of Dr Syntax in search of the picturesque. [1812], 1813 (3 edns), 1815 (6th), 1819 (9th), 1823 etc; tr German, 1820; French, 1821. Originally pbd in monthly pts in Poetical Mag 1809 as The schoolmaster's tour.
The second tour of Doctor Syntax in search of consolation: a poem. 1820, 1820, 1855, 1903. First issued in monthly pts.
The third tour of Doctor Syntax, in search of a wife: a poem. [1821], 1823, 1855. First pbd in pts.
The three tours of Dr Syntax. 3 vols 1826; ed J. C. Hotten [1869] (with biography), [1871], 3 vols 1903. Variously titled.
The Thames. 2 vols 1811.
The history of the abbey church of St Peter's Westminster. 2 vols 1812. First pbd in 16 monthly pts.
Antiquities of York. 1813.
Six poems illustrative of engravings by the Princess Elizabeth. 1813.
A history of the university of Oxford. 2 vols 1814.
The English dance of death. 2 vols 1815–16, 1903. First pbd 24 monthly pts 1815–16.
The history of the colleges [etc]. 1816. First pbd in 12 monthly pts.
The dance of life. 1817, 1903. First pbd in 8 monthly pts.
Observations on Ackermann's patent moveable axles. 1819.
Swiss scenery. 1820.
A history of Madeira. 1821.
The history of Johnny Quae Genus. 1822, 1903. First pbd in 8 monthly pts 1821–2.
Thames scenery. 1818 (for 1822). See H. W. Hamilton, Doctor Syntax, Kent Ohio 1969.
Views on the Thames. 2 vols 1822.
Letters to Marianne. 1823.
Letters between Amelia in London and her mother in the country. 1824.
For works edited, translated or contributed to by Combe, for his periodical contributions, unpbd mss and works of doubtful authenticity, see H. W. Hamilton, Doctor Syntax, below.

§ 2

Fluchère, H. Sterne et Combe. Revue Anglo-américaine 8 1931.
Curtis, L. P. Forged letters of Sterne. PMLA 50 1935.

Montgomery, F. Alexander Mackenzie's literary assistant. Canadian Historical Rev 18 1937.
— The birth and parentage of Combe. N & Q 12 April 1941.
William Combe. TLS 19 July 1941.
Barbier, C. P. Letters of an Italian nun: a bibliographical problem. Revue de Littérature Comparée 27 1954.
Hamilton, H. W. Combe and Hunter's essay on the teeth. Jnl of History of Medicine 14 1959.
— Combe and the Original letters of Sterne. PMLA 82 1967.
— Doctor Syntax: a silhouette of Combe. Kent Ohio and London 1969. With bibliography.

WILLIAM CROWE
1745–1829

§ I

A sermon preached before the University of Oxford. 1781.
On the late attempt on his Majesty's person: a sermon. Oxford 1786.
Lewesdon Hill. Oxford 1788, 1788, London 1788, 1804 (enlarged, with other poems), 1827 (corrected and much enlarged).
Oratio ex instituto Hon Dom Nathanielis Dom Crew. Oxford 1788.
Oratio Crewiana habita VIII kal. Jul. 1800 in theatro Sheldoniano. Oxford 1800.
Hamlet and As you like it: a specimen of a new edition of Shakespeare. 1819, 1820, 1829. With T. Caldecott.
A treatise on English versification. 1827.
The poems of William Collins. 1828. Ed Crowe.

§ 2

Maclean, C. M. Lewesdon hill and its poet. E & S 27 1941.
Blunden, E. C. William Crowe. Beaminster 1963.

JOHN CUNNINGHAM
1729–73

Collections

Poems chiefly pastoral. Newcastle 1766, London 1766, Dublin 1766, Newcastle 1771 (with addns).
Poetical works. Edinburgh and London 1781 (Bell's ser) (with biography).
Poetical works. [1795] etc (Cooke's edn of select British poets).
The poems of Goldsmith and Cunningham. Gotha 1807.
Poetical works. In Park's Works of the British poets vol 35, 1808.
Select poems. In Pratt's Cabinet of poetry vol 5, 1808.
Poems. In British poets vol 64, Chiswick 1822.
Select poems. In Sanford's Works of the British poets vol 32, Philadelphia 1822.
Anderson 10, Chalmers 14, Johnson (1790) 69.

§ I

Love in a mist: a farce. 1747, Dublin 1747, London 1752.
A poetical essay in manner of elegy on the death of his Majesty. Newcastle [1760].
An elegy on a pile of ruins. 1761, [Edinburgh?] 1761; rptd in J. Evans, The poetic garland, 1808 (with biographical sketch).
Day and other pastorals. Edinburgh 1761, London [c. 1825], 1855.
The contemplatist: a night piece. 1762.
Fortune: an apologue. 1765.

§ 2

O'Donoghue, D. J. In his Poets of Ireland, 1912.
Morley, E. J. John Cunningham. Essays by Divers Hands new ser 19 1942.

ERASMUS DARWIN
1731–1802

Collections

Poetical works, with philosophical notes. 3 vols 1806.
Essential writings. Ed D. King-Hele 1968.

§ I

Academiae cantabrigiensis luctus in obitum Frederici Walliae principis. Cambridge 1751. Darwin contributed an English ode.
Darwin, C., Experiments establishing a criterion. Lichfield 1780. Ed Darwin.
Linnaeus, C., The families of plants. Lichfield 1787. Tr Darwin.
The loves of the plants. Lichfield 1789, 1790 (as The botanic garden: part II, 2nd edn).
The botanic garden, a poem in two parts: part I, containing The economy of vegetables, 1791; part II, The loves of the plants. Lichfield and London 1789, 1791 (pt II dated 1790, 2nd edn), 1791 (2nd edn pt I, 3rd edn pt II), 2 vols 1794–5, Dublin 1793–6, New York 1798, London 1799 (4th edn); tr Portuguese, 1803–4; French, 1799–1800; Italian, 1805.
The golden age: a poetical epistle to T. Beddoes. 1794.
Zoonomia: or the laws of organic life. 2 vols 1794–6, 1796, Dublin 1800, 4 vols 1801, 1802, 1818; tr German, 1795–7; Italian, 1885.
A plan for the conduct of female education in boarding schools. 1797, Derby 1797.
Phytologia: or the philosophy of agriculture and gardening. 1800.
The temple of nature, or the origin of society: a poem. 1803, New York 1804; tr Russian, 1954.
Remembrance. In Poetical selections, 1812.

§ 2

Brown, T. Observations on the Zoonomia. Edinburgh 1798.
Seward, A. Memoirs of the life of Dr Darwin. 1804.
Cary, H. F. In his Lives of English poets, 1846.
Dowson, J. Erasmus Darwin. 1861.
Butler, S. In his Evolution old and new, 1879.
— In his Unconscious memory, 1880.
Krause, E. Erasmus Darwin. Tr W. S. Dallas, with preliminary note by C. Darwin 1879, Leipzig 1880 (original German).
Zoeckler, O. Darwins Grossvater als Arzt, Dichter und Naturphilosoph. Heidelberg 1880.
Darwin, C. Life of Erasmus Darwin. 1887.
Brandl, L. Erasmus Darwin's Temple of nature. Vienna 1902.
— Erasmus Darwin's Botanic garden. Vienna 1909.
Drinkwater, J. A book for bookmen. 1926.
Pryce-Jones, A. Erasmus Darwin. London Mercury July 1929.
Pearson, H. Doctor Darwin. 1930.
— Darwin. Nineteenth Century Dec 1931.
Dr Darwin. TLS 10 Dec 1931.
Crum, R. B. Scientific thought in poetry. New York 1931.
Nidecker, H. The poetical prelude of Darwin's second marriage. In Festschrift Gustav Binz dargebracht, Basle 1935.
Logan, J. V. The poetry and aesthetics of Erasmus Darwin. Princeton 1936.

Musser, R. and J. C. Krantz. Friendship of William Withering and Darwin. Bull History of Medicine 8 1940.

Emery, C. Scientific theory in the Botanic garden. Isis 33 1942.

Garfinkle, N. Science and religion in England 1790–1800: the critical response to the work of Erasmus Darwin. JHI 16 1955.

Ryskamp, C. Cowper and Darwin's Economy of vegetation. Harvard Lib Bull 11 1957.

Piper, H. The pantheistic sources of Coleridge's early poetry. JHI 20 1959.

Barlow, N. Erasmus Darwin. Notes & Records of Royal Soc 14 1959.

Gustafson, R. F. The upas tree: Pushkin and Erasmus Darwin. PMLA 75 1960.

Ritterbush, P. C. Darwin's second published poem. RES new ser 13 1962.

King-Hele, D. Erasmus Darwin. 1963.

Primer, I. Darwin's Temple of nature: progress, evolution and the Eleusinian mysteries. JHI 25 1964.

Cohen, Lord. Erasmus Darwin. Univ of Birmingham Historical Jnl 11 1967.

SAMUEL DERRICK
1724–69
Collections

A collection of original poems. 1755.

Derrick's jests: or the wit's chronicle; also a collection of poetical pieces. 1769.

§ 1

Fortune: a rhapsody. 1751.

The dramatic censor. 1752.

Sylla: a dramatic entertainment, translated from the French of the King of Prussia. 1753.

Memoirs of the Count de Beauval. 1754. Tr from the French of d'Argens.

Proposals for printing by subscription: a collection of original poems. 1754.

A voyage from the moon. 1754. From the French of C. de Bergerac.

The third satire of Juvenal translated. 1755.

The miscellaneous works of John Dryden. 4 vols 1760. Ed Derrick.

A poetical dictionary. 4 vols 1761.

The battle of Lora; with some fragments written in Erse, translated into English verse. 1762.

A collection of travels through various parts of the world. 2 vols 1762. Ed Derrick.

Letters written from Leverpoole, Chester, Corke etc. 2 vols 1767, Dublin 1767.

Preface to d'Argens's Memoirs of the Count Beauval. In Prefaces to fiction, ed B. Boyce, Los Angeles 1952 (Augustan Reprint Soc). Derrick contributed to Smollett's Critical Review: see Roper, below.

§ 2

Miller, W. H. Authorship of A general view of the stage. MLN 56 1941. Not Derrick but Thomas Wilkes.

Roper, D. Smollett's four gentlemen: the first contributors to the Critical Review. RES new ser 10 1959.

WILLIAM DODD
1729–77
Collections

Poems. 1767.

Moral pastorals, and other poems. Edinburgh 1824.

§ 1

Diggon Davy: a pastoral, on the loss of his last cow. 1747. Also recorded as A pastoral on the distemper among the horned cattle.

The African prince when in England to Zara. 1749.

Zara at the Court of Annamaboe to the African Prince. 1749.

A new book of the Dunciad. 1750.

An elegy on the death of the Prince of Wales. 1751.

A day in vacation at college: a burlesque poem. 1751.

The beauties of Shakespeare. 2 vols 1752, 1757, 3 vols 1780, 1784 etc. Ed Dodd.

An epistle to a lady concerning truths in religion. 1753.

The sisters. 2 vols 1754, 1781, 1 vol 1798. A novel.

The hymns of Callimachus translated. 1755.

Discourses on the miracles and parables. 4 vols 1757–8, 1809.

Thoughts on the epiphany of Christ: a poetical essay. 1758, 1777 (3rd edn).

Hall, J., Contemplations on the histories of the New Testament. 2 vols 1759. Ed Dodd.

Ode to the Marchioness of Granby. 1759.

Hymn to good nature. 1760.

Account of the Magdalen charity. 1761, 1766 (3rd edn), 1770, 1776.

A conference between a mystic, an Hutchinsonian, and others. 1761.

A familiar explanation of the poetical works of Milton. 1762.

The visitor, by several hands. 2 vols 1764. Ed Dodd.

The Holy Bible with a commentary and practical improvements. 3 vols 1765–70, 1770 (as A commentary on the Old and New Testaments).

A commonplace book to the Bible. 1766.

Reflections on death. 1769 (3rd edn), 1777, Preston [1780] etc.

An oration delivered at the dedication of Free-mason's Hall. 1776.

The convict's address to his unhappy brethren. 1777 (2nd edn), 1777 (3rd–4th edns).

Thoughts in prison, in five parts. 1777, Boston [1777], 1789 (3rd edn), 1793 etc.

The beauties of history: or pictures of virtue and vice. 1795 (enlarged), 1796, 1800, 1803, 1818.

Eulogium on freemasonry. In G. Oliver, The golden remains of the early masonic writers, 5 vols 1847–50, and in Oliver, The Shakespearean miscellany, 1802.

For Dodd's many religious tracts and sermons, see BM General Catalogue. *He also edited* Christian's Mag 1760–7.

§ 2

For the many 1777 accounts of Dodd's life, trial, imprisonment and death, see BM Catalogue.

Thoughts in prison. 1777. Contains biography and list of 55 works.

Johnson, S. In his Works vol 14, 1788. Papers written by Johnson for Dodd.

Bosanquet, M. An aunt's advice; to which is added a correspondence with Dodd. York 1824.

Fitzgerald, P. A famous forgery: being the story of Dodd. 1865.

Occasional papers by Dodd. TLS 7 Dec 1922.

Papers written by Dr Johnson and Dodd. Ed R. W. Chapman, Oxford 1926.

Warner, J. H. The macaroni parson. Queen's Quart 53 1946.

Foster, W. E. Samuel Johnson and the Dodd affair. Johnson Soc Address no 32 [1952].

Metzdorf, R. F. Isaac Reed and Dodd. Harvard Lib Bull 6 1952.

Fairchild, A. H. R. A Shakespearian who was hanged. Western Humanities Rev 7 1953.

Gross, R. R. Doctor Dodd. Bucknell Univ Stud 4 1953.
Willoughby, E. E. A deadly edition of Shakespeare. Shakespeare Quart 5 1954.
— The unfortunate Dr Dodd. Essays by Divers Hands new ser 29 1958.

HUGH DOWNMAN
1740–1809

Collections

The land of the Muses: a poem in the manner of Spenser; with poems on several occasions. Edinburgh 1768, Exeter 1790 (as Poems, 2nd edn), 1791.
Tragedies. Exeter 1792.

§ 1

An elegy wrote under a gallows. [1770].
The soliloquy. Edinburgh [1770].
Infancy: a poem. 1774; Book the second, 1775; Book the third, 1776; Infancy or the management of children: a didactic poem in three books, Edinburgh 1776, 1788 (4th edn), 1790, Exeter 1803 (6th edn, with additional unpbd poems), 1809 (6 bks).
The drama: a poem. 1775.
Lucius Junius Brutus, or the expulsion of the Tarquins: an historical play. 1779.
Annals of the Empire. 1781. Tr from Voltaire by D. Williams, Downman et al.
The death-song of Ragnar Lodbrach, translated. 1781; rptd in Evans's Old ballads vol 3, 1784.
The dramatic works of Voltaire. 2 vols 1781. Tr Downman and D. Williams.
Poems to Thespia. Exeter 1781, 1791, London 1805.
Editha: a tragedy. Exeter 1784.
Downman contributed to R. Polwhele, Poems chiefly by gentlemen of Devon and Cornwall, 2 vols 1792, *and to his* Essays by a society of gentlemen at Exeter, Exeter 1796.

§ 2

Critical opinions and complimentary verses on Downman. Exeter 1807.
GM Jan 1810.
Wright, W. H. K. West country poets. 1896.
Tompkins, J. M. S. The didactic lyre. In her Polite marriage, Cambridge 1938.

JOHN DUNCOMBE
1729–86

Collections

Poems. 1756.

§ 1

Academiae cantabrigiensis luctus in obitum Frederici Walliae principis. Cambridge 1751. Duncombe contributed an English ode.
An evening contemplation in a college. 1753, [1765?], 1776 (as Parody on Gray's Elegy). Also in Gray's Poems, Dublin 1768; with Gray's Elegy, Cambridge and London 1776; and in Roach's Beauties of the poets vol 1, 1794.
Horace, book 2 satire vii imitated, by Sir Nicholas Nemo. [1754].
From Vaniere's Country farm. In G. Jeffrey, Miscellanies, 1754.
The feminiad: a poem. 1754, 1757 (with An evening contemplation); Lady's Poetical Mag 4 1782.
A select collection of original letters. 2 vols 1755. Ed Duncombe.

The works of Horace in English verse by several hands. 2 vols 1757–9, 4 vols 1767. Epodes and first book of epistles tr Duncombe.
Letters by several eminent persons deceased. 2 vols 1772, 3 vols 1773.
Surry triumphant, or the Kentish men's defeat: being a parody on Chevy Chase. 1773; rptd in Evans's Old ballads vol 4, 1784.
An elegy written in Canterbury cathedral. Canterbury 1778. Rptd from An historical description of the cathedral, Canterbury 1772.
Select works of the Emperor Julian. 2 vols 1784. Tr Duncombe.
Fishing: a translation from Vaniere book xv Upon fish. 1809.
Duncombe also contributed to Dodsley's Collection, 1758 *and to* Poetical calendar, 1763. *He also pbd sermons, made other collections of letters and wrote and edited antiquarian works: see* BM General Catalogue.

§ 2

Kippis, A. In Biographia britannica vol 4, 1780.
N[ichols], J. GM 1786.

GEORGE ELLIS
1753–1815

§ 1

Bath: its beauties and amusements. 1776, Bath 1777.
Poetical tales by Sir Gregory Gander. Bath 1778.
Memoir of a map of the countries between the Black sea and the Caspian. 1788; tr French, 1797.
History of the late revolution in the Dutch republic. 1789.
Specimens of early English poets. 1790, 3 vols 1801, 1803, 1811, 1 vol 1845, 1851.
Fabliaux or tales from French manuscripts. 1796, 2 vols 1800, 3 vols 1815. Tr G. L. Way and ed Ellis.
Specimens of early English metrical romances. 3 vols 1805, 1811; rev J. O. Halliwell 3 vols 1847.
Diary of W. Windham. Ed H. Baring 1866. Contains life of Windham by Ellis.

§ 2

Holloway, O. E. Ellis, the Anti-Jacobin and the Quarterly Review.
See also under Anti-Jacobin and Rolliad, cols 698, 699, below.

WILLIAM FALCONER
1732–69

Collections

Poetical works. [1796] (Cooke's Pocket edns).
Poetical works. In Park's Works of the British poets vol 30, 1805.
The poems of Falconer, Day [etc]. In Works of the British poets vol 58, Chiswick 1822. With life by R. A. Davenport.
Select poems. In Sanford's Works of the British poets vol 27, Philadelphia 1822.
Poems. Ed J. Mitford 1836, Boston 1854, London 1866, 1870, 1895.
Poetical works of Beattie, Blair and Falconer. Ed G. Gilfillan, Edinburgh 1854, [1878].
The poetical works of Campbell and Falconer. [1880].
Anderson 10, Chalmers 14, Johnson 67.

§ 1

A poem on the death of Frederick Prince of Wales. 1751.

The shipwreck, a poem in three cantos: by a sailor.
1762, 1764 (enlarged), 1769, 1772, Philadelphia 1774
(with Viaud's voyages); ed J. S. Clarke 1804; ed R.
Dodd 1811; ed R. Carruthers 1858; ed W. H. D.
A[dams] 1887 etc. See Couchman under §2, below.
The fond lover. St James Mag 1 1762.
Ode on the Duke of York's departure. 1763.
The demagogue. 1766.
An universal dictionary of the marine. 1769, 1771, 1780,
1784, 1789 etc; ed W. Burney 1815, 1830; ed C. S. Gill
1930 (abridged as The old wooden walls).
An address to his mistress. Edinburgh Mag & Rev 1
1773.
Falconer contributed naval articles to A general dictionary
of arts and sciences, 1765–6.

§2

Campbell, A. In his An introduction to the history of
poetry in Scotland, Edinburgh 1798.
Irving, D. In his Lives of Scottish authors, 1801.
Lives of eminent Scotsmen. Vol 3, Edinburgh 1822.
Dowden, E. In Ward's English poets vol 3, 1880.
Friedrich, J. Falconer: the Shipwreck. Vienna 1901.
Dobson, A. Falconer's Shipwreck. In his Rosalba's
journal and other papers, 1915.
Joseph, M. K. William Falconer. SP 47 1950. Bio-
graphical investigation and possible contributions to
periodicals.
Couchman, G. W. Editions of Falconer's Shipwreck. N
& Q Oct 1953.

FRANCIS FAWKES
1720–77
Collections

Original poems and translations. 1761.
Anderson 13, Chalmers 16 and 20.

§1

Bramham park. 1745.
A description of May, from Gawin Douglas. 1752 (3 edns),
Edinburgh 1881 (Aungervyle Soc).
A description of winter, from Gawin Douglas. 1754.
The works of Anacreon, Sappho, Bion, Moschus and
Musaeus, translated. 1760, 1789 etc.
The complete family Bible. 2 vols 1761, 1762. Originally
issued in pts.
The poetical calendar: intended as a supplement to
Dodsley's collection. 12 vols 1763. Ed with contribu-
tions by Fawkes and W. Woty.
The poetical magazine: or the Muses' monthly companion.
1 (all pbd), 1764. Ed with contributions by Fawkes and
Woty.
The idylliums of Theocritus, translated. 1767.
Partridge-shooting: an eclogue. 1767.
The works of Horace, in English verse. 1767.
The argonautics of Appolonius Rhodius. 1780. Begun by
Fawkes and completed by H. Meen.
Fawkes contributed to Dodsley's Collection vol 4, 1755.

§2

Williams, I. A. In his Byways round Helicon, 1921.
Aldington, R. Fawkes's Brown jug. TLS 8 March 1923.
Replies 15–29 March 1923.
Hazen, A. T. and T. O. Mabbott. Dr Johnson and
Fawkes's Theocritus. RES 21 1945. On Johnson's
contributions to commentary.

JOHN HOOKHAM FRERE
1769–1846
Collections

Aristophanes: a metrical version of the Acharnians, the
Knights and the Birds. 1840, Malta 1839 (priv ptd);
ed H. Morley 1886.
Works in verse and prose. 2 vols 1872, 3 vols 1874.
Memoir by B. Frere.
Parodies and other burlesque pieces by Canning, Ellis and
Frere. Ed H. Morley 1890 (Carisbrooke Lib).
Aristophanes: four plays. Ed W. W. Merry, Oxford
[1907]. For other posthumous printings of single plays
and groups see BM General Catalogue.

§1

The microcosm. Eton 1786–7. See under Canning, col
646, above: Frere contributed 5 papers.
Ode on Æthelstan's victory. In Ellis's Specimens of the
early English poets, 1801.
Translations from the Cid. In R. Southey, Chronicle of
the Cid, 1808.
Prospectus and specimen of an intended national work by
William and Robert Whistlecraft relating to King
Arthur. Cantos 1–2, 1817, 1818, 1818; Cantos 3–4,
1818; The monks and the giants: prospectus and speci-
men, 1818, 1821 (4th edn), Bath 1842; ed R. D. Waller
1926.
Fables for five-year-olds. Malta 1830.
Aristophanes, The frogs. 1839 etc.
Psalms etc. [1839?]. A metrical paraphrase.
Theognis restitutus, the personal history of the poet
deduced from an analysis of his existing fragments: a
hundred fragments in English metre. Malta 1842, 1856
(Bohn's Lib) (as The works of Theognis).
See also under Anti-Jacobin, col 698, below.

§2

de Charmilly, V. To the British nation: the narrative of
his transactions with Frere. 1810.
Memoir. [London? 1846?].
Festing, G. Frere and his friends. 1899.
Eichler, A. von. Frere: sein Leben und seine Werke, sein
Einfluss auf Byron. Vienna 1905.

WILLIAM GIFFORD
1756–1826
Collections

The satires of Juvenal and Persius. 2 vols 1817.
The beauties of Gifford. [1834?]. Selections.

§1

The baviad: a paraphrastic imitation of the first satire of
Persius. 1791, 1793.
The maeviad, by the author of the baviad. 1795.
The baviad and maeviad. 1797, 1800 (6th edn), 1811 (8th
edn), 1813, 1827 (with Epistle to Peter Pindar).
Epistle to Peter Pindar. 1800, 1800 (with Postscript), 1800
('with considerable additions'); rptd with 1827 edn of
Baviad and Maeviad, above.
The satires of Juvenal translated. 1802, Philadelphia and
New York 1803, London 1806, 1906; ed J. Warrington
1954.
An examination of the strictures of the Critical reviewers
on the translation of Juvenal. 1803; Supplement, 1804.
The satires of Persius translated. 1821.
The illiberal! verse and prose from the north!! [1822].
Suppressed before pbn.

Autobiography. 1827. Originally prefixed to the 1802 trn of Juvenal, above, as Memoir of Gifford written by himself.
Gifford edited Quart Rev 1809–24; he also edited the works of Massinger (1805, 4 vols 1813), Jonson (9 vols 1816), Ford (2 vols 1827) and, with A. Dyce, Shirley (6 vols 1833).
See also under Anti-Jacobin, col 698, below.

§ 2

Hazlitt, W. A letter to Gifford. 1819.
—— In his Spirit of the age, 1825.
Hunt, L. Ultra-crepidarius: a satire on Gifford. 1823.
Literary Gazette 6 June 1827. Article by Eponymos [W. G. Cookesley?].
Longaker, J. The Della Cruscans and Gifford. Philadelphia 1924.
Clark, R. B. William Gifford. New York 1930. With bibliography.
Shine, H. and H. C. Shine. The Quarterly Review under Gifford. Chapel Hill 1949.
Hopkins, K. In his Portraits in satire, 1958.

JAMES GRAINGER
1721?–66
Collections

Select poems. In Park's Works of the British poets vol 4, 1808.
Select poems. In Sanford's Works of the British poets vol 27, Philadelphia 1819.
Poems. In British poets vol 59, Chiswick 1822.
Poetical works. Ed R. Anderson 2 vols Edinburgh 1836.

§ 1

Euripides, Cyclops. In The Greek theatre of Father Brumoy, 3 vols 1759. Tr Grainger.
A poetical translation of Tibullus and Sulpicia. 2 vols 1759 etc.
A letter to Smollet occasioned by his criticism upon a late translation of Tibullus. 1759.
The sugar-cane: a poem. 1764, 1766, Dublin 1766.
Grainger contributed an Ode on solitude to Dodsley's Collection vol 4, 1755 and Bryan and Percene to Percy's Reliques vol 1, 1765. He also pbd several medical works.

§ 2

Knox, R. A. A neglected poet. London Mercury May 1923.
Alleman, G. S. Mice and the muse. TLS 13 Aug 1938.
Doctor Grainger's Sugar cane. TLS 16 Feb 1951. Replies 2, 30 March 1951.

WILLIAM HAYLEY
1745–1820
Bibliographies

Barker, N. J. Some notes on the bibliography of Hayley. Trans Cambridge Bibl Soc 3 1959–62.

Collections

Poems: containing Poetical epistle to an eminent painter, Epistle on the death of John Thornton, Ode to J. Howard. Dublin 1781.
Plays of three acts written for a private theatre. 1784, Dublin 1784.
Poems and plays. 6 vols 1785, 1788.
Poetical works. 3 vols Dublin 1785.

Poems. Dublin 1786. Suppl to Dublin 1785, above.
Three plays, with a preface. 1811.
Poems on serious and sacred subjects. Chichester 1818.

§ 1

Gratulatio academiae cantabrigiensis. Cambridge 1762. Hayley contributed An English ode, rptd GM 1763.
The afflicted father. [1770?]. A play, perhaps never ptd.
A poetical epistle to an eminent painter. 1778, 1779, 1781 (as An essay on painting, in two epistles to Romney), Dublin 1781 (An essay).
An elegy on the ancient Greek model. Cambridge and London 1779, Dublin 1783.
Epistle to Admiral Keppel. 1779.
Epistle to a friend on the death of John Thornton. 1780, 1780, 1782.
An essay on history in three epistles to Gibbon. 1780, 1781, Dublin 1781, 1782.
Ode inscribed to John Howard. 1780, 1781, 1782, Philadelphia nd.
The triumphs of temper: a poem in six cantos. 1781, 1781, Dublin 1781, London 1782, Dublin 1782, London 1784, Philadelphia 1787, London 1788 (6th edn), Boston [1790?], Winchester 1792, London 1793, 1795, 1796, 1799, Newburyport [1800?], London 1801, Chichester 1803 (12th edn), Kennebunk 1804, New York 1806, Chichester 1807, London 1809, Chichester 1812, Chichester and London 1817, Chiswick 1824; tr German, 1788.
An essay on epic poetry in five epistles to Mason. 1782, Dublin 1782; ed M. C. Williamson, Gainesville 1968 (facs).
Ode to Mr Wright of Derby. Chichester 1783.
The happy prescription, or the lady relieved from her lovers: a comedy in rhyme. Calcutta 1785.
A philosophical, historical and moral essay on old maids. 3 vols 1785, 1786, Dublin 1786, London 1793; tr German, 1786; French, 1788.
The two connoisseurs: a comedy in rhyme. Calcutta 1785.
Two dialogues: containing a comparative view of the Earl of Chesterfield and Dr Johnson. 1787, 1800 (as Anecdotes of Chesterfield and Johnson).
Occasional stanzas written at the request of the Revolution Society. 1788.
Life of Crashaw. In Kippis's Biographia britannica vol 4, 1789 (2nd edn).
The young widow: or a history of Cornelia Sedley. 4 vols 1789, 2 vols Dublin 1789; tr French, 1789.
The eulogies of Howard. 1791.
An elegy on the death of Sir William Jones. 1795.
The national advocate. 1795.
The life of Milton; to which are added conjectures on the origin of Paradise lost. 1796, Dublin 1797, Basle 1799; tr German, 1797; French, 1799. First issued in short form in Boydell and Nichol's edn of Milton, 1794.
An essay on sculpture in a series of epistles to Flaxman. 1800.
Little Tom the sailor. [London?] 1800, Lambeth [1917]. Illustr Blake.
The life and posthumous writings of Cowper. 3 vols Chichester and London 1803–4, 2 vols Boston 1803, New York 1803, 3 vols Philadelphia 1805, 4 vols Chichester 1806; Supplementary pages, Chichester and London 1806; 4 vols Chichester 1809, London 1812, 3 vols 1824, 1835 etc.
The life of Cowper abridged. 1803.
The triumph of music. Chichester 1804.
Ballads founded on anecdotes relating to animals. Chichester and London 1805. First issued in pts as Designs to a series of ballads, Chichester and London 1802 etc. Illustr Blake.
An appendix to the civil and political history of Chili. New York 1808. Contains trns by Hayley.
Impromptu to the author. In F. N. C. Mundy, The fall of Needwood, Derby 1808.

Latin and Italian poems of Milton, translated by Cowper. Chichester and London 1808. Ed Hayley.
Poetical pieces by Thomas Bradford. Chichester 1808. Sonnet and epitaph by Hayley.
Stanzas to the patriots in Spain. 1808.
The life of George Romney. Chichester and London 1809.
Cowper's Milton. 4 vols Chichester and London 1810. Ed Hayley.
Select poems by John Dawes Worgan of Bristol. 1810. Ed Hayley.
A patriotic song for the Amicable club. [London?] 1814. A broadside.
Song for the Amicable fraternity of Felpham. [London?] 1817.
Hymn for the children of Petworth. In Psalms and hymns for Petworth Church, Petworth 1820.
Memoirs. 2 vols 1823. *See* under §2, below.
Letter. In Four prologues for a private theatre, Geneva [1892?].
Hayley contributed to An asylum for fugitive pieces vol 1, 1785 *and to* Extracts from the Italian poets, 1798.

§ 2

Public characters of 1799–1800. Contains account of Hayley.
Hay, A. The history of Chichester. Chichester 1804. Contains sketch of Hayley.
Lounger's common-place book vol 2. 1805. Contains account of Hayley.
Memoirs of the life and writings of Hayley written by himself, with extracts from his correspondence and unpublished poetry. Ed J. Johnson 2 vols 1823.
Cary, H. F. In his Lives of English poets, 1846.
Coldicott, H. R. S. How Cowper got his pension. Cornhill Mag April 1913.
Plowman, M. Blake and Hayley. TLS 30 April 1925.
Keynes, G. L. Blake and Hayley: a new letter. TLS 31 July 1930.
—— Blake's letters to Hayley. TLS 25 March 1955.
Sadler, E. A. Joseph Warton to Hayley. N & Q 4 April 1942.
Le Viness, W. T. The life and works of Hayley. Santa Fe 1945.
'Bishop, Morchard' (O. Stonor). Blake's Hayley. 1951.
Bentley, G. E. Blake and Johnny of Norfolk. SP 53 1956.
—— Blake, Hayley and Lady Hesketh. RES new ser 7 1956.
—— William Blake as a private publisher. BNYPL Nov 1957.
Bates, M. C. Cowper to Hayley and Rose. Harvard Lib Bull 11 1957.
Hanford, J. H. A letter to the swan of Lichfield. Newberry Lib Bull 4 1957.
Wolf, E. Four letters from Hayley to Emma Hamilton. Manuscripts 11 1959.

HENRY HEADLEY
1765–88

Collections

Fugitive pieces. 1785. Reissued with addns 1786 as Poems and other pieces; ed P. M. Spacks, Los Angeles 1966 (Augustan Reprint Soc).
Select beauties of ancient English poetry, with remarks. 2 vols 1787, 1810 (with life by H. Kett). Both edns contain Headley's poems.
Poetical works. In Park's Works of the British poets vol 41, 1808.
Poems. In British poets vol 73, Chiswick 1822.

§ 1

An invocation to melancholy: a fragment. Oxford and London 1785.

Fletcher, P. The purple island, with the critical remarks of Headley. 1816.
Headley contributed to GM 1786–7; *see* DNB.

§ 2

Wasserman, E. R. Headley and the Elizabethan revival. SP 36 1939.

FRANCIS HOYLAND
b. 1727

Poems and translations. 1763.
Poems. Strawberry Hill 1769, 1769.
Odes. Edinburgh 1783.
Poetical works. In Park's Works of the British poets vol 41, 1808.
Poems. In British poets vol 73, Chiswick 1822.

GEORGE HUDDESFORD
1749–1809

Collections

The poems, now first collected. 2 vols 1801.

§ 1

Warley: a satire. 1778.
Salmagundi: a miscellaneous combination of original poetry. 1791, 1792, 1793.
Topsy turvy, with anecdotes and observations. 1793, 1793 (3rd edn).
Bubble and squeak: a galli-maufry. 1799.
Crambe repetita: a second course of bubble and squeak. 1799.
The scum uppermost when the Middlesex porridge-pot boils over: an heroic election ballad. 1802, 1802.
Bonaparte: an heroic ballad with a sermon in its belly. 1803.
The Wiccamical chaplet: a selection of original poetry 1804. Ed Huddesford, with contributions by him.
Wood and stone: a dialogue. [London?] [1804?].
Les champignons du diable: a mock heroic poem. 1805.

§ 2

Kirby, T. F. In his Winchester scholars, 1888.

JAMES HURDIS
1763–1801

Collections

Poems by the author of the Village curate and Adriano. 1790.
Poems. 3 vols Oxford 1808.

§ 1

England's heroical epistles, by Drayton. 1788. Ed Hurdis.
The village curate: a poem. 1788, 1790, Dublin 1790, London 1792, Newburyport 1793, Bishopstone 1797, Newburyport 1808, London 1810 (with other poems and life).
Adriano: or the first of June, a poem. 1790, 1792.
A dissertation on the meaning of the word in Genesis i. 21. 1790.
Cursory remarks upon the arrangement of the plays of Shakespeare. 1792.
Sir Thomas More: a tragedy. 1792, 1793.
Reflections upon the commencement of a new year. 1793.
Select critical remarks upon the ten first chapters of Genesis. 1793.

Tears of affliction: a poem. 1794.
A poem on the marriage of the Prince of Wales. 1795.
Lectures shewing the several sources of pleasure from poetry. Bishopstone 1797.
On the nature and occasion of psalm and prophecy. 1800.
The favorite village. Bishopstone 1800, London 1810 (with another poem and Sir Thomas More).
A word or two in vindication of the University of Oxford. Wrangham nd.

Letters

Letters of Hurdis to Cowper 1791–4. Ed J. F. Tattersall, Eastbourne 1927. See also Sussex County Mag April 1927.
Clarke, W. K. L. A letter of Hurdis to Cowper. Theology 57 1954.

§ 2

Whitaker, A. P. James Hurdis. Chichester 1960.

RICHARD JAGO
1715–81
Collections

Poems, moral and descriptive. 1784. With biography by J. S. Hylton.
Poetical works. In Park's Works of the British poets vol 27, 1808.
Poems. In British poets vol 55, Chiswick 1822.
Select poems. In Sanford's Works of the British poets vol 37, Philadelphia 1822.
Anderson 11, Chalmers 17.

§ 1

The causes of impenitence consider'd. Oxford 1755. A sermon.
The nature and grounds of a Christian's happiness. Oxford 1763. A sermon.
Edge-hill, or the rural prospect delineated and moralised: a poem. 1767.
Labor and genius: a fable. 1768; rptd in Peach's collection vol 3, 1775.
Jago also contributed to Dodsley's collection vols 4–5, 1755–8.

§ 2

Bibliotheca-cornubiensis vol 3. 1822.
Poole, C. H. In his Warwickshire poets, 1914.
Lind, I. D. Jago: a study in eighteenth-century localism. Philadelphia 1945. With bibliography.

CATHERINE JEMMAT
fl. 1752–71

§ 1

Memoirs. 3 vols 1762, 2 vols 1765, 1771.
Miscellanies in prose and verse. 1766, 1771.

§ 2

Starkey, J. Two poets of old Dublin. In his Essays and recollections by Seumas O'Sullivan, Dublin 1944.

EDWARD JERNINGHAM
1727–1812
Collections

Poems on various subjects. 1767, 1774, 1779 (5th edn), Dublin 1781, 2 vols 1786, 1 vol Dublin 1790, 2 vols 1796, 4 vols 1806 (9th edn, as Poems and plays).
Fugitive poetical pieces. 1778.

§ 1

Andromache to Pyrrhus: an heroic epistle. 1761.
An elegy written among the tombs of Westminster abbey. 1762.
The nunnery: an elegy in imitation of the Elegy in a churchyard. 1762, [1763].
The magdalens: an elegy. 1763, 1763.
The nun: an elegy. 1764, 1764.
An elegy written among the ruins of an abbey. 1765, 1765.
Yarico to Inkle: an epistle. 1766.
Il latte: an elegy. 1767.
Amabella: a poem. 1768.
The deserter: a poem. 1770, 1770.
The funeral of Arabert, monk of La Trappe. 1771, 1772. Poem.
Faldoni and Teresa. 1773, 1773.
The fall of Mexico: a poem. 1775.
Margaret of Anjou: an historical interlude. 1777.
The ancient English wake: a poem. 1779.
Honoria: or the day of all souls, with other poetical pieces. 1782.
Moore, J. H. Poetical trifles. 1783 (3rd edn). Ed Jerningham.
The rise and progress of the Scandinavian poetry: a poem. 1784, 1789.
Lines written at Cossey-Hall. [London?] [1786].
Enthusiasm: a poem. 1789.
Lines on a late resignation at the Royal Academy. 1790.
The Shakespeare gallery: a poem. 1791, 1791.
Abelard to Eloisa. 1792.
Stone Henge: a poem. Norwich 1792.
The siege of Berwick: a tragedy. 1794; ed H. E. H. Jerningham 1882.
The Welch heiress: a comedy. 1795, 1795, 1796, 1798.
Peace, ignominy and destruction: a poem. 1796.
The Peckham frolic, or Nell Gwyn: a comedy. 1799.
Biographical sketches of Henrietta and Louis. 1799 (with Jerningham's trn of Bossuet's sermons), 1800, 1800 (as The funeral orations of Bossuet).
Select sermons from the French of Bossuet. 1800, 1801, 1801. Tr Jerningham, with his preface.
The mild tenour of Christianity. 1803.
The dignity of human nature: an essay. 1805.
The Alexandrian school: or a narrative of the first Christian professors in Alexandria. 1809.
The old bard's farewell. 1811, 1812.
Jerningham also contributed to Lady Miller, Poetical amusements at a villa near Bath vols 3–4, 1781 *and to* British album vol 2, 1790. *See also under Della Cruscans, below.*

§ 2

Bettany, L. Jerningham and his friends. [1919].

HENRY JONES
1721–70
Collections

Poems on several occasions. 1749, Dublin 1749.
Poems. Dublin 1756.

§ 1

Philosophy: a poem by the bricklayer. Dublin 1746.
On seeing a picture of the Prince of Wales. Dublin 1749.
Fortitude: a poem, inscribed to Colley Cibber. Dublin 1751.
An epistle to the Earl of Orrery. 1751.
The Earl of Essex: a tragedy. 1753, Dublin 1753, London 1754, Dublin 1756, London 1770 (4th edn), 1776, 1779. Also in many theatre collections.
Merit: a poem. 1753.

Verses to the Duke of Newcastle on the death of Pelham.
1754.

The relief, or day thoughts: a poem occasioned by the Complaint: or night thoughts. 1754.

The invention of letters and the utility of the press. Dublin 1755. Single sheet.

The patriotic enterprise: a poem inscribed to Pitt. 1758.

The royal vision, in an ode to peace. Dublin 1763.

Vectis, the isle of Wight: a poem. 1766, Newport 1781, London 1782.

Kew Garden: a poem. 1767.

Clifton: a poem. Bristol 1667 (for 1767), 1773 (with Ode to Shakespear).

Inoculation, or beauty's triumph: a poem. Bath 1768.

Shrewsbury quarry. Shrewsbury 1769.

The cave of Idra. Completed and pbd by P. Hiffernan as The heroine of the cave, 1775.

§ 2

Memoirs of the life of R. Devereux. 1753. On background for Earl of Essex.

Sentimental & Masonic Mag (Dublin) 1794.

O'Donoghue, D. J. In his Poets of Ireland, 1912.

Banks, J. The unhappy favourite. Ed T. M. H. Blair, New York 1939. Appendix on Earl of Essex.

SIR WILLIAM JONES
1746–94
Bibliographies

Cannon, G. H. Jones, orientalist: an annotated bibliography. Honolulu [1952].
— In his Oriental Jones: a biography, New York 1964.

Collections

Poems consisting chiefly of translations from the Asiatic languages, to which are added two essays: 1, On the poetry of the eastern nations; II, On the arts commonly called imitative. Oxford 1772, London 1777.

Works. 8 vols 1799–1801, 13 vols 1807.

Poems in three parts: part first, Latin poetry of Jones. Calcutta 1800.

Poetical works. In Park's Works of the British poets vol 42, 1808.

Poetical works. 2 vols 1810, 1816, 1818.

Three tracts. 1819. Political.

Discourse delivered before the Asiatic society. 2 vols 1821, London and Chiswick 1824. Originally pbd 1784–94 in Asiatick researches.

Select poems. In Sanford's Works of the British poets vol 35, Philadelphia 1822.

Poems. In British poets vol 74, Chiswick 1822.

Poems. Ed J. Benthall, Cambridge 1961. Selection.

Chalmers 18.

§ 1

A grammar of the Persian language. 1771, 1785, 1797 (4th), 1801, 1804, 1809, 1823, 1828; tr French, 1772.

Lettre à Monsieur A[nquetil] du P[erron]. 1771.

The history of Nader Shah. 1770 (in French, with Traité sur la poésie orientale and trns from Hafiz), 1773 (abridged); tr German, 1773.

An oration intended to have been spoken at Oxford. 1773.

Poeseos asiaticae commentariorum libri sex. 1774, Leipzig 1777.

The speeches of Isaeus concerning property. 1779. Tr Jones.

An inquiry into the legal mode of suppressing riots. 1780 (with Oration, above and speech, 1780 below).

Julii Melesigoni ad libertatem. [1780].

Letters from a tutor to his pupils. 1780.

A speech on the nomination of candidates to represent Middlesex. 1780.

An essay on the law of bailments. 1781, Dublin 1790, Boston 1796, London 1798, Philadelphia 1804, Albany 1806, Brattleboro 1807, 1813, London 1823, New York 1828, London 1833, Philadelphia 1836.

The Muse recalled: an ode. Strawberry Hill 1781, Paris 1782; rptd in An asylum for fugitive pieces vol 1, 1785.

The Moullakát: or seven Arabian poems. 1782, 1891. Tr Jones.

Muhammad, I. A., The Mahomedan law of succession. 1782. Tr Jones.

An ode on imitation of Alcaeus. [1782]. Frequently rptd in collections.

The principles of government, in a dialogue. 1782, 1783, Norwich and London 1797, [London] [1800?], 1818.

A letter to a patriot senator. 1783.

Sacontala, or the fatal ring: an Indian drama, by Calidas. Calcutta 1789, London 1790, 1792, 1796, 1855, 1870. Tr Jones.

Muhammad, I. M., Al Sirájiyyah: or the Mohammedan law of inheritance. Calcutta 1792, 1869. Tr Jones.

An ode: what constitutes a state? [1796].

Institutes of Hindu law: or the ordinances of Menu. 1796, 1825, 1863, 1869, 1880, 1911. Tr Jones.

Monthly Mag May 1804. Lines by Jones.

Testimonies in favour of the Bible. GM suppl 1815.

Ode to Pyrrha. In the Works of Samuel Parr vol 1, 1828.

A fragment of Polybius. In the Works of Franklin, Boston 1840.

Kneel to the goddess. In Autobiography of Mary Granville vol 2, 1862.

The Hindu wife and the hymns. Calcutta 1881.

Saul and David. In Thraliana, ed K. C. Balderston vol 1, Oxford 1942.

Jones was a major contributor to The Asiatick miscellany, 2 vols Calcutta 1785–6 (*rptd* Calcutta and London 1787) *and to* Asiatick researches (Calcutta) 1788–94.

Letters

European Mag 38 1800. One letter.

Monthly Mag Jan 1817. One letter.

Letters to Samuel Davis. Trans Royal Asiatic Soc 3 1831.

Thirteen inedited letters. Jnl of Amer Oriental Soc 10 1872.

The correspondence between Monboddo and Jones. Ed G. Cannon, Amer Anthropologist 70 1968.

§ 2

Shore, J. Memoirs of Jones. 1804, Philadelphia 1805, 2 vols 1806, 1 vol 1806, 1807, 1813, 1815, 2 vols 1835.

Carey, H. F. In his Lives of English poets, 1846.

Sastri, K. S. R. Jones: the man and his work. Indian Rev 22 1921.

Durga-Prasanna, R. C. Jones and his translation of Sakuntala. Calcutta 1928.

Temple, R. C. Jones: transliteration of oriental alphabets. N & Q 12 July 1930.

Aspinall, A. The work of Jones. In his Cornwallis in Bengal, Manchester 1931.

Schaffer, A. Uhland and Jones. MLN 49 1934.

Hewitt, R. M. Harmonious Jones. E & S 28 1942.

Arberry, A. J. Persian Jones. Asiatic Rev 40 1944.
— Asiatic Jones. 1946.
— The Jones tradition. Indian Art & Letters 20 1946.
— Oriental essays: portraits of seven scholars. 1960.

Bull London Univ School of Oriental & African Stud 11 1946. Pt 4 contains essays on Jones by 8 scholars.

The debt to Asiatic Jones. TLS 28 Sept 1946.

Edgerton, F. Sir William Jones. Jnl Amer Oriental Soc 66 1946.

Fan, T. C. Jones's Chinese studies. RES 22 1946.

Mahajan, J. Sir William Jones. Indian Rev 47 1946.

150th jubilee of the Royal Asiatic Society of Bengal. Calcutta 1946.

Meyerstein, E. H. W. Chatterton and Jones. N & Q 1 May 1948.

Sir William Jones: bicentenary volume. Calcutta 1948.

Waley, A. Anquetil-Duperron and Jones. History Today 2 1952.

Cannon, G. H. Jones and the Sakuntala. Jnl Amer Oriental Soc 73 1953.

— Orientalism and Jones. Quart Rev (Univ of Michigan) 42 1955.

— Freedom of the press and Jones. Journalism Quart 33 1956.

— Jones and Burke. MP 54 1957.

— Jones's Persian linguistics. Jnl Amer Oriental Soc 78 1958.

— The literary place of Jones. Jnl Asiatic Soc 2 1960.

— Jones and Franklin. Univ College Record (Oxford) 4 1961.

— Jones, Shelburne and the Indian judgeship. Ibid.

— Oriental Jones: a biography. New York 1964.

— Jones and Johnson's literary club. MP 63 1965.

Gossman, A. Harmonious Jones and Milton's invocation. N & Q Dec 1954.

Master, A. Jones and Panini. Jnl Amer Oriental Soc 76 1956.

Aarsleff, H. In his Study of language in England 1780–1860, Princeton 1967.

Mukherjee, S. N. Jones: a study in eighteenth-century British attitudes to India. Cambridge 1968.

GEORGE KEATE
1729–97
Collections

Poetical works. 2 vols 1781, 1 vol 1834.

§ 1

Ancient and modern Rome: a poem. 1760, 1763.

A short account of the republic of Geneva. 1761; tr French, 1774.

An epistle from Lady Jane Grey to Lord Dudley. 1762.

The Alps: a poem. 1763.

The ruins of Netley Abbey. 1764, 1769 (rev as Netley Abbey: an elegy); tr Latin, nd.

The temple-student: an epistle to a friend. 1765.

A poem to the memory of Mrs Cibber. 1766.

Ferney: an epistle to Voltaire. 1768.

The monument in Arcadia: a dramatic poem. 1773; rptd in A collection of new plays vol 1, 1774.

Sketches from nature in a journey to Margate. 2 vols 1779, 1 vol 1779, Dublin 1779, London 1782, 2 vols 1790, 1 vol Boston 1793, London 1802 (with memoir); tr French, 1800.

An epistle to Angelica Kauffmann. 1781. Poem.

The distressed poet: a serio-comic poem. 1787.

A probationary ode in 1785. 1787.

An account of the Pelew islands. 1788, 1788, Dublin 1788, Perth and London 1788, London 1789, Paris 1789, Philadelphia 1789, Basle 1789, Dublin 1793, Wilmington 1794, 2 vols Philadelphia 1795–6, 1 vol Nottingham 1796, New York 1796, Boston 1796, Catskill 1797, Brookfield 1800, London 1803. Nottingham, Perth and London edns as A narrative of the shipwreck of the Antelope; tr French, 1788; German, 1789; Spanish, 1805.

Keate's work appears in Bell's classical arrangement of fugitive poetry, 1797; Asylum for fugitive pieces, 1796; A collection of new plays, Altenburgh 1774–8; Pearch's collection, 1775; Universal Mag 1760, 1779, 1793; Monthly Rev 1768; Annual Register 1768; GM 1770; Hibernian Mag 1779. See Dapp, below.

§ 2

Dapp, K. G. Keate, eighteenth-century gentleman. Philadelphia 1939. With bibliography.

Horsley, P. M. Keate and the Voltaire-Shakespeare controversy. Comparative Lit Stud 16 1945.

WILLIAM KENDALL
1768–1832
Collections

Poems. Exeter 1791.
Poems. Exeter 1793.

§ 1

An analysis of the science of legislation. [1791]. From Filangieri's Italian.

§ 2

O'Donoghue, D. J. In his Poets of Ireland, 1912.

JOHN LANGHORNE
1735–79
Collections

Poems on several occasions. Lincoln 1760.

Poetical works. 2 vols 1766; ed J. T. Langhorne 2 vols 1804 (with addns).

Poetical works. [1798] (Cooke's Pocket Lib).

Poetical works. In Park's Works of the British poets vol 36, 1806.

Poems. In British poets vol 65, Chiswick 1822.

Select poems. In Sanford's Works of the British poets vol 30, Philadelphia 1822.

Anderson 11, Chalmers 16, Johnson (1790) 71.

§ 1

The death of Adonis, from Bion. 1759.

Job: a poem. 1760.

The tears of music: a poem to Handel, with an ode to the river Eden. 1760.

A hymn to hope. 1761.

Solyman and Almena: an Oriental tale. 1762, 1780, 1781, 1800; Novelist's Mag 2 1780; tr German, 1788.

Letters on religious retirement, melancholy and enthusiasm. 1762, 1772.

The Viceroy: a poem. 1762.

The visions of fancy, in four elegies. 1762.

The effusions of friendship and fancy, in several letters. 2 vols 1763, 1766 (enlarged), Dublin 1770.

The enlargement of the mind: epistle 1. 1763; Epistle 11, 1765.

The letters between Theodosius and Constantia. 1763, 1764, 1766 (4th); Correspondence, 1764, 1765, 1766; 2 vols 1770 (combined), 1778, 1782, 1 vol 1799, 1807, 1808, 1817, 1826, 1852; tr French, 1764.

Genius and valour: a Scotch pastoral. 1764, 1764.

Letters on the eloquence of the pulpit. 1765.

The poetical works of Collins. 1765, 1765, 1771, 1776, 1781, 1804, [1808], 1815, 1827, 1854. Ed Langhorne.

The fatal prophecy. 1766.

Precepts of conjugal happiness. 1767, 1769. Verse.

Sermons preached before the society of Lincoln's-Inn. 2 vols 1767 (2nd edn), 1773.

Verses in memory of a lady written at Sandgate castle. 1768.

Frederic and Pharamond: or the consolations of human life. 1769.

Letters supposed to have passed between St Evremont and Waller. 2 vols 1769.

A dialogue of the dead betwixt Lord Eglinton and Mungo Campbell. 1770.

Plutarch's lives. 6 vols 1770, 1774, 1778, 1780, 1792, 1795, London, Edinburgh and Glasgow 1798, 1801, 1805, 3 vols 1812–13. With W. Langhorne.

The fables of Flora. 1771 (3 edns), Dublin 1772, London 1773 (5th edn), 1794, 1804 (with life by F. Blagdon).

A dissertation on the ancient republics of Italy. 1773. From Denina's Italian.

The origin of the veil: a poem. 1773.

The country justice. 3 pts 1774, 1775, 1777; rptd in The late Augustans, ed D. Davie 1958.

Milton's Italian poems, translated. 1776.

The proper happiness of the ecclesiastic life: a sermon. Bristol [1776].

The love of mankind: a sermon. 1777.

Owen of Carron: a poem. 1778.

Langhorne's reviews in Monthly Rev *are listed by* B. C. Nangle, The Monthly Review, Oxford 1934.

§ 2

Macdonald, H. In Essays presented to David Nichol Smith, Oxford 1945.

Sharrock, R. Wordsworth and Langhorne's The country justice. N & Q July 1954.

FRENCH LAURENCE
1757–1809
Collections

Poetical remains of French Laurence and Richard Laurence. Dublin 1782. With memoirs by H. Cotton.

§ 1

The works of Burke. 8 vols 1792–1827, 16 vols 1803–27. Laurence co-editor until 1808.

Critical remarks on the New Testament. Oxford 1810.

Epistolary correspondence of Burke and Laurence. 1827.

Lawrence contributed to GM *and was one of the authors of* Rolliad, *below.*

EVAN LLOYD
1734–76

§ 1

The curate: a poem. 1766.

The methodist: a poem. 1766.

The powers of the pen: a poem. 1766, 1768 (with addns).

Conversation: a poem. 1767.

An epistle to Garrick. 1773. *See* Kenrick, below.

The private correspondence of Garrick. 2 vols 1831–2. Contains 2 Lloyd letters. *See also* C. J. L. Price, RES new ser 3 1952.

§ 2

[Kenrick, William?] A whipping for the Welch parson: being a comment on Lloyd's Epistle to Garrick, by Scriblerius Flagellarius; to which is superadded the parson's text. 1773.

Jones, E. A. Two Welsh correspondents of Wilkes. Y Cymmrodor 29 1919.

Price, C. J. L. A man of genius and a Welch man. Swansea 1963.

ROBERT LLOYD
1733–64
Collections

Poems. 1762.

Poetical works. Ed W. Kenrick 2 vols 1774. With life.

Select poems. In Park's Works of the British poets vol 6, 1808.

Anderson 10, Chalmers 15, Johnson (1790) 68.

§ 1

The actor: a poetical epistle. 1760, 1764 (4th), Dublin 1811; ed E. Blunden 1926.

Shakespeare: an epistle to Garrick; with an ode to genius. 1760.

The tears and triumphs of Parnassus. 1760. An interlude at Drury Lane.

Two odes. 1760, 1760. With G. Colman.

Arcadia, or the shepherd's wedding: a dramatic pastoral. 1761, [1778?].

An epistle to Churchill. 1761.

The death of Adam: a tragedy from Klopstock. 1763, 1810. Perhaps with Colman.

The New-river head: a tale in the manner of C. Denis. 1763, 1764.

The capricious lovers: a comic opera. 1764, Dublin 1764, London 1765, 1780. Based on Favart, Caprices d'amour.

Moral tales. 3 vols 1764, 1 vol 1768, Edinburgh 1768, London 1781, 1792, 4 vols Perth 1792, Manchester [1790?], 2 vols 1795, 1800. From Marmontel, with C. Denis.

Chit-chat: a poem. In Sanford's Works of the British poets vol 37, Philadelphia 1819.

Two epistles on happiness, to a young lady. Salisbury nd.

Lloyd contributed papers to Connoisseur 1754–6. *His reviews in* Monthly Rev *are listed by* B. C. Nangle, The Monthly Review, Oxford 1934. *He superintended the poetry corner in* Library: or Moral & Critical Mag April 1761–May 1762, *conducted* St James's Mag Sept 1762–March 1764, *and contributed to* North Briton 1762–4.

§ 2

Dobson, A. In his At Prior park and other papers, 1912.

Halsband, R. The poet of the North Briton. PQ 17 1938.

—— A parody of Thomas Gray. PQ 22 1943.

Weatherly, E. H. Foote's revenge on Churchill and Lloyd. HLQ 9 1946.

JOHN LOGAN
1748–88
Collections

Poems, by one of the ministers of Leith. 1781, 1782.

Sermons. 2 vols 1790–1, 1 vol 1810, Edinburgh 1739.

Poems, and Runnamede: a tragedy. Edinburgh 1805.

Poetical works. In Park's Works of the British poets vol 41, 1808.

Poems. In British poets vol 70, Chiswick 1822.

Select poems. In Sanford's Works of the British poets vol 37, Philadelphia 1822.

Anderson 11, Chalmers 18.

§ 1

Poems on several occasions by Michael Bruce. 1770. Ed Logan.

Elements of the philosophy of history. Edinburgh 1781.

Essay on the manners and government of Asia. 1782.

Runnamede: a tragedy. 1783.

A dissertation on the governments, manners and spirit of Asia. 1787.

A review of the principal charges against Warren Hastings. 1788.

§ 2

Laing, D. Ode to the cuckoo, with remarks on its authorship. Edinburgh 1873.

Matson, W. T. A complete vindication of Logan. Portsmouth 1892.

Mackenzie, J. Life of Michael Bruce. 1905. Contains letters by Logan.

EDWARD LOVIBOND
1724-75

Poems on several occasions. 1785.
Poetical works. In Park's Works of the British poets vol 33, 1807.
Poetical works. In British poets vol 63, Chiswick 1822.
Select poems. In Sanford's Works of the British poets vol 37, Philadelphia 1822.
Anderson 11, Chalmers 16.
Lovibond contributed to World.

SAMUEL MARTIN
1740-1829

§ 1

The preservation and transmission of the scriptures. Edinburgh 1779.
An epistle in verse occasioned by the death of Boswell. Edinburgh 1795; ed R. F. Metzdorf, Hamden Conn 1952.
A poetical epistle to the Princess of Wales. Edinburgh 1795.
Sinclair, J. The statistical account of Scotland. 21 vols Edinburgh 1791-9. Martin contributed the account of Monimail parish.

§ 2

Reid, H. M. B. The kirk above Dee water. Castle-Douglas 1895. With account and portrait of Martin.

WILLIAM MASON
1725-97

Bibliographies

Gaskell, P. First editions of Mason. Cambridge 1951 (Cambridge Bibl Soc).
Todd, W. B. Duplicate editions of Mason's Musaeus. PBSA 46 1952.
See Draper under §2, *below*.

Collections

Odes. Cambridge and London 1756, 1756.
Elegies. 1763, 1763.
Poems. 1764, Dublin 1764 (with 2 more poems), York 1771, 1773, 1774, 2 vols Glasgow 1774, 1 vol 1777, 2 vols Glasgow 1777, 1 vol London and York 1779, 3 vols York and London 1796-7 (with unpbd poems), London 1803, 1805.
Essays on English church music. York and London 1795.
The poetical works of the author of the heroic epistle to Chambers. 1805. 6 satirical poems.
Works. 4 vols 1811, 1816.
Poetical works. In British poets vols 77-8, Chiswick 1822. With life.
Satiric poems published anonymously by Mason, with notes by Walpole. Ed P. Toynbee, Oxford 1926.
Chalmers 18.

§ 1

Il pacifico. In Gratulatio academiae cantabrigiensis, [Cambridge] 1748.
Musaeus: a monody to the memory of Pope, in imitation of Lycidas. 1747, 1747, 1748, Dublin 1748.
Isis: an elegy. 1749, 1749, 1766. Also in The Union, Edinburgh 1753.
Ode performed in the senate house at Cambridge. Cambridge 1749. Also pbd with music by Boyce, 1749.
Elfrida: a dramatic poem. 1752 (3 edns), Dublin 1752, London 1753, Edinburgh 1755, London 1757, 1759,

1773, 1773, 1779 ('altered for theatrical representation'); tr Italian, 1774; French, 1784. Also Chorus of the dramatic poem of Elfrida as performed at the Theatre-Royal in Covent Garden, 1772.
Caractacus: a dramatic poem. 1759, 1759, 1760, Dublin 1759, London 1762, Dublin 1764, York and London 1777 ('altered for theatrical representation'); rptd in many collections; tr French, 1785; Greek and Latin, 1781; Italian, 1823. Also The lyrical part of the drama of Caractacus as altered and as spoken and sung in Covent Garden, 1776.
A supplement to Watts' psalms and hymns. Cambridge 1769, 1807.
The English garden, a poem: book the first. 1772? (priv ptd), 1772, 1772, Dublin 1772, London 1778, 1781; Second, 1776 (priv ptd), 1777, 1777; Third, London and York 1779; Fourth, London and York 1781; A poem in four books, York and London 1771-81, Dublin 1782; York and London 1783, London 1803, 1813, 1825; tr French, 1788.
An heroic epistle to Sir William Chambers. 1773 (7 edns), 1774 (5 edns), 1776, 1777.
An heroic postscript to the public. 1774 (8 edns), 1777.
The poems of Gray, [with] memoirs. York and London 1775, 1775, 2 vols Dublin 1775, 4 vols York 1778, London 1807, 1814, 1820. Ed Mason.
Ode to Mr Pinchbeck upon his newly invented patent candle-snuffers, by Malcolm McGreggor. 1776 (5 edns), 1777.
An epistle to Dr Shebbeare, [with] an ode to Sir Fletcher Norton in imitation of Horace ode VIII book IV, by Malcolm MacGregor. 1777 (4 edns).
Ode to the naval officers of Great Britain. 1779.
Ode to Eliza Ryves. 1780. By Mason?
An archaeological epistle to Jeremiah Milles. 1782, 1782 ('corrected'), Dublin 1782.
A copious collection of portions of the Psalms, [with] a critical and historical essay on cathedral music. York 1782, London 1834.
The dean and the 'squire: a political eclogue dedicated to Jenyns. 1782 (4 edns).
King Stephen's watch: a tale founded on fact. 1782.
Ode to William Pitt. 1782.
The art of painting of du Fresnoy, translated with annotations by Reynolds. York and London 1783, Dublin 1783.
Animadversions on the present government of the York lunatic asylum. York [1788].
An occasional discourse on the slave trade. York and London 1788.
Poems by William Whitehead. Vol 3, York and London 1788. Memoir by Mason.
Secular ode in commemoration of the Glorious Revolution. 1788.
Anecdotes of Reynolds. 1859.
Sappho: a lyrical drama with Italian translation by T. J. Mathias. London and Naples 1809, London 1810, 1816.
Religio clerici: a poem. 1810.
Gray, T., Ode on the pleasure arising from vicissitude. 2 vols San Francisco 1933 (facs). Ode completed by Mason.
Low, D. A., An eighteenth-century imitation of Donne's first satire. RES new ser 16 1965.
Mason contributed to Annual Register 1790, 1804; An asylum for fugitive pieces, 1788; Bell's classical arrangement of fugitive poetry, 1789-94; Hannah More's Cheap repository, Bath nd; A collection of the most esteemed pieces of poetry, 1767, 1770; Dodsley's collections of 1748, 1755, 1758, 1763, 1765, 1770, 1782, 1783; Ritson's English anthology, 1794; GM (*frequent reprints of poems*); The Muse's pocket companion, 1782; St James's Chron 1766; The new foundling hospital for wit, 1786; A select collection of poems, Edinburgh 1768.
See Draper under §2, *below*.

Letters

Hayley, W. In his Memoirs, 1823. One letter.

The private correspondence of Garrick. 2 vols 1831–2. 2 letters to Warburton.

The correspondence of Walpole and Mason. Ed J. Mitford 2 vols 1851.

The correspondence of Gray and Mason. Ed J. Mitford 1853, 1855; rptd in edns of Gray's letters.

Nichols, J. B. In his Illustrations of the literary history of the eighteenth century vol 7, 1858. 6 letters to Foster.

Prior, J. In his Life of Edmond Malone, 1860. Letter to Malone.

The correspondence of Hurd and Mason. Ed E. H. Pearce and L. Whibley, Cambridge 1932.

Nankivell, J. Extracts from destroyed letters of Hurd to Mason. MLR 45 1950.

Walpole's correspondence with Mason. Ed W. S. Lewis et al 2 vols Hew Haven 1955. Vols 28–9 of Yale edn of Walpole's correspondence.

The Harcourt papers vol 7. Ed E. W. Harcourt, Oxford nd.

§ 2

[Sheridan, R. B.] A familiar epistle to the author of the heroic epistle. 1774, 1774.

[Murray, J.] A letter to Mason concerning his edition of Gray's poems and the practices of booksellers, by a bookseller. 1777.

Cary, H. F. In his Lives of English poets, 1846.

Dobson, A. Gray's biographer. In his At Prior park and other papers, 1912.

Draper, J. W. Mason: a study in eighteenth-century culture. New York 1924. With bibliography.

Whibley, L. A satirical ode by Mason. TLS 24 Sept 1931.

Chase, I. W. Mason and Chambers's Dissertation on Oriental gardening. JEGP 35 1936.

Halsband, R. A parody of Gray. PQ 22 1943.

Day, M. S. The influence of Mason's Heroic epistle. MLQ 14 1953.

Hopkins, K. In his Portraits in satire, 1958.

Rea, R. R. Mason, Walpole and that rogue Almon. HLQ 33 1960.

JOSEPH MATHER
1737–1804

§ 1

Songs. Ed J. Wilson, Sheffield 1862.

§ 2

Armitage, W. H. G. Mather: poet of the filesmiths. N & Q 22 July 1950.

THOMAS JAMES MATHIAS
1754–1835

Collections

Odes, English and Latin. 1798.

Works of the author of The pursuits of literature. Dublin 1799, 1799.

Prose on various occasions collected from the newspapers. 1801.

Odae latinae. 1810, Naples 1819.

Poemata latina. Naples 1832.

§ 1

Qua quis ratione seipsum citra invidiam laudare possit. [Cambridge 1775].

Utrum imperium atque artes humaniores occidentali cursu nationibus sese deterant. [Cambridge 1776].

An heroic address in prose to the Rev R. Watson. 1780.

An heroic epistle to the Rev Richard Watson. 1780, 1780.

Runic odes imitated from the Norse in the manner of Gray. 1781, 1790, New York 1806 (in The garland of flowers).

An essay on the evidence relating to the poems attributed to Rowley. 1783, 1784.

Honoratissimo viro, T. Orde. [London? 1791].

The imperial epistle from Kien Long to George the Third. [1795?], 1796, 1797, 1798.

The pursuits of literature: a satirical poem in dialogue, part the first. 1794, 1796, 1796, 1797 (3 edns); Pt ii, 1796, 1796, 1797 (3 edns); Pt iii, 1796, 1796, 1797, 1797; Pt iv, 1797 (3 edns); In four dialogues, with notes, 1798 (3 edns), 1799, 1799, Philadelphia 1800, London 1801, 1803, 1805, 1808, 1812. See Brack under §2, below.

The political dramatist of the House of Commons. [1795], 1796 ('with some alterations and a postscript containing remarks on the Whig Club').

Villae Formianae, oden. [London? 1795].

An epistle in verse to the Rev Dr Randolph. [1796].

An equestrian epistle in verse to the Earl of Jersey. 1796, 1796 (with preceding as A pair of epistles in verse).

An appendix to the two epistles in verse containing the whole of the correspondence. 1796.

A letter to Buckingham on the emigrant French priests, by a layman. 1796, 1797.

An address to William Pitt. [1797].

The grove: a satire. [1798] (4th edn).

A letter to the author of Remarks on the Pursuits of literature, by a country gentleman. 1798.

The shade of Pope on the banks of the Thames. 1798, 1798, 1799, Dublin 1799.

A translation of the passages quoted in the Pursuits of literature. 1798 (3 edns).

Pandolphe attonito!: or Lord Galloway's poetical lamentation. 1800.

A letter occasioned by the death of Nicholls with an Italian ode. [1809]; rptd GM 1810.

The works of Gray. 2 vols 1814. Ed Mathias.

Observations on the writings and character of Gray. 1815. Rptd from preceding.

Lyrica sacra. Rome 1818, Naples 1819; ed F. Martin, Norwich 1835 (as Specimens of antient hymns).

Works in Italian

Componimenti lirici de' più illustri poeti d'Italia. 3 vols 1802, 4 vols Naples 1819.

Sonetti de' più illustri poeti d'Italia. 1802.

All'insigne Guglielmo Roscoe. [1803?].

Canzoni toscane. 1806, 1816, Naples 1832.

All'erudito N. Nicholls: canzone. [1807].

Aggiunta ai componimenti lirici de' più illustri poeti d'Italia. 3 vols 1808.

Canzoni e prose toscane. 1808.

Poesie liriche e prose toscane. 1810, 1816, Florence 1817, Naples 1818, 1820, 1824.

Poesie liriche italiane, inglesi e latine. Naples 1822.

Poesie liriche e varie. 3 vols Naples 1825 (new edn).

Lusitania protetta da Inghilterra: canzone. 1827.

Per la morte di F. Northe Conte di Guilford. Naples 1827, 1828.

Per la morte dell'onorevolissimo G. Drummond: canzone. 1828.

Lettera agli eruditi Inglesi. Naples 1834.

Mathias translated Akenside, J. Armstrong, J. Beattie, W. Mason, Milton, Spenser and Thomson into Italian. He pbd edns of the following Italian authors: G. M. Crescimbeni 1803, G. V. Gravina 1806, B. Menzini 1804, V. Monti 1804, F. Redi 1804, G. Tiraboschi 1803.

§ 2

Hopkins, K. In his Portraits in satire, 1958.
Brack, O. M. Mathias' The pursuits of literature. PBSA 62 1968.
For the many contemporary responses to Pursuits of litera-ture, see DNB and BM Catalogue.

MOSES MENDEZ
d. 1758

§ 1

Cervantes, Novellas exemplares. 1743. Ed Mendez.
Henry and Blanch, or the revengeful marriage: a tale from Gil Blas. 1745.
The Battiad: canto the first. 1750; In two cantos, 1751. With P. Whitehead and R. Schomberg.
The chaplet: a musical entertainment at Drury Lane. 1749, 1749 (with Boyce's score), 1750, Dublin 1750, London 1753, 1756, 1759, 1761, 1767, etc.
Robin Hood: a new musical entertainment. 1751.
The seasons, in imitation of Spenser. 1751, Dublin 1752; rptd in Pearch's collection vol 2, 1768; The poetical calendar, ed F. Fawkes and W. Woty vol 5, 1763.
The shepherd's lottery: a musical entertainment at Drury Lane. 1751, 1751 (with score by Boyce or Burney).
The squire of dames: a poem in Spenser's style. [1751]; rptd in Dodsley's collection vol 4, 1758 etc.
The double disappointment, or the fortune hunters: a comedy. 1755, 1760 (as a farce).
A collection of the most esteemed pieces of poetry, by the late Moses Mendez [et al]. 1767, 1770. Contains, with 2 other pieces, The author's account of his journey to Ireland, which is rptd Lady's Poetical Mag 1 1781.
C., W. London coffee houses. N & Q 7 Jan 1871. With poem to J. Ellis.

§ 2

Jacobs, J. and L. Wolf. Bibliotheca anglo-judaica. 1888.

JAMES MERRICK
1720–69

Collections

Poems on sacred subjects. Oxford 1763.
The psalms, in English verse. Reading 1765, 1766, London 1789, 1794, 1797, Oxford 1801, London 1804 etc.

§ 1

The Messiah: a divine essay. Reading 1734.
The destruction of Troy. Oxford 1763.
Τρυφιοδωρου 'Ιλιου 'Αλωσις. Oxford [1741]. Ed Merrick, with Latin metrical version by N. Frischlin.
A letter to Joseph Warton. Reading [1764]. On Greek indices.
Upon the thatched house. N & Q 10 Oct 1857.
Merrick also pbd devotional works and biblical exegesis: see DNB and BM General Catalogue. He contributed to Dodsley's collection vols 4–6, 1755–8; Oxford congratulatory verses 1761–2; Pearch's collection vol 1, 1768; Bell's fugitive poetry vols 12 1790, 18 1797.

§ 2

Brittain, R. E. An early model for Smart's A song to David. PMLA 56 1941. Replies by P. R. Wikelund, ELH 9 1942; A. D. McKillop, PMLA 58 1943.

ROBERT MERRY
1755–98

See also under Della Cruscans, below.

§ 1

Roberto Manners, poemetto. Florence 1785. Tr Merry.
Paulina, or the Russian daughter: a poem. 1787.
Diversity: a poem by Della Crusca. 1788.
The laurel of liberty. 1790.
The airs, duetts and choruses of the pantomime the Picture of Paris. 1790. With C. Bonner.
Lorenzo: a tragedy. 1791, Dublin 1791.
Ode for the fourteenth of July, being the anniversary of the revolution in France. 1791.
Fenelon, or the nuns of Cambray: a serious drama. 1795. From Chénier's French.
The wounded soldier: a poem by Mr M—y. [1795?].
The pains of memory. 1796.
Merry contributed to World and Oracle 1787–9, Argus and Telegraph 1793–6; and to Arno miscellany, Florence 1784; The Florence miscellany, Florence 1785; The album of Streatham, 1789; An asylum for fugitive pieces vol 3, 1789; The poetry of the world, ed E. Topham 2 vols 1788, 2 additional vols 1791; The British album, 2 vols 1790, Dublin 1790, London 1792, Boston 1793; The wild wreath, 1804. See DNB.

§ 2

Clifford, J. L. Merry: a pre-Byronic hero. Bull John Rylands Lib 27 1943.
Bostetter, E. E. The original Della Cruscans and the Florentine miscellany. HLQ 19 1956.
Adams, M. R. A newly discovered play of Merry. Manuscripts 13 1961.

WILLIAM JULIUS MICKLE
1734–88

Collections

Poems, and a tragedy. 1794. With anecdotes and letters from Lyttelton.
Poetical works. Ed J. Sim 1806. With life.
Poetical works. In Park's Works of the British poets vol 34, 1808.
Poems. In British poets vol 66, Chiswick 1822.
Select poems. In Sanford's Works of the British poets vol 34, Philadelphia 1822.
Anderson 11, Chalmers 17 and 21.

§ 1

Providence, or Arandus and Emilee: a poem. 1762.
Pollio: an elegiac ode. Oxford 1766; rptd in various collections.
The concubine: a poem in the manner of Spenser. Oxford 1767, London 1769, 1771, 1772, 1777 (as Sir Martyn), 1778.
A letter to Dr Harwood. 1768, 1769.
Voltaire in the shades. 1770.
The lusiad: or the discovery of India, from Camoens. Oxford 1776, 1778, 2 vols Dublin 1791, London 1798. 1 vol 1809, Philadelphia 1822, London 1877.
A candid examination of the reasons for depriving the East India company of its charter. 1779.
Almada hill: an epistle from Lisbon. Oxford 1781.
The prophecy of Queen Emma by Turgotus. 1782.
Mickle contributed to Donaldson's collection, Edinburgh 1761; Pearch's collection, 1772; Evans's Old ballads vols 2 and 4, 1777 and 1784, and European Mag 1785–8 (Fragments by Leo). For songs possibly by him see BM General Catalogue.

§ 2

Walter, F. In his La littérature portugaise en Angleterre, Paris 1927.

West, S. G. The work of Mickle, the first Anglo-Portuguese scholar. RES 10 1934.

— Cumnor Hall. MLR 29 1934. Mickle as probable author of this and other ballads in Evans's Old ballads, above.

— Mickle's translation of Os lusiadas. Revue de Littérature Comparée 18 1938.

Taylor, M. E. William Julius Mickle. Washington 1937. With bibliography.

ANNE, LADY MILLER
1741–81

§ 1

Poetical amusements at a villa near Bath. Bath 1775, 4 vols London and Bath 1776–81. Collected by Lady Miller, with her contributions.

Letters from Italy, by an English woman. 3 vols 1776–7, 2 vols 1777, 3 vols Dublin 1776.

On novelty and on trifles and triflers: poetical amusements at a villa near Bath. Bath 1778.

§ 2

Hesselgrave, R. A. Lady Miller and the Batheaston literary circle. New Haven 1927.

SIR JOHN HENRY MOORE
1756–80

The new paradise of dainty devises: consisting of original poems, by different hands. 1777, Bath 1778 (as Poetical trifles), 1778; ed E. Jerningham 1783. Moore wrote most of the poems.

Poetical works. In Park's Works of the British poets vol 41, 1808.

Poems. In British poets vol 73, Chiswick 1822. With life.

EDWARD PERRONET
1721–92

Collections

A small collection of hymns. Canterbury 1782.
Occasional verses moral and sacred. 1785.

§ 1

Select passages of the Old and New Testament versified. 1756.

The mitre: a sacred poem. [1757].

§ 2

Life. Methodist Mag 22 1799.
Julian, J. In his A dictionary of hymnology, 1907.

RICHARD POLWHELE
1760–1838

Collections

Discourses on different subjects. 2 vols 1788, [1791], 1 vol 1811.

Poems. 1788.

Poetic trifles. 1796.

Poems formerly published with some additional pieces. 2 vols 1798.

Poems. 3 vols 1806, 5 vols 1810.

Sermons: a new volume. London and Truro 1810.

Reminiscences in prose and verse. 3 vols 1836.

§ 1

The fate of Lewellyn: or the Druids' sacrifice; The genius of Carnbré. Bath 1777. Anon

An ode to Mrs Macaulay. Bath 1777.

The spirit of Fraser to General Burgoyne: an ode. 1778.

The castle of Tintagel: an ode. [?].

The isle of poplars: an ode. 1782.

The English orator: book the first. Exeter 1786; Books the second and third, [1787?]; A didactic poem in 4 books, [1789?], 1791. Bk 1 first pbd as The art of eloquence: a didactic poem, 1785.

An epistle from the Rev William M—n to William Pitt. 1785.

The follies of Oxford. 1785.

Pictures from nature, in twelve sonnets: the lock transformed. 1785, London and Exeter [1786] (19 sonnets).

The idyllia, epigrams and fragments of Theocritus, Bion and Moschus; with the elegies of Tyrtaeus. 1786, 2 vols 1789, Bath 1792, London 1810, 1811; rptd in Works of the Greek and Roman poets vol 7, 1813, and in British poets vol 92, Chiswick 1822. Tr Polwhele.

Poems, chiefly by gentlemen of Devonshire and Cornwall. 2 vols Bath 1792, 4 vols Bath 1794. Ed Polwhele.

A discourse preached at the parish church of Kenton. 1793.

Historical views of Devonshire. Vol 1, Exeter 1793. No more pbd.

The history of Devonshire. 3 vols London and Exeter 1793–1806.

Essays by a society of gentlemen at Exeter. 1796. Ed Polwhele.

The influence of local attachment: a poem. 1796, 1798, [London 1800?], 1810.

Sketches in verse with prose illustrations. 1796, 1797.

The old English gentleman: a poem. 1797.

The unsex'd females. 1798, New York 1800 (with A sketch of Peter Pindar).

Grecian prospects. 1799.

Anecdotes of Methodism. 1800.

Sir Aaron: or the flights of fanaticism. 1800.

A sermon preached at the assizes at Bodmin. Falmouth 1801.

Illustrations of scriptural characters. 1802.

History of Cornwall. 3 vols London and Falmouth 1803, 7 vols London et al 1816 (containing following 5 items). For the complicated bibliography of this work see Boase and Courtney, under § 2 below, BM General Catalogue and DNB.

A supplement to the first and second books of the History of Cornwall. London and Exeter 1804.

The civil and military history of Cornwall. London and Exeter 1806.

The history of Cornwall in respect to its population, and the health of its inhabitants. London and Truro 1806.

The language, literature and literary characters of Cornwall. 1806.

A Cornish-English vocabulary. London and Truro 1808, 1836.

The family picture, or domestic education: a poetic epistle. 1808.

The deserted village school. Edinburgh 1812.

The fair Isabel of Cotehele: a Cornish romance. London and Truro 1815.

An essay on evidence from scripture. 1819.

Lavington, G. The enthusiasm of Methodists and Papists considered. 1820. Ed Polwhele.

An essay on marriage, adultery and divorce. London and Truro 1823.

Epistle to an archdeacon. 1824.

Outlines of four sermons. 1826.

Traditions and recollections. 2 vols 1826.

Biographical sketches in Cornwall. 3 vols Truro and London 1831.

The rural rector. 3 vols 1831.

Polwhele contributed poems to various annuals: Forget-me-not, Amulet, Sacred Isis; *to* GM, *the* Anti-Jacobin, G. Henderson, Petrarcha 1803, European Mag, Br Critic, Orthodox Churchman's Mag, *His letters appear in* Nichols' Illustrations vols 3, 5, 7. *Poems appear in* E. Rack, Essays, letters and poems, Bath 1781, *and in* Bishop Wilson, Works vol 2, 1781. *See* DNB.

§ 2

Scott, W. Letters addressed to Polwhele. 1832. Ed Polwhele.

Boase, C. C. and W. P. Courtney. In their Bibliotheca cornubiensis vol 2, 1874.

SAMUEL JACKSON PRATT
1749–1814

Many of his writings pbd under the pseudonym Courtney Melmoth.

Collections

Miscellanies. 4 vols 1785.

Pity's gift, selected by a lady. 1798, 1798, 1801, 1807, 1816 (6th).

Harvest home: supplementary gleanings. 3 vols 1805.

§ 1

The tears of genius, occasioned by the death of Goldsmith. 1774, 1775 (subtitled An elegy on the favourite English poets lately deceased, imitative of the stile of each).

Liberal opinions or the history of Benignus. 6 vols 1775–7, 1777, 4 vols 1783.

The progress of painting. 1775.

Garrick's looking glass, or the art of rising on the stage: a poem. 1776.

Observations on the Night thoughts of Young. 1776.

The pupil of pleasure. 2 vols 1776, 1777, 1 vol Dublin 1781, 2 vols 1783; tr French, 1787; German, 1790.

Travels for the heart, written in France. 2 vols 1777, Dublin 1777–8; tr German, 1778.

The sublime and beautiful of scripture. 2 vols 1777, 1783.

An apology for the life and writings of Hume. 1777.

Supplement to the life of Hume. 1777, 1789. By Pratt?

The shadows of Shakespeare, a monody occasioned by the death of Garrick: being a prize poem written for the vase at Bath-Easton. Bath [1780?].

Shenstone-green: or the new Paradise lost. 3 vols 1779; tr German, 1780.

The tutor of truth. 3 vols 1779.

Emma Corbett: or the miseries of civil war. Dublin 1780, 2 vols London and Bath [1781] (3rd edn), 3 vols London and Bath [1781?], 2 vols 1783, 1789 (9th edn); tr French, 1798–9.

Sympathy: or a sketch of the social passion. 1781 (5 edns), 1782, London and Bury [1806?] (10th edn), 1807 (including landscapes in verse and cottage pictures).

The fair Circassian: a tragedy. 1781 (3 edns).

Landscapes in verse taken in spring. 1785, 1785.

The triumph of benevolence. 1786, 1786.

Humanity, or the rights of nature: a poem. 1788.

Ode on his Majesty's recovery. 1789.

The new cosmetic, or the triumph of beauty: a comedy. 1790.

Gleanings through Wales, Holland and Westphalia. 4 vols

1795, 1797–9 (3rd edn), 3 vols 1800 (5th edn), 1802; tr German, 1800.

Letter to the tars of old England. 1797 (6 edns).

Family secrets, literary and domestic. 5 vols 1797, 1798.

Letter to the British soldiers. 1797.

Our good old castle on the rock. 1797.

Almeria: or the penitent. In The life of a lady of the town, Portsea 1800, and in M. Henry's Observations on seduction, 1808.

Cottage pictures or the poor: a poem. 1801, 1803 (3rd edn).

Gleanings in England. 2 vols 1801 (2nd edn), 3 vols 1801–4 (3rd edn). Originally vol 4 of Gleanings through Wales, above.

The paternal present: being a sequel to Pity's gift. 1802, 1810, 1817.

Bread: or the poor. 1802.

John and Dame: or the loyal cottagers. 1803.

Classical poetry, for the use of schools. 1807, 1813 (8th edn), 1823. Ed W. F. Mavor and Pratt.

The cabinet of poetry. 6 vols 1808. Ed Pratt.

The contrast: a poem. 1808.

The sorrows of Werther: a new translation. 1809 (2nd edn), [1813?], Chiswick 1823.

Specimens of the poetry of Joseph Blacket. 1809. Ed Pratt.

The lower world: a poem. 1810.

The remains of Joseph Blacket. 2 vols 1811. Ed Pratt.

A brief account of Leamington spa charity. 1812, 1814 (enlarged as Local and literary account of Leamington), Birmingham 1814.

Pratt contributed to the Annual Register 1771; The Muse's mirror, ed E. Thompson 1783.

§ 2

Tompkins, J. M. S. In her Popular novel in England 1770–1800, 1932.

HENRY JAMES PYE
1745–1813

Collections

Elegies on different occasions. 1768.

Poems on various subjects. 2 vols 1787.

Sketches on various subjects, moral, literary and political. 1796.

Verse on various subjects written in the vicinity of Stoke Park. 1802.

Collected poems. 2 vols 1810.

§ 1

Gratulatio solemnis universitatis oxoniensis ob Georgium Fred Aug. Oxford 1762. Pye contributed an English poem.

Beauty: a poetical essay. 1766.

The triumph of fashion: a vision. 1771.

Faringdon hill: a poem. Oxford 1774, 1778 (with odes, elegies etc).

Six Olympic odes of Pindar. 1775; rptd in collections of Pindar, 1810, 1813, 1822.

The art of war. 1778. From the French of Frederick the Great.

Ode to harmony. [1780?].

The progress of refinement: a poem. Oxford 1783.

Shooting. 1784.

Æriphorion. 1784.

The poetic of Aristotle. 1788.

The spectre. 2 vols 1789.

Amusement: a poetical essay. 1790.

A commentary illustrating the Poetic of Aristotle by examples chiefly from the modern poets. 1792.

The siege of Meaux: a tragedy. 1794.

Xenophon's defence of the Athenian democracy, translated. 1794.
The democrat. 2 vols 1795, 1796.
The war elegies of Tyrtaeus imitated. 1795.
Lenore: a tale from Bürger. 1796, 1799.
The inquisitor: a tragedy, altered from the German. 1798. With J. P. Andrews.
Naucratia: or naval dominion. 1798.
The aristocrat. 2 vols 1799.
Adelaide: a tragedy. 1800.
Carmen seculare for the year 1800. 1800.
Alfred: an epic poem. 1801.
A long story. 1801. Gray's poem with a continuation.
A prior claim: a comedy. 1805, 1806. With S. J. Arnold.
Horace. 1806, 1809. Tr P. Francis and rev Pye, rptd in collections, 1812, 1822.
Comments on the commentators of Shakespeare. 1807.
The sportsman's dictionary: or the gentleman's companion. 1807 (5th edn, 'improved and enlarged' by Pye). First pbd 1735.
Summary of the duties of a justice of the peace out of sessions. 1808, 1817, 1827, 1827.
Hymns and epigrams of Homer. In Works of the Greek and Roman poets vol 4, 1810, and in British poets vol 84, Chiswick 1822.
Pye also pbd New Year and Birthday odes in Annual Register *1790-1813.*

§ 2

Austin, W. S. and J. Ralph. In their Lives of the Laureates, 1853.
Broadus, E. K. In his Laureateship, Oxford 1921.

JOSEPH RICHARDSON
1755-1803

See also under Rolliad, below.

Collections

Literary relics of the late Joseph Richardson. 1807. Ed his widow, with life by J. Taylor.

§ 1

The complete investigation of Mr Eden's treaty. 1787.
The Jekyll: a political eclogue by the authors of the Rolliad. 1788. By Richardson et al.
The fugitive: a comedy. 1792 (3 edns), Dublin 1792, Cork 1792, London 1793 (6th edn).
Richardson wrote for Morning Post *and* Citizen: *see* DNB.

WILLIAM HAYWARD ROBERTS
d. 1791

Collections

Poems. 1774, 1776.
Select poems. In Sanford's British poets vol 37, Philadelphia 1819.

§ 1

Arimant and Tamira: an eastern tale in the manner of Dryden's Fables. 1757.
Utrum diversarum gentium mores et instituta a diverso earum situ explicari possint? Cambridge 1758.
Elegia scripta in coemeterio rustico. 1762. With C. Anstey.
The poor man's prayer: an elegy. 1766.
A poetical essay on the existence of God: I, 1771, 1771; II, On the attributes of God, 1771, 1771; III, On the providence of God, 1771; 3 pts Belfast 1774.
A poetical epistle to Christopher Anstey on the English poets. 1773.

Judah restored: a poem. 2 vols 1774.
A sermon preached the 30th of April. [1782].
Corrections of various passages in the English Old Testament. 1794.

JAMES ROBERTSON
fl. 1768-88

Collections

Poems, consisting of tales, fables, epigrams by nobody. 1770, 1780, 1787.
Poems on several occasions. 1773.
A collection of comic songs, written, compiled and engraved by Robertson. 2 vols Edinburgh 1800, Peterborough [1805]. 2 distinct collections: *see* Bronson below.

§ 1

The heroine of love: a musical piece of three acts. York 1778.
Robertson also contributed to Evans's old ballads vol 2, 1777, Newcastle Chron 1768-75, *and* GM 1776-9: *see* Bronson, *below.*

§ 2

Bronson, B. H. Robertson: poet and playwright. MLN 49 1934.

MARY ROBINSON
1758-1800

Collections

Poems. 1775.
Poems. 2 vols 1791-3.
Lyrical tales. 1800.
Poetical works, including many pieces never before published. 3 vols 1806, 1826.

§ 1

Elegiac verses to a young lady on the death of her brother. 1775.
Captivity: a poem; and Celadon and Lydia: a tale. [1777].
The songs in the lucky escape. [1778].
The memoirs of Perdita. 1784.
Monody to the memory of Sir Joshua Reynolds. 1792.
Vancenza: or the daughters of credulity. 2 vols 1792 (3rd edn), 1810.
Modern manners: a poem, by Horace Juvenal. 1793.
Monody to the memory of the late Queen of France. 1793.
An ode to the harp of Louisa Hanway. 1793.
Sight, the Cavern of woe and Solitude. 1793.
Angelina: a novel. 3 vols 1796.
Hubert de Sevrac: a romance. 3 vols 1796.
Sappho and Phaon, in a series of legitimate sonnets. 1796, 1813.
The Sicilian lover: a tragedy. 1796.
The false friend: a domestic story. 4 vols 1799.
Letter to the women of England on the injustice of mental subordination. 1799.
The natural daughter: a novel. 2 vols 1799.
Ellinda: or the abbey of St Aubert. Newark [1800].
'Laura Maria', The mistletoe. 1800. Verse.
Picture of Palermo. 1800. Tr Mary Robinson.
Memoirs, with some posthumous pieces. Ed M. E. Robinson, her daughter 4 vols 1801, 2 vols 1803; ed J. F. Molloy 1895, 1930.
Walsingham: or the pupil of nature: a domestic story. 4 vols 1805 (2nd edn); tr French, 1798.
Effusions of love. nd.
Impartial reflections on the Queen of France. nd.
Thoughts on the condition of women. nd.
See also under Della Cruscans, below. Mrs Robinson contributed to Evans's old ballads vol 3, 1784, *and to* Morning Post *as 'Tabitha Bramble'.*

§ 2

Makower, S. V. Perdita: a romance in biography. 1908. With bibliography.

Mendenhall, J. C. Mary Robinson. Univ of Pennsylvania Lib Chron 4 1936.

Steen, M. The lost one: a biography of Mary Robinson. 1937.

THOMAS RUSSELL
1762–88

§ 1

Sonnets and miscellaneous poems. Ed W. Howley, Oxford 1789, 1789. With life.

Poetical works. In Park's Works of the British poets vol 41, 1808.

Sonnets. In Sanford's Works of the British poets vol 37, Philadelphia 1819.

Poems. In British poets vol 73, Chiswick 1822.

Poems of Cuthbert Shaw and Thomas Russell. Ed E. Partridge 1925. Reprint of 1789, above.

Russell contributed 2 essays to GM 1782-3

§ 2

The lounger's common-place book vol 3. 1805.

C. W. H. The Wykehamist. 1888.

FRANK SAYERS
1763–1817

Collections

Poems. Norwich 1792.

Disquisitions metaphysical and literary. 1793, Norwich 1808.

Nugae poeticae. 1803.

Poems containing sketches of northern mythology. Norwich 1803 (3rd edn), 1807.

Miscellanies, antiquarian and historical. Norwich 1805.

Collective works to which have been prefixed some biographical particulars by W. Taylor. 2 pts Norwich 1823.

Poetical works, to which have been prefixed the connected disquisitions on the rise and progress of poetry and biographical particulars by W. Taylor. 1830.

§ 1

Dramatic sketches of the ancient northern mythology. 1790, 2 vols 1792 (containing Ode to Pandora and a monodrama); tr German, 1793.

Sayer contributed to Quart Rev.

JOHN SCOTT OF AMWELL
1730–83

Bibliographies

Russell, N. Some uncollected authors XL: John Scott. Book Collector 14 1965.

See also Stewart, under §2, below.

Collections

Poetical works. 1782, 1786, 1795.

Critical essays on several English poets. 1785. With life by Hoole.

Poetical works. In Park's Works of the British poets vol 39, 1808.

Poems. In British poets vol 70, Chiswick 1822.

Select poems. In Sanford's Works of the British poets vol 32, Philadelphia 1822.

Anderson 11, Chalmers 17.

§ 1

Four elegies, descriptive and moral. 1760.

Elegy written at Amwell. 1769, 1769.

The constitution defended and the pensioner exposed, in remarks on the False alarm. 1770.

A digest of the present act for amendment of the highways. 1773.

Observations on the present state of the parochial and vagrant poor. 1773.

Remarks on the patriot. 1775.

Amwell: a descriptive poem. 1776, 1776, Dublin 1776.

Digests of the general highway and turnpike laws. 1778.

Moral eclogues. 1778.

A letter to the Critical reviewers. 1782.

Scott contributed to GM 1753–8, 1777–8; Pearch's collection vol 1, 1768, vols 1, 3–4, 1770; British Mag & Rev 1 1782; European Mag & London Rev 1782, 1799.

§ 2

Some memoirs of the last illness of Scott. [1784].

Johnson, S. In his Lives of the poets vol 4, 1854. Section completed by W. C. Hazlitt.

Liebert, H. Johnson's last literary project. New Haven 1948.

Stewart, L. D. Scott of Amwell. Berkeley 1956. With bibliography.

ANNA SEWARD
1742–1809

Collections

Variety: a collection of essays. 1788.

Original sonnets on various subjects, and odes paraphrased from Horace. 1799, 1799.

Poetical works. Ed W. Scott 3 vols Edinburgh 1810.

The beauties of Anna Seward. Ed W. C. Oulton 1813, 1822.

§ 1

Elegy on Captain Cook, to which is added an ode to the sun. 1780, 1780, 1781, Lichfield 1784 ('with additions').

Monody on Major Andre, Lichfield 1781, 1781.

Poem to the memory of Lady Miller. 1782.

Louisa: a poetical novel in four epistles. Lichfield 1784 (4 edns), 1792 (5th edn).

Ode on General Elliott's return from Gibraltar. 1787.

Llangollen vale, with other poems. 1796 (3 edns).

Memoirs of the life of Dr Darwin. 1804.

Memoirs of Abelard and Eloisa. 1805.

Blindness. Sheffield 1806.

Monumental inscriptions in Ashbourn church, Derbyshire. Ashbourn 1806. With B. Boothby.

Miss Seward's enigma. [1855].

Miss Seward also contributed to Lady Miller, Poetical amusements at a villa near Bath, 1775, 1776–81; F. N. C. Mundy, Needwood forest, Lichfield 1776; C. Shoot, Dramas for young ladies, Birmingham 1792.

Letters

Letters of Anna Seward written between 1784 to 1807. 6 vols Edinburgh 1811. A selection ptd in The swan of Lichfield, ed H. Pearson 1936.

The manuscripts of the Duke of Somerset and T. H. G. Puleston. 1898. Contains Seward letters.

Nicholson, C. A. The swan of Lichfield. Bookman (New York) Jan 1931.

The Tenbury letters. Ed E. H. Fellowes and E. Pine 1942. Contains a Seward letter.

Hanford, J. H. A letter from the Swan of Lichfield. Newberry Lib Bull 4 1957.

Rousseau, G. S. Anna Seward to William Hayley: a letter. Harvard Lib Bull 15 1967.

§ 2

Lucas, E. V. A swan and her friends. 1907.
Ashmun, M. The singing swan: an account of Anna Seward. New Haven 1931.
Lathwaite, P. Anna Seward and Dr Johnson. TLS 7 Jan 1932. Marginalia.
Addleshaw, S. The swan of Lichfield. Church Quart Rev 124 1937.
Pearson, H. The swan of Lichfield. Life & Letters 15 1936.
Monk, S. H. Anna Seward and the romantic poets. In Wordsworth and Coleridge: studies in honor of G. M. Harper, Princeton 1939.
Clifford, J. L. The authenticity of Anna Seward's published correspondence. MP 39 1942; rptd in Studies in the literature of the Augustan age, ed R. C. Boys, Ann Arbor 1952.
Scudder, H. H. Anna Seward and the Mathias family. N & Q 27 March 1943.
Myers, R. M. Anna Seward: an eighteenth-century Handelian. Williamsburg 1947.
Aldridge, A. O. Akenside, Anna Seward and colour. N & Q 24 Dec 1948.

CUTHBERT SHAW
1738–71
Collections

Poems on different occasions. 1776.
Poetical works. In Park's Works of the British poets vol 33, 1807.
Poems. In British poets vol 63, Chiswick 1822.
Select poems. In Sanford's Works of the British poets vol 31, Philadelphia 1822.
The poems of Cuthbert Shaw and Thomas Russell. Ed E. Partridge 1925.
Anderson 11.

§ I

Liberty. Darlington 1756.
Odes on the four seasons, by W. Seymour. Bury St Edmunds 1760.
The four farthing-candles: a satire. 1762.
The race, by Mercurius Spur esq, with notes by Faustinus Scriblerus. 1765, 1766.
Corruption: a satire. 1768.
Monody to the memory of a young lady who died in childbed, by an afflicted husband. 1768, 1769, 1770 (with An evening address to a nightingale), [1779]; Lady's Poetical Mag 3 1782. Both poems rptd in Pearch's collection vol 4, 1770.
An elegy on the death of Charles Yorke. 1770.
Contributions by Shaw appear in Freeholder's Mag 1769–70, European Mag 1786, Universal Mag 1759; *see Partridge's edn, above.*

§ 2

European Mag 1786.
Williams, I. A. London Mercury Oct 1925. Quotes from Four farthing-candles, not in Partridge's edn.

CHARLOTTE SMITH
1749–1806
Bibliographies

See Hilbish, under §2, below.

Collections

Elegiac sonnets and other essays. Chichester and London 1784, London 1784, 1786 ('with twenty additional sonnets'), 1786, Philadelphia 1787, London 1789 ('with

additional sonnets and other poems'), Dublin 1790, London 1792, Boston 1795, Worcester Mass 1795, London 1797, 1800, 1811, 1851; Elegiac sonnets and other poems vol 2, 1797, 1797, 1800, 1806, 1811.
Beachy head, with other poems. 1807. Unfinished.

§ I

Manon Lescaut. 2 vols 1785. From the French of Prévost.
The romance of real life. 3 vols 1787, Philadelphia 1799, Aberdeen 1847. Based on the French of Pitaval.
Emmeline, or the orphan of the castle: a novel. 4 vols 1788, 1788, Belfast nd, Philadelphia 1802, 3 vols Baltimore 1802; tr French, 1788.
Ethelinde: or the recluse of the lake. 5 vols 1789, 1790, 1814; tr French, 1799.
Celestina: a novel. 4 vols 1791, 3 vols Dublin 1791, 4 vols 1791, 1792, 1794; tr French, 1795.
Desmond, a novel. 3 vols 1792, 1792, 2 vols Dublin 1792; tr French, 1793.
The emigrants: a poem. 1793, Dublin 1793.
The old manor house: a novel. 4 vols 1793, 3 vols Dublin 1793, London 1810, 1820 (vols 26–7 of British novelists, with introd by Anna Barbauld), 4 vols 1822, 1878; ed A. H. Ehrenpreis, Oxford 1968.
D'Arcy: a novel. Dublin 1793, Philadelphia 1796.
The wanderings of Warwick. 1794. Suppl to Old manor house, above.
The banished man: a novel. 4 vols 1794, 3 vols 1795; tr French, 1803.
Rural walks, in dialogues for young persons. 2 vols 1795, 1796; tr French, 1799.
Montalbert: a novel. 3 vols 1795, 2 vols Dublin 1795, Philadelphia [1795?]; tr French, 1800.
Rambles farther. 2 vols 1796, 1 vol 1796, Dublin 1796, 2 vols 1800.
A narrative of the loss near Weymouth. 1796.
Marchmont: a novel. 4 vols 1796, 2 vols Dublin 1797.
Minor morals. 2 vols 1798, 1 vol 1799, 2 vols Dublin 1800, London 1816, 1825; tr French, 1812.
The young philosopher: a novel. 1798, 2 vols 1798; tr French, 1799.
What is she?: a comedy. 1799, Dublin 1799, London 1799, 1800; rptd in collections.
Letters of a solitary wanderer. 2 vols 1799, 5 vols 1800–2, 1801; tr French, 1799–1819 (various parts).
Conversations introducing poetry, for the use of children. 2 vols 1804, 1819, 1 vol Edinburgh and London 1863.
History of England, in a series of letters to a young lady. 3 vols 1806. Vols 1–2 by Charlotte Smith.
The natural history of birds. 2 vols 1807, 1819.

§ 2

Scott, W. In his Miscellaneous prose works vol 4, Edinburgh 1853.
Foster, J. R. Charlotte Smith, pre-romantic novelist. PMLA 43 1928.
Hilbish, F. M. A. Charlotte Smith, poet and novelist. Philadelphia 1941. With bibliography.
McKillop, A. D. Charlotte Smith's letters. HLQ 15 1952.

ANNE STEELE
1717–78

Poems on subjects chiefly devotional by Theodosia. 2 vols 1760; ed C. Evans 3 vols Bristol 1780 (with added vol as Miscellaneous pieces in verse and prose by Theodosia).
Works. 2 vols Boston 1808.
A summer journey in the west. New York 1841.
Hymns, psalms and poems, with memoir by John Sheppard. 1863, 1882.

JOHN HALL STEVENSON
1717-85
Collections

Makarony fables; Fables for grown gentlemen; Lyrick epistles; and other poems. Dublin 1772.
Crazy tales. 1762, 1764, 1769, 1780 (with Fables for grown gentlemen), 1825 ('by the late R. B. Sheridan'), 1894.
Works, corrected and enlarged, with several original poems. 3 vols 1795.

§ 1

Hymn to Miss Lawrence in the Pump-room at Bath. 1755.
A nosegay and a similie for the reviewers: a lyric epistle. 1760.
Two lyric epistles: one to my cousin Shandy on his coming to town and the other to the grown gentlewomen the Misses of ***. 1760.
Fables for grown gentlemen. 1761, 1762; Part II, 1770 ('for the year 1770').
Two lyric epistles on Margery the cook maid to the Critical Review. 1762.
A pastoral cordial preached before their Graces N[ew-castle and D[evonshire]. 1763, 1763.
A pastoral puke: a second sermon preached before the Whigs. 1764, 1764.
The sick monkey: a fable. 1765. Attributed by Horace Walpole.
Makarony fables, with the new fable of the bees, by Cosmo. 1768 (3 edns).
A sentimental dialogue between an English lady and an Irish gentleman. 1768.
Lyric consolations, with the speech of Alderman W—. 1769.
A sentimental journey through France and Italy, by Mr Yorick continued by Eugenius. 4 vols 1769, 1782, 1784, 1784, 1790, 1791, 1792.
An essay upon the King's friends, to Dr S—l J—n. 1776.
Moral tales: a Christmas night's entertainment, by Lady —. 1783, 1783.

§ 2

Cooper, W. D. Seven letters by Sterne and his friends. 1844.
See also under Sterne, col 948, below.

WILLIAM STEVENSON
1730?-83
Collections

Original poems on several subjects. 2 vols London and Edinburgh 1765.

§ 1

A method of treating the gout by blistering. Bath 1779.
An ode to peace. 1780.
Cases in medicine. Newark and Retford 1781, 1782.
An hymn to the deity. 1782.
Candid animadversions on Dr Lee's narrative; Strictures on Royal medical colleges: a summary opinion of influenza. Newark 1782.
A reply to a letter by E. Harrison. Newark 1782.
The English museum. Newark 1782-3. Ed Stevenson.
Considerations on the dangerous effects of blood-letting and drugs. 1783.
Expostulations on medical topics. Newark 1783.

§ 2

Wallis, P. J. Stevenson: a reforming physician poet. N & Q May 1953. With bibliography which lists untraced pbns.

PERCIVAL STOCKDALE
1736-1811
Collections

Six discourses. 1777.
Miscellanies in prose and verse. 1778.
Sermons on important and interesting subjects. 1784.
Poems. 2 vols 1808.

§ 1

A poetical address to the supreme being. Berwick [1764].
Churchill defended: a poem. 1765.
The constituents: a poem. 1765.
The Amyntas of Tasso, translated from the Italian. 1770.
Bos, L., Antiquities of Greece. 1772. Tr Stockdale.
The works of Waller, with the life of the author. 1772. Life by Stockdale.
The poet: a poem. 1773, 1773.
Three discourses, two against luxury and dissipation, one on universal benevolence. 1773.
Sabbathier, F., The institutions of the ancient nations. 2 vols 1776. Tr Stockdale.
An inquiry into the nature and genuine laws of poetry. 1778.
Riccobini, M. J., Letters from Rivers to Cardigan. 2 vols 1778. Tr Stockdale.
An examination of the question whether education, at a school or by private tuition, is preferable? 1782.
An essay on misanthropy. Berwick and London 1783.
Three poems: I, Siddons; II, A poetical epistle to Lever; III, An elegy on a young officer. 1784.
A sermon after the funeral of T. Knipe. Alnwick [1785].
Ximenes: a tragedy. 1788.
A letter to Sharp, suggested by the insurrection of the negroes. Durham [1791].
Thirteen sermons to seamen. 1791.
Observations on the writing and conduct of our reformers. 1792.
Poetical thoughts and views on the banks of the Wear. Durham [1792].
Two farewell letters. 1792.
Thomson, James, The seasons. 1793, 1794. Ed Stockdale.
A letter to Mr Bryant on Pope's Universal prayer. 1793.
A letter on the liberty of the press. 1794.
Poems by the late S. M. Oram. 1794. Ed Stockdale.
The invincible island: a poem. 1797.
The naval first of August. Durham 1798.
A discourse on the duties and advantages of old age. Alnwick 1801.
The reply of English truth to French gasconade. Alnwick 1801.
A remonstrance against inhumanity to animals. Alnwick 1802.
An epitaph on a very pretty and most amiable cat. Lesbury 1803.
To Mr Porter on his proposals to paint some of our principal achievements during the late war. Lesbury 1803.
A poetical tribute to Lord Nelson. Lesbury 1806.
An epitaph on Mr Pitt. Lesbury 1806.
Lectures on the truly eminent English poets. 2 vols 1809.
Stockdale edited Universal Mag *from 1771, was an editor of* Critical Rev, *contributed to* The Muse's mirror, ed E. Thompson 1783, *and contributed the* Agricola essays to Public Advertiser 1779.

Letters

Letters between Shute Bishop of Durham and Stockdale. 1792. Ed Stockdale.
A letter to P.S. on his pretended correspondence with the Bishop of Durham. 1792.

§2

D'Israeli, I. In his Calamities of authors, 1812.
Fitzgerald, E. Stockdale and Baldock Black Horse. Bibelot 10 1925.

EDWARD THOMPSON
1738?–86
Collections
The Court of Cupid. 2 vols 1770. Collected poems.

§1

The meretriciad. 1761 (2nd edn), 1763 (4th edn), 1765 (6th edn).
The temple of Venus: a gentle satire on the times: I. 1763; II, 1763.
The soldier: a poem to General Conway. 1764.
The courtezan. 1765 (3 edns).
The demi-rep. 1766.
Cooper's well. 1767. Parody of Denham, Coopers hill.
Sailor's letters written to his select friends in England. 2 vols 1767 (2nd edn).
Trinculo's trip to the jubilee. 1769.
The compositions in prose and verse of John Oldham. 3 vols 1770. Ed Thompson.
The fair Quaker, written by Mr Charles Shadwell and altered. 1773, 1775.
The case of the widows of the officers of the navy. 1775.
The works of Andrew Marvell. 3 vols 1776. Ed Thompson.
The syrens: a masque. 1776; Airs and choruses, 1776.
The seraglio: a comic poem. 1776.
The Muse's mirror: being a collection of poems. 2 vols 1777, 1783. Ed Thompson.
Paul Whitehead: poems and miscellaneous compositions and his life. 1777.
Bell Montè, or the misfortunes of Anna D'Arfet: a nautic poem. 1784.

§2

Johnson's Lives of the poets vol 4. Ed P. Cunningham 1854.
Thompson, K. F. Poet Thompson of the navy. N & Q July 1954.

BONNELL THORNTON
1724–68
§1

An ode on Saint Cecilia's day, adapted to the ancient British musick. 1749, 1763, 1767 (in Mendez's collection), nd (with Cibber's Capochio and Dorinna), nd (as Timotheus: a burlesque ode).
Catalogue: exhibition of the society of sign painters. 1754.
Poems by the most eminent ladies of Great Britain. 2 vols 1755, 1773, 1780. Ed with G. Colman.
City Latin: or remarks on the inscription of the intended new bridge. 1760, 1761.
Plain English in answer to City Latin. 1761.
Comedies of Plautus translated into familiar blank verse. 2 vols 1767, 1769, 5 vols 1774 (completed by R. Warner). With the elder Colman.
The battle of the wigs: an additional canto to Garth's Dispensary. 1768.
Thornton was sole or joint editor of Student: or the [Oxford] & Cambridge Monthly Miscellany, Oxford 1750–1; Have at You All: or the Drury Lane Jnl 16 Jan–9 April 1752; Spring-garden Jnl 16 Nov–7 Dec 1752; Con-

noisseur 31 Jan 1754–30 Sept 1756, 4 vols 1757 (3rd edn); St James's Chron 1761–2 (selections printed as Yearly chronicle for 1761); *and* Midwife 1750–5. *He contributed to* Adventurer 1751–2 (*8 essays signed A*) *and* St James Mag 1762. *See Brown, under* §2, *below*.

§2

McKillop, A. D. Thornton's burlesque ode. N & Q 23 July 1949. Reply by P. A. Scholes 29 Oct 1949.
Liebert, H. W, Whose book? Yale Univ Lib Gazette 27 1953. Reviews of Churchill by Thornton identified.
Brown, W. C. A belated Augustan. PQ 34 1955.
Ryskamp, C. Arne's music for Thornton's burlesque ode. N & Q Feb 1957.

RICHARD TICKELL
1751–93

See also Rolliad (*on Tickell's contributions to which, see* Butterfield's edn of Anticipation, *below*).

§1

Anticipation: containing the substance of his M—ty's most gracious speech. 1779 (9 edns), Dublin 1778, Philadelphia 1779, New York 1779, London 1780, 1794; ed L. H. Butterfield, New York 1942 (with bibliography).
The project: a poem. 1778 (4 edns), 1779, 1780; rptd in The new foundling hospital for wit vol 1, 1786.
The wreath of fashion: or the art of sentimental poetry. 1778 (4 edns), [1778 or 1779], Dublin 1779, London 1780; rptd in The new foundling hospital for wit vol 1, 1786 etc.
Epistle from Charles Fox, partridge-shooting, to John Townshend, cruising. 1779, 1779, Dublin 1779, London 1780; rptd in The new foundling hospital for wit vol 1, 1786.
The green box of Monsieur de Sartine. 1779 (5 edns), Dublin 1779; tr French by Tickell, 1779 etc. *See* Butterfield's edn of Anticipation, above.
Common-place arguments against administration with obvious answers. 1780 (4 edns), Dublin 1780.
Songs etc in the comic opera of the Carnival of Venice. 1781.
The select songs of the Gentle shepherd. 1781. Alteration of Ramsay's pastoral.
R. Griffith, Variety: a comedy. 1782. Prologue by Tickell.
Remarks on the commutation act. 1785 (4 edns).
A woollen draper's letter on the French treaty. 1786, 1786.
The people's answer to the Court pamphlet. 1787 (5 edns), Dublin 1787.
J. Richardson, The fugitive: a comedy. 1792. Prologue by Tickell.

JOHN TWEDDELL
1769–99
§1

Prolusiones juveniles. 1793.
Remains of Tweddell. 1815, 1816 (with An appendix and Addenda). Life by R. Tweddell.

§2

Hunt, P. A narrative respecting the literary remains of Tweddell. 1816.
'Paston, George' (E. M. Symonds). The romance of Tweddell. In her Little memoirs of the eighteenth century, 1901.

JOSEPH WARTON
1722–1800
Collections

Odes on various subjects. 1746, 1747.
Poetical works. In Park's Works of the British poets vol 37, 1805.
Poems. In British poets vol 68, Chiswick 1822.
Select poems. In Sanford's Works of the British poets vol 34, Philadelphia 1822.
The three Wartons: a choice of their verse. Ed E. Partridge 1927.
Chalmers 18.

§ I

The enthusiast: or the lover of nature. 1744.
Ranelagh house: a satire in prose. 1747.
T. Warton, Poems on several occasions. 1748. By the elder T. Warton, ed J. Warton.
An ode occasioned by reading West's translation of Pindar. 1749.
An ode to evening. 1749. English and Latin.
The works of Virgil in Latin and English. 4 vols 1753, 1763, 1778, 1 vol 1788. Eclogues, Georgics and notes throughout by Warton.
An essay on the writings and genius of Pope. I, 1756, 1762, Dublin 1764, London 1772, 1782, 1782, 1786; II, 1782, 1782; 2 vols 1806; tr German, 1763.
Sidney's Defence of poetry. 1787. Ed Warton.
The works of Pope, with notes and illustrations by J. Warton and others. 9 vols 1797, Basle 1803.
The adventurer nos 127 and 133 1754; ed E. N. Hooker, Los Angeles 1946 (with other essays on wit) (Augustan Reprint Soc).
Warton contributed 2 odes to his father's Poems on several occasions, 1748, *and miscellaneous verse to* Dodsley's museum vol 6, 1746, Dodsley's collection 3–4 1748, 1755, Pearch's collection vol 2, 1768, Adventurer 1752–4 (*24 essays*), World 1753 (*one essay*).

Letters

Sadler, E. A. Warton to Hayley. N & Q 4 April 1942.

§ 2

Wooll, J. Biographical memoirs of Warton, [with] a selection from his works and literary correspondence. Vol I (all pbd), 1806.
Gosse, E. Two pioneers of romanticism, Joseph and Thomas Warton. Proc Br Acad 7 1919.
Morley, E. J. Joseph Warton: a comparison of his essay on Pope with his edition. E & S 9 1924.
Smith, A. L. The primitivism of Warton. MLN 42 1927.
Martin, B. Some unpublished Wartoniana. SP 29 1932.
MacClintock, W. D. Warton's Essay on Pope: a history of the five editions. Chapel Hill 1933.
Trowbridge, H. Warton's classification of English poets. MLN 51 1936.
— Warton on the imagination. MP 35 1937.
Scheffer, J. D. A note on Warton and Voltaire. Bull of Citadel 7 1940.
Stern, B. H. In his Rise of romantic Hellenism, Menasha 1940.
Leedy, P. F. Genres criticism and Warton's Essay on Pope. JEGP 45 1946.
Kinsley, J. The publication of Warton's Essay on Pope. MLR 44 1949.
Baine, R. M. The first anthologies of English literary criticism. SB 3 1951.
Allison, J. Warton's reply to Johnson's Lives. JEGP 51 1952.
— Mrs Thrale's marginalia in Warton's Essay. HLQ 19 1956.

McKillop, A. D. Shaftesbury in Warton's Enthusiast. MLN 70 1955.
Schick, G. B. Delay in publication of the second volume of Warton's Essay on Pope. N & Q Feb 1955.
— Kind hints to John Nichols, by Joseph Warton and others. N & Q Feb 1956.
— Warton's conceptions of the true poet. Boston Univ Stud in Eng 3 1957.
— Warton's critical essays in his Virgil. N & Q July 1961.
Fenner, A. The Wartons romanticize their verse. SP 53 1956.
Hysham, J. Warton's reputation as a poet. Stud in Romanticism 1 1962.
Griffith, P. M. Warton's criticism of Shakespeare. Tulane Stud in Eng 14 1965.
Pittock, J. Warton and his second volume of the Essay on Pope. RES new ser 18 1967.

THOMAS WARTON the younger
1728–90
Collections

Poems: a new edition. 1777, 1777, 1779, [1789], 1791 (as Poems on various subjects).
Poetical works. Ed R. Mant 2 vols Oxford 1802. With memoir.
Poetical works. Ed T. Park 1805; also in Park's Works of the British poets vol 39, 1805, 1808.
Poems. In British poets vol 68, Chiswick 1822.
Select poems. In Sanford's Works of the British poets vol 34, Philadelphia 1822.
Poems of Gray, Parnell, Collins, Green and T. Warton. Ed R. A. Willmott 1854, 1883.
Poetical works of Goldsmith, Collins and T. Warton. Ed G. Gilfillan, Edinburgh 1854, 1874.
The three Wartons: a choice of their verse. Ed E. Partridge 1927.
Anderson 11; Chalmers 18.

§ I

Five pastoral eclogues. 1745. Attributed to Warton.
The pleasures of melancholy. 1747.
The triumphs of Isis. [1749], 1750, 1750; rptd Dodsley's collection vol 1, 1768.
A description of Winchester. [1750], 1760. See also T. Warton's Notes and corrections to his history of Winchester, Middle Hill [1857].
Newmarket: a satire. 1751.
Ode for music as performed at Oxford 1751. Oxford [1751].
The Union: or select Scots and English poems. Edinburgh 1753, London 1759, Dublin 1761, Oxford 1796. Ed Warton.
Observations on the Fairy Queen. 1754, 2 vols 1762, 1807.
Inscriptionum romanarum metricarum delectus. [1758]. Ed Warton.
A companion to the guide and a guide to the companion: a supplement to all accounts of Oxford. [1760?], [1762?], [1770?], Oxford 1806.
Mons Catharinae prope Wintoniani: poema. Oxford 1774.
The life and literary remains of Ralph Bathurst. 2 vols 1761.
The Oxford sausage: or select poetical pieces. 1764, Dublin 1766, Oxford 1772, 1777, 1804, London 1814, 1815, Oxford 1821, London 1822. Ed Warton.
Anthologiae Graecae à Constantino Cephala conditae libri tres. Oxford 1766. Ed Warton.
Theocriti Syracusii quae supersunt. 2 vols Oxford 1770.
The life of Sir Tho Pope. 1772, 1780, 1784.

The history of English poetry. 3 vols 1774–81 (2nd edn
of vol 1, 1775); ed R. Price 4 vols 1824, 3 vols 1840, 1 vol
1870 (rptd from 1st); ed W. C. Hazlitt 4 vols 1871,
[1872], [1875] (rptd from 1st). 88 pp. of unfinished vol 4
were ptd without title-page or date [1789?].

Specimen of the history of Oxfordshire. 1781, 1783 (as A
history of Kidlington), 1815.

An enquiry into the authenticity of the poems attributed to
Rowley. 1782, 1782.

Verses on Reynolds's painted window at Oxford. [1782],
1783, Oxford 1930, London 1932.

Milton, Poems upon several occasions. 1785, 1791. Ed
Warton.

Verses left under a stone. [1790?].

Milton, Comus. 1799. With essay by Warton.

Essays on gothic architecture, by T. Warton [et al]. 1800,
1802, 1808.

Satires of Joseph Hall, with the illustrations of Thomas
Warton. Chiswick 1824.

The hamlet: an ode. 1859, 1876.

A history of English poetry: an unpublished continuation.
Ed R. M. Baine, Los Angeles 1953 (Augustan Reprint
Soc).

The cestus: a mask. Ed T. B. Stroup, Gainesville 1961.
Warton possibly concerned in this piece.

Warton contributed verse to Joseph Warton, Odes on
various subjects, 1746; Dodsley's museum 1746–7;
Student 1750–1; Union 1753; Dodsley's collection vols
4, 6, 1755, 1758; the Oxford collections of 1751, 1761,
1762; The poetical calendar vols 2, 10, 1763; The
Oxford sausage 1764; Pearch's collection vol 1, 1768; J.
Warton, Poems original and translated, Salisbury 1794.
He wrote 3 papers for Idler 1758–60.

Letters

Dennis, L. The text of the Percy-Warton letters. PMLA
46 1931. Addns and corrections by I. L. Churchill 48
1933.

Correspondence of Percy and Warton. Ed M. G. Robinson and L. Dennis, Baton Rouge 1951. Vol 3 of Percy
letters, ed D. N. Smith and C. Brooks.

§ 2

[Ritson, J.] Observations on the History of English
poetry. 1782.

Dennis, J. The Wartons. In his Studies in English literature, 1876.

Ward, T. H. In English poets vol 3, 1880.

Cory, H. E. In his Critics of Spenser, Berkeley 1911.

Ker, W. P. Thomas Warton. Proc Br Acad 4 1912; rptd
in his Collected essays vol 1, 1925.

Gosse, E. Two pioneers of romanticism. Proc Br Acad 7
1919.

— The Oxford sausage. In his Selected essays vol 1,
1925.

Rinaker, C. Thomas Warton: a biographical and critical
study. Urbana 1916. With bibliography.

Broadus, E. K. In his Laureateship, Oxford 1921.

Havens, R. D. In his Influence of Milton, Cambridge
Mass 1922.

— Thomas Warton and the 18th-century dilemma. SP
25 1928; rptd in Studies in the literature of the Augustan
age, ed R. C. Boys, Ann Arbor 1952.

Woodhouse, A. S. P. Warton and the Ode to horror. TLS
24 Jan 1929. Reply by P. Parker 7 March 1929; Woodhouse 23 May 1929.

Smith, D. N. Warton's History of English poetry. Proc
Br Acad 15 1932.

— Warton's miscellany: the Union. RES 19 1943.

Hinton, P. Warton's poems. TLS 24 April 1930.

Martin, B. Some unpublished Wartoniana. SP 29 1932.

Martin, L. C. Thomas Warton and the early poems of
Milton. Proc Br Acad 20 1934.

Watkin-Jones, A. Percy, Warton and Chatterton's
Rowley poems. PMLA 50 1935.

Miller, F. S. Did Thomas Warton borrow from himself?
MLN 51 1936.

— The historic sense of Warton. ELH 5 1938.

Reid, M. J. C. In his Arthurian legend, Edinburgh
1938.

Vincent, H. P. Warton's last words on Rowley. MLR 24
1939. Correction by G. Tillotson 25 1940.

Wilson, R. H. Reed and Warton on the Old wive's tale.
PMLA 55 1940.

Montague, E. Hurd's association with Warton. Stanford
1941.

Whiting, B. J. Emerson, Chaucer and Warton. Amer Lit
17 1946.

Blakiston, J. M. G. A Dublin reprint of Warton's
History of English poetry. Library 5th ser 1 1946.

Mish, C. C. The waking mans dreame. TLS 28 Dec
1951.

Cunningham, J. S. Warton and Collins. Durham Univ
Jnl 46 1953.

McAdam, E. L. Johnson, Percy and Warton. PMLA 70
1955.

Fenner, A. J. The Wartons romanticize their verse. SP
53 1956.

Kinghorn, A. M. Warton's History and early English
poetry. E Studies 14 1963.

THOMAS SEDGWICK WHALLEY
1746-1828
Collections

Poems and translations. [1797].

§ 1

Edwy and Edilsa: a tale. 1779, 1794.

The castle of Montval: a tragedy. 1781, 1799, 1799.

The fatal kiss: a poem written in the last stage of an
atrophy by a beautiful young lady. 1781.

Verses addressed to Mrs Siddons. 1782.

Mont Blanc: an irregular epic. Bath 1788.

Animadversions on the curate of Blagdon's three publications. 1802.

Kenneth and Fenella: a legendary tale. 1809.

Letters and Diaries

Journals and correspondence. Ed H. Wickham 2 vols
1863. With memoir.

SAMUEL WHYTE
1733-1811
Collections

The shamrock, or Hibernian cresses: a collection. Dublin
1772.

A collection of poems, selected from the Shamrock. 1773,
1774.

A collection of poems on various subjects. Dublin 1792
(2nd edn), Dublin 1795 (as Poems on various subjects).

A miscellany containing remarks on Boswell's Johnson.
Dublin 1799, 1800 (as Miscellanea nova), 1801. With
E. A. Whyte.

§ 1

J. Burgh, The art of speaking. Dublin 1763. Ed Whyte.

The mourners: a sketch from life in memory of Charles
Manners. Dublin 1787.

The theatre: a didactic essay. Dublin 1790. Poem.

Treatise on the English language. 1800 (ptd 1761).

Whyte also pbd various educational books; see DNB.

§ 2

O'Donoghue, D. J. In his Poets of Ireland, 1912.
Hook, J. N. Three imitations of Spenser. MLN 55 1940.
Alspach, R. K. A Dublin Milton enthusiast. MLN 56 1941.

WILLIAM WILKIE
1721–72

Collections

Select poems. In Park's Works of the British poets vol 5, 1809.
Poems. In British poets vol 71, Chiswick 1822.
Anderson 11, Chalmers 18.

§ 1

The epigoniad: a poem. Edinburgh 1757, 1769.
Fables in verse. 1768; tr French, 1802.

§ 2

A critical essay on the Epigoniad. Edinburgh 1757.
Mossner, E. C. The forgotten Hume. New York 1943.

HELEN MARIA WILLIAMS
1762–1827

Collections

Poems. 2 vols 1786, 1791; tr French, 1808 (selection).
Poems on various subjects, with introductory remarks on France. 1823.

§ 1

Edwin and Eltruda: a legendary tale. 1782; rptd in Evans's old ballads vol 4, 1784.
An ode on the peace. 1783.
Peru: a poem. 1784.
Ode to peace. [1786?].
A poem on the bill lately passed for regulating the slave trade. 1788.
Julia: a novel, interspersed with poetical pieces. 2 vols 1790.
Letters written in France in the summer of 1790. 1790; tr French, 1791.
Letters on the French Revolution. 1790, Boston 1791, 2 vols 1792, 1796 (5th edn), Dublin 1802.
A farewell for two years to England. 1791.
Letters containing a sketch of the politics of France from May 1793 till July 1794. 2 vols Dublin 1794, London 1795, 3 vols Dublin 1796, 4 vols 1796; tr French, 1795.
J. H. B. de St Pierre, Paul and Virginia. Paris 1795, London 1796, 1799 (4th edn), [1800?], 1802, Edinburgh 1806, London 1814 (9th edn), Glasgow 1818, London 1819, Edinburgh 1820, London 1821 etc. Tr H. M. Williams.
Sonnets. In Poems moral, elegant and pathetic, 1796, 1803.
A tour in Switzerland. 2 vols 1798, Dublin 1798.
Sketches of the state of manners and opinions in the French republic in a series of letters. 3 vols 1801.
The history of Perourou. Dublin 1801, Edinburgh [1810]. Tr H. M. Williams.
The political and confidential correspondence of Lewis the sixteenth. 3 vols 1803.
Verses addressed to her two nephews. Paris 1809.
F. H. A. von Humboldt. Personal narrative of travels to the equinoctial regions of the new continent. 7 vols 1814–29. Tr H. M. Williams.
Researches concerning the institutions and monuments of the ancient inhabitants of America. 2 vols 1814. Tr H. M. Williams.

A narrative of the events in France from March 1815. 1815, 1816.
On the late persecution of the Protestants in the south of France. 1816.
J. de Maistre, The leper of the city of Aoste. 1817. Tr H. M. Williams.
The charter: lines addressed to her nephew. Paris 1819.
Letters on the events in France since the restoration in 1815. 1819.
Souvenirs de la révolution française. Paris 1827. Tr C. Coquerel.
Four new letters of Mary Wollstonecraft and Helen M. Williams. Ed B. P. Kurtz and C. C. Autry, Berkeley 1937.

§ 2

Moleville, A. F. B. de. A refutation of the libel on the late King of France. 1804.
Alger, J. E. In his Englishmen in the French Revolution, 1889.
Woodward, L. D. Une anglaise amie de la révolution française. Paris 1930.

JOHN WILLIAMS, 'ANTHONY PASQUIN'
1761–1818

Collections

Poems. 2 vols [1789], [1789].
Satires and biography. [1800].

§ 1

The children of Thespis, a poem: part first. 1786, 1786, Dublin 1786; Second part, 1787, Dublin 1787, London 1788; Third part, 1788, 1788; Three parts, 1792 (13th edn).
The lamentations of Edmund the Martyr: a poem. 1786.
The royal academicians: a farce. [1786], [1786].
The tears of Ierne: an elegiac poem upon the Duke of Rutland. 1787.
A poetical epistle from Gabrielle d'Estrees. Birmingham 1788.
A postscript to the new Bath guide. 1790.
The life and adventures of John Edwin, comedian, by an old croney. 1791, 2 vols [1791] (as The eccentricities of Edwin), Dublin 1791.
A treatise on cribbage. 1791, 1807.
Authentic memoirs of Warren Hastings. 1793.
The life of the Earl of Barrymore. 1793 (3 edns), Dublin [1794].
A serio-comic and admonitory epistle to a certain priest. [1793]. With other poems.
A crying epistle from Britannia to Col Mack. 1794.
A liberal critique on the exhibition of the Royal Academy. 1794.
Shrove Tuesday: a satiric rhapsody. 1791, [1794].
Legislative biography. 1795.
The curate of Elmwood: a tale. 1795.
An authentic history of the professors of painting, sculpture and architecture. [1796].
A critical guide to the exhibition of the Royal Academy for 1796. 1796.
Memoirs of the Royal Academicians. 1796.
The new Brighton guide. 1796 (6 edns).
The pin-basket, to the children of Thespis: a satire. 1796, 1797.
A looking glass for the royal family. 1797.
A touchstone to the present exhibition. 1797.
A critical guide to the present exhibition. 1797.
The Hamiltoniad. Boston 1804, New York 1866.
The life of Alexander Hamilton. Boston 1804, New York 1866.

Williams edited several Dublin periodicals c. 1781-4, Morning Herald 1784, Brighton guide, Federalist, New York c. 1800, Dramatic censor 1811; see DNB.

§ 2

Harper, J. A. Pasquin's Children of Thespis. N & Q 6 July 1861.

JOHN WOLCOT, 'PETER PINDAR'
1738-1819
Collections

Works. Dublin 1788, 1791, 2 vols 1792, Dublin 1792, 3 vols Dublin 1792, 4 vols 1794-6, 1809, 5 vols 1812, 4 vols 1816, 1 vol 1824, [1856].

The beauties of Pindar 1807, [1834?]. (2 different selections).

Hunt, J. H. P. Selections from Wolcot with critical notice. 1890.

Wolcot's various poems were bound together with general title-pages in one or 2 vols variously between 1790 and 1800. Besides the genuine issues there were many pirated edns. His pseudonym was usurped by several other satirists, most notably by C. F. Lawler; see BM General Catalogue.

§ I

Persian love elegies. Kingston Jamaica 1773. With another poem.

A poetical, supplicating, modest and affecting epistle to the reviewers. 1778, 1787, 1789.

Poems on various subjects. 1778.

Lyric odes to the Royal Academicians. 1782, 1784, 1786, 1787 (5th edn), 1787, 1788, 1790.

More lyric odes to the Royal Academicians. 1783, 1786 (3rd edn), 1789 (5th edn).

Lyric odes for the year 1785. 1785, 1786, 1787 (7th edn), 1791.

The lousiad: an heroi-comic poem. Canto I, 1785, 1786, 1786 (6th edn), 1787, 1788 (9th edn); Canto II, 1787, 1787, 1788, 1788 (6th edn); Canto III, 1791, Dublin 1791; Canto IV, 1792; Canto V and last, 1795, 1795; Cantos I-V, Paris [c. 1820]; tr Welsh, 1836. Edns variously combined.

Farewell odes for the year 1786. 1786 (4 edns), 1788 (5th edn).

Bozzy and Piozzi, or the British biographers: a town eclogue. 1786 (6 edns), Dublin 1786, London 1788 (9th-10th edn).

A poetical and congratulatory epistle to James Boswell. 1786 (5 edns), Dublin 1786, London 1787, 1788 (8th edn), 1789 (10th edn).

A congratulatory epistle to Peter Pindar. 1787.

Ode upon ode: or a peep at St James's. 1787 (7 edns), 1789 (9th edn).

An apologetic postscript to Ode upon ode. 1787, 1788.

Instructions to a celebrated laureat. 1787 (4 edns), 1788 (7th edn), 1790.

Brother Peter to brother Tom [Warton]: an expostulatory epistle. 1788 (3 edns), 1789 (5th edn).

Peter's pension: a solemn epistle to a sublime personage. 1788 (4 edns), 1792.

Peter's prophecy: or the president and poet. 1788.

Sir Joseph Banks and the Emperor of Morocco. 1788 (4 edns).

Tales and fables. 1788.

Expostulatory odes to a great Duke and a little lord. 1789, 1789.

Lyric odes to the academicians and subjects for painters. 1789, 1789, 1793.

A poetical epistle to a falling minister. 1789, 1789.

A benevolent epistle to Sylvanus Urban, alias John Nichols. 1790, 1790. With 2 other poems.

A complimentary epistle to James Bruce. 1790 (3 edns).

Advice to the future laureat: an ode. 1790, 1790, Dublin 1790.

Epistle to John Nichols. 1790, 1790.

A letter to the most insolent man alive. 1790.

The remonstrance; to which is added an ode to my ass. 1791, 1791, [Dublin? 1791?]. With other poems.

Odes to Mr Paine author of Rights of man. 1791, 1791.

The rights of Kings: or loyal odes to disloyal Academicians. 1791, 1791.

A commiserating epistle to James Lowther. 1791, 1791.

A pair of lyric epistles to Lord Macartney and his ship. 1792, 1792.

Odes of importance. 1792, 1792.

More money: or odes of instruction to Mr Pitt. 1792, 1792, Dublin 1792.

The tears of St Margaret. 1792, 1792, Dublin 1792. With other poems.

Odes to Kien Long. 1792, 1792. With other poems.

The captive King. [1793?]. Song on Louis XVI.

A poetical, serious and possibly impertinent epistle to the Pope. 1792. With odes.

Pindariana. 1794.

Celebration, or the academic procession to St James's: an ode. 1794.

Pathetic odes. 1794.

Hair powder: a plaintive epistle to Pitt. 1795, 1795. With another poem.

The convention bill: an ode. 1795.

Liberty's last squeak. 1795, Dublin 1796. With several poems.

The royal tour and Weymouth amusements. 1795, 1795, Dublin 1796. With other poems.

The royal visit to Exeter. 1795.

The cap: a satiric poem. [1795?].

An admirable satire on Burke's defense of his pension. 1796.

One thousand seven hundred and ninety-six. 1797.

An ode to the livery of London. 1797.

Picturesque views with poetical allusions. 1797. With engravings by Alken.

Tales of the Hoy: part the first. [1798?], 1798 (4th edn).

Nil admirari: or a smile at a bishop. 1799, 1799.

Pilkington's dictionary of painters. 1799. Ed Wolcot.

Lord Auckland's triumph: or the death of crim con. 1800. With other poems.

Odes to ins and outs. 1801, 1801.

Out at last. 1801 ('new edition'), 1801 (6th edn).

A poetical epistle to Count Rumford. 1801, 1801.

Tears and smiles. 1801, Baltimore 1802, Philadelphia 1802. Collection.

Epistle to James Lowther. 1802, 1802.

'P. Hamlin', The horrors of bribery. 1802, 1802. By Wolcot.

Pitt and his statue. 1802.

The island of innocence. 1802, 1802.

The Middlesex election. 1802, 1802.

Great cry and little wool: I, 1804, 1804; II, 1804.

An instructive epistle to the Lord Mayor. 1804.

The beauties of English poetry, selected by Dr Wolcot. 2 vols 1804. With new poems by Wolcot.

Tristia: or the sorrows of Peter. 1806.

One more peep at the Royal Academy. 1808.

The fall of Portugal, or the royal exiles: a tragedy. 1808. By Wolcot?

A solemn epistle to Mrs Clarke. 1809.

Epistle the second to Mrs Clarke. 1809.

Picture of Margate. 1809. With ode by Wolcot.

Carlton House fete: or the disappointed bard, in a series of elegies. 1811.

An address to be spoken at the opening of Drury Lane theatre by Peter Puncheon. 1813.

The Regent and the King. 1814.

Royalty fogbound. 1814.
Tom Halliard: a ballad. Penrith [1815?]. With 2 more poems.
A most solemn epistle to the Emperor of China. 1817.
Mabbott, T. O. A poem by John Wolcot. N & Q 7 Aug 1937; rptd 6 Sept 1941. Unpbd ode.

§ 2

The mousiad, an heroi-comic poem: canto 1, by Polly Pindar. 1787.
A poetical epistle from a louse to Peter Pindar. Bath 1787.
An epistle from Pindar to his pretended cousin Peter. 1788, 1788.
The history of Peter Pindar, by Tom Fact. [1788].
The King's ode in answer to Peter Pindar on his pension. [1788]. By Wolcot?
Peter provided for without a pension, by Carnaby Curry-comb. 1788, 1788. By Wolcot?
'I. Z. Zerubbabel'. The first book of the Royal Chronicle. [1788?].
The antagonists of Peter Pindar cut into atoms by Tom Plumb. 1789.
Adversity, or the tears of Britannia: a poem, by a lady. 1789.
A poetical epistle to John Wolcot. 1790.
An epistle to Peter Pindar. 1790.
Tabby to Pindar. 1790.
[Nichols, J.] A Rowland for an Oliver; also the odes songs letters etc of Peter Pindar, now first published by Sylvanus Urban. 1790.
Touchstone: or the analysis of Peter Pindar. 1795.
Anti-Jacobin July 1800.
[Gifford, W.] Epistle to Peter Pindar. 1800 (3 edns).
Peter not infallible. Cambridge 1800.
Polwhele, R. In his Unsexed females, New York 1800.
The battle of the bards, by Mauritius Moonshine. 1800.
An epistle from the devil to Peter Pindar. [London? 1800?].
Peter's Aesop: a St Giles's eclogue. 1800.
The trial of Peter Pindar for crim con, with a biographical sketch. 1807.
Hazlitt, W. Peter Pindar. Atlas 5 April 1829; rptd in Works, ed P. P. Howe, vol 20, 1934.
Reitterer, T. Leben und Werke Peter Pindars. Vienna 1900.
Gale, F. R. Peter Pindar and Canning. N & Q 9 Oct 1937.
Zall, P. M. Peter Pindar redivivus. N & Q 19 July 1952.
Hopkins, K. In his Portraits in satire, 1958.
Girtin, T. Doctor with two aunts: a biography of Peter Pindar. 1959.
Sinke, G. Wolcot and his school. Travaux de la Société des Sciences et des Lettres de Wroclaw A 79 1962.

JAMES WOODHOUSE
1735–1820

§ I

Poems on sundry occasions by James Woodhouse, a journeyman shoemaker. Birmingham 1764, London 1764, 1766.
Poems on several occasions. 1787, 1788.
Norbury park: a poem, with several others written on various occasions. 1803.
Love letters to my wife. 1804.
The life and lucubrations of Crispinus Scriblerus: a novel in verse. 2 vols 1896. Includes life and poetical works.

§ 2

Southey, R. In his Lives of uneducated poets, 1836; ed J. S. Childers, Oxford 1925.
Wink, R. In his Illustrious shoemakers, 1883.
Tinker, C. B. Nature's simple plan. Princeton 1922.

Hornbreak, K. G. New light on Mrs Montagu. In The age of Johnson: essays presented to C. B. Tinker, New Haven 1949. On her relations with Woodhouse.

ANN YEARSLEY
1756–1806

Collections

Poems on several occasions by Ann Yearsley, a milk-woman of Bristol. 1785 (3 edns), 1786.
Poems on various subjects. 1787.
The rural lyre: a volume of poems. 1796.

§ I

A poem on the inhumanity of the slave trade. [1788].
Stanzas of woe addressed to L. Eames. 1790.
Earl Goodwin: an historical play. 1791.
Reflections on the death of Louis XVI. Bristol 1793, 1793; Sequel to the Reflections, Bristol 1793.
An elegy on Marie Antoinette. [Bristol 1795?].
The royal captives. 4 vols 1795, 2 vols Dublin 1795.

§ 2

Southey, R. In his Lives of the uneducated poets, 1836; ed J. S. Childers, Oxford 1925.
Tinker, C. B. In his Nature's simple plan, Princeton 1922.
Tompkins, J. M. S. In her Polite marriage, Cambridge 1938.

THE DELLA CRUSCANS

See also Bertie Greathead, Robert Merry, William Parsons, Mrs Piozzi and Mary Robinson, above, and Hannah Cowley, below.

§ I

The Arno miscellany: a collection by a society called the Oziosi. Florence 1784.
The Florence miscellany. Florence 1785.
Diversity: a poem. 1788.
The poetry of the world. Ed E. Topham 2 vols 1788.
The album of Streatham. 1789.
The British album. 4 vols 1790, 2 vols [1790?], Dublin 1790 (with The interview by Della Crusca), 4 vols 1791, 2 vols 1792.

§ 2

Gifford, W. The baviad. 1791.
—— The maeviad. 1795.
Longaker, J. The Della Cruscans and Gifford. Philadelphia 1924.
Marshall, R. In his Italy in English literature 1755–1815, New York 1934.
Rosenfeld, S. A Della Cruscan poet. N & Q 6 Dec 1952.
Bostetter, E. E. The original Della Cruscans and the Florence miscellany. HLQ 19 1956.
Moloney, B. The Della Cruscan poets, the Florence miscellany and the Leopoldine reforms. MLR 60 1965.

THE ANTI-JACOBIN

See also under George Canning, George Ellis, John Hookham Frere and William Gifford, above, and under Rolliad, below.

§ I

The Anti-Jacobin. Nos 1–36, 20 Nov 1797–9 July 1798; 2 vols 1799 (4th edn). Ed W. Gifford.
The beauties of the Anti-Jacobin; together with explanatory notes etc. 1799.
Poetry of the Anti-Jacobin. 1799, 1800, 1801 (4th edn).

The poetry of the Anti-Jacobin. Ed C. Edmonds 1852, 1854 (with etchings by Gillray), 1890. Assigns pieces to their authors.

Parodies and other burlesque pieces, by George Canning, George Ellis and John Hookham Frere, with the whole of the poetry of the Anti-Jacobin. Ed H. Morley 1890.

The poetry of the Anti-Jacobin. Ed L. Rice-Oxley, Oxford 1924.

§ 2

Hannay, J. English political satires. Quart Rev 101 1857; rptd in his Essays, 1861.

Hayward, H. George Canning as a man of letters. Edinburgh Rev 108 1858. Review of 1854 edn.

Walker, H. In his English satire and satirists, 1925.

Hanson, L. W. Canning's copy of the Anti-Jacobin. BM Quart 11 1936.

Perkinson, R. H. The Anti-Jacobin. N & Q 6 March 1937.

THE ROLLIAD

See also under Joseph Richardson, Richard Tickell, French Laurence and Anti-Jacobin, above.

§ 1

Criticisms on the Rolliad. 1784, 1785, 1785, 1787, 1788 (8th edn), 1791; Part the second, 1785, 1790 (4 edns).

The new rolliad: number 1. 1785.

Probationary odes for the laureatship, with a preliminary discourse by Sir John Hawkins. 1785.

Poetical miscellanies. 1790.

The rolliad in two parts: probationary odes and political eclogues. 1795, 1799 (21st edn), 1812 (22nd).

The Rolliad series of poems originally appeared in Morning Herald & Daily Advertiser *for 1784 and after.*

§ 2

Satirist 1 1807.

Braybrooke, Lord. Authors of the Rolliad. N & Q 20 July 1850. Replies by H.J.M. 14 Sept 1850; W. C. Trevelyan 2 Nov 1850.

Trevelyan, W. C. The Rolliad. N & Q 22 Feb 1851. Further note by C.W., ibid.

Colquhoun, P. The Rolliad and the Anti-Jacobin. Trans Royal Soc of Lit 1883.

Whitford, R. C. Satire's view of sentimentalism. JEGP 18 1919.

— Juvenal in England 1750–1802. PQ 7 1928.

White, N. I. Shelley's Swell-foot in relation to contemporary satires. PMLA 36 1921.

Walker, H. In his English satire and satirists, 1925.

Havens, R. D. An earlier and later Rolliad. RES 3 1927.

D. S. T.

3. DRAMA

I. GENERAL INTRODUCTION

COLLECTIONS AND SELECTIONS: *Plays, Prologues and Epilogues.*
COMPILATIONS AND SURVEYS: *Dictionaries of Plays and Dramatists, General Histories of the Drama.*
CRITICAL STUDIES: *Types of Drama (Comedy of Manners, Sentimental Comedy, Heroic Play, Other Types), Origins and Influences (Native Influences, Foreign Influences), Miscellaneous Studies.*
DRAMATIC THEORY AND CRITICISM: *Anthologies and Modern Studies, Principal Works of Dramatic Criticism 1660–1800, Jeremy Collier Controversy.*

(1) COLLECTIONS OF PLAYS

Collections such as Dodsley's, which are virtually confined to the pre-Restoration period, have been excluded.

A collection of the best English plays. 10 vols [Hague 1712]. Separate title-pages and pagination.

A collection of plays by eminent hands. 4 vols 1719. Separate title-pages, pagination and dates.

Thesaurus dramaticus: containing all the celebrated passages in the English plays. 2 vols 1724, 1737 (rev as The beauties of the English stage), 3 vols 1756, 4 vols 1777 (enlarged as The beauties of the English drama).

Le théâtre anglois. Ed P. A. de la Place 8 vols 1746–9.

A select collection of English plays. 6 vols Edinburgh 1755.

A select collection of farces, as acted at London and Edinburgh. Edinburgh 1762, 6 vols Edinburgh 1786–8 (as A collection of the most esteemed farces and entertainments). *Edinburgh Farces.*

The English theatre: containing the most valuable plays which have been acted on the London stage. 8 vols 1765.

The theatre: or select works of the British dramatic poets; to which are prefixed the lives of these celebrated writers, and strictures on most of the plays. 12 vols Edinburgh 1768.

A collection of new plays by several hands. 4 vols Altenburg 1774–8.

Bell's British theatre: consisting of the most esteemed English plays. 21 vols 1776–81, 36 vols 1791–1802. *Bell.*

The new English theatre, containing the most valuable plays which have been acted on the London stage. 12 vols 1776–7. Separate plays, dated 1775–88.

The tragic and comic theatre. 8 vols 1778.

Supplement to Bell's British theatre: consisting of the most esteemed farces and entertainments. 4 vols 1784. *Bell Supplement.*

[Parsons'] The minor theatre: being a collection of the most approved farces, operas and comedies, in one, two and three acts; with some account of the respective authors. 7 vols 1794. *Minor Theatre.*

Jones's British theatre. 10 vols Dublin 1795. Separate title-pages, pagination and dates.

The beauties of modern dramatists: containing all the interesting characters, sentiments, speeches etc in the most favourite dramas. Ed W. C. Oulton 2 vols 1800.

The British drama: comprehending the best plays in the English language. 3 vols in 5 1804. *British Drama.*

Sharpe's British theatre. 18 vols 1804.

Cawthorn's minor British theatre: consisting of the most esteemed farces, operas. 6 vols 1806–7.

The British theatre: or a collection of plays with biographical and critical remarks, by Mrs Inchbald. 25 vols 1808, 20 vols 1824. *Inchbald's Theatre.*

A collection of farces and other afterpieces selected by Mrs Inchbald. 7 vols 1809, 1815. *Inchbald's Farces.*

The modern theatre. Ed E. Inchbald 10 vols 1809. *Inchbald's Modern Theatre.*

English comedy: a collection of the most celebrated dramas, since the commencement of the reformation of the stage by Sir Richard Steele and Colley Cibber. 6 vols 1810.

The modern British drama. 5 vols 1811. *Modern British Drama.*

The London theatre. Ed T. J. Dibdin 26 vols 1815–18. *Dibdin.*

A select British theatre: being a collection of the most popular stock-pieces. 8 vols 1816. Ed J. P. Kemble, who was responsible for many of the acting versions of Shakespeare et al included.

The British drama: a collection of the most esteemed dramatic productions, with biography of the respective authors, and critique on each play, by Richard Cumberland esq. 14 vols 1817.

Oxberry's new English drama. 20 vols 1818–25. *Oxberry.*

The British drama: a collection of the most esteemed tragedies, comedies, operas and farces. 2 vols 1824–6, 1828, Philadelphia 1832, 1837–8. *British Drama 1824–6.*

The London stage: a collection of the most reputed tragedies, comedies, operas, melodramas, farces and interludes. [4 vols 1824–7.] *London Stage.*

Dolby's British theatre. [8 vols] 1825. With various dates 1823–5. *Dolby.*

Duncombe's edition [of the British theatre]. [67 vols 1825–52?]. *Duncombe.*

Cumberland's British theatre, with remarks, biographical and critical [by D.G., i.e. George Daniel]. 48 vols 1826–61. *Cumberland.*

British theatre: comprising tragedies, comedies, operas and farces; with biography, critical account and explanatory notes by an Englishman [Owen Williams?]. Leipzig 1828, London 1830.

Cumberland's minor theatre; with remarks biographical and critical [by D.G., i.e. George Daniel]. 16 vols 1828–40.

The acting drama. 1834. *Acting Drama.*

Dramatists of the Restoration. Ed J. Maidment and W. H. Logan 14 vols Edinburgh 1872–9.

Representative English dramas from Dryden to Sheridan. Ed F. and J. W. Tupper, New York 1914, 1934 (enlarged).

Restoration comedies. Ed M. Summers 1921.

Types of English drama 1660–1780. Ed D. H. Stevens, Boston 1923.

Lesser English comedies of the eighteenth century. Ed A. Nicoll, Oxford 1927 (WC).

Eighteenth-century plays. Ed J. Hampden 1928.

Five Restoration tragedies. Ed B. Dobrée, Oxford 1928 (WC).

British plays from the Restoration to 1820. Ed M. J. Moses 2 vols Boston 1929.

Eighteenth-century comedy. Ed W. D. Taylor, Oxford 1929 (WC).

The best eighteenth-century comedies. Ed J. E. Uhler, New York 1929

Plays of the Restoration and eighteenth century. Ed D. MacMillan and H. M. Jones, New York 1931.

Twelve famous plays of the Restoration and eighteenth century. Ed C. A. Moore, New York 1933.
English plays 1660–1820. Ed A. E. Morgan, New York 1935.
Representative English comedies. Ed C. M. Gayley and A. Thaler. Vol 4 (Dryden and his contemporaries), New York 1936.
British dramatists from Dryden to Sheridan. Ed G. H. Nettleton and A. E. Case, Boston 1939.
Ten English farces. Ed L. Hughes and A. H. Scouten, Austin 1948.

Feasey, L. And so to the playhouse. 1951.
— On the boards of Old Drury. 1951.
Six Restoration plays. Ed J. H. Wilson, Boston 1959.
Shakespearean prompt-books of the seventeenth century. Ed G. B. Evans 4 vols Charlottesville 1960–6.
Five heroic plays. Ed B. Dobrée, Oxford 1960 (WC).
Eighteenth-century tragedy. Ed M. R. Booth, Oxford 1965 (WC).
Five Restoration adaptations of Shakespeare. Ed C. Spencer, Urbana 1965.

(2) COLLECTIONS OF PROLOGUES AND EPILOGUES ETC

A collection of the most celebrated prologues. 1727 (2nd edn).
The Court of Thespis: being a collection of the most admired prologues and epilogues. 1769.
The spouter's companion, or theatrical remembrancer: containing a select collection of prologues and epilogues. [1770?].
A compleat collection of prologues and epilogues. 1771.
The British spouter, or stage assistant: containing the most celebrated prologues and epilogues. 1773.
A collection and selection of English prologues and epilogues. 4 vols 1779
The theatrical bouquet: containing an alphabetical arrangement of the prologues and epilogues, which have been published from the time that Colley Cibber first came on the stage. 1780.

The new Thespian oracle: containing original strictures on oratory and acting, and a select collection of all the modern prologues and epilogues. 1791.
Henderson, William. The spouter's new guide: containing all the modern prologues and epilogues. 1796.
The new spouters companion: or a selection of prologues and epilogues [1798?], [1800?] ('revised by Mr Palmer').
Prologues and epilogues, celebrated for their poetical merit. Oxford [1811?].
Rare prologues and epilogues 1642–1700. Ed A. N. Wiley 1940.
Songs of the Restoration theatre. Ed P. J. Stead 1948.
Knapp, M. E. Prologues and epilogues of the eighteenth century. New Haven 1961.
Avery, E. L. Some new prologues and epilogues 1704–8. Stud in Eng Lit 1500–1900 5 1964.

(3) DICTIONARIES OF PLAYS AND DRAMATISTS, AND GENERAL HISTORIES AND SURVEYS

Dictionaries of Plays and Dramatists

See W. W. Greg, Notes on dramatic bibliographers, Malone Soc Collections vol 1 pts 4–5, 1911, vol 2 pt 3, 1931; C. S. Northup, A register of bibliographies, New Haven 1925, pp. 136–41.
Langbaine, Gerard. Momus triumphans: or the plagiaries of the English stage expos'd. 1688, 1688 (as A new catalogue of English plays).
— An account of the English dramatick poets. Oxford 1691. See A. W. Jones, E & S 21 1936.
Gildon, Charles. The lives and characters of the English dramatick poets. [1698], 1699, 1751. A revision of Langbaine, above.
A true and exact catalogue of all the plays that were ever yet printed in the English tongue. 1713, 1715 (with continuation to that year). Perhaps compiled by W. Mears, the publisher.
A compleat catologue of all the plays that were ever yet printed in the English language. 1719, 1726 (with continuation to that year). Perhaps compiled by W. Mears, the publisher.
J[acob], G[iles]. The poetical register: or the lives and characters of the English dramatick poets. 1719, 1723, 1724. Many of the accounts of Jacob's contemporaries were contributed by the dramatists themselves.
A true and exact catalogue of all the plays and other dramatick pieces that were ever yet printed in the English tongue. 1732. Perhaps compiled by W. Feales, the publisher; appended to Ben Jonson's Three celebrated plays, 1732.
[Mottley, John]. A compleat list of all the English dramatic poets. Appended to T. Whincop, Scanderbeg, 1747.
[Chetwood, W. R.] The British theatre: containing the lives of the English dramatic poets, with an account of all their plays; to which is prefixed a short view of the rise and progress of the English stage. Dublin 1750, London 1752, Dublin 1756 (in A companion to the theatre).
A compleat catalogue of all the dramatic pieces in the English language, [with] an exact list of the second titles

of every play. 1751. By Edward Cave, the publisher?
Cibber, Theophilus [and Robert Shiels]. The lives of the poets of Great Britain and Ireland, to the time of Dean Swift. 4 vols in 5 1753. Arranged in chronological order.
Theatrical records: or an account of English dramatic authors and their works. 1756, 1756 (4th edn, with Cibber's Apology). By Robert Dodsley, the publisher?
[Baker, D. E.] The companion to the playhouse: or an historical account of all the dramatic writers. 2 vols 1764.
The playhouse pocket companion: or theatrical vademecum; to which is prefixed a critical history of the English stage. 1779.
[Reed, Isaac]. Biographia dramatica: or a companion to the playhouse. 2 vols 1782. A revision of Baker, above. See L. F. Powell, George Steevens and Isaac Reed's Biographia dramatica, RES 5–6 1929–30.
Egerton's theatrical remembrancer; [with] Notitia dramatica: a chronological account of the English stage. 1788.
A new theatrical dictionary. 1792. Abridged from Reed.
Oulton, W. C. Barker's continuation of Egerton's Theatrical remembrancer, Baker's Biographia dramatica etc; also a continuation of the Notitia dramatica, to which is added a complete list of plays. [1801], [1803], 1814 (as the Drama recorded, rev to 1814).
The thespian dictionary: or dramatic biography of the eighteenth century. 1802, 1805 (enlarged).
Gilliland, T. The dramatic mirror, including a biographical and critical account of all the dramatic writers and performers and a history of the country theatres in England, Ireland and Scotland. 2 vols 1808.
Jones, Stephen. Biographia dramatica. 3 vols in 4 1812. A revision of Baker, above, divided into a dictionary of dramatists and another of plays.
[Haslewood, J.] The prompter. [London? 1814?] (priv ptd). Only known copy in Folger Lib, Washington.
Halliwell[-Phillipps], J. O. A dictionary of old English plays to the close of the 17th century. 1860.
Inglis, R. The dramatic writers of Scotland. Glasgow 1868.

Adams, W. D. A dictionary of the drama. Vol 1 (A-G), 1904.

'Clarence, R.' (H. J. Eldridge). The stage cyclopaedia: a bibliography of plays. 1909.

Summers, M. A bibliography of the Restoration drama. 1935.

Wood, F. T. Unrecorded 18th-century plays. N & Q 25 Jan, 2 May 1936, 2–16 Jan 1937, 28 May 1938. *See* D. MacMillan, 14 March 1936.

— A census of extant collections of English provincial playbills of the eighteenth century. N & Q 1 June 1946.

Harbage, A. Elizabethan and seventeenth-century play manuscripts. PMLA 50 1935, 52 1937.

— Elizabethan-Restoration palimpsest. MLR 35 1940.

— Annals of English drama 975–1700. Philadelphia 1940, London 1964 (rev S. Schoenbaum).

Babcock, R. W. Eighteenth-century comic opera manuscripts. PMLA 52 1937.

— Francis Colman's register of operas 1712–34. Music & Letters 24 1943.

— Playbills and programs: the story of a summer's quest In Studies in honor of John Wilcox, ed A. D. Wallace and W. O. Ross, Detroit 1958.

McCabe, W. H. The play-list of the English College of St Omers 1592–1762. Revue de Littérature Comparée 17 1937.

MacMillan, D. Catalogue of the Larpent plays in the Huntington Library. San Marino 1939. Corrections and addns by E. Pearce, HLQ 6 1943.

— George Steevens' contribution to Biographia dramatica. In Restoration and eighteenth-century literature, ed C. Camden, Chicago 1963.

Adams, J. Q. Hill's list of early plays in manuscript. Library 4th ser 20 1940.

Bentley, G. E. A rough check list of the University of Chicago libraries' holdings in seventeenth-century editions of plays in English. Chicago 1941.

Loewenberg, A. Annals of opera 1597–1940. Cambridge 1943; rev F. Walker 2 vols Geneva 1955.

— The theatre of the British Isles excluding London: a bibliography. 1950.

Avery, E. L. A tentative calendar of daily theatrical performances 1660–1700. Washington State Univ Research Stud 13 1945.

— and A. H. Scouten. Addenda 1700–1 to 1704–5. PMLA 63 1948.

Woodward, G. L. and J. G. McManaway. A check list of English plays 1641–1700. Chicago 1945. Supplement by F. T. Bowers, Charlottesville 1949.

Troubridge, St V. Late eighteenth-century plays. Theatre Notebook 1 1947.

Greg, W. W. A bibliography of the English printed drama to the Restoration. Vol 2, Plays 1617–89, Oxford 1951.

Laver, J. Gabrielle Enthoven and the Enthoven Theatre collection. In his Studies in English theatre history, 1952.

Hogan, C. B. Shakespeare in the theatre 1701–1800: a record of performances in London. 2 vols Oxford 1952–7.

Wilkinson, C. H. English plays in Worcester College Library. Theatre Notebook 8 1953.

Van Lennep, W. Some early English playbills. Harvard Lib Bull 8 1954.

Macleod, J. The earliest amateur playbill. Theatre Notebook 9 1954.

Pedicord, H. W. Rylands English Ms 1111: an early diary of Richard Cross (d. 1760), prompter to the theatres. Bull John Rylands Lib 37 1955.

— Course of plays 1740–2: an early diary of Richard Cross, prompter to the theatre. Bull John Rylands Lib 40 1958.

Smith, W. C. The Italian opera and contemporary ballet in London: a record of performances and players and reports from the journals of the time. 1955.

Kahn, A. M. C. Theatre collections: a symposium. [West Wickham Kent] 1955.

Langhans, E. A. The Restoration promptbook of Shirley's The sisters. Theatre Annual 14 1956.

— Three early eighteenth-century promptbooks. Theatre Notebook 20 1966.

— Restoration manuscript notes in seventeenth-century plays. Restoration & 18th-Century Theatre Research 5 1966.

— Three early eighteenth-century manuscript promptbooks. MP 65 1967.

McManaway, J. G. The theatrical collectanes of Daniel Lysons. PBSA 51 1957.

— Unrecorded performances in London about 1700. Theatre Notebook 19 1965.

White, E. W. Early theatrical performances of Purcell's operas, with a calendar of recorded performances 1690–1710. Theatre Notebook 13 1959.

Anderson, G. L. A little civil correction: Langbaine revised. N & Q June 1958.

Freedley, G. The 26 principal theatre collections in American libraries and museums. BNYPL July 1958.

Bunch, A. Playbills and programmes in Guildhall Library. Theatre Notebook 14 1960.

Nash, G. An early London playbill. Ibid.

Kerslake, J. F. Catalogue of theatrical portraits in London public collections. 1961.

Theatrical materials in the British Museum. Theatre Notebook 17 1962.

Fletcher, I. K. British playbills before 1718. Ibid.

Stratman, C. J. Unpublished dissertations in the history and theory of tragedy 1889–1957. Bull of Bibliography 23 1962.

— A survey of the Bodleian Library's holdings in the field of English printed tragedy. Bodleian Lib Record 7 1964.

— Bibliography of English printed tragedy 1565–1900. Carbondale 1966.

— Dramatic play lists 1591–1963. BNYPL Feb–March 1966.

Martin, G. The playbill: the development of its typographic style. Chicago 1963.

Grieder, T. Annotated checklist of the British drama 1789–99. Restoration & 18th-Century Theatre Research 4 1965.

Bowers, F. T. Bibliography and Restoration drama. Los Angeles 1966.

Leach, E. Playbills and programmes. Manchester Rev 11 1966.

Conolly, L. Some new Larpent titles. Theatre Notebook 23 1969.

General Histories of the Drama

[Genest, John]. Some account of the English stage, from 1660 to 1830. 10 vols Bath 1832. Analyses of nearly every acted play with miscellaneous theatrical information.

Rapp, M. Studien über das englische Theater. Tübingen 1862.

Taine, H. A. Histoire de la littérature anglaise. 4 vols Paris 1863–4; tr 2 vols Edinburgh 1871–2. Especially for Restoration comedy.

Ward, A. W. A history of English dramatic literature to the death of Queen Anne. 2 vols 1875, 3 vols 1899 (rev).

Grisy, A. de. Histoire de la comédie anglaise au dix-septième siècle 1672–1707. Paris 1878.

Matthews, B. The development of the drama. New York 1904.

Thorndike, A. H. Tragedy. Boston 1908.

— English comedy. New York 1929.

Schelling, F. E., C. Whibley and A. T. Bartholomew. The Restoration drama. CHEL 8 1912.

Nettleton, G. H. The drama and the stage. CHEL 10 1913.

—— English drama of the Restoration and eighteenth century 1642–1780. New York 1914.

Routh, H. V. The Georgian drama. CHEL 11 1914.

Archer, W. The old drama and the new. 1923.

Nicoll, A. A history of Restoration drama 1660–1700. Cambridge 1923, 1928, 1940, 1952 (rev).

—— A history of early eighteenth-century drama 1700–50. Cambridge 1923, 1929, 1952 (rev).

—— A history of late eighteenth-century drama 1750–1800. Cambridge 1927, 1937, 1952 (rev).

—— Alphabetical catalogue of plays 1660–1900. Cambridge 1959.

—— British drama: an historical survey. 1925.

Legouis, E. and L. Cazamian. Histoire de la littérature anglaise. Paris 1924; tr 2 vols 1926.

Elwin, M. The playgoer's handbook to Restoration drama. 1928.

Eaton, W. P. The drama in English. New York 1930.

Prinsen, J. Het drama in de 18ᵉ eeuw in West-Europa. Zutphen 1931.

Summers, M. The playhouse of Pepys. 1935.

Harbage, A. Cavalier drama. New York 1936.

Miller, F. S. Some eighteenth-century dramas. MLN 52 1937.

Tobin, J. E. Three eighteenth-century plays. N & Q 1 Jan 1944.

Nagler, A. M. Sources of theatrical history. New York 1952.

Boas, F. S. Introduction to eighteenth-century drama. Oxford 1953.

Lynch, J. J. Box, pit and gallery: stage and society in Johnson's London. Berkeley 1953.

Wilkinson, C. H. Theatre miscellany: six pieces connected with the seventeenth-century stage. Oxford 1953.

Clinton-Baddeley, V. C. All right on the night. 1954.

Wimsatt, W. K. (ed). English stage comedy. New York 1954, 1955.

Loftis, J. The London theatres in early eighteenth-century politics. HLQ 18 1955.

—— Comedy and society from Congreve to Fielding. Stanford 1959.

—— The politics of drama in Augustan England. Oxford 1963.

Mander, R. and J. Mitchenson. A picture history of the British theatre. 1957.

The London stage 1660–1800. Part 1 1660–1700, ed W. Van Lennep, E. L. Avery and A. H. Scouten, Carbondale 1965; Part 2 1700–29, ed E. L. Avery 2 vols Carbondale 1960; Part 3 1729–47, ed A. H. Scouten 2 vols Carbondale 1961; Part 4 1747–76, ed G. W. Stone 3 vols Carbondale 1962; Part 5 1776–1800, ed C. B. Hogan 3 vols Carbondale 1968.

Knight, G. W. The golden labyrinth: a study of English drama. 1962.

Wilson, J. H. A preface to Restoration drama. Boston 1965.

Hogan, C. B. The London theatres 1776–1800: a brief consideration. Theatre Notebook 21 1966.

Jenkins, D. C. The James Street theatre and the old tennis-court. Theatre Notebook 23 1969.

(4) STUDIES OF SPECIAL TYPES OF DRAMA

The Comedy of Manners

Hazlitt, William. A view of the English stage. 1818.

Lamb, Charles. On the artificial comedy. In his Essays of Elia, 1821.

Hunt, Leigh. The dramatic works of Wycherley, Congreve, Vanbrugh and Farquhar. 1840. Introd.

Macaulay, T. B. The dramatic works of Wycherley, Congreve, Vanbrugh and Farquhar. Edinburgh Rev 62 1841. A review of Hunt, above.

Thackeray, W. M. The English humourists of the eighteenth century. 1853.

Meredith, George. On the idea of comedy, and of the uses of the comic spirit. New Quart Mag 8 1877; 1897 (separately).

Palmer, J. The comedy of manners. 1913.

Heldt, W. A chronological and critical review of the appreciation and condemnation of the comic dramatists of the Restoration and Orange periods. Neophilologus 7–8 1922–3.

Dobrée, B. Restoration comedy. Oxford 1924.

Perry, H. T. E. The comic spirit in Restoration drama. New Haven 1925.

Lynch, K. The social mode of Restoration comedy. New York 1926.

Stoll, E. E. Literature and life. In Shakespeare studies, New York 1927.

—— Artificial comedy. TLS 5 Jan 1928.

—— Literature and life again. PMLA 47 1932.

—— The real society in Restoration comedy: hymeneal pretenses. MLN 58 1943.

Crawford, B. V. High comedy in terms of Restoration practice. PQ 8 1929.

Montgomery, G. The challenge of Restoration comedy. In California University essays in criticism, Berkeley 1929; rptd in Restoration drama, ed J. Loftis, New York 1966.

Knights, L. C. Restoration comedy: the reality and the myth. Scrutiny 6 1937; rptd in Restoration drama, ed J. Loftis, New York 1966.

Van Lennep, W. Two Restoration comedies. TLS 28 Jan 1939.

Williams, E. E. Dr James Drake and the Restoration theory of comedy. RES 15 1939.

Paine, C. S. The comedy of manners 1669–1700: a reference guide. Bull of Bibliography 17 1942.

Alleman, G. S. Matrimonial law and the materials of Restoration comedy. Wallingford Pa 1942.

Houghton, W. E. Lamb's criticism of Restoration comedy. ELH 10 1943.

Symons, J. Restoration comedy. Kenyon Rev 7 1945.

Mignon, E. Crabbed age and youth: the old men and women in Restoration comedy of manners. Durham NC 1947.

Smith, J. H. The gay couple in Restoration comedy. Cambridge Mass 1948.

Bateson, F. W. Comedy of manners. EC 1 1951.

—— Second thoughts: L. C. Knights and Restoration comedy. EC 7 1957; rptd in Restoration drama, ed J. Loftis, New York 1966.

Leech, C. Restoration comedy: the earlier phase. EC 1 1951.

Berkeley, D. S. The penitent rake in Restoration comedy. MP 49 1952.

—— The art of whining love. SP 52 1955.

—— Préciosité and the Restoration comedy of manners. HLQ 18 1955.

—— Some notes on probability in Restoration drama. N & Q June, Aug, Oct 1955.

—— The précieuse or distressed heroine in Restoration comedy. Stillwater Oklahoma 1959.

Fujimura, T. H. The Restoration comedy of wit. Princeton 1952.

Wain, J. Restoration comedy and its modern critics. EC 6 1956.

Holland, N. N. The first modern comedies: the significance of Etherege, Wycherley and Congreve. Cambridge Mass 1959.

Cecil, C. D. Libertine and précieux elements in Restoration comedy. EC 9 1959.

—— Une espèce d'éloquence abrégée: the idealized speech of Restoration comedy. Etudes Anglaises 19 1966.

—— Delicate and indelicate puns in Restoration comedy. MLR 61 1966.

—— Raillery in Restoration comedy. HLQ 29 1966.

Sharma, R. C. Conventions of speech in the Restoration comedy of manners. Indian Jnl of Eng Stud 2 1961.

—— Themes and conventions in the comedy of manners. New York 1965, 1966.

Vernon, P. F. Marriage of convenience and the mode of Restoration comedy. EC 12 1962.

Simon, I. Restoration comedy and the critics. Revue des Langues Vivantes 29 1963.

Wilkinson, D. R. M. The comedy of habit: an essay on the use of courtesy literature in a study of Restoration comic drama. 1964.

Drake, R. Manners anyone? or who killed the butler. South Atlantic Quart 63 1964.

McDonald, C. O. Restoration comedy as drama of satire: an investigation into seventeenth-century aesthetics. SP 61 1964.

Sharrock, R. Modes of satire. In Restoration theatre, ed J. R. Brown and B. Harris 1965.

Mohanty, H. P. Restoration comedy: a revaluation. Literary Criterion 7 1966.

Emery, J. P. Restoration dualism of the Court writers. Revue des Langues Vivantes 32 1966.

Sentimental Comedy

Eloesser, A. Das bürgerliche Drama: seine Geschichte im 18 und 19 Jahrhundert. Berlin 1898.

Waterhouse, O. The development of English sentimental comedy in the 18th century. Anglia 30 1907.

Bernbaum, E. The drama of sensibility. Boston 1915.

Krutch, J. W. Comedy and conscience after the Restoration. New York 1924, 1949 (rev).

Bateson, F. W. English comic drama 1700–50. Oxford 1929. Introd.

Wood, F. T. The beginnings and significance of sentimental comedy. Anglia 55 1931.

—— Sentimental comedy in the eighteenth century. Neophilologus 18 1933.

Nolte, F. O. Early middle class drama 1696–1774. Lancaster Pa 1935.

Croissant, De W. C. Early sentimental comedy. In T. M. Parrott presentation volume, Princeton 1935.

Kruuse, J. Det folsomme drama. Copenhagen 1934.

Magill, L. M. Poetic justice: the dilemma of the early creators of sentimental tragedy. Washington State Univ Research Stud 25 1957.

Sherbo, A. English sentimental drama. East Lansing 1957.

Parnell, P. E. The sentimental mask. PMLA 78 1963.

The Heroic Play

Sherwood, M. Dryden's dramatic theory and practice. Boston 1898.

Chase, L. N. The English heroic play. New York 1903.

Child, C. G. The rise of the heroic play. MLN 19 1904.

Tupper, J. W. The relation of the heroic play to the romances of Beaumont and Fletcher. PMLA 20 1905.

Grübner, W. Der Einfluss des Reims auf den Satzbau der englischen heroic plays. Königsberg 1912.

Nicoll, A. The origin and types of the heroic tragedy. Anglia 44 1920.

Poston, M. L. The origin of the English heroic play. MLR 16 1921.

Pendlebury, J. B. Dryden's heroic plays. 1923.

Clark, W. S. The sources of the Restoration heroic play. RES 4 1928.

—— The Platonic element in the Restoration heroic play. PMLA 45 1930.

—— The definition of the heroic play in the Restoration period. RES 8 1932.

Dobrée, B. Restoration tragedy. Oxford 1929.

Deane, C. V. Dramatic theory and the rhymed heroic play. 1931.

Parsons, A. E. The English heroic play. MLR 33 1938.

Valency, M. J. The tragedies of Herod and Mariamne. New York 1940.

Prior, M. E. Tragedy and the heroic play. In his Language of tragedy, New York 1947.

Wasserman, E. R. The pleasures of tragedy. ELH 14 1947.

Leech, C. Restoration tragedy: a reconsideration. Durham Univ Jnl 42 1950.

Gagen, J. Love and honor in Dryden's heroic plays. PMLA 77 1962.

Kirsch, A. C. Dryden, Corneille and the heroic play. MP 59 1962.

—— Dryden's heroic drama. Princeton 1965.

Swedenberg, H. T., jr. Dryden's obsessive concern with the heroic. SP extra ser 4 1967.

Rothstein, E. Restoration tragedy: form and process and change. Madison 1967.

Other Types

Myers, C. L. Opera in England from 1656 to 1728. Western Reserve Univ Bull 9 1906.

Marks, J. English pastoral drama 1660–1798. [1908]. With bibliography of English pastoral plays.

Ristine, F. H. English tragicomedy. New York 1910.

Wright, R. A. The political play of the Restoration. Montesano Washington 1916.

Nicoll, A. Political plays of the Restoration. MLR 16 1921.

Mark, J. Ballad opera and its significance in the history of English stage-music. London Mercury July 1923.

Baskervill, C. R. Play-lists and afterpieces of the mid-eighteenth century. MP 23 1926.

Dent, J. E. Foundations of English opera: a study of musical drama in England during the xvii century. Cambridge 1928.

Green, C. C. The neo-classic theory of tragedy in England during the eighteenth century. Cambridge Mass 1934.

Avery, E. L. Dancing and pantomime on the English stage 1700–37. SP 31 1934.

—— Vaudeville on the London stage 1700–37. Washington State Univ Research Stud 5 1937.

—— The defense and criticism of pantomimic entertainments in the early eighteenth century. ELH 5 1938.

Smith, D. F. Plays about the theatre in England from 1671 to 1737. New York 1936.

—— The critics in the audience of the London theatres from Buckingham to Sheridan: a study of neoclassicism in the playhouse 1671–1779. Albuquerque 1953.

Gagey, E. M. Ballad opera. New York 1937.

Hughes, L. Attitudes of some Restoration dramatists toward farce. PQ 19 1940

—— The early career of farce in the theatrical vocabulary. SE 1940.

—— and A. H. Scouten. John Rich and the holiday season of 1732–3. RES 21 1945.

—— Some theatrical adaptations of a picaresque tale. SE 1946.

—— A century of English farce. Princeton 1956.

Disher, M. W. Pope's angel of dulness. TLS 11 Dec 1943. On Rich and the origins of pantomime.

Davis, C. A. C. Rich as Lun. N & Q 31 May 1947.

Evans, B. Gothic drama from Walpole to Shelley. Berkeley 1947.

Vincent, H. P. Rich and the first Covent Garden Theatre. ELH 17 1950.

Clinton-Baddeley, V. C. Burlesque tradition in the English theatre after 1660. 1952.

Bowers, F. T. Ogilby's coronation entertainments 1661–89: editions and issues. PBSA 47 1953.

Rulfs, D. J. Entr'acte entertainment at Drury Lane and Covent Garden 1750–70. Theatre Annual 12 1954.

Herrick, M. T. Tragicomedy: its origin and development in Italy, France and England. Urbana 1955.

Deutsch, O. E. Handel: a documentary biography. 1955. With account of Handel's operas in London.

Speaight, G. The history of the English puppet theatre. 1955.
— A Restoration puppet show. Theatre Notebook 12 1958.
Manifold, J. S. The music in English drama from Shakespeare to Purcell. 1956.
Kerman, J. Opera as drama. 1957.
Ingram, R. W. Operatic tendencies in Stuart drama. Musical Quart 44 1958.
White, E. W. Early theatrical performances of Purcell's operas, with a calendar of recorded performances 1690–1710. Theatre Notebook 13 1958.
— The rehearsal of an opera. Theatre Notebook 14 1960.
— English opera research, the immediate past and the future: a personal viewpoint. Theatre Notebook 21 1966.
Knapp, J. M. Handel, the Royal Academy of Music and its first opera season in London 1720. Musical Quart 45 1959.
Dean, W. Handel's dramatic oratorios and masques. 1959.
Lincoln, S. Handel's music for Queen Anne. Musical Quart 45 1959.
Shaw, W. Handel's Messiah: a study of selected contemporary word-books. Ibid.
Fletcher, I. K. The history of ballet in England 1660–1740. BNYPL June 1959.

Cohen, S. J. Theory and practice of theatrical dancing in England in the Restoration and early eighteenth century as seen in the lives and works of Josias Priest, John Weaver and Hester Santlow. BNYPL Nov 1959.
Whitesell, J. E. The wits drolls: were they meant to be acted? Tennessee Stud in Lit 4 1959.
Sawyer, P. Processions and coronations on the London stage 1727–61. Theatre Notebook 14 1959.
Smith, W. C. with C. Humphries. Handel: a descriptive catalogue of the early editions. 1960.
Moore, R. E. Henry Purcell and the Restoration theatre. 1961.
Lewis, A. Purcell and Blow's Venus and Adonis. Music & Letters 44 1963.
Kimball, D. The libretto of Handel's Teseo. Ibid.
McCredie, A. D. John Christopher Smith as a dramatic composer. Music & Letters 45 1964.
Lord, P. The English-Italian opera companies 1732-3. Ibid.
Booth, M. R. English melodrama. 1963.
Green, E. M. John Rich's art of pantomime as seen in his The necromancer, or Harlequin Doctor Faustus: a comparison of the two Faustus pantomimes at Lincoln's Inn Fields and Drury Lane. Restoration & 18th-Century Theatre Research 4 1965.

(5) ORIGINS AND INFLUENCES

Native Influences

Harbeson, W. P. The Elizabethan influence on the tragedy of the late 18th and early 19th centuries. Lancaster Pa 1921.
Nicoll, A. Dryden as an adapter of Shakespeare. 1922 (Shakespeare Assoc lecture).
Summers, M. Shakespeare adaptations. 1922. Introd.
Sprague, A. C. Beaumont and Fletcher on the Restoration stage. Cambridge Mass 1926.
— Shakespeare and the actors: the stage business in the plays 1660–1905. Cambridge Mass 1944.
— Shakespearean players and performances. Cambridge Mass 1953.
— The Alchemist on the stage. Theatre Notebook 17 1962.
Wood, P. S. Native elements in English neo-classicism. MP 24 1926.
— The opposition to neo-classicism in England between 1660 and 1700. PMLA 43 1928.
Wilson, J. H. The influence of Beaumont and Fletcher on Restoration drama. Columbus 1928.
Ellehauge, M. Restoration drama: its relation to past English and past and contemporary French drama. Copenhagen 1933.
Teeter, L. The dramatic use of Hobbes's political ideas. ELH 3 1936.
Jaggard, W. Imitations of Shakespeare. N & Q 20 Nov 1937.
Ball, R. H. The amazing career of Sir Giles Overreach. Princeton 1939.
Graham, C. B. Jonson allusions in Restoration comedy. RES 15 1939.
Bentley, G. E. Seventeenth-century allusions to Jonson. HLQ 5 1941.
— Shakespeare and Jonson: their reputations in the seventeenth century compared. 2 vols Chicago 1945.
Scouten, A. H. Shakespeare's plays in the theatrical repertory when Garrick came to London. SE 1944.
— The increase in popularity of Shakespeare's plays in the eighteenth century: a caveat for interpreters of stage history. Shakespeare Quart 7 1956.
— Some assumptions behind accounts of the Elizabethan stage. In Eight essays in English literature, Pullman 1968. On the influence of these assumptions in 17th and 18th centuries.

Kermode, J. F. A note on the history of Massinger's The fatal dowry in the eighteenth century. N & Q 3 May 1947.
Rulfs, D. J. Beaumont and Fletcher on the London stage 1776–1833. PMLA 63 1948.
— Reception of the Elizabethan playwrights on the London stage 1776–1833. SP 46 1949.
Hogan, C. B. Shakespeare in the theatre 1701–1800. 2 vols Oxford 1952–7.
Hook, L. Shakespeare improv'd: or a case for the affirmative. Shakespeare Quart 4 1953.
Rosenberg, M. The refinement of Othello in the eighteenth-century British theatre. SP 51 1954.
— The masks of Othello: the search for the identity of Othello, Iago and Desdemona by three centuries of actors and critics. Berkeley 1962.
Branan, G. C. Eighteenth-century adaptations of Shakespearean tragedy. Berkeley 1956.
Avery, E. L. The Shakespeare Ladies Club. Shakespeare Quart 7 1956.
Stone, G. W., jr. Shakespeare's Tempest at Drury Lane during Garrick's management. Ibid.
Schulz, M. F. King Lear: a maverick among Shakespearian tragedies on the London stage 1700–1 to 1749–50. Tulane Stud in Eng 7 1957.
Evans, G. B. The problem of Brutus: an eighteenth-century solution. In Studies in honor of T. W. Baldwin, ed D. C. Allen, Urbana 1958.
— The Douai manuscript: six Shakespearean transcripts 1694–5. PQ 41 1962.
Lelyveld, T. Shylock on the stage. 1961.
Wells, S. A Shakespearean droll? Theatre Notebook 15 1961.
Leech, C. A projected Restoration performance of Ford's The lover's melancholy. MLR 56 1961.
— Shakespeare, Cibber and the Tudor myth. In Shakespearean essays, Knoxville 1964.
Sen, S. K. Adaptations of Shakespeare and his critics 1660–1790. Indian Jnl of Eng Stud 3 1962.
Camden, C. Songs and chorusses in the Tempest. PQ 41 1962. By Sheridan, 1777.
Nichols, J. Shakespeare as a character in drama 1679–1899. Educational Theatre Jnl 15 1963.
Price, J. G. From farce to romance: All's well that ends well 1756–1811. Shakespeare Jahrbuch 99 1963.

Tiedje, E. Die Tradition Ben Jonsons in der Restaurations-komödie. Hamburg 1963.

Marder, L. His exits and entrances: the story of Shakespeare's reputation. New York 1963.

McManaway, J. G. Richard II at Covent Garden. Shakespeare Quart 15 1964.

Dean, W. Shakespeare in the opera house. Shakespeare Survey 18 1965.

Jenkins, H. Hamlet then till now. Ibid.

Donohue, J. W. Kemble's production of Macbeth 1794. Theatre Notebook 21 1967.

Sorelius, G. The great race before the flood: pre-Restoration drama on the stage and in the criticism of the Restoration. Upsala 1966.

Gruber, C. P. Falstaff on an 18th-century battlefield. Theatre Notebook 21 1967.

Coleman, W. S. E. Post-Restoration Shylocks prior to Macklin. Theatre Survey 8 1967.

Velz, J. W. A Restoration cast list for Julius Caesar. N & Q April 1968.

Rostron, D. John Philip Kemble's Coriolanus and Julius Caesar. Theatre Notebook 23 1968.

Foreign Influences

Harvie-Jellie, W. Les sources du théâtre anglais à l'époque de la Restauration. Paris 1906.

— Le théâtre classique en Angleterre, dans l'âge de John Dryden. Montreal [1933].

Charlanne, L. L'influence française an Angleterre au dix-septième siècle. Paris 1906.

Parfitt, G. E. L'influence française dans les œuvres de Fielding et dans le théâtre anglais contemporain de ses comédies. Paris 1928.

Wray, E. English adaptations of French drama between 1780 and 1815. MLN 43 1928.

Macaulay, T. C. French and English drama in the seventeenth century: some contrasts and parallels. E & S 20 1935.

Kinne, W. A. Revivals and importations of French comedies in England 1749–1800. New York 1939.

O'Regan, M. J. Two notes on French reminiscences in Restoration comedy. Hermathena 93 1959.

Mavrocordato, A. La critique classique anglaise et la fonction de la tragédie 1660–1720. Etudes Anglaises 14 1961.

Daniels, W. M. Saint-Evremond en Angleterre. Versailles 1907.

Grobe, E. P. French librettist at the Court of Charles II. Theatre Notebook 9 1954. On Sébastien Brémond.

Humbert, C. H. Molière in England. Bielefeld 1874.

Miles, D. H. The influence of Molière on Restoration comedy. New York 1910.

Besing, M. Molières Einfluss auf das englische Lustspiel bis 1700. Leipzig 1913.

Gillet, J. E. Molière en Angleterre 1660–70. Brussels 1913.

Wilcox, J. The relation of Molière to Restoration comedy. New York 1938.

Tucker, J. E. Eighteenth-century English translations of Molière. MLQ 3 1942.

Mandach, A. de. Molière et la comédie de moeurs en Angleterre 1660–8. Neuchâtel 1946.

Loiselet, J. L. L'apport de Molière au théâtre anglais du début de la Restauration au milieu du xviii e siècle. Revue Française 6 1954.

Jones, C. E. Molière in England to 1775: a checklist. N & Q Sept 1957.

Parnell, P. E. A new Molière source for Steele's The tender husband. N & Q June 1959.

Suckling, N. Molière and English Restoration comedy. In Restoration theatre, ed J. R. Brown and B. Harris 1965.

Hill, H. W. La Calprenède's romances and the Restoration drama. Reno 1911.

Rutherford, M.-R. The Abbé Prévost and the English theatre 1730–40. Theatre Notebook 9 1955.

Mulert, A. Pierre Corneille in der englischen Übersetzungsliteratur des XVIIen Jahrhunderts. Erlangen 1900.

Canfield, D. F. Corneille and Racine in England. New York 1904.

Eccles, F. Y. Racine in England. Oxford 1922 (Taylorian lecture).

Voisine, J. Corneille et Racine en Angleterre au dix-huitième siècle. Revue de Littérature Comparée 22 1948.

Hartnoll, P. Corneille in England. Theatre Research 1 1958.

Wheatley, K. E. Racine and English classicism. Austin 1956.

Baungärtner, G. Voltaire auf der englischen Bühne des 18 Jahrhunderts. Strasbourg 1913.

Bruce, H. L. The period of greatest popularity of Voltaire's plays on the English stage. MLN 33 1918.

— Voltaire on the English stage. Berkeley 1918.

Fenger, H. Voltaire et le théâtre anglais. Orbis Litterarum 7 1949.

Perkins, M. L. Dryden's The Indian emperour and Voltaire's Alzire. Comparative Lit 9 1957.

Hume, M. Spanish influence on English literature. 1905.

Cordasco, F. Spanish influence on Restoration drama: George Digby's Elvira (1663?). Revue de Littérature Comparée 27 1953.

Loftis, J. Spanish drama in neoclassical England. Comparative Lit 11 1959.

— Restoration Hispanism and the comedy of Spanish romance. In Eight essays in English literature, Pullman 1968.

Hogan, F. T. Notes on thirty-one English plays and their Spanish sources. Restoration & 18th-Century Theatre Research 6 1967.

Nicoll, A. Italian opera in England: the first five years. Anglia 46 1922.

Walmsley, D. H. The influence of foreign opera on English operatic plays of the Restoration period. Anglia 52 1928.

Montgomery, F. Early criticism of Italian opera in England. Musical Quart 15 1929.

Smith, W. C. The Italian opera and contemporary ballet in London 1789–1820. 1955.

Kenwood, S. H. Lessing in England. MLR 9 1914.

Heineman, W. Goethe on the English stage. Pbns of Goethe Soc 4 1888.

Rea, T. Schiller's dramas and poems in England. 1906.

Cooke, M. W. Schiller's Robbers in England. MLR 11 1916.

Willoughby, L. A. English translations and adaptations of Schiller's Robbers. MLR 16 1921.

Thomson, L. F. Kotzebue: a survey of his progress in France and England. Paris 1928.

Grieder, T. The German drama in England 1790–1800. Restoration & 18th-Century Theatre Research 3 1964.

Wann, L. The Oriental in Restoration drama. Wisconsin Univ Stud 2 1918.

Morton, R. and W. M. Peterson. Peter the Great and Russia in Restoration and eighteenth-century drama. N & Q Oct 1954.

(6) MISCELLANEOUS STUDIES

B[owen], G. S. A study of the prologue and epilogue in English literature from Shakespeare to Dryden. 1884.

Duncan, C. S. The scientist as a comic type. MP 14 1916.

Landa, M. J. The Jew in English drama. 1926.

Thorp, W. The stage adventures of some Gothic novels. PMLA 43 1928.

Coleman, E. D. The Bible in English drama: an annotated list. BNYPL Oct 1930.

Maxfield, E. K. The Quakers in English plays before 1800. PMLA 45 1930.

Spencer, H. A caveat on Restoration play quartos. RES 6 1930.

Gray, C. H. Theatrical criticism in London to 1795. New York 1931.

Pfitzner, K. Die Ausländertypen im englischen Drama der Restorationszeit. Breslau 1931.

Watson, H. F. The sailor in English fiction and drama 1550–1800. New York 1931.

Praz, M. Il drama inglese della Restaurazione e i suoi aspetti pre-romantici. Cultura 12 1933.

Feen, H. R. S. van der. Jewish characters in eighteenth-century English fiction and drama. Groningen 1935.

Noyes, R. G. Songs from Restoration drama in contemporary and eighteenth-century poetical miscellanies. ELH 3 1936.

— Broadside ballad versions of the songs in Restoration drama. Harvard Stud 19 1937.

— Contemporary musical settings of the songs in Restoration dramatic operas. Harvard Stud 20 1938.

— Conventions of song in Restoration tragedy. PMLA 53 1938.

— The thespian mirror: Shakespeare in the eighteenth-century novel. Providence 1953.

— The neglected Muse: Restoration and eighteenth-century tragedy in the novel 1740–80. Providence 1956.

Parkinson, R. H. Topographical comedy in the seventeenth century. ELH 3 1936.

Stroup, T. B. Supernatural beings in Restoration drama. Archiv 61 1937.

Duggan, G. C. The stage Irishman. 1937.

Fache, E. C. Huguenots and the stage. Proc of Huguenot Soc of London 15 1937.

Silvette, H. The doctor on the stage: medicine and medical men in seventeenth-century English drama. Annals of Medical History new ser 8–9 1937–8.

Gray, P. H. Lenten casts and the Nursery: evidence for the dating of certain Restoration plays. PMLA 53 1938.

Bartley, J. O. The development of a stock character: (I) The stage Irishman to 1800; (II) The stage Scotsman and (III) the stage Welshman to 1800. MLR 37–8 1942–3.

Ramsland, C. Britons never will be slaves: Whig political propaganda in the British theatre 1700–42. Quart Jnl of Speech 28 1942.

Boas, F. S. The soldier in Elizabethan and later English drama. Essays by Divers Hands new ser 19 1942.

Avery, E. L. The dramatists in the theatrical advertisements 1700–9. MLQ 8 1947.

— Two early London playbills. N & Q 4 March 1950. Note by J. D. Aylward 15 April 1950.

— The Restoration audience. PQ 45 1966.

— Rhetorical patterns in Restoration prologues and epilogues. In Essays in honor of B. R. McElderry jr, Athens Ohio 1967.

Brown, W. C. The Near East in English drama 1775–1825. JEGP 46 1947.

Snuggs, H. L. The comic humours: a new interpretation. PMLA 62 1947.

Loftis, J. Eighteenth-century beginnings of modern drama. Emory Univ Quart 7 1951.

— The social milieu of early eighteenth-century comedy. MP 53 1955.

— Comedy and society from Congreve to Fielding. Stanford 1959.

Studies in English theatre history in memory of Gabrielle Enthoven. 1952.

Speaight, G. Powell from the Bath: an eighteenth-century puppet theatre. In Studies in English theatre history, 1952.

— Punch's opera at Bartholomew Fair. Theatre Notebook 7 1953.

— The history of the English puppet theatre. 1955.

Troubridge, St V. Theatre riots in London. In Studies in English theatre history, 1952.

Pedicord, H. W. The theatrical public in the time of Garrick. New York 1954.

— White gloves at five: fraternal patronage of London theatres in the eighteenth century. PQ 45 1966.

Gagen, J. E. The new woman: her emergence in English drama 1600–1730. New York 1954.

Walbridge, E. F. Drames à clef: a list of plays with characters based on real people. BNYPL April–June 1956.

Manifold, J. S. The music in English drama from Shakespeare to Purcell. 1956.

Scouten, A. H. The SPCK and the stage. Theatre Notebook 11 1957.

— Notes toward a history of Restoration comedy. PQ 45 1966.

Rosenthal, H. Two centuries of opera at Covent Garden. 1958.

Rubsamen, W. H. Mr Seedo, ballad opera and the Singspiel. In Miscelá nea en homenaje a Monsenôr Higinio Angles, Barcelona 1958–61.

Hopkins, R. H. Rigor mortis and eighteenth-century tragedy. N & Q Nov 1959.

Hoy, C. The effect of the Restoration on drama. Tennessee Stud in Lit 6 1961.

Peterson, W. M. and R. Morton. Mirrors on the Restoration stage. N & Q Jan–Feb 1962.

Stone, G. W. The poet and the players. Proc of Amer Philosophical Soc 106 1962.

MacMillan, D. The rise of social comedy in the eighteenth century. PQ 41 1962.

Jones, E. D. The physical representation of African characters on the English stage during the 16th and 17th centuries. Theatre Notebook 17 1962.

Bennett, G. Conventions of the stage villain. Anglo-Welsh Rev 14 1964.

Harris, B. The dialect of those fanatic times. In Restoration theatre, ed J. R. Brown and B. Harris 1965.

Preston, L. E. The noble savage: Omai or a trip around the world. Drama Critique 13 1956.

Roberts, E. V. Mr Seedo's London career and his work with Henry Fielding. PQ 45 1966.

Traugott, J. The rake's progress from Court to comedy: a study in comic form. Stud in Eng Lit 1500–1900 6 1966.

Gillespie, G. The rebel in seventeenth-century tragedy. Comparative Lit 18 1966.

Lincoln, S. The anglicization of Amadis de Gaul. In Eight essays in English literature, Pullman 1968.

Hook, L. The rape of Europa by Jupiter. Ibid.

(7) DRAMATIC THEORY AND CRITICISM

Anthologies

See also Collections and Anthologies under Literary Theory, col 43, above.

Spingarn, J. E. Critical essays of the seventeenth century. 3 vols Oxford 1908–9. With introd.

Durham, W. H. Critical essays of the eighteenth century 1700–25. New Haven 1915. With introd and bibliography.

Clark, H. B. European theories of the drama: an anthology. Cincinnati 1919, 1929 (rev).

The appreciation of Shakespeare: a collection of criticism of the eighteenth, nineteenth and twentieth centuries [1765–1939]. Ed B. N. Wagner, Washington 1949.

Dramatic essays of the neoclassical age. Ed H. H. Adams and B. Hathaway, New York 1950.

Essays of the theatre from eighteenth-century periodicals. Ed J. Loftis, Los Angeles 1960.

Restoration theatre. Ed J. R. Brown and B. Harris 1965.

Restoration drama: modern essays in criticism. Ed J. Loftis, New York 1966.

Restoration dramatists: a collection of critical essays. Ed E. Miner, Englewood Cliffs NJ 1966.

Modern Studies

The titles listed below should be supplemented by Literary Theory, col 23, above.

Friedland, L. S. The dramatic unities in England. JEGP 10 1911.

Paul, H. G. John Dennis: his life and criticism. New York 1922.

Quinlan, M. A. Poetic justice in the drama. Notre Dame 1912.

Dutton, G. B. French Aristotelian formalists and Thomas Rymer. PMLA 29 1914.

— Theory and practice in English tragedy 1650–1700. E Studien 49 1916.

Draper, J. W. Aristotelian mimesis in eighteenth-century England. PMLA 36 1921.

Raysor, T. M. The downfall of the three unities. MLN 42 1927.

Nicoll, A. The theory of drama. 1931.

Fletcher, E. G. Defoe and the theatre. PQ 13 1934.

Green, C. C. The neo-classic theory of tragedy in England during the eighteenth-century. Cambridge Mass 1934.

Larrabee, S. A. The 'closet' and the 'stage' in 1759. MLN 56 1941.

Hathaway, B. The Lucretian 'return upon ourselves' in eighteenth-century theories of tragedy. PMLA 62 1947.

Conklin, P. S. A history of Hamlet criticism 1601–1821. New York 1947.

Vowles, R. B. Dramatic theory: a bibliography. BNYPL Aug–Nov 1955.

Whitley, A. Hazlitt and the theatre. SE 34 1955.

Barber, C. L. The idea of honour in the English drama 1591–1700. Gothenburg 1957.

Nelson, R. J. Play within a play: the dramatist's conception of his art from Shakespeare to Anouilh. New Haven 1958.

Goldstein, M. Pope and the Augustan stage. 1958.

Jones, C. E. Dramatic criticism in the Critical Review 1756–85. MLQ 20 1959.

Needham, G. B. Mrs Frances Brooks: dramatic critic. Theatre Notebook 15 1961.

Rothstein, E. English tragic theory in the late seventeenth century. ELH 29 1962.

Dublin's first dramatic periodical. Restoration & 18th-Century Theatre Research 2 1963.

Stratman, C. J. Scotland's first dramatic periodical: the Edinburgh Theatrical Censor. Theatre Notebook 17 1963.

Nevo, R. Toward a theory of comedy. Jnl of Aesthetics 21 1963.

Singh, S. The theory of drama in the Restoration period. Calcutta 1963.

McDonald, C. O. Restoration comedy as drama of satire: investigation into seventeenth-century aesthetics. SP 61 1964.

Kirsch, A. C. An essay on dramatick poetry 1681. HLQ 28 1964.

Huseboe, A. R. Pope's critical views of the London stage. Restoration & 18th-Century Theatre Research 3 1964.

Simon, I. Critical terms in Restoration translation from the French. Revue Belge 42 1964.

Maurocordato, A. La critique classique en Angleterre de la Restauration à la mort de Joseph Addison. Paris 1964.

The Principal Works of Dramatic Criticism
1660–1800

Periodical criticism is excluded here, other than specifically theatrical periodicals, as well as Shakespearean criticism.

The literature of the Collier controversy has been allotted a separate section, below, and the pamphlets attacking John Home's Douglas 1757, are listed under Home, below, but no attempt has been made to include later denunciations of the drama. See also R. W. Babcock, A preliminary bibliography of eighteenth-century criticism of Shakespeare, SP extra ser 1 1929, which includes many works only incidentally connected with Shakespeare, and J. W. Draper, Eighteenth-century English aesthetics: a bibliography, Heidelberg 1931 (pt 4 on drama). C. H. Gray, Theatrical criticism in London to 1795, New York 1931, covers the periodicals minutely. Modern reprints of works by Butler, Flecknoe, Howard, Shadwell, Rymer, Dennis, Congreve Farquhar, Purney, Steele, Hume et al will be found in the main sections devoted to these writers.

Dryden, John. Essays [1664–1700]. Ed W. P. Ker 2 vols Oxford 1900; Of dramatic poesy and other critical essays, ed G. Watson 2 vols 1962 (EL).

Pepys, Samuel. Diary. Ed H. B. Wheatley 9 vols 1897–9. *See* H. McAfee, Pepys on the Restoration stage, New Haven 1916.

Butler, Samuel. Upon critics who judge of modern plays by the rules of the ancients. In his Genuine remains, ed R. Taylor vol 1, 1759.

Flecknoe, Richard. A short discourse on the English stage. Appended to his Love's Kingdom, 1664.

Howard, Sir Robert. Four new plays. 1665. Preface.

— The great favourite. 1668. Preface.

Shadwell, Thomas. The sullen lovers. 1668. Preface.

— The humourists. 1671. Preface.

Howard, Edward. The women's conquest. 1671. Preface.

Rymer, Thomas. The tragedies of the last age. 1678, 1692.

— A short view of tragedy. 1693.

— The critical works of Thomas Rymer. Ed C. A. Zimansky, New Haven 1956.

An essay on dramatick poetry. Appended to Amaryllis to Tityrus: being the first heroick harangue of Monsieur Scudéry, englished by a person of honour, 1681.

Reflections upon tragedies, comedies and operas. 1684. Tr from the French of Saint-Evremond.

The whole art of the stage now made English. 1684. Tr from D'Aubignac, La pratique du théâtre.

Mixt essays. 1685. Tr from the French of Saint-Evremond.

Dennis, John. The impartial critick: or some observations upon a late book entitled A short view of tragedy, written by Mr Rymer. 1693.

— The comical gallant; to which is added a large account of taste in poetry. 1702.

— Remarks upon Cato. 1713.

— Critical works. Ed E. N. Hooker 2 vols Baltimore 1939–43.

Tate, Nahum. A Duke and no Duke. 1693. Preface on farce.

An essay at a vindication of love in tragedies, against Rapin and Mr Rymer. In Miscellaneous letters and essays, ed Charles Gildon 1694.

Congreve, William. Letters upon several occasions, between Mr Dryden, Mr Wycherley, Mr —, Mr Congreve and Mr Dennis. Ed John Dennis 1696. Includes Congreve's letter to Dennis on humour.

A letter to A.H. esq concerning the stage. Occasional Paper no 9 1698 (anon); ed H. T. Swedenberg, Los Angeles 1946.

The works of Saint-Evremond made English. 2 vols 1700, 3 vols 1714–28.

B., W. Letters v: wherein are laid down general rules to judge of tragedy and comedy. In Letters of wit, politicks and morality, ed Abel Boyer 1701; rptd in the Dramatick works of William Burnaby, ed F. E. Budd 1931, where it is assigned to Burnaby. Sometimes ascribed to Gildon.

A comparison between the two stages, with an examen of the Generous conqueror, and other plays by Steele, Rowe [et al]. 1702; ed S. B. Wells, Princeton 1942. Sometimes attributed to Gildon.

Farquhar, George. A discourse upon comedy. In his Love and business, 1702.

Representation of the impiety and immorality of the English stage: some thoughts concerning the stage. 1704 (anon); ed E. L. Avery, Los Angeles 1947 (Augustan Reprint Soc).

Whether the dramatic poets of the last age exceeded those of this? In Athenian oracle, 1704.

Purney, Thomas. Pastorals: viz the bashful swain; and beauty and simplicity. 1717. Advertisement.

'Corinna'. Critical remarks on the four taking plays of this season. 1719. Criticism of Young, Sewell, Killigrew and Charles Johnson.

[Steele, Sir Richard]. The Theatre, by Sir John Edgar. 28 nos 2 Jan–5 April 1720; rptd J. Nichols 1791; ed J. Loftis, Oxford 1962.

The Anti-Theatre, by Sir John Falstaffe. 15 nos 15 Feb–5 April 1720; rptd J. Nichols 1791.

Letters describing the characters and customs of the English and French nations. 1726, 1726. Tr from the French of B. L. de Muralt.

Adams, George. The tragedies of Sophocles, with a defence of tragick poetry. 2 vols 1729.

[Cooke, Thomas]. Considerations on the stage. 1731. Also appended to the Triumph of love and honour, 1731.
—— The mournful nuptials: a tragedy. 1739. Includes Some observations on satire, and on the present state of our public entertainments.

Johnson, Charles. Medaea. 1731. Preface.

Trapp, Joseph. An essay upon the nature and art of moving the passions in tragedy. In Works of Virgil, 1731.

A discourse on tragedy, with reflections on the English and French drama. Tr from Voltaire and added to 1731 edn of his Essays upon the civil wars of France.

Letters concerning the English nation. 1733. Tr from the French of Voltaire.

[Hill, Aaron and William Popple]. The Prompter. 173 nos 12 Nov 1734–2 July 1736; ed W. A. Appleton and K. A. Burnim, New York 1965 (selection).

The dramatic historiographer: or the British theatre delineated, exhibiting the argument, conduct and chief incidents of the most celebrated plays. Vol I (all pbd), 1735.

An historical and critical account of the theatres in Europe. 1741, 1754 (with An introductory discourse concerning the present state of the English stage and players). Tr from the French of Luigi Riccoboni.

Morris, Corbyn. Concerning humour in comedy. Appended to his An essay towards fixing the true standards of wit, 1744.

La Place, P. A. de. Discours sur le théâtre anglois. Prefixed to Le théâtre anglois, 8 vols 1746–9.

Foote, Samuel. The Roman and English comedy consider'd and compar'd, with remarks on the Suspicious husband and an examen into the merit of the present comic actors. 1747.

A companion to the theatre: or a review of our most celebrated dramatic pieces. 1747.

An examen of the new comedy call'd the Suspicious husband, with some observations upon our dramatick poetry and authors. 1747.

Letters on the English and French nations. 2 vols 1747, Dublin 1747. Tr from J. B. le Blanc, Lettres d'un François, 1745.

Guthrie, W. Essay on English tragedy, with remarks on the Abbé Le Blanc's Observations on the English stage. 1747, 1749, 1757.

Lockman, J. A discourse on opera. With his trn of F. Vanneschi, Fetonte, 1747.

[Hippisley, John]. A dissertation on comedy, by a student of Oxford. 1750.

Betson, A. Miscellaneous dissertations on the origin and antiquity of masquerades. [1751].

[Fiquet du Boccage, P. J.] Lettre sur le théâtre anglois. 1752. Prefixed to his trns of Shadwell and Wycherley.

Derrick, Samuel. The dramatic censor. 1752.

Mason, William. Elfrida: a dramatic poem. 1752. Letter on the drama prefixed.

Hurd, Richard. Dissertation concerning the provinces of the several species of the drama. Appended to his edn of Horace, Ars poetica, 2 vols 1753.

Hume, David. Four dissertations. 1757. Includes Of tragedy.

Armstrong, John. Sketches: or essays on various subjects. 1758. Includes Of the versification of English tragedy, Of the dramatic writers.

Shirley, W. Brief remarks on the original and present state of drama. 1758.

The theatrical review for the year 1757 and the beginning of 1758. 1758.

Le train du monde: comédie en prose, traduite de l'anglois de Congreve, précédée d'une dissertation sur la comédie angloise. 1759.

Lennox, Charlotte. The Greek theatre of Father Brumoy. 3 vols 1759. Preface.

Francklin, Thomas. A disseration on ancient tragedy. 1760.

An essay upon the present state of the theatre in France, England and Italy. 1760.

Critical essays on dramatic poetry. 1761. Tr from the French of Voltaire.

Colman, George. Critical reflections on the old English dramatic writers, intended as a preface to the works of Massinger. 1761.

Moor, J. On the early tragedy according to Aristotle. 1763.

The Theatrical Review: or Annals of the Drama. 5 nos Jan–June 1763.

Warnecke, J. A. F. Harlequin: or a defence of grotesque comic performances. 1766. Tr from the German of J. Moeser.

The theatrical campaign for MDCCLXVI and MDCCLXVII. 1767. Review of plays produced 1766–7.

The [theatrical] monitor: or green-room laid open. 18 nos 17 Oct 1767–16 April 1768.

The theatrical register: or a complete list of every performer at the different theatres for the year 1769. 1769.

[Gentleman, Francis]. The dramatic censor: or critical companion. 2 vols 1770.

Hiffernan, Paul. Dramatic genius, in five books. 1770, 1772.

[Richardson, William]. Cursory remarks on tragedy, on Shakespeare and on certain French and Italian poets, principally tragedians. 1772, 1774. Sometimes ascribed to Edward Taylor or Joseph Ritson.

[Potter, John]. The theatrical review: or new companion to the Play-house, containing a critical and historical account of every tragedy, comedy, opera, farce etc, exhibited at the theatre during the last season, by a society of gentlemen. 2 vols 1772. Originally appeared in Public Ledger 25 Sept 1771–20 March 1772.

Aikin, J. and A. L. Miscellaneous pieces in prose. 1773, 1775, 1792. Includes On the province of comedy.

Cooke, William. The elements of dramatic criticism. 1775; tr German, 1777.

Hodson, W. Observations on tragedy. In his Zoraida, 1780.

[Burgoyne, John]. The Lord of the manor. 1781. Preface on comic opera.

Harris, James. Philological inquiries. 3 pts 1781–1802. Pt II on drama.

Walwyn, B. An essay on comedy. 1782.

Davies, Thomas. Dramatic miscellanies. 3 vols 1783–4, Dublin 1784, London 1785.

Brown, John. Letters upon the poetry and music of the Italian opera. Edinburgh 1789.

The Prompter. 19 nos 24 Oct–10 Dec 1789.

[Fennell, James]. The Theatrical Guardian. 6 nos 5 March–9 April 1791.

Garden, Francis [Lord Gardenstone]. Miscellanies in prose and verse, including remarks on English plays, operas and farces. Edinburgh 1792 (2nd edn).

Aikin, J. On the impression of reality attending dramatic representation. Memoirs of Manchester Literary & Philosophical Soc 4 1793.

Sayers, Frank. Of the dramatic unities. In his Disquisitions metaphysical and literary, 1793, Norwich 1808.

A complete history of the drama, from the earliest periods, by Censor dramaticus. 1793.

'Peter Pindar' (John Wolcot). The cap: a satiric poem, including most of the dramatic writers of the present day. [1795?].

[Penn, John]. Letters on the drama. 1796.

—— A translation of Ranieri di Calsabigi's Letter to Count Alfieri on tragedy. 1797.

Walker, George. On tragedy and the interest in tragical representations. Memoirs of Manchester Literary & Philosophical Soc 5 1798.

Walpole, Horace. Thoughts on comedy. In his Works vol 2, 1798.

[Walker, J. C.]. Historical memoir on Italian tragedy. 1799.

Cumberland, Richard. On dramatic style. In The artist: a collection of essays, ed P. Hoare 1810.

Barret, B. The causes of the pleasure which is derived from tragedy. Appended to his Pretentions to a final analysis of the nature of sublimity, 1812.

(8) THE COLLIER CONTROVERSY

JEREMY COLLIER
1650-1726

§ I

A short view of the immorality and profaneness of the English stage; together with the sense of antiquity upon this argument. 1698 (3 edns), 1699; tr French, 1715.

A defence of the short view of the profaneness and immorality of the English stage etc: being a reply to Mr Congreve's amendments etc and to the vindication of the author of the Relapse. 1699.

A second defence of the short view of the profaneness and immorality of the English stage etc: being a reply to a book entitled the Ancient and modern stages surveyed etc 1700.

Mr Collier's dissuasive from the play-house, in a letter to a person of quality occasion'd by the late calamity of the tempest. 1703, 1704 (with A letter written by another hand in answer to some questions sent by a person of quality).

A farther vindication of the Short view of the profaneness and immorality of the English stage, in which the objections of a late book entitled A defence of plays are consider'd. 1708.

A short view of the profaneness and immorality of the English stage etc, with the several defenses of the same. 1730, 1738. Includes all the above items except Mr Collier's dissuasive.

§ 2

J. W. Krutch, Comedy and conscience after the Restoration, New York 1924, lists several works apparently belonging to the controversy which are no longer extant. See also F. T. Wood, N & Q 11–25 Sept 1937, whose list continues to 1800.

Wright, James. Country conversations: being an account of some discourses that happen'd in a visit to the country last summer on divers subjects, chiefly of the modern comedies. 1694.

—— Historia histrionica: an historical account of the English-stage, shewing the ancient use, improvement and perfection, of dramatic representations in this nation. 1699; ed E. W. Ashbee 1872 (facs); ed W. C. Hazlitt in Dodsley's old plays vol 15 1876; ed R. W. Lowe in Colley Cibber's Apology vol 2 1889.

Blackmore, Sir Richard. Prince Arthur: an heroick poem. 1695. Preface.

—— King Arthur: an heroick poem. 1697. Preface.

—— A satyr against wit. 1700 (3 edns).

—— Essays upon several subjects. 1716. See Preface and Essay upon wit.

D'Urfey, Thomas. The campaigners: or the pleasant adventures at Brussels, with a familiar preface upon a late reformer of the stage, ending with a satyrical fable of the dog and the ottor. 1698.

[Vanbrugh, Sir John]. A short vindication of the Relapse and the Provok'd wife, from immorality and profaneness. 1698.

Congreve, William. Amendments of Mr Collier's false and imperfect citations. 1698.

A vindication of the stage, with the usefulness and advantages of dramatic representations, in answer to Mr Collier's late book. 1698. By Charles Gildon?

Animadversions on Mr Congreve's late answer to Mr Collier, in a dialogue between Mr Smith and Mr Johnson, with the characters of the present poets and some offers towards new-modelling the stage. 1698.

[Settle, Elkanah]. A defence of dramatick poetry: being a review of Mr Collier's view of the immorality and profaneness of the stage. 1698.

—— A farther defence of dramatick poetry: being the second part of the review of Mr Collier's view. 1698.

—— The city-ramble, or a play-house wedding: a comedy. 1711.

The immorality of the English pulpit, as justly subjected to the notice of the English stage, as the immorality of the stage is, to that of the pulpit, in a letter to Mr Collier. 1698.

Some remarks upon Mr Collier's Defence of his short view of English stage etc in vindication of Mr Congreve etc. 1698.

[Ridpath, George?]. The stage condemned, and the encouragement given to the immoralities and profaneness of the theatre, by the English schools, universities and pulpits, censur'd; the arguments of all the authors that have writ in defence of the stage against Mr Collier, consider'd. 1698, 1706.

A discourse of the lawfulness and unlawfulness of plays. In P. A. Motteux, Beauty in distress, 1698. Tr from François Caffero's French.

Dennis, John. The usefulness of the stage, to the happiness of mankind, to government and to religion, occasioned by a late book, written by Jeremy Collier. 1698.

—— The person of quality's answer to Mr Collier's letters. In his Original letters, 1721.

—— The stage defended from Scripture, reason, experience and the common sense of mankind, occasion'd by Mr Law's late pamphlet against stage entertainments. 1726.

—— Critical works. Ed E. N. Hooker 2 vols Baltimore 1939–43.

[Willis, Richard]. Some considerations about the danger of going to plays. Occasional Paper no 9 1698; rptd as Of plays and masquerades in A collection of the occasional papers, 1708; 1719 (separately), 1724.

[Gildon, Charles]. Phaeton: a tragedy, with some reflections on a book called A short view. 1698.

Oldmixon, John. Reflections on the stage and Mr Collier's Defence of the short view, in four dialogues. 1699.

Drake, James. The antient and modern stage survey'd: or Mr Collier's view of the immorality and profaneness of the English stage set in a true light and the comparative morality of the English stage is asserted upon the parallel. 1699.

Maxims and reflections upon plays, now made English. 1699. Brief preface by Jeremy Collier. Tr from Bossuet.

D., A. The stage acquitted: being a full answer to Mr Collier and the other enemies of the drama, with a vindication of King Charles the Martyr from the abuses of a scurrilous book called the Stage condemned; to which is added the character of the animadverter, and the animadversion on Mr Congreve's answer to Mr Collier. 1699.

Defoe, Daniel. The pacificator. 1700.

Dryden, John. Fables ancient and modern; with original poems. 1700. Preface.

Visits from the shades: or dialogues serious, comical and political. 2 pts 1704–5. Includes J. Hains' ghost and the reforming Mr Collier.

[Baker, Thomas]. An act at Oxford. 1704. Preface.

[Brown, Thomas ?]. The stage-beaux toss'd in a blanket, or hypocrasie alamode expos'd in a true picture of Jerry a pretending scourge to the English stage: a comedy, with prologue on occasional conformity and an epilogue on the reformers. 1704.

A representation of the impiety and immorality of the English stage, with reasons for putting a stop thereto; and some questions addrest to those who frequent the playhouses. 1704 (3 edns); ed E. L. Avery, Los Angeles 1947 (Augustan Reprint Soc).

Tenison, Thomas. A letter from several members of the society for the reformation of manners. 1704.

[Woodward, Josiah ?]. Some thoughts concerning the stage in a letter to a lady. 1704.

— A letter to a lady concerning the new play-houses. 1706.

Bedford, Arthur. Serious reflections on the scandalous abuse and effects of the stage, in a sermon preach'd at the parish-church of St Nicholas in the city of Bristol, on Sunday the 7th day of January 1704/5. Bristol 1705, 1705.

— A second advertisement concerning the profaneness of the play-house. Bristol 1705. Anon.

— The evil and danger of stage plays: shewing their natural tendency to destroy religion and introduce a general corruption of manners, in almost two thousand instances taken from the plays of the two last years. Bristol 1706.

— The great abuse of musick in two parts: containing an account of the use and design of musick among the antient Jews, Romans and others; and also an account of the immorality and profaneness which is occasioned by the corruption of that most noble science in the present age. 1711.

— The obligations which lie both upon magistrates and others to put the laws in execution against immorality and profaneness. 1718.

— A serious romonstrance in behalf of the Christian religion against the horrid blasphemies and impieties which are still used in the English play-houses. 1719.

The letters of Monsieur l'Abbé de Bellegarde. 1705. Includes trn of his Reflections on comedies and plays.

Esther: a sacred tragedy, with a dedication to the Lord Archbishop of York. 1705. From Racine.

Filmer, Edward. A defence of plays: or the stage vindicated, from several passages in Mr Collier's Short view etc; wherein is offer'd the most probable method of reforming our plays, with a consideration how far vicious characters may be allow'd on the stage. 1707.

A treatise of plays and stews. Tr from Prince Armand de Conti in his Works, 1711.

Stage plays justly condemned. 1720.

The conduct of the stage considered: being a short historical account of its origin, progress, various aspects and treatment in the pagan, Jewish and Christian world. 1721.

Law, William. The absolute unlawfulness of the stage entertainment fully demonstrated. 1726, 1726, 1755, 1759, 1798.

Law outlawed, written at the request of the orange-woman. 1726.

Cibber, Colley. An apology for the life of Mr Colley Cibber, comedian, written by himself. 1740; ed R. W. Lowe 2 vols 1889; ed B. R. S. Fone, Ann Arbor 1968.

Modern Studies

Macaulay, T. B. The dramatic works of Wycherley, Congreve, Vanbrugh and Farquhar. Edinburgh Rev 62 1841.

Ballein, J. Jeremy Collier's Angriff auf die englische Bühne. Marburg 1910.

Whibley, C. The Restoration drama. CHEL 8 1912.

Krutch, J. W. Comedy and conscience after the Restoration. New York 1924, 1949.

Bradley, L. J. H. Collier's Marcus Aurelius. TLS 19 Jan 1928. Reply by M. Holland 26 Jan 1928.

Anthony, R. The Jeremy Collier stage controversy 1698–1726. Marburg 1937.

Lamb, G. F. A short view of Collier. English 7 1940.

Hooker, H. M. Father John Constable on Collier. PQ 23 1944. Reply by W. K. Wimsatt 24 1945.

Meadley, T. D. Attack on the theatre c. 1580–1680. London Quart 178 1953.

— The second attack on the English stage, preliminary skirmishes. Ibid.

Mattauch, H. A propos du premier jugement sur Shakespeare en France. MLN 78 1963. On Collier's influence upon French criticism of Shakespeare.

II. THEATRES AND ACTORS

THEATRES AND THEATRICAL HISTORY: *London Stage and Theatres, Provincial Stage and Theatres*.
PRODUCTION AND RELATED TOPICS: *Costume, Scenery, Conventions, Procedure, Finance*.
THE ACTORS: *Lives of Actors, The Actor's Art*.

Lowe, R. W. A bibliographical account of English theatrical literature. 1888. Lowe lists many of the squibs and pamphlets in 18th-century theatrical history, often only of local interest. Such ephemera are not listed below.

Cameron, J. A bibliography of Scottish theatrical literature. Trans Edinburgh Bibl Soc 1 1896.

— Supplement to a Bibliography of Scottish theatrical literature. Ibid.

O'Neill, J. J. A bibliographical account of Irish theatrical literature. Dublin 1920.

Gilder, R. and G. Freedley. Theatre collections in libraries and museums: an international handbook. New York 1936.

Freedley, G. The 26 principal theatre collections in American libraries and museums. BNYPL July 1958.

(1) THE LONDON STAGE

The period 1660–1700 is covered by L. Hotson, The Commonwealth and Restoration stage, 1928, *and* E. Boswell, The Restoration Court stage. A. Nicoll, Restoration drama, Early eighteenth-century drama, *and* Later eighteenth-century drama *are useful for history and bibliography*. John Genest, Some account of the English stage, 1832, *covers the period in considerable detail*. The London stage, ed W. Van Lennep, E. L. Avery, A. H. Scouten, G. W. Stone and C. B. Hogan, *below, deals comprehensively with the daily performances and the organization and operations of the theatres. Contemporary pamphlets on Garrick's management are listed under Garrick, below*.

[Wright, James]. Historia histrionica: an historical account of the English stage, in a dialogue of plays and players. 1699; ed E. W. Ashbee 1872 (facs); rptd W. C. Hazlitt in Dodsley's Old plays vol 15, 1876; ed R. W. Lowe in Cibber's Apology vol 2, 1889; ed A. Lang in Social England illustrated, 1903.

A comparison between the two stages. 1702; ed S. B. Wells, Princeton 1942.

Downes, John. Roscius anglicanus: or an historical review of the stage. 1708; ed T. Davies 1789; ed J. Knight 1886; ed M. Summers [1928]; ed J. Loftis, Los Angeles 1969 (Augustan Reprint Soc).

Weaver, John. The history of the mimes and pantomimes. 1728.

Riccoboni, Luigi. Réflexions historiques et critiques sur les différens théâtres de l'Europe. Paris 1738; tr 1741, 1754 (with Discourse concerning the present English stage).

Cibber, Colley. An apology for the life of Mr Colley Cibber, comedian, with an historical view of the stage during his own time. 1740, 1740; ed R. W. Lowe 2 vols 1889; ed B. R. S. Fone, Ann Arbor 1968.

Betterton, Thomas. The history of the English stage, from the Restoration to the present time. 1741. By Oldys and Curll, from Betterton's notes and information supplied by Bowman.

Chetwood, W. R. A general history of the stage. 1749, Dublin 1749.

Wilkes, Thomas. A general view of the stage. 1759. Often erroneously attributed to Samuel Derrick. *See* W. J. Lawrence, TLS 26 June 1930.

Victor, Benjamin. The history of the theatres of London and Dublin, from the year 1730, [with] an annual register of plays from 1712. 2 vols 1761.

— The history of the theatres of London, from the year 1760. 1771.

Oulton, W. C. The history of the theatres of London from 1771 to 1795. 2 vols 1796.

— A history of the theatres of London 1795–1817. 3 vols 1818.

Roach's new and complete history of the stage. 1796.

Dibdin, Charles. A complete history of the English stage. 5 vols [1800].

Waldron, F. G. A compendious history of the English stage. 1800.

Gilliland, Thomas. The dramatic mirror: containing the history of the stage to the present time. 2 vols 1808.

[Genest, John]. Some account of the English stage from 1660 to 1830. 10 vols Bath 1832.

Doran, J. Their Majesties' servants: annals of the English stage from Betterton to Kean. 2 vols 1864, 1865 (rev); rev R. W. Lowe 3 vols 1888.

Fitzgerald, P. A new history of the English stage [1660–1842]. 2 vols 1882.

Aitken, G. A. Actors and managers under Queen Anne. Athenaeum 11, 25 Aug 1888.

Baker, H. B. The London stage from 1576 to 1888. 2 vols 1889, 1904 (rev to 1903).

Nicholson, W. The struggle for a free stage in London. 1906.

G., G. M. The stage censor 1544–1907. 1908.

Sharp, R. F. A short history of the English stage. 1909.

Powell, F. and F. Palmer. Censorship in England. 1913.

Odell, G. C. D. Shakespeare from Betterton to Irving. 2 vols New York 1920.

Krutch, J. W. Government attempts to regulate the stage after the Jeremy Collier controversy. PMLA 38 1923.

— Comedy and conscience after the Restoration. New York 1924, 1949.

Nicoll, A. Restoration drama. Cambridge 1923, 1928 (rev), 1940, 1952 (rev).

— Early eighteenth-century drama. Cambridge 1925, 1929, 1952 (rev).

— Late eighteenth-century drama. Cambridge 1927, 1937, 1952 (rev).

Hotson, L. The Commonwealth and Restoration stage. Cambridge Mass 1928.

White, A. F. The Office of Revels and dramatic censorship during the Restoration period. Western Reserve Univ Bull 34 1931.

Boswell, E. The Restoration Court stage. Cambridge Mass 1932.

Fuchs, M. and P. Comédiens français à Londres 1738–55. Revue de Littérature Comparée 7 1933.

MacMillan, D. Drury Lane calendar 1747–76, compiled from the playbills. San Marino 1938.

Crean, P. J. The stage licensing act of 1737. MP 35 1938.

Woehl, A. L. Plays in the repertories of the patent houses. In Studies in speech and drama in honor of A. M. Drummond, Ithaca 1944.

Vincent, H. P. John Rich and the first Covent Garden theatre. ELH 16 1950.

Stone, H. W. The authorship of Tit for tat: a manuscript source for 18th-century theatre history. Theatre Notebook 10 1955.

Rosenfeld, S. Unpublished stage documents. Theatre Notebook 11 1957.

— Goodman's Fields Theatre. Theatre Notebook 12 1957.

— Early Lyceum Theatres. Theatre Notebook 18 1964.

— Some British private theatres in the 18th century. Maske & Kothurn 10 1964.

Eddison, R. Capon and Goodman's Fields. Theatre Notebook 14 1960.

The London stage 1660–1800. Part 1 1660–1700, ed W. Van Lennep, E. L. Avery and A. H. Scouten, Carbondale 1965; Part 2 1700–29, ed E. L. Avery 2 vols Carbondale 1960; Part 3 1729–47, ed A. H. Scouten 2 vols Carbondale 1961; Part 4 1747–76, ed G. W. Stone 3 vols Carbondale 1962; Part 5 1776–1800, ed C. B. Hogan 3 vols Carbondale 1968.

Hartnoll, P. The theatre and the Licensing Act of 1737. In Silver Renaissance, ed A. Natan 1961.

Wilson, J. H. Theatre notes from the Newdigate newsletters. Theatre Notebook 15–16 1961–2.

Barker, K. M. D. The theatre proprietor's story. Theatre Notebook 18 1964.

Pedicord, H. W. The second chronicler: a tentative identification of the unknown hand in the ms diaries of the Drury Lane theatres. Theatre Survey 5 1964.

Langhans, E. A. Theatrical references in the Greenwich Hospital newsletters. N & Q Sept 1964.

— Wren's Restoration playhouse. Theatre Notebook 18 1964.

— Restoration manuscript notes in seventeenth-century plays. Restoration & 18th-Century Theatre Research 5 1966.

— The Vere Street and Lincoln's Inn Fields Theatres in pictures. Educational Theatre Jnl 20 1968.

Freehafer, J. The formation of the London patent companies in 1660. Theatre Notebook 20 1966.

(2) THE LONDON THEATRES

Saunders, George. A treatise on theatres. 1790.

Gilliland, Thomas. The dramatic mirror. 2 vols 1808. With illustrations.

[Pyne, W. H. and W. Combe]. The microcosm of London. 3 vols 1808–10. With aquatints by Pugin and Rowlandson.

Wyatt, Benjamin. Observations on the design for the Theatre Royal Drury Lane, as executed in the year 1812. 1813.

'Hood, Eu.' (Joseph Haslewood). Of the London theatres. GM Aug–Dec 1813, April, July 1814; rptd in Gentlemen's Magazine Library vol 15, 1904.

Hughson, David. Walks through London. 1817.

Wilkinson, R. Londina illustrata. 2 vols 1825.

Britton, J. Illustrations of the public buildings of London. 2 vols 1825–8.

Dibdin, C. History and illustrations of the London theatres. 1826.

Brayley, E. W. Historical and descriptive accounts of the theatres of London. 2 vols 1826.

Williams, M. Some London theatres past and present. 1883.

Brereton, A. The Lyceum and Henry Irving. 1903.

—— The story of Drury Lane. In L. N. Parker, The pageant of Drury Lane, 1918.

Maude, C. The Haymarket theatre. 1903.

Lawrence, W. J. A forgotten Restoration playhouse. E Studien 35 1904.

—— Restoration stage nurseries. Archiv 132 1914.

—— The old Duke's theatre in Dorset Garden. Architectural Rev 46 1919.

—— The early years of the first English opera house. Musical Quart 7 1921.

—— The French opera in London [1686]. TLS 28 March 1936.

Wyndham, H. S. Annals of Covent Garden theatre. 2 vols 1906.

Odell, G. C. D. Shakespeare from Betterton to Irving. 2 vols New York 1920.

Spencer, H. The Blackfriars mystery. MP 24 1926. On the supposed Blackfriars theatres 1660–1.

Wood, F. T. Goodman's Fields theatre. MLR 25 1930.

—— The account books of Lincoln's Inn Fields theatre 1724–7. N & Q 22–9 April 1933.

Jackson, A. London playhouses 1700–5. RES 8 1932.

—— The stage and the authorities as revealed in the newspapers 1700–14. RES 14 1938.

Nicoll, A. The English theatre. 1936.

Avery, E. L. and M. A. Deupree. The new theatre in the Haymarket, 1734 and 1737. N & Q July 1936.

Avery, E. L. Foreign performers in the London theatres in the early eighteenth century. PQ 16 1937.

—— Fielding's last season with the Haymarket theatre. MP 36 1939.

—— Proposals for a new London theatre in 1737. N & Q 23 May 1942. Reply by J. P. de Castro 20 June 1942.

—— Lincoln's Inn Fields 1704–5. Theatre Notebook 5 1951.

—— Private theatricals in and near London 1700–37. Theatre Notebook 13 1959.

—— A poem on Dorset Garden theatre. Theatre Notebook 18 1964.

—— The Restoration audience. PQ 45 1966.

Lowery, M. R. Performances of Shakespearean plays at Covent Garden and Drury Lane. Shakespeare Assoc Bull 16 1941.

Hughes, L. and A. H. Scouten. The new theatre in the Haymarket, 1734 and 1735. N & Q 15 Jan 1944.

Hook, L. James Brydges drops in at the theatre. HLQ 8 1945. On the Duke of Chandos's theatre-going 1697–1702.

Macqueen-Pope, W. J. Theatre Royal, Drury Lane. 1946.

—— Haymarket: theatre of perfection. 1948.

—— Pillars of Drury Lane. 1955.

Southern, R. The Georgian playhouse. 1948.

Speaight, G. Puppet theatres in London: II, Restoration to the end of the eighteenth century. Theatre Notebook 2 1948.

—— The history of the English puppet theatre. 1955.

—— Tennis court theatres. Theatre Notebook 10 1956.

Sherburn, G. A theatre party of 1729. Harvard Lib Bull 4 1950.

Rosenfeld, S. The wardrobes of Lincoln's Inn Fields and Covent Garden. Theatre Notebook 5 1951.

—— Shepherd's Market theatre and May Fair Wells. Ibid.

Bordinat, P. A new site for the Salisbury Court theatre. N & Q Feb 1956.

Scanlan, E. Reconstruction of the Duke's playhouse in Lincoln's Inn Fields 1661–71. Theatre Notebook 10 1956.

Langhans, E. A. Notes on the reconstruction of Lincoln's Inn Fields theatre. Ibid.

—— Wren's Restoration playhouse. Theatre Notebook 18 1964.

—— Pictorial material on the Bridges Street and Drury Lane theatres. Theatre Survey 7 1966.

Wilson, J. H. The Duke's theatre in March 1680. N & Q Oct 1962.

—— Six Restoration play-dates. N & Q June 1962.

—— A theatre in York House. Theatre Notebook 16 1962.

—— The Duchess of Portsmouth's players. N & Q March 1963.

—— Players' lists in the Lord Chamberlain's registers. Theatre Notebook 18 1963.

Van Lennep, W. The death of the Red Bull. Theatre Notebook 16 1962.

Kennedy-Shipton, L. Notes on a copy of William Capon's plan of Goodman's Fields theatre, 1786 and 1802, and on a copy of one of the ceiling paintings, in the Folger Shakespeare Library. Theatre Notebook 17 1963.

Cameron, K. The Monmouth and Portsmouth troupes. Ibid.

Mullin, D. C. The Queen's theatre, Haymarket: Vanbrugh's opera house. Theatre Survey 8 1967.

(3) THE PROVINCIAL STAGE AND THEATRES

Ireland, Scotland and Wales

Hitchcock, Robert. An historical view of the Irish stage. 2 vols Dublin 1788–94.

An essay on the welfare of the Irish stage. 1792.

Molloy, J. F. The romance of the Irish stage. 2 vols 1897.

O'Neil, J. J. Irish theatrical history. [1907].

Stockwell, La T. Dublin theatres and theatre customs 1637–1820. Kingston Tennessee 1938.

Bald, R. C. Shakespeare on the stage in Restoration Dublin. PMLA 56 1941.

Spencer, H. Shakespearean cuts in Restoration Dublin. PMLA 57 1942.

Van Lennep, W. The Smock Alley players of Dublin. ELH 13 1946.

Fletcher, I. K. The Smock Alley theatre, Dublin 1753–4. Theatre Notebook 6 1952.

Bartley, J. O. Teague, Shenkin and Sawney: being an historical study of the earliest Irish, Welsh and Scottish characters in English plays. Cork 1954.

Stewart, J. H. The fall of the Bastille on the Dublin stage. Jnl of Royal Soc of Antiquaries of Ireland 84 1954.

—— The French Revolution on the Dublin stage 1790–9. Jnl of Royal Soc of Antiquaries of Ireland 91 1961.

Avery, E. L. The Dublin stage 1736–7. N & Q Feb 1955.

Clark, W. S. The early Irish stage: the beginnings to 1720. Oxford 1955.

—— The Siddons in Dublin. Theatre Notebook 9 1955.

—— The Irish stage in the country towns 1720–1800. Oxford 1965.

Jackson, John. The history of the Scottish stage. Edinburgh 1793.

Logan, W. H. Fragmenta scoto-dramatica 1715–58. Edinburgh 1835.

Angus, J. K. A Scotch playhouse [Aberdeen]. 1878.

Dibdin, J. C. The annals of the Edinburgh stage. Edinburgh 1888.

Baynham, W. The Glasgow stage. [1892].

Lawson, R. The story of the Scottish stage. 1917.

Kinsley, J. A Dryden play at Edinburgh. Scottish Historical Rev 33 1954.

McKenzie, J. School and university drama in Scotland 1650–1760. Scottish Historical Rev 34 1955.

—— Shakespeare in Scotland before 1760. Theatre Notebook 11 1956.

Cameron, K. M. The Edinburgh theatre 1668–82. Theatre Notebook 17 1963.

Price, C. The English theatre in Wales in the eighteenth and early nineteenth centuries. Cardiff 1948.

English Provincial Theatres

arranged alphabetically by towns or districts

Penley, B. S. The Bath stage. 1892.

Price, C. Some movements of the Bath company 1729–34. Theatre Notebook 1 1947.

Wood, F. T. Theatrical performances at Bath in the eighteenth century. N & Q 1–15 Nov, 13–27 Dec 1947, 24 Jan, 6 March, 12 June 1948.

Pemberton, T. E. The Birmingham theatres. 1890.

Rhodes, R. C. The Theatre Royal, Birmingham 1774–1924. 1924.

Cunningham, J. E. Theatre Royal: the history of the Theatre Royal, Birmingham. Oxford 1950.

Porter, H. C. A history of the theatres at Brighton 1774–1885. Brighton 1886.

Rosenfeld, S. Duke Street theatre, Brighton 1790–1806. Theatre Notebook 8 1954.

Jenkins, Robert. Memoirs of the Bristol stage. 1826.

Watts, G. T. Theatrical Bristol. Bristol 1915.

Board, M. E. The story of the Bristol stage 1490–1925. Bristol 1925.

Rosenfeld, S. Actors in Bristol 1741–8. TLS 29 Aug 1936.

Barker, K. and R. Southern. A Bristol Theatre Royal inventory. In Studies in English theatre history, 1952.

Barker, K. The Theatre Royal, Bristol: the first seventy years. Bristol 1961.

—— The first night of the Theatre Royal, Bristol. N & Q Nov 1967.

Joseph, B. L. Famous theatres: the Theatre Royal, Bristol. Drama Survey 2 1962.

Little, B. The Theatre Royal [Bristol]: the beginnings of a bicentenary. Bristol 1964.

Rosenfeld, S. The players in Cambridge 1662–1800. In Studies in English theatre history, 1952.

Bryne, M. St C. The earliest Hamlet prompt book in an English library. Theatre Notebook 15 1960. On a Chester performance of 1785.

Rosenfeld, S. Private theatricals at Bowman's Lodge, Dartford 1795–9. Theatre Notebook 16 1962.

Doncaster old theatre. South Yorkshire N & Q 2 1901.

Rosenfeld, S. Players in Epsom. Theatre Notebook 7 1953.

Cotton, W. The story of the drama in Exeter. Exeter 1887.

Hannam-Clark, T. Drama in Gloucestershire. 1928.

Rosenfeld, S. Penkethman's Greenwich theatre. N & Q 21 Dec 1935.

Gaunt, J. The old Halifax theatre. Yorkshire N & Q 1 1904.

Sheppard, T. Evolution of the drama in Hull and district. Hull 1917.

Rosenfeld, S. An Ipswich theatre book. Theatre Notebook 13 1959.

Hodgson, N. Sarah Baker (1736–1816), governor-general of the Kentish drama. In Studies in English theatre history, 1952.

Kelly, W. Notices illustrative of the drama of the borough of Leicester. 1865.

Broadbent, R. J. Annals of the Liverpool stage. Liverpool 1908.

Wardle, A. C. Liverpool's first theatre royal. Trans Historical Soc of Lancs & Cheshire 90 1939.

Hodgkinson, J. L. and R. Pogson. The early Manchester theatre. 1960.

The Theatre Royal, Margate: its history ancient and modern. Margate 1874.

Morley, M. Margate and its theatres 1730–1965. 1966.

Tomlinson, W. W. The Newcastle theatre. Proc Newcastle Archaeological Soc 6 1893.

Dodds, M. H. The northern stage. Archaeologia Aeliana 11 1914.

Harcourt, B. The Theatre Royal, Norwich. 1903.

Burley, T. L. G. Playhouses and players of East Anglia. Norwich 1928.

Wagner, B. M. George Jolly at Norwich. RES 6 1930.

Rosenfeld, S. The players in Norwich 1669–1709. RES 12 1936.

Rhodes, R. C. The King's players at Oxford 1661–1712. TLS 21 Feb 1929. Also subsequent correspondence.

Rosenfeld, S. Some notes on the players in Oxford 1661–1713. RES 19 1943.

Knight, W. H. K. The story of the drama in Plymouth. Western Antiquary 12 1893–5.

Armstrong, W. Changeable scenery at Plymouth in 1764. Theatre Notebook 10 1955.

Bingham, F. A celebrated old playhouse [Richmond, Surrey]. [1885?].

Avery, E. L. The Richmond theatre in 1734 and 1735. N & Q 13 April 1940.

—— The summer theatrical seasons at Richmond and Twickenham 1746–53. N & Q 23 Oct–6 Nov 1937.

Hogan, C. B. The China Hall theatre, Rotherhithe. Theatre Notebook 8 1954.

The theatrical examiner for Sheffield, with a historical sketch of the beginning and progress of theatrical amusements in Sheffield. Sheffield 1825.

Broadbent, R. J. The Stanton circuit. Stage 15 Sept, 3 Nov 1932.

Steer, F. Sources of information on 18th and early 19th-century theatres in Sussex. Theatre Notebook 12 1958. *See also* C. B. Hogan, ibid.

Senior, W. The old Wakefield theatre. Wakefield 1894.

Hare, A. The Georgian theatre in Wessex. 1957.

Grice, F. Roger Kemble's company at Worcester. Theatre Notebook 9 1955.

—— The Theatre Royal at Worcester. Theatre Notebook 10 1956.

Wilkinson, Tate. The wandering patentee: or a history of the Yorkshire theatre from 1700. 4 vols York 1795.

Benson, G. The Theatre Royal and the drama in York. York 1911.

General and Miscellaneous

Holcroft, T. Alwyn: or the gentleman comedian. 2 vols 1780.

Parker, George. A view of society and manners in high life, in which is comprised a history of the stage itinerant. 2 vols 1781.

Wilkinson, Tate. Memoirs. 4 vols York 1790.

A dissertation of the country stage. European Mag 22 1762.

Memoirs of Sylvester Daggerwood, comedian etc, deceased, the whole collected by Peter Panglos. 1806, 1806.

[Winston, James]. The theatric tourist. 1808. With illustrations.

Bernard, John. Retrospections of the stage. 2 vols 1830.

Colby, E. Strolling players in the eighteenth century. N & Q 11 Dec 1915.

—— The Inchbalds strolling into Glasgow. N & Q 3 Nov 1923.

—— A supplement on strollers. PMLA 39 1924.

Hodgson, J. John Cunningham. Archaeologia Aeliana 18 1921.

Thaler, A. Strolling players and provincial drama after Shakespeare. PMLA 37 1922.

Ellis-Fermor, U. M. Studies in the eighteenth-century stage. PQ 2 1923. On English touring companies; Minor theatres of London and its environs; Theatrical booths at the London fairs.

Graves, T. S. Strolling players in the eighteenth century. N & Q 7 July 1923.

Wood, F. T. Strolling actors in the eighteenth century. E Studien 66 1931.

—— Notes on English provincial playhouses in the eighteenth century. N & Q 28 Feb–14 March 1931.

—— Some aspects of provincial drama in the eighteenth century. E Studies 14 1932.

Avery, E. L. Jonson in the provinces. N & Q 2 Oct 1937.

Rosenfeld, S. Strolling plays and drama in the provinces 1660–1765. Cambridge 1939.

Baker, H. C. Strolling actors in eighteenth-century England. SE 1941.

Price, C. An eighteenth-century theatrical agreement. Theatre Notebook 2 1948.

H., A. J. Provincial playbills of the eighteenth century. N & Q 6 March 1948.

Burner, S. A. A provincial strolling company of the 1670's. Theatre Notebook 20 1966.

Nelson, A. L. The periodicity of the Theatric tourist. Theatre Notebook 21 1967.

(4) STRUCTURE, ORGANIZATION, PROCEDURE, PRODUCTION, COSTUME ETC

A collection of letters between Mr Aaron Hill, Mr Pope and others. 1751.

The works of the late Aaron Hill esq. 4 vols 1753. With letters of theatrical interest.

Cibber, Theophilus. Cibber's two dissertations on the theatres. 3 pts [1756].

[Ralph, James]. The case of authors by profession or trade stated, with regard to booksellers, the stage and the public. 1758.

Brounsmith, J. The dramatic time-piece, or perpetual monitor: being a calculation of the length of time every act takes at the Theatres-Royal. 1767.

Garrick, David. Private correspondence. Ed J. Boaden 2 vols 1831–2.

Cook, D. A book of the play. 2 vols 1876. On Masters of the Revels, the license of play-houses, the examiner of plays, a bill of the play, strolling players, 'pay here', in the pit, the footmen's gallery, footlights, prologues, the art of making-up, paint and canvas, stage whispers, stage ghosts, half price, stage stories, doubles, benefits, 'gag', correct costumes, Harlequin and Co, epilogues etc.

—— On the stage. 2 vols 1883. On the art of acting, 'suit the action to the word', the status of the player, the reader of plays, stage doors, stage properties, stage traditions, a thespian academy, the Duke's burlesque, concerning harlequin and company, the omnibus box, of fiddlers etc.

Lawrence, W. J. The pioneers of modern English stage mounting: William Capon and De Loutherbourg. Mag of Art 17 1895.

—— The Elizabethan playhouse and other studies. 2 sers Stratford-on-Avon 1912–13. On proscenium doors, the origin of the theatre programme, early systems of admission, the origin of the English picture-stage, the persistence of Elizabethan conventionalisms etc.

—— The English theatre orchestra: its rise and early characteristics, Musical Quart 1 1913.

—— Music and song in the eighteenth-century theatre. Musical Quart 2 1916.

—— The box set. Stage 13 Aug 1925.

—— Stage and theatre-lighting [1580–1800]. Stage Year Book 1927.

—— Old theatre days and ways. 1935. On drum and trumpet, the prompter, admission systems, rehearsing, authors and their first nights, calling for tunes, the stage villain, the Royal Box, the numberer, stage sentinels, spectators in the orchestra etc.

Broadbent, R. J. Stage whispers. [1901]. Players' benefits, theatrical costume, playbills, scenery etc.

Bell, H. On three plans by Sir Christopher Wren. Architectural Record 1913.

Keith, W. G. The design for the first movable scenery on the English public stage. Burlington Mag 25 1914.

—— John Webb and the Court theatre of Charles II. Architectural Rev 57 1925.

Campbell, L. B. The rise of a theory of stage presentation in England during the eighteenth century. PMLA 32 1917.

—— A history of costuming on the English stage between 1660 and 1823. Wisconsin Univ Stud 2 1918.

—— Scenes and machines on the English stage during the Renaissance. Cambridge 1923.

Nicoll, A. Doors and curtains in Restoration theatres. MLR 15 1920. See also W. J. Lawrence, ibid and M. Summers 16 1921.

—— Scenery in Restoration theatres. Anglia 44 1920.

—— The development of the theatre. 1927.

Odell, G. C. D. Shakespeare from Betterton to Irving. 2 vols New York 1920.

Thaler, A. The 'free-list' and theatre tickets in Shakespeare's time and after. MLR 15 1920.

—— Shakspere to Sheridan: a book about the theatre. Cambridge Mass 1922.

Mackintosh, D. T. New dress'd in the habits of the times. TLS 25 Aug 1927.

—— The Restoration stage. Edinburgh Rev 248 1928.

Boswell, E. A playbill of 1687. Library 3rd ser 11 1931.

Crean, P. J. Footlights. N & Q 28 Jan 1933.

Jackson, A. Play notices from the Burney newspapers 1700–3. PMLA 48 1933.

Ross, J. L. Dramatist versus audience in the early eighteenth century. PQ 12 1933.

Summers, M. The Restoration theatre. 1934.

Avery, E. L. Dancing and pantomime on the English stage 1700–37. PS 31 1934.

—— Two French children on the English stage 1716–19. PQ 13 1934.

—— Vaudeville on the London stage 1700–37. Washington State Univ Stud 5 1937.

—— The finances of an eighteenth-century theatre. Theatre Annual 13 1955.

Rosenfeld, S. The Restoration stage in newspapers and journals 1660–1700. MLR 30 1935; PMLA 51 1936.

—— Foreign theatrical companies in Great Britain in the 17th and 18th centuries. 1955.

—— Scene designs of William Capon. Theatre Notebook 10 1956.

—— The theatre of the London fairs in the 18th century. 1960.

—— An opera house account book. Theatre Notebook 16 1962. On the season of 1716–17.

—— and E. Croft-Murray. A check-list of scene painters working in Great Britain and Ireland in the 18th century. Theatre Notebook 19–20 1964–5.

—— Scene painters at the London theatres in the 18th century. Theatre Notebook 20 1966.

—— Two comic opera scene designs. Theatre Notebook 23 1968.

Huse, W. The shipwreck. In T. M. Parrott presentation volume, Princeton 1935.

—— A noble savage on the stage. MP 33 1936.

Clark, W. S. Restoration prompt notes and stage practices. MLN 51 1936.

—— Corpses, concealments and curtains on the Restoration stage. RES 13 1937.

Stone, G. W. Garrick's presentation of Anthony and Cleopatra. RES 12 1936.

Wells, M. Spectacular scenic effects of the eighteenth-century pantomime. PQ 17 1938.

Tait, S. English theatre riots. Theatre Arts 24 1940.

Thomas, R. Contemporary taste in the stage decorations of the London theatres 1770–1800. MP 42 1944.

Speaight, G. Toy theatre lighting. N & Q 13 Jan 1945. On the first use of footlights.

Varey, J. E. On the staging of string puppets in the seventeenth and eighteenth centuries. Theatre Notebook 5 1951.

Southern, R. Changeable scenery: its origin and development in the British theatre. 1952.

Byrne, M. St C. The stage costuming of Macbeth in the eighteenth century. In Studies in English theatre history, 1952.

Croft-Murray, E. John Devoto: a baroque scene painter. 1953.

Horn-Monval, M. French troupes in England during the Restoration. Theatre Notebook 7 1953.

Bevan, I. Royal performance: the story of royal theatre-going. 1954.

Sawyer, P. The seating capacity and maximum receipts of Lincoln's Inn Fields theatre. N & Q July 1954.

Fletcher, I. K. Italian comedians in England in the 17th century. Theatre Notebook 8 1954.

Clinton-Baddeley, V. C. All right on the night. 1954.

—— A speculation on stars. Theatre Notebook 9 1955.

Armstrong, W. Changeable scenery at Plymouth 1764. Theatre Notebook 10 1955.

Hogan, C. B. An eighteenth-century prompter's notes. Ibid. On William Powell, Drury Lane in 1790s.

Francis, B. John Rich's proposals. Theatre Notebook 12 1957.

Merchant, W. M. Classical costume in Shakespearian productions. Shakespeare Survey 10 1957.

—— Costume in King Lear. Shakespeare Survey 13 1960.

Burnim, K. A. Some notes on Aaron Hill and stage scenery. Theatre Notebook 12 1957.

—— Oblique wings. Ibid.

—— Eighteenth-century theatrical illustrations in the light of contemporary documents. Theatre Notebook 14 1960.

Barrow, B. E. Macklin's costume and property notes for the character of Lovegold: some traditional elements in eighteenth-century low-comedy acting. Theatre Notebook 13 1959.

Morton, R. and W. M. Peterson. Guns on the Restoration stage. N & Q July–Sept 1959.

Cohen, S. J. Theory and practice of theatrical dancing in England in the Restoration and early eighteenth century. BNYPL Jan–Feb 1960.

Barker, K. Michael Edkins, painter. Theatre Notebook 16 1962.

Martin, L. J. From forestage to proscenium: a study of Restoration staging techniques. Theatre Survey 4 1963.

Payne, R. Stage direction during the Restoration. Theatre Annual 20 1963.

Langhans, E. A. New Restoration theatre accounts 1682–92. Theatre Notebook 17 1963.

Jackson, A. S. Restoration scenery 1656–80. Restoration & 18th-Century Theatre Research 3 1964.

Allen, R. G. Topical scenes for pantomime. Educational Theatre Jnl 17 1965.

Sorelius, G. The rights of the Restoration theatrical companies in the older drama. Studia Neophilologica 37 1965.

Oliver, A. and J. Saunders. De Loutherbourg and Pizarro 1799. Theatre Notebook 20 1965.

Mander, R. and J. Michenson. The village lawyer by Samuel De Wilder: some information on the painters. Ibid.

Highfill, P. H. Rich's 1744 inventory of Covent Garden properties. Restoration & 18th-Century Theatre Research 5 1966.

(5) OTHER SPECIAL STUDIES

Broadbent, R. J. A history of pantomime. [1901].

Nicoll, A. Political plays of the Restoration. MLR 16 1921.

—— The rights of Beeston and D'Avenant in Elizabethan plays. RES 1 1925.

Lawrence, W. J. Marionette operas. Musical Quart 10 1924.

—— Oxford Restoration prologues. TLS 16 Jan 1930.

Disher, M. W. Clowns and pantomimes. 1925.

Spencer, H. The Restoration play lists. RES 1 1925.

Baskervill, C. R. Play-lists and after-pieces of the mid-eighteenth century. MP 23 1926.

Whiting, G. W. The condition of the London theatre 1679–83. MP 25 1927.

Ham, R. G. Dryden versus Settle. MP 26 1928.

Wagner, B. M. John Rhodes and Ignoramus. RES 5 1929.

Allen, R. J. The Kit-Cat Club and the theatre. RES 7 1931.

Noyes, R. G. Contemporary musical settings of the songs in Restoration drama. ELH 1 1934.

—— Ben Jonson on the English stage 1660–1776. Cambridge Mass 1935.

Wells, M. P. Some notes on the early eighteenth-century pantomime. SP 37 1935.

Kelly, J. A. German visitors to English theatres in the eighteenth century. Princeton 1936.

Green, G. G. R. Stourbridge Fair booth. Theatre Notebook 15 1953.

Stratman, C. J. A bibliography of British dramatic periodicals 1720–1960. New York 1962.

—— Cotes weekly journal: of the English stage player. PBSA 16 1962.

Steele, R. The Theatre 1720. Ed J. Loftis, Oxford 1962.

Hammert, P. A. The Prompter: an intimate mirror of the theatre in 1789. Restoration & 18th-Century Theatre Research 3 1964.

Hayes, J. Thomas Harris, Gainsborough Dupont and the theatrical gallery at Belmont. Connoisseur 169 1968.

(6) LIVES OF ACTORS AND ACTRESSES

A few dramatists closely connected with the stage have been included.

Collection of Lives etc

Theatrical biography: or memoirs of the principal performers of the three Theatres Royal. 2 vols 1772.

The secret history of the green rooms. 2 vols 1790, 1795 (rev). By Joseph Haslewood?

The thespian dictionary: or dramatic biography of the eighteenth century. 1802, 1805 (enlarged). Includes actors as well as dramatists.

Original anecdotes respecting the stage and the actors of the old school. 1805.

Wewitzer, R. A theatrical pocket book: or brief dramatic chronology. 1814, 1817 (as A brief dramatic chronology).

Galt, John. The lives of the players. 2 vols 1831.

Fitzgerald, P. The romance of the English stage. 2 vols 1874.

Baker, H. B. Our old actors. 2 vols 1878.

Cook, D. Hours with the players. 2 vols 1881.

Brereton, A. Some famous Hamlets. 1884.

— Shakespearean scenes and characters; with descriptive notes on the plays and the principal Shakespearean players from Betterton to Irving. 1886.

Actors and actresses of Great Britain and the United States. Ed L. Hutton and B. Matthews, New York 1886.

Mantzius, K. Skuespilkunstens historie. 5 vols Copenhagen 1897–1907; tr 6 vols 1903–21. Vol 5, the great actors of the eighteenth century; 6, on periods of Sheridan, Kembles, Kean et al.

Fyvie, J. Comedy queens of the Georgian era. 1906.

— Tragedy queens of the Georgian era. 1909.

'Melville, Lewis' (L. S. Benjamin). Stage favourites of the eighteenth century. 1928.

—More stage favourites of the eighteenth century. 1929.

Lanier, H. W. The first English actresses 1660–1700. New York 1930.

Brooking, C. Actresses on the tiles. N & Q 9 Nov 1940.

— Stage folk in Dighton prints. N & Q 7 Dec 1940.

Troubridge, St V. Helena in All's well that ends well. N & Q 23 Aug 1941. A list of actresses who played the part. Further notes by A. R. Bayley and W. Jaggard 30 Aug 1941.

Crundell, H. W. Actors and actresses in eighteenth-century comedy. N & Q 18 Jan 1941.

Fea, A. Portraits of Nell Gwyn, Moss Davies and others. Connoisseur 111 1943.

Hogan, C. B. Eighteenth-century actors in the DNB: additions and corrections. Theatre Notebook 6 1952.

— Second series. Theatre Notebook 11 1957.

Jones, C. E. Isaac| Reed's Theatrical obituary. N & Q Sept 1957.

Wilson, J. H. All the King's ladies: actresses of the Restoration. Chicago 1958.

— Biographical notes on some Restoration actresses. Theatre Notebook 18 1964.

Highfill, P. R. Actors' wills. Theatre Notebook 15 1960.

Single Lives

Actors in chronological order

Gildon, C. The life of Mr Thomas Betterton. 1710.

An account of the life of that celebrated tragedian Mr Thomas Betterton. 1749.

Lowe, R. W. Thomas Betterton. 1891.

Snodgrass, A. E. The best actor in the world. Cornhill Mag Dec 1935.

Sprague, A. C. Did Betterton chant? Theatre Notebook 1 1947. Further notes by G. Bottomly and M. Sands, ibid.

Armstrong, W. A. The acting of Thomas Betterton. English 10 1954.

Van Lennep, W. Henry Harris, actor friend of Pepys. In Studies in English theatre history, 1952.

Ross, R. H. Samuel Sandford: villain from necessity. PMLA 76 1961.

Thomas, Tobyas. The life of the late famous comedian Jo Hayns. 1701.

Biswänger, R. A. Jo Haines as a fortune-teller. N & Q June 1956.

Wilson, J. H. Thomas's Life of Jo Hayns. N & Q July 1961.

Cunningham, P. The story of Nell Gwyn. 1852.

Dasent, A. I. Nell Gwynne. 1924.

Wilson, J. H. Nell Gwyn as an angel. N & Q 21 Feb 1948.

— Nell Gwyn's house in Pall Mall. N & Q 2 April 1949.

— Nell Gwyn: royal mistress. 1952.

— Nell Gwyn: two portraits. N & Q May 1956.

Van Lennep, W. Nell Gwyn's playgoing at the King's expense. Harvard Lib Bull 4 1950.

Wilson, J. H. The Marshall sisters and Anne Quin. N & Q March 1957.

— Mr Goodman the player. Pittsburgh 1964.

Taylor, A. M. Some new light on William Bowen 1666–1718: actor and customs officer. Tulane Stud in Eng 6 1956.

Hook, L. Anne Bracegirdle's first appearance. Theatre Notebook 13 1959.

— Portraits of Elizabeth Barry and Anne Bracegirdle. Theatre Notebook 15 1961.

Esar, E. The legends of Joe Miller. Amer Book Collector 13 1962.

Memoirs of the life of Robert Wilks esq. 1732 (3 edns).

[Curll, Edmund]. The life of that eminent comedian Robert Wilks esq. 1733.

Cook, T. A. Thomas Doggett deceased: a famous comedian. 1908.

An apology for the life of Mr Colley Cibber. 1740; ed R. W. Lowe 2 vols 1889; ed B. R. S. Fone, Ann Arbor 1968.

The laureat: or the right side of Colley Cibber. 1740.

Barker, R. H. Mr Cibber of Drury Lane. New York 1939.

Ashley, L. R. Colley Cibber. New York 1965.

Cibber, Theophilus. The lives of the most eminent actors and actresses, part 1: life of Barton Booth. 1753.

Eddison, R. Topless in Jerusalem. Theatre Notebook 22 1967. On Susannah Cibber.

Aston, Anthony. A sketch of the life etc of Mr Anthony Aston, commonly called Tony Aston, written by himself. Prefixed to Fool's opera 1731.

Nicholson, W. Anthony Aston, stroller and adventurer. South Haven Michigan 1920.

Graves, T. S. Some facts about Anthony Aston. JEGP 20 1921.

Rogers, Jane. The memorial of Jane Rogers humbly submitted to the town. 1711.

Sands, M. Mrs Tofts 1685?–1756. Theatre Notebook 20 1966.

Authentick memoirs of the life of Mrs Ann Oldfield. 1730 (6 edns).

'Egerton, William' (Edmund Curll?). Faithful memoirs of Mrs Anne Oldfield. 1731.

Robins, E. The palmy days of Nance Oldfield. 1898.

Gore-Brown, R. Gay was the pit: the life and times of Anne Oldfield, actress 1683–1730. 1957.

Sawyer, P. John Rich: a biographical sketch. Theatre Annual 15 1957/8.

Akerby, George. The life of Mr James Spiller, the late famous comedian. 1729.

Lawrence, W. J. A player-friend of Hogarth [Spiller]. In Elizabethan playhouse ser 2, 1913.

Halsband, R. The noble lady and the player [John Beard]. History Today 18 1968.

The life of Mr James Quin, comedian; with the history of the stage from his commencing actor. 1766, 1887.

Taylor, A. M. The patrimony of James Quin: the legend and the facts. Tulane Stud in Eng 8 1958.

Vince, S. W. E. Marie Sallé 1707–56. Theatre Notebook 12 1957.

— Camargo [Marie-Anne Cupis de Camargo] in London 1750–4. Theatre Notebook 12–13 1958.

Congreve, F. A. Authentic memoirs of the late Mr Charles Macklin, comedian. 1798.

Kirkman, J. Memoirs of the life of Charles Macklin, comedian. 2 vols 1799.

Cooke, W. Memoirs of Charles Macklin, comedian. 1804, 1806.

Parry, E. A. Macklin. 1891.

Appleton, W. W. Macklin: an actor's life. Cambridge Mass 1960.

Charke, Charlotte. A narrative of the life of Mrs Charlotte Charke, written by herself. 1755, 1929.

Speaight, G. Charlotte Charke: an unpublished letter. Theatre Notebook 12 1957.

Peary, C. D. The chimorical career of Charlotte Charke. Restoration & 18th-Century Theatre Research 8 1969.

Pearce, C. E. Polly Peachum: being the story of Lavinia Fenton. 1913.

Fitzgerald, P. Life of Mrs Catherine Clive. 1888.

Crean, P. J. Kitty Clive. N & Q 30 April 1938.

Memoirs of the celebrated Mrs Woffington. 1760.

Molloy, J. F. The life and adventures of Peg Woffington. 2 vols 1884.

Daly, A. Woffington: a tribute. Philadelphia 1888.

Dobson, A. Mrs. Woffington. In his Sidewalk studies, 1902.

Scott, W. S. Peg Woffington and her circle. New Rambler 2 1937.

Lucey, J. C. Lovely Peggy: the life and times of Margaret Woffington. 1952.

Dunbar, J. Peg Woffington and her world. 1968.

Davies, Thomas. Memoirs of the life of David Garrick esq. 2 vols 1780. For later lives of Garrick see below.

Memoirs of the life and writings of Samuel Foote esq. [1777?].

Cooke, W. Memoirs of Samuel Foote esq. 3 vols 1805, 2 vols 1806.

Bushnell, G. H. The original Lady Randolph [Sarah Ward]. Theatre Notebook 13 1959.

Tisdall, E. E. P. Mrs Pimpernel Atkyns [Charlotte Walpole Atkyns 1758–1836]: the strange story of a Drury Lane actress who was the only heroine of the French Revolution. 1965.

Hodgson, N. Sarah Baker 1736/7–1816: governess-general of the Kentish drama. In Studies in English theatre history, 1952.

[Bicknell, Alexander]. An apology for the life of George Anne Bellamy. 5 vols 1785 (3 edns), 1786.

Hartmann, C. H. Enchanting Bellamy. 1956.

Sewell, B. Bellamy. Wiseman Rev 235 1961.

Recollections of occurrences: the memoirs of Thomas Snagg. Ed H. Hobson 1951.

Grice, F. and A. Clarke. Mrs Sarah Gardner. Theatre Notebook 7 1953. See also G. Green 8 1953.

Este, Charles. My own life. 1787.

Memoirs of Richard Cumberland, written by himself. 2 vols 1807.

Mudford, W. Life of Richard Cumberland. 1812.

Steele, Elizabeth. The memoirs of Mrs Sophia Baddeley. 6 vols 1787.

Bellamy, Thomas. The life of Mr William Parsons, comedian. 1795.

The life of Mrs Abington. 1888.

Memoirs of that celebrated comedian and very singular genius Thomas Weston. 1776.

Wilkinson, Tate. Memoirs of his own life. 4 vols York 1790.

Doty, G. Anne Bruton in Bath and London. Theatre Survey 8 1967.

Memoirs of Charles Lee Lewes, written by himself. 4 vols 1805.

A sketch of the theatrical life of the late Mr John Palmer. 1798.

Spencer, D. G. Gentleman John and Jack Plausible. N & Q Feb 1961. Confusion between the two John Palmers.

— Memoirs of John Palmer esq. Restoration & 18th-Century Theatre Research 1 1962.

Ambross, —. The life and memoirs of the late Miss Ann Catley. [1790?], 1888.

McKenzie, J. James Aickin. Theatre Notebook 10 1956.

The professional life of Mr [Charles] Dibdin, written by himself. 4 vols 1803.

Speaight, G. Professional and literary memoirs of Charles Dibdin the younger, dramatist and upward of thirty years manager of minor theatres. 1956.

The strolling player: or life and adventures of William Templeton. 3 vols 1802.

Memoirs of the late Thomas Holcroft, written by himself and continued to the time of his death by W. Hazlitt. 3 vols 1816; ed C. Colby 2 vols 1925.

Davies, Thomas. A genuine narrative of the life and theatrical transactions of John Henderson, commonly called the Bath Roscius. 1777, 1778.

Ireland, John. Letters and poems by the late Mr John Henderson, with anecdotes of his life. 1786.

Recollections of the life of John O'Keeffe, written by himself. 2 vols 1826.

['Pasquin, Anthony' (John Williams)]. The life and adventures of John Edwin, comedian, by an old croney. 1791, 2 vols [1791] (as The eccentricities), Dublin [1794?].

Highfill, P. H. Charles Surface in regency retirement: some letters from Gentleman [William] Smith. SP extra ser 4 1967.

Moore, Thomas. Memoirs of the life of Richard Brinsley Sheridan. 1825. For later lives, see below.

Yoklavich, J. Hamlet in shammy shoes [Thomas Sheridan]. Shakespeare Quart 3 1952.

Sheldon, E. K. Thomas Sheridan: gentleman or actor? Theatre Survey 2 1961.

'Pasquin, Anthony' (John Williams). The life of the late Lord Barrymore, including a history of the Wargrave theatricals. 1793 (3 edns), Dublin 1794?

Boaden, James. Memoirs of Mrs Siddons. 2 vols 1827.

Campbell, Thomas. Life of Mrs Siddons. 2 vols 1834.

Parsons, Mrs Clement. The incomparable Siddons. 1909.

The reminiscences of Sarah Kemble Siddons 1773–85. Ed W. Van Lennep, Cambridge Mass 1942.

ffrench, Y. Mrs Siddons: tragic actress. 1936, 1954 (rev).

Clark, W. S. The Siddons in Dublin. Theatre Notebook 9 1955.

de la Torre, Lillian. Actress: being the story of Sarah Siddons. New York 1957.

Bernard, John. Retrospections of the stage. 2 vols 1830.

Dunlap, William. Memoirs of George Frederick Cooke. 2 vols 1813, 1815.

Boaden, James. Memoirs of the life of John Philip Kemble. 2 vols 1825.

Fitzgerald, P. An account of the Kemble family. 1871.

Baker, H. Kemble: the actor in his theatre. Cambridge Mass 1942.

Memoirs of Joseph Shepherd Munden, by his son. 1844.

Ryler, S. W. The itinerant: or memoirs of an actor. 3 sers 1808–27.

Everard, E. C. Memoirs of an unfortunate son of Thespis. 1818.

Memoirs of the present Countess of Derby [Elizabeth Farren], by Petronius Arbiter. [1797?].

Broadbent, R. J. Elizabeth Farren, Countess of Derby. nd.

Memoirs of the life of Mrs Sumbel, late Wells. 3 vols 1811.

Adolphus, John. Memoirs of John Bannister, comedian. 2 vols 1839.

Humphreys, R. The memoirs of J. Decastro, comedian. 1824.

Colman, George (the younger). Random records. 2 vols 1830.

Peake, R. B. Memoirs of the Colman family. 2 vols [1841].

Bagster-Collins, J. F. George Colman the younger 1762–1836. New York 1946.

Boaden, James. The life of Mrs Jordan. 2 vols 1831.

Fothergill, B. Mrs Jordan: portait of an actress. 1965.

Young, M. J. Memoirs of Mrs Crouch. 2 vols 1806.

Hook, Theodore. Reminiscences of Michael Kelly. 2 vols 1826.

Ellis, S. M. The life of Michael Kelly. 1930.

Reynolds, Frederick. The life and times of Frederick Reynolds. 2 vols 1826.

Dibdin, T. J. Reminiscences of the Theatre Royal, Covent Garden, Drury Lane etc. 2 vols 1827.

(7) THE ACTOR'S ART

The Theory of Acting

Gildon, Charles. The life of Mr Thomas Betterton: wherein the action and utterance of the stage, bar and pulpit are distinctly consider'd. 1710.

The Prompter. 12 Nov 1734–2 July 1736; ed W. W. Appleton and K. A. Burnim, New York 1966 (selection). A bi-weekly theatrical periodical, conducted by Aaron Hill.

[Foote, Samuel?]. A treatise on the passions, so far as they regard the stage. [1741?].

An historical and critical account of the theatres in Europe; together with an essay on action, or the arts of speaking in public. 1741. Tr from Luigi Riccoboni.

An essay on the theatres: or the art of acting, in imitation of Horace's Art of poetry. Harleian Miscellany 5 1744, Dublin 1745. In verse.

Hill, Aaron. The art of acting. Pt 1, 1746, 1801. In verse.
— An essay on the art of acting, in prose. In his Works, 4 vols 1753.

[Hill, John]. The actor: a treatise on the art of playing. 1750; tr French, 1769.
— The actor, or a treatise on the art of playing: a new work, written by the author of the former. 1755.

An essay on the stage, or the art of acting: a poem. Ed [Francis Stamper], Edinburgh 1754.

[Pickering, Roger]. Reflexions upon theatrical expression in tragedy. 1755.

Lloyd, Robert. The actor: a poetical epistle. 1760, 1764; ed E. Blunden 1926.

Boswell, James. On the profession of a player. London Mag Aug–Oct 1770; rptd 1929.

Hiffernan, Paul. Dramatic genius, in five books. 1770, 1772.

Cooke, William. The elements of dramatic criticism: containing an analysis of the stage, with some general instructions for succeeding in the art of acting. 1775; tr German, 1777.

The new thespian oracle: containing original strictures on oratory and acting. 1791.

Morris, Thomas. A letter to a friend on the poetical elocution of the theatre and the manner of acting tragedy. In his Miscellanies in prose and verse, 1791.

Kirkman, J. Memoirs of the life of Charles Macklin. 1799. Includes Macklin, Observations on the science of acting.

Downer, A. S. Nature to advantage dressed: eighteenth-century acting. PMLA 58 1943.
— Mr Dangle's defense: acting and stage history. Eng Inst Essays 1946.

Angus, W. Actors and audiences in eighteenth-century London. In Studies in speech and drama in honor of A. M. Drummond, Ithaca 1944.
— Acting Shakespeare. Queen's Quart 72 1965. On Betterton, Garrick, Macklin.

Sprague, A. C. Shakespeare and the actors: the stage business in his plays 1660–1905. Cambridge Mass 1944.
— Shakespearian players and performances. Cambridge Mass 1953.

Wasserman, E. R. The sympathetic imagination in eighteenth-century theories of acting. JEGP 46 1947.

Vardac, A. N. Stage to screen: theatrical method from Garrick to Griffith. Cambridge Mass 1949.

Wilson, J. H. Rant, cant and tone on the Restoration stage. SP 52 1955.

Joseph, B. The tragic actor. 1959.

Woodbury, L. J. Death on the romantic stage. Quart Jnl of Speech 49 1963.

Hunt, H. Restoration acting. In Restoration theatre, ed J. R. Brown and B. Harris 1965.

Schneider, B. R. The coquette-prude as an actress's line in Restoration comedy during the time of Mrs Oldfield. Theatre Notebook 22 1968.

Criticisms of Particular Actors

See also Dramatic Theory and Criticism, and Lives of Actors, above.

McAfee, H. Pepys on the Restoration stage. New Haven 1916.

A comparison between the two stages. 1702; ed S. B. Wells, Princeton 1942.

Downes, John. Roscius anglicanus: or an historical review of the stage. 1708; ed M. Summers [1928]; ed J. Loftis, Los Angeles 1969 (Augustan Reprint Soc.).

Estcourt, Richard. A letter from Dick Estcourt, the comedian, to the Spectator. 1713.

[Reynardson, Francis]. The stage: a poem, inscribed to Joseph Addison esq by Mr Webster of Christchurch, Oxon. 1713. *See* F. W. Bateson, MLN 45 1930.

[Phillips, Edward?]. The players: a satire. 1733. Verse.

Cibber, Colley. An apology for the life of Mr Colley Cibber. 1740; ed R. W. Lowe 2 vols 1889; ed B. R. S. Fone, Ann Arbor 1968.

Foote, Samuel. The Roman and English comedy considered and compar'd, with an examen into the merit of the present comic actors. 1747.

Aston, Anthony. A brief supplement to Colley Cibber esq. [1748]; rptd R. W. Lowe in Cibber's Apology vol 2, 1889.

The present state of the stage in Great Britain and Ireland. 1753.

Cibber, Theophilus. Cibber's two dissertations on theatrical subjects. 3 pts [1756]. On Garrick's acting.

Pittard, Joseph. Observations on Mr Garrick's acting. 1758.

Churchill, Charles. The Rosciad. 1761; ed R. W. Lowe 1891. Verse.
— The apology, addressed to the critical reviewers. 1761; ed R. W. Lowe 1891. Verse.

Kelly, Hugh. Thespis: or a critical examination into the merits of all the principal performers belonging to Drury-Lane theatre. 1766 (anon), 1766. Verse.
— Thespis: or a critical examination into the merits of all the principal performers belonging to Covent-Garden theatre. 1767. Verse.

L., F. B. The rational Rosciad. 1767.

Momus, a poem: or a critical examination into the merits of the performers at the Theatre Royal in the Haymarket. 1767. By G. S. Carey?

The theatres: a poetical dissection, by Sir Nicholas Nipclose. 1772, 1772.

[Downman, Hugh]. The drama: a poem. 1775.

Pilon, Frederick. An essay on the character of Hamlet, as performed by Mr Henderson. [1777?].

Davies, Thomas. Dramatic miscellanies. 3 vols 1783–4.

The new Rosciad. 1785, 1787.

An essay on the pre-eminence of comic genius; with observations on the several characters Mrs Jordan has appeared in. 1786.

'Pasquin, Anthony' (John Williams). The children of Thespis. 4 pts 1786–97. Verse.

Candid and impartial strictures on the performers belonging to Drury-Lane, Covent-Garden, and the Haymarket theatres. 1795.

Hunt, Leigh. Critical essays on the performers of the London theatres. 1807.

Betz, L. Lichtenberg as a critic of the English stage. JEGP 23 1924.

Sprague, A. C. Did Betterton chant? Theatre Notebook 1 1947. Further notes by G. Bottomly and M. Sands, ibid.

Armstrong, W. A. The acting of Thomas Betterton. English 10 1954.

Ross, R. H. Samuel Sandford: villain from necessity. PMLA 76 1961.

Stone, G. W. The poet and the players. Proc of Amer Philosophical Soc 106 1962.

III. RESTORATION DRAMA

The abbreviations used in this section and the following:
Ba burletta, Bal ballet, BO ballad opera, Bsq burlesque, C comedy, CO comic opera, D drama, DO dramatic opera, Ext extravaganza, F farce, Int interlude, M masque, MD melodrama, MF musical farce, O opera, Oa operetta, P pantomime, T tragedy, TC tragi-comedy. *For theatres:* CG Covent Garden, DG Dorset Garden, DL Drury Lane, GF Goodman's Fields, Hay Haymarket (King's and Queen's Haymarket), New Hay Little Haymarket, LIF Lincoln's Inn Fields, TR Theatre Royal, Vere Street or Brydges Street.

SIR GEORGE ETHEREGE
1653?–91

Collections

Works, containing his plays and poems. 1704, 1715, 1723, 1735.
Works: plays and poems. Ed A. W. Verity 1888.
Works. Ed H. F. B. Brett-Smith 2 vols Oxford 1927. Plays, introd and bibliography. Vol 3 unpbd.
Poems. Ed J. Thorpe, Princeton 1963.

§ 1

The comical revenge: or love in a tub. C LIF March 1664 1664, 1664, 1667, 1669, 1689, 1690, 1697.
She wou'd if she cou'd. C LIF 6 Feb 1668. 1668, 1671, 1693, 1710, [c. 1711].
The man of mode: or Sr Fopling Flutter. C DG March 1676. 1676, 1684, 1693, 1711, [c. 1711], 1733, Dublin [c. 1753], Edinburgh 1768; ed J. H. Wilson, Boston 1959; ed W. B. Carnochan, Lincoln Nebraska 1966.

Letters

Letterbook. Ed S. Rosenfeld, Oxford 1928.
Rosenfeld, S. The second letterbook of Etherege. RES new ser 3 1952.
Bracher, F. The letterbooks of Etherege. Harvard Lib Bull 15 1967.
——Etherege and his secretary. Ibid.

§ 2

Dennis, John. A defense of Sir Fopling Flutter. 1722.
Gosse, E. In his Seventeenth-century studies, 1883.
Meindl, V. Etheredge: sein Leben, seine Zeit und seine Dramen. Vienna 1901.
Palmer, J. In his Comedy of manners, 1913.
Dobrée, B. In his Restoration comedy, Oxford 1924.
—— In his Essays in biography, Oxford 1925.
Perry, H. T. E. In his Comic spirit in Restoration drama, New Haven 1925.
Foster, D. Etherege: collections. N & Q 10–31 Dec 1927, 14 Jan 1928; RES 8 1932.
Boswell, E. Etherege. RES 7 1931.
McCamie, F. S. Etherege: a study in Restoration comedy. Cedar Rapids Iowa 1931.
Rosenfeld, S. Etherege in Ratisbon. RES 10 1934.
Howarth, R. G. Untraced quotations in Etherege. N & Q 30 June 1945.
Wilson, J. H. Etherege's Julia. MLN 62 1947.
Nichol, J. W. Dame Mary Etherege. MLN 64 1949.
Sherbo, A. A note on The man of mode. MLN 64 1949.
—— Sir Fopling Flutter and Beau Hewitt. N & Q 9 July 1949.
Fujimura, T. H. In his Restoration comedy of wit, Princeton 1952.
—— Etherege at Constantinople. PMLA 62 1956.
Neville, M. Etherege and Holbein. N & Q April 1954.
Underwood, D. Etherege and the seventeenth-century comedy of manners. New Haven 1957.
Vieth, D. M. Etherege's Man of mode and Rochester's Artemisa to Cloe. N & Q Nov 1958.

Holland, N. N. In his First modern comedies, Cambridge Mass 1959.
Powell, J. Etherege and the form of a comedy. In Restoration theatre, ed J. R. Brown and B. Harris 1965.
Auffret, J. M. The man of mode and the Plain dealer: common origins and parallels. Etudes Anglaises 19 1966.
Boyette, P. E. The songs of Etherege. Stud in Eng Lit 1500–1900 6 1966.
Krause, D. The defaced angel: Satanic grace is the Man of mode. Drama Survey 7 1969.

WILLIAM WYCHERLEY
1641–1716

Collections

The works of the ingenious Mr William Wycherley. 1713, 2 vols 1720, 1 vol 1731, Dublin 1733, 2 vols 1735.
The posthumous works of William Wycherley esq in prose and verse. 2 vols 1728–9. Vol 1 ed L. Theobald, with memoir by R. Pack; vol 2 ed Pope.
The dramatic works of Wycherley, Congreve, Vanbrugh and Farquhar. Ed Leigh Hunt 1840.
William Wycherley. Ed W. C. Ward 1888 (Mermaid ser).
The country wife and the Plain dealer. Ed G. B. Churchill, Boston 1924
Complete works. Ed M. Summers 4 vols 1924.
Complete plays. Ed G. Weales, New York 1966. With introd, notes and variants.

§ 1

Hero and Leander, in burlesque. 1669. Anon.
Love in a wood: or St James's Park. C TR c. March 1671. 1672, 1693, 1694, 1711, etc.
The gentleman dancing-master. C DG c. Feb 1672. 1673, 1693, 1702.
The country-wife. C DL Jan 1675. 1675, 1683, 1688, 1688, 1695 etc; ed U. Todd-Naylor, Northampton Mass 1931; ed J. H. Wilson, Boston 1959; ed G. G. Falls, New York 1964; ed T. H. Fujimura, Lincoln Nebraska 1965.
The plain dealer. C DL Dec 1676. 1677 (3 edns), 1678, 1681, 1686, 1691, 1694, 1700, 1709, 1710, 1711 etc; ed L. Hughes, Lincoln Nebraska 1967; tr Russian, 1968 (with essay by A. Anixt).
Epistles to the King and Duke. 1683.
Miscellany poems. 1704.
The idleness of business: a satyr. 1705 (2nd edn). No known copies of first edn.
On his Grace the Duke of Marlborough. 1707.

Letters

Allen, R. J. Two Wycherley letters. TLS 18 April 1935.

§ 2

[Gildon, Charles]. Memoirs of the life of Wycherley. 1718.
Hazlitt, W. In his Lectures on the English comic writers, 1819.

Macaulay, T. B. The dramatic works of Wycherley, Congreve, Vanbrugh and Farquhar. Edinburgh Rev 72 1841.

Churchill, G. B. The relation of Dryden's State of innocence to Milton's Paradise lost and Wycherley's Plain dealer. MP 4 1906.

—— The originality of Wycherley. In Schelling anniversary papers, New York 1923.

Palmer, J. In his Comedy of manners, 1913.

Perromat, C. Wycherley: sa vie, son oeuvre. Paris 1921.

Dobrée, B. In his Restoration comedy, Oxford 1924.

Perry, H. T. E. In his Comic spirit in Restoration comedy, New Haven 1925.

Hargest, W. G. and E. Boswell. Wycherley and the Countess of Drogheda. TLS 21–8 Nov 1929.

Connely, W. Brawny Wycherley. New York 1930.

Boswell, E. Footnotes to seventeenth-century biographies. MLR 26 1931.

Granville-Barker, H. Wycherley and Dryden. In his On dramatic method, 1931.

Vincent, H. P. The date of Wycherley's birth. TLS 3 March 1932. With subsequent correspondence.

—— The death of Wycherley. Harvard Stud 15 1933.

—— Wycherley's Miscellany poems. PQ 16 1937.

—— Wycherley's Posthumous works. N & Q 3 July 1943.

Jones, H. M. Wycherley, Montaigne, Tertullian and Mr Summers. MLN 47 1932.

Seely, F. F. The last eighteenth-century performance of the Country wife. PQ 16 1937.

Williams, E. E. Furetière and Wycherley: le roman bourgeois in Restoration comedy. MLN 53 1938.

Avery, E. L. The country wife in the eighteenth century. Washington State Univ Research Stud 10 1942.

—— The plain dealer in the eighteenth century. Washington Univ Research Stud 11 1943.

Rundle, J. E. Wycherley and Calderón: a source for Love in a wood. PMLA 64 1949.

Chorney, A. H. Wycherley's Manly reinterpreted. In Essays dedicated to L. B. Campbell, Berkeley 1950.

Megaw, R. N. E. The two 1695 editions of the Country wife. SB 3 1951.

Higgins, D. Source notes for Dryden, Wycherley and Otway. N & Q July 1956.

Freeman, P. Two fragments of manuscripts. RES new ser 8 1957. A letter to Wycherley.

Taylor, A. Proverbs in the plays of Wycherley. Southern Folklore Quart 21 1957.

[Hughes, R. E.]. The country wife: no place to hide. N & Q June 1958.

Korninger, S. Wycherleys satirische Methode. Wiener Beiträge zur Englischen Philologie 66 1958.

O'Regan, M. J. Furetière and Wycherley. MLN 53 1958.

Holland, N. N. In his First modern comedies, Cambridge Mass 1959.

Craik, T. W. Some aspects of satire in Wycherley's plays. E Studies 41 1960.

Rogers, K. M. Fatal inconsistency: Wycherley and the Plain dealer. ELH 28 1961.

Zimbardo, R. The satiric design in the Plain dealer. Stud in Eng Lit 1500–1900 1 1961.

—— Wycherley's drama: a link in the development of English satire. New Haven 1965.

Auffret, J. Wycherley et ses maîtres les moralistes. Etudes Anglaises 15 1962.

—— The man of mode and the Plain dealer: common origin and parallels. Etudes Anglaises 19 1966.

Brown, T. J. English literary autographs: Wycherley. Book Collector 11 1962.

Wooton, C. The country wife and contemporary comedy: a world apart. Drama Survey 2 1963.

Bowman, J. S. Dance, chant and mask in the plays of Wycherley. Drama Survey 3 1963.

Blakeslee, R. C. Wycherley's use of the aside. Western Speech 28 1964.

Righter, A. In Restoration theatre, ed J. R. Brown and B. Harris 1965.

Mukherjee, S. Marriage as punishment in the plays of Wycherley. REL 7 1966.

Vernon, P. F. Wycherley's first comedy and its Spanish source. Comparative Lit 18 1966.

Weales, G. A Wycherley prologue. Lib Chron 32 1966.

Vieth, D. M. Wycherley's The country wife: an anatomy of masculinity. Papers on Lang & Lit 2 1966.

Berman, R. The ethic of the Country wife. Texas Stud in Lit & Lang 9 1967.

Morrissey, L. J. Wycherley's country dance. Stud in Eng Lit 1500–1900 9 1969.

Donaldson, D. The tables turned: the Plain dealer. EC 17 1967.

Friedson, A. M. Wycherley and Molière: satirical point of view in the Plain dealer. MP 64 1967.

THOMAS SHADWELL
1642?–92

Collections

The Lancashire witches; The amorous bigot. 1691. Copies of separate edns of 2 plays issued with general title.

The works of Tho Shadwell esq. 1693. A collection of various edns of the plays, except Tempest.

The dramatick works of Thomas Shadwell esq. 4 vols 1720.

Thomas Shadwell. Ed G. Sainstsbury [1903] (Mermaid ser). The sullen lovers, A true widow, The squire of Alsatia, Bury Fair.

Complete works. Ed M. Summers 5 vols 1927 (Nonesuch Press).

Epsom Wells, and The volunteers. Ed D. M. Walmsley, Boston [1930].

§ 1

The sullen lovers: or the impertinents. C LIF 2 May 1668. 1668, 1670, 1693.

The royal shepherdess. TC LIF 25 Feb 1669. 1669, 1691.

The humorists. C LIF Dec 1670. 1671, 1691.

The miser. C TR Jan 1672. 1672, 1691.

Epsom-wells. C DG Dec 1672. 1673, 1676, 1693, 1704; ed D. Walmsley, Boston [1930].

The tempest: or the enchanted island. DO DG April 1674. 1674, 1676, 1676, 1690, 1695, 1701.

Notes and observations on the Empress of Morocco. 1674. Anon. With Crowne and Dryden.

Psyche. DO DG 27 Feb 1675. 1675, 1690.

The libertine: a tragedy. C DG June 1675. 1676, 1692, 1697, 1704, 1705.

The virtuoso. C DG 25 May 1676. 1676, 1691, 1704; ed M. H. Nicolson and D. S. Rodes, Lincoln Nebraska 1966.

The history of Timon of Athens, the man-hater. T DG c. Jan 1678. 1678, 1688, 1696, 1703, [1705?].

A true widow. C DG 21 March 1678. 1679, 1689.

The woman-captain. C DG c. Sept 1679. 1680.

The Lancashire witches, and Tegue o Divelly the Irish priest. C DG c. Sept 1681. 1682, 1682, 1691, 1736.

The medal of John Bayes: a satyr against folly and knavery. 1682. Anon. See D. M. McKeithan, The authorship of the medal of John Bayes, SE 12 1932.

Satyr to his Muse, by the author of Absalom and Achitophel. 1682. Anon. Also ascribed to John, Baron Somers.

The Tory-poets: a satyr. 1682. Anon. Sometimes attributed to Shadwell.

A lenten prologue. 1683. Anon.

Some reflections upon the pretended parallel in the play called the Duke of Guise. 1683. Anon. Generally attributed to Shadwell.

The tenth satyr of Juvenal. 1687.

The squire of Alsatia. C DL May 1688. 1688, 1688, 1692, 1693, 1699, 1736 etc.
Bury-fair. C DL c. April 1689. 1689.
A congratulatory poem on his Highness the Prince of Orange his coming into England. 1689.
The amorous bigotte; with the second part of Tegue o Divelly. C DL c. March 1689. 1690, [1691 ?].
The address of John Dryden, laureat to his Highness the Prince of Orange. 1689. Anon.
A congratulatory poem to the most illustrious Queen Mary upon her arrival in England. 1689.
Ode on the anniversary of the King's birth. 1690.
Ode to the King, on his return from Ireland. [1690 ?].
The scowrers. C DL c. Dec 1690. 1691.
Votum perenne: a poem to the King on New-years-day. 1692.
Ode on the King's birth-day. 1692.
The volunteers: or the stock-jobbers. C DL Nov 1692. 1693; ed D. Walmsley, Boston [1930].

§ 2

Brady, N. A sermon preached at the funeral of Thomas Shadwell esq. 1692.
Cooke, T. The triumphs of love and honour. 1731. The appended Considerations on the stage includes a critique of Squire of Alsatia.
Shadwell's dramatic works. Retrospective Rev 2 1828.
Lawrence, W. J. Did Shadwell write an opera on the Tempest? Anglia 27 1904, 29 1906.
Ammann, E. Analysis of Shadwell's Lancashire witches. 1905.
Broadus, E. K. In his Laureateship, 1921.
Dobrée, B. In his Restoration comedy, Oxford 1924.
Thorn-Drury, G. Some notes on Dryden. RES 1 1925.
— Shadwell and the operatic Tempest. RES 3 1927.
Walmsley, D. Shadwell and the operatic Tempest. RES 2 1926.
Borgman, A. S. Shadwell: his life and comedies. New York 1928.
Lloyd, C. Shadwell and the virtuosi. PMLA 44 1929.
Bull, A. J. Shadwell's satire on Edward Howard. RES 6 1930.
Boswell, E. Footnotes to seventeenth-century biographies. MLR 26 1931.
Whitehall, H. Shadwell and the Lancashire dialect. In Essays by members of the English Department, Ann Arbor 1933.
Ward, C. E. Shadwell 1658-68. TLS 3 April 1937.
— The Tempest: a Restoration opera problem. ELH 13 1946.
Needham, F. A letter of Shadwell's. TLS 23 Oct 1930.
McKeithan, D. M. The authorship of the Medal of John Bayes. SE 12 1932.
Harris, B. The date of Shadwell's birth. TLS 10 Oct 1936. Reply by D. Walmsley 17 Oct 1936.
Iacuzzi, A. The naive theme in the Tempest as a link between Shadwell and Ramon de la Cruz. MLN 52 1937.
H., N. B. J. Shadwell: a biography. Caian 46 1938.
Stroup, T. B. Shadwell's use of Hobbes. SP 35 1938.
Evans, G. B. The source of Shadwell's character of Sir Formal Trifle in the Virtuoso. MLR 35 1940.
Hooker, H. M. Dryden's and Shadwell's the Tempest. HLQ 6 1943.
de Beer, E. S. The dramatist sons of Thomas, Earl of Berkshire. N & Q 4 Nov 1944. On the original of Lady Vaine.
Scott, F. R. News from Plimouth and Sir Positive At-All. MLR 39 1944.
Smith, R. G. Shadwell's impact on Dryden. RES 20 1944.
Milton, W. M. Tempest in a teapot. ELH 14 1947.
Smith, J. H. Shadwell, the ladies and the change in comedy. MP 46 1948.

— French sources for six English comedies 1660-1750. JEGP 47 1948. Including Woman-captain.
Jones, E. L. Robert Hooke and the Virtuoso. MLN 66 1951.
McManaway, J. G. Songs and masques in the Tempest c. 1674. In Theatre miscellany, Oxford 1953.
Vernon, P. F. Social satire in Shadwell's Timon. Studia Neophilologica 35 1963.
Pearsall, R. The case for Shadwell. Month new ser Dec 1963.
Towers, T. H. The lineage of Shadwell: an approach to MacFlecknoe. Stud in Eng Lit 1500-1900 3 1963.
Sorelius, G. Shadwell deviating into sense: Timon of Athens and the Duke of Buckingham. Studia Neophilologica 36 1964.
Love, H. R. H. The authorship of the Postscript of notes and observations on the Empress of Morocco. N & Q Jan 1966. Attributes postscript to Shadwell.
Doyle, A. Dryden's authorship of Notes and observations on the Empress of Morocco. Stud in Eng Lit 1500-1900 6 1966.
Alssid, M. W. Shadwell. New York 1967.
Edmunds, J. Shadwell and the anonymous Timon. N & Q June 1967.
Novak, M. E. Settle's attacks on Shadwell and the authorship of the operatic Tempest. N & Q July 1968.

NATHANIEL LEE
1649?-92
Bibliographies

McLeod, A. L. Restoration & 18th-Century Research 1 1962.

Collections

The works of Mr Nathaniel Lee. 1694, 2 vols 1713, 3 vols 1722, 1734, 1736 (as Dramatick works).
Works. Ed T. B. Stroup and A. L. Cooke 2 vols New Brunswick 1954-5.

§ 1

The tragedy of Nero, Emperour of Rome. DL May 1674. 1675, 1696; ed R. Horstmann, Heidelberg 1914.
Sophonisba: or Hannibal's overthrow. T DL April 1675. 1675, 1676, 1681, 1685, 1691, 1693, 1697, 1704, 1709, 1712 etc; ed B. Dobrée, Oxford 1960 (WC) (in Five heroic plays).
Gloriana: or the Court of Augustus Caesar. T DL Jan 1676. 1676, 1699 etc.
The rival Queens: or the death of Alexander the Great. T DL 17 March 1677. 1677, 1684, 1690, 1691, 1694, 1699, 1702, 1704 etc. See Colley Cibber, The rival Queans, 1729.
To the Prince and Princess of Orange upon their marriage. 1677.
Mithridates King of Pontus. T DL c. March 1678. 1678, 1685, 1693, 1697, 1702, 1711 etc.
Oedipus. T DG c. Sept 1678. 1679, 1682, 1687, 1692, [1694?], 1701, 1711. With Dryden.
Caesar Borgia, son of Pope Alexander the Sixth. T DG c. May 1679. 1679, 1680, 1696, 1711.
Theodosius: or the force of love. T DG c. Sept 1680. 1680, 1684, 1692, 1697, 1708 etc.
Lucius Junius Brutus, father of his country. T DG Dec 1680. 1681, 1708; ed J. Loftis, Lincoln Nebraska 1967.
Prologue spoken at Mithridates. 1681.
To the Duke on his return. 1682.
The Duke of Guise. T DL 28 Nov 1682. 1683, 1687, 1699. With Dryden.
Constantine the Great. T DL Nov 1683. 1684; ed W. Häfele, Heidelberg 1933.
The Princess of Cleve. TC DG 1680 or 1681. 1689, 1697.
The massacre of Paris. T DL Nov 1689. 1689, 1690.
On the death of Mrs Behn. 1689. Verse.
On their Majesties coronation. 1689. Verse.

§ 2

Biographical sketch of Lee, the poet. Monthly Mirror 13 1802.

Plays written by Lee 1722. Retrospective Rev 3 1821.

Mosen, R. Über Lees Leben und Werke. E Studien 2 1879.

Sanders, H. M. The plays. Temple Bar Dec 1901.

Resa, F. Lees Trauerspiel Theodosius. Literarhistorische Forschungen 30 1904.

Körting, G. Grundriss der Geschichte der englischen Litteratur. Münster 1905 (5th edn).

Mehr, O. Neue Beiträge zur Leekunde und Kritik insbesondere zum Cäsar Borgia und zur Sophonisba. Literarhistorische Forschungen 37 1909.

Mühlbach, E. Die englischen Nerodramen. Leipzig 1910.

Dobrée, B. In his Restoration tragedy, Oxford 1929.

Ham, R. G. Otway and Lee. New Haven 1931.

Stroup, T. B. The Princess of Cleve and sentimental comedy. RES 11 1935.

— and A. L. Cooke. The political implications in Lee's Constantine the Great. JEGP 49 1950.

— The authorship of the prologue to Lee's Constantine the Great. N & Q Sept 1954.

Fletcher, H. Lee and Milton. MLN 44 1929.

Ghosh, J. C. The prologue and epilogue to Constantine the Great. TLS 14 March 1929.

Kies, P. P. Lessing and Lee. JEGP 28 1929.

Wülker, A. Shakespeares Einfluss auf die dramatische Kunst von Lee. Emsdetten 1933.

Greene, G. Rochester and Lee. TLS 2 Nov 1935. Reply by W. J. Lawrence 9 Nov 1935.

Barbour, F. The unconventional heroic plays of Lee. SE 1940.

Evans, G. B. Milton and Lee's The rival Queens 1677. MLN 64 1949.

Bowers, F. T. A crux in the text of Lee's The Princess of Cleve 1689, II. 1. Harvard Lib Bull 4 1950.

— Lee: three probable seventeenth-century piracies. PBSA 44 1950.

— The prologue to Lee's Mithridates 1678. PBSA 44 1950.

McLeod, A. L. Lee's portrait. N & Q March 1953.

— Lee's birth date. MLN 69 1954. Suggests 1651.

— The Douai ms of Lee's Mithridates. N & Q Feb 1960.

Cross, G. Ovid metamorphosed: Marston, Webster and Lee. N & Q Jan 1956.

Peterson, W. M. (ed). Colley Cibber's The rival Queans. Painesville Ohio 1965. Appendixes contain material about Lee.

THOMAS OTWAY
1652–85

Collections

The works of Mr Thomas Otway. 1692.

The works of Mr Thomas Otway: consisting of his plays, poems and love-letters. 2 vols 1712, 1717–18, 1722, 1728, 3 vols 1757, 1768. With account of his life and works.

Plays written by Mr Thomas Otway. 2 vols 1736. Separate edns of individuals plays.

The works of Thomas Otway: consisting of his plays, poems and letters, with a sketch of his life, enlarged from that written by Dr Johnson. 2 vols 1812.

Works, with notes, critical and explanatory, and a life of the author by Thomas Thornton. 3 vols 1813.

Thomas Otway. Ed R. Noel 1888 (Mermaid ser). Includes Don Carlos, The orphan, The soldier's fortune, Venice preserved, letters.

Complete works. Ed M. Summers 3 vols 1926 (Nonesuch Press). Omits History of the triumvirates, Heroick friendship.

Works. Ed J. C. Ghosh 2 vols Oxford 1932. Plays, poems letters.

Letters

Love-letters written by the late most ingenious Mr Thomas Otway. In Familiar letters written by the Earl of Rochester, 1697.

§ 1

Alcibiades. T DG Sept 1675. 1675, 1687.

Don Carlos, Prince of Spain. T DG June 1676. 1676, 1679, 1686, 1695, 1704 etc.

Titus and Berenice. T DG c. Dec 1676. 1677, 1701 etc.

The cheats of Scapin. F. Produced and ptd with Titus and Berenice.

Friendship in fashion. C DG April 1678. 1678 etc.

The history and fall of Caius Marius. F DG Sept or Oct 1679. 1680, 1692, 1696, 1703 etc.

The orphan: or the unhappy marriage. T DG Feb or March 1680. 1680, 1685, 1691, 1696, 1703, 1705 etc, Hague 1711.

The souldiers fortune. C DG c. June 1680. 1681, 1683, 1687, 1695 etc.

The poet's complaint of his muse: or a satyr against libells. 1680.

Phaedra to Hippolytus. In Ovid's epistles translated by several hands, 1680.

Venice preserv'd: or a plot discover'd. T DG 9 Feb 1682. 1682, 1696, 1704 etc; ed C. F. McClumpha 1909; ed J. H. Wilson, Boston 1959.

Epilogue to Venice preserv'd spoken upon the Duke of York's coming to the theatre. 1682.

Prologue to the City-heiress. 1682.

Epilogue to her Highness on her return from Scotland. 1682.

The atheist: or the second part of the souldiers fortune. C DG c. July 1683. 1684.

Prologue to Constantine the Great. 1683.

Windsor Castle in a monument to our late sovereign K. Charles II. 1685. Verse.

The history of the triumvirates, written originally in French, and made English by Tho Otway, lately deceased. 1686.

Heroick friendship: a tragedy by the late Mr Otway. 1719. Perhaps by Otway.

§ 2

Derrick, Samuel. The dramatick censor. 1752.

Johnson, Samuel. In his Lives of the poets vol 1, 1781.

Davies, Thomas. In his Dramatic miscellanies, 3 vols 1784–5.

Gosse, E. In his Seventeenth-century studies, 1883.

Johnson, A. Lafosse, Otway, St Réal. Paris 1901.

Ghosh, J. C. N & Q 13–27 Dec 1924.

Ham, R. G. N & Q 15 Aug, 5 Sept 1925, 30 Jan 1926.

— Otway and Lee. New Haven 1931.

Dobrée, B. In his Restoration tragedy, Oxford 1929.

Moore, J. R. Contemporary satire in Otway's Venice preserved. PMLA 43 1928.

Babcock, R. W. The Rev Montague Summers as editor of Otway. PMLA 48 1933.

Riva, S. Otway, Saint-Réal e la Venezia Salvata. Dante June 1936.

Rich, L. M. A previous adaptation of Romeo and Juliet. Quart Jnl of Speech 23 1937.

Summers, M. A note on Otway. TLS 7 June 1941.

Mackenzie, A. A note on the date of the Orphan. ELH 12 1945.

— A note on Pierre's white hat. N & Q 8 March 1947.

— Venice preserved reconsidered. Tulane Stud in Eng 1 1949.

— (Mrs Taylor). Next to Shakespeare: Otway's Venice preserved and the Orphan and their history on the London stage. Durham NC 1950.

Goldberg, N. The two 1692 editions of Caius Marius. SB 3 1951.

Meyerstein, E. H. W. The dagger in Venice preserved. TLS 7 Sept 1951.

Higgins, D. Source notes for Dryden, Wycherley and Otway. N & Q July 1956.

Blakiston, N. Otways' friend. TLS 15 Aug 1958.

Hauser, D. R. Otway preserved: theme and form in Venice preserved. SP 55 1958.

Hughes, R. E. Comic relief in Otway's Venice preserved. N & Q Feb 1958.

McBurney, W. H. Otway's tragic muse debauched: sensuality in Venice preserved. JEGP 58 1959.

Lefevre, A. Racine en Angleterre au xviie siècle: Titus and Berenice de Thomas Otway. Revue de Littérature Comparée 34 1960.

Koziol, H. Zu Otways Venice preserved und Hugo von Hofmannsthals Das gerettete Venedig. Österreich und die Angelsächsische Welt 39 1961.

Jeune, S. Hamlet d'Otway, Macbeth de Dryden: ou Shakespeare en France en 1714. Revue de Littérature Comparée 36 1962.

Van Voris, W. Tragedy through Restoration eyes: Venice preserv'd in its own theatre. Hermathena 99 1964.

Vanhelleputte, M. Hofmannsthal und Otway: zur Struktur des Geretteten Venedig. Revue Belge 42 1964.

Fried, G. Gestalt und Funktion der Bilder im Drama Otways. Göttingen 1965.

Gillespie, G. The rebel in seventeenth-century tragedy. Comparative Lit 18 1966. Concludes with Venice preserved.

Langhans, E. A. Three early eighteenth-century prompt-books. Theatre Notebook 20 1966. The cheats of Scapin.

Stroup, T. B. Otways' bitter pessimism. In Essays in English literature presented to Dougald MacMillan, Chapel Hill 1967.

Klieneberger, H. R. Otway's Venice preserved and Hofmannsthal's Das gerettete Venedig. MLR 62 1967.

Williams, G. The sex-death motif in Otway's Venice preserv'd. Trivium 2 1967.

SIR JOHN VANBRUGH
1664–1726
Collections

Plays of Sir John Vanbrugh. 2 vols 1719, 1730, 1734, 1735, 1759, Dublin 1765, London 1776. Omits Pilgrim. The collections to 1735 also omit Country house.

The dramatic works of Wycherley, Congreve, Vanbrugh and Farquhar. Ed Leigh Hunt 1840.

Plays of Sir John Vanbrugh. Ed W. C. Ward 2 vols 1893. Omits Pilgrim.

Sir John Vanbrugh. Ed A. E. H. Swaen 1896 (Mermaid ser).

Complete works. Ed B. Dobrée and G. Webb 4 vols 1927. Includes the letters.

§ 1

The relapse: or virtue in danger. C DL 21 Nov 1696. 1697, 1698, 1708, [1709 ?], [1711 ?], 1727, 1734, 1735 etc; tr German, 1764.

Aesop. C Pt 1 DL c. Dec 1696. 1697; pt 2 DL c. March 1697. 1697, 1697 (pts 1–2), 1702, 1711, Dublin 1725, London 1730, 1735 etc.

The provok'd wife. C LIF May 1697. 1697, 1698, 1709, 1710, 1727, 1734, 1735, Dublin 1743 (with new scenes in Act iv) etc; tr French, 1726.

A short vindication of the Relapse and the Provok'd wife, from immorality and prophaneness, by the author. 1698.

The pilgrim. C DL April 1700. 1700 (anon), 1735.

The false friend. C DL c. Feb 1702. 1702. Anon.

The confederacy. C Hay 30 Oct 1705. 1705, 1734, 1751 etc.

The country house. F DL 18 Jan 1698. 1715, 1719, 1740 (as La maison rustique).

The mistake. C Hay 27 Dec 1705. 1706, Dublin 1726, London 1735.

Sir John Vanbrugh's justification, of what he depos'd in the Duchess of Marlborough's late tryal. [1718].

A journey to London. C 1728, 1730, 1735. Acted with Cibber's addns DL 10 Jan 1728 as The provok'd husband.

Squire Trelooby, of which Vanbrugh wrote one act, and the Cuckold in conceit, were not ptd. Both taken from Molière. For the former, see col 751, below.

Letters

In Complete works, ed B. Dobrée and G. Webb, 1927, above.

Vincent, H. P. Two unpublished letters of Vanbrugh. N & Q 21 Aug 1937.

Barnard, J. Two unpublished letters. HLQ 29 1966.

Rosenberg, A. New light on Vanbrugh, PQ 45 1966. 8 letters.

§ 2

Hazlitt, William. In A view of the English stage, 1818.

—— In Lectures on the English comic writers, 1819.

D'Israeli, Isaac. A second series of curiosities of literature. 3 vols 1823. Vol 2 includes Secret history of the building of Blenheim.

Dametz, M. Vanbrughs Leben und Werke. Vienna 1898.

Lovegrove, G. H. The life, work and influence of Vanbrugh. 1902. Architectural.

Palmer, J. In his Comedy of manners, 1918.

Dobrée, B. In his Restoration comedy, Oxford 1924.

—— In his Essays in biography, Oxford 1925.

Perry, H. T. E. In his Comic spirit in Restoration drama, New Haven 1925.

Mueschke, P. and J. Fleisher. A re-valuation of Vanbrugh. PMLA 49 1934.

Whistler, L. Vanbrugh, architect and dramatist 1664–1726. 1938.

—— Some unpublished drawings of Vanbrugh. New Eng Rev new ser 1–2 1948–9.

—— Blenheim: an English palace. History Today 2 1952.

—— The imagination of Vanbrugh and his fellow artists. 1954.

Boys, R. C. The architect Vanbrugh and the wits. College Art Jnl 6 1947.

—— Sir Joshua Reynolds and the architect Vanbrugh: a footnote to Boswell. Papers of Michigan Acad of Science, Arts & Letters 33 1949.

Brown, T. J. English literary autographs xli: Vanbrugh. Books Collector 6 1962.

Lloyd, C. Vanbrugh. History Today 14 1964.

Harris, B. The dialect of those fanatic times. In Restoration theatre, ed J. R. Brown and Harris 1965.

—— Vanbrugh. 1967.

Patterson, F. M. The revised scenes of the Provok'd wife. Eng Lang Notes 4 1966.

Shipley, J. B. The authorship of Cornish Squire. PQ 47 1968.

WILLIAM CONGREVE
1670–1729
Collections

The works of Mr William Congreve. 3 vols 1710, 1717, 1719–20 (adds 2 poems), Dublin 1731–29, London 1730, 1735, 1753, 1761, Birmingham 1761, Dublin 1773, 2 vols 1773, 1774 (rev text of all the plays).

Five plays written by Mr Congreve. 1710, 1712. Pirated edns of the 5 plays with general title-page.

Dramatic works. 2 vols 1773.

The dramatic works of Wycherley, Congreve, Vanbrugh and Farquhar. Ed Leigh Hunt 1840.

William Congreve. Ed A. C. Ewald 1887 (Mermaid ser). Omits operas.
Comedies. Ed G. S. Street 2 vols 1895.
William Congreve. Ed W. Archer [1912].
Complete works. Ed M. Summers 4 vols 1923.
Comedies: the Mourning bride, poems, miscellanies. Ed B. Dobrée 2 pts Oxford 1925–8 (WC).
Comedies. Ed J. W. Krutch, New York 1927.
Works. Ed F. W. Bateson 1930. With textual variorum.
Comedies. Ed N. Marshall 1948.
Complete plays. Ed H. Davis, Chicago 1967.

§ 1

Incognita, or love and duty reconcil'd: a novel. 1692, 1700, 1713, 1713; ed H. F. B. Brett-Smith, Oxford 1922; ed A. N. Jeffares 1966 (with Way of the world, below).
The old batchelour. C DL 9 March 1693. 1693 (4 'editions', re-issues with some pages re-set), 1694, 1697 ('corrected'), 1707, 1710, 1711, [1711 ?] etc.
The double dealer. C DL Oct 1693. 1694, 1706 (rev), 1711, [1711 ?], 1735, Dublin 1735, London 1739 etc.
The mourning Muse of Alexas: a pastoral, lamenting the death of Queen Mary. 1695 (3 edns), Dublin 1695.
A Pindarick ode, humbly offer'd to the King on his taking Namure. 1695.
Love for love. C LIF April 1695. 1695, 1695, 1697 (rev), 1704, 1711, [1711?], c. 1715 (2 reprints), 1733; ed E. L. Avery, Lincoln Nebraska 1966; ed A. N. Jeffares 1967; tr French, 1746 (in Le théâtre anglois vol 7).
The mourning bride. T LIF Feb 1697. 1697, 1697, 1703, 1711, [1711 ?], 1733 etc; tr French, 1746 (in Le théâtre anglois vol 6).
The birth of the Muse: a poem. 1698.
Amendments of Mr Collier's false and imperfect citations. 1698.
The way of the world. C LIF March 1700. 1700, 1706 ('revised'), 1711, [1711 ?], 1735 etc; ed W. P. Barrett 1933; ed H. T. E. Perry, New York 1951; ed J. H. Wilson, Boston 1959; ed G. G. Falls, New York 1964; ed K. Lynch, Lincoln Nebraska 1965; ed A. N. Jeffares 1966 (with Incognita, above).
The judgement of Paris. M DG March 1701. 1701.
A hymn to harmony. 1703.
The tears of Amaryllis for Amyntas: a pastoral. 1703.
A Pindarique ode on the victorious progress of her Majesties arms. 1706. With a prefatory discourse of the Pindarique ode.
Semele. In Works, 1710. An unacted opera.
The dramatic works of John Dryden. 6 vols 1717. Ed Congreve.
An impossible thing: a tale. 1720.
A letter from Mr Congreve to the Viscount Cobham. 1729.
Mr Congreve's last will and testament. 1729, 1730.
Squire Trelooby, *a trn of Molière's Monsieur de Pourceaugnac of which Congreve wrote one act, has not been preserved, though trns by Ozell 1704 and James Ralph 1734 may have been influenced by it. See* J. C. Hodges, The authorship of Squire Trelooby, RES 4 1928; J. B. Shipley, The authorship of the Cornish squire, PQ 47 1968.

Letters

Letters upon several occasions. Ed John Dennis 1696. Several letters from Congreve.
Berkeley, G. M. In his Literary relics, 1789. Includes Congreve's letters to Keally.
Congreve: letters and documents. Ed J. C. Hodges, New York 1964.

§ 2

Dryden, John. To my dear friend Mr Congreve. Prefixed to Double dealer, 1694.
'Wilson, Charles' (John Oldmixon ?). Memoirs of Congreve. 1730.

Voltaire, F. M. A. de. In his Letters concerning the English nation, 1733.
Johnson, Samuel. In his Lives of the English poets, 1779–81.
Davies, Thomas. In his Dramatic miscellanies, 3 vols 1783–4.
Walpole, Horace. Thoughts on comedy. In his Works vol 2, 1798.
Hazlitt, William. In his Lectures on the English comic writers, 1819.
Lamb, Charles. On the artificial comedy. In his Essays of Elia, 1821.
Macaulay, T. B. The dramatic works of Wycherley, Congreve, Vanbrugh and Farquhar. Edinburgh Rev 72 1841.
Hayman, Sam. New Handbook for Youghal. 1852.
Thackeray, W. M. In his Humourists of the eighteenth century, 1853.
Meredith, George. An essay on comedy. New Quart Mag 8 1877; 1897.
Gosse, E. Life of Congreve. 1888 (EML), 1924 (rev).
Bennewitz, A. Congreve und Molière. Leipzig 1890.
Schmid, D. Congreve: sein Leben und seine Lustspiele. Vienna 1897.
Palmer, J. In his Comedy of manners, 1913.
Canby, H. S. Congreve as a romanticist. PMLA 31 1916.
Dobrée, B. In his Restoration comedy, 1924.
— Congreve: a conversation between Swift and Gay. Seattle 1929.
Protopopesco, D. Un classique moderne: Congreve, sa vie, son oeuvre. Paris 1924.
— Congreve: a sheaf of poetical scraps. Bucharest [1925].
Perry, H. T. E. In his Comic spirit in Restoration drama, New Haven 1925.
Lynch, K. In her Social mode of Restoration comedy, New York 1926.
— Congreve's Irish friend, Joseph Keally. PMLA 53 1938.
— A Congreve gallery. Cambridge Mass 1951.
— References to Congreve in the Evelyn manuscripts. PQ 32 1953.
Hodges, J. C. Congreve in the government service. MP 27 1929.
— The ballad in Congreve's Love for love. PMLA 48 1933. See A. E. H. Swaen, Archiv 168 1935.
— On the date of Congreve's birth. MP 33 1935.
— The dating of Congreve's letters. PMLA 51 1936.
— Fresh manuscript sources for a life of Congreve. PMLA 54 1939.
— Congreve the man: a biography from new sources. New York 1941.
— The composition of Congreve's first play. PMLA 58 1943. Addns by R. G. Howarth 61 1946.
— The library of Congreve. New York 1955.
Taylor, D. C. Congreve. Oxford 1931.
de Beer, E. S. Congreve's Incognita: the source of its setting. RES 8 1932.
Congreve's comedies: speed, stillness and meaning. TLS 25 Sept 1937.
Wilson, J. D. Shakespeare, Milton and Congreve. TLS 16 Jan 1937.
Snider, R. Satire in the comedies of Congreve, Sheridan, Wilde and Coward. Orono Maine 1937.
Pool, E. M. A possible source of the Way of the world. MLR 33 1938.
Isaacs, J. Congreve's library. Library 4th ser 20 1940.
Lann, E. Forgotten English comedies. Theatres (USSR) 2 1941.
M., M. Congreve's Aristophanes. More Books 1942.
Avery, E. L. The première of the Mourning bride. MLN 57 1942.
— Congreve's plays on the eighteenth-century stage. New York 1951.
Potter, E. B. The paradox of Congreve's Mourning bride. PMLA 58 1943.

Smith, J. H. Thomas Corneille to Betterton to Congreve. JEGP 45 1946.

Bowers, F. T. The cancel leaf in Congreve's The double dealer 1694. PBSA 43 1949.

Robson, W. W. Hopkins and Congreve. TLS 24 Feb 1950.

Fujimura, T. H. In his Restoration comedy of wit, Princeton 1952.

Brossman, S. W. Dryden's Cassandra and Congreve's Zara. N & Q March 1956.

Brown, T. J. English literary autographs xxi: Congreve. Book Collector 6 1957.

Mueschke, P. and M. A new view of Congreve's Way of the World. Ann Arbor 1958.

Van Voris, W. Congreve's gilded carousel. Educational Theatre Jnl 10 1958.

— The cultivated stance: the designs of Congreve's plays. Dublin 1966.

Loftis, J. Comedy and society from Congreve to Fielding. Stanford 1959.

Holland, N. N. In his First modern comedies, Cambridge Mass 1959.

Noyes, R. G. Congreve and his comedies in the eighteenth-century novel. PQ 39 1960.

Leech, C. Congreve and the century's end. PQ 41 1962.

Nolan, P. T. Congreve's lovers: art and the critic. Drama Survey 1 1962.

Gosse, A. The omitted scene in Congreve's Love for love. MP 61 1963.

— Plot and character in Congreve's Double dealer. MLQ 29 1968.

Lincoln, S. The first setting of Congreve's Semele. Music & Letters 44 1963.

— Eccles and Congreve: music and drama on the Restoration stage. Theatre Notebook 18 1963.

Barnard, J. Did Congreve write A satyr against love? BNYPL May 1964. With text of poem.

Chapple, J. A. V. Manuscript texts of poems by the Earl of Dorset and Congreve. N & Q March 1964.

Gagen, J. Congreve's Mirabell and the ideal gentleman. PMLA 79 1964.

Lyons, C. E. Congreve's miracle of love. Criticism 6 1964.

Muir, K. The comedies of Congreve. In Restoration theatre, ed J. R. Brown and B. Harris 1965.

Downer, A. S. Mr Congreve comes to judgment. Humanities Assoc Bull 17 1966.

Schirmann, J. The first Hebrew translation from Hebrew literature: Congreve's Mourning bride. Scripta Hierosolymitana 19 1967.

Weales, G. The shadow on Congreve's surface. Educational Theatre Jnl 19 1967.

Simon, I. Early theories of prose fiction: Congreve and Fielding. In Imagined worlds: studies in memory of John Butt, 1968.

Williams, A. Congreve's Incognita and the contrivances of Providence. Ibid.

— Poetical justice, the contrivances of Providence and the works of Congreve. ELH 25 1968.

GEORGE FARQUHAR
1678–1707

Collections

The comedies of Mr George Farquhar. [1707], 1710, 1711, 1714, 1721, 1728, 2 vols 1736 (as Dramatick works). The earlier collections were made up from various edns of the separate plays.

The works of the late ingenious Mr George Farquhar, containing all his poems, letters, essays and comedies. 2 vols [1711] (2nd edn), [1714], 1718, 1728, 1742, 1760, 1772, Dublin 1775 (with life by T. Wilkes). The earlier collections were made up from various edns of the separate works with a general title-page.

The dramatic works of Wycherley, Congreve, Vanbrugh and Farquhar. Ed Leigh Hunt 1840.

The dramatic works of George Farquhar. Ed A. C. Ewald 2 vols 1892.

George Farquhar. Ed W. Archer [1906] (Mermaid ser). Includes The constant couple, The twin-rivals, The recruiting officer, The beaux' stratagem.

Complete works. Ed C. Stonehill 2 vols 1930.

§ 1

Love and a bottle. C DL Dec 1698. 1699, [1705?], 1735, Dublin 1761.

The adventures of Covent Garden. 1699. Anon.

The constant couple: or a trip to the Jubilee. C DL Nov 1699. 1700, 1700, 1701 (with alterations), 1704, 1710, 1711, 1732, 1735 etc.

Sir Harry Wildair: being the sequel of the trip to the jubilee. C DL c. April 1701. 1701, 1735.

The stage-coach. F LIF c. April 1701. Dublin 1704 (anon), 1705, 1709, Dublin 1719. With P. A. Motteux. See W. J. Lawrence, MLR 27 1932.

The inconstant: or the way to win him. C DL c. Feb 1702. 1702, 1718, 1736 etc.

Love and business in a collection of occasionaly verse and epistolary prose: a discourse likewise upon comedy in reference to the English stage. 1702. The Discourse rptd in Critical essays 1700–25, ed W. H. Durham, New Haven 1915.

The recruiting officer. C DL 8 April 1706. [1706] (3 edns, the 2nd 'corrected'), [1707?], 1711, 1714, 1736 etc; ed M. Shugrue, Lincoln Nebraska 1965; ed K. Tynan 1965.

The beaux' stratagem. C Hay 8 March 1707. [1707], 1707 (8 edns), 1711, 1715, 1730, 1736, 1748, 1752 etc; ed B. Dobrée, Bristol 1929; ed J. H. Wilson, Boston 1959; ed V. C. Hopper and G. B. Lahey, New York 1963; tr and ed J. Hamard as La ruse des galants, Paris 1966.

Love's catechism. 1707. An unauthorized excerpt from Beaux stratagem, above.

Barcellona, a poem: or the Spanish expedition. 1710.

Letters

Familiar and courtly letters. 2 vols 1701–1, 1718. This collection and the following contain letters by Farquhar.

Letters of wit, politicks and morality. Ed Abel Boyer 1701.

§ 2

Hazlitt, William. In his Lectures on the English comic writers, 1819.

Schmid, D. George Farquhar. Vienna 1904.

Robertson, J. G. Lessing and Farquhar. MLR 2 1907.

Palmer, J. In his Comedy of manners, 1913.

Dobrée, B. In his Restoration comedy, Oxford 1924.

Larson, M. A. The influence of Milton's divorce tracts on Farquhar's Beaux' stratagem. PMLA 39 1924.

Perry, H. T. E. In his Comic spirit in Restoration drama, New Haven 1925.

Sutherland, J. R. New light on Farquhar. TLS 6 March 1937.

Lawrence, W. J. Farquhar: Thomas Wilkes. TLS 26 June 1930.

Whiting, G. W. The date of the second edition of the Constant couple. MLN 47 1932.

Kies, P. P. Lessing's intention in Der Dorfjunker. Washington State Univ Stud 11 1943.

Kavanagh, P. Farquhar. TLS 10 Feb 1945.

Connely, W. Young George Farquhar: the Restoration drama at twilight. 1949.

Hough, R. L. An error in the Recruiting officer. N & Q Aug 1953.

— Farquhar: the Recruiting officer. N & Q Nov 1954.

Morton, R. and W. M. Peterson. The jubilee of 1700 and Farquhar's The constant couple. N & Q Dec 1955.

Spinner, K. Farquhar als Dramatiker. Berne 1956.
Pyle, F. Farquhar 1677–1707. Hermathena 92 1958.
Rosenfeld, S. Notes on the Recruiting officer. Theatre Notebook 18 1964.
Rothstein, E. Farquhar's Twin-rivals and the reform of comedy. PMLA 79 1964.
—— Farquhar. New York 1967.

Berman, R. The comedy of reason. Texas Stud in Lit & Lang 7 1965.
James, E. N. The burlesque of Restoration comedy: Love and a bottle. Stud in Eng Lit 1500–1900 5 1965.
Farmer, A. J. Farquhar. 1966.
Sharp, W. L. Restoration comedy: an approach to modern production. Drama Survey 7 1969. On Beaux' stratagem.

IV. MINOR RESTORATION DRAMA 1660–1700

This section is restricted to writers whose plays were mainly written or acted after the Restoration and who were born before 1665. One-play dramatists have normally been excluded, but a number of these will be found under Poetry, col 467 above. A key to the abbreviations will be found on col 741, above.

JOHN BANCROFT
d. 1696

The tragedy of Sertorius. DL c. March 1679. 1679.
King Edward the Third, with the fall of Mortimer, Earl of March: an historical play. DC c. Dec 1690. 1691 1691. Anon. Rptd in Six plays written by Mr Mountfort, 2 vols 1720, but attributed to Bancroft by Coxeter.
Henry the Second, King of England, with the death of Rosamond. T DL Nov 1692. 1693. Dedication signed Will Mountfort and rptd in Six plays written by Mr Mountfort, 2 vols 1720, but attributed to Bancroft by Gildon.

JOHN BANKS
c. 1650–c. 1700
§ 1

The rival Kings: or the loves of Oroondates and Statira. T DL c. June 1677. 1677.
The destruction of Troy. T DG c. Nov 1678. 1679.
The unhappy favourite: or the Earl of Essex. T DL c. May 1681. 1682, 1685, 1693, [1699], 1702, 1704, 1712; ed T. M. H. Blair, New York 1939.
Vertue betray'd: or Anna Bullen. T DG 5 April 1682. 1682, 1692, 1715, Dublin 1726, London 1727. For Banks' source, see E. N. Backus, PMLA 47 1932.
The island Queens: or the death of Mary, Queen of Scotland. T Prohibited. 1684.
The innocent usurper: or the death of the Lady Jane Gray. T Prohibited. 1694.
Cyrus the Great: or the tragedy of love. T LIF c. Dec 1695. 1696.
The Albion Queens: or the death of Mary, Queen of Scotland. T DL 1704. 1704, [1704]. An alteration of Island Queens, above.

§ 2

Bowers, F. T. The variant sheet in Cyrus the Great 1696. SB 4 1952.
Knepler, H. W. Maxwell Anderson, a historical parallel: problems for the poetic dramatist. Queen's Quart 64 1957.
Devlin, J. J. The dramatis personae and the dating of John Banks' The Albion Queens. N & Q June 1963.

APHRA BEHN
1640–89
Collections

Plays written by the late ingenious Mrs Behn. 2 vols 1702, 1716, 4 vols 1724.

The plays, histories and novels of the ingenious Mrs Aphra Behn. Ed R. H. Shepherd 6 vols 1871. Rptd from the plays of 1724 and the novels of 1725.
Works. Ed M. Summers 6 vols 1915. Omits the Pindarics.

§ 1

For the novels, see col 980, below.
The forc'd marriage: or the jealous bridegroom. TC LIF Sept 1670. 1671, 1690.
The amorous prince: or the curious husband. C LIF c. Feb 1671. 1671.
Covent Garden drollery. 1672; ed G. Thorn-Drury 1928. Perhaps ed Aphra Behn.
The Dutch lover. C DG Feb 1673. 1673.
Abdelazar: or the moor's revenge. T DG July 1676. 1677, 1693.
The town-fopp: or Sir Timothy Tawdrey. C DG c. Sept 1676. 1677, 1699.
The debauchee: or the credulous cuckold. C DG c. Feb 1677. 1677.
The rover: or the banish't cavaliers. C DG March 1677. 1677, [1697?], 1709; ed F. Link, Lincoln Nebraska 1966.
Sir Patient Fancy. C DG Jan 1678. 1678, [1681?].
The feign'd curtizans: or a night's intrigue. C DG c. March 1679. 1679.
The second part of the rover. C DG c. Jan 1681. 1681.
The revenge: or a match in Newgate. C DG c. June 1680. 1680. Anon.
The round-heads: or the good old cause. C DG c. Dec 1681. 1682, 1698.
The city-heiress: or Sir Timothy Treat-all. C DG c. March 1682. 1682, 1698.
The false count: or a new way to play an old game. C DG c. Dec 1681. 1682, 1697.
The young King: or the mistake. TC DG c. 1679. 1683, 1698.
Poems upon several occasions, with a voyage to the island of love. 1684, 1697 (with Lycidus, below).
Miscellany: being a collection of poems by several hands. 1685. Ed with preface by Aphra Behn, with her trn of La Rochefoucauld, Seneca unmasqued.
A Pindarick on the death of our late sovereign. 1685, 1685, 1686, Dublin nd.
A poem humbly dedicated to Catherine Queen Dowager. 1685.
A Pindarick poem on the happy coronation of his Sacred Majesty James II and his illustrious consort Queen Mary. 1685.
The luckey chance: or an alderman's bargain. C DL c. April 1686. 1687.
The emperor of the moon. F DG c. March 1687. 1687, 1688.
To Christopher Duke of Albemarle, on his voyage to Jamaica: a Pindarick. 1687.

To the memory of George Duke of Buckingham. 1687. Anon. *See* A. Mizener, TLS 8 May 1937.

Lycidus: or the lover in fashion, from the French [of the Abbé Tallemant]; together with a miscellany of new poems by several hands. 1688, 1697 (with Poems upon several occasions).

A discovery of new worlds, from the French [of Fontenelle]. 1688, 1700 (as The theory etc). With a prefatory essay on translated prose.

A poem to Sir Roger L'Estrange. 1688.

A congratulatory poem to her Majesty. 1688, 1688.

A congratulatory poem to the King's Most Sacred Majesty. 1688, 1688.

Two congratulatory poems to their Majesties. 1688.

The history of oracles, and the cheats of the pagan priests. 1688, 1699. Tr from Fontenelle.

A congratulatory poem to her Sacred Majesty Queen Mary. 1689.

A Pindaric poem to the Rev Dr Burnet. 1689.

The widow ranter: or the history of Bacon in Virginia. TC DL Nov 1689. 1690.

The younger brother: or the amorous jilt. C DL c. Feb 1696. 1696. With a biographical preface by Charles Gildon.

§ 2

Siegel, P. Aphra Behns Gedichte und Prosawerke. Anglia 25 1902.

Bernbaum, E. Mrs Behn's Oroonoko. In G. L. Kittredge anniversary papers, Boston 1913.

—— Mrs Behn's biography a fiction. PMLA 28 1913.

Johnson, E. D. Aphra Behn's Oroonoko. Jnl of Negro History 10 1925.

Sackville-West, V. Aphra Behn. 1927.

Jerrold, W. and C. In their Five queer women, 1929.

Platt, H. G. Astrea and Celadon: an untouched portrait of Aphra Behn. PMLA 49 1934.

Wagenknecht, E. In praise of Mrs Behn. Colophon 18 1934.

Seeber, E. D. Oroonoko in France in the xviiith century. PMLA 51 1936.

—— Oroonoko and Crusoe's Man Friday. MLQ 12 1951.

Harris, B. Bajazet to Gloriana. TLS 9 Feb 1933.

Mizener, A. Poems by Mrs Behn. TLS 8 May 1937.

Graham, C. B. An echo of Jonson in Sir Patient Fancy. MLN 53 1938.

Mathews, E. G. Montfleury's Ecole des jaloux and the False Count. MLN 54 1939.

Baker, H. Mrs Behn forgets. SE 1942.

Sypher, W. A note on the realism of Oroonoko. MLQ 3 1942.

Hill, R. M. Behn's use of setting. MLQ 7 1946.

Woodcock, G. The incomparable Aphra. 1948.

Hahn, E. Aphra Behn. 1951.

Mundy, P. D. Behn, novelist and dramatist 1640–89. N & Q May 1954. *See also* A. J. L. Ferguson, June 1954.

—— Behn 1640?–89. N & Q Jan 1955.

Turner, M. A note on the standard of English translation from the French 1685–1720. N & Q Dec 1954.

Ramsaran, J. A. Oroonoko: a study of the factual elements. N & Q April 1960.

Cameron, W. J. New light on Aphra Behn: an investigation into the facts and fictions surrounding her journey to Surinam in 1663 and her activities as a spy in Flanders in 1666. Auckland 1961.

Hargreaves, H. A. A case for Mr Behn. N & Q June 1962.

—— Mrs Behn's warning of the Dutch Thames plot. N & Q Feb 1962.

Sheffey, R. T. Some evidence for a new source of Aphra Behn's Oroonoko. SP 59 1962.

Langhans, E. A. Three early eighteenth-century prompt-books. Theatre Notebook 20 1966. On the Rover.

Link, F. M. Aphra Behn. New York 1968.

Witmer, A. and J. Freehafer. Aphra Behn's strange news from Virginia. Lib Chron 34 1968.

THOMAS BETTERTON
1635?–1710

§ 1

Appius and Virginia. T LIF May 1669. 1679. Anon.

The amorous widow: or the wanton wife. C LIF c. Nov 1670. 1706 (anon), 1710, 1714, 1725, 1729.

The counterfeit bridegroom: or the defeated widow. C DG c. Sept 1677. 1677. Anon.

The revenge: or a match in Newgate. C DG c. June 1680. 1680. Anon. Probably by Mrs Behn.

The prophetess: or the history of Dioclesian. O DG June 1690. 1690 (anon), 1719.

K. Henry IV, with the humours of Sir John Falstaff. TC LIF 9 Jan 1700. 1700. Anon.

The bondman: or love and liberty. TC DL 1719. Anon.

The sequel of Henry the Fourth; with the humours of Sir John Falstaffe. TC DL [1720].

A history of the English stage. 1741. A compilation by Oldys et al, partly based on Betterton's papers.

§ 2

Downes, John. Roscius anglicanus. 1708; ed T. Davies 1789; ed J. Knight 1886; ed M. Summers [1928]; ed J. Loftis, Los Angeles 1969 (Augustan Reprint Soc).

Gildon, Charles. The life of Mr Thomas Betterton. 1710.

Lowe, R. W. Thomas Betterton. 1891.

Summers, M. The comedies of Betterton. N & Q 27 June 1936.

Smith, J. H. Thomas Corneille to Betterton to Congreve. JEGP 45 1946.

Ward, C. E. The Tempest: a Restoration opera problem. ELH 13 1946.

Bowers, F. T. A bibliographical history of the Fletcher-Betterton play the Prophetess 1690. Library 5th ser 16 1961.

GEORGE DIGBY,
2nd EARL OF BRISTOL
1612–77

§ 1

Letters between the Ld George Digby and Sir Kenelm Digby Kt concerning religion. 1651.

Elvira: or the worst not always true. C LIF c. 1663. 1667, 1685; rptd R. Dodsley, A select collection of old plays vol 12, 1744; rev W. C. Hazlitt vol 15, 1876.

§ 2

Townshend, D. George Digby, second Earl of Bristol. 1924.

GEORGE VILLIERS,
2nd DUKE OF BUCKINGHAM
1628–87

Collections

The works of his Grace George, late Duke of Buckingham. Ed T. Brown 1704, 1704, 2 vols 1715, 1721, 1754, 1775.

§ 1

The rehearsal. Bsq TR 7 Dec 1671. 1672 (anon), 1673, 1675 (with 'amendments and large additions'), 1683, 1687, 1692, 1701, 1709 ('with a key'), 1711 etc; ed E. Arber 1869; ed M. Summers, Stratford-on-Avon 1914; ed G. G. Falls, New York 1964. Samuel Butler, Thomas Sprat and Martin Clifford are supposed to have assisted Buckingham.

A letter to Sir Thomas Osborn upon the reading of a book called the Present interest of England. 1672.

Poetical reflections on a late poem entituled Absalom and Achitophel, by a person of honour. 1681, 1682. Ascribed (wrongly?) to Buckingham by Anthony Wood.

The chances. C DL Dec 1682. 1682, 1692, 1705 etc.

A short discourse upon the reasonableness of men's having a religion. 1685.

§ 2

Niemeyer, C. Henry Killigrew and the Duke of Buckingham. RES 12 1936.

Mizener, A. Though, Phyllis, your prevailing charms. MLN 56 1941.

Chapman, H. W. Great Villiers. 1949.

Barrington, M. The reasonableness of religion. N & Q 30 Sept 1950.

Orwen, W. R. Marvell and Buckingham. N & Q 6 Jan 1951.

Wilson, J. H. A rake and his times: Villiers. New York 1954.

Reichert, J. A note on Buckingham and Dryden. N & Q June 1962.

JOHN CARYLL
1625–1711

§ 1

The English Princess: or the death of Richard the III. T LIF c. 7 March 1667. 1667 (anon), 1674.

Sir Salomon: or the cautious coxcombe. C LIF c. May 1670. 1671 (anon), 1691.

The psalms of David, translated from the Vulgat. 1700. Anon.

Caryll also contributed to Ovid's epistles translated, 1680, and to Dryden's Miscellany poems, 1683.

§ 2

Bowers, F. T. Bibliographical evidence from a resetting to Sir Salomon 1691. Library 5th ser 3 1948.

ABRAHAM COWLEY
1618–67

See vol 1, above.

JOHN CROWNE
d. 1703

Bibliographies

Winship, G. P. A bibliography of the Restoration dramatist Crowne. Cambridge Mass 1922.

Collections

Dramatic works, with memoir and notes by J. Maidment and W. H. Logan. 4 vols Edinburgh 1873–7. Omits Andromache, Misery of civil war, Henry the Sixth.

§ 1

Pandion and Amphigenia: or the history of the coy lady of Thessalia. 1665.

Juliana: or the Princess of Poland. T LIF c. June 1671. 1671.

The history of Charles the Eighth of France: or the invasion of Naples by the French. T DG c. Dec 1671. 1672, 1680.

Andromache. T DG c. Aug 1674. 1675. Anon. Rev from Racine.

The prologue to Calistho, with the chorus's between the acts. 1675.

Calisto: or the chaste nimph. M Court Feb 1675. 1675.

The countrey wit. C DG Jan 1676. 1675, 1693.

The destruction of Jerusalem by Titus Vespasian, in two parts. T DL Jan 1677. 1677, 1693, 1703; pt 1 ed B. Dobrée, Oxford 1960 (WC) (in Five heroic plays).

The ambitious statesman: or the loyal favourite. T DL c. March 1679. 1679, 1681.

The misery of civil-war. T DG c. March 1680. 1680, 1681 (as Henry the Sixth: the second part).

Henry the Sixth: the first part, with the murder of Humphrey Duke of Glocester. T DG April 1681. 1681.

Thyestes. T DL c. March 1680. 1681.

City politiques. C DL 19 Jan 1683. 1683. 1688; ed J. H. Wilson Lincoln Nebraska 1967.

Sir Courtly Nice: or it cannot be. C DL 9 May 1685. 1685, 1693, 1703; ed M. Summers 1921 (in Restoration comedies); ed C. Hughes, Hague 1966.

A poem on the death of King Charles the II. 1685.

Darius King of Persia. T DL May 1688. 1688.

The English frier: or the town sparks. C DL c. March 1690. 1690.

Dœneids, or the noble labours of the great dean of Notre-Dame in Paris: an heroique poem. 1692. From Boileau's Lutrin.

The history of the love between a Parisian lady and a young singing-man: an heroic poem. 1692.

Regulus. T DL c. June 1692. 1694.

The married beau: or the curious impertinent. C DL c. April 1694. 1694.

Caligula. T DL c. March 1698. 1698.

§ 2

White, A. F. Crowne and America. PMLA 35 1920.

—— Crowne: his life and dramatic works. Cleveland 1922.

Boswell, E. The Restoration Court stage, with a particular account of the production of Calisto. Cambridge Mass 1932.

Peterson, W. M. Sentiment in Crowne's The married beau. N & Q Nov 1953. Reply by D. S. Berkeley, April 1954.

SIR WILLIAM D'AVENANT
1606–68

See vol 1, above.

JOHN DENNIS
1657–1734

See col 1041, below.

THOMAS DILKE

The lover's luck. C LIF c. Dec 1695. 1696.

The city lady: or folly reclaim'd. C LIF c. Dec 1696. 1697.

The pretenders: or the town unmaskt. C LIF c. March 1698. 1698.

XXV select allusions to several places of Horace, Martial, Anacreon and Petron Arbit, part 1. 1698.

THOMAS DOGGETT
d. 1721

§ 1

The country-wake. C LIF c. May 1696. 1696, [1697?].

§ 2

Cook, T. A. and G. Nickalls. Thomas Doggett. 1908.

JOHN DRYDEN
1631–1700

See col 439, above.

THOMAS DUFFETT

§ 1

The Spanish rogue. C LIF c. March 1673. 1674.

The Empress of Morocco. Bsq DL c. Dec 1673. 1674. Anon.

The amorous old-woman: or 'tis well if it take. C DL c. March 1674. 1674 ('by a person of honour'), 1684 (as The fond lady). Perhaps not by Duffett.

The mock-tempest: or the enchanted castle. Bsq DL Nov 1674. 1675.

Beauties triumph: a masque, presented by the scholars of Mr Jeffery Banister and Mr James Hart at Chelsey. 1676.

New poems, songs, prologues and epilogues. 1676.

Psyche debauch'd. Bsq DL c. Aug 1675. 1678.

§ 2

Haywood, C. The songs and masques in the new Tempest: an incident in the battle of the two theatres 1674. HLQ 19 1955.

Cameron, K. M. Duffett's New poems and vacation plays. Theatre Survey 5 1964.

Lewis, P. E. The three dramatic burlesques of Duffett. Durham Univ Jnl 58 1966.

Macey, S. L. Duffett's Mock Tempest and the assimilation of Shakespeare. Restoration & 18th-Century Theatre Research 7 1968.

THOMAS D'URFEY
1653–1723

§ 1

Archerie reviv'd, or the bow-man's excellence: an heroick poem. 1676. With Robert Shotterel.

The siege of Memphis: or the ambitious Queen. T DL c. Sept 1676. 1676.

Madam Fickle: or the witty false one. C DG Nov 1676. 1677, 1682, 1691.

A fond husband: or, the plotting sisters. C DG May 1677. 1677, 1678, 1685, 1711, 1725.

The fool turn'd critick. C DL Nov 1676. 1678.

Trick for trick: or the debauch'd hypocrite. C DL c. March 1678. 1678.

Squire Oldsapp: or the night-adventurers. C DG c. June 1678. 1679.

The virtuous wife: or good luck at last. C DG c. Sept 1679. 1680.

Sir Barnaby Whigg: or no wit like a womans. C DL c. Sept 1681. 1681.

The progress of honesty, or a view of a Court and city: a Pindarique poem. 1681, 1681, 1739.

Butler's ghost, or Hudibras: the fourth part. 1682.

The royalist. C DG Jan 1682. 1682.

The injured princess: or the fatal wager. TC DL c. March 1682. 1682.

Scandalum magnatum, or Potapski's case: a satyr against Polish oppression. 1682. Anon.

A new collection of songs and poems. 1683.

Choice new songs never before printed. 1684.

Several new songs. 1684.

The malecontent, a satyr: being the sequel of the Progress of honesty. 1684.

A third collection of new songs, never printed before. 1685.

An elegy upon the late blessed monarch King Charles II; and two panegyricks upon their present Sacred Majesties King James and Queen Mary. 1685.

A common-wealth of women. C DL c. Aug 1685. 1686, 1688.

The banditti: or a ladies distress. C DL c. Feb 1686. 1686.

A compleat collection of Mr D'Urfey's songs and odes, whereof the first part never before published. 1687. The 2nd pt as A new collection of songs and poems pt II.

A poem congratulatory on the birth of the young Prince. 1688.

A fool's preferment: or the three Dukes of Dunstable; together with all the songs and notes to 'em, excellently compos'd by Mr Henry Purcell. C DG c. April 1688. 1688, 1917.

New poems: consisting of satyrs, elegies and odes. 1690.

Collin's walk through London and Westminster: a poem in burlesque. 1690, 1690.

Momus ridens: or comical remarks on the publick reports. 29 Oct 1690–11 March 1691. Anon; weekly.

Love for money: or the boarding school. C DL c. Jan 1691. 1691, 1691, 1696, 1724, 1726.

Bussy D'Ambois: or the husbands revenge. T DL c. March 1691. 1691.

A Pindarick ode on New-Year's-Day, perform'd by vocal and instrumental musick before their Sacred Majesties K. William and Q. Mary. 1691.

A Pindarick poem on the Royal Navy. 1691.

The moralist: or a satyr upon the sects. 1691. Anon.

The triennial mayor, or the new raparees: a poem. 1691. Anon.

The weesils: a satyrical fable. 1691. Anon.

The weesil trap'd: a poem. 1691. Anon.

The marriage-hater match'd. C DL Jan 1692. 1692, 1692, 1693.

A Pindarick ode upon the fleet. 1692.

The Richmond heiress: or a woman once in the right. C DL c. April 1693. 1693, 1693, 1718.

The canonical states-man's grand argument discuss'd. 1693. Anon.

The comical history of Don Quixote: part I. C DG c. May 1694. 1694, 1694, 1727, 1729, [1889].

The comical history of Don Quixote: part the second. C DG c. June 1694. 1694, 1702, 1729, [1889].

The songs to the new play of Don Quixote: part the first. 1694, 1694.

The songs to the new play of Don Quixote: part the second. 1694.

The comical history of Don Quixote: the third part. C DL c. Nov 1695. 1696, 1729, [1889].

Gloriana: a funeral Pindarique poem sacred to the blessed memory of that ever-admir'd and most excellent Princess, our late gracious soveraign Lady Queen Mary. 1695.

New songs in the third part of the comical history of Don Quixote. 1696.

A wife for any man. C 1696 or 1697. Not pbd.

A new opera call'd Cinthia and Endimion: or the loves of the deities. O DL c. Dec 1696. 1697.

The intrigues at Versailles: or a jilt in all humours. C LIF c. May 1697. 1697, 1697.

Albion's blessing: a poem panegyrical on his Sacred Majesty King William the III. 1698.

The campaigners: or the pleasant adventures at Brussels, with a familiar preface upon a late reformer of the stage, ending with a satyrical fable of the dog and the ottor. C DL c. June 1698. 1698. The preface ed J. W. Krutch, Ann Arbor 1948.

A choice collection of new songs and ballads. 1699.

The famous history of the rise and fall of Massaniello, in two parts. T DL c. May 1699. 1700. The 2nd pt dated 1699 as The famous history and fall of Massaniello: or a fisherman a prince.

An ode for the anniversary feast made in honour of St Cecilia. 1700.

The Bath: or the western lass. C DL May 1701. 1701.

The old mode and the new: or country miss with her furbeloe. C DL March 1703. [1703].

Tales tragical and comical, viz Abradatus and Panthea: or love and honour in perfection; Hell beyond hell: or the devil and mademoiselle; Female revenge: or the Queen of Lombardy; The night-adventures: or the country intrigue; Fatal piety: or the royal converts; The broken commands: or the heirs adopted. 1704.

Wonders in the sun: or the Kingdom of the birds. CO Hay April 1706. 1706, 1706, Los Angeles 1964 (Augustan Reprint Soc).

Stories moral and comical: viz, The banquet of the gods; Titus and Gisippus: or the power of friendship; The prudent husband: or cuckoldom wittily prevented: Loyalty's glory: or the true souldier of honour. [1707].

The trophies: or Augusta's glory a triumphant ode. 1707.

Honor and opes, or the British merchant's glory: a poem. 1708.

The modern prophets: or new wit for a husband. C DL May 1709. [1709].

Musa et musica: or honour and musick. [1710].

Songs compleat, pleasant and divertive. 5 vols 1719. Ed D'Urfey. Vols 1–2 contain his songs.

Wit and mirth: or pills to purge melancholy. 6 vols 1719–20. Vols 1–5 are a re-issue of Songs compleat, pleasant and divertive, above, with new title-pages and headlines. Vol 6 is dated 1720. Ed C. L. Day 3 vols New York 1959.

New opera's, with comical stories and poems, on several occasions. 1721. The two Queens of Brentford: or Bayes no poetaster, Bsq O; The Grecian heroine: or the fate of tyranny, T; Ariadne: or the triumph of Bacchus, O. All unacted.

Songs. Ed C. L. Day, Cambridge Mass 1933.

§ 2

Wit for money: or poet stutter. 1691.

Steele, R. Tatler nos 1, 4, 11, 43, 126, 214 1709–10.

— Guardian no 82 1713.

— Lover no 40 1715.

Addison, J. Spectator no 37 1711.

— Guardian nos 29, 67 1713.

Tom D'Urfey. Household Words 11 1855.

Chappell, W. The ballad literature and popular music of the olden time. 2 vols nd.

— The Roxburghe ballads. 3 vols 1871–80.

Daniel, G. Love's last labour not lost. 1863.

Besant, W. Tom D'Urfey. Belgravia 18 1872.

Ebsworth, J. W. The Bagford ballads. 2 vols 1878.

— The Roxburghe ballads. 6 vols 1883–97.

Two Court poets. All the Year Round 34 1884.

Hutchinson, W. G. Tom D'Urfey. Macmillan's Mag Nov 1901.

Baring-Gould, S. Devonshire characters and strange events. 1908.

Forsythe, R. A study of the plays of Thomas D'Urfey. 2 vols Cleveland 1916–17.

Tom D'Urfey. TLS 22 Feb 1923.

Day, C. L. Pills to purge melancholy. RES 8 1932.

— A lost play by D'Urfey. MLN 49 1934.

— Dates and performances of D'Urfey's plays. Charlottesville 1950.

Lynch, K. D'Urfey's contribution to sentimental comedy. PQ 9 1930.

Ustick, W. L. Tom D'Urfey and the graveyard. MP 36 1939.

Graham, C. B. The Jonsonian tradition in the comedies of D'Urfey. MLQ 8 1947.

Bowers, F. T. The comical history of Don Quixote 1694. PBSA 43 1949.

— The two issues of Cynthiae and Endymion 1697. Princeton Univ Lib Chron 13 1951.

Sanville, D. W. D'Urfey's Love for money: a bibliographical study. Pennsylvania Univ Lib Chron 17 1950.

Biswanger, R. A., jr. D'Urfey's Richmond heiress 1693: a bibliographical study. SB 5 1953.

— The date of D'Urfey's Richmond heiress. N & Q March 1953.

— Several words first employed in D'Urfey's The Richmond heiress. MLN 70 1955.

Ellis, W. D. D'Urfey, the Pope-Philips quarrel and the Shepherd's week. PMLA 74 1959.

Legman, G. Pills to purge melancholy: a bibliographical note. Midwest Folklore 9 1959.

Vaughan, J. A. A D'Urfey play dated. MP 64 1967. On A fond husband 1677.

— Persevering, exhausted bard: D'Urfey. Quart Jnl of Speech 53 1967.

SIR FRANCIS FANE
d. 1689?

Love in the dark: or the man of bus'ness. C DL May 1675. 1675.

A Pindarick ode on the sacred memory of King Charles II. 1685.

The sacrifice. T. Unacted. 1686, 1687, 1687.

RICHARD FLECKNOE
c. 1620–78

§ 1

The affections of a pious soule. 1640.

Miscellanea: or poems of all sorts with divers other pieces. 1653. Includes a Discourse of languages, and particularly of the English tongue.

A relation of ten years travells. [1654?], 1665 (as A true narrative).

Love's dominion. TC Unacted. 1654.

The diarium: or journall, in burlesque rhime. 1656.

Enigmaticall characters. 1658, 1665 (rev).

The idea of Oliver, late Lord Protector. 1659.

The marriage of Oceanus and Britannia. 1659. No known copy.

Heroick portraits, with other pieces. 1660.

Erminia: or the fair and vertuous lady. TC Unacted. 1661, 1665.

Love's kingdom. TC LIF c. 1664. 1664, 1674. An alteration of Love's dominion. The Short treatise of the English stage appended is rptd in W. C. Hazlitt, English drama and stage, 1869, and in J. E. Spingarn, Critical essays of the seventeenth century vol 2, Oxford 1908.

Of one that Zany's the good companion; Of a bold abusive wit. 1665 (2nd edn) etc; ed E. N. Hooker, Ann Arbor 1946.

A farrago of several pieces. 1666.

The life of Tomaso the wanderer. 1667; ed G. Thorn-Drury 1925.

Sir William Davenant's voyage to the other world. 1668.

The damoiselles a la mode. C TR Sept 1668. 1667.

Epigrams of all sorts. 1669, 1670 (expanded), 1671 (further expanded), 1673 (as A collection of the choicest epigrams and characters; adds Characters made at several times).

§ 2

Lohr, A. Flecknoe: sein Leben und seine Werke. Munich 1900.

Cox, R. S. Flecknoe and the Man of mode. MLQ 29 1968.

JOSEPH HARRIS
c. 1650–c. 1715

The mistakes: or the false report. TC DL c. Dec 1690. 1691. Includes a scene by W. Mountfort.
The city bride: or the merry cuckold. C LIF c. March 1696. 1696; ed V. A. Dearing, Los Angeles 1952 (Augustan Reprint Soc).
Love's a lottery, and a woman the prize. C LIF c. March 1699. 1699.
Love and riches reconcil'd. M. Ptd and acted with Love's a lottery, above.
Luzara: a Pindarique ode on Prince Eugenius of Savoy. 1703.
An ode inscribed to the Queen's most excellent Majesty. 1714.
Great Britain's glory. 1714.
A funeral ode to the memory of Queen Anne. [1714].
A congratulatory ode [to the] Prince of Wales. [1714].

CHARLES HOPKINS
1664–1700

§ 1

Epistolary poems on several occasions. 1694.
The history of love: a poem. 1695. Selections from Ovid's Metamorphoses.
Pyrrhus, King of Epirus. T LIF c. Aug 1695. 1695.
Neglected virtue: or the unhappy conqueror. T DL 1696. 1696.
Boadicea Queen of Britain. T LIF c. Nov 1697. 1697.
White-hall: or the Court of England. Dublin 1698, 1699 (rev as The Court-prospect).
Friendship improv'd: or the female warriour. T LIF 7 Nov 1699. 1700.
The art of love. 1700, 1704 (enlarged).

§ 2

Maxwell, B. Notes on Hopkins' Boadicea. RES 4 1928.
Jones, A. E. A note on Hopkins. MLN 55 1940.

EDWARD HOWARD
1624–c. 1700

§ 1

The usurper. T TR Jan 1664. 1668.
A panegyrick to his Highness the Duke of York, on his sea-fight with the Dutch, June 3rd 1665. 1666.
The change of crowns. TC TR 15 April 1667. Not ptd; ed F. S. Boas 1949.
The Brittish princes: an heroick poem. 1669.
The womens conquest. TC LIF c. Nov 1670. 1671.
The six days adventure: or the new utopia. C LIF March 1671. 1671. Anon.
Poems and essays; with a paraphrase on Cicero's Lælius written in heroick verse. 1674. Anon.
The man of Newmarket. C DL c. April 1678. 1678.
Spencer redivivus. 1687. Anon; see L. Bradner, RES 14 1938.
Caroloiades, or the rebellion of Forty One: a heroick poem. 1689 (anon), 1695 (as Caroloiades redivivus).

§ 2

Boas, F. S. A lost Restoration play restored. TLS 28 Sept 1946.
—— Howard's lyrics and essays. Contemporary Rev Aug 1948.

JAMES HOWARD
b. 1630?

§ 1

All mistaken: or the mad couple. C TR Sept 1667. 1672, 1710; rptd R. Dodsley, A select collection of old plays vol 12, 1744; rev W. C. Hazlitt vol 15, 1876.
The English mounsieur. C TR 30 June 1663. 1674.

§ 2

Sutherland, J. R. The date of Howard's All mistaken: or the mad couple. N & Q Sept 1964.

SIR ROBERT HOWARD
1626–98

Collections

Four new plays. 1665. The surprisal, C TR April 1662; Committee, C TR before Nov 1662, ed C. N. Thurber, Urbana 1921; The Indian Queen, T TR Jan 1664; Vestal-virgin, T TR 1664.
Five new plays. 1692, 1700 ('corrected'), 1722 (as Dramatic works). Adds Duke of Lerma.

§ 1

Poems. 1660, 1696. Includes The blind lady, C, unacted.
The duell of the stags: a poem. 1668, 1709.
The great favourite: or the Duke of Lerma. T TR 20 Feb 1668. 1668. Preface ed J. E. Springarn, Oxford 1908 (in Critical essays of the seventeenth century vol 2) (with preface to Four new plays, above); ed D. D. Arundell, Cambridge 1929 (in Dryden and Howard).
An account of the state of his Majesties revenue. 1681.
The life and reign of King Richard the Second. 1681. Anon. Not by Howard?
Historical observations upon the reigns of Edward I, II, III and Richard II. 1689 (anon), 1690 (as The history of the reigns of Edward and Richard II, written in the year 1685 by Sʳ Robert Howard).
A letter to Mr S. Johnson. 1692.
The history of religion. 1694 (anon), 1709 (as An account of the growth of deism).

§ 2

Dryden, John. Of dramatick poesie: an essay. 1668; A defence, 1668 (prefixed to The Indian Emperor); both ed W. P. Ker, Oxford 1900 (in Essays vol 1); ed G. Watson 1962 (in Of dramatic poesy vol 1) (EL).
Scott, F. R. Howard as a financier. PMLA 52 1937.
—— The marriages of Howard. MLN 55 1940.
—— The third wife of Howard. N & Q July 1947. Reply by E. S. de Beer 18 Oct 1947.
de Beer, E. S. The dramatist sons of Thomas, Earl of Berkshire. N & Q 4 Nov 1944. Reply by H.S.H. 16 Dec 1944.
Ward, C. E. An unpublished letter of Howard. MLN 60 1945.
Oliver, H. J. Howard: a critical biography. Durham NC 1963.
Roscioni, G. C. Howard's sceptical curiosity. MP 65 1967.

SIR WILLIAM KILLIGREW
1606–95

Collections

Three playes. 1664-5, 1674. Selindra TC TR March 1662; Pandora: or the converts; Ormasdes: or love and friendship, TC Unacted?

Four new playes. Oxford 1666. Adds The siege of Urbin, TC Unacted?; ed I. E. Taylor, Philadelphia 1946.

§ 1

Pandora. C TR c. 1662. 1664. Anon.
The imperial tragedy. T Unacted. 1669. Anon. Attributed to Killigrew. *See* W. H. McCabe, PQ 15 1936.
Mid-night thoughts, by a person of quality. 1681 (prose), 1684 (with addns, mainly in verse, as The artless midnight thoughts of a gentleman at Court).
Mid-night and daily thoughts, in prose and verse. 1694.

§ 2

Lawrence, W. J. Killigrew's The siege of Urbin. TLS 18 Oct 1928.

JOHN LACY
c. 1615–81
Collections

Dramatic works. Ed J. Maidment and W. H. Logan, Edinburgh 1875.

§ 1

The old troop: or Monsieur Raggou. C TR c. 1665. 1672, 1698.
The dumb lady: or the farrier made physician. C TR 1669. 1672.
Sir Hercules Buffoon: or the poetical squire. C DG c. June 1684. 1684.
Sauny the Scott: or the taming of the shrew. C TR April 1667. 1698, 1708, 1714.

JOHN LEANERD

The country innocence: or the chambermaid turn'd Quaker. C DL c. April 1677. 1677.
The rambling justice: or the jealous husbands. C DL March 1678. 1678. 1694.
The counterfeits. C DG May 1678. 1679.

MARY DE LA RIVIERE MANLEY
1663–1724

§ 1

For Mrs Manley's novels see col 983, below. For her share in Examiner and her pamphleteering activities, see DNB.
The lost lover: or the jealous husband. C DL c. April 1696. 1696.
The royal mischief. T LIF c. April 1696. 1696.
Almyna: or the Arabian vow. T Hay Dec 1706. 1707. Anon.
Lucius, the first Christian King of Britain. T DL 11 May 1717. 1717, 1720 ('corrected').
The Court legacy, by the author of the New Atlantis. BO Unacted. 1733. Perhaps not authentic.

§ 2

Anderson, P. B. Mistress Delariviere Manley's biography. MP 33 1936.
Needham, G. B. Mary de la Rivière Manley, Tory defender. HLQ 12 1949.
—— Mrs Manley: and eighteenth-century Wife of Bath. HLQ 14 1951.
Winton, C. Steele, Mrs Manley and John Lacy. PQ 62 1963.

PETER ANTHONY MOTTEUX
1663–1718
Bibliographies

Cunningham, R. N. A bibliography of the writings of Motteux. Proc Oxford Bibl Soc 3 1933.

§ 1

The gentleman's journal: or the monthly miscellany. Jan 1692–Nov 1694 (2 edns of Jan–April 1692). Ed Motteux.
The works of F. Rabelais, done out of French by Sir Tho Urchard and others. 5 bks 1694-3, 2 vols 1708, 5 vols 1737 (rev J. Ozell). Rev and concluded by Motteux.
The present state of the Empire of Morocco. 1695. From the French of Pidou de Saint Olon.
Maria: a poem occasioned by the death of her Majesty. 1695.
Christian conferences: demonstrating the truth of the Christian religion and morality. 1695. From the French of Malebranche.
Of pastorals. 1695, 2 vols 1719. From Fontenelle's French, with W.J.'s trn of Bossu, Treatise of the epick poem.
Ode De Mr Boileau Despreaux sur la prise de Namur, avec une parodie de la mesme ode et une parodie d'une scène du Cid. [1695].
Words for a musical entertainment on the taking of Namur. Int LIF 1695. [1695].
Love's a jest. C LIF c. June 1696. 1696.
The loves of Mars and Venus. Int LIF c. Nov 1696. 1697, 1722, 1735.
The novelty: every act a play. C and T LIF c. June 1697. 1697.
Europe's revels for the peace. Int LIF Nov 1697. 1697.
Beauty in distress. T LIF c. April 1698. 1698.
The island Princess: or the generous Portuguese. O DL c. Nov 1698. 1699, 1701, 1701, 1724, 1726.
The four seasons: or love in every age. Int DL c. Feb 1699. 1699; rptd with Island Princess, 1699 etc, above.
The history of the renown'd Don Quixote. 4 vols 1700-3, 1712; rev J. Ozell 4 vols 1719 etc.
The masque of Acis and Galatea, with the musical entertainments in the mad lover. DL c. March 1701. 1701, 1723.
A banquet for gentlemen and ladies. 1701, 1703, 1712, 1718, nd. A collection of novels.
The stage-coach. F LIF c. April 1701. Dublin 1704, London 1705, 1709, Dublin 1719. With Farquhar; but *see* W. J. Lawrence, MLR 27 1932.
Britain's happiness. Int DL and LIF c. Feb 1704. 1704. From Tomaso Stanzani.
Arsinoe, Queen of Cyprus. O DL 16 Jan 1705. 1705, 1705, 1707.
The amorous miser: or the younger the wiser. C Unacted? 1705. Anon. *See* A. Nicoll, N & Q Dec 1919; F. W. Bateson, RES 3 1927.
The temple of love. O Hay 7 March 1706. 1706.
Camilla. O DL 30 March 1706. 1706, 1707, 1708, 1709, 1717, 1726. Dedication signed Owen Swiny, but perhaps really by Motteux. From Silvio Stampiglia.
Farewell folly: or the younger the wiser, with the Mountebank. C DL 18 Jan 1705. 1707. A recast of the Amorous miser?
Thomyris, Queen of Scythia. O DL 1 April 1707. 1707, 1708 (as The royal Amazon), 1709, 1719.
Love's triumph. O Hay 26 Feb 1708. 1708, 1713 (as The triumph of love). From Ottoboni, La pastorella.
A poem upon tea. 1712, 1712 (both folio), 1712 (8°); rptd Bee Oct 1715.

§ 2

Charlanne, L. Un français, écrivain anglais au XVIIe siècle. Revue Bleue 26 Aug, 2 Sept 1911.

Foster, D. The earliest precursor of our present-day monthly miscellanies. PMLA 32 1917.

Cunningham, R. N. Nine tales by Motteux. MLN 46 1931.

— Motteux: a bibliographical and critical study. Oxford 1933.

Bowers, F. T. Motteux's Love's a jest 1696: a running title and presswork problem. PBSA 48 1954.

WILLIAM MOUNTFORT
1664–92

Collections

Six plays written by Mr Mountfort, [with a life]. 2 vols 1720. Omits Zelmane, and includes King Edward III and Henry the Second by John Bancroft but pbd by Mountfort.

§ 1

The injur'd lovers: or the ambitious father. T DL c. Feb 1688. 1688.

The successful strangers. TC DL c. Dec 1689. 1690, 1696.

Greenwich Park. C DL c. March 1691. 1691, [1691 ?].

The life and death of Doctor Faustus, with the humours of Harlequin and Scaramouche. F DG c. 1686. 1697.

Zelmane: or the Corinthian Queen. T LIF 1705. 1705. Left unfinished by Mountfort and completed by an unknown hand.

Mountfort also contributed a scene to J. Harris, The mistakes.

§ 2

The players tragedy, or fatal love: a new novel. 3 vols 1693.

Borgman, A. S. The life and death of Mountfort. Cambridge Mass 1935.

Avery, E. L. Lincoln's Inn Fields 1704–5. Theatre Notebook 5 1950. On Zelmane.

WILLIAM CAVENDISH,
1st DUKE OF NEWCASTLE
1592–1676

See vol 1, above.

MARGARET CAVENDISH,
DUCHESS OF NEWCASTLE
1624?–74

See vol 1, above.

ROGER BOYLE,
1st EARL OF ORRERY
1621–79

Collections

The dramatic works of Roger Boyle, Earl of Orrery; to which is added a comedy entituled As you find it, by the Honourable Charles Boyle esq. 2 vols 1739. Omits Mr Anthony.

Dramatic works. Ed W. S. Clark 2 vols Cambridge Mass 1937. Includes Tragedy of Zoroastres (from ms).

§ 1

Parthenissa that most fam'd romance. 6 vols 1654–69, 1676.

The history of Henry the Fifth. T LIF Aug 1664. 1668, 1669, 1677, 1690.

The General. T LIF Sept 1664. Ed J. O. Halliwell [-Phillipps] 1853. One ms in Plymouth Lib; another at

Worcester College, Oxford. Acted at Smock Alley, Dublin, 26 Feb 1663.

The tragedy of Mustapha, son of Solyman the magnificent. T LIF April 1665. Ptd with Henry the Fifth, above, ed B. Dobrée, Oxford 1960 (in Five heroic plays) (WC).

The Black Prince. T TR 19 Oct 1667. Ptd with Tryphon as Two new tragedies, 1669, 1672.

Tryphon. T LIF 8 Dec 1668. Ptd with Black Prince, above.

Mr Anthony. C DG c. 1671. 1690.

Guzman. C LIF April 1669. 1693.

English adventures. 1676. Incomplete.

A treatise of the art of war. 1677.

Poems on most of the festivals of the Church. 1681.

Herod the great. T Unacted. 1694, 1694 (with the earlier plays, except Mr Anthony, as Six plays).

Altemira. T Unacted. 1702. An alteration, by Charles Boyle, of General, above.

The tragedy of King Saul. T Unacted. 1703 (anon), 1739.

Letters

A collection of the state letters of Roger Boyle, the first Earl of Orrery. 1742, 2 vols Dublin 1743.

§ 2

Siegert, E. Roger Boyle, Earl of Orrery und seine Dramen. Vienna 1906.

Summers, M. Orrery's The tragedy of Zoroastres. MLR 12 1917.

Payne, F. W. The question of precedence between Dryden and Orrery with regard to the English heroic play. RES 1 1925.

Clark, W. S. RES 2 1926, 6 1930; MLN 42 1927, 44 1929.

Lynch, K. Platonic drama in Orrery and Dryden. PMLA 44 1949.

— Roger Boyle. Knoxville 1965.

Mills, L. J. The friendship theme in Orrery's plays. PMLA 53 1938.

Miller, C. W. A source note on Boyle's The general. MLQ 8 1947.

— A bibliographical study of Parthenissa. SB 2 1950.

Bogorad, S. N. Orrery's Henry the Fifth. N & Q 18 March 1950.

HENRY NEVIL PAYNE
d. c. 1710

§ 1

The fatal jalousie. T DG Aug 1672. 1673 (anon); ed W. Thorp, Los Angeles 1948 (Augustan Reprint Soc).

The morning ramble: or the town-humours. C DG Nov 1672. 1673. Anon.

The siege of Constantinople. T DG Nov 1674. 1675. Anon.

§ 2

Thorp, W. Payne: dramatist and Jacobite conspirator. In T. M. Parrott presentation volume, Princeton 1935.

SAMUEL PORDAGE
1633–91?

See col 482, above.

THOMAS PORTER
1636–80

The villain. T LIF Oct 1662. 1663, 1670, 1694.

A witty combat: or the female victor, written by T.P., gent. TC LIF April 1664? 1663.

The carnival. C TR c. 1663. 1664.
The French conjurer, written by T.P., gent. C DG c. July 1677. 1678.

GEORGE POWELL
1658?–1714

The treacherous brothers. T DL c. Dec 1689. 1690, 1696, 1699.
Alphonso King of Naples. T DL c. Dec 1690. 1691.
A very good wife. C DL March 1693. 1693, 1703.
Bonduca: or the British heroine. DO DL c. Sept 1695. 1696. Pbd by Powell, but apparently the work of a friend.
A new opera: called Brutus of Alba, or Augusta's triumph. DO DG c. Oct 1696. 1697. With John Verbruggen.
The Cornish comedy. C DG c. June 1696. 1696. Powell states that this was merely pbd by him and written by another.
The imposture defeated: or a trick to cheat the Devil. C DL c. Sept 1697. 1698.

EDWARD RAVENSCROFT
c. 1650–c. 1700

§ I

The citizen turn'd gentleman. C DG July 1672. 1672, 1675 (as Mamamouchi).
The careless lovers. C DG March 1673. 1673.
The wrangling lovers: or the invisible mistress. C DG July 1676. 1677.
Scaramouch, a philosopher, Harlequin, a school-boy, bravo, merchant and magician. C DL May 1677. 1677.
King Edgar and Alfreda. TC DL c. Oct 1677. 1677.
The English lawyer. C DL c. Dec 1677. 1678.
The London cuckolds. C DG Nov 1681. 1682, 1683, 1688, 1697; ed M. Summers 1921 (in Restoration comedies).
Dame Dobson: or the cunning woman. C DG c. May 1683. 1684.
Titus Andronicus: or the rape of Lavinia. T DL c. Dec 1686. 1687.
The Canterbury guests: or a bargain broken. C DL Sept 1694. 1695.
The anatomist: or the sham doctor. C LIF c. 14 Nov 1696. 1697, 1722.
The Italian husband. T LIF c. Nov 1697. 1698.

§ 2

McManaway, J. G. The copy for the Careless lovers. MLN 46 1931.
Noyes, E. T. The original of Ravenscroft's Anatomist. Ibid.
Norris, E. T. The Italian source for Ravenscroft's Italian husband. RES 10 1934.
Lancaster, H. C. Calderón, Boursault and Ravenscroft. MLN 51 1936. Source of Wrangling lovers.
Parshall, R. E. The source of Ravenscroft's The anatomist. RES 12 1936.
Zimansky, C. A. Ravenscroft's first play. PQ 28 1949.

THOMAS RAWLINS the younger

Tom Essence: or the modish wife. C DG c. Sept 1676. 1677. Anon.
Tunbridge-Wells: or a day's courtship. C DG c. March 1678. 1678 (by a Person of quality). Attributed by Wood to Sadley.

SIR THOMAS ST SERFE or SYDSERF

Entertainments of the cours: or academical conversations held upon the cours at Paris. 1658. Tr from Pierre de Marmet.
Σεληναρχια; or the government of the world in the moon. 1659; ed C. H. Page, New York 1899. Tr from Cyrano de Bergerac.
Tarugo's wiles: or the coffee-house. C LIF 5 Oct 1667. 1668.

THOMAS SCOTT

The mock-marriage. C DG c. Sept 1695. 1696.
The unhappy kindness: or a fruitless revenge. T DL c. July 1697. 1697

SIR CHARLES SEDLEY
1639?–1701
See col 463, above.

ELKANAH SETTLE
1648–1724
Bibliographies

Brown, F. C. Settle: his life and works. Chicago 1910. With bibliography. Addns by E. G. Fletcher, N & Q Feb 1933.

§ I

Mare clausum: or a ransack for the Dutch. 1666.
Cambyses King of Persia. T LIF c. Feb 1667. 1671, 1672, 1675 ('revised'), 1692.
The Empress of Morocco. T DG July 1673, probably produced at Court 1671. 1673, 1673, 1687, 1698; ed B. Dobrée, Oxford 1960 (in Five heroic plays) (WC).
Love and revenge. T DG Nov 1675. 1675.
Notes and observations on the Empress of Morocco revised. 1674.
The conquest of China, by the Tartars. T DG May 1675. 1676.
Ibrahim the illustrious Bassa. T DG c. March 1676. 1677, 1694; preface ed H. Macdonald, Oxford 1947 (Luttrell Soc).
Pastor Fido: or the faithful shepherd. M DG c. Dec 1676. 1677, 1689, 1694.
The female prelate: being the history of the life and death of Pope Joan. T DL 31 May 1680. 1680, 1689.
Fatal love: or the forc'd inconstancy. T DL c. Sept 1680. 1680.
The heir of Morocco, with the death of Gayland. T DL 11 March 1682. 1682, 1694.
Absalom Senior, or Achitophel transpros'd: a poem. 1682 (anon), 1682 ('revis'd, with additions'); ed H. W. Jones, Gainesville 1961.
Distress'd innocence: or the Princess of Persia. T DL c. Oct 1690. 1691.
The Fairy-Queen. O DG 2 May 1692. 1692 (anon), 1693 (rev).
The notorious impostor. 1692; Diego Redivius, 1692; both ed S. Peterson, Los Angeles 1958 (Augustan Reprint Soc).
The new Athenian comedy. C Unacted. 1693.
The ambitious slave: or a generous revenge. T DL 21 March 1694. 1694.
Philaster: or love lies a-bleeding. TC DL c. Dec 1695. 1695.
The world in the moon. O DG May 1697. 1697, 1697.
A defence of dramatick poetry. 1698.
The virgin prophetesse: or the fate of Troy. O DL 15 May 1701. 1701, 1702 (anon as Cassandra).
The siege of Troy; Droll Bartholomew and Southwark Fairs. 1707, 1715, [1716].

The city-ramble: or a play-house wedding. O DL 17 Aug 1711. [1711]. Anon.

The lady's triumph. O LIF 22 March 1718. 1718. This version is at least partly by Lewis Theobald.

For a full list of Settle's numerous complimentary poems etc, see F. C. Brown, below.

§ 2

Brown, F. C. Settle: his life and works. Chicago 1910. With bibliography. Addns by E. G. Fletcher, N & Q 18 Feb 1933.

Ham, R. G. Dryden versus Settle. MP 25 1928.

— The authorship of A session of the poets 1677. RES 9 1933.

Moss, W. E. Settle: the armorial binding expert. Book-Collector's Quart 13 1934. Postscript 14 1934.

Dunkin, P. S. Issues of the Fairy Queen 1692. Library 4th ser 26 1946.

Haviland, T. P. Settle and the least heroic romance. MLQ 15 1954.

Norton, R. An epilogue to Pastor Fido. N & Q Aug 1956.

Nixon, H. M. English bookbindings xxv: a binding by the Settle bindery 1704. Book Collector 7 1958.

Peterson, S. (ed). The Counterfeit lady unveiled and other criminal fiction of seventeenth-century England. New York 1961. Reprints Settle's Complete memoirs of the life of that notorious imposter Will Morrell, 1694.

McFadden, G. Settle and the genesis of Mac Flecknoe. PQ 43 1964.

Langhans, E. A. Three early eighteenth-century prompt-books. Theatre Notebook 20 1966. Pastor Fido c. 1706.

Doyle, A. Dryden's authorship of Notes and observations on the Empress of Morocco 1674. Stud in Eng Lit 1500–1900 6 1966.

Love, H. H. R. The authorship of the postscript of Notes and observations on the Empress of Morocco. N & Q Jan 1966.

Novak, M. E. Settle's attacks on Thomas Shadwell and the authorship of the operatic Tempest. N & Q July 1968.

THOMAS SOUTHERNE
1659–1746
Collections

The works of Mr Thomas Southerne. 2 vols 1713 (all the plays except Spartan dame and Money the mistress), 2 vols 1721 (adds Spartan dame).

Plays written by Thomas Southerne esq, now first collected. Ed T. E[vans] 3 vols 1774 (adds Money the mistress) (with life).

§ 1

The loyal brother: or the Persian Prince. T DL Feb 1682. 1682; ed P. Hamelius, Liège 1911.

The disappointment: or the mother in fashion. T DL c. April 1684. 1684.

Sir Anthony Love: or the rambling lady. C DL c. Dec 1690. 1691, 1698.

The wives excuse: or cuckolds make themselves. C DL Dec 1691. 1692, 1726, 1735.

The maid's last prayer: or any, rather than fail. C DL Jan 1693. 1693.

The fatal marriage: or the innocent adultery. T DL Feb 1694. 1694, 1732, 1735; tr French, in Le théâtre anglois vol 8, 1749.

Oroonoko. T DL c. Nov 1695. 1696, 1699, 1699, 1711, 1712, 1721, Dublin 1722, 1731, London 1735, 1736, 1740, 1744 etc.

The fate of Capua. T LIF c. April 1700. 1700.

The Spartan dame. T DL 11 Dec 1719. 1719 (3 edns), 1721 (5th edn).

Money the mistress. C LIF 19 Feb 1726. 1726.

§ 2

Hamelius, P. The source of Southerne's Fatal marriage. MLR 4 1909.

Summers, M. The source of Southerne's The fatal marriage. MLR 11 1916.

Dodds, J. W. Thomas Southerne, dramatist. New Haven 1933.

Leech, C. A cancel in Southerne's The disappointment. Library 3rd ser 13 1933.

— The political disloyalty of Southern. MLR 28 1933.

— Southerne and On the poets and actors in King Charles II's reign. N & Q 10 June 1933.

Mallery, R. D. Southerne. TLS 1 Dec 1932. Reply by C. Leech 8 Dec 1932.

Hummell, R. O. A further note on Southerne's The disappointment. Library 5th ser 1 1946.

Bowers, F. T. The supposed cancel in Southerne's The disappointment reconsidered. Library 5th ser 5 1950.

Langhans, E. A. Three early eighteenth-century manu-scripts promptbooks. MP 65 1967. On Money the mistress.

SIR ROBERT STAPYLTON
1605?–69
Collections

Works, dramatic and other. 1663.

§ 1

Dido and Aeneas: the fourthe booke of Virgil's Aeneis now englished. [1634].

Pliny's panegyricke, translated. Oxford 1644.

The first six books of Juvenal. Oxford 1644.

Ερωτοπαιγνιον: the loves of Hero and Leander, written by Musaeus, translated. Oxford 1645, 1647 (as Musaeus: on the loves of Hero and Leander, rev with annotations).

Juvenal's sixteen satyrs: or a survey of the manners and actions of mankind, with arguments, marginall notes and annotations. 1647, 1660 (as Mores hominum), 1673.

De bello belgico. 1650, 1667 (as The history of the low-countrey warres). Tr from Strada.

The slighted maid. C LIF Feb 1663. 1663.

The step mother. TC LIF c. Nov 1663. 1664. Anon.

The tragedie of Hero and Leander. T Unacted. 1669.

§ 2

Bowers, F. T. The first editions of Stapylton's The slighted maid 1663 and the Stepmother 1664. PBSA 45 1951.

NAHUM TATE
1652–1715

§ 1

Poems. 1677, 1684 ('enlarged').

Brutus of Alba: or the enchanted lovers. T DG c. July 1678. 1678.

The loyal General. T DG c. Dec 1679. 1680.

The history of King Richard the Second. T DL c. Jan 1681. 1681, 1691 (as The Sicilian usurper).

The history of King Lear. T DG c. March 1681. 1681, 1689, 1699, [1702?], 1703, 1712, 1733 etc; ed C. Spencer, Urbana 1965 (in Five Restoration adaptations of Shakespeare).

The ingratitude of a common-wealth: or the fall of Caius Martius Coriolanus. T DL c. Dec 1681. 1682.

The second part of Absalom and Achitophel. 1682. With Dryden.

A Duke and no Duke. F DL c. Aug 1684. 1685, 1693 (with a preface concerning farce).

Cuckolds-haven: or an alderman no conjurer. F DG c. July 1685. 1685.

Poems by several hands, collected by N. Tate. 1685.

On the sacred memory of our late Sovereign. 1685, 1685.

Syphilis: a poetical history of the French disease. 1686. Tr from Fracastoro.

A memorial for the learned. 1686. By J.D., ed Tate.

The Island-Princess. TC DL April 1687. 1687.

A pastoral in memory of the Duke of Ormond. 1688.

Dido and Aeneas. O At Mr Josias Priest's boarding-school at Chelsey c. Dec 1689. Ed G. A. Macfarren. 1841, 1926; 1961 (facs).

The political anatomy of Ireland. 1691. By Sir William Petty, ed Tate.

A poem occasioned by his Majesty's voyage to Holland. 1691.

A poem occasioned by the late discontents. 1691.

Characters of vertue and vice, attempted in verse from a treatise of the Reverend Joseph Hall. 1691.

An ode upon her Majesty's birth-day. 1693.

The life of Prince of Condé. 1693. Tr Tate.

A present for the ladies. 1693.

A poem on the late promotion of several eminent persons. 1694.

In memory of Joseph Washington esq: an elegy. 1694.

The four epistles of A. G. Bushbequius, done into English. 1694.

An ode upon the University of Dublin's foundation. Dublin 1694.

Mausolaeum: a funeral poem on our late Queen. 1695.

An elegy on the late Archbishop of Canterbury. 1695.

Miscellanea sacra: or poems on divine and moral subjects, collected by N. Tate. 1696, 1696, 1698 (with addns).

A new version of the psalms of David, by N. Tate and N. Brady. 1696, 1698 etc.

The original of the soul, by Sir John Davies. 1697. Ed Tate.

The innocent epicure. 1697. By J.S., ed Tate.

The anniversary ode for his Majesty's birthday. 1698.

A consolatory poem to Lord Cutts. 1698.

Elegies. 1699.

An essay of a character of Sir G. Treby. 1700.

Funeral poems. 1700.

Panacea: a poem upon tea. 1700, 1702 (as A poem upon tea).

An elegy in memory of Ralph Marshall. 1700.

A congratulatory poem on the new Parliament. 1701.

The Kentish worthies: a poem. 1701.

A monumental poem in memory of Sir George Treby. 1702.

Portrait-royal: a poem upon her Majesty's picture. 1703.

The song for new-year's-day. 1703.

The triumph: a poem on the glorious successes of the last year. 1705, 1705.

Britannia's prayer for the Queen. 1706.

Majestas imperii britannici, in Latin poems by Mr Maid-well, paraphras'd by N.T. 1706.

The triumph of union. 1707.

Injur'd love, or the cruel husband: a tragedy design'd to be acted at the Theatre Royal. 1707.

A congratulatory poem to Prince George of Denmark. 1708.

The celebrated speeches of Ajax and Ulysses, essay'd in English verse by Mr Tate and Aaron Hill gent. 1708. From Ovid.

An essay for promoting of psalmody. 1710.

The Muse's memorial of the Earl of Oxford. 1712.

The Muses bower. 1713.

The triumph of peace. 1713.

A poem sacred to the memory of Queen Anne. [1714].

Tate also collaborated in Dryden's version of Ovid, Juvenal and Lucian, and in the trn of Cowley's Latin history of plants.

§ 2

Broadus, E. K. In his Laureateship, 1921.

Scott-Thomas, H. F. The date of Tate's death. MLN 49 1934.

—— Tate and the seventeenth century. ELH 1 1934.

—— Tate, laureate: two biographical notes. MLN 56 1941.

Spencer, H. Tate and the White devil. ELH 1 1934.

Caclamanos, D. The Turkish letters of Busbeck. N & Q 24 June 1939.

Scouten, A. H. An Italian source for Tate's defence of farce. Italica 27 1950.

Golden, S. H. The three faithful Teates. N & Q Sept 1955.

—— Variations in the name of Nahum Tate. N & Q Feb 1956.

—— The late seventeenth-century writer and the laureate-ship: Tate's tenure. Hermathena 89 1957.

—— An early defence of farce. In Studies in honor of John Wilcox, Detroit 1958.

Spencer, C. A word for Tate's King Lear. Stud in Eng Lit 1500–1900 3 1963.

Hodson, G. The Tate Lear at Richmond. Drama no 81 1966. A modern production.

Williams, T. D. D. Tate's King Lear. Studia Neophilologica 38 1966.

Black, J. The influence of Hobbes on Tate's King Lear. Stud in Eng Lit 1500–1900 7 1967.

—— An Augustan stage-history: Tate's King Lear. Restoration & 18th-Century Theatre Research 6 1967.

Astor, S. L. The laureate as huckster: Tate and an early eighteenth-century example of publishing advertizing. SB 21 1968.

Sharkey, P. L. Performing Tate's King Lear [1967]. Quart Jnl of Speech 54 1968.

SIR SAMUEL TUKE
c. 1620–74

§ 1

The adventures of five hours. TC LIF 8 Jan 1663. 1663, 1664, 1671 (rev), 1704; ed R. Dodsley in Select collection of old plays vol 12, 1744; rev W. C. Hazlitt vol 15, 1876; ed A. E. H. Swaen, Amsterdam 1927 (from 1663 and 1671 edns); ed B. Van Thal and M. Summers [1927]. Swaen's edn contains a trn of the Spanish source, Coello's Los empenos de seis horas.

§ 2

Child, C. G. The rise of the heroic play. MLN 19 1904.

Gaw, A. Tuke's Adventures of five hours in relation to the Spanish plot and to Dryden. Baltimore 1917.

de Beer, E. S. Tuke. N & Q 14 Nov 1931.

JOHN WILSON
1627?–96

Collections

Dramatic works, with memoir and notes by J. Maidment and W. H. Logan. Edinburgh 1874.

§ 1

The cheats. C TR March 1663. 1664, 1671, 1684, 1693; ed M. C. Nahm, Oxford 1935.

Andronicus Comnenius. T Unacted. 1664.

The protectors. C Unacted? 1665.

Moriae encomium: or the praise of folly. 1668. Tr from Erasmus.

To his excellence Richard Earle of Arran: a poem. Dublin 1682.

A discourse of monarchy. 1684.
A Pindarique to their Sacred Majesties, James II and Queen Mary, on their joynt coronations. 1685.
Jus regium coronae. 1688.
Belphegor: or the marriage of the devil. TC DG c. Oct 1690. 1691.

§ 2

Faber, K. Wilsons Dramen: eine Quellenstudie. Wiesbaden 1904.
Boas, F. S. In his Shakespeare and the universities, 1923.

V. EARLY EIGHTEENTH-CENTURY DRAMA

A key to the special abbreviations used in this section (BO, C, M, DL, LIF etc) will be found col 741, above.

COLLEY CIBBER

1671–1757

Bibliographies

Ashley, L. R. Cibber: a bibliography. Restoration & 18th-Century Theatre Research 6 1967.

Collections

Plays written by Mr Cibber. 2 vols 1721. 10 plays, partially rev.
The dramatic works of Colley Cibber. 4 vols 1760. With anon life. Adds 6 plays.
The dramatic works of Colley Cibber. 5 vols 1777. With life by D. E. Baker. Includes all the plays below except Cinna's conspiracy and Hob, and adds John Hippisley, Flora.

§ 1

A poem on the death of our late sovereign lady Queen Mary. 1695.
Love's last shift: or the fool in fashion. C DL Jan 1696. 1696, 1702, 1711, Dublin 1725, London 1730, [1735], 1740, 1747, Dublin 1750.
Womans wit: or the lady in fashion. C DL c. Dec 1696. 1697, 1736.
Xerxes. T LIF c. Feb 1699. 1699, 1736.
The tragical history of King Richard III. T DL c. Feb 1700. [1700], 1718, Dublin [c. 1730], London 1734, 1736, 1754 etc; ed C. Spencer, Urbana 1965 (in Five Restoration adaptations of Shakespeare).
Love makes a man: or the fop's fortune. C DL 13 Dec 1700. 1701, [c. 1702], 1716, Dublin 1722, London 1726, 1735, 1745, 1751 etc.
She wou'd and she wou'd not: or the kind impostor. C DL 26 Nov 1702. 1703, 1717, 1719, 1725, 1736, 1748 etc.
The careless husband. C DL 7 Dec 1704. 1705, 1705, 1711, 1723, Dublin 1723, London 1725, 1731, 1733, 1734, 1735, 1735, Dublin 1752; rptd 1928; Amsterdam 1928; ed W. W. Appleton, Lincoln Nebraska 1966.
Perolla and Izadora. T DL 3 Dec 1705. 1706, 1736.
The school-boy: or the comical rival. F DL 1702. 1707 (anon), [1730], 1736. The subplot of Woman's wit, above.
The comical lovers. C Hay 4 Feb 1707. [1707] (anon), Dublin [1720?], London 1736, 1754.
The double gallant: or the sick lady's cure. C Hay 1 Nov 1707. [1707], 1707, 1719, 1723, Dublin 1725, London [1729], 1736, 1740 etc.
The lady's last stake: or the wife's resentment. C Hay 13 Dec 1707. [1708], 1732, 1747, Dublin 1750.
The rival fools. C DL 11 Jan 1709. [1709], 1753.
Cinna's conspiracy. T DL 1713. 1713. Anon. Not by Cibber?
Hob: or the country wake. F DL 6 Oct 1711. 1715. Anon.

A reduction of Thomas Dogget's play. Not certainly by Cibber.
The secret history of Arlus and Odolphus. 1714 (4 edns). Anon. Advertised as 'by Mr Cibber' at the end of Parnell, Poems on several occasions, 1726.
Myrtillo. M DL 5 Nov 1715. 1715, 1716, [1720] (with Venus and Adonis), 1736, 1736.
Venus and Adonis. M DL 12 March 1715. 1715, 1716, [1720] (with Myrtillo), 1736, 1736.
The non-juror. C DL 6 Dec 1717. 1718 (5 edns), 1736, 1746, Dublin 1759, London 1760.
Ximena: or the heroick daughter. T DL 28 Nov 1712. 1719, 1781.
The refusal: or the ladies philosophy. C DL 14 Feb 1721. 1721, 1722, 1735, 1736, 1737, Dublin 1749, London 1753, 1764.
Caesar in Aegypt. T DL 9 Dec 1724. 1725, 1736.
The provok'd husband: or a journey to London. C DL 10 Jan 1728. 1728, Dublin 1728 (8°), 1728 (12°), London 1729, 1730, 1734, 1735, 1741, 1743, 1748, Dublin 1748 London 1753, 1753 etc. An expansion of Vanbrugh's fragment A journey to London.
The rival queans, with the humours of Alexander the Great. Bsq Hay 29 June 1710. Dublin 1729; ed W. M. Peterson, Painesville Ohio 1965.
Love in a riddle. BO DL 7 Jan 1729. 1729 (2 issues, misprinted 1719 and with corrected date).
Damon and Phillida. BO New Hay 16 Aug 1729. [1729], 1730 (different text), Edinburgh 1732, Dublin 1733, London 1734, 1737, 1765. Altered from Love in a riddle, above.
An ode to his Majesty for the new year. 1731.
An ode for his Majesty's birth-day. 1731.
The blind boy. [c. 1735]. A broadside.
An apology for the life of Mr Colley Cibber, comedian. 1740, 1740, Dublin 1740, 2 vols 1750 (with An account of English stage and dialogue on old plays), 1756 (with list of dramatic authors); ed E. Bellchambers 1822; ed R. W. Lowe 2 vols 1889; ed B. R. S. Fone, Ann Arbor 1968.
A letter from Mr Cibber to Mr Pope. 1742, 1742, Dublin 1742, Glasgow [1743?], London 1777.
A second letter from Mr Cibber to Mr Pope. 1743.
The egotist: or Colley upon Cibber. 1743, Dublin 1743.
Another occasional letter from Mr Cibber to Mr Pope. 1744, Dublin 1744, Glasgow [1744], London 1777.
Papal tyranny in the reign of King John. T CG 15 Feb 1745. 1745, Dublin 1745.
The character and conduct of Cicero considered. 1747.
The lady's lecture: a theatrical dialogue between Sir Charles Easy and his marriageable daughter. 1748.
A rhapsody upon the marvellous arising from the first odes of Horace and Pindar. 1751. Verse.
Verses to the memory of Mr Pelham. [1754].

§ 2

The laureat: or the right side of Colley Cibber esq. 1740.

Davies, T. In his Dramatic miscellanies, 3 vols 1783–4.

D'Israeli, I. In his Quarrels of authors, 3 vols 1814.

Hazlitt, William. In his Lectures on the English comic writers, 1819.

Croissant, De W. C. Studies in the work of Cibber. Kansas City 1912.

—— A note on the Egoist: or Colley upon Cibber. PQ 3 1924.

Bernbaum, E. In his Drama of sensibility, Boston 1914.

Miles, D. H. The original of the Non-juror. PMLA 29 1914.

—— The political satire of the Non-juror. MP 13 1915.

—— A forgotten hit: the Non-juror. SP 16 1919.

Glicksman, H. The stage-history of Cibber's The careless husband. PMLA 36 1921.

Broadus, E. K. In his Laureateship, 1921.

Nichols, C. W. Fielding and the Cibbers. PQ 1 1922.

Bateson, F. W. The double gallant of Cibber. RES 1 1925.

—— In his English comic drama 1700–50, Oxford 1929.

Sprague, A. C. A new scene in Cibber's Richard III. MLN 42 1927.

Senior, F. D. The life and times of Cibber. 1928. Reprints Careless husband.

Habbema, D. M. E. An appreciation of Cibber. Amsterdam 1928. Reprints Careless husband.

MacMillan, D. The text of Love's last shift. MLN 46 1931.

Taylor, H. W. Fielding upon Cibber. MP 29 1931.

Whiting, G. W. Cibber and Paradise lost. N & Q 11 March 1933.

Vincent, H. P. Two letters of Cibber. N & Q 5 Jan 1935.

Avery, E. L. Cibber, King John and the students of the law. MLN 53 1938.

—— The Craftsman of July 2 1737 and Cibber. Washington State Univ Research Stud 7 1939.

Barker, R. H. Mr Cibber of Drury Lane. New York 1939.

Tupper, F. S. Colley and Caius Cibber. MLN 55 1940.

Wood, F. T. A letter of Cibber. N & Q 13 July 1946.

Parnell, P. E. Equivocation in Cibber's Love's last shift. SP 57 1950.

—— An incorrectly attributed speech-prefix in Love's last shift. N & Q June 1959.

Peterson, W. M. Pope and Cibber's The non-juror. MLN 70 1955.

—— Cibber's She wou'd and she wou'd not and Vanbrugh's Aesop. PQ 35 1956.

—— The text of Cibber's She wou'd and she wou'd not. MLN 71 1956.

—— Cibber's The rival Queens. N & Q May 1959.

A Cibber puff. N & Q Sept 1956.

Tucker, S. L. A note on Cibber's name. N & Q Nov 1959.

Morley, M. No apology for Cibber. New Rambler Jan 1962.

Fuller, J. Cibber, The rehearsal at Goatham and the suppression of Polly. RES new ser 13 1962.

Kalson, A. E. The chronicles in Cibber's Richard III. Stud in Eng Lit 1500–1900 3 1963.

—— Eighteenth-century editions of Cibber's Richard III. Restoration & Eighteenth-Century Theatre Research 7 1968.

Prosser, E. Cibber at San Diego. Shakespeare Quart 14 1963.

Peavy, C. D. The Pope-Cibber controversy: a bibliography. Restoration & 18th-Century Theatre Research 3 1964.

Leech, C. Shakespeare, Cibber and the Tudor myth. In his Shakespearean essays, Knoxville 1964.

Ashley, L. R. N. Cibber. New York 1965.

Gilmore, T. B. Cibber's good nature and his reaction to Pope's satire. Papers on Lang & Lit 2 1966.

Peavy, C. D. Pope, Cibber and the crown of dulness. South Central Bull (MLA) 26 1966.

NICHOLAS ROWE
1674–1718
Collections

The tragedies of Nicholas Rowe. 2 vols 1714.

The poetical works of Nicholas Rowe. 1715, 1720, 1733 (as Miscellaneous works).

The dramatick works of Nicholas Rowe. 2 vols 1720.

The works of Nicholas Rowe. 3 vols 1728.

Plays written by Nicholas Rowe. 2 vols 1736.

The works of Nicholas Rowe. Ed Anne D. Devenish 2 vols 1747, 4 vols 1756, 2 vols 1766, 1792.

The fair penitent and Jane Shore. Ed S. C. Hart, Boston 1905.

Three plays: Tamerlane, The fair penitent, Jane Shore. Ed J. R. Sutherland 1929. With detailed biographical introd and bibliography.

§ 1

The ambitious step-mother. T LIF c. Dec 1700, 1701, 1702 (with new scene), 1714, Hague 1720, Dublin 1726, London 1727, 1733, 1735 etc.

Tamerlane. T LIF c. Dec 1701. 1702, 1703, 1714, 1717, Hague 1720, London 1730, 1733, 1736, Dublin 1750 etc; ed J. R. Sutherland 1929; ed L. C. Burnes 1966; tr French, 1746 (in Le théâtre anglois vol 6).

The fair penitent. T LIF c. May 1703. 1703, 1714, 1718, Hague [1723?], Dublin 1723, London 1730, Dublin 1732, London 1733, 1735, 1742, 1747, 1750 etc; ed S. C. Hart, Boston 1907; ed J. R. Sutherland 1929; ed J. H. Wilson, Boston 1963; tr French, 1746 (in Le théâtre anglois vol 5).

The biter. F LIF 4 Dec 1704. 1705, 1720, 1726, 1736.

Ulysses. T Hay 23 Nov 1705. 1706, 1714 ('revis'd'), 1726, Dublin 1726, London 1735.

The royal convert. T Hay 25 Nov 1707. 1708, 1714 (rev), 1720, 1726, 1735, 1738 etc.

A poem upon the late glorious successes of her Majesty's arms. 1707, 1719, 1726.

The life of Pythagoras [by Dacier], with his symbols and golden verses: the golden verses translated from the Greek by N. Rowe. 1707, 1719, 1726.

Boileau's Lutrin, render'd into English verse [by J. Ozell et al]; to which is prefix'd some account of Boileau's writings, by N. Rowe. 1708, 1711, 1714, 1730.

Callipaedia: a poem written in Latin by Claudius Quillet, made English. 1712, 1720. By Rowe et al.

The works of Mr William Shakespear, revis'd and corrected. 6 vols 1709, 9 vols 1714.

The tragedy of Jane Shore. T DL 2 Feb 1714. [1714], 1714, 1720, Dublin [1720?], [Hague? 1723?], London 1728, 1733, 1735, 1736, Glasgow 1748; ed S. C. Hart, Boston 1907, ed J. R. Sutherland 1929.

Poems on several occasions. 1714 (3 issues), 1720.

The tragedy of the Lady Jane Grey. T DL 20 April 1715. 1715, [Hague?] 1718, London 1720, 1727, 1730, 1736 etc.

Ode for the new year 1716. 1716.

Lucan's Pharsalia, translated into English verse. 1718 (with life of Rowe by James Welwood), Dublin 1719, 2 vols [Hague?] 1720, London 1722.

Rowe edited the Dryden Poetical miscellanies pts 5–6 1704–9, and had a hand in the composite Metamorphoses, 1717. The 1698 trn of La Bruyère has also been attributed to him.

§ 2

For studies of Rowe's life and edn of Shakespeare see vol 1, above and col 1771, below.

A comparison between the two stages. 1702; ed S. B. Wells, Princeton 1942.

Gildon, Charles. A new rehearsal: or Bays the younger. 1714, 1715 (with addns).

Musarum lachrymae: or poems to the memory of Nicholas Rowe. 1719.

Johnson, Samuel. In his Lives of the English poets, 1779–81.

[Scott, Sir Walter]. Observer nos 88–90 1790. Comparison of Fair penitent and Massinger, The fatal dowry.

Schwarz, F. H. Rowe's Fair penitent. Berne 1907.

Intze, O. Nicholas Rowe. Leipzig [1910].

Broadus, E. K. In his Laureateship, Oxford 1921.

Jackson, A. Rowe's historical tragedies. Anglia 54 1930.

Whiting, G. W. Rowe's debt to Paradise lost. MP 32 1935.

Wright, W. G. Rowe. N & Q 21 Jan 1939.

Thorpe, W. A key to Rowe's Tamerlane. JEGP 39 1940.

Doughty, H. N. Rowe and the Widow Spann. MLQ 4 1943.

Clark, D. B. The source and characterization of Tamerlane. MLN 65 1950.

—— An eighteenth-century adaptation of Massinger. MLQ 13 1942.

Hesse, A. W. Rowe's translation of Lucan's Pharsalia 1703–18. Philadelphia 1950.

Schwarz, A. An example of eighteenth-century pathetic tragedy: Rowe's Jane Shore. MLQ 22 1961.

Wyman, L. A. The tradition of the formal meditation in Rowe's The fair penitent. PQ 42 1963.

Ingram, W. Theobald, Rowe, Jackson: whose Ajax? Lib Chron 31 1965. Rowe as probable translator of Sophocles' Ajax 1714.

Boddy, M. Tonson's loss of Rowe. N & Q June 1966.

Kearful, F. J. The nature of tragedy in Rowe's The fair penitent. Papers on Lang & Lit 2 1966.

Rowan, D. F. Shore's Wife. Stud in Eng Lit 1500–1900 6 1966.

SUSANNA CENTLIVRE or CARROLL
c. 1670–1723

Collections

The works of the celebrated Mrs Centlivre, with a new account of her life. 3 vols 1760–1, 1872 (as Dramatic works).

Another collected edn in 4 vols with a life 'by herself' is advertised in W. Taverner, The maid the mistress, 1732.

§ 1

The perjur'd husband: or the adventures of Venice. TC DL c. Oct 1700. 1700, 1737.

The beau's duel: or a soldier for the ladies. C LIF c. June 1702. 1702, 1715 ('corrected'), 1719, Dublin 1727, London 1735, 1736 etc.

The stolen heiress: or the Salamanca doctor outplotted. C LIF 31 Dec 1702. [1703]. Anon, with running title: The heiress.

Love's contrivance: or le medecin malgre lui. C DL 4 June 1703. 1703. Signed R.M.

The gamester. C LIF c. Jan 1705. 1705 (anon), 1708, 1714, Dublin 1725, London 1734, 1736, 1736, 1756, 1760 (re-issue of 1736 edn), Dublin 1765, London 1767.

Love at a venture. C Bath. 1706. Anon.

The basset-table. C DL 20 Nov 1705. 1706 (anon), [1706], 1735, 1736.

The platonick lady. C Hay 25 Nov 1706. 1707. Anon.

The busie body. C DL 12 May 1709. [1709], [1709], [c. 1715], 1727, 1732, 1741, 1746, Norwich 1746, Dublin 1747, London 1749, 1753, 1759, 1765 etc; ed J. Byrd, Los Angeles 1949 (Augustan Reprint Soc).

The man's bewitch'd: or the devil to do about her. C Hay 12 Dec 1709. [1709], 1737, 1738.

A Bickerstaff's burying: or work for the upholders. F DL 27 March 1710. [1710], Dublin 1724.

Mar-plot: or the second part of the busie-body. C DL 30 Dec 1710. 1711, 1737.

The perplex'd lovers. C DL 19 Jan 1712. 1712, 1719, Dublin 1725, London 1734, 1736.

A trip to the masquerade: or a journey to Somerset-House. 1713. Anon. English and French, in verse.

The wonder: a woman keeps a secret. C DL 27 April 1714. 1714, 1714, Dublin 1725, London 1734, 1740, 1759 etc.

The Gotham election. F Unacted. 1715, 1737 (as The humours of elections).

A wife well manag'd. F DL 1715? 1715. Anon but frontispiece of Mrs Centlivre.

A poem humbly presented to his most sacred Majesty upon his accession to the throne. 1715.

An epistle to Mrs Wallup, now in the train of the Princess of Wales. 1715.

The cruel gift. T DL 17 Dec 1716. 1717 (with running title The cruel gift: or the royal resentment), 1734, 1736.

A bold stroke for a wife. C LIF 3 Feb 1718. 1718 (in A collection of plays by eminent hands, vol 3), 1719, 1724, Dublin 1727, London 1728, 1729, 1733, 1735, 1749 etc; ed T. Stathas, Lincoln Nebraska 1967.

A woman's case, in an epistle to Charles Joye esq. 1720. Verse.

The artifice. C DL 2 Oct 1722. 1723, 1735, 1736.

§ 2

Hazlitt, William. In his A view of the English stage, 1818.

—— In his Lectures on the English comic writers, 1819.

Hohrmann, F. Das Verhältnis Susanne Centlivres zu Molière und Regnard. Zeitschrift für Vergleichende Litteratur-geschichte 14 1900.

Seibt, R. Die Komödien der Mrs Centlivre. Anglia 32–3 1909–10.

Wilson, M. In her These were Muses, 1924.

Bowyer, J. W. Susanna Freeman Centlivre. MLN 43 1928.

—— Quakers on the English stage. PMLA 45 1950.

—— The celebrated Mrs Centlivre. Durham NC 1952.

Bateson, F. W. In his English comic drama 1700–50, Oxford 1929.

Anderson, P. B. [Mrs Centlivre and Female tatler]. PQ 16 1937.

Boys, R. C. A new poem by Mrs Centlivre. MLN 57 1942.

Sutherland, J. R. The progress of error: Mrs Centlivre and the biographers. RES 18 1942.

Mackenzie, J. H. Susan Centlivre. N & Q Sept 1953.

Norton, J. E. Some uncollected authors xiv: Susanna Centlivre. Book Collector 6 1957.

McKillop, A. D. Mrs Centlivre's The wonder: a variant imprint. Book Collector 7 1958.

Neill, D. G. A poem by Mrs Centlivre. Ibid. A poem in Poetical merriment 1714–15.

Faure, J. Two poems by Susanna Centlivre. Book Collector 10 1961.

Strozier, R. A short view of some of Mrs Centlivre's celebrat'd plays, including a close accounting of the plots, subplots, asides, soliloquies etcetera contain'd therein. Discourse 7 1964.

HENRY CAREY
1687?–1743

Collections

The dramatick works of Henry Carey. 1743. Rev text, omitting Hanging and marriage. Margery appears as the Dragoness.

Songs and poems. Ed M. Gibbings 1924. A selection.

Poems. Ed F. T. Wood 1930.

§ 1

The records of love. 12 nos 1710. Anon. *See* J. R. Sutherland, TLS 25 Dec 1930.

Poems on several occasions. 1713, 1720 (enlarged), 1729 (enlarged).

The contrivances: or more ways than one. F DL 9 Aug 1715. 1715 (anon), 1719. Recast as BO DL 20 June 1729. 1729, Dublin 1731, London 1732, 1743, 1765 (7th edn) etc.

A learned dissertation on old women, male and female, spiritual and temporal; to which is added an essay on the present union of The Whig chiefs. 1720. Anon. In prose. Doubtfully attributed to Carey.

Hanging and marriage: or the dead-man's wedding. F LIF 15 March 1722. [1722]. Recast as BO, Betty: or the country bumpkin, DL 1 Dec 1732. Songs only ptd 1739. *See* F. T. Wood, RES 9 1933.

Namby-pamby: a panegyrick on the new versification, address'd to A[mbrose] P[hilips] esq. 1725. Anon. Folio sheet.

A learned dissertation on dumpling: its dignity, antiquity and excellence, with a word upon pudding, and many other useful discoveries; to which is added Namby Pamby. 1726 (3rd edn, anon), 1726 (5th edn), 1727 (7th edn). The dissertation is in prose. Doubtfully attributed to Carey.

A hue and cry after M . . . K, late Master to a Corporation in the city of Dublin. 1726. 'By the author of Namby-Pamby'. Folio sheet.

Mocking is catching: or a pastoral lamentation for the loss of a man and no man, in the simple style. 1726. 'By the author of Namby Pamby'. Folio half sheet.

Pudding and dumpling burnt to pot, by J.W., author of 684 treatises. 1727, 1727. Prose. Professes to be a key to Dissertation, above. Doubtfully attributed to Carey.

Amelia: a new English opera after the Italian manner. New Hay 13 March 1732. 1732. Anon.

Teraminta. O LIF 20 Nov 1732. 1732.

The disappointment. BO New Hay 1732? 1732, 1732. Ptd as by John Randall, but probably Carey's. *See* F. T. Wood, RES 5 1929.

The tragedy of Chrononhotonthologos. Bsq New Hay 22 Feb 1734. [1734], Edinburgh 1734, London 1743, 1744, 1753, 1760, 1765, 1770 (7th edn), 1777 etc.

The honest Yorkshireman. BO LIF 11 July 1735. 1736

(for 1735, pirated as A wonder: or an honest Yorkshire-man), 1736, 1736, Belfast 1763, Glasgow 1770, London 1777. Songs, with score, c. 1743.

Of stage tyrants: an epistle. 1735.

The dragon of Wantley. Bsq CG 26 Oct 1737. [1737] (anon), 1737 (c. 6 edns), 1738 (14th edn), 1743, [1749?], 1755, 1762, 1763, 1770, 1777, 1777. Songs and duettos, with the score, 1738.

The musical century, in one hundred English ballads. 1737, 1740, 1743. With Carey's own settings.

Margery: or a worse plague than the dragon. Bsq CG 9 Dec 1738. 1738 (3 edns), 1743.

Nancy: or the parting lovers. Int CG 1 Dec 1739. 1739, 1755 (as The press gang), 1779, 1787 (as True blue).

An ode to mankind, address'd to the Prince of Wales. 1741.

Cupid and Hymen: a voyage to the islands of love and matrimony, by the facetious Henry Carey and other persons of wit and humour; to which are added a description of the island of marriage, the batchelor's estimate of the expenses of a married life, the married man's answer, and none but fools marry, or a vindication of the batchelor's estimate. 1748. Appendixes, probably all by Carey, also ptd singly. *See* F. T. Wood, N & Q 25 Nov 1933.

§ 2

Cummings, W. H. In his God save the King, 1902.

Hudson, W. H. In his A quiet corner in a library, 1915.

Bateson, F. W. In his English comic drama 1700–50, Oxford 1929.

Wood, F. T. An eighteenth-century original for Lamb? RES 5 1929.

—— Phillipps or Carey? TLS 27 Feb 1920. *See* subsequent discussion.

Noyes, R. G. The contemporary reception of Sally in our alley. Harvard Stud 18 1935.

Ewens, J. B. Carey, John Wesley and 'Namby-Pamby'. London Quart 161 1936.

'Sally in our alley': plays of Carey. TLS 9 Oct 1943. Replies by P. A. Scholes 16 Oct; A. M. Clark 6 Nov 1943.

Hughes, L. and A. H. Scouten. The first season of the Honest Yorkshireman. MLR 40 1945.

Sands, M. The problem of Teraminta. Music & Letters 33 1952.

Oldfield, E. L. Carey and some troublesome attributions. BNYPL June 1968.

VI. MINOR DRAMA 1700–50

This section is restricted to writers born after 1664 and before 1715. A key to abbreviations will be found col 741, above.

JOSEPH ADDISON
1672–1719
See col 1098, below.

THOMAS BAKER
1680?–1710?

§ 1

The humour of the age. C DL 1 March 1701. 1701. Anon.

Tunbridge-walks: or the yeoman of Kent. C DL 27 Jan 1703. 1703 (anon), 1714, 1727 (6th edn), 1736 etc.

An act at Oxford. C Unacted. 1704. Anon.

Hampstead Heath. C DL 30 Oct 1705. 1706. Anon. Altered from An act at Oxford, above.

The lawyer's fortune: or love in a hollow tree. [1705], [1705], 1705, 1736, 1736. A comedy by William, Viscount Grimston; the anon preface is by Baker.

The fine lady's airs: or an equipage of lovers. C DL 14 Dec 1708. [1708] (anon); ed J. H. Smith, Los Angeles 1950 (Augustan Reprint Soc).

The female tatler. 8 July 1709–31 March 1710. A tri-weekly periodical.

§ 2

Anderson, P. B. The history and authorship of Mrs Crackenthorpe's Female tatler. MP 28 1931.

Graham, W. Baker, Mrs Manley and the Female tatler. MP 34 1937.

Smith, J. H. Baker and the Female tatler. MP 49 1952.

CHARLES BECKINGHAM
1699-1731

Scipio Africanus. T LIF 18 Feb 1718. 1718, 1719.
The tragedy of King Henry IV of France. T LIF 7 Nov 1719. 1720 (3 edns).
Maxims, observations and reflections, moral, political and divine, by Mr Addison. 1719. Ed Beckingham.
Musarum lachrymae: or poems to the memory of Nicholas Rowe esq, by several hands. 1719. Ed Beckingham.
Christus patiens, or the sufferings of Christ: an heroic poem, from the Latin original of Rapin. 1720, 1737.
An ode to the right honourable Sir Robert Walpole. [1725].
A poem on his most sacred Majesty King George the II[d] his accession to the throne. Dublin 1727.

JOHN DURANT BREVAL
1680?-1738
See col 538, above.

HENRY BROOKE
1703?-83
Collections

A collection of plays and poems by Henry Brooke esq. 4 vols 1778. Includes, in addition to plays listed below: The Earl of Westmorland (Dublin 1742), Little John and the giants (Dublin 1749), The female officer (Dublin 1740), The victims of love and honour (Dublin 1762), The vestal virgin, The marriage contract, Montezuma, The impostor, The contending brothers, The charitable association, Cymbeline, Antony and Cleopatra.
The poetical works of Henry Brooke esq, revised and corrected, with his life by Charlotte Brooke. 4 vols Dublin 1792.

§ 1

Universal beauty: a poem. 6 pts 1735.
Tasso's Jerusalem: an epic poem translated. 1738. Bks 1-2 only.
Gustavus Vasa, the deliverer of his country, as it was to have been acted at the Theatre-Royal in Drury-Lane. T. 1739, 1739, Dublin 1739. DL performance prohibited but acted at Dublin in 1744 as The patriot.
The Canterbury tales of Chaucer, modernis'd by several hands. 3 vols 1741, 2 vols Dublin 1742. Ed George Ogle. Brooke contributed Constantia: or the Man of Lawes tale.
Prospectus of a work to be entitled Ogygian tales: or a curious collection of Irish fables. 1743.
Fables for the female sex. 1744, 1746, 1755 (4th edn), 1766 etc; tr German, 1772. 3 fables by Brooke, the rest by Edward Moore.
A history of Ireland from the earliest times proposed. 1744.
The farmer's six letters to the Protestants of Ireland. Dublin 1745, London 1746, Dublin 1746, Manchester [1750] (as Essays against Popery).
The secret history and memoirs of the barracks of Ireland. 1745.
The last speech of John the good, vulgarly called Jack the giant queller. 1748.
New fables. 1749.
The songs in Jack the gyant queller: an antique history. Dublin 1749, 1749, London 1749, 1749, 1757. Complete text in collected works as Little John and the giants.
A new collection of fairy tales. 1750.
The Earl of Essex. T Smock Alley Dublin May 1750. 1761, Dublin 1761, Edinburgh 1761.
A new system of fairery: or a collection of fairy tales,

translated from the French of Comte de Caylus. 2 vols 1750.
A description of the College-Green Club: a satire, by the farmer. Dublin 1753.
The spirit of party. 2 pts 1753-4.
The interests of Ireland considered. Dublin 1759.
The case of the Roman Catholics of Ireland. Dublin 1760.
Tryal of the cause of the Roman Catholics. Dublin 1761, 1762, London 1762, 1764.
A proposal for the restoration of public wealth and credit. Dublin [1762?].
The fool of quality: or the history of Henry Earl of Moreland. 5 vols 1764-70 (vols 1-2 rptd 1767), 4 vols 1776, 5 vols 1777, 1781 (condensed by John Wesley) etc; ed C. Kingsley 2 vols 1859; ed E. A. Baker 1906.
Redemption: a poem. 1772.
Juliet Grenville: or the history of the human heart. 3 vols 1774; tr German, 1774.

§ 2

Wilson, C. H. Brookiana: anecdotes of Henry Brooke. 2 vols 1804.
D'Olier, Isaac. Memoirs of the life of the late excellent and pious Mr Henry Brooke. Dublin 1816.
Brooke, R. S. Henry Brooke. Dublin Univ Mag Feb 1852.
Wright, H. Brooke's Gustavus Vasa. MLR 14 1919.
Scurr, H. M. Henry Brooke. Minneapolis 1927.
Stevenson, H. M. Brooke's Universal beauty and modern thought. PMLA 43 1928.
Gillet, E. The fool of quality. London Mercury Sept 1934.
Hogl, H. Brookes Roman The fool of quality und sein Verhältnis zu den grossen Romanschriftstellern des 18 Jahrhunderts. Erlangen 1930.
Barber, F. L. John Wesley edits a novel [on Fool of quality]. London Quart 171 1946.

CHRISTOPHER BULLOCK
1690?-1724

The slip. F LIF 3 Feb 1715. 1715. Anon.
A woman's revenge: or a match in Newgate. C LIF 24 Oct 1715. 1715, 1728.
The cobler of Preston. F LIF 24 Jan 1716. 1716, 1732, 1767.
The adventures of half an hour. F LIF 19 March 1716. 1716.
Woman is a riddle. C LIF 4 Dec 1716. 1717, 1729, Edinburgh 1731, London 1759, Dublin 1760.
The per-juror. F LIF 12 Dec 1717. 1717, 1718 (3 edns), 1732.

WILLIAM BURNABY
1672?-1706
Collections

Dramatic works. Ed F. E. Budd 1931. With detailed biographical and critical introd.

§ 1

The satyr of Titus Petronius Arbiter, made English by Mr Burnaby and another hand. 1694, 1708 (with addns by T. Brown et al), 1714.
The reform'd wife. C DL March 1700. 1700 (anon), 1700 (with new scene).
The ladies visiting-day. C LIF Feb 1701. 1701 (anon), 1708.
The modish husband. C DL Jan 1702. 1702. Anon.
Love betray'd: or the agreeable disappointment. C LIF March 1703. 1703. Anon.

THEOPHILUS CIBBER
1703–58

§ I

An historical tragedy of the civil wars in the reign of King Henry VI: being a sequel to the tragedy of Humphrey Duke of Gloucester; and an introduction to the tragical history of King Richard III, alter'd from Shakespeare, in the year 1720. T DL 3 July 1723. [1723?], 1724 (as King Henry VI).

Patie and Peggie: or the fair foundling. BO DL 25 Nov 1730. 1730.

The lover. C DL 20 Jan 1731. 1730, Dublin 1731, 1731.

The harlot's progress, or the ridotto al' fresco: a grotesque pantomime entertainment. Pant DL 31 March 1733.

A letter from Theophilus Cibber, comedian, to John Highmore esq. [1733].

Romeo and Juliet, revis'd and altered from Shakespeare. T New Hay 11 Sept 1744. [1744]. Appended is a serio-comic apology, for part of the life of Mr Theophilus Cibber.

A lick at a liar, or calumny detected: being an occasional letter to a friend. [1752].

The lives and characters of the most eminent actors and actresses. Pt 1 (all pbd), 1753, Dublin 1753.

The lives of the poets of Great Britain and Ireland, to the time of Dean Swift. 5 vols 1753. Mainly compiled by Robert Shiels.

An epistle from Mr Theophilus Cibber to David Garrick esq. 1755, [1756?], 1759 (adds Dissertations).

Cibber's two dissertations on theatrical subjects. 3 pts [1756] (with Epistle to Garrick appended), 1759 (with Epistle).

The auction. F Unacted? 1757. Scenes from Fielding's Historical register.

For Cibber's share in The devil to pay, *see under Coffey, below.*

§ 2

An apology for the life Mr T. C., comedian. 1740.

Scouten, A. H. Cibber's The humourists. N & Q March 1955.

CHARLES COFFEY
d. 1745

§ I

The beggar's wedding. BO Smock Alley Dublin 24 March 1729. 1729, 1729, Dublin 1729, London [1730?], 1731, 1733, 1763.

Phebe: or the beggars wedding. BO DL 13 June 1729. 1729. Beggars wedding, above, reduced to one act.

The devil upon two sticks: or the country beau. BO DL 16 April 1729. 1745.

Southwark Fair: or the sheep-shearing. BO Southwark Fair 1729. 1729.

The female parson: or beau in the sudds. BO New Hay 27 April 1739. 1730.

The devil to pay: or the wives metamorphos'd. BO DL 6 Aug 1731. 1731 (3 acts), 1732 (one act, 3 edns), Dublin 1732, London 1733, 1736, 1738, 1748, 1748, [1777?] etc. Adapted by Coffey and John Mottley from Jevon's The devil of a wife, later reduced by Theophilus Cibber to one act.

A wife and no wife. F Unacted. [1732?].

The boarding-school: or the sham captain. BO DL 29 Jan 1733. 1733.

The merry cobler: or the second part of the Devil to pay. BO DL 6 May 1935. 1735.

§ 2

Lawrence, W. J. Early Irish ballad opera and comic opera. Musical Quart 8 1922.

THOMAS COOKE
1703–56
See col 542, above.

ROBERT DODSLEY
1703–64
Collections

Trifles. 2 vols 1745–77.

§ I

Servitude. [1729] (anon), [1731] (as The footman's friendly advice). Introd by Defoe? Verse.

An epistle from a footman to Stephen Duck. 1731. Anon. Verse.

A sketch of the miseries of poverty. 1731. Anon. Verse.

The muse in livery: or the footman's miscellany. 1732, 1732. Verse.

An entertainment for her Majesty's birthday. 1732. Anon. Verse.

An entertainment for the wedding of Governour Lowther. 1732. Anon. Verse.

The modern reasoners: an epistle to a friend. 1734. Anon. Verse.

An epistle to Mr Pope, occasion'd by his Essay on man. 1734. Verse.

Beauty: or the art of charming. 1735. Anon. Verse.

The toy-shop: a dramatick satire. CG 3 Feb 1735. 1735 (6 edns), 1737 (adds Epistles and poems on several occasions), [1739?], 1745, 1754, 1763, 1767; tr French, 1856.

The King and the miller of Mansfield: a dramatick tale. DL 29 Jan 1737. 1737, Dublin 1737, London 1745, [1751], Belfast 1764; tr French, 1756.

Sir John Cockle at Court, being the sequel of the King and the miller of Mansfield: a dramatick tale. DL 23 Feb 1738. 1738, Dublin 1738, London 1745, [1750?], Belfast 1767.

The art of preaching in imitation of Horace's Art of poetry. 1738 (anon), [1740], [1746], [1746], Glasgow 1790. Verse.

The chronicle of the Kings of England, written in the manner of the ancient Jewish historians, by Nathan Ben Saddi. 2 bks 1740–1, 1742, Dublin 1742, London 1745; tr French, 1750; German, 1744. Often ascribed to Chesterfield.

The blind beggar of Bethnal Green. BO DL 3 April 1741. 1741, 1745, Glasgow 1758, London 1761; tr French, 1756.

Colin's kisses: being twelve new songs. 1742. With and without music, anon. Verse.

Pain and patience: a poem. 1742.

A select collection of old plays. 12 vols 1744. Ed Dodsley.

Rex and Pontifex. Pant Unacted. 1745.

A collection of poems, by several hands. 3 vols 1748, 1748 (rev and enlarged, addns also separately as vol 4 1749), 1751, 2 vols Dublin 1751, 4 vols 1755 (vol 4 with new matter), 6 vols 1758 (vols 5–6 with new matter), 1763, 1765, 1766, 1770, 1775; ed I. Reed 6 vols 1782.

The triumph of peace M DL 21 Feb 1749. 1749.

The oeconomy of human life, translated from an Indian manuscript. 1751 (7 edns, anon), Dublin 1751, London 1758, 1761; tr French, 1751; German, 1752; Italian, 1752. Often ascribed to Chesterfield.

Public virtue: a poem in three books. 1753, Dublin 1754. Bk 1, Agriculture only. Verse.

Melpomene: or the regions of terror and pity. 1757. Anon. Verse.

Cleone. T CG 2 Dec 1758. 1758, 1758, 1759, Belfast 1759, London 1765, 1771, 1781, 1786.

Select fables in three books. 1761, Birmingham 1761, London, 1762, 1762, Birmingham 1764; An essay on fable, ed J. K. Welcher and R. Dircks, Los Angeles 1965 (Augustan Reprint Soc).

Fugitive pieces on various subjects. 2 vols 1761, 1762, 1765.
The works of William Shenstone. 2 vols 1764. For reprints *see* under Shenstone, col 532, above.

§ 2

Courtney, W. P. Dodsley's Collection of poetry: its contents and contributors. 1910.
Straus, R. Dodsley: poet, publisher and playwright. 1910. With bibliography of writings and pbns.
Lundeberg, O. K. The true sources of Dodsley's The King and the miller of Mansfield. MLN 39 1924.
Hill, C. J. Applause for Dodsley's Cleone. PQ 14 1935.
Lynch, J. J. An unbuplished poem by Dodsley. N & Q July 1957.
Randall, D. Dodsley's Preceptor: a window into the nineteenth century. Jnl of Rutgers Univ Lib 22 1958.
Schick, G. B. Dodsley's contributions. N & Q July–Aug 1959.
Eddy, D. D. Dodsley's Collection of poems by several hands (six volumes) 1758 index of authors. PBSA 60 1966.

RICHARD ESTCOURT
1668–1712

§ 1

The fair example: or the modish citizen. C DL 10 April 1703. 1706.
Prunella: an interlude perform'd in the Rehearsal. DL 12 Feb 1708. [1708].
A letter from Dick Estcourt, the comedian, to the Spectator. 1713.

§ 2

[Steele, Sir Richard]. Spectator 2 Jan, 21 April, 27 Aug 1712.

ELIJAH FENTON
1683–1730
See col 548, above.

HENRY FIELDING
1707–54
See col 925 below.

PHILIP FROWDE
d. 1738

Cursus glacialis, anglicè scating. 1720. First ptd in Addison, Musarum anglicanarum analecta vol 2, Oxford 1699.
The fall of Saguntum. T LIF 16 Jan 1727. 1727, Dublin 1727, London 1729, 1735.
Verses on her Majesty's birthday. 1728.
Philotas. T LIF 3 Feb 1731. 1731, 1735.

JOHN GAY
1685–1750
See col 497, above.

CHARLES GILDON
1665–1724
See col 1047, below.

RICHARD GLOVER
1712–85
See col 549, above.

GEORGE GRANVILLE, BARON LANSDOWNE
1667–1735
Collections
Three plays, viz The she-gallants, Heroick love and the Jew of Venice. 1713.
Four plays, viz Heroick love, the Jew of Venice, the She-gallants, the British enchanters. 1732.
The genuine works in verse and prose. 2 vols 1732, 3 vols 1736.
The dramatic works. Glasgow 1752.

§ 1

The she-gallants. C LIF c. Dec 1695. 1696, 1700, [1720?], 1724, 1732.
Heroick love. T LIF c. Dec 1697. 1698.
The Jew of Venice. C LIF c. May 1701. 1701 (anon), 1713; ed C. Spencer in Five Restoration adaptations of Shakespeare, Urbana 1965.
The British enchanters: or no magick like love. O Hay 21 Feb 1706. 1706 (anon), 1710, Dublin 1732 ('revis'd and enlarg'd in Poems upon several occasions), 1732.
Poems upon several occasions. 1712, 1716, 1721, 1726, Dublin 1732.
The genuine speech against repealing the occasional and schism bills. 1719.
A letter from a nobleman abroad to his friend in England. 1722.
A letter to the author of Reflexions historical and political. 1732.

§ 2

Johnson, Samuel. In his Lives of the English poets, 1779–81.
Handasyde, E. Granville the polite. Oxford 1933.
Wilson, J. H. Granville's 'Stock-jobbing Jew'. PQ 13 1934.

BENJAMIN GRIFFIN
1680–1740

§ 1

Injur'd virtue: or the virgin martyr. T Southwark 1 Nov 1714. 1715.
Love in a sack. F LIF 14 June 1715. 1715, 1719.
Complete key to the last new farce The what d'ye call it. 1715. Anon. Attributed to Griffin and Theobald.
The humours of purgatory. F LIF 3 April 1716. 1716.
The masquerade: or an evening's intrigue. F LIF 16 May 1717. 1717.
Whig and Tory. C LIF 26 Jan 1720. 1720.

§ 2

Peterson, W. M. Performances of Griffin's Whig and Tory. N & Q Jan 1957.

WILLIAM HAVARD
1710?–78

§ 1

Scanderbeg. T GF 15 March 1733. 1733.
King Charles the First, written in imitation of Shakespeare. T LIF 1 March 1737. 1737, 1765 (3rd edn) etc.

Regulus. T DL 21 Feb 1744. 1744, Dublin 1745.
Ode on the birth-day of George Prince of Wales. [1751].
The elopement. F DL 6 April 1763. Ms in Larpent collection, Huntington Lib, California.

ELIZA HAYWOOD
1693?–1756
Collections
The works of Mrs Eliza Haywood. 4 vols 1724.

§ 1

The fair captive. T LIF 4 March 1721. 1721. A revision of an unptd piece by Captain Hurst.
A wife to be lett. C DL 12 Aug 1723. 1724, 1724, 1729, 1735.
The tea table. 35 nos 21 Feb–22 June 1724. 1724.
Poems on several occasions. 1724.
The parrot. 4 nos 25 Sept–16 Oct 1728; Second ser 9 nos 2 Aug–4 Oct 1746, 1746 (with A compendium of the times).
Frederick, Duke of Brunswick-Lunenburgh. T LIF 4 March 1729. 1729, 1729, Dublin 1729.
The opera of operas: or Tom Thumb the great. Bsq New Hay 31 May 1733. 1733, 1733, 1733. Anon. Attributed to Mrs Haywood and William Hatchett.
The female spectator. 24 nos April 1744–March 1746. 4 vols Dublin 1747, London 1748, 1750, 1755, 1766; ed M. Priestley 1929 (selection).
For the novels, see col 988 f., below.

§ 2

Whicher, G. F. The life and romances of Mrs Eliza Haywood. New York 1915.
Elwood, J. R. The stage career of Eliza Haywood. Theatre Survey 5 1964.

AARON HILL
1685–1750
Collections
The works of the late Aaron Hill esq. 4 vols 1753. Poems, letters and An essay on the art of acting.
The dramatic works of Aaron Hill esq. 2 vols 1760. Includes a life of the author, subscribed I.K., all the separately ptd plays and the following short unacted pieces: Merlin in love (Pant), The Muses in mourning (O), The snake in the grass (Bsq), Saul (T), Daraxes (O).

§ 1

Camillus. 1707. Verse.
The invasion: a poem to the Queen. 1708.
The celebrated speeches of Ajax and Ulysses. 1708. Tr Hill and Tate from Ovid. Verse.
A full account of the present state of the Ottoman Empire. 1709.
Elfrid: or the fair inconstant. T DL 3 Jan 1710. [1710].
The walking statue: or the devil in the wine-cellar. F DL Jan 1710. [1710] (with Elfrid, above).
Rinaldo. O Hay 24 Feb 1711. 1711. Italian and English. Tr from G. Rossi.
The dedication of the beech-tree. 1714. Verse.
The fatal vision: or the fall of Siam. T LIF 7 Feb 1716. [1716].
The northern star. 1718, 1724, 1725, 1739 (5th edn, 'revised and corrected by the author'). Verse.
Four essays. 1718. The first essay is by Hill.
The creation: a Pindaric, with a preface concerning the sublimity of the ancient Hebrew poetry and a material and obvious defect in the English. 1720. Preface ed

G. G. Pahl, Los Angeles 1949 (Augustan Reprint Soc). Verse.
The fatal extravagance. T LIF 21 April 1721. 1720, Dublin 1721, London 1726, 1726 (enlarged to 5 acts), 1730 (one act). Given by Hill to Joseph Mitchell and ptd under Mitchell's name.
The judgment-day. 1721 (no copies extant?), [1721?]. Verse.
King Henry the Fifth: or the conquest of France by the English. T DL 5 Dec 1723. 1723, 1765 (3rd edn).
The plain-dealer. 23 March 1724–7 May 1725. A bi-weekly periodical by Hill and William Bond.
The progress of wit: a caveat, for the use of an eminent writer, by a Fellow of All-Souls. 1730. Verse.
Advice to the poets. 1731. Verse.
Athelwold. T DL 10 Dec 1731. 1731, 1732, Dublin 1732, London 1760. A recast of Elfrid, above.
The prompter. 12 Nov 1734–2 July 1736; ed W. A. Appleton and K. A. Burnim, New York 1966 (selection). A bi-weekly theatrical periodical.
The tragedy of Zara. DL 12 Jan 1736. 1736, 1736, Dublin 1737, London 1752, Edinburgh 1755, London 1758, 1760, Dublin 1762, London 1763, 1779, 1777, 1778, 1785, 1791, Dublin 1791 etc. From Voltaire.
Alzira. T LIF 18 June 1736. 1736, Dublin 1736, London 1737, 1744, 1760, 1777, 1779, 1791. From Voltaire.
The tears of the Muses. 1737. Verse.
An enquiry into the merit of assassination. 1738.
The fanciad: an heroic poem. 1743. Anon.
The impartial: an address without flattery. 1744. Verse.
The art of acting. Pt 1 (all pbd), 1746. Verse.
Free thoughts on faith: or the religion of reason. 1746. Verse.
Merope. T DL 15 April 1749. 1749, Dublin 1749, London 1750 (corrected, with additional scene), 1753, Edinburgh 1755, London 1758, Dublin 1762, London 1776, 1777, 1786. From Voltaire.
Gideon, or the patriot: an epic poem. 1749.
A collection of letters between Mr Aaron Hill, Mr Pope and others. 1751.
The Roman revenge. T Bath c. 1753. 1753, 1754, 1759, 1760. From Voltaire.
The insolvent: or filial piety. T New Hay 6 March 1758. 1758, Dublin 1760.
Hill also wrote a number of pamphlets on his beech-oil project.

Letters

A collection of letters between Mr Aaron Hill, Mr Pope and others. 1751.
The works of the late Aaron Hill esq. 4 vols 1753.
McKillop, A. D. Letters from Hill to Richard Savage. N & Q Sept 1954. Letters 1721–5.

§ 2

Ludwig, H. The life and works of Hill. [1911].
Brewster, D. Hill: poet, dramatist, projector. New York 1913.
Dobson, A. Rosalba's journal and other papers. 1915.
Havens, R. D. Hill's poem in blank verse. MLN 41 1921.
Brown, J. R. From Hill to Henry Fielding? PQ 18 1939.
Horsley, P. M. Hill: an English translator of Merope. Comparative Lit Stud 12 1944.
Hughes, L. The actor's epitome. RES 20 1944.
Dunkin, P. S. The authorship of the Fatal extravagance. MLN 60 1945.
Kies, P. P. The authorship of the Fatal extravagance. Washington State Univ Research Stud 13–14 1945–6.
— Notes on Millay's The king's henchman. Washington State Univ Research Stud 14 1946.
Sutherland, W. O. S. Polonius, Hamlet and Lear in Hill's Prompter. SP 49 1952.
Burnim, K. A. Some notes on Hill and stage scenery. Theatre Notebook 12 1957.

—— Hill's The prompter: an eighteenth-century theatrical paper. Educational Theatre Jnl 13 1961.

Burns, L. C. Three views of King Henry V. Drama Survey 1 1962.

Bergman, G. M. Hill: ein englischer Regisseur des 18 Jahrhunderts. Maske und Kothurn 18 1962.

Eddison, T. Topless in Jerusalem. Theatre Notebook 22 1967. On Zara.

BENJAMIN HOADLY
1706–57

The suspicious husband. C CG 12 Feb 1747. 1747 (3 edns), 1749, Dublin 1760, London 1761, Edinburgh 1768, London 1770, Dublin 1776, London 1777.
Hoadly also pbd a number of medical works.

JOHN HUGHES
1677–1720

See col 552, above.

SIR HILDEBRAND JACOB
1693–1739

See col 553, above.

GEORGE JEFFREYS
1678–1755

See col 553, above.

CHARLES JOHNSON
1679–1748

§ 1

The gentleman-cully. C DL c. Aug 1701. 1702. Anon.

Fortune in her wits. C Unacted. 1705. Anon. A trn of Cowley, Naufragium joculare.

Love and liberty. T Unacted. 1709.

The force of friendship. T Hay 20 April 1710. 1710.

Love in a chest. F Hay 20 April 1710. Pbd with Force of friendship, above. For both, *see* E. N. Hooker, SP 34 1937.

The generous husband: or the coffee house politician. C DL 20 Jan 1711. [1711].

The wife's relief: or the husband's cure. C DL 12 Nov 1711. 1712, 1736.

The successful pyrate. TC DL 7 Nov 1712. 1713, 1713.

The victim. T DL 5 Jan 1714. 1714, 1714, 1717.

The country lasses: or the custom of the manor. C DL 4 Feb 1715. 1715, 1732, 1735, 1753, 1768, 1779.

The cobler of Preston. F DL 3 Feb 1716. 1716 (3 edns), Dublin 1767 etc.

The Sultaness. T DL 25 Feb 1717. 1717, 1717.

The masquerade. C DL 16 Jan 1719. [1719], [1719], Dublin 1719.

Love in a forest. C DL 9 Jan 1723. 1723.

The female fortune-teller. C LIF 7 Jan 1726. 1726, 1726.

The village opera. BO DL 6 Feb 1729. 1729, 1729.

The tragedy of Medea. DL 11 Dec 1730. 1731.

Caelia: or, the perjur'd lover. TC DL 11 Dec 1732. 1733.

§ 2

Boys, R. C. Rural settings in the drama: an early example. N & Q 21 March 1936. On Country lasses.

Hooker, E. N. The force of friendship and Love in a chest: a note on tragi-comedy and licensing in 1710. SP 34 1937.

Dias, M. A satire on John Dennis 1711. RES 19 1943.

Shudofsky, M. M. Johnson and eighteenth-century drama. ELH 10 1943.

—— A dunce objects to Pope's dictatorship. HLQ 14 1951.

JOHN KELLY
1680?–1751

The married philosopher, by a gentleman of the Temple. C LIF 25 March 1732. 1732, 1732.

Timon in love: or the innocent theft, taken from the Timon misanthrope of Sieur de Lisle. BO DL 5 Dec 1733. 1733. Anon.

The plot. BO DL 21 Jan 1735. 1735. Anon.

The fall of Bob, or the oracle of gin: a tragedy by Timothy Scrub of Rag Fair esq. F Unacted? 1736. No copy extant.

The levee: a farce, as it was offer'd to, and accepted for representation by the master of the old-house in Drury-Lane, but by the inspector of farces denied a licence. BO Unacted. 1741. 1744.
For Kelly's French trns and text-books, see DNB.

THOMAS KILLIGREW
1657–1719

Chit-chat. C DL 14 Feb 1719. [1719], [1719], [Hague] 1719.
For Killigrew's Miscellanea aurea, 1720, see col 353, above.

JOHN LEIGH
1689–1726

Kensington-Gardens: or the pretenders. C LIF 26 Nov 1719. 1720.

Hob's wedding: being the sequel of the Country wake. F LIF 11 Jan 1720. 1720. Anon.

GEORGE LILLO
1693–1739
Collections

The works of the late Mr George Lillo. 1740.

The works of Mr George Lillo, with some account of his life [by T. Davies]. 2 vols 1775, 1810.

The London merchant and Fatal curiosity. Ed A. W. Ward 1906.

§ 1

Sylvia: or the country burial. O LIF 10 Nov 1730. Dublin 1730 (anon, unauthorized), London 1731 (authorized), 1731.

The London merchant: or the history of George Barnwell. T DL 22 June 1731. 1731 (3 edns), 1732, 1735 (6th edn), 1740, 1743, [1753?], 1763, Edinburgh 1768 etc: ed J. H. Wilson, Boston 1963; ed W. H. McBurney, Lincoln Nebraska 1965; ed M. R. Booth, Oxford 1965 (WC); tr French, ed J. Hamard, Paris 1962.

The Christian hero. T DL 13 Jan 1735. 1735, 1735.

Fatal curiosity. T New Hay 27 May 1736. 1737, 1762, 1768, 1780 etc; ed W. H. McBurney, Lincoln Nebraska 1966.

Marina. TC CG 1 Aug 1738. 1738.

Elmerick: or justice triumphant. T DL 23 Feb 1740. 1740.

Britannia and Batavia. M Unacted. 1740.

Arden of Feversham. T DL 12 July 1759. 1762, Dublin 1763 etc. Completed by John Hoadly.

§ 2

Hudson, W. H. In his A quiet corner in a library, 1915.

Benn, T. V. Notes sur la fortune du George Barnwell de Lillo en France. Revue de Littérature Comparée 6 1926.

Griffith, R. H. Early editions of Lillo's London merchant. SE 15 1935.

Lossack, G. Lillo und seine Bedeutung für die Geschichte des englischen Dramas. Göttingen 1939.

Pallette, D. B. Notes for a biography of Lillo. PQ 19 1940.

Pendell, W. D. The London merchant and La Mierre's Barnevelt. MLN 56 1941.

Prince, L. M. George Barnwell on the German stage. Monatshefte für Deutschen Unterricht 35 1943.

—— The Bassewitz translation of the London merchant. JEGP 43 1944.

—— George Barnwell aboard. Comparative Lit 2 1950.

Rodman, G. B. Sentimentalism in the London merchant. ELH 12 1945. Reply by R. D. Havens, ibid.

Hallowell, R. E. Claude-Joseph Dorat: opponent of the 'drame bourgeois' and the critic of the English theatre. French Rev 25 1952.

Bremner, G. Millwood, Lady Milford and Maria Stuart. German Life & Letters 11 1957.

Virtanen, R. Camus' Le malentendu and some analogues. Comparative Lit 10 1958. On Fatal curiosity.

Carson, H. L. The play that would not die: Lillo's The London merchant. Quart Jnl of Speech 49 1963.

Daunicht, R. Die Entstehung des bürgerlichen Trauerspiels in Deutschland. Berlin 1963. Ch 5 on London merchant.

Hamard, J. Le drame bourgeois: l'influence de Lillo. Revue de Littérature Comparée 39 1965.

McBurney, W. H. What Lillo read: a speculation. HLQ 29 1966.

Burgess, C. F. Further notes for a biography of Lillo. PQ 46 1967.

DAVID MALLET
1705?–65
See col 556, above.

FRANCIS MANNING

A pastoral essay lamenting the death of our most gracious Queen Mary, of blessed memory. 1695.

A congratulatory poem, humbly offered to the King upon his return home, after the taking of Namur. 1695.

Greenwich-Hill: a poem. 1697.

To his sacred Majesty King William III: a panegyrick, presented to the Earl of Portland. 1698, 1698.

The generous choice. C LIF c. Feb 1700. 1700.

The shrine: a poem sacred to the memory of King William III. 1702.

All for the better: or the infallible cure. C DL c. Nov 1702. 1703. Anon.

Manning also pbd trns of historical works by Fléchier and Cassius Dio, and collaborated in the version of Saint Evremond's essays.

BENJAMIN MARTYN
1699–1763

Timoleon. T DL 26 Jan 1730. 1730, 1730, Dublin 1730.

Reasons for establishing the colony of Georgia, with some account of the country. 1733, 1733.

The life of Shaftesbury. [1790?]; ed G. W. Cooke 2 vols 1836.

MOSES MENDEZ
d. 1758
See col 673, above.

JAMES MILLER
1706–44
Collections

Miscellaneous works in verse and prose. Vol 1 (all pbd), 1741. Includes Miller's first 4 plays.

§ 1

The humours of Oxford. C DL 9 Jan 1730. 1730, 1730. Anon.

Harlequin-Horace: or the art of modern poetry. 1731 (anon), 1735 (expanded), 1735.

The mother-in-law: or the doctor the disease. C New Hay 12 Feb 1734. 1734 (anon), 1734 (adds new scene).

The man of taste. C DL 6 March 1735. 1735 (anon), 1735 (anon), 1744.

Seasonable reproof: a satire. 1735. Anon.

The universal passion. C DL 28 Feb 1737. 1737. Anon.

The coffee-house. C DL 26 Jan 1738. 1737 (anon), 1743, 1781.

Art and nature. C DL 16 Feb 1738. 1738. Anon.

Of politeness: an epistle. 1738. Anon.

An hospital for fools. C DL 15 Nov 1739. 1739 (anon), 1781.

The works of Molière. 10 vols 1739. Tr Miller and H. Baker.

The art of life, in imitation of Horace's art of poetry: epistle the first. 1739.

Are these things so? 1740 (anon), 1740 (corrected), Dublin 1740.

Joseph and his brethren: a sacred drama. Unacted 1744.

Mahomet the impostor. T DL 25 April 1744. 1744, 1745, Dublin 1745, Edinburgh 1759, London 1765, 1766, Edinburgh 1773, London 1776 (rev David Garrick), 1777, 1778. In collaboration with John Hoadly.

The picture: or the cuckold in conceit. BO DL 11 Feb 1745. 1745.

Vanelia: or the amours of the great. BO Unacted. 1732 (6 edns). Also attributed to Miller by DNB.

CHARLES MOLLOY
d. 1767

The perplex'd couple: or mistake upon mistake. C LIF 16 Feb 1715. 1715. Anon.

The coquet: or the English chevalier. C LIF 19 April 1718. 1718.

The half-pay officers. F LIF 11 Jan 1720. 1720. Anon.

Common sense: or the Englishman's journal. 342? nos 5 Feb 1737–29 Aug 1743?, 2 vols 1738–9. Conducted and mainly written by Molloy.

EDWARD MOORE
1712–57
See col 558, above.

JOHN MOTTLEY
1692–1750

The imperial captives. T LIF 29 Feb 1720. 1720 (3 edns).

Antiochus. T LIF 13 April 1721. 1721, 1721.

Penelope. BO New Hay 8 May 1728. 1728. Anon. Assisted by Thomas Cooke.

The craftsman, or weekly journalist: a farce. BO New Hay 15 Oct 1728. 1729. Anon.

The widow bewitch'd. C GF 8 June 1730. 1730. Anon.

Joe Miller's jests: or the wit's vade-mecum. 1739 (3 edns), 1740, 1742.

A compleat list of all the English dramatic poets. Appended to Thomas Whincop, Scanderbeg, 1747. Attributed to Mottley on internal evidence.

The history of the life of Peter I, Emperor of Russia. 3 vols 1739, 1740, Dublin 1740.

The history of the life and reign of the Empress Catharine of Russia. 2 vols 1744.

For The devil to pay, see under Coffey, above.

THOMAS ODELL
1691–1749

The chimera. C LIF 19 Jan 1721. 1721. Anon.
The patron: or the statesman's opera. BO New Hay 7 May 1729. [1729], Dublin [1729].
The smugglers. F New Hay 7 May 1729. 1729, Dublin 1729 (with Soame Jenyns, The art of dancing).
An ode sacred to the nuptials of their Highnesses the Prince and Princess of Orange and Nassau. 1733, 1733.
The prodigal: or recruits for the Queen of Hungary. C New Hay 11 Oct 1744. 1744.

GABRIEL ODINGSELLS
1690–1734

The Bath unmask'd. C LIF 27 Feb 1725. 1725, Dublin 1725.
The capricious lovers. C LIF 8 Dec 1725. 1726.
Bays's opera. BO DL 30 March 1730. 1730.
Monumental inscriptions: or a curious collection of epitaphs, serious and humourous. 1742. Ed Odingsells.

JOHN OLDMIXON
1673–1742
See col 1708, below.

AMBROSE PHILIPS
1674–1749
See col 562, above.

WILLIAM PHILIPS
d. 1734

The revengeful Queen. T DL c. June 1698. 1698. Anon.
St Stephen's Green: or the generous lovers. C Dublin. Dublin 1700 (anon), London 1720.
Hibernia freed. T LIF 13 Feb 1722. 1722 (anon), Dublin 1722.
Belisarius. T LIF 14 April 1724. 1724, 1758, 1758.

EDWARD PHILLIPS

The chambermaid. BO DL 10 Feb 1730. 1730 (anon), 1735.
The mock lawyer. BO CG 27 April 1733. 1733 (no known copy), Dublin 1737.
The livery rake and country lass: an opera. BO DL 5 May 1733. 1733.
The stage mutineers: or a play-house to be lett. F CG 27 July 1733. 1733. Anon.
The nuptial masque: or the triumphs of Cupid and Hymen. M CG 16 March 1734. 1734.
A new dramatic entertainment called the royal chace: or Merlin's cave. Pant CG 23 Jan 1736. 1736.
Britons, strike home! or the sailor's rehearsal: a farce. BO DL 31 Dec 1739. 1739, Glasgow 1758.
The players: a satire, 1733 (anon) *is a poem doubtfully attributed to Phillips.*

MARY PIX
1666–1720?

§ 1

Ibrahim the thirteenth Emperour of the Turks. T DL c. May 1696. 1696.
The Spanish wives. C DL c. Sept 1696. 1696. *See* J. M. Edmunds, MLN 48 1933.

The innocent mistress. C LIF c. June 1697. 1697.
The deceiver deceived. C LIF c. Dec 1697. 1698.
Queen Catharine: or the ruines of love. T LIF c. June 1698. 1698.
The false friend: or the fate of disobedience. T LIF c. May 1699. 1699.
The beau defeated: or the lucky younger brother. C LIF c. March 1700. [1700].
To the Right Hon the Earl of Kent, Ld Chamberlain. [1700?]. A poem.
The double distress. T LIF c. March 1701. 1701.
The Czar of Muscovy. T LIF c. March 1701. 1701.
The different widows: or intrigue all-a-mode. C LIF c. Nov 1703. [1703]. Anon.
Violenta: or the rewards of virtue, turn'd from Boccace into verse. 1704.
The conquest of Spain. T Hay May 1705. 1705. Anon.
The adventures in Madrid. C Hay c. June 1706. [1706]. Anon.

§ 2

Bowers, F. T. Underprinting in Mary Pix, The Spanish wives. Library 5th ser 9 1954.

WILLIAM POPPLE
1701–64

The lady's revenge: or the rover reclaim'd. C CG 9 Jan 1734. 1734, Dublin 1734.
The double deceit: or a cure for jealousy. C CG 25 April 1735. 1736.
The prompter. 173 nos 12 Nov 1734–2 July 1736; ed W. W. Appleton and K. A. Burnim, New York 1966 (selection). With Aaron Hill, above.
Horace's Art of poetry translated. 1753.

JAMES RALPH
1705?–62

§ 1

The tempest, or the terror of death: a poem. 1727.
The Muses address to the King: an ode. 1728.
Night: a poem. 1728, Dublin 1728.
Sawney: an heroic poem, occasion'd by the Dunciad. 1728.
The touchstone: or historical, critical, political, philosophical and theological essays on the reigning diversions of the town. 1728 (anon), 1731 (as The taste of the town).
Clarinda, or the fair libertine: a poem. 1729.
The loss of liberty: or the fall of Rome. 1729. Verse.
Miscellaneous poems, by several hands, publish'd by Mr Ralph. 1729, 1743 (as A present for a young lady).
Zeuma, or the love of liberty: a poem. 1729.
Miscellaneous poems. 4 pts 1729–8. The following pieces with collective title-page: Night, Zeuma, Clarinda, The Muses address.
The fashionable lady: or Harlequin's opera, in the manner of a rehearsal. Bsq GF 2 April 1730. 1730.
The fall of the Earl of Essex, alter'd from the Unhappy favourite of Mr Banks. T GF 1 Feb 1731. 1731. Anon.
The Cornish squire, done from the French by the late Sir John Vanbrugh. F DL 3 Jan 1734. From Molière's Monsieur de Pourceaugnac. On the relation of this version to that by Congreve, Vanbrugh and Walsh (LIF 30 March 1704), *see* J. C. Hodges, RES 4 1928; J. B. Shipley, PQ 47 1968.
A critical review of the publick buildings, statues and ornaments in London and Westminster. 1734, 1783 (expanded by another). Doubtfully attributed to Ralph.
The other side of the question, by a woman of quality. 1742, 1744. Retort to Hooke, Account of the conduct of the Duchess of Marlborough.

A critical history of the administration of Sir Robert Walpole, by a gentleman of the Middle Temple. 1743.
The case of our present theatrical disputes fairly stated. 1743. Anon.
The lawyer's feast. F DL 12 Dec 1743. 1744.
The astrologer. F DL 3 April 1744. 1744. Anon.
Of the use and abuse of parliaments. 2 vols 1744. Anon.
The history of England during the reigns of King William, Queen Anne and George I, by a lover of truth and liberty. 2 vols 1744–6.
The case of authors by profession or trade stated, with regard to booksellers, the stage and the public, no matter by whom. 1758 (anon), 1762 (signed).
Ralph also conducted or contributed largely to the following periodicals: Universal Spectator (1728–46), Champion (1739–44), Remembrancer (1747–51), Protester (1753).

§ 2

Kenny, R. W. Ralph's Case of authors: its influence on Goldsmith and Isaac D'Israeli. PMLA 52 1937.
— Ralph: an eighteenth-century Philadelphia in Grub Street. Pennsylvania Mag of History & Biography 64 1940.
Shipley, J. B. Garrick and Ralph: remarks on a correspondence. N & Q Sept 1958.
— Franklin attends a book auction. Pennsylvania Mag of History & Biography 80 1956. On purchases from Ralph's library.
— Publick buildings. TLS 8 May 1959.
— Ralph, Prince Titi and The black box of Frederick, Prince of Wales. BNYPL March 1967.
— The authorship of the Cornish Squire. PQ 47 1968.
— The authorship of the Touch-stone 1728. PBSA 62 1968.
Lowens, I. The touch-stone (1928): a neglected view of London opera. Musical Quart 45 1959.
McKillop, A. D. Ralph in Berkshire. Stud in Eng Lit 1500–1900 1 1961. Letters.
Bastian, J. M. Ralph's second adaptation from John Banks. HLQ 25 1962. On Anna Bullen (c. 1735), neither performed nor pbd.

RICHARD SAVAGE
1697?–1742
See col 565, above.

CHARLES SHADWELL
d. 1726
Collections

Five new plays. 1720, Dublin 1720. (1) The hasty wedding; (2) The sham prince; or news from Passau, C; (3) Rotherick O'Connor, King of Connaught: or the distress'd Princess, T; (4) The plotting lovers: or the dismal squire, F; (5) Irish hospitality: or virtue rewarded, C. All had been acted at Dublin.
The works of Charles Shadwell. 2 vols Dublin 1720.

§ I

The fair Quaker of Deal: or the humours of the navy. C DL 25 Feb 1710. 1710, 1715, 1723.
The humours of the army. C DL 29 Jan 1713. 1713.
The hasty wedding: or the intriguing squire. F Dublin. 1717.

WILLIAM SHIRLEY

The parricide: or innocence in distress. T CG 17 Jan 1739. 1739.

Edward the Black Prince, or the battle of Poictiers: an historical tragedy, attempted after the manner of Shakespear. T DL 6 Jan 1750. 1750, 1779 etc.
King Pepin's campaign. Bsq DL 15 April 1745. 1755, [1778?].
Brief remarks upon the original and present state of the drama. 1758. Anon.
A bone for the chroniclers to pick: a poem. 1758. Anon.
Observations on a pamphlet lately published [concerning a Portuguese conspiracy]. 1759.
Electra. T Prohibited CG Jan 1763. 1765.
The birth of Hercules. M Unacted. 1765 (with Electra).

EDMUND SMITH
1672–1710
Collections

The works, [with] a character of Mr Smith by Mr Oldisworth. 1714, 1719, 1729 (rev Dr Adams). Pocockius, first pbd here, was tr anon from Latin [1750?] as Thales: a monody.

§ I

Phaedra and Hippolitus. T Hay April 1707. [1707], 1711, 1719, [1720], 1745, Dublin 1751 etc. Based on Racine, Phèdre.
A poem on the death of Mr John Philips. [1710?].
Oratio in laudem T. Bodleii. 1711. Delivered in 1701.

§ 2

Johnson, Samuel. In his Lives of the English poets, 1779–81.
Geffen, E. M. The expulsion from Oxford of Edmund ('Rag') Smith. N & Q 6 June 1936.
— [Biographical notes]. RES 14 1938.
Wheatley, K. E. The relation of Phaedra and Hippolitus to Racine's Phèdre and Bajazet. Romanic Rev 37 1946.

SIR RICHARD STEELE
1672–1729
See col 1112, below.

WILLIAM TAVERNER
d. 1731

The faithful bride of Granada. T DL c. May 1704. 1704. Anon.
The maid the mistress. C DL 5 June 1708. 1708 (anon), 1732, 1736.
The female advocates: or the frantick stock-jobber. C DL 6 Jan 1713. 1713. Anon.
Presumptuous love. M LIF 10 March 1716. [1716].
The artful husband. C LIF 11 Feb 1717. [1717], [1717], 1721, Dublin 1725.
The artful wife. C LIF 3 Dec 1717. 1718.
'Tis well if it takes. C LIF 28 Feb 1719. 1719.

LEWIS THEOBALD
1688–174

§ I

The Persian Princess: or the royal villain. T DL 31 May 1708. 1715 (anon), 1717.
The perfidious brother. T LIF 21 Feb 1716. 1715, 1715.
Pan and Syrinx. O LIF 14 Jan 1718. 1718.
Decius and Paulina. M LIF March 1718. 1718 (in The entertainments for the Lady's triumph), 1718 (appended to Lady's triumph, by Settle), 1719 (expanded).

The tragedy of King Richard the II. LIF 10 Dec 1719. 1720.

Harlequin a sorcerer: with the loves of Pluto and Proserpine. Pant LIF 21 Jan 1725. 1725. Anon.

Vocal parts of an entertainment called Apollo and Daphne: or the burgomaster trick'd. Pant LIF 15 Jan 1726. 1726 (anon), 1729, 1731, 1734.

The rape of Proserpine. Pant LIF 13 Feb 1727. 1727 (anon, 4 edns), 1731.

Double falshood: or the distrest lovers, written originally by W. Shakespeare, and now revised. T DL 13 Dec 1727. 1728, 1728, 1767; ed W. Graham, Cleveland 1920.

Perseus and Andromeda. Pant LIF 2 Jan 1730. 1730 (anon), 1730 (rev, 3 edns), 1731.

Orestes. O LIF 3 April 1731. 1731.

The vocal parts of an entertainment call'd Merlin: or the devil of Stone-Henge. Pant DL 12 Dec 1734. 1734.

The fatal secret. T CG 4 April 1733. 1735.

Orpheus and Eurydice. Pant CG 12 Feb 1740. 1739. Anon.

The happy captive, with an interlude, in two comick scenes. New Hay 16 April 1741. 1741. Interlude, tr from Italian? rptd separately 1745 (with addns) as The temple of dullness, and abridged in Capochio and Dorinna, nd, attributed to Colley Cibber. *See* G. W. Whiting, RES 10 1934.

For Theobald's non-dramatic writings, see col 1745, below.

§ 2

Muir, K. Cardenio. Etudes Anglaises 11 1958. On Double falshood.

Kaul, R. K. What Theobald did to Webster. Indian Jnl of Eng Stud 2 1961.

Ingram, W. H. Theobald, Rowe, Jackson: whose Ajax? Lib Chron 21 1965.

Woods, C. B. Theobald and Fielding's Don Tragedio. Eng Lang Notes 2 1965.

Frazier, H. C. Theobald's The double falshood: a revision of Shakespeare's Cardenio? Comparative Drama 1 1967.

—— The rifling of beauty's stores: Theobald and Shakespeare. Neuphilologische Mitteilungen 69 1968.

Langhans, E. Three early eighteenth-century manuscript prompt-books. MP 65 1967. On Perfidious brother.

Freehafer, J. Cardenio, by Shakespeare and Fletcher. PMLA 84 1969. On Double falshood.

JAMES THOMSON
1700–48
See col 527, above.

JOSEPH TRAPP
1679–1747
See col 571, above.

CATHARINE TROTTER, late COCKBURN
1679–1749

Olinda's adventures: or the amours of a young lady. 1693 (in Letters of love and gallantry), 1694, 1718 (in Familiar letters of love, gallantry vol 2); ed R. A. Day, Los Angeles 1969 (Augustan Reprint Soc).

Agnes de Castro. T DL c. Dec 1695. 1696. Anon.

Fatal friendship. T LIF c. May 1698. 1698.

Love at a loss: or most votes carry it. C DL 23 Nov 1700. 1701.

The unhappy penitent. T DL 4 Feb 1701. 1701.

The revolution of Sweden. T DL 11 Feb 1706. 1706.

For the philosophical works, see col 1860, below.

EDWARD YOUNG
1683–1765
See col 493, above.

VII. LATER EIGHTEENTH-CENTURY DRAMA

In this section italicized abbreviations have been employed for the principal contemporary collections of plays (e.g. Bell, Inchbald's Farces, Acting Drama etc); the full titles will be found on col 701, above. The note 'Larpent ms' means that the ms submitted to the licenser for the original English production is now in the Larpent Collection at the Huntington Library, California. A key to the other abbreviations used will be found on col 741, above.

DAVID GARRICK
1717–79
Bibliographies

Knapp, M. E. A checklist of verse by Garrick. Charlottesville 1955.

Collections

The dramatic works of David Garrick esq. 3 vols 1768, 2 vols 1774. 16 plays, 9 original and 7 adapted.

The poetical works of David Garrick, with explanatory notes [by G. Kearsley]. 2 vols 1785.

The dramatic works of David Garrick esq, to which is prefixed a life of the author. 3 vols 1798. Includes all the pbd plays except Neck or nothing, Cymon, and A Christmas tale, and all of the adaptations except Chances, Tempest, Antony and Cleopatra, A midsummer night's dream, King Lear, The country girl, Alfred, Albumazar, and Alchymist.

Three farces: The lying valet, A peep behind the curtain, Bon ton. Ed L. B. Osborn, New Haven 1925.

Three plays: Harlequin's invasion, The jubilee, The meeting of the company, or Bayes's art of acting. Ed E. P. Stein, New York 1926.

§ 1

The lying valet. F GF 30 Nov 1741. Dublin 1741, London 1742, 1743; *British Drama 5.*

Mr Garrick's answer to Mr Macklin's case. 1743. Attributed by Murphy, Life of Garrick vol 1, to William Guthrie, but probably by Garrick.

An essay on acting, in which will be considered the mimical behaviour of a certain fashionable faulty actor. 1744.

Lethe: or Aesop in the shades. F DL 15 April 1745. 1745 (pirated), 1749 (as Lethe a dramatic satire), Dublin 1749, London 1755, 1757 ('with additional character of Lord Chalkstone'), 1767, Glasgow 1767; *Bell* (*suppl 1*), *Edinburgh Farces 1* 1768, *Modern British Drama 5.*

Miss in her teens; or the medley of lovers. F CG 17 Jan 1747. 1747 (anon), Dublin 1747, 1747, London 1748, 1749, 1759, 1771, Belfast 1775, London 1777; *Bell* (*suppl 1*), *Edinburgh Farces 1* 1786, *Minor Theatre 6*, *British Drama 5*, *Modern British Drama 5*, *Dibdin 8.*

Romeo and Juliet, by Shakespear, with alterations and an additional scene. T DL 29 Nov 1748. 1750, 1778, [1780], 1788, 1793, 1807, 1814; *Oxberry 6*.

The diary of Garrick: being a record of his trip to Paris in 1751. Ed R. C. Alexander, New York 1928.

Every man in his humour, by Ben Jonson, with alterations and additions. C DL 29 Nov 1751. 1752, 1754, 1755, 1759, Dublin 1759, Edinburgh 1768 (in Theatre vol 2), London 1769, Edinburgh 1774, London 1777; *Bell 2 1776, 4 1797*; Dublin 1792; *Dibdin 17, Oxberry 16, London Stage 3, Acting Drama*.

An ode on the death of Mr Pelham. 1754, Dublin 1754. Also rptd in London Mag 1754, Dodsley's Collection of poems vol 1, and Murphy, Life of Garrick vol 2. Erroneously ascribed to Edward Moore.

The chances, by Beaumont and Fletcher, with alterations. C DL 7 Nov 1754. 1773, 1774, 1777 (in New English Theatre 11); *London Stage 4, Acting Drama*.

The fairies, taken from A midsummer night's dream, written by Shakespear; the songs from Shakespear, Milton, Dryden, Waller, Lansdown, Hammond. O DL 3 Feb 1755. 1755, 1755.

Catherine and Petruchio, alter'd from Shakespear's Taming of the shrew. C DL 21 Jan 1756. 1756, 1786; *Bell (suppl 3), Minor Theatre 4, Inchbald's Farces 4, Cumberland 18*.

King Lear, alter'd from Shakespeare. T DL 28 Oct 1756. 1786 (Bell's Shakespeare).

Florizel and Perdita: a dramatic pastoral, alter'd from the Winter's tale of Shakespear. DL 21 Jan 1756. 1758, 1762; Larpent ms.

The tempest, taken from Shakespear; the songs from Shakespear, Dryden etc. O DL 11 Feb 1756. 1756; Larpent ms.

Lilliput: a dramatic entertainment. Int DL 3 Dec 1756. 1757.

The male coquette: or seventeen fifty seven. F DL 24 March 1757 as The modern fine gentleman. 1757, Dublin 1758; *British Drama 5, Modern British Drama 5*, Larpent ms.

Isabella, or the fatal marriage: a play alter'd from Southern. T DL 2 Dec 1757. 1757, 1758, Dublin 1769, Edinburgh 1773, London 1776 (in New English theatre vol 12); *Bell (5, 1776, 1780, 1797)*; 1777, 1779, 1783 (in New English theatre vol 12), 1784, Dublin 1785, London 1789, 1790, 1792, 1792, 1800, Dublin 1803; *Modern British Drama 2 1804* (in Sharp's British theatre vol 3), 1806; *Inchbald's Theatre 7, Dibdin 22, British Drama 1, London Stage 1, Cumberland 9*.

The gamesters, alter'd from Shirley. C DL 22 Dec 1757. 1758; *Bell (19 1778, 6 1792)*, Larpent ms.

Antony and Cleopatra: an historical play, written by Shakespear, fitted for the stage by abridging only. DL 3 Jan 1759. 1758. Abridged by Garrick and Edward Capell.

The guardian. C DL 3 Feb 1759. 1759, 1759, 1771, 1773, 1779; *Bell (suppl 1), Inchbald's Farces 4*, Larpent ms.

High life below stairs. F DL 31 Oct 1759. 1759 (4 edns), 1775, 1787, 1795; *British Drama 5, Morgan*, Larpent ms. Ptd as by James Townley, but *see* A. Murphy, Life of Garrick vol 1, 1801, p. 343.

Harlequin's invasion: a Christmas gambol, after the manner of the Italian comedy. Int DL 31 Dec 1759. Larpent ms.

Reasons why David Garrick esq should not appear on the stage, in a letter to John Rich esq. 1759. Generally ascribed to Garrick himself.

The enchanter, or love and magic: a musical drama. Int DL 13 Dec 1760. 1760; Larpent ms.

The fribbleriad. 1761. Verse.

Cymbeline, by Shakespear, with alterations. T DL 28 Nov 1761. 1762, 1767, 1770, 1784, 1795.

The farmer's return from London. Int DL 30 March 1762. 1762 (3 edns); *Minor Theatre 1, Inchbald's Farces 5*, Larpent ms.

A midsummer night's dream, written by Shakespear, with alterations and additions. C DL 23 Nov 1763. 1763; Larpent ms.

The clandestine marriage. *See under Colman, col 812, below.*

The sick monkey: a fable. 1765.

Neck or nothing. F DL 18 Nov 1766. 1766, 1767, 1774; *Bell (suppl 2), Edinburgh Farces 2, British Drama 1824*.

The country girl, alter'd from Wycherley. C DL 25 Oct 1766. 1766, 1790, 1791; *Bell (1797) 13, Inchbald's Theatre 16, Modern British Drama 3, Dibdin 19, Oxberry 13, Cumberland 21*, Larpent ms.

Cymon: a dramatic romance. DL 2 Jan 1767. 1767, 1767, 1768, 1770, Dublin 1771, London 1778; *Bell (suppl 1), Edinburgh Farces 3, [1792]*, 1792 ('with additional airs' for revival 31 Dec 1791), 1815, 1816 (songs only), Larpent ms.

Linco's travels. Int DL 6 March 1767. Larpent ms.

A peep behind the curtain: or the new rehearsal. Bsq DL 23 Oct 1767. 1767 (3 edns), 1770, 1772, 1778, 1786, Larpent ms (as The new rehearsal).

The elopement. Pant DL 26 Dec 1767. Not ptd.

An ode upon dedicating a building and erecting a statue to Shakespeare at Stratford upon Avon. 1769.

Shakespeare's garland being a collection of the new songs, ballads, roundelays, catches, glees, comic-serenatas etc performed at the Jubilee at Stratford-upon-Avon. 1769. 7 songs by Garrick.

The Jubilee. Int DL 14 Oct 1769. 1769, 1770, 1776, 1778 (songs only), Waterford 1773 (pirated, as The jubilee in honour of Shakespeare as performed at Waterford with additions).

King Arthur: or the British worthy, by Mr Dryden. M DL 13 Dec 1770. 1770, 1770, 1781, 1784 (abridged as Arthur and Emmeline), 1786.

The institution of the Garter: or Arthur's round table restored. M DL 28 Oct 1771. 1771 (songs and 'serious dialogue' only), Larpent ms (as The Order of the Garter). Based on Gilbert West, The institution of the Garter: a dramatic poem, 1742.

The Irish widow. F DL 23 Oct 1772. 1772, 1772, 1773, 1774, 1781, 1787; *Edinburgh Farces 5, Inchbald's Farces 1, British Drama 5, Dibdin 1, London Stage 3*.

Hamlet, as altered from Shakespear. T DL 18 Dec 1772. Not ptd. Garrick's copy now in Folger Lib, Washington. *See* G. W. Stone, PMLA 49 1934. An earlier acting version by Garrick was ptd 1763, 1755 (for 1765), 1767, 1768, 1770.

Alfred, by Thomson and Mallet, as it is now revised. M DL 9 Oct 1773. 1773, Dublin 1774. Doubtfully ascribed to Garrick.

Albumazar, as it is now revived with alterations. C DL 19 Oct 1773. 1773, 1773, Dublin 1773, Larpent ms.

A Christmas tale: a dramatic entertainment. DL 27 Dec 1773. [1773] (songs only), 1774 (in 5 pts, 3 edns), Dublin 1774, London 1776 (in 3 acts), Larpent ms.

Bon ton: or high life above stairs. F DL 18 March 1775. 1775, 1776, 1781, 1784, Dublin 1785; *Bell (suppl 1), Edinburgh Farces 4 1793, Minor Theatre 2, British Drama 5, Inchbald's Modern Theatre 5, Modern British Drama 5, British Drama 1824, London Stage 3, Acting Drama*, Larpent ms.

The theatrical candidates: a musical prelude. DL Sept 1775. 1775 (appended on May day).

May Day, or the little gipsy: a musical farce. DL 28 Oct 1775. 1775, 1775 (songs only), 1776 (songs only), 1777 (songs only); *Edinburgh Farces 6*, Larpent ms.

Rule a wife and have a wife, as altered from Beaumont and Fletcher by Garrick. C DL 14 Feb 1776. 1786 (in New English theatre 3), 1820, 1822; *London Stage 1*, Garrick emphatically denied altering this play. *See* Biographia dramatica vol 3, p. 232. The adaptation was pbd 1811 as by James Love.

The alchymist as altered from Ben Jonson. C DL 1766? 1777; *Bell (1777) 17*.

Journal describing his visit to France and Italy in 1763. Ed G. W. Stone, New York 1939.

Letters

The private correspondence of David Garrick. [Ed J. Boaden] 2 vols 1831–2, 1835. 242 letters by Garrick.

Morning Post 24 Aug–7 Oct 1786. 17 letters by Garrick.

Biographical memoirs of Joseph Warton, by John Wooll. 1806. 6 letters by Garrick.

The life of Arthur Murphy esq, by Jesse Foot. 1811. 13 letters by Garrick.

Letters to Colman the elder. Ed G. Colman (the younger) 1820. 37 letters by Garrick, rptd below.

Memoirs of the Colman family. Ed R. B. Peake 2 vols 1841. Contains the same 37 letters.

Memoirs of Hannah More. Ed W. Roberts 2 vols 1834. 6 letters by Garrick.

Some unpublished correspondence of Garrick. Ed G. P. Baker, Boston 1907. 35 letters by Garrick.

A cosmopolitan actor: Garrick and his French friends, by F. A. Hedgcock. [1912]. 24 letters by Garrick.

Mrs Montagu, Queen of the blues. Ed R. Blunt 2 vols 1923. 8 letters by Garrick.

Williams, C. R. Two unpublished letters 1765. Cornhill Mag March 1929.

Pineapples of finest flavour. Ed D. M. Little, Cambridge Mass 1930. 43 letters by Garrick.

Babler, O. F. Two letters of Garrick. N & Q 26 May 1934.

Pedicord, H. W. Mr and Mrs Garrick: some unpublished correspondence. PMLA 60 1945.

Price, C. Some Garrick letters. N & Q May 1955.

Letters of Garrick and Georgiana, Countess Spencer 1759–79. Ed Earl Spencer and C. Dobson, Cambridge 1960.

Letters. Ed D. M. Little and G. R. Kahrl 3 vols Cambridge Mass 1963.

§ 2

A clear stage and no favour, occasion'd by the emulation of David [Garrick] and Goliah [Quin]. [1742].

The case of Charles Macklin, comedian. 1743. Ascribed to Corbyn Morris, who denied its authorship. Probably by Macklin himself.

Mr Macklin's reply to Mr Garrick's answer. 1743; rptd with the previous item and Garrick's Answer as The case of Charles Macklin, comedian, 1743, and in Murphy's Life of Garrick, vol 2, below.

[Foote, Samuel]. A treatise on the passions, with a critical enquiry into the theatrical merit of Mr G—k, Mr Q—n and Mr B—y. [1747].

A letter of compliment to the ingenious author of a Treatise on the passions. [1747].

A letter to Mr Garrick on his having purchased a patent for Drury Lane play-house. [1747].

F., E. Mr Garrick's conduct as a manager considered. [1747].

[Lancaster, N.] The pretty gentleman: or softness of manners vindicated from Garrick's farce of Miss in her teens, by Philautus. 1747; ed E. Goldsmid, Edinburgh 1885.

D—ry-L-ne p—yh—se broke open in a letter to Mr G—. 1748.

[Moore, Edward]. An ode to David Garrick esq upon the talk of the town. 1749.

A letter to Mr Garrick relative to his treble capacity of manager, actor and author, with some remarks upon Lethe. 1749.

Lethe rehears'd or a critical discussion. 1749.

[Gentleman, F.] Fortune: a rhapsody to Mr Garrick. 1751.

—— The Stratford jubilee: a new comedy. 1769.

The theatrical manager: a satire. 1751, Dublin 1751.

A poetical epistle from Shakespear in Elysium to Mr Garrick at Drury Lane theatre. 1752.

An epistle from Mr Theophilus Cibber to David Garrick esq. 1755.

The dancers damn'd: or the devil to pay at the old house. 1755. Occasioned by the riot at Chinese festival.

The visitation: of an interview between the ghost of Shakespeare and D–v–d G–rr–k esq. 1755. Against pantomimes, in the controversy following Chinese festival.

[Colman, George]. A letter of abuse to D—d G—k esq. 1757.

—— Man and wife, or the Shakespeare jubilee: a comedy. 1770.

A letter to Mr Garrick on the opening of the theatre. 1758.

Pittard, Joseph. Observations on Mr Garrick's acting in a letter to the Earl of Chesterfield. 1758.

[Shirley, William]. Brief remarks upon the original and present state of the drama; to which is added Hecate's prophecy. 1758.

—— A bone for the chroniclers to pick: a poem. 1758.

[Ralph, James]. The case of authors by profession. 1758.

[Hill, John]. A letter to the author of the Rout; to which is subjoined an epistle to Mr G—k with an appendix on the new-reviv'd play of Antony and Cleopatra. 1759.

—— To David Garrick esq: the petition of I. in behalf of herself and her sisters. 1759.

[Purdon, Edward]. A letter to David Garrick on opening the theatre in which is told with great freedom how he ought to behave. 1769 (for 1759).

A defence of Mr Garrick in answer to the letter-writer, by a dramatic author. [1759].

[Lloyd, Robert]. Shakespeare: an epistle to Mr Garrick. 1760.

P., A. A letter to David Garrick occasioned by the intended representation of the Minor at Drury Lane theatre. 1760, Edinburgh 1776 (3rd edn).

[Fitzpatrick, Thomas]. An enquiry into the real merit of a certain popular performer, in a series of letters with an introduction to David Garrick esq. 1760. Rptd from Letters by X.Y.Z. in Craftsman.

Fizgig or the modern Quixote: a tale relative to the late disturbances. 1763. Satirizing Fitzpatrick.

Theatrical disquisitions: or a review of the late riot at Drury Lane Theatre, by a lady. 1763.

An appeal to the public in behalf of the manager. 1763.

Three original letters on the late riot. 1763.

An historical account of the late riots. 1763.

[Hiffernan, Paul]. A letter from the rope-dancing monkey in the Hay-Market to the acting monkey of Drury Lane on the Earl of Warwick [by Thomas Francklin]. 1767.

Warner, Richard. A letter to David Garrick esq concerning a glossary to Shakespeare. 1768.

An ode on dedicating a building, and erecting a statue to Le Stue, cook to the Duke of Newcastle, with notes by Martinus Scriblerus. Oxford 1769.

Garrick's vagary: or England run mad. 1769. On the Jubilee.

[Thompson, Edward]. Trinculo's trip to the Jubilee. 1769.

Anti-Midas. A Jubilee preservative from unclassical, ignorant, false and invidious criticism. 1769.

Garrick: oder die englischen Schauspieler. Copenhagen 1771.

[Combe, William]. Sanitas, daughter of Aesculapius, to David Garrick esq: a poem. 1772.

[Kenrick, William]. Love in the suds, a town eclogue: being the lamentation of Roscius for the loss of his Nyky [Isaac Bickerstaffe]. 1772; rptd in A letter to David Garrick esq from William Kenrick, 1772 (3rd edn), 1772 (5th edn, 'with annotations').

—— A letter to David Garrick esq occasioned by his having moved the Court of King's Bench against the publisher of Love in the suds. 1772.

—— A whipping for the Welch parson: being a comment upon the Rev Mr Evan Lloyd's Epistle to David Garrick esq. 1773.

'Ariel'. The Kenrickad: a poem. 1772.

The recantation and confession of Dr Kenrick. 1772. A mock recantation. Kenrick's genuine apology appeared in Publick Advertiser 23 Nov 1772.

[Williams, David]. A letter to David Garrick esq on his conduct at Drury Lane. 1772, 1773.

Miles, William Augustus. A letter to Sir John Fielding occasioned by his request to Mr Garrick for the suppression of the Beggar's opera. 1773.

Lloyd, Evan. An epistle to David Garrick esq. 1773.

R., T. An appeal to the publick from the judgment of a certain manager, with original letters and the drama [Politician reformed], which was refused representation. 1774.

Garrick's looking-glass or the art of rising on the stage: a poem. 1776, Dublin 1776.

Pursuit after happiness; to which is added an ode to Mr Garrick on his quitting the stage. 1777.

[More, Hannah]. Ode to Dragon Mr Garrick's house-dog at Hampton. 1777.

The poetical review, a poem: being a satirical display of the literal characters of Mr G—r—ck [et al]. [1778?].

Meyler, William. A monody on the death of David Garrick. Bath 1779.

[Pratt, Samuel Jackson]. Shadows of Shakespeare: a monody by Courtney Melmoth. Bath 1779, [1780?].

Sheridan, Richard Brinsley. Verses to the memory of Garrick. 1779, 1779, Dublin 1780 (as The tears of genius).

[Tasker, William]. An elegy on the death of David Garrick. 1779.

Garrick in the shades: or a peep into Elysium, a farce never offered to the managers of the Theatres Royal. 1779.

The apotheosis of Punch: a satirical masque with a monody on the death of Mr Punch acted at the Patagonian theatre, Exeter Change. 1779. An attempt to ridicule Sheridan's monody, usually ascribed to Leonard MacNally.

The life and death of David Garrick, the celebrated English Roscius, by an old comedian. 1779, 1779 ('with additions').

Davies, Thomas. Memoirs of the life of David Garrick esq. 2 vols 1780, 1780, 1781, 1784; rev S. Jones 2 vols 1808.

Anderson, J. W. The manner in which the Common Prayer was read by the late Mr Garrick for the instruction of a young clergyman. 1797; ed R. Cull 1840.

Murphy, Arthur. Life of David Garrick esq. 2 vols 1801, Dublin 1801.

Wilkinson, Tate. Original anecdotes with remarks on Mr Murphy's Life of Garrick. [1805]. Rptd from Monthly Mirror.

Reynolds, Sir Joshua. Johnson and Garrick. 1816; ed R. B. Johnson 1927.

Daniel, G. Garrick in the green room: a biographical and critical analysis of a picture painted by William Hogarth and engraved by William Ward. 1829.

Fitzgerald, P. The life of Garrick. 2 vols 1868, 1899 (rev).

Hitchman, F. In his Eighteenth-century studies, 1881.

Knight, J. David Garrick. 1894.

Dobson, A. Exit Roscius. In his Eighteenth-century vignettes ser 3, 1896.

—— Garrick's grand tour. In his At Prior Park, 1912.

Gaehde, C. Garrick als Shakespeare-darsteller. Berlin 1904.

Martin, T. In his Monographs, 1906.

Parsons, Mrs C. Garrick and his circle. 1906.

Hedgcock, F. A. Garrick et ses amis français. Paris 1911; tr and enlarged as A cosmopolitan actor: Garrick and his French friends, [1912].

Williams, I. A. Garrick's epitaph on William Hogarth. London Mercury May 1922.

Nicoll, A. Garrick's lost Jubilee: a manuscript copy. Times 25 June 1927.

Klercker, E. af. David Garrick. Stockholm 1928.

Williams, C. R. Garrick, actor-manager. Cornhill Mag March 1929.

MacMillan, D. Garrick as critic. SP 31 1934.

—— Garrick, manager: notes on the theatre as a cultural institution in England in the eighteenth century. SP 45 1948.

Stone, G. W. Garrick's presentation of Antony and Cleopatra. RES 13 1937.

—— A midsummer night's dream in the hands of Garrick and Colman. PMLA 54 1939.

—— Garrick and an unknown operatic version of Love's labour's lost. RES 15 1939.

—— Garrick's handling of Macbeth. SP 38 1941.

—— Garrick's production of Lear: a study in the temper of the eighteenth-century mind. SP 45 1948.

—— The god of his idolatry: Garrick's theory of acting and dramatic composition with especial reference to Shakespeare. In J. Q. Adams memorial studies, Washington 1948.

—— Garrick's significance in the history of Shakespearean criticism: a study of the impact of the actor upon the change of critical focus during the eighteenth century. PMLA 65 1950.

—— The poet and the players. Jnl of Amer Philosophical Soc 106 1962.

—— Romeo and Juliet: the source of its modern stage career. Shakespeare Quart 15 1964.

—— Garrick and Othello. PQ 45 1966.

—— Bloody, cold and complex Richard: Garrick's interpretation. In Eight essays in English literature, Pullman 1968.

Stein, E. P. Garrick, dramatist. New York 1938.

Whibley, L. Garrick's verses to Gray. TLS 12 Feb 1938.

Angus, W. An appraisal of Garrick: based mainly on contemporary sources. Quart Jnl of Speech 25 1939.

C., T. C. Garrick's Christmas tale. N & Q 30 Dec 1939.

Fischer, W. Ein unbekannter Brief Garricks an Samuel Richardson. Anglia 63 1939.

Wecter, D. Garrick and the Burkes. PQ 18 1939.

Garrick the author. TLS 18 Oct 1941.

Rosenfeld, S. Garrick and private theatricals. N & Q 25 Oct 1941. Reply by J. P. de Castro 25 April 1942.

Martz, L. L. and E. M. Some manuscripts relating to Garrick. RES 19 1943.

W[ind], E. Harlequin between tragedy and comedy. Jnl of Warburg & Courtauld Inst 6 1943. On Theatrical candidates.

Motter, T. H. V. Garrick and the private theatres, with a list of amateur performances in the eighteenth century. ELH 11 1944.

Knapp, L. M. Smollett and Garrick. In Elizabethan studies in honor of G. F. Reynolds, Boulder 1945.

Weatherley, E. H. The personal and literary relations of Charles Churchill and Garrick. In Studies in honor of A. H. R. Fairchild, Columbia Missouri 1946.

Barton, M. Garrick. 1948.

Lancaster, H. C. Garrick at the Comédie Française, June 9 1757. MLN 63 1948.

Knapp, M. E. Garrick's last command performance. In The age of Johnson: essays presented to C. B. Tinker, New Haven 1949.

—— Garrick's verses to Rockingham. PQ 29 1950.

Mann, I. R. The Garrick Jubilee at Stratford. Shakespeare Quart 1 1950.

Bergman, F. L. Garrick and the Clandestine marriage. PMLA 67 1952.

—— Garrick's Zara. PMLA 74 1959.

Price, C. Garrick and Evan Lloyd. RES new ser 3 1952.

—— Chesterfield and Garrick. TLS 23 Oct 1953.

Greene, G. Notes on an unpublished letter and on Messink. Theatre Notebook 8 1953.

Malnick, B. Garrick and the Russian theatre. MLR 50 1955.

Garrick and the London cuckolds. N & Q June 1956.

England, M. W. Garrick's Stratford Jubilee: reactions in France and Germany. Shakespeare Survey 9 1956.

—— The grass roots of bardolatry. BNYPL March 1959.

—— Garrick and Stratford. New York 1962.

—— Garrick's Jubilee. Columbus 1964.

Gerber, H. The Clandestine marriage and its Hogarthian associations. MLN 72 1957.

Wallace, A. D. Le Texier's early years in England 1775–9. In Studies in honor of John Wilcox, Detroit 1958.

Oman, C. Garrick. 1958.

Shipley, J. B. Garrick and James Ralph: remarks on a correspondence. N & Q Sept 1958.

Burnim, K. A. Garrick's quarrel with Lacy in 1745. Yale Univ Lib Gazette 33 1958.

—— The significance of Garrick's letters to Hayman. Shakespeare Quart 9 1958.

—— Garrick as director of Shakespeare's plays. Shakespeare Newsletter 9 1959.

—— David Garrick, director. Pittsburgh 1961.

—— The theatrical career of Giuseppe Galli-Bibiena. Theatre Survey 6 1965.

—— Garrick's early will. Theatre Research 7 1965.

—— Garrick, Johnson and Lichfield. New Rambler June 1966.

Mander, R. and J. Mitchenson. The Derby figure of Garrick. Theatre Notebook 13 1959.

Evans, G. B. Garrick's The fairies 1755: two editions. N & Q Nov 1959.

Sawyer, P. The Garrick-Mrs Cibber relationship. N & Q Aug 1960.

—— Garrick, Joseph Reed and Dido. Restoration & 18th-Century Theatre Research 6 1967.

Haywood, C. William Boyce's Solemn dirge in Garrick's Romeo and Juliet production of 1750. Shakespeare Quart 11 1960.

Tait, H. Garrick, Shakespeare and Wilkes. BM Quart 24 1961.

McNamara, B. The Stratford Jubilee: dram to Garrick's vanity. Educational Theatre Jnl 14 1962.

Boulton, J. T. Garrick. Burke Newsletter 4 1962.

Highfill, P. A real bill of mortality. Theatre Notebook 16 1962.

Jennings, J. Garrick and 'Nicholas Nipclose'. Educational Theatre Jnl 16 1964.

Stochholm, J. M. Garrick's folly: the Shakespeare Jubilee of 1769 at Stratford and Drury Lane. 1964.

Lloyd-Evans, G. Garrick and the 18th-century theatre. Trans of Johnson Soc Dec 1965.

Gottesman, L. Garrick's Institution of the Garter. Restoration & 18th-Century Theatre Research 6 1967.

Hafter, R. Garrick and Tristram Shandy. Stud in Eng Lit 1500–1900 7 1967.

Pentzell, R. J. Garrick's costuming. Theatre Survey 10 1969.

SAMUEL FOOTE

1720–77

Collections

The works of Samuel Foote esq. 4 vols 1786. Plays variously dated 1770–86. Also issued as Dramatic works, nd.

The dramatic works of Samuel Foote esq; to which is prefixed a life of the author. 2 vols [1797?]. Plays variously dated.

The dramatic works of Samuel Foote esq; to which is prefixed a life of the author. 2 vols 1797, 1809.

Works. 2 vols 1799.

Works, with remarks on each play and an essay on the life, genius and writings of the author by Jon Bee esq [John Badcock]. 3 vols 1830.

Dramatic works. Ed M. M. Belden, New Haven 1929.

§ 1

Genuine memoirs of Sir John Dinely Goodere, Bart who was murdered by his own brother near Bristol Jan 19

1740, by S. Foote of Worcester College, Oxford, nephew of the late Sir John D. Goodere. 1740, Worcester 1782. Foote's authorship has been doubted.

A treatise on the passions, so far as they regard the stage, with a critical enquiry into the theatrical merit of Mr G—k, Mr Q—n, and Mr B—y. [1747]. Anon.

The Roman and English comedy consider'd and compar'd, with remarks on The suspicious husband, and an examen into the merit of the present comic actors. 1747.

Taste. C DL 11 Jan 1752. 1752, 1753, Dublin 1762, London 1765, [1772], 1778, 1781; Bell (suppl 1); 1799; British Drama 5, Larpent ms (dated 1761).

The Englishman in Paris. C CG 24 March 1753. 1753, Dublin 1753, London 1763, 1765, 1778, 1783; Bell (suppl 3), British Drama 5,

The knights. C DL 9 Feb 1754. 1754, Dublin 1754, Glasgow 1758, London [1778], 1787; Bell (suppl 1), British Drama 5, Larpent ms. Based on Two knights from the Land's End, acted New Hay 1749 but not ptd.

The Englishman returned from Paris: being the sequel to the Englishman in Paris. F CG 3 Feb 1756. 1756, Dublin 1756, London [1780], 1780, 1788; Bell (suppl 3), British Drama 5.

The author. C DL 5 Feb 1757. 1757, Dublin 1757, London 1760, [c. 1760], 1778, 1782, 1794; British Drama 5, Larpent ms.

The diversions of the morning: an entertainment. DL 17 Oct 1758. Act 2 ptd by Tate Wilkinson, The wandering patentee vol 4, 1795; W. Cooke, Memoirs of Foote vol 3, 1805; and Works of Foote, ed J. Badcock vol 1, 1830. Act 1 altered from Taste, above.

The minor. C Crow Street, Dublin 28 Jan 1760, and with alterations New Hay 28 June 1760. 1760 (4 edns), Dublin 1760, Belfast 1760, London 1761, 1762, 1764, 1767, 1778, 1781, 1792; Bell (2 1797), British Drama 5, Larpent ms.

A letter from Mr Foote to the reverend author [Martin Madan] of the Remarks critical and Christian on the Minor. 1760.

Modern tragedy. Bsq DL 6 April 1761. Pbd as Tragedy a la mode in Tate Wilkinson, The wandering patentee vol 1, 1795; and as Lindamira in Thomas Matthews, Thespian gleanings, 1805. Based on William Whitehead, Fatal constancy, 1754.

The orators. C New Hay 30 Aug 1762. 1762, Dublin 1762, London 1767, 1777, 1780, 1788; Bell (suppl 4), British Drama 5.

The comic theatre: being a free translation of all the best French comedies, by Samuel Foote esq and others. 5 vols 1762. 'The first only, The young hypocrite, is to be attributed to him', Life of Foote, in Works, [1797].

The mayor of Garratt. C New Hay 20 June 1763. 1763 (no copy extant?), 1764, Dublin 1764, London 1769, Dublin 1774, London 1776, 1780, 1783, 1797; Bell (suppl 2), British Drama 5, Oxberry 9, British Drama 1824, Larpent ms.

The tryall of Samuel Foote esq for a libel on Peter Paragraph. F New Hay 18 May 1763. Pbd in Tate Wilkinson, The wandering patentee vol 4, 1795; and W. Cooke, Memoirs of Foote vol 6, 1805.

The lyar. C CG 12 Jan 1762. 1764, 1764, Dublin 1764, London 1769, 1776, 1780, 1786, Dublin 1793; Bell (suppl 2), British Drama 5, 1805, Oxberry 15, London Stage 2, Larpent ms.

The patron. C New Hay 26 June 1764. 1764, 1764, Dublin 1764, London 1774, 1780, 1781; British Drama 5.

The commissary. C New Hay 10 June 1765. 1765, 1765, Dublin 1765, London 1773, 1779, 1782; British Drama 5.

An occasional prologue in prose. New Hay 29 May 1767. Monthly Mirror 1804; in W. Cooke, Memoirs of Foote vol 3, 1805. Extracts in London Mag July 1767.

The taylors: a tragedy for warm weather. Bsq New Hay 2 July 1767. 1778 (anon); ed R. Ryan 1836. Foote disclaimed authorship, not necessarily with truth. Rev Colman, who was responsible for pbn.

The Devil upon two sticks. C New Hay 30 May 1768. 1778, 1778, Dublin 1788, London 1794; *British Drama 5*, Larpent ms.

Wilkes: an oratorio, as performed at the great room in Bishopsgate-Street, written by Mr Foote; the music by Signor Carlos Francesco Baritini. [1769]. Political burlesque of doubtful authorship. *See* M. M. Belden, Dramatic works of Foote, 1929.

The lame lover. C New Hay 22 June 1770. 1770, Dublin 1770, London 1794; *British Drama 5*, Larpent ms.

An apology for the Minor in a letter to Mr Baine. Edinburgh 1771, 1771.

The maid of Bath. C New Hay 26 June 1771. 1771 (unauthorized, copy noted by E. Green, Bibliotheca Somersetensis vol 1, Taunton 1902), 1778 (authorized), 1778, Dublin 1778, London [c. 1780]; *British Drama 5*, Larpent ms.

The nabob. C New Hay 26 June 1772. 1778, 1795; Larpent ms.

Piety in pattens. C New Hay 15 Feb 1773. Larpent ms (as The handsome housemaid); synopsis in S. Jones, Biographia dramatica vol 3, 1812.

The bankrupt. C New Hay 21 July 1773. 1776, 1776, 1782; Larpent ms.

The cozeners. C New Hay 15 July 1774. 1778, 1778, Dublin 1778, London 1795; Larpent ms.

A trip to Calais. C Unacted. 1778, 1788, 1795. Prohibited by the Lord Chamberlain on a protest from the Duchess of Kingston.

The capuchin. C New Hay 19 Aug 1776. Larpent ms. Altered from A trip to Calais, above, with which it is pbd.

§2

Memoirs of the life and writings of Samuel Foote esq, the English Aristophanes; to which are added the bon mots, repartees and good things said by that great wit and excentrical genius. [1777].

Wit for the ton! the convivial jester: or Sam Foote's last budget opened, with authentic remarks on his life and writings. 1777.

Cooke, William. Memoirs of Samuel Foote esq, containing a collection of his genuine bon mots, anecdotes, opinions etc, mostly original, and three of his dramatic pieces not published in his works. 3 vols 1805, 2 vols 1806. The 'pieces' are The diversions of the morning (1758), An occasional prelude (1767), The trial of Samuel Foote (1763).

Forster, John. In his Historical and biographical essays vol 2, 1858.

Bon mots of Foote and Theodore Hook. Ed W. Jerrold 1894.

Fitzgerald, P. Foote: a biography. 1910.

Belden, M. M. The dramatic work of Foote. New Haven 1929.

Wimsatt, W. K. Foote and a friend of Boswell's: The nabob. MLN 57 1942.

Weatherley, E. H. Foote's revenge on Churchill and Lloyd. HLQ 9 1945.

Sinko, G. Foote: the satirist of rising capitalism. Wroclaw 1950.

Comstock, H. Gainsborough's portrait of Foote. Connoisseur 128 1951.

Corner, B. C. Dr Melchisedeck Broadbrim and the playwright. Jnl of History of Medicine 7 1952.

Scouten, A. H. On the origin of Foote's matinees. Theatre Notebook 8 1953.

Berveiller, M. Anglais et français de comédie chez Louis de Boissy et Foote. Comparative Lit Stud 2 1965.

Wharton, R. V. The divided sensibility of Foote. Educational Theatre Jnl 17 1965.

Wood, C. An eighteenth-century satire on the art market. Connoisseur 163 1966.

Bogorad, S. N. Prospects for a life and works. Restoration & 18th-Century Research 6 1967.

GEORGE COLMAN the elder
1732–94

Collections

The dramatick works of George Colman. 4 vols 1777. Includes all the original plays to 1776, and adaptations except A fairy tale, Comus and Achilles in petticoats.

§1

The connoisseur. 140 nos 31 Jan 1754–30 Sept 1756. 4 vols 1757, 1793. Conducted and largely written by Colman and Bonnell Thornton.

Poems by eminent ladies. 2 vols 1755, Dublin 1757, London 1773, 1780. Ed Colman and Thornton.

A letter of abuse to D—d G—k esq. 1757. Anon.

Two odes: 1, To obscurity; 2, To oblivion. 1760. With Robert Lloyd.

Polly Honeycombe: a dramatick novel. F DL 5 Dec 1760. 1760, 1761, Dublin 1761, London 1762 ('with alterations'), 1778; *Bell (suppl 3), Edinburgh Farces 3, Dibdin 24, London Stage 2*, Larpent ms.

The jealous wife. C DL 12 Feb 1761. 1761, 1761, Dublin 1761, Oxford 1763, [1764], London 1775, Dublin 1775, London 1789, 1789, *Bell (20 1797), British Drama 4, Inchbald's Theatre 16, Dibdin 11, Oxberry 1, Cumberland 7*.

The genius. 15 essays contributed to St James's Chron 11 June 1761–9 Jan 1762.

Critical reflections on the old English dramatick writers. 1761. Also prefixed to some sets of Coxeter's Massinger, 4 vols 1761.

The musical lady. F DL 6 March 1762. 1762, Dublin 1762, London 1778; *Bell (suppl 2), Edinburgh Farces 2*, Larpent ms.

Terrae filius. 4 nos Oxford 5–8 July 1763.

Philaster, written by Beaumont and Fletcher with alterations. T DL 8 Oct 1763. 1763, Dublin 1763, London 1764, 1764, 1780.

The deuce is in him. F DL 4 Nov 1763. 1763, 1764, Dublin 1764, London 1769, 1776; *Bell (suppl 1), Edinburgh Farces 1, British Drama 5, Inchbald's Farces 6, Modern British Drama 5, British Drama 1824, London Stage 3*, Larpent ms.

A fairy tale, taken from Shakespeare. Int DL 26 Nov 1763. 1763, 1777 (altered); Larpent ms. From A midsummer night's dream via Garrick, The fairies, 1755.

The comedies of Terence translated into familiar blank verse. 1765, 1766 ('revised and corrected', with an appendix), 1802, 1810.

The clandestine marriage. C DL 20 Feb 1766. 1766 (3 edns), Dublin 1766, Edinburgh 1766, London 1770, 1778, Dublin 1788, London 1789; *Bell 15 1797; 1800; British Drama 4, Inchbald's Theatre 16, Modern British Drama 4, Dibdin 12, Oxberry 5, British Drama 1824, London Stage 1, Duncombe 40, Cumberland 7, Acting Drama, Morgan*. With Garrick. *See* the younger Colman, Posthumous papers relating to the proportionate shares of authorship to be attributed to the elder Colman and Garrick, 1820.

The English merchant. C DL 21 Feb 1767. 1767, 1767, Dublin 1767; *Inchbald's Theatre 9*.

The Oxonian in town. C CG 7 Nov 1767. 1770 (for 1769), Dublin 1679; Larpent ms.

The history of King Lear. T CG 20 Feb 1768. 1768.

A true state of the differences [between the proprietors of Covent Garden Theatre]. 1768, 1768.

An epistle to Dr Kenrick. 1768.

T. Harris dissected. 1768.

Man and wife: or the Shakespeare Jubilee. C CG 9 Oct 1769. 1770 (3 edns), Dublin 1770; Larpent ms.

The portrait: a burletta. CG 22 Nov 1770. 1770, 1770, 1772; Larpent ms as The portrait: or a painter's easel.

The fairy prince from Ben Jonson. M CG 12 Feb 1771. 1771; Larpent ms. From Jonson, Masque of Oberon, with songs by Shakespeare, Dryden and Gilbert West.

Comus, altered from Milton. M CG 16 Oct 1773. 1772, 1774, 1780; *Inchbald's Farces* 5, 1815; *Cumberland* 32.

Achilles in petticoats, written by Mr Gay with alterations. BO CG 16 Dec 1773. 1774.

The man of business. C CG 29 Jan 1774. 1774 (4 edns), Dublin 1774, London 1775; Larpent ms.

The gentleman. 6 essays in London Packet 10 July–4 Dec 1775.

An occasional prelude. CG 21 Sept 1772. 1776; Larpent ms.

The spleen: or Islington Spa. F DL 24 Feb 1776. 1776; Larpent ms.

Epicoene: or the silent woman, written by Ben Jonson with alterations. C DL 13 Jan 1776. 1776.

New brooms! an occasional prelude. DL 21 Sept 1776. 1776; Larpent ms. With Garrick.

Polly: being a sequel to the Beggar's opera written by Mr Gay with alterations. BO New Hay 19 June 1777. 1777.

The sheep shearing: a dramatic pastoral taken from Shakespeare's A winter's tale. New Hay 18 July 1777. 1777.

The Spanish barber: or the fruitless precaution. C New Hay 30 Aug 1777. Larpent ms. From Beaumarchais.

The works of Beaumont and Fletcher. 10 vols 1778. Preface by Colman.

The suicide. C New Hay 11 July 1778. Larpent ms.

Bonduca, written by Beaumont and Fletcher, with alterations. T New Hay 30 July 1778. 1778 (3 edns), 1801, 1808.

The separate maintenance. C New Hay 31 Aug 1779. Larpent ms.

The manager in distress: a prelude. New Hay 30 May 1780. [1780?], 1820; Larpent ms.

The genius of nonsense: an extravaganza. New Hay 2 Sept 1780. 1781 (songs only); Larpent ms.

Preludio to the Beggar's opera. New Hay 8 Aug 1781. Larpent ms.

Harlequin Teague: or the giant's causeway. Pant New Hay 17 Aug 1782. 1782 (songs only); Larpent ms. With John O'Keeffe.

Fatal curiosity: a true tragedy, written by George Lillo, with alterations. New Hay 29 Aug 1782. 1783.

Q. Horatii Flacci epistola de arte poetica. 1783. English version and commentary, together with Latin text.

The election of the managers: a prelude. New Hay 2 June 1784. Larpent ms.

Tit for tat: or the mutual deception. C New Hay 29 Aug 1786. 1788, 1788; Larpent ms. From Joseph Atkinson, The mutual deception, 1785, an adaptation of Marivaux, Le jeu de l'amour et du hasard.

Poems on several occasions, accompanied by some pieces in verse. 3 vols 1787. Includes all the above, together with prologues and epilogues, except the contributions to Connoisseur, Terence, the 1768 pamphlets and Horace.

Ut pictura poesis! or the enraged musicians: a musical entertainment founded on Hogarth. New Hay 18 May 1789. 1789.

Some particulars of the life of George Colman, written by himself. 1795. Chiefly concerning affairs of 1767.

Colman also pbd in 1778 six of Foote's posthumous plays.

Letters

Posthumous letters addressed to Francis Colman and George Colman the elder. Ed G. Colman the younger 1820.

Peake, R. B. Memoirs of the Colman family, including their correspondence with the most distinguished personages of their time. 2 vols 1841.

§ 2

Posthumous letters addressed to Francis Colman and George Colman the elder. Ed George Colman the younger 1820.

Peake, R. B. Memoirs of the Colman family, including their correspondence with the most distinguished personages of their time. 2 vols 1841.

Beatty, J. M. Garrick, Colman and the Clandestine marriage. MLN 36 1921.

Lynch, K. M. Pamela Nubile, L'écossaise and the English merchant. MLN 47 1932.

Page, E. R. George Colman the elder. New York 1935.

Knochen H. Der Dramatiker Colman. Göttingen 1935.

Stone, G. W. A midsummer night's dream in the hands of Garrick and Colman. PMLA 54 1939.

Vincent, H. P. Colman, 'lunatick'. RES 18 1942.

Halsband, R. A parody of Thomas Gray. PQ 22 1943.

Bergman, F. L. Garrick and the Clandestine marriage. PMLA 67 1952.

Preston, T. R. Smollett and the benevolent misanthrope type. PMLA 79 1964. On English merchant.

Scott, W. Polly Honeycomb and circulating library fiction in 1760. N & Q Dec 1968.

RICHARD CUMBERLAND
1732–1811

§ 1

An elegy written on Saint Mark's eve. 1754. Anon.

Lucani Pharsalia. 1760. Ed Cumberland.

The banishment of Cicero. T Unacted. 1761, Dublin 1741 (for 1761).

The summer's tale. CO CG 6 Dec 1765. 1765, Dublin 1766, London 1771; Larpent ms.

A letter to the Bishop of O—d, containing some animadversions upon a character of the late Dr Bentley. 1767, 1767.

Amelia. CO CG 12 April 1768. 1768, 1771 ('with alterations'). An abbreviation of Summer's tale, above.

The brothers. C CG 2 Dec 1769. 1770, Dublin 1770, London 1775, 1777, 1778, Perth 1792; *Bell 12 1797, British Drama 4, Inchbald's Theatre 18, Modern British Drama 4, Dibdin 5, British Drama 1826, London Stage 2*, Larpent ms.

The West Indian. C DL 19 Jan 1771. 1771 (several edns), Dublin 1771, London 1773, 1774, Dublin 1774, London 1775, Dublin 1775, Perth 1790, London 1792, Boston 1794; *Bell 19 1797*; Paris 1804; *British Drama 4, Inchbald's Theatre 18, Modern British Drama 4, Dibdin 2, Oxberry 1, British Drama 1826, London Stage 1, Cumberland 2, Acting Drama, Morgan*, Larpent ms; tr German, 1772; French, 1822.

Timon of Athens: a tragedy altered from Shakespear. DL 4 Dec 1771. 1771, Dublin 1772; Larpent ms.

The fashionable lover. C DL 20 Jan 1772. 1772 (3 edns), Dublin 1772, London 1774, 1781, Perth 1790; *Bell 18 1797, Dibdin 6, London Stage 2*, Larpent ms.

The note of hand; or trip to Newmarket. F DL 9 Feb 1774. 1774, Dublin 1774; Larpent ms.

The choleric man. C DL 19 Dec 1774. 1775 (3 edns), Dublin 1775; *Bell 4 1797, British Drama 4*, Larpent ms.

Odes. 1776, Dublin 1776.

Miscellaneous poems: consisting of elegies, odes, pastorals; together with Calypso: a masque. 1778.

The battle of Hastings. T. DL 24 Jan 1778. 1778, Dublin 1778; *Bell 6 1797*.

Calypso. M CG 20 March 1779. 1779, 1784, 1785; Larpent ms. Adapted from versions in Miscellaneous poems, 1778.

The widow of Delphi: or the descent of the deities. CO CG 1 Feb 1780. 1780 (songs only); Larpent ms.

The Walloons. C CG 20 April 1782. In Posthumous works vol 1, 1813; Larpent ms.

Anecdotes of eminent painters in Spain during the sixteenth and seventeenth centuries. 2 vols 1782.

A letter to Richard, Lord Bishop of Llandaff. 1783.

The mysterious husband. T CG 28 Jan 1783. 1783, Dublin 1783, London 1785; *Inchbald's Theatre 5, London Stage 3*, Larpent ms.

The Carmelite. T DL 2 Dec 1784. 1784, 1785, 1785, Dublin 1785; *Bell 16 1797, London Stage 4*, Larpent ms.

The natural son. C DL 22 Dec 1784. 1785, 1785, Dublin 1785; *Bell 20 1797, Inchbald's Theatre 5*, Larpent ms.

The Arab. T CG 8 March 1785. In Posthumous works vol 2, 1813 as Alcanor; Larpent ms.

The observer. 40 nos 1785, 5 vols 1788, 6 vols 1798 (with trn of Clouds), 1802–3; ed A. Chalmers, British essayists vols 38–40, 1817, 1823, 1856.

The character of the late Viscount Sackville. 1785.

An accurate catalogue of the paintings in the King of Spain's palace at Madrid. 1787.

Arundel: a novel. 1789, 1795.

The impostors. C DL 26 Jan 1789. 1789 (3 edns), Dublin 1789, 1790; Larpent ms.

The school for widows. C CG 8 May 1789; Larpent ms. Not pbd. Previously acted as The country attorney, New Hay 7 July 1787.

Curtius rescued from the gulph: or the retort courteous to the Rev Dr Parr. 1792.

Calvary or the death of Christ: a poem. 1792, 2 vols 1800, 1803, 1808, 1811.

The clouds of Aristophanes. [1793], 1798 (with Observer, above).

The armourer. CO CG 4 April 1793. 1793 (songs only); Larpent ms.

The box-lobby challenge. C New Hay 22 Feb 1794. [1794] (7 edns), Dublin 1794; *Inchbald's Theatre 5*, Larpent ms.

The Jew. C DL 8 May 1794. 1794, 1794 (pirated), Dublin 1794, London 1795 (3 edns), Dublin 1796, London 1797, 1797, 1801; *Inchbald's Theatre 18, London Stage 1, Cumberland 38, Acting Drama*; Larpent ms; tr German, 1798.

The wheel of fortune. C DL 28 Feb 1795. 1795 (4 edns), Dublin 1795, London 1796, Dublin 1801, London 1805; *Inchbald's Theatre 18, London Stage 1, Cumberland 14*, Larpent ms.

First love. C DL 12 May 1795. 1795, 1795, Dublin 1795, London 1796, 1799; *Inchbald's Theatre 18, London Stage 3*, Larpent ms.

The defendant. C DL 20 Oct 1795. Not pbd; Larpent ms.

Henry: a novel. 1795, 1798, 1821 (with preface by Sir Walter Scott).

The days of yore: a drama. CG 13 Jan 1796. 1796; Larpent ms.

Don Pedro: a play. New Hay 23 July 1796. In Posthumous works vol 2, 1813; Larpent ms.

The last of the family. C DL 8 May 1797. In Posthumous works vol 2, 1813; Larpent ms.

The village fete. Int CG 18 May 1797. Larpent ms. Not pbd and not certainly by Cumberland.

False impressions. C CG 23 Nov 1797. 1797, Dublin 1798; *Inchbald's Theatre 5, London Stage 4*.

The eccentric lover. C CG 30 April 1798. In Posthumous works vol 2, 1813; Larpent ms.

A word for nature. C DL 5 Dec 1798. In Posthumous works vol 1, 1813 as The passive husband; Larpent ms.

Joanna of Montfaucon: a dramatic romance. CG 16 Jan 1800. 1800, 1800, [1800] (songs only). Adapted from Maria Geisweiler's trn of Kotzebue.

A few plain reasons why we should believe in Christ. 1801, 1826 (as The Anti Carlile).

A poetical version of certain psalms of David. 1801.

Lover's resolutions. C DL 2 March 1802. In Posthumous works vol 1, 1813; Larpent ms.

The sailor's daughter. C DL 7 April 1804. 1804 (3 edns); Larpent ms.

The victory and death of Lord Viscount Nelson: a spectacle. DL 11 Nov 1805. 1805; Larpent ms. Cumberland wrote a similar piece for CG, which was interdicted.

A hint to husbands. C CG 8 March 1806. 1806 (4 edns); Larpent ms. In verse.

Memoirs of Richard Cumberland written by himself. 2 pts 1806–7, 1 vol New York 1806, 2 vols 1807; ed H. Flanders, Philadelphia 1856.

The exodiad: a poem, by the authors of Calvary and Richard the First [i.e. Sir James Bland Burgess]. 1807, 1808.

The Jew of Mogodore. CO DL 3 May 1808. 1808; Larpent ms.

The London review. 2 vols 1809. Conducted by Cumberland.

John de Lancaster: a novel. 3 vols 1809.

The widow's only son. C CG 7 June 1810. Not pbd; Larpent ms.

Retrospection: a poem in familiar verse. 1811.

The sybil, or the elder Brutus: a drama. DL 3 Dec 1818. In Posthumous works vol 1, 1813.

The posthumous dramatick works of the late Richard Cumberland. 2 vols 1813. Preface by Cumberland's daughter, Frances Marianne Jansen. Includes, in addition to those above, the following unacted pieces: vol 1, The confession, Torrendal; 2, Tiberius in Capreae, The false Demetrius.

§2

Mudford, William. The life of Richard Cumberland, embracing a critical examination of his various writings. 1812.

'Paston, George' (E. M. Symonds). In her Little memoirs of the eighteenth century, 1901.

Fehler, K. Cumberland: Leben und dramatische Werke. Erlangen 1911.

Williams, S. T. Cumberland: his life and dramatic works. New Haven 1917. With bibliography.

—— Cumberland's West Indian. MLN 35 1920.

—— The early sentimental dramas of Cumberland. MLN 36 1921.

—— The dramas of Cumberland 1779–85. MLN 36 1921.

Landa, M. J. The grandfather of melodrama. Cornhill Mag Oct 1925.

Caskey, J. H. Cumberland's mission in Spain. PQ 9 1930.

Fletcher, I. K. The Princess of Parma. TLS 15 March 1934.

Rosenfeld, S. The Princess of Parma. TLS 16 April 1938.

Todd, W. B. Press figures and book reviews as determinants of priority: a study of Hume's Douglas 1757 and Cumberland's The brothers 1770. PBSA 45 1951.

Parnell, P. E. The sentimental mask. PMLA 78 1963. Includes West Indian.

RICHARD BRINSLEY SHERIDAN

1751–1816

Bibliographies

Nettleton, G. H. In his Sheridan's major dramas, Boston 1906.

—— TLS 11 Oct 1934, 28 March 1935, 21 Dec 1935. On early edns.

Sichel, W. In his Sheridan vol 2, 1909.

Williams, I. A. In his Seven xviiith-century bibliographies, 1924.

Rhodes, R. C. In his edn of Plays and poems of Sheridan, 3 vols Oxford 1928.

—— The early editions of Sheridan: 1, The duenna; 2, The school for scandal. TLS 17–24 Sept 1925.

—— Sheridan: a study in theatrical bibliography. London Mercury Feb 1927.

— Some aspects of Sheridan bibliography. Library 3rd ser 9 1928.

Ryan, M. J. The text of the School for scandal. TLS 22–9 March 1928. *See also* subsequent correspondence.

Bateson, F. W. The text of Sheridan. TLS 28 Nov, 5 Dec 1929. *See also* subsequent correspondence.

— The text of two Sheridan plays: the Camp and the Critic. RES 16 1940.

Purdy, R. L. A gift of Sheridan manuscripts. Yale Univ Lib Gazette 22 1947.

Vincent, H. P. An attempted piracy of the Duenna. MLN 62 1947.

Shuttleworth, B. Early editions of the School for scandal. Theatre Notebook 6 1952, 8 1954.

Van Lennep, W. The Chetwynd manuscript of the School for scandal. Theatre Notebook 6 1952.

Collections

Jones's British theatre. Vol 5, Dublin 1795. Includes, with continuous pagination, School for scandal (1792), Critic (1793), Rivals (1793), A trip to Scarborough (1793). Governess (1793) is in vol 6.

The dramatic works of Sheridan. [1797], 1798 (reissue, with A short life).

Speeches of the late Right Honourable Richard Brinsley Sheridan, several corrected by himself. Ed a constitutional friend 5 vols 1816, 3 vols 1842.

The works of the late Right Honourable Richard Brinsley Sheridan. 2 vols 1821, 1 vol Leipzig 1833; ed R. G. White 2 vols New York 1883. The first authorized collection, with preface by Thomas Moore.

Dramatic works. Greenock 1828. With Observations upon his personal and literary character.

Dramatic works. Ed Leigh Hunt 1840, 1846, 1765.

Speeches. Modern Orator 1 1845.

Dramatic works. Ed G. G. S[igmond] 1848, 1889, 1902.

Works, with a memoir by J. P. Browne. 2 vols 1873, 1 vol 1873, 2 vols 1884, 1891.

Works: dramas, poems, translations, speeches and unfinished sketches. Ed F. Stainforth 1874.

Plays. Ed H. Morley 1883 etc.

Sheridan's comedies: the Rivals and the School for scandal. Ed B. Matthews, Boston 1885, New York 1904 (rev).

Plays. Ed R. Dircks [1891].

School for scandal and the Rivals. Ed A. Birrell 1896.

Plays. [Ed A. W. Pollard] 1900 etc.

Sheridan's plays now printed as he wrote them. Ed W. F. Rae 1902. Partly from ms drafts.

Plays. Ed E. Gosse 3 vols 1905.

Sheridan's major dramas. Ed G. H. Nettleton, Boston 1906. Text from Rae, above.

Sheridan's plays. Ed J. Knight, Oxford 1906.

Plays. Ed I. A. Williams 1926.

Plays. Ed C. Hamilton, New York 1926.

Plays and poems. Ed R. C. Rhodes 3 vols Oxford 1928.

§ I

The ridotto of Bath: a panegyric written by a gentleman, resident in that city, published originally in the Bath Chronicle October 10th 1771. Bath 1771; rptd in Rival beauties, Bath 1773; and in Clio's protest, 1819.

The rival beauties: a poetical contest. London and Bath 1772. Contains The Bath picture [by Miles Peter Andrews?] and Clio's protest: or the picture varnished addressed to the Lady M[a]rg[a]r[e]t F[o]rd[y]ce [by Sheridan]. Clio's protest was previously pbd as a broadside, but no copy is known.

The rival beauties: a poetical contest; to which is added the Ridotto of Bath. Bath 1773.

Clio's protest: or the picture varnished, with other poems, [including Ridotto of Bath], by the late Right Honourable R. B. Sheridan. 1819.

The love epistle of Aristaenetus, translated from the Greek into English metre. 1771, 1773 ('corrected'); rptd in Erotica, 1854 (Bohn's Classics), 1883. With Nathaniel Brassey Halhed.

A familiar epistle to the author of the Heroic epistle to Sir William Chambers, and of the heroic postscript to the public. 1774, 1774; rptd in Plays and poems, ed R. C. Rhodes vol 3, Oxford 1928. Ascribed to Sheridan in European Mag Feb 1892.

The rivals. C CG 17 Jan 1775. 1775, 1775, Dublin 1775, 1775, London 1776 ('corrected'), [1785], Dublin 1788, London 1791, Dublin 1793 (from 1st edn), 1793 (corrected), London 1798, Dublin 1802; *British Drama 4*; New York 1807; *Inchbald's Theatre 19*, *Modern British Drama 4*; Edinburgh [1814]; *Dibdin 1, Oxberry 2, Dolby 2, London Stage 1, Cumberland 2*, Larpent ms. The Larpent version, ed R. L. Purdy, Oxford 1935, is that used for the first performance; the ptd texts all derive from the rev version, first produced CG 28 Jan 1775; ed A. S. Downer, New York 1953; ed A. N. Jeffares 1967.

St Patrick's day: or the scheming Lieutenant. F CG 2 May 1775. Dublin 1788, 1789; *Cumberland 28*, Larpent ms.

The duenna. CO CG 21 Nov 1775. The songs, duets, trios etc in The duenna: or the double elopement, 1775 (at least 6 edns), 1776 (at least 6 edns), Tamworth [1776?], London 1777 (at least one edn), Dublin 1777, London 1778 (25th edn), 1780 (27th edn), 1783 (29th edn), 1801. These edns only contain the words. The music was issued separately, [1776], [1776?], [1794?].

The governess. Dublin 1777 (anon), London 1783 (as The duenna), [Dublin?] 1784, London 1785, Dublin 1785, 1786, 1786, 1788 (as The governess). This spurious text may have been the 'imitation' concocted by Tate Wilkinson (Wandering patentee vol 1; Memoirs vol 2) and acted at York as The duenna 9 April 1776. It was acted as The governess with new names for the characters at Crow St Dublin 31 Jan 1777.

The duenna: a comic opera, in three acts. 1794, Dublin 1794, [1795], New York 1808 ('second edition, from the original prompt book'); *Inchbald's Theatre 19*; Edinburgh [1814]; *Oxberry 10*; Boston 1822 (from *Oxberry*); *London Stage 1*, [1825] (Duncombe), *Cumberland 2*; Edinburgh 1828; *Dolby 2*.

The general fast: a lyric ode, with a form of prayer proper for the occasion and a dedication to the King, by the author of the Duenna. 1776; rptd in W. Sichel, Sheridan vol 1, 1909. R. C. Rhodes ascribes to the author of the parody called The duenna.

A trip to Scarborough, altered from Vanbrugh's Relapse: or virtue in danger. C DL 24 Feb 1777. 1781, Dublin 1781; *Dibdin 14*, *Dolby* ('in three acts'), *Oxberry 20*, *Cumberland 4*, Larpent ms.

The school for scandal. C DL 8 May 1777. Dublin 1780, 1781 (3 edns), 1782, 1782, Philadelphia 1782 (as The real and genuine school for scandal; *see* G. H. Nettleton, TLS 28 March 1935), London 1783 (as The real and genuine school for scandal), Dublin 1783, 1785, 1786, 1786, New York 1786, Dublin 1787, 1788, [Dublin?] 1788, Guernsey 1788, Paris 1789, Philadelphia 1789, Guernsey 1789, Dublin 1792, Boston 1792, Dublin 1793, London 1798, [1799?] ('for J. Ewing'; this edn used to be considered the first, but that has now been shown to be typographically impossible), Dublin 1799 ('taken from a correct copy'), 1800, Paris 1804, New York 1807, Dublin 1818, New York 1820, London 1823, Washington 1824; *London Stage 4*, *British Drama 1826*; Philadelphia 1827. *Cumberland 14*, 1825 (Duncombe), *Acting Drama etc*; ed G. A. Aitken 1897 (Temple Dramatists); ed R. C. Rhodes, Oxford 1930; ed J. H. Wilson, Boston 1963; ed J. Loftis, New York 1966; ed A. N. Jeffares 1967; tr German, 1782; French, 1788, 1789, 1807, 1822, 1824; Italian 1796, 1818. The pbd texts fall into 5 groups: (1) a corrupt piratical version—represented by the great majority of the early edns; on the early Dublin edns, *see* G.H. Nettleton, TLS 11 Oct 1934; (2) a less corrupt Amer version—represented by Amer edns of 1786, 1789, 1824 and 1827; *see* G.H. Nettleton, TLS 21 Dec 1935, and F.W. Bateson's reply; (3) the Dublin edn of 1799, a genuine text; (4) the acting version, represented by *London Stage, Cumberland* and *Duncombe;* (5) Sheridan's final revision—first pbd in the 1821 works and represented by the 1823 and modern edns.

The camp: a musical entertainment. DL 15 Oct 1778; 1795; *Cumberland 32,* Larpent ms. Sheridan's authorship was denied by Moore, who ascribed it to Richard Tickell. As stated by Linley in the preface to the pbd music, 1778, many of the songs were borrowed from Thomas Hull, The royal merchant, 1767.

Verses to the memory of Garrick spoken as a monody. 1779, 1779, Dublin 1780 (as The tears of genius: a monody on the death of Mr Garrick). The Airs and Chorusses in the monody on the death of Mr Garrick were also pbd separately [1779].

Sheridan also contributed prologues to William Woodfall, Sir Thomas Overbury, 1777, *and* Samuel Jackson Pratt, The fair Circassian, 1781; *see* I.A. Williams, London Mercury Aug 1924; *and epilogues to* Thomas Hull, Edward and Eleonora, 1775, George Edward Ayscough, Semiramis, 1776, Hannah More, The fatal falsehood, 1779, *and* Lady Craven, The miniature picture, 1781.

The critic: or a tragedy rehearsed. Bsq 30 Oct 1779, 1781 (engraved title-page retained in authorized edns and copied in at least 2 unauthorized edns), Dublin 1781, 1785, 1790, 1806, New York, 1807, London 1811; *Modern British Drama 5, Inchbald's Farces 3, Minor Theatre 6, Dibdin 8, English Theatre 4, Oxberry 9, London Stage 1, Cumberland 15,* Larpent ms; tr French, 1963.

Robinson Crusoe: or Harlequin Friday. Pant DL 29 Jan 1781. A short account of the situations and incidents 1781; overture, comic-tunes and song, [1781].

An ode to scandal. [Cambridge?] 1781, London 1781, 1819 (with Stanzas on fire by the late R.B. Sheridan), 1819; ed R.C. Rhodes, Oxford 1927 (ascribed to Sheridan). The Ode is possibly by George Tierney, under whose name it appeared in Bath Herald 18 June 1803. The Stanzas on fire are from Walter Chamberlain, The travellers.

The statesman. BM Add ms 25939. Extracts in W. Sichel, Sheridan vol 1, 1809, who ascribes it to Sheridan. The author was John Dent.

The legislative independence of Ireland vindicated in a speech of Mr Sheridan's on the Irish propositions in the British House of Commons. Dublin 1785.

The genuine speech of Mr Sheridan delivered in the House of Commons on a charge etc against Warren Hastings esquire, late Governor-General of Bengal, for extortion, perfidy and cruelty to the Princesses and other branches of the royal family of Oude: faithfully reported. [1787].

The speech of R.B. Sheridan in bringing forward the fourth charge [in the House of Commons] relative to the Begums of Oude. 1787, 1787 ('second edition enlarged').

The celebrated speech of Richard Brinsley Sheridan in Westminster Hall on his summing of the evidence on the Begum charge against Warren Hastings. 1788.

Speech before the High Court of Parliament in summing up the evidence on the Begum charge against Warren Hastings. 1788.

A short memoir of the life of the Right Honourable Richard Brinsley Sheridan; to which is added a report of his celebrated speech delivered in Westminster Hall. 1816.

Speeches in the trial of Warren Hastings. Ed A.E. Bond 4 vols 1859–61. From Gurney's original shorthand notes.

A comparative statement of the two bills for the better government of India brought into Parliament by Mr Fox and Mr Pitt, with explanatory observations. 1788 (4 edns). *See* John Scott, Observations upon Mr Sheridan's pamphlet intituled, Comparative statement of the two bills, 1788.

The glorious First of June: an entertainment for the benefit of the widows and orphans of the brave men who fell in the late engagement under Lord Howe. DL 2 July 1794. Larpent ms. Dialogue chiefly by James Cobb, with assistance from Sheridan. Songs by the Duke of Leeds, Lord Mulgrave, Mrs Robinson et al. Songs, duets, choruses etc, 1794.

Cape St Vincent: or British valour triumphant, altered from a dramatical performance performed in 1794 [i.e. The glorious First of June]. DL March 1797. Songs, duets, chorusses etc, 1797.

Speech in the House of Commons on the 21st of April 1798 on the motion to address his Majesty on the present alarming state of affairs. [London?] 1798.

Speech of R.B. Sheridan in the House of Commons, in reply to Mr Pitt's speech on the union with Ireland. Dublin 1799.

Pizarro: a tragedy taken from the German drama of Kotzebue adapted to the English stage. DL 24 May 1799. 1799 (at least 20 edns), Dublin 1799, 1799, Cork 1799, Philadelphia 1799, London 1800 (at least 4 edns), 1804 (27th edn), Paris 1804, London 1807, 1811, 1814, 1823, *Dolby, Oxberry 20, Cumberland 4;* 1856 (with historical notes by Charles Kean); tr German, 1800; music, [1800].

Speech of Richard Brinsley Sheridan esquire in the House of Commons in reply (December 8 1802) on the motion for the army establishment for the ensuing year. 1802, 1803.

The speech of R.B. Sheridan in the House of Commons, December 8th 1802, on the army estimates. Birmingham [1802].

The forty thieves: a grand romantic drama, in two acts, by R.B. Sheridan and Colman the younger. DL 8 April 1806. New York 1808, Philadelphia 1808, Boston 1810 (fuller text), Dublin 1814 (as Ali Baba: or the forty thieves), New York 1825; *Cumberland 27,* [*1830*] (*Duncombe*), [*1833*] (*Duncombe*). Sheridan wrote the scenario; the dialogue was by Charles Ward, rev younger Colman. The songs and the music both issued [1806].

Death of Mr Fox: an elogium delivered by Mr Sheridan at the Crown and Anchor Tavern on Thursday, September 13th 1806. Nottingham 1806.

Crazy tales, by the late Richard Brinsley Sheridan. 1825. By John Hall Stevenson. First pbd 1762.

Letters

Letters. Ed C.J.L. Price 3 vols Oxford 1966.

Sheridaniana
Parodies and Adaptations of the Plays

The duenna: a comic opera, as it is performed by his Majesty's servants. 1776, 1776, Dublin 1776, London [1777?]. Political. By Israel Pottinger?

La governante, or the duenna: a new comic opera; the poetry by Mr Badini; the music by Signor Bertoni. 1779. King's Theatre, Haymarket, 15 May 1779.

The school for scandal: a comedy. 1779. Political.

The school for scandal, as it is performed by his Majesty's servants. 1784. Political.

The critick anticipated: or the humours of the green room. 1779.

The critic, or tragedy rehearsed: a literary catchpenny. 1779.

The critic: or a tragedy rehearsed, by the author of the Duenna [Israel Pottinger?]. 1780. Political.

Pamphlets on Sheridan

An epistle from Joseph Surface esq to Richard Brinsley Sheridan. 1780.

Independence: a poem, in Hudibrastic verse addressed to Richard Brinsley Sheridan esq. 1783.

The struggles of Sheridan: or the ministry in full cry. 1790.

Account of the proceedings of a meeting of the inhabitants of Westminster in Palace-yard, Nov 26 1795. Including the substance of the speeches of the Duke of Bedford, Mr Sheridan et al 1795.

[Mathias, Thomas James]. The political dramatist in November 1795: a poem. 1795.

[Stewart, C. B.] A second letter to Mr Sheridan, with strictures on the general conduct of opposition, by a Suffolk freeholder. Bury St Edmunds 1796.

Cobbett, William. The political Proteus: a view of the public character and conduct of R. B. Sheridan. 1804.

'Patricus'. The impostor unmasked: or the new man of the people, with anecdotes illustrative of the character of Bardolph Sheridan. 1806.

Mr Fox's title to patriot disputed, and the political character of Mr Sheridan scrutinised. 1806.

An address to R. B. Sheridan on the public and private proceedings during the late election for Westminster, by the author of Mr Fox's title to patriot disputed. 1807.

Authentic memoirs of the life and death of R. B. Sheridan, with an estimate of his character and talents. 1816.

The life of R. B. Sheridan with the remarks of Pitt, Fox and Burke on his most celebrated speeches: second edition, including an account of the funeral. [1816?].

Lines on the death of —. 1816.

Concanen, Matthew. Lines supposed to be written on the death of the late R. B. Sheridan esq. [1816], 1816.

The literary bazaar, by Peter Pepperpod; with a pic-nic elegy on Richard Brinsley Sheridan. 1816.

Philips, Charles. A garland for the grave of Richard Brinsley Sheridan. [1816].

[Byron, George Gordon, Baron]. Monody on the death of the Rt Hon R. B. Sheridan, written at the request of a friend, to be spoken at Drury Lane theatre. 1816.

Gent, Thomas. Monody to the memory of Sheridan. 1816.

§ 2

Watkins, John. Memoirs of the public and private life of the Right Honourable R. B. Sheridan. 2 vols 1817, 1818 (3rd edn).

Lefanu, Alicia. Memoirs of Mrs Frances Sheridan, with remarks upon a late life [by Watkins] of R. B. Sheridan. 1824.

Moore, Thomas. Memoirs of the life of the Right Honourable Richard Brinsley Sheridan. 2 vols 1825 (also large paper, 1 vol), 1827 (5th edn, with new preface).

Sheridaniana: or anecdotes of the life of Richard Brinsley Sheridan, his table talk and bon mots. 1826.

Smyth, William. A memoir of Mr Sheridan. Leeds 1840.

[Earle, William?]. Sheridan and his times, by an octogenarian who stood by his knee in youth and sat at his table in manhood. 2 vols 1859.

Oliphant, Margaret. Sheridan. 1883 (EML).

Fitzgerald, P. Lives of the Sheridans. 2 vols 1886.

Sanders, L. C. Life of Sheridan. [1890]. With bibliography by J. P. Anderson.

Rae, W. F. Sheridan: a biography. 2 vols 1896.

Sichel, W. Sheridan, from new and original material. 2 vols 1909.

Sadleir, T. H. The political career of Sheridan. Oxford 1912.

Gabriel, M. and P. Mueschke. Two contemporary sources of Sheridan's The rivals. PMLA 43 1928.

Hinton, P. F. A Sheridan pamphlet. TLS 28 June 1928.

'Sheridan'. Sheridan: ou l'insoucieux. Paris 1930.

MacMillan, D. Sheridan's share in the Stranger. MLN 45 1930.

Butler, E. M. Sheridan: a ghost story. 1931.

F., R. The Sheridan papers. BM Quart 7 1932.

Fijn van Draat, P. Sheridan's Rivals and Ben Jonson's Every man in his humour. Neophilologus 18 1932.

Darlington, W. A. Sheridan. 1933.

Rhodes, R. C. Harlequin Sheridan: the man and the legends. Oxford 1933.

Parsons, C. Smollett's influence on Sheridan's The rivals. N & Q 21 Jan 1933.

Legouis, P. Buckingham et Sheridan: ce que le Critique doit à la Répétition. Revue Anglo-américaine 1934.

Snider, R. Satire in the comedies of Congreve, Sheridan, Wilde and Coward. Orono Maine 1937.

Foss, K. Here lies Sheridan. 1939.

Glasgow, A. Sheridan of Drury Lane. New York 1940.

Loewenberg, A. The songs in the Critic. TLS 28 March 1942.

— An uncollected poem of Sheridan. N & Q 1 Jan 1944.

Nettleton, G. H. Robinson Cruso: Sheridan's Drury Lane pantomime. TLS 25 Dec 1943, 1 Jan 1944. Further notes by S. Rosenfeld 4 March; G. H. Nettleton 15 April 1944, 23–30 June 1945.

— Sheridan's introduction to the American stage. PMLA 65 1950.

Harding, H. F. The listener on eloquence 1750–1800. In Studies in honor of A. M. Drummond, Ithaca 1944.

Moore, J. R. Sheridan's 'Little Bronze Pliny'. MLN 59 1944.

Daghlian, P. B. Sheridan's minority waiters. MLQ 6 1945.

Gibbs, L. Sheridan. 1947.

— Sheridan against Warren Hastings. Quart Jnl of Speech 34 1948. Reply by G. H. Nettleton 35 1949.

Reid, L. D. Sheridan's speech on Mrs Fitzherbert. Quart Jnl of Speech 33 1947.

Sinko, G. Sheridan and Kotzebue: a comparative essay. Wroclaw 1949.

Williams, G. W. A new source of evidence for Sheridan's authorship of the Camp and the Wonders of Derbyshire. SP 47 1950.

Van Lennep, W. The Chetwynd manuscript of the School for scandal. Theatre Notebook 6 1951.

Matlow, M. English versions of Die Spanier in Peru. MLQ 16 1955.

— Adultery analyzed: the history of the Stranger. Quart Jnl of Speech 43 1957.

— This is tragedy! the history of Pizarro. Ibid.

Price, J. B. Sheridan 1751–1816. Contemporary Rev Sept 1956.

Schiller, A. The school for scandal: the Restoration unrestored. PMLA 62 1956.

Landfield, J. B. Sheridan's maiden speech: indictment by anecdote. Quart Jnl of Speech 43 1957.

— The triumph and failure of Sheridan's speeches against Hastings. Speech Monographs 28 1961.

— Sheridan. Quart Jnl of Speech 48 1962.

Moore, J. R. Lydia Languish's library. N & Q Feb 1957.

Price, C. Hymen and Hirco: a vision. TLS 11 July 1958.

— The text of the first performance of the Duenna. PBSA 53 1959.

— The Columbia manuscript of the School for scandal. Columbia Lib Columns 11 1961.

— Another Crewe ms of the School for scandal? PBSA 57 1963.

— Sheridan's doxology. TLS 4 May 1962.

— Noverre and Sheridan 1776. Theatre Research 7 1965.

— The Larpent manuscript of St Patrick's day. HLQ 29 1966.

—— Sheridan-Linley documents. Theatre Notebook 21 1967.

Woehl, A. L. Sheridan, parliamentarian. In The historical idiom, ed D. C. Bryant, Ithaca 1958.

Sen, S. K. Sheridan's literary debt: the Rivals and Humphry Clinker. MLQ 21 1960.

Sherwin, O. Uncorking old sherry: the life and times of Sheridan. New York 1960.

Sheridan, Elizabeth. Betsy Sheridan's journal: letters from Sheridan's sister 1748–86 and 1786–90. Ed W. L. Fanu 1960.

Trainer, J. Tieck's translation of the Rivals. MLQ 21 1960.

Jackson, J. R. de J. The importance of witty dialogue in the School for scandal. MLN 76 1961.

Donaldson, I. New papers of Henry Holland and Sheridan: 1, Holland's Drury Lane 1794; 2, The Hyde Park Corner operas and the dormant patent. Theatre Notebook 16 1962.

Deelman, C. The original cast of the School for scandal. RES new ser 13 1962.

Delpech, J. Sheridan, le Beaumarchais anglais. Nouvelles Littéraires 17 May 1962.

Dulck, J. Les comédies de Sheridan. Paris 1962.

Skinner, Q. Sheridan and Whitbread at Drury Lane 1809–15. Theatre Notebook 17 1963.

Nussbaum, R. D. Poetry and music in The duenna. Westerley no 1 1963.

Pryce-Jones, A. The school for scandal. Theatre Arts 47 1963.

Sprague, A. C. In defense of a masterpiece: the School for scandal re-examined. In English studies today: 3rd series, Edinburgh 1964.

Phare, E. E. Lydia Languish, Lydia Bennet and Dr Fordyce's sermons. N & Q May 1964. See also F. W. Bradbrook, Nov 1964.

Mahoney, J. L. Sheridan on Hastings: the classical oration and eighteenth-century politics. Burke Newsletter 6 1965.

Oliver, A. and J. Saunders. De Loutherbourg and Pizarro 1799. Theatre Notebook 20 1965.

Tillett, J. (ed). Shakespeare, Sheridan, Shaw. 1965.

Rodway, A. Goldsmith and Sheridan: satirists of sentiment. In Renaissance and modern essays, ed G. R. Hibbard 1966.

Lutaud, O. Des acharniens d'Aristophane au Critique de Sheridan. Les Langues Modernes 60 1966.

Tucker, S. I. Notes on Sheridan's vocabulary. N & Q May 1967.

Price, C. J. L. The completion of the School for scandal. TLS 28 Dec 1967.

VIII. MINOR DRAMA 1750–1800

This section is restricted to writers, with one or two exceptions, who were born between 1715 and 1765. Italicized abbreviations have been employed for the principal contemporary collections of plays (e.g. Bell etc); the full titles will be found on col 701, above. The note Larpent ms means that the ms submitted to the licenser for the original English production is now in the Larpent Collection at the Huntington Library, California. A key to the abbreviations used (C, CO etc) will be found on col 741, above. No attempt has been made to record edns of songs and music of comic operas, pantomimes etc, except in cases where the whole play has not been pbd. Acted plays have been arranged in the chronological order of production.

MILES PETER ANDREWS
d. 1814

§ 1

The conjuror. F DL 29 April 1774. Larpent ms.

A new musical interlude called the Election. DL 21 Oct 1774. 1774, 1780; Larpent ms.

Belphegor: or the wishes. CO DL 16 March 1778. Dublin 1788; Larpent ms.

Summer amusement: or an adventure at Margate. CO New Hay 1 July 1779. 1780 (songs only), 1780 (songs only), 1781; Larpent ms. With W. A. Miles.

Fire and water! Co New Hay 8 July 1780. 1780; Larpent ms.

Dissipation. C DL 10 March 1781. 1781, 1781; Larpent ms.

The Baron Kinkvervankotsdorsprakingatchdern: a new musical comedy. New Hay 9 July 1781. 1781; Larpent ms.

The best bidder. F DL 11 Dec 1782; Larpent ms.

The reparation. C DL 14 Feb 1784. 1784, 1784; Larpent ms.

The enchanted castle. Pant CG 26 Dec 1786. 1786 (songs only).

For Better late than never, 1790, *and* The mysteries of the castle, 1795, *see under Frederick Reynolds, col 857, below.*

§ 2

Rosenfeld, S. A Della Cruscan poet. N & Q 6 Dec 1952.

RICHARD BENTLEY the younger
1708–82

A full and true account of the dreadful and melancholy earthquake which happened on Thursday the fifth instant, with an exact list of such persons as have hitherto been found in the rubbish. 1750 (6th–7th edns); 1887 (Aungervyle Soc). Signed P.D. Also attributed to Paul Whitehead. A second letter, 1750.

A petition to the Right Hon Mr — [Henry Pelham] in favour of Mr Maclean, by a lady. 1750.

An attempt towards an apology for the R— H— the D— [of Cumberland]. 1751. Anon.

A true and faithful account of the greatest wonder produced by nature, Mr Manpferdt, the surprizing centaur. 1751. Anon.

Designs by Mr Richard Bentley for six poems by Mr T. Gray. Strawberry Hill 1753. Drawings.

A journey into England, by Paul Hentzner, in the year mdxcviii. Strawberry Hill 1757. Tr Bentley.

The wishes: or Harlequin's mouth open'd. C DL 27 July 1761. Larpent ms.

Patriotism: a mock-heroic in five cantos. 1763 (anon), 1765 ('in six cantos').

Philodamus. T CG 14 Dec 1782. 1767.

The prophet. CO CG 15 Dec 1788. 1788 (songs only).

A letter to the Rt Hon Charles James Fox. 1793. Anon.

ISAAC BICKERSTAFFE
d. 1812?

§ 1

Leucothoe: a dramatic poem. 1756.

Thomas and Sally, or the sailor's return: a musical entertainment. CG 28 Nov 1760. 1761, 1765 (3rd edn), Dublin 1767, Belfast 1767, London 1780 ('with alterations'); *Edinburgh Farces 2, London Stage 4, Acting Drama.*

Love in a village. CO CG 8 Dec 1762. 1763 (7 edns), Dublin 1763, London 1764 (10th edn), 1765, 1767, 1776, [1780], 1787, Dublin 1791; *Bell 12 1797;* Manchester 1799; *British Drama 5, Inchbald's Theatre 17, Modern British Drama 5, Dibdin 3, Oxberry 2;* 1821 (with preface by Elliston); *Duncombe 1, Dolby 5, Cumberland 5, British Drama 1826, Acting Drama.*

The maid of the mill. CO CG 31 Jan 1765. 1765 (6 edns), Dublin 1765, London 1783, Dublin 1791; *Bell 8 1791–7;* 1798; *British Drama 5, Inchbald's Theatre 17, Modern British Drama 5, Dibdin 5, Oxberry 2, Cumberland 8, London Stage 1.*

Daphne and Amintor. CO DL 8 Oct 1765. 1765 (5 edns), 1766, 1788; *Edinburgh Farces 5.* Altered from The oracle of St Foix and Mrs Cibber.

The plain dealer, with alterations from Wycherley. C DL 7 Dec 1765. 1766, 1767; *Bell 23 1797, British Drama 3,* Larpent ms.

Love in the city. CO CG 21 Feb 1767. 1767, 1767, Dublin 1767.

Lionel and Clarissa. CO CG 25 Feb 1768. 1748 (for 1768), 1768 (3rd edn), Dublin 1769, London 1770, Dublin 1770, 1774; *Bell 21 1797, Inchbald's Theatre 17, Dibdin 7, Oxberry 2, London Stage 1, British Drama 1826, Acting Drama,* Larpent ms.

The absent man. F DL 21 March 1768. 1768, Dublin 1768; *Edinburgh Farces 6,* Larpent ms.

The padlock. CO DL 3 Oct 1768. 1768 (3 edns), 1769, Dublin 1770 ('with alterations'); *Edinburgh Farces 3, Bell suppl 3, British Drama 5, Modern British Drama 5, Cawthorn 4, Dibdin 12, Inchbald's Farces 4, Cumberland 3, London Stage 1, British Drama 1824,* Larpent ms; tr French, 1822.

The royal garland: a new occasional interlude in honour of his Danish Majesty. CG 10 Oct 1768. 1768, Larpent ms (as An occasional interlude: or the King of Denmark when in England).

The hypocrite taken from Molière and Cibber. C DL 17 Nov 1768. 1769, 1769, Dublin 1769; *Bell 21 1797, Dibdin 9, Oxberry 1, British Drama 1824, London Stage 1, Cumberland 3, Acting Drama.* Based on Colley Cibber, The nonjuror.

Dr Last in his chariot. C New Hay 21 June 1769. 1769 (misprinted mdccxvix), Dublin 1769; *British Drama 5.* One scene by Samuel Foote.

The captive. CO New Hay 21 June 1769. 1769.

The Ephesian matron, or the widow's tears: a comic serenata after the manner of the Italian. New Hay 31 Aug 1769. 1769, 1786; *Edinburgh Farces 6.*

The life and adventures of Ambrose Gwinnett, written by himself. 1770 (anon), [1771], [1775], [1780], [1800]. Ascribed to Bickerstaff on the slight evidence of a note in BM copy of 1st edn.

The school for fathers. CO DL 8 Feb 1770. 1770, 1773. Altered from Lionel and Clarissa, above.

Tis well it's no worse. C DL 24 Nov 1770. 1770; Larpent ms.

The recruiting serjeant: a musical entertainment. DL 1770. 1770, 1787; *Edinburgh Farces 6, Dibdin 18, London Stage 3, British Drama 1824;* New York 1824.

He wou'd if he cou'd, or an old fool worse than any: a burletta. DL 12 April 1771. 1771; *Edinburgh Farces 5.*

The sultan: or a peep into the seraglio. F DL 12 Dec 1775. 1787, 1787; *Edinburgh Farces 1, Bell suppl 1, Minor Theatre 3, Inchbald's Farces 3, Dibdin 25, London Stage 3,* Larpent ms.

The spoiled child. F DL 22 March 1790. Dublin 1792, 1795, 1799, London [1800]; *Cumberland 14,* Larpent ms. Assigned to 'the exile Bickerstaff' on very conjectural reasoning by James Boaden, but ascribed at the time to Mrs Jordan. Other attributions are Sir Richard Ford, Prince Hoare and Mrs Inchbald.

§ 2

Guiet, R. An English imitator of Favart: Bickerstaffe. MLN 38 1923.

Macmillan, E. The plays of Bickerstaffe in America. PQ 5 1926.

Emerson, E. H. The date of Bickerstaffe's death. N & Q 8 Nov 1952.

Eddy, D. O. John Hawkesworth: book reviewer in the Gentleman's Magazine. PQ 43 1964. Review of 'Tis well if's no worse.

HANNAH BRAND
d. 1821

Plays and poems. Norwich 1798. The plays are 3 tragedies: (1) Adelinda (unacted); (2) The conflict: or love, honour and pride (unacted); (3) Huniades: or the siege of Belgrade, King's Hay 18 Jan 1792. Larpent ms of Huniades, also of last scene when altered as Agmunda, King's Hay 2 Feb 1792.

FRANCES BROOKE
1724–89

See col 000, below.

JOHN BROWN
1715–66

Bibliographies

Roberts, S. C. Some uncollected authors xxiv: 'Estimate' Brown. Book Collector 9 1960.

—— Bibliography of 'Estimate' Brown. Book Collector 10 1961.

Collections

Works of the British poets vol 10. [Ed R. Anderson], Edinburgh 1794.

§ 1

Honour: a poem. 1743; rptd in Dodsley's Collection vol 3, 1748.

An essay on satire occasion'd by the death of Mr Pope. 1745, 1749; rptd in Dodsley's Collection vol 3, 1748, and Warburton's edn of Pope, 1751.

On liberty: a poem. 1749.

Essays on the Characteristics [of Shaftesbury]. 1751, 1752, Dublin 1752, London 1755 (4th edn), 1764.

Barbarossa. T DL 17 Dec 1754. 1755, 1755, Dublin [1755?], 1757, London [1760?] (4th edn), 1770, 1770, 1777; *Bell 10 1777, Brtiish Drama 2, Inchbald's Theatre 15, London Stage 2, Cumberland 17,* Larpent ms.

Athelstan. T DL 27 Feb 1756. 1756; Larpent ms.

An estimate of the manners and principles of the times. 1757 (6 edns), 1758 (7th edn), Boston 1758; tr French, 1758; vol 2, 1758.

An explanatory defence of the Estimate. 1758.

An additional dialogue of the dead between Pericles and Aristides: being a sequel to [Lyttleton's] Dialogue between Pericles and Cosmo. 1760, 1760.

The cure of Saul: a sacred ode. 1763, 1767.

A dissertation on the rise, union and power, the progressions, separations and corruptions, of poetry and music; to which is prefixed the Cure of Saul. 1763, Dublin 1764; tr French, 1768; German, 1769; Italian, 1772.

The history of the rise and progress of poetry, through its several species. Newcastle 1764. A recast of the Dissertation 'for the sake of such classical readers as are not particularly conversant with music'.

Sermons on various subjects. 1764.

Thoughts on civil liberty, on licentiousness and faction. Newcastle 1765, London 1765.

A letter to the rev Dr Lowth, occasioned by his late letter to the author [Warburton] of the Divine legation of Moses. Newcastle 1766 (4 edns).

Brown also pbd a number of sermons.

§ 2

Flasdieck, H. M. Brown und seine Dissertation on poetry and music. Halle 1924.

Templeman, W. D. Warburton and Brown continue the battle over ridicule. HLQ 17 1953.

JOHN BURGOYNE
1722-92
Collections

Jones's British theatre. 10 vols Dublin 1795-8. Contains The lord of the manor, The heiress, The maid of the oaks and Richard Coeur de Lion—each with separate title-page dated 1794.

The dramatic and poetical works; to which is prefixed memoirs of the author. 2 vols 1808.

§ 1

The maid of the oaks: a new dramatic entertainment. DL 5 Nov 1774. 1774, 1774, 1775. 1777, 1778; *Edinburgh Farces 6, Inchbald's Farces 6, London Stage 3, Acting Drama,* Larpent ms; tr German, 1776.

The substance of General Burgoyne's speeches, with an appendix containing General Washington's letter to General Burgoyne. 1778 (3 edns).

A letter from Lieut Gen Burgoyne to his constituents upon his late resignation. 1779 (5 edns).

The state of the expedition from Canada as laid before the House of Commons. 1780, 1780.

A supplement to the state of the expedition from Canada, containing General Burgoyne's orders respecting the siege of Ticonderoga. 1780, New York 1865.

The lord of the manor. CO DL 27 Dec 1780. 1781 (anon), Dublin 1781; *Dibdin 11, London Stage 2, Cumberland 13,* Larpent ms.

The heiress. C DL 14 Jan 1786. 1786 (7 edns), Dublin 1786, London 1787 (5 edns), Dublin 1801; *Inchbald's Theatre 22, London Stage 3,* Larpent ms; tr German, 1788; French, 1822.

Fonblanque, E. B. de. Political and military episodes derived from the life and correspondence of Burgoyne. 1786.

Richard Coeur de Lion: an historical romance from the French of Sedaine. DL 24 Oct 1786. 1786 (3 edns), [1789] (8th edn), 1804, 1806; *Minor Theatre 5, Inchbald's Farces 6, Dibdin 4,* Larpent ms. With help from Mrs Sheridan.

The orderly book of Lieut General John Burgoyne from his entry in the State of New York until his surrender at Saratoga. Ed E. B. O'Callaghan, New York 1860.

§ 2

Hudleston, F. J. Gentleman Johnny Burgoyne. Garden City NY 1927.

GEORGE SAVILE CAREY
1743-1807

The inoculator: a comedy. 1766, 1766 (as The flights of fancy).

CATHERINE CLIVE
1711-85

§ 1

The case of Mrs Clive submitted to the publick. 1744.

The rehearsal: or Bays in petticoats. Bsq. DL 15 March 1750. 1753.

Every woman in her humour. F DL 20 March 1760. Larpent ms.

The island of slaves. F DL 26 March 1761. Larpent ms. This trn from Marivaux is not certainly by Mrs Clive.

The sketch of a fine lady's return from a rout. F DL 21 March 1763. Larpent ms.

The faithful Irishwoman. F DL 18 March 1765. Larpent ms.

§ 2

Fitzgerald, P. Life of Mrs Catherine Clive. 1888.

Crean, P. J. N & Q 30 April 1938.

JAMES COBB
1756-1818

Hurly burly: or the fairy of the well. Pant DL 1785. [1785]; Larpent ms. With Thomas King.

The strangers at home. CO DL 8 Dec 1785. 1786, 1786, Dublin 1786, 1787; Larpent ms.

The first floor. F DL 13 Jan 1787. 1787 (3 edns), Dublin 1787, London 1789; *Inchbald's Farces 6, British Drama 2 1824, London Stage 3, Cumberland 41,* Larpent ms; tr German, 1792.

English readings: a comic piece. New Hay 7 Aug 1787. 1787, Dublin 1788; Larpent ms.

Love in the East: or adventures of twelve hours. CO DL 25 Feb 1788. 1788, 1788, Dublin 1788, [Dublin 1789].

The doctor and the apothecary: a musical entertainment. DL 25 Oct 1788. 1788, 1792; *Inchbald's Farces 6, British Drama 1 1824, London Stage 2.*

The haunted tower. CO DL 24 Nov 1789. [Dublin 1790] (pirated), London 1793, [1796], 1819, 1824; *London Stage 2, Duncombe 9, Cumberland 30,* Larpent ms.

The siege of Belgrade. CO DL 1 Jan 1791. [Dublin 1792] (pirated), London [1815], 1818; *London Stage 4, Cumberland 20, Acting Drama,* Larpent ms.

The pirates. CO King's Hay 21 Nov 1792. 1792 (songs only); Larpent ms.

The Cherokee. CO DL 20 Dec 1794. 1795 (pirated); Larpent ms.

Ramah Droog. CO CG 12 Nov 1798. 1800; *Inchbald's Modern Theatre 6,* Larpent ms.

Paul and Virginia: a musical entertainment. CG 1 May 1800. [Dublin 1800] (pirated); *London Stage 4, Cumberland 20.*

8 early short pieces, unpbd, are preserved among the Larpent mss. For Cobb's later plays, mainly comic operas, see Nicoll, Early nineteenth-century drama vol 2, Cambridge 1930.

GEORGE COLMAN the younger
1762-1836
Collections

Dramatic works, with an original life of the author by J. W. Lake. 4 vols Paris 1827.

§ 1

Two to one. CO New Hay 19 June 1784. Dublin 1785;
Larpent ms (dated 1783).
A Turk and no Turk. CO New Hay 9 July 1785. 1785
(songs only); Larpent ms.
Inkle and Yarico. CO New Hay 4 Aug 1787. [1787], 1788,
Dublin 1788, London 1789, Dublin 1789, London 1792,
1806, New York 1806, Dublin 1807; *Inchbald's Theatre
20, Cumberland 16*, Larpent ms.
Ways and means: or a trip to Dover. C New Hay 16 July
1788. 1788, 1788, Dublin 1788, London 1805, 1806;
Inchbald's Farces 7, British Drama 1824, London Stage 3.
The battle of Hexham. C New Hay 11 Aug 1789. 1790
(pirated text), Dublin 1790, London 1808 (authorized
text); *Inchbald's Theatre 20, Cumberland 37*, Larpent ms.
The surrender of Calais: a play. New Hay 30 July 1791.
Dublin 1792 (pirated), London 1808 (authorized);
Inchbald's Theatre 20, Larpent ms.
Poor old Haymarket, or two sides of the gutter: a prelude.
New Hay 15 June 1792. 1792; Larpent ms.
The mountaineers: a play. New Hay 3 Aug 1793. 1794
(pirated), Dublin 1794, London 1795 (authorized, 3
edns), 1802, 1805, Dublin 1806, 1808; *Inchbald's
Theatre 21, Duncombe 37, Cumberland 35*, Larpent ms.
New Hay at the old market: an occasional drama. New
Hay 9 June 1795. 1795, 1808 (altered, as Sulvester
Daggerwood); *Duncombe 1, Cumberland 26*, Larpent ms.
The iron chest: a play. DL 12 March 1796. 1796 ('with
a preface', attacking J. P. Kemble), 1796 ('with a preface
and a postscript'), 1796 (without preface or postscript),
Dublin 1796, London 1798, 1808; *Inchbald's Theatre 21,
Duncombe 37, Cumberland 35*, Larpent ms; ed M. A.
Booth, Oxford 1965 (WC) (in Eighteenth-century
tragedy).
My night-gown and slippers or talks in verse. 1797;
Larpent ms. Recited DL 28 April 1797.
The heir at law. C New Hay 15 July 1797. Dublin 1800
(pirated), 1806, London 1808 (authorized); *Inchbald's
Theatre 21, Cumberland 38*, Larpent ms.
Blue Beard: or female curiosity! a dramatick romance.
DL 16 Jan 1798. 1798 (4 edns), Dublin 1798, London
1799, [1800], New York 1803, 1806, London 1808, 1811;
Cumberland 36, Larpent ms.
Blue devils. F CG 24 April 1798. 1808, 1811; *Oxberry 15,
Cumberland 39*, Larpent ms.
Feudal times, or the banquet-gallery: a drama. DL 19 Jan
1799. [1799], Dublin [1799], London 1808; Larpent ms.
The review: or the wags of Windsor. CO New Hay 2 Sept
1800. Dublin 1801 ('by Arthur Griffinhoofe'), New
York 1804, London 1808; *Oxberry 13, Cumberland 36,
Duncombe 53*, Larpent ms.
The poor gentleman. C CG 11 Feb 1801, 1802, 1804,
1806, Dublin 1806; *Inchbald's Theatre 21, Duncombe 39,
Cumberland 37*, Larpent ms.
Broad grins: comprising with additional tales those pub-
lished under the title of My nightgown and slippers.
1802, 1804, 1807, 1811 (5th edn), 1819 (7th edn), 1839.
Broad grins, my night-gown and slippers and other
humorous works, with life and anecdotes of the author.
Ed G. B. Buckstone [1872].
John Bull: or the Englishman's fireside. C CG 5 March
1803. Dublin 1803 (pirated), London 1805 (authorized);
Inchbald's Theatre 21, Duncombe 37, Cumberland 36,
Larpent ms; tr French, 1803.
Love laughs at locksmiths: an operatic farce. New Hay 25
July 1803. 1803 ('by Arthur Griffinhoofe'; pirated),
Dublin 1803, London 1808 (authorized); *Oxberry 13,
Cumberland 39*, Larpent ms.
The gay deceivers, or more laugh than love: an operatic
farce. New Hay 22 Aug 1804. 1808 ('by Arthur
Griffinhoof'); Larpent ms.
Who wants a guinea? C CG 18 April 1805. 1805, 1805;
Inchbald's Theatre 3, Cumberland 20, Larpent ms.

We fly by night or long stories: an opera farce. CG 25 Jan
1806. 1806 ('by Arthur Griffinhoofe'); Larpent ms.
The forty thieves. *See under Sheridan, col 820, above*.
The Africans, or love, war and duty: a musical drama.
New Hay 29 July 1808. 1808; *Cumberland 43*, Larpent
ms.
XYZ. F CG 11 Dec 1810. 1820; *Cumberland 25*, Larpent
ms.
The quadrupeds of Quedlinburgh: or the rovers of
Weimar. Bsq New Hay 26 July 1811. Larpent ms.
Palmer, John, Like master like man: a novel. 2 vols 1811.
Preface by Colman.
Poetical vagaries. 1812, 1814 (with Vagaries vindicated),
1818.
Vagaries vindicated: or hypocritick hypercriticks. 1813,
1814 (with Poetical vagaries). A reply to the Quart Rev
notice, 8 1812. Reply Quart Rev 9 1813.
Doctor Hocus Pocus, or Harlequin wash'd white: a pre-
lude. New Hay 12 Aug 1814. Larpent ms.
Eccentricities for Edinburgh. Edinburgh [1816].
The actor of all work: or first and second floor. F New
Hay 13 Aug 1817. Larpent ms.
Posthumous papers relative to the proportionate shares of
authorship [of the Clandestine marriage] to be attributed
to the elder Colman and Garrick. 1820.
The law of Java: a musical drama. CG 11 May 1822.
1822; Larpent ms.
Stella and Leatherlungs: or a star and a stroller. Int DL 1
Oct 1873. Larpent ms.
Random records. 2 vols 1830. An autobiography to c.
1790. The Circle of anecdote and wit, by George
Coleman esq, 1821 *etc is disclaimed by Colman in the*
Advertisement *to* Random records vol 1.

Letters

Posthumous letters addressed to Francis Colman and
George Colman the elder, with annotations by George
Colman the younger. 1820.

§ 2

Peake, R. B. Memoirs of the Colman family. 2 vols 1841.
With list of Colman's plays.
Vincent, H. P. Colman the younger: adopted son. PQ 15
1936.
Bagster-Collins, J. F. Colman the younger. New York
1946.
Parsons, C. O. Francis and Mary Colman: biographical
glimpses 1690–1776. N & Q 12, 26 July 1947.

HANNAH COWLEY
1743–1809
Bibliographies

Norton, J. E. Some uncollected authors: Cowley. Book
Collector 7 1958. *See* W. B. Todd, ibid.

Collections

Works of Mrs Cowley: poems and dramas. 3 vols 1813.
With life. Includes all the pbd plays.

§ 1

The runaway. C DL 15 Feb 1776. 1776, 1776; Larpent
ms.
Who's the dupe? F DL 10 April 1779. 1779, 1779, 1780,
1812; *Minor Theatre 4, Inchbald's Farces 1, Oxberry 2,
London Stage 1, British Drama 1826*, Larpent ms.
Albina, Countess Raymond. T New Hay 31 July 1779.
1779, 1779, Dublin 1779, London 1780 (4th edn); *Bell
29 1797;* 1812; Larpent ms.
The belle's stratagem. C CG 22 Feb 1780. Dublin 1781,
1781, London 1782, Dublin 1783, London 1787, 1806,

1812; *Inchbald's Theatre 19, Dibdin 4, Oxberry 6, British Drama 1824, Cumberland 2,* Larpent ms; ed T. H. Lacy 1867 (from incomplete ms).

The school for eloquence. Int DL 4 April 1780. Larpent ms.

The maid of Arragon: a tale. Pt 1, 1780. Verse.

The world as it goes: or a party at Montpellier. C CG 24 Feb 1781. Larpent ms.

Which is the man? C CG 9 Feb 1782. 1782, 1783, 1783, 1784, 1785, 1812; *Inchbald's Theatre 10, Dibdin 23, London Stage 2,* Larpent ms.

A bold stroke for a husband. C CG 25 Feb 1783. 1784 (5 edns), 1812; *Inchbald's Theatre 19, London Stage 3, Cumberland 36,* Larpent ms.

More ways than one. C CG 6 Dec 1783. 1784 (3 edns), Dublin 1784.

A school for greybeards: or the mourning bride. C DL 25 Nov 1786. 1786, 1787, Dublin 1787; Larpent ms.

The Scottish village or Pitcairne Green. 1786. Verse.

The poetry of Anna Matilda. 1788. Verse.

The fate of Sparta: or the rival kings. T DL 31 Jan 1788. 1788, 1788, Dublin 1788; Larpent ms.

A day in Turkey: or the Russian slaves. CO CG 3 Dec 1791. 1792 (4 edns); Larpent ms; tr German, 1788.

Edwina. In William Hutchinson, History of Cumberland vol 2, Carlisle 1794. Verse.

The town before you. C CG 6 Dec 1794. 1795, 1795, Dublin 1799; Larpent ms (as The town as it is).

The siege of Acre: an epic poem. 1801 (6 bks), 1810 (4 bks). First pbd in 4 bks in Annual Register 1799.

See also under the Della Cruscans, col 698, above.

§ 2

Rhodes, R. C. The belle's stratagem. RES 5 1929.

JOSEPH CRADOCK
1742–1826

Collections

Literary and miscellaneous memoirs. Ed J. B. Nichols 4 vols 1828. Includes all the items listed below.

§ 1

Letters from Snowdon, descriptive of a tour through the northern counties of Wales. 1770 (anon), Dublin 1770, London 1777 (enlarged).

Zobeide. T CG 11 Dec 1771. 1771, 1772, Dublin 1772.

The life of John Wilkes esq in the manner of Plutarch. 1773. Anon.

Village memoirs, in a series of letters between a clergyman and his family in the country. 1774 (anon), Dublin 1775.

An account of some of the most romantic parts of North Wales. 1777; tr German, 1781.

Four dissertations: moral and religious. 1815.

Fidelia. 1821.

The Czar: an historical tragedy. Unacted. 1824.

Literary and miscellaneous memoirs. 2 vols 1826.

§ 2

Dobson, A. Mr Cradock of Gumley. In his Old Kensington Palace and other papers, 1910.

ELIZABETH, BARONESS CRAVEN,
later MARGRAVINE of ANSPACH
1750–1828

§ 1

The sleep-walker, translated from the French. C Newbury. Strawberry Hill 1778.

Modern anecdotes of the ancient family of Kinkvervankotsdarsprakengotchderns: a tale for Christmas. [1779] (anon), 1781, 1781.

The miniature picture. C DL 24 May 1780. 1781. Anon.

The silver tankard: or the point at Portsmouth. F New Hay 18 July 1781. Larpent ms.

A journey through the Crimea to Constantinople. 1789, 1789; tr German, 1789.

Le philosophe moderne. C Unacted. 1790.

The Princess of Georgia. CO Brandenburg House. 1798 (songs only, priv ptd).

Love rewarded. Past Unacted. [1799]. Italian and English.

The soldier of Dierenstein, or love and mercy: an Austrian story. Newbury 1802.

Letters from Lady Craven to the Margrave of Anspach in 1785 and 1786. 1814 (2nd enlarged edn).

Memoirs of the Margravine of Anspach, written by herself. 2 vols 1826; ed A. M. Broadley and L. Melville 2 vols 1914 (with detailed introd).

Also 7 pieces priv acted, which have not survived.

§ 2

'Paston, George' (E. M. Symonds). In her Little memoirs of the eighteenth century, 1901.

Ley, H. Die litterarische Tätigkeit der Lady Craven. Erlangen 1904.

JOHN DELAP
1725–1812

Marcellus: a monody. 1751.

Elegies. 1760.

Hecuba. T DL 11 Dec 1761. 1762 (anon), Dublin 1762, 1782; Larpent ms.

The royal suppliants. T DL 17 Feb 1781. 1781 (3 edns); Larpent ms.

The captives. T DL 9 March 1786. 1786 (anon); Larpent ms.

Dramatic poems, comprising the following tragedies: Grinilda, Usurper, Matilda and Abdalla. Lewes 1803.

Elegy on the death of the Duke of Rutland. 1788.

CHARLES DIBDIN
1745–1814

§ 1

For a complete list of plays etc, see E. R. Dibdin, A Dibdin bibliography, Liverpool 1937 *(priv ptd), which describes unpbd as well as all the pbd works.*

The shepherd's artifice: a dramatic pastoral. CG 21 May 1764. 1765; Larpent ms.

The deserter: a new musical drama. DL 2 Nov 1773. 1773, 1773, Dublin 1775, London 1776, Dublin 1789; *Bell 4 1784, Inchbald's Farces 2, Oxberry 11, London Stage 1,* Larpent ms.

The waterman: or the First of August. BO New Hay 8 Aug 1774. 1774 (anon), 1776, 1777, 1783, Dublin 1785; *Inchbald's Farces 7, London Stage 4, Duncombe 5, Cumberland 23,* Larpent ms.

The cobler: or a wife of ten thousand. BO DL 9 Dec 1774. 1774, Dublin 1775, 1776.

The Quaker. CO DL 7 Oct 1777. 1777 (anon), 1778, 1780, Belfast 1782, London 1784 (5th edn), 1787; *Dibdin 2, Inchbald's Farces 4, Oxberry 11, British Drama 1;* 1824; *London Stage 1, Cumberland 37.*

Poor Vulcan. Bsq CG 4 Feb 1778. 1778, 1778, Belfast 1784, [Dublin 1789] (as by O'Keefe); Larpent ms.

The Chelsea pensioner. CO CG 6 May 1779. 1779 (anon), 1779 (anon), Dublin 1779; Larpent ms.

The harvest-home. CO New Hay 16 May 1787. 1787, Dublin 1788; Larpent ms.

The musical tour. Sheffield 1788.

The bystander: or universal weekly expositor. 22 nos 15 Aug 1789–6 Feb 1790.

Hannah Hewit; or the female Crusoe. 3 vols (1792). Anon.

The younger brother: a novel. 3 vols 1793.

How do you do? 8 nos 30 July–5 Nov 1796. With F. G. Waldron.

A complete history of the English stage. 5 vols [1800].

Observations on a tour through Scotland and England. 2 vols [1801–2].

The professional life of Mr Dibdin, written by himself; together with the words of six hundred songs. 4 vols 1803, 6 vols 1809 (800 songs).

§ 2

Kitchener, W. A brief memoir of Dibdin, with some letters and documents supplied by his grand-daughter. [1884].

Bennett, W. Dibdin on theorists. Monthly Musical Record 1938.

Dibdin, E. R. Dibdin as a writer. Music & Letters 19 1938.

Sear, H. G. Dibdin. Music & Letters 26 1945.

ALEXANDER DOW
d. 1779

Zingis. T DL 17 Dec 1768. 1769, 1769, Dublin 1769, London 1773; Larpent ms.

Tales translated from the Persian of Inatulla of Delhi. 1768.

The history of Hindostan, translated from the Persian of Ferishta. 1768, 1772 (continuation).

Sethona. T DL 19 Feb 1774. 1774, Dublin [1774], London 1775; Larpent ms.

HUGH DOWNMAN
1740–1809
See col 653, above.

SIR HENRY BATE DUDLEY,
earlier BATE
1745–1824

§ 1

Henry and Emma. Int CG 13 April 1774. 1774.

The rival candidates. CO DL 1 Feb 1775. 1775, Dublin 1775, London [1775]; *Bell suppl 4*, Larpent ms.

The blackamoor wash'd white. CO DL 1 Feb 1776. 1776 (songs only); Larpent ms.

The flitch of bacon. CO New Hay 17 Aug 1778. 1779, Dublin 1779, London 1780; Larpent ms.

The dramatic puffers: a prelude. CG 9 Feb 1782. 1782.

The magic picture: a play altered from Massinger. CG 8 Nov 1783. 1783, 1783.

The woodman. CO CG 26 Feb 1791. 1791 (3 edns), Dublin 1791, London 1794; *London Stage 4*, Larpent ms.

The travellers in Switzerland. CO CG 25 Feb 1794. 1794, 1794; Larpent ms.

For Dudley's journalistic activities, pamphlets and sermons, see DNB.

§ 2

Fyvie, J. In his Noble dames and notable men of the Georgian era, 1910.

PHILIP FRANCIS
1708?–73
See col 548, above.

THOMAS FRANCKLIN
1721–84

Translation: a poem. 1753, 1754.

Truth and falsehood: a tale. 1755. Anon.

The orphan of China. T Unacted. 1756, 1756, 1761 (6th edn).

The Centinel. 27 nos 6 Jan–6 July 1757. 1757, 2 vols 1758 (extended to 31 Dec 1757).

The Earl of Warwick. T DL 13 Dec 1766. 1766, 1766, 1767, 1769; *Bell 17* 1797, *Inchbald's Theatre 19, Modern British Drama 2, Dibdin 23, London Stage 3*.

The works of Mr de Voltaire. 25 vols 1761–5, 38 vols 1778–81. Includes (1) Orestes, T CG 18 March 1769; (2) Electra, T DL 15 Oct 1774.

Matilda. T DL 21 Jan 1775. 1775, Dublin 1775; *Modern British Drama 2, Inchbald's Modern Theatre 8*.

The contract. F New Hay 12 June 1776. 1776; Larpent ms.

Mary, Queen of Scots: an historical play. Unacted. 1837.

Also many sermons and pamphlets, trns and regular contributions to Critical Rev.

FRANCIS GENTLEMAN
1728–84

Fortune: a rhapsody. 1751. Anon.

Sejanus, as it was intended for the stage. T Bath. 1752. From Jonson.

The sultan: or love and fame. T Bath c. 1754. 1770.

Narcissa and Eliza: a dramatic tale. 1754.

The tobacconist, altered from Ben Jonson. C Edinburgh c. 1760. 1771; *Dibdin 13, Oxberry 13, London Stage 2*.

Oroonoko: or the royal slave. T Edinburgh c. 1760. Glasgow 1760. Adapted from Southerne.

The modish wife; to which is prefixed a summary view of the stage, with biographical anecdotes of Messrs Mossop, Dexter, Derrick and the author. C Chester 1761. [1774] (anon), [1775].

The General: a poem. 1764. Anon.

A trip to the moon, by Sir Humphrey Lunatic, Bart. 2 vols York 1764–5.

Characters: an epistle. 1766.

Royal fables. 1766.

The Stratford Jubilee: a new comedy, to which is prefixed Scrub's trip to the Jubilee. Unacted. 1769.

The dramatic censor: or critical companion. 2 vols 1770. Anon.

The orator: an essay on reading and declamation. Edinburgh 1771.

Cupid's revenge: an Arcadian pastoral. New Hay 27 July 1772. 1772 (anon); Larpent ms.

The Pantheonites: a dramatic entertainment. New Hay 3 Sept 1773. 1773 (anon); Larpent ms.

Gentleman was also responsible for Bell's edn of Shakespeare's plays, 1774.

RICHARD GLOVER
1712–85
See col 549, above.

OLIVER GOLDSMITH
1728–74
See col 1191, below.

ELIZABETH GRIFFITH
1720?–93

Bibliographies

Norton, J. E. Some uncollected authors: Elizabeth Griffith. Book Collector 8 1959.

§ 1

A series of genuine letters between Henry and Frances. 4 vols 1757–66 (vols 1–2 enlarged 1761), 6 vols 1766–70, 1786. 'Henry's' letters by Richard Griffith (1714?–1788). See J. M. S. Tompkins, The polite marriage, Cambridge 1938.
Amana: a dramatic poem, by a lady. 1764.
The platonic wife, by a lady. C DL 24 Jan 1765. 1765, 1765, Dublin 1765; Larpent ms.
The double mistake. C CG 9 Jan 1766. 1766 (anon, 3 edns); Larpent ms.
The school for rakes. C DL 4 Feb 1769. 1769 (anon, 3 edns), Dublin 1770, London 1795; Bell 30 1797.
The history of Lady Barton: a novel, in letters. 3 vols 1771, 1773.
A wife in the right. C CG 5 March 1772. 1772; Larpent ms (as Patience the best remedy: or a wife in the right).
The barber of Seville: or the useless precaution. C Unacted. 1776.
The morality of Shakespeare's drama illustrated. 1775, 2 vols Dublin 1777.
The story of Lady Juliana Harley: a novel, in letters. 2 vols 1776.
A collection of novels, selected and revised. 3 vols 1777. Ed Mrs Griffith.
The times. C DL 2 Dec 1779. 1780, Dublin 1780; Larpent ms.
Essays addressed to young married women. 1782, 1782.
Also several trns from French.

§ 2

Tompkins, J. M. S. In her Polite marriage, Cambridge 1938.

HALL HARTSON
d. 1773

The Countess of Salisbury. T Dublin 2 May 1765. 1767 (3 edns), 1769, Belfast 1771, Dublin 1775, London 1784, 1793; Bell 18 1797, Inchbald's Theatre 16, Modern British Drama 2, Larpent ms.
Youth: a poem. 1773, Dublin 1773.

JOHN HAWKESWORTH
1715?–73

§ 1

The adventurer. 7 Nov 1752–9 March 1754, 2 vols 1763–4, 4 vols 1756, 2 vols Dublin 1760, London 1766, 4 vols 1770, 1778, 1 vol 1796, 4 vols 1797. 140 nos, of which Hawkesworth, the editor, wrote at least 70.
The works of Jonathan Swift, accurately revised, with some account of the author's life and notes historical and explanatory. 12 vols 1754–5. For later edns of this, and of Swift's Letters, below, see under Swift, col 000, below.
Amphitryon: or the two Sosias altered from Dryden. C DL 15 Dec 1756. 1756, 1780; Bell 11 1776, 21 1797, Larpent ms.
Oroonoko, by Thomas Southerne, with alterations. T DL 1 Dec 1759. 1759, 1775, 1776, 1776 (in New English theatre vol 6); Bell 6 1776, 19 1797; 1777, 1778, 1785

(in New English theatre vol 6); 1785, 1785, 1791; British Drama 1, Inchbald's Theatre 7, Modern British Drama 1824, London Stage 2, Cumberland 25, Acting Drama, Larpent ms.
Edgar and Emmeline: a fairy tale in a dramatic entertainment. DL 31 Jan 1761. 1761, [1777]; Bell suppl 4, Inchbald's Farces 6.
Almoran and Hamet: an Oriental tale. 2 vols 1761 (anon), 1761 (anon), 1780, 1789, 1795, 1796.
Letters written by the late Jonathan Swift 1703–40, with notes explanatory and historical. 3 vols 1766.
An account of the voyages undertaken in the Southern Hemisphere, drawn up from the journals which were kept by the several commanders and from the papers of Joseph Banks esq. 3 vols 1773, 2 vols Dublin 1775, 4 vols Perth 1789; tr Dutch, 1774.
The fall of Egypt: an oratorio. DL. 1774.
Zimri: an oratorio. [1780?].
Hawkesworth also pbd a trn of Fénelon's Telemachus. For his GM activities, see DNB.

§ 2

Kies, P. P. Lessing and Hawkesworth. Washington State Univ Research Stud 8 1940.
Eddy, D. D. Hawkesworth: book reviewer in the Gentleman's Magazine. PQ 43 1964.

WILLIAM HAWKINS
1722–1801

Collections

Tracts in divinity [etc]. 3 vols Oxford 1758. Vol 1, theological works; 2, plays and poems; 3, lectures in Latin delivered as Professor of Poetry at Oxford.

§ 1

The thimble: an heroi-comical poem, in four cantos, by a gentleman of Oxford. 1744. First pbd in 2 cantos 1743, expanded to 5 cantos in Tracts in divinity vol 2, Oxford 1758.
Henry and Rosamond. T Birmingham 1761. 1749, Dublin 1749.
The siege of Aleppo. T Unacted. In Tracts in divinity vol 2, Oxford 1758.
Cymbeline: a tragedy, altered from Shakespeare. TC CG 15 Feb 1759. 1759; Larpent ms. First pbd in Tracts in divinity vol 2.
A review of the works of the Rev Mr W. Hawkins, by an impartial reader. 1760 (signed Veridicus). Hawkins's retort to the unfavourable reviews, particularly Goldsmith's, Critical Rev Aug 1759, of collected works.
Poems on various subjects. Oxford 1781.
Also sermons and theological works, and a trn of Virgil's Aeneid bks 1–4.

WILLIAM HAYLEY
1745–1820

See col 657, above.

ROBERT HITCHCOCK
d. 1809

The macaroni. C York c. 1773. York 1773 (anon), 1773, Dublin 1774; Larpent ms.
The coquette: or the mistakes of the heart. C York and Hull c. 1776. Bath 1777 (anon); Larpent ms.
An historical view of the Irish stage, from the earliest period down to 1788, interspersed with theatrical anecdotes. 2 vols Dublin 1788–94. Ends 1774.

PRINCE HOARE
1755–1834

The tears of virtue: or such things were. T Bath 1 Jan 1788. Larpent ms.

No song, no supper: an opera. DL 16 April 1790. Dublin 1792; *London Stage 4;* [1830]; *Cumberland 24,* Larpent ms.

The cave of Trophonius: an opera. DL 3 May 1791. 1791 (songs only); Larpent ms.

Dido Queen of Carthage: an opera, with the masque of Neptune's prophecy. King's Haymarket 23 May 1792. 1792.

The prize, or 2, 5, 3, 8: a musical farce. King's Haymarket 11 March 1793. Dublin 1793, London 1798; *Cumberland 26,* Larpent ms.

My grandmother: a musical farce. New Hay 16 Dec 1793. 1794, Dublin 1795, London 1796, 1796, New York 1806; *Cumberland 26,* Larpent ms.

Love's victim: or the hermit's story. 1793. Verse.

The three and the deuce: a comic drama. New Hay 2 Sept 1795. 1806, 1809, 1823; *Cumberland 38,* Larpent ms.

Lock and key: a musical entertainment. CG 2 Feb 1796. 1796, 1797; *Inchbald's Farces 3, Cumberland 24,* Larpent ms (as Lock and key: or Bamboozell).

Mahound: a musical romance. DL 30 April 1796. 1796 (songs only); Larpent ms.

A friend in need is a friend indeed. CO DL 9 Feb 1797. [1797] (music only); Larpent ms.

The Italian villagers. CO CG 25 April 1797. Larpent ms.

The captive of Spilsburg, altered from the French drama called Le Souterrain. DL 14 Nov 1798. 1799 ('with a preface by the translator'); Larpent ms.

Sighs: or the daughter, taken from the German drama of Kotzebue, with alterations. C New Hay 30 July 1799. 1799, 1799, Dublin 1802.

Children, or give them their way: an operatic farce. DL 28 April 1800. Larpent ms.

Indiscretion. C DL 10 May 1800. 1800 (3 edns), Dublin 1803; Larpent ms.

Chains of the heart, or the slave by choice: an opera. CG 9 Dec 1801. 1802; Larpent ms (as Chains for the heart: or the slaves of Ceuta).

Extracts from a correspondence with the academies of Vienna and St Petersburg on the cultivation of painting, sculpture and architecture. 1802. Hoare was Secretary of the Royal Academy.

Academic correspondence 1803. 1804.

The paragraph: a musical entertainment. CG 18 March 1804. 1804.

The partners. C New Hay 8 June 1805. Larpent ms.

An enquiry into the art of design in England. 1806.

Something to do. C DL 22 Jan 1808. Larpent ms.

The artist. 2 vols 1809–10. Ed Hoare, who contributed several essays.

Academic annals 1805 to 1809. 1810.

Epochs of the arts including the progress of painting and sculpture in Great Britain. 1813.

Memoirs of Granville Sharpe, composed from his own manuscripts and other authentic documents. 6 pts 1820, 2 vols 1828.

THOMAS HOLCROFT
1745–1809

Bibliographies

Colby, E. A bibliography of Holcroft. BNYPL June, Aug–Sept 1922.

Stallbaumer, V. R. N & Q 4 Dec 1937. Against some attributions of trns.

§1

Elegies: 1, On the death of Samuel Foote; 2, On age. 1777.

A plain and succinct narrative of the late riots and disturbances with an account of the commitment of Lord George Gordon to the Tower and anecdotes of the life by William Vincent [i.e. Holcroft]. 1780. The anecdotes by John Perry.

Alwyn: or the gentleman comedian. 2 vols 1780. With assistance from William Nicholson.

Duplicity. C CG 13 Oct 1781. 1781, 1781, 1782, Dublin 1782; *Inchbald's Theatre 4, London Stage 4, Acting Drama,* Larpent ms.

The trial of the Hon George Gordon at the Court of King's Bench, taken in shorthand by William Vincent. 1781.

Human happiness, or the sceptic: a poem. 1783.

The family picture: or domestic dialogues on amiable subjects. 2 vols 1783.

The noble peasant. CO New Hay 2 Aug 1784. 1784, Dublin 1784; Larpent ms.

The follies of a day: or the marriage of Figaro, from the French of M. de Beaumarchais. C CG 14 Dec 1784. 1785, 1785; *Oxberry 13, London Stage 2, Acting Drama,* Larpent ms (as The marriage of Figaro).

Philosophical essays with observations on the laws and customs of several Eastern nations, written in French by M. Foucher d'Osbornville. 1784.

Memoirs of the life of Voltaire, translated from the French. 1784. Anon. Attributed by Colby, but doubtful.

Tales of the castle: being Les veillées du château, written by la Comtesse de Genlis. 5 vols 1785, 4 vols Dublin 1785, 5 vols 1787 (3rd edn), 1806 (8th edn), 2 vols 1817.

Memoirs of Baron de Toth, containing the state of the Turkish Empire and the Crimea. 2 vols 1785. Anon. Attributed by Colby.

The choleric fathers. CO CG 10 Nov 1785. 1785, Dublin 1786; Larpent ms.

Sacred dramas written in French by la Comtesse de Genlis. 1786, Dublin 1786. A selection from Le théâtre à l'usage des jeunes personnes.

Caroline of Lichtfield: a novel, translated from the French. 2 vols 1786, New York 1798, 3 vols 1817. From the French of Baroness de Montolieu.

Letter on Egypt by Mr Savary. 2 vols 1786, Dublin 1787.

An amorous tale of the chaste loves of Peter the Long and his most honoured friend Dame Blanche Bazu, imitated from the original French. 1786.

Historical and critical memoirs of the life and writings of M. de Voltaire, from the French of Dom Chaudon. 1786. From Chaudon, Mémoirs de M. de Voltaire, Amsterdam 1785. Ascribed by Colby.

Seduction. C DL 12 March 1787. 1787 (3 edns), Dublin 1787; *Inchbald's Theatre 4, London Stage 4, Acting Drama,* Larpent ms.

The present state of the Empire of Morocco, from the French of M. Chenier. 2 vols 1788.

The life of Baron Frederick Trenck, translated from the German. 3 vols 1788, 1795, 1800, 1817, 1835, 2 vols 1886.

The secret history of the Court of Berlin. 2 vols 1789. Anon.

Essays on physiognomy written in German by J. C. Lavater. 3 vols 1789, 1793 (abridged), 1850 (7th edn), 1867 (13th edn). Tr from German. *See* V. R. Stallbaumer, TLS 23 Jan 1937.

Posthumous works of Frederick King of Prussia. 13 vols 1789.

The German hotel. C CG 11 Nov 1790. 1790, 1790, Dublin 1791; Larpent ms. Attributed to James Marshall on first production, and probably his.

The school for arrogance. C CG 4 Feb 1791. 1791, 1791, Dublin 1791, New York 1807; *Inchbald's Theatre 4, London Stage 4,* Larpent ms.

The road to ruin. C CG 18 Feb 1792. 1792 (11 edns), Dublin 1792, New York 1792, 1806; *Inchbald's Theatre 24*; Edinburgh 1813, New York 1819; *Oxberry 7* (with preface by Hazlitt), *London Stage 1, Cumberland 4*, Larpent ms; tr German, 1793, 1794; Dutch, 1794; Danish, 1828.

Anna St Ives: a novel. 7 vols 1792.

The adventures of Hugh Trevor: a novel. 6 vols 1794, 4 vols 1801 (3rd edn); tr French, 1798. Largely autobiographical.

Love's frailties. C CG 5 Feb 1794. 1794, New York 1794; Larpent ms (as Love's frailties: or precept against practice).

The rival queens', or Drury Lane and Covent Garden: a prelude. CG 15 Sept 1794. Larpent ms.

The deserted daughter. C CG 2 May 1795. 1795 (4 edns), 1806, New York 1806; *Inchbald's Theatre 24, London Stage 3, Cumberland 34*, Larpent ms.

A narrative of facts relating to a prosecution for high treason, including the defence the author had prepared. 2 pts 1795.

A letter to the Right Honourable William Windham on the intemperance and danger of his public conduct. 1795.

The man of ten thousand. C DL 23 Jan 1796. 1796 (3 edns); Larpent ms.

The force of ridicule. C DL 6 Dec 1796. Larpent ms.

Travels through Germany, Switzerland and Italy, translated from the German of Frederick Leopold Count Stolberg. 2 vols 1796–7, 1797.

Knave or not? C DL 25 Jan 1798. 1798, Dublin 1798; Larpent ms.

He's much to blame. C CG 13 Feb 1798. 1798 (4 edns), Dublin 1798; *London Stage 4*. Also attributed to 'Mr Fenwick'; *see* J. Genest, English stage vol 7, 1832.

The inquisitor: a play. New Hay 23 June 1798. 1798 (4 edns); Larpent ms.

The old clothesman. Int CG 3 April 1799. Larpent ms. 'Ascribed to Holcroft, but not acknowledged by him', S. Jones, Biographia dramatica vol 3, 1812.

Herman and Dorothea: a poem from the German of Goethe. 1801.

Deaf and dumb, or the orphan protected: an historical drama, taken from the French of M Bouilly. DL 24 Feb 1801. 1801 (5 edns), 1802; *Oxberry 6, London Stage 1, Acting Drama, Cumberland 15*, Larpent ms.

A tale of mystery: a melodrama. CG 13 Nov 1802. 1802, 1802, New York 1803, 1808, London 1813 (4 edns), *Cumberland 8*, Larpent ms.

Hear both sides. C DL 12 Feb 1803. 1803 (4 edns), Philadelphia 1803; Larpent ms.

Travels from Hamburg through Westphalia, Holland and the Netherlands. 2 vols 1804, 1 vol Glasgow 1804 (abridged).

Memoirs of Bryan Perdue: a novel. 3 vols 1805.

The lady of the rock: a melo-drama. DL 12 Feb 1805. 1805, 1805, New York 1807; Larpent ms.

The theatrical recorder, edited by Thomas Holcroft. 2 vols 1805–6. Originally issued in 12 pts 1805; suppl 1806.

The vindictive man. C DL 20 Nov 1806. 1806, 1807; Larpent ms.

Memoirs of the late Thomas Holcroft, written by himself and continued (by William Hazlitt) to the time of his death from his diary, notes and other papers. 3 vols 1816, 1 vol 1852, 2 vols 1857; ed A. R. Waller and A. Glover in Hazlitt's Works vol 2, 1902; ed E. Colby 2 vols 1925, 1 vol Oxford 1926 (WC); ed P. P. Howe in Hazlitt's Works vol 3, 1932.

§ 2

Colby, E. Holcroft: man of letters. South Atlantic Quart 22 1923.

—— Financial accounts of Holcroft's plays. N & Q 19–26 Jan 1924.

—— Holcroft: translator of plays. PQ 3 1924.

Benn, T. V. Holcroft en France. Revue de Littérature Comparée 6 1926.

Stallbaumer, V. R. Holcroft: a satirist in the stream of sentimentalism. ELH 3 1936.

—— Holcroft's German. TLS 23 Jan 1937. Reply by O. Teichman 6 Feb 1937; V.R. Stallbaumer 20 March 1937.

—— Translations by Holcroft. N & Q 4 Dec 1937.

—— Holcroft as a novelist. ELH 15 1948.

—— Holcroft's influence on Political justice. MLQ 14 1953.

Hennig, J. Trenck and Britain. MLR 41 1946.

Eva, J. Mrs Inchbald and Holcroft in Canterbury 1777. N & Q April 1954.

Morgan, S. S. The damning of Holcroft's Knave or not? and O'Keefe's She's eloped. MLQ 32 1958.

Ter-Abramova, V. G. Roman Tomase Xolkrofta Anna Sent-Iv. Filologiceskie Nauki 7 1964.

Baine, R. M. Holcroft and the revolutionary novel. Athens Georgia 1965.

JOSEPH GEORGE HOLMAN
1764–1817

Abroad and at home. CO CG 19 Nov 1796. 1796 (5 edns), Dublin 1797, London 1801, 1802; *London Stage 4*, Larpent ms.

The votary of wealth. C CG 12 Jan 1799. 1799 (4 edns). *Inchbald's Modern Theatre 3, London Stage 4*, Larpent ms.

The Red-Cross Knights: a play, founded on the Robbers of Schiller. New Hay 21 Aug 1799. 1799; Larpent ms.

A statement of the differences subsisting between the proprietors and performers of the Theatre-Royal Covent-Garden. 1800 (3rd edn). Anon.

What a blunder! Co New Hay Aug 1800. 1800.

The gazette extraordinary. C CG 23 April 1811. 1811.

JOHN HOME
1722–1808
Collections

The dramatick works of John Home. 1760. Douglas, The siege of Aquileia, Agis.

Dramatic works. 2 vols Edinburgh 1798. Complete.

Works now first collected, to which is prefixed an account of his life by Henry Mackenzie. 3 vols Edinburgh 1822. Plays and History of the Rebellion. Mackenzie's Life was also issued separately.

§ 1

Douglas. T Edinburgh Dec 1756, CG 14 March 1757. 1757, Edinburgh 1757 (fuller text), Belfast 1758, Dublin 1761, London 1764; *Bell 20 1776; 1777, 1780, 1783; Bell 3 1791, British Drama 2, Inchbald's Theatre 16*; Edinburgh 1813, *Dibdin 3, Oxberry 12, London Stage 1, Cumberland 1, Dolby 1, British Drama 1824, Acting Drama*; ed H. J. Tunney, Lawrence Kansas 1924; tr French, 1822.

Agis, by the author of Douglas. T DL 21 Feb 1758. 1758, Dublin 1758; Larpent ms.

The siege of Aquileia. T DL 21 Feb 1760. 1760. Edinburgh 1760, Dublin 1760; Larpent ms.

The fatal discovery. T DL 23 Feb 1769. 1769, Dublin 1769, London 1772.

Alonzo. T DL 27 Feb 1773. 1773, 1773, Dublin 1773; Larpent ms.

Alfred. T CG 21 Jan 1778. 1778, 1778; Larpent ms.

Le caffé, ou l'écossaise: comédie par Mr Hume pasteur de l'Église d'Édimbourg, traduite en français, Londres 1760, *has nothing to do with Home. It is by Voltaire and was pbd at Geneva.*

The history of the Rebellion in 1745. 1802.

The Douglas Controversy

Address to the moderator of the presbytery of Haddington. Edinburgh 1757.

Address to the Synod of Lothian and Tweedale concerning Mr Home's tragedy. Edinburgh 1757.

Advice to writers in defence of Douglas. Edinburgh 1757.

Apology for the writers against Douglas. Edinburgh 1757.

An argument to prove that Douglas ought to be publickly burnt at the hands of the hangman. Edinburgh 1757.

The deposition, or fatal miscarriage: a tragedy. Edinburgh 1757.

Douglas weighed and found wanting. Edinburgh 1757.

The immorality of stage-plays in general and Douglas in particular. Edinburgh 1757.

Ferguson, A. The morality of stage plays seriously considered. Edinburgh 1757.

The philosopher's opera. Edinburgh 1757.

The player's scourge: or a detection of the ranting profanity of stage-plays, and especially against the nine prophane pagan priests falsely called ministers of the Gospel, who countenanced the thrice accursed tragedy called Douglas. Edinburgh 1757.

[Harper, —]. Some serious remarks [in answer to Player's scourge]. Edinburgh 1757.

The seven champions of the stage: an old fashion'd song to the tune of Gill Morrice. Edinburgh 1757.

A letter to Mr David Hume on the tragedy of Douglas, by an English critic. 1757.

The theatrical examiner; with a short consideration of Douglas. 1757.

The second part of the Player's scourge. Edinburgh 1758.

§ 2

Gipson, A. E. Home: a study of his life and works, with special reference to the tragedy of Douglas and the controversies which followed its first representations. Caldwell Idaho 1917.

MacMillan, D. The first editions of Home's Douglas. SP 26 1929.

Troubridge, St V. 'Norval'. N & Q 13 Sept 1941. See L. R. M. Strachan 20 Sept 1941; 'Hibernicus' 27 Sept 1941.

Boas, F. S. Home's first two plays. Fortnightly Rev Nov 1950.

Todd, W. B. Press figures and book reviews as determinants of priority: a study of Home's Douglas 1757 and Cumberland's The brothers 1770. PBSA 45 1951.

Bushnell, G. H. The original Lady Randolph. Theatre Notebook 13 1959. In Douglas.

Stratman, C. J. Scotland's first dramatic periodical: The Edinburgh theatrical censor. Theatre Notebook 17 1963. On Douglas.

Eddy, D. O. John Hawkesworth: book reviewer in the Gentleman's Magazine. PQ 43 1964. On Fatal discovery.

Emslie, M. Home's Douglas and Willy Shakespeare. Stud in Scottish Lit 2 1964.

JOHN HOOLE
1727–1803

§ 1

A monody to the memory of Mrs Margaret Woffington. 1760. Anon.

Jerusalem delivered: an heroic poem translated from the Italian. 2 vols 1763, 1767 (3rd edn), 1783 (5th edn), 1797, 1802–3, 1807, 1809. From Tasso.

The works of Metastasio, translated from the Italian. 2 vols 1767, 3 vols 1800 (enlarged as Dramas and other poems of the Abbé Pietro Metastasio).

Cyrus. T CG 3 Dec 1868. 1768, 1772 (3rd edn); Bell 24 1797, Larpent ms.

Timanthes. T CG 24 Feb 1770. 1770 (3 edns), 1771; Bell 34 1797, Larpent ms.

Cleonice, Princess of Bithynia. T CG 2 March 1775. 1775; Bell 24 1797.

Orlando Furioso, translated into English verse. 5 vols 1783, 1785, 1791, 6 vols 1807, 1813, Philadelphia 1816, 1 vol 1818, 1819. From Ariosto. 'Reduced to 24 books', 2 vols 1791.

Rinaldo: a poem in xii books. 1792. From Tasso.

§ 2

Hoole, Samuel. Anecdotes respecting the life of the late Mr Hoole; [with] some pieces written by the deceased, never before printed. 1803.

Sägesser, A. Hoole: his life and his tragedies. Berne 1922.

THOMAS HULL
1728–1808

Mr Hull's case, addressed to the consideration of the public. Bath 1759.

Pharnaces, altered from the Italian. O DL 15 Feb 1765. 1765; Larpent ms. From A. M. Lucchini, Farnace.

The Spanish lady: a musical entertainment founded on the plan of the old ballad. CG 2 May 1765. [1765]; Larpent ms.

All in the right. F. Larpent ms.

The perplexities. C CG 31 Jan 1767. 1767, Dublin 1767; Larpent ms. Adaptation of Tuke, Adventures of five hours.

The fairy favour. M CG 31 Jan 1767. 1766; Larpent ms.

The royal merchant, founded on Beaumont and Fletcher. CO CG 14 Dec 1767. 1768, Dublin 1768; Larpent ms.

The history of Sir William Harrington. 4 vols 1771, 1772, 1797; tr German, 1771; French, 1773.

Genuine letters from a gentlewoman [J. Preston] to a young lady, her pupil. 2 vols 1772. Ed and rev Hull.

Henry the Second: or the fall of Rosamond. T CG 1 May 1773. 1774 (3 edns), York 1775, London 1795; Bell 28 1797, Inchbald's Modern Theatre 9, Larpent ms.

The prodigal son: an oratorio. 1773, 1777.

Richard Plantagenet: a legendary tale. [1774], [1774?] (6th edn, 'corrected').

Edward and Eleonora, altered from James Thomson. T CG 18 March 1775. 1775.

Love finds the way. CO CG 18 Nov 1777. 1777 (songs only), 1777 (songs only). Adaptation of Murphy, The school for guardians.

Select letters between the late Duchess of Somerset, Lady Luxborough and others, including a sketch of the manners etc of the Republic of Venice. 2 vols 1778. Ed Hull.

The comedy of errors. C CG 22 Jan 1779. 1811 ('revised by J. P. Kemble').

A collection of poems and translations in English and Latin. Bath [1780?], Reading nd.

The fatal interview. T DL 16 Nov 1782. Larpent ms.

Moral tales in verse. 2 vols 1797.

Disinterested love. C CG 30 May 1798. Larpent ms. Adaptation of Massinger, The bashful lover.

Elisha: or the woman of Shunem, a new sacred oratorio. 1801.

The advantages of repentance: a moral tale attempted in blank verse. nd, nd.

ELIZABETH INCHBALD,
née SIMPSON
1753–1821

Bibliographies

Joughin, G. L. An Inchbald bibliography. SE 14 1934.

§ 1

The fruitless repentance: or the history of Kitty Le Fever. 1769. Anon. The attribution is uncertain.

A mogul tale: or the descent of the balloon. F New Hay 6 July 1784. Dublin 1788, London 1796; *London Stage 4*; New York 1827; *Cumberland 42*, Larpent ms.

I'll tell you what. C New Hay 4 Aug 1785. 1786, 1786, 1787, Dublin 1787; *Inchbald's Modern Theatre 7*, Larpent ms; tr German, 1792.

Appearance is against them. F CG 22 Oct 1785. 1785, Dublin 1786; *London Stage 4*, Larpent ms.

The widow's vow. F New Hay 20 June 1786. 1786, Dublin 1786, New York 1787.

Emily Herbert, or perfidy punished: a novel, in a series of letters. 1786. Anon. The attribution is uncertain.

Such things are: a play. CG 10 Feb 1787. 1788, 1788, Dublin 1788, 1790, London 1800 (12th edn), 1805; *Inchbald's Theatre 23*, *London Stage 1*, Larpent ms.

The midnight hour: or war of wits, translated from the French. F CG 22 May 1787. 1787, Dublin 1787, London 1788, Dublin 1788, Boston 1795; *Inchbald's Farces 1*; New York 1811; *Oxberry 13*, *London Stage 1*, *Cumberland 15*, Larpent ms.

All on a summer's day. C CG 15 Dec 1787. Larpent ms.

Animal magnetism. F CG 29 April 1788. Dublin [1788?], 1789, 1792, New York 1808; *Cumberland 14*, *London Stage 4*, *Acting Drama*.

The child of nature: a dramatic piece from the French of the Marchioness of Sillery, formerly Countess of Genlis. CG 28 Nov 1788. 1788, 1789, Dublin 1789, Philadelphia 1790, London 1794, 1800 (6th edn), New York 1806; *Inchbald's Farces 1*, *London Stage 2*, *Cumberland 11*.

The married man, from Le philosophe marié of Mr Nericault Destouches. C New Hay 15 July 1789. 1789, Dublin 1789; Larpent ms.

The hue and cry. F DL 11 May 1791. Larpent ms.

Next door neighbours, from the French dramas L'indigent [by L. S. Mercier] and Le dissipateur [by Destouches]. 1791, Dublin 1791; *Inchbald's Modern Theatre 7*, Larpent ms.

A simple story. 4 vols 1791, 2 vols Dublin 1791, 4 vols 1793 (3rd edn), 1799, 1 vol 1801, 2 vols Dublin 1804, 1 vol 1823, 1831 etc; ed W. B. Scott 1880; ed G. L. Strachey 1908; ed J. M. S. Tompkins, Oxford 1967; tr French, 1792; German, 1792.

Every one has his fault. C CG 29 Jan 1793. 1793 (5 edns), Dublin 1793, London 1794, 1794, Philadelphia 1794, Dublin 1795, London 1805; *Inchbald's Theatre 23*; Boston 1809; *Oxberry 16*, *Dolby 1824*, *London Stage 2*, *Cumberland 7*, Larpent ms.

The wedding day. C DL 1 Nov 1794. 1794, Dublin 1795, London 1806; *Inchbald's Farces 1*; New York 1819; *Oxberry 5*, *London Stage 2*, *Cumberland 39*, Larpent ms.

Nature and art. 2 vols 1796, Philadelphia 1796, London 1797, 1 vol 1810, 1821, 1823, 1824; ed W. B. Scott 1886; tr French, 1797. A novel.

Wives as they were and maids as they are. C CG 4 March 1797. 1797 (6 edns), Dublin 1797, Cork 1797, London 1806; *Inchbald's Theatre 23*; New York 1813; *London Stage 2*, *Dolby 1825*, *Cumberland 10*, Larpent ms (as The primitive wife and modern maid).

Lovers' vows: a play, from the German of Kotzebue. CG 11 Oct 1798. 1798 (11 edns), Dublin 1798, London 1799, 1799, Boston 1799, Cork 1799, London 1804, 1805, Dublin 1806; *Inchbald's Theatre 23*, *London Stage 3*, *Cumberland 17*, *Acting Drama*, Larpent ms.

The wise men of the East: a play, from the German of Kotzebue. CG 30 Nov 1799. 1799 (4 edns), Dublin 1800; *Inchbald's Modern Theatre 8*, Larpent ms.

To marry or not to marry. C CG 16 Feb 1805. 1805, 1805, Baltimore 1805; *Inchbald's Theatre 23*, Larpent ms.

The British theatre: or a collection of plays with biographical and critical remarks. 25 vols 1808, 20 vols 1824.

A collection of farces and other afterpieces. 7 vols 1809, 1815.

The modern theatre. 10 vols 1809.

§ 2

Boaden, James. Memoirs of Mrs Inchbald, including her familiar correspondence; to which are added the Massacre and A case of conscience now first published. 2 vols 1833.

Littlewood, S. R. Elizabeth Inchbald and her circle. 1921.

Reitzel, W. Mansfield Park and Lovers' vows. RES 9 1933.

McKee, W. Elizabeth Inchbald, novelist. Baltimore 1935.

Stebbins, L. P. In her London ladies: true tales of the eighteenth century, New York 1952.

Eva, J. Mrs Inchbald and Thomas Holcroft in Canterbury 1777. N & Q April 1954.

Beer, E. S. de. Lovers' vows: the dangerous insignificance of the butler. N & Q Nov 1962.

ROBERT JEPHSON

1736–1803

§ 1

Considerations upon the augmentation of the army. Dublin 1768.

Epistle to Gorges Edward Howard esq with notes by Alderman Faulkner. Dublin 1771 (3rd edn), 1772 ('with considerable additions').

Epistle from G— E— H—d esq to Alderman Faulkner. Barataria [Dublin] 1772.

Select essays from the Bachelor. Dublin 1772, London 1773 (as Essays from the Bachelor by the author of the Epistle to Gorges Edward Howard). Signed Geoffrey Wagstaffe, and written with John Courtenay.

A speech on the bill for the encouragement of persons professing the Popish religion to become Protestants. Dublin 1774.

Braganza. T DL 17 Feb 1775. 1775, 1775, Dublin 1775, London 1776; *Inchbald's Modern Theatre 6*, *London Stage 4*.

The law of Lombardy. T DL 8 Feb 1779. 1779, Dublin 1779; *Inchbald's Modern Theatre 6*, *London Stage 4*, Larpent ms.

The count of Narbonne. T CG 17 Nov 1781. 1781, Dublin 1782, London 1787 ('corrected'), Dublin 1788; *Inchbald's Theatre 20*, Larpent ms. Founded on Horace Walpole, The Castle of Otranto.

The hotel: or the servant with two masters. F Smock Alley Dublin May 1783. Dublin 1784. Altered from Thomas Vaughan, The hotel: or the double valet, 1776.

The campaign: or love in the East Indies. CO Smock Alley Dublin Jan 1784, CG 12 May 1785. 1785 (songs only), Larpent ms.

Julia: or the Italian lover. T DL 17 April 1787. 1787, 1787, Dublin 1788, London [1802]; Larpent ms.

Two strings to your bow. F CG 16 Feb 1791. 1791, 1791; *Minor Theatre 3*, *Inchbald's Farces 2*, *London Stage 3*, *Cumberland 30*. Altered from Hotel, above.

Roman portraits. 1794. Verse.

The confessions of Jacques Baptiste Couteau. 2 vols 1794.

Conspiracy. T DL 15 Nov 1796. Dublin 1796; Larpent ms.

§ 2

Walpole, Horace. In Thoughts on tragedy. In his Works vol 2, 1798. On Braganza.

Peterson, M. S. Jephson: a study of his life and works. Lincoln Nebraska 1930.

EDWARD JERNINGHAM

1727–1812

See col 662, above.

HENRY JONES

1721–70

See col 662, above.

HUGH KELLY

1739–77

Collections

The works of Hugh Kelly, to which is prefixed his life. 1778.

§ 1

The prater. 1757. Anon. 35 nos 13 March–6 Nov 1756. Not certainly by Kelly.

L'amour a-la-mode: or love-a-la-mode. F Unacted. 1760. Anon.

An elegy to the memory of the Right Honourable William, late Earl of Bath. 1765 (2nd edn).

Thespis: or a critical examination into the merits of all the principal performers belonging to Drury-Lane theatre. 1766, 1766 (rev); Book the second, 1767.

The babler: containing a careful selection from those essays which have given so much satisfaction under that title in Owen's Weekly Chronicle. 2 vols 1767. Anon. 123 nos 12 Feb 1763–5 June 1767.

Memoirs of a Magdalen: or the history of Louisa Mildmay. 2 vols 1767 (anon), 1782, 1784; tr French, [1800].

False delicacy. C DL 23 Jan 1768. 1768 (4 edns), Dublin 1770; *Bell 30 1797*, Larpent ms.

A word to the wise. C DL 3 March 1770. 1770, Dublin 1770, London 1773, 1775; *Bell 30 1797*, Larpent ms.

Clementina. T CG 23 Feb 1771. 1771 (anon), 1771 (anon), Dublin 1771; Larpent ms.

The school for wives. C DL 11 Dec 1773. 1774 (4 edns), Belfast 1774, London 1775; *Bell 7 1797, Inchbald's Modern Theatre 9, London Stage 4*, Larpent ms; tr German, 1776. Assisted by Sir William Addington.

The romance of an hour. C CG 2 Dec 1774. 1774, 1774, Dublin 1775; Larpent ms.

Also some poetical pamphlets and much journalism, particularly in the Court Mag, Lady's Museum and Public Ledger—all ed Kelly.

§ 2

Schorer, M. Kelly: his place in the sentimental school. PQ 12 1933.

Rawson, C. J. Some remarks on eighteenth-century 'delicacy', with a note on Kelly's False delicacy (1768). JEGP 61 1962.

Eddy, D. O. John Hawkesworth: book reviewer in the Gentleman's Magazine. PQ 43 1964. On A word to the wise.

JOHN PHILIP KEMBLE

1757–1823

§ 1

Belisarius or injured innocence. T Liverpool and Hull 1778. Larpent ms.

The female officer. F Manchester 1778. Larpent ms (rev as The projects, DL 18 Feb 1786, also in Larpent ms).

Oh! it's impossible. C York 1780. Larpent ms.

Fugitive pieces. York 1780, nd (facs). Verse.

The maid of honour. C DL 27 Jan 1785. Larpent ms. Adapted from Massinger.

The pilgrim, with additions. C DL 26 Oct 1787. 1788. Vanbrugh's adaptation of Fletcher.

Shakespear's King Lear, as altered by N. Tate, newly revised. T DL 21 Jan 1788. 1788, 1800, 1808, 1815.

The pannel: an entertainment, altered from the comedy of 'Tis well it's no worse. F DL 28 Nov 1788. 1789, [1789]; *London Stage 4*. From Bickerstaffe.

The farm house. F DL 1 May 1789. 1789, 1789, Dublin 1789; *Inchbald's Farces 6*. From Charles Johnson, The country lasses.

King Henry V: or the conquest of France. T DL 1 Oct 1789. 1789, 1801, 1806, 1815.

The tempest: or the enchanted island with additions from Dryden. C DL 13 Oct 1789. 1789, 1806 (with further alterations).

Love in many masks, as altered from Mrs Behn's Rover. C DL 8 March 1790. [1790]; Larpent ms.

Lodoiska. O DL 9 June 1794. [1794], [1794], 1801; *Inchbald's Farces 7, Oxberry 20, London Stage 2, Cumberland 41*.

Macbeth. T DL 21 April 1794. [1794], [1794], 1803, 1814.

Shakespeare's All's well that ends well, with alterations. C DL 12 Dec 1794. 1793, 1815.

The Roman actor: a piece in two acts. T DL. Larpent ms. From Massinger.

Otway's tragedy of Venice preserv'd. DL 21 Oct 1795. 1795, 1811, 1814.

Lee's tragedy of Alexander the Great. DL 23 Nov 1795. 1796, 1815.

Wycherley's comedy of the Plain dealer. DL 27 Feb 1796. 1796, 1815.

The merry wives of Windsor. C DL. 1797, 1804, 1815.

Celadon and Florimel: or the happy counterplot. C DL 23 May 1796. Larpent ms. Cibber's adaptation of Dryden.

Much ado about nothing. C DL 12 Oct 1799. 1799, 1810, 1815.

A select British theatre: being a collection of the most popular stock-pieces. 8 vols 1816. Includes many of Kemble's later adaptations of Fletcher, Massinger, Lee, Otway, Southerne, Congreve, Rowe, Addison, Young, Moore, Murphy and Holcroft 1800–15.

Macbeth and Richard the Third: an essay, in answer to Remarks on some of the characters of Shakespeare [by T. Whateley]. 1817. The Macbeth essay was pbd separately 1786.

§ 2

Boaden, J. Memoirs of the life of John Philip Kemble esq. 2 vols 1825.

Fitzgerald, P. The Kembles. 2 vols [1871].

Donohue, J. W. Kemble's production of Macbeth 1794. Theatre Notebook 21 1967.

Rosron, D. Kemble's Coriolanus and Julius Caesar: an examination of the prompt copies. Theatre Notebook 23 1968.

WILLIAM KENRICK

1725?–79

§ 1

The town: a satire. 1748.

The kapélion: or poetical ordinary, consisting of great variety of dishes, in prose and verse; by Archimagirus Metaphoricus. 6 nos Aug 1750–Jan 1751. Ed Kenrick.

The grand question debated: or an essay to prove that the soul of man is not, neither can it be, immortal: by Ontologos. Dublin 1751. Answered by Kenrick himself in A reply to the grand question debated, 1751.

A monody to the memory of his Royal Highness Frederick Prince of Wales. 1751, 1751.

The so much talk'd of and expected Old woman's Dunciad, by Mary Midnight. 1751 (3 edns). *See* R. P. Bond, MLN 43 1928.

Fun: a parodi-tragi-comical satire. Unacted. 1752. Anon.

The pasquinade, with notes variorum: book the first [all pbd]. 1753. Anon.

The whole duty of woman, by a lady. 1753 (3 edns).

Epistles to Lorenzo. 1756 (anon), 1759 (rev as Epistles philosophical and moral), 1773 (4th edn, as Epistles to Lorenzo). Defended by Kenrick in A scrutiny: or the criticks criticis'd, 1759.

A review of Doctor Johnson's new edition of Shakespeare, in which the ignorance, or inattention, of that editor is exposed. 1765. Defended (by Kenrick himself?) against James Barclay, Examination in a defence of Mr Kenrick's review, by a friend, 1766 (signed R.R.).

Falstaff's wedding: being a sequel to the second part of the play of King Henry the Fourth, written in imitation of Shakespeare. C DL 12 April 1766. 1760 (for 1766), 1766, 1766, Dublin 1766, London 1773, 1781; Bell 31 1797, Modern British Drama 4, Larpent ms.

The widow'd wife. C DL 5 Dec 1767. 1767, 1768, Dublin 1768; Larpent ms.

An epistle to G. Colman. 1768, 1768.

An epistle to James Boswell esq occasioned by his having transmitted the moral writings of Dr Samuel Johnson to Pascal Paoli, by W.K. esq. 1768.

Poems ludicrous, satirical and moral. 1768, 1770 ('with additions').

Love in the suds, a town eclogue: being the lamentations of Roscius for the loss of his Nyky. 1772 (5 edns, some with additional matter, both as above and as A letter to David Garrick esq from William Kenrick LID).

A letter to David Garrick esq, occasioned by his having moved the Court of King's Bench against the publisher of Love in the suds. 1772.

A whipping for the Welch parson: being a comment upon the Rev Mr Evan Lloyd's epistle to David Garrick esq. 1773. Anon.

The duellist. C CG 20 Nov 1773. 1773 (3 edns), Dublin 1774; Larpent ms.

Introduction to the school of Shakespeare. [1774].

The London review of English and foreign literature. 10 vols 1775–9. Ed and largely written by Kenrick.

The lady of the manor. CO CG 23 Nov 1778. 1778 (3 edns), Dublin 1779; Larpent ms.

The spendthrift: or a Christmas gambol. F 21 Dec 1778. Larpent ms.

Also pamphlets on divorce, mechanics and Christian evidences, an English dictionary, an account of Robert Lloyd prefixed to Lloyd's Poetical works, 1774, and trns of Gesner, Rousseau, Voltaire, Buffon and Millot.

§ 2

McCusker, H. Doctor Kenrick of Grub Street. More Books 14 1939.

Sewall, R. B. Kenrick as translator and critic of Rousseau. PQ 20 1941.

Brewer, G. E. and P. Fussell. The birth date of Kenrick. N & Q 4 Feb 1950.

Fussell, P. Kenrick's 'courtesy' book. PMLA 66 1951.

—— Kenrick: eighteenth-century scourge and critic. Jnl of Rutgers Univ Lib 20 1957.

Irwin, W. R. Kenrick: volunteer moralist. PMLA 67 1952.

THOMAS KING
1730–1805

Love at first sight: a ballad farce. BO DL 17 Oct 1763. 1763 (anon); Larpent ms.

Wit's last stake. F DL 14 April 1768. 1769, 1769, 1803 (4th edn); Larpent ms.

Hurly burly: or the fairy of the well. Pant DL 1785. [1785]; Larpent ms. With James Cobb.

Lovers' quarrels, or like master like man: an interlude in one act altered from the Mistake of Sir J. Vanbrugh. *London Stage 3.*

SOPHIA LEE
1750–1824
See col 1007 f., below.

CHARLOTTE LENNOX
1720–1804

§ 1

Poems on several occasions, written by a young lady. 1747.

The life of Harriot Stuart, written by herself. 2 vols 1751. Anon. A novel.

The female Quixote: or the adventures of Arabella. 2 vols 1752 (anon), 1752 ('corrected'), Dublin 1752, 1 vol [1752?] (abridged as Entertaining history of the female Don Quixote), 2 vols Dublin 1763, London 1783, [1799]; tr German, 1754; French, 1773; Spanish, 1808.

Shakespear illustrated: or the novels and histories, on which the plays of Shakespear are founded, collected and translated. 3 vols 1753–4.

Henrietta. 2 vols 1758, Dublin 1758, London 1761 ('corrected'), 1787; tr French, 1760.

Philander: a dramatic pastoral. Unacted. 1757, Dublin 1758.

The lady's museum. 11 nos 1 March 1760–1 Jan 1761. 2 vols 1760–1. Ed and mainly written by Mrs Lennox.

Sophia. 2 vols 1762. Rptd from Lady's Museum. A novel.

The history of the Marquis of Lussan and Isabella. Dublin 1764; tr French, 1770. Rptd, with many changes, from Lady's Museum.

The sister. C CG 18 Feb 1769. 1769, 1769; Larpent ms; tr German, 1776. Dramatized from Henrietta, above.

Old city manners, altered from the original Eastward Hoe. C DL 9 Nov 1775. 1775; Larpent ms.

Euphemia. 4 vols 1790. A novel.

The history of Sir George Warrington: or the political Quixote. 3 vols 1797, 1797 (2nd edn). A novel.

For Mrs Lennox's numerous trns from French etc, see M. R. Small, Charlotte Ramsay Lennox, New Haven 1935, appendix 6.

§ 2

Dobson, A. In his Eighteenth-century vignettes ser 1, 1892.

Wilson, M. In her These were Muses, 1924.

Small, M. R. Charlotte Ramsay Lennox: an eighteenth-century lady of letters. New Haven 1935.

Troxell, J. C. The history of Sir George Warrington. TLS 2 Sept 1939.

Maynadier, G. H. The first American novelist? Cambridge Mass 1940.

Eddy, D. O. John Hawkesworth: book reviewer in the Gentleman's Magazine. PQ 43 1964. On the Sister.

ROBERT LLOYD
1733–64
See col 667, above.

CHARLES MACKLIN
1697?-1797
Collections

The man of the world; Love à la mode. 1793. Subscription edn, organized by Arthur Murphy.
The plays of Charles Macklin: The man of the world, The true born Irishman, Love à la mode. Dublin 1793. Also issued as part of Jones's British theatre, Dublin 1795-6.

§ 1

The case of Charles Macklin, comedian. 1743.
Mr Macklin's reply to Mr Garrick's answer. 1743. For this item, and the preceding one, see under Garrick, col 805, above.
Henry the Seventh: or the Popish impostor. T DL 18 Jan 1746. 1746.
A will and no will: or a bone for the lawyers. C DL 23 April 1746. Larpent ms; ed J. B. Kern, Los Angeles 1967 (Augustan Reprint Soc).
The new play criticiz'd: or the plague of envy. F DL 24 March 1747. Larpent ms; ed J. B. Kern, Los Angeles 1967 (Augustan Reprint Soc).
Covent Garden theatre: or Pasquin turn'd Drawcansir, censor of Great Britain. Bsq CG 8 April 1752. Larpent ms; ed J. B. Kern, Los Angeles 1965 (facs) (Augustan Reprint Soc). See E. M. Raushenbush, Macklin's lost play about Fielding, MLN 51 1936.
Epistle from Tully in the shades to Orator M—n in Covent Garden. 1755.
Love à la mode. F DL 12 Dec 1759. [Dublin?] 1784 (pirated), Dublin 1785, 1785, London 1786, 1793 (authorized), Dublin 1793; Minor Theatre 4, Inchbald's Farces 1; Edinburgh [1811]; Modern British Drama 1826, London Stage 3, Acting Drama. See W. Matthews, The piracies of Macklin's Love à-la-mode, RES 10 1934.
The true born Irishman: or the Irish fine lady. C Crow Street Dublin 14 May 1762. Dublin 1793; Larpent ms (for CG performance 28 Nov 1767 as The Irish fine lady.)
An apology for the conduct of Mr Charles Macklin, comedian. 1773.
The genuine arguments of the Council why an information should not be exhibited against Thomas Leigh [et al] for a conspiracy to deprive Charles Macklin of his livelihood. 1774.
Riot and conspiracy: the trial of Thomas Leigh and others for conspiring to ruin in his profession Charles Macklin. [1775].
The man of the world. C CG 10 May 1781. Dublin 1785 (pirated), London 1786, Dublin 1791, London 1793 (authorized), Dublin 1793; Bell 27 1797, Inchbald's Theatre 14; 1809; Dibdin 5, Oxberry 14; New York 1824; British Drama 1824, London Stage 1, Cumberland 5, Acting Drama, Larpent ms; ed D. MacMillan, Los Angeles 1951 (Augustan Reprint Soc). Altered from Macklin's unpbd The true born Scotchman, Crow Street Dublin 26 Dec 1764.

§ 2

Congreve, F. A. Authentic memoirs of the late Mr Charles Macklin, comedian. 1798.
Kirkman, J. T. Memoirs of the life of Charles Macklin. 2 vols 1799.
Cooke, W. Memoirs of Charles Macklin, comedian. 1804, 1806.
Parry, E. A. Charles Macklin. 1891.
Matthews, W. The piracies of Macklin's Love-à-la-mode. RES 10 1934.
MacMillan, D. The censorship in the case of Macklin's The man of the world. Huntington Lib Bull no 10 1936.

Raushenbush, E. M. Macklin's lost play about Henry Fielding. MLN 51 1936.
Barrow, B. E. Macklin's costume and property notes for the character of Lovegold: some traditional elements in eighteenth-century low-comedy acting. Theatre Notebook 13 1958.
Findlay, R. R. Macklin's legitimate acting version of Love à-la-mode. PQ 45 1966.
— The comic plays of Macklin: dark satire at mid eighteenth century. Educational Theatre Jnl 20 1968.
Bartley, J. O. Macklin: appearances outside London. Theatre Notebook 22 1967.

LEONARD MacNALLY
1752-1820

An heroic epistle from Richard Twiss at Rotterdam. 1776. Probably by William Preston.
Seventeen hundred and seventy seven. 1777. Probably by Preston.
The apotheosis of Punch: a satirical masque with a monody on the death of Master Punch acted at the Patagonian Theatre, Exeter Change. 1779. Anon. The ascription to MacNally is doubtful.
The claims of Ireland and the resolutions of the volunteers vindicated. 1782.
Retaliation. F CG 7 May 1782. 1782 (3 edns), Dublin 1782.
Tristram Shandy: a sentimental, Shandean bagatelle. C CG 26 April 1783. 1783, 1783; Larpent ms.
Coalition: a musical piece. CG 19 May 1783. Larpent ms.
Robin Hood: or, Sherwood Forest. CO CG 17 April 1784. 1784, 1787 ('with alterations'), 1787 (5th edn), Dublin 1788 ('with additional songs'), London 1789; Larpent ms.
Fashionable levities. C CG 2 April 1785. 1785, 1785, Dublin 1786; Inchbald's Modern Theatre 10, Larpent ms.
Abstract of acts passed in Parliament from Jan 26 to Oct 27 1786. 1786.
April Fool: or the follies of a night. F CG 1 April 1786. Larpent ms.
Richard Coeur de Lion, taken from the French comedy by M. Sedaine. CO CG 16 Oct 1786. 1786; Larpent ms.
Critic upon critic: a dramatic medley. Unacted? 1788 (2nd edn), 1792 ('as it is acted at Covent Garden').
The rules and evidence on pleas of the Crown illustrated from printed and manuscript trials. 2 vols 1802-3.
The Justice of the Peace for Ireland. 2 vols 1808, 4 vols Dublin 1820.

WILLIAM MASON
1724-97
See col 669, above.

MOSES MENDEZ
d. 1758
See col 673, above.

HANNAH MORE
1745-1833
See col 1598, below.

THOMAS MORTON
1764?-1838

Columbus, or a world discovered: an historical play. O CG 1 Dec 1792. 1792, 1792, Dublin 1793, London 1799; Larpent ms.

The children in the wood: a musical piece. New Hay 1 Oct 1793. Dublin 1794 (pirated), London 1796 (said to be rptd from priv ptd edn of 1794, anon); *Cumberland 17*, Larpent ms.

Zorinski: a play. O New Hay 20 June 1795. 1795, Dublin 1796, London 1800; *Inchbald's Modern Theatre 3*.

The way to get married. C CG 23 Jan 1796. 1796, Dublin 1797, London 1800, 1805; *Inchbald's Theatre 25, Cumberland 20*, Larpent ms.

A cure for the heart-ache. C CG 10 Jan 1797. 1797, 1797, Dublin 1797, London 1799, 1800, 1805; *Inchbald's Theatre 25, Cumberland 16*, Larpent ms.

Secrets worth knowing. C CG 11 Jan 1798. 1798, Dublin 1798, London 1802; *Inchbald's Modern Theatre 3, Cumberland 18*, Larpent ms.

Speed the plough. C CG 8 Feb 1800. 1800 (10 edns), Dublin 1800, London 1801, 1805; *Inchbald's Theatre 25, Cumberland 15, British Drama 1826*, Morgan (collated with Larpent ms), Larpent ms.

The blind girl: or a receipt for beauty. CO CG 22 April 1801. Larpent ms.

Beggar my neighbour: or a rogue's a fool. C New Hay 10 July 1802. Larpent ms.

The school of reform: or how to rule a husband. C CG 15 Jan 1805. 1805; *Inchbald's Theatre 25;* New York 1814; *Cumberland 17*, Larpent ms.

Town and country. C CG 10 March 1807. 1807, 1815; *Cumberland 23*.

The knight of Snowdoun: a musical drama. CG 5 Feb 1811. 1811, Larpent ms.

Education. C CG 27 April 1813. 1813; *Cumberland 16*, Larpent ms.

The slave: a musical drama. CG 12 Nov 1816. 1816, 1818 ('with additional songs'); *Cumberland 22*.

Who's my father? F CG 13 April 1818. Larpent ms (as My father! methinks I see my father!).

A Roland for an Oliver. F CG 29 April 1819. 1819; Larpent ms.

Henri Quatre, or Paris in the olden time: a musical romance. CG 22 April 1820. [1820]; Larpent ms.

A school for grown children. C CG 9 Jan 1827. 1827, 1827.

The invincibles: a musical farce. CG 28 Feb 1828. *Cumberland 36*.

Also 3 pieces 1828–30, preserved among the Lord Chamberlain's mss in the Office of Works. The farces etc in Duncombe and T. H. Lacy's Acting edition of plays 1850, ascribed to Morton in DNB and elsewhere, are by his son Thomas Morton.

ARTHUR MURPHY

1727–1805

Collections

The works of Arthur Murphy esq. 7 vols 1786. Vols 1–4 include the plays listed below, except Spouter, Arminius, and Hamlet with alterations.

The way to keep him and five other plays by Murphy. Ed J. P. Emery, New York 1956.

New essays. Ed A. Sherbo, East Lansing 1963.

§ 1

The Gray's Inn Journal, by Charles Ranger. 2 vols 1756, Dublin 1756. 104 nos originally issued weekly in 52 nos 29 Sept 1753–21 Sept 1754.

The apprentice. F DL 2 Jan 1756. 1756, 1756, Dublin 1756, London 1764, Belfast 1773; *Bell suppl 1, Edinburgh Farces 1;* [1803]; *British Drama 5, Minor Theatre 2, Inchbald's Farces 3, Modern British Drama 5, Dibdin 14, British Drama 1824, London Stage 4*.

The Englishman from Paris. F DL 3 April 1756. Ed S. Trefman, Los Angeles 1969 (Augustan Reprint Soc).

The spouter: or the triple revenge. F Unacted. 1756. Anon. Attributed to Murphy by D. E. Baker, Companion to the playhouse, 1764, but probably not Murphy's.

The upholsterer: or what news? F DL 30 March 1758. 1758, 1760, 1763, 1765, 1769 ('with alterations and additions'), Newry 1786, London 1793; *Bell suppl 1, Edinburgh Farces 1, British Drama 5, Modern British Drama 5*, Larpent ms.

The orphan of China. T DL 21 April 1759. 1759, 1759, Dublin 1759, 1761, London 1772, Dublin 1787; *Bell 24 1797;* [1803]; *British Drama 2, Modern British Drama 2, Dibdin 17, London Stage 2*, Larpent ms. Based on the play by Voltaire, who pbd A letter to the author of the Orphan of China, 1759.

The desert island: a dramatic poem in three acts. DL 24 Jan 1760. 1760, Dublin 1760, London 1762, 1786; tr Dutch, 1774.

A letter to M. de Voltaire on the Desert island. 1760.

A poetical epistle to Samuel Johnson. 1760.

The way to keep him. C DL 24 Jan 1760. 1760, 1760, Dublin 1760, London 1761 (4th edn, enlarged from 3 to 5 acts, as performed DL 10 Jan 1761, and with song by Garrick), Dublin 1765, London 1765, 1770, 1770, 1785, [1787]; *Bell 17 1797;* 1802; *British Drama 4, Inchbald's Theatre 15, Modern British Drama 4, Dibdin 10, Oxberry 3, London Stage 1, British Drama 1826, Cumberland 3*, Larpent ms; ed J. P. Emery, New York 1956; tr French, 1818.

All in the wrong. C DL 15 June 1761. 1761, Dublin 1762, Cork 1765, Dublin 1765, London 1775, 1787, Cork 1795; *Bell 12 1797, British Drama 4, Inchbald's Theatre 15, Dibdin 10, Oxford 20, London Stage 2, Cumberland 6, Morgan*, Larpent ms; tr German, 1788.

The old maid. F DL 2 July 1761. 1761, 1761, [1761], Dublin 1762, Belfast 1769; *Bell Suppl 2, Edinburgh Farces 2, British Drama 5, Inchbald's Farces 7, Modern British Drama 5;* tr German, 1842.

The citizen. F DL 2 July 1761. 1763, Dublin 1763, London 1766, 1770, Dublin 1774, London 1784; *Bell suppl 3, Edinburgh Farces 3;* [1803]; *British Drama 5, Minor Theatre 2, Modern British Drama 5, Inchbald's Farces 4, Dibdin 16, Oxberry 11, London Stage 1, Cumberland 24*.

An ode to the Naiads of Fleet Ditch. 1761. A reply to Churchill's Rosciad.

The examiner. 1761. A reply to Murphiad: a mock heroic poem by Philim Maculloch, 1761.

A letter from a Right Honourable Person [the elder Pitt] and the answer to it [by William Beckford] translated into verse. 1761. Anon. Also attributed to Philip Francis.

A letter from the anonymous author of the Letters versified to the anonymous writer of the Monitor. 1761. Anon. Also attributed to Philip Francis.

An essay on the life and genius of Henry Fielding. In Works of Fielding vol 1, 1762.

The auditor. 43 nos 15 July 1762–16 May 1763.

No one's enemy but his own. C CG 9 Jan 1764. 1764, Dublin 1764; Larpent ms.

What we must all come to. F CG 9 Jan 1764. 1764 ('as it was intended to be acted'), [1776] (as Three weeks after marriage: or what we must all come to, as revived CG 30 March 1776), 1776, [1778]; *Bell suppl 1784, Edinburgh Farces 4, British Drama 5, Minor Theatre, Inchbald's Farces 4, Dibdin 7, Oxberry 9, British Drama 1824, London Stage 1*, Larpent ms; tr German, 1786.

The choice. C DL 23 March 1765. In Works vol 1, 1786, Larpent ms.

The school for guardians. C CG 10 Jan 1767. 1767; *Bell 33 1797*, Larpent ms.

Zenobia. T DL 27 Feb 1768. 1768 (4 edns), Dublin 1784; *Bell 33 1797, British Drama, 2 Modern British Drama 2*, Larpent ms.

The Grecian daughter. T DL 26 Feb 1772. 1772, 1772, Dublin 1774, London 1776, 1777, 1787, 1792, 1796; *Bell 4 1797, British Drama 2, Inchbald's Theatre 15, Modern British Drama 2;* Edinburgh [1814], London 1815 (rev J. P. Kemble); *Dibdin 15, Oxberry 14, London Stage 3, Cumberland 25*, Larpent ms; tr Italian, 1787.

Alzuma. T CG 23 Feb 1773. 1773 (3 edns), 1774; Larpent ms.

News from Parnassus: a prelude. CG 23 Sept 1776. In Works vol 4, 1786; Larpent ms.

Know your own mind. C CG 22 Feb 1777. 1778, 1787, [1800]; *Inchbald's Theatre 15*, *Oxberry 14*, *London Stage 2*, *Cumberland 8*, Larpent ms.

Seventeen hundred and ninety-one: a poem in imitation of the thirteenth satire of Juvenal. 1791.

An essay on the life and genius of Samuel Johnson. 1792.

The works of Tacitus with notes, supplements etc. 4 vols 1793, 8 vols 1811, 2 vols 1813.

The rival sisters, adapted for theatrical representation. T King's Haymarket 18 March 1793. 1793, 1793, Dublin 1793; Larpent ms; first pbd in Works vol 7, 1786.

The history of Catiline's conspiracy; with the four orations of Cicero, by George Frederick Sydney. 1795. *See* J. H. Caskey, The first edition of Murphy's Sallust, PQ 13 1934.

Arminius. T Unacted. 1798, [1800] (as Arminius: or the champion of liberty).

The bees: a poem from the fourteenth book of Vaniere's Praedium rusticum. 1799.

The life of David Garrick. 2 vols 1801, Dublin 1801.

The works of Sallust translated. 1807.

Hamlet with alterations: a tragedy in three acts. Bsq Unacted. In J. Foot, Life of Murphy, 1811. Satirizing Garrick; dated 15 Dec 1772.

The game of chess: a poem translated from the Latin [of Vida]. Amsterdam 1876.

§ 2

Foot, Jesse. The life of Arthur Murphy esq. 1811. *See* review by John Foster, Eclectic Rev 14 1811.

Caskey, J. H. Murphy and the war on sentimental comedy. JEGP 30 1931.

—— The first edition of Murphy's Sallust. PQ 13 1934.

—— Murphy's common-place book. SP 37 1940.

Emery, J. P. An unpublished letter from Murphy to Goldsmith concerning She stoops to conquer. PQ 17 1938.

—— Murphy's criticisms in the London Chronicle. PMLA 54 1939.

—— Murphy: an eminent English dramatist of the eighteenth century. Philadelphia 1946.

—— Murphy's authorship of the Notes of Smart's Hilliad. MLN 61 1946.

Bradford, C. B. Murphy's meeting with Johnson. PQ 18 1939.

Botting, R. B. Bolingbroke and Aboulcasem. MLQ 5 1944.

—— The textual history of Murphy's Gray's Inn Journal. Washington State Univ Research Stud 25 1957.

Dunbar, H. H. The dramatic career of Murphy. New York 1946.

New essays by Murphy. Ed A. Sherbo, East Lansing 1963.

—— Imitation of concealment: who wrote the Entertainer essays? BNYPL Sept 1965. *See* H. K. Miller, ibid.

Trefman, S. Murphy's long lost Englishman from Paris: a manuscript discovered. Theatre Notebook 20 1966.

Lehnert, M. Murphys Hamlet-parodie 1772 auf David Garrick. Sh Jb 102 1966.

WILLIAM O'BRIEN
d. 1815

Cross purposes. F CG 5 Dec 1772. [1772] (anon), [1772] (anon), [1773], Dublin 1773, London 1783; *London Stage 2*, Larpent ms.

The duel: a play. DL 8 Dec 1772. 1772 (anon), 1773; Larpent ms.

Lusorium: being a collection of convivial songs, lectures etc. 1782.

KANE O'HARA
1714?–82

§ 1

Midas: an English burletta. Dublin 22 Jan 1762. 1764, 1764, Dublin 1764, London 1766, 1767, 1768, Cork 1770, Dublin 1770, London 1771, Perth 1777, London 1795, 1812; *Bell suppl 2*, *Modern British Drama 5*, *Dibdin 9*, *Inchbald's Farces 7*, *Oxberry 15*, *British Drama 1824*, *London Stage 12*, Larpent ms.

The golden pippin: an English burletta. CG 6 Feb 1773. 1773, 1773, 1776, 1777, 1787; *Bell suppl 3*, Larpent ms.

The two misers: a musical farce. CG 21 Jan 1775. 1775; *Modern British Drama 5*, *Dibdin 19*, *London Stage 3*.

April-Day. Bsq New Hay 22 Aug 1777. 1777, 1778.

Tom Thumb, altered from Henry Fielding. Bsq CG 3 Oct 1780. [1805], 1806, 1810, 1830; *Inchbald's Farces 6*, *British Drama 1824*, *London Stage 2*, *Cumberland 23*.

§ 2

Maxwell, M. F. Olympus at Billingsgate: the burlettas of O'Hara. Educational Theatre Jnl 15 1963.

JOHN O'KEEFFE
1747–1833

Collections

The dramatic works of John O'Keeffe, prepared for the press by the author. 4 vols 1798. 29 plays, including all those previously pbd in authorized edns except She gallant. It omits the Haymarket pieces—The agreeable surprise, The son-in-law, The dead alive, Peeping Tom of Coventry, The young Quaker—the copyright of which belonged to the younger Colman. These 5 plays had been pirated in Dublin; the earliest authentic texts are those in *Cumberland*.

§ 1

The she gallant: or square toes outwitted. F Smock Alley Dublin 14 Jan 1767. Dublin [1767], London 1767.

Tony Lumpkin in town. F New Hay 2 July 1778. 1780 (authorized), Dublin 1780.

The son-in-law: a musical farce. New Hay 14 Aug 1779. Dublin 1783, 1788; *Cumberland 31*, Larpent ms.

The dead alive: a musical farce. New Hay 16 June 1781. Dublin 1783, Belfast 1784; Larpent ms (as Edward and Caroline: or the dead alive).

The agreeable surprise. CO New Hay 3 Sept 1781. Newry 1783, Dublin 1784, 1785, 1786, 1787, 1792; *Cumberland 31*, Larpent ms.

The banditti: or love's labyrinth. CO CG 28 Nov 1781. 1781 (songs only); Larpent ms.

The positive man. F CG 16 March 1782. 1798 (in O'Keeffe's works vol 2), 1800; *Inchbald's Farces 2*, Larpent ms.

Harlequin Teague: or the giant's causeway. Pant New Hay 17 Aug 1782. 1782 (songs only); Larpent ms.

The castle of Andalusia. CO CG 2 Nov 1782. Dublin 1783 ('with additional songs by Sig Tenducci'), 1788, 1794, London 1794 (authorized); *Inchbald's Theatre 22*, *Cumberland 32*, Larpent ms.

Lord Mayor's Day: or a flight from Lapland. Pant CG 25 Nov 1782. 1782 (songs only); Larpent ms.

The maid the mistress: a burletta. CG 15 Feb 1783. 1783 (songs only); Larpent ms (as The servant mistress).

The Shamrock: or St Patrick's Day. C Crowe Street Dublin 15 April 1777. Larpent ms (for CG performance 7 March 1783, as The Shamrock, or anniversary of St Patrick: a pastoral romance).

The young Quaker. C New Hay 26 July 1783. Dublin 1784, 1784, 1788; *Cumberland 37*, Larpent ms.

The birth-day, or the Prince of Arragon: a dramatick piece with songs. New Hay 12 Aug 1783. Dublin 1783 (authorized); Larpent ms.

Gretna Green. CO New Hay 28 Aug 1783. Dublin [1791]; Larpent ms (as New Gretna Green). By Charles Stuart, with alterations and additional songs by O'Keeffe.

The poor soldier. CO CG 4 Nov 1783. Dublin 1785 ('a new edition corrected'), 1786, 1788, London 1798 (in O'Keeffe's works vol 1); 1800; *Inchbald's Farces 2, Cumberland 20*, Larpent ms.

Friar Bacon: or Harlequin's adventures in Lilliput, Brobdinnag etc. Pant CG 23 Dec 1783. [1784] (music only); Larpent ms.

Peeping Tom of Coventry. CO New Hay 6 Sept 1784. Dublin 1785, 1786, 1787, 1792, Coventry 1815; *Cumberland 21*, Larpent ms.

Fontainebleau: or our way to France. CO CG 16 Nov 1784. Dublin 1785, 1787, 1790, London 1798 (in O'Keeffe's works vol 2); *Inchbald's Theatre 20, Cumberland 32*, Larpent ms.

The blacksmith of Antwerp: a musical farce. CG 7 Feb 1785. In O'Keeffe's works vol 2, 1798; Larpent ms.

A beggar on horseback: an operatic farce. New Hay 16 June 1785. In O'Keeffe's works vol 3, 1798; Larpent ms.

Omai: or a trip around the world. Pant CG 20 Dec 1785. 1785 (songs and synopsis); Larpent ms.

Patrick in Prussia: or love in a camp. CO CG 17 Feb 1786. Dublin 1786 ('from the author's original manuscript'), 1792, London 1798 (in O'Keeffe's works vol 4 as Love in a camp), 1800; Larpent ms.

The siege of Curzola. CO New Hay 12 Aug 1786. 1786 (songs only); Larpent ms.

The man milliner: an operatic farce. CG 27 Jan 1787. In O'Keeffe's works vol 4; Larpent ms.

The farmer. CO CG 31 Oct 1787. Dublin 1788, 1789, 1792, London 1798 (in O'Keeffe's works vol 4); 1800; *Cumberland 27*.

Tantara Rara rogues all: an afterpiece. CG 1 March 1788. 1798 (in O'Keeffe's works vol 3); Larpent ms.

The prisoner at large. F New Hay 2 July 1788. 1788 (authorized), Dublin 1789, 1792, London 1800; *Cumberland 26*.

The Highland reel. CO CG 6 Nov 1788. Dublin 1789, 1790, [1791], London 1798 (in O'Keeffe's works vol 4); 1800; *Inchbald's Farces 2, Cumberland 18*.

Aladdin: or the wonderful lamp. Pant CG 26 Dec 1788. Larpent ms.

The toy: or the life of a day. C CG 3 Feb 1789. 1798 (in O'Keeffe's works vol 3); Larpent ms (as The toy: or Hampton Court frolics).

The faro table. C CG 4 April 1789. Larpent ms. An alteration of Mrs Centlivre, Gamester.

The little hunch-back: or a frolic in Bagdad. F CG 14 April 1789. 1789; Larpent ms.

Le grenadier: a musical play, intended to have been performed at the Haymarket. 1789, 1798 (in O'Keeffe's works vol 1). Prohibited.

The Czar Peter. CO CG 8 March 1790. 1798 (in O'Keeffe's works vol 3); Larpent ms.

Modern antiques: or the merry mourners. F CG 14 March 1791. Dublin 1792, 1792, London 1798 (in O'Keeffe's works vol 1); 1800; *Cumberland 29*, Larpent ms (as The merry musicians).

Wild oats: or the strolling gentleman. C Dublin 1791. Dublin 1792, 1794, London 1794 (authorized), 1806; *Cumberland 34*, Larpent ms.

Sprigs of laurel. CO CG 11 May 1793. 1793 (authorized), 1804; *Cumberland 39*, Larpent ms (as Sprigs of laurel or royal example).

The London hermit: or rambles in Dorsetshire. C New Hay 29 June 1793. 1793 (authorized, 3 edns), Dublin 1794, London 1798, Larpent ms.

The world in a village. C CG 23 Nov 1793. 1793 (authorized), Larpent ms.

Jenny's whim: or the roasted emperor. F Unacted. Larpent ms. Advertised for New Hay 1 Sept 1794 but prohibited.

Oatlands or the transfer of the laurel: a poem. 1795.

Life's vagaries. C CG 19 March 1795. 1795 (authorized), 1795, 1810; Larpent ms.

The Irish mimic, or Blunders at Brighton: a musical piece. CG 23 April 1795. 1795 (authorized), 1797.

Merry Sherwood: or Harlequin forrester. Pant CG 21 Dec 1795. 1795 (songs only); Larpent ms (as The merry forester).

The lie of the day. C CG 9 March 1796. 1798 (in O'Keeffe's works vol 3); 1800; *Inchbald's Modern Theatre 10*. A revision of Toy, above.

The Wicklow gold mines: or the lad of the hills. CO CG 13 April 1796. Dublin 1814; Larpent ms.

The doldrum: or 1803. F CG 23 April 1796. 1798 (in O'Keeffe's works vol 4), Larpent ms (as The sleeper: or AD 1803).

Alfred, or the magic banner: a drama. New Hay 22 June 1796. Dublin 1796, London 1798 (in O'Keeffe's works vol 4), Larpent ms (as The magick banner: or two wives in a house).

The Wicklow Mountains. CO CG 17 Oct 1796. Dublin 1797, London 1798 (in O'Keeffe's works vol 2). A revision of Wicklow gold mines, above.

Olympus in an uproar: or the descent of the deities. Bsq CG 5 Nov 1796. Larpent ms. Adapted from Kane O'Hara, The golden pippin.

Our wooden walls, or all to St Paul's: an interlude. CG 19 Dec 1797. Larpent ms.

The eleventh of June or the Daggerwoods at Dunstable. F DL 5 June 1798. Larpent ms.

Nosegay of weeds: or new servants in old places. F DL 6 June 1798. Larpent ms.

Recollections of the life of John O'Keeffe, written by himself. 2 vols 1826.

A father's legacy to his daughter: being the poetical works of the late John O'Keeffe edited by Adelaide O'Keeffe. 1834.

§ 2

Babcock, R. W. Adelaide O'Keeffe. TLS 9 Jan 1937.

Morgan, S. S. The damning of Holcroft's Knave or not? and O'Keeffe's She's eloped. HLQ 22 1958.

FREDERICK PILON
1750–88

The drama: a poem. 1775. Anon.

An essay on the character of Hamlet, as performed by Mr Henderson. [1777], [1777]. Anon.

The invasion: or a trip to Brighthelmstone. F CG 4 Nov 1778. 1778, 1778, 1782; Larpent ms.

The Liverpool prize. F CG 22 Feb 1779. 1779; Larpent ms.

Illumination, or the glazier's conspiracy: a prelude. CG 12 April 1779. 1779; Larpent ms.

The device: or the deaf doctor. F CG 27 Sept 1779. Larpent ms.

The deaf lover. F CG 2 Feb 1780. 1780, 1780, 1781, 1793, Dublin 1802, London 1811; *London Stage 3*. An alteration of Device, above.

The siege of Gibraltar: a musical farce. CG 25 April 1780. 1780, 1780.

The humours of an election. F CG 19 Oct 1780. 1780, 1780; Larpent ms.

Thelyphthora: or more wives than one. F CG 8 March 1781. Larpent ms.

The fair American. CO DL 18 May 1782. 1785, Dublin 1785; Larpent ms.

Ærostation: or the Templar's stratagem. F CG 29 Oct 1784. 1784, Dublin 1785; Larpent ms.

Barataria: or Sancho turn'd governor. F CG 29 March 1785. 1793 ('new edition').

A lecture of heads, by G. A. Stevens. Expanded by Pilon, 1785.

He would be a soldier. C CG 18 Nov 1786. 1786, 1786, 1787, Dublin 1787; *British Drama 1826, London Stage 3*, Larpent ms.

SAMUEL JACKSON PRATT
1749–1814

See col 677, above.

HENRY JAMES PYE
1745–1813

See col 678, above.

JOSEPH REED
1723–87

A British philippic, inscribed to the Earl of Granville. 1756. Anon.

Madrigal and Trulletta: a mock-tragedy, with notes by the author and Dr Humbug, critick and censor-general. Bsq CG 6 July 1758. 1758; Larpent ms.

A sop in the pan for a physical critick, in a letter to Dr Sm*ll*t, occasion'd by a criticism on Madrigal and Truletta, by a halter-maker. 1759.

The register-office. F DL 25 April 1761. 1761, Dublin 1761, London 1771; *Bell suppl 3, Inchbald's Farces 3, London Stage 4, Acting Drama*, Larpent ms.

Dido. T DL 28 March 1767. 1808; Larpent ms.

Tom Jones. CO CG 14 Jan 1769. 1769, 1769, Dublin 1769; Larpent ms.

The impostors: or a cure for credulity. F CG 19 March 1776. Larpent ms.

Saint Peter's lodge: a serio-comi-legendary tale, in Hudibrastic verse. 1786. Anon.

The retort courteous: or a candid appeal to the public. 1787. On the rejection of Reed's Dido by the DL management.

FREDERICK REYNOLDS
1764–1841

Werter. T Bath 25 Nov 1785, CG 14 March 1786. Dublin 1786, London 1796, 1802; Larpent ms.

Eloisa. T CG 20 Dec 1786. Larpent ms.

The dramatist: or stop him who can. C CG 15 May 1789. Dublin 1790 (pirated), London 1793 (authorized); *Inchbald's Theatre 20, Cumberland 39*, Larpent ms.

The Crusade: an historical romance. CG 6 May 1790. 1790 (songs only); Larpent ms.

Better late than never. C DL 17 Nov 1790. 1790, Dublin 1791; Larpent ms. With M. P. Andrews.

Notoriety. C CG 5 Nov 1791. Dublin 1792, London 1793; *Inchbald's Modern Theatre 1, Cumberland 26*, Larpent ms.

How to grow rich. C CG 18 April 1793. 1793 (3 edns); *Inchbald's Modern Theatre 1, Cumberland 30*, Larpent ms.

The rage. C CG 23 Oct 1794. 1795 (5 edns), Dublin 1795, London 1797; *Inchbald's Modern Theatre 1*, Larpent ms.

The mysteries of the castle: a dramatic tale. CG 31 Jan 1795. 1795; Larpent ms. With M. P. Andrews.

Speculation. C CG 7 Nov 1795. 1795, 1796, 1800; Larpent ms.

Fortune's fool. C CG 29 Oct 1796. 1796, Dublin 1797; *Inchbald's Modern Theatre 2*, Larpent ms.

The will. C DL 19 April 1797. 1797 (3 edns), Dublin 1797, London 1806; *Inchbald's Modern Theatre 1*; 1815; *Cumberland 21*.

Cheap living. C DL 21 Oct 1797. 1797 (3 edns), Dublin 1798; Larpent ms.

Laugh when you can. C CG 8 Dec 1798. 1799, Dublin 1799, London 1802; *Inchbald's Modern Theatre 2, Cumberland 23*.

Management. C CG 31 Oct 1799. 1799 (4 edns), 1800; Larpent ms.

Life. C CG 1 Nov 1800. 1801 (6 edns), Dublin 1801; *Inchbald's Modern Theatre 1*, Larpent ms.

Folly as it flies. C CG 29 Oct 1801. 1801, 1801; *Inchbald's Modern Theatre 2, Cumberland 27*, Larpent ms.

Delays and blunders. C CG 30 Oct 1802. 1803, 1805; Larpent ms.

The caravan, or the driver and his dog: a serio comic romance. DL 5 Dec 1803, 1803 (3 edns); Larpent ms.

The blind bargain: or hear him out. C CG 24 Oct 1804. 1805; *Cumberland 28*.

The delinquent: or seeing company. C CG 14 Nov 1805. 1805; *Inchbald's Modern Theatre 2, Cumberland 40*, Larpent ms (as Seeing company).

The deserts of Arabia: a spectacle. CG 20 Nov 1806. 1806 (songs only); Larpent ms.

Arbitration, or free and easy: a musical farce. CG 11 Dec 1806. Larpent ms.

Begone dull care: or how will it end? C CG 9 Feb 1808. 1808.

The free knights, or the edict of Charlemagne: a drama interspersed with music. CG 8 Feb 1808. 1810; Larpent ms (dated 1810 as The edict of Charlemagne: or the free knights).

The exile, or the deserts of Siberia: an operatic play. CG 10 Nov 1808. *Cumberland 29*, Larpent ms.

The bridal ring: a dramatic romance. CG 16 Oct 1810. Larpent ms.

The virgin of the sun: an operatic drama. CG 31 Jan 1812. 1812 (4 edns); Larpent ms.

The renegade: a historical drama founded on Dryden's Don Sebastian, King of Portugal. CG 2 Dec 1812. 1812, 1812, 1813; Larpent ms.

A midsummer night's dream: a comic opera. CG 17 Jan 1816. 1816. From Shakespeare.

The humorous lieutenant: or Alexander's successors. C CG 18 Jan 1817. Larpent ms.

The Duke of Savoy, or wife and mistress: a melo-drama. CG 29 Sept 1817. Larpent ms.

The father and his children: a melo-drama. CG 25 Oct 1817. Larpent ms.

The illustrious traveller, or the forges of Kanzell: a melo-drama. CG 3 Feb 1818. Larpent ms.

The burgomaster of Sardaam, or the two Peters: a melo-drama. CG 23 Sept 1818. Larpent ms.

The comedy of errors. CO CG 11 Dec 1819. 1819. From Shakespeare.

Don John: or the two Violettas. CO CG 20 Feb 1821. 1821. From Buckingham's adaptation of John Fletcher, The chances.

The life and times of Frederick Reynolds written by himself. 2 vols 1826, 1827.

A playwright's adventures. 1831. A novel.

Reynolds' later plays were not pbd. The mss of 6 of them 1828-40 are among the Lord Chamberlain's papers in the Record Office.

FRANCES SHERIDAN
1724–66

Bibliographies

Russell, N. H. Some uncollected authors xxxviii: Frances Sheridan. Book Collector 13 1964.

§ 1

Memoirs of Miss Sidney Bidulph, extracted from her own journal. 3 vols 1761 (anon), 5 vols 1767 (expanded), 3 vols 1767, 1 vol 1786, 5 vols 1796; tr French, 1762; German, 1762. A novel.

The discovery, written by the editor of Miss Sidney Bidulph. C DL 3 Feb 1763. 1763, 1763, Dublin 1763, Edinburgh 1763; Larpent ms.
The dupe, by the author of the Discovery. C DL 10 Dec 1763. 1764; Larpent ms.
A trip to Bath. C Unacted. Ed F. Rae as A journey to Bath in Sheridan's plays as he wrote them, 1902. Rae's text is apparently an incomplete revision by another hand, possibly R. B. Sheridan's c. 1774. The play was originally written in 1765.
The history of Nourjahad, by the editor of Sidney Bidulph. 1767, 1788, 1827, 1828; tr Polish, 1784; French, 1785.

§ 2

Lefanu, Alicia. Memoirs of the life and writings of Mrs Frances Sheridan. 1824.
Fitzgerald, P. The lives of the Sheridans. 2 vols 1886.
Wilson, M. In her These were Muses, 1924.
Chew, S. P. Prévost's Mémoires pour servir à l'histoire de la vertu. MLN 54 1939. On the French version of Miss Sidney Bidulph.
— The Dupe: a study in the 'low'. PQ 18 1939.

TOBIAS SMOLLETT
1721–71
See col 962, below.

GEORGE ALEXANDER STEVENS
1710–84
See col 569, above.

RICHARD TICKELL
1751–93
See col 688, above.

JAMES TOWNLEY
1714–78

High life below stairs. F DL 31 Oct 1759. *See under Garrick, col 803, above.*
False concord. F CG 20 March 1764. Larpent ms.
The tutor. F DL 4 Feb 1765. Larpent ms.
Also sermons.

THOMAS VAUGHAN
fl. 1761–1820

The retort. 1761. Anon. A reply to Churchill's Rosciad.
Love's vagaries, or the whim of the moment: a dramatic piece. F DL 15 April 1776, as Love's metamorphoses. 1791.
The hotel: or the double valet. F DL 21 Nov 1776. 1776, [1777], Dublin 1777; Larpent ms.
Fashionable follies: a novel, containing the history of a Parisian family. 2 vols 1781, 3 vols 1810 (enlarged).
Deception. F DL 28 Oct 1784. Larpent ms.
Playful translations, from the Greek and Roman classics, adapted to men, manners and things, with some prologues, epilogues [etc]. No 1 (all pbd?), 1804.
Vaughan's The Triumvirate, by Veritas, 1761, is said to be extant only in fragments.

FRANCIS GODOLPHIN WALDRON
1744–1818

The maid of Kent. C DL 17 May 1773. 1778; Larpent ms. Anon.

The sad shepherd, with a continuation, notes and an appendix. Past Unacted. 1783; ed W. W. Greg in Bang's Materialien vol 11, Louvain 1905. Jonson's fragment completed.
The King in the country: a dramatic piece. Richmond and Windsor 1788. 1789. From Thomas Heywood, Edward IV.
The literary museum: or ancient and modern repository, comprising scarce and curious tracts. 1792.
The prodigal: a dramatic piece. New Hay 2 Dec 1793. 1794; Larpent ms. From J. Mitchell, The fatal extravagance.
Heigho for a husband. C New Hay 14 Jan 1794. 1794; Larpent ms.
Love and madness. TC New Hay 21 Sept 1795. 1795 (songs only); Larpent ms. From Two noble kinsmen.
'Tis a wise child knows its own father. C New Hay 21 Sept 1795. Larpent ms.
The biographical mirrour. 3 vols 1795–8. Lives mainly by Waldron.
Free reflections on miscellaneous papers and legal instruments under the hand and seal of William Shakespeare, in the possession of Samuel Ireland; to which are added extracts from an unpublished ms play called the Virgin Queen, written by or in imitation of Shakespeare. 1796.
The Virgin Queen, attempted as a sequel to Shakespeare's Tempest. C Unacted. 1797.
The man with two wives: or wigs for ever! a dramatic fable. Bsq Royalty 24 March 1798. 1798.
A compendious history of the English stage. 1800. Ed Waldron.
A collection of miscellaneous poetry. 1802.
The Shakespearean miscellany. 4 pts 1802.
The miller's maid. CO New Hay 25 Aug 1804. [1804] (songs only); Larpent ms.
Waldron also produced edns of Downes's Roscius Anglicanus, Lodge's Rosalynde and extracts from Kynaston's commentary on Chaucer's Troilus and Criseyde. He assisted in Charles Dibdin's How do you do?

WILLIAM WHITEHEAD
1715–85

Collections

Plays and poems by William Whitehead esq, Poet Laureat. 2 vols 1774; Poems vol 3; to which are prefixed Memoirs of his life and writings by W. Mason, York 1788.
The works of the British poets. Vols 72–3, 1790.
The poets of Great Britain. [Ed R. Anderson] vol 11, Edinburgh 1793.
The works of the English poets. Ed A. Chalmers vol 17, 1810.

§ 1

The danger of writing verse. 1741, 1748 (rptd in Dodsley's Collection vol 2).
Anne Boleyn to Henry the Eighth: an epistle. 1743.
An essay on ridicule. 1743, 1753.
Atys and Adrastus: a tale, in the manner of Dryden's Fables. 1744, 1744.
On nobility; an epistle to the Earl of ****** [Ashburnham]. 1744.
The Roman father. T DL 24 Feb 1750. 1750, 1750, Dublin 1750, London 1754 (in Poems on several occasions), 1766, 1769, 1776 (in New English theatre vol 12), 1777; *Bell 20 1778, 3 1797, British Drama 2, Inchbald's Theatre 14, Modern British Drama 2, Dibdin 12, London Stage 3, British Drama 1826.*
A dissertation on the Shield of Aeneas. In Works of Virgil in English, ed J. Warton 4 vols 1753 etc.
An hymn to the nymph of Bristol Spring. 1751.
Poems on several occasions, with the Roman father. 1754.
Fatal constancy. T Unacted. In Poems on several occasions, 1754.

Creusa, Queen of Athens. T DL 20 May 1754. 1754, Dublin 1755; *Bell 20 1778, 34 1797, British Drama 2,* Larpent ms.

Elegies, with an ode to the Tiber, written abroad. 1757, 1757.

Verses to the people of England. 1758, 1758.

A charge to the poets. 1762.

The school for lovers. C DL 10 Feb 1762. 1762, Dublin 1762, London 1763, 1770 (4th edn); *Bell 7 1797;* tr German, 1771.

A trip to Scotland. F DL 6 Jan 1770. 1770 (anon); *Edinburgh Farces 6.*

Variety: a tale for married people. 1776 (4 edns), 1777, [1784?].

The goat's beard: a fable. 1777, 1777, Dublin 1777.

§ 2

Dobson, A. Laureate Whitehead. In his Old Kensington Palace and other papers, 1910.

Broadus, E. K. In his Laureateship, Oxford 1921.

Bitter, A. Whitehead: poeta laureatus. Halle 1933.

Todd, W. B. A hidden edition of Variety 1776. PBSA 45 1951.

IX. ADAPTATIONS AND TRANSLATIONS

(1) CORNEILLE, RACINE AND VOLTAIRE ON THE ENGLISH STAGE

Critical Studies

Mulert, A. Pierre Corneille in der englischen Übersetzungsliteratur. Munich 1900.

Canfield, D. F. Corneille and Racine in England. New York 1904. With bibliography.

Baumgärtner, Georg. Voltaire auf der englischen Bühne des 18 Jahrhunderts. Strasbourg 1913.

Bruce, H. L. The period of greatest popularity of Voltaire's plays on the English stage. MLN 33 1918.

— Voltaire on the English stage. Berkeley 1918. With bibliography.

Eccles, F. Y. Racine in England. 1921.

Brenner, C. D. Dramatizations of French short stories in the eighteenth century. Berkeley 1947. Especially La Fontaine, Marmontel and Voltaire.

Crowley, F. J. Voltaire at Stationers' Hall. Library 5th ser 10 1955.

Gooch, G. P. Voltaire in England. Contemporary Rev June–Sept 1959.

Adaptations of Corneille

For the unacted versions and literal trns, see col 1504, below.

Dancer, John. Nicomede. TC Theatre Royal Dublin. 1671.

The mistaken beauty: or the lyar. C DL c. Sept 1684. 1685.

[Cibber, Colley?]. Cinna's conspiracy. T DL 19 Feb 1713. 1713.

Cibber, Colley. Ximena: or the heroick daughter. T DL 28 Nov 1712. 1719. From Le Cid.

Whitehead, William. The Roman father. T DL 24 Feb 1750. 1750 etc. From Horace.

Foote, Samuel. The lyar. C CG 12 Jan 1762. 1764 etc.

Adaptations of Racine

The literal and unacted versions are listed col 1527, below.

[Crowne, John]. Andromache. T DG c. Aug 1674. 1675.

Otway, Thomas. Titus and Berenice. T DL c. Dec 1676. 1677 etc.

Boyer, Abel. Achilles: or Iphigenia in Aulis. T DL c. Dec 1699. 1700 etc.

Smith, Edmund. Phaedra and Hippolitus. T Hay April 1707. [1707] etc.

Philips, Ambrose. The distrest mother. T DL 17 March 1712. 1712 etc. From Andromaque.

Johnson, Charles. The victim. T DL 5 Jan 1714. 1714 etc. From Iphigénie.

— The Sultaness. T DL 25 Feb 1717. 1717 etc. From Bajazet.

[Robe, Jane]. The fatal legacy. T LIF 23 April 1723. 1723. From La Thébaïde.

Adaptations of Voltaire

The literal and unacted versions are listed col 1534, below.

Fenton, Elijah. Mariamne. T LIF 22 Feb 1723. 1723 etc.

Duncombe, William. Junius Brutus. T DL 25 Nov 1734. 1735 etc.

Hill, Aaron. The tragedy of Zara. DL 12 Jan 1736. 1736 etc.

— Alzira. T LIF 18 June 1736. 1736 etc.

— Merope. T DL 15 April 1749. 1749 etc.

— The Roman revenge. T Bath c. 1753. 1753 etc. From La mort de César.

Miller, James and John Hoadley. Mahomet the impostor. T DL 25 April 1744. 1744 etc.

Murphy, Arthur. The orphan of China. T DL 21 April 1759. 1759 etc.

— No one's enemy but his own. C CG 9 Jan 1764. 1764 etc. From L'indiscret.

— Alzuma. T CG 23 Feb 1773. 1773 etc.

Colman, George, the elder. The English merchant. C DL 21 Feb 1767. 1767 etc. From L'écossaise.

Francklin, Thomas. Orestes. T CG 13 March 1769. 1762 (in Works of Mr de Voltaire vol 3), 1776, 1787 (as Electra).

— Matilda. T DL 21 Jan 1775. 1775, 1775, Dublin 1775. From Le Duc de Foix.

[Celesia, Dorothea]. Almida. T DL 12 Jan 1771. 1771, 1771. From Tancrède.

[Cradock, Joseph]. Zobeide. T CG 11 Dec 1771. 1771, 1772, 1762 (for 1772), Dublin 1772. From Les Scythes.

Ayscough, G. E. Semiramis. T DL 14 Dec 1776. 1776.

Macklin, Charles. The man of the world. C CG 10 May 1781. 1785 etc. Partly fron Nanine.

(2) LESSING, GOETHE, SCHILLER AND KOTZEBUE ON THE ENGLISH STAGE

Critical Studies

Brandl, A. Die Aufnahme von Goethes Jungwerken in England. Goethe-Jahrbuch 1882.

Rea, T. Schiller's poems and dramas in England. 1906.

Rullman, W. Schillers Räubern. Schriften der Gesellschaft für Theatergeschichte 15 1910.

Todt, W. Lessing in England. Heidelberg 1912.

Kenwood, S. H. Lessing in England. MLR 9 1914.

Buyers, G. The influence of Schiller in England 1780–1830. E Studien 48 1915.

Cooke, M. W. Schiller's Robbers in England. MLR 11 1915.

Willoughby, L. A. English translations and adaptations of Schiller's Robbers. MLR 16 1921.

Williams, L. A. Schiller's Kabale und Liebe in English translations. Pbns of Eng Goethe Soc 1924.

Thomson, L. F. Kotzebue: a survey of his progress in France and England. Paris 1928.

Ewen, F. The prestige of Schiller in England 1788–1859. New York 1932.

Waterhouse, G. Schiller's Räuber in England before 1800. MLR 30 1935.

Gosch, M. 'Translators' of Kotzebue in England. Monatshefte für Deutschen Unterricht 31 1939.

Schiller in England 1787–1960: a bibliography. Ed R. Pick 1961.

Adaptations and Translations of Lessing

Raspe, Rudolph Erich. Nathan the Wise: a philosophical drama. Unacted. 1781.

Johnstone, James. The disbanded officer: or the Baroness of Bruchsal. C New Hay 24 July 1786. 1786, Dublin 1786. Adapted from Minna von Barnhelm.

Taylor, William. Nathan the Wise. Unacted. Norwich 1791, London 1805.

The school for honour: or the chance of war. Unacted. 1799. A trn of Minna von Barnhelm.

Adaptations and Translations of Goethe

Reynolds, Frederick. Werter. T Bath 25 Nov 1785. Dublin 1786, London 1796, 1802.

Taylor, William. Iphigenia of Tauris. T Unacted. 1793, 1794.

Leftley, Charles. Clavidgo. T Unacted. 1798.

Scott, Sir Walter. Goetz of Berlichingen, with the Iron hand. T Unacted. 1799.

Lawrence, Rose. Goetz of Berlingen. Unacted. 1799.

Adaptations and Translations of Schiller

Tytler, A. F. The robbers. T Unacted. 1792, 1795, 1797, 1800.

[Timaeus, J. J. C.] Cabal and love. T Unacted. 1795, 1796, 1797.

Noehden, Georg Heinrich and J. Stoddart. Fiesco: or the Genoese conspiracy. T Unacted. 1796, 1798, 1798.

— Don Carlos. T Unacted. 1798.

Lewis, M. G. The minister. T Unacted. 1797, 1798. From Kabale und Liebe.

Thompson, Benjamin. Don Carlos. Unacted. 1798.

[Craven, Keppel]. The robbers, translated and altered. Brandenburgh House 1797. 1799.

Holman, J. G. The Red-cross knights: a play founded on the Robbers of Schiller. New Hay 21 Aug 1799. 1799.

Render, William. The robbers. Unacted. 1799.

Adaptations and Translations of Kotzebue

The Corsicans: a drama. Unacted. 1796, 1799, Dublin 1799.

The negro slaves: a dramatic historical piece. Unacted. 1796.

Inchbald, Elizabeth. Lovers' vows: a play. CG 11 Oct 1798. 1798 (11 edns). From Das Kind der Liebe.

— The wise man of the East: a play. CG 30 Nov 1799. 1799 (3 edns). From Das Schreibepult.

Papendick, George. The stranger: or misanthropy and repentance. T Unacted. 1798 (4 edns). From Menschenhass und Reue.

Plumptre, Anne. The Count of Burgundy: a play. Unacted. 1798 (3 edns), Dublin 1799.

— The natural son: a play. Unacted. 1798 (4 edns), Dublin 1798.

— The force of calumny: a play. Unacted. 1799, 1799.

— La-Peyrouse: a drama. Unacted. 1799.

— The Spaniards in Peru: or the death of Rolla. T Unacted. 1799 (6 edns).

— The virgin of the sun: a play. Unacted. 1799 (5 edns).

— The widow and the riding horse: a dramatic trifle. Unacted. 1799.

Porter, Stephen. Lover's vows, or the child of love: a play. Unacted. 1798.

Render, William. Count Benyowsky: or the conspiracy of Kamtschatka. TC Unacted. 1798, 1798.

Schinck, A. The stranger, freely translated from Kotzebue's Misanthropy and repentance. Unacted. 1798 (5 edns), 1799, 1799.

Thompson, Benjamin. The stranger. DL 24 March 1798. 1798.

— Adelaide of Wulfingen. T Unacted. 1798.

— La Perouse. Unacted. 1799.

— The happy family: a drama. Unacted. 1799, Dublin 1800.

— The virgin of the sun. Unacted. 1799.

Dibdin, T. J. The horse and the widow. F CG 4 May 1799. 1799, Dublin 1799. From Die Witwe and das Reitpferd.

Dutton, Thomas. Pizarro in Peru: or the death of Rolla. T Unacted. [1799].

Geisweiler, Maria. The noble lie: a drama. Unacted. 1799.

— Poverty and nobleness of mind: a play. Unacted. 1799.

— Joanna of Montfaucon: a drama. Unacted. 1799.

Heron, Robert. Pizarro: or the death of Rolla. T Unacted. 1799.

Hoare, Prince. Sighs: or the daughter. C New Hay 30 July 1799. 1799, 1799, Dublin 1802. From Die edle Lüge.

Ludger, C. The peevish man: a drama. Unacted. 1799.

— The reconciliation: or the birth-day. C Unacted. 1799 (4 edns).

Sheridan, R. B. Pizarro. T DL 24 May 1799. 1799 (26 edns). Adapted from Die Spanier in Peru.

Neuman, H. Family distress, or self-immolation: a play. New Hay 15 June 1799. 1799, Dublin 1799 (as Self-immolation).

West, Matthew. Pizarro. Unacted. 1799.

The East Indian. C Unacted. 1799.

The writing-desk, or youth in danger: a drama. Unacted. 1799.

E. L. A.

4. THE NOVEL

1. GENERAL WORKS

(1) BIBLIOGRAPHIES

Esdaile, A. A list of English tales and prose romances printed before 1740. 1912 (Bibl Soc).

Baker, E. A. A guide to the best fiction in English. 1913; rev J. Packman 1932 (enlarged).

Rolfe, F. On the bibliography of seventeenth-century prose fiction. PMLA 49 1934.

Bernbaum, E. Recent works on prose fiction before 1800. MLN 51–2 1936–7.

— Recent works on prose fiction before 1800. MLN 55 1940.

Bourne, J. A. Some English translations of seventeenth-century Spanish novels. MLR 31 1936.

Block, A. The English novel 1740–1850: a catalogue including prose romances, short stories and translations of foreign fiction. 1939, 1961 (rev).

Blakey, D. The Minerva Press 1790–1820. 1939 (Bibl Soc). Chronological list 1773–1820; popular fiction.

Black, F. G. The epistolary novel in the late eighteenth century: a descriptive and bibliographical study. Eugene Oregon 1940.

Summers, M. A Gothic bibliography. [1941].

Gove, P. B. The imaginary voyage in prose fiction: a history of its criticism and a guide to its study with an annotated check-list of 215 imaginary voyages from 1700 to 1800. New York 1941.

Black, R. K. The Sadleir-Black Gothic collections. Charlottesville 1949.

Rouse, H. B. A selective and critical bibliography of studies in prose fiction. JEGP 48–51 1949–52.

Cordasco, F. The eighteenth-century novel. Brooklyn 1950.

Mish, C. C. English prose fiction 1600–1700: a chronological checklist. Charlottesville 1952, 1967 (rev).

Gecker, S., F. Schmalbach and R. Duncombe. English fiction to 1820 in the University of Pennsylvania Library. Philadelphia 1954.

Sloane, W. Children's books in England and America in the seventeenth century: a history and a checklist. New York 1955.

Tucker, J. E. Wing's short-title catalogue and translations from the French 1641–1700. PBSA 49 1955. Many addns and corrections in translated fiction.

Jones, C. E. Modern books dealing with the novel in English. Bull of Bibliography 22 1957.

Wiles, R. M. Serial publication in England before 1750. Cambridge 1957. Much on minor fiction, including chronological list of titles.

Bell, I. F. and D. B. The English novel 1578–1956: a checklist of twentieth-century criticisms. Denver 1959.

Sherbo, A. Eighteenth-century English fiction in print: an uncritical census. College Eng Nov 1959.

McBurney, W. H. A check-list of English prose fiction 1700–39. Cambridge Mass 1960.

Neuburg, V. E. Chapbooks: a bibliography of reference to English and American chapbook literature of the eighteenth and nineteenth centuries. 1964.

McBurney, W. H. and C. Taylor. English prose fiction 1700–1800 in the University of Illinois library. Urbana 1965. 966 items.

Day, R. A. In his Told in letters, Ann Arbor 1966.

(2) HISTORIES AND STUDIES

Huet, P. D. Essai sur l'origine des romans. 1670; trn rptd in The continental model, ed S. Elledge and D. Schier, Minneapolis 1960.

Reeve, C. The progress of romance. Colchester 1785.

de Staël, Mme. In her De l'Allemagne, Paris 1800.

Bonald, C. de. In his Du style et de la littérature pt 1, Paris 1806.

Barbauld, A. L. On the origin and progress of novel writing. In British novelists vol 1, 1810.

Scott, W. The lives of the novelists. 10 vols 1821–4.

Tocqueville, A. de. In his La démocratie en Amérique, 2 vols Paris 1835, 1840; tr H. Reeve 2 vols 1835.

Green, T. H. Estimate of the value and influence of works of fiction in modern times. 1862; rptd in his Works vol 3, ed R. L. Nettleship 1888.

James, H. The art of fiction (1884). In his Partial portraits, 1888.

— The future of the novel (1899). In his Future of the novel, ed L. Edel, New York 1956.

Lanier, S. The English novel: the development of personality. New York 1883.

Jusserand, J. J. Le roman anglais: origine et formation des grandes écoles de romanciers du 18e siècle. Paris 1886.

Dunlop, J. C. A history of prose fiction. Ed H. Wilson 2 vols 1888 (rev).

Taine, H. In his History of English literature, 1863; tr 1890.

Raleigh, W. The English novel. 1894, 1929 (rev).

Cross, W. L. The development of the English novel. New York 1899.

Williams, H. Two centuries of the English novel. 1911.

Morgan, C. E. The rise of the novel of manners 1600–1740. New York 1911.

Saintsbury, G. The English novel. 1913.

Tieje, A. J. A peculiar phase of the theory of realism in pre-Richardsonian prose fiction. PMLA 27 1913.

Bernbaum, E. The Mary Carleton narratives 1663–73. Cambridge Mass 1914.

Johnson, R. B. The women novelists. 1918.

Huffman, C. H. The eighteenth-century novel in theory and practice. Dayton [1920].

Lubbock, P. The craft of fiction. 1921, 1954 (with new preface).

Lukács, G. Die Theorie des Romans. Berlin 1920.

— Studies in European realism. Tr 1950.

Prinsen, J. De roman in de 18e eeuw in West Europa. Groningen 1925.

Prothero, R. E. The light reading of our ancestors. 1927.

Forster, E. M. Aspects of the novel. 1927 (Clark lectures).

Muir, E. The structure of the novel. 1928.

Ford, F. M. In his English novel from the earliest days to the death of Conrad, 1930.

Baker, E. A. The history of the English novel vol 3: The later romances and the establishment of realism. 1930; vol 4: Intellectual realism from Richardson to Sterne, 1930; vol 5: The novel of sentiment and the Gothic romance, 1934.

Leavis, Q. D. Fiction and the reading public. 1932.

Lovett, R. M. and H. S. Hughes. The history of the novel in England. Boston 1932.

Tompkins, J. M. S. The popular novel in England 1770–1800. 1932, 1962.

Edgar, P. In his Art of the novel, New York 1933.

Rickword, E. A note on fiction. In his Towards standards of criticism, 1933; rptd in Forms of modern fiction, ed W. V. O'Connor, Bloomington 1959.

Singer, G. F. The epistolary novel. Philadelphia 1933.

Tieghem, P. van. Le roman sentimental en Europe de Richardson à Rousseau. Revue de Littérature Comparée 20 1940.

Elistratov, A. Iz istorii angliskogo realisma. Moscow 1941.

MacCarthy, B. G. Women writers: their contribution to the English novel 1621–1744. Cork 1945.

— The later women novelists 1744–1818. Cork 1947.

Liddell, R. A treatise on the novel. 1947.

— Some principles of fiction. 1953.

Schorer, M. Technique as discovery. Hudson Rev 1 1948.

— Fiction and the analogical matrix. Kenyon Rev 2 1949.

— In his World we imagine, New York 1968.

Foster, J. R. History of the pre-romantic novel in England. New York 1949.

Aldridge, A. O. Polygamy in early fiction. PMLA 65 1950.

Ebiike, S. A study of English novels in the eighteenth century. Tokyo 1950.

Church, R. The growth of the English novel. 1951.

Kettle, A. An introduction to the English novel. Vol 1, 1951.

— Puritanism and the rise of the novel. Kwartalnik Neofilologiczny (Warsaw) 1965.

Ransom, J. C. The understanding of fiction. Kenyon Rev 12 1950.

Boyce, B. (ed). Prefaces to fiction. Los Angeles 1952 (Augustan Reprint Soc).

Britton, W. E. Fiction and disillusionment. Papers of Michigan Acad of Science, Arts & Letters 38 1952.

Allen, W. The English novel: a short critical history. 1954.

— Six great novelists. 1955.

Mish, C. C. Best sellers in seventeenth-century fiction. PBSA 47 1953.

O'Connor, J. J. A note on the meaning of 'novel' in the seventeenth century. N & Q Nov 1953.

Black, S. J. Eighteenth-century 'histories' as a fictional mode. Boston Univ Stud in Eng 1 1955.

McKillop, A. D. The early masters of English fiction. Lawrence Kansas 1956.

Tillyard, E. M. W. The novel as a literary kind. E & S 42 1956.

— The epic strain in the English novel. 1958.

Jones, C. E. (ed). Prefaces to three eighteenth-century novels. Los Angeles 1957 (Augustan Reprint Soc).

— The English novel: a Critical view 1756–85 (notices of fiction in the Critical Review). MLQ 9 1958.

Watt, I. The rise of the novel: studies in Defoe, Richardson and Fielding. 1957.

Kennedy, M. The outlaws on Parnassus. 1958.

— The novelist and his public. Trans Royal Soc of Lit 32 1963.

Woolf, V. Style in prose fiction. In her Granite and rainbow, 1958.

Allott, M. Novelists on the novel. 1959. An anthology.

Grundy, J. and G. I. James. The mode of the novel. EC 9 1959.

Krutch, J. W. Five masters: a study in the mutations of the novel. Bloomington 1959.

Pascal, R. The autobiographical novel and the autobiography. EC 9 1959.

Shapiro, C. (ed). Twelve original essays on great English novels. Detroit 1960.

Mudrick, M. Character and event in fiction. Yale Rev 50 1960.

Pabst, W. Literatur zur Theorie des Romans. Deutsche Vierteljahrschrift 34 1960.

Weimann, R. Romanheld und Wirklichkeit. Zeitschrift für Anglistik und Amerikanistik 8 1960.

Lever, K. The novel and the reader. 1961.

Stevenson, L. The English novel: a panorama. 1961.

Gregor, I. and B. Nicholas. The moral and the story. 1962.

Danziger, M. K. The eighteenth-century novel: a comparative approach. College Eng May 1962.

Hartley, L. P. The novelist's responsibility. E & S 15 1962.

Mayo, R. D. The English novel in the magazines 1740–1815. Evanston 1962.

Putt, S. G. In his Scholars of the heart, 1962.

Sacks, S. Fiction and the shape of belief. Los Angeles 1964.

Wolff, E. Der englische Roman im 18 Jahrhundert: Wesen und Formen. Göttingen 1964.

May, G. Le dilemme du roman au 18e siècle. New Haven and Paris 1964.

Spector, R. D. (ed). Essays on the 18th-century novel. Bloomington 1964.

Würzbach, N. Die Struktur des Briefromans und seine Entstehung in England. Munich 1964; tr 1969 (as The novel in letters).

Dyson, A. E. In his Crazy fabric: essays in irony, 1965.

Gillie, C. In his Character in English literature, 1965.

Harvey, W. J. Character and the novel. 1965.

Steeves, H. R. Before Jane Austen: the shaping of the English novel in the eighteenth century. New York 1965.

Bradbrook, F. W. Jane Austen and her predecessors. Cambridge 1966.

Lodge, D. Language of fiction: essays in criticism and verbal analysis of the English novel. 1966.

Spearman, D. The novel and society. 1966.

Donovan, R. A. Shaping vision: imagination in the English novel from Defoe to Dickens. 1966.

Park, W. Change in the criticism of the novel after 1760. PQ 46 1967.

Paulson, R. Satire and the novel in eighteenth-century England. New Haven 1967.

Borinski, L. Der englische Roman des 18 Jahrhunderts. Frankfurt 1968.

Richetti, J. J. Popular fiction before Richardson: narrative patterns 1700–39. 1969.

Williams, I. The novel and romance 1700–1800: a documentary record. 1969.

Technique

Wicklein, E. Das 'Ernsthafte' in dem englischen komischen Roman des 18 Jahrhunderts. Dresden 1908.

Dibelius, W. Englische Romankunst. Berlin 1910.

Crawford, B. V. The use of formal dialogue in narrative. PQ 1 1922.

Lee, V. The handling of words and other studies in literary psychology. 1923.

Birkhead, E. Sentiment and sensibility in the eighteenth-century novel. E & S 2 1925.

Black, F. G. The technique of letter-fiction in English from 1740 to 1800. Harvard Stud 15 1933.

Zeller, H. Die Ich-Erzählung im englischen Roman. Breslau 1933.

Wright, W. F. Sensibility in English prose fiction 1760–1814. Urbana 1937.

Taylor, H. W. Modern fiction and the doctrine of uniformity. PQ 19 1940.

Sherwood, I. Z. The novelists as commentators. In The age of Johnson: essays presented to C. B. Tinker, New Haven 1949.

Booth, W. C. The self-conscious narrator in comic fiction before Tristram Shandy. PMLA 67 1952.

— The rhetoric of fiction. Chicago 1961.

— Distance and point-of-view. EC 11 1961.

Tate, A. Techniques of fiction. In Critiques and essays on modern fiction, ed A. O. Aldridge, New York 1952.

Van Ghent, D. The English novel: form and function. 1953.

Tillotson, K. The tale and the teller: a lecture on the place of the narrator in fiction. 1959; rptd in her Mid-Victorian studies, 1965.

Lange, V. Erzählformen im Roman des achtzehnten Jahrhunderts. In Stil- und Formprobleme, ed P. Böckman, Heidelberg 1959.

Stanzel, F. Die typischen Formen des englischen Romans und ihre Entstehung im achtzehnten Jahrhundert. Ibid.

Bland, D. S. Endangering the reader's neck: background description in the novel. Criticism 3 1961.

Pascal, R. Tense and novel. MLR 57 1962.

Romberg, B. Studies in the narrative techniques of the first-person novel. Stockholm 1962.

Weimann, R. Erzählerstandpunkt und 'point of view': zu Geschichte und Asthetik der Perspektive im englischen Roman. Zeitschrift für Anglistik und Amerikanistik 10 1962.

Kluge, W. Die Szene als Bauelement des Erzählers im englischen Roman des achtzehnten Jahrhunderts. Munich 1966.

Characterization

Tieje, A. J. The theory of characterization in prose fiction prior to 1740. Minneapolis 1916.

Oster, E. Das Verhältnis von Mutter und Kind im englischen Roman von 1700–1860. Bonn 1923.

Gutermuth, E. Das Kind im englischen Roman von Richardson bis Dickens. Giessener Beiträge 2 1924.

Watson, H. F. The sailor in English fiction and drama 1550–1800. New York 1931.

Crane, R. S. Suggestions towards a genealogy of 'the man of feeling'. ELH 1 1934; rptd in Studies in the literature of the Augustan age: essays in honor of A. E. Case, Ann Arbor 1952.

van der Feen, H. R. S. Jewish characters in eighteenth-century English fiction and drama. Groningen 1935.

Utter, R. P and G. B. Needham. Pamela's daughters. New York 1937.

Slagle, K. C. The English country squire as depicted in English prose fiction from 1740 to 1800. Philadelphia 1938.

Sypher, W. The West-Indian as a 'character' in the eighteenth century. SP 36 1939.

Richmond, H. The naval officer in fiction. E & S 30 1944.

Sams, H. W. Anti-stoicism in seventeenth and early eighteenth-century England. SP 41 1944.

Taylor, H. W. 'Particular character': an early phase of a literary evolution. PMLA 60 1945.

Mack, E. C. Pamela's step-daughters: the heroines of Smollett and Fielding. College Eng March 1947.

Watt, I. The naming of characters in Defoe, Richardson and Fielding. RES 25 1949.

Galbraith, L. H. The established clergy as depicted in English prose fiction from 1740 to 1800. Philadelphia 1950.

Graham, J. Character and description in the romantic novel. Stud in Romanticism 5 1966.

Types of Fiction

Romances

Haviland, T. P. The roman de longue haleine on English soil. Philadelphia 1931.

Cooke, A. L. Fielding and the writers of heroic romance. PMLA 62 1947.

Mish, C. C. (ed). Short fiction of the seventeenth century. New York 1963. With text of Fortunatus.

Macaree, D. Three early eighteenth-century prose romances. Book Collector 11 1962.

Baker, S. The idea of romance in the eighteenth-century novel. Stud in Eng Lit 1500–1900 3 1963.

Picaresque Novel

Head, R. and F. Kirkman. The English rogue. 1665, 1666, 1671; rptd 1928.

Kollman, W. Nash's Unfortunate traveller und Head's English rogue. Anglia 22 1899.

Schneider, E. Die Entwicklung des Seeromans in England im 17 und 18 Jahrhundert. Leipzig 1901.

Chandler, F. W. The literature of roguery. Boston 1907.

Habel, U. Die Nachwirkung des picaresken Romans in England von Nash bis Fielding und Smollett. Breslau 1930.

Birnbaum, J. Die 'Memoirs' um 1700: eine Studie zur Entwicklung der realistischen Romankunst vor Richardson. Halle 1934.

Renwick, W. L. Comic epic in prose. E & S 32 1946.

Koike, S. English picaresque novels. Tokyo 1962.

Alter, R. Rogue's progress: studies in the picaresque novel. Cambridge Mass 1964.

Parker, A. A. Literature and the delinquent: the picaresque novel in Spain and Europe 1599–1763. Edinburgh 1967. On Defoe, Smollett.

Epistolary Novel

Hughes, H. S. English epistolary fiction before Pamela. In J. M. Manly anniversary studies, Chicago 1923.

Singer, G. F. The epistolary novel: its origin, development, decline and residuary influence. Philadelphia 1933.

Würzbach, N. Die Struktur des Briefromans und seine Entstehung in England. Munich 1964; tr 1969.

Day, R. A. Told in letters. Ann Arbor 1966.

Jost, F. Le roman épistolaire et la technique narrative au xviiie siècle. Comparative Lit Stud 3 1966.

Gothic Novel

Müller-Fraureuth, C. Die Ritter und Räuber Romane. Halle 1894.

Mobius, H. The Gothic romance. Leipzig 1902.

— Die englischen Rosenkreuzromane und ihre Vorläufer während des 18 und 19 Jahrhunderts. Hamburg 1911.

Killen, A. M. Le roman terrifiant ou roman noir de Walpole à Ann Radcliffe et son influence jusqu'en 1840. Paris 1920.

Birkhead, E. The tale of terror: a study of the Gothic romance. 1921.

McIntyre, C. The later career of the Elizabethan villain-hero. PMLA 40 1925.

Railo, E. The haunted castle: a study of the elements of English romanticism. 1927. Tr from Italian.

Sadleir, M. The Northanger novels. Edinburgh Rev 144 1927; 1927 (Eng Assoc pamphlet).

Brauchli, J. Der englische Schauerroman um 1800. Weida 1928.

Watt, W. W. Shilling shockers of the Gothic school. Cambridge Mass 1932.

Heine, M. Le Marquis de Sade et le roman noir. Nouvelle Revue Française 41 1933.

Praz, M. In his Romantic agony, Oxford 1933, 1951 (enlarged). Tr from Italian.

Mehrotra, K. K. Horace Walpole and the English novel 1764–1820. Oxford 1934.

Summers, M. The Gothic quest. [1938].

Tuttle, D. R. Christabel sources in Percy's Reliques and the Gothic romances. PMLA 53 1938.

Heilman, R. B. Fielding and 'the first Gothic revival'. MLN 57 1942.

Mayo, R. D. The Gothic short story in the magazines. MLR 37 1942.

— How long was Gothic fiction in vogue? MLN 58 1943.

— Gothic romance in the magazines. PMLA 65 1950.

Tarr, M. M. Catholicism in Gothic fiction 1762–1820. Washington 1946.

Cooke, A. L. Some side lights on the theory of the Gothic romance. MLQ 12 1951.

Patterson, C. J. The authenticity of Coleridge's reviews of Gothic romances. JEGP 50 1951.

Penzoldt, P. The supernatural in fiction. 1952.

Frankl, P. The Gothic: literary sources and interpretations through eight centuries. Princeton 1960.

Henderson, J. The Gothic novel in Wales 1790–1820. Nat Lib of Wales Jnl 2 1960.

Nelson, L., jr. Night thoughts on the Gothic novel. Yale Rev 52 1962.

Lévy, M. Shakespeare et le roman 'gothique'. Caliban new ser 1 1965.

Other Types

Conant, M. P. The oriental tale in England in the eighteenth century. New York 1908.

Binkert, D. Historische Romane vor Walter Scott. Berlin 1915.

Thälmann, M. Der Trivialroman des 18 Jahrhunderts und der romantische Roman. Berlin 1923.

Buck, G. Die Vorgeschichte des historischen Romans in der modernen englischen Literatur. Hamburg 1931.

Black, F. G. The continuations of Pamela. Revue Anglo-américaine 13 1936.

Lukács, G. Der historische Roman. Moscow 1937, Budapest 1960; tr 1962 (as The historical novel).

Shepperson, A. B. The novel in motley: a history of the burlesque novel in English. Cambridge Mass 1936.

Giles, E. L. Shipwrecks and desert islands. N & Q 23 Sept 1939. Reply by J. T. Hardyman 7 Oct 1939.

Boyce, B. News from hell: satiric communications with the nether world in English writing of the seventeenth and eighteenth centuries. PMLA 58 1943.

— English short fiction in the eighteenth century: a preliminary view. Stud in Short Fiction 5 1968.

Lawlor, J. Radical satire and the realistic novel. E & S new ser 8 1955.

Leland, T. Longworth, Earl of Salisbury: an historical romance. Ed J. C. Stephens jr, New York 1947.

Moussa-Mahmoud, F. Orientals in picaresque: the oriental tale in England. Cairo Stud in Eng 1962.

Jones, C. E. Satire and certain English satirists of the Enlightenment. Trans of First International Congress on Enlightenment 1963.

Füger, W. Die Entstehung des historischen Romans aus der fiktiven Biographie in Frankreich und England. Munich 1963.

Mack, M. (ed). Imagined worlds: essays on some English novels and novelists in memory of John Butt. 1968.

Foreign Influences and Relationships

Schmidt, E. Richardson, Rousseau und Goethe. Jena 1875, 1924.

Furst, R. Die Vorläufer der modernen Novelle im 18 Jahrhundert: ein Beitrag zur vergleichenden Litteraturgeschichte. Halle 1897.

Macaulay, G. C. Richardson and his French predecessors. MLR 8 1913. See R. S. Crane, MP 16 1919, MLR 17 1922.

Gregory, A. The French Revolution and the English novel. 1915.

Hughes, H. S. Translations of the Vie de Marianne and their relation to contemporary English fiction. MP 15 1917.

— Notes on eighteenth-century fictional translations. MP 17 1919.

Havens, G. R. L'Abbé Prévost and English literature. Princeton 1921.

van Tieghem, P. La sensibilité et la passion dans le roman européen au 18e siècle. Revue de Littérature Comparée 6 1926.

Foster, J. R. The Abbé Prévost and the English novel. PMLA 42 1927.

Wilcox, F. H. Prévost's translations of Richardson's novels. California Univ Pbns in Modern Philology 12 1927.

Bourne, J. A. Some English translations of seventeenth-century Spanish novels. MLR 31 1936.

Warner, J. H. Eighteenth-century English reactions to the Nouvelle Héloise. PMLA 52 1937.

— Emile in eighteenth-century England. PMLA 59 1944.

Kany, C.-E. The beginnings of the epistolary novel in France, Italy and Spain. Berkeley 1937.

Engel, C. E. English novels in Switzerland in the eighteenth century. Comparative Lit Stud 14–15 1944.

Tucker, J. E. The earliest English translations of Scarron's nouvelles. Revue de Littérature Comparée 24 1950.

Halsband, R. An imitation of Perrault in England: Lady Mary Wortley Montagu's Carabosse. Comparative Lit 3 1951.

Phelps, N. F. The queen's invalid. Baltimore 1951. On Scarron's influence on English literature.

Price, L. M. The English domestic novel in Germany 1740–99. In Libris et litteris, ed C. Voigt, Hamburg 1959.

Wahba, M. Madame de Genlis in England. Comparative Lit 13 1961.

Bundy, J. Fréron and the English novel. Revue de Littérature Comparée 36 1962.

May, G. The influence of English literature on the French mid-eighteenth-century novel. In Aspects of the eighteenth century, ed E. R. Wasserman, Baltimore 1965.

Starkie, W. F. Miguel de Cervantes and the English novel. Essay by Divers Hands new ser 34 1966.

Jones, G. L. Lessing and Amory. German Life & Letters 20 1967.

Special Topics

Tieje, A. J. The expressed aim of the long prose fiction 1579–1740. JEGP 11 1912.

MacIntyre, C. F. Were the Gothic novels Gothic? PMLA 36 1921.

Hughes, H. S. The middle-class reader and the English novel. JEGP 25 1926.

Heidler, J. B. The history of English criticism of prose fiction 1700–1800. Urbana 1928.

Proper, C. B. A. Social elements in English prose fiction between 1700 and 1832. Amsterdam 1929.

Horner, J. M. English women novelists and their connection with the femininist movement 1688–1797. Northampton Mass 1930.

Newlin, C. M. The English periodicals and the novel 1709–40. Pbns of Michigan Acad of Science, Arts & Letters 16 1931.

Smith, W. H. Architecture in English fiction 1760–1800. Baton Rouge 1937.

Brown, W. C. Prose fiction and English interest in the Near East 1775–1825. PMLA 53 1938.

Gallaway, W. F. The conservative attitude toward fiction 1770–1830. PMLA 55 1940.

Taylor, J. T. Early opposition to the English novel: the popular reaction from 1760 to 1830. New York 1943.

Heilman, H. B. America in English fiction 1760–1800. Baton Rouge 1943.

Drummond, A. L. English nonconformity in fiction. London Quart 169 1944.

Seeber, E. D. Ideal languages in the French and English imaginary voyage. PMLA 60 1945.

Parkinson, C. N. Portsmouth point: the navy in fiction 1793–1815. 1948.

Koller, K. The Puritan preacher's contribution to fiction. HLQ 2 1948.

Davis, R. G. The sense of the real in English fiction. Comparative Lit 3 1951.

Foster, J. R. A forgotten noble savage: Tsonnonthouan. MLQ 14 1953.

Lockhead, M. Social history in miniature: domestic tales for children. Quart Rev 291 1953.

Noyes, R. G. The Thespian mirror: Shakespeare in the eighteenth-century novel. Providence 1953.

—— The neglected Muse: Restoration and eighteenth-century tragedy in the novel. Providence 1958.

Melchiori, G. Joyce and the eighteenth-century novelists. Eng Miscellany (Rome) 2 1951.

Mish, C. C. Black letter as a social discriminant in the seventeenth century. PMLA 48 1953. On fiction.

—— A note on the fiction reprint market in the early eighteenth century. Newberry Lib Bull 3 1954.

—— Reynard the Fox in the seventeenth century. HLQ 17 1954.

McKillop, A. D. On the acquisition of minor English fiction. Newberry Lib Bull 4 1956.

Scott, W. Mottoes from the English poets as chapter-headings in the novel. N & Q Nov 1957.

Bond, R. P. (ed). Studies in the early English periodical. Chapel Hill 1957.

McBurney, W. H. Edmund Curll, Mrs Jane Barker and the English novel. PQ 37 1958.

Kaufman, P. Borrowings from the Bristol library 1773–84: a unique record of reading vogues. Charlottesville 1960.

Boyce, B. The effect of the Restoration on prose fiction. Tennessee Stud in Lit 6 1961.

Bredvold, L. I. In his Natural history of sensibility, Detroit 1962.

Horn, A. Byron's Don Juan and the eighteenth-century English novel. Swiss Stud in Eng 51 1962.

Mylne, V. Changing attitudes towards truth in fiction. Renaissance & Modern Stud 7 1963.

Seigel, J. P. Puritan light reading. New England Quart 37 1964.

Foxon, D. F. Libertine literature in England 1660–1745. 1965.

Pierce, R. B. Moral education in the novel of the 1750's. PQ 44 1965.

Starr, G. A. Escape from Barbary: a seventeenth-century genre. HLQ 29 1965.

Halsband, R. Lady Mary Wortley Montagu and eighteenth-century fiction. PQ 45 1966.

Newell, A. G. Early evangelical fiction. Evangelical Quart 38 1966. Mostly on Hannah More.

Park, W. Fielding and Richardson. PMLA 81 1966. On their similarities with Shebbeare, Charlotte Lennox et al.

Studies of Minor Novelists

Whicher, G. F. The life and romances of Mrs Eliza Haywood. New York 1915.

Hughes, H. S. A precursor of Tristram Shandy. JEGP 17 1918. On Life and memoirs of Mr Ephraim Tristram Bates, 1756.

Foster, J. R. Charlotte Smith: pre-romantic novelist. PMLA 43 1928.

Anderson, P. B. The history and authorship of Mrs Crackanthorpe's Female tatler. MP 28 1931.

—— Delariviere Manley's prose fiction. PQ 13 1934.

—— Mistress Delariviere Manley's biography. MP 33 1936.

Cunningham, R. N. Nine tales by Motteux. MLN 46 1931.

Thompson, H. W. A Scottish man of feeling: some account of Henry Mackenzie. Oxford 1931.

Crittenden, W. M. The life and writings of Mrs Sarah Scott, novelist 1723–95. Philadelphia 1932.

Giguilliat, G. W. The author of Sandford and Merton: a life of Thomas Day. New York 1932.

Vail, R. W. Susanna Haswell Rowson, the author of Charlotte Temple: a bibliographical study. Proc Amer Antiquarian Soc 42 1932.

Macgregor, M. E. Amelia Alderson Opie: worldling and Friend. Northampton Mass 1933.

Platt, H. G. Astrea and Celadon: an untouched portrait. PMLA 49 1934.

Black, F. G. Edward Kimber: anonymous novelist of the mid-eighteenth century. Harvard Stud in Eng 17 1935.

Ellison, L. M. Gaudentio di Lucca: a forgotten Utopia. PMLA 50 1935.

McKee, W. Elizabeth Inchbald, novelist. Baltimore 1935.

Sells, A. L. The history of Francis Wills: a literary mystery. RES 11 1935.

Small, M. R. Charlotte Ramsay Lennox: an eighteenth-century lady of letters. New Haven 1935, 1969.

Tompkins, J. M. S. In her Polite marriage, Cambridge 1938. On Richard and Elizabeth Griffith; Ann Yearsley; and John Carter, The Scotch parents.

Pritchett, V. S. The Quaker coquette. In his In my good books, 1942. On Amelia Opie.

—— The crank. In his Living novel, 1946. On Thomas Day.

Sypher, W. A note on the realism of Mrs Behn's Oronooko. MLQ 3 1942.

Bald, R. C. Francis Kirkman: bookseller and author. MP 41 1943.

Boyce, B. Introd to his edn of Adventures of Lindamira: a lady of quality, Minneapolis 1949.

Woodcock, G. The incomparable Aphra. 1948.

Fletcher, T. T. F. Robert Bage: a representative revolutionary novelist. New York 1949.

Carswell, J. The prospector: the life and times of Rudolf Erich Raspe 1737–94. 1950.

Hahn, E. Aphra Behn. 1951.

Needham, G. B. Mrs Manley: an eighteenth-century wife of Bath. HLQ 14 1951.

Barbier, C. P. Letters of an Italian nun and an English gentleman 1781: a bibliographical problem. Revue de Littérature Comparée 28 1954.

Hamnet, I. Elizabeth Inchbald. Blackfriars 35 1954.

Mundy, P. D. Aphra Behn: novelist and dramatist. 1640?–89. N & Q May 1954.

Sutherland, J. H. Bage's supposed Quaker upbringing. N & Q Jan 1953.

—— Robert Bage: novelist of ideas. PQ 36 1957.

Furbank, P. N. Godwin's novels. EC 5 1955.

McBurney, W. H. Mrs Penelope Aubin and the early eighteenth-century English novel. HLQ 20 1957.

—— Mary Davys: forerunner of Fielding. PMLA 74 1959.

—— Four before Richardson: selected English novels 1720–7. Lincoln Nebraska 1963.

Cruttwell, P. On Caleb Williams. Hudson Rev 11 1958.

Alekseev, M. P. In his Iz istorii angliyskoy literatury, Moscow and Leningrad 1960. On Godwin.

Parreaux, A. The publication of the Monk. Paris 1960.

Ware, M. Mrs Radcliffe's 'picturesque embellishment'. Tennessee Stud in Eng 5 1960.

—— Sublimity in the novels of Ann Radcliffe. Copenhagen 1963.

Cameron, W. J. New light on Aphra Behn: an investigation into her journey to Surinam in 1763 and her activities as a spy in Flanders in 1666. Auckland 1961.

Peck, L. F. A life of Matthew Gregory Lewis. New York 1961.

Haden, H. J. Words in the Spiritual Quixote. N & Q Jan 1962.

Sheffey, R. T. Some evidence for a new source of Aphra Behn's Oronooko. SP 59 1962.

Erickson, J. P. Evelina and Betsy Thoughtless. Tulane Stud in Eng 6 1964.

Hartley, K. H. Un roman philosophique anglais: Hermsprong. Revue de Littérature Comparée 38 1964.

Kramer, D. The structural unity of the Man of feeling. Stud in Short Fiction 1 1964.

Morrissey, L. J. and B. Slepian. Fanny and Moll. N & Q Feb 1964.
— What is Fanny Hill? EC 14 1964.
Thomas, D. The first poetess of romantic fiction: Ann Radcliffe 1764–1823. English 15 1964.
Foxon, D. F. In his Libertine literature in England, 1965.

Baine, R. M. Holcroft and the revolutionary novel. Athens Georgia 1965.
Dumas, D. G. Things as they were: the original ending of Caleb Williams. Stud in Eng Lit 1500–1900 6 1966.
Richetti, J. J. Mrs Elizabeth Rowe: the novel as polemic. PMLA 82 1967.

R. S.

II. THE PRINCIPAL NOVELISTS

JOHN BUNYAN
1628–88

Bibliographies

A catalogue-table of Mr Bunyan's books. In Works, ed Charles Doe 1692.
A catalogue of all Mr Bunyan's books, being sixty, with the title-pages at length. In Heavenly footman, 1698.
Harrison, F. M. A bibliography of the works of Bunyan. 1932 (Bibl Soc).
Catalogue of the Bunyan library (Frank Mott Harrison collection in the Bedford Public Library). Bedford 1938.
Sotheby catalogue of the Harmsworth sale. 1947.

Collections

The works of that eminent servant of Christ, Mr John Bunyan. Ed Charles Doe, with prefatory epistle by E. Chandler and J. Wilson 1692. Vol 1 only pbd.
Works. Ed E. Gardner with a preface by S. Wilson 2 vols 1736–7.
Works with a preface by George Whitefield, including the Divine emblems and other works not collected in 1692. 2 vols 1767–8.
Works. 6 vols Edinburgh 1769, 1784.
Works. 3 vols 1805–6.
Complete works. Ed H. Stebbing 4 vols 1859.
Complete works. Ed G. Offor 3 vols Glasgow, Edinburgh and London 1860–2.
God's knotty log. Ed H. A. Talon, Cleveland and New York 1961. Includes only Pilgrim's progress and Heavenly footman.
Grace abounding and the Pilgrim's progress. Ed R. Sharrock, Oxford 1966 (OSA).

§ I

Some gospel-truths opened according to the Scriptures. London and Newport Pagnell 1656.
A vindication of the book called some gospel-truths opened. London and Newport Pagnell 1657.
A few sighs from Hell: or the groans of a damned soul. London (and Newport Pagnell?) 1658, London [1666?], [1672], 1674, 1675, nd (6th edn), [1686?], 1692, 1700, 1702, 1707 etc; tr Welsh, 1766.
The doctrine of the law and grace unfolded. London and Newport Pagnell 1659, London 1685, 1701, 1708 etc; tr Welsh, 1767; Gaelic, 1781.
Profitable meditations fitted to mans different condition. (1661?]; ed G. Offor 1862.
I will pray with the spirit, and I will pray with the understanding also. 1663 (2nd edn), nd (3rd edn), 1685, 1692; rptd 1818 from 2nd edn; tr Welsh, 1790. Also in Works 1692, above.
Christian behaviour: or the fruits of true Christianity. [1663], 1680, [1690?]; tr Welsh, 1784.
A mapp shewing the order and causes of salvation and damnation. [1664?], 1691 (broadside). Also in Works 1692, above.
One thing is needful: or serious meditations upon the four

last things. [1665?] (no known copy), 1688 (3rd edn), [1700?]; tr Welsh, 1767.
The holy city: or the new Jerusalem. 1665 (2 imprints), 1669; tr Welsh, 1789.
Prison meditations. 1665 (broadside), 1688 (with One thing is needful); tr Welsh, 1765.
The resurrection of the dead. [1665?].
Grace abounding to the chief of sinners: or a brief and faithful relation of the exceeding mercy of God in Christ to his poor servant John Bunyan. 1666, nd (2nd edn, 'corrected and much enlarged'), probably 1672, 1680, 1688, 1692, 1695, Glasgow 1697, London 1701, Edinburgh 1707, 1716 etc; ed E. Venables, Oxford 1879; rev M. Peacock, Oxford 1900; ed J. Brown 1888, Cambridge 1907 (from 1688); ed A. Smellie 1897; ed R. Sharrock, Oxford 1962; tr Dutch, 1689; Welsh, 1737.
A confession of my faith and a reason of my practice. 1672.
A Christian dialogue. [1672?]. No known copy.
A new and useful confordance to the Holy Bible. [1672?]. No known copy; advertised in 1672.
A defence of the doctrine of justification by faith in Jesus Christ. 1672, 1673.
Differences in judgment about water-baptism. 1673.
The barren fig-tree: or the doom and downfall of the fruitless professor. 1673, 1688, 1692, 1695, Glasgow 1697, 1698, 1709, Glasgow 1717; tr Welsh, [1760?].
Peaceable principles and true: or a brief answer to Mr D'Anvers and Mr Paul's books. [1674]. No known copy; answered by John Denne in 1674.
Light for them that sit in darkness. 1675.
Instruction for the ignorant. 1675, 1728 (6th edn).
Saved by grace: or a discourse of the grace of God. [1676?]. No known copy; entered in Term Catalogue 1676 and ptd in Works, 1692, above; tr Welsh, 1791.
The strait gate: or great difficulty of going to heaven. 1676; tr Dutch, 1727; Welsh, 1791.
The pilgrim's progress from this world to that which is to come, delivered under the similitude of a dream wherein is discovered, the manner of his setting out, his dangerous journey, and safe arrival at the desired countrey; printed for Nath Ponder at the Peacock in the Poultrey near Cornhil. 1678, 1678, 1679, 1680 (2 issues), 1680 (5th edn), 1682 (called 'fifth edn, 2 issues), 1681 (6th edn), Boston 1681, London 1682 (also called 'sixth edn'), 1681, 1682, 1683 (9th edn), 1684 (also called 'ninth edn'), 1685, 1688 etc; ed R. Southey 1830; ed G. Offor 1847, 1856; ed C. Kingsley 1860; ed E. Venables, Oxford 1866, 1879 (with Grace abounding, rev M. Peacock 1900); ed J. Brown 1887, 1895, Cambridge 1907; ed C. H. Firth 1898; ed G. K. Chesterton 1908; ed C. Whibley 1926; N. Douglas 1928 (facs of 1st edn); ed J. B. Wharey, Oxford 1928, rev R. Sharrock, Oxford 1960, corrected 1968; tr Dutch, 1682; French-Flemish, 1685; Welsh 1688; German, 1699; Polish, 1728; Swedish, 1743; French, 1773.
Come and welcome, to Jesus Christ. 1678, 1684, 1685 (3rd edn), 1686 (also called 'third edn'), 1688, 1690, 1691, 1694, 1697 (8th edn), 1700 (8th–9th edns), 1702, 1707, 1715, 1719 etc; tr Dutch, 1689; German, 1698; Welsh, [1719?].
A treatise of the fear of God. 1679; tr Dutch, 1727.

The life and death of Mr Badman presented to the world in a familiar dialogue between Mr Wiseman, and Mr Attentive. Printed by J.A. for Nath Ponder at the Peacock in the Poultrey neer the church. 1680, 1685, 1688 ('second edn'), 1698, [1734?]; ed J. Froude 1900; ed J. Brown, Cambridge 1905; ed G. B. Harrison 1928; tr Dutch, 1683; Welsh, 1731.

The holy war made by Shaddai upon Diabolus for the regaining of the metropolis of the world: or the losing and taking again of the town of Mansoul. Printed for Dorman Newman at the Kings Arms in the Poultry; and Benjamin Alsop at the Angel and Bible in the Poultry. 1682, 1684, 1696, [1700?], Edinburgh 1703, London 1707, Edinburgh 1707, 1711, 1718, London 1719, Glasgow 1720, London 1721, 1724 etc; ed J. Brown 1887, Cambridge 1905; ed M. Peacock, Oxford 1892 (with Heavenly footman); ed J. F. Forrest, Toronto 1967; tr Dutch, 1685; German, 1694; Welsh, 1744.

The greatness of the soul and unspeakableness of the loss thereof. 1683, 1691, 1717, 1728, 1730.

A case of conscience resolved. 1683.

A holy life, the beauty of Christianity. 1684, 1689.

Seasonable counsel: or advice to sufferers. 1684.

The pilgrim's progress from this world to that which is to come: the second part, delivered under the similitude of a dream wherein is set forth the manner of the setting out of Christian's wife and children, their dangerous journey and safe arrival at the desired country. Printed for Nathaniel Ponder at the Peacock in the Poultry, near the church. 1684, 1685, 1686, 1687, 1690, 1693, 1696, 1702, 1708, 1712, 1717, 1719, 1723, 1726, 1728, 1732 etc; ed J. Wesley 1743 (abridged); ed G. Offor 1847; ed E. Venables, Oxford 1866; ed J. Brown 1887, Cambridge 1907; ed C. H. Firth 1898; ed J. B. Wharey, Oxford 1928, rev R. Sharrock, Oxford 1960, corrected 1968, 1966 (OSA); tr Welsh, [1713].

A caution to stir up to watch against sin. [1684]. Broadside.

A discourse upon the pharisee and the publicane. 1685, 1704 (3rd edn), [1704] (5th edn), 1703 (also called 'fifth edn'), [1720?] (12th edn) etc; tr Welsh, 1775.

Questions about the nature and perpetuity of the seventh-day-sabbath. 1685.

A book for boys and girls: or country rhimes for children. 1686, 1701 (subtitled Or temporal things spiritualized), 1724 (9th edn; this and subsequent edns as Divine emblems: or temporal things spiritualized), 1732, 1757, 1770, [1780?], 1793 etc; ed A. Smith nd; ed J. Brown 1889 (facs of 1686); ed E. S. Buchanan, New York 1928.

Good news for the vilest of men. 1688, 1689 (as The Jerusalem sinner saved), 1691, 1697 ('third edn'), 1700, 1715, 1728 etc; tr Welsh, 1721.

The advocateship of Jesus Christ clearly explained and largely improved. 1688 (2 issues, 2nd as The work of Jesus Christ as an advocate), 1703 etc.

A discourse of the building, nature, excellency and government of the house of God. 1688.

The water of life. 1688, 1756 etc.

Solomon's temple spiritualiz'd: or gospel light fetcht out of the temple at Jerusalem. 1688, 1691, 1698, 1706, 1707, 1727, 1728 etc; tr Welsh, 1725?; Dutch, 1731.

The acceptable sacrifice. 1689, 1691, 1698, 1702, 1718 etc; tr Welsh, 1767.

Mr John Bunyan's last sermon. 1689, [1708?]; tr Welsh, 1744.

The following works were first pbd in Works, 1692, above:
An exposition of the first ten chapters of Genesis;
Of justification by imputed righteousness;
Paul's departure and crown;
Of the Trinity and a Christian;
Of the law and a Christian;
Israel's hope encouraged;
The desire of the righteous granted;
The saint's knowledge of Christ's love;
Of the house of the forest of Lebanon;
Of Antichrist and his ruine.

The heavenly footman. 1698, 1700, Edinburgh 1702, London 1708, 1724 etc; ed M. Peacock, Oxford 1892; ed H. A. Talon in God's knotty log, New York and Cleveland 1961; tr Welsh, 1765.

A relation of the imprisonment of Mr John Bunyan. 1765; rptd in subsequent edns of Grace abounding.

§2

A continuation of Mr Bunyan's life. In Grace abounding, 1692 (7th edn).

Doe, C. The struggler. In Works, 1692.

— A collection of experience of the work of grace. [1700?].

An account of the life and actions of Mr Bunyan. 1692. In spurious 3rd pt of Pilgrim's progress.

An account of the life and death of Mr Bunyan. In Heavenly footman, ed C. Doe 1698.

Ivimey, J. The life of Mr Bunyan. 1809.

Cheever, G. B. Lectures on the Pilgrim's progress and on the life and times of Bunyan. 1828.

Southey, R. Life of Bunyan. In his edn of 1830.

Scott, W. Quart Rev 38 1830. Review of Southey's Life above.

Macaulay, T. B. John Bunyan. Edinburgh Rev 51 1830, Encyclopaedia britannica 1854. Review of Southey's Life, above.

Coleridge, S. T. In his Literary remains, 2 vols 1836–9.

Philip, R. Life of Bunyan. 1839.

Jukes, J. A brief of Bunyan's church. 1849.

Offor, G. Life of Bunyan. In edn of Works vol 6, 1832.

Gilfillan, G. In his Literary portraits, 2 vols 1856.

Hill, N. The ancient poem of G. de Guilleville, entitled Le pèlerinage de l'homme, compared with the Pilgrim's progress of John Bunyan. 1858.

Tulloch, J. In his English puritanism and its leaders, Edinburgh 1861.

Whittier, J. G. In his Prose works, 1866.

Grier, J. B. Studies in the English of Bunyan. Philadelphia 1872.

Holyoake, G. J. The literary genius of Bunyan: a lecture. 1874.

Widholm, A. E. Grammatical notes on the language of Bunyan. Jonkoping 1877.

Froude, J. A. Bunyan. 1880 (EML).

Brown, J. Bunyan: his life, times and work. 1885 etc; rev F. M. Harrison 1928.

Hales, J. W. In his Folia litteraria, 1893.

Whyte, A. Bunyan characters. 4 vols Edinburgh 1893.

Blatchford, R. In his My favourite books, 1900.

Dowden, E. In his Puritan and Anglican, 1900.

Whitley, W. T. Trans of Baptist Historical Soc 1901–2 etc.

Shaw, G. B. In his Man and superman, 1903.

— In his Dramatic opinions and essays, 2 vols 1907.

Wharey, J. B. The sources of Bunyan's allegories. Baltimore 1904.

— Bunyan's Mr Badman. MLN 36 1921.

— Bunyan's Mr Badman and the picaresque novel. Texas Univ Stud 4 1924.

White, W. H. ('Mark Rutherford'). John Bunyan. 1905.

— Last pages from a journal. Oxford 1915.

Marcault, E. Le 'cas Bunyan' et le tempérament psychologique. In Mélanges littéraires de Clermont-Ferrand, 1910.

Firth, C. H. John Bunyan. 1911 (Eng Assoc lecture).

— Bunyan's Holy war. Jnl of Eng Stud 1 1913.

Kelman, J. The road: a study of Bunyan's Pilgrim's progress. 2 vols 1912.

Glover, T. R. In his Poets and Puritans, 1915.

Mackail, J. W. The pilgrim's progress: a lecture delivered at the Royal Institution of Great Britain. 1924.

Draper, J. W. Bunyan's Mr Ignorance. MLR 22 1927.

Griffith, G. O. John Bunyan. 1927.

Emmison, F. G. The writer of the warrant for the arrest of Bunyan. Bedfordshire Historical Record Soc 12 1928.

Guppy, H. Bull John Rylands Lib 12 1928.

Harper, C. G. The Bunyan country. 1928.

Harrison, F. M. Nathaniel Ponder: the publisher of the Pilgrim's progress. Library 4th 15 1934.

— Editions of the Pilgrim's progress. Library 4th ser 22 1942.

— Notes on the early editions of Grace abounding. Baptist Quart 11 1943.

Harrison, G. B. Bunyan: a study in personality. 1928.

— (ed). The Church book of Bunyan meeting 1751 and onwards. 1928.

— (ed). The narrative of the persecution of Agnes Beaumont in 1674. 1929.

Knox, E. A. Bunyan and the England of his time. 1928.

Noyes, A. In his Opalescent parrot, 1929.

Golder, H. Bunyan's valley of the shadow. MP 27 1929.

— Bunyan and Spenser. PMLA 45 1930.

— Bunyan's Giant Despair. JEGP 30 1931.

Withington, R. Notes on Bunyan's Pilgrim's progress part i. Northampton Mass 1929.

Lowes, J. L. In his Of reading books, 1930.

Thiel, G. Bunyans Stellung innerhalb der religiosen Strömungen seiner Zeit. Breslau 1931.

Tindall, W. Y. Bunyan, mechanick preacher. New York 1934, 1967.

Bridges, R. Bunyan's Pilgrim's progress. In his Collected essays vol 17, Oxford 1934.

Gibson, D. On the genesis of Pilgrim's progress. MP 32 1935.

Sachs, S. W. Der typisch-puritanische Ideengehalt in Bunyans Life and death of Mr Badman. Leipzig 1936.

Crump, W. B. Greatheart's map. TLS 4 Feb 1939.

Dugdale, C. E. Bunyan's Court scenes. SE 1941.

Law, R. A. 'Muck-rakers' before Bunyan. MLN 57 1942.

Willcocks, M. P. Bunyan calling. 1943.

Sharrock, R. Bunyan and the English emblem writers. RES 21 1945.

— Spiritual autobiography in the Pilgrim's progress. RES 24 1948.

— The trial of vices in Puritan fiction. Baptist Quart 19 1951.

— John Bunyan. 1954.

— Mathew's pills and the Pilgrim's progress. N & Q June 1954.

— Personal vision and Puritan tradition in the Pilgrim's progress. Hibbert Jnl 56 1957.

— An anecdote in Bunyan's Mr Badman. TLS 25 July 1958.

— The origin of A relation of the imprisonment of Mr Bunyan. RES 35 1959.

— The pilgrim's progress. 1966.

Lamont, D. Bunyan's Holy war: a study in Christian experience. Theology Today 3 1947.

Prices for Pilgrim's progress. TLS 1 Feb 1947.

Godber, J. The imprisonment of Bunyan. Trans Congregational Historical Soc 16 1949.

Talon, H. A. Bunyan: l'homme et l'œuvre. Paris 1948; tr 1951.

— Space and the hero in the Pilgrim's progress. Etudes Anglaises 14 1961.

Hussey, M. Mr Ignorance. MLR 44 1949.

— The life and death of Mr Badman. Congregational Quart 28 1950.

Brittain, V. In the steps of Bunyan. 1950.

Johnson, W. S. Hawthorne and the Pilgrim's progress. JEGP 50 1951.

Sann, A. Bunyan in Deutschland. Giessen 1951.

Leavis, F. R. In his Common pursuit, 1952.

— In his Anna Karenina and other essays, 1968.

Lerner, L. D. Bunyan and the Puritan culture. Cambridge Jnl Jan 1954.

Donnell, N. F. O. Shaw, Bunyan and Puritanism. PMLA 72 1957.

Blondel, J. Allégorie et réalisme dans le Pilgrim's progress. Archives des Lettres Modernes 1958.

— The pilgrim's progress: est-il l'œuvre d'une angoisse? Annales de la Faculté des Lettres d'Aix 36 1960.

Curtis, E. The house beautiful. Elstow Moot Hall Leaflet 5 1958.

Honig, E. In his Dark conceit: the making of allegory, Evanston 1959.

Weintraub, W. Bunyan in Poland. Canadian Slavonic Papers 4 1959.

Brown, T. J. English literary autographs xxxiii: Bunyan. Book Collector 9 1960.

Iser, W. Bunyan's Pilgrim's progress: die kalvinistische Heilsgewissheit und die Form des Romans. In Festschrift für Walther Bulst, Heidelberg 1960.

Frye, R. M. In his God, man and Satan, Princeton 1960.

Arnold, R. Ein neues Kapitel in der Geschichte der Bunyans-Ausgabe. Zeitschrift für Anglistik und Amerikanistik 9 1961.

Winslow, O. E. John Bunyan. New York 1961.

Chew, S. C. In his Pilgrimage of life, New Haven 1962.

Lewis, C. S. The vision of Bunyan. Listener 13 Dec 1962.

Smith, D. E. The publication of Bunyan's works in America. BNYPL Dec 1962.

— Illustrations of American editions of the Pilgrim's progress to 1870. Princeton Univ Lib Chron 26 1964.

Forrest, J. F. Mercy with her mirror. PQ 42 1963.

— Bunyan's Ignorance and the Flatterer. SP 60 1963.

Haferkamp, B. Bunyan als Künstler: stilkritische Studien zu seinem Hauptwerk The pilgrim's progress. Tübingen 1963.

King, B. Pilgrim's progress and the Protestant tradition. Venture 3 1963.

Roppen, G. and R. Sommer. In their Stranger and pilgrims: an essay on the metaphor of journey. Bergen and Oslo 1964.

Greaves, R. L. Bunyan and Reprobation asserted. Baptist Quart 21 1965.

— Bunyan and Covenant thought in the 17th century. Church History 36 1967.

Huisinga, D. John Bunyan. Utrecht 1965.

MacNeice, L. In his Varieties of parable, 1965.

Pascal, R. The present tense in the Pilgrim's progress. MLR 60 1965.

Stokes, E. E. Bernard Shaw's debt to Bunyan. Shaw Rev 8 1965.

Watson, M. R. The drama of Grace abounding. E Studies 46 1965.

McMillan, S. G.B.S. and Bunyan's Badman. Shaw Rev 9 1966.

Kaufmann, U. M. The Pilgrim's progress and traditions in Puritan meditation. New Haven 1966.

R. S.

DANIEL DEFOE

1660–1731

Bibliographies

This section includes articles primarily devoted to ascribing works to Defoe. Lists of Defoe's writings are also included in the biographies of Chalmers, Wilson, Lee, Wright, Dottin, under §2, below, and in Hazlitt's edn.

Boyer, A. Political State April 1716, Feb, June 1717. Reply by Defoe, Mercurius Politicus July 1717. On Defoe's authorship of certain works. *See also* J. Crossley, Defoe's pamphlet on the septennial bill, N & Q 19 June 1852.

Stace, M. An alphabetical catalogue of the writings of De Foe. 1829. Includes writings on Defoe.

Aitken, G. A. Defoe and Mist's Weekly Journal. Athenaeum 26 Aug 1893.

— Defoe's library. Athenaeum 1 June 1895.

Bülbring, K. D. An autograph manuscript of Defoe's in the British Museum. Academy 13 Oct 1894.

Ulrich, H. Robinson und Robinsonaden: Bibliographie, Geschichte, Kritik. Weimar 1898.

— Unbekannte Übersetzungen von Schriften Defoes. Zeitschrift für Bücherfreunde 4 1900.

Trent, W. P. CHEL vol 9, Cambridge 1912.

— Bibliographical notes on Defoe. Nation (New York) 6 June, 11 July, 15, 29 Aug 1907.

Davis, A. M. A bibliographical puzzle. Pbns of Colonial Soc of Mass 13 1910.

Lloyd, W. S. Catalogue of various editions of Robinson Crusoe and other books by and referring to Defoe. Philadelphia 1915.

Gückel, W. and E. D. Günther. Defoes und J. Swifts Belesenheit und literarische Kritik. Leipzig 1925.

Hutchins, H. C. Robinson Crusoe and its printing 1719–31. New York 1925.

— Two hitherto unrecorded editions of Robinson Crusoe. Library 2nd ser 8 1927.

— Robinson Crusoe at Yale. Yale Univ Lib Gazette 11 1936.

Hubbard, L. L. Text changes in the Taylor editions of Robinson Crusoe. PBSA 20 1928.

Moore Smith, G. C. An unrecognized work of Defoe's? RES 5 1929.

Burch, C. E. Defoe's connections with the Edinburgh Courant. Ibid.

— [Robert] Wodrow's list of Defoe's pamphlets on the Union. MP 28 1930.

— The authorship of A Scots poem 1707. PQ 21 1942.

— Defoe and his northern printers. PMLA 60 1945.

— Defoe's first Seasonable warning 1706. RES 21 1945.

— A discourse concerning the Union: an unrecorded Defoe pamphlet? N & Q 16 June 1945.

— An unassigned Defoe pamphlet in the Defoe-Clark controversy. N & Q 5 May 1945. Ascribes to Defoe A reproof to Mr Clark and A brief vindication of Mr De Foe.

— The authorship of A letter concerning trade from several Scots gentlemen that are merchants in London etc 1706. N & Q 6 March 1948.

— Defoe's Some reply to Mr Hodges and some other authors. N & Q 21 Feb 1948.

Haraszti, Z. A great Defoe library. More Books 6 1931.

Schutt, J. H. Hermann Ulrich: a bibliography. E Studies 13 1931. A list of his pbns on Defoe.

Fletcher, E. G. The London and Edinburgh printings of Defoe's Review. SE 14 1934.

Greenough, C. N. Defoe in Boston. Pbns of Colonial Soc of Mass 28 1935.

Callendar, G. The authorship of the History of the pirates 1724. Mariner's Mirror 26 1940.

Gove, P. B. Robert Drury. N & Q 2 March 1940. List of edns.

Secord, A. W. Defoe and Robert Drury's journal. JEGP 44 1945. Replies by J. R. Moore, N & Q 30 June 1945; Secord 3 Nov 1945.

'Friday'. Defoe at Yale. Yale Univ Lib Gazette 22 1948.

— The true-born Englishman at Yale. Yale Univ Lib Gazette 23 1950.

Moore, J. R. Defoe's lost letter to a dissenter. HLQ 14 1951.

— Defoe's hand in A journal of the Earl of Marr's proceedings 1716. HLQ 17 1954.

— Defoe's Essay upon projects: an unrecorded issue. N & Q March 1955.

— The canon of Defoe's writings. Library 5th ser 11 1956.

— A checklist of the writings of Defoe. Bloomington 1960, 1962 (rev). Ms revisions in BM copy 1966.

— John Robert Moore: a bibliography. Bloomington 1961. Full list of Moore's writings on Defoe.

— Defoe acquisitions at the Huntington Library. HLQ 28 1964.

— Defoe's Queries upon the foregoing act. In Essays in history and literature presented to S. Pargellis, ed H. Bluhm, Chicago 1965.

Watt, I. Considerations upon corrupt elections of members

to serve in Parliament 1701: by Anthony Hammond, not Defoe. PQ 31 1952.

Maslen, K. I. The printers of Robinson Crusoe. Library 5th ser 7 1952.

Healey, G. H. Defoe's handwriting. TLS 19 Dec 1952.

Defoe: an excerpt from the general catalogue of printed books in the British Museum. 1953.

Oldham, E. M. Problems of a Defoe cataloguer. Boston Public Lib Quart 7 1955.

Brown, T. J. English literary autographs 24: Defoe. Book Collector 6 1957.

Peterson, S. A sonnet not Defoe's. N & Q May 1957.

— A lost edition (1745) of Defoe's Roxana. Book Collector 7 1957.

Brigham, C. S. Bibliography of American editions of Robinson Crusoe to 1830. Proc of Amer Antiquarian Soc 67 1958.

Tucker, J. On the authorship of the Turkish spy. PBSA 52 1958.

O'Donovan, A. Sale catalogue of Defoe's library. Book Collector 205 1960.

Defoe: 1960 commemoration in Stoke Newington of the tercentenary of his birth. 1960 (Stoke Newington Public Lib).

Foxon, D. F. Defoe: a specimen of a catalogue of English verse 1701–50. Library 5th ser 20 1965.

Snyder, H. L. Defoe, the Duchess of Marlborough and the Advice to the electors of Great Britain. HLQ 29 1965.

Alden, J. A catalogue of the Defoe collection in the Boston Public Library. Boston 1966.

Baine, R. M. Defoe's imaginary voyages to the moon. PMLA 81 1966.

— Chalmers' first bibliography of Defoe. Texas Stud in Lang & Lit 10 1969.

Ivanyi, B. G. Defoe's prelude to the Family instructor. TLS 7 April 1966.

Shipley, J. B. Defoe and Henry Baker: some of their correspondence. Bodleian Lib Record 7 1967.

Collections

A collection of the writings of the author of the True-born Englishman. 1703. Collected by Defoe, though he claimed it was pirated.

A true collection of the writings of the author of the True born English-man, corrected by himself. 1703, 1705 ('corrected and enlarg'd by himself'). Vol 2 as A second volume of the writings of the author of the True-born Englishman, 1705. Both vols reissued as A true collection etc, [1710], [1713], [1721] (as The genuine works of Mr Daniel D'Foe) (with 'a compleat key to the whole work').

[A selection from the works]. 3 vols 1790.

Novels. Ed W. Scott 12 vols Edinburgh 1810.

Novels and miscellaneous works, with prefaces attributed to Sir Walter Scott. 20 vols Oxford 1840–1.

Works. Ed W. Hazlitt 3 vols 1840–3.

Novels and miscellaneous works. 7 vols 1854–67. (Bohn).

Life and recently discovered writings 1716–29. Ed W. Lee 3 vols 1869.

Works, carefully selected. Ed J. S. Keltie, Edinburgh 1869. With Chalmers's life.

The earlier life and chief earlier works. Ed H. Morley 1889.

Selections from Defoe's minor novels. Ed G. Saintsbury, New York 1892.

Romances and narratives. Ed G. A. Aitken 16 vols 1895.

Works. Ed G. H. Maynadier 16 vols New York 1903–4.

Novels. 8 vols Philadelphia 1906.

[Selection]. Ed J. Masefield 1909.

[Selection]. Ed G. K. Chesterton 1913.

Selections. Ed H. K. Hawkins [1922].

Novels and selected writings. 14 vols Oxford 1927–8.

A journal of the plague year and other pieces. Ed A. W. Secord, New York 1935.

The best of Defoe's Review: an anthology. Ed W. L. Payne, New York 1951.

Selections from the prose. Ed R. Manvell 1953, 1966.

[Selection]. Ed J. T. Boulton 1965.

Selected poetry and prose. Ed M. Shugrue, New York 1968.

Robinson Crusoe and other writings. Ed J. Sutherland, Boston 1968.

§ I

The canon of Defoe's writings is not yet fixed. Some titles will eventually be removed from the following list, and more added. The increase in the number of ascriptions from 75 certain and 20 doubtful titles suggested by Chalmers to the 560 suggested by J. R. Moore has sometimes been regarded sceptically; but there can be little doubt of the authenticity of many of the ascriptions of Trent on the basis of style, of Burch on the basis of new knowledge of Defoe's activities in Scotland, and of Moore on the basis of internal evidence.

In the following list undiscovered works such as the tract on the Turks are omitted. Evidence of ascription, whether internal or external, has usually been indicated. Many works attributed to Defoe, both in his own time and during the nineteenth and twentieth centuries, have been omitted for lack of evidence. Others, such as The history of Prince Mirabel's infancy *or* Some memoirs of the amours and intreagues of a certain Irish Dean, *have been dropped on grounds of style.*

A letter to a Dissenter from his friend at the Hague, concerning the penal laws and the test. [1688]. Probably by Defoe.

Reflections upon the late great revolution, written by a layhand in the country. 1689. Probably by Defoe.

The advantages of the present settlement, and the great danger of a relapse. 1689. Probably by Defoe.

An account of the late horrid conspiracy to depose their present Majesties K. William and Q. Mary, to bring in the French and the late King James, and ruine the city of London, with a relation of the miraculous discovery thereof, 1691. Probably by Defoe.

A new discovery of an old intreague: a satyr level'd at treachery and ambition, calculated to the nativity of the Rapparee plott, and the modesty of the Jacobite clergy. 1691; rptd in A true collection, 1705 and in M. E. Campbell, Defoe's first poem, Bloomington 1938.

To the Athenian Society. In C. Gildon, History of the Athenian Society, [1692?]; rptd by J. Dunton in successive edns of The Athenian oracle.

A dialogue betwixt Whig and Tory. 1693, 1710. Probably by Defoe.

The Englishman's choice, and true interest, in a vigorous prosecution of the war against France; and serving K. William and Q. Mary, and acknowledging their right. 1694. Almost certainly by Defoe.

Some seasonable queries on the third head, viz: a general naturalization. 1697? Probably by Defoe. See J. R. Moore, Newberry Lib Bull 6 1965.

The character of the late Dr Samuel Annesley, by way of elegy; with a preface. 1697; rptd in A true collection, 1703.

Some reflections on a pamphlet lately publish'd entituled An argument shewing that a standing army is inconsistent with a free government, and absolutely destructive to the Constitution of the English monarchy. 1697, 1697. Reply to J. Trenchard.

An essay upon projects. 1697; reissued as Essays upon several projects, 1702. (Same sheets issued 4 to 7 times); rptd H. Morley.

An enquiry into the occasional conformity of Dissenters, in cases of preferment, with a preface to the Lord Mayor, occasioned by his carrying the sword to a conventicle. 1697 (for 1698), Dublin 1698, 1701 (for 1700) (with preface to Mr How); rptd in A true collection, 1703; and in G. M. Trevelyan, Select documents for Queen Anne's reign, Cambridge 1929.

An argument shewing that a standing army, with consent of Parliament, is not inconsistent with a free government. 1698; rptd in A true collection, 1703.

A brief reply to the History of standing armies in England, with some account of the authors. 1698, 1698. A reply to J. Trenchard and W. Moyle.

Some queries concerning the disbanding of the army. 1698, 1698. Perhaps by Defoe.

The poor man's plea for a reformation of manners and suppressing immorality in the nation. 1698, 1698, 1700; rptd in Collection, 1703 and in A true collection, 1703.

The interests of the several princes and states of Europe consider'd, with respect to the succession of the crown of Spain, and the titles of the several pretenders thereto examin'd. 1698.

Lex talionis: or an enquiry into the most proper ways to prevent the persecution of the Protestants in France. 1698; rptd in Collection, 1703.

An encomium upon the Parliament (1699). In Poems on affairs of State vol 2, 1703. Perhaps by Defoe.

The pacificator: a poem. 1700; rptd in A true collection vol 2, 1705.

The two great questions consider'd: I. what the French King will do, with respect to the Spanish monarchy; II. what measures the English ought to take. 1700, 1700, 1700, 1700; tr French, 1701; rptd in A true collection, 1703.

The two great questions further considered, with some reply to the remarks. 1700; rptd in A true collection, 1703; tr French, 1701.

Reasons humbly offer'd for a law to enact the castration of popish ecclesiastics. 1700. Perhaps by Defoe. See G. C. Moore Smith, RES 5 1929.

The six distinguishing characters of a Parliament-man, address'd to the good people of England. 1700 (for 1701); rptd in A true collection, 1703.

The danger of the Protestant religion consider'd, from the present prospect of a religious war in Europe. 1701; rptd in A true collection, 1703.

The true-born Englishman: a satyr. 1700 (for 1701). Foxon lists 30 edns before 1750. Preface added and text rev, 9th edn 1701; rptd in Collection, 1703; rptd in A true collection, 1703; further revisions adapting the poem to the reign of George I, 1716; frequently rptd in contemporary miscellanies; ed A. C. Guthkelch, E & S 4 1913.

The succession to the crown of England, considered. 1701.

The free-holders plea against stock-jobbing elections of parliament men. 1701, 1701 (with addns); rptd in A true collection, 1703.

A letter to Mr How, by way of reply to his considerations of the preface to An enquiry into the occasional conformity of Dissenters, by the author of the said Preface and Enquiry. 1701; rptd in Collection, 1703, and in A true collection, 1703.

The livery man's reasons, why he did not give his vote for a certain gentleman either to be Lord Mayor: or Parliament man for the city of London. 1701.

The villainy of stock-jobbers detected, and the causes of the late run upon the bank and bankers discovered and considered. 1701, 1701; rptd in A true collection, 1703.

The apparent danger of an invasion, briefly represented in a letter to a Minister of State, by a Kentish gentleman. 1701. Perhaps by Defoe.

The present state of England and the Protestant interest. 1701. Perhaps by Defoe.

[Legion's memorial]. [1701]; rptd in Somers tracts vol 11, 1814, and in An English garner, ed E. Arber vol 7, 1883.

Ye true-born Englishmen proceed [first line of first stanza]. [1701]. Known by a variety of titles, but most commonly as The ballad. Foxon lists 11 edns in 1701. Almost certainly by Defoe.

The history of the Kentish petition. 1701, Edinburgh 1701; rptd in Somers tracts vol 11, 1814, and in An English garner, ed E. Arber vol 7, 1883.

The present state of Jacobitism considered, in two querys: 1, What measures the French King will take with respect to the person and title of the pretended Prince of Wales; 2, What the Jacobites in England ought to do on the same account. 1701. Preface signed D.F.

An argument, shewing that the Prince of Wales, tho' a Protestant, has no just pretensions to the crown of England. 1701.

Reasons against a war with France: or an argument shewing that the French King's owning the Prince of Wales as King of England, Scotland and Ireland is no sufficient ground of a war. 1701; rptd in A true collection, 1703.

Legion's new paper: being a second memorial to the gentlemen of a late House of Commons, with Legion's humble address to his Majesty. 1702 (for 1701). Also as Legion's second memorial; rptd in Somers tracts vol 11, 1814. Chiefly a reply to J. Drake, A short defence of the last Parliament, [1701 ?].

The original power of the collective body of the people of England, examined and asserted. 1702 (for 1701); rptd in A true collection, 1703.

The mock-mourners: a satyr, by way of elegy on King William. 1702. Foxon lists 12 edns in 1702, including 2 pbd in Dublin; Edinburgh 1703; rptd in Collection, 1703; and in A true collection, 1703.

Reformation of manners: a satyr. 1702, 1702; rptd in Collection, 1703; rptd in A true collection, 1703.

A new test of the Church of England's loyalty: or Whiggish loyalty and church loyalty compar'd. 1702, 1702, [Edinburgh] 1703; rptd in Collection, 1703, and in A true collection, 1703; 1715 (as A defence of Mr Withers' History of resistance); in Somers tracts vol 9, 1813.

Good advice to the ladies: shewing that as the world goes, and is like to go, the best way is for them to keep unmarried, by the author of the True born Englishman. 1702, 1705, 1709, 1727, 1728 (as A timely caution). Probably by Defoe, though mistakenly thought to have been disowned by him. See A. M. Wilkinson, N & Q 24 June 1950.

The Spanish descent: a poem, by the author of the True-born Englishman. 1702, 1703; rptd in Collection, 1703; and in A true collection, 1703.

An enquiry into occasional conformity, shewing that the Dissenters are no way concern'd in it, by the author of the preface to Mr Howe. 1702; rptd in Collection, 1703, and in A true collection, 1703; reissued 1703, 1704 (as An enquiry into the occasional conformity bill).

The opinion of a known Dissenter on the bill for preventing occasional conformity. 1703 (for 1702 ?).

The shortest way with the Dissenters: or proposals for the establishment of the Church. 1702; rptd in Collection, 1703, and in A true collection, 1703; rptd in English garner, ed E. Arber vol 7, 1883.

A brief explanation of a late pamphlet, entituled the Shortest way with the Dissenters. [1703]; rptd in Collection, 1703; in A true collection, 1703; and in G. M. Trevelyan, Select documents for Queen Anne's reign, Cambridge 1929.

A dialogue between a Dissenter and the observator, concerning the Shortest way with Dissenters. 1703; rptd in Collection, 1703.

King William's affection to the Church of England examin'd. 1703 (5 edns).

More reformation: a satyr upon himself, by the author of the True born English-man. 1703; rptd in A true collection vol 2, 1705.

The shortest way to peace and union, by the author of the Shortest way with the Dissenters. 1703, 1703; rptd in A true collection, 1703, 1704.

A hymn to the pillory. 1703 (3 edns), [1703 ?], [1703 ?], 1708, [1721 ?], [1748]; rptd in A true collection vol 2, 1705.

The sincerity of the Dissenters vindicated, from the scandal of occasional conformity, with some considerations on a late book entitul'd Moderation a vertue [by J. Owen]. 1703.

A hymn to the funeral sermon. 1703 (3 edns).

The case of Dissenters as affected by the late bill proposed in Parliament for preventing occasional conformity. 1703; rptd in Somers tracts vol 12, 1814.

An enquiry into the case of Mr Asgil's general translations shewing that 'tis not a nearer way to heaven than the grave, by the author of the True born English-man. 1704 (for 1703).

A challenge of peace, address'd to the whole nation, with an enquiry into ways and means for bringing it to pass. 1703; rptd in A true collection vol 2, 1705.

Some remarks on the first chapter in Dr Davenant's Essays. 1704 (for 1703), 1704 (as The reasonableness of appeals to the people).

Peace without union, by way of reply, to Sir H[umphrey] M[ackworth']s Peace at home. 1703 (4 edns); rptd with preface in A true collection vol 2, 1705.

The Dissenters answer to the High-Church challenge. 1704; rptd in A true collection vol 2, 1705. Reply to C. Leslie, The wolf stript of his Shepherd's cloathing.

An essay on the regulation of the press. 1704; ed J. R. Moore, Oxford 1948.

A serious inquiry into this grand question, whether a law to prevent the occasional conformity of Dissenters, would not be inconsistent with the Act of Toleration, and a breach of the Queen's promise. 1704; rptd in A true collection vol 2, 1705.

The paral[l]el: or persecution of Protestants the shortest way to prevent the growth of popery in Ireland. Dublin 1705 (for 1704 ?); rptd in A true collection vol 2, 1705.

The lay-man's sermon upon the late storm, held forth at an honest coffee-house-conventicle. 1704.

Royal religion: being some enquiry after the piety of princes, with remarks on a book entituled A form of prayers us'd by King William. 1704, 1704; rptd in A true collection vol 2, 1705.

Moderation maintain'd, in defence of a compassionate enquiry into the causes of the Civil War etc in a sermon preached the thirty-first of January, at Aldgate-Church by White Kennet. 1704.

Legion's humble address to the Lords. [1704]; rptd in Legion's humble address to the Lords answered paragraph by paragraph, [1704].

The Christianity of the High-Church consider'd, dedicated to a noble peer. 1704.

More short-ways with the Dissenters. 1704; rptd in A true collection vol 2, 1705.

The address. [1704]; rptd in Poems on affairs of State vol 4, 1707. Perhaps by Defoe.

The Dissenter[s] misrepresented and represented. [1704]; rptd in A true collection vol 2, 1705.

A new test of the Church of England's honesty. 1704, Edinburgh 1705; rptd in A true collection vol 2, 1705.

The storm: or a collection of the most remarkable casualties and disasters which happen'd in the late dreadful tempest, both by sea and land. 1704.

An elegy on the author of the True-born English-man, with an essay on the late storm, by the author of the Hymn to the pillory. 1704, 1704 (as The live man's elegy), Dublin 1704, 1708; rptd in A true collection vol 2, 1705.

A true state of the difference between Sir George Rook Knt and William Colepeper esq. Part 1, 1704. Probably partly by Defoe.

A hymn to victory. 1704 (4 edns), [Edinburgh ?] 1704; rptd in A true collection vol 2, 1705.

The Protestant Jesuite unmask'd, in answer to the two parts of Cassandra, wherein the author and his libels are laid open, with my service to Mr Lesley. 1704.

Giving alms no charity, and employing the poor a grievance to the nation. 1704; rptd in A true collection vol 2, 1705; rptd in A select collection of scarce and valuable economic tracts, ed J. R. McCulloch 1859.

Queries upon the bill against occasional conformity. [1704].

The double welcome: a poem to the Duke of Marlbro. 1705, 1705; rptd in A true collection vol 2, 1705.

Persecution anatomiz'd: or an answer to the following questions [4 questions on the High Church and Dissenters]. 1705.

The consolidator: or memoirs of sundry transactions from the world in the moon, translated from the lunar language, by the author of the True-born English man. 1705, 1705. Extracts from Consolidator, perhaps pirated, perhaps abridged by Defoe to reach a wider audience, were pbd under the following titles: A journey to the world in the moon, [1705]; A letter from the man in the moon, [1705]; A second, and more stragne voyage to the world in the moon, [1705].

The experiment, or the shortest way with the Dissenters exemplified: being the case of Mr Abraham Gill, a Dissenting Minister in the Isle of Ely. 1705, 1707 (for 1706?) (as The honesty and sincerity of those worthy English gentlemen, commonly called High-Church men).

A hint to the Blackwell-hall factors: being the true state of the case between Mr Samuel Weatherhead, Blackwell-hall factor and Mr John Hellier, merchant. 1705. Perhaps by Defoe.

Advice to all parties, by the author of the True-born Englishman. 1705, 1705.

The dyet of Poland: a satyr. 1705, 1705, Dublin 1705; rptd in The dyet of Poland consider'd paragraph by paragraph, 1705.

The ballance: or a new test of the High-Fliers of all sides. 1705.

The High-Church legion, or the memorial examin'd: being a new test of moderation as 'tis recomended to all that love the Church of England and the Constitution. 1705.

Party-tyranny: or an Occasional Bill in miniature, as now practised in Carolina humbly offered to the consideration of both Houses of Parliament. 1705.

An answer to the L[or]d H[aver]sham's speech, by Daniel D'Foe. 1705; rptd Review 24 Nov 1705.

Declaration without doors. [1705].

A hymn to peace, occasion'd by the two Houses joining in one address to the Queen, by the author of the True-born English-man. 1706, 1706, [1706?], 1709.

A reply to a pamphlet entituled the L[or]d H[aversham]'s vindication of his speech etc, by the author of the Review. 1706.

The case of Protestant Dissenters in Carolina, shewing how a law to prevent occasional conformity there, has ended in the total subversion of the Constitution in church and state, recommended to the serious consideration of all that are true friends to our present establishment. 1706.

Remarks on the bill to prevent frauds committed by bankrupts, with observations on the effect it may have upon trade. 1706.

Remarks on the letter to the author of the State-memorial. 1706. Defence of J. Toland and attack on W. Stephens.

An essay at removing national prejudices against a union with Scotland, to be continued during the treaty here. Part I, 1706, [Edinburgh] 1706.

An essay on the great battle at Ramellies, by the author of the Review. 1706; rptd Review 21 May 1706.

Jure divino: a satyr in twelve books, by the author of the True-born-Englishman. 1706 (4 edns).

An essay at removing national prejudices against a union with Scotland, to be continued during the treaty here. Part II, 1706, [Edinburgh] 1706.

Preface to De Laune's plea for the Non-conformists. 1706 (9 edns), 1709 (as Dr Sacheverell's recantation), 1720.

Daniel Defoe's hymn for the thanksgiving. 1706; rptd Review 27 June 1706.

A true relation of the apparition of one Mrs Veal. 1706, 1707, 1710; rptd in C. Drelincourt, The Christian's defence against the fears of death, 1706 (over 20 edns before 1800).

An essay, at removing national prejudices against a union with England. Part III, by the author of the two first, [Edinburgh] 1706.

A letter from Mr Reason, to the high and mighty prince the mob. [Edinburgh 1706].

An answer to my Lord Beilhaven's speech, by an English gentleman. [Edinburgh?] 1706.

The vision: a poem. [Edinburgh 1706] (3 edns), 1706.

A fourth essay, at removing national prejudices; with some reply to Mr H[o]dges and some other authors, who have printed their objections against an union with England. [Edinburgh] 1706.

Observations on the fifth article of The treaty of union, humbly offered to the consideration of the Parliament, relating to foreign ships. [Edinburgh 1706]. Probably by Defoe.

Considerations in relation to trade considered, and a short view of our present trade and taxes, compared with what these taxes may amount to after the union etc reviewed. [Edinburgh] 1706.

A seasonable warning or the Pope and King of France unmasked. [Edinburgh] 1706.

A reply to the Scots answer, to the British vision (by Lord Beilhaven). [Edinburgh 1706] (3 edns).

Caledonia: a poem in honour of Scotland, and the Scots nation, in three parts. Edinburgh 1706, 1706, London 1707, Dublin 1707, London 1748.

The state of the excise after the union, compared with what it is now. [Edinburgh] 1706. Perhaps by Defoe. See Burch, MP 28 1930.

The state of the excise etc vindicated from the remarks of the author of the Short view etc, wherein other escapes of that author are likewise taken notice of. [Edinburgh 1706]. Perhaps by Defoe. See Burch, MP 28 1930.

A short letter to the Glasgow-men. [Edinburgh 1706]; rptd Review 2 Jan 1707.

The rabbler convicted: or a friendly advice to all turbulent and factious persons, from one of their own number. [Edinburgh 1706]. Almost certainly by Defoe.

The advantages of Scotland by an incorporate union with England, compar'd with these of a coalition with the Dutch, or league with France, in answer to a pamphlet call'd the Advantages of the act of security etc. 1706. Almost certainly by Defoe. See Burch, MP 28 1930.

A letter concerning trade, from several Scots-gentlemen that are merchants in England, to their country-men that are merchants in Scotland. [Edinburgh 1706]. Probably by Defoe.

An enquiry into the disposal of the equivalent. [Edinburgh 1706].

A Scots poem: or a new-years gift, from a native of the universe, to his fellow-animals in Albania. Edinburgh 1707.

A fifth essay, at removing national prejudices; with a reply to some authors, who have printed their objections against an union with England. [Edinburgh?] 1607 (for 1707).

Two great questions considered: being a sixth essay at removing national prejudices against the union. [Edinburgh] 1707.

The dissenters in England vindicated from some reflections in a late pamphlet entitled Lawful prejudices [by J. Webster]. [Edinburgh 1707].

Passion and prejudice, the support of one another, and both destructive to the happiness of this nation, in church and state; being a reply to the vindicator of Mr W[ebste]r's Lawful prejudices. Edinburgh 1707.

Proposals for printing by subscription a compleat history of the Union, by the author of the True-born-Englishman. [1707].

A discourse upon an union of the two Kingdoms of England and Scotland. 1707. Perhaps by Defoe.

Queries upon the foregoing act. In The copy of an act lately pass'd in Carolina, [1707].

Remarks upon the Lord Haversham's speech in the House of Peers, Feb 15 1707. [Edinburgh 1707]. Probably by Defoe.

A short view of the present state of the Protestant religion in Britain, as it is now profest in the Episcopal Church in England, the Presbyterian Church in Scotland, and the Dissenters in both. Edinburgh 1707, London 1707 (as The Dissenters vindicated: or a short view).

The true-born Britain, written by the author of the True-born Englishman. 1707. Perhaps by Defoe.

A voice from the south: or an address from some Protestant Dissenters in England to the Kirk of Scotland. [Edinburgh 1707]; rptd Review 10, 15 May 1707.

A modest vindication of the present ministry; from the reflections publish'd against them in a late paper entitled the Lord Haversham's speech. 1707.

The trade of Britain stated: being the substance of two papers published in London on occasion of the importation of wine and brandy from North-Britain. [Edinburgh 1707]; rptd from Review 10, 12 June 1707.

An historical account of the bitter sufferings, and melancholly circumstances of the Episcopal Church in Scotland, under the barbarous usage and bloody persecution of the Presbyterian Church government. Edinburgh 1707, 1707 (as Presbyterian persecution examined).

De Foe's answer to Dyer's scandalous news letter. [Edinburgh 1707].

Dyers news examined as to his Sweddish memorial against the Review. [Edinburgh 1707].

Reflections on the prohibition act, wherein the necessity, usefulness and value of that law are evinced and demonstrated. 1708.

A memorial to the nobility of Scotland, who are to assemble in order to choose the sitting peers for the Parliament of Great Britain. Edinburgh 1708. Probably by Defoe.

Scotland in danger: or a serious enquiry into the dangers which Scotland has been in, or may be in since the Union; with some humble proposals for the remedy. [1708]. Probably by Defoe.

An answer to a paper concerning Mr De Foe, against his History of the Union. Edinburgh 1708.

The Scot's narrative examin'd: or the case of the Episcopal ministers in Scotland stated. 1709.

A brief history of the poor Palatine refugees, lately arrived in England. 1709, Dublin 1709; ed J. R. Moore, Los Angeles 1964 (Augustan Reprint Soc).

The history of the Union of Great Britain. Edinburgh 1709, London 1711, 1712 (both as A collection of original papers and material transactions concerning the Union between England and Scotland), 1786 (with appendix of original papers), Dublin 1799 (selection).

Parson Plaxton of Barwick. [1709]; ed S. Peterson, HLQ 19 1955.

A letter to Mr Bisset, eldest brother of the Collegiate Church of St Catherines; in answer to his remarks on Dr Sacheverell's sermon. 1709.

A letter from Captain Tom to the mobb, now rais'd for Dr Sacheverel. [1710].

A reproof to Mr Clark, and a brief vindication of Mr De Foe. [Edinburgh 1710].

Advertisement from Daniel De Foe, to Mr Clark. [Edinburgh 1710?].

A speech without doors. 1710.

The age of wonders: to the tune of Chivy chase. 1710 (3 edns), Edinburgh 1710. Attributed by J. R. Moore, but doubtful.

Greenshields out of prison and toleration settled in Scotland: or the case of Mr Greenshields, farther examin'd. 1710.

A vindication of Dr Henry Sacheverell, by D. D'F. esq: or otherwise etc. [1710].

Instructions from Rome, in favour of the Pretender, inscrib'd to the most elevated Don Sacheverellio, and his brother Don Higginisco. [1710].

The recorder of B[anbu]ry's speech to Dr Sach[eve]rell. 1710. Attributed by J. R. Moore.

The Ban[bur]ly apes: or the monkeys chattering to the magpye, in a letter to a friend in London. [1710] (4 edns).

A collection of the several addresses in the late King James's time: concerning the conception and birth of the pretended Prince of Wales. [1710].

Dr Sacheverell's disappointment at Worcester: being a true account of his cold reception there, in a letter from a gentleman in that city to his friend in London. 1710. Attributed by J. R. Moore.

A new map of the laborious and painful travels of our blessed High Church apostle: giving a true account of the many strange, miraculous cures and wonders that he has perform'd both on dumb and blind persons throughout the countreys wheresoever he went. 1710. Probably by Defoe.

High-Church miracles: or modern inconsistencies. 1710 (3 edns). Perhaps by Defoe.

A short historical account of the contrivances and conspiracies of the men of Dr Sacheverell's principles, in the late reigns. [1710]. Probably by Defoe.

Seldom comes a better, or a tale of a lady and her servants: qui capit ille facit. 1710. Perhaps by Defoe.

A letter from a Dissenter in the city of a Dissenter in the country, advising him to a quiet and peaceable behaviour in this present conjuncture. 1710. Attributed by J. R. Moore, but doubtful.

An essay upon publick credit. 1710 (3 edns), 1797; rptd in Somers tracts vol 13, 1815; and in A select collection of tracts on the national debt, ed J. R. McCulloch 1857; tr Dutch, 1710.

A new test of the sence of the nation: being a modest comparison between the addresses to the late King James, and those to her present Majesty. 1710.

A letter from a gentleman at the Court of St Germains, to one of his friends in England: containing a memorial about methods for setting the Pretender on the throne of Great Britain. 1710. Perhaps Defoe but also ascribed to Maynwaring.

A condoling letter to the Tattler: on account of the misfortunes of Isaac Bickerstaff esq, a prisoner in the [——] on suspicion of debt. [1710].

Queries to the new hereditary right-men. 1710. Probably by Defoe.

An essay upon loans, by the author of the Essay upon credit. 1710; rptd in Somers tracts vol 13, 1815.

A word against a new election: that the people of England may see the happy difference between English liberty and French slavery; and may consider well before they make the exchange. 1710.

A supplement to the faults on both sides: containing the compleat history of the proceedings of a party ever since the Revolution; in a familiar dialogue between Steddy and Turn-Round, two displac'd officers of State. (5 edns). Also as Faults on both sides: the second part.

The British visions. [Newcastle 1710], London 1711.

Atalantis Major, printed in Olreeky, the chief city of the north part of Atalantis Major. 1711 (for 1710).

R[ogue]'s on both sides, in which are the characters of some R[ogue]'s not yet describ'd; with a true description of an old Whig, and a modern Whig; an old Tory, and a modern Tory; High-flyer: or motly; as also of a Minister of State. 1711.

A short narrative of the life and actions of his Grace John D. of Marlborough, from the beginning of the Revolution to this present time, by an old officer in the army. 1711.

Counter queries. [1711?].

The Quaker's sermon: or a holding-forth concerning Barabbas. 1711. Perhaps by Defoe.

Captain Tom's remembrance to his old friends the mob of London, Westminster, Southwark and Wapping. [1711]. Probably by Defoe.

A seasonable caution to the general assembly, in a letter from a member of Parliament of North-Britain to a minister in Scotland, occasioned by the House of Lords reversing the sentence of Mr Greenshiels. 1711.

A spectators address to the Whigs, on the occasion of the stabbing Mr Harley. 1711. Probably by Defoe.

The secret history of the October Club, from its original to this time, by a member. 1711, 1711; pt 2, 1711.

The succession of Spain consider'd: or a view of the several interests of the princes and powers of Europe, as they respect the succession of Spain and the Empire. 1711. Probably by Defoe.

Eleven opinions about Mr H[arle]y, with observations. 1711.

The re-representation: or a modest search after the great plunderers of the nation. 1711. Perhaps by Defoe.

The representation examined: being remarks on the state of religion in England. 1711, Edinburgh 1711. Perhaps by Defoe.

Reasons for a peace: or the war at an end. 1711.

An essay upon the trade to Africa. 1711.

The Scotch medal decipher'd, and the new hereditary-right men display'd: or remarks on the late proceedings of the faculty of advocates at Edinburgh, upon receiving the Pretender's medal. 1711. Probably by Defoe.

A speech for Mr D[unda]sse Younger of Arnistown, if he should be impeach'd of h[igh] t[reaso]n for what he said and did about the Pretender's medal, lately sent to the Faculty of Advocates at Edinburgh. 1711.

A true account of the design and advantages of the South-Sea trade; with answers to all the objections rais'd against it; a list of all the commodities proper for that trade, and the progress of the subscription towards the South-Sea Company. 1711.

An essay on the South-Sea trade, by the author of the Review. 1712 (for 1711).

The true state of the case between the government and the creditors of the Navy etc, as it relates to the South-Sea trade, and the justice of the transactions on either side impartially enquired into. 1711.

Reasons why this nation ought to put a speedy end to this expensive war; with a brief essay, at the probable conditions on which the peace now negotiating, may be founded. 1711 (3 edns), Edinburgh 1711.

Reasons why a party among us, and also among the Confederates, are obstinately bent against a treaty of peace with the French at this time, by the author of the Reasons for putting an end to this expensive war. 1711 (3 edns).

Armageddon: or the necessity of carrying on the war, if such a peace cannot be obtained as may render Europe safe, and trade secure. [1711] (3 edns).

The ballance of Europe: or an enquiry into the respective dangers of giving the Spanish monarchy to the Emperour as well as to King Phillip, with the consequences that may be expected from either. 1711.

Worcestershire-queries about peace, by Tom Flockmaker, clothier of Worcester. 1711. Attributed by J. R. Moore, but little internal evidence.

An essay at a plain exposition of that difficult phrase a good peace, by the author of the Review. 1711.

The felonious treaty: or an enquiry into the reasons which moved his late Majesty King William of glorious memory, to enter into a treaty at two several times with the King of France for the partition of the Spanish monarchy, by the author of the Review. 1711.

An essay on the history of parties, and persecution in Britain: beginning with a brief account of the Test-Act and an historical enquiry into the reasons, the original and the consequences of the occasional conformity of Dissenters. 1711.

A defence of the Allies and the late ministry: or remarks on the Tories new idol [Swift]. 1712.

A justification of the Dutch from several late scandalous reflections: in which is shewn the absolute necessity of preserving a strict and inviolable friendship betwixt Great-Britain and the States-General; with the fatal consequences that must attend a war with Holland. 1712.

No queen, or no general: an argument, proving the necessity her Majesty was in, as well for the safety of her person as of her authority, to displace the D[uke] of M[arl]borough. 1712.

The conduct of parties in England, more especially of those Whigs who now appear against the new Ministry and a treaty for peace. 1712.

Peace or poverty: being a serious vindication of her Majesty and her Ministers consenting to a treaty for a general peace, shewing the reasonableness, and even necessity, there was for such a procedure. 1712. Probably by Defoe.

The case of the poor skippers and keel-men of Newcastle. [1712?]. Probably by Defoe.

A farther case relating to the poor keel-men of Newcastle. [1712]. Probably by Defoe.

The history of the Jacobite clubs; with the grounds of their hopes from the p[resen]t m[inistr]y; as also a caveat against the Pretender. 1712. Perhaps by Defoe.

Imperial gratitude, drawn from a modest view of the conduct of the Emperor Ch[arl]es VI and the King of Spain Ch[arl]es III; with observations on the difference etc: being a farther view of the deficiencies of our confederates. 1712. Probably by Defoe.

The Highland visions, or the Scots new prophecy: declaring in twelve visions what strange things shall come to pass in the year 1712. 1712.

Plain English, with remarks and advice to some men who need not be nam'd. 1712. Perhaps by Defoe.

Wise as serpents: being an enquiry into the present circumstances of the Dissenters, and what measures they ought to take in order to disappoint the designs of their enemies. 1712.

The present state of the parties in Great Britain: particularly an enquiry into the state of the Dissenters in England, and the Presbyterians in Scotland. 1712.

Reasons against fighting: being an enquiry into this great debate, whether it is safe for her Majesty, or her ministry, to venture an engagement with the French, considering the present behaviour of the Allies. 1712.

The present negotiations of peace vindicated from the imputation of trifling. 1712. Almost certainly by Defoe.

The validity of the renunciations of former powers enquired into, and the present renunciation of the Duke of Anjou impartially considered. 1712.

An enquiry into the danger and consequences of a war with the Dutch. 1712.

A further search into the conduct of the Allies and the late Ministry as to peace and war; containing also a reply to the several letters and memorials of the States-General, with a vindication of the British Parliament in their late resolves and address relating to the deficiences of the Dutch. 1712. Some copies as A farther search.

The justice and necessity of a war with Holland, in case the Dutch do not come into her Majesty's measures, stated and examined. 1712.

An enquiry into the real interest of princes in the persons of their ambassadors. 1712.

A seasonable warning and caution against the insinuations of Papists and Jacobites in favour of the Pretender: being a letter from an Englishman at the Court of Hannover. 1712.

Hannibal at the gates: or the progress of Jacobitism, with the present danger of the Pretender. 1712, 1714 (rev).

A strict enquiry into the circumstances of a late duel, with some account of the persons concern'd on both sides. 1713. On Hamilton and Mohun.

Reasons against the succession of the House of Hanover, with an enquiry how far the abdication of King James, supposing it to be legal, ought to affect the person of the Pretender. 1713 (4 edns).

Not[tingh]am politicks examin'd: being an answer to a pamphlet lately publish'd intitul'd Observations upon the state of the nation. 1713. Probably by Defoe.

The second-sighted Highlander, or predictions and foretold events, especially about the peace, by the famous Scots Highlander: being ten new visions for the year 1713. 1713.

And what if the Pretender should come? or some considerations of the advantages and real consequences of the Pretender's possessing the Crown of Great-Britain. 1713.

An answer to a question that no body thinks of, viz But what if the Queen should die? 1713.

An essay on the Treaty of Commerce with France. 1713, 1713.

An account of the abolishing of duels in France: being extracts out of the edicts of the Kings, the regulations of the Marshals, and the records of the Parliaments of France, with the resolutions of the Archbishops, Bishops and the clergy there, in relation to that matter. 1713.

Union and no union: being an enquiry into the grievances of the Scots, and how far they are right or wrong, who alledge that the union is dissolved. 1713.

Considerations upon the Eighth and Ninth Articles of the Treaty of Commerce and Navigation, now publish'd by authority, with some enquiries into the damages that may accrue to the English trade from them. 1713.

Some thoughts upon the subject of commerce with France, by the author of the Review. 1713.

A general history of trade, and especially consider'd as it respects the British commerce. 4 pts 1713.

The honour and prerogative of the Queen's Majesty vindicated and defended against the unexampled insolence of the author of the Guardian, in a letter from a country Whig to Mr Steele. 1713, 1713. Probably by Defoe.

Memoirs of Count Tariff etc. 1713.

A brief account of the present state of the Afr ican trade. 1713.

Reasons concerning the immediate demolishing of Dunkirk: being a serious enquiry into the state and condition of that affair. 1713. Probably by Defoe.

A letter from a member of the House of Commons to his friends in the country, relating to the Bill of Commerce, with a true copy of the Bill, and an exact list of all those who voted for and against engrossing it. 1713, 1713. Probably by Defoe.

Whigs turn'd Tories, and Hanoverian-Tories, from their avow'd principles, prov'd Whigs: or each side in the other mistaken. 1713.

A view of the real dangers of the succession, from the peace with France: being a sober enquiry into the securities proposed in the Articles of Peace, and whether they are such as the nation ought to be satisfy'd with or no. 1713, 1714 (as A view of the real danger of the Protestant succession), Dublin 1714.

A letter to the Dissenters. 1713, 1714 (with new preface).

Proposals for imploying the poor in and about the city of London, without any charge to the publick. 1713.

A letter to the Whigs, expostulating with them upon their present conduct. 1714.

Memoirs of John Duke of Melfort: being an account of the secret intrigues of the Chevalier de S. George, particularly relating to the present times. 1714, 1714.

The Scots nation and union vindicated; from the reflections cast on them, in an infamous libel, entitl'd the Publick spirit of the Whigs etc. 1714.

Reasons for im[peaching] the L[or]d H[igh] T[reasure]r, and some others of the p[resent] m[inistry]. [1714].

A letter to Mr Steele, occasion'd by his letter to a member of Parliament, concerning the bill for preventing the growth of schism, by a member of the Church of England. 1714. Probably by Defoe.

The remedy worse than the disease: or reasons against passing the bill for preventing the growth of schism. 1714.

The weakest go to the wall, or the Dissenters sacrific'd by all parties. 1714.

A brief survey of the legal liberties of the Dissenters, and how far the bill now depending consists with preserving the toleration inviolably, wherein the present bill is publish'd; and also the Toleration Act at large, that they may be compar'd with one another. 1714, Edinburgh 1714.

The Schism act explain'd: wherein some methods are laid down how the Dissenters may teach their schools and academies as usual, without incurring the penalties of the said act. 1714. See B. G. Ivanyi, TLS 7 April 1966.

The secret history of the white staff: being an account of affairs under the conduct of some late Ministers, and of what might probably have happened if her Majesty had not died. 1714 (4 edns); pt II, 1714 (3 edns), Dublin 1714; pt III, 1715. The 3 pts were subsequently included in one pamphlet.

Advice to the people of Great Britain, with respect to two important points of their future conduct: I, What they ought to expect from the King; II, How they ought to behave by him. 1714, Dublin 1714.

A secret history of one year. 1714; rptd in Somers tracts vol 13, 1815.

Tories and Tory principles ruinous to both prince and people: being a specimen of the inconsistency of their pretended principles and real practices. 1714. Probably by Defoe.

Impeachment, or no impeachment: or an enquiry how far the impeachment of certain persons, at the present juncture, would be consistent with honour and justice. 1714. Probably by Defoe.

The Bristol riot: containing I, A full and particular account of the riot in general, with several material circumstances preceding, and contributing to it; II, The whole proceedings relating to the tryal of the rioters, before Judge Powys, Judge Tracey and Mr Baron Price, by a gentleman who attended the Commission. 1714. Perhaps by Defoe.

The pernicious consequences of the clergy's intermedling with affairs of state, with reasons humbly offer'd for passing a bill to incapacitate them from the like practice for the future. [1714?].

A full and impartial account of the late disorders in Bristol, to which is added the compleat tryals of the rioters before Mr Justice Powys, Mr Justice Tracey and Mr Baron Price. 1714. Perhaps by Defoe.

The secret history of the secret history of the white staff, purse and mitre. 1715.

Strike while the iron's hot: or now is the time to be happy, humbly propos'd upon his Majesty's late most gracious injunction. 1715.

Memoirs of the conduct of her late Majesty and her last Ministry, relating to the separate peace with France, by the Right Honourable the Countess of ——. 1715.

Treason detected, in an answer to that traiterous and malicious libel, entitled English advice to the freeholders of England humbly offer'd to the consideration of all those freeholders who have been poyson'd with that malignant pamphlet. 1715, 1715.

The immorality of the priesthood: being an historical account of the factious and insolent behaviour of the inferior clergy, ever since the Reformation, shewing how troublesome and dangerous they have been to the State, and the many mischiefs that have happen'd for want of a due restraint of the licentiousness of the pulpit. 1715. Also pbd without preface as The justice and necessity of restraining the clergy in their preaching. Perhaps by Defoe.

The secret history of state intrigues in the management of the scepter, in the late reign. 1715. Also pbd as The secret history of the scepter.

The candidate: being a detection of bribery and corruption as it is just now in practice all over Great Britain, in order to make members of Parliament, humbly recommended to all those who are now keeping Christmas at the expence of their representatives; they that will buy, will sell. 1715.

A reply to a traiterous libel entituled English advice to the freeholders of Great Britain. 1715.

The Protestant jubilee: a thanksgiving sermon on that doubly remarkable day the 20 of January, appointed for celebrating the praises of God, for our wonderful deliverance, by the happy accession of his most gracious Majesty King George to the throne of Great Britain, when we were just at the brink of ruin. 1714 (for 1715).

A letter to a merry young gentleman intituled Tho. Burnet esq, in answer to one writ by him to the right honourable the Earl of Halifax: by which it plainly appears, the said Squire was not awake when he writ the said letter. 1715 (3 edns). Sometimes attributed to W. Oldisworth.

Burnet and Bradbury: or the confederacy of the press and pulpit for the blood of the last ministry. 1715, 1715.

A view of the present management of the Court of France, and what new measures they are like to take. 1715.

The fears of the Pretender turn'd into the fears of debauchery, propos'd, without ceremony, to the consideration of the lords spiritual and temporal; with a hint to Richard Steele esq. 1715 (3 edns).

A friendly epistle by way of reproof from one of the people called Quakers, to Thomas Bradbury, a dealer in many words. 1715 (6 edns).

Reflections upon Sacheverell's sermons of January 20 and 31 1715: a sermon preach'd January 11 1714/5, by Henry Sacheverell DD Rector of St Andrew's Holborn, as it was taken in short hand by one of his parishioners; to which is added a postscript containing notes of another sermon, preach'd on the twentieth of the same month. 1715. Remarks, preface and postscript by Defoe.

An appeal to honour and justice, tho' it be of his worst enemies, by Daniel De Foe: being a true account of his conduct in publick affairs. 1715; rptd in English garner, ed E. Arber vol 7, 1883.

Some reasons offered by the late ministry in defence of their administration. 1715. Probably by Defoe.

The family instructor, in three parts, with a recommendatory letter by the Reverend Mr S. Wright. Newcastle 1715, London 1715 (corrected by the author), 1720 (8th edn), 1725 (10th edn), 1766 (16th edn) etc; vol 2, in two parts, 1718, 1727 (3rd edn), 1766 (8th edn); rptd 5 pts Bungay 1816. The 2 vols were often sold together. See also A new family instructor, 1727, below.

A sharp rebuke from one of the people called Quakers to Henry Sacheverell, the high-priest of Andrew's Holbourn, by the same friend that wrote to Thomas Bradbury. 1715.

An apology for the army, in a short essay on fortitude etc, written by an officer. 1715.

The second-sighted Highlander: being four visions of the eclypse, and something of what may follow. 1715.

Some methods to supply the defects of the late peace without entring into a new war. [1715].

A remonstrance from some country Whigs to a member of a secret committee. 1715. Probably by Defoe.

The happiness of the Hanover succession, illustrated from the conduct of the late administration, wherein their designs are farther expos'd, and publick justice demanded upon the betrayers of our Constitution. 1715. Perhaps by Defoe.

An attempt towards a coalition of English Protestants, from the weakness of the pretensions of the several parties, for being either better Christians, or better subjects, upon any principles wherein they differ; to which is added reasons for restraining the licentiousness of the pulpit and press. 1715.

A seasonable expostulation with, and friendly reproof unto James Butler who, by the men of this world, is stil'd Duke of O[rmon]d, relating to the tumults of the people, by the same friend that wrote to Thomas Bradbury, the dealer in many words, and Henry Sacheverell, the high-priest of St Andrew's Holbourn. 1715.

His Majesty's obligations to the Whigs plainly proved, shewing that he can neither with safety, reason or gratitude depart from them. 1715. Probably by Defoe.

A brief history of the pacific campaign in Flanders anno 1712, and of the fatal cessation of arms. 1715.

Some considerations on the danger of the Church from her own clergy, humbly offer'd to the lower-house of Convocation. 1715.

A letter from a gentleman of the church of England, to all the high-flyers of Great Britain. [London 1715], Dublin 1716.

An humble address to our soveraign lord the people. 1715.

The history of the wars, of his present Majesty Charles XII, King of Sweden. 1715, 1720 (with A continuation to the time of his death).

An account of the conduct of Robert Earl of Oxford. 1715, 1717 (as Memoirs of some transactions during the late Ministry of Robert E. of Oxford).

A hymn to the mob. 1715.

Hanover or Rome: shewing the absolute necessity of assisting his Majesty. 1715, Dublin 1715.

An account of the great and generous actions of James Butler (late Duke of Ormond), dedicated to the famous University of Oxford. [1715].

A view of the Scots rebellion; with some enquiry what we have to fear from them? 1715.

The traiterous and foolish manifesto of the Scots rebels, examin'd and expos'd paragraph by paragraph. 1715.

Bold advice: or proposals for the entire rooting out of Jacobitism in Great Britain, address'd to the present M[inistr]y. 1715. Almost certainly by Defoe.

An address to the people of England, shewing the unworthiness of their behaviour to King George. 1715. Perhaps by Defoe.

A trumpet blown in the North, and sounded in the ears of John Eriskine, call'd by the men of the world Duke of Mar, by a ministring friend of the people call'd Quakers. 1716 (for 1715).

A letter from one clergy-man to another, upon the subject of the rebellion. 1716 (for 1715). Probably by Defoe.

A conference with a Jacobite, wherein the clergy of the Church of England are vindicated from the charge of hypocrisy and perjury, in praying for the King, and taking the oaths of allegiance and abjuration. 1716. Probably by Defoe.

[Letter from General Forster to the Earl of Mar]. [1715]. In A. Boyer, Political state vol 10, 1715. Attributed by J. R. Moore on doubtful reference to Defoe at the end.

Proper lessons for the Tories, to be read throughout the year: but more particularly upon June 10, the birth-day of the Pretender, alias the fugitive hero. 1716. Sometimes as Proper lessons written by a Quaker. Almost certainly by Defoe.

Some account of the two nights court at Greenwich, wherein may be seen the reason, rise and progress of the late unnatural rebellion, against his sacred Majesty King George and his government. 1716.

The case of the Protestant Dissenters in England, fairly stated, humbly inscrib'd to all true lovers of religion, liberty and their country. 1716. Perhaps by Defoe.

The address of the Episcopal clergy of the Diocese of Aberdeen, to the Pretender, with remarks upon the said address. [1716]. Attributed by J. R. Moore.

The address of the magistrates and Town Council of Aberdeen, to the Pretender, with remarks upon the said address. [1716]. Attributed by J. R. Moore.

Some thoughts of an honest Tory in the country, upon the late dispositions of some people to revolt. 1716.

The declaration of the free-holders of Great Britain, in answer to that of the Pretender. [1716]. Attributed tentatively by J. R. Moore.

The conduct of some people, about pleading guilty, with some reasons why it was not thought proper to shew mercy to some who desir'd it. 1716.

An account of the proceedings against the rebels, and other prisoners, tried before the Lord Chief Justice Jefferies, and other judges, in the West of England in 1685 for taking arms under the Duke of Monmouth. 1716 (3 edns).

The proceedings of the government against the rebels, compared with the persecutions of the late reigns. [1716].

Remarks on the speech of James late Earl of Derwent-water, beheaded on Tower-Hill for high-treason, February 24, 1715/16. 1716. Perhaps by Defoe.

An essay upon buying and selling of speeches in a letter to a worshipfull Justice of the Peace, being also a member of a certain worshipfull society of speech-makers. 1716.

Some considerations on a law for triennial Parliaments, with an enquiry I, Whether there may not be a time when it is necessary to suspend the execution, even of such laws as are most essential to the liberties of the people?; II, Whether this is such a time or no? 1716, 1716, Edinburgh 1716, Dublin 1716.

The Triennial Act impartially stated. 1716. Ascribed by Boyer in Political State April 1716; denied by Defoe, Mercurius Politicus July 1717.

Arguments about the alteration of triennial elections of Parliament, in a letter to a friend in the country. 1716. Unlike Defoe's style, but claimed by him in Mercurius Politicus July 1717.

The ill consequences of repealing the Triennial Act in a letter to Mr Sh[ippe]n. 1716. Probably by Defoe.

A dialogue between a Whig and a Jacobite, upon the subject of the late rebellion and the execution of the rebel-lords etc, occasion'd by the phaenomenon in the skie, March 6 1715–1716. 1716. Probably by Defoe.

A true account of the proceedings at Perth; the debates in the street council there; with the reasons and causes of the suddain finishing and breaking up of the rebellion, written by a rebel. 1716, 1716, Edinburgh [1716] (abstract); rptd in Spottiswoode miscellany vol 2, 1845 (attributed to the Master of Sinclair).

A journal of the Earl of Marr's proceedings, from his first arrival in Scotland, to his embarkation for France. [1716]. Introd by Defoe.

Remarks on the speeches of William Paul Clerk, and John Hall of Otterburn esq, executed at Tyburn for rebellion, the 13th of July 1716. 1716 (3 edns).

The annals of King George, year the second: being a faithful history of the affairs of Great Britain for the year MDCCXVI, containing also a full and complete history of the rebellion. 1717 (for 1716). Vol 2 as The annals of King George, but the general history of Europe during that time, 1718 (for 1717). Written in part and ed Defoe.

The layman's vindication of the Church of England, as well against Mr Howell's charge of schism, as against Dr Bennett's pretended answer to it. 1716.

Secret memoirs of the new treaty of alliance with France, in which some of the first steps in that remarkable affair are discovered, with some characters of persons. 1716, Dublin 1716.

Secret memoirs of a treasonable conference at S[omerset] House, for deposing the present Ministry and making a new turn at Court. 1717, 1717.

Some national grievances considered in a letter to R[obert] W[alpole]. 1717. Perhaps by Defoe.

The danger of Court differences: or the unhappy effects of a motley ministry, occasion'd by the report of changes at Court. 1717.

The quarrel of the school-boys at Athens, as lately acted at a school near Westminster. 1717.

Faction in power: or the mischiefs and dangers of a High-Church magistracy. 1717. Probably by Defoe.

An impartial enquiry into the conduct of the Right Honourable Charles Lord Viscount T[ownshend]. 1717.

An argument proving that the design of employing and enobling foreigners is a treasonable conspiracy against the Constitution, dangerous to the Kingdom, an affront to the nobility of Scotland in particular and dishonourable to the peerage of Britain in general. 1717.

An account of the Swedish and Jacobite plot, with a vindication of our government from the horrid aspersions of its enemies. 1717. Probably by Defoe.

A curious little oration deliver'd by Father Andrew. 1717, 1717.

An expostulatory letter, to the B[ishop] of B[angor] concerning a book lately publish'd by his Lordship entitul'd A preservative against the principles and practices of the Nonjurors etc. [1717].

Fair payment no spunge: or some considerations on the unreasonableness of refusing to receive back money lent on publick securities, and the necessity of setting the nation free from the insupportable burthen of debt and taxes. 1717.

What if the Swedes should come? with some thoughts about keeping the army on foot, whether they come or not. 1717.

The question fairly stated, whether now is not the time to do justice to the friends of the government as well as to its enemies? 1717.

Christianity no creature of the state: or if it be made one, reasons why it should be abolish'd, by the author of the Case of the Protestant Dissenters in England. 1717. Perhaps by Defoe.

The danger and consequences of disobliging the clergy consider'd, as it relates to making a law for regulating the universities, and repealing some laws which concern the Dissenters. 1717.

Reasons for a royal visitation, occasion'd by the present great defection of the clergy from the government. 1717. Probably by Defoe.

Memoirs of the Church of Scotland, in four periods, with an appendix of some transactions since the union. 1717, 1734.

A farther argument against ennobling foreigners, in answer to the two parts of the state anatomy; with a short account of the anatomizer. 1717.

The conduct of Robert Walpole esq, from the beginning of the reign of her late Majesty Queen Anne to the present time. 1717.

The report reported: or the weakness and injustice of the proceedings of the convocation in their censure of the Ld Bp of Bangor examin'd and expos'd. 1717, 1717. Probably by Defoe.

A short view of the conduct of the King of Sweden. [1717].

A general pardon consider'd, in its circumstances and consequences, particularly relating to the exceptions said to be now in debate, and to the reason why it came out no sooner. 1717. Probably by Defoe.

Observation on the Bishop's answer to Dr Snape, by a lover of truth. 1717.

A vindication of Dr Snape, in answer to several libels lately publish'd against him. [1717]. Probably by Defoe.

A reply to the remarks upon the Lord Bishop of Bangor's treatment of the clergy and convocation, said to be written by Dr Sherlock. 1717.

Minutes of the negotiations of Monsr Mesnager at the Court of England towards the close of the last reign. 1717.

Memoirs of some transactions during the late Ministry of Robert E. of Oxford. 1717.

A declaration of truth to Benjamin Hoadly, one of the high priests of the land, and of the degree whom men call Bishops, by a ministring friend, who writ to Tho. Bradbury, a dealer in many words. 1717.

A history of the clemency of our English monarchs, from the Reformation, down to the present time, with some comparisons. 1717. Probably by Defoe.

The conduct of Christians made the sport of infidels, in a letter from a Turkish merchant at Amsterdam to the Grand Mufti at Constantinople, on occasion of some of our national follies, but especially the late scandalous quarrel among the clergy. 1717.

The old Whig and modern Whig revived, in the present divisions at Court: or the difference betwixt acting upon principle and interest exemplified by some of our present patriots. 1717. Probably by Defoe.

A letter to Andrew Snape, occasion'd by the strife that lately appeared among the people call'd, clergy-men, by the author of the Declaration of truth. 1717.

The case of the war in Italy stated: being a serious enquiry how far Great-Britain is engaged to concern it self in the quarrel between the Emperor and the King of Spain. 1718 (for 1717).

Considerations on the present state of affairs in Great-Britain. 1718, 1718 (as The juncture: or considerations on his Majesty's speech).

The defection farther consider'd, wherein the resigners, as some would have them stil'd, are really deserters. 1718, 1718.

Some persons vindicated against the author of the Defection etc [Tindal], and that writer convicted of malice and falsehood R[obert] W[alpole] esq. 1718.

Memoirs of the life and eminent conduct of that learned and reverend divine Daniel Williams DD. 1718.

Mr de la Pillonniere's vindication: being an answer to the two schoolmasters, and their boys tittle tattle, wherein the dispute between Dr Snape and Mr Pillonniere is set in a true light, by the author of the Lay-man's vindication. 1718.

A brief answer to a long libel: being an examination of a heap of scandal, published by the author of the scourge, entituled the Danger of the Church's establishment, from the insolence of Protestant Dissenters. 1718. Perhaps by Defoe.

A letter from the Jesuists to Father de la Pillonniere, in answer to the letter sent to them by that Father, and published by Dr Snape in his Vindication etc. 1718.

A golden mine of treasure open'd for the Dutch, by a lover of Britain. 1718. Probably by Defoe.

Miserere cleri, or the factions of the Church: being a short view of the pernicious consequences of the clergy inter-medling with affairs of State. [1718], 1718.

Some reasons why it could not be expected the government wou'd permit the speech or paper of James Shepheard, which he delivered at the place of execution, to be printed. 1718. Probably by Defoe.

The Jacobites detected, in the methods they made use of to draw young men into an association against his Majesty King George. 1718. Perhaps by Defoe.

Dr Sherlock's vindication of the Test Act examin'd, and the false foundations of it exposed, in answer to so much of his book against the Bishop of Bangor, as relates to the Protestant Dissenters. 1718. Perhaps by Defoe.

A brief comment upon his Majesty's speech: being reasons for strengthening the Church of England by taking off the penal laws against Dissenters, by one called a Low-Church-Man. 1718. Perhaps by Defoe.

A vindication of the press: or an essay on the usefulness of writing, on criticism, and the qualification of authors. 1718; ed O. C. Williams, Los Angeles 1951 (Augustan Reprint Soc).

A letter from some Protestant dissenting laymen, in the behalf of that whole body, to their friends of the British Parliament, concerning their treatment under the present administration. 1718. Probably by Defoe.

Memoirs of publick transactions in the life and ministry of his Grace the D. of Shrewsbury. 1718.

A letter from Paris, giving an account of the death of the late Queen Dowager, and of her disowning the Pretender to be her son, with some observations. 1718. Probably by Defoe.

A history of the last session of the present Parliament, with a correct list of both Houses. 1718.

A letter to the author of the Flying-post, in answer to a most malicious false story of his from Edinburgh; and to a celebrated deistical letter of his from the Grecian coffee-house. 1718.

A continuation of Letters written by a Turkish spy at Paris. 1718.

The history of the reign of King George, from the death of her late Majesty Queen Anne, to the first of August 1718, collected from the most authentick vouchers, to be continued yearly. 1719 (for 1718).

The memoirs of Majr Alexander Ramkins, a High-land-officer, now in prison at Avignon: being an account of several remarkable adventures during about twenty eight years service in Scotland, Germany, Italy, Flanders and Ireland. 1719 (for 1718).

A friendly rebuke to one Parson Benjamin [Hoadly]; particularly relating to his quarreling with his own church, and vindicating the Dissenters. 1719.

Observations and remarks upon the declaration of war against Spain, and upon the manifesto publish'd in the name of the King of France, explaining the said declaration. 1719. Probably by Defoe.

Merry Andrew's epistle to his old master Benjamin, a mountebank at Bangor-Bridge, on the River Dee, near Wales. 1719. Perhaps by Defoe.

The life and strange surprizing adventures of Robinson Crusoe, of York, mariner, written by himself. 1719 (4 edns: 25 April, 9 May, 4 June, 7 Aug), 1720, 1722 etc; ed A. Dobson 1883 (facs); tr French, 1720, 1721, 1722 etc; German, 1720, 1721 etc; Dutch, 1720, 1721, 1735; Italian, 1731, 1738 etc; Danish, 1774.

A letter to the Dissenters. 1719.

The anatomy of exchange-alley: or a system of stock-jobbing, proving that scandalous trade, as it is now carry'd on, to be knavish in its private practice, and treason in its publick, by a jobber. 1719, 1719; rptd J. Francis in Chronicles and characters of the stock exchange, 1849.

Some account of the life and most remarkable actions of George Henry Baron de Goertz, Privy-Counsellor and Chief Minister of State, to the late King of Sweden. 1719.

The just complaint of the poor weavers truly represented. 1719.

The farther adventures of Robinson Crusoe: being the second and last part of his life. 1719, 1719, 1722 etc; tr French, 1720, 1721, 1722 etc; German, 1720, 1721 etc; Dutch, 1721, 1722, 1736 etc; Italian, 1734, 1742 etc; Danish, 1745.

A brief state of the question, between the printed and painted callicoes and the woollen and silk manufacture, as far as it relates to the wearing and using of printed and painted callicoes in Great-Britain. 1719, 1719, 1720.

Charity still a Christian virtue: or an impartial account of the tryal and conviction of the Reverend Mr Hendley for preaching a charity-sermon at Chisselhurst. 1719.

The dumb philosopher: or Great Britain's wonder, containing 1: A faithful and very surprizing account how Dickory Cronke, a tinner's son in the county of Cornwal, was born dumb, and continued so for 58 years; and how some days before he died, he came to his speech. 1719, 1719. Always attributed to Defoe but not certainly his.

[The petition of Dorothy Distaff etc to Mrs Rebecca Woollpack]. [1719?]; rptd in Mercurius Politicus Dec 1719.

The king of pirates: being an account of the famous enterprises of Captain Avery, the mock King of Madagascar, with his rambles and piracies; wherein all the sham accounts formerly publish'd of him, are detected. 1720 (for 1719), 1720.

An historical account of the voyages and adventures of Sir Walter Raleigh, with the discoveries and conquests he made for the crown of England. 1719 (for 1720).

The chimera: or the French way of paying national debts laid open. 1720.

The case of the fair traders, humbly represented to the honourable the House of Commons: being a clear view and state of clandestine trade, as now carry'd on in Great Britain. [1720]. Attributed to Defoe by J. R. Moore.

The trade to India critically and calmly consider'd, and prov'd to be destructive to the general trade of Great Britain as well as to the woollen and silk manufacturers in particular. 1720.

The case fairly stated between the Turky Company and the Italian merchants, by a merchant. 1720, 1720.

The compleat art of painting: a poem translated from the French of M. du Fresnoy, by D.F. gent. 1720. Defoe's initials and one of his publishers, but few other signs of his hand.

A letter to the author of the Independent Whig, wherein the merits of the clergy are consider'd, the good vindicated, and the bad expos'd. 1720. Perhaps by Defoe.

The history of the life and adventures of Mr Duncan Campbell, a gentleman who, tho' deaf and dumb, writes down any stranger's name at first sight; with their future contingencies of fortune. 1720, 1720, 1732, 1739, 1748; tr German, 1742; 1728 (as The supernatural philosopher by William Bond). Always attributed to Defoe, perhaps in part or entirely by Bond.

Memoirs of a Cavalier: or a military journal of the wars in Germany, and the wars in England, from the year 1632 to the year 1648. [1720], Edinburgh 1759, 1766, 1788; tr German, 1785–6.

The life, adventures and pyracies of the famous Captain Singleton. 1720, 1721, 1737, 1768, 1810, 1887 etc, 1800 (abridged).

Serious reflections during the life and surprising adventures of Robinson Crusoe, with his vision of the angelick world. 1720; tr French, 1721, 1735, 1770; German, 1721; Dutch, 1722, 1736, 1752.

The South-Sea scheme examin'd; and the reasonableness thereof demonstrated. 1720 (3 edns). Probably by Defoe.

A true state of the contracts relating to the third money-subscription taken by the South-Sea Company. 1721.

A vindication of the honour and justice of Parliament against a most scandalous libel entituled the Speech of John A[islabie] esq. [1721].

Brief observations on trade and manufactures; and particularly of our mines and metals and the hard-ware works. 1721.

Some account of the life of Sir Charles Sedley by an eminent hand. Prefixed to vol 1 of Works of Sir Charles Sedley, 1722 (for 1721).

The case of Mr Law, truly stated, in answer to a pamphlet, entitul'd A letter to Mr Law. 1721.

A collection of miscellany letters, selected out of Mist's weekly journal. 4 vols 1722, 1722, 1727, 1727. Defoe contributed to and probably edited this work.

The fortunes and misfortunes of the famous Moll Flanders, written from her own memorandums. 1721 (for 1722), 1722, 1722 (rev), 1723, 1740, 1741, 1759 etc; 1723 (abridged, with added ch), 1730 (as Fortune's fickle distribution) (with continuation of the lives of her husband and governess), 1776 (as The history of Laetitia Atkins); chap-books c. 1750, c. 1760, c. 1770 etc; ed H. Davis, Oxford 1961 (WC) (from 1721); tr German, 1723, 1745; Dutch, 1752; French, 1761.

Due preparations for the plague as well for soul as body: being some seasonable thoughts upon the visible approach of the present dreadful contagion in France. 1722.

Religious courtship: being historical discourses, on the necessity of marrying religious husbands and wives only. 1722, 1729, 1734, 1735, 1737 etc, 1789 ('21st edn'), 1797 etc.

A journal of the plague year: being observations or memorials of the most remarkable occurrences, as well publick as private, which happened in London during the last great visitation in 1665. 1722, 1754 (as The history of the great plague in London), 1832, 1832?, 1835, 1840, 1863 etc; 1795 (abridged), 1824, 1886 etc; ed L. A. Landa, Oxford 1969.

A brief debate upon the dissolving the late Parliament. 1722.

An impartial history of the life and actions of Peter Alexowitz, the present Czar of Muscovy, from his birth down to this present time, written by a British officer in the service of the Czar. 1723 (for 1722), 1725 (with addns, as A true, authentick and impartial history of the Czar).

The history and remarkable life of the truly honourable Col Jacque, commonly call'd Col Jack. 1723 (for 1722), 1723, 1724, 1738, 1810 etc; 1809 (abridged), 1813; ed S. H. Monk, Oxford 1965; tr Dutch, 1729; German, 1740.

A memorial to the clergy of the Church of England, relating to their conduct since the Revolution; together with some advice to them upon the present state of affairs, by a clergyman. 1723. Probably by Defoe.

The fortunate mistress: or a history of the life and vast variety of fortunes of Mademoiselle de Beleau, afterwards call'd the Countess de Wintselsheim, in Germany, being the person known by the name of the lady Roxana, in the time of King Charles II. [1724], [1745?], 1750 (with anon continuation partly from E. Hayward's British recluse), 1755, 1923; ed W. Cather, New York 1924; ed R. B. Johnson [1926]; ed J. Jack, Oxford 1964; 1765 (abridged), 1766; tr German, 1736.

The great law of subordination consider'd; or the insolence and unsufferable behaviour of servants in England duly enquir'd into, in ten familiar letters. 1724, 1726 (reissued as The behaviour of servants in England inquired into).

A general history of the robberies and murders of the most notorious pyrates, and also their policies, discipline and government, from their first rise and settlement in the island of Providence, in 1717, to the present year 1724, by Captain Charles Johnson. 1724, 1724, 1725 (reissued with addns), 1726 etc; Dublin 1727 (abridged); ed P. Gosse 1925; tr Dutch, 1725; German, 1728; French, 1744, 1775; Vol 2 as The history of the pyrates, 1728, 1729; ed L. Hayward 1926. Both vols frequently abridged and sections added to lives of criminals and pirates. A fictional section excerpted as Of Captain Misson, ed M. E. Novak, Los Angeles 1961 (Augustan Reprint Soc.)

A tour thro' the whole island of Great Britain, divided into circuits or journies: giving a particular and diverting account of whatever is curious and worth observation, by a gentleman. [Vol 1] 1724; vol 2, 1725; vol 3, 1727; 3 vols 1738 (rev S. Richardson?), 4 vols 1742, 1748, 1753, 1762, 1769, 1778; ed G. D. H. Cole 2 vols 1927.

The royal progress: or a historical view of the journeys or progresses, which several great princes have made to visit their dominions. 1724.

[Letter about the King's intended progress]. Rptd in Political State, ed A. Boyer, June 1724.

A narrative of the proceedings in France, for discovering and detecting the murderers of the English gentlemen, September 21 1723, near Calais, translated from the French. 1724, 1724, 1725.

A narrative of all the robberies, escapes etc of John Sheppard: giving an exact description of the manner of his wonderful escape from the castle in Newgate, written by himself during his confinement. 1724 (8 edns); ed H. Bleackley as Jack Sheppard, [1933]; tr French, 1725.

Some farther account of the original disputes in Ireland, about farthings and halfpence, in a discourse with a Quaker of Dublin. 1724.

The history of the remarkable life of John Sheppard, containing a particular account of his many robberies and escapes. [1724] (3 edns), [1724?]; ed H. Bleackley as Jack Sheppard, [1933].

A new voyage round the world, by a course never sailed before. 1725 (for 1724), 3 vols 1787, 2 vols Edinburgh 1810.

An epistle from Jack Sheppard to the late L[or]d C[hance]l-l[o]r of E[nglan]d, who when Sheppard was try'd, sent for him to the Chancery Bar. [1725]. Perhaps by Defoe.

The life of Jonathan Wild, from his birth to his death, containing his rise and progress in roguery, by H.D. late clerk to Justice R——. 1725, 1725.

Every-body's business is no-body's business: or private abuses, publick grievances; exemplified in the pride, insolence and exorbitant wages of our women-servants, footmen etc, by Andrew Moreton esq. 1725 (5 edns, 5th edn with a preface).

The true and genuine account of the life and actions of the late Jonathan Wild, not made up of fiction and fable, but taken from his own mouth. 1725; ed W. Follett, New York 1926 (with Fielding's novel).

An account of the conduct and proceedings of the late John Gow alias Smith, Captain of the late pirates. [1725]; ed J. R. Russell 1890.

The complete English tradesman, in familiar letters; directing him in all the several parts and progressions of trade. 1726 (for 1725), Dublin 1726, 1727 (for 1726) (with suppl; suppl issued separately, dated 1727), 1732; vol 2, 1727 (as The compleat English tradesman). Both vols 1732, 1738, 1745, Edinburgh 1839 (with notes).

A general history of discoveries and improvements, in useful arts, particularly in the great branches of commerce, navigation and plantation, in all parts of the known world. 4 monthly pts Oct 1725–Jan 1726; 1727 (for 1726) (bound together as The history of the principal discoveries and improvements, in the several arts and sciences).

A brief case of the distillers, and of the distilling trade in England, shewing how far it is the interest of England to encourage the said trade. 1726.

A brief historical account of the lives of the six notorious street-robbers, executed at Kingston, viz William Blewet, Edward Bunworth, Emanuel Dickenson, Thomas Berry, John Higges and John Legee. 1726.

An essay upon literature: or an enquiry into the antiquity and original of letters; proving that the two tables, written by the finger of God in Mount Sinai, was the first writing in the world. 1726.

The political history of the Devil, as well ancient as modern: in two parts. 1726, 1727 (with new preface), 1734 etc; tr French, 1729; German, 1730, 1733, etc.

Unparallel'd cruelty: or the tryal of Captain Jeane of Bristol, who was convicted at the Old Bailey for the murder of his cabbin-boy. 1726.

The friendly daemon, or the generous apparition: being a true narrative of a miraculous cure, newly perform'd upon that famous deaf and dumb gentleman Dr Duncan Campbell, by a familiar spirit that appear'd to him in a white surplice, like a cathedral singing boy. 1726.

The four years voyages of Capt George Roberts: being a series of uncommon events, which befell him in a voyage to the islands of the Canaries, Cape de Verde and Barbadoes, from whence he was bound to the coast of Guiney. 1726.

Mere nature delineated, or a body without a soul: being observations upon the young forester lately brought to town from Germany; also a brief dissertation upon the usefulness and necessity of fools, whether political or natural. 1726.

Some considerations upon street-walkers, with a proposal for lessening the present number of them, in two letters to a Member of Parliament. [1726].

The Protestant monastery: or a complaint against the brutality of the present age, particularly the pertness and insolence of our youth to aged persons, by Andrew Moreton esq. 1727 (for 1726), 1731 (for 1730) (with new preface and postscript as Chickens feed capons: or a dissertation on the pertness of our youth in general) (4 edns).

A system of magick, or a history of the black art: being an historical account of mankind's most early dealing with the Devil; and how the acquaintance on both sides first began. 1727 (for 1726), 1728, 1729, 1731.

The evident approach of a war, and something of the necessity of it, in order to establish peace and preserve trade. 1727, 1727.

Conjugal lewdness: or matrimonial whoredom. 1727 (re-issued as A treatise concerning the use and abuse of the marriage bed); ed M. E. Novak, Gainesville 1967; tr German, 1734.

The evident advantages to Great Britain and its allies from the approaching war, especially in matters of trade. 1727.

A brief deduction of the original, progress and immense greatness of the British woolen manufacture. 1727.

An essay on the history and reality of apparitions. 1727, 1728 (as The secrets of the invisible world disclos'd: or an universal history of apparitions), 1729, 1735, 1738, 1740 etc.

A new family instructor, in familiar discourses between a father and his children, on the most essential points of the Christian religion, in two parts, with a poem upon the divine nature of Jesus Christ, in blank verse, by the author of the Family instructor. 1727, 1742.

Parochial tyranny: or the house-keeper's complaint against the insupportable exactions, and partial assessments of select vestries etc, by Andrew Moreton esq. [1727].

Some considerations on the reasonableness and necessity of encreasing and encouraging the seamen, founded on the gracious expressions, in their favour, contain'd in his Majesty's speech from the throne. 1728.

Augusta triumphans: or the way to make London the most flourishing city in the universe. 1728, 1731 (for 1730) (rev as The generous projector: or a friendly proposal to prevent murder and other enormous abuses).

A plan of the English commerce: being a compleat prospect of the trade of this nation, as well the home trade as the foreign, in three parts. 1728, 1730 (with appendix on foreign trade).

The memoirs of an English officer who serv'd in the Dutch war in 1672, to the peace of Utrecht in 1713, by Capt George Carleton. 1728, 1740 (as A true and genuine history of the last two wars), 1743 (as The memoirs of Cap George Carleton); ed W. Scott 1808. Always attributed to Defoe but possibly in part by a real G. Carleton.

Atlas maritimus and commercialis: or a general view of the world, so far as it relates to trade and navigation; describing all the coasts, ports, harbours and noted rivers, according to the latest discoveries and most exact observations. 1728. A compilation but certainly by Defoe.

An impartial account of the late famous siege of Gibraltar; to which are added most accurate plans of the town, and of the approaches and camp of the Spaniards, with many remarkable transactions never made publick before, by an officer. 1728.

Second thoughts are best: or a further improvement of a late scheme to prevent street robberies; by which our streets will be so strongly guarded, and so gloriously illuminated, that any part of London will be as safe and pleasant at midnight as at noonday; and burglary totally impracticable, by Andrew Moreton esq. 1729 (for 1728).

Street-robberies consider'd: the reason of their being so frequent, with probable means to prevent 'em, written by a converted thief; to which is prefix'd some memoirs of his life. [1728].

Reasons for a war, in order to establish the tranquillity and commerce of Europe. 1729.

The unreasonableness and ill consequences of imprisoning the body for debt, prov'd from the laws of God and nature, human policy and interest, address'd to a noble lord. 1729.

An humble proposal to the people of England, for the encrease of their trade, and encouragement of their manufactures; whether the present uncertainty of affairs issues in peace or war, by the author of the Compleat tradesman. 1729.

An enquiry into the pretensions of Spain to Gibraltar, together with a copy of a letter (said to be sent) to his Catholick Majesty. 1729, 1729.

Some objections humbly offered to the consideration of the hon House of Commons, relating to the present intended relief of prisoners. 1729.

The advantages of peace and commerce; with some remarks on the East-India trade. 1729.

Madagascar: or Robert Drury's journal, during fifteen years captivity on that island, written by himself, digested into order, and now publish'd at the request of his friends. 1729, 1731, 1743, 1750 etc. Edited and written in part by Defoe.

A brief state of the inland or home trade of England, and of the oppressions it suffers and the dangers which threaten it from the invasion of hawkers, pedlars and clandestine traders of all sorts. 1730.

The perjur'd Free Mason detected, and yet the honour and antiquity of the Society of Free Masons preserv'd and defended, by a Free Mason. 1730.

An effectual scheme for the immediate preventing of street robberies, and suppressing all other disorders of the night. 1731 (for 1730).

The compleat English gentleman. Ed K. D. Bülbring 1890.

Of royall educacion: a fragmentary treatise. Ed K. K. Bülbring 1895.

The meditations (1681). Ed G. H. Healey, Cummington Mass 1946.

Periodicals

Vols 2–3 of Lee's Life, 1869 contain selections from Defoe's contributions to periodicals during the reign of George I. Although most are unquestionably by Defoe, Lee tended to include news items which appeared in approximately the same form in almost all the journals of the time. There is no evidence that Defoe wrote these. For journals like Review and Manufacturer, Defoe probably wrote almost every line; for the journals of Mist and Applebee, he was only an occasional contributor and editor.

A review of the affairs of France: and of all Europe. 9 vols 19 Feb 1704–11 June 1713; ed A. W. Secord 22 vols New York 1938; Index by W. L. Payne, New York 1948. With several changes of name, including A review of the state of the British nation, and simply The review for last vol. In addition to the regular London edn, one vol and part of another were rptd at Edinburgh. On several occasions individual issues were rptd as separate pamphlets with appropriate titles. Regular issues were supplemented by special issues as Appendix, Supplement and The little review. See Secord's introd to vol 1 of his edn.

The London post. 25 Sept 1704?–8 June 1705. Defoe's hand is not evident until 6 Dec 1704.

The Edinburgh courant. 24 Sept 1708–July 1709 (and perhaps for a period after 15 May 1710).

The London post-man. 1706–8. Occasional contributions.

The Newcastle gazette: or northern courant. Dec 1710. Some connection with Defoe.

The Scots postman. 27 Oct–end of 1710.

The observator. 19 July–11 Oct 1710.

Mercator: or commerce retrieved. 26 May 1713–20 July 1714.

The monitor. 22 April–21 Aug 1714.

The flying post: and medley. 27 July–21 Aug 1714.

The flying post. Occasional contributions? See [Two letters to the author of the flying-post], rptd in Political

State, ed A. Boyer, Aug 1724. J. R. Moore also attributes a letter in Flying Post 22 Jan 1715.

Mercurius politicus. May 1716–Oct 1720.

[Dormer's news letter. June 1716–Aug 1718?]. Suppositious title and dates for a journal Defoe edited at this time.

The weekly-journal: or Saturday's evening post. (Mist's weekly-journal). c. Feb 1717–24 Oct 1724.

The weekly journal: being an auxiliary packet to the Saturday's post. 25 Sept–23 Oct 1717.

Mercurius britannicus. Jan 1718–March 1719.

The White-Hall evening post. 18 Sept 1718–c. 14 Oct 1720.

The daily post. 3 Oct 1719–c. 27 April 1725.

The manufacturer. 30 Oct–17 Feb 1720.

The commentator. 1 Jan–16 Sept 1720.

The original weekly journal (later called Applebee's original weekly journal). 25 June 1720–14 May 1726 (and occasionally after).

The director. 5 Oct 1720–16 Jan 1721. In part and perhaps wholly by Defoe.

The citizen. 18 Sept–17 Nov 1727. Perhaps Defoe.

The universal spectator and weekly journal. 12 Oct 1728.

Fog's weekly journal. 11 Jan 1729.

The political state of Great-Britain. Dec 1729–Oct 1730.

Letters

Letters. Ed G. H. Healey, Oxford 1955. Includes a number of reports to Harley and others on various national problems: Of the fleet and Sir Geo Rook; Methods of mannagement of the Dissenters; An abstract of my journey; Of the Seamen etc. These have sometimes been listed as separate titles among Defoe's works.

§ 2

A complete bibliography of attacks on Defoe is being prepared by W. L. Payne; only representative examples are listed below.

Howe, J. Some consideration of a preface to an Enquiry concerning the occasional conformity of Dissenters. 1700.

Englishmen no bastards. 1701.

The fable of the cuckoo. 1701.

The female critick; with a letter to the author of a satyr called the True-born Englishman. 1701.

The true-born Englishman answer'd paragraph by paragraph. 1701.

The ballad answered stanza by stanza, with the Memorial, alias Legion, reply'd to paragraph by paragraph. 1701.

Animadversions on the succession to the crown of England consider'd. 1701.

An answer to the Mock mourners. 1702.

The fox with his fire-brand unkenell'd and insnar'd. 1703.

Leslie, C. The New Association. Pt 2, 1703.

—— Rehearsal 19 June–28 Sept 1706.

Reflections upon a late scandalous and malicious pamphlet entitul'd the Shortest way with the Dissenters. 1703.

The reformer reform'd: or the shortest way with Daniel D'Fooe. 1703.

The safest way with the Dissenters. 1703.

The scribler's doom: or the pillory in fashion. 1703.

The shortest way with whores and rogues. 1703.

The true-born hugonot: or Daniel de Foe. 1703.

An answer paragraph by paragraph to Legion's humble address to the Lords. 1704.

Astell, M. A fair way with the Dissenters and their patrons. 1704.

Virgil the epic poet, and De Foe the hymnist. In Visits from the shades, 1704.

The republican bullies, in a dialogue between Mr Review and the Observator. 1705.

An equivalent for De Foe. [Edinburgh? 1706].

Jure divino toss'd in a blanket. 1706.

The moderation, justice and manners of the Review. 1706.

Observations on the bankrupts bill, occasion'd by the many false misrepresentations of Mr Daniel De Foe. 1706.

Remarks on the Review. 1706.

The Review and Observator review'd. 1706.

The sourse of our present fears discover'd. 1706.

Black, W. A reply to the authors of the Advantages of Scotland by an incorporate union. [Edinburgh] 1707.

A character of a turn-coat. 1707.

The Review review'd. [1707].

Webster, J. The author of the Lawful prejudices against Union defended in answer to [Defoe's] Dissenters in England vindicated. [Edinburgh 1707].

Clark, J. A paper concerning Daniel De Foe. Edinburgh 1708.

—— A just reprimand to Daniel Defoe. 1710.

A dialogue between Lewis le petite and Harlequin le grand. [1708].

The Welsh-monster: or the rise and downfall of that late upstart the r—t h—ble Innuendo Scribble. 1708.

'Robin-hog'. A hue and cry after Daniel Defoe, for denying the Queen's hereditary right. 1711.

The three false brethren. 1711. Cartoon with poem attacking Defoe.

Judas discuver'd and catch'd at last: or Daniel de Foe in lob's pound. 1713.

Oldmixon, J. Remarks on a scandalous libel entitl'd A letter from a Member of Parliament etc relating to the bill of commerce. 1713.

Remarks on the Letter to the Dissenters. 1714.

A vindication of the Earl of Nottingham. 1714.

Pittis, W. Queen Anne vindicated from the base aspersions of some late pamphlets. 1715.

A dream by a gentleman in imitation of Quevedo's Vision of h—l. Read's Weekly Jnl 1 Nov 1718. Read ptd numerous attacks on Defoe during Oct–Nov.

Gildon, C. The life and surprising adventures of D— D— F—. 1719; ed P. Dottin as Robinson Crusoe examin'd and criticis'd, 1923.

'Comb-brush, C.' Every man mind his own business: being an answer to Every-body's business is no-body's business. 1725.

Every-body's business is no-body's business answered by a committee of woman-servants and footmen. [1725].

Dodsley, R. Servitude: a poem. 1729. Postscript attacks Defoe's Every-body's business is no-body's business.

Cibber, T. and R. Shiels. In his Lives of the poets vol 4, 1753.

Rousseau, J.–J. In his Emile, Amsterdam 1762. On Crusoe.

Chalmers, G. Life of Defoe. 1785, 1790 (first separate edn with author's name and bibliography); also prefixed to his edn of Defoe's History of the Union, 1786; appended to vol 2 of Stockdale edn of Robinson Crusoe, 1790 etc.

Memoirs of the life and writings of De Foe. Universal Mag of Knowledge & Pleasure 92 1793.

De Foe's Memoirs of a Cavalier. Retrospective Rev 3 1821.

Scott, W. In his Miscellaneous works vol 4, Edinburgh 1827.

Wilson, W. Memoirs of the life and times of Defoe. 3 vols 1830. With contributions by C. Lamb.

Charles, P. Les romans de De Foe. In his Le dix-huitième siècle en Angleterre vol 2, Paris 1846.

Daniel De Foe. Chambers' Papers for the People 7 1851; rptd Philadelphia 1854.

Daniel De Foe. Dublin Univ Mag 48 1856; rptd Littell's Living Age 14 1856.

De Foe as a novelist. Nat Rev 3 1856.

The works of de Foe. Br Quart Rev 27 1856.

Tuckerman, H. T. De Foe: writer for the people. In his Essays biographical and critical, Boston 1857.

Forster, J. Charles Churchill; Daniel Defoe. 1855. Rptd

with addns from Edinburgh Rev 82 1845; in his Historical and biographical essays vol 2, 1858.

Jeaffreson, J. C. In his Novels and novelists vol 1, 1858.

Chadwick, W. Life and times of Defoe. 1859.

Windsor, A. L. De Foe and the rise of pamphleteering. In his Ethica, 1860.

Russell, W. Daniel De Foe. In his Eccentric personages, 1864, New York 1866.

Stephen, L. Defoe's novels. In his Hours in a library ser 1, 1874. Rptd from Cornhill Mag 1868.

A gentleman of the press. All the Year Round 2 1869.

A great Whig journalist. Blackwood's Mag Oct 1869.

Lee, W. Defoe: his life and recently discovered writings 1716–29. 3 vols 1869.

Dennis, J. In his Studies in English literature, 1876.

Ireland, M. E. The Defoe family in America. Scribner's Mag May 1876.

Minto, W. Daniel Defoe. 1879 (EML).

London Quart Rev 57 1882.

Hale, E. E. Defoe and Thomas Shepard. Atlantic Monthly July 1885.

Dawson, G. In his Biographical lectures, ed G. St Clair 1886.

Jusserand, J.–J. Le roman anglais et la réforme littéraire de Defoe. Brussels 1887.

Parneil, A. Defoe and the Memoirs of Captain Carleton. Athenaeum 2 March 1889.

Robinson, E. F. Defoe in Stoke Newington. 1889.

Aitken, G. A. Defoe's birth and marriage. Athenaeum 23 Aug 1890.

—— The wife of Defoe. Contemporary Rev Feb 1890.

—— Defoe's brick-kilns. Athenaeum 13 April 1889.

—— Defoe in trouble. 1703. Athenaeum 22 Dec 1894; More state papers, 12 Jan 1895.

—— Defoe and Malthus. Social Economist 7 1894.

—— Defoe's apparition of Mrs Veal. Nineteenth Century Jan 1895.

Murray, J. O. The author of Robinson Crusoe. Presbyterian & Reformed Rev 1 1890.

Rannie, D. W. Daniel Defoe. Oxford 1890.

Bülbring, K. D. Defoe and Mary Astell. Academy 14 March 1891.

Roe, J. E. The mortal moon: or Bacon and his masks. 1891. On Bacon as author of Crusoe etc.

Geissler, P. H. Is Robinson Crusoe an allegory? Pirna 1839.

—— Defoes Theorie über Robinson Crusoe. Halle 1896.

Harrison, H. The political career of Defoe: its influence on English history. Westminster Rev 135 1893.

Oliphant, M. O. W. The author of Robinson Crusoe. Century 24 1893.

Wright, T. Life of Defoe. 1894, 1931 (rev and enlarged).

Vogüé, E.-M. de. Le livre anglais: Robinson Crusoë. Revue des Deux Mondes 1 Oct 1895.

Day, G. Daniel Defoe, the tile-maker of Tilbury. Essex Rev 5 1896.

Hadden, J. C. The making of Robinson Crusoe. Century 58 1899.

A masterly lie. Academy 9 Sept 1899. On Defoe's narrative in Mist's Jnl 5 July 1718, of the reported blowing up of the Island of St Vincent.

Bateson, T. The relations of Defoe and Harley. EHR 15 1900.

Cockburn, J. D. Defoe in Scotland. Scottish Rev 56 1900.

Whitten, W. Daniel Defoe. Boston 1900.

Roscoe, E. S. Harley and De Foe 1703–14. In his Robert Harley Earl of Oxford ,1902.

Wells, C. Defoe and Selkirk at Bristol. Academy 30 Dec 1905.

Wherry, A. Daniel Defoe. 1905.

Baker, E. A. Defoe as sociological novelist. Academy 26 May 1906.

Staverman, W. H. Robinson Crusoe in Nederland. Groningen 1907.

Trent, W. P. and A. Matthews. Defoe and Woodward. Nation (New York) 15 Aug 1907.

Trent, W. P. New light on Defoe's life. Nation (New York) 17 Sept 1908.
— Defoe: the newspaper and the novel. CHEL 9 1913.
— Defoe: how to know him. Indianapolis [1916].
Masefield, J. Defoe: the man and the writer. Fortnightly Rev Jan 1909.
Günther, M. Entstehungsgeschichte von Defoes Robinson Crusoe. Greifswald 1909.
Wackwitz, F. Entstehungsgeschichte von Defoes Robinson Crusoe. Berlin 1909.
Lannert, G. L. An investigation into the language of Robinson Crusoe as compared with that of other 18th-century works. Upsala 1910.
Hastings, W. T. Misprints in Defoe. Nation (New York) 18 May 1911.
— Errors and inconsistencies in Defoe's Robinson Crusoe. MLN 27 1912.
Pilon, E. Daniel de Foë. Nouvelle Revue Française 7 1912.
— Daniel De Foe. Paris 1913.
Purves, W. L. Literary output of Defoe. Library 2nd ser 3 1912.
Wyatt, E. De Foe, author of Robinson Crusoe. North Amer Rev 198 1913.
Horten, F. Studien über die Sprache Defoes. Bonn 1914.
Minet, W. Defoe and Kent: a chapter in Capel-le Ferne history. Archaeologia Cantiana 31 1914.
Mann, W. E. Robinson Crusoé en France: étude sur l'influence de cette œuvre dans la littérature française. Paris 1916.
Schreiber, M. Defoe: sein Leben und seine Werke. Salzburg 1916.
Stevens, D. H. Defoe and the Earl of Oxford: party politics and English journalism 1702–42. Menasha 1916.
Moffatt, J. Religion of Robinson Crusoe. Contemporary Rev Aug 1919.
Nicholson, W. Historical sources of Defoe's Journal of the Plague Year. Boston 1919.
Bellessort, A. Les romans picaresques de Defoe. Revue Bleue 58 1920.
Fernsemer, O. F. W. Defoe and the Palatine emigration of 1709: a new view of the origin of Robinson Crusoe. JEGP 19 1920.
Hübener, G. Der Kaufmann Robinson Crusoe. E Studien 54 1920.
Lüthi, A. Defoe und seine Fortsetzungen zu Robinson Crusoe. Stuttgart 1920.
Ulrich, H. Einführung in das Studium Defoes. Zeitschrift für Französischen und Englischen Unterricht 19 1920.
— Defoes Robinson Crusoe: die Geschichte eines Weltbuches. Leipzig 1924.
— Zum Defoeproblem. E Studien 56 1922.
Giraudoux, J. Suzanne et le Pacifique. Paris 1921; tr 1923. On Crusoe.
Hubbard, L. L. A Dutch source for Robinson Crusoe: the narrative of the El-ho Sjouke Gabbes by Hendrik Smeeks, 1708, translated from the Dutch and compared with the Story of Robinson Crusoe. Ann Arbor 1921.
Maanen, W. van. Defoe and Swift. E Studies 3 1921.
Liljegren, S. B. Defoes Robinson. E Studien 56 1922.
Davies, W. H. Moll Flanders. New Statesman 23 June 1923.
Dottin, P. De Foe et les sciences occultes. Revue Anglo-américaine 1 1923.
— De Foe, mystificateur: ou des faux mémoires de Mesnager. Revue Germanique 14 1923.
— De Foe et ses romans. 3 vols Paris 1924; vol 1 tr New York 1929.
— Les sources de la Roxana de De Foe. Revue Anglo-américaine 4 1927.
— De Foe et la France. E Studies 8 1931.
— La correspondence de Defoe. Etudes Anglaises 8 1955.
— Les relations de voyage remaniées par Defoe. Caliban 3 1966.

Utter, R. P. On the alleged tediousness of Defoe and Richardson. Univ of California Chron 25 1923.
Fischer, W. Defoe und Milton. E Studien 58 1924.
Schmidt, R. Der Volkswille als realer Faktor des Verfassungslebens und Defoe. Berichte über die Verhandlungen der Sächsischen Akademie (Leipzig) 1924.
Secord, A. W. Studies in the narrative method of Defoe. Urbana 1924.
— Defoe in Stoke Newington. PMLA 66 1951.
— A September day in Canterbury: the Veal-Bargrave story. JEGP 54 1955.
— The correspondence of Defoe. MP 54 1956.
— Robert Drury's journal and other studies. Urbana 1961.
Law, M. H. Oliver Twist and Defoe's History of the Devil. PMLA 11 1925.
Parker, G. The allegory of Robinson Crusoe. History 10 1925.
Thompson, T. A. Theology of Robinson Crusoe. Holborn Rev 67 1925.
Woolf, V. In her Common reader, 1925.
— Robinson Crusoe. In her Second common reader, 1932.
Williams, O. Roxana. In his Some great English novels, 1926.
Birrell, A. Daniel Defoe. Nation (London) 7 May 1927.
Forster, E. M. In his Aspects of the novel, 1927. On Moll Flanders as a novel of character.
Howes, R. F. Robinson Crusoe: a literary accident. Eng Jnl 16 1927.
Lindsay, W. B. Defoe's Review: forerunner of modern journalism. Ibid.
Weil, A. Wesen und Ursprung von Defoes Vorstellungen der übersinnlichen Welt. Freiburg 1927.
Flasdieck, H. M. Robinson Crusoe im Lichte der neueren Forschung. Deutsche Rundschau 214 1928.
Hirn, Y. Ön i världshavet. Helsinki 1928. On Robinson Crusoe and island utopias.
Levett, A. E. In The social and political ideas of some thinkers of the Augustan age, ed F. J. C. Hearnshaw 1928.
Pollert, H. Defoes Stellung zum englischen Kolonialwesen. Münster 1928.
Burch, C. E. Defoe's views on education. London Quart Rev 40 1930.
— Attacks on Defoe in Union pamphlets. RES 6 1930.
— British criticism of Defoe as a novelist 1719–1860. E Studien 67 1932.
— Defoe's British reputation 1869–94. E Studien 68 1934.
— An equivalent for Defoe. MLN 44 1929.
— Notes on the contemporary popularity of Defoe's Review. PQ 16 1937.
— Benjamin Defoe at Edinburgh University 1710–11. PQ 19 1940.
— Defoe and the Edinburgh Society for the Reformation of Manners. RES 16 1940.
Jacob, E. G. Defoe, Essay on projects 1697: eine wirtschafts- und sozialgeschichtliche Studie. Leipzig 1922; Kölner Anglistische Arbeiten 8 1929.
— Defoe als Kolonialpolitiker. Uebersee- und Kolonialzeitung 43 1931.
— Parlamentssouveränität und Volkssouveränität in der Staatslehre Defoes. Zeitschrift für Öffentliches Recht 13 1933.
— Defoe als Sozialreformer. Leuvese Bijdragen 40 1950.
— Das Problem der Impersonation bei Defoe. Forschungen und Fortschritte Jan 1951.
— Die medizingeschichtliche Bedeutung des Robinsondichters Defoe. Wissenschaftliche Zeitschrift der Karl-Marx-Universität (Leipzig) 4 1955.
— Zum 300 Jährigen Defoe-Jubiläum 1660–1960. Archiv für das Studium der Neueren Sprachen 197 1960.
— Die medizingeschichtliche Bedeutung des Robinsondichters. Die Medizinsche Welt 1 1962.

—— Der englische Robinsondichter in seiner medizin-geschichtlichen Bedeutung. Aktuelle Probleme aus der Geschichte der Medizin, ed R. Blaser und H. Buess, Basle 1966.

Martin, B. Defoe's conception of poetry. MLN 44 1929.

Morris, F. D. Pilloried pamphleteer. Mentor 17 1929.

Ritterbusch, P. Parlamentssouveränität und Volkssouveränität in der Staats- und Verfassungsrechtslehre Englands, vornehmlich in der Staatslehre Defoes. Leipzig 1929.

Roorda, G. Realism in De Foe's Narrative of adventure. Wageningen 1929.

Swann, G. R. In his Philosophical parallelisms in six English novelists: the conception of good, evil and human nature, Philadelphia 1929.

Thomas, G. Defoe's England. Contemporary Rev Aug 1929.

De la Mare, W. Desert islands and Robinson Crusoe. 1930.

Beeck, P. van. Der psychologische Gehalt in den Romanen Defoes. Münster 1931.

Blass, A. Die Geschichtsauffassung Defoes. Heidelberg 1931.

Blunden, E. In his Votive tablets, 1931.

Firth, C. H. Defoe's True relation of the apparition of Mrs Veal. RES 7 1931.

Gardiner, D. What Canterbury knew of Mrs Veal and her friends. Ibid.

Harlan, V. Defoe's narrative style. JEGP 30 1931.

Herting. Die Idioten- und Geistekrankenfürsorge des Robinsondichters Defoe. Zeitschrift für Kinderforschung 38 1931.

MacDonald, W. L. Daniel Defoe. Queen's Quart 38 1931.

Marriott, J. A. R. Daniel Defoe. Cornhill Mag May 1931.

Praviel, A. Le père de Robinson: de Foë. Le Correspondant 328 1931.

Praz, M. De Foe and Cellini. E Studies 13 1931.

Staverman, W. H. Robinson Crusoe in Holland. E Studies 13 1931.

Watson, F. Defoe: father of modern journalism. Bookman (London) April 1931.

—— Daniel Defoe. 1952.

—— Robinson Crusoe: fact and fiction. Listener 15 Oct 1959.

—— Robinson Crusoe. History Today Nov 1959. Replies by G. M. D. Henderson-Howat and Watson, Dec 1961.

Maxfield, E. K. Defoe and the Quakers. PMLA 47 1932.

Potter, G. R. Henry Baker FRS 1689–1744. MP 29 1932. On Defoe's son-in-law.

Hatfield, T. M. Moll Flanders in Germany. JEGP 32 1933.

Röhnsch, M. Defoes Stellung zu den religiösen Strömungen seiner Zeit. Breslau 1933.

Sutherland, J. R. Some early troubles of Defoe. RES 9 1933.

—— A note on the last years of Defoe. MLR 29 1934.

—— Defoe. 1937, 1954 (rev).

—— Defoe. 1954 (Br Council pamphlet).

—— The relation of Defoe's fiction to his non-fictional writings. In Imagined worlds, ed M. Mack and I. Gregor 1968.

Bonner, W. H. In his Captain William Dampier: some account of English travel literature in the early eighteenth century, Stanford 1934.

—— Moll, Knapton and Defoe: a note on early serial publication. RES 10 1934.

Fletcher, E. G. Defoe and the theatre. PQ 13 1934.

—— Defoe on Milton. MLN 50 1935.

Graham, W. Defoe's Review and Steele's Tatler: the question of influence. JEGP 33 1934.

Deneke, O. Robinson Crusoe in Deutschland: die Frühdrucke 1720–80. Göttingen 1935.

Häusermann, H. W. Aspects of life and thought in Robinson Crusoe. RES 11 1935.

Moore, J. R. Defoe and modern economic theory. Bloomington 1935.

—— Defoe in the pillory and other studies. Bloomington 1939.

—— Defoe's use of personal experience in Colonel Jack. MLN 54 1939.

—— A Defoe allusion in Gulliver's travels. N & Q 3 Feb 1940.

—— Defoe's history of the pirates: its date. N & Q 6 July 1940.

—— Defoe and the Rev James Hart: a chapter in high finance. PQ 19 1940.

—— Defoe's political propaganda in the Dumb philosopher. HLQ 4 1940.

—— Defoe, Selkirk and John Atkins. N & Q 21 Dec 1940.

—— Evidence for Defoe's authorship of the Memoirs of Captain Carleton. MLN 55 1940.

—— Defoe and Scott. PMLA 56 1941.

—— Defoe's religious sect. RES 17 1941.

—— Defoe and the eighteenth-century pamphlets on London. PQ 20 1941. Replies by P. B. Anderson and Moore 21 1942.

—— Defoe, Stevenson and the pirates. ELH 10 1943.

—— Defoe's sources for Robert Drury's journal. Bloomington [1943].

—— A rare tract by Defoe. Indiana Quart for Bookman 1 1945.

—— The tempest and Robinson Crusoe. RES 21 1945.

—— Defoe's workshop. More Books 23 1948.

—— Defoe, Steele and the demolition of Dunkirk. HLQ 13 1950.

—— Gildon's attack on Steele and Defoe in the Battle of the authors. PMLA 66 1951.

—— Defoe, ambidextrous Mercury. Periodical Postboy 11 1952.

—— Defoe and the South Sea Company. Boston Public Lib Quart 5 1953.

—— Defoe: star reporter. Boston Public Lib Quart 6 1954.

—— Defoe's project for lie-detection. Amer Jnl of Psychology 68 1955.

—— Robin Hog Stephens: messenger of the press. PBSA 50 1956.

—— Defoe's lampoon: a speech of a stone chimney piece. Boston Public Lib Quart 11 1957.

—— Lydia Languish's library. N & Q Feb 1957. On influence of Family instructor.

—— Defoe: citizen of the modern world. Chicago 1958.

—— Defoe: precursor of Samuel Richardson. In Restoration and eighteenth-century literature, ed C. Camden, Chicago 1963.

—— Defoe and Shakespeare. Shakespeare Quart 19 1968.

Klingender, F. P. Coleridge on Robinson Crusoe. TLS 1 Feb 1936.

Main, C. F. The German Princess: or Mary Carleton in fact and fiction. Huntington Lib Bull 10 1936.

Meyerstein, E. H. W. Daniel, the Pope and the Devil: a caricaturist's portrait of the true Defoe. TLS 15 Feb 1936.

Mullett, F. The English plague scare of 1720–3. Osiris 2 1936.

Pritchett, V. S. In English novelists, ed D. Verschoyle 1936.

Stamm, R. G. Defoe: an artist in the Puritan tradition. PQ 15 1936.

—— Der aufgeklärte Puritanismus Defoes. Zürich 1936.

Cole, G. D. H. In From Anne to Victoria, ed B. Dobrée 1937.

Praz, M. In his Studi e svaghi inglesi, Florence 1937.

Campbell, M. E. Defoe's first poem. Bloomington 1938.

Luithlen, G. Der Realismus des Robinson Crusoe. Cologne 1938.

Mundy, P. D. The ancestry of Defoe. N & Q 12 Feb 1938, 16 July 1938, 30 Aug 1952, June 1957, July 1958. Replies by A. V. Ellison 9 April 1938; R.S.B. 30 July 1938; F. J. Dallet, Oct 1958.

Newton, T. F. M. The civet-cats of Newington Green: new light on Defoe. RES 13 1937. Reply by J. R. Moore 14 1938.

Singer, H. Defoe, A tour through England and Wales: eine kulturgeschichtle Studie. Munich 1938.

Giles, E. Shipwrecks and desert islands. N & Q 23 Sept 1939.

Mégroz, R. L. The real Robinson Crusoe: being the life and strange surprising adventures of Alexander Selkirk of Largo, Fife, mariner. [1939].

Mühlhaupt, F. Das Kaufmänn und Puritan-element in den Abenteuerromanen Defoes. Freiburg 1939.

Morgan, W. Defoe's Review as a historical source. Jnl of Modern History 12 1940.

— The versatility of Defoe. More Books 21 1946.

Wright, H. G. Defoe's writings on Sweden. RES 16 1940.

Anderson, H. H. The paradox of trade and morality in Defoe. MP 39 1941.

Ross, J. F. Swift and Defoe: a study in relationship. Berkeley 1941.

Keys, T. The plague in literature. Bull of Medical Lib Assoc 32 1944.

Nettleton, G. R. Robinson Crusoe: Sheridan's Drury Lane pantomime. TLS 25 Dec 1944. Replies by F. S. Boas 29 Jan 1944; S. Rosenfeld 4 March 1944.

Sherwin, O. Defoe reviews World War II. JHI 5 1944.

Dobrée, B. Daniel Defoe. Neophilologus 30 1946.

— Some aspects of Defoe's prose. In Pope and his contemporaries: essays presented to George Sherburn, Oxford 1949.

— The writing of Defoe. Jnl of Royal Soc of Arts 108 1960.

Laird, J. Robinson Crusoe's philosophy. In his Philosophical incursions into English literature, Cambridge 1946.

Apollonio, M. Defoe. Brescia 1946.

Reeve, J. Defoe and the Quakers. Friends Intelligencer 103 1946.

Atkinson, A. D. Goldsmith borrows. TLS 25 Jan 1947.

Murray, J. J. Defoe: news commentator of northern European affairs. Indiana Quart for Bookman 3 1947.

Payne, W. L. Mr Review: Defoe as author of the Review. New York 1947.

Sen, S. De Foe: his mind and art. Calcutta 1948.

Kronenberger, L. Defoe: an island and a plague. Saturday Rev 32 1949.

L'Ami, C. E. The philosophy of journalism. Dalhousie Rev 29 1949.

Watt, I. The naming of characters in Defoe, Richardson and Fielding. RES 25 1949.

— Defoe and Richardson on Homer. RES new ser 3 1952.

— Robinson Crusoe as myth. EC 1951.

— Defoe as novelist. In A Pelican guide to English literature vol 4, ed B. Ford 1954.

— In his Rise of the novel, 1957.

— The recent critical fortunes of Moll Flanders. Eighteenth-century Stud 1 1967.

— Serious reflections on the Rise of the novel. Novel 1 1968.

Cadbury, H. J. Defoe, Bugg and the Quakers. Jnl of Friends Historical Soc 42 1950.

Davies, G. Defoe's A tour thro' the whole island of Great Britain. MP 48 1950.

Freeman, W. The incredible Defoe. 1950.

Schorer, M. A study in Defoe: moral vision and structural form. Thought 25 1950.

Swallow, A. Defoe and the art of fiction. Western Humanities Rev 4 1950.

Wilkinson, A. M. Defoe's New discovery and Pacificator. N & Q 11 Nov 1950.

— Good advice to the ladies: a note on Defoe. N & Q 29 June 1950.

— The meditations of Defoe. MLR 46 1951.

Benjamin, E. B. Symbolic elements in Robinson Crusoe. PQ 30 1951.

Bishop, J. Knowledge, action and interpretation in Defoe's novels. JHI 13 1951.

Honig, E. Crusoe, Rasselas and the suit of clothes. Univ of Kansas City Rev 18 1951.

Price, E. J. The projects of Defoe. Congregational Quart 29 1951.

Scholte, J. H. Robinsonades. Neophilologus 35 1951.

Seeber, E. D. Oroonoko and Crusoe's man Friday. MLQ 12 1951.

Gates, W. B. A note on Cooper and Robinson Crusoe. MLN 67 1952.

Hobman, D. L. Defoe the journalist. Fortnightly Rev Sept 1952.

Peterson, S. Defoe's Abdy, Harvy in A new discovery of an old intreague. N & Q 24 May 1952. Replies by F. W. Steer 5 July 1952; G. O. Rickword 19 July 1952.

— The matrimonial theme of Defoe's Roxana. PMLA 70 1955.

— Defoe's Yorkshire quarrel. HLQ 19 1956.

— Defoe and city customs. N & Q Sept 1958.

— Johnsonian News Letter Dec 1958. Fielding's comments on Defoe.

Peterson, W. M. Gide and Defoe. N & Q 10 May 1952.

Quennell, P. C. In his Singular preference, 1952.

Robins, H. F. How smart was Robinson Crusoe? PMLA 67 1952.

Boyce, B. The question of emotion in Defoe. SP 50 1953.

Girdler, L. Defoe's education at Newington Green Academy. SP 50 1953.

Raleigh, J. H. Style and structure and their impact in Defoe's Roxana. Univ of Kansas City Rev 20 1953.

Rodway, A. E. Moll Flanders and Manon Lescaut. EC 3 1953.

Van Ghent, D. Moll Flanders. In her English novel: form and function, New York 1953.

Baine, R. M. The apparition of Mrs Veal: a neglected account. PMLA 69 1954.

— Defoe and Mrs Bargrave's story. PQ 33 1954.

— Defoe and the History and reality of apparitions. Proc of Amer Philosophical Soc 106 1962.

— Defoe and the angels. SE 9 1967.

— Defoe and the supernatural. Athens Georgia 1968.

Fitzgerald, B. Defoe: a study in conflict. 1954.

Allen, W. E. In his Six great novelists, 1955.

Boreham, F. W. The gospel of Robinson Crusoe. 1955.

Maclaine, A. H. Robinson Crusoe and the Cyclops. SP 52 1955.

Scouten, A. H. An early printed report on the Apparition of Mrs Veal. RES new ser 6 1955.

— The loyal post: a rare Queen Anne newspaper and Defoe. BNYPL April 1955.

— At that moment of time: Defoe and the early accounts of the apparition of Mistress Veal. Ball State Teachers College Forum 2 1962.

Berne, E. The psychological structure of space with some remarks on Robinson Crusoe. Psychoanalytic Quart 25 1956.

McKillop, A. D. In his Early masters of English fiction, Lawrence Kansas 1956.

Pafford, J. H. P. Defoe's Proposals for printing the history of the Union. Library 5th ser 11 1956.

Parsons, C. O. Ghost stories before Defoe. N & Q July 1956.

Pire, G. Jean-Jacques Rousseau et Robinson Crusoe. Revue de Littérature Comparée 30 1956.

Gifford, G. E. Defoe and Maryland. Maryland Historical Mag 52 1957.

Izzo, C. Su Defoe. Letterature Moderne 7 1957.

Main, C. F. Defoe, Swift and Captain Tom. Harvard Lib Bull 11 1957.

Mauriac, F. En relisant Moll Flanders. Figaro Littéraire 20 July 1957.

Wölken, F. Major Rankin's memoirs, Defoe und die Anfänge des realistischen Ich-Romans. Anglia 75 1957.

Baird, T. The world turned upside down. Amer Scholar 77 1958. On Defoe's style.

Bastian, F. Defoe and the Dorking district. Surrey Archaeological Collection 55 1958.

— James Foe, merchant, father of Defoe. N & Q March 1964.

— Defoe's Journal of the plague year reconsidered. RES new ser 16 1965.

— Defoe's Tour and the historian. History Today Dec 1967.

Clark, P. O. Lapponia, Lapland and Laputa. MLQ 7 1958.

Memorabilia. N & Q Nov 1958. On Defoe's tombstone.

Rosenberg, A. Defoe's Pacificator reconsidered. PQ 37 1958.

Swados, H. Robinson Crusoe: the man alone. Antioch Review 18 1958.

Tillyard, E. M. W. In his Epic strain in the English novel, 1958.

West, A. In his Mountains in the sunlight, 1958.

Andrews, J. H. A case of plagiarism in Defoe's Tour. N & Q Nov 1959.

— Defoe and the source of his Tour. Geographical Jnl 126 1960.

— Defoe's Tour and Macky's Journey. N & Q Aug 1960.

Little, B. Crusoe's captain: being the life of Woodes Rogers. 1960. On Defoe as writer for Rogers.

Novak, M. E. Defoe and the machine smashers. N & Q Aug 1960.

— Colonel Jack's 'thieving roguing' trade to Mexico and Defoe's attack on economic individualism. HLQ 24 1961.

— Moll Flanders' first love. Papers of Michigan Acad 46 1961.

— The problem of necessity in Defoe's fiction. PQ 40 1961.

— Robinson Crusoe's fear and the search for natural man. MP 57 1961.

— Robinson Crusoe's original sin. Stud in Eng Lit 1500–1900 1 1961.

— Crusoe the king and the political evolution of his island. Stud in Eng Lit 1500–1900 2 1962.

— Economics and the fiction of Defoe. Berkeley 1962.

— Defoe and the nature of man. Oxford 1963.

— Defoe, Thomas Burnet and the Deistical passages of Robert Drury's Journal. PQ 42 1963.

— Robinson Crusoe and economic utopia. Kenyon Rev 25 1963.

— Conscious irony in Moll Flanders. College Eng Dec 1964.

— Defoe's theory of fiction. SP 61 1964.

— Simon Forecastle's weekly journal: notes on Defoe's conscious artistry. SE 6 1965.

— Crime and punishment in Defoe's Roxana. JEGP 55 1966.

— Defoe's Shortest way with the Dissenters: hoax, parody, paradox, fiction, irony and satire. MLQ 27 1966.

— and H. Davis. The uses of irony: Defoe and Swift. Ed H. T. Swedenberg, Los Angeles 1966.

Wassermann, C. R. John Norris and the Veal-Bargrave story. MLN 63 1960.

Béranger, J. Defoe pamphletaire 1716–20. Etudes Anglaises 14 1961.

— Du nouveau sur Defoe. Etudes Anglaises 18 1965.

Ganzel, D. Chronology in Robinson Crusoe. PQ 40 1961.

Jack, J. H. A new voyage round the world: Defoe's roman à thèse. HLQ 24 1961.

Martin, T. The unity of Moll Flanders. MLQ 22 1961.

Johnson, C. A. Two mistakes of geography in Moll Flanders. N & Q Dec 1962.

McBurney, W. H. Colonel Jacque: Defoe's definition of the complete gentleman. Stud in Eng Lit 1500–1900 2 1962.

Michel-Michot, P. The myth of innocence. Revue des Langues Vivantes 28 1962.

Weimann, R. Defoe: eine Einführung in das Romanwerk. Halle 1962.

Columbus, R. Conscious artistry in Moll Flanders. Stud in Eng Lit 1500–1900 3 1963.

Cook, I. Defoe and Swift: contrasts in satire. Dalhousie Rev 43 1963.

— Mr Examiner and Mr Review: the Tory apologetics of Swift and Defoe. HLQ 29 1966.

Donoghue, D. The values of Moll Flanders. Sewanee Rev 71 1963.

Füger, W. Die Entstehung des historischen Romans aus der fiktiven Biographie in Frankreich und England, unter besonderer Berücksichtung von Courtilz de Sandras und Defoe. Munich 1963.

— Der betrunkene Pfeifer. Archiv für das Studium der Neueren Sprachen 202 1965. On Journal of plague year.

Hunter, J. P. Friday as a convert: Defoe and the accounts of Indian missionaries. RES new ser 14 1963.

— The reluctant pilgrim. Baltimore 1966.

Koonce, H. L. Moll's muddle: Defoe's use of irony in Moll Flanders. ELH 30 1963.

Plumb, J. H. In his Men and places, 1963.

Poston, L. Defoe and the peace campaign 1710–15. HLQ 27 1963.

Schonhorn, M. Accounts of the apparition of Mrs Veal. Los Angeles 1965 (Augustan Reprint Soc).

— Defoe's pirates: a new source. RES new ser 14 1963.

— Defoe's Journal of the plague year: topography and intention. RES new ser 19 1968.

Schücking, L. L. Die puritanische Familie in literatur-soziologischer Sicht. Berne 1963.

Scrimgeour, G. J. The problem of realism in Defoe's Captain Singleton. HLQ 27 1963.

Sgard, B. Un aspect de la révolution romantique: la traduction de Robinson Crusoe par Pétrus Borel. Moderna Språk 57 1963.

Stockum, C. van. Von Friederich Nicolai bis Thomas Mann: Aufsätze zur deutschen und vergleichenden Literaturgeschichte. Groningen 1963.

Alter, R. In his Rogue's progress: studies in the picaresque novel, Cambridge Mass 1964.

Artizzu, L. Motivi economici e morali nei romanzi di Defoe. Economica e Storia 11 1964.

Dennis, N. On Swift and satire. Encounter March 1964.

Gerber, R. Zur Namengebung bei Defoe. Festschrift Hübner 24 1964.

Halewood, W. H. Religion and invention in Robinson Crusoe. EC 14 1964.

Joyce, J. Daniel Defoe. Tr J. Prescott, Buffalo 1964.

Kettle, A. In defence of Moll Flanders. In Of books and humankind: essays presented to Bonamy Dobrée, ed J. Butt 1964.

Rawson, C. J. The phrase 'legal prostitution' in Fielding, Defoe and others. N & Q Aug 1964.

Skydsgaard, N. J. En studie i Defoe jeg-roman. Copenhagen 1964.

Uchida, T. Robinson Crusoe: a reconsideration. Stud in Eng Lit (Tokyo) 41 1964.

Watson, T. G. Defoe's attitude toward marriage and the position of women revealed in Moll Flanders. Southern Quart 3 1964.

Arnold, H. L. Robinson Crusoe: Notizen zu einer Illusion. Antaios 6 1965.

Krajewska, W. Defoe: The dyet of Poland. Kwartalnik Neofilologiczny 12 1965.

Schwoerer, L. G. The literature of the standing army controversy. HLQ 28 1965.

— Chronology and authorship of the standing army tracts. N & Q Oct 1966.

Starr, G. A. Defoe and spiritual autobiography. Princeton 1965.

— From casuistry to fiction: the importance of the Athenian Mercury. JHI 28 1967.

Stein, W. B. Robinson Crusoe: the trickster tricked. Centennial Rev 9 1965.

Amakawa, J. Defoe as an economist. Karan sei Gakuin Univ Stud 15 1966.

Black, S. A. Defoe's The shortest way. Amer N & Q 5 1966.

Greif, M. J. The conversion of Robinson Crusoe. Stud in Eng Lit 1500-1900 6 1966.

Mirimsky, I. V. Stati o klassikach. Moscow 1966. On Defoe's realism.

Oda, M. Allegory and history: a study of Defoe's Roxana. Memoirs of Osaka Gakugei Univ 15 1966.

Echeruo, M. J. Robinson Crusoe, Purchas his pilgrimes and the 'novel'. Eng Stud in Africa 10 1967.

Goldberg, M. A. Moll Flanders: Christian allegory in a Hobbesian mode. Univ Rev 33 1967.

Nordon, P. Robinson Crusoe: unité et contradictions. Paris 1967.

Pilgrim, K. Zu Defoes Weltverständnis im 3 Teil von Robinson Crusoe. Die Neueren Sprachen 16 1967.

Rocks, J. E. Camus reads Defoe. Tulane Stud in Eng 15 1967.

Barringer, G. M. Defoe's A tour thro' the whole island of Great Britain. Thoth 9 1968.

Howard, W. J. Truth preserves her shape: an unexplored influence on Defoe's prose style. PQ 47 1968. On libel laws.

Howson, G. Who was Moll Flanders? TLS 18 Jan 1968.

Shinagel, M. Defoe and middle-class gentility. Cambridge Mass 1968.

—— The maternity theme in Moll Flanders. Cornell Lib Jnl 7 1969.

Tsuchiya, S. Robinson Crusoe as a moral fable. In Collected essays by the faculty of Kyoritsu women's junior college vol 11, Kyoritsu 1968.

Brooks, D. Moll Flanders: an interpretation. EC 19 1969.

Ellis, F. H. (ed). Twentieth-century interpretations of Robinson Crusoe. Englewood Cliffs NJ 1969.

M. E. N.

SAMUEL RICHARDSON
1689-1761

Bibliographies

Sale, W. M. Richardson: a bibliographical record of his literary career with historical notes. New Haven 1936.

Cordasco, F. Richardson: a list of critical studies 1896-1946. Brooklyn 1948.

Collections

The works, with a sketch of life and writings by E. Mangin. 19 vols 1811.

The novels; to which is prefixed a memoir of the life of the author [by Sir Walter Scott]. 3 vols 1824 (Ballantyne's Novelist's Lib vols 6-8).

The works, with a prefatory chapter of biographical criticism by L. Stephen. 12 vols 1883.

The novels, with a life of the author and introductions by W. M. Phelps. 19 vols New York 1902.

The novels. Ed E. M. M. McKenna 20 vols 1902.

The novels. 18 vols Oxford 1929-31.

§ I

The apprentice's vade mecum. 1734 (for 1733).

A seasonable examination of the pleas and pretensions of the proprietors of, and subscribers to, play-houses, erected in defiance of the royal licence. 1735.

Aesop's fables. 1740 (for 1739), [1747?], [1753].

The negotiations of Sir Thomas Roe, in his embassy to the Ottoman Porte. 1740. Co-edited by Richardson, the dedication signed by him.

Pamela: or virtue rewarded. 2 vols 1741 (for 1740), 1741 (4 edns); vols 3 and 4 (Pamela in her exalted condition), 1742 (for 1741); 4 vols 1742, [1746?], 1754, 1762 (for 1761), 1767, 1772; abridged [1769?], Edinburgh 1817, 1845; tr French, 2 vols 1741, 4 vols 1742-3; Dutch, 1742-4; German, 1742; Danish, 1743-6, Italian, 1744-6; Russian 1787; Spanish, 1794-5; Welsh, 1818. Introduction to Pamela, ed S. W. Baker, Los Angeles 1954 (Augustan Reprint Soc).

Letters written to and for particular friends, directing the requisite style and forms to be observed in writing familiar letters. 1741, 1742, 1746, 1750, 1752, 1755; ed B. W. Downs 1928 (as Familiar letters on important occasions).

A tour thro' the whole island of Great Britain [by Defoe]; with very great additions, improvements and corrections [by Richardson]. 4 vols 1742, 1748, 1753, 1761-2.

Clarissa: or the history of a young lady. 7 vols 1748 (for 1747-8), 1749, 8 vols (in which many passages and some letters are restored from the original manuscripts), 1751, 1751, 1759, 1764, 1768, 1774, 1784; abridged [1769?]; J. H. Emmert, Göttingen 1792; E. Dallas 1868; Mrs Ward 1868; C. H. Jones, New York 1874; J. Burrell, New York 1950; G. Sherburn, Boston 1962; tr German, 1748-52; French, 1751; Dutch, 1752-5; Italian, 1783-6; Danish, 1783-8; Russian, 1791-2; Spanish, 1794-?; Portuguese, 1804-18.

Clarissa: preface, hints of prefaces, and postscript, ed R. Brissenden, Los Angeles 1964 (Augustan Reprint Soc).

Answers to the remarks on the history of Clarissa. GM Aug 1749.

Answer to the letter of a gentleman objecting to the warmth of a particular scene in the history of Clarissa. 1749.

Meditations collected from the sacred books mentioned in the history of Clarissa. 1750.

Rambler no 97 1751.

Letters and passages restored to Clarissa. 1751.

The history of Sir Charles Grandison. 7 vols 1754 (3 edns), 1762, 1766, 1770, 1776, 1781, 1783, 1796; abridged [1769?]; J. H. Emmert, Göttingen 1792; M. Howitt 1873; G. Saintsbury 1895; T. Archer [1924?]; tr German, 1754-5; French, 1755-6; Dutch, 1756-7; Swedish, 1779-1800; Danish, 1780-2; Italian, 1784-9; Russian, 1793-4; Spanish, 1798.

The case of Samuel Richardson of London, printer. 1753.

Letter to a lady, who was solicitous for an additional volume to the history of Sir Charles Grandison. 1754.

Answer to a letter from a friend, who had objected to Sir Charles Grandison's offer to allow his daughters to be educated Roman Catholics. 1754.

An address to the public, on the treatment which the editor of the history of Sir Charles Grandison has met with. 1754.

A collection of the moral and instructive sentiments contained in the histories of Pamela, Clarissa and Sir Charles Grandison. 1755; tr German, 1757.

The paths of virtue delineated: or the history in miniature of the celebrated Pamela, Clarissa Harlowe and Sir Charles Grandison, familiarized and adapted to the capacities of youth. 1756, 1813 (as Beauties of Richardson); tr German, 1765; Dutch, 1805.

Six original letters upon duelling. Candid Rev & Literary Repository 1 1765.

Samuel Richardson. 1912. Selected by S. Kaye-Smith.

Letters

The correspondence of Richardson, selected from the original manuscripts, to which are prefixed a biographical account of the author and observations on the writings. Ed A. L. Barbauld 6 vols 1804.

A series of original letters of the late Mr Richardson to Miss Wescomb. European Mag 53-4 1808.

Original letters of Miss Elizabeth Carter and Mr Richardson. Monthly Mag July 1812.

One hundred and forty-eight original letters between Dr Edward Young and Mr Richardson. Monthly Mag Dec 1813–March 1819.

Correspondence of Smollett and Richardson. Monthly Mag Nov 1819.

Letters of Dr George Cheyne to Richardson 1733–43. Ed C. F. Mullett, Columbia Missouri 1943.

McKillop, A. D. A letter from Richardson to Alexis Claude Clairaut. MLN 63 1948.

McAdam, E. L. A new letter from Fielding. Yale Rev 38 1949. A letter to Richardson on Clarissa, dated 15 Oct 1748.

Bishop, A. Richardson discusses his Clarissa and Grandison. Boston Public Lib Quart 4 1952. Letter to Lady Echlin dated 17 May 1754.

Selected letters. Ed J. Carroll, Oxford 1964.

The Richardson-Stinstra correspondence and Stinstra's prefaces to Clarissa. Ed W. Slattery 1969.

For an account of the Forster collection of Richardson's correspondence in the Victoria and Albert Museum, see McKillop, Samuel Richardson, *below, and* Selected letters, ed Carroll, *above.*

Spurious Sequels, Skits, Adaptations, Dramatizations etc

An apology for the life of Mrs Shamela Andrews, in which the many notorious falshoods and misrepresentations of a book called Pamela are exposed and refuted, by Mr Conny Keyber. 1741, 1741; ed R. B. Johnson 1926; ed B. W. Downs, Cambridge 1930; ed S. W. Baker, Berkeley 1953; ed I. Watt, Los Angeles 1956 (Augustan Reprint Soc); ed M. C. Battestin, Cambridge Mass 1961. By Fielding. *For his Joseph Andrews, see col 929, below.*

Pamela's conduct in high life. 2 vols 1741 (vol 1 rptd 1741 and Dublin 1741). By John Kelly.

Pamela in high life. 1741.

The life of Pamela. 1741.

Anti-Pamela: or feign'd innocence detected. 1741, 1742; tr French, 1743. By Eliza Haywood?

The true anti-Pamela: or memoirs of Mr James Parry. 1741, 1741, Dublin [1741], London 1742.

Pamela: a comedy. 1741, 1742. By Henry Giffard.

Pamela: or virtue triumphant. 1741. Dramatization by James Dance.

Bennet, George. Pamela, or virtue rewarded: a heroick poem. 1741.

Edge, —. Pamela: an opera. 1742.

Antipamela ou mémoires de M. D***. 1742, 1743. By C. Villaret?.

Godard d'Aucourt, C. La déroute de Pamela. Paris 1744.

W—, J—. Pamela: or the fair impostor. 1744.

Boissy, L. de. Paméla en France: ou la vertu mieux éprouvée. Paris 1745.

Den belønneded dyd, eller Pamela sødskende barn. Copenhagen 1751.

Edward Grandison: Geschichte in Görlitz. Berlin 1755.

Goldoni, C. Pamela: a comedy. 1756. An English trn.

History of Sir Charles Grandison spiritualized. 1760.

Grandison der Zweite. 3 vols Eisenach 1760–1. By J. C. A. Musäus.

La Chausée, P. C. Nivelle de. Pamela. Paris 1762. Dramatization produced in 1743.

Fanny: ou la nouvelle Paméla. Paris 1767 (3rd edn of Fanni ou l'heureux repentir 1764); tr Dublin 1777. By F. T. Baculard d'Arnaud.

Steffens, J. H. Clarissa: ein bürgerliches Trauerspiel. Zelle 1765.

La nouvelle Clarice. 1767; tr 1768. By J. M. Leprince de Beaumont.

Histoire de Pamela en liberté. 1770.

Lovelace og Clarissa elder den dramatiske bortførelse. Copenhagen 1780.

Clarissa: a tragedy. 1788. By R. Porrett.

Le petit Grandisson: traduction libre du hollandois par [in fact written by] A. Berquin. 1795.

Clarisse Harlow: drame. Paris 1833. By 'Pierre Dinaux', P. P. Goubaux.

Lacy, T. H. and J. Courtney. Clarissa Harlow: a tragic drama adapted from the French [of Jules Janin]. In Lacy's acting edn of plays vol 77, 1850 etc.

A sequel to Sir Charles Grandison. 1878

Barbier, P. J. and P. Choudens. Clarisse Harlowe: opera. Paris 1896.

Sinclair, U. Another Pamela. New York 1950.

§2

Pamela censured: shewing that under the specious pretence of cultivating the principles of virtue the most artful and alluring amorous ideas are convey'd. 1741.

Povey, C. The virgin in Eden; to which are added Pamela's letters proved to be immodest romances. 1741, 1767.

Lettre sur Pamela. 1742.

Remarks on Clarissa. 1749.

Remarks on the history of Clarissa. GM June, Aug 1749.

A candid examination of the history of Sir Charles Grandison. 1754, 1755. By Francis Plumer?

Critical remarks on Sir Charles Grandison, Clarissa and Pamela, by a lover of virtue. 1754; ed A. D. McKillop, Los Angeles 1950 (Augustan Reprint Soc).

Diderot, D. Eloge de Richardson. Journal Etranger Jan 1762.

L. (probably E. Bridgen). Memoirs of the life and writings of Mr Samuel Richardson. Universal Mag 78 1786.

Jeffrey, F. Samuel Richardson. Edinburgh Rev 5 1804; rptd in his Contributions to the Edinburgh Review vol 1, 1844.

Hazlitt, W. On the English novelists. In his Lectures on the English comic writers, 1819.

Forman, H. B. Richardson as artist and moralist. Fortnightly Rev 1 Oct 1869.

Stephen, L. Richardson's novels. In his Hours in a library ser 1, 1874.

Schmidt, E. Richardson, Rousseau und Goethe. Jena 1875.

Crompton, S. Richardson's Clarissa annotated. N & Q Aug 1877.

Lang, L. Morals and manners in Richardson. Nat Rev Nov 1889.

Gassmeyer, G. Richardson's Pamela: ihre Quellen und ihr Einfluss auf die englische Litteratur. Leipzig 1890.

Magnussen, J. Samuel Richardson. Copenhagen 1891.

Birrell, A. In his Res judicatae, 1892.

Dobson, A. Richardson at home. In his Eighteenth-century vignettes ser 2, 1894.

— Samuel Richardson. 1902 (EML)

Texte, J. Jean-Jacques Rousseau et les origines du cosmopolitisme littéraire. Paris 1895; tr 1899.

Donner, J. Richardson in der deutschen Romantik. Zeitschrift für Vergleichende Litteraturgeschichte 10 1896.

Thomson, C. L. Richardson: a biographical and critical study. 1900.

Thorne, W. A famous printer: Richardson. Library 2nd ser 2 1901.

Vreeland, W. U. D. Etude sur les rapports littéraires entre Genève et l'Angleterre jusqu'à la publication de la Nouvelle Héloïse. Geneva 1901.

Canby, H. S. Pamela abroad. MLN 18 1903.

Uhrström, W. P. Studies on the language of Richardson. Upsala 1907.

Poetzsche, E. Richardsons Belesenheit. Kiel 1908.

Boas, F. S. Richardson's novels and their influence. E & S 2 1911; rptd in his From Richardson to Pinero, 1936.

Ward, H. Richardson's character of Lovelace. MLR 7 1912.

Cazamian, L. Richardson. CHEL 10 1913.

Macaulay, G. C. Richardson and his French predecessors. MLR 8 1913.

Hughes, H. S. Characterization in Clarissa Harlowe. JEGP 13 1914.

— Translations of the Vie de Marianne and their relation to contemporary English fiction. MP 15 1917.

— Richardson and Warburton. MP 17 1919.

Schroers, C. Ist Richardsons Pamela von Marivauxs Vie de Marianne beeinflusst? E Studien 49 1916.

Danielowski, E. Richardsons erster Roman. Berlin 1917.

Crane, R. S. A note on Richardson's relation to French fiction. MP 16 1919.

— Richardson, Warburton and French fiction. MLR 17 1922.

Richardson's illustrators. TLS 16 Dec 1920.

Digeon, A. Autour de Fielding. Revue Germanique 11 1920.

Reade, A. Richardson and his family circle. N & Q Sept 1922–June 1923.

Williams, I. A. Two kinds of Richardsons. London Mercury Feb 1923.

Grimm, C. Encore une fois la question Marivaux-Richardson. Revue de Littérature Comparée 4 1924.

Schücking, L. Die Grundlagen des Richardson'schen Romans. Germanisch-romanische Monatsschrift 12 1924.

McKillop, A. D. Richardson, Young and the Conjectures. MP 22 1925.

— The personal relations between Fielding and Richardson. MP 28 1931.

— Richardson's early years as a printer. RES 9 1933.

— Richardson, printer and novelist. Chapel Hill 1936.

— Richardson's advice to an apprentice. JEGP 42 1943.

— The mock marriage device in Pamela . PQ 26 1947.

— Wedding bells for Pamela. PQ 28 1949.

— Epistolary technique in Richardson's novels. Houston 1951 (Rice Inst pamphlet); rptd in Studies in the literature of the Augustan age in honor of A. E. Case, Ann Arbor 1952.

— Richardson's early writings: another pamphlet. JEGP 53 1954. Evidence of authorship of pamphlet of 1734 on the playhouses.

— Two eighteenth-century 'first works'. Newberry Lib Bull 4 1955.

— In his Early masters of English fiction, Lawrence Kansas 1956.

— Supplementary notes on Richardson as a printer. SB 12 1959.

Birkhead, E. Sentiment and sensibility in the eighteenth-century novel. E & S 11 1925.

Price, L. Richardson in the moral weeklies of Germany. Wisconsin Univ Stud 22 1925.

— On the reception of Richardson in Germany. JEGP 25 1926.

— Richardson, Wetzlar and Goethe. In Mélanges offerts à Fernand Baldensperger vol 2, Paris 1930.

Prinsen, J. De roman in de 18e eeuw in West-Europa. Groningen 1925.

Binz-Winiger, E. Erziehungsfragen in den Romanen von Richardson, Fielding, Smollett, Goldsmith und Sterne. Zürich 1926.

Facteau, B. A. Les romans de Richardson sur la scène française. Paris [1927].

Schlichting, H. M. von. Frauengestalten bei Richardson. Freiburg 1927.

Wilcox, F. H. Prévost's translations of Richardson's novels. Berkeley 1927.

Downs, B. W. Richardson. 1928.

Thomsen, E. Studier i Richardsons romaner. Copenhagen 1928.

Lanzisera, F. I romanzi di Richardson in Italia. Annalis del R. Istituto Orientale di Napoli 7 1928–9.

Beckstein, J. Pamela nach ihrem Gedenkengehalt betrachtet. Bremen 1929.

Dottin, P. L'accueil fait à Pamela. Revue Anglo-américaine 7 1930.

— Les continuations de Pamela. Revue de l'Enseignement des Langues Vivantes 47 1930.

— Richardson, imprimeur de Londres. Paris 1931.

— Richardson et le roman épistolaire. Revue Anglo-américaine 13 1936.

Krutch, J. W. In his Five masters, New York 1930.

Brown, H. Richardson and Sterne in the Massachusetts Magazine. New England Quart 5 1932.

MacCarthy, D. In his Criticism, 1932. On Richardson and Proust.

Black, F. G. The technique of letter fiction in English from 1740 to 1800. Harvard Stud 15 1933.

— The continuations of Pamela. Revue Anglo-américaine 13 1936.

Lefever, C. Richardson's paradoxical success. PMLA 48 1933.

Singer, G. In his Epistolary novel, Philadelphia 1933.

Sale, W. M. Sir Charles Grandison and the Dublin pirates. Yale Univ Lib Gazette 7 1933.

— The first dramatic version of Pamela. Yale Univ Lib Gazette 9 1935.

— Richardson and Sir William Harrington. TLS 29 Aug 1935.

— Richardson's house at Fulham. N & Q 24 Aug 1935.

— The Singer copy of Sir Charles Grandison. Univ of Pennsylvania Lib Chron 3 1935.

— A bibliographical note on Richardson's Clarissa. Library 4th ser 16 1936.

— From Pamela to Clarissa. In The age of Johnson: essays presented to C. B. Tinker, New Haven 1949.

— Samuel Richardson, master printer. Ithaca 1950.

Hornbeak, K. G. The complete letter-writer in English 1568–1800. Northampton Mass 1934.

— Richardson's familiar letters and the domestic conduct books: Richardson's Aesop. Northampton Mass 1938.

Riva, S. Pamela a Venezia. Annuario 1933–4 del R. Istituto Tecnico Provinciale Pareggioto Jacopo Riccotti di Treviso, Treviso 1934.

Coe, A. M. Richardson in Spain. Hispanic Rev 18 1935.

Ronte, H. Richardson und Fielding: Geschichte ihres Ruhms. Leipzig 1935.

Ewald, E. Abbild und Wunschbild der Gesellschaft bei Richardson und Fielding. Cologne 1935.

Mitrani, C. Richardson and Mme de Souza. West Virginia Univ Stud 1 1936.

Liljegren, S. The English sources of Goethe's Gretchen tragedy. Lund 1937.

Utter, R. P. and G. B. Needham. Pamela's daughters. New York 1937.

Purdie, E. Some adventures of Pamela on the continental stage. In German studies presented to H. G. Fiedler, Oxford 1938.

Taupin, R. Richardson, Diderot et l'art de conter. French Rev 12 1939.

White, W. Richardson: idealist or realist? MLR 34 1939.

Tieghem, P. van. Le roman sentimental en Europe de Richardson à Rousseau 1740–61. Revue de Littérature Comparée 20 1940.

Pettit, H. The text of Edward Young's letters to Richardson. MLN 57 1942.

Eaves, T. C. D. The Harlowe family by Joseph Highmore: a note on the illustration of Clarissa. HLQ 7 1943.

— An unrecorded children's book. Library 5th ser 5 1950. An abridgement of Pamela.

— Graphic illustrations of the novels of Richardson 1740–1810. HLQ 14 1951.

— and B. Kimpel. The publisher of Pamela and its first audience. BNYPL March 1960.

— Johnson's letters to Richardson. PMLA 75 1960.

— Richardsoniana. SB 14 1961.

— Richardson's London houses. SB 15 1962

— Richardson and his family circle. N & Q June–Dec 1964, Dec 1968.

— Cowper's An ode on reading Mr Richardson's History of Sir Charles Grandison. N & Q Dec 1966.

— Richardson's revisions of Pamela. SB 20 1967.

— Richardson's helper in creating the character of Elias Brand. N & Q Nov 1967.

— The composition of Clarissa and its revision before publication. PMLA 83 1968.

— Richardson's connection with Sir William Harrington. Papers on Lang & Lit 4 1968.

— Two notes on Richardson: Richardson's chapel rules; the printer of the Daily Journal. Library 5th ser 23 1968.

Baker, C. H. C. Joseph Highmore, Richardson and Lady Bradshaigh. HLQ 7 1944.

Pritchett, V. S. Clarissa. In his Living novel, 1946.

Mack, E. Pamela's stepdaughters: the heroines of Smollett and Fielding. College Eng March 1947.

Roddier, H. Robert Challes, inspirateur de Richardson et de l'abbé Prévost. Revue de Littérature Comparée 21 1947.

Carter, A. E. The greatest English novelist. UTQ 17 1948.

Moore, J. The London address of Richardson's father. N & Q 17 April 1948.

Watt, I. The naming of characters in Defoe, Richardson and Fielding. RES 25 1949.

— Defoe and Richardson on Homer. RES new ser 3 1952.

— In his Rise of the novel, 1957.

— In The novelist as innovator, ed W. Allen 1965.

Kermode, J. F. Richardson and Fielding. Cambridge Jnl Nov 1950.

Van Ghent, D. Clarissa and Emma as Phedre. Partisan Rev 17 1950.

— On Clarissa Harlowe. In her English novel, New York 1953.

Bonnard, G. A. Richardson and Guillaume-Antoine de Luc. MLR 46 1951.

Erämetsa, E. Notes on Richardson's language. Neuphilologische Mitteilungen 53 1952.

— Der sprachliche Einfluss Richardsons auf Goethes Werther. Neuphilologische Mitteilungen 57 1956.

Lesser, S. O. A note on Pamela. College Eng Oct 1953.

Shaw, E. Malesherbes, the abbé Prévost and the first French translation of Sir Charles Grandison. MLN 69 1954.

Shipley, J. B. Richardson and Pamela. N & Q Jan 1954.

Hill, C. Clarissa Harlowe and her times. EC 5 1955.

Daiches, D. In his Literary essays, 1956.

Rabkin, N. Clarissa: a study in the nature of convention. ELH 23 1956.

Bradbrook, F. W. In Pelican guide to English literature, ed B. Ford, vol 4 1957.

— Richardson and Joseph Conrad. N & Q March 1958.

Duncan-Jones, E. E. Proposals of marriage in Pride and prejudice and Pamela. N & Q Feb 1957.

— The Misses Selby and Steele. TLS 10 Sept 1964.

Keast, W. R. The two Clarissas in Johnson's dictionary. SP 54 1957.

Reid, B. L. Justice to Pamela. Hudson Rev 9 1957.

Sherbo, A. Time and place in Richardson's Clarissa. Boston Univ Stud in Eng 3 1957.

Brissenden, R. Samuel Richardson. 1958.

Newcomb, R. Benjamin Franklin and Richardson. JEGP 57 1958.

Kinkead-Weekes, M. Clarissa restored? RES new ser 10 1959.

McWatters, K. Stendhal, Richardson et l'Edinburgh Review. Stendhal Club 1 1959.

Fiedler, L. In his Love and death in the American novel. New York 1960. Includes chapters on the influence of Richardson.

Kreissman, B. Pamela-Shamela: a study of criticisms, burlesques, parodies and adaptations of Richardson's Pamela. Lincoln Nebraska 1960.

Nachtigall, E. Die Memoires der Marguerite de Valois als Quelle zu Richardsons Clarissa. Bonn 1960.

Wendt, A. Clarissa's coffin. PQ 39 1960.

Griffith, P. Fire-scenes in Richardson's Clarissa and Smollett's Humphry Clinker: a study of a literary relationship in the structure of the novel. Tulane Stud in Eng 11 1961.

Pons, C. Richardson et la Nouvelle Héloïse. Etudes Anglaises 14 1961.

Ten Harmsel, H. The villain-hero in Pamela and Pride and prejudice. College Eng Nov 1961.

Tucker, S. I. Predatings from Richardson's Familiar letters. N & Q Feb 1961.

— Richardsonian phrases. N & Q Dec 1966.

Mojašević, M. Richardsonovi romani i Goetheov Werther. Filologija 3 1962.

Sherburn, G. Richardson's novels and the theatre: a theory sketched. PQ 41 1962.

— Writing to the moment: one aspect. In Restoration and eighteenth-century literature: essays in honor of A. D. McKillop, Chicago 1963.

Carroll, J. Richardson on Pope and Swift. UTQ 33 1963.

— Richardson: a collection of critical essays. Englewood Cliffs NJ 1969.

Drew, E. In her Novel, New York 1963. On Clarissa.

Farrell, W. The style and the action in Clarissa. Stud in Eng Lit 1500–1900 3 1963.

Golden, M. Richardson's characters. Ann Arbor 1963.

— Richardson's repetitions. PMLA 82 1967.

Hughes, L. Theatrical convention in Richardson: some observations on a novelist's technique. In Restoration and eighteenth-century literature; essays in honor of A. D. McKillop, Chicago 1963.

Southam, B. C. Jane Austen and Clarissa. N & Q May 1963.

McKenzie, D. Richardson, Mr W. and Lady T.— N & Q Aug 1964.

Price, M. Clarissa and Lovelace. In his To the palace of wisdom, New York 1964.

Rawson, C. 'Nice' and 'sentimental': a parallel between Northanger Abbey and Richardson's correspondence. N & Q May 1964.

Schulte, E. Pamela e le sue origini. Annali Istituto Universitario Orientali Napoli, Sezione Germanica 7 1964.

Van Heyningen, C. Clarissa: poetry and morals. Pietermaritzburg 1964.

Wilson, S. The first dramatic version of Clarissa. Eng Lang Notes 2 1964.

Bullen, J. Time and space in the novels of Richardson. Logan Utah 1965.

Jenkins, O. Richardson's Pamela and Fielding's 'vile forgeries'. PQ 44 1965.

Lyles, A. Pamela's trials. College Lang Assoc Jnl 8 1965.

Slattery, W. Richardson and the Netherlands: early reception of his work. Papers on Eng Lang & Lit 1 1965.

— and Cain, R. Richardson's role in an attack on Hume and Bolingbroke. Papers on Lang & Lit 4 1968.

Day, R. A. Richardson, Aaron Hill and Johnson's Life of Savage. N & Q June 1966.

— Told in letters: epistolary fiction before Richardson. Ann Arbor 1966.

Donovan, R. A. The problem of Pamela. In his Shaping vision, Ithaca 1966.

Dussinger, J. Conscience and the pattern of Christian perfection in Clarissa. PMLA 81 1966.

— Richardson's 'Christian vocation'. Papers on Lang & Lit 3 1967.

— Richardson's tragic muse. PQ 46 1967.

— Richardson and Johnson: critical agreement on Rowe's The fair penitent. E Studies 49 1968.

Hilles, F. W. The plan of Clarissa. PQ 45 1966.

Kearney, A. Richardson's Pamela: the aesthetic case. REL 7 1966.

— Clarissa and the epistolary form. EC 16 1966.

— Samuel Richardson. 1968.

— Pamela and Joseph Andrews. EC 18 1968. Replies to Brooks, below.

Konigsberg, I. The tragedy of Clarissa. MLQ 27 1966.

— Richardson and the dramatic novel. Lexington Kentucky 1968.

— The dramatic background of Richardson's plots and characters. PMLA 83 1968.

Park, W. Fielding *and* Richardson. PMLA 81 1966.

Sharrock, R. Richardson's Pamela: the Gospel and the novel. Durham Univ Jnl 27 1966.

Zirker, M. Richardson's correspondence: the personal letter as private experience. In The familiar letter in the eighteenth century, ed H. Anderson, P. Daghlian and I. Ehrenpreis, Lawrence Kansas 1966.

Brooks, D. Richardson's Pamela and Fielding's Joseph Andrews. EC 17 1967.

— Pamela and Joseph Andrews. EC 18-19 1968-9. Replies to Kearney, above.

Muecke, D. C. Beauty and Mr B. Stud in Eng Lit 1500-1900 7 1967.

Ball, D. Pamela II: a primary link in Richardson's development as a novelist. MP 65 1968.

Battestin, M. C. On the contemporary reputations of Pamela, Joseph Andrews and Roderick Random: remarks by an 'Oxford scholar' 1748. N & Q Dec 1968.

Beer, G. Richardson, Milton and the status of evil. RES new ser 19 1968.

MacIntosh, C. Pamela's clothes. ELH 35 1968.

Pierson, R. The revisions of Richardson's Sir Charles Grandison. SB 21 1968.

Reed, J. A new Richardson manuscript. Yale Univ Lib Gazette 42 1968.

Barker, G. The complacent paragon: exemplary characterization in Richardson. Stud in Eng Lit 1500-1900 9 1969.

Cowler, R. Twentieth-century interpretations of Pamela. Englewood Cliffs NJ 1969.

J. C.

HENRY FIELDING

1707-54

No mss of Fielding's pbd works appear to have survived. Autograph copies of 2 unpbd poems, however, have recently been discovered at Sandon Hall, Stafford, among the papers of Fielding's cousin, Lady Mary Wortley Montagu (Harrow-by ms 81 [Wortley viii], ff 57-8, 64-5, 172-80, 182-5). The first, written c. 1729-30, is an unfinished imitation of Dun-ciad, satirizing Pope and the circle of Tory wits, including Swift, Gay, Bolingbroke and Nicholas Amherst; the 2nd, An epistle to Mr Lyttleton occasioned by two lines in Mr Pope's paraphrase on the first satire of the 2d Book of Horace (1733), is a further attack on Pope elicited by his abuse of Lady Mary.

Miscellaneous documents relating to Fielding are listed in W. L. Cross, History of Fielding, New Haven 1918, iii. 358-66. These include indentures and a deed pertaining to the sale of Fielding's estate at East Stour (1737-8); legal notes; Fielding's will (1754); and receipts or copyright assignments for the Despairing debauchee and Covent-Garden tragedy (1732), for Joseph Andrews, Miss Lucy in town, and A full vindication of the Dutchess Dowager of Marlborough (1742), and for Tom Jones (1748-9). See also F. H. Dudden, Fielding, Oxford 1952, ii. 1135-7. Several minor Fielding mss are in private collections or on deposit in BM, Harvard, Huntington Library etc. See H. Amory on the Fielding collection of Mrs Donald Hyde in Four Oaks library, ed G. Austin, Somerville NJ 1967; and A pre-liminary census of Fielding's legal manuscripts, PBSA 62 1968.

Bibliographies

Henley, W. E. In his edn of the Complete works vol 16, 1903. On first edns.

Dickson, F. S. Fielding's dramatic works. Philadelphia 1912.

Cross, W. L. In his History of Fielding vol 3, New Haven 1918. On pbd works, works of doubtful author-ship, works mistakenly attributed, dramas on Fielding or his works, letters and mss.

Banerji, H. K. In his Fielding: his life and works. Oxford 1929. On works, collected edns of works and of novels, selections, biographies, criticism.

Dudden, F. H. In his Fielding vol 2, Oxford 1952. On pbd works, letters and documents, collections, separate edns, selections, early trns, works mistakenly attributed, notices.

Levidova, I. M. [Fielding: a bio-bibliographical guide in honour of the 250th anniversary of his birth]. Moscow 1957. Contains bibliographies of Russian trns and criticism.

Collections

Miscellanies. 3 vols 1743. Vol 1, Poems [Of true great-ness, Of good-nature, Liberty, To a friend on the choice of a wife, To John Hayes esq etc]; Essay on conver-sation; Essay on the knowledge of the characters of men; Essay on nothing; Some papers proper to be read before the Royal Society; The first Olynthiac of Demosthenes; Of the remedy of affliction for the loss of our friends; A dialogue between Alexander the Great and Diogenes the Cynic; An interlude between Jupiter, Juno, Apollo and Mercury; vol 2, A journey from this world to the next; Eurydice: a farce; The wedding day: a comedy; vol 3, The life of Mr Jonathan Wild the Great.

Dramatick works. 2 vols [1745]. Vol 1, Love in several masques; The intriguing chambermaid; The miser; The modern husband; The lottery; The virgin un-mask'd; The universal gallant; Don Quixote in Eng-land; The coffee-house politician; vol 2, The author's farce; The Temple beau; The tragedy of tragedies; The letter-writers; The old debauchees; The mock-doctor; Pasquin; The Covent-Garden tragedy; Tumble-down Dick; The historical register for the year 1736; Eury-dice hiss'd.

Works, with the life of the author [by Arthur Murphy]. 4 vols 1762, 8 vols 1762, 12 vols 1766, 8 vols 1771, 12 vols 1771 etc, 1783 (vol 4 adds The fathers: or the good-natured man) etc.

Works. Ed A. Chalmers 10 vols 1806. Revision of Murphy, above.

Novels. Ed W. Scott 1821 (Ballantyne's Novelist's Lib).

Novels. Ed T. Roscoe 1831-2. Illustr G. Cruikshank.

Works. Ed T. Roscoe 1840.

Works. Ed J. P. Browne 10 vols 1871 (from Chalmers); vol 11, 1872 (Miscellanies and poems).

Writings. Ed D. Herbert, Edinburgh 1872. The novels only.

Works. Ed L. Stephen 10 vols 1882.

Works. Ed G. Saintsbury 12 vols 1893, 1902 (as Temple edn).

Works. Ed E. Gosse 12 vols, Westminster and New York 1898-9.

Complete works. Ed W. E. Henley 16 vols 1903, New York 1967.

Works. Ed G. H. Maynadier 12 vols, New York and Cambridge Mass [1903].

Complete works. Ed A. Trimble 7 vols Boston 1904.

Works. 6 vols [1917] (International Lib). The novels only.

Works. Ed G. Saintsbury 12 vols [1926] (Navarre Soc). Illustr G. Cruikshank. The novels only.

Fielding's novels. 10 vols Oxford 1926 (Shakespeare Head edn).

Works. Ed W. B. Coley et al, Oxford and Middletown Conn 1967 (Wesleyan edn). In progress.

Tr French, 23 vols 1804 (vols 11-14 contain Smollett, Roderick Random; vols 18-20 Sarah Fielding, David Simple); 1964 (the novels, omitting Amelia); Russian, 1954 (selected comedies).

Selections

The beauties of Fielding. 1782.

The beauties of Fielding. Ed A. Howard [1829 ?]. Vol 29 of Howard's Beauties of literature.

Episodes of fiction: or choice stories from the great novelists. Edinburgh 1870. Fielding, pp. 51–67.

Selected essays. Ed G. H. Gerould [1905].

Wise sayings and favorite passages from the works of Fielding, including his Essay on conversation. Ed C. W. Bingham, Cedar Rapids 1909.

Fielding. Ed G. Saintsbury 1909.

The Fielding calendar: a quotation from the works of Fielding for every day in the year. Ed J. Kirby 1913.

The genius of Fielding. Ed H. H. Harper, Boston 1919.

Selections, with essays by Hazlitt, Scott, Thackeray. Ed L. Rice-Oxley, Oxford 1923.

Fielding: scenes and characters. Ed J. Hadfield 1950.

Fielding. Ed C. J. Rawson 1968.

Tr Russian, 1954.

§ 1

The masquerade: a poem, inscribed to C[oun]t H[ei]d-[eg]g[e]r, by Lemuel Gulliver, poet laureat to the King of Lilliput. 1728, 1731 (with the Grub-street opera, dedication added); ed C. E. Jones, Liverpool 1960 (in his edn of Female husband and other writings).

Love in several masques: a comedy. (Drury Lane 16 Feb 1728). 1728; tr German, 1782.

The Temple beau: a comedy. (Goodman's Fields 26 Jan 1730). 1730; tr German, 1782.

The author's farce; and the pleasures of the town, written by Scriblerus Secundus. (Haymarket 30 March 1730). 1730 (2 printings), 1730, 1750 (text of rev version performed in 1734); ed C. B. Woods, Lincoln Nebraska 1966.

Tom Thumb: a tragedy. (Haymarket 24 April 1730). 1730, 1730 ('written by Scriblerus Secundus', rev), 1730, 1731 (rev as The tragedy of tragedies: or the life and death of Tom Thumb the Great, with the annotations of H. Scriblerus Secundus (Haymarket 24 March 1731), 1737, 1751 etc; ed F. Lindner, Berlin 1899; ed J. T. Hillhouse, New Haven 1918; ed J. Hampden 1925.

Rape upon rape, or the justice caught in his own trap: a comedy. (Haymarket 23 June 1730). 1730, 1730 (as The coffee-house politician).

A dialogue between a beau's head and his heels, taken from their mouth as they were spoke at St James's Coffee-house. 1731 (in The musical miscellany: being a collection of choice songs and lyrications vol 6). See H. S. Hughes, PQ 1 1922; H. P. Vincent, N & Q 13 March 1943.

The letter-writers, or a new way to keep a wife at home: a farce, written by Scriblerus Secundus. (Haymarket 24 March 1731). 1731, 1750; tr German, 1781.

Epilogue to Lewis Theobald's Orestes. (Lincoln's-Inn Fields 3 April 1731). 1731. See C. B. Woods, PQ 28 1949.

The Welsh opera: or the grey mare the better horse, written by Scriblerus Secundus. (Haymarket 22 April 1731). [1731], 1731 (rev as The genuine Grub-street opera), 1731 (as The Grub-street opera; to which is added The masquerade: a poem, printed in 1728); ed E. V. Roberts, Lincoln Nebraska 1968.

The lottery: a farce. (Drury Lane 1 Jan 1732). 1732, 1732, 1732, 1733, 1748 etc.

Epilogue to Charles Bodens' The modish couple. (Drury Lane 10 Jan 1732). 1732.

The modern husband: a comedy. (Drury Lane 14 Feb 1732). 1732, 1732; tr German, 1781.

The Covent-Garden tragedy. (Drury Lane 1 June 1732). 1732, 1754 etc.

The old debauchees: a comedy. (Drury Lane 1 June 1732). 1732, 1732, 1745 (as The debauchees: or the Jesuit caught), 1746, 1750 etc; tr Russian, 1956.

The mock doctor, or the dumb lady cur'd: a comedy done from Molière. (Drury Lane 23 June 1732). 1732, 1732 (rev), 1734, 1742, 1753 etc; ed J. Hampden [1931]. From Molière, Le médecin malgré lui.

Letter signed 'Philalethes'. Daily Post 31 July 1732. Possibly by Fielding; see Cross i. 135–9.

Epilogue to Charles Johnson's Caelia: or the perjur'd lover. (Drury Lane 11 Dec 1732). 1733 (for 1732).

The miser: a comedy taken from Plautus and Molière. (Drury Lane 17 Feb 1733). 1733, 1744, 1754 etc. From Plautus, Aulularia, and Molière, L'avare.

[Deborah: or a wife for you all]. (Drury Lane 6 April 1733). Never pbd. See E. V. Roberts, BNYPL Nov 1962.

The intriguing chambermaid: a comedy of two acts, taken from the French of Regnard. (Drury Lane 15 Jan 1734). 1734, 1750 etc; tr German, 1782. From Regnard, Le retour imprévu.

Don Quixote in England: a comedy. (Haymarket 5 April 1734). 1734, 1754 etc.

An old man taught wisdom, or the virgin unmask'd: a farce. (Drury Lane 6 Jan 1735). 1735, 1735 (with fewer songs), 1742, 1749 etc.

The universal gallant, or the different husbands: a comedy. (Drury Lane 10 Feb 1735). 1735.

Pasquin, a dramatick satire on the times: being the rehearsal of two plays, viz a comedy call'd the Election; and a tragedy call'd the Life and death of Common-Sense. (Haymarket 5 March 1736). 1736, 1737, 1740, 1754.

Tumble-down Dick, or Phaeton in the suds: a dramatick entertainment of walking, in serious and foolish characters, interlarded with burlesque, grotesque, comick interludes call'd Harlequin a pick-pocket, invented by the ingenious Monsieur Sans Esprit; the musick compos'd by the harmonious Signior Warblerini, and the scenes painted by the prodigious Mynheer Van Bottom-Flat. (Haymarket 29 April 1736). 1736, 1744.

Prologue to George Lillo's Fatal curiosity. (Haymarket 27 May 1736). 1737.

Eurydice, a farce: as it was d–mned at the Theatre-Royal in Drury-Lane. (Drury Lane 19 Feb 1737, as Eurydice: or the devil hen-peck'd). 1743 (in Miscellanies vol 2); tr German, 1759 (with Wedding-day), 1790.

The historical register for the year 1736; to which is added a very merry tragedy called Eurydice hiss'd: or a word to the wise. (Haymarket 21 March 1737, Historical register; 13 April 1737, Eurydice hiss'd). [1737], [1737] (rev), 1741, 1744; ed W. W. Appleton, Lincoln Nebraska 1967.

Eurydice hiss'd: or a word to the wise. See Historical register, above.

Letter signed 'Pasquin'. Common Sense 21 May 1737; rptd in London Mag May 1737; Common Sense vol 1 1738. See Cross i. 220–2 and C. W. Nichols, MLN 34 1919.

The military history of Charles XII, King of Sweden, by M. Gustavus Alderfeld, translated into English. 3 vols 1740. See J. E. Wells, JEGP 11 1912.

Of true greatness: an epistle to the Right Honourable George Dodington esq. 1741, 1743 (in Miscellanies vol 1).

ΤΗΣ ΟΜΗΡΟΥ VEPNON-ΙΑΔΟΣ, ΡΑΨΩΔΙΑῆ ΓΡΑΜΜΑ Α': the Vernon-iad, done into English from the original Greek of Homer, lately found at Constantinople, with notes in usum etc, book the first. 1741.

An apology for the life of Mrs Shamela Andrews, by Mr Conny Keyber. 1741, 1741; ed R. B. Johnson 1926; ed B. W. Downs, Cambridge 1930; ed S. W. Baker, Berkeley 1953; ed I. Watt, Los Angeles 1956 (Augustan Reprint Soc); ed M. C. Battestin, Boston 1961 (with Joseph Andrews, below).

The crisis: a sermon on Revel XIV 9, 10, 11, necessary to be preached in all churches before the next general election, by a lover of his country. 1741, 1741. Possibly by Fielding: see J. E. Wells, MLN 27 1912; G. E. Jensen, 31 1916.

The opposition: a vision. 1742 (for 1741).

The history of the adventures of Joseph Andrews and of his friend Mr Abraham Adams, written in imitation of the manner of Cervantes, author of Don Quixote. 2 vols 1742, 1742 ('revised and corrected with alterations and additions by the author'), 1743 (illustr J. Hulett), 1749 (for 1748), 1751 etc; illustr G. Cruikshank 1832 (Novelist's Lib); illustr 'Phiz' 1857; ed G. Saintsbury, illustr H. Railton and E. J. Wheeler 1902; ed Saintsbury 1910 (EL); ed L. Rice-Oxley, Oxford 1929 (WC); ed J. P. de Castro 1929; ed J. B. Priestley, illustr N. Tealby 1929; ed B. M. McCullough, New York 1930; ed H. H. Harper, illustr H. Jones, Boston 1931 (Bibliophile Soc); ed H. M. Jones, New York 1939 (Modern Lib); ed M. Mack, New York [1948]; illustr D. Harris 1953 (Folio Soc); ed M. E. Chase, New York [1958]; ed C. Baker, New York [1960]; ed I. Ehrenpreis, New York 1960; ed M. C. Battestin, Boston 1961 (with Shamela, above); ed A. R. Humphreys 1963 (EL); ed I. Watt, New York 1966; ed M. C. Battestin, Oxford and Middletown Conn 1967 (Wesleyan edn, textual preface by F. T. Bowers); tr French, 1743, 1807; Dutch, 1744; German, 1745; Danish, 1749; Italian, 1752–3, 1951; Russian, 1772, 1949.

A full vindication of the Dutchess Dowager of Marlborough, both with regard to the account lately published by her Grace and to her character in general. 1742, 1742.

Miss Lucy in town, a sequel to the virgin unmasqued: a farce, with songs. (Drury Lane 6 May 1742). 1742 etc. A collaboration with Garrick? See C. B. Woods, PQ 41 1962.

Plutus, the god of riches: a comedy translated from the original Greek of Aristophanes, with large notes explanatory and critical. 1742. With W. Young.

Some papers proper to be read before the Royal Society concerning the Terrestrial Chrysipus, Golden-Foot or Guinea, collected by Petrus Gualterus, but not published till after his death. 1743, 1743 (in Miscellanies vol 1, postscript added).

The wedding-day: a comedy. (Drury Lane 17 Feb 1743). 1743, 1743 (in Miscellanies vol 2); tr German, 1759 (with Eurydice), 1764, 1781.

A journey from this world to the next. 1743 (in Miscellanies vol 2); illustr D. Tegetmeier 1930; tr German, 1759; Russian, 1766; Danish, 1769; French, 1784; Swedish, 1785.

The life of Mr Jonathan Wild the Great. 1743 (in Miscellanies vol 3), 1754 ('with considerable corrections and additions'); illustr 'Phiz' 1840; ed J. Macy [1926]; ed W. Follett, New York 1926 (with Defoe, Life of Jonathan Wild); Oxford [1932] (WC); ed G. Saintsbury [1932] (EL) (with Journal of a voyage to Lisbon); illustr D. Tegetmeier 1932; ed L. Kronenberger, illustr T. M. Cleland, New York 1943 (Limited Edns Club); ed J. H. Plumb, New York 1961; illustr F. Martin 1966 (Folio Soc); tr German, 1750; Dutch, 1757; Danish, 1759; French, 1763, 1947; Russian, 1772–3; Norwegian, 1932; Italian, 1943; Czech, 1961.

Preface to Sarah Fielding's Adventures of David Simple. Vol 1, 1744 (2nd edn); tr French, 1784.

An attempt towards a natural history of the Hanover rat. 1744. See G. E. Jensen, Yale Univ Lib Gazette 10 1935.

The charge to the jury: or the sum of the evidence on the trial of A.B.C.D. and E.F. all M. D. for the death of one Robert at Orfud before Sir Asculapius Dosem. 1745. See R. C. Jarvis, MLR 41 1946.

The history of the present rebellion in Scotland, taken from the relation of James Macpherson, who was an eye-witness of the whole. 1745, 1745; ed I. K. Fletcher, Newport 1934.

A serious address to the poeple of Great Britain, in which the certain consequences of the present rebellion are fully demonstrated. 1745 (2 printings), 1745 ('corrected'; with A calm address to all parties in religion, not by Fielding; see R. C. Jarvis, N & Q Jan 1957), 1745.

A dialogue between the devil, the Pope and the Pretender. 1745.

The female husband: or the surprising history of Mrs Mary, alias Mr George Hamilton, taken from her own mouth since her confinement. 1746; ed C. E. Jones, Liverpool 1960. See J. P. de Castro, N & Q 5 March 1921; S. Baker, PMLA 74 1959.

Ovid's Art of love paraphrased and adapted to the present time, with notes and a most correct edition of the original, book 1. 1747, Dublin 1759 (as The lover's assistant); ed C. E. Jones, Los Angeles 1961 (Augustan Reprint Soc).

Preface and letters 40–44 of Sarah Fielding's Familiar letters between the principal characters in David Simple and some others. 2 vols 1747.

A dialogue between a gentleman of London, agent for two Court candidates, and an honest alderman of the Country Party, earnestly address'd to the electors of Great Britain. 1747, 1747.

A proper answer to a late scurrilous libel, entitled An apology for the conduct of a late celebrated second-rate minister, by the author of the Jacobite's journal. 1747, 1748.

The history of Tom Jones, a foundling. 6 vols 1749, 1749, 4 vols 1749 (rev), 1750 (for 1749) (rev) etc; illustr Rowlandson, Edinburgh 1805; illustr G. Cruikshank 1831; ed G. H. T[ownsend] [1867]; ed J. E. M. Fielding 1896 (expurgated by novelist's grand-daughter); 1900 (bibl note by A. W. Pollard); ed B. E. Stevenson, New York 1904 (abridged); ed S. Lee 1905; ed G. Saintsbury 1909 (EL); ed W. L. Cross, New York 1924; ed J. B. Priestley, illustr A. King, New York 1931 (Limited Edns Club); illustr W. Chappell, New York 1943 (Modern Lib); ed W. S. Maugham, illustr H. Diamond 1948 (abridged); ed G. Sherburn, New York 1950 (Modern Lib); ed L. Kronenberger, illustr T. M. Cleland, New York 1952 (Limited Edns Club); illustr D. Harris 1959 (Folio Soc); ed W. S. Maugham, introd by B. Evans 1962 (abridged); ed A. R. Humphreys 1962 (EL); ed R. H. Singleton, New York 1963; ed F. Kermode, New York 1964; illustr L. B. Smith 1964; ed R. P. C. Mutter 1966 (Penguin); ed J. Macalpine 1966; ed A. Sherbo, New York 1967; tr French, 1750 (illustr Gravelot), 1796, 1804, 1833, 1833; Dutch, 1749–50, 1862; German, 1750, 1786–8, 1853; Italian, 1756–7, 1954; Polish, 1783; Spanish, 1796; Russian, 1787, 1849, 1935, 1938, 1960; Czech, 1872, 1958; Finnish, 1959.

A charge delivered to the Grand Jury at the sessions of the peace held for the City and Liberty of Westminster etc on Thursday the 29th of June 1749. 1749.

A true state of the case of Bosavern Penlez, who suffered on account of the late riot in the Strand. 1749.

An enquiry into the causes of the late increase of robbers etc with some proposals for remedying this growing evil. 1751, 1751.

Amelia. 4 vols 1752 (for 1751), 1762 (rev, in Murphy's edn of Fielding's Works) etc; ed S. S. Wilkinson [1815?] ('epitomized'); illustr G. Cruikshank 1832; illustr 'Phiz' 1857; ed G. Saintsbury 1930 (EL); tr German, 1752; Dutch, 1758; French, 1762, 1782; Russian, 1772–85; Italian, 1782; Spanish, 1795–6; Czech, 1959.

A plan of the Universal Register office. 1752 (for 1751), 1753 etc. With John Fielding.

Examples of the interposition of Providence in the detection and punishment of murder, with an introduction and conclusion, both written by Henry Fielding esq. 1752 etc.

A proposal for making an effectual provision for the poor, for amending their morals and for rendering them useful members of the society. 1753.

A clear state of the case of Elizabeth Canning, who hath sworn that she was robbed and almost starved to death for which one Mary Squires now lies under sentence of death. 1753, 1753, 1754.

The journal of a voyage to Lisbon (with A fragment of a comment on L. Bolingbroke's essays). 1755 (edited text, really 2nd edn), 1755 (original text, really 1st edn) etc; ed A. Dobson 1892, 1907 (WC); ed H. Bennett 1907; ed J. H. Lobban 1913; ed H. E. Pagliaro, New York 1963; tr German, 1764; French, 1783.

Plain truth. 1758 (in J. Dodsley's Collection of poems in six volumes by several hands vol 5).

A treatise on the office of constable. 1761 (in Sir John Fielding's Extracts from such of the penal laws as particularly relate to the peace and good order of this metropolis).

The fathers, or the good-natur'd man: a comedy. (Drury Lane 30 Nov 1778). 1778. Originally written by Fielding c. 1737.

An original song written on the first appearance of The beggars opera [1728]. 1788 (in Country magazine for the years 1786 and 1787, Salisbury and London 1788). See H. P. Vincent, N & Q 13 March 1943.

Periodicals

The champion: or the British Mercury, by Capt Hercules Vinegar of Hockley in the Hole. 15 Nov 1739–June 1741 (with James Ralph); rptd 2 vols 1741 (essays of 15 Nov 1739–19 June 1740 only), 1743, 1766. On the identification of Fielding's contributions, see J. E. Wells, MLR 7 1912, E Studien 46 1912–13, MLR 8 1913, MLN 35 1920; and J. B. Shipley, N & Q Nov 1953, June, Aug 1955, PQ 42 1963. Excerpt: The voyages of Mr Job Vinegar, ed S. J. Sackett, Los Angeles 1958 (Augustan Reprint Soc).

The true patriot: and the history of our own times. 5 Nov 1745–17 June 1746; ed M. A. Locke, University Alabama 1964 (facs).

The Jacobite's journal, by John Trottplaid esq. 5 Dec 1747–5 Nov 1748.

The Covent-Garden journal, by Sir Alexander Drawcansir, Knt Censor of Great Britain. 4 Jan–25 Nov 1752; ed G. E. Jensen, New Haven 1915.

Letters

Only 21 letters by Fielding are generally known to exist; they have never been collected and pbd. One is to Davidge Gould (15 July 1740), one to Richardson (15 Oct 1748), one to George Lyttelton (29 Aug 1749), one to Hutton Perkins (25 Nov 1750); 2 are to Lady Mary Wortley Montagu (4 Sept [1730], [Feb–March 1732]), 3 to John Nourse (6 March 1738, 9 July 1739, 20 April 1741), 2 to Lord Chancellor Hardwicke (21 July 1749, 6 Dec 1753); 3 are to the Duke of Bedford (13 Dec 1748, 3 July 1749, 14 May 1750), 3 to the Duke of Newcastle (15 Jan 1751, 14, 27 April 1753); and 4 are to John Fielding (12, 22 July, [Sept] 1754); see J. P. de Castro, TLS 15 Jan 1920. See Dudden ii. 1133–4; Cross iii. 358–64. By far the largest single collection of Fielding's correspondence—his letters to James Harris—has not yet been made available.

§2

For bibliographies of secondary works on Fielding, see F. T. Blanchard, Fielding the novelist, New Haven 1926; and F. Cordasco, Fielding: a list of critical studies published from 1895 to 1946, Brooklyn 1948. Corrections and addns to Cordasco are in PQ 29 1950, pp. 273–5.

Desfontaines, P. F. G. Lettre d'une dame angloise à Madame *** Maitresse des Comptes de Montpellier. In his trn of Joseph Andrews, Amsterdam 1744 (2nd edn).

'Orbilius'. An examen of the History of Tom Jones, a foundling. 1749.

La Place, P.–A. de. Traduction d'une lettre. In his trn of

Tom Jones, Amsterdam 1750. See also GM March 1750.

An apology for the life of Mr Bampfylde-Moore Carew, commonly call'd the King of the Beggars. '2nd edn' [in fact, a later edn, pbd Nov 1751]. Includes 'parallel' between Tom Jones and Carew and a dedication 'To the worshipful Justice Fielding'.

Monthly Rev Dec 1751. On Amelia.

[Coventry, F.?] An essay on the new species of writing founded by Mr Fielding; with a word or two upon the modern state of criticism. 1751; ed A. D. McKillop, Los Angeles 1962 (Augustan Reprint Soc).

—— The history of Pompey the Little: or the life an d adventures of a lap-dog. 1752 (3rd edn). Dedication to Fielding.

[Smollett, T.?] A faithful narrative of the base and inhuman arts that were lately practised upon the brain of Habbakuk Hilding, by Drawcansir Alexander. 1752.

Clément, P. Lettres 50 (Paris, 28 Feb 1750) and 91 (London, 1 Jan 1752). In his Les cinq années littéraires, vols 2–3, Hague 1754. On Tom Jones and Amelia.

From Joseph Addison to the author of Tom Jones (Letter 16). In Admonitions from the dead in epistles to the living, 1754.

A catalogue of the entire and valuable library of books of the late Henry Fielding esq, which will be sold by auction. [1755]. In BM; rptd in E. M. Thornbury, Fielding's theory of the comic prose epic, [Madison 1931].

Murphy, A. An essay on the life and genius of Henry Fielding esq. 1762. Prefixed to his edn of Fielding's Works.

[Baker, D. E.] In his Companion to the play-house vol 2, 1764.

[Burnet, J. (Lord Monboddo)]. In his Of the origin and progress of language vol 3, Edinburgh 1776. Pp. 296–8 on Tom Jones.

Beattie, J. On fable and romance. In his Dissertations moral and critical, 1783. Pp. 571–3.

Reeve, C. In her Progress of romance vol 1, Colchester 1785. Pp. 139–41.

Aikin, J. et al. General biography vol 4, 1803.

Murray, H. In his Morality of fiction, Edinburgh 1805.

Watson, W. The life of Fielding. Edinburgh 1807.

Drake, N. Essays biographical, critical and historical illustrative of the Rambler, Adventurer and Idler and of the various periodical papers. Vol 1 1809. Pp. 79–91 on Champion.

Barbauld, A. L. Preface to Joseph Andrews. In British novelists vol 18, 1810.

Mudford, W. Critical observations [on Fielding's fiction]. In British novelists vols 4–5, 1811.

Nichols, J. In his Literary anecdotes of the eighteenth century vol 3, 1812.

Chalmers, A. In his General biographical dictionary, 1814.

Suard, J. B. A. In his Biographie universelle vol 14, Paris 1815.

Hazlitt, W. In his Lectures on the English comic writers, 1819. Lecture 6 a revision of essay in Edinburgh Rev 24 1815.

Scott, W. In his Lives of the novelists, 1825. Rptd from essay in Ballantyne's Novelist's Lib 1821.

Cruikshank, G. Illustrations of Smollett, Fielding and Goldsmith. 1832.

Planche, G. Fielding. Revue des Deux Mondes 5 1832.

Cunningham, G. In his Lives of eminent and illustrious Englishmen vol 5, Glasgow 1837.

Roscoe, T. The life and works of Fielding. 1840. Prefixed to his edn of Fielding's Works. See review by Thackeray, Times 2 Sept 1840.

[Whipple, E. P.] North Amer Rev Jan 1849.

Thackeray, W. M. In his English humourists of the eighteenth century, 1853.

[Elwin, W.] Fielding. Quart Rev 98 1855; rptd in his Some eighteenth-century men of letters, 1902.

Lawrence, F. The life of Fielding; with notices of his writings, his times and his contemporaries. 1855. Rptd from Sharpe's London Mag Feb–June 1854.

P., P. T. Woodfall's ledger 1734–47. N & Q 2 June 1855. On the printing of Fielding's works.

[Patmore, C.] Fielding and Thackeray. North Br Rev Nov 1855.

Jeaffreson, J. C. In his Novels and novelists from Elizabeth to Victoria vol 1, 1858.

Keightley, T. On the life and writings of Fielding. Fraser's Mag Jan–Feb, June 1858; ed F. S. Dickson, Cleveland 1907.

— Tom Jones. N & Q 30 May 1863.

Masson, D. British novelists of the eighteenth century. In his British novelists and their styles, Cambridge 1859.

[Lewes, G. H. ?] A word about Tom Jones. Blackwood's Mag March 1860.

Spalding, W. In his Handbook of biography, 1863.

Taine, H. In his Histoire de la littérature anglaise vol 4, Paris 1863; tr Edinburgh 1871.

Forsyth, W. In his Novels and novelists of the eighteenth century, in illustration of the manners and morals of the age, 1871.

Browne, J. P. Prefaces to his edn of Fielding's Works, 11 vols 1871–2.

Clarke, C. C. Fielding, Smollett and Sterne. GM May 1872.

Smith, G. B. Our first great novelist. Macmillan's Mag May 1874; rptd in his Poets and novelists, 1875.

Jesse, J. H. In his Memoirs of celebrated Etonians vol 1, 1875.

Latreille, F. Fielding and Timothy Fielding. N & Q 26 June 1875.

Stephen, L. In his History of English thought in the eighteenth century vol 2, 1876.

— Fielding's novels. Cornhill Mag Feb 1877; rptd in his Hours in a library 3rd ser, 1879.

— Memoir of Fielding. 1882. Prefixed to his edn of Fielding's Works.

Bobertag, F. Zur Charakteristik Fieldings. E Studien 1 1877.

Hettner, H. J. T. In his Literaturgeschichte des achtzehnten Jahrhunderts, Brunswick 1879.

Dobson, A. Tom Jones on the French stage. N & Q 10 Sept 1881. See also T. Child 8 Oct 1881.

— Fielding. 1883 (EML), 1889 (rev), 1900 (rev).

— Fieldingiana. N & Q 1 Sept 1883.

— Fielding's Voyage to Lisbon. In his Eighteenth-century vignettes 1st ser, 1892.

— Fielding's library. In his Eighteenth-century vignettes 3rd ser 1896. Rptd from Bibliographica 1 1895.

— The Covent-Garden journal. In his Sidewalk studies, 1902. Rptd from Nat Rev May 1901 and Living Age 29 June 1901.

— Fresh facts about Fielding. In his De libris, 1908. Rptd from Macmillan's Mag April 1907.

— A Fielding find. In his At Prior Park, 1912. Rptd from Nat Rev Aug 1911.

— A new dialogue of the dead. In his Rosalba's journal, 1915. Rptd from Nat Rev Dec 1912.

— Fielding and Andrew Millar. Library 3rd ser 7 1916.

Tuckerman, B. In his A history of English prose fiction from Malory to George Eliot, 1882.

Lowell, J. R. Address at unveiling of Fielding's bust at Taunton, 4 Sept 1883; rptd in his Democracy and other addresses, Boston 1887.

— Inscription for a memorial bust of Fielding. Atlantic Monthly Sept 1890.

Perry, T. S. In his English literature in the eighteenth century, New York 1883. On Tom Thumb and Joseph Andrews.

Traill, H. D. Richardson and Fielding. In his New Lucian, 1884.

Gray, G. J. Fielding's Covent-Garden journal. Book-Lore Nov 1885.

Jusserand, J. J. In his Le roman anglais, Paris 1886.

Noble, J. A. In his Morality in English fiction, Liverpool [1886].

Gosse, E. In his A history of eighteenth-century literature 1660–1780, 1889.

— Introd to his edn of Fielding's Works, 1898–9.

— The character of Fielding. In his Books on the table, 1921.

Lang, A. In his Letters on literature, 1889.

Aitken, G. A. Fielding. Athenaeum 1 Feb 1890. Prints Fielding's will.

Henley, W. E. Views and reviews: literature. 1890. Revision of reviews of Stephen's edn (Athenaeum 4 Nov 1882) and of Dobson's Fielding (Athenaeum 28 April 1883).

— Essay on the life, genius and achievement of Fielding. In his edn of Fielding's Complete works vol 16, 1903.

Péronne, J. Ueber englische Zustände im 18 Jahrhundert nach den Romanen von Fielding und Smollett. 1890.

Stapfer, P. Le grand classique du roman anglais: Fielding. Revue des Deux Mondes 15 Sept 1890.

Saintsbury, G. Introd to his edn of Fielding's Works, 1893.

— In English prose selections, ed H. Craik vol 4, 1894.

— Fielding. Bookman (London) April 1907.

— Introduction to Fielding. 1909.

— The four wheels of the novel wain. In his English novel, 1913.

Moriarty, G. P. The political world of Fielding and Smollett. Macmillan's Mag Jan 1894.

Raleigh, W. Richardson and Fielding. In his English novel, 1894.

Wilson, F. Dickens in seinen Beziehungen zu den Humoristen Fielding und Smollett. Leipzig 1894.

Lindner, F. Fieldings dramatische Werke. Leipzig and Dresden 1895.

Wood, A. Einfluss Fieldings auf die deutsche Literatur. Yokohama 1895.

Clarke, C. H. Fielding und der deutsche Sturm und Drang. Freiburg 1897.

'P'. Reputations reconsidered: Fielding. Academy 29 Jan 1898.

Thomson, C. A note on Fielding's Amelia. Westminster Rev Nov 1899.

Cross, W. L. In his Development of the English novel, New York 1899.

— The new Fielding collection. Yale Alumni Weekly 21 Feb 1913. On the Dickson donation.

— The secret of Tom Jones. Bookman (New York) Sept 1918.

— The legend of Fielding. Yale Rev 8 1918.

— The history of Fielding. 3 vols New Haven 1918.

Homann, W. Fielding als Humorist. Marburg 1900.

Ohnsorg, R. John Lacys Dumb lady, Mrs Centlivres Love's contrivance und Fieldings Mock doctor in ihrem Verhältnis zu einander und zu ihrer gemeinschaftlichen Quellen. Hamburg 1900.

Forman, H. B. Richardson, Fielding and the Andrews family. Fortnightly Rev 1 Dec 1901.

Whittuck, C. A. The good man of the eighteenth century. 1901. Pt 3 on Parson Adams and Allworthy.

Becker, G. Die Bedeutung des Wortes 'romantic' bei Fielding und Smollett. Archiv 110 1903.

— Der Einfluss des Don Quijote auf Fielding. In his Die Aufnahme des Don Quijote in die englische Literatur 1605–c. 1770, Berlin 1906.

Maynadier, G. H. Introd to his edn of Fielding's Works, New York and Cambridge Mass [1903].

Schacht, H. R. Der gute Pfarrer in der englischen Literatur bis zu Goldsmiths Vicar of Wakefield. Berlin 1904. On Joseph Andrews and Amelia.

Prideaux, W. F. Fielding's Journal of a voyage to Lisbon 1755. N & Q 28 July 1906. See also St Swithin 11 Aug 1906.

'Ranger'. Fielding. Bookman (London) Feb 1906.

Swaen, A. E. H. Fielding and Goldsmith at Leyden. MLR 1 1906.

Waldschmidt, C. Die Dramatisierungen von Tom Jones. Wetzlar 1906.

The Fielding Bicentenary prompted the following notices: Academy 20 April 1907; Bookman (New York) April 1907; Literary Digest 4 May 1907; Saturday Rev 20 April 1907; C. H. Gaines, Harper's Weekly 20 April 1907; J. H. Lobban, Blackwood's Mag April 1907; H. C. Minchin, Fortnightly Rev April 1907; G. Saintsbury, Bookman (London) April 1907; T. Seccombe, Cornhill Mag June 1907.

Dickson, F. S. Biographies of Fielding. In his edn of T. Keightley, Life and writings of Fielding, Cleveland 1907.

— William Makepeace Thackeray and Fielding. North Amer Rev April 1913.

— Fielding's Tom Jones: its geography. N & Q 5 Sept 1914. *See also* J. P. de Castro 26 Sept 1914; E. Bensly 10 Oct, 7 Nov 1914.

— Fielding and Richardson on the continent. N & Q 6 Jan 1917.

— The early editions of Fielding's Voyage to Lisbon. Library 3rd ser 8 1917. Comments by A. W. Pollard and J. P. de Castro, ibid.

— The chronology of Tom Jones. Library 3rd ser 8 1917. Rev from N & Q 30 May 1914.

— Errors and omissions in Tom Jones. Library 3rd ser 9 1918.

Yardley, E. Fielding and Shakespeare. N & Q 8 June 1907. Allusions in Tom Jones.

Berger, T. W. Der Einfluss des Don Quixote auf Fieldings Roman. In his Don Quixote in Deutschland und sein Einfluss auf den deutschen Roman 1613–1800, Heidelberg 1908.

Bosdorf, E. Entstehungsgeschichte von Fieldings Joseph Andrews. Berlin 1908.

Chesterton, G. K. Tom Jones and morality. In his All things considered, 1908.

News for bibliophiles. Nation (New York) 24 Dec 1908. On Tom Jones.

Wicklein, E. Das 'Ernsthafte' in dem englischen komischen Roman des xviii Jahrhunderts. Dresden 1908.

Bispham, G. T. Fielding's Jonathan Wild. In Eighteenth-century literature: an Oxford miscellany, Oxford 1909.

Blake, W. B. Tom Jones in France. South Atlantic Quart 8 1909.

Burton, R. Eighteenth-century beginnings: Fielding. In his Masters of the English novel, New York 1909.

Godden, G. M. Fielding: some unpublished letters and records. Fortnightly Rev Nov 1909.

— Fielding: a memoir. 1910.

Green, E. Fielding, his works: an independent criticism. 1909.

Dibelius, W. Fielding. In his Englische Romankunst, Berlin 1910.

Düber, R. Beiträge zu Fieldings Romantechnik. Halle 1910.

Robbins, A. F. Jonathan Wild the Great: its germ. N & Q 1 Oct 1910. *See also* J. P. de Castro 2 Dec 1916.

Swain, C. R. Amelia Booth and Lucy Feverel. Nation (New York) 10 Nov 1910.

Metcalf, J. C. Fielding, critic. Sewanee Rev 19 1911.

Williams, H. In his Two centuries of the English novel, 1911.

Holliday, C. In his English fiction from the fifth to the twentieth century, New York 1912.

Wells, J. E. A few details of Fielding's life. Nation (New York) 25 April 1912.

— Fielding and The crisis. MLN 27 1912.

— Fielding and the history of Charles XII. JEGP 11 1912.

— Fielding's signatures in the Champion and the date of his Of good nature. MLR 7 1912.

— The Champion and some unclaimed essays by Fielding. E Studien 46 1913.

— Fielding's Champion and Captain Hercules Vinegar. MLR 8 1913.

— Fielding's political purpose in Jonathan Wild. PMLA 28 1913.

— Some new facts concerning Fielding's Tumble-down Dick and Pasquin. MLN 28 1913.

— Fielding's first poem to Walpole and his garret in 1730. MLN 29 1914.

— Fielding's Miscellanies. MLR 13 1918.

— Fielding's Champion: more notes. MLN 35 1920.

Child, H. Fielding and Smollett. In CHEL vol 10, 1913.

Pope, F. J. Fielding's boyhood. Br Archivist Jan 1914.

—-Fielding's ancestors at Sharpham Park, Somerset. N & Q Feb 1920.

Lücker, H. Die Verwendung der Mundart im englischen Roman des 18 Jahrhunderts (Fielding, Smollett). Darmstadt 1915.

Schönzeler, H. Fieldings Verhältnis zu Lesage und zu anderen Quellen. Weimar 1915.

de Castro, J. P. Did Fielding write Shamela? N & Q 8 Jan 1916. *See also* C. R. Greene, MLN 59 1944; J. C. Maxwell, N & Q 21 Aug 1948.

— Fielding and the Collier family. N & Q 5 Aug 1916.

— Fielding at Boswell Court. N & Q 1 April 1916.

— Fieldingiana. N & Q 17 June 1916, 2 Dec 1916, 10 March, Nov 1917.

— Fielding's Parson Adams. N & Q 18 March 1916.

— John Ranby: Fielding. N & Q 1 July 1916.

— Fielding's last voyage. Library 3rd ser 8 1917. *See also* F. S. Dickson and A. W. Pollard, ibid.

— Fielding as a publicist. N & Q Nov 1919.

— Tom Jones. N & Q 10 April 1920. On Fielding's grandfather.

— The printing of Fielding's works. Library 4th ser 1 1921.

— Fielding's pamphlet The female husband. N & Q 5 March 1921.

— Edmund Fielding. N & Q 26 Aug 1922. Fielding's father's 4th marriage.

— A forgotten Salisbury surgeon. TLS 13 Jan 1927. *See also* A. E. DuBois 19 March 1931; de Castro 26 March 1931.

— Fielding and Lyme Regis. TLS 4 June 1931. *See also* W. W. Gill, N & Q 3 Oct 1936.

— Ursula Fielding and Tom Jones. N & Q 9 March 1940. Letter of Fielding's sister 25 Oct 1748.

— Derham. N & Q 15 Feb 1941. Allusion in Voyage to Lisbon.

— Gravelot. N & Q 1 Feb 1941. Illustrator of French trn of Tom Jones.

Jensen, G. E. An apology for the life of Mrs Shamela Andrews 1741. MLN 31 1916.

— The Crisis: a sermon. Ibid.

— Fashionable society in Fielding's time. PMLA 31 1916.

— The Covent-Garden journal extraordinary. MLN 34 1919.

— An Address to the electors of Great Britain: possibly a Fielding tract. MLN 40 1925. *See also* A. L. Greason, PQ 33 1954; W. B. Coley 36 1957.

— A Fielding discovery. Yale Univ Lib Gazette 10 1935. Fielding's An attempt towards a natural history of the Hanover rat 1744.

— Proposals for a definitive edition of Fielding's Tom Jones. Library 4th ser 18 1937.

Phelps, W. L. Fielding, Smollett, Sterne. In his Advance of the English novel, New York 1916.

Frölich, A. Fieldings Humor in seinen Romanen. Leipzig 1918.

Kurrelmeyer, W. A German version of Joseph Andrews. MLN 33 1918.

Whiteford, R. N. Samuel Richardson, Fielding, Sarah Fielding and Tobias Smollett. In his Motives in English fiction, New York 1918.

Harrison, F. Bath-Somerset-Fielding. Fortnightly Rev Nov 1919; rptd in his De senectute, 1923.

Loomis, R. S. Tom Jones and Tom-mania. Sewanee Rev 27 1919.

Nichols, C. W. Fielding notes. MLN 34 1919. On Pasquin, The historical register, and pbd letter of 21 May 1737.

— The date of Tumble-down Dick. MLN 36 1921.

— Fielding and the Cibbers. PQ 1 1922.

— Fielding's Tumble-down Dick. MLN 38 1923.

— A new note on Fielding's Historical register. Ibid.

— Social satire in Fielding's Pasquin and the Historical register. PQ 3 1924.

— Fielding's satire on pantomime. PMLA 46 1931.

Biron, H. C. A famous magistrate. Nat Rev Jan 1920; rptd in Living Age 7 Feb 1920.

Digeon, A. Autour de Fielding. Revue Germanique 11 1920. On Fielding's relationship with his sister Sarah.

— Les romans de Fielding. Paris 1923; tr 1925.

— Le texte des romans de Fielding. Paris 1923.

— La condemnation de Tom Jones à Paris. Revue Anglo-américaine 4 1927.

— Fielding a-t-il écrit le dernier chapitre de A journey from this world to the next? Revue Anglo-américaine 8 1931. By Sarah Fielding?

Blanchard, F. T. Coleridge's estimate of Fielding. In C. M. Gayley anniversary papers, Berkeley 1922.

— Fielding the novelist. New Haven 1926.

Hughes, H. S. Fielding's indebtedness to James Ralph. MP 20 1922.

Roberts, W. Fielding in French. Nat Rev July 1922.

Marr, G. S. Developments in journalism of the period and the work of Fielding. In his Periodical essayists of the eighteenth century, 1923.

Van Doren, C. The greatest English man of letters. Nation (New York) 6 June 1923.

— Tom Jones and Philip Carey: heroes of two centuries. Century May 1925.

Birrell, A. Fielding and the literary tradition. In his More obiter dicta, 1924.

George, M. D. The sale of Fielding's farm. TLS 26 June 1924. Reply by J. P. de Castro 17 July 1924.

Deinhardt, M. Beziehungen der Philosophie auf die Romane Fieldings. In her Beziehungen der Philosophie zu dem grossen englischen Roman des achtzehnten Jahrhunderts, Hamburg 1925.

MacLaurin, C. In his Mere mortals: medico-historical essays, New York 1925.

Priestley, J. B. Parson Adams. In his English comic characters, 1925.

— Tom Jones. In V. W. Brooks et al, A book of prefaces, New York 1941.

Prinsen, J. In his De roman in de 18e eeuw in West-Europa, Hague 1925.

Stonehill, C. Fielding's The miser. TLS 22 Oct 1925. Bibliographical.

Binz-Winiger, E. Erziehungsfragen in den Romanen von Samuel Richardson, Fielding, Tobias Smollett, Oliver Goldsmith und Laurence Sterne. Zürich 1926.

Ernle, Lord. Founders of the modern novel: Fielding. Edinburgh Rev 243 1926.

Fielding's Charge to the jury 1745. TLS 4 March 1926. Bibliographical.

Radtke, B. Fielding als Kritiker. Leipzig 1926.

Williams, O. Tom Jones. In his Some great English novels, 1926.

Balderston, K. C. Goldsmith's supposed attack on Fielding. MLN 42 1927.

Bennett, J. O. Fielding's Tom Jones. In his Much loved books, 1927.

McCutcheon, R. P. Amelia: or the distressed wife [1751]. MLN 42 1927. Against its influence on Fielding.

Cobb, L. Pierre-Antoine de La Place: sa vie et son œuvre 1707-93. Paris 1928. On Fielding's translator.

Fornelli, G. Fielding e la sua epoca. Annali delle Università Toscane 12 1928.

Köhler, F. Fieldings Wochenschrift The champion und das englische Leben der Zeit. Münster 1928.

Parfitt, G. E. L'influence française dans les oeuvres de Fielding et dans le théâtre anglais contemporain de ses comédies. Paris 1928.

Banerji, H. K. Fielding: playwright, journalist and master of the art of fiction, his life and works. Oxford 1929.

Bateson, F. W. In his English comic drama 1700-50, Oxford 1929.

Proper, C. B. A. In his Social elements in English prose fiction between 1700-1832, Amsterdam 1929.

Swann, G. R. Fielding and empirical realism. In his Philosophical parallelism in six English novelists, Philadelphia 1929.

Graham, W. In his English literary periodicals, New York 1930. On Fielding's journalism.

Habel, U. In his Die Nachwirkung des picaresken Romans in England (von Nash bis Fielding und Smollett), Breslau 1930.

R., E. An advertisement of Fielding's. N & Q 1 Nov 1930. Denying authorship of Battle of the poets.

Thomsen, E. Studier i Fieldings romaner. Copenhagen 1930.

Huxley, A. Tragedy and the whole truth. In his Music at night and other essays, 1931. On Tom Jones.

McKillop, A. D. The personal relations between Fielding and Richardson. MP 28 1931.

— An iconographic poem on Tom Jones. PQ 17 1938. On The fan, 1749.

— In his Early masters of English fiction, Lawrence Kansas 1956.

— Some recent views of Tom Jones. College Eng Oct 1959.

Read, S. E. Fielding's Miser. Huntington Lib Bull 1 1931.

Taylor, H. W. Fielding upon Cibber. MP 29 1931.

Thornbury, E. M. Fielding's theory of the comic prose epic. Madison 1931.

van der Voorde, F. P. Fielding: critic and satirist. Hague 1931.

Collins, N. In his Facts of fiction, 1932.

Joesten, M. Die Philosophie Fieldings. Leipzig 1932.

Bissell, F. O. Fielding's theory of the novel. Ithaca 1933.

Fischer, H. Das subjektive Element in den Romanen Fieldings. Breslau 1933.

Jones, B. M. Fielding: novelist and magistrate. 1933.

Edgar, P. Fielding and Tom Jones. In his Art of the novel from 1700 to the present time, New York 1933.

Avery, E. L. An early performance of Fielding's Historical register. MLN 49 1934.

— Some notes on Fielding's plays. Research Stud of State College of Washington 3 1935.

— Fielding's Universal gallant. Research Stud of State College of Washington 6 1938.

— Fielding's last season with the Haymarket Theatre. MP 36 1939.

Beatty, R. C. Criticism in Fielding's narratives and his estimate of critics. PMLA 49 1934.

Ewald, E. Abbild und Wünschbild der Gesellschaft bei Richardson und Fielding. Cologne 1935.

Mundy, P. D. Fielding's Tom Jones. N & Q 28 Dec 1935. Joseph Spence's letter, 15 April 1749, on pbn of the novel.

Ronte, H. Richardson und Fielding: Geschichte ihres Ruhms. Leipzig 1935.

Seymour, M. Fielding's History of the Forty-five. PQ 14 1935. The work, however, is not by Fielding: see R. C. Jarvis, N & Q 8 Sept 1945; Sept, Nov 1956; Jan 1957.

Coolidge, A. C. A Fielding pamphlet? TLS 9 May 1936. Against attribution to Fielding of Stultus versus sapientem.

Haage, R. Charakterzeichnung und Komposition in Fieldings Tom Jones in ihrer Beziehung zum Drama. Britannica 13 1936.

Lind, L. R. Lucian and Fielding. Classical Weekly 20 Jan 1936.

Raushenbush, E. M. Charles Macklin's lost play about Fielding. MLN 51 1936.

Shepperson, A. B. Richardson and Fielding: Shamela and Shamelia. In his Novel in motley, Cambridge Mass 1936.

—— Fielding on liberty and democracy. Univ of Virginia Stud 4 1951.

—— Additions and corrections to facts about Fielding. MP 51 1954. On Fielding's legal career.

Sherburn, G. Fielding's Amelia: an interpretation. ELH 3 1936.

—— Fielding's social outlook. PQ 35 1956.

Smith, D. F. The rise and fall of Fielding, Grand Mogul of satirical farce. In his Plays about the theatre in England from the Rehearsal in 1671 to the Licensing Act in 1737, Oxford 1936.

Streeter, H. W. In his Eighteenth-century English novel in French translation, New York 1936.

Studt, A. Fieldings Charakterromane. Britannica 13 1936.

Chandler, K. Two 'Fielding' pamphlets. PQ 16 1937. Satires against Pope, 1742, not by Fielding.

Esdaile, Mrs. Fielding's Danish translator: Simon Charles Stanley the sculptor. TLS 3 April 1937.

Fox, R. The novel as epic. In his Novel and the people, 1937.

Greene, G. Fielding and Sterne. In From Anne to Victoria: essays by various hands, ed B. Dobrée 1937; rptd in his Lost childhood, 1951.

Woods, C. B. Notes on three of Fielding's plays. PMLA 52 1937. On The letter-writers, The modern husband, and Eurydice hiss'd.

—— Fielding and the authorship of Shamela. PQ 25 1946.

—— Fielding's epilogue for Theobald. PQ 28 1949.

—— The 'Miss Lucy' plays of Fielding and Garrick. PQ 41 1962.

—— The folio text of Fielding's The miser. HLQ 28 1964.

—— Cibber in Fielding's Author's farce: three notes. PQ 44 1965.

—— Theobald and Fielding's Don Tragedio. Eng Lang Notes 2 1965.

'Alain' (E. Chartier). En lisant Fielding. Nouvelle Revue Française March 1939.

Brown, J. R. From Aaron Hill to Fielding? PQ 18 1939. If the letter is to Fielding, he may be author of the play Rehearsal of kings.

—— Fielding's Grub-street opera. MLQ 16 1955.

Iyengar, K. R. S. Fielding's Tom Jones. Jnl of Univ of Bombay 8 1939.

'Olybrius'. A presentation inscription by Fielding. N & Q 27 April 1940. Reply by J. P. de Castro 11 May 1940.

Rogers, W. H. The significance of Fielding's Temple beau. PMLA 55 1940.

—— Fielding's early aesthetic and technique. SP 40 1943.

Vincent, H. P. The childhood of Fielding. RES 16 1940.

—— Fielding in prison. MLR 36 1941.

Wallace, R. M. Fielding manuscripts. TLS 18 May 1940. Reply by J. P. de Castro 1 June 1940.

—— Fielding's knowledge of history and biography. SP 44 1947.

Buck, G. 'Written in imitation of the manner of Cervantes'. Germanisch-romanische Monatsschrift 29 1941. On Joseph Andrews.

Elistratov, A. Fielding's realism. In Iz istorii Anliskogo realizma [On the history of English realism], Moscow 1941.

—— Fielding. Soviet Lit Oct 1954.

Hammond, G. E. Evidences of the dramatist's technique in Fielding's novels. Bull of Univ of Wichita 16 1941.

Irwin, W. R. The making of Jonathan Wild: a study in the literary method of Fielding. New York 1941.

—— Satire and comedy in the works of Fielding. ELH 13 1946.

Jaggard, W. Revivals of Fielding's plays. N & Q 4 Jan 1941.

Mead, H. R. [Variant issues of Coffeehouse politician 1730]. PBSA 35 1941.

Gerould, G. H. In his Patterns of English and American fiction, Boston 1942.

Heilman, R. B. Fielding and 'the first Gothic revival'. MLN 57 1942.

Humphreys, A. R. Fielding's irony: its methods and effects. RES 18 1942.

Price, L. M. The works of Fielding on the German stage 1762–1801. JEGP 41 1942.

Randall, D. A. and J. T. Winterich. Fielding: the history of Tom Jones. Publishers' Weekly 21 March 1942.

Jonathan Wild. TLS 14 Aug 1943. Reply by B. W. Downs 11 Sept 1943.

Hill, R. M. Setting in the novels of Fielding. Bull of Citadel 7 1943.

Pons, E. Fielding, Swift et Cervantes. Studia Neophilologica 15 1943.

Wagenknecht, E. Fielding and the prose epic. In his Cavalcade of the English novel, New York 1943.

C., T. C. Fielding and Bentley. N & Q 20 May 1944. On Amelia x. i.

Swaen, A. E. H. Fielding's The intriguing chambermaid. Neophilologus 29 1944.

Van Doren, M., K. A. Porter and A. Tate. Fielding: Tom Jones. In The new invitation to learning, ed Van Doren, New York 1944.

Eaves, T. C. D. The publication of the first translations of Fielding's Tom Jones. Library 4th ser 26 1945.

—— and B. D. Kimpel. Fielding's son by his first wife. N & Q June 1968.

Hughes, L. The influence of Fielding's milieu upon his humor. SE 1944.

Jarvis, R. C. Fielding, Dodsley, Marchant and Ray: some fugitive histories of the '45. N & Q 8 Sept 1945.

—— The death of Walpole: Fielding and a forgotten cause célèbre. MLR 41 1946. On Fielding's authorship of A charge to the jury, 1745.

—— Fielding and the 'Forty-Five'. N & Q Sept, Nov 1956, Jan 1957. On the Fielding canon.

Graham, W. H. Fielding's Tom Jones. Contemporary Rev March 1946.

Pritchett, V. S. The ancestor. In his Living novel, 1946.

Tillett, N. S. Is Coleridge indebted to Fielding? SP 43 1946. On Biographia literaria. See also E. N. Dilworth, N & Q Jan 1958.

Cooke, A. L. Fielding and the writers of heroic romance. PMLA 62 1947.

Jenkins, E. Fielding. 1947.

Mack, E. C. Pamela's stepdaughters: the heroines of Smollett and Fielding. College Eng March 1947.

Maugham, W. S. Ten best novels: Tom Jones. Atlantic Monthly Dec 1947.

Weide, E. Fieldings Komödien und die Restaurationskomödie. Hamburg 1947.

Willcocks, M. P. A true-born Englishman: being the life of Fielding. 1947.

Renwick, W. L. Comic epic in prose. E & S 32 1946.

Touster, E. B. The literary relationship of Thackeray and Fielding. JEGP 46 1947.

Moore, R. E. Hogarth's literary relationships. Minneapolis 1948.

—— Dr Johnson on Fielding and Richardson. PMLA 66 1951.

Our immortal Fielding. TLS 24 Jan 1948.

Stephens, J. C. The verge of the court and the arrest for debt in Fielding's Amelia. MLN 63 1948.

Glättli, W. In his Die Behandlung des Affekts der Furcht im englischen Roman des 18 Jahrhunderts, Zürich 1949.

Sherwood, I. Z. The novelists as commentators. In The age of Johnson: essays presented to C. B. Tinker, New Haven 1949.

Watt, I. P. The naming of characters in Defoe, Richardson and Fielding. RES 25 1949.
— In his Rise of the novel, 1957. *See also* his Serious reflections on the Rise of the Novel, Novel 1 1968.
Work, J. A. Fielding, Christian censor. In The age of Johnson: essays presented to C. B. Tinker, New Haven 1949.
Crane, R. S. The plot of Tom Jones. Jnl of General Education 4 1950; rev as The concept of plot and the plot of Tom Jones in Critics and criticism ancient and modern, ed Crane, Chicago 1952.
Elwes, W. The Feilding album. 1950. The family to which Fielding is related.
Halsband, R. Fielding: the Hogarth of fiction. Sat Rev of Lit 30 Sept 1950.
Jackson, T. A. Pamela and Tom Jones. In his Old friends to keep, 1950.
Kermode, F. Richardson and Fielding. Cambridge Jnl Nov 1950.
Peterson, W. Satire in Fielding's An interlude between Jupiter, Juno, Apollo and Mercury. MLN 65 1950.
Willy, M. Portrait of a man: Fielding. In her Life was their cry, 1950.
Davis, J. L. Criticism and parody. Thought 26 1951. On Shamela.
Newton, W. The poetics of the rogue-ruined. Bull of Oklahoma Agricultural & Mechanical College 48 1951. On Jonathan Wild.
Rothschild, N. M. V. The history of Tom Jones, a changeling. Cambridge 1951. Report of lawsuit relating to copy of first edn.
Shipley, J. B. Fielding and the Plain truth 1740. N & Q 22 Dec 1951.
— On the date of the Champion; Essays from Fielding's Champion. N & Q Oct–Nov 1953.
— Fielding's Champion and a publisher's quarrel. N & Q Jan 1955.
— The 'M' in Fielding's Champion. N & Q June, Aug 1955.
— A new Fielding essay from the Champion. PQ 42 1963.
— Ralph, Ellys, Hogarth and Fielding. Eighteenth-Century Stud 1 1968. Reply by W. B. Coley 2 1969.
Antal, F. The moral purpose of Hogarth's art. Jnl of Warburg & Courtauld Inst 15 1952. Compares Hogarth and Fielding.
Booth, W. C. The self-conscious narrator in comic fiction before Tristram Shandy. PMLA 67 1952.
— 'Fielding' in Tom Jones. In his Rhetoric of fiction, Chicago 1961.
Brogan, H. O. Fiction and philosophy in the education of Tom Jones, Tristram Shandy and Richard Feverel. College Eng Dec 1952.
Dudden, F. H. Fielding: his life, works and times. 2 vols Oxford 1952.
Frey, B. Shaftesbury und Fielding. Berne 1952.
Goggin, L. P. Development of techniques in Fielding's comedies. PMLA 67 1952.
— Fielding and the Select comedies of Mr de Molière. PQ 31 1952.
— Fielding's The masquerade. PQ 36 1957.
Iser, W. Die Weltanschauung Fieldings. Tübingen 1952.
Knapp, L. M. Fielding's dinners with Dodington 1750–2. N & Q 20 Dec 1952.
Longhurst, J. E. Fielding and Swift in Mexico. Modern Lang Jnl 36 1952. Tom Jones not proscribed by the Inquisition 1803.
Masengill, J. A. Variant forms of Fielding's Coffeehouse politician. SB 5 1953.
Praz, M. Hogarth e Fielding. In his La casa della fama, Milan 1952.
Robertson, O. Fielding as satirist. Contemporary Rev Feb 1952. On Journey from this world to the next.
Todd, W. B. Press figures. Library 5th ser 7 1952. On the printing of Amelia.

— Three notes on Fielding. PBSA 47 1953. On An apology for the life of Mr T[heophilus] C[ibber]; A dialogue between a gentleman of London etc; and Amelia.
Baker, S. W. Fielding and Stultus versus sapientem. N & Q Aug 1953. Argues against Fielding's authorship.
— Fielding and the cliché. Criticism 1 1959.
— Fielding's The female husband: fact and fiction. PMLA 74 1959. *See* correction, N & Q Nov 1959.
— Fielding's comic romances. Papers of Michigan Acad 45 1960.
— Fielding's Amelia and the materials of romance. PQ 41 1962.
— Political allusion in Fielding's Author's farce, Mock doctor and Tumble-down Dick. PMLA 77 1962.
— Bridget Allworthy: the creative pressures of Fielding's plot. Papers of Michigan Acad 52 1967.
— Fielding and the irony of form. Eighteenth-Century Stud 2 1968.
Boas, F. S. In his An introduction to eighteenth-century drama 1700–1800, Oxford 1953.
Malone, K. Fielding's Tom Jones. In Literary masterpieces of the western world, ed F. H. Horn, Baltimore 1953.
Spilka, M. Comic resolution in Fielding's Joseph Andrews. College Eng Oct 1953.
Van Ghent, D. On Tom Jones. In her English novel, New York 1953.
Butt, J. Fielding. 1954 (Br Council pamphlet), 1959 (rev).
England, D. Fielding. Contemporary Rev Oct 1954.
Fielding. TLS 8 Oct 1954.
Greason, A. L. Fielding's An address to the electors of Great Britain. PQ 33 1954. *See* W. B. Coley 36 1957.
— Fielding's The history of the present rebellion in Scotland. PQ 37 1958.
Numéro spécial pour le 200ᵉ anniversaire de la mort d'Henry Fielding. Lettres Françaises 30 Sept–7 Oct 1954. Articles by A. Villelaur, P. Daix and R. Merle.
Stanzel, F. Tom Jones und Tristram Shandy. Eng Miscellany (Rome) 5 1954.
— Der auktoriale Roman: hauptsächlich dargestellt am Tom Jones. In his Die typischen Erzählsituationen im Roman, Vienna 1955.
Towers, A. R. Amelia and the state of matrimony. RES new ser 5 1954.
— Fielding and Dr Samuel Clarke. MLN 70 1955. A source for Amelia.
Allen, W. In his Six great novelists, 1955.
Kronenberger, L. Fielding: Tom Jones and Jonathan Wild. In his Republic of letters, New York 1955.
Pracht, E. Fielding zu Fragen der Romantheorie. Zeitschrift für Anglistik und Amerikanistik (East Berlin) 3 1955.
— Die gnoseologischen Grundlagen der Romantheorie Fieldings. Berlin 1957.
— Probleme der Entstehung des Romans. Zeitschrift für Anglistik und Amerikanistik 6 1958.
— Bittere Enttäuschung und erschütterter Optimismus in Fieldings Spätwerk? Zeitschrift für Anglistik und Amerikanistik 7 1959.
Pringle, P. Hue and cry: the story of Henry and John Fielding and their Bow Street runners. New York 1955.
Cauthen, I. B. Fielding's digressions in Joseph Andrews. College Eng April 1956.
Imbert, H.-F. Stendhal et Tom Jones. Revue de Littérature Comparée 30 1956.
Murry, J. M. In defence of Fielding. In his Unprofessional essays, 1956.
Parker, A. A. Fielding and the structure of Don Quixote. Bull of Hispanic Stud 33 1956.
Powers, L. H. The influence of the Aeneid on Fielding's Amelia. MLN 71 1956.
— Tom Jones and Jacob de la Vallée. Papers of Michigan Acad 47 1962.

Rader, R. W. Ralph Cudworth and Fielding's Amelia. MLN 71 1956.
— Thackeray's injustice to Fielding. JEGP 56 1957.
Stern, G. Fielding and the sub-literary German novel: a study of Opitz, Wilhelm von Hohenberg. Monatshefte Nov 1956.
— A German imitation of Fielding: Musäus, Grandison der Zweite. Comparative Lit 10 1958.
Coley, W. B. The authorship of An address to the electors of Great Britain. PQ 36 1957. Against Fielding's authorship.
— The background of Fielding's laughter. ELH 26 1959.
— Gide and Fielding. Comparative Lit 11 1959.
— Fielding's 'lost' law book. MLN 76 1961.
— Fielding and the two Covent-Garden journals. MLR 57 1962.
— The 'remarkable queries' in the Champion. PQ 41 1962.
— Fielding, Hogarth and three Italian masters. MLQ 24 1963.
— Fielding's two appointments to the magistracy. MP 63 1965.
— Fielding and the two Walpoles. PQ 45 1966.
— Hogarth, Fielding and the dating of the March to Finchley. Jnl of Warburg & Courtauld Inst 30 1967.
Dyson, A. E. Satiric and comic theory in relation to Fielding. MLQ 18 1957.
— Fielding: satiric and comic irony. In his Crazy fabric, 1965.
Erzgräber, W. Das Menschenbild in Fieldings Roman Amelia. Die Neueren Sprachen 6 1957.
Hunting, R. S. Fielding's revisions of David Simple. Boston Univ Stud in Eng 3 1957.
Jones, C. E. Fielding's True patriot and the Henderson murder. MLR 52 1957.
— Fielding as translator. In Langue et littérature, Paris 1961.
Shaw, E. P. A note on the temporary suppression of Tom Jones in France. MLN 72 1957. Reply by B. P. Jones 76 1961.
Shea, B. Machiavelli and Fielding's Jonathan Wild. PMLA 72 1957.
Taylor, D. Joseph as hero in Joseph Andrews. Tulane Stud in Eng 7 1957.
Wendt, A. Fielding and South's 'luscious morsel': a last word. N & Q June 1957. Reply by A. Sherbo, Sept 1957.
— The moral allegory of Jonathan Wild. ELH 24 1957.
— The naked virtue of Amelia. ELH 27 1960.
'West, Rebecca' (C. I. Andrews). The great optimist. In her Court and the castle, 1957.
Carver, W. The worlds of Tom and Tristram. Western Humanities Rev 12 1958.
Dooley, D. J. Some uses and mutations of the picaresque. Dalhousie Rev 37 1958.
Empson, W. Tom Jones. Kenyon Rev 20 1958. Reply by C. J. Rawson, N & Q Nov 1959.
Erämetsä, E. Über den englischen Einfluss auf den deutschen Wortvorrat des 18 Jahrhunderts. Neuphilologische Mitteilungen 59 1958.
Nathan, S. The anticipation of nineteenth-century ideological trends in Fielding's Amelia. Zeitschrift für Anglistik und Amerikanistik (East Berlin) 6 1958. Reply by E. Pracht 7 1959.
Sherbo, A. Fielding and Chaucer—and Smart. N & Q Oct 1958. Argues that Smart contributed to Covent-Garden Jnl.
— The time-scheme in Amelia. Boston Univ Stud in Eng 4 1960.
Tillyard, E. M. W. In his Epic strain in the English novel, 1958. On Tom Jones.
Battestin, M. C. The moral basis of Fielding's art: a study of Joseph Andrews. Middletown Conn 1959.
— Fielding's changing politics and Joseph Andrews. PQ 39 1960.

— Fielding's revisions of Joseph Andrews. SB 16 1963.
— Lord Hervey's role in Joseph Andrews. PQ 42 1963.
— Fielding and 'master Punch' in Panton Street. PQ 45 1966. Fielding as puppet-showman 1748.
— Osborne's Tom Jones: adapting a classic. Virginia Quart Rev 42 1966; rptd in Man and the movies, ed W. R. Robinson, Baton Rouge 1967. On the film of the novel.
— Fielding and Ralph Allen: benevolism and its limits as an eighteenth-century ideal. MLQ 28 1967.
— Pope's 'magus' in Fielding's Vernoniad: the satire of Walpole. PQ 46 1967.
— Tom Jones and 'his Egyptian majesty': Fielding's parable of government. PMLA 82 1967.
— Fielding's definition of wisdom: some functions of ambiguity and emblem in Tom Jones. ELH 35 1968.
— (ed). Tom Jones: a collection of critical essays. Englewood Cliffs NJ 1968. Reprints essays by F. R. Leavis, I. Watt, W. Empson, A. Wright, R. S. Crane, W. C. Booth and R. Alter.
— On the contemporary reputations of Pamela, Joseph Andrews and Roderick Random. N & Q Dec 1968.
Caliumi, G. Il romanzo di Fielding. Milan 1959.
Carroll, J. J. Fielding and the 'trunk-maker'. N & Q June 1959. Tom Jones IV. vi and Spectator no 235.
Johnson, M. The device of Sophia's muff in Tom Jones. MLN 74 1959.
— Fielding's art of fiction: eleven essays on Shamela, Joseph Andrews, Tom Jones and Amelia. Philadelphia 1961.
Loftis, J. In his Comedy and society from Congreve to Fielding, Stanford 1959.
Lynch, J. J. Structural techniques in Tom Jones. Zeitschrift für Anglistik und Amerikanistik (East Berlin) 7 1959.
McBurney, W. H. Mrs Mary Davys: forerunner of Fielding. PMLA 74 1959.
Sackett, S. J. Fielding and Pope. N & Q June 1959. See also M. C. Battestin, PQ 42 1963.
Schmidt-Hidding, W. In his Sieben Meister des literarischen Humors in England und Amerika, Heidelberg 1959.
Smith, R. A. The 'great man' motif in Jonathan Wild and the Beggar's opera. College Lang Assoc Jnl 2 1959.
Coolidge, J. S. Fielding and 'conservation of character'. MP 57 1960.
Ehrenpreis, I. Fielding's use of fiction: the autonomy of Joseph Andrews. In Twelve original essays on great English novels, ed C. Shapiro, Detroit 1960.
— Fielding: Tom Jones. 1964.
Feil, J. P. Fielding's character of Mrs Whitefield. PQ 39 1960. Letter of 3 April 1749 concerning Tom Jones.
Fleissner, R. F. Kubla Khan and Tom Jones: an unnoticed parallel. N & Q March 1960.
Harris, K. Beiträge zur Wirkung Fieldings in Deutschland 1742–92. Göttingen 1960.
Johnston, A. Fielding, Hearne and merry-andrews. N & Q Aug 1960. Proposes source for Joseph Andrews I. ii.
Jordan, R. M. The limits of illusion: Faulkner, Fielding and Chaucer. Criticism 2 1960.
Kreissman, B. Pamela-Shamela: a study of the criticisms, burlesques, parodies and adaptations of Richardson's Pamela. Lincoln Nebraska 1960.
Miller, H. K. Fielding's satire on the Royal Society. SP 57 1960.
— Essays on Fielding's Miscellanies: a commentary on volume one. Princeton 1961. Incorporates notes: Benjamin Stillingfleet's Essay on conversation 1737 and Fielding, PQ 33 1954; Fielding and Lady Mary Wortley Montagu: a parallel, N & Q Oct 1958.
— Some functions of rhetoric in Tom Jones. PQ 45 1966.
Taube, M. Tom Jones with French words and music. Southern Speech Jnl 26 1960. Comic opera of 1764.

Tichý, A. Remarks on the flow of time in the novels of Fielding. Brno Stud in Eng 2 1960.

Allott, M. A note on Fielding's Mr Square. MLR 56 1961.

Freedman, W. A. Joseph Andrews: clothing and concretization of character. Discourse 4 1961.

Johnson, E. D. H. Vanity Fair and Amelia: Thackeray in the perspective of the eighteenth century. MP 59 1961.

Lane, W. G. Relationships between some of Fielding's major and minor works. Boston Univ Stud in Eng 5 1961.

Murray, P. B. Summer, winter, spring and autumn in Tom Jones. MLN 76 1961.

Roberts, E. V. Eighteenth-century ballad opera: the contribution of Fielding. Drama Survey 1 1961.

—— Fielding's lost play Deborah, or a wife for you all (1733): consisting partly of facts and partly of observations upon them. BNYPL Nov 1962.

—— Possible additions to Airs 6 and 7 of Fielding's ballad opera The lottery 1732. N & Q Dec 1962.

—— Fielding's ballad opera The lottery 1732 and the English state lottery of 1731. HLQ 27 1963.

—— Fielding and Richard Leveridge: authorship of the Roast beef of old England. Ibid.

—— Mr Seedo's London career and his work with Fielding. PQ 45 1966.

Smith, L. W. Fielding and Mandeville: the 'war against virtue'. Criticism 3 1961.

—— Fielding and 'Mr Bayles's' Dictionary. Texas Stud in Lit & Lang 4 1962.

Tannenbaum, E. A note on Tom Jones and the Man of the Hill. College Lang Assoc Jnl 4 1961.

Dircks, R. J. Some notes on Fielding's Proposal for the poor. N & Q Dec 1962.

—— The perils of Heartfree: a sociological review of Fielding's adaptation of dramatic convention. Texas Stud in Lit & Lang 8 1966.

Eddy, D. D. The printing of Fielding's Miscellanies 1743. SB 15 1962.

Greenberg, B. L. Fielding's 'humane surgeon'. N & Q Dec 1962. Allusion in Tom Jones.

Horn, A. Social morality: Fielding. In his Byron's Don Juan and the eighteenth-century English novel, Berne 1962.

Paulson, R. (ed). Fielding: a collection of critical essays. Englewood Cliffs NJ 1962. Reprints essays by A. R. Humphreys, W. H. Rogers, I. Watt, M. Mack, M. Spilka, A. Digeon, A. Gide, A. Kettle, J. M. Murry, W. Empson, G. Sherburn and J. S. Coolidge.

—— Fielding the satirist; the anti-romanticist; the novelist. In his Satire and the novel in eighteenth-century England, New Haven 1967.

—— and T. Lockwood (ed). Fielding: the critical heritage. 1969. Anthology of 18th-century criticism.

Bliss, M. Fielding's bill of fare in Tom Jones. ELH 30 1963.

Drew, E. Tom Jones. In her Novel, New York 1963.

Plumb, J. H. Fielding and Jonathan Wild. In his Men and places, 1963.

—— Fielding: the journey through Gin Lane. Horizon 6 1964.

Rolle, D. Fielding und Sterne: Untersuchungen über die Funktion des Erzählers. Münster 1963.

Thomas, D. S. The publication of Fielding's Amelia. Library 5th ser 18 1963.

—— Fortune and the passions in Fielding's Amelia. MLR 60 1965.

Alter, R. The picaroon domesticated. In his Rogue's progress: studies in the picaresque novel, Cambridge Mass 1964. On Tom Jones.

—— On the critical dismissal of Fielding: post-Puritanism in literary criticism. Salmagundi 1 1966.

—— Fielding and the nature of the novel. Cambridge Mass 1968. Incorporates Fielding and the uses of style, Novel 1 1967.

Broich, U. Fieldings Shamela und Pamela, or the fair impostor: zwei Parodien von Richardsons Pamela. Anglia 82 1964.

Cazenave, M. A propos de Tom Jones. Nouvelle Revue Française Nov 1964.

Chandler, S. B. A Shakespeare quotation in Fielding and Manzoni. Italica 41 1964. In Tom Jones.

Ferguson, O. W. Partridge's vile encomium: Fielding and honest Billy Mills. PQ 43 1964.

Goldberg, H. Comic prose epic or comic romance: the argument of the preface to Joseph Andrews. PQ 43 1964.

—— The interpolated stories in Joseph Andrews or 'the history of the world in general' satirically revised. MP 63 1966.

—— The art of Joseph Andrews. Chicago 1969.

Kishler, T. C. Heartfree's function in Jonathan Wild. Satire Newsletter 1 1964.

McCullen, J. T. Fielding's Beau Didapper. Eng Lang Notes 2 1964.

Maxwell, J. C. Hazlitt and Fielding. N & Q Jan 1964. Parallels with Joseph Andrews, III. v. See also S. R. Swaminathan, May 1964.

Price, M. Fielding: the comedy of forms. In his To the palace of wisdom, New York 1964.

Rawson, C. J. The phrase 'legal prostitution' in Fielding, Defoe and others. N & Q Aug 1964.

—— Gentlemen and dancing-masters: thoughts on Fielding, Chesterfield and the genteel. Eighteenth-Century Stud 1 1967.

—— Tom Jones and Michael: a parallel. N & Q Jan 1967.

Sacks, S. Fiction and the shape of belief: a study of Fielding with glances at Swift, Johnson and Richardson. Berkeley 1964.

Stevick, P. T. Fielding and the meaning of history. PMLA 79 1964.

Wright, K. D. Fielding and the Theatres Act of 1737. Quart Jnl of Speech 50 1964.

Bort, B. D. Incest theme in Tom Jones. Amer N & Q Feb 1965.

Deppe, W. G. History versus romance: ein Beitrag zur Entwicklungsgeschichte und zum Verständnis der Literaturtheorie Fieldings. Münster 1965.

Haslinger, A. Die Funktion des Stadt-land-themas in Fieldings Tom Jones und Joseph Andrews. Die Neueren Sprachen March 1965.

Herman, G. Fielding defends Allworthy. Iowa Eng Yearbook no 10 1965.

Hutchens, E. N. Irony in Tom Jones. University Alabama 1965. Incorporates 'Prudence' in Tom Jones: a study of connotative irony, PQ 39 1960; Verbal irony in Tom Jones, PMLA 77 1962.

Jenkins, O. Richardson's Pamela and Fielding's 'vile forgeries'. PQ 44 1965.

Lavin, H. St C. Rhetoric and realism in Tom Jones. Kansas City Univ Rev 32 1965.

Levine, G. R. Fielding's 'defense' of the stage licensing act. Eng Lang Notes 2 1965.

—— Fielding and the dry mock: a study of the techniques of irony in his early works. Hague 1967.

Mazza, A. Coincidenze. Vita e Pensiero Jan 1965. On Promessi sposi and Tom Jones.

Roscoe, A. A. Fielding and the problem of Allworthy. Texas Stud in Lit & Lang 7 1965.

Schilling, B. Fielding's preface and Joseph Andrews; Slipslop, Lady Booby and the ladder of dependence. In his Comic spirit, Boccaccio to Thomas Mann, Detroit 1965.

Smith, J. O. Masquerade and marriage: Fielding's comedies of identity. Ball State Univ Forum 6 1965.

Smith, R. The ironic structure of Fielding's Jonathan Wild. Ibid.

Wright, A. Fielding: mask and feast. 1965. Incorporates Joseph Andrews, mask and feast, EC 13 1963.

Dolbier, M., G. D. Crothers and G. Westcott. Fielding: Tom Jones. In Invitation to learning, ed G. D. Crothers, New York 1966.

Donovan, R. A. Joseph Andrews as parody. In his Shaping vision, Ithaca 1966.

Farrell, W. J. The mock-heroic form of Jonathan Wild. MP 63 1966.

— Fielding's familiar style. ELH 34 1967.

Golden, M. Fielding's moral psychology. [Amherst] 1966.

Hopkins, R. H. Language and comic play in Fielding's Jonathan Wild. Criticism 8 1966.

Koljević, S. Fildingov Tom Dzons i ljubavna etika evropskog romana. Izraz (Sarajevo) 10 1966.

Milburn, D. J. The philosophy of wit in Fielding's Tom Jones and in Laurence Sterne's Tristram Shandy. In his Age of wit 1650–1750, 1966.

Park, W. Fielding and Richardson. PMLA 81 1966.

Preston, J. The ironic mode: a comparison of Jonathan Wild and the Beggar's opera. EC 16 1966.

— Tom Jones and 'the pursuit of true judgment'. ELH 33 1966.

— Plot as irony: the reader's role in Tom Jones. ELH 35 1968.

Spearman, D. In her Novel and society, 1966.

Taylor, D. Fielding's England. 1966.

Zirker, M. R. Fielding's social pamphlets: a study of An enquiry into the causes of the late increase of robbers and A proposal for making an effectual provision for the poor. Berkeley 1966.

— Fielding and reform in the 1750's. Stud in Eng Lit 1500–1900 7 1967.

Amory, H. Fielding's epistles to Walpole: a reexamination. PQ 46 1967.

— Two lost Fielding manuscripts. N & Q May 1967. Documents of 1737 and 1753 mentioned in auction catalogues.

Bloch, T. Bampfylde-Moore Carew and Fielding's King of the gypsies. N & Q May 1967. Reply by A. M. Fraser, Nov 1967; see also M. C. Battestin, PMLA 82 1967.

Brooks, D. Richardson's Pamela and Fielding's Joseph Andrews. EC 17 1967. See exchanges with A. M. Kearney, EC 18–19 1968-9.

— Abraham Adams and Parson Trulliber: the meaning of Joseph Andrews, book ii, chapter 14. MLR 63 1968.

— The interpolated tales in Joseph Andrews again. MP 65 1968.

Evans, D. L. The theme of liberty in Jonathan Wild. Papers on Lang & Lit (Southern Illinois Univ) 3 1967.

Carrière, M. Fielding dramaturge se veut-il moraliste. Caliban 3 1967.

Hassall, A. J. The authorial dimension in the plays of Fielding. Komos 1 1967.

Irwin, M. Fielding: the tentative realist. Oxford 1967.

Jason, P. K. Samuel Jackson Pratt's unpublished comedy of Joseph Andrews. N & Q Nov 1967.

LePage, P. V. The prison and the dark beauty of Amelia. Criticism 9 1967.

Macallister, H. Fielding. 1967.

Penner, A. R. Fielding's adaptation of Cervantes' knight and squire. Revue de Littérature Comparée 41 1967.

Price, J. V. Sex and the foundling boy: the problem in Tom Jones. REL 9 1967.

Reid, B. L. Utmost merriment, strictest decency: Joseph Andrews. Sewanee Rev 75 1967.

Rexroth, K. Tom Jones. Saturday Rev 1 July 1967.

Schneider, D. J. Sources of comic pleasure in Tom Jones. Connecticut Rev 1 1967.

Combs, W. W. The return to Paradise Hall: an essay on Tom Jones. South Atlantic Quart 67 1968.

Driskell, L. V. Interpolated tales in Joseph Andrews and Don Quixote: the dramatic method as instruction. South Atlantic Bull 33 1968.

Duncan, J. L. The rural ideal in eighteenth-century fiction. Stud in Eng Lit 1500–1900 8 1968. On Fielding, Smollett, Goldsmith and Sterne.

Edwards, P. D. Education and nature in Tom Jones and the Ordeal of Richard Feverel. MLR 63 1968.

Hatfield, G. W. Fielding and the language of irony. Chicago 1968. Incorporates Puffs and pollitricks: Jonathan Wild and the political corruption of language, PQ 46 1967; Quacks, pettyfoggers and parsons: Fielding's case against the learned professions, Texas Stud in Lit & Lang 9 1967; The serpent and the dove: Fielding's irony and the prudence theme of Tom Jones, MP 65 1967.

Hilles, F. W. Art and artifice in Tom Jones. In Imagined worlds: essays in honour of John Butt, ed M. Mack and I. Gregor 1968.

Mandel, J. The Man of the Hill and Mrs Fitzpatrick: character and narrative technique in Tom Jones. Papers on Lang & Lit (Southern Illinois Univ) 4 1968.

Rothstein, E. The framework of Shamela. ELH 35 1968.

Schonhorn, M. Fielding's digressive-parodic artistry: Tom Jones and the Man of the Hill. Texas Stud in Lit & Lang 10 1968.

Simon, I. Early themes of prose fiction: Congreve and Fielding. In Imagined worlds: essays in honour of John Butt, ed M. Mack and I. Gregor 1968.

Wolff, C. G. Fielding's Amelia: private virtue and public good. Texas Stud in Lit & Lang 10 1968.

M. C. B.

LAURENCE STERNE
1713–68

The mss of A sentimental journey vol 1 *and of* Journal to Eliza *are in BM; and Pierpont Morgan Library, New York has* A sentimental journey vols 1–2 *in a fair copy not by Sterne, as well as his Letter-book and Fragment in the manner of Rabelais. See also* W. L. Cross, Life and times of Sterne, New Haven 1929 (rev); *L. P. Curtis, Letters, Oxford 1935; and G. D. Stout (ed), A sentimental journey, Berkeley 1967.*

Bibliographies etc

A catalogue of a collection of books, among which are included the entire library of the late Sterne, which will begin to be sold on Tuesday, August 23 1768, by J. Todd and H. Sotheran. [York 1768]; ed C. Whibley 1930 (facs).

Cross, W. L. In his Life and times of Sterne, New Haven 1929 (rev).

Cordasco, F. Sterne: a list of critical studies published from 1896 to 1946. Brooklyn 1948.

Fluchère, H. In his Sterne, Paris 1961.

Hartley, L. Sterne in the twentieth century: an essay and a bibliography of Sternean studies 1900–65. Chapel Hill 1966, 1968 (corrected).

The following lists of edns do not aim at completeness after 1800:

Collections

Works. 5 vols 1769, 1773, 1774, 5 and 6 vols Philadelphia 1774, 7 vols Dublin 1770, 1774, 8 vols Dublin 1774–6, 5 vols Dublin 1775, 7 vols 1775, 7 and 8 vols Dublin 1779, 5 and 10 vols 1780, 5 and 7 vols Dublin 1780, 7 and 10 vols 1783, 8 vols 1784, 10 vols 1788, 5, 8 and 10 vols 1790, 5 and 10 vols 1793, 8 vols 1794, 1795, 10 vols 1798, Perth 1798, 8 vols 1799, Edinburgh 1799, Berwick 1800, 7 and 10 vols 1802, 4 and 8 vols 1803, 8 vols Glasgow 1803, 5 vols Harrisburg 1804–5, 4 vols 1808, 7 vols 1810, 6 vols New York 1813–14, 4 vols 1815, 1819, 1823, 6 vols 1823, 1833, 1 vol Philadelphia 1839, London 1839, 1847, Philadelphia 1848 (illustr Darley, rptd), 2 vols 1857, New York 1859, 1 vol New York 1860, London [1868], 1869 (Globe edn); ed D. Herbert, Edinburgh 1872; ed J. P. Browne 4 vols 1873, 1885; ed G. Saintsbury 6 vols 1894 (illustr E. J. Wheeler); ed W. L. Cross 12 vols New York 1904; ed Cross 12 vols Cambridge Mass 1906 (illustr) (Jenson Soc); 7 vols Oxford 1926–7 (Shakespeare Head edn); tr French, 1787.

A sentimental journey; Letters from Yorick to Eliza; A letter to Eugenius. Dublin 1776.

A sentimental journey; Letters from Yorick to Eliza; Letters to his friends; History of a watch-coat. Dublin 1780.

A sentimental journey; Appendix containing several pieces written by the author of the Sentimental journey. 2 vols Vienna 1795, 1798.

Select works. 8 vols Vienna 1798.

A sentimental journey; Letters from Yorick to Eliza. Paris 1800 (Didot, stereotype edn), 1811, 1817, 1822.

A sentimental journey; Appendix containing several pieces by the author of the Sentimental journey; Letters from Yorick to Eliza. Paris 1802.

Novels; prefatory memoir [by Sir W. Scott]. 1823 (in Ballantyne's Novelist's Lib vol 5).

The life and opinions of Tristram Shandy; A sentimental journey. 2 vols 1832 (illustr Cruikshank).

The life and opinions of Tristram Shandy; A sentimental journey; A political romance; A fragment in the manner of Rabelais; Memoirs. 2 vols 1900. With bibliographical note by A. W. Pollard.

A sentimental journey, with selections from the journals, sermons and correspondence. Ed W. L. Cross, New York 1926, 1942.

A sentimental journey; Journal to Eliza. Ed G. Saintsbury 1926 (EL); ed D. George [1960] (EL).

Novels. 4 vols [1926] (illustr Cruikshank) (Navarre Soc).

Memoirs; The life and opinions of Tristram Shandy; A sentimental journey; Selected sermons and letters. Ed D. Grant 1950 (Reynard Lib).

A sentimental journey; Journal to Eliza; A political romance. Ed I. Jack, Oxford 1968.

Selections

The beauties of Sterne. 1782 (several edns), 1783 (7th edn), Dublin 1784 (8th edn), London 1785 (8th edn), 1787 (10th edn), Philadelphia 1789 (10th edn), 1790, London 1790 (11th edn), Philadelphia 1791, Boston 1793 (11th edn, 2 issues), London 1793 (12th edn), 1799 (13th edn), Dublin 1802, Boston 1807, London 1809 (illustr Rowlandson), 1810, 1811, Amsterdam 1836, London 1905; tr French, [1800]; Russian, 1801.

The whole story of the sorrows of Maria, selected from various works of Sterne. Salem 1793, Boston 1793.

Gleanings from the works of Sterne. 1796.

The stories of Le Fevre, of poor Maria and of the dead ass. New London Conn 1806.

Extracts from the Tristram Shandy and Sentimental journey of Sterne. Poughnill nd, Stourport 1812. In the multi-volume ser Literary miscellany or selections and extracts.

Frammenti scelti delle opere di Sterne. Chieti 1836.

Other vols of (or containing) selections or extracts:

New universal story-teller. [Ed S. J. Pratt] [1777?].

Select English pieces in prose and poetry. 4 vols Upsala 1792-8.

The literary miscellany. 2 vols Philadelphia 1795.

The selector: or miscellaneous pieces from the best English authors. 1798.

The speaker: or miscellaneous pieces selected from the best English writers by W. Enfield. Liverpool 1804.

Elegant extracts from classical English authors, collected by J. C. Frick. Vol 1, Erlangen 1804.

Classic tales, serious and lively. [Ed Leigh Hunt] vol 5, 1807.

Fiori e glorie della letteratura inglese offerti nelle due lingue inglese ed italiana da M. Mazzoni. 2 vols Milan 1844.

§ I

Various contributions to newspapers (see L. P. Curtis, The politicks of Sterne, Oxford 1929), of which the following are known in separate printings:

A paragraph taken from the York-Courant, June 9th 1741. Broadside.

To the Rev Mr James Scott at Leeds. [1741]. Broadside.

Query upon query: being an answer to J.S.'s letter printed in the York-Courant, October 20. York 1741; also in York Courant 27 Oct 1741, Daily Gazetteer 28 Oct 1741, Leeds Mercury 3 Nov 1741.

An answer to J.S.'s letter, address'd to a freeholder of the county of York. [1741]. Broadside; also in York Courant 10 Nov 1741.

The unknown world: verses. GM July 1743; rptd Scots Mag July 1743, Ladies Mag 10 Aug 1751; T. Gill, Vallis eboracensis, 1852, pp. 199-200; set to music in The hymns, anthems and tunes with the ode used at the Magdalen Chapel, [c. 1765] (etc).

Dialogue ('How imperfect the joys of the soul'). In Joseph Baildon's Collection of new songs sung at Ranelagh, [c. 1765] and The laurel: a collection of English songs bk 2 (New Musical Mag no 93) [c. 1785]. For authorship *see* Cross, Life and times of Sterne, New Haven 1929, pp. 218-19.

On a lady's sporting a somerset. 4-line epigram attributed to Sterne in Muse's mirrour, 2 vols 1778.

The dream, to Mr Cook. Ptd as Fragment inédit by P. Stapfer, Sterne: sa personne et ses ouvrages, Paris 1870.

Sermons

The case of Elijah and the widow of Zerephath. York 1747.

The abuses of conscience. York 1750.

The sermons of Mr Yorick. Vols 1-2, [1760], 1760 (2nd and 3rd edns), Dublin 1760, London 1761 (4th edn), 1 vol Dublin 1761, London 1763 (5th edn vol 1), 1764 (5th edn vol 2, 6th edn vols 1-2), 1765 (7th edn), [1766?] ('new edn'), 1 vol Dublin 1766 ('3rd edn'), London 1767 (8th edn), 1768 (9th edn), 1771 (10th edn), 1773 (11th edn), 1775 (12th edn), 1777 ('new edn'); vols 3-4, 1766, Dublin 1766, London 1767, 1768 ('new edn'), 1770 ('new edn'), 1773 ('new edn'); vols 5-7, 1769 (2 edns) (as Sermons by the late Rev Mr Sterne).

Vols 1-4, 1 vol (4 pts) Dublin 1767 (pts 1-2, '3rd edn', pts 3-4 '4th edn', pt 2 dated 1766); vols 1-7, 2 vols 1769, (6 pts) Dublin 1775; vols 3-7, 4 vols 1776; vols 1-7, 1 vol (7 pts) Altenburg 1777, 6 vols 1777; vols 3-7, 4 vols 1779 ('new edn'); vols 1-7, 6 vols 1784 ('new edn'), 3 vols 1784, 2 vols (6 pts) 1785, 1 vol 1787, 2 vols 1794; tr Dutch, 1779, French, 1770, 1786 (Sermons choisis); German, 1766-73; Italian, 1831.

3 sermons rptd in The practical preacher, 1762; *2 in* The English preacher, 1773.

A political romance addressed to — — esq of York. York 1759 (rptd W. L. Cross, Club of Odd Volumes, Boston 1914), London 1769. Rptd in collections as The history of a good warm watch-coat.

The life and opinions of Tristram Shandy, gentleman. Vols 1-2, [York] 1760, London 1760 (3 edns), 1 vol (2 pts) Dublin 1760 ('3rd edn'), London 1763 (5th edn), 1767 (6th edn); vols 3-4, 1761, 1761, 1 vol (2 pts) Dublin 1761; vols 5-6, 1762, 1767 (2nd edn, 3 settings of vol 5); vols 7-8, 1765, 1765; vol 9, 1767, Dublin 1767; vols 1-4, 1 vol Dublin 1761, 1765 ('2nd edn'); vols 5-8, 1 vol Dublin '1765'; vols 1-9, 3 vols '1760'-67.

Vol 1, 1768 (7th edn); vols 3-4, 1768 ('new edn'); vol 2, 1769 (7th edn); vols 3-4, 6, 1769 ('new edn'); vols 1-9, 2 vols 1769, 6 vols 1770 (vols 1-2 8th edn); vol 2, 1772 (9th edn); vols 4-6, 1772 ('new edn'); vols 1-9, 6 vols Altenburg 1772, London 1773 (vol 1 9th edn, vol 3 'new edn'), 3 vols 1774, 6 vols 1775 (vols 1-2 10th edn), 2 vols Dublin 1776 ('4th edn'), 6 vols 1777, 2 vols ('5th edn') and 3 vols 1779, 3 vols Dublin 1779, 2 vols 1780, 6 vols 1781, 1 vol 1781 (Novelists Mag, illustr Stothard), 3 and 6 vols 1782, 3 vols 1786, 1 vol 1791 (Novelists Mag, illustr Stothard), 2 vols Basle 1792, Gotha 1792, 2 and 6 vols London

1793, 3 vols 1794, 4 vols Vienna 1798, 2 vols Basle 1803, Leipzig 1849 (Tauchnitz), 2 vols 1883 (illustr Furniss); ed H. Morley 1884; ed C. Whibley 2 vols 1894 (Henley's Eng Classics); ed W. Jerrold 1899 (Temple Classics); Oxford 1903 (WC); ed W. L. Cross 4 vols New York 1904; ed G. Saintsbury 1914 (EL); ed Cross, New York 1925; ed J. B. Priestley 1928 (illustr J. Austen); Waltham St Lawrence 3 vols 1929–30 (Golden Cockerel, illustr Laboureur); ed C. Morley 2 vols New York 1935 (Limited Edns Club, illustr T. M. Cleland); ed J. A. Work, New York 1940 (with commentary); ed P. C. Quennell 1948 (Chiltern Lib, illustr Cruikshank); ed J. C. Powys 1949; ed S. H. Monk, New York 1950; ed G. Weales, New York [1960]; ed A. D. McKillop 1962; ed I. Watt, Boston 1965; ed G. Petrie, introd by C. Ricks 1967 (Penguin); tr German, 1763–7; Dutch, 1776–9; French, 1776–85, 1784 (extracted as Nouveau voyage en France); Danish, 1794; Russian, 1804; Italian, 1829 (selections); Hungarian, 1956; Czech, 1963; Japanese, 1966; Rumanian, 1969. *See also Collections, above.*

A sentimental journey through France and Italy, by Mr Yorick. 2 vols 1768 (3 edns), Dublin 1768, 1768, [Boston] 1768, Dublin 1769, 1 vol (4 pts) 1769, 2 vols 1770, 1 vol (2 pts) [Philadelphia] 1770, 2 vols 1771, 1 vol (2 pts) Leipzig 1771, Altenburg 1771, 2 vols 1773, 1774, 1 vol (4 pts) 1774, 2 pts Dublin 1775, 4 pts 1775, 2 pts Altenburg 1776, 2 vols 1778, 1 vol Göttingen 1779, 2 vols 1780, 1780, 1782, 1 vol 1782, 1782 (Novelists Mag no 9, illustr), [1782], [1782], 2 vols 1783, 1 vol Paris 1783, 1783, 4 pts 1784, 1784, 2 pts [1787?], Göttingen 1787, London 1790, 1790, Philadelphia 1790, London 1791, 1791, Philadelphia 1791, London 1792 (illustr Stothard), 4 pts 1792, 2 pts Norwich Conn 1792, Basle 1792, 2 pts Worcester Mass 1793, London 1794 (3 edns), Halle 1794, New York 1795, London '1795' (illustr Newton), New York 1796, Basle 1800, Lund 1800, Dublin [1800?], [London 1800?] (Henshall's Pocket Lib), London 1801 (illustr Stothard), 1803, 1804 (illustr Austin), Edinburgh 1806 (illustr Campbell), London 1809 (illustr Rowlandson), Brattleboro Vermont [1810], Philadelphia [c. 1810], [c. 1810], Copenhagen 1815, Chiswick 1821, London 1826 (Jones's Diamond Classics), New York 1827 (illustr), London [1839] (illustr Jacque and Fussell), [1859] (illustr Johannot), 1882 (illustr Hédouin), 1885 (illustr Leloir), 1894 (Guillaume's Nelumbos); ed W. Jerrold 1899 (Temple Classics); ed H. Paul 1902; ed F. Bickley [1922]; 1927 (illustr Vera Willoughby); Waltham St Lawrence 1928 (Golden Cockerel, illustr Laboureur; ed V. Woolf, Oxford 1928 (WC); Paris 1929 (Black Sun Press, illustr Polia Chentoff); London 1929 (illustr V. Angelo); ed H. Read 1929; ed W. L. Cross, High Wycombe 1936 (Limited Edns Club, illustr Tegetmeier); 2 vols Stamford Conn 1936; 1 vol 1938 (Penguin, illustr G. Raverat); ed P. G. Gaye 1948 (Camden Classics, illustr Marian), ed O. Warner 1949 (Folio Soc, illustr N. Lambourne); ed G. Petrie, introd by A. Alvarez 1967 (Penguin); ed G. D. Stout, Berkeley 1967; ed P. F. Kirby, Milan 1968; tr German, 1768 (by Bode), 1769 (by Mittelstedt), 1801 (by Benzler); French, 1769 (by Frénais), 1788 (by Michel), 1801 (by Crassous), 1828 (by Moreau-Christophe), 1841 (3 trns by Defauconpret, Janin, Wailly), 1866 (by Fournier), 1875 (by Hédouin), 1884 (by Blémont): bilingual edns, Aix 1796, Paris 1796, 2 vols (4°) and 3 vols (18°) Paris [1799/1800] (illustr Monsiau), 3 vols Strasbourg 1800; Danish, 1775 (by Birch), 1841 (by Magnus); Dutch, 1778 (by Brunius), 1837 (by Geel); Swedish, 1790–1; Italian, 1792 (by Vianello), 1813 (by Foscolo); Russian, 1793; Hungarian, 1815; Polish, 1817, 1845; Spanish, 1821, 1843 (illustr Jacque and Fussell), 1890; Czech, 1903; Serbocroat, 1926; Japanese, 1947. *See also Collections, above; and for continuations see Sterneana, below.*

Letters

Letters from Yorick to Eliza. 1773, Philadelphia 1773, London 1775 (6 edns of which 3 are 'a new edn'), Dublin 1775, Burlington NJ 1792, Manchester 1794; with Letters from Eliza to Yorick (fictitious), Montego Bay 1786, Vienna 1795, 1797, Giessen 1802, London 1807, 1815; tr German, 1775; French, 1776; Russian, 1789; Italian, 1792; Swedish, 1797; Hungarian, 1815, 1828. *See also Collections, above.*

Sterne's Letters to his friends on various occasions, to which is added his History of a watch coat. 1775, 1775, Dublin 1775; tr German, 1775. 12 letters, of which 8 are fabrications presumably by William Combe. *See also Collections, above.*

Letters of the late Rev Mr L. Sterne to his most intimate friends, with a fragment in the manner of Rabelais; to which are prefix'd memoirs of his life and family written by himself, published by his daughter Mrs Medalle. 3 vols 1775, 1776, 1 vol (3 pts) Dublin 1776, Altenburg 1776, 3 vols Philadelphia 1778, 1 vol 1794; tr German, 1776.

Letters from Yorick to Eliza, Letters on various occasions. Dublin 1776, Altenburg 1776; Letters from Yorick to Eliza, Letters on various occasions, Letters to his most intimate friends, 1790; Letters from Yorick to Eliza, Letters on various occasions, Letters to his most intimate friends, An appendix of xxxii letters, i.e. Original letters of the late Rev Mr L. Sterne, 1788 (*see Supposititious Works, below*) 2 vols Vienna 1797.

In Elegant epistles, [ed V. Knox] 1790 etc.

Seven letters written by Sterne and his friends, hitherto unpublished. Ed W. D. Cooper 1844.

Unpublished letters of Sterne. In Miscellanies of the Philobiblon Soc vol 2, 1855–6.

Sterne's letter to the Rev Mr Blake. St Louis 1915. Priv ptd from original in possession of W. K. Bixby.

Letters, selected. Ed R. B. Johnson 1927.

Letters. Ed L. P. Curtis, Oxford 1935, 1965. Includes all attributable letters previously pbd with addns, and Journal to Eliza. For new letters *see* MLN 66 1951, 76 1961; Virginia Quart Rev 30 1954; TLS 8 April 1965, 14 March 1968.

Supposititious Works

The life and opinions of Tristram Shandy. Vol 3, 1760. Spurious. By J. Carr.

The life and opinions of Tristram Shandy. Vol 9, 1766, 1766. Spurious.

Murray, J. Sermons to asses. 1768. Attributed to Sterne in German trns (Reden an Esel), 1769, 1795.

The posthumous works of a late celebrated genius deceased. 2 vols 1770, 1775, Philadelphia 1778, London 1785, Vienna 1795, 1798; tr German, 1771, 1778. By R. Griffith. Also entitled The Koran.

La quinzaine angloise à Paris: ouvrage posthume du docteur Stearne. Londres 1776; tr (but without attribution to Sterne) 1777. By J. J. Rutledge.

Letters supposed to have been written by Yorick and Eliza. 2 vols 1779, 1780, (2 pts) Dublin 1780, Savannah 1787, Burlington 1792; tr German, 1780. By W. Combe, but accepted as genuine and ed M. R. B. Shaw, Second journal to Eliza, 1929.

Original letters of the late Rev Mr L. Sterne. 1788, Dublin 1788; tr French, 1788, 1789. 39 letters, of which 3 or 4 may be substantially genuine, fabricated by W. Combe.

Versifications

Timbury, J. The story of Le Fevre put into verse. 1797.
Verses in:

On beneficence: a poetical essay. 1764.

Clark, E. Miscellaneous poems. Whitehaven 1779.

Air-balloon: or Blanchard's triumphal entry into the etherial world. [1785].

A collection of poems, by a young lady. Rochester 1792.

Tasset, A. Le voyage sentimental suivi de fragments d'un premier voyage en France par L. Sterne, traduits en vers français. Paris 1866.

Collin D'Harleville, J. F. L'Anglais à Montreuil: traduction littérale d'un chapitre du Voyage sentimental de Sterne. In Almanach des muses, 1789, and in various edns of his Works.

Dramatizations

MacNally, L. Tristram Shandy: a sentimental Shandean bagatelle in two acts. 1783, 1783.

Forbin, A. and P. H. Révoil. Sterne à Paris, ou le voyageur sentimental: comédie mêlée de vaudevilles. Paris [1799/1800].

Dunlap, W. Sterne's Maria, or the vintage: opera produced in New York 1799. Not pbd, but 3 songs ptd in Yankee doodle-doo, ed G. Vernon, New York 1927. *See also* below, Songs: music by J. Moulds.

Songs

Music by M. Arne:
2 songs ('Let eloquence boast of her pow'r', 'What tho' my tongue did never move') sung at the performance of L. MacNally's play Tristram Shandy. 1783.

Music by Thomas Billington:
Maria's evening service. [c. 1790].
Sterne's soliloquy on hearing Maria. [c. 1795].

Music by William Carnaby:
Yorick at the grave of Maria. [c. 1795].

Music adapted from Haydn:
Yorick's fille de chambre. [c. 1785].

Music by John Moulds:
Moulines Maria ('Twas near a thicket's calm retreat', also entitled Sterne's Maria). [c. 1785] (3 edns), Dublin [c. 1785], [c. 1785], 1791; in The whole story of the sorrows of Maria, Boston 1793, The American musical miscellany, Northampton Mass 1798, The American mock-bird, New York 1801, The temple of harmony, Baltimore 1801, The vocal medley, Alexandria Virginia 1801, S. Larkin, The nightingale, Portsmouth NH 1804 (2 versions); incorporated in W. Dunlap's unpbd opera Sterne's Maria: or the vintage, produced in New York in 1799.
Sterne at the tomb of Moulines Maria. [c. 1790].
The starling. [c. 1790].
The peasant. [c. 1795].
The handkerchief. [c. 1795].
La Fleur. [c. 1796].

Anon:
Tristram Shandy ('Have you not read a book call'd Tristram Shandy, ma'am'). [1760?].
Tristram Shandy's ghost ('Her eyes like liquid flint arise'). [c. 1775].
Maria's urn, as sung at the Dillitanti concerts, supposed to be set to music by Sterne. [c. 1790].

Other Sterneana to 1800

excluding imitations (but not professed continuations) of Sentimental Journey

Two lyric epistles: on to my cousin Shandy. 1760. By J. Hall-Stevenson.

Explanatory remarks upon the Life and opinions of Tristram Shandy, by Jeremiah Kunastrokius. 1760.

The clockmakers outcry against the author of The life and opinions of Tristram Shandy. 1760 (4 edns).

The history of Tom Fool. 2 vols 1760. Dedicated to Tristram Shandy.

A letter from one of the jolly sons of Comus to the author of Tristram Shandy. 1760.

Dialogues of the living, by Littleton Shandy. 1760.

Tristram Shandy in a reverie. 1760.

The cream of the jest: or the wits out-witted, dedicated to poor Yorick. 1760.

Tristram Shandy's bon mots, repartees, odd adventures and humorous stories. 1760.

The life and opinions of Miss Sukey Shandy. 1760.

Tristram Shandy at Ranelagh. 1760.

The life and opinions of Jeremiah Kunastrokius. 1760.

Yorick's meditations upon various subjects. 1760, Dublin 1760; tr German, 1769.

A supplement to the Life and opinions of Tristram Shandy, by the author of Yorick's meditations. 1760.

A Shandean essay on human passions, by Caleb McWhim. 1760.

Whitfield, G. A letter to the Rev L. Sterne, the supposed author of the Life and opinions of Tristram Shandy. 1760, 1761.

A genuine letter from a Methodist preacher in the country to L. Sterne. 1760.

Tristram Shandy ('Early one summer morning, it was down by Portsmouth ferry O!'). [1760?]. Slip ballad.

Ways to kill care: a collection of original songs, written by young D'Urfey. 1761. By F. Forrest. Dedicated to Tristram Shandy.

Explanatory remarks upon the third and fourth volumes of the Life and opinions of Tristram Shandy. Vol 2, by the author of the first. 1761.

The life and opinions of Bertram Montfichet. 2 vols [1761].

A funeral discourse occasioned by the death of Mr Yorick, by Christopher Flagellan. 1761, 'Aretopolis' 1761.

An admonitory letter to the Rev Mr S— upon the publication of his fifth and sixth volumes of Tristram Shandy, by a layman. 1761.

Jack and his whistle; to which is added a paper dropt from Tristram Shandy's pocket-book. Edinburgh 1762.

Tristram Shandy's description of general elections and septennial parliaments. Dublin 1762.

The life, travels and adventures of Christopher Wagstaff, grandfather to Tristram Shandy. 2 vols 1762, 1763. Based on John Dunton, Voyage round the world, 1691.

The life and amours of Hafen Slawkenbergius. 1762.

Miss C—y's cabinet of curiosities, or the green room broke open, by Tristram Shandy gent. 'Utopia' 1765.

A sentimental dialogue between two souls, in the palpable bodies of an English lady of quality and an Irish gentleman. [1768]. Signed Tristram Shandy. By J. Hall-Stevenson.

Occasional verses on the death of Mr Sterne. 1768.

Sentiments on the death of the sentimental Yorick, by one of Uncle Toby's illegitimate children. 1768.

Veni, vidi, vici, ivi: or he's gone! Who? Yorick! 1768.

Yorick's Sentimental journey continued, by Eugenius [J. Hall-Stevenson?]. First ptd in unauthorized edns of A sentimental journey 1769, subsequently in edns of 1774, 1775, 1782, 1784, 1784, 1790, 1791, 1792, Basle 1792, London 1794, New York 1795, 1796, Basle 1800; separately pbd 1902 (Georgian Soc).

Sentimental lucubrations, by Peter Pennyless. 1770, Dublin 1770, Philadelphia 1793; tr German, 1770.

Yorick turned trimmer. [1770?].

An humble tribute to the memory of Mr Sterne, by a lady. 1775.

Letters from Eliza to Yorick. 1775, 1775, 1801; tr German, 1775.

Yorick's skull: or College oscitations, by the author of A monstrous good lounge. 1777.

The Shandymonian. 1779, 1779.

A familiar epistle to Roger Kenyon esq in memory of Sterne, by Rowley Thomas. Shrewsbury 1779, 1785 (3rd edn as The frolics of fancy: a familiar epistle characteristic of Tristram Shandy).

Sterne's witticisms: or Yorick's convivial jester. [1782].

Unfortunate sensibility: or the life of Mrs L****, written by herself in a series of sentimental letters, dedicated to Mr Yorick in the Elysian fields. 1784.

Gorgy, J. C. Nouveau voyage sentimental, par M. de Gorjy (sous le nom d'Yorik). 1784; tr Russian, 1794.

The Whitsun donative: being a hasty sketch of an intended publication under the title of the Life and opinions of Tristram's papa. 1787.

Continuation of Yorick's Sentimental journey. 1788.

Dunlap, W. The father, or American Shandyism: a comedy. New York 1789. Later edns as The father of an only child.

The letters of Maria, to which is added an account of her death. 1790; tr German, 1791.

Gorgy, J. C. Ann'quin Bredouille: ou Le petit cousin de Tristram Shandy. 6 vols Paris 1791–2.

Tableau sentimental de la France depuis la révolution, par Yoryck sous le nom de Sterne, pour servir de suite au Voyage sentimental. Londres 1792.

A sentimental journey intended as a sequel to Mr Sterne's, by Mr Shandy. Southampton 1793; tr German, 1794; Swedish, 1797.

Fragments in the manner of Sterne [by I. Brandon]. 1797, 1798, Leipzig nd (as The lady's and gentleman's pocket-book); tr French, 1799; tr German, 1800.

Sterne's Maria, with an account of her death at the castle of Valerine. [1800?].

§2

Baster, W. An essay on rheumatism; to which are added observations on the medical treatment of Sterne during his last illness. 1776, Devizes 1776.

Ferriar, J. Illustrations of Sterne. 1798, 2 vols 1812.

Whyte, D. The fallacy of French freedom and dangerous tendency of Sterne's writings. 1799.

Scott, W. Prefatory memoir to Sterne. Ballantyne's Novelist's Lib 5 1823; rptd in his Lives of the novelists, ed A. Dobson 1906 (WC).

Coleridge, S. T. In his Literary remains vol 1, 1836.

Sterne. Dublin Univ Mag 8 1836.

Thackeray, W. M. In his English humourists of the eighteenth century, 1853.

Elwin, W. Sterne. Quart Rev 94 1854. Review article with Sterne inédit, tr A. Hédouin.

Bagehot, W. Sterne and Thackeray. Nat Rev 18 1864; rptd in his Collected works, ed N. St John Stevas vol 2, 1965.

Fitzgerald, P. The life of Sterne. 2 vols 1864, 1896; rptd by W. L. Cross in Works of Sterne, New York 1904; 1906. An earlier version pbd as Sterne and his day, Dublin Univ Mag 60–2 1862–3.

Hill, A. S. Laurence Sterne. North Amer Rev 107 1868.

Stapfer, P. Sterne: sa personne et ses ouvrages. Paris 1870.

Gibbs, T. W. Some memorials of Sterne. Bath [1878]. See Athenaeum 30 March 1878.

Stephen, L. Sterne. Cornhill Mag July 1880; rptd in his Hours in a library vol 3, 1892.

Traill, H. D. Sterne. 1882 (EML).

Merwin, H. C. The philosophy of Sterne. Atlantic Monthly Oct 1894.

Hewins, W. A. S. The Whitefoord papers. Oxford 1898. Anecdotes of Sterne.

Baker, T. S. The influence of Sterne upon German literature. Americana Germanica 2 1899.

Czerny, J. Sterne, Hippel und Jean Paul. Berlin 1904.

Heinrich, F. Sterne und Edward Bulwer. Buttstädt 1904.

More, P. E. In his Shelburne essays ser 3, New York 1905.

Thayer, H. W. Sterne in Germany. New York 1905.

— Thümmel's Reise and Sterne. MLN 24 1909.

Cross, W. L. The life and times of Sterne. New York 1909, 2 vols New Haven 1925, 1 vol 1929 (rev with addns).

— Sterne in the twentieth century. Yale Rev 15 1926.

Woolf, V. Sterne. TLS 12 Aug 1909; rptd in her Granite and rainbow, 1958.

— Eliza and Sterne. TLS 14 Dec 1922; rptd ibid.

— The sentimental journey. In her Common reader ser 2, 1932; rptd from her WC edn, 1928.

'Melville, Lewis' (L. S. Benjamin). The life and letters of Sterne. 2 vols 1910.

Sichel, W. Sterne: a study, to which is added the Journal to Eliza. 1910.

Williams, H. Sterne, sentimentalist. Westminster Rev 174 1910.

Barton, F. B. Etude sur l'influence de Sterne en France au dix-huitième siècle. Paris 1911.

— Sterne and Charles Nodier. MP 14 1917.

— Sterne and Théophile Gautier. MP 16 1919.

Rabizzani, G. Lorenzo Sterne. Genoa 1914.

— Sterne in Italia. Rome 1920.

Hughes, H. S. A precursor of Tristram Shandy. JEGP 17 1918.

Pinger, W. R. R. Sterne and Goethe. Berkeley 1920.

Shklovsky, V. Tristram Shendi: Sterna i teoriya romana. Petrograd 1921.

— Evgeny Onegin: Pushkin i Stern. Berlin 1923.

Birrell, A. In his Collected essays and addresses vol 1, 1922.

Wright, A., and W. L. Sclater. Sterne's Eliza. 1922.

De Froe, A. Sterne and his novels in the light of modern psychology. Groningen [1925].

Pottle, F. A. Bozzy and Yorick. Blackwood's Mag March 1925.

Priestley, J. B. The brothers Shandy. In his English comic characters, 1925, 1963.

Bensly, E. Sterne and Lord Aboyne. N & Q 23 Jan 1926.

Ollard, S. L. Sterne as a young parish priest. TLS 18 March 1926.

— Sterne as parish priest. TLS 25 May, 1 June 1933.

Curtis, L. P. Sterne and 'sentimental'. TLS 23 June 1927.

— The printer of Sterne's Political romance. TLS 28 Feb 1929.

— The politicks of Sterne. Oxford 1929.

— Sterne in Bond-Street. TLS 24 March 1932.

— The first printer of Tristram Shandy. PMLA 47 1932.

— Forged letters of Sterne. PMLA 50 1935.

— New light on Sterne. MLN 76 1961.

Glaesener, H. Sterne et Xavier de Maistre. Revue de Littérature Comparée 7 1927.

Read, H. Laurence Sterne. TLS 26 May 1927; rptd in his Sense of glory, Cambridge 1929; Collected essays in literary criticism, 1938.

— Alas, poor Yorick! In his Contrary experience, 1963.

Shaw, M. R. B. Sterne's 'Letters to his wife'. TLS 21 July 1927.

— Letters of Sterne. TLS 6 June 1935.

— Sterne: the making of a humorist 1713–62. 1957.

Klingemann, G. Goethes Verhältnis zu Sterne. Marburg 1929.

Tompkins, J. M. S. Triglyph and Tristram. TLS 11 July 1929.

Gallaway, W. F. Boswell and Sterne. Letters 5 1931.

Muir, E. Laurence Sterne. Amer Bookman 73 1931; rptd in his Essays on literature and society, 1949.

Reitzel, W. Cobbett and Sterne. TLS 10 Dec 1931.

Brown, H. R. Richardson and Sterne in the Massachusetts Magazine. New England Quart 5 1932.

— In his Sentimental novel in America 1789–1860, Durham NC 1940.

Behrmann, F. Samuel Paterson and Sterne. N & Q 7 Oct 1933.

— Sterne und sein Einfluss auf die englische Prosa des achtzehnten Jahrhunderts. Lachen 1936.

Baird, T. The time-scheme of Tristram Shandy and a source. PMLA 51 1936.

Hallamore, G. J. Das Bild Sternes in Deutschland. Berlin 1936.

Maack, R. Sterne im Lichte seiner Zeit. Hamburg 1936.

MacLean, K. In his John Locke and English literature of the eighteenth century, New Haven 1936.

— Imagination and sympathy: Sterne and Adam Smith. JHI 10 1949.

Urbahn, T. Die Geste in Sternes Tristram Shandy. Britannica 12 1936.

Greene, G. Fielding and Sterne. In From Anne to Victoria, ed B. Dobrée 1937; rptd in his Lost childhood, 1951.

Pressly, I. P. In her A York miscellany, 1938.

Vertsman, I. Lorens Stern. Literaturny Kritik July 1938.

Buisman-de Savornin Lohman, F. L. W. M. Sterne en de Nederlandse schrijvers van c. 1780–1840. Wageningen 1939.

Watkins, W. B. C. In his Perilous balance: the tragic genius of Swift, Johnson and Sterne, Princeton 1939, Cambridge Mass 1960.

Putney, R. D. S. The evolution of A sentimental journey. PQ 19 1940.

— Alas, poor Eliza! MLR 41 1946.

— Sterne's Eliza. TLS 9 March 1946.

— Sterne: apostle of laughter. In The age of Johnson: essays presented to C. B. Tinker, New Haven 1949; rptd in Eighteenth-century English literature: modern essays in criticism, ed J. L. Clifford, New York 1959.

Lehman, B. H. Of time, personality, and the author: a study of Tristram Shandy. In Studies in the comic, Berkeley 1941.

Hartley, L. This is Lorence: a narrative of the Reverend Laurence Sterne. Chapel Hill 1943.

— Tristram and the angels. College Eng 9 1948.

— From Crazy Castle to the House of Usher. Stud in Short Fiction 2 1965.

— Sterne and the eighteenth-century stage. Papers on Lang & Lit 4 1968.

— The Eustace-Sterne correspondence. Eng Lang Notes 5 1968.

Eaves, T. C. D. George Romney: his Tristram Shandy paintings and trip to Lancaster. HLQ 7 1944.

Pearce, R. H. Sterne and sensibility in American diaries. MLN 59 1944.

Sclater, W. L. Letters addressed by Eliza Draper to the Strange family 1776–8. N & Q 22 April, 6 May 1944, 1–29 July 1944.

Connolly, C. Sterne and Swift. Atlantic Monthly June 1945.

Quennell, P. C. In his Four portraits, 1945. First pbd Horizon Nov–Dec 1943, July 1944.

Russell, H. K. Tristram Shandy and the technique of the novel. SP 42 1945; rptd in Studies in language and literature, ed G. R. Coffman, Chapel Hill 1945.

Yoseloff, T. A fellow of infinite jest. New York 1945, London 1948 (as Sterne, a fellow of infinite jest).

Laird, J. Shandean philosophy. In his Philosophical incursions into English literature, Cambridge 1946.

Yorick at Yale. Yale Univ Lib Gazette 20 1946.

Lang, D. M. Sterne and Radishchew. Revue de Littérature Comparée 21 1947.

Seidlin, O. Sterne's Tristram Shandy and Thomas Mann's Joseph the provider. MLQ 8 1947; rptd in his Essays in German and comparative literature, Chapel Hill 1961.

Varese, C. Linguaggio sterniano e linguaggio foscoliano. Florence 1947.

Watson, W. The fifth commandment: some allusions to Sir Robert Filmer's writings in Tristram Shandy. MLN 62 1947.

Dilworth, E. N. The unsentimental journey of Sterne. New York 1948.

Hammond, L. Van der H. Sterne's Sermons of Mr Yorick. New Haven 1948.

Lamborn, E. A. G. Great Tew: a link with Sterne. N & Q 27 Nov 1948.

Yoklavich, J. M. Notes on the early editions of Tristram Shandy. PMLA 63 1948.

Monk, S. H. Sterne at Princeton. Princeton Univ Lib Chron 10 1949.

Brunskill, E. Eighteenth-century reading: some notes on the people who frequented the library of York Minster. York 1950.

Macaffee, C. H. G. The obstetrical aspects of Tristram Shandy. Ulster Medical Jnl 19 1950.

Thompson, K. F. The authorship of Yorick's Sentimental journey continued. N & Q 22 July 1950.

Booth, W. C. Did Sterne complete Tristram Shandy? MP 48 1951.

— Thomas Mann and eighteenth-century comic fiction. Furioso 6 1951.

— The self-conscious narrator in comic fiction before Tristram Shandy. PMLA 67 1952.

— In his Rhetoric of fiction, Chicago 1961.

Boys, R. C. Tristram Shandy and the conventional novel. Papers of Michigan Acad 37 1951.

Cornu, D. Shandy in America. N & Q 23 June 1951.

Erämetsä, E. In his A study of the word 'sentimental' and of other linguistic characteristics of eighteenth-century sentimentalism in England, Helsinki 1951.

Jefferson, D. W. Tristram Shandy and the tradition of learned wit. EC 1 1951.

— Laurence Sterne. 1954 (Br Council pamphlet).

Wasserman, E. R. Unedited letters by Sterne, Hume and Rousseau. MLN 66 1951.

— Byron and Sterne. MLN 70 1955.

Mendilow, A. A. In his Time and the novel, 1952.

Monkman, K. An annotated copy of Sterne's Sentimental journey. Antiquarian Booksellers Assoc Annual 1952.

— Some new Sterne letters. TLS 6 May 1965.

— and J. Diggle. Yorick and his flock: a new Sterne letter. TLS 14 March 1968.

Monkman, K. The bibliography of the early editions of Tristram Shandy. Library 5th ser 25 1970.

Oates, J. C. T. On collecting Sterne. Book Collector 1 1952.

— Notes on the bibliography of Sterne, I: Letters from Eliza to Yorick, 1775; II: Letters from Yorick to Eliza, 1775. Trans of Cambridge Bibl Soc 2 1958.

— Shandyism and sentiment. Cambridge 1968. Bicentenary lecture.

Price, L. M. Sterne and the sentimental novel. In his English literature in Germany, Berkeley 1953.

Pritchett, V. S. Tristram Shandy. In his Books in general, 1953.

Van Ghent, D. On Tristram Shandy. In her English novel: form and function, New York 1953.

McKillop, A. D. The reinterpretation of Sterne. Etudes Anglaises 7 1954.

— In his Early masters of English fiction, Lawrence Kansas 1956.

Shepperson, A. B. Yorick as ministering angel. Virginia Quart Rev 30 1954.

Stanzel, F. K. Tom Jones und Tristram Shandy. Eng Miscellany (Rome) 5 1954.

Traugott, J. Tristram Shandy's world: Sterne's philosophical rhetoric. Berkeley 1954.

— (ed). Sterne: a collection of critical essays. New York 1968.

Cash, A. H. The Lockean psychology of Tristram Shandy. ELH 22 1955.

— The sermon in Tristram Shandy. ELH 31 1964.

— Some new Sterne letters. TLS 8 April 1965.

— Sterne's comedy of moral sentiments. Pittsburgh 1966.

— Who was Sterne's mother? N & Q May 1967.

— The birth of Tristram Shandy. In Studies in the eighteenth century, ed R. F. Brissenden, Canberra 1968.

— and J. M. Stedmond (ed). The winged skull: papers from the Sterne bicentenary conference. Kent Ohio 1971.

Corbellini, M. La versione foscoliana de Viaggio di Sterne. Ulisse 9 1955.

Fredman, A. G. Diderot and Sterne. New York 1955.

Harper, K. E. A Russian critic [V. Shklovsky] and Tristram Shandy. MP 52 1955.

Legnani, E. S. L'avventura milanese di Sterne con la 'Marquesina di F***' fu 'fabbricata di pianta'. Eng Miscellany (Rome) 6 1955.

Sallé, J. C. A source of Sterne's conception of time. RES new ser 6 1955.

Hicks, J. H. The critical history of Tristram Shandy. Boston Univ Stud in Eng 2 1956.

Milic, L. T. Sterne and Smollett's Travels. N & Q Feb 1956.

— A Sterne letter re-dated. N & Q May 1956.

Reid, B. L. The sad hilarity of Sterne. Virginia Quart Rev 32 1956.

— Sterne and the absurd homunculus. Virginia Quart Rev 43 1967.

Speaight, G. Battles and raree-shows. N & Q March 1956.

Brown, R. C. Sterne and Virginia Woolf. Univ of Kansas City Rev 26 1959.

Stedmond, J. M. Uncle Toby's 'campaigns' and raree-shows. N & Q Jan 1956.

— Genre and Tristram Shandy. PQ 38 1959.

— Sterne as plagiarist. E Studies 41 1960.

— Satire and Tristram Shandy. Stud in Eng Lit 1500–1900 1 1961.

— The comic art of Sterne. Toronto 1967.

Holland, N. N. The laughter of Sterne. Hudson Rev 9 1957.

Rawson, C. J. Two notes on Sterne. N & Q June 1957.

— Tristram Shandy and Candide. N & Q May 1958.

Towers, A. R. Sterne's cock and bull story. ELH 24 1957.

Brown, T. J. Laurence Sterne. Book Collector 7 1958.

Carver, W. The worlds of Tom [Jones] and Tristram [Shandy]. Western Humanities Rev 12 1958.

Connely, W. Sterne as Yorick. 1958.

Findeisen, H. Lorenzo-Kult in Seifersdorf. Zeitschrift für Anglistik und Amerikanistik 6 1958.

Howes, A. B. Yorick and the critics: Sterne's reputation in England 1760–1868. New Haven 1958.

Kleinstück, J. Zur Form und Methode des Tristram Shandy. Archiv 194 1958.

Meyer, H. Zitat und Plagiat im Tristram Shandy. In Amor librorum: a tribute to A. Horodisch, Amsterdam 1958.

— In his Das Zitat in der Erzählkunst, Stuttgart 1961; tr as The poetics of quotation in the European novel, Princeton 1968.

Reeve, F. D. Through hell on a hobby-horse: notes on Gogol and Sterne. Symposium 13 1959.

Cook, A. S. Reflexive attitudes: Sterne, Gogol, Gide. Criticism 2 1960; rptd in his Meaning of fiction, Detroit 1960.

Jackson, W. A. The curse of Ernulphus. Harvard Lib Bull 14 1960.

Kaufman, P. Mr Yorick and the Minster Library. N & Q Aug 1960.

— A true image of Sterne. BNYPL Dec 1962.

Parish, C. A table of contents for Tristram Shandy. College Eng 22 1960.

— The nature of Mr Tristram Shandy, author. Boston Univ Stud in Eng 5 1961.

Tave, S. M. In his Amiable humorist: a study in the comic theory and criticism of the eighteenth and early nineteenth centuries, Chicago 1960.

Ulanov, B. Sterne and Fielding: the allegory of irony. In his Sources and resources: the literary traditions of Christian humanism, Westminster Maryland 1960.

Weales, W. Tristram Shandy's anti-book. In Twelve original essays on great English novels, ed C. Shapiro, Detroit 1960.

Wedel, E. L. N. Tolstojs Übersetzung von Sternes A sentimental journey. Welt der Slaven 5 1960.

Burckhardt, S. Tristram Shandy's law of gravity. ELH 28 1961.

Fluchère, H. Sterne: de l'homme à l'oeuvre. Paris 1961;

tr and abridged as Sterne from Tristram to Yorick, Oxford 1965.

Piper, W. B. Tristram Shandy's digressive artistry. Stud in Eng Lit 1500–1900 1 1961.

— Tristram Shandy's tragi-comical testimony. Criticism 3 1961.

— Laurence Sterne. New York 1966.

Dyson, A. E. Sterne: the novelist as jester. Critical Quart 4 1962; rptd in his Crazy fabric: essays in irony, 1965.

Kroeger, F. P. Uncle Toby's pipe and whistle. Papers of Michigan Acad 47 1962.

McCormick, C. A. Foscolo's two theories of translation and the version of the Sentimental journey. AUMLA 18 1962.

Mayo, R. D. The imitators of Sterne. In his English novel in the magazines 1740–1815, Evanston 1962.

Mayoux, J.-J. Sterne parmi nous. Critique 18 1962.

Michelsen, P. Sterne und der deutsche Roman des achtzehnten Jahrhunderts. Göttingen 1962.

Griffin, R. J. Tristram Shandy and language. College Eng 23 1962.

Pons, C. Sterne ou le génie de l'humeur. Cahiers du Sud no 367 1962.

Rauter, H. Eine Anleihe Sternes bei George Herbert. Anglia 80 1962.

Tuveson, E. Locke and Sterne. In Reason and the imagination: studies in the history of ideas 1600–1800, ed J. A. Mazzeo, New York 1962.

Wickler, F. J. Rabelais und Sterne. Bonn 1962.

Farrell, W. J. Nature versus art as a comic pattern in Tristram Shandy. ELH 30 1963.

Fasano, P. L'amicizia Foscolo-Sterne e la traduzione didimea del Sentimental journey. Eng Miscellany (Rome) 14 1963.

Hall, J. J. The hobbyhorsical world of Tristram Shandy. MLQ 24 1963.

Landa, L. A. The Shandean homunculus. In Restoration and eighteenth-century literature: essays in honor of A. D. McKillop, Chicago 1963.

Rolle, D. Fielding und Sterne. Münster 1963.

Stout, G. D., jr. Yorick's Sentimental journey: a comic Pilgrim's progress for the Man of feeling. ELH 30 1963.

— Sterne's borrowings from Bishop Hall's Quo vadis? Eng Lang Notes 2 1965.

— Some borrowings in Sterne from Rabelais and Cervantes. Eng Lang Notes 3 1966.

Brandi-Dohrn, B. Der Einfluss Sternes auf Jean Paul. Munich 1964.

Brissenden, R. F. Sterne and painting. In Of books and humankind: essays and poems presented to B. Dobrée, ed J. Butt 1964.

Lockridge, E. H. A vision of the sentimental absurd: Sterne and Camus. Sewanee Rev 72 1964.

Price, M. Sterne: art and nature. In his To the palace of wisdom, Garden City NY 1964.

Ridgeway, A. Two authors in search of a reader. James Joyce Quart 1 1964.

Warning, R. Fiktion und Wirklichkeit in Sternes Tristram Shandy und Diderots Jacques le fataliste. In Nachahmung und Illusion, ed H. R. Jauss, Munich 1964.

— Illusion und Wirklichkeit in Tristram Shandy und Jacques le fataliste. Munich 1965.

Chatterjee, A. Dramatic technique in Tristram Shandy. Indian Jnl of Eng Stud 6 1965.

Johnson, M. A comic homunculus before Tristram Shandy. Lib Chron 31 1965.

Kuist, J. M. New light on Sterne: an old man's recollection of the young Vicar. PMLA 80 1965.

Ricks, C. The novelist as innovator: Sterne. Listener 11 Feb 1965; rptd in The novelist as innovator, ed W. Allen 1965.

Grebeníčková, R. La méthode de Sterne (Sternianstvo) dans le roman russe avant Dostoievski. In Proc of 4th Congress of International Comparative Lit Assoc (Paris) 1966.

Hnatko, E. Tristram Shandy's wit. JEGP 65 1966.

Holtz, W. Time's chariot and Tristram Shandy. Michigan Quart Rev 5 1966.

—— Yorick and the Rotary Club. Yale Univ Lib Gazette 41 1967.

—— The journey and the picture: the art of Sterne and Hogarth. BNYPL Jan 1967.

—— Pictures for parson Yorick. Eighteenth-Century Stud 1 1968.

James, O. P. The relation of Tristram Shandy to the life of Sterne. Hague 1966.

Miller, D. M. The reader-characters in Tristram Shandy. Mankato State College Stud 1 1966.

Rudy, P. Young Lev Tolstoj's acquaintance with Sterne's Sermons and Griffith's The Koran. Slavic & East European Jnl 4 1966.

Stobie, M. Walter Shandy: generative grammarian. Humanities Assoc Bull 17 1966.

Theobald, D. W. Philosophy and imagination: an eighteenth-century example. Personalist 47 1966.

Alvarez, A. The delinquent aesthetic. Hudson Rev 19 1967; rptd in A sentimental journey, ed G. Petrie 1967.

Anderson, H. A version of pastoral: class and society in Tristram Shandy. Stud in Eng Lit 1500–1900 7 1967.

—— Sterne's letters: consciousness and sympathy. In The familiar letter in the eighteenth century, ed H. Anderson, P. B. Daghlian and I. Ehrenpreis, Lawrence Kansas 1966.

—— Associationism and wit in Tristram Shandy. PQ 48 1969.

Giddey, E. Le jeu de la découverte et du sentiment dans Tristram Shandy. Etudes de Lettres 10 1967.

Goodin, G. The comic as a critique of reason: Tristram Shandy. College Eng Dec 1967.

Hafter, R. Garrick and Tristram Shandy. Stud in Eng Lit 1500–1900 7 1967.

Hamilton, H. W. William Combe and the Original letters of the late Reverend Mr Sterne 1788. PMLA 82 1967; rptd Times Saturday Rev 20 April 1968 (abridged).

Harvey, J. H. A lost link with Sterne. Yorks Archaeological Jnl 42 1967.

Paulson, R. In his Satire and the novel in eighteenth-century England, New Haven 1967.

Petrie, G. Note on the novel and the film: flashbacks in Tristram Shandy and the Pawnbroker. Western Humanities Rev 21 1967.

Ryan, M. Sterne and Hogarth's Analysis of beauty. N & Q Nov 1967.

Skoumal, A. Sternovské stopy v díle K. H. Máchy. In Realita slova Máchova, ed F. Grebeníčková, O. Králík, Prague 1967.

Thomson, J. E. P. The morality of Sterne's Yorick. AUMLA 27 1967.

Wagoner, M. S. Satire of the reader in Tristram Shandy. Texas Stud in Lit & Lang 8 1967.

Watt, I. The comic syntax of Tristram Shandy. In Studies in criticism and aesthetics 1660–1800: essays in honor of S. H. Monk, Minneapolis 1967.

Alter, Robert. Tristram Shandy and the game of love. Amer Scholar 37 1968.

Duncan, J. L. The rural ideal in eighteenth-century fiction. Stud in Eng Lit 1500–1900 8 1968.

Rousseau, G. S. Harvard's holdings in Sterne. Harvard Lib Bull 16 1968.

Singleton, M. K. Deduced knowledge as Shandean nub. Zeitschrift für Anglistik und Amerikanistik 16 1968.

—— Trismegistic tenor and vehicle in Sterne's Tristram Shandy. Papers on Lang & Lit 4 1968.

Stewart, J. F. Romantic theories of humor relating to Sterne. Personalist 49 1968.

Doherty, F. Sterne and Hume: a bicentenary essay. E & S new ser 22 1969.

Downey, J. The eighteenth-century pulpit: a study of the sermons of Butler, Berkeley, Secker, Sterne, Whitefield and Wesley. Oxford 1969.

Fabian, B. Sterne-Tristram Shandy. In Der englische Roman vom Mittelalter zur Moderne, Düsseldorf 1969.

New, M. Two notes on Sterne. N & Q Sept 1969.

—— Sterne and Swift: sermons and satire. MLQ 30 1969.

—— Sterne as satirist: a reading of Tristram Shandy. Gainesville 1969.

Simmen, E. Sterne's A political romance: new locations, new copies. N & Q Sept 1969.

J. C. T. O.

TOBIAS GEORGE SMOLLETT
1721–71

For mss see Letters ed L. M. Knapp, Oxford 1970.

Bibliographies

Anderson, J. P. In D. Hannay, Life of Smollett, 1887.

Cordasco, F. Smollett criticism 1925–45. New York 1947; Smollett criticism 1770–1924, New York 1948.

Isaacs, J. H. In Roderick Random, Peregrine Pickle and Humphry Clinker, 1895.

Joliat, E. Bibliographie des traductions de Smollett. In his Smollett et la France, Paris 1935.

Boege, F. W. Smollett's reputation as a novelist. Princeton 1947.

Newman, F. B. Bibliographical problems connected with the first edition of Humphry Clinker. PBSA 44 1950.

Collections

Select works. 8 vols Dublin 1775–6.

Miscellaneous works. 6 vols Edinburgh 1790.

Works. 10 vols 1793–4.

Miscellaneous works. Ed R. Anderson 6 vols Edinburgh 1796, 1800, 1806, 1811, 1817, 1820.

Works. Ed J. Moore 8 vols 1797.

Miscellaneous works. 5 vols Edinburgh 1809, 6 vols Dublin 1816, 12 vols 1824.

Select works. 2 vols Philadelphia 1833, 1836.

Ausgewählte humoristische Romane. 15 vols Stuttgart 1839–41, 6 vols Stuttgart 1846.

Miscellaneous works. Ed T. Roscoe 1841, 1844, 1845, 1849, 1851, 1852, 1853, 1856, 1858, 1860, 1887, 1889.

Works. Ed D. Herbert 1870, 1871, 1872, 1873, 1876, 1881, 1883, 1903.

Works. Ed J. P. Browne 8 vols 1872.

Works. Ed W. E. Henley and T. Seccombe 12 vols 1899–1901.

Works. Ed G. Saintsbury 12 vols 1889–1900, 1895, 1900–3, 1902, [1925].

Works. Ed G. H. Maynadier 12 vols New York 1902, 1905, 1907, 1911.

Novels. 2 vols 1810 Novelists, ed W. Mudford, vols 1–2).

Novels. 2 vols 1821 (Ballantyne's Novelist's Lib vols 2–3).

Novels. 6 vols 1884, 1890, 1890–2, 1894.

Novels. 11 vols Oxford 1925–6.

Plays and poems. 1777, 1784, 1796.

§ I

The tears of Scotland. In The land of cakes, c. 1746; in Thrush, 1749; in Craftsman, c. 1750; in Mitre and Crown, 1750, and in The Union, ed T. Warton 1753, 1759, 1766. In A collection of the most esteemed pieces of poetry, 1767; and The beauties of English poesy, ed O. Goldsmith 1767.

Advice: a satire. 1746, 1748 (with Reproof, below).

Reproof: a satire. 1747, 1748 (with Advice).

The adventures of Roderick Random. 2 vols 1748, 1748 (frontispieces by F. Hayman and C. Grignion), Dublin 1748–9, London 1750, 1752, 1754, Dublin 1755, London 1762, 1760, 1763, 1764, 1766, Dublin 1768, London 1769, 1770, Dublin 1773, London 1774, 1775. 1777, 1778, Edinburgh 1778, London 1780, 1781, Novelist's Mag 2 1781, 1783 (illustr R. Dodd); 2 vols

1784, Edinburgh 1784, 1791, Dublin 1791 (abridged), London 1792; illustr T. Rowlandson and A. M. Stadler 2 vols 1793; 2 vols Philadelphia 1794, 1794 etc; Gotha 1805; ed J. H. Isaacs 1895 (Bohn's Lib illustr G. Cruikshank); ed H. W. Hodges [1927] (EL); Oxford [1930] (WC); tr French, 1751, 1782, 1784, 1786, 1948, 1964; German, 1754, 1755, 1790, 1805, 1915; Danish, 1802–3; Dutch, 1805; Polish, 1956; Estonian, 1957.

The regicide, or James the First of Scotland: a tragedy. 1749 (by subscription), 1749, Dublin 1749.

The adventures of Peregrine Pickle, in which are included Memoirs of a lady of quality. 4 vols 1751, 3 vols Dublin 1751, 4 vols 1758 (rev), 1765, Dublin 1768–9, 1769 (frontispieces by H. Fuseli and C. Grignion), 1773, 1776, 1778, 3 vols Edinburgh 1779, 4 vols 1781 (illustr T. Stothard); Novelist's Mag 6 1781, 1782, 1792; 4 vols 1784 (illustr R. Dodd), Edinburgh 1793, [1794] (illustr R. Corbould and J. Allen), 1805 (illustr T. Rowlandson), 3 vols Harrisburg Pennsylvania 1813 etc; ed J. H. Isaacs 2 vols 1895; 2 vols New York [1929], London [1930] (EL), New York 1936 (Limited Edns Club); ed J. L. Clifford, Oxford 1964; tr French, 1753, 1776, 1787, 1799; German, 1753, 1769, 1785, 1789, 1917, [1966]; Danish, 1787, 1797–1817, 1833, 1884; Russian, 1788 (first 35 chs), 1934, 1955; Dutch, 1815.

An essay on the external use of water in a letter to Dr ****, with particular remarks upon the present method of using the mineral waters at Bath in Somersetshire and a plan for rendering them more safe, agreeable and efficacious. 1752, 1767, 1770; ed C. E. Jones, Baltimore 1935.

The adventures of Ferdinand Count Fathom. 2 vols 1753 (ptd for W. Johnston), 1753 (pirated?; ptd for T. Johnson), Dublin 1753, London 1760, 1771, Dublin 1772, London 1780, 1782; Novelist's Mag 7 1782 (illustr T. Stothard); 2 vols 1789, [1795] (illustr R. Corbould), 1796 etc; ed E. Boyd, New York 1926; tr German, 1770–1, 1803; Italian, 1791; French, 1798.

The reprisal, or the tars of Old England: a comedy of two acts. 1757 ('printed for R. Baldwin'), 1757 (pirated?; 'printed for Paul Vaillant'), 1758, Dublin 1757, London 1761, Belfast 1767, London 1774, 1776.

The life and adventures of Sir Launcelot Greaves. Br Mag Jan 1760–Dec 1761 (serially); 2 vols 1762, 1 vol Dublin 1762, 1763, 1769, 1783, Cork 1767, 2 vols 1774, 1780, 1782; Novelist's Mag 9 1782 (illustr T. Stothard); 2 vols 1783, Edinburgh 1783, London 1793, [1793] (illustr R. Corbould), 1796, Liverpool [1800] (in Mirror of amusement); tr German, 1772, 1791; Danish, 1790; French, 1824.

The history and adventures of an atom. 2 vols 1749 (for 1769), Dublin 1769, Edinburgh 1784, London 1786; Novelist's Mag 21 1786 (illustr R. Corbould); 2 vols [1795].

A complete history of England, deduced from the descent of Julius Caesar to the Treaty of Aix la Chapelle 1748: containing the transactions of one thousand eight hundred and three years. 4 vols 1757–8, 11 vols 1758–60 etc; tr French, 19 vols 1759–64. Often rptd as a continuation of Hume's History.

Continuation of the Complete history of England. 4 vols 1760–1; vol 5, 1765.

Travels through France and Italy: containing observations on character, customs, religion, government, police, commerce, arts and antiquities, with a particular description of the town, territory and climate of Nice; to which is added a register of the weather, kept during a residence of eighteen months in that city. 2 vols 1766, 1766, Dublin 1766, 1772, London 1767, 1769, 1778; ed W. F. Mavor (in General collection of voyages and travels vol 17, 1813); ed T. Seccombe, Oxford [1907] (WC); ed O. Sitwell [1949]; 1968; tr German, 1767.

The expedition of Humphry Clinker. 3 vols 1771 (vol 1, '1671') (several issues), 2 vols Dublin 1771, 3 vols 1772, 2 vols Dublin 1774, 3 vols 1681 (for 1781), 2 vols Dublin 1781, 3 vols 1683 (for 1783), 2 vols 1784, Dublin 1784, 1785, London 1685 (for 1785), 1785; Novelist's Mag 19 1785 (illustr E. F. Burney); 2 vols 1788, Edinburgh 1788, Leith 1788, Dublin 1790, 3 vols 1792, 1793 (illustr T. Rowlandson), Dublin 1793, London 1793, 1795, Boston 1813 etc; ed J. H. Isaacs 1895; ed L. Rice-Oxley, Oxford [1925] (WC); ed A. Machen, New York [1929]; ed H. M. Jones and C. Lee 1943 (EL); ed R. G. Davis [1950]; ed V. S. Pritchett 1954; ed L. M. Knapp, Oxford 1966; ed A. Ross [1967] (Penguin); ed A. Parreaux 1968; tr German, 1772, 1775, 1785; Dutch, 1779, 1780; Russian, 1789, 1953; Danish, 1796–8; French, 1826, 1955; Swedish, 1855; Czech, 1909.

Ode to independence. Glasgow 1773, London 1774; Pennsylvania Mag July 1776; Glasgow 1794; in Poetry original and selected, Glasgow 1796.

Editions etc by Smollett

Smellie, W. A treatise on the theory and practice of midwifery. 1751.
— A collection of cases and observations in midwifery. 1754.
— A collection of preternatural cases and observations in midwifery. 1764.

Drummond, A. Travels through different cities of Germany, Italy, Greece and several parts of Asia. 1754.

A compendium of authentic and entertaining voyages, digested in a chronological series. 7 vols 1756. Vol 5 includes Smollett's An account of the expedition against Carthagene, besieged by the English in the year 1741.

The modern part of an universal history, by the authors of the ancient part. 44 vols 1759–66.

The present state of all nations: containing a geographical, natural, commercial and political history of all the countries in the known world. 8 vols 1768–9.

Uncertain Attributions

A faithful narrative of the base and inhuman arts that were lately practised upon the brain of Habbakkuk Hilding, justice, dealer and chapman, who now lies at his house in Covent-Garden in a deplorable state of lunacy, by Drawcansir Alexander. 1752. An attack on Henry Fielding.

The orientalist: a volume of tales after the Eastern taste, by the author of Roderick Random, Sir Launcelot Greaves etc and others. Dublin 1764, 1769, 1773.

Wonderful prophecies, particularly those worthy of notice by Richard Brothers and a memorable prophecy of Dr Smollet, just before his death. 1795 (3rd edn enlarged).

Wonderful prophecies: among which are Dr Smollet's celebrated letter. 1795 (5th edn), [1795?] (6th edn).

Translations

The adventures of Gil Blas of Santillane. 4 vols 1748 (no known copy), 1749, 1750, Dublin 1759, 1767, London 1761, 1764, 1766, 1768, Edinburgh 1771, 1773, London 1773, 1778, 1780, 1781; Novelist's Mag 4 1781; 4 vols 1782, 1785, Dublin 1785, London 1789, 1792, 1794, 1797. Numerous edns after 1800; ed J. Fitzmaurice-Kelly 2 vols Oxford [1907] (WC); ed J. B. Priestley 2 vols 1937 (Limited Edns Club).

The history and adventures of the renowned Don Quixote, translated from the Spanish of Miguel De Cervantes Saavedra. 2 vols 1755 (illustr Francis Hayman), 4 vols 1761 (corrected), 1765, Dublin 1765, London 1770, 1782; Novelist's Mag 8 1782; 4 vols 1786, 1792, 1793, 1794, 1795, Dublin 1796, Philadelphia 1803.

Select essays on commerce, agriculture, mines, fisheries and other useful subjects. 1754.

The works of M. de Voltaire, translated from the French, with notes, historical and critical, by Dr Smollet and others. 38 vols 1761–74, 39 vols 1761–74 etc; Arouet edition, 22 vols 1927 (rev with additional trns by W. F. Fleming).

The adventures of Telemachus, the son of Ulysses, translated from the French of Messire François Salignac de la Mothe-Fenelon, Archbishop of Cambray. 2 vols 1776, Dublin 1777, 1793, London 1786, 1787, 1792.

Select essays: containing the manner of raising and dressing flax and hemp, collected from the Dictionary of arts and sciences. Philadelphia 1777. Several of the essays probably by Smollett.

Periodicals

Monthly Review 1751–2. For Smollett's contributions, see B. C. Nangle, The Monthly Review first series 1749–89: indexes of contributors and articles, Oxford 1934.

Critical Review: or Annals of Literature, by a Society of Gentlemen. Jan–Feb 1756–Dec 1790. Smollett was doubtless editor-in-chief and contributed many reviews until 1763, and a few after.

British Magazine: or Monthly Repository for Gentlemen and Ladies. 8 vols Jan 1760–Dec 1767. Vols 1–2 contain the first pbn of Launcelot Greaves.

Briton. 29 May 1762–12 Feb 1763.

Letters

Letters. Ed E. S. Noyes, Cambridge Mass 1926.

Noyes, E. S. Another Smollett letter. MLN 42 1927.

Knapp, L. M. Smollett's Works as printed by William Strahan, with un unpublished letter of Smollett to Strahan. Library 3rd ser 13 1932.

— More Smollett letters. MLN 48 1933.

— An important Smollett letter. RES 12 1936.

— Smollett's letter to Philip Miller. TLS 24 June 1944.

— Smollett's letter to Samuel Mitchelson. N & Q June 1956.

— Another letter from Smollett to Dr William Hunter. N & Q Aug 1960.

— The letters of Smollett. Oxford 1970.

Jones, C. E. A Smollett letter. MLN 50 1935. To William Huggins.

Meikle, H. W. New Smollett letters. TLS 24–31 July 1943. 7 letters to Dr Alexander Carlyle.

Powell, L. F. William Huggins and Smollett. MP 34 1936. Letters of Smollett to Huggins and Gatehouse.

Letters of Smollett: a supplement to the Noyes collection. Ed F. Cordasco, 'Madrid' 1950. Contains 31 letters, 5 pbd for the first time: letters 19, 26, 29–31. The authenticity of these 5 questioned by L. M. Knapp and L. de la Torre, PQ 30 1951; see also 31 1952, where Cordasco admits them to be forgeries.

§2

Henderson, A. A second letter to Samuel Johnson, with an impartial character of Doctor Smollett. [c. 1775].

Tytler, A. F. (Lord Woodhouselee). Essay on the principles of translation. 1791. Ch 12 compares Smollett's trn of Don Quixote with those by Jarvis and Motteux.

Anderson, R. The life of Smollett. In A complete edition of the poets of Great Britain vol 10, 1795. Rev and enlarged versions of this Life appeared in Anderson's edns of Miscellaneous works, 1796, 1800, 1806, 1811, 1817, 1820.

— The life of Smollett. 1796, Edinburgh 1803, 1806.

Moore, J. The life of Smollett. In his edn of Works of Smollett vol i, 1797.

Hazlitt, W. In his Lectures on the English comic writers, 1819.

Scott, W. A memoir of the life of Smollett. Prefixed to

Novels of Smollett in Ballantyne's Novelist's Lib vol 2, 1821.

Thackeray, W. M. In his English humourists of the eighteenth century, 1853.

[Hannay, J.] Tobias Smollett. Quart Rev 103 1858.

Irving, J. Some account of the family of Smollett of Bonhill; with a series of letters, hitherto unpublished, written by Smollett. Dumbarton 1859.

Chambers, R. Smollett: his life and a selection from his writings. 1867.

Wershoven, F. Smollett et Lesage. Berlin 1883.

Hannay, D. Life of Smollett. 1887.

Dobson, A. The typography of Humphry Clinker. In his Eighteenth-century vignettes: second series, 1894.

Smeaton, O. Tobias Smollett. Edinburgh [1897].

Seccombe, T. Smelfungus goes South. Cornhill Mag Aug 1901.

Burton, R. The vigorous Dr Smollett. Dial 32 1902.

Leuschel, M. Autobiographisches in Smolletts Roderick Random. Leipzig 1903.

Ford, D. Admiral Vernon and the Navy. 1906.

Robinson, C. N. The British tar in fact and fiction. 1909.

Fischer, A. Autobiographisches in Smolletts Humphry Clinker. Coburg 1913.

Chancellor, E. B. Smollett as a traveller. Fortnightly Rev March 1921.

Cross, W. L. Smollett two centuries after. Literary Rev 1 1921.

Pottle, F. A. A North Briton extraordinary. N & Q 11 Oct, 6 Dec 1924.

Buck, H. S. A study in Smollett, chiefly Peregrine Pickle, with a complete collation of the first and second editions. New Haven 1925.

— Smollett as poet. New Haven 1927.

— A Roderick Random play 1748. MLN 43 1928.

— Smollett and Dr Akenside. JEGP 31 1932.

— A new Smollett anecdote. MLN 47 1932.

Drinker, C. Doctor Smollett. Annals of Medical History 7 1925.

Whitridge, A. Smollett: a study of his miscellaneous works. [1925].

'Melville, Lewis' (L. S. Benjamin). The life and letters of Smollett. [1926].

Noyes, E. S. A note on Peregrine Pickle and Pygmalion. MLN 41 1926.

Read, H. In his Reason and romanticism, 1926.

McKillop, A. D. Notes on Smollett. PQ 7 1928.

— Smollett's first comedy. MLN 45 1930.

— In his Early masters of English fiction, Lawrence Kansas 1956.

Ellison, L. M. Elizabethan drama and the works of Smollett. PMLA 44 1929.

Knapp, L. M. Ann Smollett, wife of Tobias Smollett. PMLA 45 1930.

— Smollett's verses and their musical settings in the eighteenth century. MLN 41 1931.

— A rare satire on Smollett. TLS 8 Oct 1931.

— Smollett and Le Sage's The Devil upon crutches. MLN 47 1932.

— A sequel to Humphry Clinker. TLS 6 Oct 1932.

— Elizabeth Smollett, daughter of Smollett. RES 8 1932.

— Smollett's Works as printed by William Strahan. Library 3rd ser 13 1932.

— The naval scenes in Roderick Random. PMLA 49 1934.

— The publication of Smollett's Complete history and Continuation. Library 3rd ser 16 1935.

— Smollett and the case of James Annesley. TLS 28 Dec 1935.

— Smollett's friend Smith. TLS 9 Oct 1943.

— Rex versus Smollett: more data on the Smollett-Knowles libel case. MP 41 1944.

— Smollett and the elder Pitt. MLN 59 1944.

— Smollett and Garrick. In Elizabethan studies in honor of G. F. Reynolds, Boulder 1945.

—— Smollett? doctor of men and manners. Princeton 1949.
—— Smollett's self-portrait in the expedition of Humphry Clinker. In The age of Johnson: essays presented to C. B. Tinker, New Haven 1949.
—— and L. de la Torre. Smollett and Fizes. MLN 67 1952.
Knapp, L. M. Forged 'Smollett' letters. N & Q April 1953.
—— Abridgements of Smollett for children. N & Q Nov 1954.
—— and L. de la Torre. Smollett, MacKercher and the Annesley claimant. Eng Lang Notes 1 1963.
Knapp, L. M. The keys to Smollett's Atom. Eng Lang Notes 2 1964.
—— The prophecy attributed to Smollett. RES new ser 16 1965.
—— Comments on Smollett by the Rev Dr Thomas Birch. N & Q June 1965.
—— Smollett's translation of Fénelon's Télémaque. PQ 44 1965.
—— Early Scottish attitudes toward Smollett. PQ 45 1966.
—— Smollett and Johnson, never cater-cousins? MP 66 1968.
Lawrence, A. L'influence de Lesage sur Smollett. Revue de Littérature Comparée 12 1932.
Purcell, J. M. A note on Smollett's language. MLN 47 1932.
—— A note on Smollett's language. TLS 14 April 1932.
—— Smollett on oats as food for Scots. PMLA 53 1938.
Grant, A. J. Smollett and billiards. TLS 16 Nov 1935.
Joliat, E. Smollett et la France. Paris 1935.
—— Millin's use of Smollett's Travels. Revue de Littérature Comparée 71 1938.
—— Smollett, editor of Voltaire. MLN 54 1939.
Kahrl, G. M. The influence of Shakespeare on Smollett. In T. M. Parrott presentation volume, Princeton 1935.
—— Captain Robert Stobo. Virginia Mag of History & Biography 49 1941.
—— Smollett: traveler-novelist. Chicago [1945].
Carmichael, M. Smollett a Livorno. In Liburni civitas: rassegna di attività municipale, [Leghorn] 1936.
Roberts, W. Gainsborough and Smollett. TLS 18–25 Sept 1937. Replies by L. Rice-Oxley 2 Oct; M. H. Grant 9 Oct; and L. F. Powell 16 Oct 1937.
Underwood, E. Medicine and science in the writings of Smollett. Proc Royal Soc of Medicine 30 1937.
Bélanger, J. Note sur Roderick Random et L'expédition de Carthagène. Etudes Anglaises 3 1939.
Taylor, W. D. Smollett, MD, Aberdeen 1750. Aberdeen Univ Rev 26 1939.
Viets, H. R. Smollett, the War of Jenkins's Ear and An account of the expedition to Carthagena 1743. Bull of Medical Lib Assoc June 1940.
Vincent, H. P. Smollett's assault on Gordon and Groom. RES 16 1940.
Martz, L. L. Smollett and the expedition to Carthagena. PMLA 56 1941.
—— Smollett and the Universal history. MLN 56 1941.
—— The later career of Smollett. New Haven 1942.
Norwood, L. F. The authenticity of Smollett's Ode to independence. RES 17 1941.
—— Smollett's Ode to independence. Colby Lib Quart no 15 1946.
—— Imposition on a half-sheet in duodecimo [Humphry Clinker]. Library 5th ser 1 1946.
Foster, J. R. Smollett's pamphleteering foe Shebbeare. PMLA 57 1942.
—— Peregrine Pickle and the Memoirs of Count Grammont. MLN 66 1951.
—— Smollett and the Atom. PMLA 68 1953.
—— A forgotten noble savage, Tsonnonthouan. MLQ 14 1953.
Jones, C. E. Smollett studies. Berkeley 1942. Smollett and the Navy; Smollett and the Critical Review; with appendixes and bibliography.

—— Smollett: the doctor as man of letters. Jnl of History of Medicine 12 1957.
Parker, A. Smollett and the law. SP 39 1942.
Putney, R. D. S. The plan of Peregrine Pickle. PMLA 60 1945.
—— Smollett and Lady Vane's Memoirs. PQ 25 1946.
Heilman, R. B. Falstaff and Smollett's Micklewhimmen. RES 22 1946.
Pritchett, V. S. The shocking surgeon. In his Living novel, 1947.
Young, P. M. Observations on music by Smollett. Music & Letters 27 1946.
Mack, E. C. Pamela's stepdaughters: the heroines of Smollett and Fielding. College Eng March 1947.
Oppenheimer, J. M. A note on William Hunter and Smollett. Jnl of History of Medicine 2 1947.
Cordasco, F. A Peregrine Pickle play 1929. N & Q 3 April 1948.
—— Smollett's creditor Macleane identified. Ibid.
—— Smollett and his detractor Hugh Blair, with an unpublished Smollett letter. N & Q 10 July 1948.
—— Smollett and the translation of Don Quixote: important unpublished letters. N & Q 21 Aug 1948.
—— Smollett and the translation of Don Quixote: a critical bibliography. N & Q 4 Sept 1948.
—— The ascription of A sorrowful ditty to Smollett affirmed. N & Q 2 Oct 1948.
—— J. B. Browne's edition of Smollett's Works. Ibid.
—— Robert Anderson's edition of Smollett. N & Q 11 Dec 1948.
—— Smollett and the translation of Fénelon's Telemachus. N & Q 24 Dec 1948.
—— Smollett and the death of King William III. MLN 64 1949.
—— Smollett and the translation of Gil Blas. MLQ 10 1949.
—— Smollett's register of the weather. N & Q 16 April 1949.
—— Two notes on Smollett. N & Q 24 Dec 1949.
—— Smollett's medical degree. MLN 65 1950.
—— An unrecorded medical translation by Smollett. N & Q 25 Nov 1950.
—— Smollett and the translation of Don Quixote. MLQ 13 1952.
Deutsch, O. E. Poetry preserved in music: bibliographical notes on Smollett and Oswald, Handel and Haydn. MLN 63 1948.
Kline, J. Three doctors and Smollett's lady of quality. PQ 27 1948.
Linsalata, C. R. Smollett's translation of Don Quixote. Texas Univ Lib Chron 3 1948.
—— Smollett's indebtedness to Jarvis' translation of Don Quijote. Symposium 4 1950.
—— Smollett's hoax: Don Quixote in English. Stanford 1956.
Graham, W. H. Humphry Clinker. Contemporary Rev July 1949.
Matthews, W. Tarpaulin Arabic in the days of Pepys. In Essays dedicated to L. B. Campbell, Berkeley 1950. On nautical speech in fact and fiction.
Orr, J. Did Smollett know Spanish? MLR 45 1950.
Brander, L. Tobias Smollett. [1951].
Lancaster, H. C. The death of William III: a correction. MLN 67 1952.
Almiral, C. L. Smollett's 'Gothic': an illustration. MLN 68 1953.
Harder, K. B. Genealogical satire in Humpry Clinker. N & Q Oct 1955.
Knowles, E. B. A note on Smollett's Don Quixote. MLN 16 1955.
Scott, W. Smollett, Dr John Hill and the failure of Peregrine Pickle. N & Q Sept 1955.
—— Smollett's The tears of Scotland: a hitherto unnoticed printing and some comments on the text. RES new ser 8 1957.

Spector, R. D. Smollett and Admiral Byng. N & Q Feb 1955.
— Eighteenth-century political controversy and linguistics. N & Q Sept 1955.
— Further attacks on the Critical Review. N & Q Dec 1955, March, 1957, July 1958, Aug 1960.
— Smollett's use of Tsonnonthouan. N & Q March 1959.
— Tobias George Smollett. New York 1968.
Wasserman, E. R. Smollett's satire on the Hutchinsonians. MLN 70 1955.
Hunter, R. A. and I. Macalpine. Smollett's reading in psychiatry. MLR 51 1956.
— Smollett MD and William Battie MD. Jnl of History of Medicine 1956.
Roper, D. Smollett and the Founders of his Review. Call Number (Oregon) 19 1957.
— Smollett's Four gentlemen: the first contributors to Critical Review. RES new ser 10 1959.
— The politics of the Critical Review 1756–1817. Durham Univ Jnl 53 1961.
Taylor, A. Proverbial materials in Smollett, The adventures of Sir Launcelot Greaves. Southern Folklore Quart 21 1957.
Orowitz, M. Smollett and the art of caricature. Spectrum 2 1958.
Strauss, A. B. On Smollett's language: a paragraph in Ferdinand Count Fathom. In Style in prose fiction, New York 1959 (Eng Inst Essays).
Boggs, W. A. Hassock of hair. N & Q Feb 1960.
— Win Jenkins' malapropisms. Jammu & Kashmir Univ Rev 4 1961.
— Smollett's coinages in the Win Jenkins' letters. Univ of Southern Florida Lang Quart 2 1963.
— A Win Jenkins' lexicon. BNYPL May 1964.
— Shakespeare and Win. Amer N & Q June 1965.
— Some standard eighteenth-century usages. Quart Jnl of Speech 51 1965.
— Win Jenkins' first citations in the OED. Word Study 41 1965.
— Win Jenkins' archaisms and proverbial phrases. Univ of Southern Florida Lang Quart 4 1965.
— Dialectical ingenuity in Humphry Clinker. Papers on Eng Lang & Lit (Illinois) 1 1965.
— Win Jenkins' addenda to Mr Murray's dictionary. Discourse 9 1966.
— 'Birthday suit' and 'cheese-toaster'. N & Q Dec 1966.
McCombie, F. Count Fathom and El Buscón. N & Q Aug 1960.
Paulson, R. Satire in the early novels of Smollett. JEGP 59 1960.
— Smollett and Hogarth: the identity of Pallet. Stud in Eng Lit 1500–1900 4 1964.
— In his Satire and the novel in eighteenth-century England, New Haven 1967.
Sen, S. K. Sheridan's literary debt, the Rivals and Humphry Clinker. MLQ 21 1960.
Baker, S. Humphry Clinker as comic romance. Papers of Michigan Acad of Science, Arts & Letters 46 1961.
Compan, A. Smollett et le dialecte Niçois. Nice-Matin L'Espoir 11 May 1961.
Griffith, P. M. Fire-scenes in Richardson's Clarissa and Smollett's Humphry Clinker. Tulane Stud in Eng 11 1961.
Webster, G. Smollett and Shaw: a note on a source for Heartbreak House. Shaw Rev 4 1961.
Aubrun, C. Smollett et Cervantes. Etudes Anglaises 15 1962.
Maxwell, J. C. French borrowings in Ferdinand Count Fathom. N & Q Jan 1962.
Clifford, J. L. Pallet in Peregrine Pickle. N & Q Dec 1963.
Gassman, B. The Briton and Humphry Clinker. Stud in Eng Lit 1500–1900 3 1963.
— Religious attitudes in the world of Humphry Clinker. Brigham Young Univ Stud 6 1965.

Hunting, R. Footnote to a comparative study: Smollett and Ibsen. N & Q June 1963.
Piper, W. B. The large diffused picture of life in Smollett's early novels. SP 60 1963.
Bruce, D. Radical Doctor Smollett. 1964.
Preston, T. R. Smollett and the benevolent misanthrope type. PMLA 79 1964.
Boucé, P.-G. Smollett's libel. TLS 30 Dec 1965.
— Les procédés du comique dans Humphry Clinker. Etudes Anglaises 25 1966.
— Smollett criticism 1770–1924: corrections and additions. N & Q May 1967.
— The 'Chinese pilot' and 'Sa-Rouf' in Smollett's Atom. Eng Lang Notes 4 1967.
— Smollett and the expedition against Rochefort 1757. MP 65 1967.
— A note on Smollett's Construction of the complete history of England. RES new ser 20 1969.
Klukoff, P. J. A Smollett attribution in the Critical Review. N & Q June 1965.
— Two Smollett attributions in the Critical Review: the Reverie and Tristram Shandy. N & Q Dec 1966.
— Smollet and the Critical Review: criticism of the novel 1756–63. Stud in Scottish Lit 4 1966.
— New Smollett attributions in the Critical Review. N & Q Nov 1967.
— Smollett and the Sackville controversy. Neuphilologische Mitteilungen 59 1968.
Reid, B. L. Smollett's healing journey. Virginia Quart Rev 41 1965.
Stevick, P. The Augustan nose. UTQ 34 1965.
Bevis, R. W. Smollett and the Israelites. PQ 45 1966.
Garrow, S. A study of the organization of Smollett's The expedition of Humphry Clinker. Southern Quart 4–5 1966.
Park, W. Fathers and sons: Humphry Clinker. Lit & Psychology 16 1966.
Wagoner, M. On the satire in Humphry Clinker. Papers in Lang & Lit 2 1966.
Bloch, T. Smollett's quest for form. MP 65 1967.
Driskell, L. V. Looking for Dustwich. Texas Stud in Lit & Lang 9 1967.
Giddings, R. The tradition of Smollett. [1967].
Grant, D. J. Unpublished additions to Smollett's Travels. N & Q May 1967.
Korte, D. M. Smollett's Advice and Reproof. Thoth 8 1967.
Kent, J. P. Smollett's translation of Gil Blas: a question of text. Eng Lang Notes 5 1967.
Musher, D. M. The medical views of Smollett. Bull of History of Medicine 41 1967.
Rousseau, G. S. Smollett, Sir Launcelot Greaves and the lunatics. Stud on Voltaire & Eighteenth Century 29 1967.
— Smollett's acidum vagum. Isis 58 1967.
— Matt Bramble and the sulphur controversy in the xviiith century: medical background of Humphry Clinker. JHI 28 1967.
Bertrand, C.-J. Humphry Clinker: a 'so-called Methodist'. Bulletin de la Faculté des Lettres de Strasbourg Jan 1969.
Hopkins, R. The function of grotesque in Humphry Clinker. HLQ 32 1969.   L. M. K.

FRANCES BURNEY, later D'ARBLAY
1752–1840

Bibliographies

Sale catalogue of Fanny Burney's library, Sotheby's 12 Jan 1883.
Scholes, P. A. Works of Fanny Burney, published and unpublished. In his Great Dr Burney vol 2, 1948.

Hemlow, J. The Burney manuscripts: a tentative summary. In her History of Fanny Burney, Oxford 1958. Lists mss of 8 unpbd plays.
— A catalogue of the Burney family correspondence 1749–1878. New York 1970.

§ 1

Evelina: or the history of a young lady's entrance into the world. 3 vols 1778, 1779 (3 edns), 2 vols Dublin 1779, 1780, 3 vols 1783, 1784, 2 vols Dublin 1784, 3 vols Dresden 1788, 2 vols 1791, 1793, 1794, 1798, 1801, 1808, 1810, 1814 (with biographical sketch), 1815 etc; ed A. R. Ellis 1881, 2 vols [1903], 1904; ed R. B. Johnson 2 vols 1893; ed A. Dobson [1903]; ed F. D. Mackinnon, Oxford 1930; ed E. A. Bloom, Oxford 1968; tr French, 1779, 1780, 1784, 1797; German, 1779; Dutch, 1780–5.
Cecilia: or memoirs of an heiress. 5 vols 1782, 1783, 3 vols Dublin 1783, 5 vols 1784, 3 vols Dublin 1784, 5 vols 1786, Dresden 1790, 1791; 3 vols Dublin 1795, 5 vols 1796, 1802 (8th edn), Birmingham 1809, 3 vols 1810 etc; ed A. R. Ellis 2 vols 1882, 1904; ed R. B. Johnson 3 vols 1893; tr French, 1783, 1784.
Brief reflections relative to the emigrant French clergy. 1793.
Camilla: or a picture of youth. 5 vols 1796, 3 vols Dublin 1796, 5 vols 1802, 3 vols 1840; tr French, 1797; German, 1798.
The wanderer: or female difficulties. 5 vols 1814; tr French, 1814.
Memoirs of Dr Burney. 3 vols 1832.
Edwy and Elgiva. Ed M. J. Benkovitz, Hamden Conn 1957.

Letters, Diaries etc

A complete edn from the mss of her correspondence and journals is in preparation under the general editorship of Prof Joyce Hemlow.

The diary and letters of Madame d'Arblay 1778–1840. Ed C. Barrett 7 vols 1842–6 (2 issues of vols 1–2), 1854, 4 vols 1876, 1891; ed W. C. Ward 3 vols 1890–1; ed C. Barrett and A. Dobson 6 vols 1904–5; [selections] ed L. B. Seeley 1890, 1895; ed C. B. Tinker 1912 (as Dr Johnson and Fanny Burney); ed M. Masefield 1931; ed L. Gibbs 1940 (EL); ed C. Lloyd 1948; ed J. Wain 1961.
The early diary of Frances Burney 1768–78. Ed A. R. Ellis 2 vols 1889, 1907 (rev), 1913.
The Queeney letters: being letters addressed to Hester Maria Thrale by Dr Johnson, Fanny Burney and Mrs Thrale-Piozzi. Ed Marquis of Lansdowne 1934. 18 letters by Fanny Burney.
Gates, W. B. An unpublished Burney letter. ELH 5 1938.
Sambrook, A. J. Fanny Burney's first letter to Dr Johnson. RES new ser 14 1963.

§ 2

[Rivers, D.] In his Literary memoirs of living authors of Great Britain vol 1, 1798.
Hazlitt, W. Edinburgh Rev 24 1815. A review of Wanderer. Rev in his English comic writers, 1819.
Croker, J. W. Quart Rev 49 1833. A review of Memoirs of Dr Burney.
— Quart Rev 70 June 1842. A review of Diary and letters.
Macaulay, T. B. Edinburgh Rev 75 1843. A review of Diary and letters.
Shuckburgh, E. S. Fanny Burney's Edwy and Elgiva. Macmillan's Mag Feb 1890.
'Paston, George' (E. M. Symonds). A Burney friendship; with unpublished letters from Madame d'Arblay and Dr Burney to Mrs Waddington. Monthly Rev Sept 1902; rptd in her Side-lights on the Georgian period, 1902.
Dobson, A. Fanny Burney. 1903 (EML).

Hill, C. Juniper Hall. 1904. Contains letters by Fanny Burney and Dr Burney.
— The house in St Martin's Street: being chronicles of the Burney family. 1907.
— Fanny Burney at the Court of Queen Charlotte. 1912.
Hutton, W. H. Burford papers: being letters of Samuel Crisp to his sister. 1905.
More, P. E. In his Shelburne essays: fourth series, New York 1906.
Kershaw, S. W. Fanny Burney and Surrey. In Memorials of old Surrey, ed J. C. Cox 1911.
Hale, W. T. Madame d'Arblay's place in the development of the English novel. Indiana Univ Stud 3 1916.
Danz, K. Frances Burneys Evelina und das Aufkommen der Frauenromane. Anglia 36 1924.
Buttner, C. Die Sprache in Fanny Burneys Evelina. Giessen 1924.
Morley, E. J. Fanny Burney. 1925 (Eng Assoc lecture). Contains 2 letters to Mrs Thrale.
Johnson, R. B. Fanny Burney and the Burneys. 1926.
A great-niece's journals: being extracts from the journals of Fanny Anne Burney (Mrs Wood) 1830–42. Ed M. S. Rolt 1926.
Masefield, M. The story of Fanny Burney. Cambridge 1927.
Roberts, W. W. Charles and Fanny Burney in the light of the new Thrale correspondence in the John Rylands Library. Bull John Rylands Lib 16 1932.
Overman, A. A. An investigation into the character of Fanny Burney. Amsterdam 1933.
Delachaux, E. Fanny Burney: intermédiaire manquée entre l'Angleterre et la France. Revue de Littérature Comparée 15 1935.
Lloyd, C. Fanny Burney. 1936.
Tourtellot, A. B. Be loved no more: the life and environment of Fanny Burney. New York 1938.
Dugdale, E. T. S. Madame d'Arblay. Quart Rev 274 1940.
Fanny Burney: a life in a world of fantasy. TLS 6 Jan 1940.
Gooch, G. P. In his Courts and cabinets, 1944.
Cecil, D. Fanny Burney's novels. In Essays on the eighteenth century presented to David Nichol Smith, Oxford 1945.
— In his Poets and story-tellers, 1949.
Coolidge, T. Family concerns of Fanny Burney. More Books 21 1946.
Lincoln, E. T. A breakfast at Streatham. N & Q 15 Feb 1947.
Eaves, T. C. D. Edward Burney's illustrations to Evelina. PMLA 62 1947.
Graham, W. H. Evelina. Contemporary Rev June 1947.
Edwards, A. Fanny Burney: a biography. 1948.
Scholes, P. A. The great Dr Burney: his life, his travels, his works, his family and his friends. 2 vols 1948.
Blakeney, T. S. A minor character in Fanny Burney's diary identified. N & Q 24 Dec 1949. On Edward Blakeney.
Montagu, E. and L. L. Martz. Evelina. In The age of Johnson: essays presented to C. B. Tinker, New Haven 1949.
Hemlow, J. Fanny Burney and the courtesy books. PMLA 65 1950.
— Fanny Burney: playwright. UTQ 19 1950.
— Dr Johnson and Fanny Burney: some additions to the record. BNYPL Feb 1951.
— The history of Fanny Burney. Oxford 1958.
— Dr Johnson and the young Burneys. In New light on Dr Johnson, ed F. W. Hilles, New Haven 1959.
— Dr Johnson and Fanny Burney: some additions to the record. In Johnsonian studies, ed Magdi Wahba, Cairo 1962.
— Preparing a catalogue of the Burney family correspondence 1749–1878. BNYPL Oct 1967.
— Letters and journals of Fanny Burney: establishing the text. In Editing eighteenth-century texts, ed D. I. B. Smith, Toronto 1968.

Hahn, E. A degree of prudery. 1951. A biography.
Johnson's little Burney. TLS 13 June 1932.
Fanny Burney: an identification. N & Q Aug 1954.
Quennell, P. C. Bas bleu. Spectator 28 March 1958.
Benkovitz, M. J. Dr Burney's memoirs. RES new ser 10 1959.
White, E. Fanny Burney, novelist. Hamden Conn 1960.
Gérin, W. The young Fanny Burney: a biography. 1961.
Bugnot, A. The wanderer de Fanny Burney: essai de réhabilitation. Etudes Anglaises 15 1962.
The real Fanny Burney. TLS 9 March 1962.
Laski, M. Antedatings of OED in Evelina. N & Q July 1962.
Erickson, J. P. Evelina and Betsy Thoughtless. Texas Stud in Lit & Lang 6 1964.
Lonsdale, R. H. Dr Charles Burney: a literary biography. Oxford 1965.
Malone, K. Evelina revisited. Papers on Eng Lang & Lit 1 1965.
Moler, K. L. Fanny Burney's Cecilia and Jane Austen's Jack and Alice. Eng Lang Notes 3 1965.
Kamm, J. M. The story of Fanny Burney. 1966.

R. H. L.

WILLIAM BECKFORD
1760–1844

Bibliographies

Chapman, G. and J. Hodgkin. A bibliography of Beckford of Fonthill. 1930.
Hunter, A. O. Le Vathek de Beckford: historique des éditions françaises. Revue de Littérature Comparée 15 1935.
Carter, J. The Lausanne edition of Beckford's Vathek. Library 3rd ser 17 1937.
—— Two Beckford collections. Colophon 1 1939.
Parreaux, A. Un Vathek ignoré. Bulletin du Bibliophile 5 1957.
—— Beckford's Vathek, Londres 1791. Book Collector 7 1958.
Gottlieb, H. B. Beckford of Fonthill. New Haven 1960. Catalogue of Yale Univ Library exhibition.
Gemmett, R. J. An annotated checklist of the works of Beckford. PBSA 61 1967.
—— Beckford: bibliographical addenda. Bull of Bibliography 25 1967.

§ I
Vathek

In French

Vathek. Lausanne 1787 (for 1786), 1791 (as Les caprices et les malheurs du calife Vathek), Paris 1787 (rev as Vathek: conte arabe), 1815 (final revision), nd [1828?]; ed S. Mallarmé, Paris 1876 (from Paris 1787, with a few misreadings), 1893 (rev); ed G. Chapman (from Paris 1787); ed J. B. Brunius, Paris 1948 (from Paris 1787); ed E. Giddey, Lausanne 1962 (from Paris 1787).

In English

An Arabian tale, from an unpublished manuscript, with notes critical and explanatory. 1786 (tr Samuel Henley, unauthorized from unknown French ms), 1809, 1816 ('revised and corrected'), Philadelphia 1816, London 1823 ('revised and corrected'), 1834, 1849, 1852, 1856, 1868, 1882; ed G. T. Bettany 1891; ed R. Garnett 1893, 1900; ed R. B. Johnson 1922; Vathek: a new translation by H. B. Grimsditch 1929 (text as 1815 edn), 1953 (with new introd); ed R. H. Lonsdale, Oxford 1970 (text of 1816, with original notes).

German translations

Der Thurm von Samarah. Leipzig 1788 (from Lausanne 1787), Mannheim 1788, Vienna 1788 (from Paris 1787).

Episodes of Vathek

The episodes of Vathek. Tr F. T. Marzials 1912 (includes French text); [1922] (English trn only, in Abbey Classics); Vathek with the episodes of Vathek, ed G. Chapman 2 vols 1929 (French text only); Vathek et les épisodes, ed J. B. Brunius, Paris 1948.

Other Works

Biographical memoirs of extraordinary painters. 1780, 1824, 1834.
Dreams, waking thoughts and incidents, in a series of letters, from various parts of Europe. 1783 (suppressed by Beckford except for 6 copies); ed G. T. Bettany 1891 (with Vathek); ed G. Chapman 1928 (The travel diaries vol 1).
Modern novel writing: or the elegant enthusiast; and interesting emotions of Arabella Bloomville: a rhapsodical romance; interspersed with poetry, by the Right Hon Lady Harriet Marlow. 2 vols 1796.
Azemia: a descriptive and sentimental novel, interspersed with pieces of poetry, by Jaquetta Agneta Mariana Jenks. 2 vols 1797, 1798; Arnold et la belle musulmane, Paris 1808 (French trn).
The story of Al Raoui: a tale from the Arabic. 1799 (with German version and a few poems), 1799.
A dialogue in the shades. [1819], 1821.
Epitaphs, some of which have appeared in the Literary Gazette of March and April 1823. [1825].
Italy; with sketches of Spain and Portugal, by the author of Vathek. 2 vols 1834, 1834 (rev), Paris 1834, Philadelphia 1834, 2 vols 1835, 1 vol 1840 (with Recollections of an excursion); ed G. T. Bettany 1891 (with Vathek); ed G. Chapman 1928 (The travel diaries vol 2).
Recollections of an excursion to the monasteries of Alcobaça and Batalha. 1835, Philadelphia 1835, 1840 (rev) (with Italy); ed G. T. Bettany 1891 (with Italy); ed G. Chapman 1928 (The travel diaries vol 2); ed A. Parreaux, Paris 1956 (from 1840, with French trn; not from 1835, as wrongly stated on title-page).
The vision; Liber veritatis. Ed G. Chapman 1930.

Letters, Diaries etc

Journal in Portugal and Spain 1787–8. Ed B. Alexander 1954.
Life at Fonthill 1807–22, from the correspondence of Beckford. Tr (mostly from the Italian) and ed B. Alexander 1957.
1794 journal. Ed B. Alexander, New Haven 1960 (in Beckford of Fonthill).

§ 2

Hazlitt, W. Fonthill Abbey. London Mag Nov 1822.
—— Pictures at Wilton, Stourhead etc. London Mag Oct 1823.
Lockhart, J. G. Quart Rev 51 1834. Review of Italy.
Redding, C. Recollections of the author of Vathek. Colburn's New Monthly Mag June–July 1844.
—— Memoirs of Beckford. 2 vols 1859.
Conant, M. P. In her Oriental tale in England in the 18th century, New York 1908.
'Melville, Lewis' (L. S. Benjamin). Life and letters of Beckford. 1910.
Delattre, F. L'orientalisme dans la littérature anglaise. Le Beffroi Aug 1912.
—— De Byron à Francis Thompson. Paris 1913.
Larbaud, V. The episodes of Vathek. Nouvelle Revue Française Jan, April, June 1913.
May, M. La jeunesse de Beckford et la genèse de son Vathek. Paris 1928.
Belloc, H. A conversation with an angel. 1928.
Sitwell, S. Beckford and Beckfordism. 1930.

Oliver, J. W. The life of Beckford. 1932.

Morgulis, G. Un épisode de la vie de Beckford. Revue de Littérature Comparée 14 1934. On Beckford in Paris 1793.

Parreaux, A. Le Portugal dans l'oeuvre de Beckford. Paris 1935.

— Beckford en Italie. Revue de Littérature Comparée 33 1959.

— Beckford: auteur de Vathek. Paris 1960.

— Les peintres extraordinaires de Beckford. Revue du Nord 43 1961.

Chapman, G. Beckford. 1937, 1952.

— Beckford the caliph. TLS 6 May 1944.

Macaulay, R. In her They went to Portugal, 1946.

Andersen, J. Giant dreams. Eng Miscellany (Rome) 3 1952.

T'Serstevens, A. Le Vathek de Beckford. Revue Palladienne 19–20 1952.

Thomson, K. F. Henley's share in Vathek. PQ 31 1952.

Brockman, H. A. N. The caliph of Fonthill. 1956.

Mahmoud, F. M. (ed). Beckford of Fonthill: bicentenary essays. Cairo 1960.

Mayoux, J.-J. La damnation de Beckford. Eng Miscellany (Rome) 12 1961.

[Lonsdale, R. H.] The mask of Beckford. TLS 10 Feb 1961.

Alexander, B. England's wealthiest son. 1962.

Rieger, J. H. Au pied de la lettre: stylistic uncertainty in Vathek. Criticism 4 1962.

Folsom, J. K. Beckford's Vathek and the tradition of oriental satire. Criticism 6 1964.

Grimm, R. Vathek in Deutschland. Revue de Littérature Comparée 38 1964.

Giddey, E. La vision créatrice de Vathek. In Mélanges offerts à Georges Bonnard, Geneva 1966.

Oldman, C. B. Beckford and Mozart. Music & Letters 47 1966.

Gemmett, R. J. The composition of Beckford's Biographical memoirs of extraordinary painters. PQ 47 1968.

— The critical reception of Beckford's Fonthill. Eng Miscellany (Rome) 19 1968.

Crallan, H. Beckford in Bath. Architectural Rev March 1968.

Mouret, F. J. L. Le Vathek de Beckford et le Voyage d'Urien d'André Gide. MLR 64 1969.

A. P.

III. MINOR FICTION

The following list is selective, representing less than one-fifth of the total output of fiction in the period. In the 1730's alone, for example, nearly 200 new or rptd works of fiction appeared; over 1,000 works of epistolary fiction were pbd 1660–1800. Standards for inclusion have been early or unusual developments in fictional technique or in quality; popularity and influence, irrespective of literary merit; modern edns, reprints, studies; and interest as illustrating popular movements in fiction. Short fiction, chap-books, reprints, serializations, with a few exceptions, are not included. For fuller bibliographies, see Mish, McBurney, Wiles, Mayo, Neuburg, cols 866, 868, above. Secondary works listed are strictly supplementary to those above, col 865. With many trns, where the English title renders the original French or Spanish closely, the latter is not given. Entries, both of original and translated works, are arranged by year of first authenticated appearance; within the year they are arranged alphabetically, with anon works first by title, then according to the author of the original work. No attempt at a complete recording of edns has been made; if more than 2 are known this information is usually summarized.

Brusoni, Girolamo. Arnaldo: or the injur'd lover. 1660. Trn of B's Italian version of Diego de San Pedro, Tractado de amores de Arnalte y Lucenda, c. 1492; late medieval romance, with emphasis on psychology of lovers.

Ingelo, Nathaniel. Bentivolio and Urania. 1660–4; 5 edns by 1682. Preface ed C. Davies, Los Angeles 1953 (Augustan Reprint Soc). Religious-allegorical romance.

Mackenzie, Sir George. Aretina: or the serious romance. Edinburgh 1660, 1661. Preface ed with above. Romance; political allegory.

d'Ortigue, Pierre, sieur de Vaumorière. The grand Scipio. 2 vols 1660–1. Heroic and historical romance.

Sadler, John. Olbia: the new iland lately discovered. 1660. Perhaps a burlesque of Hartlib, Macaria.

Eliana: a new romance formed by an English hand. 1661. Ornate and derivative; little action.

The Princess Cloria: or the royal romance. 2 pts 1653–4 (as Cloria and Narcissus), 1 vol 1661, 1665. Heroic, allegorical; may refer to exile of Charles II.

Dauncey, John. The English lovers: a romance. 1661–2. Version of Heywood, The fair maid of the west.

[Flatman, Thomas]. Don Juan Lamberto: or a comical history of late times. 1661 (3 edns), 1664, 1665, 1667. Satirical roman à clef; ridicules Commonwealth notables; Anthony Wood ascribes to Flatman.

Sorel, Charles. The most delightful and pleasant history of Francion. 1661. Apparently a new trn of Francion, 1622; early example of humorous realism; anti-romantic.

The noble birth and gallant atchievements of Robin Hood. 1662; 5 edns by 1700.

La Calprenède, Gauthier de Costes, sieur de. Pharamond: or the history of France. 4 pts 1662, 1 vol 1677, 12 pts 1684. Tr John Davies; see col 140, above.

Howard, Thomas. The history of the seven wise mistresses of Rome. 1663, 1684, 1688 (4th edn). Based on popular Seven wise masters; see C. C. Mish, Howard's Seven wise mistresses, N & Q April 1960.

Lucian. Part of Lucian made English from the originall. Oxford 1663, 1664. First pbn of trn by Jasper Mayne.

The triumph of truth. 1664; ed S. Peterson in The counterfeit lady unveiled, Garden City NY 1961. Rogue biography.

Bulteel, John. Birinthea: a romance. 1664. Version of Xenophon, Cyropaedia.

Newcastle, Margaret Cavendish, Duchess of. CCXI sociable letters. 1664, 1718. Primitive letter-fiction depicting domestic life. See D. Grant, Margaret the first, 1956.

Castillo Solorzano, Alonso de. La picara: or the triumphs of female subtilty. 1665, [1700?]. Tr John Davies of Kidwelly. Other versions: The life of Donna Rosina, 1703–8; Three ingenious Spanish novels, 1712; The Spanish pole-cat, 1717; Spanish amusements, 1727. Clever anti-heroine Rufina; inserted romantic tales.

Crowne, John. Pandion and Amphigenia. 1665. Romance modelled on Sidney, Arcadia.

Head, Richard and Francis Kirkman. The English rogue described in the life of Meriton Latroon. 4 pts 1665–80, 1 vol 1693, 1697 (4th edn). Many edns to 1786; ed M. Shinagel, Boston 1961 (Head's pt only). See S. Gibson, A bibliography of Kirkman, Oxford 1950. Sensational patchwork; many sources.

Patrick, Simon. The parable of the pilgrim. 1665; 7 edns by 1687. Bunyanesque; a possible source of Pilgrim's progress.

Scarron, Paul. The comical romance: or a facetious history of a company of stage-players. 1665, 1676. Tr John Bulteel; rev T. Brown and J. Savage 1700; 6 edns by 1759. *See* A. W. Secord, Scarron's roman comique and its English translators, in Robert Drury's journal and other studies, Urbana 1961.

— Scarron's novels, rendred into English by John Davies of Kidwelly. 1665, 1667; 3 more edns by 1700. 7 lively picaresque tales; *see* J. E. Tucker, The earliest English translation of Scarron's nouvelles, Revue de Littérature Comparée 24 1950.

La Fayette, Marie Madeleine, comtesse de. The Princess of Montpensier. 1666. Pseudo-historical romance of sentiment.

Newcastle, Margaret Cavendish, Duchess of. The description of a new world called the blazing world. 1666, 1668. *See* K. Prasad, Margaret Cavendish's Blazing world: a seventeenth-century Utopia, in Essays presented to Amy G. Stock, Jaipur 1965.

Head, Richard. The life and death of Mother Shipton. 1667; 6 edns by 1697. Pseudo-biography of the legendary prophetess.

Quevedo y Villegas, Francisco de. Visions, made English by R[oger] L[Estrange]. 1667; 11 edns by 1715; ed J. M. Cohen, Fontwell and Carbondale 1963. Satirical pictures of city life; sharpers.

Nevile, Henry. The isle of pines. 1668, 1668 (with 2nd pt), 1704; ed W. C. Ford, Boston 1920; pt 1, 1930 (EL). Narrator populates deserted island with progeny, founds commonwealth; *see* G. Bullough, Polygamy among the reformers, in Renaissance and modern essays presented to V. de S. Pinto, 1966.

Boyle, Roger, Earl of Orrery. Parthenissa. 1669 (last pt; others appeared 1651–6), 1676 (complete); other edns in 18th century. Preface ed C. Davies, Los Angeles 1953 (Augustan Reprint Soc). Lengthy imitation of Greek and French romances; *see* K. Lynch, Roger Boyle, Knoxville 1965; C. W. Miller, A bibliographical study of Parthenissa, SB 2 1949.

Salas Barbadillo, Alonso Jeronimo. The fortunate fool. 1670, [c. 1712] (as The lucky idiot), 1736. Humorous picaresque.

Villiers, Claude Deschamps, sieur de. The gentleman apothecary. 1670; 9 edns by 1740. Trn by L'Estrange. Bawdy, realistic tale of amorous contretemps.

Furetière, Antoine. Scarron's city romance made English. 1671. Actually trn of Furetière, Roman bourgeois.

Panton, Edward. Speculum juventutis. 1671. Didactic; story of a misguided youth.

Quevedo y Villegas, Francisco de. The novels of Dom Francisco de Quevedo Villegas. 1671, 1707, 1709. Satirical realism.

Schooten, Hendrik van (pseudonym?). The hairy giants: or a description of two islands in the south sea. 1671. Apparently a trn; Utopian.

The annals of love: containing select histories of the amours of divers princes courts. 1672. 20 brief tales, pseudo-historical; loves and adventures of European royal and noble personages; apparently a trn of Ville-dieu, Annales galantes, 1670; *see* B. Morrissette, The life and works of Marie-Catherine Desjardins, St Louis 1947.

The French rogue: being a pleasant history. 1672; 5 edns by 1716. Picaresque.

Cervantes Saavedra, Miguel de. The second part of the history of Don Quixote of the Mancha. 1672–5. Shelton's trn; *see* cols 202–3, *above*.

Desjardins, Marie-Catherine, Mme de Villedieu. The memoires of the life and rare adventures of Henrietta Silvia Moliere. 2 vols 1672–7. Pseudo-autobiography; love and fantastic adventures.

Head, Richard. The floating island: or a new discovery.

1673. Satire on London low life in the manner of a voyage.

Kirkman, Francis. The counterfeit lady unveiled. 1673, 1679; ed S. Peterson, Garden City NY 1961; see C. F. Main, The German Princess: or Mary Carleton in fact and fiction, Harvard Lib Bull 10 1956.

— The unlucky citizen; with several choice novels. 1673. Autobiography mixed with fiction; London life.

Le Pays, René. The drudge: or the jealous extravagant. 1673. Satirical comedy.

Head, Richard. The western wonder: or O Brazeel, an in-chanted island discovered. 1674, 1675 (as O-Brazile); ed I. M. Westcott, Los Angeles 1958 (Augustan Reprint Soc).

Abu Bakr Ibn Al-Tufail, Abu Jafar. An account of the oriental philosophy, shewing the profound wisdom of Hai Ebn Yokdan. 1674 (tr G. Keith), 1686 (tr G. Ashwell) etc; ed A. S. Fulton 1929. From E. Pococke's Latin version, 1671. Numerous edns and versions through 18th century. Autodidact reared on desert island.

Saint-Réal, César Vichard de. Don Carlos. 1674, 1676. *See* Croxall, 1720, below. Psychological love-tragedy; source of Don Carlos theme.

Scudéry, Madeleine de. Ibrahim: or the illustrious bassa. 1674. Complete work; trn by Henry Cogan. *See col 144, above.* Preface rptd by B. Boyce, Los Angeles 1952 (Augustan Reprint Soc).

Barnes, Joshua. Gerania: or a new discovery of pigmies. 1675, 1750. Utopian romance.

Shirley, John. The famous history of Aurelius, the valiant London prentice. 1675; 4 edns by 1700. Continuation of Dick Whittington tradition. *See* B. L. Magaw, The work of Shirley, an early hack writer, PBSA 56 1962.

Vairasse d'Allais, Denis. The history of the Sevarites or Sevarambi. 1675–9, 1700, 1738. Important early Utopia; *see* G. Atkinson, The extraordinary voyage in French literature before 1700, New York 1920.

The right pleasant and variable tragical history of Fortun-atus. 1676, 1679; other versions and abridgments to 1700; ed C. C. Mish in Short fiction of the seventeenth century, New York 1963. First datable prose version of popular folk tale of marvels, of German origin.

Tachmas, Prince of Persia: an historical novel. 1676. Tr P. Porter. Early use of Oriental setting.

Boyle, Roger, Earl of Orrery. English adventures. 1676. Early attempt at historical novel; on Henry VIII.

Brémond, Gabriel de. Hattige: or the amours of the king of Tamaran. 1676, 1680 etc. *See* Croxall, 1720, below. Actually a scandal-novel on amours of Charles II.

Saint-Réal, César Vichard de. The memoires of the Dutchess Mazarine. 1676, 1676, 1690. Tr P. Porter. Scandal-novel with interpolated letters.

Voiture, Vincent. Zelinda. 1676, 1678, 1692. *See* C. W. Miller, Zelinda and Voiture, PQ 22 1943; C. C. Mish, Voiture's Alcidalis et Zélide in English, N & Q Oct 1957. Trn burlesques original.

Brémond, Gabriel de. The happy slave. 1677; 4 edns by 1699. *See* Croxall, 1720, below. Influential; exotic adventure.

Camus, Jean Pierre. A true tragical history of two illus-trious Italian families. 1677, 1678 (as Forced marriage). Trn of Camus, Alcime.

Scudéry, Madeleine de. Almahide: or the captive Queen. 1677, 1702, 1728. Tr J. Phillips. *See col 144, above.*

Five love-letters from a nun to a cavalier. 1678; at least 12 edns by 1716. Tr Sir Roger L'Estrange; rptd N. Würzbach in The novel in letters, 1969. Widely influential for epistolary fiction. Probably by G. J. L. de Guilleragues. *See* F. C. Green, Who was the author of the Lettres portugaises?, MLR 21 1926; F. Deloffre and J. Rougeot, introd to Guilleragues, Lettres portu-gaises, Paris 1962.

The lives of sundry notorious villains. 1678. Rogue bio-graphies, realistic; wrongly attributed to Aphra Behn.

Curli, — de. Tudor, a Prince of Wales: an historical novel. 1678, 1751 (as The life and amours of Owen Tideric). Tr from French.

La Fayette, Marie Madeleine de. Zayde: a Spanish history. 1678, 1690; rptd Richard Aldington in Great French romances, New York 1946. See Croxall, 1720, below. Tr P. Porter; another trn by Elizabeth Griffiths, 1777, 1780. Attributed to Jean Segrais, who collaborated.

La Roche-Guilhem, Mlle de. Almanzor and Almanzaida. 1678. Oriental setting; author attributes romance to Sir Philip Sidney.

Subligny, Adrien Thomas Perdou de. The mock Clelia. 1678, 1705 etc. Satire on French romances in manner of Cervantes.

The amorous convert. 1679. Story of a Christian's amorous intrigues among the Jewish community of Amsterdam.

The penitent hermit: or the fruits of jealousie. 1679. Love-story in fairly realistic English setting.

Carleton, Rowland. Diana, Duchess of Mantua: or the persecuted lover. 1679, 1681. Romantic tale, complicated intrigue.

Desjardins, Marie Catherine, Mme de Villedieu. The unfortunate heroes: or the adventures of ten famous men. 1679, 1726 (as The exiles of the Court of Augustus Caesar), 1728, 1729 (as The secret history of the Court of Augustus Caesar). Trn of Les exilés, 1675; romantic treatment of Ovid et al.

La Fayette, Marie Madeleine, comtesse de. The Princess of Cleves. 1679, 1688 etc. Many edns to 1777; then a new trn by Elizabeth Griffith. Highly esteemed throughout 18th century.

Don Tomazo: or the juvenile rambles of Thomas Dangerfield. 1680; ed S. Peterson in The counterfeit lady unveiled, Garden City NY 1961. Pretended autobiography of Dangerfield; consciously picaresque.

The secret history of the most renowned Queen Elizabeth and the Earl of Essex. 1680, 1681; 6 edns by 1700. Source of John Banks, The unhappy favourite.

[d'Aulnoy, Marie Catherine Jumelle de Berneville, comtesse?]. The novels of Elizabeth, Queen of England 2 pts 1680–1. Romanticized pseudo-history. Tr Spencer Hickman.

Brémond, Gabriel de. The Princess of Montferrat. 2 pts 1680–1. Novel of sentiment.

Montfaucon de Villars. The Count of Gabalis. 1680, 1680. 2 trns, by Philip Ayres and Archibald Lovell. Satire on cabalists, Rosicrucians; source of machinery in Pope, Rape of the lock.

Grimalkin: or the rebel-cat. 1681. Satire against Shaftesbury in form of beast-fable.

Lisander: or the souldier of fortune. 1681, 1688 (as The history of the loves of Lysander and Sabina). Early example of realism; good technique.

Seven Portuguese letters. 1681, 1693. Trn of anon, inferior French continuation of Lettres portugaises.

Gracián y Morales, Baltasar. The critick. 1681. Tr Sir Paul Rycaut; philosophical romance.

Grenadine, Sebastian (pseudonym?). Homais Queen of Tunis: a novel. 1681. Tale of love and intrigue.

Bernard, Catherine. The female Prince: or Frederick of Sicily. 1682. Tr Ferrand Spence; sex-disguise plot.

Bussy-Rabutin, Roger de. Loves empire: or the amours of the French Court. 1682, 1684 (with different title, added material). Tr from Histoire amoureuse des Gaules, archetype of the scandal-novel.

Loredano, Giovanni Francesco. The novells of Loredano. 1682. Trn of 9 of the Novelle amorose; brief, with intrigue-plots.

Marsh, A. The ten pleasures of marriage. 2 pts 1682–3. Fictional development of the character genre.

Oldys, Alexander. The fair extravagant: or the humorous bride. 1682. English domestic setting.

Préchac, Jean de. The Princess of Fess: or the amours of the Court of Morocco. 2 pts 1682. Tr P. Bellon; French manner, oriental background; secret history.

S., T. The perplex'd Prince. 1682, 1692 etc. Key-novel, defending legitimacy of Duke of Monmouth; 'answered' in The fugitive statesman, 1683.

The Dutch rogue: or Gusman of Amsterdam. 1683. Variation on familiar formula of Alemán, Guzman de Alfarache.

Eromena: or the noble stranger. 1683. Prose version of Chamberlayne, Pharonnida.

Five love-letters written by a cavalier. 1683; 5 edns by 1716. Trn of Réponse aux lettres portugaises, anon.

Barrin, Jean. Venus in the cloyster: or the nun in her smock. 1683; numerous surreptitious edns. Tr R. Samber 1724, 1725. One of earliest pornographic fictions.

Behn, Aphra. Love letters between a nobleman and his sister. 3 pts 1683–7 (pt 3, as Amours of Philander and Sylvia); at least 16 edns by 1765; rptd in N. Würzbach, The novel in letters, 1969 (pt 1); see R. A. Day, Told in letters, Ann Arbor 1966.

Cespedes y Meneses, Gonzalo de. The famous history of Auristella. 1683. Picaresque adventures.

['D'Argences']. The Countess of Salisbury: or the most noble Order of the Garter. 1683, 1692. Tr Ferrand Spence; proto-historical novel.

Dunton, John. The informer's doom: or an amazing and seasonable letter from Utopia, directed to the man in the moon. 1683.

G., D. A Sundays adventure: or walk to Hackney. 1683. Realistic tale of London life.

Keach, Benjamin. The travels of True Godliness from the beginning of the world to the present day. 1683, 1684 (3 edns), 1700. Many edns through 18th century. Bunyanesque allegory.

S., R. The travels of Don Francesco de Quevedo through Terra Australis Incognita. 1683. No connection with Quevedo; Utopian romance.

Dunton, John. The pilgrim's guide from the cradle to his death-bed, with his glorious passage from thence to the new Jerusalem. 1684. Allegory in manner of Bunyan.

Keach, Benjamin. The progress of sin. 1684, 1685, 1700. Religious allegory; resembles Bunyan in method and atmosphere.

Lucian. Works, translated from the Greek. 3 vols 1684; vols 4–5, 1685. Tr Ferrand Spence from French.

Préchac, Jean de. The amours of Bonne Sforza, Queen of Polonia. 1684. Historical novel in manner of period; intrigues and disguises; tr P. Bellon.

[Stretser, Thomas]. Erotopolis: the present state of Betty-land. 1684, 1741. Numerous surreptitious edns probable. Mild pornography; geographical terms for female anatomy.

A discovery of houses under ground. 1685; ed I. M. Westcott, Los Angeles 1958 (Augustan Reprint Soc). Fantastic tale.

Courtilz de Sandras, Gatien. The amorous conquests of the great Alcander. 1685. Secret history; Alcander is Henry IV of France.

Le Vayer de Boutigny, Rolland. The famous romance of Tarsis and Zelie. 1685, 1728. Tr Charles Williams. Romance in manner of La Calprenède.

Préchac, Jean de. The chaste seraglian: or Yolanda of Sicily. 1685, 1692. Romance of oriental adventure.

[Reynolds, John?]. Delightful and ingenious novels: being choice and excellent stories of amours tragical and comical. 1685, 1685, 1686, 1686. 6–8 tales of love and intrigue, with middle-class characters; see C. Morgan, The rise of the novel of manners, New York 1911, 1963 for descriptions.

Wright, Thomas. The glory of God's revenge against the sins of murther and adultery; to which are annexed the Triumphs of friendship and chastity. 1685, 1686 etc. Numerous edns through 18th century. Abridgment with addns of J. Reynolds, Gods revenge against murder. *See* R. A. Day, Told in letters, Ann Arbor 1966; C. C. Mish, Short fiction of the seventeenth century, New York 1963.

Loves posie: or a collection of seven and twenty letters. 1686. Trn of anon Le commerce galant. Epistolary novel of sentiment and wit.

Bonnecorse, Balthasar de. La montre: or the lover's watch. Tr Aphra Behn 1686. Fictional conduct book for lovers.

Cervantes Saavedra, Miguel de. The famous history of Don Quixote de la Mancha. 1686; 5 edns by 1699. Various versions of an abridgment. *See col 202, above*; E. B. Knowles, Don Quixote abridged, PBSA 51 1957.

Heliodorus. The Æthiopian history. 1686, 1687 (as The triumphs of love and constancy). Trn by Nahum Tate and another; first appearance of this version.

Cynthia; with the tragical account of the unfortunate loves of Almerin and Desdemona. 1687, 1700; over 10 edns in 18th century. Episodic and moralizing; *see* C. C. Mish, A note on the fiction reprint market in the early eighteenth century, Newberry Lib Bull 3 1954.

Boyle, Robert, Earl of Orrery. The martyrdom of Theodora and of Didymus. 1687, 1703. Historical and psychological romance. Preface ed C. Davies, Los Angeles 1953 (Augustan Reprint Soc).

Cervantes Saavedra, Miguel de, and Castillo Solorzano. The Spanish Decameron: or ten novels. 1687, 1720. Tr Sir Roger L'Estrange; selected from both authors.

Cyrano de Bergerac, Hercule Savinien de. The comical history of the states and empires of the worlds of the moon and the sun. 1687. Tr A. Lovell; not the first English trn.

[Marana, Giovanni Paolo?]. Letters writ by a Turkish spy, who lived five and forty years undiscovered at Paris. 1687–94 (various edns of 8 vols); at least 13 edns by 1753. Foundation of immensely popular genre of alien spy letters; authorship and translators much disputed; *see* W. H. McBurney, The authorship of the Turkish spy, PMLA 72 1957; J. E. Tucker, On the authorship of the Turkish spy, PBSA 52 1958; —, The Turkish spy and its French background, Revue de Littérature Comparée 32 1958; G. Almansi, L'esploratore turco e la genesi del romanzo pseudo-orientale, Studi Secenteschi 7 1966.

The pleasant adventures of the witty Spaniard Lazarillo de Tormes; to which is added the life and death of young Lazarillo. 1688, 1693. A new version of a novel popular throughout 17th century.

Behn, Apha. The fair jilt. 1688, 1688 (in Three histories), 1696 (in Histories and novels, below); ed M. Summers in Works of Aphra Behn, 1915, New York 1967. *See* R. A. Day, Aphra Behn's first biography, SB 22 1969.

— Oroonoko: or the royal slave. 1688, 1696. For pbn *see* above; R. M. Hill, Aphra Behn's use of setting, MLQ 7 1946; E. D. Seeber, Oroonoko and Crusoe's man Friday, MLQ 12 1951; J. A. Ramsaran, Oroonoko: a study of the factual elements, N & Q April 1960; R. Sheffey, Some evidence for a new source of Aphra Behn's Oroonoko, SP 59 1962.

Blackbourn, Richard. Clitie: a novel. 1688. Preface by Nahum Tate; young lovers overcome obstacles, misunderstandings.

Brillac, J. B. de. The fatal beauty of Agnes de Castro. 1688, 1696. Tr or adapted by Aphra Behn; for pbn *see* The fair jilt, above.

[Claude, Isaac?] The Count d'Soissons: a gallant novel. 1688, 1731 (as Amours of Count of Soissons). Psychological novel.

The amours of Messalina, late Queen of Albion. 1689; pt 2, with title The royal wanton, 1689, 1690. Scandal-novel concerning supposed intrigues of Mary of Modena with Louis XIV.

The amours of the Sultana of Barbary. 1689, 1690 (as Secret history of the Duchess of Portland), 1697. Lively dialogue.

Love letters between Polydorus, the Gothick King, and Messalina, late Queen of Albion. 1689. Psychological-epistolary novel; *see* R. A. Day, Love letters between Polydorus and Messalina, Seventeenth-century News 14 1956.

Peppa: or the reward of constant love. 1689. Trn from French.

Behn, Aphra. The history of the nun: or the fair vowbreaker. 1689, 1696 (in Histories and novels; *see* below).

— The lucky mistake. 1689, 1696 (in Histories and novels; *see* below).

Bellon, Peter. The Court secret. 1689. Intrigues at James II's Court, disguised as oriental tale.

L'Epy, Heliogenes de [pseudonym?]. A voyage to Tartary: containing a curious description of that country. 1689. Utopian society of sun-worshippers.

The cabinet open'd: or the secret history of the amours of Madam de Maintenon with the French King. 1690. Tr from [P. Lenoble?], La cassette ouverte; epistolary scandal-novel.

The frauds of Romish monks and priests. 1690, 1691 (3 edns); 9 edns by 1726. Trn of Gavin, Histoire des tromperies des prestres, 1690; autobiographical travel-letters devoted to anticlerical anecdotes.

The Irish rogue: or the comical history of Teague O'Divelley. 1690. Picaresque tale; by J. Shirley?

The pagan prince: or a comical history of the Palatine of Eboracum. 1690. Satire on James II and the Catholic party.

Cox, H. Lisarda: or the travels of love and jealousy. 1690, 1693 (with second title only). Brief romance.

La Roche Guilhem, Mlle de. The great Scanderbeg. 1690; *see* Croxall, 1720, below. Historical-sentimental romance.

d'Aulnoy, Marie, comtesse. The ingenious and diverting letters of the lady —'s travels into Spain. 1691, 1692; 10th edn by 1735; ed R. Foulché-Delbosc, Paris 1926; tr 1930. Trn of Relation du voyage d'Espagne: highly popular, founds genre of lively epistolary travel-narratives.

Dunton, John. A voyage round the world: the rare adventures of Don Kainophilus. 1691. Eccentric novel; anticipates Sterne.

Modern novels. 1692-3. 12-vol collection of 46 novels issued by Bentley & Magnes; sometimes cited as edns; all are issues, bound up to produce vols: *see* C. Morgan, The rise of the novel of manners, New York 1911, 1963.

The siege of Mentz: or the German heroin. 1692. Love and war; woman tests hero in male disguise.

d'Aulnoy, Marie, comtesse. Memoirs of the Court of France. 1692, 1697. Romanticized, loosely connected tales of court amours.

— Memoirs of the Court of Spain. 1692, 1701. Tr Thomas Brown; contents resemble those of preceding entry.

Congreve, William, Incognita: or love and duty reconcil'd. 1692, 1700; 5 edns by 1730; 1930 (EL); ed A. N. Jeffares 1966. *See* I. Simon, Early theories of prose fiction: Congreve and Fielding; A. Williams, Congreve's Incognita and the contrivances of Providence; both in Imagined worlds, ed M. Mack and I. Gregor 1968.

Daniel, Gabriel. A voyage to the world of Cartesius. 1692, 1694. Tr T. Taylor; philosophical romance; moon voyage, attacks Cartesian theories.

Gildon, Charles. The post-boy rob'd of his mail: or the pacquet broke open. 1692-3, 1706. Variety of characteristic letters, some in narrative sequences; derived from Préchac, La valize ouverte and Pallavicino, Il corriere svaligiato.

La Roche Guilhem, Mlle de. Zingis: a Tartarian history. 1692. Historical-romantic treatment of oriental material.

Settle, Elkanah. The notorious impostor. 1692; ed S. Peterson, Los Angeles 1958 (Augustan Reprint Soc) (with Settle, Diego redivivus). Rogue biography; the confidence-man William Morrell.

The players tragedy: or fatal love. 1693. Realistic story of backstage intrigue, based on actual amour of Mrs Bracegirdle, Lord Mohun and murder of actor Mountfort. Competent fictional technique.

Virtue rewarded: or the Irish Princess. 1693. Combines military, domestic, political, sentimental material; realistic treatment; by Mrs Mary Manley?

d'Aulnoy, Marie, comtesse. The present Court of Spain. 1693, 1698. Several novels; varied content; one, The enamored Teresa, is epistolary-psychological.

Foigny, Gabriel de. A new discovery of Terra Incognita Australis: or the southern world. 1693. Utopian; see J. M. Patrick, A consideration of La terre australe connue by Gabriel de Foigny, PMLA 61 1946.

Trotter, Catherine. Olinda's adventures. 1693 (in Letters of love, gallantry and several occasions), 1718, 1724 (in Familiar letters of love); ed R. A. Day, Los Angeles 1969 (Augustan Reprint Soc). Excellent domestic novel in letters.

The adventures of the Helvetian hero with the young Countess of Albania: or the amours of Armadorus and Vincentia. 1694. Novel of contemporary life; well developed plot.

Scarron incens'd: or his appearing to Madam Maintenon. 1694. Tr from Scarron apparu à Mme de Maintenon, 1694; purports to be inside story of her career and to include authentic documents.

The unhappy lovers: or the timorous fair one. 1694. Realistic novel in letter form; has been attributed to Mrs Mary Manley.

Petronius, Titus. The satyr of Titus Petronius Arbiter. 1694; 7 edns by 1736. Trn of the Satyricon by W. Burnaby and another.

Sergeant, John. An historical romance of the wars. 1694. Secret history of Revolution of 1688; Jacobite; uses allegory.

Settle, Elkanah. The complete memoirs of the life of that notorious impostor Will Morrell. 1694, 1698; ed S. Peterson in The counterfeit lady unveiled, Garden City NY 1961; see S. Peterson, William Morrell and late seventeenth-century fiction, PQ 42 1963. Rogue biography.

Crouch, Nathaniel. The unfortunate Court favourites of England. 1695; 6 edns by 1729. Collection of brief popularized biographies, pseudo-historical fiction.

The French convert. 1696; numerous edns through 19th century. Huguenot propaganda; probably trn of a French work, semi-fictional, autobiographical. Tr Charles Gildon?

Behn, Aphra. The histories and novels [reprints Oroonoko, The fair jilt, Agnes de Castro, The lover's watch, The lucky mistake [see above]; adds Mrs Behn's letters and fictional biography]. 1696, 1697 (with The King of Bantam, The nun, The black lady); at least 10 edns by 1751. See R. A. Day, Aphra Behn's first biography, SB 22 1969.

Courtilz de Sandras, Gatien. The memoirs of the Count de Rochefort. 1696, 1700, 1705. Pseudo-authentic, picaresque account of French Court and military life. See W. Füger, Courtilz de Sandras, der französische Defoe, Die Neueren Sprachen 12 1963.

Le Noble de Tennelière, Eustache. Abra-Mulè: or a true history of the dethronement of Mahomet IV. 1696. Romanticized history; tr 'J.P.'.

Manley, Mary de la Riviere. Letters written by Mrs Manley, to which is added a letter from a suppos'd nun in Portugal. 1696, 1713, 1725 (as A stage-coach journey to Exeter), 1735 (in Mr Pope's literary correspondence). Lively account of a journey, imitating Mme d'Aulnoy's methods, based on actual correspondence; much imitated in next decades.

Pix, Mary. The inhumane cardinal: or innocence betray'd. 1696. Lurid, lengthy novel of amorous intrigue in Rome.

Quevedo Villegas, Francisco de. Fortune in her wits: or

the hour of all men. 1697, 1707 (in Comical works); at least 7 edns by 1800. Tr Capt John Stevens.

Behn, Aphra. The unfortunate bride: or the blind lady a beauty; The unfortunate happy lady; The wandring beauty. 1698 (as separate pamphlets?), 1700 (bound into Histories, novels and translations). The only appearance of these novels, ptd posthumously by S. Briscoe; ed M. Summers in Works of Aphra Behn, 1915, New York 1967.

Ward, Edward. The London spy. 18 pts, 2 vols 1698–1700, 1 vol 1700; 7 or more edns by 1724; ed K. Fenwick 1955. See H. W. Troyer, Ned Ward of Grubstreet, Cambridge Mass 1946; W. J. Cameron, Bibliography of Ned Ward, N & Q July 1953; S. H. Ward, The works of Ward, N & Q Oct 1953. Lively account of rambles through London's districts.

A collection of novels. 2 vols 1699-1700. 7 novels in all, including Brémond, The viceroy of Catalonia, The happy slave; Congreve, Incognita. Probably unsold copies bound into volumes.

The compleat mendicant or unhappy beggar: being the life of an unfortunate gentleman. 1699, 1700 etc. Realistic pseudo-autobiography.

Woman's malice. 1699. Supposed account of amours of Louis Duras, Earl of Faversham.

d'Aulnoy, Marie, comtesse. Tales of the fairys. 1699, 1716 (new trn). First appearance in English of several famous fairy tales; at least 15 edns by 1800.

Farquhar, George (?). The adventures of Covent Garden in imitation of Scarron's City romance. 1699. Realistic tale of London life; based on Furetière, Roman bourgeois, not on Scarron. See G. Stonehill, Complete works of Farquhar, 1930.

Fénelon, François. The adventures of Telemachus the son of Ulysses. 1699 (incomplete), 1700; numerous edns through century; highly esteemed. First English trn, by I. Littlebury and A. Boyer.

Winstanley, William. The Essex champion: or the famous history of Sir Billy of Billerecay. 1699 (an earlier edn, perhaps 1690). The adventures of an English Quixote, bemused by romances.

The amours of Edward the IV. 1700. Perhaps a trn; follows pattern of French romanticized histories; introduces Richard III.

Bateman's tragedy: or the perjured bride justly rewarded. [1700?]. Lurid tale of revenge; urban setting; bourgeois characters.

Behn, Aphra. The dumb virgin; The unhappy mistake. 1700 (in Histories, novels and translations: also separately?). The only appearance of these tales; see The unfortunate bride, 1698, above.

Brown, Thomas. Amusements serious and comical, calculated for the meridian of London. 1700; at least 10 edns by 1760; ed A. L. Hayward 1927; see B. Boyce, Tom Brown of facetious memory, Cambridge Mass 1939. Uses ingénu device for social satire.

Courtilz de Sandras, Gatien. The French spy: or the memoirs of John Baptist de la Fontaine. 1700, 1703. Autobiographical memoir of soldier of fortune; purports to reveal secret history.

Cr[awford], D[avid]. Several letters, containing: The unfortunate Dutchess, Love after enjoyment, The unhappy mistake. 1700. First tale rptd separately, 1739; second separately, 1735. Epistolary fiction in manner of French romances. See D. Macaree, Crawfurd: a for gotten man of Scottish letters, Stud in Scottish Lit 5 1967.

Ward, Edward, et al. A pacquet from Will's. 1701, 1705 (in Works of Voiture vol 2), 1724 (in Familiar letters of love). Miscellany of narrative letters, humorous and satirical.

The adventures of Lindamira, a lady of quality. 1702, 1703, 1713 (as The lover's secretary) etc; ed B. Boyce, Minneapolis 1949. Epistolary domestic novel of excellent quality; ascription to Thomas Brown unjustified.

The perfidious P—: being letters from a nobleman to two ladies. 1702, 1704. Dramatic epistolary novel; excellent technique and characterization.

Russen, David. Iter-lunare: or a voyage to the moon. 1703, 1707. Whimsical Utopian romance.

Boccalini, Traiano. Secretaria di Apollo: or letters from Apollo. 1704. Early example of satirical genre of letters from the dead to the living. Tr Martin Bladen; see G. L. Brodersen, A Boccalini translation identified, N & Q April 1953.

Davys, Mary. The amours of Alcippus and Leucippe. 1704. Domestic comedy of manners; commonsense realism.

Avellaneda, Alonso Fernandez de. A continuation of the comical history of the most ingenious knight Don Quixote. 1705. Trn of a version by Le Sage of the Spanish original.

Davys, Mary. The fugitive. 1705, 1725 (in Works). Humorous, loosely organized tale, based on own life.

Manley, Mary Delariviere. The secret history of Queen Zarah and the Zarazians. 1705; 5 edns by 1749. Sensational account of Sarah, Duchess of Marlborough. Preface ed B. Boyce, Los Angeles 1952 (Augustan Reprint Soc).

The jilted bridegroom: or the London coquet. 1706. Domestic epistolary tale; London middle-class life; unusual realism.

Galland, Antoine. The Arabian nights entertainments: consisting of one thousand and one stories. 1706; 8 edns listed by 1736; numerous edns through century in 3–12 vols. Pts 1–6 of French version had appeared by 1704, the remainder by 1717.

The pleasant intrigues and surprising adventures of an English nobleman at the last carnival at Venice. 1707. Complex plot of adventure; anticipates modern novel of espionage.

The Spanish libertines: or the lives of Justina, Celestina and Estevanillo Gonzales. 1707, 1709. New trns of 3 famous Spanish novels by Capt John Stevens.

d'Aulnoy, Marie, comtesse. The diverting works of the Countess D'Anois. 1707; at least 4 edns by 1749, varying from 1–3 vols. Includes her fairy tales, a fictionalized autobiography, Spanish histories.

—— The history of the Earl of Warwick, sirnam'd the Kingmaker. 1707, 1708. Trn of Le comte de Warwick, love story with slight historical content.

—— Memoirs of the Court of England. 1707, 1708. Trn by J.C.; amorous history of the Court of Charles II.

La Chapelle, Jean de. The adventures of Catullus, and history of his amours with Lesbia. 1707, 1708. Trn of romanticized biographical novel of 1680–1, interspersed with Catullus's poems.

Manley, Mary Delariviere. The lady's pacquet of letters, taken from her by a French privateer in her passage to Holland. 1707, 1708. Pt 1, ptd with d'Aulnoy, Memoirs of the Court of England; Pt 2, ptd with d'Aulnoy, History of the Earl of Warwick, 1711 (complete, 41 letters, as Court intrigues). Epistolary fiction of several varieties, excellent technique; see P. B. Anderson, Delariviere Manley's prose fiction, PQ 13 1934. Letter 33 ed N. Würzbach in The novel in letters, 1969.

An account of some remarkable passages in the life of a private gentleman, with reflections thereon. 1708, 1711, 1715 (as An abstract of the remarkable passages). Autobiographical; much realistic self-analysis; anticipates Defoe. See G. A. Starr, Defoe and spiritual autobiography, Princeton 1965.

A voyage to the new island Fonseca, near Barbadoes. 1708. Imaginary letters by 2 travellers satirizing life in England and the colonies.

Alemán, Mateo. Guzman de Alfarache. 1708. Preface ed C. E. Jones, Los Angeles 1957 (Augustan Reprint Soc).

d'Aulnoy, Marie, comtesse. Hypolitus Earl of Douglas, with the secret history of Mack-Beth; the amours of Count Schlick. 1708; 5 edns by 1768; 1773 (another trn). Hypolitus is a typical pseudo-historical novel; Count Schlick is a new version of Aeneas Sylvius (Pope Pius II), Historia de duobus amantibus, 1444, a Renaissance roman à clef.

Gildon, Charles. The new metamorphosis: being the golden ass of Lucius Apuleius. 1708; 5 edns by 1733. May be original or trn; popularized adaptation.

Lesage, Alain René. Le diable boiteux: or the Devil upon two sticks. 1708; 6th edn 1729; numerous edns through century. Early example of non-human spy genre.

Misson, François. A new voyage to the east-Indies by Francis Leguat and his companions. 1708. Partly Utopian; ed P. Oliver 1891; see G. Atkinson, A French desert island novel of 1708, PMLA 36 1921.

Pétis de la Croix, François. Turkish tales. 1708. See The Persian and the Turkish tales, 1714, below.

The life and adventures of Capt John Avery, the famous English pirate. 1709. Fictitious biography, in manner of Defoe.

Gildon, Charles. The golden spy: or a political journal of the British nights entertainments. 2 vols 1709–10, 1 vol [1724?]. Inanimate spy; gold piece explores many social levels; early example of popular genre.

Manley, Mary Delariviere. Secret memoirs and manners of several persons of quality of both sexes from the new Atalantis. 1709; at least 7 edns by 1736. Alleged secrets of numerous contemporary notables; the archetypal scandal novel; highly popular.

Olivier, J., abbé. Memoirs of the life and adventures of Signor Rozelli. 1709; 5 edns by 1725; continuation, 1724. Picaresque adventures; anti-Catholic propaganda. Trn has been doubtfully assigned to Defoe.

[Cibber, Colley?]. The secret history of Arlus and Odolphus, ministers of state to the Empress of Grandinsula. 1710 (3 edns). Thinly-veiled political satire, pro-Harley, anti-Godolphin. One of several similar works in a controversy using the same names.

Manley, Mary Delariviere. Memoirs of Europe, towards the close of the eighth century. 1710, 1711 etc, 1720 (with New Atalantis as Secret memoirs); 7th edn by 1736. Continuation of scandal-chronicle of contemporary personages.

The generous rivals: or love triumphant. 1711, 1713, 1716. Comedy; misunderstandings of lovers; colloquial style; set in London.

The tell-tale: or the invisible witness. 1711. Whimsical satire on beaux and belles; narrator spies, invisible.

Bordelon, Laurent, abbé. A history of the ridiculous extravagances of Monsieur Oufle. 1711, 1754. Trn of satirical account of adept deluded by books on magic.

The history of Prince Mirabel's infancy, rise and disgrace; with the sudden promotion of Novicius. 1712, 1712. Political satire on Marlborough and Harley.

The history of the proceedings of the mandarins and proatins of the Britomartian empire. 1712, 1713. Pretended secret history of maneuvers of chief Whigs and Tories.

Oldmixon, John. The secret history of Europe. 1712; 4 edns by 1724. Secret history with Whig bias.

The infernal congress: or news from below. 1713, 1713. Letter from the dead to the living; social and political satire.

Letters of Abelard and Heloise; to which is prefix'd a particular account of their lives, amours and misfortunes. 1713, 1714 etc; 10 edns by 1765; serialized 1734–5. Trn by John Hughes of DuBois, Histoire des amours et infortunes d'Abélard et d'Héloïse, romanticized account with versions of their letters. Highly popular; 1722 edn rptd 1904 (Temple Classics).

A new voyage to the island of fools, representing the policy, government and present state of the Stultitians. 1713, 1715. Ramble through London; satire of manners. Attributed to Edward Ward; resembles his manner in London spy.

Barker, Jane. Love's intrigues: or the history of the amours of Bosvil and Galesia. 1713; at least 4 edns by 1750 (with other titles, and in Barker, Entertaining novels). Moralizing romance.

Bland, Captain. The northern Atalantis: or York spy. 1713, 1713. Scandal-chronicle of Yorkshire gentry.

Smith, Alexander. The history of the lives and robberies of the most noted highway-men. 1713; 6 edns by 1720 (2–3 vols); 1734 (with Charles Johnson, General history of the pyrates); ed A. L. Hayward, New York 1926; see A. W. Secord, Captain Alexander Smith, TLS 19 April 1934. Collection of short rogue biographies, male and female; lively and often obscene; highly popular.

[Walpole, Sir Robert ?]. The present state of fairy-land. 1713. Anti-Tory propaganda in form of a letter to Louis XIV from an English squire; replies to attack on Walpole, The Testimonies of several citizens of Fickleborough. See J. H. Plumb, Sir Robert Walpole, 1956.

The Court of Atalantis. 1714, 1717, 1732 (as Court tales). Scandal-chronicle; short tales of court amours and political satire, anti-Tory; may be by John Oldmixon.

The ladies tale, exemplified in the virtues and vices of the quality. 1714; 3 edns by 1741. Short stories in a frame narrative.

The rover. Br Mercury 1714. First long fiction to have first pbn in instalments; picaresque. See C. E. Jones, The Rover 1714, N & Q May 1956.

Hamilton, Anthony. Memoirs of the life of the Count de Grammont. 1714, 1719; at least 4 edns by 1760. Tr Abel Boyer; ed and tr N. Deakin 1965. See J. R. Foster, Peregrine Pickle and the Memoirs of Count Grammont, MLN 46 1951; C.-E. Engel, Le véritable chevalier de Gramont, Revue des Deux Mondes May 1960; H. Drion, Mémoires du chevalier de Grammont, Tirade 8 1964.

Manley, Mary Delariviere. The adventures of Rivella. 1714, 1717, 1725. Lively fictionalized autobiography; secret history, scandal.

Pétis de la Croix, François. The Persian and the Turkish tales, compleat. 1714, 1718 etc; 6 edns by 1750. Tr William King et al from Les Mille et un jours, and Histoire de la sultane de Perse, contes turcs; Ambrose Philips' version of the former, 1714, had 5 edns by 1738. Extremely popular and influential; see 1708, above.

The fatal effects of arbitrary power. 1715. Secret history of Philip II of Spain in form of memoir by a Minister.

The German Atalantis. 1715, 1719, 1721 (as Hanover tales). Scandal-chronicle of German and English Courts of George I.

The history of Menuthia; with an account of the chief transactions in that kingdom. Nottingham 1715. Hanoverian politics, disguised as a letter from Madagascar.

Barker. Jane. Exilius: or the banish'd Roman; written after the manner of Telemachus. 1715, 1719–50 (in Entertaining novels). Short romance, with inserted histories; modest, moralizing tone.

Renneville, René Auguste. The French inquisition: or the history of the Bastille in Paris. Tr from L'Inquisition françoise, 1715. Sensational memoir in manner of Defoe; anti-clerical.

Smith, Alexander. The secret history of the lives of the most celebrated beauties. 1715, 1716 (as The school of Venus and The Court of Venus), 1730 (vol 2 as Court intrigues). Large collection of brief lives of famous courtesans and royal favourites; lively, anecdotal style; inserted letters.

'Symson, William'. A new voyage to the East Indies. 1715, 1720, 1732. A probable source of Gulliver's travels. See R. W. Frantz, Gulliver's Cousin Sympson, HLQ 1 1938.

DuNoyer, Anne Marguerite Petit. Letters from a lady at Paris to a lady at Avignon. 1716, 1716, 1717. Tr from Lettres historiques et galantes; lively imitated correspondence with Court gossip and good characterization.

Lesage, Alain René. The history and adventures of Gil Blas of Santillane. 1716; 5 edns by 1744 (2–4 vols). Trn of Histoire de Gil Blas, 1715–35; superseded by Smollett's trn, 1749.

Lyly, John. Euphues and Lucilla: or the false friend and inconstant mistress. 1716; 5 edns by 1732. Modernized version, rewritten and recast, of Euphues.

Theobald, Lewis. The history of the loves of Antiochus and Stratonice. 1717, 1721. Retelling of legend, probably with French novel as intermediary.

The double captive: or chains upon chains. 1718; ed N. Würzbach in The novel in letters, 1969. Epistolary tale, ostensibly by prisoner in Newgate; realistic pictures of prison life.

Hearne, Mary. The lover's week: or the six days adventures of Philander and Amaryllis. 1718, 1718, 1720 (in Honour the victory and love the prize), 1724 (serialized in Original London Post), 1726; ed N. Würzbach in The novel in letters, 1969. Epistolary autobiographical tale; excellent characterization.

Le Noble de Tennelière, Eustache. Pure love, a novel: being the history of the princess Zulima. 1718, 1719 (as Zulima), 1725, 1750 (as Pure love). Tr M.B. from Zulima, 1694 or 1718. Sentimental novel in French historical mode.

Moncrif, François Augustin Paradis de. Indian tales: or the adventures of Zeloide and Amanzarifdine. 1718; ed C. K. Scott-Moncrieff 1929.

Quintana, Francisco de. The most entertaining history of Hyppolito and Aminta: being a collection of delightful novels. 1718, 1721 etc. Tr John Stevens from Spanish novel of 1627.

Passionate love-letters between a Polish princess and a certain chevalier. 1719. Epistolary novel; purports to be correspondence of the Old Pretender and Maria Clementina of Poland. See R. A. Day, Told in letters, Ann Arbor 1966.

The secret history of the Prince of the Nazarenes and two Turks; The fatal amour between a beautiful lady and a young nobleman. 1719, 1721 (3rd edn). First tale appears to be political satire; second an epistolary, realistic tale of adultery.

Barker, Jane. The entertaining novels of Mrs Jane Barker. 1719; 3 edns by 1736; 1750. Consists of Exilius, Bosvil and Galesia; see above, 1713, 1715.

Butler, Sarah. Milesian tales: or instructive novels for the happy conduct of life. 1719, 1727. May have appeared 1716 as Irish tales; perhaps by Charles Gildon.

Gildon, Charles. The post-man robb'd of his mail: or the packet broke open. 1719. Epistolary miscellany containing psychological novel, The lover's sighs. See R. A. Day, Told in letters, Ann Arbor 1966.

Haywood, Eliza. Love in excess: or the fatal enquiry. 1719; at least 9 edns by 1750. Sensationally popular; melodramatic romance of passion and intrigue.

Hearne, Mary. The female deserters. 1719, 1720 (with The lover's week; see 1718, above), 1731 (in A collection of curious novels). Sequel to The lover's week; inserted histories.

The German rogue. 1720. Trn of contemporary version of Tyl Eulenspiegel tale.

A select collection of novels in six volumes. 1720, 1725, 1729 (with 9 novels added); 6 edns by 1740. Ed Samuel Croxall; 26 titles, mostly trns, of best and most popular short fiction of previous century; authors include Cervantes, Machiavelli, Mme de La Fayette, Lesage, Brémond, Scarron, Saint-Réal, Alemán, Mlle de La Roche-Guilhem, Fénelon; Huet's essay on romances in vol 1.

Blackamore, Arthur. The perfidious brethren: or the religious triumvirate, displayed in three ecclesiastical novels. 1720. Attacks priests, Presbyterians, Anabaptists; see R. B. Davis, Blackamore: the Virginia colony and the early English novel, Virginia Mag of History & Biography 75 1967.

Chetwood, William Rufus. The voyages, dangerous adventures and imminent escapes of Capt R. Falconer. 1720; 6 edns by 1769. Manner of Defoe.

Gildon, Charles. Miscellanea aurea: or the golden medley. 1720. Epistolary miscellany, moral in tone; contains 2 utopian imaginary voyages and a psychological novel in letters.

Manley, Mary Delariviere. The power of love, in seven novels. 1720, 1741. Free adaptations from Bandello, perhaps from versions in Painter, Palace of pleasure.

P., W. (William Pittis?). The Jamaica lady: or the life of Bavia. 1720; ed W. H. McBurney in Four before Richardson, Lincoln Nebraska 1963. Female rogue.

The secret history of Pythagoras. 1721, 1722. Tr Dr James Walker; subtitle may have inspired Walpole's title, The Castle of Otranto.

Aubin, Penelope. The life of Madam de Beaumont, a French lady. 1721, 1728; several other edns; c. 1770 (as Belinda). Adventure, romance, religion; see R. B. Dooley, Penelope Aubin: forgotten Catholic novelist, Renascence 11 1959.

—— The strange adventures of the Count de Vinevil and his family. 1721, 1728 etc, 1739 (in A collection of entertaining histories and novels). Sensational adventures; Turkish setting.

Boursault, Edmé. Letters from a lady of quality to a chevalier. 1721, 1724 (also in Works of Mrs Haywood). Tr Eliza Haywood from Lettres nouvelles, 1699; sentimental-psychological epistolary novel: little action.

Chamberlen, Paul. Love in its empire, illustrated in seven novels. 1721. First is original; others trns from La Roche-Guilhem, La foire de Beaucaire, 1708 etc; novels of intrigue.

Le Noble de Tennelière, Eustache. Ildegerte, Queen of Norway. 1721, 1722. Tr John Cavendish from Histoire d'Ildegerte, 1695, romanticized history, ultimately from Saxo Grammaticus.

Armeno, Christoforo. The travels and adventures of three Princes of Sarendip. 1722; ed T. G. Remer, Norman Oklahoma 1965. Tr from French version by Mailly, 1719; see B. E. Schaar, Serendipity, N & Q Oct 1960. Fantastic adventures; Horace Walpole's favourite.

Aubin, Penelope. The life and amorous adventures of Lucinda, an English lady. 1722, 1739. Autobiography; heroine captured by Barbary pirates.

—— The noble slaves: or the lives and adventures of two lords and two ladies. 1722, 1729; numerous edns through century. Similar in plot to Lucinda, above.

Courtilz de Sandras, Gatien de. The unfortunate marriage. 1722. Trn of Mémoires de Mme la marquise de Fresne, 1701. Separated spouses, Turkish captivity.

Haywood, Eliza. The British recluse: or the secret history of Cleomira, suppos'd dead. 1722; 4 edns by 1732. Imitation of Mrs Aubin's romances.

Montesquieu, Charles de Secondat, baron de. Persian letters. 1722, 1730; 6 edns by 1773. Tr John Ozell; epistolary; pioneering psychological, sociological fiction; influential and much imitated.

Love letters between a certain late nobleman and the famous Mr Wilson. 1723. Epistolary scandal-chronicle; see R. A. Day, Told in letters, Ann Arbor 1966.

Aubin, Penelope. The life of Charlotta Du Pont. 1723, 1733; 6 edns by 1800. Abduction and adventure in North and South America.

Barker, Jane. A patch-work screen for the ladies. 1723. Stories in frame, with poems; mild romances of country life.

Blackamore, Arthur. Luck at last: or the happy unfortunate. 1723, 1737 (as The distress'd fair); ed W. H. McBurney, in Four before Richardson, Lincoln Nebraska 1963. Decorous and domestic; heroine disguised as servant.

Haywood, Eliza. Idalia: or the unfortunate mistress. 1723; 4 edns by 1732. The Haywood formula established; amorous misadventures.

—— Lasselia: or the self-abandon'd. 1723; 4 edns by 1732.

Thibault, gouverneur de Talmont. The life of Pedrillo del Campo. 1723. Tr Ralph Brookes; Spanish picaresque modified for French taste as roman comique.

Walker, Capt Charles. Authentick memoirs of the life intrigues and adventures of the celebrated Sally Salisbury. 1723, 1724. Lively memoir of famous courtesan; inserted letters from her clients; combines jestbook with rogue biography.

Love upon tick: or implicit gallantry. 1724, 1725. Foolish fop duped by feigned love letters; clever satire; style and details suggest Mary Manley as author.

A narrative of all the robberies, escapes etc of John Sheppard. 1724 (8 edns). Feigned autobiography of famous highwayman.

A., Ma. The prude. 3 pts 1724-6 (4 edns). Interesting mixture of character study and adventure; girl a secret libertine.

Davys, Mary. The reform'd coquet. 1724, 1725; at least 8 edns by 1785. Exemplary novel; humour; good characterization, plotting.

E., G. Authentick memoirs of the life and surprizing adventures of John Sheppard. 1724. Rogue biography in series of letters.

Gomez, Madeleine, dame de. La belle assemblée: or the adventures of six days. 1724, 1725; 8 edns by 1765. Tr Eliza Haywood from Les journées amusantes; collection of novels in a frame story. See C. C. Mish, Mme de Gomez and La belle assemblée, Revue de Littérature Comparée 34 1960.

Haywood, Eliza. The fatal secret: or constancy in distress. 1724; 4 edns by 1732. Novel of passion; melodramatic psychology.

—— The masqueraders: or fatal curiosity. 1724; 6 edns by 1732. Intrigue in high life.

—— A spy upon the conjurer. 1724-5 (several issues). Secret history, largely epistolary, of Duncan Campbell, a famous soothsayer of the period.

—— The works of Mrs Eliza Haywood. 1724; 8 novels, together with poems and plays, rptd in 4 vols.

'Johnson, Capt Charles'. A general history of the robberies and murders of the most notorious pyrates. 1724, 1724; 6 edns by 1734 (combined with Smith's History of highwaymen, 1713). Often reissued, adapted and abridged.

—— The history of the life and intrigues of that celebrated courtezan and posture-mistress, Eliz Mann. 1724. Hack biography hastily compiled; plagiarism from jestbooks.

Bussy-Rabutin, Roger de. The amorous history of the Gauls. 1725, 1727. New trn, probably by Samuel Humphreys, of the archetypal scandal-novel. See 1682, above.

Davys, Mary. The works of Mrs Davys. 1725. 2 vols, containing works listed above, 1704, 1705, 1724, with The cousins and Familiar letters betwixt a gentleman and a lady. Last item ed R. A. Day, Los Angeles 1955 (Augustan Reprint Soc).

Gueulette, Thomas Simon. Chinese tales: or the wonderful adventures of the mandarin Fum-Hoam. 1725, 1740; 4 edns by 1800; ed L. C. Smithers 1894. Tr J. Macky; 2 other versions recorded in same year.

Haywood, Eliza. Bath-intrigues. 1725 (3 edns), 1727 (in Secret histories). Lively epistolary scandal chronicle.

—— Fantomina: or love in a maze. 1725, 1732 (in Secret histories). Clever story of amorous stratagems.

—— Memoirs of a certain island adjacent to the kingdom of Utopia. 1725, 1726. Scandal chronicle of politics and amours in high life, in manner of New Atalantis, with key.

—— Secret histories, novels and poems. 4 vols 1725; 4 edns by 1742. Reissue of 11 novels.

Segrais, Jean Regnauld de. Five novels. 1725 (2 formats); 4 edns by 1736. Tr from Nouvelles françaises, reissued 1722. Condensed romances.

Aubin, Penelope. The life and adventures of the lady Lucy. 1726, 1728, 1739 (in collection). Separated spouses, fantastic adventures; historical matter involving Irish rebellion under James II.

Barker, Jane. The lining for the patch-work screen. 1726. Tales as a sequel; see 1723; one continues story of Portuguese nun.

Chetwood, William Rufus. The voyages and adventures of Captain Robert Boyle. 1726, 1727; at least 13 edns by 1800. Extremely popular; adventure, sentiment, hazard; resembles manner of Defoe, but lacks moral tone; partly set in America.

Haywood, Eliza. The city jilt: or the alderman turn'd beau. 1726 (3 edns), 1727 (in Secret histories). Clever plot; realistic depiction of middle-class life.

—— The mercenary lover: or the unfortunate heiresses. 1726, 1726, 1728. Primitive psychological novel.

St Hyacinthe, Themiseul de. The adventures of Pomponious, a Roman knight. 1726. Tr S. Macky; scandal novel of French court; see C. C. Mish, A voyage to the moon, N & Q Dec 1955.

Smith, Alexander. Memoirs of the life and times of the famous Jonathan Wilde. 1726. One of several rogue biographies of Wild.

'Brunt, Samuel'. A voyage to Cacklogallinia. 1727; ed M. H. Nicolson, New York 1940. Satire imitative of Swift.

Chasles, Robert. The illustrious French lovers. 1727, 1739 (one episode as The unnatural mother, 1734). Tr Penelope Aubin from Les illustres Françoises, 1722; 7 interlinked realistic tales. See F. Deloffre, edn of original, Paris 1959.

Davys, Mary. The accomplish'd rake: or modern fine gentleman. 1727, 1756; ed W. H. McBurney in Four before Richardson, Lincoln Nebraska 1963. Satiric, realistic, humorous; much indebted to Restoration comedy.

Haywood, Eliza. Cleomelia: or the generous mistress. 1727, 1727. Passion, adventure, intrigue.

—— The fruitless enquiry. 1727; 5 edns by 1800. Stories linked by framework of a quest for happiness.

—— Letters from the palace of fame. 1727 (also in Secret histories). Epistolary scandal chronicle of political figures.

—— The life of madam de Villesache, written by a lady, who was an eye-witness of the greatest part of her adventures. 1727. Probably trn of unidentified French source; unusually good analysis of heroine's feelings, motivations.

—— Love in its variety. 1727. 6 novels, said to be trns from Bandello; more probably original or very freely adapted.

—— The perplex'd Dutchess, or treachery rewarded: being some memoirs of the Court of Malfy. 1727, 1727, 1728. No connection with Webster's play; intrigues of a scheming parvenue.

—— Philidore and Placentia: or l'amour trop delicat. 1727; ed W. M. McBurney in Four before Richardson, Lincoln Nebraska 1963. Highflown tale of love and adventure.

—— The secret history of the present intrigues of the Court of Caramania. 1727, 1727. Love and politics at the English Court; a key-novel.

Longueville, Peter. The hermit: or the unparalled sufferings and surprising adventures of Mr Philip Quarll, an Englishman. 1727 (2 versions); 13 edns by 1800. Highly successful exploitation of Crusoe idea; extreme variety of adventures; many versions, including chap-book abridgements.

Plantin, Arabella. Two novels: the ingrateful; Love led astray. 1727, 1731 (as a filler in miscellanies relating to Duke of Wharton). Romances with a moral tone.

The illegal lovers: a true secret history. 1728. Unusual anticipation of psychological novel. See R. A. Day, Told in letters, Ann Arbor 1966.

Some memoirs of the amours and intrigues of a certain Irish dean. 1728, 1730 (3rd edn). Attack on Swift and the Blount sisters combined with tale of extravagant passion; see R. A. Day, An anonymous attack on Swift, N & Q Dec 1955.

The velvet coffee-woman. 1728. Supposed biography of the notorious Mrs Anne Rochford, composed entirely of plagiarisms from works of popular fiction; see R. A. Day, How to write a shilling biography, Newberry Lib Bull 6 1970.

Beauchamps, Pierre François Godart de. The history of King Apprius, translated from a Persian manuscript. 1728, 1728, 1739. Trn of Histoire du prince Apprius 1728. Obscene account of sexual matters using anagrams; Apprius is Priapus, etc.

Haywood, Eliza. The agreeable Caledonian: or memoirs of signiora di Morella, a Roman lady. 2 pts 1728, 1729, 1 vol 1768 (as Clementina). Intrigues and adventures in Italy; heroine abducted from convent.

—— Irish artifice: or the history of Clarina. 1728. Grimly realistic story of a fortune-hunter and his victim.

Préchac, Jean de. The disguis'd Prince: or the beautiful Parisian. 1728, 2 pts 1729, 1 vol 1733. Tr Eliza Haywood from L'illustre Parisienne, 1679; free rendition; amusing version of student-prince theme.

Rowe, Elizabeth. Friendship in death. 3 pts 1728–32; at least 18 edns by 1800. Letters from the dead to the living device for pious instruction; see H. S. Hughes, Elizabeth Rowe and the Countess of Hertford, PMLA 49 1944; J. J. Richetti, Mrs Elizabeth Rowe: the novel as polemic, PMLA 82 1967.

Bignon, Jean Paul. Adventures of Abdalla, son of Hanif. 1729; 4 edns by 1733. Tr W. Hatchett; fantastic adventures, with inserted histories in manner of romances.

Haywood, Eliza. The fair Hebrew. 1729, 1729. Use of Jewish characters for exoticism; realistic plot becomes sensational.

Lussan, Marguerite de. The life of the Countess de Gondez. 1729. Tr Penelope Aubin; adventure and morality.

Perrault, Charles? Tales of Mother Goose. 1729; several edns by 1800; many titles, versions, selections; tr Robert Samber. Authorship now questioned; see M. Soriano, Les contes de Perrault, Paris 1968.

Rowe, Elizabeth. Letters moral and entertaining. 3 pts 1729–33; numerous later edns; see Friendship in death, 1728, above. Similar, but better as fiction.

The brothers: or treachery punish'd. 1730. Spanish setting; romance plot with interpolated stories.

The unnatural mother and ungrateful wife. [1730?]. Domestic-realistic tale of family treachery; epistolary.

[Campbell, John?]. The polite correspondence: or rational amusement. [1730?]. 6 series of letters; one, domestic novel of intrigue with complex plot, ed N. Würzbach in The novel in letters, 1969.

Haywood, Eliza. Love-letters on all occasions lately passed between persons of distinction. 1730. Collection ranging in scope from single narrative letters to short letter novels.

L., S. The amours of Philaris and Olinda: or the intrigues of Windsor. 1730; also undated edn as Windsor tales. Short romance in domestic setting; inserted letters.

A view of the beau monde: or memoirs of the celebrated Coquetilla. 1731. Picaresque secret history; detailed setting at Bath.

Winter evenings tales. 1731, Dublin 1733–4, 1737 (6th edn), 1738 (3 of the tales as French novels). 17 stories told by members of group, as in La belle assemblée.

Costeker, John Littleton. The constant lovers. 1731. 2 old-fashioned romances; the second, Alexis and Sylvia, ed N. Würzbach in The novel in letters, 1969.

Desfontaines, Pierre François Guyot. The travels of Mr John Gulliver, son to Capt Lemuel Gulliver. 1731. Tr John Lockman from Le nouveau Gulliver, 1730.

Prévost d'Exiles, Antoine François, abbé. The life of Mr Cleveland, natural son of Oliver Cromwell. 1731, 1734–5 etc, [Dublin] 1736. Numerous edns through century; several different trns, from Le philosophe anglais, 1731–9. Sensibility and deism; complex series of adventures; hero autodidact. Extremely popular and influential; much imitated; *see* G. Sherburn, MP 25 1928.

Valdory, Guillaume de. The adventures of the celebrated Madam de Muci. 1731. Epistolary; adventures, disguises, amorous intrigues; trn of Histoire de Madame de Muci, 1731.

The fair concubine: or the secret history of the beautiful Vanella. 1732 (3 edns). Scandal history of Miss Vane, mistress of Prince Frederick.

Memoirs of love and gallantry. 1732; also issued as Love in all shapes. Secret history of extreme complexity; vivid characters.

The perjur'd citizen: or female revenge. 1732. Sensational but realistic plot; pictures of bourgeois life; seems based on actual events.

Boyd, Elizabeth. The happy-unfortunate: or the female-page. 1732, 1737 (as Female page). Highly romantic tale of disguise and adventure; written entirely in blank verse rhythm.

Terrasson, Jean. The life of Sethos. 1732. Tr Thomas Lediard from Sethos, 1731; historical novel with moral purpose in imitation of Fénelon, Télémaque.

The finished rake: or gallantry in perfection. 1733. Unusually realistic autobiographical narrative; semi-picaresque; sympathetic treatment of hero's childhood.

Love without artifice: or the disappointed peer. 1733, 1734, 1736. Based on contemporary scandal; blend of fact and fiction; uses supposedly authentic letters as documentation.

The secret history of Mama Oella, Princess Royal of Peru. 1733. Key novel based on marriage of Anne, daughter of George II.

Fontanieu, Gaspard Moise de. Rosalinda: a novel. 1733, 1741. Trn of French version of a work by Bernardo Morando; mixed texture, numerous interpolated histories: moralizing romance.

Madden, Samuel. Memoirs of the twentieth century: being original letters of state under George the Sixth. 1733, 1763 (as The reign of George VI); ed C. Oman 1899. Satire against George II and Court; 6 vols projected, suppressed after vol 1.

Marini, Giovanni Ambrogio. The desperadoes; an heroick history. 1733. Trn of French version, Les désespérés, 1732; tale of mistaken identities and melodramatic adventure.

Tyssot de Patot, Simon. The travels and adventures of James Massey. 1733, 1743 (another version). Tr Stephen Whatley; *see* S. G. Andrews, The Wandering Jew and The travels and adventures of James Massey, MLN 72 1957.

Gomez, Madeleine, dame de. L'entretien des beaux esprits. 1734. Tr Eliza Haywood from Les cent nouvelles nouvelles, 1732. 13 stories in frame; emphasis on plot surprises.

Gueulette, Thomas Simon. Peruvian tales, related in one thousand and one hours. 1734, Dublin 1734, London 1735; at least 6 edns by 1800. Tr Samuel Humphreys and John Kelly from Les mille et une heures, 1733–4; variation on Arabian nights themes.

The English nobleman: or peasant of quality. 1735. Tr of My lord ***, 1702, evidently to profit from vogue of Marivaux, Paysan parvenu.

Crébillon, Claude Prosper Jolyot de, fils. Letters from the Marchioness de M*** to the Count de R***. 1735. Tr Samuel Humphreys; epistolary novel of extreme sensibility, action almost totally suppressed, psychological analysis.

— The skimmer: or the history of Tanzai and Néadarné. 1735, 1742, 1748. Fantasy with 'Japanese' setting; wit, eroticism, political and religious satire.

Lyttelton, George, Baron. Letters from a Persian in England to his friend at Ispahan. 1735 (4 edns); spurious continuation in same year, as The Persian letters continued; at least 11 edns by 1800. Influential; much imitated; foreign commentator on English institutions derived from Montesquieu, Lettres persanes.

Marivaux, Pierre Carlet de Chamblain de. Le paysan parvenu: or the fortunate peasant. 1735. Contains only the first 4 pts of the French original, all that had then appeared.

Celenia: or the history of Hyempsal king of Numidia. 1736, 1740. Pt 1 had appeared with The Persian letters continued, 1735, above. May be trn of Levesque, Célénie, 1732; allegorical apologue.

The history of Autonous. 1736. Account of autodidact living on desert island; one of many borrowings from Ibn Al-Tufail, 1674.

Letters from a Moor at London to his friends at Tunis. 1736. 24 letters combining travelogue with satire on English manners.

Cordonnier, Hyacinthe. The history of Prince Titi, a royal allegory. 1736. Tr Eliza Stanley; another trn, The memoirs and history of Prince Titi, in same year by James Ralph. Scandal novel concerning prince Frederick; *see* J. B. Shipley, James Ralph, Prince Titi and the black box of Frederick, Prince of Wales, BNYPL March 1967.

Gueulette, Thomas Simon. Mogul tales: or the dreams of men awake. 1736, 1743. Trn of Les Sultanes de Guzarate, 1732; had appeared in Applebee's Weekly Jnl 1733–5.

Haywood, Eliza. Adventures of Eovaai, Princess of Ijaveo. 1736, 1741 (as The unfortunate Princess). Pretended trn; secret history and satire attacking Walpole.

Locatelli, Francesco. Lettres moscovites: or Muscovian letters. 1736. Tr William Musgrave; 11 long letters of travel and adventure in Russia, mingling fact and fiction.

Marivaux, Pierre Carlet de Chamblain de. The life of Marianne: or the adventures of the Countess of ***. 3 vols 1736–42. Extremely popular and influential; many edns, other trns; *see* below, 1742, 1747, 1755.

A letter from Mrs Jane Jones, alias Jenny Diver. 1737. Ironic autobiography and advice to courtesans; ed N. Würzbach in The novel in letters, 1969; *see* TLS 25 Sept 1969.

Berington, Simon. The memoirs of Sigr Gaudentio de Lucca. 1737, 1738; 8 edns by 1800. Not a trn; Utopian voyage; *see* L. M. Ellison, Gaudentio de Lucca: a forgotten Utopia, PMLA 50 1935.

Lesage, Alain René. The bachelor of Salamanca: or memoirs of Don Cherubim de la Ronda. 2 vols 1737–9, 1767, Dublin 1784. Tr John Lockman; picaresque.

Pöllnitz, Karl Ludwig. Les amusemens de Spa: or the gallantries of the Spaw in Germany. 1737, 1737, 1739, 1740, 1745. Travelogue, anecdotes, secret histories.

Lediard, Thomas. The German spy, in familiar letters. 1738, 1740. Said to be a trn; more likely Lediard's own letters, enlarged and including anecdote and fiction.

Prévost d'Exiles, Antoine François, abbé. Memoirs of a man of quality. 1738, 1740; 5 edns by 1770 (with other titles). Autobiographical; pathos and sentiment.

Vega, Lope de. The pilgrim: or the stranger in his own country. 1738. Tr from Peregrino en su patria, 1604; collection of novels, with Montemayor and Gil Polo, Diana; already pbd in Applebee's Original Weekly Jnl.

The life and adventures of Mrs Christian Davies, commonly call'd Mother Ross. 1739. Fictionalized biography of woman who served in disguise as a soldier.

The unfortunate Dutchess: or the lucky gamester. 1739; *see* David Crawford, 1700, above.

d'Argens, Jean Baptiste de Boyer, marquis. The Jewish spy: being a philosophical, historical and critical correspondence. 5 vols 1739–40, 1744; 5 edns by 1766. Trn of Lettres juives, 1736; imitated correspondence on manners of several European countries.

Mottley, John. Joe Miller's jests: or the wit's vade-mecum. 1739 (3 edns); many further edns and versions; ed R. Hutchinson, New York 1963. The classic jestbook of the period; some anecdotes approach short fiction.

Mouhy, Charles de Fieux, Chevalier de. The fortunate country maid: being the entertaining memoirs of the present celebrated Marchioness of L.V. 1740, 1741; at least 5 edns by 1792. Trn of La paysanne parvenue, 1738; Eliza Haywood's trn as The virtuous villager, 1742. Distressed heroine; theme of Pamela and Marianne.

Tencin, Claudine Alexandrine Guérin de. The siege of Calais by Edward of England. 1740; 4 edns by 1751. Romantic treatment of history; unusual amount of historical detail, setting; tr Charles Dennis?

The true anti-Pamela: or memoirs of Mr James Parry, late organist of Ross. 1741, 1742, [Dublin] 1770. See W. J. T. Collins, A scandal of old Monmouthshire, Monmouthshire Rev 1 1933.

d'Argens, Jean Baptiste de Boyer, marquis. Chinese letters. [1739?], 1741, 1743, 1751 (as Chinese spy). Repeats method and manner of author's Lettres juives.

Chetwood, William Rufus. Five new novels. 1741. The twins ptd separately, 1742-3; Six historical relations, Dublin 1755, adds a novel. Probably trns; novels of love, adventure.

[Haywood, Eliza?]. Anti-Pamela: or feign'd innocence detected, in a series of Syrena's adventures. 1741, 1741. Typical Haywood tale; title a catchpenny device.

Kelly, John. Pamela's conduct in high life, publish'd from her original papers. 1741. A spurious sequel which appeared before Richardson's second part.

Lyttelton, George, Baron. The Court-secret: a melancholy truth. 1741 (5 edns); 2 more by 1743. Pseudo-oriental scandal chronicle; see W. B. Todd, Multiple editions of Lyttelton's The Court secret, PBSA 47 1953.

Collyer, Mary. The virtuous orphan: or the life of Marianne. 1742; ed W. H. McBurney and M. F. Shugrue, Carbondale 1965; 1746 (with changes as The life and adventures of Indiana). Very free adaptations of Marivaux, Vie de Marianne.

Crébillon, Claude Prosper Jolyot de, fils. The sofa. 1742; 18 edns by 1800. Salacious adaptation of the inanimate spy device.

Haywood, Eliza. The busy body: a successful spy. 1742. Adaptation of de Mouhy, La Mouche, 1736.

Holberg, Ludwig. A journey to the world underground, by Nicholas Klimius. 1742, 1746 etc. Imaginary voyage; Utopian satire on contemporary life.

Prévost d'Exiles, Antoine François, abbé. The dean of Coleraine. 1742-3, 1752 etc. Popular and esteemed; benevolence and morality combined with lurid adventure.

The lady's drawing room. 1744, Dublin 1746; 5 edns by 1799. Frame-stories; includes True history of Henrietta de Bellgrave, whose heroine is shipwrecked and lives among the Indians.

The travels and adventures of Mademoiselle de Richelieu. 1744. Epistolary; heroine travels over Europe in male disguise; said to be trn by Mr Erskine, may be original.

Collyer, Mary. Felicia to Charlotte: being letters from a young lady in the country to her friend in town. 2 vols 1744-9, 1755, 1788. Popular and influential; sentiment and delicacy; see H. S. Hughes, An early romantic novel, JEGP 15 1916.

Fielding, Sarah. The adventures of David Simple. 3 vols 1744-53, 1744 (1-2 rev Henry Fielding), 5 vols Dublin 1761; 3 more edns by 1792; ed M. Kelsall, Oxford 1969. The natural man; sentiment and adventure; see R. S. Hunting, Fielding's revisions of David Simple, Boston Univ Stud in Eng 3 1957.

Haywood, Eliza. The fortunate foundlings: being the genuine history of Colonel M—rs and his sister Madam Du P—y. 1744; 4 edns by 1761. Distresses in the manner of Marivaux; moral. Another version, The

happy orphans, 1759; 3 edns by 1770, is a trn by Edward Kimber of a French version with addns by Crébillon.

The life and adventures of Bampfylde-Moore-Carew. 1745 (also as The accomplished vagabond); several other versions, many edns by 1775. Rogue biography of real person; later versions influenced by Tom Jones; see T. Bloch, Bampfylde-Moore-Carew and Fielding's King of the gypsies, N & Q May 1967.

Fielding, Sarah. Familiar letters between the characters in David Simple. 1747, 1752. A sequel.

Cleland, John. Memoirs of a woman of pleasure. 2 vols 1748-9, 1750 (a reworking); numerous surreptitious edns; ed P. C. Quennell 1963. See J. Hollander, The old last act, Encounter Oct 1963; D. Foxon, Libertine literature in England 1660-1745, 1965. Epistolary-autobiographical; the classic of English pornography.

Graffigny, Françoise d'Issembourg d'Happoncourt. Letters written by a Peruvian Princess. 1748; many edns through century; other trns, 1752, 1774; 1749, sequel by R. Roberts. Very popular; theme of child of nature; sentimental primitivism, feminism.

Haywood, Eliza. Life's progress through the passions: or the adventures of Natura. 1748. Education of the heart by a series of encounters.

The history of Charlotte Summers, the fortunate parish girl. 1749, 1750 (corrected), Dublin 1753 etc. Popular and esteemed; female Tom Jones as heroine; sentimental; introduces Lady Bountiful.

The history of Tom Jones, the foundling, in his married state. 1749, 1750 (corrected), 1786.

Diderot, Denis. Les bijoux indiscrets: or the indiscreet toys. Paris 1749. Pornographic.

Fielding, Sarah. The governess, or the little female academy: being the history of Mrs Teachum and her nine girls. 1749; at least 7 edns by 1800; ed J. E. Gray, Oxford 1968. Didactic; advocates educational ideas of Locke.

Marivaux, Pierre Carlet de Chamblain de. Pharsamond: or the knight errant. 1749, 1750. Tr Lockman from Pharsamon, 1737; satire on modes of traditional French romance.

Hill, 'Sir' John. The adventures of Mr Loveill. 1750. Series of exemplary amorous encounters.

Kimber, Edward. The life and adventures of Joe Thompson. 1750, Dublin 1750; 6 edns by 1783. Lively, picaresque; see F. G. Black, Edward Kimber, anonymous novelist, Harvard Stud in Eng 17 1935.

Lennox, Charlotte. The life of Harriot Stewart, written by herself. 1750, 1751. Uses skeleton of Clarissa plot; autobiographical; troubled love; American scenes. See G. H. Maynadier, The first American novelist?, Cambridge Mass 1940.

Scott, Sarah. The history of Cornelia. 1750. Resembles Marianne, but more melodramatic.

Constantia: or a true picture of human life. 1751; preface rptd G. L. Barnett, Eighteenth-century novelists on the novel, New York 1968. 14 tales, 11 of foreign origin.

Cleland, John. Memoirs of a coxcomb: or the history of Sir William Delamere. 1751, 1782, New York 1963. Fictional autobiography; amorous adventures.

Coventry, Francis. The history of Pompey the little: or the life and adventures of a lap-dog. 1751; at least 10 edns by 1800; rptd 1926; preface ed C. E. Jones, Los Angeles 1957 (Augustan Reprint Soc). See W. Scott, N & Q June 1968. Entertaining satire of manners; toy dog as spy figure.

Haywood, Eliza. The history of miss Betsy Thoughtless. 1751, Dublin 1751; at least 8 edns by 1800. Girl matures, learns prudence; Haywood's best work. See J. P. Erickson, Evelina and Betsy Thoughtless, Texas Stud in Lit & Lang 6 1964.

Hill, 'Sir' John. The adventures of Mr George Edwards, a Creole. 1751, 1751, 1788. Exemplary experiences; West Indian setting; resembles Tom Jones.

—— The history of a lady of quality: or the adventures of Lady Frail. 1751. The story of Lady Vane, rushed into print before Smollett's version in Peregrine Pickle.

Morris, Ralph. A narrative of the life and astonishing adventures of John Daniel. 1751, 1770, 1926. Imaginary voyage; desert island; lunar flight.

Paltock, Robert. The life and adventures of Peter Wilkins, a Cornish man. 1751, Dublin 1751; at least 5 edns by 1800; 1915 (EL). Utopian voyage to a world within the earth; highly popular; dramatized; influenced Scott, Coleridge, Shelley; see A. N. Wilkins, Robert Paltock and the Bishop of Chester, N & Q Oct 1958.

[—— ?]. Memoirs of the life of Parnese, a Spanish lady of vast fortune. 1751. Story of adventure; heroine disguised as man.

The adventures of a valet; written by himself. 1752. Sprightly, realistic; hero goes on stage, to prison, is rescued etc.

The life of Patty Saunders, written by herself. 1752. Heroine has variety of highly romantic adventures.

Memoirs of the life and actions of Charles Osborne esq, natural son to the E—l of A—e. 1752. Hero enters on evil courses, reforms.

Chaigneau, William. The history of Jack Connor. 1752, Dublin 1752, 1753, 1766. Realistic, semi-picaresque.

Coyer, Gabriel François. A supplement to Lord Anson's voyage round the world: containing a discovery of the island Frivola. 1752, 1752, Dublin 1752. Imaginary voyage ridiculing French society of the period.

Gellert, Christian Fürchtegott. The history of the Swedish Countess of G—. 1752, 1757; new trn 1776; 2 more edns by 1780. Epistolary in part; attempts to blend Richardson with Prévost; teaches Christian resignation toward accidental bigamy, incest.

Goodall, William?. The adventures of Captain Greenland. 1752. Nautical adventures; life on a deserted island.

Lennox, Charlotte. The female Quixote: or the adventures of Arabella. 1752, Dublin 1752 (and an abridgment), 1783; 7 edns by 1800; ed M. Dalziel, Oxford 1969. Heroine bedazzled by reading romances; locus classicus of type.

Mozeen, Thomas. Young Scarron. 1752. Lively imitation of Roman comique; pictures life of English strolling players.

The history of Betty Barnes. 1753. Heroine is a housemaid, imitates Pamela. Attributed to Sarah Fielding.

Memoirs of Sir Charles Goodville and his family. 1753, 1778. Series of anecdotal letters to a friend; exemplary, written upon plan of Grandison to anticipate it.

Modern characters illustrated by histories in real life, and address'd to the polite world. 1753. Variety of short tales.

The travels and adventures of William Bingfield esq. 1753, 1799. Comic; fantastic and ridiculous adventures.

Haywood, Eliza. The history of Jenny and Jemmy Jessamy. 1753, Dublin 1753, London 1769, 1785 (Novelists' Mag). Hero escapes wiles of pretended innocent; she becomes debauched.

Smythies, Miss, of Colchester. The stage-coach: containing the characters of Mr Manley and the history of his fellow travellers. 1753, 1755, Berwick 1789, London 1791. See F. G. Black, A lady novelist of Colchester, Essex Rev 64 1935.

Wollaston, George. The life and history of a pilgrim. 1753, Dublin 1753. Picaresque.

Chit chat: or natural characters and the manners of real life. 1754. Novel of sensibility.

The history and adventures of Frank Hammond. 1754, 1755. Oxonian shifts for himself; satire of various livelihoods.

The history of Jasper Banks, commonly call'd the handsome man. 1754. Cautionary on marriage, parents, children; picaresque life.

d'Argens, Jean Baptiste de Boyer, marquis. Memoirs of the count du Beauval. 1754. Deals with the Dukes of Wharton and Ormond; preface to trn by Samuel Derrick ed B. Boyce, Los Angeles 1952 (Augustan Reprint Soc).

Dodd, William. The sisters: or the history of Lucy and Caroline Sanson. 1754, 1798. Exemplary; one sister rises, one falls; realistic scenes of London low life.

Guthrie, William. The friends: a sentimental history. 1754, 1759, 1761. Vicissitudes of love; preface discusses problem of making Grandisonian good man interesting.

Kimber, Edward. The history of the life and adventures of Mr Anderson. 1754. Adventures of a noble Indian chieftain in Europe; see M. W. Bingman, Mr Anderson: a novel of the late 18th century, Duke Univ Bibl Notes 34 1959.

Scott, Sarah. Agreeable ugliness. 1754. Sisters foreshadow sense and sensibility theme; probably a trn of P.-A. de la Place, La laideur aimable; see G. Onderwyzer, Sarah Scott's Agreeable ugliness: a translation, MLN 70 1955.

Shebbeare, John. The marriage act. 1754, 1755 (as Matrimony), 1766. Against Presbyterians and the act to prevent runaway matches; see J. R. Foster, Smollett's pamphleteering foe Shebbeare, PMLA 57 1942.

Smythies, Miss, of Colchester. The history of Lucy Wellers. 1754. Servant-girl heroine sacrifices passion to delicacy, rewarded.

The devil upon crutches in England. 1755; 7 edns by 1772. Imitation of Lesage, Le diable boiteux; spirit allows narrator to spy on variety of social types.

The history of Lavinia Rawlins. 1755, 1756. Sentimental, epistolary.

Memoirs of the Shakespear's-Head in Covent-Garden. 1755. Ghost of Shakespeare frames collection of picaresque tales.

Amory, Thomas. Memoirs: containing the lives of several ladies of Great Britain. 1755, 1769 (as Memoirs of several ladies). Didactic, uneven, idiosyncratic; fantasy voyage with female paragons.

Charke, Charlotte. The history of Henry Dumont esq and Miss Charlotte Evelyn. 1755, 1756 (3rd edn). Sentimental, epistolary.

Haywood, Eliza. The invisible spy. 1755, Dublin 1755. Epistolary scandal-chronicle.

Kidgell, John. The card. 1755. Epistolary burlesque; satire on technique of Richardson and of Edward Young.

Kimber, Edward. The life and adventures of James Ramble esq. 1755, 1770. Virtuous hero is involved in uprising of 1715.

Prévost d'Exiles, Antoine François, abbé. The history of a fair Greek who was taken out of a seraglio at Constantinople and brought to Paris. 1755 (2nd edn), 2 vols 1761. Trn of Histoire d'une Grecque moderne, 1740; narrator's relations with heroine; based on Mlle Aïssé.

Shebbeare, John. Letters on the English nation, by Batista Angeloni, a Jesuit. 1755. In tradition of spy letters; polemics.

—— Lydia: or filial piety. 1755, 1769, 1786 (Novelists' Mag). Shebbeare's best novel; Indian observes English manners; satire on variety of topics.

Victor, Benjamin. The widow of the wood. 1755, Dublin 1755. Story based on a contemporary scandal.

Emily: or the history of a natural daughter. 1756. Heroine has picaresque adventures; some satire. Delicacy rewarded; heroine discovers noble parents.

The life and memoirs of Mr Ephraim Tristram Bates, commonly called corporal Bates. 1756. Eccentric self-conscious narrator: see H. S. Hughes, A precursor of Tristram Shandy, JEGP 17 1918.

Memoirs of the noted Buckhorse. 1756. Realistic tale of a prize-fighter.

Memoirs of an Oxford scholar, written by himself. 1756. Picaresque ramble.

Amory, Thomas. The life of John Buncle. 2 vols 1756–66, 4 vols 1770; ed E. A. Baker 1904. Eccentric, extravagant narrator; much admired; pioneer in romantic description of landscape; *see* G. L. Jones, Lessing and Amory, German Life & Letters 20 1967.

'Bannoc, Adolphus'. The history of my own life. 1756, Dublin 1760 (as The history of Miss Biddy Farmer). Parental tyranny.

Kimber, Edward. The juvenile adventures of David Ranger esq. 1756. Roman à clef concerning Garrick.

Pery, E. S., Viscount. Letters from an Armenian in Ireland. 1756. *See* A. S. Crisafulli, A neglected English imitation of Montesquieu's Lettres persanes, MLQ 14 1953.

Toldervy, William. The history of two orphans. 1756. Wandering adventures of brothers; faintly picaresque.

Woodfin, Mrs A. Northern memoirs: or the history of a Scotch family. 1756. Extremely complex plot of personal relationships.

The sedan. 1757. Use of inanimate object as spy-narrator.

'Bannoc, Adolphus'. The fortunate villager: or memoirs of Sir Andrew Thompson. 1757. Free variation on Marivaux, Paysan parvenu.

Fielding, Sarah. The lives of Cleopatra and Octavia. 1757, 1758; ed R. B. Johnson 1928. Moralizing hybrid of history and fiction.

Griffith, Elizabeth, and Richard. A series of genuine letters between Henry and Frances. 6 vols 1757–70 (several edns), 1786. Borderline fiction; letters fictionalized; extreme delicacy of feeling emphasized; *see* J. M. S. Tompkins, The polite marriage, Cambridge 1938.

Long, Edward. The anti-Gallican: or the history and adventures of Henry Cobham esq. 1757.

Caraccioli, Charles. Chiron: or the mental optician. 1758. Another variation on spy theme.

Lennox, Charlotte. Henrietta. 1758; 4 edns by 1798. Vicissitudes of orphan; much praised; dramatized as The sister.

Smythies, Miss, of Colchester. The brothers. 1758. Author professes to imitate Richardson, with characters of less perfection and lower social station.

The juvenile adventures of Miss Kitty F—r. 1759. Spicy biography of the celebrated Kitty Fisher.

Memoirs of the celebrated Miss Fanny M—. 1759 (2nd edn). Imitation of Fanny Hill; less indecent.

Rosalind: or an apology for the history of a theatrical lady. Dublin 1759. Scandalous biography of Ann Crawford, a noted actress.

Fielding, Sarah. The history of the Countess of Dellwyn. 1759. Heroine corrupted by pride and town life; good characterization.

Lewis, Robert. Adventures of a rake, in the character of a public orator. 1759. Excellent picaresque novel; stage life; strolling players.

Voltaire, François Marie Arouet de. Candidus: or the optimist. 1759. Tr W. Rider; also as Candid: or all for the best. At least 6 edns, various reprints, various titles and versions by 1800.

The life and adventures of a cat. 1760, 1760, 1781. Animal observer; social satire. By William Guthrie?

The life and opinions of Miss Sukey Shandy of Bow Street, gentlewoman, in a series of letters to her dear brother Tristram Shandy gent. 1760. One of many imitations and sequels.

Fielding, Sarah. The history of Ophelia. 1760, 1785, 1787. Sufferings of orphan; pioneering use of Gothic elements; epistolary.

Johnstone, Charles. Chrysal: or the adventures of a guinea. 4 vols 1760–5; perhaps 20 edns by 1800; ed E. A. Baker 1908. Immense success; gold coin as spy; satire of manners, politics; depicts many famous contemporaries in all walks of life.

Riccoboni, Marie-Jeanne. Letters from Juliet, Lady Catesby, to her friend Lady Henrietta Campley. 1760 (2 trns, one by Frances Brooke); 6 edns by 1780. Highly successful and influential; lengthy descriptions of the agonies of extreme sensibility.

Stevens, George Alexander. The history of Tom Fool. 1760. Fictionalized autobiography.

Woodfin, Mrs A. The auction. 1760. Seduction and ruin of heroine; she becomes a prostitute.

The adventures of Sylvia Hughes, written by herself. 1761. Imitates manner of Fielding; clergyman's daughter educated by life.

Hau Kiou Choaan: or the pleasing history. 1761. Ed Thomas Percy from fragmentary trn, part English, part Portuguese, of Hao Ch'iu Chuan (The story of an ideal marriage); first Chinese fiction in English; virtuous lovers overcome obstacles to marriage.

The life and opinions of Bertram Montfichet esq, written by himself. 1761. Eccentric narrator; imitates Sterne.

Hawkesworth, John. Almoran and Hamet: an oriental tale. 1761, 1761; 6 edns by 1796. Influenced by Rasselas; treacherous brother's magical powers defeated by virtue.

Rousseau, Jean Jacques. Eloisa: or a series of letters. 1761. Dublin 1761; at least 8 edns by 1800. Several versions and abridgments of Nouvelle Héloïse; earliest by William Kenrick.

Sheridan, Frances. Memoirs of Miss Sidney Bidulph, extracted from her own journal. 5 vols 1761–7, Dublin 1761–7; at least 5 edns by 1796. Highly influential and esteemed; sentimental tale of considerable merit; excessive tribulations of innocent heroine.

A history of the matrimonial adventures of a banker's clerk with the pretended Lady Ann Frances Caroline Boothby. 1762. Epistolary.

The life, travels and adventures of Christopher Wagstaff, gentleman. 1762. Imitation of Tristram Shandy; criticizes it adversely.

Johnstone, Charles. The reverie: or a flight to the paradise of fools. 1762; at least 6 edns by 1800. Political satire; attacks Bute, other prominent political figures.

Langhorne, John. Solyman and Almena: an oriental tale. 1762; 5 edns by 1800. Sentimental, moralistic; descriptions of Eastern scenery.

Leland, Thomas. Longsword, Earl of Salisbury. 1762, Dublin 1766; ed J. C. Stephens jr, New York 1957. Called first English historical novel; actually pre-Gothic, sentimental.

Lennox, Charlotte. Sophia. 1762. Sense and sensibility theme.

Rousseau, Jean Jacques. Emilius and Sophia: or a new system of education. 4 vols 1762–3. Tr William Kenrick. Several other trns, numerous edns by 1800 (also Dublin, Edinburgh). A sequel, Emilius and Sophia: or the solitaires, 1783.

Scott, Sarah. A description of Millennium Hall and the country adjacent. 1762; 4 edns by 1778; ed W. M. Crittenden, New York 1955. Life histories of ladies in a secular convent; philanthropic schemes, varied social comment.

The history of the gay Bellario and the fair Isabella. 1763. Written as memoir of Oxford student, exemplary against vice.

The peregrinations of Jeremiah Grant esq, the West-Indian. 1763, 1768. Absorbing picaresque; chapters imitate Smollett, Fielding, Sterne.

Brooke, Frances. The history of lady Julia Mandeville. 1763; 10 edns by 1792; ed E. P. Poole 1930. Highly regarded; sentimental; tragic conclusion.

Langhorne, John. The letters that passed between Theodosius and Constantia, after she had taken the veil. 1763; at least 8 edns by 1800. A sequel, Correspondence of Theodosius and Constantia, 1765, ptd with this. Sentimental distress.

Marmontel, Jean François. Moral tales. 3 vols 1763–5. 3 trns, several selections, numerous edns; Gloucester, Edinburgh, Manchester, New York. Edifying exempla on social and family problems, correction of minor vices; immense success.

The adventures of Charles Careless. 1764. Illegitimate hero must seek fortune; education of sentiments by wise benefactor.

Beaumont, Mme Elie de. The history of the marquis de Roselle. 1764, 1765, 1766. A trn; hero escapes designing actress; epistolary technique imitative of Richardson.

Gentleman, Francis. A trip to the moon, containing an account of the island of Noibla [Albion]. York 1764-5. Imitation of Swift, Sterne; satire of religion, politics.

Gibbes, Phebe. The life and adventures of Mr Francis Clive. Dublin 1764. Plot resembles Amelia.

Griffith, Richard. The triumvirate: or the authentic memoirs of A[ndrew], B[eville] and C[arewe]. 1764. Imitates Sterne.

Gunning, Susannah Minifie. Family pictures, a novel: containing curious and interesting memoirs of several persons of fashion of W[arwickshire]. 1764, Dublin 1764. Complex plot of relationships, misunderstandings.

Ridley, James. Tales of the Genii. 1764; at least 7 edns by 1800. Pretended trn of Persian ms; didactic; laden with oriental paraphernalia.

Memoirs of a coquet: or the history of Miss Harriot Airy, by the author of Emily Willis: or the natural daughter. 1765. Comedy of manners. See 1756, above.

Brooke, Henry. The fool of quality: or the history of Henry, Earl of Moreland. 5 vols 1765-70; numerous edns; ed E. A. Baker 1906. Abridged by Wesley, 1780; see F. L. Barber, John Wesley edits a novel, London Quart 171 1946; further abridged as The history of a reprobate, 1789, 4 edns by 1797. Highly popular thesis novel; hero educated in virtue.

Cleland, John. The surprises of love, exemplified in the romance of a day. 1765.

Marishall, Jean. The history of Miss Clarinda Cathcart and Miss Fanny Renton. 1765, 1767 (3rd edn). Sentimental; distresses of lovers.

Scott, Sarah. The man of real sensibility: or the history of sir George Ellison. 1765, 2 vols 1766; at least 5 more edns by 1800; several American edns. Didactic; has an episode at author's Millenium Hall.

Walpole, Horace. The castle of Otranto: a Gothic story. 1765; ed W. S. Lewis, Oxford 1964. See col 1589, below.

The adventures of Jack Wander. 1766. In picaresque manner; hero travels in England and abroad.

The history of little Goody Twoshoes. 1766 (3 edns); many English and American edns and versions.

The history of Miss Delia Stanhope, in a series of letters to Miss Dorinda Boothby. 1766, Dublin 1766, London 1767.

d'Arnaud, François Baculard. Fanny: or injured innocence. 1766; numerous edns and versions. Highly popular; exaggerated distresses, moralizing tone, extreme sensibility.

Goldsmith, Oliver. The vicar of Wakefield. 2 vols 1766. See col 1197, below.

Kelly, Hugh. Memoirs of a magdalen: or the history of Louisa Mildmay. 1766; at least 4 edns by 1800. Distressed heroine; her steadfastness after a slip rewarded with marriage; epistolary.

Minifie, Margaret and Susannah. The picture. 1766. Improving tale intended for young ladies.

Young, Arthur. The history of Sir Charles Beaufort. 1766. Reverses usual distress theme; hero victim of wicked woman.

The adventures of an author, written by himself and a friend. 1767. Education of a young man in the ways and wiles of society.

The female American: or the adventures of Unca Eliza Winkfield. [1767?], 2 vols 1768; American edns. Adventures among the Indians; heroine abandoned in wilderness; praise of primitivism.

The generous guardian: or the history of Horatio Saville esq and Miss Louisa C—. 1767. Sensibility; domestic entanglements.

The history of Miss Pittborough. 1767. Series of letters from several persons; mild satire of manners: orphaned heroine visits polite world.

Boswell, James. Dorando: a Spanish tale. 1767, 1930. The adultery case of Jane Douglas, disguised in fiction; see col 1211, below.

Gibbes, Phebe. The woman of fashion: or the history of Lady Diana Dormer. 1767. Growth of sensibility.

Higgs, Henry. High life, a novel: or the history of Miss Falkland. 1767, Dublin 1768. Novel of manners; anticipates Evelina.

Jenner, Charles. Letters from Altamont in the capital to his friends in the country. Dublin 1767. Social comment; sketches and essays.

Marmontel, Jean François. Belisarius. 1767, Dublin 1767; 10 more edns by 1800. Thesis novel; historical; one ch on religious persecution made it a sensational success.

Paterson, Samuel. Another traveller! or cursory remarks and critical observations made upon a journey through part of the Netherlands. 1767, 1769. Imitation of Sterne, Sentimental journey.

Sheridan, Frances. The history of Nourjahad. 1767, Dublin 1767, London 1787; several more edns by 1800. Pseudo-oriental tale; the uselessness of riches and worldly pleasures.

Young, Arthur. The adventures of Emmera: or the fair American. 1767, Dublin 1767. Primitivism; idealized American setting in Pennsylvania wilderness; child of nature.

The adventures of Oxymel Classic esq. 1768. Oxford student, expelled, with variety of experiences.

Flagel: or a ramble of fancy through the land of electioneering, in the manner of the devil upon two sticks. 1768.

The vanity of human wishes: or the history of Sir James Scudamore bart. 1768, Dublin 1768. Epistolary.

Donaldson, William. The life and adventures of Sir Bartholomew Sapskull baronet. 1768. Eccentric; imitates Sterne.

Gunning, Susannah Minifie. Barford Abbey: a novel in a series of letters. 1768, 1771. Heroine, disfigured by smallpox, rewards hero with riches.

Voltaire, François Marie Arouet de. L'ingénu: or the sincere Huron. 1768, 1771 (as The pupil of nature); tr F. Ashmore 1786 etc.

The fruitless repentance: or the history of Kitty Le Fever. 1769. Persecuted heroine; trials resemble Clarissa's.

Private letters from an American in England to his friends in America. 1769. Spy device; England in ruins at close of century.

The wanton widow. 1769. Roman à clef; Lord Bute and the mother of George III.

Brooke, Frances. The history of Emily Montague. 1769, 1777, 1784, 1786. Sentimental; trials of love end happily; set in Canada.

Cooper, Maria Susannah. The exemplary mother: or letters between Mrs Villars and her family. 1769, 1784. Close imitation of Frances Sheridan, Sidney Bidulph.

Griffith, Elizabeth, and Richard. Two novels in letters, by the authors of Henry and Frances. 1769-70, 1775. See 1757, above. Novels are The delicate distress, The Gordian knot. Extreme sensibility; semi-autobiographical.

Lawrence, Herbert. The life and adventures of common sense: an historical allegory. 1769, 1771 (3rd edn). Unusual device: common sense personified travels through time, comments on ancient and modern history.

Musgrave, Sir W. The female captive: a narrative of facts which happened in Barbary in the year 1756. 1769. Autobiographical; heroine captured by Moors, escapes after many trials; narrator represented with unusual realism.

Potter, John. The history of the adventures of Arthur O'Bradley. 1769. Experiences of a young man seeking his fortune; variety of characters encountered relate their histories.

Tooke, William. The loves of Othniel and Achsah, translated from the Chaldee. 1769. Romanticism influenced by Sterne, Ossian.

Treyssac de Vergy, Pierre Henri. The mistakes of the heart. 3 vols 1769; vol 4, 1771. Epistolary; amorous intrigues; *see* B. Sutherland, Pierre Henri Treyssac de Vergy c. 1738–74, MLQ 4 1943.

The fortunate blue-coat boy. [1770?]. Story of benevolence; Christ's Hospital.

The life, adventures, intrigues and amours of the celebrated Jemmy Twitcher. [1770?]. Scandal novel concerning the Earl of Sandwich.

The younger brother. 1770–2. Fictional attack on George Colman the elder.

Bancroft, Edward. The history of Charles Wentworth esq. 1770. Sentimental deism; epistolary; primitive paradise in Guiana, hero marries Indian maiden.

Bridges, Thomas. The adventures of a bank-note. 1770–1. Inanimate spy; picaresque blended with sentiment.

Jenner, Charles. The placid man: or memoirs of Sir Charles Beville. 1770, Dublin 1770, London 1773 (with addns). Imitates style of Fielding, sentiments of Sterne.

Skinn, Mrs Anne (Masterman). The old maid: or the history of Miss Ravensworth. 1770. Epistolary, realistic; against double standard, mercenary marriages.

The adventures of a Jesuit. 1771. Hero's mysterious guardian good early example of Svengali type; theme of Inquisition's secret power.

The disguise: a dramatic novel. 1771. Entirely in dialogue form.

Memoirs of Lady Woodford, written by herself. 1771. Young girl flees to London, experiences city life.

Dubois-Fontenelle, Jean Gaspard. The shipwreck and adventures of M. Pierre Viaud. 1771. Tr Elizabeth Griffith; substantially based on fact; *see* C. Fox, The shipwreck of Monsieur Pierre Viaud, N & Q June 1958.

Griffith, Elizabeth. The history of Lady Barton. 1771, 1773. Married heroine torn between fidelity and inclination. *See* J. E. Norton, Some uncollected authors xxii: Elizabeth Griffith 1727–93, Book Collector 8 1959.

Lawrence, Herbert. The contemplative man: or the history of Christopher Crab esq of north Wales. 1771, Dublin 1772. Reflective irony in the manner of Fielding; echoes of Smollett.

Mackenzie, Henry. The man of feeling. Edinburgh and Dublin 1771, 1771; at least 9 edns by 1800; ed B. Vickers, Oxford 1967. Hero paralyzed by extreme sensibility; *see* D. G. Spencer, Mackenzie: a practical sentimentalist, Papers in Lang & Lit 3 1967.

Meades, Anne. The history of Sir William Harrington. 1771, 1772, 1797. Imitates Grandison; not rev Richardson, as stated, though some of his suggestions were used. *See* T. C. D. Eaves and B. D. Kimpel, Richardson's connection with Sir William Harrington, Papers in Lang & Lit 4 1968.

Treyssac de Vergy, Pierre Henri. The palinode: or the triumphs of virtue and love. 1771. Fashionable persons and scandals.

Ermina: or the fair recluse. 1772. Series of letters by a lady; sentimental.

The feelings of the heart: or the history of a country-girl, written by herself and addressed to a lady of quality. 1772.

The precipitate choice: or the history of Lord Ossory and Miss Rivers. 1772, 1783. Lurid plot involves murder, rape, canonical incest.

Bonhote, Elizabeth. The rambles of Mr Frankly, published by his sister. 4 vols 1772–6, 2 vols 1773, Dublin 1773, London 1799. Collection of eccentric characters, city types; modelled on Sterne, Sentimental journey.

Briscoe, Sophia. The fine lady. 1772. Heroine's pride leads to downfall.

Hull, Thomas. Genuine letters from a gentleman to a young lady his pupil. 1772. Didactic; recommends course of reading; shows high admiration of Shakespeare.

Mercier, Sebastien. Memoirs of the year two thousand five hundred. 1772, Philadelphia 1795, 1802. Dreamer wakes in Utopia of the future; influenced Holcroft. Tr W. Hooper from L'an deux mille quatre cent quarante, 1770.

Reeve, Clara. The phoenix. 1772. A new trn of Barclay, Argenis, 1621.

Scott, Sarah. The test of filial duty. 1772. Epistolary; 2 girls with differing inclinations.

[Treyssac de Vergy, Pierre Henri?]. Memoirs of an hermaphrodite. 1772. Witty scandal-chronicle; involves Chevalier d'Éon.

The history of Miss Pamela Howard. 1773, Dublin 1773. Epistolary; imitates method of Richardson, ideas of Prévost; includes scenes clearly borrowed from Fielding, Sterne.

The mercenary marriage: or the history of Miss Shenstone. 1773.

The prudential lovers: or the history of Harry Harper. 1773. Education of a young man in social behaviour.

'Twas right to marry him: or the history of Miss Petworth. 1773. Serious consideration of social problem of a girl's damaged reputation.

'Twas wrong to marry him: or the history of Lady Dursley. 1773. Appears to have precipitated previous item.

Aikin, Anna Letitia. Sir Bertram. 1773. Influenced by Castle of Otranto; many reprints, imitations; a simulated 'fragment'.

d'Arnaud, François Baculard. The tears of sensibility. 1773, 1783. 4 novels; melodrama and sentiment; tr J. Murdoch from Les épreuves du sentiment.

Brooke, Henry. Juliet Grenville: or the history of the human heart. 1773, 1774. Adventure and extravagant sentiment; nature overcomes nurture.

Chater, John. The history of Tom Rigby. 1773. Includes serious treatment of problem of incest.

Duff, William. The history of Rhedi, the hermit of Mount Ararat: an oriental tale. 1773.

Graves, Richard. The spiritual Quixote: or the summer's ramble of Mr Geoffrey Wildgoose. 1773; at least 6 edns by 1800; ed C. R. Tracy, Oxford 1967. Dilemmas of idealism exemplified; satire on Methodists.

Mackenzie, Henry. The man of the world. 1773, 1773, 1783, 1787; several other edns. Influential; written as antithesis to Man of feeling, 1771, above; life of wicked squire.

Wieland, Christopher Martin. Reason triumphant over fancy; exemplified in the singular adventures of Don Sylvio de Rosalva. 1773; ed E. A. Baker 1904. Variation on Don Quixote theme; satire of society, of fairy tales; sustained frivolity.

—— The history of Agathon. 1773; tr John Richardson. Anticipates modern Bildungsroman, autobiographical; philosophical education of a youth in ancient Athens.

The history of Lord Stanton. 1774, Dublin 1780. Epistolary.

The modern fine gentleman. 1774. Epistolary; sensibility; a libertine is punished.

The news-paper wedding: or an advertisement for a husband. 1774. Epistolary; autobiography of heroine.

Cradock, Joseph. Village memoirs, in a series of letters between a clergyman and his family in the country and his son in town. 1774. Popular didacticism.

Helvétius, Claude. The child of nature. 1774 (also as The philosophy of pleasure).

Johnstone, Charles. The history of Arsaces, Prince of Betlis. 1774, Dublin 1775. Comment on America, using oriental allegory; criticizes policy of founding colonies.

The correspondents: an original novel. 1775, 1775, 1776, 1784. Epistolary; influence of Sterne; sensibility; reputed correspondence of Lord Lyttelton and Miss Peach; *see* R. M. Davis, The correspondents, PMLA 51 1936.

The delicate objection: or sentimental scruple. 1775. Epistolary.

The general election: a series of letters chiefly between two female friends. 1775.

Bicknell, Alexander. The benevolent man: or the history of Mr Belville. 1775. Imitation of Clarissa.

Cooper, Maria Susanna. The history of Fanny Meadows. 1775. Epistolary; imitation of Pamela.

Johnstone, Charles. The pilgrim: or a picture of life. 1775, Dublin 1775. Chinese spy comments on English life to friends.

Pratt, Samuel Jackson, 'Courtney Melmoth'. Liberal opinions upon animals, man and Providence. 1775–7, 1777, 1783 (as Liberal opinions: or the history of Benignus). Didactic; benevolent man disillusioned by ungrateful world.

Young, Arthur. Julia Benson: or the sufferings of innocence. 1775, 1776, Dublin 1784 (as History of Julia Benson). Strong-minded girl escapes seducers, flees city, comes to bad end.

Emma: or the child of sorrow. 1776. Epistolary.

Memoirs of a demi-rep of fashion: or the private history of Miss Amelia Gunnersbury. 1776.

Bicknell, Alexander. The history of Lady Anne Neville, sister to the great Earl of Warwick. 1776. Historical fiction, but sentimental, influenced by manner and works of Prévost, Mme d'Aulnoy.

Cogan, Thomas. John Buncle junior, gentleman. 1776–8. Epistolary; thesis novel; some satire of Amory, John Buncle.

Griffith, Elizabeth. The story of Juliana Harley. 1776, 1786. Epistolary; forced, loveless marriage; distress and death.

Pratt, Samuel Jackson, 'Courtney Melmoth'. The pupil of pleasure: or the new system illustrated. 1776; at least 5 edns by 1800. Against Chesterfieldian education; its product, a libertine, punished.

Walker, Lady Mary (Hamilton). Munster village. [1776?], 1778, Dublin 1779. Depicts a Utopian social community experiment.

The history of Miss Maria Barlowe. 1777. Sentimental, epistolary.

'Squire Randal's excursion round London. 1777. Series of letters home; lively pictures; tricks of the town.

Brooke, Frances. The excursion. 1777, 1785. Epistolary; man corrupted by Chesterfieldian education attempts heroine, reforms, is refused.

Mackenzie, Henry. Julia de Roubigné. 1777; at least 8 edns by 1800. Epistolary; pre-Gothic; doomed marriage, wife torn between love and fidelity.

Pratt, Samuel Jackson, 'Courtney Melmoth'. Travels for the heart, written in France. 1777. Imitates Sterne, Sentimental journey.

Reeve, Clara. The champion of virtue: a Gothic story. Colchester 1777; later titled The old English baron; at least 10 edns by 1800; ed J. Trainer, Oxford 1967. Sentiment and terror; supernatural; didactic emphasis.

—— [Castle Connor, c. 1787]. Ms lost; ptd as Fatherless Fanny, 1819; see J. K. Reeves, The mother of Fatherless Fanny, ELH 9 1942.

Thistlethwaite, James. The child of misfortune: or the history of Mrs Gilbert. 1777. Sentiment, distress; Welsh setting.

Walker, Lady Mary (Hamilton). Memoirs of the Marchioness de Louvoi. 1777. Epistolary; illustrates strength of female mind.

Letters of Momus from Margate. 1778. Satire in imitation of Humphry Clinker.

The travels of Hildebrand Bowman esq. 1778. Imaginary voyage; fantastic adventures; reflects voyage of Capt Cook.

Way, Gregory Lewis. Learning at a loss: or the amours of Mr Pedant and Miss Hartley. 1778. Humorous; university scenes; satire of several social types.

The sylph. 1779, 1779, Dublin 1779, London 1783, 1784, Dublin 1784. By Georgiana, Duchess of Devonshire? See TLS 15 Sept 1918, 21 June 1934. Sentimental; persecuted heroine.

Combe, William. Letters supposed to have been written by Yorick and Eliza. 1779; several edns. Spurious continuation; see col 952, above; H. W. Hamilton, Dr Syntax, 1969.

Goethe, Johann Wolfgang von. The sorrows of Werter. 1779; 30 or more edns by 1800; several trns; first (incomplete) by Richard Graves. See col 180, above; A. D. McKillop, MLN 43 1928; C. J. Hill 47 1932.

Graves, Richard. Columella: or the distressed anchoret. 1779. Satire on Shenstone's ideas of retiring to the country.

Keate, George. Sketches from nature, taken and coloured on a journey to Margate. 1779; 4 edns by 1790. Imitates Sentimental journey; see K. G. Dapp, George Keate, Philadelphia 1939.

Pratt, Samuel Jackson, 'Courtney Melmoth'. Shenstone-Green: or the new Paradise lost. 1779. Satire on Utopian communal living, specifically of Munster village; see 1776, above.

—— The tutor of truth. 1779, 1781, Dublin 1784. Epistolary, didactic, concerning educational methods.

Masquerades: or what you will. 1780. Novel of manners; diversions of the nobility.

Croft, Sir Herbert. Love and madness: a story too true, in a series of letters. 1780; 4 edns by 1786. Based on Hackman's murder of Martha Ray, mistress of Earl of Sandwich; digressions on Chatterton and Werther.

Holcroft, Thomas. Alwyn: or the gentleman comedian. 1780. Episodes include autobiography in fictional form. See V. R. Stallbaumer, Holcroft as a novelist, ELH 15 1948; Holcroft's influence on [Godwin's] Political justice, MLQ 14 1953.

Palmer, Charlotte. Female stability: or the history of Miss Belville. 1780. Heroine refuses to marry after death of lover.

Pratt, Samuel Jackson, 'Courtney Melmoth'. Emma Corbett: or the miseries of civil war. 1780, Dublin 1780; 9 edns by 1789. Sentimental; tragic ending; set in American revolution.

The adventures of a hackney coach. 1781, Dublin 1781; as many as 7 edns by 1800. Pictures of society include Goldsmith, other persons of note; topical content; manner of Chrysal. Attributed to Dorothy Kilner.

Combe, William. Letters of an Italian nun and an English gentleman; translated from the French of J. J. Rousseau. 1781; numerous edns, 9 by 1800. Highly popular; depiction of passion, persecuted lovers; not by Rousseau; see Barbier, col 874, above.

Johnstone, Charles. The history of John Juniper esq. 1781. Follows Fielding, Jonathan Wild.

The philosophical Quixote: or memoirs of Mr David Wilkins, in a series of letters. 1782. Burlesque of recent philosophical theories.

Bage, Robert. Mount Henneth. 1782, 1788. Philosophical novel; pictures community dedicated to benevolence; histories of its members. See S. Piggot, The Roman camp and three authors, REL 7 1966.

Scott, Helenus. The adventures of a rupee. 1782, Dublin 1782, 1783, 1783, 1790. Coin sees both Asia and Europe; various reforms advocated, notably in medicine.

Memoirs of the Manstein family. 1783. Thesis novel on variety of subjects; partly epistolary.

Berquin, Arnaud. The children's friend. 24 vols 1783, 6 vols 1783–4; 15 edns by 1800. Moral tales.

Day, Thomas. The history of Sandford and Merton. 3 vols 1783–9; 7 edns by 1795. Classic improving work for children; see S. H. Scott, The exemplary Mr Day, New York 1935.

Genlis, Stéphanie-Félicité de. Adelaide and Theodore: or letters on education. 1783, 1796 (4th edn). Predominantly didactic.

Lee, Sophia. The recess: or a tale of the times. 1783–5, 1804 (5th edn). Popular and influential; mingles historical, Gothic elements; involves Elizabeth and Essex, Mary Stuart, Leicester.

Reeve, Clara. The two mentors; a modern story. 1783, Dublin 1783, 1803 (3rd edn). Epistolary; false education cannot eradicate natural goodness; good and bad advisers; hero becomes infidel, then Christian, through reading.

[Thomson, William ?] The man in the moon: or travels into the lunar regions by the man of the people. 1783, 1787 etc. Satire on republican ideas, notably of Charles James Fox.

The history of Lord Belford and Miss Sophia Woodley. 1784. Epistolary; characters modelled on those of Grandison.

Bage, Robert. Barham Downs. 1784, 1788. Thesis novel; against religious bigotry; rakes produce distresses.

Bromley, Eliza Nugent. Laura and Augustus. 1784. Epistolary, West Indian setting; extravagant melancholy, melodrama; lovers prove siblings; may be principal work satirized in Jane Austen, Love and friendship.

Godwin, William. Imogen: a pastoral romance from the ancient British. 1784; ed J. W. Marken, New York 1963 (with several studies).

—— Italian letters: or the history of the Count de St Julian. 1783 (anon); ed B. R. Pollin, Lincoln Nebraska 1965. Thought lost; sentiment and passion. See J. De Palacio, La 'fortune' de Godwin en France, Revue de Littérature Comparée 41 1967; B. R. Pollin, Godwin criticism: a synoptic bibliography, Toronto 1967; *col 1249, below*.

Laclos, Choderlos de. Dangerous connections. 1784. Trn of Les liaisons dangereuses; apparently little noticed in England; see D. R. Thelander, Laclos and the epistolary novel, Geneva 1963.

Parry, Catherine. Eden vale. 1784. Epistolary; partly set in colonies during Revolution.

The aerostatic spy: or adventures with an air-balloon. 1785, 1786 (as The balloon). Spy genre adapted to reflect fame of Lunardi's ascent; faint anticipations of modern science fiction.

d'Arnaud, François Baculard. Warbeck: a pathetic tale. 1785, 1786, Dublin 1786. Trn by Sophia Lee of historical novel; sentimental treatment of Perkin Warbeck.

Bennett, Agnes Maria. Anna: or memoirs of a Welch heiress interspersed with the anecdotes of a nabob. 1785, 1796 (4th edn). Imitates manner of Cecilia and of Charlotte Summers.

Blower, Elizabeth. Maria. 1785. One of the better imitations of Evelina; ridicules Ossian, learned ladies, affectations.

Genlis, Stéphanie-Félicité de. Tales of the castle: or stories of instruction and delight. 1785, 1785 etc. Moral tales intended for children; tr Thomas Holcroft.

Graves, Richard. Eugenius: or anecdotes of the golden vale. 1785, 1786. Utopian; comment on schemes thought extravagant.

Peacock, Lucy. The adventures of the six princesses of Babylon in their travels to the temple of virtue: an allegory. 1785, 1786.

Raspe, Rudolf Eric. Baron Munchausen's narrative of his marvellous travels and campaigns in Russia. [1785?], Oxford 1786 (also as Gulliver revived, with addns), 1792 (as The surprising travels and adventures); at least 9 edns of enlarged version by 1800. Raspe wrote only shorter original version.

Cartwright, Mrs H. The platonic marriage. 1786, 1787. Epistolary; unrealistic platonism hinders love.

Harley, Mrs M. St Bernard's priory: an old English tale. 1786, 1787, 1789 (as Priory of St Bernard). Historical; imitates The recess; includes account of tournament.

[Johnstone, Charles ?]. The adventures of Anthony Varnish. 1786. Social satire, picaresque; great variety of lively scenes in Ireland, England.

Lee, Harriet. The errors of innocence. 1786. Thesis novel; injustices of women; perceptive treatment of girlhood; good characterization.

Montolieu, Jeanne Isabelle, baronne de. Caroline of Lichtfield: a novel. 1786, Dublin 1786, London 1795, 1797. Tr Thomas Holcroft; explores sentiment and custom.

Moore, John. Zeluco: various views of human nature. 1786; at least 7 edns by 1800. Psychology of character development; principal character forerunner of Ann Radcliffe's Schedoni. See S. N. Ray, Moore: a forgotten favourite of the eighteenth century, Calcutta Rev 69 1938.

Bage, Robert. The fair Syrian. 1787. Thesis novel: sentimental psychology; resembles manner of Prévost; girl rescued from harem, describes her life.

Burke, Mrs Adela. Ela: or the delusions of the heart. 1787, 1788. Sentimental; heroine in predicament of Griselda.

Helme, Elizabeth. Louisa: or the cottage on the moor. 1787 (4 edns); 9 edns by 1789. Bestseller; persecuted heroine analysed in manner of Marivaux.

Keir, Susanna Harvey. The history of Miss Greville. 1787. A second attachment can succeed.

The amicable Quixote: or the enthusiasm of friendship. 1788. Unusual interest in exploration of character.

Powis Castle: or anecdotes of an antient family. 1788. Gothic.

Bage, Robert. James Wallace. 1788. Epistolary; middleclass setting; caricature and social satire; influence of Humphry Clinker.

Blower, Elizabeth. Features from life: or a summer visit. 1788. Foolish delicacy corrected; her best novel.

Cambon, Maria Gertruida de. Young Grandison: a series of letters from young persons to their friends. 1788, 1790. Improving juvenile; trn attributed to Mary Wollstonecraft.

Godwin, Mary Wollstonecraft. Mary: a fiction. 1788, [1790?]. Emphasizes spiritual development of heroine.

Hervey, Elizabeth. Melissa and Marcia, or the sisters: a novel. 1788, 1789, 1796. May be among novels satirized by Beckford.

Léonard, Nicolas-Germain. The correspondence of two lovers, inhabitants of Lyons. 1788. Persecution, suicide; influence of Werther.

Reeve, Clara. The exiles: or memoirs of the Count de Cronstadt. 1788, 1789, Dublin 1789. Epistolary; melodramatic distresses.

Renwick, William. The solicitudes of absence. 1788. Written in behalf of sailors and naval surgeons; autobiographical, dominated by author's personal feelings, prejudices.

Rowson, Susanna. The inquisitor: or invisible rambler. 1788. Adaptation of spy device for social comment.

Sandham, Elizabeth. The twin sisters: or the effects of education. 1788. Epistolary, didactic; education can produce opposite characters in twins.

Smith, Charlotte. Emmeline: or the orphan of the castle. 1788, 1789 (3rd edn). Gothic; mistreated heroine. See F. M. A. Hilbish, Charlotte Smith: poet and novelist, Philadelphia 1941; A. D. McKillop, Charlotte Smith's letters, HLQ 15 1952.

Thomson, Mrs (Harriet Pigott). Fatal follies: or the history of the Countess of Stanmore. 1788. Epistolary; inserted histories; Scottish setting.

The Bastile: or history of Charles Townly, a man of the world. 1789 (apparently 3 edns), Dublin 1789. Original title, Memoirs of Charles Townly, changed after fall of Bastille; comic, Smollettian.

The fair Hibernian. [1789?], 1790, Dublin 1790, 1794. Irish setting not exploited for local color.

Bernardin de Saint-Pierre, Jacques Henri. Paul and Mary: an Indian story. Tr Daniel Malthus 1789; tr Helen Maria Williams 1795 (as Paul and Virginia); tr C. Barrett 1795 (as The shipwreck); several edns of each version by 1800. Influential; sentimental primitivism.

Cumberland, Richard. Arundel. 1789; 3 edns by 1795. Epistolary; adventures of young scholar in the world; realism.

Fuller, Anne. The son of Ethelwolf: an historical tale. 1789, 1800. King Alfred's wars with Danes as setting.

Goldborne, Sophia. Hartly house, Calcutta. 1789, Dublin 1789. Interesting pictures of domestic life in India from a young English girl's point of view.

Hayley, William. The young widow: or the history of Cornelia Sedley. 1789. Didactic; influence of Grandison; see W. T. Le Viness, The life and works of Hayley, Santa Fe 1945.

Heriot, John. The half-pay officer. 1789. Based on author's distresses as naval officer involuntarily retired.

Mathews, Mrs. Argus: the house-dog at Eadlip. 1789. Epistolary; competent, realistic; complicated affairs of two families.

Radcliffe, Ann. The castles of Athlin and Dunbayne: a Highland story. 1789, 1793, 1793, 1799. Gothic; Scotland in the Middle Ages. See R. D. Mayo, Ann Radcliffe and Ducray-Duminil, MLR 36 1941; W. Sypher, Social ambiguity in a Gothic novel, Partisan Rev 12 1945; W. Ruff, Ann Radcliffe: or the hand of taste, in The age of Johnson, New Haven 1949; R. D. Havens, Ann Radcliffe's nature description, MLN 46 1951; F. L. Beaty, Mrs Radcliffe's fading gleam, PQ 42 1963; J. De Cottignies, A l'occasion centenaire de la naissance d'Ann Radcliffe, Revue des Sciences Humaines 116 1964.

Ryves, Elizabeth. The hermit of Snowden: or memoirs of Albert and Lavinia. 1789, 1793. Partly autobiographical; purports to be copied from old ms.

Smith, Charlotte. Ethelinda: or the recluse of the lake. 1789, 1790, Dublin 1790; 5 edns by 1800. Influential; distresses of love; extensive descriptions of scenery.

White, James. Earl Strongbow. 1789. Historical; pictures conquest of Ireland; includes burlesque, satire of contemporary manners. See J. M. S. Tompkins, A forgotten humourist, RES 3 1927.

Ballin, Rossetta. The statue room. 1790. Historical, melodramatic; Elizabeth I cast as villain.

Cambon, Maria Gertruida de. Letters and conversations between several young ladies. [1790?], 1792. Tr from Die kleine Klarissa; improving work for children, based closely on Richardson.

Combe, William. The devil upon two sticks in England. 6 vols 1790. Adaptation of device in Lesage, Le diable boiteux; demon assists narrator-spy; structure approaches a miscellany of tales.

Graves, Richard. Plexippus: or the aspiring plebian. 1790. Set in Cheltenham, Wales, London; sober, pleasant tale of two young men's love affairs.

Knight, Ellis Cornelia. Dinarbas, a tale: being a continuation of Rasselas. 1790; 4 edns by 1800. See B. Luttrell, The prim Romantic, 1965; C. J. Rawson, The continuation of Rasselas, in Bicentennial essays on Rasselas, Cairo 1959.

Lennox, Charlotte. Euphemia. 1790. Epistolary; detailed American setting; noble savages, trials of patient wife.

Radcliffe, Ann. A Sicilian romance. 1790; 8 edns by 1826. Gothic; landscape, sensibility, many borrowings from earlier fiction.

Rowson, Susanna. Charlotte: or a tale of truth. 1790, 1791 etc; ed C. M. and R. Kirk, New York 1964. As Charlotte Temple in most edns; heroine elopes with officer, is deserted, bears his child, dies in misery; American setting.

White, James. The adventures of John of Gaunt, Duke of Lancaster. 1790. Historical; personages include the Black Prince, Chaucer; see W. L. Cross, Chaucer as a character in fiction, Anglia 25 1902.

Benedicta. 1791. Examines true and false delicacy, scruples and morality in young women.

Berquin, Arnaud. The history of little Grandison. 1791. For children; follows Richardson closely; impeccable boy as hero.

Inchbald, Elizabeth. A simple story. 1791, Dublin 1791; 4th edn 1799; ed J. M. S. Tompkins, Oxford 1967. Highly regarded; plausible events, good motivation and character.

Purbeck, Elizabeth and Jane. William Thornborough: the benevolent Quixote. 1791.

Radcliffe, Ann. The romance of the forest. 1791; at least 10 edns by 1800. Highly popular; Gothic 17th-century setting, melodrama, persecuted heroine; see G. Humphrey, Victor ou l'enfant de la forêt et le roman terrifiant, French Rev 33 1959.

Reeve, Clara. The school for widows. 1791. 3 interlinked retrospective memoirs; puzzle story, proto-detective fiction.

Sadler, —, of Chippenham. Wanley Penson: or the melancholy man. 1791, 1792. Hero crippled by excessive sensibility; point of view interesting; story put together from several differing accounts.

Smith, Charlotte Turner. Celestina. 1791, 1791, Dublin 1791, London 1792. Extremely romantic dilemmas; highly complicated plot.

Bage, Robert. Man as he is. 1792, 1796; 6 edns by 1800. Social comedy and satire; variety of sharply-drawn characters.

Florian, J. P. Claris de. New tales. 1792; many separate reprints in periodicals. 6 stories, each set in a different country.

Gunning, Susannah Minifie. Anecdotes of the Delborough family. 1792, 1792, Dublin 1792. Begun years earlier; pictures of high life.

Holcroft, Thomas. Anna St Ives. 7 vols 1792, 1800. Epistolary; includes journals; set in French Revolution; thesis novel with revolutionary moral code; problems of marriage.

Hutchinson, William. The doubtful marriage. 1792. Idealistic meddling by clergyman in Gretna Green marriage brings disaster to all concerned; epistolary.

Mackenzie, Anna Maria. Slavery: or the times. 1792, 1793, Dublin 1793. Letters and journals; African chief is informed of his son's progressive disgust with European manners and morals.

Raithby, John. Delineations of the heart: or the history of Henry Bennet. 1792. Comedy and satire in an attempted imitation of Fielding.

Robinson, Mary. Vancenza: or the dangers of credulity. 1792, Dublin 1792; 5 edns by 1794. Popularity largely due to 'Perdita' as author. Heroine dies on discovering intended her half-brother; much description of romantic scenery.

Smith, Charlotte Turner. Desmond. 1792, 1792, Dublin 1792. Epistolary; favours French Revolution, praises platonic attachments, satirizes aristocrats, conservatives.

West, Jane. The advantages of education: or the history of Maria Williams. 1792. The fates of several girls determined by the characters of their chosen lovers; humour as antidote to sensibility.

The minstrel. 1793. Unusual anticipation of manner of Scott; detailed, accurate 15th-century background.

Gunning, Susannah Minifie. Memoirs of Mary. 1793, 1794, 1794, Dublin 1794. Faithful but unskilful imitation of Richardson's epistolary techniques.

Imlay, Gilbert. The emigrants. 1793, 1794, 1796; ed R. R. Hare, Gainesville 1964 (on ascription to Mary Wollstonecraft). Thesis novel; encourages easy divorce, emigration to America.

Parsons, Eliza. The castle of Wolfenbach. 1793; ed D. P. Varma 1968. Gothic; one of the Northanger novels.

Peacock, Lucy. The knight of the rose. 1793. Collection of fairy tales.

Smith, Charlotte. The old manor house. 1793, Dublin 1793; several edns after 1800; ed A. H. Ehrenpreis, Oxford 1969. Her best work; realistic English atmosphere and setting; influence of Radcliffe tales of terror.

Caroline de Montmorenci: a tale founded in fact. 1794. Perhaps a trn; pathetic, tragic ending; correspondence between prioress and former charge.

The offspring of Russell. 1794. Gothic; sensibility.

Bennett, Agnes Maria. Ellen, Countess of Castle Howell. 1794, Dublin 1794. Persecuted heroine rewarded.

Cullen, Stephen. The haunted priory: or the fortunes of the house of Rayo. 1794. Gothic setting, supernatural horrors, but with unusual poetic effects, descriptions.

Flammenberg, Lawrence. The necromancer: or the tale of the Black Forest. 1794; ed D. P. Varma 1968. Lurid romance, poorly constructed.

Godwin, William. Things as they are: or the adventures of Caleb Williams. 1794, 1797 (3rd edn); ed G. Sherburn, New York 1960. *See col 1249, below:* R. F. Storch, Metaphors of private guilt and social rebellion in Caleb Williams, ELH 34 1967; E. E. Rothstein, Allusion and analogy in the romance of Caleb Williams, UTQ 37 1967.

Holcroft, Thomas. The adventures of Hugh Trevor. 6 vols 1794–7; 1–3 rptd 1794, Dublin 1795; 4–6, 1797. Realistic; general condemnation of society, notably the professions.

Naubert, Benedicte. Herman of Unna: a series of adventures of the fifteenth century. 1794, 1794, Dublin 1794, 1796. Important early example of novel dealing with a secret society; first of influential German romances to appear.

Radcliffe, Ann. The mysteries of Udolpho. 1794, 1794, 1795, Dublin 1800; many edns in next decades; ed B. Dobrée, Oxford 1966. *See* M. Levy, Une nouvelle source d'Ann Radcliffe, Caliban 1 1964; M. L. Allen, The black veil: three versions of a symbol, E Studies 47 1966.

Robinson, John. Sydney St Aubyn, in a series of letters. 1794. Remarkable for extreme and frequent miseries of hero.

Robinson, Mary Elizabeth. The shrine of Bertha. 1794. Epistolary; partly set in Swiss convent; vivid pictures of society.

Robert and Adela: or the rights of women best maintained by the sentiments of nature. 1795, Dublin 1795. Against the new morality.

Susanna: or traits of a modern miss. 1795. Female Quixote device; variety of targets burlesqued: pastoral, Gothic, Methodist, romantic cottage life, Bardolatry, Clarissa. Attributed to Susanna Bullock.

Bird, John. The castle of Hardayne: a romance. 1795, Liverpool 1795. In the Radcliffe tradition.

Cumberland, Richard. Henry. 1795, 1798 (3rd edn). Deliberately simple style; imitates Joseph Andrews, Roderick Random.

Edgeworth, Maria. Letters for literary ladies. 1795. Exemplary; illustrate contrast of sense and sensibility.

Hanway, Mary Anne. Ellinor: or the world as it is. 1795, 1798. Influenced by Bage's treatment of fiction.

Hedgeland, Isabella Kelly. The abbey of St Asaph. 1795. Romantic novel; *see* E. R. Loomis, The problem of the Gothic novel in Wales, Nat Lib of Wales Jnl 13 1963.

Lewis, Matthew Gregory. The monk. 1795, 1796, 1796, Dublin 1796, London 1797 etc; ed L. F. Peck, New York 1952; *see* H. Koziol, E. T. A. Hoffmans Die Elixire und M. G. Lewis, The monk, Germanisch-romanische Monatsschrift 26 1938; W. B. Todd, The early editions and issues of the Monk, SB 2 1950; W. Moss, Lewis and Mme de Staël, E Studies 34 1953; L. F. Peck, The monk and Musäus' Die Entführung, PQ 32 1953; The monk and Le diable amoureux, MLN 68 1953.

Meek, Mary. The abbey of Clugny. 1795. Gothic romance.

Parsons, Eliza. The voluntary exile. 1795. First historical novel on American Revolution; interpolated histories; rambling.

Pye, Henry James. The democrat, interspersed with anecdotes of well-known characters. 1795, 1796. Satire; French libertarian visits America, England; his practice belies his principles.

Rowson, Susanna. Trials of the human heart. 1795. Convent-bred girl discovers the world, writes to cloistered friend; detailed depiction of reactions.

Schiller, Johann. The ghost-seer or apparitionist: an interesting fragment found among the papers of Count O—. 1795, 1796, 1800 (as Armenian), Dublin 1800. Tr rom Der Geisterseher, 1789, by Robert Huish.

Smith, Charlotte Turner. Montalbert. 1795. Gothic; Alpine setting; influence of Radcliffe.

Yearsley, Ann. The royal captives. 1795. Based on mystery of the man in the iron mask; *see* J. M. S. Tompkins, The polite marriage, 1938.

Arville Castle. 1796. Highly romanticized history; Queen Boadicea.

Berkeley Hall: or the pupil of experience. 1796, 1803. Set in America; general satire; romanticized primitives, life of nature explored, disillusioning of idealistic travellers.

Interesting tales. 1796. 6 stories from the German.

Bage, Robert. Hermsprong: or man as he is not. 1796, 1799; ed V. Wilkins 1951. Child of nature visits England; satire, varied social comment; lively style.

Burke, Mrs Anne. The sorrows of Edith: or the hermitage on the cliff. 1796. Epistolary; close imitation of Werther.

Ducray-Duminil, François-Guillaume. Ambrose and Eleanor: or the adventures of two children deserted on an uninhabited island. 1796, 1797. Tr Lucy Peacock from Lolotte et Fanfan; fantastic tale for children.

Edgeworth, Maria. The parent's assistant: or stories for children. 3 vols 1796, 6 vols 1800 (3rd edn).

Grosse, Carl, Marquis von Pharnusa. Horrid mysteries. 1796; ed D. P. Varma 1968. Also tr in 1796 as The genius. Concentrated horror in manner of Lewis; society of anarchists.

Hamilton, Elizabeth. Letters of a Hindoo rajah. 1796, Dublin 1797. Variation on the spy theme.

Hays, Mary. Memoirs of Emma Courtney. 1796. Epistolary; semi-autobiographical; feminist. The woman does the courting; dangers of surrendering to impulse. *See* M. R. Adams, Mary Hays: disciple of William Godwin, PMLA 55 1940.

Helme, Elizabeth. The farmer of Inglewood forest. 1796. Pathos and melodrama; story of an innocent girl ruined.

Inchbald, Elizabeth. Nature and art. 1796, 1797; several edns after 1800. Goodness of natural impulses; cultivated man evil.

Moore, John. Edward: various views of human nature. 1796, 1797, Dublin 1797, 1798. Tender-hearted hero buffeted by world.

Parsons, Eliza. The mysterious warning. 1796; ed D. P. Varma 1968. Gothic; a Northanger novel.

Roche, Regina Maria. The children of the abbey. 1796–1800 (4th edn); 10 edns by 1825. Very popular; persecution, sentiment, scenery.

Smith, Charlotte. Marchmont. 1796. Radcliffian; young man opposed by mysterious villains.

Walker, George. Theodore Cyphon: or the benevolent Jew. 1796; 3 edns by 1800. Thesis novel; resembles Caleb Williams.

West, Jane. A gossip's story, and a legendary tale. 1796, 1799 (4th edn). 2 sisters exemplify over-refinement and sense; *see* M. Melander, An unknown source of Jane Austen's Sense and sensibility, Studia Neophilologica 22 1950.

The history of Sir George Warrington: or the political Quixote. 1797. Hero reads Paine, Rights of man, becomes temporarily insane. Not by Mrs Lennox, as stated.

Bennett, Agnes Maria. The beggar girl and her benefactors. 7 vols 1797, 3 vols Dublin 1798, 5 vols 1799. Sensibility; poor but virtuous girl rewarded.

Bonhote, Elizabeth. Bungay Castle. 1797. Gothic; interesting use of detailed local color.

Diderot, Denis. The nun. 1797. Trn of La religieuse.

D'Israeli, Isaac. Flim-flams: or the life of my uncle. 3 vols 1797–1805, 1806. Whimsical imitation of Tristram Shandy.

—— Vaurien: or sketches of the times. 1797. Satire on follies of society; satanic protagonist.

Fox, Joseph. Santa-Maria: or the mysterious pregnancy. 1797. Over-strenuous effort at horror.

Hervey, Elizabeth. The church of Saint Siffrid. 1797, 1798. A Gothic tale.

Lee, Harriet and Sophia. Canterbury tales. 5 vols 1797–1801. 12 tales in all, of popular types; sentimental doctrines.

Leigh, Sir Samuel Egerton. Munster abbey: a romance. Edinburgh 1797.

Radcliffe, Ann. The Italian. 1797, 1811 (3rd edn); ed F. Garber, Oxford 1968. The villain Schedoni is unusually well presented and analysed; involves Inquisition; complex adventures.

Robinson, Mary. Walsingham: or the pupil of nature. 1797, 1805. Epistolary; exquisite sensibility causes hero's sufferings; cautionary against surrender to impulse.

Brydges, Sir Samuel Egerton. Arthur Fitz-Albini: a novel. 1798, 1799. Super-refined hero, last of ancient race, collapses totally from contact with the mundane. See M. K. Woodworth, The literary career of Brydges, Oxford 1935.

Fortnum, Sophia. Waldorf: or the dangers of philosophy. 1798. Abstract doctrines put into practice ruin several persons.

Godwin, Mary Wollstonecraft. The wrongs of woman: or Maria. 1798 (incomplete; in Posthumous works), Philadelphia 1799 (as Maria). Thesis novel; women crushed by poverty, matrimonial despotism.

Kotzebue, August Friedrich Ferdinand von. Ildegarte, Queen of Norway. 1798, Philadelphia 1800. Based on Saxo Grammaticus, but romanticized with Ossianic elements.

Lathom, Francis. The midnight bell. 1798; ed D. P. Varma 1968. Tale of terror.

Lloyd, Charles. Edmund Oliver: a novel. Bristol 1798. Rebellion on Godwinian principles leads to madness and suicide; hero based on Coleridge.

Moore, Frances. The subterranean cavern: or memoirs of Antoinette de Montflorence. 1798. Epistolary; set in French Revolution; parental tyranny and fate persecute lovers; Gothic elements.

Patrick, Mrs F. C. More ghosts! 1798. Satire of Gothic horrors.

Roche, Regina Maria. Clermont. 1798; ed D. P. Varma 1968. Gothic features in abundance; primitivism; good quality.

Sleath, Eleanor. The orphan of the Rhine. 1798; ed D. P.

Varma 1968. Modifies the ecclesiastical calumnies of Gothic fiction with a Roman Catholic view.

Surr, Thomas Skinner. George Barnwell: a novel. 1798, Dublin 1798. Lillo's character translated to genteel high life.

The natural son. 1799. Novel-version of play by Diderot; incest threatened but averted.

Charlton, Mary. Rosella: or modern occurrences. 1799, Dublin 1800. Reacts against sensibility, Gothicism.

Godwin, William. St Leon: a tale of the sixteenth century. 1799, 1800, Dublin 1800; several edns in 19th century. Romance, philosophy, psychology; Faustian hero estranged from mankind. Parodied, 1800, in E. DuBois, St Godwin. See W. A. Flanders, Godwin and Gothicism: St Leon, Texas Stud in Lang & Lit 8 1967.

Hays, Mary. The victim of prejudice. 1799. Persecuted heroine refuses to marry reformed ravisher.

Lafontaine, Augustus. The man of nature: or nature and love. 1799, 1807. Trn from German; indebted to Rasselas, Nouvelle Héloïse, Werther.

Reeve, Clara. Destination: or memoirs of a private family. 1799, Dublin 1800. Didactic; education propaganda; young man should be free to choose his way of life.

Walker, George. The vagabond: or whatever is just is equal, but equality not always just. 1799, 1800 (4th edn). Against new social ideas; see H. H. MacMullan, The satire of Walker's Vagabond on Rousseau and Godwin, PMLA 52 1937.

Henry of Northumberland, or the hermit's cell: a tale of the fifteenth century. 1800, Dublin 1800. Fictional development of Bishop Percy's ballad The hermit of Warkworth.

Edgeworth, Maria. Castle Rackrent: an Hibernian tale. 1800, 1800 etc; ed G. Watson, Oxford 1964. Noted for realism and excellence; first regional novel in English; see W. H. G. Armytage, Little women, Queen's Quart 56 1949; I. C. Clarke, Maria Edgeworth, 1950; P. H. Newby, Maria Edgeworth, 1950; P. Leyris, Château-Rackrent, Mercure de France 340 1963; J. Newcomer, Castle Rackrent: its construction and its irony, Criticism 8 1966; W. B. Coley, An early 'Irish' novelist, in Minor British novelists, ed C. A. Hoyt 1967.

Hamilton, Elizabeth. Memoirs of modern philosophers. 1800; 3 edns by 1802. Female Quixote device; satirizes contemporary radical thought and thinkers, notably Godwin circle.

Moore, John. Mordaunt: being sketches of life, character and manners in various countries. 1800, Dublin 1800; ed W. L. Renwick, Oxford 1965. Detailed use of French Revolution as background; portraits of Robespierre etc.

Pilkington, Mary Hopkins. New tales of the castle, or the noble emigrants: a story of modern times. 1800, 1803.

Walker, George. The three Spaniards: a romance. 1800, Dublin 1800. Tale of terror in Gothic manner.

R. A. D.

IV. CHILDREN'S BOOKS

This section consists primarily of books intended to be read by children in their leisure hours for enjoyment. It does not include books produced for school or educational use as such (see under Education, *below), or books of manners (see* Courtesy Books *under* Education, *below), books of practical advice, or moral, religious or other purely didactic works. It admits 'readers' and books of information (e.g. natural history for children) only when they are pioneer works in their class and of consequence to the development of children's literature as a whole. Even within these limits, the list is not comprehensive. The number of books produced for juvenile reading in the eighteenth century was considerable. The titles given here are of the works of the best known writers of the period or of the books which had the most enduring popularity. Most are books which were rptd over and over again, in many cases fresh edns still being called for 30 years or more after their first pbn. No attempt is made to list reprints; but new edns are given when significant alterations have been made in the text or noteworthy illustrations added.*

The dating of some of these little books, particularly those which appeared anonymously or pseudonymously, can present peculiar difficulty. Some were not merely undated when they first appeared and undated when rptd, but the reprints may bear no specific indication that they are not the original edn. Further, in some cases no copy of the original edn is known to have survived. In such cases dates have been deduced from the text of later edns, from contemporary reviews or from advertisements; but owing to the unreliability of publishers' announcements in the eighteenth century, dates so derived are given with a question-mark, and when a work was advertised at the end of the year, or 'to be published in the Christmas holidays', the date is given of both the old year and the new. Where the date is conjectural, or where no copy of the original edn is known, the conjectural date is followed where possible by the date of the earliest extant dated edn.

Certain categories of books which supplied much of the reading matter enjoyed by children in the eighteenth century were not originally intended for the young, and are outside the scope of this section. The chief of these categories are as follows:

1. *Books written for adults which quickly became favourites with the young either as a whole or in abridged edns, in particular*: John Bunyan, The pilgrim's progress, 1678; Arabian nights' entertainments, 1706?–1717; Daniel Defoe, Robinson Crusoe, 1719; Jonathan Swift, Gulliver's travels, 1726; Peter Longueville, The hermit: or the adventures of Philip Quarll, 1727; Robert Paltock, Life and adventures of Peter Wilkins, 1751; Rudolph Erich Raspe, Baron Munchausen's marvellous travels, 1785.

2. *Books written for adults which were unsuitable for children in their original edns, but which were subsequently issued abridged for children. The dates below are those of juvenile edns*: Henry Fielding, History of Tom Jones, [1768 or 1769];—History of Joseph Andrews, 1769; Samuel Richardson, Pamela: or virtue rewarded, 1769;—History of Clarissa Harlowe, [1769?];—History of Sir Charles Grandison, [1769?].

3. *Selections from Aesop and other fabulists, the versions most frequently rptd for juvenile use during this period being those of Sir Roger L'Estrange (1692); Samuel Croxall (1722); Robert Dodsley (1761); and T. Saint, Newcastle 1776, with cuts by T. Bewick.*

4. *Cheap reprints or abridgements of traditional and popular literature, produced for sale by the itinerant chapmen, some of the titles most read by the young being*: The history of Jack and the giants; The history of Guy, Earl of Warwick; The history of Valentine and Orson; The life and death of Sir Bevis of Southampton; The life and merry exploits of Robin Hood; The pleasant history of Jack Horner; The famous history of Tom Thumb; The history of Sir Richard Whittington; The history of two children in the wood; The life and death of St George; The merry tales of the wise men of Gotham; The cries of London; A whetstone for dull wits, or a poesy of riddles; and The death and burial of Cock Robin. *See* F. J. H. Darton, Children's books in England, 1932, ch 5 *and works cited under* Special Subjects, *below*.

(1) BIBLIOGRAPHIES AND HISTORIES

General Works

Trimmer, Sarah. The guardian of education. 5 vols 1802–6. Criticism of current works for children, with comment on many earlier works.

The juvenile review: or moral and critical observations on children's books, intended as a guide to parents and teachers in their choice of books of instruction and amusement. 1817. Pt I, books for children under eight; pt II, for children 8–12. A summary and criticism of over 300 books of the Georgian era.

Hugo, Thomas. The Bewick collector: a descriptive catalogue of the works of Thomas and John Bewick. 2 vols 1866–8.

Yonge, C. M. A storehouse of stories. 2 vols 1870. Selections, 18th and 19th centuries, with historical introd.

Welsh, C. A bookseller of the last century: being some account of the life of John Newbery, and of the books he published, with a notice of the later Newberys. 1885.

Tuer, A. Pages and pictures from forgotten children's books. 1898.

—— Stories from old-fashioned children's books. 1899.

Field, L. F. The child and his book: some account of the history and progress of children's literature in England. [1891].

Lucas, E. V. Old fashioned tales. [1905]. Selections, with introd.

—— Forgotten tales of long ago. 1906. Selections, with introd.

Barry, F. V. A century of children's books. 1922.

Andreae, G. The dawn of juvenile literature in England. Amsterdam 1925.

Gumuchian et Cie. Les livres de l'enfance du XVe au XIXe siècle; préface de Paul Gavault. 2 vols Paris [1930], 1 vol 1967 (with fewer plates). A bookseller's catalogue which is virtually a bibliography. English collations etc in English. Many facs.

Darton, F. J. H. Children's books in England: five centuries of social life. Cambridge 1932, 1958 (2nd edn, with introd by K. Lines).

James, P. Children's books of yesterday. Ed C. G. Holme, Studio (special no) 1933.

Rosenbach, A. S. W. Early American children's books; with bibliographical descriptions of the books in his private collection; foreword by A. Edward Newton. Portland Maine 1933, New York 1966. Includes comments on English edns which preceded American.

Moore, A. E. Literature old and new for children. Boston [1934].

Johnson, E., and C. E. Scott. Anthology of children's literature. Cambridge Mass 1935, 1948; ed E. Johnson, E. R. Sickels and F. C. Sayers 1959 (enlarged).

Smith, E. S. The history of children's literature: a syllabus with bibliographies. Chicago 1937.

Muir, P. H. Children's books of yesterday. Cambridge 1946. Annotated catalogue of a loan exhibition sponsored by the National Book League.

—— English children's books 1600–1900. 1954.

Kiefer, M. American children through their books 1700–1835. Philadelphia 1948. Many of the books are of English origin.

Smith, J. A. Children's illustrated books. 1948.

Meigs, C. et al. A critical history of children's literature from earliest times to the present. New York 1953.

Cahoon, H. Children's literature, books and manuscripts. New York 1954. Annotated catalogue of a loan exhibition at the Pierpont Morgan Library.

Sloane, W. Children's books in England and America in the seventeenth century: a history and a checklist. New York 1955.

Targ, W. (ed). Bibliophile in the nursery. Cleveland 1957. Mainly rptd chs from works listed above, or below under Special Subjects.

St John, J. The Osborne Collection of early children's books 1566–1910. Toronto 1958. Library catalogue with extensive annotations and appendices.

Thwaite, M. F. From primer to pleasure: an introduction to the history of children's books in England. 1963.

Welch, d'A. A. A bibliography of American children's books printed prior to 1821. 6 pts, Proc of Amer Antiquarian Soc 1963–8. Includes descriptions of preceding parallel English edns.

Vries, L. de. Flowers of delight culled from the Osborne collection of early children's books 1765–1830. 1965.

Roscoe, S. A provisional check-list of books for children and young people, issued under the imprints of John Newbery and his family 1742-1802. Harrow 1966.

Good, D. A catalogue of the Spencer Collection of early children's books and chapbooks, presented to the Harris Public Library. Preston 1967.

Special Subjects

Keightley, T. Fairy mythology. 1828, 1847 (enlarged).

Halliwell [-Phillipps], J. O. The nursery rhymes of England. 1842, 1843, 1844, 1846, 1853, c. 1860 (all enlarged).

— Popular rhymes and nursery tales. 1849.

— Notices of fugitive tracts and chap-books. 1849.

John Cheap the Chapman's library: the Scottish chap literature of last century. 1878.

Ashton, J. Chapbooks of the eighteenth century. 1882.

Chap-books and folk-lore tracts. Ed G. L. Gomme and H. B. Wheatley 5 pts 1885. Thomas Hickathrift; The seven wise masters of Rome; Mother Bunch's closet newly broke open (charms, dreams and fortune-telling); Patient Grisel; Sir Richard Whittington.

Cunningham, R. H. Amusing prose chap-books, chiefly of last century. 1889.

Lang, A. The blue fairy book. 1889. Introd in large-paper edn only.

Pearson, E. Banbury chapbooks and nursery toy book literature of the eighteenth and early nineteenth centuries. 1890.

Hartland, E. S. The science of fairy tales. 1891.

Cox, M. E. R. Cinderella: 345 variants. 1893. Introd by A. Lang.

Fables of Aesop. Ed J. Jacobs 1894.

Tuer, A. History of the horn-book. 2 vols 1896, 1 vol 1897.

Lane, W. C. Catalogue of English and American chapbooks in Harvard College Library. Cambridge Mass 1905.

Eckenstein, L. Comparative studies in nursery rhymes. 1906.

Conant, M. P. The oriental tale in England in the 18th century. New York 1908.

Yearsley, M. The folklore of fairy-tale. 1924.

Mahony, B. E., L. P. Latimer and B. Folmsbee. Illustrators of children's books 1744-1945. Boston 1947.

Opie, I. and P. The Oxford dictionary of nursery rhymes. Oxford 1951.

— The Oxford nursery rhyme book. Oxford 1955.

Williams-Ellis, A. Fairy tales from the British Isles. 1960.

Neuburg, V. E. The penny histories: a study of chapbooks for young readers over two centuries. Oxford 1968.

(2) 1660-1700

Youths lookinglass, wherein they may behold the frailties and vanities of all things under the sun. [c. 1660].

Vernon, John. The compleat scholler: or a relation of the life of Caleb Vernon. 1666.

Janeway, James (1636?-74). A token for children, being an exact account of the conversion, holy and exemplary lives and joyful deaths of several young children. Pt I, [1671?], 1676; pt II, [1672?], 1673.

Chear, Abraham (d. 1668), Henry Jessey (1601-1663) and H.P. [H. Punchard]. A looking-glass for children: being a narrative of God's gracious dealings with some little children. 1672, 1673 (corrected), 1708 (enlarged).

Keach, Benjamin (1640-1704). War with the Devil: or the young mans conflict with the powers of darkness. 1673.

— Instructions for youth: or the childs and youths delight. [1693?], New York 1695, London 1696 (4th edn enlarged), 1715 (9th edn further enlarged), 1763 (30th edn). Title varies in different edns.

J., W. [William Jole (fl. 1660-1710)]. The father's blessing penn'd for the instruction of his children: containing godly and delightful verses, riddles, fables, jests, stories, proverbs, rules of behaviour and other useful matters to allure children to read. [1674], 1696.

White, Thomas (d. c. 1672). A little book for little children: wherein are set down several directions for little children, and several remarkable stories. [c. 1674], 1702 (12th edn).

Crossman, Samuel (1624-84), and Nathaniel Crouch (1632?-1725?). The young man's calling: or the whole duty of youth, together with remarks upon the lives of several young persons. 1678.

Harris, Benjamin (fl. 1673-1716) (ed?). The Protestant tutor, instructing children to spel and read English. 1679.

B., J. [John Bunyan (1628-88)]. A book for boys and girls: or country rhimes for children. 1686, 1701 (shortened), 1707 (illustr). The 9th edn 1724 and after as Divine emblems: or temporal things spiritualized; ed J. Brown 1889 (facs of 1686).

B., R. ['Richard Burton', Nathaniel Crouch (1632?-1725?)]. Youth's divine pastime: containing forty remarkable scripture stories, turned into common English verse. 1691 (3rd edn); pt II, 'forty more histories', [c. 1720] (2nd edn), 1729 (4th edn).

Russell, Robert. A little book for children and youth. [c. 1691]; A little book for children: the second part, [c. 1696].

The child's recreation: containing a necessary catechism, also easie directions for speedy teaching children to spell and read true English. 1692.

Mason, John (1646?-94). A little catechism, with little verses and little sayings for little children. 1692.

G., J. A play-book for children, to allure them to read as soon as then can speak plain. 1694.

(3) 1701-1800

Ronksley, William. The child's weeks-work: or a little book, so nicely suited to the genius and capacity of a little child, both for matter and method, that it will infallibly allure and lead him on into a way of reading. 1712.

W., T. A little book for little children: wherein are set down, in a plain and pleasant way, directions for spelling, and other remarkable matters. [c. 1712]. Not a reprint of Thomas White, Little book for little children, above.

Watts, I[saac] (1674-1748). Divine songs attempted in easy language for the use of children. 1715, 1740 (16th edn, with addns), 1787 (as Dr Watts's divine and moral songs for children). For list of edns, see W. M.

Stone, Divine and moral songs of Watts, New York 1918; supplement, 1929; and d'A. A. Welch, Bibliography of American children's books vol 6, 1968.

Amusements serious and comical: or a new collection of bon-mots, keen-jests, ingenious thoughts, pleasant tales and comical adventures. Hague 1719. Text in English and French.

H., T. A guide for the child and youth in two parts: first for children, containing plain and pleasant directions to read English; the second, for youth. 1723.

Wright, John. Spiritual songs for children: or poems on several subjects and occasions. 1727.

Foxton, Thomas (fl. 1721-36). Moral songs composed for the use of children. 1728, 1731 (corrected).

Emblems for the entertainment and improvement of youth: containing hieroglyphical and enigmatical devices, engraved on 62 copper plates. c. 1730, 1788 (rev). Not the same work as Wynne's (or Riley's) Choice emblems, 1772.

[Boreman, Thomas?]. A description of three hundred animals, viz beasts, birds, fishes, serpents and insects, extracted from the best authors and adapted to the use of all capacities. 1730, New York 1968 (facs of 1786 edn).

—— A description of a great variety of animals and vegetables, adapted to the use of all capacities, but more particularly for the entertainment of youth. 1736.

—— A description of some curious and uncommon creatures, omitted in the Description of three hundred animals. [1739?].

—— The gigantic history of the two famous giants and other curiosities in Guildhall, London. 1740; The gigantick history, volume the second: which completes the history of Guildhall, 1740.

—— The history and description of the famous cathedral of St Paul's, London. 2 vols 1741.

—— Curiosities in the Tower of London. 2 vols 1741.

—— The history of Cajanus, the Swedish giant. 1742.

—— Westminster Abbey. Vols 1–2, 1742; vol 3, 1743.
The above 5 titles were issued in matching vols, and were in print as a set in 1753. See W. M. Stone, The gigantick histories of Boreman, Portland Maine 1933.

[Spateman, Thomas]. The school-boy's mask, design'd for the diversion of youth and their excitement to learning. 1742.

The child's new play-thing: being a spelling-book intended to make the learning to read a diversion. [1742], 1743.

'Lovechild, Nurse'. Tommy Thumb's song book for all little masters and misses. [1744] (same contents? as Worcester Mass 1788, facs by F. G. Melcher, New York 1946); Tommy Thumb's pretty song book vol 2, [1744].

—— Nancy Cock's pretty song book for all little masters and misses. [1744?], [c. 1781].

[Newbery, John (1713–67)]. *The authorship of the books pbd for children by Newbery is speculative; but it seems probable he wrote, wholly or partly, some of the works below, and that he edited or materially influenced others. They are grouped together under his name for convenience.*

—— A little pretty pocket-book, intended for the instruction and amusement of little Master Tommy and pretty Miss Polly. [1744], 1760 (10th edn); ed M. F. Thwaite, Oxford 1966 (facs of 1767).

—— A museum for young gentlemen and ladies: or a private tutor for little masters and misses. [1750?], 1758 (2nd edn).

—— Nurse Truelove's Christmas box: or the golden plaything for little children. [1750?], 1776.

—— Nurse Truelove's New-Year's-gift: or the book of books for children. [1750?], [c. 1770].

—— A pretty book of pictures for little masters and misses: or Tommy Trip's history of beasts and birds; to which is prefix'd the history of little Tom Trip himself, of his dog Jowler and of Woglog the great Giant. 1752, Newcastle 1779 (woodcuts by John Bewick); ed E. Pearson 1867 (facs). Newbery's authorship is suggested by Goldsmith in Vicar of Wakefield ch 18.

—— 'Tommy Trapwit', Be merry and wise: or the cream of the jests and the marrow of maxims for the conduct of life. [1753?], 1761 (5th edn).

—— 'Tommy Tagg', A collection of pretty poems for the amusement of children three foot high. 1756. First edn is numbered 'fifty-fourth', and numbering runs consecutively thereafter up to 'sixtieth' edn 1768.

—— 'John-the-Giant-Killer', Food for the mind: or a new riddle book, compiled for the use of the great and the little good boys and girls in England, Scotland and Ireland. [1756 or 1757], 1759 (3rd edn); ed A. W. Tuer 1899 (facs of 1778).

—— 'Abraham Aesop', Fables in verse for the improvement of young and old; to which are added Fables in verse and prose by Woglog the great giant. 1757.

—— Short histories for the improvement of the mind, extracted chiefly from the works of the celebrated Joseph Addison esq, Sir Richard Steele and other eminent writers. 1760.

—— A pretty plaything for children of all denominations. [1760?], 1762.

—— 'Tom Telescope', The Newtonian system of philosophy adapted to the capacities of young gentlemen and ladies: being the substance of six lectures read to the Lilliputian Society. 1761. Sometimes called The philosophy of tops and balls.

—— The renowned history of Giles Gingerbread, a little boy who lived upon learning. 1764.

—— The Easter gift: or the way to be very good, a book very much wanted. 1764.

—— The Whitsuntide gift: or the way to be happy. 1764.

—— The Valentine's gift: or the whole history of Valentine's Day. 1765.

—— The fairing: or golden toy for children, in which they can see all the fun in the fair. [1765?], 1767.

—— The history of little Goody Two-Shoes, otherwise called Mrs Margery Two-Shoes; with the means by which she acquired her learning and wisdom. 1765, 1766 (enlarged); ed C. Welsh 1881 (facs of 3rd edn 1766). *See* W. M. Stone, History of little Goody Two-Shoes, Proc Amer Antiquarian Soc 49 1939; R. J. Roberts, BM Quart 29 1965.

—— The important pocket book: or the Valentine's ledger. [c. 1766].

—— The rival pupils: or a new holiday gift for a boarding-school. [c. 1766].

—— The Twelfth-Day gift: or the grand exhibition, containing a curious collection of pieces in prose and verse by a society of young gentlemen and ladies. 1767, 1788 (newly illustr).

—— Six-pennyworth of wit: or stories for little folks of all denominations. [c. 1767].

—— Tom Thumb's folio: or a new penny plaything for little giants. [1767?], 1768.
See above, Bibliographies and Histories; C. Welsh, A bookseller of the last century, 1885; *and* S. Roscoe, A provisional check-list, Harrow 1966.

The child's New-Years gift: being a collection of chaste and significant riddles upon the most familiar subjects. [1744 or 1745?].

A Christmas-box for masters and misses: consisting of stories proper to form the opening minds of children. [1745?].

Select tales and fables with prudential maxims in prose and verse. 2 vols 1746. With engravings by B. Cole after S. Wale.

The trifle, or gilded toy, to humour every girl and boy. [Birmingham 1748?] (3rd edn), 1755 (4th edn).

Little master's miscellany: or divine and moral essays in prose and verse, containing dialogues; to which is added select fables, moral songs and useful maxims. Birmingham 1748 (2nd edn).

A new play book for children: or an easy and natural introduction to the art of reading. 1749.

[Fielding, Sarah (1710–68)]. The governess, or little female academy: being the history of Mrs Teachum and her nine girls, by the author of David Simple. 1749, 1749 (2nd edn rev); recast by Mrs Sherwood 1820; ed J. E. Grey, Oxford 1968 (facs of 1st edn).

Youth's entertaining and instructive calendar for the jubilee year 1750. [1749]. Tales, verses, maxims and information, arranged calendrically.

[Cotton, Nathaniel (1705–88)]. Visions in verse, for the entertainment and instruction of younger minds. 1751, 1752 (3rd edn 'revis'd and enlarg'd'), 1798 (with plates [by John Thurston]).

Marchant, John. Puerilia: or amusements for the young, consisting of a collection of songs. 1751.

—— Lusus juveniles: or youth's recreation. 1753.

[Fisher, Anne (Mrs Thomas Slack fl. 1750–75)]. The pleasing instructor or entertaining moralist: consisting of select essays, relations, visions and allegories. 1757, Newcastle-upon-Tyne 1760 (3rd edn enlarged). Preface signed A. Fisher from 1770.

The moral miscellany: or a collection of select pieces in prose and verse for the instruction and entertainment of youth. 1758, 1768 (3rd edn 'enlarged').

The famous Tommy Thumb's little story-book, containing his life and surprising adventures; to which are added fables and pretty stories [nursery rhymes]. [c. 1760].

The top book of all, for little masters and misses, containing the choicest stories, prettiest poems and most diverting riddles; to which is added a new play of the wide mouth waddling frog. [c. 1760].

A present for children, containing [extracts from Isaac Watts' Catechisms and divine and moral songs, and] familiar dialogues, with proverbs, riddles, amusing questions, fables etc. Edinburgh 1761 (2nd edn).

The polite academy: or school of behaviour for young gentlemen and ladies. 1762.

The cries of London: or child's moral instructor. 3 vols [1765 or 1766].

The world turned up-side down, or the comic metamorphoses: a work entirely calculated to excite laughter in grown persons, and promote morality in the young ones. [c. 1766].

Entertaining fables for the instruction of children. [c. 1768].

'Winlove, Solomon'. Moral lectures on the following subjects: pride, envy, avarice, anger [etc.]. 1769.

—— A collection of the most approved entertaining stories calculated for the instruction and amusement of all little masters and misses in this vast Empire. [1768 and 1769], 1770 (2nd edn).

The mother's gift: or a present for little children who are good. 1769; pt 2, 1773; pt 3, 1775; 2 vols 1783.

The brother's gift: or the naughty girl reformed. [c. 1769], 1777.

The sister's gift: or the naughty boy reformed. [c. 1769], 1793.

Mrs Lovechild's golden present. [1769?].

Robin Goodfellow: a fairy tale, written by a fairy for the amusement of all the pretty little faies and fairies. 1770.

[Johnson, Richard (1733?–93)]. The little female orators: or nine evenings' entertainments, with observations. 1770, 1772 (corrected).

—— Letters between Master Tommy and Miss Nancy Goodwill. 1770, 1786 (rev).

—— 'Littleton, Master Tommy'. Juvenile trials for robbing orchards, telling fibs and other high misdemeanours. 1772.

—— Tea-table dialogues between Miss Thoughtful, Miss Sterling, Miss Prattle [and others], wherein is delineated the charms of innocence and virtue and the pleasures of rural amusements. 1772. Partly rewritten as Tea-table dialogues between a Governess and Miss Sensible [et al], [1776?], 1779.

—— 'Angelo, Master Michael'. The drawing school for little masters and misses. 1773.

—— 'Angelo, Master Michel'. Juvenile sports and pastimes; to which are prefixed Memoirs of the author. [1773 or 1774], 1776 (2nd edn corrected).

—— The picture exhibition: containing the original drawings of eighteen little masters and misses; to which are added Moral and historical explanations, published under the inspection of Master Peter Paul Rubens. 1774.

—— 'Gulliver, Lilliputius'. The Lilliputian library: or Gulliver's museum. 10 vols [1779].

—— The entertaining traveller: giving a brief account of the voyages and travels of Master Tommy Columbus in search of the Island of Wisdom. [1780 or 1781].

—— The holiday spy: being the observations of little Tommy Thoughtful. [1780 or 1781].

—— The juvenile biographer: containing the lives of little masters and misses, by a little biographer. [1780 or 1781].

—— 'J., R.' The little moralists: or the history of Amintor and Florella, the pretty little shepherd and shepherdess of the Vale of Evesham. 1786.

—— 'J., R.' The little wanderers; or the surprising history and miraculous adventures of two pretty orphans. 1786.

—— The adventures of a silver penny. [1786 or 1787].

—— 'J., R.' The village tattlers: or anecdotes of the rural assembly. [1786 or 1787].

—— 'J., R.' The flights of a lady-bird: or the history of the winged rambler. 1787.

—— The foundling: or the history of Lucius Stanhope. 1787.

—— The history of a little boy found under a haycock. [1786 or 1787].

—— 'J., R.' False alarms: or the mischievous doctrine of ghosts and apparitions, exploded from the minds of every miss and master. [1787 or 1788], 1796.

—— Rural felicity: or the history of Tommy and Sally. [1787 or 1788].

—— 'J., R.' The toy-shop, or sentimental preceptor: containing some choice trifles, for the instruction and amusement of every little miss and master. [1787 or 1788].

—— The hermit of the forest and the wandering infants. 1788.

—— The history of Tommy Careless: or the misfortunes of a week. 1788.

—— The blossoms of morality intended for the amusement and instruction of young ladies and gentlemen. 1789, 1796 (2nd edn, with cuts by J. Bewick).

—— The youthful jester, or repository of wit and innocent amusement: containing moral and humourous tales, merry jests, laughable anecdotes and smart repartees. [1789 or 1790].

—— The adventures of a bee. 1790.

—— A fortnight's tour through different parts of the country, by Master Tommy Newton, including original anecdotes. 1790.

—— Moral sketches for young minds. 1790.

—— Choice scraps, historical and biographical: consisting of pleasing stories, most of them short to prevent their being tiresome. [1790?].

—— The history of Jacky Idle and Dicky Diligent. [1790?].

—— The visits of Tommy Lovebook to his neighbouring little misses and masters. 1792.

—— 'Cooper, Rev Mr'. Poetical blossoms being a selection of short poems. 1793.

—— 'Meanwell, Miss Nancy'. The history of a doll: containing its origin and progress through life. [1794?].

Johnson's educational works and trns appeared under the name of, or were advertised as by 'The Rev Mr Cooper'.

See M. J. P. Weedon, Richard Johnson and the successors to John Newbery, Library 5th ser 4 1950.

[Smart, Christopher (1722–71)]. Hymns for the amusement of children. [1771?]; ed E. B. (Edmund Blunden), Oxford 1947 (facs of 1775).

The sugar plum: or sweet amusements for leisure hours. 1771.

The cries of London, as they are daily exhibited in the streets, with an epigram in verse, adapted to each. [1771?], 1775.

'Ticklepitcher, Toby'. The hobby-horse or Christmas companion: containing among other interesting particulars, the song of a cock and a bull. [1771?], 1784.

The puzzling cap: being a collection of choice riddles. [c. 1771], 1786.

[Wynne, John Huddlestone (1743–88)]. Choice emblems, natural, historical, fabulous, moral and divine, for the improvement and pastime of youth. 1772, 1775 (with addns). 1779, 1781 as Riley's emblems (after George Riley, the original publisher).

—— J.H.W., Tales for youth: in thirty poems. 1794. With woodcuts by John Bewick.

'Bunyano, Don Stephano'. The prettiest book for children: being the history of the enchanted castle, situated in one of the fortunate isles and governed by the giant instruction. 1772.

A poetical description of beasts, with moral reflections for the amusement of children. 1773.

A poetical description of song birds, interspersed with entertaining songs, fables and tales. [1773?], 1779.

'Chatter, Charley'. A Lilliputian auction, to which all little masters and misses are invited. [1773?], 1777.

Youth's instructive and entertaining story-teller: being a choice collection of moral tales, deduced from real life. Newcastle-upon-Tyne 1774 (with cuts by T. Bewick).

The history of little King Pippin; with an account of the melancholy death of four naughty boys, who were devoured by wild beasts. [1774 or 1775], 1783.

'Prattle, Goody'. A companion for the nursery: containing a variety of pretty things, to please the nurses and the children too. Salisbury [c. 1775].

'Hurlothrumbo, Doctor'. The fortune-teller, by which young gentlemen and ladies can easily foretel a variety of important events. [c. 1775], 1785.

The amusing instructor: or tales and fables in prose and verse for the improvement of youth. 1777.

'Goose, Mother'. The mirror: or a looking-glass for young people of both sexes, consisting of a choice collection of fairy tales [from various sources]. Newcastle-upon-Tyne 1778 (woodcuts by T. Bewick?).

Filial duty, recommended and enforc'd by a variety of instructive and entertaining stories of children. [c. 1778].

Wright, George. The young moralist: consisting of allegorical and entertaining essays by various authors. [c. 1778], 1782 (3rd edn enlarged), 1819 (5th edn with notes).

The history of young Edwin and little Jessy, by Margery who lives at the foot of Parnassus. [c. 1779], 1797.

Trimmer, Sarah (b. Kirby, 1741–1810). An easy introduction to the knowledge of nature and reading the Holy Scriptures. 1780, 1789 (with addns). Not a school text book.

—— Fabulous histories, designed for the instruction of children, respecting their treatment of animals. 1786. In nineteenth century known as The history of the robins, or The robins.
  See Some account of the life and writings of Mrs Trimmer, 2 vols 1814. *Also above*, Bibliographies and Histories, The guardian of education, 1802–6.

'Sobersides, Solomon'. Christmas tales, for the amusement and instruction of young ladies and gentlemen in winter evenings. [c. 1780], Newcastle-upon-Tyne [c. 1781] (with cuts by T. Bewick).

'Teachem, Toby'. The orphan: or the entertaining history of little Goody Goosecap, containing a variety of adventures calculated to amuse and instruct the Lilliputian world. [c. 1780], [1788] (as The entertaining history).

Mother Goose's melody: or sonnets for the cradle. [1780 or 1781], [Worcester Mass 1786], London 1791; ed W. F. Prideaux 1904 (facs); ed J. Barchilon and H. Pettit as The authentic Mother Goose, 1960; Worcester Mass 1794; ed W. H. Whitmore as The original Mother Goose, 1892 (facs); ed F. G. Melcher 1945 (facs).

The adventures of Master Headstrong and Miss Patient in their journey towards the land of happiness. [1780 or 1781].

Virtue and vice: or the history of Charles Careful and Harry Heedless. [1780 or 1781].

B., A. L. [Barbauld, Anna Laetitia (b. Aikin 1743–1825)]. Hymns in prose for children. 1781, 1814 ('much enlarged').

[Barbauld, Anna Laetitia, and Aikin, John (1747–1822)]. Evenings at home: or the juvenile budget opened. 6 vols 1792–6, 4 vols 1826 (14th edn rev Arthur Aikin).

The friends: or the history of Billy Freeman and Tommy Truelove. [c. 1781].

Jacky Dandy's delight: or the history of birds and beasts, in prose and verse. [c. 1781].

[Kilner, Dorothy (1755–1836)]. All works anon or signed 'M.P.', later 'M. Pelham'.

—— The first principles of religion explained in a series of dialogues adapted to the capacity of the infant mind. 2 vols [1781?]. Abridged by Sarah Trimmer as Sunday school dialogues, [c. 1790].

—— The history of a great many little boys and girls of four and five years of age. [1781].

—— The holiday present: containing anecdotes of Mr and Mrs Jennett and their little family. [1781?].

—— Dialogues and letters on morality, oeconomy and politeness, for the improvement and entertainment of young female minds. [c. 1781]; vols 2–3, 1787.

—— Little stories for little folk, in easy lessons of one, two and three syllables. [c. 1781].

—— Anecdotes of a boarding-school: or an antidote to the vices of those useful seminaries. 2 vols [1782?].

—— The good child's delight: or the road to knowledge. [c. 1782].

—— The histories of more children than one: or goodness better than beauty. [c. 1782].

—— Short conversations: or an easy road to the temple of fame. [c. 1782].

—— A father's advice to his son. [1783]. A collection of stories linked by dialogue.

—— The village school: or a collection of entertaining histories. 2 vols [c. 1783].

—— Poems on various subjects, for the amusement of youth. [c. 1783]. With others.

—— The life and perambulations of a mouse. 2 vols [1783–4?].

—— Letters from a mother to her children, on various important subjects. 2 vols [c. 1785], 1787 (2nd edn).

—— The Rotchfords: or the friendly counsellor, written for the amusement of the youth of both sexes. 2 vols [1785?].

—— The rational brutes: or talking animals. 1799.

—— First going to school: or the story of Tom Brown. 1804.

—— Jingles: or original rhymes for children. 1806.

—— The review, or three days' pleasure: a story written in the last century. 1820.

[Kilner, Mary Ann (b. Maze, 1753–1831)]. All works anon or signed 'S.S.'.

Familiar dialogues for the instruction and amusement of children four and five years of age. [c. 1782].

—— The adventures of a pincushion, designed chiefly for the use of young ladies. [1782].

—— Memoirs of a peg-top: an entertaining history. [1782?].

—— Jemina Placid: or the advantage of good nature, exemplified in a variety of familiar incidents. [1783].

—— William Sedley: or the evil day deferred. [1783].

More, Hannah (1745–1833). Sacred dramas, chiefly intended for young persons. 1782. *See also col 1599, below.*

Little Robin Red breast: a collection of pretty songs for children, entirely new. 1782.

[Fenn, Lady Eleanor (b. Frere, 1743–1813)]. All works anon or under pseudonyms 'Mrs Teachwell' and 'Mrs Lovechild', or thus ascribed in advertisements.

—— School occurrences: supposed to have arisen among a set of young ladies under the tuition of Mrs Teachwell, and to be recorded by one of them. [1782].

—— Juvenile correspondence: or letters suited to children from four to above ten years of age. 1783.

—— Cobwebs to catch flies: or dialogues in short sentences. 2 vols [1783].

—— Rational sports, in dialogues passing among the children of a family, suited to children from five to twelve years of age. [1783].

—— School dialogues for boys, by a lady. 2 vols [1783]. Dialogues about school events.

—— Fables by Mrs Teachwell, in which the morals are drawn incidentally in various ways, suited to children from five to seven years of age. [1783].

—— Fables in monosyllables by Mrs Teachwell, suited to children from four to six years of age. [1783].

—— Morals to a set of fables by Mrs Teachwell. [1783]. Issued separately from preceding, but also sold with it.

—— The female guardian: designed to correct some of the foibles incident to girls, and supply them with innocent amusement for their hours of leisure, by a lady. 1784.

—— The rational dame: or hints towards supplying prattle for children. [1786].

—— The fairy spectator: or the juvenile monitor, by Mrs Teachwell and her family. 1789.

—— The juvenile Tatler, by a society of young ladies under the tuition of Mrs Teachwell. 1789.

—— Lilliputian spectacle de la nature: or nature delineated, in conversations and letters passing between the children of a family. 3 vols [c. 1789]. Or as Nature displayed. Not a trn. Vols 1–2 in dialogues; vol 3 a ser of letters.

—— A miscellany in prose and verse for young persons, designed particularly for the amusement of Sunday scholars. [1795].

—— The village matron: or anecdotes of Mrs Lovechild. Norwich [1795?].

—— The family miscellany, in prose and verse for children of various ages. 1805.

The renowned history of Primrose Prettyface, who by her love of learning was raised to great riches. [c. 1782].

[Day, Thomas (1748–99)]. The history of Sandford and Merton: a work intended for the use of children. [Vol 1], 1783, 1784 (corrected); vol 2, 1786; vol 3, 1789; [1790] (abridged [by Richard Johnson]); 1794 (7th edn, selections), 1808 (with an account of the author).

—— The children's miscellany. 1788, 1790 (enlarged with cuts by J. Bewick). No contemporary record found of an edn of 1787.

—— The history of little Jack. 1788. Extracted from the above, with cuts by J. Bewick.

—— The grateful Turk (extracted from Sandford and Merton) in Moral tales by esteemed writers. [c. 1800]. See G. W. Gignilliat, The author of Sandford and Merton, 1932; S. H. Scott, The exemplary Mr Day, 1935.

J., S. [Stephen Jones? (1763–1827)]. The history of Tommy Play-Love and Jacky Love-Book, written by a friend. 1783.

—— The life and adventures of a fly, supposed to have been written by himself. [c. 1789]. With woodcuts by John Bewick.

[Ritson, Joseph (1752–1803)]. Gammer Gurton's garland, or the nursery Parnassus: a choice collection of pretty songs and verses. Stockton [1784], [c. 1799] (with addns], London 1810 (much enlarged).

Peacock, Lucy. The adventures of the six princesses of Babylon, in their travels to the temple of virtue: an allegory. 1785.

—— The rambles of fancy: or moral and interesting tales. 2 vols 1786.

—— The knight of the rose: an allegorical narrative. 1793, 1807 (enlarged).

—— The visit for a week: or hints on the improvement of time. 1794, 1795 (rev).

—— The little emigrant: a tale, interspersed with amusing anecdotes and instructive conversations. 1799.

—— Friendly labours: or tales and dramas for the amusement and instruction of youth. Brentford 1815.

—— Emily: or the test of sincerity. 1816.

See also Magazines, below, The Juvenile magazine 1788.

The adventures of a whipping-top: illustrated with stories of many bad boys who themselves deserve whipping, and of some good boys who deserve plum pudding. [c. 1785].

Moral and instructive tales for the improvement of young ladies. 1786. The preface, by another hand, signed H.C.

The happy family: or memoirs of Mr and Mrs Norton, intended to shew the delightful effects of filial obedience. [1786].

—— Mrs Norton's story book, composed for the amusement of her children; to which are added Instructions for the proper application of the stories. [1786].

Holiday entertainment: or the good child's fairing, containing the plays and sports of Charles and Billy Welldon. [c. 1786], 1793.

The history of Tommy Titmouse. [1786 or 1787].

May-Day: or anecdotes of Miss Lydia Lively, intended to improve and amuse the rising generation. 1787.

Mother Chit-Chat's curious tales and puzzles: or master and miss's entertaining companion. Newcastle-upon-Tyne 1787 (7th edn 'enlarged').

[Darton, William (1755–1819)]. All works illustrated and copper-plates engraved by the author, who was also the publisher.

—— Little truths better than great fables. 2 vols 1787. Illustr anecdotes.

—— A present for a little girl. 1797, 1806 (enlarged); ed E. Norman-Stahli 1965 (facs).

—— A present for a little boy. 1798.

—— The first [second and third] chapter of accidents and remarkable events, containing caution and instruction for children. 3 vols 1801.

—— City scenes. 1801, 1806 (rev Ann and Jane Taylor).

—— Rural scenes. 1801, 1806 (rev Ann and Jane Taylor).

—— ? Youthful sports. 1801.

The wren, or the fairy in the green-house: consisting of song, story and dialogue: founded upon actual incidents. [1787]. With woodcuts by John Lee; rptd 1843 with preface by author's son.

Virtue in a cottage: or a mirror for children in humble life. [c. 1787].

The new instructive history of Miss Patty Proud: or the downfall of vanity. [c. 1787]. Titles vary slightly with different publishers.

A birth-day present: or nine days conversation between a mother and a daughter on interesting subjects, for the use of young persons from ten to fourteen years of age. 1788.

The history of the three brothers. 1788. Extracted from The children's miscellany, above, illustr John Bewick, and issued with A sketch of universal history, or with other matter.

Midsummer holydays: or a long story written for the improvement and entertainment of young folk. 1788.

History of a school boy, with other pieces. 1788.

Wollstonecraft, Mary (afterwards Godwin) (1759–97). Original stories from real life, with conversations, calculated to regulate the affections and form the mind to truth and goodness. 1788, 1791 (with plates by William Blake); ed E. V. Lucas, Oxford 1906. See also below, Translations, C. G. Salzmann, and col 1254, below.

M., A. The history of the family at Smiledale, presented to all little boys and girls who wish to be good and make their friends happy. [c. 1788]. Woodcuts probably by J. Bewick.

Youthful recreations, containing amusements of a day as spent by Master Freelove and his companions. 1789. Tales and intellectual amusements.

The interesting and affecting history of Prince Lee Boo, a native of the Pelew Islands, brought to England by Captain Wilson. 1789.

Anecdotes of a little family, interspersed with fables, stories and allegories. [c. 1789].

[Beloe, William (1756–1817)]. Incidents of youthful life: or the true history of William Langley. 1790.

The oracles, containing some particulars of the history of Billy and Kitty Wilson. [c. 1790].

The Tom Tit's song book: being a collection of old songs, with which most young wits have been delighted. [c. 1790]. Nursery rhymes.

'John, Little'. The history of little Dick. [c. 1790].

Tommy Trip's Valentine gift; to which is added Some account of old Zigzag and of the horn which he used to understand the language of birds, beasts, fishes and insects. Gainsborough 1791.

[Pinchard, Mrs, of Taunton]. The blind child: or anecdotes of the Wyndham family, written for the use of young people by a lady. 1791.

—— Dramatic dialogues for the use of young persons. 2 vols 1792.

—— The two cousins: a moral story for the use of young persons. 1794.

—— Family affection: a tale for youth. Taunton 1816.

S., H. The history of the Davenport family. 2 vols [1791], 1 vol 1798.

—— Anecdotes of Mary: or the good governess. 1795.

'Puzzlewell, Peter'. A choice collection of riddles, charades, rebuses etc: part the first. 1792; pt 2, 1796; pt 3, 1796; 1 vol 1835.

Evans, John (1767–1827). Juvenile pieces designed for the youth of both sexes. 1794 (2nd edn enlarged).

Wakefield, Priscilla (b. Bell, 1751–1832). Mental improvements: or the beauties and wonders of nature and art. 2 vols 1794.

[——] Leisure hours: or entertaining dialogues between persons eminent for virtue and magnanimity. 2 vols 1794–6.

—— Juvenile anecdotes, collected for the amusement of children. 2 vols 1795–8, 1 vol 1821 (6th edn), 4 vols 1840.

—— An introduction to botany in a series of familiar letters. 1796.

—— The juvenile travellers: containing the remarks of a family during a tour through Europe. 1801, [1842] (18th edn enlarged).

—— A family tour through the British Empire [i.e. United Kingdom]. 1804.

—— Domestic recreation: or dialogues illustrative of natural and scientific subjects. 1805.

—— Excursions in North America, described in letters. 1806, 1819 (3rd edn 'improved').

—— Sketches of human manners, delineated in stories. 1807.

—— Perambulations in London and its environs. 1809, 1814 (2nd edn 'improved').

—— Variety: or selections and essays. 1809.

—— Instinct displayed: well-authenticated facts exemplifying the sagacity of the animal creation. 1811.

—— The traveller in Africa. 1814.

—— An introduction to the natural history of insects, in a series of letters. 1816.

—— The traveller in Asia. 1817.

[Andrews, Eliza]. The brothers: a novel for children. Henley 1795 (2nd edn).

—— The history of a pin, as related by itself, interspersed with a variety of anecdotes. 1798.

Mitchell, M. (later Mrs Ives Hurry). Tales of instruction and amusement, written for the use of young persons. 2 vols 1795.

[——?]. The silver thimble. 1799.

—— The faithful contrast: or virtue and vice accurately delineated in a series of moral and instructive tales. 1804.

—— Rational amusement for leisure hours, consisting of interesting tales for the mental improvement of youth. 1804.

Smith, Charlotte (1749–1806). Rural walks, in dialogues intended for the use of young persons. 2 vols 1795.

—— Rambles farther: a continuation of rural walks. 2 vols 1796.

—— Minor morals, interspersed with original stories. 2 vols 1798.

—— Conversations introducing poetry: chiefly on subjects of natural history. 2 vols 1804.

For her novels and education works, see col 683 above.

Edgeworth, Maria (1767–1849). The parent's assistant: or stories for children. 3 vols 1795 (anon), 1796 (2nd edn, with addn), 6 vols 1800 (3rd edn, signed, with 8 new stories). *See* also vol 3.

Mavor, William Fordyce (1758–1837)]. The juvenile olio, or mental medley: consisting of original essays, tales, fables etc, written by a father. 1796.

—— Youth's miscellany: or a father's gift to his children. 1798.

—— A father's gift to his children. 2 vols 1805. Enlarged edn of The juvenile olio and Youth's miscellany.

See also col 1799, below.

[Fanshawe, Althea]. Easter holidays. Bath 1797.

The force of example: or the history of Henry and Caroline. 1797.

The history of Solomon Serious and his dog Pompey: containing many pleasing particulars of Solomon's life, his rapid progress in learning, his wonderful discoveries with the microscope. 1797.

The selector: being a new and chaste collection of visions, tales and allegories. 1797.

Pilkington, Mary (b. Hopkins, 1766–1839). Obedience rewarded and prejudice conquered: or the history of Mortimer Lascells. 1797.

—— Edward Barnard: or merit exalted, containing the history of the Egerton family. 1797.

[——] Tales of the hermitage: written for the instruction and amusement of the rising generation. 1798.

—— Tales of the cottage: or stories, moral and amusing, for young persons. 1798.

—— Historical beauties for young ladies. Also as A mirror for the female sex. 1798, 1799 (reset, both with woodcuts by T. Bewick).

—— The spoiled child: or indulgence counteracted. 1799.

—— Biographies for boys: or characteristic histories. 1799.

—— Biography for girls: or moral and instructive examples. 1799.

—— Henry, or the foundling; to which are added Tales calculated to improve the mind and morals of youth. 1799.

—— The Asiatic princess. 2 vols 1800.

—— Edward: a tale for young persons. 1800. Founded on John Moor, Edward, 1796.

—— New tales of the castle: or the noble emigrants. 1800.

—— Marvellous adventures: or the vicissitudes of a cat. 1802.

—— Mentorial tales for the instruction of young ladies just leaving school. 1802.

—— Violet Vale: or stories for the entertainment of youth. 1806.

—— The calendar: or monthly recreations, chiefly consisting of dialogues between an aunt and her nieces. 1807.

—— The disgraceful effects of falsehood, and the fruits of early indulgence: exemplified in the histories of Percival Pembroke and Augustus Fitzhue. 1807.

—— A reward for attentive studies: or moral and entertaining stories. [1810?].

—— The sorrows of Caesar: or the adventures of a foundling dog. 1813.

Also didactic works and novels. See also Translations, *below, under* Marmontel *and* Genlis.

Griffin, Elizabeth. The friends, or the contrast between virtue and vice: a tale designed for the improvement of youth. Oxford 1798.

Moral amusement: or a selection of tales, histories and interesting anecdotes. Bath 1798.

Pratt, Samuel Jackson (1749–1814). Pity's gift: a collection of interesting tales, to excite the compassion of youth for the animal creation, from the writings of Mr Pratt, selected by a lady. 1798.
— The paternal present: being a sequel to Pity's gift, chiefly selected from the writings of Mr Pratt. 1802.

Kendall, Edward Augustus (1776?–1842).
[—] 'E.A.K.' Keeper's travels in search of his master. 1798.
[—] The sparrow. 1798.
[—] The canary bird: a moral fiction. 1799.
— The crested wren. 1799.
[—?] The hare: or hunting incompatible with humanity. 1799.
— The stories of Senex: or little histories of little people. 1800.
— The swallow: a fiction interspersed with poetry. 1800.
[—] 'E.A.K.' Burford Cottage and its robin-red-breast. 1835.
[—] The English boy at the Cape: an Anglo-African story. 3 vols 1835.

Helme, Elizabeth. Instructive rambles in London and the adjacent villages. 2 vols 1798.
— Instructive rambles extended in London and the adjacent villages. 2 vols 1800.
— Maternal instruction: or family conversations on moral and entertaining subjects. 2 vols 1802.
— History of England related in familiar conversations, by a father to his children. 2 vols 1804.
— History of Scotland related in familiar conversations, by a father to his children. 2 vols Brentford 1806.
See below, Translations, *under* Campe.

Helme jun, Elizabeth (afterwards Somerville). James Manners, little John and their dog Bluff. 1799.
— Flora: or the deserted child. 1800.
— The village maid: or Dame Burton's moral stories for the instruction and amusement of youth. 1801.

English, Harriet. Conversations and amusing tales for the youth of Great Britain. 1799. Illustr with aquatints; frontispiece by Bartolozzi.
— The faithful mirror. 1799.

Memoirs of the Danby family, designed for the improvement of young persons: by a lady. 1799.

The budget: or moral and entertaining fragments. 1799.

Choice tales: consisting of an elegant collection of delightful little pieces for the instruction and amusement of young persons. 1799.

Hamlain, or the hermit of the beach: a moral reverie calculated for the instruction and amusement of youth. 1799.

'Puzzlebrains, Peregrine'. Christmas amusement, or the happy association of mirth and ingenuity: being an elegant collection of original riddles, charades etc. 1799.

Sandham, Elizabeth
[—] The happy family at Eason house, exhibited in the amiable conduct of the little Nelsons and their parents. 1799.
[—] Trifles, or friendly mites: being a collection of original stories. 1800.
[—] Juliana: or the affectionate sisters. 1800.
[—] The boys' school, or traits of character in early life: a tale. [1800].
[—] More trifles for the benefit of the rising generation. 1804.
[—] The twin sisters: or the advantages of religion. [c. 1807], 1810 (4th edn).
— The adventures of poor puss. 1809.
[—] The adventures of a bullfinch. 1809.
[—] Deaf and dumb. 1810.
[—] Alithea Woodley: or the advantages of an early friendship founded on virtue. [c. 1810].
— The perambulations of a bee and a butterfly. 1812, 1824 (as The bee and the butterfly).
— The adopted daughter: a tale for young persons. 1815.
— The history of William Selwyn. 1815.
[—] Conversations on natural history. [c. 1815].
— The grandfather: or the Christmas holidays. 1816.
[—] The school-fellows: a moral tale. 1818.
— Pleasure and improvement blended. 1819.
— The history of Elizabeth Woodville: or the wars of the House of York and Lancaster. 1822.
[—] Providential care: a tale founded on facts. 1825.
Several other works have been attributed to Elizabeth Sandham.

Smith, Thomas (c. 1775–1830). The shepherd's son: or the wish accomplished. 1800.
— Lucinda, or virtue triumphant: a moral tale. 1801.

Visits to the aviary for the instruction of youth. 1800.

Memoirs of Dick, the little poney, supposed to be written by himself. 1800.
— The dog of knowledge: or memoirs of Bob, the spotted terrier. 1801.

Brewer, George (b. 1766). The life of Rolla: a Peruvian tale with moral inculcations for youth. 1800.
— The juvenile lavator: or a familiar explanation of the Passions of Le Brun, interspersed with tales. [1812].

The triumphs of goodnature, exhibited in the history of Master Harry Fairborn and Master Trueworth. [c. 1800].

Bisset, James (1762–1832). Juvenile reduplications: or the new House that Jack built. Birmingham 1800.
— The orphan boy. Birmingham [c. 1800].

(4) MAGAZINES

The Lilliputian magazine: or the young gentleman and lady's goldenl ibrary. [1752]. First monthly pt advertised Feb 1751, 2 pts issued.

The juvenile magazine: or an instructive and entertaining miscellany. Ed Lucy Peacock Jan–Dec 1788.

The minor's pocket-book. [Annually 1796?–1815?]. During its later years ed Ann Taylor.

The young gentleman's and lady's magazine: or universal repository of knowledge, instruction and amusement. Jan–Dec 1799.

The children's magazine: or monthly repository of instruction and delight. Jan 1799–Dec 1800.

The monthly preceptor: or juvenile library. 1800–2.
See W. E. A. Axon, Library 2nd ser 2 1901.

The picture magazine: or monthly exhibition for young people. [1800–1?].
See S. A. Egoff, Children's periodicals of the nineteenth century, 1951.

(5) TRANSLATIONS

Aulnoy, Marie Catherine La Mothe (1650/1–1705). Les contes des fées. 1698; Les contes nouveaux ou les fées à la mode, 3 vols 1698–1711.
Tales of the fairys, translated from the French. 1699.
The diverting works of the Countess D'Anois, pt IV:

Tales of the fairies in three parts compleat, 1707, 1715 (illustr).
The history of the tales of the fairies, newly done from the French. 1716. A different trn; dedication signed B.H.

A collection of novels and tales of the fairies, written by that celebrated wit of France, the Countess D'Anois. 3 vols 1728 (2nd edn; dedication signed W.C.).

The Court of Queen Mab: containing a select collection of only the best, most instructive and entertaining tales of the fairies; to which are added a fairy tale by Dr Parnell, and Queen Mab's song. 1752.

Mother Bunch's fairy tales, published for the amusement of all those little masters and misses who, by duty to their parents, and obedience to their superiors, aim at becoming great lords and ladies. 1773.

The palace of enchantment: or entertaining and instructive fairy tales. 1788.

See Fairy tales by the Countess d'Aulnoy, tr J. R. Planché 1855; The fairy tales of Madame d'Aulnoy, newly done into English by Miss A. Macdonell and Miss Lee, with an introduction by Anne Thackeray Ritchie, 1892; M. E. Storer, La mode des contes de fées, 1928.

Perrault, Charles (1628–1703). Histoires ou contes du temps passé; avec des moralitez. 1698.

Histories: or tales of past times: viz I The little Red Riding-hood; II The fairy; III The Blue Beard; IV The sleeping beauty in the wood; V The master cat or puss in boots; VI Cinderella or the little glass slipper; VII Riquet a la houpe; VIII Little Poucet and his brothers; IX The discreet princess, with morals. Tr Robert Samber 1729; ed J. Barchilon and H. Pettit, The authentic Mother Goose, Denver 1960 (facs); 1737 (2nd edn corrected).

Tales of passed times by Mother Goose, with morals, englished by R.S. 1764 (6th edn corrected, with French and English texts).

Histories or tales of past times told by Mother Goose, with morals, englished by G. M. Gent. Salisbury 1763 (3rd edn). Probably by G.M., gentleman. In fact Samber's corrected edn, with minor revisions.

The histories of passed times: or the tales of Mother Goose, with morals. 2 vols 1785. French and English texts.

One or more tales were included in several children's books pbd in the second half of the century, or separately under various titles. An edn of the tales misdated 1719, should read 1799; See Opie, Oxford dictionary of nursery rhymes, pp. 39–40. For notes on the tales, see J. R. Planché, Four and twenty fairy tales, 1858; A. Lang, Perrault's popular tales, 1888; P. Saintyves (Emile Nourry), Les contes de Perrault, 1923; J. Barchilon, Perrault's tales of Mother Goose, 2 vols 1956.

Le Prince de Beaumont, Jeanne Marie (1711–80). Magasin des enfans. 1756; Contes moraux, 1774.

The young misses magazine, containing dialogues between a governess and several young ladies of quality. 2 vols 1761. Tales from this work frequently rptd elsewhere.

Moral tales. 2 vols 1775.

Marmontel, Jean François (1723–1799). Contes moraux. 1761.

Select moral tales, translated by a lady [R. Roberts]. 1763.

Marmontel's tales, selected and abridged by [Mary] Pilkington. 1799. With woodcuts by T. Bewick.

Marmontel's moral tales. Ed G. Saintsbury 1895.

Richer, Adrien. Les grands évémemens par les petites causes. 1758; Great events from little causes: or a selection of interesting stories; tr Griffith Jones (1722–1786) 1767.

Genlis, Stéphanie-Félicité de (afterwards Brulart de Sillery) (1746–1830). Théâtre d'éducation. 1779–80; Les veillées du château, 1782.

The theatre of education. 4 vols 1781, 1787 ('a new translation'). Plays for children.

Sacred dramas. Tr Thomas Holcroft 1786. A trn of vol I only.

Tales of the castle: or stories of instruction and delight. Tr Thomas Holcroft 5 vols 1785.

See W. M. Kerby, The educational ideas and activities of Madame la Comtesse de Genlis, Paris 1926.

Campe, Joachim Heinrich (1746–1818). Robinson der Jüngere. 2 vols 1779–80; Die Entdeckung von Amerika, 3 pts 1790–1.

Robinson the younger. Hamburg 1781. Tr author.

The new Robinson Crusoe: an instructive and entertaining history for the use of children of both sexes, translated from the French [of J. H. Campe's trn from the German]. 4 vols 1788, 2 vols 1789, 1 vol 1789, 1789 (abridged). With woodcuts by J. Bewick.

The new Robinson Crusoe, translated from the original German [by Richard Johnson]. 1790.

The discovery of America, for the use of children and young persons, translated from the German. 1799.

Cortes, or the discovery of Mexico: being a continuation of the Discovery of America. 1800. Companion to above.

Pizarro, or the conquest of Peru: being a continuation of the Discovery of America. 1800. Companion to above.

Columbus, or the discovery of America, as related by a father to this children, translated by Elizabeth Helme. 2 vols 1799, 1 vol 1811 (corrected).

Cortez, or the conquest of Mexico, translated by Elizabeth Helme. 2 vols 1799.

Pizarro, or the conquest of Peru, translated by Elizabeth Helme. 2 vols 1800.

Berquin, Arnauld (1749?–91). L'ami des enfans. 24 monthly pts Jan 1782–Dec 1783; Le petit Grandisson, 1787.

The children's friend, translated from the French of Mr Berquin. 24 vols? 1783–4. Issued twice a month from 15 Nov 1783.

The children's friend: consisting of apt tales, short dialogues and moral dramas, translated by Mark Anthony Meilan. 24 vols 1786. A different trn.

The children's friend. [Tr Lucas Williams] 4 vols 1787, 1788 (corrected), 6 vols 1793 (with addns and new illustrations; signed).

Select stories for the instruction and entertainment of children. 1787. A selection from the 4-vol edn, above.

The looking-glass for the mind, or intellectual mirror: being an elegant collection of the most delightful little stories and interesting tales, chiefly translated from L'ami des enfans [by Richard Johnson]. 1787, 1792 (with cuts by J. Bewick); ed C. Welsh 1885.

The children's friend: being a selection from the works of M. Berquin. 1788.

The history of little Grandison. 1791 (frontispiece by J. Bewick). Also in The friend of youth, 2 vols 1788 (for older children).

The mountain piper: or the history of Edgar and Matilda. [1788?]. Extracted from The children's friend.

The family book, or children's journal: consisting of moral and entertaining stories from [Berquin], interspersed with poetical pieces written by the translator, Miss Stockdale. 1798.

Weisse, Christian Felix (1726–1804). Kleine lyrische Gedichte. 1772.

Moral songs for children, translated from the German. 1789.

Salzmann, Christian Gotthilf (1744–1811). Moralisches Elementarbuch. 1785.

Elements of morality, for the use of children [tr Mary Wollstonecraft]. 2 vols 1790, 2 vols 1791 (some plates by William Blake?).

[Masson, Charles François Philbert (1762–1807)]. Elmine. 1790.

Elmina, or the flower that never fades: a tale for young people. 1791.

Ducray-Duménil, François Guillaume (1761–1819). Lolotte et Fanfan. 1796.

Ambrose and Eleanor: or the adventures of two children deserted on an uninhabited island, translated from the French, with alterations [by Lucy Peacock]. 1796.

The new children's friend: or pleasing incitements to wisdom and virtue, conveyed through the medium of anecdote, tale and adventure, translated chiefly from the German. 1797.

I. and P. O.

5. PROSE

1. ESSAYISTS AND PAMPHLETEERS

SIR ROGER L'ESTRANGE
1616–1704

§ 1

To a gentleman, a member of the House of Commons. 1646 (8 July).

L'Estrange his appeale from the Court Martiall to the Parliament. 1647 (April).

L'Estrange his vindication to Kent. 1649.

The liberty of the imprisoned royalist. [1649]. Anon; verse.

The fanatique powder-plot. 1660 (24 March). Anon.

Peace to the nation. [Feb 1660]. Anon.

Let me speake too? or eleven queries. 1659.

No blinde guides, in answer to Milton's Brief notes upon a late sermon. 1660 (20 April).

Physician cure thyself: or an answer to Eye-salve for the English army. 1660 (23 April).

Sir Politique uncased: or a sober answer to A letter intercepted. [1660?]. Anon.

L'Estrange his apology; with a short view of some late and remarkable transactions. 1660. Includes the following pamphlets, almost all of which appear to have been first ptd separately: (1) The declaration of the City, to the men at Westminster; (2) The engagement and remonstrance of the City of London, 12 Dec 1659; (3) The final protest, and sense of the City, [1659]; (4) The resolve of the City, 23 Dec 1659; (5) A free parliament proposed by the City to the nation (dated 6 Dec 1659, but apparently combined with a letter To the Honorable the Commissioners of the City of London, which is dated 3 Jan 1659, i.e. 1660); (6) A plain case, 24 Jan 1659; (7) To his Excellency General Monck: a letter from the gentlemen of Devon (dated 18 Jan 1659); (8) The sense of the army (dated 2 Feb 1659); (9) The citizens declaration for a free parliament (dated 2 Feb 1659); (10) For his Excellency General Monck (dated 4 Feb 1659); (11) A narrative (dated 12 Feb 1659, untitled); (12) A word in season, to General Monck, the city and the nation (dated 18 Feb 1659); (13) A seasonable word; (14) Quaere for quaere; (15) No fool to the old fool (dated 16 March 1659); (16) A paper against the faction (dated 24 March 1659, untitled); (17) A necessary and seasonable caution, concerning elections (dated 27 March 1660); (18) Treason arraigned, in answer to Plain English, 1660; (19) Double your guards, in answer to an alarum to the armies of England, Scotland and Ireland (dated 4 April 1660). Some copies of L'Estrange his apology also contain No blinde guides and Physician cure theyself.

An appeal in the case of the late King's party. 1660. Anon.

A plea for a limited monarchy. 1660. Anon. Rptd Harleian miscellany vol 1, 1744, 1808.

A caveat to the cavaliers, dedicated to the author [James Howell] of A cordial for the cavaliers. 1661 (4 edns).

A modest plea for the caveat, and the author of it. 1661 (Aug), 1661, 1662.

Interest mistaken: or the holy cheat. 1661, 1661, 1662, 1662, 1682 (as The holy cheat).

The relaps'd apostate: or notes upon a petition for peace. 1661 (Nov) ('1641'), 1661, 1681.

To the Right Hon Edward Earl of Clarendon, Lord High Chancellor. 1661 (3 Dec).

State divinity: or a supplement to the Relaps'd apostate. 1661 (4 Dec).

A memento directed to all those that truly reverence the memory of King Charles the Martyr: the first part. 1662 (April), 1682 (omits last 3 chs; as A memento treating of the rise, progress and remedies of sedition).

Truth and loyalty vindicated, from the reproches and clamours of Mr Edward Bagshaw. 1662 (7 June).

The visitation: or long look'd-for comes at last. 1662. Anon.

A whipp, a whipp for the schismatical animadverter [Bagshaw] upon the Bishop of Worcester's letter. 1662 (Feb), 1662.

Toleration discuss'd. 1663, 1670, 1673 ('enlarged'), 1681.

Considerations and proposals in order to the regulation of the press, together with diverse instances of treasonous and seditious pamphlets. 1663 (3 June).

The intelligencer, published for the satisfaction and information of the people, with privilege. 31 Aug 1663–29 Jan 1666. A weekly, pbd on Monday.

The newes, published for the satisfaction and information of the people, with privilege. 3 Sept 1663–29 Jan 1666. Originally a distinct weekly periodical, pbd on Thursday, but from 1664 a Thursday suppl to Intelligencer, above, with numbering and pagination continuous throughout both papers.

Publick intelligence, with sole privilege. No 1 (all issued). 28 Nov 1665.

Publick advertisements (with privilege). No 1 (all issued?), 25 June 1666.

The visions of Quevedo, made English. 1667, 1668 (3rd edn), 1708 (10th edn) etc; rptd 1904, Fontwell 1963.

A guide to eternity. 1672 (anon), 1680, 1680, 1688, 1694, 1709, 1712, 1722; ed J. W. Stanbridge 1900. From the Latin of Cardinal J. Bona.

A discourse of the fishery. 1674, 1695.

The city mercury. 1675. Licensed, and possibly ed L'Estrange.

The parallel: or an account of the growth of knavery under the pretended fears of arbitrary government and popery. 1677. (Also issued as An account of the growth of knavery, with a parallel betwixt the reformers of 1677 and those of 1641), 1678, 1679, 1681, 1681.

A treatise of wool and cattel. 1677.

A register of the nativity of the present Christian princes. 1678.

Tyranny and popery lording it over King and people. 1678 (anon), 1680, 1681.

The gentleman 'pothecary: a true story done out of the French. 1678, 1726.

Five love letters from a nun to a cavalier, from the French. 1678, 1686, 1693, 1701.

Seneca's Morals by way of abstract. 1678, 1682, 1693 (5th edn), 1696, 1699, 1702, 1711, 1718, 1722, 1729 etc.

The history of the plot: or a brief and historical account of the charge and defence of Edward Coleman esq [and 16 others], by authority. 1679 (anon), 1680; tr French, 1679.

An answer to The appeal [by Charles Blount] from the country to the city. 1679, 1681, 1684.

The case put, concerning the succession of his Royal Highness the Duke of York. 1679 (anon), 1679 ('enlarged'), 1680.

The reformed Catholique: or the true Protestant. 1679, 1679 ('corrected').

The free-born subject: or the Englishman's birthright. 1679 (anon), 1680, 1681.

Citt and Bumpkin, in a dialogue over a pot of ale, concerning matters of religion and government. 1680 (anon, 4 edns), 1681; ed B. J. Rahn, Los Angeles 1965 (Augustan Reprint Soc).

Citt and Bumpkin, the second part: or a learned discourse upon swearing and lying, and other laudable qualities tending to a thorow reformation. 1680 (3 edns), 1681.

A seasonable memorial in some historical notes upon the liberties of the presse and pulpit. 1680, 1681 (3rd edn).

A further discovery of the plot. 1680 (3 edns), 1681.

L'Estrange's narrative of the plot, set forth for the edification of his Majesty's liege people. 1680 (3 edns).

The casuist uncas'd in a dialogue betwixt Richard and Baxter, with a moderator between them for quietnesse sake. 1680, 1680, 1681.

Discovery upon discovery, in a defence of Dr Oates against B.W.'s libellous vindication of him. 1680, 1680.

A letter to Miles Prance. 1680.

L'Estrange's case in a civil dialogue between 'Zekiel and Ephraim. 1680, 1680 ('with additions').

A short answer to a whole litter of libels. 1680. Some copies have 'libellers'.

To the Rev Dr Thomas Ken. 1680 (1 Feb).

The committee: or popery in masquerade. 1680, 1681. Verse 'explanation' of an engraving.

A compendious history of the most remarkable passages of the last fourteen years. 1680. Anon.

Goodman country to his worship the City of London. 1680. Anon.

The presbyterian sham. 1680.

The state and interest of the nation, with respect to the Duke of York. 1680.

Twenty select colloquies out of Erasmus Roterodamus. 1680, 1689 (adds 2 colloquies), 1699 (with 7 further colloquies tr Thomas Brown), 1711, 1725.

Tully's Offices. 1680, 1681, 1684, 1688, 1699, 1720 etc; rptd 1900 (Temple Classics).

The character of a papist in masquerade, in answer to the Character of a popish successor. 1681.

A reply to the second part of the Character of a popish successor. 1681.

L'Estrange his appeal humbly submitted to the King's most excellent Majesty and the Three Estates. 1681.

L'Estrange no papist, in answer to a libel entituled L'Estrange a papist. 1681, 1685.

An apology for the protestants, done out of French into English. 1681.

Machiavil's advice to his son, newly translated. 1681. Anon; verse.

Seven Portuguese letters. 1681. Tr L'Estrange.

The Observator in question and answer. 13 April 1681–9 March 1687.

The dissenter's sayings, in requital for L'Estrange's sayings: published in their own words, for the information of the people. 1681 (3 edns), 1683; tr French, 1683.

Dissenters sayings: the second part, dedicated to the Grand-Jury of London, August 29 1681. 1681, 1681.

Notes upon Stephen College, grounded principally upon his own declarations and confessions. 1681, 1681.

The reformation reformed: or a short history of new-fashioned Christians. 1681.

A word concerning libels and libellers, humbly presented to the Right Hon Sir John Moor, Lord-Mayor of London. 1681, 1681.

The shammer shamm'd, in a plain discovery. 1681.

A letter out of Scotland. 1681. Anon ('R.L.').

A new dialogue between some body and no body: or the Observator observed. 1681.

Dialogue upon dialogue: or L'Estrange no papist nor jesuite, but the dog Towzer. 1681. By 'Philo-Anglicus'; L'Estrange?

The account clear'd, in answer to a libel intituled A true account from Chichester. 1682.

The apostate protestant, a letter to a friend. 1682 (July). Anon.

Remarks on the growth and progress of non-conformity. 1682. Anon.

Reflections upon two scurrilous libels called Speculum crapegownorum. 1682. Anon.

A sermon prepared to be preach'd. 1682.

Considerations upon a printed sheet entituled the Speech of the late Lord Russel to the sheriffs; together with the paper delivered by him to them on July 21 1683. 1683. Anon; rptd 1882 (Clarendon Historical Soc).

The lawyer outlaw'd. 1683, 1683.

Theosebia: or the churches advocate. 1683.

The whore's rhetorick, calculated to the meridian of London. 1683. Anon; by L'Estrange?

Five love letters written by a cavalier. 1683, 1694.

The observator defended, by the author of the Observator. 1685.

An answer to a letter [by Halifax] to a dissenter, upon occasion of his Majestie's late gracious declaration of indulgence. 1687.

A brief history of the times. 3 pts 1687–8.

A reply to the reasons of the Oxford clergy against addressing. [c. 1687]; rptd W. Scott in Somers tracts vol 9, 1809.

Two cases submitted to consideration. 1687, 1709.

Notice to the reader. In Fairfax's Tasso, 1687.

The Spanish Decameron: or ten novels made English. 1687, [1700], 1712, 1720. 5 novels by Cervantes and 5 by A. del Castillo Solorzano.

Heraclitus ridens redivivus: or a dialogue between Harry [Henry Care] and Roger [L'Estrange] concerning the times. Oxford 1688.

A dialogue between Sir R.L. and T.O.D. [Oates]. 1689.

Some queries concerning the election of members for the ensuing Parliament. 1690. Reply by James Harrington with similar title.

The fables of Aesop and other eminent mythologists, with morals and reflexions. 1692, 1694, 1704. This was followed by Fables and storyes moralized: being a second part of the fables of Aesop, 1699; rptd 2 vols 1703, 1708, 1714, 1715, 1724, 1730, 1738.

Terence's comedies made English. 1694, 1698, 1705, 1718, 1724, 1733, 1741. 'By several hands', including L'Estrange.

The works of Flavius Josephus. 1702, 1708 (abridged), 1709, 1725 (4th edn) etc.

A poem upon imprisonment, written by Sir Roger L'Estrange, when in Newgate, in the days of Oliver Cromwell's usurpation. 1705.

Key to Hudibras. In Samuel Butler, Posthumous works, 1715.

The Spanish pole-cat: or the adventures of Seniora Rufina. 1717, 1727 (as Spanish amusements). From the Spanish of A. del Castillo Solorzano; begun by L'Estrange and completed by J. Ozell.

§ 2

Whibley, C. Writers of burlesque and translators. CHEL vol 9 1912; rptd in Literary studies, 1919 (as An underworld of letters).

Kitchin, G. L'Estrange: a contribution to the history of the press in the seventeenth century. 1923.

Sensabaugh, G. F. Adaptations of Areopagitica. HLQ 13 1950.

Allen, C. G. Roger L'Estrange. TLS 11 April 1958.

Ketton-Cremer, R. W. A letter of L'Estrange. TLS 13 March 1959.

SIR WILLIAM TEMPLE
1628–99

Collections

Works. 2 vols 1720, 1731, 1740, 1750, 4 vols Edinburgh 1754, 1757, 1770, 1814.

Miscellanies, in four essays by Sir William Temple.

Glasgow 1761. Contains Ancient and modern learning; Of gardens; Of heroic virtue; Of poetry.

Select collection of poems 1780–2. Ed J. Nichols. Vol 2, Essays; 2 vols 1821 (vol 4 of British prose-writers, 1819–21).

Essays on ancient and modern learning and on poetry. Ed J. E. Spingarn, Oxford 1909.

Essays. Ed J. A. Nicklin 1903.

Early essays and romances, with the life and character by his sister Lady Giffard. Ed G. C. Moore Smith, Oxford 1930.

Upon the garden of Epicurus, with other xviith-century garden essays. Ed A. F. Sieveking 1908.

Three essays. Ed F. J. Fielden, Oxford 1939. Contains Of poetry; Of popular discontents; Of health and long life.

Five miscellaneous essays. Ed S. H. Monk, Ann Arbor 1963. Contains Upon the gardens of Epicurus; Ancient and modern learning; Some thoughts upon reviewing Ancient and modern learning; Of heroic virtue; Of poetry.

§ I

Upon the death of Mrs Catherine Philips. 1664. Anon; verse.

Lettre d'un marchand de Londres a son amy a Amsterdam. [1666]. Anon.

Poems by Sir W.T. [1670?] (priv ptd). A copy with ms corrections by the author in BM.

An essay upon the advancement of trade in Ireland. Dublin [1673].

Observations upon the United Provinces of the Netherlands. 1673, 1673, 1676, 1680, 1690, 1693, 1696, 1705, Edinburgh 1747; ed G. N. Clark, Cambridge 1932; tr Dutch, 1673; French, 1674.

Miscellanea: the first part. 1680, 1681 ('augmented'), 1691, 1693, 1697, 1705; tr French, 1693.

Miscellanea: the second part. 1690, 1690, 1692 ('augmented'), 1696, 1705; tr French, 1693.

Miscellanea: the third part, published by Jonathan Swift. 1701; tr French, 1704.

An essay upon the original and nature of government. In Miscellanea pt 1, 1680; ed R. C. Steensma, Los Angeles 1964 (Augustan Reprint Soc).

Memoirs of what past in Christendom, from the war begun in 1672 to the peace concluded 1679. 1692, 1692, 1693, 1694, 1700, 1709; tr French, 1692.

An essay upon taxes. 1693.

An answer to a scurrilous pamphlet, lately printed, intituled A letter from Monsieur de Cros to the Lord —. 1693. Anon.

An introduction to the history of England. 1659, 1699 ('corrected'), 1708; tr French, 1695.

The temple of death. 1695 (2nd edn). Verse.

Memoirs: part III, from the peace concluded 1679 to the time of the author's retirement from publick business, publish'd [with preface] by Jonathan Swift. 1709, 1709; tr French, 1729.

Letters

Letters written by Sir William Temple during his being Ambassador at the Hague to the Earl of Arlington and Sir John Trevor. 1699.

Letters written by Sir W. Temple Bart and other ministers of State, published by Jonathan Swift. 2 vols 1700; tr French, 1700.

Letters to the King, the Prince of Orange: being the third and last volume, published by Jonathan Swift. 1703. Continuation of above.

Select letters to the Prince of Orange, King Charles the IId and the Earl of Arlington; to which is added an Essay upon the state and settlement of Ireland. 1701.

[Osborne, Dorothy, afterwards Lady Temple]. Letters from Dorothy Osborne to Sir William Temple. Ed E. A. Parry, Edinburgh 1888, 1888, 1903 (rev), [1914]; ed G. C. Moore Smith, Oxford 1928.

§ 2

[Boyer, A.] Memoirs of the life and negotiations of Temple. 1714.

[Giffard, Martha, Lady]. The life and character of Sir William Temple Bart, by a particular friend. 1728.

Lüden, H. Temple: Biographie. In his Kleine Aufsätze vol 2, Göttingen 1808.

Moumergué, L. J. N. Notice sur le Chevalier Temple et sur ses Mémoires. In C. B. Petitot, Collection des mémoires relatifs à l'histoire de France, ser 2, vol 64, Paris 1827.

Courtenay, T. P. Memoirs of the life, works and correspondence of Temple. 2 vols 1836. Reviewed by T. B. Macaulay, Edinburgh Rev 68 1838.

Hirschberg, C. Temples Antheil an der Gründung der Tripleallianz. Rostock 1875.

Emerton, E. Temple und die Tripleallianz vom Jahre 1688. Berlin 1877.

Herriot, F. I. Temple on the origin and nature of government. Philadelphia [1893].

Beaven, M. L. R. Sir William Temple. Oxford 1908.

Lyttel, E. S. Sir William Temple. Oxford 1908.

Bensly, E. The library at Moor Park. N & Q 19 July 1930.

Marburg, C. Temple: seventeenth-century 'libertin'. New Haven 1932.

Allen, R. J. Swift's earliest political tract and Temple's essays. Harvard Stud 19 1937.

Douglas, D. C. In his English scholars 1660–1730, 1939, 1951 (rev).

Woodbridge, H. E. Temple: the man and his work. New York 1940.

Macpherson, C. B. Temple, political scientist? Canadian Jnl of Economics 9 1943.

Hanson, L. Temple, pamphleteer. TLS 15 Jan 1944.

Case, A. E. Swift and Temple: a conjecture. MLN 60 1945.

Pevsner, N. and S. Lang. Temple and Sharawaggi. Architectural Rev 106 1949.

Gogarty, O. St J. Dean Swift as a human being. Atlantic Monthly Oct 1950.

Williams, H. China to Peru. N & Q 27 Oct 1951.

Rowen, H. J. John de Witt and the Triple Alliance. Jnl of Modern History 26 1954.

Jarrell, M. L. The handwriting of the Lilliputians. PQ 37 1958.

Ehrenpreis, I. In his Jonathan Swift vol 1, 1962.

Roberts, W. Temple on Orinda: neglected publications. PBSA 57 1963.

Halewood, W. M. Young Temple and young Swift. CLA Jnl 10 1966.

GEORGE SAVILE, 1st MARQUIS OF HALIFAX
1633–95

Collections

Foxcroft, H. C. The life and letters of Halifax, with a new edition of his works. 2 vols 1898.

Complete works. Ed W. Raleigh, Oxford 1912. Omits Observations upon a late libel.

Works. Ed J. P. Kenyon 1969 (Pelican).

§ I

Observations upon a late libel. [1681?]; ed H. Macdonald, Cambridge 1940.

A letter to a dissenter upon occasion of his Majesties late gracious declaration of indulgence, by T.W. 1687 (6 edns); 1689 (in Fourteen papers); rptd W. Scott in Somers tracts vol 9, 1813; tr French, 1687.

A letter from a clergyman in the city to his friend in the country, containing his reasons for not reading the Declaration. [1688]. Anon.

The character of a trimmer, by the Honourable Sir W[illiam] C[oventry]. 1688, 1689, 1689, 1689 ('by Mss H.'), 1697, 1699. Circulated in ms 1685.

The anatomy of an equivalent. 1688, 1689 (in Fourteen papers), 1706.

The lady's new-year gift: or advice to a daughter. 1688, 1688 ('corrected'), 1688, Edinburgh 1688, London 1692, 1696, 1699, 1701, 1707, 1734 (11th edn) etc; ed B. Dobrée 1927; tr French, 1692; Italian, 1734.

Maxims [33] found amongst the papers of the Great Almanzor. 1693.

A rough draft of a new model at sea. 1694; rptd A. F. Pollard 1897 (in Political pamphlets).

Some cautions to those who are to chuse members to serve in Parliament. 1695, 1695, 1701, 1734; rptd A. F. Pollard 1897 (with above).

Miscellanies. 1700, 1704, 1717. Includes Advice to a daughter; Character of a trimmer; Anatomy of an equivalent; Letter to a dissenter; Cautions for choice of parliament men; A rough draught; Maxims [33] of state; A letter to C. Cotton upon his new translation of Montaigne's Essays. The last had already appeared in Cotton's Montaigne, 1693.

A character of King Charles the Second, and political, moral and miscellaneous thoughts and reflections. 1750, Dublin 1750; rptd 1927.

Letters

Savile correspondence. Ed W. D. Cooper 1858 (Camden Soc).

Some unpublished letters of Savile to Gilbert Burnet. Ed D. L. Poole, EHR 26 1911.

The Rochester-Savile letters 1671-80. Ed J. H. Wilson, Columbus 1941. Includes 14 letters to Rochester.

§2

Foxcroft, H. C. The life and letters of Halifax. 2 vols 1898, 1 vol Cambridge 1946 (rev as A character of the trimmer).
— New light on Halifax the trimmer. History 26 1941.

Paul, H. In his Men and letters, 1901.

Gooch, G. P. In his Political thought from Bacon to Halifax, 1914.

Whibley, C. In his Political portraits: second series, 1923.

Reed, A. W. In The social and political ideas of some English thinkers, ed F. J. C. Hearnshaw 1928.

Klose, K. George Savile, Marquis von Halifax. Breslau 1936.

Stapleton, L. Halifax and Raleigh. JHI 2 1941.

James, D. G. In his Life of reason, 1949.

Alington, C. A. The Marquess of Halifax. Quart Rev 289 1951.

Moore, J. R. Defoe's lost Letter to a dissenter. HLQ 14 1951. On a tract often confused with Halifax's Letter to a dissenter.

Newcomb, R. Poor Richard's debt to Lord Halifax. PMLA 70 1955. On Franklin's Poor Richard sayings.

Goodison, J. W. Cambridge portraits II. Connoisseur 140 1957.

Gathorne-Hardy, R. Halifax's Character of a trimmer: some observations in the light of a manuscript from Ickworth. Library 5th ser 14 1959.

Buranelli, V. The King and the Quaker. Philadelphia 1962.

Benson, D. R. Halifax and the trimmers. HLQ 27 1964.

JOHN DENNIS
1657-1734
Collections

Critical works. Ed E. N. Hooker 2 vols Baltimore 1939-43.

§ 1

Poems in burlesque. 1692.

Poems and letters upon several occasions. 1692.

The passion of Byblis. 1692. Tr from Ovid.

The impartial critick: or some observations upon A short view of tragedy, written by Mr Rymer. 1693; rptd in Critical essays of the seventeenth century vol 3, ed J. E. Spingarn, Oxford 1909.

Miscellanies in verse and prose. 1693, 1697 (as Miscellany poems, with Passion of Byblis, above).

The court of death: a pindarique poem, to the memory of Queen Mary. 1695, 1695.

Remarks on a book entitul'd Prince Arthur. 1696. On Blackmore.

The nuptials of Britain's genius and fame: a pindarick poem on the peace. 1697.

A plot and no plot: a comedy. (Drury Lane, 8 May 1697). [1697].

The annals and history of Cornelius Tacitus. 1698. Vol 3. The 5th bk was tr Dennis. Other translators included Dryden, William Bromley and John Potenger.

The usefulness of the stage. 1698. A reply to Jeremy Collier.

Rinaldo and Armida: a tragedy. (Lincoln's Inn Fields, c. Nov 1698). 1699.

Iphigenia: a tragedy. (Lincoln's Inn Fields, Dec 1699). 1700.

[The seamen's case]. [1700?]. The only known copy, in Bodley, is without title-page.

The advancement and reformation of modern poetry: a critical discourse in two parts. 1701.

The comical gallant, or the amours of Sir John Falstaffe: a comedy. (Drury Lane, 1702). 1702. An adaptation of Merry wives.

The danger of priestcraft to religion and government. 1702.

An essay on the navy. 1702, 1702.

A large account of the taste in poetry and the causes of the degeneracy of it. Prefixed to The comical gallant, 1702; rptd in Critical essays 1700-25, ed W. H. Durham, New Haven 1915.

The monument: a poem to the memory of William the Third. 1702.

A proposal for putting a speedy end to the war. 1703.

Britannia triumphans. 1704.

Liberty asserted: a tragedy. (Lincoln's Inn Fields, 24 Feb 1704). 1704.

The person of quality's answer to Mr Collier's letter. 1704.

The grounds of criticism in poetry, contain'd in some new discoveries never made before. 1704; rptd in Critical essays 1700-25, ed W. H. Durham, New Haven 1915.

Gibraltar, or the Spanish adventure: a comedy. (Drury Lane, 16 Feb 1705). 1705.

The battle of Ramillia. 1706.

An essay on the operas after the Italian manner. 1706.

Orpheus and Eurydice: a masque. (Unacted). 1707.

Appius and Virginia: a tragedy. (Drury Lane, 5 Feb 1709). [1709].

An essay upon publick spirit: being a satyr in prose upon the manners and luxury of the times. 1711.

Reflections critical and satyrical upon a late rhapsody, call'd An essay upon criticism. [1711]; rptd in Critical essays 1700-25, ed W. H. Durham, New Haven 1915.

An essay upon the genius and writings of Shakespear. 1712.

Remarks upon Cato: a tragedy. 1713.

A poem upon the death of Queen Anne and the accession of King George. 1714.

Priestcraft distinguish'd from Christianity. 1715.

A true character of Mr Pope and his writings. 1716 (anon), 1717.

Remarks upon Mr Pope's translation of Homer, with two letters concerning Windsor Forest and the Temple of fame. 1717.

Select works. 2 vols 1718, 1718–21 (with Coriolanus).
Proposals for printing by subscription were issued in
1717.
The characters and conduct of Sir John Edgar and his
three deputy governours. 1720. Attacks Steele and the
Drury Lane management.
The characters and conduct of Sir John Edgar, in a third
and fourth letter. 1720.
The invader of his country, or the fatal resentment: a
tragedy. (Drury Lane, 11 Nov 1719). An adaptation of
Coriolanus.
A defense of Sir Fopling Flutter. 1722.
Julius Caesar acquitted and his murderers condemn'd.
1722.
A short essay towards an English prosody. In J. Green-
wood, Essay towards a practical English grammar, 1722
(2nd edn).
Remarks on a play call'd the Conscious lovers: a comedy.
1723.
Vice and luxury public mischiefs: or remarks on a book
intitul'd the Fable of the bees. 1724.
The stage defended from scripture, reason, experience and
the common sense of mankind. 1726. A reply to
Law.
Miscellaneous tracts in two volumes. Vol 1 (all pbd), 1727.
Proposals for printing by subscription were issued [1721].
The faith and duties of Christians. [1728?]. Tr from T.
Burnet's Latin.
Remarks on Mr Pope's Rape of the lock, in several letters
to a friend; with a preface. 1728.
Remarks upon several passages in the preliminaries to the
Dunciad, and in Pope's preface to his translation of
Homer's Iliad. 1729.
A treatise concerning the state of departed souls. 1733,
1739. From T. Burnet's Latin.

Letters

Letters upon several occasions. 1696 (to and from Dennis
Dryden, Wycherley, Congreve et al, with trns from
Voiture; ed Dennis), 1700 (in Voiture's Familiar and
courtly letters pt 2), 1705 (in Works of Voiture vol 1).
Original letters, familiar, moral and critical. 2 vols 1721.
Plain Dealer nos 57, 60, Oct 1724; 96, Feb 1725.

§ 2

[Pope, A.] The narrative of Dr Robert Norris concerning
the frenzy of Mr J. Denn–. 1713.
The critical specimen. 1715. Also by Pope?; rptd in
Pope's prose works, ed N. Ault, Oxford 1936.
The life of Mr John Dennis. 1734.
[Talfourd, T. N.] Dennis's works. Retrospective Rev 1
1820.
Paul, H. G. Dennis: his life and criticism. New York
1911.
Lenz, H. Dennis: sein Leben und seine Werke. Halle 1913.
Hooker, E. N. An unpublished autograph manuscript of
Dennis. ELH 1 1934.
—— Pope and Dennis. ELH 7 1940.
Thorpe, C. de W. Two Augustans cross the Alps: Dennis
and Addison on mountain scenery. SP 32 1935.
Tupper, F. S. Notes on the life of Dennis. ELH 5 1938.
Graham, C. B. The Jonsonian tradition in the comedies of
Dennis. MLN 56 1941.
Dias, M. A satire on Dennis. 1711. RES 19 1943. On
Charles Johnson's play The generous husband.
Atkins, J. W. H. In his English literary criticism, 17th and
18th centuries, 1951.
Lynch, K. M. A Congreve gallery. Cambridge Mass 1951.
Davis, H. Musical entertainments in Rinaldo and Armida.
In his Miscellany: six pieces connected with the 17th-
century stage, Oxford 1953.
Haun, E. Dennis' Rinaldo and Armida confused with
Handel's Rinaldo. N & Q June 1954. Corrects the
above.

Wilkins, A. N. A prologue by Dennis. N & Q Dec 1955.
—— Dennis' stolen thunder. N & Q Oct 1956.
—— Dennis and poetic justice. N & Q Oct 1957.
—— Dennis on love as a tragical passion. N & Q Sept–
Oct 1958.
—— Tragedy and The true politicks. N & Q Nov 1959.
Singh, A. The argument on poetic justice: Addison versus
Dennis. Indian Jnl of Eng Stud 3 1962.
Kline, R. B. Prior and Dennis. N & Q June 1966.
Heffernan, J. A. W. Wordsworth and Dennis: the dis-
crimination of feelings. PMLA 87 1967.
Kramer, D. Passion in poetic theory: Dennis and Words-
worth. Neuphilologische Mitteilungen 69 1968.

THOMAS BROWN
1663–1704
Collections

A collection of miscellany poems, letters etc. 1699, 1699,
1700 (with addns).
A collection of all the dialogues written by Mr Thomas
Brown. 1704. Includes the unpbd Democratici
Vapulantes.
Works. 2 vols 1707 (3rd vol added later, dated 1708 but
advertised Sept 1707), 3 vols 1708, 1709, 4 vols 1711–12,
1715 (vols 1–2 described as 4th edn, vols 3–4 as 3rd edn),
5 vols 1719–20, 4 vols 1730 (7th edn), 1744, 1760,
Dublin 1778–9.
Remains, collected from scarce papers and original manu-
scripts. 1720. Also issued dated 1718 and 1721.
The beauties of Tom Brown. Ed C. H. Wilson 1808.
Amusements serious and comical, calculated for the
meridian of London. 1700, 1702 (enlarged), 1704; ed
A. L. Hayward 1927. Based upon C. R. Dufresny,
Amusemens sérieux et comiques, 1699.

§ 1

The reasons of Mr Bays changing his religion, considered
in a dialogue between Crites, Eugenius and Mr Bays.
1688 (anon), 1691 (with addns).
The weesils: a satirical fable. 1691. Anon; verse. Satire
on William Sherlock.
The late converts exposed, or the reasons of Mr Bays's
changing his religion: part the second. 1690. Anon.
The reasons of Mr Joseph Hains the player's conversion
and reconversion: being the third and last part of the
dialogue of Mr Bays. 1690 (anon), 1691.
The reasons of the new convert's taking the oaths to the
present government. 1691. Anon.
Wit for money: or poet stutter. 1691. Anon. Satire, prob-
ably by Brown, on D'Urfey's comedy Love for money.
Novus reformator vapulans: or the Welch Levite tossed in
a blanket. 1691 (anon), 1691.
The London Mercury [later Lacedemonian Mercury]. 32
nos 1 Feb–30 May 1692. Brown was assisted by William
Pate et al.
Marguetel de Sain Denis, C, Seigneur de Saint-Evre-
mond, Miscellaneous essays etc. 1692. Vol 2 tr Brown
et al.
Memoirs of the Court of Spain done into English by T.
Brown. 1692, 1701.
The Salamanca wedding, in a letter. [1693]. A squib on
Titus Oates's marriage.
Du Plessis, A. J. Cardinal, Duke de Richelieu, The life of
the famous Cardinal Duke de Richelieu, translated from
the French. 1695.
A new and easy method to understand the Roman history,
done out of French, with very large additions and
amendments. 1695, 1731.
Le Clerc, Jean of Amsterdam, Twelve dissertations out of
Monsieur Le Clerc's Genesis done out of Latin. 1696.
Familiar letters written by the Earl of Rochester. 2 vols
1697, 1699, 1705. Vol 1 ed Brown.

Erasmus, D., Seven new colloquies translated out of Erasmus Roterodamus, as also the life of Erasmus. 1699.

Commendatory verses, on the author [Blackmore] of the two Arthurs, and the Satyr against wit; by some of his particular friends. 1700, 1702 (with addns). Dedication and several poems by Brown.

A description of Mr D[ryde]n's funeral: a poem. 1700 (anon), 1700, 1700.

The infallible astrologer: or Mr Silvester Partridge's prophesies. 18 nos 16 Oct–24 Feb 1701. Anon. Brown wrote nos 1–11 and Ned Ward nos 12–18. Selections entitled A comical view of London and Westminster rptd, with authors named, in A legacy for the ladies, 1705.

Scarron, P., The whole comical works of Monsr Scarron, translated by Mr Brown and others. 1700, 1703, 1727, 1892.

Laconics: or new maxims of state and conversation. 1701 (anon), 1705. Mainly by Brown.

Advice to the Kentish long-tails, by the wise-men of Gotham. 1701. Anon; rptd as Brown's in Buckingham's works vol 2, 1705.

The adventures of Lindamira, written with her own hand. 1702, 1703, 1713 (as The lover's secretary), 1734, Dublin 1745, 1751. Ed Brown.

A dissertation upon the Mona of Caesar and Tacitus. In William Sacheverell, An account of the Isle of Man, 1702; rptd 1859 (Manx Soc).

Letters from the dead to the living. 3 pts 1702–3, 1707, 1708. Only signed portions by Brown. Pt 2 first pbd in Certamen epistolare, 1703, as Suppl to 2nd pt.

Miscellanea aulica: or a collection of state-treatises. 1702.

Certamen epistolare: or viii letters between an attorney and a dead person. 1703. With other letters. Certamen epistolare had already appeared in Brown's trn of Select epistles or letters out of Cicero, 1702.

Gelli, G., The Circe of Signor Giovanni Battista Gelli, done out of Italian by Mr T. Brown. 1702; ed R. M. Adams, New York 1963.

Trogus Pompeius, Justin's history of the world, made English by Mr T. Brown. 1702, 1712.

The mourning poet. 1703.

The miscellaneous works of the Duke of Buckingham. 2 vols 1704, 1705, 1715. Ed Brown, with a memoir of Buckingham.

The dying thoughts and last reflections, in a letter to a friend. 1704.

Garcia, C., France and Spain naturally enemies, englished with large additions and improvements by Mr T. Brown. 1704.

Goya, L. de, A looking-glass for married people: or the fantastick adventures of Sir E— H— with his seven wives, put into modern English by Mr Brown. 1704.

The stage-beaux toss'd in a blanket: or hypocrisie alamode, expos'd in a true picture of Jerry [Jeremy Collier]. 1704. Anon.

A legacy for the ladies: or characters of the women of the age, by T. Brown; with a comical view of London and Westminster: or the merry quack, in two parts, the first part by Mr Tho Brown; the second part by Mr Edw Ward [with a character of Brown by Dr Drake]. 1705.

The works of Monsieur Voiture, made English by John Dryden, T. Brown etc. 1705.

Petronius Arbiter, T., The satirical works made English by Mr Wilson, Mr Brown and several others. 1708, 1713, 1899.

Azarias: a sermon held forth in a Quakers meeting. 1710.

Erasmus, Twenty two select colloquies; to which are added seven more dialogues, with the life of the author by Mr T. Brown. 1711.

Lucian, The works translated from the Greek by several eminent hands. 4 vols 1711, 1745.

§ 2

Tom Brown arrested by the Devil. 1698.

A full and terrible account of a terrible fight between Tom Brown the poet and a bookseller. [1700?].

K[ingston], R[ichard]. Impudence, lying and forgery, detected and chastiz'd in a rejoinder to a reply, written by that infamous town-poet, Tom Brown, and father'd by Matt Smith. 1700.

Memoirs relating to the late famous Mr Tho Brown. 1704.

A letter from the dead Thomas Brown to the living Heraclitus. 1704.

T— B—'s last letter to his witty friends and companions. [1704?].

Thompson, E. N. S. Brown and eighteenth-century satirists. MLN 32 1917.

Reed, E. B. Gulliver's travels and Brown. MLN 33 1918.

Eddy, W. A. Brown and Tristram Shandy. MLN 44 1929.

— Brown and Partridge the astrologer. MP 28 1930.

Webster, C. M. Brown and the Tale of a tub. TLS 18 Feb 1932. Reply by E. K. Linton 25 Feb 1932.

Boyce, B. Two debits for Brown, with a credit for Addison. PQ 14 1935.

— Brown and Elia. ELH 4 1937.

— Brown of facetious memory. Cambridge Mass 1939.

Boys, R. C. Sir Richard Blackmore and the Wits: a study of contemporary verses on the author of the two Arthurs and the Satyr against wit 1700. Ann Arbor 1949.

Wilson, J. H. Thomas's Life of Jo Hayns. N & Q July 1961. Against Brown's authorship of Life of the late famous comedian Jo Hayns.

WILLIAM KING
1662–1712

Collections

Remains of the late learned and ingenious Dr William King. 1732, 1734 (as Posthumous works), 1739. Ed Joseph Browne, with some account of King and his writings.

Original works. 3 vols 1776. Ed with detailed memoir by John Nichols, assisted by Isaac Reed.

Poetical works, with the life of the author. 2 vols Edinburgh 1781.

§ 1

Reflections upon Mons Varillas's History of heresy. 1688. With Edward Hannes.

The meditations of M. Aurelius Antoninus, 5th edition; to which is added the life of Antoninus, with some select remarks upon the whole, by Monsieur and Madame Dacier. 1692. The life of Antoninus tr King.

An answer to a book which will be publish'd next week, upon Dr Sherlock's book, in vindication of the Trinity. 1693. Anon.

Langlade, J. de, Baron de Saumières, New memoirs and characters of the two great brothers, the Duke of Bouillon and Mareschal Turenne, made English. 1693.

Animadversions on a pretended account of Danmark. 1694. Anon.

A journey to London in the year 1698, after the ingenious method of that made by Dr Martin Lister to Paris in the same year, written originally in French by Monsieur Sorbière. 1698 (anon), 1700 ('corrected'), 1700; ed K. N. Colvile in A miscellany of the Wits, 1920.

Dialogues of the dead, relating to the present controversy concerning the Epistles of Phalaris. 1699 (anon); ed K. N. Colvile, with above.

The furmetary: a very innocent and harmless poem in three cantos. 1699. Anon.

The transactioneer, with some of his philosophical fancies, in two dialogues. 1700. Anon; satire on Sir Hans Sloane.

Mully of the Mountown: a poem. 1702 (for 1704) ('by the author of the Tale of a tub'), 1704.

The fairy feast. 1704 ('by the author of the Tale of a tub, and the Mully of Mountown').

Some remarks on the Tale of a tub; to which are annexed Molly of Mountown and Orpheus and Eurydice [The fairy feast]. 1704. Anon. This is the only complete and authorized edn of these 2 poems.

Miscellanies in prose and verse. 2 vols [1707?]. Contains Animadversions on a pretended account of Danmark; Dialogues of the dead; Orpheus and Eurydice; Reflections upon Monsieur Varillas; Miscellaneous poems; The art of cookery; The art of love; Useful transactions in philosophy. Some copies lack the last.

The art of cookery, in imitation of Horace's Art of poetry, with some letters to Dr Lister and others. [1708], [1708] (both anon), 1708 (unauthorized edn of Art of cookery alone), 1709.

The art of love, in imitation of Ovid, with a preface containing the life of Ovid. [1709], [1709].

Useful transactions in philosophy and other sorts of learning, for the months of January [–September], 1709. 3 pts 1709. Anon.

The present state of physick in the island of Cajamai, to the members of the R.S. No 1 (all pbd), [1709?].

A friendly letter from honest Tom Boggy to the Rev Mr G[oddard]. 1710. Anon.

A second letter to Mr Goddard. 1710. Anon.

A vindication of the Rev Dr Henry Sacheverell. [1711]. With Charles Lambe.

Mr B[isset]'s recantation. 1711. Anon.

An answer to a second scandalous book that Mr B[isse]t is now writing. 1711. Anon.

An historical account of the heathen gods and heroes. [1711], [1711], 1727 (4th edn), 1731, 1761; rptd 1965.

Nandé, G., Political considerations upon refin'd politicks, translated by Dr King. 1711.

Rufinus: or an historical essay on the favourite ministry under Theodosius the Great and his son Arcadius. 1712. Anon; an attack on Marlborough.

Britain's Palladium: or my Lord Bolingbroke's welcome from France. 1712.

Useful miscellanies: containing 1, A preface; 2, The tragicomedy of Joan of Hedington, in imitation of Shakespeare; 3, Some account of Horace his behaviour in Cambridge. Pt 1 (all pbd), 1712.

The northern Atalantis: or York spy, the whole interspersed with poetical amusements, among which is Apple-pye, or instructions to Nelly: a poem written by Dr W. King. 1713; rptd [1893?].

The Persian and the Turkish tales, compleat, translated into French by M. Pétis de la Croix and now into English by Dr King. 1714, 1718.

[Hall, Joseph]. A fragment of Joseph Hall's Mundus alter et idem, translated by Dr W. King. 1885 (in Henry Morley, Ideal Commonwealth).

§ 2

Johnson, S. In his Lives of the poets vol 2, 1781.

Williams, G. G. Dr William King, humorist. Sewanee Rev 35 1927.

Horne, C. J. Early parody of scientific jargon: some notes for OED. N & Q 30 Jan 1943.

—— The Phalaris controversy: King versus Bentley. RES 22 1946.

CHARLES GILDON

1665–1724

§ 1

The history of the Athenian society. [1691]; rptd with revisions in The Athenian oracle vol 4, 1710, 1728.

A letter to Mr D'Urfey, occasioned by his play called the Marriage-hater match'd. 1692. Prefixed to D'Urfey's play, 1692, 1693.

Nuncius infernalis: or a new account from below. 1692. Anon. With preface by D'Urfey. Both dialogues rptd in Works of Tom Brown, 1715, 1719, and 2nd in the 1730 and 1749 edns.

Dacier, A., An essay upon satyr. Tr Gildon in Miscellany poems, 1692.

Miscellany poems upon several occasions. 1692. Ed Gildon.

The post-boy rob'd of his mail: or the pacquet broke open. 1692. Signed C.G.

The second volume of the post-boy robb'd of his mail: or the pacquet broke open. 1693. Signed C.G. A one-vol edn, adding a few letters but discarding more, appeared in 1706.

The oracles of reason. 1693. By Gildon, Charles Blount et al.

Chorus poetarum: or poems on several occasions. 1694, 1696 (as Poems on several occasions), 1698 (as Poetical remains of the Duke of Buckingham, Mrs Behn and others). Ed Gildon.

Miscellaneous letters and essays on several subjects in prose and verse. 1694, 1697 (as Letters and essays). Ed and partly written by Gildon; 2 essays rptd in Critical essays 1700–25, ed W. H. Durham, New Haven 1915, and a short letter in Critical essays of the seventeenth century vol 3, ed J. E. Spingarn, Oxford 1909.

The miscellaneous works of Charles Blount. 1695. Ed Gildon. Includes The oracles of reason and a life of Blount.

The younger brother, or the amorous jilt: a comedy. (Drury Lane, 1696). 1696. By Aphra Behn; rewritten and pbd by Gildon.

The histories and novels of the late ingenious Mrs Behn. 1696, 1697 (3rd edn), 1700, 1705, 1718, 2 vols 1722, 1735. Ed Gildon.

Familiar letters written by the Earl of Rochester. 2 vols 1697, vol 1, 1697, 2 vols 1699, 1705. Vol 2 ed Gildon.

The Roman bride's revenge: a tragedy. (Drury Lane, 1697). 1697. Anon.

Phaeton, or the fatal divorce: a tragedy. (Drury Lane, 1698). 1698. Anon.

The lives and characters of the English dramatick poets. 1699, nd. Anon. Revision and continuation of Langbaine's Account.

Measure for measure, or beauty the best advocate: a comedy. (Lincoln's Inn Fields, 1699). 1700. Anon. An adaptation of Shakespeare. 'With additions of several entertainments of musick'.

Love's victim, or the Queen of Wales: a tragedy. (Lincoln's Inn Fields, 1701). 1701. Anon.

A new miscellany of original poems, on several occasions. 1701. Anon. Ed Gildon.

A comparison between the two stages. 1702 (anon); ed S. B. Wells, Princeton 1942.

Examen miscellaneum, consisting of verse and prose. 1702. Anon. Ed Gildon.

The patriot, or the Italian conspiracy: a tragedy. (Drury Lane, 1703). 1703. Anon; an adaptation of Lee's Lucius Junius Brutus.

Ovid Britannicus: or love epistles in imitation of Ovid. 1703. By David Craufurd, ed Gildon.

The deist's manual. 1705.

A letter from the Princess Sophia to the Archbishop of Canterbury, with another from Hanover. 1706 (anon), 1706, [1706?], 1714. Rptd by Gildon from a continental edn.

A review of her Royal Highness the Princess Sophia's letter to the Lord Archbishop of Canterbury: or a Jacobite plot against the Protestant succession discover'd. [1706].

Threnodia Virginea, or the apotheosis: a poem. 1708. Signed C.G.

Libertas triumphans. 1708. Poem on Marlborough's victory.

The new metamorphosis, or the pleasant transformation: being the Golden Ass of Lucius Apuleius of Medaura, the second edition. 2 vols 1709. (anon), 1724, 1821. First edn c. 1708? Purports to be from the Italian of Carlo Monte Socio.

The golden spy: or a political journal of the British nights entertainments of war and peace, and love and politics. 1709. Anon. Attempted serial pbn abandoned after 2 nos 1710; rptd in vol 2 of The new metamorphosis, 1724.

An essay on the art, rise and progress of the stage in Greece, Rome and England: remarks on the plays of Shakespear; remarks on the poems of Shakespear. Included in the vol of Shakespear's poems pbd by Curll in 1710 as suppl to Rowe's Works of Shakespear, pbd by Tonson; rptd 1714, 1725, Dublin 1726, 1728, in various edns of Shakespeare.

The life of Mr Thomas Betterton. 1710. Also issued anon, and with The amorous widow: a comedy, written by Mr Betterton, 2 vols 1710.

Plutarch's Lives. 1710, 1713, 1718. Abridged by Gildon from the Dryden version.

A grammar of the English tongue. 1711 (anon), 1712 ('improved'), 1714, nd (6th edn). Known as Brightland's Grammar from the publisher. Preface by Steele.

The works of Lucian. 4 vols 1711. Gildon translated 2 dialogues in vol 2.

A new rehearsal: or Bays the younger. 1714. Anon; an attack on Rowe and Pope.

Trojan tales. 1714. Anon. Advertised 1724; another edn?

Canons, or the vision: a poem. 1717.

The complete art of poetry. 2 vols 1718. Vol 1 contains specimens of Shakespear's beauties; vol 2 other poets' Beauties. Vol 1, pt 2, is rptd in Critical essays 1700–25, ed W. H. Durham, New Haven 1915.

Memoirs of the life of William Wycherley esq. 1718. Anon.

The post-man robb'd of his mail: or the packet broke open. 1719. Anon.

The life and strange surprizing adventures of Mr D[aniel] DeF[oe]. 1719 (anon), 1719, Dublin 1719; rptd P. Dottin 1923 (with an essay on Gildon's life).

Miscellanea aurea: or the golden medley. 1720. Also issued anon. Ed Gildon.

A new project for the regulation of the stage. 1720, 1720. With Dennis.

All for the better: or the world turn'd upside down. 1720. Also issued anon.

The battle of the authors. 1720.

The laws of poetry, as laid down by the Duke of Buckinghamshire, the Earl of Roscommon and by the Lord Lansdowne. 1721.

Milesian tales: or instructive novels for the happy conduct of life, written by Mrs Butler. 1727. Ed Gildon. Reissued 1735 as Irish tales. Curll advertised Irish tales in 1714, 1717, and Milesian tales in 1719.

§ 2

Wells, S. B. An eighteenth-century attribution. JEGP 38 1939.

Litz, F. E. The sources of Gildon's Complete art of poetry. ELH 9 1942.

Grove, P. B. Gildon's Fortunate shipwreck as background for Gulliver's travels. RES 18 1942.

Moore, J. R. The groans of Great Britain: an unassigned tract by Gildon. PBSA 40 1946.

— Gildon's attack on Steele and Defoe in the Battle of the authors. PMLA 66 1951.

Griffiths, R. H. Isaac Bickerstaff's Grammar. N & Q 20 Aug 1949.

Boyce, B. Pope, Gildon and Salamanders. N & Q 8 Jan 1949.

Maxwell, J. C. Gildon and the quarrel of the ancients and moderns. RES new ser 1 1950.

Atkins, J. W. H. In his English literary criticism, 17th and 18th centuries, 1951.

Anderson, G. L. Gildon vs Prior. N & Q Feb 1954.

— Lord Halifax in Gildon's New rehearsal. PQ 33 1954.

— Gildon's Total academy. JHI 16 1955.

— The authorship of Cato examin'd 1713. PBSA 51 1957.

— A little civil correction: Langbaine revised. N & Q June 1958.

Wright, H. B. Prior and Gildon. N & Q Jan 1956.

Goldstein, M. Gildon's New rehearsal again. PQ 36 1957.

Scheurweghs, G. Brightland's or Steele's Grammar. E Studies 40 1959.

Honoré, J. Gildon rédacteur du British Mercury 1711–12: les attaques contre Pope, Swift et les Wits. Etudes Anglaises 15 1962.

— Gildon et la grammaire de Brightland. Etudes Anglaises 18 1965.

JOHN ARBUTHNOT
1667–1735
Collections

The miscellaneous works of the late Dr Arbuthnot. 2 vols Glasgow 1751, 1751 (with addns), 1770 (with a short life of Arbuthnot).

Aitken, G. A. The life and works of Arbuthnot. Oxford 1892. Contains chief satirical pieces, together with some attributed works.

§ I

Of the laws of chance. 1692. Anon; trn of Huygens, De ratiociniis in ludo aleae.

Theses medicae de secretione animali, pro gradu doctoratus in medicina consequendo. [St Andrews] 1696.

An examination of Dr Woodward's account of the deluge, by J.A. MD; with a letter to the author concerning an abstract of Agostino Scilla's book on the same subject, by W.W. FRS. 1697, 1741 (as A philosophico-critical history of the deluge, by Dr Arbuthnot and Dr Wotton).

An essay on the usefulness of mathematical learning, in a letter from a gentleman in the city to his friend in Oxford. Oxford 1701, 1721, 1745. Anon.

Tables of the Grecian, Roman and Jewish measures, weights and coins, reduc'd to the English standard. [1705], 1707, 1709.

A sermon preach'd to the people at the Mercat Cross of Edinburgh on the subject of the Union. [Edinburgh] 1706 (anon), Dublin [1706], [Edinburgh? 1707?], 1707, 1707, [1745?].

An argument for Divine Providence, taken from the constant regularity observed in the births of both sexes. Philosophical Trans of Royal Soc 27 1710.

Law is a bottomless-pit. 1712 (6 March; 5 further edns 1712, all anon), Edinburgh 1712.

John Bull in his senses: being the second part of Law is a bottomless-pit. 1712 (18 March; 3 further edns 1712, all anon), Edinburgh 1712.

John Bull still in his sense: being the third part of Law is a bottomless-pit. 1712 (17 April; 3 further edns 1712, all anon), Edinburgh 1712.

An appendix to John Bull still in his senses: or Law is a bottomless-pit. 1712 (9 May; 3 further edns 1712, all anon), Edinburgh 1712.

Lewis Baboon turned honest and John Bull politician: being the fourth part of Law is a bottomless-pit. 1712 (31 July; one further edn 1712, both anon), Edinburgh 1712.

The history of John Bull [the above 5 pamphlets collected]. Edinburgh 1712 (anon), 1727 (in The Pope-Swift Miscellanies in prose and verse vol 2), Glasgow 1766; ed E. Arber 1883 (English garner vol 6); ed H. Morley 1889; ed K. N. Colvile in A miscellany of Wits 1920; ed H. Teerink, Amsterdam 1925; tr French, 1753.

Proposals for printing a very curious discourse, in two volumes in quarto, entitled ΨΕΥΔΟΛΟΓΙΑ ΠΟΛΙΤΙΚΗ or a treatise of the art of political lying. 1712 (anon), 1712, Edinburgh 1746; ed A. F. Pollard 1897 (in Political pamphlets).

Concerning the peace. In L. M. Beattie, John Arbuthnot, Cambridge Mass 1935.

To the Right Honourable the Mayor and aldermen of the City of London: the humble petition of the colliers. 1716. Anon; single sheet.

Three hours after marriage: a comedy. 1717. Gay was assisted by Pope and Arbuthnot.

Annus mirabilis, by Abraham Gunter, Philomath. 1722 (21 Dec).

Reasons humbly offer'd by the company of upholders, against part of the Bill, for the better receiving drugs. 1724. Anon.

A poem address'd to the Quidnunc's, at St James's Coffee-house, London. 1724. Anon; single sheet.

It cannot rain but it pours: or London strow'd with rarities. 1726. Anon. Begun by Arbuthnot, completed by another.

The Craftsman 1726-7. Contributions by Arbuthnot.

Miscellanies in prose and verse. 4 vols 1727-32. Preface signed by Swift and Pope. Vol 2 contains The history of John Bull and The art of political lying; vol 3 The humble petition of the colliers, An essay concerning the origin of the sciences, It cannot rain but it pours.

Tables of ancient coins, weights and measures, explain'd and exemplify'd in several dissertations. 1727 (anon), 1754 (with Appendix, containing Observations on Dr Arbuthnot's Dissertation by Benjamin Langwith); tr Latin, 1756.

Oratio anniversaria Harvaeana. 1727.

The Dunciad, variorum; with prolegomena of Scriblerus. 1729. Contributions by Arbuthnot.

Virgilius restauratus. In Dunciad variorum, above.

A brief account of Mr John Ginglicutt's treatise concerning the altercation or scolding of the Ancients. 1731 (Feb). Anon.

An essay concerning the nature of aliments, and the choice of them, according to the different constitutions of human bodies. 2 vols 1731, Dublin 1731, London 1731-2 (with Practical rules of diet, also sold separately), 1735-6, 1751, 1756; tr German, 1744.

An epitaph on Francis Chartres. London Mag April 1732; GM April 1732.

An essay of the learned Martinus Scriblerus concerning the origin of species. In Miscellanies vol 3, 1732.

An essay concerning the effects of air on human bodies. 1733, 1751, 1756, 1851; tr French, 1742; Latin, 1753.

A supplement to Dr Swift's and Mr Pope's works, now first collected into one volume. Dublin 1739. Contains The history of John Bull; Proposals for printing the Art of political lying; The humble petition of the colliers; Reasons humbly offer'd by the upholders; Annus mirabilis; An essay concerning the origin of sciences; Virgilius restauratus; It cannot rain but it pours; Epitaph of Fr—s Ch—is; and other pieces attributed to Arbuthnot.

Miscellanies by Dr Arbuthnot. Dublin 1746. Contains the above pieces, etc.

ΓΝΩΘΙ ΣΕΑΥΤΟΝ, know yourself: poem. 1734. Anon; rptd in Dodsley's Collection of poems by several hands vol 1, 1748.

Memoirs of the extraordinary life, works and discoveries of Martinus Scriblerus. In Works of Pope in prose vol 2, 1741; rptd Dublin 1741 as 'by Mr Pope'.

Miscellanies in prose and verse, by Dr Arbuthnot: a new edition corrected. Glasgow 1766.

A burlesque of Pope's Lines sung by Durastanti. Annual Register 18 1775.

Works Attributed to Arbuthnot

Unauthentic pieces included in Miscellaneous works of the late Dr Arbuthnot, above.

The longitude examin'd, by Jeremy Thacker of Beverley in Yorkshire. 1714.

Notes and memorandums of the six days, preceding the death of a late Right Reverend —. 1715.

The state quacks: or the political botchers. 1715.

A letter to the Reverend Mr Dean Swift, occasion'd by a satire said to be written by him, entitled A dedication to a great man. 1719. Signed P.A. 30 Jan 1718-19.

An account of the sickness and death of Dr W—dw—rd, by Dr Technicum. 1719.

The life and adventures of Don Bilioso de L'Estomac, translated from the original Spanish into French, done from the French into English; with a letter to the College of Physicians. 1719.

An epitaph on a greyhound. [?].

A supplement to Dean Sw—t's Miscellanies, by the author. 1723.

The most wonderful wonder that ever appeared to the wonder of the British nation. 1726 (2nd edn).

The manifesto of Lord Peter. 1726. Signed Solomon Andrian.

A learned dissertation on dumpling: its dignity, antiquity and excellence. 1726. By Henry Carey?

The devil to pay at St James's. 1727.

The masquerade: a poem inscribed to C—t H—d—g—r, by Lemuel Gulliver. 1728. By Henry Fielding.

Kiss my a— is no treason: or an historical and critical dissertation upon the art of selling bargains. 1728.

Gulliver decypher'd; with some probable conjectures concerning the real author. [1728], [1728?].

An account of the state of learning in the empire of Lilliput. 1728. Satire on Richard Bentley.

The congress of bees: or political remarks on the bees swarming at St James's. [1728].

Harmony in an uproar: a letter to F—d—k H—d—l esq. [1731].

The freeholder's political catechism. 1733, 1769 ('written by Dr Arbuthnot').

Critical remarks on Capt Gulliver's travels, by Doctor Bantlay. Cambridge 1735, 1735, Dublin 1735.

The history of John Bull: part three. 1744.

Other Attributions

A letter from the famous Sir Humphry Polesworth to the author of the Examiner. Examiner 8-15 May 1712.

The story of the St Alb—ns ghost: or the apparition of Mother Haggy. 1712, 1712 (5th edn).

An invitation to peace: or Toby's preliminaries to Nestor Ironside. [1713].

A letter from the facetious Dr Andrew Tripe at Bath, to his loving brother. 1719.

Esther: an oratorio. [1732?], 1733 (4th edn), Dublin 1742, 1756, 1757, [1760?], 1761. 'By Arbuthnot and Pope, with additions by S. Humphreys', BM catalogue.

The country post, from Tuesday August the 12th to Thursday August the 14th; rptd in Miscellanies, Glasgow 1766.

Letters

The practices of the Pretender and his agents at Paris and Rome. London Mag June 1732. Contains letter from Robert Arbuthnot to John Arbuthnot.

Extracts of original letters from Dr Arbuthnot to Mr Watkins. GM Dec 1787.

Berkeley, George Monck. In his Literary relics, 1789. Letters from Berkeley to Arbuthnot.

Letters written by eminent persons in the seventeenth and eighteenth centuries. 3 vols 1813. Letters from Arbuthnot to Dr Charlett.

Croker, J. W. Letters to and from Henrietta Countess of Suffolk. 2 vols 1824. Letters from Arbuthnot.

Baily, Francis. An account of the Revd John Flamsteed, the first Astronomer Royal. 1835. Contains correspondence with Arbuthnot.

Strickland, A. Lives of the Queens of England. 12 vols 1840–8. Vol 8 contains letters to Arbuthnot.

Montagu, Lady Mary Wortley. Letters and works. Ed W. M. Thomas 2 vols 1861. Contains letters to Arbuthnot.

Pope, Alexander. Works. Ed M. and W. J. Courthope 10 vols 1871–89. Letters to and from Arbuthnot.

Aitken, G. A. The life and works of Arbuthnot. Oxford 1892.

Swift, Jonathan. Correspondence. Ed F. E. Ball 6 vols 1910–14. Letters to and from Arbuthnot.

The reports of the Royal Commission on historical manuscripts; Marquis of Bath mss, Stuart mss, Laing mss, Duke of Portland mss, and Earl of Mar and Kellie mss. 1891. Letters to and from Arbuthnot and his brother Robert.

'Melville, Lewis' (L. S. Benjamin). Lady Suffolk and her circle. 1924. Letter from Arbuthnot.

Papers from the collection of Sir William Fraser. Pbns of Scottish Historical Soc 3rd ser 5 1924.

The Chandos letterbooks, Stowe mss in Huntington Lib California contain unpbd correspondence between Arbuthnot and the first Duke of Chandos.

§ 2

A complete key to the three parts of Law is a bottomless pit, and the story of the St Alban's ghost. 1712, 1712 ('corrected'), 1712 ('to the four parts'), 1712 ('enlarged'), 1713 (6th edn, 'enlarged').

'Parker, E. Philomath'. A complete key to the new farce, call'd Three hours after marriage, with an account of the authors. 1717.

'Drub, Timothy'. A letter to Mr John Gay concerning his late farce entituled A comedy. 1717.

'Gay, Joseph' (J. D. Breval). The confederates. 1717.

Smith, William. Literae de re nummaria, with some remarks on Dr Arbuthnot's book and tables. 1729.

The practices of the Pretender and his agents at Paris and Rome. London Mag June 1732.

Langwith, Benjamin. Observations on Doctor Arbuthnot's Dissertations on coins, weights and measures. 1747, 1754.

Kippis, Andrew. In Biographia britannica vol 1, 1778 (2nd edn).

Mahon, Viscount. Letters of Philip Dormer Stanhope, Earl of Chesterfield. 1845. Vol 2 contains Character of Arbuthnot, 'now first printed'.

D[ennis], J[ohn]. Dr Arbuthnot. Cornhill Mag Jan 1879.

Cartwright, J. J. In his Wentworth papers 1705–39, 1883.

Richardson, B. W. Arbuthnot the medical scholar. Asclepiad 4 1887; rptd in his Disciples of Aesculapius, 2 vols 1900.

Aitken, G. A. The life and works of Arbuthnot. Oxford 1892.
—— Arbuthnot's brother. Athenaeum 18 June 1892.
—— Dr Arbuthnot. Athenaeum 17 June 1893.

Hausen, A. En engelsk forfattergruppe. Copenhagen 1892.

Sichel, W. Bolingbroke and his times. 2 vols 1901–2.

Teerink, H. (ed). The history of John Bull, with an investigation into its composition, publication and authorship. Amsterdam 1925.

Sherburn, G. The fortunes and misfortunes of Three hours after marriage. MP 24 1926.

Simpson, A. A. le M. The originator of John Bull. London Mercury Nov 1928.

Mayo, T. F. The authorship of the History of John Bull. PMLA 45 1930.

Beattie, L. M. Arbuthnot: mathematician and satirist. Cambridge Mass 1935.

Memoirs of Martinus Scriblerus. Ed C. Kerby-Miller, New Haven 1950.

Cooke, A. L. The shadow of Martinus Scriblerus in Hawthorne's The prophetic pictures. New England Quart 17 1944.

Steeves, E. L. (ed). The art of sinking in poetry; with bibliographical notes on the last volume of the Swift-

Pope Miscellanies by R. H. Griffith and E. L. Steeve. New York 1952.

[Hilles, F. W.] Johnson on Dr Arbuthnot. 1957 (priv ptd). On alterations in Life of Pope.

Köster, P. J. Arbuthnot's use of quotations and parody in his account of the Sacheverell affair. PQ 48 1969.

D. A. L.

JONATHAN SWIFT
1667–1745

The principal ms collections are in BM, Victoria & Albert Museum, Trinity College Cambridge, Trinity College Dublin, Pierpont Morgan Library, New York, Houghton Library at Harvard and Huntington Library, San Marino Cal.

Bibliographies

Lane-Poole, S. Notes for a bibliography of Swift. Bibliographer Nov 1884; rptd separately 1884.

Wagner, H. R. Irish economics 1700–83: a bibliography with notes. 1907. Contains descriptions of Swift tracts and Swiftiana of the 1720's and 1730's dealing with Irish economic affairs.

Jackson, W. S. Bibliography of Swift's works. In Prose works, ed T. Scott vol 12, 1908.

Hubbard, L. L. Contributions towards a bibliography of Gulliver's travels. Chicago 1922.

Williams, H. The Motte editions of Gulliver's travels. Library 4th ser 6 1925; rptd separately 1925.

Dobell, P. J. A catalogue of works by Swift, together with contemporary works relating to or illustrative of the life and works of the Dean of St Patrick's, Dublin. 1933.

Teerink, H. A bibliography of the writings in prose and verse of Swift. Hague 1937, Philadelphia 1963 (rev H. Teerink, ed A. H. Scouten).

Catalogue of the exhibition held in the library of Trinity College, Dublin from October 19 to November 23 1945 to commemorate the bicentenary of the death of Swift. Dublin 1945.

Hayward, J. A catalogue of printed books and manuscripts by Swift exhibited in the Old Schools in the University of Cambridge to commemorate the 200th anniversary of his death. Cambridge 1945. See H. Williams, TLS 20 Oct 1945.

Landa, L. A. and J. E. Tobin. Swift: a list of critical studies published from 1895 to 1945. New York 1945.

Wiley, A. N. Swift: an exhibition of printed books at the University of Texas, October 19–December 31 1945. Austin 1945.

[Swift collection]. In The Rothschild library vol 2, Cambridge 1954.

Stathis, J. A bibliography of Swift studies 1945–65. Nashville 1967.

Lenfest, D. S. A checklist of illustrated editions of Gulliver's travels 1727–1914. PBSA 62 1968.

Collections

The works of J.S., DD, DSPD. 4 vols Dublin 1735 (8°), 1735 (12°), 6 vols Dublin 1738, 8 vols Dublin 1746, 11 vols Dublin 1763 (8°), 20 vols Dublin 1772. Pbd by Faulkner. The first attempt at a complete Swift and important textually. Series, dates, issues and edns irregularly combined in later reprints.

A supplement to Dr Swift's and Mr Pope's works. Dublin 1739. Adds nothing new.

The works of Dr Jonathan Swift. 14 vols 1751.

The works of Dr Jonathan Swift. 10 vols Edinburgh 1752.

A supplement to the works of Dr Swift. 1752.

The works of Jonathan Swift DD, Dean of St Patrick's, Dublin, accurately revised. 6 vols 1755 (4°), 12 vols 1755 (8°). Ed J. Hawkesworth for Bathurst in opposition to Faulkner's Dublin edns. The 4° edn was completed by 8 additional vols 1764–79 (including the letters) and the 8° edn by 13 vols. Also pbd 27 vols in 18°.

The works of Dr Jonathan Swift. 8 vols Edinburgh and Glasgow 1756.

Satyrische und ernsthafte Schriften von Dr Jonathan Swift. 8 vols Hamburg and Zürich 1756–66.

The works of Dr Jonathan Swift. 8 vols Edinburgh 1757.

The works of Dr Jonathan Swift. 8 vols Edinburgh 1761.

The works of Dr Jonathan Swift. 17 vols Dublin 1767.

An appendix to Dr Swift's works with literary correspondence, improved from an edition printing by Mr Faulkner. 1767. Contains letters, verses, and for the first time, Observations on Heylyn's History of the Presbyterians.

The works of Dr Jonathan Swift, Dean of St Patrick's, Dublin, with the author's life and character: more complete than any preceding edition. 13 vols Edinburgh (also Dumfries) 1768.

The works of Jonathan Swift, DD, DSPD, with notes historical and critical by J. Hawkesworth LlD and others. 15 vols Dublin 1774. Claims to be the first edn to arrange the letters chronologically.

A supplement to Dr Swift's works, containing miscellanies in prose and verse by the Dean, Dr Delany, Dr Sheridan, Mrs Johnson and others, with explanatory notes by the editor [John Nichols]. 1779 (4°), 2 vols 1779 (8°).

The works of the Rev Dr Swift, Dean of St Patrick's, Dublin, arranged, revised and corrected with notes by Thomas Sheridan AM. 17 vols 1784, 1787. Vol 1 contains Sheridan's Life. Follows the Hawkesworth text.

Miscellaneous pieces, in prose and verse, by the Rev Dr Swift, not inserted in Mr Sheridan's edition of the Dean's works. 1789.

The works of the Rev Jonathan Swift DD, Dean of St Patrick's, Dublin. 19 vols 1801, 24 vols 1803, 19 vols 1808. Sheridan's edn augmented by J. Nichols.

The works of Jonathan Swift DD, Dean of St Patrick's, Dublin: containing additional letters, tracts and poems, not hitherto published; with notes and a life of the author. Ed Sir W. Scott 19 vols Edinburgh 1814, 1824.

The works of Jonathan Swift DD, with memoir of the author, by Thomas Roscoe. 2 vols 1841.

The prose works of Jonathan Swift DD, with a biographical introduction by W. E. H. Lecky. Ed T. Scott 12 vols 1897–1908.

Prose works. Ed H. Davis 14 vols Oxford 1939–68.

Vol I: A tale of a tub, with other early works 1696–1707. 1939.

Vol II: Bickerstaff papers and pamphlets on the church. 1939.

Vol III: The examiner and other pieces written in 1710–11. 1940.

Vol IV: A proposal for correcting the English tongue, Polite conversation etc. Ed Davis and L. A. Landa 1957.

Vol V: Miscellaneous and autobiographical pieces. fragments and marginalia. 1962.

Vol VI: Political tracts 1711–13. 1951.

Vol VII: History of the four last years of the Queen. 1951. Introd by H. Williams.

Vol VIII: Political tracts 1713–19. Ed Davis and I. Ehrenpreis 1953.

Vol IX: Irish tracts 1720–3 and sermons. Ed L. A. Landa 1948.

Vol X: The Drapier's letters and other works 1724–5. 1941, 1959 (rev).

Vol XI: Gulliver's travels 1726. 1941, 1959 (rev). Introd by H. Williams.

Vol XII: Irish tracts 1728–33. 1955.

Vol XIII: Directions to servants and miscellaneous pieces 1733–42. 1959.

Vol XIV: Index to the prose writings. Ed Davis and I. Ehrenpreis 1968.

Miscellanies

Miscellanies in prose and verse. 1711, 1713. Pbd by Morphew. Contains 25 early pieces.

Miscellanies by Dr Jonathan Swift. 1711. Unauthorized; pbd by Curll.

Miscellaneous works comical and diverting by T.R.D. J.S.D. O.P. I.I., in two parts. 1720. Pirated; ptd in Holland.

A second collection of miscellanies, written by Jonathan Swift DD. 1720. Pbd by Roberts. Only in part by Swift.

Miscellanies in prose and verse. Dublin 2721 (for 1721) (4th edn). Unauthorized. Contains pieces ptd in 1711 Miscellanies, above, with 2 addns and others not by Swift.

Miscellanies written by Jonathan Swift DD, Dean of St Patrick's, Dublin. 1722 (4th edn, also issued without the general title-page).

Miscellanea never before published. 2 vols 1727. Unauthorized Curll pbn. Part of vol 2 appeared separately as Swifteana: consisting of poems by Dean Swift and several of his friends, 1727.

Miscellanies in prose and verse. 3 vols 1727. Called First, Second and Last volume. Variously rptd 3 vols (8° and 12°), 1728–33. Pbd by Motte, with pieces by Pope, Gay, Arbuthnot et al.

Miscellanies in prose and verse. 4 vols Dublin 1728–35.

Miscellanies: the third volume. 1732, 1732, 1733, 1736, 1738. Pbd by Motte and Gilliver. Prose and verse by Swift, Pope, Arbuthnot and Gay.

The Drapier's miscellany. Dublin 1733 (3 edns).

Miscellanies: consisting chiefly of original pieces in prose and verse, by D—n S—t, never before published in this Kingdom; Dublin printed, London reprinted. 1734, 1734. Unauthorized. Not wholly by Swift.

A new miscellany for the year 1734. Pt I, [1734]. Contains 4 poems by Swift.

Miscellanies in prose and verse: volume the fifth. 1735. Pbd by C. Davis. Supplements the 4 vols 1727–32, above, by adding pieces from Faulkner's edn of the works.

A collection of poems etc omitted in the fifth volume of miscellanies. 1735. A separately issued supplement, intended to be bound up with the previous item.

Miscellanies. 6 vols 1736. With slight variations contains the matter of 5 vols 1727–32–35, above.

Miscellanies in prose and verse by Dr Swift. Vol VII [and VIII] 1742. Pbd by Cooper. Intended as a supplement to Miscellanies, 6 vols 1736.

Miscellanies in four volumes by Dr Swift, Dr Arbuthnot, Mr Pope and Mr Gay: the fourth edition corrected. 1742. Pbd by C. Bathurst, and based on the earlier Motte Miscellanies. Extended to 13 vols of varying combinations of edns and dates 1742–53.

The sermons of Dr J. Swift, to which is prefixed the author's life; together with his Prayer for Stella, his Thoughts on and Project for the advancement of religion. 2 vols [1790?].

The Drapier's letters to the people of Ireland. Ed H. Davis, Oxford 1935, 1965 (with rev bibliography).

Poems

The poetical works of J.S., DD, DSPD, reprinted from the second Dublin edition. 1736.

The poetical works of Dr Jonathan Swift, Dean of St Patrick's, Dublin. 2 vols [1760's?]. See Teerink no 59. A trade edn based on the successive Miscellanies.

A supplement to the works of the most celebrated minor poets, to which are added, pieces omitted in the works of Dean Swift. Pt III of Works of the minor poets vol 3, 1750.

The British poets vols 31–2. Edinburgh 1773–6.

The poetical works of Dr Jonath Swift, with the life of the author. 4 vols Edinburgh 1778.

The works of the English poets vols 39–40. Ed S. Johnson 1779–81.

The works of the British poets vol 9. [Ed R. Anderson], Edinburgh 1792–5.

The poetical works of Jonathan Swift. Ed T. Park 4 vols 1806–7.
The works of the English poets vol 11. Ed A. Chalmers 1810.
The British poets vols 37–9. Chiswick 1822.
The poetical works of Jonathan Swift. Ed J. Mitford 3 vols 1833–4, 1853, 1866 (Aldine edn).
The poems of Jonathan Swift DD. Ed W. E. Browning 2 vols 1910.
Miscellaneous poems by Jonathan Swift. [Ed R. E. Roberts] 1929.
Poems. Ed H. Williams 3 vols Oxford 1937, 1958.
Collected poems. Ed J. Horrell 2 vols 1958 (ML).
Poetical works. Ed H. Davis, Oxford 1967 (OSA).

Selections

Political tracts by the author of Gulliver's travels. 2 vols 1738.
The historical works of the Rev Dr Jonathan Swift. 3 vols Glasgow 1769.
Dean Swift's tracts on the repeal of the Test Act. 1790.
Select works. 5 vols 1823–5, 1826.
Works, carefully selected by D. L. Purves. 1869.
The choice works of Dean Swift in prose and verse. 1876.
Selections from the prose writings. Ed S. Lane-Poole 1884.
Letters and journals. Ed S. Lane-Poole 1885.
The Tale of a tub and other works. Ed H. Morley 1889.
Gulliver's travels and other works. Ed H. Morley 1890, 1906.
Swift: selections from his works. Ed H. Craik 2 vols 1892–3.
Select letters. Ed W. D. Taylor 1925.
Selected essays. Ed R. E. Roberts 1925.
Selections chosen by W. J. Halliday. 1929.
Satires and personal writings. Ed W. A. Eddy 1932.
Gulliver's travels and selected writings in prose and verse. Ed J. Hayward 1934 (Nonesuch Press), 1949 (corrected).
Selected prose writings of Swift. Ed J. Hayward 1949.
Swift on his age: selected prose and verse. Ed C. J. Horne 1953.
Gulliver's travels and other writings. Ed L. A. Landa, Cambridge Mass 1960.
Oeuvres. Ed E. Pons et al, Paris 1965 (Pléiade).
Ausgewählte Werke. Ed A. Schlösser 3 vols Berlin 1967.

§ 1

Supplement to the fifth volume of the Athenian gazette. 1691–2. Contains a letter from Swift and his Ode to the Athenian Society.
Letters written by Sir W. Temple Bart and other Ministers of State, published by Jonathan Swift, domestick chaplain to his Excellency the Earl of Berkeley. 2 vols 1700. The dedication to William III and publisher's epistle to the reader in vol 1 are by Swift.
Miscellanea: the third part, by the late Sir William Temple Bar, published by Jonathan Swift AM, prebendary of St Patrick's, Dublin. 1701. The Publisher to the reader is by Swift.
A discourse of the contests and dissensions between the nobles and the commons in Athens and Rome. 1701; ed F. H. Ellis, Oxford 1967 (see E. Rosenheim jr, MP 66 1968); tr French, 1733.
Letters to the King, the Prince of Orange, the chief ministers of State and other persons by Sir W. Temple Bart: being the third and last volume, published by Jonathan Swift DD. 1703. The Preface is by Swift.
A tale of a tub, written for the universal improvement of mankind; to which is added An account of a battel between the antient and modern books in St James's Library. 1704 (3 edns), 1705. Includes The battel of the books and A discourse concerning the mechanical operation of the spirit.
A tale of a tub: the fifth edition, with the author's

apology and explanatory notes, by W. W—tt—n BD and others. 1710. Contains the Apology, the footnotes and 8 plates for the first time. The unsigned footnotes are by Swift.
An apology for the tale of a tub. 1711. A suppl to earlier edns.
A tale of a tub. 1711 (4 edns). No place. Does not contain the Apology or footnotes. Pirated and set from 3rd edn.
Miscellaneous works, comical and diverting, by T.R.D. J.S.D. O.P. I.I. in two parts, 1: The tale of a tub; 11: Miscellanies in prose and verse; London, printed by order of the Society de Propagando etc. 1720. Pirated. Ptd in Holland. Adds The history of Martin (not by Swift).
A tale of a tub. 1724, 1727, 1733, 1739, 1743, (reissued 1751), 1747, 1751 (as vol 1 of Works, 14 vols), 1755 etc.
A tale of a tub. 1734. Pirated, and set from the edn of 1720, with a bookseller's advertisement and some additional notes.
    Dublin edns: 1705 (4th edn), 1726 (7th edn), 1741 (8th edn). Also Edinburgh 1750, Glasgow 1753. Trns: French, 1721, 1721; German, 1729, 1758, 1787; Dutch, 1735. Modern annotated edns: T. Scott (Prose works vol i, 1897); A. Guthkelch and D. N. Smith, Oxford 1920, 1958; Guthkelch 1902 (as The battle of the books, with selections from the literature of the Phalaris controversy).
Predictions for the year 1708: wherein the month and day of the month are set down, the persons named and the great actions and events of next year particularly related, as they will come to pass, written to prevent the people of England from being further impos'd on by vulgar almanack-makers, by Isaac Bickerstaff esq. 1708 (and several pirated edns under the same title, or as Esquire Bickerstaff's most strange and wonderful predictions for the year 1708); tr German, 1708; Dutch, 1708.
The accomplishment of the first of Mr Bickerstaff's predictions: being an account of the death of Mr Partrige, the almanack-maker, upon the 29th inst, in a letter to a person of honour. 1708.
An elegy on Mr Patrige, the almanack-maker, who died on the 29th of this instant March 1708. 1708, Edinburgh 1708. Broadside.
A vindication of Isaac Bickerstaff esq against what is objected to him by Mr Partridge, by the said Isaac Bickerstaff esq. 1709.
A famous prediction of Merlin, the British wizard: written above a thousand years ago and relating to this present year, with explanatory notes by T. N. Philomath. 1709, 1708 (for 1709; pirated), Edinburgh 1709, 1740.
A project for the advancement of religion, and the reformation of manners, by a person of quality. 1709, 1709, Edinburgh 1709.
A letter from a Member of the House of Commons in Ireland, to a Member of the House of Commons in England, concerning the sacramental test. 1709, Dublin 1709.
The tatler, by Isaac Bickerstaff esq. 1709–11. No 230 and nos 5 and 20 in Harrison's continuation by Swift. For other nos attributed wholly or in part, see Davis, Prose works vol 2.
Memoirs: part III, from the peace concluded 1679 to the time of the author's retirement from publick business, by Sir William Temple Baronet, publish'd by Jonathan Swift DD. 1709, 1709. The Preface is by Swift.
Baucis and Philemon, imitated from Ovid. 1709. No place; 4 leaves.
Baucis and Philemon: a poem; together with Mrs Harris's earnest petition, by the author of the Tale of a tub; as also an Ode upon solitude by the Earl of Roscommon. 1708 (for 1709), 1709, 1710. Pbd by Hills. Baucis and Philemon was also included, together with Mrs Biddy Floyd, in Poetical miscellanies: the sixth part, 1709, pbd by Tonson.

A meditation upon a broom-stick, and somewhat beside, of the same author's. 1710, 1710.

The virtues of Sid Hamet the magician's rod. 1710. Half sheet.

The examiner. 1710. Swift's principal contributions are in vol 1.

The examiners for the year 1711; to which is prefix'd A letter to the examiner. 1712.

A short character of his Ex T.E. of W[harton]. L.L. of I——; with an account of some smaller facts. 1711 (3 edns), 1711 (without title-page), [1715?] (with omissions and alterations), nd, nd.

The spectator. 1711. Swift's contributions were very slight. See H. Davis, Prose works vol 2.

Some remarks upon a pamphlet entitl'd A letter to the seven Lords of the committee appointed to examine Gregg, by the author of the Examiner. 1711, Dublin 1711.

A new journey to Paris; together with some secret transactions between the Fr—h K—g and an Eng— gentleman, by the Sieur du Baudrier, translated from the French. 1711 (3 edns); tr French, 1711

An excellent new song: being the intended speech of a famous orator against peace. 1711. Half sheet.

The W—ds—r prophecy. 1711 (3 broadside edns).

The conduct of the allies, and of the late ministry, in beginning and carrying on the present war. 1712 (for 1711; 5 edns), 1712–13, Edinburgh 1712, Dublin 1712; tr French, 1712; Spanish, 1712.

A fable of the widow and her cat. 1711 (for 1712), 1712, 1712, Dublin 1712. Broadsides and half sheet. Partly by Swift.

The fable of Midas. 1711 (for 1712). Half sheet.

Some advice humbly offer'd to the members of the October Club in a letter from a person of honour. 1712, 1712, Dublin 1712.

Some remarks on the barrier treaty between Her Majesty and the States-General by the author of the Conduct of the allies. 1712, 1712, Edinburgh 1712, Dublin 1712, 1712; tr Dutch, 1712; French, 1712; Spanish. 1712.

A proposal for correcting, improving and ascertaining the English tongue, in a letter to the most honourable Robert Earl of Oxford and Mortimer, Lord High Treasurer of Great Britain. 1712, 1712. The half title reads: Dr Swift's letter to the Lord High Treasurer.

Some reasons to prove that no person is obliged by his principles as a Whig to oppose Her Majesty or her present Ministry, in a letter to a Whig-Lord. 1712, Dublin 1712.

T——nd's invitation to Dismal, to dine with the Calves-head Club. 1712 (broadside, no place), [Edinburgh?] 1712.

A hue and cry after Dismal: being a full and true account, how a Whig Lord was taken at Dunkirk, in the habit of a chimney-sweeper, and carried before General Hill. 1712 (broadside), 1712 (as Dunkirk to be let with a hue and cry after Dismal).

Peace and Dunkirk: being an excellent new song upon the surrender of Dunkirk to General Hill. 1712. Broadside.

Dunkirk still in the hands of the French. 1712. Mentioned by Swift, Journal to Stella, 17 July 1712, and advertised in Examiner of that date. No known copy.

A letter from the pretender to a Whig-Lord. 1712. Broadside.

A letter of thanks from my Lord W**** n to the Lord Bp of S. Asaph. 1712, 1712.

Remarks on the Bp of S. Asaph's Preface. Examiner 24 July 1712.

An appendix to the Conduct of the allies; and Remarks on the Barrier Treaty. Examiner 16 Jan 1713.

Mr C—n's discourse of free-thinking, put into plain English, by way of abstract, for the use of the poor, by a friend of the author. 1713.

A complete refutation of the falsehoods alleged against Erasmus Lewis esq. Examiner 2 Feb 1713.

The address of the House of Lords to the Queen. 10 April 1713. Ptd in Journals of the House of Lords, 11 April 1713.

Part of the seventh epistle of the first book of Horace imitated, and address'd to a noble peer. 1713 (3 edns), Dublin 1713.

The importance of the Guardian considered, in a second letter to the bailiff of Stockbridge, by a friend of Mr St—le. 1713.

A preface to the B—p of S—r—m's introduction, to the third volume of the history of the reformation of the Church of England, by Gregory Misosarum. 1713, 1713, Dublin 1714.

The first ode of the second book of Horace paraphras'd, and address'd to Richard St—le esq. 1713 (for 1714), 1714, Dublin 1714.

The publick spirit of the Whigs, set forth in their generous encouragement of the author of the Crisis; with some observations on the Seasonableness, candor, erudition and style of that treatise. 1714. Pbd 23 Feb 1714. At least 7 further edns, London and Dublin, in the same year. A long passage offensive to the Scots Lords was expunged after 1st issue. Copies of the 1st and 2nd edns occur censored and uncensored. Tr French, 1714; Dutch, 1714; German, 1714.

A rebus written by a lady, on the Rev D—n S—t, with his answer. [1714–20?]. Half sheet.

Letters, poems and tales: amorous, satyrical and gallant, which passed between several persons of distinction. 1718. Contains A decree for concluding the treaty between Dr Swift and Mrs Long.

The works of Sir William Temple, Bart, in two volumes. 1720. Prefaces etc by Swift.

An elegy on the much lamented death of Mr Demar, the famous rich man, who died the 6th of this inst July, 1720. [Dublin] [1720], [1720]. Broadside.

A proposal for the universal use of Irish manufacture, in cloaths and furniture of houses etc, utterly rejecting and renouncing every thing wearable that comes from England. Dublin 1720.

A letter from a lay-patron to a gentleman, designing for holy orders. Dublin 1720, London 1721 (as A letter to a young gentleman, lately enter'd into holy orders, by a person of quality), 1721; tr German, 1782.

Epilogue to be spoke at the Theatre-Royal this present Saturday being April the 1st, in the behalf of the distressed weavers. Dublin [1721] (broadside), Dublin [1721] (as An epilogue, as it was spoke by Mr Griffith at the Theatre-Royal on Saturday the first of April in the behalf of the distressed weavers). Ptd on the verso of A prologue spoke by Mr Elrington.

The bubble: a poem. 1721, Dublin 1721; rptd in Miscellanies: the last volume, 1727, as The South Sea.

Subscribers to the bank plac'd according to their order and quality, with notes and queries. Dublin [1721]. Probably by Swift.

A letter to the K[ing] at arms from a reputed esquire one of the subscribers to the bank. Dublin [1721]. Half sheet; probably by Swift.

The run upon the bankers. [Dublin 1720?]. No known copy, but a Cork broadside of 1721 was probably rptd from a Dublin issue.

The wonderful wonder of wonders. [Dublin 1721?], 1722 (amplified as Being an accurate description of the birth, education, manner of living, religion, politicks, learning etc of mine a—se, by Dr Sw—ft). Probably by Swift. Rptd as his in Miscellanies: the third volume, 1732, and in Faulkner's edn of Works, 1735.

The wonder of all the wonders that ever the world wondered at. [Dublin 1721?], 1722. Probably by Swift. Rptd as his in Miscellanies: the third volume, 1732, and in Faulkner's edn of Works, 1735.

The bank thrown down. Dublin 1721, 1721. Broadside.

The journal. [Dublin 1721?] (broadside), [Dublin 1722] (half sheet; on verso, A description in answer to the journal); rptd in Curll's Miscellanea, 1727, and in Gulliveriana, 1728. Appears as The country life in the Miscellany vols.

The last speech and dying words of Ebenezor Elliston, who is to be executed this second day of May 1722: publish'd at his desire for the common good. Dublin [1722].

The first of April: a poem, inscribed to Mrs E.C. [1723?]

Some arguments against enlarging the power of Bishops in letting of leases, with remarks on some queries lately published. Dublin 1723.

A letter to the shop-keepers, tradesmen, farmers and common-people of Ireland, concerning the brass half-pence coined by Mr Woods, with a design to have them pass in this kingdom, by M. B. Drapier. Dublin [1724] (folio and 2 8° edns), [Limerick 1724].

A letter to Mr Harding the printer, upon occasion of a paragraph in his news-paper of Aug 1st relating to Mr Woods's half-pence, by M. B. Drapier. Dublin [1724], [1724], Limerick [1724] (as An answer to Mr Wood's proposal).

Some observations upon a paper call'd The Report of the committee of the most honourable the Privy-Council in England, relating to Wood's half-pence, by M. B. Drapier. Dublin [1724] (at least 3 edns).

A letter to the whole people of Ireland, by M. B. Drapier. Dublin [1724], [1724].

Seasonable advice: since a bill is preparing for the Grand-Jury to find against the printer of the Drapier's last letter, there are several things to be considered before they determine upon it. [Dublin] 1724. Broadside.

An extract out of a book entituled An exact collection of the debates of the House of Commons held at Westminster, October 21 1680. Pag 150. [Dublin 1724].

The presentment of the Grand-Jury of the County of the City of Dublin. Dublin 1724. Half sheet.

His Grace's answer to Jonathan. Dublin 1724. Broadside.

To his Grace the Arch-bishop of Dublin: a poem. Dublin [1724]. Broadside.

An excellent new song upon his Grace our good Lord Archbishop of Dublin, by honest Jo, one of his Grace's farmers in Fingal. Dublin 1724. Broadside.

Prometheus, a poem. Dublin 1724. Broadside.

A letter to the Right Honourable the Lord Viscount Molesworth, by M. B. Drapier, author of the letter to the shop-keepers etc. Dublin [1724].

A serious poem upon William Wood, brasier, tinker, hardware-man, coiner, counterfeiter, founder and esquire. Dublin [1724]. Half sheet.

Sphinx: a poem ascrib'd to certain anonymous authors. Dublin 1725. This is the Ode to the Athenian society under another title.

Fraud detected, or the Hibernian patriot: containing all the Drapier's letters to the people of Ireland on Wood's coinage etc. Dublin 1725. See Hibernian patriot, 1730, below.

The birth of manly virtue, from Callimachus. Dublin 1725 (folio and 8°).

A riddle by Dr S—t to my Lady Carteret. [Dublin 1725]. Broadside. Followed by Answered by Dr S—g.

Cadenus and Vanessa: a poem. 1726. Contains the complete text. Pbd by J. Roberts. 7 edns, N. Blandford, London, in the same year; also T. Warner, London; and Dublin and Edinburgh edns.

Travels into several remote nations of the world, in four parts, by Lemuel Gulliver, first a surgeon, and then a captain of several ships. Vol I, 1726.

Travels into several remote nations of the world, by Captain Lemuel Gulliver, pt III: A voyage to Laputa, Balnibarbi, Glubbdubdrib, Luggnagg and Japan; pt IV: A voyage to the Houyhnhnms. 1726. Frontispiece and 6 plates. Oval round the portrait blank, and the inscription 'Captain Lemuel Gulliver, of Redriff Ætat

suæ 58' in 2 lines below. Some copies, however, have the portrait in the 2nd state with inscription round oval. Pbd on large and small paper, copies of the latter representing the earlier printing.

Travels into several remote nations. 2 vols 1726 (vol II The second edition), 1726 (no indication of edn), 1727 (12°, reissued 1731), 1727 (8°, vol II The second edition, corrected), 1 vol 1742 (4th edn), 1747 (5th edn), 2 vols 1748, 1751 (5th edn, distinct from 1747 edn), 1 vol 1751 (12°), 1751 (6th edn), 1755 (4° and 8°, both rev Hawkesworth in opposition to the text of Faulkner's Dublin edns), 2 vols 1757, 1760, 1765, 1766, 1767, 1768, 1777; ed T. Sheridan 1784. These edns were all pbd either by Motte or his successor Bathurst.

Travels into several remote nations. Dublin 1726, 1727, 2 vols in 1 1727, 1 vol 1735 (8°, as vol III of Works, and embodying important textual revision), 1735 (12°, as vol III of Works, 1738, 1743, 1752, 1756, 1759 (with textual changes in mistaken deference to the Preface to Bathurst's 1755 edn), 1763, 1772.

Other London edns: The Penny London Post nos 251 [252]– 267, 25 Nov–30 Dec 1726 (part of Lilliput only); Parker's Penny Post nos 246–390, 28 Nov 1726–3 Nov 1727; 1727 (faithfully abridged); 66 nos [1740?]; 1766. *Scottish edns*: Edinburgh 1757, 1761, 1768, Glasgow 1765. Trns: French 1727, 1727; Dutch, 1727; German, 1727; etc.

Modern annotated edns: G. A. Aitken 1896 (Temple Classics); G. R. Dennis 1899 (in Prose Works, ed T. Scott vol 8); H. Williams 1926; A. E. Case, New York 1938; P. Dixon and J. Chalker 1967 (Penguin).

The furniture of a woman's mind, written by Dr Swift. Written 1727. Quarter sheet broadside of later date.

A short view of the state of Ireland. Dublin 1727–8, [1728]; rptd, with preface by Sheridan, as Intelligencer no 15.

An answer to a paper called A memorial of the poor inhabitants, tradesmen and labourers of the Kingdom of Ireland, by the author of the short view of the state of Ireland. Dublin 1728.

The intelligencer. Numb 1, Saturday May 11, to be continued weekly. Dublin 1728. 20 nos. By Swift and Sheridan. Pbd as vol, 1729 (19 nos), 1730 (20 nos). No 19 was separately rptd as A letter from the Revd J.S. DSPD to a country gentleman in the north of Ireland, printed in the year 1736.

A modest proposal for preventing the children of poor people from being a burthen to their parents or the country, and for making them beneficial to the publick. Dublin 1729, London 1729, Dublin 1730, London 1730 (3 edns).

The journal of a Dublin lady, in a letter to a person of quality. Dublin [1729], 1729, London 1740 (as The journal of a modern lady). Also half sheet edn of later date. Rptd 1730, 1731, 1743, in 2nd–4th edns of The metamorphosis of the town.

On Paddy's character of the Intelligencer. [Dublin 1729?]. Broadside.

A panegyric on the Reverend Dean Swift. [Dublin] 1729–30, London 1730.

An apology to the Lady C—R—T on her inviting Dean S—F—T to dinner. [Dublin?] 1730.

Lady A—S—N weary of the Dean. [Dublin?] 1730. Broadside.

An epistle to his Excellency John Lord Carteret, Lord Lieutenant of Ireland. Dublin [1730] (folio and 8°).

An epistle upon an epistle from a certain doctor to a certain great Lord: being a Christmas-box for D. D—ny. Dublin 1730.

An epistle to his Excellency John Lord Carteret, Lord Lieutenant of Ireland; to which is added An epistle upon an epistle: being a Christmas-box for Doctor D—ny. Dublin 1730.

A libel on D—D— and a certain great Lord. [Dublin] 1730, 1730, London 1730 (4 edns), 1730 (as A satire on Dr D—NY, by Dr Sw—T).

To Doctor D—l—y on the libels writ against him. London printed and Dublin reprinted in the year 1730. Dublin 1730. The imprint is deliberately misleading. The first printing was in Dublin.

An answer to Dr D—y's fable of the pheasant and the lark. [Dublin?] 1730.

An excellent new ballad: or the true En—sh D—n to be hang'd for a R—pe. [Dublin 1730]. Half sheet.

A vindication of his Excellency the Lord C—T, from the charge of favouring none but Tories, High-Churchmen and Jacobites, by the Reverend Dr S—T. 1730, Dublin 1730.

Horace, book 1 ode XIV, paraphrased and inscribed to Ir—d. [Dublin] 1930 (for 1730).

Traulus: the first part, in a dialogue between Tom and Robin. [Dublin] 1730, 1730.

Traulus: the second part. [Dublin] 1730.

The Hibernian patriot: being a collection of the Drapier's letters to the people of Ireland, concerning Mr Wood's brass half-pence, printed at Dublin. London reprinted 1730. A reprint of Fraud detected, 1725, above, with slight alterations.

Memoirs of Capt John Creichton, written by himself. 1731, Glasgow 1768. The Advertisement to the reader is by Swift.

Helter skelter: or the hue and cry after the attornies, going to ride the circuit. [Dublin 1730, 1731]. Broadside.

The place of the damn'd, by J.S., DD, DSPD. [Dublin] 1731. Broadside.

'With favour and fortune fastidiously blest'. [London? 1731?]. Quarter sheet.

A soldier and a scholar: or the lady's judgment upon those two characters in the persons of Captain— and D—n S—T. 1732 (pbd Jan by Roberts), 1732 (reissued as 2nd edn), 1732 (3rd edn, reissued as 4th edn), Dublin 1732 (as The grand question debated: whether Hamilton's bawn should be turn'd into a barrack, or a malthouse; according to the London edition, with notes). Last edn adds a paraphrase of Horace, bk 1 ode XIV.

Considerations upon two bills sent down from the R—H— the H— of L— to the h—ble H— of C— relating to the clergy of I******D. 1732, 1732 (as Considerations upon two bills, by the Rev Dr Swift DSPD; to which is added A proposal for an Act of Parliament to pay off the debt of the nation, by A— P—, esq).

An examination of certain abuses, corruptions and enormities in the city of Dublin. Dublin 1732, London 1732 (as City cries instrumental and vocal: or an examination of certain abuses, corruptions and enormities in London and Dublin).

The lady's dressing room; to which is added A poem on cutting down the old thorn at Market Hill, by the Rev Dr S—T. 1732, 1732, Dublin 1732 (3 edns).

The advantages propos'd by repealing the sacramental test, impartially considered. Dublin 1732, London 1732 (To which is added Remarks on a pamphlet intitled The nature and consequences of the sacramental test consider'd).

Quæries wrote by Dr J. Swift in the year 1732, very proper to be read (at this time) by every member of the established Church. [Dublin? 1732]. Half sheet. Advantages, above, and Quæries were rptd in The dispute adjusted (by Gibson, Bishop of London), 1733.

An elegy on Dicky and Dolly. Dublin 1732.

An answer to a late scandalous poem, wherein the author most audaciously presumes to compare a cloud to a woman. Dublin 1733. With T. Sheridan, A new simile for the ladies.

Some considerations humbly offered to the Right Honourable the Lord-Mayor, the Court of Aldermen and Common Council of the honourable City of Dublin, in the choice of a recorder. [Dublin] 1733. Half sheet.

Advice to the freemen of the city of Dublin. [Dublin] 1733. Broadside.

The life and genuine character of Doctor Swift, written by himself. 1733 (folio and 8°), Dublin 1733, 1739 (rev and extended as Verses on the death of Doctor Swift).

A serious and useful scheme to make an hospital for incurables of universal benefit to all his Majesty's subjects; to which is added A petition of the footmen in and about Dublin, by a celebrated author in Ireland. 1733, Dublin 1733, 1733, 1734. Only the Petition is by Swift. A serious and useful scheme is probably by M. Pilkington.

The Presbyterians plea of merit in order to take off the test impartially examined. Dublin 1733, London [1733?], [1733?].

On poetry: a rapsody. 1733, [1734?], Dublin 1734.

Reasons humbly offered to the Parliament of Ireland for repealing the sacramental test etc in favour of the Catholics, otherwise called Roman Catholics, and by their ill-willers Papists, written in the year 1733. [1734?].

Some reasons against the bill for settling the tyth of hemp, flax etc by a modus. Dublin 1724 (for 1734).

An epistle to a lady who desired the author to make verses on her, in the heroick stile; also a poem occasion'd by reading Dr Young's Satires called The universal passion. Dublin, printed and re-printed at London. 1734.

Poems on several occasions [by Mary Barber]. 1734, 1735, 1736. Contains a commendatory letter by Swift to John, Earl of Orrery.

A beautiful young nymph going to bed, written for the honour of the fair sex; to which are added Strephon and Chloe; and Cassinus and Peter. Dublin printed, London reprinted. 1734.

The Rev Dean Swift's reasons against lowering the gold and silver coin. Ptd on verso of title of Reasons why we should not lower the coins now current in this Kingdom, Dublin [1736].

A proposal for giving badges to the beggars in all the parishes of Dublin, by the Dean of St Patrick's. Dublin 1737, London 1737.

Some thoughts on the tillage of Ireland. 1737, Dublin 1738. By Alexander M'Aulay. Prefatory letter by Swift.

An imitation of the sixth satire of the second book of Horace: the first part done in the year 1714 by Dr Swift; the latter part now first added, and never before printed. 1738. Completed by Pope.

The beasts confession to the priest on observing how most men mistake their own talents, written in the year 1732. Dublin 1738, 1738, London 1738 (3 edns).

A complete collection of genteel and ingenious conversation, according to the most polite mode and method now used at court, and in the best companies of England, in three dialogues, by Simon Wagstaff esq. 1738, Dublin 1738; ed E. Partridge, New York 1963.

Verses on the death of Dr Swift, written by himself Nov 1731. 1739 (5 folio edns), London (for Edinburgh?) 1739 (8°), Dublin 1739 (5 edns), London (for Edinburgh?) 1741, Dublin 1741.

Some free thoughts upon the present state of affairs, written in the year 1714. Dublin 1741, 1741, London 1741, 1741.

Three sermons, I: On mutual subjection; I: On conscience; III: On the Trinity, by the Reverend Dr Swift, Dean of St Patrick's. 1744, 1744 (with a 4th sermon, The difficulty of knowing one's self, added [not by Swift?], Dublin 1744, 1760 (as Four sermons); tr German, 1758.

Directions to servants in general; and in particular to the butler, cook, by the Reverend Dr Swift DSPD. 1745, 1746, 1749, Dublin 1745, 1746; tr German, 1748.

The story of the injured lady: being a true picture of Scotch perfidy, Irish poverty and English partiality, with letters and poems never before printed, by the Rev Dr Swift DSPD. 1746, Dublin 1749.

The last will and testament of Jonathan Swift DD. Dublin printed, London reprinted 1746.

A true copy of the late Rev Dr Jonathan Swift's will, taken from, and compar'd with, the original. [Dublin? 1746?], London 1746, Dublin 1747. An authentic copy of the last will and testament of the Reverend Dr Swift, sold by J. Oldcastle, nd, is a satire.

Brotherly love: a sermon, preached in St Patrick's Church on December 1st 1717, by Dr Jonathan Swift, Dean of St Patrick's, Dublin. Dublin 1754, London 1754.

The history of the four last years of the Queen, by the late Jonathan Swift DD, DSPD. 1758, Dublin 1758 (as vol 9 of Works, and as The history of the last session of Parliament, and of the Peace of Utrecht, written at Windsor in the year 1713); tr French, 1765.

An enquiry into the behavior of the Queen's last Ministry. Ed I. Ehrenpreis, Bloomington 1956. First pbd 1765 in vol 8 of Hawkesworth's 4° edn of Works.

Letters

Letters to and from Dr J. Swift DSPD from the year 1714 to 1738. Dublin 1741. Pbd by Faulkner; also issued as vol VII of his edn of Works.

Dean Swift's literary correspondence, for twenty-four years from 1714 to 1738. 1741. Curll. Follows above with some variations.

Letters written by the late Jonathan Swift DD, Dean of St Patrick's, Dublin; and several of his friends. Ed J. Hawkesworth 1766, 1766, 1767, 1768, 1769; ed Hawkesworth and D. Swift 6 vols 1768–9. Part of Hawkesworth's edn of Works, 1755–79. Letters 1 and 41–65 of the Journal to Stella were first pbd by Hawkesworth in Works, vol 10, 1766. Letters 2–40 were first pbd by D. Swift in Works vol 12 1768. The best modern annotated edns of the Journal to Stella are G. A. Aitken 1901; F. Ryland (vol 2, Prose works, ed T. Scott 1905); J. K. Moorhead 1924 (EL); H. Williams 2 vols Oxford 1948.

Literary relics: containing Original letters from Swift; to which is prefixed An inquiry into the life of Dean Swift. [Ed G. M. Berkeley] 1789, 1792. Contains 7 letters by Swift.

Unpublished letters of Dean Swift. Ed G. B. Hill 1899.

The correspondence of Swift, with an introduction by J. H. Bernard. Ed F. E. Ball 6 vols 1910–14.

Vanessa and her correspondence with Swift. Ed A. M. Freeman 1921.

The letters of Swift to Charles Ford. Ed D. N. Smith, Oxford 1935.

The correspondence of Swift. Ed H. Williams 5 vols Oxford 1963–5.

Works Attributed to Swift

See also H. Teerink, Bibliography, ed Scouten pp. 389–404 and Rothschild library pp. 595–608.

An answer to a scurrilous pamphlet lately printed, entitled A letter from M. de Cros to the Lord . . . 1693. Attributed to Temple on doubtful grounds, possibly by Swift; see H. Woodbridge, Temple, New York 1940 p. 227.

A poem occasioned by the hangings in the Castle of Dublin. [Dublin 1701?].

The fairy feast written by the author of A tale of a tub and the Mully of Mountown. 1704. Unauthorized edn of W. King, Orpheus and Euridice.

Mully of Mountown: a poem by the author of the Tale of a tub. 1704. By W. King.

The Swan tripe-club in Dublin. 1706.

A trip to Dunkirk: or a hue and cry after the pretended Prince of Wales. 1708.

Jack Frenchman's lamentation. 1708. Broadside. 3 other broadside edns. Also attributed to Prior and Congreve.

Mr Baron L—'s charge to the Grand Jury for the County of Devon: the famous speech-maker of England. 1710.

The tale of a nettle. Cambridge 1710 (broadside), 1710 (half sheet, as Still more advice).

The London tale, by the author of the Tale of a nettle. 1710. Broadside.

A learned comment upon Dr Hare's excellent sermon preach'd before the D. of Marlborough on the surrender of Bouchain, by an enemy to peace. 1711, 1711. By Swift and Mrs Manley.

A true narrative of what pass'd at the examination of the Marquis de Guiscard. 1711. By Mrs Manley, with hints from Swift.

The reasons which induc'd Her Majesty to create the Right Honourable Robert Harley esq, a peer of Great-Britain. 1711.

Dublin April 25th 1709, The recorder's speech to the Lord Wharton; Dublin July 4th 1711, The recorder's speech to his Grace the Duke of Ormonde; The R—r's s—ch explain'd. [Dublin 1711]. The explanation in verse is attributed to Swift. Another edn with the verses only.

A true relation of the several facts and circumstances of the intended riot and tumult on Queen Elizabeth's birthday. 1711, 1711, Edinburgh 1711. By Mrs Manley from Swift's hints.

It's out at last: or French correspondence clear as the sun. 1712.

The story of the St Alb—ns ghost. 1712. By William Wagstaffe?

The character of Richard St—le esq, with some remarks, by Toby, Abel's kinsman. 1713. By William Wagstaffe?

A modest enquiry into the reasons of the joy expressed by a certain sett of people upon the spreading of a report of her Majesty's death. 1714, Dublin 1714, Edinburgh 1714. By Mrs Manley with Swift's assistance.

Essays divine, moral and political, by the author of the Tale of a tub. 1714, 1715 ('collected from the Works of J. S—t, D— of St P—, and author of the Tale of a tub'). By Thomas Burnet.

Saint Patrick's purgatory: or Dr S—t's expostulation with his distressed friends. 1716.

The speech of the P—st of T—y C—ge to his Royal Highness, Prince of Wales. [1716].

Doctor Sw—t's circular letter to the clergy of the diocese of Dublin. [1716?].

An argument to prove that the abolishing of Christianity in England may, as things now stand, be attended with some inconveniences. 1717. A retouched version.

Ars punica, sive flos linguarum: the art of punning; or the flower of languages, by the labour and industry of Tom Pun-Sibi etc. Dublin 1719, London 1719, 1720 (3 edns). Mainly by Thomas Sheridan.

D—n S—t's prologue to Hyppolitus, spoken by a boy of six years old. [1720]. By Dr Helsham.

The swearers-bank: or parliamentary security for establishing a new bank in Ireland, wherein the medicinal use of oaths is considered; (with The best in Christendom: a tale), written by Dean Swift. Dublin [1720], 1721, London 1720. The 2nd pt of The swearers bank, with new reasons to encourage that project, Dublin 1720.

An account of the short life, sudden death and pompous funeral of Michy Windybank etc. [Dublin? 1720–1?].

The last speech and dying words of the Bank of Ireland which was executed at College-Green on Saturday the 9th inst. Dublin [1721].

A letter from a lady in town to her friend in the country, concerning the bank: or the list of the subscribers farther explain'd. Dublin 1721.

A letter of advice to a young poet; together with a proposal for the encouragement of poetry in this Kingdom. Dublin 1721, London 1721, 1721; tr German, 1738.

A supplement to Dean Sw—t's Miscellanies, by the author, containing 1: A letter to the students of both universities; 11: An essay upon an apothecary; 111: An account of a surprizing apparition, October 20 1722. 1723.

Jove's ramble. Dublin 1723. Broadside.

Memoirs of the life of Scriblerus, by D. S—t. 1723.

Ireland's warning: being an excellent new song upon Woods's base half-pence. Dublin [1724]. Broadside.

To the citizens. Dublin 1724.

An excellent new song upon the late Grand-Jury. Dublin 1724.

A new poem ascrib'd to the Honble the gentlemen of the late Grand-Jury. Dublin [1724].

An excellent new song upon the declarations of the several corporations of the City of Dublin against Wood's half-pence. [Dublin 1724].

The fifth and last letter to the people of Ireland in reference to Wood and his brass. Dublin 1724. Signed 'Hibernicus'.

The sixth letter to the whole people of Ireland, by an ancient patriot. Dublin 1724. Signed 'Well Wisher'.

A letter to William Woods esq, from his only friend in Ireland. Dublin 1724. Signed 'Hibernicus'.

Wood's plot discovered by a member of his society. Dublin 1724.

A letter from a lady of quality to Mr Harding the printer. Dublin 1724.

A poem address'd to the Quidnuncs. 1724. Broadside. Probably by Arbuthnot.

A defence of the conduct of the people of Ireland. Dublin 1724, 1724.

A letter from the grand mistress of the female Free-Masons to Mr Harding the printer. Dublin 1724.

The true state of the case between the Kingdom of Ireland of the one part and Mr William Wood of the other part. Dublin [1724].

Some considerations on the attempts made to pass Mr Wood's brass-money in Ireland. Dublin [1724].

Some reasons shewing the necessity the people of Ireland are under for continuing to refuse Mr Wood's coinage, by the author of the Considerations. Dublin 1724. Dedication signed 'D.B.', probably David Bindon.

Punch's Petition to the ladies. [Dublin 1724?].

A letter from a friend to the Right Honourable —. 1724. Half sheet. Dated 'Dec the first 1724' and signed 'N.N.'.

A second letter from a friend to the Right Honourable —. 1725. Dated 'Jan 4 1724-5' and signed 'N.N.'. This and the preceding letter have been attributed to Robert Lindsay, but without probability. The author may have been St John Brodrick (see Correspondence, ed Williams vol 3, p. 50). Also A third letter, and Fourth letter, signed 'N.N.'.

Apollo's edict. [Dublin? c. 1725?]. 4°; no imprint or date. By Mary Barber?

Blue-Skin's ballad, to the tune of Packington's pound. 1725. Broadside. Other broadside edns in the same year as Newgate's garland, one with imprint of J. Baker, London, another without imprint. Possibly by Gay, with stanzas 6–7 added by Swift.

Tom Punsibi's dream. Dublin 1725. Possibly by Thomas Sheridan.

An elegy on the universally lamented death of the Right Honourable Robert Lord Vis. Molesworth, by M.B. [1725].

On wisdom's defeat in a learned debate. Dublin [1725].

Woods reviv'd: or a short defence of his proceedings in Bristol, London etc. [Dublin?] 1724-5.

An essay on gibing, with a project for its improvement. Dublin 1725.

A letter from D. S—t to D. S—y. [1725].

A poem upon R—r, a lady's spaniel. [1725].

A history of poetry by the Revd D— S—t. Dublin 1726.

Travels into several remote nations of the world, by Capt Lemuel Gulliver. Vol 3, 1727. Contains A second voyage to Brobdingnag, a voyage to Sporunda, and a voyage to Sevarambia, the last taken from Denis Vairasse d'Alais, Histoire des Sévarambes.

A poem to his Majesty King George II on the present state of affairs in England, by the Rev Dr J. Swift, Dean of St Patrick's. Dublin 1727.

Considerations on two papers lately published. Dublin 1728, 1729. Possibly by Arthur Dobbs.

Gulliveriana, or a fourth volume of miscellanies: being a sequel of the three volumes, published by Pope and Swift. 1728. Largely by Jonathan Smedley. Contains genuine pieces by Swift.

Dean Jonathan's parody on the 4th chap of Genesis. 1729.

The Drapier's advice to the freemen and freeholders of the city of Dublin. [Dublin 1729].

P—em by D— S— on the scheme propos'd to the people of Ireland, humbly address'd to the skilfull and ingenious Mr Maculla. Dublin [1729].

To his Excellency John, Lord Carteret, Lord Lieutenant of Ireland. Dublin 1729. Broadside. An altered version, addressed to 'Humphry French esq', was ptd in the London edn of The Presbyterians plea of merit, 1733.

A letter to the people of Ireland, by M. B. Draper. Dublin 1729.

A vindication of the Libel: or a new ballad written by a shoe-boy. [Dublin] 1729–30, London 1730. By William Dunkin.

The present state of Ireland consider'd. Dublin 1730, London 1730.

Some seasonable advice to Doctor D—n—y. 1730.

An infallible scheme to pay the publick debt of this nation in six months. [Dublin] 1731, London 1732. By M. Pilkington.

A proposal humbly offer'd to the P—T, for the more effectual preventing the further growth of Popery, by Dr S—t; to which is added The humble petition of the weavers and venders of gold and silver lace, embroiderers etc; As also two poems, viz Helter skelter and The place of the damn'd. Dublin 1731, London 1731, 1732. Only the poems by Swift.

A sermon preached at St Patrick's Church on St Cæcilia's Day, by Thomas Sheridan DD. Dublin 1731. Introductory letter To the Reverend Dr Thomas Sheridan by Swift?

An enquiry whether the Christian religion is of any benefit or only an useless commodity to a trading nation. 1732.

A modest defence of the lady's dressing-room. Dublin 1732.

The correspondent. No 1 [–6], [Dublin] 1733. By William Tisdall, though nos 3–4 were rptd in the 2nd London edn of The Presbyterians plea of merit.

Human ordure, botanically considered, by Dr S—t. Printed at Dublin and reprinted at London. 1733. Attributed to Dr Chamberlayne.

Some queries upon the demand of the Presbyterians to have the sacramental test repealed at this session of the Parliament. [Dublin] 1733. Broadside.

Ten reasons for repealing the Test Act. [Dublin 1733]. Broadside.

Ub-Bub-A-Boo: or the Irish-howl in heroic verse, by Dean Swift. 1735.

Bounce to Fop: an heroick epistle from a dog at Twickenham to a dog at court, by Dr S—t. Dublin printed, London reprinted. 1736. Attributed also to Gay, but most probably by Pope.

The humours of the age: or Dean Swift's new evening-post. Numb 1 (to be continued weekly). [15–21 Oct 1738].

Dean Swift's copy of that most strange, wonderful and surprizing prophecy written by Saint Patrick above a thousand years ago. 1740.

A modest address to the wicked authors of the present age, by H.F. esq. 1765 (for 1745?), nd (as Dean Swift's legacy to the wicked authors of the present age).

The Drapier's letter to the good people of Ireland. Dublin 1745. Followed by a Second letter shortly afterwards.

D—n Sw—t's medley. Dublin printed, London reprinted [1749].

The mishap: a poem written by the late Rev D.J.S., DD, DSPD. [1750?].

Some account of the Irish, by the late J.S., DD, DSPD. 1753. A reprint of A brief character of Ireland, 1692 (anon).

Swiftiana

See also H. Teerink, Bibliography, ed Scouten, pp. 405–31, and Rothschild library pp. 630–43.

The source of our present fears discover'd: or plain proof of some late designs against our present constitution and government. 1703, 1706. Contains criticisms of Swift's Discourse of the contests and dissensions.

[King, William]. Some remarks upon the Tale of a tub. 1704.

Wotton, William. A defence of the reflections upon ancient and modern learning, with observations upon the Tale of a tub. 1705.

Bickerstaffe's prediction confirm'd in the death of Partridge. 1708.

A continuation of the pr[e]dictions for the remaining part of the year 1708. 1708.

Mr Partridge's answer to Esquire Bickerstaff's strange and wonderful predictions for the year 1708. 1708.

Esquire Bickerstaff's reply to Dr Patridge's pretended answer. Dublin re-printed at the Old Post Office in Fish shamble street. [1708?].

Bickerstaff's almanack: or a vindication of the stars from all the false imputations and erroneous assertions of the late John Partridge. 1710.

A complete key to the Tale of a tub. 1710.

Remarks on a false, scandalous and seditious libel intituled the Conduct of the allies and of the late Ministry. 1711.

Remarks upon remarks: or the Barrier Treaty and the Protestant succession vindicated. 1711, 1712.

[Hare, Francis]. The allies and the late Ministry defended against France. 1711.

A full answer to the Conduct of the allies; to which is added Some observations on the remarks on the Barrier Treaty, by the same author. 1712.

The tryal and condemnation of Don Prefatio D'Asaven'. 1712. Contains a reference to Swift's Letter of thanks from my Lord W***n to the Lord Bp of St Asaph.

Reflections on Dr Swift's Letter to the Earl of Oxford, about the English tongue. [1712]. By Oldmixon.

The British Academy: being a new-erected society for the advancement of wit and learning. 1712. By Mainwaring et al.

The fable of the shepherd and his dog, in answer to the fable of the widow and her cat. 1711, 1712.

When the cat's away the mice may play: a fable humbly inscribed to Dr Swift. [1712?].

Two letters concerning the authour of the Examiner. 1713.

A genuine epistle from M—w P—r esq at Paris to the Reverend J—n S—t DD at Windsor. 1714.

[Defoe, Daniel]. The Scots nation and union vindicated from the reflections cast on them in an infamous libel entitl'd the Publick spirit of the Whigs. 1714.

[Diaper, William]. An imitation of the seventeenth epistle of the first book of Horace, address'd to Dr S—ft. 1714.

An hue and cry after Dr S—t. 1714; A farther hue and cry after Dr Sw—t. 1714.

The enigmatical Court: being the characters of those men whose actions are a mystery. 1714. Swift appears under the heading of 'Smut'.

Dr S—'s real diary. 1715.

A letter from the Lord V—t B—ke to the Rev Dr S—t. 1715.

Saint Patrick's purgatory: or Dr S—t's expostulation with his distressed friends in the Tower and elsewhere. 1716.

A letter to the Rev Dean Swift occasion'd by a satire said to be written by him entitled A dedication to a great man, by a sparkish pamphleteer. 1719.

A defence of English commodities: being an answer to the Proposal for the universal use of Irish manufactures. Printed at Dublin and reprinted at London. 1720.

Hibernia's passive obedience. Dublin 1720. Contains references to Swift's letter concerning the sacramental test.

A description in answer to the journal. Dublin 1722.

The drapier anatomized, a song: a new song sung at the club at Mr Taplin's the sign of the Drapier's Head in Truck-Street. Dublin 1724.

An express from Elisium, with advice how to manage (and some observations on) M. B. Drapier. Dublin 1724.

An express from Parnassus to the Reverend Dr Jonathan Swift Dean of St Patrick's. [1724].

The present state of Ireland consider'd, in a letter to the Rev Dean Swift. [Dublin?] 1724.

A letter from Aminadab Firebrass Quaker merchant to M. B. Drapier. Dublin [1724].

The Drapier demolished and set out in his own proper colours, by William Wood esq. Dublin [1724].

Seasonable advice to M. B. Drapier. [Dublin? 1724].

A letter to M. B. Drapier, author of a Letter to the Ld Molesworth etc. Dublin 1725.

The Donore ballad, inscrib'd to the praise of the worthy M. B. Drapier. Dublin 1725.

A poem to D— S—. Dublin 1725.

A second poem, to Dr Jo—n S—t. Dublin 1725.

A second song, sung at the club at Mr Taplin's. Dublin 1725.

The Drapier's ballad to the tune of the London 'prentice. Dublin 1725. By T. Sheridan?

A congratulatory poem on Dean Swift's return to town. Dublin 1725.

Ashton, Robert. A congratulatory poem to the Reverend Dean Swift. Dublin 1725.

Scourge for the author of the satyr, Gibing on Trinity College, and on the Reverend Dean Swift, Hibernia's Apollo. [Dublin] 1725.

Trinity Colledge vindicated: or a short defence of the Reverend Dean Swift. Dublin 1725.

To His Excellency the Lord Carteret, occasion'd by seeing a poem intituled the Birth of manly virtue. Dublin 1725.

A poem inscrib'd to the author of the Birth of manly virtue. Dublin 1725.

A poem delivered to the Reverend Doctor Swift, Dean of St Patrick's Dublin, by a young nobleman, November 30 1725, being the Dean's birth-day. [1725?]. By Lord Mountcashell, or Lord Orrery?

[Smedley, Jonathan). A satyr. [Dublin?] 1725.

Satyr satiris'd, an answer to a Satyr on the Reverend D—n S—t. [Dublin 1725?].

A letter from a clergyman to his friend, with an account of the travels of Capt Lemuel Gulliver. 1726.

A true and faithful inventory of the goods belonging to D. Sw—t, Vicar of Lara Cor. [1726?]. Probably by Thomas Sheridan.

Account of the Journey-men weavers grateful congratulation of the Rev Dr. Swift. [Dublin] 1726.

Lemuel Gulliver's travels into several remote nations of the world, compendiously methodized. 1726. Another title: A key, being observations and explanatory notes, upon the Travels.

Gulliver decypher'd. [1727?]. Attributed to Arbuthnot, but not likely to be his.

A voyage to Cacklogallinia, by Samuel Brunt. 1727.

The anatomist dissected, by Lemuel Gulliver, surgeon and anatomist to the Kings of Lilliput and Blefuscu. 1727.

Tom Punsibi's letter to Dean Swift. Dublin 1727. Probably by Thomas Sheridan.

The metamorphosis: or the canine appetite, demonstrated in the person of P—p—e and Sw—t. 1728. By Jonathan Smedley.

An account of the state of learning in the Empire of Lilliput. 1728. Attributed to Arbuthnot.

The characters of the times. 1728.

Some memoirs of the amours and intrigues of a certain Irish dean, part I. [1728]; Part II, 1728.

A supplement to the profound. 1728.

A compleat collection of all the verses, essays, letters and advertisements, which have been occasioned by the publication of three volumes of miscellanies by Pope and company. 1728.

An appeal to the Reverend Dean Swift by way of reply to the observer on Seasonable remarks. Dublin 1728. By John Browne.

A letter in answer to a paper, intitled An appeal to the Reverend Dean Swift. Dublin 1728.

To the R—d Dr J—n S—t, The memorial of the poor inhabitants, tradesmen and labourers of the Kingdom of Ireland. Dublin [1728]. By John Browne?

An answer to the Christmas-Box, in defence of Doctor D—n—y, by R—t B—r. 1729. Probably not by Rupert Barber but by Thomas Sheridan.

[Delany, Patrick]. The pheasant and the lark. Dublin 1730.

Advice to a certain Dean. 1730.

An epistle to a certain Dean, written originally in Italian. 1730.

The travels of Mr John Gulliver, son to Capt Lemuel Gulliver, translated from the French, by J. Lockman. 2 vols 1731. From a sequel in French by Desfontaines.

An answer to Hamilton's bawn: or a short character of Dr S—t. 1732.

The gentleman's study in answer to the Lady's dressing room. 1732.

A vindication of the Protestant dissenters, from the aspersions cast upon them in a late pamphlet intitled The Presbyterians plea of merit. [1733].

The Dean's provocation for writing the Lady's dressing-room. 1734. By Lady Mary Wortley Montagu.

A rap at the Rapsody. 1734.

[Arbuckle, James]. Momus mistaken: a fable, occasioned by the publication of the works of the Revd Dr Swift DSPD in Dublin. 1735.

Critical remarks on Capt Gulliver's travels, by Doctor Bantley. 1735, Dublin 1735. Possibly by Arbuthnot.

A brush to the curry-comb of truth. Dublin 1736.

The old woman and her goose, inscrib'd to the Revd Jonathan Swift. Dublin 1736.

S—t contra omnes: an Irish miscellany. [1736]. Contains Swift's Legion Club.

A collection of Welsh travels, and memoirs of Wales, containing I: The Briton describ'd, or a journey thro' Wales: being a pleasant relation of D—n S—t's journey to that ancient Kingdom. 1738.

An epistle to Dean Swift: a poem, by a gentleman in the Army. Hereford 1739.

The enthusiasm: a poem, with a character of Dr Jonathan Swift. By Mr P.H. author of the Poet. Dublin 1739.

A catalogue of books: the library of the late Rev Dr Swift. Dublin 1745.

Memoirs of the life and writings of Jonathan Swift DD, Dean of St Patrick's Dublin etc. 1752. A reworked piracy of Orrery's Remarks, with additonal anecdotes. By Henry Jones?

Swift's vision, or the women's hue and cry against Alexander Pope, for the loss of their characters: a poem. Dublin 1757.

§ 2

Pilkington, L. Memoirs written by herself. 3 vols 1748–54; ed J. Isaacs 1928.

Orrery, Earl of. Remarks on the life and writings of Swift. 1752. Reply by P. Delany, Observations upon Lord Orrery's Remarks, 1754.

Amory, T. Memoirs of several ladies of Great Britain. 1755.

Hawkesworth, J. Life of Swift. 1755, Dublin 1755.

Swift, D. Essay upon the life, writings and character of Swift. 1755.

'C.M.P.G.N.S.T.S.' GM Nov 1757. On Stella.

Dilworth, W. H. Life of Swift. 1758, 1760.

Johnson, S. In his Lives of the poets vol 3, 1781.

Sheridan, T. Life of Swift. 1784.

Berkeley, G. M. In his Literary relics, 1789.

Beddoes, T. In his Hygeia: or essays moral and medical vol 3, 1803.

[Wilson, C. H.] Swiftiana. 2 vols 1804.

Barrett, J. Essay on the earlier part of the life of Swift. 1808.

Craufurd, Q. Essai historique sur Swift. Paris 1808.

Nichols, J. In his Literary anecdotes of the eighteenth century, 9 vols 1812–15.

—— In his Illustrations of the literary history of the eighteenth century, 8 vols 1817–58.

Scott, W. Memoirs of Swift. 1814.

Jeffrey, F. The works of Swift. Edinburgh Rev 27 1816.

Hazlitt, W. In his Lectures on the English poets, 1818.

[Berwick, E.] A defence of Swift. 1819.

Mason, W. M. The history and antiquities of the collegiate church of St Patrick. Dublin 1820.

Spence, J. In his Anecdotes, observations and characters, ed S. W. Singer 1820; ed J. Osborn 2 vols Oxford 1966.

Account of the skull of Swift recently disinterred at Dublin. Phrenological Jnl & Miscellany 9 1836.

Houston, J. On the authenticity of the skulls of Swift and Stella. Ibid.

Macaulay, T. B. Sir William Temple. Edinburgh Rev 68 1838.

—— The life and writings of Addison. Edinburgh Rev 78 1843.

Wilde, W. R. The closing years of Swift's life. Dublin 1849.

Thackeray, W. M. In his English humourists of the eighteenth century, 1853.

Masson, D. In his Essays, chiefly on English poets, 1856.

Prévost-Paradol, L. Swift: sa vie et ses oeuvres. Paris 1856.

Rigault, H. In his Histoire de la querelle des Anciens et des Modernes, Paris 1856.

Taine, H. Swift, son génie et ses oeuvres. Revue des Deux Mondes 15 Aug 1858; rptd in his Histoire de la littérature anglaise vol 4, Paris 1863.

Reynald, H. Biographie de Swift. Paris 1860.

Lecky, W. E. H. The leaders of public opinion in Ireland. 1861.

—— Biographical introduction. In Prose works, ed T. Scott vol 1, 1897.

Caro, J. Lessing und Swift. Jena 1869.

Forster, J. Life of Swift. Vol 1 (all pbd), 1875.

Ward, A. W. Swift's love story in German literature. Macmillan's Mag Feb 1877.

Chamberlain, B. H. Wasaubiyauwe, the Japanese Gulliver. Trans Asiatic Soc of Japan 7 1879.

Bucknill, J. C. Swift's disease. Brain 4 1882.

Craik, H. Life of Swift. 1882, 2 vols 1894.

Stephen, L. Swift. 1882 (EML). Also article in DNB, 1898.

Roberts, W. Swiftiana published by Curll. Antiquarian Mag & Bibliographer 7 1885.

Solly, E. Swift's Cadenus and Vanessa. Ibid.

—— Swift's Conduct of the allies. Ibid.

Flach, J. Swift: son action politique en Irlande. Paris 1886.

Meyer, R. M. Swift und G. C. Lichtenberg. Berlin 1886.

Hönncher, E. Quellen zu Swift's Gulliver's travels. Anglia 10 1888.

Parnell, A. Swift and the Memoirs of Captain Carleton. EHR 6 1891.

Borkowsky, T. Quellen zu Swifts Gulliver. Anglia 15 1892.

Collins, J. C. Swift: a biographical and critical study. 1893.

Moriarty, G. P. Swift and his writings. 1893.

Simon, M. Swift: étude psychologique et littéraire. Paris 1893.

Birrell, A. In his Essays about men, women and books, 1894.

— In his Collected essays and addresses 1880–1920 vol 1, 1922.

Dobson, A. In his Eighteenth-century vignettes ser 2, 1894. On Journal to Stella.

King, R. A. Swift in Ireland. 1895.

Le Fanu, T. P. Swift's library. Jnl Royal Soc of Antiquaries of Ireland 26 1896.

— Catalogue of Swift's library in 1715, with an inventory of his personal property in 1742. Proc Royal Irish Acad 37 1927.

Lane-Poole, S. In his Eighteenth-century letters, 1897.

— The alleged marriage of Swift and Stella. Fortnightly Rev Feb 1910.

— Swift's correspondence. Quart Rev 218 1913.

Thierkopf, P. Swifts Gulliver und seine französischen Vorgänger. Magdeburg 1899.

White, N. B. Swiftiana in Marsh's Library. Hermathena 11 1901; rptd in his An account of Archbishop Marsh's library, Dublin 1926.

Cork and Orrery, Countess of. The Orrery papers. 2 vols 1903.

Meye, R. Die politische Stellung Swifts. Leipzig 1903.

Brown, A. C. L. Gulliver's travels and an Irish folk-tale. MLN 19 1904.

Ainger, A. In his Lectures and essays, 1905.

Bernard, J. H. Swift in Dublin. Blackwood's Mag Nov 1906.

— The relations between Swift and Stella. In Prose works of Swift, ed T. Scott vol 12, 1908.

— The cathedral church of St Patrick, with a short account of the Deans. Dublin and Cork 1940.

Toldo, P. Les voyages merveilleuses de Cyrano de Bergerac et de Swift et leurs rapports avec l'oeuvre de Rabelais. Revue des Études Rabelaisiennes 4–5, 1906–7.

Cordelet, H. Swift. Paris 1907.

Falkiner, F. On the portraits, busts and engravings of Swift and Stella. In Prose works of Swift, ed T. Scott vol 12, 1908.

The Lady of the House 1908 (Xmas). Article on Swift and Stella, and facs of last page of Stella's will.

Dickens, L. and M. Stanton. An eighteenth-century correspondence: being the letters of Swift etc. 1910.

Hanford, J. H. Plutarch and Swift. MLN 25 1910.

Longe, J. G. Martha, Lady Giffard: life and letters. 1910.

Smith, S. S. Swift. 1910.

Hofmann, H. Swift's Tale of a tub. Leipzig 1911.

Lauchert, F. Die pseudo-swiftische Reise nach Kaklogallinien [S. Brunt] und in den Mond in der deutschen Literatur. Euphorion Zeitschrift für Literaturgeschichte 18 1911.

O'Donoghue, D. J. Swift as an Irishman. Irish Rev June–Aug 1912.

Reid, E. C. Manifestations of manic-depressive insanity in literary genius. Amer Jnl of Insanity 68 1912.

Becker, H. P. Die Satire Swifts. Halle 1913.

Guthkelch, A. C. The tale of a tub revers'd and Characters and criticisms upon the ancient and modern orators etc. Library 4 1913.

— Swift's Tale of a tub. MLR 8–10 1913–15.

Jacobson, A. C. Literary genius and manic-depressive insanity. Scientific Amer (suppl) 4 Jan 1913.

Woods, M. L. Swift, Stella and Vanessa. Nineteenth Century Dec 1913.

Gillot, H. In his La querelle des Anciens et des Modernes en France, Paris 1914.

Dargan, H. M. The nature of allegory as used by Swift. SP 13 1916.

Thomas, J. M. Swift and the Stamp Act of 1712. PMLA 31 1916.

Thompson, E. N. S. Tom Brown and eighteenth-century satirists. MLN 32 1917.

Whibley, C. Swift. 1917.

— Gulliver's travels. Blackwood's Mag Oct 1926.

Lawlor, H. J. The graves of Swift and Stella. EHR 33 1918.

— The fasti of St Patrick's, Dublin. Dundalk 1930.

— The deaneries of St Patrick's. Jnl Royal Soc of Antiquaries of Ireland 62 1932.

Reed, E. B. Gulliver's travels and Tom Brown. MLN 33 1918.

Firth, C. The political significance of Gulliver's travels. Proc Br Acad 9 1919.

— Dean Swift and ecclesiastical preferment. RES 2 1926.

— A story from Gulliver's travels. Ibid.

— The canon of Swift. Ibid. See H. Williams, 3 1927.

Ball, F. E. Swift and Prince Butler. N & Q 20 Nov 1920.

— Swift's verse. 1929.

Burlingame, A. E. The Battle of the books in its historical setting. 1920.

Elder, L. W. The pride of the Yahoo. MLN 35 1920.

Jones, R. F. The background of the Battle of the books. Washington Univ Stud 7 1920.

— Ancients and moderns: a study of the background of the Battle of the books. St Louis 1936.

Eddy, W. A. A source for Gulliver's travels. MLN 36 1921.

— Rabelais: a source for Gulliver's travels. MLN 37 1922.

— A source for Gulliver's first voyage. Ibid.

— Cyrano de Bergerac and Gulliver's travels. MLN 38 1923.

— Gulliver's travels: a critical study. Princeton 1923.

— The anatomist dissected, by Lemuel Gulliver. MLN 41 1926.

— Gulliver's travels and le théâtre italien. MLN 44 1929.

— Ned Ward and Lilliput. N & Q 1 March 1930.

— Tom Brown and Partridge the astrologer. MP 28 1930.

— The wits vs John Partridge, astrologer. SP 29 1932.

Huxley, A. Polite conversation. In his On the margin, 1923.

— In his Do what you will, 1929.

Goulding, S. Swift en France. Paris 1924.

Darnall, F. M. Traditional notions about Swift. Eng Jnl Sept 1925.

— Swift's religion. JEGP 30 1931.

— Swift's belief in immortality. MLN 47 1932.

— Was Swift ambitious? Eng Jnl Nov 1932.

— Old wine in new bottles. South Atlantic Quart 41 1942. On Swift's ethical ideas.

Gückel, W. and E. D. Günther. Defoes und Swifts Belesenheit und literarische Kritik. Leipzig 1925.

Pons, E. Swift: les années de jeunesse et le Conte du Tonneau. Strasbourg 1925.

— Rabelais et Swift à propos du Lilliputien. In Mélange Abel Lefranc, Paris 1936.

— Du nouveau sur le Journal à Stella. Etudes Anglaises 1 1937.

— Swift et Pascal. Langues Modernes 4 1951.

— Note complémentaire: Swift. Etudes Anglaises 5 1952.

— Swift, créateur linguistique: à propos du Lilliputien. Cahiers du Sud 46 1958.

— Gulliver: ou l'utopie-bouffe. Etudes de Littérature Etrangère et Comparée 50 1964.

Teerink, H. The history of John Bull. Amsterdam 1925.

— Swift's ordination. Dublin Mag 13 1947.

— Cadenus and Vanessa. Harvard Lib Bull 2 1948. See 3 1949.

— The publication of Gulliver's travels. Dublin Mag 23 1948.

—— A source book for A tale of a tub from Swift's own library. Irish Book Lover Oct 1949.
—— Swift's Contests and dissensions in Athens and Rome. Library 5th ser 4 1949.
—— Swifte of Rotherham. N & Q 21 Jan 1950.
—— Swift's Verses on the death of Doctor Swift. SB 4 1951. *See* 7 1954.
Digeon, A. Gulliver and La Bruyère. Revue Anglo-américaine 3 1926.
Metzger, F. Swifts Gulliver's travels und irische Sagen. Archiv 151 1926.
Wedel, T. O. On the philosophical background of Gulliver's travels. SP 23 1926.
Williams, H. The canon of Swift. RES 2–3 1926–7.
—— Gulliver's travels: further notes. Library 4th ser 9 1928.
—— Dean Swift's library. 1932.
—— Swift and the Four last years of the Queen. Library 4th ser 16 1935.
—— Miscellanies in prose and verse, second edition 1713. Bibl N & Q 2 1938.
—— and Lord Rothschild. The grand question debated. RES 15 1939.
—— Swift, Hawkesworth and the Journal to Stella. In Essays on the eighteenth century presented to David Nichol Smith, Oxford 1945.
—— Old Mr Lewis. RES 21 1945.
—— Swift and Shakespeare. N & Q 1 May 1948.
—— Swift's early biographers. In Pope and his contemporaries: essays presented to George Sherburn, Oxford 1949.
—— The text of Gulliver's travels. Cambridge 1952. *See* exchange with W. B. Todd, Library 5th ser 8–9 1953–4.
Ferenczi, S. Gulliver-Phantasien. Internationale Zeitschrift für Psychoanalyse 13 1927.
Hearsey, M. New light on the evidence for Swift's marriage. PMLA 42 1927.
Hubbard, L. L. Notes on The adventures of James Dubourdien and his wife: a source for Gulliver's travels. Ann Arbor 1927.
Bennett, R. E. A note on the Cyrano-Swift criticism. MLN 43 1928.
Dark, S. Five deans. 1928.
Leslie, S. The skull of Swift. 1928.
—— The script of Swift and other essays. Philadelphia 1935.
—— The Swift manuscripts in the Morgan Library. In Studies in art and literature for Bella da Costa Greene, Princeton 1954.
Moore, J. B. The role of Gulliver. MP 25 1928.
Read, H. In his Sense of glory, Cambridge 1929.
Rovillain, E. E. Swift's A voyage to Lilliput and the Thousand and one quarters of an hour, Tartarian tales of T. S. Gueulette. MLN 44 1929.
Mayo, T. F. The authorship of the History of John Bull. PMLA 45 1930.
Van Doren, C. Swift. New York 1930.
Davis, H. Swift's view of poetry. In Studies in English Toronto 1931.
—— Verses on the death of Dr Swift. Book-Collector's Quart 2 1931.
—— Swift and the Four last years of the Queen. Library 4th ser 16 1935.
—— The poetry of Swift. College Eng Nov 1940.
—— Stella. New York 1942.
—— The canon of Swift. Eng Inst Annual (New York) 1942.
—— Swift and the pedants. Oriel Rev 1 1943.
—— The conciseness of Swift. In Essays on the eighteenth century presented to David Nichol Smith, Oxford 1945.
—— Remarks on some Swift manuscripts in the United States. In J. E. Tobin and L. A. Landa, Swift: a list of critical studies published from 1895 to 1945, New York 1945.
—— The satire of Swift. New York 1947.

—— The manuscript of Swift's Sermon on brotherly love. In Pope and his contemporaries: essays presented to George Sherburn, Oxford 1949.
—— Some free thoughts of a Tory Dean. Virginia Quart Rev 28 1952.
—— The manuscripts of Swift's Directions to servants. In Studies in art and literature for Bella da Costa Greene, Princeton 1954.
—— Alecto's whip. REL 3 1962.
—— A modest defence of the Lady's dressing room. In Restoration and eighteenth-century literature: essays in honor of A. D. McKillop, Chicago 1963.
—— Swift's use of irony. In The uses of Irony: papers on Defoe and Swift, Los Angeles 1966.
—— Swift's character. In Swift: a Dublin tercentenary tribute, ed P. Edwards and R. McHugh, Dublin 1967.
Doorn, C. van. An investigation into the character of Swift. Amsterdam 1931.
Frantz, R. W. Swift's Yahoos and the voyagers. MP 29 1931.
—— Gulliver's 'Cousin Sympson'. HLQ 1 1938.
Lawton, H. W. Bishop Godwin's Man in the moone. RES 7 1931.
Webster, C. M. Swift and the Royal Society's Philosophical Transactions. N & Q 8 Aug 1931. *See* 12 Sept 1931.
—— Temple, Casaubon and Swift. N & Q 6 June 1931.
—— Hudibras and Swift. MLN 47 1932.
—— Notes on the Yahoos. MLN Ibid.
—— The Puritan's ears in A tale of a tub. MLN 47 1932.
—— Swift's Tale of a tub compared with earlier satires of the Puritans. PMLA 47 1932.
—— Tom Brown and the Tale of a tub. TLS 18 Feb 1932.
—— A possible source for A tale of a tub. MLN 48 1933.
—— Swift and some earlier satirists of Puritan enthusiasm. PMLA 48 1933.
—— The satiric background of the attack on the Puritans in Swift's A tale of a tub. PMLA 50 1935.
—— A source for Swift's meditation upon a broom-stick. MLN 51 1936.
Babcock, R. W. Swift's conversion to the Tory Party. Univ of Michigan Pbns in Lang & Lit 8 1932.
Glaser, H. Swifts Kritik an der englischen Irlandpolitik. Breslau 1932.
Rossi, M. M. Essay on the character of Swift. Life & Letters Sept 1932.
—— and J. M. Hone. Swift: or the egoist. 1934.
—— Notes on the eighteenth-century German translation of Gulliver's travels. Lib Chron of Univ of Pennsylvania 25 1959.
Woolf, V. Swift's Journal to Stella. In her Second common reader, 1932.
Beattie, L. M. The authorship of the Quidnuncki's. MP 30 1933.
—— The lighter side of Swift. In Six satirists, Pittsburgh 1965.
Brown, H. In his Rabelais in English literature, Cambridge Mass 1933.
Gregory, A. Stella, Vanessa and Swift. Nineteenth Century June 1933.
Gulick, S. L. Swift's The day of judgement. PMLA 48 1933.
Gwynn, S. The life and friendships of Dean Swift. 1933.
Taylor, W. D. Swift. 1933.
Dege, C. Utopie und Satire in Swifts Gulliver's travels. Frankfurt 1934.
Heidenhain, A. Ueber den Menschenhass: eine pathographische Untersuchung ueber Swift. Stuttgart 1934.
Hone, J. M. Berkeley and Swift as national economists. Studies 23 1934.
—— The story of Damer gold. Studies 39 1950. On Swift's Elegy on the death of Damer.
Leavis, F. R. The irony of Swift. Scrutiny 2 1934; rptd in his Determinations, 1934; and in his Common pursuit, 1952.

McCracken, G. Homerica in Gulliver's travels. Classical Jnl 29 1934.

Morrison, F. A note on the Battle of the books. PQ 13 1934.

Boyce, B. Predecessors of the Tale of a tub. N & Q 16 Feb 1935.

Korn, M. A. Die Weltanschauung Swifts. Jena 1935.

Looten, C. La pensée religieuse de Swift et ses antinomies. Lille 1935.

McCain, J. W. Swift and Heywood. N & Q 6 April 1935.

O'Conor, C. George Faulkner and Swift. Studies 24 1935.

Reimers, H. Swift, Gedanken und Schriften über Religion und Kirche. Hamburg 1935.

Rockwell, F. S. A probable source for Gulliver's travels. N & Q 24 Aug 1935.

Smith, D. N. Swift: some observations. Trans Royal Soc of Lit 14 1935.

Goodwin, A. Wood's halfpence. EHR 51 1936.

Handro, L. Swift, Gulliver's travels: eine Interpretation im Zusammenhang mit den geistesgeschichtlichen Beziehungen. Hamburg 1936.

McCue, G. S. A seventeenth-century Gulliver. MLN 50 1935. Comment by A. W. Secord 51 1936.

Quintana, R. The mind and art of Swift. New York 1936, 1953 (with additional notes and bibliography).

— Recent discussions of Swift. College Eng Oct 1940.

— Situational satire: a commentary on the method of Swift. UTQ 17 1948.

— Swift: an introduction. 1955.

— Emile Pons and the modern study of Swift's Tale of a tub. Etudes Anglaises 18 1965.

— Gulliver's travels: the satiric intent and execution. In Swift: a Dublin tercentenary tribute, ed P. Edwards and R. McHugh, Dublin 1967.

— A modest appraisal: Swift scholarship and criticism 1945–65. In Fair liberty was all his cry: a tercentenary tribute to Swift, ed A. M. Jeffares 1967.

Van Lennep, W. Three unnoticed writings of Swift. PMLA 51 1936.

Wilson, M. Swift's Polite conversation. English 1 1936.

Allen, R. J. Swift's earliest political tract and Sir William Temple's essays. Harvard Stud 19 1937.

— Swift's Contests and dissensions in Boston. New England Quart 29 1956.

Duff, I. F. G. A onesided sketch of Swift. Psychoanalytic Quart 6 1937.

Gold, M. B. Swift's marriage to Stella. Cambridge Mass 1937.

Linn, I. Swift, Pope Innocent and Oliver Wendell Holmes. PQ 16 1937. Comment by G. P. Smith 17 1938.

Newman, B. Swift. 1937.

Nicolson, M. H. and N. M. Mohler. The scientific background of Swift's Voyage to Laputa. Annals of Science 2 1937.

— Swift's flying island in the Voyage to Laputa. Ibid.

Nicolson, M. H. Voyages to the moon. New York 1948.

Jourdan, G. V. The religion of Swift. Church Quart Rev 126 1938.

Krappe, E. S. A 'lapsus calami' of Swift. MLN 53 1938.

Private libraries iv: Lord Rothschild. TLS 6 Aug 1938; v: Harold Williams, 27 Aug 1938.

Rothschild, Lord. The publication of the first Drapier letter. Library 4th ser 19 1938.

Sherburn, G. Methods in books about Swift. SP 35 1938.

— The Swift-Pope Miscellanies of 1732. Harvard Lib Bull 6 1952.

— Errors concerning the Houyhnhnms. MP 56 1958.

— The 'copies of verses' about Gulliver. Texas Stud in Lang & Lit 3 1961.

Thompson, P. V. The canon of Swift. RES 14 1938. Reply by H. Williams, ibid.

— Swift and the Wagstaffe papers. N & Q 30 July 1938.

— An unpublished letter from Swift [to Delany, 11 July 1726]. Library 5th ser 22 1967.

— Swift's 'poor Mr Davis'. N & Q June 1968.

Trench, W. F. and K. B. Garratt. John Macky's memoirs with Swift's notes. TLS 13–20 Aug 1938.

— On Swift's marginalia in Macky's memoirs. Library 4th ser 19 1939.

Baughan, D. E. Swift's source of the Houyhnhnms reconsidered. ELH 5 1938. Reply by R. W. Frantz, 6 1939.

— Swift and Gentillet. SP 37 1940.

Brawner, J. P. Swift and the Harley-St John ministry. West Virginia Univ Bull Philological Stud 3 1939.

Cornu, D. Swift, Motte and the copyright struggle: two unnoticed documents. MLN 54 1939.

Jackson, R. W. Swift, Dean and pastor. 1939.

— Dean Swift's tour of Munster. Dublin Mag 18 1943.

— Swift and his circle. Dublin 1945.

Knight, G. W. Swift and the symbolism of irony. In his Burning oracle, Oxford 1939; rptd in his Poets of action, 1967.

Mack, M. The first printing of the letters of Pope and Swift. Library 4th ser 19 1939. Reply by V. A. Dearing, 24 1943.

Matthews, A. The Iroquois virtuosi. N & Q 10 June 1939.

Petitjean, A. M. Présentation de Swift. Paris 1939.

Sutherland, J. R. Dr Swift in London. In his Background for Queen Anne, 1939.

— Forms and methods in Swift's satire. In Swift: a Dublin tercentenary tribute, ed P. Edwards and R. McHugh, Dublin 1967.

Watkins, W. B. C. Absent thee from felicity. In his Perilous balance: the tragic genius of Swift, Johnson and Sterne, Princeton 1939.

Wilson, T. G. Swift's deafness and his last illness. Irish Jnl of Medical Science June 1939; rptd in Annals of Medical History 2 1940.

— Swift's personality and death-masks. REL 3 1962.

Freyer, G. Swift and Machiavelli. TLS 8 June 1940.

McKenzie, G. Swift: reason and some of its consequences. California Univ Pbns in Eng 8 1940.

Moore, J. R. A Defoe allusion in Gulliver's travels. N & Q 3 Feb 1940.

— The geography of Gulliver's travels. JEGP 40 1941.

— A new source for Gulliver's travels. SP 38 1941.

— The Yahoos of the African travellers. N & Q 29 April 1950.

— Swift as historian. SP 49 1952.

— A possible model for the organization of A tale of a tub. N & Q July 1954.

Ross, J. F. The character of Poor Richard: its source and alteration. PMLA 55 1940.

— The final comedy of Lemuel Gulliver. In Studies in the comic, California Univ Stud in Eng 8 1941.

— Swift and Defoe: a study in relationship. Berkeley 1941.

Alton, E. H. Some fragments of college history. Hermathena May, Nov 1941. On Swift and Delany.

Berwick, D. M. The reputation of Swift 1781–1882. Philadelphia 1941.

Clubb, M. D. The criticism of Gulliver's Voyage to the Houyhnhnms 1726–1914. Stanford Stud in Lang & Lit 1941.

de C[astro], J. P. Swift: the groaning elmboard. N & Q 8 March 1941.

Gove, P. B. The imaginary voyage in prose fiction. New York 1941.

— Gildon's Fortunate shipwreck as background for Gulliver's travels. RES 18 1942.

Johnston, D. The mysterious origin of Dean Swift. Dublin Hist Record 3 1941. Reply by H. Williams, TLS 29 Nov 1941.

— In search of Swift. Dublin 1959.

Manch, J. Swift and women. Univ of Buffalo Stud 16 1941.

Potter, G. R. Swift and natural science. PQ 20 1941.

Karpman, B. Neurotic traits of Swift, as revealed in Gulliver's travels. Psychoanalytic Rev 29 1942.

Landa, L. A. A modest proposal and populousness. MP 40 1942.

—— Swift's economic views and mercantilism. ELH 10 1943.

—— Swift, the mysteries and deism. SE 1944.

—— Swift and charity. JEGP 44 1945.

—— Swift. Eng Inst Essays (New York) 1946.

—— Swift's deanery income: a new document. In Pope and his contemporaries: essays presented to George Sherburn, Oxford 1949.

—— The insolent rudeness of Dr Swift. MLN 68 1953.

—— Swift and the Church of Ireland. Oxford 1954.

—— Swift: 'not the gravest of divines'. In Swift: a Dublin tercentenary tribute, ed P. Edwards and R. McHugh, Dublin 1967.

Maxwell, J. C. Demigods and pickpockets: the Augustan myth in Swift and Rousseau. Scrutiny 11 1942.

—— The text of A tale of a tub. E Studies 36 1955.

Neumann, J. H. Swift and English pronunciation. Quart Jnl of Speech 28 1942.

—— Swift and the vocabulary of English. MLQ 4 1943.

—— Swift and English spelling. SP 41 1944.

Pritchett, V. S. The Dean. In his In my good books, 1942.

—— Swift to Stella. In his Books in general, 1953.

Westgate, R. I. W. and P. L. MacKendrick. Juvenal and Swift. Classical Jnl 37 1942.

Barnett, G. L. Gay, Swift and Tristram Shandy. N & Q 4 Dec 1943.

Brooks, E. St J. A poem of Swift's. TLS 10 July 1943.

—— Swift and Dr Wilson. TLS 7 Aug 1943.

—— 'The Cheshire Sheaf': Swift's lodgings in Chester. N & Q 15 Dec 1945. See W. Taggard 12 Jan 1946.

Davies, G. Swift's The story of the injured lady. HLQ 6 1943.

—— A new edition of Swift's The story of the injured lady. HLQ 8 1945.

Hand, G. Swift and marriage. California Univ Pbns in Eng 14 1943.

Horrell, J. What Gulliver knew. Sewanee Rev 51 1943.

Wittkowsky, G. Swift's Modest proposal: the biography of an early Georgian pamphlet. JHI 4 1943. Reply by L. A. Landa, PQ 23 1944.

Ault, N. Pope and Gulliver. Nat Rev 122 1944.

Bracher, F. The maps in Gulliver's travels. HLQ 8 1944.

—— The name 'Lemuel Gulliver'. HLQ 12 1949.

Hornbeak, K. Swift's Letter to a very young lady. HLQ 7 1944.

Montagu, M. F. A. Tyson's 'orang-outang' and Gulliver's travels. PMLA 54 1944.

Rowse, A. L. In his English spirit, 1944.

—— Swift at Letcombe. In his English past, 1951.

Case, A. E. Four essays on Gulliver's travels. Princeton 1945.

—— Swift and Sir William Temple: a conjecture. MLN 60 1945.

—— Swift's supposed ingratitude towards his uncle Godwin: a surmise. In Pope and his contemporaries: essays presented to George Sherburn, Oxford 1949.

Dobrin, M. B. Lilliput revisited: Reynolds, Fronde, dimensional analysis and Swift. Technology Rev 47 1945.

Gould, S. H. Gulliver and the moons of Mars. JHI 6 1945.

Grennan, M. R. Lilliput and Leprecan: Gulliver and the Irish tradition. ELH 12 1945.

Hogan, J. J. Bicentenary of Swift. Studies 34 1945.

Kliger, S. The unity of Gulliver's travels. MLQ 6 1945.

Scouten, A. H. Swift at the moving pictures. N & Q 27 Jan 1945.

—— Materials for the study of Swift at the University of Pennsylvania. Lib Chron of Univ of Pennsylvania 23 1957. The Teerink collection.

—— The earliest London printings of Verses on the death of Doctor Swift. SB 15 1962.

Briggs, H. E. Swift and Keats. PMLA 61 1946.

Scott-Thomas, L. M. The vocabulary of Swift. Dalhousie Rev 25 1946.

Ehrenpreis, I. Swift and Mr John Temple. MLN 62 1947.

—— Swift's father. N & Q 15 Nov 1947.

—— Swift's 'little language' in the Journal to Stella. SP 45 1948.

—— Swift's Enquiry. N & Q 20 Aug 1949.

—— Lady Betty Butler to Swift. TLS 15 Dec 1950.

—— Swift's voyages. MLN 65 1950.

—— The date of Swift's Sentiments. RES new ser 3 1952.

—— Swift and satire. College Eng March 1952.

—— Swift on liberty. JHI 13 1952.

—— Swift's History of England. JEGP 51 1952.

—— Swift's April Fool for a bibliophile. Book Collector 2 1953.

—— Swift's first poem [Ode to the King]. MLR 49 1954.

—— Four of Swift's sources. MLN 70 1955.

—— The pattern of Swift's women. PMLA 70 1955.

—— and J. L. Clifford. Swiftiana in Rylands English ms 659 and related documents. Bull John Rylands Lib 37 1955.

—— The origins of Gulliver's travels. PMLA 72 1957.

—— The personality of Swift. Cambridge Mass 1958.

—— The literary side of a satirist's work. Minnesota Rev 2 1962. On An argument against abolishing Christianity.

—— The meaning of Gulliver's last voyage. REL 3 1962.

—— Swift: the man, his works, and the age, vol 1: Mr Swift and his contemporaries. 1962; vol 2: Dr Swift, 1967. A 3rd vol is in progress.

—— Personae. In Restoration and eighteenth-century literature: essays in honor of A. D. McKillop, Chicago 1963.

—— Dr S***t and the Hibernian Patriot. In Swift: a Dublin tercentenary tribute, ed P. Edwards and R. McHugh, Dublin 1967.

—— Swift and the comedy of evil. In The world of Swift, ed B. Vickers, Oxford 1968.

—— Letters of advice to young spinsters. In his Lady of letters in the eighteenth century, Los Angeles 1969. On Swift's attitude to women.

Fink, Z. S. Political theory in Gulliver's travels. ELH 14 1947.

Griffith, R. H. Swift's Contests 1701: two editions. N & Q 22 March 1947. Reply by H. Teerink, Library 5th ser 4 1949.

Craig, M. J. (ed). The legacy of Swift: a bicentenary record of St Patrick's Hospital, Dublin. Dublin 1948.

Honig, E. Notes on satire in Swift and Jonson. New Mexico Quart Rev 18 1948.

—— Dark conceit: the making of allegory. Evanston 1959.

Limouze, A. S. Vergil and the Battle of the books. PQ 27 1948.

Mackenzie, A. Another note on Gulliver's travels pt 1, ch 3. N & Q 11 Dec 1948.

Mundy, P. D. The Dryden-Swift relationship. N & Q 30 Oct 1948. For his other notes on Swift's ancestry, see 4 March, 22 July 1950, 1 Sept 1951, 16 Aug 1952, June 1954.

Wiley, A. N. Unrecorded printings of Thomas Sheridan's 'inventory' of Swift's goods at Laracor. N & Q 7 Feb, 1 May 1948.

Beckett, J. C. Swift as an ecclesiastical statesman. In Essays in British and Irish history in honour of J. E. Todd, 1949.

Bredvold, L. I. The gloom of the Tory satirists. In Pope and his contemporaries: essays presented to George Sherburn, Oxford 1949.

Clifford, J. L. Swift's Mechanical operation of the spirit. Ibid.

—— and I. Ehrenpreis. New light on Swift and his family. TLS 21 April 1966.

Elliott, R. C. Swift's 'little' Harrison. SP 46 1949.
—— Swift's Tale of a tub: an essay in problems of structure. PMLA 66 1951.
—— Gulliver as literary artist. ELH 19 1952.
—— Swift and Dr Eachard. PMLA 69 1954.
—— Gulliver's travels. In his Power of satire, Princeton 1960.

Hardy, E. The conjured spirit: Swift. 1949.

Green, D. B. Keats, Swift and Pliny the Elder. N & Q 11 Nov 1950.

Jensen, J. V. Swift og Oehlenschläger. Copenhagen 1950.

Johnson, M. O. The sin of wit: Swift as a poet. Syracuse 1950.
—— A literary chestnut: Dryden's 'Cousin Swift'. PMLA 67 1952. Replies by J. R. Moore and Johnson, 68 1953.
—— Swift's renunciation of the muse. N & Q 24 May 1952.
—— Swift and 'the greatest epitaph in history'. PMLA 68 1953.
—— The structural impact of A modest proposal. Bucknell Rev 7 1958.
—— Remote regions of man's mind: the travels of Gulliver. Univ of Kansas City Rev 27 1961.

Joost, N. Gulliver and the Free-thinker. MLN 45 1950.

Kermode, J. F. Yahoos and Houyhnhnms. N & Q 22 July 1950.

Leyburn, E. D. Certain problems of allegorical satire in Gulliver's travels. HLQ 13 1950.
—— Swift's view of the Dutch. PMLA 66 1951.
—— Swift's language trifles. HLQ 15 1952.
—— Satiric allegory: mirror of man. New Haven 1956.
—— Gulliver's clothes. Satire Newsletter 1 1964.

'Orwell, George' (E. Blair). Politics vs literature: an examination of Gulliver's travels. In his Shooting an elephant and other essays, 1950.

Starkman, M. K. Swift's satire on learning in A tale of a tub. Princeton 1950.
—— Quakers, phrenologists and Swift. JHI 20 1959.
—— Swift's rhetoric: the 'overfraught pinnace'? South Atlantic Quart 68 1969.

Tuveson, E. Swift and the world-makers. JHI 11 1950.
—— Swift: the Dean as satirist. UTQ 22 1953.

A book from Swift's library. Bodleian Lib Record 3 1951.

French, D. P. The title of A tale of a tub. N & Q 27 Oct 1951.
—— Swift and Hobbes: a neglected parallel. Boston Univ Stud in Eng 3 1957.
—— Swift, the non-jurors and Jacobitism. MLN 72 1957.
—— Swift, Temple and A digression on madness. Texas Stud in Lang & Lit 5 1963.
—— The Swift-Gulliver litigation. N & Q Feb 1964.
—— The identity of C.M.P.G.N.S.T.N.S. In Swift: tercentenary essays, ed W. Weathers and T. F. Staley, Tulsa 1967.

Hunting, R. S. Gulliver among the Brobdingnagians: a real-life incident (?). N & Q 15 Sept 1951.

Kelling, H. D. Some significant names in Gulliver's travels. SP 48 1951.
—— Gulliver's travels: a comedy of humours. UTQ 21 1952.
—— Reason and madness in A tale of a tub. PMLA 69 1954.

Kulischeck, C. L. Hudibrastic echoes in Swift. N & Q 4 Aug 1951.
—— Swift's octosyllabics and the Hudibrastic tradition. JEGP 53 1954.

Sampson, E. C. Gulliver's travels: book III. N & Q 27 Oct 1951.

Todd, W. B. Another attribution to Swift. PBSA 45 1951.

Williams, K. M. Gulliver's voyage to the Houyhnhnms. ELH 18 1951.
—— Animal rationis capax: a study of certain aspects of Swift's imagery. ELH 21 1954.
—— Swift and the age of compromise. Lawrence Kansas 1958.
—— Swift's Laputans and 'mathematica'. N & Q June 1963.
—— Restoration themes in the major satires of Swift. RES new ser 16 1965.
—— Jonathan Swift. 1968.

Brain, W. R. The illness of Swift. Irish Jnl of Medical Science Aug 1952.

Burian, O. Da Vinci and Swift. N & Q 11 Oct 1952.

Olson, R. C. Swift's use of the Philosophical transactions in section v of A tale of a tub. SP 49 1952.

Rosenheim, E. W., jr., A 'source' for the rope-dancing in Gulliver's travels. PQ 31 1952.
—— The fifth voyage of Lemuel Gulliver: a footnote. MP 60 1962.
—— Swift and the satirist's art. Chicago 1963.

Stephens, J. C. '7 penny papers of my own'. N & Q 29 March 1952. Reply by H. Williams 10 May 1952.

Block, E. A. Lemuel Gulliver: middle-class Englishman. MLN 68 1953.

Bullitt, J. M. Swift and the anatomy of satire. Cambridge Mass 1953.

Clark, P. O. A Gulliver dictionary. SP 50 1953.
—— Lapoonia, Lapland and Laputa. MLQ 19 1958.

Dearing, V. A. Swift or William Wagstaffe? Harvard Lib Bull 7 1953.

Ferguson, O. W. Swift, Tisdall and A narrative. N & Q Nov 1953.
—— The authorship of Apollo's edict. PMLA 70 1955.
—— Swift, Freeman of Dublin. MLN 71 1956.
—— Swift's sæva indignatio and A modest proposal. PQ 38 1959.
—— Swift and Ireland. Urbana 1962.
—— 'Nature and friendship': the personal letters of Swift. In The familiar letter in the eighteenth century, ed H. Anderson, P. B. Daghlian and I. Ehrenpreis, Lawrence Kansas 1966.

Preu, J. A. Swift and the common man. Florida State Univ Stud 11 1953.
—— Swift's influence on Godwin's doctrine of anarchism. JHI 15 1954.
—— The Dean and the anarchist [William Godwin]. Tallahassee 1959.
—— The case of the mysterious manuscript. Eng Jnl 52 1963. On Gulliver's travels.

Price, M. Swift's rhetorical art. New Haven 1953.
—— Swift: order and obligation. In his To the palace of wisdom, New York 1964.

Yost, G., jr. Well-filled silences: the case of Swift and Vanessa. Florida State Univ Stud 11 1953.

Baker, F. Swift and the Wesleys. London Quart 179 1954.

Brown, J. Swift as moralist. PQ 33 1954.

Clark, J. K. Swift and the Dutch. HLQ 17 1954.

Ewald, W. B. The masks of Swift. Oxford 1954.

Fiore, J. D. Swift and the American episcopate. William & Mary Quart 11 1954.

Frye, R. M. Swift's Yahoos and the Christian symbols for sin. JHI 15 1954. Reply by W. A. Murray, ibid.

Mayhew, G. P. A draft of ten lines from Swift's poem to John Gay. Bull John Rylands Lib 37 1954.
—— Swift's Anglo-Latin games and a fragment of Polite conversation in manuscript. HLQ 17 1954; rptd in his Rage or raillery, San Marino 1967.
—— Swift's games with languages in Rylands English ms 659. Bull John Rylands Lib 36 1954.
—— Swift's manuscript version of On his own deafness. HLQ 18 1954; expanded in his Rage or raillery, above.
—— Two burlesque invitations by Swift. N & Q Feb 1954.
—— Swift's first will and the first use of the provost's negative at T.C.D. HLQ 21 1958; rptd in his Rage or raillery, above.
—— A missing leaf from Swift's Holyhead journal. Bull John Rylands Lib 41 1959.
—— 'Rage or raillery': Swift's Epistle to a lady and On poetry: a rapsody. HLQ 23 1960; rptd in his Rage or raillery, above.

—— The early life of John Partridge. Stud in Eng Lit 1500–1900 1 1961.

—— Swift's notes for his The history of the four last years, book IV. HLQ 24 1961; rptd in his Rage or raillery, above.

—— Two entries of 1702–3 for Swift's Polite conversation 1738. N & Q Feb 1961.

—— Swift's hoax of 1722 upon Ebenezor Elliston. Bull John Rylands Lib 44 1962.

—— Swift's Bickerstaff hoax as an April Fool's joke. MP 61 1964.

—— Some dramatizations of Polite conversation 1738. PQ 44 1965.

—— A portrait of Swift. HLQ 29 1966.

—— Swift and the tripos tradition. PQ 45 1966.

—— The Swift mss at the Huntington Library. In his Rage or raillery, above.

—— Swift's Letter to a young lady on her marriage. Ibid.

—— Swift's 'Prefermts of Ireland' 1713–14. HLQ 30 1967.

Murry, J. M. Swift: a critical biography. 1954.

Ong, W. J. Swift on the mind: the myth of Asepsis. MLQ 15 1954.

Smith, R. M. Swift's little language and nonsense names. JEGP 53 1954. Replies by P. O. Clark and Smith 56 1957.

Aden, J. M. Dryden and Swift. N & Q June 1955.

—— Corinna and the sterner muse of Swift. Eng Lang Notes 4 1966.

—— Swift, Pope and 'the sin of wit'. PBSA 62 1968.

Elwood, J. R. Swift's 'Corinna' [Mrs E. Haywood?]. N & Q Dec 1955.

Greenacre, P. Swift and Carroll: a psychoanalytic study of two lives. New York 1955.

Herrde, D. Die Satire als Form der Gesellschaftskritik dargestellt am Werke Swifts. Leipzig 1955.

Lawlor, J. Radical satire and the realistic novel. E & S new ser 8 1955.

Monk, S. H. The pride of Lemuel Gulliver. Sewanee Rev 63 1955; rptd in Eighteenth-century English literature: modern essays in criticism, ed J. L. Clifford, New York 1959.

Morris, H. C. The dialogues of Hylas and Philonous as a source in Gulliver's travels. MLN 70 1955.

Nemser, W. Linguistic economy in Lagado. History of Ideas News Letter 1 1955.

Taylor, A. M. Cyrano de Bergerac and Gulliver's Voyage to Brobdingnag. Tulane Stud in Eng 5 1955.

—— Swift's use of the term 'canary bird'. MLN 71 1956.

—— Sights and monsters and Gulliver's Voyage to Brobdingnag. Tulane Stud in Eng 7 1957.

Baker, S. Swift, 'Lilliputian' and Catullus. N & Q Nov 1956.

Colie, R. L. Gulliver, the Locke-Stillingfleet controversy and the nature of man. History of Ideas News Letter 2 1956.

Holloway, J. The well-filled dish: an analysis of Swift's satire. Hudson Rev 9 1956.

—— Dean of St Patrick's: a view from the letters. In The world of Swift, ed B. Vickers, Oxford 1968.

Jarrell, M. L. The proverbs in Polite conversation. HLQ 20 1956.

—— Joyce's use of Polite conversation in the 'Circe' episode of Ulysses. PMLA 72 1957.

—— The handwriting of the Lilliputians. PQ 37 1958.

—— Swiftiana in Finnegans wake. ELH 26 1959.

—— A new Swift attribution: the preface to Sheridan's sermon on St Cecilia's Day. PMLA 78 1963.

—— 'Jack and the Dane': Swift traditions in Ireland. Jnl of Amer Folklore 77 1964.

—— Ode to the King: some contests, dissensions and exchanges among Swift, John Dunton and Henry Jones. Texas Stud in Lang & Lit 7 1965.

Loomis, C. G. Superstitions and beliefs in Swift. Western Folklore 15 1956. On A complete collection of genteel conversation.

Miller, H. K. The paradoxical encomium with special reference to its vogue in England 1600–1800. MP 53 1956. On A tale of a tub in the tradition of paradoxical encomia.

Quinlan, M. J. Swift's Project for the advancement of religion. PMLA 71 1956.

—— Swift and the prosecuted Nottingham speech. Harvard Lib Bull 11 1957.

—— Lemuel Gulliver's ships. PQ 46 1967.

—— The prosecution of Swift's Public spirit of the Whigs. Texas Stud in Lang & Lit 9 1967.

—— Swift's use of literalization as a rhetorical device. PMLA 82 1967.

Watt, I. and J. R. Sutherland. The ironic tradition in Augustan prose from Swift to Johnson. In Restoration and Augustan prose, Los Angeles 1956.

Woodring, C. R. The aims, audience and structure of the Drapier's fourth letter. MLQ 17 1956.

Baker, D. C. Tertullian and Swift's A modest proposal. Classical Jnl 52 1957. See J. W. Johnson, MLN 73 1958.

—— Metaphors in A tale of a tub and Middleton's The family of love. N & Q March 1958.

Barroll, J. L. Gulliver in Luggnagg: a possible source. PQ 36 1957.

—— Gulliver and the Struldbruggs. PMLA 73 1958.

Benjamin, E. B. The King of Brobdingnag and Secrets of state. JHI 18 1957.

Geering, R. G. Swift's Struldbruggs: the critics considered. Jnl of Australian Universities Lang & Lit Assoc 7 1957.

Miner, E. R. A poem by Swift and W. B. Yeats' Words upon the window-pane. MLN 72 1957.

Seronsy, C. C. Some proper names in Gulliver's travels. N & Q Nov 1957.

—— Sir Politic Would-Be in Laputa. Eng Lang Notes 1 1963.

Stedmond, J. M. Another possible analogue for Swift's Tale of a tub. MLN 72 1957.

Sutherland, J. N. A reconsideration of Gulliver's third voyage. SP 54 1957.

Ure, P. Laputans and Eleutheri: Swift and the Vindicator of the clergy. N & Q April 1957.

Adams, R. M. Swift and Kafka. In his Strains of discord, Ithaca 1958.

—— Jonathan Swift, Thomas Swift and the authorship of A tale of a tub. MP 64 1967. Reply by D. Nandy 66 1969.

Byers, J. R., jr. Another source for Gulliver's travels. JEGP 57 1958.

Canseliet, E. L'hermétisme dans la vie de Swift et dans ses Voyages. Cahiers du Sud 46 1958.

Danchin, P. Le lecteur anglais d'aujourd'hui peut-il connaître Gulliver's travels? Etudes Anglaises 11 1958.

—— The text of Gulliver's travels. Texas Stud in Lang & Lit 2 1960.

Dyson, A. E. Swift: the metamorphosis of irony. E & S new ser 11 1958; rptd in his Crazy fabric, 1965.

Jones, M. Further thoughts on religion: Swift's relation to Filmer and Locke. RES new ser 9 1958.

Manly, F. Swift's marginalia in Howell's Medulla historiae anglicanae. PMLA 73 1958.

Richer, J. Swift au pays de kabbale. Cahiers du Sud 46 1958.

Wasiolek, E. Relativity in Gulliver's travels. PQ 37 1958.

Wilson, J. R. Swift, the psalmist and the horse. Tennessee Stud in Lit 3 1958.

—— Swift's Alazon. Studia Neophilologica 30 1958.

—— Encountering vice with mirth. In His firm estate: essays in honor of F. J. Eikenberry, Tulsa 1967.

Ball, A. Swift and the animal myth. Trans of Wisconsin Acad of Sciences, Arts & Letters 48 1959.

Barker, E. Gelli's Circe and Swift. Cesare Barbieri Courier 2 1959.

Brown, N. O. The excremental vision. In his Life against death, Middletown Conn 1959.

Fussell, P., jr. Speaker and style in A letter to a young poet and the problem of attribution. RES new ser 10 1959.

— The frailty of Lemuel Gulliver. In Essays in literary history presented to J. M. French, New Brunswick 1960.

— In his Rhetorical world of Augustan humanism, Oxford 1965.

McCue, D. L., jr. A newly discovered broadsheet of Swift's Last speech of Ebenezor Elliston. Harvard Lib Bull 13 1959.

Merle, R. Les desseins de Gulliver. Revue de Paris April 1959.

— L'amère et profonde sagesse de Swift. Europe Nov 1967.

Papajewski, H. Swift and Berkeley. Anglia 77 1959.

Pinkus, P. Swift and the Ancients-Moderns controversy. UTQ 29 1959.

— A tale of a tub and the Rosy Cross. JEGP 59 1960.

— Satire and St George. Queens Quart 70 1963.

— The upside-down world of A tale of a tub. E Studies 44 1963.

— Sin and satire in Swift. Bucknell Rev 13 1965.

Powell, W. S. A Swift broadside from the opposition. Virginia Mag of History & Biography 67 1959.

Sams, H. W. Swift's satire of the second person. ELH 26 1959.

— Swift's proposal concerning the English language: a reconsideration. SP extra ser 4 1967.

Tilton, J. W. Gulliver's travels as a work of art. Bucknell Rev 8 1959.

— The two modest proposals: a dual approach to Swift's irony. Bucknell Rev 14 1966.

Beaumont, C. A. Swift's classical rhetoric in A modest proposal. Georgia Rev 14 1960.

— Swift's classical rhetoric. Athens Georgia 1961.

— Swift's use of the Bible. Athens Georgia 1965.

Dircks, R. J. Gulliver's tragic rationalism. Criticism 2 1960.

Dustin, J. E. The 1735 Dublin edition of Swift's Poems. PBSA 54 1960.

Gray, J. The modernism of Swift. Queen's Quart 67 1960.

Greenberg, R. A. A modest proposal and the Bible. MLR 54 1960.

Hart, J. The ideologue as artist: some notes on Gulliver's travels. Criticism 2 1960.

Horne, C. J. and H. Powell. A German analogue for A tale of a tub. MLR 55 1960.

Kallich, M. Three ways of looking at a horse: Swift's voyage to the Houyhnhnms again. Criticism 2 1960.

McNelis, J. (ed). Journey of Niels Klim to the world underground. Lincoln Nebraska 1960. Introd on Swift and Holberg.

O Hehir, B. Meaning in Swift's Description of a city shower. ELH 27 1960.

Paulson, R. Swift, Stella and permanence. ELH 27 1960.

— Theme and structure in Swift's Tale of a tub. New Haven 1960.

— Swift: the middleman and the Dean. In his Fictions of satire, Baltimore 1967.

Peake, C. Swift and the passions. MLR 4 1960.

— Swift's Satirical elegy on a late famous general. REL 3 1962.

Reiss, E. The importance of Swift's Glubbdubdrib episode. JEGP 59 1960.

Ricks, C. Notes on Swift and Johnson. RES new ser 11 1960.

Stavrou, C. N. Gulliver's voyage to the land of the Dubliners. South Atlantic Quart 59 1960.

— The love songs of Swift, G. B. Shaw and J. A. A. Joyce. Midwest Quart 6 1965.

Winton, C. Conversion on the road to Houyhnhnmland. Sewanee Rev 68 1960.

Woolley, D. The canon of Swift. Johnsonian News Letter June 1960.

Cook, R. I. Dryden's Absalom and Achitophel and Swift's political tracts 1710–14. HLQ 24 1961.

— The 'several ways of abusing one another': Swift's political journalism. Speech Monographs 29 1962.

— Swift as a Tory rhetorician. Texas Stud in Lang & Lit 4 1962.

— The uses of sæva indignatio: Swift's political tracts 1710–14 and his sense of audience. Stud in Eng Lit 1500–1900 2 1962.

— Swift's polemical characters. Discourse 6 1963.

— The audience of Swift's Tory tracts 1710–14. MLQ 24 1963.

— Defoe and Swift: contrasts in satire. Dalhousie Rev 43 1963.

— 'Mr Examiner' and 'Mr Review': the Tory apologetics of Swift and Defoe. HLQ 29 1966.

— Swift as a Tory pamphleteer. Seattle 1967.

Corder, J. Gulliver in England. College Eng Nov 1961.

Crane, R. S. The rationale of the fourth voyage. In Swift: Gulliver's travels, New York 1961.

— The Houyhnhnms, the Yahoos and the history of ideas. In Reason and the imagination: studies in the history of ideas 1600–1800, ed J. A. Mazzeo, New York 1962.

Goldgar, B. A. The curse of party: Swift's relations with Addison and Steele. Lincoln Nebraska 1961.

Harth, P. Swift and Anglican rationalism. Chicago 1961.

Hughes, R. E. The five fools in A tale of a tub. Lit & Psychology 11 1961.

Johnson, J. W. That neo-classical bee. JHI 22 1961.

— Swift's historical outlook. Jnl of Br Stud 4 1965.

McAleer, J. J. Gulliver at Greenwich. Eng Record 12 1961.

— Swift's Letcombe admonition to Bolingbroke. College Lang Assoc Jnl 4 1961.

Seelye, J. D. Hobbes' Leviathan and the giantism complex in the first book of Gulliver's travels. JEGP 60 1961.

Tallman, W. Swift's fool: a comment upon satire in Gulliver's travels. Dalhousie Rev 40 1961.

Traugott, J. A voyage to nowhere with Thomas More and Swift: Utopia and the voyage to the Houyhnhnms. Sewanee Rev 69 1961.

— Swift's allegory: the Yahoo and the man-of-mode. UTQ 33 1963.

— Swift our contemporary. Univ Rev (Dublin) 4 1967.

Yunck, J. A. The skeptical faith of Swift. Personalist 42 1961.

Béranger, J. Swift en 1714: position politique et sentiments personnels. Etudes Anglaises 15 1962.

Calderwood, J. L. Structural parody in Swift's Fragment. MLQ 23 1962.

Chiasson, E. J. Swift's clothes philosophy in the Tale and Hooker's concept of law. SP 59 1962.

Harlow, B. C. Houyhnhnmland: a Utopian satire: McNeese Rev 13 1962.

Hitt, R. E. Antiperfectionism as a unifying theme in Gulliver's travels. Mississippi Quart 15 1962.

Honoré, J. Charles Gildon rédacteur du British Mercury 1711–12: les attaques contre Pope, Swift et les Wits. Etudes Anglaises 15 1962.

Johnston, O. Swift and the common reader. In In defense of reading, ed R. Brower and R. Poirier, New York 1962.

Le Brocquy, S. Cadenus. Dublin 1962.

Mercier, V. In his Irish comic tradition, Oxford 1962.

— Swift and the Gaelic tradition. REL 3 1962.

— Swift's humour. In Swift: a Dublin tercentenary tribute, ed P. Edwards and R. McHugh, Dublin 1967.

Mortenson, R. A note on the revision of Gulliver's travels. Lib Chron of Univ of Pennsylvania 28 1962.

Rawson, C. J. Swift's certificate to Parnell's Posthumous works. MLR 57 1962.

—— A phrase of John Gay in Swift's Modest defence of the lady's dressing-room? RES new ser 16 1965.

—— Gulliver and the gentle reader. In Imagined worlds: essays in honour of John Butt, 1968.

Slepian, B. When Swift first employed George Faulkner. PBSA 56 1962.

—— The ironic intention of Swift's verses on his own death. RES new ser 14 1963.

—— The publication history of Faulkner's edition of Gulliver's travels. PBSA 57 1963.

—— Some forgotten anecdotes about Swift. BNYPL Jan 1964.

—— George Faulkner's Dublin journal and Swift. Lib Chron of Univ of Pennsylvania 31 1965.

Taylor, Dick, jr. Gulliver's pleasing visions: self-deception as a major theme in Gulliver's travels. Tulane Stud in Eng 12 1962.

Tracy, C. The unity of Gulliver's travels. Queen's Quart 68 1962.

Voigt, M. Swift and psychoanalytic criticism. Western Humanities Rev 16 1962.

—— Swift and the twentieth century. Detroit 1964.

Andreasen, N. J. C. Swift's satire on the occult in A tale of a tub. Texas Stud in Lang & Lit 5 1963.

Bond, R. P. Isaac Bickerstaff esq. In Restoration and eighteenth-century literature: essays in honor of A. D. McKillop, Chicago 1963.

—— John Partridge and the company of stationers. SB 16 1963.

Bruckmann, P. Gulliver cum grano salis. Satire Newsletter 1 1963.

Carnochan, W. B. The complexity of Swift: Gulliver's fourth voyage. SP 60 1963.

—— Gulliver's travels: an essay on the human understanding? MLQ 25 1964.

—— Some roles of Lemuel Gulliver. Texas Stud in Lang & Lit 5 1964.

—— Lemuel Gulliver's mirror for man. Berkeley 1968.

Carroll, J. Richardson on Pope and Swift. UTQ 33 1963.

Gilbert, J. G. The Drapier's initials. N & Q June 1963.

—— Swift, romantic and cynic moralist. Austin 1966.

Klima, S. A possible source for Swift's Struldbruggs? PQ 42 1963.

Stanzel, F. K. Gulliver's travels: Satire, Utopie, Dystopie. Die Moderne Sprachen 7 1963.

Steensma, R. C. Swift on standing armies: a possible source. N & Q June 1963.

—— Swift's apologia: Verses on the death of Dr Swift. Proc Utah Acad of Sciences, Arts & Letters 42 1965.

—— Swift's model for Lord Munodi. N & Q June 1965.

Stephens, L. A digression in praise of digressions as a classical oration: rhetorical satire in section vii of A tale of a tub. Tulane Stud in Eng 13 1963.

Torchiana, D. T. W. B. Yeats, Swift and liberty. MP 61 1963.

West, P. Swift and dry religion. Queen's Quart 70 1963.

Bloom, A. An outline of Gulliver's travels. In Ancients and Moderns: essays in honor of L. Strauss, New York 1964.

Brown, W. J. Gulliver's passage on the Dutch Amboyna. Eng Lang Notes 1 1964.

Frédérix, P. Swift le véritable Gulliver. Paris 1964.

Hopkins, R. H. The issue of anonymity and the beginning of the Steele-Swift controversy of 1713–14: a new interpretation. Eng Lang Notes 2 1964.

—— The personation of Hobbism in Swift's Tale of a tub and Mechanical operation of the spirit. PQ 45 1966.

Ohlin, P. Cadenus and Vanessa: reason and passion. Stud in Eng Lit 1500–1900 4 1964.

Pagliaro, H. E. Paradox in the aphorisms of La Rochefoucauld and some representative English followers. PMLA 79 1964.

Peterson, L. D. On the keen appetite for perpetuity of life. Eng Lang Notes 1 1964.

—— Swift's Project [for the advancement of religion]: a religious and political satire. PMLA 82 1967. See exchange with P. Harth 84 1969.

Schuster, Sister M. F. Clothes philosophy in Gulliver's travels. Amer Benedictine Rev 15 1964.

Smith, C. C. Metaphor structure in A tale of a tub. Thoth 5 1964.

Banks, L. O. Moral perspective in Gulliver's travels and Candide. Forum 4 1965.

Dennis, N. Swift: a short character. 1965.

Erickson, R. A. Situations of identity in the Memoirs of Martinus Scriblerus. MLQ 26 1965.

Halewood, W. H. Plutarch in Houyhnhnmland: a neglected source of Gulliver's fourth voyage. PQ 44 1965.

—— and M. Lynch. Houyhnhnm est animal rationale. JHI 26 1965.

—— Gulliver's travels 1 vi. ELH 33 1966.

—— Young William Temple and young Swift. College Lang Assoc Jnl 10 1966.

Meyers, J. Swift, Johnson and the Dublin MA. Amer N & Q 4 1965.

—— The sermons of Swift and Johnson. Personalist 47 1966.

Reichard, H. M. Gulliver the pretender. Papers on Eng Lang & Lit 1 1965.

—— Satiric snobbery: the Houyhnhnms' man. Satire Newsletter 4 1967.

Roscelli, W. J. A tale of a tub and the 'cavils of the sour'. JEGP 64 1965.

San Juan, E. The anti-poetry of Swift. PQ 44 1965.

Smith, R. J., jr. The 'character' of Lemuel Gulliver. Tennessee Stud in Lit 10 1965.

—— Swift's Utopias. Discourse 9 1966.

Suits, C. The role of the horses in A voyage to the Houyhnhnms. UTQ 34 1965.

Sutherland, W. O. S., jr. Satire and the use of history: Gulliver's third voyage. In his Art of the satirist: essays on the satire of Augustan England, Austin 1965.

Tyne, J. L., SJ. Gulliver's maker and gullibility. Criticism 7 1965.

Waingrow, M. Verses on the death of Dr Swift. Stud in Eng Lit 1500–1900 5 1965.

Zimansky, C. A. Gulliver, Yahoos and critics. College Eng Oct 1965.

André, R. Les instruments d'optique du doyen. Nouvelle Revue Française 14 1966.

Cruttwell, P. Swift, Miss Porter and the 'dialect of the tribe'. Shenandoah 17 1966.

Dussinger, J. A. 'Christian' vs 'Hollander': Swift's satire on the Dutch East India traders. N & Q June 1966.

E[ddy], D. D. Swift's copy of the Comoediae sex of Terence. Cornell Lib Jnl 1 1966.

England, A. B. World without order: some thoughts on the poetry of Swift. EC 16 1966.

Irwin, A. B. Swift as translator of the French of William Temple and his correspondents. Stud in Eng Lit 1500–1900 6 1966.

Levine, S. A. The design of A tale of a tub. ELH 33 1966.

McManmon, J. J. The problem of a religious interpretation of Gulliver's fourth voyage. JHI 27 1966.

Merton, R. C. The 'motionless' motion of Swift's flying island. JHI 27 1966.

Milic, L. T. Unconscious ordering in the prose of Swift. In The computer and literary style, ed J. Leed, Kent Ohio 1966.

—— A quantitative approach to the style of Swift. Hague 1967.

—— Swift and syntactical connection. In Literary English since Shakespeare, ed G. Watson, New York 1970.

Novarr, D. Swift's relation with Dryden and Gulliver's annus mirabilis. E Studies 47 1966.

Snyder, H. L. The identification of Sir James of the Peake: a corrigendum to the editions of Swift's correspondence. Books & Libraries at Univ of Kansas 4 1966.

Van Tine, J. The risks of Swiftian sanity. Univ Rev (Kansas City) 4 1966.

White, J. H. Swift's Trojan horses: 'reasoning but to err'. Eng Lang Notes 3 1966.

Whitley, E. M. Contextual analysis and Swift's little language of the Journal to Stella. In In memory of J. R. Firth, 1966.

Yeomans, W. E. The Houyhnhnm as Menippean horse. College Eng March 1966.

Arinshtein, L. M. Swift's literary reputation in Russia. Univ Rev (Dublin) 4 1967.

Asselineau, R. Satire et humour noir. Europe Nov 1967.

Barbé, S. Langue et langage dans la prose de Swift. Ibid.

Bouvier-Ajam, M. Swift et son temps. Ibid.

Buckley, M. Key to the language of the Houyhnhnms in Gulliver's travels. In Fair liberty was all his cry: a tercentenary tribute to Swift, ed A. N. Jeffares 1967.

Chateauneu, R. Nous sommes Gulliver. Europe Nov 1967.

Clarke, A. The poetry of Swift. In Swift: a Dublin tercentenary tribute, ed P. Edwards and R. McHugh, Dublin 1967.

Coudert, M. Les trois rires: Rabelais, Swift, Voltaire. Europe Nov 1967.

Dobrée, B. The jocose Dean. In Fair liberty was all his cry: a tercentenary tribute to Swift, ed A. N. Jeffares 1967.

Donoghue, D. Swift's perspective. Studies 56 1967.
— Swift: a critical introduction. Cambridge 1969.

Easthope, A. The disappearance of Gulliver: character and persona at the end of the Travels. Southern Rev (Adelaide) 2 1967.

Falle, G. Walter Scott as editor of Dryden and Swift. UTQ 36 1967.

Fluchère, H. Satire et mystification. Europe Nov 1967.

Frost, W. The irony of Swift and Gibbon: a reply to F. R. Leavis. EC 17 1967.

Gaucheron, J. Mon cousin Swift, mon copain Gulliver. Europe Nov 1967.

Goldberg, G. Y. Swift and contemporary Cork. Cork 1967.

Greene, D. On Swift's 'scatological' poems. Sewanee Rev 75 1967.

Griffith, P. M. Dr Johnson's 'diction of common life' and Swift's Directions to servants. In Swift: tercentenary essays, ed W. Weathers and T. F. Staley, Tulsa 1967.

Halsband, R. Swift and Swiftiana at Columbia. Columbia Univ Columns 16 1967.

Hamilton, D. Swift, Wagstaff and the composition of Polite conversation. HLQ 30 1967.

Hunting, R. Swift. New York 1967.

Lengeler, R. Desunt caetera: Swifts Tonnenmärchen als Fragment. Germanisch-romanische Monatsschrift new ser 48 1967.

Luce, J. V. A note on the composition of Swift's epitaph. Hermathena 104 1967.

McDowell, R. B. Swift as political thinker. In Swift: a Dublin tercentenary tribute, ed P. Edwards and R. McHugh, Dublin 1967.

McHugh, R. The woven figure: Swift's Irish context. Univ Rev (Dublin) 4 1967.

Moore, J. N. P. Swift's philanthropy. In Swift: a Dublin tercentenary tribute, ed P. Edwards and R. McHugh, Dublin 1967.

Moreau, P. L'homme-cheval. Europe Nov 1967.

Osborn, J. M. Swiftiana in the Osborn collection at Yale. Univ Rev (Dublin) 4 1967.

Passon, R. H. Legal satire in Gulliver from John Bull. Amer N & Q March 1967. See also P. Köster, Swift, Arbuthnot and the law, Feb 1969.

Pons, J. and M. Pons, Les clés du langage imaginaire dans l'oeuvre de Swift. Europe Nov 1967.

Schlösser, A. Gulliver in Houyhnhnmland. Zeitschrift für Anglistik und Amerikanistik 15 1967; also in Dublin Mag 6 1967; and as introd to Ausgewählte Werke vol 3, Berlin 1967.

Schwandt, J. A. The love of learning and the lust for the marketplace: reflections on Swift and the Grand Academy of Lagado. Discourse 10 1967.

Shipley, J. B. A note on the authorship of the Whale. RES new ser 18 1967.

Soriano, M. Comment et pourquoi les deux premières parties des voyages de Gulliver sont devenues un livre pour la jeunesse. Europe Nov 1967.

Speck, W. A. Swift's politics. Univ Rev (Dublin) 4 1967; rev as From principles to practice: Swift and party politics, in The world of Swift, ed B. Vickers, Oxford 1968.

Stathis, J. J. Diminution in the pulpit: Swift's sermon Upon the martyrdom of King Charles I. Tennessee Stud in Lit 12 1967.
— Swift and the rhetoric of the Anglican Via Media. In Rhetoric: theories for application, ed R. W. Gorrell, Champaign 1967.

Stéphane, N. Nous ne sommes pas Gulliver. Europe Nov 1967.

Strang, B. Swift and the English language: a study in principles and practice. In To honor R. Jakobson, 3 vols Hague 1967 (Janua Linguarum).

Thacker, C. Swift and Voltaire. Hermathena 104 1967.

Thomas, L. H. C. Swift in German literature. Ibid.

Walton, J. K. The unity of the Travels. Ibid.

Watson, S. Swift and Ovid: the development of meta-satire. Humanities Assoc Bull 18 1967.

Weathers, W. A technique of irony in A tale of a tub. In Swift: tercentenary essays, ed W. Weathers and T. F. Staley, Tulsa 1967.

Weedon, M. An uncancelled copy of the first collected edition of Swift's poems. Library 5th ser 22 1967.

Wolper, R. S. Swift's enlightened gulls. Stud on Voltaire & Eighteenth Century 58 1967.

Zimmerman, L. F. Lemuel Gulliver. In Swift: tercentenary essays, ed W. Weathers and T. F. Staley, Tulsa 1967.

Ahrends, G. Theorie der Dichtung und der literarischen Kritik in Swifts Battle of the books. Germanisch-romanische Monatsschrift new ser 18 1968.

Allison, A. W. Concerning Houyhnhnm reason. Sewanee Rev 76 1968.

Berrie, F. Swift et l'Ecosse. Les Langues Modernes 62 1968.

Brown, L. W. The person of quality in the eighteenth century: aspects of Swift's social satire. Dalhousie Rev 48 1968.

Davies, H. S. Irony and the English tongue. In The world of J. Swift, ed B. Vickers, Oxford 1968.

Dixsaut, J. Le sanglier du Parnasse. Les Langues Modernes 62 1968.

Fitzgerald, R. P. The allegory of Luggnagg and the Struldbruggs in Gulliver's travels. SP 65 1968.

Gilmore, T. B., jr. Swift's Modest proposal: a possible source. PQ 47 1968.

Hall, B. 'An inverted hypocrite': Swift the churchman. In The world of J. Swift, ed B. Vickers, Oxford 1968.

Hill, G. Swift: the poetry of 'reaction'. Ibid.

Horne, C. J. 'From a fable form a truth': a consideration of the fable in Swift's poetry. In Studies in the eighteenth century; papers presented at the D. N. Smith memorial seminar, Canberra 1968.

Jenkins, C. The Ford changes and the text of Gulliver's travels. PBSA 62 1968.

Korshin, P. J. The Earl of Orrery and Swift's early reputation. Harvard Lib Bull 16 1968.

Lawry, J. S. Dr Lemuel Gulliver and 'the thing which was not'. JEGP 67 1968.

Matlack, C. S. and W. F. Matlack. A statistical approach to problems of attribution: A letter of advice to a young poet. College Eng May 1968.

McKenzie, A. T. Proper words in proper places: syntax and substantive in The conduct of the Allies. Eighteenth-Century Stud 1 1968.

Munro, J. M. Book III of Gulliver's travels once more. E Studies 49 1968.

Nordon, P. L'effet de glissement dans Gulliver's travels. Les Langues Modernes 62 1968.

Probyn, C. T. The source for Swift's Fable of the bitches. N & Q June 1968.

Rafroidi, P. Swift et l'Irlande. Les Langues Modernes 62 1968.

Reichert, J. F. Plato, Swift and the Houyhnhnms. PQ 47 1968.

Rogers, P. Swift and the idea of authority. In The world of J. Swift, ed B. Vickers, Oxford 1968.

Ross, A. The social circumstances of certain remote nations. Ibid.

Savage, R. Swift's fallen city: A description of the morning. Ibid.

Smith, F. N. Dramatic elements in Swift's Journal to Stella. Eighteenth-Century Stud 1 1968.

Söderlind, J. The word Lilliput. Studia Neophilologica 40 1968.

Thomas, W. K. Satiric catharsis. Univ of Windsor Rev 3 1968. Largely on the Struldbruggs and Gulliver bk IV.

Traldi, I. D. Gulliver the 'educated fool': unity in the voyage to Laputa. Papers on Lang & Lit 4 1968.

Vickers, B. Swift and the Baconian idol. In The world of Swift, ed Vickers, Oxford 1968.

— The satiric structure of Gulliver's travels and More's Utopia. Ibid.

Warncke, W. Samuel Johnson on Swift: the life of Swift and Johnson's predecessors in Swiftean biography. Jnl of Br Stud (Hartford Conn) 7 1968.

Champion, L. S. Gulliver's voyages: the framing events as a guide to interpretation. Texas Stud in Lang & Lit 10 1969.

Graham, E. Smedley and Swift: 'further reasons for their enmity'. PQ 48 1969.

Kelsall, M. M. Iterum Houyhnhnm: Swift's sextumvirate and the horses. EC 19 1969.

New, M. Sterne and Swift: sermons and satire. MLQ 30 1969.

Potter, L. H. The text of Scott's edition of Swift. SB 22 1969.

Wood, J. O. Gulliver and the monkey of Tralee. Stud in Eng Lit 1500–1900 9 1969.

Zirker, H. Lemuel Gullivers Yahoos und Swifts Satire. Anglia 87 1969.

O. W. F.

EDWARD WARD
1667–1731

Most of Ward's works were anon or 'by the author of the London Spy'.

Bibliographies

Troyer, H. W. In his Ned Ward of Grubstreet, Cambridge Mass 1946.

Jones, C. E. Short-title check-list of works attributed to Ward. N & Q 6 April 1946.

Cameron, W. J. Bibliography of Ned Ward. N & Q July 1953.

Ward, S. H. The works of Ward. N & Q Oct 1953.

Collections

The writings of the author of the London-Spy. Vol 1, 1703, 1704 (The London-spy compleat).

Vol 2, 1703, 1704, 1706, 1709, 1717 (as A collection of the writings of Mr Edward Ward). Contains The poet's ramble after riches; Sot's paradise; Ecclesia et factio; Modern religion and ancient loyalty; A walk to Islington; The insinuating bawd; The revels of the gods; Battle without bloodshed; O raree-show, o pretty show; The cock-pit combat; A hue and cry after a man-midwife; The Dutch guards farewel; A trip to Jamaica; A trip to New-England; A frolick to horn-fair; The dancing-school; A step to stir-bitch fair; The humours of a coffee-house; The infallible predictor; The rise and fall of madam coming-sir; An elegy on White Hall (not in 1704 and 1717 edns).

Vol 3, Consisting of poems on divers subjects. 1706. Contains A journey to Hell; The wealthy shop-keeper; All men mad; Helter skelter; Honesty in distress; A satyr against wine; A poem in praise of small-beer; On the success of the Duke of Marlborough; Fortune's bounty; a protestant scourge; A musical entertainment; Bribery and simony; A dialogue between Britannia and prudence; Pinkman—prologue and epilogue; A song; A song; The libertine's choice; The religious turncoat; Upon the alteration of coin; The mad-song.

Vol 4, 1709. Contains remainders, The London Terraefilius, 1707–8, The diverting muse, 1707. Satyrical reflections on clubs, 1710, has 'vol 5' on title-page. *During 1717–18 the earlier vols of Writings were rptd with new title-pages by A. Bettesworth as Miscellanies.*

§ I

The school of politicks: or the humours of a coffee-house. 1690, 1691 (enlarged).

The poet's ramble after riches: or a night's transactions upon the road burlesqu'd. 1691, 1692, 1698, 1699, 1700, 1701, 1720, Dublin 1724.

The miracles perform'd by money. 1692.

Female policy detected: or the arts of a designing woman laid open. 1695, 1702, 1704, 1712, 1716, [1720], 1749, 1755, 1828, Baltimore 1830, Glasgow 1835. Authorship later denied by Ward.

Ecclesia et factio: a dialogue between Bow-steeple dragon and the Exchange grasshopper. 1698.

The London Spy. 18 monthly pts 1698–1700. Pts 1–2, 1700 (3rd edn).

The London-Spy compleat in eighteen-parts, by the author of the Trip to Jamaica. 1703, 1704 (enlarged), 1706 (3rd edn, as The London-Spy compleat in eighteen parts: the first volume of the author's writings), 1709, 1718, 1753 ('revis'd'); ed R. Straus 1924; ed A. L. Hayward 1927 (expurgated); ed K. Fenwick 1955.

O raree-show, o pretty-show: or the city feast. 1698.

Sot's paradise: or the humours of a Derby ale-house, with a satyr upon the ale. 1698, 1699, 1700.

A trip to Jamaica, with a true character of the people and the island, by the author of Sot's paradise. 1698 (3 edns), 1699 (3 edns), 1700, 1702; New York 1933 (facs).

The cockpit combat: or the baiting of the tiger. 1699.

The Dutch-guards farewel to England. 1699. A broadside.

A hue and cry after a man-midwife. 1699.

A frolick to the horn-fair with a walk from cuckold's point thro' Deptford and Greenwich. 1699, 1700, 1702, 1704.

The insinuating bawd and the repenting harlot. 1699, 1700, 1755, 1758.

Modern religion and ancient loyalty: a dialogue. 1699.

A trip to New-England, with a character of the country and people, both English and Indians. 1699; New York 1933 (facs).

A walk to Islington, with a description of New Tunbridge Wells and Sadler's musick-house. 1699, 1701.

The weekly comedy as it is dayly acted at most coffee houses. 10 weekly nos 10 May–12 July 1699. Re-issued, with general title and Epilogue, 1699, as The humours of a coffee-house: a comedy.

The world bewitched: a dialogue between two astrologers and the author. 1699.

The dancing school with the adventures of the Easter holydays. 1700.

The English nun: or a comical description of a nunnery. [1700].

The reformer exposing the vices of the age in several characters. 1700.

The grand mistake: or all men happy if they please. [1700?].

Labour in vain: or what signifies little or nothing. 1700.

Laugh and be fat, or an antidote against melancholy. 1700, 1733, 1741 (12th edn), 1761.

The metamorphosed beau: or the intrigues of Ludgate. 1700, 1703.

The pleasures of single life or the miseries of matrimony. [1700?], 1709.

The rambling rakes: or London libertines. 1700.

A step to the Bath, with a character of the place. 1700, 1700.

A step to stir-bitch-fair, with remarks upon the University of Cambridge. 1700.

The infallible astrologer: or Mr Silvester Partridge's prophesies. 18 weekly nos 16 Oct 1700–24 Feb 1701. Tom Brown wrote nos 1–11, Ward nos 12–18. Selections entitled A comical view of London and Westminster were rptd in A legacy for the ladies, 1705.

The wealthy shop-keeper: or the charitable citizen, a poem. 1700, 1702 (rev as The character of a covetous citizen).

Aesop at Paris: his life and letters. 1701.

Battle without bloodshed: or martial discipline buffoon'd by the city train-bands. 1701.

A collection of the writings hitherto extant of Mr Edward Ward. 1701 (13 folio works with general title), 1702 (with addns).

The revels of the gods: or a ramble thro' the heavens. 1701.

Three nights adventures or accidental intrigues. 1701.

Bribery and simony: or a satyr against the corrupt use of money. 1703.

A journey to Hell: or a visit paid to the Devil. 3 pts 1700–5; pt 1, 1700; rptd later as The infernal vision.

The rise and fall of madam coming sir. 1703.

Female dialogues: or ladies conversations, by the author of the London spy. 1704.

The secret history of the Calves-head Clubb: or the republican unmasqu'd. 1703 (3 edns), 1704, 1705, Dublin 1705, 1706 ('with large improvements'), 1707, 1709, 1713 (as The Whig's unmasked: being the secret history of the Calf's head Club), 1714, 1721; rptd in Harleian Miscellany vol 6, 1744.

All men mad: or England a great Bedlam. 1704.

The dissenting hypocrite: or occasional conformist. 1704.

Helter skelter: or the devil upon two sticks. 1704.

The libertine's choice: or the mistaken happiness of the fool in fashion. 1704, 1709.

Fair shell but a rotten kernel: or a bitter nut for a facetious monkey. 1705.

Honesty in distress, but relieved by no party. 1705, 1708 (3 edns), 1710, 1725.

Hudibras redivivus: or a burlesque poem on the times. 24 pts 1705–7, 2 vols 1707, 1708, 1710 ('with an apology and some other improvements throughout the whole; to which is added the Rambling fuddle caps: or a tavern struggle for a kiss'), 1715.

A legacy for the ladies, or characters of the women of the age, by T. Brown, with a comical view of London and Westminster: or the merry quack, in two parts; the first part by Mr Tho Brown; the second part by Mr Edw Ward. 1705.

A pacquet from Will's. In Works of Monsieur Voiture: second edition vol 2, 1705. 4 letters by Ward.

A satyr against wine, with a poem in praise of small beer. 1705.

A trip to Germany: or the poet turn'd carbineer. 1705.

The barbecue-feast: or the three pigs of Peckham, broil'd under an apple-tree. 1706.

The rambling fuddle-caps: or a tavern struggle for a kiss. 1706, 1709.

Mars stript of his armour: or the army display'd in all its true colours. 1707, 1708, 1709, [1710], 1765, 1779.

The humours of a coffee-house: a comedy. 7 nos 25 June–6 Aug 1707.

The London Terraefilius: or the satyrical reformer. 6 pts 1707–8.

The weekly comedy: or the humours of a coffee-house. 24 nos 13 Aug 1707–22 Jan 1708.

The wooden world dissected in the character of a ship of war. 1707, 1708, 1709, 1711, 1749, 1756, 1760, 1801, Chatham 1807, 1929.

The forgiving husband and adultress wife: or a seasonable present to the unhappy pair in Fenchurch-street. 1708, [1710].

Marriage-dialogues: or a poetical peep into the state of matrimony. 1708, 1709, 1710 (as Matrimony unmask'd), 2 vols 1710 (expanded as Nuptial dialogues and debates), 1723, 1737, 1759.

The modern world disrob'd: or both sexes stript of their pretended vertue. 1708, [1710] (as Adam and Eve stripped of their furbelows) (partly verse), 1714; tr German, 1720.

The satyrical works of Titus Petronius Arbiter. 3 pts 1708. Pt 3 contains That the dog of hell was a lawyer; On a wife; Concerning our choice in marriage; The rope dancer.

The wars of the elements: or a description of a sea storm. 1708, 1709, 1709, 1730.

The history of the London clubs: or the citizen's pastime. Pt 1, 1709, 1711; The second part of the London clubs, [1720?]; 2 pts 1709, 1709, 1710 (as The secret history of clubs), 1745 (enlarged to 31 clubs, as A compleat and humorous account of all the remarkable clubs and societies in the cities of London and Westminster), 1756; rptd 1896 (from original edns).

The diverting works of the famous Miguel de Cervantes. 1710. Introd by Ward.

Vulvus britannicus: or the British Hudibras, in fifteen cantos, the five parts compleat in one volume. 1710, 1710, 1711.

Wine and wisdom, or the tipling philosophers: a lyrick poem. 1710, 1710, 1719, Dublin 1751.

The life and notable adventures of that renown'd knight Don Quixote de la Mancha translated into Hudibrastic verse. 2 vols 1711–12, Edinburgh 1804.

The poetical entertainer: or tales, satyrs, dialogues etc serious and comical. 5 nos 1712.

The quack-vintners: or a satyr against bad wine. 1712.

The history of the Grand Rebellion: containing the most remarkable transactions from the beginning of the reign of King Charles I to the happy restoration. 3 vols 1713–15.

The field spy: or the walking observator. 1714.

The Hudibrastic brewer: or a preposterous union between malt and meter. 1714, 1727. Included in A collection of historical and state poems, 1717.

The mourning prophet: or faction revived by the death of Queen Anne. 1714.

The republican procession, or the tumultuous cavalcade: a merry poem. 1714, 1714 (enlarged), 1727 ('to which is added An answer by the same author'), 1730.

The Lord Whiglove's elegy, with a pious epitaph upon the late Bishop of Addlebury. 1715.

St Paul's church: or the protestant ambulators. 1716.

British wonders: or a poetical description of the several prodigies and most remarkable accidents that have happened in Britain since the death of Queen Anne. 1717, 1717.

A collection of the best English poetry, by several hands. 1717. Contains The rambling fuddle-caps; The libertine's choice; The forgiving husband and the adultress wife.

A seasonable sketch of an Oxford reformation. 1717. Tr from J. Allibone's Latin.

The Tory Quaker: or Aminadab's new vision in the fields. 1717.

The vanity of upstarts. [1717]. A poem.

The delights of the bottle: or the complete vintner; to which is added a South Sea song. 1720, 1720, 1721, 1721, 1743.

A south-sea ballad: or merry remarks upon exchange-alley bubbles. Mercurius Politicus Sept 1720.

The merry travellers, or a trip upon ten-toes, from Moor-fields up to Bromley: an humorous poem, intended as the wandering spy. Pt 1, 1721, [1722], 1723 (as The wandering spy or the merry travellers), 1724; The wandering spy: or the merry travellers, pt 2, 1722; The wandering spy: or the merry observator, 6 pts 1724.

The northern cuckold: or the garden house intrigue. 1721, 1721.

The parish gutt'lers: or the humours of a select vestry. 1722, 1732.

The dancing devils, or the roaring dragon: a dumb farce. 1724.

The amorous bugbears: or the humours of a masquerade. 1725.

The batchelor's estimate of the expenses of a married life. [1725], 1729, [1729], [1730]. By Ward?

News from Madrid: the Spanish beauty or the tragi-comical revenge. 1726.

Apollo's maggot in his cups, or the whimsical creation of a little satirical poet: a lyrick ode. 1729.

Durgen: or a plain satyr upon a pompous satirist, inscribed to those gentlemen misrepresented in the Dunciad. 1729, 1742 (as The cudgel: or a crab-tree lecture).

A fidler's fling at roguery. 1730.

To the Right Honourable Humphrey Parsons: a congratulatory poem. 1730.

Five travel scripts commonly attributed to Ward. Ed H. W. Troyer, New York 1933 (facs).

§2

The Devil's journey to London: or the visit repaid Ned W.D. 1700.

The shoemaker beyond his last: or a satyr upon scurrilous poets, especially Ned W..D. 1700.

Cibber, T. In his Lives of the poets vol 4, 1755.

Jones, S. In his Biographica dramatica vol 1 pt 2, 1812.

London in 1699: scenes from Ned Ward. GM Oct 1857.

Whibley, C. Writers of burlesque and translators. CHEL vol 9 1912; rptd as An underworld of letters, in his Literary studies, 1919.

Jackson, A. Defoe, Ward, Brown and Tutchin. N & Q 11 June 1932.

Allen, R. J. Ned Ward and the Weekly comedy. Harvard Stud 17 1935.

Matthews, W. The character-writings of Ward. Neophilologus 21 1936.

Bourne, R. The wooden world dissected. Pacific Historical Rec 14 1945.

Troyer, H. W. Ned Ward of Grubstreet: a study of sub-literary London in the eighteenth century. Cambridge Mass 1946.

Kawai, M. The scurrilous language of the London Spy. Anglica (Osaka) 5 1962.

BERNARD MANDEVILLE

1670–1733

Bibliographies

Kaye, F. B. The writings of Mandeville. JEGP 20 1921.

—— The Mandeville canon: a supplement. N & Q 3 May 1924. See also introd and appendices to his edn of Fable of the bees, 2 vols Oxford 1924.

§1

Bernardi à Mandeville de medicina oratio scholastica. Rotterdam 1685.

Disputatio philosophica de brutorum operationibus. Leyden 1689.

Some fables after the easie and familiar method of Monsieur de la Fontaine. 1703, 1704 (with addns, as Æsop dress'd: or a collection of fables writ in familiar verse); ed J. S. Shea, Los Angeles 1966 (Augustan Reprint Soc).

The pamphleteers: a satyr. 1703. Anon. Advertised in Flying Post 17 June 1703 as 'by the author of Some fables after the familiar method of Mr de la Fontaine', but not certainly by Mandeville.

Typhons, or the wars between the gods and giants: a burlesque poem in imitation of the comical Mons Scarron. 1704.

The grumbling hive: or knaves turn'd honest. 1705, 1705, 1714 (in The fable of the bees pt 1); rptd Boston 1811.

The virgin unmask'd: or female dialogues betwixt an elderly maiden lady and her niece. 1709, 1714 (as The mysteries of virginity), 1724, 1731, 1742, 1757.

Lucinda-Artesia papers [32]. Female Tatler 2 Nov 1709–31 March 1710.

A treatise of the hypochondriack and hysterick passions, vulgarly call'd the hypo in men and vapours in women. 1711, 1711, 1715, 1730 (enlarged as A treatise of the hypochondriack and hysterick diseases in three dialogues), 1730.

Wishes to a godson, with other miscellany poems. 1712.

The fable of the bees: or private vices, publick benefits. Pt 1, 1714, 1714, 1723 (much enlarged), 1724 (rev and slightly enlarged), 1725, 1728, 1729, 1732; pt 2, 1729, 1730, 1730; pts 1–2, [1734?], Edinburgh 1755, 'London 1734', Edinburgh 1772, London 1795, 1795, 1806; ed F. B. Kaye 2 vols Oxford 1924; ed I. Primer, New York 1962; tr French, 1740; German, 1761, 1818, 1957.

The mischiefs that ought justly to be apprehended from a Whig-government. 1714, [1715?] (advertised Jan 1715 as Non-resistance an useless doctrine in just reigns). Probably by Mandeville.

Free thoughts on religion, the Church and national happiness. 1720, 1721, 1723, 1729 (rev and enlarged), [1733?]; tr French, 1722; Dutch, 1723; German, 1726.

[Vindication of Fable of the bees]. London Jnl 10 Aug 1723; 1723 (with other documents), 1724 etc (in Fable, above).

A modest defence of publick stews: or an essay upon whoring as it is now practis'd in these kingdoms. 1724, 1725, 1740, 1740; tr French, 1727.

An enquiry into the causes of the frequent executions at Tyburn. 1725. Originally pbd in British Jnl Feb–April 1725; ed M. R. Zirker, Los Angeles 1964 (Augustan Reprint Soc).

Remarks upon two late presentments of the Grand-Jury of the county of Middlesex. 1729. Probably by Mandeville.

An enquiry into the origin of honour, and the usefulness of Christianity in war. 1732.

A letter to Dion [Berkeley], occasion'd by his book call'd Alciphron: or the minute philosopher. 1732; ed J. Viner, Los Angeles 1953 (Augustan Reprint Soc); ed B. Dobrée, Liverpool 1954.

The divine instinct recommended to men, translated from the French [of B. L. de Muralt by B. de Mandeville]. 1751, 1781.

§2

Controversy over Fable of the bees

Dennis, John. Vice and luxury publick mischiefs. 1724.

Fiddes, Richard. A general treatise of morality, form'd upon the principles of natural reason only. 1724.

Law, William. Remarks upon a late book entitul'd the Fable of the bees. 1724.

[Bluet, George]. An enquiry whether a general practice of virtue tends to the wealth or poverty, benefit or disadvantage of a people? 1725.

Hendley, W. A defence of the charity-schools. 1725.

Hutcheson, Francis. An inquiry into the original of our ideas of beauty and virtue. 1725.

— Reflections upon laughter, and remarks upon the Fable of the bees. 1750. Originally pbd in Dublin Jnl 5–19 Feb 1726.

Thorold, John. A short examination of the notions advanc'd in a (late) book, intitul'd the Fable of the bees. 1726.

The true meaning of the Fable of the bees. 1726.

Barnes, W. G. Charity and charity schools defended: a sermon [preached 6 March 1724]. 1727.

Chandler, Sam. Doing good recommended from the example of Christ. 1728.

Innes, Alexander. ΑΡΕΤΗ-ΛΟΓΙΑ: or an enquiry into the original of moral virtue. Westminster 1728. Only a Prefatory introduction, in a Letter to the author of the Fable of the bees, and a few notes were by Innes; the body of the book was by Archibald Campbell, who reissued it in 1733, below.

Watts, Isaac. An essay towards the encouragement of charity schools. 1728.

London Jnl 7–21 June 1729.

Berkeley, George. Alciphron: or the minute philosopher. 1732.

[Hervey, John, Baron]. Some remarks on the minute philosopher. 1732.

Campbell, Archibald. An enquiry into the original of moral virtue. 1733. See under Innes, above.

Rutherforth, T. An essay on the nature and obligations of virtue. Cambridge 1744.

[Skelton, Philip]. Deism revealed. 1749, 1751.

Brown, John. Essays on the characteristics. 1751.

Stephen, L. Mandeville's Fable of the bees. In his Essays on freethinking and plainspeaking, 1873.

— History of English thought in the eighteenth century. 2 vols 1876, 1881, 1902.

Robertson, J. M. In his Essays towards a critical method, 1889; expanded in his Pioneer humanists. 1907.

Sakmann, P. Bernard de Mandeville und die Bienenfabel-controverse. Freiburg 1897.

Wilde, N. Mandeville's place in English thought. Mind 7 1898.

Schatz, A. Bernard de Mandeville. Vierteljahrsschrift für Social-und Wirtschaftsgeschichte 1 1903.

Morize, A. L'Apologie du luxe au xviii° siècle et le mondain de Voltaire. Paris 1909.

Kaye, F. B. The influence of Mandeville. SP 19 1922.

— Mandeville on the origin of language. MLN 39 1924.

Rogers, A. K. The ethics of Mandeville. International Jnl of Ethics 36 1925.

Lamprecht, S. P. The fable of the bees. Jnl of Philosophy 23 1926.

Lecler, J. Libéralisme, économique et libre pensée au xviii° siècle: Mandeville et La fable des abeilles. Etudes 230 1930.

Gordon, W. H. An unnoted poem by Mandeville. RES 7 1931.

Anderson, P. B. Splendor out of scandal. PQ 15 1936. On Mandeville and Female Tatler.

— Innocence and artifice: Mrs Centlivre and the Female Tatler. PQ 16 1937.

— Bernard Mandeville. TLS 28 Nov 1936. New attributions.

— Cato's obscure counterpart in the British Journal 1722–5. SP 34 1937.

— Mandeville on gin. PMLA 54 1939.

Deckelmann, W. Untersuchungen zur Bienenfabel Mandevilles und zu ihrer Entstehungsgeschichte im Hinblick auf die Bienenfabelthese. Hamburg 1939.

Grégoire, F. Mandeville et la Fable des abeilles. Nancy 1947.

Maxwell, J. C. Ethics and politics in Mandeville. Philosophy 26 1951.

Alpers, P. J. Pope's To Bathurst and the Mandevillian state. ELH 25 1958.

Goretti, M. Il paradosso Mandeville. Florence 1958. On Fable of the bees.

Miner, E. R. Dr Johnson, Mandeville and 'publick benefits'. HLQ 21 1958.

Young, J. D. Mandeville: a popularizer of Hobbes. MLN 74 1959.

Jones, H. L. Holberg on Mandeville's Fable of the bees. CLA Jnl 4 1960.

Saccenti, M. Illuministi inglesi: il paradosso Mandeville. Convivium 29 1961.

Preu, J. A. Private vices—public benefits. Eng Jnl 52 1963.

Rosenberg, M. Mandeville and laissez-faire. JHI 24 1963.

Edwards, T. R. Mandeville's moral base. ELH 31 1964.

Scott-Taggart, M. J. Mandeville: cynic or fool. Philosophical Quart 16 1966.

Vichert, G. S. Some recent Mandeville attributions. PQ 45 1966.

Primer, I. A bibliographical note on Mandeville's Free thoughts. N & Q May 1969.

D. A. L.

JOSEPH ADDISON
1672–1719

Bibliographies etc

Wheeler, W. The Spectator: a digest-index. 1892, 1897 (as A concordance).

Greenough, C. N. In Selections from the writings of Addison, ed B. Wendell and C. N. Greenough, Boston [1905].

Humphreys, A. R. Steele, Addison and their periodical essays. 1959 (Br Council pamphlet).

Collections

The works of the Right Honourable Joseph Addison esq. Ed T. Tickell 4 vols 1721, Dublin 1722–3, London 1730, 1741, Birmingham 1761, 6 vols 1804, New York 1811 (omitting Spectator); ed R. Hurd 6 vols 1811, 1854–6 (Bohn); ed G. W. Greene 6 vols New York 1856, 1857, Philadelphia 1880, 3 vols New York 1859. Vol 1: Poems on several occasions (32 pieces, with Notes on some of the foregoing stories in Ovid's Metamorphoses and An essay on Virgil's Georgics); Rosamond; Cato; Poemata (8 pieces); Dialogues upon the usefulness of ancient medals. Vol 2: Remarks on several parts of Italy etc in the years 1701, 1702, 1703; The tatler, by Isaac Bickerstaff esq (62 essays, chosen from nos 20–267); The spectator (51 essays, chosen from nos 1–89). Vol 3: The spectator (181 essays, chosen from nos 90–505). Vol 4: The spectator (18 essays from nos 507–50, and 24 essays from nos 556–600, of the 1714 series); The guardian (53 essays from nos 67–167); The lover, by Marmaduke Myrtle gent (2 essays, nos 10, 39); The present state of the war and the necessity of an augmentation considered; The late tryal and conviction of Count Tariff; The Whig examiner (complete, 5 essays); The freeholder (complete, 55 essays); Of the Christian religion. The Dublin edn omits Spectator, Guardian and Freeholder. The Birmingham edn ptd by Baskerville adds Drummer and 'a complete index'. Hurd's edn adds A discourse on ancient and modern learning, critical footnotes and a lengthy index to each vol. The 1854–6 edn adds letters, new poems, trns of the Latin poems, Latin prose pieces, some official documents, 'Addisoniana' and a complete index. Greene's edn retains Hurd's notes and adds new ones; it includes 92 letters, The old Whig and the related nos of Steele's Plebeian, 6 poems from Spectator and 1 from Guardian, and reprints Swift's notes on Freeholder from Scott's edn.

Miscellaneous works, in verse and prose. 3 vols 1726, Dublin 1735, London 1736, 1746, 1753, 4 vols 1765, 3 vols 1766, 1777, 4 vols Oxford 1830; ed A. C. Guthkelch 2 vols 1914. Vols 1–2 of the 1726 edn reprint vol 1 of Tickell's edn of 1721 and add Prologue to Phaedra and Hippolitus, and Drummer; Vol 3: Dialogues upon medals, The present state of the war, and Of the Christian religion. Vol 1 of Guthkelch's edn: Poems and Poemata arranged chronologically (adding those not in Tickell), Rosamond, Cato, Drummer; Vol 2: prose pieces as in Tickell, adding the Latin works but not including the periodical essays.

Poetical works. Glasgow 1750.

Poems on several occasions. Glasgow 1751.

Poetical works. Glasgow 1760.

Poems on several occasions. Glasgow 1770.

The British poets vol 23. Edinburgh 1773.

The poets of Great Britain vol 66. Edinburgh 1778.

The works of the English poets vol 23. Ed S. Johnson 1779.

Poems on several occasions, with Cato. Paris 1780.

The poets of Great Britain vol 7. Ed R. Anderson, Edinburgh 1793.

The works of the British poets vol 10. Ed T. Park 1807; suppl, 1809.

The works of the English poets vol 9. Ed A. Chalmers 1810.

The works of the British poets vol 14. Ed E. Sanford, Philadelphia 1819.

The British poets vol 26. Chiswick 1822.

Poetical works [with Gay and Somerville]. Ed G. Gilfillan, Edinburgh 1859, 1875.

These collections are all incomplete, though they vary in their inclusions and exclusions. The best edn of Addison's poems is in Miscellaneous works, ed A. C. Guthkelch vol 1, 1914.

Dramatic works: containing Cato, Rosamond, the Drummer. Glasgow 1750.

Dramatick works, with the author's poems on several occasions. Boston 1808.

Selections from the writings of Addison. Ed B. Wendell and C. N. Greenough, Boston [1905].

Selections from the works of Addison. Ed E. B. Reed, New York 1906.

For selections from the essays, see below.

§ I

Vota oxoniensia pro serenissimis Guilhelmo rege et Maria regina nuncupata. Oxford 1689. Includes Addison's poem Inauguratio regis.

Academiae oxoniensis gratulatio pro regis Guilielmi ex Hibernia reditu. Oxford 1690. Includes Addison's Gratulatio.

Examen poeticum: being the third part of miscellany poems. Ed J. Dryden 1693, 1716. Includes Addison's poem To Mr Dryden.

Nova philosophia veteri praeferenda. In Theatri oxoniensis encaenia: sive comitia philologica 1693 celebrata, Oxford 1693; rptd in The altar of love: consisting of poems and other miscellanies, 1727; tr as An oration in defense of the new philosophy in W. Gardiner, English version of Fontenelle's Plurality of worlds, 1728, 1737, 1757, 1769, 1783.

The annual miscellany for the year 1694: being the fourth part of miscellany poems. Ed J. Dryden 1694, 1716. Includes A translation of all Virgil's fourth Georgick, except the story of Aristaeus; A song for St Cecilia's day at Oxford (rptd in Cupid's bee-hive: or the sting of love, translated from Bonefonius, by several hands, with some original poems 1721); The story of Salmacis and

Hermaphroditus, from the fourth book of Ovid's Metamorphoses [omitted from the 1716 edn, but rptd with alterations in the trn of Ovid, ed S. Garth 1717]; An account of the greatest English poets, to Mr H.S., April 3 1694.

A poem to his Majesty, presented to the Lord Keeper. 1695, 1716 (in Miscellany poems).

An essay on Virgil's Georgics. In The works of Virgil, translated by Mr Dryden, 1697 etc.

Examen poeticum duplex: sive musarum anglicanarum delectus alter. 1698. Contains unauthorized versions of 7 Latin poems by Addison: Barometri descriptio; ΠΥΓΜΑΙΟ–ΓΕΡΑΝΟΜΑΧΙΑ: sive praelium inter pygmaeos et grues commissum: Resurrectio delineata ad altare Col Magd Oxon [English trn by N. Amhurst pbd separately 1718]; Sphaeristerium; Ad medicum et poetam ingeniosum (rptd in Musarum anglicanarum analecta vol 2, Oxford 1699 as Ad D. D. Hannes, insignissimum medicum et poetam); Machinae gesticulantes: anglice A puppet-show; Ad insignissimum virum D. Tho. Burnettum, Sacrae theoriae telluris autorem.

Musarum anglicanarum analecta: sive poemata quaedam, melioris notae, seu hactenus inedita, seu sparsim edita. 2 vols Oxford 1699. Vol 2, ed Addison, contains the 7 Latin peoms ptd in 1698, above, with considerable alterations; also Pax Gulielmi auspiciis Europae reddita 1697. The dedication to vol 2 is signed by Addison. The lines Ad D. Tho. Burnettum are rptd in The sacred theory of the earth, translated from Burnet's Latin, 1719, 1722, 1726, 1727. A trn by Thomas Newcomb of these lines and of those Ad D. D. Hannes was issued by Curll in 1718 as Two poems written by Mr Addison. Trns of the Praelium inter pygmaeos et grues, the Machinae gesticulantes and Sphaeristerium had appeared in 1716 in Miscellaneous translations from Bion, Ovid, Moschus and Mr Addison. For reprints of these trns and trns of Addison's other Latin poems, see below. William Warburton, Miscellaneous translations from Roman poets, orators and historians, 1724 includes a trn of the Praelium inter pygmaeos et grues 'In imitation of Milton's style'.

Poetical miscellanies: the fifth part. Ed J. Dryden [and N. Rowe] 1704, 1716. Contains Addison's A letter from Italy, 1703; Milton's stile imitated, in a translation of a story out of the third Æneid; two stories, with notes, translated from Book II of Ovid's Metamorphoses, and nine stories, with notes, translated from Book III. The 1716 edn excludes all but Milton's stile imitated. A letter from Italy was rptd by Hills in 1709, where it is dated 1701, and was also included in A collection of the best English poetry, 1717, and in the 2nd edn of Addison's Remarks on Italy 1718; tr Latin, 1799.

The campaign: a poem to his Grace the Duke of Marlborough. 1705 (3 edns), Edinburgh 1705, 1708 (with Latin trn), 1710, 1713, 1713, Dublin 1713, 1725 etc. Also rptd in Poetical miscellanies pt 6, 1716 (2nd edn).

Remarks on several parts of Italy etc in the years 1701, 1702, 1703. 1705, 1718 (rev), Hague 1718, London 1726, 1733, 1736, 1745, 1753, Glasgow 1755, London 1761, 1767, Dublin 1773 etc; tr French, 1722.

The tender husband. 1705 etc. By Steele. Prologue by Addison.

The British enchanters: or no magick like love. 1706 etc. By George Granville. Epilogue by Addison.

The Muses Mercury. 1707. The Feb issue contains Addison's Horace ode 3, bk 3, rptd with alterations in Poetical miscellanies: the sixth part, ed N. Rowe 1709, 1716; the March issue contains the prologue and epilogue to Rosamond.

Rosamond: an opera, humbly inscrib'd to her Grace the Dutchess of Marlborough. 1707, 1707, 1713, Dublin 1743 (with Fielding's Tom Thumb), Glasgow 1746, 1751, 1758, London 1765, 1767, 1778 etc. Also rptd in Poetical miscellanies: the sixth part, 1709.

The present state of the war and the necessity of an augmentation considered. 1708.

Phaedra and Hippolitus. 1709 etc. By Edmund Smith. Prologue by Addison.

The tatler, by Isaac Bickerstaff esq. 271 nos (12 April 1709–2 Jan 1711). About 42 nos by Addison alone, 20 by Addison and Steele. For reprints and selections see under Steele, below.

The Whig examiner. 5 nos (14 Sept–12 Oct 1710). All 5 nos by Addison; rptd in The medleys for the year 1711, to which are prefixed the five Whig-examiners, 1712.

The spectator. 555 nos (1 March 1711–6 Dec 1712); nos 556–635 (18 June–20 Dec 1714); 8 vols 8° and 12° 1712–15 (vols 1–4, 1712; vols 5–7, 1713; vol 8, 1715 [vol 3, 8° and vol 4, 12° are dated 1713]); 1713–4, 1714, 1718, 1720, 1723, 1724 (16 vols), 1726, 1729, 1729, 1733, 1738–9 (12th edn) etc; ed J. Nichols 8 vols 12° 1788, 1788, 8 vols 8° 1789; ed R. Bisset 8 vols 1793–4; ed A. Chalmers 8 vols 1802 (British Essayists), 1806 etc; ed H. Morley 1868 etc; ed G. Gregory Smith 8 vols 1897–8, 1907 (EL); ed G. A. Aitken 8 vols 1898, 1905; ed D. F. Bond 5 vols Oxford 1965; tr French, 1714–26 etc; German, 1739–43, 1757; Dutch, 1720–44.

The guardian. 175 nos (12 March–1 Oct 1713). 53 nos by Addison. For reprints see under Steele, below.

Cato: a tragedy, as it is acted at the Theatre-Royal in Drury-Lane, by Mr Addison. 1713 (8 authorized edns), Dublin 1713, Hague 1713, Edinburgh 1713, London 1721 (10th edn), 1722, 1725 (11th edn), 1730, Dublin 1732, London 1733 (13th edn), 1734, 1735, Göttingen 1737, 1739, 1744, 1746 (in English miscellanies, ed J. Thompson, vol 2), Glasgow 1748, London 1750, Dublin 1750, etc; tr Italian, 1715, 1715, 1725, [1776]; French, 1713, 1749, 1767, 1789, 1789, 1814, 1815, 1871; German, 1735, 1763; Dutch, 1715, 1725, 1742; Latin, 1764, 1794.

The late tryal and conviction of Count Tariff. 1713, 1714.

The lover, by Marmaduke Myrtle gent. 40 nos (25 Feb–27 May 1714). Nos 10, 39 by Addison. For reprints see under Steele, below.

The free-holder: or political essays. 55 nos (23 Dec 1715–29 June 1716); 1 vol 1716 (12° and 8°), Dublin 1716, London 1723, 1729, 1732, 1739, 1744, 1751 etc; tr French, 1727. Entirely by Addison.

The drummer, or the haunted-house: a comedy, as it is acted at the Theatre-Royal in Drury-Lane. 1716 (anon, with brief preface by Steele), 1716 ('2nd edn'), 1722 (2nd edn, 'with a preface by Sir Richard Steele, in an epistle dedicatory to Mr Congreve, occasioned by Mr Tickell's preface to the four volumes of Mr Addison's works'), 1722 (3rd edn), Hague [1725?], Dublin 1725, London 1733 (4th edn), Dublin 1734, London 1735, Glasgow 1749, London 1751, Glasgow 1751, London 1759, 1765 etc; tr French, 1736, 1737, 1737, 1765; Dutch, nd; German, 1741, 1765; Italian, 1750.

Epilogue spoken at the Censorium on the King's birthday. In Steele's Town-talk no 4, 6 Jan 1716.

Poetical miscellanies pt 5, 1716 (2nd edn). Includes Verses written for the toasting-glasses of the Kit-Kat Club in the year 1703; Lady Manchester, by Mr Addison.

To her Royal Highness the Princess of Wales, with the tragedy of Cato, Nov 1714; To Sir Godfrey Kneller, on his picture of the King. 1716, 1716 (4th edn); rptd in Cato, 1716 etc.

Ovid's Metamorphoses translated. Ed S. Garth 1717 etc. Contains Addison's trns of 19 stories from Books 2–4, including the 12 already ptd in Dryden's Miscellanies, and notes.

A dissertation upon the most celebrated Roman poets, written originally in Latin by Joseph Addison esq, made English by Christopher Hayes. 1718 (Latin and English texts); rptd in Poems on several occasions, 1719, 1721, 1736, below.

The resurrection: a poem written by Mr Addison. 1718 (3rd edn), 1728 (6th edn). Rptd from Resurrectio delineata ad altare col Magd Oxon, with English translation by Nicholas Amhurst. This and the succeeding items were pbd by Curll; see L. Bradner, MP 35 1938.

Poems on several occasions, with a dissertation upon the Roman poets, by Mr Addison. 1719, 1719. Addison's 8 Latin poems, rptd with English trns. The translators' names are given in Miscellanies in verse and prose, 1725. The trns are rptd in Miscellanies of prose and verse, 1721 (4th edn).

The old Whig. 2 nos 19 March, 2 April 1719; 1 vol 1720 (3rd edn); ed J. Nichols 1789.

Dialogues upon the usefulness of ancient medals, especially in relation to the Latin and Greek poets. Probably written 1703–5. First pbd in Tickell's edn of Works vol 1, 1721.

Miscellanies in verse and prose, written by the Right Honourable Joseph Addison esq. 1725. Contains (1) Poems on several occasions 1724 (2nd edn), including an Ode for St Cecilia's day, and trns of Addison's 8 Latin poems by Thomas Newcomb, George Sewell and Nicholas Amhurst; (2) Serino: or the character of a fine gentleman, in which are inserted five poems written by Mr Addison [from Spectator] 1723 (2nd edn); (3) Mr Addison's Dissertation upon the most celebrated Roman poets; to which is added An essay upon Mr Addison's writings, by R. Young esq, 1721; (4) Tentamen de scriptis Addisonianis, authore R. Young.

The Christian poet: a miscellany of divine poems, all written by the late Mr Secretary Addison, with memoirs of Mr Addison's life and writings. 1728. Reprints Amhurst's trn of Addison's Resurrectio and the 5 poems from Spectator.

The evidences of the Christian religion, by the Right Honourable Joseph Addison esq; to which are added several discourses against atheism and infidelity and in defence of the Christian revelation, occasionally published by him and others. 1730, 1733, 1742, Glasgow 1745, Edinburgh 1751, London 1753, Dublin 1755, 1758, Glasgow 1759, Dublin 1761, Edinburgh 1772, London 1776, Edinburgh 1792, London 1796 [?1800], Oxford 1801, Edinburgh 1806, London 1807 ('with the notes of the learned Gabriel Seigneux de Correvon, translated by Richard Purdy'); rptd in Richard Watson, Collection of theological tracts vol 5, 1785, 1791. First pbd in Tickell's edn of Works vol 4, 1721. 12 of the addns are signed with one of the letters of the word CLIO, attributed to Addison. His version of the 23rd Psalm, first pbd in Spectator, is rptd unsigned. Edns pbd Glasgow 1745, Edinburgh 1751, Glasgow 1759, Dublin 1761, Edinburgh 1772, 1792, contain 5 additional essays not in London edns; tr French, 1757, 1772.

A discourse on antient and modern learning, by the late Right Honourable Joseph Addison esq, published from an original manuscript of Mr Addison's, prepared and corrected by himself. 1734, 1739 (9th edn).

Some portions of essays contributed to the Spectator by Mr Joseph Addison, now first printed from his ms notebook. Ed J. D. C[ampbell], Glasgow 1864 (facs). See J. D. Campbell, Addison's Spectator mss, Athenaeum 1 Nov 1890.

A fragment [on friendship] by Addison [BM Add ms 33, 441]. Ed R. P. Bond, RES 5 1929.

Selections from essays (see also under Steele, below)

Maxims, observations and reflections, moral, political and divine, by Mr Addison. [Ed C. Beckingham] 2 pts 1719, 1720; 1 vol 1737.

Notes upon the twelve books of Paradise lost, collected from the Spectator, written by Mr Addison. 1719, 1731, 1738 etc; ed E. Arber 1868, 1895; ed A. S. Cook, Boston 1892; ed H. Morley 1889 etc; tr French, 1721, 1721, 1736, 1740, 1742–3, 1748, 1755, 1765, 1778, 1805, 1810; tr German, 1740.

A collection of all the odes and hymns out of the Spectators and set to music by J. Sheels. 1741.

The beauties of the Spectators, Tatlers and Guardians, connected and digested under alphabetical heads. 2 vols 1753, 1763, Dublin 1757, 1767, London 1773, 1787, 1792 (3rd edn corrected), 1 vol Paris 1816, 1819.

Histories, fables, allegories and characters, selected from the Spectator and Guardian. 1753 (4th edn), 1765 (8th edn).

Réduction du Spectateur anglais à ce qu'il renferme de meilleur, de plus utile et de plus agréable. Ed Mlle Hubert 3 vols Amsterdam 1753.

Scelta delle più belle ed utili speculazioni inglesi dello Spettatore, Ciarlatore e Tutore, tradotte in italiano. Leghorn 1753. 74 Spectators, 15 Tatlers, one Guardian.

Short histories for the improvement of the mind, extracted chiefly from the works of the celebrated Joseph Addison esq, Sir Richard Steel and other eminent writers. 1760.

The tatler, by the Right Honourable Joseph Addison esq. Glasgow 1760, 2 vols 1777. Addison's contributions, pbd separately.

A collection from the Spectator, Tatler etc. Ed J. Warden, Newcastle 1761.

L'esprit d'Addisson: ou les beautés du Spectateur, du Babillard et du Gardien, consistant principalement dans une collection des feuilles de Mr Addisson, avec un précis de sa vie; ouvrage nouvellement traduit de l'anglais par Mr J.P.A. 3 vols Yverdon 1777.

Auszug des englischen Zuschauers, nach einer neuen Uebersetzung. 8 vols Berlin 1782–3.

The select Spectator: or a selection of moral and religious papers from the Spectator, alphabetically arranged. 2 vols 1789, Stourbridge 1789.

The papers of Joseph Addison esq in the Tatler, Spectator, Guardian and Freeholder; to which are prefixed extracts from Dr Johnson's remarks on his prose writings, with original notes. 4 vols Edinburgh 1790.

The story of Theodosius and Constantia, from the Spectator. Manchester 1793.

Les beautés du Spectateur: ou choix des morceaux les plus élégants, les plus agréables et les plus instructifs de cet ouvrage célèbre et principalement de ceux écrits par Addisson, en anglais et en français. Paris 1804.

Selections from the Spectator, Tatler, Guardian and Freeholder. Ed A. L. Barbauld 3 vols 1804 etc; ed Mrs Herbert Martin 1899, [1920].

The spectator in miniature: being a collection of the principal religious, moral, humorous, satyrical and critical essays contained in that celebrated publication. Ed F. Prevost and F. W. Blagdon 2 vols 1806, 1808, New York 1833, Exeter 1840.

The famous history of the whimsical Mr Spectator. Edinburgh [1809?]. A chap-book.

Essays on the pleasures of the imagination, originally published in the Spectator. 1813.

Beautés du Spectateur, du Babillard et du Tuteur: ou recueil des morceaux les plus intéressants, extraits de ces trois ouvrages, par G. Hamonière, en anglais et en français. 2 vols Paris 1819.

Encyclopédie morale: ou choix des essais du Spectateur, du Babillard et du Tuteur, traduits par M. L. Mézières. 2 vols Paris 1826.

A selection from the Spectator, printed for the use of Charter-House School . 1827 (2nd edn).

Select beauties of the Spectator, with a sketch of the life of Addison. By J. W. Lake, Paris 1827, 1829.

Selections from the papers of Addison in the Spectator and Guardian, for the use of young persons. Ed E. Berens 2 pts 1827–8.

The beauties of Addison. Ed A. Howard [1829?].

Addison's essays from the Spectator. 2 vols 1830.

La visione di Mirza, dall' inglese di Addison. Leghorn 1831.

Essays on taste and the pleasures of the imagination, from the Spectator. 1834.

Essais sur Milton et sur l'imagination, par Addison. Paris 1841.

Sir Roger de Coverley. Ed W. H. Wills 1850 etc.

Selections from the essays in the Spectator. Glasgow [1862].

Addison's humorous essays selected from the Spectator, with a memoir of the author. [1863].

Wisdom, wit and allegory, selected from the Spectator. Edinburgh 1864, [1870].

Addison's essays from the Spectator. [1870], 1876, [1882], 1894 (Lubbock's Hundred Books).

Essay on the imagination, from the Spectator. 1871. Arranged in 11 chs.

Addison's Sir Roger de Coverley, from the Spectator. 1872.

Selections from Addison's papers in the Spectator. Ed O. Airy 1874.

Beautés d'Addison. Ed A. de Grisy, Paris 1875.

Selections from Addison's papers contributed to the Spectator. Ed T. Arnold, Oxford 1875 etc.

Sir Roger de Coverley and other essays from the Spectator. Ed W. N. Dew 1875 etc.

Sir Roger de Coverley: papers originally published in the Spectator. Ed J. Haberton, New York 1877.

Selections from the Spectator. Ed T. Morrison 1879.

Essays. Ed J. R. Green 1880 etc.

Sir Roger de Coverley, reprinted from the Spectator. [1882].

Readings from the Spectator. [1884], [1910].

Days with Sir Roger de Coverley. 1886, [1892].

Sir Roger de Coverley and the Spectator's club. Ed H. Morley 1886 etc.

Sir Roger de Coverley, by Addison and Steele, reprinted from the Spectator. 4 pts Edinburgh 1886–8.

Sir Roger de Coverley: essays from the Spectator. Ed D. Salmon 1886.

The spectator: choice selections. Ed H. R. Haweis 1886.

The spectator: selected essays. Ed A. C. Ewald 1886.

The lover and other papers of Steele and Addison. Ed W. Lewin 1887.

Essays and tales (from the Tatler and Spectator). 1888 etc.

Sir Roger de Coverley, from the Spectator. 1889.

Addison: De Coverley papers. Ed S. Thurber, Boston 1892 etc.

Select essays. Ed S. Thurber, Boston 1892.

Selections from the Spectator. Ed K. Deighton 1892.

The Sir Roger de Coverley papers from the Spectator. New York 1892.

An essay on the pleasures of the garden. 1893. Spectator 477.

Papers on Sir Roger de Coverley from the Spectator. Ed F. E. Wilcroft 1893.

The Sir Roger de Coverley papers. Boston 1893.

Selected essays, ethical and religious, contributed to the Spectator. [1895].

Coverley papers from the Spectator. Ed K. Deighton 1896.

Sir Roger de Coverley papers. Ed D. O. S. Lowell, New York 1896.

The spectator in London: essays by Addison and Steele. 1896.

Addison's Sir Roger de Coverley. Ed J. R. and A. A. Large [1897].

Selections from the Spectator. Ed H. Evans, Dublin 1897.

Sir Roger de Coverley. New York [1897].

Sir Roger de Coverley papers. Ed A. S. Twombly, New York 1897.

Sir Roger de Coverley: papers from the Spectator. Halifax Nova Scotia [1898].

The Sir Roger de Coverley papers. Ed H. V. Abbott, Chicago 1898.

Sir Roger de Coverley. Ed Z. Gray, New York 1899 etc; rev H. Y. Moffatt, New York 1910.

The Sir Roger de Coverley papers. Ed W. H. Hudson, Boston 1899, 1907.

Sir Roger de Coverley papers. Ed L. J. Wylie, New York 1900.

The De Coverley essays. 1901.

Sir Roger de Coverley papers. Ed F. L. Bliss and M. M. Post, Boston 1902.

The Sir Roger de Coverley papers from the spectator. Ed C. E. T. Dracass, Chicago 1902.

The Sir Roger de Coverley essays from the Spectator. Ed J. W. Samuel 1902.

Addison's Sir Roger de Coverley papers from the Spectator. Ed W. Raybould [1903].

Sir Roger de Coverley: papers reprinted from the Spectator. 1903.

Sir Roger de Coverley papers. Ed C. T. Winchester, New York 1904.

Essays from Addison. Ed J. H. Fowler 1905 etc.

Selections from Addison's essays. [1905].

Selections from the De Coverley papers. Ed E. A. Arnold 1905.

Sir Roger de Coverley and other essays from the Spectator. Ed A. Symons 1905.

Sir Roger de Coverley: selected essays. 1905.

Essays of Addison. Ed R. D. Gillman [1906].

Essays: selected, with biographical introduction by H. Bennett. 1906.

Selected essays, with introduction by A. Dobson. 1906.

Sir Roger de Coverley. 1906.

Sir Roger de Coverley papers. Ed E. H. L. Turpin and C. Beare, New York 1906.

The Sir Roger de Coverley papers. Ed R. G. Watkin 1906.

The Spectator: essays I–L. Ed J. Morrison 1908.

Sir Roger de Coverley. 1908.

The Coverley papers from the Spectator. Ed O. M. Myers, Oxford 1908.

Selections from the Spectator. Ed J. H. Lobban, Cambridge 1909.

Essays from the Spectator. Ed W. H. D. Rouse 1910.

Sir Roger de Coverley papers from the Spectator. Ed J. C. Metcalf, Richmond Va 1910.

Sir Roger de Coverley. [1911].

Sir Roger de Coverley papers. Ed H. K. Underwood, New York 1911.

The De Coverley essays from the Spectator. Ed C. L. Thomson [1913].

Selections from the Tatler and the Spectator. Ed H. V. Abbott, Chicago 1914.

Sir Roger de Coverley papers from the Spectator. Ed N. E. Griffin, New York 1914.

Essays. Ed J. G. Frazer 2 vols 1915.

Sir Roger de Coverley papers. Ed H. V. Abbott, Chicago 1919.

Streatfeild, G. S. The mind of the Spectator under the editorship of Addison and Steele. 1923.

Sir Roger de Coverley papers. Ed M. E. Litchfield, Boston 1925.

Sir Roger de Coverley papers from the Spectator. Ed H. Bement, New York 1925.

The story of Sir Roger de Coverley from the Spectator. 1925.

Selected essays. Ed G. A. Sheldon 1926.

Sir Roger de Coverley: select essays from the Spectator. Ed A. D. Innes 1926.

Selections from the Tatler, the Spectator and their successors. Ed W. Graham, New York 1928.

Sir Roger de Coverley papers. Ed M. A. Weaver, Boston 1928.

Essays (selected). Ed T. O. Wedel, New York 1929.

Sir Roger de Coverley papers, from the Spectator. Ed H. G. Paul, New York 1930.

An essay on friendship. Birmingham 1932.

Sir Roger de Coverley and other papers. Ed A. Compton-Rickett 1937.

Sir Roger de Coverley. 1937.

Narrative and descriptive essays by Addison and Goldsmith. Ed V. H. Collins and H. A. Treble, Oxford 1938.

An original issue of the Spectator, together with the story of the famous English periodical and of its founders, by E. Partridge. San Francisco 1939.

The De Coverley papers from the Spectator. Ed J. C. Dent 1939.

The Coverley papers. Ed R. Wilson 1941.

Selected essays. In R. Wilson, Four essayists, 1942.

Sir Roger de Coverley papers. New York 1946.

The Coverley papers from the Spectator. Ed F. B. Pinion [1947], [1954].

Selected essays from the Tatler and the Spectator. Ed W. L. Fleischauer, Chicago 1956.

Selections from the Tatler and the Spectator. Ed R. J. Allen, New York 1957, 1969.

Critical essays from the Spectator. Ed D. F. Bond, Oxford 1970.

Doubtful Works

Praelium navale. Included in Examen poeticum duplex, 1698 and Musarum anglicanarum analecta vol 2, 1699 as by Hugh Parker. See L. Bradner, MP 35 1938.

Cursus glacialis, anglice, scating. Included in Musarum anglicanarum analecta vol 2, 1699 as by Philip Frowde; rptd by Curll with tr in Poems on several occasions, 1719. In 1720 he rptd it as Scating: a poem, by Mr Addison, with a preface by Thomas Newcomb: 'This poem, though under the name Mr Philip Frowde of Magdalen College, a pupil of Mr Addison's, was written by the late excellent Mr Addison'. See L. Bradner, MP 35 1938.

A description of the play-house in Dorset-Garden. 1706. Anon. A single folio sheet. Rptd in Poetical works of Sir C. Sedley, 1707 etc as The play-house, by J. Addison esq. See C. N. Greenough, Harvard Stud 17 1935, rptd in his Collected studies, 1940.

The thoughts of a Tory author concerning the press. 1712. Anon.

An answer to a pamphlet [by F. Atterbury] entituled An argument to prove the affections of the people of England to be the best security of government, by the author of the Freeholder. 1716.

[Preamble to the patent creating Sir Thos Parker, Baron Macclesfield]. 1716. Advertised by Curll as 'Mr Addison's Preamble to the Lord Parker's patent'.

Arguments about the alteration of triennial elections of Parliament, in a letter to a friend in the country. In Abel Boyer, The political state of Great Britain, 1716. See J. Crossley, N & Q 19 June 1852.

The Vestal: Ovid De fastis lib III, El 1. In The pleasures of coition, 1721, and Miscellanies in prose and verse, 1725.

Fragment of a tragedy, probably written by Addison. In Epistolary correspondence of Sir R. Steele, ed J. Nichols vol 1, 1809.

Letters

Letters. Ed W. Graham, Oxford 1941.

Klibansky, R. Leibniz's unknown correspondence with English scholars and men of letters. Medieval & Renaissance Stud 1 1941. 2 letters to Addison 1708.

§ 2

A table of the principal matters contained in Mr Addison's Remarks on several parts of Italy. [1705?], 1706; rptd in Somers tracts vol 1 1748, vol 12 1809. A satire.

G[ay], J[ohn]. The present state of wit. 1711; ed E. Arber in An English garner vol 6, 1877; ed D. F. Bond, Los Angeles 1947 (Augustan Reprint Soc).

A spy upon the Spectator pt 1. 1711.

The Spectator inspected: or a letter to the Spectator from an officer of the army in Flanders, touching the use of French terms, in relations from the army, occasioned by the Spectator of the 8th of Sept 1711. 1711.

[Wagstaffe, Walter]. A comment upon the history of Tom Thumb. 1711.

The British censor: a poem. 1712.

Dennis, J. Essays upon Shakespear; with some letters to the Spectator. 1712; rptd in his Original letters, 1721.

Dennis, J. Remarks upon Cato: a tragedy. 1713.

Mottoes in five volumes of the Tatler and to the two volumes of Spectators, Latin and English. 1712.

Flying-post: or the post-master. 2 May 1713. In praise of Cato.

[Gildon, C.] Cato examin'd. 1713.

The life and character of Marcus Portius Cato Uticensis, design'd for the readers of Cato: a tragedy. 1713, 1713.

Mr Addison turn'd Tory: or the scene inverted, by a gentleman of Oxford. 1713. An attack on Marlborough.

Sewell, G. Observations upon Cato: a tragedy, in a letter to ***. 1713, 1713.

— A vindication of the English stage, exemplified in the Cato of Mr Addison. 1716.

Tickell, T. The prologue to the University of Oxford [for a performance of Cato]. 1713.

The unfortunate general, together with a key or explanation of the new-play called Cato: a tragedy. [1713?].

A letter from Will Honeycomb to the Examiner, occasioned by the revival of the Spectator. 1714.

A letter to the late author the spectator, occasion'd by his paper of Monday Dec 6 1714. 1714.

des Champs, F. M. C. Caton d'Utique: tragédie. Paris 1715; tr 1716 ('to which is added A parallel betwixt this piece and the tragedy of Cato written by Mr Addison').

Grumbler 20 May 1715. Defends Cato against des Champs.

LeClerc, J. Mr Addison's travels through Italy epitomiz'd, with some remarks. 1715.

An epilogue written for the new comedy, The drummer, but not spoke. In State poems, 1716.

Huddesford, W. A congratulatory letter to Addison upon his being appointed one of his Majesty's Principal Secretaries of State. Oxford 1717.

Memoirs of the life of the Right Honourable Joseph Addison esq, with a particular account of his writings. 1719.

Walpole, R. Some reflections upon a pamphlet call'd the Old Whig. 1719.

Weekly Medley: or Gentleman's Recreation 4 July 1719.

Young, E. A letter to Mr Tickell, occasioned by the death of the Right Honourable Joseph Addison. 1719.

Cobden, E. A poem on the death of the Rt Hon J. Addison. 1720.

Dennis, J. Original letters. 2 vols 1721.

Tickell, T. The works of Addison. 4 vols 1721. Preface.

Steele, R. Dedication to Congreve. In Addison, The drummer, 1722 (2nd edn); rptd in Steele's Correspondence, ed R. Blanchard 1941.

J[acob?], G[iles]. Memoirs of the life and writings of the Right Honourable Joseph Addison esq, with his character by Sir Richard Steele, and a true copy of his last will and testament. 1724.

Young, R. Tenamten de scriptis Addisonianis. In Miscellanies in prose and verse, 1725. With trn.

Lillie, C. Original and genuine letters sent to the Tatler and Spectator, none of which have been before printed. 2 vols 1725.

Ralph, J. Remarks on the Account of the English poets. London Jnl Sept 1728.

Budgell, E. Memoirs of the family of the Boyles. 1732.

The life of J. Addison [by T. Birch and J. Lockman], extracted from the General Dictionary; to which is prefixed the Life of Dr Lancelot Addison. 1733.

The mottoes to the Spectators, Tatlers and Guardians, translated into English; to which is added the mottoes of the Freeholder. 1737.

Bodmer, J. J. Critische Abhandlung des Gedichtes J. Miltons von dem verlohrnen Paradiese; der beygefüget

ist Joseph Addisons Abhandlung von den Schönheiten in demselben Gedichte. Zürich 1740.

Biographia britannica. Vol 1, 1747; rev A. Kippis 1778 (2nd edn).

Yart, abbé. In his Idée de la poésie angloise, 8 vols Paris 1749–56.

Cibber, T. and R. Shiels. In their Lives of the poets vol 3, 1753.

Young, E. Conjectures on original composition. 1759.

Johnson, S. In his Lives of the English poets vol 5, 1781.

Blair, H. In his Lectures on rhetoric and belles lettres, 2 vols 1783. On Addison's style in Spectator.

Tyers, T. An historical essay on Mr Addison. 1783.

A catalogue of the valuable library of the late celebrated Right Hon Joseph Addison, sold at auction by Leigh and Sotheby. 27–31 May 1799.

Phillips, R. Addisoniana. 2 vols 1803.

Drake, N. Essays, biographical, critical and historical, illustrative of the Tatler, Spectator and Guardian. 3 vols 1805.

Scolari, F. Saggio di critica sul Paradiso perduto e sulle annotazioni a quello di G. Addisson. Venice 1818.

Spence, J. In his Observations, anecdotes and characters, ed S. W. Singer 1820; ed J. M. Osborn 2 vols Oxford 1966.

Ogle, N. The life of Addison. 1826.

Aikin, L. The life of Addison. 2 vols 1843.

Macaulay, T. B. The life and writings of Addison. Edinburgh Rev 78 1843.

Bates, W. Addison's Latin dissertation upon the most celebrated Roman poets. N & Q 21 April 1866.

Maschmeier, C. Addisons Beiträge zu den moralischen Wochenschriften. Rostock 1872.

Milberg, E. Die moralischen Wochenschriften des 18 Jahrhunderts. Meissen [1880].

Kawcynski, M. Studien zur Literaturgeschichte des xviii Jahrhunderts: moralische Zeitschriften. Leipzig 1880.

Beljame, A. In his Le public et les hommes de lettres en Angleterre au dix-huitième siècle 1660–1744, Paris 1881; tr 1948.

Koch, M. Über die Beziehungen der englischen Literatur zur deutschen im 18 Jahrhundert. Leipzig 1883.

Courthope, W. J. Addison. 1884 (EML).

Doble, C. E. The dedication of Addison's Greatest English poets. Academy 10 May 1884.

Vetter, T. Der Spectator als Quelle der Discurse der Maler. Frauenfeld 1887.

Hartshorne, A. Mr Addison: an unpublished note. Athenaeum 2 Nov 1889.

Axon, W. E. A. The literary history of the Drummer. 1895.

Worsfold, W. B. In his Principles of criticism, 1897.

Crawley-Boevey, A. W. The 'perverse widow'. 1898.

Winter, A. Addison als Humorist in seinem Einfluss auf Dickens Jugendwerke. Anglia 21 1899.

Duke, R. E. H. Reflections on the character and doings of the Sir Roger de Coverley of Addison. 1900.

Sander, C. Die Franzosen und ihre Literatur im Urteil der moralischen Zeitschriften Steeles und Addisons. Strasbourg 1903.

Baldwin, E. C. La Bruyère's influence upon Addison. PMLA 19 1904.

— Marivaux's place in the development of character portrayal. PMLA 27 1912.

Wood, H. Addison's connexion with Ireland. Jnl of Royal Soc, Antiquaries of Ireland 34 1905.

Legouis, E. Les deux Sir Roger de Coverley, celui de Steele et celui d'Addison. Revue Germanique 2 1906; rptd in his Dernière gerbe, Paris 1940.

Broadus, E. K. Addison's Discourse on ancient and modern learning. MLN 22 1907.

— Addison's influence on the development of interest in folk-poetry in the eighteenth century. MP 9 1910.

Reed, E. B. Some unpublished notes of Lord Macaulay. MLN 23 1908. On Cato.

Reed, E. B. Two notes on Addison. MP 6 1908. Text revisions; papers on ballads.

Lewis, L. The advertisements of the Spectator. Boston 1910.

Northup, C. S. Addison and Gay as travellers. In Studies in language and literature in honor of J. M. Hart, New York 1910.

Umbach, E. Die deutschen moralischen Wochenschriften und der Spectator von Addison und Steele. Strasbourg 1911.

Hegnauer, A. G. Der Einfluss von Addisons Cato auf die dramatische Literatur Englands und des Continents in der ersten Hälfte des 18 Jahrhunderts. Hamburg 1912.

Murray, J. R. H. Addison in Ireland: some unpublished letters. Nineteenth Century May–June 1914.

Rand, B. Berkeley and Addison. Athenaeum 6 March 1915.

Turkin-Lerch, E. Die Forderungen an das Drama und die Bühne Englands im Tatler, Spectator und Guardian. Frauenfeld 1918.

Joseph Addison 1672–1719. Athenaeum 20 June 1919.

Frazer, J. G. Sir Roger de Coverley and other literary pieces. 1920; tr French, 1922.

Göricke, W. Das Bildungsideal bei Addison und Steele. Bonn 1921.

Law, F. H. Social degeneration and the De Coverley papers. Independent 1 April 1922.

Marr, G. S. In his Periodical essayists of the 18th century, 1923.

McCutcheon, R. P. Addison and the Muses Mercury. SP 20 1923.

— Another burlesque of Addison's ballad criticism. SP 23 1926.

Neumann, J. H. Shakespearean criticism in the Tatler and the Spectator. PMLA 39 1924.

Dobrée, B. In his Essays in biography 1680–1726, Oxford 1925.

Graham, W. In his Beginnings of English literary periodicals 1665–1715, 1926.

— Addison's travel letters in the Tatler and Guardian. PQ 15 1936.

— Addison's letters to Joshua Dawson. PQ 16 1937.

Bolton, J. H. A commentary and questionnaire on the Coverley papers in Addison and Steele. 1927.

Chandler, Z. E. An analysis of the stylistic technique of Addison [et al]. Iowa City 1928.

Budde, R. Der Toleranz- und Kompromissgedanke der englischen Aufklärung in den moralischen Wochenschriften Steeles und Addisons. Marburg 1930.

Heinrich, J. Die Frauenfrage bei Steele und Addison. Leipzig 1930.

Papenheim, W. Die Charakterschilderungen im Tatler, Spectator und Guardian: ihr Verhältnis zu Theophrast, La Bruyère und den englischen Character-Writers des 17 Jahrhunderts. Leipzig 1930.

Segrè, C. Il viaggio dell' Addison in Italia. Nuova Antologia 270 1930.

Heilman, L. W. Addison's The drummer. TLS 1 Oct 1931.

Anderson, P. B. Addison's Letter from Italy. MLN 47 1932.

Gustafson, W. W. The influence of the Tatler and Spectator in Sweden. Scandinavian Stud & Notes 12 1932.

Garrison, F. H. Medicine in the Tatler, Spectator and Guardian. Bull of Inst History of Medicine 2 1934.

Michéa, R. Le Président de Brosses en Italie. Revue de Littérature Comparée 14 1934.

Zeitvogel, A. Addisons Cato. Hamm 1934.

Boyce, B. Two debits for Tom Brown, with a credit from Addison. PQ 14 1935.

Case, A. E. Pope, Addison and the Atticus lines. MP 33 1935.

Thorpe, C. D. Addison and Hutcheson on the imagination. ELH 2 1935.

— Two Augustans cross the Alps: Dennis and Addison on mountain scenery. SP 32 1935.

— Addison's theory of the imagination as perceptive response. Papers of Michigan Acad 21 1936.

— Addison and some of his predecessors on 'novelty'. PMLA 52 1937.

— Addison's contribution to criticism. In The seventeenth century: studies by R. F. Jones and others Stanford 1951.

Gelobter, H. Le Spectateur von Pierre Marivaux und die englischen moralischen Wochenschriften. Limburg 1936.

Moody, D. Johnson's translation of Addison's Battle of the cranes and pygmies. MLR 31 1936.

Peterson, H. Notes on the influence of Addison's Spectator and Marivaux's Spectateur français upon El Pensador. Hispanic Rev 4 1936.

Carritt, E. F. Addison, Kant and Wordsworth. E & S 22 1937.

Hamm, V. M. Addison and the pleasures of the imagination. MLN 52 1937.

— Antonio Conti and English aesthetics. Comparative Lit 8 1956.

Bradner, L. The composition and publication of Addison's Latin poems. MP 35 1938.

— An earlier text of Addison's Ode to Dr Hannes. MLN 53 1938.

Cardwell, G. A., jr. The influence of Addison on Charleston periodicals 1795–1860. SP 35 1938.

Shawcross, I. Addison as a social reformer. Contemporary Rev May 1938.

Hubbell, J. B. Some uncollected poems by Addison. MP 36 1939.

Saer, H. A. Notes on the use of themes taken from the Spectator in eighteenth-century French plays. Modern Languages 21 1939.

Sutherland, J. In his Background for Queen Anne, 1939.

Noack, F. E. Die bürgerlichen Züge in Addisons Cato. Berlin 1940.

Ault, N. Pope and Addison. RES 17 1941.

Atkins, S. Addison's Cato 1. i. 47–53. PQ 21 1942.

Mays, M. J. Johnson and Blair on Addison's prose style. SP 39 1942.

Morris, R. L. Addison's mixt wit. MLN 57 1942.

Aldridge, A. O. The eclecticism of Akenside's The pleasures of imagination. JHI 5 1944.

Bond, D. F. Pope's contributions to the Spectator. MLQ 5 1944.

— The first printing of the Spectator. MP 47 1950.

— The Spectator. Newberry Lib Bull 2nd ser 8 1952.

— The text of the Spectator. SB 5 1953.

— Addison in perspective. MP 54 1956.

Betz, S. A. E. The operatic criticism of the Tatler and Spectator. Musical Quart 31 1945.

Bond, R. P. The Spectator: two notes. SP 42 1945.

— The business of the Spectator. Univ of North Carolina Extension Bull 32 1953.

— New letters to the Tatler and Spectator. Austin 1959.

Kallich, M. The association of ideas and critical theory: Hobbes, Locke and Addison. ELH 12 1945.

Lewis, C. S. In Essays on the eighteenth century presented to David Nichol Smith, Oxford 1945.

Jackson, R. W. An unrecorded Tatler. TLS 7 Dec 1946.

Watson, M. R. The Spectator tradition and the development of the familiar essay. ELH 13 1946.

Freeman, P. Who was Sir Roger de Coverley? Quart Rev 285 1947. Suggests William Walsh.

Horn, R. D. Addison's Campaign and Macaulay. PMLA 63 1948.

— The early editions of Addison's Campaign. SB 3 1951.

Bloom, L. D. Addison as translator: a problem in neoclassical scholarship. SP 46 1949.

Elliott, R. C. Swift's 'little' Harrison: poet and continuator of the Tatler. SP 46 1949.

Bloom, E. A. and L. D. Addison's 'enquiry after truth': the moral assumptions of his proof for divine existence. PMLA 65 1950.

— Addison and eighteenth-century 'liberalism'. JHI 12 1951.

— Addison on 'moral habits of the mind'. JHI 21 1960.

Evans, G. B. Addison's early knowledge of Milton. JEGP 49 1950.

Halsband, R. Addison's Cato and Lady Mary Wortley Montagu. PMLA 65 1950.

Wheatley, K. E. Addison's portrait of the neo-classical critic [the Tatler no 165]. RES new ser 1 1950.

Lannering, J. Studies in the prose style of Addison. Upsala 1951.

Cooke, A. L. Addison vs Steele 1708. PMLA 68 1953.

— Addison's aristocratic wife. PMLA 72 1957.

— Addison and the Duke of Somerset. N & Q July 1957.

Turner, M. The influence of La Bruyère on the Tatler and the Spectator. MLR 48 1953.

Brown, F. A. Addison's 'imagination' and the Gesellschaft der Mahlern. MLQ 15 1954.

Crum, M. C. A manuscript of essays by Addison. Bodleian Lib Record 5 1954.

Hodgart, M. J. C. The eighth volume of the Spectator. RES new ser 5 1954.

Smithers, P. The life of Addison. Oxford 1954, 1968 (rev).

Dédéyan, C. Marivaux à l'école d'Addison et de Steele. Annales de l'Université de Paris 25 1955.

Garai, P. R. Addison and the 'fiction' of color. History of Ideas News Letter 1 1955.

Loftis, J. The London theaters in early eighteenth-century politics. HLQ 18 1955.

— In his Politics of drama in Augustan England, Oxford 1963.

Edelen, G. Joseph Glanvill, Henry More and the phantom drummer of Tedworth. Harvard Lib Bull 10 1956.

Anderson, G. L. The authorship of Cato examined 1713. PBSA 51 1957.

Kingsbury, D. G. Bilton Hall: its history and literary association. [1957].

Brown, T. J. English literary autographs xxv: Steele; Addison. Book Collector 7 1958.

Brunner, K. Addisons umfassende Interessen. Wiener Beiträge zur Englischen Philologie 66 1958. Mainly on the Remarks on Italy.

Rau, F. Texte, Ausgaben und Verfasser des Tatler und Spectator: Forschungsbericht. Germanisch-romanische Monatsschrift new ser 8 1958.

— Zur Gestalt des Tatler und Spectator: kritischer Bericht. Germanisch-romanische Monatsschrift new ser 10 1960.

Baker, D. C. Witchcraft, Addison and the Drummer. Studia Neophilologica 31 1959.

Chambers, R. D. Addison at work on the Spectator. MP 56 1959.

Humphreys, A. R. Steele, Addison and their periodical essays. 1959 (Br Council pamphlet).

Friedman, A. B. Addison's ballad papers and the reaction to metaphysical wit. Comparative Lit 12 1960.

Klotz, G. Das Werturteil des Erzählers: Formen der Bewertung der epischen Gestalten im Tatler und Spectator. Halle 1960.

Lonsdale, R. Dr Burney, John Weaver and the Spectator. BNYPL May 1960.

Tuveson, E. L. The imagination as a means of grace: Locke and the aesthetics of romanticism. Berkeley 1960.

Goldgar, B. A. The curse of party: Swift's relations with Addison and Steele. Lincoln Nebraska 1961.

Kenney, W. Addison, Johnson and the 'energetick' style. Studia Neophilologica 33 1961.

Marsh, R. Akenside and Addison: the problem of ideational debt. MP 59 1961.

Papajewski, H. Addison, Vergil und die Chevy Chase Ballade. Anglia 80 1962.

Schuch, G. Addison und die lateinischen Augusteer. Cologne 1961.

Singh, A. The argument on poetic justice: Addison versus Dennis. Indian Jnl of Eng Stud 3 1962.

Elioseff, L. A. The cultural milieu of Addison's literary criticism. Austin 1963.

Osborn, J. M. Addison's tavern companion and Pope's 'Umbra'. PQ 42 1963. On Walter Carey.

Winton, C. Addison and Steele in the English enlightenment. Trans First International Congress on Enlightenment (Geneva) 1963.

Beaty, F. L. 'Ae spark o' nature's fire'. Eng Lang Notes 1 1964.

Dust, A. I. An aspect of the Addison-Steele literary relationship. Ibid.

Wilkinson, J. Some aspects of Addison's philosophy of art. HLQ 28 1964.

Erskine-Hill, H. The medal against time: a study of Pope's Epistle to Mr Addison. Jnl of Warburg & Courtauld Inst 28 1965.

Possin, H. J. Natur und Landschaft bei Addison. Tübingen 1965.

Stephens, J. C., jr. Addison as social critic. Emory Univ Quart 21 1965.

Colombo, R. M. Lo Spectator e i giornali veneziani del settecento. Bari 1966.

Jackson, W. Addison: empiricist of the moral consciousness. PQ 45 1966.

Kelsall, M. M. The meaning of Addison's Cato. RES new ser 17 1966.

Little, F. M. Addison's Cato in the colonies. William & Mary Quart 23 1966.

Mahoney, J. L. Addison and Akenside: the impact of psychological criticism on early English romantic poetry. Br Jnl of Aesthetics 6 1966.

Campbell, H. J. Addison's 'Cartesian' passage and Nicolas Malebranche. PQ 46 1967.

— The sale catalogue of Addison's library. Eng Lang Notes 4 1967.

Françon, Marcel. Montaigne et The spectator. Bulletin de la Société des Amis de Montaigne 12 1967.

Hansen, D. A. Addison on ornament and poetic style. In Studies in criticism and aesthetics 1660–1800: essays in honor of S. H. Monk, Minneapolis 1967.

Kinsley, W. Meaning and format: Mr Spectator and his folio half-sheets. ELH 34 1967.

Battersby, J. L. Johnson and Shiels: biographers of Addison. Stud in Eng Lit 1500–1900 9 1969.

D. F. B.

SIR RICHARD STEELE

1672–1729

Bibliographies

Aitken, G. A. In his Richard Steele, 2 vols 1889. Appendix v.

Carpenter, G. R. In his Selections from the works of Steele, Boston 1897.

Collections

The Funeral and the Tender husband. 1711, 1712, Hague 1712, London 1717.

The Funeral, the Lying lover and the Tender husband. 1712.

Political writings. 1715; tr French, 1715.

Dramatick works. 1723. The 3 early comedies.

Dramatick works. [1733?], 1734, 1736, [1748?] etc. 4 comedies.

Works. Dublin 1759. The 4 comedies and The Christian hero.

Steelens Lustspiele. Tr C. H. Schmid, Leipzig 1767.

Dramatic works. Ed G. A. Aitken 1894, 1903 (Mermaid Ser). The 4 comedies and fragments of 2 plays.

The Lover, to which is added the Reader. 1715 (8° and 12°), 1718, 1723; ed J. Nichols 1789.

The Lover and Reader; to which are prefixed the Whig-examiner and a selection from the Medley. Ed J. Nichols 1789.

Town talk, the Fish pool, the Plebeian, the Old Whig, the Spinster etc. Ed J. Nichols 1789, 1790 (with addns), Dublin 1790 (pirated).

The Theatre, Steele's case with the Lord Chamberlain, the Crisis of property, with the sequel; Two Pasquins etc. Ed J. Nichols 1791, 2 vols 1791 (with slightly different notes).

The Tatler and the Guardian. 1814, Cincinnati 1860, London 1861, Edinburgh 1880.

The Lover and other papers of Steele and Addison. Ed W. Lewin 1887.

The lover and selected papers from the Englishman, Town talk, the Reader and the Spinster. Boston 1889.

Tracts and pamphlets. Ed R. Blanchard, Baltimore 1944.

Occasional verse. Ed R. Blanchard, Oxford 1952.

Steele's periodical journalism 1714–16: the Lover, the Reader, Town talk in a letter to a lady in the country, Chit-chat in a letter to a lady in the country. Ed R. Blanchard, Oxford 1959.

Selections. See also under Addison, *above.*

Extracts of remarkable passages out of Mr Steele's writings. [1714].

Recueil de quelques pièces de Mr Steele. Amsterdam 1714, 1734.

Der getreue Hofmeister, sorgfältige Vormund und neue Mentor. Frankfurt 1725.

Extracts from Steele's Crisis. 1746.

Auszug des englischen Zuschauers. 8 vols Berlin 1782–3.

History, opinions and lucubrations of Isaac Bickerstaff, from the Tatler. Ed H. R. Montgomery 1861.

Eighteenth-century essays. Ed A. Dobson 1882.

Steele: selections from the Tatler, Spectator and Guardian. Ed A. Dobson, Oxford 1885, 1896.

Sir Roger de Coverley and the Spectator's Club. Ed H. Morley 1886.

Isaac Bickerstaff, physician and astrologer: papers from Steele's Tatler. Ed H. Morley 1887.

The Tatler: selected essays. Ed E. C. Ewald 1888.

Essays and tales. Ed H. Morley 1888, 1905.

Selections from Steele's contributions to the Tatler. Ed L. E. Steele 1896.

Selections from the works of Steele. Ed G. R. Carpenter, Boston 1897.

Eighteenth-century letters. Ed R. B. Johnson 1897.

Essays. Ed L. E. Steele 1902.

Toasts, rakes and cits: being portraits of maids, men and matrons. [Ed P. B. M. Allan] 1920. From Tatler.

Letters. Ed R. B. Johnson 1927. A selection.

The Tatler. Ed L. Gibbs 1953 (EL). A selection.

Essays from the Tatler, the Spectator and the Guardian. Ed E. Chinol, Milan [1960].

§ I

For songs from the plays, verses and trns in the periodical essays, tentative attributions and poems of doubtful author-ship, lost poems, and poems wrongly attributed, see The occasional verse of Steele, *ed R. Blanchard, Oxford 1952. The minor prose works are mainly collected in her edn of* Tracts and pamphlets, *Baltimore 1944.*

The procession: a poem on her Majesty's funeral, by a gentleman of the army. 1695; rptd in Poetical miscel-lanies, 1714.

Commendatory verses on the author of the Two Arthurs and the Satyr against wit. 1700. Includes To the mirrour of British knighthood [a satire on Sir Richard Blackmore] by Steele. Rptd in Works of Mr Thomas Brown vol 4, 1711.

The Christian hero: an argument proving that no prin-ciples but those of religion are sufficient to make a great man. 1701, 1701 ('with additions'), 1710, 1711, 1711, 1712 etc; ed R. Blanchard, Oxford 1932 (with biblio-graphy); tr French, 1729.

A new collection of poems on several occasions. Ed C. Gildon 1701, 1701 (another issue as A new miscellany of original poems). Includes To Mr Congreve, occasion'd by the Way of the world. Rptd in Abel Boyer's Letters of wit, politicks and morality, 1701, and Congreve's Collected works vol 2, 1710.

The funeral, or grief à-la-mode: a comedy, as it is acted at the Theatre Royal in Drury-Lane. 1702, 1710, 1712, 1717, 1721, 1723, Dublin 1725, London 1730 (6th edn) etc; tr Italian, 1742; French, 1749.

The lying lover, or the ladies friendship: a comedy, as it is acted at the Theatre Royal by her Majesty's servants. 1704, 1712, 1717, 1723, Dublin 1725, London 1732 (5th edn) etc.

The diverting post no 2 (4 Nov 1704). Contains Steele's Imitation of the sixth ode of Horace apply'd to his Grace the Duke of Marlborough. Rptd in Oxford and Cam-bridge miscellany poems, ed E. Fenton 1708 etc.

The tender husband, or the accomplish'd fools: a comedy, as it is acted at the Theatre-Royal in Drury-Lane. 1705, 1711, 1712, 1717, 1723, Dublin 1725, London 1731 (5th edn) etc; ed C. Winton, Lincoln Nebraska 1967.

The mistake. 1706. By Vanbrugh. Prologue by Steele.

A prologue to the University of Oxford. 1706. Folio half-sheet. Rptd in Muses Mercury Sept 1707.

The Muses Mercury. 1707. Jan issue contains To a young lady who had marry'd an old man; Feb contains Song; both by Steele.

The tatler, by Isaac Bickerstaff esq. 271 nos (12 April 1709–2 Jan 1710/11), 1710 (nos 1–100 a piracy), 4 vols (8° and 12°) 1710–11, 1712, 1713, 1716, 1720 etc; ed J. Nichols 6 vols 1786, 1788, 4 vols 1789, 1797; ed R. Bisset 4 vols 1797; ed A. Chalmers 1803 (Br Essayists vols 1–5), 1806 etc; ed G. A. Aitken 4 vols 1898–9; tr French, 1724–5, 1735, 1737, 1737–8; Dutch, 1733–52; German, 1756. About 188 nos by Steele alone, 20 by Steele and Addison.

The medley. 1710–11. Part of no 23 (5 March 1711) by Steele; rptd in Tracts and pamphlets, ed R. Blanchard, Baltimore 1944.

The spectator. 555 nos (1 March 1711–6 Dec 1712), nos 556–653 (18 June–20 Dec 1714). Steele contributed 251 papers to first ser, none to second. For reprints *see* under Addison, above.

[Gildon, Charles]. A grammar of the English tongue, printed for John Brightland. 1711. Pbd Nov 1710. Contains a preface by Steele.

The distrest mother. 1712. By Ambrose Philips. Pro-logue by Steele.

The Englishman's thanks to the Duke of Marlborough. 1712.

The guardian. 175 nos (12 March–1 Oct 1713), 2 vols 1714 (8° and 12°), 1723, 1726, 1729 etc; ed J. Nichols 2 vols 1789, 1797; ed A. Chalmers 1802 (Br Essayists vols 16–18) etc; tr Dutch, 1723, 1730–1; French, 1723, 1725, 1727; German, 1749. 82 nos by Steele.

The Englishman.

The Englishman: being the sequel of the Guardian. 56 nos (6 Oct 1713–11 Feb 1714); 1714 (8° and 12°), Dublin 1713 (40 nos), London [1723?].

The Englishman: being the close of the paper so called [no 57, 15 Feb 1714]; with an epistle concerning the Whiggs, Tories and new converts. 1714 (3 edns), Dublin 1714; tr French, 1714.

The Englishman: second series. 38 nos (11 July–21 Nov 1715); 1716, 1737. Ed R. Blanchard, Oxford 1955 (complete).

Cato. 1713 (7th edn). By Addison; verses to Addison prefixed.

A letter to Sir M. W[arton] concerning occasional peers. 1713.

The importance of Dunkirk consider'd in defence of the Guardian of August the 7th. 1713 (4 edns), 1730; tr Dutch, 1714; French, 1715.

The crisis; with some seasonable remarks on the danger of a Popish successor. 1714 [pbd 19 Jan; some copies dated 1713 (Old Style)], 1714 (8°, pirated edn), Edinburgh 1714, Dublin 1714; ed H. Morley 1886 (Famous pamphlets); tr French, 1714, 1714; Dutch, 1714; German, 1714, 1716.

The French faith represented in the present state of Dunkirk. 1714.

The ladies library. 3 vols 1714, 1722 (3rd edn), 1732 etc; tr French, 1717, 1719, 1724; Dutch, 1764. Ed Steele.

A letter to a Member of Parliament concerning the bill for preventing the growth of schism. 1714, 1714, Dublin 1714, Edinburgh 1714; tr French, 1714.

The lover, written in imitation of the Tatler by Marmaduke Myrtle gent. 40 nos (25 Feb–27 May 1714).

Mr Steele's apology for himself and his writings, occasioned by his expulsion from the House of Commons. 1714.

Mr Steele's speech upon the proposal of Sir Thomas Hanmer for Speaker. 1714.

Poetical miscellanies, consisting of original poems and translations. 1714, 1727. Ed Steele.

The reader. 9 nos (22 April–10 May 1714).

The Romish ecclesiastical history of late years. 1714 (with and without cancelled leaf F8); tr French, nd. Partly by Steele.

An account of the state of the Roman-Catholick religion throughout the world, written for the use of Pope Innocent XI by Monsignor Cerri, now first translated. 1715, 1716; tr French, 1716. Partly by Steele.

A letter from the Earl of Mar to the King. 1715, Edinburgh 1715, Glasgow 1715; ed J. Nichols 1790; tr French, nd. Rptd in Somers Tracts vol 4, 1751, and at end of some copies of Englishman vol 2, 1716, 1737.

Town-talk, in a letter to a lady in the country. 9 nos (17 Dec 1715–13 Feb 1716).

The British subject's answer to the Pretender's declaration. 1716. Single-sheet folio. Also as Town-talk no 5 (13 Jan 1716). Rptd in Somers Tracts vol 4, 1751.

Chit-chat, in a letter to a lady in the country, by Humphrey Philroye. 3 nos (March 1716). 2 nos extant: no 2 (10 March), no 3 (16 March).

The tea table. 3 nos (Feb–March 1716). No known copy. The Lover, the Reader, Town-talk and Chit-chat. Ed R. Blanchard, Oxford 1959 (as Steele's periodical journalism 1714–16).

A letter to a Member etc concerning the condemn'd Lords. 1716; ed J. Nichols 1789, 1790.

Sir Richard Steele's speech for repealing of the Triennial Act and his reasons for the Septennial Bill. 1716, Dublin 1716; ed J. Nichols 1789, 1790.

Sir Richard Steele's account of Mr Desagulier's new-invented chimneys. 1716.

The Drummer [by Addison]. 1716 (with preface by Steele), 1722 (2nd edn, with preface and dedication to Congreve by Steele).

Lucius. 1717. By Mrs Manley. Prologue by Steele. Rptd, enlarged, in Theatre no 10 (2 Feb 1720).

An account of the fish pool, by Sir Richard Steele and Mr Joseph Gillmore. 1718; ed J. Nichols 1789, 1790.

The antidote, in a letter to the Free-thinker. 1719.

The antidote no 2. In a letter to the Free-thinker. 1719.

The joint and humble address of the Tories and Whiggs, concerning the intended Bill of Peerage. 1719.

A letter to the Earl of O——d concerning the bill of Peerage. 1719 (3 edns); ed J. Nichols 1789, 1790; rptd in The orphan revived: or Powell's weekly journal, 2 Jan 1720.

The plebeian, by a member of the House of Commons. 4 nos (March–April 1719), 1 vol 1719 (6th edn); ed J.

Nichols 1789, 1790; ed R. Hurd 1856 (Addison's works vol 5).

The spinster, in defence of the woollen manufactures. No 1 1719.

The crisis of property. 1720, 1720; ed J. Nichols 1791.

A nation a family, being the sequel of the crisis of property: or a plan for the improvement of the South-Sea proposal. 1720; ed J. Nichols 1791.

The state of the case between the Lord-Chamberlain and the governor of the Royal Company of Comedians. 1720, 1720; ed J. Nichols 1791.

The theatre. 1720. Includes in no 10 (2 Feb) Prologue intended for All for love reviv'd; in no 13 (13 Feb) Prologue intended for the players at Hampton Court.

The theatre, by Sir John Edgar. 28 nos (2 Jan–5 April 1720); ed J. Nichols 1791; ed J. Loftis, Oxford 1962.

A prologue to the town [by L. Welsted], with an Epilogue [by Steele]. 1721; rptd in Welsted's Works, 1787.

The conscious lovers: a comedy, as it is acted at the Theatre Royal in Drury-Lane. 1723 (3 issues), Dublin 1725 etc, London 1730, 1733 (4th edn), 1735 etc; tr Italian, 1724; French, 1736, 1778, 1784; German, 1752, 1767.

Pasquin. [1722–4]. Nos 46, 51 (9, 26 July 1723) by Steele.

The school of action, and the gentleman. Unacted fragments. Pbd by J. Nichols in Epistolary correspondence, 1809; and by G. A. Aitken in Dramatic works, 1894, 1903.

Prologue and epilogue to Rowe's Tamerlane revived. *See* R. Blanchard, PMLA 47 1932.

Letters

Correspondence. Ed R. Blanchard, Oxford 1941, 1968 (with appendix of addns).

§ 2

See also under Addison, *above.*

A comparison between the two stages. 1702; ed S. B. Wells, Princeton 1942.

Dennis, J. Remarks on a play called the Conscious lovers. 1723.

Steele and the Conscious lovers vindicated. 1723.

[Curll, E.?] Memoirs of the life and writings of Sir Richard Steele. 1731.

Biographia britannica vol 6 pt i. 1763.

F., T. C. Abrégé de la vie de Monsieur le Chevalier Richard Steele. Amsterdam 1767.

Victor, B. Original letters, dramatic pieces and poems. Vol 1, 1776.

[Dalrymple, D.] Remarks on the Tatler. GM Aug 1790.

Hazlitt, W. In his Lectures on the English comic writers, 1819.

Hunt, L. In his A book for a corner vol 2, 1849.

Thackeray, W. M. In his English humourists of the eighteenth century, 1853.

Forster, J. In his Historical and biographical essays vol 2, 1858.

Montgomery, H. R. Memoirs of the life and writings of Steele. 2 vols Edinburgh 1865.

Dilke, C. W. In his Papers of a critic, 2 vols 1875.

Dennis, J. In his Studies in English literature, 1876.

Hartmann, H. Steele als Dramatiker. Königsberg 1880.

Kawczyński, M. Studien zur Literaturgeschichte des XVIIIten Jahrhunderts: moralische Zeitschriften pt 2: über den Tatler. Leipzig 1880.

Ricken, W. Bemerkungen über Anlage und Erfolge der wichtigsten Zeitschriften Steeles und den Einfluss Addisons auf die Entwicklung derselben. Elberfeld 1884.

Dobson, A. Richard Steele. 1886.

—— The latest life of Steele. In his A paladin of philanthropy, 1899.

Aitken, G. A. Richard Steele. 2 vols 1889. Supplemented by Aitken's articles in Athenaeum 27 Dec 1890, 6 June 1891, 5 Dec 1891, 19 Nov 1892.

Hartmann, F. Thackeray's lecture on Steele. Berlin 1900.

Wendt, O. Steeles litterarische Kritik über Shakespeare im Tatler und Spectator. Rostock 1901.

Forsythe, R. S. Shadwell's contributions to She Stoops to conquer and to the Tender husband. JEGP 11 1912.

Young, M. V. Voiture and Steele. MLR 8 1913.

Greenough, C. N. The development of the Tatler, particularly in regard to news. PMLA 31 1916.

Strahan, J. A. Swift, Steele and Addison. Blackwood's Mag Oct 1920.

Hendrix, W. S. Quevedo, Guevara, Le Sage and the Tatler. MP 19 1921.

Graham, W. Some predecessors of the Tatler. JEGP 24 1925.

— Defoe's Review and Steele's Tatler: the question of influence. JEGP 33 1934.

Williams, S. T. The English sentimental drama from Steele to Cumberland. Sewanee Rev 33 1925.

Bateson, F. W. In his English comic drama 1700–50, Oxford 1929.

— The errata in the Tatler. RES 5 1929.

Blanchard, R. Steele and the status of women. SP 26 1929.

— Steele's Christian hero and the errata in the Tatler. RES 6 1930.

— Was Steele a Freemason? PMLA 63 1948.

— The songs in Steele's plays. In Pope and his contemporaries: essays presented to George Sherburn, Oxford 1949.

— Steele's Maryland story. Amer Quart 10 1958.

— Steele and the Secretary of the SPCK. In Restoration and eighteenth-century literature: essays in honor of A. D. McKillop, Chicago 1963.

[Blunden, E.] Richard Steele. TLS 29 Aug 1929; rptd in his Votive tablets, 1931.

Hazard, P. Une source anglaise de l'Abbé Prévost. MP 27 1930. The conscious lovers.

Allen, R. J. The Kit-cat Club and the theatre. RES 7 1931.

— Steele and the Molesworth family. RES 12 1936.

— Contemporary allusions in the Tatler. MLN 55 1940.

Dobrée, B. In his Variety of ways, Oxford 1932.

Connely, W. Sir Richard Steele. 1934.

Hawkes, C. P. Authors-at-arms: the soldiering of six great writers. 1934.

Sharp, R. L. Lines in the Guardian. TLS 8 March 1934.

McCoy, R. F. Hygienic recommendations of the Ladies library. Bull Inst of History of Medicine 4 1936.

Price, L. M. Inkle and Yarico album. Berkeley 1937.

Summers, M. Santon Barsisa. N & Q 3 Sept 1938.

Friedman, A. Goldsmith and Steele's Englishman. MLN 55 1940.

Luce, A. A. Berkeley's essays in the Guardian. Mind 52 1943.

Smith, J. H. Tony Lumpkin and the country booby type in antecedent English comedy. PMLA 58 1943. The tender husband.

Horne, C. J. Notes on Steele and the Beef-steak club. RES 21 1945.

Jackson, R. W. An unrecorded Tatler. TLS 7 Dec 1946.

The theatre (1720), by 'Sir John Falstaffe'. Ed J. Loftis, Los Angeles 1948 (Augustan Reprint Soc). Nos 16–18, 20–6, a continuation of the 15 nos of Anti-theatre, also by 'Sir John Falstaffe', written in opposition to Steele's periodical Theatre.

Aubin, R. A. Behind Steele's satire on undertakers. PMLA 64 1949.

Loftis, J. Steele, Drury Lane and the Tories. MLQ 10 1949.

— 'Sir John Falstaffe's' Theatre. JEGP 48 1949. See 53 1954.

— The genesis of Steele's The conscious lovers. In Essays critical and historical dedicated to L. B. Campbell, Berkeley 1950.

— Steele's Censorium. HLQ 14 1950.

— The Blenheim papers and Steele's journalism 1715–18. PMLA 66 1951.

— Steele at Drury Lane. Berkeley 1952.

Moore, J. R. Steele's unassigned tract against the Earl of Oxford. PQ 28 1949.

— Defoe, Steele and the demolition of Dunkirk. HLQ 13 1950.

— Gildon's attack on Steele and Defoe in The battle of the authors. PMLA 66 1951.

Baine, R. M. The publication of Steele's Conscious lovers. SB 2 1950.

Fineman, D. A. The motivation of Pope's Guardian 40. MLN 67 1952.

Stephens, J. C., jr. Steele and the Bishop of St Asaph's Preface. PMLA 67 1952.

— [Allusions in Guardian]. N & Q June 1956.

Foxon, D. F. A piracy of Steele's The lying lover. Library 5th ser 10 1955.

White, R. B., jr. The Hepburn Tatler, Edinburgh 1711. N & Q Aug 1955.

— A 'new' continuation of the Tatler. N & Q March 1956.

— Character of the Tatler. PQ 45 1966. On dating of a sheet with this title, 1709.

Achurch, R. W. Steele: gazetteer and Bickerstaff. In Studies in the early English periodical, ed R. P. Bond, Chapel Hill 1957.

Winton, C. Steele, the Junto and the Tatler no 4. MLN 72 1957.

— Steele and the fall of Harley in 1714. PQ 37 1958.

— Steele, Mrs Manley and John Lacy. PQ 42 1963.

— Captain Steele: the early career of Steele. Baltimore 1964; The later career, Baltimore 1970.

Furlong, E. J. How much of Steele's Guardian no 39 did Berkeley write? Hermathena 89 1957.

Ellis, W. D., jr. Thomas D'Urfey, the Pope-Philips quarrel and the Shepherd's week. PMLA 74 1959.

Parnell, P. E. A new Molière source for Steele's The tender husband. N & Q June 1959. On L'avare.

— A source for the duel scene in the Conscious lovers. N & Q Jan 1962. On Cibber's Woman's wit.

Scheurweghs, G. Brightland's or Steele's Grammar. E Studies 40 1959.

Kaufman, P. Establishing Berkeley's authorship of Guardian papers. PBSA 54 1960.

Mayhew, G. P. The early life of John Partridge. Stud in Eng Lit 1500–1900 1 1961.

Grotegut, E. K. Bodmer contra Gellert. MLQ 23 1962. Inkle and Yarico.

Todd, W. B. Early editions of the Tatler. SB 15 1962.

Bond, D. F. Armand de la Chapelle and the first French version of the Tatler. In Restoration and eighteenth-century literature: essays in honor of A. D. McKillop, Chicago 1963.

Bond, R. P. Isaac Bickerstaff esq. Ibid.

— The pirate and the Tatler. Library 5th ser 18 1963.

— Mr Bickerstaff and Mr Wortley. In Classical, mediaeval and Renaissance studies in honor of B. L. Ullman, Rome 1964.

— and M. N. Bond. The Tatler and the Spectator and the development of the early periodic press in England: a checklist of the collection of Richmond P. Bond and Marjorie N. Bond. Chapel Hill 1965.

Hopkins, R. H. The issue of anonymity and the beginning of the Steele-Swift controversy of 1713–14: a new interpretation. Eng Lang Notes 2 1964.

— A further note on Steele's authorship of the dedication to Bickerstaff's Almanack 1709. N & Q Dec 1965.

Dixon, P. Pope and Steele. Ibid.

Honoré, J. Charles Gildon et la grammaire de Brightland. Etudes Anglaises 18 1965.

Kenny, S. S. Two scenes by Addison in Steele's Tender husband. SB 19 1966.
— Eighteenth-century editions of Steele's Conscious lovers. SB 21 1968.
Bloom, E. A. and L. D. Steele in 1719: additions to the canon. HLQ 31 1968.
Green, E. M. Three aspects of Steele's theory of comedy. Educational Theatre Jnl 20 1968.
Kline, R. B. Tory Prior and Whig Steele: a measure of respect? Stud in Eng Lit 1500–1900 9 1969.
Snyder, H. L. The identity of Monoculus in the Tatler. PQ 48 1969.

D. F. B.

HENRY ST JOHN, VISCOUNT BOLINGBROKE
1678–1751

Bibliographies

Lettres historiques. 3 vols Paris 1808. Contains a Catalogue raisonné and details of French trns.
Barber, G. Some uncollected authors 41: Bolingbroke. Book Collector 14 1965.

Collections

Works. Ed D. Mallet 5 vols 1754, 1777, 11 vols 1786 ('ghost' edn?), 5 vols Dublin 1793, 8 vols 1809, 4 vols Philadelphia 1841, London 1844 (re-issue of preceding with new title-page; rptd 1967). The 1754 edn omits many items below, but prints for the first time: Letters to Mr de Pouilly; A letter occasioned by one of Archbishop Tillotson's sermons; Letters or essays addressed to Pope.
Philosophical works. 5 vols 1754.
Miscellaneous works. 4 vols Edinburgh 1768, 1773.
Pensées. Amsterdam 1771.
Beauties of Hume and Bolingbroke. 1782, 1782.
Extracts from the political writings. 1897.

§ 1

A letter to the Examiner. 1710, 1710 (both anon), Edinburgh 1710; rptd in Somers tracts, ed W. Scott vol 13, 1815, and in J. Swift, The examiner, ed H. J. Davis, Oxford 1940.
Examiner 3 Aug 1710–26 July 1714. Contributions by Bolingbroke.
Considerations upon the Secret history of the White Staff. [1714]. Anon; sometimes attributed to Bolingbroke.
A copy of my Lord Bolingbroke's letter to my Lord —, Dover, March 27 1715. 1715, 1715 (as A true copy of a letter from Dover), Edinburgh [1715] (as A letter of my Lord Bollingbrokes to his friend at London); rptd in Somers tracts, ed W. Scott vol 13, 1815.
The representation of the Lord Viscount Bolingbroke. 1715, 1715.
The craftsman, by Caleb Danvers. 5 Dec 1726–c. 1747.
The occasional writer. 1727, 1727 (both anon), Edinburgh 1727.
The occasional writer no 2. 1727, 1727 (both anon), Edinburgh 1727.
The occasional writer no 3. 1727.
Observations on the public affairs of Great-Britain, in a letter from W. Raleigh to Caleb D'Anvers. 1729 (2nd edn). Anon; sometimes attributed to Bolingbroke.
The craftsman extraordinary: containing an answer to the Defence of the Enquiry into the reasons of the conduct of Great Britain, in a letter to the Craftsman by John Trot, yeoman, publish'd by Caleb D'Anvers esq. 1729.
A letter to Caleb D'Anvers esq concerning the state of affairs in Europe as published in the Craftsman, January 4 1728–9, by John Trott, yeoman. 1730, Anon; rptd from Craftsman, above.
The case of Dunkirk faithfully stated and impartially considered, by a member of the House of Commons. 1730 (3 edns). Anon.
The monumental inscription on the column at Blenheim-House. 1731. Anon; first pbd in Craftsman, above.
A final answer to the Remarks on the Craftsman's vindication. 1731 (anon), 1731 (8th edn); tr French, 1731.
The freeholder's political catechism. 1733 (anon), Dublin 1733, [place?] 1757, New London 1769, London 1774. Rptd from Craftsman, above.
The craftsman extraordinary: or the late dissertation on parties continued. 1733. Anon; rptd from Craftsman, above.
The craftsman extraordinary. 30 June 1734. No known copy: attributed to Bolingbroke in Mémoires du Maréchal de Berwick, Paris 1737.
A dissertation on parties, in several letters to Caleb D'Anvers. 1735, 1735 (so-called 2nd and 3rd edns, anon), Dublin 1735, London 1739 (5th edn), 1743, 1749, Dublin 1749 ('10th' edn), London 1754 (8th edn), 1771, 1775, 1786. Rptd from Craftsman.
The famous dedication to the pamphlet entitled A dissertation upon parties. [1735] (anon); tr French, 1739.
Letters to a young nobleman on the study and use of history. 1738. Priv ptd by Pope at Bolingbroke's direction; unique copy in Harvard Library.
The idea of a patriot king. [c. 1740?], [c. 1740?] (both anon); tr French, 1790; tr German, 1765, 1922; rptd in Letters on the spirit of patriotism, below. On the relation between the 3 known copies, see G. Barber, Library 5th ser 19 1964.
Remarks on the history of England from the minutes of Humphrey Oldcastle esq. 1743, Dublin 1743, London 1747, Dublin 1752, London 1754, [1780?], Basle 1794, 1795; tr Italian, 1814. Rptd from Craftsman, above. On the printing of first edn see H. J. Davis, Book Collector 2 1953.
A collection of political tracts. 1748, 1748 (both anon), Dublin 1748, London 1769, 1775, 1788. Contains Occasional writers; Craftsman (nos 16, 29, 131, 154, 324–6, 371, 375, 406, 430); Remarks on a late pamphlet intitled Observations on the conduct of Great Britain; An answer to the Defence of the inquiry [i.e. Craftsman extraordinary]; Freeholder's political catechism; Case of Dunkirk consider'd; A final answer to the Remarks on the Craftsman's vindication.
Good Queen Anne vindicated, by the author of the Dissertation upon parties. 1748. Sometimes attributed to Bolingbroke.
Letters on the spirit of patriotism; on the idea of a patriot king; and on the state of the parties at the accession of King George the First. 1749 (anon), Dublin 1749, Philadelphia 1749, London 1750, 1752, 1767 ('new edition'), 1775, 1783, 1831; ed A. Hassall, Oxford 1917, 1926; tr French, 1750, 1750, 1790; tr German, 1765, 1922.
The last will and testament of the late Right Honourable Henry St John, Lord Viscount Bolingbroke. 1752, Dublin 1752.
Letters on the study and use of history. Ed D. Mallet 2 vols 1752, 1 vol 1752 ('corrected'), 2 vols Dublin [1752], 1 vol 1770, Edinburgh 1777, 1779, Basle 1788, London 1791, 1792, Paris 1808, London 1870, [1881], 1889?, 1932 (Letters 6–8 only); tr French 2 vols 1752, 1752 (with 2 suppl vols containing Reflexions sur l'exil and Lettre de mylord Bolingbroke à mylord Bathurst), 1752, 1753, 1753, 1754, 1755; tr German, 1758, 1774, 1779, 1794; tr Italian, 1770, 1803.
Reflections concerning innate moral principles, written in French by the late Lord Bolingbroke and translated into English. 1752. Advertisement attributes to Bolingbroke.
A letter to Sir William Windham 11: A letter to Mr Pope. 1753, 1753, Dublin 1753, London 1787, 1889; tr French, 1754, 1754, 1754, 1754, 1754, 1755, 1756, 1766, 1784 (for 1754?).
A tract of the late Viscount Bolingbroke, illustrated with

notes and adapted to the present times, with an appendix containing some remarks on the conduct of a late court-martial. [1759?]. Rptd from Craftsman no 371 in connection with death of Admiral Byng.

Letters

There is no complete edn of the correspondence; in addition to those noted below, letters also appear in the pbd correspondence of others.

Letters of Lord Bolingbroke to Dr Jonathan Swift DSPD. Glasgow 1752.

Letters and correspondence, public and private, of Viscount Bolingbroke during the time he was Secretary of State to Queen Anne. Ed G. Parke 2 vols 1798 (4°), 4 vols 1798 (8°).

Lettres historiques, politiques, philosophiques et particulières de lord vicomte Bolingbroke depuis 1710 jusqu'en 1736. 3 vols Paris 1808. Includes a Catalogue raisonné, bibliographical notes on French trns and letters to Alari and Mme de Ferriol.

Original letters from Richard Baxter, Matthew Prior, Lord Bolingbroke [et al]. Ed R. Warner 1817.

Davies, G. and M. Tinling. Letters of Henry St John to James Brydges. Huntington Lib Bull no 8 1935; Brydges to Bolingbroke, no 9 1936.

Lettres inédites de Bolingbroke à Lord Stair 1716-20. Ed P. Baratier, Trévoux 1939.

§2

[Warburton, W.] A letter to the editor of the Letters on the spirit of patriotism etc, occasioned by the editor's advertisement. 1749.

— A view of Lord Bolingbroke's philosophy: four letters. 1754.

To the author of a libel entitled A letter to the editor of the Letters on the spirit of patriotism. 1749.

A familiar epistle to the most impudent man living. 1749.

Memoirs of the life and ministerial conduct of the late Lord Bolingbroke. 1752.

An examination of Lord Bolingbroke's Letters on history. 1753 (2nd edn).

'Philalethes'. Some remarks on the famous letter to Sir William Windham. 1753.

Critical remarks upon Letters on the study and use of history. 1754.

Francklin, R. A short state of the case with relation to a claim on David Mallet. [1754].

Philologus Cantabrigiensis. The freethinker's criteria exemplified, in a vindication of M. Tullius Cicero and the late Duke of Marlborough, against the censure of the late Lord Bolingbroke. 1755.

The life of Henry St John, Viscount Bolingbroke. 1770.

Cooke, G. W. Memoirs of Lord Bolingbroke. 2 vols 1835, 1836.

Macknight, T. Life of Henry St John, Viscount Bolingbroke. 1863.

Remusat, C. In his L'Angleterre au xviiie, Paris 1865.

Brosch, M. Lord Bolingbroke und die Whigs und Tories seiner Zeit. Frankfurt 1883.

Harrop, R. Bolingbroke: a political study and criticism. 1884.

Collins, J. C. Bolingbroke: a historical study. 1886.

Hassall, A. Life of Viscount Bolingbroke. 1889, Oxford 1915 (rev).

Sichel, W. Bolingbroke and his times. 1901.

— A sequel. 1902. With bibliography and selection of letters.

Butler, G. G. In his Tory tradition: Bolingbroke, Burke, Disraeli, Salisbury, 1914.

Hurn, A. S. Voltaire et Bolingbroke. Paris 1914.

Robertson, J. M. Bolingbroke and Walpole. 1919.

Whibley, C. Bolingbroke. Criterion 1 1923.

Ratchford, F. E. Pope and the patriot king. SE 6 1926.

Ludwig, W. Lord Bolingbroke und die Aufklärung. Heidelberg 1928.

Dahle, A. Disraelis Beziehungen zu Bolingbroke. Quakenbrück 1931.

Humphreys, A. L. Bucklebury: a Berkshire parish, the home of Bolingbroke. 1932.

Sherburn, G. Bolingbroke's Fragments and the Essay on man. PQ 12 1933.

Fieldhouse, H. N. St John and Savoy in the War of Spanish Succession. EHR 50 1935.

— Oxford, Bolingbroke and the Pretender's place of residence. EHR 52 1937.

— Bolingbroke's share in the Jacobite intrigue of 1700-14. Ibid.

— Bolingbroke and the d'Iberville correspondence 1714-15. Ibid.

— Bolingbroke and the idea of non-party government. History 23 1938.

Hopkinson, M. R. Married to Mercury: a sketch of Lord Bolingbroke and his wives. 1936.

Petrie, C. Bolingbroke. 1937.

— Bolingbroke and his influence on English politics. Quart Rev 289 1951.

Baratier, P. Bolingbroke: ses écrits politiques. Paris 1939.

— A propos du style de Bolingbroke. Études Anglaises 11 1958.

Cable, M. H. The Idea of a patriot king in the propaganda of the opposition to Walpole 1735-9. PQ 18 1939.

Butterfield, H. Bolingbroke and Machiavelli. In his Statecraft of Machiavelli, 1940.

Botting, R. B. Bolingbroke and Murphy's Aboulcasem. MLQ 5 1944.

Wimsatt, W. K. Johnson's treatment of Bolingbroke in the Dictionary. MLR 43 1948.

Merrill, W. M. From statesman to philosopher: a study in Bolingbroke's Deism. New York 1949.

James, D. G. In his Life of reason: Hobbes, Locke, Bolingbroke, 1949.

Shackleton, R. Montesquieu, Bolingbroke and the separation of power. French Stud 3 1949.

Williams, M. An eighteenth-century correspondence. English 9 1952.

Davis, H. J. Reprinting the Craftsman. Book Collector 2 1953.

Harkness, D. Bolingbroke: the man and his career. 1957.

Hedges, W. L. Knickerbocker, Bolingbroke and the fiction of history. JHI 20 1959.

Faber, R. Beaconsfield and Bolingbroke. 1961.

Burns, J. H. Bolingbroke and the concept of constitutional government. Political Stud 10 1962.

Nadel, G. H. New light on Bolingbroke's Letters on history. JHI 23 1962.

Barber, G. Bolingbroke, Pope and the Patriot king. Library 5th ser 19 1964.

Hart, J. P. Viscount Bolingbroke: Tory humanist. 1965.

Mansfield, H. C. In his Statesmanship and party government: a study of Burke and Bolingbroke, 1965.

Fletcher, D. J. The fortunes of Bolingbroke in France in the eighteenth century. Stud on Voltaire & Eighteenth Century 47 1966.

Jackman, S. W. Man of mercury: an appreciation of the mind of Bolingbroke. 1966.

What of Bolingbroke? TLS 12 May 1966.

Krammick, I. Bolingbroke and his circle. Cambridge Mass 1968.

Smallwood, F. The Bolingbroke inscriptions at Battersea. N & Q June 1968.

J. B.

SAMUEL JOHNSON
1709-84

Mss of the whole of Irene and of the Welsh and French diaries are in BM, as well as notes for the Life of Pope, others of which are in Victorian & Albert. The collection of

Mrs Donald Hyde at Somerville NJ includes parts of London *and* Irene, *the* Vanity of human wishes, *the* Life of Rowe, 2 *dedications for John Hoole and many minor pieces. The complete ms of the* Life of Pope *is in the Pierpont Morgan Library, New York. Prayers and diaries are at Pembroke College, Oxford; various minor mss are in BM, Bodley, Rylands Library Manchester, Yale, Harvard and Huntington. For mss of letters see* Letters, ed R. W. Chapman 3 vols Oxford 1952.

Bibliographies

Courtney, W. P. and D. N. Smith. A bibliography of Johnson. Oxford 1915, 1925 (with facs), 1968.

Catalogue of the Johnsonian collection of R. B. Adam. Buffalo 1921 (priv ptd).

The R. B. Adam library relating to Johnson and his era. 4 vols 1929–30.

Chapman, R. W. Johnsonian bibliography. Colophon 12 1932, 14 1934.

— and A. T. Hazen. Johnsonian bibliography: a supplement to Courtney. Proc Oxford Bibl Soc 5 1939.

Liebert, H. W. This harmless drudge. New Colophon 1 1948.

Clifford, J. L. Johnsonian studies 1887–1950: a survey and bibliography. Minneapolis 1951.

Manuscripts

Broadley, A. M. In his Chats on autographs, 1910.

Tyson, M. Unpublished manuscripts. Bull John Rylands Lib 15 1931.

Guppy, H. Library notes. Bull John Rylands Lib 16 1932.

Chapman, R. W. Hyde collection of Johnsonian mss. TLS 23 Sept 1949.

— Manuscript hunting in two continents. New Colophon 2 1950.

— The Congreve manuscripts. Bodleian Lib Record 5 1955.

Hyde, M. C. The history of the Johnson papers. PBSA 45 1951.

Taylor, F. Johnsoniana from the Bagshawe muniments. Bull John Rylands Lib 35 1952.

Brown, T. J. English literary autographs vi: Johnson. Book Collector 2 1953.

Fleeman, J. D. Preliminary handlist of manuscripts and documents by Johnson. Oxford 1967 (Oxford Bibl Soc).

Exhibition Catalogues

The bicentenary of the birth of Johnson: official guide [and exhibition catalogue]. Lichfield 1909.

Catalogue of an exhibition commemorative of the bicentenary of the birth of Johnson. New York 1909.

Catalogue of an exhibition of manuscripts, first editions, early engravings and various literature relating to Johnson, arranged by C. B. Tinker. New Haven 1909.

List of books and articles relating to Johnson compiled on the occasion of the exhibition held at the Yale University Library, Nov 1–6 1909. New Haven 1909.

Johnson: a list of books with references to periodicals in the Brooklyn Public Library. Brooklyn 1909.

[R. W. Chapman]. Notes on a loan collection of Johnsonian books and mss shown at Amen House, July 1925. Oxford 1925.

Catalogue of an exhibition of literary material pertaining to Doctor Johnson and James Boswell. Cambridge Mass 1928.

Catalogue of an exhibition of the private papers of James Boswell from Malahide Castle. New York 1931.

An exhibition of original manuscripts, autograph letters and books of and relating to Johnson, from the collection of Dr A. S. W. Rosenbach. Philadelphia 1934.

A Johnson exhibition. Bodleian Quart Record 7 1934.

A Johnson exhibition. Harvard Lib Notes 3 1935.

Hazen, A. T. and E. L. McAdam. A catalogue of an exhibition of first editions of the works of Johnson in the Library of Yale University, 8 November to 30 December 1935. New Haven 1935.

— First editions of Johnson. Yale Univ Lib Gazette 10 1936.

Dr Johnson in Texas. Austin 1940.

Johnson's books: catalogue of an exhibition of books in the Birmingham Library. Birmingham 1959.

Johnson: an exhibition of books, manuscripts, views and portraits arranged jointly by the Reference Library and the Museum and Art Gallery, 14th September to 4th October 1959. Birmingham 1959.

Cahoon, H. Johnson: an exhibition of first editions, manuscripts, letters and portraits to commemorate the 250th anniversary of his birth, and the 200th anniversary of the publication of his Rasselas, September 22–November 28 1959. New York 1959 (Pierpont Morgan Lib).

City and County of Lichfield. Johnson 250th anniversary: Johnson and the Lichfield circle. Lichfield 1959.

An exhibit of books and manuscripts from the Johnsonian collection formed by Mr and Mrs Donald F. Hyde at the Houghton Library, Harvard University. Cambridge Mass 1966.

Special Collections

Johnsoniana in the library of Robert B. Adam. Buffalo NY 1895 (priv ptd).

Osgood, C. G. Catalogue of the Johnsonian collection of R. B. Adam. Buffalo NY 1922.

A Johnsonian collection. TLS 20 April 1922.

Merritt, E. Piozzi on Boswell and Johnson. Harvard Lib Notes 2 1926.

Johnson and his birthplace. Lichfield 1933.

Gilchrist, D. B. Johnsonian Library in the University of Rochester. E Studien 71 1937.

Abbott, C. C. A catalogue of papers relating to Boswell, Johnson and Sir William Forbes found at Fettercairn House. Oxford 1936.

Gomme, L. The Robert B. Adam library relating to Johnson and his era. New York 1945 (priv ptd).

The Rothschild library: a catalogue of the collection of 18th-century books and mss formed by Lord Rothschild. 2 vols Cambridge 1954 (priv ptd).

Hyde, D. and M. The Hyde collection. Book Collector 4 1955.

Metzdorf, R. F. The Tinker library: a bibliographical catalogue of the books and manuscripts collected by Chauncey Brewster Tinker. New Haven 1959.

Sales and Booksellers' Catalogues

A catalogue of the valuable library of books of the late learned Samuel Johnson esq LlD, deceased. Christie's 16 Feb 1785, 1892 (facs for Johnson Club); ed A. E. Newton 1925 (facs).

Collecteana Johnsoniana: catalogue of the library etc of Mrs Hester Lynch Piozzi at the Emporium Rooms, Manchester, by Mr Broster. 17 Sept 1823.

Bibliotheca Boswelliana. James Boswell jr. Sotheby 24 May 1825.

Edward Skegg. Sotheby 4 April, 17, 19 June 1842, 12 Aug 1847.

G. J. Squibb. Puttick 9 July 1859.

Robert Cole. Puttick 29 July 1861.

Lewis Pocock. Sotheby 10 May 1875.

Major Ross. Christie 5 June 1888.

William Chisholme. Sotheby 27 Nov 1889.

Sotheby 14 Dec 1901.

[Major E. P. Salusbury]. Sotheby 5 Dec 1904.

Sotheby 22 Jan 1907.

[Major Salusbury]. Sotheby 2 June 1908.

Mrs Colmer. Sotheby 30 Jan 1918.

Catalogue of books by or relating to Dr Johnson and members of his circle. 1925 (Elkin Mathews Ltd). Introd by John Drinkwater.

The books of a busted bibliophile, alias A. Edward Newton. New York. Anderson Galls 29 Nov 1926.

The important collection of xviith and xviiith century books formed by Lt-Colonel Ralph H. Isham. New York Amer Art Assoc 7 Jan 1927.

The works of Johnson. New York, Brick Row Bookshop 1927.

The library of Jerome Kern. 7–10, 21 Jan 1929. New York, Anderson Galls 1929.

Brett, O. A note on Dr Johnson's first editions. Life & Letters 3 1929.

The renowned library of Lt-Col R. H. Isham. New York, Anderson Galls 4 May 1933.

The valuable library of Charles T. Jeffrey. Philadelphia, Freeman 14th April 1936.

Rare books, original drawings, autograph letters and manuscripts collected by the late A. Edward Newton pt ii. New York, Parke-Bernet Galls 14 May 1941.

The collection of books by or relating to Johnson and James Boswell formed by R. W. Chapman. Sotheby 1 June 1945.

Sotheby (G. Madan). 29 June 1948.

The Great Cham. Maggs Bros catalogue 809, 1952.

Johnson's Library

Hutton, A. W. Dr Johnson's library. [1892] (priv ptd).

Dobson, A. Johnson's library. In his Eighteenth-century vignettes ser 2, 1894.

Gove, P. B. Johnson's copy of Hammond's Elegies. MLQ 5 1944.

Mahoney, J. L. Dr Johnson at work: observations on a Columbia rare book. Columbia Lib Columns 10 1960.

Roberts, S. C. Johnson's books. London Mercury Oct 1927. *See* Dr Johnson's library, TLS 4 July, 11–18 July 1942.

Johnsonian Handlists

Johnsoniana. Book-Lore 1 1885.

Harrison, R. The bibliography of Johnson. Bookworm 1 1888.

Simms, R. Bibliotheca Staffordiensis, Lichfield. 1894.

Memorials of Dr Johnson. Church Quart Rev 50 1900.

Moulton, C. W. Samuel Johnson. In Library of literary criticism vol 3, Buffalo NY 1902.

Johnson and Johnsoniana: being some account of the books by or about Dr Johnson published by the Oxford University Press. Ed R. W. Chapman 1926.

Struble, M. C. A Johnson handbook. New York 1933.

Clifford, J. L. et al (ed). Johnsonian news letter. New York 1941–.

— Johnsonian-studies 1887–1950: a survey and bibliography. Minneapolis 1951.

Clifford, J. L. and D. J. Greene. Supplement 1950–60. Johnsonian Stud (Cairo) 1962.

Davis, H. Recent studies of Swift and Johnson. In Sprache und Literatur Englands und Amerikas vol 3, Tübingen 1959.

Collections

An account of the life of Mr Richard Savage, to which are added the Lives of Sir Francis Drake and Admiral Blake. 1767 (3rd edn), 1769, 1775.

The idler, by the author of the Rambler, with additional essays [Essay on epitaphs, Dissertation on the epitaphs of Pope, Essay on the bravery of the English common soldier]. 1767 (3rd edn), 1783, 1790, 1790 etc.

Miscellaneous and fugitive pieces. [Ed T. Davies]. Vols 1–2, Dec 1773, 1774; vol 3, 1774; 2 vols Dublin 1774, Sheffield 1804. 2 issues of 1–2 with variant imprints. Vol 1 consists wholly of pieces of Johnson; vol 2 is mainly his; vol 3 contains a few pieces by him.

Works, together with his Life, and notes on his Lives of the poets, by Sir John Hawkins. 11 vols 1787. The Latin poems in vol 11 ed Bennet Langton; Hawkins wrote the Life in vol 1 and annotated the Lives in vols 2–4; the remainder is virtually unedited. Vols 12–13 (Debates), [ed George Chalmers] 1787; vol 14 (Miscellaneous pieces) [ed Isaac Reed] 1788, 1792; vol 15 (Miscellaneous pieces) [ed George Gleig] 1789.

Works: a new edition in twelve volumes, with an essay on his life and genius by Arthur Murphy. 1792 (vols 13–14 a reissue of Debates, 1787), 6 vols Dublin 1793, 12 vols 1793, 1801, 1806, Boston 1809–12, London 1810 (vols 13–14, Debates, 1810), 1816 8° and 12°), 8 vols Dublin 1816, 12 vols 1820, 1823 (8° and 12°), 1824, 6 vols Philadelphia 1825, 2 vols New York 1834, London 1834, 1835, 1836, 1837, 1838, 1840, 1843, 1846, 1851, 1856, 1857, 1859, 1 vol 1877, 1881. Edns of 1806, 1810, 1816 and 1823 by Alexander Chalmers.

Works: a new edition, with a life of the author. 15 vols Edinburgh 1806.

Works: a new edition. 10 vols Alnwick 1816, London 1818.

Works. [Ed F. P. Walesby] 9 vols Oxford 1825; vols 10–11, Debates, Oxford 1825.

Works. Ed R. Lynam 6 vols 1824, 1825.

Works. 2 vols 1825, Glasgow 1825.

Works. 2 vols 1850 (Bohn's Lib).

Works. 16 vols New York 1903.

Works. Ed A. T. Hazen et al, New Haven 1958–.

Poems

Poetical works. [Ed G. Kearsley] 1785, 1785, 1789 (enlarged).

Poetical works. London and Gainsborough 1785.

Poetical works. Dublin 1785.

Works of the English poets. 1790 (vol 72).

Works of the British poets. Ed R. Anderson vol 11, Edinburgh 1794.

Cooke's pocket edition of select British poets vol 10 1797. With a life.

Works of the British poets. Ed T. Park vol 37, suppl vol 6. 1805–12.

Poetical works, with his life. Philadelphia 1805.

Poems. Ed F. W. Blagdon 1807, 1808, 1815.

Bell's poets of Great Britain vol 60. 1807.

The laurel, with a life by F. W. Blagdon. 1808.

The works of the English poets vol 16. Ed A. Chalmers 1810. With a life.

Poetical works, with an account of the author. Charlestown Mass 1810.

Poetical works. Ed T. Park 1811.

Lives of the most eminent English poets, with Johnson's poetical works vol 4. Edinburgh 1815.

Poetical works. Burlington NJ 1816.

Poems, to which is prefixed a life of the author. 1820.

The British poets: Chiswick edition vol 67. 1822. With a life by S. W. Singer.

The British anthology: or poetical library vol 7. 1825.

Poetical works. Ed G. Gilfillan, Edinburgh 1855.

Poetical works of Goldsmith, Smollett, Johnson and Shenstone. 1853, 1855, 1880.

Poetical works of Johnson, Parnell, Gray and Smollett. Ed G. Gilfillan, Edinburgh 1855, 1862, 1863, 1868.

Cassell's library edition of British poets pt 95. 1878.

Poems of Johnson, Goldsmith, Gray and Collins. Ed T. Methuen Ward [1905] (ML).

Poems. Ed D. N. Smith and E. L. McAdam, Oxford 1941, 1951, 1962 (rev).

The Yale edition of the works vol 6: Poems. Ed E. L. McAdam and G. Milne, New Haven 1964.

Selections

The beauties of Johnson. 2 pts 1781–2.

The beauties of Johnson. 1787.

The life of Johnson, with maxims and observations. Boston 1833.

The beauties of literature vol 28. 1834.
The life and writings of Johnson. Ed W. Page 2 vols New York 1840, 1844, 1855.
The beauties, with biographical anecdotes. 1885.
The wisdom and genius of Johnson. Ed W. A. Clouston 1876.
Wit and wisdom of Johnson. Ed G. B. Hill, Oxford 1888.
Dr Johnson's table talk. Ed J. P. Briscoe 1900 (Bibelot ser).
Table talk. Ed W. A. L. Bettany, Boston 1904.
Samuel Johnson. Ed W. Stead 1905.
Selections. [1905].
Sayings. 1908.
Wit and wisdom of Dr Johnson and his friends. [Ed A. E. Newton], Philadelphia 1908.
Wit and sagacity of Dr Johnson. Ed N. J. Davidson 1909.
Selections from the works. Ed C. G. Osgood, New York 1909.
Sir, said Dr Johnson. Ed C. Biron 1911.
Extracts from his writings. Ed A. Meynell and G. K. Chesterton 1911.
Selections from Johnson's writings, with Macaulay's life. Ed N. C. Greenough, New York 1912.
The Johnson calendar. Ed A. M. Bell, Oxford 1916.
Aphorisms on authors. Ed A. Birrell 1917.
Prose and poetry. Ed R. W. Chapman, Oxford 1922 (WC).
Critical opinions. Ed J. E. Brown, Princeton 1926.
Johnson, writer. Ed S. C. Roberts 1926.
Selections from Johnson. Ed W. V. Reynolds [1936].
The reader's Johnson. Ed C. H. Conley, New York 1940.
The portable Johnson and Boswell. Ed L. Kronenberger, New York 1947.
Dr Johnson: some observations and judgements upon life and letters. Ed J. Hayward 1948.
The wisdom of Johnson. Ed C. Maxwell 1948.
Selected writings. Ed J. Symons 1949.
A selection. Ed M. Wilson 1950 (Reynard Lib), 1967 (rev).
Rasselas and selected prose and poetry. Ed B. H. Bronson, New York 1952, 1958 (enlarged).
Selections. Ed R. W. Chapman, Oxford 1955.
A Johnson sampler. Ed H. D'A. Curwen, Cambridge Mass 1963.
A Johnson reader. Ed E. L. McAdam and G. Milne, New York 1964.
Selected poems of Johnson and Goldsmith. Ed A. Rudrum and P. Dixon 1965.
Selected writings. Ed R. T. Davies 1965.
A Johnson selection. Ed F. R. Miles 1965.
Rasselas and essays. Ed C. Peake 1967.

Special Selections (in order of canon)

The narrative companion: or entertaining moralist. 2 vols 1760. From Rambler.
Miscellaneous letters, essays etc by Pope, Atterbury, the Rambler etc. Leipzig 1763.
The beauties of the Rambler, Idler etc. 2 vols 1787, 1796.
The wisdom of the Rambler, Adventurer and Idler. 1848.
Essays. Ed S. J. Reid [1885].
Select essays. Ed G. B. Hill 2 vols 1889.
Essays from the Rambler and Idler. New York 1901.
Selections from Rambler. Ed W. H. White, Oxford 1907.
Papers from the Idler. Ed S. C. Roberts, Cambridge 1921.
Selections from the Rambler, including essays from the Idler. Ed B. B. Evans, Evanston 1940.
The Rambler, selected by S. C. Roberts. 1953 (EL).
Johnson's Dictionary: a modest selection. Ed E. L. McAdam and G. Milne 1963.
Shakespearean criticism textual and literary from Dryden to the end of the 18th century. Ed E. Welder, Bradford 1895.
Eighteenth-century essays on Shakespeare. Ed D. N. Smith, Glasgow 1903.
Johnson on Shakespeare. Ed W. Raleigh, Oxford 1908, 1925 (corrected).

Johnson on Shakespeare. Ed W. K. Wimsatt, New York 1960.
Political writings. Ed J. P. Hardy 1968.
The six chief lives of Johnson's Lives of the poets. Ed M. Arnold 1878, 1892.
Selections from the Lives of the poets. Ed W. L. Fleischauer, Chicago 1955, 1964 (rev).
Lives of the poets. Ed S. C. Roberts 1963 (selected).
Selections from the Lives of the poets and Preface to Shakespeare. Ed E. Fuller, New York 1965.
Selected letters. Ed R. W. Chapman, Oxford 1925, 1951 (rev) (WC).
His life in letters. Ed D. Littlejohn, Englewood Cliffs NJ 1965.
Prefaces and dedications. Ed A. T. Hazen, New Haven 1937.

§ I

Life: James Boswell, The life of Johnson, ed G. B. Hill, rev L. F. Powell 6 vols Oxford 1934–64.

A voyage to Abyssinia, by Father Jerome Lobo, a Portuguese Jesuit, with a continuation of the history of Abyssinia down to the beginning of the eighteenth century, and fifteen dissertations by Mr Legrand, from the French. 1735, 1735, 1789 (to which are added various other tracts by the same author; sometimes known as Works vol 15 and with half-title to that effect; *see* above); rptd J. Pinkerton in A general collection of voyages and travels vol 15, 1814; ed H. Morley 1886, 1887, 1893.
The history of the Council of Trent, translated from the Italian of Father Paul Sarpi; with the author's life and notes etc from the French. Proposals issued Oct 1738; *see* below. 'Some sheets were printed off, but the design was dropt'. See Life 1 p. 135.
London: a poem in imitation of the third satire of Juvenal. 1738 (3 edns), 1738 ('2nd edn'), Dublin 1738, London 1739, 1750; rptd in Dodsley's collection of poems vol 1, 1748 etc; as Two satires by Samuel Johnson AM Oxford, 1759; in Goldsmith's beauties of English poesy, 1767; in A select collection of poems, Edinburgh 1768; in Miscellaneous and fugitive pieces vol 2, 1773 etc (*see* above); in Juvenal, ed V. Knox 1784. Common in later anthologies and edns of Juvenal; ed T. S. Eliot 1930 (with Vanity, below).
Marmor Norfolciense: or an essay on an ancient prophetical inscription, in monkish rhyme, lately discover'd near Lynn in Norfolk, by Probus Britanicus. 1739, 1775 (with notes and a dedication to Samuel Johnson LlD by Tribunus [i.e. Francis Webb, DNB]) 1820 (from 1739).
A compleat vindication of the licensers of the stage from the malicious and scandalous aspersions of Mr Brooke, author of Gustavus Vasa, with a proposal for making the office of licenser more extensive and effectual, by an impartial hand. 1739.
A commentary on Mr Pope's Principles of morality: or essay on man, by Mons Crousaz. 1739, 1742. Tr and annotated by Johnson. See Life 4, 494–6.
The life of Admiral Blake. 1740. Rptd from GM June 1740. See E. L. McAdam, TLS 14 March 1936. Added to Life of Savage, 1767 etc. See Savage, below.
An account of the life of Mr Richard Savage, son of the Earl Rivers. 1744, 1748, 1767 (with additional lives), 1769, 1777.
The works of Richard Savage esq, with an account of the author, by Samuel Johnson LlD. Vol 1, 1775, 1777, Dublin 1777, 1822; Bell's British poets 1780, 1791, 1807; in Poetical works of Richard Savage, 1795, 1801, New York 1805, London 1806, 1807. Rev and included in Johnson's Lives of the poets, below.
Histoires de Richard Savage et de J. Thompson [i.e. James Thomson], traduites de l'anglois par M. Le Tourneur. Paris 1771.

An account of the life of John Philip Barretier, who was master of five languages at the age of nine years. 1744. A conflation of GM Dec 1740, Feb 1741, May 1742.

Miscellaneous observations on the tragedy of Macbeth, with remarks on Sir T. H[anmer]'s edition of Shakespear; to which is affix'd Proposals for a new edition of Shakespear with a specimen. 1745. The Proposals are ptd on a half-sheet folio folded into 4 and inserted at the conclusion. *See* Proposals, below.

A sermon preached before the sons of the clergy, second of May 1745, by the Honourable and Reverend Henry Hervey Aston AM. [1745]; ed J. L. Clifford, Los Angeles 1955 (Augustan Reprint Soc). *See* Life 5, 483–4.

The plan of a dictionary of the English language, addressed to the Right Honourable Philip Dormer, Earl of Chesterfield, one of his Majesty's Principal Secretaries of State. 1747, 1755; rptd in Harrison's edn of Dictionary, 1786. *See* J. H. Sledd and G. J. Kolb, Dr Johnson's Dictionary, Chicago 1955 ch 2.

Prologue and epilogue, spoken at the opening of the Theatre in Drury-Lane. 1747 (2 states of title, with and without price 6d; 'printed by E. Cave'), 1747 ('printed by W. Webb'); ed A. Dobson and A. S. W. Rosenbach, New York 1902 (facs of Cave); ed R. W. Chapman, Oxford 1924 (facs of Webb). Prologue rptd GM Oct 1747, and collected poems. The Epilogue was by Garrick.

The vanity of human wishes: the tenth satire of Juvenal, imitated by Samuel Johnson. 1749, 1750 (5th edn); W. Hoskins 1851; ed J. P. Fleming 1876; ed E. J. Payne, Oxford 1876; ed F. Ryland 1893; Oxford 1927 (facs), Los Angeles 1950 (Augustan Reprint Soc); rptd in Dodsley's collection vol 4, 1755 etc as Two satires, Oxford 1759 (with London). Common in anthologies and edns of Juvenal; ed T. S. Eliot 1930 (with London). *See* Collections *and* London, above.

Irene: a tragedy, as it is acted at the Theatre Royal in Drury-Lane. 1749, Dublin 1749, 8° 1754, 1781; in Bell's British theatre 1796 etc. *See* D. N. Smith, Johnson's Irene, E & S 14 1928, 1929 (separately with addns).

The rambler, price 2d: to be continued on Tuesdays and Saturdays. No 1 (20 March 1750)–no 208 (14 March 1752); 2 vols 1751 (with Contents & mottoes 1753), 8 vols Edinburgh 1750–2; vols 1–4 Edinburgh 1751–3 (superintended by James Elphinstone and originally sold in penny nos); 6 vols 1752 (2 issues), Dublin 1752, 4 vols 1756 (rev), 1761, 1763, 1767, 1771, Edinburgh 1772, 1776, London 1779, Edinburgh 1781, London 1783, 1784, Dublin 1785; in Harrison's British classicks vol 1, 1785, 1792, 1795, 1796; 1789, 1791, 2 vols 1791; in Parson's Select British classics, 1793, 1795–6; 1793, 3 vols 1794, 4 vols Edinburgh 1794, 1795; Cooke's edn, 3 vols [c. 1795]; 4 vols 1796, 1798, Edinburgh 1798, 1799; in British Classics vol 1 1800; 4 vols Montrose 1800, New York 1800, London 1801; ed A. Chalmers 4 vols 1802, 1803–4, 1806, 1807–8, New York 1811, 1817, 3 vols 1823, 3 vols Philadelphia 1803, 1805, Berwick 1805, 1806, 1806, Edinburgh 1806; in British Classics 1809; 1810 etc; ed A. B. Strauss and W. J. Bate, New Haven 1969 (in Works); tr German, 4 vols 1754–5; French, 4 vols 1786, 5 vols 1827.

> Individual essays frequently found in prose collections and anthologies as well as in contemporary magazines etc. The 'four billets' in no 10 were by Hester Mulso, afterwards Mrs Chapone; no 30 by Catherine Talbot; nos 44 and 100 by Elizabeth Carter; no 97 by Samuel Richardson; and the 2nd letter in no 107 by Joseph Simpson. The 2nd letter in no 15 was supposed to be by Garrick. *See* D. N. Smith, Bodleian Quart Record 7 1934. Nos 186–7 were versified in Anne Penny, Anningait and Ajutt, 1761. Bonnell Thornton, A rambler, number 99999, Drury-Lane Jnl 30 Jan 1752; Nathan

Drake, Essays illustrative of the Rambler, Adventurer and Idler, 2 vols 1809.

A new prologue spoken by Mr Garrick, Thursday April 5 1750 at the representation of Comus for the benefit of Mrs Elizabeth Foster, Milton's grand-daughter, and only surviving descendant. 1750, Oxford 1925 (facs), Edinburgh 1750; GM April 1750. In most anthologies: *see* Collections, above.

A dictionary of the English language, in which the words are deduced from their originals and illustrated in their different significations by examples from the best writers; to which are prefixed a history of the language and an English grammar, by Samuel Johnson AM. 2 vols 1755, New York 1967 (facs); 1755–6 (in weekly nos at sixpence); 2 vols 1765, 1773 (rev 4th edn), Dublin 1775, 1777, London 1784, 1785 (also issued in weekly nos), 1785 (based on revision of 1773); Harrison's edn 1786; 2 vols 1786, 1787, Dublin 1797–8, 1798, London 1799; incorporated in Encyclopaedia Perthensis 23 vols [1806]; reissued as New encyclopaedia, Perth 1807; ed H. J. Todd 5 vols 1818; 4 vols Philadelphia 1818, London 1828 (stereotyped), Heidelberg 1827–8; ed R. G. Latham 1866–70 (in fascicles and 2 vols in 2 pts each). *See* J. H. Sledd and G. J. Kolb, Dr Johnson's Dictionary, Chicago 1955; R. C. Alston, A bibliography of the English language, vol 5, 1966. The Preface to the first folio edn was pbd Cleveland 1934.

A dictionary of the English language abstracted from the folio edition. 2 vols 1756, Dublin 1758, London 1760, Dublin 1764, London 1766, Dublin 1768, London 1770, 1773, 1778, 1778, 1783, 1786, 1 vol 1790, 1792, 1792, 1794, 1794, Edinburgh 1797, London 1798, 1799, Montrose 1802, Philadelphia 1805; abridged by W. Mavor, Glasgow 1809; abridged by A. Chalmers 1820. Many miniature edns pbd in 12° claim to be Johnson's Dictionary, but are of no interest save that they reproduce his portrait and show that his name was synonymous with an English dictionary.

> Translations. The abridged Dictionary was frequently the basis upon which bilingual dictionaries were constructed: Italian and French, 1777, 1791, 1795; German, 1783, 1852; Italian 1819; Bengali, 1822, 1828, 1834, 1851, 1856, 1872; French, 1846; Welsh, 1867. A French trn of the Preface is included in Oeuvres de F. G. J. S. Andrieux, 1823; and an Italian version Prefazione di S. Jonson ab suo Dizionaro, tradotta in Toscano, 1813.

The Prince of Abissinia: a tale. 2 vols 1759, 1759 (rev), Dublin 1759, London, 1760, 1766; The history of Rasselas, Prince of Abissinia: an Asiatic tale, Philadelphia 1768, London 1775, Dublin 1777, 1783; [Parallel English & German], Metz and Frankfurt 1785, London 1786; Harrison's Novelist's Mag 23 1787; Wenman's edn 1787, Dublin 1787, Edinburgh 1789, London 1790, 1790; Philadelphia 1791, London 1792, 1793, Wenman's edn, 1794; Literary Assoc, 1795, 1796; Dublin [1795]; New York 1795 (with Dinarbas), Harding's edn, 1796; Cooke's edn, [1797]; 1798, 1799; Cook's edn [1799] etc. An English or American edn has appeared roughly every year since 1759. Of some interest are:

> Bristol 1802, Cork 1803, Banbury ('Rusher's edn', 2 states) 1804; illustr A. Raimbach 1805, 1819; Liverpool 1813, Leeds 1814, York 1815, Oxford 1816, Lanark 1819, Belfast 1821, Derby [c. 1830]; Manchester 1845; 'Lundun', Pitman's phonetic edn, 1849; Vathek and Rasselas, 1883; facs of 1st edn, ed J. Macaulay 2 vols 1884; ed G. B. Hill, Oxford 1887; ed O. F. Emerson, New York 1895; Birmingham 1898; ed G. K. Chesterton 1926; ed R. W. Chapman 1927 (with valuable introd); Hartford Conn 1803, Cambridge Mass 1804, Boston 1808, Bridgeport Conn 1809 (variant titles), Baltimore 1810, Fredericktown Md 1810, Philadelphia 1811, Brattleborough Vt 1813, New York 1834, Ithaca 1841, Chicago [1878], New York 1886,

Rahway NJ [1899], Wausau Wis 1902; tr Dutch, in De Hollandsche Wysgeer vol 4, 1760, 1824, 1828, 1838, 1843, 1845, 1857; French, 1760, 1768, 1787, 1788, 1797, 1798, 1799, 1802, 1803, 1804, 1817 (with Dinarbas), 1818, 1818, 1819, 1820, 1821, 1822, 1823, 1825, 1827, 1829, 1830, 1831, 1832, 1833, 1834, 1835, 1840, 1842, 1845, 1846, 1847, 1850, 1853, 1860, 1863, 1867, 1873, 1882, 1886, [1896], 1905; German, 1762, 1785, 1786, 1787, 1826, 1827, 1829, 1832, 1836, 1840, 1841, 1842, 1844, 1846, [1855?], 1862, 1874, 1884; Italian, 1764, 1797, 1823, 1825, 1828, 1852, 1883; Russian, in Dobroe namerenie 1764, 1795, 1875; Spanish, 1798, 1817, 1834, 1860, 1945, 1951; Polish, 1803, 1838–40; Danish, 1809; Greek, 1817, 1861; Armenian, 1826; Bengali, 1833, 1907, 1912; Hungarian, 1840; Japanese, 1886, 1890, 1890, 1905, 1948; Marathi, 1900; Arabic, 1923, 1959.

The idler. 104 nos (nos 2–105, 15 April 1758–5 April 1760) in Universal Chron or Weekly Gazette. In the collected edns the original of no 22 was omitted; this essay was rptd by Basil Montagu in his Enquiries respecting the Insolvent Debtor's Bill, 1815, and the subsequent essays renumbered, leaving a total of 103. Johnson disclaimed the authorship of nos 9, 15 (Bonnell Thornton), 33 (Thomas Warton), 42, 54, 67 (Bennet Langton), 76 (Joshua Reynolds), 79 (Reynolds), 82 (Reynolds,) 93 (Warton), 96 (Warton) and 98 (William Emonson); he did not remember the authors of 9, 42 and 54. See D. N. Smith, Bodleian Quart Record 7 1934. 2 vols 1761 (an offprint of Reynolds's 3 essays was specially taken from this edn), Dublin 1762 (partly rptd from Universal Chron and so accidentally retaining the original 104 essays), 2 vols 1767 ('with additional essays', viz An essay on epitaphs, rptd from GM 1740; A dissertation on the epitaphs written by Pope, rptd from Universal Visiter 1756; The bravery of the English common soldier, rptd from British Mag 1760); 1783; Harrison's British Classicks vol 8 1787, 1792, 1795, 1796; 1790; Parsons's edn 1793, 1795, 1798; Cooke's edn [c. 1799], Alnwick 1800; 1801; ed A. Chalmers (British essayists vols 33–4) 1802; Philadelphia 1803; ed W. J. Bate and J. M. Bullitt, New Haven 1963.

The plays of William Shakespeare, with the corrections and illustrations of various commentators; to which are added notes by Sam Johnson. 8 vols 1765, 1765 (an offprint of the Preface was taken from this 2nd edn), 10 vols Dublin 1766, 8 vols 1768, 12 pts Dublin 1771, 10 vols 1773 ('To which are added notes by Samuel Johnson and George Steevens, with an appendix'); 10 vols 1778 ('revised and augmented'; Supplement, ed E. Malone 2 vols 1780), 1785 ('revised and augmented by the editor of Dodsley's collection of old plays', i.e. Isaac Reed); 1793. For later edns and revisions see under Shakespeare, vol 1.

Mr Johnson's preface to his edition of Shakespear's plays. 1765. From the 2nd edn of 1765; distinguished from 1st in that the Preface is paginated. A similar separate issue of the Preface was made from the 1785 edn in 1788; rptd in Eighteenth-century essays on Shakespeare, ed D. N. Smith 1903; Johnson on Shakespeare, ed W. Raleigh, Oxford 1908.

The false alarm. 1770, Dublin 1770, London 1770 (3 edns). See W. B. Todd, Concealed editions of Johnson, Book Collector 2 1953; D. J. Greene, SB 13 1960.

Thoughts on the late transactions respecting Falkland's Islands. 1771 (leaf K2 is cancelled in most copies, but some retain the original reading on p. 68. See Life 2 p. 135), 1771, Dublin 1771, New York 1771, London 1948.

The patriot, addressed to the electors of Great Britain. 1774, 1774, 1775, Dublin 1775, 1790.

Taxation no tyranny: an answer to the resolutions and address of the American Congress. 1775, 1775 (3 edns). See W. B. Todd, Book Collector 2 1953; D. J. Greene,

SB 13 1960; tr German, Amerikanisches Archiv 2 1777 (see R. F. Metzdorf, MLN 68 1953).
The preceding 4 pieces collected and rev in one vol as Political tracts, 1775, Dublin 1777; ed J. P. Hardy 1967.

A journey to the Western Islands of Scotland. 1775 (with 2 cancelled leaves D8 affecting p. 48, and U4 p. 296; also a leaf of 11 errata), 1775 (no cancels, and a leaf of only 6 errata), Dublin 1775 (3 edns pbd by Leathley, Walker and Williams), London 1775 (3 edns pbd J. Pope, another issue of Williams), 1785, 1791, Edinburgh 1792, 1795, 1798; ed W. Mavor, Br Tourist 2 1798, [1800], 1809, Alnwick 1800, Baltimore 1810, Edinburgh 1811, Glasgow (with McNicol's Remarks, below), 1812, New York 1812, London 1813, 1816 (2 states), Glasgow (with McNicol) 1817, 1822, Philadelphia 1817, Edinburgh 1819, London 1824, Glasgow (with McNicol) 1825, London 1876; ed H. Morley 1886; New York 1887, London 1892; ed E. J. Thomas [1904]; ed D. T. Holmes, Paisley [1906]; ed R. W. Chapman, Oxford 1924 (with Boswell's Tour), 1930 (corrected) (OSA); ed J. Freeman 1924; London 1925, Boston 1925; ed D. L. Murray 1931; tr German 1775, 1889; French, 1784, 1804.

Prefaces, biographical and critical, to the works of the English poets, by Samuel Johnson. 10 vols 1779–81 (vols 1–4, 1779); rptd 1 vol Dublin 1779, London 1780, 1781; vols 5–6, 1781; rptd Dublin as vols 2–3, 1781 (as The lives of the English poets, and a criticism of their works); 4 vols 1781 (as The lives of the most eminent English poets; with critical observations on their works); 1783 (rev), 6 vols 1790 (as Prefaces), 1790–1, 1793, 1794, Dublin 1795, Montrose 1800, London 1801, Philadelphia 1803, Dublin 1804; ed A. Chalmers 1806; Charleston 1810, New York 1811, Edinburgh 1815, Halifax 1835, Glasgow 1839, Aberdeen 1847; ed P. Cunningham 3 vols 1854; Leipzig 1858 (Tauchnitz); ed Mrs A. Napier and J. W. Hales 3 vols 1890; ed J. H. Millar 3 vols 1896; ed A. Waugh 6 vols 1896; ed G. B. Hill 3 vols Oxford 1905, 2 vols Oxford 1906 (WC); tr German, 1781–3, 1797 (abridged); French, 1842.

Six chief lives. Ed M. Arnold 1878.

The principal additions and corrections in the third edition of Dr Johnson's Lives of the poets, collected to complete the second edition (compiled by John Nichols). 1783.

Prayers and meditations, composed by Samuel Johnson LlD, and published from his manuscripts, by George Strahan. 1785, Dublin 1785, London 1785 (with additional prayers), 1796 (with additional prayer), Dublin 1796, London 1806, 1807, 1813, 1817, Dorchester 1821, London 1823, 1826, Dorchester 1826, London 1836, Lichfield 1840, Glasgow 1846, Lichfield 1860, New York 1902; ed H. Higgins and A. Birrell [1904]; 1906, [1928], Lichfield 1927, Mount Vernon NY 1937; ed E. Trueblood 1945; ed G. B. Hill in Johnsonian Miscellanies vol 1, Oxford 1897, 1967; ed D. and M. Hyde with E. L. McAdam in Diaries, prayers and annals, New Haven 1958.

Debates in Parliament, by Samuel Johnson LlD. 2 vols 1787 (ed George Chalmers; see Life 1 pp. 152, 501–12; and B. B. Hoover, Johnson's parliamentary reporting, Berkeley 1953) (rptd from GM 1740–3, and pbd as supplementary vols to Sir John Hawkins's edn of Works, 1787, with half-title to that effect, 1811 (as supplementary vols to Works, 1810), 2 vols 1812 (ed J. Wright in Cobbett's parliamentary history of England to the year 1803, vols 11–12); Oxford 1825 (as supplementary vols to Works).

Letters to and from the late Samuel Johnson LlD; to which are added some poems never before printed, published from the original mss in her possession by Hester Lynch Piozzi. 2 vols 1788, Dublin 1788. Mrs Piozzi's is the first major collection of Johnson's letters; others are included in T. Wilson, An archaeological dictionary, 1793 (2nd edn); Rev James Grainger, Letters, ed J. P. Malcolm 1805; Original letters, ed R. Warner, Bath 1817; George Colman the younger, Posthumous letters, 1820; Letters of Johnson, Edinburgh 1822; Literary recollections by Richard Warner, 1830.

Original letters of Johnson, communicated by Sir John Simeon. In Philobiblon Miscellany vol 6, 1860–1. 13 letters.

Sir Joshua Reynolds's notes with some unpublished letters of Dr Johnson. Ed William Cotton 1859.

Letters of Samuel Johnson LlD. Ed G. B. Hill 2 vols Oxford 1892, New York 1892; [additional letters] in Johnsonian Miscellanies, ed Hill vol 2, Oxford 1897; Eighteenth-century letters, ed R. B. Johnson 2 vols 1898; Letters of literary men, ed F. A. Mumby 2 vols [1906]; Johnson: some unpublished letters, ed C. K. Shorter 1915 (priv ptd).

Selected letters. Ed R. W. Chapman, Oxford 1925 (WC), 1951 (rev).

A letter of Dr Johnson and some eighteenth-century imprints of the House of Longman, by C. J. Longman. 1928 (priv ptd).

Johnson, Boswell and Mrs Piozzi: a suppressed passage restored. Ed R. W. C[hapman] 1929.

Forty-four letters from Johnson. Ed L. D'O. Walters, Chelsea 1931.

Johnson and Queeney: letters from Dr Johnson to Queeney Thrale from the Bowood Papers. Ed Marquis of Lansdowne 1932.

Some unpublished letters to and from Dr Johnson, from the originals now in the possession of the John Rylands Library. Ed J. D. Wright, Manchester 1932.

Illustrations of Jacobite relics etc inherited by Alexander Pelham Trotter. 2 vols Salisbury 1933–4 (priv ptd).

The Queeney letters: being letters addressed to Hester Maria Thrale by Dr Johnson, Fanny Burney and Mrs Thrale-Piozzi. Ed Marquis of Lansdowne 1934; English letters of the xviii century, ed Aitkin 1946.

The letters of Johnson, with Mrs Thrale's genuine letters to him. Ed R. W. Chapman 3 vols Oxford 1952. For further letters see M. Hyde, Not in Chapman, in Johnson, Boswell and their circle, 1965.

A sermon [on St John xi 25–6] written by the late Samuel Johnson LlD for the funeral of his wife, published by the Rev Samuel Hayes. 1788; rptd in The mourner comforted, ed J. Abercrombie, Philadelphia 1812; and Sermons on different subjects, left for publication by John Taylor LlD, ed S. Hayes 2 vols 1788–9; 1790 (vol I); 1792 (complete), Dublin 1793, 2 vols 1795, 1800; 1806; Walpole NH 1806, 1812, 1812, 1812, Boston 1821, Ripon 1835. Sermons also included in British prose Writers vol 15, 1819. See Life 3, p. 181.

For other sermons see 1745, above; and Life 5 p. 484.

The celebrated letter from Samuel Johnson LlD to Philip Dormer Stanhope, Earl of Chesterfield, now first published, with notes, by James Boswell esq. 1790 (for 1791).

A conversation between his Most Sacred Majesty George III and Samuel Johnson LlD, illustrated with observations, by James Boswell esq. 1790 (for 1791); Christmas greetings, ed R. B. Adam, Buffalo 1927 (facs). Both pieces are offprints taken with slight alterations in type from the same setting of text as in Boswell's Life 2 vols 1791; see F. A. Pottle, Literary career of Boswell, 1929, pp. 134–41.

An account of the life of Dr Samuel Johnson, from his birth to his eleventh year, written by himself; to which are added original letters to Dr Samuel Johnson by Miss Hill Boothly, from the mss preserved by the Doctor and now in possession of Richard Wright [the editor]. 1805. Partly rptd in Johnsonian miscellanies, ed G. B. Hill vol 1, 1897; rptd in Diaries, prayers and annals, ed M. and D. Hyde with E. L. McAdam, New Haven 1958.

Parliamentary logick, by the Right Hon William Gerard Hamilton, with an appendix containing Considerations on the Corn Laws by Samuel Johnson LlD, never before printed. [Ed E. Malone] 1808. Originally written c. 1766; ms in Hyde Collection; added to Diary of a tour in North Wales, below, Philadelphia 1817. Not included in subsequent edns or trns of Parliamentary logick.

A diary of a journey into North Wales in the year 1774, by Samuel Johnson LlD. Ed R. Duppa 1816 (variant states). Included in Life 5 and in Diaries, prayers and annals, New Haven 1958; ms in BM.

Dr Johnson and Mrs Thrale, including Mrs Thrale's unpublished Journal of the Welsh tour made in 1774, by A. M. Broadley, with an introductory essay by Thomas Seccombe. 1910.

The French journals of Mrs Thrale and Dr Johnson. Ed M. Tyson and H. Guppy, Manchester 1932.

Proposals

Angeli Politiani poemata latina, quibus notas cum historia latinæ poeseos, a Petrarchæ ævo ad Politiani tempora deducta, et vita Politiani fusius quam antehac enarrata, addidit Sam Johnson. Issued 5 Aug 1734; see Life 1 p. 90. No known copy.

Proposals for printing the History of the Council of Trent, translated from the Italian of Father Paul Sarpi; with the author's life, and notes theological, historical and critical, from the French edition of Dr Le Courayer; to which are added observations on the history and notes, and illustrations from various authors, both printed and manuscript, by S. Johnson. Issued 11 Oct 1738, 2 leaves 4°. See J. A. V. Chapple, John Rylands Lib Bull 45 1963. Unique copy at Manchester Univ.

Proposals for printing a medicinal dictionary: designed as a body of physic and surgery both with regard to theory and practice, compiled from the best writers ancient and modern, with useful observations, illustrated with copper plates, by R. James MD. Dated 24 June 1741. 2 leaves folio. A general account of the work, pp. 3, 4. Also issued as wrappers on nos of James's Dictionary; see below.

Proposals for printing, by subscription, the two first volumes of Bibliotheca Harleiana: or a catalogue of the library of the late Earl of Oxford, purchased by Thomas Osborne, bookseller, in Gray's-Inn. Dated 1 Nov 1742. 2 leaves folio. Rptd GM Dec 1742; ed R. W. C[hapman] 1926 (facs). An account of the Harleian Library, pp. 2–3 by Johnson. Rptd as An essay on the origin and importance of small tracts and fugitive pieces in Harleian catalogue vol 1, 1787, and in Literary pamphlets vol 1, ed E. Rhys 1897.

Proposals for printing, by subscription, the Harleian Miscellany: or a collection of scarce, curious and entertaining tracts and pamphlets found in the late Earl of Oxford's Library. 2 issues: 2 leaves 4°, probably 30 Dec 1743; 2 leaves folio with list of subscribers. Rptd GM 1743 and in Catalogus Harleianae vol 3; also ptd on wrappers of weekly numbers of Harleian Miscellany as An account of this undertaking.

Proposals for printing every fortnight (price sixpence) the Publisher: containing miscellanies in prose and verse, collected by J. Crokatt, bookseller. Dated 'September 24th, 1744', folio. Unique copy in Rothschild Collection; ed R. W. Chapman, Oxford 1930 (facs). An account of the design; rptd Publisher no 1 1745.

Proposals for publishing the debates of the House of Commons, from the year 1667 to the year 1694, collected by the Hon Anchitell Grey esq. First issue 1745; rptd GM March 1745; a second issue appeared in 1762, one leaf 8°. Unique copy in John Johnson Collection, Oxford.

Proposals for printing a new edition of the plays of William Shakespeare, with notes critical and explanatory, by the author of the Miscellaneous observations on the tragedy of Macbeth. One leaf folio; bound in with the Miscellaneous observations, 1745, and also issued separately; rptd in Works vol 14, 1788.

Proposals for printing by subscription Hugonis Grotti Adamus Exsul, tragoedia; with an English version by William Lauder. Dated 5 Sept 1747, 2 leaves 8°; rptd GM Sept 1747, and with alterations as preface to Lauder's Essay on Milton, 1750.

Proposals for printing by subscription Essays in verse and prose by Anna Williams. Dated 25 Sept 1750, 2 leaves 4°; rptd GM Sept 1750, where the work is announced as 8°; possibly another issue of these proposals in 8°, but no copy known. Strahan's ledgers record the proposals under March 1766 as ptd 'at different times'.

[Proposals for the second edition of the folio Dictionary, published in sixpenny weekly numbers. Strahan's ledgers record 5,000 folio proposals and 24,000 in 4° ptd June 1755. No copies known.]

Proposals for printing, by subscription, the dramatick works of William Shakespeare, corrected and illustrated by Samuel Johnson. 4 leaves 8°. Dated 1 June 1756; rptd London Chron 12–14 April 1757; ed R. W. C[hapman], Oxford 1923 (facs).

[Proposals for Richard Rolt's dictionary of trade and commerce, to be published in weekly numbers. Strahan ptd 16,000 proposals Jan 1757. Johnson's part in them is merely presumptive, as no copies are known.]

Proposals for printing by subscription the English works of Roger Ascham, Preceptor to Queen Elizabeth; with notes and observations, and the author's life, by Mr James Bennet, Master of the Boarding-School at Hoddesdon in Hertfordshire. 2 issues: Dec 1757 (unique copy in BM seems to be of this issue, 2 leaves 4°), and Aug 1760 when pbn was delayed; see Boswell, Life 1, pp. 550–2.

Proposals for printing by subscription Le poesie di Giuseppe Baretti. 2 leaves 4°. Ptd in 1758 according to Strahan's ledgers; Baretti's work never pbd.

Announcement of the forcoming publication of the World displayed in [20] monthly volumes by John Newbery. 1 leaf 8°, dated 23 Oct 1759. 'To the public' (p. 2); unique copy in John Johnson Collection, Oxford.

[Proposals for Hoole's translation of Tasso's Jerusalem delivered. William Bowyer's ledgers record the printing of 1,500 in April 1761. Johnson's part in them is merely presumptive, as no copies are known.]

Proposals for publishing the works of Mrs Charlotte Lennox, in three volumes quarto. 1775. 1 leaf 4° dated 14 Feb 1775; the project was abortive. Unique copy at Yale.

Proposals for printing by subscription, inscribed by permission, to the Right Honourable the Earl of Eglinton: An analysis of the Scotch Celtic language, by William Shaw, native of one of the Hebrides; the book will be elegantly printed in one volume in quarto, price half a guinea, to be paid at the time of subscribing; the books will be delivered in November 1777, by J. Murray, Fleet Street [et al]. 1 leaf 4° dated March 1777; see Life 3 pp. 107, 488.
   See also H. G. Pollard and A. Ehrman, The distribution of books by catalogue, 1965 (Roxburghe Club) pp. 196–7.

Contributions to Periodicals etc

Adventurer

The adventurer. 3 leaves folio, published bi-weekly (Tuesday & Saturday) from 7 Nov 1752 to 9 March 1754; 140 nos. First pbd thus, and in 2 folio vols with titles 1753, 1754, lists of contents and mottoes. Ed John Hawkesworth. Other contributors include Joseph Warton, Earl of Orrery, Bonnell Thornton and R. Bathurst.

Nos 34, 39, 41, 45, 50, 53, 58, 62, 67, 69, 74, 81, 84, 85, 92, 95, 99, 102, 107, 108, 111, 115, 119–20, 126,

128, 131, 137–8. From 3 March 1753 to 2 March 1754. Signed T. (some copies of no 84 lack this signature). Johnson's sole authorship of nos 34, 41, 53, 62, which are letters signed Misargyrus, has been questioned: see Life 1 p. 254. According to Hawkins, Johnson 'did not himself write' no 81 (on 'Admirable Crichton'), but 'dictated' it to Hawkesworth: see Life 1787 pp. 294, 309. See L. F. Powell, Johnson's part in the Adventurer, RES 3 1927 and his edn of Johnson's papers in Yale edn of Works vol 2, New Haven 1963.

4 vols 1754 (2nd edn), Dublin 1754, London 1756 (3rd edn), 2 vols Dublin 1760, 4 vols 1762, 1766, 1770, 2 vols Dublin 1770, 4 vols 1774, 1777, 1778, 4 vols Dublin 1778 etc.

Birmingham Journal

'Some numbers of a periodical essay printed in the newspaper, of which Warren was proprietor'.
Life 1 p. 85. The only known no (no 28, 21 May 1733) contains nothing Johnsonian.

British Magazine: or Monthly Repository

The bravery of the English common soldiers. Jan 1760. Added to 3rd edn of Idler, 1767 etc.
The fountains: a fairy tale. May–June 1766. An adumbration from Miscellanies in prose and verse by Anna Williams. 1766. See below.

Critical Review (ed T. Smollett)

[Review of Hawkesworth's revision of Southerne's Oronooko, Dec 1759?]
Review of Graham's Telemachus: a mask. April 1763.
Review of Grainger's Sugar-cane. Oct 1764. See also London Chronicle, below.
Review of Goldsmith's Traveller. Dec.

Daily Advertiser

Letter signed 'Edward Cave' on Sarpi's History. 21 Oct 1738. See E. Ruhe, N & Q Oct 1954.
Sherbo, A. Two additions to the Johnson canon. JEGP 52 1953.
Letter of 13 April 1739.
Election addresses for Henry Thrale. 4 Oct, 6 Oct?, 14 Oct 1774. See Public Advertiser, below.

Daily Gazetteer

Three letters on the plans for Black-friars bridge [for J. Gwynne the architect]. 1, 8, 15 Dec 1759.

Dodsley's Museum 3 vols 1746–7

To Miss — [Carpenter] playing on a Harpsicord. Vol 2 pp. 178–9.
On a sprig of myrtle. Vol 2 p. 429.

Gazetteer & New Daily Advertiser

Election address for Henry Thrale. 4–8 March 1768. See Johnson, Boswell and their circle, 1959.
Letter to the printer. 13 March 1769. See ibid.

General Advertiser

Letter announcing the representation of Comus for the benefit of Milton's grand-daughter. 4 April 1750.

Gentleman's Magazine

[Latin verse on GM by 'Rusticus'? p.ii. 1736].
Advertisement for Edial School. June–July 1736.
[Latin verses on the Gin Act by 'Ardelio'? July 1736].
To the Reader. Prefixed to vol 8 1738.
Latin verses: Ad Urbanum, by 'S.J.' March 1738.
Latin verses: Ad Ricardum Savage. April 1738.
Greek and Latin verses on Eliza [Elizabeth Carter]. Ibid. These verses relate to Eliza's Riddle of Feb 1738, which produced several solutions and replies.

[Latin verses: to a lady who spoke in defence of liberty [i.e. Molly Aston]. Ibid].

[Latin epigram with English trn 'Venus in armour'? Ibid].

[Latin verses: Ex cantico Solomonis? Ibid].

[Latin verses: The logical warehouse? May 1738].

[Introduction to the debates in the Senate of Magna Lilliputia? June 1738].

[Political questions. i–xvi? Ibid].

[Examination of a question [no 1] proposed in the Magazine of June, by 'Pamphilus'? July 1738]. See J. Leed, MP 54 1957; D. J. Greene, PMLA 74 1959.

[Letter to Mr Urban on Chinese political manners? Ibid].

[Latin verses: Ad Elisam? Ibid].

Translation of verses on Eliza plucking Laurel in Mr Pope's Gardens, by 'Urbanus'. Aug 1738.

To Lady F[irebra]ce at Bury Assizes. Sept 1738.

[Letter on Gay's monument by 'Pamphilus'? Oct 1738]. See MP 54 1957, PMLA 74 1959.

Life of Father Paul Sarpi, by 'S.J.' Nov 1738.

Greek verses on Rev Thomas Birch. Dec 1738.

Advertisement concerning debates in Senate of Lilliput. Suppl 1738.

Proposals for printing Anagrammata rediviva. Ibid; and on separate leaf in some copies of vol 8 or 9.

Letter to Mr Urban. Jan 1739.

Latin verses: in Birchium. Ibid.

The life of Dr Herman Boerhaave. Jan–April 1793.

[Editorial note? Feb 1739].

An appeal to the publick. March 1739.

[Editorial note? Ibid].

To the reader. May 1739.

Latin verses: Post-Genitis [from Marmor Norfolciense]. Ibid.

[Extract from Trapp's Four sermons? June 1739; unfinished].

Verses: To Posterity Post-Genitis. Ibid.

[Letter to Mr Urban on poetry. Nov 1739].

Preface to vol 10 1740.

[Prefatory essay on the Acta diurna of the Old Romans? Jan 1740].

[Part of Extract of Mr Gulliver's Memoirs? March, May 1740].

[Letter to Mr Urban on swearing, by 'S.J.'? April 1740].

The life of Admiral Blake. June 1740.

Announcement of forthcoming Life of Drake. July 1740.

Life of Sir Francis Drake. Aug–Oct, Dec–Jan 1740.

Epitaph on Claudy Philips, by 'G'. Sept 1740.

[Translation of a Welch epitaph on Prince Madoc, by 'I'? Oct 1740].

An essay on epitaphs. Dec 1740.

Life of John Philip Barretier. Dec 1740, Feb 1741.

Preface to vol 11, 1741.

A debate upon the petition of Parliament to Cromwell to assume the title of King. Feb–March 1741.

Editorial note. April 1741.

A dissertation on the Amazons. Ibid (first paragraph). See J. L. Abbott, PQ 44 1965.

A panegyric on Dr Morin. July 1741 (with footnotes).

[Monthly articles: Foreign History, Aug–Dec 1741].

The jests of Hierocles. Sept 1741.

[Monthly articles: Foreign Books. Nov–Dec 1741].

[Remarks on considerations on the embargo upon the provision of victual? Dec 1741].

Preface to vol 12, 1742.

Debates in the Senate of Lilliput. Jan–Dec suppl.

[Monthly articles: Foreign History? Jan, March, Aug, Nov, Dec 1742].

[Monthly articles: Foreign books? Jan–May, July–Aug, Oct–Dec 1742].

Review of Account of the conduct of the Duchess of Marlborough. March, April?, May–June 1742. By 'Britannicus'. See J. Leed, N & Q May 1957.

[Cryptographia denudata? March–May, Sept 1742].

Life of Peter Burman. April 1742.

Additional account of the life of Barretier. May 1742.

Essay on DuHalde's Description of China. June–July 1742.

Life of Dr Sydenham. Dec 1742. Rptd from Sydenham's Works, ed John Swan 1742; see below.

An account of the Harleian Library. Ibid. Rptd from Proposals for the Harleian catalogue, 1 Nov 1742; see above.

Preface to vol 13, 1743.

Debates in the Senate of Lilliput. Jan–Dec suppl.

[Editorial note on Grazier's advocate? Jan 1743].

Letter to Mr Urban on Controversy between Crousaz and Warburton. March, Nov 1743.

[Articles: Foreign books. March, May, Aug–Sept 1743].

[Foreign history? April 1743].

Friendship: an ode. July 1743.

Latin verses: Ad Lauram parituram epigramma. Ibid.

The young author. Ibid.

Translation of Horace, Odes 1, xxii. Ibid.

Letter to Mr Urban on forthcoming Life of Savage. Aug 1743.

Latin translation of Pope's verses on his grotto. Oct 1743.

[Advertisement of Bibliotheca Harleiana? Ibid.]

Preface to vol 14, 1744.

Debates in the Senate of Lilliput. Jan–March 1744.

[Letter and introduction to excerpts from Delaney's Fifteen sermons. July 1744].

Revision of Walmesley's Latin translation of Byrom's poem. Feb 1745. See TLS 9 Dec 1953.

Proposals for publishing Grey's Debates. March 1745. See above.

[Life of Nicholas Rienzy? Jan–Feb 1747].

On Lord Lovat's execution. April 1747.

Translation of Latin Epitaph on Sir Thomas Hanmer. May 1747.

To Miss — on her giving the author a gold and silk network purse, of her own weaving. Ibid.

Stella in mourning. Ibid.

The winter's walk. Ibid.

An ode (Stern winter now, by spring repress'd). Ibid.

To Lyce, an elderly lady. Ibid. See J. Reeding, TLS 11 Sept 1937.

[A song ('Not the soft sigh of vernal gales'). June 1747].

Proposals for printing Hugonis Grotii Adamus Exsul. Aug 1747. Also pbd separately; see above.

Prologue spoken at the opening of Drury Lane Theatre. Oct 1747. Also pbd separately; see above.

[Foreign history? Nov 1747]. See A. Sherbo, JEGP 52 1953.

[Life of Sir Thomas de Veil? Dec 1747].

[The natural beauty: to Stella? Feb 1748].

Life of the Earl of Roscommon. May 1748.

[Supplement to the Life of M. Burman? Sept 1748].

[Foreign history? Nov 1748].

Letter to Mr Urban on the fireworks, by 'O.N.' Jan 1749.

Foreign history. Feb 1749.

Three introductory paragraphs to Abridgement of Anson's Voyages. Sept–Oct, Dec 1749; Feb–March 1750.

[An evening ode: to Stella? Jan 1750].

[Remarks on the tragedy called the Black Prince? Feb 1750].

[The vanity of wealth: an ode to a friend? Ibid].

Prologue to Comus. April 1750; also pbd separately; see above.

Proposals for Essays in verse and prose by Anna Williams. Sept 1750. Also pbd separately at different times: see above.

Editorial note on Some account of the controversy concerning Milton's imitation of the Moderns. Dec 1750.

[Foreign history? Ibid].

[Notice of Charlotte Lennox's Life of Harriot Stuart? Ibid].
[Preface to vol 21, 1751? p. iii].
[Some account of Shirley's Black Prince? Ibid].
[Extract from the Scribleriad? Jan 1751].
[Review of Edward Moore's Gil Blas? Feb 1751].
[Notice of Feijo on the practice of physic. Ibid].
[Notice of the Scribleriad? Ibid].
[Notice of Ayloffe's translation of Diderot and D'Alembert's Encyclopaedia? Jan 1752].
[Notice of the Abuse of poetry? Ibid].
Sparks: or small poems morally turned? Feb 1752.
Mrs Cibber's translation of The Oracle? March 1752.
Review of Charlotte Lennox's The female Quixote. Ibid.
[Some account of Elfrida, by Mr Mason? May 1752].
[Notice of Mason's Elfrida? Ibid].
Notice of Grey's Hudibras? Ibid.
[Notice of Robson's account of six years in Hudson's Bay? June 1752].
[Notice of G. A. Steven's Distress upon distress? July 1752].
[Notice of Hill's The impertinent? August 1752].
Preface to vol 23, 1753.
Some account of Moore's The gamester. Feb 1753.
[Some account of Young's The brothers? March 1753].
[Notice of Dyer's Carnation? Ibid].
[Notice of Charlotte Lennox's Shakespear illustrated? May 1753].
[Notice of Baker's microscope? Ibid].
[Moral and religious aphorisms? June 1753].
[Foreign history: para 1 of Persia? Nov 1753].
[Notice of Richardson's Grandison? Ibid].
[Notice of Glover's Boadicea? Dec 1753].
[Notice of Hogarth's Analysis of beauty? Ibid].
[Reflections on the Tragedy of Boadicea? Ibid].
Notice of death of Edward Cave. After Index to vol 23.
Preface to A general index to the first twenty volumes of the Gentleman's Magazine. See below.
Preface to vol 24, 1754.
[Some account of the Principles of beauty? Jan 1754].
[Corrections to Anna Williams's verses on Richardson's Grandison. Ibid. See Life 2 pp. 25-6, 479. The ms addns in the separate pamphlet in the Victoria & Albert Museum are not in Johnson's hand].
Life of Edward Cave. Feb 1754; rev at Nichols's request in 1781 in 2nd edn of Biographia britannica.
[Plan of Philoclea? Ibid].
[Some account of the new plays: Virginia. March 1754].
[Notices of books: Observations on the office of a constable by Saunders Welsh; the Feminiad by John Duncombe; the Choice of an husband by N. Weeks; The triumph of death: a poem; the Immortality of the soul by William Hay. March, 1754].
[Notice of book: another translation of Mr Browne's poem by Dr Grey? Ibid].
[Some account of Constantine: a new tragedy. April 1754].
[Notice of the History of Pudica, a lady of N–rf—k? Ibid.].
[Notice of a Letter to Thomas Shadwell? Ibid].
[Some account of Creusa: a new tragedy by Mr William Whitehead. May 1754].
[Notices of Pomery Hill: a poem; Narcissa and Eliza? Ibid].
[List of foreign books? June 1754].
[Notices of the Lay of Doom? Ibid].
[Notice of the Day of Judgement: a poem? Aug 1754].
[List of foreign books? Sept 1754].
[Notice of Barbadoes: a poem by Mr Weekes? Ibid].
[Notice of A dissertation upon genius by W. Sharpe; A descriptive poem by Dr Dalton? Dec 1754].
[Notice of Miscellanies in prose and verse by C. Hallifax? Ibid].
[An account of foreign books? Suppl 1754].
[Notice of Select epitaphs? Jan 1755].

[Notice of An account of an attempt to ascertain the longitude, by Zachary Williams? Ibid].
[Notice of T. Edwards's New English translation of the Psalms? Feb 1755].
[Notice of An essay towards a translation of Homer's works, by J. N. Scot? March 1755].
[Notice of the History of Margaret of Anjou? April 1755].
[An account of the best foreign books? Sept 1755].
[Notice of foreign books? March 1756].
[Notice of foreign books. Suppl 1757].
[Review of the Reduction of Louisbourg; and the Prisoner: or nature's complaint against justice? Dec 1758].
Review of Tytler's Defence of Mary Queen of Scots. Oct 1760.
[Review of the Honour and advantage of agriculture? July 1760].
[Foreign history: opening paragraph? Sept 1760].
Account of the detection of the imposture in Cock-lane. Feb 1762.
Prologue to Goldsmith's Good-natur'd man. Feb 1768. See below.
[Notice of R. Deane's Essay on the future life of brute creatures? April 1768. Attributed by Croker in his edn of Boswell's Life, 1831].
[Account of the actions of Sir Joseph Mawbey MP for Southwark? March 1769. Johnson's letter on this subject was partly quoted in this piece, from Gazetteer].
[Review of Ruffhead's Life of Pope by 'X'? May 1769].
Life of Francis Cheynel. March–April 1775. See Student July–Sept 1751.
Prologue to Hugh Kelly's A word to the wise. June 1777. See London Chron May, and most newspapers for May, and magazines for June.
On the death of Dr Robert Levet. August 1783.
Epitaphs on Michael, Sarah and Nathanael Johnson. Jan 1784.
Rules of the Essex Head Club. Feb 1784.
Account of Styan Thirlby. April 1784.
Letter on the Universal history. Dec 1784.
A speech dictated after the expedition to Rochefort. Oct 1785.

Hereford Journal

Address by T[homas] T[albot] on the establishment of the Hereford Infirmary. 20 Oct 1774. See below.

Literary Magazine: or Universal Review

Johnson seems to have been part editor with William Faden, the printer, as promoter of the Magazine.
See D. J. Greene, RES new ser 1956.
Preliminary address. May 1756.
Historical memoirs. Ibid.
[Anatomy of a Manatee? Ibid].
An introduction to the political state of Great Britain. Ibid.
Observations added to An authentic account of the present state of Lisbon. Ibid.
[Description of a Sea Bear? June 1756].
Commentary on a letter from Joseph Ames. Ibid.
Observations on the Militia Bill. Ibid.
Observations on A letter from a French refugee. Ibid. See D. J. Greene, The Johnsonian canon: a neglected attribution, PMLA 65 1950.
Observations on his Britannick Majesty's treaties with her Imperial Majesty of all the Russias and the Landgrave of Hesse-Cassel. July 1756.
Abstract of the charge and defence of Alexander Bower. Ibid.
[Account of the Channel Islands? Ibid].
Observations on the present state of affairs. Aug 1756.
[A hint to the publick (on the price of corn)? Nov 1756].
Memoirs of the King of Prussia. Nov 1756–Jan 1757.

Memoirs of Charles Frederick, King of Prussia, with notes and a continuation by Mr Harrison. 1786. Originally ptd in Literary Mag 1756; rptd in Miscellaneous and fugitive pieces vol i, 1773. The continuation said to be 'by Mr Harrison' was written by William Mavor, 1787, Liverpool [1787?].

Reviews

Birch's History of the Royal Society. May 1756.
White's Collateral bee-boxes. Ibid.
Murphy's Gray's Inn Journal. Ibid.
Warton's Essay on the writings and genius of Pope. Ibid.
Hampton's Polybius. Ibid.
Blackwell's Natural history of Aleppo. June 1756.
Newton's Letters to Bentley containing arguments in proof of a Deity. Ibid.
Borlase's Observations on the islands of Scilly. Ibid.
Home's Experiments on bleaching. July 1756.
Browne's Christian morals. Ibid.
Hales on distilling sea-water, the great benefit of ventilators, and curing an ill-taste in milk. Ibid.
Lucas's Essays on waters. Aug–Sept 1756.
Whalley's edition of Works of Ben Jonson. Aug 1756.
Keith's Catalogue of the Bishops of Scotland. Ibid.
Brown's History of Jamaica. Ibid.
Free's Sermon before the Antigallicans. Ibid.
Parkin's Account of the invasion under William Duke of Normandy. Ibid.
A scheme for preventing a further increase of the National Debt. Ibid.
An account of the conferences between Sir William Johnson and the Mohawks. Ibid.
Philosophical transactions, vol 49. Ibid.
Lovett's The subtile medium proved. Sept 1756.
Hoadly and Wilson's Observations on a series of electrical experiments. Ibid.
Keysler's Travels. Ibid.
Mrs Lennox's translation of Sully's Memoirs. Oct 1756.
Miscellanies by Elizabeth Harrison. Ibid.
Evans's Map and account of the middle colonies in America. Ibid.
Letter on the case of Admiral Byng. Ibid.
Appeal to the people concerning Admiral Byng. Ibid.
Hanway's eight days journey, to which is added an essay on tea. Nov 1756, May 1757.
The Cadet: a military treatise. Nov 1756.
Further particulars relating to the case of Admiral Byng. Ibid.
The conduct of the ministry impartially examined. Ibid.
Soame Jenyns's A free inquiry into the nature and origin of evil. May–July 1757.
Reply to a paper in the gazetteer of May 26 1757 [by Hanway]. June 1757.

London Chronicle

Introduction. 1 Jan 1757.
Advertisement concerning the World Displayed. 13 Nov 1759. *See* Public Ledger, below; and under Proposals, above.
Review of Grainger's Sugar-cane. 5 July 1754. With Thomas Percy. *See* Critical Review, above.
Character of the Rev Zachariah Mudge. 2 May 1769, rptd in Life 4 p. 77.
Vindication of Dr James's Fever powders. 20 Feb 1777, rptd in 8th edn of R. James, Dissertation on fevers, 1778.
Observations on the propriety of pardoning Dr [William] Dodd. 24–5 June 1777.

London Evening Post

[Advertisement for reprint of Pilgrim's progress in weekly parts. 27 Nov 1755]. *See* G. J. Kolb, Stud in Eng Lit 1500–1900 1 1961.

London Gazette

The address of the painters, sculptors and architects to King George III on his accession to the throne. 6–10 Jan 1761.

London Magazine

Elegy on the death of Mr Levet. Sept 1783. 'Incorrect copies of this effusion of the most friendly regard have been distributed; that which you will now receive, is genuine', p. 229.

Morning Chronicle

[Election address for Henry Thrale? 20 Nov 1775].
See Johnson, Boswell and their circle, 1965.
Communication showing that a passage in the Rambler no 85 did not favour suicide. 29 May 1782. *See* GM Feb 1786.

Public Advertiser

[Election address for Henry Thrale? 24 Sept 1765].
See Johnson, Boswell and their circle, 1965.
[Election address for Henry Thrale? 1 Oct 1765].
Election address for Henry Thrale 24 Dec 1765.
Election address for Henry Thrale. 3 March 1768. 9, 15 and 23 March 1768?
Election address for Henry Thrale. 1 Oct 1774. 7, 14 Oct 1764?
Advertisement of new edition of the Spectator. 14 Dec 1776. *See* Life 2 p. 503.
Election address for Henry Thrale. 7 Sept 1780. 5, 6, 11 Sept 1780?

Public Ledger

Advertisement of the World displayed. 14 Jan 1760. *See* Life 1 p. 546, *but see also* London Chron 13 Nov 1759 and under Proposals, above.
Weekly correspondent. 2, 9, 16 Dec 1760. *See* E. L. McAdam, RES 18 1942.

St James's Chronicle

Epigram on Lord Anson's Temple of the winds. 1 Jan 1785.
[Election address for Henry Thrale? 26 Sept 1765].
See Johnson, Boswell and their circle, 1965.

The Student: or the Oxford & Cambridge Monthly Miscellany. Vol 2, 1751.

The life of Dr Francis Cheynel, by 'S. J—n'. July–Sept 1751; rptd GM March–April 1775.

Universal Chronicle & Weekly Gazette

Introduction, in part. 8 April 1758. *See* A. T. Hazen, Johnson's prefaces and dedications, New Haven 1937, pp. 205–13.
Idler 15 April 1758–5 April 1760. *See* above.
Green, B. Possible additions to the Johnson canon. Yale Univ Lib Gazette 16 1942. The text of 5 articles, Observations, 19 Aug–30 Sept 1758.
Advertisement against reprinting the Idler without leave. 5 Jan 1759.
Advertisement for Public Ledger. 12 Jan 1760. *See* G. J. Kolb, SB 12 1958.

Universal Magazine

The convict's address, by William Dodd. June 1777. Abridged.

Universal Museum & Complete Magazine

[Essay on elegies? 3 1767]. *See* A. Sherbo and E. G. Fogel, BNYPL Jan, July 1959.

Universal Visiter & Memorialist for the Year 1756

Further thoughts on agriculture. March.
[Latin verses beginning Nequiquam Danaen includit ahenea turris? Ibid].

Reflections on the present state of literature. April.

A dissertation on the epitaphs written by Pope. May. Added to Idler 1767 (3rd edn) etc and to Lives of poets, under Pope.

All signed**; other contributions signed ** are clearly not Johnson's.

[Some account of the life and writings of Chaucer? Jan].

[Reflections upon the state of Portugal? Feb].

[Song: The silver rain, the pearly dew? April].

[The rise, progress and perfection of architecture? June]. *See* R. B. Botting, MP 36 1939.

Unidentified newspapers or magazines

Obituary notice of Zachariah Williams (d. 12 July 1755).

Obituary notice of Coleborne Hancock (d. 13 Feb 1783). The notice gives the date 16 April 1783.

Contributions to Books and Assistance to Other Writers

Johnson's prefaces and dedications, ed A. T. Hazen, New Haven 1937, *reprints with critical comments most of the prefaces and dedications Johnson contributed to others' books.*

A miscellany of poems by several hands, published by J. Husbands AM, Fellow of Pembroke-College, Oxon. Oxford 1731. Messia, pp. 111–17; 'the translation of Mr Pope's Messiah was deliver'd to his tutor as a college exercise, by Mr Johnson, a Commoner of Pembroke-College in Oxford, and 'tis hoped will be no discredit to the excellent original,' Preface. Poem tr as The Messiah: a poem, translated from the Latin of Dr Johnson, by W. Meickle, 1843. On Husbands, *see* R. S. Crane, MLN 37 1922.

Poems on several occasions by Mary Masters. 1733. According to Boswell (Life 4 p. 246) Johnson revised her volumes. *See* A. Sherbo, MLR 50 1955.

Dedication to King George II of Henry Hervey Aston's English translation of a Latin epitaph on the death of Queen Caroline by Lord John ('Sporus') Hervey, unpublished but written 1738. Ms copy of 1769 in Bodley, MS Add A.190. Dedication ascribed by J. L. Clifford, Young Samuel Johnson, 1955.

Prologue to Garrick's Lethe, 1740 (ms copy in Folger); ascribed by M. E. Knapp, TLS 4 Jan 1947.

The works of Dr Thomas Sydenham, newly made English from the original Latin, by John Swan MD. 1742. The prefatory Life of Sydenham, rptd in GM Dec 1742; 1749 (2nd edn) (Life rev), 1753, 1763, 1769; ed G. Wallis 1788.

Monarchy asserted to be the best, most antient and legall form of government. 1660, 1742. Probably Johnson.

A medicinal dictionary, by Robert James MD. 3 vols 1743–5. Issued at first in fortnightly and then in weekly pts. Variant titles to vol 1. Tr French, 3 vols 1746–8. Dedication to Dr Mead. 'I helped in writing the proposals for his Dictionary, and also a little in the Dictionary itself'. *See* Life 3 p. 22, and A. T. Hazen, Johnson and Dr Robert James, Bull Inst of History of Medicine 4 1936, 7 1939. L. C. McHenry, Johnson's medical biographies, Jnl of History of Medicine 14 1959.

Miscellaneous correspondence: containing essays on various subjects, sent to the Gentleman's Magazine. 9 pts 1742–8. Attributed by Yale Univ Lib catalogue.

Catalogus bibliothecæ Harleianæ. 5 vols 1743–4. Vol 5 repeats unsold items. An account of the Harleian Library vol 1 already ptd in Proposals for printing Bibliotheca Harleiana. Preface to vol 3. Johnson is said to have catalogued the Latin books and Oldys the English; Hazen pp. 43–4.

The Harleian miscellany. 8 vols 1744–6; vol 1, 1744, 1753. Introd, afterwards entitled An essay on the origin and importance of small tracts and fugitive pieces; ed J. Malham 12 vols 1808–11; ed T. Park 10 vols 1808–13.

Johnson's Essay rptd in Literary pamphlets vol 1, ed E. Rhys 1897. *See also* D. J. Greene, Johnson and the Harleian Miscellany, N & Q July 1958.

The publisher: containing miscellanies in prose and verse. 4 pts 1745. Johnson's Account of the design rptd from his Proposals on p. iii of no 1.

Boulter's monument: a panegyrical poem, sacred to the memory of that great and excellent prelate and patriot, Dr Hugh Boulter, late Lord-Archbishop of Ardmagh [by Samuel Madden]. 1745 (2 issues), Dublin 1745. 'Castigated' by Johnson at the author's request: *see* Life 1 p. 318; and Hawkins, Life 1787 p. 391.

A sermon preached at the Cathedral Church of St Paul, before the sons of the clergy, on Thursday the second of May 1745 by the Honourable and Reverend Henry Hervey Aston. 1745.

Attributed by L. F. Powell, Times 25 Nov 1938; *see also* Life 3 p. 507; ed J. L. Clifford, Los Angeles 1955 (Augustan Reprint Soc).

The preceptor: containing a general course of education. 1748. Vol 1, Preface; vol 2, The vision of Theodore, the Hermit of Teneriffe; 2 vols 1754, 1758, 1763, Dublin 1761 ('4th edn'), London 1764, 1769, 1775, 1783, Dublin 1786 ('8th edn'), London 1793; tr German, 2 vols 1765–7.

Vision of Theodore rptd in Harrison's New Novelist's Magazine or Entertaining Library vol 1, 1786, and in Rasselas, Philadelphia 1850; tr Dutch, in De Hollandsche Wysgeer pt 1, 1759. *See* Rasselas, above; also R. P. McCutcheon, Johnson and Dodsley's Preceptor 1748, Tulane Stud in Eng 3 1952.

[The interest of England with regard to foreign alliances explained by Sir Walter Raleigh Knt, now first published from his original manuscript. 1750. *See* Johnson's Letter to Birch 12 May 1750, and European Mag Jan 1785. Johnson's part in the book, if any, is uncertain].

An essay on Milton's use and imitation of the moderns in his Paradise lost [by William Lauder]. 1750. Preface and postscript. The preface is a reprint of most of the text of Lauder's Proposals of 1747, above. When his fraud was exposed by Douglas, the booksellers continued to issue the Essay with addn of a New preface of 2 leaves dated 1 Dec 1750, and yet again with a further New postscript of 2 leaves dated 2 Jan 1751. *See* Hazen 77 f.

A letter to the Reverend Mr Douglas, occasioned by his Vindication of Milton, by William Lauder. Beginning dictated by Johnson.

The female Quixote: or the adventures of Arabella, by Charlotte Lennox. 2 vols 1752. Dedication to the Earl of Middlesex; the 2nd last chapter, i.e. bk 9 ch 11, 'the best chapter in this history.' Also 2 vols Dublin 1752, London 1752, Dublin 1763; Harrison's edn 1783; Novelist's Magazine 1787; Cooke's edn 1799; ed Mrs Barbauld in British Novelists vol 24–5, 1810, 1820; tr German, as Don Quixote in Reifrocke, 1754; tr Spanish as Don Quixote un Faldas, 1808.

A general index to the first twenty volumes of the Gentleman's Magazine. 1753. Preface by Johnson, attributed by J. Nichols, General indexes to the GM, 1831, p. xlviii; also L. F. Powell, E & S 28 1942.

[T. Warton]. The Union: or select Scots and English poems. 'Edinburgh' [=Oxford] 1753. The sprig of myrtle, p. 117, by 'Mr Hammond'.

Shakespear illustrated, by the author of the Female Quixote. 2 vols 1754; vol 3, 1754; 1753. Dedication to the Earl of Orrery; rptd Philadelphia 1809.

The works of Virgil. Ed Joseph Warton 4 vols 1753. Johnson's help is acknowledged 1, xxx. *See* A. Sherbo, Johnsonian Newsletter Dec 1958.

[Baretti, Joseph. The voice of discord: or the battle of the fiddles. 1753. Samuel Johnson's assistance is suggested by C. J. M. Lubbers van der Brugge, Eng Miscellany (Rome) 10 1959.

Familiar letters and poems on several occasions, by Mary Masters. 1755. 'Mrs Masters, the poetess, whose volumes he revised'. Life 4 pp. 246, 525. *See* under 1733, above.

An account of an attempt to ascertain the longitude at sea, by an exact theory of the variation of the magnetical needle, by Zachariah Williams. 1755. Written for Williams by Johnson; with an Italian trn ptd on the right-hand pages, by Baretti. In the Bodley copy, which was presented by Johnson, there are 3 notes in Johnson's handwriting, and an unidentified newspaper cutting about Williams, evidently written by Johnson.

An introduction to the Italian language by Giuseppe Baretti. 1755. Preface, perhaps in part; also pp. 48 and 198.

Christian morals by Sir Thomas Browne of Norwich MD, with a life of the author by Johnson and explanatory notes: second edition. 1756, 1761; ed S. Wilkin 1836, 1856 (in Browne's Works), 1845, 1863, 1904; ed S. C. Roberts, Cambridge 1927.

An introduction to the game of draughts, by William Payne. 1756, '1756' (for c. 1800). Dedication to the Earl of Rochford; and Preface.

A new dictionary of trade and commerce, by Richard Rolt. 1756, 1761. Preface.

Memoirs of Maximilian de Bethune, Duke of Sully, translated from the French [by Mrs Lennox]. 3 vols 1756, 5 vols 1757, Edinburgh 1760, 3 vols 1761, 6 vols 1763, 5 vols Edinburgh 1770, 1773, London 1778, 6 vols Dublin 1781, London 1810, Edinburgh 1812, London 1812, Philadelphia 1817, Edinburgh 1819, 4 vols 1856. Dedication to Duke of Newcastle: *see* Hazen, p. 110.

The Italian library, by Giuseppe Baretti. 1757. A history of the Italian tongue (in part).

Designs of Chinese buildings, furniture, dresses, machines, utensils etc, by William Chambers. 1757. 'The first two paragraphs'; *see* Life 1 p. 21, 4 p. 188. Some portions rptd in T. Percy, Miscellaneous pieces relating to the Chinese, 2 vols 1762; tr French, 1757, 1776. *See also* B*** de la Malpière, La Chine: moeurs, usages etc d'après Chambers, 1825.

The evangelical history of our Lord Jesus Christ, harmonized, explained and illustrated etc by a society of gentlemen [i.e. John Lindsay (Hazen 116)]. 2 vols [1757]. Dedication to the Lords Spiritual and Temporal and Commons. Johnson's authorship of this Dedication was denied by Boswell. *See* Life 4 p. 383. But *see* 4 p. 549, and R. Anderson, Life of Johnson, 1815, pp. 257–8.

The works of Horace in English verse, by several hands, collected and published by Mr Duncombe. 2 vols 1757. No doubt trn in vol 1 of Ode 1, xxii, 'by S.J.'.

Memoirs for the history of Madame de Maintenon, translated by the author of the Female Quixote [Mrs Charlotte Lennox]. 5 vols 1757, 3 vols Dublin 1758. Dedication.

New tables of interest, by John Payne. 1758. Preface.

Philander: a dramatic pastoral, by the author of the Female Quixote. 1758, Dublin 1758. Dedication to Viscount Charlemont; *see* Hazen 102.

[Stenography]: or short-hand improved, by John Angell. [1758]. Dedication to the Duke of Richmond. 'I remember one Angel, who came to me to write for him a preface or dedication to a book upon short-hand.' But the Preface is mostly taken from P. Gibbs, Compendious and swift writing, 1736. Life 2 p. 224 and p. 504. If Johnson helped with the Dedication, it cannot have been ptd as he wrote or dictated it.]

A proposal to render effectual a plan to remove the nuisance of common prostitutes from the streets of this metropolis [by Saunders Welch]. 1758. Attributed by E. L. McAdam, RES new ser 4 1953.

The Greek theatre of Father Brumoy, translated by Mrs Charlotte Lennox. 3 vols 1759. Dedication to the Prince of Wales; tr from A dissertation upon the Greek comedy, and from The general conclusion.

The world displayed: or a curious collection of voyages and travels, selected from the writers of all nations. 20 vols 1759–61. Introd vol 1. Rptd several times in the course of production both in London and Dublin; 8 vols Philadelphia 1795–6, Baltimore 1797.

The monthly melody: being a collection of vocal and instrumental music composed by Dr Arne. 1760. Dedication to Prince Edward, Duke of York. 'He once dedicated some musick for the German flute to Edward, Duke of York,' Life 2 p. 2; but this identification is doubtful.

A dictionary of the English and Italian languages, by Joseph Baretti. 2 vols 1760 (variant imprints), 1771. Dedication. Subsequent edns of this Dictionary are numerous, but none contains Johnson's Dedication.

A treatise of canine madness, by Robert James. 1760. Dedication to the Duke of Kingston? The sentiments may be compared with Idler 17. It is doubtful that it is ptd as Johnson wrote it.

Flloyd, Thomas. Bibliotheca biographica. 3 vols 1760. Dedication to Earl of Corke and Orrery?

Address of the painters, sculptors and architects to George III on his accession to the throne of these kingdoms. 1760. Written by Johnson, *see* Life 1 p. 252; ptd in London Gazette 6–10 Jan 1761.

Proceedings of the Committee appointed to manage the contributions begun at London, December 18 1759, for cloathing French Prisoners of War. 1760. Introd. The Committee was established at the instigation of Thomas Hollis.

The English works of Roger Ascham, with notes and observations and the author's life by James Bennet. 1761, [1767]. Dedication to the Earl of Shaftesbury; the Life of Ascham; notes mainly by Johnson. *See* Life 1 pp. 550–2. Johnson's Life of Ascham rptd in Ascham's English works, 1815. Ed J. H. Carlisle, Boston 1886, Syracuse NY 1890.

Thoughts on the Coronation of his present Majesty King George the Third, by John Gwynn. 1761. Corrections and improvements. *See* Life 1 pp. 21, 361.

Henrietta, by Mrs Charlotte Lennox: the second edition 1761. Dedication (added to 2nd edn) to Duchess of Newcastle; *see* Hazen 100. First edn of 1758 had no Dedication. Rptd in Harrison's edn, 1788; Cooke's edn [1805?].

An enquiry into the nature and origin of literary property. 1762.

A complete system of astronomical chronology, by John Kennedy. 1762. Dedication to the King; and concluding paragraph.

Chronological tables of universal history, by Abbé Lenglet du Fresnoy. [Tr Thomas Flloyd] 2 vols 1762. Preface: *see* A. T. Hazen, TLS 28 June 1934, and Prefaces and dedications, p. 84.

Catalogue of the pictures exhibited by the Society of Artists. 1762. Preface. *See* Life 1 p. 367. Johnson's Preface rptd in W. Sandby, History of the Royal Academy, 1862.

Debates of the House of Commons, from the year 1667 to the year 1694, collected by the Honble Anchitell Grey, in ten volumes. 1763, 10 vols 1769. Perhaps editorial assistance from Johnson; he wrote the Proposals, 1745, 1762.

Jerusalem delivered: an heroic poem translated by John Hoole. 2 vols 1763, 1764, 1767, 1772. Dedication to the Queen.

See T. O. Mabbott, The text of Dr Johnson's dedication of Hoole's Tasso, N & Q 3 Nov 1945.

The poetical calendar: containing a collection of scarce and valuable pieces of poetry, with variety of originals and translations, by the most eminent hands, written and selected by Francis Fawkes MA and William Woty. 12 vols 1763, 1764. Some account of the life and writings of Mr William Collins in vol 12 for December. Rptd in GM Jan 1764 and included in Lives of the poets.

The traveller: or a prospect of society by [Oliver Goldsmith]. 1764, 1765 (3 edns) etc. Lines 420, 429–34, 437–8. *See* Life 2 p. 6.

Reliques of ancient English poetry. 3 vols 1765. Dedication to the Countess of Northumberland. All subsequent edns omit Johnson's Dedication, except 3 vols Dublin 1766; tr German, 1766. Partly Johnson: *see* Anderson, Life of Johnson, 1815, p. 309; G. B. Hill, Boswell's proof-sheets, Johnson Club Papers 1899, p. 69; L. F. Powell, Percy's Reliques, Library 3rd ser 9 1938; R. M. Baine, Harvard Lib Bull 5 1951.

Election addresses for Henry Thrale, Sept–Dec 1765. Assistance, *see* Johnson, Boswell and their circle, 1965, pp. 170–89.

Miscellanies in prose and verse, by Anna Williams. 1766. Advertisement; several poems, including the Ant, the Fountains: a fairy tale, rptd with Rasselas, Philadelphia 1850; London 1927. 'Most of the pieces in this volume have evidently received additions from his superiour pen' (Life 2 p. 26); besides Johnson and Mrs Williams, other contributors were Thomas Percy, Mrs Thrale, Frances Reynolds and John Hoole; *see* Hazen p. 214.

Dissertations on the ancient history of Ireland, by Charles O'Conor. 1766 (2nd edn). 'The first hints have been communicated by Dr Samuel Johnson' for this rev edn (first edn 1753). *See* Letters, ed Chapman i, 101; Johnson to O'Conor, 9 April 1757.

London and Westminster improved, illustrated by plans, by John Gwynn. 1766. Dedication to the King.

A treatise describing and explaining the construction and use of new celestial and terrestrial globes, by George Adams. 1766, 1769, 1772, 1777, 1782, Philadelphia 1800. Dedication to the King.

An introduction to geometry: containing the most useful propositions in Euclid, and other authors, by William Payne. 1767, 1768. Dedication to the Duke of York. *See* The R. B. Adam Library vol 2, 1929, p. 18 and Life 2 pp. 481–2; Hazen 151–2.

The works of Metastasio, translated from the Italian by John Hoole. 2 vols 1767. Dedication to the Duke of Northumberland.

The Idylliums of Theocritus, translated from the Greek by Francis Fawkes. 1767. 'The celebrated Mr Samuel Johnson has corrected part of this work, and furnished me with some judicious remarks', Preface p. xx. *See* R. W. Chapman, Johnsonian bibliography supplement, 1938 and A. T. Hazen and T. O. Mabbott, RES 21 1945.

Election address for Henry Thrale, March 1768. *See* Johnson, Boswell and their circle, 1965, pp. 170–89.

The good-natur'd man: a comedy by Oliver Goldsmith. 1768. *See* W. B. Todd, SB 11 1958. Prologue.

Cyrus: a tragedy, by John Hoole. 1768, 1768, 1769, Dublin 1769, London 1772. Dedication to the Duchess of Northumberland. *See* Hazen 60.

1768–9 collaboration with Robert Chambers on the Vinerian Law Lectures in Oxford. *See* E. L. McAdam, Dr Johnson and the English law, 1951; S. Krishnamurti, Dr Johnson and the law lectures of Sir Robert Chambers, MLR 44 1949; E. L. McAdam, Dr Johnson's law lectures for Chambers: an addition to the canon, RES 15–16 1939–40.

The deserted village [by Oliver Goldsmith]. 1770. The last 4 lines. *See* Life 2 p. 7; and W. B. Todd, SB 6 1954.

Elements of trigonometry, plain and spherical for the use of learners, by William Payne. 1772. Dedication to the Earl of Rochford. *See* Hazen 152–4.

Introduction to the most useful European languages, by Giuseppe Baretti. 1772. 2 chs of Rasselas are included.

The present state of the East India Company's affairs [by John Hoole]. 1772. Assistance with the Preface? *See* Hazen 60n.

A dictionary of ancient geography, by Alexander Macbean. 1773. Preface.

An address to the nobility, gentry and clergy of the County of Hereford [on the founding of the Hereford Infirmary, 3 Oct 1774] in Hereford Journal 20 Oct 1774; rptd as Three addresses to the inhabitants of the County of Hereford in favour of the establishment of a publick informary, by Thomas Talbot, 1774. Assistance: *see* A. T. Hazen and E. L. McAdam, HLQ 3 1940.

Election address for Henry Thrale, March 1774. *See* Johnson, Boswell and their circle, 1965, pp. 170–89.

Easy phraseology for the use of young ladies, who intend to learn the colloquial part of the Italian language, by Joseph Baretti. 1775. Preface. Another very rare state as Small talk for the use of young ladies.

Annals of Scotland, by Sir David Dalrymple, Lord Hailes. 2 vols 1776, 1779, 3 vols Edinburgh 1797, London 1819. Revision of proofs.

The Lusiad, translated by William Julius Mickle. 1776, 1778, 1798, Dublin 1791. Sentence in introd, p. cliii. *See* Life 4 p. 251.

A general history of music, by Charles Burney. 2 vols 1776–82. Vol 1, dedication to the Queen; vol 2, p. 340, trn of lines from Euripides' Medea. *See* Life 4 pp. 546–7.

A general history of music, by Charles Burney, MusD, FRS. 4 vols 1776, 1787, 1789, 1789. A 2nd edn of vol 1 only 1789, and of vol 2 '1782' (for 1809).
Dedication to the Queen, verses in 2, 340, and apology at end of vol 2. *See* Hazen 24–6.

A word to the wise. Prologue spoken 29 May 1777. Ptd in GM June 1777 and in Works of Hugh Kelly 1778.

The convict's address to his unhappy brethren: being a sermon preached by the Rev Dr Dodd, Friday, June 6 1777, in the Chapel of Newgate. 1777 (24 pp.), 1777 (28 pp.); other edns pbd in Dublin, Salisbury, Gainsborough, Newcastle, Taunton, Whitehaven; and several unauthorized edns with varying titles. Included in subsequent edns of Dodd's Thoughts in prison. Johnson marked for Boswell 'such passages as were added by Dr Dodd'. *See* Life 3 p. 142.

Occasional papers by the late William Dodd LlD. Unique copy in BM. Suppressed, but rptd in Life of Johnson (attributed to Cooke), pbd by Kearsley in 1785, pp. 130–40. The pamphlet contains, besides editorial matter, Dr Dodd's account of himself; a Declaration inclosed by Dodd in a letter to a friend; his Letter to the Lord Chancellor; his Letter to the Earl of Mansfield; his petition to the King; and Mrs Dodd's petition to the Queen. All were written by Johnson, except Dodd's account of himself, which he revised. Johnson wrote also Dodd's speech to the Recorder of London; a petition from the City of London, which 'they mended'; Dodd's last solemn declaration and observations on the propriety of pardoning Dodd, sent by Johnson to the public papers, and ptd in the Life pbd by Mearsley, 1785, pp. 139, 140. *See* Life 3 pp. 141, 496, 497. Various of Johnson's pieces for Dodd were pbd in the contemporary newspapers, and in topical tracts and pamphlets on the trial, execution and life of Dodd.

Papers written by Dr Johnson and Dr Dodd in 1777 printed from the originals in the possession of A. Edward Newton esq, with an introduction and notes by R. W. Chapman. Oxford 1926. The 'originals' are now in the Hyde Collection.

Poems and plays of Oliver Goldsmith [by Edmond Malone]. Dublin 1777. The first printing of Johnson's epitaph on Goldsmith, p. ix; the epitaph was rptd by Thomas Campbell in his A philosophical survey of the south of Ireland, 1777, Dublin 1778.

A commentary, with notes, on the Four Evangelists and the Acts of the Apostles, by Zachary Pearce. Ed John Derby 2 vols 1777. Dedication to the King; and Additions to Pearce's autobiography. *See* Life 3 pp. 489–90, and Hazen 154.

A dissertation on fevers: 8th edition, by the late R. James MD. 1778. Advertisement to the Vindication of James's fever powders, previously ptd in London Chron 20 Feb 1777. *See* Hazen 71.

Seven discourses delivered in the Royal Academy by the President Sir Joshua Reynolds. 1778; rptd Cassell's Nat Lib no 109 1888 and 1891; ed E. Gosse 1884; ed R. R. Wark 1959; tr Italian, 1778 (by Baretti, without Dedication). Dedication to the King. *See* Hazen 195.

Sir Eldred of the Bower, and the Bleeding Rock: two legendary tales, by Miss Hannah More. 1778 (2nd edn). *See* H. W. Liebert in New light on Dr Johnson, 1959. Johnson revised the text of the work for this 2nd edn; it was first pbd in 1776.

Poems and miscellaneous pieces, with a free translation of the Oedipus Tyrannus of Sophocles, by the Rev Thomas Maurice. 1779. Preface (pp. 149–52) to the 'free translation'; Johnson may also have helped with the Dedication to the Duke of Marlborough. *See* Hazen 136.

Poems to her Majesty; to which is added a new tragedy entitled the Earl of Somerset, by Henry Lucas AM. 1779. Dedication to the Queen. *See* H. W. Liebert, PBSA 41 1947.

The Carmen seculare of Horace [by Joseph Baretti]. [1779]; rptd for the ceremony of the installation of the Knights of the Bath, 1788, [1788] ('set to music by Mr Philidor'). Trn of the Epilogue.

[Henry Thrale's election address] To the worthy Electors of the Borough of Southwark. 5 Sept 1780. *See* Life 3, p. 440; and Johnson, Boswell and their circle, 1965, pp. 170–89.

Memoirs of the life of David Garrick, by Thomas Davies. 2 vols 1780 (first 2 sentences), 1780, Dublin 1780, London 1781, 1784, 1808, Boston 1808, 1818; tr German, 1782.

A guide through the Royal Academy, by Joseph Baretti. [1781]. Opening sentences, *see* Hazen 11.

An enquiry into the authenticity of the poems ascribed to Ossian, with a reply to Mr Clark's answer by W. Shaw. 1782, Dublin 1782, London 1782. Appendix, containing A reply to Mr Clark; several paragraphs.

Rev James Compton, 'your book'. Unidentified; *see* Johnson's letter to Compton 7 Nov 1782 relating to a Dedication.

The village, by the Rev George Crabbe. 1783. Lines 15–18 and 20; and general revision. *See* Life 4 p. 175.

A system of vegetables, by a Botanical Society of Lichfield. 1783. 2 vols [1782]. 'Advice in the formation of the botanic language' (p. 11).

An account [by Charles Burney] of the musical performances in Westminster Abbey, and the Pantheon, May and June 1784, in commemoration of Handel. 1785, Dublin 1785, London 1834, Amsterdam 1964; tr German, 1785. Dedication to the King. *See* Life 4 pp. 544–6.

Simpson, Joseph. The patriot: a tragedy, from a manuscript of the late Dr Samuel Johnson, corrected by himself. 1785. *See* Life 3 p. 28. Johnson's part remains doubtful.

An enquiry concerning the principles of taste, and of the origin of our ideas of beauty [by Frances Reynolds]. 1785; ed J. L. Clifford, Los Angeles 1951 (Augustan Reprint Soc). Assistance.

Letter to Samuel Johnson LlD on the subject of a future state, by John Taylor. 1787; rptd in T. Taylor, Life of John Taylor, 1911. For Johnson's contributions *see* R. W. Chapman, Dr Johnson and Dr Taylor, RES 2 1926.

British synonomy: or an attempt at regulating the choice of words in familiar conversation [by Mrs Piozzi]. 2 vols 1794, Dublin 1794, London and Paris 1804. Verses on Sir John Lade, 1 359–60.

A treatise of estates and tenures, by the late Sir Robert Chambers. Ed Sir Charles Harcourt Chambers 1824. Based on Chambers's Vinerian lectures 1768–9, above.

Subscription Books

Angell, John. Stenography: or shorthand improved. [1758].

Beattie, James. Essays on poetry and music. Edinburgh 1776.

Boyce, Samuel. Poems on several occasions. 1757.

Brooke, Henry. Gustavus Vasa: the deliverer of his country. 1739. 2 issues: only first lists subscribers.

Burney, Charles. History of music. 4 vols 1776–89. Johnson's copy of vols 1–2—all he lived to receive—is in Berg Collection, New York Public Library.

Carter, Elizabeth. All the works of Epictetus. 1758.

Davies, Thomas. Dramatic miscellanies. 3 vols 1784.

Davy, Charles and Frederick. A relation of a journey to the glaciers, translated from M. T. Bourrit. 1776 (2nd edn).

Derrick, Samuel. Collection of original poems. 1755.

Deverell, Mary. Theodora and Didymus. 1784.

Elphinston, James. The epigrams of Martial. 1782.

Fawkes, Francis. Original poems and translations. 1761.

— The Idylliums of Theocritus. 1767.

Handel, George Frederick. Messiah. 1767.

Harrison, Elizabeth. Miscellanies on moral and religious subjects. 1756.

Hill, Aaron. The works of the late Aaron Hill esq. 4 vols 1753.

Hoole, John. Jerusalem delivered, translated from the Italian of Torquato Tasso. 2 vols 1763. Hoole's present to Johnson is in Hyde Collection.

— Orlando Furioso, from the Italian of Ariosto. 5 vols 1783.

Lloyd, Robert. Poems, by Robert Lloyd AM. 1762.

Lucas, Henry. Poems to her Majesty; to which is added a new tragedy entitled the Earl of Somerset. 1779.

Lye, Edward. Dictionarium saxonico-et-gothico-latinum. 1772.

Masters, Mary. Familiar letters and poems. 1755.

Maurice, Thomas. Poems and miscellaneous pieces. 1779.

— Westminster-Abbey: an elegiac poem. 1784.

Merrick, James. The Psalms, translated or paraphrased. Reading 1765.

Mickle, William Julius. The Lusiad: or the discovery of India, translated from Camoes. Oxford 1776.

Musgrave, Samuel. Two dissertations. 1782. Johnson's copy in Hyde Collection.

Penny, Anne. Poems with a dramatic entertainment. 1771.

Ridley, Gloster. Melampus: a poem in four books. 1781.

Rucellai, Giovanni. Rosamunda tragedia. Ed Giovanni Pavoleri 1779. Dedicated to Mrs Thrale.

Shaw, Rev William. A Galic and English dictionary. 2 vols 1780.

Virgil. Bucolica, Georgica et Aeneis. Birmingham 1757.

Walters, John. Poems with notes. Oxford 1780.

Woty, William. The shrubs of Parnassus, by J. Copywell. 1760.

— The poetical works of Mr William Woty. 2 vols 1770.

Dedications to Johnson

(*see* Life 4 p. 421 etc)

A refutation of a pamphlet called Thoughts on Falkland's Islands. 1771. Ironic.

Davies, Thomas. Life of Massinger. 1789.

Francklin, Thomas. Demonax. In Works of Lucian, 1780.

Goldsmith, Oliver. She stoops to conquer. 1773.

[Matthews, John]. An ode to Cloacina. 1782. Ironic.

Murphy, Arthur. Seventeen hundred and ninety one. 1791. In memoriam.

Penny, Anne. Anningait and Ajutt. 1761. Rambler 186–7.

Stevenson, John Hall. An essay upon the King's friends. 1776. Ironic.

Walker, John. Elements of elocution. 2 vols 1781.
—— A rhetorical grammar. 1785.
Wilson, Rev Thomas. An archaeological dictionary. 1782, 1793.
Woty, William. The shrubs of Parnassus. 1760.

§ 2

Notices and reviews in periodicals such as GM, London Mag, Monthly Rev, Edinburgh Rev, London Rev, Annual Register *and* Critical Rev *are not listed below.*

Irene

An essay on tragedy, with a critical examen of Mahomet and Irene. 1749. By John Hippisley, d. 1767?
A criticism of Mahomet and Irene. 1749. *See* R. F. Metzdorf, Harvard Lib Bull 4 1950.
[Chetwood, W. R.] The British theatre: containing the lives of the English dramatic poets. 1752.
[Chetwood, Thomas?] Theatrical records: or an account of English dramatic authors and their works. 1756.
The theatres: a poetical dissection by Sir Nicholas Nipclose. 1772, 1772. Attributed to David Garrick; denied by Halkett and Laing.

Rambler and Periodical Essays

[Poetic address] To the author of the Rambler. Daily Advertiser 20 Aug 1750.
[Campbell, Archibald]. Lexiphanes, a dialogue imitated from Lucian and suited to the present times: being an attempt to restore the English tongue to its ancient purity, and to correct, as well as expose, the affected style, hard words and absurd phraseology of many late writers, and particularly of our English Lexiphanes, the Rambler. 1767, 1767, Dublin 1774, 1783, Philadelphia 1805. *See* R. C. Whitford: Lexiphanes: satire's view of Dr Johnson, South Atlantic Quart 19 1920.
K[enrick], W[illiam]. An epistle to James Boswell esq occasioned by his having transmitted the moral writings of Dr Samuel Johnson, to Pascal Paoli. 1768.
Colman, George. Prose on several occasions vol 2. 1787. Includes letter from Lexiphanes (4 Dec 1770) and a Sketch of Dr Johnson, by Chiaro Oscuro, from the London Packet 22 Dec 1775.
Chalmers, Alexander. Essays on the Rambler and Idler in British essayists vols 19, 33, 1802.
Drake, Nathan. Essays illustrative of the Rambler, Adventurer and Idler. 2 vols 1809.

Dictionary

See S. Rypins, PQ 4 1925, and G. E. Noyes, MP 52 1955.
Wilkes, John. A letter to the printer [of Public Advertiser]. 1755 (one leaf 4°).
A letter from a friend in England to Mr [John] Maxwell, with a character of Mr Johnson's English dictionary, lately published, and Mr Maxwell's justification of himself. Dublin 1755.
Murphy, Arthur. A poetical epistle to Mr Samuel Johnson AM. 1760.
[Kenrick, William]. Free thoughts on seduction, adultery and divorce, by a civilian. 1771.
Sauseuiul, Chevalier de. An analysis of the French orthography. 1772.
Tooke, Horne. In his Diversions of Purley, 1786 etc.
Croft, Herbert. An unfinished letter to the Rt Hon William Pitt concerning the new dictionary of the English language. 1788.
Withers, P. Aristarchus. 1789.
Walker, John. A critical pronouncing dictionary. 1791. Preface.
Thornton, William. Cadmus: or a treatise on the elements of written language. Philadelphia 1793.
Adelung, J. C. On the relative merits and demerits of

Johnson's English dictionary. Essay 3 in A. F. M. Willich, Elements of the critical philosophy, 1798.
Mason, George. A supplement to Johnson's English dictionary. 1801, New York 1803.
Pegge, Samuel. Anecdotes of the English language. 1803.
Boucher, Jonathan. A supplement to Dr Johnson's dictionary. 1807.
Webster, Noah. A letter to Dr David Ramsay etc. New Haven 1807.
Maver, William. An appendix to Johnson's dictionary. 1809.
Richardson, Charles. Illustrations of English philology. 1815, 1817, 1826.
Seager, John. A supplement to Dr Johnson's dictionary. 1819.
Jodrell, R. P. Philology of the English language. 1820.

Shakespeare

Kenrick, William. A review of Doctor Johnson's new edition of Shakespeare, in which the ignorance, or inattention, of that editor is exposed, and the poet defended from the persecution of his commentators. 1765.
[Barclay, James]. An examination of Mr Kenrick's Review of Mr Johnson's edition of Shakespeare. 1766.
A defence of Mr Kenrick's Review, by a Friend ['R.R.' = W. Kenrick?]. 1766.
[Campbell, Archibald]. The sale of authors: a dialogue in imitation of Lucian's Sale of philosophers. 1767.
Ritson, Joseph. Remarks on the last edition of Shakespeare. 1783.
Mason, John Monck. Comments on the last edition of Shakespeare's plays. Dublin 1785, 1807.
Chedworth, Lord John. Notes upon some of the obscure passages in Shakespeare's plays. 1805.

Political Tracts

[Rosenhagen, Philip]. The crisis, in answer to the False alarm. 1770.
[Scott, John]. The constitution defended and pensioner exposed. 1770.
[Stockdale, Rev Percival]. The remonstrance: a poem. 1770, 1770.
[Wilkes, John]. A letter to Samuel Johnson LlD. 1770.
A refutation of a pamphlet called Thoughts on the late transactions respecting Falkland's Islands, in a letter addressed to the author and dedicated to Dr Samuel Johnson. 1771.
Letters concerning the present state of England. 1772. Letter 30.
Baillie, Hugh. An appendix to a letter to Dr Shebbeare. 1775.
[Scott, John]. Remarks on the Patriot. 1775.
[Towers, Joseph]. A letter to Dr Samuel Johnson, occasioned by his late political publications. 1775; rptd in Tracts on political subjects vol 1, 1796.
Wesley, John. A calm address to the American colonies. [1775]. An adumbration of Taxation no tyranny.
An answer to a pamphlet entitled Taxation no tyranny, addressed to the author and to persons in power. 1775.
A defence of the resolutions and address of the American congress, in reply to Taxation no tyranny, by the author of Regulus. [1775].
The pamphlet entitled Taxation no tyranny, candidly considered, and its arguments, and pernicious doctrines exposed and refuted. [1775]. Wrongly attributed to Edmund Burke; *see* W. B. Todd, Bibliography of Burke, pp. 289-90.
A plain state of the argument between Great Britain and her colonies. 1775.
The present crisis with respect to America considered. 1775.
Resistance no rebellion, in answer to Doctor Johnson's Taxation no tyranny. 1775.

Taxation, tyranny. Addressed to Samuel Johnson LlD. 1775.

Tyranny unmasked: an answer to a late pamphlet entitled Taxation no tyranny. 1775.

[Stevenson, John Hall]. An essay upon the King's friends, with an account of some discoveries made in Italy, and found in a Virgil, concerning the Tories, to Dr S—l J—n. 1776; rptd in Stevenson's Works vol 1, 1795.

A short appeal to the people of Great Britain upon the unavoidable necessity of the present war. 1776.

Hypocrisy unmasked. 1776 (3 edns). Wrongly attributed to Johnson by Halkett and Laing.

Tyranny the worst taxation. 1778.

Unanimity: a poem inscribed to the Duke of Leinster. 1780. By John Macaulay.

Journey to Western Isles

Remarks on a Voyage to the Hebrides, in a letter to Samuel Johnson LlD. 1775.

Henderson, Andrews. A letter to Dr Samuel Johnson, on his Journey to the Western Isles. [1775].

A second letter to Dr Samuel Johnson, in which his wicked and opprobrious invectives are shewn etc. [1775].

[Hanway, Mary Ann]. A journey to the Highlands of Scotland, with occasional remarks on Dr Johnson's Tour, by a Lady. [1776].

Topham, Capt Edward. Letters from Edinburgh. 1776.

Remarks on Dr Samuel Johnson's Journey to the Hebrides, by Donald M'Nicol, Minister of Lismore in Argyleshire. 1779, 1817 (with Johnson's Journey), Glasgow 1852. See Journey, ed R. W. Chapman 1926, appendix 3.

Two songs in Gaelic on Dr Johnson by Rev Donald Mac-Nicol. Glasgow 1781. See E. G. Cox, The case of Scotland vs Johnson, Trans Gaelic Soc of Inverness 32 1932.

Extracts from the publications of Mr Knox, Dr Anderson, Mr Pennant and Dr Johnson. 1787.

A cure for the blue devils. 1809.

Inch Kenneth: a poem in three cantos. Dublin 1830.

Lives of the Poets

[Blackburne, Francis]. Remarks on Johnson's Life of Milton; to which are added Milton's Tractate on education and Areopagitica. 1780; rptd from Memoirs of Thomas Hollis vol 2, 1780.

A cursory examination of Dr Johnson's strictures on the lyric performances of Gray. 1781. By 'Rev Mr Fitzthomas' (Letters of Anna Seward vol 2, 1811, p. 146).

[Callander, J. T.] Deformities of Dr Samuel Johnson, selected from his Works. Edinburgh 1782, 1782.

[Tindal, William?] Remarks on Dr Johnson's life and critical observations on the works of Mr Gray. 1782.

Remarks on Doctor Johnson's Lives of the most eminent English poets, by a Yorkshire Freeholder. 1782. By Rev Dr Beilby of Ferriby.

[Beville, William]. Observations on Dr Johnson's Life of Hammond. 1782. See Anderson's Life of Johnson, 1815, p. 401; GM 1822.

Blair, Hugh. Lectures on rhetoric and belles lettres. 1783.

[Callander, J. T.] A critical review of the works of Johnson: containing a particular vindication of several eminent characters. Edinburgh 1783, 1783, 1787.

Potter, Robert. An inquiry into some passages in Dr Johnson's Lives of the poets, particularly his observations on lyric poetry and the odes of Gray. 1783.

[Young, John]. A criticism on the Elegy written in a country church yard: being a continuation of Dr J—n's criticism on the poems of Gray. 1783, Edinburgh 1810. Ms in Strahan papers in BM.

A dialogue between Dr Johnson and Dr Goldsmith in the shades relative to the former's strictures on the English poets, particularly Pope, Milton and Gray. 1785.

[Palmer, Samuel]. The life of Isaac Watts, by Samuel Johnson LlD, with notes containing animadversions and additions. 1785.

Turner, Daniel. Devotional poetry vindicated, in some occasional remarks on the late Dr Samuel Johnson's animadversions upon that subject in his Life of Waller. Oxford [1785].

Wright, J. Elegia scripta in sepulchreto rustico. 1786.

Poems written while the author was at college. 1787.

Potter, Robert. The art of criticism, as exemplified in Dr Johnson's Lives of the most eminent English poets. 1789. See H. G. Wright, Robert Potter as a critic of Dr Johnson, RES 12 1936.

Sinclair, A. G. The critic philosopher. 1789, 1791 ('5th edn', a reissue).

Palmer, Samuel. A vindication of the modern dissenters. 1790.

Stockdale, Percival. Lectures on the truly eminent English poets. 2 vols 1807.

White, T. H. A review of Johnson's criticism on the style of Milton's English prose. 1818.

General

For Boswell's Life of Johnson etc 1791, the standard edn is ed G. B. Hill, rev L. F. Powell 6 vols Oxford 1934–64, cited as Life.

Useful collections of miscellaneous newspaper cuttings and articles are in Birmingham Public Library (78131, 249901), Bristol Central Library (2 vols collected by J. Taylor), Johnson House, in London (5 vols), and the Hyde Collection, Somerville NJ.

For recent articles and studies, see:

Johnsonian studies 1887–1950, ed J. L. Clifford, Minneapolis 1951;

in Johnsonian studies 1950–60, ed M. Wahba, Cairo 1962;

Johnsonian news-letter, ed J. L. Clifford and J. H. Middendorf, New York (quarterly).

Cibber, Theophilus. Lives of the poets. 5 vols 1753. Miscellaneous extracts from Johnson's early works.

Murphy, Arthur. A poetical epistle to Mr Johnson. 1760.

[Rider, William]. A historical and critical account of the lives and writings of the living authors of Great Britain, wherein their respective merits are discussed with the utmost candour and impartiality. 1762. Mr Johnson, pp. 7–10.

Churchill, Charles. Poems. 1763. Johnson attacked in Rosciad and Ghost.

[Baker, David Erskine]. The companion to the play-house. 2 vols 1764; rev Isaac Reed as Biographia dramatica, 1782, Dublin 1782; rev Stephen Jones 3 vols 1812. See Irene, above.

[Shaw, Cuthbert]. The race, by Mercurius Spur esq. 1765, 1766. See Life 2 p. 31 and Monthly Rev April 1766.

[Lloyd, Evan]. The powers of the pen: a poem addressed to John Curre esq. 1766.

Sketches and characters of the most eminent and most singular persons now living. Bristol 1770.

A short character of Dr S. Johnson. Scots Mag (and London Mag) March 1773; rptd in Weekly Mag (Edinburgh) 8 April 1773.

[Tytler, James?]. An account of the life, character and writings of Dr Samuel Johnson. Gentleman & Lady's Weekly Mag (Edinburgh) 28 Jan 1774.

An impartial account of the life, character, genius and writings of Dr Samuel Johnson. 1774. See Westminster Mag Sept 1774.

Some anecdotes of the celebrated Doctor S—l J—n, during his late tour through Scotland with a few observations, reprinted from the Aberdeen Journal. 22 April 1774. Lond reply signed R[obert?] S[haw?], 11 May 1774.

Whitaker, John. The history of Manchester vol 2. 1775.

Johnsoniana: or a collection of Bon Mots etc by Dr Johnson and others; together with the choice sentences of Publius Syrius. 1776 ('considerably enlarged and improved: being the only jest book extant, proper to be read in families, in which no obscenity, or profane oath is to be found'), 1776, 1820.

The sixteenth ode of the third book of Horace imitated. 1777. Dedication signed 'S—l J—n'.

[Mason, William]. An epistle to Dr Shebbeare, by Malcolm Macgregor. 1777 (4 edns).

The watch: an ode inscribed to the Rt Hon the Earl of M[ans]f[iel]d. 1778.

[Coutts, Barton]. Modern characters for 1778, by Shakespeare. 1778, 1778.

Tickell, R. The project: a poem. 1778.

Parsons, Philip. Dialogues of the dead with the living. 1779. Dialogue 7: Johnson and Addison.

The Abbey of Kilhampton. 1780 etc.

Dunbar, James. Essays on the history of mankind. 1780, 1781.

[Bodini, Joseph]. The flames of Newgate. 1782.

[Matthews, John]. An ode to Cloacina upon the most fashionable model, with a card to Dr J—ns—n. 1782. Dedicated to Johnson.

Newton, Thomas. An account of his own life. In his Works, 1782.

Tasker, William. Annus mirabilis, or the eventful year 1782: an historical poem. 1783.

Several biographical accounts were pbd shortly after Johnson's death on 13 Dec 1784 in newspapers and magazines; notable are those in GM Dec 1784, European Mag Dec 1784, Jan–April 1785; St James's Chron 13–18 Jan 1785 *(by George Steevens) etc.*

T[yers], T[homas]. A biographical sketch of Johnson. GM Dec 1784; 1785; ed G. D. Meyer, Los Angeles 1952 (Augustan Reprint Soc).

A catalogue of the valuable library of books of the late learned Samuel Johnson esq LlD, deceased, which will be sold by auction, by order of the executors by Mr Christie, at his Great Room in Pall Mall on Wednesday, February 16 1785 and three following days. [1785]; 1892 (facs) (Johnson Club); ed A. E. Newton 1923 (facs).

One glass of Helicon: or a short flight to Parnassus. Norwich 1785.

Johnson's laurel, or a contest of the poets: a poem. 1785.

An ode on the much lamented death of Johnson, written the 18th December 1784. [1785].

Dr Johnson's table talk: or conversations of the late Samuel Johnson LlD on a variety of useful and entertaining subjects (arranged in alphabetical order, after the manner of Selden's Table talk). 1785, 1798, 1807, 1818, Edinburgh 1868, London [1907]. Compiled by [Stephen?] Jones (Anderson, Life of Johnson, 1815, p. 625); or by D. E. McDonnell?

Boswell, James. The journal of a tour to the Hebrides with Samuel Johnson LlD. 1785. *See col 1213, below.*

[Butt, George]. A dialogue between the Earl of C[hesterfiel]d and Mr Garrick in the Elysian shades. 1785.

[Cooke, William]. The life of Samuel Johnson LlD with occasional remarks on his writings and an authentic copy of his will, and a catalogue of his works; to which are added some papers written by Dr Johnson in behalf of a late unfortunate character [William Dodd], never before published. 1785, Dublin 1785, London 1785 ('with considerable additions and corrections; to which is added Johnsoniana: or a selection of Dr Johnson's Bon-Mots, Observations etc, most of which were never before published'). First Preface dated Dec 1784; 2nd Feb 1785. The author was 'Conversation' Cooke, also probably compiler of the Beauties in 1782, and a member of the Essex Head Club. *See* John Nichols, Illustrations of literary history vol 7, p. 467.

Fordyce, James. Addresses to the Deity. 1785, 1786. Address 6 on the death of Johnson.

Hobhouse, Thomas. Elegy to the memory of Doctor Samuel Johnson. 1785, 1785.

[Percy, Thomas]. Verses on the death of Dr Samuel Johnson. 1785. By the Bishop's nephew.

[Shaw, William]. Memoirs of the life and writings of the late Dr Samuel Johnson: containing many valuable original letters, and several interesting anecdotes both of his literary and social connections; the whole authenticated by living evidence. 1785. The attribution to Shaw is supported by the full description of the Ossian controversy, in which Shaw apparently had Johnson's assistance.

—— A collection of interesting biography: containing 1, the life of Johnson, abridged by Sir Andrew Anecdote. 1791, Dublin 1792.

[Wolcot, James, 'Peter Pindar']. A poetical and congratulatory epistle to James Boswell. 1785.

Anecdotes of the learned pig, with notes critical and explanatory, and illustrations from Bozzy, Piozzi etc. 1786.

A monody on the much lamented death of Samuel Johnson LlD. 1786.

A poetical epistle from the ghost of Dr Johnson, to his four friends: the Rev Mr Strahan, James Boswell esq, Mrs Piozzi, J. Courtenay esq MP, from the original copy in the possession of the editor. 1786.

Courtenay, John. A poetical review of the literary and moral character of Johnson, with notes. 1786 (3 edns), Dublin 1786, London 1787.

Graves, Richard. Lucubrations. 1786.

[Heathcote, Ralph]. Sylva, or the wood: a collection of anecdotes, by a society of the learned. 1786. Ch 85.

Moody, Elizabeth. Johnson's ghost. 1786; rptd in her Poetic trifles, 1798.

Piozzi, Hester Lynch (Mrs Thrale). Anecdotes of the late Samuel Johnson LlD during the last twenty years of his life. 1786 (4 edns), Dublin 1786, London 1822, 1826, 1831, 1835, 1856, 1887, 1888. In Johnsoniana, ed R. Napier 1884, 1892; in Johnsonian miscellanies, ed G. B. Hill 1897, 1967; ed S. C. Roberts, Cambridge 1925, 1932.

Towers, Joseph. An essay on the life, character and writings of Johnson. 1786. Also issued anon.

[Wolcot, John]. Bozzy and Piozzi: a town eclogue by Peter Pindar. 1786 etc.

[Callender, J. T.] A critical review of the works of Johnson: containing a particular vindication of several eminent characters. 1787.

Burrowes, Robert. Essay on the style of Johnson. Trans Royal Irish Acad 1 1787.

[Harwood, Thomas]. Observations on the writings and genius of Dr Johnson. 1787.

Hawkins, Sir John. The life of Johnson. 1787, 1787 (rev), Dublin 1787. Also issued as vol 1 in Works, 1787; ed B. H. Davis 1961 (abridged).

[Hayley, William]. Two dialogues: containing a comparative view of the lives, characters and writings of Philip, the late Earl of Chesterfield and Dr Samuel Johnson. 1787, 1800 (as Anecdotes of Chesterfield and Johnson).

The olla podrida [a periodical conducted by Thomas Monro, Magdalen College, Oxford] 9 June 1787. By George Horne, President of Magdalen [afterwards Bishop of Norwich]. This Character of Johnson repeated in Gleaner [a series of periodical essays] vol 3, 1811.

'Barber, Francis'. More last words of Dr Johnson: consisting of important anecdotes and a curious letter from a medical gentleman. 1787. By a 'Mr Francis', who had been Johnson's barber.

Chalmers, Alexander. The character of Dr Johnson. GM 1788.

Moir, James. Gleanings: or fugitive pieces. 2 vols [c. 1790]. Vol 1, Johnson.

'Merry, J.' The witticisms, anecdotes, jests and sayings, of Dr Samuel Johnson, collected from Boswell, Piozzi, Hawkins and other gentlemen, and a full account of Dr Johnson's conversation with the King; to which is added a great number of jests, in which the most distinguished wits of the present century bore a part. 1791, 1793, 1797.

Murphy, Arthur. Seventeen hundred and ninety-one. 1791. Dedicated to Johnson.

— An essay on the life and genius of Samuel Johnson LlD. Prefaced to Works, 12 vols 1792; 1792, 1793, 1820. Prefixed to almost all subsequent edns of Johnson's collected works.

A dialogue between Dr Johnson and Mrs Knowles. GM June 1791; 1799, 1805.

Reflections on the last scene of the late Dr Johnson's life, as exhibited by his biographer Sir John Hawkins. 1791.

Grose, Francis. The olio. 1792.

[Temple, William Johnston]. The character of Doctor Johnson, with illustrations from Mrs Piozzi, Sir John Hawkins and Mr Boswell. 1792. See F. A. Pottle, TLS 22 May 1930.

Alves, Robert. A character of Dr Johnson. In his Sketches for a history of literature, 1794.

Beattie, James Hay. Dialogues of the dead: I, Addison and Johnson; II, Socrates, Johnson etc. In Essays and fragments, Edinburgh 1794.

'Gale, Gustavus'. Miscellanies in prose and verse. 1794.

Anderson, Robert. The life of Johnson, with critical observations on his works. 1795, 1815 (3rd edn, enlarged with anecdotes by Bishop Percy). Percy's notes in Bodley.

Seward, William. Anecdotes of distinguished persons. 4 vols 1795; A supplement to the anecdotes, 1797 (5th vol).

— In his Biographiana, 1799.

[Gleig, George]. Life of Johnson. In Encyclopaedia britannica vol 9, Edinburgh 1797.

[Jones, Stephen]. Dr Johnson's table-talk: containing aphorisms on literature, life and manners; with anecdotes of distinguished persons, selected and arranged from Mr Boswell's Life of Johnson. 1798, 2 vols 1807.

S., G. Moral biography: or the worthies of England. 1798.

Walpole, Horace. A general criticism of Dr Johnson's writings. In his Works vol 4, 1798. BM Add 37728.

Hoole, John. Narrative of what passed in the visits paid by J. Hoole to Dr. Johnson in his last illness. European Mag Sept 1799. Ms Sotheby 20 May 1968/369–70.

Knight, Lady Philippina. European Mag Oct 1799.

Stevens, George Alexander. A lecture on heads. 1799.

Whyte, Samuel. Miscellanea nova: containing remarks on Boswell's Johnson. Dublin 1799, London 1800, Dublin 1801. See M. J. Quinlan, Dartmouth College Lib Bull 1963.

Agutter, William. On the difference between deaths of the righteous and the wicked: Johnson and Hume. 1800.

[Mudford, William]. A critical enquiry into the moral writings of Johnson; to which is added an appendix containing a dialogue between Boswell and Johnson in the shades, by Attalus. 1802, 1803, 1806.

The Thespian dictionary: or dramatic biography. 1802, 1805.

Brookiana [Henry Brooke]. Ed C. H. W[ilson] 2 vols 1804.

Two new dialogues of the dead: the first between Handel and Braham, the second between Johnson and Boswell. 1804.

An account of the life of Johnson, from his birth to his eleventh year, written by himself. [Ed Richard Wright] 1805.

Forbes, William. In his Life of James Beattie, 1806, 1810.

Wooll, John. In his Memoirs of Joseph Warton vol 1 (all pbd), 1806.

Cumberland, R. In his Memoirs, 1807.

Pennington, Montagu. In his Memoirs of Mrs Carter, 2 vols 1808.

Stockdale, Percival. In his Memoirs, 2 vols 1809.

Seward, Anna. Letters. 6 vols 1810.

Northcote, J. In his Memoirs of Sir Joshua Reynolds, 1813.

Buds of genius: or some account of the early lives of celebrated characters. 1816, 1818.

Reynolds, Sir Joshua. Johnson and Garrick. 1816 (priv ptd); ed R. B. Johnson 1927; ed F. W. Hilles, New York 1952.

— The character of Dr Johnson. In Life of Reynolds vol 2, ed Beloe, W. Sexagenarian. 1817. Leslie and Taylor 1865.

Bingley, W. In his Biographical conversations, 1818, 1821 (3rd edn).

Boswell, James (the younger). The talk of Johnson: comprising his most interesting remarks and observations. 2 vols 1818.

[Turner, Baptist N.] An account of Dr Johnson's visit to Cambridge in 1765. New Monthly Mag 1819.

Singer, S. W. The life of Johnson. [1820].

Nichols, J. The rise and progress of the Gentleman's Magazine: being a prefatory introduction to the general index of that work from 1787 to 1818. 1821.

Scott, W. Life of Johnson. 1821 (ms in Signet Library, Edinburgh); Lebensbeschreibungen berühmter brittischer Dichter und Prosaisten von Walter Scott, Vienna 1826.

Hawkins, L. M. Anecdotes, biographical sketches and memoirs. 1822.

— In her Memoirs, 1824.

Servois, J. P. Notice sur la vie et les ouvrages du Dr Johnson. 1823.

The Englishman's library. 1824.

Byroniana, Bozzies and Piozzies. 1825.

Gisborne, T. Reflections on recent occurrences at Lichfield, including an illustration of the opinions of Johnson on slavery. 1826.

Letters from the late Lord Chudworth to the Rev Thomas Crompton 1780–95. 1826.

Cradock, J. In his Literary memoirs, 4 vols 1828. Ms in Hyde Collection.

Smith, J. T. Nollekens and his times. 1828; ed E. Gosse 1895.

— A book for a rainy day. 1845.

Roscoe, Henry. Anecdotes of literary society in the age of Johnson. c. 1830 (unpbd ms in Victoria & Albert Museum, Forster 301).

[Macaulay, T. B.]. Essay on Boswell's Life, ed J. W. Croker. Edinburgh Rev 54 1831.

— Life of Johnson. In Encyclopaedia britannica vol 12, 1856 (8th edn); ed D. Nichol Smith, Edinburgh 1900; ed C. N. Greenough, New York 1912.

Carlyle, T. Essay on Boswell's Life. Fraser's Mag May 1832.

— The hero as man of letters. Lecture 5 of On heroes, hero-worship and the heroic in history, 1841.

— Samuel Johnson. 1853.

D'Arblay, Frances (Fanny Burney). In her Memoirs of Dr Burney, 1832.

Taylor, J. In his Records of my life, 2 vols 1832.

Roberts, W. In his Memoirs of Hannah More, 2 vols 1834.

Graphic illustrations of the life and times of Johnson. 1835, 1837.

Mackintosh, R. J. In his Memoirs of Sir James Mackintosh, 1835.

Johnsoniana: or supplement to Boswell. Ed J. W. Croker 1836, Philadelphia 1842, London 1845, 2 vols 1859.

Select thoughts of Johnson. Boston 1837 (6th edn).

Prior, J. In his Life of Oliver Goldsmith, 1837.

— In his Life of Edmond Malone, 1860.

The life and writings of Johnson. Ed W. P. Page, New York 1840, 1844, 1855, 1900.

Russell, J. F. The life of Dr Sam Johnson. 1847.

Anderson, J. M. In his Addresses on miscellaneous subjects, 1849.

Armitage, R. Dr Johnson: his religious life and death. 1850.

[Campbell, Thomas]. A diary of a visit to England in 1775. By an Irishman. With notes by Samuel Raymond MA, Prothonotary of the Supreme Court of New South Wales, Sydney 1854. On the authenticity of this diary see Edinburgh Rev Oct 1859; Life 2 p. 338. Extracts in G. B. Hill, Johnsonian Miscellanies, 1897, below. Ed J. L. Clifford [from the ms], Cambridge 1947.

Reynald, H. Johnson: étude sur sa vie et sur ses principaux ouvrages. Paris 1856.

The autobiography of Sylvanus Urban. GM July–Sept, Nov–Dec 1856, Jan–April 1857.

Elwin, W. The early life of Johnson. Quart Rev 103 1858.

De Quincey, T. On Johnson's Life of Milton. In his Works vol 4, ed D. Masson 1859.

Kaye, J. W. (ed). Autobiography of Miss Cornelia Knight. 1861.

Hayward, A. (ed). Autobiography of Mrs Piozzi. 1861.

Windham, W. Diary. 1866; ed R. W. Ketton-Cremer 1930.

Main, A. Life and conversations of Johnson. 1874. Preface by G. H. Lewes.

The life of Johnson and various original pieces. Otley [1877].

Hill, G. B. Dr Johnson: his friends and his critics. Oxford 1878.

—— Dr Johnson as a Radical. Contemporary Rev June 1889.

—— Footsteps of Dr Johnson. 1890.

—— Johnsonian miscellanies. 2 vols Oxford 1897, 1967. See TLS 24 Aug 1967.

Jewitt, L. Unpublished episodes in the life of Dr Johnson. GM Dec 1878. Langley correspondence, mss in Bodley.

Stephen, L. Samuel Johnson. 1878 (EML).

—— In DNB, 1892.

Mason, E. T. Johnson: his words and his ways. New York 1879.

Waller, J. F. Boswell and Johnson: their companions and contemporaries. 1881.

Twining, T. In his Recreations and studies of a country clergyman of the 18th century, ed R. Twining 1882.

Courthope, W. J. In English poets vol 3, ed T. H. Ward 1884.

Croker, J. W. Correspondence. 1884. Original papers in Clements Lib, Ann Arbor, Michigan.

Hay, J. Johnson: his characteristics and aphorisms. 1884, Paisley 1889, London 1895.

Macaulay, J. Dr Johnson: his life, works and table-talk. 1884.

Mazzinghi, T. J. Dr Johnson's early life. N & Q 1884.

Welsh, C. A bookseller of the last century: being some account of the life of John Newbery. 1885.

Grant, F. R. C. Life of Johnson, with a bibliography by J. P. Anderson. 1887.

Spofford, H. P. Sam Johnson's boyhood. Harper's Young People 12 1890.

Dobson, A. A garret in Gough Square. In his Eighteenth-century vignettes vol 1, 1892.

—— Johnson's library. In his Eighteenth-century vignettes vol 2, 1894.

—— Dr Johnson's haunts and habitations. Introd to Boswell, ed A. Glover 1901; rptd in his Side-walk studies, 1902.

Napier, R. Johnsoniana, newly collected and edited. 1892.

Craik, H. Johnson's prose. In his English prose vol 4, 1894.

Lang, A. In his Cock-Lane and common-sense, 1894.

Sims, R. In his Bibliotheca Staffordiensis, 1894

Jowett, B. In his Essays on men and manners, 1895.

Macleane, D. In his History of Pembroke College, 1897.

Sargeant, J. Dr Johnson's politics. Bookman (New York) 1898.

Spurgeon, C. F. E. The works of Johnson. 1898.

Barker, W. R. Dr Johnson as representative of the character of the eighteenth century. 1899.

Emerson, O. F. The text of Johnson's Rasselas. Anglia 22 1899.

Seccombe, T. The age of Johnson. 1899.

Johnson Club papers by various hands, 1899; 2nd ser, 1920.

Bouchier, J. Johnson's father and Elizabeth Blaney. N & Q 7 July 1900.

Hoste, J. W. Johnson and his circle. [1900].

Murray, J. A. H. The evolution of English lexicography. Oxford 1900 (Romanes lecture).

Life of Johnson, compiled chiefly from Boswell's biography. Madras 1900.

Luckock, H. M. A popular sketch of Dr Johnson's life and works. Lichfield 1902, 1923.

Hutton, W. H. The religion of Dr Johnson. In his Burford papers, 1905.

Parrott, T. M. The personality of Dr Johnson. New York 1906.

Ramage, A. An essay on Dr Johnson. 1906.

Reade, A. L. The Reades of Blackwood Hill and Dr Johnson's ancestry. 1906.

—— Johnsonian gleanings. 11 pts 1909–52.

—— Johnsonian gleanings: some unsolved problems. N & Q 4 June 1938.

—— Parson Ford. TLS 6 Aug 1938.

—— Michael Johnson and Lord Derby's Library. TLS 17 July 1940.

—— The early career of Johnson's father. TLS 17 June 1949. Reply by E. Howe 24 June 1949.

Hill, J. In his Bookmakers of old Birmingham, Birmingham 1907.

Raleigh, W. Samuel Johnson. 1907 (Leslie Stephen lecture).

—— Johnson on Shakespeare. Oxford 1908, 1925 (corrected).

—— Six essays on Johnson. Oxford 1910, 1927.

Shorter, C. K. In his Immortal memories, 1907.

Wheatley, H. B. Dr Johnson as a bibliographer. Library 2nd ser 8 1907.

—— Johnson's edition of Shakespeare. Athenaeum 11 Sept 1909.

Collins, J. C. Dr Johnson's Lives of the poets. Quart Rev 208 1908.

—— In his Posthumous essays, 1912.

Conant, M. P. In her Oriental tale in England in the eighteenth century, New York 1908.

Primrose, A. P. (Earl of Rosebery). Dr Johnson: Lichfield bicentenary address. 1909.

Sargisson, C. S. Dr Johnson's ancestry. Bookman (London) 1909.

Bi-centenary of the birth of Dr Samuel Johnson: commemoration festival at Lichfield, Sept 15–19 1909. Ed J. T. Raby 1909.

Long, P. W. English dictionaries before Webster. PBSA 4 1910.

Broadley, A. M. Doctor Johnson and Mrs Thrale, including Mrs Thrale's unpublished journal of the Welsh tour made in 1774 and much hitherto unpublished correspondence of the Streatham coterie. 1910.

Cross, A. Dr Johnson. [1911].

Braithwaite, B. Dr Johnson and his times. Epsom 1912.

Bailey, J. Dr Johnson and his circle. 1913, 1944 (rev).

Nichol Smith, D. Johnson and Boswell. CHEL 10 1913.

—— Johnson's Irene. E & S 14 1929.

—— Johnson's poems. RES 19 1943.

—— Johnsonians and Boswellians. Lichfield 1949 (Johnson Soc).

Saintsbury, G. In his Peace of the Augustans, 1916.

Birrell, A. In his Aphorisms on authors, 1917.

Chapman, R. W. Johnson in Scotland. TLS 3 Oct 1918.

—— Johnson, Boswell and Mrs Piozzi: a suppressed passage restored. Oxford 1929.

—— Johnson's works: a lost piece and a forgotten piece. London Mercury March 1930.

—— In his Cancels, 1930. *See* Library 4th ser 4 1923.
—— Johnson's Journey 1775. RES 7 1932.
—— Sermon by Dr Johnson? Times 29 Sept 1933.
—— Johnson's letters. RES 13 1937. A list of his extant letters; for addns *see* 16 1940.
—— Johnson's letters: notes on Boswell's text. TLS 25 Feb, 4 March 1939.
—— Johnson's letters to Taylor. RES 15–16 1939–40.
—— Baretti's Carmen seculare. TLS 16 Aug 1941.
—— Johnson's letters to Boswell. RES 18 1942. A calendar; for a calendar of Boswell's letters to Johnson *see* N & Q 17 July 1943, 15 Jan 1944.
—— Emendations in Johnson's letters. TLS 26 Sept 1942.
—— Did Johnson destroy Mrs Thrale's letters? N & Q 28 Aug 1943.
—— Johnson's journey. TLS 27 March 1943.
—— Johnson's literary earnings: a problem. RES 19 1943.
—— The sale of Johnson's Idler. N & Q 24 April 1943.
—— The formal parts of Johnson's letters. In Essays presented to David Nichol Smith, Oxford 1945.
—— Two centuries of Johnsonian scholarship. Glasgow 1945.
—— 'Doctor' Johnson. N & Q 23 Feb 1946. On the use of the title before 1775.
—— Mrs Piozzi's omissions from Johnson's letters to Thrale. RES 22 1946.
—— Mrs Thrale's letters to Johnson published by Mrs Piozzi in 1788. RES 24 1948.
—— Crousaz on Pope. RES 25 1949.
—— Johnsonian and other essays. Oxford 1953.
The character and opinions of Dr Johnson, by Algernon Charles Swinburne. Ed T. J. Wise 1918.
Rivington, S. The publishing family of Rivington. 1919.
Roberts, S. C. The story of Dr Johnson. Cambridge 1919, 1922.
—— On the death of Dr Robert Levet: a note on the text. RES 3 1927. *See also* W. H. G. Flood 4 1928.
—— Johnson in Grub Street; Johnson's books; The focus of the Lichfield lamps. In An 18th-century gentleman: notes and other essays, Cambridge 1930.
—— Dr Johnson. 1935.
—— Johnson's library. TLS 4 July 1942. Replies 11–18 July 1942.
—— Johnson. Proc Br Acad 30 1944.
—— Samuel Johnson. 1954, 1955, 1965 (Br Council pamphlet, with reading list).
Hirn, Yrjo. Dr Johnson och James Boswell. Helsinki 1922.
Alexander, S. Dr Johnson as a philosopher. Cornhill Mag Oct 1923.
Christie, O. F. Johnson the essayist. New York 1923.
Houston, P. H. Dr Johnson. Cambridge Mass 1923, 1963.
Asquith, H. H. (Earl of Oxford). Dr Johnson and Fanny Burney. 1923; rptd in his Studies and sketches, 1924.
Spittal, J. K. Contemporary criticisms of Dr Samuel Johnson, his works and his biographers. 1923.
Williams, I. A. Dr Johnson in poetry. Cornhill Mag 1923.
Young, K. Johnson on Shakespeare. Wisconsin Univ Stud 18 1923.
Gennadius, J. Dr Johnson and Homer. 1924.
Tinker, C. B. Rasselas in the New World. Yale Rev 14 1924; New Haven 1925.
Rolleston, H. Medical aspects of Johnson. Glasgow Medical Jnl April 1924.
Rypins, S. Johnson's Dictionary reviewed by his contemporaries. PQ 4 1925.
Silvester, J. The Great Cham of literature. Clacton 1925.
Laithwaite, P. A short history of Lichfield Grammar School. Lichfield 1925.
Hutchison, R. Johnson and medicine. Edinburgh Medical Jnl Aug 1925. *See* Lancet 9 May 1925; Br Medical Jnl 9 May 1925.
Brown, J. E. The critical opinions of Johnson. 1926, 1960.
—— Johnson: a man of faith. Shiling [1926].

Gissing, A. Appleby School: an extra-illustration to Boswell. Cornhill Mag April 1926.
Powell, L. F. Dr Johnson and the Encyclopédie. RES 2 1926.
—— Dr Johnson and Dr James. TLS 3 Jan 1929.
—— Johnson and a friend. Times 25 Nov 1938. Attributes a sermon by Rev Hervey Aston, 1745; *see* Life 5 pp. 483–4.
—— Johnson's DCL diploma. Bodleian Quart Record 5 1938.
—— The history of St Kilda. RES 16 1940.
—— A task ended. Lichfield 1950 (Johnson Soc).
—— An addition to the canon of Johnson's writings. E & S 28 1943.
—— A friend of Dr Johnson: Dr Birkbeck Hill. New Rambler Jan 1960.
—— Edmund Southwell: his sisters and Dr Johnson. TLS 30 Dec 1960.
—— For Johnsonian collectors. TLS 20 Sept 1963.
Cuming, A. A copy of Shakespeare's works which formerly belonged to Dr Johnson. RES 3 1927.
Green, J. In his Suite anglaise, Paris 1927.
Babbitt, I. Dr Johnson and imagination. Southwest Rev 13 1927.
Whibley, C. Johnson: man of letters. Blackwood's Mag May 1927.
—— Dr Johnson and the universities. Blackwood's Mag Sept 1929.
Lynd, R. Dr Johnson and company. New York 1928.
George, D. England in Johnson's day. 1928.
Roscoe, E. S. Aspects of Dr Johnson. 1928.
Hollis, C. Doctor Johnson. 1928.
Blunden, E. New light on Dr Samuel Johnson. Living Age 136 1929.
Buchan, J. In his Midwinter, 1929.
Eliot, T. S. Introd to London and Vanity of human wishes, 1930; rptd in English critical essays: twentieth century, ed P. M. Jones, Oxford 1933 (WC).
McKinlay, R. Some notes on Dr Johnson's Journey. Records of Glasgow Bibl Soc 8 1930.
Segar, M. Dictionary making in the early eighteenth century. RES 7 1931.
Smith, F. M. Some friends of Dr Johnson. [1931].
Christiani, S. Johnson als Kritiker. Leipzig 1931.
Gow, A. S. F. The unknown Johnson. Life & Letters Sept 1931.
Haight, G. S. Johnson's copy of Bacon's works. Yale Univ Lib Gazette 6 1932.
Laithwaite, P. Dr Johnson's Lichfield forbears. Trans North Staffs Field Club 66 1932.
'Kingsmill, Hugh' (H. K. Lunn). Samuel Johnson. 1933.
Reynolds, W. V. Johnson's opinions on prose style. RES 9 1933.
—— The reception of Johnson's prose style. RES 11 1935.
Struble, M. C. A Johnson handbook. New York 1933.
Turberville, A. S. (ed). Johnson's England. 2 vols Oxford 1933.
Mathews, M. M. A survey of English dictionaries. 1933.
Tillotson, A. Dr Johnson and the Life of Goldsmith. MLR 28 1933.
Evans, B. Dr Johnson's theory of biography. RES 10 1934.
Brain, W. R. A post-mortem on Dr Johnson. London Hospital Gazette 37 1934; 1934. *See also* Br Medical Jnl 8 Sept 1934.
—— Johnson on science. London Hospital Gazette 2nd ser 1 1947.
—— Johnson and the kangaroo. E & S new ser 4 1951.
—— Some reflections on genius. 1960.
—— Dr Johnson and his doctors. New Rambler Jan 1962.
Barnonw, A. J. Rasselas in Dutch. TLS 11 April 1935. *See* L. F. Powell 20 Sept 1963.
Tillotson, G. Rasselas and the Persian tales. TLS 29 April 1935; rptd in his Essays in criticism and research, Cambridge 1942.
—— Johnson's Dictionary. Spectator 29 April 1955.

—— Imlac and the business of a poet. In Studies in criticism and aesthetics 1660–1800, ed H. Anderson and J. S. Shea, Minneapolis 1967.

Boyle, E. Johnson and Sir John Hawkins. In his Biographical essays 1790–1890, Oxford 1936.

Clifford, J. L. Further letters of the Johnson circle. Bull John Rylands Lib 20 1936.

—— Johnson's Mr Thrale. TLS 30 Dec 1939.

—— Thomas Coxeter the younger to Johnson. N & Q 12 April 1941.

—— The authenticity of Anna Seward's correspondence. MP 39 1949. On her revision of Johnsonian passages.

—— Young Samuel Johnson. 1955, New York 1955 (as Young Sam Johnson).

Leavis, F. R. English poetry in the eighteenth century. Scrutiny 5 1936; rptd in his Revaluation, 1936.

—— Johnson as critic. Scrutiny 12 1944.

—— Johnson. Kenyon Rev 8 1946.

—— Johnson and Augustanism; Johnson as poet. Both in his Common pursuit, 1952.

Macdonald, A. Johnson as lexicographer. Edinburgh Univ Jnl 8 1936.

Watkins, W. B. C. Johnson and English poetry before 1660. Princeton 1936.

—— In his Perilous balance, Princeton 1939.

—— Johnson on the imagination. RES 22 1946.

Boas, G. Johnson on schools and schoolmasters. English 1 1937.

Cooper, L. Johnson on oats and other grains. PMLA 52 1937.

Gray, W. F. Johnson in Edinburgh. Quart Rev 269 1937.

Powys, L. Johnson: Idler, Rambler and Straggler. Dublin Mag 12 1937.

Reading, J. Poems by Johnson. TLS 11 Sept 1937.

Smith, N. G. The piety of Johnson. Queen's Quart 44 1937.

Brown, S. G. Johnson and the religious problem. E Studies 20 1938.

—— Johnson, poetry and imagination. Neophilologus 23 1938.

Sewall, R. B. Rousseau's second discourse in England from 1755 to 1762. PQ 17 1938.

Hart, C. W. Johnson's 1745 Shakespeare proposals. MLN 53 1938.

Hazen, A. T. Johnson's Shakespeare: a study in cancellation. TLS 24 Dec 1938. See Bodleian Lib Record 1 1939.

—— The beauties of Johnson. MP 35 1938.

—— The cancels in Johnson's Journey 1775. RES 17 1941. See SB 6 1954; PBSA 58 1964.

—— and T. O. Mabbott. Johnson and Francis Fawkes's Theocritus. RES 21 1945.

—— New styles in typography. In The age of Johnson: essays presented to C. B. Tinker, New Haven 1949.

Lewis, F. R. New facts about Johnson. TLS 25 June 1938.

Osborn, J. M. Lord Hailes and Johnson: the Lives of the poets. TLS 16–23 April 1938.

—— In his Dryden: some biographical facts and problems, New York 1940.

—— Dr Johnson and the contrary converts. New Haven 1954 (priv ptd). On Rev James Compton and John Walker.

Wecter, D. A letter from Johnson. TLS 2 July 1938.

—— Johnson, Mrs Thrale and Boswell: three letters. MLN 56 1941.

Williams, H. Johnson's favourite pursuits. Nineteenth Century May 1938.

Botting, R. B. Johnson, Smart and the Universal Visiter. MP 36 1939.

Bradford, C. B. The Edinburgh Ramblers. MLR 34 1939.

—— Johnson's revision of the Rambler. RES 15 1939.

—— Arthur Murphy's meeting with Johnson. PQ 18 1939.

McAdam, E. L. Johnson's law lectures for Chambers: an addition to the canon. RES 15–16 1939–40.

—— and A. T. Hazen. Johnson and the Hereford Infirmary. HLQ 3 1940.

—— New essays by Johnson. RES 18 1942. 3 from Public Ledger 1760.

—— Johnson's lives of Sarpi, Blake and Drake. PMLA 58 1943.

—— Pseudo-Johnsoniana. MP 41 1944.

—— Johnson and Saunders Welch's Proposals. RES new ser 4 1953.

—— Dr Johnson and the English law. Syracuse 1951.

—— Johnson and the King's Library. New York 1955 (priv ptd). Facs of letter of 28 May 1768 in BM.

—— A Johnsonian retort. TLS 21 July 1961. Reply by D. J. Greene 13 Oct 1961.

Metzdorf, R. F. Notes on Johnson's Plan of a dictionary. Library 4th ser 9 1939.

—— A newly recovered criticism of Irene. Harvard Lib Bull 4 1950.

Alexander, S. Johnson as a philosopher. In his Philosophical and literary pieces, 1939.

Gove, P. B. Notes on serialization and competitive publishing: Johnson's and Bailey's dictionaries 1755. Proc Oxford Bibl Soc 5 1939.

—— Johnson and the works of the Bishop of Sodor and Man. RES 16 1940.

—— Johnson's copy of Hammond's elegies. MLQ 5 1944.

Hanes, F. M. The particularities of Johnson. South Atlantic Quart 39 1940.

Hare, K. Lord Chesterfield and Johnson. Quart Rev 274 1940.

Jenkins, H. D. Some aspects of the background of Rasselas. In Studies in English in honor of R. D. O'Leary and S. L. Whitcomb, Lawrence Kansas 1940.

Johnson without Boswell: a contemporary portrait. Ed 'Hugh Kingsmill' (H. K. Lunn) 1940.

Levy, H. L. H. P. Sturz and Dr Johnson. TLS 10 Feb 1940.

Leyburn, E. D. The translations of the mottoes and quotations in the Rambler. RES 16 1940.

—— Bishop Berkeley: metaphysician as moralist. In The age of Johnson: essays presented to C. B. Tinker, New Haven 1949.

—— 'No romanticka bsurdities or incredible fictions'. PMLA 70 1955.

—— Two allegorical treatments of man: Rasselas and La Peste. Criticism 4 1962.

Noyes, A. Johnson. In his Pageant of letters, New York 1940.

Osgood, C. G. In his Poetry as a means of grace. Princeton 1941.

—— Lady Phillipina Knight and her circle. Princeton Lib Chron 4 1943.

—— Johnson and Macrobius. MLN 69 1954.

Pottle, F. A. The dark hints of Sir John Hawkins and Boswell. MLN 56 1941.

Stauffer, D. A. In his Art of biography in eighteenth-century England, Princeton 1941.

Wimsatt, W. K. The prose style of Johnson. New Haven 1941. See also A. Friedman, PQ 21 1942; replies 22 1943.

—— Johnson and Scots. TLS 9 March 1946.

—— Johnson on electricity. RES 23 1947.

—— Johnson's treatment of Bolingbroke in the Dictionary. MLR 43 1948.

—— Philosophic words: a study of style and meaning in the Rambler and Dictionary of Johnson. New Haven 1948.

—— and M.H. Self-quotations and anonymous quotations in Johnson's Dictionary. ELH 15 1948.

Wimsatt, W. K. Johnson and Dryden's Du Fresnoy. SP 48 1951.

—— and C. Brooks. In their Literary criticism: a short history, New York 1957.

Wimsatt, W. K. James Boswell: the man and the journal. Yale Rev 49 1959.
— A Philadelphian meets Dr Johnson. TLS 1 Jan 1960.
Abrams, M. H. Unconscious expectations in the reading of poetry. ELH 9 1942.
Mays, M. J. Johnson and Blair on Addison's prose style. SP 39 1942.
Schinz, A. Les dangers du cliché littéraire: Johnson et Rousseau. MLN 57 1942.
Thraliana: the diary of Mrs Thrale 1776–1809. Ed K. C. Balderston 2 vols Oxford 1942, 1952 (corrected).
Cameron, K. N. Rasselas and Alastor: a study in transmutation. SP 40 1943.
Esdaile, A. Johnson and the young. English 3 1943.
Hagstrum, J. H. The sermons of Johnson. MP 40 1943.
— On Dr Johnson's fear of death. ELH 14 1947.
— Johnson's conception of the beautiful, the pathetic and the sublime. PMLA 64 1949.
— The nature of Johnson's nationalism. ELH 17 1950.
— Johnson's literary criticism. Minneapolis 1952.
Havens, R. D. Johnson's distrust of the imagination. ELH 10 1943.
— Time, Johnson and Shakespeare. N & Q 27 March 1943.
— Solitude and the Neoclassicists. ELH 21 1945.
Mossner, E. C. Hume and Johnson. In his Forgotten Hume, New York 1943.
— Johnson 'in partibus infidelium'. MLN 63 1948.
Bronson, B. H. Johnson and Boswell: three essays. Berkeley 1944. Johnson Agonistes, Boswell's Boswell and Irene.
— Personification reconsidered. ELH 14 1947.
— The double tradition of Dr Johnson. ELH 18 1951; rptd in Eighteenth-century English literature: modern essays in criticism, ed J. L. Clifford, New York 1959.
Coleman, W. H. The Johnsonian conversational formula. Quart Rev 282 1944.
Krutch, J. W. Johnson. New York 1944.
— Johnson and his friends. Amer Scholar 13 1944.
— On the talk of Johnson and his friends. Ibid.
— Johnson as critic. Nation (New York) 19 Feb 1944.
McCutcheon, R. P. Johnson and Boswell today. In Addresses made before the friends of the Howard-Tilton Library, New Orleans 1944.
Pyles, T. The romantic side of Johnson. ELH 11 1944.
Stenberg, T. Quotations from Pope in Johnson's Dictionary. SE 1944.
Fan Tsen-Chung. Johnson and Chinese culture. China Soc Occasional Papers new ser 6 1945.
Kilbourne, H. R. Johnson and war. ELH 12 1945.
Mabbott, T. O. The text of Johnson's dedication of Hoole's Tasso. N & Q 3 Nov 1945
Schmitz, R. M. Johnson and Blair's sermons. MLN 60 1945.
Tracy, C. R. Johnson and the art of anecdote. UTQ 15 1945.
— Democritus arise! a study of Johnson's humor. Yale Rev 39 1949.
— The artificial bastard [Richard Savage]. Cambridge Mass 1953.
— Johnson's Journey to the Western Islands of Scotland: a reconsideration. Stud on Voltaire 58 1967.
Wallis, J. E. W. Johnson and his Dictionary. Lichfield 1945 (Johnson Soc).
Brown, J. J. Johnson and the first roller-spinning machine. MLR 41 1946. Replies, ibid; TLS 15 May 1946.
Bate, W. J. Johnson and Reynolds: the premise of general nature. In his From classic to romantic, Cambridge Mass 1946.
— The achievement of Johnson. New York 1955.
Cairns, W. T. The religion of Johnson. In his Religion of Johnson and other essays, Oxford 1946.
Hudson, V. B. Johnson and the Scots. TLS 13 April 1946.
Jones, C. E. Johnson and Mrs Montagu: two letters. N & Q 7 Sept 1946.

Reed, Isaac. Diaries 1762–1804. Ed C. E. Jones, Berkeley 1946.
Rush, B. Reminiscences of Boswell and Johnson. Ed L. H. Butterfield, Somerville NJ 1946.
Starnes, D. T. and G. E. Noyes. The English dictionary from Cawdrey to Johnson. Chapel Hill 1946.
Vulliamy, C. E. Ursa Major: a study of Johnson and his friends. 1946.
Bergler, E. Johnson's Life of Savage: a paradigm for a type. Imago 4 1947.
Brown, W. C. Johnson as poet. MLQ 8 1947.
Hallett, H. F. Johnson's refutation of Berkeley. Mind 56 1947.
Liebert, H. W. Addition to the bibliography of Johnson. PBSA 41 1947.
— Johnson's last literary project. New Haven 1948 (priv ptd).
— Reflections on Johnson. JEGP 47 1948.
— This harmless drudge. New Colophon 1 1948.
— New letters from Dr Johnson to Dr Taylor. Harvard Lib Bull 3 1949.
— Johnson and Gay. N & Q 12 May 1951. See 20 Jan 1951.
— Johnson's first book. Yale Lib Gazette 25 1950.
— Johnson's Dictionary 1755–1955. Yale Lib Gazette 30 1955.
— Johnson's head. New Haven 1960 (priv ptd).
— Boswell's Life of Johnson 1791. Amer N & Q 1 1962.
Marshall, C. Doctor Johnson. 1947.
Quinlan, M. J. An intermediary between Cowper and Johnson. RES 24 1948.
— The rumour of Johnson's conversion. Rev of Religion 12 1948.
— Franklin meets Johnson. Pennsylvania Mag of History 73 1949.
— The reaction to Johnson's Prayers and meditations. JEGP 52 1953.
— Samuel Johnson: a layman's religion. Madison 1964.
— Samuel Whyte's anecdotes about Dr Johnson. Dartmouth College Lib Bull 5 1963.
Bloom, E. A. Johnson on copyright. JEGP 47 1948.
— Johnson on a free press. ELH 16 1949.
— The allegorical principle. ELH 18 1951.
— Symbolic names in Johnson's periodical essays. MLQ 13 1952.
— Johnson in Grub Street. Providence 1957.
— Johnson's divided self. UTQ 31 1964.
— The vanity of human wishes: reason's images. EC 15 1965.
Davies, G. Johnson on history. HLQ 12 1948.
Eastman, A. M. Johnson's Shakespearean labors in 1765. MLN 63 1948.
— Johnson's Shakespeare and the laity: a textual study. PMLA 65 1950.
— The texts from which Johnson printed his Shakespeare. JEGP 49 1950.
— In defence of Dr Johnson. Shakespeare Quart 8 1957.
McNair, A. Johnson and the law. Cambridge 1948.
McCue, G. S. Johnson's word-hoard. MLN 63 1948.
McNulty, J. B. The critic who knew what he wanted. College Eng 9 1948.
Tinker, C. B. Johnson: II, Literary monarch; I, The unaccountable companion. In his Essays in retrospect, New Haven 1948.
Sherburn, G. In A literary history of England, ed A. C. Baugh, New York 1948.
— Rasselas returns to what? PQ 38 1959.
Atkinson, A. D. Notes on Johnson's dictionary. N & Q 15 Oct 1949, 21 Jan, 4 Feb, 15 April, 10 June 1950.
— Johnson and Science. N & Q 5 Aug, 25 Nov, 9, 23 Dec 1950.
— Donne quotations in Johnson's dictionary. N & Q 1 Sept 1951.
— William Derham. Annals of Science 8 1952.
— Johnson and the Royal Society. Notes & Records of Royal Soc 10 1953.

—— Dr Johnson and Newton's Opticks. RES new ser 2 1951.

—— Johnson and Sweden. English 8 1951.

The age of Johnson: essays presented to C. B. Tinker. Ed F. W. Hilles, New Haven 1949.

Brunner, K. Did Johnson hate Scotland and the Scottish? E Studies 30 1949.

Emden, C. S. Rhythmical features in Johnson's prose. RES 25 1949.

—— Johnson and imagery. RES new ser 1 1950.

—— Dr Johnson's ménage. Quart Rev 304 1966.

Emery, C. Johnson on Dr Hill. MLN 64 1949.

Evans, G. B. The text of Johnson's Shakespeare 1765. PQ 28 1949.

Gulick, S. L. Johnson, Chesterfield and Boswell. In The age of Johnson: essays presented to C. B. Tinker, New Haven 1949. See also B. Boyce, Johnson and Chesterfield once more, PQ 32 1953.

Kolb, G. J. Johnson's dissertation on flying and John Wilkins' Mathematical magick. MP 47 1949.

—— The structure of Rasselas. PMLA 56 1951.

—— The use of Stoical doctrines in Rasselas. MLN 68 1953.

—— and J. H. Sledd. Johnson's Dictionary and lexicographical tradition. MP 50 1953.

—— The Reynolds copy of Johnson's Dictionary. Bull John Rylands Lib 37 1955.

—— Dr Johnson's Dictionary. Chicago 1955.

Kolb, G. J. A note on the publication of Johnson's proposals for printing the Harleian Miscellany. PBSA 48 1954.

—— The address of Dr Johnson's last letter to Windham. N & Q May 1957.

—— The Paradise in Abyssinia and the Happy Valley in Rasselas. MP 56 1958.

—— Dr Johnson and the Public Ledger. SB 11 1958.

—— Notes on four letters by Dr Johnson: addenda to Chapman's edition. PQ 38 1959.

—— More attributions to Dr Johnson. Stud in Eng Lit 1500–1900 1 1961.

—— Rasselas: purchase price, proprietors and printings. SB 15 1962.

Krishnamurti, S. Johnson and the law lectures of Sir Robert Chambers. MLR 44 1949.

—— Frequency-distribution of nouns in Dr Johnson's prose works. Jnl of Univ of Bombay 20 1951.

—— Vocabulary tests. Jnl of Univ of Bombay 21–2 1952–3.

Moore, J. R. Johnson and Roman history. HLQ 12 1949.

—— Johnson as poet. Boston Lib Quart 2 1950.

—— Rasselas and the early travellers to Abyssinia. MLQ 15 1954.

Magnus, P. Unpublished Burke papers. TLS 30 Dec 1949.

Sewall, R. B. Johnson, Rousseau and reform. In The age of Johnson: essays presented to C. B. Tinker, New Haven 1949.

Stockdale, P. Elegy on the death of Hodge. Ed H. W. Liebert, New Haven 1949.

Tate, A. Johnson on the Metaphysicals. Kenyon Rev 11 1949.

Williams, H. Swift's early biographers. In Pope and his contemporaries, Oxford 1949.

Baker, C. The Cham on horseback. Virginia Quart Rev 26 1950. On Johnson and natural scenery.

Cornu, D. On Johnson at Fort Augustus: Captain Lewis Ourry. MLQ 11 1950.

—— The historical authenticity of Johnson's Speaking cat. RES 2 1951.

Hart, E. Some new sources of Johnson's Lives. PMLA 65 1950. On John Nichols.

—— The contributions of John Nichols to Boswell's Life of Johnson. PMLA 67 1952.

Hyde, D. and M. Johnson and journals. New Colophon 3 1950.

—— The history of the Johnson papers. PBSA 45 1951.

—— Johnson's second wife. Somerville NJ 1953 (priv ptd).

—— The Hyde collection. Book Collector 4 1955.

Jack, I. The choice of life in Johnson and Matthew Prior. JEGP 49 1950.

—— Tragical satire: the Vanity of human wishes. In his Augustan satire, Oxford 1952.

Keast, W. R. Johnson's criticism of the metaphysical poets. ELH 17 1950.

—— The theoretical foundations of Johnson's criticism. In Critics and criticism, ed R. S. Crane, Chicago 1952.

—— The preface to A dictionary: Johnson's revision of the text. SB 5 1953.

—— Some emendations in Johnson's preface to the Dictionary. RES new ser 4 1953.

—— Johnson's Plan of a dictionary: a textual crux. PQ 35 1954.

—— The two Clarissas in Johnson's Dictionary. SP 54 1957.

Petrie, C. Dr Johnson and the Forty-five. Eng Rev Mag 4 1950.

Scudder, H. H. Johnson at Chatsworth. N & Q 28 Oct 1950.

Tillotson, K. Arnold and Johnson. RES new ser 1 1950.

Atkins, J. W. H. The Great Cham of literature. In English literary criticism, 17th and 18th centuries, 1951.

Chase, P. P. The ailments and physicians of Johnson. Yale Jnl of Biology & Medicine 23 1951.

Darbishire, H. Milton's Paradise Lost. Oxford 1951 (Bryce lecture). On Johnson's criticism.

Hemlow, J. Johnson and Fanny Burney: some additions to the record. BNYPL Feb 1951.

Hudson, W. M. Whitaker's attack on Johnson's etymologies. HLQ 14 1951.

Lascelles, M. Rasselas reconsidered. E & S 4 1951.

—— 'A physician in a great city'. Lichfield 1951 (Johnson Soc).

Lubbers-Van der Brugge, C. J. M. Johnson and Baretti. Groningen 1951.

—— A lost pamphlet of Giuseppe Baretti. Eng Miscellany (Rome) 10 1959.

Moore, R. E. Johnson on Fielding and Richardson. PMLA 66 1951.

Morgan, E. 'Strong lines' and strong minds: reflections on the prose of Browne and Johnson. Cambridge Jnl May 1951.

Spector, R. D. Johnson's swallows. N & Q 22 Dec 1951.

Sherbo, A. Johnson on Macbeth: 1745 and 1765. RES new ser 2 1951.

—— Father Lobo's Voyage to Abyssinia and Ramblers 204 and 205. N & Q 1 Sept 1951.

—— The making of Ramblers 186 and 187. PMLA 67 1952.

—— The translation of mottoes and quotations. N & Q 10 Nov 1951, 21 June 1952.

—— Two additions to the Johnson canon. JEGP 52 1953.

—— Johnson's revision of his Dictionary. PQ 31 1952.

—— The proof-sheets of Johnson's Preface to Shakespeare. Bull John Rylands Lib 35 1952.

—— Johnson's Dictionary and Warburton's Shakespeare. PQ 33 1954.

—— The text of the Vanity of human wishes. N & Q 10 May 1952.

—— Dr Johnson marks a book list. N & Q 22 Nov 1952.

—— Dr Johnson's Dictionary: a preliminary puff. PQ 31 1952.

—— The cancels in Dr Johnson's Works, Oxford 1825. PBSA 47 1953.

—— Two additions to the Johnson canon. JEGP 52 1953.

—— Two notes on Johnson's revisions. MLR 50 1955.

—— A possible addition to the Johnson canon. RES new ser 6 1955.

—— Johnson: editor of Shakespeare, with an essay on the Adventurer. Urbana 1956.

—— Johnson and certain poems in the May 1747 Gentleman's Magazine. RES new ser 17 1966.

—— Johnson's intent in the Journey to the Western Islands of Scotland. EC 16 1966.

—— Johnson's essay on Du Halde's Description of China. Papers on Lang & Lit 2 1966.

Springer-Miller, F. Johnson and Boileau. N & Q 10 Nov 1951.

Waingrow, M. Johnson's degree diplomas. Bodleian Lib Record 3 1951.

Allison, J. Joseph Warton's reply to Johnson's Lives. JEGP 51 1952.

Greene, D. J. Was Johnson theatrical critic of the Gentleman's Magazine? RES new ser 2 1952.

—— Yeats' Byzantium and Johnson's Lichfield. PQ 33 1954.

—— Johnson's contributions to the Literary Magazine. RES new ser 7 1956

—— Johnson and the Harleian Miscellany. N & Q July 1958.

—— Some notes on Johnson and the Gentleman's Magazine. PMLA 79 1959.

—— The false alarm and Taxation no tyranny: some further observations. SB 13 1960.

—— The politics of Johnson. New Haven 1960.

—— Johnsonian critics. EC 10 1960.

—— The development of the Johnson canon. In Restoration and eighteenth-century literature: essays presented to A. D. McKillop, Chicago 1964.

—— Johnson. EC 14 1964.

—— (ed). Johnson: a collection of critical essays. Garden City NY 1965.

Hopkins, M. A. Dr Johnson's Lichfield. New York 1952.

Hilles, F. W. Dr Johnson rebuked: a hitherto unrecorded incident in his life as revealed in a letter from Dr S. Glasse. 1952 (priv ptd).

—— Johnson on Dr Arbuthnot. In his On poetry and poets, New Haven 1957 (priv ptd).

—— (ed). New light on Johnson: essays. New Haven 1959.

Metzdorf, R. F. Isaac Reed and the unfortunate Dr Dodd. Harvard Lib Bull 6 1952.

—— The first American Rasselas and its imprint. PBSA 47 1953.

—— Johnson in Brunswick. MLN 68 1953.

Reynolds on Johnson. In Sir Joshua Reynolds, Portraits, ed F. W. Hilles, New York 1952.

Sledd, J. H. and G. J. Kolb. Johnson's definitions of Whig and Tory. PMLA 67 1952.

—— Dr Johnson's Dictionary. Chicago 1955.

—— The Reynolds copy of Johnson's Dictionary. Bull John Rylands Lib 37 1955.

Taylor, F. Johnsoniana from the Bagshawe Muniments in the Rylands Library. Bull John Rylands Lib 35 1952.

Beattie, P. H. The ocular troubles of Johnson and Pepys. Proc Royal Soc of Medicine 46 1953.

Fletcher, E. G. Mrs Piozzi on Boswell's and Johnson's Tour. SE 32 1953.

Graham, W. H. Dr Johnson's Rambler. Contemporary Rev July 1953.

Hanson, L. W. Johnson, Percy and Sir William Chambers. Bodleian Lib Record 4 1953.

Hoover, B. B. Johnson's parliamentary reporting. Berkeley 1953.

Perkins, D. Johnson on wit and metaphysical poetry. ELH 20 1953.

Mild, W. Johnson and Lauder. MLQ 14 1953.

Monaghan, T. J. Johnson's additions to his Shakespeare for the edition of 1773. RES new ser 4 1953.

Sarason, B. D. George Croft and Johnson. N & Q March 1953. See also Letters vol 1, ed R. W. Chapman, pp. 207, 426.

Scholes, P. A. Life and activities of Sir John Hawkins, musician, magistrate and friend of Johnson. 1953.

Ruhe, E. Hume and Johnson. N & Q March 1953.

—— The two Samuel Johnsons. N & Q Oct 1954.

—— Birch, Johnson and Elizabeth Carter. PMLA 73 1958.

Schoff, F. G. Johnson on Juvenal. N & Q July 1953.

Todd, W. B. The concealed editions of Johnson. Book Collector 2 1953. False alarm and Taxation no tyranny.

—— The printing of Johnson's Journey. SB 6 1954.

—— Cowper's commentary on the Life of Johnson. TLS 15 March 1957.

—— Variants in Johnson's Dictionary. Book Collector 14 1965.

Adams, S. F. Boswell's Life of Johnson. Yale Lib Gazette 29 1954.

Donner, H. W. Dr Johnson as a literary critic. Edda (Oslo) 54 1954.

Fleming, L. Dr Johnson's use of authorities in compiling his Dictionary. N & Q June–Aug 1954.

—— Johnson, Burton and Hale. N & Q April 1957.

Gray, J. Johnson and the King of Ashbourne. UTQ 23 1954.

Osborn, J. M. Dr Johnson and the contrary converts. 1954 (priv ptd); rev in New light on Johnson, ed F. W. Hilles, New Haven 1959.

—— Johnson to Taylor no 90. TLS 24 Dec 1964.

Chapin, C. F. In his Personification in 18th-century English poetry, 1955.

—— Dr Johnson's approval for a passage in Rousseau. N & Q Nov 1959.

—— Johnson's prayer for Kitty Chambers. MLN 76 1964.

—— Johnson and the 'proofs' of Revelation. PQ 40 1964.

—— Johnson's religious development. Stud in Eng Lit 1500–1900 4 1964.

de Beer, E. S. Johnson's θφ. N & Q Dec 1955.

Fifer, C. N. Dr Johnson and Bennet Langton. JEGP 54 1955.

Gifford, H. The vanity of human wishes. RES new ser 5 1955.

Joyce, M. Samuel Johnson. 1955.

Laithwaite, P. Johnson and his birthplace. Lichfield 1955.

Noyes, G. E. The critical reception of Johnson's Dictionary. MP 52 1955.

Watt, I. Johnson after 250 years. Listener 24 Sept 1955.

Wellek, R. Dr Johnson. In his A history of modern criticism vol 1, New Haven 1955.

Boyce, B. Johnson's Life of Savage and its literary background. SP 53 1956.

Carnie, R. H. Lord Hailes's notes on Johnson's Lives of the poets. N & Q Feb–Nov 1956.

Ketton-Cremer, R. W. Johnson's last gifts to Windham. Book Collector 5 1956.

Moran, B. The Irene story and Dr Johnson's sources. MLN 61 1956.

Sutherland, R. Dr Johnson and the collect. MLN 17 1956.

Lascelles, M. M. Johnson's last allusion to Mary Queen of Scots. RES new ser 8 1957.

Leed, J. Johnson and the Gentleman's Magazine. N & Q May 1957.

—— Two new pieces by Johnson in the Gentleman's Magazine? MP 54 1957.

Maxwell, J. C. Othello and Johnson's Irene. N & Q April 1957.

—— 'Talk dead': Pope and Johnson. N & Q June 1963.

Tucker, S. I. and H. Gifford. Johnson's On the death of Levet. Explicator 15 1957.

—— Johnson's Latin poetry. Neophilologus 41 1957.

—— The steeps of fate. N & Q Aug 1957.

—— Johnson's poetic imagination. RES new ser 8 1957.

Hemlow, J. In her History of Fanny Burney, Oxford 1958.

Miner, R. E. Dr Johnson, Mandeville and Public Benefits. HLQ 21 1958.

Pearson, H. Johnson and Boswell. 1958.

Ricks, C. B. Wolsey in the Vanity of human wishes. MLN 73 1958.

—— Notes on Swift and Johnson. RES new ser 11 1960.

—— Johnson's poetry. New Statesman 6 Aug 1965.

— Johnson's battle of the Pygmies and Cranes. EC 16 1966.

Hart, C. R. Johnson: a portrait. 1959.

Jones, M. Housman and Johnson. Trans Lichfield Johnson Soc 1959.

McHenry, L. C. Johnson's medical biographies. Jnl of History of Medicine 14 1959.

— Medical case notes on Johnson in the Heberden manuscripts. New Rambler 15 1964.

— Johnson's The life of Dr Sydenham. Medical History 8 1964.

— and R. McKeith. Johnson's childhood illnesses and the King's Evil. Medical History 10 1966.

— Johnson's tics and gesticulations. History of Medicine 12 1967.

Morgan, H. A. Johnson's Life of Savage. Contemporary Rev Jan 1959.

Wahba, M. (ed). Bicentenary essays on Rasselas. Cairo 1959.

— Johnsonian studies. Oxford 1962.

Adler, J. H. Johnson's He that imagines this. Shakespeare Quart 11 1960.

Balderston, K. C. Dr Johnson's use of William Law in the Dictionary. PQ 39 1960.

— Dr Johnson and William Law. PMLA 80 1960.

Bradbrook, F. W. Dr Johnson and Jane Austen. N & Q March 1960.

Comyn, J. R. G. Two letters of Dr Johnson. TLS 26 Aug 1960.

Davis, B. H. Johnson before Boswell. New Haven 1960.

Eaves, T. C. D. Dr Johnson's letters to Richardson. PMLA 75 1960.

Elder, A. T. Irony and humour in the Rambler. UTQ 30 1960.

— A Johnson borrowing from Addison? N & Q Feb 1961.

— Thematic patterning and development in Johnson's essays. SP 42 1965.

Hart, J. Johnson's A journey to the Western Islands: history as art. EC 10 1960.

Leed, J. Two notes on Johnson and the Gentleman's Magazine. PBSA 54 1960.

Mahoney, J. L. Dr Johnson at work. Columbia Lib Columns 10 1960.

Middendorf, J. H. Dr Johnson and mercantilism. JHI 21 1960.

— Dr Johnson and Adam Smith. PQ 40 1961.

Rawson, C. J. Johnson's bibliotheque. N & Q Feb 1960.

— The vanity of human wishes line 73. N & Q Jan 1965.

Scholes, R. W. Dr Johnson and the bibliographical criticism of Shakespeare. Shakespeare Quart 11 1960.

Aden, J. M. Pope's Horace in Johnson's Juvenal. N & Q July 1961.

— Rasselas and the Vanity of human wishes. Criticism 3 1961.

Fleeman, J. D. Dr Johnson in the Highlands. TLS 29 Sept 1961. See F. G. Sleigh 15 Dec 1961, and Scots Mag Nov 1961.

— A letter of Dr Johnson. TLS 22 June 1962.

— Some proofs of Johnson's Prefaces to the poets. Library 5th ser 17 1962.

— The reprinting of Rambler no 1. Library 5th ser 18 1963.

— Some of Dr Johnson's preparatory notes for his Dictionary 1755. Bodleian Lib Record 7 1964.

— Johnson's Journey 1775 and its cancels. PBSA 58 1964. See also L. H. Kendall, A note on Johnson's Journey 1775, 59 1965.

— The making of Johnson's Life of Savage. Library 5th ser 22 1967.

— Some notes on Johnson's Prayers and meditations, RES new ser 19 1968.

Fox, R. C. The imaginary submarines of Dr Johnson and Richard Owen Cambridge. PQ 40 1961.

Hamilton, H. W. Boswell's suppression of a paragraph in Rambler 60. MLN 76 1961.

Hyde, M. C. Two distinguished Dr Johnsons. Columbia Lib Columns 10 1961.

Kenney, W. Addison, Johnson and the 'energetick' style. Studia Neophilologica 33 1961.

Knieger, B. The moral essays of Johnson. Personalist 42 1961.

Strauss, A. B. English and American celebrations of Johnson's 250th birthday. Books Abroad 35 1961.

— The dull duty of an editor: on editing the text of Johnson's Rambler. Bookmark (Chapel Hill) 35 1965.

Voitle, R. Johnson the moralist. Cambridge Mass 1961.

West, P. Rasselas: the humanist as Stoic. English 13 1961.

Addison, W. Dr Johnson on crime and punishment. New Rambler June 1962.

Chapple, J. A. V. A Johnson discovery. TLS 25 May 1962.

— Johnson's Proposals for printing the history of the Council of Trent [1738]. Bull John Rylands Lib 45 1963.

Daniel, R. W. Johnson on literary textures. In Studies in honor of J. C. Hodges and A. Thaler, Knoxville 1962.

Downes, R. R. Johnson's theory of language. REL 3 1962.

Eddy, D. D. The publication date of the first edition of Rasselas. N & Q Jan 1962.

— Johnson's editions of Shakespeare 1765. PBSA 56 1962.

Halsband, R. Rasselas: an early allusion. N & Q Dec 1962.

Hodgart, M. Johnson and his times. 1962.

Kaul, R. K. Johnson on imagery and description. Literary Criterion (Mysore) 1962.

— The philosopher of nature in Rasselas xxii. Indian Jnl of Eng Stud 3 1962.

— The unities again: Dr Johnson and delusion. N & Q July 1962.

— A journey to the Western Isles re-considered. EC 13–14 1963–4.

— Dr Johnson on the emotional effect of tragedy. Cairo Stud in Eng 1963–6.

Knox, T. M. Notes on R. W. Chapman's edition of Johnson's letters. N & Q July 1962.

Mitchell, S. O. Johnson and Cocker's Arithmetic. PBSA 56 1962.

Nagashima, D. On Johnson's London. Stud in Eng Lit 1500–1900 2 1962.

— Johnson's Dictionary reconsidered. Stud in Eng Lit (Tokyo) 41 1964.

Reed, J. W. Noah Webster's debt to Johnson. Amer Speech 37 1962.

Ryskamp, C. A letter and a portrait of Dr Johnson. Princeton Univ Lib Chron 24 1962.

Sorelius, G. The unities again: Dr Johnson and delusion. N & Q 19 1962.

Torbarina, J. The meeting of Bošković with Dr Johnson. Studia Romanica & Anglica (Zagreb) no 13–14 1962.

Winnett, A. R. Trinity College, Dublin, in the age of Johnson. New Rambler 12 1962.

— Johnson and Hume. New Rambler 17 1966.

Buckley, V. Johnson: the common condition of men. Melbourne Critical Rev 6 1963.

Curtis, L. P. and H. W. Liebert. Esto perpetua: the Club of Dr Johnson and his friends 1764–84. Hamden Conn 1963.

Critchley, M. Johnson's Aphasia. Medical History (London) 6 1963.

Irwin, M. G. Doctor Johnson's troubled mind. Lit & Psychology 13 1963.

Lasser, M. L. Johnson in Scotland: new life amid the Ruins of Iona. Midwest Quart 4 1963.

Lockhart, D. M. 'The fourth son of the mighty Emperor': the Ethiopian background of Johnson's Rasselas. PMLA 78 1963.

Sachs, A. Johnson on the vacuity of life. Stud in Eng Lit 1500–1900 3 1963.
—— Reason and unreason in Johnson's religion. MLR 59 1964.
—— Generality and particularity in Johnson's thought. Stud in Eng Lit 1500–1900 5 1965.
—— Johnson on idle solitude and diabolical imagination. E Studies 47 1966.
—— Johnson on the art of forgetfulness. SP 43 1966.
—— Passionate intelligence. Baltimore 1967.
Sambrook, A. J. Fanny Burney's first letter to Johnson. RES new ser 14 1963.
Schultz, M. F. Coleridge's 'debt' to Dryden and Johnson. N & Q May 1963.
Bernard, F. V. A stylistic touchstone for Johnson's prose. N & Q Feb 1964.
—— A note on two attributions to Johnson. N & Q Feb, May 1964.
—— A new note on Johnson's London. N & Q Aug 1964.
—— 'The fierce Croatian' in the Vanity of human wishes. N & Q Nov 1964.
—— Johnson's address to the reader. N & Q Dec 1965.
—— Johnson and the authorship of Four debates. PMLA 77 1967.
—— A possible source for Johnson's Life of the King of Prussia. PQ 47 1968.
Bowers, F. T. The text of Johnson. MP 61 1964.
Cochrane, J. A. Dr Johnson's printer. 1964.
Hoyt, C. A. On Johnson, who wrote against Scotland. Amer Book Collector 14 1964.
Illo, J. The polymathic Dictionary. West Humanities Rev 18 1964.
Johnston, A. Dr Johnson, John Dyer and the Ruins of Rome. New Rambler 14 1964.
Leicester, J. H. Dr Johnson and Isaac Watts. New Rambler 15 1964.
Link, F. M. A new Johnson letter. N & Q Feb 1964.
McDonald, D. The ribaldry of Dr Johnson. Amer N & Q 2 1964.
Rothenberg, G. E. 'The fierce Croatian' in the Vanity of human wishes. N & Q Aug 1964.
Sacks, S. Fiction and the shape of belief. 1964.
Simmons, J. S. G. Johnson on the banks of the Wolga. Oxford Slavonic Papers 11 1964.
Stanley, E. G. Dr Johnson's use of the word 'also'. N & Q Aug 1964.
Watson, T. G. Johnson and Hazlitt on the imagination in Milton. Southern Quart 2 1964.
Abbott, J. L. Dr Johnson, Fontenelle, Le Clerc and six French lives. MP 12 1965.
—— Dr Johnson and the Amazons. PQ 44 1965.
—— Dr Johnson and the making of the Life of Father Paul Sarpi. Bull John Rylands Lib 48 1966.
—— Johnson's panegyric on Dr Morin. Romance Notes 8 1966.
—— Dr Johnson and the Society of Arts. Jnl Royal Soc of Arts April 1967.
—— 'No dialect of France': Johnson's translations from the French. UTQ 37 1967.
Akiyama, H. The romantic elements in Dr Johnson. Stud in Eng Lit 1500–1900 41 1965.
Cannon, G. Sir William Jones and Dr Johnson's literary club. MP 43 1965.
Currie, H. M. Johnson and the classics. New Rambler 17 1965.
Draper, F. W. M. Johnson's friend Baretti. Ibid.
Findlay, R. R. Johnson: a transitional view of mixing tragedy and comedy. Ohio Speech Jnl 3 1965.
Fisher, S. T. Johnson on flying. TLS 4 Nov 1965.
Gardner, H. Johnson on Shakespeare. New Rambler 17 1965.
Gold, J. J. Johnson's translation of Lobo. PMLA 75 1965.

Isles, D. E. Unpublished Johnson letters. TLS 29 July, 5 Aug 1965.
—— Johnson and Charlotte Lennox. New Rambler 19 1967.
Lonsdale, R. In his Dr Charles Burney, Oxford 1965.
Lustig, I. S. Boswell on politics in the Life of Johnson. PMLA 75 1965.
Meyers, J. Swift, Johnson and the Dublin MA. Amer N & Q Sept 1965.
From sensibility to romanticism: essays presented to F. A. Pottle. New Haven 1965.
Johnson, Boswell and their circle: essays presented to L. F. Powell. Oxford 1965.
San Juan, E. The actual and the ideal in the making of Johnson's Dictionary. UTQ 35 1965.
Wesling, D. An ideal of greatness: ethical implications in Johnson's critical vocabulary. UTQ 35 1965.
Alston, R. C. In his Bibliography of the English language vol 5, 1966.
Baker, S. Rasselas: psychological irony and romance. PQ 45 1966.
Boyle, E. Johnson's attitude to the American colonies. Trans Johnson Soc of Lichfield 1966.
Butt, J. Biography in the hands of Walton, Johnson and Boswell. Los Angeles 1966.
Hardy, J. P. Johnson and Don Bellianis. RES new ser 18 1966.
—— The poet of nature and self-knowledge. UTQ 37 1967.
Kahrl, G. M. Garrick, Johnson and Lichfield. New Rambler 18 1966.
Kallich, M. Johnson's principles of criticism and Imlac's dissertation upon poetry. Jnl of Aesthetics 24 1966.
Manzalaoui, M. A textual crux in the concluding chapter of Rasselas. Cairo Stud in Eng 1963–6.
Alkon, P. Johnson and moral discipline. Evanston 1967.
Fox, A. Johnson's strictures on pious poetry. New Rambler 19 1967.
Grant, D. Johnson: satire and satirists. Ibid.
Hamilton, H. W. The relevance of Johnson's Lives of the poets. In English studies today: 4th series, Oxford 1967.
Jones, E. L. The artistic form of Rasselas. RES new ser 18 1967.
Lams, V. J. The 'A' papers in the Adventurer. SP 64 1967.
O'Flaherty, P. Johnson as satirist. ELH 34 1967.
Trickett, R. In her Honest Muse: a study in Augustan verse, Oxford 1967.
Weinbrot, H. D. Dr Johnson's poems etc. N & Q Nov 1967.
Ingham, P. Dr Johnson's elegance. RES new ser 19 1968.
Meier, T. K. Pattern in Johnson's A journey to the Western Islands. Stud in Scottish Lit 5 1968.
Walker, I. C. Dr Johnson and the Weekly Magazine. RES new ser 19 1968.
Wiles, R. M. The contemporary distribution of Johnson's Rambler. Eighteenth-Century Stud 2 1968.

RICHARD GRAVES
1715–1804

§ I

The festoon: a collection of epigrams, ancient and modern, with an essay on that species of composition. 1766 (for 1765) (anon), 1767 (expanded), nd (4th edn).
The spiritual Quixote, or the summer's ramble of Mr Geoffrey Wildgoose: a comic romance. 3 vols 1773 (anon), 1774, 2 vols Dublin 1774, 3 vols 1783 ('with corrections and additions by the author'), 1792, 2 vols 1808, 1810 (vols 32–3 of British Novelists), 1816 (Walker's Br Classics), Providence 1816, London 1926; ed C. Tracy, Oxford 1967; tr German, 1773; Dutch, 1798–9.

The love of order: a poetical essay in three cantos. 1773. Anon.

The progress of gallantry: a poetical essay in three cantos. 1774. Anon.

Galateo: or a treatise on politeness and delicacy of manners, from the Italian of Monsig Giovanni De La Casa. 1774. Anon.

Euphrosyne: or amusements on the road of life, by the author of the Spiritual Quixote. 2 vols 1776–80 (vol 1 rptd 1780), 1783 (adds Pieces written for the Poetical Society at Bath-Easton).

Columella, or the distressed anchoret: a colloquial tale, by the editor of the Spiritual Quixote. 2 vols 1779.

The sorrows of Werter: a German story. 2 vols 1779, 1780, 1782, 1 vol 1785, 1786 (adapted), 2 vols 1794. Tr Graves from a French version of Goethe's Werther.

Fleurettes, containing an Ode on solitude, On the Pleasures of retirement, The origin of sculpture, translated from the French. 1784. No known copy.

Eugenius: or anecdotes of the golden vale, an embellished narrative of real facts. 2 vols 1785 (anon), 1786.

Lucubrations: consisting of essays, reveries etc in prose and verse, by the late Peter of Pontefract. 1786.

A letter from a father to his son at the university relative to a late address to young students etc. Oxford 1787.

Recollections of some particulars in the life of the late William Shenstone esq in a series of letters from an intimate friend of his to — — esq FRS [William Seward]. 1788. P. 195 signed R.G.

The rout: or a sketch of modern life, from an academic in the metropolis to his friend in the country. 1789. Anon.

The heir apparent: or the life of Commodus, translated from the Greek of Herodian. 1789. Anon.

Plexippus: or the aspiring plebeian. 2 vols 1790. Anon.

The meditations of the Emperor Marcus Aurelius Antonius: a new translation, with a life, notes etc. Bath 1792, Stourport 1811, Halifax 1826, 1905.

Hiero on the condition of royalty: a conversation from the Greek of Xenophon, by the translator of Antoninus's Meditations. Bath 1793.

The reveries of solitude: consisting of essays in prose, a new translation of the Muscipula, and original pieces in verse, by the editor of Columella, Eugenius etc. Bath 1793.

The coalition, or the opera rehears'd: a comedy in three acts by the editor of the Spiritual Quixote. Bath 1814 (for 1794).

The farmer's son: a moral tale inscribed to Mrs Hannah More by the Rev P.P.M.A. Bath 1795.

Sermons; to which is added A letter from a father to his son at the university. Bath 1799.

Senilities: or solitary amusements in prose and verse, with a cursory disquisition on the future condition of the sexes, by the editor of the Reveries of solitude etc. 1801.

The invalid; with the obvious means of enjoying health and a long life, by a nonagenarian, editor of the Spiritual Quixote etc. 1804.

The triflers: consisting of trifling essays, trifling anecdotes and a few poetical trifles, by an adept in the art of trifling; to which is added the Rout, corrected by the author, also the Farmer's son. 1805, 1806.

Shenstone's Miscellany 1759–63. Ed I. A. Gordon, Oxford 1953. Contains some epigrams by Graves.

§ 2

Hutton, W. H. In his Burford papers, 1905.

Ellis, H. Richard Graves and the Spiritual Quixote. Nineteenth Century April 1915.

Richard Graves. TLS 11 May 1922.

Hill, C. J. Shenstone and Graves's Columella. PMLA 49 1934.

— The literary career of Graves. Northampton Mass 1934. With bibliography.

— Applause for Dodsley's Cleone. PQ 14 1935. Several letters from Graves to Dodsley.

Haden, H. J. Words in the Spiritual Quixote. N & Q Jan 1962.

J. B.

SIR JOSHUA REYNOLDS
1723–92

Bibliographies

Hilles, F. W. A bibliography of Sir Joshua's writings. Appendix 4 to his Literary career of Reynolds, Cambridge 1936.

Todd, W. B. Reynolds's Discourses 1769–91. Book Collector 7 1958.

Collections

Works, containing his Discourses, Idlers, A journey to Flanders and Holland (now first published) and his commentary on du Fresnoy's Art of painting, printed from his revised copies [with] an account of the life and writings of the author. Ed E. Malone 2 vols 1797, 3 vols 1798 ('corrected'), 1801, 1809, 1819 (with memoir by J. Farington; here and hereafter as Literary works), 1824, 2 vols 1835 (with memoir by H. W. Beechey), 1 vol 1845 (Bohn's Lib), 1867.

§ 1

A discourse, delivered at the opening of the Royal Academy, January 2 1769, by the President. 1769; tr French, 1769.

A discourse delivered to the students of the Royal Academy on the distribution of the prizes, December 11 1769, by the President. 1769.

The first 2 discourses were followed by 13 more, with titles like 2nd above: 3rd discourse, 1771 (2 states); 4th, 1772, 1772; 5th, 1773, 1773; 6th, 1775; 7th, 1777; 8th, 1779; 9th and 10th (together), 1781; 11th, 1783; 12th, 1785; 13th, 1787; 14th, 1789; 15th, 1791.

Seven discourses delivered in the Royal Academy by the President. 1778; ed H. Morley 1888; tr German, 1781; tr Italian, 1778, 1787. 13 discourses tr French, 2 vols 1787.

The [15] discourses of Reynolds. 2 vols 1820, 1 vol Boston 1821, London 1837; ed J. Burnet 1842; ed E. Gosse 1884; ed E. G. Johnson 1891; ed R. Fry 1905; ed A. Dobson, Oxford 1907 (WC); ed W. R. M. Lamb 1924; ed E. Olson, Chicago [1945] (with trn of Longinus, On the sublime); ed R. P. Wark, San Marino 1959; tr French, ed L. Dimier, Paris 1909; tr German, ed E. Leisching 1893.

The art of painting of Charles Alphonse du Fresnoy: translated into English verse by William Mason MA, with annotations by Reynolds verse by William Mason MA, with annotations by Reynolds. York 1783, Dublin 1783.

Johnson and Garrick. 1816 (priv ptd); ed R. B. Johnson 1927.

Characters of the most celebrated painters of Italy. 1816.

Notes and observations on pictures. Ed W. Cotton 1859. Letters from Johnson, Malone, Boswell et al, with transcript of Reynolds' account book.

Portraits by Reynolds. Ed F. W. Hilles, New York 1952 (Private papers of Boswell, vol 3).

Journey from London to Brentford, now first published. In D. Hudson, Reynolds: a personal study, 1958.

Letters

Letters. Ed F. W. Hilles, Cambridge 1929. 161 letters by Reynolds.

§ 2

Blake's annotated copy of Malone's edn of Reynolds's Works, 1798, *is in BM*: *the marginalia are ptd in* Complete writings of William Blake, ed G. L. Keynes 1957.

Northcote, J. Memoirs of Reynolds. 1813; Supplement, 1815; 2 vols 1818.

Hazlitt, W. On certain inconsistencies in Reynolds's Discourses. In his Table talk vol 1, 1821.

Cotton, W. Reynolds and his works. Ed J. Burnet 1856.

Leslie, C. R. and T. Taylor. The life and times of Reynolds. 2 vols 1865.

Hine, J. Reynolds of Plympton. 1887.

Phillips, C. Sir Joshua Reynolds. 1894.

Graves, A. and W. V. Cronin. A history of the works of Reynolds. 4 vols 1899–1901.

Armstrong, W. Sir Joshua Reynolds. 1900.

Edgecumbe, R. The parentage and kinsfolk of Reynolds. 1901.

Gower, R. S. Reynolds: his life and art. 1902.

Baldry, A. L. Sir Joshua Reynolds. 1903.

Boulton, W. B. Sir Joshua Reynolds. 1905.

Thompson, E. M. S. The Discourses of Reynolds. PMLA 32 1917.

Radcliffe, A. M. Sir Joshua's nephew. 1930.

Wind, E. Humanitätsidee und heroisiertes Porträt in der englischen Kultur des 18 Jahrhunderts. In Vorträge der Bibliothek Warburg 1930–1, Leipzig 1932.

— Charity: the case history of a pattern. Jnl of Warburg Inst 1 1938.

— Borrowed attitudes in Reynolds and Hogarth. Jnl of Warburg Inst 2 1939.

— A lost article on David. Jnl of Warburg & Courtauld Inst 6 1943.

— Reynolds and Pope on composite beauty. Ibid.

— A source for Reynold's parody of the School of Athens. Harvard Lib Bull 3 1949.

Steegman, J. Joshua Reynolds. 1933.

— Portraits of Reynolds. Burlington Mag 80 1942.

Templeman, W. D. Reynolds on the picturesque. MLN 47 1933.

Greenway, L. Alterations in the Discourses of Reynolds. New York 1936 (priv ptd).

Hilles, F. W. The literary career of Reynolds. Cambridge 1936.

— Sir Joshua's prose. In The age of Johnson: essays presented to C. B. Tinker, New Haven 1949.

Tinker, C. B. A new portrait of Omai. Yale Bull of Fine Arts 7 1937.

Waterhouse, E. K. A review of Reynolds. Burlington Mag 70 1937.

— Reynolds. 1941.

Chance, B. Reynolds and his blindness and death. Annals of Medical History 1 1939.

Trowbridge, F. H. Platonism and Reynolds. E Studies 21 1939.

Wecter, D. Reynolds and the Burkes. PQ 18 1939.

Mandowsky, E. Reynolds' conception of truth. Burlington Mag 77 1940.

Gombrich. E. H. Reynolds's theory and practice of imitation. Burlington Mag 80 1942.

Mitchell, C. Three phases of Reynolds's method. Ibid.

Burke, J. Hogarth and Reynolds: a contrast in English art theory. Oxford 1943.

Clough, W. O. Reason and genius: an eighteenth-century dilemma. PQ 23 1944.

Bate, W. J. Johnson and Reynolds: the premise of general nature. In his From classic to romantic, Cambridge Mass 1946.

Boys, R. C. Reynolds and the architect Vanbrugh. Michigan Acad of Science, Arts & Letters 33 1947.

Grigson, G. In his Essays from the air, 1951.

Macklem, M. Reynolds and the ambiguities of neo-classical criticism. PQ 31 1952.

Hipple, W. J. General and particular in the Discourses of Reynolds: a study in method. Jnl of Aesthetics 11 1953; rptd in his Beautiful, the sublime and the picturesque, Carbondale 1957.

Gwynne-Jones, A. The life and works of Reynolds PRA. Jnl of Royal Soc of Arts 104 1956.

Will, F. Blake's quarrel with Reynolds. Jnl of Aesthetics 15 1957.

Hudson, D. Reynolds: a personal study, with Reynolds's Journey from London to Brentford now first published. 1958.

Ferrara, F. Presagi del romanticismo in Reynolds. Eng Miscellany (Rome) 9 1958.

Gerber, H. E. Reynold's pendulum figure and the watchmaker. PQ 38 1959.

Elliott, E. C. Reynolds and Hazlitt. Jnl of Aesthetics 21 1962.

Trawick, L. M. Hazlitt, Reynolds and the ideal. Stud in Romanticism 4 1965.

Goldstein, H. D. Ut pictura poesis: Reynolds on imitation and imagination. Eighteenth-Century Stud 1 1968.

Rosenburg, J. In his On quality in art, Princeton 1967.

J. B.

'JUNIUS'
probably SIR PHILIP FRANCIS
1740–1818

For an account of the controversy surrounding the identity of Junius, along with new evidence in support of Francis, see A. Ellegård, A statistical method for determining authorship: the Junius Letters, Stockholm 1962; *and* Who was Junius? Stockholm 1962.

For accounts of Francis's other writings see Ellegård, Who was Junius? *and* BM catalogue.

The first of the Letters of Junius *appeared in* Woodfall's Public Advertiser *in London,* 21 Jan 1769. *Further letters appeared irregularly until 21 Jan 1772. The series attracted enough attention to make it profitable for various booksellers to bring out edns of the* Letters *before the series was concluded. At least 16 of these unauthorized partial edns were pbd before the end of 1771. In addition, individual letters were pbd in other political collections. In 1772, with Junius's authorization, Woodfall pbd the first complete edn with a dedication and preface by the author. Frequent edns of this authorized version were issued by various publishers in England, Scotland, Ireland and America between 1772 and 1812. This version contained 69 letters, of which 42 bear the signature of Junius, 16 that of Philo Junius, 5 that of Sir William Draper, 3 that of John Horne, and 3 are unsigned.*

Lists of the persons to whom the authorship has been attributed appear in Cushing's Initials, Halkett and Laing's Dictionary, Allibone's Dictionary and Everett's edn of the Letters, *below.*

Many bibliographical notes occur in the nineteenth century in N & Q. For a detailed account of the frequent later edns not recorded here, see Cordasco, Bibliography, below.

Bibliographies

Edmands, J. A. A Junius bibliography. Bull of Mercantile Lib of Philadelphia July 1890–Jan 1892.

Lowndes, W. T. In his Bibliographer's manual of English literature vol 3, 1864 (rev H. G. Bohn).

Cordasco, F. A Junius bibliography, with a preliminary essay on the political background, text and identity. New York 1949.

— Supplement to the Junius bibliography. Bull of Bibliography 21 1953; Addendum, 22 1957.

Bowyer, T. H. A bibliographical examination of the earliest editions of the Letters of Junius. Charlottesville 1957.

§ 1
Incomplete Early Editions of Letters

The political contest [pt 1]: containing a series of letters between Junius and Sir William Draper; also the whole of Junius's letters to his Grave the D— of G—, brought into one point of view [ptd for F. Newbery]. [1769] (3 edns), Dublin 1769 ('3rd' edn, including letters from pts 1–2, with 3 new letters, making total of 24; ptd for J. Potts). Contains 14 letters, the last dated 8 July 1769.

The political contest [pt 2]: being a continuation of Junius's letters from the 8th of July last to the present time. [1769]. Contains 7 later letters, ending with that of 25 Sept 1769.

Two letters from Junius to the D— of G—; to which is added a letter from Junius, containing an address supposed to have been made to a great personage, taken from the Public Advertiser. 1769.

Junius's supposed address to a great personage. [Dec 1769 or early 1770].

A collection of the letters of Atticus, Lucius, Junius and others. 1769, 1769 ('a new edition continued to the end of October 1769'), 1769 (as preceding but with addns of Modestus's answer to Letter 30, and Letters 32–3). All ptd for J. Almon.

A complete collection of Junius's letters with those of Sir William Draper. 1770 (4? issues, each adding further material, the first with 29 letters, the last with 33; all ptd for A. Thomson).

The letters of Junius [ptd for J. Wheble]. 1770, 1770, 1771.

Letters of Junius [ptd for J. Wheble]. 2 vols 1770–4. The first vol, dated 1770, is closely associated with the preceding item.

Bref til konugen i England: ifran auctoren til Weckoskriften Junius. Stockholm 1770. Apparently circulated as a pamphlet in the current Swedish controversy.

The political contest: containing Junius's letter to the K— and Modestus's answer. Dublin 1770.

Two remarkable letters of Junius and the Freeholder, addressed to the K—. 1770. Only known copy owned by Library Company of Philadelphia.

The state of the nation as represented to a certain great personage by Junius and the Freeholder. 1770.

The letters of Junius. 2 vols 1771–2. Ptd for J. Wheble: contains dedication and all the letters except the first 7 of Philo Junius.

The letters of Junius. 1771. Ptd for W. Morison.

The genuine letters of Junius; to which are prefixed anecdotes of the author. 1771, 1771. Contains 50 letters; Burke is presumed to be the author.

Complete Editions

Junius: stat nominis umbra, printed for Henry Sampson Woodfall. 2 vols 1772 (2 issues: first lacks table of contents and index, which appear in 2nd), nd (2nd edn closely resembling preceding, but with table of contents and index; thought by Cordasco et al to be first edn, but see Bowyer's Bibliographical examination, 1957), Dublin 1772, 1772, London 1775, 1771 (for after 1775), 1 vol 1779, 1783, 2 vols 1783, 1 vol 1784, 1786, 1787, Dublin 1787, 1788, 1788, 1789, 1791, Philadelphia 1791, 2 vols 1792 (3 edns), 1 vol Edinburgh 1793, London 1794, 2 vols 1794, 1 vol Philadelphia 1795, Basle 1795, London, 1796 (3 edns), 2 vols 1796 (with 16 portraits), 1797 (with portraits), 1 vol 1797 (5 edns), 2 vols 1797 (with 21 portraits), 1797 ('new and complete'), 1 vol Huddersfield 1798, London 1798, 2 vols 1798 (with 10 portraits), 1799 (with 21 portraits), 1800 (with 10 portraits), 1801 (with 16 portraits), 1801 (21 portraits) etc; tr French, 1791, 1823.

The letters of Junius: stat nominis umbra, with notes and illustrations, historical, political, biographical and critical. Ed R. Heron [2 vols 1801?], 1802, 1804, Boston 1804, Philadelphia 1804, New York 1804. A good edn, used by later editors for its notes. Attributes authorship to Dunning.

The letters of Junius: prodesse civibus. 1806.

The letters of Junius complete, [with a] prefatory enquiry respecting the real author of John Almon. 2 vols 1806. Attributes authorship to Hugh Boyd.

Junius: including letters by the same writer under other signatures (now first collected); to which are added his confidential correspondence with Mr Wilkes, and his private letters addressed to Mr H. S. Woodfall. 3 vols 1812. Introductory essays by Mason Good. It is improbable that Junius wrote any of the miscellaneous essays in vol 3; see C. W. Dilke in his Papers of a critic vol 2, 1875; and C. W. Everett's edn of the Letters, 1927.

Letters of Junius; with preliminary dissertation and copious notes by Atticus Secundus. Edinburgh 1822. The editor, John McDiarmid, argues for Francis as author.

The letters of Junius. 2 vols Paris 1822. Contains essay by J. W. Lake favouring the authorship of Francis.

Junius: a new and enlarged edition, with new evidence as to authorship. Ed J. Wade 1850 etc. 3rd edn of Mason Good's edn of 1812, above. Wade's revision was frequently rptd, and was part of Bohn's Lib. Wade argues for Francis's authorship. The editing and essay were severely criticized by Dilke in his Papers of a critic vol 2, 1875.

The letters of Junius. Ed C. W. Everett 1927. Argues for Lord Shelburne's authorship.

Writings by Francis

Francis was an extensive minor writer. His work includes letters to newspapers, pamphlets and the ptd versions of his parliamentary speeches. Many of these pieces are uncertainly attributed to him. For further information, see A. Ellegård, Who was Junius? Stockholm 1962; DNB; and BM catalogue.

A state of the British authority in Bengal under the government of Mr Hastings. 1780. Anon; attributed to Francis.

A short account of the resignation of Warren Hastings. 1781. Anon. Attributed to Francis.

Extract of an original letter from Calcutta relative to the administration of Sir E. Impey. 1781. Anon; attributed to Francis.

Original minutes of the Governor General and Council of Fort William on the appointment of Sir E. Impey to be Judge of the Sudder Duauny Adawlet. 1781. Ed Francis?

Original minutes of the Governor-General and Council of Fort William on the settlement and collection of the revenues of Bengal. 1782. Anon.

State of India, in two letters from Warren Hastings esq to the Court of Directors, and one from the Nabob Asuful Dowla, Subadar of Owde, to which are added a series of explanatory facts and remarks. 1782. Ed Francis.

Ninth report from the Select Committee appointed to take into consideration the state of the administration of justice in the provinces of Bengal. 1783. Drawn up in part by Francis?

Speech [on the East India Company] in the House of Commons, July 2 1784. 1784.

Two speeches in the House of Commons on the original East-India Bill and on the amended Bill, on the 16th and 26th of July 1784. 1784; tr French, 1784.

A letter from Warren Hastings esq with remarks. 1786. Anon; sometimes attributed to Francis.

Speech in the House of Commons, 7 March 1786 [on the affairs of the East India Company]. 1786, 1786.

Observations on the defence made by Warren Hastings. 1787. Anon.

Answer of P. Francis esq to the charge brought against Sir J. Clavering, Colonel G. Monson and Mr Francis at the Bar of the House of Commons on 4 February 1788 by Sir E. Impey. 1788.

Draught of a resolution and plan intended to be proposed to the Society of Friends of the People. [1792?]. Anon.

Heads of Mr F.'s speech in the House of Commons on the 7th of May 1793, on Mr Grey's notion for a reform in Parliament. 1793.

Letter from Mr F. to Lord North [on the government of India]. [1793?].

Mr Francis's speech on the order of the day for the second reading of the Bill for preventing bribery at Stockbridge election. [1793].

The speech of Mr F. on the tenth of April in favour of a radical reform with observations by Merlin. 1793.

Proceedings in the House of Commons on the slave trade and state of the negroes in the West India islands. 1796.

The question as it stood in March 1798. 1798. Anon.

Mr F.'s speeches on the affairs of India delivered in the House of Commons on the 29th of July 1803. 1803.

Speeches in the House of Commons on the war against the Marhattas. 1805.

Mr F.'s speech in the House of Commons, 28 May 1806, against the exemption of foreign property in the funds from the duty on income. 1806.

A letter from P.F. to Lord Viscount Howick on the state of the East India Company. 1807, 1807.

Reflections on the abundance of peper in circulation and the scarcity of specie. 1810, 1810.

Letter to Earl Grey [occasioned by the blockade of the ports of Norway by the English fleet]. Pamphleteer 4 1813; 1814, 1814.

Plan of a reform in the election of the House of Commons, adopted by the Society of the Friends of the People in 1795; with a new introduction and other documents, republished. Pamphleteer 9 1813; 1817. Anon.

A letter missive from Sir P.F. to Lord Holland [on Irish politics]. 1816, 1816.

Memoirs of Francis, with his correspondence and journals. Ed J. Parkes and H. Merivale 2 vols 1867.

The Francis letters, by Sir Philip Francis and other members of the family. Ed B. Francis and E. Keary 2 vols [1901].

§ 2

Only a selected list of the writings on Junius is given. The Letters provoked immediate response in contemporary periodicals, and the guesses as to Junius's identity continued throughout the 19th century. For a fuller list see F. Cordasco, Junius bibliography, New York 1949.

Thicknesse, P. Junius discovered. 1789. Attributes authorship to John Horne Tooke.

The miscellaneous works of Hugh Boyd, the author of the letters of Junius. 2 vols 1800.

The letters of Junius. Ed R. Heron 2 vols 1802 etc. Attributes authorship to J. Dunning.

The letters of Junius complete. Ed J. Almon 2 vols 1806. Attributes authorship to Hugh Boyd.

Girdlestone, T. Reasons for rejecting the presumptive evidence of Mr Almon that Hugh Boyd was the writer of Junius, with passages selected to prove the real author of the Letters of Junius. 1807, 1813, New York 1818. Attributes authorship to General Charles Lee.

— Facts tending to prove that General Lee was never absent from this country, and that he was the author of Junius. 1813.

Blakeway, J. B. An attempt to ascertain the author of the Letters of Junius. 1813. Attributes authorship to Tooke.

— The sequel of an Attempt to ascertain the author of the Letters of Junius. 1815.

Taylor, J. A discovery of the author of the Letters of Junius, founded on such evidence and illustrations as explain all the mysterious circumstances and apparent contradictions which have contributed to the conceal-

ment of this 'most important secret of our times'. 1813. Attributes authorship to Dr Francis, and says that help was given by his son Sir Philip Francis.

— The identity of Junius with a distinguished living character established. 1816. Changes his view that Dr Francis was the author in favour of the son Sir Philip Francis.

— A supplement to Junius identified. 1817.

Roche, J. An inquiry, concerning the author of the Letters of Junius, in which it is proved that they were written by the late Right Hon Edmund Burke. 1813.

Serres, O. W. The life of the author of the Letters of Junius, the Rev James Wilmot DD. 1813.

— Junius, Sir Philip Francis denied! a letter addressed to the British nation. 1817. According to C. W. Everett, Mrs Serres was an impostor who invented her evidence.

[Duppa, R.] An inquiry concerning the author of the Letters of Junius. 1814. Attempts to prove from the Memoirs by Richard Glover that Glover was author.

Johnston, A. G. Letters to a nobleman, proving a late Prime Minister to have been Junius. 1816. Attributes authorship to the Duke of Portland.

Wraxall, N. W. Historical memoirs of my own time. 1815; ed R. Askham 1904. Inconclusive.

Busby, T. Arguments and facts demonstrating that the Letters of Junius were written by John Lewis DeLolme. 1816.

Junius unmasked. 1819. Attributes authorship to Gibbon.

Butler, C. In his Historical memoirs vol 3, 1821. On Francis as Junius's amanuensis.

Cramp, W. The author of Junius discovered in the person of the celebrated Earl of Chesterfield. 1821.

Mackintosh, J. Authorship of Junius. 1824. Against claim for Sackville.

Coventry, G. A critical enquiry regarding the real author of the Letters of Junius, proving them to have been written by Lord Viscount Sackville. 1825. An excellent analysis of the conflicting claims for the authorship of the Letters.

Kelly, P. Junius proved to be Burke. 1826.

Allen, W. Junius unmasked. 1828. Attributes authorship to Sackville.

Barker, E. H. The claims of Sir Philip Francis KB to the authorship of Junius's Letters disproved: some enquiry into the claims of the late Charles Lloyd esq to the composition of them. 1828. First pbd as a series of single letters, Thetford 1826–7.

Swinden, J. An attempt to prove that Lord Chatham was Junius. 1830.

— Junius Lord Chatham, and the miscellaneous letters proved to be spurious. 1833.

Newhall, I. Letters on Junius showing that the author was Earl Temple. Boston 1831.

Coleridge, S. T. Notes on Junius. In his Literary remains vol 1, 1836. No attempt to solve authorship.

Chatham, William Pitt, Earl of. In his Correspondence, 4 vols 1838.

Macaulay, T. B. Warren Hastings. Edinburgh Rev Oct 1841; rptd in his Collected essays, 1843. Attributes authorship to Francis.

Jacques, J. The history of Junius and his works; and a review of the controversy. 1843. Attributes authorship to Sackville.

Britton, J. The authorship of the Letters of Junius elucidated; including a biographical memoir of Lt-Col Barré MP. 1848. 1848.

Coulton, D. T. Junius. Quart Rev 90 1851. Attributes authorship to Thomas Lyttleton.

The Grenville papers. Ed W. J. Smith 4 vols 1852–3. Attributes authorship to Earl Temple.

Hayward, A. More about Junius: the Franciscan theory unsound, reprinted from Fraser's Magazine with additions. 1868. Hayward also contributed the article on Junius to the 9th edn of the Encyclopaedia britannica, 1881.

Dilke, C. W. In his Papers of a critic vol 2, 1875. Articles and reviews dealing with the controversy, rptd chiefly from Athenaeum.

Brockhaus, F. Die Briefe des Junius. Leipzig 1876.

Lecky, W. E. H. In his History of England in the eighteenth century vol 3, 1887 (3rd edn). Attributes authorship to Francis.

Rae, W. F. Facts about Junius and Francis: Mr Leslie Stephen on Sir Philip Francis; theories about Junius; Walpole's hints for discovering Junius; more letters of Junius. Articles in Athenaeum from 1888.

Grafton, A. F. H., 3rd Duke of. Autobiography and political correspondence. Ed Sir W. Andon 1898. On Lord Temple as director of policy in the Letters.

The Francis letters by Sir Philip Francis and other members of the family. Ed B. Francis and E. Keary 2 vols 1901. Contains a short article by C. F. Keary arguing for Francis.

Smith, J. Junius unveiled. 1909. Attributes authorship to Gibbon.

The letters of Junius. Ed C. W. Everett 1927. Contains a list of the various claimants for the authorship, and supports Lord Shelburne.

Monaghan, F. A new document on the identity of Junius. Jnl of Modern History 4 1932. On Thomas Mante. See also H. B. Bates, Some notes on Thomas Mante, ibid.

Rowse, A. L. The letters of Junius. In his English spirit, 1944.

Cordasco, F. Colonel Macleane and the Junius controversy. ELH 16 1949.

—— The first American edition of Junius. N & Q April 1949.

—— A monody on the death of Junius. N & Q Jan 1950.

—— Laughlin Macleane: further information on the Junius mystery. N & Q April 1950.

—— Junius and Milton. N & Q June 1950.

—— John Miller: associate with Woodfall in the printing of the Junius. N & Q July 1950.

—— Juniana in the Earl of Shelburne's library. N & Q Nov 1950.

—— Junius's motto: stat nominis umbra. N & Q June 1951.

—— An obscene elegy by Junius. N & Q July 1951.

—— Did John Wilkes correct the ms of Junius's letters: a note on John Almon's edition. Ibid.

—— Junius as the author of the North Briton: a note on the Rev Allen's Junius unmasked. N & Q Sept 1951.

—— Edward Bocquet's illustrated edition of Junius. PBSA 46 1952.

—— Letters of Junius. Book Collector 1 1952.

—— Two Junius problems solved. Neophilologus 37 1953.

—— Thomas Paine and the history of Junius: a forgotten cause célèbre. JEGP 52 1953.

—— Gibbon and the authorship of Junius. N & Q Nov 1959.

—— Junius on vellum. N & Q Oct 1959.

—— Junius collection of Francis Place. N & Q Feb 1961.

—— The Twistleton Junius: a suppressed passage restored. N & Q Feb 1961.

Rea, R. R. Bookseller as historian. Indiana Quart for Bookmen 5 1949.

Spector, R. D. The American publication of Heron's edition of the Letters of Junius. N & Q June 1952.

Evans, G. B. The missing third edition of Wheble's Junius 1771. SB 13 1960.

Boulton, J. T. The letters of Junius. Durham Univ Jnl 54 1962.

Ellegård, A. A statistical method for determining authorship: the Junius letters 1769–72. Stockholm 1962 (Gothenburg Stud in Eng 13).

—— Who was Junius? Stockholm 1962. Attributes authorship to Francis.

J.B.

EDMUND BURKE
1729–97

For the locations of mss see Correspondence, ed T. W. Copeland et al, Cambridge 1958– (*introds*). *Many letters and photostats of letters are in Sheffield City Lib.*

Bibliographies

Cordasco, F. Burke: a handlist of critical notices and studies. New York 1950.

Copeland, T. W. and M. S. Smith. A checklist of the correspondence of Burke. Cambridge 1955 (Index Soc).

Todd, W. B. A bibliography of Burke. 1964 (Soho Bibliographies).

Stanlis, P. J. A bibliography of Burke 1748–1968. 1972.

Collections

Political tracts and speeches. Dublin 1777.

The beauties of Fox, North and Burke. Ed G. Chalmers 1784.

The deformities of Fox and Burke. Ed G. Chalmers 1784.

Works. Ed F. Laurence and W. King 8 vols 1792–1827 (4°; vols 1–4 ed Laurence, vols 5–8 ed King), 8 vols 1801 (8°), 16 vols 1803–27, 8 vols 1854–7, rptd to 1889, 12 vols Boston 1865–7.

Posthumous works. 1798. Nonce title for separate issues.

The beauties of Burke. [Ed C. H. Wilson] 2 vols 1798.

Maxims and opinions. 1804.

Speeches in the House of Commons, and in Westminster-Hall. 4 vols 1816.

Extracts from Mr Burke's table-talk at Crewe Hall. [Ed R. M. Milnes], Philobiblon Miscellany 7 1863.

Select works. Ed E. J. Payne 3 vols Oxford 1874–8.

Letters, speeches, and tracts on Irish affairs. Ed M. Arnold 1881.

Selections and extracts, with essays by Hazlitt, Arnold and others. Ed A. M. D. Hughes, Oxford 1921.

Selected prose. Ed P. Magnus 1948.

Burke's politics: selected writings and speeches on reform, revolution and war. Ed R. J. S. Hoffman and P. Levack, New York 1949.

The philosophy of Burke: a selection. Ed L. I. Bredvold and R. G. Ross, Ann Arbor 1960, 1967.

Selected writings and speeches. Ed P. J. Stanlis, Garden City NY 1963.

§ I

The reformer. Dublin 1747–8. Ed Burke. Unique ser at Pearse St Library, Dublin; ed A. P. I. Samuels in his Early life of Burke, Cambridge 1923.

A vindication of natural society in a letter to Lord ****, by a late noble writer. 1756 (anon), 1757 (with new preface); tr French, 1776, 1781.

An account of the European settlements in America. 2 vols 1757, 1758; tr Italian, 1763; French, 1767, 1780; German, 1778. Burke revised and contributed to this work, written by his kinsman William Burke.

A philosophical enquiry into the origin of our ideas of the sublime and beautiful. 1757 (anon), 1759 (adds Introductory discourse concerning taste); ed J. T. Boulton 1958; tr French, 1765, 1803; German, 1773, 1956; Italian, 1804, 1804; Spanish, 1807.

An essay towards an abridgment of the English history [1757]. [1812].

The annual register. 1759–88. Burke edited this annual till 1766 and probably contributed in later years. Some of the historical surveys were rptd in 1761 as A complete history of the present war, and in later compilations.

A short account of a late short administration. 1766.

Observations on a late state of the nation. 1769, 1769.

Thoughts on the cause of the present discontents. 1770 (4 edns).

Burke's speech [13 Oct]. Bristol 1774.

To the gentlemen of Bristol [13 Oct]. Bristol 1774.

To the gentlemen of Bristol [3 Nov]. Bristol 1774.

Speech to the electors [3 Nov]. Bristol 1774.

To the gentlemen of Bristol [16 Nov]. Bristol 1774. Unique copy at Bristol Central Library.

Burke's speeches at his arrival at Bristol. 1774, 1775.

Speech on American taxation April 19 1774. 1775.

The speech on moving his resolutions for conciliation with the colonies March 22 1775. 1775 (3 edns); tr French, 1776; German, 1777.

The letters of Valens. 1777. With occasional contributions by Burke.

A letter to John Farr and John Harris, the sheriffs of Bristol, on the affairs of America [3 April]. Bristol 1777, London 1777 (3 edns).

Two letters to gentlemen in the City of Bristol on Ireland. [23 April, 2 May 1778]. 1778.

An authentic copy of the trial of Keppel. 1779; rev as Proceedings of the court-martial of Keppel, 1779. Burke prepared the formal defence.

Substance of the speeches made in the House of Commons on Wednesday 15 December 1779. 1779.

The Yorkshire question. 1780. Apparently with Burke's assistance.

Speech on presenting to the House of Commons 11th of February 1780 a plan of public oeconomy. 1780. Pirated edn, followed by the authentic sequence: Speech on presenting to the House of Commons the 11th of February 1780 a plan for the oeconomical reformation of the civil and other establishments, 1780 (4 edns).

A letter from Burke in vindication of his conduct with regard to the affairs of Ireland. Dublin 1780, London 1780.

To the gentlemen of Bristol [1 Sept]. Bristol 1780.

To the gentlemen of Bristol [6 Sept]. Bristol 1780.

Bristol, 9th Sept [speech beginning 'I decline the election']. Bristol 1780.

To the gentlemen of Bristol [9 Sept]. Bristol 1780.

Speech at the Guildhall in Bristol upon his parliamentary conduct [6 Sept]. 1780.

Heads of objections to Paul Benfield [of the East India Company with] Benfield's answers. [1780].

Report[s] from the Select Committee [on India]. 1782–3. Burke was sole author of reports 9 and 11, and doubtless assisted in the preparation of others.

Letter to a peer of Ireland [Kenmare] on the penal laws [21 Feb]. 1782; ed H. C. Clifford 1824.

Burke's speech on the 1st December 1783 upon the question for the Speaker's leaving the chair, in order for the House to resolve itself into a committee on Mr Fox's East India Bill [1 Dec 1783]. 1784.

A representation to his Majesty, moved in the House of Commons and seconded by William Windham, June 14. 1784.

Burke's speech, on the motion made for papers relative to the Nabob of Arcot's debts. 1785.

Articles of charge of high crimes and misdemeanours, against Warren Hastings, late Governor-General of Bengal, presented to the House of Commons on the 4th day of April [–5th day of May] 1786. 1786.

Articles of impeachment against Warren Hastings. 1787, 1787.

A letter to Philip Francis. 1788.

Substance of the speech in debates upon the Army Estimates. 1790 (3 edns); tr French, 1790 (6 edns).

Reflections on the Revolution in France, and on the proceedings in certain societies in London relative to that event. 1790 (7 edns); ed E. J. Payne 1875; ed T. H. D. Mahoney 1955; ed W. B. Todd, New York 1959 (from 7th edn); ed C. C. O'Brien 1969 (Pelican); tr French, 1790–1 (12 edns); German, 1791–4 (4 edns); Italian, 1791–8 (3 edns), 1930; Spanish, 1826.

Lettre à un membre de l'Assemblée Nationale de France. [Paris] 1791; rev and tr 1791; tr Italian, 1793.

Two letters on the French Revolution. 1791.

An appeal from the new to the old Whigs, in consequence of some late discussions in Parliament relative to the Reflections on the French Revolution. 1791 (4 edns); tr French, 1791.

Lettre à l'Archevêque d'Aix. [Paris? 1791].

Lettre to [Rivarol] sur les affaires de France. [Paris? 1791].

Traduction d'un article [from Evening Mail 19 Sept as Case of the suffering clergy of France]. [Paris?] 1792.

Burke's speech in Westminster-Hall 18th and 19th of February 1788. 1792.

J. P. Brissot to his constituents. 1794 (3 edns). Burke supplied the preface and assisted in translating an earlier French edn.

Report from the committee of the House of Commons on the trial of Warren Hastings. 1794.

Substance of the speech in answer to certain observations in the report of the Committee of Managers [of the impeachment of Warren Hastings], representing that report to have been a libel on the judges. 1794, 1794.

A letter to a noble Lord on the attacks made upon him and his pension in the House of Lords by the Duke of Bedford and the Earl of Lauderdale. 1796 (14 edns); tr French, 1796 (4 edns); German, 1796.

Thoughts on the prospect of a regicide peace. 1796. Pirated edn followed by the authentic series: Two letters addressed to a member of the present Parliament on the proposals for peace with the regicide directory of France, 1796–[1800] (13 edns); tr French, 1797 (4 edns); German, 1797, 1798. A third letter on the proposals for peace with France, 1797. 4th letter, written before all the others (Xmas 1795) was not pbd until 1812, when it was included in vol 5 of Laurence and King's 4° edn of Works.

A letter to the Duke of Portland. 1797. Pirated edn followed by the authentic series: Two letters on the conduct of our domestick parties, 1797 (3 edns). Consists of Letter to the Duke of Portland on the conduct of the minority, 1793; Letter concerning Lord Fitzwilliam, 1795.

[Address to the King]. Monthly Mag July 1797.

Three memorials on French affairs written 1791, 1792 and 1793. 1797 (3 edns); tr French, 1797, 1799; German, 1798, 1798, 1804, 1815.

Thoughts and details on scarcity. 1800. Written 1795.

The Catholic claims. Dublin 1807, London 1807.

Speech of the late Burke on reform in the House of Commons, 1782; with extracts from the speech of the late W. Windham on Mr Curwen's reform bill 1809. 1831.

Speech in opening the impeachment of Warren Hastings 15 Feb 1788. Ed E. A. Bond 1859.

Letters and Notebooks

Epistolary correspondence of Burke and French Laurence. 1827.

Correspondence 1744–97. Ed Earl Fitzwilliam and R. Bourke 4 vols 1844.

Correspondence of Burke and William Windham. Ed J. P. Gilson 1910 (Roxburghe Club).

A note-book [1750–6]. Ed H. V. F. Somerset, Cambridge 1957.

Correspondence. Ed T. W. Copeland et al 10 vols Cambridge 1958–.

See also A. P. I. Samuels, below.

§ 2

Mackintosh, J. Vindiciae gallicae: defence of the French Revolution against Burke. 1791, Dublin 1791, London 1837.

Paine, T. Rights of man: being an answer to Mr Burke's attack on the French Revolution. 2 pts 1791–2 etc.

Priestley, J. Letters to Burke occasioned by his Reflections on the French Revolution. 1791.

McCormick, C. Memoirs of Burke. 1797.

Bissett, R. The life of Burke. 1798, 2 vols 1800.

A catalogue of the collection of antique statues and other marbles and Italian pictures the property of Burke. 1812.

Prior, J. Memoir of the life and character of Burke. 1812, 1854 (5th edn), 1967.

Burney, Frances (later D'Arblay). In her Diary and letters 1778–1840, 7 vols 1842–6.

Macknight, T. History of the life and times of Burke. 3 vols 1858–60.

Leadbeater, M. The Leadbeater papers. 1862.

Napier, J. Burke: a lecture. Dublin 1863; rptd in Lectures, essays and letters, Dublin 1888.

Dilke, C. W. In his Papers of a critic vol 2, 1875. On Burke's debts.

Weare, G. E. Burke's connection with Bristol 1774–80. Bristol 1894.

Windham papers, with an introduction by the Earl of Rosebery. 2 vols 1913. See Windham's Diary 1784–1810, ed Mrs H. Baring 1866.

Braune, F. Burke in Deutschland. Heidelberg 1917.

Samuels, A. P. I. The early life, correspondence and writings of Burke. Cambridge 1923. Prints for the first time much of Burke's early writings.

Cobban, A. Burke and the revolt against the eighteenth century. 1929, 1961.

Hearnshaw, F. J. C. Social and political ideas of some representative thinkers of the revolutionary era. 1930.

Barker, E. Burke and Bristol 1774–80. Bristol 1931.

Sutherland, L. S. Burke and the first Rockingham ministry. EHR 47 1932.

Bryant, D. C. Burke's opinions of some orators of his day. Quart Jnl of Speech 20 1934.

—— Burke and his literary friends. St Louis 1939.

—— The frustrated opposition: Burke, Barré and their audiences. Washington Univ Stud new ser 20 1951.

—— Burke: new evidence, broader view. Quart Jnl of Speech 38 1952.

—— Burke's Present discontents: the rhetorical genesis of a party testament. Quart Jnl of Speech 42 1956.

—— Burke: the new images 1966. Quart Jnl of Speech 52 1966.

Einaudi, M. Burke e l'indirizzo storico nelle scienze politiche. Turin 1930.

—— The British background of Burke's political philosophy. Political Science Quart 49 1934.

Wecter, D. Burke's birthday. N & Q 19 June 1937.

—— The missing years in Burke's biography. PMLA 53 1938.

—— Four unpublished letters from Boswell to Burke. MP 36 1938.

—— Four letters from Crabbe to Burke. RES 14 1938.

—— Goldsmith and the Burkes. TLS 12 Feb 1938.

—— Adam Smith and Burke. N & Q 30 April 1938.

—— Burke and his kinsmen. Boulder 1939.

—— Garrick and the Burkes; Sir Joshua Reynolds and the Burkes. PQ 18 1939.

—— Horace Walpole and Burke. MLN 54 1939.

—— Burke, Franklin and Samuel Petrie. HLQ 3 1940.

—— Burke's error regarding sugar-crystals. MLN 55 1940. On a passage in Sublime and beautiful.

—— Burke's theory of words, images and emotion. PMLA 55 1940.

Copeland, T. W. Our eminent friend Edmund Burke: six essays. New Haven 1949.

—— Unpublished Burke letters. TLS 30 Sept 1949. 3 letters from Boswell to Burke.

—— Unpublished Burke papers. TLS 30 Dec 1949. 2 letters from Johnson to Burke.

—— Burke's first patron. History Today 2 1952.

—— Burke's friends and the Annual Register. Library 5th ser 18 1963.

Clifford, J. L. Fanny Burney meets Burke. TLS 23 July 1938.

Krieger, H. Die Bedeutung des Organischen im englischen Volks- und Staatsbegriff (Burke, Freeman, Seeley, Froude). Die Neueren Sprachen 46 1938.

Sewall, R. B. Rousseau's Second discourse in England from 1755 to 1762. PQ 17 1938. Demonstrates Burke's use of Rousseau in Vindication.

Magnus, P. Burke: a life. 1939.

—— The finances of Burke: unpublished documents. TLS 6 May 1939.

—— Burke. Oriel Rev [1 1943].

—— The character and private life of Burke. E & S ('English Studies') new ser 2 1949.

Robert, J. Toleration for Catholics: the mind of Burke. Thought 14 1939.

Osborn, A. M. Rousseau and Burke: the idea of liberty. Oxford 1940.

Young, G. M. An essay by Burke. TLS 3 Aug 1940. Reply by P. Magnus 10 Aug 1940.

—— In his Today and yesterday, 1948.

Dunn, W. C. Adam Smith and Burke: complementary contemporaries. Southern Economic Jnl 7 1941.

Luhn, K. Die Berichterstattung über die Ereignisse der französischen Revolution bei Burke, Paine, Mackintosh und Young. Frankfurt 1941.

Maugham, W. S. On style, after reading Burke. Decision 1 1941.

—— After reading Burke. In his Vagrant mood, 1953.

Millar, M. F. X. Burke and the moral basis of political liberty. Thought 16 1941.

Carver, P. L. Burke and the totalitarian system. UTQ 12 1942.

Hutchins, R. M. The theory of oligarchy: Burke. Thomist 5 1943.

—— The theory of the state: Burke. Rev of Politics 5 1943.

Clough, W. O. Reason and genius: an eighteenth-century dilemma (Hogarth, Hume, Burke, Reynolds). PQ 23 1944.

Hamm, V. M. Burke and metaphysics. New Scholasticism 18 1944.

Bernstein, S. English reactions to the French Revolution. Science & Soc 9 1945.

Cone, C. B. Burke the farmer. Agricultural History 19 1945.

—— Burke's art collection. Art Bull 29 1947.

—— Burke's library. PBSA 44 1950.

—— Pamphlet replies to Burke's Reflections. In The making of English history, ed R. L. Schuyler, New York 1952.

—— Burke and the nature of politics. 2 vols Lexington Kentucky 1957–64.

—— Burke and the European social order. Thought 39 1964.

Barker, E. Burke and his Bristol constituency; Burke on the French Revolution. In his Essays on government, Oxford 1945.

Oliver, R. T. Four who spoke out: Burke, Fox, Sheridan, Pitt. Syracuse 1946.

Burke's empire. TLS 20 Dec 1947.

Greenough, H. Burke on the beautiful. In his Form and function, Berkeley 1947.

Laski, H. J. Burke. Dublin 1947.

Reynolds, E. E. Burke: Christian statesman. 1948.

Brenlan, C. Burke and our present discontents. Thought 24 1949.

Fasnacht, G. E. Lord Acton on nationality and Socialism (with an appendix on Burke based on the Acton mss). Oxford 1949.

Himmelfarb, G. American revolution in the political theory of Lord Acton. Jnl of Modern History 21 1949. On his estimate of Burke.

Hoffman, R. J. S. The Wentworth papers of Burke, Rockingham and Fitzwilliam. Proc Amer Philosophical Soc 94 1950.

—— Burke, New York agent. Philadelphia 1956. Includes some 200 unpbd letters to and from Burke.

Horne, C. J. Burke, Boswell and the life of Johnson. N & Q 11 Nov 1950.

Kirk, R. How dead is Burke? Queen's Quart 57 1950.

—— Burke and natural rights. Rev of Politics 8 1951.

—— The Anglican mind of Burke. Church Quart Rev 153 1952.

—— Burke and the principle of order. Sewanee Rev 60 1952.

—— Burke and the philosophy of prescription. JHI 14 1953.

—— Burke and the politics of prescription. In his Conservative mind, New York 1953.

—— The conservative revolution of Burke. Catholic World Aug 1958.

—— Burke: a genius reconsidered. New Rochelle NY 1967.

White, H. B. Burke on political theory and practice. Social Research 17 1950.

Blanchard, L. L'évolution de la notion du bien publique dans la pensée de Burke. Revue d'Histoire Economique et Sociale 29 1951.

Boulton, J. T. An unpublished letter from Paine to Burke. Durham Univ Jnl 42 1951.

—— The Reflections: Burke's preliminary draft and methods of composition. Durham Univ Jnl 45 1953.

—— Exposition and proof: the apostrophe in Burke's Reflections. Renaissance & Modern Stud 2 1958.

—— Burke's Letter to a noble Lord: apologia and manifesto. Renaissance & Modern Stud 8 1966.

—— The letters of Burke: 'manly liberty of speech'. In The familiar letter in the eighteenth century, ed H. Anderson et al, Kansas City 1966.

Pollard, A. Two new letters of Crabbe [to Burke]. RES new ser 2 1951.

Barry, L. Our legacy from Burke. Cork 1952.

Frisch, M. J. Rational planning versus unplanned becoming. Classical Jnl 47 1952.

—— The classical attack on the French Revolution. Classical Jnl 48 1953.

—— Burke on theory. Cambridge Jnl Feb 1954.

Levack, A. P. Burke, his friends and the dawn of Irish Catholic emancipation. Catholic Historical Rev 37 1952.

Schmitt, H. A. and J. C. Weston. Ten letters to Burke from the French translator of the Reflections. Jnl of Modern History 24–5 1952–3.

Sarason, B. D. Burke and the two Annual Registers. PMLA 68 1953.

—— A sketch of Burke by his executors. N & Q Feb 1954.

—— Burke's burial place. N & Q Feb 1955.

—— Editorial mannerisms in the early Annual Register. PBSA 52 1958.

—— Burke's two notes on America. Burke Newsletter 6 1965.

Stanlis, P. J. Burke and the law of nations. Amer Jnl of International Law 47 1953.

—— Burke and the natural law. Ann Arbor 1958.

—— Burke and the sensibility of Rousseau. Thought 36 1961.

—— The basis of Burke's political conservatism. Modern Age 5 1961.

—— Burke in the twentieth century. Bucknell Rev 7 1964.

—— (ed). The relevance of Burke. New York 1964.

—— (ed). Burke, the Enlightenment and the modern world. Detroit 1967.

Vincitorio, G. L. Burke and Charles Lucas. PMLA 68 1953.

Crowley, P. J. Burke and scholasticism. New Scholasticism 28 1954.

Cambray, P. G. Towards an abridgement of English history. TLS 27 May 1955.

Fay, C. R. Burke and Adam Smith. Belfast 1956.

Gottschalk, L. Reflections on Burke's Reflections. Proc Amer Philosophical Soc 100 1956.

Mahoney, T. H. D. Burke's imperial mentality and the proposed Irish absentee tax of 1773. Canadian Historical Rev 37 1956.

—— Burke and Rome. Catholic Historical Rev 43 1958.

—— Burke and Ireland. Cambridge Mass 1960.

—— Burke and the American Revolution: the repeal of the Stamp Act. Burke Newsletter 8 1966.

Parkin, C. The moral basis of Burke's political thought. Cambridge 1956.

Skalweit, S. Burke und Frankreich. Cologne and Oplanden 1956.

—— Burke und sein 'Prussian Gentleman'. In Spiegel der Geschichte, ed K. Repgen and S. Skalweit, Münster 1964.

Snow, V. F. Robert C. Johnson's appraisal of Burke's eloquence. Quart Jnl of Speech 42 1956.

Cannon, G. H. Sir William Jones and Burke. MP 54 1957.

Rogow, A. A. Burke and the American liberal tradition. Antioch Rev 17 1957.

Utley, T. E. Burke. 1957 (Br Council pamphlet).

Weston, J. C. Burke's authorship in Dodsley's Annual Register. PBSA 51 1957.

—— An essay by Burke. TLS 17 May 1957. Reply by W. B. Todd 14 June 1957; reply by Weston 19 July 1957.

—— The ironic purpose of Burke's Vindication vindicated. JHI 19 1958.

—— Burke's view of history. Rev of Politics 23 1961.

—— Burke's Irish history: a hypothesis. PMLA 77 1962.

—— Burke's wit. REL 4 1963.

—— Predecessors to Burke's and Dodsley's Annual Register. SB 17 1964.

Mazlish, B. The conservative revolution of Burke. Rev of Politics 20 1958.

Rothbard, M. N. A note on Burke's Vindication of natural society. JHI 19 1958.

Underdown, P. T. Burke, the commissary of his Bristol constituents 1774–80. EHR 73 1958.

—— Henry Cruger and Burke. William & Mary Quart 3rd ser 15 1958.

—— Bristol and Burke. Bristol 1961.

Canavan, F. P. Burke's conception of the role of reason in politics. Jnl of Politics 21 1959.

—— The political reason of Burke. Durham 1960.

Macpherson, C. B. Burke and the new conservatism. Science & Soc 22 1958.

—— Burke. Proc Royal Soc of Canada 53 1959.

Brooke, J. Burke in the 1760's. South Atlantic Quart 58 1959.

Davidson, J. F. Natural law and international law in Burke. Rev of Politics 21 1959.

—— Wit and politics: Burke. Tennessee Stud in Lit 9 1964.

Eulau, H. et al. The role of the representative: some empirical observations on the theory of Burke. Amer Political Science Rev 53 1959.

Johnson, S. F. Hardy and Burke's 'sublime'. In Style in prose fiction, New York 1959.

Love, W. D. New studies of Burke. Emory Univ Quart 15 1959.

—— Burke, Charles Vallancey and the Sebright manuscripts. Hermathena 95 1960.

—— Burke's idea of the body corporate: a study in imagery. Rev of Politics 27 1965.

—— Burke's transition from a literary to a political career. Burke Newsletter 6 1965.

—— 'Meaning' in the history of conflicting interpretation of Burke. Burke Newsletter 8 1966.

Lucas, F. L. In his Art of living, 1959.

May, G. Diderot and Burke: a study in aesthetic affinity. PMLA 75 1960.

Pocock, J. G. A. Burke and the ancient constitution. Historical Jnl 3 1960.

Graubard, S. R. Burke, Disraeli and Churchill: the politics of perseverance. Cambridge Mass 1961.

Phillips, N. C. Burke and the county movement 1779–80. EHR 76 1961.

Torchiana, D. T. Senator Yeats, Burke and able men. Newberry Lib Bull 5 1961.

Brady, F. Prose style and the 'Whig' tradition. BNYPL Sept 1962.

Courtney, C. P. Burke and Petrus Camper. E Studies 48 1962.

—— Montesquieu and Burke. Oxford 1963.

The Burke-Paine controversy: texts and criticism. Ed R. B. Browne, New York 1963.

Fennessy, R. R. Burke, Paine and the rights of man: a difference of political opinion. Hague 1963.

Ware, M. Sublimity in the novels of Ann Radcliffe. Upsala and Copenhagen 1963. On influence of Burke's Enquiry.

Hodgart, M. Radical prose in the late eighteenth century. In The English mind, ed H. S. Davies and G. Watson, Cambridge 1964. Burke's influence on Paine and Godwin.

Schumann, H. G. Burkes Anschauungen vom Gleichgewicht in Staat und Staatensystem, mit einer Burke-Bibliographie. Meisenheim 1964.

Wood, N. The aesthetic dimension of Burke's political thought. Jnl of Br Stud 4 1964.

Fitzgerald, J. J. The logical style of Burke's Thoughts on the cause of the present discontents. Burke Newsletter 7 1965.

—— Burke's neglected masterpiece. Discourse 8 1965. On Letter to a noble Lord.

Fuchs, M. Burke et Augustus Keppel. Etudes Anglaises 18 1965.

Mansfield, H. C. Statesmanship and party government: a study of Burke and Bolingbroke. Chicago 1965.

Ripley, R. Adams, Burke and conservatism. Political Science Quart 80 1965.

Robbins, C. Burke's rationale of Cabinet government. Burke Newsletter 7 1965.

Schneider, F. Das Rechts- und Staatsdenken Burkes. Bonn 1965.

Skelton, R. Britannia's Muse revisited. Massachusetts Rev 6 1965.

Smith, R. A. Burke's crusade against the French Revolution. Burke Newsletter 7 1965.

Reitan, E. A. Burke and the Civil List 1769–82. Burke Newsletter 8 1966.

Sutherland, L. S. and J. A. Woods. The East India speculations of Burke. Proc Leeds Philosophical & Literary Soc (Literary & Historical Section) 11 1966.

Wyss, W. von. Burke, Denker, Redner und Warner. Munich 1966.

Chapman, G. W. Burke: the practical imagination. Cambridge Mass 1967.

Guttman, A. In his Conservative tradition in America, Oxford 1967.

Hart, J. Burke and radical freedom. Rev of Politics 29 1967.

Joy, N. R. Burke's Speech on conciliation. Stud in Burke 9 1967.

O'Brien, C. C. Burke and Marx. New Amer Rev 1 1967.

Wilkins, B. T. The problem of Burke's political philosophy. Oxford 1967.

Goodwin, A. The political genius of Burke's Reflections. Bull John Rylands Lib 50 1968.

Kallich, M. Horace Walpole against Burke. Stud in Burke 9 1968. Reply by J. W. Johnson 10 1968.

Sutherland, L. S. Burke and the relations between Members of Parliament and their constituents. Stud in Burke 10 1968.

W. B. T.

OLIVER GOLDSMITH

1730?–74

For mss see Balderston, below.

Bibliographies etc

Anderson, J. P. In A. Dobson, Life of Goldsmith, 1888.

Williams, I. A. In his Seven xviiith-century bibliographies, 1924.

Balderston, K. C. A census of the manuscripts of Goldsmith. New York 1926.

Sotheby and Co. Catalogue of the very extensive collection of the writings of Goldsmith, the property of W. Swanston. 1926.

Dix, E. R. McC. The works of Goldsmith: hand list of Dublin editions before 1801. Trans Bibl Soc of Ireland 3 1928.

An exhibition in the Yale University Library of the works of Goldsmith. New Haven 1928.

Scott, T. Goldsmith bibliographically and biographically considered. New York 1928. Based on the collection of W. M. Elkins now in Free Library, Philadelphia.

Paden, W. D. and C. K. Hyder. A concordance to the poems of Goldsmith. Lawrence Kansas 1940.

Collections

Miscellaneous works: consisting of his essays, poems, plays &c. 2 vols Edinburgh 1791, Perth 1791, Glasgow 1795.

Miscellaneous works: containing the Citizen of the world, the Vicar of Wakefield, essays, poems and plays. 4 vols Edinburgh 1792.

Miscellaneous works, now first uniformly collected. 7 vols Perth 1792.

Miscellaneous works: a new edition. 4 vols 1801, 1806, 6 vols 1809, 4 vols Boston 1809, London 1812, Glasgow 1816, London 1820, 1821, 6 vols 1823. On the history of this edn see K. C. Balderston, The history and sources of Percy's Memoir of Goldsmith, Cambridge 1926.

Miscellaneous works. Ed Washington Irving 4 vols Paris 1825, Philadelphia 1834, 1836, 1837, Paris 1837.

Miscellaneous works. Ed J. Prior 4 vols 1837, New York 1850, Philadelphia 1865.

Works. Ed H. G. Bohn 4 vols 1848.

Works. Ed P. Cunningham 4 vols 1854, New York 1881.

Works, with introductory memoir by W. Spalding. 1858.

Miscellaneous works. Ed D. Masson 1869 (Globe edn).

Works. Ed J. W. M. Gibbs 5 vols 1884–6.

Selected works. Ed R. Garnett 1950 (Reynard Lib).

Collected works. Ed A. Friedman 5 vols Oxford 1966.

Poems

A collection of the most esteemed pieces of poetry. 1767. Contains The gift and The hermit: a ballad.

Four poems. Altenburgh 1773. Contains The deserted village and The traveller.

Select poems. 1775. *See* A. Williams, London Mercury Oct 1922.

Poems. Belfast 1775.

Poetical works. 1784, 1785, 1788, 1792.

Poems. 1786, Philadelphia 1791, Manchester 1798, London 1799, 1800.

Poems. In The works of the English poets, ed S. Johnson vol 70, 1790.

Poetical works. 1793. Other edns with the same title, Hereford 1794, 1795, Manchester 1795, London 1795, [1795], 1796, 1798, Cheltenham 1798, Hereford 1799, Paris 1803, London 1804 (3 edns), 1805, 1806, Gloucester 1809, Alnwick 1812, Philadelphia 1813, London 1816, 1817, 1818, Chiswick 1818, 1822.

Poetical works. In A complete edition of the poets of Great Britain, ed R. Anderson vol 10, 1794.

Poems by Goldsmith and Parnell. [Ed I. Reed] 1795, 1804.

Poems: a new edition adorned with plates. 1800.

Poetical works. In Works of the British poets, ed T. Park vol 37, 1805.

Poetical works. In S. Rogers, The pleasures of memory, Paris 1805.
Poems of Goldsmith and Cunningham. Gotha 1807.
Poems. In Works of the English poets, ed A. Chalmers vol 16, 1810.
Poetical works, with remarks attempting to ascertain the actual scene of the Deserted village, by R. H. Newell. 1811, 1820.
The traveller, the Deserted village and other poems. 1816, 1817, 1819, 1822.
Poems. In Works of the British poets, ed E. Sanford and R. Walsh vol 30, Philadelphia 1822.
Poems. In The British poets vol 64, Chiswick 1822.
Poésies choisies, traduites en vers français par F. Guide. Paris 1829.
Poetical works. Ed J. Mitford 1831, 1866 (rev); rev A. Dobson 1895 (Aldine edn).
Poetical works. Ed B. Corney 1846.
Poetical works, with a notice by E. F. Blanchard [1858].
Poems. Ed R. A. Willmott 1859.
Selected poems. Ed A. Dobson, Oxford 1887, 1906 ('extended and revised' as Complete poetical works).
Selected poems. In Selected poems of Johnson and Goldsmith, ed A. Rudrum and P. Dixon 1965.

Poems and Essays

Miscellaneous works, containing all his essays and poems. 1775, 1778, 1780, 1782, 1784, 1786, 1789, Edinburgh 1792, London [1792], 1793, Boston 1793, Glasgow 1795, Brookfield Mass 1795.
Retaliation. 1776 (8th edn). Contains other poems and 2 essays. Reissued 1777, still as '8th edn', with additional poems.
Essays and poems. Edinburgh 1802, Salem Mass 1804, Edinburgh 1806, 1807, London 1807, 1819.
Essays [and 2 poems]. 1804.
Poetical works and essays. 1817, 1819, 1824.

Poems and Plays

Poems and plays. Dublin 1777, London 1780, Dublin 1785.
Poetical and dramatic works. 2 vols 1780, 1786, 1791.
Poems and plays. Ed A. Dobson 2 vols 1889.

Essays

For collections by Goldsmith himself see under §1, below.
The beauties of the magazines and other periodical works. 1772. Contains 11 essays ascribed to Goldsmith.
Novellettes selected for the use of young ladies and gentlemen, written by Dr Goldsmith, Mrs Griffith etc. 1780. Contains 2 essays by Goldsmith from Westminster Mag.
Essays and criticisms. 3 vols 1798. Prepared by T. Wright with the assistance of I. Reed. Of the 37 essays and reviews here first ascribed to Goldsmith, many are almost certainly not his. *See* R. S. Crane, New essays, 1927, pp. xii–xv.
Essays. New York 1809.
Essays. 1819.
Essays and the Bee. In Select edition of the British prose writers vol 3, Boston 1820.
Selected essays. Ed J. H. Lobban, Cambridge 1910.
The Bee and other essays, together with the Life of Nash. Oxford 1914.
New essays. Ed R. S. Crane, Chicago 1927. Prints 18 new ascriptions; nos 1 and 13 are doubtful.

Vicar of Wakefield and Other Works

Select works containing the Vicar of Wakefield, the Traveller and the Deserted village. Berlin 1803.
The Vicar of Wakefield, to which is added a choice collection of essays. Hanover [1805].

The Vicar of Wakefield, essays and poems. Edinburgh 1823.
The Vicar of Wakefield and other writings. Ed F. W. Hilles, New York 1955.

Plays

Plays. Ed A. Dobson 1893, 1901.
The good natur'd man and She stoops to conquer. Ed A. Dobson and G. P. Baker, Boston 1905.
Plays. Ed C. E. Doble, Oxford 1909.
Two plays. Ed G. Boas and M. Willy 1962.

'Beauties'

The beauties of Goldsmith: or the moral and sentimental treasury of genius. 1782 (2nd edn), Dublin 1783, 1790, London 1801 (with new sub-title and rearranged contents), 1803.

§1

The monthly review: or literary journal. 1757, 1758, 1763. *The following list of Goldsmith's contributions is based on the editor R. Griffiths's notes in his copy of the* Review *now in Bodley. See* B. C. Nangle, The Monthly Review: first series 1749–89, Oxford 1934.
Mallet's Remains of the mythology and poetry of the Celtes (April 1757). *See* C. F. Tupper, MLN 45 1930.
Home's Douglas: a tragedy (May).
The Connoisseur (May).
A catalogue of foreign publications (May).
Literary news (May).
Burke's A philosophical enquiry into the origin of our ideas of the sublime and beautiful (May).
Smith's The history of the province of New York (June).
A review of the military operations in North America (June).
Count Saxe's Reveries: or memoirs upon the art of war (June).
Smollett's A compleat history of England (June).
Charlevoix's Histoire du Paraguay (June).
Keysler's Travels through Germany, Bohemia, Hungary, Switzerland, Italy etc (appendix to vol 16).
Layard's An essay on the nature, causes and cure of the contagious distemper among the horned cattle in these kingdoms (July).
Polignac's Anti-Lucretius, of God and nature: a poem (July).
Hanway's A journal of eight days journey from Portsmouth to Kingston upon Thames (July).
Rabener's Satirical letters (Aug).
Letters from an Armenian in Ireland to his friends at Trebisonde (Aug).
Voltaire's Universal history (Aug).
The contest in America between Great-Britain and France (Aug).
Wilkie's The Epigoniad (Sept).
Gray's Odes (Sept).
Brief notices in the Monthly Catalogue (April–July). 37 of these are marked as Goldsmith's in Griffiths's copy; rptd in Collected works, ed A. Friedman.
Wise's Some enquiries concerning the first inhabitants, language, religion, learning and letters of Europe (Dec 1758).
Bayly's An introduction to languages, literary and philosophical (Dec).
Burton's Πενταλογια: sive tragœdiarum Græcarum delectus (Dec.)
The Tusculan disputations of Cicero: a new translation (Dec).
Brookes's A new and accurate system of natural history (Oct 1763).
The memoirs of a Protestant, condemned to the galleys of France for his religion. 2 vols 1758 (9 March), Dublin 1765; ed A. Dobson 1895. Tr Goldsmith from the French of J. Marteilhe.

The critical review: or annals of literature. 1759, 1760, 1763. *On the following and other attributions see* A. Friedman, MP 44 1946.
Marriott's Female conduct (Jan 1759).
Barrett's trn of Ovid's Epistles (Jan).
Langhorne's The death of Adonis (March).
Ward's A system of oratory (April).
Murphy's The orphan of China: a tragedy (May).
Formey's Philosophical miscellanies (June).
Van Egmont and Heyman's Travels through part of Europe, Asia Minor etc. (June).
Marriott's The twentieth epistle of Horace to his book, modernized (July).
Massinger's Dramatic works (July).
Guicciardini's The history of Italy (Aug).
The works of Mr William Hawkins (Aug).
Jemima and Louisa (Aug).
Thyer's The genuine remains in verse and prose of Mr Samuel Butler (Sept). This review is of the prose; the review of the verse (July) is not by Goldsmith.
Kedington's Critical dissertations upon the Iliad of Homer (Jan 1760).
A review of the Works of the Rev Mr W. Hawkins, by an impartial reader (March).
Dunkin's An epistle to the Earl of Chesterfield (March).
Brookes's A new and accurate system of natural history (Aug, Oct 1763).
An enquiry into the present state of polite learning in Europe. 1759 (4 April), 1774 (30 July, rev); tr French, 1762.
The bee. Nos i–viii, 6 Oct–24 Nov 1759. Reissued in book form 1759 (15 Dec), reissued c. 1800 with new title-page, new edn 1819.
The busy body. 1759.
Description of various clubs (no iii 13 Oct); rptd in Essays by Mr Goldsmith, 1765.
(?) The logicians refuted (no v 18 Oct). Attributed to Swift in Busy body; to Goldsmith in Poetical and dramatic works, 1780.
On public rejoicings for victory (no vi 20 Oct); Prior, Life 1 p. 335.
(?) On the taking of Quebec (no vii 23 Oct); Poetical and dramatic works, 1780.
The weekly magazine: or gentleman and lady's polite companion. 1759, 1760. *For the following and other possible contributions see* A. Friedman, MP 32 1935; Collected works 3 pp. 22–3.
A description of the manners and customs of the native Irish (no i 29 Dec 1759).
Some thoughts preliminary to a general peace (no i); rptd with changes in Lady's Mag Oct 1761; *see* Crane, New essays pp. 89–97.
Some original memoirs of the late famous Bishop of Cloyne (no i, no ii 5 Jan 1760).
The life of the Hon Robert Boyle (no ii).
Serious reflections on the life and death of the late Mr T— C—, by the ordinary of Newgate (no ii); rptd in Essays by Mr Goldsmith, 1765.
The double metamorphosis: a tale (no ii); rptd in Essays by Mr Goldsmith, 1765.
A sublime passage in a French sermon (no iii 12 Jan).
The futility of criticism (no iii).
On the present state of our theatres (no iii).
The royal magazine: or gentleman's monthly companion. 1759, 1760.
The proceedings of providence vindicated: an eastern tale (Dec 1759); rptd in Essays by Mr Goldsmith, 1765.
A comparative view of races and nations (June, supplement to vol 2 (26 July), July, Sept 1760); Crane, New essays.
The public ledger. 1760, 1761.
Chinese letters. 119 essays pbd between 24 Jan 1760 and 14 Aug 1761; rptd as Citizen of the world, 1762.

(?) Translations from Voltaire (27 Aug, 12 Nov 1760). *See* Works, ed Gibbs, 3 p. 28; Crane, New essays pp. 136–7.
Preface to a series of literary essays (19 Aug 1761); New essays.
New fashions in learning (22 Aug); New essays.
Avenbrugger's discovery of percussion (27 Aug); New essays.
The progress of the arts in Switzerland (29 Aug); New essays.
South American giants (5 Sept); New essays.
The taste for shows and processions deplored (10 Sept); New essays.
From a common-council-man (17 Sept); Essays by Oliver Goldsmith, 1766.
To the printer (24 Sept); Essays by Oliver Goldsmith, 1766.
The British magazine: or monthly repository. 1760. On the 'Belles-lettres' ser, *see* C. F. Tupper, Essays erroneously attributed to Goldsmith, PMLA 39 1924; on other attributions *see* Friedman, Collected works 3 pp. 87–90.
On the different schools of music (Feb, April).
A reverie at the Boar's-Head-Tavern in Eastcheap (Feb, March, April).
The effect which climates have upon men and other animals (May).
A dream [The fountains of fine sense and of good sense] (May). *See* A. Friedman, MLN 53 1938.
The distresses of a common soldier (June).
The history of Carolan, the last Irish bard (July).
A true history for the ladies (July).
A dream [The mansions of poetry and taste] (July). *See* R. S. Crane, TLS 1 March 1934.
The history of Miss Stanton (July).
The adventures of a strolling player (Oct).
The lady's magazine: or polite companion for the fair sex. 1760, 1761.
Of the assemblies of Russia (Sept 1760); Essays by Mr Goldsmith, 1765.
A lady of fashion in the times of Anna Bullen compared with one of modern times (Oct); Crane, New essays pp. 131–2; Friedman, MP 30 1933.
Some remarks on the modern manner of preaching (Dec); Essays by Mr Goldsmith, 1765.
Memoirs of M. de Voltaire (Feb–Nov 1761). Identified by Prior with the life of Voltaire to which Goldsmith referred in his letter to Henry Goldsmith of c. 13 Jan 1759.
Lloyd's evening post and British chronicle. 1762.
The author's motives for writing (20–22 Jan); Crane, New essays.
The author's club (25–27 Jan); Essays by Mr Goldsmith, 1765; New essays.
The state of literature (29 Jan–1 Feb); New essays.
Specimen of a magazine (8–10 Feb); Essays by Mr Goldsmith, 1765.
The revolution in low life (14–16 June); R. S. Crane, TLS 8 Sept 1927; New essays.
To the editor [in defence of The life of Nash], signed A.B. (22–24 Nov); Friedman, Collected works 3 pp 392–8.
The mystery revealed: containing a series of transactions and authentic testimonials respecting the supposed Cock-Lane ghost. 1762 (23 Feb), misdated 1742; rptd Westport Conn 1928. *See* Prior, Life 1 pp. 387–8; N & Q 24 Jan 1852, 13 May 1865.
The citizen of the world: or letters from a Chinese philosopher residing in London to his friends in the East. 2 vols 1762 (1 May), Dublin 1762, 1769, London 1774 (1 July, called 3rd edn), Dublin 1775, London 1776, 1782, 1785, 1786, Dublin 1789, London 1790, 1792, 1793, 1793–4, 1794, Albany NY 1794, London 1799, 1800, Philadelphia 1804, Edinburgh 1805, London 1809, Baltimore 1816, Belfast 1818, Chiswick

1819, Bungay 1823, London 1824 etc; ed C. Knight 1840; ed A. Dobson 1891, 1893, 1900; tr French, 1763; German, 1763.

Plutarch's Lives, abridged from the original Greek, illustrated with notes and reflections. 7 vols 1762 (beginning of each month May–Nov). Goldsmith prepared vols 1–4 but was unable to complete 5.

The life of Richard Nash of Bath esq, extracted principally from his original papers. 1762 (14 Oct), 1762 (9 Dec), Dublin 1762.

A new and accurate system of natural history, by R. Brookes. 6 vols 1763–4 (beginning of each month Aug 1763–Jan 1764), 1772. Goldsmith wrote Preface and Introductions to vols 1–4; see Friedman, Collected works 5 pp. 229–30.

A general history of the world from the creation to the present time, by W. Guthrie, J. Gray and others. 12 vols and index vol 1764–7. Goldsmith wrote Preface to vol 1, pbd 2 April 1764.

An history of England in a series of letters from a nobleman to his son. 2 vols 1764 (26 June), Dublin 1767, London 1769, 1770, 1771, 1772, 1774, 1776, 1780, 1783, 1784, 1786, 1787, 1788, Paris 1788, London 1790, 1792, 1793, 1799, Basle 1800, London 1803, 1807, 1808, 1812, 1817, 1821, 1823 etc; tr French, 1786.

A complete English grammar on a new plan, by C. Wiseman. 1764. Goldsmith wrote Preface.

An history of the lives, actions, travels, sufferings and deaths of the most eminent martyrs and primitive fathers of the Church. 1764 (26 Dec). See R. W. Seitz, Goldsmith's Lives of the fathers, MP 26 1929.

The traveller: or a prospect of society. 1765 (19 Dec 1764; on the 4 states of the 1st edn, 2 dated 1764, see W. B. Todd, SB 7 1955), 1765 (14 March), 1765, 1765 (6 Aug), 1768 (25 Feb), 1770 (6th edn corrected 29 June), 1770 (8 Dec), 1770 (29 Feb 1772; see A. Friedman, SB 13 1960), 1774, 1778, 1786. All pbd by Newbery or his successors. Rptd by other publishers Dublin 1767, Philadelphia 1768, Dublin 1769, [1770?], London 1770, [1780?], Edinburgh 1782, London [1785?], 1787, Manchester 1793, 1794; ed G. B. Hill, Oxford 1888; ed W. B. Todd as A prospect of society, Cambridge 1954, Charlottesville 1956; tr Italian, [1832?]. A set, now in BM, of uncorrected proof-sheets of lines 73–92 and 103–400 of first edn of the poem was discovered by and ed B. Dobell as A prospect of society: being the earliest form of the Traveller, 1902. For an explanation of these proof-sheets see W. B. Todd, SB 7 1955; L. W. Hanson, Library 5th ser 10 1955; Todd 11 1956.

The geography and history of England, in two parts; the second contains A concise history of England: or the revolutions of the British constitution. 1765 (23 March). For Goldsmith's authorship of the Concise history see R. W. Seitz, N & Q 2 July 1927, MP 28 1931.

Essays by Mr Goldsmith. 1765 (with engraved title-page, 4 June), 1765 (with ptd title-page, probably a piracy; see A. Friedman, SB 5 1953), 1766 (2nd edn as Essays by Oliver Goldsmith, with 2 additional essays), Dublin 1767, 1772, Altenburgh 1774, London 1775, 1775, 1783, 1789, Dublin 1793, London 1799; tr French, 1788 (in part). See R. S. Crane, Goldsmith's Essays: dates of original publication, N & Q 27 Aug 1927.

Edwin and Angelina: a ballad by Mr Goldsmith, printed for the amusement of the Countess of Northumberland. [1765], Philadelphia 1964 (facs). Rptd in Vicar of Wakefield, 1766, and in Poems for young ladies, 1767; set to music [1782].

The Vicar of Wakefield: a tale. 2 vols 1766 (27 March), 1766 (31 May), 1766 (27 Aug), 1766 (pirated edn), Cork 1766, Dublin 1766, 1767, 1767, London 1768, Berlin 1769, London 1770 (4th edn 9 Dec 1769), 1770, Philadelphia 1772, London 1773 (5th edn 2 April 1774), 1774, Berlin 1776, London 1777, 1778, 1779 (6th edn), Paris 1779, 1780, London 1780, 1780, 1781, 1781, 1783, 1784, Paris 1784, Berlin 1784, London 1785, 1785,

1786, 1787, Halle 1787, Berlin 1789, London 1789, 1789, 1790, Glasgow 1790, Dublin [c. 1790], 1791, Perth 1791, Philadelphia 1791, Norwich Conn 1791, London 1791, 1791, 1792 (4 edns), Providence RI 1792, London 1793, Dublin 1793, Vienna 1796, London [1796?], 1797, Paris 1797, Berlin 1797, Hereford 1798, Vienna 1798, Paris [1799], 1800, London 1800, 1800, Edinburgh 1800, Salem Mass 1801, Manchester 1802, London 1803, Paris 1803, Bath 1803–4, Edinburgh 1804, 1806, London 1806, 1806, Paris 1806, Philadelphia 1807, New York 1807, Hanover [1807?], London 1808, 1809, Wellington 1809, Philadelphia 1809, Baltimore 1809, Walpole NH 1809, London 1810, Edinburgh 1810, Birmingham 1811, London 1812, [1812?], Edinburgh 1812, Alnwick 1812, Pittsburgh 1812, London 1813, 1814, 1815, Sheffield 1815, Paris 1815, New York 1816, Berlin 1816, London 1816, 1817, 1818, Belfast 1818, Boulogne 1818, Paris 1818, Derby 1819, Chiswick 1819, London 1819, 1820, Philadelphia 1820, London 1823 etc; ed A. Dobson 1883, 1885; ed G. Saintsbury 1886; ed H. James, New York 1900; ed C. E. Doble, Oxford 1909; ed O. Doughty 1928; tr French, 1767, 1796, 1802, 1803; German, 1767, 1776, 1781, 1818; Dutch, 1768, 1827; Spanish, 1833. On the date of composition of the novel and the sale of the ms, see Friedman, Collected works 4.

A concise history of philosophy and philosophers, by M. Formey. 1766 (24 June). Tr Goldsmith.

Poems for young ladies in three parts: devotional, moral and entertaining. 1767 (15 Dec 1766), 1770 (a reissue), 1785.

The beauties of English poesy, selected by Oliver Goldsmith. 2 vols 1767 (6 April), Dublin 1771.

St James's Chron 23–5 July 1767. Signed letter by Goldsmith answering the charge that he had taken Edwin and Angelina from a ballad by Percy.

Essay on friendship. In H. Kelly's Babler: containing a careful selection from essays in Owen's weekly chronicle, 1767. See Universal Mag April 1774; A. Friedman, PQ 35 1956.

The good natur'd man: a comedy. 1768 (5 Feb; all the 'editions' for W. Griffin in 1768 may be distinguished as 5 impressions of the same edn; see W. B. Todd, SB 11 1958), Dublin 1768, 1770, 1784, London 1792, 1797, [1807]. Produced at Covent Garden 29 Jan 1768.

The present state of the British Empire in Europe, America, Africa and Asia. 1768 (13 May). See I. A. Williams, London Mercury Oct 1924; R. W. Seitz, MLN 45 1930.

The sister: a comedy, by Mrs Charlotte Lennox. 1769 (3 March). Produced at Covent Garden 18 Feb 1769. Goldsmith wrote the epilogue.

The Roman history, from the foundation of the city of Rome to the destruction of the Western Empire. 2 vols 1769 (18 May), Dublin 1769, London 1770, Dublin 1771, 1773, 1775–6, London 1775, 1781, Dublin 1781, 1786, London 1786, 1789, 1793, 1797, Dublin 1798, 1799, London 1799, Cork 1800, London 1809, 1812, Edinburgh 1812, London 1817 (12th edn), 1820, 1821, 1822, 1823, 1824 etc; tr German, 1795–1802; French, 1805.

The deserted village. 4° edns: 1770 (26 May), 1927 (facs), New York 1934 (facs), 1770 (2nd–6th edns 6, 13, 28 June, 8 Aug, 4 Oct), 1772, 1775, 1779, 1783, Springfield Mass 1783, London [1784], 1786 (14th edn). 12° edns: 1770 (4 edns, some thought to antedate the 1st 4°, but all piracies; see W. B. Todd, The 'private issues' of the Deserted village, SB 6 1954), 1777, [1783], Dublin 1784. 8° edns: Dublin 1770, 1770, Philadelphia 1771, Altenburgh 1773, London 1775, [1784] (3 edns), Providence RI 1784. 18° edn: Manchester 1793. Tr French, [1770?] (see E. D. Seeber and H. H. H. Remak, MLR 41 1946), 1772, 1805; German, 1772, 1812; Latin, 1789; Italian, 1825; Welsh, 1831. See bibliography of unauthorized British edns by W. B. Todd, SB 6 1954.

Poems on several occasions, written by Dr Thomas Parnell; to which is prefixed the Life of Dr Parnell, written by Dr Goldsmith. 1770 (19 June), 1772, 1773, Dublin 1773. Separate edn of Life of Thomas Parnell, 1770 (5 July); rptd in Davies's Miscellaneous and fugitive pieces vol 3, 1774; rptd abridged in Poems by Goldsmith and Parnell, ed I. Reed 1795.

A dissertation upon parties, by Henry St John, Lord Viscount Bolingbroke; to which is prefixed the Life of the author [by Goldsmith]. 9th edn 1771 (1 Dec 1770), 1775 (10th edn), 1786. Life issued separately as Life of Henry St John, Lord Viscount Bolingbroke, 1770 (4 Dec; see A. Friedman, SB 13 1960); rptd in Davies's edn of Bolingbroke's Works, 1774, and in Davies's Miscellaneous and fugitive pieces vol 3, 1774.

The history of England, from the earliest times to the death of George II. 4 vols 1771 (6 Aug), 1774 (17 Dec, corrected), 1784 (4th edn), 1786, 1787, Dublin 1789, London 1790, 1794, Dublin 1796, London 1800, 1805, Bungay 1807 (for c. 1815), London 1815, 1819 (11th edn with continuation to 1815), 1823 (with continuation to 1820) etc.

Zobeide: a tragedy. 1771 (19 Dec), 1772, 1774. By J. Cradock. Produced at Covent Garden 11 Dec 1771. Goldsmith wrote the prologue.

Threnodia augustalis: sacred to the memory of the Princess Dowager of Wales. 1772 (20 Feb). On the composition of this piece see K. C. Balderston, Collected letters, pp. xxxiii–vii. For a description of its only performance see A series of letters of the first Earl of Malmesbury vol 1, 1870 pp. 253–4.

Dr Goldsmith's Roman history, abridged by himself for the use of schools. 1772 (1 Dec), Dublin 1773, 1781, London 1786 (4th edn), 1790, Philadelphia 1795, London 1796, 1799, Edinburgh 1801, London 1802, Trenton NJ 1802, Troy NY 1804, London 1807, Philadelphia 1808, Otsego NY 1808, Edinburgh 1809, Baltimore 1811, London 1814, Gainsborough 1814, Edinburgh 1815, London 1816, Poughkeepsie NY 1816, Derby 1817, New York 1817, Lyons 1817, Baltimore 1818, Pittsburgh 1818 (2nd Pittsburgh edn), New York 1820, Canandaigua 1820, London 1822, 1823 etc; tr Italian, [1810?]; French, 1812; Spanish, 1829.

The Westminster magazine. 1773.
The history of a poet's garden (1 Jan); Essays and criticisms, 1798.
An essay on the theatre: or a comparison between laughing and sentimental comedy (1 Jan); Essays and criticisms.
The history of Cyrillo Padovano, the noted sleepwalker (Feb, pbd 1 March); Novellettes, 1780; Essays and criticisms.
A register of Scotch marriages (Feb); Novellettes; Essays and criticisms.

She stoops to conquer, or the mistakes of a night: a comedy. 1773 (25 March), 1773 (2nd–5th edns; all the 'editions' ptd for F. Newbery dated 1773 may be distinguished as 6 impressions of a single edn; see W. B. Todd, SB 11 1958), Belfast 1773, Philadelphia 1773, Dublin 1773, 1774, London 1774, 1775, 1783, Dublin 1784, 1785, London 1785, 1786, 1791, Dublin 1792, London 1797, [1806], [1816], 1820, 1823 etc; ed G. G. Urwin 1956; ed A. Friedman, Oxford 1968; tr German, 1773; French, 1823. Produced at Covent Garden 15 March 1773. 2 epilogues by Goldsmith intended for the play ptd in Miscellaneous works, 1801. Song intended for the play ptd by J. Boswell, London Mag June 1774; ptd from ms in Private papers of Boswell vol 10, 1930. The Larpent ms of the play is described by C. O. Parsons, MP 40 1942. See also K. C. Balderston, Collected letters, pp. xxxviii–li.

The daily advertiser. 31 March 1773. On the occasion of this signed letter, see Percy Memoir, 1801, pp. 103–10.

Epilogue spoken by Mr Lee Lewes in the character of Harlequin at his benefit, May 7 1773. London Chron 28–30 April 1774; Poetical and dramatic works, 1780.

The grumbler: a farce. Performed once at Covent Garden 8 May 1773. One scene ptd by Prior, Miscellaneous works, 1837. Ed from Larpent ms by A. I. P. Wood, Cambridge Mass 1931. An adaptation of Sir Charles Sedley's trn of Brueys's Le grondeur.

Retaliation: a poem. 1774 (19 April), 1774 (2nd–7th edns; the 2nd issue of 4th edn adds Postscript probably not by Goldsmith); 1776, 1777.

The Grecian history, from the earliest state to the death of Alexander the Great. 2 vols 1774 (14 June), Dublin 1774, London 1785, 1796, 1798, 1800, Washington 1800, 1804, London 1805, Dublin 1806, Philadelphia 1808, London 1809 (10th edn), 1812, Dublin 1812–14, Edinburgh 1813, Belfast 1814, New York 1816, London 1817, Philadelphia 1817, Hallowell Maine 1818, London 1820, Dublin 1821, London 1823, New York 1823 etc. Abridged edns 1787, 1798 (3rd edn), 1801, 1804, 1805, 1809, 1811, Gainsborough 1814, London 1816, Derby 1817, London 1818, Dublin 1819, London 1821 etc; tr German, 1792; French, 1802, 1812; Greek, 1806; Italian, 1807; Spanish, 1822.

An history of the earth and animated nature. 8 vols 1774 (1 July), 1774 (probably ptd much later and misdated to deceive buyers; see Friedman, Collected works 5 p. 349), Dublin 1776–7, London 1779, Dublin 1782, London 1790, 1791, 4 vols Philadelphia 1795, London 1797, 6 vols 1805, 4 vols New York 1808, Liverpool 1810, Thetford [1810?], 8 vols Dublin 1812–14, 6 vols 1816, 4 vols 1822, 5 vols Philadelphia 1823–4, 3 vols 1824 etc; abridged 1807. For Goldsmith's original plan of the work, see Critical Rev 38 1774, rptd by C. E. Jones, N & Q 21 Sept 1946.

An abridgement of the history of England from the invasion of Julius Caesar to the death of George II. 1774 (23 Sept), 1777, Dublin 1779, 1789, London 1793 (7th edn), Philadelphia 1795, London 1796, Dublin 1797, London 1798, Air 1799, Philadelphia 1802, Edinburgh 1803, London 1805 (13th edn), Philadelphia 1806, Gainsborough 1807, Wellington 1810, Dublin 1810, London 1812, Winchester 1812, Gainsborough 1813, New York 1813, London 1814, 1815, Derby 1816, Baltimore 1816, Lyons 1817, London 1818, Derby 1819, 1820, Baltimore 1822, Edinburgh 1823, Paris 1823, Boston 1824 etc; tr French, 1788, 1801, 1807; Bengali, 1820; Spanish, 1853.

The comic romance of Monsieur Scarron, translated by Oliver Goldsmith. 2 vols 1775, Dublin nd. See H. Stein, MLN 49 1934.

The haunch of venison: a poetical epistle to Lord Clare. 1776, 1776 (with 'additions and corrections'), Dublin 1776. Written in 1770 or 1771. Ms in New York Public Library.

A survey of experimental philosophy, considered in its present state of improvement. 2 vols 1776.

The captivity: an oratorio. In Miscellaneous works vol 2, 1820; 1836 (separately). 2 of the songs first pbd in Haunch of venison, 1776, above. On the relationship between the 2 mss of the oratorio see A. Friedman, Collected works 4.

The political view of the result of the present war with America upon Great Britain, France, Prussia, Germany and Holland. In Miscellaneous works, ed Prior 1837 as Preface and introduction to the history of the Seven Years' War. Written c. 1760–1. The ms is in the Huntington Lib. See J. W. Oliver, TLS 18 May 1922.

Spurious, Doubtful and Lost Works

The art of poetry on a new plan. 2 vols 1762. Mentioned in Percy Memoir, 1801, as 'corrected and revised' by Goldsmith. Of 25 chs 12 are largely from Art of Poetry made easy, 1746; others show no clear signs of his hand.

The Christian's magazine: or a treasury of divine knowledge. 1760–7. See J. Prior, Life 1 pp. 409–13, 479–80, 488; 2 p. 102; R. S. Crane, New essays pp. 140–1; R. W. Seitz, MP 26 1929 pp. 303–5.

A description of Millenium Hall and the country adjacent, by a gentleman on his travels. 1762 (28 Oct), 1764, 1767, 1778. Prior, Life 1 pp. 468–9, records a tradition that the work was rev Goldsmith. The authors were Lady Barbara Montagu and Sarah Scott.

The fair thief. Poem was attributed to Goldsmith in A collection of poems mostly original by several hands, Dublin 1789, but first pbd in GM Dec 1746. See M. H. Addington, N & Q 24 June 1933.

The gentleman's journal: or weekly register of news, politics, literature and amusement. Nos i–ii 19–26 Nov 1768. According to Cooke, European Mag 24 1793 p. 171, Goldsmith was one of the contributors to this short-lived periodical. No copy of the nos seems to be known.

The history of little Goody Two-Shoes. 1765 (advertised as in press 1 Jan), 1766 (3rd edn), 1772 etc; ed C. Welsh 1881. An attribution apparently first suggested by William Godwin; see Prior, Life 2 pp. 100–1. On this and other children's books pbd by Newbery and ascribed to Goldsmith on inconclusive grounds, see N & Q 20 July 1861, 16 Dec 1871, 6 Jan 1872, 25 March 1893, 24 Sept 1904; Athenaeum 25 March 1871; C. Welsh, A bookseller of the last century, 1885; and his Goldsmith and Mother Goose in Bibliographer 1 1902; Gibbs, Works, 5 pp. 356, 405–8.

The history of Mecklenburgh, from the first settlement of the Vandals in that country to the present time. 1762 (26 Feb), 1762. By Sarah Scott; mentioned among Goldsmith's writings in Westminster Mag April 1774 p. 167. See Prior, Life 1 pp. 388–9.

The history of Pamela: or virtue rewarded, abridged from the works of Samuel Richardson. 1769; ed A. E. Newton, Berwyn Pa 1929. A purely conjectural attribution.

The history of the Chevalier des Grieux. 2 vols 1767. This trn of Prévost, Manon Lescaut ascribed to Goldsmith by R. S. Garnett, Blackwood's Mag Dec 1931. But see F. C. Green, Minuet, 1935 p. 474.

An history of the life of our Lord and Saviour Jesus Christ. This work, for which Goldsmith acknowledged the receipt of 10 guineas 11 Oct 1763, was advertised by Newbery in Dec 1764. It was listed among their pbns by Carnan and Newbery in 1769, and it was advertised with other books in Morning Chron 15 June 1774 as by Goldsmith. No copy seems to be known. See R. W. Seitz, MP 26 1929.

The life of Asclepiades, from the Italian of Antonio Cocchi. 1762. Ascribed to Goldsmith without supporting reasons by D. A. Stauffer in his Art of biography in eighteenth-century England, Princeton 1941.

The Lilliputian magazine: or the young gentleman and lady's golden library. nd. Attributed to Goldsmith in BM catalogue and elsewhere, but pbd in 1752.

Lines attributed to Dr Goldsmith inserted in the Morning Chronicle of April 3 1800. 2 quatrains ptd under this heading in several early 19th-century edns of Goldsmith's Poetical works, including Mitford's in 1831 and rejected by later editors. It is doubtful whether the correspondent who inserted them in the Morning Chron intended to ascribe them to Goldsmith.

The literary magazine. 1757–8. 7 articles or sers of articles between Dec 1757 and July 1758 have been ascribed to Goldsmith—4 in 1837 by Prior, Life 1 pp. 233–6; the others in 1885 by Gibbs, Works 3 pp. 450–9, 4 pp. 417–62; see M. Golden, N & Q Oct–Nov 1956. For arguments against Goldsmith's authorship see R. W. Seitz, RES 5 1929; R. S. Crane, PQ 9 1930; A. Friedman, PQ 36 1957.

The march of intellect. Dublin 1802. A ballad of 9 stanzas beginning 'Oh learning's a very fine thing',

ascribed to Goldsmith by C. O Lochlainn, Irish Times 2 April 1960; see his More Irish street ballads, Dublin 1965.

The martial review: or a general history of the late wars. 1763 (Sept). Ascribed to Goldsmith in BM catalogue. Based on a series of articles ptd in Oxford Gazette and Reading Mercury beginning 25 Jan 1762. See Prior, Life 1 pp. 477–8.

Memoirs of my Lady B. According to an undated receipt Goldsmith was paid 10 guineas by R. Griffiths to translate this work. Pbn announced in GM Jan 1761, but no copy known; see Prior, Life 1 p. 279; Balderston, Census, pp. 26–7; Collected letters, p. 51.

Memorial to Lord Bute. [1762?]. Mentioned by Percy in letter to Malone in 1786; now lost. See Balderston, The history and sources of Percy's Memoir of Goldsmith, p. 27.

Museum rusticum et commerciale. 1763–8. Prior's conjecture in Life 2 p. 103 that Goldsmith wrote for this periodical seems to have rested merely on the circumstances that Newbery was a publisher and that it served as an organ for Society of Arts, of which Goldsmith became a member 17 Nov 1762.

A new history of England by question and answer. [1761?] (11th edn). The '79 leaves of the History of England' mentioned in a Newbery memorandum of 1764 or 1765 were identified by Prior in Life, 1 p. 402 with addn of 5 sheets dealing with the reign of George II in 11th edn of this work; but see R. W. Seitz, MP 28 1931.

The Newtonian system of philosophy. 1761. Listed as by Goldsmith in An exhibition in the Yale University Library of the works of Goldsmith, New Haven 1928.

On the several conditions of life. Reformer (Dublin) no 4 1748. Poem of 18 lines conjectured to be Goldsmith's by A. P. I. Samuels, The early life, correspondence and writings of Edmund Burke, Cambridge 1923 pp. 170, 308.

A poetical dictionary: or the beauties of the English poets alphabetically displayed. 4 vols 1761. Attributed to Goldsmith by J. Crossley, N & Q 5 June 1852. The compiler was really Samuel Derrick.

Prospectus for An universal dictionary of arts and sciences. [1773?]. See Westminster Mag April 1774 p. 167 and Percy Memoir, 1801 pp. 112–13. No copy known; perhaps never pbd.

Select fables of Æsop and others; to which are prefixed the life of Æsop and an essay upon fable: a new edition improved. Newcastle 1784. The essay upon fable, the poetical 'applications' and the Fables in verse are ascribed to Goldsmith by Edwin Pearson in his Bewick's Select fables of Æsop and others, [1871], preface. His reasons do not appear.

A spelling dictionary of the English language on a new plan: the eleventh edition, to which is prefixed a compendious English grammar, with a concise historical account of the language. 1766. In the Sotheby catalogue of the third portion of the Thorn-Drury library, Nov 1931, this work is identified with the 'short English grammar' mentioned in a Newbery memorandum of 28 Dec 1766. The 'compendious English grammar' had, however, been ptd with A spelling dictionary from at least the 5th edn 1755.

The triumph of benevolence: or the history of Francis Wills. 2 vols 1772 (no known copy), Dublin 1772 (copy in Univ of Chicago Lib), Berlin 1786, Upsala 1799; tr French 1773, 1774 (as Histoire de François Wills: ou le triomphe de la bienfaisance, par l'auteur du Ministre de Wakefield). See Gibbs, Works 1 pp. 238–40; B. Neuendorff, Goldsmiths verlorener Roman, Anglia 32 1909; A. L. Sells, RES 11 1935; C. B. Suits, PQ 43 1964.

Universal museum and complete magazine. 1764–5. M. Golden, N & Q Aug 1957, Nov 1958 ascribes several essays in this periodical to Goldsmith.

Verses written by the late Dr Goldsmith addressed to a friend. W. Jerrold, Bookman (New York) Nov 1914. 68 lines beginning 'O Firm in virtue, as of soul sincere', from a scrapbook clipping of unidentified periodical of late 18th century. The verses express some of Goldsmith's characteristic ideas and may be authentic, though rejected by Prior in his Life, 1837.

Vida's Game of chess translated. Attributed to Goldsmith by Forster; *see* Life and times, 1877, 2 pp. 234–42. First pbd by Cunningham in his edn of the Works, 1854, from ms then in the possession of Bolton Corney. The sole ground for the ascription was the mistaken belief that the ms was in Goldsmith's hand.

Letters

Collected letters. Ed K. C. Balderston, Cambridge 1928.

Private papers of James Boswell from Malahide Castle. Ed G. Scott and F. A. Pottle. Vols 8–9, New York 1930. 2 letters not available to Miss Balderston, above.

Seitz, R. W. Goldsmith to Sir William Chambers. TLS 26 Sept 1936. 2 letters of 1773.

Bald, R. C. A note from Goldsmith [to Sir William Chambers]. Bulletin [of Cornell Univ Lib Associates] winter 1945.

Balderston, K. C. New Goldsmith letters. Yale Univ Lib Gazette 39 1964. 2 letters of 1766 to John Bindley.

§ 2

The motives for writing: a dream. Court Mag Dec 1761. Perhaps the first mention of Goldsmith's name in print.

[Rider, W.] In his An historical and critical account of the lives and writings of the living authors of Great-Britain, 1762.

The history of the Robin Hood Society. 1764 (24 Oct). Contains a short characterization of Goldsmith.

Humorous anecdotes of Dr Goldsmith. Westminster Mag March 1773.

Percy, T. Memoirs of Dr Goldsmith (chiefly from his own mouth, 1773). 28 April. Frequently called the Percy Memorandum. Ed K. C. Balderston in The history and sources of Percy's Memoir of Goldsmith, Cambridge 1926.

Hawes, W. An account of the late Dr Goldsmith's illness. 1774 (26 April).

'Melmouth, Courtney' (S. J. Pratt). The tears of genius occasioned by the death of Dr Goldsmith. 1774 (28 April).

Literary anecdotes of the late Dr Goldsmith. Westminster Mag April 1774; rptd in Walker's Hibernian Mag May 1774.

G[lover]. Authentic anecdotes of the late Dr Goldsmith. Universal Mag May 1774; rptd in Annual Register 1774; in Poems by the late Dr Goldsmith, Belfast 1775. *See* Malone, below.

[Tait, John]. The druid's monument: a tribute to the memory of Goldsmith. 1774 (10 June).

An impartial character of Goldsmith, with a word to his encomiasts. 1774 (22 June).

A monody on the death of Goldsmith. 1774 (30 June).

The life of Goldsmith, written from personal knowledge, authentic papers and other indubitable authorities. 1774 (13 July). A paraphrase of Glover's Anecdotes, above, with some omissions and a few additional facts and observations. Erroneously ascribed to Percy by Halkett and Laing.

A catalogue of the household furniture, with the select collection of books, late the library of Dr Goldsmith. 1774 (July); rptd by Prior, Life of Goldsmith vol 2, 1837; by Forster, Life and times of Goldsmith vol 2, 1854.

Spilsbury, F. Free thoughts on quacks and their medicines, occasioned by the death of Dr Goldsmith and Mr Scawen. 1776.

[Malone, E.] The life of Goldsmith. In Poems and plays, Dublin 1777, London 1780; Poetical and dramatic works, 1780; Miscellaneous works, Perth 1792 etc. A reprint with corrections and addns of Glover's Anecdotes, above. *See* I. Reed, below.

[Campbell, T.] In his A philosophical survey of the south of Ireland, 1777.

—— Diary. Ed J. L. Clifford, Cambridge 1947. On Campbell's part in Percy Memoir.

—— Memoirs of the life and writings of Goldsmith. BM Add Ms 42517. Prepared by Campbell under Percy's direction; never pbd. Contains notations in Percy's hand; important for the genesis of Percy Memoir.

Davies, T. In his Memoirs of the life of David Garrick, 2 vols 1780.

Anecdotes of Goldsmith. Universal Mag Aug 1780; rptd in Public Advertiser 29 Sept 1780.

Anecdote of Goldsmith, never published. European Mag Jan 1784.

Scott, J. In his Critical essays on some of the poems of several English poets, 1785. Contains essay on Deserted village.

Piozzi, H. L. In her Anecdotes of the late Samuel Johnson, 1786.

—— In her Autobiography, letters and literary remains of Mrs Piozzi, ed A. Hayward 2 vols 1861 (2nd edn).

—— In her Thraliana, ed K. C. Balderston 2 vols Oxford 1942, 1951 (corrected).

Hawkins, J. In his Life of Samuel Johnson, 1787.

Boswell, James. In his Life of Samuel Johnson, 2 vols 1791.

—— In his Private papers from Malahide Castle in the collection of Lt-Colonel R. H. Isham, ed G. Scott and F. A. Pottle 19 vols New York 1928–37.

—— In his London journal 1762–3, ed F. A. Pottle, New York 1950; Boswell on the grand tour 1765–6, ed F. Brady and Pottle, New York 1955; Boswell in search of a wife 1766–9, ed Brady and Pottle, New York 1956; Boswell for the defense 1769–74, ed W. K. Wimsatt and Pottle, New York 1959.

Anecdotes of Dr Goldsmith. European Mag Feb 1792.

[Cooke, W.] Dr Goldsmith. European Mag Aug–Oct 1793.

—— In his Memoirs of Samuel Foote, 3 vols 1805.

Anderson, R. The life of Goldsmith. In Works of the British poets vol 10, 1795.

[Reed, I.] Life of Goldsmith. In Poems by Goldsmith and Parnell, 1795. A revision with some new material of the life by Malone, above.

Aikin, J. [Essay on Goldsmith's poetry]. In Poetical works of Goldsmith, 1796.

—— In his General biography vol 4, 1803.

[Percy, T. et al]. The life of Goldsmith. In Miscellaneous works of Goldsmith vol 1, 1801. Usually called Percy Memoir. See K. C. Balderston, History and sources of Percy's Memoir of Goldsmith, Cambridge 1926; T. Shearer and A. Tillotson, Library 3rd ser 15 1934; and under T. Campbell, above.

Evans, J. [Original anecdotes of Goldsmith]. In Poetical works of Goldsmith, 1804 (pbd by T. Hurst). *See* European Mag May 1808; GM March 1817 p. 277.

Cumberland, R. In his Memoirs written by himself, 2 vols 1807.

Mangin, E. In his An essay on light reading, 1808. Contains letter on Goldsmith by Annesley Strean.

Stockdale, P. In his Memoirs of the life and writings of Stockdale, 1809.

Chalmers, A. The life of Goldsmith. In Works of the English poets vol 16, 1810. Largely based on the Percy Memoir of 1801.

Newell, R. H. [Remarks on the scene of Deserted village]. In Poetical works of Goldsmith, 1811.

Northcote, J. In his Memoirs of Sir Joshua Reynolds, 1813, 2 vols 1818 (as Life of Reynolds).

—— In his Conversations by William Hazlitt, 1830. Originally pbd in New Monthly Mag 1826–7.

Mason, W. S. In his A statistical account or parochial survey of Ireland, 3 vols Dublin 1814–19.

Campbell, T. In his Specimens of the British poets vol 6, 1819.

Posthumous letters from various celebrated men, addressed to Francis Colman and George Colman the elder. 1820.

Cradock, J. In his Literary and miscellaneous memoirs, 1826, 4 vols 1828.

Colman, G. (the younger). In his Random records, 2 vols 1830.

Garrick, D. In his Private correspondence with the most celebrated persons of his time, 2 vols 1831.

Taylor, J. In his Records of my life, 1832.

Weld, I. In his Survey of Roscommon, 1832.

Prior, J. The life of Goldsmith from a variety of original sources. 2 vols 1837.

C., S.P. Pedigree of the poet Goldsmith. GM March 1837.

Willmott, R. A. Goldsmith and Gray. Church of England Quart Rev 1 1837.

Irving, W. The life of Goldsmith, with selections from his writings. 1844, 1850 (rev and enlarged as Goldsmith: a biography).

Forster, J. The life and adventures of Goldsmith. 1848, 2 vols 1854 (with notes as The life and times of Goldsmith).

Bohn, H. G. The life of Goldsmith. In his edn of Works of Goldsmith, 1848; rptd with corrections and addns in Works, ed Gibbs vol 1, 1884.

Thackeray, W. M. In his English humourists of the eighteenth century, 1853.

Macaulay, T. B. Encyclopedia britannica 10 1856.

Leslie, C. R. and T. Taylor. In their Life and times of Sir Joshua Reynolds, 2 vols 1865.

Black, W. Oliver Goldsmith. 1878 (EML).

The deserted village. N & Q 3 Aug, 12 Oct 1878. On the tradition that the poem was written at Springfield Essex.

Ford, E. Names and characters in the Vicar of Wakefield. Nat Rev 1 1883.

O., W. H. and J. W. M. G[ibbs]. A plagiarism of Goldsmith's. Athenaeum 21 July, 4 Aug 1883.

Welsh, C. A bookseller of the last century. 1885. On John Newbery.

Dobson, A. Life of Goldsmith. 1888.

—— In his Eighteenth-century vignettes ser 1, 1892. Contains essays on Citizen of the world, John Newbery, Goldsmith's library.

—— In his Miscellanies, 1898. Contains essays on Goldsmith's poems and plays, Vicar of Wakefield and its illustrators.

—— Old Kensington Palace and other papers. 1910. Contains paper on Goldsmith and Percy.

—— Oliver Goldsmith. CHEL 10 1913.

Burney, F. In her Early diary 1768–78, ed A. R. Ellis 2 vols 1889.

d'Alviny, R. G. In his Le Cosmopolite de Goldsmith: lettres choisies, Le Havre 1891. On Goldsmith's borrowings from the Marquis d'Argens in Citizen of the world.

Charlemont, James 1st Earl of. In his Manuscripts and correspondence, 1891.

Cox, M. F. The country and kindred of Goldsmith. Jnl of Nat Lit Soc of Ireland 1 1900.

Henderson, W. A. The birthplace of Goldsmith. N & Q 19 Oct 1901.

Ferguson, R. Goldsmith and the notions Grille and Wandrer in Werthers Leiden. MLN 17 1902. See J. A. Walz, 18 1903.

Fischer, W. Goldsmiths Vicar of Wakefield. Anglia 25 1902; Halle 1902 (separately).

Neuendorff, B. Entstehungsgeschichte von Goldsmiths Vicar of Wakefield. Berlin 1903. See W. Fischer, Anglia 27 1904.

Sollas, H. Goldsmiths Einfluss in Deutschland im 18 Jahrhundert. Heidelberg 1903.

Schacht, H. Der gute Pfarrer in der englischen Literatur bis zu Goldsmiths Vicar of Wakefield. Berlin 1904.

Hering, R. Goldsmiths Vicar of Wakefield. Dessau 1905.

Kelly, J. J. The early haunts of Goldsmith. Dublin [1905].

Swaen, A. E. H. Fielding and Goldsmith in Leyden. MLR 1 1906.

Osgood, C. G. Notes on Goldsmith. MP 5 1907.

Conant, M. P. In her Oriental tale in England in the eighteenth century, New York 1908.

Gaussen, A. C. C. In her Percy: prelate and poet, 1908.

Leichsering, A. S. C. Über das Verhältniss von Goldsmiths She stoops to conquer zu Farquhars The beaux' stratagem. Cuxhaven 1909.

King, R. A. Oliver Goldsmith. [1910].

Moore, F. F. The life of Goldsmith. 1910.

Lowes, J. L. Wordsworth and Goldsmith. Nation (New York) 23 March 1911.

Mendt, A. Goldsmith als Dramatiker. Leipzig 1911.

Forsythe, R. S. Shadwell's contribution to She stoops to conquer and to the Tender husband. JEGP 11 1912.

Barnouw, A. J. Goldsmith's indebtedness to Justus van Effen [and to Voltaire]. MLR 8 1913.

Clarke, E. The medical education and qualifications of Goldsmith. Proc Royal Soc of Medicine 7 1914.

—— Goldsmith as a medical man. Nineteenth Century April 1914.

—— The family letters of Goldsmith. Trans Bibl Soc 15 1920.

Annals of the Club 1764–1914. 1914.

Crawfurd, R. Goldsmith and medicine. Proc Royal Soc of Medicine 8 1915.

Patton, J. In his English village: a literary study 1750–1850, New York 1919.

Crane, R. S. and H. J. Smith. A French influence on Goldsmith's Citizen of the world. MP 19 1921. The Lettres chinoises of the Marquis d'Argens.

—— and J. H. Warner. Goldsmith and Voltaire's Essai sur les mœurs. MLN 38 1923.

—— The Deserted village in prose 1762. TLS 8 Sept 1927.

—— The text of Goldsmith's Memoirs of M. de Voltaire. MP 28 1930.

—— 'Oliver Goldsmith MB'. MLN 48 1933.

—— and A. Friedman. Goldsmith and the Encyclopédie. TLS 11 May 1933.

—— A neglected mid-eighteenth-century plea for originality and its author. PQ 13 1934.

—— Goldsmith and Justus van Effen. TLS 1 March 1934.

Davidson, L. J. Forerunners of Goldsmith's The citizen of the world. MLN 36 1921.

Oliver, J. W. Johnson, Goldsmith and the History of the Seven Years' War. TLS 18 May 1922.

Tupper, C. F. Essays [in British Magazine] erroneously attributed to Goldsmith. PMLA 39 1924.

—— Goldsmith and 'the gentleman who signs D'. MLN 45 1930.

Pitman, J. H. Goldsmith's Animated nature. New Haven 1924.

Sells, A. L. Les sources françaises de Goldsmith. Paris 1924.

—— Goldsmith's influence on the French stage. Durham Univ Jnl 33 1941.

[Goldsmith's signature on the Roll Book of the Medical Society of Edinburgh]. N & Q 25 July 1925.

Anson, E. and F. Mary Hamilton, afterwards Mrs John Dickenson, from letters and diaries 1756 to 1816. 1925. See pp. 181–3.

Marcus, H. Goldsmith über Deutschland. Archiv 149 1925.

Binz-Winiger, E. Erziehungsfragen in den Romanen von Richardson, Fielding, Smollett, Goldsmith und Sterne. Zürich 1926.

Balderston, K. C. The history and sources of Percy's Memoir of Goldsmith. Cambridge 1926.

—— Goldsmith's supposed attack on Fielding. MLN 42 1927.

—— (ed). The collected letters of Goldsmith. Cambridge 1928. Contains the full text of Mrs Hodson's narrative of Goldsmith's youth and studies of several biographical problems.

—— The birth of Goldsmith. TLS 7 March 1929. *See* R. S. Crane, PQ 9 1930; Balderston 10 1931; A. Friedman, N & Q 1 Sept 1951.

—— A manuscript version of She stoops to conquer. MLN 45 1930.

Brown, J. E. Goldsmith's indebtedness to Voltaire and Justus van Effen. MP 23 1926.

—— Goldsmith and Johnson on biography. MLN 42 1927.

Duméril, E. L'élément autobiographique dans The traveller. Revue de l'Enseignement des Langues Vivantes 43 1926.

Milner-Barry, A. A note on the early literary relations of Goldsmith and Thomas Percy. RES 2 1926. *See* L. F. Powell, ibid.

Smith, H. J. Goldsmith's The citizen of the world: a study. New Haven 1926.

Seitz, R. W. Goldsmith and A concise history of England. N & Q 2 July 1927.

—— Goldsmith and the Literary Magazine. RES 5 1929.

—— Goldsmith's Lives of the fathers. MP 26 1929.

—— Goldsmith and the Present state of the British Empire. MLN 45 1930.

—— Goldsmith and the English lives. MP 28 1931.

—— Goldsmith and the Annual Register. MP 31 1933.

—— Goldsmith to Sir William Chambers. TLS 26 Sept 1936.

—— The Irish background of Goldsmith's social and political thought. PMLA 52 1937.

—— Some of Goldsmith's second thoughts on English history. MP 35 1938.

Scott, T. Goldsmith bibliographically and biographically considered. New York 1928.

Tinker, C. B. Figures in a dream. Yale Rev 17 1928. On Deserted village.

Ingalls, G. V. A. Some sources of Goldsmith's She stoops to conquer. PMLA 44 1929.

Baudin, M. Une source de She stoops to conquer. PMLA 45 1930.

Chapman, R. W. An unconsidered trifle. Colophon 3 1930. On Goldsmith's use of D. Fenning, The young man's book of knowledge.

Paschal, Father. Goldsmith as a social philosopher. Irish Ecclesiastical Record 35 1930.

Price, L. M. The reception of English literature in Germany. Berkeley 1932.

—— The works of Goldsmith on the German stage 1776–95. MLQ 5 1944.

Friedman, A. An essay by Goldsmith in the Lady's Magazine. MP 30 1933.

—— Goldsmith and the Weekly Magazine. MP 32 1935.

—— Goldsmith's Life of Bolingbroke and the Biographia britannica. MLN 50 1935.

—— Goldsmith and the Marquis d'Argens. MLN 53 1938.

—— The immediate occasion of Goldsmith's Citizen of the world letter xxxviii. PQ 17 1938.

—— Goldsmith and Jean Rousset de Missy. PQ 19 1940.

—— Goldsmith and Steele's Englishman. MLN 55 1940.

—— Goldsmith's contributions to the Critical Review. MP 44 1946.

—— Goldsmith and Hanway. MLN 66 1951.

—— The first edition of Essays by Mr Goldsmith 1765. SB 5 1953.

—— Goldsmith and the jest-books. MP 53 1955.

—— Goldsmith's Essay on friendship: its first publication and the problem of authorship. PQ 35 1956.

—— The first edition of Goldsmith's Bee, no I. SB 11 1958.

—— The problem of indifferent readings in the eighteenth century, with a solution from the Deserted village. SB 13 1960.

—— The time of composition of Goldsmith's Edwin and Angelina. In Restoration and eighteenth-century literature, ed C. Camden, Chicago 1963.

Kent, E. E. Goldsmith and his booksellers. Ithaca 1933.

Schorer, M. She stoops to conquer: a parallel. MLN 48 1933.

Tillotson, A. Dr Johnson and the Life of Goldsmith. MLR 28 1933.

Rocher, M. L. Goldsmith l'éternel vagabond. Revue Anglo-américaine 11 1933.

Roberts, W. Goldsmith in France. TLS 30 Nov, 28 Dec 1933.

Gallaway, W. F. The sentimentalism of Goldsmith. PMLA 48 1933.

[Woolf, V.] Oliver Goldsmith. TLS 1 March 1934; rptd in her Captain's death bed, 1950.

Stein, H. Goldsmith's translation of the Roman comique. MLN 49 1934.

Gwynn, S. Oliver Goldsmith. 1935.

Fraser-Harris, D. F. Goldsmith on his teachers. Dalhousie Rev 16 1936.

Magnus, P. Goldsmith and the Burkes. TLS 11 Dec 1937. Replies 18 Dec 1937, 12 Feb 1938.

Kenny, R. W. Ralph's Case of authors: its influence on Goldsmith and Isaac d'Israeli. PMLA 52 1937.

Emery, J. P. An unpublished letter from Arthur Murphy to Goldsmith concerning She stoops to conquer. PQ 17 1938.

Reynolds, W. V. Goldsmith's critical outlook. RES 14 1938.

Howarth, R. G. Proverbs in the Good-natured man. N & Q 2 April 1938.

Chên Shou-yi. Goldsmith and his Chinese letters. T'ien Hsia Monthly 8 1939.

Haydon, F. M. Goldsmith as a biographer. South Atlantic Quart 39 1940.

Heilman, R. B. The sentimentalism of Goldsmith's Good-natured man. In Studies for W. A. Read, Baton Rouge 1940.

McAdam, E. L. New essays by Dr Johnson. RES 18 1942. An essay by Johnson, not Goldsmith.

—— Goldsmith: the good-natured man. In The age of Johnson: essays presented to C. B. Tinker, New Haven 1949.

Bell, H. J. Goldsmith and the pickle-shop. MLN 57 1942.

—— The deserted village and Goldsmith's social doctrines. PMLA 59 1944.

Lynskey, W. Pluche and Derham: new sources of Goldsmith. PMLA 57 1942.

—— The scientific sources of Goldsmith's Animated nature. SP 40 1943.

—— Goldsmith and the warfare in nature. PQ 23 1944.

—— Goldsmith and the chain of being. JHI 6 1945. *See* A. O. Lovejoy 7 1946.

Parsons, C. O. Textual variants in a manuscript of She stoops to conquer. MP 40 1942.

Moore, J. R. Goldsmith's degenerate song-birds. Isis 34 1943.

Smith, J. H. Tony Lumpkin and the country booby type in antecedent English comedy. PMLA 58 1943.

Knight, D. Two issues of Goldsmith's Bee. N & Q 16 Dec 1944.

Krause, G. Goldsmiths Stellung zum Bauerntum. Anglia 67–8 1944.

Starkey, J. Goldsmith's birthplace. In his Essays and recollections by Seumas O'Sullivan, Dublin 1944. *See* A. Friedman, PQ 24 1945.

MacDermot, H. E. Goldsmith as a talker. Queen's Quart 51 1944.

Hammer, C. Goethe's estimate of Goldsmith. JEGP 44 1945.

Seeber, E. D. Goldsmith's American tigers. MLQ 6 1945.
—— and H. H. H. Remak. The first French translation of the Deserted village. MLR 41 1946.
Jones, C. E. Goldsmith's natural history: a plan. N & Q 21 Sept 1946.
Atkinson, A. D. Goldsmith borrows. TLS 25 Jan 1947. In Life of Nash. See A. Friedman 8 Nov 1956.
Thorpe, J. Issues of the first edition of the Vicar of Wakefield. PBSA 42 1948.
Angus-Butterworth, L. M. Goldsmith as historian. South Atlantic Quart 48 1949; rptd in his Ten master historians, Aberdeen 1961.
Jefferson, D. W. Observations on the Vicar of Wakefield. Cambridge Jnl July 1950.
Barbier, C. P. Goldsmith en France au xviii° siecle. Revue de Littérature Comparée 25 1951.
Blum, H. T. Goldsmith: eine Studie über die Anfänge seines Humors. Constance 1951.
Sands, M. Goldsmith and music. Music & Letters 32 1951.
Jackson, R. W. Goldsmith: essays towards an interpretation. Dublin 1951.
Freeman, W. Oliver Goldsmith. 1952.
Reynolds, J. Reynolds on Goldsmith. In his Portraits, ed F. W. Hilles, New York 1952.
Harth, P. Goldsmith and the Marquis d'Argens. N & Q Dec 1054.
Todd, W. B. The 'private issues' of the Deserted village. SB 6-7 1954-5.
—— Quadruple imposition: an account of Goldsmith's Traveller. SB 7 1955. See L. W. Hanson, Library 4th ser 10 1955; Todd 11 1956.
—— The first editions of the Good natur'd man and She stoops to conquer. SB 11 1958.
Davie, D. The deserted village: poem as virtual history. Twentieth Century Aug 1954.
Eichenberger, K. Goldsmith: das Komische in den Werken seiner Reifeperiode. Berne 1954.
Golden, M. [Notes on the canon of Goldsmith's essays]. N & Q April, Sept–Oct 1955, Aug 1956, Jan 1958; MLN 74 1959.
—— Goldsmith attributions in the Literary Magazine. N & Q Oct–Nov 1956.
—— Goldsmith and the Universal Museum and Complete Magazine. N & Q Aug 1957, Nov 1958.
—— The family-wanderer theme in Goldsmith. ELH 25 1958.
—— The broken dream of the Deserted village. Lit & Psychology 11 1959.
—— Image frequency and the split in the Vicar of Wakefield. BNYPL Sept 1959.
—— The time of writing the Vicar of Wakefield. BNYPL Sept 1961.
Hennig, J. The Auerbachs Keller scene and She stoops to conquer. Comparative Lit 7 1955.
Sherbo, A. A manufactured anecdote in Goldsmith's Life of Nash. MLN 70 1955.
Wardle, R. M. Oliver Goldsmith. Lawrence Kansas 1957.
Dahl, C. Patterns of disguise in the Vicar of Wakefield. ELH 25 1958.
Lucas, F. L. In his Search for good sense: four eighteenth-century characters, 1958.
Jeffares, A. N. Oliver Goldsmith. 1959.
—— A critical commentary on She stoops to conquer. 1966.
Miner, E. The making of the Deserted village. HLQ 22 1959.
Rawson, C. J. Some unpublished letters of Pope and Gay and some manuscript sources of Goldsmith's Life of Parnell. RES new ser 10 1959.
Gassman, B. French sources of Goldsmith's The good natur'd man. PQ 39 1960.
Montague, J. Tragic picaresque: Goldsmith. Studies 49 1960.
—— The sentimental prophecy: a study of the Deserted village. Dolmen Miscellany 1 1962.

Adelstein, M. E. Duality of theme in the Vicar of Wakefield. College Eng Feb 1961.
Sherwin, O. Goldy: the life and times of Goldsmith. New York 1961.
Arthos, J. The prose of Goldsmith. Michigan Quart Rev 1 1962.
Schwegel, D. M. The American couplets in the Deserted village. Georgia Rev 16 1962.
Emslie, M. Goldsmith: the Vicar of Wakefield. 1963.
Quintana, R. The deserted village: its logical and rhetorical elements. College Eng Dec 1964.
—— Goldsmith's achievement as a dramatist. UTQ 34 1965.
—— Goldsmith as a critic of the drama. Stud in Eng Lit 1500–1900 5 1965.
—— Goldsmith: a Georgian study. New York [1967].
Suits, C. B. Who wrote the History of Francis Wills? PQ 43 1964. Not Goldsmith.
Ferguson, O. W. The materials of history: Goldsmith's Life of Nash. PMLA 80 1965.
—— Goldsmith. South Atlantic Quart 66 1967.
Eversole, R. The oratorical design of the Deserted village. Eng Lang Notes 4 1966.
Rodway, A. Goldsmith and Sheridan: satirists of sentiment. In Renaissance and modern essays, ed G. R. Hibbard 1966.
Kirk, C. M. Oliver Goldsmith. New York [1967].
Dussinger, J. A. Goldsmith: citizen of the world. Stud on Voltaire & Eighteenth Century 55 1967.
Le Breton, M. Goldsmith et l'Italie. Caliban 3 1967.
Jaarsma, R. J. Satiric intent in the Vicar of Wakefield. Stud in Shorter Fiction 5 1968.
Hopkins, R. H. The true genius of Goldsmith. Baltimore [1969].

A. F.

JAMES BOSWELL
1740–95

References

*	Attributions made on internal evidence only.
?	Attributions made somewhat doubtfully on internal evidence only.
BP	Private papers of Boswell from Malahide Castle in the collection of Lt-Col R. H. Isham. Ed G. Scott and F. A. Pottle 18 vols Mt Vernon 1928–34 (priv ptd).
C778, M318, P100 etc	File numbers of items or groups of items in the unpbd catalogue of the Boswell papers at Yale. P122 was generally labelled by Boswell 'Publick Advertiser 1792–3'.
Corsica	Boswell, An account of Corsica, the journal of a tour to that island and memoirs of Pascal Paoli.
Journ	Boswell's journal, between BP and Yale edn.
Life	Boswell, The life of Samuel Johnson. When vol and p. are cited, the reference is to edn of G. B. Hill, rev L. F. Powell 6 vols Oxford 1934–64.
Lit Car	F. A. Pottle, The literary career of Boswell, Oxford 1929, 1966.
Murray	J. Murray, Notes on Johnson's movements in Scotland N & Q 6 Jan 1940; Boswell in the Caledonian Mercury, N & Q 16 March 1940.
Nangle	B. C. Nangle, The Monthly Review 1st series 1749–89, Oxford 1934; The Monthly Review 2nd series 1790–1815, Oxford 1955.
Tour	Boswell, The journal of a tour to the Hebrides with Samuel Johnson.
Werkmeister	L. Werkmeister, Jemmie Boswell and the London daily press 1785–95, BNYPL Feb–March 1963.

Authorities for attribution are briefly cited when the items in question do not appear in Lit Car or when attributions have been confirmed by evidence discovered since 1929.

Bibliographies

Pottle, F. A. The literary career of James Boswell esq: being the bibliographical materials for a life of Boswell. Oxford 1929, 1966.
—— and M. S. The private papers of Boswell from Malahide Castle in the collection of Lt-Col R. H. Isham: a catalogue. New York 1931.
Abbott, C. C. A catalogue of papers relating to Boswell, Johnson and Sir William Forbes found at Fettercairn House. Oxford 1936.
Chapman, R. W. (ed). The Johnson-Boswell correspondence. Appendix B vol 3 of Letters of Samuel Johnson, 3 vols Oxford 1952. A calendar of Boswell's side of the correspondence.
Clifford, J. L. Johnsonian studies 1887-1950: a survey and bibliography, part 4. Minneapolis 1951. Works by and about Boswell relating to Johnson.
—— and D. J. Greene. A bibliography of Johnsonian studies 1950-60, with additions and corrections 1887-1950, items 303-94 and part 4. In Johnsonian studies, Cairo 1962. Works by and about Boswell relating to Johnson.
Brown, A. E. Boswellian studies. Cairo Stud in Eng 1964.

§ 1

A view of the Edinburgh theatre during the summer season 1759, by a society of gentlemen. 1760. Lit Car pp. 284–91; Boswell to John Johnston 26 Sept 1759, in Correspondence of Boswell and John Johnston, ed R. S. Walker 1966; F. A. Pottle, Boswell: the earlier years, 1966 p. 467.
Observations good or bad stupid or clever serious or jocular on Squire Foote's dramatic entertainment intitled the Minor, by a genius. Edinburgh 1760, London 1761.
An elegy on the death of an amiable young lady, with an epistle from Menalcas to Lycidas [i.e. Lycidas to Menalcas]; to which are prefixed three critical recommendatory letters. Edinburgh 1761; rptd in Caledoniad vol 1, 1775.
An ode to tragedy, by a gentleman of Scotland. Edinburgh 1661 (for 1761).
A collection of original poems by Scotch gentlemen. Vol 2, Edinburgh 1762. Boswell's contributions are listed Lit Car p. 13. Boswell revised proofs of this vol.
The cub at Newmarket: a tale. 1762.
Critical strictures on the new tragedy of Elvira written by Mr David Malloch. 1763; ed F. A. Pottle, Los Angeles 1952 (Augustan Reprint Soc). By Boswell, Andrew Erskine and George Dempster.
Disputatio juridica de supellectile legata quam publicae disquisitioni subjicit Jacobus Boswell ad diem 26 Julii. Edinburgh 1766.
The Douglas cause. [Edinburgh 1767]. 2 pp. on one side of a quarter sheet.
Dorando: a Spanish tale. 1767, 1767, Edinburgh 1767, London 1930.
The essence of the Douglas cause, to which is subjoined Some observations on a pamphlet lately published, intitled Considerations on the Douglas cause. 1767 (issued also with the same title-page but without Observations, which were not by Boswell), 1767 (imprint London but probably a Scots piracy); latter reissued 1769, probably at Edinburgh, with Observations on the Douglas cause in general, by Francis Douglas.
Letters of the Right Hon Lady Jane Douglas with several other important pieces of private correspondence. 1767. Boswell may not have been the sole editor.
An account of Corsica; The journal of a tour to that island, and memoirs of Pascal Paoli, by James Boswell esq. Glasgow 1768, London 1768, 1769, Dublin 1768, 1768, 1769. About half the book rptd in Universal Mag Feb–Aug 1768. Abridgement of Account 1794. Journal

of a tour, ed G. B. Hill 1879 (with Letters between the Hon Andrew Erskine and James Boswell esq); ed S. C. Roberts, Cambridge 1923; ed 'Morchard Bishop' 1951; ed F. Brady and F. A. Pottle in Boswell on the Grand Tour: Italy, Corsica and France, 1955; tr German [by A. E. Klausing; see J. K. Bostick, A. E. Klausing's translation of Boswell's Corsica, Oxford 1931 (priv ptd)] 1768, 1769, 1770, 1789; abridged German [by H. A. Mertens], 1769; tr Dutch, 1769; French, by [Gabriel] S[eigneux] d[e] C[orrevon], 'London' (actually Lausanne) 1769, 1769; French by J. P. I. Dubois, Hague 1769; Italian, 2 vols 'London' 1769.
British essays in favour of the brave Corsicans by several hands, collected and published by James Boswell esq 1769 (for Dec 1768). The known authors besides Boswell were Sir John Dick, Edward Dilly and Gen Oglethorpe; Boswell's own marked copy at Johnson Birthplace, Lichfield.
Verses in the character of a Corsican at Shakespeare's jubilee at Stratford-upon-Avon, by James Boswell esq. [Stratford] 6 Sept 1769; Birmingham 7 Sept 1769. Folio half-sheet ptd on one side.
The works of Shakespear. 8 vols Edinburgh 1771, 1771 (for 1773 or later). The dedication to Garrick in vol 1 is by Boswell.
Reflections on the late alarming bankruptcies in Scotland. Edinburgh 1772.
The decision of the Court of Session upon the question of literary property in the cause John Hinton of London bookseller against Alexander Donaldson and John Wood booksellers in Edinburgh and James Meurose bookseller in Kilmarnock, published by James Boswell esq, advocate. Edinburgh 1774, 1774.
The mournful case of poor misfortunate and unhappy John Reid now lying under sentence of death in the Tollbooth of Edinburgh, taken from his own mouth on Wednesday night the 7th of September 1774, being the day fixed for his execution. [Edinburgh 10 Sept 1774]. Folio half-sheet ptd on one side. Journ 7, 14 Sept 1774.
The patriotic Chamberlain: an excellent new song for Midsummer Day 1776. [June 1776]. Long narrow strip ptd on one side. 8 stanzas and refrain urging the liverymen of London to vote for John Wilkes for Chamberlain. Woodcut head of Wilkes at top. Journ 27–8 May 1776; Register of letters June 1776.
St Cecilia: or the lady's and gentleman's harmonious companion. [Ed Charles Wilson], Edinburgh 1779. Contains Boswell's song The Court of Session garland: to the tune of Logan water, pts 1 and 2, 10 stanzas each. Rptd with slight variations in Robert Chambers, Traditions of Edinburgh, 1825 etc. Another version corresponding stanza for stanza but not divided into pts and showing much verbal variation was ptd separately in an octavo half-sheet, editor and place of pbn unknown, on paper water-marked 1816. This version is followed in the same half-sheet by 'Part 2, by Lord Dreghorn'. John Maclaurin, Lord Dreghorn, is indeed supposed to have had a hand in the Court of Session garland, but these 9 stanzas are an independent poem. A transcript of the Garland in the Mansfield Manuscript (see F. Miller, The Mansfield manuscript, Dumfries 1935) consists of 10 stanzas corresponding to St Cecilia's pt 1; another ms in an unidentified hand in the Nat Lib of Scotland dates the piece 1770, entitles it Song to the tune of Logan water and attributes it to Boswell. This corresponds to St Cecilia pt 1, but consists of 13 stanzas. From ms evidence it seems probable that Boswell wrote pt 1 and stanza 5 of pt 2 of St Cecilia, and Maclaurin the rest.
To the printer of the Public Advertiser. Letter signed 'Tantalus', 6 April. [c. 8 April 1779]. Offprint on long narrow slip, blank verso, of letter occupying nearly a column of Public Advertiser 8 April 1779, below. A complaint of the niggardliness of provision of wine and music at the ball at the Mansion House given by Samuel

Plumbe, Lord Mayor. Copy at Yale has a marginal gloss in Boswell's hand.

A letter to Robert Macqueen, Lord Braxfield on his promotion to be one of the judges of the High Court of Justiciary. Edinburgh 1780.

An excellent new war song, the words adapted to Mr Muschet's quick march for the Edinburgh Defensive Band. [Edinburgh 16 July 1782]. Long narrow strip ptd on one side. 4 stanzas and notes. Journ 16 July 1782.

A letter to the people of Scotland on the present state of the nation, by James Boswell esq. Edinburgh 1783, London 1784, 1784 (anon, as A letter to the people on the present state of the nation).

A letter to the people of Scotland on the alarming attempt to infringe the Articles of Union and introduce a most pernicious innovation by diminishing the number of the Lords of Session, by James Boswell esq. 1785.

For the Public Advertiser: Mr Boswell's answer to a letter to this paper signed An Ayrshireman. [Signed] James Boswell, Upper Seymour-street, Portman-square, no 1, 25 July 1785. [c. 27 July 1785]. Offprint of Boswell's letter to Public Advertiser 27 July 1785, below. The newspaper type, which in the Public Advertiser had occupied most of 2 columns of front page, is rearranged in one col and ptd on long narrow slip of paper with blank verso.

Opinion of English counsel on the bill for diminishing the number of the Lords of Session in Scotland, sent to Mr Boswell by Capel Lofft esq of Lincoln's Inn. [Probably London c. 27 Aug 1785]. Single squarish leaf ptd in 2 columns on one side. Letters of Lofft dated 7 June and 17 Aug 1785; at end, 'Mr Boswell begs leave to communicate this opinion to the counties and boroughs of Scotland. London, Aug 27 1785'. Also in St James's Chron 30 Aug 1785, perhaps first pbd there. Rptd in Edinburgh Advertiser 6 Sept 1785.

The journal of a tour to the Hebrides with Samuel Johnson LlD, by James Boswell esq: containing some poetical pieces by Dr Johnson relative to the tour and never before published. 1785, 1785, Dublin 1785, London 1786, 1807, New York and Boston 1810; ed J. W. Croker in his Life of Johnson, 1831, 1835, 1848; ed R. Carruthers 1852; ed G. B. Hill in his edn of Life of Johnson, Oxford 1887, rev L. F. Powell, Oxford 1950, 1964; ed R. W. Chapman in his edn of Johnson's Journey, Oxford 1924; ed F. A. Pottle and C. H. Bennett 1936 (from ms), rev Pottle, New York 1961, London 1963; ed L. F. Powell 1955 (EL); tr French, 1786 (in part); German, 1787 (abridged); German, 1951 (abridged and combined with the Life of Johnson).

Two new songs: Houses shut up, or Rowland in the dumps; Rowland deceived, a Carlisle song. [Probably Carlisle c. 12 Dec 1786]. Single leaf printed on one side. Like the 2 pieces following, a campaign squib in the Carlisle election 1786 directed against Rowland Stephenson, the Duke of Norfolk's candidate against Edward Knubley, supported by the Earl of Lonsdale. Journ 11 Dec 1786.

December 12, 1786: To Rowland Stephenson esq banker in London and candidate for Carlisle, the address and remonstrance of independent old freemen. [Carlisle c. 12 Dec 1786]. Folio leaf ptd on one side. A satirical complaint implying that some 200 of Stephenson's voters think they are not paid enough. A copy at Yale contains pen-and-ink correction by Boswell.

Grand committee, Bluebell, Carlisle 13 Dec 1786. Modest proposals for chairing Mr Rowland Stepenson in case he shall lose his election. [Carlisle c. 13 Dec 1786]. Folio leaf ptd on one side. Ludicrous and belittling descriptions of Stephenson's supporters as they will appear in the proposed procession. Proof and revise at Yale bear extensive revisions in Boswell's hand.

*Carlisle, Dec 14, 1786. Attempt to chair Mr Stephenson. [Carlisle c. 14 Dec 1786]. Single leaf ptd on one side.

Sharp and contemptuous anon warning that chairing of Stephenson will not be suffered. Style and relation to other documents in this series.

*Carlisle. Whereas chairing any candidate . . . [signed] J. Senhouse Mayor. [Carlisle c. 14 Dec 1786]. Single leaf ptd on one side. Proclamation prohibiting the chairing of any candidate before the conclusion of the poll. Boswell was counsel for the Mayor.

Case of chairing: opinion of James Boswell esq of the Inner Temple barrister at law . . . [signed] James Boswell. [Carlisle c. 15 Dec 1786]. Folio leaf ptd on one side. Chairing an unsuccessful candidate is declared to be a defiance to established authority and persons assembling for such purpose constitute a mob. A copy at Yale shows a one-word correction in Boswell's hand.

Ring lost: lost on Wednesday evening 30th of April. . . . [London 1 May 1788]. Small handbill ptd on one side. Journ 30 April–1 May 1788.

Ode by Dr Samuel Johnson to Mrs Thrale upon their supposed approaching nuptials. 1784. Actually pbd a few days after 9 May 1788. See Journ.

Small paper book lost: lost out of a gentleman's pocket on Monday the 2nd of November . . . [London c. 3 Nov 1789]. Small handbill ptd on one side. Assumed to be Boswell's from presence of a copy among his papers and similarity to the last item but one. 1789 is the only year when 2 Nov was a Monday and Boswell in London.

William Pitt the grocer of London: an excellent new ballad written by James Boswell esq and sung by him at Guildhall on Lord Mayor's Day 1790. c. 11 Nov 1790.

No abolition of slavery: or the universal empire of love, a poem. [16 April] 1791.

The celebrated letter from Samuel Johnson LlD to Philip Dormer Stanhope, Earl of Chesterfield, now first published by James Boswell esq. 1790. Actually pbd 12 May 1791. Cutting of advertisement from Public Advertiser 30 April 1791 in P100 at Yale.

A conversation between his most sacred Majesty George III and Samuel Johnson LlD illustrated with observations by James Boswell esq. 1790. Actually pbd 12 May 1791. See preceding item.

The life of Samuel Johnson LlD: comprehending an account of his studies and numerous works, a series of his correspondence and conversations with many eminent persons, and various original pieces of his composition never before published, the whole exhibiting a view of literature and literary men in Great Britain for near half a century during which he flourished, by James Boswell esq. 2 vols 1791, 3 vols Dublin 1792, London 1793 ('revised and augmented'); ed Edmond Malone 4 vols 1799 ('revised and augmented'), 1804, 1807, 1811, 5 vols 1811, Boston 3 vols 1807; ed A. Chalmers 4 vols 1822; [ed F. P. Walesby] 4 vols Oxford 1826; ed J. W. Croker 5 vols 1831 (with Tour); rev J. Wright 10 vols 1835 (with Tour); ed J. W. Croker 1848 (with Tour); ed P. Fitzgerald 3 vols 1874 (with Tour), 1888 (with A bibliography of Life by H. R. Tedder); ed A. Napier 5 vols 1884 (with Tour), 6 vols 1884; ed G. B. Hill 6 vols Oxford 1887 (with Tour); rev L. F. Powell 6 vols Oxford 1934–40 1964; ed R. Ingpen 2 vols 1907 (illustr), 3 vols Bath 1925; ed S. C. Roberts 2 vols 1949 (EL); ed R. W. Chapman, with introd by C. B. Tinker, Oxford 1953 (OSA); tr German, 1797 (abridged and unfinished), 1951 (abridged, with Tour); Russian, 1851 (abridged, with Tour); Swedish, 4 vols 1926–30 (to 1778); Italian, 1939 (selections, rearranged), 3 vols 1954; Danish, 1942 (abridged); Norwegian, 1951 (abridged); French, 1954 (abridged); Serbo-Croat 1958 (abridged).

Song for the glorious 26th of June: being the anniversary of Mr Alderman [William] Curtis's election as one of the Members of Parliament for the City of London, by James Boswell esq [26 June 1792]. Folio leaf ptd on both sides. 7 stanzas with chorus, followed by Appendix, 5 stanzas with chorus, 'sung on the anniversary

1792'. A note preceding the title shows that Boswell sang the song on 26 June 1791, was asked to sing it annually, and that John Nichols engaged to produce ptd copies for 1792.

Proposals for publishing a new and improved edition of Shakespeare illustrated by Charlotte Lennox. [c. Feb 1793]. Folio leaf ptd on one side. Mrs Lennox to Boswell 5 Feb 1793; his endorsement on the letter.

It is impossible for me an enthusiastic Tory. [c. 17 May 1793]. Single leaf ptd on one side, 11-line paragraph in italic type. Offprint of a passage set in type for inclusion in the Advertisement of the 2nd edn of Life of Johnson but removed before printing because of the sharp remonstrance of Malone. Malone to Boswell 13 May 1793; Boswell to Malone 17 May 1793. See also J. M. Osborn, By appointment to his Ma'esty biographer of Johnson, New Haven 1964 (priv ptd).

The principal corrections and additions to the first edition of Mr Boswell's Life of Dr Johnson. 1793. Pbd soon after 9 Aug; see Journ for that date.

*For the European Evening Post: Too true a prophesy, written some time ago. [Signed 'Through']. [c. 1794]. Single small leaf ptd in 2 cols, backed up with same type inverted; if cut down middle would produce 2 copies of a pretended newspaper-cutting of a 6-stanza song with advertisements on the verso. The song is a scurrilous prediction that the Earl of Eglinton's second Countess will bear him heirs not of his begetting, probably written c. 1783. A ms copy from the print in an unidentified hand among the Boswell papers at Yale is written on paper watermarked 1794. Lady Eglinton, divorced by her husband in 1788 for adultery with the Duke of Hamilton, remarried 29 Nov 1794; Lord Eglinton died 30 Oct 1796. No external evidence except the presence of at least 2 copies among the Boswell papers. Evidence of style is very strong.

Song to an Irish air, by the late James Boswell esq. Edinburgh 1802. P. 17 of Songs chiefly in the Scottish dialect, by Alexander Boswell. Inspired by a connexion with Margaret Caroline Rudd. Also in Alexander Boswell's Songs, etc 1803 and the Poetical works of Sir Alexander Boswell, ed R. H. Smith 1871.

The laird of Glenlee. Glasgow 1803. Pp. 24–6 of A collection of songs and poems by Isabel Pagan. There is a copy of the song in the Mansfield ms. See F. Miller, The Mansfield manuscript, Dumfries 1935.

The Justiciary garland: being the form of trial before a criminal court. Edinburgh 1813. Pp. 140–4 of Carminum rariorum macaronicorum delectus: editio altera emendata et aucta, ed A. Duncan. Rptd in various edns of James Maidment's Court of Session garland. Composition of the piece was begun at the Princes street coffee-house by Boswell, Andrew Crosbie and John Maclaurin on 4 March 1776 after the acquittal that day in the Court of Justiciary of their clients Andrew Gibson et al on the charge of assaulting an exciseman. Crosbie and Boswell made more songs on 16 March 1778 (Journ). A ms at Yale appears to show that others were contributed by Robert Cullen, Robert Sinclair and Alexander Wight. No complete ms has been recovered. Duncan's version records the work after 37 years of oral transmission and topical adaptation.

[Notes for the life of Lord Kames]. Edinburgh 1814. Pp. 14, 19, 61, 65, 82, 123 of the 2nd vol of Memoirs of the life and writings of the Hon Henry Home of Kames, by A. F. Tytler of Woodhouselee, 2nd edn 3 vols. 6 footnotes ponderously paraphrased from Boswell's unpbd materials for writing a life of Kames.

Songs in the Justiciary opera composed fifty years ago by C[rosbie], M[aclaurin] and B[oswell]. Auchinleck 1816. Ed and largely composed by Alexander Boswell. See Justiciary garland, above. Another memorial reconstruction with large acknowledged addns.

[Song on the Earl of Cassillis and the Misses Cooper]. Edinburgh 1839. In J. Johnson (ed), The Scottish musical museum, 1839, 'Additional illustrations' by David Laing, 4.410*. The song, which Boswell composed with some help from John Hamilton of Sundrum, is to the tune of 'Johny Faa', which relates how a Countess of Cassillis eloped with a gipsy. Laing took it from the Mansfield ms; Journ 7 Nov 1782; F. Miller, The Mansfield manuscript, Dumfries 1935.

Remarks on the Journey to the western islands of Scotland. 1848. Pp. 825–6 of J. W. Croker's 3rd edn of Life of Johnson, ptd from a ms in the hand of Boswell's clerk, John Lawrie, then in the Anderdon collection; a few insertions in this ms are in Boswell's hand.

Specimen of Parliament: a poem. 1891. In P. Fitzgerald's Life of Boswell 1.82, from Boswell's ms among Wilkes papers in BM. Also (2 stanzas only) in Letters of Boswell, ed C. B. Tinker, Oxford 1924, 2.519.

[Proof-sheets of the Life]. Boston 1894. Extracts in G. B. Hill, Boswell's proof-sheets, Atlantic Monthly Nov 1894, rptd in G. Whale and J. Sargeaunt (ed), Johnson Club papers by various hands, 1899. Much fuller text by R. W. Chapman, London Mercury Nov–Dec 1926, rptd in D. N. Smith et al, Johnson and Boswell revised, Oxford 1928.

Song to Lord Kames. 1925. Ptd by F. A. Pottle from Bodleian Douce ms 193 in Three new legal ballads by Boswell, Juridical Rev 37 1925. Dated 1766 in ms.

The bl[aeph]lum: S[cots song]. New York 1952. Ptd in L. de la Torre, The heir of Douglas, pp. 211–12. A Douglas cause ballad composed May 1767. Correspondence of Boswell and John Johnston of Grange, ed R. S. Walker, 1966, pp. 229–30.

Letters between the Hon Andrew Erskine and James Boswell esq. 1763; ed G. B. Hill 1879 (with Journal of a tour to Corsica); in Letters of Boswell to Temple 1857, 1908 (selected).

Boswelliana. 1856 (Miscellanies of Philobiblon Soc vol 2 no 15). A small selection ed R. M. Milnes, later Lord Houghton, from Boswell's ms then in his possession; rptd as Thoughts on family and friends, by James Boswell, Bookman's Jnl May 1925.

Boswelliana: folium reservatum. 1856. 8 pp. ed R. M. Milnes for private distribution. Other anecdotes, mainly coarse, from Boswell's ms.

Letters of Boswell addressed to the Rev W. J. Temple, now first published from the original mss. [Ed Philip Francis] 1857 (for 1856); ed T. Seccombe 1908.

Boswelliana: the commonplace book of Boswell. Ed C. Rogers 1874 (Grampian Club). A much fuller pbn than Milnes's, above, but not quite complete.

[Boswell's note-book 1776–7]. 1893. Ptd in Collection of autograph letters and historical documents formed by Alfred Morison, 2nd ser 1; ed R. B. Adam [1919]. The R. B. Adam Library, Oxford 1929 2.51 ff; ptd in Catalogue of the Johnsonian collection of R. B. Adam, Buffalo 1921; ed R. W. Chapman, Oxford 1923 (with corresponding passages from Life on opposite pages).

[Boswell's consultation book]. Edinburgh 1922. Extracts in T. B. Simpson, Boswell as an advocate, Juridical Rev 34 1922. Ms in the National Library of Scotland.

Letters of Boswell. Ed C. B. Tinker 2 vols Oxford 1924. The first and only collected edn.

Poetical epistle to Tristram Shandy. 1925. Portions of Bodleian Library Douce ms 193 quoted in F. A. Pottle, Bozzy and Yorick, Blackwood's Mag March 1925.

[Verse letter to Lady Mackintosh]. New York 1925. Ptd from Bodleian Library Douce ms 193 in F. A. Pottle, Bozzy was a bold young blade, New York Times Book Rev 23 Aug 1925.

Private papers of Boswell from Malahide Castle in the collection of Lt-Col R. H. Isham. Ed G. Scott (vols 1–6) and F. A. Pottle (vols 7–18) Mt Vernon 1928–34 (priv ptd). Index by F. A. Pottle, Joseph Foladare, J. P. Kirby et al, Oxford 1937. Vol 1: General introduction,

early papers 1754–63, especially Journal of my jaunt, harvest 1762, 1928; vol 2: Correspondence with Belle de Zuylen, inviolable plan, journal in Holland 1764, 1929; vol 3: Tour of the German courts 1764, 1928; vol 4: Boswell with Rousseau and Voltaire 1764, 1928; vol 5: Love letters in Italy, other records of the Italian tour 1765, 1929; vol 6: The making of the Life of Johnson, 1929; vol 7: Journal 1765–8, development of Corsica, 1930; vol 8: Journal 1769, love-letters of Boswell and Margaret Montgomerie, 1930; vol 9: Journal 1772–4, letter from Goldsmith concerning She stoops to conquer 1773, efforts to save John Reid 1774, 1930; vol 10: Journal 1774–5, threatened duel with William Miller 1774, birth of Alexander 1775, 1931; vol 11: Journal 1775–6, meeting with Mrs Rudd 1776, 1931; vol 12: Journal 1776–7, last interview with Hume 1776, 1931 (interview rptd by N. K. Smith (ed) in Hume's dialogue concerning natural religion, Oxford 1935; annotated trn of the interview by G. Beaulavon, Revue de Métaphysique et de Morale 46 1939; vol 13: Journal 1777–9, at Ashbourne with Johnson 1777, 1932; vol 14: Journal 1779–81, David Boswell's return 1780, 1932; vol 15: Journal 1781–3, death of Lord Auchinleck 1782, materials for life of Kames, 1932; vol 16: Journal 1783–6, death of Johnson 1784, pbn of Tour and quarrel with Lord Macdonald 1785, admission to the English bar 1786, 1932; vol 17: Journal 1786–9, removal to London 1786, work on Life, elected recorder of Carlisle 1788, death of Mrs Boswell 1789, 1933; vol 18: Journal 1789–94, quarrel with Lonsdale 1790, pbn of Life 1791, 1934.
The Yale editions of the private papers of Boswell. Ed F. W. Hilles, H. W. Liebert, F. A. Pottle, E. C. Aswell, Edward Kuhn, F. E. Taylor. In progress. 2 edns are projected, the 'trade' and the 'research', consisting in all of more than 30 vols. Of the 'trade' edn the following have appeared:
Boswell's London journal 1762–3. Ed F. A. Pottle 1950, 1951 (enlarged de luxe edn, reset, with Journal of my jaunt harvest 1762 and additional illustrations), 1951 (text of 1950 rptd Reprint Soc), New York 1956, London 1958, New York 1963, London 1966 (Penguin); tr Danish, 1951; Swedish, 1951; Finnish, 1952; French, 1952; (extracts in Revue de Paris June 1952); German, 1953; Italian, 1954.
Boswell in Holland 1763–4. Ed F. A. Pottle, New York 1952, 1963, London 1952, 1952 (de luxe impression with additional illustrations); tr Danish, 1952.
Portraits by Sir Joshua Reynolds. Ed F. W. Hilles, New York 1952, London 1952. Includes new Boswell-Reynolds letters and a biographical note by Boswell on Reynolds.
Boswell on the Grand Tour: Germany and Switzerland 1764. Ed F. A. Pottle, New York 1953, 1963, London 1953, 1953 (de luxe impression with additional illustrations); tr French, 1955, extracts in Revue de Paris April 1955; German, 1955.
Boswell on the Grand Tour: Italy, Corsica and France. Ed F. Brady and F. A. Pottle, New York 1955, London 1955, 1956 (de luxe impression with additional illustrations); tr French, Revue de Paris Sept 1956 (Journal of a tour to Corsica only, abridged).
Boswell in search of a wife 1766–9. Ed F. Brady and F. A. Pottle, New York 1956, London 1957, 1957 (de luxe impression with additional illustrations); tr French, 1959.
Boswell for the defence 1769–74. Ed W. K. Wimsatt and F. A. Pottle, New York 1959, 1963, London 1960, 1960 (de luxe impression with additional illustrations).
Boswell's journal of a tour to the Hebrides with Samuel Johnson LID 1773. Ed F. A. Pottle and C. H. Bennett, New York 1961 (from ms), London 1963. New impression of plates of 1936, as above under Journal of a tour to the Hebrides, with new introd and additional notes by Pottle.

Boswell: the ominous years 1774–6. Ed C. Ryskamp and F. A. Pottle 1963.
Boswell in extremes 1776–8. Ed C. McC. Weis and F. A. Pottle 1970.

Of the research edn the following have appeared:
The correspondence of Boswell and John Johnston of Grange. Ed R. S. Walker 1966.
The correspondence of Boswell relating to the making of the Life of Johnson. Ed M. Waingrow 1969.

Printed Legal Papers

Perhaps as many as 200 of Boswell's ptd legal papers have survived; see W. H. Bond and D. E. Whitten, Boswell's Court of Session papers: a preliminary checklist, in Eighteenth-century studies in memory of Donald F. Hyde, New York 1970, for bibliography of 80 titles in the Yale, Hyde and Harvard collections. The Signet Library, Edinburgh has 66 titles (catalogue also at Yale), about half not in Bond-Whitten. Occasional examples are in most other Boswell collections, public and private. The Session Papers in the Advocates' Library, Edinburgh (the largest single collection) have not been searched for papers by Boswell.

Contributions to Periodicals

Boswell was a voluminous contributor of signed and unsigned articles to newspapers and magazines. But failing the recovery of marked files or of lists kept by himself, much of his pbn will always remain untraced. Apart from the difficulty of assembling complete files of the newspapers to which he contributed and the time required to search them systematically, his practice of writing on both sides of questions and in many dramatic modes makes complete recovery difficult. His own marked and partially indexed file of the London Chron 1767–75, now at Yale, provides a large and trustworthy specimen of his methods. His journal identifies many of his anonymous or pseudonymous periodical paragraphs. Finally, several collections of newspapers and newspaper cuttings among the Boswell papers at Yale, some of them labelled (Paragraphs relative to my Life of Dr Johnson, Newspaper paragraphs by myself or relating to me etc) furnish valuable but tantalizingly inexplicit information of his dealings with the periodical press, especially in his later years.

Scots Magazine
2 files, perhaps marked by Boswell, have not been reported since sold by Sotheby, Wilkinson & Hodge in the sale of the Auchinleck library 23–5 June 1893, lots 586–7.
An evening walk in the abbey-church of Holyroodhouse. Aug 1758. This and the next 3 items rptd in Original poems by Scotch gentlemen, 1762. Boswell's first known pbn.
On hearing that Theophilus Cibber was drowned. Nov 1758.
Epigram on a marriage. Dec 1758.
Epitaph on the Rev John Campbell. April 1761.
An original letter from a gentleman of Scotland to the Earl of [Eglinton] 25 Sept 1761. Sept 1761.
Letter from Turin 6 Jan. Feb 1766. Rptd from an unidentified newspaper. Part of the letter appears in London Chron 13 Feb 1766.
The H[amilton] cause. March 1767.
*A conference between Signor Romanzo and Lord Shelburne. April 1767. Rptd from a newspaper, not London Chron.
Publications relating to the Douglas cause taken into consideration as disrespectful of the Court of Session. July 1767. Useful collection rptd from Caledonian Mercury, Edinburgh Evening Courant, Edinburgh Weekly Jnl, Edinburgh Advertiser, London Chron.
Prologue at the opening of the Theatre Royal in Edinburgh. Nov 1767. Possibly first pbn of these widely ptd verses. Earliest printing otherwise Caledonian Mercury 14 Dec 1767; also in London Mag Dec 1767,

Edinburgh Evening Courant 16 Dec 1767; Edinburgh Advertiser 18 Dec 1767; Public Advertiser 18, 22 Dec 1767, 12 Jan 1768; St James's Chron 19 Dec 1767; London Chron 19 Dec 1767, 5 Jan 1768.

Extracts from the Essence of the Douglas cause. Dec 1767, Nov 1768.

Article on the French invasion of Corsica communicated by means of Boswell, Corte 4 June. July 1768. Probably merely tr Boswell.

*Letter submitting a character of Francis Stewart, signed D. May 1770. The character probably written by Boswell's brother David; David Boswell to Boswell 28 April 1767.

An imitation of Chaucer's style. Sept 1770.

Extracts from the Decision of the Court of Session in the matter of literary property. Jan–Feb 1774.

Questions by Sir Alexander Dick concerning the making of cider with answer by W. J. Temple. Communicated by Boswell. May 1779.

*Note on the adjournment of the Court of Session, so many of the judges being absent or ill with the influenza that a quorum for the next day seemed unlikely. July 1782.

*Account of the meeting of the freeholders of the county of Ayr 25 Oct 1785. Oct 1785.

London Magazine

From 1769 to its demise in 1785 Boswell was part owner and regular contributor. A file in which he may have marked his contributions has not been reported since sold by Sotheby, Wilkinson & Hodge in the sale of the Auchinleck library 23–5 June 1893, lot 344.

*An account of the armed Corsican chief at the Stratford jubilee, incorporating verses by Boswell in the character of an armed Corsican chief. Sept 1769 (with portrait); account rptd in London Chron 5 Oct 1769, Edinburgh Advertiser 13 Oct 1769. The verses were pbd as a broadside (*see* above) 6 Sept 1769 and were ptd in London Chron 12 Sept 1769, Edinburgh Advertiser 15 Sept 1769, Scots Mag Sept 1769.

On the profession of a player. Aug–Oct 1770. 3 essays. Collected and rptd 1929.

*An authentick account of Gen Paoli's tour to Scotland autumn 1771. Sept 1771; rptd in Scots Mag Sept 1771.

Sketch of the character of the celebrated Mr Gray. March 1772. The character itself was by W. J. Temple.

A sketch of the constitution of the Church of Scotland. April–May 1772; rptd in Scots Mag April–May 1772 with added notes and some rearrangement. Journ 17–18 April 1772.

*Sceptical observations upon a late character of Dr Robertson. June 1772.

*Some anecdotes of the late voyage of Mr Banks and Dr Solander in the northern seas. Nov 1772.

Debates in the General Assembly of the Church of Scotland [1772 and 1771, not 1773]. April–May 1773.

Notes of Dr Johnson's tour to Scotland and the Western Isles. Jan 1774.

*An essay on masquerade, with an account of one given at Edinburgh by Lady Macdonald 15 Jan 1773. Feb 1774.

*Memoirs of the Edinburgh theatre during the winter season 1773-4. May 1774.

Letter signed, communicating an unpublished song by Goldsmith. June 1774.

Some account of the travels of the celebrated Mr Bruce. Aug–Sept 1774; rptd in London Chron 8 Sept, 4 Oct 1774; Scots Mag Sept 1774, notes added from 'Philo' in London Chron 20 Sept 1774. Journ 16 Aug 1774.

*A short account of Alexander Lockhart. March 1775; rptd in Scots Mag March 1775.

Remarks on the life and writings of Gray. May 1775.

A cure requested for occasional impotence of mind. Nov 1775. Journ 16 Oct 1775.

An account of the chief of the Mohock Indians who lately visited England. July 1776 (with portrait); rptd in London Chron 6 Aug 1776; Caledonian Mercury 12 Aug 1776. Journ 18, 20 April 1776.

Consolation under impotence of mind. Signed 'Medicus Mentis'. Nov 1776. Journ 8 Nov 1776.

Hypochondriack 1–70. Monthly essays Oct 1777–Aug 1783. Nos 47, 49, 68 were rptd from Public Advertiser; ed M. Bailey 2 vols Stanford 1928, 1 vol 1951 (with reduced annotation as Boswell's column).

Letter 15 Dec 1779, signed, to the Bishop of Derry concerning the Union of Ireland and Great Britain. March 1784; rptd in London Chron 10 Sept 1785; GM Sept 1785.

*Letter, signed R, submitting various letters concerning Johnson, including one by himself 18 Jan 1785, signed, denying his authorship of a letter in St James's Chron. April 1785. The letter of 18 Jan was rptd from St James's Chron 25 Jan 1785.

Gentleman's Magazine

Extracts from Corsica. April 1768.

*Letter signed J.B. on the omission of certain Scots authors in the new edn of the Biographical dictionary. May 1785.

*Letter signed B.J. submitting an Ode to Edmund [sic] Malone (probably by John Courtenay). Jan 1786; rptd Scots Mag Dec 1786.

*Epitaph on [Soame Jenyns], with a note signed 'Mercutio'. Aug 1786.

?On Mason's abuse of Johnson in the Memoirs of Billy Whitehead. Jan 1788.

*Obituary of David Ross the player. Sept 1790. *See* Boswell to Temple 15 Sept 1790, and below under London Chron 21 Sept 1790.

Advertisement of the Life of Johnson. Paper wrapper of March 1791. Edmond Malone to Boswell 14 April 1791.

Ode to Charles Dilly. Signed. April, June 1791. Also in Scots Mag April 1791, European Mag July 1791.

*To the man of letters; To the man of fashion. Both signed 'Querist'. July 1791.

Letter, 16 Jan, signed, defending the justice of Johnson's animadversions on Mr and Mrs Gastrell. Jan 1792.

?Letter, 10 Jan, signed 'Philalethes', defending Malone's Shakespeare from the aspersions of the Critical Review. Jan 1792.

*Obituary of Ackerman, keeper of Newgate. Nov 1792.

*Letter, Dublin 5 Oct, signed Z, urging some friend of Sir Joshua Reynolds to collect his works and publish a biography. Suppl 1792.

On observing a lock of Miss B[al]d[wi]n's hair. Signed. May 1793; rptd in Scots Mag May 1793.

?Letter, 7 Sept, signed J.B., defending Mavor's New description of Blenheim. Sept 1793.

Letter, Great Portland Street, 16 Nov 1793, signed, replying to Anna Seward. Nov 1793.

Letter, Great Portland Street, 20 Jan, replying to a second letter of Anna Seward's. Jan 1794.

European Magazine

*Extract of a letter, Edinburgh, 23 July, reporting Sir William Forbes's assertion of his right as a juror to judge a point of law. Aug 1782.

*Letter, Edinburgh, 19 April 1784, signed J.B., communicating a correspondence between John Garden and Archbishop Secker. April 1784.

Extract from a review of Anna Seward's Louisa. Aug 1784; rptd from some newspaper as yet unidentified.

Memoirs of James Boswell esq. May, June 1791 (with portrait); rptd in Lit Car pp. xxix–xliv.

?Letter to John Wilkes, Edinburgh 1 March 1769, signed, urging Wilkes to procure a pardon for two Irishmen condemned for murder. Submitted by X as by Boswell or in his character. July 1795. *See* below under Caledonian Mercury 25 March 1769.

London Chronicle

Review of Letters between the Hon Andrew Erskine and James Boswell esq. 28 April 1763. Memoranda 21, 29 April 1763.

'The island of Corsica is now become . . .' 7 Jan 1766. Boswell's notation 'Mr Wilkie' in his Register of letters 23 Dec 1765, 23 Jan 1766 with the marked cutting of the next item indicates authorship of this and the other items to 13 Feb 1766.

Extract of a letter from Rome, 5 Dec 1765. 9 Jan 1766; rptd in Scots Mag Jan 1766. Marked cutting in P116.

Mr Boswell's compliments to Paoli on being presented to him. 11 Jan 1766; rptd in Scots Mag Jan 1766.

Description of Paoli and account of the gifts he made to Mr Boswell. 14 Jan 1766. 2 paragraphs.

Notice of Mr Symonds's intention of visiting Corsica. 16 Jan 1766.

Notice of Mr Symonds's meeting Boswell. 18 Jan 1766.

Foreign intelligence, Florence 16 Dec. 23 Jan 1766.

Extract of a letter from Genoa, 2 Jan. 6 Feb 1766.

Extract of a letter from Leghorn, 3 Jan. 11 Feb 1766.

Extract of a letter from Turin, 6 Jan. 13 Feb 1766. Apparently rptd from some other newspaper. Scots Mag Feb 1766 prints a longer version.

Notice of Boswell's arrival in London. 15 Feb 1766. The notice appeared in Lloyd's Evening Post 14 Feb 1766. Journ 20 Feb 1766.

Notice of an attempt to assassinate Paoli and that Rousseau plans to write a history of Corsica. 8 April 1766. Register of letters 31 March 1766.

Extract of a letter from Leghorn, 1 March. 10 April 1766. Boswell used almost identical language in his Corsica.

*Extract of a letter from Lucca, 5 April. 3 May 1766.

*Opening paragraph of an unsigned letter consisting mainly of a long quotation against capital punishment from the Vicar of Wakefield. 21 Sept 1766. Unmarked cutting of the opening paragraph only in P116.

Postscript signed 'A country gentleman' concerning the repeal of the embargo on Corsica. 27 Sept 1766. Rptd in Edinburgh Advertiser 3 Oct 1766. David Boswell to Boswell 1 Oct 1766.

*M. Suard is to write the history of Corsica; Rousseau is incapacitated for the task by ill health and his quarrel with Hume. 27 Sept 1766. Unmarked cutting in P116.

*Mention of Boswell's arrival at Sollacarò on 10 Nov 1765 from the Corsican Gazette. 27 Sept 1766.

Extract of a letter from Rome, 19 June, with an alleged letter from Voltaire announcing his intention of visiting Corsica. 30 Sept 1766. Annotated cutting in P116, David Boswell to Boswell 31 Oct 1766.

Extract of a letter from Leghorn, 15 July: the Corsicans are building flat-bottomed boats to make a descent on Genoa; if the French recall their troops from Corsica, the Genoese will seek the protection of a certain northern potentate. 2 Oct 1766. Marked cutting in P116.

Invention concerning Dr Brown's intention to publish a memorial in favour of the Corsicans. 11 Oct 1766. Journ 26 March 1772. Marked cutting in P116.

*Notice that Boswell is soon to publish an Account of Corsica. 11 Oct 1766.

*It is confidently reported that the embargo on British ships trading to Corsica will be taken off. 14 Oct 1766.

See Lit Car pp. 237–48 *for a list of Boswell's contributions 1767–75, over 150, based upon his own marked and* partially indexed file of London Chron *now at Yale. The items range in length from a line to a full page. Many of them were rptd in other newspapers and in* Scots Mag. *The list provided by the file for the period June 1770–Dec 1775 is probably incomplete; it certainly fails to include the following item.*

The Boston bill: a ballad. 23 July 1774. Journ 6–7, 19 July 1774.

Letter, Edinburgh 19 Jan, signed 'Borax', on the apathy of the people of Scotland concerning the American war. 25 Jan 1776. Journ 16 Jan 1776.

The Long Island prisoners. 21 Nov 1776. Journ 11 Nov 1776.

*Letter signed 'An Edinburgh correspondent' with reflections on the true character of Hume. 25 Nov 1776. Rptd in Scots Mag Nov 1776; London Mag Jan 1777.

Letter signed 'A constant correspondent' urging publication of a memoir of Derrick. 22 Aug 1780. M76. Unmarked cutting n P119.

*Letter enclosing a compliment to Dr Johnson from the Shamrock: or Hibernian cresses. 26 Aug 1780.

*Letter signed 'A constant reader' asking for a recipe for detecting and destroying bookworms. 20 Oct 1781.

*Extract of a letter, Edinburgh, 19 March, giving an account of a meeting of the county of Ayr to address the King, with a resolution moved by Boswell. 25 March 1784. For the address, which Boswell drafted, *see* London Gazette 3 April 1784.

*Advertisement for Letter to the people of Scotland. 2 June 1785.

Address to the King by the tenants of Auchinleck. 7 July 1785. Alex Miller to Boswell 4 June 1785.

Letter, London, 27 July 1785, signed, enclosing Sir Richard Maitland's Complaint aganis the lang lawsutes. 30 July 1785. Boswell to John Pinkerton 23 May 1785.

*First advertisement for the Tour. 13 Sept 1785.

Resolutions proposed for the counties and boroughs of Scotland previous to the meeting of Parliament. 13 Sept 1785. *See under* Edinburgh Advertiser 28 Oct 1785.

Piozzian rhymes, signed 'Old Salisbury briar'. 20 April 1786. Also in Public Advertiser 20 April 1786; rptd in Morning Herald 21 April 1786 (Werkmeister p. 86); St James's Chron 27 April 1786 (rev); J. Debrett, Asylum for fugitive pieces 1786 2.288–9. *See also* F. Foster, TLS 30 March 1933, E. K. Willing-Denton 20 April 1933. Journ 20 April 1786; Lit Car p. 266.

Obituary of David Ross. 21 Sept 1790. Abridgement and rearrangement of account that appears more fully in GM Sept 1790. *See* that entry, above.

Letter, signed, enclosing Paoli's speech to the General Assembly of Corsica. 30 Nov 1790; rptd in GM suppl 1790.

Edinburgh Advertiser

*Announcement that the Corsican Gazette, pubd by authority, will be presented to readers of the Edinburgh Advertiser. 3 Oct 1766. Also in London Chron 4 Oct 1766. *See* David Boswell to Boswell 1 Oct 1766.

Extract of a letter from Berwick, 15 June, concerning certain short hand reporters. 16 June 1767; rptd in Caledonian Mercury 17 June 1767.

Advertisement of Dorando. 16 June 1767.

*Ballad on Dorando. 19 June 1767.

Extract of a letter from Berwick, 18 June, with descriptions of the shorthand reporters. 19 June 1767; rptd in Caledonian Mercury 20 June 1767; abridged in London Chron 20 Oct 1767.

*Communication hinting that the author of Dorando is a clergyman [Principal Robertson]. 23 June 1767.

Review of Dorando. 26 June 1767. Expanded from Caledonian Mercury 20 June 1767.

Extract of a letter from Berwick, 25 June, enclosing a letter from one of the shorthand reporters. 26 June 1767; rptd in Caledonian Mercury 27 June 1767; Public Advertiser 8 July 1767; abridged in London Chron 3 Sept 1767.

*Scots publishers summoned to appear before the Court of Session. 3 July 1767.

*Extract of a letter from Berwick, 6 July, enclosing a letter from another of the shorthand reporters. 7 July 1767.

*Advertisement of the 3rd edn of Dorando. 7 July 1767.

Account of the trial of the Edinburgh publishers. 28 July 1767; rptd in London Chron 3 Sept 1767.

Verses on the equestrian statue of Charles II in the Parliament Close being painted white, by 'the author of Dorando'. 25 Sept 1767; rptd in Scots Mag Sept 1767; Caledonian Mercury 26 Sept 1767; London Chron 13 Oct 1767; Donaldson's Collection of poems, 1768, 2.251; European Mag April 1790.

*Verses signed 'Brito' on the verses by 'The author of Dorando'. 29 Sept 1767.

*Review of Reflections on the late alarming bankruptcies. 20 Nov 1772.

*Account of the determination of Scruton v. Gray. 4 Dec 1772.

*Account of the determination of Fullarton v. Dalrymple. 25 Dec 1772. See Juridical Rev 52 1940 p. 231.

*Account of a masked ball given by Sir Alexander and Lady Macdonald. 19 Jan 1773.

Account of the determination of Jack v. Cramond. 27 Dec 1776. Journ 22 Jan 1777.

Extract from the Letter to the people of Scotland quoted by Dundas in the House of Commons. 23 Jan 1784.

*Account of a meeting of the county of Ayr to address the King. 23 March 1784; rptd in Whitehall Evening Post 30 March 1784; abridged in Edinburgh Evening Courant 20 March 1784. Journ 17 March 1784.

Account of a dinner given by the Town Council of Edinburgh to J. Hunter Blair, with one stanza of the Midlothian address, a ballad composed and sung by Boswell. 2 April 1784; rptd in Gazetteer 8 April 1784.

Addendum to Boswell's account of the meeting at York. 6 April 1784. See below, Edinburgh Evening Courant 31 March 1784.

*Account of the installation of Burke as Lord Rector of the University of Glasgow. 13 April 1784; rptd in Whitehall Evening Post 20 April 1784.

Letter, Edinburgh, 18 Jan 1785, signed, urging the counties of Scotland to petition Parliament in the matter of nominal and fictitious votes. 21 Jan 1785.

Letter, London, 12 May 1785, signed, promising the people of Scotland that he will oppose the bill for diminishing the number of the Lords of Session. 17 May 1785. Probably also in Caledonian Mercury and Edinburgh Evening Courant.

Resolutions, 25 Oct 1785, signed Hugh Montgomerie, accepted at the meeting of the county of Ayr concerning the bill for diminishing the number of the Lords of Session. 28 Oct 1785. Next item below says that Boswell drafted and prepared these resolutions.

*Account of the meeting of the county of Ayr. 28 Oct 1785.

Letter, Lancaster, 6 April 1786, signed, urging the people of Scotland to petition Parliament for the restoration of trial by jury in civil suits. 11 April 1786; rptd in London Chron 22 April 1786.

*Anecdote concerning Boswell's defence of a prisoner named Margaret Montgomerie at the Lancaster Assizes. 15 May 1786.

*Account of a meeting at Ayr at which nominal and fictitious votes were removed from the rolls. 7 Oct 1791.

Public Advertiser

*Letter signed 'A constant correspondent' referring to Letters between Andrew Erskine and James Boswell. 16 April 1763.

Gilbert Long-nose: a Scotch character. 23 July 1763. Verse. Boswell to Andrew Erskine 26 July 1763; George Dempster to Boswell 23 Aug 1763.

Letter from A gentleman of Scotland to a friend in France. 25 Sept 1767. Edward Dilly to Boswell 10, 24 Sept, 13 Oct 1767; rptd in Caledonian Mercury 30 Sept 1767.

An essay on travelling signed 'Britannus'. 20 Nov 1767; rptd in Caledonian Mercury 28 Nov 1767; London Mag Nov 1767. Marked leaf in P114.

Essay signed J.B. on identification by numbers. 22 Jan 1768; rptd as Hypochondriack no 49, London Mag Oct 1781.

Notice that Boswell is expected in town. 29 Feb 1768; rptd in London Chron 1 March 1768.

Notice of Boswell's arrival in town. 24 March 1768. In London Chron same day.

Notice that church bells are to be sent to Corsica. 19 April 1768; rptd in London Chron 21 April 1768; Scots Mag April 1768.

Extract of a letter, Berlin, 2 April, concerning Corsica and the King of Prussia. 20 April 1768; rptd in London Chron 21 April 1768.

Verses on reading that church bells are to be sent to Corsica. 20 April 1768; rptd in London Chron 21 April 1768.

*Extract of a letter, Genoa, 23 March, and other items relating to Corsica. 20 April 1768.

Letter signed 'Mortalis' on the execution of Gibson and Payne. 26 April 1768; rptd as Hypochondriack no 68, London Mag May 1783.

Invention as to a treaty between the Dutch and Corsica. 26 April 1768; rptd in London Chron 28 April 1768. Marked cutting in P116.

A Corsican agent in London has commissioned British manufactures worth several thousand pounds. 26 April 1768. Marked cutting in P116.

Letter signed 'A constant reader' enclosing a letter, Bristol, April 1768, on France and Corsica. 3 May 1768; rptd as British essays in favour of the brave Corsicans nos 1–2. See above under that title.

Letter signed O.P. urging the merchants of London to make a subscription for Corsica. 6 July 1768; rptd as British essays in favour of the brave Corsicans no 12. See above under that title.

Letter, Dublin, 8 June, giving an account of Boswell's visit to Ireland. 7 July 1769; abridged in London Chron 11 July 1769.

Letter signed J.B. giving an account of the Stratford jubilee. 16 Sept 1769; rptd in London Mag Sept 1769; Scots Mag Sept 1769; abridged in London Chron 16 Sept 1769. Journ 6 Sept 1769.

Letter, Old Bond Street, 12 Oct, signed J.B. denying that he has made any reply to 'Anti-Gnatho'. 13 Oct 1769. See Lit Car p. 257. Anti-Gnatho's reply to D.C. is in Public Advertiser 29 Sept 1769.

Series of occasional essays signed 'Rampager'. 14 April, 12 May, 16 June, 7 July 1770 (rptd in Caledonian Mercury 16 July 1770), 20 May 1771 (rptd in Caledonian Mercury 8 July 1771), 25 Nov 1771, 15 May 1773, 23 Feb, 16 Aug 1774, 11 March, 14 Aug 1775, 9 March 1776, 21, 27 Aug 1777, 21 March, 18 April 1778, 14 Aug 1779. 23 Aug 1780, 23 April 1782. See also Public Advertiser 23 April 1774 for an answer to Rampager by 'A Feather's man'. Journ 24 Aug 1774. Copies of all but 3, with Boswell's annotations, are in P152. Systematic search in a complete file of Public Advertiser would probably reveal more.

Essay on the new freezing discovery signed J. 2 June 1770; rptd as Hypochondriack no 47, London Mag Aug 1781.

*Account of a masquerade—the first in Edinburgh—given by Sir Alexander and Lady Macdonald. 23 Jan 1773.

Letter signed 'A lover of decency' in reply to 'A lover of wit', censuring Nathaniel Hone and defending Sir Joshua Reynolds. 20 May 1775. Marked copy in P114.

Letter signed 'A warm friend to the brave', proposing that the ministry publish the names of soldiers wounded and killed. 18 Nov 1776. Copy of Public Advertiser 19 Nov 1776 containing a reply to this letter by 'A friend to sinking', with a note by Boswell identifying himself as 'A warm friend to the brave', is in P114.

Epigram signed 'Defiance' on the prospect of a French invasion. 23 Nov 1776. Marked copy in P114.

Irregular verses on the reception of the British commissioners by the Americans. 26 Aug 1778. Marked copy in P114.

Letter about the mutiny at Edinburgh of a body of the Seaforth Highlanders. 22, 23, 24, 29 Sept 1778. Journ 22, 23 Sept 1778.

Letter about the mutiny at Edinburgh, 25 Sept 1778, 1 Oct 1778.

Letter signed 'Tantalus', 6 April, complaining of the niggardliness of provision of wine and music at the ball at the Mansion House given by Samuel Plumbe, Lord Mayor. 8 April 1779. See also above under the year 1779 in the section of books, pamphlets etc.

Account which Boswell gave Mr Booth of Hackman's trial. 19 April 1779. See BP 13. 241.

Denial of the report that Boswell attended Hackman to Tyburn. 21 April 1779. See BP 13.243–4.

Characters from Fielding's Tom Thumb, signed J.B. 24 Dec 1779. Journ 10 April 1778.

Suggestion by an Edinburgh correspondent that if Sir Joseph Mawbey is made a peer, the title of Lord Bacon might appropriately be revived for him. 23 April 1782. Marked copy in P152.

*Sam Johnson in Latin. 1783 or later. Letter submitting a Latin trn of Johnson's character of Gilbert Walmesley from Henry Bright's Praxis: or a course of English and Latin exercises, Oxford 1783. Unmarked cutting in P119. See GM May 1803 p. 476.

Letter, Edinburgh, 23 Feb 1784, signed, replying to 'Clarendon'. 18 March 1784. Clarendon's letter attacking Boswell's Letter to the people of Scotland 1783 appeared in Public Advertiser 10 Feb 1784.

Letter, signed, disclaiming authorship of certain newspaper paragraphs. 17 March 1785.

Execution intelligence. 7 July 1785. Account of the execution of Peter Shaw and others. Rptd in Morning Chron 8 July 1785; abridged in London Chron 7 July 1785. Journ 6 July 1785.

Letter, Upper Seymour Street, Portman Square, no 1, 25 July 1785, signed, replying to 'An Ayrshireman'. 27 July 1785. An Ayrshireman's attack appeared in Public Advertiser 14 July 1785. See under Books, Pamphlets etc, 1785 above.

*Execution intelligence. 18 Aug 1785. See Journ 17 Aug 1785.

*Boswell has quitted London and is to visit John Lee at Staindrop. 30 Sept 1785. Unmarked cutting in P116. See Journ 24 Sept 1785; Lee to Boswell 3 Oct 1785; Boswell to Lee 7 Nov 1785.

*Mr Boswell's retort courteous to the stiletto postscript has played the devil with the bluestockings. 21 April 1786. Unmarked cutting in P119.

*The report of a coldness between Boswell and Wilkes is malicious. Wilkes was a guest at Boswell's dinner on

being admitted to the English bar. 3 May 1786. Unmarked cutting in P116.

*Letter signed 'A hungry correspondent' on the appointment by the City of London of a committee to consider the causes of the high price of provisions. 16 Aug 1786. Unmarked cutting in P119. In style of Boswell's Rampagers.

Home circuit shows how many Scots there are at the English bar. 4 Nov 1786. Cutting in P119 with a ms correction by Boswell.

*On the reversal of judgment in Sutton v. Johnstone. 27 Nov 1786. Unmarked cutting in P119. See Domestic occurrences, GM Nov 1786.

*Letter to George Kearsley signed 'Detector' pointing out that certain passages in the Beauties of Johnson said to be from the Tour are not in that work. 29 Nov 1786. Unmarked cutting in P119. Cutting of Kearsley's reply, Public Advertiser 1 Dec 1786, also in P119.

*Letter signed 'Antiwellstop' commending Love's Falstaff. 29 Nov 1786. In the same cutting as preceding.

Johnson's biographers: Boswell and Hawkins each delaying so as to see the other's book. 9 Feb 1787. Marked cutting in P119. This and one other acknowledged item show that Boswell did not strictly keep the promise he made on 25 Jan 1785. See below under Public Advertiser, 12 May 1788 and under St James's Chron 25 Jan 1785, 19 Oct 1790.

On the late Judge Willes. 9 Feb 1787. Marked cutting in P119.

Ecclesiastical bon mot on Henry Beaufoy; Hasting's prosecution; flattery and the Commercial treaty; repeal of the Test and Corporation acts dangerous to the articles of Union [sequence of 6 paragraphs]. 27 March 1787. Cutting in P119 with ms correction in one paragraph by Boswell.

*Repeal of the Test [epigram on Boswell and Henry Beaufoy]. 30 March 1787, receipt acknowledged in Public Advertiser 28 March 1787. Unmarked cutting in P119.

Letter signed 'Domesticus' replying to 'Indignation' and 'More indignation', whose letters are in Public Advertiser 21 Jan, 3 March 1788, asserting the right to criticize John Howard. 12 March 1788. Marked cutting in P116, with annotation 'P.A. 1788'.

*The Lord Provost of Edinburgh presents Boswell with the freedom of that city, granted him in 1784. 18 April 1788. Rptd with some abridgement in London Chron 17–19 April 1788. Unmarked cutting in P116.

Second letter signed 'Domesticus' replying to 'More Indignation', 20 March 1788. Extended strictures on Howard's 'prison schemes'. 12 May 1788. Marked cutting in P116 with annotation 'P.A. 1788'.

Boswell's appointment as recorder of Carlisle will result in his not contesting the county of Ayr at the next general election. 12 May 1788. Marked cutting in P116 with annotation 'P.A. 1788'.

Did Johnson court Mrs Thrale and was he enraged at being rejected for Piozzi? Does Boswell know? 12 May 1788. Marked cutting in P116 with annotation 'P.A. 1788'.

Remarkable increase in the number of lawyers, especially of Scots solicitors in London. 12 May 1788. Marked cutting in P116 with annotation 'P.A. 1788'.

Hastings's accusers are using very coarse and blunt weapons. 13 May 1788. Marked cutting in P116 with annotation 'P.A. 1788'.

The Earl of Lonsdale has recovered from an illness. 13 May 1788. Marked cutting in P116 with annotation 'P.A. 1788'.

On the remarkable number of recorders elected during the year. 13 May 1788. Marked cutting in P116 with annotation 'P.A. 1788'.

Epigram on two late Lonsdale promotions, Scotch Street, Carlisle, May 1788. 13 May 1788. Marked cutting in P116 with annotation 'P.A.'. *See* Lit Car p. xlii.

A Thralian epigram. 13 May 1788. Marked cutting in P116 with annotation 'P.A. 1788'.

Bishop Douglas, Boswell, Lords Kenyon and Cathcart at the anniversary service in Westminster Abbey, 30 Jan 1790; Malone's Shakespeare; Frith Street and King Street; Fox and the dissenters [5 consecutive paragraphs]. 8 Feb 1790. Marked cutting in P117 with annotation 'Publick Advertiser Feb 1790'.

The dissenters: an impromptu, purporting to have been sent from Brighton [Michael Lort praised for tolerance as compared with some 'fiery churchman']. 8 Feb 1790. Marked cutting in P117 with annotation 'Publick Advertiser Feb 1790'.

Johnson's monument. George Nichol's subscription mentioned. 22 Feb 1790. Marked cutting in P117 with annotation 'Publick Advertiser 1790'. Journ 5 Jan 1790.

The celebrated stone-eater was in reality Boswell of Auchinleck ('field of stones'). 2 March 1790. Marked cutting in P117.

Boswell's tragedy Favras. Epigram on Burke and Boswell [2 paragraphs]. 24 March 1790. One cutting in P117, so dated by Boswell, both items marked.

Paoli sets out for Corsica, Boswell gives a dinner for him. 2 April 1790. Marked cutting in P117 with annotation 'Publick Advertiser 1790'.

Lord Mayor elect's feast. 9 Nov 1790. Marked cutting in P117. Dates the feast on 'Tuesday the second instant'.

Boswell sings his ballad William Pitt the grocer of London at the Lord Mayor's feast. 11 Nov 1790. Marked cutting in P117 with annotation 'P.A. 1790'. Account of the feast preceding the song and its introductory paragraph is not by Boswell.

*Paragraph on Warren Hastings. 9 Dec 1790. Cutting in P117 with annotation 'P.A.' merely.

Col MacLeod, Johnson's characterization of him. 22 Dec 1790. Marked cutting in P117 with annotation 'P.A.' merely.

Paragraph speculating as to authorship of No abolition of slavery. 16 April 1791. Marked cutting in P117 with annotation 'P.A. 1791'.

Letter signed 'A cautious man' concerning Johnson's monument. 16 April 1791. Marked cutting in P117.

Johnson's monument suspended like Mahomet's coffin. 16 April 1791. Marked cutting in P117 with annotation 'P.A. 1791'.

*Announcement that A conversation between George III and Samuel Johnson and the Letter from Samuel Johnson to Chesterfield will be pbd on 12 May, price half a guinea each. 30 April 1791. Unmarked cutting in P100. *See* E. K. Willing-Denton, TLS 1 Dec 1932.

Johnson and Burke, 'Non equidem invideo' etc. 14 May 1791. Unmarked cutting in P100 with annotation 'P.A. 14 May 1791'. *See* Life 3. 310 n. 4.

On Boswell's remarks in the Life concerning Warren Hastings. 16 May 1791. Marked cutting in P100 with annotation 'P.A. 16 May 1791'.

*Literary property. Boswell has printed Johnson's conversation with the King and his letter to Chesterfield separately and has entered them in Stationers' Hall. 17 May 1791. *See* E. K. Willing-Denton, TLS 1 Dec 1932; C. J. Horne N & Q 8 July 1950.

Quakers. Boswell's great regard for Lloyd of Birmingham. 18 May 1791. Marked cutting in P100, largely a quotation from the Life.

Johnson's remarks in the Life on insolvent debtors. 19 May 1791. Marked cutting in P100 with annotation 'P.A. 19 May 1791'.

Earl of Abercorn. Contrary to Abercorn's saying,

Johnson lives again in the Life. 20 May 1791. Marked cutting in P100 with annotation 'P.A. 20 May 1791'.

Portable soup. The Life is portable soup of lion's marrow. 21 May 1791. Marked cutting in P100 with annotation 'P.A. 21 May 1791'.

Dilly and Dodsley [a poetical altercation over the respective merits of Boswell and Burke as authors]. 26 May 1791. Marked cutting in P100. *See* C. J. Horne, N & Q 11 Nov 1950.

Letter signed 'The author', correcting a printer's error in Dilly and Dodsley; the poem an imitation of a song by Congreve. 27 May 1791. Marked cutting in P100. *See* C. J. Horne, N & Q 11 Nov 1950.

Boswell has so many invitations he may be said to live on his deceased friend. 27 May 1791. Marked cutting in P100.

*Bennet Langton the character perhaps most highly held forth in the Life to the regard of the world. 1 June 1791. Largely a quotation from the Life. Unmarked cutting in P100.

Friendly patronage. Reynolds has given Boswell not only his portrait of Johnson reproduced in the Life but also his portrait of Boswell. Boswell's *magnum opus* is rather an *opera*. Boswell's retort on the request of European Magazine to print memoirs of him. 18 June 1791. Marked cutting in P100; 2nd paragraph rptd by Werkmeister p. 105.

Celebration of the French Revolution [ironical]. Letters of invitation were first signed by 'Lt Frith in Newgate' and afterwards by 'poor Stone in Bedlam'. 13 July 1791. Marked cutting in P117.

*Extract of a letter from Portsmouth. 19 Aug. Counsellors Towers and Boswell visit the Grand Fleet. 23 Aug 1791. Cutting in P121 with annotation 'P.A. 1791'.

Verses on the election of Bishop Hinchliffe to The Club. 10 April 1792. Marked cutting in P122.

*Weldon enclosure bill, Boswell counsel for the rector before a committee of the House of Lords. 1 May 1792. Unmarked cutting in P121 with annotation 'P.A. 1 May 1792'.

*Weldon enclosure bill. Boswell cross-examines witnesses. 10 May 1792. Unmarked cutting in P121.

Weldon enclosure bill, Boswell finishes cross-examining, Perceval and Graham sum up. 22 May 1792. Marked cutting in P122.

Alderman Macaulay and Boswell may be styled Alderman Curtis's *chairmen*. 4 July 1792. Marked cuttings in P122. *See below* under Diary, Curtis's election.

Another play of words on Macauley and Boswell being Curtis's *chairmen*. 5 July 1792. Marked cutting in P122. *See below* under Diary, Curtis's election.

*Boswell's songs [ironical critique of the song sung by Boswell at the anniversary of Alderman Curtis's election]. 6 July 1792. Rptd by Westminster pp. 173-6. Unmarked cutting in P118. Exactly in the style of the 'recommendatory letters' prefixed to Elegy on an amiable young lady. *See* Lit Car p. 6.

Boswell kisses hands on his appointment as secretary for foreign correspondence to the Royal Academy. 7 July 1792. Marked cutting in P122.

To James Boswell, verses signed 'Old Stingo' defending Boswell's song for the anniversary of Alderman Curtis's election. 7 July 1792. Rptd by Werkmeister pp. 176-7. Marked cutting in P122.

?A card. Alderman Curtis entreats Boswell to expunge from his song the line 'Hie to Curtis, my boys, he'll discount all your bills'. 9 July 1792. Rptd by Werkmeister p. 177.

Essex assizes. Boswell as counsel for Lord Petre presents a plea for mercy for two men capitally convicted on Lord Petre's prosecution. 31 July 1792. Marked cutting in P121.

Mr Boswell to his wine merchant. c. 7 Aug 1792.
Verses, 7 Aug 1792, signed.

New police defended by a gentleman lately knocked down by a street robber. 9 July 1793. Marked cutting in P122. Verso shows that this item immediately preceded the next following item. *See* note on 2nd following item.

Bennet Langton and his son made Doctors of Laws at Oxford. 9 July 1793. Verses. Marked cutting in P122. Date of 9th provided by the next following item. George Langton's degree was conferred 4 July 1793. *See* next item.

Oxoniana: correction. George Langton only an MA. Soon after 9 July 1793. Verses. Marked cutting in P122. Dates 2 preceding items. No known file of Public Advertiser for this period.

Caledonian Mercury

Advertisement of Dorando. 15 June 1767.

*Review of Dorando. 17 June 1767.

Review of 2nd edn of Dorando. 20 June 1767. Expanded in Edinburgh Advertiser 26 June 1767; abridged in London Chron 20 Oct 1767.

*Advertisement of the 2nd edn of Dorando. 20 June 1767.

*Verses on Dorando signed 'Episcopus'. 24 June 1767.

*Advertisement of 3rd edn of Dorando. 29 June 1767.

Prologue spoken at the opening of the Theatre Royal, Edinburgh. 14 Dec 1767. Perhaps the first printing of these verses. *See above* under Scots Mag Nov 1767.

?Letter to John Wilkes, Edinburgh, 1 March 1767, signed J.B. urging Wilkes to use his influence in procuring a pardon for [Balfe and McQuirk] two Irishmen condemned for a murder committed at the election at Brentford. 25 March 1769; rptd in European Mag July 1795. Complete copy in P32, 2 misprints corrected with pen and ink, apparently by Boswell. *See* GM 1769 pp. 52, 108, 135, 161. Probably an imitation or satire rather than a genuine composition of Boswell's.

*Letter signed 'Your constant reader J.B.' suggesting that Digges produce Cumberland's Fashionable lover. 27 Jan 1772. Murray.

*Masquerade intelligence extraordinary, New Town, 18 January. 18, 20 Jan 1773. Ibid.

*Letter signed 'Scotus', Edin. 6 March 1773, defending the Scots theatre. 8 March 1773.

*Report on the trial of Cameron and Tosh. 17 March 1773, rptd in Scots Mag June 1773. Murray.

*Report of the trial of Richard Robertson. 17 March 1773; abridged in Scots Mag June 1773. Ibid.

*Report of the trial of Thomas Gray. 26 July 1773; rptd in Scots Mag Aug 1773. Ibid.

*Departure of Boswell and Johnson for Skye. 18 Aug 1773. Ibid.

*Route followed by Boswell and Johnson. 23 Aug 1773. Ibid.

*Extract of a letter from Inveraray on Boswell's and Johnson's tour. 30 Oct 1773. Ibid.

*Return of Boswell and Johnson to Edinburgh. 10 Nov 1773. Ibid.

*Boswell and Johnson visit Lord Elibank. 13 Nov 1773. Ibid.

*Johnson's engagements in Edinburgh. 17 Nov 1773. Ibid.

*Johnson's stay in Edinburgh and his departure. 27 Nov 1773. Ibid.

*Scottish literary intelligence: announcement, with other titles, of the forthcoming publication of the Decision of the Court of Session upon literary property. 27 Nov 1773.

*John Reid brought to Edinburgh. 11 Jan 1774. Murray.

*Trial of Margaret and Agnes Adam. 24 Jan 1774. Ibid.

*Advertisement announcing that the Decision of the Court of Session upon literary property will be pbd on 2 Feb. 31 Jan 1774.

Opinions of the judges of the Court of Session upon literary property, extracted from the Decision etc. 5, 7, 9, 12, 14 Feb 1774. Murray.

*Correction of a report of Lord Auchinleck's decision in a cause involving the game laws. 16 Feb 1774. Ibid.

*Report of the trial of Andrews, Wilson and Love. 16 March 1774. Ibid.

Account of the execution of John Reid. 21 Sept 1774. Also in Edinburgh Evening Courant, same date. Expanded version in London Chron 29 Sept 1774. Journ 21 Sept 1774.

*Letter signed 'Vetustus', 26 Jan 1776, condemning the affectation of calling the Parliament Close the Parliament Square. 27 Jan 1776; rptd in Scots Mag appendix 1775.

Letter signed 'Hypodidasculus' complaining of the obscurity of certain of the Mercury's articles. 5 Oct 1776. Marked copy in P114.

Letter signed 'Trumpetarius' defending trumpets. 23 Nov 1776. Marked copy in P114.

Letter signed 'Medicus' concerning Dr Memis's cause. 23 Nov 1776. Marked copy in P114.

*Letter signed 'An advocate' giving the true reasons why the Faculty of Advocates declined to subscribe to the Edinburgh regiment. 17 Jan 1778; rptd in Scots Mag Jan 1778.

Letter signed 'An old correspondent' introducing an ironical letter on Johnson's diet while in Scotland. 10 March 1779. Annotated copy in P120. The ironical letter was by Lt John Boswell.

Report of a meeting of the Faculty of Advocates at which it was voted to contribute to repair the damages of the Roman Catholics. 22 Jan 1780; rptd in Edinburgh Advertiser 25 Jan 1780. Journ 22 Jan 1780.

Letter signed 'Lelius' urging a meeting of jurymen to take Boswell's Letter to Lord Braxfield under consideration. 8, 26 July 1780. Journ 22 May 1780. Robert Syme's letter, signed 'An enemy to faction', appeared 17 July 1780.

Defence of the Town guard signed 'An Old Town citizen'. 26 Feb 1781. Copy of this number in P114. 'Town guard' written by Boswell on p. 1.

*Anon letter replying to 'Common sense' (Caledonian Mercury 7 Jan 1782), pleased that the Fleshers have not been removed from the town. 12 Jan 1782. *See* next following item.

*Letter signed 'Simplex munditiis', replying to 'Candidus' (Caledonian Mercury 16 Jan 1782) continuing the debate. 21 Jan 1782. Candidus replied, Caledonian Mercury 28 Jan 1782. *See* Boswell to Edmund Burke 18 March 1782; Journ 15 Dec 1781.

Speech at the Ayr quarter sessions. 16 Nov 1782. H. W. Meikle, Scotland and the French Revolution, Glasgow 1912. pp. xix note, 16 note.

Advertisement for a meeting of freeholders of Midlothian to address the King. 8 March 1784. Slightly variant advertisements in Edinburgh Evening Courant 8 March 1784, Edinburgh Advertiser 9 March 1784. Journ 8 March 1784.

St James's Chronicle

Account of Hackman's trial with a copy of his speech to the court. 17 April 1779. Journ 16 April 1779.

Letter signed J.B. concerning Hackman. 17 April 1779. Journ 16 April 1779. Unmarked cutting in P119.

The English barrister to his mistress signed J.B. 24 April 1781. Marked copy in P51.

Letter, Edinburgh, 18 Jan 1785, signed, referring to a communication [by George Steevens] recommending him to be biographer of Johnson. He has printed no article on the subject in the newspapers and will print none without signing it. 25 Jan 1785; rptd in London

Mag April 1785. Journ 30 Dec 1784–23 March 1785. Cutting in P100.

Letter, London, 12 May 1785, signed, promising the people of Scotland that he will oppose the bill for diminishing the number of the Lords of Session. 12 May 1785; rptd in Edinburgh Advertiser 17 May 1785. Journ 12 May 1785.

Notice of publication of A letter to the people of Scotland. 4 June 1785. 2 paragraphs quoted.

*Account of Boswell's exhibition of his Chinese gong at the Mansion House. 14 June 1785; rptd in London Chron 16 June 1785.

Letter 27 August 1785 communicating the opinion of Capel Lofft on the bill for diminishing the number of the Lords of Session. 30 Aug 1785; rptd in Edinburgh Advertiser 6 Sept 1785. Perhaps the first pbn. *See above* under books, pamphlets, broadsides etc.

Ode on Mr Boswell's gong. 22 Sept 1785. Copy of this number in P131, Boswell's gong' written by Boswell on p. 1.

Dinner given by Lord Lonsdale at the London Tavern. 15 Dec 1789. 3 paragraphs. Marked cutting in P117, date and source recorded by Boswell.

Letter, London, 18 Oct, signed, announcing that he will no longer refrain from sending to the press anonymous contributions concerning the Life. 19 Oct 1790. Also in Gazetteer 20 Oct 1790. *See above* under St James's Chron 25 Jan 1785 and Public Advertiser 9 Feb 1787.

Account of Boswell's singing his ballad the Grocer of London at the Lord Mayor's feast, with text of the ballad. 11 Nov 1790; also in Public Advertiser 11 Nov 1790; rptd in General Evening Post 13 Nov 1790 (abridged); Edinburgh Advertiser 16 Nov 1790. Marked cutting from Public Advertiser in P117.

Impromptu by Boswell at a rehearsal of M. P. Andrews's Better late than never. 18 Nov 1790. Also in Gazetteer 18 Nov 1790; rptd in Diary 19 Nov 1790. Copy of Diary in P66.

*Boswell's compliment to 'a certain enchanting comic actress' [Mrs Jordan]. 18 Nov 1790.

Another extempore by Boswell addressed to M. P. Andrews. 27 Nov 1790. M119.1 No 1 p. 57.

Boswell's advice to Thomas Warton concerning an ode for the King's recovery. 15 Jan 1791. Marked cutting in P117, date and source recorded by Boswell.

Retort of the highwayman who robbed Pepper Arden. 15 Jan 1791. Marked cutting in P117, date and source recorded by Boswell.

*Boswell observes that a certain M. P. [M. A. Taylor?] need not have relinquished one of the two places for which he was returned. 8 March 1791.

*Boswell has taken the critics in with indifferent rhymes. 12 April 1791. Cutting in P117 with annotation 'St J. Chron. 1791' merely.

*Announcement of publication of No abolition of slavery. 16 April 1791.

*Boswell has rescued Johnson from the inaccuracy of Hawkins and Thrale but illiberal Scots still have enough to growl at. 17 May 1791. Cutting in P100, date and source recorded by Boswell.

Literary property. Apology of London Packet for reprinting Johnson's conversation with the King and his letter to Lord Chesterfield. 21 May 1791. Marked cutting in P100, date and source recorded by Boswell. *See* J. B. Nichols (ed), Illustrations of the literary history of the 18th century 7. 344; E. K. Willing-Denton, TLS 1 Dec 1932.

*Anecdote of Johnson's ambition from the Life. 23 May 1791. Unmarked cutting in P100.

Burke and Boswell: Boswell's book, allowing for the difference in price, is outselling Burke's Reflections. 28 May 1791. Rptd in Morning Chron 30 May 1791. Marked cutting in P100. Source and date from C. J. Horne, N & Q 11 Nov 1950.

*Dr Johnson and Burke: Johnson denied Burke wit. 28 May 1791. Unmarked cutting in P100. Mainly a quotation from the Life.

*Account of a meeting at the Crown and Anchor. 4 June 1791.

*Hastings's letters to Johnson in the Life show him capable of having composed his defence himself. 4 June 1791. Unmarked cutting in P100.

*Presentiment: Johnson on ghosts; anecdote of Prendergast in the Life. 30 June 1791. Unmarked cutting in P100.

*Extract of a letter from Chelmsford 5 August: encomiums on Donald Cameron High Sheriff; Boswell gives a toast. 6 Aug 1791. Rptd with 2 other paragraphs by Boswell in an unidentified newspaper, cutting from which is in P121. *See below* in Unidentified section c. 8 Aug 1791.

*Boswell elected Secretary for foreign correspondence to the Royal Academy. 17 Nov 1791.

Weldon enclosure bill, Boswell counsel for the rector. 5 May 1792. Marked cutting in P124.

*Boswell attends the Royal Academy for the first time as Secretary for foreign correspondence, makes a laudatory speech on President West. 5 May 1792.

Epigram on the French national troops. 10 May 1792. Rptd in Scots Mag May 1792; European Mag May 1792; Edinburgh Advertiser 15 May 1792.

*Weldon enclosure bill, Boswell examines witnesses. 10 May 1792.

*Mrs Broadhed's grand masquerade in Portland Place. 12 May 1792.

*Malone's letter to Farmer commended. 12 May 1792.

*Weldon enclosure bill: Boswell cross-examines, Perceval and Graham sum up. 19 May 1792. Unmarked cutting in P121.

*Chelmsford assizes: Boswell recommends to mercy two men capitally convicted of stealing cattle. 31 July 1792. Unmarked cutting in P124.

Literary intelligence: Boswell recovering from the wounds inflicted by a robber; Croft will not proceed with his dictionary; Malone has gone to Oxford for materials for his Dryden. 6 July 1793. Marked cutting in P124.

Edinburgh Evening Courant

Advertisement of Dorando. 17 June 1767.

Review of 2nd edn of Dorando. 22 June 1767.

Reply by 'The author of the Essence of the Douglas cause' to a letter by the Hon Margaret Primrose in the Courant for 20 June. 22 June 1768; rptd in Scots Mag July 1768; Edinburgh Advertiser 22 July 1768.

Reply by 'The author of the Essence of the Douglas cause' to a letter by Miss Primrose in the Courant for 18 July, enclosing a letter by the Duchess of Douglas. 10 Aug 1768; rptd in Scots Mag Aug 1768; Edinburgh Advertiser 12 Aug 1768.

Reply by 'The author of the Essence of the Douglas cause' to a letter by Miss Primrose in the Courant for 29 Aug. 31 Oct 1768; rptd in Scots Mag Oct 1768; Edinburgh Advertiser 1 Nov 1768.

Account of John Reid's execution. 21 Sept 1774. Also in Caledonian Mercury 21 Sept 1774. Journ 21 Sept 1774.

*Account of the general meeting of the County of Ayr to address the King. 20 March 1784. Shorter version than in Edinburgh Advertiser 23 March 1784. Journ 17 March 1784.

*Further account of the meeting of the County of Ayr. 24 March 1784; rptd in Edinburgh Advertiser 26 March 1784.

Letter, Auchinleck, 19 March 1784, signed, to the real freeholders of the County of Ayr, offering himself as candidate in the next election if Col Montgomerie shall not stand. 24 March 1784. Same in Edinburgh Advertiser 26 March 1784.

Letter, 30 March 1784, giving an account of the meeting at York to address the King. 31 March 1784. Same in Edinburgh Advertiser 2 April 1784.

Letter, London, 19 Dec 1785, signed, denying authorship of certain writings in Scottish newspapers and apologizing for any intemperance in the Letter to the people of Scotland. 24 Dec 1785. Same in Edinburgh Advertiser 27 Dec 1785. Unmarked cutting in P116.

Address to the Prince of Wales from the Justices of the Peace for Ayrshire. 21 May 1789. Prefaced by a hostile covering letter not by Boswell. Rptd in Star c. 26 May 1789. Ptd with concluding sentence and signature, from minutes of the Quarter sessions in P. Fitzgerald, Life of Boswell 2.61. Copy of Courant and undated cutting from Star in P6.

Edinburgh Weekly Journal

Extracts from Dorando, with remarks, and letters concerning certain shorthand reporters. 24 June 1767. The remarks on Dorando may be original. The other material is from Edinburgh Advertiser 16, 19 June 1767. See Scots Mag 29.337, 341.

Edinburgh Chronicle

Letter on theatrical criticisms, with a review of the performance of Oroonoko, 20 June. 23 June 1759. Collected, with the 4 following articles, in A view of the Edinburgh theatre during the summer season, 1759.

Review of the performance of Hamlet, 23 June. 28 June 1759.

Review of the performance of the Beaux's stratagem, 25 June, and the Provoked husband, 27 June. 30 June 1759.

Review of the performance of Romeo and Juliet, 30 June, and the Careless husband, 2 July. 7 July 1759.

Letter signed 'Censor' protesting against the performance of Amphytrion. 7 July 1759.

London Gazette

Address of the County of Ayr on the East India bill. 3 April 1784. See under London Chron 25 March 1784, above.

Lloyd's Evening Post

No attempt has been made to list Boswell's items, since with one exception, below, they all appear to have been copied from other papers. It may often, however, be usefully consulted when the original sources are not available. The exception is:

Notice that James Boswell arrived in town 'yesterday' from his travels. 14 Feb 1766.

Gazetteer and New Daily Advertiser

Letter, London, 17 April, signed, replying to the postscript of Mrs Piozzi's Anecdotes. 17 April 1786. Also in Public Advertiser 18 April 1786, St James's Chron 18 April 1786; rptd in European Mag June 1786; GM April 1786; London Chron 20 April 1786; Morning Chron 24 April 1786. Sent to Alex Donaldson c. 20 April 1786 for insertion in Edinburgh Advertiser (Register of letters).

World

*Boswell is at work upon a tragedy on the death of Favras. 13 March 1790. Werkmeister p. 96; M84.

*Boswell in his forthcoming Life presents Johnson's opinion concerning libels on the dead and comments on a case of that sort [King v. Topham] tried in Trinity term last. 2 Nov 1790. Cutting in P100, date and source recorded by Boswell.

Lord Mayor's feast. Boswell sings his ballad, William Pitt the grocer of London. 12 Nov 1790. Marked cutting in P117 with annotation 'World 1790'.

Letter, signed, referring to his ballad the Grocer of London and denying that he showed servility in singing it. 25 Nov 1790; rptd in William Gifford, Baviad, 1791 p. 2.

*Letter signed 'An old courtier' complaining of the current mode of announcing presentations at Court. 16 May 1793. Unmarked cutting in P118.

Times

State paper extraordinary. 13 July 1791. Ironical correspondence between the celebrators of the anniversary of the French Revolution and Lord George Gordon. Marked cutting in P117, name of paper but not date recorded by Boswell.

*Songs, parodies and choruses for the celebration of the glorious revolution in France, 14 July 1791. Cutting in P118 on which Boswell has merely written 'Times'. His authorship indicated by the song given to William Bosville and Boswell to Andrew Kippis 11 July 1791.

Morning Post

Mrs Piozzi traduced as to the generosity of her subscription to Johnson's monument. 23 Feb 1790. Ironical. Marked cutting in P117, date and source recorded by Boswell.

The entertainment to be given when Mrs Piozzi revisits Thrale's brewhouse at Southwark. c. 1 March 1790. Ironical. Marked cutting in P117 with annotation 'Morning Post 1790'. In the preceding item the fete is said to be for 3 March 1790. No known file of Morning Post for this period.

General Evening Post

Song sung by Boswell at the meeting of the Humane Society. 1 April 1790; rptd in Edinburgh Advertiser 9 April 1790.

Lines to Lady [Mary Lindsay], with introductory unsigned letter, Ayrshire. 29 June 1790. M318, L576, L577.

Diary: or Woodfall's Register

Account of the Lord Mayor's feast with Boswell's song the Grocer of London. 11 Nov 1790; rptd Werkmeister p. 98, somewhat abridged. The account is probably not by Boswell.

Commemoration of Alderman Curtis's election as one of the representatives of the City of London with the song sung by Boswell on the occasion and an appendix of new verses. 27 June 1792; rptd in Werkmeister p. 169. Only the verses appear to be by Boswell. They appear also in Morning Chron 5 July 1792. 2 unmarked cuttings, one incomplete, in P117.

Whitehall Evening Post

The Helicon bag: [verses] written by a gentleman while shaving himself, Loch-Gordon, Currie-Grange. 15 Sept 1770. Marked cutting in P116.

*Extract from a letter, Edinburgh, 20 Jan, quoting Lord Monboddo's interlocutor in favour of Boswell in his cause against Sir Adam Fergusson. 2 Feb 1790. Abridged in London Chron 6 Feb 1790. Cutting in P118, on which Boswell has recorded the date and source.

Morning Chronicle

*Announcement that A conversation between George III and Samuel Johnson and the Letter from Johnson to Chesterfield will be pbd on 12 May, price half a guinea each. 2 May 1791. See E. K. Willing-Denton, TLS 1 Dec 1932.

Mr Boswell's song. 5 July 1792. Song for the anniversary of Alderman Curtis's election: see under Diary, above. Prefaced by brief notice of dinner signed 'Geo. M. Macaulay, chairman' and introd probably not by Boswell.

*Song on Benjamin West for the Royal Academy dinner in honour of the Queen's birthday. 22 Jan 1793; rptd with date in Werkmeister p. 180. M331, a very similar song on West composed for a Royal Academy dinner in honour of the King's birthday.

Morning Herald

Letter, 9 March 1786, signed, denying that Lord Macdonald has forced him to suppress passages in the Tour. 11 March 1786. Rptd in St James's Chron 14 March 1786; GM April 1786; European Mag June 1786.

Newspaper cuttings preserved by Boswell, sources not identified; they appear not to be from Public Advertiser, St James's Chron, Morning Post, Times, World.

Grand dinner by Earl Fife for Burke, Boswell present. Shortly after 8 May 1791. Marked cutting in P117, date and source not recorded. Date of dinner from Palmer's index to Times. *See also* A. and H. Tayler, Lord Fife and his factor, 1925 p. 235 (letter of 10 May 1791 wrongly ptd under 1792).

Boswell, having resigned the recordship of Carlisle, returns to the semi-annual feast of the counsel on the home circuit. Probably 6–9 Aug 1791. Marked cutting in P121, date and source not recorded. Dinner reported to have been held 'on Saturday se'nnight'. News item on verso with date-line 'Vienna, July 3' appears verbatim in Morning Post 8 Aug 1791. *See* next item.

*Essex assizes, containing extract of a letter 5 August, much mention of Boswell and Donald Cameron, high sheriff. Probably 6–9 Aug 1791. Unmarked cutting in P121, date and source not recorded. The extract of a letter also appears in St James Chron 6 Aug 1791. This cutting appears from its verso to have been removed from the same newspaper page as that immediately preceding.

*Weldon enclosure bill. c. 1 May 1792. Unmarked cutting in P121, date and source not recorded. Apparently from the same newspaper as 2 preceding items.

§ 2

GM Feb 1760 (rptd in Scots Mag Feb 1760); Monthly Rev March 1760. Reviews of A view of the Edinburgh theatre.

Monthly Rev Dec 1760; Critical Rev Jan 1761. Reviews of Observations on the Minor.

Br Mag May 1762; Critical Rev June 1762; Monthly Rev Sept 1762. Reviews of Original poems by Scotch gentlemen.

Monthly Rev March 1762; Critical Rev March 1762. Reviews of the Cub at Newmarket.

Monthly Rev Jan 1763 (by Ralph Griffiths: Nangle); Critical Rev Feb 1763. Reviews of Critical strictures.

Public Advertiser 15, 19, 28 April 1763 (by Bonnell Thornton: Journ 24 May 1763); London Chron 28 April 1763 (by Boswell: Memoranda 21, 29 April 1763); Critical Rev May 1763; Monthly Rev June 1763 (by Ralph Griffiths: Nangle). Reviews of Letters between Andrew Erskine and James Boswell.

Caledonian Mercury 17, 20, 29 June 1767 (by *Boswell, partially rptd in Scots Mag July 1767 and London Chron 20 Oct 1767); Edinburgh Advertiser 26 June 1767 (by *Boswell); London Chron 2 July 1767 (by Boswell); Critical Rev July 1767; GM July 1767; Monthly Rev July 1767; Scots Mag appendix 1767. Reviews of Dorando.

Critical Rev Nov 1767; Scots Mag 1767 (rptd from Critical Rev), Dec 1767 (extracts), Nov 1768 (extracts); Monthly Rev Dec 1767. Reviews of Essence of the Douglas cause.

Critical Rev Nov 1767; Monthly Rev Dec 1767. Reviews of Letters of Lady Jane Douglas.

A.B. (John Wilkes). To the editor of the Political Register. Political Register extraordinary No 12 between March and April 1768. Rptd in Correspondence of Wilkes, ed J. Almon 1805, the passage dealing with Boswell abridged.

K[enrick], W[illiam]. An epistle to James Boswell esq occasioned by his having transmitted the moral writings of Dr Samuel Johnson to Pascal Paoli. 1768. An answer to this pamphlet was advertised in Public Advertiser 4 July 1768.

London Mag Feb 1768; Critical Rev March 1768 (by William Guthrie: Journ 25 March 1768) (rptd in Scots Mag Feb 1768); GM April 1768; Monthly Rev July–Aug 1768 (by Ralph Griffiths: Nangle); [Edward Gibbon and Georges Deyverdun], Mémoires littéraires de la Grande Bretagne pour l'an 1768, 1769. Reviews of An account of Corsica.

Critical Rev Jan 1769; Monthly Rev Jan 1769. Reviews of British essays in favour of the brave Corsicans.

Edinburgh Advertiser 20 Nov 1772 (by *Boswell). Review of Reflections on the late alarming bankruptcies.

Monthly Rev Aug 1774 (by William Enfield: Nangle); Scots Mag Jan–Feb 1774 (extracts). Reviews of the Decision of the Court of Session on literary property.

Scots Mag April 1780 (extracts). Review of A letter to Lord Braxfield.

Critical Rev Jan 1784; Monthly Rev Jan 1784 (by John Noorthouck: Nangle); Eng Rev Feb 1784; European Mag Feb 1784. Reviews of A letter to the people of Scotland 1783.

'An Ayrshireman'. To James Boswell esq. Letter, Public Advertiser 14 July 1785. Boswell replied in his own name, 27 July 1785.

[Correspondence concerning the Tour in GM]. 'Byblius', Dec 1785; D.H. ibid; 'Johnsonophilus', ibid; 'Anti-Stiletto', Jan 1786; 'Gratian', Feb 1786; T., March, May 1786; Boswell on Lord Macdonald and Mrs Piozzi, April 1786; 'Philanthopus', ibid; 'Pro me, si merear, in me', May 1786; E.R.R., Sept 1786; 'Bristolensis', ibid; I.D.I., suppl 1786. *See also* Anna Seward, 1786, below.

Critical Rev June 1785; Eng Rev June 1785; Monthly Rev June 1785 (by John Noorthouck: Nangle); Scots Mag June 1785 (mainly extracts). Reviews of A letter to the people of Scotland 1785.

Critical Rev Nov 1785; Eng Rev Nov 1785; GM Nov 1785; Oct, Dec 1785, Jan 1786 (extracts); European Mag Dec 1785, March, May–June 1786; Oct–Dec 1785, Jan–Feb 1786 (extracts); Scots Mag Dec 1785 (rptd from GM), Sept 1785 (extract); Monthly Rev April 1786 (by Samuel Badcock: Nangle). Reviews of the Tour.

[Malone, Edmond]. St James's Chron 8 Oct 1785. Letter signed 'An enemy to nonsense and slander'. Defends Boswell and George Strahan. Proof in P82, Malone's initials added in his own hand.

— St James's Chron 20 Oct 1785. Letter reprinting Johnson's remarks on Ossian from the Tour. Proof in P82, Malone's initials added in his own hand.

— GM June 1795. Unsigned obituary letter. Editorially identified as 'a correspondent whom we believe to be Mr Malone'.

'Momus'. Westminster Mag Nov 1785. *See* M. R. Watson, 'Momus' and Boswell's Tour, JEGP 48 1949.

'Verax'. Remarks on the Journal of a tour to the Hebrides in a letter to James Boswell esq. 1785. Reply by [Walter James], A defence of Mr Boswell's Journal in a letter to the author of Remarks signed Verax, 1785. Another reply, anon: The remarker remarked: or a parody on the Letter to Mr Boswell on his Tour to the Hebrides, 1786. 'Verax' and the author of the Remarker remarked remain unidentified. 'W. James' acknowledged the Defence in a letter to Boswell 26 Dec 1785. C. Ryskamp has shown that he was Walter James Head, later Sir Walter James Bt.

Q. Mr Boswell's gong. GM Nov 1785. *See above* under Boswell's contributions to periodicals, St James's Chron 14 June, 22 Sept 1785.

Anecdotes of the learned pig, with notes critical and explanatory and illustrations from Bozzy, Piozzi etc. 1786.

Collings, S. and T. Rowlandson. Picturesque beauties of Boswell. 1786. 20 caricatures illustrating the Tour.

'A lady'. Dr Johnson's ghost. General Evening Post 21 March 1786. Parody of Mallet, William and Margaret. Unmarked copy in P120.

'Pindar, Peter' (John Walcot). A poetical and congratulatory epistle to James Boswell on his Journal of a tour to the Hebrides. 1786, 10th edn 1789.

— Bozzy and Piozzi: or the British biographers. 1786, 9th edn 1788.

A poetical epistle from the ghost of Dr Johnson to his four friends: Rev Mr Strahan, Boswell, Mrs Piozzi, Courtenay. 1786.

[Seward, Anna]. GM Feb, April 1786, Aug 1787. Letters signed 'Benvolio' concerning the Tour and Johnson's biographers. Authorship acknowledged GM Dec 1793.

— GM Oct, Dec 1793. Letters, signed, on Johnson's Verses on a sprig of myrtle. Replies by Boswell, signed, Nov 1793, Jan 1794.

Monthly Rev June 1788; Critical Rev Sept 1788. Reviews of Ode by Dr Samuel Johnson to Mrs Thrale 1788.

Epistle to James Boswell esq occasioned by his long-expected and now speedily-to-be-published Life of Dr Johnson. 1790. K. F. Thompson, N & Q 16 April 1949, suggests that Boswell may have written this himself. The attribution seems unlikely. The piece is un-Boswellian in style and advocates principles of biography to which Boswell was opposed.

'Causidicus' (probably T. E. Tomlins). A poetical epistle to James Boswell esq on his Life of Johnson. St James's Chron 9 June 1791; also in Public Advertiser signed merely 'C'. 10 June 1791. Unmarked cutting from Public Advertiser in P101. Journ 14 Feb 1791, 3 Oct 1793, DNB under Tomlins. 'Causidicus', who gives evidence of knowing the Boswell family, was a regular contributor of letters on legal subjects to St James's Chron, e.g. 11 Dec 1790, 9 June 1791.

[Chalmers, Alexander]. Lesson in biography: or how to write the life of one's friend. Morning Herald 5 July 1791; rptd in Public Advertiser 6 July 1791; Town and County Mag July 1791 (abridged); 1798 (pamphlet); included in all Croker's edns of the Life; rptd with typefacs of title-page of 1798 in Aungervyle Soc Reprints 4th ser 1887. Nichols, Illustrations, above, 7. 344. Cutting from Morning Herald in P101, date entered in an unidentified hand.

[Correspondence concerning the Life in GM up to Boswell's death]. A.Z., June 1791; 'A constant reader of the GM', Sept 1791; death notice of Mrs Gastrell, Dec 1791, Boswell's signed reply, Jan 1792; 'Sciolus' (J. B. Blakeway: see Percy-Malone Correspondence, ed A. Tillotson 1944, p. 86) Feb–March 1792; 'Academicus', March 1793; J. Henn, May 1793; 'Bob Short', June 1793; * B, Jan 1794; Will Faulkner, Feb 1794; H. White, March 1794; B.B.S., ibid; L.X., ibid; W & D, April 1794; E.E.A., May 1794; 'Eboracensis', June 1794; T.W., July 1794; 'Protoplastides', July 1794, Jan 1795; E., Aug 1794; G., Nov 1794; S. Parr, March 1795; D.H., April 1795. *See also* John Nichols, 1791, and Anna Seward, 1786, above.

GM April 1791; Monthly Rev April 1791; Critical Rev June 1791. Reviews of No abolition of slavery.

'A lover of extraordinary extracts'. Johnson and Bozzy on power and prerogative. St James's Chron 17 Nov 1791. Cutting in P101, annotated by Boswell 'Ludicrous imitation of Johnsonian dialogue'.

[Nichols, John]. Letter signed J.N. on Johnson's verses on a sprig of myrtle. GM May 1791.

— Letter signed J.N. with additions for the Life. GM June 1791.

— Letter, 8 June, signed 'M. Green'. GM June 1795.

— Additions and corrections: Boswell preparing a reply to Dr Parr; inscription on his coffin-plate. Ibid.

— In his Literary anecdotes of the 18th century, 9 vols 1812–15.

— In his Illustrations of the literary history of the 18th century, 8 vols (vols 7–8 ed J. B. Nichols) 1817–58. *See* in general E. Hart, Contributions of John Nichols to Boswell's Life of Johnson, PMLA 67 1952.

St James's Chron 16 May 1791 (by T. E. Tomlins: cutting in P100, authorship indicated by Boswell); GM May–June, Sept, suppl 1791, Jan 1792; July 1791 (extracts); Oracle 23 June 1791 (rptd by Werkmeister p. 105; she thinks written by Peter Stuart or James Boaden); Critical Rev July, Nov 1791, March 1792; Eng Rev July–Aug 1791; European Mag Aug–Sept, Nov 1791, Jan, March–May, Aug–Oct 1792, with letter signed G.H. Jan 1792; Monthly Rev (by Ralph Griffiths: Nangle) Jan, Feb, May 1792; Scots Mag Jan 1792, extracts May 1792. Reviews of the Life of Johnson.

Supplement to the Life of Johnson. Morning Chron 20 Sept 1791. Unmarked copy in P101. Another parody, much in Chalmers's style. If by him, it probably appeared first in Morning Herald.

Extract from memoirs of the life of the orang outang, intended to be published. Public Advertiser 19 Jan 1792. Unmarked cutting in P101. Close parody of Life 16 May 1763.

[Greville, Fulke]. A letter to James Boswell esq with some remarks on Johnson's dictionary and on language. 1792. Attributed confidently to Greville in the office copy of the Monthly Rev in Bodley.

[Correspondence in GM concerning the Corrections and additions]. N.Y., Nov 1793, Jan 1794; M—s, Feb 1794; Αἰσχυνεο σεαυτόν, ibid; 'Mastigophoros', ibid; Henry White, March 1794; G.S., ibid; 'Scrutator', ibid; 'Libra', April 1794. *See also* Anna Seward, 1786, above.

European Mag Oct 1793 (extracts); Critical Rev Nov 1793; GM Nov 1793, Jan 1794. Reviews of Corrections and additions to the Life of Johnson.

GM Nov 1793; 63 pt 1 1793, last p. of index (extract). Review of the Life, 1793 (2nd edn).

'Biographicus'. Letter dated 29 July, GM Aug 1795. Certainly not W. J. Temple as suggested. If one can trust a letter signed 'William', GM Feb 1797, 'Biographicus' was 'a Scottish lady, well educated; who knew Mr B from his youth, and had been in intimacy and correspondence with him till near the time of his death'.

C. Letter, 3 June. GM June 1795. Describes himself as 'an old correspondent'. From C 778, apparently author's revised draft of about half this letter in a hand as yet unidentified but certainly not Alexander Chalmers's, one would infer that 'C' was a Scot with a rather old-fashioned cast of language who knew the Boswell family personally. Perhaps James Chalmer, Scots solicitor in London from 1776.

'Filiolus'. Dr Parr, Mr Boswell and Dr Johnson. GM May 1795.

GM May 1795; True Briton 23 May 1795, rptd by Werkmeister p. 182, John Taylor suggested as author; Oracle 25 May 1795, rptd by Werkmeister p. 183, Peter Stuart suggested as author. Obituaries.

J.B.R. Memoirs of James Boswell esq. GM June 1795.

Martin, Samuel. An epistle in verse occasioned by the death of James Boswell esquire of Auchinleck. 1795; ed R. F. Metzdorf, Hamden Conn 1952 (facs).

Whyte, E. A. Remarks on Boswell's Life of Johnson. Attached to 3rd edn of Samuel Whyte, Poems on various subjects, Dublin 1795, 1797 (separately); included in A miscellany by S. and E. A. Whyte, Dublin 1799, reissued as Miscellanea nova, Dublin 1800, 1801.

'Attalus' (William Mudford). A critical inquiry into the moral writings of Dr Samuel Johnson. Appendix containing a dialogue between Boswell and Johnson in the shades. 1802, 1803. Rptd from Porcupine 3 Oct–26 Dec 1801.

J.B. Two new dialogues of the dead: the first between Handel and Braham; the second between Johnson and Boswell. 1804.

Rush, Benjamin. Johnson's conversations, recorded by Rush 22 April 1793. Portfolio, Philadelphia 15 Dec 1804. Submitted with introductory letter by J. Abercrombie, who had sent another copy to Boswell 17 May 1793. See Osgood, 1942, Butterfield, 1946, below.

Ireland, W. H. Confessions. 1805.

Forbes, W. An account of the life and writings of Beattie. 2 vols 1806, 3 vols 1807.

Holcroft, T. Memoirs. 3 vols 1816, 1 vol 1852, Oxford 1926.

Hawkins, L. M. Memoirs. 3 vols 1822–4. Extracts in Croker's Boswell 1831, 1835 (rptd in Johnsoniana 1836); in Johnsonian miscellanies, ed G. B. Hill 2 vols Oxford 1897; selections as Gossip about Dr Johnson and others, ed F. H. Skrine 1926.

Macaulay, T. B. Edinburgh Rev 54 1831. Collected as Essay on Boswell's Life of Johnson in his Critical and historical essays, 3 vols 1843 etc. Reply [by Croker and John Wilson] in Wilson's Noctes ambrosianae, Blackwood's Mag Nov 1831, rev and separately pbd as Answers to Mr Macaulay's criticism on Mr Croker's edition of Boswell's Life of Johnson, 1856. Review of J. W. Croker's edn of the Life.

— Samuel Johnson. Encyclopaedia britannica 1856. Collected in Miscellaneous writings of Lord Macaulay, ed T. F. E[llis] 2 vols 1860 etc.

d'Arblay, Frances Burney. In Memoirs of Dr Burney, 3 vols 1832.

— Diary and letters ed by her niece. 7 vols 1842–6 etc; ed A. Dobson 6 vols 1904–5.

Carlyle, T. Biography: Boswell's Life of Johnson. Fraser's Mag April–May 1832. Collected in his Critical and miscellaneous essays, 4 vols 1839 etc.

Lockhart, J. G. Croker's edition of Boswell. Quart Rev 46 1832.

Taylor, J. In his Records of my life, 2 vols 1832.

Roberts, W. Memoirs of the life and correspondence of Hannah More. 4 vols 1834.

Shelton, F. W. Boswell the biographer. Knickerbocker Mag Feb 1851. Perhaps the first extended reply to Macaulay's characterization.

Bozzies. Eliza Cook's Mag 26 Feb 1853; rptd in Eclectic Mag July 1853.

Campbell, T. Diary of a visit to England in 1775, with notes by Samuel Raymond. Sydney 1854, 1854; rptd in Johnsoniana, ed R. Napier 1884, 1884; extracts in Johnsonian miscellanies, ed G. B. Hill 2 vols Oxford 1897; ed J. L. Clifford, Cambridge 1947 (from ms).

[Elwin, Whitwell]. Boswell; early life of Johnson. Quart Rev 103 1858.

Prior, J. Life of Edmond Malone. 1860.

Rogers, C. Memoir. Prefixed to Boswelliana, 1874. The first extended life.

Hill, G. B. Dr Johnson, his friends and critics. 1878.

— Footsteps of Dr Johnson. 1890.

— The centenary of Boswell. Macmillan's Mag May 1891; rptd in Living Age 4 July 1891; rptd in Johnson Club papers by various hands, ed G. Whale and J. Sargeaunt 1899.

— Boswell's proof-sheets. Atlantic Monthly Nov 1894; rptd in Johnson Club papers by various hands, ed G. Whale and J. Sargeaunt 1899.

— The Boswell centenary 19 May 1895. Illustr London News 25 May 1895; 1895 (priv ptd for members of the Johnson Club).

Fitzgerald, P. Croker's Boswell and Boswell. 1880.

— Editing à la mode: an examination of Dr Birkbeck Hill's new edition of Boswell's Life of Johnson. 1891. Enlarged and rptd from Time Sept 1890.

— Further examination of Dr Birkbeck Hill's edition of Boswell's Life of Johnson. 1891.

— Life of Boswell. 2 vols 1891.

— More editing à la mode: being a further examination of Dr Birkbeck Hill's edition of Boswell's Life of Johnson. 1892.

— Some new lights on Bozzy. New Century Rev 2 1897.

— A critical examination of Dr G. B. Hill's Johnsonian editions. 1898. Collects material from his previous strictures. Reply by L. Stephen, 1898, below.

— Some Bozzyana. GM Feb 1902.

— Boswell's autobiography. 1912. Earlier sketch in Quart Rev 214 1911.

Boswell and his editors. Church Quart Rev 27 1889.

Henley, W. E. Boswell. In his Views and reviews: essays in appreciation, 1890, 1892; in his Works 1908 vol 5. Rptd from Athenaeum.

Layard, G. S. Johnson's Boswell. Universal Rev Aug 1890.

Saintsbury, G. Some great biographies. Macmillan's Mag June 1892; rptd in his Essays in English literature 1780–1860 2nd ser, 1895; also in vol 1 of his Collected essays and papers, 1923.

Shuckburgh, E. S. Corsica Boswell. Macmillan's Mag Oct 1892; rptd in Living Age 3 Dec 1892.

Johnson, L. P. Bustling breathless bragging Boswell. Academy 18 Sept 1897; rptd in his Post liminium, ed T. Whittemore 1911.

Leask, W. K. James Boswell. 1897.

Stephen, L. Johnsoniana. Nat Rev Sept 1897; rptd with added note in reply to Fitzgerald in his Studies of a biographer, 4 vols 1898.

B.H.L. Boswell's last London residence. N & Q 11 June 1898. See also Boswell memorial in London, 1915, below.

Dobson, A. Boswell's predecessors and editors. In his Miscellanies, New York 1898, also in his A paladin of philanthropy, 1899.

Birrell, A. The transmission of Dr Johnson's personality. In Johnson Club papers by various hands, ed G. Whale and J. Sargeaunt 1899.

— Boswell as biographer. In his In the name of the Bodleian, 1905; also in his Collected essays and addresses, 1922.

— Introd to vol 2 of Temple Bar edn of the Life, 1922.

— Johnson's Journey and Boswell's Journal. Nation (London) 9 Aug 1924.

— Boswell disrobed. In his Et cetera, 1930.

Stobart, M. A. Boswell in Corsica: the perfect journalist on his travels. Pall Mall Mag Oct 1901.

Chesterton, G. K. Boswell's Johnson. Introd to Life abridged and ed G. N. Bankes and H. Higgins, 1903; rptd in Good Words Nov 1903; also in G.K.C. as M.C., ed J. P. de Fonseka 1929.

— Introd to vol 4 of Temple Bar edn of the Life, 1922.

Bicknell, P. F. A prince of interviewers. Dial 1 March 1905.

Caldwell, J. W. A brief for Boswell. Sewanee Rev 13 1905.

Henderson, J. S. Boswell and his practice at the bar. Juridical Rev 17 1905.

Filon, A. Boswell's love story. Fortnightly Rev new ser 80 1906. First presentation in English of the Belle de Zuylen episode.

Godet, P. Madame de Charrière et ses amis. 2 vols Geneva 1906. First account of Boswell's courtship of Belle de Zuylen.

Brown, J. T. T. The youth and early manhood of Boswell. Proc of Royal Philosophical Soc of Glasgow 41 1910.

— Boswell: an episode of his grand tour. Trans of Glasgow Archaeological Soc new ser 7 pt 2 1920. First complete printing of Boswell's letter to Belle de Zuylen 9 July 1764.

— Boswell as essayist. Scottish Historical Rev 17 1921.

Raleigh, W. Johnson without Boswell. In his Six essays on Johnson, Oxford 1910.

Lee, S. Principles of biography. Cambridge 1911 (Leslie Stephen lecture).

Mallory, G. Boswell the biographer. 1912.

Bailey, J. C. Chs 2–3 of his Dr Johnson and his circle, 1913 etc, 1944 (rev with bibliography by L. F. Powell).

Nicoll, W. R. The six best biographies. In his A bookman's letters, 1913.

Cosulich, G. Johnson's affection for Boswell. Sewanee Rev 22 1914.

A Boswell memorial in London [Boswell's residence in Great Queen St]. Outlook 24 March 1915. See also B.H.L., 1898, above.

Glover, T. R. In his Poets and puritans, 1915.

Tinker, C. B. Boswell and the art of intimate biography. In his Salon and English letters, New York 1915.

— Young Boswell. 1922. 4 chs had appeared in Atlantic Monthly May 1921, Jan–March 1922.

— A new nation. In his Nature's simple plan, Princeton 1922. On Boswell and Corsica.

— Introd to vol 4 of Temple Bar edn of the Life, 1922.

— and F. A. Pottle. A new portrait of Boswell. Cambridge Mass 1927.

Tinker, C. B. The great diarist and some others. In his Essays in retrospect, New Haven 1948. Rptd from Atlantic Monthly.

Dunn, W. H. In his English biography, 1916.

— Jamie Boswell's thorn in the flesh. South Atlantic Quart 28 1929. On John Wolcot ('Peter Pindar')

Barker, F. W. E. Boswell's record of Johnson's table talk. Papers of Manchester Literary Club 43 1917.

Newton, A. E. Boswell: his book. In his Amenities of book collecting, Boston 1918, London 1920. Some chs had appeared in Atlantic Monthly.

— Introd to vol 5 of Temple Bar edn of the Life, 1922. When Boswell dared to differ. TLS 9 Jan 1919.

Thayer, W. R. In his Art of biography, New York 1920.

F.D.M. Boswell: executions, a query. TLS 13 April 1922. Boswell accused by H. Croft of renting by the year a window in the Grassmarket.

Hirn, Y. Dr Johnson och James Boswell. Helsingfors 1922.

The life of Samuel Johnson. Ed C. Shorter 10 vols New York 1922 (Temple Bar edn). Original introds by A. L. Reade, A. Birrell, W. P. Trent, G. K. Chesterton, A. E. Newton, J. Drinkwater (rptd in his Muse in council 1925), R. B. Adam, W. de la Mare, C. B. Tinker and R. A. King. Bibliographical introd by C. Shorter.

Murry, J. M. Was Boswell a fool? Nation (London) 7 Oct 1922.

Roberts, S. C. Dr Johnson in Cambridge: essays in Boswellian imitation. Cambridge 1922.

— More Boswell letters. TLS 1 Jan 1954. Letters from Boswell to Robert Boswell, now at Yale.

— Pepys and Boswell. In his Dr Johnson and others, Cambridge 1958.

Simpson, T. B. Boswell as an advocate. Juridical Rev 34 1922.

Smith, M. S. Ms notes by Mme Piozzi in a copy of Boswell's Life of Johnson. London Mercury Jan 1922; rptd in Living Age 4 March 1922.

Roth, G. Boswell and Rousseau. London Mercury Sept 1923.

Whibley, L. Boswell's journals. Blackwood's Mag March 1923.

— Boswell without Johnson. Blackwood's Mag Feb 1925.

Bacon, L. Evening in Great Portland street: Boswell speaks to his son Alexander, a poem. Literary Rev 15 March 1924.

Cross, W. L. In his Outline of biography from Plutarch to Strachey, New York 1924. Rptd from Yale Rev 11 1922.

Murdock, K. Earl Percy dines abroad: a Boswellian episode. Boston 1924.

Pottle, F. A. Bozzy and Yorick. Blackwood's Mag March 1925.

— The incredible Boswell. Blackwood's Mag Aug 1925.

— The part played by Walpole and Boswell in the quarrel between Rousseau and Hume. PQ 4–5 1925–6. Superseded by rev and greatly expanded version in Horace Walpole: writer, politician and connoisseur, ed W. H. Smith, New Haven 1967.

— Three new legal ballads by Boswell. Juridical Rev 37 1925.

— See under C. B. Tinker, 1927, above.

— Boswell's shorthand. TLS 28 July 1932.

— Printer's copy in the 18th century [illustr by Isham ms of Tour]. PBSA 27 1933.

— Boswell and the girl from Botany Bay. New York 1937, London 1938; rptd in A. Woolcott, Second reader, New York 1937.

— The dark hints of Sir John Hawkins and Boswell concerning Johnson. MLN 56 1941. Superseded by rev and enlarged version in New light on Dr Johnson, ed F. W. Hilles, New Haven 1959.

— and C. H. Bennett. Boswell and Mrs Piozzi. MP 39 1942.

Pottle, F. A. The power of memory in Boswell and Scott. In Essays on the eighteenth century presented to David Nichol Smith, Oxford 1945.

— The life of Boswell. Yale Rev 35 1946.

— James Boswell, journalist. In The age of Johnson: essays presented to C. B. Tinker, New Haven 1949.

— Notes on the importance of private legal documents for the writing of biography [illustr with transcripts of Boswell legal documents collected by R. H. Isham in the Fettercairn litigation]. Proc of Amer Philosophical Soc 106 1962.

— Boswell as Icarus [as member of the Collegio d'Arcadia; the Arcadian calendar]. In C. Camden (ed), Restoration and 18th-century literature: essays in honor of A. D. McKillop, Chicago 1964.

— Boswell revalued. In C. Camden (ed), Literary views: critical and historical essays, Chicago 1964.

— Boswell's university education. In Johnson, Boswell and their circle: essays presented to L. F. Powell, Oxford 1965.

— Boswell: the earlier years. 1966.

Scott, G. The portrait of Zelide. 1925, New York 1927, 1959.

— The making of the Life of Johnson. Mt Vernon NY 1929 (priv ptd). Vol 6 of Private papers.

Strachey, L. Boswell. Nation (London) 31 Jan 1925, also in New Republic 4 Feb 1925; rptd in his Portraits in miniature, 1931.

Van Doren, M. First glance. Nation (New York) 25 March 1925.

— and R. H. Isham and J. W. Krutch. Boswell: the Life of Johnson. In his New invitation to learning, New York 1942. Transcript of unrehearsed radio dialogue.

Chapman, R. W. Boswell's proof-sheets. London Mercury Nov–Dec 1926; rptd in Johnson and Boswell revised by themselves and others, by D. N. Smith, L. F. Powell and Chapman, Oxford 1928.

— Johnson, Boswell and Mrs Piozzi. Oxford 1929.

— The making of the Life of Johnson. TLS 6 Feb 1930; rptd in his Johnsonian and other essays and reviews, Oxford 1953.

— Boswell's archives. E & S 17 1932.

— Two centuries of Johnsonian scholarship. Glasgow 1945.

— Boswell's editors. TLS 14 Sept 1946.

— Johnsonian and other essays and reviews. Oxford 1953.

Duke, W. Boswell among the lawyers. Juridical Rev 38 1926.

Lynd, R. In his Dr Johnson and company, 1927; rptd in his Essays on Life and literature, 1951 (EL).

Macphail, J. R. James Boswell, esq. Cornhill Mag July 1927.

Nicolson, H. The Boswell formula. In his Development of English biography, 1927.

Boswell and his father. Blackwood's Mag March 1928.

Pleadwell, F. L. Lord Mountstuart, Boswell's Maecenas. Amer Collector 5 1928.

Powell, L. F. The revision of Dr Birkbeck Hill's Boswell. In D. N. Smith et al, Johnson and Boswell revised by themselves and others, Oxford 1928.

— Boswell's original journal of his tour to the Hebrides and the printed version. E & S 23 1938.

— A task ended. 1950 (Johnson Soc, Lichfield).

— A Boswellian identification. TLS 30 March 1967. Richard How identified, name restored in Life 4. 181 n.

Buxton, C. R. Boswell's Life of Johnson. In his A politician plays truant, 1929.

Conjugal fidelity. 1929 (priv ptd, 30 copies), rptd in Life & Letters 5 1930. Text of original Qq3 of vol 2 of Life 1791.

Macphail, A. Johnson's life of Boswell. Quart Rev 253 1929.

Notes on sales: Boswell and Shakespeare problems. TLS 16 May 1929. Qq3 of vol 2 of Life 1791 alleged to exist in 3 states.

Salpeter, H. Dr Johnson and Mr Boswell. New York 1929.

Chauvet, P. L'Angleterre et la Corse. Revue Anglo-américaine 7 1930.

Fortescue-Brickdale, C. Dr Johnson and Mrs Macaulay: the credibility of Boswell. N & Q 16 Aug 1930.

Gould, R. T. The making of Boswell's Johnson. TLS 27 Feb 1930. Is Malone's 'burned' in a note in the 5th edn of the Life a misprint for 'buried'? See also F. A. Pottle, Boswell's executors, TLS 3 Nov 1927; J. N. Bryson 6 Oct 1927.

Inge, C. C. Two more Boswell letters. TLS 27 March 1930. To Ralph Churton.

Pearson, H. Ventilations. 1930. On Boswell's biographical method.

— Boswell as artist. Cornhill Mag Dec 1932. Adapted from preceding.

— and 'Hugh Kingsmill' (H. K. Lunn). Skye high: a tour through Scotland in the wake of Johnson and Boswell. 1937.

Pearson, H. Johnson and Boswell. 1958.

Blunden, E. C. A Boswellian error. In his Votive tablets, 1931.

Longaker, J. M. Boswell's Life of Johnson. In his English biography in the 18th century, Philadelphia 1931.

Cox, J. E. The independent Boswell and the capricious Dr Johnson. Quart Jnl of Univ of North Dakota 22 1932.

Elovson, H. Mr Kristrom in Boswell's Life of Johnson. MLR 27 1932.

Gallaway, W. F. Boswell and Sterne. Letters 5 1932.

Reilly, J. J. Bozzy: the man who made Johnson. In his Dear Prue's husband and other people, New York 1932.

Roughead, W. Boswell's queer client. In his In Queer Street, Edinburgh 1932; also in his Rascals revived, Edinburgh 1940. Boswell's professional association with James Gilkie.

Vulliamy, C. E. James Boswell. 1932.

— Ursa major: a study of Dr Johnson and his friends. 1946.

Kirwan, H. N. The Boswell supplement. London Mercury Feb 1933.

Rait, R. S. Boswell and Lockhart. Essays by Divers Hands 12 1933.

Schinz, A. Documents nouveaux sur Rousseau et Voltaire. Revue de Paris 15 May 1933, 1 June 1933. See also June 1952 (André Maurois); July 1953 (Maurois); April 1955 (extracts from French trn of Tour of the German courts by Célia Bertin); Sept 1956 (René Lalou).

Radecki, S. von. Englische Lieblingsbücher. Hochland Dec 1935.

Smith-Dampier, J. L. Who's who in Boswell? Oxford 1935.

Warnock, R. Boswell and Wilkes in Italy. ELH 3 1936.

— Boswell and Bishop Trail. N & Q 15 Jan 1938.

— Boswell and some Italian literati. Interchange Fortnightly 26 July 1940.

— Boswell and Andrew Lumisden. MLQ 2 1941.

— Boswell on the grand tour. SP 39 1942.

— Nuove lettere inedite di Giuseppe Baretti. Giornale Storico della Letteratura Italiana 131 1954.

Wecter, D. The soul of Boswell. Virginia Quart Rev 12 1936.

— Roving among the Hebrides. Yale Rev new ser 26 1937.

— Four unpublished letters from Boswell to Burke. MP 36 1939.

— Dr Johnson, Mrs Thrale and Boswell: three letters. MLN 56 1941.

Johnson, E. Eighteenth-century apogee. In his One mighty torrent: the drama of biography, New York 1937.

Young, G. M. Boswell—and unashamed. In his Daylight and champaign, 1937.

Fletcher, E. G. (ed). The life of Samuel Johnson with marginal comments and markings by H. L. Piozzi. 3 vols 1938. Combines marginalia from 2 copies.

— Mrs Piozzi on Boswell's and Johnson's tour. SE 32 1955.

Gray, W. F. New light on Boswell. Juridical Rev 50 1938.

— Boswell in the newer light. Quart Rev 283 1945.

Haraszti, Z. The life of Johnson. More Books March 1938.

Ramsay, J. Boswell's first criminal case. Juridical Rev 50 1938.

Bryant, D. C. In his Edmund Burke and his literary friends, St Louis 1939.

Hazen, A. T. Boswell's cancels in the Tour to the Hebrides. Bibl N & Q 2 1939.

Morley, E. J. Boswell in the light of recent discoveries. Quart Rev 272 1939. Based on Year's Work in Eng Stud 10–17 1929–36.

Roubíček, K. Strukturální povaha Boswellova Životopisu doctora Johnsona. Časopis pro moderní filologii, Prague 25 1939. Provided with English summary.

Togawa, S. Boswell's Life of Johnson as the theme of biographical study. Studies in English literature by the English Literary Soc of Japan, Tokyo 19 1939. In Japanese, title only translated.

Belloc, H. In his Silence of the sea and other essays, 1940.

Esdaile, A. Boswell in his diaries. In his Autolycus' pack, 1940. Rptd from Library Assoc Record Feb 1934.

— Boswell redivivus. Quart Rev 291 1953.

— and E. Esdaile. Boswell on the grand tour. Quart Rev 294 1956.

Keith, A. Boswell's Boswell. Listener 7 Nov 1940.

Murray, J. Some civil cases of Boswell 1772–4. Juridical Rev 52 1940.

— Notes on Johnson's movements in Scotland. N & Q 6 Jan 1940.

— Boswell in the Caledonian Mercury. N & Q 16 March 1940.

— Boswell and his ego: some bi-centenary reflections. TLS 26 Oct 1940. Anon.

Stauffer, D. A. In his Art of biography in 18th-century England, 2 vols Princeton 1941.

Wimsatt, W. K. Foote and a friend of Boswell's. MLN 57 1942.

— Boswell: the man and the journal. Yale Rev 49 1959; rptd in his Hateful contraries, 1965.

De Castro, J. P. Laetitia Hawkins and Boswell. N & Q 18 Dec 1943. Letters by Boswell et al to Francis Barber, seen by her in 1827.

Osgood, C. G. Lady Knight and her Boswell. Princeton Univ Lib Chron 4 1943. Anecdotes of the Johnsonian circle written by Lady Knight in her daughter's copy of the Life.
— An American Boswell. Princeton Univ Lib Chron 5 1944. *See* Rush, 1804, above, and Butterfield, 1946, below.
Bronson, B. H. Boswell's Boswell. In his Johnson and Boswell: three essays, Berkeley 1944; rptd in his Johnson agonistes and other essays, Cambridge 1946; also in his Facets of the Enlightenment: studies in English literature and its contexts, Berkeley 1968.
McCutcheon, R. P. Johnson and Boswell today. In Addresses made before the Friends of the Howard-Tilton Library of Tulane University, New Orleans 1944.
Hegeman, D. van B. Boswell and the Abt Jerusalem. JEGP 44 1945.
— Boswell's interviews with Gottsched and Gellert. JEGP 46 1947.
Meier, W. Johnson und Boswell. In Freundesgabe für Eduard Korrodi, Zürich 1945.
Quennell, P. C. Four portraits. 1945. On Boswell, Gibbon, Sterne and Wilkes. Boswell portion adapted from Boswell's progress, Horizon Dec 1942, June–July 1943.
— Books in general. New Statesman 21 Dec 1946.
— My admirable Margaret. Spectator 12 July 1957.
Abbott, C. C. Boswell. Literary & Philosophical Soc (Newcastle) 1946.
— New light on Johnson and Boswell. Listener 19 May 1949.
— Boswell's London journal. Listener 28 Dec 1950.
— Romantic Boswell. Listener 6 Oct 1955.
— Boswell for the defence. Listener 13 Oct 1960.
— Boswell's Journal of a tour to the Hebrides. Listener 26 Dec 1963.
Butterfield, L. H. Benjamin Rush's reminiscences of Boswell and Johnson. Princeton 1946 (priv ptd). Collects, expands and comments on matter in Rush, 1804, and Osgood, 1944, above. *See also* Autobiography of Benjamin Rush, ed G. W. Corner, Princeton 1948.
Hamm, V. M. Boswell's interest in Catholicism. Thought 21 1946. Collects nearly all the documentation in the journal.
Lewis, D. B. W. The hooded hawk. 1946, 1952 (as Boswell: a short life).
Tucker, W. J. Prince of biographers. Catholic World June 1946.
Carew Hunt, R. N. A fragment of Boswelliana. Nineteenth Century Nov 1947. Letters between Alexander, James and Euphemia Boswell and John Heaviside, surgeon.
Hetherington, J. The tour to the Hebrides: its value to the social historian. 1947 (Johnson Soc, Lichfield).
MacCarthy, B. G. Boswell: a problem. Studies 36 1947.
Price, C. Meetings with Boswell. TLS 8 March 1947. Reminiscences of Boswell by Richard Fenton.
Hitschmann, E. Boswell: the biographer's character. Psychoanalytic Quart 17 1948; rptd in his Great men: psychoanalytic studies, New York 1956.
Liebert, H. W. New York Times 8 Nov 1948. On the Boswell papers.
— Boswell's Life of Johnson 1791. Amer N & Q Sept 1962. Full list of cancels, press-numbers, incorrect foliation and textual 'points'.
The Malahide and Fettercairn papers. TLS 18 Dec 1948. *See also* The Boswell papers, TLS 12 Aug 1949.
Mossner, E. C. Dr Johnson in partibus infidelium? MLN 63 1948. On location of Boswell's house in Edinburgh at the time of Johnson's visit.
Copeland, T. W. Boswell's portrait of Burke. In The age of Johnson: essays presented to C. B. Tinker, New Haven 1949; extended in his Our eminent friend Edmund Burke, New Haven 1949.

— Unpublished Burke papers. TLS 30 Sept 1949. 3 letters from Boswell to Burke.
Gulick, S. L. Johnson, Chesterfield and Boswell. In The age of Johnson: essays presented to C. B. Tinker, New Haven 1949.
Spalding, P. A. In his Self-harvest: a study of diaries and the diarist, 1949.
Wells, M. Boswell and the modern dilemma. South Atlantic Quart 48 1949.
Altick, R. D. The secret of the ebony cabinet. In his Scholar adventurers, New York 1950.
Auden, W. H. Young Boswell. New Yorker 25 Nov 1950.
Basso, H. Boswell detective story. Life 4 Dec 1950. Abridged in Reader's Digest March 1951.
Horne, C. J. Malone and Steevens. N & Q Feb 1950.
Lowry, W. Boswell, Scots advocate and English barrister. Stanford Law Rev 2 1950.
Smith, D. N. Johnsonians and Boswellians. 1950 (Johnson Soc, Lichfield).
Stevenson, R. The rivals: Hawkins, Burney and Boswell. Musical Quart 36 1950.
Wright, A. Defeating the forces of oblivion. Virginia Quart Rev 27 1951.
Baldwin, L. The conversation in Boswell's Life of Johnson. JEGP 51 1952.
De la Torre, L. The heir of Douglas. 1952.
Krutch, J. W. Close-up of Boswell. Nation (New York) 24 May 1952.
Leigh, R. A. Boswell and Rousseau. MLR 47 1952.
Plumb, J. H. Boswell abroad. History Today Aug 1952.
Yoklavich, J. Hamlet in shammy shoes. Shakespeare Quart 3 1952. Boswell's journal shows Thomas Sheridan to have been the first irresolute Hamlet.
Hoover, A. G. Boswell's first London visit. Virginia Quart Rev 29 1953. First pbn of a long letter from Boswell to Sir David Dalrymple 22 March 1760.
— Boswell's letters at Newhailes. UTQ 22 1955.
Muir, M. Dear Mrs Boswell. 1953. A novel based on Boswell's journal and letters.
Pritchett, V. S. Boswell's London. In his Books in general, 1953.
— Bachelor Boswell. New Statesman 6 July 1957.
— Boswell's Scottish conscience. New Statesman 29 Oct 1960.
Taylor, F. Johnsoniana from the Bagshawe muniments in the John Rylands Library: Boswell's use of the Caldwell minute. Bull John Rylands Lib 35 1953.
Cairnie, R. H. A letter [27 June 1764] from Lord Hailes to Boswell in Holland. N & Q Feb 1954.
— Boswell's projected history of Ayrshire. N & Q June 1955.
Garton, C. Boswell and Dr Gordon. Durham Univ Jnl 46 1954.
— Boswell's favourite lines from Horace. N & Q July 1958.
McLaren, M. The Highland jaunt. 1954.
— Corsica Boswell. 1966.
Shepperson, A. B. Boswell the lion hunter. Virginia Quart Rev 30 1954.
Denvir, B. Guillaume Martin. TLS 4 Nov 1955. On Boswell's companion in Rome.
Fifer, C. N. Dr Johnson and Bennet Langton. JEGP 54 1955.
— Boswell's Langton and the river Wey. N & Q Aug 1956.
— Boswell and the decorous bishop [Percy]. JEGP 61 1962.
Gregory, H. That impossible young man in Italy. New York Times Book Rev 22 May 1955.
Irving, W. H. The providence of wit in the English letter-writers. Durham NC 1955.
Kolb, G. J. Boswell and Johnson. Virginia Quart Rev 31 1955.
Kronenberger, L. Johnson and Boswell. In his Republic of letters, New York 1955.

'Maurois, André' (E. S. W. Herzog). La jeunesse de Boswell. In his Portraits, 1955. Rev and rptd from Revue de Paris June 1952, July 1953 and the prefaces of the French trns of Boswell's London journal, 1952 and Boswell on the grand tour: Germany and Switzerland, 1955.

Collins, P. A. W. James Boswell. 1956 (Br Council pamphlet).

— Boswell's contact with Johnson. N & Q April 1956.

Duesberg, J. Boswell l'incorrigible. Synthèses March 1956.

Reid, B. L. Johnson's Life of Boswell. Keynon Rev 18 1956.

Sheldon, E. K. Boswell's English in the London journal. PMLA 71 1956.

Sherbo, A. Gleanings from Boswell's notebook. N & Q March 1956.

Stucley, E. F. A Hebridean journey with Johnson and Boswell. 1956.

Edel, L. In his Literary biography, 1957.

Garraty, J. A. In his Nature of biography, New York 1957.

Todd, W. B. Cowper's commentary on the Life of Johnson. TLS 15 March 1957.

Corrigan, B. Guerrazzi, Boswell and Corsica. Italica 35 1958.

Dilworth, E. N. Boswell in America. N & Q May 1958. Extracts from Corsica in Bickerstaff's Boston Almanack for 1769.

Lucas, F. L. In his Search for good sense: Johnson, Chesterfield, Boswell, Goldsmith, 1958.

Morgan, H. A. Boswell and Macaulay. Contemporary Rev Jan 1958.

de Beer, E. S. Macaulay and Croker: the review of Croker's Boswell. RES new ser 10 1959.

Frank, T. Two notes on Giuseppe Baretti in England, 1: Baretti and Boswell. Annali Instituto Universitario Orientale Napoli (Sezione Germanica) 2 1959.

Gray, J. Boswell's brother confessor W. J. Temple. Tennessee Stud in Lit 4 1959.

Hyde, D. and M. Dr Johnson's second wife. In New light on Dr Johnson, ed F. W. Hilles, New Haven 1959.

Lonsdale, R. Dr Burney and the integrity of Boswell's quotations. PBSA 53 1959.

Davis, B. H. Johnson before Boswell: a study of Sir John Hawkins' Life of Johnson. New Haven 1960.

Hart, F. R. Boswell and the Romantics: a chapter in the history of biographical theory. ELH 27 1960.

Lyall, A. The case of Dr Memis. Medical History 4 1960.

Hamilton, H. W. Boswell's suppression of a paragraph in Rambler 60. MLN 76 1961.

Morgan, L. Boswell's portrait of Goldsmith. In Studies in honor of J. C. Hodges and Alwin Thaler, ed R. B. Davis and J. L. Livesay, Knoxville 1961.

Stewart, M. M. Boswell's denominational dilemma. PMLA 76 1961.

— Boswell and the infidels. Stud in Eng Lit 1500–1900 4 1964.

— James Hervey's influence on Boswell. Amer N & Q 4 1966.

— Boswell and the National Church of Scotland. HLQ 30 1967.

Verosky, Sr M. V. John Walker's 'one clergyman'. N & Q April 1961. On Life 4. 206.

Dankert, C. E. Adam Smith and Boswell. Queen's Quart 68 1962.

Fussell, P. F. The force of literary memory in Boswell's London journal. Stud in Eng Lit 1500–1900 2 1962.

— The memorable scenes of Mr Boswell. Encounter May 1967.

Hodgart, M. J. C. Samuel Johnson and his times. 1962.

Kiley, F. S. Boswell's literary art in the London journal. College Eng May 1962.

McElderry, B. R. Boswell in 1790–1: two unpublished comments. N & Q July 1962. By Mrs Boscawen and Mrs Alison in letters to Mrs Montagu.

Mitchell, S. O. Johnson and Cocker's Arithmetic. PBSA 56 1962.

Tillinghast, A. J. The moral and philosophical basis of Johnson's and Boswell's idea of biography. In Johnsonian studies, ed M. Wahba, Cairo 1962.

— Boswell playing a part. Renaissance & Modern Stud 9 1965.

Balliett, W. Johnson père, Boswell fils. New Yorker 29 June 1963.

Molin, S. E. Boswell's account of the Johnson-Wilkes meeting. Stud in Eng Lit 1500–1900 3 1963.

Trevor-Roper, H. Noble prospects. New Statesman 26 July 1963.

Werkmeister, L. Jemmie Boswell and the London daily press. BNYPL Feb–March 1963.

Day, D. Boswell, Corsica and Paoli. E Studies 45 1964.

Golden, J. L. Boswell on rhetoric and belles-lettres. Quart Jnl of Speech 50 1964.

Greene, D. J. Reflections on a literary anniversary. Queen's Quart 70 1964. Deplores the effect of the Life on Johnson's reputation.

Ross, I. Boswell in search of a father? or a subject? REL 5 1964.

Brady, F. Boswell's political career. New Haven 1965.

Isles, D. E. Other letters in the Lennox collection. TLS 5 Aug 1965.

Jack, I. Two biographers: Lockhart and Boswell. In Johnson, Boswell and their circle: essays presented to L. F. Powell, Oxford 1965.

Lascelles, M. Notions and facts: Johnson and Boswell on their travels. Ibid.

Lustig, I. S. Boswell on politics in the Life of Johnson. PMLA 80 1965.

— Boswell's literary criticism in the Life of Johnson. Stud in Eng Lit 1500–1900 6 1966.

Pettit, H. Boswell and Young's Night thoughts. N & Q Jan 1965. Passage referred to in Life 4. 61 wrongly identified.

Rae, T. I. and W. Beattie. Boswell and the Advocates' Library. In Johnson, Boswell and their circle: essays presented to L. F. Powell, Oxford 1965.

Brooks, A. R. The Scottish education of Boswell. Stud in Scottish Lit 3 1966.

Burbank, P. N. The moment's fool. Listener 1 Sept 1966.

Burgess, A. A biographer for a biographer. Guardian 5 Aug 1966.

Butt, J. Biography in the hands of Walton, Johnson and Boswell. Los Angeles 1966 (Ewing lectures). Portion on Boswell incorporates part of Butt's inaugural lecture at Edinburgh 1959.

Jaarsma, R. J. Boswell the novelist: structural rhythms in the London journal. North Dakota Quart 34 1966.

Morris, J. N. In his Versions of the self, New York 1966.

Reed, J. W. Boswell and the Major [James George Semple]. Kenyon Rev 28 1966.

— In his English biography in the early 19th century, New Haven 1966.

Reiberg, R. Boswell's personal correspondence: the dramatized quest for identity. In The familiar letter in the 18th century, ed H. Anderson et al, Lawrence Kansas 1966.

Wain, J. A singular being. New York Rev of Books 9 June 1966.

Cole, R. C. The Sitwells and Boswell: a genealogical study. Genealogists' Mag 15 1967. Common descent from Sir John Cochrane of Ochiltree, d.c. 1707.

Cruttwell, P. Pottle's Boswell. Hudson Rev 19 1967.

Davis, E. C. An epigram on Boswell. N & Q May 1967. On the Tour, from Jackson's Oxford journal.

Schalit, A. E. Literature as product and process: two differing accounts of the same trip [the Hebridean tour]. Serif 4 1967.

Brinitzer, C. Dr Johnson und Boswell: Begegnung und Freundschaft. Mainz 1968.

Core, G. Boswellian aether. Sewanee Rev 76 1968.

Hartley, L. A late-Augustan circus: Macaulay on Johnson, Boswell and Walpole. South Atlantic Quart 67 1968.

Rader, R. W. Literary form in factual narrative: the example of Boswell's Johnson. In Essays in 18th-century biography, ed P. B. Daghlian, Bloomington 1968.

Alkon, P. K. Boswell's control of aesthetic distance. UTQ 38 1969.

Amory, H. Boswell in search of the intentional fallacy. BNYPL Jan 1969.

McAdam, E. L. Johnson and Boswell: a survey of their writings. Boston 1969.

F. A. P.

WILLIAM GODWIN
1756–1836

Bibliographies etc

[Sotheby's]. Catalogue of the curious library of William Godwin esq. 1836.

Cordasco, F. Godwin: a handlist of critical notices and studies. Brooklyn 1950.

Shirai, A. Godwin kenkyu bunken i–iv. Mita Jnl of Economics (Tokyo) 52–3 1959–60.

Pollin, B. R. In his Education and enlightenment in the works of Godwin, New York 1962.

— Godwin criticism: a synoptic bibliography. Toronto 1967.

§ I

The history of the life of William Pitt, Earl of Chatham. 1783, 1783 (both anon), Dublin 1783, 1783; rptd in New annual register for the year 1783, 1784.

A defence of the Rockingham party, in their late coalition with Lord North. 1783 (anon); ed B. R. Pollin, Gainesville 1966 (in Four early pamphlets).

An account of the seminary that will be opened on Monday the fourth day of August at Epsom in Surrey. 1783 (anon); ed Pollin, with above.

Italian letters: or the history of the Count de St Julian. 1783; ed B. R. Pollin, Lincoln Nebraska 1965. Only known copy of 1783 in Bristol Public Library.

The herald of literature. 1784 (anon); ed B. R. Pollin, Gainesville 1967 (in Four early pamphlets).

Sketches of history in six sermons. 1784 (anon), 2 vols Alexandria Virginia 1801, 1802.

Damon and Delia. 1784? No known copy.

Imogen: a pastoral romance. 2 vols 1784. 2 known copies; see BNYPL Jan–June 1963 and col 1007, above.

Instructions to a statesman, humbly inscribed to the Earl Temple. 1784 (anon); ed B. R. Pollin, Gainesville 1966 (in Four early pamphlets).

History of the internal affairs of the United Provinces. 1787. Anon. Attributed to Godwin by J. W. Marken, PQ 45 1966.

An enquiry concerning the principles of political justice, and its influence on general virtue and happiness. 2 vols 1793, Dublin 1793, London 1796 ('corrected'), New York nd, London 1842; ed H. S. Salt 1890; ed R. A. Preston 2 vols New York 1926 (abridged); ed F. E. L. Priestley 3 vols Toronto 1946 (facs of 3rd edn with variant readings from 1st–2nd); tr German, 1803, 1904, 1948; Spanish, 1948.

Cursory strictures on the charge delivered by Lord Chief Justice Eyre to the Grand Jury, Oct 2 1794. 1794. Anon. Rptd from Morning Chron 21 Oct 1794; attributed to Godwin by B. R. Pollin.

A reply to an answer to Cursory strictures by the author of Cursory stricutures. 1794. Attributed to Godwin by Pollin.

Things as they are: or the adventures of Caleb Williams. 3 vols 1794, 2 vols Dublin 1795, 3 vols 1796 (2nd edn 'corrected'), 1797, 2 vols Philadelphia 1802, 3 vols 1816, 2 vols Philadelphia 1818, 1 vol 1824, 1826, 3 vols 1830,

1 vol 1831, 2 vols New York 1831, 1832, 1 vol New York 1838, Edinburgh 1839, London 1849, 1853, 1903, [1904]; ed V. Wyck Brooks, New York 1936; ed G. Sherburn, New York 1960; tr French, 1794, 1794, 1795, 1795, 1796, 1796, 1797, 1813, 1846–7, 1868, 1945; German, 1795, 1797–8, 1931, 1931; Polish, 1954; Russian, 1838, 1949. A play entitled The iron chest, founded on Caleb Williams by George Colman jr, was first acted at Drury Lane in 1796.

Considerations on Lord Grenville's and Mr Pitt's Bills concerning treasonable and seditious practices. [1795]. Anon.

The enquirer: reflections on education, manners and literature. 1797, Dublin 1797, Edinburgh and London 1823.

Memoirs of the life of Simon, Lord Lovat. 1797. Tr Godwin.

Memoirs of the author of a vindication of the rights of woman. 1798, 1798 ('corrected'), Dublin 1798, Philadelphia 1799, 1802, 1804; ed W. C. Durrant 1927 (with addns); ed J. M. Murry 1930; tr French, 1802; German, 1799, 1912.

Posthumous works of the author of a vindication of the rights of women. 4 vols in 2 1798. Godwin was the anon editor.

St Leon: a tale of the sixteenth century. 4 vols 1799, 1800, 2 vols Dublin 1800, Alexandria Virginia 1801, 1802, 4 vols 1816, 1 vol 1831, 1829, 1849, 1850; tr French, 1799, 1800; German, 1800.

Antonio: a tragedy in five acts. 1800, New York 1806.

Thoughts occasioned by Dr Parr's spital sermon. 1801.

Life of Geoffrey Chaucer the early English poet, including memoirs of John of Gaunt, Duke of Lancaster. 2 vols 1803, 4 vols 1804; tr German, 1812.

Fables ancient and modern adapted for the use of children. 1805, 1821 (9th edn) etc; tr French, 1806. By 'Edward Baldwin'.

Fleetwood: or the new man of feeling. 3 vols 1805, 2 vols New York 1805, Alexandria Virginia 1805, 1 vol 1832 (vol 22 of Standard Authors, 'revised with a new preface'), 1849, 1853; tr French, 1805; German, 1806.

The looking glass: a true history of the early years of an artist. 1805, 1885 (facs). By 'Theophilus Marcliffe'.

The history of England. 1806 etc. By 'Edward Baldwin'.

The life of Lady Jane Grey and of Guildford Dudley her husband. 1806, 1809, 1815, 1824. By 'Theophilus Marcliffe'.

Faulkener: a tragedy. 1807.

Essay on sepulchres. 1809, New York 1809.

The lives of Edward and John Philips, nephews and pupils of Milton. 1815.

Letters of Verax to the editors of the Morning Chronicle on the question of a war to be commenced for the purpose of putting an end to the possession of the supreme power in France by Napoleon Buonaparte. 1815. Anon.

Mandeville: a tale of the seventeenth century in England. 3 vols Edinburgh and London 1817, 2 vols New York 1818, Philadelphia 1818; tr French, 1818.

Letter of advice to a young American. 1818.

Of population: an answer to Mr Malthus's essay. 1820; tr French, 1821.

Valperga: a novel by Mary Shelley. 1823. Rev and pbd by Godwin.

History of the commonwealth of England from its commencement to the Restoration of Charles the Second. 4 vols 1824–8.

Cloudesley: a tale. 3 vols 1830, 1830, 2 vols New York 1830; tr French, 1830.

Thoughts on man, his nature, productions and discoveries. 1831.

Deloraine. 3 vols 1833, 2 vols Philadelphia 1833.

Lives of the necromancers. 1834, New York 1835, 1847, London 1876, New York 1876.

The moral effects of aristocracy. [1835?] (with W. Hazlitt, The spirit of monarchy).

An essay on trades and professions. Manchester 1842. Rptd from Enquirer II.v.

Essays never before published. Ed C. K. Paul 1873.

The elopement of Percy Bysshe Shelley and Mary Wollstonecraft Godwin, as narrated by William Godwin. Ed H. Buxton Forman 1911, [Boston] 1912 (both priv ptd).

Uncollected writings 1785–1822. Ed J. Marken and B. R. Pollin, Gainesville 1968.

Godwin also pbd other children's books and elementary historical works by 'Edward Baldwin'.

Letters

Koszul, A. and G. Bresch. Une lettre de Godwin. Revue Anglo-américaine 6 1929.

Tragical consequences: or a disaster at Deal. Ed E. Blunden 1931. An unpbd letter dated 18 Nov 1789.

Letter to David Booth. Bodleian Lib Record 1 1941.

Loveman, S. Godwin and Shelley. TLS 23 March 1951. Replies.

Fleisher, D. Godwin to Shelley. TLS 27 April 1951.

Green, D. B. Letters of Godwin and Thomas Holcroft to William Dunlap. N & Q Oct 1956.

Cook, W. Two letters of Godwin. Keats-Shelley Jnl 15 1966.

Godwin and Mary: letters of Godwin and Mary Wollstonecraft. Ed R. M. Wardle, Lawrence Kansas 1966.

§2

For further articles and reviews, see B. R. Pollin, Godwin criticism, Toronto 1967.

Proby, W. C. Modern philosophy and barbarism: or a comparison between the theory of Godwin and the practice of Lycurgus. [1798?].

Malthus, T. An essay on the principle of population, with remarks on the speculations of Mr Godwin, Mr Condorcet and other writers. 1798 etc.

Green, T. An examination of the leading principle of the new system of morals in Mr Godwin's Enquiry concerning political justice. [1799].

Findlater, C. Liberty and equality: a sermon; to which is subjoined an appendix containing an analysis of Godwin's system of society in his Political justice. Edinburgh 1800.

[Fenwick, J.] Biographical sketch. In his Public characters, 1800; rptd Monthly Mirror 1805.

Scott, W. Godwin's Fleetwood. Edinburgh Rev 6 1805; rptd in his Miscellaneous prose works vol 18, 1835.

Shelley, P. B. (signed 'E.K.'). Remarks on Mandeville and Mr Godwin. Examiner 28 Dec 1817; rptd in his Prose works, ed R. H. Shepherd 2 vols 1888.

Lockhart, J. G. (signed 'T'). Remarks on Godwin's new novel Mandeville. Blackwood's Mag Dec 1817; rptd in Lockhart's literary criticism, ed M. C. Hildyard, Oxford 1931.

Remarks on Mr Godwin's Enquiry concerning population. 1821.

Rosser, H. B. Godwin against Malthus. 1821.

Place, F. Illustrations and proofs of the principle of population; including a reply to the objections of Mr Godwin. 1822.

Everett, A. H. New ideas on population; with remarks on the theories of Malthus and Godwin. 1823.

Hazlitt, W. In his Spirit of the age, 1825.

— Mr Godwin. Edinburgh Rev April 1830.

Hunt, L. Notices of new books. Tatler 7 April 1831; rptd in his Literary criticism, ed L. H. Houtchens and C. Washburn, New York 1956. Includes Caleb Williams.

[Shelley, Mary]. Memoirs of Godwin. New York nd. A reprint of prefatory memoir to Bentley's Standard Novels, 1831 etc, Paris 1832 (signed).

Cunningham, A. In his Biographical and critical history of the British literature of the last fifty years, Paris 1834.

Gilfillan, G. In his Literary portraits, Edinburgh 1845, 2 vols 1856.

Paul, C. K. Godwin: his friends and contemporaries. 2 vols 1876.

Stephen, L. William Godwin. Fortnightly Rev Oct 1876.

— Godwin and Shelley. Cornhill Mag March 1879.

— Godwin's novels. Nat Rev Feb 1902; rptd in Studies of a biographer: 2nd ser vol 3, 1902.

Salt, H. S. In his Literary sketches, 1888.

Kingsland, W. G. Shelley and Godwin. Poet Lore 10 1898.

Elsner, P. Percy Bysshe Shelleys Abhängigkeit von Godwins Political justice. Berlin 1906.

Meyer, J. Godwins Romane. Leipzig 1906.

Ramus, P. Godwin der Theoretiker des kommunistischen Anarchismus: eine biographische Studie mit Auszügen aus seiner Schriften. Leipzig 1907.

Saitzeff, H. Godwin und die Anfänge des Anarchismus im XVIII Jahrhundert. Altenberg 1907.

Gourg, R. Godwin: sa vie, ses œuvres principales. Paris 1908.

Simon, H. Godwins Ethik. Zukunft 17 1909.

— Godwin and Mary Wollstonecraft. Munich 1909.

Rogers, A. K. Godwin and Political justice. International Jnl of Ethics 22 1911.

Harper, G. M. Rousseau, Godwin and Wordsworth. Atlantic Monthly May 1912.

Brailsford, H. N. Shelley, Godwin and their circle. [1913] (Home Univ Lib).

Roussin, H. William Godwin. Paris 1913.

Jensen, A. Godwin, anarkismens förste vetenskaplige teoretiker och apostel. Falköping 1916.

Allen, B. S. The reaction against Godwin. MP 16 1918.

— Godwin as sentimentalist. PMLA 33 1918.

— Godwin and the stage. PMLA 35 1920.

— Godwin's influence upon John Thelwall. PMLA 37 1922.

Saintsbury, G. Bolshevism in its cradle. New World Nov 1919; rptd in his Collected essays and papers, 1923.

Brown, F. K. The life of Godwin. 1926.

— Notes on Skinner Street. PMLA 54 1939.

Kareyev, N. I. Godwin and his Political justice. Uchenyye Zapiski (Moscow) 3 1929.

Sen, A. Godwin and Shelley. Jnl of Dept of Letters of Univ of Calcutta 19 1930.

Brodtman, C. N. Godwin: der Theoretiker des individualischen Anarchismus. Kaldenkirchen 1931.

Partington, W. English papers and marginalia: Letter of advice to a young American. Bookman (New York) Aug 1931.

Roberts, C. W. Influence of Godwin on Wordsworth's Letter to the Bishop of Llandaff. SP 29 1932.

— Wordsworth, the philanthropist and Political justice. SP 31 1934.

Storr, M. S. L'amour et le mariage chez Godwin. Revue Anglo-américaine 10 1932.

Michaltschaff, T. Grundzüge, Stellung und Entwicklung der Philosophie der Godwins. Hamburg 1935.

Johns, D. S. Godwin, sentimentalist. Congregational Quart 17 1936.

Murry, J. M. Godwin: apostle of universal benevolence. TLS 4 April 1936. Anon; rev and rptd in his Heaven and earth, 1938.

MacMullan, H. H. Satire of George Walker's Vagabond 1799 on Rousseau and Godwin. PMLA 52 1937.

Woehler, E. Das Bevölkerungsproblem bei Malthus in seinem Gegensatz zu den Theorien von Godwin. Hamburg 1938.

Adams, M. R. Mary Hays, disciple of Godwin. PMLA 55 1940.

Evans, F. B. Shelley, Godwin, Hume and the doctrine of necessity. SP 37 1940.

Merchant, W. M. Wordsworth's Godwinian period. Comparative Lit Stud 4 1942.

Norman, F. A Godwin pamphlet. TLS 28 July 1942. On Letters of Berax, 1815.

Priestley, F. E. L. Platonism in Political justice. MLQ 4 1943.

Wilcox, S. C. A Hazlitt borrowing from Godwin. MLN 58 1943.

Deen, F. H. The genesis of Martin Faber in Caleb Williams. MLN 59 1944.

Glasheen, A. E. Shelley's first published review of Mandeville. MLN 59 1944.

Taylor, S. M. J. Godwin and Co: juvenile library and publication house in the early nineteenth century. Hornbook 20 1944.

Woodcock, G. Godwin. Politics 3 1946.

— Godwin: a biographical study. 1946.

— William Godwin. Univ Libertarian 3 1957.

Aldridge, A. O. Jonathan Edwards and Godwin on virtue. Amer Lit 18 1947.

Stone, E. Caleb Williams and Martin Faber: a contrast. MLN 62 1947.

Ewen, D. R. Godwin and Shelley. TLS 6 April 1951.

Fleischer, D. Godwin: a study in liberalism. 1951.

— On Godwin. TLS 27 April 1951.

Wilson, A. The novels of Godwin. World Rev June 1951.

Davenport, W. H. Shelley and Godwin's Essay on sepulchres. N & Q 15 March 1952.

Rodway, A. E. Godwin and the age of transition. 1952.

Cole, G. D. H. Godwin, Paine and Charles Hall. In his Socialist thought: the forerunners, 1953.

Day, H. A l'école de Godwin: la non-violence comme technique de libération. Brussels 1953.

Erdman, D. V. 'Blake' entries in Godwin's diary. N & Q Aug 1953.

— Blake and Godwin. N & Q Feb 1954.

Godwin, philosophe de la justice et de la liberté. Brussels 1953.

Grylls, R. G. Godwin and his world. 1953.

Koszul, A. Un disciple inconnu de Godwin. Etudes Anglaises 6 1953. On John Horseman.

Marken, J. W. Godwin's writing for the New Annual Register. MLN 68 1953.

— The canon and chronology of Godwin's early works. MLN 69 1954.

— Godwin's Instructions to a statesman. Yale Univ Lib Gazette 34 1959.

— Joseph Bevan and Godwin. Georgia Historical Quart 43 1959.

— Godwin and the Political Herald and Review. BNYPL June 1961.

— Godwin's Imogen rediscovered. BNYPL Jan 1963.

— Godwin's History of the United Provinces. PQ 45 1966.

Monro, D. H. Godwin's moral philosophy. 1953.

Patton, L. The Shelley-Godwin collection of Lord Abinger. Duke Univ Lib Notes 27 1953.

Stallbaumer, V. R. Holcroft's influence on Political justice. MLQ 14 1953.

Zaccaria, C. Godwin le constructeur: fédérations de personnes. Paris and Brussels 1953.

Preu, J. Swift's influence on Godwin's doctrines of anarchism. JHI 15 1954.

— Antimonarchism in Swift and Godwin. Florida State Univ Stud 19 1955.

— The Dean and the anarchist. Tallahassee 1959.

Albrecht, W. P. and C. E. Pulos. Godwin and Malthus. PMLA 70 1955.

Furbank, P. N. Godwin's novels. EC 5 1955.

Kuic, R. Revolucionarna misao persi bis selija a njegovim proznim i poetskim delima, njeni izvori razvoj i odnos prema idejama Godvina i Tomasa Pejna. Ljubliana 1956.

Blunden, E. Godwin's library catalogue. Keats-Shelley Memorial Bull 9 1958.

Cruttwell, P. On Caleb Williams. Hudson Rev 11 1958.

Kaymer, G. Der gesellschaftliche Optimus Godwins in seiner literarischen Darlegung. Cologne 1958.

Werkmeister, L. Coleridge and Godwin on the communication of truth. MP 55 1958.

Gross, H. The pursuer and the pursued: a study of Caleb Williams. Texas Stud in Lang & Lit 1 1959.

Marshall, W. H. Caleb Williams and the Cenci. N & Q July 1960.

Cameron, K. N. (ed). Shelley and his circle 1773-1872. 2 vols Cambridge Mass 1961.

Collins, H. William Godwin. Socialist Rev 8 1961.

Deen, L. W. Coleridge and the sources of Pantisocracy: Godwin, the Bible and Hartley. Boston Univ Stud in Eng 5 1961.

Pollin, B. R. Education and enlightenment in the works of Godwin. New York 1962.

— Primitivism in Imogen. BNYPL March 1963.

— Godwin's Letters of Verax. JHI 25 1964.

— Godwin's Fragment of a romance. Comparative Lit 16 1964.

— Verse satires on Godwin in the Anti-Jacobin period. Satire News Letter 2 1964.

— Poe and Godwin. Nineteenth-Century Fiction 20 1966.

— Godwin's letter to Ogilvie, friend of Jefferson and the Federalist propaganda. JHI 28 1967.

— Nicholson's lost portrait of Godwin: a study in phrenology. Keats-Shelley Jnl 16 1967.

Sharrock, R. Godwin on Milton's Satan. N & Q Dec 1962.

Sherburn, G. Godwin's later novels. Stud in Romanticism 1 1962.

Boulton, J. T. In his Language of politics in the age of Wilkes and Burke, 1963.

England, M. W. Further discussion of Godwin's Imogen: felix culpa. BNYPL Feb 1963.

Primer, I. Further discussion of Godwin's Imogen: some implications of irony. BNYPL April 1963.

McCelvey, G. Godwin's novels: theme and craft. Durham NC 1964.

Shirai, A. Godwin kenkyu. Tokyo 1964.

— On Godwin. Keio Economic Stud (Tokyo) 3 1965.

Duerkson, R. A. Caleb Williams, Political justice and Billy Budd. Amer Lit 38 1967.

Dumas, D. Things as they were: the original ending of Caleb Williams. Stud in Eng Lit 1500-1900 6 1966.

Farouk, M. O. Mandeville, a tale of the seventeenth century: historical novel or psychological study? In Essays in honour of William Gallacher, Berlin 1966.

Smith, E. E. and E. G. William Godwin. New York 1966.

Flanders, W. A. Godwin and Gothicism: St Leon. Texas Stud in Lit & Lang 8 1967.

Grob, A. Wordsworth and Godwin: a reassessment. Stud in Romanticism 6 1967.

Palacio, J. de. Etat present des études Godwiniennes: à propos deux livres récents. Etudes Anglaises 20 1967.

Rothstein, E. Allusion and analogy in the romance of Caleb Williams. UTQ 37 1967.

Storch, R. F. Metaphors of private guilt in Godwin's Caleb Williams. ELH 34 1967.

Rosen, F. Godwin and Holcroft. Eng Lang Notes 5 1968.

J. B.

MARY WOLLSTONECRAFT, Mrs WILLIAM GODWIN

1759-97

Collections

Posthumous works. Ed W. Godwin 4 vols 1798. Vols 1-2, The wrongs of woman; vols 3-4, Letters and miscellanies.

Select works, abridged by C. Jebb. [1912].

§ 1

Thoughts on the education of daughters. 1787.

Mary: a fiction. 1788 (anon), [1790?].

Original stories from real life. 1788, 1791 (illustr William Blake); ed E. V. Lucas, Oxford 1906.

Of the importance of religious opinions, translated from the French. 1788, 1791. Trn of J. Necker, De l'importance des opinions religieuses.

A vindication of the rights of men in a letter to Edmund Burke. 1790, 1790; ed E. L. Nicholes, Gainesville 1960.

Elements of morality for the use of children, translated from the German of C. G. Salzmann. 2 vols 1790, 1793, 3 vols 1791, 1792, Baltimore 1811, Edinburgh 1821.

A vindication of the rights of woman. Vol 1 (all pbd), 1792, 1792, Dublin 1793; ed E. R. Pennell 1892; tr French, 1792.

The emigrants. 1793, Dublin 1794; ed R. R. Hare, Gainesville 1964. Normally attributed to Gilbert Imlay before Hare's edn.

An historical and moral view of the origin and progress of the French Revolution. Vol 1 (all pbd), 1794.

Letters

Letters written during a short residence in Sweden, Norway and Denmark. 1796; ed H. Morley 1889.

Mary Wollstonecraft: letters to Imlay. Ed C. K. Paul 1879 (with prefatory memoir).

Love letters to Gilbert Imlay. Ed R. Ingpen 1908 (with prefatory memoir).

Thornton, R. H. A letter of Mary Wollstonecraft [1790?]. N & Q 28 April 1928.

Four new letters of Mary Wollstonecraft and Helen Maria Williams. Ed B. P. Kurtz and C. C. Autrey, Berkeley 1937.

Godwin and Mary: letters of William Godwin and Mary Wollstonecraft. Ed R. M. Wardle, Lawrence Kansas 1966.

§ 2

Colls, I. H. A poetical epistle addressed to Miss Wollstonecraft, occasioned by reading her essay on the rights of man. [1793?].

Godwin, W. Memoirs of the author of a Vindication of the rights of woman. 1798 etc, 1927, 1928.

D—N, citoyen. Vie et mémoires de Marie Wollstonecraft Godwin. 1802.

A defence of the character and conduct of the late Mary Wollstonecraft Godwin. 1803.

Pennell, E. R. Mary Wollstonecraft Godwin. 1885.

Rauschenbusch-Clough, E. A study of Mary Wollstonecraft and the rights of woman. 1898.

Robertson, J. M. In his Pioneer humanists, 1907.

Simon, H. William Godwin und Mary Wollstonecraft: eine biographisch-soziologische Studie. Munich 1909.

Taylor, G. R. S. Mary Wollstonecraft: a study in economics and romance. 1911.

Peabody (later Marks), J. P. A portrait of Mrs W.: a play. 1922.

Durant, W. C. Mary Wollstonecraft. TLS 28 June 1923.

—— Mary Wollstonecraft and Gilbert Imlay. N & Q 30 June 1923.

Routen, F. Mary Wollstonecraft and the beginnings of female emancipation in France and England. 1923.

Rusk, R. L. The adventures of Gilbert Imlay. Indiana Univ Stud 10 1923.

Linford, M. Mary Wollstonecraft 1759–1797. 1925.

James, H. R. Mary Wollstonecraft: a sketch. Oxford 1932.

Storr, M. S. Mary Wollstonecraft et le mouvement féministe dans la littérature anglaise. Paris 1932.

Woolf, V. Four figures 3: Mary Wollstonecraft. In her Second common reader, 1932.

'Preedy, G. R.' (G. M. V. Campbell). This shining woman: Mary Wollstonecraft Godwin. 1937.

Jeffry, S. Fuseli and Mary Wollstonecraft. TLS Feb 1941.

Nitchie, E. An early suitor of Mary Wollstonecraft. PMLA 58 1943.

Wardle, R. M. Mary Wollstonecraft, analytical reviewer. PMLA 62 1947. Reply by D. Roper, N & Q Jan 1958.

—— Mary Wollstonecraft. Lawrence Kansas 1952.

Harper, G. M. Mary Wollstonecraft's residence with Thomas Taylor the Platonist. N & Q Dec 1962.

J. B.

II. PERIODICAL PUBLICATIONS

The determining feature for inclusion is periodicity, whether the interval be a day or a year. With the exception of calendars, almanacs, annual reports of societies, army lists and books issued in pts, practically all pbns known or believed to have appeared in the British Isles at regular intervals at any time between 1 Jan 1660 and 31 Dec 1800 are listed, regardless of subject-matter.

R. M. Wiles, Serial publication in England before 1750, Cambridge 1957, explains how hundreds of books were issued in weekly, fortnightly or monthly 'numbers'; several sers of complete single plays were issued weekly, some newspapers issued regular supplements, and works of history, geography, biography and fiction appeared as instalments in many newspapers. These are not listed here; but it would be absurd not to include Goldsmith's Chinese letters, Johnson's Idler essays and other sers of essays which appeared regularly in newspapers. Yet a ser of essays, though numbered consecutively, does not comprise a periodical if those essays first appeared all together on the same date: Country common sense 1738 can properly be listed here only because nos 1–2 were ptd as original essays in Gloucester Jnl; 3–25 did not come out fortnightly but were pbd, with the rptd first 2 nos, in 3 vols 1738, 1739. Similarly Vicesimus Knox, Essays moral and literary 1782, though numbered consecutively, did not appear at periodic intervals and are not listed here. No attempt has been made to enumerate the many sers of written newsletters, but as they served the same purpose as newspapers a few references are given.

Some papers contain little or nothing that could be called either news or journalistic comment on current affairs but cannot be classed as periodical essays, magazines or reviews. For that reason the London section includes a group of papers under 'Miscellaneous'.

Where possible, the precise dates of first and final issues, if before 1 Jan 1801, are given; elsewhere the dates given are those of issues known to have survived, uncertainty concerning dates of first and last issues being indicated by interrogation marks. A dash followed by a full-stop indicates that the pbn is known to have continued either to the next date given (with altered title) or beyond Dec 1800. Dates prior to the change of the calendar in Sept 1752 are adjusted so that papers pbd between 1 Jan and 24 March are shown as belonging to the same year as those pbd in the 9 months which followed March.

A. BIBLIOGRAPHIES, HISTORY OF THE PRESS AND GENERAL STUDIES

Special studies of individual periodical pbns are listed immediately after the titles. Bibliographies and general studies referring exclusively to provincial, Scottish or Irish periodical pbns are listed in the respective sections below.

A compleat catalogue of all the stitch'd books and single sheets printed since the first discovery of the popish plot. 1680. 2 continuations.

Dunton, J. Dunton's whipping post: or a satire upon everybody; also the secret history of the weekly writers. 1706; rptd with The life and errors of John Dunton, ed J. Nichols 1818.

[Gay, J.] The present state of wit, in a letter to a friend in the country. 1711; rptd Los Angeles 1947.

The case of the coffee-men of London and Westminster, by a coffee-man. [1728].

The case between the proprietors of the news-papers and the coffee-men of London fairly stated. 1729.

Observations on the first six of the morning and evening papers, published by the subscribing coffee-men. 1729.

Verres and his scribblers: a satire. 1732.

GM Feb 1733.

'Marforio'. An historical view of the principles, characters, persons etc of the political writers of Great Britain. 1740; rptd Los Angeles 1958.

Oldmixon, J. Memoirs of the press, historical and political, for thirty years past, from 1710 to 1740. 1742.

The rise and utility of newspapers. Monthly Miscellany March 1774.

On the use and abuse of newspapers. Westminster Mag March 1785.

Crabbe, G. The newspaper. 1785. A poem.

[Almon, J.] Biographical, literary and political anecdotes of several of the most eminent persons of the present age. 3 vols 1797.

[Jones, S.] The spirit of the public journals. 14 vols 1800–14.

[Whitefoord, C.] Advice to the editors of newspapers. 1799.

Savage, J. An account of the London daily papers and of the manner in which they are conducted. 1811.

Nichols, J. Literary anecdotes of the eighteenth century. 9 vols 1812–16, New York 1967.

—— Illustrations of the literary history of the xviiith century. 8 vols 1817–58.

Hazlitt, W. On the periodical essayists. In his Lectures on the English comic writers, 1819.

—— The periodical press. Edinburgh Rev 1823.

Parkes, S. An account of the periodical literary journals which were published in Great Britain and Ireland from 1681 to 1749. Quart Jnl of Science, Lit & Arts 13 1822.

The periodical press of Great Britain and Ireland. Edinburgh 1824.

Lamb, C. Newspapers thirty-five years ago. Englishman's Mag Oct 1831; rptd in his Last essays of Elia, 1833.

Fifth report of the commissioners appointed to enquire into the management of the Post office. 1836. An account of price currents.

[West, W.] Fifty years' recollections of an old bookseller. 1837.

[Peters, A.] Historical sketches of British periodicals prior to the present century. Amer Eclectic 1 1841.

Timperley, C. H. An encyclopædia of literary and typographical anecdote. 1842.

Crossley, J. Works of the learned. N & Q 6 Nov 1852.

Advertisements. Quart Rev 97 1855.

Hunt, F. K. The fourth estate: contributions towards a history of newspapers and of the liberty of the press. 2 vols 1850. *See* review by T. K. Hunt, Eclectic Rev 27 1850; and The London daily press, Westminster Rev 64 1855.

Clarigny, C. Histoire de la presse en Angleterre et aux Etats-Unis. Paris 1857.

Andrews, A. The history of British journalism from the foundation of the newspaper press in England to the repeal of the Stamp act in 1855. 2 vols 1859.

Public Record Office. Calendar of state papers. Domestic series of the reign of Charles II [1660–85]. Ed M. A. E. Green et al 27 vols 1860–1938.

—— Calendar of state papers. Domestic series of the reign of William III [1689–1702]. Ed W. S. Hardy et al 1896–1937.

—— Calendar of state papers. Domestic series of the reign of Queen Anne [1702–4]. Ed R. P. Mahaffy 2 vols 1916–25.

The newspaper press of the present day: its birth and growth throughout the United Kingdom from 1665. 1860.

Knight, C. Shadows of the old booksellers. 1865, 1927.

[Burn, J. H.] Catalogue of a collection of early newspapers and essayists, formed by the late John Thomas Hope esq and presented to the Bodleian library by the late Rev Frederick William Hope. Oxford 1865.

Lee, W. Forgotten periodical publications. N & Q 20 Jan 1866.

—— Periodical publications during the twenty years 1712 to 1732. N & Q 27 Jan–3 Feb 1866.

Rowland, W. Cambrian bibliography: containing an account of books printed in the Welsh language or relating to Wales from the year 1546 to the end of the 18th century. 1869.

The newspaper press: its early history. Tinsley's Mag April 1871.

Grant, J. The newspaper press: its origin—progress—and present position. 3 vols 1871–2.

Rayner, W. Sunday newspapers. N & Q 14 Feb 1874.

—— The Caxton exhibition. N & Q 28 July 1877.

Sampson, H. A history of advertising. 1875.

Caxton collection: catalogue of the loan collection. Ed G. Bullen 1877.

Catalogue of periodicals contained in the Bodleian library. 2 vols Oxford 1878–80.

Public Record Office. Calendar of state papers. Home office papers [1760–5]. Ed J. Redington et al 4 vols 1878–99.

[Nicoll, D.] Publicity: an essay on advertising. 1878.

Scudder, S. H. Catalogue of scientific serials of all countries, including the transactions of learned societies in the natural, physical and mathematical sciences, 1633–1876. Cambridge Mass 1879, 1966.

Pebody, C. English journalism and the men who have made it. 1882.

Jackson, M. The pictorial press: its origin and progress. 1885.

Bourne, H. R. F. English newspapers. 2 vols 1887, New York 1966.

Stevenson, E. Early reviews of the great writers 1786–1832. 1890.

Stephen, L. The evolution of editors. Nat Rev 26 1896; rptd in his Studies of a biographer, 1898.

Hamelius, P. Die moralischen Zeitschriften und ihre Verfasser: die Kritik in der englischen Literatur des 17 und 18 Jahrhunderts. Leipzig 1897.

Bolton, H. C. A catalogue of scientific and technical periodicals 1665–1895. Washington 1897 (2nd edn).

Chaney, J. B. The historical value of newspapers. Minnesota Historical Soc Collections 8 1898.

British Museum catalogue of printed books: periodical publications. 1899–1900, Ann Arbor 1946, London 1963.

Davis, N. D. British newspaper accounts of Braddock's defeat. Pennsylvania Mag of History & Biography 23 1899.

[Edmond, J. P.]. Bibliotheca Lindesiana: collations and notes no 5: catalogue of English newspapers 1641–1666. Aberdeen 1901.

Cholmondeley, M. An art in its infancy [advertising]. Monthly Rev June 1901.

Marston, E. Sketches of the booksellers of other days. 1901.
— Sketches of the booksellers of the days of Dr Johnson. 1902.

Bowen, E. W. The essay in the eighteenth century. Sewanee Rev 10 1902.

Growoll, A. Three centuries of English booktrade bibliography. New York 1903.

Ames, J. G. The English literary periodical of morals and manners. Mt Vernon Ohio 1904.

Baldwin, E. C. The relation of the seventeenth-century character to the periodical essay. PMLA 19 1904.

Eckhart, J. H. Die moralischen Wochenschriften: die ältesten deutschen Nachahmungen der englischen moralischen Wochenschriften. Grenzboten 64 1905.

Catalogue of the pamphlets, books, newspapers, and manuscripts relating to the Civil war, the Commonwealth and Restoration, collected by George Thomason 1640–61. 1908.

'Williams, J. B.' (J. G. Muddiman). The newsbooks and letters of news of the Restoration. EHR 23 1908.
— A history of English journalism to the foundation of the Gazette. 1908.

[Muddiman, J. G.] Tercentenary handlist of English and Welsh newspapers, magazines and reviews. 1920, 1966. For addns and corrections see N & Q 29 Jan–5, 26 Feb, 26 March 1921, 11–18 March 1922.
— The King's journalist. 1923.

Barwick, G. F. Some magazines of the eighteenth century. Trans of Bibl Soc 10 1909.

Wellcome, H. S. The evolution of journalism. 1909.

Dix, E. R. McC. Rare ephemeral magazines of the eighteenth century. Irish Book Lover 1 1910.

Blair, E. H. Annotated catalogue of newspaper files in the library of the State Hist Soc of Wisconsin. Madison 1911.

Escott, T. H. S. Masters of English journalism. 1911.

Mainzer, P. Die schöne Literatur Englands und die literarische Kritik in einigen der kleineren englischen Zeitschriften des 18 Jahrhunderts. Leipzig 1911.

Origin and growth of the British newspaper. Times 10 Sept 1912.

Chancellor, E. B. The annals of Fleet street. 1912.

Dibblee, G. The newspaper. 1912.

Bell, W. G. Fleet street in seven centuries. 1912.

The history of advertising down to 1695. Times 10 Sept 1912.

Scott-James, R. A. The influence of the press. 1913.

Kitchin, G. Sir Roger L'Estrange: a contribution to the history of the press in the xviith century. 1913.

Symon, J. D. The press and its story. 1914.

Sell, H. A descriptive catalogue of some of the earliest newspapers collected by Mr Henry Sell. [1914].

News-books, newspapers, and periodical publications. 1914 (Ellis's winter catalogue no 156).

[Ellis]. A catalogue of old newspapers and periodicals of the 17th, 18th and early 19th centuries. No 276 1930.

Walker, H. The English essay and essayists. 1915.

Peet, H. W. A bibliography of journalism. 1915.

Haskell, D. C. Checklist of newspapers and official gazettes in the New York Public Library. New York 1915.
— A check list of cumulative indexes to individual periodicals in the New York Public Library. New York 1942.

Bleackley, H. A bibliography of forgotten magazines. N & Q 19 Aug 1916.

[Meyer, H. H. B.] List of references on advertising. Special Libraries 7 1916.

Stevens, D. H. Party politics and English journalism 1702–42. Menasha 1916.

Seitz, D. C. Paul Jones: his exploits in English seas: contemporary accounts collected from English newspapers. New York 1917.

Simonis, H. The street of ink. 1917.

Robbins, A. F. Evening papers: their evolution. N & Q 14 April 1917.

Durham, W. H. Some forerunners of the Tatler and the Spectator. MLN 33 1918.

Schmid, A. Die Stellung der englischen Frau nach den Zeitschriften zum Anfang des 18 Jahrhunderts. Zürich 1919.

McAra, T. W. English newspapers: their origin and development. Caxton Mag & British Stationer 21 1919.

[Peddie, R. A.] St Bride Foundation. Catalogue of the technical reference library of works on printing and the allied arts. 1919.

Sugden, E. H. Some references to Methodism in the periodical literature of the eighteenth century. Proc of Wesley Historical Soc 12 1920.

Gerould, J. T. Newspapers. In his Sources of English history of the seventeenth century 1603–89 in the University of Minnesota library, Minneapolis 1921.

Levy, L. Der Einfluss des moralischen Wochenschriften auf Richardsons Romane. Königsberg 1921.

Davidson, L. J. Forerunners of Goldsmith's Citizen of the world. MLN 36 1921.

Brown, J. T. T. James Boswell as essayist. Scottish Historical Rev 18 1921.

Silberling, N. J. British prices and business cycles 1779–1850. Rev of Economic Statistics 5 1923. On price currents.

Cannon, C. L. Journalism: a bibliography. BNYPL Feb–July 1923; New York 1924 (with addns).

Salmon, L. M. The newspaper and the historian. New York 1923.

Marr, G. S. The periodical essayists of the eighteenth century. 1923, New York 1924.

Tupper, C. F. Essays erroneously attributed to Goldsmith. PMLA 39 1924.

Graham, W. Some predecessors of the Tatler. JEGP 24 1925.
— English literary periodicals. New York 1930, 1967.

Leigh, A. Some old news letters 1727–8. Nat Rev 85 1925.

Hinkhouse, F. J. The preliminaries of the American revolution as seen in the English press 1763–75. New York 1926.

Crane, R. S. and F. B. Kaye. A census of British newspapers and periodicals 1620–1800. Chapel Hill 1927, 1967. See W. Graham, JEGP 28 1929; J. G. Muddiman, N & Q 3–24 Jan 1931 (replies, 7 March 1931).

Sherburn, G. Edward Young and book advertising. RES 4 1928.

McCutcheon, R. P. John Dunton's connection with book-reviewing. SP 25 1928.

Davies, G. Journalism. In his Bibliography of British history: Stuart period 1603–1714, Oxford 1928.

Laprade, W. T. The power of the English press in the eighteenth century. South Atlantic Quart 27 1928.
— Public opinion and politics in eighteenth-century England to the fall of Walpole. New York 1936.

Romer, C. Eighteenth-century advertisements. Nineteenth Century 1929.

Presbrey, F. The history and development of advertising. Garden City NY 1929.

Thompson, J. W. The origin and development of the newspaper. Rice Inst Pamphlet 17 1930.

Caskey, J. H. Truth and fiction in eighteenth-century newspapers. MLN 45 1930.

Birrell and Garnett Ltd. Catalogue 26: early newspapers. 1930. Also Catalogues 31 1931, 44 [1934].

Bleyer, W. G. Answers to correspondents in early English journalism. Journalism Quart 7 1930.
— The beginnings of English journalism. Journalism Quart 8 1931.

Gray, C. H. Theatrical criticism in London to 1795. New York 1931, 1964.

Gabler, A. J. Check list of English newspapers and periodicals before 1801 in the Huntington library. Huntington Lib Bull 2 1931.

Isaacs, G. A. The story of the newspaper printing press. 1931.

Newlin, C. M. The English periodicals and the novel 1709–40. Papers of Michigan Acad of Science, Art & Letters 16 1931.

Reesink, H. J. L'Angleterre et la littérature anglaise dans les trois plus anciens périodiques français de Hollande de 1684 à 1794. Amsterdam 1931.

Morison, S. The English newspaper. Cambridge 1932.
— The bibliography of newspapers and the writing of history. Library 5th ser 9 1954.
— The origins of the newspaper. 1954.

Bömer, K. International Bibliographie des Zeitungswesens. Leipzig 1932.

[Stewart, A.] Catalogue of an exhibition illustrating the history of the English newspaper through three centuries [Press Club]. 1932.
— The evolution of the English newspaper from its origin to the present day as illustrated by the catalogue of the Press Club collection. 2 vols 1935–46.

Stearns, B. M. Early English periodicals for ladies 1700–60. PMLA 48 1933.

Hatfield, T. M. John Dunton's periodicals. Journalism Quart 10 1933.

Richardson, Mrs H. The old English newspaper. 1933.

Smith, D. N. The newspaper. In Johnson's England, ed A. S. Turberville 2 vols Oxford 1933.

Stutterheim, K. von. Die englische Presse von ihren Anfängen bis zur Gegenwart. Berlin 1933; tr W. H. Johnson as The press in England, 1934.

Jackson, A. Play notices from the Burney newspapers 1700–3. PMLA 48 1933.
— The stage and the authorities 1700–14 (as revealed in the newspapers). RES 14 1938.

Hooker, E. N. The reviewers and the new criticism 1754–70. PQ 13 1934.
— The discussion of taste from 1750 to 1770 and the new trends in criticism. PMLA 49 1934.

Price, M. B. and L. M. The publication of English literature in Germany in the eighteenth century. Univ of California Pbns in Modern Philology 17 1934.

Sutherland, J. R. The circulation of newspapers and literary periodicals 1700–30. Library 4th ser 15 1934.
— Lost journals. Periodical Post Boy 6 March 1950.

Garrison, F. H. The medical and scientific periodicals of the 17th and 18th centuries, with a revised catalogue and check-list. Bull of Inst of History of Medicine 2 1934.

Barnes, S. B. The scientific journal 1665–1730. Scientific Monthly March 1934.
— The editing of early learned journals. Osiris 1 1936.

Weill, G. Le journal. Paris 1934.

Pollard, H. G. Serial fiction. In New paths in book collecting, ed J. Carter 1934; rptd separately 1938.

Lang, W. J. British and Irish newspapers before 1801. Irish Book Lover 22 1934.

Tubbs, F. A. Circulation of xvii-century newspapers. N & Q 5 Oct 1935. See also E. S. Chalk 9 Nov 1935.

Rosenfeld, S. The Restoration stage in newspapers and journals 1660–1700. MLR 30 1935.
— Dramatic advertisements in the Burney newspapers 1660–1700. PMLA 51 1936.

Hawke, E. G. A brief history of the British newspaper press. Bull of International Committee of Historical Sciences 7 1935.

Gelobter, H. Le Spectateur von Pierre Marivaux und die englischen Wochenschriften. Limburg 1936.

Milford, R. T. and D. M. Sutherland. A catalogue of English newspapers and periodicals in the Bodleian library 1622–1800. Oxford 1936.

Newton, T. F. M. William Pittis and Queen Anne journalism. MP 33 1936.

Grünbeck, M. Die Presse Grossbritanniens. 2 vols Leipzig 1936.

Newspapers in libraries of Chicago. Chicago 1936.

Sper, F. The theatrical press of London. Boston 1937.

Carlson, C. L. Richard Lewis and the reception of his work in England. Amer Lit 9 1937.

Roupell, M. G. Union catalogue of the periodical publications in the university libraries of the British Isles. 1937.

Le Fanu, W. R. British periodicals of medicine. Bull of Inst of History of Medicine 5 1938.

Henderson, J. M. James Fraser 1645–1731 [successor to L'Estrange]. Aberdeen Univ Rev 25 1938.

Tobin, J. E. Eighteenth-century English literature and its cultural background: a bibliography. New York 1939. Addns by D. F. Bond, Lib Quart 10 1940.

Bond, R. P. Some early English newspapers and periodicals at Yale. Yale Univ Lib Gazette 13 1939.
— Notes on advertising in early newspapers and periodicals. Antiquarian Booksellers' Assoc Annual: Books & the Man 1953.
— Contemporaries of the Tatler and Spectator. Los Angeles 1954.
— Studies in the early English periodical. Chapel Hill 1957. Introd.
— Growth and change in the early English press. Lawrence Kansas 1969.

The oldest newspaper. Newspaper World 1939. A ser of articles.

Grose, C. L. A select bibliography of British history 1660–1760. Chicago 1939.

Quinlan, M. J. Anti-Jacobin propaganda in England 1792–4. Journalism Quart 16 1939.

Stonehill, C. A., Ltd. English newspapers 1643–1869. Catalogue 138 [1939?]. See also later catalogues.

Joshi, K. L. Some conditions of the production of periodical literature about the year 1720. Bombay Univ Jnl 8 1939.

Periodicals, including newspapers and annuals. In W. T. and C. S. Morgan, A bibliography of British history 1700–15 vol 3, Bloomington 1939. Suppl in vol 5, 1942.

Goan, F. E. Union list of serials in Indiana libraries. Lafayette Indiana 1940.

Graham, R. X. A bibliography in the history and background of journalism. Pittsburgh 1940.

Lehmann, E. H. et al. Handbuch der Zeitungswissenschaft. Leipzig 1940.

Brittain, R. E. Christopher Smart in the magazines. Library 4th ser 21 1941.

Clark, D. E. News and opinion concerning America in English newspapers 1754–63. Pacific Historical Rev 10 1941.

Mayo, R. D. The Gothic short story in the magazines. MLR 37 1942.
— Gothic romances in the magazines. PMLA 65 1950.
— The English novel in the magazines 1740–1815; with a catalogue of 1375 magazine novels and novelettes. Evanston 1962.

French, J. M. Seventeenth-century English news-books. Jnl of Rutgers Univ Lib 7 1943.

Burnett, V. S. Seventeenth-century English newspapers and periodicals. Ibid.

Jaryc, M. Studies of 1935–42 on the history of the periodical press. Jnl of Modern History 16 1943.

Bragg, M. J. American news in English periodicals 1783–1800. HLQ 8 1945.

Aronson, A. The anatomy of taste: a note on eighteenth-century periodicals literature. MLN 61 1946.

Watson, M. R. The Spectator tradition and the development of the familiar essay. ELH 13 1946.
— Magazine serials and the essay tradition. Baton Rouge 1956.

Weed, K. K. and R. P. Bond. Studies in British newspapers and periodicals from their beginning to 1800: a bibliography. Chapel Hill 1946.

Babcock, R. W. A note on genius, imagination and enthusiasm in some late eighteenth-century periodicals. N & Q 8 March 1947.

— Benevolence, sensibility and sentiment in some eighteenth-century periodicals. MLN 62 1947.

Aspinall, A. Statistical accounts of the London newspapers in the eighteenth century. EHR 63 1948.

— Politics and the press c. 1780–1850. 1949.

— The reporting and publishing of House of Commons debates 1771–1834. In Essays presented to Sir Lewis Namier, ed R. Pares and A. J. P. Taylor 1956.

The periodical post boy. No 1, March 1948–?

Grayland, E. C. The value of newspaper sources for historical and other research. Auckland 1948.

Rochedieu, C. A. Bibliography of French translations of English works 1700–1800. Ed D. F. Bond, Chicago 1948.

Morgan, B. Q. and A. R. Hohlfeld. German literature in British magazines 1750–1860. Madison 1949.

Smith-Manden, W. H. Old English newspapers 1745–1825. Quart Rev 257 1949.

Fan, T. C. Chinese fables and anti-Walpole journalism. RES 25 1949.

Cordasco, F. A register of 18th-century bibliographies and references: a chronological quarter-century survey relating to English literature, newspapers, periodicals, printing and publishing. Chicago, Milan, Rome and Paris 1950.

Stewart, R. British newspapers and periodicals 1632–1800: a descriptive catalogue of a collection at the University of Texas. Austin 1950.

Berg, V. Holdings of 17th- and 18th-century English newspapers in the University of Illinois Library, Urbana. Coranto 2 1950.

Butress, F. A. Agricultural periodicals of the British Isles 1681–1900 and their location. Cambridge 1950.

Stone, G. W. Shakespeare in the periodicals 1700–40. Shakespeare Quart 2–3 1951–2.

Todd, W. B. Press figures and book reviews as determinants of priority. PBSA 45 1951.

— Bibliography and the editorial problem in the eighteenth century. SB 4 1952.

— On the use of advertisements in bibliographical studies. Library 5th ser 8 1953.

— The printing of xviith-century periodicals; with notes on the Examiner and the World. Library 5th ser 10 1955.

Mallaber, K. A. and P. M. de Paris. London union list of periodicals. 1951. Excludes those ending before 1800.

Herd, H. The march of journalism: the story of the British press from 1622 to the present day. 1952.

Brown, F. A. On education: John Locke, Christian Wolff and the 'moral weeklies'. Berkeley 1952.

Price, L. M. English literature in Germany. Berkeley 1953; tr German, 1961.

Blackburn, R. H. A joint catalogue of the serials in the libraries of the city of Toronto. Toronto 1953 (5th edn).

Ward, W. S. Index and finding list of serials published in the British Isles 1789–1832. Lexington Kentucky [1953].

Moore, J. R. On the use of advertisements as bibliographical evidence. Library 5th ser 9 1954.

Dukes, G. The beginnings of the English newspaper. History Today 4 1954.

Stewart, J. D. et al. British union-catalogue of periodicals: a record of periodicals of the world, from the seventeenth century to the present day, in British libraries. 4 vols 1955–1958 (with suppls).

Broome, H. H. Pierre Desmaizeaux, journaliste: les nouvelles littéraires de Londres entre 1700 et 1740. Revue de Littérature Comparée 29 1955.

Brown, W. C. A belated Augustan: Bonnell Thornton esq. PQ 34 1955.

Mellor, G. R. History from newspapers. Amateur Historian 2 1956.

Ewald, W. B. The newsmen of Queen Anne. Oxford 1956, Boston 1956 (as Rogues, royalty, and reporters).

Walcott, R. English politics in the early eighteenth century. Cambridge Mass 1956.

Check list of newspapers of the British Isles 1665–1800 in the American Antiquarian Society. Worcester Mass 1956.

Fraser, P. The intelligence of the secretaries of state and their monopoly of licensed news 1660–88. Cambridge 1956.

Bloom, E. A. Labours of the learned: neoclassic book reviewing aims and techniques. SP 54 1957.

— Samuel Johnson in Grub street. Providence 1957.

Williams, F. Dangerous estate: the anatomy of newspapers. 1957.

A complete list of the seventeenth-century newspapers in the Guildhall library. Guildhall Miscellany 8 1957.

Schwegmann, G. A. Newspapers on microfilm. Washington 1957 (3rd edn).

Union list of scientific serials in Canadian libraries. Ottawa 1957.

Peter Murray Hill, Ltd. Early newspapers and periodicals: catalogue 58 1957, 78 1961 etc.

Wiles, R. M. Serial publication in England before 1750. Cambridge 1957.

— Perfect diurnalls. Dalhousie Rev 42 1962.

Price, J. M. A note on the circulation of the London press 1704–14. Bull of Inst of Historical Research 31 1958.

Hill, P. M. Two Augustan booksellers: John Dunton and Edmund Curll. Lawrence Kansas 1958.

Thomas, P. D. G. The beginning of parliamentary reporting in newspapers 1768–74. EHR 74 1959.

Tilmouth, M. A calendar of references to music in newspapers published in London and the provinces 1660–1719. 1961.

Frank, J. The beginning of the English newspaper 1620–60. Cambridge Mass 1961.

[Haig, R. L.] News and advertisements. TLS 3 March 1961.

Werkmeister, L. Some account of Robert Burns and the London newspapers, with special reference to the spurious Star 1789. BNYPL Oct 1961.

— The London daily press 1772–92. Lincoln Nebraska 1963.

— Jemmie Boswell and the London daily press 1785–95. New York 1963.

— Chatterton and the London daily press 1792–6. N & Q Jan 1965.

— Collins and the London daily press 1788–98. N & Q June 1965.

— Thomson and the London daily press 1789–97. MP 62 1965.

— A newspaper history of England 1792–3. Lincoln Nebraska [1967].

Sackett, S. J. English literary criticism 1726–50. Fort Hays Stud, Lit Ser 1 1962.

Reid, L. Charles Fox and the London press. Quart Jnl of Speech 47 1961; also in Parliamentary Affairs 15 1962.

Stratman, C. J. Preparing a bibliography of English dramatic periodicals 1720–1960. BNYPL June 1962.

— A bibliography of British dramatic periodicals 1720–1960. New York 1962.

Hand-list of music published in some British and foreign periodicals between 1787 and 1848 now in the British Museum. 1962.

Kronick, D. A. A history of scientific and technical periodicals: the origins and development of the scientific and technological press 1665–1790. New York 1962.

— Scientific journal publication in the eighteenth century. PBSA 59 1965.

Shugrue, M. The rise of the weekly journal. N & Q July 1962.

[Gemmell, J.] The Mitchell library, Glasgow: catalogue of periodicals. Glasgow 1962.

Bole, R. and G. S. Darlow. A union list of periodicals in the learned libraries of Durham. Durham 1962.

Perry, T. W. Public opinion, propaganda and politics in eighteenth-century England. Cambridge Mass 1963.

Hanson, L. W. Contemporary printed sources for British and Irish economic history 1701–50. Cambridge 1963.

Rea, R. R. The English press in politics 1760–74. Lincoln Nebraska 1963.

Ritcheson, C. R. The London press and the first decade of American independence 1783–93. Jnl of Br Stud 2 1963.

Riffe, N. L. Contributions to a finding list of eighteenth-century British periodicals. BNYPL Sept 1963.

— Milton in the eighteenth-century periodicals: 'Hail, wedded love'. N & Q Jan 1965.

— Milton's minor poetry in British periodicals before 1740. N & Q Dec 1965.

Hart, J. Political writers of eighteenth-century England. New York 1964.

Freitag, R. S. Union list of serials: a bibliography. Washington 1964.

Sen, S. K. English literary criticism in the second half of the eighteenth century: a reconsideration. Calcutta 1965.

Titus, E. B. Union list of serials in libraries of the United States and Canada. 5 vols New York 1965 (3rd edn).

Bond, R. P. and M. N. Bond. The Tatler and the Spectator and the development of the early periodic press in England: a checklist of the collection of Richmond P. Bond and Marjorie N. Bond. Chapel Hill 1965.

Thomas, D. The story of newspapers. [1965].

Non-Scandinavian newspapers in libraries of Denmark, Finland, Norway and Sweden 1750–1963. Oslo 1966.

Spence, J. Observations, anecdotes and characters of books and men. Ed J. M. Osborn 2 vols Oxford 1966.

Whitford, H. C. Expos'd to sale: the marketing of goods and services in seventeenth-century England as revealed by advertisements in contemporary newspapers and periodicals. BNYPL Oct–Nov 1967.

Snyder, H. L. The reports of a press spy for Robert Harley: new bibliographical data for the reign of Queen Anne. Library 5th ser 22 1967.

— The circulation of newspapers in the reign of Queen Anne. Library 5th ser 23 1968.

Levin, Y. D. Angliyskaya prosvetitel'skaya zhurnalistika v russkoy literature xviii veka [English enlightenment journalism in Russian translations of the 18th century] In Epokha prosvescheniya [The epoch of the Enlightenment]. Ed M. P. Alekseev, Leningrad 1967. Appendix II has Materials for a bibliography of English journalism in Russian trns of the eighteenth century.

Pinkus, P. Grub street stripped bare. 1968.

B. PRINTERS, PRINTING AND RESTRICTIONS ON THE PRESS

The original returns of the Commissioners of Stamp Taxes up to 1855 were scheduled for destruction under the Public Record Office Act of 1877.

L'Estrange, R. Considerations and proposals in order to the regulation of the press. 1663.

Blount, C. Reasons humbly offered for the liberty of un-licens'd printing. 1693.

Gregory, F. A modest plea for the due regulation of the press. 1698.

Tindal, M. A letter to a Member of Parliament: shewing that a restraint on the press is inconsistent with the Protestant religion and dangerous to the liberties of the nation. 1698.

— Reasons against restraining the press. 1704.

A letter to a Member of Parliament: shewing the necessity of regulating the press. Oxford 1699.

Defoe, D. An essay on the regulation of the press. 1704; ed J. R. Moore 1948.

— A vindication of the press 1718. Ed O. C. Williams, Los Angeles 1951.

Reasons humbly offer'd to the Parliament in behalf of several persons concern'd in paper making, printing and publishing the halfpenny news papers, against the bill now depending for laying a penny stamp. [1712].

The printers proposal for a regulation of the press. [1712].

The printers' case, humbly offer'd to the honourable House of Commons. [1712].

The case of the poor paper makers and printers further stated. [1712].

The case of the manufacturers of paper, the stationers, printers etc of this Kingdom relating to several duties on paper and printing, now voted in the House; humbly represented to the honourable House of Commons. [1712].

The case of the company of parish clerks relating to the duties on pamphlets etc, humbly offer'd to the honourable House of Commons. [1712].

The case of the members of the Sun-fire-office, London, relating to the duties on newspapers. [1712].

[Addison, J.] The thoughts of a Tory author concerning the press; with the opinion of the ancients and moderns about freedom of speech and writings. 1712.

A collection of statutes now in force relating to the stamp duties. 2 vols 1716–22; Index by P. Pinckney, 1722.

[Toland, J.] Proposal for regulating ye news-papers. c. 1717 (BM Add ms 4295); rptd in L. Hanson, Government and the press 1695–1763, 1936, 1967.

State law: or the doctrine of libels, discussed and examined. 1729 (2nd edn).

A letter to a great man concerning the liberty of the press. 1729.

Arnall, W. The case of the opposition stated between the Craftsman and the people. 1731.

The doctrine of innuendo's discuss'd, or the liberty of the press maintain'd: being some thoughts upon the present treatment of the printer and publishers of the Craftsman. 1731.

The Craftsman's doctrine and practice of the liberty of the press explained to the meanest capacity. 1732.

Treachery, baseness and cruelty display'd to the full, in the hardships and sufferings of Mr Henry Haines, late printer of the Country Journal: or the Craftsman. 1740.

A complete alphabetical list of the stamp duties. 1745.

Smith, J. The printer's grammar. 1755, 1965.

A digest of the law concerning libels. 1765.

The freedom of speech and writing upon public affairs considered. 1766.

Luckombe, P. The history of the art of printing. 1771, 1966.

Pendred, J. The London and country printers, booksellers and stationers vade mecum. 1785, ed H. G. Pollard, 1955.

[Bell, J.] The new duty on paper. Oracle & Public Advertiser 21 April 1794.

An account of the rise and progress of the dispute between the masters and journeymen printers. 1799.

George, J. A treatise on the offence of libel; with a disquisition on the right benefits and proper boundaries of political discussion. 1812.

Holt, F. L. The law of libel. 1812, 1816 (enlarged).

Tournachon de Montvéran, J. E. De la législation anglaise sur la libelle, la presse et les journaux. Paris 1817.

Timperley, C. H. A dictionary of printers and printing. 1839, 1842 (as Encyclopaedia of literary and typographical anecdote).

Tilsley, H. Treatise on the stamp laws in Great Britain and Ireland. 1849 (2nd edn).

Routledge, J. Chapters in the history of popular progress chiefly in relation to the freedom of the press and trial by jury 1660–1820. 1876.

Dowell, S. The history and explanation of the stamp duties. 1878.

— The history of taxation and taxes in England. 4 vols 1888. Vol 3.

Paterson, J. The liberty of the press, speech, and public worship. 1880.

Katalog der Bibliothek des Börsenvereins der deutschen Buchhändler. 3 vols Leipzig 1885–1902. List of pamphlets on libel.

Böddecker, K. Die öffentliche Meinung und ihr Ausdruck in England im 16–17 Jahrhundert. Heidelberg 1886.

Ford, D. M. The growth of the freedom of the press. EHR 4 1889.

Fisher, J. R. and J. A. Strahan. The law of the press. 1891, 1898 (enlarged).

Collet, C. D. History of the taxes on knowledge, their origin and repeal. 2 vols 1899, 1933 (abridged).

Macfarlane, J. The paper duties of 1696–1713: their effect on the printing and allied trades. Library 1 1900.

— Pamphlets and the pamphlet duty of 1712. Ibid.

Select statutes, cases and documents to illustrate English constitutional history 1660–1832. Ed C. G. Robertson 1904, 1919, 1923 (4th edn, rev).

Foster, G. A. Pre-Victorian postage stamps and franks. 1910.

Morley, W. Catalogue and price list of the newspaper tax stamps of Great Britain and Ireland. 1912.

Thomas, J. M. Swift and the Stamp Act of 1712. PMLA 31 1916.

Shroeder, T. Free speech bibliography. New York 1922.

Plomer, H. R. et al. A dictionary of the printers and booksellers who were at work in England, Scotland and Ireland from 1668 to 1725. 1922.

— A dictionary of the printers and booksellers who were at work in England, Scotland and Ireland from 1726 to 1775. 1932.

Pollard, A. W. Some notes on the history of copyright in England 1662–1774. Library 2nd ser 3 1923.

Wickwar, W. H. Struggle for the freedom of the press. 1928.

Young, K. and R. D. Lawrence. Bibliography on censorship and propaganda. Eugene Oregon 1928.

Oswald, J. C. A history of printing: its development through five hundred years. New York 1928.

Morison, S. John Bell 1745–1831. Cambridge 1930.

Mumby, F. A. Publishing and bookselling: a history from the earliest times to the present day. [1930].

Caskey, J. H. The two issues of the World. MLN 45 1930.

Isaacs, G. A. Story of the newspaper printing press. 1931.

Thomson, M. A. The secretaries of state 1681–1782. Oxford 1932.

Clyde, W. M. The struggle for the freedom of the press from Caxton to Cromwell. 1934.

Turner, S. R. The newspaper tax stamps of Great Britain. 1936.

— Caricatures of the newspaper tax stamps of Great Britain and America 1765–1842. 1941.

— Some notes on the stamps of the Stamp Act 1765–6. 1945.

Siebert, F. S. Regulation of the press in the seventeenth century: excerpts from the records of the court of the Stationers' Company. Journalism Quart 13 1936.

— Taxes on publications in England in the eighteenth century. Journalism Quart 21 1944.

— Freedom of the press in England 1476–1776. Urbana 1952.

McKillop, A. D. Samuel Richardson, printer and novelist. Chapel Hill 1936.

Hazen, A. T. Eighteenth-century quartos with vertical chainlines. Library 4th ser 16 1936.

— Eustace Burnaby's manufacture of white paper in England. PBSA 48 1954.

Hanson, L. Government and the press 1695–1763. Oxford 1936, 1967.

Laprade, W. T. The freedom of the press: an outworn shibboleth? South Atlantic Quart 35 1936.

Jenkins, R. T. J. Lewis, the printer and his family. Proc of Wesley Historical Soc 21 1938.

McDowell, R. B. The Irish government and the provincial press. Hermathena 53 1939.

Plant, M. The English book trade. 1939, 1965 (rev).

Hughes, E. The English stamp duties 1664–1764. EHR 56 1941.

Pollard, H. G. Notes on the size of the sheet. Library 4th ser 22 1942.

Henderson, A. J. London and the national government 1721–42. Durham NC 1945.

Howe, E. The London compositor: documents relating to wages, working conditions and customs of the London printing trades 1781–1900. 1947.

Aspinall, A. Statistical accounts of the London newspapers in the eighteenth century. EHR 63 1948.

Povey, K. and I. J. C. Foster. Turned chain-lines. Library 5th ser 5 1950.

Sale, W. M. Samuel Richardson: master printer. Ithaca 1950.

Walker, J. The censorship of the press during the reign of Charles II. History 35 1950.

Bond, D. F. The first printing of the Spectator. MP 47 1950.

Dickerson, O. M. British control of American newspapers on the eve of the Revolution. New England Quart 24 1951.

Updike, D. B. Printing types, their history, forms and use. Cambridge Mass 1951 (2nd edn).

Rostenberg, L. John Martyn: printer to the Royal Society. PBSA 46 1952.

— Robert Stephens, messenger of the press: an episode in 17th-century censorship. PBSA 49 1955.

— Nathaniel Thompson: Catholic printer and publisher of the restoration. Library 5th ser 10 1955.

— Literary, political, scientific, religious and legal publishing, printing and bookselling in England 1551–1700. 2 vols New York 1965.

Smith, W. C. New evidence concerning John Walsh and the duties on paper 1726. Harvard Lib Bull 6 1952.

Stephens, J. C. Seven penny papers of my own. N & Q 29 March 1952. Replies 10 May 1952.

Labarre, E. J. Dictionary and encyclopaedia of papermaking. Amsterdam and London 1952 (2nd edn).

[Morison, S.] Printing the Times since 1785: some account of the means of production and changes of dress of the newspaper. 1953.

Inglis, B. The freedom of the press in Ireland 1784–1841. 1954.

Todd, W. B. The printing of eighteenth-century periodicals; with notes on the Examiner and the World. Library 5th ser 10 1955.

— Early editions of the Tatler. SB 15 1962.

Steinberg, S. H. Five hundred years of printing. 1955 (Pelican), 1961 (rev).

Balston, T. William Balston, paper maker 1759–1849. 1955.

Fraser, P. The intelligence of the secretaries of state and their monopoly of licensed news 1660–88. Cambridge 1956.

Ransom, H. The first copyright statute: an essay on An act for encouragement of learning 1710. Austin 1956.

Hetherington, J. R. Robert Walker, printer c. 1755. Library 5th ser 11 1956.

Haig, R. New light on the King's printing office. SB 8 1956.

Gaskell, P. The Strahan papers. TLS 5 Oct 1956.

Shorter, A. H. Paper mills and paper makers in England 1485–1800. Hilversum 1957.

Chandler, J. H. The story of the Stamford mercury postage and revenue stamps. Stamford [1958].

Coleman, D. C. The British paper industry 1495–1860. 1958.

Price, J. M. A note on the circulation of the London press 1704–14. Bull of Inst of Historical Research 31 1958.

Jarvis, R. C. The paper-makers and the excise in the eighteenth century. Library 5th ser 14 1959.

Thomas, P. D. G. John Wilkes and the freedom of the press 1771. Bull of Inst of Historical Research 33 1960.

Musson, A. E. Newspaper printing in the industrial revolution. Economic Historical Rev 10 1960.

Handover, P. M. Printing in London from 1476 to modern times: competitive practice and technical invention in the trade of book and Bible printing, periodical production etc. 1960.

— Red and black: the duty and postage stamps impressed on newspapers 1712–80, and on the Times or its postal wrappers from 1785 to 1962. 1962.

Bloom, E. A. Neoclassic 'paper wars' for a free press. MLR 56 1961.

Dowding, G. An introduction to the history of printing types from 1440 up to the present day. 1961.

Smith, A. H. John Nichols, printer and publisher. Library 5th ser 18 1963.

Bronson, B. H. Printing as an index of taste in eighteenth-century England. BNYPL Aug–Sept 1958; New York 1958.

Fleeman, J. D. 18th-century printing ledgers. TLS 19 Dec 1963.

— The reprint of Rambler no 1. Library 5th ser 18 1963.

Dreyfus, J. Type specimen facsimiles: reproductions of fifteen type specimen sheets issued between the sixteenth and eighteenth centuries. 1963.

Cochrane, J. A. Dr Johnson's printer: the life of William Strahan. 1964.

Clair, C. A history of printing in Britain. 1965.

Povey, K. Working to rule 1600–1800: a study of pressmen's practice. Library 5th ser 20 1965.

Berry, W. T. and H. E. Poole. Annals of printing: a chronological encyclopedia from the earliest times to 1950. 1966.

Thwaite, M. F. John Newbery: publisher and bookseller. Private Lib 8 1967.

Hernlund, P. William Strahan's ledgers: standard charges for printing 1738–85. SB 20 1967.

Davies, A. E. Paper-mills and paper-makers in Wales 1700–1900. Nat Lib of Wales Jnl 15 1967.

Snyder, H. L. The reports of a press spy for Robert Harley: new bibliographical data for the reign of queen Anne. Library 5th ser 22 1967.

— The circulation of newspapers in the reign of Queen Anne. Library 5th ser 23 1968.

Lambert, S. Printing for the House of Commons in the eighteenth century. Ibid.

Eaves, T. C. D. and B. D. Kimpel. The printer of the Daily Journal. In his Two notes on Samuel Richardson, Ibid.

McKenzie, D. F. and J. C. Ross. A ledger of Charles Akers, printer of the London Magazine. Oxford 1968.

Representative mss:

Public Record Office. T. 1/129/4 fols 147–8.

— Report of the inspector of franks. Chatham mss 196.

BM. Portland deposit. Harley mss list 2 miscellaneous mss ix nos 83, 90–107.

— Loan 29/162. Harley miscellany folder 60.

C. PERIODICAL ESSAYS PUBLISHED IN LONDON BY THEMSELVES, IN NEWSPAPERS, OR IN MAGAZINES AND MISCELLANIES

In addition to named series of essays, selected newspapers containing essays are included in present list, their titles marked in square brackets.

Belles lettres and other literary matter will be found in many of the early pbns listed as Miscellaneous and in those listed as Magazines, Miscellanies, Learned Journals and Reviews.

The philosophical observator. No 1, 22 Jan 1695; rptd in S. Morison, Ichabod Dawks. Cambridge 1931 (facs).

The weekly entertainment. No 1, 24 Oct 1700.

[The daily courant. 1702–35.]

Mercure scandale: or advice from the scandalous club. In A weekly review of the affairs of France, ed D. Defoe, no 2, 26 Feb 1704–. Continued as Advice from the scandal club, no 18, 5 May 1704–c. May 1705.

The little review: or an inquisition of scandal, consisting in answers of questions and doubts, remarks, observation, and reflection, by D. Defoe. No 1, 6 June 1705–no 23, 22 Aug 1705.

The wandering spy: or the way of the world inquired into. No 1, 9 June 1705–no 4, 30 June 1705.

Mercurius politicus: or an antidote to popular misrepresentations, by J. Drake. Vol 1 no 1, 12 June 1705–vol 2 no 51, 4 Dec 1705.

The tatler, by R. Steele, J. Addison et al. No 1, 12 April 1709–no 271, 2 Jan 1711. Continuations: (1) ?–no 272 4 Jan 1711–no 273, 6 Jan 1711 (sold by J. Baker); (2) nos 272–3, 6 Jan 1711–no 330, 19 May 1711 (sold by J. Morphew); (3) by W. Harrison, no 1, 13 Jan 1711–no 6, 30 Jan 1711 (pbd by Mrs A. Baldwin) and no 285, 3 Feb 1711–no 330, 19 May 1711, nos 285–330 being the same as nos 285–330 of continuation (2).

Oldisworth, W. Annotations on the Tatler, by W. Wagstaffe. 1710.

Original and genuine letters sent to the Tatler and Spectator during the time those works were publishing. Ed C. Lillie 1725.

Drake, N. Essays illustrative of the Tatler, Spectator and Guardian. 3 vols 1805.

Greenough, C. N. The development of the Tatler particularly in regard to news. PMLA 31 1916.

Durham, W. H. Some forerunners of the Tatler and the Spectator. MLN 33 1918.

Hendrix, W. S. Quevedo, Guevara, Lesage and the Tatler. MP 19 1921.

Neumann, J. H. Shakespearean criticism in the Tatler and the Spectator. PMLA 39 1924.

Graham, W. Some predecessors of the Tatler. JEGP 24 1925.

— Defoe's Review and Steele's Tatler: the question of influence. JEGP 33 1934.

— Addison's travel letters in the Tatler and the Guardian. PQ 15 1936.

Bateson, F. W. The errata in the Tatler. RES 5 1929.

Blanchard, R. Steele's Christian hero and the errata in the Tatler. RES 6 1930.

Papenheim, W. Die Charakterschilderungen im Tatler, Spectator und Guardian. Leipzig 1930.

Heinrich, J. Die Frauenfrage bei Steele und Addison. Leipzig 1930.

Gustafson, W. W. The influence of the Tatler and Spectator in Sweden. Scandinavian Stud & Notes 12 1933.

Garrison, F. H. Medicine in the Tatler, Spectator and Guardian. Bull of History of Medicine 2 1934.

Allen, R. J. Steele and the Molesworth family. RES 12 1936.

—— Contemporary allusions in the Tatler. MLN 55 1940.

Betz, S. A. E. The operatic criticism of the Tatler and Spectator. Musical Quart 31 1945.

Jackson, R. An unrecorded Tatler. TLS 7 Dec 1946.

Elliott, R. C. Swift's 'little' Harrison, poet and continuator of the Tatler. SP 44 1949.

Wheatley, K. E. Addison's portrait of the neo-classical critic. RES new ser 1 1950.

Loftis, J. The Blenheim papers and Steele's journalism PMLA 66 1951.

Turner, M. The influence of La Bruyère on the Tatler and the Spectator. MLR 48 1953.

White, R. B. A 'new' continuator of the Tatler. N & Q March 1956.

—— Character of the Tatler. PQ 45 1966.

Todd, W. B. Early editions of the Tatler. SB 15 1962

Achurch, R. W. Richard Steele, gazetteer and Bickerstaff. In Studies in the early English periodical, ed R. P. Bond, Chapel Hill 1957.

Bond, R. P. (ed). New letters to the Tatler and Spectator. Austin 1959.

—— The pirate and the Tatler. Library 5th ser 18 1963.

—— Mr Bickerstaff and Mr Wortley. In Classical and mediaeval and Renaissance studies in honor of Berthold Louis Ullman, Rome 1964.

—— Isaac Bickerstaff esq. In Restoration & eighteenth-century literature, ed C. Camden, Chicago 1964.

Humphreys, A. R. Steele, Addison and their periodical essays. [1959].

Klotz, G. Das Werturteil des Erzählers: Formen der Bewertung der epischen Gestalten im Tatler und Spectator. Halle 1960.

Goldgar, B. A. The curse of party: Swift's relations with Addison and Steele. Lincoln Nebraska 1961.

Winton, C. Steele, Mrs Manley and John Lacy. PQ 42 1963.

Bond, D. F. Armand de la Chapelle and the first French version of the Tatler. In Restoration and eighteenth-century literature, ed C. Camden. Chicago 1964.

Dixon, P. Pope and Steele. N & Q Dec 1965.

Gibson, G. H. and J. C. Gibson. The influence of the Tatler and the Spectator on the Monitor. Furman Stud 14 1966.

The female tatler, by Mrs Crackenthorpe, a lady that knows everything [T. Baker]. No 1, 8 July 1709–no 111, 31 March 1710.

Anderson, P. B. The history and authorship of Mrs Crackenthorpe's Female Tatler. MP 28 1931.

—— Splendor out of scandal: the Lucinda-Artesia papers in the Female Tatler. PQ 15 1936.

—— La Bruyère and Mrs Crackenthorpe's Female Tatler. PMLA 52 1937.

—— Innocence and artifice: or Mrs Centlivre and the Female Tatler. PQ 16 1937.

Milford, R. T. The Female Tatler. MP 29 1932.

Graham, W. Thomas Baker, Mrs Manley and the Female Tatler. MP 34 1937.

Smith, J. H. Thomas Baker and the Female Tatler. MP 49 1952.

Vichert, G. S. Some recent Mandeville attributions. PQ 45 1966.

The female tatler, by Mrs Crackenthorpe a lady that knows everything. No 19 (first issued), 17 Aug 1709–no 44, 17 Oct 1709. Spurious rival of the paper of the same name beginning 8 July 1709.

The whisperer, by Mrs Jenny Distaff, half-sister to Isaac Bickerstaff esq. No 1, 11 Oct 1709; rptd in Contemporaries of the Tatler and Spectator, ed R. P. Bond, Los Angeles 1954 (facs).

Titt for tatt, by Jo Patridge esq. No 1, 2 March 1710–no 6 [14 March 1710?]; rptd Los Angeles 1954 (facs).

The moderator. No 1, 22 May 1710–no 50, 10 Nov 1710.

The examiner: or remarks upon papers and occurrences. Ed W. King et al. Vol 1 no 1, 3 Aug 1710–. Continued as Examiner, no 4, 24 Aug 1710–vol 6 no 19, 26 July

1714. Second series: vol 1 no 1, 3 Nov 1714–vol 3 no 52, 10 March 1716. Pbn interrupted 26 July–6 Dec 1711; rptd seriatim in Dublin 1710–13. Nos 13–45 ed H. Davis, Oxford 1940.

Allen, R. J. William Oldisworth: the author of the Examiner. PQ 26 1947.

Needham, G. B. Mary de la Rivière Manley, Tory defender. HLQ 12 1949.

Todd, W. B. The printing of eighteenth-century periodicals: with notes on the Examiner and the World. Library 5th ser 10 1955.

Cook, R. I. The 'several ways of abusing one another': Jonathan Swift's political journalism. Speech Monographs 29 1962.

—— 'Mr Examiner' and 'Mr Review': the Tory apologetics of Swift and Defoe. HLQ 29 1966.

Serious thoughts: or a golden chain of contemplations. No 1, 15 Aug 1710–no 2, 17 Aug 1710; no 2 rptd Los Angeles 1954 (facs).

The visions of Sir Heister Ryley, with other entertainments, by C. Povey. No 1, 21 Aug 1710–no 80, 21 Feb 1711.

The Whig examiner, by J. Addison. No [1, as Examiner no 7], 14 Sept 1710–no 5, 12 Oct 1710; rptd 1712 (with Medley), 1789.

The medley. Ed A. Maynwaring et al. No 1, 5 Oct 1710–no 45, 6 Aug 1711; rptd 1712 (as Medleys for the year 1711), 1789 (in part). Some nos rptd Dublin 1711.

The Tory tatler. No 1, 27 Nov 1710–no 16, 3 Jan 1711.

The silent monitor. No 1, 18 Jan 1711–no 4, 24 March 1711. No 2 rptd in Contemporaries of the Tatler and Spectator, ed R. P. Bond. Los Angeles 1954 (facs).

The grouler: or Diogenes robb'd of his tub. No 1, 27 Jan 1711–no 6, 15 Feb 1711. Nos 1–2 rptd Los Angeles 1954 (facs).

The spectator, by R. Steele, J. Addison et al. No 1, 1 March 1711–no 555, 6 Dec 1712. Continued with no 556, 18 Jun 1714–no 635, 20 Dec 1714. For reprints see above, cols 000.

Drake, N. Essays illustrative of the Tatler, Spectator and Guardian. 3 vols 1805.

Wheeler, W. The spectator: a digest-index. 1892, 1897 (as A concordance to the Spectator).

Child, M. Mr Spectator and Shakespeare. Library 6 1905.

Legouis, E. Les deux 'Sir Roger de Coverley'; celui de Steele et celui d'Addison. Revue Germanique 2 1906.

Lewis, L. The advertisements of the Spectator. Boston 1909.

Umbach, E. Die deutschen moralischen Wochenschriften und der Spectator von Addison und Steele. Strasbourg 1911.

Salmon, D. The spectator. N & Q 21 Aug 1920.

Göricke, W. Das Bildungsideal bei Addison und Steele. Bonn 1921.

Streatfield, G. S. The mind of the Spectator under the editorship of Addison and Steele. New York 1923.

Neumann, J. H. Shakespearean criticism in the Tatler and the Spectator. PMLA 39 1924.

Casson, T. E. Wordsworth and the Spectator. RES 3 1927.

Heinrich, J. Die Frauenfrage bei Steele und Addison. Leipzig 1930.

Papenheim, W. Die Charakterschilderungen im Tatler, Spectator und Guardian. Leipzig 1930.

Tickell, R. Thomas Tickell and the eighteenth-century poets 1685–1740. 1931.

Gustafson, W. W. The influence of the Tatler and Spectator in Sweden. Scandinavian Stud & Notes 12 1933.

Garrison, F. H. Medicine in the Tatler, Spectator and Guardian. Bull of History of Medicine 2 1934.

Thorpe, C. De W. Addison's theory of the imagination as 'perceptive response'. Papers of Michigan Acad 21 1935.

—— Addison and Hutcheson on the imagination. ELH 2 1935.

Boyce, B. Two debits for Tom Brown, with a credit from Joseph Addison. PQ 14 1935.

Peterson, H. Notes on the influence of Addison's Spectator and Marivaux' Spectateur français upon El Pensador. Hispanic Rev 4 1936.

Price, L. M. Inkle and Yarico album. Berkeley 1937.

Saer, H. A. Notes on the use of themes taken from the Spectator in eighteenth-century French plays. Modern Languages 21 1939.

Bond, D. F. Pope's contributions to the Spectator. MLQ 5 1944.

—— The first printing of the Spectator. MP 47 1950.

—— The Spectator. Newberry Lib Bull 8 1952.

—— The text of the Spectator. SB 5 1953.

—— Introduction to the Spectator. 5 vols Oxford 1965.

Betz, S. A. E. The operatic criticism of the Tatler and Spectator. Musical Quart 31 1945.

Davis, K. A note on the Spectator 459. MLN 60 1945.

Bond, R. P. The Spectator: two notes. SP 42 1945.

—— A letter to Steele on the Spectator. MLQ 18 1957.

—— (ed). New letters to the Tatler and Spectator. Austin 1959.

Lewis, C. S. Addison. In Essays on the eighteenth century presented to David Nichol Smith, Oxford 1945.

Freeman, P. Who was Sir Roger de Coverley? Quart Rev 285 1947.

Atkinson, A. D. The Spectator no 543. N & Q 24 June 1950.

Stephens, J. C. Addison and Steele's Spectator [no 384]. TLS 15 Dec 1950.

—— Addison as a social critic. Emory Univ Quart 21 1965.

Lannering, J. Studies in the prose style of Joseph Addison. Upsala 1951.

Turner, M. The influence of La Bruyère on the Tatler and the Spectator. MLR 48 1953.

Hodgart, M. J. C. The eighth volume of the Spectator. RES new ser 5 1954.

Crum, M. C. A manuscript of essays by Joseph Addison. Bodleian Lib Record 5 1954.

Brauer, G. C. Recommendations of the Spectator for students during the eighteenth century. N & Q May 1955.

Kenney, W. The morality of the Spectator. N & Q Jan 1957.

—— Addison, Johnson and the 'energetick' style. Studia Neophilologica 33 1961.

Brunner, K. Joseph Addisons umfassende Interessen. Wiener Beiträge zur Englischen Philologie 66 1958.

Chambers, R. D. Addison at work on the Spectator. MP 56 1959.

Humphreys, A. R. Steele, Addison and their periodical essays. [1959].

Klotz, G. Das Werturteil des Erzählers: Formen der Bewertung der epischen Gestalten im Tatler und Spectator. Halle 1960.

Lonsdale, R. Dr Burney, John Weaver and the Spectator. BNYPL May 1960.

Friedman, A. B. Addison's ballad papers and the reaction to metaphysical wit. Comparative Lit 12 1960.

Bloom, E. A. and L. D. Bloom. Addison on 'moral habits of the mind'. JHI 21 1960.

Papajewski, H. Addison, Vergil und die Chevy Chase ballade. Anglia 80 1962.

Ito, H. The language of the Spectator, chiefly concerning the aspect of double meaning. Anglica 5 1962.

Morpurgo Tagliabue, G. La nozione di 'gusto' nel secolo xviii: Shaftesbury e Addison. Rivista di Estetica 7 1962.

Winton, C. Addison and Steele in the enlightenment. Studies on Voltaire & Eighteenth Century 27 1962.

Osborn, J. M. Addison's tavern companion and Pope's Umbra. PQ 42 1963.

Lovett, R. W. Mr Spectator in Bleak House. Dickensian 59 1963.

Elioseff, L. A. The cultural milieu of Addison's literary criticism. Austin 1963.

Dust, A. A. An aspect of the Addison-Steele literary relationship. Eng Lang Notes 1 1964.

Stevick, P. Familiarity in the Addisonian familiar essay. College Composition & Communication 16 1965.

Possin, H.-J. Natur und Landschaft bei Addison. Studien zur Englischen Philologie 8 1965.

Gibson, G. H. and J. C. Gibson. The influence of the Tatler and the Spectator on the Monitor. Furman Stud 14 1966.

Colombo, R. M. Le Spectator e i giornali veneziani del settecento. Bari 1966.

Jackson, W. Addison: empiricist of the moral consciousness. PQ 45 1966.

Hopkins, R. H. 'The good old cause' in Pope, Addison and Steele. RES new ser 17 1966.

Hansen, D. A. Addison on ornament and poetic style. In Studies in criticism and aesthetics, 1660–1800 presented to S. H. Monk, Minneapolis 1967.

Campbell, H. H. Addison's 'Cartesian' passage and Nicholas Malebranche. PQ 46 1967.

Kinsley, W. Meaning and format: Mr Spectator and his folio half-sheets. ELH 34 1967.

Gay, P. The spectator as actor: Addison in perspective. Encounter Dec 1967.

The miscellany. No 1, 28 April 1711–no 7, 9 June 1711; nos 1 and 6 rptd in Contemporaries of the Tatler and Spectator, ed R. P. Bond, Los Angeles 1954 (facs).

The pilgrim, by Don Diego Picolomini. No 1, 22 June 1711; rptd Los Angeles 1954 (facs).

The inquisitor. No 1, 26 June 1711; rptd Los Angeles 1954 (facs).

The hermit. No 1, 4 Aug 1711–no 30, 23 Feb 1712; 1714.

The surprize, by 'Humphry Armstrong'. [No 1, 16 Aug 1711]–no 4, 6 Sept 1711; no 4 rptd Los Angeles 1954 (facs).

The restorer, by F. Hoffman. No 1, 17 Aug 1711; rptd Los Angeles 1954 (facs).

The free-thinker. No 1, 17 Nov 1711–no 6, 3 Dec 1711. Nos 1–2, 5–6 rptd Los Angeles 1954 (facs).

A cry from the wilderness. No 1, 1 Jan 1712–no 3, 15 Jan 1712. No 2 rptd Los Angeles 1954 (facs).

The rhapsody. No 1, 1 Jan 1712–no 30, 8 March 1712.

The historian. No 1, 2 Feb 1712–no 13, 1 March 1712.

The rambler. [No 1, 1712]–no 4, 19 March 1712; no 4 rptd Los Angeles 1954 (facs).

The plain dealer, by W. Wagstaffe? No 1, 12 April 1712–no 17, 2 Aug 1712.

The medley. No 1, 3 March 1712–no 43, 28 July 1712.

The medley. No 21, 12 May 1712–no 45, 4 Aug 1712. Rival to contemporary of same name, above.

Poston, M. L. The Medleys of 1712. Library 5th ser 13 1958.

The medley, in the Flying-post from Paris and Amsterdam. No 3,255, 9 Aug 1712–no 3323, 15 Jan 1713.

The Christian's gazette, by J. Dunton. Jan 1713–April 1713.

Britain. No 1, 6 Jan 1713–no 37, 13 May 1713.

The monitor. No 1, 2 March 1713–no 21, 24 April 1713.

The guardian, by R. Steele, J. Addison et al. No 1, 12 March 1713–no 175, 1 Oct 1713. For reprints see col 1114, above.

Drake, N. Essays illustrative of the Tatler, Spectator and Guardian. 3 vols 1805.

Papenheim, W. Die Charakterschilderungen im Tatler, Spectator und Guardian. Leipzig 1930.

Garrison, F. H. Medicine in the Tatler, Spectator and Guardian. Bull of History of Medicine 2 1934.

Graham, W. Addison's travel letters in the Tatler and the Guardian. PQ 15 1936.

Templeman, W. D. Joseph Addison's 'man-planter'. N & Q 21 Nov 1942.

Luce, A. A. Berkeley's essays in the Guardian. Mind 52 1943.

Fineman, D. A. The motivation of Pope's Guardian 40. MLN 67 1952.

Stephens, J. C. Joseph Addison's 'man-planter'. N & Q Aug 1958.

De Stasio, C. Pope, Berkeley e il Guardian. Acme 19 1966.

The reconciler. No 1, 30 April 1713–no 25, 22 June 1713.

The Englishman: being the sequel of the Guardian, by R. Steele. No 1, 6 Oct 1713–no 57, 15 Feb 1714. Second series: no 1, 11 July 1715–no 38, 21 Nov 1715. First ser rptd 1714, second 1716; ed R. Blanchard, Oxford 1955. Some nos rptd seriatim in Dublin 1715.

Friedman, A. Goldsmith and Steele's Englishman. MLN 55 1940.

Hopkins, R. H. The issue of anonymity and the beginning of the Steele–Swift controversy of 1713–14: a new interpretation. Eng Lang Notes 2 1964.

The lay-monk, by R. Blackmore and J. Hughes. No 1, 16 Nov 1713–no 40, 15 Feb 1714; rptd as the Lay-monastery, 1714, 1727, 1754.

The balm of Gilead: or the healer of divisions, by T. Smith. No 1, 4 Jan 1714–no 10, 5 Feb 1714.

The lover, by R. Steele. No 1, 25 Feb 1714–no 40, 27 May 1714; ed R. Blanchard, 1959 (in Steele's periodical journalism 1714–16).

Dunton's ghost: or his speeches to the most remarkable persons in church and state, by J. Dunton. No 1, 4 March 1714–no 2, [20 March 1714?].

The patriot. Ed J. Harris. No 1, 20 March 1714–vol 3 no 25, 22 Jan 1715.

The reader, by R. Steele. No 1, 22 April 1714–no 9, 10 May 1714; ed R. Blanchard 1959 (in Steele's periodical journalism 1714–16).

The monitor. No 1, 22 April 1714–no 47, 7 Aug 1714.

Gibson, G. H. and J. C. Gibson. The influence of the Tatler and the Spectator on the Monitor. Furman Stud 14 1966.

The high-German doctor. Ed P. Horneck. Vol 1 no 1, 4 May 1714–vol 2 no 50, 12 May 1715; the High-German doctor concluded, 16 Aug 1715; rptd 2 vols 1715–19.

The muscovite. No 1, 5 May 1714–no 5, 2 June 1714.

The idler. No 1, 23 June 1714–no 5, 28 July 1714.

The controller: being a sequel to the Examiner. No 1, 8 Oct 1714–no 2, 15 Oct 1714–?

The spectator. Ed W. Bond. No 636, 3 Jan 1715–no 696, 3 Aug 1715.

The grumbler, by 'Squire Gizzard' [T. Burnet]. No 1, 24 Feb 1715–no 34, 15 July 1715.

Joost, N. Burnet's Grumbler and Ambrose Philips. N & Q 7 Aug 1948.

The observator: being a sequel to the Englishman. No 1, 25 Feb 1715–no 3, 4 March 1715.

The censor, by L. Theobald et al. No 1, 11 April 1715–no 30, 17 June 1715, and no 1, 1 Jan 1717–no 66, 1 June 1717. Latter ser rptd 1717 as nos 31–96.

The medley: or daily tatler, by 'Jeremy Quick' [J. Oldmixon et al]. No 1, 21 April 1715–no 15, 7 May 1715.

[The weekly journal: or British gazetteer. 1715–61.]

The daily benefactor. No 1, 2 May 1715–. Continued as Benefactor, no 13, 17 May 1715–no 24, 11 June 1715.

[The original weekly journal. 1715–37.]

Town talk, in a letter to a lady in the country, by R. Steele. No 1, 17 Dec 1715–no 9, 13 Feb 1716; rptd 1789, 1790; ed R. Blanchard 1959 (in Steele's periodical journalism 1714–16).

The tea table, by R. Steele? No 1, 17 Dec 1715–no 3, 2 March 1716.

The free-holder: or political essays, by J. Addison. No 1, 23 Dec 1715–no 55, 29 June 1716; rptd 1716, 1723, 1732, 1739, 1744, 1751, 1758; rptd seriatim, Dublin 1715–16; tr French, 1727.

McDonald, D. The 'logic' of Addison's Freeholder. Papers on Lang & Lit 4 1968.

The political tatler, by 'J. Standfast'. No 1, 19 Jan 1716.

Chit-chat, in a letter to a lady in the country, by 'Humphrey Philroye' [R. Steele]. No 1, 6 March 1716–no 3, 16 March 1716; ed R. Blanchard 1959 (in Steele's periodical journalism 1714–16).

Essays for the month of December 1716 [etc], by a Society of Gentlemen. Dec 1716–Jan 1718–?

The charitable mercury and female intelligence. No 1, 7 April 1716.

The weekly observator. No 1, 28 May 1716–no 11, 11 July 1716–?

The spectator. No 1, 13 June 1716–no 9, 8 Aug 1716.

The citizen. No 1, 22 June 1716–no 9, 20 July 1716.

The occasional paper, by S. Browne et al. Vol 1 no 1, 1716–vol 3 no 12, 1719. The 'Bagweel papers'. A few nos rptd 1717, 1718, 1719.

[The weekly journal or: Saturday's post 1716–37. Selected letters rptd 1722, 1732.]

The freeholder extraordinary. [No 1, Jan 1717?]–no 2, 29 Jan 1717–no 20, 7 June 1718.

The scourge, designed as a modest vindication of the Church of England, by T. Lewis. No 1, 4 Feb 1717–no 43, 25 Nov 1717; rptd 1717, 1720.

The wanderer, by J. Fox and D. Hanchet. No 1, 9 Feb 1717–no 26, 1 Aug 1717; rptd 1718.

The entertainer: containing remarks upon men, manners, religion and policy. No 1, 6 Nov 1717–no 43, 27 Aug 1718; rptd 1718, 1734.

The reprisal. No 1, 22 Nov 1717–no 4, 11 Dec 1717.

The occasional courant. Nos 1–30, 1717.

The critick, by T. Brereton. No 1, 6 Jan 1718–no 22, 28 May 1718; rptd 1719.

The free-thinker. Ed A. Philips. No 1, 24 March 1718–no 350, 28 July 1721; rptd 1722–3 (nos 1–159), 1733, 1739, 1740 (nos 1–159).

Joost, N. Henry Stephens [contributor to Free-thinker]. N & Q 3 Sept 1949.

— The Fables of Fénelon and Philips's Free-thinker. SP 47 1950.

— Gulliver and the Free-thinker. MLN 45 1950.

— Plain-dealer and Free-thinker. Amer Lit 23 1951.

— The authorship of the Free-thinker. In Studies in the early English periodical, ed R. P. Bond, Chapel Hill 1957.

The free-thinker extraordinary. No 1, 18 April 1718–no 6, 1 April 1719.

The weekly medley: or the gentleman's recreation. No 1, 26 July 1718–no 79, 23 Jan 1720.

The doctor. No 1, 6 Aug 1718–no 6, 22 Aug 1718.

The honest gentleman. No 1, 5 Nov 1718–no 25, 22 April 1719.

The Whigg. 1718.

The tea-table tatler: or the ladies delight. In the Orphan reviv'd: or Powell's weekly journal, 1719–20.

The mirrour. No 1, 5 Feb 1719–no 12, 23 April 1719.

The plebian, by R. Steele. No 1, 14 March 1719–no 4, 6 April 1719; rptd 1719, 1789, 1790.

Bloom, E. A. and L. D. Bloom. Steele in 1719: additions to the canon. HLQ 31 1968.

The old Whig, by J. Addison. No 1, 19 March 1719–no 2, 2 April 1719; rptd 1789, 1790.

The patrician; being considerations on the peerage, in answer to the Plebian, by Viscount Molesworth. No 1, 21 March 1719–no 4, 11 April 1719; rptd 1719, 1789, 1790.

The moderator, by R. Steele? No 1, 4 April 1719; rptd 1789, 1790.

The free-thinker extraordinary, to the Free-thinker in ordinary. No 7, 2 Dec 1719.

[The London journal. 1719–44.]

The commentator, by D. Defoe. No 1, 1 Jan 1720–no 74, 16 Sept 1720.

The theatre, by 'Sir John Edgar' [R. Steele]. No 1, 2 Jan 1720–no 28, 5 April 1720; rptd 1720, 1791; rptd Oxford 1962.

The British Harlequin. No 1, 5 Jan 1720–no. 2, 12 Jan 1720. Perhaps continued as the Merry-Andrew: or British Harlequin, no 3, nd 1720.

The independent Whig. Ed J. Trenchard and T. Gordon. No 1, 20 Jan 1720–no 53, 4 Jan 1721; rptd 1721, 1722, 1726, 1732 (with new matter), 1735 (nos 54–74 added as vol 3), 1741 (nos 54–74), 1743, 1747 (vol 4, nos 1–32), 1753, 1816.

The anti-theatre, by 'Sir John Falstaffe'. No 1, 15 Feb 1720–no 15, 4 April 1720. Continued as Theatre, by 'Sir John Falstaffe', no 16, 9 April 1720–no 26, 14 May 1720. Nos 1–15 rptd 1791; nos 9–26 rptd Los Angeles 1948.

Loftis, J. 'Sir John Falstaffe's' Theatre. JEGP 48 1949.

The Muses' gazette. Applebee's Original Weekly Jnl, 12 March 1720–9 July 1720.

The dependent Whig. [March 1720].

Sutherland, J. R. Lost journals. Periodical Post Boy March 1950.

The director. No 1, 5 Oct 1720–no 30, 16 Jan 1721.

Letters by 'Cato' in the London journal and in the British Journal. 144 nos 5 Nov 1720–27 Dec 1723.

Anderson, P. B. Cato's obscure counterpart in the British Journal 1722–5. SP 34 1937.

The advocate: or a vindication of the Christian religion. No 1, 9 Nov 1720–no 18, 8 March 1721.

Interviews in the realm of death, to be continued monthly: written originally in High-Dutch. 3 nos c. 1720.

Terrae filius, by N. Amhurst. No 1, 11 Jan 1721–no 52, 12 July 1721. Nos 1–50 rptd 1726, 1754.

The projector. No 1, 6 Feb 1721–no 8, 3 March 1721.

The fairy tatler. Weekly Jnl: or British Gazetteer Dec 1721–March 1722.

The freeholders journal. No 1, 31 Jan 1722–no 76, 18 May 1723.

The trifler, by 'Timothy Scribbler esq.' [No 1, ?]–no 6, 28 Nov 1722.

Pasquin, by G. Duckett et al. No 1, 28 Nov 1722–no 120, 26 March 1724; rptd 1791.

The true Briton, by Philip, Duke of Wharton. No 1, 3 June 1723–no 74, 17 Feb 1724; rptd 1723–4, 1732.

Allen, R. J. William Oldisworth: the author of the Examiner. PQ 26 1947.

The visiter. No 1, 18 June 1723–no 51, 31 Jan 1724.

The Briton. No 1, 7 Aug 1723–no 30, 26 Feb 1724; rptd 1724.

The instructor. No 1, 8 Jan 1724–no 7, 19 Feb 1724.

The tea-table, by E. Haywood. No 1, 21 Feb 1724–no 36, 22 June 1724.

The plain dealer, by A. Hill et al. No 1, 23 March 1724–no 117, 7 May 1725; rptd 1730, 1734.

McKillop, A. D. Peter the Great in Thomson's Winter. MLN 67 1952.

The inquisitor. No 1, 8 July 1724–no 2, 15 July 1724.

The monitor. No 1, 31 July 1724–no 5, 5 Sept 1724.

The speculatist, by M. Concanen. London Jnl and Br Jnl, 3 July 1725–26 Oct 1728; rptd 1730.

The advocate. No 1, 17 Feb 1725–?

Letters of 'Momus' in the London Journal. 1725.

The country gentleman, by E. Philips. No 1, 11 March 1726–no 84, 26 Dec 1726; rptd 1751. Some nos rptd seriatim in Dublin, no 1, 30 March 1725–?

[The craftsman. Ed N. Amhurst et al. 5 Dec 1726–1752?; rptd 1721–7.]

Essays on the vices and follies of the times, by N. Amhurst. Pasquin and London Jnl 1726.

The ladies journal. No 1, 17 Jan 1727–no 22, 29 June 1727.

The seasonable writer. No 1, 8 Sept 1727–no 2, 15 Sept 1727.

The citizen. [No 1, ?]–no 3, 15 Sept 1727–no 21, 27 Nov 1727.

The tatler reviv'd, by 'Isaac Bickerstaff esq'. No 1, 16 Oct 1727–no 27, 15 Jan 1728.

The occasional writer, by H. St John, Lord Bolingbroke. Nos 1–4 1727.

The senator, by 'A. Standfast' [E. Roome?]. No 1 [9 Feb 1728]–no 32, 28 May 1728.

The parrot, by E. Haywood et al. No 1, 25 Sept 1728–no 4, 16 Oct 1728.

[The universal spectator and weekly journal, by 'Henry Stonecastle, of Northumberland, esq.' [Henry Baker et al]. No 1, 12 Oct 1728–no 907, 22 Feb 1746; selections rptd 1736, 1747, 1756.]

Bond, R. P. A fragment by Addison. RES 5 1929.

Potter, G. R. Henry Baker FRS 1698–1774. MP 29 1932.

The knight-errant. No 1, 27 Feb 1729–no 12, 15 May 1729.

The free Briton, by 'Francis Walsingham of the Inner Temple esq.' [W. Arnall]. No 1, 4 Dec 1729–no 294, 26 June 1735.

An xviiith century journalist. TLS 16 Aug 1923.

The free Briton: or the opinion of the people. Ed John, Lord Hervey? Nos 1–2, 1727.

Carlson, C. L. The free Briton: or the opinion of the people, and F. Walsingham's Free Briton. N & Q 7 Sept 1935.

[The Grub-street journal. Ed R. Russel and J. Martyn. No 1, 8 Jan 1730–no 418, 29 Dec 1737; selections rptd 1731, 1737 (as Memoirs of the society of Grub-street).]

Hillhouse, J. T. The Grub-street Journal. Durham NC 1928.

Williamson, R. John Martyn and the Grub-street Journal. Medical History 5 1961.

The hyp-doctor, by 'Sir Isaac Ratcliffe of Elbow-Lane' [J. Henley]. No 1, 15 Dec 1730–no 534, 20 Jan 1741. Nos 156–170 are entitled the Free-mason, nos 1–15. Subtitles of others vary.

[The weekly register: or universal journal. 1730–4.]

[The miscellany (continued as the Weekly miscellany). Ed W. Webster. No 1, 16 Dec 1732–no 444, 27 June 1741; rptd in part 1736, 1738.]

The auditor. No 1, 9 Jan 1733–no 34, 4 May 1733. Pbn resumed with no 36, 28 Nov 1733–no 45, 30 Jan 1734.

[The bee: or universal weekly pamphlet. Ed E. Budgell. No 1, 3 Feb 1733–no 118, 14 June 1735.]

The British Nestor: or weekly entertainer. [No 1, June 1733]–no 2, [June 1733]–?

The what-d'ye-call-it. No 1, 24 Nov 1733–no 22, 18 April 1734.

[The weekly amusement: or universal magazine. No 1, 9 Nov 1734–no 45, 13 Sep 1735.]

The prompter. Ed A. Hill et al. No 1, 12 Nov 1734–no 173, 2 July 1736. Some nos rptd seriatim Dublin 1735.

Brewster, D. Aaron Hill: poet, dramatist, projector 1685–1750. New York 1913.

Sutherland, W. O. S. Polonius, Hamlet, and Lear in Aaron Hill's Prompter. SP 49 1952.

—— Essay forms in the Prompter. In Studies in the early English periodical, ed R. P. Bond, Chapel Hill 1957.

Burnim, K. A. Aaron Hill's the Prompter: an eighteenth-century theatrical paper. Educational Theatre Jnl 13 1961.

[The weekly oracle: or universal library. No 1, 7 Dec 1734–no 108, Jan 1737.]

The old Whig: or the consistent Protestant. Ed S. Chandler et al. No 1, 13 May 1735–no 160, 30 March 1738; rptd 1739.

Essays by 'R. Freeman' in the London Journal. 1735.

[The daily gazetteer. 1735–48.]

Occasional paper upon the subject of religion and the Church Establishment. Nos 1–8, 1735–6.

Common sense: or the Englishman's journal, by the Earl of Chesterfield et al. No 1, 5 Feb 1737–no 359, 31 Dec 1743–? Nos 1–104 rptd 1738–9.

The weekly essay: or Middlesex journal. No 1, 5 Nov 1737–no 19, 11 March 1738.

Fan, T. C. Chinese fables and anti-Walpole journalism. RES 25 1949.

Common sense: or the Englishman's journal. No 40 (first issued), 5 Nov 1737–. Continued as Old common sense: or the Englishman's journal, no 43, 26 Nov 1737–no 123, 16 June 1739. Rival to the earlier Common sense, with serial nos and dates parallel.

The nonsense of Common-sense, by Lady M. W. Montagu. No 1, 16 Dec 1737–no 8, 21 Feb 1738; rptd Evanston 1961.

Ransom, H. H. Mary Wortley Montagu's newspaper. SE 26 1947.

The literary courier of Grub-street. No 1, 5 Jan 1738–no 30, 27 July 1738.

The British censor. No 1, 16 March 1738.

The occasional writer. Nos 1–4, 1738.

[The champion: or British mercury, by 'Capt. Hercules Vinegar, of Pall-Mall' [H. Fielding and J. Ralph]. No 1, 15 Nov 1739–3 April 1744?; rptd in part 1741, 1743.]

Hughes, H. S. Fielding's indebtedness to James Ralph. MP 20 1923.

Shipley, J. B. Essays from Fielding's Champion. N & Q Nov 1953.

The prattler. No 1, 30 Dec 1740.

Occasional paper. Nos 1–4, 1740–1.

Essays in the Westminster journal. 28 Nov 1741–8 Jan 1743; rptd 1747.

[Old England: or the constitutional Journal [subtitle varies]. 1743–53.]

[The true patriot: and the history of our own times. Ed H. Fielding. No 1, 5 Nov 1745–no 32, 10 June 1746–no 33; rptd University Alabama 1964, London 1965.]

The occasional spectator. 6 essays in British magazine by J. Hill. March 1746–Sept 1746.

The fool. 93 essays in Daily gazetteer. 10 July 1746–25 Feb 1747; rptd 1748.

The parrot: with a compendium of the times. By E. Haywood et al. No 1, 2 Aug 1746–no 9, 4 Oct 1746.

The visiter. Essays in British magazine. Sept 1746–?

The moralist. 56 essays in British magazine. Oct 1746–May 1751.

[The Jacobite's journal. Ed H. Fielding. No 1, 5 Dec 1747–no 49, 5 Nov 1748.]

The remembrancer, by 'George Cadwallader gent.' [J. Ralph]. No 1, 12 Dec 1747–51. Nos 1–12 rptd 1748.

[The London gazetteer. 1748–53.]

The whimsical philosopher. 5 essays in London magazine. May 1749–Dec 1750.

Occasional letters. 201 nos in Universal magazine. June 1749–Feb 1784.

The Covent garden journal. No 1, 5 Dec 1749.

[The midwife: or old woman's magazine. Ed Christopher Smart. 1750–3.]

The tatler reviv'd. No 1, 13 March 1750–no 6, 24 March 1750–?

Resupinus. The tatler revived. N & Q 28 Nov 1857.

The rambler, by S. Johnson. No 1, 20 March 1750–no 208, 17 March 1752. For reprints see col 1129.

Drake, N. Essays illustrative of the Rambler, Adventurer and Idler. 2 vols 1809.

Christie, O. F. Johnson the essayist: his opinions on man, morals and manners: a study. 1924.

Smith, D. N. The contributors to the Rambler and the Idler. Bodleian Quart Record 7 1934.

Murphy, M. J. The Rambler no 191. PMLA 50 1935.

Powys, L. Dr Johnson: idler, rambler and straggler. Dublin Mag 12 1937.

Pratt, W. W. Leigh Hunt and the Rambler. SE 18 1938.

Bradford, C. B. The Edinburgh Ramblers. MLR 34 1939.

— Johnson's revisions of the Rambler. RES 15 1939.

Leyburn, E. D. The translations of the mottoes and quotations in the Rambler. RES 16 1940.

Wimsatt, W. K. Philosophical words: a study of style and meaning in the Rambler and Dictionary by Johnson. New Haven 1948; rptd in Samuel Johnson: a collection of critical essays, ed D. J. Greene, Englewood Cliffs NJ 1965.

Sherbo, A. The making of Ramblers 186 and 187. PMLA 67 1952.

— The translations of mottoes and quotations in Johnson's Rambler. N & Q 21 June 1952.

Bloom, E. A. Symbolic names in Johnson's periodical publications. MLQ 13 1952.

— Samuel Johnson in Grub street. Providence 1957.

Balderston, K. C. Doctor Johnson and William Law. PMLA 75 1960.

Elder, A. T. Irony and humour in the Rambler. UTQ 30 1960.

— Thematic patterning and development in Johnson's essays. SP 62 1965.

Hamilton, H. W. Boswell's suppression of a paragraph in Rambler 60. MLN 76 1961.

Fox, R. C. The imaginary submarines of Dr Johnson and R. O. Cambridge. PQ 40 1961.

Kenney, W. Addison, Johnson and the 'energetick' style. Studia Neophilologica 33 1961.

Grange, K. M. Samuel Johnson's account of certain psychoanalytic concepts. Jnl of Nervous & Mental Disease 135 1962; rptd in Samuel Johnson: a collection of critical essays, ed D. J. Greene, Englewood Cliffs NJ 1965.

Fleeman, J. D. The reprint of Rambler no 1. Library 5th ser 18 1963.

Misenheimer, J. B. Dr Johnson on the essay. New Rambler 18 1966.

Alkon, P. K. Samuel Johnson and moral discipline. Evanston 1967.

Kelly, R. Johnson among the sheep. Stud in Eng Lit 1500–1900 3 1968.

Wiles, R. M. Contemporary distribution of Johnson's Rambler. Eighteenth-Century Stud 2 1968.

Ingham, P. Dr Johnson's 'elegance'. RES new ser 19 1968.

[The true Briton. 2 Jan 1751–6 June 1753.]

Libertine, by 'Hilario'. 4 essays in Magazine of Magazines. March–May 1751.

The inspector, by J. Hill. 152 essays in London daily advertiser. March 1751–; rptd 1753.

The cabinet for wit: or an infallible recipe to cure stupidity by 'Timothy Sharpe'. No 1, nd 1751.

[The Covent-garden journal, by H. Fielding. 4 Jan 1752–25 Nov 1752; rptd seriatim in part, Dublin 1752–3; rptd in part, 1752, New Haven 1915, 1964.]

Coley, W. B. Fielding and the two Covent-garden journals. MLR 57 1962.

New essays by A. Murphy. Ed A. Sherbo, East Lansing 1963.

[Have at you all: or the Drury lane journal, by B. Thornton. 16 Jan–9 April 1752.]

Essays in the Lady's magazine. 7 nos 13 June 1752–30 Sept 1752.

The patriot; The trifler; The critic. Essays in General Review: or Impartial Register. No 1 [May 1752]–no 5 [July 1752].

Essays by A. Murphy in the Craftsman: or Gray's inn journal. 21 Oct 1752–Sept 1753; rptd with 52 from the Gray's inn journal, 1756.

The adventurer. Ed J. Hawkesworth. No 1, 7 Nov 1752–no 140, 9 March 1754; rptd 1754, 1756, 1762, 1770, 1778, 1788; rptd (those by Johnson) New Haven 1963.

Drake, N. Essays illustrative of the Rambler, Adventurer and Idler. 2 vols 1809.

Powell, L. F. Johnson's part in the Adventurer. RES 3 1927; rptd with corrections and addns in Samuel Johnson: the Idler and the Adventurer, New Haven 1963.

Sherbo, A. Two notes on Johnson's revisions. MLR 50 1955.

Griffith, P. M. The authorship of the papers signed 'A' in Hawkesworth's Adventurer: a stronger case for Dr Richard Bathurst. Tulane Stud in Eng 12 1963.

Lams, V. J. The 'A' papers in the Adventurer: Bonnell Thornton, not Dr Bathurst, their author. SP 64 1967.

The new female spectator. In the Spring-garden journal nos 2, 23 Nov 1752 and 4, 7 Dec 1752. By B. Thornton.

The scourge. No 1, 28 Nov 1752–no 81, 2 June 1753.

The lady's curiosity: or weekly Apollo, by 'Nestor Druid'. Nos 1–13, nd 1752.

The world, by 'Adam Fitz-Adam' [E. Moore et al]. No 1, 4 Jan 1753–no 209, 30 Dec 1756. Followed by A world extraordinary, by 'Vandyke' [H. Walpole]; rptd 1755–1756, 1757, 1761, 1763, 1767, 1772, 1774; Edinburgh 1776, 1793, 1794.

Caskey, J. H. The life and works of Edward Moore. New Haven 1927.

— The two issues of the World. MLN 45 1930.

Todd, W. B. Bibliography and the editorial problem in the eighteenth century. SB 4 1952.

— The printing of eighteenth-century periodicals; with notes on the Examiner and the World. Library 5th ser 10 1955.

— The first edition of the World. Library 5th ser 11 1956.

— The printing history of the World. In Studies in the early English periodical, ed R. P. Bond, Chapel Hill 1957.

[The gazetteer and London daily advertiser. 1753–64.]

The protester, on behalf of the people, by 'I. Barebone' [J. Ralph]. No 1, 2 June 1753–no 24, 10 Nov 1753.

[The Gray's inn journal. Ed A. Murphy. No 1, 29 Sept 1753–no 52, 21 Sept 1754; rptd 1756 with 52 nos which had been pbd in the Craftsman: or Gray's inn journal, 21 Oct 1752–Sept 1753.]

The spectator. No 1, 3 Nov 1753–no 19, 5 Jan 1754.

The tatler, by 'William Bickerstaff esq, nephew to the late Isaac Bickerstaff esq.' No 1, 20 Dec 1753–no 4, 10 Jan 1754.

The connoisseur, by 'Mr Town, critic and censor-general' [G. Colman and B. Thornton]. No 1, 31 Jan 1754–no 140, 30 Sept 1756; rptd 1757, 1761, 1793, 1795; rptd Oxford 1767, 1774.

Page, E. R. George Colman the elder 1732–94. New York 1935.

Sherbo, A. Cowper's Connoisseur essays. MLN 70 1955.

The entertainer, by 'Charles Mercury esq.' No 1, 3 Sept 1754–no 12, 19 Nov 1754.

New essays by Arthur Murphy. Ed A. Sherbo, East Lansing 1963.

Sherbo, A. Imitation or concealment: who wrote the Entertainer essays? BNYPL Sept 1965. Reply by H. K. Miller, ibid.

The retrospector, by 'Valentine Veteran, Esq.' No 1, 31 Dec 1754–no 2, 7 Jan 1755.

Man: a paper for ennobling the species. Ed P. Shaw. No 1, 1 Jan 1755–no 53, 31 Dec 1755.

The friend. No 1, 5 Jan 1755–no 10, 9 March 1755.

The Devil upon crutches in England: or night scenes in London. No 1, 8 Jan 1755–no 20, 31 May 1755; rptd 1759 (4th edn).

The Devil, by J. Slade. No 1, 18 Jan 1755–no 25, 5 July 1755.

[The monitor: or British freeholder. Ed R. Beckford and J. Entinck. No 1, 9 Aug 1755–no 504, 20 March 1765; rptd 1756 (in part), 1757, 1760.]

The old maid, by 'M. Singleton' [F. Brooke et al]. No 1, 15 Nov 1755–no 37, 24 July 1756; rptd 1764.

The young lady, by 'Euphrosine'. No 1, 6 Jan 1756–no 7, 17 Feb 1756.

The prater, by 'Nicholas Babble' [J. Holcombe]. No 1, 13 March 1756–no 35, 6 Nov 1756.

The test, by A. Murphy and H. Fox, Lord Holland. No 1, 6 Nov 1756–no 35, 9 July 1757.

The con-test, by O. Ruffhead et al. No 1, 23 Nov 1756–no 38, 6 Aug 1757.

[The London chronicle. 1757–.]

The centinel, by T. Francklin. No 1, 6 Jan 1757–no 27, 6 July 1757; rptd 1758 (nos 1, 6 Jan 1757–140, 31 Dec 1757).

[The rhapsodist. No 1, 24 Jan 1757–no 8, 14 March 1757.]

The microcosm: a new paper, by 'Francis Fashion esq.' No 1, 7 March 1757–no 2, 14 March 1757.

The mirror. Vol 1 no 1, 22 March 1757.

The humanist. No 1, 26 March 1757–no 15, 2 July 1757.

The theatre: essays in the London chronicle. 1757–8.

The crab-tree. No 1, 26 April 1757–no 14, 26 July 1757.

The constitution. Nos 1–3, nd 1757.

The idler, by S. Johnson. Universal Chronicle: or Weekly Gazette 15 April 1758–5 April 1760; rptd New Haven 1963. For earlier reprints see col 1131, above.

Drake, N. Essays illustrative of the Rambler, Adventurer and Idler. 2 vols 1809.

Smith, D. N. The contributors to the Rambler and the Idler. Bodleian Quart Record 7 1934.

Chapman, R. W. The sale of Johnson's Idler. N & Q 24 April 1943.

Elder, A. T. Thematic patterning and development in Johnson's essays. SP 62 1965.

Rhodes, R. D. Idler no 24 and Johnson's epistemology. MP 64 1966.

[Owen's weekly chronicle: or universal journal. 1758–67.]

[Universal chronicle: or weekly gazette. 1758–60.]

Green, B. Possible additions to the Johnson canon. Yale Univ Lib Gazette 16 1942.

Letters by 'Probus' in the Gazetteer and London daily advertiser. 1758–9.

[The bee. Ed O. Goldsmith. 6 Oct 1759–24 Nov 1759.]

The busy body, by O. Goldsmith et al. No 1, 9 Oct 1759–no 12, 3 Nov 1759.

Chinese letters, by O. Goldsmith. Public Ledger 24 Jan 1760–14 Aug 1761; rptd 1762 (as The citizen of the world, 123 nos), 1774, 1776, 1782, 1785, 1790, 1792, 1793–4, 1794, 1796, 1799, 1800, Dublin 1765, 1775; ed A. Friedman, Oxford 1966 (in Collected works); tr French and German, 1763.

Crane, R. S. and H. J. Smith. A French influence on Goldsmith's Citizen of the world. MP 19 1921.

Davidson, L. J. Forerunners of Goldsmith's The citizen of the world. MLN 36 1921.

Smith, H. J. Goldsmith's Citizen of the world. New Haven 1926.

Reding, K. A study of the influence of Goldsmith's Citizen of the world upon the Cartas Marruecas of José Cadalso. Hispanic Rev 2 1934.

Friedman, A. The immediate occasion of Goldsmith's Citizen of the world, letter xxxviii. PQ 17 1938.

— Goldsmith and Steele's Englishman. MLN 55 1940.

— (ed). The collected works of Goldsmith. 5 vols Oxford 1966.

Chên Shou-yi. Goldsmith and his Chinese letters. T'ien Hsia Monthly Jan 1939.

[The public ledger. 1760–.]

McAdam, E. L. New essays by Dr Johnson. RES 18 1942.

The meddler. 10 essays in Royal female magazine. March 1760–Dec 1760.

The trifler. 11 essays by C. Lennox in the Lady's museum. March 1760–Jan 1761.

The schemer: or universal satirist, by 'Helter van Scelter' (J. Ridley). 33 essays in the London chronicle. 13 May 1760–28 Dec 1762; 1763.

The British commonwealthsman. Essays in Gazetteer and London daily advertiser. Nov 1760–?

The cottager. 3 essays in Royal magazine. Feb–March, July 1761.

Life. 14 essays in the Library. April 1761–May 1762.

The genius. 15 essays by G. Colman in the St James's chronicle. 11 June 1761–9 Jan 1762; rptd in Colman's Prose on several occasions, 1787.

[St James's chronicle: or British evening-post. 1761–. Selected pieces pbd 1762 as the Yearly chronicle for 1761.]

On the study of the belles lettres. 14 essays by T. Smollett [?] in the British magazine. July 1761–Jan 1763.

The green room. Essays in the Court magazine. Sept 1761 and later.

The free-enquirer, by P. Annet. No 1, 17 Oct 1761–no 9, 12 Dec 1761.

The philosopher. 3 essays in the Library. Jan–April 1762.

The town. 6 essays in the Universal museum. Jan–June 1762.

The author. 16 essays in the Universal museum. Jan 1762–July 1763.

The reader. 4 essays in the British magazine. April–Oct 1762.

The Briton. Ed T. G. Smollett. No 1, 29 May 1762–no 38, 12 Feb 1763; rptd in Political controversy 1762–3.
Gassman, B. The Briton and Humphry Clinker. Stud in Eng Lit 1500–1900 3 1963.

The north Briton. Ed J. Wilkes. No 1, 5 June 1762–no 46, 28 May 1763. Continuation by J. W. Brooke, no 47, 4 June 1763–no 235, 6 Dec 1766. Continuation by W. Bingley, no 47, 10 May 1768–no 218, 11 May 1771. Continuation in Bingley's journal: or the universal gazette. Many issues of North Briton extraordinary. Nos 1–46 rptd 1763, 1766, 1769, 1772, Dublin 1764–5. Bingley's continuation rptd in Political controversy 1762–3.
Bleackley, H. The life of John Wilkes. 1917.
Pottle, F. A. A North Briton extraordinary. N & Q 11 Oct, 6 Dec 1924.
Halsband, R. The poet of the North Briton. PQ 17 1938.
Nobbe, G. The North Briton. New York 1939.
Thomas, P. D. G. John Wilkes and the freedom of the press 1771. Bull of Inst of Historical Research 33 1960.

The patriot. No 1, 17 June 1762–no 5, 17 July 1762; rptd in Political controversy 1762–3.

The occasional writer. No 1, 26 June 1762.

The auditor, by A. Murphy. No 1, 15 July 1762–no 43, 16 May 1763; rptd in Political controversy 1762–3.

Political controversy: or a weekly magazine of ministerial and anti-ministerial essays, consisting of the Monitor, Briton, North Briton, Auditor and Patriot entire, with select pieces from the newspapers. Ed J. Wilkes. Reprints also Aylesbury journal, 20 Nov 1762, Champion, 30 April 1763–21 May 1763, Contrast, nos 1–10, Fumbler, 4 Aug 1762–18 Aug 1762, Lying intelligencer, 12 Feb 1763–26 Feb 1763, Plain dealer, 14 May 1763–3 Sept 1763, Politician, nos 1–2, South Briton, 2 May 1763, Trimmer, 4 Sept 1762–11 Sept 1763. Vol [1] no 1, 1762–vol 2 no 1, 14 Oct 1762–vol 5 no 8, 6 Sept 1763. Title from vol 4 no 1 is Weekly magazine.

The investigator. A. Ramsay. Nos 1–4, 1762.

The lying intelligencer. 2 essays in the Gentleman's magazine. Jan–Feb 1763; rptd in Political controversy 1762–3.

The babler, by H. Kelly. 123 essays in Owen's weekly chronicle: or universal journal 12 Feb 1763–5 June 1767.

The plain dealer. No 1, 14 May 1763–no 50, 21 April 1764; rptd (in part) in Political controversy 1762–3.

The champion. 1763; rptd in Political controversy 1762–3.

The contrast. No 1, 29 June 1763–no 24, 14 Dec 1763; nos 1–10 rptd in Political controversy 1762–3, 1765 (nos 1–24, with corrections).

Terrae-filius, by G. Colman. No 1, 5 July 1763–no 4, 8 July 1763; rptd 1787.

The witting's chronicle. 3 essays in the Universal museum. Aug–Oct 1763.

The moderator. No 1, 19 Nov 1763–?

[The gazetteer and new daily advertiser. 1764–97.]

Terrae-filius. No 1, 16 March 1764–no 5, 6 April 1764; Terrae filius extraordinary, 27 March [1764].

The scrutator, by J. Scott. No 1, 5 April 1764–no 38, 20 Dec 1764.

The traveller. Essays in the Complete magazine April 1764–?

The hermit in town. 10 essays in the Universal museum Nov 1764–Nov 1765.

The trifler. 2 essays in the Universal museum Dec 1765.

The spendthrift, by H. Fox, Lord Holland. No 1, 29 March 1766–no 20, 9 Aug 1766.

The batchelor: or speculations of 'Jeoffrey Wagstaffe esq.' [J. Courtenay et al]. No 1, 29 March 1766–no 139, 30 Jan 1768. Extracts rptd Dublin 1773, London 1773.

The medley. Nos 1–18. 1766.

[The monitor: or green-room laid open. No 1, 17 Oct 1767. Continued as the Theatrical monitor: or stage management and green-room laid open. No 2, 24 Oct 1767–no 18, 16 April 1768.]

The visionary. 3 essays in the Royal magazine. Oct–Dec 1767.

The miscellany, by N. F. Horne. No 1, 1 Jan 1768.

The extraordinary North Briton, by W. Moore. No 1, 16 May 1768–no 91, 27 Jan 1770. Spurious nos 89–90 by T. Brayne; rptd in 2nd–5th edns.

The Englishman. No 1, 11 June 1768–no 12, 20 Aug 1768–?

The occasionalist. No 1, 12 Aug 1768–no 14, 11 Nov 1768.

Letters of 'Junius' in the Public advertiser. 21 Nov 1768–19 Dec 1769.

The national mirror. 24 essays in the Gazetteer and new daily advertiser Dec 1768–9; rptd 1771.

The critic. Nos [1]–3, Jan 1769.

The constitutionalist. 20 essays by J. Burgh in the Gazetteer and new daily advertiser July 1769–May 1770.

The parliamentary spy. No 1, 21 Nov 1769–no 23, 25 May 1770. No 23 as Parliamentary spy extraordinary.

The tuner: a periodical paper on popular topics. No 1, [9 Dec 1769?].

Euphrasy, by T. Green. Nos 1–12, c. 1769.

Letters from the dead. 18 essays in the Court and city magazine Jan 1770–June 1771.

The whisperer, by W. Moore. No 1, 17 Feb 1770–no 100, 11 Jan 1772. Several extraordinary issues. Nos 1–25 rptd 1770.

The king's fool. 11 essays in the Gazetteer and new daily advertiser 9 Aug 1770–25 Oct 1770.

The tickler. No 1, 20 Oct 1770–no 8, 8 Dec 1770.

The volunteer. Essays in the Gazetteer and new daily advertiser 30 Oct 1770–?

Letters of 'Modestus' in the Gazetteer and new daily advertiser. 1770.

The scourge. No 1, 23 Jan 1771–no 2, 30 Jan 1771.

The man of pleasure. 165 essays in the Town and country magazine March 1771–March 1785.

Letters. 10 nos in the Gazetteer and new daily advertiser. 11 March 1771–28 March 1771.

The Court mirrour. 2 essays in the Lady's magazine. April–May 1771.

The lady's counsellor, by 'A young philanthropist'. 7 essays in the Lady's magazine. July 1771–April 1772.

The theatrical review, by J. Potter. Essays on the theatre in the Public ledger 21 Sept 1771–10 April 1772; rptd 1772 as the Theatrical review: or new companion to the playhouse.

Advice to a sister, by 'Frater'. 12 essays in the Town and country magazine Oct 1771–Sept 1772.

Letters by 'Attorney general to the Gazetteer'. In the Gazetteer and new daily advertiser 1771.

Essays by 'Hortensia' in the Gazetteer and new daily advertiser. 1771.

The Scotchman. No 1, 21 Jan 1772–no 21, 6 June 1772.

The moralist. 3 essays in the British magazine and general review Jan–March 1772.

On the education of the fair sex. 10 essays in the Lady's magazine Sept 1772–May 1773.

The taste and critical observations of J. H[ope?]. 8 essays in Westminster magazine Dec 1772–Dec 1773.

Momus: or the laughing philosopher. 100 essays in the Westminster magazine Dec 1772–April 1782, Jan 1785–Nov 1785.

The Harlequin. 29 essays in London magazine Jan 1733–suppl 1775.

The reasoner. 22 essays in Lady's magazine March 1773–Aug 1775.

The lady's monitor. 3 essays in Lady's magazine May–Aug 1773.

A friend to the fair sex. 14 essays in Lady's magazine June 1773–June 1774.

The observer. 195 essays in Town and country magazine June 1773–March 1790.

The skeptic: or unbeliever. No 1, Oct [?] 1773.

The templar and literary gazette, by S. Paterson. No 1, 6 Nov 1773–no 14, 22 Dec 1773.

The physician of the heart. 21 essays in Sentimental magazine Nov 1773–July 1775.

The speculatist: or the entertaining and instructive philosopher. 6 essays in the Sentimental magazine Nov 1773–May 1774.

The reasoner. 22 essays in Sentimental magazine Nov 1773–Aug 1775.

The sentimental philosopher. 7 essays in Sentimental magazine Dec 1773–May 1774.

The censor, by 'Reuben Rustick'. 7 essays in Lady's magazine Jan–Oct 1774.

The scribbler. 11 essays in Monthly miscellany Jan–Oct 1774.

The leveller, by J. Hope. 14 essays in Westminster magazine Jan 1774–March 1776; rptd in Thoughts in prose and verse, 1780.

The matron, by 'Mrs Martha Grey'. 224 essays in Lady's magazine Jan 1774–April 1791; rptd (in part) in New lady's magazine Jan 1790–suppl 1795.

Original letters from a young American gentleman in London to his friend in South Carolina. 6 essays in the Town and country magazine. Feb 1774–July 1774.

The man of fancy. 6 essays in St James's magazine Feb–Dec 1774.

The picture, by 'Charles Contour esq.' 8 essays in St James's magazine April–Nov 1774.

Letters of 'Ibrahim to Osman Hope'. 6 nos in Gazetteer and new daily advertiser May–June 1774.

The book-worm. 9 essays in Monthly miscellany. July 1774–Oct 1775.

The speculator. 12 essays in Monthly ledger. July 1774–Nov 1775.

The speculatist. 17 essays in Westminster magazine. July 1774–Dec 1775.

The young lady's preceptor. 14 essays in Lady's magazine. July 1774–suppl 1775.

The English Marmontel. 3 essays in St James's magazine Oct–Dec 1774.

Essays by 'Regulus' in the Gazetteer and new daily advertiser 1774–9.

The crisis, by W. Moore? No 1, 20 Jan 1775–no 91, 12 Oct 1776; The crisis extraordinary, 9 Aug 1775.

The archer. 4 essays in Matrimonial magazine Feb–May 1775.

Essays on several subjects. 21 essays in Lady's magazine Feb 1775–suppl 1776.

The gentleman. 6 essays in Universal magazine June suppl 1775–Dec 1775.

Essays by 'Gentleman'. In London packet 10 July 1775–4 Dec 1775.

The censor. 6 essays in Monthly ledger Aug 1775–Jan 1776.

The impartialist. 2 essays in Lady's magazine Aug–Sept 1775.

The matrimonial preceptor. 3 essays in Westminster magazine Aug–Nov 1775.

Essays on various subjects. 18 essays in Town and country magazine Sept 1775–March 1778.

Letters of 'Roderic M'Alpin'. In Gazetteer and new daily advertiser Nov 1775–May 1779.

The plain dealer. No 1, 25 Dec 1775–no 8, 12 Feb 1776.

Essay on friendship, by Lubbock Thornley. 5 nos in Lady's magazine Dec 1775–Aug 1776.

The plagiarist. 7 essays in Gazetteer and new daily advertiser 1775.

The allegorical preceptor, by 'Francis Fiction esq.' 5 essays in Lady's magazine 1775 suppl–Sept 1776.

The dreamer, by 'Samuel Shadow, Esq.' 7 essays in Town and country magazine 1775 suppl–Jan 1777.

The female reformer, by 'Bob Short jr.' 39 essays in Lady's magazine March 1776–June 1782.

The philosopher. 2 essays in Town and country magazine Aug–Sept 1776.

The oriental fabulist. 2 essays in Lady's magazine Aug, Nov 1776.

The saunterer. 3 essays in Lady's magazine Nov 1776–March 1777.

Characters. 34 nos in Gazetteer and new daily advertiser Nov 1776–Feb 1778; rptd 1777.

The chamelion. 2 essays in Lottery magazine July–Aug 1777.

The philosopher, by T. Holcroft. 12 essays in Town and country magazine Sept 1777–Feb 1779.

The hypochondriack, by J. Boswell. 70 essays in London magazine Oct 1777–Aug 1783; rptd Stanford 1928.

Essays on various subjects. 30 nos in London magazine Jan 1778–Nov 1781.

The fortune teller. 3 essays in Westminster magazine Aug–Dec 1778.

The literary fly, by H. Croft. No 1, 18 Jan 1779–no 17, 8 May 1779.

The Englishman, by C. J. Fox et al. No 1, 13 March 1779–no 17, 2 June 1779.

Occasional letters to 'Bob Short'. 4 nos in Lady's magazine Feb–Sept 1779.

Adventures in an easy chair. 2 essays in Westminster magazine. April, July 1779.

The buck below stairs. 2 essays in Westminster magazine June 1779.

Select essays relating to the genius and writings of Shakespeare. 6 essays in Lady's magazine July–Dec 1779.

The Whig, by H. Boyd. In London courant 25 Nov 1779–?

Letters by 'Democraticus' in the Public advertiser, by H. Boyd? 1779.

The scourge. No 1, 20 Jan 1780–no 19, 3 June 1780.

The actor, by T. Holcroft. 5 essays in Westminster magazine Jan–May 1780.

The delineator. 66 essays in Town and country magazine Jan 1780–Feb 1785.

The speculator, by P. Reid. 11 essays in GM Oct 1780–Sept 1781.

The traiteur, by M. Madan. No 1, 18 Nov 1780–no 20, 31 March 1781.

Periodical essays, by R. Nares. No 1, 2 Dec 1780–no 14, 3 March 1781; rptd 1810.

The reformer. Nos 1–4, 1780.

The coffee house. 70 essays in Town and country magazine Jan 1781–Nov 1786.

The scribbler. 8 essays in GM Feb–Sept 1781.

The babbler. 2 essays in GM Aug–Sept 1781.

The termagant, by 'Mrs Xantippe'. 6 essays in Town and country magazine Oct 1781–March 1782.

The lucubrator. 9 essays in Westminster magazine Dec 1781–Nov 1782.

The link boy. 8 essays in London magazine Jan–Aug 1782.

The poetical inspector. 8 essays in Town and country magazine Jan–Nov 1782.

The man of the town. 16 essays in European magazine Jan 1782–Dec 1783.

The knight-errant, by 'Victor Amadeus'. 12 essays in Town and country magazine March 1782–April 1783.

The essayist, by 'Castalio'. 27 essays in Lady's magazine April 1782–5 suppl.

The dabbler. 2 essays in European magazine June–July 1782.

The busy-body. 11 essays in British magazine and review July 1782–June 1783.

The country curate. 7 essays in European magazine. Sept 1782–June 1783.

The prisoner. No 1, 30 Nov 1782.

The budget. 23 essays in Lady's magazine. Nov 1782–Nov 1784.

The Jesuit. No 1, 8 Feb 1783–no 4, 29 Feb 1784.

The wanderer, by 'Plummericus, the Wanderer'. 13 essays in Lady's magazine Feb 1783–Aug 1784.

The mental counsellor. 2 essays in European magazine March, June 1783.

The friend of the people. [No 1, ?]–no 3, 15 April 1783.

The traveller, by 'Humphrey Ramble'. 2 essays in Lady's magazine April–May 1783.

The critic, by J. Hodson. 8 essays in Lady's magazine June 1783–Feb 1784.

The touchstone, by 'Solomon Sagebaro'. 4 essays in British magazine and review Aug–Nov 1783.

The occasional and miscellaneous critic. 2 essays in European magazine. Aug 1783, Jan 1784.

[The Sunday London gazette and weekly monitor. 1783–.] Country. 1783–9.

The reasoner. No 1, 1 Jan 1784.

The story-teller, by T. Holcroft. 5 essays in Wit's magazine Jan–May 1784.

The new spectator; with the sage opinions of John Bull, by H. Robson. No 1, 3 Feb 1784–no 25, 17 Jan 1786.

The town-talker. 3 essays in Wit's magazine Feb–April 1784.

The night-walker. 8 essays in Wit's magazine July 1784–March 1785.

The Rolliad. Essays in Morning herald 1784; rptd 1785 etc.

The traveller. 4 essays in Wit's magazine Jan–March 1785.

The nutshell. 3 essays in Westminster magazine Jan, May, July 1785.

Original letters, moral and entertaining. 6 nos in Westminster magazine Feb 1785–Oct 1785.

The contemplative philosopher, by R. Lobb. 78 essays in Universal magazine Aug 1784–Dec 1792.

The rover. 12 essays in Lady's magazine Dec 1785–6 suppl.

The trifler. 12 essays in GM Jan–Dec 1786.

The female rambler. 5 essays in New lady's magazine Aug–Dec 1786.

The essayist, by 'Academicus'. 3 essays in New London magazine. Aug–Oct 1786.

[The Devil: containing a review and investigation of all public subjects, by C. Dibdin? Vol 1 no 1, 2 Oct 1786–vol 2 no 9, 26 Feb 1787.]

Pharos. No 1, 7 Nov 1786–no 50, 28 April 1787; rptd 1787.

[The Devil's pocket-book. Nos 1–10, 1786–7.]

The busy body, by W. C. Oulton. No 1, 2 Jan 1787–no 25, 26 Feb 1787; rptd 1789.

The contemplator. 2 essays in New London magazine March–April 1787.

The clown. 12 essays in New lady's magazine March 1787–May 1788.

The juvenile instructress. 7 essays in New lady's magazine. March 1787–Oct 1788.

The plenipotentiary, by a society of ladies and gentlemen. No 1, 2 June 1787–no 4, 23 June 1787–?

The lady's librarian. 14 essays in New lady's magazine Aug 1787–8 suppl.

The scribbler, by W. Holland. 11 essays in Lady's magazine Oct 1787–Aug 1788.

Moral tales, by S. Trimmer. 26 nos in Family magazine. Jan 1788–June 1789.

The female monitor. 3 essays in Lady's magazine Feb, Oct, Dec 1788.

The friend. 25 essays in General magazine and impartial review Feb 1788–June 1792.

Moral sketches, by 'Fidelio'. 2 nos in Court, city and country magazine March–April 1788.

The citizen. No 1, 15 April 1788–no 5, 13 May 1788.

The lounger's miscellany, by C. Gower. No 1, 31 May 1788–no 20, 7 March 1789.

The trifler, by R. Oliphant et al. No 1, 31 May 1788–no 43, 21 March 1789.

The peeper, by J. Watkins. 27 essays in European magazine Sept 1788–Dec 1791. 21 of these rptd in Universal magazine and review, Jan 1789–Jan 1792.

The heteroclite. 13 essays in European magazine. Oct 1788–April 1791.

Occasional papers, by 'Nestor'. 28 essays in Lady's magazine Feb 1789–July 1791.

The index, by 'Marmaduke Mastiz'. 22 essays in Lady's magazine March 1789–April 1791.

The visitant. 4 essays in Universal magazine and review. July–Sept 1789.

Moral reflector, by J. Reynolds. 3 essays in General magazine and impartial review July, Dec 1789, Sept 1791.

The by-stander: or universal weekly expositor, by C. Dibdin. No 1, 15 Aug 1789–no 26, 6 Feb 1790; rptd 1790.

The prompter: a theatrical paper. No 1, 24 Oct 1789–no 19, 10 Dec 1789.

Hummert, P. A. The prompter: an intimate mirror of the theater in 1789. Restoration & 18th-Century Theatre Research 3 1964.

The censor: or friendly female monitor. 14 essays in Lady's magazine Nov 1789–Nov 1791.

The actor. 15 essays in Attic miscellany Dec 1789–May 1791.

The hive: a hebdomadal selection of literary tracts. Nos 1–10, 1789.

The spy. 6 essays in Universal magazine and review Jan–Feb 1790.

The lady's friend. 4 essays in New lady's magazine Jan–May 1790.

The physiogno-magnetic mirror. 16 essays in Attic miscellany Jan 1790–Nov 1791.

The moralist. 4 essays in New lady's magazine Feb–May 1790.

The depictor. 7 essays in New lady's magazine Feb–Aug 1790.

The speculator, by N. Drake and W. Frend. No 1, 27 March 1790–no 26, 22 June 1790; rptd London and Dublin 1791.

The spirit of the times: in a series of observations on the important events of the age. Nos 1–8, 1790.

The undertaker. 2 essays in Lady's magazine Oct–Nov 1790.

The guardian angel. 15 essays in Universal magazine Jan 1791–Feb 1794.

The adventurer. 43 essays in Bon ton magazine March 1791–April 1795.

The English freeholder. No 1, 1 June 1791–no 21, 20 Nov 1791.

The scribbler, by 'Pisano'. 6 essays in Universal magazine and review July–Dec 1791.

The medical spectator. Vol 1 no 1, 1 Oct 1791–vol 3 no 48, 1796. An extraordinary issue 10 Nov 1792.

The collector: containing useful and entertaining histories, tales, anecdotes etc, by 'Ardmes'. 6 nos in New lady's magazine Nov 1791–Nov 1792.

Olla-podrida. 11 essays in New lady's magazine Dec 1791–2 supplement.

The grumbler. 1791.

The crisis. 41 essays in Public advertiser 11 Jan 1792–31 Oct 1793; rptd 1794.

The observer, by 'Ardmes'. 5 essays in New lady's magazine Feb–Nov 1792.

Academic. 7 essays in GM Feb 1792–Aug 1793.

The flagellant, by R. Southey and G. Bedford. No 1, 1 March 1792–no 9, [26 April 1792].

The looker-on: a periodical paper, by the Rev Simon Olive-Branch [W. Roberts et al]. No 1, 10 March 1792–no 86, 21 Dec 1793; rptd 1794, 1795 (extended to no 93, with alterations of nos and dates), 1797.

The moralist. 10 essays in County magazine. March–Dec 1792.

The patriot: or political, moral and philosophical repertory. Vol 1 no 1, 3 April 1792–vol 3, no 10 [1793].

The patriot [different ser from the preceding?]. No 1, 12 May 1792–no 16, 15 June 1793.

The vagarist. 6 essays in Sentimental and masonic magazine July 1792–Jan 1793.

The country spectator. No 1, 9 Oct 1792–no 33, 21 May 1793.

The academician. 2 essays in County magazine Oct, Dec 1792.

The associator. 13 Dec 1792.

The argus. 2 essays in New lady's magazine. 1792 suppl–Jan 1793.

The farrago. 1792.

The anti-leveller. No 1, 10 Jan 1793.

The universal monitor: or friendly censor, by H. F. Offley. 12 essays in Lady's magazine April 1793–1795 suppl.

The critic. 2 essays in Thespian magazine. May 1793 suppl–June 1793.

Christian philosophy. 4 essays in Evangelical magazine. July 1793–June 1794.

The actor. 4 essays in Thespian magazine. Sept 1793–Dec 1794.

A picture of the times in a series of letters addressed to the people of England by a lover of peace. Nos 1–31, 1795.

The new olla-podrida. 3 essays in New lady's magazine. Jan–April 1794.

The voluptuary. 14 essays in Bon ton magazine. 1794–June 1795.

Essays (6 nos) in European magazine April–Dec 1794.

The loyalist. 5 essays in New London magazine 1794.

On the abuse of terms, by 'Probus'. 4 essays in Evangelical magazine Oct 1794–Oct 1795.

The glancer, by 'Tobias Hint'. 3 essays in Lady's magazine Jan–March 1795.

The freemason. 7 essays in Freemason's magazine Jan–July 1795.

The philanthropist: or philosophical essays on politics, government, morals and manners. No 1, 16 March 1795–no 43, 25 Jan 1796.

The whisperer: or tales and speculations. No 1, 28 May 1795–no 24, Nov 1795; rptd 1798.

The essayist. 8 nos in Bon ton magazine. July 1795–Mar 1796.

The sylph. No 1, 22 Sept 1795–no 40, 30 April 1796.

Glances at life, by 'Sam Squint' et al. 11 essays in Monthly mirror Dec 1795–Oct 1800.

The dramatic guardian, by 'Leonardo'. 9 essays in Monthly mirror Dec 1795–Dec 1802.

Brotherly love. 7 essays in Evangelical magazine Feb–March 1796.

The enquirer, by W. Enfield et al. 41 essays in Monthly magazine Feb 1796–May 1820.

Coldicutt, D. Was Coleridge the author of the Enquirer series in the Monthly magazine 1796–9? RES 15 1939.

Patton, L. Coleridge and the Enquirer series. RES 16 1940.

The friend: a weekly essay, by W. Fox. No 1, 23 April 1796–no 23 nd.

The dangler. 6 essays in Lady's magazine. May–Oct 1796.

[How do you do?, by C. Dibdin and F. G. Waldron. No 1, 30 July 1796–no 8, 5 Nov 1796.]

The censor, by 'Seneca'. 5 essays in Monthly mirror Aug 1796–Feb 1797.

The progress of plagiarism. 5 essays ibid.

The loiterer: or universal essayist. No 1, 12 Nov 1796–no 8, 31 Dec 1796.

The projector, by 'Plume Aircastle, esq.' 6 essays in Cabinet magazine Nov 1796–April 1797.

The quiz. Ed T. F. Dibdin et al. No 1, Nov 1796–no 51, 1798. Nos 1–38 rptd 1797.

The lynx. Nos 1–7, 1796.

The parental monitor. Nos 1–4, 1796.

The reflector. 7 essays in Monthly visitor Jan 1797–April 1803.

The plaintiff. 12 essays in Monthly visitor Feb 1797–May 1798.

Characters, by J. C. Smedley. 5 nos in Monthly mirror. July 1797–1802.

[The anti-Jacobin: or weekly examiner. Ed W. Gifford. No 1, 20 Nov 1797–no 36, 9 July 1798; rptd 1799 (4th edn).]

Hawkins, E. Authors of the poetry of the Anti-Jacobin. N & Q 3 May 1851.

Poetry of the Anti-Jacobin. Ed L. Rice-Oxley, Oxford 1924.

Clark, R. B. William Gifford: Tory satirist, critic and editor. New York 1931.

Holloway, O. E. George Ellis, the Anti-Jacobin and the Quarterly Review. RES 10 1934.

Perkinson, R. H. The Anti-Jacobin. N & Q 6 March 1937.

The wanderer. 18 essays in European magazine April 1798–Oct 1799.

The old woman. 115 essays in Lady's monthly museum July 1798–April 1808.

The gleaner. 46 essays in Universal magazine. July 1798–March 1803.

The moralizer. 8 essays in European magazine. March 1799–April 1800.

Literary leisure: or the recreation of Solomon Saunter esq. No 1, 26 Sept 1799–no 60, 18 Dec 1800.

The sylphid. Nos 1–14, 1799.

The leptologist. 9 essays in British magazine Feb–Oct 1800.

Essays after the manner of Goldsmith, by G. Brewer. 22 nos in European magazine Nov 1800–Dec 1802.

The governess. 3 essays in Young gentleman's and lady's magazine 1800.

The burnisher. No 1, 20 Dec 1800–.

D. MAGAZINES, MISCELLANIES, LEARNED JOURNALS AND REVIEWS PUBLISHED IN LONDON 1660–1800

For magazines, miscellanies, learned journals and reviews pbd in the English provinces, in Scotland and in Ireland, see below. Studies of individual magazines etc are listed under their titles.

Royal Soc of London. Philosophical transactions. Ed H. Oldenburg et al. 6 March 1665–. Abridgements pbd in pts 1738–41, 1749–56.

McCutcheon, R. P. The Journal des Sçavans and the Philosophical Transactions of the Royal Society. SP 21 1934.

Lloyd, L. S. Musical theory in the early Philosophical Transactions. Notes & Records of Royal Soc 3 1941.

Olson, R. C. Swift's use of the Philosophical Transactions in section V of A tale of a tub. SP 49 1952.

Hulls, L. G. Philosophical transactions: the first fifty years. Discovery June 1960.

Porter, J. R. The scientific journal: 300th anniversary. Bacteriological Rev 28 1964.

Andrade, E. N. da C. The birth and early days of the Philosophical Transactions. Notes & Records of Royal Soc 20 1965.

Philosophical collections. Ed R. Hooke. No 1, 1679–no 3, 10 Dec 1681–no 7, April 1682.

Mercurius librarius: or a faithful account of all books and pamphlets. No 1, 16 April 1680–no 3, 29 April 1680.

A collection of letters for the improvement of husbandry and trade, by J. Houghton. No 1, 8 Sept 1681–Jan 1684; rptd in part, 1728.

McCutcheon, R. P. John Houghton: a seventeenth-century editor and book-reviewer. MP 20 1923.

Lacy, M. G. An early agricultural periodical. Annual Report of Amer Historical Assoc 1 1923.

Weekly memorials for the ingenious: or an account of books lately set forth in several languages. Ed? Beaumont? No 1, 16 Jan 1682–no 50, 15 Jan 1683.

Weekly memorials for the ingenious: or an account of books lately set forth in several languages. No 1, 20 March 1682–no 29, 25 Sept 1682. No 1 has same text as no 10 of a paper with similar title beginning 16 Jan 1682.

Medicina curiosa: or a variety of new communications in physick, chirurgery [etc]. No 1, 17 June 1684–no 2, 23 Oct 1684.

The universal historical bibliotheque: or an account of most of the considerable books printed in all languages. Ed J. C. de la Crose. [No 1], Jan 1687–[no 3], March 1687. Partly based on Bibliotheque universelle by J. Le Clerc, ptd at Hague.

Modern history: or a monethly account of all considerable occurrences, civil, ecclesiastical and military, with all natural and philosophical productions and transactions. Ed J. Phillips. [Vol 1 no 1, Oct 1687]. Continued as Monethly account, no 2, Nov 1687–[vol 3] no 5, Feb 1689–[1690?].

Godwin, W. The lives of Edward and John Phillips. 1815.

Weekly memorials: or an account of books lately set forth, with other accounts relating to learning. No 1, 19 Jan 1689–no 2, 23 Jan 1689.

The politicks of Europe: or a rational journal concerning the affairs of the time. No 1, 3 July 1690–no 17, 3 Oct 1691.

The present state of Europe: or the historical and political monthly mercury, giving an account of all the publick and private occurrences, civil, ecclesiastical and military. Ed J. Phillips [and Fonvive?]. Tr from Mercure historique et politique, by G. de Courtilz de Sandras, pbd at Hague. Vol 1 no 0, July 1690–vol 47 no 12, Dec 1738. Early issues rptd London, Edinburgh, Dublin.

Godwin, W. The lives of Edward and John Phillips. 1815.

Blagden, C. Henry Rhodes and the Monthly Mercury, 1702 to 1720. Book Collector 5 1956.

Supplement to the Athenian mercury. By J. Dunton. [No 1], May 1691–[no 5], 30 Jan 1692.

The history of learning: or an abstract of several books lately published as well abroad as at home. Ed J. C. de la Crose. [No 1, July 1691]. Continued as the Works of the learned: or an historical account and impartial judgment of books newly printed, both foreign and domestick. No 1, Aug 1691–no 9, April 1692. Succeeded by Compleat library.

McCutcheon, R. P. John Dunton's connection with book-reviewing. SP 25 1928.

McEwen, G. D. 'What is a conger?' John Dunton and Scottish booksellers. Stud in Scottish Lit 1 1963.

Parks, S. John Dunton and the Works of the learned. Library 5th ser 23 1968.

Hatfield, T. M. John Dunton's periodicals. Journalism Quart 10 1933.

Mercurius eruditorum: or news from the learned world. [No 1, 5 Aug 1691]–no 2, 12 Aug 1691.

The gentleman's journal: or the monthly miscellany by way of letter to a gentleman in the country consisting of news, history, philosophy, poetry, musick [etc]. Ed P. A. Motteux. No 1, Jan 1692–Nov 1694.

Foster, D. The earliest precursor of our present-day monthly miscellanies. PMLA 32 1917.

Cunningham, R. N. Peter Anthony Motteux: a biographical and critical study. Oxford 1933.

—— A bibliography of the writings of Peter Anthony Motteux. Proc Oxford Bibl Soc 3 1933.

Wieder, P. Pierre Motteux et les débuts du journalisme en Angleterre au xviie siècle. Paris 1944.

Physical and mathematical memoirs, extracted from the registers of the Royal Academy of Sciences at Paris. 31 Jan 1692–?

The present state of Europe: or the monthly account of all occurrences, ecclesiastical, civil and military. No 1, April 1692. Continued as Memoirs of the present state of Europe, no 2, May 1692–vol 2 no 12, Dec 1693–6. Trn of Lettres historiques, pbd at Hague 1692–1736.

The compleat library, or news for the ingenious: containing an historical account of the choicest books printed in England and in the forreign journals. Ed J. Dunton and R. Woolley. No 1, May 1692–June 1694.

Memoirs for the ingenious: containing several curious observations in philosophy, mathematicks, physick, philology and other arts and sciences. Ed J. C. de la Crose. No 1, Jan 1693–no 12, Dec 1693.

Memoirs for the ingenious: or the universal mercury. No 1, Jan 1694.

The history of learning, giving a succinct account and narrative of the choicest new books. No 1, May 1694.

Miscellaneous letters, giving an account of the works of the learned, both at home and abroad. No 1, 17 Oct 1694–no 25, March 1696.

The night walker: or evening rambles in search after lewd women, by J. Dunton. [No 1], Sept 1696–[no 8], April 1697.

Miscellanies over claret: or the friends to the tavern the best friends to poetry. Ed W. Pittis et al. Nos 1–2, 1697.

Newton, T. F. M. William Pittis and Queen Anne journalism. MP 33 1936.

The political state of Europe: with an account of new books. Nos 1–2, 1697.

The occasional paper: containing reflexions on books, by R. Willis. No 1, 1697–no 10, 1698.

Theosophical transactions of the Philadelphian society. No 1, March 1697–no 2, April 1697–no 5 [July 1697?].

Mercurius musicus. Ed H. Playford. No 1, Jan 1699–Jan 1702.

The history of the works of the learned: or an impartial account of books lately printed in all parts of Europe. Ed S. Parker et al. No 1, Jan 1699–March 1712. Nos 4–12 rptd at Edinburgh as nos 1–8, April–Nov 1699.

  Blagden, C. An early literary periodical. TLS 3 Dec 1954.

Mercurius theologicus: or the monthly instructor. Nos 1–12, 1700–1.

A general view of the world: or the marrow of history. Jan 1700–May 1702.

The monthly account of the present state of affairs. [No 1, Jan 1700]–no 3, March 1700.

The post-angel. Ed J. Dunton. No 1, Jan 1701–. Continued as the Post-angel: or universal entertainment, no 3, March 1701–Sept 1702.

  Dunton, J. The life and errors of John Dunton, written by himself. 1705; ed J. Nichols, 1818.

  Moore, C. A. John Dunton: pietist and imposter. SP 22 1925.

  See also The history of learning, 1691.

Memoirs for the curious: or an account of what occurs that's rare, secret, extraordinary, prodigious or miraculous throughout the world, whether in nature, art, learning, policy or religion. Nos 1–2, 1701.

The pacquet from Parnassus: or a collection of papers. Vol 1 nos 1–2, 1702.

The poetical observator. 1702–3.

The poetical observator revived, to be continued monthly. 1703.

The monthly register: or memoirs of the affairs of Europe. Ed? Buckley? No 1, Jan 1703–vol 5 no 12, Dec 1707.

Monthly masks of vocal musick: containing all the choicest songs. Ed H. Playford? 1703–17.

Cassandra (but I hope not), by C. Leslie. Nos 1–2, 1704; rptd 1704, 1750. No 2 rptd 1704.

The monthly journal of the affairs of Europe. No 1, July 1704–?

The diverting post. Ed H. Playford. No 1, 28 Oct 1704–no 36, 30 June 1705. Continued Jan 1706–Feb 1706.

The poetical courant. Ed S. Phillips. No 1, 26 Jan 1706–[no 30, 17 Aug 1706].

The British intelligencer. [Nov 1706]–?

The diverting muse: or the universal medly. Pt 1, 1707.

The London terrae filius: or satyrical reformer. Ed E. Ward. No 1, [Sept 1707]–no 6, [Feb] 1708.

The Muses mercury: or the monthly miscellany. Ed J. Oldmixon et al. Vol 1 no 1, Jan 1707–vol 2 no 1, Jan 1708.

  McCutcheon, R. P. Addison and the Muses Mercury. MP 20 1923.

The monthly miscellany: or memoirs for the curious, containing an epitome of books and news, lives and characters of famous persons. No 1, Jan 1707–Sept 1710.

Censura temporum: the good or ill tendencies of books, sermons, pamphlets etc impartially considered, by S. Parker. Vol 1 no 1, Jan 1708–Nov 1710.

A help to history: or a short memorial of the most material matters of fact and passages domestick and foreign. No 1, Jan 1709–Dec 1714; 1715 (abridged).

Useful transactions in philosophy and other sorts of learning. Ed W. King. No 1, Jan–Feb 1709–no 3, May–Sept 1709.

The monthly amusement. Ed J. Ozell. No 1, April 1709–no 6, Sept 1709.

The records of love: or weekly amusements for the fair sex. Ed H. Carey? No 1, 7 Jan 1710–no 12, 25 March 1710.

  Sutherland, J. R. Carey: an ascription. TLS 25 Dec 1930.

Memoirs of literature: containing an account of the state of learning both at home and abroad. Ed M. de la Roche. No 1, 13 March 1710–Sept 1714. Pbn resumed Jan 1717–April 1717 with subtitle English and foreign library; rptd 1722.

Delights for the ingenious: or a monthly entertainment for the curious of both sexes. Ed J. Tipper. No 1, Jan 1711–no 8, Oct–Dec 1711.

The political state of Great Britain. Ed A. Boyer et al. No 1, Jan 1711–Dec 1740. Vols 1–8 rptd 1718–20.

The poetical entertainer: or tales, satyrs, dialogues, and intrigues etc, serious and comical. Nos 1–5, 1712–13.

The general history of trade. Ed D. Defoe. No 1, July 1713–no 4, May 1714.

News from the dead: or the monthly packet of true intelligence from the other world. No 1, Nov 1715–no 7 [i.e. 8], Aug [1716]; rptd 1756.

The historical register: containing an impartial relation of all transactions, foreign and domestick. Ed J. Meres. 1716–38.

Mercurius politicus: being monthly observations on the affairs of Great Britain. Ed D. Defoe. No 1, May 1716–Dec 1720.

Essays for the month of December [January]. [No 1], Dec 1716–[no 2], Jan 1717.

The critick: a review of authors and their productions, by T. Brereton. No 1, 6 Jan 1718–no 22, 3 June 1718; rptd 1719.

Mercurius Britannicus: being collections of publick intelligence, by W. Campbell. No 1, Jan 1718–Dec 1718.

The Court miscellany in prose and verse. Nos 1–2, 1719.

The Delphick oracle, set forth by the most learned scholars in the most famous universities of Europe. No 1, Sept 1719–no 7, March 1720; rptd 1720.

The Athenian spy: or a packet for the virtuosi, by J. Dunton. No 1, Jan 1720.

The monthly register of experiments and observations in husbandry and gardening, by R. Bradley. June 1722–July 1722–?

Bibliotheca literaria: being a collection of inscriptions, medals, dissertations etc. Ed S. Jebb. Nos 1–10, 1722–4.

Monthly London journal. [No 1, Oct 1722?]–no 2, Nov 1722.

The monthly packet of advice from Parnassus, established by Apollo's express authority and sent direct to England. Ed M. Earbery. No 1, Nov 1722–3.

New memoirs of literature. Ed M. de la Roche. No 1, Jan 1725–Dec 1727.

The Athenian library: or a universal entertainment for lovers of novelty, by J. Dunton. No 1, March 1725.

The universal mercury. No 1, Jan 1726–no 4, April 1726.

A general history of the principal discoveries and improvements in useful arts. Ed D. Defoe. No 1, Oct 1726–no 4, Jan 1727.

The political mercury. No 1, Jan 1727–no 2, Feb 1727.

Advice from Parnassus, by 'Trojano Boccalini' [M. Earbery]. No 1, March 1727–no 4, June 1727.

The weekly miscellany for the improvement of husbandry, trade, arts and sciences, by R. Bradley. 1727–?

The monthly chronicle. Ed I. Kimber. No 1, Jan 1728–March 1732–[May 1732].

The present state of the republick of letters. Ed M. de la Roche, A. Reid. No 1, Jan 1728–Dec 1736. Superseded by the History of the works of the learned, beginning Jan 1737.

The mirrour. No 1, 18 Dec–21 Oct 1730; rptd 1733.

The new political state of Great Britain. No 1, Jan 1730–May 1730–?

A literary journal: or a continuation of the Memoirs of literature. Ed M. de la Roche. No 1, Jan 1730–vol 3 no 6, June 1731.

Historia litteraria: or an exact and early account of the most valuable books. Ed A. Bower. Vol 1 no 1, 1730–vol 4 no 23, 1734.

The occasional historian, by M. Earbery. No 1, 1730–no 4, 1732.

The monthly remembrancer: or an historical and chronological diary of the affairs of Europe. No 1, 1730.

Miscellaneous observations upon authors ancient and modern. Ed J. Jortin. Vol 1 no 1, Jan 1731–vol 2 no 24, 1732; tr Latin and continued, Amsterdam 1732–4.

The gentleman's magazine: or monthly intelligencer, by 'Sylvanus Urban' [E. Cave et al]. Vol 1 no 1, Jan 1731–. Continued as the Gentleman's magazine and historical chronicle, Jan 1736–. Many nos rptd.

[Johnson, S.] To the reader. GM 8 1738 (attached to annual vol).

— The life of Edward Cave. GM Feb 1754; rptd in Biographia britannica, 1784 (2nd edn), and in Johnson's works.

Kimber, E. [List of books, with annual indexes and the index to the first twenty years, 1752]; rptd London 1966.

Bond, D. Friendship strikingly exhibited in letters between D. Henry and J. Nichols, managing proprietors of the Gentleman's Magazine, and D. Bond, late printer of that monthly miscellany. 1781.

Ayscough, S. A general index to the first 56 vols from 1731 to 1786. 2 vols 1789.

A list of plates, maps etc in the Gentleman's Magazine, 1731–1813. 1814.

[St Barbe, C.] A complete list of the plates and woodcuts in the Gentleman's Magazine 1731–1818. 1821.

Nichols, J. An account of the rise and progress of the Gentleman's magazine. In Index vol 3, 1821.

— A general index to the Gentleman's Magazine from 1787 to 1818. 1821.

Nichols, J. G. A memoir of John Nichols. 1858; rptd in Literary illustrations vol 8, 1858.

N. Royal paper copies of the Gentleman's Magazine. N & Q 4 May 1861.

[Blacker, B. H.] Gloucestershire engravings in the Gentleman's Magazine 1731–1818. Gloucestershire N & Q 2 1882.

The Gentleman's Magazine library: being a classified collection of the chief contents of the Gentleman's Magazine from 1731 to 1868. Ed G. L. Gomme 29 vols in 30 1883–1905.

Blaydes, F. A. and J. G. Raynes. Index of references to articles in the Gentleman's Magazine relating to Bedfordshire. Bedfordshire N & Q 1 1884.

Farrar, R. H. Index to the obituary and biographical notices 1731–80. Index Soc 15 [1886].

— An index to the biographical and obituary notices in the Gentleman's Magazine 1731–80. 1891.

Genealogical notes extracted from the Gentleman's Magazine 1731–56. Bedfordshire N & Q 2 1888.

Swiftiana in the Gentleman's Magazine. Bookworm 2 1889.

Roberts, W. The Gentleman's Magazine and its rivals. Athenaeum 26 Oct 1889.

— The history of the Gentleman's Magazine. Bookworm 3 1890.

Haverfield, F. Extracts from the Gentleman's Magazine relating to Oxford 1731–1800. In Collectanea, ed M. Burrows, Oxford 1890.

Extracts from the Gentleman's Magazine relating to Wiltshire. Wiltshire N & Q 1–2 1894–7, 8 1916.

Hutton, A. W. Dr Johnson and the Gentleman's magazine. Eng Illustr Mag 17 1897; rptd in Johnson Club papers, 1899.

Hope, H. G. The Gentleman's Magazine. N & Q 25 Feb 1899. See also J. C. Francis 25 March, 15 April 1899.

Adler, J. Die Shakespeare-Kritik im Gentleman's Magazine. In his Zur Shakespeare-Kritik des 18 Jahrhunderts. Königsberg 1906.

Sylvanus Urban. TLS 2 Feb 1906.

Bullen, A. H. An account of the Gentleman's Magazine. GM Feb 1906.

McR., A. T. The Gentleman's Magazine and Scotland in 1749. Scottish N & Q Aug 1923.

Roberts, S. C. Johnson in Grub street. Cornhill Mag 1928.

A literary competition. TLS 20 March 1930.

Blunden, E. The Gentleman's Magazine 1731–1907. In his Votive tablets, 1931.

The Gentleman's Magazine 1731–1907. TLS 11 June 1931. See also R. B. McKerrow 18 June 1931; E. Whitaker 25 June 1931.

Lewis-Melville, A. R. Henry Fielding. TLS 27 July 1933.

Johnsonian gleanings pt 6. Ed A. L. Reade 1933.

Reade, A. L. The Seatonian prize at Cambridge. N & Q 23 Feb 1946.

Yost, C. D. The poetry of the Gentleman's Magazine: a study in eighteenth-century literary taste. Philadelphia 1936.

Carlson, C. L. The first magazine: a history of the Gentleman's Magazine. Providence 1938.

Bond, D. F. The Gentleman's Magazine. MP 38 1941.

Powell, L. F. An addition to the canon of Johnson's writings. E & S 28 1942.

Aylward, J. D. The Gentleman's Magazine. N & Q 4 Oct 1947.

Limouze, A. S. A note on Edward Cave's early London career. N & Q 7 Aug 1948.

Greene, D. J. The Johnsonian canon: a neglected attribution. PMLA 65 1950.

— Was Johnson theatrical critic of the Gentleman's Magazine? RES new ser 3 1952.

— Some notes on Johnson and the Gentleman's Magazine. PMLA 74 1959.

— Johnsonian attributions by Alexander Chalmers. N & Q May 1967.

Hart, E. The contributions of John Nichols [in GM] to Boswell's Life of Johnson. PMLA 67 1952.

— An ingenious editor: John Nichols and the Gentleman's Magazine. Bucknell Rev 10 1962.

Hoover, B. B. Samuel Johnson's parliamentary reporting: debates in the senate of Lilliput. Berkeley 1953.

Leed, J. Two new pieces by Johnson in the Gentleman's Magazine. MP 54 1957.

— Two notes on Johnson and the Gentleman's Magazine. PBSA 54 1960.

— Some reprintings of the Gentleman's Magazine. SB 17 1964.

Bloom, E. A. Samuel Johnson in Grub street. Providence 1957.

Fox, R. C. The imaginary submarines of Dr Johnson and Richard Owen Cambridge. PQ 40 1961.

Kolb, G. J. More attributions to Dr Johnson. Stud in Eng Lit 1500–1900 1 1961.

Lonsdale, R. Christopher Smart's first publication in English. RES new ser 12 1961.

Sherbo, A. Samuel Johnson and the Gentleman's Magazine. In Johnsonian studies, ed M. Wahba, Cairo 1962.

— Samuel Johnson and certain poems in the May 1747 Gentleman's Magazine. RES new ser 17 1966.

Eddy, D. D. John Hawkesworth: book reviewer in the Gentleman's Magazine. PQ 43 1964.

Bernard, F. V. New evidence on the Pamphilus letters. MP 62 1964.

— Johnson's address 'To the reader'. N & Q Dec 1965.

— Common and superior sense: a new attribution to Johnson. N & Q May 1967.

— Johnson and the authorship of four debates. PMLA 82 1967.

Todd, W. B. A bibliographical account of the Gentleman's Magazine. SB 18 1965.

The London magazine: or gentleman's monthly intelligencer. Ed I. Kimber (1732–55) and E. Kimber (1755–69). No 1, April 1732–. Continued as London magazine and monthly chronologer, 1736–. Continued as London magazine enlarged and improved, July 1783–5. Followed by New London magazine, beginning July 1785; rptd seriatim Dublin as London and Dublin magazine, Jan–June 1734, and as London magazine and monthly chronicle, 1742–83.

Kimber, I. Memoirs of the life and writings of Isaac Kimber. In his Sermons on the most interesting religious, moral, and practical subjects, 1756.

[Kimber, E.] The general index to the first 27 volumes 1732–58. 1750, 1966.

The hypochondriack: being the seventy essays by James Boswell appearing in the London magazine from November 1777 to August 1783. Ed M. Bailey 2 vols Stanford 1928.

Pottle, F. A. The literary career of James Boswell esq. Oxford 1929.

Kimber, S. A. The relation of a late expedition to St Augustine, with biographical and bibliographical notes on Isaac and Edward Kimber. PBSA 28 1934.

Wendlund, I. Der Einfluss der Politik auf das London Magazine und seine Hauptbeiträger, Emsdetten 1937.

Tave, S. M. Some essays by James Beattie in the London Magazine 1771. N & Q 6 Dec 1952.

The monthly catalogues from the London magazine 1732–66; with the index for 1732–58 compiled by E. Kimber. 1966.

Sambrook, A. J. Another early version of Shenstone's Pastoral ballad [in London Mag Dec 1751]. RES new ser 18 1967.

McKenzie, D. F. and J. C. Ross. A ledger of Charles Akers, printer of the London Magazine. Oxford 1968.

The comedian: or philosophical enquirer, by T. Cooke. No 1, April 1732–no 9, March 1733.

The friendly writer and register of truth, by 'Ruth Collins'. No 1, Sep 1732–no 8, April 1733.

The bee: or universal weekly pamphlet. Ed E. Budgell. Vol 1 no 1, 10 Feb 1733–no 13, 5 May 1733. Continued as Bee: or universal weekly pamphlet reviewed, vol 2 no 14, nd–. Continued as Bee revived: or the universal weekly pamphlet, no 17–vol 9 no 118, 14 June 1735. Remainders issued as 'second edition', with textual changes in nos 1–2 only.

Herd, H. In his Seven editors, 1955. On E. Budgell.

The lady's magazine: or universal repository. No 1, March 1733–[no 5, July 1733]–?

The weekly amusement: or universal magazine. No 1, 9 Nov 1734–[no 62], 10 Jan 1736.

The literary magazine: or select British library. Ed E. Chambers. No 1, Jan 1735–. Continued as The literary magazine: or the history of the works of the learned, July 1735–Dec 1736–. Continued as History of the works of the learned, Jan 1737–Dec 1743. For E. Chambers see Universal Mag of Knowledge & Pleasure Jan 1785.

Queen Anne's weekly journal: or the ladies magazine. No 1, 15 Nov 1735–. Continued as Queen Anne's weekly magazine: or the ladies library, no 6, 20 Dec 1735–no 175, 17 March 1739.

Sutherland, J. R. Lost journals. Periodical Post Boy 6 March 1950.

The gentleman's magazine and monthly oracle, by 'Merlin the Second'. [No 1, March 1736]–no 7, Sept 1736–?

Roberts, W. The Gentleman's Magazine and its rivals. Athenaeum 26 Oct 1889.

The Oxford magazine: or family companion. Nos 1–2, May–June 1736–?

Sutherland, J. R. Lost journals. Periodical Post Boy 6 March 1950.

The distillers universal magazine. Ptd by J. Stanton. No 1, 25 Sept 1736–? Continued as Distillers magazine ?–no 10, 27 Nov 1736–?

Sutherland, J. R. Lost journals. Periodical Post Boy 6 March 1950.

The country magazine: or the gentleman and lady's pocket companion. [No 1, March 1736]–[No 2], April 1736–May 1737–?

The British librarian, exhibiting a compendious view of our most scarce, valuable and useful books, by W. Oldys. No 1, Jan 1737–no 6, June 1737; rptd 1738.

The Oxford magazine: or universal library. No 1, 8 Jan 1737–?

The lady's magazine: or the compleat library. ?–no 18, 3 Feb 1739–?

The universal spy: or London weekly magazine, by 'Timothy Truepenny'. No 1, 13 April 1739–no 26, 5 Oct 1739.

The Spanish spy: or the unfortunate merchant's magazine. No 1, 1 Sept 1739–no 24, 9 Feb 1740.

The country magazine: or weekly pacquet. [No 1, c. 14 Nov 1739]–?

The entertaining correspondent. 1739.

The history of our own times. No 1, 1 Jan 1741–no 4, 5 March 1741.

The publick register: or the weekly magazine. No 1, 3 Jan 1741–no 24, 13 June 1741.

Miscellaneous correspondence: containing essays sent to the author of the Gentleman's Magazine, which could not be conveniently inserted. No 1, 1742–no 8, 1748.

The general magazine: containing something to hit every body's taste. No 1, 29 Oct 1743–?

The modern husbandman: or the practice of farming, by W. Ellis. Jan–March 1744.

The political cabinet: or an impartial review of the most remarkable occurrences of the world. Vol 1 no 1, July 1744–vol 2 no 12, June 1745.

The publisher: containing miscellanies in prose and verse. Ed. J. Crokatt. Nos 1–4, 1745.

Proposals for printing every fortnight, price sixpence, the Publisher containing miscellanies in prose and verse. 1744, Oxford 1930.

Chapman, R. W. Johnson's works: a lost piece and a forgotten piece. London Mercury March 1930.

The female spectator, by E. Haywood. No 1, April 1744–no 24, May 1746; rptd 1748, 1750, 1755, 1766, 1771, Dublin 1746. Portions rptd 1929.

Whicher, G. F. The life and romances of Mrs Eliza Haywood. New York 1915.

Hodges, J. The female spectator: a courtesy periodical. In Studies in the early English periodical, ed R. P. Bond, Chapel Hill 1957.

The British magazine. Ed J. Hill. No 1, March 1746–Dec 1750.

Kennedy, J. Some remarks on the life and writings of Dr J— H—, Inspector General of Great Britain. 1752.

A short account of the life, writings and character of sir John Hill. 1779.

Herd, H. In his Seven editors, 1955. On John Hill.

The lists of books from the British magazine 1746–50, collected with annual indexes. Farnborough 1965.

The museum: or the literary and historical register. Ed M. Akenside. No 1, 29 March 1746–no 39, 12 Sept 1747.

Cunningham, P. Dr Akenside. GM Feb 1853. On agreement with Dodsley for editing.

Seymour, M. The Museum. N & Q 14 Nov 1931.

— Fielding's History of the forty-five. PQ 14 1935.

Addington, M. H. The Museum. N & Q 16 Jan 1932.

Blunden, E. Collins and Dodsley's Museum. TLS 8 Aug 1935.

Roberts, W. Verses in Dodsley's Museum. N & Q 18 Nov 1939.

Ryskamp, C. J. G. Cooper and Dodsley's Museum. N & Q May 1958.

The penny medley: or weekly entertainer. Nos 1–12, 1746.

The literary register. Jan–March 1947.

The lady's weekly magazine, by 'Mrs Penelope Pry'. [E. Haywood]. No 1, 19 Feb 1747–?

The universal magazine of knowledge and pleasure. Ed P. Stockdale. No 1, June 1747–. With suppls.

The memoirs of the life and writings of Percival Stockdale. 1809.

Clark, A. Essex in the Universal magazine 1750. Essex Rev 24 1915.

Friedman, A. Goldsmith's Essay on friendship: its first publication and the problem of authorship. PQ 35 1956.

The oratory magazine. Ed J. Henley. [Nos 1–3, 1748]–?

Mitre and crown: or Great Britain's true interest. No 1, Oct 1748–Feb 1751.

The travellers magazine: or gentleman and lady's agreeable companion. No 1, Jan 1749–no 12, Dec 1749–[Dec 1750]–?

Mazazin de Londres. ?–March 1749–?

The monthly review. Ed R. Griffiths et al. Vol 1 no 1, May 1749–vol 81, Dec 1789. Continued as Monthly review: or literary journal, vol 1 no 1, Jan 1790–vol 33, Dec 1800–.

A complete catalogue of all the books and pamphlets published for ten years past, with their prices and references to their characters in the Monthly Review: the whole forming a general index to all the articles in the first 20 vols of the said Review. 1760.

An apology for the Monthly Review with an appendix in behalf of the Critical. 1763.

Ayscough, S. A general index from the commencement to the end of the seventieth volume. 1786.

— A continuation from the 71st to the 81st volume. 1796.

A general index from Jan 1790 to Dec 1816. 1818.

Aikin, L. Memoirs of John Aikin. 1823.

Robberds, J. W. Memoir of William Taylor. 1843.

Knight, C. Shadows of the old booksellers. 1865.

'George Paston' (E. M. Symonds). The Monthly Review in the xviiith century. Monthly Rev Aug 1902; rptd in her Sidelights on the Georgian period, 1903.

Spittal, J. K. (ed). Contemporary criticism of Dr Samuel Johnson [articles rptd from Monthly Review 1775–96]. New York 1923.

Hawkins, A. Some writers on the Monthly Review. RES 7 1931.

The Monthly Review. TLS 5 April 1934.

Nangle, B. C. The Monthly Review, first series 1749–89: indexes of contributors and articles. Oxford 1934.

— The Monthly Review, second series 1790–1815: indexes of contributors and articles. Oxford 1955.

Carlson, C. L. Edward Cave's club and its project for a literary review. PQ 17 1938.

Knapp, L. M. Ralph Griffiths, author and publisher 1746–50. Library 4th ser 20 1940.

— Griffiths' Monthly Review as printed by Strahan. N & Q May 1958.

Spector, R. D. The Monthly and its rival. BNYPL March 1960.

Lonsdale, R. William Bewley and the Monthly Review: a problem of attribution. PBSA 55 1961.

— Dr Burney and the Monthly Review. RES new ser 14–15 1963–4.

The London review: or weekly entertainer. [No 1, 14 Oct 1749]–no 2, 21 Oct 1749–?

The ladies magazine: or the universal entertainer, by 'Jasper Goodwill, of Oxford esq.' Vol 1 no 1, 18 Nov 1749–vol 4 no 23, 10 Nov 1753.

The student: or Oxford monthly miscellany. Ed C. Smart et al. Vol 1 no 1, 30 Jan 1750–. Continued as the Student: or the Oxford and Cambridge monthly miscellany, vol 1 no 6, 30 June 1750–vol 2 no [10], July 1751.

Gray, G. J. A bibliography of the writings of Christopher Smart, with biographical references. Trans of Bibl Soc 6 1901.

Botting, R. B. Christopher Smart in London. Research Stud of State College of Washington 6 1939.

— Christopher Smart's association with Arthur Murphy. JEGP 43 1944.

Brittain, R. E. Christopher Smart in the magazines. Library 4th ser 21 1941.

Ainsworth, E. G. and C. E. Noyes. Christopher Smart: a biographical and critical study. Columbia Missouri 1943.

Sherbo, A. Christopher Smart, scholar of the university. East Lansing 1967.

The bee newly revived. No 1, [Jan] 1750–no 12, [Dec] 1750. Vol pbd as Bee revived: or the prisoners magazine.

Mercure historique, politique, littéraire et galant. [No 1], Jan 1750.

The magazine of magazines, composed from original pieces. No 1, July 1750–1.

The grand magazine of magazines: or a public register of literature and amusement, by R. Woodville. No 1, July 1750–no 2, Sept 1750–?

The kapélion: or poetical ordinary, consisting of great variety of dishes in prose and verse, by A. Metaphoricus [W. Kenrick]. No 1, [Aug 1750]–no 6, [Jan 1751].

Le nouveau magasin français: ou bibliothèque instructive et amusante. Ed J. L. de Beaumont. [No 1, Aug 1750]–July 1751–[1752; 1755].

The midwife: or old woman's magazine. Ed C. Smart. No 1, [16] Oct 1750–vol 3 no 2, [Nov] 1751–no 3–no 4, [April 1753]. Selections rptd in Nonpareil 1757.

See under Student, beginning 30 Jan 1750, above.

The royal magazine: or quarterly bee. No 1, Oct 1750–June 1751.

The living world: or the history of the last fortnight. Nos 1–3, 1750.

The Westminster magazine. No 1, 24 Nov 1750–no 27, 23 Nov 1751–?

The theological magazine. ?–Dec 1750–?

The dissenting gentleman's magazine. ?–Dec 1750–?

The true Briton. No 1, [2 Jan] 1751–vol 5 no 20, 6 June 1753.

The universal librarian: containing a copious account of new books. No 1, April–June 1751.

The Lilliputian magazine. No 1, [?]–no 2, June 1751–?; rptd 1783.

Botting, R. B. Christopher Smart and the Lilliputian Magazine. ELH 9 1942.

The new universal magazine: or gentleman and lady's polite instructor. No 1, Sept 1751–[1759]. Possibly continued as New royal and universal magazine: or the gentleman and lady's companion. ?–vol 16 no 4, Oct 1759–no 5, Nov 1759–?

The general review: or impartial register. No 1, [May] 1752–no 5, [July] 1752.

Repository: containing a succinct and clear view of the most considerable transactions and publications both at home and abroad. [Nos 1–2], 1752.

The lady's curiosity: or weekly Apollo, by 'Nestor Druid gent.' Nos 1–20, 1752.

The general magazine of arts and sciences, philosophical, philological, mathematical and mechanical, by B. Martin. Jan 1755–65.

The universal visiter and monthly memorialist. Ed C. Smart et al. No 1, Jan 1756–Dec 1758.

Swann, J. H. Christopher Smart. Papers of Manchester Literary Club 21 1902.

Pigott, S. New light on Smart. TLS 13 June 1929.

Jones, C. E. Smart, Richard Rolt and the Universal Visiter. Library 4th ser 18 1938.

Botting, R. B. Johnson, Smart, and the Universal Visiter. MP 36 1939.

Sherbo, A. Smart and the Universal Visiter. Library 5th ser 10 1955.

New essays by A. Murphy. Ed A. Sherbo, East Lansing 1963.

The critical review: or annals of literature. Ed T. Smollett et al. No 1, Jan 1756–.

For studies of Smollett see cols 965, above.

An apology for the Monthly review with an appendix in behalf of the Critical. 1763.

Zeitlin, J. Southey's contributions to the Critical Review. N & Q Feb–May 1918.

Jones, C. E. Smollett and the Critical review. In his Smollett studies, Berkeley 1942.

— Contributors to the Critical Review 1756–85. MLN 61 1946.

— Poetry and the Critical Review. MLQ 9 1948.

— The Critical Review's first thirty years 1756–85. N & Q Feb 1956.

— The Critical Review and some major poets. N & Q March 1956.

— Dramatic criticism in the Critical Review 1756–85. MLQ 20 1959.

Friedman, A. Goldsmith's contributions to the Critical Review. MP 44 1946.

Patterson, C. I. The authenticity of Coleridge's reviews of Gothic romances. JEGP 50 1951.

Spector, R. D. Language control in the eighteenth century [in Critical Review]. Word Study 27 1951.

— Attacks on the Critical Review. Periodical Post Boy 1955.

— Further attacks on the Critical Review. N & Q Dec 1955.

— Additional attacks on the Critical Review. N & Q Oct 1956.

— Attacks on the Critical review 1764–5. N & Q March 1957.

— Attacks on the Critical Review in the Court Magazine. N & Q July 1958.

— Attacks on the Critical Review in the Literary Magazine. N & Q Aug 1960.

— The Monthly and its rivals. BNYPL March 1960.

Roper, D. Smollett's four gentlemen: the first contributors to the Critical Review. RES new ser 10 1959.

— Coleridge and the Critical Review. MLR 55 1960.

— The politics of the Critical Review 1756–1817. Durham Univ Jnl 53 1961.

Erdman, D. V. Immoral acts of a library cormorant: the extent of Coleridge's contributions to the Critical review. BNYPL Sept–Nov 1959.

Klukoff, P. J. A Smollett attribution in the Critical Review. N & Q June 1965.

— Two Smollett attributions in the Critical review: The reverie and Tristram Shandy. N & Q Dec 1966.

— New Smollett attributions in the Critical Review. N & Q Nov 1967.

— Smollett and the Critical Review: criticism of the novel 1756–63. Stud in Scottish Lit 4 1967.

Boucé, P.-G. Smollett's libel. TLS 30 Dec 1965.

The monthly and critical review. No 1, Jan 1756–no 6, June 1756.

The repository: or general review. No 1, 13 March 1756–no 5, 15 May 1756.

The literary magazine: or universal review. Ed W. Faden et al. No 1, May 1756–no 27, July 1758. No 21, Jan 1758 as Literary and anti-Gallican magazine.

Hutton, A. W. Dr Johnson and the Gentleman's magazine. Eng Illustr Mag 17 1897; rptd in Johnson Club Papers 1899.

Seitz, R. W. Goldsmith and the Literary Magazine. RES 5 1929.

Sherbo, A. A possible addition to the Johnson canon. RES new ser 6 1955.

— Two pieces newly ascribed to Christopher Smart. MLR 62 1967.

Golden, M. Goldsmith attributions in the Literary Magazine. N & Q Oct–Nov 1956.

Greene, D. J. Johnson's contributions to the Literary Magazine. RES 7 1956.

— Johnsonian attributions by Alexander Chalmers. N & Q May 1967.

Spector, R. D. Attacks on the Critical Review in the Literary Magazine. N & Q Aug 1960.

New essays by Arthur Murphy. Ed A. Sherbo, East Lansing 1963.

Bernard, F. V. A possible source for Johnson's Life of the King of Prussia. PQ 47 1968.

The literary miscellany. 1756–7.

The grand magazine of universal intelligence and monthly chronicle of our own times. No 1, Feb 1758–Dec 1760.

Harlan, R. D. The publishing of the Grand Magazine of universal intelligence and monthly chronicle of our own times. PBSA 59 1955.

The weekly magazine and literary review. Ed Nicholas Spencer (pseudonym?). No 1, 15 April 1758–no 16, 29 July 1758.

The magazine of magazines: or universal register. No 1, July 1758–no 16, Dec 1758. Continued as Grand magazine of magazines: or universal register, Jan 1759– vol 3 no 18, Dec 1759.

Suttor, W. H. The grand magazine of magazines. N & Q 19 Sept 1891. Comments 17 Oct, 5 Dec 1891, 30 Jan 1892.

The royal magazine: or gentleman's monthly companion. No 1, July 1759–no 21, Dec 1771.

New essays by Oliver Goldsmith. Ed R. S. Crane, Chicago 1927.

The historical and political mercury. No 1, Sept 1759.

The lady's magazine: or polite companion for the fair sex. Ed O. Goldsmith. [No 1, Sept or Oct 1759]–Dec 1763.

New essays by Oliver Goldsmith. Ed R. S. Crane, Chicago 1927.

Walker, H. A. The Lady's Magazine. N & Q 20 Dec 1930.

Friedman, A. An essay by Goldsmith in the Lady's Magazine. MP 30 1933.

The bee. Ed O. Goldsmith. No 1, 6 Oct 1759–no 8, 24 Nov 1759. Some essays rptd 1765, 1766. All rptd 1966.

Friedman, A. The first edition of Essays by Mr Goldsmith. SB 5 1953.

— (ed). The collected works of Oliver Goldsmith vol 1. Oxford 1966.

Knight, D. Two issues of Goldsmith's Bee. N & Q 16 Dec 1944.

Starkey, J. Goldsmith and the Bee. In his Essays and recollections by Seumas O'Sullivan, Dublin 1944.

The impartial review: or literary journal. No 1, 1 Nov 1759.

The weekly magazine: or gentleman and lady's polite companion. No 1, [29 Dec 1759]–no 4, [19 Jan 1760]– [no 5, 26 Jan 1760].

Friedman, A. Goldsmith and the Weekly magazine. MP 32 1935.

Golden, M. Goldsmith attributions in the Weekly magazine. N & Q Aug 1956.

The weekly magazine and memoirs of modern literature. ?–Jan 1760–?

The British magazine: or monthly repository for gentlemen and ladies. Ed T. G. Smollett. No 1, Jan 1760– Dec 1767.

Tupper, C. F. Essays erroneously attributed to Goldsmith. PMLA 39 1924.

New essays by Oliver Goldsmith. Ed R. S. Crane. Chicago 1927.

Golden, M. Two essays erroneously attributed to Goldsmith. MLN 74 1959.

The imperial magazine: or complete monthly intelligencer. No 1, Jan 1760–Dec 1762.

The royal female magazine. Ed 'Charles Honeycombe esq' (R. Lloyd). No 1, Jan 1760–Dec 1760.

The public magazine. No 1, 26 Jan 1760–?

The lady's museum. Ed C. Lennox. Feb 1760–Feb 1761.
Small, M. R. Charlotte Ramsay Lennox: an eighteenth century lady of letters. New Haven 1935.
The musical magazine. No 1, Feb 1760–?
The universal review: or a critical commentary on the literary productions of these kingdoms. No 1, March 1760.
The monthly melody: or gentlemen and ladies polite amusement. [No 1, March 1760?]–no 2, April 1760–?
The new magazine of knowledge: concerning heaven and hell, and the universal world of nature. Vol 1, April 1760–Dec 1760.
The Christian's magazine: or a treasury of divine knowledge. Ed W. Dodd. No 1, May 1760–vol 8, 1767.
[Reed, I.] Historical memoirs of the life and writings of Dr Dodd. 1777.
Fitzgerald, P. A famous forgery: being the story of the unfortunate Dr Dodd. 1865.
Warner, J. H. The macaroni parson. Queen's Quart 53 1946.
Sherbo, A. Two pieces newly ascribed to Christopher Smart. MLR 62 1967.
The spiritual magazine: or the Christian's grand treasure. 1760–. Merged with the Gospel magazine, 1784.
The Protestant's Magazine. No 1, Feb 1761.
Sedgwick, D. Protestant Magazine. N & Q 12 Jan 1861.
The library: or moral and critical magazine. Ed A. Kippis. No 1, April 1761–May 1762.
The lawyers's magazine: or attorney's and solicitor's universal library. No 1, [April] 1761–2.
The mathematical magazine: and philosophical repository. Ed G. Witchell et al. No 1, April 1761–?
The Court magazine: or royal chronicle. Ed H. Kelly. No 1, Sept 1761–. Continued as the Court and city magazine, March 1763–. Continued as the Court, city and country magazine, Feb 1764–Nov 1765.
Spector, R. D. Attacks on the Critical Review in the Court Magazine. N & Q July 1958.
The universal museum: or gentleman's and lady's polite magazine of history, politics and literature. Ed A. Young, J. Seally. No 1, Jan 1762–. Continued as the Universal museum and complete magazine of knowledge and pleasure, Nov 1764–70.
Golden, M. Goldsmith and the Universal Museum and Complete Magazine. N & Q Aug 1957.
The London register: or historical notes of the present time. No 1, Jan 1762–June 1762.
The beauties of all the magazines selected. No 1, Jan 1762–Dec 1764.
The political controversy: or weekly magazine of ministerial and anti-ministerial essays. Ed J. Wilkes. Vol 1 no 1, 17 July 1762–. Continued as the Weekly magazine, vol 4 no 1–vol 5 no 8, 3 Sept 1763.
The fortnight's register: or a chronicle of interesting and remarkable events, foreign and domestic. No 1, 11 Aug 1762–no 22, 4 June 1763.
The St James's magazine. Ed R. Lloyd, W. Kenrick. No 1, Sept 1762–June 1764.
Kenrick, W. An account of the life and writings of the author [R. Lloyd]. In Poetical works of Robert Lloyd, 1774.
The country magazine calculated for the gentleman; the farmer and his wife. No 1, Jan 1763–?
The theatrical review: or annals of the drama. No 1, Jan 1763–no 6, June 1763.
The gentleman's museum. ?–April 1763–?
The medical museum: or a repository of cases, experiments, researches and discoveries collected at home and abroad. 1763–4; rptd 1781.
Museum rusticum et commerciale: or select papers on agriculture, commerce, arts and manufactures. No 1, Sept 1763–June 1766.
The weekly amusement: or an useful and agreeable miscellany of literary entertainments. No 1, 24 Dec 1763–26 Dec 1767. Fortnightly suppls.

Price, C. An early publication of one of Chesterfield's letters to his son. Neuphilologische Mitteilungen 67 1966.
The poetical magazine: or the muses' monthly companion. Ed F. Fawkes and W. Woty. No 1, Jan 1764–no 6, June 1764.
The general magazine. No 1, Jan 1764–no 7, July 1764–?
The complete magazine. No 1, April 1764–Oct 1764. Merged with the Universal museum and continued as the Universal museum and complete magazine of knowledge and pleasure, Nov 1764–1770.
Golden, M. Goldsmith and the Universal Museum and Complete Magazine. N & Q Aug 1957.
The wonderful magazine: or marvellous chronicle. 1764–6.
Literary annals: or the reviewers reviewed. No 1, Jan 1765–?
The candid review and literary repository. No 1, Jan 1765–June 1765.
The Court miscellany: or ladies new magazine. Ed H. Kelly. No 1, July 1765–. Continued as the Court miscellany: or gentleman and lady's new magazine, Aug 1766–71.
The jester's magazine: or the monthly merrymaker. No 1, Oct 1765–Dec 1766.
The gospel magazine: or spiritual library. No 1, Jan 1766–Dec 1773.
The monthly record of literature. No 1, Jan 1767–Dec 1767.
The political register: and impartial review of new books. Ed J. Almon. Vol 1 no 1, May 1767–June 1772.
The trial of John Almon. 1770.
Memoirs of a late eminent bookseller. 1790.
Rea, R. R. John Almon: bookseller to John Wilkes. Indiana Quart for Bookmen 4 1948.
The Oxford magazine: or university museum. No 1, Jan 1768–Dec 1776.
The constitutional magazine: or complete treasure of politics and literature. 1768–9.
The musical companion: or songster's magazine. 1768.
The town and country magazine: or a universal repository of knowledge, instruction and pleasure. Ed A. Hamilton. No 1, Jan 1769–Dec 1796.
Critical memoirs of the times: containing a summary view of the popular pursuits, political debates and literary productions of the present age. Ed W. Kenrick? No 1, Jan 1769–no 9, Dec 1769.
The freeholder's magazine: or monthly chronicle of liberty. Ed J. Seally. No 1, Sept 1769–Dec 1770.
The repository: or half-yearly register: containing whatever is remarkable in the history, politics, literature and amusements of the year 1768. 1769.
The gentleman's journal: or weekly register of news, politics, literature and amusement. No 1, 19 Nov 1769–no 2, 26 Nov 1769.
The London museum of politics, miscellanies and literature. No 1, Jan 1770–Dec 1771.
The repository: or treasury of politics and literature. 1770.
The lady's magazine: or entertaining companion for the fair sex. Ed J. H. Wynne. No 1, July 1770–.
Mayo, R. D. How long was Gothic fiction in vogue? MLN 58 1943.
— To our correspondents. Periodical Post Boy 12 1952.
Pollard, H. G. The early poems of George Crabbe and the Lady's Magazine. Bodleian Lib Record 5 1955.
The gentleman's museum and grand imperial magazine. No 1, July 1770–Dec 1771.
The Court and city magazine: or a fund of entertainment for the man of quality. Vol 1 Jan 1770–Dec 1771.
Every man's magazine: or the monthly repository of science, instruction and amusement. July 1771–June 1772.

The British magazine and general review of the literature, employment and amusements of the times. No 1, March 1772–Dec 1772.

The Covent garden magazine: or amorous repository. No 1, July 1772–Dec 1774.

The macaroni and theatrical magazine: or monthly register of the fashions and diversions of the times. No 1, Oct 1772–. Continued as the Macaroni, savoir vivre and theatrical magazine, no 7, April 1773–no 15, Dec 1773. Walford, E. The macaroni magazine. N & Q 27 Sept 1879.

The Westminster magazine: or the pantheon of taste. Vol 1 no 1, Jan 1773–vol 13 no [158], July 1785.

The sentimental magazine: or general assemblage of science, taste and entertainment. No 1, March 1773–Dec 1777.

The medical magazine. No 1, Dec 1773–?

The biographical magazine. 1773–6.

The lawyer's magazine. 1773.

The monthly ledger: or literary repository. 1773–5.

The monthly miscellany: or gentleman and lady's compleat magazine, wherein every valuable production in the several magazines, reviews and other periodical publications is regularly and carefully collected. No 1, Jan 1774–1775–[1776?].

Moore, J. Extracts from the Monthly Miscellany for the year 1774. Gloucestershire N & Q 4 1889.

The gospel magazine: or treasury of divine knowledge. Ed A. M. Toplady. No 1, Jan 1774–Jan 1784. Merged with Spiritual magazine.

The St James's magazine: or memoirs of our times. Vol 1 no 1, Feb 1774–vol 3 no 34, July 1776.

The whimsical repository: or general receptacle of wit, humour and entertainment. No 1, Aug 1774–no 3, Oct 1774–?

The copper plate magazine: or monthly treasure for the admirers of the imitative arts. No 1, Aug 1774–no 42, Jan 1778.

The builder's magazine: or monthly companion for architects, carpenters, masons, bricklayers etc. No 1, Sept 1774–?

The monthly miscellany: or gentleman and lady's compleat magazine. 1774–6.

The new musical and universal magazine. No 1, Oct 1774–no 17, Feb 1776–?

The parliamentary register: or history of the proceedings and debates of the House of Commons (and the House of Lords). Ed J. Almon. Nov 1774–.

The London review of English and foreign literature. Ed W. Kenrick and W. S. Kenrick. No 1, Jan 1775–Dec 1780.

The trader's magazine and monthly treasury of trade, commerce, arts, manufactures and mechanics. No 1, Jan 1775–?

The general review of foreign literature. Ed Winstanley et al. No 1, Jan 1775–no 3, March 1775.

The matrimonial magazine: or monthly anecdotes of love and marriage for the Court, the city and the country. No 1, Jan 1775–June 1775. Merged with the Westminster magazine, which began in 1773.

The cathedral magazine: or divine harmony. No 1, April 1775–no 12, March 1776–?

The classical magazine: or monthly repository for persons of real taste. Ed M. Jacob. No 1, Aug 1775–?

The convivial magazine and polite intelligencer. 1775.

The new universal magazine. 1775.

The remembrancer: or impartial repository of public events. Ed J. Almon. 1775–84.

The general magazine: or compleat repository of arts, sciences, politics and literature. No 1, Jan 1776–Dec 1776.

The biographical magazine: or complete historical library. No 1, April 1776–?

The farmer's magazine and useful family companion, by 'Agricola Sylvan'. No 1, April 1776–80.

The lottery magazine: or compleat fund of literary, political and commercial knowledge. No 1, July 1776–Dec 1777.

Le magazin du monde politique, galant et littéraire: or the gentleman and lady's magazine in French and English. Ed C. de Missy? Nos 1–3, 1776.

The selector. Ed J. Calder. No 1, Nov 1776–no 5, 2 Jan 1777.

Monthly museum: comprehending a political and parliamentary remembrancer, a classical miscellany, a poetical kalendar, a critical catalogue, a theatrical diary and an historical register for the year. [No 1], 1776.

The theatrical magazine. ?–no 3, Jan 1777–81.

The gentleman and lady's museum. No 1, Jan 1777–Jan 1778–?

The magazine a la mode: or fashionable miscellany. Jan 1777–Dec 1777.

The young gentleman's magazine: or monthly repository of science, moral and entertaining matter. No 1, Jan 1777–June 1777.

The American magazine: or lottery magazine of literature, politics and pleasure, by 'Philanthropos'. 1777.

Journal étranger de littérature, des spectacles et de politique. No 1, July 1777–May 1778.

The musical companion: or songster's magazine. 1777.

The moral and entertaining magazine: or literary miscellany of instruction and amusement. 1777–9.

The Arminian magazine: consisting of extracts and original translations on universal redemptions. Ed J. Wesley et al. No 1, Jan 1778–. Continued as Methodist magazine, Jan 1798–.

Green, R. Bibliography of John and Charles Wesley. 1896.

Harrison, A. W. The Arminian magazine. Proc of Wesley Historical Soc 12 1920.

Wallington, A. The Arminian and Methodist magazine: British and Irish editors. Proc of Wesley Historical Soc 13 1921.

Herbert, T. W. John Wesley as editor and author. Princeton 1940.

The vocal magazine: or British songster's miscellany. Nos 1–9, 1778.

The British miscellany. No 1, Jan 1779–?

The gospel magazine and moral miscellany. No 1, Jan 1779–?

The whig magazine: or patriot miscellany. No 1, May 1779–?

The foreign medical review. No 1, July 1779.

The poetical magazine. 1779.

The political magazine and parliamentary, naval, military and literary journal. No 1, Jan 1780–Dec 1791.

The Protestant magazine. No 1, March 1780–no 6, Dec 1780–no 3, 1783.

The novelist's magazine. 1780–8.

Letters and papers on agriculture [etc]. 1780, 1783–.

Bibliotheca topographic Britannica. 1780–90. Continued as Miscellaneous antiquities, 1791–3.

Esprit des gazettes. Vol 1, 1780–vol 35, 1797. Continued as Echo des feuilles politiques et littéraires, vol 36, 1798–vol 38, 1799. Continued as Le compilateur des nouvelles nationales, politiques et littéraires, 2 April 1799–.

The new musical magazine: or compleat library of vocal and instrumental music. c. 1780.

The London medical journal. Ed S. F. Simmons. Vol 1 no 1, Jan 1781–. Continued as Medical facts and observations, 1791–1800.

The vocal magazine: or compleat British songster. Nos 1–9, 1781.

The lady's poetical magazine: or beauties of British poetry. 1781–2.

The European magazine and London review. Ed J. Perry et al. No 1, Jan 1782–.

European Mag & London Rev Sept 1818. On J. Perry. BM Add MS 38728.

A new review, with literary curiosities and literary intelligence. Ed P. H. Maty. No 1, Jan 1782–vol 10 no 3, Sept 1786.

The new Christian's magazine: being an universal repository of divine knowledge. No 1, Oct 1782–no 50 [1786].

The British magazine and review: or universal miscellany of arts, sciences, literature, history, poetry, politics, manners, amusements and intelligence foreign and domestick. Ed W. Wood. No 1, July 1782–Dec 1783.

The repository: containing various political, philosophical and miscellaneous articles. 1782–9.

The English review: or an abstract of English and foreign literature. Ed Whitaker and G. Stuart. No 1, Jan 1783–. Continued as English review of literature, science, discoveries and contests, Jan 1796–Dec 1796. Incorporated in Analytical review, which began in 1788.

The rambler's magazine: or the annals of gallantry, glee, pleasure and the bon ton. No 1, Jan 1783–Feb 1791.

The new spiritual magazine: or evangelical treasury of experimental religion. No 1, July 1783–no 60, Dec 1785.

The theological miscellany, and review of books on religious subjects. Ed C. de Coetlogon. No 1, Jan 1784–Dec 1789.
> GM Oct 1820. On Coetlogon.

The wit's magazine: or library of Momus. Ed T. Holcroft. No 1, Jan 1784–May 1785–?
> The life of Thomas Holcroft, written by himself. Ed W. Hazlitt 3 vols 1816; ed E. Colby 2 vols 1925.
> Colby, E. A biography of Thomas Holcroft. New York 1922.
> Stallbaumer, V. R. Thomas Holcroft: a satirist in the stream of sentimentalism. ELH 3 1936.

Annals of agriculture and other useful arts. Ed Arthur Young. 1784–. Pbd at Bury St Edmunds from 1790.
> Annals of Agriculture 1 1784, 15 1791. On Young.

The vocal magazine: or British songster. Nos 1–9, 1784.

The intrepid magazine. Ed W. Hamilton. 1784.

The weekly amusement. 1784.

The historical chronicle. [No 1, Jan 1785]–June 1786–?

The artists' repository and drawing magazine. Ed F. Fitzgerald. 1785–94.

The political herald and review. Ed G. Stuart and W. Thompson. No 1, July 1785–no 18, Dec 1786.
> Marken, J. W. William Godwin and the Political Herald and Review. BNYPL Oct 1961.

The new London magazine, being an universal and complete monthly repository of knowledge, instruction and entertainment. No 1, July 1785–92.

The new lady's magazine: or polite and entertaining companion for the fair sex. Ed C. Stanhope. No 1, Feb 1786–Dec 1795.
> Tillotson, G. The new lady's magazine of 1786. London Mercury 1931; rptd in his Essays in criticism and research, Cambridge 1942.

The new novelist's magazine: or entertaining library of pleasing and instructive histories, tales, romances. 1786–7.

The fashionable magazine: or lady and gentleman's recorder of new fashions. 1786.

Dramatic magazine: or tragic, comic and operatical library. No 1, Dec 1786–no 2, 1787–?

Affaires du temps. No 1, 1786–no 23, 1789.

The new town and country magazine: or general monthly repository of knowledge and pleasure. No 1, Jan 1787–Dec 1788.

The humourist's magazine. No 1, Jan 1787–?

The olla podrida: a periodical work. Ed T. Monro. No 1, 17 March 1787–no 44, 12 Jan 1788. Pbd Oxford and London.
> Walford, E. The Olla podrida and its author. N & Q 20 Nov 1886.

The plenipotentiary. No 1, 2 June 1787–no 4, 23 June 1787.

The general magazine and impartial review. June 1787–Dec 1792.

The botanical magazine: or flower garden displayed. Ed W. Curtis. No 1, June 1787–.
> Tonks, E. General index to the Latin names and synonyms of the plants depicted in vols 1–107. 1883.
> Curtis, W. H. William Curtis 1746–99. Winchester 1942.
> Hunkin, J. W. William Curtis, founder of the Botanical Magazine. Endeavour 5 1946.
> Synge, P. M. The Botanical Magazine. Jnl of Royal Horticultural Soc Jan 1948.

The English lyceum: or choice of pieces selected from the best periodical papers and other British publications. No 1, July 1787–vol 3 no 9, June 1788. Pbd Hamburg and London.

The repository: containing various political, philosophical, literary and miscellaneous articles. [No 1, Jan 1788]–no 3, 1 Feb 1788–1 Jan 1789–?

Kemmish's new weekly miscellany: or amusing companion. 1787.

The humourist's magazine: or monthly banquet of wit, whim, mirth and fancy, calculated for the entertainment and amusement of both sexes. No 1, Jan 1788–no 5, May 1788.

The Court, city and country magazine: or gentleman and lady's universal and polite instructor. No 1, Jan 1788–no 4, April 1788.

The family magazine: or a repository of religious instruction and rational amusement, by S. Trimmer. No 1, Jan 1788–June 1789.
> The life and writings of Mrs [Sarah] Trimmer. 2 vols 1814, 1825 (3rd edn).

The new universal magazine of knowledge, pleasure and amusement: or gentleman's grand imperial magazine. No 1, Jan 1788–Dec 1788.

The juvenile magazine: or an instructive and entertaining miscellany for youth of both sexes. No 1, Jan 1788–Dec 1788.

The templar: or monthly register of legal and constitutional knowledge. No 1, Feb 1788–Jan 1789.

The Philadelphian magazine. No 1, Feb 1788–no 22, Nov 1789.

The cosmopolitan: a periodical miscellany by gentlemen of the University of Oxford. No 1, 15 April 1788–?

The analytical review: or history of literature domestic and foreign. Ed Thomas Christie. No 1, May 1788–June 1799.
> Nichols, J. In his Literary anecdotes of the eighteenth century vol 4, 1812. On Christie.
> Wardle, R. M. Mary Wollstonecraft: analytical reviewer. PMLA 62 1947.

The trifler: a new periodical miscellany, by 'Timothy Touchstone of Saint Peter's College, Westminster' [J. H. Allen et al?]. No 1, 31 May 1788–no 43, 21 March 1789.

The lounger's miscellany: or the lucubrations of 'A. Slug' [C. Gower]. No 1, 31 May 1788–no 20, 7 March 1789.

The literary and biographical magazine and British review. No 1, July 1788–June 1794.

The royal magazine. Aug 1788.

The historical magazine: or classical library of public events. Ed R. Bisset. No 1, [Nov 1788]–vol 4 no 50, Dec 1792.

The lady's musical magazine: or monthly repository of new vocal music. 1788.

The gentleman's musical magazine. 1788.

The biographical and imperial magazine. Ed J. Thelwall. No 1, Jan 1789–92.
> The life of John Thelwall by his widow. 1837.

Il mercurio italico: o sia ragguaglio generale intorno alla letteratura di tutta l'Italia. The Italian mercury: or a general account concerning the literature, fine arts, useful discoveries etc of all Italy. Ed F. Sastres. No 1, Jan 1789–Jan 1790.

The naturalist's miscellany. Ed G. Shaw and R. P. Nodder. 1789-.

The hive: a hebdomadal selection of literary tracts. No 1, June 1789-no 10, Nov 1789.

The Attic miscellany: or characteristic mirror of men and things. Ed T. Holcroft. No 1, Oct 1789-Aug 1792.

The topographer containing a variety of original articles, by E. Bydges and S. Shaw. Vol 1 no 1, April 1789-vol 4 no 27, June 1791. Continued as Topographical miscellanies containing ancient histories and modern descriptions of mansions, churches, monuments and families throughout England, vol 1 [no 1, Aug 1791]-[no 7, Feb 1792].

[An unidentified monthly magazine of 1789]. See G. S. Gibbons, N & Q 27 June 1936.

The genius of Albion: or weekly biographical, political, law and literary repository. No 1, Jan 1790-?

The new Jerusalem magazine. No 1, Jan 1790-no 6, June 1790.

The lawyer's and magistrate's magazine, in which is included an account of every important proceeding in the courts of Westminster. Vol 1, Feb 1790-vol 6 1794. Vols 1-3 rptd Dublin.

The Christian's magazine: or gospel repository. Ed J. Priestley. 1790-2.

The new magazine of knowledge concerning heaven and hell and the universal world of nature. Vol 1 no 1, April 1790-vol 2 no 20, Oct 1791.

The bon-ton magazine: or microscope of fashion and folly. Vol 1 no 1, March 1791-vol 5 no 61, March 1796.

Oriental repertory. April 1791-April 1797.

The conjurer's magazine: or magical and physiognomical mirror. No 1, Aug 1791-. Continued as the Astrologer's magazine and philosophical miscellany, Aug 1793-4.

Monthly extracts: or beauties of modern authors. No 1, Sept 1791-Nov 1792.

The political state of Europe. No 1, Jan 1792-Dec 1795.

Monthly register of literature: or magazin des savans. Jan 1792-June 1792-?

The Carlton house magazine: or annals of taste, fashion and politeness. No 1, Jan 1792-Feb 1798.

The Christian miscellany: or religious and moral magazine. No 1, Jan 1792-no 8, Aug 1792.

The copper plate magazine: or monthly cabinet of picturesque prints, consisting of views in Great Britain and Ireland. Ed J. Walker. No 1, Feb 1792-.

The new London medical journal. 1792-3.

The new Jerusalem journal: or treasury of divine knowledge. Ed R. Hindmarsh. Nos 1-10, 1792.

The patriot: or political, moral and philosophical repository. No 1, 3 April 1792-3.

The Thespian magazine and literary repository. Vol 1 no 1, June 1792-vol 3 no 24, Sept 1794.

The Covent garden monthly recorder. 1792.

The sporting magazine: or monthly calendar of the transactions of the turf, the chase etc. No 1, Oct 1792-.
Index of engravings in the Sporting Magazine from 1792 to 1870. 1892.

The weekly repository of letters on historical, moral and theological subjects. Nos [1]-18, 1792.

Mathematical, geometrical and philosophical delights. 1792-8.

Monthly beauties: or the cabinet of literary genius. Ed S. Jones. No 1, Jan 1793-?

The wonderful magazine and marvellous chronicle: or new weekly entertainer. Vol 1 no 1, Jan 1793-. Continued as New wonderful magazine: or marvellous chronicle, no 3, March 1793-no 60, [1794].

The British critic: a new review. Ed W. Beloe and R. Nares. No 1, May 1793-.
[Ayscough, S.] A general index to the first 20 vols. 1804.

The free-mason's magazine: or general and complete library. June 1793-. Continued as the Scientific magazine and freemason's repository, Jan 1797-Dec 1797.

The Britannic magazine: or entertaining repository of heroic adventures. Vol 1 no 1, Jan 1793-.

The general magazine: or epitome of useful knowledge. 1793.

Monthly communications: being a collection of tracts on all subjects. Ed J. Trusler. 1793.
The memoirs of the Rev Dr Trusler. Bath 1806.

The evangelical magazine. Ed T. Williams, M. Wilks. No 1, July 1793-.
Index to the first 24 vols. 1817.
Lindsay, J. The evangelical magazine. TLS 12 Nov 1938.

The military magazine. 1793.

Bellamy's picturesque magazine and literary museum. 1793.

The Bacchanalian magazine: or vehicle of monstrous good things. 1793.

One pennyworth of pig's meat: or lessons for the swinish multitude. Ed T. Spence. 1793. Continued as Pig's meat: or lessons for the swinish multitude, 1793-5.
Davenport, A. The life, writings and principles of Thomas Spence. [1836].
Waters, A. W. The trial of Thomas Spence; also a brief life. Leamington 1917.

Hog's wash: or a salmagundy for swine. Ed D. I. Eaton. No 1, 9 Sept 1793. Continued as Hog's wash, no 2, 5 Oct 1793-. Continued as Hog's wash: or politics for the people, No 6, 2 Nov 1793. Continued as Politics for the people, no 7, 9 Nov 1793-[Jan] 1795.

The constitutional magazine and true Briton's friend: containing a weekly register of public affairs, foreign and domestic. 1793.

The Protestant dissenter's magazine. 1794-9.

The biographical magazine. 1 March 1794-2 May 1796.

Gallery of fashion. No 1, April 1794-.

The register of the times: or political museum. No 1, 21 June 1794-vol 5, 30 June 1795. Continued as Register of the times and literary review, vol 6, 15 July [1795]-vol 8, June 1796.

The repertory of arts and manufactures. No 1, July 1794-.
An analytic index to the sixteen volumes of the first series 1794-1802. 1802.

The medical and chirurgical review: or compendium of medical literature, foreign and domestic. Ed H. Clutterbuck. No 1, July 1794-.

The pocket magazine: or elegant repository of useful and polite literature. No 1, Aug 1794-no 17, Dec 1795.

The political magazine. Sept 1794.

The literary review and political journal. No 1, 1 Oct 1794-no 15, [15] May 1795.

History of the curiosities and rarities in nature and art. 1794-.

The lady's new and elegant pocket magazine: or polite and entertaining companion for the fair sex. 1795.

The tribune: a periodical publication consisting chiefly of the political lectures of J. Thelwall. Vol 1 no 1, 14 March 1795-vol 2 no 32, 2 Oct 1795-no 50, 15 April 1796.

The gentleman's new and elegant pocket magazine: or polite repository of useful and entertaining literature. Ed C. F. Russell. No 1, March 1795-?

Paris pendant l'année. Ed J. G. Peltier. Vol 1 no 1, 6 June 1795-.

The argus: or general observer: a political miscellany. Ed S. Perry. Vol 1 no [1], [29 Oct 1795]-[no 24, 18 May 1796]. Contains material from the Argus of 1789-91.

The Italian magazine. No 1, Nov 1795-no 2, Dec 1795. Continued as Italian tracts, 1796.

The monthly mirror, reflecting men and manners; with strictures on their epitome, the stage. Dec 1795-.

Fashions of London and Paris. 1795-.

Mathematical and philosophical repository. Nos 1-8. 1795-?

The bouquet: or blossoms of fancy. Vol 1 no 1, 1795-vol 2 no 12, 1796.

Ranger's magazine: or the man of fashion's companion. 1795.

Revolutionary magazine: history of the French revolution. Nos 1–7, 1795.

New copper plate magazine. 1795.

The new print magazine: being a collection of picturesque views. Nos 1–5, 1795.

The scientific receptacle: containing problems, anagrams etc. Ed T. Whiting. 1795–.

The magic and conjuring magazine and wonderful chronicle. 1795–.

The Cambrian register. 1795.

Juvenile olio: or monthly medley. Ed W. F. Mavor. Jan 1796–Dec 1796.

The monthly magazine: or British register. Ed J. Aikin et al. Vol 1 no 1, Feb 1796–. Continued as Monthly magazine and British register, no 1, May 1796. Continued as the Monthly magazine, no 5, June 1796–.

   Coldicutt, D. Was Coleridge the author of the Enquirer series in the Monthly magazine 1796–9? RES 15 1939.

   Patton, L. Coleridge and the Enquirer series. RES 16 1940.

   Carnall, G. The Monthly Magazine. RES new ser 5 1954.

The comick magazine: or compleat library of mirth, humour, wit, gaiety and entertainment. [No 1, April 1796]–no 2, May 1796–no 6, Sept 1796.

The moral and political magazine of the London corresponding society. Ed T. Hardy. No 1, June 1796–Dec 1796.

The Thespian telegraph: or dramatic mirror. No 1, [June?] 1796.

The universal politician and periodical reporter of the most interesting occurrences. No 1, July 1796–Dec 1796.

The English magazine and commercial repository. No 1, July 1796–7.

The cabinet magazine: or literary olio. No 1, Nov 1796–July 1797.

The gospel magazine and theological review. Ed W. Row. 1796–.

The Methodist monitor. 1796.

The pianoforte magazine. 1796–.

The new, general and complete weekly magazine: or entertaining miscellany. 1796.

Medical extracts. 1796–7.

The monthly visitor and entertaining pocket companion. No 1, Jan 1797–.

A journal of natural philosophy, chemistry and the arts. Ed W. Nicholson. No 1, April 1797–.

The oriental collections: consisting of original essays illustrating the history and literature of Asia. Ed W. Ouseley. 1797–9.

The universalists' miscellany: or philanthropist's museum; intended chiefly as an antidote against the anti-Christian doctrine of endless misery. Ed W. Vidler. 1797–.

Monthly epitome and catalogue of new publications. 1797–.

The philosophical magazine: comprehending the various branches of science, the liberal and fine arts, agriculture, manufactures and commerce. Ed A. Tilloch. No 1, June 1798–.

   Imperial Mag (Liverpool) 1825; Annual Biography & Obituary 1826. On Tilloch.

The lady's monthly museum: or polite repository of amusement and instruction. No 1, July 1798–.

The anti-Jacobin review and magazine: or monthly political and literary censor. Ed J. R. Green and R. Bisset. No 1, July 1798–.

The British mercury: or historical and critical views of the events of the present times. Ed J. M. du Pan. No 1, Sept 1798–1800. Also issued in French; Italian trn began in 1799.

The British military library: or journal comprehending a complete body of military knowledge. No 1, Oct 1798–.

The general Baptist magazine. Ed D. Taylor. 1798–1800. Underwood, W. Life of Daniel Taylor. [1870].

The soldier's pocket magazine. Nos 1–3, 1798.

The magazine of female fashions of London and Paris. 1798.

The monthly collector of elegant anecdotes and other curiosities of literature. 1798.

Naturalists' pocket magazine: or compleat cabinet of the curiosities and beauties of nature. 1798–.

Selections from the most celebrated foreign literary journals and other periodical publications. 1798–?

The children's magazine: or monthly repository of instruction and delight. No 1, Jan 1799–Dec 1800.

The new London review: or monthly report of authors and books. No 1, Jan 1799–no 18, June 1800. Continued as the London review and biographia literaria, no 19, July 1800–no 20, Aug 1800.

The naval chronicle: containing a general and biographical history of the royal navy of the United Kingdom. Ed J. S. Clarke, S. Jones. No 1, Jan 1799–.

The historical, biographical, literary and scientific magazine. Ed R. Bisset. No 1, Feb 1799–Dec 1800.

The medical and physical journal: containing the earliest information on subjects of medicine, surgery, pharmacy, chemistry and natural history. Ed T. Bradley and A. F. M. Willich. No 1, March 1799–.

   Physich-medicinsches Journal nach Bradley und Willich für Deutschland bearbeitet. Leipzig 1800–2. Index to vols 1–40. 1820.

The Aurora: or dawn of genuine truth. No 1, May 1799–.

The commercial and agricultural magazine. No 1, Aug 1799–.

Il mercurio britannico. Ed J. M. du Pan. [No 1, Aug 1799?]–[no 32, 10 Jan 1800]–? Trn of British mercury, which began 1798.

The meteors. Vol 1 no 1, 30 Nov 1799–vol 2 no 12, 3 May 1800.

The young gentleman's and lady's magazine: or universal repository of knowledge, instruction and amusement. Ed W. F. Mavor. 1799–1800.

The London medical review and magazine. Ed W. Blair. 1799–.

Recreations in agriculture, natural history, the arts and miscellaneous literature. Ed J. Anderson. 1799–.

The weekly review: or literary journal. 1799.

The naval magazine: or maritime miscellany. 1799.

The British magazine. Vol 1 no 1, Jan 1800–.

The monthly preceptor: or juvenile library. No 1, [Jan] 1800–. Continued as the Juvenile library, [no 6, June 1800]–.

The German museum: or monthly repository of the literature of Germany, the north and the Continent in general. No 1, Jan 1800–.

The nose, a periodical publication, by 'Caraquallfa'. Jan 1800–July 1800.

The social magazine: or monthly cabinet of wit. 1800.

The dramatic censor, or weekly theatrical report: comprising a complete chronicle of the British stage and a regular series of theatrical criticism in every department of the drama. Ed T. Dutton. Vol 1 no 1, 4 Jan 1800–.

Mercure de France: ou recueil historique, politique et littéraire. 1800–.

The novel reader. 1800.

Landscape magazine: containing preceptive principles of landscapes. Nos 1–12, c. 1800–?

E. ANNUALS

Reports of societies, diaries and almanacs are not included.

The whole proceedings of the sessions of the peace, and oyer and terminer for the City of London and County of Middlesex. ?–1674–.

A compleat history of Europe: or a view of the affairs thereof, civil and military, for the year 1701 [etc]. 1702–11.

The history of the reign of Queen Anne digested into annals. Ed A. Boyer. 1702–13.

Lives and characters of the most illustrious persons who died in the year, by J. Le Neve. 1712–14.

Annals of King George. Ed A. Boyer. 1716–21.

Ephemeris: or an astronomical state of the heavens, by G. Kingsley. No 1, 1717–no 7, 1723.

The British telescope. 1724–49.

An historical list of horse races. [Pbd fortnightly April–Nov each year and rptd in annual pocket vols]. [1729]–[68].

A new miscellany for the year 1724 [etc]. Ed J. Swift et al. 1734–9.

The annual advertiser. 1739–40.

The annals of Europe for the year 1739 [etc]. 1739–44.

The gentleman's diary: or mathematical repository. 1741–.

The palladium: or appendix to the ladies diary. Ed J. Tipper. 1749–. Continued as Gentleman and lady's palladium, 1752–. Continued as Gentleman and lady's military palladium, 1759–. Continued as Gentleman and lady's palladium, 1760–. Continued as Palladium extraordinary, 1763–. Continued as Palladium enlarged, 1764–. Continued as Palladium of fame: or annual miscellany, 1765–. Continued as Fame's palladium: or annual miscellany, 1766–. Continued as British palladium, 1768–79.

The sporting calendar: containing a distinct account of what plates and matches have been run for in 1751 [etc], by J. Pond. 1751–[57]–?

An historical list of horse matches, cock matches, by R. Heber. 1752–68.

The Court and city register. [1746?]–? Continued as Court and city calendar: or gentleman's register, ?–1758–? Continued as Court and city register: or gentleman's complete annual calendar, ?–1779–? Continued as London kalendar: or city and Court register, ?–1783–1797–?

Theatrical review for the year 1757 and beginning of 1758. 1758.

The annual register: or a view of the history, politics and literature for the year 1758 [etc]. Ed E. Burke. 1759–. A rival series was pbd from 1792 (i.e. for 1791) to 1826.
General index 1758–80. 1783–4.
General index to 1792. 1796.
General index 1758–1819. 1826.

Copeland, T. W. Burke and Dodsley's Annual Register. PMLA 54 1939.

—— Edmund Burke and the book reviews in Dodsley's Annual Register. PMLA 57 1942.

—— Our eminent friend Edmund Burke. New Haven 1949, London 1950 (as Edmund Burke: six essays).

—— Edmund Burke's friends and the Annual Register. Library 5th ser 18 1963.

H.A.M. The annual register: a bibliographical note. N & Q 13 Feb 1943.

Havens, R. D. A theft in the Annual register. PQ 29 1950.

Bryant, D. C. New light on Burke. Quart Jnl of Speech 39 1953.

—— Edmund Burke: a generation of scholarship and discovery. Jnl of Br Stud 2 1962.

Sarason, B. D. Edmund Burke and the two Annual Registers. PMLA 68 1953.

—— Editorial mannerisms in the early Annual Register. PBSA 52 1958.

The Annual Register. TLS 29 May 1959.

Todd, W. B. A bibliographical account of the Annual Register 1758–1825. Library 5th ser 16 1961.

Weston, J. C. Predecessors to Burke's and Dodsley's Annual Register. SB 17 1964.

Mémoires littéraires de la Grande Bretagne, by E. Gibbon and G. Deyverdun. 1768–9.

The sporting calendar: containing an account of the plates, matches and sweepstakes that have been run for in Great Britain and Ireland, by W. Tuting and T. Fawconer [by T. Fawconer in 1773 and 1774]. 1769–74.

An historical list of horse matches, by B. Walker. 1770–1.

The racing calendar: containing an account of the plates, matches and sweepstakes, by J. Weatherby. 1773–.

Annales politiques, civiles et littéraires du 18ᵉ siècle. Vol 1 1777–vol 19 1792. Paris and London.

The annals of Europe: or regal register shewing the succession of sovereigns. 1779.

The London mercury. Ed G. Stuart? 1780–[3].

The new annual register: or general repository of history, politics and literature. Ed A. Kippis et al. 1781–.

Marken, J. W. William Godwin's writing for the New Annual Register. MLN 67 1953.

The Baptist Annual Register: including sketches of the state of religion among different denominations, by J. Rippon. 1790–.

A companion to the Gentleman's diary: or a preparative to that useful work. Ed W. Davis. No 1, 1798. Continued as Gentleman's mathematical companion, no 2, 1799–.

Spirit of the public journals for 1797 [etc]. 1798–.

British public characters, 1798 [etc]. 1799–.

The new register book of shipping. 1799–.

The Asiatic annual register: or a view of the history of Hindustan and the politics, commerce and literature of Asia. 1799–.

Annual necrology for 1797–8: including also various articles of neglected biography. 1800.

F. LONDON NEWSPAPERS

Mercurius politicus. Ed M. Nedham et al. No 1, 13 June 1650–no 615, 12 April 1660.

Bond, R. P. Mercurius politicus. Newberry Lib Bull 6 1966.

Nouvelles ordinaires de Londres. Ed H. Muddiman. 1650–66?

The publick intelligencer. Ed M. Nedham, J. Canne. No 1, 8 Oct 1655–9 April 1660.

The weekly bill of mortality. ?–1658–.

The faithful scout. ?–no 3, 13 May 1659–. Continued as National scout, 16 July 1659–. Continued as Loyall scout, 22 July 1659–no 78, 17 June 1660.

The weekly post. Ed D. Border? No 1, 10 May 1659–no 42, 21 Feb 1660.

The weekly intelligencer of the commonwealth. No 1, 10 May 1659–no 43, 17 April 1660.

A particular advice from the office of intelligence. Ed O. Williams et al. No 1, 30 June 1659–. Continued as An exact accompt of the daily proceedings in Parliament, 6 Jan 1660–6 July 1660.

Occurrences from foreign parts. Ed O. Williams et al. No 1, 5 July 1659–no 88, 18 May 1660–?

The weekly intelligencer of the commonwealth. No 1, 26 July 1659–no 43, 17 April 1660.

The faithful post. [1659?]–no 53, 8 May 1660.

The Kingdoms intelligencer. [1659?]–no 49, 29 May 1660–no 56, 3 July 1660.

Perfect occurrences. [1659?]–no 41, 18 May 1660.

Al-a-mode of Paris: or the diurnall in verse. ?–29 Dec 1659–?

The parliamentary intelligencer. Ed H. Muddiman and G. Dury. No 1, 26 Dec 1659–no 53, 31 Dec 1659. Continued as The Kingdomes intelligencer, no 1, 7 Jan 1661–. Continued as The Kingdoms intelligencer, no 1, 6 Jan 1662–31 Aug 1663.

Mercurius pragmaticus. ?–no 2, 30 Dec 1659–?

The monthly intelligencer. No 1, 1 Jan 1660.

Mercurius publicus. Ed H. Muddiman and G. Dury. Vol 1 no 1, 5 Jan 1660–3 Sept 1663.

Mercurius fumigosus: or the smoaking nocturnal. Ed J. Crouch. No 1, 18 Jan 1660–28 March 1660.

Londons diurnal. No 1, 8 Feb 1660–no 18, 13 June 1660.

A perfect diurnal of every dayes proceedings in Parliament. Ed O. Williams et al. No 1, 21 Feb 1660–. Continued as A perfect diurnal: or the dayly proceedings in Parliament, no 5, 25 Feb 1660–no 21, 16 March 1660.

The London-apprentices grand politick informer. ?–no 3, 5 March 1660.

Mercurius phanaticus: or Mercury temporizing. 4 March 1660–23 May 1660.

A perfect diurnall: or the daily proceedings in the conventicle of the phanatiques. No 1, 19 March 1660.

Mercurius honestus: or Tom Tell-truth. No 1, 21 March 1660.

The phanatick intelligencer. No 1, [24 March 1660].

Mercurius civicus: or the cities intelligencer. No 1, 26 March 1660–no 2, 2 April 1660; also no 2, 24 April 1660–no 11, 3 July 1660.

The royal informer. No 1, 4 April 1660.

Mercurius aulicus: or the royal intelligencer. No 1, 16 April 1660–? continued as Mercurius aulicus: or the Court mercury. ?–no 12, 25 June 1660.

The publick intelligencer. Ed O. Williams et al. No 1, 16 April 1660–no 19, 25 June 1660. Alternated with Mercurius politicus, below.

Mercurius politicus. Ed O. Williams. No 1, 19 April 1660–no 22, 5 July 1660. Alternated with the Publick intelligencer, above.

The man in the moon. No 1, 26 April 1660; also no 1, 20 Aug 1660 and no 2, 12 May 1663.

Perfect occurrences, by H. Walker? No 4, 18 May 1660.

Merlinus phanaticus. No 1, 23 May 1660.

London's intelligencer. ?–no 6, 8 June 1660.

Mercurius veridicus. No 1, 5 June 1660–no 2, 12 June 1660.

Mercurius democritus in querpo. ?–no 9, 14 June 1660.

The votes of both Houses. Ed O. Williams. No 1, 20 June 1660.

Mercurius poeticus. No 1, 16 July 1660.
Weber, H. H. The Mercurius poeticus of 1660. N & Q 28 Dec 1935.

Mercurius Caledonius. No 1, 8 Jan 1661–? Reprint of Edinburgh paper.

Mercurius democritus: or the smoaking nocturnal, by J. Crouch. No 1, 22 May 1661.

A monthly intelligencer relating the affairs of the people called Quakers. No 1, Sept 1662.

The intelligencer. Ed R. L'Estrange. No 1, 31 Aug 1663–29 Jan 1666.
Kitchin, G. Sir Roger L'Estrange: a contribution to the history of the press in the seventeenth century. 1913.

The newes. Ed R. L'Estrange. No 1, 3 Sept 1663–18 Jan 1666. From 7 Jan 1664 issued as Thursday supplement to the Intelligencer, with continuous numbering and pagination.

Intelligence from the south borders of Scotland. ?–no 8, 24 April 1664.

The London gazette. Ed H. Muddiman et al. Began as Oxford gazette, pbd at Oxford from 16 Nov 1665 to 29

Jan 1666 and continued in London, no 24, 5 Feb 1666– Some nos reset once or twice. Some issues rptd seriatim in Dublin, ?–4 Dec 1700–1703–? Tr as Gazette de Londres, ?–no 288, 16 Aug 1669–4100, 6 Dec 1705–?
Muddiman, J. G. The King's journalist 1659–89. 1923.
Seymour, M. Fielding's history of the Forty-five [use of the London Gazette]. PQ 14 1935.
Hatton, R. The London Gazette in 1718: supply of news from abroad. Bull of Inst of Historical Research 18 1941.
Leach, D. E. B. Batten and the London Gazette report on King Philip's war. New England Quart 34 1963.
Handover, P. M. A history of the London Gazette 1665–1965. 1965.
H. H. The London Gazette 1665–1965. Manchester Rev 10 1965.
Snyder, H. L. The circulation of newspapers in the reign of Queen Anne. Library 5th ser 23 1968.

Publick intelligence. Ed R. L'Estrange. No 1, 28 Nov 1665.

The current intelligence. Ed H. Muddiman. No 1, 4 Jun 1666–no 24, 23 Aug 1666.

Publick advertisements. Ed R. L'Estrange. No 1, 25 June 1666.

The true character of Mercurius urbanicus and rusticus. No 1, 10 June 1667. Continued as the City and countrey mercury, no 2, 13 June 1667–. Continued as Mercury, publishing advertisements of all sorts, no 14, 25 July 1667–. Continued as the City mercury, no 22, 19 Aug 1667–no 34, 31 Oct 1667. Pbd alternately with Country mercury, below.

The country mercury. No 23, 22 Aug 1667–no 32, 17 Oct 1667. Pbd alternately with City mercury, above.

The prices of merchandise in London. ?–8 July 1667–30 Dec 1685–?

Prix courant des marchandises à Londres. ?–7 May 1668–22 June 1699–?

The London mercury. No 1, 6 Jan 1669–no 2, 27 Jan 1669.

The city mercury: or advertisements concerning trade. No 1, 4 Nov 1675–? Continued as Mercury: or advertisements concerning trade, ?–no 119, 21 Feb 1678–. Continued as City mercury: from the office of the Royal Exchange, no 252, 21 Oct 1680–no 279, 16 June 1681.

The merchant's remembrancer, by J. Whiston, F. Robinson. ?–no 7, 16 Feb 1679–23 May [1681]–? Continued as Whiston's merchant's weekly remembrancer, ?–17 June 1689–? Continued as Whiston's merchant's weekly remembrancer of the present money prices of their goods ashoar in London, ?–26 Oct 1691–7 July 1707–? Probably continued as Robinson's merchant's weekly remembrancer of the present money prices of their goods ashoar in London, ?–no 264, 1712–?

Domestick intelligence: or news both from city and country. Ptd for B. Harris. No 1, 7 July 1679–. Continued as Protestant (domestick) intelligence, no 56, 16 Jan 1680–no 82, 16 April 1680–no 83, 28 Dec 1680–no 114, 15 April 1681. See True Protestant (domestick) intelligence, April 1680.
Monaghan, F. Benjamin Harris: printer, bookseller and the first American journalist. Colophon 12 1932.

The English intelligencer. No 1, 21 July 1679–no 8, 30 Aug 1679.

The faithfull mercury, imparting news domestick and forein. No 1, 22 July 1679–[no 2, 25 July 1679].

The domestick intelligence: or news both from city and country. Ptd by N. Thompson. No 15 (first issued), 26 Aug 1679–. Continued as True domestick intelligence, no 19, 9 Sept 1679–no 90, 14 May 1680.

The friendly intelligence. No 1, 7 Sept 1679–no 4, 2 Oct 1679.

The English currant: or advice domestick and forreign. No 1, 8 Sept 1679.

Mercurius anglicus: or the weekly occurrences faithfully transmitted. No 1, 20 Nov 1679–. Continued as True news: or mercurius anglicus, no 11, 27 Dec 1679–no 51, 15 May 1680.

The weekly intelligence: communicating news from city and country. No 1, 5 Dec 1679.

The Haerlem courant truly rendred into English. No 1, 29 Dec 1679–no 11 (i.e. 12), 19 Feb 1680.

The currant intelligence: or an impartial account of transactions both forraign and domestick. No 1, 14 Feb 1680–. Continued as Smith's currant intelligence: or an impartial account of transactions both forraign and domestick, no 10, 16 March 1680–no 24, 4 May 1680.

Mercurius publicus: being a summary of the whole weeks intelligence. No 1, 28 Feb 1680–no 2, 18 March 1680.

Catholick intelligence: or infallible news both domestick and forreign, published for the edification of Protestants. No 1, 1 March 1680–no 5, 29 March 1680.

The currant intelligence: or an impartial account of transactions both forreign and domestick. No 1, 13 March [1680]. Continued as Banks's currant intelligence: or an impartial account of transactions both forreign and domestick, no 2, 20 March [1680]–no 4, 3 April 1680.

The loyal intelligence: or news both from city and country. No 1, 16 March 1680–no 3, 10 April 1680.

The city mercury: from the office at the Royal Exchange. Ptd by R. Everingham. 17 March 1680.

Mercurius civicus: or a true account of affairs both forreign and domestick. No 1, 22 March 1680–. Continued as Mercurius civicus: or an account of affairs both forreign and domestick, no 5, 3 April 1680–no 14, 6 May 1680. Perhaps continued as Mercurius civicus: or the city mercury, no 241, 12 May 1680–no 244, 11 June 1680.

The true Protestant (domestick) intelligence: or news both from city and country. No 1, 23 April 1680–no 7, 14 May 1680–?

The Rotterdam's courant. 7 June 1680. Reprint of Rotterdam paper.

Votes of the House of Commons. ?–21 Oct 1680–no 1, 1 Nov 1680–no 62, 28 March 1681. Nos 59–62 also ptd at Oxford. Variant issues of some other nos.

The city mercury. Ptd by T. James. ?–Nov 1680–?

The English gazette. No 1, 22 Dec 1680–no 7, 12 Jan 1681. Continued as the Westminster gazette, no 8, 15 Jan 1681.

The true Protestant mercury: or occurrences forein and domestick. No 1, 28 Dec 1680–no 188, 25 Oct 1682.

Mercurius veridicus, communicating the best and truest intelligence from all parts of England. Ed W. Henchman. No 1, 7 Jan 1681.

Smith's Protestant intelligence, domestick and forein. No 1, 1 Feb 1681–no 22, 14 April 1681.

An account of the injurious proceedings of Sir George Jeffries against Francis Smith, bookseller. [1680].

The case of Francis Smith. Ptd as appendix to [Anthony Ashley Cooper, 1st Earl of Shaftesbury] The speech of a noble peer, 1689 (3rd edn).

The loyal Protestant and true domestick intelligence. No 1, 9 March 1681–no 234, 16 Nov 1682–no 235, 20 Feb 1683–no 247, 20 March 1683.

The trial of N. Thompson, W. Pain and J. Farwell. 1682; rptd in State trials vol 8, ed W. Cobbett 1810.

The Protestant Oxford intelligence: or occurrences forraign and domestick. No 1, 10 March [1681]–no 7, 31 March [1681]. Continued as Impartial London intelligence, no 1, 4 April [1681]–no 4, 14 April [1681].

Votes of the House of Commons at Oxford. No 1, 21 March 1681–no 5, 28 March 1681.

A new news-book: or occurrences foreign and domestick. [No 1], 23 April 1681.

The currant intelligence. No 1, 26 April 1681–no 70, 24 Dec 1681.

The true Protestant mercury: or occurrences foreign and domestick. No 1, 27 April 1681–. Continued as

Impartial Protestant mercury: or occurrences foreign and domestick, no 5, 7 May 1681–no 115, 30 May 1682.

The domestick intelligence: or news both from city and country impartially related. No 1, 13 May 1681–no 155, 16 Nov 1682.

The universal intelligence: comprizing the substance of the most remarkable passages weekly published by others. No 1, 18 May 1681.

Mercurius anglicus. No 1, 10 Oct 1681–no 3, 17 Oct 1681.

Le memorial des marchands à Londres. Ed J. Whiston. ?–14 Nov 1681–8 June 1682–? Continued as Memorial des marchands estant le prix des marchandises comptant à terre à Londres, ?–12 Feb 1683–[1691]–?

The monthly recorder of all true occurrences both foreign and domestick. No 1, 1 Jan 1682–no 5, 1 May 1682.

The Haerlem courant, truly rendred into English. No 1, [17 Jan] 1682. Continued as the Compleat mercury: or the Haerlem courant truly rendred into English, no 2, 21 Jan 1682–no 4, 28 Jan 1682.

The London mercury. No 1, April 1682–no 56, 17 Oct 1682.

The Protestant courant, imparting news forreign and domestick. No 1, 24 April 1682–no 6, 13 May 1682.

The loyal impartial mercury: or news both forreign and domestick. No 1, 9 June 1682–no 46, 17 Nov 1682.

The loyal London mercury: or the moderate intelligencer. No 1, 14 June 1682–no 20, 19 Aug 1682. Continued as Moderate intelligencer, no 21, 23 Aug 1682–no 37, 23 Oct 1682.

Stewart, P. Typographical peculiarities of the Loyal London Mercuries. N & Q 19 March 1949.
— The Loyal London Mercuries. SE 28 1949.

The conventicle-courant, by J. Hilton. No 1, [24 July] 1682–no 30, 14 Feb 1683.

The loyal London mercury: or the currant intelligence. No 1, 23 Aug 1682–no 25, 15 Nov 1682. See Loyal London mercury, which began in June 1682.

The epitome of the weekly news. No 1, 28 Aug 1682–no 2, 4 Sept 1682.

L'état présent de l'Europe, suivant les gazettes d'Angleterre, France, Hollande etc. 5 nos, 25 Sept–16 Oct 1682.

London imported. ?–[1683]–no 1, 2 Jan 1694–no 268, 23 Dec 1694–.

Domestick intelligence published gratis every Thursday for the promoting of trade. No 1, [22 March] 1683–no 27, 19 Dec 1683.

The jockies intelligencer: or weekly advertisements of horses and second-hand coaches to be bought or sold. [No 1, 28 June] 1683–no 11, 10 Jan 1684.

From the Mercury office, at Charing cross. ?–no 5, nd [1685?] Apparently began as From the office, at Charing cross. For buying and selling of estates.

Publick occurrences truely stated, by H. Care and E. Settle. No 1, 21 Feb 1688–no 34, 2 Oct 1688.

Cowan, W. The Holyrood press 1686–8. Edinburgh Bibl Soc Pbns 6 1904.

A true and impartial account of the remarkable accidents in city and country. No 1, [25 May] 1688–no 11, 25 Aug 1688.

The universal intelligence. No 1, 11 Dec 1688–no 14, 18 Feb 1689.

The London courant. No 1, 12 Dec 1688–no 9, 8 Jan 1689.

The English currant. No 1, 12 Dec 1688–no 9, 9 Jan 1689.

The London mercury: or moderate intelligencer. No 1, 15 Dec 1688–. Continued as the London mercury: or the Orange intelligence, no 7, 3 Jan 1689–. Continued as the London mercury: or moderate intelligencer, no 10, 10 Jan/6 Feb 1689–no 13, 18 Feb 1689.

The observer. No 1, [24 Dec 1688?].

The Orange gazette. No 1, 31 Dec 1688–no 18, 9 March 1689.

The London intelligence. No 1, 15 Jan 1689–no 10, 16 Feb 1689.

The Harllum currant. No 1, 14 Feb 1689–no 2 (as Harlem currant), 19 Feb 1689.

An account of the proceedings of the meeting of the Estates in Scotland. No 1, [15 March 1689]. Continued as A continuation of the proceedings of the convention of the Estates in Scotland, no 2, 19 March 1689–no 147, 18 Oct 1690.

Speech made by a member of the convention of the States in Scotland. No 1, nd 1689.

Account from Scotland and London-derry of the proceedings against the Duke of Gordon. No 1, 7 June [1689].

The true Protestant mercury: or an impartial history of the times. No 1, 6 Dec 1689–no 4, 27 Dec 1689. Continued as True Protestant mercury: containing three general heads, no 1, 3 Jan 1690–no 6, 7 Feb 1690.

Votes of the House of Commons. No 1, 21 March [1690]–no 47, 23 May 1690. Continued in each following session, with fresh numbering.

Bellot, H. H. Parliamentary printing 1660–1837. Bull of Inst of Historical Research 11 1933.

The weekly packet of advice from Ireland. No 1, 4 April 1690–no 2, 11 April 1690.

The coffee-house mercury, by J. Dunton. No 1, 11 Nov 1690–no 3, 25 Nov 1690.

Compendio mercuriale. 29 Feb 1691–?

The city mercury, published (gratis) every Monday for the promotion of trade. [No 1, 7 March 1692]–no 18, 4 July 1692–no 53, 27 March 1693–?

The Scottish mercury: giving a true account of the daily proceedings and occurrences in Scotland. No 1, 8 May 1692–no 5, 22 May 1692.

Votes of the House of Commons in Ireland. No 1, 5 Oct 1692–no 7, 17 Oct 1692. Reprint of Dublin paper.

The proceedings of the Parliament of Scotland. No 1, 29 April 1693–no 3, 6 May 1693.

Proctor's price-courant. [1693?]–no 622, 19 Sept 1706–?

An account of the publick transactions in Christendom. No 1, 11 Aug 1694. Continued as An historical account of the publick transactions, no 2, 18 Aug 1694–no 5, 8 Sept 1694, no 6, 4 May 1695–no 14, 15 June 1695. Continued as Holland pacquet-boat: or an historical account of the publick transactions in Christendom, no 15, 17 June 1695. Amalgamated with Post boy, foreign and domestick, and continued as Post boy and historical account, no 16, 19 June 1695–no 71, 22 Oct 1695. For subsequent titles see Post-man, Oct 1695.

Mercurius mediterraneus: or the streights weekly mercury. No 1, 28 Nov 1694.

The London newsletter, with foreign and domestick occurrences. No 1, 29 April 1695–[no 156, 27 April 1696]–no 1, 29 April 1696–no 20, 12 June 1696–?

Intelligence domestick and foreign. No 1, 14 May 1695–. Continued as Intelligence domestick and foreign, with the flying post-boy from the camp in Flanders, no 8, 7 June 1695–no 14, 28 June 1695. Continued as Foreign and domestick news; with the pacquet boat from Holland and Flanders: being an historical account of the publick transactions of Europe, no 1, 2 July 1695. Continued as Pacquet-boat from Holland and Flanders, no 2, 5 July 1695–no 3, 9 July 1695–?

The post boy, foreign and domestick. Ed A. Roper, E. Thomas et al. No 1, 16 May 1695–. Continued as Post boy, with foreign and domestick news, no 3, 21 May 1695–no 15, 18 June 1695. Amalgamated with Holland pacquet-boat: or an historical account of the publick transactions in Christendom; and continued as Post boy and historical account, no 16, 19 June 1695–no 60, 26 Sept 1695. Continued as Post boy, no 61, 28 Sept 1695–no 6,130, 30 Sept 1728. Continued as Daily post boy, no 6,131, 1 Oct 1728–no 8,004, 31 Dec 1735–6 May 1736–? Nos 2,766–7 as Pax, pax: or a pacifick postboy. Nos 2,806–9 as Pax, pax, pax: or a pacifick postboy. Postscript to the post-boy issued separately. ?–no 12, 11 June 1695–no 2,923, 3 Feb 1714–? No 2,751, as Pacifick postscript to the post boy, 29 Dec 1712.

The case of Mr Abel Boyer. 1709.

Tory annals faithfully extracted out of Abel Roper's famous writings vulgarly called Post-boy. 1712.

[King, E.?] Some memoirs of the life of Abel, Toby's uncle, by 'Dr Andrew Tripe'. 1725.

Memoir of Abel Boyer. Political State of Great Britain 38 1729.

The flying-post from Paris and Amsterdam. Ed G. Ridpath et al. No 1, [7 or 11 or 18 May 1695]–no 53, 17 Sept 1695. Continued as Flying-post, no 54, 19 Sept 1695–no 121, 22 Feb 1696. Continued as Flying-post: or the post-master, no 122, 25 Feb 1696–no 6,081, 25 Dec 1733. Some nos rptd 1696. Postscript to Flying-post, ?–25 June 1695–11 Aug 1711–?

Account of the proceedings and sentence against Mr George Redpath. 1713.

The trial and conviction of Mr George Redpath. 1713.

The English courant. No 1, 25 May 1695–no 2, 29 May 1695–?

The Harlem's courant. No 1, 28 May 1695–no 2, nd–? Trn of paper pbd at Haarlem.

The weekly news-letter. No 1, 6 July 1695–no 2, 13 July 1695–?

The post-man: and the historical account. Ed J. de Fonvive. No 72 (first issued), 24 Oct 1695–21 Feb 1730. Continued as Oedipus: or the post-man remounted, no 1, 24 Feb 1730–no 29 (i.e. 24), 18 April 1730. Postscripts to Post-man pbd separately occasionally 1706–10–? Some rptd seriatim in Dublin 1707–8.

The London mercury, published for the promoting of trade. No 1, 30 Dec 1695–21 June 1697.

The Protestant mercury: occurrences forein and domestick. No 1, 9 March 1696–no 545 (sic), 18 Dec 1700.

The London news-letter, with foreign and domestick occurrences. No 1, 29 April 1696–no 22, 17 June 1696.

The London mercury: or mercure de Londres. No 1, 3 June 1696–no 12, 13 July 1696. English and French in parallel columns.

The old post-master. No 1, 23 June 1696–no 12, 21 July 1696–?

Dawks's news-letter. Ed I. Dawks. [No 1, 23 June 1696]–no 23, 13 Aug 1696–22 Dec 1716.

Morison, S. Ichabod Dawks and his news-letter. Cambridge 1931.

Lloyd's news. [No 1, 1 Sept 1696?]–no 8, 17 Sept 1696–no 76, 23 Feb 1697.

Votes of the House of Commons. No 1, 20 Oct 1696–no 145, 16 April 1697.

An historical journal: or an impartial account in English and French of the most considerable occurrences in Europe. 3 Feb 1697–17 Feb 1697–?

The course of the exchange. No 1, 26 March 1697–.

The London post with the newest intelligence both forreign and domestick. No 1, 17 May 1697–no 11, 8 June 1697.

The foreign post. [No 1, 17 May 1697]–no 3, 21 May 1697–no 66, 22 Oct 1697. Continued as Foreign post: or historical narrative, no 67, 25 Oct 1697–no 95, 31 Jan 1698–?

The Amsterdam slip. [No 1?], 5 July 1697.

The London slip of news, both foreign and domestick. Ed D. Defoe 1704–5. No 1, 6 June 1699. Continued as London post, with intelligence foreign and domestick, no 2, 9 June 1699–no 1,011, 1 Jan 1705. Continued as London post, no 1,012, 3 Jan 1705–no 1,035, 26 Feb 1705–no 1, 28 Feb 1705–no 44, 8 June 1705–?

The English spy: or the weekly observator. No 1, 18 Aug 1699.

The English post: giving an authentick account of the transactions of the world. Ed N. Crouch. No 1, 14 Oct 1700–no 27, 13 Dec 1700. Continued as the English post; with news foreign and domestick, no 28, 16 Dec 1700–no 1,191, 19 May 1708–?

The new express; with an account of the chiefest novelties, both foreign and domestick. 24 Jan 1701.

The new state of Europe, both as to publick transactions and learning. No 1, 23 May 1701–no 14, 29 July 1701–?

The new state of Europe: or a true account of publick transactions and learning. No 1, 20 Sept 1701–no 54, 22 Jan 1702–?

The daily courant. Ed S. Buckley. No [1], 11 March 1702–no 6,002, 28 June 1735. 2 consecutive issues combined for country edn. ?–no 33, 27 May 1702–no 6,001, 27 June 1735. Some nos rptd seriatim Dublin 1716.

Rosenberg, M. The rise of England's first newspaper. Journalism Quart 30 1953.

Merchants news letter. Nos 1–18, 1703.

Le post-man: ou relation historique de ce qui passe de plus considérable dans l'Europe etc, traduit de l'anglois. Ed R. Roger. No 1, 4 July 1704–?

The mercury of England: giving an account of all publick events with historical observations. [No 1, 21 July 1704?]–no 6, 25 Aug 1704–?

The Paris gazette english'd. [No 1, 20 Sept 1704?]–no 17, 10 Jan 1705; rptd Dublin. No 1, 7 Feb 1705–?

Mercurius politicus: or an antidote to popular mis-representations, by J. Drake. No 1, 12 June 1705–no 51, 4 Dec 1705.

The general remark on trade. Ed C. Povey. [No 1, 23 Oct 1705?]–no 9, 20 Nov 1705–no 213, 7 July 1707. Continued as General remark on trade: with an extract of foreign news and observations on publick affairs, no 214, 9 July 1707–no 250, 1 Oct 1707–? Continued as General remark: or miscellanies, ?–no 430, 1 Dec 1708–no 440, 24 Dec 1708–?
Relton, F. B. An account of the fire insurance companies; also of Charles Povey. 1893.

The loyal post; with foreign and inland intelligence. Ed J. Harris or N. Crouch. No 1, 23 Nov 1705–?
The loyal post: a rare queen Anne newspaper and Daniel Defoe. BNYPL April 1955.

The poetical courant. Ed S. Philips. Vol 1 no 1, 26 Jan 1706–no 23, 29 June 1706.

The evening post, with the historical account. [No 1, 24 Aug 1706]–no 3, 29 Aug 1706–no 5, 3 Sept 1706–?

The country gentleman's courant: or universal intelligence. No 1, 12 Oct 1706–7?

The generous advertiser: or weekly information of trade and business. [No 1, 25 Jan 1707?]–no 14, 18 March 1707–no 21, 11 April 1707–?

The supplement [to Post boy]. Ed G. James. [No 1, 19 Jan 1708]–no 13, 16 Feb 1708–no 753, 30 July 1712–?

The British Apollo: or curious amusements for the ingenious, by A. Hill and M. Smith. No 1, 13 Feb 1708–vol 4 no 20, 11 May 1711. Suppls. Rptd 1726, 1740.
Belcher, W. F. The sale and distribution of the British Apollo. In Studies in the early English periodical, ed R. P. Bond. Chapel Hill [1957].

The tatler, by R. Steele, J. Addison et al. No 1, 12 April 1709–no 271, 2 Jan 1711. Continuations: (1) ?–no 272, 4 Jan 1711–no 273, 6 Jan 1711 (sold by J. Baker); (2) no 272–3, 6 Jan 1711–no 330, 19 May 1711 (sold by J. Morphew); (3) by W. Harrison, no 1, 13 Jan 1711–no 6, 30 Jan 1711 (pbd by Mrs A. Baldwin) and no 285, 3 Feb 1711–no 330, 19 May 1711, nos 285–330 being the same as nos 285–330 of continuation (2). For reprints see col 1114, above.
Greenough, C. N. The development of the Tatler particularly in regard to news. PMLA 31 1916.
Graham, W. Defoe's Review and Steele's Tatler: the question of influence. JEGP 33 1934.
Allen, R. J. Contemporary allusions in the Tatler. MLN 55 1940.
Elliott, R. C. Swift's 'little' Harrison: poet and continuator of the Tatler. SP 44 1949.
Todd, W. B. Early editions of the Tatler. SB 15 1962.
Achurch, R. W. Richard Steele, gazetteer and Bickerstaff. Studies in the early English periodical, ed R. P. Bond, Chapel Hill, [1957].

The post boy. Ed A. Boyer. No 2225 (first issued), 18 Aug 1709–no 2,320, 23 March 1710. Continued as True post boy, no 2,322, 25 March 1710–no 2,324, 1 April 1710–?

The evening post. No 1, 6 Sept 1709–no 3,511, 5 Feb 1732. Continued as B. Berington's evening post, 8 Feb 1732–29 Aug 1740.

The rehearsal revivd, by E. Stacey. [No 1, 22 Sept 1709]–11 Nov 1709.

The general postscript, by E. Stacey. No 1, 27 Sept 1709–no 20, 11 Nov 1709.

The city intelligencer. ?–1709–?

The British mercury. Ed A. Hill et al. [No 1, 27 March 1710]–no 2, 29 March 1710–no 497, 12 Jan 1715. Continued as British weekly mercury, no 498, 15 Jan 1715–no 566, 2 May 1716.
Lewis, H. History of the British mercury from 1715 to 1886. Bristol [1887?].
Baumer, E. The early days of the Sun Fire office. 1910.
Honoré, J. Charles Gildon rédacteur du British Mercury 1711–12: les attaques contre Pope, Swift et les Wits. Etudes Anglaises 15 1962.

The moderator. No 1, 22 May 1710–no 50, 10 Nov 1710.

The medley. Ed A. Maynwaring et al. No 1, 5 Oct 1710–no 45, 6 Aug 1711. Some nos rptd Dublin 1711. Rptd 1712.

Votes of the new parliament of women. No 1 [10 Oct 1710]–?

The Tory tatler. No 1, 27 Nov 1710–no 16, 3 Jan 1711.

Le mercurie britannique. ?–10 Jan 1711–12?

The useful intelligencer for promoting of trade and commerce. [No 1, 2 March 1711?]–no 39, 10 July 1711–no 51, 21 Aug 1711–no 10, 11 Jan 1712.

The marine intelligencer: or an account of sea affairs. No 1, 28 April 1711.

The evening courant. No 1, 17 July 1711–no 5, 26 July 1711–?

The general post. No 1, 19 July 1711–no 46, 2 Nov 1711–?

The night post. [No 1, July 1711?]–no 68, 1 Jan 1712–Nov 1713?

The Protestant postboy. No 1, 4 Sept 1711–no 123, 12 July 1712–? Some nos rptd seriatim Dublin 1712.

The weekly post: or a just account of all the principal news. No 1, 1 Dec 1711–no 3, 15 Dec 1711–?

The medley. No 1, 3 March 1712–no 43, 28 July 1712. Pbd A. Baldwin.

The medley. No 1, 3 March 1712–no 45, 4 Aug 1712. Pbd J. Baker.

The weekly packet. [No 1, 12 July 1712]–no 5, 9 Aug 1712–no 473, 29 July 1721–?

The weekly journal, with fresh advices foreign and domestick. No 1, 8 Jan 1714–no 53, 1 Jan 1715–no 1, 8 Jan 1715–no 50, 17 Jan 1715–[31 Dec 1715?]. Suppl 4 Jan 1716.

The flying-post and medley, by D. Defoe. No 1, 27 July 1714–no 3, 31 July 1714. Continued as Flying-post, no 5, 5 Aug 1714–no 25, 21 Sept 1714.

A weekly journal, with fresh advices, foreign and domestick. No 1, 9 Oct 1714–. Continued as Original weekly journal, 11 June 1715–. Continued as Applebee's original weekly journal, 16 July 1720–24 Dec 1737–?
Shugrue, M. Richard Savage in the columns of Applebee's original weekly journal. N & Q Feb 1961.
— Applebee's original weekly journal: an index to eighteenth-century taste. Newberry Lib Bull 6 1964.

The supplement to the weekly journal. [No 1, Jan 1715?]–3 Aug 1715–14 Dec 1715–? Perhaps continued as Supplement by way of postscript to the weekly journal and other weekly accounts, no 1, 4 Jan 1716–?

The St James's post. Ed A. Boyer? [No 1, 21 Jan 1715]–no 14, 25 Feb 1715–no 1,176, 30 July 1722–[1734?].

The weekly journal, or British gazetteer: being the freshest advices foreign and domestick. 5 Feb 1715–24 April 1725–no 1, 1 May 1725–no 282, 15 Aug 1730. Continued as Read's weekly journal: or British gazetteer, no 283, 22 Aug 1730–no 798, 22 Dec 1739–no 1,331, 2 May 1761. Continued as London spy and Read's weekly journal, 9 May 1761–no 38, 26 Dec 1761. Followed by Baldwin's London journal 2 Jan 1762.

The London post; with the best account of the whole week's news, foreign and domestick, with room to write into the country without the charge of double postage. [No 1, 23 April 1715?]–no 39, 14 Jan 1716–no 57, 19 May 1716–? Nos 51–2 as London post: or weekly intelligencer.

St James's evening post. Ed A. Boyer? [No 1, 22 June 1715]–no 24, 26 July 1715–no 8,069, 16 June 1757–[1760?]

The penny-post. No 1, 19 July 1715.

The daily oracle. No 1, 1 Aug 1715–no 10, 11 Aug 1715. Continued as Oracle, no 11, 12 Aug 1715–no 17, 26 Aug 1715.

The London post. [No 1, 15 Oct 1715]–no 11, 12 Jan 1716–[1717?].

Weekly remarks and political reflections upon the most material news foreign and domestick. Vol 1 no 1, 3 Dec 1715–15 Sept 1716–?

St James's evening post: or nightly pacquet. No 1, 20 Dec 1715–no 14, 19 Jan 1716–?

The news letter. Ed N. Storer. No 1, 7 Jan 1716–no 10, 10 March 1716–?

The general post. No 1, 15 Jan 1716–?

The Protestant packet: containing the freshest account of all occurrences foreign and domestick. No 1, 21 Jan 1716–no 4, 11 Feb 1716–?

The evening weekly packet. [No 1, 11 Feb 1716]–no 9, 3 March 1716–no 10, 10 March 1716–? A postscript to the evening packet [pbd separately], ?–no 6, 25 Feb 1716–no 8, 1 March 1716–?

Robin's last shift: or weekly remarks and political reflexions. Ed G. Flint. No 1, 18 Feb 1716–no 11, 26 April 1716. Continued as Shift shifted: or weekly remarks and political reflexions, no 1, 5 May 1716–no 22, 29 Sept 1716–[9 Feb 1717?]. Perhaps continued as Shift's last shift: or weekly journal, no 1, 16 Feb 1717–? Nos 1–11 rptd 1717.

Weekly remarks and political reflections upon the most material news foreign and domestick. Vol 1 no 14, 1 March 1716 (spurious issue of Weekly remarks vol 1 no 14, 3 March 1716).

The general post. [No 1, 15 March 1716]–no 2, 17 March 1716–no 9, 3 April 1716. Continued as Evening general post, no 10, 5 April 1716–no 115, 6 Dec 1716–?

The orphan; with reflections political and moral upon all material occurrences foreign and domestick. No 1, 21 March 1716–?

The weekly general post. No 1, 31 March 1716–no 49, 2 March 1717–?

The charitable mercury and female intelligence: being a weekly collection of all the material news foreign and domestick. No 1, 7 April 1716–?

The political courier. No 1, 25 April 1716–?

The Whitehall-courant. No 1, 2 May 1716–no 39, 30 July 1716–?

The weekly-journal. No 1, 26 May 1716–no 8, 14 July 1716–?

Great Britain's weekly pacquet. [No 1, 23 June 1716]–no 17, 13 Oct 1716–?

The Saturday's post. No 1, 29 Sept 1716–[No 11], 8 Dec 1716–before Nov 1717.

Jones's evening news letter. No 1, 29 Oct 1716–no 13, 26 Nov 1716.

The weekly journal: or Saturday's post, with freshest advices foreign and domestick. Ed N. Mist et al. No 1, 15 Dec 1716–no 339, 24 April 1725. Continued as Mist's weekly journal, no 1, 1 May 1725–no 179, 21 Sept 1728. Continued as Fog's weekly journal, no 1, 28 Sept 1728–no 445, 28 May 1737–no 1, 4 June 1737–no 22, 29 Oct 1737. Excerpts rptd 1722–7, 1732.

Anderson, P. B. Bernard Mandeville. TLS 28 Nov 1936. On Mandeville's contributions to Weekly Journal.

Limouze, A. S. Burlesque criticism of the ballad in Mist's Weekly Journal. SP 47 1950.

Novak, M. E. Simon Forecastle's Weekly Journal: some notes on Defoe's conscious artistry. SE 6 1965.

The loyal weekly journal, the phoenix or Sir Roger reviv'd: containing the whole weeks news foreign and domestick; to which will be added an amusement of a paragraph or two. [No 1, 5 Jan 1717?]–no 4, 26 Jan 1717.

The penny post: or tradesman's select pacquet. No 1, 13 March 1717–no 3, 18 March 1717–?

The London post, or the tradesman's intelligence: being a collection of the freshest advices, foreign and domestick. [No 1, 31 March 1717]–no 4, 8 April 1717–no 113, 18 Dec 1717–? Continued as Original London post: or Heathcote's intelligence, ?–no 125, 7 Oct 1719–no 633, 28 Dec 1722–12 June 1723–Oct 1733–?

The plain dealer. No 1, 22 May 1717–no 9, 17 July 1717.

The weekly review: or the Wednesday's post. No 1, 14 Aug 1717–?

The Protestant medley, or weekly courant: containing news foreign and domestick. No 1, 17 Aug 1717–no 2, 24 Aug 1717–[1720?].

St James's weekly journal. No 1, 7 Sept 1717–no 13, 30 Nov 1717–?

The Wednesday's journal: being an auxiliary to the Saturday's post. No 1, 25 Sept 1717–no 5, 23 Oct 1717–?

The weekly packet; with the price courant. No 1, 22 March 1718–no 34, 15 Nov 1718–?

The weekly medley, or the gentleman's recreation: containing an historical account of all news foreign and domestick; together with observations on the writings and manners of the age. No 1, 26 July 1718–no 79, 23 Jan 1720.

The Whitehall evening post. Ed D. Defoe. No 1, 18 Sept 1718–no 7,719, 30 April 1796–? BM Egerton ms 2236.

The Church-man. No 1, 29 Oct 1718–?

The orphan reviv'd: or Powell's weekly journal, containing all remarkable occurrences foreign and domestick. Ed W. Pittis. [No 1, 9 Nov 1718?]–no 9, 17 Jan [1719]–no 76, 20 Feb [1720].

Votes of the House of Commons. No 1, 11 Nov 1718–no 117, 18 April 1719.

Parker's London news: or the impartial intelligencer. [No 1, Nov 1718?]–no 38, 18 Feb 1719–no 1,005, 25 April 1725. Continued as Parker's penny post, no 1, 28 April 1725–no 1,302, 24 Aug 1733–?

The Oxford post: or the ladies new tatler. [No 1, 17 Dec 1718?]–no 21, 3 Feb 1719–?

Britain's genius: or the weekly correspondent. No 1, 5 Feb 1719–no 8, 9 April 1719.

The London mercury: or Great Britain's weekly journal. No 1, 14 March 1719–?

The Thursday's journal. Ed J. Pitt. No 1, 6 Aug 1719–no 21, 24 Dec 1719. Continued as London journal: or the Thursday's journal, no 22, 26 Dec 1719–no 41, 7 May 1720. Continued as London journal, no 42, 14 May 1720–no 991, 12 Aug 1738–17 March 1744. Excerpts rptd as Cato's letters 1721, 1722, 1724, 1725, 1750–4, and other portions as Speculatist 1730.

Bullock, J. M. Thomas Gordon: 'the independent Whig'. Aberdeen 1918.

Realey, C. B. The London Journal and its authors 1720–3. Humanities Stud of Univ of Kansas 5 1935.

Joshi, K. L. The London Journal 1719–38. Bombay Univ Jnl 9 1940.

The Jesuite, with political reflections on the most material occurrences foreign and domestick. [No 1, 8 Aug 1719]–no 2, 15 Aug 1719–no 9, 3 Oct 1719–?

The daily post. Ed D. Defoe. No 1, 3 Oct 1719–no 8,255, 14 Feb 1746.

The manufacturer: or the British trade truly stated, by D. Defoe. [No 1, 30 Oct 1719?]–no 3, 6 Nov 1719–no 31, 17 Feb 1720.

The St James's weekly journal: or Hanover postman. No 1, 31 Oct 1719–no 24, 16 April 1720. 2 issues dated 16 April 1720.

The British merchant: or a review of the trade of Great Britain. No 1, 10 Nov 1719–no 12, 11 Feb 1720.

The daily journal. [No 1, 23 Jan 1720]–no 2, 24 Jan 1720–no 5,977 (ptd 9,577), 9 April 1737–42.

The churchman's last shift: or loyalist's weekly journal. No 1, 14 May 1720–no 22, 29 Oct 1720. Continued as Church-man: or loyalist's weekly journal, no 23, 5 Nov 1720–no 35, 28 Jan 1721–?

The postmaster: or the loyal mercury. [No 1, 19 Aug 1720?]–no 6, 2 Sept 1720–23 Dec 1720–[1722].

The weekly journal: or general post. ?–11 Sept 1720–?

The penny weekly journal: or Saturday's entertainment. No 1, 29 Oct 1720–no 15, 4 Feb 1721. Continued as London mercury: or Great Britain's weekly journal with the freshest advices foreign and domestick, no 16, 11 Feb 1721–no 59 (i.e. 86), 8 June 1722–?

The spy. [No 1, 16 Nov 1720?]–no 5, 14 Dec 1720–no 13, 8 Feb 1721.

The exchange evening-post. No 1, 16 Jan 1721–no 26, 15 March 1721.

The daily packet: or the new London day post. No 1, 20 Jan 1721–no 2, 21 Jan 1721.

The patriot. No 1, 6 March 1721–no 9, 7 April 1721.

The gentleman's journal and tradesman's companion. No 1, 1 April 1721–no 18, 29 July 1721.

The moderator. Ed A. Hammond. No 1, 21 April 1721–no 15, 24 May 1721.

The freeholder's journal. No 1, 31 Jan 1722–no 76, 18 May 1723.

The St James's journal, with memoirs of literature. No 1, 3 May 1722–no 56, 18 May 1723.

The London post: the freshest and most remarkable occurrences at home and abroad. [No 1], 11 May 1722–26 Feb 1725–?

Baker's news: or the Whitehall journal. Ed J. Smedley. No 1, 29 May 1722–no 24, 30 Oct 1722. Continued as Whitehall journal, no 25, 6 Nov 1722–no 53, 21 May 1723. A supplement to Baker's news: or the Whitehall journal, no 12, 9 Aug 1722.

The Irishman's journal. [No 1 announced in the St James's journal no 6, 7 June 1722].

The Englishman's journal. No 1, 6 June 1722–no 12, 22 Aug 1722–?

The British journal. Ed J. Trenchard et al. No 1, 22 Sept 1722–no 277, 13 Jan 1728. Continued as British journal: or the censor, no 1, 20 Jan 1728–no 151, 23 Nov 1730. Continued as British journal: or the travel-ler, no 152, 30 Nov 1730–no 168, 20 March 1731–?

Anderson, P. B. Cato's obscure counterpart in the British Journal. SP 34 1937.

Vichert, G. S. Some recent Mandeville attributions. PQ 45 1966.

The loyal observator reviv'd: or Gaylard's journal. Ed Dr Gaylard. No 1, 8 Dec 1722–no 33, 20 July 1723. Continued as Loyal observator: or Collins's weekly journal, no 34, 27 July 1723–no 47, 26 Oct 1723–?

Limouze, A. S. Doctor Gaylard's Loyal observator reviv'd. MP 48 1950.

The news journal English and French. No 1, 28 Feb 1723–no 18, 27 June 1723. Continued as English and French news journal, no 19, 4 July 1723–no 28, 5 Sept 1723. Continued as English and French journal, no 29, 12 Sept 1723–no 31, 26 Sept 1723–?

Clifton's Oxford post: or the ladies new tatler reviv'd. [No 1, 9 July 1723?]–no 46, 24 Oct 1723–?

The universal journal. No 1, 11 Dec 1723–no 38, 29 Aug 1724.

The Protestant intelligence, with news foreign and domestick. No 1, 1 Jan 1724–no 2, 8 Jan 1724.

The honest true Briton. No 1, 21 Feb 1724–no 32, 15 June 1724.

The Protestant intelligence. [No 1, 26 Sept 1724]–no 3, 10 Oct 1724–no 27, 27 March 1725–?

The half-penny London journal, with freshest advices at home and abroad. ?–no 8, 3 Nov 1724–no 15, 19 Nov 1724–? Pbd by W. Parks and F. Lightbody.

The Protestant advocate, with remarks upon popery, serious and comical. No 1, 14 Dec 1724–no 3, 21 Dec 1724.

The half-penny London journal: or the British oracle. [No 1, 22 Dec 1724?]–no 10, 12 Jan 1725–no 17, 28 Jan 1725–? Pbd by T. Read.

The original half-penny London journal. ?–no 55, 23 Feb 1725–?

The London post: containing the freshest and most remarkable occurrences at home and abroad. ?–no 13, 6 Jan 1725–?

The observator. ?–no 7, 18 Jan 1725–no 8, 21 Jan 1725–?

The penny London post. [No 1, April 1725?]–no 109, 3 Jan 1726–no 211, 5 Sept 1726–1734.

The British spy: or weekly journal. No 1, 25 Sept 1725–?

The censor: or muster-master-general of all the news-papers printed in Great Britain and Ireland. [No 1, 6 April 1726?]–no 2, 13 April 1726–?

Lloyd's list. [1726]–no 560, 2 Jan 1740–.

The craftsman. Ed N. Amhurst et al. No 1, 5 Dec 1726–no 44, 8 May 1727. Continued as Country journal: or the craftsman, no 45, 13 May 1727–no 1,111, 10 Oct 1747–? Several issues of Craftsman extraordinary. Pbn resumed ?–no 1,124, 20 Jan 1750–no 1,159, 15 Sept 1750–[1752?]. Some nos rptd seriatim Dublin 1739.

Arnall, W. The case of the opposition stated, between the Craftsman and the people. 1731.

The grand accuser the greatest of all criminals. 1735.

Treachery, baseness and cruelty displayed to the full in the hardships and sufferings of Mr Henry Haines, late printer of the Country journal: or the craftsman. 1740.

Avery, E. L. The Craftsman of July 2 1737 and Colley Cibber. Research Stud of State College of Washington 7 1939.

Davis, H. Reprinting the Craftsman. Book Collector 2 1953.

The evening entertainment. [No 1, 20 Jan 1727]–no 3, 27 Jan 1727–no 4, 30 Jan 1727–?

The monitor. No 1, 26 Jan 1727–no 2, 2 Feb 1727–?

The evening journal. No 1, 1 Dec 1727–no 62, 12 Feb 1728.

The London evening post. No 1, 12 Dec 1727–.

Deacon, E. The family of Meres. Bridgeport Conn 1891.

Cranfield, G. A. The London evening post, 1727–44: a study in the development of the political press. Historical Jnl 6 1963.

—— The London evening post and the Jew bill of 1753. Historical Jnl 8 1965.

The flying-post. No 5,447 [first issued], 30 Dec 1727–no 5,455, 18 Jan 1728. Pbd by T. Warner as rival to the Flying-post: or the post-master, which he had formerly ptd.

The Free Briton: or the opinion of the people. 1727–?

Proctor's price-courant reviv'd. [No 1, Jan 1728?]–no 182. 1 July 1731–?

The flying-post: or the weekly medley, French and English. Ed J. M. Smith, J. Ralph. No 1, 5 Oct 1728–no 43, 26 July 1729. Continued as Weekly medley, no 44, 2 Aug 1729–no 55, 18 Oct 1729–? Continued as Weekly medley and literary journal, no 57, 1 Nov 1729–no 83, 2 May 1730–?

The universal spectator and weekly journal. Ed H. Baker, W. Guthrie. No 1, 12 Oct 1728–no 907, 22 Feb 1746. Excerpts rptd 1736, 1747, 1756.

Potter, G. R. Henry Baker. MP 29 1932.

La staffetta italiana: or the Italian post. [No 1, 19 Dec 1728?]–no 3, 2 Jan 1729–no 7, 30 Jan 1729–?
The coffee-house evening post. No 1, 1 Jan 1729–?
The coffee-house morning post. ?–28 April 1729–?
The Grub-street journal. Ed R. Russel and J. Martyn. No 1, 8 Jan 1730–no 418, 29 Dec 1737. Continued as Literary courier of Grub-street, no 1, 5 Jan 1738–no 30, 27 July 1738. Nos from 8 Jan 1730 to 24 Aug 1732 rptd as Memoirs of the society of Grub-street, 1737.
   Hillhouse, J. T. The Grub-street journal. Durham NC 1928.
The daily advertiser. No 1, 3 Feb 1730–. Incorporated with Oracle and public advertiser and continued as Oracle and daily advertiser, 10 Sept 1798–.
   'Sternhold, Thomas'. The Daily Advertiser in metre. 1781.
The weekly news and daily register. Ed T. Birch? [No 1, 17 April 1730]–no 6, 22 May 1730–. Continued as Weekly news and register, no 9, 12 June 1730–. Continued as Weekly register, no 27, 17 Oct 1730–. Continued as Weekly register: or universal journal, no 106, 22 April 1732–no 301, 6 Dec 1735.
The mountebank, by 'Democritus Sindercombe'. No 1, 5 Jan 1732–no 9, 1 March 1732.
The historical journal. No 1, 10 Jan 1732–no 12, 26 Aug 1732–?
The universal spy: or Aesop the fabulist. No 1, 25 March 1732–no 4, 15 April 1732–?
The universal spy: or the Royal oak journal reviv'd, by 'John Perspective'. No 1, 29 April 1732–no 12, 22 Sept 1732.
The St James's weekly packet. No 1, 1 July 1732–no 5, 29 July 1732–?
The miscellany: giving an account of the religion, morality and learning of the present time, by 'Richard Hooker, of the Temple esq.' [W. Webster]. No 1, 16 Dec 1732–no 2, 23 Dec 1732. Continued as Weekly miscellany: giving an account of the religion, morality and learning of the present time, no 3, 30 Dec 1732–. Continued as Weekly miscellany, no 13, 10 March 1733–no 444, 27 June 1741. Nos 1–101 rptd 1736–8, 1738. 52 issues rptd Dublin: no 1, 10 Jan 1734–no 52, 4 Jan 1735.
The London crier. [Jan 1733]–? Excerpts quoted in Bee, 1733.
The British observator. No 1, 10 March 1733–no 113, 12 April 1735; rptd 1735.
The bee: or universal weekly pamphlet. Ed E. Budgell. No 1, 3 (10) Feb 1733–no 13, 5 May 1733. Continued as Bee: or universal weekly pamphlet reviv'd, vol 2 no 14, nd–. Continued as Bee reviv'd: or the universal weekly pamphlet, vol 2 no 17–vol 9 no 118, 14 June 1735; rptd 1737.
   Herd, H. In his Seven editors. 1955. On Budgell.
   Riffe, N. L. Budgell's Bee 1733–4. N & Q Feb 1964.
The compleat historian: or the Oxford penny-post. [No 1, 12 Sept 1733?]–no 2, 14 Sept 1733–?
The British mercury: or weekly pacquet. [No 1, 15 Sept 1733?]–?
The Englishman. Ed W. Prynn. No 1, 18 June 1733–no 2, 23 June 1733.
Osborn's penny post: or the London mercury. [No 1, 9 July 1733?]–no 103, 4 March 1734–no 125, 24 April 1734–?
The oeconomist: or Edlin's weekly journal. No 1, 1 Sept 1733–?
The general evening post. No 1, 2 Oct 1733–. Rival paper with same title pbd 12 March 1771–July 1771. BM Add. ms 38729.
The corn-cutter's journal. No 1, 2 Oct 1733–no 78, 25 March 1735.
Cotes's weekly journal: or the English stage player. No 1, 11 May 1734–no 9, 6 July 1734.
   Milford, R. T. Cotes's Weekly Journal. TLS 19 March 1931.

Stratman, C. J. Cotes's weekly journal: or the English stage-player. PBSA 56 1962.
The penny i[ntelligencer?]. ?–30 Sept 1734–?
The weekly amusement: or the universal magazine. Vol 1 no 1, 9 Nov 1734–vol 5 no 62, 10 Jan 1736–? Some nos rptd seriatim Dublin 1735.
The London daily post and general advertiser. Ed T. Cibber. No 1, 4 Nov 1734–. Continued as General advertiser, no 2,909, 12 March 1744–. Continued as Public advertiser, no 5,645, 1 Dec 1752–no 18,632, 28 Feb 1794. Incorporated with Oracle and continued as Oracle and public advertiser, no 18,633, 1 March 1794–. Combined with Daily advertiser and continued as Oracle and daily advertiser, [10 Sept 1798]–. BM Add. ms 38169.
   [Bell, J.] The new duty on paper. Oracle & Public Advertiser 21 April 1794.
   The Whitefoord papers. Ed W. A. S. Hewins, Oxford 1898.
The tell tale, by 'Timothy Tattle gent.' [No 1, 20 Nov 1734]–no 7, 1 Jan 1735–?
The weekly oracle: or universal library. No 1, 7 Dec 1734– no 70, 29 May 1736–[1737].
The gentleman's journal. [No 1, Dec 1734?]–no 55, 27 Dec 1735–?
Walker's half-penny post. ?–no 82, 21 March 1735–?
The old Whig: or the consistent Protestant. Ed B. Avery et al. No 1, 13 March 1735–no 160, 30 March 1738; rptd 1739.
The daily gazetteer. Ed W. Arnall et al. No 1, 30 June 1735–. Continued as Daily gazetteer: or London advertiser, [1746]–15 April 1748. Continued as London gazetteer, no 1, 5 Dec 1748–. Merged with London daily advertiser and continued as Gazetteer and London daily advertiser, 1 Nov 1753–. Continued as Gazetteer and new daily advertiser. No 10,960, 27 April 1764–. Continued as Gazetteer, Nov 1796–. Absorbed by Morning post, Sept 1797.
   BM Add ms 38729, 38730.
   Jack Ramble's account of setting up the Daily gazetteer. Craftsman 2 Aug 1735; rptd GM Aug 1735.
   Crane, V. W. (ed). Benjamin Franklin's letters to the press 1758–75. Chapel Hill 1950.
   Haig, R. L. The last years of the Gazetteer. Library 5th ser 7 1953.
   Haig, R. L. The Gazetteer 1735–97: a study in the eighteenth-century English newspaper. Carbondale 1960.
The independent London journalist. Ed C. Middleton et al. No 1, 19 July 1735. Continued as Independent London journal, no 2, 26 July 1735–no 29, 24 Jan 1736–?
Queen Anne's weekly journal: or the ladies magazine. No 1, 15 Nov 1735–. Continued as Queen Anne's weekly magazine: or the ladies library, no 6, 20 Dec 1735–no 175, 17 March 1739.
   Sutherland, J. R. Lost journals. Periodical Post Boy 6 1950.
Rayner's morning advertiser. [No 1, 23 Dec 1735?]–no 57, 3 May 1736–no 189, 7 March 1737–? Continued as London morning advertiser, ?–no 938, 4 Sept 1741–. Continued as Generous London morning advertiser, no 978, 21 Dec 1741–? Continued as Rayner's London morning advertiser, ?–no 117 [i.e. 1,186], 15 Sept 1742–. Continued as London morning advertiser, no 1,224, 17 Dec 1742–no 1,272, 4 May 1743–?
The parrot: or pretty Poll's morning post. Dec 1735.
   Sutherland, J. R. Lost journals. Periodical Post Boy 6 1950.
The Oxford journal: or the tradesman's intelligencer. Jan 1736.
   Sutherland, J. R. Lost journals. Periodical Post Boy 6 1950.
The weekly spectator and English theatre. Nos 1–2, July 1736.

Sutherland, J. R. Lost journals. Periodical Post Boy 6 1950.

The London spy revived, by 'Democritus Secundus of the Fleet'. [No 1, 28 July 1736?]–no 5, 6 Aug 1736–no 257, 15 March 1738–?

Walker's half-penny London spy, by 'Democritus Secundus, the laughing philosopher of the Fleet'. [No 1, 2 Aug 1736]–no 15, [30 Aug 1736?]–? Pbd in opposition to London spy revived, above.

The London tatler. ?–6 Nov 1736–4 Dec 1736–?

[Dormer's] country tatler. [1736].

Common sense: or the Englishman's journal, by the Earl of Chesterfield et al. No 1, 5 Feb 1737–no 359, 31 Dec 1743–? Nos 1–104 rptd 1738–9.

Barnard, F. V. Common and superior sense: a new attribution to Johnson. N & Q May 1967.

Common sense: or the Englishman's journal. No 40, 5 Nov 1737 (first issued)–. Continued as Old common sense: or the Englishman's journal, no 43, 26 Nov 1737–no 123, 16 June 1739. Rival to Common sense: or the Englishman's journal, above, with serial numbers and dates parallel.

The Saturday's evening-post: or universal journal. [No 1, 18 June 1737]–?

[Newspaper issued as cover to Exposition on the common-prayer, pbd in pts by L. Clarke.] [No 1, 20 July 1737]–no 3, 3 Aug 1737–no 87, 10 Jan 1739–?

The Warwick and Staffordshire journal; with the exposition on the common-prayer. [No 1, 20 Aug 1737]–no 3, 3 Sept 1737–. Continued as Warwick and Staffordshire journal; with the history of the Holy Bible, 29 Oct 1737–. Continued as Warwick and Staffordshire journal; with the history of the life of Jesus Christ, 25 June 1740–June 1743.

The weekly essay: or Middlesex journal. No 1, 5 Nov 1737–no 19, 11 March 1738.

The Shropshire journal; with the history of the Holy Bible. [No 1, 19 Dec 1737?]–no 73, 12 Feb 1739–?

The nonsense of common-sense, by Lady M. W. Montagu. No 1, 20 Dec 1737–no 9, 14 March 1738; rptd Evanston 1948.

The halfpenny London spy. 1737.

The Englishman. [No 1, May 1738?]–no 147, 21 Feb 1741–?

The Derbyshire journal; with the history of the Holy Bible. [No 1, 24 May 1738?]–no 2, 31 May 1738–?

The Lancashire journal; with the history of the Holy Bible. [No 1, 6 July 1738?]–no 3, 20 July 1738–no 142, 16 March 1741–? From no 12, 18 Sept 1738, ptd in Manchester.

[Newspaper issued without title]. [No 1, 17 July 1738]–no 4, 24 July 1738. Continued as Original London post: or Heathcote's intelligence, no 17, 23 Aug 1738–no 41, 18 Oct 1738–?

The new half-penny post. [No 1, 2 Aug 1738]–[no 12, 28 Aug 1738?]–?

The humours of the age: or Dean Swift's new evening-post. No 1, 21 Oct 1738–? Facetious.

The London farthing post. 14 Dec 1738–3 April 1739–?

Lady's curiosity: or weekly Apollo. [1738].

News from the dead: or a weekly packet of intelligence piping-hot from the other world. ?–[1 Jan 1739?]–?

The London and country journal; with the history of the Old and New Testament [later subtitle: with the freshest news foreign and domestick]. 6 different sers appeared: (a) the Tuesday series: [no 1, 2 Jan 1739?]–no 8, 20 Feb 1739–no 149, 3 Nov 1741–no 1, 10 Nov 1741–no 7, 22 Dec 1741–?; (b) the first Wednesday ser: [no 1, 23 May 1739?]–no 3, 6 June 1739–no 122, 16 Sept 1741–?; (c) the second Wednesday ser; [no 1, 23 July 1740?]–no 3, 6 Aug 1740–no 100, 16 June 1742–?; (d) the Thursday ser: [no 1, 24 May 1739?]–no 3, 7 June 1739–no 142, 4 Feb 1742–?; (e) the second Thursday ser: [no 1, 24 July 1740?]–no 15, 30 Oct 1740–no 138, 10 March 1743–?; (f) the Friday ser: [no 1, 13 Nov 1741?]–no 32,

18 June 1742–no 33, 25 June 1742–? There may also have been an earlier Friday ser beginning 5 Oct 1739.

The citizen: or the weekly conversations of a society of London merchants on trade and other publick affairs, by W. Keith. No 1, 9 Feb 1739–no 25, 27 July 1739; rptd 1740.

The universal spy: or London weekly magazine, by 'Timothy Truepenny'. No 1, 13 April 1739–no 26, 5 Oct 1739.

All-alive and merry: or the daily farthing post. ?–April 1739–? Continued as All-alive and merry: or the London morning post?–? Continued as All-alive and merry: or the London daily post ?–20 April 1743–?

All-alive and merry: or the London daily post. ?–Sept 1741–10 Nov 1741–? Rival to other paper of the same title, above.

The universal weekly journal. ?–5 May 1739–8 Sept 1739–?

The country magazine: or weekly packet. No 1, ? Nov 1739–?

Country correspondent: or the stage monitor. No 4, ? 1739–?

The champion: or British mercury, by 'Capt Hercules Vinegar, of Pall-Mall' [H. Fielding et al]. No 1, 15 Nov 1739–. Continued as Champion: or evening advertiser, no 64, 10 April 1740–31 Aug 1742–? Continued as British champion: or the impartial advertiser, ?–no 54, 18 Aug 1743–no 70, 15 Sept 1743–?; rptd 1741, 1743.

Wells, J. E. Fielding's choice of signature for the Champion. MLR 7 1912.

—— Fielding's signatures in the Champion and the date of his Of good-nature. MLR 7 1912.

—— News for bibliophiles. Nation (New York) 16 Jan 1913.

—— The Champion and some unclaimed essays by Henry Fielding. E Studien 46 1913.

—— Fielding's Champion and Captain Hercules Vinegar. MLR 8 1913.

—— Fielding's Champion: more notes. MLN 35 1920.

Cross, W. L. The history of Henry Fielding. 3 vols New Haven 1918.

Hughes, H. S. Fielding's indebtedness to James Ralph. MP 20 1923.

Köhler, F. Fieldings Wochenschrift the Champion und das englische Leben der Zeit. Münster 1928.

Banerji, H. K. Henry Fielding: playwright, journalist and master of the art of fiction. Oxford 1929.

Kenny, R. W. James Ralph: an eighteenth-century Philadelphian in Grub street. Pennsylvania Mag of History & Biography 64 1940.

Dudden, F. H. Henry Fielding. 2 vols Oxford 1952.

Shipley, J. B. On the date of the Champion. N & Q Oct 1953.

—— Essays from Fielding's Champion. N & Q Nov 1953.

—— Fielding's Champion and a publishers' quarrel. N & Q Jan 1955.

—— The 'M' in Fielding's Champion. N & Q June, Aug 1955.

—— A new Fielding essay from the Champion. PQ 42 1963.

Sackett, S. J. (ed). The voyages of Mr J. Vinegar from the Champion. Los Angeles 1958.

Coley, W. B. The 'remarkable queries' in the Champion. PQ 41 1962.

Levine, G. H. Henry Fielding and the dry mock. Hague 1967.

The Englishman's evening post and universal advertiser. Ed W. Guthrie et al. [No 1, 1 Jan 1740?]–no 32, 13 March 1740–no 60, 17 May 1740–?

The Methodist's journal. No 1, 2 Aug 1740–?

The Christian's amusement: containing letters concerning the progress of the gospel both at home and abroad. No 1, Sept 1740–no 27, [1740]. Continued as Weekly history: or an account of the most remarkable particulars relating to the present progress of the gospel, no 1 [containing same material as no 27 of the Christian's amusement], 11 April 1741–no 84, 13 Nov 1742.

The prattler. No 1, 30 Dec 1740.

The publick register: or the weekly magazine. No 1, 3 Jan 1741–no 24, 13 June 1741.

The Northamptonshire journal with the history of the Old and New Testament. ?–19 March 1741–?

Robinson Crusoe's daily London evening post. 20 May 1741–? Continued as Robinson Crusoe's London daily evening post, ?–21 Sept 1742–18 Nov 1742–?

The new weekly miscellany, by 'Richard Hooker' [W. Webster]. No 1, 18 July 1741–no 19, 21 Nov 1741. Continued as Westminster journal: or the new weekly miscellany, by 'Thomas Touchit, of Spring-gardens, esq', no 20, 28 Nov 1741–no 898, 7 April 1759–? Combined with Universal chronicle: or weekly gazette, vol 3 no 92 [no 937 of Westminster journal], 5 Jan 1760–no 105 [no 950 of Westminster journal], 5 April 1760–? Continued as Royal Westminster journal and London political miscellany, 1 Jan 1763–[1764?]. Continued as Westminster journal and London political miscellany, by 'Simon Gentletouch, of Pall-Mall, esq' [1764?–no 1,329, 25 Aug 1770–no 2,149, 1 July 1786–[1794?]. Continued as Westminster journal and old British spy, [1794?]–.

Letters from the Westminster journal, 28 Nov 1741–8 Jan 1743; rptd 1747.

The weekly packet. [No 1, July 1741?]–no 133, 22 Jan 1744–1 Oct 1744–?

The country oracle: a weekly newspaper containing answers to all questions in all sciences. March 1741.

Admiral Vernon's weekly journal. [Oct 1741]–? Given as cover with weekly nos of books pbd in pts by W. Rayner.

The London morning penny advertiser. [No 1, 18 Jan 1742?]–no 15, 19 Feb 1742–. Continued as London morning advertiser, no 47, 5 May 1742–[1743?].

Old England: or the constitutional journal, by 'Jeffrey Broadbottom, of Covent-garden, esq' [W. Guthrie]. No 1, 5 Feb 1743–. Continued as Old England: or the Broadbottom journal, no 140, 17 Jan 1747–. Continued as Old England: or the national gazette, 6 April 1751–. Continued as Old England's journal, no 1, 24 Feb 1753–no 7, 7 April 1753.

The universal London morning advertiser. [No 1, 2 May 1743?]–no 11, 25 May 1743–. Continued as Penny London morning advertiser, no 109, 9 Jan 1744–. Continued as Penny London post: or the morning advertiser, no 203, 15 Aug 1744–no 1,403, 5 April 1751–. Continued as London morning penny post, no 1,416, 6 May 1751–?

The general London evening mercury. [No 1, 3 May 1743?]–no 94, 6 Dec 1743–no 573, 30 Dec 1746–?

The British intelligencer: or universal advertiser. ?–no 10, 23 May 1743–. Continued as Penny London morning advertiser, Aug 1744–?

The London journal and country craftsman. [No 1, 7 May 1743?]–no 34, 24 Dec 1743–no 46, 17 March 1744–?

The express: or evening gazette. ?–May 1743–?

The London courant. [No 1, 2 May 1745?]–no 47, 17 Aug 1745–? Continued as London courant: or new advertiser, ?–no 494, 28 Jan 1747–no 1,021, 4 Oct 1748–? Continued as London courant and Westminster chronicle, ?–25 Nov 1779–. Continued as London courant, Westminster chronicle and daily advertiser, [10 Oct 1781]–. Continued as London courant, noon gazette and daily advertiser, [21 Jan 1782]–. Continued as London courant and daily advertiser, [9 April 1782]–. Continued as London courant, Westminster chronicle and daily advertiser, [15 April 1782]–. Continued as London courant and daily advertiser, [6 Sept 1782]–?

The true patriot: and the history of our own times. Ed H. Fielding. No 1, 5 Nov 1745–no 32, 10 June 1746–no 33; rptd University Alabama 1964, London 1965.

The West Indian monthly packet of intelligence. No 1, 30 Nov 1745.

The penny medley: or weekly entertainer. Nos 1–12, 1746.

The Whitehall evening post: or London intelligencer. Ed T. Wright, S. Jones. [No 1, Feb 1746?]–no 174, 24 March 1747–.

Mercurius latinus: or the Latin mercury, by 'Agricola Candidus AM'. No 1, 15 March 1746–no 31, 11 Oct 1746.

The national journal: or the country gazette. No 1, 22 March 1746–no 43, 28 June 1746; rptd in part, 1748.

The museum: or the literary and historical register. Ed R. Dodsley. Vol 1 no 1, 29 March 1746–vol 3 no 39, 12 Sept 1747.

The parrot; with a compendium of the times, by E. Haywood. No 1, [2 Aug 1746]–no 9, [4 Oct 1746].

The Jacobite's journal. Ed H. Fielding. No 1, 5 Dec 1747–no 49, 5 Nov 1748.

The tatler reviv'd. No 1, 13 March 1750–no 6, 24 March 1750–?

The living world: or the history of the last fortnight. Nos 1–3, 1750.

The true Briton: in which the state, constitution and interest of Great-Britain will be considered. Vol 1 no 1, [2 Jan 1751]–vol 5 no 20, 6 June 1753.

The London advertiser and literary gazette. Ed J. Hill. No 1, 4 March 1751–. Continued as London daily advertiser and literary gazette, no 40, 18 April 1751–. Continued as London daily advertiser, no 228, 25 Nov 1751–no 738, 21 July 1753.

Leslie-Melville, A. R. Henry Fielding. TLS 27 July 1933.

The dramatic censor: being remarks upon the conduct of our most celebrated plays. No 1, [1751].

The Covent-garden journal, by 'Sir Alexander Drawcansir Knt, Censor of Great Britain' [H. Fielding]. No 1, 4 Jan 1752–no 72, 25 Nov 1752; rptd seriatim in part, Dublin 1752–3; rptd in part, 1752, New Haven 1915, 1964. Spurious Covent-garden journal extraordinary in the Spring-garden journal and in Have at you all: or the Drury lane journal.

The British spy: or new universal London weekly journal. [No 1, 15 Feb 1752?]–no 209, 21 Feb 1756–no 235, 21 Aug 1756–? Perhaps continued with faulty numbering or resumed after interval as Old British spy: or newsman's weekly journal, ?–no 242, 8 Jan 1757–? Perhaps continued as the Old British spy, ?–no 2,037, 26 June 1779–no 2,255, 4 Jan 1783–[1794?]. Incorporated with Westminster journal and continued as the Westminster journal and old British spy, [1794?]–.

Have at you all: or the Drury lane journal, by 'Madam Roxana Termagant' [B. Thornton]. No 1, 16 Jan 1752–no 13, 9 April 1752.

The general review: or impartial register. No 1, [May 1752]–no 5, [July 1752].

The craftsman: or Gray's inn journal. 21 Oct 1752–? Continued as Craftsman: or Say's weekly journal [sometimes gazetteer], ?–no 353, 11 Sept 1762–.

The Spring-garden journal, by 'Miss Priscilla Termagant' [B. Thornton]. No 1, [16 Nov] 1752–no 4, 7 Dec 1752.

The scourge. No 1, 28 Nov 1752–no 81, 2 June 1753.

The protester on behalf of the people, by 'I. Barebone' [J. Ralph]. No 1, 2 June 1753–no 24, 10 Nov 1753.

The Gray's-inn journal. Ed A. Murphy. No 1, 29 Sept 1753–no 52, 21 Sept 1754; rptd 1756, with 52 nos which had been pbd in the Craftsman: or Gray's-inn journal.

The patriot: or the Irish packet open'd. No 1, 25 Oct 1753–no 7, 6 Dec 1753; rptd 1754.

Canning's farthing post. [No 1], 1753–no 65, 1754.

The evening advertiser. Ed E. Kimber. [No 1, 3 March 1754]–no 2, 5 March 1754–no 641, 15 April 1758.

Kimber, S. A. The relation of a late expedition to St Augustine. PBSA 28 1934.

The monitor: or British freeholder. Ed R. Beckwith and J. Entinck. No 1, 9 Aug 1755–no 504, 20 March 1765; rptd 1756, 1757, 1760.

The citizen: or morning post. No 1, 16 Sept 1756–. Continued as Citizen: or general advertiser, 7 Sept 1757–31 Dec 1757.

The new daily advertiser. [No 1, 6 Oct 1756]–no 5, 11 Oct 1756–no 29, 8 Nov 1756.

The reformer, by 'Walter Wagbucket'. No 1, 19 Nov 1756–no 3, 3 Dec 1756.

The London chronicle: or universal evening post. Ed Spens. No 1, 1 Jan 1757–. Continued as London chronicle, 2 July 1765–. Weekly version began 7 Jan 1758.

Pottle, F. A. The incredible Boswell. Blackwood's Mag Aug 1925.

Bodleian Quart Record 7 1935.

Emery, J. P. Murphy's criticism in the London Chronicle. PMLA 54 1939.

Aldridge, A. O. Franklin's deistical Indians. Proc Amer Philosophical Soc 94 1950.

New essays by Arthur Murphy. Ed A. Sherbo. East Lansing 1963.

Lloyd's evening post and British chronicle. No 1, 22 July 1757–.

Rivington, S. The publishing family of Rivington. 1919.

New essays by Oliver Goldsmith. Ed R. S. Crane, Chicago 1927.

The herald: or patriot-proclaimer, by 'Stentor Tell-truth'. No 1, 17 Sept 1757–no 30, 6 April 1758; rptd 1758.

A Briton. No 1, nd [1757?].

The London chronicle. No 1, 7 Jan 1758–no 20, 20 May 1758–? Weekly version of the London chronicle, which began 1 Jan 1751.

The universal chronicle: or weekly gazette. No 1, 8 April 1758–. Continued as Payne's universal chronicle: or weekly gazette, no 5, 6 May 1758–. Continued as Universal chronicle: or weekly gazette, no 40, 6 Jan 1759–. Continued as Universal chronicle and Westminster journal, no 92 of Universal chronicle and no 937 of Westminster journal, 5 Jan 1760–no 105 of Universal chronicle and no 950 of Westminster journal, 5 April 1760.

Green, B. Possible additions to the Johnson canon. Yale Univ Lib Gazette 16 1942.

Kolb, G. J. John Newbery, projector of the Universal Chronicle: a study of the advertisements. SB 11 1958.

The new weekly chronicle: or universal journal. No 1, 8 April 1758. Continued as Owen's weekly chronicle: or universal journal, no 2, 15 April 1758–[10 Nov 1768]–? Excepts rptd as Babler, by H. Kelly, 1767.

Gove, P. B. Early numbers of the Morning Chronicle and Owen's Weekly Chronicle. Library 4th ser 20 1940.

— No 1 of Owen's Weekly Chronicle. Library 4th ser 21 1941.

The London weekly chronicle. No 1, 8 July 1758–no 4, 29 July 1758.

The comptroller, in English and French. No 1, 20 Sept 1759–?

The public ledger: or daily register of commerce and intelligence. Ed J. Newbery, G. Jones, A. Chalmers. No 1, 12 Jan 1760–. Continued as Public ledger, 3 Nov 1761–.

Welsh, C. A bookseller of the last century: being some account of the life of John Newbery. 1885.

Records of the House of Newbery. 1911.

New essays by Oliver Goldsmith. Ed R. S. Crane, Chicago 1927.

Thwaite, M. F. John Newbery: publisher and bookseller 1713–67. Private Lib 8 1967.

The St James's chronicle: or British evening post. Ed N. Thomas. [No 1, 12 March 1761]–no 17, 21 April 1761–. Selected pieces pbd 1762 as Yearly chronicle for 1761.

Some particulars of the life of George Colman. 1795.

Page, E. R. George Colman the elder 1732–94. New York 1935.

Vincent, H. P. Christopher George Colman, 'lunatick'. RES 18 1942.

The royal gazette and universal chronicle. No 1, 22 May 1761–. Continued as Royal gazette, no 13, 19 June 1761–?

Baldwin's London journal: or British chronicle. No 1, 2 Jan 1762–? Continued as Baldwin's London weekly journal, ?–1791–.

The royal chronicle and the British evening post. No 1, 15 Jan 1762–17 March 1762.

The Briton. No 1, 29 May 1762.

The fortnight's register: or a chronicle of interesting and remarkable events, foreign and domestick. No 1, 12 Aug 1762–no 22, 4 June 1763.

Topics of the day: or London-correspondent. No 1, 16 Feb 1764–no 8, 5 April 1764.

The East-India observer. Nos 1–7, [1766].

The East India examiner. No 1, [6 Sept 1766]–no 11, 19 Nov 1766.

The monitor: or green-room laid open. No 1, 17 Oct 1767. Continued as Theatrical monitor: or stage management and green-room laid open, no 2, 24 Oct 1767–no 18, 16 April 1768.

The Covent-garden chronicle. ?–no 2, 9 March 1768.

The gentleman's journal: or weekly register of news, politics, literature and amusement. No 1, 19 Nov 1768–no 2, 26 Nov 1768–?

Critical memoirs of the times. No 1, 25 Jan 1769–no 3, 25 Feb 1769–?

The Middlesex journal: or chronicle of liberty. Ed W. Beckford. No 1, 4 April 1769–. Continued as Middlesex journal: or universal evening post, no 508, 2 July 1772–. Continued as Middlesex journal and evening advertiser, no 729, 30 Nov 1773–? Continued as Middlesex journal and London evening-post, ?–no 2,269, 21 Oct 1783–no 2,530, 4 June 1785–[1790?].

Bryant, D. C. Rhetorical criticism in the Middlesex Journal 1774. Quart Jnl of Speech 50 1964.

The morning chronicle and London advertiser. Ed W. Woodfall, J. Perry. [No 1, 28 June 1769]–no 184, 3 Jan 1770–? Continued as Morning chronicle, [1789 or 1790]–.

Memoirs of James Perry. European Mag 1818; Bell's Weekly Messenger 7 Dec 1821.

Gove, P. B. Early numbers of the Morning Chronicle and Owen's Weekly Chronicle. Library 4th ser 20 1940.

The independent chronicle. No 1, 29 Sept 1769–. Continued as Independent chronicle: or the freeholders evening-post, no 102, 23 May 1770–no 104, 28 May 1770–?

The case of William Bingley, bookseller, compiled by a barrister of the Middle Temple. 1773.

[Bingley, W.] A sketch of English liberty. 1790.

The London packet. Ed A. Chalmers et al. [No 1, Oct 1769?]–no 91, 28 May 1770–no 207, 20 Feb 1771–? Continued as London packet: or new evening post, ?–no 210, 1 March 1771–. Continued as London packet: or new Lloyd's evening post, no 387, 17 April 1772–. No 464, 14 Oct 1772, as London packet and general hue and cry.

MB Add mss 38728–9.

Marston, E. Sketches of some booksellers of the time of Dr Johnson. 1902.

Bingley's journal: or the universal gazette. No 1, 9 June 1770–. Continued as Bingley's journal, no 56, 29 June 1771–. Continued as Bingley's London journal, no 118, 5 Sept 1772–25 Feb 1775–[1790].

Independent Chron 1769. On Bingley.

The constitutional guardian. No 1, 20 Oct 1770–no 6, 24 Nov 1770.

The general evening post. [March 1771–July 1771]. Issued as rival to paper of same name established 1733.

The historical register of publick occurrences, foreign and domestick. No 1, 1 Sept 1772–8 April 1774–?

The morning post and daily advertising pamphlet. Ed H. Bate et al. No 1, 2 Nov 1772–. Continued as Morning post: or cheap daily advertiser, no 14, 17 Nov 1772–? Continued as Morning post and daily advertiser, ?–no 886, 29 Aug 1775–no 4,121, 16 May 1792–? Continued as Morning post and gazetteer, ?–no 9,029, 16 Dec 1797–.

The trial of the Rev Henry Bate for a libel on the Duke of Richmond. 1781.

An account of Henry Bate Dudley. GM March 1824.

Taylor, J. Records of my life. 2 vols 1832.

Wilkinson, T. and J. F. Tattersall. Memories of Hurstwood. Burnley 1889.

Letters of the Lake poets to Daniel Stuart. 1889.

Roberts, W. Memorials of Christie's. 2 vols 1897.

Francis, J. C. The Morning Post 1772–1916. N & Q 14–28 Oct 1916.

Ferguson, M. T. The Morning Post 1772–1922: the triple jubilee of a great newspaper. Nat Rev Jan 1922.

Hindle, W. The Morning Post 1772–1937. 1937.

Woof, R. S. Wordsworth's poetry and Stuart's newspapers 1797–1803. SB 15 1962.

The independent chronicle and universal evening post. [Vol 1 no 1?]–no 76, 20 Sept 1773–?

The whole proceedings on the King's Commission of the Peace, oyer and terminer, and gaol delivery for the City of London. Dec 1775–Oct 1776.

The craftsman: or London intelligencer. ?–no 121, 25 Aug 1778–?

British gazette and public advertiser. ?–1776–1797–?

The general advertiser and morning intelligencer. Ed W. Cooke. [1776?]–no 135, 10 April 1777–no 1297, 18 Dec 1780–? Continued as Parker's general advertiser and morning intelligencer, ?–no 1,789, 3 July 1782–no 1,937, 20 Jan 1783–[23 Nov 1784]. Continued as General advertiser, [24 Nov 1784]–[May 1789]. Continued as Patriot and general advertiser, no 3,908, 3 June 1789–16 Aug 1790–?

Memoirs of John Almon, bookseller of Piccadilly. 1790.

The London price courent. [1776]–no 488, 30 Sept 1785–no 704, 8 Oct 1789–? Continued as Prince's London price courant, ?–1 Jan 1796–no 1,238, 27 Dec 1799–?

American gazette, by several gentlemen from America. [No 1]?–no 2, Feb 1776–no 4, March 1776.

The citizen and weekly register. No 1, 24 Feb 1776–no 2, 2 March 1776–?

Courier de l'Europe. Ed D. de la Tour et al. [No 1, July 1776?]–vol 9 no 50, 22 June 1781–. Continued as Courier de Londres, 29 Feb 1787–.

Hatin, E. Histoire de la presse politique et littéraire en France. Paris 1859.

Robiquet, P. Theveneau de Morande. Paris 1882.

Brissot de Warville, J. I. Mémoires. Ed C. Perroud 2 vols Paris 1912.

The morning post and daily advertiser. No 2,000 (first issued), 5 Nov 1776–no 2,007, 11 Nov 1776. Continued as New morning post, no 2,008, 12 Nov 1776–no 35, 14 Dec 1776–[Feb 1777?].

The fall of Britain, by T. Stephens et al. No 1, 9 Nov 1776–no 15, 15 Feb 1777.

The Westminster gazette: or constitutional evening post. [No 1, Nov 1776?]–no 82, 13 May 1777–no 124, 30 Aug 1777–?

Courier politique et littéraire: or French evening post. Ed H. Bate. [No 1, 23 May 1777?]–vol 1 no 53, 21 Nov 1777–vol 2 no 17, 27 Feb 1778–no 44, 2 June 1778–?

The Englishman. Ed C. J. Fox et al. No 1, 13 March 1779–no 17, 2 June 1779.

The English chronicle. [No 1], 2 Jan 1779–no 133, 6 Nov 1779–[29 March 1781?]. Continued as English chronicle and universal evening-post, [31 March 1781?]–no 401, 24 July 1781–no 3,240, 25 Feb 1800–.

The London courant and Westminster chronicle. 25 Nov 1779–. Continued as London courant, Westminster chronicle and daily advertiser, 10 Oct 1781–. Continued as London courant, noon gazette and daily advertiser, 21 Jan 1782–. Continued as London courant, morning gazette and daily advertiser, 11 March 1782–. Continued as London courant and daily advertiser, 9 April 1782–. Continued as London courant, Westminster chronicle and daily advertiser, 15 April 1782–. Continued as London courant and daily advertiser, 6 Sept 1782–?

The British gazette and Sunday monitor. [No 1, 26 March 1780]–no 66, 24 June 1781–no 171, 9 Feb 1783–? Continued as E. Johnson's British gazette and Sunday monitor, ?–no 220, 6 June 1784–.

The morning herald and daily advertiser. Ed H. Bate, A. Chalmers. No 1, 1 Nov 1780–no 6,330, 31 Dec 1800–. Subtitle varies. By 1796 title is Morning herald.

The hypocrite unmasked, by W. Moore. No 1, 11 Nov 1780.

The British mercury and evening advertiser. No 1, 16 Nov 1780–no 27, 16 Dec 1780–?

The aurora and universal advertiser. No 1, 15 Jan 1781–no 42, 3 March 1781.

The noon gazette and daily spy. ?–10 Dec 1781–26 Dec 1781–? Incorporated with London courant, Jan 1782.

The freeman's journal. No 1, 25 April 1781–3.

The abstract and brief chronicle of the time. No 1, 7 Dec 1782–?

Ayre's Sunday London gazette and weekly monitor. [No 1], 27 April 1783–22 March 1795–[1800?].

The London recorder or Sunday gazette. [No 1], 27 July 1783–. Apparently absorbed Sunday reformer and universal register and continued as London recorder and Sunday reformer. ?–.

The freeholder. No 1, 9 March 1784–no 2, 16 March 1784–?

Journal politique et littéraire d'Angleterre. [No 1, 7 June 1784]–no 13, [28 Aug] 1784.

von Feilitzen, O. Journal politique et littéraire d'Angleterre, 1784. Library 5th ser 1 1946.

The universal London price-courant. [1784?]–no 174, 26 June 1787–no 287, 25 Aug 1789–[1795]–?

The daily universal register. No 1, 1 Jan 1785–. Continued as Times: or the daily universal register, 1 Jan 1788–. Continued as Times, 18 May 1788–.

Makomer, S. V. Some notes on the history of the Times 1785–1904. 1904.

The history of the Times: 'the Thunderer' in the making 1785–1841. New York 1935.

Haig, R. L. William Finey and the Times. TLS 4 April 1952.

[Morison, S.] Printing the Times since 1785: some account of the means of production and changes of dress of the newspaper. 1953.

The new London price courant. ?–14 April 1786–.

The world, fashionable advertiser. Ed E. Topham et al. No 1, 1 Jan 1787–. Continued as World, no 272, 27 Nov 1787–no 2,342, 30 June 1794.

Este, C. My own life. 1787.

Memoirs of the life of Mrs Sumbel, late Wells. 3 vols 1811.

Heriot, J. GM Aug 1833. A memoir.

Morison, S. Capt Edward Topham and the 'Keep-the-line' Club. Colophon 6 1932; rptd Cambridge 1933.

Werkmeister, L. The first publication of Chatterton's verses To Miss C. on hearing her play the harpsichord. N & Q July 1962.

The British mercury: or annals of history, politics, manners, literature etc. Vol 1 no 1, 4 April 1787–25 Dec 1790.

The county chronicle and weekly advertiser for Essex, Herts, Kent, Surrey, Middlesex, Berks. No 1, 29 May 1787–no 440, 22 Nov 1796–.

The Sunday chronicle. No 1, 30 March 1788–no 94, 7 June 1789–no 144, 20 June 1790–[1791?].

The evening star and grand weekly advertiser. No 1, 1 April 1788–. Continued as Original star and grand weekly advertiser, no 5, 7 May 1788–?

The star and evening advertiser. Ed A. Macdonald, A. Tilloch. No 1, 3 May 1788–. Continued as Star, no 187, 6 Dec 1788–.

Tilloch, A. Imperial Mag (Liverpool) 7 1825. A memoir.

Werkmeister, L. Some account of Robert Burns and the London newspaper, with special reference to the spurious Star 1789. BNYPL Oct 1961.

Stuart's star and evening advertiser. Ed P. Stuart. No 1, 13 Feb 1789–no 64, 27 April 1789. Continued as Morning star, no 65, 28 April 1789–no 106, 16 June 1789–Oct 1789–?

The evening mail. [No 1, Feb 1789?]–no 62, 20 July 1789–.

The Argus. Ed S. Perry. No 1, 9 March 1789. Continued as Argus of the constitution, 27 Jan 1792–. Continued as Argus of the people, 13 Oct 1792–no 1,168, 4 Dec 1792. Excerpts rptd in Argus: or general observer, vol 1 no 1, [29 Oct 1795]–no [24], [18 May 1796].

The diary: or Woodfall's register. No 1, 30 March 1789–no 1,452, 31 Aug 1793.

Lady's gazette and evening advertiser. No 1, 5 May 1789–no 12, 13 June 1789–?

The oracle, Bell's new world. Ed J. Boaden. No 1, 1 June 1789–? Continued as Oracle, ?–no 875, 16 March 1792–28 Feb 1794. Combined with Public advertiser and continued as Oracle and public advertiser, no 18,633, 1 March 1794–[8 Sept 1798]. Combined with Daily advertiser and continued as Oracle and daily advertiser, [10 Sept 1798]–no 22,232, 27 Feb 1800–.

Mackintosh, R. J. The life of Sir James Macintosh. 2 vols 1836.

Boaden, J. GM April 1839. A memoir.

Morison, S. John Bell. Cambridge 1930.

The review and Sunday advertiser. No 1, 21 June 1789–no 301, 22 March 1795–[1796?]. Continued as Sunday review, [1796?]–no 574, 19 Aug 1798–.

Lettres à Monsieur le Comte de B. sur la Révolution. No 1, 12 July 1789–no 51, 28 March 1790.

Journal de l'Europe, by D. de la Tour. No 1, 4 Aug 1789–no 16, 25 Sept 1789.

Mitchell's Sunday London gazette and weekly monitor. [9 May 1790?]–no 16, 22 Aug 1790.

The comet: or evening gazette. ?–14 June 1790–16 June 1790–?

The Sunday herald. [?–1790–?]

The Westminster evening herald. 11 Sept 1790–14 Sept 1790–?

The senator: or Clarendon's parliamentary chronicle. No 1, 25 Nov 1790–.

The theatrical guardian. Ed J. Fennell. No 1, 5 March 1791–no 6, 9 April 1791.

The hue and cry and police gazette. [1791?]–.

Journal de Middlesex. No 1, 15 April 1791–no 6, 3 May 1791–?

The observer. No 1, 4 Dec 1791–.

The observer 1791–1921: a short record of 130 years. 1921.

The county herald and weekly advertiser for one hundred miles round London, particularly for the counties of Surrey, Bucks, Beds, Herts, Essex, Kent, Middlesex, Sussex, Berks, Oxon, Camb, Suffolk, Norfolk, Hants etc. [1791?]–no 1,383, 3 Jan 1818–?

The cabinet. No 1, 2 Jan 1792–no 36, 11 Feb 1792–?

Jordan's parliamentary journal. 1792–5.

The unsuspected observer. Nos 1–2, 1792.

The Paris mercury and continental chronicle. No 1, 28 May 1792–16 June 1792–?

The courier and evening gazette. Ed J. Perry. [No 1, July 1792?]–no 86, 31 Dec 1792–.

The sun. Ed J. Heriot. No 1, 1 Oct 1792–.

Memoir of J. Heriot. GM Aug 1833.

The true Briton. Ed J. Taylor. No 1, 1 Jan 1793–.

Taylor, J. Records of my life. 1832.

The Sunday reformer and universal register. [No 1, 14 April 1793]–no 11, 23 June 1793–no 307, 3 March 1799–? Apparently absorbed by London recorder and Sunday gazette, and continued as London recorder and Sunday reformer.

Correspondance française: ou tableau de l'Europe. Ed J. G. Peltier. No 1, 2 Nov 1793. Continued as Correspondance politique: ou tableau de l'Europe, no 2, 5 Nov 1793–no 118, 2 Aug 1794.

The morning advertiser. Ed J. Scott. No 1, 8 Feb 1794–. Morning Advertiser. Centenary no 8 Feb 1894.

Impartial report of the debates that occur in the two Houses of Parliament. 1794–.

The express and evening chronicle. [No 1, Sept 1794?]–no 439, 8 July 1797–no 517, 11 Jan 1798–? Perhaps continued as Express and the London herald, ?–no 1,324, 29 Aug 1799–?

The politician. No 1, 13 Dec 1794–no 4, 3 Jan 1795–?

The telegraph. Ed D. E. Macdonnel. No 1, 30 Dec 1794–18 March 1797–? United with Morning post.

Electioneering and parliamentary review. Vol 1 no 1, 1795.

The tomahawk: or censor general. No 1, 27 Oct 1795–no 113, 7 March 1796–?

The selector: or Say's Sunday reporter. [No 1, Nov 1795?]–no 161, 9 Dec 1798–no 287, 28 Dec 1800–.

An historical detail of the most remarkable public occurrences and newest political intelligence. No 1, 8 Jan 1796–. Continued as A complete historical detail of the most remarkable public occurrences, no 3, 5 Feb 1796–no 8, 15 April 1796–?

The mirror of the times. [No 1, April 1796?]–no 92, 6 Jan 1798–.

Bell's weekly messenger. No 1, 1 May 1796–. Selections rptd as Bell's annual messenger, 1798, 1799.

The London herald and evening post. [No 1, July 1796?]–no 400, 9 Feb 1799–no 402, 16 Feb 1799–? Perhaps united with Express and evening chronicle.

The reporter: or the general observer. No 1, 5 Oct 1797.

The anti-Jacobin: or weekly examiner. Ed W. Gifford. No 1, 20 Nov 1797–no 36, 9 July 1798; rptd 1799.

Albion: a new weekly paper. Ed A. M'Leod. [Dec 1797?]–? Continued as Albion and evening advertiser, ?–no 106, 9 Jan 1800–.

Journal de France et d'Angleterre. Nos 1–3, 1797.

Leith commercial list. 1797–.

The brazen trumpet. No 1, 10 Feb 1798–no 6, 17 March 1798.

The weekly register. By D. Brewman. No 1, 11 April 1798–.

Mercure britannique: ou notices historiques et critiques sur les affaires du temps. Ed J. M. du Pan. Vol 1 no 1, Aug 1798–vol 4 no 36, 25 March 1800.

Il mercurio britannico: ossia notizie storico-critiche sugli affari attuali. Ed J. M. du Pan. No 1, Aug 1798–25 March 1800.

The British mercury: or historical and critical views of the events of the present time. Ed J. M. du Pan. Vol 1 no 1, 1798–vol 4 no 36, 31 March 1800.

Mallet, B. Mallet du Pan and the French Revolution. 1902.

The old Englishman and anti-Jacobin examiner. No 1, 5 Dec 1798–no 14, 10 Feb 1799–?

General post office. Daily statement of the packet boats. Ed T. Johns. [1798]–.

Eighth report of the commissioners appointed to enquire into the management of the Post Office department. 1837.

The country porcupine. ?–13 July 1799–15 July 1799–?

The dramatic censor: or weekly theatrical report. By T.

Dutton. Vol 1 no 1, 4 Jan 1800–. Continued as Dramatic censor: or monthly epitome of taste, fashion and manners, vol 3 no 27, July 1800–no 32, Dec 1800–.
The porcupine. Ed W. Cobbett, J. R. Green. No 1, 30 Oct 1800–.
  Cole, G. D. H. The life of William Cobbett. 1924.
  Reitzel, W. The progress of a ploughboy to a seat in Parliament. 1933.

Clark, M. E. Peter Porcupine in America. Philadelphia 1939.
Muirhead, A. M. An introduction to a bibliography of William Cobbett. Library 4th ser 20 1940.
Pemberton, W. B. William Cobbett. 1949.
Pearl, M. L. Cobbett: a bibliographical account. Oxford 1953.

G. MANUSCRIPT NEWSLETTERS

Most of the hand-written newsletters by Muddiman, Williamson, Dyer, Fox, Wye, Dormer, Stanley, Miller, Jackson, Le Bourdery, Delpouch and many other professional news writers have not been preserved; but important collections exist in the Public Record Office, the BM, Bodley, the Folger Shakespeare Lib and the Press Club in London. Numerous extracts can be found in the provincial newspapers as late as the 1740s.

Nichols, J. G. Manuscript news letters. N & Q 3 Dec 1859.
Public Record Office. Calendar of state papers, domestic series of the reign of Charles II [1660–83]. Ed M. A. E. Green and F. H. B. Daniell 23 vols 1860–1932.
Historical Manuscripts Commission. First report, appendix: Lord Mostyn's collection of newsletters. 1870.
  — Twelfth report, appendix: the manuscripts of S. H. Le Fleming esq of Rydal Hall. 1890.
  — Fourteenth report, pt 2, appendix, vols 3–6. Harley mss of the Duke of Portland. 1894–1901.
Newdigate–Newdegate, Lady. Cavalier and puritan in the days of the Stuarts. New York 1901. [Has extracts from newsletters.]
News letters of 1715–16. Ed A. F. Stewart. London and Edinburgh 1910.
Merritt, E. P. News-letters sent by Sir Joseph Williamson,

1664–5. Colonial Soc of Massachusetts. Transactions 1915–16 18 1917.
Newton, Lady. Lyme letters, 1660–1760. 1925.
Leigh, A. Some old newsletters. Nat Rev Aug 1925.
Newsletters and early newspapers. TLS 11 Jan 1934.
B., R. S. The Aston hall news-letters. Cheshire Sheaf 29 1934.
Muddiman, J. G. The Dutch at Chatham in 1667. Draft newsletters of Henry Muddiman from 2 April to 18 June 1667. N & Q 11–18 April 1936.
Wilson, J. H. Theatre notes from the Newdigate newsletters. Theatre Notebook 15 1961.
Langhans, E. A. Theatrical references in the Greenwich Hospital newsletters. N & Q Sept 1964.
Snyder, H. L. Dyer's news letters–a new source for the study of the early Augustan period. Books and Libraries at the Univ of Kansas 2 1964.

H. MISCELLANEOUS LONDON SERIALS

Question-and-answer journals, dialogue papers, periodical lists of books and serials not easily classified.

The wandering whore: a dialogue, by J. Garfield. ?–No 2, [5 Dec 1660]–no 5, [nd 1661].
Mercurius librarius: or a catalogue of books. Ed J. Starkey and R. Clavell. No 1, Michaelmas term 1668–no 8, Trinity term 1670. Continued as A catalogue of books continued, no 1, Easter term 1670–Easter and Trinity terms 1709–Easter term 1711; rptd 1903, 1964.
  Arber, E. Contemporary printed lists of books produced in England. Bibliographica 3 1897.
Weekly advertisements of things lost and stollen, with catalogue of books newly come forth. No 1, nd–no 2, 25 Jan [1669]–no 3, 1 Feb [1669].
Poor Robin's intelligence. Ed H. Care [or W. Winstanley?] No 1, 23 March 1676–. Continued as Poor Robin's memoirs, no 1, 10 Dec 1677–no 17, 8 April 1678.
Poor Gillian: or mother Redcap's weekly advice to city and country. [No 1], 23 Nov 1677–no [4], 14 Dec 1677.
A pacquet of advice from Rome. Vol 1 no 1, 3 Dec 1678. Continued as Weekly pacquet: or advice from Rome, vol 1 no 2, 10 Dec 1678–vol 3 no 4, 25 June 1680. Continued as New anti-Roman pacquet, no 1, nd–no 2, 16 July 1680–no 4, 30 July 1680. Continued as Anti-Roman pacquet, no 5, 6 Aug 1680–no 21, 26 Nov 1680. Continued as Weekly pacquet of advice from Rome restored, vol 3 no 26, 3 Dec 1680–vol 5 no 47, 13 July 1683. Rival pbn with different text by W. Salmon issued as vol 5 no 1, 25 Aug 1682–vol 5 no 36, 27 April 1683.
The weekly pacquet of advice from Germany, by H. Care. No 1, 3 Sept 1679–no 19, 4 Feb 1680; rptd as History of the Protestant reformation as it was begun by Luther in Germany, 1680.
Poor Robin's intelligence newly revived. Ed H. Care or W. Winstanley. No 1, 4 Sept 1679–. Continued as Poor Robin's intelligence revived, no 4, 24 Sept 1679–no 38, 12 May 1680.

The snotty-nose gazette: or coughing intelligence. No 1, 24 Nov 1679.
The weekly character: being the character of a Pope. No 1, 1679.
Mercurius infernus: or news from the other world discovering the cheats and abuses of this. No 1, [4 March 1680]–no 6, [8 April 1680].
Heraclitus ridens: or a discourse between Jest and Earnest. Ed E. Rawlins? No 1, 1 Feb 1681–no 82, 22 Aug 1682; rptd 1713. Nos 1–3 rptd Edinburgh 1681.
  Newton, T. F. M. The mask of Heraclitus: a problem in Restoration journalism. Harvard Stud 16 1934.
News from Parnassus. No 1, 2 Feb 1681. Continued as Advice from Parnassus, no 2, 2 (i.e. 6) Feb 1681–no 4, 18 Feb 1681.
The weekly discovery of the mystery of iniquity: in the rise, growth, methods and ends of the unnatural rebellion in England, anno 1641. No 1, [5 Feb] 1681–no 30, 27 Aug 1681. No 3 rptd Edinburgh 1681.
The weekly discoverer strip'd naked: or Jest and Earnest expos'd to publick view in his proper colours, by H. Care? No 1, 16 Feb 1681–no 6, 23 March 1681.
Mercurius bifrons: or the English Janus, the one side true and serious, the other jocular. No 1, [17 Feb 1681]–no 3, 3 March 1681.
News from the land of chivalry: containing the pleasant and delectable history of don Rugero de Strangemento [R. L'Estrange]. No 1, [21 Feb 1681]–no 3, [7 March 1681].
Democritus ridens, or Comus and Momus: a new Jest and Earnest pratling concerning the times. No 1, 17 March 1681–no 13, 13 June 1681.
The observator, in question and answer, by R. L'Estrange. Vol 1 no 1, 13 April 1681–no 29, 2 July 1681. Continued as Observator in dialogue, no 30, 6 July 1681–no 112, 16 March 1682. Continued as Observator, no 113, 18 March 1682–vol 3 no 246, 9 March 1687.

The popish mass display'd: or the superstitions and fopperies of the Romish church discovered. No 1, 20 April 1681–no 2, 27 April 1681.

The weekly visions of the late popish plot. No 1, [22 April] 1681–no 7, 3 June 1681.

The observator observ'd: or Protestant observations upon anti-Protestant pamphlets. No 1, 6 May 1681–no 3, [16 June] 1681.

The history of reformation, in a dialogue between Philanax and Erasmus. No 1, 12 May 1681.

The weekly pacquet of advice from Geneva: or the history of the reformation. No 1, 20 May 1681–no 2, 26 May 1681.

The Protestant observator: or Democritus flens in a dialogue. No 1, 19 Nov 1681–no 10, 24 Dec 1681.

A new dialogue between some body and no body: or the Observator observed. No 1, 25 Nov 1681–no 5, 19 Dec 1681.

The mock-press: or the encounter of Harry Lungs and Jasper Hem, two running stationers. No 1, 1681.

England's monitor: or the history of separation. No 1, 30 March 1682–no 3, 13 April 1682.

The English Guzman: or captain Hilton's memoirs. No 1, [27 Jan 1683]–no 2, [1 Feb 1683].

Scots memoirs, by way of dialogue between John and Elymas. No 1, 20 Feb 1683. Continued as Scotch memoirs, no 2, 27 Feb 1683–no 5, [1 April] 1683.

The weekly pacquet of advice from Geneva: or the history of presbytery. Nos 1–3, 1683.

Lucian's dialogues (not) from the Greek, done into English burlesque. [No 1, 25 Dec 1683]–no 10, 26 Feb 1684.

Hippocrates ridens: or joco-serious reflections on quacks and illiterate pretenders to physick. No 1, 26 April 1686–no 4, 17 May 1686.

Observations on the weekly bill, with directions how to avoid the diseases now prevalent. No 1, 9 Aug 1686–no 3, 28 Aug 1686.

A friendly debate upon the next elections of Parliament. No 1, nd [1687?].

The test-paper. No 1, [9 May] 1688. Continued as Weekly test-paper, no 2, 16 May 1688–no 4, 30 May 1688. Nos 1–2 rptd Edinburgh 1688.

Poor Robin's publick and private occurances and remarks. No 1, [12 May] 1688–no 8, 4 July 1688.

The pacquet of advice from Rome restored, by H. Care. Vol 6 no 1, 5 Jan 1689–no 3, 8 Feb 1689.

When all is done [so text begins]. No 1, 10 Jan 1689.

The dilucidator: or reflections upon modern transactions. No 1, 15 Jan 1689–no 7, nd.

The Roman postboy: or weekly account from Rome, by J. Mumford? No 1, nd–no 2, 23 March [1689]–no 4, 15 April [1689].

Mercurius reformatus: or the new observator, by J. Welwood. No 1, 15 May 1689–vol 5 no 1, 7 Nov 1691. Continued as Weekly observator, vol 5 no 2, 9 Jan 1692–no 12, 1 April 1692. Continued as Mercurius britannicus: or the weekly observator, vol 5 no 13, 15 April 1692–no 29, 23 July 1692–[1694?]. Some early issues rptd Edinburgh. Early issues tr Dutch, 1690.

The new Heraclitus ridens: or an old dialogue between Jest and Earnest revived. No 1, 24 May 1689–no 3, 7 June 1689.

The geographical intelligence, for the better understanding of foreign news. No 1, 19 June 1689.

A ramble round the world: or the travels of Kainophilus, a lover of novelties, by J. Dunton. No 1, [6 Nov] 1689–no 2, 8 Nov 1689.

The life and errors of Mr John Dunton. 1705; ed J. Nichols 1818.

Moore, C. A. John Dunton: pietist and impostor. SP 22 1925.

Hatfield, T. M. John Dunton's periodicals. Journalism Quart 10 1933.

A dialogue between two friends concerning the present revolution. No 1, 12 Nov 1689–no 2, 19 Nov 1689.

The weekly lampoon: or satirical reflections on the last weeks publick news letters and Observator. [No 1, 29 Oct 1690?]–? Continued as Momus ridens: or comical remarks on the publick reports?–no 7, 10 Dec 1690–no 18, 25 Feb 1691–[no 19, 11 March 1691].

Mercurius britannicus: or the London intelligencer turn'd solicitor. No 1, 11 Nov 1690–no 2, 27 Nov 1690.

The Athenian gazette: or casuistical mercury resolving all the most nice and curious questions proposed by the ingenious. Ed J. Dunton et al. No 1, 17 March 1691. Continued as Athenian mercury [etc], no 2, 21 March 1691–14 June 1697. Suppls. Rptd (in part) as Athenian oracle, 3 vols 1704, 1728.

Bodleian library. Rawlinson mss miscellany 72, folios 65, 67.

Gildon, C. History of the Athenian society. 1710.

Steeves, H. R. The Athenian virtuosi and the Athenian society. MLR 7 1912.

Starr, G. A. From casuistry to fiction: the importance of the Athenian Mercury. JHI 28 1967.

The weekly remarks on the transactions abroad, by J. Welwood. No 1, 25 March 1691–no 5, 13 May 1691.

The pacquet of advice from France. No 1, 6 April 1691–no 6, 27 April 1691.

Poor Robin's intelligence: or news from city and country. No 1, 8 July 1691–no 2, 17 July 1691.

Mercurius reformatus: or the true observator. No 1, 10 Dec 1691.

The weekly memorial: or political observations on England's benefits by the war with France. No 1, 13 Jan 1692.

The introduction to the London mercury. Ed T. Brown. No 1, 1 Feb 1692. Continued as London mercury, no 5, 5 Feb 1692–no 8, 4 March 1692. Continued as Lacedemonian mercury, no 9, 7 March 1692–vol 2 no 1, 30 May 1692.

Boyce, B. Tom Brown of facetious memory. Cambridge Mass 1939.

A collection for improvement of husbandry and trade. Ed J. Houghton. Vol 1 no 1, 30 March 1692–vol 20 no 583, 24 Sept 1703; rptd 1727.

Lacy, M. G. An early agricultural periodical. Annual Report of Amer Historical Assoc 1 1923.

The moderator. No 1, 9 June 1692–no 4, 30 June 1692.

Merlin: the weekly monitor predicting England's grandeur. No 1, 15 June 1692.

The jovial mercury: containing the choicest and most pleasant questions in every art and science. No 1, [24 Feb] 1693–no 4, 17 March 1693.

The ladies mercury. No 1, 28 Feb 1693–no 4, 17 March 1693.

Stearns, B. M. The first English periodical for women. MP 27 1930.

Observations upon the most remarkable occurrences in our weekly news. No 1, 31 May 1693.

The gentleman's journal for the war. No 1, 13 July 1693–no 8, 30 Aug 1693; rptd 1694.

The news-expositour: being a brief explanation of the places and things contain'd in the Gazette, Harlemcourant, News-letters and other papers of intelligence. No 1, 16 June 1694.

The monthly account of the land-bank. [No 1, ?]–no 2, 3 Sept 1695–no 5, 3 Dec 1695.

Pegasus, with news, an observator and a Jacobite courant. No 1, 15 June 1696–14 Sept 1696.

The weekly survey of the world: or the gentleman's solid recreation. No 1, 29 Oct 1696.

The English Lucian: or weekly discoveries of the witty intrigues in town and country. [No 1], 18 Jan 1698–no 15, 18 April 1698.

The London spy, by E. Ward. Nov 1698–April 1700; rptd 1701–2, 1703, 1709, 1718, 1753, 1924, 1955.

Boyce, B. Two debits for Tom Brown, with a credit from Joseph Addison. PQ 14 1935.

Matthews, W. The character writings of Edward Ward. Neophilologus 21 1936.

The English Martial. No 1, Jan 1699.

The weekly comedy, as it is dayly acted at most coffee-houses in London, by E. Ward. No 1, 10 May 1699–no 10, 12 July 1699.

Bibliotheca annua: the annual catalogue for the year 1699 [1700–3]. Vol 1 1700–vol 4 1704; rptd 1965.

The infallible astrologer: or Mr Silvester Partridge's prophecie of what shall infallibly happen in and about the Cities of London and Westminster every day this week. [No 1, 15 Oct 1700]–no 2, nd–no 3, 29 Oct 1700–no 15, 3 Feb 1701. Continued as Astrological observator, no 16, 10 Feb 1701. Continued as Jesting Astrologer: or the merry observator, no 17, 17 Feb 1701–no 18, 24 Feb 1701.

The weekly entertainment. No 1, 24 Oct 1700–no 3, 7 Nov 1700.

The Dutch prophet: or the devil of a conjurer, being infallible predictions of what shall happen in and about the cities of London and Westminster from Tuesday the 26th of November to Tuesday the 3rd of December 1700, by 'Peter Nicholas Vangrin'. [26 Nov] 1700.

The merry mercury: or a farce of fools. No 1, 29 Nov 1700.

The compleat courtier: or the morals of Tacitus. 1700.

A new observator on the present times. No 1, 1 Jan 1701–no 15, 9 April 1701.

The weekly miscellany, by C. Cibber. No 1, 1 Feb 1701–no 3, 22 Feb 1701.

The politick spy: or the weekly reflections on the state and present dangers of Christendom. No 1, 30 July 1701–no 5, 27 Aug 1701.

The observator. By J. Tutchin et al. No 1, 1 April 1702–30 July 1712.

   The trial and examination of Mr John Tutchin for writing a certain libel called the Observator. [1704].

The secret mercury: or the adventure of seven days, by J. Dunton. No 1, 9 Sept 1702–no 4, 30 Sept 1702.

The weekly remembrancer shewing the best way to thrive, and to provide for the poor, in a dialogue between a churchman and a mystic. [No 1]–nos 2–4. Continued as Weekly remembrancer and discoverer: or truths spiritual and temporal, no 5. Continued as Tell-truth remembrancer, no 6, nd [1702–3].

The poetical observator. [1702]–vol 2 no 9, 12 Jan 1703–? Continued as Poetical observator reviv'd, 1703.

Heraclitus ridens in [sometimes at] a dialogue between Jest and Earnest concerning the times. Ed W. Pittis. Vol 1 no 1, [3 Aug 1703]–vol 3 no 3, 14 March 1704.

   Newton, T. F. M. William Pittis and Queen Anne journalism. MP 33 1936.

A new observator. No 1, 7 Jan 1704–no 5, 4 Feb 1704.

A dialogue between master Truth and master Honesty. [Jan 1704]. Perhaps continued as Truth and honesty, ?–no 27, 1705.

The loyal observator. Vol 1 no 1, 12 Jan 1704.

A weekly review of the affairs of France, by D. Defoe. No [1], 19 Feb 1704–no 7, 28 March 1704. Continued as A review of the affairs of France, no 8, 1 April 1704–vol 2 no 127, 27 Dec 1705. Continued as A review of the state of the English nation, vol 3 no 1, 1 Jan 1706–no 172, 6 Feb 1707–. Continued as A review of the state of the British nation, vol 4 no 12, 8 March 1707–11 June 1713. Issues of March 1709–10 pbd in advance in Edinburgh; ed A. W. Secord 9 vols New York 1938 (complete).

For studies of Defoe see col 906, above.

Couper, W. J. Mrs Anderson and the royal prerogative in printing. Proc of Royal Philosophical Soc of Glasgow 48 1917.

Fletcher, E. G. Some notes on Defoe's Review. N & Q 31 March 1934.

—— The London and Edinburgh printings of Defoe's Review vol 6. SE 14 1934.

Graham, W. Defoe's Review and Steele's Tatler: the question of influence. JEGP 33 1934.

Burch, C. E. Notes on the contemporary popularity of Defoe's Review. PQ 16 1937.

Morgan, W. T. Defoe's Review as a historical source. Jnl of Modern History 12 1940.

Murray, J. J. Defoe: news commentator and analyst of northern European affairs. Indiana Quart for Bookmen 3 1947.

Payne, W. L. Mr Review: Defoe as author of the Review. New York 1947.

Hobman, D. L. Defoe the journalist. Fortnightly Rev Sept 1952.

Moore, J. R. Defoe: ambidextrous mercury. Periodical Post Boy 11 1952.

—— Defoe: citizen of the modern world. Chicago 1958.

—— A checklist of the writings of Defoe. Bloomington 1960.

A catalogue of the Defoe collection in the Boston Public Library. Boston 1966.

Cook, R. I. 'Mr Examiner' and 'Mr Review': the Tory apologetics of Swift and Defoe. HLQ 29 1966.

The observator, by C. Leslie. No 1, 5 Aug 1704. Continued as Rehearsal [sometimes Rehearsal of observator], no 2, 12 Aug 1704–vol 4 no 48, 26 March 1709; rptd 6 vols 1750.

The Athenian catechism, by J. Dunton. [No 1, 23 Aug 1704?]–no 17, 13 Dec 1704–no 20, [3 Jan 1705?].

A supplementary journal to the advice from the scandal club. [No 1], Sept 1704–[no 5], Jan 1705. Suppl to Defoe's Weekly review of the affairs of France.

The observator reformed: in a dialogue between the Observator and Heraclitus ridens, with a moderator between them. No 1, 20 Sept 1704–no 17, 11 Jan 1705.

The diverting post, by H. Playford. No 1, 28 Oct 1704–no 36, 30 June 1705.

The casual observator. No 1, 7 Nov 1704–no 5, 24 Nov 1704.

The town spy. 1704.

The little review: or an inquisition of scandal, consisting in answers of questions and doubts, remarks, observations and reflection, by D. Defoe. No 1, 6 June 1705–no 23, 22 Aug 1705.

The moderator: published for promoting of peace. No 1, 16 May 1705–no 7, 27 June 1705.

The whipping-post: or a new session of oyer and terminer, for the weekly scribblers. Ed W. Pittis. No 1, 12 June 1705–no 20, 23 Oct 1705.

   Newton, T. F. M. William Pittis and Queen Anne journalism. MP 33 1936.

The monthly weather-paper. 1705.

The elixir. [No 1, Jan 1706?]–no 8, 26 Jan 1706–no 21, 2 March 1706–?

The rehearsal rehears'd in a dialogue between Bayes and Johnson. No 1, 27 Sept 1706.

Mercurius romanus. No 1, 1706–no 36, 1707. In Latin.

The humours of a coffee house: a comedy as it is dayly acted, by E. Ward and W. Oldisworth. [No 1], 25 June 1707–no 7, 6 Aug 1707. Continued as Weekly comedy: or the humours of a coffee house, no 1, 13 Aug 1707–no 24, 22 Jan 1708.

   Allen, R. Ned Ward and the Weekly comedy. Harvard Stud 17 1935.

The observator reviv'd. No 1, 27 Sept 1707.

The phenix: or a revival of scarce and valuable pieces. Vol 1 no 1, 1707–vol 2 no 30, 1708.

The British Apollo: or curious amusements for the ingenious, by A. Hill and M. Smith. No 1, 13 Feb 1708–vol 4 no 20, 11 May 1711. Suppls. Rptd 1726, 1740.

   Belcher, W. F. The sale and distribution of the British Apollo. In Studies in the early English periodical, ed R. P. Bond, Chapel Hill 1957.

The Scots observator being some remarks upon the affairs of the north of Britain. [No 1, 14 March 1708]–no 2, 17 March 1708–no 12, 25 April 1708.

The gazette-a-la-mode: or Tom Brown's ghost. No 1, 12 May 1709–no 5, 9 June 1709. Nos 1, 3, 5 rptd Los Angeles 1954 (facs).

The tatling harlot: or a dialogue between Bess o' Bedlam and her brother Tom, by 'Mother Bawdycoat'. No 1, 22 Aug 1709–no 3, [27 Aug 1709?]. No 1 rptd Los Angeles 1954 (facs).

The Christian's gazette: or news chiefly respecting the invisible world, by J. Dunton. [No 1], 1709. Next issue 1713.

Athenian news: or Dunton's oracle, by J. Dunton. No 1, 7 March 1710–no 27, 6 June 1710–?

The friendly couriere, by way of letters from persons in town. No 1, 1711.

The monthly weather-paper. 27 Feb 1711–July 1711.

The Christian's gazette: or nice and curious speculations, by J. Dunton; to which is added the Lame-poet [and] the Court-spy. Jan 1713–April 1713; rptd 1713.

Mercator: or commerce retrieved, by D. Defoe et al. No 1, 26 May 1713–no 181, 20 July 1714.

The British merchant: or commerce preserv'd in answer to the Mercator, by C. King et al. No 1, 7 Aug 1713–no 103, 30 July 1714; rptd 1721, 1743, 1748.

Dunton's ghost, or his speeches to the most remarkable persons in church and state: being the Hanover courant or merry observator, by J. Dunton. No 1, 4 March 1714–no 2, [March 1714].

The monthly catalogue. No 1, May 1714–no 8, Dec 1714–15; rptd 1964.

Arber, E. Contemporary printed lists of books produced in England. Bibliographica 3 1897.

McKillop, A. D. Lintot's Monthly catalogue. Newberry Lib Bull 6 1963.

The daily oracle. No 1, 1 Aug 1715–no 17, 26 Aug 1715.

The weekly observator. [No 1, 28 April 1716]–no 2, 5 May 1716–no 11, 11 July 1716.

The British physician. No 1, 30 May 1716–no 5, nd. Nos 3–4 as Great Britain's rules of health: or the British physician; no 5 as Great Britain's rules of health.

Heraclitus ridens: a discourse between Jest and Earnest

concerning the times. No 1, 30 Jan 1718–no 31, 28 Aug 1718.

The weaver: or the state of our home manufacture considered. No 1, 23 Nov 1719–no 8, 11 Jan 1720.

The casuist: or a dialogue between Pasquin and Marforio. No 1, 25 Nov 1719–no 15, 2 March 1720.

The spinster: in defence of the woollen manufactures, by R. Steele. No 1, [19 Dec] 1719; rptd in Town talk etc, Dublin 1790.

The Christian priest. [No 1, 27 May 1720?]–no 2, 3 June 1720–no 3, 10 June 1720.

The monthly catalogue: or a general register of books, sermons, plays and pamphlets. No 1, March 1723–no 80, Dec 1729. Continued in Monthly chronicle. Rptd 1964.

Arber, E. Contemporary printed lists of books produced in England. Bibliographica 3 1897.

Cook, D. F. Register of books 1732. Book Collector 16 1967.

News from the fairy island, where knaves and fools are painted in their proper colours, by Dr Censor and Volatile Oleosum. ?–no 3, 14 April 1726–no 5, 29 April 1726.

An historical list of horse races. [1729]–[68]. Pbd fortnightly April–Nov and rptd annually.

Lloyd's register of shipping. c. 1730–?
Annals of Lloyd's register. 1884.

The Christian's amusement. 1740.

Miscellanea curiosa mathematica. By F. Holliday. Vol 1 no 1, 1745–vol 2 no 5, [1749].

The register book of shipping. [1760?]–1776–.

The universal catalogue for the year 1772 [1773, 1774].

A register of the trade of the port of London, with a list of the ships entered inwards and cleared outwards, by C. Whitworth. No 1, Jan–March 1776–?

The lives and traits of the bon ton theatricals. No 1, 14 June 1790.

The monthly epitome and catalogue of new publications. Jan 1797–.

Protestant dissenters' register. Dec 1800.

I. PERIODICAL PUBLICATIONS: ENGLISH PROVINCES

(1) BIBLIOGRAPHIES AND GENERAL STUDIES

Local bibliographies and regional studies are listed under the name of the place; studies of individual magazines and newspapers are listed with them.

Grant, J. The newspaper press. 3 vols 1871–2.

Worth, R. N. Notes on the history of printing in Devon. Report & Trans of Devonshire Assoc for Advancement of Science, Literature & Art 11 1879.

Wallis, A. A sketch of the early history of the printing press in Derbyshire. Jnl of Derbyshire Archaeological & Natural History Soc 3 1881.

Hems, H. The press in the west. Western Antiquary 2 1883.

Gray, C. J. List of Cambridge periodicals. 1885.

A series of articles on the provincial press in Effective Advertiser. 1887.

Paterson, A. Yorkshire journalism, past and present. Barnsley 1901.

Gilbert, H. M. and G. N. Godwin. Bibliotheca Hantoniensis. Southampton [1891].

Edwards, F. A. A list of Hampshire newspapers. Hampshire Antiquary & Naturalist 1–2 1891–2.

Allnutt, W. H. English provincial presses, III. Bibliographica 2 1896.

— Notes on the introduction of printing-presses into the smaller towns of England and Wales after 1750 to the end of the eighteenth century. Library 2 1901.

Hyett, F. A. and W. Bazeley. The bibliographer's manual of Gloucestershire literature vol 3, Gloucester 1897.

Madan, F. Oxford periodicals 1651–80. In Oxford books:

a bibliography of printed works relating to the university and city of Oxford, Oxford 1912–31.

Williams, J. B. The first English provincial newspaper. N & Q 29 July, 9 Sept, 7 Oct 1916. Reply by R. P. Chope 19 Aug 1916.

Humphreys, A. L. A handbook to county bibliography. 1917.

Slade, J. J. and H. Richardson. Wiltshire newspapers: past and present. Wiltshire Archaeological & Natural History Mag 40–1 1922.

Local catalogue of material concerning Newcastle and Northumberland. Newcastle 1932.

The oldest newspapers. Newspaper World 18 March 1939–28 Oct 1939.

Weed, K. K. and R. P. Bond. Studies of British newspapers and periodicals from their beginning to 1800: a bibliography. Chapel Hill 1946.

Hudson, D. Three hundred years of university journalism. Oxford 7 1940.

Barnes, F. and J. L. Hobbs. Handlist of newspapers published in Cumberland, Westmorland and north Lancashire. Kendal 1951.

Cranfield, G. A. A hand-list of English provincial newspapers and periodicals 1700–60. Cambridge 1952.

— Additions and corrections. Trans of Cambridge Bibl Soc 2 1956. See also Wiles 1958, below.

— The development of the provincial newspaper 1700–60. Oxford 1962.

Burton, K. G. The early newspaper press in Berkshire 1723–1855. Reading 1954.

Thwaite, M. F. Hertfordshire newspapers 1772–1955. [no place] 1956.

Read, D. North of England newspapers c. 1700–c. 1900 and their value to historians. Proc of Leeds Philosophical Soc (Literary Historical Section) 8 1957.

—— Press and people 1790–1850: opinion in three English cities [Leeds, Manchester, Sheffield]. 1961.

Wiles, R. M. Further additions and corrections to G. A. Cranfield's Hand-list of English provincial newspapers and periodicals 1700–60. Trans of Cambridge Bibl Soc 2 1958.

—— Freshest advices: early provincial newspapers in England. Columbus Ohio 1965. Contains a Register of English provincial newspapers 1701–60.

—— Crowd-pleasing spectacles in eighteenth-century England. Jnl of Popular Culture 1 1967.

—— Weekly entertainments for the mind. Jnl of Popular Culture 2 1968.

Laughton, G. E. and L. R. Stephen. Yorkshire newspapers: a bibliography with locations. [Harrogate] 1960.

Brooke, L. E. J. Somerset newspapers 1725–1960. Yeovil 1960.

Myson, W. Surrey newspapers: a handlist and tentative bibliography. Wimbledon 1961.

Clare, D. The local newspaper press and local politics in Manchester and Liverpool 1780–1800. Trans of Lancashire & Cheshire Antiquarian Soc 73–4 1964.

Smith, R. E. G. Newspapers first published before 1900 in Lancashire, Cheshire and the Isle of Man: a union list of holdings in libraries and newspaper offices within that area. 1964.

O'Rourke, D. T. Early provincial newspapers in Reading University library. Trans of Cambridge Bibl Soc 4 1966.

Fraser, D. The press in Leicester c. 1790–1850. Leicestershire Archaeological & Historical Soc Trans 42 1967.

(2) PERIODICAL ESSAYS

Newspapers and magazines in which original essays are to be found are marked by square brackets.

Bath

The theatrical review. Pope's Bath Chron Oct 1767–March 1768.

The scribbler. 33 essays in Archer's Bath Chron 1768–9.

The remembrancer: essays and dissertations. 1771.

Salmon's mercury: or entertaining repository. Vol 1 no 1, 1 Nov 1777–vol 3 no 130, 11 May 1781.

Birmingham

[The Birmingham journal. 1732–3.]

Brentford

The ranger, by M. Hawke and R. Vincent. Vol 1 no 1, 1 Jan 1794–vol 2 no 40, 21 March 1795.

Bristol

The Bristol spectator. Bee, and Sketchley's Weekly Advertiser 3 Nov 1777–30 Dec 1777.

The bee and Sketchley's weekly advertiser. Vol 1 no 1, 27 Oct 1777–no 10, 30 Dec 1777–?

The bee: or entertaining repository. No 1, 1 Nov 1777–?

The morning visitor. Bristol & Bath Mag 1782–3.

The observer. 7 essays in Bristol & Bath Mag 1782–3.

The censor, by 'Roderic Random'. Bristol & Bath Mag 1783.

The crier. Vol 1 no 1, 24 Dec 1785–no 15, 29 July 1786–?; rptd [1786?].

The watchman, by S. T. Coleridge. No 1, 1 March 1796–no 10, 13 May 1796.

The Bristol spectator. [No 1, 9 Oct 1800 ?]–no 5, 6 Nov 1800–?

Cambridge

[The Cambridge chronicle. 1762.]

The occasional respondent. No 1, 12 April 1764.

The reformer. No 1, 6 April 1776–no 7, 18 May 1776.

Canterbury

The Kentish spectator. 22 essays in Kentish Post 1738–9.

The Kentish repository for miscellaneous essays, literary, moral, political etc. Kentish Gazette 1768–.

Chester

[The Chester weekly journal. 1721–33.]

[Adams's weekly courant. 1732–.]

Deptford

The sylph. Vol 1 no 1, 22 Sept 1795–no 40, 30 April 1796.

Exeter

[The Post-master. 1717–25.]

[Brice's weekly journal. 1725–31–?]

Gainsborough

The country spectator, by T. F. Middleton et al. No 1, 9 Oct 1792–no 33, 21 May 1793.

Gloucester

Country common sense, by a gentleman of Wilts. Nos 1–2 in Gloucester Jnl 1738: rptd 1738–9 (with 23 additional essays).

Kendal

[The Kendal weekly courant. 1732–6.]

Leicester

The selector. No 1, 28 Aug [1783]–no 23, 29 Jan [1784].

Liverpool

The recluse, by W. Roscoe and Dr Currie. Liverpool & Lancaster Herald 1790.

Manchester

[Whitworth's Manchester magazine 1737–60.]

The hermit. Orion Adams's Weekly Jnl 1752.

Norwich

The cabinet, by a society of gentlemen. Vol 1 no 1, 11 Oct 1794–vol 3 1795.

Graham, W. The authorship of the Norwich Cabinet. N & Q 23 April 1932.

Oxford

Letters in defence of religion. Student: or Oxford Monthly Miscellany March 1750–Oct 1750.

A new system of castle-building, by 'Chimaericus Cantabrigiensis'. Student: or Oxford Monthly Miscellany June 1750–Aug 1751.

The female student. Student: or Oxford Monthly Miscellany 1751.

Essays. 8 nos in Student: or Oxford Monthly Miscellany 1751.

The scribbler, by 'Jonathan Eyebright esq'. Oxford Mag Nov–Dec 1768.

A series of letters on English grammar. 11 nos in Oxford Mag July 1768–Sept 1769.

The police, by 'Senex'. 14 essays in Oxford Mag July 1769–Feb 1772.

The censor. 15 essays in Oxford Mag Aug 1769–Mar 1772.

The looker-on: a periodical paper, by 'Rev S. Olive-Branch' [W. Roberts et al]. No 1, 10 March 1792–no 86, 21 Dec 1793; rptd with additional papers 1794, 1795, 1797.

Reading

The fund: or literary entertainer. Oxford Gazette & Reading Mercury April 1767–June 1767.

Salisbury

[The Salisbury journal 1736–.]

Whitby

Anomaliae: being desultory essay on miscellaneous subjects. No 1, 24 Oct 1797–no 34, 12 June 1798.

Windsor

The microcosm, by George Griffin of the College of Eton [G. Canning et al]. No 1, 6 Nov 1786–no 40, 30 July 1787; rptd 1787, 1788, 1790, 1793, 1809.

York

The trifler. 11 essays in Yorkshire Mag Jan–Dec 1786.

(3) MAGAZINES AND MISCELLANIES

Alston

The Alston miscellany: or gentleman's magazine. April 1799–.

Bath

The Bath miscellany for the year 1740. 1741.
Remembrancer: essays and dissertations. 1771.
The Bath and Bristol magazine. No 1, April 1776–Dec 1776–?
Bath and west of England agricultural society: correspondence. 1780–.
Bath and west and southern counties society: letters and papers on agriculture etc. 1780–.

Birmingham

The Birmingham register: or entertaining museum. No 1, 10 May 1764–[6 June 1765]–? Alternated with Coventry museum.
The repository: or the weekly general entertainer. 1770; rptd 1772 (as Repository: or winter evening's entertainer).
The theological repository: consisting of original essays, hints, queries etc, by J. Priestley. Vol 1 1769–vol 6 1788. Vol 1 rptd 1773; vol 2 1770; vols 1–2 1795; vol 3 1795.
The Birmingham magazine: or lady's and gentlemen's weekly amusement. No 1, Oct 1770–?
The British museum: or universal register of literature, politics and poetry. Vol 1 1771–?

Bristol

The Bristol and Bath magazine: or instructive and entertaining miscellany. Vol 1 no 1, July 1782–[June 1783?]
The monitor: consisting principally of original essays, both in prose and verse. 1790.
Zion's trumpet: a theological miscellany, by a society of gentlemen. June 1798–.
Hey, J. The important question at issue between the editors of a periodical publication entitled Zion's trumpet, and a nonconformist. 1801.
Annual anthology. Ed R. Southey. Vols 1–2 1799–1800.

Bury St Edmunds

Annals of agriculture and other useful arts. Ed A. Young. Ptd London 1784–. Ptd Bury St Edmunds 1790–.

Cambridge

University magazine. No 1 Jan 1795–no 2 Feb 1795.

Canterbury

The genius of Kent: or county miscellany. No 1 Sept 1792–no 28 1795.
The Kentish register and monthly miscellany. Vol 1 no 1 Aug 1793–vol 3 no 29 Dec 1795.

Carlisle

The Carlisle museum. ?–13 July 1776–27 July 1776–?
The satellite: or repository of literature. No 1 10 Nov 1798–no 6 June 1800. Nos 4–6 pbd at Newcastle.

Chelmsford

The monthly magazine. 1800.

Chester

Y geirgrawn: neu drysorfa gwybodaeth. 1796.
The bee-hive: or Chester magazine. Vol 1 28 Feb 1798–15 Aug 1798.
Y drysorfa ysprydol. 1799.
Y creal. 1800.

Coventry

Jones's Coventry, Warwick and Birmingham magazine. [Jan 1764]–28 July 1764–?
The universal museum: or the entertaining repository, for gentlemen and ladies. [Jan 1764]–Oct 1765–?
The Coventry museum: or the universal entertainer. No 1 17 May 1764–? Fornightly, alternating with Birmingham register.

Ewood Hall (near Halifax)

Miscellanea sacra: or the theological miscellany. 1797–9.

Exeter

Remembrancer. Jan–Feb 1797.

Faringdon

The Berkshire chronicle: or the gentleman's, sportsman's, husbandman's and tradesman's repository. Ed L. Piggot. Vol 1 no 1 2 Jan 1798–?

Huddersfield

British poetical miscellany. Nos 1–30 1797.

Ipswich

The Ipswich magazine. Ed J. Bransby. Feb 1799–Feb 1800–?

Kendal

The agreeable miscellany: or something to please every man's taste. 13 May 1749–26 Oct 1750.

Leeds

The monthly miscellany. ?–Jan 1734–Feb 1734–?
The Leeds magazine. 1738.
The Methodist monitor: or moral and religious repository. Ed A. Kilham. Vol 1 no 1 [1796]–vol 2 no 18 [1797]
The Methodist magazine: or evangelical repository. 1798.

Leicester

Museum. Nos 1–12 1795–?

Liverpool

The Liverpool weekly magazine. Vol 1 no 1 6 Oct 1774–no 3 20 Oct 1774–?
The student: containing many curious essays. No 1 1797–no 4 1800.
The caterer. No 1 1798.
The new theological repository. No 1 July 1800.

Maidenhead

The Berkshire repository. Vol 1 nos 1–2 1797 (prose); vol 1 no [1] 1797 (verse).

Manchester

The humourist: or magazine of magazines. [No 1, 6 Oct 1750?]–no 3, 3 Nov 1750–?

The Lancashire magazine: or Manchester museum. [No 1, 15 March 1763?]–no 52, 21 Feb 1764. No 52 as Lancashire magazine: or Manchester weekly amusement.

Harland, J. The Lancashire magazine: or Manchester museum. Manchester Collectanea 2 1899.

The Manchester and Liverpool museum: or the beauties of all magazines selected. Vol 1, Aug 1779–?

Manchester literary and philosophical society memoirs. 1785–.

Newark

The lady and gentleman's scientifical repository. 1782–4.

The Briton. Vol 1 no 1 23 Jan 1793–no 54 12 Feb 1794.

Newcastle

The Newcastle general magazine. No 1 Jan 1747–Dec 1760.

The literary register: or weekly miscellany. Vol 1 no 1 1769–vol 5 no 52 1773.

The freemens' magazine: or the constitutional repository. Ed J. Murray. No 1 [April] 1774–no 4 [July] 1774.

The Newcastle weekly magazine: or compendium of politics, literature and amusement. 31 July 1776–25 Dec 1776–?

The magazine of ants: or pismire Journal. Ed J. Murray. No 1 [26 July] 1777–no 6 1777.

The evangelical magazine: or Christian library. No 1 3 Aug 1780–78.

The Protestant packet: or British monitor. Ed J. Murray. No 1 4 Aug 1780–vol 2 no 27 18 May 1781.

The Newcastle magazine: or, monthly journal. No 1 Jan 1785–Feb 1786.

The oeconomist: or Englishman's magazine. Ed T. Bigge et al. Vol 1 no 1 Jan 1798–vol 2 no 24 Dec 1799.

Literary and philosophical society of Newcastle-upon-Tyne: reports. 1793.

Newmarket

The eclipses: or luminaries involved in darkness; an universal repository for questions. Ed J. Pharaoh et al. 1795–7.

Northampton

The Northampton miscellany: or monthly amusements. No 1 31 Jan 1721–no 6 30 June 1721.

Norwich

The Norwich journal: or historical chronicle. ?–Aug 1741–?

The budget: or Norfolk, Suffolk and Essex entertaining weekly miscellany. No 1, 5 May 1779–no 7, 17 June 1779.

The cabinet, by a society of gentlemen. Vol 1 no 1 11 Oct 1794–vol 3 1795.

Oxford

The student: or the Oxford monthly miscellany. Ed C. Smart, B. Thornton et al. Vol 1 no 1 31 Jan 1750–; as Student: or the Oxford and Cambridge monthly miscellany no 6 30 Jan 1750–vol 2 no [10] 3 July 1751.

The loiterer: a periodical work. Ed J. Austen. Vol 1 no 1, 31 Jan 1789–vol 2 no 60, 20 March 1790; rptd Dublin 1792.

Plymouth

The Plymouth magazine: or the universal intelligencer. No 1, 23 Oct 1758–?

Wright, W. H. K. The Plymouth magazine. Western Antiquary 5 1886.

Brushfield, T. N. Extinct Devonshire periodicals, 2: the Plymouth magazine. Western Antiquary 9 1890.

The industrious bee: or the Devonshire and Cornwall chronicle. [30 Oct 1758]–?

The Plymouth magazine. 1772.

Reading

Alter et idem: a new review. Ed R. Deverell. No 1 1794.

Salisbury

The Salisbury magazine: given gratis with the Salisbury and Winchester journal. 1773.

The county magazine, by a society of gentlemen. Vol 1 no 1, Jan 1786–. Continued as the Western county magazine, vol 3 1790–vol 6 1792.

The detector. 1786–7.

Sherborne

An appendix to the Sherborne mercury: or the weekly magazine. Vol 1 no 1 6 Jan 1772–vol 2 20 Sept 1773.

The weekly miscellany: or instructive entertainer. No 1 4 Oct 1773–no 483 30 Dec 1782; as Weekly entertainer or agreeable and instructive repository, no 1 6 Jan 1783.

Southampton

Masquerade. 1798–9.

Stockport

Virtue's friend: consisting of essays. Vol 1 no 1 April 1798–vol 2 no 48 Sept 1978; rptd Ormskirk 1808, 1816.

Stockton-on-Tees

The Stockton bee: or monthly miscellany. Vol 1 Jan 1793–vol 3 Dec 1795.

Stourport

The literary miscellany: or selections and extracts, classical and scientific. 1800.

Whitehaven

Beauties of the magazines. 1775–6.

The Cumberland magazine: or Whitehaven monthly miscellany. Vol 1 1778–vol 5 1781.

Winchester

The annual Hampshire repository: or historical, economical and literary miscellany. Vol 1 1798–. Vol 2 as Hampshire repository.

Windsor

The microcosm. Ed G. Canning. No 1 6 Nov 1786–no 40 30 July 1787; rptd 1788, 1790, 1793, 1809.

York

Miscellaneæ curiosæ: or entertainments for the ingenious of both sexes. Ed T. Turner. [No 1] March 1734–[No 6] July, Aug, Sept 1735. No 2–as Miscellanea curiosa: or entertainments for the ingenious of both sexes.

The Yorkshire magazine. Vol 1 Jan 1786–Dec 1786–?

Sportsmans and breeders vade mecum. Vol 1 1786–vol 12 1797.

(4) NEWSPAPERS

Aylesbury

Aylesbury journal. ?–20 Nov 1762–? Rptd, perhaps first pbd, in Political controversy: or weekly magazine of ministerial and anti-ministerial essays, 1762–3.

Bath

Lewis, H. The beginnings of the Bath newspaper press: a paper read before the Bath Natural History and Antiquarian Field Club, Jan 18th 1882. Bath nd; also in Proc of Bath Natural History & Antiquarian Field Club 5 1885.

Green, E. Bibliotheca Somersetensis. 3 vols Taunton 1902.

The Bath journal. [Vol 1 no 1, 27 Feb 1744]–no 2, 5 March 1744–? Continued as Boddely's Bath journal, ?–29 Nov 1756–. Continued as Bath journal, 8 March 1773–.

The Bath advertiser. Vol 1 no 1, 18 Oct 1755–. Continued as Bath chronicle: or universal register, 16 Oct 1760–. Continued as Martin's Bath chronicle, 15 Sept 1763–?

Farley's Bath journal. [No 1, 27 Sept 1756]–18 Oct 1756–?

The Bath chronicle and weekly gazette. Vol 1 no 1, 16 Oct 1760–. Continued as Pope's Bath chronicle and weekly gazette, vol 2 no 7, 26 Nov 1761–. Continued as Pope's Bath chronicle, no 175, 16 Feb 1764–. Continued as Archer's Bath chronicle, no 407, 4 Aug 1768–. Continued as Bath and Bristol chronicle, 29 Sept 1768–. Continued as R. Cruttwell's Bath and Bristol chronicle, 25 Jan 1770–. Continued as Bath chronicle, no 517, 13 Sept 1770–.

The Bath courant. No 1, 1 May 1773–?

The Bath gazette. ?–8 June 1778–?

The Bath register and western advertiser. No 1, 3 March 1792–no 83, 28 Sept 1793. Merged with Bath herald and general advertiser.

The Bath herald and general advertiser. No 1, 3 March 1792–. Absorbed Bath register and western advertiser and continued as Bath herald and register, 5 Oct 1793–. Continued as Bath herald, 2 Jan 1800–.

The history of the Bath Herald from 1792 to its centenary 1892. Bath 1892.

Birmingham

The Birmingham journal. [No 1, 9 Nov 1732?]–no 28, 21 May 1733–?

The Warwick and Staffordshire journal. Ptd in London, but by Nov 1741 some issues may have been ptd in Birmingham.

The Birmingham gazette: or the general correspondent. No 1, 16 Nov 1741–. Continued as Aris's Birmingham gazette: or the general correspondent, no 16, 1 March 1742–.

Bennett, W. On the first issue of the Birmingham gazette. Book Collector's Quart 10 1933.

The Birmingham register. Vol 1, 10 May 1764–28 March 1765–?

The Birmingham and Wolverhampton chronicle. [No 1, 23 March 1769?]–vol 2 no 56, 12 April 1770–?

The Warwickshire weekly journal. Introductory issue, 6 April 1769–no 1, 13 April 1769. Continued as Warwickshire journal, no 2, 20 April 1769–. Continued as Warwickshire journal and Hereford mercury, 10 May 1770–. Continued as Birmingham chronicle and Warwickshire journal, 22 Nov 1770–. Continued as Swinney's Birmingham and Stafford chronicle, 16 Aug 1773–? Continued as Swinney's Birmingham and Stafford chronicle and Piercy's Coventry gazette, ?–1778–? Continued as Swinney's Birmingham and Stafford chronicle: and Coventry gazette, ?–vol 14 no 638, 12 April 1781–? Continued as Swinney's

Birmingham chronicle: and Warwickshire and Staffordshire advertiser, ?–[1792]–.

Blackburn

The Blackburn mail and Lancashire weekly advertiser. 29 May 1793–.

Bristol

Mathews, E. R. N. A catalogue of the books, pamphlets, collectanea etc relating to Bristol contained in the Central Reference Library. Bristol 1916.

Early Bristol newspapers: a detailed catalogue of Bristol newspapers published up to and including the year 1800 in the Bristol Reference Library. Bristol 1956.

The Bristol post-boy. [1702?]–no 91, 12 Aug 1704–no 340, 26 Aug 1710–[1712?].

Sam Farley's Bristol post man: or weekly intelligence. [Feb 1713?]–[no 24, 25 July 1713]–no 29, 28 Jan 1716–? Perhaps continued as Farley's Bristol newspaper, 1725.

The Bristol weekly mercury. [Oct 1715?]–no 61, 1 Dec 1716–[1727?]

Lewis, H. The history of the Bristol mercury from 1715 to 1886. Bristol [1887?].

Farley's Bristol news-paper. [No 1, 8 May 1725?]–no 20, 18 Sept 1725–? Continued as Sam Farley's Bristol news-paper, ?–30 March 1734–? Continued as Farley's Bristol journal, ?–29 Aug 1741–?

The oracle: or Bristol weekly miscellany. Vol 1 no 1, 3 April 1742–. Continued as Oracle: or Bristol weekly miscellany, by A. Hooke esq. No 16, 17 July 1742–no 40, 31 Dec 1742.

The Bristol, Bath and Somersetshire journal. [May 1742?]–no 58?, 4 June 1743–no 68, 13 Aug 1743–?

The Bristol oracle and country intelligencer, by Andrew Hooke esq. Vol 1 no 1, 8 Jan 1743–vol 3 no 60, 6 April 1745. Pbd fortnightly, alternating with Bristol oracle and country advertiser.

The Bristol oracle and country advertiser. Vol 1 no 1, 15 Jan 1743–vol 3 no 60, 13 April 1745. Pbd fortnightly, alternating with Bristol oracle and country intelligencer.

F. Farley's Bristol journal. [No 1, 3 Dec 1743?]–no 17, 24 March 1744–. Continued as S. Farley's Bristol journal, 16 Jan 1748–. Continued as Farley's Bristol journal, 30 Jan 1748–. Continued as Bristol journal, 26 March 1748–. Continued as Sarah Farley's Bristol journal, 19 July 1777–. Pbd fortnightly from 3 Dec 1743 to 23 Aug 1746, alternating with Farleys Bristol advertiser, below.

Farleys Bristol advertiser. [No 2, 10 Dec 1743?]–no 18, 31 March 1744–no 111, 23 Aug 1746. Continued as F. Farley's Bristol advertiser,–no 1,599, 23 Jan 1748.

The Bristol oracle. Vol 1 no 1, 20 April 1745–vol 3 no 65, 16 Sept 1749. Pbd fortnightly, alternating with Country advertiser, below.

The country advertiser. Vol 1 no 1, 27 April 1745–. Continued as oracle country advertiser, 25 May 1745–vol 3 no 64, 9 Sept 1749. Pbd fortnightly, alternating with British oracle, above.

The Bristol mercury. ?–no 24, 20 Oct 1748–[Sept 1749?]

The Bristol weekly intelligencer. No 1, 23 Sept 1749–no 487, 3 Feb 1759–?

Felix Farley's Bristol journal. ?–2 May 1752–.

The Bristol chronicle: or universal mercantile register. Vol 1 no 1, 5 Jan 1760–vol 2 no 96, 7 Nov 1761–?

The Bristol gazette and public advertiser. ?–vol 1 no 19, 24 Dec 1767–.

Bonner and Middleton's Bristol journal. ?–vol 1 no 8, 1 Oct 1774–.

Wells, C. History of the Bristol Times and mirror 1713–1913. Bristol 1913.

Bristol presentments: exports for the year. No 1, 1 Jan 1770–no 51, 17 Dec 1770–.

Bristol presentments: imports for the year. No 1, 3 Jan 1770–no 112, 24 Dec 1774–?

The constitutional chronicle. No 1, 7 Dec 1780–no 69, 4 April 1782.

The Bristol mercury and universal advertiser. Vol 1 no 1, March 1790–.

Bury St Edmunds

The Suffolk mercury: or St Edmund's-Bury post. ?–no 43, 3 Feb 1718–vol 22 no 40, 4 Oct 1731–? Continued as Suffolk mercury: or Bury post, ?–vol 24 no 67, 9 April 1733–[July 1752?]–? Between 1742 and 1752 title may have been Bury journal.

The Bury post and universal advertiser. No 1, 11 July 1782–. Continued as Bury post: or Suffolk and Norfolk advertiser, no 143, 30 March 1785–no 182, 28 Dec 1785–? Continued as Bury and Norwich post ?–no 242, 21 Feb 1787–? Continued as Bury and Norfolk advertiser ?–no 548, 2 Jan 1793–.

Cambridge

Bowes, R. On the first and other early Cambridge newspapers. Proc of Cambridge Antiquarian Soc 8 1895.

Fenton, W. A. Cambridge periodicals 1750–1931. Cambridge Public Lib Record & Book List 3 1931.

The Cambridge journal and weekly flying post. [Vol 1 no 1, 22 Sept 1744?]–no 26, 16 March 1745–. Continued as Cambridge journal. 14 July 1753–Dec 1766.

Cranfield, G. A. The first Cambridge newspaper. Proc of Cambridge Antiquarian Soc 45 1952.

The Cambridge chronicle. No 1, 30 Oct 1762–. Absorbed Cambridge journal and continued as Cambridge chronicle and journal, 3 Jan 1767–.

The Cambridge intelligencer. ?–no 2, 17 July 1793–.

Canterbury

The Kentish post: or the Canterbury news-letter. [No 1, 16 Oct 1717]–no 2, 23 Oct 1717–no 5,281, 20 July 1768.

Plomer, H. R. James Abree: printer and bookseller, of Canterbury. Library 2nd ser 4 1913.

Cock, F. W. The Kentish post of the Canterbury news letter. Ibid.

The Kentish gazette. No 1, 4 May 1768–.

The Kentish weekly post: or Canterbury journal. Introductory issue, 12 Sept 1768–no 1, 19 Sept 1768–. Continued as Kentish post and Canterbury journal, no 35, 15 May 1769–. Continued as Canterbury journal, vol 2 no 81, 3 April 1770–. Continued as Kentish chronicle and Canterbury journal, no 1,028, 27 May 1788–. Continued as Kentish chronicle, no 1,187, 17 June 1791–.

The Kentish herald and universal register. ?–no 18, 10 Nov 1792–?

Carlisle

The Carlisle journal. No 1, 27 Oct 1798–.

Chelmsford

The Chelmsford and Colchester chronicle. [No 1, 10 Aug 1764]–no 3, 24 Aug 1764–no 346, 29 March 1771. Continued as Chelmsford chronicle, no 1, 5 April 1771–no 1,434, 18 May 1798–.

The Essex herald and weekly advertiser. [1800]–.

Chester

Stewart-Brown, R. The stationers, booksellers and printers of Chester to about 1800. Trans of Historical Soc of Lancashire and Cheshire 83 1931.

The Chester weekly journal. [No 1, May 1721?]–no 105, 9 May 1723–vol 36 no 8, 18 July 1733–?

Adams's weekly courant. [No 1, 29 Nov 1732?]–no 51,

14 Nov 1733–? Continued as Chester courant and Anglo-Welsh gazette, ?–1793–. Selected articles rptd in Manchester vindicated, Chester 1749, in The Chester miscellany, Chester 1750, and in A collection of political tracts, Edinburgh 1747.

Taylor, H. Chester's oldest newspaper. Chester & North Wales Archaeological & Historical Soc Jnl 27 1915.

The industrious bee: or weekly entertainer. [No 1, 1 Aug 1733?]–[no 23, 9 Jan 1734]–?

The Chester weekly tatler: containing the freshest advices foreign and domestick, with a new voyage round the world. [No 1, 28 Aug 1734?]–[no 4, 18 Sept 1734]–?

The Chester chronicle: or commercial intelligencer [subtitle varies]. Vol 1 no 1, 2 May 1775–? Continued as Chester chronicle and general advertiser, ?–no 499, 6 Jan 1785–.

Hand, C. R. John Fletcher. Trans of Historical Soc of Lancashire & Cheshire 76 1924.

The Eaton chronicle: or the salt-box. Ed W. Gifford. No 1, 30 Aug 1788–no 20, [Sept 1788]; rptd 1789.

Cirencester

Norris, H. E. The booksellers and printers of Cirencester. Cirencester 1912.

The Cirencester post: or Gloucestershire mercury. [No 1, 17 Nov 1718]?–no 18, 16 March 1719–vol 6 no 5, 9 Dec 1723–?

The Cirencester flying-post and weekly miscellany. [No 1, Dec 1740?]–no 42, 5 Oct 1741–. Continued as Cirencester flying-post, no 149, 24 Oct 1743–no 313, 15 Dec 1746–[1750?]

Austin, R. The Cirencester flying-post. N & Q 24 Oct 1914.

Colchester

The Essex mercury: or Colchester weekly journal. [No 1, 17 March 1733?]–no 173, 3 July 1736–? Continued as Pilborough's Colchester journal: or the Essex mercury, ?–no [306], 3 Feb 1739–. Continued as Pilborough's Colchester journal: or the Essex weekly mercury, no 310, 3 March 1739–? Continued as Colchester journal: or Essex advertiser, ?–no 333, 11 Aug 1739–no 340, 29 Sept 1739–[1751?].

Coventry

Jopson's Coventry mercury: or the weekly country journal. No 1, 20 July 1741–. Continued as Jopson's Coventry and Northampton mercury: or the weekly country journal, 21 Feb 1743–. Continued as Jopson's Coventry mercury: or the weekly country journal, 4 July 1743–no 864, 23 Jan 1758–? Continued as Jopson's Coventry and Warwick mercury, ?–no 1,826, 19 Aug 1776–? Continued as Jopson's Coventry mercury: or the British advertising gazette ?–no 1,888, 27 Oct 1777–no 1,984, 16 Aug 1779–? Continued as Jopson's Coventry mercury: or the Warwickshire weekly chronicle, ?–? Continued as Coventry mercury, ?–29 Oct 1787–.

Luckman and Sketchley's Coventry gazette: or the weekly country magazine. [No 1, March 1757?]–? Continued as Luckman and Sketchley's Coventry gazette and Birmingham chronicle, ?–vol 5 no 234, 16 Sept 1761–? Continued as Coventry, Birmingham and Worcester chronicle, ?–vol 6 no 289, 23 Sept 1762–?

Jones's Coventry and Warwick ledger: or the weekly register of news, trade and commerce. ?–no 14, 24 Aug 1765–no 22, 19 Oct 1765–?

Darlington

The Darlington pamphlet: or county of Durham intelligencer. No 1, 22 May 1772–20 Nov 1772. Continued as Darlington mercury, no 1, 27 Nov 1772–no 5, 25 Dec 1772.

Derby

Wallis, A. A sketch of the early history of the printing press in Derbyshire. Derbyshire Archaeological & Natural Historical Soc Jnl 3 1881; rptd Derby 1881.

The Derby post-man. [No 1, 1 Dec 1720?]–no 8, 19 Jan 1721–[1724]–?

Jewitt, L. An historical and descriptive note on the first Derby newspaper. Reliquary 21 1881.

The British spy: or Derby post-man. No 1, 6 April 1727–no 203, 22 April 1731–?

The Derby mercury. Introductory issue, 23 March 1732–vol 1 no 1, 30 March 1732–. Continued as Drewry's Derby mercury, [1769?]–? Continued as Derby mercury, ?–no 2,959, 1 Jan 1789–.

Harrison's Derby journal. No 1, 2 Aug 1776– Nov 1776?] Continued as Harrison's Derby and Nottingham journal: or Midland advertiser, [Nov 1776?]–[1781?]

The Derby herald: or Derby, Nottingham and Leicester advertiser. [1792].

Devizes

The Salisbury journal and Devizes mercury. ?–no 596, 12 June 1749–no 744, ? April 1752–? Local edn of Salisbury journal.

Doncaster

The Doncaster flying-post: or Hull and Sheffield weekly advertiser. [No 1, 30 April 1754?]–no 37, 7 Jan 1755–. Amalgamated with Lister's Sheffield weekly journal, Aug 1755.

The Yorkshire journal and general weekly advertiser. [No 1, 19 Aug 1786?]–no 6, 23 Sept 1786–? Continued as Yorkshire journal, ?–no 207, 31 July 1790–? Continued as Doncaster journal and Yorkshire advertiser, ?–vol 6 no 335, 12 Feb 1791–no 748, 15 Dec 1797.

The Yorkshire, Nottinghamshire and Lincolnshire gazette and universal advertiser. No 1, 4 Jan 1794–? Continued as Doncaster, Retford and Gainsborough gazette and universal advertiser, ?–no 11, 4 April 1795–? Continued as the Doncaster, Retford and Gainsborough gazette and Yorkshire, Nottingham and Lincolnshire advertiser, no 81, 18 July 1795–? Continued as Doncaster, Nottingham and Lincoln gazette, Yorkshire, Nottinghamshire and Lincolnshire advertiser, ?–no 173, 21 April 1797–.

Durham

The Durham courant. [1733?]–[40?]

Eton

The Eton journal: or early intelligencer. [No 1, 7 Oct 1745?]–no 14, 21 Nov 1745–? Continued as Windsor and Eton journal, ?–no 33, 27 Jan 1746–no 170 9 June 1748–?

The earliest Eton journal. Etoniana 12 April 1916.

Leigh, R. A. A. Joseph Pote of Eton. Library 3rd ser 17 1936.

Exeter

Brushfield, T. N. Andrew Brice and the early Exeter newspaper press. Report & Trans of Devonshire Assoc for Advancement of Science, Literature & Art 20 1888; rptd Exeter 1888.

The anniversary of the Devon and Exeter gazette, 5 March 1910: being the completion of the 138th year of the uninterrupted existence of the paper. Exeter 1910.

Sam Farley's Exeter post-man: or weekly intelligence. ?–no 556, 10 Aug 1711–23 Sept 1715.

Jos. Bliss's Exeter post-boy. [No 1, 8 April 1790?]–no 211, 4 May 1711–no 241, 17 Aug 1711–?

The Exeter mercury: or weekly intelligence of news. No 1, 24 Sept 1714–no 553, 23 Jan 1722–?

The Protestant mercury: or the Exeter post-boy. ?–no 4, 7 Oct 1715–28 Nov 1718–?

The post-master: or the loyal mercury. [1717]?– 28 Nov 1718]–no 6, 2 Sept 1720–no 223, 23 April 1725.

Farley's Exeter journal. [No 1, May 1723?]–no 104, 14 May 1725–no 286, 8 Nov 1728–?

Brice's weekly journal. No 1, 30 April 1725–no 325, 4 June 1731–?

Brice's weekly collection of intelligence. [1736?]–no 134, 8 Dec 1738–?

Farley's Exeter weekly journal. [No 1, 1 May 1741?]–no 33, 11 Dec 1741–?

Andrew Brice's old Exeter journal: or the weekly advertiser. [1746?]–no 326, 17 April 1752–no 53, 7 July 1758–?

The old Exeter journal and weekly advertiser. ?–12 Sept 1755–? Continued as Old Exeter journal: or weekly advertiser, ?–vol 65 no 3,363, 13 Sept 1781–? Continued as Brice's old Exeter journal: or western advertiser, ?–vol 73 no 3,757, 23 April 1789–no 3,780, 1 Oct 1789. Continued as Brice & Co's old Exeter journal, no 3,781, 8 Oct 1789–[24 Nov 1791].

[A newspaper pbd by T. Brice]. ?–[Sept 1755]–?

The Exeter flying post. ?–[1760]–?

The Exeter chronicle: or universal register. [No 1, 15 Sept 1760?]–no 32, 10 April 1761–?

The Exeter mercury: or west-country advertiser. No 1, 2 Sept 1763–. Continued as Exeter evening post, no 98, 11 July 1765–. Continued as Exeter evening post: or Plymouth and Cornish advertiser, no 211, 18 Sept 1767–. Continued as Trewman's Exeter evening post, no 293, 28 April 1769–. Continued as Trewman's Exeter flying post, no 380, 28 Dec 1770–.

Carrington, A. Trewman's flying post. N & Q July 1917.

The Exeter gazette. [1772]–? Continued as Woolmer's Exeter and Plymouth gazette, ?–no 1,025, 28 June 1792–.

The Devon and Exeter gazette. ?–1792–1794–?

The Exeter journal. ?–1792–[Nov 1797].

Gloucester

The Gloucester journal. No 1, 9 April [1722]–.

Gregory, A. Robert Raikes: journalist and philanthropist. 1877.

Austin, R. Robert Raikes the elder and the Gloucester journal. Library 4th ser 6 1915.

—— The Gloucester journal 1722–1922. N & Q 15 April 1922.

—— History of the Gloucester journal 1722–1922. Gloucester Jnl Bicentenary Suppl 8 April 1922.

Chance, H. G. The bicentenary of the Gloucester Journal, 9 April 1722–8 April 1922. Gloucester 1922.

Kendall, G. Robert Raikes: a critical study. 1939.

The Gloucester gazette: and South Wales, Worcester and Wiltshire advertiser. [No 1, Aug 1782?]–vol 2 no 100, 8 July 1784–18 Nov 1796–?

Halifax

The union journal: or Halifax advertiser. No 1, 6 Feb 1759–no 84, 9 Sept 1760–?

Hereford

Morgan, F. C. Herefordshire printers and booksellers. Trans of Woolhope Naturalists' Field Club, Herefordshire, vol for 1939–41, 1942.

The Hereford journal: with the History of the world given gratis. [No 1, 26 June 1739?]–no 12, 11 Sept 1739–?

The British chronicle: or Pugh's Hereford journal. [No 1, Oct 1770?]–vol 1 no 34, 28 March 1771–.

Hertford

The Hartford mercury. [No 1, 22 May 1772?]–no 18, 18 Sept 1772–?

Hull

Hunt, W. Hull newspapers. Hull 1880.
Page, W. G. B. Notes on early Hull authors, printers, booksellers and stationers. Hull 1930.
The Hull courant. [No 1, 24 Nov 1739]–no 368, 19 Aug 1746–no 518, 11 Aug 1749–[1750].
The Hull journal. ?–[1750].
The Hull courant. [No 1, 7 Oct 1755?]–no 34, 25 May 1756–no 183, 20 March 1759–?
The Hull packet and Humbrian gazette. [No 1, 29 May 1787?]–vol 1 no 25, 13 Nov 1787–. Continued as Hull packet, vol 2 no 32, 1 Jan 1788–.
The Hull advertiser. No 1, 5 July 1794–.
Index to Hull advertiser: vol 1, July 1794 to Dec 1825. Hull 1955.

Ipswich

The history of the Ipswich journal for 150 years. Ipswich 1875. Rptd from Ipswich Jnl 28 Dec 1875.
Watson, S. F. Some materials for a history of printing and publishing in Ipswich. Ipswich 1949.
—— History of printing and publishing in Ipswich. Proc of Suffolk Inst of Archaeology & Natural History 24 1949.
The Ipswich journal: or the weekly mercury. [No 1, 20 Aug 1720?]–no 14, 19 Nov 1720–? Continued as Ipswich gazette, ?–vol 13 no 650, 27 Jan 1733–no 902, 26 Nov 1737–?
The Ipswich weekly mercury. [No 1, 22 Feb 1735?]–?
The Ipswich journal. No 1, 17 Feb 1739–no 1,874, 29 Oct 1774–? Continued as Original Ipswich journal, ?–no 1,880, 17 Dec 1774–? Continued as the Ipswich journal, ?–no 1,883, 31 Dec 1774–.
A critical review of the Ipswich journal: or candid remarks on the disputes, both religious and political, which occur in that paper. No 1, Jan 1790–no 3, March 1790.

Kendal

Nicholson, C. The annals of Kendal. 1861.
Local chronology: being notes of the principal events published in the Kendal newspapers since their establishment. 1865.
The Kendal weekly courant. [No 1, 1 Jan 1732]–no 2, 8 Jan 1732–no 240, 14 Aug 1736–[Dec 1736?].
The Kendal weekly mercury. [No 1, 8 Feb 1735?]–no 13, 3 May 1735–no 429, 19 March 1743–no 90, 26 Sept 1747–?

Leeds

The Leeds mercury. [No 1, May 1718?]–vol 2 no 28, 17 Nov 1719[–no 1,816, 17 June 1755]. Extracts rptd in Pbns of Thoresby Soc: Miscellanea 22–40 1913–53.
The Leedes intelligencer. No 1, 2 July 1754–. Extracts rptd in Pbns of Thoresby Soc: Miscellanea 4 1895, 22–40 1922–53.
Beckwith, F. The Leedes intelligencer 1754–1866. Pbns of Thoresby Soc 40 1953.
Gibb, M. A., and F. Beckwith. The Yorkshire post two centuries. Leeds 1954.
The Leeds mercury. [1767?]–vol 17 no 896, 13 April 1784–.

Leicester

Herne, F. S. An old Leicestershire bookseller. Leicester Literary & Philosophical Soc Trans 1893.
Leicester journal. [No 1, May 1753?]–[Nov 1755]. Continued as Leicester and Nottingham journal, ?–no 132, 8 Nov 1755–no 1,773, 23 Dec 1786–? Continued as Leicester journal, ?–no 1,795, 26 May 1795–.
The Leicester herald. No 1, 5 May 1792–no 160, 22 May 1795–[Oct 1795?].
The Leicester chronicle. ?–1792–?

Lewes

The Lewes newsmen's new year verses. [1786]–.
Lower, M. A. Notes on a volume of newspaper cuttings relating to Sussex, with a brief bibliographical note on Sussex newspapers. Sussex Archaeological Collections 24 1872.
Beckett, A. The first Sussex newspaper. Sussex County Mag 15 1941.
The Sussex weekly advertiser: or Lewes journal. [No 1, 9 June 1746?]–no 5, 7 July 1746–.
The Lewes and Brighthelmston pacquet and weekly advertiser for the county of Sussex. 1789–90.

Lincoln

Corns, A. R. Bibliotheca Lincolniensis. Lincoln 1904.
The Lincoln gazette: or weekly-intelligencer. [No 1, 12 Dec 1728?]–vol 1 no 14, 9 March 1729–no 45, 23 Oct 1729–?
Lincoln journal. [No 1, 4 Aug 1744?]–[no 16, 17 Nov 1744]–?

Liverpool

Morley, J. C. The newspaper-press and periodical literature of Liverpool. Liverpool 1887. Rptd from Liverpool Mercury.
The Leverpoole courant: being an abstract of the London and other news. ?–no 18, 18 July 1712–?
Williamson's Liverpool advertiser and mercantile register. Vol 1 no 1, 28 May 1756–. Continued as Williamson's Liverpool advertiser and mercantile chronicle, 7 Sept 1759–. Continued as Billinge's Liverpool advertiser and marine intelligencer, [1792]–.
Harris, J. R. and B. L. Anderson. The founding of an eighteenth-century newspaper: the partnership agreement of Williamson's Liverpool advertiser. Historic Soc of Lancashire & Cheshire: Trans 116 1964.
The Liverpool chronicle and marine gazetteer. No 1, 6 May 1757–no 121, 24 Aug 1759–?
The general advertiser. No 1, 27 Dec 1765–vol 14 no 711, 13 Aug 1779–? Continued as Gore's Liverpool general advertiser, ?–vol 23 no 1,177, 17 July 1788–? Continued as Gore's general advertiser, ?–[1788]. Continued as Liverpool general advertiser, ?–11 March 1790–.
The Liverpool chronicle. [Vol 1 no 1, 17 March 1767?]–no 22, 14 April 1768–?
The Liverpool herald. [1788]–. Continued as Liverpool and Lancaster herald, –? Continued as the Liverpool and Lancashire weekly herald, ?–March 1790–? Possibly continued as Liverpool weekly herald, ?–1792–?
Thomas, M. G. Edward Rushton. 1949.
The Liverpool phoenix. [1790]–25 July 1795–?
The Liverpool trade list. [1794]–no 234, 26 July 1798–.

Ludlow

The Ludlow post-man: or the weekly journal. No 1, 9 Oct 1719–no 22, 4 March 1720–?
Wroth, L. C. William Parks: printer and journalist of England and colonial America. Richmond Va 1926.

Lynn

The Lynn and Wisbech packet: or the Norfolk, Suffolk, Cambridge and Lincolnshire advertiser. No 1, 7 Jan 1800–.

Maidstone

The Maidstone mercury. [No 1, 4 March 1725?]–no 6, 22 March 1725–no 25, 27 May 1725–?
The Maidstone journal. [No 1, 22 Sept 1737?]–no 3, 6 Oct 1737–?

The Maidstone journal and Kentish advertiser. No 1, 25 Jan 1786–no 284, 28 June 1791–.

Manchester

Leary, F. The Manchester press: a history. Manchester Monthly 1 1894.

Harland, J. Collectanea relating to Manchester vol 2, Manchester 1899.

Axon, W. E. A. Newspapers in 1738–9: echoes of old Lancashire. 1899.

Axon, G. R. Roger and Orion Adams, printers. Trans of Lancashire & Cheshire Antiquarian Soc 39 1921.

News from abroad: or the Manchester weekly news letter. [No 1, Jan 1719?]–no 201, 17 Nov 1722–? Continued as Manchester news-letter, ?–no 291, 6 Aug 1724–. Continued as Manchester weekly journal, no 293, 20 Aug 1724–no 325, 25 March 1725–?

Axon, G. R. A note on the first Manchester newspaper. Trans of Lancashire & Cheshire Antiquarian Soc 41 1924.

—— A further note on the first Manchester newspaper 1719–25. Trans of Lancashire & Cheshire Antiquarian Soc 68 1958.

Read, D. Manchester news-letter. Manchester Rev 8 1957. Rptd from Manchester Guardian 31 Aug 1956.

Wiles, R. M. Manchester's first newspaper: news from abroad 1722. Manchester Rev 11 1968.

The Manchester gazette. [No 1, 22 Dec 1730]–? Continued as Manchester magazine, ?–20 Dec 1737–? Continued as Whitworth's Manchester magazine: with the history of the Holy Bible, ?–no 105, 2 Jan 1739–? Continued as Manchester magazine, ?–no 182, 24 June 1740–? Continued as Whitworth's Manchester magazine, ?–no 3,002, 26 Dec 1752. Continued as Whitworth's Manchester magazine: or universal advertiser, 29 April 1755–. Continued as Whitworth's Manchester magazine and weekly advertiser, 9 Dec 1755–. Continued as Whitworth's Manchester advertiser and weekly magazine, 20 July 1756–no 3,414, 25 March 1760.

Manchester weekly courant. ?–2 July 1733–?

The Manchester journal. [No 1, 30 March 1736?]–no 22, 24 Aug 1736–?

The Lancashire journal: with the history of the Holy Bible. [No 1, 6 July 1738?]–no 3, 20 July 1738–. Continued as Lancashire journal, no 57, 30 July 1739–. Continued as Lancashire journal; with a description of the Spanish territories in America, no 91, 24 March 1740–. Continued as Lancashire journal, 22 Dec 1740–no 142, 16 March 1741–?

Orion Adams's weekly journal: or the Manchester advertiser. [No 1, 7 Jan 1752?]–no 3, 21 Jan 1752–. Continued as Orion Adams's Manchester journal: or the Lancashire and Cheshire advertiser, no 13, 31 March 1752–no 27, 7 July 1752–?

Harrop's Manchester mercury. No 1, 3 March 1752–. Continued as Harrop's Manchester mercury and general advertiser, no 9, 28 April 1752–. Continued as Manchester mercury and Harrop's general advertiser, no 278, 12 July 1757–.

The Manchester journal. [No 1, 2 March 1754?]–no 2, 9 March 1754–?

The Manchester chronicle: or Anderton's universal advertiser. No 1, 13 July 1762–no 25, 28 Dec 1762–?

Prescott's Manchester journal. No 1, 23 March 1771–? Continued as Manchester journal: or Prescott's Lancashire advertiser, ?–vol 10 no 493, 26 Aug 1780–8 Dec 1781–?

The Manchester chronicle. No 1, 23 June 1781. Continued as Wheeler's Manchester chronicle: or weekly advertiser, no 2, 30 June 1781–? Continued as Wheeler's Manchester chronicle, ?–3 Jan 1789–.

The Manchester herald. No 1, 31 March 1792–no 52, 23 March 1793.

The Manchester gazette. [No 1, Oct 1795?]–no 7, 2 Jan 1796–? Continued as Cowdroy's Manchester gazette and weekly advertiser, ?–no 75, 27 April 1797–.

Marlborough

The Marlborough journal. [No 1, 30 March 1771]–no 2, 5 April 1771–no 171, 2 July 1774.

Middlewich

Schofield's Middlewich journal: or general advertiser. [No 1, 13 July 1765?]–no 5, 10 Aug 1756–? Continued as Schofield's Middlewich journal: or Cheshire advertiser, ?–no 46, 24 May 1757–?

Newark

B[lagg], T. M. Newark as a publishing town. Newark 1898.

The Newark herald. No 1, 5 Oct 1791–. Continued as the Midland mercury. No 1, Oct? 1794–no 25, March? 1795.

Holt, D. A vindication of the conduct and principles of the printer of the Newark Herald. Newark 1794.

Newcastle

Tomlinson, W. W. The advertisement columns of old newspapers. Proc of Soc of Antiquaries of Newcastle-upon-Tyne 6 1893.

Welford, R. Early Newcastle typography 1639–1800. Archaeologia Aeliana 3 1907; 4 1908.

Pierpont, R. Newcastle and Durham papers. N & Q 31 March 1923.

The press in Newcastle-upon-Tyne in the eighteenth century. Proc of Wesley Historical Soc 1924.

The Newcastle gazette: or the northern courant. [No 1, 29 July 1710?]–no 308, 14 July 1712–?

The Newcastle courant; with news forreign and domestick. [No 1, 1 Aug 1711?]–no 2, 4 Aug 1711 (subtitle varies)–? Continued as Newcastle weekly courant, ?–no 16, 8 Oct 1720. Continued as Newcastle courant, no 193, 29 Feb 1724–.

The Newcastle weekly mercury. [No 1, 14 July 1722?]–no 30, 2 Feb 1723–no 41, 20 April 1723. Continued as New-castle weekly journal, No 42, 27 April 1723–no 44, 11 May 1723–[no 45, 18 May 1723?].

The north country journal: or the impartial intelligencer. [No 1, 17 Aug 1734?]–no 17, 7 Dec 1734–no 160, 10 Sept 1737–[1738].

The Newcastle journal. No 1, 7 April 1739–? Continued as Newcastle journal: or general advertiser, ?–no 1,907, 10 Feb 1776–[9 Aug 1788].

The Newcastle gazette: or Tyne-Water journal. [No 1, 20 June 1744?]–no 9, 15 Aug 1744–? Continued as Newcastle gazette, ?–no 74, 13 Nov 1745–[1755?].

The Newcastle intelligencer. [No 1, 15 Oct 1755?]–no 7, 26 Nov 1755–no 190, 30 May 1759.

The Newcastle chronicle: or general weekly advertiser. No 1, 24 March 1764–? Continued as Newcastle chronicle: or weekly advertiser and register of news, commerce and entertainment, ?–30 July 1785–.

The provincial press, no 16: the Newcastle chronicle. Effective Advertiser 1 June 1887.

Hodgson, J. Thomas Slack of Newcastle: printer, 1723–84, founder of the Newcastle Chronicle. Archaeologia Aeliana 17 1920.

The Protestant packet: or British monitor. No 1, 4 Aug 1780–no 27, 18 May 1781–?

The Newcastle advertiser: or general weekly post. No 1, 18 Oct 1788–.

Northampton

Northampton mercury: or the Monday's post. Vol 1 no 1, 2 May 1720–. Continued as the Northampton mercury. 24 July 1721–.

Wilkins, H. C. Robert Raikes of Northampton. Gloucestershire N & Q 3 1885.

The provincial press no 5: the Northampton mercury. Effective Advertiser 1 July 1886.

History of the Northampton mercury. Northampton 1901. Rptd from Northampton Mercury.

The early history of an old provincial newspaper. Antiquary 37 1901.

Hadley, W. W. The bi-centenary record of the Northampton Mercury. Northampton [1920].

The Northampton Mercury 1720–1920. Sell's World Press 1921.

Northampton journal. [No 1, 7 July 1722]–[no 2, 14 July 1722]–?

The Northamptonshire journal with the history of the Old Testament. ?–19 March 1741–? Ptd at London?

Taylor, J. The Northamptonshire journal. N & Q 11 July 1885.

T[aylor], J. The Northamptonshire journal. Northamptonshire N & Q 1 1885.

Jopson's Coventry and Northampton mercury: or the country journal. ?–21 Feb 1743–?

Norwich

E[uren], A. D. The first provincial newspaper. Norwich 1924. Rptd from Norwich Mercury.

[Payne, M.] The Norwich Post: its contemporaries and successors. Norwich 1951.

The Norwich post. [No 1, 8 Nov 1701?]–no 287, 3 May 1707–no 594, 5 July 1712–?

The Norwich gazette: or the accurate weekly intelligencer. No 1, 7 Dec 1706–. Continued as Norwich gazette: or the loyal packet, 8 Feb 1717–. Continued as Norwich gazette no 2,236, 30 Dec 1749–? 'Williams, J. B.' (J. G. Muddiman). Henry Crossgrove: Jacobite, journalist and printer. Library 2nd ser 5 1914.

The Norwich post-man. [No 1, 28 Dec 1706?]–vol 2 no 68, 10 April 1708–vol 3 no 135, 30 July 1709–[Feb 1710?].

The transactions of the universe: or the weekly mercury. [Vol 1 no 1, 1713?]–vol 2 no 29, 17 July 1714–? Continued as Weekly mercury: or the Protestant packet, ?–22 Oct 1722–. Continued as Norwich mercury, 26 Feb 1726–.

The Norwich courant: or weekly packet. [1714?]–[4 Feb 1716]–[1718]–?

The Norwich journal: or weekly intelligencer. ?–vol 3 no 401, 2 June 1753–?

The Norwich gazette and Norfolk weekly advertiser. No 1, 18 July 1761–no 24, 26 Dec 1761. Continued as Norwich gazette or the Norfolk advertiser, no 1, 2 Jan 1762–. Continued as Norwich gazette or the Norfolk and Suffolk advertiser, no 14, 3 April 1762–no 183, 26 Jan 1765–. Continued as Norfolk chronicle or the Norwich gazette, No 1, 8 April 1796–.

Norwich and Bury post. ?–1784–.

The Norwich mercury, and Yarmouth, Lynn and Ipswich herald. ?–1796–?

Nottingham

Clark, W. J. Early Nottingham printers and printing. Nottingham 1942, 1953 (rev).

The Nottingham post. [No 1, 4 Oct 1710?]–no 42, 18 July 1711–no 65, 19 (for 14) Dec 1711–?

The weekly courant. [No 1, 7 Aug 1712?]–vol 4 no 21, 22 Dec 1715–? Continued as Nottingham weekly courant, ?–vol 24 no 52, 1 June 1749–? Continued as Ayscough's Nottingham courant, ?–vol 32 no 68, 29 Jan 1757–vol 51 no 332, 27 March 1762, then combined with Creswell's Nottingham journal.

The new mercury. [No 1, 1 Jan 1714?]–no 18, 30 April 1714–. Continued as the Nottingham mercury [subtitle varies], 16 Dec 1715–16 March 1727–?

The Nottingham post. [1730?]–vol 9 no 449, 3 Aug 1738–vol 12 no 617, 24 Oct 1741–?

The Leicester and Nottingham journal. *See* under Leicester, above.

Creswell's Nottingham journal. [No 1, 10 Jan 1756?]–no 5, 7 Feb 1756–. Combined with Ayscough's Nottingham courant as Nottingham journal: or Creswell's weekly advertiser, 3 April 1762–? Continued as Creswell's Nottingham journal, ?–27 Aug 1763–vol 9 no 432, 7 April 1770. Continued as Creswell's Nottingham and Newark journal: or the weekly advertiser, vol 9 no 433, 14 April 1770–. Continued as Creswell's Nottingham, Newark, Retford and Worksop journal: or the weekly advertiser, vol 33, no 3,638, 21 May 1774–vol 36 no 3,696, 24 June 1775. Continued as Creswell and Burbage's Nottingham journal: or the Newark, Gainsborough, Retford and Worksop general advertiser, vol 36 no 3,687, 1 July 1775–. Continued as Nottingham journal: or the Newark, Gainsborough, Retford, Worksop, Mansfield, Chesterfield, Grantham and Sheffield general advertiser, no 6,040, 20 Jan 1787–.

Burbage's Nottingham chronicle: or the British weekly intelligencer. 29 Feb 1772–vol 4 no 173, 24 June 1775. Incorporated with Creswell's Nottingham, Newark, Retford and Worksop journal.

The Nottinghamshire gazette. No 1, 23 Dec 1780–no 34, 11 Aug 1781.

Oxford

The Oxford gazette. No 1, 16 Nov 1665–no 23, 1 Feb 1666. Continued as London gazette, no 24, 5 Feb 1666–.

Handover, P. M. A history of the London gazette 1665–1965. 1965.

The Oxford journal: or the tradesman's intelligencer. [1735–36?]. Ptd in London?

The Oxford flying weekly journal and Cirencester gazette. [No 1, 6 Sept 1746]–vol 2 no 79, 7 March–[June 1749].

Jackson's Oxford journal. No 1, 5 May 1753–.

Mordaunt, E. A. B. Index to obituary and biographical notices in Jackson's Oxford Journal. 1904.

Townsend, J. News of a country town: being extracts from Jackson's Oxford journal relating to Abingdon 1753–1835. 1914.

The birch. No 1, 1 May 1795–no 4, 1 June 1795. Spurious no 5, June 1796.

The Oxford mercury and midland county chronicle. No 1, 5 Aug 1795–no 40, 4 May 1796–?

Plymouth

The Plymouth weekly-journal: or general post. [No 1, 3 Jan 1718?]–no 36, 5 Sept 1718–vol 2 no 32, 12 March 1725–?

The Plymouth gazette. [1759?–Jan 1760?]

Plymouth and Exeter gazette. ?–1760–?

Plymouth chronicle and general advertiser for the west of England. [1780–2].

Portsmouth

The Portsmouth and Gosport gazette. ?–April 1750. Wiles, R. M. The earliest Hampshire newspaper. N & Q June 1966.

The Portsmouth and Gosport gazette and Salisbury journal. ?–no 640, 16 April 1750–no 768, 13 Nov 1752–? Local edn of Salisbury journal.

The Hampshire chronicle: or Portsmouth, Winchester and Southampton gazette. Pbd in Southampton Sept 1778–. Transferred to Portsmouth 1780–no 121, 6 Jan 1781–1786.

The Portsmouth gazette and weekly advertiser. No 1, 8 July 1793–.

The Portsmouth telegraph: or Mottley's naval and military journal. No 1, 14 Oct 1799–.

Preston

Preston weekly journal. [No 1, 3 Oct 1740?]–no 16, 16 Jan 1741–? Continued as Preston journal, ?–no 120, 14 Jan 1743–? Continued as Smith's Preston journal, ?–23 Aug 1745–? Continued as Preston journal, ?–18 Oct 1745–no 307, 5 Sept 1746–? Perhaps continued as Preston journal and Croft's Lancashire general advertiser, ?–.

The true British courant: or Preston journal. [No 1, 11 Jan 1745?]–no 11, 22 March 1745–no 414, 26 Jan 1753–?

The Preston review and county advertiser. Vol 1 no 1, 1 June 1793–no 43, 29 March 1794–?

Reading

The Reading mercury: or weekly entertainer. No 1, 8 July 1723–? Continued as Reading post: or the weekly mercury, ?–no 96, 10 July 1727–? Continued as Reading mercury: or the London spy, ?–30 Aug 1736–? Continued as Reading mercury: or weekly post, ?–6 Feb 1738–. Continued as Reading mercury and Oxford gazette, 21 Oct 1745–. Continued as Oxford gazette and Reading mercury, 18 Nov 1745–? Continued as Reading mercury and Oxford gazette, ?–13 July 1767–.

The Reading journal. [No 1, 27 Sept 1736?]–no 128, 5 March 1739–? Continued as Reading journal: or weekly review, ?–no 42, 23 July 1744–? Continued as Henry's Reading journal: or weekly review, ?–no 125, 10 March 1746–no 231, 15 Feb 1748–? Local edn pbd as Henry's Winchester journal: or weekly review. See Winchester, below.

St Ives

The St Ives post. [No 1, 18 March 1717]–vol 2 no 1, 20 Jan 1718–vol 2 no 21, 16 June 1718–?

The St Ives post boy: or the loyal packet. [No 1, 16 June 1718]–no 2, 23 June 1718–no 36, 16 Feb 1719–?

St Ives mercury: or the impartial intelligencer. [No 1, 12 Oct 1719?]–no 6, 16 Nov 1719–?

Salisbury

Richardson, Mrs H. 1729–1929. Suppl to Salisbury & Winchester Jnl 7 June 1929.

The story of the Salisbury and Winchester journal 1729 to 1939. Salisbury 1939.

The Salisbury post man: or packet of intelligence. No 1, 27 Sept 1715–[no 40, 1 March 1716]–?

The Salisbury journal. [No 1, 2 June 1729?]–no 58, 6 July 1730.

The Salisbury journal. No 1, 27 Nov 1736–. Continued as Salisbury journal: or weekly advertiser, vol 2 no 57, 27 Feb 1739–. Continued as Salisbury journal, 11 June 1750–. Continued as Salisbury and Winchester journal, 7 Dec 1772–. Local edns pbd in Devizes and Portsmouth. See under Devizes and Portsmouth, above.

Sheffield

Porter, W. S. Old Sheffield newspapers. Trans of Hunter Archaeological Soc 1 1914.

Lister's Sheffield weekly journal. [No 1, 23 April 1754?] –no 42, 18 Feb 1735–. Amalgamated with Doncaster flying-post Aug 1755. Continued as Sheffield weekly journal: or Doncaster flying post [Aug 1755]–no 90, 20 Jan 1756–no 172, 16 Aug 1757–[1759?].

The public advertiser (Sheffield). [No 1, 29 April 1760?]–no 11, 8 July 1760–no 35, 23 Dec 1760–? Continued as Sheffield public advertiser, ?–no 141, 4 Jan 1762 [i.e. 1763]–7 June 1793. Continued as Sheffield courant, 10 June 1793–4 Aug 1797.

The Sheffield register: or the Yorkshire, Derbyshire and Nottinghamshire general advertiser. No 1, 9 June 1787–. Continued as Iris: or Sheffield advertiser for the northern counties, 4 July 1794–. Continued as Iris: or Sheffield advertiser, 31 Jan 1800–.

Armytage, W. H. G. The editorial experiences of Joseph Gales 1786–1794. North Carolina Historical Rev 28 1951.

The spy: or political inspector. Nos 1–16 1795.

Sherborne

The Sherborne mercury: or weekly advertiser. [No 1, 21 Feb 1737]–no 16, 7 June 1737–vol 12 no 623, 23 Jan 1749. Amalgamated with Western flying post: or Yeovil mercury and continued as the Western flying-post: or Sherborne and Yeovil mercury, vol 1 no 1, 30 Jan 1749–. Continued as Western flying post: or Sherborne and Yeovil mercury and general advertiser, 23 Sept 1765–.

Rogers, W. H. H. A hundred and twenty years since. Western Antiquary 8 1889.

Cruttwell's Sherborne journal. No 1, 1 Dec 1764–? Continued as Cruttwell's Sherborne, Shaftesbury and Dorchester journal: or Yeovil, Taunton, and Bridgewater chronicle, ?–vol 4 no 163, 15 Jan 1768–? Continued as Sherborne weekly journal, ?–vol 4 no 193, 12 Aug 1768–? Continued as Sherborne journal, ?–8 July 1773–? Continued as Sherborne journal and western advertiser, ?–11 Jan 1781–? Continued as Dorchester and Sherborne journal and western advertiser, ?–14 Sept 1792–.

Shrewsbury

Lloyd, L. C. The Book-trade in Shropshire. Trans of Shropshire Archaeological & Natural Historical Soc 48 1936.

A collection of all the material news. [1705?]–no 68, 21 Dec 1706–?

The Shrewsbury mercury. [1706?]–no 27, 26 April 1707–?

The Shropshire journal; with the history of the Holy Bible. [No 1, 19 Dec 1737]–[no 73, 12 Feb 1739]–? Ptd in London.

Axon, W. E. A. Shropshire newspaper printed in London. N & Q 9 July 1910.

The Shrewsbury chronicle: or Wood's British commercial pamphlet. [No 1, 23 Nov 1772]–? Continued as Shrewsbury chronicle: or Wood's British gazette, ?–vol 2, no 7, 20 Feb 1773–? Continued as Shrewsbury chronicle: or Wood's British advertising gazette, ?–vol 4 no 119, 15 April 1775–? Continued as Shrewsbury chronicle and Shropshire, Montgomeryshire, Denbighshire, Merionethshire, Flintshire etc general advertiser, ?–vol 17 no 816, 26 Jan 1788–.

T. Wood and the Shrewsbury Chronicle: the trials of an eighteenth-century newspaper man. Times 10 Nov 1961.

The Salopian journal and courier of Wales. [No 1, 29 Jan 1794?]–.

Southampton

The Hampshire chronicle: or Southampton, Winchester and Portsmouth mercury. [No 1, 24 Aug 1772]–no 3, 7 Sept 1772–. Continued as Hampshire chronicle: or Winchester, Southampton and Portsmouth mercury, vol 1 no 6, 28 Sept 1772–? Continued as Hampshire chronicle, ?–vol 4 no 157, 21 Aug 1775–vol 6 no 301, 25 May 1778. Transferred to Winchester with no 302, 1 June 1778–.

Davies, T. L. O. An old Southampton newspaper. Hants Field Club Papers & Proc 6 1907.

The Hampshire chronicle: or Portsmouth, Winchester and Southampton gazette. [No 1, 18 Sept 1778]–no 16, 2 Jan 1779–no 89, 27 May 1780–? Transferred to Portsmouth 1780–6.

Stafford

The Staffordshire advertiser and political, literary and commercial gazette. No 1, 3 Jan 1795–.
The centenary of the Staffordshire advertiser, 5 Jan 1895. Stafford nd.

Stamford

The Stamford-post. [No 1, 8 June 1710?]–[no 82, 3 Jan 1712]–no 112, 31 July 1712–?
The Stamford mercury. [No 1, 1713?]–vol 3 no 43, 13 May 1714–vol 39 no 9, 2 March 1732–[no ?, 13 July 1732]–[1732].
Adcock, A. Stamford mercury: earliest provincial newspaper. N & Q 14 June 1913.
Evans, H. L. History of the Stamford Mercury. Stamford nd.
Howgrave's Stamford mercury. No 1, 15 June [1732]–. Continued as Stamford mercury, no 202, 22 April 1736–no 2,766, 12 March 1784. Continued as Lincoln, Rutland and Stamford mercury, no 2,767, 19 March 1784–.
The loyal intelligencer: or Lincoln, Rutland, Leicester, Cambridge and Stamford advertiser. [No 1, 1793?]–no 65, 10 June 1794–?

Stratford-upon-Avon

The Stratford, Shipston and Aulcester journal. Vol 1 no 1, 5 Feb 1750–? Continued as Keating's Stratford and Warwick mercury: or Cirencester Shipston and Alcester weekly journal, ?–vol 3, no 114, 9 March 1752–vol 4 no 210, 12 Nov 1753–?
Morgan, P. The earliest Stratford newspaper. N & Q 4 Feb 1950.

Taunton

The Taunton-journal. [No 1, 21 May 1725?]–20th week, 1 Oct 1725–. Continued as Norris's Taunton-journal, 30th week, 10 Dec 1725–138th week, 5 Jan 1728–?
The Taunton herald and weekly advertiser. 2 March 1793–23 June 1797. Title may have been altered to Somersetshire herald.

Warrington

Eyres's weekly journal: or the Warrington advertiser. [No 1, 23 March 1756?]–no 7, 4 May 1756–no 19, 27 July 1756–?
Kendrick, J. The Eyres' printing press at Warrington. Warrington Guardian Jan–May 1881.

Whitby

The Whitby spy. No 2, 4 Sept 1784–no 28, 4 Dec 1784–?

Whitehaven

The Whitehaven weekly courant. [No 1, 16 Dec 1736?]–[no 6, 20 Jan 1737]–?
The Cumberland pacquet and Ware's Whitehaven advertiser. No 1, 20 Oct 1774–.
The Cumberland chronicle and Whitehaven public advertiser. [Vol 1 no 1, 5 Nov 1776]–no 2, 12 Nov 1776–15 July 1779–?
Nolan, J. B. A British editor reports the American Revolution. Pennsylvania Mag of History & Biography 80 1956.

Winchester

The Winchester journal: or the weekly review. [Oct 1743?]–[no 84, 3 June 1745]–? Continued as Henry's Winchester journal: or weekly review, ?–no 128, 31 March 1746–no 166, 8 Dec 1746–? Local ed of the Reading journal: or weekly review.
The Hampshire chronicle: or Winchester, Southampton and Portsmouth mercury. Transferred from Southampton to Winchester with no 302, 1 June 1778–.

Continued as Salisbury and Winchester journal and Hampshire chronicle, 5 Jan 1784–. Continued as Hampshire chronicle and Portsmouth and Chichester journal, no 690, 5 Dec 1785–. Continued as Hampshire chronicle: or Winchester, Southampton, Portsmouth and Chichester journal, vol 26 no 1,381, 31 March 1800–.
The Hampshire journal and county register. No 1, 6 March 1790–no 46, 15 Jan 1791–?

Wokingham

The Berkshire chronicle. [No 1, 8 Jan 1771]–vol 1 no 27, 8 July 1771–vol 5 no 256, 1 Dec 1775–.

Wolverhampton

The Wolverhampton chronicle. [No 1, 2 Sept 1789]–no 108, 21 Sept 1791–.

Worcester

The Worcester post-man. [No 1, 17 June 1709?]–no 85, 2 Feb 1711–? Continued as Worcester post: or western journal, ?–no 687, 25 Aug 1722–? Continued as Weekly Worcester-journal, ?–no 827, 30 April 1725–? Continued as Worcester journal, ?–no 2,021, 14 April 1748–. Continued as Berrow's Worcester journal, no 2,306, 11 Oct 1753–.
The oldest English newspaper. Rptd from Berrow's Worcester Jnl, Worcester 1890.
Muddiman, J. G. Berrow's Worcester Journal. N & Q 11–18 July 1914.
Bennett, W. A note on 'the Worcester post-man'. Book Collector's Quart 14 1934.
Berrow's Worcester journal. No 12,888, 28 Dec 1940. Special anniversary issue. See correction in Times Jan 1941.
Griffith, I. Berrow's Worcester Journal. Worcester 1941.
The new Worcester journal. [No 1, Nov 1753]–?
The Worcester herald. No 1, 4 Jan 1794–.

Yarmouth

The Yarmouth gazette. [May 1707?]–? Perhaps a local ed of Norwich gazette.
[The Yarmouth post] ?–[no 351, 22 May 1708]–? Probably a local edition of Norwich post.
The Yarmouth gazette extraordinary. No 1, 28 March 1784–?

Yeovil

The Western flying post: or Yeovil mercury. [No 1, 30 July 1744]–vol 5 no 213, 22 Aug 1748–. Amalgamated with Sherborne mercury: or weekly advertiser and continued as the Western flying-post: or Sherborne and Yeovil mercury, ptd in Sherborne. Vol 1 no 1, 30 Jan 1749–.

York

Gent, T. The life of Thomas Gent, printer of York. 1832.
Davies, R. A memoir of the York Press. Westminster 1868.
York mercury: or a general view of the affairs of Europe. Vol 1 no 1, 23 Feb 1719–. Continued as York journal, no 1, 23 Nov 1724–? Continued as York journal: or the weekly courant, ?–11 Jan 1725–? Continued as Original York journal: or weekly courant, ?–13 June 1727–. Continued as Original mercury, York journal: or weekly courant, 2 Jan 1728–no 327, 16 Nov [1731]–1740?].
The York courant. [No 1, 14 Sept?]–no 171, 17 Dec 1728–.
Shipley, J. B. Essays from Fielding's Champion [in the York Courant]. N & Q Nov 1953.
The York gazetteer. [No 1, 10 March 1741]?–no 41, 14 Dec 1741–1752.
The York journal: or the weekly advertiser. No 1, 26

Nov 1745-. Continued as York journal: or the Protestant courant, no 18, 25 March 1746-? Continued as Protestant York courant, ?-12 Dec 1749-no 383, 3 April 1753-?

The York chronicle: and weekly advertiser. No 1, 18 Dec 1772-. Continued as Etherington's York chronicle, no 56, 7 Jan 1774-. Continued as Etherington's York chronicle: or the northern flying post, 5 July 1776-. Continued as York chronicle: or the northern flying post and general advertiser, 31 Jan 1777-. Continued as York chronicle and general advertiser, 21 Feb 1777-. Continued as York chronicle, 7 Jan 1785-.

Racing calendar. Pbd fortnightly from April to Nov each year. [April 1773?]-No 16, 11 Nov 1784-? Accumulated lists of each season rptd in annual vol.

The Yorkshire freeholder, by Lancelot Lackrent esq [C. Wyvill?]. No 1, 20 Jan 1780-no 19, 25 May 1780.

The theatrical register. No 1, 4 Feb 1788-no 18, 27 May 1788.

The York herald. No 1, 2 Jan 1790-? Continued as York herald and county advertiser, ?-no 329, 16 April 1796-.

The Yorkshire herald: jubilee number. 2 Jan 1905.

J. SCOTLAND

(1) BIBLIOGRAPHIES, BIOGRAPHIES AND GENERAL STUDIES

Special studies of individual periodicals are listed immediately after the titles.

Political review of Edinburgh periodical publications. No 1, 20 Jan 1792-no 7, 1 Aug 1792.

Chalmers, G. The life of Thomas Ruddiman AM. 1794.

Meek, T. A bibliographical sketch of the life of James Tytler. Edinburgh 1805.

Tytler, A. F. (Lord Woodhouselee). Memoirs of the life and writings of Henry Home of Kames. 2 vols Edinburgh 1807.

Kerr, R. Memoirs of the life, writings and correspondence of William Smellie, late printer in Edinburgh. 2 vols Edinburgh 1811.

Fugitive pieces. Edinburgh 1815 (2nd edn).

[Duncan, W. J.] Notices and documents illustrative of the literary history of Glasgow. Glasgow 1831.

The newspaper press of Scotland. Fraser's Mag 1838.

Documents relative to the printers of early Scottish newspapers 1686-1705. Maitland Club Miscellany 2 1840.

A short memoir of Gavin Hamilton, bookseller in Edinburgh in the eighteenth century. Edinburgh 1840.

Lamb, A. D. Bibliography of Dundee periodicals. Scottish N & Q Dec 1889.

Bullock, J. M. Chronological list of Aberdeen newspapers and magazines. Aberdeen 1889.

—— Files of the local Aberdeen press, past and present. Scottish N & Q April 1896.

Scott, J. W. A bibliography of Edinburgh periodical literature. Scottish N & Q July 1891 etc.

Norrie, W. Edinburgh newspapers past and present. Earlston 1891.

Rae, J. The life of Adam Smith. 1895.

Gibb, J. S. James Watson, printer: notes of his life and work 1697-1722. Edinburgh Bibl Soc Pbns 1 1896.

Wallace, W. Early Scottish journalists and journalism. Stirling 1899.

Three northern newspapers: their rise and progress. Aberdeen 1900.

Minto, J. A notable publishing house: the Morisons of Perth. Library 1 1900.

Johnstone, G. H. The Ruddimans in Scotland: their history and works. Edinburgh 1901.

Carrick, J. C. William Creech: Robert Burns's best friend. Dalkeith 1903.

Aldes, H. G. A list of books printed in Scotland before 1700. Edinburgh 1904.

Sinclair, G. A. Periodical literature of the 18th century. Scottish Historical Rev 2 1905.

Graham, M. The early Glasgow press. Glasgow 1906.

Couper, W. J. The Edinburgh periodical press. 2 vols Stirling 1908.

—— James Watson, King's Printer. Scottish Historical Rev 7 1910.

—— Mrs Anderson and the royal prerogative in printing. Proc of Royal Philosophical Soc of Glasgow 48 1917.

—— A bibliography of Edinburgh periodical literature. Scottish N & Q Oct 1930-April 1931.

M'Lean, H. A. R. Urie, printer in Glasgow. Records of Glasgow Bibl Soc 3 1913.

Hilson, J. L. Kelso typography. Proc of Berwickshire Naturalists' Club 22 1915.

Craig, M. E. The Scottish periodical press 1750-89. Edinburgh 1931.

Dale, C. The Glasgow periodical press in the eighteenth century. Scottish N & Q Nov 1935.

Ferguson, J. P. S. Scottish newspapers held in Scottish libraries. Edinburgh 1956.

Carnie, R. H. Publishing in Perth before 1807. Abertay Historical Soc Pbns, Dundee 1960.

—— Scottish printers and booksellers 1668-1775. SB 14-15 1961-2.

—— Scottish printers and booksellers 1688-1775: a study of source-material. Bibliotheck 4-5 1966-7.

[Gemmell, J.] (compiler). Mitchell Library, Glasgow: catalogue of periodicals. Glasgow 1962.

Duncan, D. Thomas Ruddiman: a study in Scottish scholarship of the early eighteenth century. Edinburgh and London 1965.

(2) PERIODICAL ESSAYS

Included in this list are some newspapers and magazines marked in square brackets in which original essays are to be found.

Edinburgh

The tatler, by R. Steele and J. Addison. No 1 [no 130 of original] 13 Feb 1710-no 142 [no 271 of original], 9 Jan 1711. Rptd from London paper.

The north tatler. No 1, 1 April 1710.

The tatler, by 'Donald MacStaff of the north' [R. Hepburn]. No 1, 13 Jan 1711-no 40, 30 May 1711.

White, R. B. The Hepburn Tatler, Edinburgh 1711. N & Q Aug 1955.

The mercury: or the northern reformer, by 'Duncan Tatler esq'. No 1, 1 Jan 1717-no 7, 12 Feb 1717.

[The echo [from no 3, eccho]: or Edinburgh weekly journal. No 1, 10 Jan 1729-no 277 (i.e. 278), 10 April 1734.]

The conjurer. No 1, 8 Nov 1735-no 11, 16 Jan 1736-?

The reveur. Ed R. Wallace. No 1, 18 Nov 1737-no 28, 26 May 1738.

Letters of the critical club. No 1, Jan 1738-no 6, June 1738.

[The patriot. No 1, 3 June 1740–no 23, 6 Nov 1740.]

The Rambler. By S. Johnson. No 1, [27 March] 1750–no 104. Seriatim reprint of London originals.

[The Scots spy: or critical observer, by P. Williamson. Vol 1 no 1, 8 March 1776–vol 2 no 11, 15 Nov 1776].

[The new Scots spy: or critical observer, by P. Williamson. Vol 1 no 1, 29 Aug 1777–no 12, 14 Nov 1777.]

The Mirror. Ed H. Mackenzie. No 1, 23 Jan 1779–no 110, 27 May 1780. Rptd Edinburgh 1779, 1781, London 1783, 1787, 1790, 1792, 1793, 1794, Dublin 1790.

Hudson, R. Henry Mackenzie, James Beattie et al and the Edinburgh Mirror. Eng Lang Notes 1, 1963.

The weekly mirror: being a collection of original essays, by J. Tytler. No 1, 22 Sept 1780–no 26, 23 March 1781.

The lounger. Ed H. Mackenzie. No 1, 5 Feb 1785–no 101, 6 Jan 1787. Early nos rptd 1785; rptd Edinburgh 1787, London 1787, 1788, New York 1789.

[The bee: or literary intelligencer. Ed J. Anderson. No 1, 22 Dec 1790–no 163, 21 Jan 1794.]

The trifler, by 'Richard Maw-worm esq.' No 1, 19 Dec 1795–no 33, 1 Aug 1796; rptd Edinburgh 1797.

The ghost, by 'Felix Phantom' [R. Heron]. No 1, 25 April 1796–no 46, 16 Nov 1796; rptd Edinburgh 1796.

The adviser: a new periodical paper. Ed A. Briarcliff. No 1, 11 Feb 1797–no 16, 27 May 1797.

[The Edinburgh weekly journal. Ed W. Brown. [No 1, 3 Jan 1798]–.

[The gleaner. 15 essays in Edinburgh Mag Nov 1798–Jan 1800.]

Aberdeen

[The northern gazette, literary chronicle and review. Ed J. Chalmers. No 1, 6 April 1787–no 39, 27 Dec 1787. Followed by Aberdeen magazine or literary chronicle and review, Jan 1788–Dec 1791–?]

Dumfries

[The Dumfries weekly magazine. No 1, 16 March 1773–?]

Glasgow

The observer, by J. Tytler. Nos 1–26, 1786.

(3) MAGAZINES, MISCELLANIES, LEARNED JOURNALS AND REVIEWS

Edinburgh

Bibliotheca universalis: or an historical account of books and translations. Ed J. Cockburn. Jan 1688–?

The present state of Europe: or the historical and political mercury. No 1, Oct 1690–Aug 1695. Rptd from London trn of Mercure historique et politique, pbd at Hague.

The history of the works of the learned. 1699. Rptd from London pbn.

Medical essays and observations. 1733–44. Rptd 1737–38, 1747, 1752.

The Scots magazine. Ed W. Smellie et al. No 1, Jan 1739–.

Niven, G. W. The bibliography of the Scots Magazine. Library 10 1898.

Cook, D. Burns and the Scots Magazine. Scots Mag 20 1934.

Imrie, D. S. M. The story of the Scots magazine 1739–1826. Scots Mag Jan–June 1939.

Elliott, R. C. The early Scots magazine. MLQ 11 1950.

The Christian monthly history: or an account of the revival and progress of religion, abroad and at home. Ed J. Robe. No 1, Nov 1743–no 10, Jan 1746.

Austin, R. The Christian monthly history. Proc of Wesley Historical Soc 12 1919.

The British magazine: or the London and Edinburgh intelligencer. Vol 1 no 1, Jan 1747–vol 2 no 12, Dec 1748.

Highland gentleman's magazine. 1751.

Philosophical society of Edinburgh: essays and observations. Vol 1 1754–vol 3 1771.

The Edinburgh review: containing an account of all the books and pamphlets published in Scotland. No 1, July 1755–no 2, Jan 1756.

View of the Edinburgh review, pointing out the spirit and tendency of that paper. Edinburgh 1756.

New groat's worth of wit for a penny: or an analysis or compend of the view of the Edinburgh review. [1756].

The Edinburgh magazine. Ed W. Ruddiman. Vol 1 1757–vol 6 Dec 1762.

The religious magazine: or Christian's storehouse. No 1, July 1760–no 2, Aug 1760.

The Edinburgh museum: or north-British magazine. No 1, Jan 1763–Dec 1764.

The weekly magazine: or Edinburgh amusement, containing the essence of all the magazines, reviews etc. Ed J. Anderson (or W. Ruddiman?) No 1, 7 July 1768–23 Dec 1779. Continued as Edinburgh magazine: or literary amusement, 30 Dec 1779–11 Jul 1782. Continued as Edinburgh weekly magazine, 3 July 1783–10 June 1784–[24 June 1784].

The Scots farmer. 1 Sept 1772.

Medical and philosophical commentaries. Vol 1 no 1, 1773–9. Continued as Medical commentaries, 1780–95. Continued as Annals of medicine, 1796–.

The Caledonian weekly magazine: or Edinburgh intelligencer. No 1, 1 June 1773–28 July 1773.

The Edinburgh magazine and review. Ed W. Smellie and G. Stuart. No 1, Oct 1773–Aug 1776.

The gentleman and lady's weekly magazine. Ed J. Tytler. No 1, 28 Jan 1774–vol 5 no 13, 29 March 1775.

The Edinburgh repository: or fortnight's magazine. No 1, 2 March 1774–?

The Scots weekly magazine: or grand repository containing the substance of all the magazines, reviews, and news-papers. Vol 1 no 1, 3 Oct 1775–vol 2 26 March 1776–?

The north British intelligencer: or constitutional miscellany. Ed R. Dick and A. Belshis. Vol 1 no 1, 3 April 1776–vol 5 no 13, 25 June 1777.

The new Scots spy: or critical observer. ?–no 9, 7 Sept 1777–?

The Scots town and country magazine. Vol 1 no 1, 7 July 1778–vol 2 25 May 1779–[Aug 1779?]

The Edinburgh eighth day magazine: or Scots town and country intelligencer. Vol 1 no 1, 1 Sept 1779–no 16 (i.e. 30), June 1780.

The gentleman and lady's pocket register: or fortnight's intelligencer. No 1, 27 July 1780–3 Oct 1780.

The north British magazine: or Caledonian miscellany. Ed J. Murray. No 1, 16 Oct 1782–vol 2 no 6, 24 Oct 1783.

The Edinburgh magazine: or literary miscellany. Ed J. Sibbald et al. No 1, Jan 1785–.

The Royal Society of Edinburgh: transactions. 1788–.

The beauties of the magazines, reviews and other periodical publications. Jan 1788–March 1789.

The bee: or literary weekly intelligencer. Ed J. Anderson. No 1, 22 Dec 1790–21 Jan 1794.

GM Dec 1808. On Anderson.

Cook, D. The editor of the Bee. TLS 27 Aug 1920.

Currie, A. W. Literary views of Adam Smith. N & Q July 1962.

Mullett, C. F. A village Aristotle and his harmony of interests: James Anderson 1739–1808 of Monks Hill. Jnl of Br Stud 8 1968.

The young misses magazine. Vols 1–3 1791.

The historical register: or Edinburgh monthly intelligencer. Ed J. Tytler. Vol 1 no 1, July 1791–July 1792. Continued as Universal monthly intelligencer, 1792–?

The political review of Edinburgh periodical publications. Ed J. Thomson? No 1, 20 June 1792–no 7, 1 Aug 1792.

The Edinburgh repository for polite literature. No 1, Sept 1792.

The Scottish register: or general view of history, politics and literature. No 1, March 1794–no 6, June 1795.

The gleaner: containing original essays in prose and verse, with extracts from various publications. Ed J. Graham. No 1, 14 Feb 1795.

The missionary magazine. Ed G. Ewing. Vol 1 no 1, 18 July 1796–.

The vocal magazine: containing a selection of the most esteemed English, Scotch and Irish songs. 1797–9.

The Christian magazine: or evangelical repository. No 1, 6 Feb 1797–.

The Edinburgh quarterly magazine: intended to promote the knowledge, belief and influence of divine revelation. No 1, 31 March 1798–28 June 1800.

The farmer's magazine. Ed R. Brown. No 1, Jan 1800–.

Aberdeen

The Aberdeen magazine. No 1, Jan 1761–no 12, Dec 1761. Suppl.

The Caledonian magazine: or Aberdeen repository. Ed A. Leighton and A. Shirrefs. No 1, 6 Oct 1786–5 Oct 1787.

The Caledonian magazine: or Aberdeen repository. Ed A. Shirrefs. No 1, Jan 1788–Dec 1790.

The Aberdeen magazine, literary chronicle and review. No 1, 17 Jan 1788–[1798]–?

The Aberdeen magazine: or universal repository. Vol 1 no 1, June 1796–vol 3, Dec 1798.

Arbroath

The Arbroath magazine: or repository of literature. No 1, Oct 1799–Oct 1800.

Berwick-on-Tweed

The Berwick museum: or monthly literary intelligencer. No 1, Jan 1785–Dec 1787.

Dumfries

The Dumfries weekly magazine. No 1, 16 March 1773–vol 18 no 10, 22 July 1777.

Dundee

The Dundee magazine. [Dec 1757]–19 Jan 1758–?

The Dundee magazine: or a history of the present times. No 1, 11 Aug 1775. Continued as Dundee weekly magazine: or a history of the present times, no 2, 18 Aug 1775–20 June 1777–[1778].

The north British miscellany: or Dundee amusement. No 1, June 1778–23 June 1780.

The Dundee repository of political and miscellaneous information. Ed W. Brown. No 1, 15 Feb 1793–vol 2 no 13, 21 Feb 1794.

The Dundee magazine and journal of the times. Vol 1 no 1, Jan 1799–.

Glasgow

The Glasgow magazine. No 1, 10 Jan 1770.

The Glasgow universal magazine of knowledge and pleasure. No 1, 13 Aug 1772–no 24, 3 Feb 1773.

The Glasgow museum: or weekly instructor. No 1, 11 Jan 1773–10 July 1773.

The Glasgow magazine and review: or universal miscellany. No 1, Oct 1783–May 1784.

The weekly magazine of instruction and entertainment. Vol 1 no 1, 1789–vol 6 no 156, 1792. Continued as Phoenix: or weekly miscellany improv'd, vol 1 no 1, 4 July 1792–vol 4 no 104, 2 July 1794–? Continued as Asylum: or weekly miscellany, ?–vol 3 no 53, 14 Oct 1795–no 78, 14 April 1796.

The Glasgow magazine. Vol 1 June–Dec 1795.

The young misses magazine: containing dialogues between a governess and several young ladies of quality. Vol 1 ?–vol 2 1800.

The polyhymnia: being a collection of poetry, original and selected. Nos 1–20, 1799 or 1800.

Montrose

The literary mirror. Ed Murray. 1793–.

Perth

The Perth magazine of knowledge and pleasure. Ed R. Morison and G. Johnston. Vol 1 no 1, 3 July 1772–vol 5 24 Dec 1773.

The Caledonian magazine and review. No 1, March 1783–no 2, 21 March 1783.

(4) NEWSPAPERS

Edinburgh

Mercurius politicus. [Pbn began at Leith 1653; transferred to Edinburgh Nov 1654]–Jan 1660–. Continued as Mercurius publicus, 18 April 1660–[1663?]. Rptd from London paper.

The faithfull intelligencer from the Parliaments army in Scotland. No 1, 3 Dec 1659. Continued as Mercurius britannicus, no 2, 15 Dec 1659–no 6, 6 Jan 1660.

Mercurius Caledonius. Ed T. Sydserf. 31 Dec 1660–no 10, 28 March 1661. Rptd seriatim in London.

The Kingdoms intelligencer, Ed R. Mein. 30 Oct 1661–15 Dec 1664–[1668?]. Began as reprint of Kingdomes intelligencer, London; continued independently from 1663.

The Edinburgh gazette. No 1, 7 Dec 1680–no 4, 28 Dec 1680.

Ferguson, F. S. The Edinburgh gazette 1680. Pbns of Edinburgh Bibl Soc 12 1925.

The weekly journal from London. [No 1, 2 May 1688]–no 4, 30 May 1688–?

The test paper. No 1, nd. Continued as Weekly test paper, no 2, 16 May 1688–? Rptd from London paper.

Public occurrences truely stated. ?–29 May 1688–? Rptd from London paper.

Gowan, W. The Holyrood press 1686–8. Edinburgh Bibl Soc Pbns 6 1905.

Orange gazette. 22 Feb 1689–5 March 1689. Rptd from London paper.

The London gazette. ?–18 March 1689–? Rptd from London paper.

Mercurius reformatus: or the new observator. 4 June 1690–5 June 1691. Rptd from London paper.

Dublin intelligence: giving a true account of the killing of several rapparees in Ireland. No 38, 16 June 1691. Rptd from Dublin paper.

The Edinburgh gazette. Ed J. Donaldson and J. Bisset. No 1, 2 March 1699–16 Dec 1707–? Continued as Edinburgh gazettee ?–no 114, 31 Aug 1708. Continued as Scots postman: or the new Edinburgh gazette, No 1, 7 Sept 1708–no 143, 16 Aug 1709. Continued as Edinburgh gazette, no 144, 18 Aug 1709–Dec 1709. Also continued as Scots post-man, no 144, 18 Aug 24–24 Dec 1709. Continued as Scots post-man: or the new Edinburgh gazette, no 1, 27 Dec 1709–no 140, 21 Nov 1710. Continued as New Edinburgh gazette, no 141 (i.e. 1), 23 Nov 1710–. Continued as Evening post: or the new Edinburgh gazette, no 1, 7 Dec 1710–no 229, 24 May 1712–? Continued as Scots post-man: or the Edinburgh gazette, no 141, 23 Jan 1711–no 336, 12 July 1712–. Continued as Edinburgh gazette: or Scots postman, no 1, 11 March 1714–no 76 (i.e. 77), 15 March 1715–?

The Edinburgh courant. Ed A. Boig and J. Muirhead. No 1, 19 Feb 1705–. Continued as Scots courant, no 707, 22 March 1710–no 2,251, 22 April 1720.

Observator: or a dialogue between a country-man and a Landwart school-master. No 1, nd–no 2, 6 April 1705–no 9, 23 July 1705–no 10, 25 May 1706.

The Paris gazette. No 1, nd–no 2, 15 Feb 1706–[1708]?

The Edinburgh flying post. No 1, 20 Feb 1707–no 2, 25 Feb 1707. Possibly continued as Edinburgh courant revived, no 1, 6 March 1707.

A review of the state of the British nation. Ed D. Defoe. 27 March 1709–1710. Advance issues of London paper, A weekly review, 1704.

The Edinburgh courant. Ed D. Defoe. No 1, 20 March 1710–no 2, 22 March 1710.

Burch, C. E. Defoe's connections with the Edinburgh Courant. RES 5 1929.

Republican queries answer'd paragraph by paragraph. No 1, ?–no 2, nd 1710.

The examiner: or remarks upon papers and occurrences. No 1, 2 Sept 1710–vol 2 no 31, 3 July 1712–? Rptd from London paper.

Miscellany numbers. Nos 1–29, 1712.

The freeholder and the weekly packet. 5 April 1716–26 June 1716. Rptd from selected issues of 2 London papers, Freeholder nos 27–41 and Weekly packet nos 1–12.

The Edinburgh evening courant. No 1, 15 Dec 1718–.

The Caledonian mercury. Ed W. Rolland, J. Grant et al. No 1, 28 April 1720–.

Murray, J. Notes on Johnson's movements in Scotland: suggested attributions to Boswell in the Caledonian Mercury. N & Q 16 March 1940.

—— Boswell and the Caledonian Mercury. Ibid.

The Edinburgh news-letter. ?–no 5, 8 Aug 1722–?

The echo [from no 3: eccho]: or Edinburgh weekly journal. No 1, 10 Jan 1729–no 277 (i.e. 278), 10 April 1734.

The thistle, by 'Sir William Wallace, Knight' [from no 21 'By Sir John De Graham, Knight']. No 1, 13 Feb 1734–no 105, 11 Feb 1736.

The patriot. No 1, 3 June 1740–no 23, 4 Nov 1740.

The Edinburgh weekly journal. [1757?]–vol 2 no 1, 17 Feb 1758–vol 14 no 15, 7 Feb 1770–[1775?]

The moderator, by J. Home. No 1, ? no 2, nd 1757.

The Edinburgh chronicle: or universal intelligencer. No 1, 22 March 1759–vol 3 no 173, 8 Oct 1760–?

The Edinburgh advertiser. No 1, 3 Jan 1764–.

The citizen. No 1, nd 1764.

The Scots spy: or critical observer, by P. Williamson. Vol 1 no 1, 8 March 1776–no 11, 15 Nov 1776.

The Caledonian gazetteer. No 1, 31 May 1776–no 13, 28 June 1776.

The spectator. Nos 1–8, 1776.

Ruddiman's weekly mercury. Ed W. Ruddiman. No 1, 3 July 1777–18 Dec 1782–[1784].

The new Scots spy: or critical observer, by P. Williamson. Vol 1 no 1, 29 Aug 1777–no 12, 14 Nov 1777.

The Edinburgh gazette. Ed. T. Robertson. No 1, 1 Feb 1780–no 26, April 1780–[July 1780].

The Edinburgh evening post. [No 1, May ? 1780]–Oct 1781–no 474, 26 Nov 1784–?

The weekly review. Ed J. Tytler. 1780.

The Edinburgh herald. Ed J. Sibbald, W. Brown. No 1, 15 March 1790–? Continued as Edinburgh herald and chronicle, ?–no 1,066, 2 Jan 1796–.

Constitutional letters. No 1, 4 June 1792–no 8, 23 July 1792.

The Caledonian chronicle. No 1, 9 Oct 1792–25 June 1793.

The Edinburgh gazetteer. Ed W. Johnston, A. Scott. No 1, 16 Nov 1792–no 87, 29 Jan 1794 (for Feb 1794).

The Edinburgh gazette. No 1, 2 July 1793–.

The observer: or a delineation of the times. No 1, 28 Sept 1793.

The patriots' weekly chronicle. Ed W. Brown. [No 1, 3 April 1794?]–no 107, 14 April 1796–?

The Scots chronicle. Ed J. Morthland. No 1, 1 March 1796.

The Edinburgh weekly journal. Ed W. Brown. [No 1, 3 Jan 1798]–.

The Wednesday packet. No 1, 3 Jan 1798–.

The Edinburgh review: or weekly report of sermons. No 1, 10 Nov 1799–.

Aberdeen

Aberdeen's journal. Ed J. Chalmers. No 1, 5 Jan 1748–. Continued as Aberdeen journal, no 9, 1 March 1748–. Absorbed Aberdeen intelligencer 1757. Continued as Aberdeen journal and north-British magazine, no 1,078, 5 Sept 1768–. Continued as Aberdeen journal, no 1,774, 7 Jan 1782–.

The Aberdeen Journal and its history. Aberdeen 1894.

The Aberdeen Journal: our 150th year. Aberdeen 1897.

The Aberdeen intelligencer. Ed F. Douglas. No 1, 3 Oct 1752–22 Feb 1757. Incorporated with Aberdeen journal, above.

[Boyle's paper]. 1770–? Scottish N & Q June 1889.

The northern gazette, literary chronicle and review. Ed J. Chalmers. No 1, 6 April 1787–no 39, 27 Dec 1787. Followed by Aberdeen magazine: or literary chronicle and review, Jan 1788–Dec 1791–?

The Aberdeen chronicle. 1787. Scottish N & Q June 1889.

Dumfries

The Dumfries mercury. ?–no 18, 8 May 1721–? Couper, W. J. The date of the Dumfries Mercury. Records of Glasgow Bibl Soc 4 1915.

The Dumfries weekly magazine. No 1, 16 March 1773–?

The Dumfries weekly journal. Ed R. Jackson and J. Mayne. No 1, 29 July 1777–.

Republican journal: and Dumfries weekly advertiser. ?–2 May 1795–14 April 1796–?

Dundee

The Dundee weekly intelligencer. ?–30 May 1755–?

The Dundee mail. Ed J. Chalmers. No 1, 1798–?

Angus intelligencer. 1799–?

Glasgow

The Glasgow courant. No 1, 14 Nov 1715–. Continued as West country intelligence, no 4, 25 Nov 1715–no 67, 1 May 1716.

Stewart, W. The first Glasgow newspaper. Glasgow 1924.

The Glasgow journal. Ed A. Stalker et al. No 1, 20 July 1741–. Absorbed the 1745 Glasgow courant in 1760. Absorbed Glasgow chronicle in 1779.

The Glasgow weekly history relating to the history of the gospel at home and abroad. Ed W. McCullock. No 1, 18 Nov 1741–[1743?]

The Glasgow courant. Ed M. Simpson. No 1, 14 Oct 1745–1760. Absorbed by Glasgow journal in 1760.

Exhortation to the inhabitants of the south parish of Glasgow, by J. Gillies. No 1, 26 Sept 1750–no 21, 10 April 1751.

The Glasgow chronicle: or weekly intelligencer. [1766?] –29 Jan 1767–12 March 1778–. Absorbed by Glasgow journal in 1779.

The Glasgow mercury. Ed R. Chapman. No 1, 8 Jan 1778–27 Sept 1796.

The Glasgow advertiser. Ed J. Mennons. No 1, 27 Jan 1783–? Continued as Glasgow advertiser and evening intelligencer, ?–29 June 1789–. Continued as Glasgow advertiser, 24 Jan 1794–.

[Stewart, W.] The Glasgow Herald. Glasgow 1911.

G[ourlay], J. An early Glasgow journalist [J. Mennons]. [Glasgow? 1929?]

The Glasgow courier. No 1, 1 Sept 1791–.

The culler. No 1, 12 Aug 1795–no 20, 23 Dec 1795.

The torch. No 1, 13 Jan 1796–no 5, 10 March 1796–?

The rush-light. No 1, 15 Feb 1800–.

Greenock

The Greenock advertiser. [1799]–.

Kelso

The Kelso chronicle. Ed J. Palmer. No 1, 7 March 1783–. Continued as the British chronicle: or union gazette, [1784]–.

The Kelso mail and border gazette. No 1, 13 April 1797–.

K. IRELAND

(1) BIBLIOGRAPHIES, BIOGRAPHIES AND GENERAL STUDIES

Special studies of individual periodicals are listed immediately after their titles.

Power, J. List of Irish periodical publications (chiefly literary) from 1729 to the present time. [1866].

Madden, R. R. The history of Irish periodical literature. 2 vols 1867, 1968.

Campbell, A. A. Early Strabane newspapers and magazines. Ulster Jnl of Archaeology 7 1901.

— Belfast newspapers, past and present. Belfast 1921.

Dix, E. R. McC. List of books, pamphlets and Newspapers printed in Strabane, Co Tyrone, in the eighteenth century. Irish Bibl Pamphlets 1 1901.

— The earliest periodical journals published in Dublin. Royal Irish Acad 6 1902.

— List of books, pamphlets, and newspapers printed in the city of Cork in the XVIIth and XVIIIth centuries. Cork 1904.

— List of books, pamphlets and newspapers printed in Drogheda, Co Louth, in the eighteenth century. Irish Bibl Pamphlets 3 1904.

— List of books, pamphlets and newspapers printed in Monaghan in the eighteenth century. Irish Bibl Pamphlets 4 1908.

— Rare ephemeral magazines of the eighteenth century. Irish Book Lover 1 1910.

— Irish bibliography: tables relating to some Dublin newspapers of the eighteenth century. Dublin 1910.

— List of books, pamphlets and newspapers printed in Ennis, Co Clare, in the eighteenth century. Irish Bibl Pamphlets 8 1912.

— List of books, pamphlets and newspapers printed in Limerick to 1800. Irish Bibl Pamphlets 5 1912 (2nd edn).

— Some rare Dublin magazines of the eighteenth century. Irish Book Lover 8 1916.

Brindley, L. H. A study of some old newspapers. New Ireland Rev 16 1901.

Buckley, J. Some account of the earliest Limerick printing. Cork 1902.

P[ower], P. A bundle of old Waterford newspapers. Jnl of Waterford & South East of Ireland Archaeological Soc 10 1907, 12–13 1909–10.

Casaide, S. A guide to old Waterford newspapers. Waterford 1917.

— A history of the periodical literature of Cork from the beginning to AD 1900. Cork 1943.

O'Neill, J. J. A bibliographical account of Irish theatrical literature. Bibl Soc of Ireland 1 1920.

Crone, J. S. Some rare Dublin periodicals. Irish Book Lover 12 1921.

Lang, W. J. British and Irish newspapers before 1801. Irish Book Lover 22 1934.

Brown, S. J. The Dublin newspaper press: a bird's eye view 1659–1916. Studies 25 1936.

McManus, M. J. The first Limerick newspaper. Irish Book Lover 24 1936.

McDowell, R. B. The Irish government and the provincial press. Hermathena 53 1939.

Irish newspapers prior to 1750 in Dublin libraries now available for purchase in positive microfilm form. Ann Arbor 1950.

Irish periodicals: a list of Irish newspapers, periodicals, annual and serial publications in Northern Ireland libraries. Belfast 1953.

Inglis, B. The freedom of the press in Ireland 1784–1841. 1954.

Munter, R. L. A hand-list of Irish newspapers 1685–1750. 1960.

— The history of the Irish newspaper 1685–1760. Cambridge 1967.

Eager, A. R. A guide to Irish bibliographical material. 1964.

(2) PERIODICAL ESSAYS

Newspapers and magazines in which original essays are to be found are marked in square brackets.

Dublin

The tatler, by R. Steele and J. Addison. No 1 [no 154 of original], 1 April 1710–no 10, 10 May 1710–? Rptd from London paper.

Jackson, R. W. An unrecorded Tatler. TLS 7 Dec 1946.

Essays by 'Hibernicus' [J. Arbuckle] in Dublin weekly journal. 1725–?; rptd Dublin 1734.

[The country gentleman. No 1, 30 March 1726–no 2, 4 April 1726–?]

[The intelligencer. Ed J. Swift and T. Sheridan. 1728–9].

[The temple-oge intelligence. Nos 1–6, 1728.]

The plain dealer's intelligencer. No 1, 7 Aug 1728–no 26, 2 Jan 1729.

[The plain dealer. 1728–[9?].]

The tribune. Ed P. Delany. No 1, [10 Oct ?] 1729–no 2, 13 Oct 1729–no 21, 20 Dec 1729; rptd 1729.

The meddler, by W. R. Chetwood? No 1, 5 Jan 1744–no 26, 28 June 1744.

The reformer, by E. Burke. No 1, 28 Jan 1748–no 13, 21 April 1748; rptd in appendix of A. P. I. Samuel, Early life of Burke, Cambridge 1923.

The tickler. Ed P. Hiffernan. No 1, 18 Feb 1748–no 35, 20 Oct 1749–? Nos 1–7 rptd Dublin 1748.

[Brett's miscellany, by P. Brett. 1748.]

[The censor: or the citizen's journal, by 'Frank Some-body esq' [C. Lucas]. No 1, 3 June 1749–no 28, 28 July 1750. Nos 1–24 rptd London 1751.]

The play-house journal. No 1, 18 Jan 1750–?

[The Covent-garden journal. Vol 1 no 1, 25 Jan 1752–6.]

[The universal advertiser: or a collection of essays. ?–no 9, 3 Feb 1753–no 1,030, 27 Nov 1762–?]

The Dublin spy. No 1, 13 Aug 1753–no 55, 27 May 1754.

The shepherd. No 1, 16 Jan 1759–July 1760–?

Speculations of 'Geoffrey Wagstaffe esq' in the Dublin mercury. 1770.

The gleaner. Nos 1–6, 1793.

The flapper, by W. C. Smith et al. Vol 1 no 1, 2 Feb 1796–vol 2 no 75, 10 Sept 1797. Nos 1–13 rptd Dublin 1796.

Graham, W. The authorship of the Flapper 1796. N & Q 9 Jan, 2 April 1932.

Milford, R. T. The authorship of the Flapper. N & Q 13 Feb 1932.

The wanderer. 6 essays in Dublin magazine Dec 1798–June 1799.

Cork

The modern monitor, by H. Sheares et al. Hibernian Chron 26 March 1770–1 Nov 1770; rptd 1771.

(3) MAGAZINES, MISCELLANIES, LEARNED JOURNALS AND REVIEWS

Dublin

The weekly magazine. No 1, 2 Jan 1733–Jan 1734.

The Dublin magazine: or the gentleman's new miscel-lany. 1733.

The Dublin literary journal. No 1, Oct 1734.

The London and Dublin magazine. Jan 1734–Dec 1735–?

The weekly amusement: or universal magazine. Nos 1–2, 1735.

Exshaw's magazine. Jan 1741–July 1793.

The London magazine and monthly chronicler. ?–May 1741–? Continued as Gentleman's and London magazine, ?–[1752]–1794.

A literary journal. Ed J. P. Droz. No 1, Oct–Dec 1744–June 1749.

Brett's miscellany, by P. Brett. 1748.

The compendious library. Ed V. Desvoeux. No 1, Dec 1751–no 3, April 1752.

The Dublin literary magazine. May 1761.

The Dublin magazine. Jan 1762–1765.

The repository: or library of fugitive pieces. 1763.

The monstrous magazine. 1770.

The Hibernian magazine: or compendium of entertain-ing knowledge. No 1, Jan 1771–? Continued as Sequin's Hibernian magazine, ?–1773–. Continued as Walker's Hibernian magazine: or compendium of entertaining knowledge, Jan 1786–.

The Dublin weekly magazine. 1778.

The weekly magazine and literary review. Vol 1 no 1, 2 Jan 1779–?

The town and country magazine and Irish miscellany. ?–July 1784–vol 1 no 16, 30 July 1785–vol 2 no 3, 21 Jan 1786–?

The town and country weekly magazine. Vol 1 no 1, 16 April 1785–?

The Dublin magazine and Irish monthly register. 1788–1800.

The universal magazine and review: or repository of literature. No 1, Jan 1789–June 1793.

The geographical magazine: or the universe displayed. 1790–2.

The patriot. 1792–3.

The lawyer's and magistrates magazine. 1790–2. Reprint of London periodical, vols 1–3.

The sentimental and masonic magazine. Vol 1, no 1, July 1792–vol 6 Dec 1795–?

Anthologia hibernica: or monthly collections of science, belles lettres and history. No 1, Jan 1793–Dec 1794.

The weekly magazine and historical register. No 1, 3 Feb 1793–no 7, 17 March 1793.

The Minerva magazine of knowledge, instruction and entertainment, and complete monthly register of foreign and domestic occurrences, including the beauties of all the London magazines, immediately after publication. No 1, June 1793–no 7, Dec 1793.

The parlour window. Nos 1–8, 1795.

The Irish agricultural magazine. 1798–.

The Dublin magazine and Irish monthly register. 1798–1800.

The universal magazine. Vol 1 no 1, April 1798.

The new magazine: or moral and entertaining miscel-lany. No 1, Jan 1799–1800

McKenzie's loyal magazine. No 1, Jan 1800.

The monitor: or useful miscellany. No 1, 1800.

The olio: or anything Arian magazine. 1800.

Belfast

The Ulster miscellany. 1753.

The literary museum: or weekly magazine. 1793.

Bolg an tsolair: or Gaelic magazine. No 1, 1795.

The microscope: or minute observer. Vol 1 no 1, May 1799–vol 2 no 8, Aug 1800–?

Cork

The weekly repository. No 1, 1 Feb 1779–no 12, 19 April 1779.

The museum. No 1, 9 March 1796–no 23, 14 Dec 1796.

The monthly miscellany: or Irish review and register. No 1, April 1796–[March 1797].

The casket: or hesperian magazine. Ed R. A. Millikin. No 1, April 1797–no 10, Feb 1798.

Dungannon

The Dungannon weekly magazine. Vol 1 no 5, 27 Feb 1800–.

Kennedy, F. M. The Dungannon weekly magazine. Irish Book Lover 5 1914.

Limerick

The magazine of magazines. No 1, Jan 1751–Dec 1761. Reprint of London periodical?

The Limerick magazine. 1752.

The Limerick weekly magazine: or miscellaneous repository. No 1, 19 June 1790–no 26, 11 Dec 1790.

Monaghan

Goggin's Ulster magazine: a weekly journal. ?–[no 5], 12 Jan 1799–5 Dec 1800–?

Strabane

The new magazine. No 1, Jan 1800–no 6, June 1800. Continued as Strabane magazine, no 7, July 1800–no 12, Dec 1800.

Campbell, A. A. The Strabane magazine. Irish Book Lover 3 1912.

(4) NEWSPAPERS

Dublin

An account of the chief occurrences of Ireland. No 1, 22 Feb 1660–no 5, 19 March 1660–?

Mercurius hibernicus: or the Irish intelligencer. No 1, 20 Jan 1663–no 15, 28 April 1663–?

News letter. ?–25 July 1685–no 92, 25 Feb 1686–[Sept 1688?].

The Dublin gazette. April 1689.

The Dublin intelligence. No 1, 30 Sept 1690–no 142, 14 Oct 1693.

Votes of the House of Commons [Ireland]. No 1, 5 Oct 1692–no 152, 14 Oct 1693.

The flying post: or the post master. ?–7 March 1699–7 Jan 1713–? Continued as Flying post by 26 Jan 1719–30 Dec 1724–?

The London gazette. ?–4 Dec 1700–1 March 1703–? Reprint of London paper.

The Dublin intelligence [or Oxman-Town news; after 1725: and Royal Irish journal; or weekly gazette]. ?–no 7, 13 June 1702–13 May 1723.

Munter, R. L. A hand-list of Irish newspapers 1685–1750, 1960 gives title of a few issues in 1728 as the Old Dublin intelligence, Irish journal or weekly gazette.

The Dublin intelligence. No 1, 18 July 1702–no 13, 29 Aug 1702.

The Dublin castle. ?–18 Nov 1702–?

The Dublin post. No 1, 21 Nov 1702–?

The post-man and the historical account. ?–2 Feb 1703–? Rptd from London paper.

The Dublin courant. ?–no 20, 8 April 1703–[26 May 1705]–?

Impartial occurrences. ?–vol 1 no 61, 26 Dec 1704–? Continued as Pue's occurrences ?–30 March 1714–1792.

Whalley's flying post. [No 1, Jan? 1704]–no 7, 14 Feb 1704–? Continued as Flying post: or the post-master, ?–9 July 1705–13 May 1708–?

The flying post: or the post-master. [No 1?], 11 April 1704–1 April 1713–?

Whitehall. ?–26 June 1704–1July 1704–?

The flying post: or the post-master. [No 1?], 28 Aug 1704–5 Oct 1704–?

The Paris gazette Englished. No 1, 7 Feb 1705–? Rptd from London paper.

The flying post: or the post-master. ?–10 March 1705–21 May 1705–?

The Dublin courant: or the diverting post. ?–no 3, 26 May 1705–?

The Dublin gazette. [1705]–no 129, 13 July 1706–no 2,659, 23 Feb 1726–?

Hammond, J. W. The Dublin gazette 1705–1922. Dublin Historical Record 13 1953.

The Dublin mercury. [1705]–no 22, 1 Jan 1706–no 85, 10 Aug 1706–[Dec 1707]–?

Whitehall. ?–16 May 1706–?

The flying-post: or the post-master. [No 1?], 31 March 1707–29 March 1708. Continued as Flying post: or the post msater's news, no 1, 12 April 1708–28 Aug 1710.

The post-man and the historical account. ?–no 7, 23 June 1707–no 226, 1 Oct 1713–4 Oct 1714–?

The London-postman: or the historical account. [June 1707?]–[Sept 1708?] Reprint of London paper.

Votes of the House of Commons [Ireland]. No 1, 1 July 1707–no 16, 23 July 1707.

The post man and the historical account. ?–no 94, 7 Oct 1708–?

Dublin, 19 April 1708. ?–19 April 1708–?

The Dublin intelligence. ?–no 4, 22 May 1708–no 29, 19 Feb 1709. Continued as Edward Waters' Protestant Dublin intelligence. No 31, 26 Feb 1709–no 46, 4 May 1709. Continued as Dublin weekly intelligence, no 1, 24 June 1710–no 18, 27 Aug 1710.

The Dublin castle. ?–12 July 1708–?

The diverting post. ?–no 5, 1 Oct 1709–Oct 1709–?

Dublin, September the 10th, 1708. ?–10 Sept 1708–?

The medley. No 1, 5 Oct 1710–no 45, nd 1711–? Reprint of London paper.

The Dublin spy. Vol 1 no 1, 27 May 1710–[1715].

The flying post: or the post-master. ?–3 April 1710–9 Nov 1714–? Perhaps continued as Flying-post: or the post-boy, ?–15 March 1715–2 Aug 1722. Perhaps continued as Flying post, ?–18 March 1723–14 Aug 1729–?

Lloyd's news-letter. [June 1710?]–no 61, 3 Jan 1713–no 206, 13 March 1714–[no 221, 8 May 1714]–?

'Scaramuccio' (W. J. Lawrence). Dublin two hundred years ago: the story of a forgotten newspaper. Irish Life 12–19 Dec 1913.

The examiner. No 1, 14 Aug 1710–4 Nov 1712–? Reprint of London paper.

The evening post. ?–[Feb 1712?]–27 Nov 1713–?

The Protestant post-boy. ?–no 89, 27 March 1712–?

The post boy. [No 1, July 1712?]–no 2, 4 Aug 1712–15 Nov 1716.

The post man. ?–13 Oct 1712–12 Oct 1712–?

The Englishman. Vol 1 no 1, 11 Jul 1715–22 Aug 1715–? Reprint of London paper.

The London post boy. ?–22 May 1713–? Reprint of London paper.

Votes of the House of Commons [Ireland]. ?–no 7, 2 Dec 1713–?

The Dublin post-man: and the historical account. [No 1, Feb 1714?]–no 4, 18 Feb 1714–12 Sept 1715. Continued as Needham's post-man: and the historical account, Sept 1715–25 Feb 1720–? Continued as Needham's post-man by no 2, 25 May 1724–? Continued as Dublin post-man (sometimes as R. Dickson's Dublin post-man) by 13 Nov 1724–? Continued as Post-man by 9 March 1727–? Continued as Dublin post-man by 16 Aug 1727–? Continued as Post-man by 4 Nov 1727.

Dublin, February 18 1714. ?–18 Feb 1714–?

Dublin, March 27 1714. ?–27 March 1714–?

The Dublin weekly mercury. ?–1 Sept 1714–?

Whalley's news-letter. [No 1?], 2 July 1714–28 Aug 1723–?

The Dublin-post: or the post-master. ?–18 July 1714–? Continued as Dublin general post-man by 5 May 1715–? Continued as Dublin post-man, and the historical account by 23 May 1715–? Continued as Whalley's Dublin post-man, and the historical account by 2 July 1715–? Continued as Whalley's Dublin post-man by 6 Feb 1716–? Continued as Whalley's general post-man by 2 April 1716–? Continued as Whalley's general post-man: containing an impartial historical account by 9 July 1716–? Continued as General post-man: containing an impartial historical account by 20 July 1719–17 Aug 1719–?

Whally's news-letter. ?–no 34, 31 Aug 1714–?

Dublin, Octob 29 1714. ?–29 Oct 1714–9 Feb 1716 (date as title)–?

The Dublin news-letter. [No 1, 26 March 1715]–no 2, 29 March 1715–no 140, 24 July 1716–?

Dublin, November the 21st 1715. ?–21 Nov 1715–8 Feb 1716 (date as title)–?

Votes of the House of Commons [Ireland]. ?–17 Dec 1715–18 Dec 1737–?

The free-holder. No 1, 23 Dec 1715–no 55, 29 June 1716–? Reprint of London paper.

This day arrived a packet from north-Britain with the following advice. ?–22 Feb 1716–7 March 1716–?

Thomas Humes the Dublin intelligence. No 1, 22 May 1716–? Continued as Thomas Humes the Dublin courant by no 5, 9 June 1716–no 1,058, 17 Aug 1726. Continued as Dublin gazette: or weekly courant by no 1,060, 23 Aug 1726–no 13,323 (sic), 2 Sept 1729.

The post-man: and the historical account. [No 1, 12 Aug ? 1716]–no 12, 21 Sept 1716–no 331, 9 Jan 1724–? Continued as Dublin post-man by 30 May 1926.

The daily courant. ?–no 4,652, 17 Sept 1716–no 4,676, 15 Oct 1716–? Reprint of London paper.

Harding's Dublin impartial news letter [sometimes as Harding's weekly impartial news letter, sometimes Harding's impartial news letter]. [No 1, Jan 1717?]–no 110, 6 Jan 1719–9 March 1725.

The post-boy. ?–23 June 1718–27 Jan 1720–? Continued as Flying post: or the post-boy by 5 Dec 1720–1 March 1721–? Continued as Dublin journal by 29 March 1722–24 Dec 1722–? Continued as Post-boy by 31 July 1724–?

The Dublin evening-post. No 1, 27 Jan 1719–31 Jan 1719–? Continued as Dublin-post by no 31, 4 April 1719–11 Dec 1719.

The St James's evening-post. ?–3 July 1719–31 Oct 1726–?

The weekly pacquet: or the impartial post-boy. No 1, 25 March 1720–?

Irish news-tatler. ?–10 June 1720–?

The Dublin intelligence. No 2,249, 9 July 1720–22 Aug 1724–?

The new Dublin mercury: or Irish gazetteer. No 1, 14 Oct 1721–?

The Quakers Dublin weekly oracle. ?–[Nov 1721]–? M[ortimer], R. S. The Quakers Dublin Weekly Oracle 1721. Jnl of Friends Historical Soc 49 1961.

The London post-man. [No 1, April 1722?]–no 3, 7 May 1722–no 50, 31 May 1724–?

The Dublin mercury. [No 1, 24 Nov 1722?]–no 11, 29 Dec 1722–no 153, 13 May 1724–?

A supplement to the Dublin mercury. ?–no 2, 2 Jan 1723–no 104, 27 Jan 1724–?

The Dublin journal. Ed C. Faulkner et al. No 1, 27 March 1725–. Continued as George Faulkner's Dublin journal, ?–11 Jan 1729–.
Fitzgibbon, H. M. A Dublin newspaper of 1769. Irish Monthly 1934.
Slepian, B. When Swift first employed George Faulkner. PBSA 56 1962.
—— George Faulkner's Dublin Journal and Jonathan Swift. Lib Chron 31 1965.

The dictator. ?–[May 1725]?–

The Dublin weekly journal. Ed J. Arbuckle et al. No 1, 3 April 1725–[1750]–?

The diverting post. [No 1, 18 Oct 1725?]–no 2, 25 Oct 1725–no 9, 13 Dec 1725–?

The Dublin post-boy: or a supliment to the Dublin weekly journal. No 1, 19 Feb 1730–no 4, 20 March 1730–?

Faulkner's Dublin post boy [sometimes as Dublin post boy]. [No 1, 13 Dec 1725?]–no 3, 20 Dec 1725–23 Feb 1744–?

The Dublin mercury: or impartial weekly news-letter. No 1, 13 Jan 1726–8 March 1727–? Continued as Walsh's Dublin weekly impartial news-letter, ?–29 March 1728–? Followed by Dublin impartial news-letter [sometimes as Walsh's impartial news-letter], no 1, 24 March 1731–24 May 1732–?

Dublin intelligence. No 1, 22 Aug 1724–?

The Dublin mercury: or the weekly impartial news-letter. ?–no 3, 14 April 1726–no 26, 25 Aug 1726–[24 March 1717]–?

The castle courant. [No 1, 19 Jan 1726 ?]–no 2, 24 Jan 1726–6 Feb 1727–?

The country gentleman. No 1, 30 March 1726–no 2, 4 April 1726–? Reprint of London paper.

The castle courant. ?–no 14, 4 July 1726–?

The Dublin gazetteer. No 1, 5 Aug 1726–?

The flying post-man. ?–no 79, 9 Sept 1726–?

The White-hall gazette [sometimes as R. Dickson's White-hall gazette]. [No 1, 30 Sept? 1726]–no 2, 3 Oct 1726–10 Nov 1727–?

The Dublin postman. No 1, 10 Oct 1726–?

The ladies journal. No 1, [17 Jan] 1727–no 22, 29 June 1727–?

Anburey's weekly journal. [No 1, 8 March 1727]–no 3, 22 March 1727–?

The London post-man. ?–24 March 1727–30 March 1727–?

Walsh's Dublin post-boy. ?–29 March 1727–9 Aug 1723–[22 June 1734]–? Issue of 3 Jan 1729 as Dublin post-boy.

The Dublin gazette. [No 1, 6 June 1727]–no 3, 10 June 1727–no 7, 24 June 1727–? Continued as Dickson's news letter by no 10, 4 July 1727–no 40, 7 Nov 1727. Continued as Dickson's the Dublin news letter by no 42, 14 Nov 1727–no 46 28 Nov 1727–?

A supplement to the Dublin gazette. ?–no 2, 8 June 1727–no 8, June 1727–?

The flying-post. [No 1, 5 June? 1727]–no 12, 10 July 1727–no 37, 11 Dec 1727.

The Dublin gazette. No 1, 21 June 1727–no 1726, 10 April 1744.

The temple-oge intelligence. Nos 1–6, 1728.

The Silver Court gazzette. [No 1, Feb 1728?]–no 94, 1 Jan 1729–no 127, 3 April 1728–?

The intelligencer. Ed J. Swift and T. Sheridan. No 1, 11 May 1728–no 20, 14 Dec 1728. Nos 1–19 rptd 1729; nos 1–20 rptd 1730, Edinburgh 1730.

The plain dealer. No 1, 15 Sept 1728–no 7, 27 Oct 1728–[no 26, 2 Jan 1729?]–?

No 99 D—n Sw—ts intelligencer. ?–[no 20, Dec? 1728]–?

The weekly post: or the Dublin impartial news letter. No 1, 18 Feb 1729–23 April 1729–? A supplement to the Dublin news-letter, 12 March 1729–20 March 1729–?

The Dublin post boy. ?–4 March 1729–?

The flying post: or the Dublin post-man. ?–1 April 1729–30 May 1729–?

The flying post. ?–16 May 1729–?

The Dublin journal. ?–14 June 1729–no 6, 1 July 1729.

The second craftsman extraordinary. [1730?]. Reprint of London paper.

The Dublin journal. [No 475, 9 May 1730]–no 479, 23 May 1730–[no 1,341, 8 Aug 1738]–? J. Hoey's independent continuation of Dublin journal which began 27 March 1725.

The Dublin post-boy. ?–17 July 1732–30 Aug 1734–?

The Dublin packet. ?–1 June 1730–?

The universal advertiser. [1731]–no 1,030, 27 Nov 1762–[1766].

The Dublin evening post. Vol 1 no 1, 10 June 1732–vol 3 no 7, 31 March 1739–[11 July 1741?]–?
Shipley, J. B. A new Fielding essay from the Champion. PQ 42 1963.

The correspondent. Nos 1–7, nd 1733–?

The weekly miscellany. No 1, 10 Jan 1734–no 52, 4 Jan 1735. Reprints of London paper.

Dalton's Dublin impartial news letter. [No 1, 31 Aug? 1734]–no 5, 15 Sept 1734–no 24, 23 Nov 1734–?

A supplement to the Dublin impartial news letter, 12 Sept 1734.

The prompter. ?–28 Jan 1735–? Reprint of London paper.

The weekly oracle: or universal library. No 1, 3 May 1735. Continued as Weekly oracle: or Reilly's universal library, no 2, 6 May 1735–28 Feb 1736. Continued as Reilly's weekly oracle, vol 2 no 1, 3 March 1736–no 53, 31 Aug 1736–?

The country journal. No 1, 5 June 1735–no 58, 3 March 1736–?

The Dublin news-letter. ?–vol 1 no 9, 2 Oct 1736–no 30, 14 Dec 1736–?

The Dublin daily advertiser. No 1, 6 Oct 1736–no 497, 6 May 1738–[31 Oct? 1738]–? Suppl 17 Jan, 4 Feb 1737.

The scribler. [Nos 1–3, Oct 1736]–?

The Dublin news-letter. Vol 1 no 1, 4 Jan 1737–31 Dec 1743–? Suppl 23 March 1744.

The general advertiser. ?–13 Jan 1737–?

The Dublin daily post, and general advertiser. ?–vol 2 no 319, 11 Jan 1739–vol 3 no 756, 10 June 1740–?

The Dublin Society's weekly observations. No 1, 4 Jan 1737–no 52, 4 April 1738.

The craftsman. ?–no 684, 18 Aug 1739–no 690, 29 Sept 1739–? Reprint of London paper.

The general post office advertiser. ?–22 July 1741–23 Nov 1741–?

The general correspondent. ?–[No 9, 5 Aug 1740]–?

The Dublin mercury. ?–no 2, 26 Jan 1742–no 70, 21 Sept 1742–?

The flying post. ?–31 March 1744–3 May 1744–?

The Dublin courant. No 1, 24 April 1744–no 613, 24 March 1750–?

The general news-letter. ?–vol 1 no 10, 3 Oct 1744–no 11, 14 Oct 1744–? Continued as Esdall's news-letter, ?–[no 13, 5 Feb 1746]–10 July 1747–?

The universal journal. ?–no 174, 17 Feb 1747–?

The Dublin gazette. ?–no 16, 29 April 1746–[May 1748]–? Suppl 19 May 1749.

The impartial examiner: or the faithful representer of the various and manifold misrepresentations imposed on the Roman Catholics of Ireland, by the scribblers of the Farmer's Merchant's and Drapier's letters, the editors of the magazines, and by the printers of the journals, courants, news-letters, gazettes etc. No 1, nd 1746. Continued as Examiner, nos 2–8, nd 1746.

The patriot. No 1, 3 Nov 1748–no 2, 22 Nov 1748–?

The censor: or the citizen's journal, by 'Frank Somebody esq.' (C. Lucas). Vol 1 no 1, 3 June 1749–vol 1 no 28, 28 July 1750. Nos 1–24 rptd London 1751.

The censor extraordinary. ?–vol 1 no 11, 7 Aug 1749–vol no 23, 25 Oct 1749–?

The Cork surgeon's antidote against the Dublin apothecary's poyson, by 'Anthony Litten' (R. Cox). Nos 1–7, 1749.

The apologist: or the alderman's journal. No 1, nd–no 2, 21 July 1749–no 13, 9 Oct 1749–?

The political manager: or the invasion of the music-hall. No 1, 2 Oct 1749–?

A bone to pick for somebody. nd 1749.

A breakfast for the freeman. No 1, nd 1749–no 2, 24 Oct 1749–no 3, 24 Oct (sic) 1749–?

The church-monitor. No 1, 27 Oct 1749–no 2, 1 Nov 1749–?

The Dublin gazette. No 1, 21 Aug 1750–no 311, 21 Aug 1753?–

The nettle. No 1, 24 Oct 1751.

The mirror. No 1, 8 Nov 1750–no 2, 15 Nov 1750–?

The Covent-garden journal. Vol 1 no 1, 25 Jan 1752–? Continued as Covent-garden journal: or the censor, ?–vol 2 no 77, 14 June 1753–? Continued as Censor: or Covent garden journal ?–no 83, 26 July 1753–? Continued as Censor, ?–vol 5 no 234, 10 June 1756. In part rptd from London paper.

The universal advertiser: or a collection of essays. ?–no 9, 3 Feb 1743–no 1030, 27 Nov 1762–?

The city watchman. No 1, 31 May 1754–no 2, 7 Jun 1754–?

An address to friends and foes. Nos 1–2, nd 1754.

The curry-comb. No 1, 1755.

Saunders' news-letter. [1755]–[28 Sept 1769]–no 5,115, 11 March 1775–. Continued as Saunders' news-letter and daily advertiser, [1 Jan 1784]–no 8,815, 23 June 1785–.

Hue and cry. ?–no 3, 18 June 1755–?

The Dublin evening post. ?–26 Oct 1756–?

The Dublin intelligencer. ?–17 June 1756–?

The London chronicle. 1 Jan 1758–7 July 1758–? Rptd from London paper?

The Dublin courier. [1758]–no 201, 7 Jan 1760–no 1,423, 30 Dec 1766–?

The public gazetteer [also known as Sleater's gazetteer]. No 1, 23 Sept 1758–15 Dec 1772–[1783]–?

[Hunter's] Dublin chronicle: or universal journal. ?–vol 3 no 204, 7 Oct 1762–[1771]–?

The public register: or Freeman's journal. Ed H. Brooke et al. No 1, 10 Sept 1763–.

Every man's journal. Nos 1–5, 1765.

The public prompter and Irish journal. No 1, 1 Nov 1765–no 9, 22 Nov 1765.

The Dublin mercury. No 1, 18 March 1766–no 1,006, 1 April 1773.

The universal journalist. ?–1 June 1768–?

The Dublin spectator. Vol 1 no 38, 1 June 1768?

The publick journal. ?–no 208, 13 Feb 1771–no 214, 27 Feb 1771–? Continued as Peter Hoey's publick journal, ?–[1771]–?

The independent Irishman. –no 3, 16 Nov 1770–? Continued as Dublin evening post, ?–no 26, 11 Jan 1771–no 64, 8 April 1771–?

The Dublin evening packet. [1770]–no 102, 27 Nov 1770–no 192, 27 June 1771–?

The public monitor: or new Freeman's journal. [No 1, Sept? 1772]–?

The Hibernian journal: or chronicle of liberty [1771]– Vol 3 no 43, 9 April 1773–.

The public advertiser: or the theatrical chronicle. ?–vol 1 no 67, 14 Feb 1774–no 68, 16 Feb 1774–?

Mercure de France. No 1, April 1775–July 1775.

Stewart's Dublin weekly journal: or the universal intelligencer. ?– Vol 3 no 109, 27 April 1776–?

The independent chronicle and universal advertiser. No 1, 1 March 1777–no 33, 15 May 1777–?

Magee's weekly packet: or Hope's lottery journal of news, politics and literature. No 1, 21 June 1777–? Continued as Magee's weekly packet, ?–no 544, 19 April 1788–1795.

The Dublin evening journal. ?–Feb 1778–9 July 1778.

The Dublin evening post. ?–no 79, 4 Aug 1778–no 6,595, 30 Dec 1800–?

The general evening post. ?–[May 1781]–vol 1 no 107, 3 Jan 1782–vol 4 no 516, 31 July 1784–?

The new evening post. Vol 1 no 1, 15 Oct 1782–no 25, 10 Dec 1782–?

The volunteer's journal: or Irish herald. ?–no 2, 15 Oct 1783–no 170, 10 Nov 1784–?

The volunteer evening post. No 1, 11 Nov 1783–no 357, 18 Feb 1786–?

The evening chronicle. ?–no 50, 31 March 1784–?

The edile: or a review of the Dublin stage. Nos 1–5, Nov 1784.

M'Donnel's Dublin weekly journal. [1785]–vol 10 no 7, 14 Feb 1795–?

The evening herald: or general advertiser. ?–no 19, 17 May 1786–no 587, 31 Dec 1789–?

The Dublin chronicle. No 1, 3 May 1787–no 1040, 19 Dec 1793–?

The Dublin evening packet. ?–no 2, 8 May 1788–? Continued as The town: or Dublin evening packet, ?–no 80, 6 Nov 1788–[1794]–?

The Dublin packet: or weekly advertiser. ?–no 154, 10 May 1788–?

The rights of Irishmen: or national evening star. ?–10 Nov 1791–no 214, 21 March 1793–no 215, 23 March 1793–?

The morning post: or Dublin courant. ?–vol 1 no 42, 26 April 1788–[31 Dec 1798]–?

The Phenix: or Griffith's new morning post. ?–13 Nov 1789–8 Jan 1790–?

New Phoenix. ?–vol 1 no 59, 1791.

The national journal. ?–no 5, 4 April 1792–?

The morning star. ?–13 Feb 1793–no 180, 1794–?

The Freemason's journal: or Pasley's universal intelligencer. 1795–7.

The Hibernian telegraph: or morning star. ?–18 March 1795–no 322, 25 March 1795–.

The morning chronicle and public advertiser. ?–22 April 1796–[1799].

The Sunday gazette. [No 1, 3 June 1796]–? Probably continued as the Oracle: or Sunday gazette, ?–vol 2 no 3, 22 Oct 1797?

Carey's general evening post. ?–[22 April 1797]–?

The press. No 1, 28 Sept 1797–no 69, 13 March 1798.

The union star. Nos 1–2, 1798.

The torch: or a light to enlighten the nations of Europe. No 1, 1798.

The anti-union. No 1, 27 Dec 1798–no 32, 9 March 1799.

The storm: being a periodical paper. No 1, 1798.

The lantern. No 1, 26 Feb 1799–no 6, 9 March 1799.

The shamroc. Ed D. Taafe. ?–no 2, 8 Feb 1799–. Continued as Taaffee's national shamroc, no 5, 18 Feb 1799–no 10, 8 March 1799.

The constitution: or anti-union evening post. No 1, 9 Dec 1799–no 101, 31 July 1800–?

The detector. No 1, 30 Jan 1800–no 36, 20 May 1800–?

Athlone

The Athlone chronicle. [1770?]–vol 19 no 56, 16 July 1788–?

The Athlone herald. 1785–.

The Athlone sentinel. 1798–.

Belfast

The Belfast news-letter and general advertiser. No 1, 1 Sept 1737–. Continued as Belfast news-letter, 22 July 1769–.

The Belfast courant. ?–[31 Dec 1745]–19 July 1746–?

The Belfast mercury: or Freeman's chronicle and political repository. [Aug 1783]–vol 1 no 73, 9 April 1784–vol 3 no 63, 6 March 1786–? Continued as Belfast evening post, ?–Jun 1786–?

The northern star. No 1, 4 Jan 1792–19 May 1797. Bigger, F. J. The northern star. Ulster Jnl of Archaeology 1 Sept 1894.

Birr

The Birr weekly journal. [1774].

Carlow

The Carlow journal: or Leinster chronicle. ?–1773–?

Carrick-on-Suir

The Carrick recorder: or weekly collation. [1792].

Cashel

Lord's Munster herald: or general advertiser. No 1, 24 March 1788–31 Dec 1789–?

Clonmel

The Hibernian gazette: or universal advertiser. [1772?] –? Continued as Clonmel gazette: or Hibernian advertiser, ?–4 Oct 1781–vol 22 no 77, 22 Dec 1792– [Feb 1795]–?

The herald. [1800]–?

Cork

The idler. [No 1, 1 Feb 1715]–?

The free-holder. ?–no 24, 31 May 1716–?

Cork intelligence. ?–[13 March 1718]–?

The Cork news-letter. ?–[no 828, 1723]–1725–?

Welsh's impartial news-letter. ?–[18 Nov 1736]–?

The medley. [No 1, 16 Feb 1738]–[no 22, 15 July 1738]–?

The serio-jocular medley. ?–[19 April 1738]–?

The Cork journal. ?–[21 Jan 1746]–?

George Swiney's Corke journal. [1754]–31 Aug 1769–?

The Cork evening post. 1754–vol 19, no 66, 18 Aug 1774–25 Dec 1788–? Continued as the New Cork evening post, ?–1791–vol 7 no 67, 17 Aug 1797–23 Dec 1799–.

The Cork chronicle: or universal register. ?–vol 2 no 31, 10 Feb 1765–?

The Cork chronicle: or free intelligencer. ?–30 Sept 1768–vol 9 no 1, 2 Jan 1792–?

The Hibernian chronicle. 1768–vol 22 no 61, 2 Aug 1790–. Extracts pbd as Modern monitor: or Flynn's speculations, 1771.

The Hibernian morning post: or literary chronicle. 1776.

The Cork general advertiser. No 1, 10 Oct 1776–25 June 1778–?

The Cork journal. No 1, 4 June 1778–9 Nov 1778–? Continued as Cork weekly journal, ?–Jan 1779–21 Feb 1780–?

The volunteer journal: or independent gazetteer. ?–7 Nov 1782–vol 3 no 1, 1 Jan 1784–? Continued as John and Robert Baldwin's volunteer journal: or independent gazetteer, ?–vol 3 no 30, 12 April 1784–? Continued as John Baldwin's volunteer journal: or weekly advertizer, ?–vol 4 no 70, 2 Jan 1786–June 1787–?

The Cork gazette: and general advertiser. ?–no 185, 11 April 1792– 16 Sept 1797.

The Cork packet. No 1, 17 Jan 1793–?

The Cork courier. Vol 1 no 1, 23 July 1794–no 73, 1 April 1795–?

The Cork herald: or Munster advertiser. No 1, 10 Feb 1798–10 Jan 1799.

The harp of Erin. No 1, 7 March 1798–no 4, 17 March 1798–?

The Cork advertiser and commercial register. ?–no 75, 20 July 1799–.

Drogheda

The Drogheda journal: or Meath and Louth advertiser. ?–vol 15 no 1,378, 13 Dec 1778–vol 29 no 30, 15 April 1797–.

The Drogheda news letter. ?–April 1800–.

Ennis

The Clare journal. ?–vol 2 no 13, 15 Feb 1779–.

The Enniss chronicle and Clare advertiser. ?–vol 2 no 116, 14 Feb 1785–vol 17 no 1,758, 29 Dec 1800–.

Galway

Connaught journal: or Galway advertiser [subtitle varies]. No 1, 1754–. May be same paper as Martin Burke's Connaught journal, ?–vol 19 no?, 13 May 1779–.

Galway chronicle. ?–[1775]–?

Galway evening post. [1782]–[1791]–?

Kilkenny

Finn's Leinster journal. ?–[24 Jan 1767]–no 1,079, 21 May 1777–vol 28 no 2, 4 Jan 1794–? Continued as Leinster journal, ?–25 Dec 1799–.

Limerick

The Limerick news letter. ?–4 May 1716–?

The Limerick journal. ?–vol 3 no 46, 11 Aug 1741–vol 8 no 16, 19 May 1746–? Continued as Munster journal, ?–vol 11 no 15, 15 May 1749–vol 40 no 82, 13 Oct 1777–?

[Ferrar's] Limerick chronicle. ?–no 19, 13 Oct 1768–no 2,460, 28 March 1792–? Continued as Watson's Limerick chronicle, ?–no 3,023, 23 March 1793–no 3,144, 5 Nov 1794–? Continued as Limerick chronicle, ?–no 3,600, 7 Oct 1795–.

The Limerick journal. ?–23 April 1781–vol 20 no 3,121, 14 Aug 1799–?

The Limerick herald. [1787]. Perhaps continued as Limerick herald and Munster advertiser, ?–29 May 1788–19 Dec 1795–?

The Sligo morning herald. ?–29 May 1793–? Madden says ptd by J. O'Connor, Limerick.

Londonderry

The Londonderry journal and general advertiser. No 1, 3 June 1772–vol 19 no 1,488, 27 Dec 1791–? Continued as Londonderry journal and Donegal and Tyrone advertiser, ?–vol 21 no 1,546, 9 April 1793–.

Loughrea

The Connaught mercury: or universal register. ?–no 64, 24 May 1770–?

The Connaught gazette. No 1, 21 Aug 1797–no 26, 6 Nov 1797–?

Mullingar

The Westmeath journal. [1783]–.

Newry

The Newry journal. [1775]–[1777]–?

Gordon's merry chronicle and universal advertiser. [1795].

Roscrea

Roscrea southern star: or general advertiser. No 1, 19 Aug 1795–?

Sligo

The Sligo journal. [1771]–.

Strabane

The Strabane journal: or the general advertiser. [May 1771]–2 May 1785–.

The Strabane news-letter. ?–[May 1788]–?

Tralee

The Kerry evening post. [1774]–.

The Western mercury: or Kerry herald. [1793].

Tuam

The Connaught advertiser. [1774]–[1796]. Perhaps continued as the Western chronicle: or Connaught advertiser. ?–.

The Tuam gazette. [June or July 1799]–.

Waterford

The Waterford flying post. ?–21 Aug 1729–?

The Waterford news-letter. ?–[Jan 1742]–?

The Waterford journal. [1765]–[1771?].

The Waterford chronicle. [1765]–no 178, 1 Jan 1772–? Continued as Ramsay's Waterford chronicle, ?–no 1,899, 20 July 1787–.

The Munster packet: or general advertiser. No 1, 14 Jan 1788–.

The Waterford herald. No 1, 3 Feb 1791–no 907, 10 March 1796–?

Carey's Waterford packet. No 1, 20 Aug 1791–?

Wexford

The Wexford journal. ?–[1774]–?

The Wexford chronicle. 1782–16 Aug 1784–?

The Wexford herald. [1788]–vol 2 no 55, Dec? 1799–.

L. PERIODICALS IN WELSH

Chester

Y geirgrawn. No 1, Feb 1796–July 1796–?

Carmarthen

Trysorfa gwybodaeth, neu yr eurgrawn Cymraeg. Ed J. Rees. No 1, 3 March 1770–no 15, 15 Sept 1770.

Holyhead

Tlysau yr hen oesoedd. Ed L. Morris. No 1, 1735.

Mold

Trysorfa ysprydol. No 1, April 1799–no 6, July 1800.

M. CHANNEL ISLES

St Helier

Magazin de l'Ile de Jersey. 1784–?

Gazette de l'Ile de Jersey. Vol 1 no 1, 5 Aug 1786–.

St Peter Port

Gazette de Guernsey. Vol 1 no 1, Jan 1791–.

R. M. W.

III. TRAVEL

BIBLIOGRAPHIES

Manwaring, G. E. A bibliography of British naval history. 1929.

Cox, E. G. A reference guide to the literature of travel [in English]. 3 vols Seattle 1935–49. This lists with descriptions and bibliography the travel narratives pbd in English of travellers of all nations before 1800: vol 1, The Old World; 2, The New World; 3, Britain.

An annual bibliography of studies and edns of travel literature of geographical interest was included in the Histoire de géographie section of the Bibliographie géographique internationale, originally called, from 1893, vols 1–22, Annales de géographie; from 1913 to 1930, vols 23–40, Bibliographie géographique. The historical section is omitted since vol 70 1964.

COLLECTIONS AND HISTORIES

Regional collections are listed under appropriate sections below.

Evelyn, John. Navigations and commerce, their original and progress: containing a succinct account of traffick in general, of discoveries, wars and conflicts at sea, with special regard to the English nation. 1674; rptd in his Miscellaneous writings, 1825; rptd in J. R. McCulloch, A select collection of scarce and valuable tracts on commerce, 1859.

Ray, John (ed). A collection of curious travels and voyages, in two tomes: the first, Dr Leonhart Rauwolff's itinerary into the eastern countries, as Syria etc; the second taking in many parts of Greece, Asia Minor etc, from the observations of Mr Belon [to] Thevenot's collections. 2 vols 1693, 1705, 1738.

An account of the several late voyages and discoveries to the south and north by Sir John Narborough [to the South-sea 1669], Captain Jasmen Tasman [to the south Terra Incognita (Australia) 1642], Captain Wood [to Nova Zembla 1676] and Frederick Marten [to Spitsbergen and Greenland 1671]. 1694, 1711.

Hacke, William (ed). A collection or original voyages: i, Capt [Ambrose] Cowley's voyage round the globe [1683]; ii, Capt [Bartholomew] Sharp's journey over the Isthmus of Darien [1679]; iii, Captain [John] Wood's voyage through the Streights of Magellan [1669]; iv, Mr — Roberts' adventures among the corsairs of the Levant. 1699; rptd in William Dampier, A collection of voyages vol 4, 1729; *see* below.

Commelin, Isaak. A collection of voyages undertaken by the Dutch East India Company, with an account of several attempts to find out the North East Passage, and their discoveries in the East Indies and the South Seas: translations from the French version by Constantin de Renneville of the Dutch original [1646]. 1703.

Churchill, Awnsham and John. A collection of voyages and travels, some now first printed, others translated and now first publish'd in English, some few reprinted. 4 vols 1704, 6 vols 1732 (expanded), 1744–6, 8 vols 1752 (with Thomas Osborne collection, 1745, below). Originally 26 narratives, many extensive, of travels to all parts of the world; the new vols 5–6 added 13 more narratives and 2 historical surveys.

Harris, John (ed). Navigantium atque itinerantium bibliotheca: a complete collection of voyages and travels, consisting of above 400 writers. 2 vols 1705; rev John Campbell 1715, 1744; again as by Harris, 1744–8, 1764. Digests of pbd narratives arranged to form a history of European travel to Africa and the Indies, to Russia and China, to the Americas etc. The enlarged edn adds some later narratives, also in digest.

Du Perier, M. A general history of all voyages and travels. 1708. *See under* Voyages to America, *below*.

Miscellanea curiosa: a collection of some of the principal Phaenomena in nature. Vol III, containing a collection of curious travels, voyages and natural histories of countries, as they have been delivered in to the Royal Society. 1708, 1726. 15 recent narratives or observations, mostly in Europe and Asia, mostly brief.

[Stevens, John (editor-translator)]. A new collection of voyages and travels, with historical accounts of the discoveries, none before printed in English. 2 vols 1708–10, 1711. 7 narratives of some size and importance, apparently pbd separately, and here assembled with original separate pagination.

The travels of several learned missioners of the Society of Jesus into divers parts of the Archipelago, India, China and America: translation from French [1713]. 1714. Compiled from the annual missionary letters.

A collection of voyages: containing i, Captain William Dampier's voyage round the world [pbd 1697]; ii, The voyages of Lionel Wafer and his being left on the Isthmus of America among the Indians [pbd 1699]; iii, A

voyage round the world of Captain Dampier, by William Funnell, Mate [pbd 1707]; iv–vii, ed William Hacke as A collection, 1699, above; 4 vols 1729, 2 vols 1776 (rearranged chronologically).

Barclay, Patrick. The universal traveller: or a complete account of the most remarkable voyages and travels of our own and other nations to the present time. 1735, Dublin 1735.

A collection of voyages and travels [rptd]: i, Captain Thomas James to the Northwest Passage [pbd 1633, rptd in Churchill vol 2, 1704]; ii, Pontis' voyage to America, also the taking of Carthagena by the French in 1697 [pbd 1698]; iii, Daniel Coxe, A description of Carolina [pbd 1722], 1741.

The curious traveller: being a choice collection of remarkable histories, voyages, travels. 1742. Curiosities only.

Lockman, John. Travels of the Jesuits into various parts of the world, compiled from their letters. 2 vols 1743, 1762 (with An account of the Spanish settlements in America).

Campbell, John. Lives of the Admirals and other eminent British seamen, with a new and accurate naval history from the earliest time. 4 vols 1742–4, 1750, 1761, 1779, 1781, 1785, 8 vols 1812–17; condensed 1849 etc.

Osborne, Thomas (ed). A collection of voyages and travels of authentic writers in our own tongue, compiled from the library of the late Earl of Oxford. 2 vols 1745; rptd 1752 as vols 7–8 of the A. and J. Churchill collection, 1704 above. Most of the 38 items were pbd before 1660. In addn to this collection, 24 travel items are scattered through the 8 vols of the Harleian Miscellany 1744–6, which is a collection of reprints of pamphlets from the same library, largely pre-1660.

Astley, Thomas. A new general collection of voyages and travels. 4 vols 1745–7. Largely abstracts, ed Thomas Green for the publisher Astley. The work was the basis of the French collection by the Abbé Prévost d'Exiles, Histoire générale des voyages, 18 vols 1746–68, and was used for the German collection, ed J. J. Schwabe as Allgemeine Historie der Reisen, 21 vols 1747–74.

Osorio da Fonseca, Jeronimo. The history of the Portuguese during the reign of Emmanuel [1495–1521], containing all their discoveries from the coast of Affrick to the farthest parts of China: translation from Latin [of 1571] by James Gibbs. 2 vols 1752.

A new universal history of voyages and travels, everything worthy of observation in the four quarters of the globe. 3 vols 1754.

Barrow, John. A chronological abridgement or history of discoveries by Europeans in different parts of the world. 3 vols 1756, 1764–5 (as A collection of authentic, useful and entertaining voyages and discoveries), 1783; tr French, 1766; German, 1767.

Smollett, Tobias. A compendium of authentic and entertaining voyages digested in a chronological series. 7 vols 1756, 1766, 9 vols 1784.

A compendium of the most approved modern travels. 4 vols 1757 (pbd for J. Scott). Recent travels to Europe and the Middle East, largely British, rptd.

Newbery, John. The world displayed: or a curious collection of voyages and travels. 20 vols 1759–61, 1760, 1767, 1774–8, 1790; tr German, 1764.

The naval chronicle: or voyages, travels, exploits of English navigators and commanders to 1759. 1760.

A new and complete collection of voyages and travels, comprising whatever is valuable in this kind. 1760.

Derrick, Samuel. A collection of travels through various parts of the world. 2 vols 1762.

Knox, John. A new collection of voyages, discoveries and travels, containing whatever is worthy of notice in Europe, Asia, Africa and America, consisting of such foreign authors as are in most esteem. 7 vols 1765–7. Mostly abstracts.

Drake, Edward Cavendish. A new universal collection of authentic and entertaining voyages and travels from the earliest accounts to the present time. 1768, 1770, 1771.

The modern traveller: being a collection of useful and entertaining travels lately made into various countries, the whole carefully abridged. 6 vols 1776–7 (pbd by Thomas Lowndes). Mainly on Europe and Asia.

Moore, John Hamilton. A new and complete collection of voyages and travels describing Europe, Asia, Africa and America. 1778, 2 vols 1785. A compilation, though with much direct quotation.

Adams, John. The flower of modern travels: being elegant, entertaining and instructive extracts. 1788, Boston 1797.

Richardson, W. (publisher). A general collection of voyages and discoveries made by the Portuguese and Spaniards during the fifteenth and sixteenth centuries. 1789.

Curious and entertaining voyages undertaken either for discovery, conquest, or the benefit of trade, commencing with Prince Henry of Portugal and 58 different Portuguese and Spanish voyages. 1790.

An interesting account of the early voyages made by the Portuguese and Spaniards to Africa, East and West Indies. 1790.

Mavor, William. An historical account of voyages, travels and discoveries from the time of Columbus to the present. 26 vols 1796–1802, 28 vols 1810, 1813–15. A compilation.

Pinkerton, John. A general collection of the best and most interesting voyages and travels in all parts of the world. 17 vols 1808–14. The most ambitious collection, reprints with much abridgement: vols 1–6, Europe; 7–11, Asia; 12–14, America; 15–16, Africa; 17, history and bibliography; some 140 items altogether, many of great length.

GENERAL STUDIES

Beazley, C. R. Exploration 1642–1742, 1742–84, 1784–1802. In H. D. Traill, Social England vol 5, 1896.

Clowes, W. L. The Royal Navy: a history. Vols 2–4, 1897–1903.

Heawood, E. A history of geographical discovery in the seventeenth and eighteenth centuries. Cambridge 1912.

Kirkpatrick, F. A. The literature of travel 1700–1900. CHEL 14 1917.

Rose, J. H. Sea power and expansion 1660–1763. In The Cambridge history of the British Empire vol 1, Cambridge 1928.

Baker, J. N. L. A history of geographical discovery and exploration. 1931.

Williamson, J. A. Exploration and discovery. In Johnson's England, ed A. S. Turberville vol 1, Oxford 1933.

Brown, W. C. English travel books 1775–1825. PQ 16 1937.

Dilke, O. A. W. The English literature of exploration in the eighteenth century. Mariner's Mirror 32 1946.

Charliat, Pierre-Jacques. Le temps des grands voiliers [17th–18th centuries]. Vol 3 of L.-H. Paris (ed), Histoire universelle des explorations, Paris 1955.

Adams, P. G. Travelers and travel liars 1660–1800. Berkeley 1962.

Fussell, P., jr. Patrick Brydone: the eighteenth-century traveler as representative man. BNYPL June 1962.

Bissell, B. The American Indian in English literature of the eighteenth century. New Haven 1925.

Lowes, J. L. The road to Xanadu: a study in the ways of the imagination. Boston 1927, 1930 (rev).

Fairchild, H. N. The noble savage: a study in romantic naturalism. New York 1928.

Eugenia, Sr. Coleridge's scheme of pantisocracy and American travel accounts. PMLA 45 1930.

Frantz, R. W. Swift's Yahoos and the voyagers. MP 29 1931.

— The English traveller and the movement of ideas 1660–1732. Lincoln Nebraska 1934.

Watson, H. F. The sailor in English fiction and drama 1550–1800. New York 1931.

Bonner, W. H. Captain William Dampier. Stanford 1934. Chs on the influence of travel literature on Defoe and Swift.

Aubin, R. A. Topographical poetry in eighteenth-century England. New York 1936.

Hauser, S. Die Entwicklung der Landschaftsschau in der englischen Reiseliteratur [1700–1850]. Thayngen 1937.

Moore, J. R. Defoe in the pillory and other studies. Indiana Univ Pbns, Humanities ser 1 1939. Authoritative studies of pseudo-narratives of travel now assigned to Defoe.

— Defoe's sources for Robert Drury's Journal. Ibid 9 1943.

Gove, P. B. The imaginary voyage in prose fiction: a history of its criticism and a guide to its study, [listing] 215 imaginary voyages 1700 to 1800. New York 1941.

Appleton, W. W. A cycle of Cathay: the Chinese vogue in England during the seventeenth and eighteenth centuries. New York 1951.

Coe, C. N. Wordsworth and the literature of travel. New York 1953.

Parks, G. B. The turn to the romantic in the travel literature of the eighteenth century. MLQ 25 1964.

Literary Influences of Travel

Woolley, M. E. The development of the love of romantic scenery in America. Amer Historical Rev 3 1898.

Cooper, Lane. Wordsworth's sources. Athenaeum 22 April 1905.

— A glance at Wordsworth's reading. MLN 22 1907.

Tinker, C. B. Nature's simple plan: a phase of radical thought in the mid-eighteenth century. Princeton 1922.

Secord, A. W. Studies in the narrative method of Defoe. Univ of Illinois Stud 9 1924.

(1) GENERAL

Barlow, Edward. Journal of his life at sea in King's ships, East and West India-men and other merchantmen from 1659 to 1703. Ed B. Lubbock 2 vols 1934 (with Barlow's drawings). Voyages in home waters, the Mediterranean, East and West Indies.

Roch, Capt Jeremy. Journals of some remarkable [naval] voyages and adventures at sea [1665–1700]. Ed B. S. Ingram 1936 (in Three sea journals of Stuart times).

F., R., esq. A true and faithfull account of what was observed in ten years travells into the principal places of Europe, Asia etc. 1665.

Fox, George. A journal or historical account of the life, travels, sufferings. Ed Thomas Ellwood, preface by William Penn, vol 1 1694 etc; ed N. Penney 1921 (from ms). The travels were mostly in England, from 1647, but included a voyage to the West Indies 1671–2, and journeys to Holland and Germany in 1677, and to Holland in 1681.

— The short journal. Ed N. Penney 1925.

— Journal 1694–8. Ed J. L. Nickalls, Cambridge 1952.

Struys, Jans (properly Jans Janszoon Strauss). The voiages and travels through Italy, Greece, Muscovy, Tartary,

Media, Persia, East-India, Japan and other countries in Europe, Africa and Asia [1647–72], translated from Dutch by John Morrison. 1684.

Martin, Capt Stephen. Life 1666–1740. Ed C. R. Markham 1895 (Navy Records Soc). Voyages 1686–1714 in home and Mediterranean waters, with one voyage to Newfoundland.

Mocquet, John. Travels and voyages [from 1611] into Africa, Asia and America, the East and West-Indies, Syria, Jerusalem and the Holy Land, translated from French [of 1617] by Nathaniel Pullen. 1696.

C., T. The new atlas: or travels or voyages in Europe, Asia, Africa and America, from England to the Dardanelles, thence to Aegypt, Palestine, Syria, Mesopotamia, Chaldea, Persia, East India, China, Tartary, Muscovy and Poland. 1699. A compilation.

Cremer, Capt John. Ramblin' Jack, the Journal 1700–74. Ed R. R. Bellamy 1936. Voyages in European and Mediterranean waters.

Rogers, Francis. The diary of a London merchant kept on his voyages to the East Indies, the West Indies and elsewhere 1703 and 1704. Ed B. S. Ingram 1936 (in Three sea journals of Stuart times).

Roberts, Capt George. Four years voyages to Africa and Barbadoes. 1726; ed A. W. Lawrence 1930. Ascribed to Defoe.

Uring, Capt Nathaniel. A history of the voyages and travels [in Europe and America], with new draughts of the Bay of Honduras. 1726, 1727, 1739, 1745, 1749; ed A. Dewar 1928.

Atkins, John. A voyage to Guinea, Brazil and the West-Indies in his Majesty's ships. 1735.

Wesley, John. Journals [1735–90]. 4 vols 1827 etc; ed N. Curnock 8 vols 1909–16 (from ms). In the American colonies 1735–8, Germany 1738, Ireland from 1747, Scotland from 1751, and in England throughout.

Thompson, Charles. The travels: containing his observations on France, Italy, Turkey in Europe, the Holy Land, Arabia, Egypt and many other parts of the world. 3 vols Reading 1744, 4 vols Dublin 1744, 3 vols 1748, 2 vols 1754, 1767.

Lambert, Abbé. Curious observations upon the manners, customs of the nations of Asia, Africa and America, translated from French by John Dunn. 1751, 1755, 1760.

Holme, Benjamin. An account of his life and travels in the work of the ministry through several parts of Europe and America. In A collection of the epistles and works, 1753, 1754. Especially in America 1715–20, chs 4–5.

Houston, James, MD. The works, containing memoirs of his life and travels in Asia, Africa, America and most parts of Europe, giving a particular account of the Scottish expedition to Darien in America. 1753.

Drummond, Alexander. Travels through different cities of Germany, Italy, Greece and several parts of Asia as far as the Euphrates. 1754.

Thompson, Thomas. An account of two missionary voyages, the one to New Jersey, the other from North America to Guiney. 1758.

Walker, Commodore George. The voyages and cruises during the late Spanish and French wars. 2 vols 1760, Dublin 1762; ed H. S. Vaughan 1928. Privateering voyages.

Kelly, Samuel. An eighteenth-century seaman, whose days [1764–95] have been few and evil: an autobiography. Ed C. Garstin 1925.

Thompson, Lieut Edward. Sailor's letters written during his voyages in Europe, Asia, Africa and America, in 1754–9. 1766, 2 vols 1767.

Le Poivre, M. The travels of a philosopher: or observations on manners and arts of various nations in Africa and Asia, translated from French. 1769, 1769, Glasgow 1770, Dublin 1770.

Robertson, Robert. A physical journal during three voyages to Africa and the West Indies. 1777.

Pasley, Admiral Sir Thomas. Private sea journals 1778–82. Ed R. M. S. Pasley 1931.

Bruce, Peter Henry. Memoirs of a military officer in the services of Prussia, Russia and Great Britain: his travels in Germany, Russia, Tartary, Turkey, the West Indies etc. 1782, Dublin 1783.

MacIntosh, W. Travels in Europe, Asia and Africa: containing various remarks on the commercial interests of Great Britain. 2 vols 1782.

The polite traveller: being a modern view of part of Germany, France, Italy, Spain, Portugal and Africa, Russia, Turkey and Asia, and of the thirteen United States of America. 4 vols 1783.

Jardine, Lieut-Col Alexander. Letters from Barbary, France, Spain and Portugal. 2 vols 1788, Dublin 1789, London 1790, 1793, 1794; tr German, 1790.

Equiano, Olaudah. The interesting narrative of the life of Olaudah Equiaino or Gustavus Vassa the African [in Africa, America and England]. 2 vols 1789, 1789, 1790, New York 1791, London 1793 (6th edn), 1793, Norwich 1795, Belper 1809, Halifax 1814, Leeds 1814, London 1963 (as Equino's travels).

Macdonald, John. Travels in various parts of Europe, Asia and Africa during thirty years [1745–79], at first as a footman. 1790; ed J. Beresford 1927.

Stewart, John. Travels over the most interesting parts of the globe to discover the source of moral motion. 1792. Travels between England and India, part on foot.

Bisani, Alessandro. A picturesque tour through part of Europe, Africa and Asia, with remarks on the present state of society, remains of ancient edifices. 1793; French version (as Lettres sur divers endroits parcourus en 1788 et 1789), presumably the original, rptd London 1799.

Thunberg, Carl P. Travels in Europe, Africa and Asia [especially Japan] 1770–9, translated from Swedish. 3 vols 1793, 4 vols 1795 (adding Journies into Caffraria). The Caffraria (South Africa) portion rptd in John Pinkerton, A collection vol 16, 1814. Vol 1, southern Europe and Cape of Good Hope; vol 2, South Africa, Java; vol 3, Japan.

Thomson, Alexander, MD. Letters of a traveller on the various countries of Europe, Asia and Africa. 1798.

Macpherson, Charles. Memoirs of his life and travels in Asia, Africa and America, written chiefly between 1773 and 1790. Edinburgh 1800.

Moore, Mordaunt. Sketches of life, characters and manners in various countries. 3 vols 1800.

(2) BRITISH ISLES

Bibliographies

Anderson, J. P. The book of British topography: a classified catalogue of the topographical works in the library of the British Museum. 1881.

Mitchell, A. A list of travels and tours in Scotland 1296–1900. Proc Soc Antiquaries of Scotland 35, 39, 44 1902–10.

—— and C. G. Cash. A contribution to the bibliography of Scottish topography. Pbns of Scottish Historical Soc 2nd ser 14–15 1917.

Humphreys, A. L. A handbook of county bibliography: being a bibliography of bibliographies relating to the counties and towns of Great Britain and Ireland. 1917.

Fordham, H. G. The road-books and itineraries of Ireland. Dublin 1923.

—— The road-books and itineraries of Great Britain 1570–1850. Cambridge 1924.

—— The road-books of Wales. Cambridge 1927.

Chubb, T. The printed maps in the atlases of Great Britain and Ireland: a bibliography 1579–1870. 1927.

Fussell, C. E. Travel and topography in seventeenth-century England: a bibliography of sources for social and economic history. Library 4th ser 13 1932.

—— The exploration of England: a select bibliography of travel and topography 1570–1815. 1935.

Cox, E. G. A reference guide to the literature of travel. Vol 3, Great Britain. Seattle 1949. Vol 4, to be devoted to Ireland, was not pbd.

Robson-Scott, W. D. German travellers in England 1400–1800. Oxford 1953. With extensive bibliography.

Collections

Mavor, W. The British tourist: or traveller's pocket companion. 5 vols 1799, 6 vols 1800. Reprints of extracts.

Pinkerton, J. A collection of voyages and travels. Vol 2, 1808 (travels in England); vol 3, 1809 (travels in Scotland and Ireland).

Brown, P. H. Early travellers in Scotland [1265–1689]. Edinburgh 1891.

—— Scotland before 1700 from contemporary documents. Edinburgh 1893.

§ I

The Cox bibliography, above, makes it unnecessary to list here either the innumerable local descriptions of places or the extensive geographical studies included. This list includes genuine travels, and descriptions resulting from travels, beyond the boundaries of a single city or county; but it does not include the numerous guide-books or the collections of prints of the later eighteenth century, for which see Cox.

Mundy, Peter. Travels in south-west England and western India, with a diary of events in London 1658–63, and in Penryn 1664–7. Vol 5 of Travels, ed R. C. Temple and L. M. Anstey 1936 (Hakluyt Soc).

Browne, Edward. Journal of a tour into Derbyshire in 1662. In Works of Sir Thomas Browne vol 1, Norwich 1836.

Mandelslo, J. Albert de. [His reception in England on return from India 1639–40]. In Voyages and travels into the East Indies, translated by John Davies of Kidwelly, 1662.

Sorbière, Samuel de. [Relation d'un voyage en Angleterre, où sont touchées plusieurs choses qui regardent l'estat des sciences et de la religion. Paris 1664 etc]; tr as A voyage to England, 1709. The book at once called forth the protest: Thomas Sprat, Observations on Monsieur de Sorbier's Voyage into England, 1665, 1668, 1672, 1677, rptd in 1709 trn. It also provoked the humorous reply: Samuel de Sorbière, A journey to London in the year 1698, 1698, written by Dr William King, below.

Magalotti, Lorenzo. Travels of Cosmo the Third, Grand Duke of Tuscany, through England [in 1668]. 1821. Trn of part of Italian ms.

Jorevin de Rocheford. Description of England and Ireland [1668]. In F. Grose, Antiquarian repertory vol 4, 1809.

[Mercer, William]. The moderate cavalier: or the soldier's description of Ireland. [Cork?] 1675.

Ogilby, John. Britannia: or an illustration of the Kingdom of England and Dominion of Wales [with maps and road-maps]. 1675, 1675, 1698, 1720 (enlarged as Britannia depicta: or Ogilby improv'd), 1724, 1736, 1750, 1764; Amsterdam 1969 (facs of first edn); numerous reprints also of the epitome or road-book. *See* H. G. Fordham, John Ogilby his Britannia, Library 4th ser 6 1926.

An account of a tour in Scotland 1677. Ed J. Hunter in Diary of Ralph Thoresby, appendix, 1830; ed P. H. Brown with Kirk, below.

Englands Remarques, giving an exact account of the several shires, counties and islands. 1678, 1682.

Kirk, Thomas. A modern account of Scotland by an English gentleman. 1679, 1699; rptd in Cleveland, The rebel Scot, [c. 1720]; in Harleian Miscellany vol 7, 1746; ed P. H. Brown, Tours in Scotland 1677 and 1681, Edinburgh 1892 (with Account, above).

—— Journeyings through Northumberland and Durham 1677. In Reprints of rare tracts and imprints of ancient mss, Newcastle 1847.

Baskerville, Thomas. Journeys in England [from 1681]. In Portland mss vol 2, 1893 (Historical Manuscripts Commission).

Dineley, Thomas. Observations in a voyage through the Kingdom of Ireland in 1681. Ed J. Graves, Kilkenny Archaeological Jnl 1870.

—— The official progress of Henry Duke of Beaufort through Wales in 1684. Ed C. Baker 1864; facs edn of ms, 1888.

Thoresby, Ralph. Travel in Scotland in 1681. Ed J. Hunter in Diary of Ralph Thoresby, 1830; ed P. H. Brown 1891.

—— The wayfarings in the north of England. Ed J. Hunter, with above.

R[ichard], W[illiam]. Wallography, or the Briton described: being a pleasant relation of a journey into Wales. 1682, 1753 (as Dean Swift's ghost); rptd in Reprints of rare tracts and imprints of ancient mss, Newcastle 1845.

Wheeler, Adam. Iter bellicosum, Adam Wheeler his account of 1685. Ed H. E. Malden 1910 (Camden Soc Miscellany). On Monmouth rebellion.

Fiennes, Celia. The Diary [including travels in England 1685–1703]. Ed as Through England on a side-saddle, 1888 (from ms); ed C. Morris as Journeys, 1947, 1949.

Davies, Rev Rowland, Dean of Cork. The journal 1688–91 [of his travels in England and Ireland during the Revolution]. Ed R. Caulfield 1857 (Camden Soc).

Stevens, John. The journal: containing a brief account of the war in Ireland 1689–91. Ed R. H. Muncey, Oxford 1912.

Eachard, Laurence. An exact description of Ireland. 1691.

Lewkenor, John. Metellus his dialogues: the first part, containing a description of a journey to Tunbridge-Wells; also a description of the wells and place. 1693.

Fox, George. A journal or historical account of the life, travels, sufferings, Christian experience and labours of love in the work of the ministry. 1694 etc; ed N. Penney and T. E. Harvey 2 vols 1911 (from ms); with later abridgements; rev J. L. Nickalls, Cambridge 1952. The travels in England begin c. 1643; other travels to Scotland, 1657; Ireland, 1659; West Indies and North America, 1671–2; Holland, 1677, 1684.

—— Itinerary journals. Ed N. Penney (with Short journal) 1925. Travels in and about London after 1681.

Franck, Richard. Northern memoirs: wherein the cities, citadels, sea-ports, castles, forts, fortresses, rivers and rivulets are compendiously described. 1694; ed W. Scott 1821; ed P. H. Brown, Early travellers in Scotland, 1891.

Brome, Rev James. An historical account of Mr Rogers's three years travels over England and Wales; giving a true and exact description of all the chiefest cities, towns and corporations etc. 1694 (anon), 1697, 1700 (signed, and as Travels over England, Scotland and Wales), 1707, 1726; ed P. H. Brown, Edinburgh 1892.

King, Dr William. A journey to London 1798. 1698, 1699, 1704. Ostensibly by Sorbière, 1664 above.

—— A journey to England, with some account of the manners and customs of that nation. 1700.

Martin, Martin. A late voyage to St Kilda, the remotest of the Hebrides. 1698, 1716, 1749, 1753, 1774; in Miscellanea scotica vol 2, Glasgow 1818; ed D. J. Macleod, Stirling 1935.

—— A description of the western isles of Scotland, with a brief description of the isles of Orkney and Shetland. 1703, 1716; rptd in Pinkerton vol 3, 1808; Glasgow 1884; ed D. J. Macleod 1935 (with preceding).

Dunton, John. An account of Ireland. 1699.

A journey to Scotland, giving a character of that country, the people and their manners, by an English gentleman. 1699.

[Ward, Edward]. A trip to Ireland. 1699; rptd in Five travel scripts, New York 1933 (facs).

Haydock, Roger. A collection of the Christian writings, labours, travels and sufferings of Roger Haydock. 1700. Travels in Scotland and Ireland 1680.

Brand, John. A brief description of Orkney, Zetland, Pightland, Firth and Caithness, with a short journal of the author's voyage thither. Edinburgh 1701, London 1703; rptd in Pinkerton vol 3, 1808; Edinburgh 1883.

The new description and state of England: containing the [53] mapps of the counties of England and Wales. 1701.

Sacheverell, William. An account of the Isle of Man, with a voyage to I-Columb-kill. 1701, 1702; ed J. G. Cumming, Pbns Manx Soc 1 1859.

Morer, Rev Thomas. A short account of Scotland. 1702, 1706, 1715.

Adair, John. The description of the sea coast and islands of Scotland, with large and exact maps for the use of seamen. Edinburgh 1703.

The North of England and Scotland in 1704. Edinburgh 1818.

Taylor, Joseph. A journey to Edenborough in Scotland 1705. Ed W. Cowan, Edinburgh 1903.

Dunois, Countess of [for D'Aulnoy, Marie Catherine La Mothe, comtesse]. Memoirs of the Court of England, translated by J.C. from French. 1707, 1708; tr Mrs W. H. Arthur, ed G. D. Gilbert, as Memoirs of the Court of England in 1675, 1913, 1927. Fiction.

An account of a journey from Lancashire into Scotland. GM April 1766.

K., T. Account of a journey through North Wales. GM Dec 1767.

Nouveau théâtre de la Grande Bretagne. 1708 (with 80 engravings); Supplément, 5 vols 1720-9; tr as Britannia illustrata: or views of the royal palaces as also of the principal seats of the nobility and gentry, 2 vols 1720-40.

Calamy, Rev Edmund. [A visit to Scotland 1709, and to the west of England 1713]. In An historical account of my own life, ed J. T. Rutt 2 vols 1829.

Molyneux, T. Journey to Connacht. 1709; rptd Irish Archaeological Soc Miscellany 50 1846.

Sorbière, Samuel de. A voyage to England, translated from French. 1709. See 1664, above.

Davies, Richard. An account of the convincement, exercises, services and travels [especially] in North Wales. 1710, 1765, Philadelphia 1771, London 1790, 1794, 1825, 1844, 1849, Newtown 1928; tr Welsh, 1840.

Smith, J. E. A tour to Hafod. 1710.

Von Uffenbach, Zacharias Conrad. [The travels in Germany, Holland and England 1702-10]. Pbd as Merkwürdige Reisen, 3 vols Frankfurt, Leipzig and Ulm 1753-4. Part of the English travels pbd in trn as follows: Cambridge under Queen Anne, ed and tr J. E. B. Mayor, Cambridge 1911; Oxford in 1710, ed W. H. and W. J. C. Quarrell 1928; London in 1710, tr and ed W. H. Quarrell and M. Mare 1934.

Erndtel, Christian Heinrich. The relation of a journey into England and Holland in 1706 and 1707 by a Saxon physician, translated from Latin [of 1710]. 1711.

Chancel, A. D. A new journey over Europe, from France thro' Savoy, Switzerland, Germany, Great Britain and Ireland. 1714.

Macky, John. A journey through England in familiar letters to a friend abroad. 2 vols 1714, 1722-3, 3 vols 1723-4 (with Journey through Scotland, below), 1732.

— A journey through Scotland. 1723, 1724 (with preceding), 1729.

Misson de Valbourg, Henri. Memoirs and observations in his travels over England, with some account of Scotland and Ireland, translated from French [1698] by John Ozell. 1719.

Cox, Thomas, and Anthony Hall. Magna Britannia et Hibernia, antiqua et nova. 6 vols 1720-31. Based on Camden's Britannia, 1586.

Gratton, John. A journal of the life of that ancient servant of Christ, of his labours, travels and sufferings. 1720, 1779, 1795, Stockport 1823.

Harley, Edward Lord (later Earl of Oxford). Journies and tours in the eastern counties [1723-38]. Historical Manuscripts Commission Portland Mss vol 6, 1901.

La Mottraye, Aubry de. Travels through Europe, Asia and into part of Africa, translated from French. 3 vols 1723-32, rptd 1732. See General Travels. Includes travels in England.

Defoe, Daniel. A tour thro' the whole island of Great Britain. 3 vols 1724-7, 1738, 4 vols 1742, 1748, 1753, 1755, 1762, 1769, 1778; ed G. D. H. Cole 2 vols 1928 (from 1724-7).

Moll, Herman. A new description of England and Wales, with a new set of maps of each country. 1724, 1736, 1739, 1753.

Stukeley, Dr William. Itinerarium curiosum: or an account of the antiquitys and remarkable curiositys in nature and art observ'd in travels thro' Great Britain. Centuria I, 1724; 1776 (with Centuria II).

Saussure, César de. A foreign view of England in the reigns of George I and George II [1726-9 and 1738], translated from French by Madame van Muyden. 1902. A number of letters.

Gordon, Alexander. Itinerarium septentrionale: or a journey through most of the counties of Scotland and those in the north of England. 1726, 1732 (with addns); tr Latin, 1731.

Muralt, Beat Louis de. Letters describing the character and customs of the English and French nation, translated from French [of 1725]. 1726, 1726.

Buchan, Alexander. A description of St Kilda, the most remote western isle of Scotland. Edinburgh 1727, 1741, 1752, 1774; rptd in Miscellanea scotica, Glasgow 1818.

Prévost, Antoine François. Adventures of a man of quality, translated from French [of 1729] by Mysie E. I. Robertson. 1930. Vol 5 of the Mémoires et aventures, dealing with life in London.

Careri, John Francesco Gemelli. Travels through Europe, in Churchill, A collection vol 6, 1732. Includes England.

A curious and diverting journey through the whole island of Great Britain. 1734.

A journey from London to Scarborough, with an account of the nature and use of the Scarborough Spaw-water. 1734.

Voltaire, François Arouet de. Letters concerning the English nation (Lettres philosophiques), translated from French by John Lockman. 1733, Dublin 1733, London 1735, Dublin 1735, London 1741, Glasgow 1752, 1759, London 1760, 1767, 1889 (Cassell's Nat Lib), 1910 (Harvard Classics); ed C. Whibley 1926. See A. Ballantyre, Voltaire's visit to England 1726-9, 1919; and D. Flower (ed), Voltaire's England, 1950 (selections from Letters and other works).

Wesley, John. Journals. Ed N. Curnock 8 vols 1909-16, 1938. Records countless journeys in Great Britain from 1735, Ireland from 1747, Scotland 1751. Numerous extracts from the journals were pbd in 18th century; a 4-vol edn was pbd in 1827 etc.

Pöllnitz, Karl Ludwig, Baron von. The memoirs: being the observations in his late travels from Prussia through Germany, Italy, France, Flanders, Holland, England, translated from French [of 1734]. 4 vols 1737, 5 vols 1739, 1745. See Travels on the Continent, below. He was in England in 1721.

Torbuck, John (ed). A collection of Welsh travels and memoirs of Wales. 1738, 1742, Dublin 1743, London 1749, 1752, 3 vols 1764-7.

A journey to Llandrindod Wells in Radnorshire, with a particular description of those wells. 1744, 1746.

Carew, Bampfylde-Moore. The life and adventures of the noted Devonshire stroller and dog-stealer as related by himself. Exeter 1745. *See* Robert Goadby, printer, An apology for the life of Mr Carew, as taken from his own mouth. [1749], [1750], [1760?], [c. 1760], 1768, 1775, 1779, [1785?], 1788, 1798, 1804, 1811, 1812, 1813 etc, also in chap-books; ed C. H. Wilkinson as The King of the Beggars, Oxford 1931.

Gonzalez, Don Manoel. The voyage of Don Manoel (late merchant) of the city of Lisbon to Great Britain, translated from Portuguese ms, in Osborne, A collection of voyages vol 1, 1745; rptd in Pinkerton, A collection vol 2, 1808.

Maxwell, James. A narrative of Charles Prince of Wales's expedition to Scotland in 1745. Edinburgh 1841 (Maitland Club).

Dodsley, Robert. England illustrated: or a compendium of the natural history, geography, topography and antiquities of England and Wales. 2 vols 1746.

Journal of an English medical officer who attended the Duke of Cumberland's army as far north as Inverness during the rebellion. 1746; rptd in The contrast: Scotland as it was in 1745 and in the year 1819, 1825.

A journey through part of England and Scotland along with the army of the Duke of Cumberland, by a volunteer. 1746.

Simpson, Samuel. The agreeable historian: or the complete English traveller, giving a geographical description of every county in England. 3 vols 1746.

LeBlanc, Abbé Jean Bernard. Letters on the English and French nations, translated from French (1745). 2 vols Dublin 1747, London 1747.

A tour through Ireland in several entertaining letters. 1746.

Pococke, Richard, Bishop of Meath. Travels in Scotland 1747, 1750, 1760. Ed D. W. Kemp, Edinburgh 1887 (Scottish Historical Soc).

—— Travels through England during 1750, 1751, and later years [to 1764]. Ed J. J. Cartwright 2 vols 1888-9 (Camden Soc).

—— Tour in Ireland in 1752. Ed G. T. Stokes, Dublin, 1891.

—— Northern journeys [in 1760]. 1914 (Surtees Soc).

Story, Thomas (Quaker). Journal of the life and of his travels and labours in the service of the Gospel. Newcastle 1747. Travels, especially to Scotland.

Kalm, Pehr. Account of his visit to England on his way to America in 1748, translated from Swedish by Joseph Lucas. 1893.

A tour through Ireland by two English gentlemen. 1748.

Ray, James, A compleat history of the rebellion, likewise the natural history and antiquities of the several towns thro' which the author pass'd with his Majesty's army, York 1749, Bristol 1750, 1752, Whitehaven 1754, London 1757.

Mackenzie, Murdoch. Orcades: or a geographic and hydrographic survey of the Orkney and Lewis Islands. 1750.

Windham, William. The early life and diaries 1750-85. Ed R. W. Ketton-Cremer 1930. Including travels in England and Ireland.

A voyage to Shetland, the Orkneys and the Western Isles of Scotland. 1751.

Campbell, John. A full and particular description of the Highlands of Scotland. 1752.

Loveday, J. Diary of a tour 1752 through parts of England, Wales, Ireland and Scotland. Edinburgh 1890 (Roxburghe Club).

Narrative of the journey of an Irish gentleman through England in 1752. Ed W. C. Hazlitt 1869.

Davies, Rev Samuel. Diary of a journey to England and Scotland [from New Jersey] 1753-5. Ed G. W. Pilcher, Urbana 1968 (as The Reverend Samuel Davies abroad).

Burt, Captain Edward. Letters from a gentleman in the north of Scotland containing the description of a capital town [Inverness] and an account of the Highlands. 2 vols 1754, Dublin 1755, London 1759, 1815; ed R. Jamieson 2 vols 1818; tr Dutch, 1758; German, 1760.

Hanway, Jonas. A journal of eight days journey from Portsmouth to Kingston-upon-Thames, to which is added an essay on tea. 1756, 2 vols 1757.

Lyttelton, Lord George. An account of a journey into Wales. Bristol 1756; rptd in Annual Register 17 1774; rptd with Henry Wyndham, 1778 below, 1781.

Patching, Resta. Four topographical letters 1755 upon a journey thro' Bedfordshire, Northamptonshire, Leicestershire, Nottinghamshire, Derby and Warwick. Newcastle 1757.

Richardson, John. An account of the life, giving a relation of his trials and exercises in the work of the ministry in England, Ireland, America. 1757, 1774 (3rd edn), 1791, 1825.

Hepburn, Thomas. A letter from Orkney 1757: containing the true causes of the poverty of that country. 1885.

English, John. Travels through Scotland. 1762. Abusive.

Kielmannsegge, Friedrich Graf von. Diary of a journey to England in 1761-2, translated from German ms by Countess Kielmannsegge. 1902.

Cole, Rev William. A tour with Walpole 1763. In Horace Walpole, Correspondence vol 2, appendix, New Haven 1941.

Casanova de Seingalt, Giacomo. Casanova in England in 1763-4. Ed H. Bleakley 1923.

An account of a journey from Lancashire into Scotland. GM April 1766.

The beauties of England: or a comprehensive view of the chief villages, market-towns, cities. 1767.

Derrick, Samuel. Letters written from Leverpoole, Chester, Corke, the Lake of Killarney, Dublin, Tunbridge Wells, Bath. 2 vols Dublin 1767.

K., T. Account of a journey through North Wales. GM Dec 1767.

Young, Arthur. A six weeks' tour through the southern counties of England and Wales. 1768, 1769, Dublin 1771, London 1772.

—— A six months' tour through the north of England. 4 vols 1770, 1771, New York 1967. An abridgement of this and preceding, Dublin 1771.

—— A farmer's tour through the east of England. 4 vols 1771.

—— A tour in Ireland in 1776, 1777 and 1778. 1780; ed A. W. Hutton 2 vols 1880, 1892, 1968.

—— A tour to the west. Annals of Agriculture 6 1766.

—— A tour in Wales. Annals of Agriculture 8 1787.

—— A tour in Sussex. Annals of Agriculture 11 1789.

—— A month's tour in Northamptonshire, Leicestershire etc. Annals of Agriculture 16 1791.

—— A farming tour in the south and west of England. 1796. Annals of Agriculture 28-31 1797-8.

Grimston, Lord (Earl of Verulam). A northern tour from St Albans, 1768; A tour in Wales 1769. Historical Manuscripts Commission, Earl of Verulam mss, 1906.

Bielfeld, Baron Jacob Friedrich von. Letters [including account of a journey to England in 1740-1], translated from German [1763] by Mr Hooper. 4 vols 1768-70.

Brown, Dr John. Letter to Lord Lyttelton [describing the Lake Country]. In Pearch's Continuation of Dodsley's Collection of poems, 1768-70.

England displayed: a new, complete and accurate survey by a society of gentlemen. 2 vols 1769.

Cradock, Joseph. Letters from Snowdon, descriptive of a tour through the northern counties of Wales. 1770, 1777.

—— An account of some of the most romantic parts of North Wales 1776. 1777.

Bocage, Madame Fiquet du. Letters concerning England [in 1750], Holland and Italy, translated from French. 2 vols 1770.

Forbes, Rt Rev Robert. Journals of the episcopal visitations of the dioceses of Ross and Caithness, and of Ross and Argyll 1762 and 1770. 1770.

Lichtenberg, Georg Christoph. Lichtenberg's visits to England [1770, 1774–5] as described in his letters and diaries, translated from German by Margaret L. Mare and W. H. Quarrell. Oxford 1938.

Pennant, Thomas. A tour in Scotland 1769. Chester 1771, London 1772, Warrington 1774, London 1774, 1790; rptd in Pinkerton, A collection vol 3, 1809.

—— A tour in Scotland and voyage to the Hebrides 1772. 2 vols Chester 1774, 3 vols Chester 1775; rptd with preceding, London 1776 etc; tr German, 1779.

—— A tour in Wales in 1770. 1778, Dublin 1779; rptd with next item, 2 vols 1781, 3 vols 1784, 1810; tr Welsh, 1883.

—— A journey to Snowdon. 1781; rptd with the preceding item, 2 vols 1781.

—— The journey from Chester to London. 1782, Dublin 1783. See The literary life of Pennant, by himself, 1793; and C. Price in Welsh Anvil 8 1958.

Smollett, Tobias. The expedition of Humphry Clinker. 3 vols 1771.

Grosley, Pierre Jean. A tour to London: or new observations on England and its inhabitants, translated from French by Thomas Nugent. 2 vols 1772, 3 vols Dublin 1772.

Quincey, Thomas. A short tour in the midland counties of England 1772. GM May–Sept 1774; 1775 (separately, adding A short tour of the same 1774).

Gray, Thomas. The traveller's companion in a tour through England and Wales. Ed W. Mason 1773 (from notes in an atlas), 1789.

—— Journal of the Lakes. In W. Mason, Life and memoirs of Gray, 1775.

Herring, Bishop. An account of two journies into Wales 1737 and 1739. Annual Register 16 1773.

Macartney, George (later Earl). An account of Ireland by a late Chief Secretary. 1773.

Murray, James. The travels of the imagination: a true journey from Newcastle to London in a stage coach. 1773.

A new display of the beauties of England: or a description of public edifices, royal palaces, noblemen's and gentlemen's seats. 2 vols 1773–4 (2nd edn), 1777–6, 1787.

Banks, Joseph. Letter on Staffa. In Thomas Pennant, A tour in Scotland, Chester 1774, above; rptd in Annual Register 20 1777; also in Uno von Troil, Letters on Iceland, 1780 etc.

'Collier, Joel' (George Veal). Musical travels through England. 1774, 1775, 1775, 1776, 1785.

Hutchinson, Thomas. Diary and letters vol 2. 1886. On his life in England 1774–80.

Hutchinson, William. An excursion to the lakes in Westmoreland and Cumberland 1773. 1774, 1776 (with A tour through part of the northern counties).

—— A view of Northumberland, with an excursion to the Abbey of Mailross in Scotland [1776]. 2 vols Newcastle 1778. See J. C. Hodgson, William Hutchinson FSA, Archaeologia Aeliana new ser 12 1916.

Johnson, Samuel. A diary of a journey into North Wales in 1774. Ed R. Duppa, aided by Mrs Piozzi 1816; rptd in G. B. Hill (ed), Boswell's Life of Johnson vol 5, 1885. See Mrs Thrale's account of same journey, 1774 below.

—— A journey to the western islands of Scotland in 1773. 1775, Dublin 1775, London 1791; in William Mavor, The British tourist vol 2, 1798; ed R. W. Chapman 1924 (with Boswell's Journal). See Donald M'Nichol, Remarks on Johnson's Journey to the Hebrides, 1779; G. B. Hill, In the footsteps of Dr Johnson in Scotland, 1896; E. Stucley, A Hebridean journey with Johnson and Boswell, 1956.

Low, Rev George. A tour through the islands of Orkney and Shetland: containing hints relative to the ancient, modern and natural history collected in 1774. Ed J. Anderson, Kirkwall 1879.

Thrale, Mrs Hester. Journal of the Welsh tour in 1774

[with Johnson]. Ed A. M. Broadley, in Dr Johnson and Mrs Thrale, 1910.

Quincy, John. London journal 1774–5. Proc Mass Historical Soc 50 1917.

Brereton, Owen Salusbury. Observations in a tour through South Wales, Shropshire etc [of archaeological matters]. Archaeologia 3 1775.

Campbell, T. Diary of a visit to England in 1775 by an Irishman. Ed S. Raymond, Sydney 1854; rptd in Johnsoniana, ed R. Napier 1884.

—— A philosophical survey of the south of Ireland. 1777.

Curwen, Samuel. Journal and letters of an American refugee in England from 1775 to 1784. Ed G. A. Ward 1842.

Hanway, Mrs Mary Anne. A journey to the Highlands of Scotland, with remarks on Dr Johnson's tour. 1775, 1777, 1800.

Wyndham, Henry Penruddocke. A gentleman's tour through Monmouthshire and Wales 1774. 1775, Salisbury 1781 (with A journey into Wales 1777), London 1781 (with Lord Lyttelton's tour into Wales, 1756 above); in William Mavor, The British tourist vol 3, 1800.

—— A picture of the Isle of Wight in 1793. 1794.

Topham, Edward. Letters from Edinburgh containing some observations on the Scotch nation. Edinburgh 1776, 2 vols Dublin 1780; tr German, 1777.

Twiss, R. A tour in Ireland in 1775. Dublin 1776.

Bray, Rev William. Sketch of a tour into Derbyshire and Yorkshire etc. 1777, 1783, 1798; in William Mavor, The British tourist vol 2, 1800; in John Pinkerton, A collection vol 2, 1808.

Britannia curiosa: or a description of the most remarkable curiosities, natural and artificial. 6 vols 1777, [1780].

Description of Keswick Lake in Cumberland. GM Oct 1777.

Heard, ——. A sentimental journey to Bath, Bristol and their environs. 1778.

Lock, D. A tour through most of the trading towns and villages of Scotland. Edinburgh 1778.

Van Shaack, H. C. The life of Peter van Shaack [an American loyalist in England 1778–85]. New York 1842.

Watkinson, J. Philosophic survey of South Ireland. 1778.

Keate, George. Sketches from nature, taken and coloured in a journey to Margate. 2 vols 1779 etc.

Cordiner, Rev Charles. Antiquities and scenery of the north of Scotland, in a series of letters to Thomas Pennant. 1780, 1790.

A diary kept in an excursion to Littlehampton near Arundel and Brighthelmston 1778 and 1779. 2 vols 1780.

Gough, Richard. British topography. 2 vols 1780.

—— (ed). Camden's Britannia. 3 vols 1789, 1806 (much enlarged).

Luckombe, P. Tour through Ireland. 1780.

Sullivan, Richard. Observations made during a tour through parts of England, Scotland and Wales. 1780, 2 vols 1785, Dublin 1785; in William Mavor, The British tourist vol 3, 1800; tr German, 1781 (with John Hutton, below).

Byng, Hon John (Viscount Torrington). The Torrington diaries: containing the tours through England and Wales 1781–94. Ed C. Bruyn Andrews 4 vols 1934–8.

Hutton, John. A tour to the caves in the environs of Ingleborough and Settle in the West Riding of Yorkshire. 1781 (2nd edn); tr German, 1781 (with Sullivan, above).

A journal of first thoughts, observations, characters, anecdotes in a journey to Scarborough 1779. 1781.

A month's tour in North Wales, Dublin and its environs, with observations on men, manners and police in 1780. 1781.

Parker, George. A view of society and manners in high and low life: being the adventures in England, Ireland, Scotland, Wales, France etc, with a history of the stage itinerant. 2 vols 1781.

Gilpin, Rev William. Observations on the river Wye and several parts of South Wales etc, relative chiefly to picturesque beauty 1770. 1782, 1800 (4th edn); tr French, 1800.
— Observations relative chiefly to picturesque beauty 1772, particularly the mountains and lakes of Cumberland and Westmoreland. 2 vols 1786, 1788, 1792; tr French, 1789, 1801.
— Observations relating chiefly to picturesque beauty, particularly in the Highlands of Scotland. 2 vols 1789.
— A tour in Hampshire, Sussex and Kent in 1774. 1789.
— Remarks on forest scenery and other woodland views, illustrated by the scenes in the New-Forest in Hampshire. 2 vols 1791, 1794.
— Observations on the western parts of England, relative chiefly to picturesque beauty. 1798.
— Observations on the coasts of Hampshire, Sussex and Kent, relative chiefly to picturesque beauty in 1774. 1804.
Douglas, Francis. A general description of the east coast of Scotland. Paisley 1782.
D'Amour, Matthias. Memoir. Ed P. Rodgers 1836. Including travels in Scotland 1782–5.
Watson, Elkanah. Journal of a visit to England 1782–4. In Men and times of the Revolution, ed W. C. Watson 1856.
Hutcheson, Charles. Journal to Arran in 1783. Ed W. P. Ker, Scottish Historical Rev 16 1918.
Moreau, Simeon. A tour to Cheltenham Spa: or Gloucestershire displayed. Bath 1783, 1786, 1788, 1789, 1793, 1793, 1797, 1873.
Lunardi, Vincent. An account of the first aerial voyage [balloon] in England. 1784, 1784.
— An account of five aerial voyages in Scotland. 1786.
Mirabeau, Count de. Mirabeau's letters during his residence in England 1784–5, translated from French. 2 vols 1832 (from ms).
Rochefoucauld, François de la. A Frenchman in England 1784: being the Mélanges sur l'Angleterre. Ed and tr S. C. Roberts, Cambridge 1933 (from ms).
Walpoole, G. A. The new British traveller. 1784.
Adams, Abigail. Journal and correspondence of Miss Adams, daughter of John Adams, written in France and England in 1785. New York 1841.
Boswell, James. The journal of a tour to the Hebrides with Samuel Johnson LlD. 1785 etc; tr German, 1787. See A defence of Mr Boswell's journal, 1786; Peter Pindar, A poetical and congratulatory epistle to James Boswell esq, 1786; Remarks on a journal of a tour to the Hebrides, 1786; The remarker remarked: or a parody on the letter to Mr Boswell, 1786; Thomas Rowlandson, Twenty humourous illustrations of Boswell's tour, 1786.
Hutton, William. A journey from Birmingham to London. 1785, 1818.
— A description of Blackpool in Lancashire frequented for sea-bathing 1788. Ed R. S. France, Liverpool 1944.
A pocket vade-mecum through Monmouthshire and part of South Wales in 1785. 1785.
Jeffries, Dr John. A narrative of the two aerial voyages 1784 London into Kent, and 1785 England into France. 1786.
La Roche, Sophie von. Sophie in London 1786, translated from German 1788 by Clare Williams. 1933.
Thornton, T. A sporting tour through the north parts of England and great part of the Highlands of Scotland [in 1786]. 1804.
Burns, Robert. Journal of a tour in the Highlands in 1787. Ed J. C. Ewing 1927 (ms facs).
Clarke, James. Survey of the lakes of Cumberland, Westmoreland and Lancashire. 1787, 1789.
Knox, John. A tour through the Highlands of Scotland and the Hebrides in 1786. 1787; tr French, 1790.
A tour in England and Scotland in 1784 by an English gentleman. 1788.

Dibdin, Charles. The musical tour in a series of 107 letters. Sheffield 1788.
Newte, Thomas. A tour in England and Scotland in 1785. 1788, 1791 (enlarged as Prospects and observations on a tour etc). Also ascribed to William Thomson.
Shaw, Rev Stebbing. A tour in 1787 from London to the western Highlands of Scotland, including excursions to the lakes of Westmoreland and Cumberland. 1788; rptd in John Pinkerton, A collection vol 2, 1808.
— A tour to the west of England in 1788. 1789.
Archenholz, Wilhelm von. A picture of England, translated from German of part of England und Italien 1785. 2 vols 1789, 1791.
Warner, Richard. A companion in a tour round Lymington, the New Forest, Isle of Wight, Southampton, Christchurch etc. Southampton 1789.
Fisher, Jonathan. A picturesque tour of Killarney, in twenty views engraved in aquatints 1789. Dublin 1790.
— The scenery of Ireland, in prints of select views. 2 pts Dublin 1795–6.
Hassell, J. A. A tour of the Isle of Wight (30 aquatints). 1790.
Wigstead, Henry and Thomas Rowlandson. An excursion to Brighthelmstone 1789. 1790.
— Remarks on a tour to north and south Wales in 1797. 1800. 22 plates.
Willis, R. L. Journal of a tour from London to Elgin made about 1790. Ed J.T., Edinburgh 1897.
Bowden, C. T. A tour through Ireland. Dublin 1791.
Townley, Richard. A journal kept in the Isle of Man [1789–90]. 2 vols Whitehaven 1791.
Wendeborn, G. F. A. A view of England toward the close of the eighteenth century, translated from German 1785–8. 1791. His account of his travel in England in 1791 has not been translated.
An account of a voyage to the Hebrides by a committee of the British Fishery Society in 1787. Bee 8–9 1792.
Budworth, Joseph. A fortnight's ramble to the Lakes in Westmoreland, Lancashire and Cumberland, by a rambler. 1792, 1795, 1810.
A tour from London to the lakes in 1791. 1792.
Gibson, W. A sketch of a two months' tour in Scotland performed on horseback in 1773. GM Jan, April–Aug, Oct 1792, March, May–June, Aug–Sept, Nov 1793 (suppl), March–April, June–July 1794.
Walker, A. Remarks made in a tour from London to the lakes of Westmoreland and Cumberland in 1791. 1792.
Buchanan, Rev John. Travels in the western Hebrides from 1782 to 1790. 1793.
Clarke, Dr. E. D. A tour through the south of England, Wales and part of Ireland in 1791. 1793.
— Tour in Scotland in 1797. In W. Otter, Life and remains of Edward D. Clarke, 2 vols 1825.
Cozens, Z. A tour through the Isle of Thanet and some other parts of east Kent. 1793.
Heron, Robert. Observations made in a journey through the western counties of Scotland in 1792. 2 vols Perth 1793.
— Scotland described: or a topographical description of all the counties of Scotland, with the northern and western isles. Edinburgh 1797, 1799.
Wordsworth, William. An evening walk: an epistle to a young lady from the Lakes of the north of England. 1793.
Lettice, John. Letters on a tour through various parts of Scotland in 1792. 1794.
The new and complete English traveller: or a new historical survey and modern description of England and Wales, Scotland, Ireland, revised by William Hugh Dalton. 1794.
Robertson, David. A tour through the Isle of Man. 1794, 1798; rptd in William Mavor, The British tourist vol 5, 1800; in John Pinkerton, A collection vol 2, 1808; tr French, 1800.

Wallis, —. A tour through England and Wales: a new geographical pastime. 1794.

Huck, J. Pedestrian tour through north Wales [with Coleridge]. 1795.

Letocnaye, M. de. Promenade autour de la Grande Bretagne. Edinburgh 1795.

—— Promenade d'un Français dans l'Irlande. Dublin 1797; tr 2 vols 1799, [Belfast] 1917.

MacRitchie, Rev William. Diary of a tour through Great Britain in 1795. Antiquary 32–3 1896–7.

Morgan, Mrs Mary. A tour to Milford Haven in 1791. 1795.

Moritz, Carl Philip. Travels, chiefly on foot, through several parts of England in 1782, translated from German (1783) by a lady. 1795; rptd in William Mavor, The British tourist vol 4, 1798; ed P. E. Matheson 1926.

Pratt, Samuel Jackson. Gleanings through Wales, Holland and Westphalia, with views of peace and war at home and abroad. 4 vols 1795, 1796, 2 vols 1797, 3 vols 1800. Vol 1 on Wales, vol 4 England.

Radcliffe, Ann. Observations during a tour of the lakes of Lancashire, Westmoreland and Cumberland. 1795. Added to her Journey made in the summer of 1794 through Holland and the western frontier of Germany.

Skrine, Henry. Three successive tours in the north of England and great part of Scotland. 1795.

—— Two successive tours throughout the whole of Wales. 1798, 1812; in William Mavor, British tourist vol 5,1800.

Ferrar, John. A tour from Dublin to London in 1795 through the Isle of Anglesey, Bangor, Conway etc. Dublin 1796.

Fisher, J. The scenery of Ireland. Dublin 1795–6.

Jones, J. G. A. A sketch of a political tour through Rochester, Chatham, Maidstone, Gravesend etc. 1796.

Tomkins, Charles. A tour to the Isle of Wight (80 aquatint views). 2 vols 1796.

Aikin, Arthur. A journal of a tour through North Wales and part of Shropshire, with observations in mineralogy. 1797.

A collection of Welsh tours: or a display of the beauties of Wales. 1797, 1797, 1798 (with A tour of the River Wye).

A descriptive account of the Devil's Bridge, Hafod, Strata Florida Abbey and other scenery in Cardiganshire. Hereford 1797.

Holmes, G. Sketches of some of the southern counties of Ireland. 1797.

Maton, Dr W. G. Observations relative to the natural history, picturesque scenery and antiquities of the western counties of England in 1794 and 1796. 2 vols Salisbury 1797.

M'Nayr, James. A guide from Glasgow to some of the most remarkable scenes in the highlands of Scotland, and to the falls of the Clyde. 1797.

Penhouet, A. B. L. Maudet de. Letters describing a tour through part of South Wales by a pedestrian traveller. 1797.

Feltham, John. A tour through the Isle of Mann in 1797 and 1798. 1798.

Grant, Johnson. A London journal of a three weeks' tour in 1797 through Derbyshire to the Lakes. 1798; rptd in William Mavor, The British tourist vol 5, 1800.

Haldane, R. A journal of a tour through the northern counties of Scotland and the Orkney Isles in 1797 to promote the knowledge of the Gospel. Edinburgh 1798, 1798. See Rev Gavin Mitchell, Remarks upon the journal of a tour in 1797, Aberdeen 1799.

Jameson, Robert. An outline of the mineralogy of the Shetland Islands and of the Island of Arran, with mineralogical observations made in a tour through the mainland of Scotland. 1798.

Journal of a tour to Scarborough in the summer of 1798. Wisbech 1798.

Shepard, Charles, jr. A tour through Wales and the central parts of England. GM April–July 1798, June, Sept–Dec 1799 (suppl).

Thompson, G. A sentimental tour from Bewbiggin near Penrith to London by way of Cambridge and by way of Oxford. 1798.

A tour of the river Wye and its vicinity. Chester 1798.

Warner, Rev Richard. A walk through Wales in 1797. Bath 1798, 1798, 1799.

—— A second walk through Wales in 1798. Bath 1799.

—— Excursions from Bath to Stourhead, Wardour Castle and Charlton Park. Bath 1800.

—— A walk through some of the western counties of England. Bath 1800.

—— Tour through the northern counties of England and borders of Scotland. 2 vols Bath 1802.

Douglas, N. Journal of a mission to parts of the Highlands of Scotland in 1797 by appointment of the Relief Synod, designed to show the state of religion in that country. Edinburgh 1799.

Faujas de Saint Fond. Travels in England, Scotland and the Hebrides, undertaken for the purpose of examining the state of the arts, the sciences, natural history and manners, translated from French (1790). 1799; ed A. Geikie 1907.

Heath, C. Excursion down the Wye from Ross to Monmouth, Wilton and Goodrich Castles etc. Monmouth 1799, 1827 (10th edn).

Hill, Rev Rowland. Journal of a tour through the north of England and parts of Scotland, with remarks on the present state of the Established Church of Scotland. 1799. See John Jamieson DD, Remarks on the Rev Rowland Hill's journey, Edinburgh 1799.

—— Extract of a journal of a second tour from London through the Highlands of Scotland and the north western parts of England. 1800.

Lipscomb, G. A journey into Cornwall from Hampshire, interspersed with remarks moral, historical, literary and political. 1799.

Meister, Jakob Heinrich. Letters written during a residence in England: manners, government, theatres etc, translated from French (1798). 1799.

Murray, S. A companion to the beauties of Scotland, lakes of Westmoreland etc. 1799, 1803 (enlarged), 1810.

Bingley, Rev William. A tour round North Wales in 1798. 2 vols 1800.

A companion to the watering and bathing places of England. 1800.

Cooper, George. Letters on the Irish nation in 1799. 1800.

Dunsford, M. Miscellaneous observations in the course of two tours through several parts of the west of England. Tiverton 1800.

Garnett, Dr Thomas. Observations on a tour through the Highlands and part of the western isles of Scotland. 1800 (with aquatints); tr German, 1802.

Housman, John. A descriptive tour and guide to the lakes, caves, mountains and other natural curiosities in Cumberland, Westmoreland, Lancashire and a part of the West Riding of Yorkshire. Carlisle 1800.

Leyden, J. Journal of a tour in the Highlands and western islands in 1800. Ed J. Sinton 1903.

Love, David. His journey to London and his return to Nottingham. Nottingham 1800.

A tour of health and pleasure: or a visit to the principal sea-bathing places and mineral waters in England. In William Mavor, The British tourist vol 6, 1800.

Roland de la Platière, Mme Jeanne Marie. The works, her philosophical and literary essays, her correspondence and her travels, translated from French. 1800. Including an account of her visit to England in 1784.

§ 2

Kelly, J. A. England and the Englishman in German literature of the eighteenth century. New York 1921.

—— German visitors to English theatres in the eighteenth century. Princeton 1936.

Beatty, J. M. and J. R. The English Lake District before Wordsworth. South Atlantic Quart 22 1923.

Parkes, J. Travel in England in the seventeenth century. Oxford 1925.

Spiller, R. E. The American in England during the first half century of independence. New York 1926.

Hussey, C. The picturesque: a study in a point of view. 1927.

Fordham, H. G. Notable surveyors of the sixteenth, seventeenth, and eighteenth centuries and their work. Cambridge 1929.

Matheson, P. E. German visitors to England 1770–95. Oxford 1930.

Anderson, R. M. C. The roads of England: being a review of the roads, of travellers and traffic in England. 1932.

Beales, H. L. Travel and communications. In Johnson's England vol 1, ed A. S. Turberville, Oxford 1933.

Aubin, R. Topographical poetry in the eighteenth century 1640–1840. New York 1936.

Willan, T. S. The English coasting trade. Manchester 1938.

Addison, W. English spas. 1951.

Bayne-Powell, R. Travellers in eighteenth-century England. 1951.

Robson-Scott, W. D. German travellers in England 1400–1800. Oxford 1953.

(3) THE CONTINENT

Collections

Carrington, D. The travellers' eye. 1947. Extracts from travel-narratives, 16th to 19th centuries.

Morrison, H. The golden age of travel: literary impressions of the Grand Tour. New York 1951.

Putnam, P. Seven Britons in Imperial Russia 1698–1812. Princeton 1952. Extracts from narratives of John Perry, Jonas Hanway, William Richardson, Sir James Harris, Archdeacon William Coxe, Robert Ker Porter and General Sir Robert Thomas Wilson.

§ I

A narrative of the successe of the embassy of [Heneage Finch] the Earl of Winchelsea to Turkey. 1661.

Howell, James. La perambulación de Espana y Portugál: The perambulation of Spain and Portugal, which may serve for a director how to travel through those countries. 1662.

Olearius, Adam. Voyages and travels of the ambassadors to the Great Duke of Muscovy and the King of Persia. 1662, 1662.

Browne, Edward, MD. Journal of a visit to Paris in 1664. Ed G. L. Keynes 1923.

— A brief account of travels in Hungaria, Servia, Bulgaria, Macedonia, Thessaly, Austria, Styria, Carinthia, Carniola and Friuli, through a great part of Germany and the Low Countries, through Marca Trevisana and Lombardy. 1673, 1685 (with next item as A brief account of some travels in divers parts of Europe), 1687; rptd in Works of Sir Thomas Browne vol 1, ed S. Wilkin 1836; tr French, 1674.

— An account of several travels through a great part of Germany in four journeys. 1677; rptd with preceding, 1685, 1836.

Corraro, Angelo. Rome exactly described as to the present state of it under Pope Alexander the Seventh: a relation of the Court of Rome made in 1661, translated from Italian by J.B. gent, with A new relation of Rome as to the government of the city, translated by J.T. 1664, 1668.

Clarke, Samuel. A description of the present state of Germany. 1665.

— A description of the seaventeen provinces commonly called the Low Countries. 1672.

Montagu, Edward, Earl of Sandwich. The journal 1659–65. Ed R. C. Anderson 1929 (Navy Records Soc).

Carr, William. Pietas parisiensis: or a short description. [1666].

— Remarks of the government of severall parts of Germanie, Denmark, Sweedland, Hamburg, Lubeck and Hansiactique townes, but more particularly of the United Provinces. Amsterdam 1688, London 1688, 1691 (as An accurate description of the United Netherlands), 1695 (as The travellours guide: being the sixteen years travells), 1697, 1725 (as Travels through Flanders, Holland, Germany, Sweden and Denmark), Amsterdam 1744 (8th edn).

Europae modernae speculum: or a view of the empires, kingdoms and commonwealths from 1648. 1666.

Palmer, Roger, Earl of Castlemaine. An account of the present war between the Venetians and the Turks, with the state of Candia. 1666.

Gailhard, Jean. The present state of the princes and republicks of Italy. 1668, 1671.

— The present state of the republick of Venice. 1669.

Rycaut, Paul. The present state of the Ottoman Empire. 1668, 1668, 1670, 1675, 1680, 1682, 1686, 2 vols 1687 (with Richard Knolles, The Turkish Empire); tr French, 1670, 1678, 1696; Italian, 1672; Polish, 1678; German, 1694.

Aglionby, William. The present state of the United Provinces of the Low Countries. 1669, 1671.

Finch, Heneage, Earl of Winchelsea. A true relation of the late prodigious earthquake and eruption of Mount Aetna or Monte-Gibello. 1669, Cambridge Mass 1669, London 1775; rptd in Somers tracts vol 3, 1750; 1775 (with W.B.E., below).

Miège, Guy. The Earl of Carlisle's relation of three embassies to the Duke of Muscovy, the King of Sweden and the King of Denmark in 1663 and 1664. 1669, 1926 (abridged); tr French, 1670, 1683.

— The present state of Denmark, translated from French [of 1670]. 1683.

Brunel, Antoine de, and Francois van Aerssen. A journey into Spain, translated anonymously from French [of 1665]. 1670.

Lassels, Richard. The voyage of Italy: or a compleat journey through Italy. Paris 1670, 1670, London 1685, 1698, 1705 (in John Harris, Navigantium vol 2); tr French, 1671.

A description of Candia: its ancient and modern state, with an account of the siege thereof. 1670.

[Besogne, Nicolas]. The present state of France: containing the orders, dignities, and charges of the kingdom, translated anonymously from French. 1657, 1687, 1691.

[Burbury, John]. A relation of a journey of Lord Henry Howard from London to Vienna and thence to Constantinople. 1671.

Collins, Samuel. The present state of Russia, in a letter to a friend. 1671; tr French, 1679.

Santos, Frey Francisco de los. The Escurial: or a description of that wonder of the world lately consumed by fire, translated by a servant of the Earl of Sandwich [George Thompson]. 1671, 1760.

Chevalier, Pierre. A discourse of the original, countrey, manners, government and religion of the Cossacks, with another of the Procopian Tartars, translated from French by Edward Browne. 1672.

W., T. An exact survey of the United Provinces of the Netherlands. 1672.

A description of the seven United Provinces of Netherland. 1673.

Ray, John. Observations (topographical, moral and physiological) made in a journey through part of the Low Countries, Germany, Italy and France, with a

catalogue of plants. 1673, 1705 (in John Harris, Navigantium vol 2), 2 vols 1738.
—— A collection of curious travels and voyages. 1693. *See* Collections, above.

Temple, Sir William. Observations of the United Provinces of the Netherlands. 1673, 1673, 1676, 1680, Amsterdam 1680, London 1690, 1693, 1705; in Works, 1720, 1770.

Willughby, Francis. A relation of a voyage made through Spain. In John Ray, Observations, 1673 above.

W., F. News from the Channel: or the discovery and perfect description of the Isle of Serke. 1673; rptd in Harleian miscellany, vol 3 1744.

Wilson, Elias. Strange and wonderful news from Italy: or the travels, adventures and martyrdom of four eminent Quakers of York-shire, who in 1672 travelled through France, Italy and Turkey to propagate their religion, also of their voyage to Constantinople, and of their most barbarous, cruel and bloody death. 1673.

A discourse of the Dukedom of Modena. 1674.

Smith, Thomas. Epistolae de moribus et institutis Turcarum; accessit brevis Constantinopoleos notitia. Oxford 1674 (in Quatuor epistolae); tr as Remarks upon the manners, religion, and government of the Turks, 1678.

La Martinière, Pierre Martin de. Travels into the northern countries: being a description of Norwegians, Laponians, Kilops, Borandians, Siberians, Samiedes, Zemblans and Icelanders, translated from French [of 1671]. 1674, 1706 (as A new voyage to the north).
—— A particular relation of the Court of the Czar, of the religion and customs of the Muscovites, and a short history of Muscovy, translated from French [of 1671]. 1706 (with preceding).

Scheffer, John. The history of Lapland, translated from Latin [Upsala 1670]. Oxford 1674, London 1703 (with Olof Rudbeck, The travels of the King of Sweden's mathematicians into Lapland), 1751.

[Clenche, John]. A tour of France and Italy made by an English gentleman 1675-6. 1676; rptd in Thomas Osborne, Collection vol 1, 1745.

Debes, Luces Jacobson. Fœroæ et Fœroa reserata: that is, a description of the islands and inhabitants of Fœroa, translated from Danish [of 1673] by J[ohn] S[terpin]. 1676.

La Guillatière, M. de [Guillet de Saint-George, Georges]. An account of a late voyage to Athens: containing the estate, both ancient and modern, of that famous city, and of the present empire of the Turks, translated from French [of 1675]. 1676.

Samber, Robert. Roma illustrata: or a description of the most beautiful pieces of painting, sculpture and architecture at and near Rome. 1676, 1722, 1723.

Barri, Giacomo. The painter's voyage of Italy, in which all the famous paintings are particularised, translated from Italian by Thomas Lodge. 1678.

Georgirenes, Archbishop of Samos. Description of the present state of Samos, Nicaria, Pathmos and Mount Athos, translated from demotic Greek by Henry Denton. 1678.

Covel, Dr John. Extracts from the diaries 1670-9. Ed J. T. Bent in Early voyages in the Levant, 1892 (Hakluyt Soc).

Popery and tyranny: or the present state of France in relation to the government, trade, manner of their people, and nature of the country, in a letter from an English gentleman abroad. 1679.

Teonge, Henry. Diary 1675-9. Ed G. E. Manwaring 1927 (Navy Records Soc).

Pitt, Moses. The English atlas: containing the description of Muscovy, Poland, Sweden, Denmark and the Netherlands. 4 vols Oxford 1680-3.

Finch, Sir John. [A record of his embassy 1674-81]. Ed G. F. Abbott as Under the Turk in Constantinople, 1920.

[Leti, Gregorio]. The present state of Geneva, with a brief description of that city, and several changes and alterations from the first foundation thereof, translated from Italian. 1681, 1687.

Milton, John. A brief history of Moscovia, and of other less known countries lying eastward of Russia as far as Cathay. 1682; rptd in the collected prose works vol 2, 1698; vol 2, 1738; vol 2, 1753; vol 4, 1806; vol 2, 1809, 1835; vol 2, 1847; complete works, 1851; vol 5, 1853; ed D. Mirsky 1929; New York 1932 (Columbia edn, vol 10); ed R. R. Cawley, Princeton 1941.

Wheler, George, and Jacob Spon. A journey into Greece. 1682, 1688, 1693; tr French (in part) 1678, 1689. *See* R. W. Ramsey, Wheler and his travels in Greece 1650-1724, Essays by Divers Hands new ser 19 1942.

Pierreville, G. The present state of Denmark, and reflections upon the ancient state thereof. 1683.

Pontier, R. A new survey of the present state of Europe: containing remarks upon Italy, France, Lorrain, Germany, Spain, translated from Latin by W. Beaumont. 1683.

The present state of the German and Turkish empires, with memoirs of the siege of Vienna by an eminent officer. 1683.

Taafe, Francis, Count. Letters from the Imperial camp giving an account of the actions both before and at the raising the siege of Vienna, together with the campagne against the Turks in Hungary. 1684.

Trevelyan, Mr. A true and exact relation of the imperial expedition in Hungaria, with a journal of the siege and taking of Buda. 1685, 1687 (journal pbd separately).

Burnet, Gilbert. Some letters containing an account of what seemed most remarkable in travelling through Switzerland, Italy and parts of Germany. Rotterdam 1686, Amsterdam 1686, Rotterdam 1687, London 1689 (as Travels, with next item); 1705 etc in Harris vol 2; 1708, 1724, 1750, 1758; tr French, 1687 (3 edns), 1688.
—— Three letters concerning the present state of Italy. Rotterdam 1688, 1688, London 1689 etc (with preceding item).

[Brice, Germain]. A new description of Paris, translated from French by James Wright. 1686, 1688, 1698.

Randolph, Bernard. The present state of the Morea, anciently called Peloponnesus. 1686, 1687, 1689.
—— The present state of the islands in the Archipelago. Oxford 1687.

Coronelli, P. M. An historical and geographical account of the Morea, Negropont and the maritime places as far as Thessalonica, translated from Italian by R.W. gent. 1687.

Ferrier, Major Richard. Journal while travelling in France in 1687. 1895 (Camden Miscellany).

The present state of Hungary: or a geographical and historical description of that kingdom, to which is added a short account of Transylvania. 1687.

Spon, Isaac. The history of the city and state of Geneva from its first foundation to the present time. 1687.

A journal of the Venetian campaigne 1687. 1688.

A modern view of such parts of Europe that have lately been and still are the places of great transactions (Italy, Germany, Spain). 1689.

[Whittie, John]. An exact diary of the late expedition of the Prince of Orange from the Hague to his landing at Torbay, and from thence to Whitehall. 1689.

A journal of the late motions and actions of the confederate forces against the French in the United Provinces and Spanish Netherlands, with remarks on the most considerable cities, towns and fortifications, written by an English officer. 1690.

The present state of Germany, or an account of that empire, the prerogatives of the Emperour and the privileges of the electors, princes and free cities. 1690.

Strutton, Richard. A true relation of the cruelties and barbarities of the French upon the English prisoners of war: being a journal of their travels from Dinan in Britanny to Thoulon and back again. 1690.

Acton, William. A new journal of Italy: containing the antiquities of Rome, Savoy, Naples, with observations on strengths, beauty and situation of the other towns, together with the best painting, carving, limning and other both natural and artificial curiosities. 1691.

D'Aulnoy, Marie-Catherine de la Mothe, Countess. The ingenious and diverting letters of the Lady —'s travels into Spain, translated anonymously from the French [of 1691]. 1691, 1692 (with 2 new pts) etc; 1708 (7th edn), 1774 (12th edn), 16 edns to 1800; ed R. Foulché-Delbosc 1930. Fiction.

A description of Holland, with directions for travel. Pt 1 of An exact relation of the entertainment of William III at the Hague, 1691 (3rd edn).

Eachard, Laurence. The Duke of Savoy's dominions most accurately described. 1691.

—— Flanders: or the Spanish Netherlands described. 1691, 1692, 1693.

'd'Emiliane, Gabriel' (Antonio Gavin). Observations on a journey to Naples, in which the frauds of Romish monks and priests are set forth in eight letters. 1691 (3 edns), 1692, 1704, 1710, 1725, 1727, 1817, 1827; tr French, 2 vols 1727.

A late voyage to Holland, with brief relations of the transactions at the Hague. 1691; rptd in Harleian Miscellany vol 2, 1744.

Wolley, R. Galliae notitia, or the present state of France: containing a general description of that kingdom, translated from French. 1691.

Bromley, William. Remarks in the grand tour. 1692, 1693 (as Remarks made in travels through France and Italy with many publick inscriptions), 1705.

—— Several years travels through Portugal, Spain, Italy, Germany, Prussia, Sweden, Denmark and the United Provinces. 1702; rptd in John Harris, Navigantium vol 2, 1705; abridged in later edns.

S., J. A description of France in its several governments. 1692.

La Ferr, M. de. Voyages and travels over all Europe, translated from French. 4 vols 1693–6. Vol 2, Spain and Portugal; vol 3, Italy; vol 4, Holland.

Crull, Jodocus, MD. Denmark vindicated: being an answer to a late treatise [by Molesworth, below], called An account of Denmark in 1692. 1694.

—— The antient and present state of Muscovy: containing a geographical, historical and political account. 2 vols 1698.

—— The present condition of the Muscovite Empire till the year 1699, in two letters. 1699 (with Joachim Bouvet, The present emperor of China; see Travels to Asia, below).

—— Memoirs of Denmark: containing the life and reign of the late King Christian V. 1700.

Fox, George. [Travels in Holland in 1677, 1684]. In A journal: or historical account of the life, 1694. See under General Travels, above.

La Croze, Jean Cornann de. An historical and geographical description of France. 1694.

Molesworth, Robert, Viscount. An account of Denmark as it was in the year 1692. 1694 (3 edns), 1697, 1738. See answers: William King, Animadversions on a pretended account of Denmark, 1694; and Jodocus Crull, Denmark vindicated, 1694.

Penn, William. An account of William Penn's travails in Germany and Holland 1676 for the service of the gospel of Christ. 1694, 1694, 1695 (rev). See O. Seidensticker, Pennsylvania Mag of History 2 1878.

Robinson, John, Bishop. An account of Sweden, with an extract of the history of that Kingdom. 1694.

Misson, Maximilian. A new voyage to Italy, with a description of the chief towns, churches, tombs, libraries, palaces, statues and antiquities, translated anonymously from French [of 1691]. 2 vols 1695, 1699 (enlarged), 1714 (4th edn), 1739; rptd in Harris, Navigantium vol 2, 1705.

Du Mont, Jean, Baron de Carlscroon. A new voyage to the Levant: containing an account of the most remarkable curiosities in Germany, France, Malta and Turkey, translated anonymously from French. 1696, 1702, 1703 (4th edn).

Kennett, Basil. Romae antiquae notitia, or the antiquities of Rome: I, Rise, progress and decay of the commonwealth; II, Description of the city. 1696, 1699 (enlarged) etc, 1763 (13th edn), 1776 (15th edn).

Mountague, William. The delights of Holland: or a three months travel about that and the other provinces. 1696.

Patin, Charles. Travels through Germany, Bohemia, Swisserland, Holland, and other parts of Europe; translated anonymously from French [of 1673]. 1696, 1697.

The ancient and present state of Poland drawn out of their best historians. 1697.

Travels through Denmark and some parts of Germany, translated from French. 1697.

Bilberg, John. A voyage of the late King of Sweden, and another of mathematicians sent by him [for astronomical observations] in the northern parts. 1698. Tr from Latin.

Bowrey, Thomas. Diary of a six weeks tour in 1698 in Holland and Flanders. Ed R. C. Temple 1925 (Hakluyt Soc).

C., T. A new atlas: or travels and voyages in Europe. 1698.

Connor, Bernard. The history of Poland: giving an account of the ancient and present state of that kingdom, historical, geographical, physical, political and ecclesiastical. 2 vols 1698; part rptd in John Harris, Navigantium vol 2, 1705.

'De Hauteville, M.' (Gaspard de Tende). An account of Poland: containing a geographical description of the country, the manners etc. 1698.

An historical account of Russia: containing the customs and manners of the people and a description of the vast dominions subject to the Czar of Muscovia. 1698.

Allison, Thomas. An account of a voyage from Archangel in 1697 [to the North Cape], also remarkable observations of the climate, country and inhabitants. 1699; rptd in John Pinkerton, A collection vol 1, 1808.

An answer to a late ill-natured libel, call'd A trip to Holland, by a Dutch merchant. 1699.

Dorrington, Theophilus. Observations concerning the present state of religion in the Romish church, made in a journey through some provinces of Germany. 1699.

Harris, Dr Walter. A description of the King's royal palace and gardens at Loo, with a short account of Holland, in which are some observations relating to their diseases. 1699, 1699.

La Neuville, Foy de. An account of Muscovey, as it was in the year 1689, and the troubles from the present Czar Peter's election to the throne, translated from French [of 1699]. 1699.

Lister, Dr Martin. A journey to Paris in 1698. 1699 (3 edns); rptd in John Pinkerton, A collection vol 4, 1808; ed G. Henning 1823; tr French, 1873.

Roberts, —. Adventures among the corsairs of the Levant, with a description of the Archipelago islands. In William Hacke, A collection, 1699.

A succinct description of France dedicated to Dr Martin Lister. 1699. Satire of Lister, above.

[Ward, Edward]. A trip to Holland: being a description of the country, people and manners. 1699; in Five travel scripts, New York 1933 (facs).

A pilgrimage to the grand jubilee at Rome in 1700. 1700, 1701.

Blomberg, Baron Carl Johann von. An account of Livonia, with a relation of the Marian Teutonick order [and] the author's journey from Livonia to Holland in 1698. 1701; tr French, 1705.

A new account of Italy, with a particular description of Rome, Venice and other cities. 1701.

A new description of Holland and the rest of the United Provinces. 1701.

Veryard, Ellis, MD. An account of divers choice remarks taken in a journey through the Low-Countries, France, Italy and part of Spain, with the isles of Sicily and Malta, as also a voyage to the Levant. 1701.

A view of Paris and places adjoining, with an account of the court of France and of the late King James. 1701, 1706.

Campagna miravigliosa: or an exact journal of the Imperial Army's advance into and incampments in Italy, by an officer of the German army, translated by William Barton. 1702.

A curious survey of France. 1702.

Fanshaw, Sir Richard. Original letters during his embassies in Spain and Portugal. 1702, 2 vols 1724.

A new description of Spain and Portugal, as also of the city of Lisbon and other places remarkable in Portugal. 1702.

Northleigh, John. Topographical descriptions, with historico-political and medico-physical observations made in two several voyages through most parts of Europe. 1702; part dealing with France rptd in John Harris, Navigantium vol 2, 1705.

Rooke, Sir George. The journal of the Admiral of the Fleet 1700–2. Ed O. Browning 1897 (Navy Records Soc).

— A narrative of his late voyage to the Mediterranean, with a description of Gibraltar, and an account of the naval battell. 1704.

Savage, John. The antient and present state of the Empire of Germany, and an account of the Empire and all its dependencies. Vol 2 of Complete history of Germany, 1702.

Several years' travels through Portugal, Spain, Italy, Germany, Prussia, Sweden, Denmark and the United Provinces. 1702.

A compleat history of the Cevennes, giving a particular account of the people and country, by a Doctor of the Civil Laws. 1703.

An impartial account of the Grand Fleet and land forces 1702, with a relation of the expedition at Cadiz and the victory at Vigo, by an officer that was present. 1703.

B., C. M. A journal of the expedition of her Majesty's fleet under Sir George Rooke from Lisbon to the Bay of Altea 1704. 1704.

Levasseur, Guillaume Beauplan, sieur de. A description of Ukraine, translated from French [of 1660]. In A. and J. Churchill, A collection vol 1, 1704.

Merin, John Baptist. Journey to the mines of Hungary 1615, translated from Latin. With above, vol 4, 1704.

Rudbeck, Dr Olof. The travels of the King of Sweden's mathematicians into Lapland, also a journey into Lapland and Finland, translated anonymously from Swedish. 1704 (added to John Scheffer, The history of Lapland, 2nd edn of 1674 trn from Latin).

S., C. A trip to Portugal: or a view of their strength by sea and land, in a letter from a voluntier at Lisbon. 1704.

The travels of an English gentleman from London to Rome on foot. 1704, 1718, 1728 (5th edn).

Addison, Joseph. Remarks on several parts of Italy, in the years 1701, 1702, 1703. 1705, 1718, Hague 1718, London 1726, 1733, 1745; in Somers tracts vol 1, 1748, Glasgow 1755, London 1761, 1767; in The world displayed vol 19, 1778; in John H. Moore, A new collection, 1785; in William Mavor, An historical account vol 12, 1797; in Miscellaneous Works vol 1, 1914. See also his letters, many written about his travels; and for commentary, 1715 below.

A geographical and historical account of the Principality of Catalonia and Earldom of Barcelona. 1705.

The present state of Europe: or a genealogical, political description of all the kingdoms, states and principalities thereof. 1705, 1706.

Toland, John. An account of the courts of Prussia and Hannover. 1705, 1706, 1714.

— A faithful account of his travels in Germany, Holland. In An historical account of the life and writings, 1723.

A trip to Spain: or a true description of the comical humors of the Spaniards, in a letter from an officer in the Royal Navy. 1705.

The ancient and present state of Portugal: containing the description of that Kingdom. 1706.

A description of all the seats of the present wars of Europe, in Netherlands, Piedmont, Lombardy, Germany, Hungary, Poland, Spain and Portugal. 1707 (3 edns).

Freind, John, MD. An account of the Earl of Peterborow's conduct in Spain, chiefly since the raising of the siege of Barcelona. 1706, 1707 (with The campagne of Valencia), 1707, 1708.

Hill, Aaron. A full and just account of the present state of the Ottoman Empire from serious observations taken in many years' travels thro' those countries. 1709, 1710, 1733.

Letters to a nobleman from a gentleman travelling through Holland, Flanders and France, with a description of Ghent, Lisle, and the Courts of Versailles and St Germain. 1709.

Montagu, Ralph, Duke of. Life, containing his travels abroad. 1709.

Leonhard, Johann. An account of the Grisons: or a description of the free and independent commonwealth of the three Rhætish leagues, translated from Latin. 1711.

Brome, James. Travels through Portugal, Spain and Italy [about 1708]. 1712.

Montfaucon, Father Bernard de. The travels from Paris thro' Italy in 1698, 1699, 1700, containing an account of many antiquities, translated anonymously from Latin [of 1702]. 1712, 1725 (as The antiquities of Italy).

Chancel, A. D. A new journey over Europe, from France thro' Savoy, Switzerland, Germany, Great Britain and Ireland. 1714, 1717.

Stanyan, Abraham. An account of Switzerland. 1714, Edinburgh 1756; tr French, 1714, 1756.

Whitelock, Bulstrode. Account of his embassy to Sweden delivered to the Parliament in 1654. 1714. A pamphlet, supposed not by Whitelock, for whose journal see 1772, below.

LeClerc, J. Observations on Mr Addison's travels through Italy. 1715.

A new journey to France, with an exact description of the sea-coast, from London to Calais. 1715.

The present state of his Majesty's dominions in Germany, containing an exact description of the same. 1715.

Damato, Juan Bautista. The ancient and modern history of the Balearick islands, with their natural and geographical description, translated Colin Campbell from Spanish. 1716, 1719.

Dryden, John (the younger). A voyage to Sicily and Malta 1700 and 1701. 1716, 1776.

Perry, Captain John. The state of Russia under the present Czar, also an account of those Tartars and other people on the eastern and extreme northern parts. 1716.

South, Dr Robert. An account of his travels into Poland with the Earl of Rochester in 1674. In his Posthumous works, 1717.

Leopold, J. F. Relatio epistolica de itinere suo Suecico anno 1707 facto, ad J. Woodward. 1720.

Versailles illustrated: or divers views of the royal palace and gardens. [1720?].

Richardson, Jonathan, sr and jr. An account of some of the statues, bas-reliefs, drawings and pictures in Italy, France. 1722, 1754.

Weber, Friedrich Christian. The present state of Russia, being the journal of a foreign minister, with a description of Petersburg and Cronstot, translated anonymously from German. 2 vols 1722–3.

La Mottraye, Aubry de. Travels through Europe, Asia and into part of Africa, containing geographical, topographical and political observations on Italy, Turkey, Greece, Crim and Noghaian Tartaries, Circassia, Sweden and Lapland, translated anonymously from French. 3 vols 1723, 1730–3 (vol 3 pbd in Hague) (in French and English).

Macky, John. A journey through the Austrian Netherlands: containing the modern history and description of all the provinces, towns, castles, palaces. 1725, 1732.

Saint-Maure, Charles de. A new journey through Greece, Aegypt, Palestine, Italy, Swisserland, Alsatia and the Netherlands 1721–3 by a French officer, translated anonymously from French. 1725.

Breval, John Durant. Remarks on several parts of Europe, relating chiefly to the history, antiquities and geography of France, the Low Countries, Lorrain, Germany, Savoy, Tyrol, Switzerland, Italy and Spain. 2 vols 1726, 1738.

— Calpe, or Gibraltar: a poem. 1727.

Letters describing the character and customs of the English and French nations, with a curious essay on travelling and a criticism on Boileau's description of Paris. 1726.

Salmon, Thomas. The modern history, or the present state of all the nations (Asia and Europe). 3 vols Dublin 1727, 2 vols 1752 (as The universal traveller).

Burrish, Onslow. Batavia illustrata: or a view of the policy and commerce of the United Provinces. 2 vols 1728, 1731.

Corbett, T. An account of the expedition of the British fleet to Sicily in the years 1718, 1719, 1720, collected from the Admiral's mss. 1729.

Gyllius, Petrus (Pierre Gilles). The antiquities of Constantinople, translated from Latin [of 1561] by John Ball. 1729.

Behrens, Georg Henning. The natural history of Hartz-Forest in his Majesty's German dominions, translated from Latin by John Andree. 1730.

Wright, Edward. Some observations made in travelling through France, Italy etc in 1720–2. 2 vols 1730, 1764, 1 vol 1764 (without plates).

Careri, Dr John Francis Gemelli. Travels through Europe [1686] in several letters. In A. and J. Churchill, A collection vol 6, 1732. Travels in Italy, France, England, Low Countries and Germany.

Rolamb, Nicholas. A relation of a journey to Constantinople for the King of the Swedes, translated from Swedish. In A. and J. Churchill, A collection vol 5, 1732.

Skippon, Philip. An account of a journey made thro' part of the Low Countries, Germany, Italy and France [1663, with John Ray; see above 1673]. In A. and J. Churchill, A collection vol 6, 1732.

Cantemir, Demetrius, Prince of Moldavia. The history of the growth and decay of the Ottoman empire, translated from Latin ms by N. Tindal. 1734.

A particular description of the city of Dantzick, its fortifications, extent, trade, by an English merchant. 1734.

Dick, Sir Alexander (then Cunningham). A journey from London to Paris in 1736 [and to Rome]. GM Jan–March, June 1853.

Frankz, Thomas. A tour through France, Flanders and Germany. 1735.

Strahlenberg, Philip Johann von. An historico-geographical description of the north and eastern part of Europe and Asia, but more particularly of Russia, Siberia, and Great Tartary, translated from German [of 1730]. 1736, 1738.

Pöllnitz, Charles-Louis, Baron de. Les amusemens de Spa, or the gallantries of the Spaw in Germany: containing the virtues of every spring, translated from French by Hans de Veil. 1737.

— The memoirs: being the observations he made in his late travels from Prussia through Germany, Italy, France, Flanders, Holland, England, translated from French [of 1737] by Stephen Whatley. 4 vols 1737, 2 vols 1737, 4 vols 1739, 5 vols 1745.

Lediard, Thomas. The German spy, in familiar letters from Munster, Paderborn, Osnaburg, Minden, Bremen, Hamburg, Gluckstadt, Helgoland, Stade, Lubeck and Rostock. 1738.

Wesley, John. [Travels in Germany, 1738]. In Journals. See General Travels, above, 1735.

Byng, Sir George, Viscount Torrington. An account of the expedition to Sicily in 1718, 1719 and 1720, from the Admiral's manuscripts. 1739.

Justice, Elizabeth. A voyage to Russia: describing the laws, manners and customs of that great empire. York 1739, London 1746.

Montagu, John, Earl of Sandwich. A voyage round the Mediterranean 1738–9, with memoirs of the author's life by John Cooke. 1738, 1739.

Whatley, Rev Robert. Three letters giving an account of his travels into Germany in 1721–2. 1739.

Gray, Thomas, and Horace Walpole. [Journey to Italy]. See F. C. Roe, Le voyage de Gray et Walpole en Italie [1739–41], Revue de Littérature Comparée 6 1926.

Ripperda, Jan Willem, Duke van. Memoirs of the Duke de Ripperda, first embassador from the States-General to his most Catholic Majesty, afterwards Prime Minister to the Emperor of Fez and Morocco, containing an account of events between 1715 and 1736. 1740 (2nd edn).

Roe, Sir Thomas. The negotiations in his embassy to the Ottoman Porte 1621 to 1628. 1740.

Whatley, Stephen. A short account of a late journey to Tuscany, Rome and other parts of Italy. 1741.

Poole, Robert, MD. A journey from London to France and Holland: or the traveller's useful vade mecum. 2 vols 1742, 1746–50.

A description of Holland: or the present state of the United Provinces. 1743, 1745, Leyden 1765 (4th edn).

Blainville, M. de. Travels through Holland, Germany, Switzerland and other parts of Europe, but especially Italy, translated from French [of 1713] by George Turnbull and William Guthrie. 3 vols 1743–5, 1757.

Thompson, Charles. The travels of the late Charles Thompson, containing his observations on France, Italy, Turkey in Europe, the Holy Land, Arabia, Egypt. 3 vols Reading 1744, 4 vols Dublin 1744, 3 vols 1748, 2 vols 1754, 1767, Glasgow 1798.

Windham, William, and Peter Martel. An account of the glaciers or ice Alps in Savoy, in two letters: one from [Windam] to his friend at Geneva, the other from Peter Martel to [Windam], translated from French. 1744. The Windam letter rptd in G. R. de Beer, Early travellers in the Alps, 1930.

A description of Moscovy [Written 1698?]. In Thomas Osborne, A collection vol 1, 1745.

Flanders delineated: or a view of the Austrian and French Netherlands by an officer of the allied army now in Flanders, with a concise account of Bavaria, Bohemia. 1745.

Story, John. Travels through Sweden [1632]: containing a short survey of the kingdom. In Thomas Osborne, A collection vol 1, 1745.

The theatre of the present war in the Netherlands and upon the Rhine: containing a description of all the divisions. 1745.

Butler, Alban. Travels through France and Italy 1745–6. Ed C. Butler, Edinburgh 1803.

Douglas, John. Journal of a tour through Germany, Holland and France, 1748 to 1749. In Select works, ed W. Macdonald, Salisbury 1820.

Nugent, Thomas. The Grand Tour: or a journey through the Netherlands, Germany, Italy and France. 1749; rptd, adding The European itinerary, 4 vols 1756, 1778.

— Travels through Germany, with a particular account of the Court of Mecklenburgh. 2 vols 1768; tr German, 1781–2, 1935.

The present state of Holland: or a description of the United Provinces. Hague 1749.

ap Rhys, Udal. An account of the most remarkable places and curiosities in Spain and Portugal. 1749.

Clancy, Michael, MD. Memoirs containing his observations on many countries in Europe. 2 vols Dublin 1750.

Gori, Antonio Francisco. Memoirs concerning Herculaneum: giving a particular account of the buildings, statues, paintings, medals and other curiosities, translated from Italian [of 1748]. 1750.

[Lucas, William]. A five weeks tour to Paris, Versailles etc. 1750, 1752, 1754, 1765.

[Russell, James]. Letters from a young painter abroad to his friends in England. 2 vols 1750, 1750. Mainly from Italy.

A trip to the jubilee, by a gentleman that was at the late grand one in Rome, containing a diverting account of his most remarkable travels through France, Milan. 1750.

Cleghorn, George. Observations on the epidemical diseases in Minorca from 1744 to 1749, to which is prefixed a short account of the islands. 1751, 1768, 1815 (5th edn).

Garrick, David. The diary: being a record of his trip to Paris in 1751. Ed R. C. Alexander, New York 1928.

— Journal describing his visit to France and Italy in 1763. Ed G. W. Stone, New York 1939.

Armstrong, John. The history of the island of Minorca, trade, customs, antiquities. 1752, 1756, 1782 (as Letters from Minorca), Dublin 1782; tr French, 1769.

— A short ramble through some parts of France and Italy. 1771.

Campbell, John. The present state of Europe, explaining the interests, connections, political and commercial view of its several powers. 1752, 1757 (5th edn).

Bellicard, Jérôme Charles, and Charles Nicolas Cochin. Observations upon the antiquities of Herculaneum, translated from French. 1753.

A brief account of the Vaudois, his Sardinian Majesty's Protestant subjects in the valleys of Piedmont, in a letter from a gentleman on his travels in Italy. 1753.

Hanway, Jonas. An historical account of the British trade over the Caspian Sea, with a journal of travels through Russia into Persia, and back through Russia, Germany and Holland. 4 vols 1753, 2 vols 1754, Dublin 1754, London 1762; tr German, 1754.

The traveller's companion and guide through France, Flanders, Brabant and Holland. 1753.

Drummond, Alexander. Travels through different cities of Germany, Italy, Greece and several parts of Asia as far as the banks of the Euphrates. 1754.

Ducarel, Andrew Coltee. A tour through Normandy. 1754, 1767 (enlarged as Anglo-Norman antiquities considered in a tour through part of Normandy); tr French, 1823-5.

Major, Thomas. The ruins of Paestum otherwise Posidonia, in Magna Graecia. 1754, 1768 (with French version), Paris 1769 (also with French).

Fielding, Henry. Journal of a voyage to Lisbon. 1755, 1755, Dublin 1756, London 1785; rptd in Mavor vol 11; 1892, Boston 1902; ed A. Dobson, Oxford 1907; tr German, 1764.

Pontoppidan, Erik, Bishop of Bergen. The natural history of Norway, translated anonymously from Danish [of 1752-4]. 1755.

Calderwood, Margaret. Letters from England, Holland and the Low Countries in 1756. Ed A. Ferguson, Edinburgh 1884.

Keysler, Johan Georg. Travels through Germany, Bohemia, Hungary, Switzerland, Italy and Lorraine, translated anonymously from German [of 1740]. 4 vols 1756, 1758, 1760; in The world displayed vol 19, 1761.

Stevens, Sacheverell. Miscellaneous remarks made on the spot in a late seven years' tour through France, Germany and Holland. 1756; rptd in The world displayed vol 19, 1761.

Horrebov, Niels. The natural history of Iceland, interspersed with an account of the island by Mr Anderson, translated by Mr Anderson from Danish [of 1750]. 1758.

Whitworth, Charles Lord. An account of Russia as it was in 1710. Strawberry Hill 1758; rptd in his Fugitive pieces vol 2, 1761, 1762, 1765, 1771.

LeRoy, Julien David. The ruins of Athens, with remains and other valuable antiquities in Greece, translated from French by Robert Sayer. 1759.

Jefferys, Thomas. A description of the maritime parts of France: containing a particular account of all the fortified towns, forts, harbours, bays and rivers. 2 vols 1761, 1764.

Keate, George. A short account of the ancient history, present government, and laws of the republic of Geneva. 1761.

Taylor, John. The history of the travels and adventures of the Chevalier John Taylor, Ophthalmiater Pontifical-Imperial and Royal. 3 vols 1761-2.

Venuti, Rudolfini. A collection of some of the finest prospects in Italy, engraved by various celebrated engravers at Rome. 2 vols 1762 (captions in English, Italian and French).

Antonini, abbé Annibale. A view of Paris, describing all the churches, palaces, public buildings and fine paintings. 2 vols 1763 (in French and English; the French original 1734, 1744).

Clarke, Rev Edward. Letters concerning the Spanish nation, written at Madrid in 1760 and 1761. 1763; tr German, 1765; French, 2 vols 1770.

La Condamine, Charles de. Journal of a tour to Italy, translated from French. 1763.

Maihows (or Matthews), Dr. Travels in France, Italy and the Archipelagus: or letters written from several parts of Europe in 1750. 4 vols 1763; tr French, 2 vols 1763, 1767, 1881 (in part).

Montagu, Lady Mary Wortley. Letters written during her travels in Europe, Asia and Africa. 1763, 1765 (3rd edn); tr French, 1763. See col 1584, below.

Boswell, James. Boswell in Holland 1763-4. Ed F. A. Pottle, New York 1952 (from ms).

— Boswell on the Grand Tour, Germany and Switzerland 1764; ed F. A. Pottle, New York 1953 (from ms).

— An account of Corsica: the journal of a tour to that island and memoirs of Pascal Paoli. 1768, 1768; ed S. C. Roberts, Cambridge 1923.

Gibbon, Edward. Le journal de Gibbon à Lausanne 1763-4. Ed G. Bonnard, Lausanne 1945 (from ms, in French).

— Journey from Geneva to Rome: his journal 1764. Ed G. Bonnard 1961. See also Autobiography, ed Lord Sheffield in Miscellaneous works, 1796; ed G. Bonnard 1966.

Adam, Robert. A picturesque journey in Istria and Dalmatia. 1764.

An account of the southern maritime provinces of France, representing the distress to which they are reduced at the conclusion of the war in 1748. 1764.

Cole, William. A journal of my journey to Paris in 1765. Ed F. G. Stokes and H. Waddell 1931.

Pennant, Thomas. Tour on the Continent 1765. Ed G. R. de Beer 1948 (from ms).

Northall, Captain John. Travels through Italy [1752], containing new and curious observations on that country. 1766.

Sharp, Samuel, MD. Letters from Italy, describing the customs and manners of that country in the years 1765 and 1766. 1766, 1767, 1767.

— A view of the customs, manners, drama of Italy, as they are described in the Frustra Litteraria and in the account of Italy in English written by Mr Baretti, compared with the Letters from Italy, written by Mr Sharp. 1768.

Smollett, Tobias, Dr. Travels through France and Italy: containing observations on character, customs, religion, government, police, commerce, arts and antiquities, with a particular description of Nice. 2 vols 1766, 1766, Dublin 1766, 1772, London 1767 etc; tr German, 1767. *See col 963, above*; and G. M. Kahrl, Smollett: traveler-novelist, Chicago 1945.

Thicknesse, Philip. Observations on the customs and manners of the French nation, in a series of letters in which that nation is vindicated from the misrepresentations of some late writers. 1766, Dublin 1767, London 1779, 1789 (enlarged).

—— Remarks on the character and manners of the French, in a series of letters written during a residence of twelve months in Paris and its environs. 1767, 2 vols 1770.

—— Useful hints to those who make the tour of France in letters written from that Kingdom. 1768, 1770.

—— A year's journey through France and part of Spain. 2 vols 1777, Dublin 1777, London 1778, 1789; tr German, 1789.

—— A year's journey through the Pais Bas and Austrian Netherlands. Vol 1 (all pbd), 1784, 1786 (enlarged).

Blankett, John (or Philadelphia Stephens). 150 views in Italy, etched by various artists and amateurs on the spot. 1767.

—— Letters from Portugal on the late and present state of that Kingdom. [1777]; tr German, 1782; French, 1797.

Calvert, Frederick, Baron Baltimore. A tour to the east in years 1763 and 1764, with remarks on the city of Constantinople and the Turks. 1767, Dublin 1768.

'Coriat Junior' (Samuel Paterson). Another traveller! or cursory remarks and critical observations made upon a journey through part of the Netherlands in 1766. 2 vols 1767, 1769.

Baretti, Joseph. An account of the manners and customs of Italy, with observations on the mistakes of some travellers with regard to that country. 2 vols 1768, 1769 (with Appendix in answer to Mr Sharp's reply), Dublin 1769.

—— A journey from London to Genoa through England, Portugal, Spain and France. 2 vols 1770 (3 edns), 1969. Developed and expanded from an Italian original, Lettere familiari, 2 vols Milan 1761.

Macartney, George, Earl Macartney. An account of the embassy to Russia [in 1764]. 1768. *See also* British Isles, *above*, 1773; Asia, *below*, 1781–5.

Porter, Sir James. Observations on the religion, laws, government and manners of the Turks. 1768, 1771; tr French, 1768.

—— Turkey: its history and progress, from the journals and correspondence, with a memoir. 2 vols 1854.

Sterne, Laurence. A sentimental journey through France and Italy by Mr Yorick. 2 vols 1768. *See col 951, above.*

Wolf, John. Sketches and observations taken in a tour through a part of the south of Europe in 1757. 1768.

Grosley, Pierre Jean. New observations on Italy, translated from French [of 1764] by Thomas Nugent. 2 vols 1769, 4 vols 1770 (in French as Observations sur l'Italie et sur les Italiens).

Letters concerning the present state of the French nation. 1769.

Stevenson, John Hall. Yorick's sentimental journey continued. 2 vols in 1 1769.

An account of the character and manners of the French. 1770.

Fiquet du Boccage, Marie Anne. Letters concerning England, Holland and Italy, translated from French. 2 vols 1770.

Millard, John. The gentleman's guide in his tour through France by an officer in the Royal Navy. Bristol [1770?], 1787 (9th edn).

A review of the characters of the principal nations in Europe. 2 vols 1770.

Wilkinson, J. L. Excursions in France. 1770, 2 vols 1775.

Burney, Dr Charles. The present state of music in France and Italy: or the journal of a tour undertaken to collect materials for a general history of music. 1771, 1773; tr German, 1772.

—— The present state of music in Germany, the Netherlands and the United Provinces. 2 vols 1773; tr German, 1773; Dutch, 1786. Parts of the two journals which deal with the musical experiences were ed C. H. Glover as Continental travels 1770–2, 1927.

James, Thomas, Lieut-Colonel. The history of the Herculean Straits, now called the Straits of Gibraltar, including those parts of Spain and Barbary that lie adjacent thereto. 2 vols 1771.

Talbot, Sir R. Letters on the French nation considered in its different departments, translated from French. 2 vols 1771.

Travels into France and Italy, in a series of letters to a lady. 2 vols 1771.

An authentic narrative of the Russian expedition against the Turks by sea and land [1770], compiled by an officer on board the Russian fleet. 1772.

Guys, Pierre Augustin. A sentimental journey through Greece in a series of letters written from Constantinople, translated from French [Un voyage littéraire, 1771]. 3 vols 1772.

Hamilton, Sir William. Observations on Mount Vesuvius, Mount Etna and other volcanos. 1772, 1773, 1774; tr German, 1773; partly in French in J. H. von Riedesel, Voyage en Sicile et dans la Grande Grèce, 1773.

—— Campi Phlegraei: observations on the volcanos of the Two Sicilies. 2 vols Naples 1776 (in English and French); with suppl as An account of the eruption of Mount Vesuvius 1779, Naples 1779.

Marshall, Joseph. Travels through Holland, Flanders, Germany, Denmark, Sweden, Lapland, Russia, the Ukraine and Poland in 1768, 1769 and 1770, [with] the present state of their agriculture, population, manufactures, commerce, the arts and useful undertakings. 3 vols 1772, 1792.

—— Travels through France and Spain in the years 1770 and 1771. Vol 4 of Travels, 1776; tr German, 1778.

[Peckham, Harry]. A tour through Holland, Dutch Brabant, the Austrian Netherlands and part of France, [and] a description of Paris and its environs. 1772, 1788, 1793.

Whitelock, Bulstrode. A journal of the Swedish embassy in 1653 and 1654. Ed C. Morton 2 vols 1772; ed H. Reeve 1855; tr Swedish, 1777.

Wraxall, Sir Nathaniel William. A tour through the western, southern and interior provinces of France. 1772, 1777 (as Memoirs of the kings of France, with a tour), 1784; tr French, 1777.

—— Cursory remarks made in a tour through some of the northern parts of Europe, particularly Copenhagen, Stockholm and Petersburgh. 1775, 1776 (as A tour etc), 1807 (as A tour round the Baltic).

—— Memoirs of the courts of Berlin, Dresden, Warsaw and Vienna 1777–9. 2 vols 1800.

—— Historical memoirs of my own time from 1772 to 1784. 2 vols 1815. Contains much travel material.

Antiquities of Herculaneum. Translated from Italian by Thomas Martyn and John Lettice. 1773.

Boyle, John, Earl of Cork and Orrery. Letters from Italy in the years 1754–5, with notes by Rev John Duncombe. 1773, 1774.

Brydone, Patrick, FRS. A tour through Sicily and Malta, in a series of letters to William Beckford. 2 vols 1773, 1774, 1774, Dublin 1775, London 1776, Paris 1780, London 1790, Perth 1799, London 1807 etc; tr French, 1776. In 1782 the Comte de Borch pbd Lettres sur la Sicile et l'Isle de Malte, pour servir de Supplément au voyage de Brydone. *See* P. Fussell jr, Brydone the eighteenth-century traveler as representative man, BNYPL June 1962.

Essex, James. Journal of a tour through part of Flanders and France in 1773. Ed W. M. Fawcett 1888 (Cambridge Antiquarian Soc).

Letters from an English gentleman during his travels through Denmark. 1773.

Lind, John, FRS. Letters concerning the present state of Poland. 1773.

Riedesel, Johann Hermann, Baron von. Travels through Sicily and Magna Graecia, and a tour through Egypt, translated from German [of 1771] by J. R. Forster. 1773. The French version, 1773, includes parts of Sir William Hamilton, Observations on Mount Vesuvius, 1772 above.

[Young, Sir William]. A journal of a summer's excursion to Naples and from thence over parts of Italy, Sicily and Malta. [1773?].

The roads of Italy, engraved on 26 copper plates from the ms drawings of a nobleman of distinction. 1774.

Blaikie, Thomas. Journal: excursions d'un botaniste écossais dans les Alpes et le Jura en 1775, translated into French by L. Seylaz. Neuchâtel 1935.

— The diary of a Scotch gardener at the French Court 1775-92. Ed F. Birrell 1931.

A brief account of the roads of Italy. 1775.

Bourrit, Marc Théodore. A relation of a journey to the glaciers in the Duchy of Savoy, translated from French [of 1771] by C. and F. Davy. Norwich 1775, London 1776, Dublin 1776. The later Nouvelle description, Geneva 1783-5, was not pbd in England.

E., W. B. A letter to the late Lord Lyttelton on the eruption of Mount Aetna in 1766. 1775 (with reprints of Heneage Finch, Relation of late eruption, 1669, above).

Johnson, Samuel. Journal of his tour in France 1775. In James Boswell, Life of Samuel Johnson, 1791. *See* Mrs Thrale, 1775, *below*.

Percy, Elizabeth, Duchess of Northumberland. A short tour [in the Netherlands] in 1771. 1775.

Thrale, Hester Lynch (later Piozzi). The French journals of Mrs Thrale and Dr Johnson [describing the journey in France in 1775]. Ed M. Tyson and H. Guppy, Manchester 1932.

— Observations and reflections made in the course of a journey through France, Italy and Germany. 1789, Dublin 1789; tr German, 1790.

Twiss, Richard. Travels through Portugal and Spain in 1772 and 1773. 1775, 2 vols Dublin 1775; tr French, 1776; German, 1776.

— A trip to Paris in 1792. 1793.

Chandler, Richard. Travels in Greece. Oxford 1776, Dublin 1776. *See* his Travels in Asia Minor, 1775, *under* Asia, *below*.

Ferber, J. J. Travels through Italy 1771 and 1772 described in letters on the natural history, particularly the mountains and volcanos of that country, translated from German [of 1773] by Rudolph Erich Raspe. 1776.

— Mineralogical history of Bohemia, translated from German [of 1774] by the same. In Baron Inigo Born, Travels, 1777, below.

Knight, Lady Philippina. Letters from France and Italy 1776-95. Ed Lady Elliott-Drake 1905.

Palmer, Dean Joseph. A four months' tour through France. 2 vols 1776, Dublin 1776.

Raspe, Rudolph Erich. An account of some German volcanos and their productions. 1776.

Riggs, Anna (Lady Anne Millar). Letters from Italy, describing the manners, customs, antiquities, paintings, in 1770 and 1771. 1776, 2 vols 1776 (rev).

Born, Baron Inigo. Travels through the Bannat of Temeswar, Transylvania and Hungary in 1770, letters on the mines and mountains. Also J. J. Ferber, Mineralogical history of Bohemia, translated from German by R. E. Raspe, 1777.

Carter, Francis. A journey from Gibraltar to Malaga, with a view of that garrison and its environs, a particular account of the towns in the hoya of Malaga, the ancient and natural history of those cities, of the coast between them, and the mountains of Ronda. 3 vols 1777, 1778, 2 vols 1780; tr German, 1779.

Cayley, Cornelius. A tour through Holland, Flanders and part of France 1772. Leeds 1777 (2nd edn).

Dalrymple, Major William. Travels through Spain and Portugal in 1774, with a short account of the Spanish expedition against Algiers in 1775. Dublin 1777, rptd in J. H. Moore, A new and complete collection vol 2, 1777; tr German, 1778, 1784; French, 1783, 1787.

The Englishman's fortnight in Paris: or the art of ruining himself there in a few days, by an observer, translated from French. 1777. Also London 1766 in French, subtitled Ouvrage posthume du Docteur Stearne traduit de l'Anglois.

Howard, John. The state of the prisons in England and Wales, and an account of some foreign prisons and hospitals [in France, Holland, Low Countries, Germany and Switzerland]. Warrington 1777, 1780 (enlarged), 1784 (with Observations in Scandinavia and Russia, and in Spain and Portugal), 1792; 1929 (abridged) (EL).

— An account of the principal lazarettos in Europe. Warrington 1789, 1791; tr French, 1799.

Jones, Rev William. Observations in a journey to Paris by way of Flanders 1776. 2 vols 1777.

'Melmoth, Courtney' (Samuel Jackson Pratt). Travels for the heart, written in France. 2 vols 1777.

— Gleanings through Wales, Holland and Westphalia, with views of peace and war at home and abroad. 4 vols 1795, 1797-9 (3rd edn), 1800 (5th edn), 1802 (6th edn); tr German, 1800 (in part). *See* Gleanings through Wales and in England, 1795, *under* British Isles, *above*.

Sandby, Paul. Sixteen views in Naples and other parts of Italy. 1777.

Williams, J. The rise, progress and present state of the northern governments, viz United Provinces, Denmark, Sweden, Russia and Poland: or observations on the nature, constitution, religion, laws, policy, customs and commerce of each government. 2 vols 1777.

Ayscough, George L. Letters from an officer in the Guards: containing some accounts of France and Italy. 1778.

Dutens, Louis. Itinéraire des routes les plus fréquentées: ou journal d'un voyage aux villes principales de l'Europe en 1768, 1769, 1770, et 1771. Paris 1777, London 1778 (with Un voyage en Espagne), Paris 1783, London 1786, 1793 (with Un tour d'Angleterre); tr John Hightower as Journal of travels made through the principal cities of Europe, with an account of the best inns, 1782.

Fortis, Abbé Alberto. Travels into Dalmatia: containing general observations on the natural history of that country and the neighboring islands, in letters to the Earl of Bute, translated from Italian [of 1774]. 1778. Includes the Latin text by Antal Verancsics, Iter Buda Hadrianapolim 1553, ed Fortis.

Hull, Thomas. Selected letters between the late Duchess of Somerset, Lady Luxborough, Miss Dolman, Mr Whistler, Mr R. D. Dodsley, Wm Shenstone esq and others, including a sketch of the manners, laws etc of the Republic of Venice. 2 vols 1778.

King, Rev John Glen. A letter to the Bishop of Durham containing some observations on the climate of Russia and the northern countries. 1778.

Coxe, Archdeacon William. Sketches of the natural, civil and political state of Swisserland. 1779; tr French, 1781 (enlarged by the translator Ramond de Carbonnières), 2 vols 1782, 1787.

— An account of the Russian discoveries between Asia and America, to which is added the conquest of Siberia and the history of the commerce between Russia and China. 1780, 1780, 1787 (with Supplement: A comparative view of the Russian discoveries with those made by Captains Cook and Clerke), 1804; tr German, 1783.

—— An account of the prisons and hospitals in Russia, Sweden and Denmark. 1781.

—— Travels into Poland, Russia, Sweden and Denmark. 3 vols 1784, 5 vols 1787–91, 3 vols 1792, 1802, 1803; tr French, 4 vols 1786, 2 vols 1791.

—— Travels in Switzerland and in the country of the Grisons. 3 vols 1789, 1791, 1794, 1801, Basle 1802 (with the Ramond addns translated into English); rptd in John Pinkerton, A general collection vol 5, 1809; tr French, 1790.

Moore, Dr John. A view of society and manners in France, Switzerland and Germany, with anecdotes relating to some eminent characters. 2 vols 1779, 1780 (3rd edn), 3 vols Dublin 1792 (4th edn), 1786 (6th edn), 2 vols 1800 (9th edn); tr German, 2 vols 1779; French, 2 vols 1781.

—— A view of society and manners in Italy. 1781, 1783, Philadelphia 1783, Dublin 1786, 1792, London 1795.

—— A journal during a residence in France from August to December 1792. 2 vols 1793 (2nd edn), Boston 1794; tr German, 1794.

Sherlock, Martin. Lettres d'un voyageur anglois. [Geneva?] 1779, London and Paris 1780; tr Rev John Dunscombe as Letters from an English traveller, written from Berlin, Dresden, Vienna, Rome, Naples and France in 1776, 1777 and 1778. 1779, 1780 (rev, with New letters), 1781, 1802 (enlarged); tr German, 1780.

—— Nouvelles lettres d'un voyageur anglois. London and Paris 1780, London 1780; tr Sherlock as New letters from an English traveller 1780 (with preceding), 1781 (separate). The first collection included 27 letters out of 200; the New letters numbered 44.

Swinburne, Henry. Travels through Spain in 1775 and 1776, in which monuments of Roman and Moorish architecture are illustrated by drawings taken on the spot. 1779, 2 vols Dublin 1783–6, 1787 (with A journey from Bayonne to Marseilles); tr French 1787. The drawings were engraved by Thomas Bensley and pbd as Views in Spain, 1794 (in English and French).

—— Travels in the Two Sicilies 1777, 1778, 1779 and 1780. 2 vols 1783–5, 4 vols 1790, 1795; tr French, 1785.

—— A journey from Bayonne to Marseilles. 1787, 1787 (with Travels through Spain, above).

Dillon, Sir John Talbot. Travels through Spain, with a view to illustrate the natural history and physical geography of that kingdom. 1780, Dublin 1781, London 1782; rptd in C. Pelham, The world vol 2, 1808; tr German, 1782.

—— Letters from an English traveller in Spain in 1778 on the origin and progress of poetry in that Kingdom. 1781.

Georgi, J. G. Russia: or a complete historical account of all the nations which comprise that extensive nation, translated from German [of 1777] by William Tooke. 4 vols 1780–3.

Peyron, Jean-François. Nouveau voyage en Espagne fait en 1777 et 1778. Geneva 1780, 2 vols London and Paris 1782, London and Liège 1783. Partly tr in Jean-Francois de Bourgoing, Travels in Spain, 1789, below.

Richard, John. A tour from London to Petersburgh and Moscow, and return to London by Courland, Poland, Germany and Holland. 1780, Dublin 1781.

Troil, Uno von. Letters on Iceland: containing observations on the civil, literary, ecclesiastical and natural history, antiquities, volcanoes, basaltes, hot springs; customs, dress, manners of the inhabitants, made during a voyage 1772 by Joseph Banks esq, Dr Solander, Dr J. Lind, Dr Uno von Troil, translated from Swedish [of 1777]. 1780, 1780, Dublin 1780 (rev), London 1783; rptd in John Pinkerton, A collection vol 1, 1808.

Richard, Abbé Jérôme. Historical and critical description of Italy, translated from French [of 1766 etc]. 1781.

Charington, Lord. Memoirs: containing a genuine description of the government and manners of the present Portuguese. 1782.

Sheridan, T. R. A full and genuine account of the revolution in the Kingdom of Sweden, [and] facts concerning the extent, power, government, religion, literature and manners of the Swedish nation. 1782.

The traveller's vade mecum through the Netherlands and parts of France and Germany. Canterbury 1783.

The American wanderer through various parts of Europe, in a series of letters to a lady. 1783, Dublin 1783.

Beckford, William. Dreams, waking thoughts and incidents in a series of letters from various parts of Europe. 1783, 2 vols 1834 (rev as Italy, with sketches of Spain and Portugal).

—— Letters written through France and Italy. 1786, 2 vols 1834 (rev in Italy, with preceding).

—— The journal in Portugal and Spain 1787–8. Ed B. Alexander 1954.
The travel-writings were collected by G. Chapman in Travel diaries, 2 vols Cambridge 1928.

The female spy: or Mrs Tonkin's journey through France in the late war, under taken by the express order of the Rt Hon Chas. Jas. Fox, for which she has been refused any compensation. 1783.

An accurate description of the island and kingdom of Sicily. Falkirk 1784, 1786 (with A narrative of Sardinia, and translated by D. Macnab). The BM catalogue notes the source as Pierre d'Avity, Les empires, royaumes, estatz du monde, 1614.

Habesci, Elias. The present state of the Ottoman empire, including a particular description of the Court and seraglio of the Grand Signor, translated from French ms. 1784.

Parminter, Jane. Extracts from a Devonshire lady's notes of travel in France 1784. Ed O. J. Reichel, Trans Devonshire Assoc for Advancement of Science 34 1902.

Randolph, —. Observations on the present state of Denmark, Russia and Switzerland. 1784.

[Richardson, William]. Anecdotes of the Russian empire, in a series of letters written from St Petersburgh. 1784.

Hervey, Christopher. Letters from Portugal, Spain, Italy and Germany, in 1759 to 1761. 3 vols 1785.

Tott, Francis, Baron de. Memoirs of the Turks and Tartars, translated from French [of 1784]. 2 vols 1785, Dublin 1785, London 1786 (as Memoirs containing the state of the Turkish empire and the Crimea during the late war with Russia, adding Strictures by M. Charles de Peyssonnel).

A tour to Ermenonville: containing an account of Chantilly. 1785.

[Becket, Andrew]. A trip to Holland: containing sketches of the characters. 2 vols 1786.

Drinkwater, Capt John. The history of the siege of Gibraltar [1779–83] with a description and account of that garrison. 1786, 1786, 1844, 1905.

Fleuriot, Jean-Marie-Jérôme (called Marquis de Langle). A sentimental journey through Spain, translated from French [Le voyage de Figaro en Espagne, 1784]. 2 vols 1786.

—— A picturesque description of Switzerland, translated from French. [1791?].

Letters and observations written in a short tour through France and Italy by a gentleman. 1786.

[Russell, Francis, Duke of Bedford]. A descriptive journey through the interior parts of Germany and France. 1786.

Shaw, James. Sketches of the history of the Austrian Netherlands, with remarks on the general state of these provinces. 1786.

Beckford, Peter. Familiar letters from Italy in 1787. 2 vols Salisbury 1805.

Costigan, Arthur William. Sketches of society and manners in Portugal. 2 vols 1787, 1788; tr German, 1788–9; French, 1804.

General observations regarding the present state of Denmark. [1787?].

General observations regarding the present state of the Russian empire. [1787?].

General observations regarding the political circumstances of the Kingdom of Sweden drawn up in a tour in 1786. [1787?].

A hasty sketch of a tour through part of the Austrian Netherlands and great part of Holland. 1787.

Martyn, Thomas. The gentleman's guide in his tour through Italy. 1787, 1791 (as A tour through Italy); tr French, 1791.

— Sketch of a tour through Swisserland, with a catalogue of paintings etc in Italy. 1787, 1797.

Muirhead, Lockhart. Journals of travels in parts of the late Austrian Low Countries, France, the Pays de Vaud and Tuscany in 1787 and 1789. 1803.

Risbeck, Johann Caspar. Travels through Germany, translated from German by Paul Henry Maty. 1787; rptd in John Pinkerton, A collection vol 6, 1809.

Boruwlaski, Joseph. Memoirs of the celebrated dwarf: containing an account of his birth, education, marriage, travels and voyages, translated from French by Mr des Carrières. 1788 (with parallel French and English), Birmingham 1792 (separate French and English edns), Durham 1820; ed R. H. Heatley as Life and Love letters of a dwarf, 1902.

Bowdler, Thomas, FRS. Letters written in Holland in September and October 1787, with other papers relating to the journey of the Princess of Orange on June 28th. 1788.

Gardnor, Rev John. Views taken on and near the river Rhine at Aix-la-Chapelle, and on the river Maese, engraved in aqua-tinta by William and Elizabeth Ellis (32 large plates). 1788, 1792.

Jardine, Alexander, Lieut-Colonel. Letters from Barbary, France, Spain and Portugal. 1788, Dublin 1789, London 1790, 1793, 1794; tr German, 1790.

Letters from several parts of Europe and the east. 3 vols 1788.

Lusignan, S. [A journey overland from Constantinople to England]. In Letters addressed to Sir William Fordyce FRS, containing a voyage from England to Smyrna etc, 1788. See Asia, below.

Mercier du Paty, C. M. J. B., President. Travels through Italy in letters written in 1785, translated by an English gentleman from French [of 1788]. 1788, 1789. Another trn by J. Povoleri as Sentimental letters on Italy, 2 vols 1789.

Peckham, Harry. Travels through Holland, Dutch Brabant, the Austrian Netherlands and part of France. 1788 (4th edn), 1793 (5th edn).

Pownall, Thomas. Notices and descriptions of antiquities of the Provincia Romana of Gaul, now Provence, and an appendix describing the Roman baths discovered in 1784 at Badenweiler. 1788.

Savary, Claude Etienne. Letters on Greece: containing travels through Rhodes, Crete and other islands, translated from French [of 1788]. 1788. See his Letters on Egypt, 1787, under Asia, below.

A tour sentimental and descriptive through the United Provinces, the Austrian Netherlands and France. 2 vols 1788.

Bourgoing, Jean François de. Travels in Spain: containing a comprehensive view of the present state of that country, with copious extracts from the Essays on Spain of M. Peyron [see 1782, above], translated from French [of 1789]. 1789; retr in John Pinkerton, A collection vol 5, 1809.

Consett, Matthew. A tour through Sweden, Swedish-Lapland, Finland and Denmark. 1789, Stockton 1815; tr German, 1790.

Craven, Lady Elizabeth, Margravine of Brandenburg-Anspach. A journey through the Crimea to Constantinople in 1786. 1789, Dublin 1789, London 1814; tr French, 1789; German, 1789.

[Paris, John]. Six days tour in Normandy, with a short account of Havre de Grace, Caen etc. 1789.

Richard de Saint-Non, Jean Claude. [Picturesque voyage, a description of the kingdoms of Naples and Sicily, translated from French, 5 vols 1781–6]. 1789. Listed by Pinkerton, A collection vol 17.

Rigby, Dr Edward. Letters from France in 1789. Ed his daughter Lady Eastlake. 1880.

[Villiers, John Charles, Earl of Clarendon]. A tour through part of France: containing a description of Paris, Cherbourg and Ermenonville. 1789.

Drevon, I. F. H. A journey through Sweden written by a Dutch officer, translated from French [of 1789] by W. Radcliffe. 1790.

Ireland, Samuel. A picturesque tour through Holland, Brabant and part of France in 1789. 2 vols 1790, 1796.

Sutherland, Capt David. A tour up the Straits from Gibraltar to Constantinople, with the leading events in the present war to 1789. 1790, 1790.

Walker, Adam. Ideas suggested on the spot in a late excursion through Flanders, Germany, Italy and France. 1790.

— A sketch of an excursion to Paris in 1785. 1792 (in Remarks made in a tour from London to the Lakes).

Williams, Helen Maria. Letters written in France in the summer of 1790. 1791, Boston 1791 (as Letters on the French Revolution written in France); tr French, 1791.

— Letters from France concerning the events of 1790, 1791, 1792, 1793. 2 vols Dublin 1794.

— Letters containing a sketch of the politics of France from May 1793 to July 1794. 2 vols 1795, Dublin 1796; tr French, [1795?].

— New travels in Switzerland: containing a picture of the country. 2 vols 1796, 1798 (as A tour in Switzerland: or a view of those countries).

— A residence in France, described in letters from an English lady. Ed 'John Gifford' (J. R. Green) 2 vols 1797, 1797.

— Sketches of the state of manners and opinion in the French Republic toward the close of the eighteenth century in a series of letters. 2 vols 1801.

Other travel works follow after 1800.

Garden, Francis, Lord Gardenstone. Travelling memorandums made in a tour upon the continent of Europe 1786–8. 3 vols Edinburgh 1791–5; vols 1–2 rptd Edinburgh 1792.

Temple, Henry, Viscount Palmerston. Diary in France July 6–August 31 1791. Ed O. Browning in Despatches of Earl Gower 1790–2, Cambridge 1885.

Townsend, Rev Joseph. A journey through Spain in the years 1786 and 1787, with attention to the agriculture, manufactures, commerce, population and revenues, and remarks in passing through a part of France. 3 vols 1791, 1792, Bath 1814; tr German, 1791; French, 3 vols 1800.

Albanis de Beaumont, Jean François. An historical and picturesque description of the country of Nice (12 etchings colored), translated from French [of 1787]. 1792.

— Travels through the Rhaetian Alps in 1786, from Italy to Germany through Tyrol (10 large aquatint views, from drawings by the author). 1792.

— A picturesque tour from Geneva to the Pennine Alps, translated from French [of 1787]. 1794.

— Travels (in 1794) through the Maritime Alps from Italy to Lyons across the Col de Tende by way of Nice, Provence and Languedoc (18 aquatints); Select views of the antiquities and harbours in the south of France (13 aquatints). 2 vols in 1 1794–5.

— Travels from France to Italy through the Lepontine Alps: or an itinerary of the road from Lyons to Turin by way of the Pays-de-Vaud, the Vallais and the Monts Great St Bernard, Simplon and St Gothard (27 aquatint views). 1800, 1806.

Hill, Rev Brian. Observations and remarks in a journey through Sicily and Calabria in 1791. 1792.

Plescheef, F. (Sergyei Plyeschchyeev). A survey of the Russian empire, translated by James Smirnove. 1792.

Smith, John. Select views in Italy (72 engraved plates by Landseer and others after Smith). 2 vols in 1 1792–6.

Swinton, Andrew. Travels into Norway, Denmark and Russia 1788–91. 1792, Dublin 1792; tr French, 1798; German, 1793.

Watkins, Thomas. Travels in 1787–9 through Swisserland, Italy, Sicily, the Greek islands, to Constantinople; through part of Greece, Ragusa and the Dalmatian isles. 2 vols 1792, 1794.

Weston, Stephen, FRS. Letters from Paris during the summer of 1791. 1792.

— Letters from Paris during the summer of 1792. 1793.

Young, Arthur, FRS. Travels during the years 1787, 1788 and 1789, undertaken with a view of ascertaining the cultivation, wealth, resources and national prosperity of the Kingdom of France; added, the register of a tour into Spain. 2 vols Bury St Edmunds 1792, Dublin 1793, London 1794; rptd in John Pinkerton, A collection vol 4, 1809; ed M. B. Edwards 1889; 1915 (EL); ed C. Maxwell, Cambridge 1929; tr French, 3 vols 1793, 1794 etc; German, 1793–4.

Letters from Paris during the summers of 1791 and 1792. 2 vols 1793.

Moore, Dr Edward. The journal of a residence in France from August to the middle of December 1792. 2 vols 1793; tr French, German, Dutch.

A ramble through Holland, France and Italy 1793. 2 vols 1793.

Smith, Sir James Edward. A sketch of a tour on the Continent in the years 1786 and 1787. 3 vols 1793, 1807.

A tour through Germany: containing full directions for travelling in that interesting country. 1793.

A tour through the theatre of war [France] in November and December 1792, January 1793, and accounts of the death of Louis XVI. 1793, 1793.

Wordsworth, William. Descriptive sketches in verse taken during a pedestrian tour in the Italian, Grison, Swiss and Savoyard Alps. 1793.

Astley, Philip. A description and historical account of the places now the theatre of war in the Low Countries. 1794, Dublin 1794, London 1794, 1794.

Chantreau, P. N. Philosophical, political and literary travels in Russia 1788 and 1789, translated from French [of 1794]. 2 vols 1794, 1794.

[Cogan, Thomas, MD.] The Rhine: a journey from Utretch to Francfort 1791–2, with 24 views in aqua tinta. 2 vols 1793, 1794.

Courtenay, John, MP. The present state of the manners, arts and politics of France and Italy, in a series of poetical epistles from Paris, Rome and Naples in 1792 and 1793. 1794, 1794.

Este, Charles. A journey in the year 1793 through Flanders, Brabant and Germany to Switzerland. 1794, 1795, 1800.

Gray, Robert, Bishop of Bristol. Letters during the course of a tour through Germany, Switzerland and Italy in 1791 and 1792, with reflections on the manners, literature and religion. 1794.

Pausanias. The description of Greece, translated from Greek by Thomas Taylor. 3 vols 1794, 1824.

A peep into Paris: amusing and incidental French anecdotes, with a description of the Parisian theatres. 1794.

Rocques de Montgaillard, J. G. M., Count. The state of France in May 1794, translated Joshua L. Wilkinson. [1794].

Frederick, Col. Description of Corsica, with an account of its union to the crown of Great Britain. 1795.

Murphy, James Cavanah, architect. Travels in Portugal through the provinces of Entre Douro e Minho, Beira, Entremaduro and Alem-Tejo in 1789 and 1790. 1795; tr German, 1794.

— A general view of the state of Portugal: containing a topographical description thereof, compiled from the best Portuguese writers and from notices obtained in the country. 1798.

Radcliffe, Ann. A journey made in the summer of 1794 through Holland and the western frontier of Germany, with a return down the Rhine, with observations during a tour to the lakes of Lancashire, Westmoreland and Cumberland. 1795.

Spallanzani, Abbé Lazzaro. Tour to Vesuvius, Aetna. 1795.

— Travels in the Two Sicilies and some parts of the Apennines, translated from Italian [of 1788]. 4 vols 1798; retr in John Pinkerton, A collection vol 5, 1809.

Wilkinson, Joshua Lucock. The wanderer: or a collection of anecdotes and incidents, with reflections political and religious, during two excursions in 1791 and 1793 in France, Germany and Italy. 2 vols 1795, 1798.

Hobhouse, Sir Benjamin. Remarks on several parts of France, Italy etc in 1783, 1784, 1785. Bath 1796, Trowbridge 1796.

Hunter, William. Travels in 1792 through France, Turkey and Hungary to Vienna, concluding with an account of that city. 1796, 2 vols 1798 (enlarged), 1803 (with Several tours in Hungary 1799 and 1800).

Journal du voyageur neutre depuis son départ de Londres pour Paris le 18 novembre 1795 jusqu'à son retour à Londres 16 février 1796. 1796.

Letters from Scandinavia on the past and present state of the northern nations of Europe. 2 vols 1796.

Merigot, J. Views and ruins in Rome and its vicinity, from drawings made upon the spot in 1791 (62 aquatint plates, descriptions in French and English). 1796, 1797–9 (with plates in ser).

Owen, Rev John. Travels into different parts of Europe in the years 1791–2, with familiar remarks on places, men and manners. 1796.

Select views in Italy, with topographical and historical descriptions in English and French (india proof engravings drawn by J. Smith). 1796.

Stolberg, Frederick Leopold zu, Graf. Travels through Germany, Switzerland, Italy and Sicily, translated from German [of 1794] by Thomas Holcroft. 2 vols 1796–7.

Tench, Watkin. Letters written in France to a friend in London 1794–5. 1796.

Wollstonecraft, Mary. Letters written during a short residence in Sweden, Norway and Denmark. 1796, Wilmington 1796, London 1889.

Dallaway, James. Constantinople, ancient and modern, with excursions to the shores and islands of the Archipelago and to the Troad (10 colored aquatints). 1797; tr French, 1799.

'Gifford, John' (John Richard Green). A residence in France. See Helen Maria Williams, 1791 above.

Lumisden, Andrew. Remarks on the antiquities of Rome and its environs: being a classical and topographical survey of the ruins. 1797, 1812.

Reynolds, Sir Joshua. A journey to Flanders and Holland in 1781. In Works, ed Edmond Malone 2 vols 1797 etc.

Sketches and observations made in a tour through various parts of Europe in 1792–4. 1797.

Southey, Robert. Letters written during a short residence in Spain and Portugal, with some account of Spanish and Portugueze poetry. Bristol 1797, 1799, London 1808.

Townson, Robert. Travels in Hungary, with a short account of Vienna in 1793. 1797.

[Brooke, N., MD]. Observations on the manners and customs of Italy, with remarks on British commerce on that Continent, also of the explosion of Mount Vesuvius in 1794. Bath 1798.

Clubbe, Rev William. The Omnium: containing the journal of a late three days' tour into France. Ipswich 1798.

Coleridge, Samuel Taylor. Satyrane's letters [selections from letters written home from Germany 1798–9]. Friend Nov–Dec 1809; rptd in Biographia literaria, 2 vols 1817; Collected letters vol 1, ed E. L. Griggs, Oxford 1956.

Eton, William. A survey of the Turkish empire. 1798, 1799.

Salmon, J. A description of the works of art of ancient and modern Rome, with a tour through the environs. 2 vols 1798–1800.

—— An historical description of ancient and modern Rome, [and] a tour through the cities and towns in the environs of the metropolis and an account of the antiquities found at Gabia. 2 vols 1800, 1816.

A sketch of modern France in letters to a lady of fashion in 1796 and 1797 during a tour through France by a lady. Ed C. L. Moody 1798.

Croker, Capt Richard. Travels through several provinces of Spain and Portugal. 1799.

Matthison, Friedrich von. Letters written from various parts of the Continent [Germany, Switzerland, southern France etc], translated from German by A. Plumptre. 1799.

Montagu, John, Earl of Sandwich. A voyage round the Mediterranean in 1738 and 1739. 1799.

Tooke, Rev William. A view of the Russian empire during the reign of Catherine II and to 1798: manufactures, commerce. 3 vols 1799, 1800; tr French, 1801.

Hager, Dr. Pictures of Palermo, translated from German [of 1799] by Mrs Robinson. 1800.

Mercier, Louis Sébastien. New pictures of Paris, translated from French [of 1782 etc]. 1800; retr W. and E. Jackson 1929.

Walsh, Edward, MD. A narrative of the expedition to Holland in the autumn of 1799. 1800.

Pennington, Rev Thomas. Continental excursions: or tours into France, Switzerland and Germany in 1782, 1787 and 1789. 2 vols 1809.

§ 2

Klenze, C. von. The interpretation of Italy during the last two centuries. Chicago 1907.

Mead, W. E. The Grand Tour in the eighteenth century. New York 1914.

Beza, M. English travellers in Rumania. EHR 32 1917.

de Beer, G. R. Early travellers in the Alps. 1930.

—— Travellers in Switzerland 941–1945. 1947. With lists and bibliographies.

Maxwell, C. The English traveller in France 1698–1915. 1932.

Peyre, H. Les voyageurs anglais en Bourgogne au xviiie siècle. Annales de Bourgogne 4 1932.

Wood, K. L. The French theatre in the xviiith century according to some contemporary English travellers. Revue de Littérature Comparée 12 1932.

Marshall, R. Italy in English literature 1755–1815: origins of the romantic interest in Italy. New York 1934.

Thorpe, C. D. Two Augustans cross the Alps: Dennis and Addison on mountain scenery. SP 32 1935.

Lambert, R. S. Grand Tour: a journey in the tracks of the age of aristocracy. 1937.

—— The fortunate traveller: a short story of touring and travel for pleasure. 1950.

Bruford, W. H. Germany and the Germans: eighteenth-century English travellers' tales. German Life & Letters 1 1937.

Kirby, P. F. The grand tour in Italy 1700–1800. New York 1952.

Stoye, J. W. English travellers abroad 1604–1667. 1952.

Spencer, T. J. B. Fair Greece sad relic: literary philhellenism from Shakespeare to Byron. 1954.

Osborn, J. M. Travel literature and the rise of neo-Hellenism in England. BNYPL May 1963.

Sells, A. Lytton. The paradise of travellers: the Italian influence on Englishmen in the eighteenth century. 1964.

Trease, G. The Grand Tour. 1967.

Parks, G. B. The decline and fall of the English renaissance admiration of Italy. HLQ 31 1968.

(4) ASIA

Mandelslo, Johann Albrecht von. The voyage and travels into the East Indies 1638 to 1640: containing a description of the Great Mogul's empire, the kingdoms of Deccan, Zeilan, Coromandel, Pegu, Japan and China, translated from German [of 1658] by John Davies of Kidwell. 1662 (with next item), 1669; condensed in John Harris, Navigantium vol 2, 1705 etc; Bombay 1931 (complete).

Olearius, Adam. Voyages and travels of the ambassadors of Holstein to the Great Duke of Muscovy [1633–5] and the King of Persia [1635–9], translated from German [of 1647] by John Davies. 1662 (with preceding), 1669; rptd in John Harris, Navigantium vol 2, 1705 etc.

Caron, Frans, and Joost Schouten. A true description of the mighty kingdoms of Japan and Siam, translated from Dutch [of 1636] by Capt Roger Manley. 1663, 1671; ed C. R. Boxer 1925.

Della Valle, Pietro. The travels into East India and Arabia deserta [1614–24], translated from Italian [of 1650–8] by G. Havers. 1665 (with Sir Thomas Roe, Voyage into the East Indies, rptd from 1655); ed E. Grey 2 vols 1891 (Hakluyt Soc).

Nieuhof, Jan. An embassy [of Peter de Goyer and Jacob de Keyzer] from the [Dutch] East India Company to the Grand Tartar Cham Emperour of China, translated from Dutch [of 1665] by John Ogilby. 1669, 1671; tr in John Pinkerton, A collection vol 7, 1811 (from French version of 1665).

Montanus, Arnoldus. Atlas Japannensis: containing a description of their territories etc, translated from Dutch [of 1669] by John Ogilby. 1670.

—— Atlas chinensis: being a second part of remarkable passages in two embassies to the Vice Roy Sing La

Mong and General Taysing Lipovi and to Ka-Konchi Emperor of China and East Tartary, translated from Dutch by John Ogilby. 1671 (as vol 2 of Nieuhof item, above), 1673 (as vol 2 following Atlas japannensis).

Bernier, François. The history of the late revolution of the empire of the Great Mogol, with a letter touching the extent of Indostan, the riches, forces and justice of the same and the principal cause of the decay of the states of Asia: a continuation of the memoirs of Monsieur de Bernier, translated from French [of 1659] by H[enry] O[ldenbourg]. 2 vols 1671, 1676, 1684 (with Tavernier, below); rptd in Thomas Osborne, A collection vol 2, 1745; in John Pinkerton, A collection vol 8, 1811; as Travels in the Mogul Empire 1656–68, retr I. Brock 2 vols 1826; rptd 1891, Calcutta 1904, London 1914.

A journey to Jerusalem: or a relation of the travels of fourteen Englishmen 1669 from Scanderoon to Tripoly, Jerusalem, Bethlem, Jericho and back to Aleppo. 1672; rptd in R.B., Two journeys to Jerusalem, 1683, 1685, 1692, 1715, 1759, 1786; tr Welsh, 1690.

Marshall, John. John Marshall in India: notes and observations in Bengal 1668–72. Ed S. A. Kahn 1927.

—— A letter from the East Indies on the heathen priests commonly called Bramines. Philosophical Trans 22 1702; rptd in Miscellanea curiosa vol 3, 1708.

Smith, Thomas. Epistolae duae, altera de moribus ac institutis Turcarum agit, altera septem Asiae ecclesiarum notitiam continet. Oxford 1672, 1674 (expanded Epistolae quatuor, duae de moribus Turcarum, duae septem Asiae ecclesiarum ac Constantinopoleos notitiam continet). These letters rptd separately as follows:

—— Septem ecclesiarum notitia. 1676, Utrecht 1694; in Opuscula, 1716, below.

—— De graecae ecclesiae hodierno statu epistola. Oxford 1676, 1678, Utrecht 1698; London 1680 (tr as An account of the Greek church as to its doctrine and rites of worship).

—— Remarks upon the manners religion and government of the Turks, and a brief description of Constantinople. 1678.

—— A journal of a voyage from England to Constantinople 1668 with an account of Brusa. In Miscellanea curiosa vol 3, 1708.

—— Opuscula ex itinere ipsius turcico sive septem ecclesiarum notitia. Rotterdam 1716.

Varenius, Bernard. Descriptio regni Japoniae et Siam, item de Japoniorum religione et Siamensium. Cambridge 1673 (from original edn of Amsterdam 1629).

[Grueber, Johann]. China and France: or two treatises, the one of the present state of China, published by the French King's cosmographer, the other the life of Lewis the XIV, translated from French. 1676.

—— Travels from China to Europe in 1661. In Thomas Astley, A collection vol 4, 1745; rptd in J. H. Moore, A collection, 1785.

Tavernier, Jean Baptiste, Baron d'Aubonne. The six voyages through Turkey into Persia and the East Indies for the space of forty years, with a new description of the Seraglio, translated from French [of 1676] by John Phillips, with a description of the kingdoms which encompass the Euxine and Caspian seas by an English traveller. 1677, 1678, 2 vols 1684 (with Bernier, 1671 above), 1688, 1690, Calcutta 1905; retr V. Ball 1889, 1925.

—— A collection of several relations and treatises not printed among the first six voyages, translated from French [of 1679] by Edward Everard. 1680, 1684 etc (with preceding).

—— A new relation of the inner part of the Seraglio. 1684 (separate from Six voyages).

Bowrey, Thomas. A geographical account of the Bay of Bengal 1669–79. Ed R. C. Temple 1905 (Hakluyt Soc).

Knox, Robert. An historical relation of the island Ceylon, with the detaining in captivity the author and divers other Englishmen. 1681; rptd with continuation in John Harris, Navigantium vol 2, 1705; rptd in History of Ceylon, 1817; rptd in An English garner: voyages and travels vol 2, ed C. R. Beazley 1903; rptd Colombo 1908, Glasgow 1911; tr French, 1684, 1693; Dutch, 1692; German 1747.

Glanius, W. Relation of an unfortunate voyage to the Kingdom of Bengala and the loss of their ship. 1682. Tr from Dutch?

—— A new voyage to the East Indies: containing an account of several of those countries, and more particularly of the Kingdom of Bantam, and likewise of the Kingdom of Siam, of the isles of Japan and Madagascar. 1682, 1682. Tr from Dutch?

Struys, Jan Janszoon. The voiages and travels [1647–72] through Italy, Greece, Muscovy, Tartary, Media, Persia, East-India, Japan and other countries, translated from Dutch [of 1670] by John Morrison. 1684.

Chardin, Sir John. Travels into Persia and the East-Indies, with the author's voyage from Paris to Ispahan, translated from French [London 1686]. 1686, 1689, 1691, 1711; ed N. M. Penzer 1925.

—— A new and accurate description of Persia and other eastern nations, translated from enlarged French work [vols 3–4 of 10 vols 1711] by Edmund Lloyd. 2 vols 1724.

Verbiest, Ferdinand. Two journeys of the present Emperour of China into Tartary in 1682 and 1683. 1686 (with reprint of Fernando de Soto, Relation of the invasion and conquest of Florida, original Portuguese 1557, tr 1609, 1611).

Chaumont, Alexandre de. A relation of the late embassy to the Court of the King of Siam, translated from French [of 1687]. 1687, 1688 (incorporated in Tachard, 1688 below).

Hedges, William. Diary during his agency in Bengal as well as on his voyage out and return overland 1681–7. Ed R. Barlow with notes by Sir H. Yule 3 vols 1886–8 (Hakluyt Soc).

Thevenot, Jean. The travels into the Levant: I, Turkey; II, Persia; III, The East Indies, translated from French [of 1684] by David Lovell. 1687, 1687; Pt III rptd Delhi 1949 (India Records Soc).

Magaillans [Magalhaes], Gabriel, SJ. A new history of China: containing a description of that vast empire: language, government, manufactures, translated from the French version of [1688] of the unpublished Portuguese [written 1668] by William Ogilby. 1688.

Tachard, Guy, SJ. A relation of the voyage to Siam, performed by six Jesuits sent by the French King 1685, with the astrological observations, and their remarks of natural philosophy etc, translated from French [of 1686]. 1688. The account of a second voyage vol 2, 1689, was not translated.

Heliogenes del Epy. A voyage into Tartary: containing a curious description of that country, with part of Greece and Turkey. 1689.

A new history of the empire of China: containing a description of the politick, government, towns, manners and customs, translated from French. 1689. This may be Magaillans, 1688 above.

A relation of the revolution in Siam: being the substance of letters writ in 1688 and 1689 from Siam and the coast of Coromandel, translated from French. 1690; rptd in Thomas Osborne, A collection vol 2, 1745.

Avril, Philippe, SJ. Travels into divers parts of Europe and Asia to discover a new way by land into China, together with a description of Great Tartary, translated from French [of 1692]. 1693.

La Loubère, Simon de. A new historical relation of the Kingdom of Siam 1687, 1688, translated from French [of 1692] by A.P., FRS. 1693.

Rauwolff, Dr Leonhart. Itinerary into the eastern countries, as Syria, Palestine, Armenia, Mesopotamia, translated from German [of 1581] by Nicholas Staphorst, in John Ray, A collection vol 1, 1693. Vol 2 of Ray contains extracts from many travellers to the Levant, from Belon [1550] to Thevenot.

Busbecq, Ogier Ghiselin de. Travels into Turkey: containing the most accurate account of the Turks and neighboring nations, translated from the Latin [of 1589 etc, including a Latin edn, Oxford 1660] of the letters from Turkey 1554–62. 1694, 1744, Glasgow 1761; retr as Life and letters, ed C. T. Forster and F. H. B. Daniell 2 vols 1881; retr as Turkish letters by E. S. Forster, 1927. The Paris dispatches of Busbecq 1574–6, not translated in 1694 etc were tr R. E. Jones and B. C. Weber, New York 1962.

Faria y Sousa, Manuel de. The Portuguese Asia: or the history of the discovery and conquest of India by the Portuguese, translated from Portuguese [of 1666] abridged by John Stevens. 3 vols 1695.

Sanson, Nicolas. The present state of Persia, translated from French [of 1695] by John Savage. 1695.

Duquesne, Abraham. A new voyage to the East Indies in 1690 and 1691: being a full description of the isles of Maldive, Cocos, Andamans and all the forts and garrisons of the French, translated from French [of 1692]. 1696.

Mocquet, Jean. Travels and voyages into Africa, Asia and America, the East and West-Indies, Syria, Jerusalem and the Holy-land, translated from French [of 1617] by Nathaniel Pullen. 1696.

Ovington, John. A voyage to Suratt 1689, giving a large account of that city and its inhabitants and of the English factory there. 1696; ed H. G. Rawlinson 1929; tr French, 1725.

Seller, Abednego. The antiquities of Palmyra, with critical observations on the manners, religion and government of that country. 1696.

Halifax, William. A relation of a voyage from Aleppo to Palmyra in Syria. 1691. Philosophical Trans 19 1695-7; rptd separately 1705; and in Miscellanea curiosa vol 3, 1708; ed C. R. Condee as A relation of a voyage to Tadmor 1691, 1890 (from ms).

Le Comte, Louis Daniel. Memoirs and observations topographical, physical, mathematical, mechanical, natural, civil, ecclesiastical made in a late journey through the empire of China, translated from French [of 1696]. 1697, 1698, 1699 (rev), 1737, 1738.

Brand, Adam. Journal of the embassy from the emperors of Muscovy over land into China to Peking by Everard Isbrand [Ides] 1693-5, translated from German [of 1697]. 1698. See Ides' own relation, 1706 below.

Dandini, Girolamo. A voyage to Mount Libanus: an account of the customs, manners of the Turks, with remarks upon the Turks and Maronites, translated from Italian [of 1656]. 1698; rptd in Thomas Osborne, A collection vol 1, 1745; in John Pinkerton, A collection vol 10, 1814.

Fryer, John. A new account of East-India and Persia: being nine years' travels 1672-81. 1698; rptd with Sir Thomas Roe, Travels, 1873; ed W. Crooke 3 vols 1909-15 (Hakluyt Soc); tr Dutch, 1700.

C., T. The new Atlas: or travels and voyages in Europe, Asia, Africa and America, to Aegypt, Palestine, Syria, Mesopotamia, Chaldea, Persia, East India, China, Tartary, with the pilgrimages to Mecca and Medina in Arabia [and back through Europe] performed by an English gentleman. 1698, 1699.

Bouvet, Joachim, SJ. The life of the present Emperor of China. 1699. Trn from French of 1697 or Latin of 1699. With Jodocus Crull, The present condition of the Muscovite empire.

—— The journey from Pe-king to Kanton in 1693. In Thomas Astley, A collection vol 3, 1745.

Dellon, Gabriel. A voyage to the East Indies [1669-76]: giving an account of Madagascar, Suratte, the coast of Malabar, of Goa, Gameron, Ormus and the coast of Brazil, translated from French [of 1688]. 1699.

Greaves, John. [Journey to Italy, Constantinople and Egypt 1637-9.] In Thomae Smithi, Joannis Gravii vita: de illis studiis, itineribus in Italiam, ad Constantinopolim et in Egyptis, 1699; rptd in Vitae illustrium virorum, 1707; in Miscellaneous works, 1737. Professor Greaves had pbd his Pyramidographia: or a description of the pyramids, 1646.

Ziegenbalg, Bartholomew. An account of the religion, manners and learning of the people of Malabar in letters written by learned men of that country to the Danish missionaries, translated from German by J. T. Phillips. 1699, 1717. Account of the Danish missionaries were pbd in 1711, 1715, 1719: see Cox, 1.281-2.

Fryke, Christopher, and Christopher Schweitzer. A relation of two several voyages made to the East Indies, describing those countrys under the Dutch, translated from two separate works in German [Schweitzer travels 1675-81; Friken travels 1680-5] by S.L. 1700; ed C. E. Fayle 1929.

An historical description of the Kingdom of Macassar in the East Indies. 1701.

Veryard, Ellis. A voyage to the Levant: a description of Candia, Egypt, the Red-Sea, the deserts of Arabia, Mount-Horeb and Mount-Sinai, the coasts of Palestine, Syria and Asia-Minor. In An account of a journey (through Europe to Constantinople) in thirteen years travels, 1701.

Daniel, William. A journal or account of his late expedition from London to Surrat in India [but only as far as Mocha]. 1702.

Bruin, Cornelis de (called Corneille Le Brun). A voyage to the Levant [in 1674] including Egypt, Syria and the Holy Land, translated from French version [1700] of the Dutch original, by W.J. 1702; rptd 3 vols 1720 (with his Travels into Muscovy, below), 2 vols 1737.

—— Travels into Muscovy, Persia and the East Indies, translated from French [of 1718]. 3 vols 1720 (with preceding); retranslated by a gentleman of Oxford 1759.

Baldaeus, Philip. A true and exact description of the East-India coasts of Malabar and Coromandel, as also of the isle of Ceylon, translated from Dutch [of 1672]. 1703; rptd in A. and J. Churchill, A collection vol 3, 1704 etc.

Barlow, Edward. Journal of his life at sea in King's ships, east and west India-men and other merchantmen, from 1659 to 1703. Ed B. Lubbock 2 vols 1934 (from ms).

Maundrell, Henry. A journey from Aleppo to Jerusalem at Easter 1697. Oxford 1703, 1707, 1714 (with A journey to Mesopotamia), 1721, 1732, 1740, 1749, Perth 1800, London 1810; rptd in The world displayed vol 11, 1774; in J. H. Moore, A new collection, 1780; in John Pinkerton, A collection vol 10, 1811; tr French, 1705; Dutch, 1792; German, 1792.

Baumgarten, Martin. The travels through Egypt, Arabia, Palestine and Syria 1507-8, translated from Latin [of 1594]. In A. and J. Churchill, A collection vol 1, 1704 etc.

Cunningham, James. Part of two letters giving an account of his voyage (to Chusan, China). Philosophical Trans 23 1704; rptd in Miscellanea curiosa vol 3, 1708.

Hamel, Henry. An account of the shipwreck of a Dutch vessel [1653] on the coast of the isle of Quelpaert [off Korea], together with the description of the Kingdom of Corea, translated from a French version of the Dutch original [of 1668]. In A. and J. Churchill, A collection vol 4, 1704 etc; rptd in John Pinkerton, A collection vol 7, 1811.

Navarette, Fr Domingo Fernandez. An account of the empire of China, historical, political, moral and religious, translated from Spanish [of 1676]. In A. and J. Churchill, A collection vol 1, 1704 etc; retr and ed J. S. Cummins 1862 (Hakluyt Soc).

Pitts, Joseph. A true and faithful account of the religion and manners of the Mahometans, with a particular relation of their pilgrimage to Mecca (and an account of his captivity in Africa). Exeter 1704, 1717, London 1731; rptd in The world displayed vol 17, 1774; rptd with Maundrell, 1703 above, 1810.

Roe, Sir Thomas. The journal of the Embassador [1615-19] from James the First to the mighty Emperor of India the Great Mogul. Ed in A. and J. Churchill, A collection vol 1, 1704 etc (from ms). A badly edited version of the narrative had been pbd by Samuel Purchas in Purchas his pilgrimes vol 1, 1625. Another narrative by the chaplain Edward Terry had been pbd in 1655, and rptd in collections. An authoritative edn of the journal was first made by William Foster in 1899 (Hakluyt Soc), 1926 (rev).

Ides, Everard Ysbrants. Three years travels from Moscow overland to China [1693], with a description of China by a Chinese author (Dionysius Kao), translated from Dutch [of 1704]. 1706.

An extract of the journals of two several voyages of the English merchants of the factory of Aleppo to Tadmor, anciently called Palmyra, in 1678, 1691. In Miscellanea curiosa vol 3, 1708. Edmund Halley adds some account of the ancient state of Palmyra, with its inscriptions.

Leguat, François. Voyage et avantures en deux isles désertes des Indes Orientales. 2 vols 1708, 1720; tr as A new voyage to the East-Indies, 1708 (with descriptions of the Cape of Good Hope etc, for which see Africa, below); tr Dutch, 1708; German, 1805 (as Der französische Robinson). The voyage is argued to be fictitious by G. Atkinson, The extraordinary voyage in French fiction, New York 1922.

Leonardo y Argensola, Bartolome. The discovery and conquest of the Molucco and Philippine Islands, translated from the Spanish [of 1609] by John Stevens. 1708; also in A new collection, 1708.

A letter [with inscriptions from Persepolis taken 1667, with drawings by N. Witsen]. In Miscellanea curiosa vol 3, 1708.

A voyage of the emperour of China into the eastern Tartary 1682, into the western Tartary 1683. In Miscellanea curiosa vol 3, 1708.

Manucci, Niccolao. The general history of the Mogul Empire to the late Emperor Orangzeb, extracted from the memoirs [in Portuguese] of M. Manouchi, chief physician to Orangzeb, by François Catrou, translated from French [of 1705]. 1709 (2 of 3 pts), 1826, Calcutta 1907, Bhowanipou 1908. The original work by Manucci was tr William Irvine as Storia do Mogor or Mogul India 1653–1708, 4 vols 1907–8 (India Texts Soc), 1 vol 1913 (abridged).

Hill, Aaron. A full and just account of the present state of the Ottoman Empire from serious observations taken in many years' travels. 1709, 1710, 1733.

Teixeira, Pedro. The travels [1601–5 overland to and from India]. Part tr from Spanish [of 1610] by John Stevens in A new collection, 1710. Complete trn by the same as The history of Persia with a curious account of India, China, Tartary, Kermon, Arabia, 1715. A retrn by W. F. Sinclair as The journey from India to Italy by land 1604–5, with the chronicle of the kings of Ormuz, was pbd 1901 (Hakluyt Soc).

Lockyer, Charles. An account of the trade in India, with descriptions of Fort St George, Acheen, Malacca, Condore, Canton, Aujengo, Muskat, Cape of Good Hope, St Helena. 1711.

Burnell, John. An account of the island of Bombay 1710?–13. Ed S. T. Sheppard in Bombay in the days of Queen Anne, 1933 (Hakluyt Soc).
— Adventures in Bengal. 1712; ed W. Foster 1933 (with above).

Vaughan, Walter. The adventures of five Englishmen from Pulo Condoro, a factory in the East Indies, who were shipwreckt upon Jehore. 1714.

Symson, William. A new voyage to the East-Indies, to Suratte and the coast of Arabia and the Maldive islands, with an account of the French factories. 1715, 1720.

d'Arvieux, Laurent. Travels in Arabia the desert: giving an account of the Bedouins, or Arabian Scenites, with a general description of Arabia by Sultan Ishmael Abulfeda, translated from French [of 1717]. 1718, 1723, 1732. The portion of the Abulfeda Geography (c. 1300) was apparently tr from Arabic into French by M. de la Roque.

Beeckman, Daniel. A voyage to and from the island of Borneo in the East Indies, also a description of the islands of Canary, Cape Verd, Java, Madura. 1718; rptd in John Pinkerton, A collection vol 11, 1812.

Pitton de Tournefort, Joseph. A voyage into the Levant: the state of the islands, Constantinople, Armenia, Georgia, the frontiers of Persia and Asia Minor, translated from French [of 1717] by John Ozell. 2 vols 1718, 3 vols 1741.

Cornwall, Capt Henry. Observations upon several voyages to India, out and home. 1720, 1724.

Lange, Lorenz. Travels through Russia to China and Siberia, translated from German. In F. C. Weber, The present state of Russia vol 2, 1723. Retrn by John Bell as Journal of M. de Lange, resident of Russia at Pekin, in John Bell, Travels vol 2, Glasgow 1763.

de la Roque, Jean. A voyage to Arabia the happy by the western ocean and the streights of the Red Sea 1708–10, with a journey from Moka to the King of Yemen 1711–13, also an account of the coffee-tree, translated from French [of 1716]. 1726, 1732, 1742.

Hamilton, Alexander. A new account of the East Indies, his trading and travelling 1688 to 1723 between the Cape of Good Hope and the island of Japan. 2 vols Edinburgh 1727, London 1737, Edinburgh 1739, London 1744; rptd in John Pinkerton, A collection vol 8, 1811; ed W. Foster 2 vols 1930 (Hakluyt Soc).

Kaempfer, Engelbert. The history of Japan: giving an account of the present state and government of that empire and of their trade and commerce, with a description of Siam, translated from German by J. G. Scheuchzer. 2 vols 1727, 1728 (vol 1 only, adding A journal of a voyage to Japan made by the English 1673); ed A. Geikie 3 vols Glasgow 1906; Kyoto 1929 (facs of 1727); tr French, 1729 (from English).
— Travels in Persia and other countries of the east. 1736. Part trn of the Amoenitates exoticae et descriptiones rerum persicarum, 1712.
— Icones selectae plantarum quas in Japonia collegit et delineavit. 1791. Pbd by Sir Joseph Banks.

Arrian. History of Alexander's expedition, translated from Greek [Anabasis] by John Rooke. 2 vols 1729, 1812, 1813.
— The voyage of Nearchus from the Indus to the Euphrates, translated from Greek [Indika] by William Vincent. 1797, 1807.

General history of the Turks, Moguls and Tatars, vulgarly called Tartars, together with a description of the countries they inhabit, translated from French [of 1726]. 2 vols 1729–30.

Forbin, Count de. Memoirs of the voyages he made to the East Indies etc, translated from French. 1731.

Baron, Samuel. A description of the Kingdom of Tonqueen, by a native thereof. In A. and J. Churchill, A collection vol 6, 1732; rptd in John Pinkerton, A collection vol 9, 1811.

An historical relation of the island of Ceylon in the East Indies. 1732.

Mas'udi, Abul Hasan ibn Ali. Ancient accounts of India and China by two Mohammedan travellers who went to those parts in the ninth century, translated from a French version by Eusebius Renaudot of a part of the Arabic Meadows of Gold (10th century). 1733.

Green, John. A journey from Aleppo to Damascus in 1725, with a description of those two capital cities and the neighbouring parts of Syria, and an account of the Maronites inhabiting Mount Libanus. 1736.

Du Halde, Jean Baptiste. The general history of the empire of China, Chinese Tartary, Corea and Thibet, including an exact account of their customs, translated from French [of 1735] by R. Brookes. 4 vols 1736, 2 vols 1738–41.

Strahlenburg, Philipp Johann von. An histori-geographical description of the north and eastern part of Europe and Asia, but more particularly of Russia, Siberia and great Tartary, translated from German [of 1730]. 1736, 1738.

Downing, Clement. A compendious history of the Indian wars [1715–23], with an account of John Plantain, a notorious pirate at Madagascar. 1737; ed W. Foster, Oxford 1924.

Shaw, Thomas. Travels or observations relating to several parts of Barbary and the Levant [Syria and Arabia Petraea]. Oxford 1738, 1757, 2 vols Edinburgh 1808 (rev); rptd in John Pinkerton, A collection vol 15, 1814; tr French, 1743; German, 1765; Dutch, 1773.

Persepolis illustrata: or an account of the ancient and royal palace destroyed by Alexander the Great. 1739.

Spilman, James. A journey through Russia into Persia by two English gentlemen 1739 from Petersburgh. 1742.

Lockman, John. Travels of the Jesuits into various parts of the world compiled from their letters [and including China and the East Indies]. 2 vols 1743, 1762.

Perry, Charles, MD. A view of the Levant, particularly of Constantinople, Syria, Egypt and Greece. 1743, 3 vols 1770; tr German, 1754, 1765.

Pococke, Richard, Bishop. Description of the east, and some other countries: Egypt, Palestine, Mesopotamia, Cyprus, Candia, Asia Minor. 2 vols 1743–5, 1771; rptd in John Pinkerton, A collection vols 10, 15, 1811–14; tr German, 1754–5; French, 1772–3; Dutch, 1776–86.

Thompson, Charles. The travels of the late Charles Thompson: containing his observations on France, Italy, Turkey in Europe, the Holy Land, Arabia, Egypt, with a curious description of Jerusalem. 3 vols Reading 1744, 2 vols 1754, 1767, Glasgow 1798.

Beawes, William. A journey from Aleppo to Basra in 1745. Ed D. Carruthers in The desert route to India, 1929 (Hakluyt Soc).

Journal or narrative of the Boscawen's voyage to Bombay in the East-Indies 1749 [for an attack on Pondicherry]. 1750, 1751, Edinburgh 1756.

Dalton, Richard. [A collection of 52 engraved plates from his drawings of antiquities in Sicily, Greece, Asia Minor and Egypt]. 1751.

Gmelin, Johann Georg. Travels through Siberia 1733-43, translated from German [of 1751-2]. 4 vols Haarlem 1752-7.

Falconer, David. A journey from Joppa to Jerusalem in May 1751. 1753.

Hanway, Jonas. An historical account of the British trade over the Caspian Sea, with the author's journals of travels through Russia into Persia, and back. 4 vols 1753, 2 vols 1754 (rev), Dublin 1754, 1762 (rev); tr German, 1754.

Wood, Robert. The ruins of Palmyra, otherwise Tedmor, in the desert. 1753, 1827; tr French, 1753, 1819.

—— The ruins of Balbec, otherwise Heliopolis, in Coelo-Syria. 1757.

Drummond, Alexander. Travels through different cities of Germany, Italy, Greece and several parts of Asia as far as the banks of the Euphrates. 1754.

A voyage to the island of Ceylon on board a Dutch India-man 1747 written by a Dutch gentleman. 1754. Trn from Dutch.

Russell, Alexander, MD. The natural history of Aleppo and parts adjacent, with the climate, inhabitants and diseases. 1756, 2 vols 1794; tr Dutch, 1762.

Grose, John Henry. A voyage to the East Indies begun 1750. 2 vols 1757, 1766 (with observations till 1764), 1772 (with Mr Carmichael, A journey from Aleppo to Busserah); rptd in The world displayed vol 9, 1761 etc; tr French, 1758.

Guyon, Abbé Claude Marie. A new history of the East Indies, ancient and modern, containing the chorography, natural history etc, translated from French [of 1744]. 2 vols 1757.

Plaisted, Bartholomew. A journal from Calcutta in Bengal by sea to Busserah, from thence across the great desert to Aleppo and thence to Marseilles and England in 1750. 1757, 1758; ed D. Carruthers in The desert route to India, 1929 (Hakluyt Soc).

Travels in Egypt, Turkey, Syria and the Holy-Land by an English merchant. 1758.

Nijenburg, Jan Egidius van Egmont van der and John Heyman. Travels through part of Europe, Asia Minor, Syria, Palestine, Egypt, Mount Sinai, translated from Dutch [1757-8]. 2 vols 1759, 1772.

A voyage to the East Indies in 1747 and 1748: Java, Batavia, the Dutch government, Canton and China. 1762.

Bell, John. Travels from St Petersburg in Russia to divers parts of Asia [1715-38 to Persia, China and Turkey]. 2 vols Glasgow 1763, Dublin 1764, Edinburgh 1788, London 1806; rptd in John Pinkerton, A collection vol 7, 1811; tr French, 1766; German, 1787.

Krasheninnikof, Stephen Petrovitch. The history of Kamtschatka and the Kurilsky islands, with the countries adjacent, translated from Russian [of 1755] by John Grieve. 1763, Gloucester 1764.

Orme, Robert. A history of the military transactions of the British nation in Indostan from 1745, with the establishments made by Mahomedan conquerors in Indostan. 2 vols 1763-78; vol 1 rptd 1775, 1780, 1803; 2 vols Madras 1861-2; tr French 1765 (in part).

—— Historical fragments of the Mogul empire, of the Morattoes and of the British concerns in Indostan. 1782, 1805, Calcutta 1905.

Holwell, John Zephaniah, FRS. India tracts, including the narrative of the Black Hole at Calcutta, defense of Vansittart, East India Company affairs 1752-60. 1764, 1774.

—— Interesting historical events relating to the provinces of Bengal and the empire of Indostan, as also the mythology of the Gentoos, followers of the Shastah. 1765, 1766-7; tr German, 1767; French, 1768.

—— A familiar epistolary journal of a voyage from Bengal in 1757. 1791.

Lyttleton, Charles. An account of the plague at Aleppo. 1765.

Carmichael, John. A journal from Aleppo over the desert to Basserah 1751. In John Henry Grose, A voyage to the East Indies, 1766 (2nd edn); ed D. Carruthers 1929 (Hakluyt Soc).

Hasselquist, Frederick. Voyages and travels in the Levant 1749-52: natural history, particularly in the Holy Land, physick, agriculture, translated from Swedish [of 1757]. 1766.

Lally Tollendal, Thomas Arthur de, Count. Memoirs from his embarking for the East Indies as Commander in chief of the French forces to his being sent prisoner of war to England. 1766.

Vansittart, Henry. A narrative of the transactions in Bengal during the government of Vansittart 1760-4, by himself. 3 vols 1766.

Chandler, Richard. Ionian antiquities, published by order of the Society of the Dilettanti. 1769; vol 2, 1797; rev Nicholas Revett 2 vols Oxford 1825.

—— Inscriptiones antiquae in Asia Minori et Graeciae praesertim Athenis. Oxford 1774.

—— Travels in Asia Minor: or an account of a tour made at the expense of the Society of Dilettanti. Oxford 1775, 1776, Dublin 1775-6, 2 vols 1817 (with The travels in Greece), Oxford 1825; tr French, 3 vols 1806 (both works). See L. Cust, History of the Society of Dilettanti, 1914.

Chappe d'Auteroche, Abbé Jean. A journey into Siberia: containing an account of the manners and customs of the Russians with the natural history and geographical description of their country, translated abridged from French [of 1768]. 1770. See the commentary on this work said to be inspired by the Empress Catherine: The antidote: or an inquiry into the merits of a journey into Siberia, translated into English by a lady, 1772.

Cook, John, MD. Voyages and travels through the Russian empire, Tartary and Persia. 2 vols Edinburgh 1770.

Ellis, John, FRS. Directions for bringing over seeds and plants from the East-Indies and other distant countries. 1770.

—— An historical account of coffee, with a botanical description of the tree. 1774.

—— A description of the mangostan and the bread-fruit, the first esteemed one of the most delicious, the other the most useful of all the fruits in the East-Indies. 1775.

Osbeck, Peter. Voyage to China and the East Indies, with a voyage to Suratte by Olaf Toreen, and an account of the Chinese husbandry by Capt C. G. Eckeberg, with a Faunula and Flora Sinensis, translated from a German version of the Swedish [of 1757] by J. R. Forster. 2 vols 1771.

Bolts, William. Considerations on India affairs, particularly respecting the present state of Bengal and its dependencies. 3 vols 1772-5. Part (vol 1) tr French, 1778, 1858.

—— Civil, political and commercial state of Bengal. 2 vols 1773; tr French, 1775.

Dalrymple, Alexander. A collection of charts and memoirs [of eastern waters and seacoasts]. 7 pts 1772, 1786. For numerous pamphlets—charts, reports of brief voyages in eastern waters, discussions of East India Company affairs—see BM Catalogue.

— Journal of a voyage to the East Indies in the Grenville 1775. 1779.

— An account of the loss of the Grosvenor Indiaman 1782. 1783, 1785. *See* William Hubberly, An appendix containing the report of one of the survivors, 1786.

Verelst, Harry. A view of the rise, progress and present state of the English government in Bengal, including a reply to the misrepresentations of Mr Bolts and other writers. 1772.

Ives, Edward. A voyage from England to India 1754; also a journey from Persia to England by an unusual route: an historical narrative of the operations of the squadron and army in India 1755–7. 1773.

Rennell, Major James. A description of the roads in Bengal and Behar etc. 1778.

— Memoir of a map of Hindostan: or the Mogul's empire. 1783, 1785 (enlarged), 1788, 1792, 1793; tr German, 1785; French, 1788, 1800.

— A Bengal atlas: containing maps of the theatre of war and commerce on that side of Hindostan. 1791.

— The marches of the British armies in the peninsula of India during the campaigns of 1790–1. 1792, 1792.

— Observations on the topography of the plain of Troy. 1814.

— A treatise on the comparative geography of western Asia. 2 vols 1831.

Forrest, Thomas. Voyage to New Guinea and the Moluccas, including an account of the Magindano, Sooloo and other islands, in the Tartar galley 1774–6. 1779, Dublin 1779, London 1780; tr French, 1780; German, 1782.

— A treatise on the monsoons in East India. Calcutta 1782, London 1783; rptd 1792 with his last work, below.

— A journal of the Esther brig from Bengal to Quedah. 1788.

— Voyage from Calcutta to the Merguy archipelago; also an account of the islands of Jan-Seylan, Pulo-Pinang and the port of Quedas, the present state of Achem, an account of the island of Celebes and a treatise on the monsoon. 1792.

Coxe, William. An account of the Russian discoveries between Asia and America, with the conquest of Siberia and history of the transactions and commerce between Russia and China. 1780, 1780, 1787 (with Supplement, below), 1804.

— Supplement: comparative view of the Russian voyages with those made by Captains Cook and Clerke. 1787 (with preceding).

Irwin, Eyles. A series of adventures in a voyage up the Red Sea, on the coasts of Arabia, and of a route through the desarts of Thebais hitherto unknown to the European traveller, in 1777. 1780, 1781 (with A voyage from Venice to Latichea and a route through the desarts of Arabia to Busrah 1780–1), 2 vols 1784, 1787; tr German, 1781; French, 1792.

Pinnell, R. Journal of the Jane from Banjar to Timor and back. Ed Alexander Dalrymple 1781.

Porter, Lt John. Remarks on the Bloachee, Broadia and Arabian coasts. Ed Alexander Dalrymple 1781, 1787.

[Hastings, Warren.] A narrative of the late transactions at Benares. Calcutta 1782.

— Memoirs relative to the state of India. 1786, 1787.

Macintosh, William. Travels in Europe, Asia and Africa 1777–81, delineating a new system for the government and improvement of the British settlements in the East Indies. 2 vols 1782; tr German, 1785; French, 1786, 1792.

Capper, Capt James. Observations on the passage to India through Egypt and across the Great Desert. 1783, 1784, 1785, 1788 (in James Rennell, Memoirs of a map of Hindostan, 1788 above); tr French, 1792, 1797.

Lusignan, S. A description of several celebrated places in Egypt, Palestine and Syria, also the journal of a gentleman who travelled from Aleppo to Bassora. In his

History of the revolt of Ali Bey against the Ottoman Porte, 1783 (under Africa, below).

— Letters addressed to Sir William Fordyce FRS: containing a voyage from England to Smyrna, from thence to Constantinople and overland to England, with an appendix on the Holy Land. 1788.

Marsden, William. The history of Sumatra: containing an account of the governments, laws, customs and manners of the native inhabitants, with a description of the natural productions. 1783, 1784, 1811.

Rooke, Major Henry. Travels to the coast of Arabia Felix, and from thence by the Red Sea and Egypt to Europe. 1783, 1784, Leghorn 1788; tr German, 1787; French, 1788. *See also under* Africa, *below*.

Evers, Samuel. A journal kept on a journey from Bessora to Bagdad through the Little-Desert to Aleppo, Cyprus, Rhodes, Zante, Corfu and Otrante 1779. Horsham 1884.

Forster, George. Sketches of the mythology and customs of the Hindoos. 1785.

— A journey from Bengal to England through Kashmire, Afghanistan and Persia, and into Russia by the Caspian Sea. Vol 1, Calcutta 1790; vols 1–2, 1798; tr French, 1802.

G[ough], R[ichard]. A comparative view of the antient monuments of India, particularly those in the island of Salset, described by different writers. 1785.

Hunter, William, MD. A concise account of the Kingdom of Pegu [Burma]: its climate, produce, manners and customs. Calcutta 1785; tr French, 1793.

Macartney, George, Earl. The private correspondence of the Governor of Madras 1781–5. Ed C. C. Davies 1950 (Camden Soc).

The first British embassy to China 1792–4 was reported in several contemporary records as follows. See T. Besterman, A bibliography of Lord Macartney's embassy to China, 1928.

Anderson, Aeneas. A narrative of the British embassy to China, with accounts of the manners and customs of the Chinese. 1795, 1795; tr German, 1795.

Staunton, Sir George L. An authentic account of an embassy to the Emperor of China, taken chiefly from the papers of the Earl Macartney and Sir E. Gower. 2 vols 1797, 3 vols 1798; tr French, 1798; German, 1798, 1798–9. The official account.

Holmes, Samuel. The journal during his attendance as one of the guard on Lord Macartney's embassy to China and Tartary. 1798; tr German, 1805.

[Winterbotham, W.] A genuine and copious account of Earl Macartney's embassy. In A complete view of the Chinese Empire, 1798. *See* H. H. Robbins, Our first ambassador to China: an account of the life, with the narrative of his experiences in China as told by himself, 1908.

Wolf, Johann Christoph. The life and adventures of the late principal secretary of state at Jaffanapatam in Ceylon, with a description of that island and its inhabitants, translated from German [Reise nach Zeilan, 1782–4]. 1785.

A description of the holy places of Jerusalem and the objects visited by pilgrims in Judea and Galilee, by the reverend fathers of the Latin convent at Jerusalem, translated from Latin by William Wittman. 1786.

Hodges, William. Select views in India, engraved in aqua-tint. 1786–8 (text in English, French and Latin).

— Travels in India 1780–3. 1793; tr French, 1865.

Fullarton, William. A view of the English interests in India, and an account of the military operations in the southern parts of the peninsula 1782 to 1784. 1787.

Volney, Constantin François de, Comte. Travels through Syria and Egypt 1783–5: containing observations of their commerce, arts and politics, translated from French [of 1787]. 2 vols 1787, 1788, Dublin 1788, New York 1798.

Ellis, George. Memoir of a map of the countries between the Black Sea and the Caspian, with an account of the Caucasian nations. 1788; tr French, 1797.

Howel, Thomas, MD. A journal of the passage from India by a route partly unfrequented through Armenia and Natolia or Asia Minor. 1788, 1790; tr French, 1797.

Francklin, Capt William. Observations on a tour from Bengal to Persia 1786–7, with a short account of the remains of the palace of Persepolis. Calcutta 1788, London 1790.

— The history of the reign of Shah Aulun, the present Emperor of Hindostan: containing the transactions of the Court of Delhi for thirty-six years. 1798.

— Remarks and observations on the plain of Troy 1799. 1800.

Grosier, Abbé J. B. G. A general description of China: containing the topography of the fifteen provinces, of Tartary, the isles and other tributary countries, translated from French [of 1787]. 2 vols 1788, 1795.

Trapaud, Elisha. A short account of the Prince of Wales's Island: or Pulo Peenang in the East Indies. 1788; tr German 1790.

Benyowsky, Móricz August, Count. The memoirs and travels in Siberia, Kamchatka, Japan, the Liukiu islands and Formosa. 2 vols 1789, 1790, Dublin 1790, London 1794; ed P. Oliver 1893, 1904; tr German, 1790; French, 1791, 1863; Dutch, 1793; Hungarian, 1888–91; Polish, 1898. Tr William Nicholson from French.

[Larkins, Capt John P.] An account of the passage of the ship Warren Hastings by the Macclesfield Strait on the east of Banka. 1789.

Munro, Innes. A narrative of the military operations on the Coromandel coast against the French, Dutch and Hyder Ally Cawn 1780 to 1784. 1789.

[Crauford, Quintin]. Sketches chiefly relating to the history, religion, learning and manners of the Hindoos, with the present state of the native powers of Hindostan. 1790, 2 vols 1792 (rev); tr French, 1791.

LeCouteur, General John. Letters chiefly from India [with an account of the war on the Malabar coast], translated from French. 1790.

Lesseps, J. B. B. de, Baron. Travels in Kamtschatka 1787–8, translated from French [of 1790]. 2 vols 1790. For the falsifications in the book see P. G. Adams, Travelers and travel liars, Berkeley 1962, ch 5.

Jenner, Matthew. The route to India through France, Germany, Hungary, Turkey, Natolia, Syria and the desert of Arabia. 1791.

Mariti, Giovanni. Travels through Cyprus, Syria and Palestine [1760–8], with a general history of the Levant, translated from a French version of the Italian [of 1769–76]. 3 vols 1791–2; vol 1, Dublin 1792.

Bristow, James. A narrative of the sufferings of James Bristow, belonging to the Royal Artillery, during ten years' captivity with Hyder Ali and Tippoo Saheb. Calcutta 1792, London 1793, 1794, Calcutta 1828.

Emin, Joseph. Life and adventures [including time spent in Armenia]. 1792.

Niebuhr, Carsten. Travels through Arabia and other countries in the East: Hedjas, Yemen, Oman, translated from German [of 1774] by Robert Heron. 2 vols Edinburgh 1792, London 1799.

Stahl, Dr Wilhelm. The authentic memoirs and sufferings of a German physician: containing his travels, observations and interesting narrative during four years' imprisonment at Goa. 1792 (2nd edn).

Dirom, Alexander, General. A narrative of the campaign in India which terminated the war with Tippoo Sultan in 1792. 1793.

Mackenzie, Major Roderick. A sketch of the war with Tippoo Sultan. 2 vols Calcutta 1793–4.

Matthew, J. M. Nine letters from a very young officer serving in India. 1793.

Moor, Major Edward. A narrative of the operations of Captain Little's detachment and of the Mahratta army against Tippoo Sultan. 1794.

Thunberg, C. P. Travels in Europe, Africa and Asia 1770–9, translated from Swedish. 4 vols 1794. Especially on Japan.

'Campbell, Donald' (S. C. Carpenter). A journey overland to India: comprehending his shipwreck and imprisonment with Hyder Alli. 1795, 1796, 1796 (abstract), 1797, 1798 etc; also chap-book [1800?].

Cleghorn, Hugh. The Cleghorn papers: being the diary 1795–6 of the first colonial secretary of Ceylon 1796–1800. Ed W. Neil 1927.

Winterbotham, William. An historical, geographical and philosophical view of the Chinese Empire. 2 vols 1795. Including an account of the Macartney embassy, see 1785 above.

James, Silas. Narrative of a voyage to Arabia, India 1781–4. 1797.

Braam Houckgeest, André Everard van. An authentic account of the embassy of the Dutch East-India Company to the Court of the Emperor of China 1794 and 1795 [taken from his diary by L. E. Moreau de St Méry], translated from French [of 1797]. 1798.

— Icones plantarum sponté Chinâ nascentium. 1821.

Stavorinus, Admiral Jan Splinter. Voyage to the East Indies [1768–71]: comprising a full account of the possessions of the Dutch in India and at the Cape, translated from Dutch [of 1793] by S. H. Wilcocke. 3 vols 1798.

Jackson, John, FSA. A journey from India towards England 1797 over-land through Curdistan, Diarbek, Armenia and Natolia in Asia and Romalia, Bulgaria, Wallachia and Transylvania in Europe. 1799; tr German, 1804.

Popham, Sir Home Riggs. Description of Prince of Wales Island in the Streights of Malacca, with its advantages as a marine establishment. 1799, 1805.

Taylor, John, Lt-Col. Travels to India in 1789 by way of the Tyrol, Venice, Scandaroon, Aleppo and the Great Desert to Bussora. 2 vols 1799.

— Letters from India. 1800.

Boyd, Hugh. A journal of an embassy from the government of Madras to the King of Candy in Ceylon 1782. In Miscellaneous works vol 2, 1800.

Ibn Haukal. The oriental geography of an Arabian traveller of the tenth century, translated from Arabic by Sir William Ouseley. 1800. Now known to be not by Ibn Haukal but by Al-Farisi.

Leckie, Daniel Robinson. Journal of a route to Nagpore 1790, with an account of Nagpur and a journal from that place to Benares. 1800.

Paolino da San Bartolomeo, Fra. A voyage to the East Indies, with an account of the manners, customs of the natives 1776–89, translated from a German version of the Italian [of 1796] by W. Johnston, with notes by J. R. Forster. 1800.

The Periplus of the Erythraean Sea [Indian Ocean]. Ed and tr from Greek by William Vincent 2 pts 1800–5.

Symes, Michael. An account of an embassy to the Kingdom of Ava from the Governor-General of India in 1795. 1800, 4 vols 1800 (rev); tr French, 1800; German, 1801.

Turner, Capt Samuel. An account of an embassy to the Court of the Teshoo Lama in Tibet [1783–5]: describing a journey through Bootan and part of Tibet. 1800; tr French, 1800; German, 1801.

White, Capt William. Journal of a voyage from Madras to Columbo and Da Lagoa Bay on the east coast of Africa 1798. 1800. French trn with the Symes narrative, 1800 above.

§ 2

Oaten, J. T. European travellers in India during the fifteenth, sixteenth and seventeenth centuries. 1909.

Cambridge History of India. Vol 4, British India 1497–1958. Ed H. H. Dodwell, Cambridge 1929. Also vol 4 of the Cambridge History of the British Empire.

Brown, W. C. The popularity of English travel books about the Near East 1775–1825. PQ 15 1936.

Wheeler, J. T. European travellers in India [1600–1700]. Calcutta 1956.

Hachicho, Mohamad Ali. English travel books about the Arab Near East in the eighteenth century. Die Welt des Islams 9 1964.

(5) AFRICA

Collections

African Association. Proceedings for promoting the discovery of the interior parts of Africa: the journeys of Ledyard and Lucas. 1790.

—— Proceedings containing an abstract of Mr Park's account of his travels, with geographical illustrations by Major Rennell. 1798; Park and Houghton travels tr French, 1798.

Leyden, John. An historical and philosophical sketch of the discoveries and settlements of Europeans in northern and western Africa at the close of the eighteenth century. 1798; tr German, 1802.

The modern traveller: containing compressed travels of Mungo Park and others in Africa. 4 vols 1800.

Murray, Hugh. Historical account of discoveries and travels in Africa. 2 vols Edinburgh 1818. Based on preceding item.

Axelson, E. (ed). South African explorers. Oxford 1951 (WC).

Howard, C. and J. H. Plumb (ed). West African explorers. Oxford 1954 (WC).

Richards, C. and J. Place (ed). East African explorers. Oxford 1960 (WC).

§ I

The golden coast: or a description of Guinney in four rich voyages to that coast. 1665.

D'Aranda, Emanuel. The history of Algiers and its slavery, with many remarkable particularities of Africk, by [one] sometime a slave there. 1666. Trn from Latin [of 1657] by John Davies of Kidwelly.

[Lobo, Fr Jeronimo]. A short relation of the river Nile. 1669, 1673, 1791, 1798; tr Latin, 1669; French, 1673. Trn from Portuguese ms for Royal Soc by Sir Peter Wyche. A portion of Voyage to Abyssinia, 1735 below.

Ogilby, John. An accurate description of Africa. 1669.

—— Africa: being an accurate description of Aegypt, Barbary, Lybia and Billedulgerid, the land of the negroes, Guinee, Aethiopia and the Abyssines. 1670.

Baratti, Giacomo. The late travels into the remote countries of the Abissins, or of Ethiopia interior. 1670. Trn from Italian by G.D.

Dapper, Olfert. Africa: being an accurate description of the regions of Egypt, Barbary, Libyia and Billedulgoria etc. 1670. Probably a trn from the German, 1670.

L., S. A letter from a gentleman of the Lord Ambassador Howard's retinue dated at Fez, of the present state of countries under the power of Morocco. 1670.

S[mith], T. The adventures of an English merchant taken prisoner by the Turks of Argiers, with a description of the Kingdom of Argiers. 1670.

Villaut, Nicolas, Sieur de Bellefond. A relation of the coasts of Africa called Guinea, collected in a voyage 1666 and 1667. 1670, 1670, 1709. Trn from French of 1669.

Addison, Lancelot. West Barbary: or a short narrative of the revolutions of the Kingdoms of Fez and Morocco. Oxford 1671; rptd in John Pinkerton, A general collection vol 15, 1814.

—— The present state of the Jews, more particularly those in Barbary. 1675, 1676, 1682.

—— The Moores baffled: being a discourse concerning Tanger under the government of the Earl of Teviot. 1681, 1685 (as A discourse of Tangier), 1738.

Balthorpe, John. The streights voyage: or St David's penman, a description of the first expedition against the

Turks of Argier, Sir John Harmon commander, 1699 to 1671. 1671.

[Charant,] A[ntoine]. A letter concerning the religion, manners and customs of the countrys of Muley Arxid. Trn from French, included in next item, 1671.

Frejus, Roland. The relation of a voyage made into Mauritania in 1666 to Muley Arxid, King of Tafiletta. 1671. Trn from French of 1670, with preceding.

Murtadi ibn Gaphiphus [Murthadá ibn al Khalif]. The Egyptian history: treating of the pyramids, the inundation of the Nile and other prodigies according to the traditions of the Arabians. 1672, 1672. Trn from the French version of the Arabic by Pierre Vattier 1666.

Watts, John. A true relation of the inhumane actions and barbarous murders of Negroes or Moors, committed on three Englishmen in Old Calabar, in Guinny. 1672; rptd in Thomas Osborne, A collection vol 2, 1745.

Alcafarado, Francisco. An historical relation of the first discovery of the isle of Madera. 1675. Trn from the 1671 French version of the Portuguese. Retr William Mulgrave in Capt Richard Falconer, Voyages, dangerous adventures and imminent escapes, 1720 (ascribed to W. R. Chetwood, see under Americas, below).

Okeley, William. Eben-ezer: or a small monument of great mercy appearing in the miraculous deliverance of William Okeley, William Adams etc from the miserable slavery of Algiers. 1675, 1676, 1684.

P[hilips], G[eorge]. The present state of Tangier; to which is added the present state of Algiers. 1676, 1678, 1680.

Blome, Richard. The present state of Algiers. 1678, 1687. Added to 2nd edn of A description of the island of Jamaica, first pbd 1672.

Vansleb, John Michael. The present state of Egypt: or a new relation of a voyage into that Kingdom in 1672–3. 1678. Tr M.D. from the 1677 French version of the Latin original. The name was actually Johann Michael Wansleben.

Glanius, W. A faithful narrative of the isles of Japan and Madagascar etc. In A new voyage to the East Indies, 1682, 1682.

Ludolphus, Hiob. A new history of Aethiopia: being a full and accurate description of the kingdom of Abessinia. 1682, 1684, 1684. Trn from Latin of 1681 by J. P. Gent.

Pepys, Samuel. Journal towards Tangier 1683. In The Tangier papers of Samuel Pepys, ed E. Chappell 1935 (Navy Records Soc).

Phelps, Thomas. A true account of the captivity at Machaness in Barbary and of his strange escape [1685]. 1685; rptd in Thomas Osborne, A collection vol 2, 1745.

B., R. [Robert Burton?]. A description of the island of St Helena, the bay of Soldania. In A view of the English acquisitions in Guiana and the East Indies, 1686.

Wilkinson, William. Systema Africanum: or a treatise discovering the intrigues of the Guiney Company, together with a true account of their fortifications. 1690.

S[adleir], [Sir] E[dward]. The history of the Jacobites of Egypt, Lybia and Nubia: their origins, religion, ceremonies, laws and customs. 1691.

Brooks, Francis. Barbarian cruelty: being a true history of Christian captives under the tyranny of Muly Ishmael, Emperor of Morocco. 1693, Boston 1700; tr Dutch, 1708.

Pidou de Saint Olon, François. The present state of the Empire of Morocco, wherein the scituation of the country, the manners, customs, government and religion are fully described. 1695. Trn from French of 1694.

Le Maire, Jacques Joseph. A new description of the Canary Islands, Cape Verd, Senegal and Gambia. In Abraham Duquesne, A new voyage to the East Indies, 1696 (trn from French of 1692); rptd in Thomas Osborne, A collection vol 2, 1745.

Geddes, Michael. The church-history of Ethiopia. 1696.

Ovington, John. A description of Madeira, St Jago, St Helena, Johanna, Bombay, the Cape of Good Hope. In A voyage to Suratt 1689, 1696; ed H. G. Rawlinson 1929; tr French, 1725.

Dampier, William. A new voyage round the world. 1697 etc. See Voyages round the World, above. Each vol contains accounts of a part of South Africa and of the islands from the Canaries to St Helena.

Dellon, Charles. An account of the isles of Madagascar and Mascareigne [Réunion]. In his A voyage to the East Indies, 1698.

Froger, François. A relation of a voyage made in the years 1695 to 1697 on the coasts of Africa [and in South America], by a squadron of French men of war. 1698; rptd in Thomas Osborne, A collection vol 2, 1745. Trn from French of 1698.

Montauban, Sieur de. The adventures of the captain of the French buccaneers on the coast of Guinea in 1695. In Chevalier [Henri de] Tonti, An account of Monsieur de la Salle's last expedition and discoveries in the North America, 1698 (trn from French of 1697); rptd in John Esquemeling, History of the Bucaniers of America, 1699 (2nd edn); rptd in Raveneau de Lussan, Journal of a voyage into the South Sea, 1742.

Fryke, Christophe and Christophe Schweitzer. [Descriptions of the Cape of Good Hope and of the island Mauritius]. In A relation of two several voyages made in to the East Indies, 1700, 1929. Tr from Dutch of 1694 by S.L.

Angelo, Fr Michael and Fr Denis de Carli. A curious and exact account of a voyage to Congo in 1666 and 1667. In A. and J. Churchill, A collection vol 1, 1704 etc. Trn from French version of Italian.

Pitts, Joseph. A faithful account of the religion and manners of the Mahometans and of their pilgrimage to Mecca and Medina, as likewise of Algiers, Alexandria, Grand Cairo etc, with an account of his being taken captive and of his escape [in 1694]. Exeter 1704, London 1731; rptd in The world displayed vol 17, 1774; rptd with Henry Maundrell, A journey from Aleppo to Jerusalem, 1810 (see Voyages to Asia, 1703, above).

Ten Rhyne, William. An account of the Cape of Good Hope 1673. In A. and J. Churchill, A collection vol 4, 1704 etc. Trn from Latin.

Bosman, William. A new and accurate description of the coast of Guinea, divided into the Gold, the Slave and the Ivory Coasts. 1705, 1721; rptd in John Pinkerton, A collection vol 16, 1814; rptd 1907, 1967; tr French, 1705. Trn from Dutch.

Leguat, François. [A description of the Cape of Good Hope and of the islands St Helena and Mauritius]. In A new voyage to the East Indies, 1708. See Voyages to Asia, 1708, above.

Maxwell, John. An account of the Cape of Good Hope. Philosophical Trans 25 1708.

A view of the state of the trade to Africa: wherein is laid down the present condition of the English settlements there. 1708.

Poncet, Charles Jacques. A voyage to Aethiopia, made in 1698–1700. 1709; rptd in John Lockman, Travels of the Jesuits, 1743 etc; in John Pinkerton, A collection vol 15, 1814. Trn from French.

Cauche, François. A voyage to Madagascar. In John Stevens, A collection, 1710. Trn from French of 1651.

Moüette, Germain. The travels in Fez and Morocco during his eleven years' captivity. In John Stevens, A collection, 1710. Trn from French of 1683.

Telles, Fr Balthasar. The travels of the Jesuits in Ethiopia [a collection]. In John Stevens, A collection, 1711. Trn from Portuguese of 1660. The work is an abridgement by Fr Telles of the Historia geral do Ethiopia a Alta of Fr Manuel de Almeida.

Ockley, Simon. An account of south-west Barbary, the territories of the King of Fez and Morocco, written by a person who had been a slave there. 1713, 1713; tr French, 1726.

Beeckman, Daniel. [A description of the islands of Canary etc and of the Cape of Good Hope and the Hottentots]. In A voyage to and from the island of Borneo, 1718; rptd in John Pinkerton, A collection vol 11, 1812.

Houstoun, John. Some new and accurate observations of the coast of Guinea, so far as relates to the improvement of that trade. 1725.

Windhus (or Windus), John. A journey to Mequinez, the residence of the present Emperor of Morocco on the occasion of Commodore Stewart's embassy for the redemption of British captives in 1721. 1725, Dublin 1725; rptd in John Pinkerton, A collection vol 15, 1814.

Roberts, George. The four years voyages [to the Canary and Cape Verde islands]. 1726; rptd in Thomas Astley, A collection vol 1, 1745; rptd 1930. Now known to be fiction by Defoe.

Hamilton, Capt Alexander. [An account of the maritime countries and islands of the east coast of Africa]. In A new account of the East Indies, 1727 etc. See Voyages to Asia, above.

Braithwaite, Capt John. The history of the revolutions in the Empire of Morocco upon the death of the late Emperor Muley Ishmael. 1729; tr French, 1731.

Drury, Robert. Madagascar: or Robert Drury's journal during fifteen years captivity on that island. 1729, 1731, [1739], 1743, 1743, 1807, 1826; ed Capt P. Oliver 1890, 1897 (author shown as Defoe, the work fiction); tr French, 1906.

Morgan, John. A complete history of Algiers. 2 vols 1729–30, 1750.

Kolben (for Kolb), Peter. The present state of the Cape of Good Hope: or a particular account of the several nations of the Hottentots. 2 vols 1731, 1738. Trn from German of 1719 by Mr Medley.

Barbot, Jean. A description of the coasts of north and south Guinea and of Ethiopia Inferior, vulgarly Angola; Jacques Barbot, A voyage to New Calabar or Rio Real in 1699; Jacques Barbot the younger, Abstract of a voyage to Congo River and to Cabinde in 1700. In A. and J. Churchill, A collection vol 5, 1732 etc.

Everard, Robert. A relation of three years sufferings upon the coast of Assada near Madagascar, in a voyage to India 1686. In A. and J. Churchill, A collection vol 6, 1732 etc.

Merolla da Sorrento, Fr Girolamo. A voyage to Congo and several other countries chiefly in Southern-Africk. In A. and J. Churchill, A collection vol 1, 1732 etc. Trn from Italian of 1692.

Phillips, Capt Thomas. A journal of a voyage made in the Hannibal of London 1693–4 to Cape Momseradoc in Africa and thence along the coast of Guiney and so forward to Barbadoes. In A. and J. Churchill, A collection vol 6, 1732 etc.

Bluett, Thomas. Some memoirs of the life of Job, the son of Solomon, the high priest of Boonda in Africa. 1734; tr German, 1747.

Snelgrave, Capt William. A new account of some parts of Guinea and the slave trade, with a relation of the author's being taken by pirates in 1719. 1734, 1754.

Atkins, John. [A description of the Guinea coast]. In A voyage to Guinea, Brasil and the West Indies, 1735, 1737.

Lobo, Fr Jeronymo. A voyage to Abyssinia. 1735, 1789, 1887. Trn abridged by Samuel Johnson from the 1728 French version of Portuguese original.

Philémon de la Motte, Fr. A voyage to Barbary [1720] for the redemption of captives, with lists of more than 400 slaves ransomed from Mequeniz, and the history ancient and modern of Oran. 1735. Trn by Joseph Morgan from French of 1721.

Morgan, John. Several voyages to Barbary, with hardships, sufferings and manner of redeeming Christian slaves. 1736.

Downing, Clement. An account of John Plantain, a notorious pyrate at Madagascar. In A history of the Indian wars, 1737.

Moore, Francis. Travels into the inland parts of Africa up the river Gambia, with a particular account of Job Ben Solomon, who was in England 1733; Captain Stibbs' voyage up the Gambia in 1723. 1738, [1740?]; rptd in John Newbery, The world displayed vol 17, 1778; tr German, 1747.

Shaw, Thomas, DD. Travels: or observations of Barbary and the Levant. Oxford 1738, 1757, 2 vols Edinburgh 1808; rptd in J. H. Moore, A new collection, 1778 etc; tr French, 1743; German, 1765; Dutch, 1773; A supplement (answering criticisms by Pococke), Oxford 1746; A further vindication, Oxford 1747.

Brown, Edward. [Travels in Egypt and Abyssinia]. In The travels and adventures, 1739.

Thomson, William. Mammuth: or human nature displayed in a tour with the thinkers into the island parts of Africa. 2 vols 1739.

Pellow, Thomas. The history of the long captivity in South Barbary, carry'd to Mequinez, his various adventures for twenty-three years. [1740?], [1740], [1890].

Norden, Friderik Ludvig. Drawings of some ruins and colossal statues at Thebes in Egypt. 1741, 1792 (as The antiquities, natural history, ruins and other curiosities in Egypt, Nubia and Thebes, in near 200 drawings).
— and Martin Teuscher (engraver). Alexandria, plan and 15 views. 1744.
— Travels in Egypt and Nubia, with 159 large copper engravings. 2 vols 1757, 1757; rptd in J. H. Moore, A new collection, 1778 etc. Trn by Peter Templeman from 1750–5 French version of Danish mss, with the original plates.

Leach, John. Travels on the Nile. 1742.

Pococke, Bishop Richard. [Journey in Egypt 1737–8]. In his Description of the East, 1743–5.
— Dissertatio de geographia Aegypti. 1743.

Smith, William. A new voyage to Guinea, describing whatever is memorable among the inhabitants. [1744], 1745; tr French, 1751; German, 1747.

Laugier de Tassy. A complete history of the piratical states of Barbary. 1750. Trn by Joseph Morgan from the French of 1725.

Journal of a voyage from Grand Cairo to Mount Sinai and back [1722], from a ms written by the [Franciscan] Prefetto of Egypt, with remarks on the origin of hieroglyphics. 1751, 1753 (rev); rptd in John Pinkerton, A collection vol 10, 1811; tr German, 1754; French, 1759.

Troughton, Thomas et al. Barbarian cruelty: a narrative of slavery under Muley Abdullah 1745–50. 2 vols 1751; rptd Exeter 1788 (adding A relation of a shipwreck on the Barbary coast in 1758).

Dalton, Richard. [A collection of 52 engraved plates entitled] Antiquities and views in Sicily, Greece, Asia Minor and Egypt, from drawings made 1749. 1751–2.
— A series of prints relative to the present inhabitants of Egypt. 1781.
— The explanation of a series of prints relative to the present inhabitants of Egypt from drawings made 1749. 1781.
— Remarks on prints. 1781, 1790 (enlarged).

Owen, Nicholas. A view of some remarkable axcedents on the coast of Africa 1746 to 1757. Ed Eveline Martin 1930 (as The journal of a slave dealer).

Thompson, Rev Thomas. [The voyage from North America to Guiney]. In An account of two missionary voyages, 1758, 1937 (facs). See General Voyages, above.
— The African trade for negro slaves shown to be consistent with humanity and religion. Canterbury [1772].
— Memoirs of an English missionary to Guinea. 1788.

Adanson, Michel. A voyage to Senegal, the isle of Goree and river Gambia. 1759, Dublin 1759; rptd in John Pinkerton, A collection vol 16, 1814. Trn from French, Histoire naturelle du Sénégal, 1757.

Lindsey, Rev John. A voyage to the western coast of Africa: containing an account of the expedition commanded by Keppel. 1759.

Sutherland, James. A narrative of the loss of the Litchfield on the coast of Africa. 1761, 1768, Exeter 1788 (rptd with Thomas Troughton, 1751 above).

Benezet, Anthony. A short account of that part of Africa inhabited by the Negroes, extracted from divers authors. 1762, Philadelphia 1762, 1762, London 1763, 1768; tr German, 1763, 1783, 1791.
— Some historical account of Guinea, with an inquiry into the slave trade. Philadelphia 1771, London 1788.

Abreu de Galindo, Juan de. The history of the discovery and conquest of the Canary Islands. 1764, Dublin 1767; rptd in John Pinkerton, A collection vol 16, 1814. Trn from Spanish ms of 1632 by Capt George Glas, adding a description of the islands.

Drew, Richard. Copy of a letter from the late governor of Annamaboe Fort touching the state of the trade to the Gold Coast of Africa. 1768.

Tourtechot de Granger, Sieur. A journey through Egypt 1730, with the most remarkable particulars on natural history. 1773 (with J. H. von Riedesel, Travels through Sicily). Trn from French of 1745 by John Reinhold Forster.

Bernardin de Saint-Pierre, Jacques Henri. A voyage to the island of Mauritius, the isle of Bourbon, the Cape of Good Hope. 1775, 1800. Trn abridged from French of 1772 by John Parish.

Kindersley, Mrs [Jemima]. Letters from the island of Teneriffe, Brazil, the Cape of Good Hope and the East Indies. 1777.

Robertson, Robert. A physical journal to the coast of Africa and the West Indies 1772–4. 1777.

Dalrymple, Alexander (ed). An account of the loss of the Grosvenor Indiaman on the coast of Africa. 1783, 1785. See William Hubberley, An appendix to the account of the loss of the Grosvenor by one of the survivors, 1786; George Carter, A narrative of the loss of the Grosvenor East Indiaman, 1791; Edward Riou, 1790, below.

L[usignan], S. Κοσμοπολιτης: history of the revolt of Ali Bey against the Ottoman Porte, including an account of the government of Egypt, together with a description of Grand Cairo. 1783.
— A short answer to Volney's contradictions on Ali Bey's history and revolt. In his Letters addressed to Sir William Fordyce, 1788. See Asia, above.

Rooke, Major Henry. An expedition undertaken against the Cape of Good Hope. In Travels to the coast of Arabia Felix, 1783 etc. See Asia, above.

Sparrman, André. A voyage to the Cape of Good Hope, towards the Antarctic Polar Circle, and around the world, but chiefly into the country of the Hottentots and Caffres 1772–6. 1785, Dublin 1785, London 1786, Perth 1789. Trn from Swedish of 1783 by George Forster. A relation of 2nd voyage of Captain James Cook, principally on South Africa.

Savary, Claude Étienne. Letters on Egypt: containing a parallel between the manners of its ancient and modern inhabitants. 2 vols 1786. Trn from French of 1785.

Stanley, Edward. Observations on the city of Tunis and the adjacent country. 1786.

Volney, Constantin de. Travels through Syria and Egypt. 1787. See Asia, above.

Chenier, Louis de. The present state of the empire of Morocco. 2 vols 1788. Trn from French, Recherches historiques sur les Maures vol 3, 1787.

Falconbridge, Alexander. An account of the slave trade on the coast of Africa. 1788.

Hollingsworth, S. A dissertation on the manners, governments and spirit of Africa, with observations on the present application to Parliament for abolishing Negro slavery in the British West India. Edinburgh 1788; tr German, 1789.

Matthews, John, RN. A voyage to the river Sierra-Leone: containing an account of the country and of the customs and manners of the people. 1788; tr French, 1797.

Norris, Robert. Memoirs of the reign of Bossa Ahadee, King of Dahomy, with the author's journey to Abomey, the capital. 1789.

Stanfield, James Field. Observations on a Guinea voyage. 1788.

— The Guinea voyage: a poem. 1789, Bath 1807, Edinburgh 1807 (with Observations).

Paterson, William. A narrative of four journeys into the country of the Hottentots and Caffraria 1777-1779. 1789, 1790; tr German, 1790; French, 1790 (in trn of James Bruce, 1790 below).

African Association. Proceedings for promoting the discovery of the interior parts of Africa, the journeys of Ledyard and Lucas etc. 1790. Summarizing the first 2 expeditions for the Association.

— Proceedings: containing an abstract of Mr [Mungo] Park's account of his travels, with geographical illustrations by Major Rennell. 1798; Park and Houghton travels tr French, 1798.

Benyowsky, Mauritius Augustus, Count de. An account of the French settlement he was appointed to form upon the island of Madagascar. In Memoirs and travels, 1790. See Asia, above.

Brisson, Pierre Raymond de. An account of shipwreck and captivity: containing a description of the deserts of Africa from Senegal to Morocco. 1790; rptd with Saugnier narrative, 1792 below; rptd 1827. Trn from French of 1789.

Bruce, James. Travels [in Egypt, Arabia, Abyssinia and Nubia] to discover the source of the Nile 1768-73. 5 vols Edinburgh and London 1790, 7 vols Edinburgh 1805 (enlarged), 1813. Many abridgements from 1790; tr French, 1790-2, 1790-2; German, 1790-1. See Richard Wharton, Observations on the authenticity of Bruce's travels, Newcastle 1800.

LeVaillant, François. Travels into the interior parts of Africa by the way of the Cape of Good Hope 1780-5. 2 vols 1790, Dublin 1790, Perth 1791, London 1796. Trn from French of 1790. Another bowdlerized trn by Elizabeth Helme, 2 vols 1790.

Rennell, James. Sketch of the northern part of Africa, exhibiting the geographical information collected by the African Association. 1790.

Riou, Capt Edward. The log of the Guardian 1789-90 [wrecked off South Africa]. Ed L. Kennedy 1952 (from ms) (Navy Records Soc).

— Journal of a voyage from the Cape of Good Hope in search of the wreck of the Grosvenor. 1792.

Clarkson, Thomas. Letters on the slave trade, and the state of the natives in those parts of Africa which are contiguous to Fort St Louis and Goree, with a map of the travels of Mr [Geoffrey] de Villeneuve from the river Sallum to Senegal. 1791.

Lempriere, William, MD. A tour from Gibraltar to Tangier, Sallee, Mogadore, Santa-Cruz, Tarudant, and thence over Mount Atlas to Morocco. 1791, 1793, 1800, Newport 1813; rptd in John Pinkerton, A collection vol 15, 1814; tr German, 1792, 1798; Portuguese, 1794. A 'corrective supplement' pbd 1794.

Poiret, Abbé Jean Louis Marie. Travels through Barbary, the ancient Numidia 1785-6. [1791]. Trn from French of 1789.

Saugnier, — and Pierre Raymond de Brisson. Voyages to the coast of Africa, with shipwreck on board different vessels and subsequent slavery; an account of the Arabs of the desert. 1792. Trn of Saugnier narrative from French of 1791, with reprint of Brisson from 1789.

Dalzel, Archibald. The history of Dahomey compiled from authentic memoirs. 1793.

Rochon, Alexis. Voyage to Madagascar and the East Indies. 1793; rptd in John Pinkerton, A collection vol 16, 1814; tr German, 1792, 1805. Trn from French by Joseph Trapp.

Rye, Peter. An excursion to the peak of Teneriffe in 1791. 1793.

Falconbridge, Anna Maria. Two voyages to Sierra Leone 1791-3. 1794, 1802.

Montefiore, Joshua. An authentic account of the late expedition to Bulam on the coast of Africa, with a description of Sierra Leone. 1794.

Thunberg, Carl P. A description of the region of the Cape of Good Hope. In Travels in Europe, Asia and Africa vols 1-2, 1793. See General Travels, above.

An account of the colony of Sierra Leone, from its first establishment in 1793. 1795; tr German, 1799.

Hanno. The voyage [to the west coast of Africa c. 500 BC]. Ed and tr Thomas Falconer 1797, 1835.

Stout, Capt Benjamin. Narrative of the loss of the ship Hercules on the coast of Caffraria 1796; also travels through the southern deserts and the colonies to the Cape of Good Hope. New York 1797, London 1798, 1800, 1819, 1820. [1830?]; tr French, 1842.

Leyden, John. An historical and philosophical sketch of the discoveries and settlements of Europeans in northern and western Africa at the close of the eighteenth century. 1798; tr German, 1802. The work provides the basis of Hugh Murray, Historical account of discoveries and travels in Africa, 2 vols Edinburgh 1818.

Park, Mungo. Travels in the interior districts of Africa performed under the direction and patronage of the African Association 1795-7. 1798, 1799, 1799; rptd in John Pinkerton, A collection vol 16, 1814; 1907 (EL). See L. G. Gibbon, Niger: the life of Mungo Park, Edinburgh 1934.

Browne, William G. Travels in Africa, Egypt and Syria 1792-8. 1799, 1806; tr Dutch, 1800; French, 1800; German, 1801.

Sonnini de Manoncourt, Charles Nicolas Sigisbert. Travels in upper and lower Egypt, undertaken by order of the government of France. 3 vols 1799, 1800, 1807. Trn by H. Hunter from French of 1799.

Antes, John. Observations on the manners and customs of the Egyptians, the overflowing of the Nile and its effects, written during a residence of twelve years in Cairo and its vicinity. 1800.

Norry, Charles. An account of the French expedition to Egypt. 1800. Trn from French of 1799.

The periplus of the Erythrean Sea. 2 pts 1800-5. Ed and tr from Greek by William Vincent.

Ripault, Louis Madeleine. Report of the commission of arts to the First Consul Bonaparte on the antiquities of upper Egypt and the present state of all the temples, palaces etc. 1800. Trn by William Combe from French.

White, Capt William. Journal of a voyage from Madras to Columbo and Da Lagoa Bay on the east coast of Africa in 1798, with the manners and customs of the inhabitants of Da Lagoa Bay. 1800; tr French, 1800.

§ 2

Murray, H. Historical account of discoveries and travels in Africa from the earliest ages to the present time. 2 vols Edinburgh 1818. Based on John Leyden, 1798 above.

Mott, A. J. On the literature of expeditions to the Nile. Proc of Literary & Philosophical Soc of Liverpool, 56th session 21 1866-7.

Ancelle, J. Les explorations au Sénégal et dans les contrées voisines depuis l'antiquité jusqu'à nos jours. Paris 1886.

Theal, G. M. History and ethnography of Africa south of the Zambesi 1505–1795. 3 vols 1907–10.

Budge, E. W. A history of Ethiopia. 1928.

Starr, G. A. Escape from Barbary: a seventeenth-century genre. HLQ 29 1965.

(6) THE AMERICAS

Bibliographies

Sabin, J. Bibliotheca americana: a dictionary of books relating to America. 29 vols New York 1872–1936 (completed by W. Eames and R. W. G. Vail), Amsterdam 1961–2.

Cox, E. G. A reference guide to the literature of travel. Vol 2, The new world, Seattle 1938.

Collections and Histories

Acunha, Christoval de, et al. Voyages and discoveries in South America: the first up the river of the Amazons to Quito in Peru and back again to Brazil [1637–9]; the second up the river of Plata and thence by land to the mines of Potosi by M. Acarete (du Biscay); the third from Cayenne into Guiana by M. Grillet and Bechamel. 1698. Trn from Spanish and French. The Acarete narrative rptd separately 1716; the Acunha narrative rptd in Expeditions into the valley of the Amazon, 1859 (Hakluyt Soc). The Acunha narrative originally in Spanish, 1641; the Acarete narrative originally in French, 1632; the Guiana narrative of Jean Grillet and François Béchamel was taken from Jesuit letters, presumably in French.

Du Perier, M. A general history of all voyages and travels throughout the old and new world. 1708, 1711 (as A complete collection of voyages made into North and South America, the whole extracted from the works of considerable travellers by M. l'abbé Bellegarde. Trn from French of 1702.

Solis y Ribadeneyra, Antonio de. The history of the conquest of Mexico by the Spaniards. 1724, Dublin 1727; rev Nathaniel Hooke 2 vols 1738, 1753. Trn from Spanish of 1684 by Thomas Townsend.

Herrera, Antonio de. The general history of the vast continent and islands of America from the first discovery thereof, collected from the original relations sent to the King of Spain. 6 vols 1725–6. Trn from Spanish Historia de los hechos de los Castellanos en las islas i tierra firma del mar oceano, 8 vols in 4 1601–15, by John Stevens.

Jenkins, Capt Charles. England's triumph, or Spanish cowardice expos'd: being a compleat history of the [naval] victories of Great Britain for the term of four hundred years past. 1739. Mainly on encounters in the Americas.

Campbell, John. A concise history of Spanish America, of the discovery and settlement of its several colonies, of their situation, extent, commodities, trade; together with an exact description of Paraguay. 1741, 1742, 1747; tr Dutch, 1745–6, 1750; German, 1763.

A collection of voyages and travels: i, Captain Thomas James to the Northwest Passage [pbd 1633]; ii, Pontis' voyage to America, also the taking of Carthagena by the French in 1697 [pbd 1698]; iii, Daniel Coxe (ed), A description of Carolina [pbd 1722]. 1741.

The American traveller: being a new historical collection of voyages and travels. 1743.

Burke, Edmund. An account of the European settlements in America. 2 vols 1758, 1758, 1760, Dublin 17—, London 1765, 1770, 1777; tr German, 1758; French, 1767.

Calder, Isabel M. (ed). Colonial captivities, marches and journeys [1745–71]. New York 1935, Port Washington NY 1968.

Dalrymple, Alexander. A collection of voyages chiefly in the South Atlantic Ocean [1698–1767]. 1775.

Raynal, abbé Guillaume Thomas. A philosophical and political history of the settlements and trade of the Europeans in the East and West Indies. 4 vols 1776, 5 vols 1776, 4 vols Dublin 1776; tr from augmented edn, 5 vols 1777, Edinburgh 1779 (with A history of the present war in America), 6 vols Edinburgh 1782 (with The revolution in America), 8 vols 1783. Trn from French [of 1770] by J. Justamont.

Robertson, William. The history of America. 2 vols 1777, 1778, Cork 1778 etc, 3 vols 1800 (9th edn); tr Italian, 1777–8; French, 1778; Polish, 1789.

Edwards, Bryan. The history civil and commercial of the British Colonies in the West Indies. 2 vols 1793, Dublin 1793, 3 vols 1794, 4 vols 1801 (with An historical survey of the French colony in St Domingo), 5 vols 1819 (with A continuation to the present); tr French, 1801.

Winterbotham, William. Historical, geographical, commercial and philosophical view of the American United States and of the European settlements in America and the West Indies. 4 vols 1795.

Mereness, Newton D. (ed). Travels in the American colonies. New York 1916.

Morrison, A. J. (ed). Travels in Virginia in revolutionary times. Lynchburg 1922. Extracts from the writings of 12 travellers.

§ I

Maverick, Samuel. A briefe description of New England [c. 1660]. 2nd ser Proc Massachusetts Historical Soc 1 1885.

Hickeringill, Edward. Jamaica viewed, with all the ports, harbours, towns and settlements, its climate, fruitfulness of the soils and its suitablenesse to English complexions. 1661, 1661, 1705.

Pagan, Blaise François de, Count of Merveilles. An historical and geographical description of the great county and river of the Amazones in America, drawn out of diverse authors. 1661. Trn from French of 1656 by William Hamilton.

G[ray], R[obert]. Virginia's cure: or an advisive narrative concerning Virginia. 1662; rptd in Peter Force, Tracts vol 3, Washington 1844.

Berkeley, Sir William. A discourse and view of Virginia. [1663]; ed W. H. Smith, Norwalk Conn 1914.

Hilton, William. A relation of a discovery lately made on the coast of Florida. 1664; rptd in Peter Force, Tracts vol 4, Washington 1846.

Alsop, George. A character of the province of Maryland: i, The scituation, and plenty of the province; ii, The laws, customs and natural demeanour of the inhabitants; iii, The worst and best usage of a Mary-Land servant, opened in view; iv, The traffique and vendable commodities of the countrey; also the wilde and naked Indians (or Susquehanokes). 1666; ed N. D. Mereness, Cleveland 1902.

A brief description of the province of Carolina. 1666; rptd in Historical collections of South Carolina vol 2, 1886; ed J. T. Lanning, Charlottesville 1944 (facs).

[Rochefort, Charles César de]. The history of Barbados. 1666. Trn from French.

— The history of the Caribby-Islands: viz Barbados, St Christophers, St Vincents, Martinico, Domenico, Barbouthos, Monserrat, Mevis, Antego etc. 1666. Trn from French Histoire des Iles Antilles, 1658.

Sandford, Robert. A relation of a voyage on the coast of Caroline in 1666. In Narratives of early Carolina, ed A. S. Salley, New York 1911.

Warren, George. An impartial description of Surinam upon the continent of Guiana. 1667; rptd in Thomas Osborne, A collection vol 2, 1745.

Shrigley, Nathaniel. A true relation of Virginia and Mary-Land, with the commodities therein. [1669]; rptd in Peter Force, Tracts vol 3, Washington 1844.

Clarke, Samuel. A true and faithful account of the four chiefest plantations of the English in America, to wit, of Virginia, New England, Bermudus, Barbados, with the temperature of the air, the nature of the soil etc, as also of the natives of Virginia and New England. 1670; also included in his Geographical description of all the countries of the known world, 1670–1 (4th edn).

Denton, Daniel. A brief description of New-York. 1670; ed F. Neumann, Cleveland 1902; New York 1937 (facs).

Ogilby, John. America: being the latest and most accurate description of the new world. 1670, 1671. Actually a trn from the Dutch of Arnoldus Montanus, 1671.

Anderson, William Wemyss. A description and history of the island of Jamaica. 1671.

Fallam, Robert. A journal from Virginia beyond the Apailachian mountains in 1671. Ed C. W. Alvord and L. Bidgood in First explorations of the Trans-Allegheny region, Cleveland 1912.

H[ardy], J[ohn]. A description of the last voyage to Bermudas in the ship Marigold 1670–1. 1671. Verse.

Blome, Richard. A description of the island of Jamaica, with the other isles and territories in America to which the English are related, taken from the papers of Sir Thomas Linch Governor of Jamaica. 1672, 1678, 1687 (as The present state of his Majesty's isles and territories in America); tr French, 1688, 1715; German, 1697.

Josselyn, John. New-Englands rarities discovered in birds, beasts, fishes, serpents and plants of that country, together with the remedies of the natives. 1672, 1675; ed E. Tuckerman, Boston 1865.

— An account of two voyages to New-England. 1674, 1675; rptd in 3rd ser Massachusetts Historical Soc Collections vol 3, 1833.

Lederer, John. The discoveries in three several marches from Virginia to the west of Carolina 1669–70. 1672. Trn from Latin by Sir William Talbot; rptd Cincinnati 1879, Rochester NY 1902; in C. W. Alvord and L. Bidgood, The first explorations of the Trans-Allegheny region, Cleveland 1912; ed W. P. Cumming, Charlottesville 1948.

Gookin, Daniel. Historical collections of the Indians in New England in 1674. In Massachusetts Historical Soc Collections vol 1, 1792.

Glover, Thomas. An account of Virginia. Philosophical Trans 11 1676.

Trapham, Thomas. A discourse on the state of health in Jamaica. 1679.

Barlow, Edward. [2 voyages to the West Indies 1678–8]. In Journal of his life at sea 1659–1703, ed B. Lubbock 2 vols 1934.

Penn, William. Some account of the province of Pennsilvania in America lately granted under the great seal of England. 1681; tr Dutch, 1681. For further pamphlets pbd 1682–5 to interest prospective settlers, see E. G. Cox, Reference guide to travel literature vol 2, 1938, pp. 76–80.

— A brief account of the province of Pennsylvania. 1681, 1681; tr Dutch, 1685.

A[sh], T[homas]. Carolina: or a description of the present state of that country and the natural excellencies thereof. 1682; rptd in Historical collections of South Carolina vol 2, 1836.

A description of New England in general, with a description of the town of Boston in particular. 1682.

Rowlandson, Mary. A true history of the captivity and restoration, with the cruel and inhumane usage she underwent amongst the heathens for eleven weeks time, and her deliverance from them. Boston 1682, London 1682, Boston 1930.

W., J. A letter from New England concerning their customs, manners and religion. 1682, Providence 1905 (with Edward Ward 1699, below).

[Wilson, Samuel]. An account of the province of Carolina. 1682, 1682.

[Crafford, John]. A new and most exact account of the fertile and famous colony of Carolina; also an account of the islands of Bermudas, the whole being a compendious account of a voyage. Dublin 1683.

Poyntz, John. The present prospect of the famous and fertile island of Tobago. 1683, 1695.

The present state of Jamaica, with an account of Sir Henry Morgan's voyage to and famous siege and taking of Panama from the Spaniards. 1683.

Carolina described more fully than heretofore from divers letters from the Irish settled there. Dublin 1684.

Esquemeling, John. The bucaniers of America: or a true account of the most remarkable assaults upon the coasts of the West-Indies by the bucaniers of Jamaica and Tortuga, both England and French. 1684, 1684. Trn from a Spanish version of the original Dutch of 1678. On Francis L'Ollonais and Henry Morgan.

— The second volume: the dangerous voyage and bold attempts of Captain Bartholomew Sharp and others, written by Mr Basil Ringrose. 1685. Both vols pbd thereafter under the name of Esquemeling, as follows: 1695, 1699 (rev trn, adding Lussan and Montauban, below), 1704, 1704, 1741, Dublin 1741, London 1774, 1810, Dublin 1821, 3 vols New York 1826, 1836, 1840, Boston 1856; ed H. Powell 1893, 1967; ed W. S. Stallybrass 1928 (rev).

Sharp, Capt Bartholomew. The voyages and adventures in the South Sea; also Captain Van Horn with his bucanieres surprizing of la Vera Cruz, and Sir Henry Morgan his expedition against the Spaniards in the West Indies and his taking Panama, together with President of Panama's account of the same translated out of Spanish. 1684; the Sharp voyage rptd in William Hacke, A collection, 1699, above; tr French, 1712.

Budd, Thomas. Good order established in Pennsilvania and New Jersey in America: being a true account of the country. 1685; ed F. J. Shepard, Cleveland 1902.

Burton, Richard. The English empire in America: or a prospect of his Majesty's possessions in the West-Indies [and in Newfoundland and the mainland]. 1685, 1692, 1695, 1698, 1704, 1711, 1728, Dublin 1729, 1735, London 1739.

Jeaffreson, Christopher. A young squire of the seventeenth century from his papers [1676–86]. Ed J. C. Jeaffreson 2 vols 1878. His letters from the West Indies are in vol 1.

Garcilaso de la Vega. The royal commentaries of Peru [part 1, The Inca regime; part 2, The Spanish conquest]. 1688 (4 issues). Trn from Spanish of 1609 by Sir Paul Ricault; tr C. R. Markham 2 vols 1869–71 (Hakluyt Soc).

Widders, Robert. The life and death, travels [in America] and sufferings of Robert Widders of Kellet in Lancashire. 1688. The travels described by George Fox and James Lancaster.

Pitman, Henry. A relation of the great sufferings and strange adventures [in Barbadoes and Central America]. 1689; rptd in E. Arber, An English garner vol 7, 1883.

Burnyeat, John. The truth exalted in the writings of John Burnyeat. 1691. Journal of his travels in the English colonies.

A true and faithful relation of the forces of their Majesties in their expedition against the French in their Caribby Islands in the West Indies. 1691.

Frame, Richard. A short description of Pennsylvania. Philadelphia 1692; ed H. G. Jones, Philadelphia 1867.

Kelsey, Henry. Journal 1691–2. Ed C. N. Bell in Trans of Historical & Scientific Soc of Manitoba no 4 1928.

Lodwick, Charles. Account of New Yorke 1692. In New York Historical Society collections: ser 2, vol 2, 1848.

Gordon, Patrick. The present state of the European plantations in the East and West Indies [added to his Geography anatomiz'd: or the geographical grammar]. 1693, 1699, 1702 etc, 1749 (19th edn).

Crisp, Stephen. A memorable account of the Gospel labours, travels [in America] and sufferings. 1694.

Fox, George. A journal or historical account of the life, travels [in America 1671–2] etc. 1694. *See* General Travels, *above*.

Hammond, Lawrence. Diary 1677–94. 2nd ser Massachusetts Historical Soc Proc 7 1892.

Narborough, Sir John. Voyage to the South-Sea [and to the coast of Chile 1669]. In An account of the several late voyages and discoveries. 1694, 1711, 1724. *See* Collections, *above*. The Narborough voyage rptd in John Callander, Terra Australis vol 2, 1767 (*see* Collections, Voyages to the Pacific, *below*); tr French, 1722. Another account of this voyage by John Wood, 1699. below.

Wadsworth, Benjamin. Journal 1694. 4th ser Massachusetts Historical Soc Collections 1 1852.

Clayton, John. A letter giving an account of several observables in Virginia. Philosophical Trans 17–18, 1694–5; rptd in Peter Force, Tracts vol 3, Washington 1844.

Miller, John. New Yorke considered 1695. Ed V. H. Paltsits, Cleveland 1903.

Brinley, Francis. Briefe narrative of the Nanhiganset countrey 1696. Pbns of Rhode Island Historical Soc 8 1900.

Sloane, Sir Hans. Catalogus plantarum in insula Jamaica. 1696.

—— A voyage to the islands Madera, Barbados, Nieves, S. Christophers and Jamaica, with the natural history of the last. 2 vols 1707–25.

Dampier, William. For his voyages to the West Indies and Central and South America, *see* Voyages to the Pacific, *below*, 1697.

An account of the present state of Virginia [c. 1698]. Massachusetts Historical Soc Collections 5 1798.

Froger, François. A relation of a voyage 1695–7 on the coasts of Africa, Straights of Magellan, Brasil, Cayenna and the Antilles by a squadron of French men of war under M. de Gennes. 1698. Trn from French of 1698.

Hennepin, Louis. A new discovery of a vast country in America between New France and New Mexico [La Salle in Mississippi valley]. 1698, 1698, 1699; an abstract, [1720?]; ed R. G. Thwaites 2 vols Chicago 1903. Trn from French of 1697, 1698. For falsifications in the narrative, *see* A. H. Greenly, Father Hennepin: his travels and his books, PBSA 51 1957; P. G. Adams, Travelers and travel liars, Berkeley 1962, ch 3.

Pontis, Louis de. An account of the taking of Carthagena by the French in the year 1697. 1698, 1699, 1699, 1740; rptd in A collection, 1741. Trn from French of 1698. *See* Collections under Americas, *above*.

Rose, Hugh. Journal during the Scots African and Indian fleet in their voyage from Madera to America 1698. Ed F. R. Hart in his Disaster of Darien, New York 1929.

[Tonti, Henri de]. An account of Monsieur de la Salle's last expedition and discoveries in North America. 1698; trn from French Dernières découvertes, 1697. Rptd in Collections New York Historical Soc 2 1814; tr M. B. Anderson, Chicago 1898 (Caxton Club), with French text; ed I. J. Cox with the other journals of the La Salle discoveries, 2 vols 1922. The 1698 vol includes an account of the Sieur de Montauban and the French buccaneers on the Guinea coast in 1695, tr from French of 1698; *see* Voyages to Africa, *above*, 1698.

Ward, Edward. A trip to Jamaica, with a true character of the people and island. 1698, 1699 etc, 1700 (7th edn), 1702 (8th edn); rptd in Collection of the writings hitherto extant, 1700, 1701, 1702, 1717; ed H. W. Troyer in Five travel scripts, New York 1933 (facs of 7th edn).

—— A trip to New-England with a character of the country and people, both English and Indians. 1699, 1704; rptd in Collections, 1700, 1701, 1702, 1717; ed G. P. Winship in his Boston in 1682 and 1699, Providence 1905; ed H. W. Troyer 1933 (facs) (with preceding). *See* bibliography in H. W. Troyer, Ned Ward, Cambridge Mass 1946.

B[lackwell], I[saac]. A description of the province and bay of Darien. 1699.

Dickinson, Jonathan. God's protecting Providence man's surest help and defence in the remarkable deliverance from the sea and the canibals of Florida [in a voyage Jamaica to Philadelphia 1696–7]. Philadelphia 1699, London 1700, 1700, 1720, 1759, 1787, 1790; ed C. M. and E. W. Andrews, New Haven 1945.

The history of Caledonia, or the Scots colony in Darien. 1699, Dublin 1699 (with 7 other pieces).

A letter giving a description of the Isthmus of Darien. Edinburgh 1699. For other pieces on the Darien colony, *see* E. G. Cox, Reference guide to the literature of travel vol 2, 1938, pp. 244–7.

Raveneau de Lussan, Sieur. A journal of a voyage made into the South-Sea by the bucaniers or freebooters of America 1684–9. 1699 (added to the 2nd edn of John Esquemeling, The bucaniers of America, 1684–5 above); rptd separately 1742 (with The voyage of Montauban, in Voyages to Africa, above, 1698). Trn from French of 1689.

Wafer, Lionel. A new voyage and description of the Isthmus of America, the form and make of the country, the Indian inhabitants, with remarkable occurrences in the South Sea and elsewhere. 1699, 1704 (with addns); ed G. P. Winship, Cleveland 1903; ed L. E. Elliott Joyce 1933 (with addns) (Hakluyt Soc).

Wood, Capt John. Voyage through the Straits of Magellan. In William Hacke, A collection, 1699; tr French, 1712. On Narborough voyage, 1694, above.

Paterson, William. Central America [1701]. Ed S. Bannister 1857.

Wolley, Charles. A two years' journal in New York 1701. Ed E. G. Bourne, Cleveland 1902.

Davis, Nathaniel. The expedition of a body of Englishmen to gold mines of Spanish America 1702. In Lionel Wafer, A new voyage, 1704, (*see* 1699, *above*); rptd with Wafer, 1933 (Hakluyt Soc).

Burchett, Josiah. Memoirs of transactions at sea during the war with France 1688–97. 1703; tr French, 1704. *See* Col Luke Lillingston, Reflections on Mr Burchett's memoirs, 1704; and Josiah Burchett, Mr Burchett's Justification, 1704. *See also* Burchett, A complete history, 1720, under Collections, *above*.

Clarke, George. Voyage to America. [1703]; ed E. B. O'Callaghan, Albany NY 1867.

Lahontan, Louis Armand, Baron de. New voyages to North-America: containing an account of the several nations of that vast continent. 2 vols 1703, 1735; ed R. G. Thwaites 2 vols Chicago 1905; ed S. Leacock, Ottawa 1932. Trn from French of 1703. For the falsifications, *see* P. G. Adams, Travelers and travel liars, Berkeley 1962, ch 3.

Knight, Sarah K. The private journal kept on a journey from Boston to New-York 1704. Ed G. P. Winship, Boston 1920.

Nieuhoff, John. The voyages and travels into Brazil [1640–9] and the East Indies. In A. and J. Churchill, A collection vol 2, 1704 etc. Trn from Dutch of 1682.

Ovalle, Alonso de, S. J. An historical relation of the Kingdom of Chile. In A. and J. Churchill, A collection vol 3, 1704 etc; rptd in John Pinkerton, A collection vol 14, 1814. 6 of 8 bks translated from Spanish of 1646 by a member of Royal Society.

Sepp, Anthony, and Anthony Behme SJ. A voyage from Spain to Paraquaria [Paraguay] 1691. In A. and J. Churchill, A collection vol 4, 1704 etc. Trn from German of 1696.

Techo, Nicholas de, SJ. The history of the provinces of Paraguay, Tucuman, Rio de la Plata etc, and of the Kingdom of Chili. In A. and J. Churchill, A collection vol 4, 1704 etc. Trn abridged from Latin of 1673.

Beverley, Robert. The history and present state of Virginia. 1705, 1722 (rev); ed C. Campbell, Richmond Va 1855; ed L. B. Wright, Chapel Hill 1947; tr French, 1707, 1712.

Dunton, John. The life and errors (with his life in New England). 1705; ed J. B. Nichols 2 vols 1818 (enlarged). Extracts on his American visit 1686 rptd in 2nd ser Collection Massachusetts Historical Soc vol 2, 1815.
— Letters written from New England 1686 in which are described his voyages by sea, his travels by land, and his friends and acquaintances. Ed W. H. Whitmore, Boston 1867 (Prince Soc) (from ms).

Narrative of a voyage to Maryland 1705–6. Amer Historical Rev 12 1906–7.

Keith, George. A journal of travels from New-Hampshire to Caratuck in Carolina. 1706; rptd in Protestant Episcopal Church Historical Soc vol 1, New York 1851.

An account of Jamaica and its inhabitants by a gentleman long resident in the West Indies. [1707?], 1708, [1708?].

Archdale, John. A new description of that fertile and pleasant province of Carolina. 1707; rptd Charleston 1822; in Historical collections of South Carolina, 1836; in A. S. Salley, Narratives of early Carolina 1670–1708, 1911.

Clayton, John. Letters from Virginia 1688 on several observables. In Miscellanea curiosa vol 3, 1708; rptd in Peter Force, Tracts vol 3, 1836.

Cook, Ebenezer. The sot-weed factor, or a voyage to Maryland: a satyr in burlesque verse. 1708, Annapolis 1731; ed J. G. Shea, New York 1865.

Graves, John. A memorial: or a short account of the Bahama Islands. 1708.

Oldmixon, John. The British Empire in America: containing the history of all the British colonies with an account of the country, soil, climate, products and trades. 2 vols 1708, 1741 (rev).

Cieza de Léon, Pedro de. The seventeen years travels [1532–50] through the mighty Kingdom of Peru from the city of Panama to the frontiers of Chile. In A new collection, 1709; tr as Travels 1532–50 by C. R. Markham, 1864 (Hakluyt Soc), who also translated pts 2–4 on the Peruvian wars, not pbd until the 19th century, in 1883, 1913, 1918–23. Trn from Spanish La crónica del Perú 1553 by John Stevens.

Lawson, John. A new voyage to Carolina: containing the exact description and natural history of that country, together with a journal of a thousand miles travel'd thro' several nations of Indians. In John Stevens, A new collection, 1709; 1714 (as The history of Carolina etc), 1718, Dublin 1737 (as by John Brickell); 1743; rptd Raleigh NC 1860; Charlotte NC 1903; ed F. L. Harriss, Richmond Va 1937, 1952; ed H. T. Lefler, Chapel Hill 1967; tr German, 1712, 1722. The 1737 text ed J. B. Grimes, Raleigh NC 1911.

Taylor, John. An account of some of the labours, exercises, travels and perils by sea and land [to America] by way of journal [1656–1705]. 1709, York 1830 (as Memoirs etc).

Nairn, Capt Thomas. A letter from South-Carolina, giving an account of the soil, air, productions, trade, government, laws, religion, inhabitants, military strength, written by a Swiss gentleman. 1710, 1732.

Langman, Christopher et al. A true account of the voyage of the Nottingham-galley of London, J. Dean commander, to New-England [with shipwreck and ensuing cannibalism]. 1711; rptd Mag of History no 59 1917.

A view of the coasts, countries and islands within the limits of the South-Sea Company from the river Aranoca to Terra del Fuego and from thence through the South Sea. 1711, 1711. For the numerous South Sea Company pamphlets, see BM catalogue.

Norris, John. Profitable advice for rich and poor in a dialogue containing a description of South Carolina. 1714.

Selkirk, Alexander. Providence displayed: or a very surprising account written with his own hand. 1712; rptd in Harleian miscellany vol 5, 1745 etc; 1800 (as by Isaac James). The account is a nearly verbatim extract from Woodes Rogers, A cruising voyage round the world, 1712. The 4-year isolation on Juan Fernandez Island was also noticed at length in the Edward Cooke account of the circumnavigation, 1712; and by Richard Steele in an interview reported in Englishman no 26 1714.

Edmundson, William. A journal of the life, travels [to North America], sufferings. 1713, 1715, Dublin 1715, London 1774, Dublin 1820; rptd in the Friends' Library, 1833 etc; and Philadelphia 1838.

Sharpe, John. Journal 1704–13. Pennsylvania Mag of History 40 1916.

Joutel, Henri. A journal of the last voyage by Monsr de la Sale to the Gulph of Mexico to find out the mouth of the Missisipi River. 1714, 1715, 1719; rptd in Historical Collection of Louisiana vol 1, 1846; Chicago 1896 (Caxton Club); ed I. J. Cox 1905 (with other La Salle narratives); ed H. R. Stiles, Albany NY 1906. Trn from French of 1713.

The present state of the sugar plantations considered, but more especially that of the island of Barbadoes. 1714.

A relation of the new mission to the Moxos Indians in Peru, with their life and customs. In The travels of Missioners of the Society of Jesus, 1714, under Collections, above. The Relation originally written in Spanish.

Grantham, Sir Thomas. An account of some memorable actions particularly in Virginia. 1716; ed R. A. Brock, Richmond Va 1882.

M., Mr R. A relation of a voyage to Buenos Ayres, and by land to Potosi. 1716.

Frezier, Amédée François. A voyage to the South-Sea and along the coasts of Chili and Peru 1712–14. 1717. Trn from French of 1716.

Knight, James. The founding of Churchill: being the journal of James Knight 1717. Ed J. F. Kenney, Toronto 1932.

Parker, George. The West-India almanac for the year 1719, with an account of New England or Virginia and the West Indies. 1719.

Chetwood, W. R. Voyages, dangerous adventures and imminent escapes of Captain Richard Falconer, with the manners of the Indians in America, and the voyages of Thomas Randal, taken by the Indians of Virginia. 1720, 1724, 1734, 1764, 1769.

A description of the Golden Islands, with an account of the undertaking for making a settlement there. 1720. One of several pamphlets advertising the islands off the coast of present Georgia: see E. G. Cox, Reference guide vol 2, 95–6.

Neal, Daniel. The history of New England to 1700, with the present state of New England. 2 vols 1720, 1747 (enlarged).

Walker, Sir Hovenden. A journal: or full account of the late expedition to Canada [1711]. 1720. With an appendix of documents, including the court-martial proceedings.

Coxe, Daniel. A description of the English province of Carolana, by the Spaniards call'd Florida, and by the French La Louisiane, as also of the great and famous river Meshacebe or Missisipi, the five vast navigable lakes of fresh water and the parts adjacent. 1722, 1726, 1727, 1741; rptd St Louis 1840; in Historical collections of Louisiana vol 2, 1746.

B.M.R., S. A general survey of that part of the island of St Christopher's now yielded up to Great Britain. 1722.

Jones, Hugh. The present state of Virginia, of Indian, English and Negroe inhabitants of that colony. 1724, New York 1865.

Chicken, George. Journal of the commissr for Indian affairs on his journey to the Cherokees 1725. Ed N. D. Mereness in Travels in the American colonies, 1916; see Collections, above.

Fitch, Tobias. Journal to the Creeks 1725. 1916 (with preceding).

Goddard, Edward. Journal of the peace commission to the eastern Indians 1726. Pbns of Colonial Soc of Massachusetts 20 1920.

Penhallow, Samuel. The history of the wars of New-England. Boston 1726; rptd in New Hampshire Historical Soc collections vol 1, 1824.

The state of the island of Jamaica, chiefly in relation to its commerce and the conduct of the Spaniards in the West-Indies. 1726.

Colden, Cadwallader. The history of the five Indian nations of Canada depending on the province of New-York. New York 1727, London 1747, 1750, 1755; ed J. G. Shea, New York 1866, 1902, 1904.

Hartwell, Henry et al. The present state of Virginia and the college [of William and Mary]. 1727; rptd in Collections of Massachusetts Historical Soc 5 1835 (from ms); ed H. D. Farish, Williamsburg 1940.

Wharton, Philip, Duke of. Some modern observations upon Jamaica, its natural history, improvements, trade and manner of living [1726]. In Whartoniana or miscellanies in verse and prose vol 2, 1727; rptd in Poetical works vol 2, 1731; in Works vol 2, 1740.

Catesby, Mark. The natural history of Carolina, Florida and the Bahama Islands. 2 vols 1731–43 (French and English), 1754, 1764 (augmented), 1771; tr German, 1749 (in part).

—— Hortus britanno-americanus: the produce of the British colonies in North America. 1763.

—— Hortus Europae americanus: a collection of 85 curious trees and shrubs. 1767.

Catesby's drawings of American fauna were pbd as Piscium, serpentum insectorum etc, Nuremberg 1750, *with text in Latin and German.*

Cuming, Sir Alexander. Journal. Historical Register 61 1731; ed S. C. Williams in Early travels in the Tennessee country, Johnson City 1928.

Hall, F. Ayrer. The importance of the British plantations in America to this Kingdom, with the state of their trade, as also a description of the several colonies there. 1731.

Comer, John. Diary 1704–32. Ed C. E. Burrows and J. W. Willmarth, in Rhode Island Historical Soc collections vol 8, 1893.

Du Guay-Trouin, René. The memoirs of M. du Gué-Trouin, chief of a squadron in the Royal Navy of France: containing all his sea-actions with the English, Dutch and Portugueze. 1732. Trn from a surreptitious Dutch version 1730 of the French by a sea-officer. The first French edn was in 1740.

May, Charles. An account of the wonderful preservation of the ship Terra Nova of London, homeward bound from Virginia 1688. In A. and J. Churchill, A collection vol 6, 1732 etc.

Norwood, Colonel. A voyage to Virginia [in 1649]. 1732 (with preceding).

Oglethorpe, James Edward. An account of the colony in Georgia and an essay on plantations. 1732, 1733.

—— A new and accurate account of the provinces of South Carolina and Georgia. 1732, 1733; rptd in Georgia Historical Soc collections vol 1, 1840.

—— An impartial inquiry into the state and utility of the province of Georgia. 1741; rptd 1840 (with preceding).

—— An impartial account of the late expedition against St Augustine under General Oglethorpe. 1742. See Campbell, 1744, *below*, for another account.

W., M. The Mosqueto Indian and his Golden River: a familiar description of the Mosqueto kingdom in [Central] America [1699]. In A. and J. Churchill, A collection vol 6, 1732 etc.

Martyn, Benjamin. Reasons for establishing the colony of Georgia, with regard to the trade of Great Britain, with some account of the country. 1733, 1733; rptd in Georgia Historical Soc collections vol 1, 1840.

Von Reck, Baron P. G. F., and John Martin Bolzius. An extract of the journals of Mr Commissary von Reck who conducted the first transport of Saltsburgers to Georgia, and of Rev Mr Bolzius, giving an account of their voyage and settlement. 1734; rptd in Peter Force, Tracts vol 4, 1846.

Atkins, John. A voyage to Guinea, Brasil and the West-Indies in HMS the Swallow and Weymouth: describing the several island and settlements. 1735, 1737; tr German, 1748.

Cockburn, John et al. A journey overland from the Gulf of Honduras to the great South-Sea. 1735, 1740, 1742, 1773, 1794, 1799, 1810.

Gyles, John. Memoirs of odd adventures, strange deliverances in the captivity in the district of Maine. Boston 1736, Cincinnati 1869; Massachusetts Historical Soc 1936 (photostat).

Brickell, John. The natural history of North-Carolina etc. 1737. See John Lawson, 1709 *above*.

Whitefield, George. A journal of a voyage from London to Savannah in Georgia. 1738; 6 edns to 1741, and 6 continuations pbd separately 1739–44. For full bibliography, *see* J. Sabin, Dictionary of books relating to America. *See* particularly T. Robert, A narrative of the life and travels, 1770.

A description of the Windward Passage and Gulf of Florida, with the course of the British trading-ships to and from the island of Jamaica. 1739.

Leslie, Charles. A new and exact account of Jamaica, with the ancient and present state of that colony and a particular account of the sacrifices, libations etc in use among the Negroes. Edinburgh 1739, 1740, 1740 (as A new history of Jamaica), Dublin 1741; tr French, 1751 (in part). The 3rd edn adds An account of Admiral Vernon's success at Porto Bello and Chagre.

Gonzales Carranza, Domingo. A geographical description of the coasts, harbours and sea ports of the Spanish West-Indies, written 1718. 1740. Trn from Spanish.

Seward, William. A journal of a voyage from Savannah to Philadelphia and to England 1740. 1740. With George Whitefield.

A description of Georgia by one of the first settlers. 1741; rptd in Peter Force, Tracts vol 2, Washington 1838.

A ranger's report of travels with General Oglethorpe 1739–42. Ed N. D. Mereness in Travels in the American Colonies, 1916; *see* Collections, *above*.

Stephens, William. A journal of the proceedings in Georgia, to which is added a state of that province. 2 vols 1742, Atlanta 1906.

For the Anson voyage to South America on his circumnavigation and the accounts of 1743–68, see Voyages to the Pacific and round the world, below.

Lockman, John. Travels of the Jesuits into various parts of the world with an account of the Spanish settlements in America. 2 vols 1743, 1762.

Moraley, William. The infortunate: or the voyage and adventures [of an indentured servant] in the provinces of Pensilvania and New Jersey. Newcastle 1743.

Dobbs, Arthur. An account of the countries adjoining to Hudson's Bay in the north-west part of America; showing the benefit to be made by settling colonies and opening trade in those parts, with an abstract of all the discoveries which have been published of the islands and countries adjoining to the great Western Ocean, with an extract of Captain Middleton's journal. 1744, 1764. For controversial remarks on Middleton, *see* BM catalogue.

—— Observations upon the Russian discoveries. *See* N.N., A letter, 1754, *below*.

Hamilton, Alexander, MD. Hamilton's itinerarium: being a narrative of a journey from Annapolis, Maryland, through Delaware to New Hampshire 1744. Ed A. B. Hart, St Louis 1907; ed C. Bridenbaugh, Chapel Hill 1945.

'Campbell, G. L.' (Edward Kimber). A relation or journal of a late expedition to St Augustine. 1744; ed S. A. Kimber, Boston 1935.

—— Itinerant observations in America. London Mag 1745–6; rptd Savannah 1878.

—— History of the life and adventures of Mr Anderson in Europe and America. 1754, Dublin 1754, Berwick 1782, Glasgow 1799, London [1800?]. Fiction.

Moore, Francis. A voyage to Georgia 1735: containing a description of the soil, birds, beasts, trees, rivers, islands, also a description of Savannah. 1744; rptd in Georgia Historical Soc collections vol 1, 1840.

The present state of Louisiana: containing the garrisons, forts and forces, price of all manner of provisions and liquors, and a list of the country goods and those proper to be sent to the natives, by an officer at New Orleans. 1744. Trn from captured French documents.

Dickinson, James. A journal of the life, travels and ministry [in Pennsylvania]. 1745; rptd in Thomas Wilson, Journals, 1847; Philadelphia 1848 (Friends' Lib).

Logan, William. Journal of a journey to Georgia 1745. Pennsylvania Mag of History 27 1903.

Norris, Isaac. Journal during a trip to Albany 1745. Ibid.

Smith, William. A natural history of Nevis and the rest of the English Leeward Charibee islands in America. Cambridge 1745.

Douglass, William. A summary of the first planting, progressive improvements and present state of the British settlements in North America. 2 vols Boston 1747–50, London 1755, 1760.

La Condamine, Charles Marie de. A succinct abridgement of a voyage made within the inland parts of South America from the coasts of the South Sea to the coasts of Brazil and Guiana down the River of the Amazons. 1747; rptd in John Pinkerton A collection vol 14, 1814. Trn from French of 1745.

Pepperell, Sir William. An accurate journal and account of the New-England land forces against the French settlements on Cape Breton to the surrender of Louisbourg. Exeter 1747, London 1758.

Story, Thomas. A journal of the life, as also of his travels and labours in the service of the Gospel [in Pennsylvania]. Newcastle 1747, Philadelphia 1848 (Friends' Lib). *See* E. E. Moore, Travelling with Thomas Story, 1947.

Lozano, Pedro. A relation of the dreadful earthquake at Lima, the capital of Peru, and the port of Callao 28 October 1746. 1748. Trn from Spanish of 1746, and adding A description of Peru in general.

Walcot, James. The new pilgrim's progress: or the pious Indian convert baptis'd George James, with a narrative of his laborious and dangerous travels among the savage Indians [of Carolina] for their conversion. 1748, 1763.

Brainerd, Rev David. Journal while among the Indians in New Jersey [before his death in 1747]. Ed Jonathan Edwards in An account of the life, collected from his diary, Boston 1749, Edinburgh 1765, Glasgow 1798, London 1818, New Haven 1822 etc; ed 2 vols 1902 (as Diary). Many extracts and abridgements.

Chalkley, Thomas. A journal or historical account of the life, travels and Christian experiences. In his Works, Philadelphia 1749, London 1751, Philadelphia 1754, London 1766, 1791; 1818 (separately), Lindfield 1832, 1835, Philadelphia 1842, 1850.

A geographical history of Nova Scotia. 1749; tr French, 1755.

Report from the committee appointed to inquire into the state and condition of the countries adjoining to Hudson's Bay, and of the trade carried on there. 1749. An appendix adds a report by Joseph la France on a visit to Quebec and Montreal.

Stevens, Phineas. Journal of journey to Canada 1749. New Hampshire Historical Soc Collections 5 1837.

—— Journal of journey to Canada 1752. Ed N. D. Mereness in Travels in the American colonies, New York 1916.

Hughes, Rev Griffith. The natural history of Barbadoes. 1750.

Nicholson, Thomas. Journal 1746–50. Pbns of Southern Historical Assoc (Washington) 4 1900.

Tabago: or a geographical description, natural and civil history, of that famous island. 1750, 1750.

Birket, James. Some cursory remarks made in his voyage to North America 1750–1. New Haven 1916.

Bartram, John. Observations on the inhabitants, climate, soil, rivers, production, animals and other matters in his travels from Pensilvania to Onondago, Oswego and the Lake Ontario; annex'd, a curious account of the cataracts of Niagara by Mr Peter Kalm. 1751; ed W. F. Humphrey, Geneva NY 1895.

—— A journal kept upon a journey from St Augustine up the river St Johns as far as the lakes. In William Stork, An account of East Florida, [1766] etc, below; ed F. Harper as Diary of a journey through the Carolinas, Georgia and Florida 1765–6, in Trans Amer Philosophical Soc new ser 33 1942 (from ms).

Gist, Christopher. Journal of a tour through Ohio and Kentucky in 1751. Ed J. S. Johnston in First explorations of Kentucky, Louisville 1898.

—— Journal of a journey [in Maryland, Virginia and North Carolina]. In Thomas Pownall, A topographical description of the middle British colonies, 1776. These and other journals were collected and ed W. M. Darlington, Pittsburgh 1893.

Knyveton, John. The diary of a surgeon 1751–2 [on a naval voyage to the West Indies]. Ed E. Gray 1937.

Robson, Joseph. An account of six years residence in Hudson's-Bay 1733–6 and 1744–7. 1752.

Courte de la Blanchardière, abbé René. A voyage to Peru by the Conde de St Malo 1745–9, with an appendix containing the present state of the Spanish affairs in America in respect to mines, trade and discoveries. 1753. Trn from French of 1751.

Fothergill, John. An account of the life and travels in the work of the ministry. 1753, Philadelphia 1754, London 1773.

Holme, Benjamin. An account of his life and travels. In his A collection of the epistles and works, 1753. Chs 4–5 on his travels in the British colonies in North America 1715–20.

Houston, James, MD. The works: containing memoirs of his life and travels from 1690, giving a particular account of the Scottish expedition to Darien in America, the late expedition to the Spanish West-Indies, the taking and restitution of Cape Breton. 1753.

Livingston, William. A brief consideration of New York. Independent Reflector 1753; ed E. G. Swem, Metuchen NJ 1925.

MacSparran, James. America dissected: being a full and true account of all the American colonies, shewing the intemperance of the climates, danger from enemies, but above all the dangers to the souls of the poor people that remove thither. Dublin 1753; rptd in W. Updike, History of the Episcopal Church in Narragansett, New York 1847, 3 vols Boston 1907.

Poole, Robert, MD. The beneficent bee: or a voyage from London to Barbadoes, Antigua etc. 1753.

N., N. A letter from a Russian sea-officer, with remarks upon Mr De l'Isles chart and memoir relative to the new discoveries northward and eastward from Kamtschatka, together with observations by Arthur Dobbs. 1754. Trn from the French of G. F. Müller. *See* the Arthur Dobbs entry, 1744 *above*.

Some account of the North American Indians: their genius, characters, customs and dispositions. 1754.

Stiles, Ezra. Diary 1754. Massachusetts Historical Soc Proc 2nd ser 7 1892.

Washington, George. The journal of Major George Washington [on reconnaissance west of the Alleghenies 1754]. Williamsburg 1754, London 1754, New York 1765. Often rptd in collections and edns of his writings.

Atkin, Edmund. Indians of the southern colonial frontier 1754. Ed W. R. Jacobs, Columbia SC 1954 (from ms).

Evans, Lewis. A brief account of Pennsylvania. Ed L. H. Gipson in Lewis Evans, Philadelphia 1939.

— Geographical, historical, philosophical and mechanical essays: the first containing an analysis of a general map of the middle British colonies in America and of the country of the confederate Indians etc. Philadelphia 1755, 1755–6; rptd in L. H. Gipson, above (facs).

The expedition of Major General Braddock to Virginia: being extracts from letters of an officer giving a lively idea of the nature of the country. 1755.

Fisher, Daniel. Extracts from the diary 1755. Pennsylvania Mag of History 17 1893.

Smith, William, DD. A brief state of the province of Pennsylvania, in which the true cause of the continual encroachments of the French displayed. 1755, 1755, 1756, 1765, New York 1865.

— A brief view of the conduct of Pennsylvania 1755, particularly the expedition under the late General Braddock. 1756; tr French, 1756.

— An historical account of the expedition against the Ohio Indians in 1764, with some account of the Indian country. Philadelphia 1765, London 1766, Dublin 1769, Cincinnati 1868; tr French, 1769.

Bownas, Samuel. An account of the life, travels and Christian experience in the work of the ministry [in America from 1702]. Ed J. Besse 1756; Philadelphia 1759 (in Journals of the lives and travels of Samuel Bownas and John Richardson); London 1761, 1795, Stamford 1805, London 1826, Philadelphia 1839 (Friends' Lib), London 1846.

Browne, Patrick, MD. The civil and natural history of Jamaica: foreign trade, revenue, vegetable productions, quadrupeds, birds, fishes. 1756, 1759.

Rolt, Richard. A new and accurate history of South America, with a full description of Chili, Paraguay, Peru and Terra Firma, of Guiana, Cayenne, Brazil and the various nations of Indians. Vol 1 (all pbd), 1756.

Burke, William and Edmund. An account of the European settlements in America. 2 vols 1757, 1758, 1762, Dublin 17—, London 1765, 1766, 1770, 1777, 1808, Boston 1835, London 1839 (in Works vol 9); tr German, 1758; Italian, 1763; French, 1767.

A review of the military operations in North America, from the commencement of the French hostilities on the borders of Virginia 1753 to the surrender of Oswego 1756. 3 vols 1757.

Smith, William. The history of the province of New-York from the first discovery to 1732, with a description of the country and the inhabitants. 1757, 1776, Albany NY 1814, New York 1829; tr French, 1767.

Williamson, Peter. French and Indian cruelty exemplified during his captivity among the Indians. York 1757, London 1758, York 1758, London 1759, Dublin 1766, Edinburgh 1792.

Juan, Jorge, and Antonio de Ulloa. A voyage to South-America: describing at large the Spanish cities, towns, provinces, together with the natural history of the country. 2 vols 1758, Dublin 1758, London 1760, 1772, 1806, 1807; rptd in John Pinkerton, A collection vol 14, 1814. Trn from Spanish of 1748 by John Adams.

Thompson, Thomas. An account of two missionary voyages, the one to New Jersey in North America, the other from America to the coast of Guiney. 1758; rptd 1937 (Soc for Propagation of Gospel) (facs).

Bradstreet, John. An impartial account of his expedition to Fort Frontenac, by a volunteer. 1759.

Gardiner, Richard. An account of the expedition to the West Indies against the Leeward Islands. 1759, 1760, 1762; tr French, 1762.

Kenny, James. Journal to ye westward 1758–9. Pennsylvania Mag of History 37 1931.

— Journal 1761–3. Ibid.

Moncrief, Major. A short account of the expedition against Quebec commanded by Major General Wolfe 1759, by an engineer. 1759.

Montresor, James. Journals 1757–9. New York Historical Soc Collections 14 1881.

Muratori, L. A. A relation of the missions of Paraguay. 1759, 1788 (as The Jesuits travels in South America, Paraguay, Chile). Trn from a French version of the Italian of 1743.

Venegas, Fr Miguel. A natural and civil history of California, with an accurate description of that country and the customs of the inhabitants. 2 vols 1759. Trn from Spanish Noticia de la California y de su conquista temporal y espiritual, 1757.

Amherst, William. Journal in America 1758–60. Ed J. C. Webster [1928].

Jefferys, Thomas. The natural and civil history of the French dominions in north and south America, illustrated. 1760, 1761.

— A description of the Spanish islands and settlements on the coast of the West Indies, compiled from authentic memoirs. 1762, 1774.

— A general topography of North America and the West Indies. 1768.

— The American atlas: or a geographical description of the whole continent of America. 1776 (with 30 maps). As geographer to the King, Jefferys had a hand in much map-making for himself and to illustrate the writings of others, such as the following.

— A journal of the siege of Quebec [with maps etc] drawn from the original surveys taken by the engineers of the army, engraved by Thomas Jefferys. 1760.

Montresor, Capt John. Journal of a march on snowshoes from Quebec to New England [1760]. New England Historical & Genealogical Register 1882.

— The journals [of a British engineer officer] 1757–78. Ed G. D. Scull, in New York Historical Soc Collections 14 1882.

— Journal 1777–8. Pennsylvania Mag of History 5–6 1881–2.

Patrick, J. Quebec: a poetical essay on the glorious expedition against Canada 1759. 1760.

Pichon, T. Genuine letters and memoirs relating to the history of the islands of Cape Breton and St John to 1758. 1760. Trn from French of 1760.

Charlevoix, Fr Pierre François Xavier de. Journal of a voyage to North America: containing the geographical description and natural history of that country, particularly Canada. 2 vols 1761, 1 vol 1763 (as Letters to the Dutchess of Lesdiguieres), 2 vols Dublin 1766; abridged in J. H. Moore, A new collection, 1778; trn of History by J. G. Shea 6 vols New York 1866–72, 1900; trn of Journal by L. P. Kellogg 2 vols Chicago 1923. Trn from French of 1744, vols 5–6 of Histoire de la nouvelle France.

— The history of Paraguay, with an account of the establishment formed there by the Jesuits. 2 vols 1769, Dublin 1769. Trn from French of 1756.

Glen, Dr James. A description of South Carolina. 1761; rptd in Historical Collections of South Carolina 2 1836.

An account of the Spanish settlements in America, in four parts. Edinburgh 1762.

The American gazetteer: containing a distinct account of all the parts of the new world. 3 vols 1762; tr Italian, 1763.

Bossu, J. B. Travels in the interior of North America 1751–62. Ed and tr from French by S. Feiler, Norman Oklahoma 1962.

Forbes, Eli. Diary 1762. Proc Massachusetts Historical Soc 2nd ser 54 1922.

Rodney, George Brydges, Baron. A description of the Caribee islands 1762. Ibid.

Amherst, Jeffery. Journal in America 1758–63. Ed J. C. Webster, Toronto 1931.

Complete history of the origin and progress of the late war to 1763: naval and land campaigns of the French and British in America. 2 vols 1763.

Gorrell, James. Journal 1761–3. State Historical Soc of Wisconsin Collections 1 1855.

Le Page du Pratz. The history of Louisiana, or of the western parts of Virginia and Carolina: containing a description of the countries that lye on both sides of the river Missisipi. 2 vols 1763, 1764. Trn from French of 1758.

Roberts, William (ed). An account of the first discovery and natural history of Florida, with a geographical description by Thomas Jefferys. 1763.

Mifflin, Benjamin. Journal 1764. Pennsylvania Mag of History 52 1928.

Croghan, George. Letters and journals relating to tours into the western country 1750–65. Ed N. D. Mereness in Early western travels, New York 1916.

Gordon, Lord Adam. Journal of an officer in the West Indies and North America in 1764 and 1765. Ibid.

Gregory, William. Journal from Fredericksburg to Philadelphia 1765. William & Mary College Quart Historical Mag 13 1905.

Rogers, Col Robert. A concise account of North America: containing a description of the several British colonies and an account of the several nations and tribes of Indians. 1765, Dublin 1770; tr German, 1767.

— Journals: containing an account of the several excursions he made under the generals in North America. 1765, Dublin 1769; ed F. B. Hough, Albany NY 1883.

Timberlake, Lt Henry. The memoirs: containing whatever he observed during his travels to and from that [Cherokee] nation. 1765; ed S. C. Williams, Johnson City Tennessee 1927; tr German, 1767.

Webster, Pelatiah. Journal of a voyage to Charlestown 1765. Ed T. P. Harrison in Southern Historical Assoc Pbns 2 1898.

Williams, Capt Griffith. An account of the island of Newfoundland: its trade and fishery. 1765.

Gordon, Harry. Journal 1766. In Thomas Pownall, A topographical description, 1776, below; ed N. D. Mereness in Travels in the American colonies, New York 1916.

Jennings, John. A journal from Fort Pitt to the Illinois country 1766. Pennsylvania Mag of History 21 1907.

— A journal to New Orleans 1768. Ibid.

Stork, William. An account of East Florida, with a journal kept by John Bartram upon a journey from St Augustine up the river St Johns. [1766], 1769. For Bartram item see Bartram, above, under 1751.

Campbell, Thomas. An account of the Creek nation 1767. Florida Historical Soc Quart 8 1930.

Coyer, abbé Gabriel François. A letter to Doctor Matay: containing an abstract of the relations of travellers concerning the Patagonians, with the several discoveries of the latest French and English navigators relative to this gigantic race of men. 1767. A satire. Trn from French of 1767. See Horace Walpole's satirical pamphlet, An account of the giants lately discovered, 1766, rptd in his Works vol 2, 1798; and the discussion of the giant hoax by P. G. Adams, Travellers and travel liars, 1962, ch 2.

Journal from New York to Canada 1767. New York History 13 1932.

Singleton, John. A general description of the West-Indian islands. Barbados 1767, Dublin 1766, London 1776, 1777 (as A description of the West Indies: a poem).

Beatty, Charles. The journal of a two-months tour with a view of promoting religion among the frontier inhabitants of Pennsylvania. 1768. First pbd with David Brainerd, under 1749, above.

Coffin, Paul. Tours 1760–8. Maine Historical Soc Collections 4 1856.

Lees, John. Journal 1768. 1911 (Soc of Colonial Wars of Michigan).

Swindrage, Theodore. An account of a discovery of part of the coast and inland country of Labrador 1753. In The great probability of a North West passage, 1768, under Voyages to the Arctic, below.

Williamson, Peter. The travels among the different nations and tribes of savage Indians in America. Edinburgh 1768.

Bancroft, Edward. An essay on the natural history of Guiana, with an account of its Indian inhabitants. 1769.

[Cluny, Alexander]. The American traveller: containing observations on the present state, culture and commerce of the British colonies in America. 1769, 1770, Philadelphia 1770; rptd in Mag of History 41 1930; tr French, 1782.

Cook, Lt James. Remarks on a passage from the river Balise in the Bay of Honduras to Merida, relative to the logwood cutters in the Bay 1765. 1769; rptd New Orleans 1935 (facs). For Cook's surveys used for the North American Pilot, see BM catalogue. His later voyage to the northwest coast of North America is listed under Voyages to the Pacific, below.

Knox, Capt John. An historical journal of the campaigns in North America 1757–60, particularly the two sieges of Quebec. 1769; ed A. G. Doughty 3 vols Toronto 1914–16 (Champlain Soc).

Smith, Richard. A tour of four great rivers: the Hudson, Mohawk, Susquehanna and Delaware 1769. Ed F. W. Halsey, New York 1906.

Johnston, George Milligen. A short description of the province of South Carolina in 1763. 1770; rptd in Historical Collections of South Carolina vol 2, 1836.

Pittman, Philip. The present state of the European settlements on the Missisippi, with a geographical description of that river. 1770; ed F. H. Hodder, Cleveland 1906.

Bossu, Nicolas. Travels through that part of North America formerly called Louisiana, with notes relative chiefly to natural history. 2 vols 1771. Trn from French of 1768 by John Reinhold Forster, with his Flora Americae Septentrionalis.

Forster, John Reinhold. Catalogue of animals of North America. 1771.

Kalm, Pehr. Travels into North America: containing its natural history with the civil, ecclesiastical state of the country. 2 vols Warrington 1770–1, London 1772 (slightly abridged); rptd in J. H. Moore, A new collection, 1778; in John Pinkerton, A collection vol 13, 1814; tr A. B. Benson, New York 1937 (with addns), 2 vols 1966. Trn from Swedish of 1753–61 by John Reinhold Forster.

Loefling, Peder. [Travels through Spain and Cumana in South America 1751–6: an abstract of the most useful articles by John Reinhold Forster in Nicolas Bossu, 1771 above]; trn from Swedish of 1758 or from the German version of 1766.

Owen, Capt William. Narrative of the American voyages and travels 1766–71. Ed V. H. Paltsits, New York 1942.

Pernety, Dom Antoine Joseph. The history of the voyage [of Louis de Bougainville] to the Malouine [Falkland] islands in 1763–4, and of two voyages to the streights of Magellan, with an account of the Patagonians. 1771, 1773. Trn from French of 1769.

Richardson, William. Journal [to] Labrador in 1771. Canadian Historical Rev 16 1935.

Taylor, G. A voyage to North America, with the author's manner of trading with the Indians. Nottingham 1771.

Adams, John. A voyage to South America describing the Spanish cities, towns, provinces. 2 vols 1772.

Hulton, Henry. Journal 1772 [of the Commissioner of Customs, Boston]. In Ann Hulton, Letters of a loyalist lady, Cambridge Mass 1927.

Mante, Thomas. The history of the late war in North-America and the islands of the West Indies. 1772.

Stanton, Daniel. A journal of the life, travels and Gospel labours [in Pennsylvania]. Philadelphia 1772, London 1799, Philadelphia 1848 (Friends' Lib).

Taitt, David. Journal of travels from Pensacola, West Florida, to and through the country of the Creeks 1772. Ed N. D. Mereness in Travels in the American colonies, New York 1916.

Cocking, Matthew. Journal from York factory to the Blackfeet country 1772-3. Ed L. J. Burpee in Trans Royal Soc of Canada 3rd ser 2 1909.

A brief account of the mission established among the Esquimaux Indians on the coast of Labrador by the Church of the Brethren or Unitas Fratrum. 1774, 1779.

C., W. Memoirs of a gentleman who resided several years in the West Indies. 1774.

Falkner, Fr Thomas. A description of Patagonia, and the adjoining parts of South America, and some particulars relating to Falkland's Islands. Ed W. Combe, Hereford 1774, London 1777; ed A. E. S. Neumann, Chicago 1935 (facs). An abstract by Thomas Pennant, Of the Patagonians, 1788.

Finlay, Hugh. Journal of a survey of the post offices [in Maine and Georgia] 1773-4. Ed F. H. Norton, Brooklyn 1867.

Fowler, John. A summary account of the present flourishing state of the respectable colony of Tobago. 1774, 1777.

— A general account of the late tremendous hurricanes and earthquakes in the West-India islands. 1781.

Jones, Rev David. A journal of two visits to the Indians on the west side of the river Ohio 1772-3. Burlington NJ 1774, New York 1865.

Long, Edward. The history of Jamaica: a general survey of the antient and modern state, with reflections on its settlements etc. 3 vols 1774.

Robinson, John, and Thomas Rispin. A journey through Nova Scotia: containing a particular account of the country and its inhabitants. York 1774.

Smethurst, Gabriel. A narrative of an extraordinary escape out of the hands of the Indians in the gulph of St Lawrence. 1774; ed W. F. Ganong, New Brunswick Historical Collections 2 1905.

Woolman, John. A journal of his life and travels in the service of the Gospel [pt i of his Works]. Philadelphia 1774, 1775, London 1775 etc; Dublin 1776 etc (separately); ed A. M. Gummere 1922 (as Journal and essays) (from ms).

Adair, James. The history of the American Indians, particularly those nations adjoining to the Mississippi, East and West Florida, Georgia, South and North Carolina, and Virginia; also a description of the Floridas and Mississippi lands. 1775; ed S. C. Williams, Johnson City Tennessee 1930.

Burnaby, Andrew. Travels through the middle settlements in North America 1759-60, with observations upon the state of the colonies. 1775, 1775, Dublin 1775, London 1798 (expanded); rptd in John Pinkerton, A collection vol 13, 1814; ed R. R. Wilson, New York 1904 (from 1798 edn); tr German, 1776; French, 1778.

Harvey, Col Alexander. Journal 1774-5. Vermont Historical Soc Proc 1924.

A journal of the march of a party of provincials from Carlisle to Boston and thence to Quebec June to December 1775, with an account of the attack and engagement at Quebec. Glasgow 1775. A company of colonial riflemen taken prisoner.

Penrose, Bernard. An account of the expedition to Port Egmont in Falkland's Islands 1772. 1775.

Romans, Bernard. A concise natural history of East and West Florida, with directions to navigators. New York 1775.

Harrower, John. Diary 1773-6. Amer Historical Rev 6 1901.

Rymer, James. A description of the island of Nevis, with an account of its principal diseases. 1775.

M'Robert, Patrick. A tour through part of the north provinces of America 1774 and 1775: being a series of letters. Edinburgh 1776; rptd Pennsylvania Mag of History 1935.

Pownall, Thomas. A topographical description of the middle British colonies in North America, with journals of six travellers [1743 to 1766 from New Hampshire to Illinois and North Carolina]. 1776, 1779 (rev), 1800; ed L. Mulkearn, Pittsburgh 1949. An enlargement of Lewis Evans, 1755, above.

Reckitt, William. Some account of the life and gospel labours [from 1758]. 1776, Philadelphia 1783, London 1799; rptd Philadelphia 1845 (Friends' Lib).

[Schaw, Janet, or 'Jen' Shaw]. Journal of a lady of quality in a journey from Scotland to the West Indies, North Carolina and Portugal 1774-6. Ed E. W. and C. M. Andrews, New Haven 1921.

Cresswell, Nicholas. The journal during a trip to his Majesty's late colonies in North America 1774-7. New York 1924, London 1925.

Jamaica: a poem in three parts written 1776, with a poetical epistle from that island. 1777.

Robertson, Robert. A physical journal during three voyages to Africa and the West Indies 1772-4. 1777.

André, Major John. André's journal: an authentic record of the movements of the British Army in America from June 1777 to November 1778. Ed H. C. Lodge 2 vols Boston 1903.

Barclay, James. The voyages and travels: containing surprising adventures and interesting narratives. 1778.

Carver, Capt Jonathan. Travels through the interior parts of North America 1766-8. 1778, 1779, Dublin 1779, London 1781, Philadelphia 1784, 1789, 1792, Boston 1794, Philadelphia 1795, 1796, Boston 1797, Edinburgh 1798, Charlestown 1802, Edinburgh 1807, 1808, Walpole NH 1813, 1838; tr German, 1780; French, 1784; Dutch, 1796. For falsifications see E. G. Bourne, The travels of Carver, Amer Historical Rev 11 1906; and L. P. Kellogg, The mission of Carver, Wisconsin Mag of History 12 1929.

Chappe d'Auteroche, Jean. A voyage to California to observe the transit of Venus [1769], with an historical description of the route through Mexico; also a voyage to Newfoundland and Sallee by Monsieur de Cassini. 1778. Trn from French of 1772.

Hutchins, Thomas. A topographical description of Virginia, Pennsylvanis, Maryland and North Carolina. 1778; ed F. C. Hicks, Cleveland 1904.

— Historical narrative and topographical description of Louisiana and West Florida. Philadelphia 1784; rptd in Gilbert Imlay, A topographical description, 1793 below.

The present state of the West Indies, with an accurate description of what parts are now possessed by the several powers in Europe. 1778.

Griffith, John. Journal of the life, travels and labours in the work of the ministry in the British colonies in North America [1726-66]. 1779, Philadelphia 1780, York 1830, Philadelphia 1841.

[Hewatt, Dr Alexander]. An historical account of the rise and progress of South Carolina and Georgia. 2 vols 1779; rptd in B. R. Carroll, Historical collections vol 2, New York 1836.

Sullivan, Major-Gen John. Journals of the military expedition against the Six Nations of Indians in 1779. Ed F. Cook, Auburn NY 1887.

Burgoyne, Lt-Gen John. A state of the expedition from Canada, as laid down before the House of Commons, written and collected by himself. 1780, 1780, 1780-1.

— A supplement to the state of the expedition from Canada: containing General Burgoyne's orders respecting the principal movements and operations of the army. 1780. *See* anon, A brief examination of the plan and conduct of the northern expedition and of the surrender, 1779; and An enquiry into and remarks upon the conduct of Lt Gen Burgoyne, 1780. Burgoyne's letters written during the campaign were pbd in Massachusetts Historical Soc Collections vol 2, 1795.

Fleming, William. Journal in Kentucky 1779 to 1780. Ed N. D. Mereness in Travels in the American colonies, New York 1916.

— Journal in Kentucky from January 4th to April 22nd 1783. Ibid.

Hall, Capt William Cornwallis. The history of the civil war in America. Vol 1, the campaigns of 1775-7, 1780.

Maurelle, Francisco Antonio. Journal of a voyage in 1775 to explore the coast of America northward of California. 1780, 1781 (in Daines Barrington, Miscellanies).

Murray, Sir James. Letters from America 1773-80. Ed E. Robson, Manchester 1951 (from ms).

Suckling, George. An historical account of the Virgin Islands in the West Indies. 1780.

Fermin, Philippe. An historical and political view of the colony of Surinam in South America, with the settlements of Demerary and Issequibo. 1781. Trn from French of 1769.

Bruce, Peter Henry. Memoirs of a military officer. 1782, Dublin 1783. Includes travels in the West Indies, and among the Greek and Cherokee Indians.

Crevecoeur, Michel Guillaume Saint Jean de. Letters from an American farmer, describing certain provincial situations, manners and customs not generally known. 1782, Dublin 1782, London 1783, Belfast 1793, Philadelphia 1793, New York 1904, London 1912 (EL), New York [1963] (with next item); tr French, 1784; German, 1784.

— Sketches of eighteenth-century America. Ed S. T. Williams, New Haven 1925 (from ms), New York [1963] (with preceding). Essays written at the same time as the preceding, but unpbd.

— Voyage dans la haute Pensylvanie et dans l'état de New-York. Paris 1801; Selections, tr P. G. Adams, Lexington Kentucky [1961]; tr Ann Arbor 1964 (complete).

Filson, John. The discovery, settlement and present state of Kentucke, and the adventures of Col Daniel Boon. Wilmington 1784, London 1793, 1797 (incorporated in Gilbert Imlay, A topographical description, 1793 etc), Louisville 1929 (facs of 1784), 1930; tr French, 1785; German, 1790. *See* J. W. Coleman, John Filson esq: Kentucky's first historian and topographer, Lexington Kentucky 1954.

Jefferson, Thomas. Notes on the state of Virginia. Paris 1784-5, 1785, London 1787, Philadelphia 1788, 1794, Baltimore 1800, 1800, Philadelphia 1801 etc; ed P. L. Ford, Brooklyn 1894, New York 1964; ed W. Peden, Chapel Hill 1955.

Smyth, J. F. D. A tour in the United States of America, with an account of the present situation of the country, the population, agriculture, commerce etc. 2 vols 1784, Dublin 1784; tr French, 1791. A journey through the southern states 1784.

Umfreville, Edward. Nipigon to Winnipeg: a canoe voyage 1784. Ed H. Douglas, Ottawa 1929.

— The present state of Hudson's Bay, and a journal of a journey from Montreal to New York. 1790; tr German, 1791.

Walton, William. A narrative of the captivity and sufferings of Benjamin Gilbert and his family, taken by the Indians on the frontiers of Pennsylvania 1780-3. Philadelphia 1784, 1785, 1790, London 1790, Philadelphia 1813, 1848; rptd in Narratives of Indian captivities, Cleveland 1904.

Booth, W. Journal 1785. In Report of Public Archives of Nova Scotia, 1933.

Hadfield, Joseph. An Englishman in America in 1785: being the diary. Ed D. S. Robertson, Toronto 1933.

Heart, Capt Jonathan. Journal on the march with his company from Conncticut to Fort Pitt 1785. Ed C. W. Butterfield, Albany NY 1885.

— Observations on the ancient works, the native inhabitants of the western country. In Gilbert Imlay, A topographical description, 1792.

Hunter, John. An account of a visit made to Washington at Mount Vernon by an English gentleman in 1785. Pennsylvania Mag of History 17 1893.

Roch, John. The surprizing adventures of a mariner of Whitehaven, with a genuine account of his long captivity amongst the Indians and imprisonment by the Spaniards in South America. Liverpool 1785, Dumfries 1788.

Hollingsworth, S. An account of the present state of Nova Scotia, with a brief account of Canada and the British islands on the coast of North America. Edinburgh 1786, 1787; tr French, 1787.

Hunter, Robert. Quebec to Carolina in 1785-6. Ed L. B. Wright and M. Tinling, San Marino 1944 (from ms).

Varlo, Charles. A twelve months' tour thro' America. In his Essence of agriculture, 1786; rptd in Miscellany of knowledge, 1792, 1792; rptd in his Nature displayed, 1793, 1794.

Chastellux, François Jean, Marquis de. Travels in North America 1780 to 1782. 2 vols 1787, 1787, Dublin 1787, New York 1827, 1828 (abridged). Trn from French of 1785 by George Greive. The original French was followed by an Examen critique, written by Brissot de Warville, 1786; the English trn was followed by General Simcoe's critical Remarks, 1787, below.

Clavigero, Francesco Saverio, SJ. The history of Mexico, collected from Spanish and Mexican historians, with critical dissertations on the land, the animals, and inhabitants of Mexico. 2 vols 1787, 1807. Trn from Italian of 1780-1 by Charles Cullen.

Moseley, Benjamin, MD. A treatise on tropical diseases and on the climate of the West Indies. 1787, 1792, 1793, 1803, 1806.

Simcoe, General John Graves. A journal of the operation of the Queen's Rangers 1777 to 1783. Exeter [1787]; rptd New York 1844.

— Remarks on the travels of the Marquis de Chastellux in North America. 1787, in Mag of History 172 1931.

Tarleton, Sir Banastre. A history of the campaigns of 1780 and 1781 in the southern provinces of North America. 1787, Dublin 1787, London 1796.

MacLean, Capt Neil. The complaint to the Honourable the Commons of Great Britain in Parliament assembled. [c. 1788]. Includes a lengthy narrative of his military experiences during the American war of independence.

Penn, John. Journal 1788. Pennsylvania Mag of History 3 1879.

Warder, Ann. Extracts from her diary 1786-8. Pennsylvania Mag of History 17-18 1893.

Anburey, Thomas. Travels through the interior parts of America [as a British officer in War of Independence]. 2 vols 1789, 1790, 1791, Boston 1923; tr French, 1790, 1792, 1793.

Coke, Rev Dr Thomas. A journal of his visit to Jamaica and of his third tour on the continent of America. 1789.

— Journal of his third tour through the West-Indies and fourth tour of the continent of North America. 1791-2.

— Extracts of the journals of three visits to America 1790, and of five visits to America. 1793.

— A history of the West Indies: containing the natural, civil and ecclesiastical history of each island. 3 vols Liverpool and London 1808-11.

Fitzgerald, Lord Edward. Letters 1788-9. In Thomas Moore, The life and death of Lord Edward Fitzgerald vol 1, 1831. Written on journey from New Brunswick to New Orleans via Detroit.

Hughes, Ensign Thomas. A journal for his amusement [of his military service in North America 1778–89]. Ed E. A. Benians, Cambridge 1947 (from ms).

Luffman, John. A brief account of the island of Antigua, together with the customs and manners of its inhabitants. 1789, [1790].

Morse, Jedediah. The American geography: or a view of the present situation of the United States of America. Elizabeth Town NJ 1789, London 1792, Dublin 1792, London 1794 (enlarged), Edinburgh 1795, London 1798.

Beckford, William. A descriptive account of the island of Jamaica, with remarks upon the cultivation of the sugar-cane. 2 vols 1790.

Costanso, Miguel. An historical journal of the expedition by sea and land to the north of California 1768 to 1770, when Spanish establishments were first made at San-Diego and Monte-Rey. 1790; ed and tr F. J. Teggert, Berkeley 1910 (as A narrative of the Portolá expedition). Trn from a Spanish ms by William Revely.

Moreton, J. B. Manners and customs in the West India islands [by a negro]. 1790, 1793.

A short journey in the West Indies, in which are interspersed curious anecdotes and characters. 2 vols 1790.

Atwood, Thomas. History of the island of Dominica, with a description of its situation, climate, extent, mountain, rivers and natural productions. 1791.

Bartram, William. Travels [1773–4] through North and South Carolina, Georgia, East and West Florida, the Cherokee country, the Creek confederacy and the country of the Choctaws. Philadelphia 1791, London 1792, Dublin 1793, London 1794; ed M. Van Doren, New York 1928; tr German, 1793; Dutch, 1794–7; French, 1799–1801. The original journal from which this account was developed was ed F. Harper, Trans Amer Philosophical Soc new ser 33 1943. For commentary, see N. B. Fagin, Bartram: interpreter of the American landscape, Baltimore 1933.

Colnett, Capt James. Journal aboard the Argonaut [to Vancouver] 1788–91. Ed F. W. Howay, Toronto 1940 (Champlain Soc) (from ms).

—— A voyage to the South Atlantic and round Cape Horn for the purpose of extending the spermaceti whale fisheries, compiled by William Combe from Colnett's notes. 1798, Amsterdam 1968 (facs).

Long, John. Voyages and travels [1768–88] of an Indian interpreter and trader: describing the manners and customs of the North American Indians, with an account of the posts situated on the river St Laurence and Lake Ontario. 1791; ed R. G. Thwaites in Early western travels vol 2, Cleveland 1904; ed M. M. Quaife, Chicago 1922; tr German, 1791, 1792; French, 1794, 1802.

Mair, John. Journal 1791 [of sea and land voyage Charleston to Quebec]. Amer Historical Rev 12 1907.

Morris, Capt Thomas. Journal of Captain Thomas Morris of his Majesty's XVII regiment of infantry in 1764. In Miscellanies of prose and verse, 1791; rptd in Mag of History 76 1922; ed R. G. Thwaites in Early western travels vol 1, Cleveland 1904.

Fidler, Peter. Journal 1791–2. In Journals of Samuel Hearne 1934 (Champlain Soc).

Pagès, Pierre-Marie François de. Travels round the world in the years 1767–71. 3 vols 1791–2, 1793–2. Trn from French of 1782. The first 2 vols relate his travels up the Mississippi and thence south to Mexico and across the Pacific. Vol 3 relates voyages toward the South and North Poles.

Brissot de Warville, Jacques Pierre. New travels in the United States of America 1788. 1792, Dublin 1792, New York 1792, London 1794, 2 vols 1794, Boston 1797. Trn from French of 1791 by Joel Barlow. See Brissot's Examen critique des voyages dans l'Amérique septentrionale de M. le marquis de Chastellux, 1786.

Cartwright, George. A journal during a residence of nearly sixteen years on the coast of Labrador. 3 vols Newark 1792; ed C. W. Townsend 1911.

Eddis, William. Letters from America, historical and descriptive: comprising occurrences from 1769 to 1777. 1792.

Imlay, Gilbert. A topographical description of the western territory of North America. 1792, Dublin 1793, New York 1793, London 1793 (with John Filson, The discovery of Kentucke, 1784 above), 1797 (with Filson etc, viz: An account of the Indian nations inhabiting with in the limits of the XIII states; The culture of Indian corn etc; Major Jonathan Heart, Observations on the ancient works, the native inhabitants of the western country (see his Journal, 1785 above); Thomas Hutchins, Historical narrative and topographical description of Louisiana and West-Florida (under 1778 above); An account of the soil, particularly in the Genesee tract; Dr Franklin, Remarks for those who wish to become settlers in America (first pbd 1784); Thomas Hutchins, Topographical description of Virginia etc (1778 above); Patrick Kennedy, Journal up the Illinois River; Description of the state of Tenasee; official documents of the Territory of Tennessee). The original work tr German, 1793.

R[andall], M[aria]. Voyages to the Madeira and Leeward Caribbean isles. Edinburgh 1792, Salem 1802. The author has also been thought to be Maria Riddell.

Stewart, James. A brief account of the negroes in Jamaica. Bath 1792.

Turnor, Philip. Journals 1778–92. Ed J. B. Tyrrell in Journal of Samuel Hearne, Toronto 1934 (Champlain Soc).

Campbell, Patrick. Travels in the interior inhabited parts of North America 1791 and 1792 [in eastern Canada, New York and New England]. Edinburgh 1793; ed H. H. Langton and W. F. Ganong, Toronto 1937 (Champlain Soc).

Edwards, Bryan. The history civil and commercial of the British colonies in the West Indies. 2 vols 1793, Dublin 1793, 3 vols 1794, 4 vols 1801 (with An historical survey of the French colony in St Domingo), 5 vols 1819 (with continuation to the present); tr French, 1801.

Macdonell, John. Diary 1793. Ed C. M. Gates in Five fur traders of the Northwest, Minneapolis 1933.

Mackenzie, Alexander. First man west: journal of his voyage to the Pacific coast of California in 1793. Ed W. Sheppe, Berkeley and Montreal 1962. The Mackenzie narratives of his journeys of 1789 and 1793 were originally pbd 1801, rptd 1931; tr French, 1802; German, 1802.

Coxe, Tench. A view of the United States of America, in papers written between 1787 and 1794 of exports, imports, fisheries, navigation, ship-building, manufactures and general improvement. Philadelphia 1794, London 1795, Dublin 1795.

Hodgkinson, —. Letters on emigration by a gentleman lately returned from America. 1794. An account of an emigrant voyage, with a description of Kentucky.

Loskiel, Georg Heinrich. History of the mission of the United Brethren among the Indians in North America [in New York and Pennsylvania]. 1794. Trn from German of 1789 by Christian Ignatius La Trobe.

Stedman, C. The history of the origin, progress and termination of the American war by [one] who served under Sir W. Howe etc. 2 vols 1794.

Hearne, Samuel. A journey from Prince of Wales's Fort in Hudson's Bay to the northern ocean in 1769–72. 1795, Dublin 1796, Philadelphia 1802; ed R. Glover 1958; Amsterdam 1963 (facs); tr German, 1797, 1797; Dutch, 1798; Swedish, 1798; French, 1799.

Kelly, Samuel. Samuel Kelly: an eighteenth-century seaman. Ed C. Garstin 1925. Journal of voyages to West Indies and North America 1764–95.

M'Gillivray, Duncan. Journal at Fort George on the Saskatchewan 1794–5. Ed A. S. Morton, Toronto 1929.

Winterbotham, William. Historical, geographical, commercial and philosophical view of the American United

States and of the European settlements in America and the West-Indies. 4 vols 1795, Philadelphia 1795–6, New York 1796, London 1799, 1819.

Simcoe, Mrs John G. Diary of the wife of the first Lieut-Gov of Upper Canada 1792–6. Ed J. R. Robertson, Toronto 1911.

Stedman, John Gabriel. Narrative of a five years' expedition against the revolted negroes of Surinam 1772–7. 2 vols 1796, 1806, 1813; tr German, 1797, 1797; French, 1798, 1799, 1799; Dutch, 1799, 1801; Italian, 1818.

Wansey, Henry. The journal of an excursion to the United States of North America in the summer of 1794. Salisbury 1796, 1798; tr German, 1797.

Baily, Francis. Journal of a tour in unsettled parts of North America 1796–7. Ed A. De Morgan 1856; ed S. C. Williams in Early travels in the Tennessee country, Johnson City 1928.

Crespel, Emanuel. Travels in North America, with a narrative of his shipwreck and extraordinary hardships on the island of Anticosti. 1797.

Decalves, Alonso. Travels to the westward: or the unknown parts of America 1786 and 1787 to the westward of the river Missisippi. Rutland Vermont 1797.

Wimpffen, Baron de. A voyage to St Domingo 1788 to 1790. 1797. Trn from French ms by J. Wright (George Gifford?). French edn 1793.

Black, John. An authentic narrative of the mutiny on board the ship Lady Shore, with particulars of a journey through part of Brazil. 1798.

Willyams, Rev Cooper. An account of the campaign in the West Indies 1794, with the reduction of the islands of Martinique, St Lucia, Guadalupe, Marigalante etc. 1798.

Gregory, William. A visible display of divine Providence: or the journal of a captured missionary, captured off Cape Frio, with every occurrence in Paraguay, Spanish South America and in Portugal in 1798 and 1799. 1799, 1800, [1801].

Hill, Thomas. A journey on horseback from New Jersey to Pennsylvania in 1799. Pennsylvania Mag of History 14 1890.

La Rochefoucault-Liancourt, François Alexandre Stanislas, Duc de. Travels through the United States of America, the country of the Iroquois, and Upper Canada 1795–7, with an authentic account of Lower Canada. 2 vols 1799, 4 vols 1800, 1803. Trn from French of 1797 by H. Newman.

Lempriere, William. Practical observations on the diseases of the army in Jamaica 1792 to 1797, on the situation, climate and diseases of that island. 2 vols 1799.

Smyth, David William. A short topographical description of Upper Canada. 1799, 1813.

Weld, Isaac. Travels through the states of North America and the provinces of upper and lower Canada 1795–7.

1799, 2 vols 1799, 1800, 1800, 1807; tr French, 1800; Italian, 1819.

Aimé, J. J. Narrative of the deportation to Cayenne and shipwreck on the coast of Scotland, with observations on the present state of that colony and of the negroes. 1800. Trn from French of 1800.

Barry, Thomas. Narrative of the singular adventures and captivity among the Munsipi Indians 1797 to 1799, including the manners, customs etc of that tribe. 1800. Probably fiction.

Macpherson, Charles. Memoirs of the life and travels in Asia, Africa and America, with investigation of the nature, treatment and improvement of the negro in the British and French West India islands. Edinburgh 1800.

§ 2

Tuckerman, H. T. America and her commentators, with a critical sketch of travel in the United States. New York 1864.

Winsor, J. In his Narrative and critical history of America vols 3, 5, 8 Boston 1884–9. On the history of discovery.

Williams, G. History of the Liverpool privateers. 1897.

Cooper, L. Travellers and observers 1763–1846. In Cambridge history of American literature vol 1, 1917.

Burpee, L. J. The search for the western sea: the story of the exploration of northwestern America. Toronto 1905.

Haring, C. H. The buccaneers in the West Indies in the seventeenth century. New York 1910.

Alvord, C. W. and L. Bidgood. The first explorations of the trans-Allegheny region by the Virginians 1650–74. Cleveland 1912.

Winship, G. P. Travellers and explorers 1583–1763. In Cambridge history of American literature vol 1, 1917.

Mesick, J. L. The English travellers in America 1785–1835. New York 1922.

Nevins, A. American social history as recorded by British travellers. New York 1923.

Crouse, N. M. In quest of the western ocean. New York 1928.

Hart, F. R. The disaster of Darien: the story of the Scots settlement and the causes of its failure 1699–1701. Boston 1929.

Chatterton, E. K. English seamen and the colonization of America. 1930.

Brebner, J. B. The explorers of North America 1492–1806. 1933, 1955.

Mackay, D. The honourable company: a history of the Hudson's Bay Company. 1937.

Rich, E. E. History of Hudson's Bay Company 1670–1870. Vol 1, 1670–1763, 1958 (Hudson's Bay Record Soc).

Gerhard, P. Pirates on the west coast of New Spain 1675–1742. Glendale Cal 1960.

(7) VOYAGES ROUND THE WORLD, AND OTHER VOYAGES ACROSS THE PACIFIC AND TO AUSTRALASIA

Collections and Histories

Callander, John. Terra australis cognita: or voyages to the southern hemisphere during the sixteenth, seventeenth and eighteenth centuries. 3 vols Edinburgh 1766–8. Based on Charles de Brosses, Histoire des navigations aux terres australes, 2 vols 1756. Both De Brosses and Callander were rptd Amsterdam 1967 (facs).

Dalrymple, Alexander. An account of the discoveries made in the South Pacific Ocean prior to 1764. 1767.

— An historical collection of several voyages and discoveries in the South Pacific Ocean: being chiefly from Spanish writers. 2 vols in 1 1770–1, 1775; rptd Amsterdam 1967 (facs); tr French, 1774; German, 1786.

Hawkesworth, John. An account of the voyages undertaken for discoveries in the Southern Hemisphere [from

Byron to Cook]. 3 vols 1773, 1773, Dublin 1773, 1775, Perth 1789; tr Dutch, 1774; French, 1774; German, 1775; Italian, 1784 (with Cook's later voyages). This was the official history compiled from the journals of the voyagers: vol 1 reporting on Byron, Wallis and Carteret; vol 3 on Cook's first voyage, rptd New York 1774. The collection ed Anderson, 1784 below, was based on Hawkesworth.

Henry, David. An historical account of all the voyages round the world performed by English navigators [from Drake to Cook]. 5 vols 1773–5; vol 6, 1786 (completing the Cook voyages); tr German, 1775–80.

New discoveries concerning the world and its inhabitants comprehending all the discoveries made in the several voyages [to the Pacific]. 1778.

Anderson, G. W. A new, authentic and complete collection of voyages round the world by Capt Cook, together with Drake's, Byron's, Carteret's, Wallis's and other voyages. 1784-6 (in pts), 4 vols 1790. Largely derived from Hawkesworth, 1773 above.

The voyages and travels of Columbus, Magellan, Drake, Cavendish, Dampier, Cowley, Cook, Clipperton and Shelvocke. Edinburgh 1786.

Hogg, Capt. A collection of [British] voyages round the world. 1790.

Discoveries of the French in 1768-9 to the south-east of New Guinea, with the subsequent visits by English navigators. 1791.

Burney, James. A chronological history of the South Sea or Pacific Ocean. 5 vols 1803-17, Amsterdam 1967 (facs).

Fitzpatrick, K. (ed). Australian explorers: a selection from their writings. Oxford 1958 (WC).

Dunsmore, J. French explorers in the Pacific. Vol 1, Oxford 1965.

§ 1

Sharp, Capt Bartholomew. The voyages and adventures in the South Sea. 1684. See Voyages to America, above.

Narbrough, Sir John. Voyage to the South-sea. 1694. See ibid.

Rembrantse, Dirke. A relation of a voyage made [1642] towards the South Terra Incognita extracted from the journal of Captain Abel Jansen Tasman. Ed R. Hooke in Philosophical Collections, 1681-2; rptd with Sir John Narbrough, Voyage, 1694. See General collections. Trn from Dutch of 1678. An abstract in John Harris, Navigantium vol 1, 1704, and in John Callander vol 2, 1756. Tasman's journal was pbd in trn by C. G. Woide from a longer ms version in J. Burney, A chronological history vol 3, 1803. The full original journal was ed and tr J. E. Heeres, Amsterdam 1898.

Dampier, Capt William. A new voyage round the world. 1697, 1698, 1699, 1703; rptd in John Harris, Navigantium vol 1, 1705 etc; rptd with the 3 items following, 3 vols 1717, 4 vols 1729, 2 vols 1776; ed J. Masefield 2 vols 1906 (with next item); ed A. Gray 1927 (Argonaut Press); ed P. G. Adams, New York 1968 (from 1927); tr French, 1698.

— Voyages and descriptions vol 2 (A supplement with descriptions of Tonquin, Malacca etc; two voyages to Campeachy, New Spain; a discourse of trade winds in the torrid zone and an account of Natal). 1699, 1700, 1705; rptd with preceding; ed B. Wilkinson 1931 (Argonaut Press); tr French, 1701.

— A voyage to New Holland in 1699. 1703 (as vol 3); rptd to 1776; rptd 1937 (facs of 1729 edn); ed J. A. Williamson 1939.

— A continuation of a voyage to New Holland. 1709 (as vol 3, pt 2); rptd to 1776. For Dampier, see C. Wilkinson, Dampier: explorer and bucaneer, 1929; W. H. Bonner, Captain Dampier: bucaneer-author, 1934.

Cowley, Capt Ambrose. A voyage round the globe in 1683. Ed W. Hacke, A collection of original voyages, 1699; see Collections, General, above.

Careri, John Francesco Gemelli. A voyage round the world 1693-9. In A. and J. Churchill, A collection vol 4, 1704 etc. Trn from Italian.

Funnell, William. A voyage round the world: containing an account of Captain Dampier's expedition into the south seas 1703 and 1704, together with the author's voyage from Mexico to the East India. 1707; rptd in vol 4 of Dampier edn 1729, above; in John Harris, Navigantium vol 1, 1744; in John Callander, Terra Australis vol 3, 1768. See pamphlet, Captain Dampier's vindication of his voyage, with observations on Mr Funnell's chimerical relation, 1707.

Cooke, Capt Edward. A voyage to the South Sea and round the world 1708-11; wherein an account is given of Mr Alexander Selkirk upon Juan Fernandes. 1712, 2 vols 1712 (expanded).

Rogers, Capt Woodes. A cruising voyage round the world 1708-11. 1712, 1718, 1722, 1726; rptd in John Callander, Terra Australis vol 3, 1768; in The world displayed vol 6, 1777, 1806, 1889, 1894; ed G. E. Manwaring 1928; tr Dutch, 1715; French, 1716; German, 1747. Also containing the account of Alexander Selkirk.

Frezier, Amédée François. A voyage to the South-Seas and along the coasts of Chile and Peru in 1712-14. 1717. See Voyages to America, above.

Shelvocke, Capt George. A voyage round the world by the way of the great South Sea 1719-22. 1726, 1757 (rev); rptd abridged in John Callander, Terra Australis vol 3, 1768; in J. H. Moore, A new and complete collection, 1778; ed W. G. Perrin 1928, 1930; tr German, 1787.

Betagh, William. A voyage round the world begun in 1719; relating the true historical facts [of the Shelvocke voyage]. 1728. Part on Peru rptd in John Harris, Navigantium vol 1, 1744; in John Pinkerton, A collection vol 14, 1813.

Relations of the circumnavigation 1740-4 of Lord Anson.

Bulkeley, John and John Cummins. A voyage to the South Seas 1740-1: containing a faithful narrative of the loss of the Wager. 1743, 1743, Philadelphia 1757; ed A. D. Howden Smith 1927 (Argonaut Press).

Philips, John. An authentic journal of the last expedition under the command of Anson. 1744, 1767.

An authentic account of Commodore Anson's expedition. 1744, Dublin 1745.

A voyage to the South Seas by Commodore Anson, by an officer. 1744.

Thomas, Pascoe. A true and impartial journal of a voyage to the South Seas and round the globe. 1745.

Campbell, Alexander. The sequel to Bulkeley and Cummins's voyage to the South-Seas: containing the unparallel'd sufferings [of the marooned] gentlemen and others. 1747.

Walter, Richard and Benjamin Robins. A voyage round the world 1740-4 compiled from the papers of George Lord Anson. 1748 (4 edns); 16 edns to 1781 etc; ed J. Masefield 1911 (EL); ed G. S. Laird Clowes 1928; tr French, 1749; Dutch, 1749; German, 1749; Italian, 1756. The official account of the voyage by the chaplain.

Young, John. An affecting narrative of the unfortunate voyage and catastrophe of the Wager. 1751.

Morris, Isaac. A narrative of the dangers and distresses which befell him and seven more of the crew belonging to the Wager store-ship. [1750].

Byron, John. The narrative of the Honorable John Byron (Commodore in a late voyage round the world): containing an account of the great distresses suffered from 1740 to 1746, with a relation of the loss of the Wager man of war. 1768, 1768, Dublin 1768, London 1769, 1778, 1780, 1782, 1784, 1785 etc (with abridgements); tr French, 1799; Spanish, 1901.

Documents relating to Anson's voyage round the world 1740-4. Ed G. Williams 1967 (Navy Records Soc).

Coyer, abbé Gabriel François. A supplement to Lord Anson's voyage round the world: containing a discovery and description of the island of Frivola. 1752, 1752; Dublin 1752. A jeu d'esprit. Trn from French. For Anson's voyage, see W. V. Anson, The life of Admiral Lord Anson, 1912; and H. B. T. Somerville, Commodore Anson's voyage into the South Seas and around the world, 1934.

Clipperton, Capt John. The voyage round the world [1719] from an authentic journal. Abstract in John Harris, Navigantium vol 1, 1744; rptd as Voyage to Magellanica and round the world in John Callander, Terra Australis vol 3, 1768; abstract in J. H. Moore, A new collection, 1778.

Commodore [Jacob] Roggewein's expedition for the discovery of southern lands [1721-3] under the direction of the Dutch East India Company. In John Harris,

Navigantium vol 1, 1744 (trn from Dutch of 1728); rptd as Voyage to Polynesia and Australasia in John Callander, Terra Australis vol 3, 1768. Other accounts of the voyage were tr from separate pbns in French and German by Alexander Dalrymple, A collection of voyages, 1775, above.

Voyage round the world in the years 1764–6 in the Dolphin, commanded by the Honorable Commodore Byron, written by an officer. 1767, Dublin 1767; part rptd in John Callander, Terra Australis vol 3, 1768; tr French, 1767; Italian, 1768; German, 1769; Spanish, 1769, 1769.

—— An account of a voyage round the world by Commodore Byron, compiled from his papers by John Hawkesworth, An account of the voyages in the southern hemisphere vol 1, 1773.

—— Byron's Journal of his circumnavigation. Ed R. E. Gallagher 1964 (Hakluyt Soc).

Wallis, Capt Samuel. An account of a voyage round the world [1766–8]. Ed John Hawkesworth in An account of the voyages vol 1, 1773. See Collections, above.

—— A journal of the voyage by George Robertson. Ed H. Carrington 1948 (Hakluyt Soc) (from ms).

Bougainville, Louis Antoine de. A voyage round the world 1766–9. 1772, Dublin 1772, London 1773, Amsterdam 1967 (facs of 1772 edn). Trn from French of 1772 by John Reinhold Forster.

Carteret, Capt Philip. An account of a voyage round the world 1766–9. Ed John Hawkesworth in An account of the voyages vol 1, 1773; ed H. Wallis 2 vols 1965 (Hakluyt Soc). See Collections, above.

The three voyages of Captain James Cook 1768–79. The monumental edn by J. C. Beaglehole of Journals of Captain Cook, 4 vols in 5 1955–, *in progress, includes all important accounts by participants, mostly from ms, and supersedes all earlier relations. Those pbd at the time are listed here. The authoritative study is the* Bibliography of Cook, Sydney 1928 (Public Lib of New South Wales).

A journal of a voyage round the world in the Endeavour 1768–71. 1771, Amsterdam 1967 (facs). Actually a compilation.

An account of a voyage round the world by Lieutenant James Cook [1768–71]. Ed John Hawkesworth from the journals of Cook and of Sir Joseph Banks in An account of the voyages vols 2–3, 1773, New York 1774.

Parkinson, Sydney. A journal of a voyage to the South Sea in the Endeavour. 1773; rptd in David Henry, An historical account vols 3–4, 1773; rptd 1784 (enlarged); tr French, 1795.

The official journal of the first voyage was ed W. J. L. Wharton as Captain Cook's journal during his first voyage, 1893. *It was ed R. T. Gould in* The first edition of the three voyages, 8 vols 1931 (Argonaut Press); *ed J. C. Beaglehole in* Journals vol 1, 1955 (*with other relations*); The journal of Sir Joseph Banks was ed J. D. Hooker 1896 (*from ms*); ed J. C. Beaglehole 1962.

Marra, John. A journal of the Resolution's voyage 1771–5 on discovery to the southern hemisphere; also a journal of the Adventure's voyage 1772–4. 1775, Dublin 1776, Amsterdam 1967 (facs).

A second voyage round the world 1772–5 in the Resolution. 1776, 1781.

Forster, John Reinhold. Characteres generum plantarum quas in itinere ad insulas maris Australis collegerunt. 1776.

Cook, James. A voyage towards the South Pole and round the world in the Resolution and Adventure in 1772–5. 2 vols 1777, 1778, 1779, 1784; tr French, 1777, 1778; Dutch, 1778. The official account.

Forster, Johann Georg Adam. Voyage round the world in the Resolution 1772–5. 2 vols 1777, Dublin 1777; tr German, 1779–80. The ensuing controversy brought forth the next 3 items.

Wales, William. Remarks on Mr Forster's account of

Captain Cook's last voyage round the world in 1772–5. 1778.

Forster, George. Reply to Mr Wales's remarks. 1778.

—— A letter to the Earl of Sandwich, first Lord Commissioner of the Board of Admiralty. 1778.

Forster, John Reinhold. Observations made during a voyage round the world on physical geography, natural history and ethical philosophy. 1778; tr French, 1778 (with the official account); Italian, 1784–5.

Wales, William and William Bayly. Original astronomical observations made in the course of a voyage of Captain Cook 1772–5. 1778, 1784; rptd Chicago 1963; ed J. C. Munford, Corvallis Oregon 1963; tr French, 1778 (with official account).

Sparrman, André. A voyage to the Cape of Good Hope [in Cook's 2nd expedition] towards the Antarctic polar circle, and round the world, but chiefly into the country of the Hottentots and Caffres. 1785. Trn from Swedish of 1783. See Voyages to Africa, *above.*

Forster, Johann Reinhold. Tagebuch einer Entdeckungsreise nach der Südsee 1776 bis 1780. Berlin 1781.

Ledyard, John. A journal of Captain Cook's last voyage to the Pacific Ocean on discovery 1776–9. 1781, Hartford Conn 1783, London 1784 (rev); tr French, 1782. Derived from next item.

Rickman, John. Journal of Captain Cook's last voyage to the Pacific Ocean on discovery. 1781, Dublin 1781; rptd Philadelphia 1783 (as by William Ellis), Amsterdam 1967 (facs).

Zimmerman, Heinrich. Reise um die Welt mit Captain Cook. Mannheim 1781; tr U. Tewsley, Wellington 1926.

Bayly, William. Astronomical observations made in a voyage to the north Pacific Ocean 1776–80. 1782.

Ellis, William. An authentic narrative of a voyage performed by Captain Cook and Captain Clerke 1776–80. 2 vols 1782, 1783, 1784; tr German, 1783.

Cook, James, and James King. Voyage to the Pacific Ocean for making discoveries in the northern hemisphere. [Vols 1–2, by Capt Cook, 3 by Capt Clerke, rev Capt King and ed Bishop Douglas as the official account after their deaths]. 3 vols 1784, 1785, 1785; later abridgements and compilations; tr French, 1785; German, 1786; Dutch, 1787; Russian, 1788; Italian, 1794–5 (abridged).

Anderson, George William. A new authentic and complete collection of Captain Cook's voyages round the world. 1784, 1787.

Samwell, David. A narrative of the death of Captain Cook. 1786.

Anderson, George W. and [J.] R. Foster. A catalogue of the different specimens of cloth collected in the three voyages of Captain Cook. 1787.

Kippis, Andrew. The life of Captain James Cook [describing the 3 voyages]. 1788, Dublin 1788, London 1791; tr French, 1789; German, 1789.

See William Coxe, Comparative view of the Russian voyages with those made by Captains Cook and Clerke, 1787 (suppl to 3rd edn of An account of the Russian discoveries between Asia and America, 1780, 1780, 1787), 1804 (ibid); *also* J. A. Williamson, Cook and the opening of the Pacific, 1946.

Inglefield, Capt [John N.] Narrative concerning the loss of the Centaur, and the miraculous preservation of the pinnace in a traverse of near 390 leagues on the great western Ocean. 1783 (3 edns), Bath [1795] (abridged), London 1818.

An historical narrative of the discovery of New Holland [by the Dutch] and New South Wales [by Capt Cook] and a particular description of Botany Bay. [1786], [1786].

Eden, William, later Lord Auckland. The history of New Holland from its first discovery to the present time, with a particular account of its produce and inhabitants, and a description of Botany Bay. 1787, 1787, 1808.

Strange, James. Journal and narrative of the commercial expedition from Bombay to the north-west coast of America [1785-7]. Ed A. V. Venkatarama Ayyar, Madras 1929 (from ms).

Keate, George. An account of the Pelew islands situated in the western part of the Pacific Ocean: composed from the journals of Captain Henry Wilson shipwrecked there 1783. 1788, 1788, Dublin 1788, Perth 1788 (a chapbook), London 1789, Dublin 1793, Nottingham 1796, London 1803 (with suppl); tr French 1788, 1793; Dutch, 1789.

Gilbert, Thomas. Voyage from New South Wales to Canton 1788. 1789, Amsterdam 1968 (facs).

An authentic and interesting narrative of the late expedition to Botany Bay of Commodore Phillip. 1789.

The voyages of Governor Phillip to Botany Bay, with the establishment of the colonies of Port Jackson and Norfolk Island, compiled from authentic papers [and] journals. 1789, 1790, 1790; rptd in C. Pelham, The world vol 1, 1806-8, Melbourne 1950 (facs); tr German, 1789, 1794; French, 1791.

Portlock, Capt Nathaniel and Capt George Dixon. A voyage round the world, but more particularly to the north-west coast of America in 1785-88. 1789, 1789, Amsterdam 1968 (facs); tr French, 1789; German, 1789, 1791; Dutch, 1795. Separate narratives by the 2 captains, the 2nd written however by W[illiam] B[eresford], and rptd separately 1789.

Shortland, Lt John. The voyage of Governor Phillip to Botany Bay. 1789; rptd in Voyages of Governor Phillip, 1789 above.

Tench, Capt Watkin. A narrative of the expedition to Botany Bay, with an account of New South Wales. 1789, 1789, Dublin 1789; tr French, 1789.
—— A complete account of the settlement at Port Jackson in New South Wales. 1793; tr German, 1794.

The Bounty narratives

Bligh, Lt William. A narrative of the mutiny aboard the Bounty, and the subsequent voyage in the ship's boat to Timor. 1790, Dublin 1790; tr French, 1790; Dutch, 1790.
—— A voyage to the South Sea in the Bounty, including an account of the mutiny. 1792, Dublin 1792, London 1794. Ed Laurence Irving 1936 (as Bligh and the Bounty); ed G. Mackaness 1938 (as Book of the Bounty and selections from Bligh's writings) (EL); tr French, 1792; German, 1793. The official account.
—— The voyage of the Bounty's launch as related in William Bligh's dispatch to the Admiralty, and the journal of John Fryer. Ed O. Rutter 1934 (from ms).
—— The journal of James Morrison, boatswain's mate. Ed O. Rutter 1935.
—— The log of the Bounty. Ed O. Rutter 2 vols 1936-7 (from ms).
—— Bligh's voyage in the Resource from Coupang to Batavia; together with the log of his subsequent passage to India in the Dutch packet Vlydt and his remarks on Morrison's journal. Ed O. Rutter 1937 (from ms).
—— Captain Bligh's second voyage to the South Sea [1791-3, and continuing to the West Indies], partly retold from logs etc by Ida Lee. 1920.
See also the fictitious Letters from Mr Fletcher Christian, 1796; Voyages and travels of Fletcher Christian, 1798; and Alexander Smith (later John Adams), The life of the Captain of the Island of Pitcairn, Boston 1815. For secondary accounts, *see* Sir John Barrow, The eventful history of HMS Bounty, 1831 etc, Oxford 1914 (WC); G. Mackaness, The life of Vice-Admiral William Bligh, 2 vols Sydney 1931; H. S. Montgomerie, Bligh of the Bounty in fact and fable, 1937.

Meares, John. Voyages made in the years 1788 and 1789 from China to the north-west coast of America, with a voyage performed in 1786 from Bengal in the ship Nootka. 1790, 2 vols 1791, Amsterdam 1967 (facs); tr French, 1794; German, 1796; Italian, 1796.
—— Mr Mears's memorial [on the capture of his vessels by the Spaniards in Nootka Sound]. 1790, 1790. *See* Capt George Dixon, Remarks on the voyages of John Meares, 1790; John Meares, An answer, 1791; George Dixon, Further remarks, 1791. The 3 pamphlets were ed F. W. Howay, Toronto [1929].

White, John. Journal of a voyage to New South Wales, to Botany Bay, Port Jackson, in 1787-9, with plates of nondescript animals. 1790; tr German, 1791; Swedish, 1793; French, 1795.

Claret de Fleurieu, Charles Pierre. Discoveries of the French in 1768 and 1769 to the south-east of New Guinea, with the subsequent visits by English navigators, who gave them new names. 1791. Trn from French of 1790.

Mortimer, Lt George. Observations and remarks made during a voyage to the Sandwich Islands, Otaheite, Tinian, the north west coast of America and Canton, commanded by John Henry Cox. 1791, Dublin 1791; tr German, 1791; Dutch, 1793.

Phillip, Arthur. Extracts of letters, with a description of Norfolk Island by P. G. King. 1791.
—— Copies and extracts of letters from Governor Phillip: giving an account of the nature and fertility of the land in New South Wales. 1792.

Pagès, Pierre Marie François de. Travels round the world in the years 1767-71, together with the voyages toward the South and North Poles [ostensibly 1773-6]. 3 vols 1791-2; vols 1-2 1793 (rev). Trn from French [of 1783].

Bartlett, John. Narrative of events during voyages to Canton and the northwest coast of America 1790-3. Ed E. Snow in The sea, the ship and the sailor, Salem 1925.

Easty, John. Memorandum of the transactions of a voyage from England to Botany Bay 1787-93: a first fleet journal. Sydney 1965.

Hamilton, George, RN. A voyage round the world in the Pandora, Captain Edwards commander, 1790-2. Berwick 1793; ed B. Thomson 1915 (with the narrative of Capt Edwards); tr German, 1794. Voyage in search of the mutineers of the Bounty, wrecked on the Great Barrier Reef.

Hunter, Admiral John. An historical journal of the transactions at Port Jackson and Norfolk Islands, with the discoveries made in New South Wales and in the southern ocean since [1789], including the journal of Governor Phillip and [Lt] King and Lt Ball, and voyages from the first sailing of the Sirius in 1787 to the return of that ship's company to England in 1792. 1793, 1793 (abridged); ed J. Bach, Sydney 1968 (Royal Australian Historical Soc).

'Barrington, George' (Waldron). A voyage to Botany Bay, with a description of the natives; to which is added his life and trial. 1794, 1795, 1796, 1801; tr French [1798?].

Parker, Mary Ann. A voyage round the world in the Gorgon man of war [1791], written by the captain's widow. 1795.

A new and correct history of New Holland, with a description of Botany Bay and Port Jackson, by a society of gentlemen. Glasgow 1796.

Collins, David. An account of the English colony in New South Wales. 2 vols 1798-1802 (with account of New Zealand etc), 1 vol 1804 (abridged), Christchurch [1911].

Flinders, Matthew. Narrative of his voyage [to Australia] in the schooner Francis 1798. Ed G. Rawson 1947.

Galaup de La Pérouse, Jean François. A voyage round the world in 1785-8. 3 vols 1798, 1799; Amsterdam 1968 (facs of 2nd edn). Trn from French of 1797. 2 other trns were pbd by other publishers in the same years; an edn of the original French was also pbd London 1799.

Vancouver, George and John. A voyage of discovery to the North Pacific Ocean and round the world 1790–5. 3 vols 1798, 6 vols 1801 (rev), Amsterdam 1968 (facs of 1798); tr Danish, 1799; German, 1799, 1800; French, 1800. Part of the Vancouver journal relating to Puget Sound in 1792 was cd E. Meany, New York 1907 (from ms), Seattle 1914–15. The Journal of Archibald Menzies April to September 1792 was ed C. F. Newcombe and J. Forsyth, Victoria 1923 (from ms). For Vancouver, see G. Godwin, Vancouver: a life 1757–98, 1930.

Bishop, Charles. The journal and letters on the northwest coast of America, in the Pacific and in New South Wales 1794–9. Ed M. Roe 1967 (Hakluyt Soc) (from ms).

Wilson, William (ed). A missionary voyage to the southern Pacific Ocean 1796–8 in the ship Duff, commanded by Captain James Wilson: compiled from journals of the officers and missionaries [at Tahiti]. 1799; tr German, 1800.

History of the Otaheitan Islands from their first discovery to the present time, with an account of the mission [of the Duff]. Edinburgh 1800.

Labillardière, Jacques Julien Houton de. Voyage in search of La Pérouse 1791–4. 1800. Trn from French of 1799–1800.

§ 2

Burney, James. A chronological history of the discoveries in the South Sea. 5 vols 1803–17, Amsterdam 1966 (facs).

Wood, G. A. The discovery of Australia. 1922.

Williamson, J. A. The exploration of the Pacific. In Cambridge history of the British Empire vol 7, 1923.

— Exploration and discovery. In Johnson's England, ed A. S. Turberville vol 1, 1933.

Henderson, C. C. The discoverers of the Fiji Islands: Tasman, Cook, Bligh, Wilson, Bellingshausen. 1933.

Beaglehole, J. C. The exploration of the Pacific. 1934, 1947, 1968.

— The discovery of New Zealand. Wellington 1939, 1961.

Wroth, L. C. The early cartography of the Pacific [to 1798]. PBSA 38 1944.

Dilke, O. A. W. The English literature of exploration in the eighteenth century. Mariner's Mirror 32 1946.

Lloyd, C. Pacific horizons: the exploration of the Pacific before Cook. 1946.

Appleton, M. They came to New Zealand: an account of New Zealand to the middle nineteenth century. 1958.

Pownall, Eve. Exploring Australia. 1958.

Sharp, A. The discovery of the Pacific Islands. Oxford 1960.

— The discovery of Australia. Oxford 1963.

Smith, B. European vision and the South Pacific 1768–1850: a study in the history of art and ideas. Oxford 1960.

(8) ARCTIC

Collections and Histories

Müller, Samuel [actually Gerhard Friedrich Müller]. Voyages from Asia to America to complete the discoveries of the north-west coast of America, with a summary of the voyages of the Russians on the Frozen-Sea. 1761, 1764. Trn from German of 1758, by Thomas Jefferys. Containing reports of the voyages of Deshnev round the northeast point of Asia, and of the Bering voyages in the Sea and Strait named after him.

Coxe, William. An account of the Russian discoveries between Asia and America. 1780, 1780, 1787 (with next item), 1804; tr French 1781; German, 1783.

— Comparative view of the Russian voyages with those made by Captain Cook and Captain Clerke. 1787, 1787 (with preceding).

[Pickersgill, Richard]. A concise account of the voyages for the discovery of a north-west passage undertaken for finding a route to the East Indies. 1782.

Forster, John Reinhold. The history of the voyages and discoveries made in the North. 1786. Trn from German of 1784.

§ I

Martens, Friedrich. Observations on his voyage to Spitzbergen and Greenland [in 1671]. In An account of several late voyages, 1694 etc, under General Collections, above; ed A. White 1856 (Hakluyt Soc). Trn from German of 1675.

Wood, Captain John. A relation of a voyage for the discovery of a passage by the North-East [to Nova Zembla 1676]. In An account, 1694 (with preceding).

Allison, Capt Thomas. An account of a voyage from Archangel in Russia 1697. 1699; rptd in John Pinkerton, A collection vol 1, 1808.

La Peyrere, Isaac de. An account of Iseland 1644. In A. and J. Churchill vol 2, 1704. Trn from French of 1647.

— An account of Greenland 1646. In A. and J. Churchill, A collection vol 2, 1704 etc; rptd 1856 (Hakluyt Soc). Trn from French of 1647.

Isham, James. Observations on Hudson's Bay 1743. Ed E. E. Rich, Toronto 1949 (Champlain Soc) (from ms).

— Notes and observations on a voyage to Hudson's Bay. Ed Rich (with preceding). On the Henry Ellis account, see 1748 below.

Middleton, Capt Christopher. An account of his voyage for the discovery of the North-West Passage 1741–3. In John Harris, Navigantium vol 2, 1744. Extracts from the log of the voyage were ed J. Barrow 1852 (Hakluyt Soc). For the pamphlet controversy over the good faith of Middleton, see E. G. Cox, Reference guide to travel literature vol 2; and for the story of the mystifications involved, see P. G. Adams, Travels and travel liars ch 4.

Egede, Bishop Hans. A description of Greenland: shewing the natural history, boundaries and face of the country, ancient and modern inhabitants. 1745, 1818. Trn from Danish of 1729 by Richard Norcliffe.

Ellis, Henry. A voyage to Hudson's Bay 1746–7 in the Dobbs galley and the California for discovering a North-West Passage. 1748, 3 vols 1748 (combined with next item), Dublin 1749; rptd in John Newbery, The world displayed vol 10, 1761 etc; tr French, 1749; Dutch, 1750; German, 1750.

[Swaine, Charles]. An account of a voyage for the discovery of a North-West Passage 1745 and 1747 in the California. 2 vols 1748, 3 vols 1748 (combined with preceding), Dublin 1749.

— The great probability of a north west passage. 1768. With accounts of Admiral de Fuentes on the northwest coast of North America 1640; and of a voyage to Labrador in 1753.

Coats, Capt William. The geography of Hudson's Bay: being the remarks made in many voyages to that locality 1727 to 1751. Ed J. Barrow 1852 (Hakluyt Soc).

Robson, Joseph. An account of six years' residence in Hudson's Bay 1733–6 and 1744–7. 1752.

A letter from a Russian sea-officer with remarks upon Mr de l'Isle's chart and memoir of the new discoveries northward and eastward from Kamtschatka. 1754. Trn from French version 1753 of the Russian.

Crantz, David. The history of Greenland: containing a description of the country and its inhabitants, and particularly a relation of the mission of the Unitas Fratrum. 2 vols 1767, 1780 (as The antient and modern history of the Brethren). Trn from German of 1765.

The journal of a voyage for making discoveries towards the North Pole by Commodore Phipps [in 1773], with an account of the [earlier] voyages for the discovery of the North-East Passage. 1773, 1774. The account of the earlier voyages was rptd in G. W. Anderson, A collection of voyages round the world, 1784, in Voyages round the world, Collections, above.

Phipps, Commodore Constantine John (later Lord Mulgrave). A voyage from June 4 to September 24 1773 to determine how far navigation was practicable to the North Pole. 1774, Dublin 1775; rptd in John Hawkesworth, An account of the voyages, Dublin 1775. See Voyages round the world, Collections, above; rptd in G. W. Anderson, A collection, 1784 (as in preceding); rptd in John Pinkerton, A collection vol 1, 1808; tr German, 1774; French, 1775. The voyage was stopped by ice beyond Spitzbergen.

LeRoy, Pierre Louis. A narrative of the adventures of four Russian sailors who were cast away on the desert island of East-Spitzbergen. In next item, 1774; rptd in John Pinkerton, A collection vol 1, 1808. Trn from German of 1760. A French version of the English was pbd in 1767: hence an earlier edn of the English is indicated.

Stählin[-Storcksburg], Jacob von. An account of the new northern archipelago lately discovered by the Russians in the seas of Kamtschatka and Anadir [in 1765–7]. 1774. Trn from German of 1774 by C. Heidinger, rev M. Maty. Includes an account of earlier Russian voyages, and also the LeRoy item above.

Barrington, Daines. The probability of reaching the North Pole discussed. 1775–6, 1780 (enlarged); in his Miscellanies, 1781, 1818 (as The possibility of approaching the North Pole asserted).

Cook, Capt James. For his 3rd voyage 1776–80, which explored the region of the Bering Sea, see Voyages round the world, above, from 1781.

Pennant, Thomas. Arctic zoology. 2 vols and suppl 1784–7, 2 vols 1792; tr German, 1787; French, 1789.

Pagès, Pierre Marie François. Voyages toward the South and North Poles [in 1773–4 and 1776]. Vol 3 of Travels round the world, 1792. Trn from French of 1782.

Goldson, William. Observations on the passage between the Atlantic and Pacific Oceans in two memoirs on the Straits of Anian and the discoveries of De Fonte. Portsmouth 1793.

Hearne, Samuel. A journey from Hudson's Bay to the Northern Ocean [overland 1770–2 to the mouth of the Coppermine River]. 1795. See under Voyages to the Americas, above.

Bacstrom, John. An account of a voyage to Spitzbergen in 1780. Philosophical Mag July 1799; rptd in John Pinkerton, A collection vol 1, 1808.

§ 2

Barrow, J. A chronological history of voyages into the Arctic regions. 1818.

Markham, C. R. The lands of silence: a history of Arctic and Antarctic exploration. Cambridge 1921.

Mirsky, J. To the north! New York 1934, 1948 (rev as To the Arctic!).

G. B. P.

IV. TRANSLATIONS INTO ENGLISH

Translations from the Greek and Latin Classics; Translations from French; Translations from German; Translations from Italian.

A. TRANSLATIONS FROM THE CLASSICS

(1) BIBLIOGRAPHIES

Brueggemann, L. W. A view of the English editions, translations and illustrations of the ancient Greek and Latin authors. Stettin 1797.

Moss, J. W. A manual of classical bibliography. 2 vols 1825, 1 vol 1830, 2 vols 1837 (rev).

Foster, F. M. K. English translations from the Greek. New York 1918.

Smith, F. S. The classics in translation. 1930.

Evans, F. B. Platonic scholarship in eighteenth-century England. MP 41 1943. With a bibliography of English edns and trns of Plato 1670–1804.

Benham, A. R. Horace and his Ars poetica in English: a bibliography. Classical Weekly Oct 1955.

Morgan, B. Q. A critical bibliography of works on translation. In On translation, ed R. A. Brower, Cambridge Mass 1959.

Fleischmann, W. B. Lucretius and English literature 1680–1740. Paris 1964. Ch 3, Translations of De rerum natura published in England before 1740.

Parks, G. B. and R. Z. Temple. The literatures of the world in English translation: a bibliography. Vol 1, The Greek and Latin literatures, New York 1968.

(2) THE THEORY OF TRANSLATION

General Discussions

Dryden, John. Ovid's epistles, translated by several hands. 1680. Preface.

—— The works of Virgil. 1697. Dedication.

Dillon, Wentworth, Earl of Roscommon. An essay on translated verse. 1684, 1685 (enlarged), 1709.

Behn, Aphra. A discovery of new worlds, made English [from Fontenelle]; to which is prefixed a preface by way of essay on translated prose. 1688.

[Wright, James]. Country conversations, chiefly of the modern comedies, of drinking, of translated verse. 1694.

Lucian's Charon: or a survey of the follies of mankind, with a prefatory dialogue in vindication of translations. [1700?].

Brady, N. Proposals for a translation of Virgil's Aeneis in blank verse. 1713.

Pope, Alexander. The Iliad of Homer. Vol 1, 1715. Preface.

Parnell, Thomas. Homer's battle of the frogs and mice. 1717. Preface.

Spence, Joseph. An essay on Mr Pope's Odyssey. 2 pts Oxford 1726–7.

Trapp, Joseph. The works of Virgil in English verse. 3 vols 1731. Dedication.

Benson, William. Letters concerning poetical translations. 1739.

Francklin, Thomas. Translation: a poem. 1753.
Principles of translation. Edinburgh 1760. A trn from the French of Batteux.
Stockdale, Percival. The Amyntas of Tasso. 1770. Preface.
Macpherson, James. The works of Ossian. 2 vols 1773 (4th edn). Preface.
Mickle, W. J. The Lusiad: or the discovery of India. 1776. Introduction.
Tytler, A. F., Baron Woodhouselee. Essay on the principles of translation. 1791, 1797, Edinburgh 1813; rptd [1907] (EL).
Beattie, James. A letter to the Rev Hugh Blair on the improvement of psalmody in Scotland. 1839. Written 1778.

Amos, F. R. Early theories of translation. New York 1920.
Draper, J. W. The theory of translation in the eighteenth century. Neophilologus 6 1921.

The Translation of Particular Authors

Arnold, Matthew. On translating Homer: three lectures. 1861.
Conington, J. The English translators of Virgil. Quart Rev 110 1861.
Henkel, W. Ilias und Odyssee und ihre Übersetzer in England von Chapman bis auf Lord Derby. Hersfeld 1867.
Fehlauer, F. Die englischen Übersetzungen von Boethius De consolatione philosophiae. Berlin 1909.
Bridges, R. Ibant obscuri. Oxford 1916. On Virgil trns.
Rosenberg, A. Longinus in England bis zum Ende des 18 Jahrhunderts. Berlin 1917.

Wild, F. Die Batrachomyomachia in England. Vienna 1918.
Craig, H. Dryden's Lucian. Classical Philology 16 1921.
Duckett, E. S. Catullus in English poetry. Northampton Mass 1925.
Bush, D. English translations of Homer. PMLA 41 1926.
— Musaeus in English verse. MLN 43 1928.
Whitford, R. C. Juvenal in England 1750–1802. PQ 7 1928.
Herrick, M. T. The poetics of Aristotle in England. New Haven 1930.
Bottkol, J. M. Dryden's Latin scholarship. MP 40 1943.
Hooker, H. M. Dryden's Georgics and English predecessors. HLQ 9 1945.
George Stepney's translations of the eighth satire of Juvenal. Ed T. and E. Swedenberg, Berkeley 1948.
Knight, D. Pope and the heroic tradition: a critical study of his Iliad. New Haven 1951.
Callan, N. Pope's Iliad: a new document. RES new ser 4 1953.
Frost, W. Dryden and the art of translation. New Haven 1955.
Sühnel, R. Homer und die englische Humanität: Chapmans und Popes Übersetzungskunst im Rahmen der humanistischen Tradition. Tübingen 1958.
Riddehough, G. B. Thomas Hobbes' translations of Homer. Phoenix 12 1958.
Proudfoot, L. Dryden's Aeneid and its seventeenth-century predecessors. Manchester 1960.
Gallagher, M. Dryden's translation of Lucretius. HLQ 28 1965.
Zimmerman, H.-J. Alexander Popes Noten zu Homer: eine Manuskript- und Quellenstudie. Heidelberg 1966.
Sherbo, A. Christopher Smart's three translations of Horace. JEGP 66 1967.

(3) CLASSICAL GREEK LITERATURE

Unless otherwise stated, trns of poetry are in verse and of prose in prose. The lists are intended to be complete for the authors included, except for paraphrases, adaptations and trns of occasional passages and short poems.

Aelian

Stanley, Thomas. Aelianus Claudius, his various history. 1665, 1666, 1670, 1677.

Aeschines

Dawson, Thomas. The orations of Aeschines and Demosthenes concerning the Crown. 1732.
Portal, Abraham. The orations of Aeschines against Ctesiphon, and Demosthenes De corona. Oxford 1755.
See also Thomas Leland *under* Demosthenes, *below*.

Aeschylus

Morell, Thomas. Prometheus in chains. 1773. With Greek text and Latin trn.
Potter, Robert. The tragedies. Norwich 1777, 1779, Oxford 1808, Weybridge 1809, 1812 etc.

Aesop

Philipot, Thomas. Aesop's fables in English, French and Latin. 1665, 1666, 1687, 1703. Also includes verse paraphrases by Aphra Behn. The French and Latin versions are by Robert Codrington.
The fables in English. 1672, 1676, 1700.
Ayres, Philip. Mythologia ethica: or three centuries of Aesopian fables. 1689, 1690.
L'Estrange, Sir Roger. The fables of Aesop and other eminent mythologists. 2 pts 1692–9; 1694 (pt I); 2 vols 1703; 1704 (pt I); 2 vols 1708, 1714, 1715, 1724, 1730, 1738.

Hoole, Charles. Aesop's fables. 1695, 1700, 1731. English and Latin.
[Locke, John]. Aesop's fables, in English and Latin. 1703, 1723.
Toland, John. The fables. 1704.
Arwaker, Edmund. Truth in fiction or morality in masquerade: a collection of select fables. 1708. Verse.
J[ackson], J[ohn]. A new translation of Aesop's fables. 1708, 1715 (enlarged), 1734.
Croxall, Samuel. Fables of Aesop and others. 1722, 1724, 1728, 1731, 1737, 1740, 1746, 1747, 1757, 1770, 1778 etc.
Dodsley, Robert. Select fables of Esop and other fabulists. Birmingham 1761, London 1762, Birmingham 1764, London 1765, 1784, 1786, 1797 etc.
Clarke, H. Fabulae Aesopi selectae. 1774, Boston 1787, London 1789, Exeter NH 1799, Walpole NH 1802. Latin and English.

Alciphron

[Monro, Thomas and William Beloe]. Alciphron's epistles, now first translated from the Greek. 1791.

Anacreon

Willis, Francis, Cowley, Abraham, Oldham, John and Thomas Wood. Anacreon done into English. Oxford 1682.
Odes of Anacreon. In Examen miscellaneum, 1702.
S[ewell], G[eorge] et al. The works of Anacreon and Sappho, done from the Greek by several hands. 1713. Based on the 1683 version, with addns.
Addison, John. The works. 1735. With Greek. Sappho's poems are appended.
[Fawkes, Francis]. The works of Anacreon, Sappho, Bion, Moschus and Musaeus. 1760, 1789.

[Greene, Edward Burnaby]. The works of Anacreon and Sappho. 1768.
Urquhart, David Henry. The odes. 1787, 1810 (enlarged).
The odes, literally translated into English prose. York 1796.
Moore, Thomas. The odes. 1800, 2 vols 1802, 1 vol Dublin 1803, 2 vols 1804, 1805, 1806, 1815, 1820 etc.
See also W. Green *under* Pindar, *below*.

Apollonius Rhodius

Ekins, Jeffrey. The loves of Medea and Jason. 1771, 1772, 1810.
Fawkes, Francis. The Argonautics. 1780. Completed by H. Meen.
[Greene, Edward Burnaby]. The Argonautic expedition. 2 vols 1780.

Appian

D[avies], John. The history. 1679, 1692, 1703.

Aristophanes

Theobald, Lewis. The clouds. 1715.
—— Plutus: or the world's idol. 1715.
Fielding, Henry and William Young. Plutus: the god of riches. 1742.
[White, James]. The clouds. 1759.
Dunster, Charles. The frogs. Oxford [1780?].
Cumberland, Richard. The clouds. 1797, 1798.

Aristotle

Hobbes, Thomas. A briefe of the art of rhetorique. 1637, 1651. The art of rhetoric 1681, commonly ascribed to Hobbes, is not his: see W. J. Ong, Trans Cambridge Bibl Soc 1 1949–52.
C., H. Aristotle's Rhetoric. 1686, 1693.
Aristotle's book of problems. 1690, 1710.
Aristotle's Art of poetry. 1705, 1709, 1713, 1714. From Dacier's French version.
Pargiter, E. Aristotle of morals to Nicomachus. 1745. Bk 1 only.
Aristotle's Poetics. 2 pts 1775.
Ellis, William. A treatise on government. 1776, 1778.
Pye, Henry James. The poetics. 1788, 1792 (with commentary).
Twining, Thomas. Aristotle's treatise on poetry. Oxford 1789, 2 vols 1812.
Gillies, John. Aristotle's Ethics and Politics. 2 vols 1797, 1804, 1813, 1823.

Arrian

Rooke, [John]. Arrian's History of Alexander's expedition. 2 vols 1729.
Vincent, William. The voyage of Nearchus. 1797, Oxford 1809.

Marcus Aurelius

Collier, Jeremy. The Emperor Marcus Antonius his conversation with himself. 1701, 1708, 1726.
Moor, James and Francis Hutcheson. The meditations. Glasgow 1742, 1749, 1752, 1764.
Thomson, James. The commentaries. 1747, Glasgow 1747, London 1755, Glasgow 1766.
Graves, Richard. The meditations. Bath, 1792, Stourport 1811, Halifax 1826; rptd 1905.

'Batrachomyomachia'

See Samuel Parker, Thomas Parnell, Samuel Wesley, H. Price *and* William Cowper *under* Homer, *below*.

Bion

Langhorne, John. The death of Adonis: a pastoral elegy. 1759.
See Francis Fawkes *under* Anacreon, *above*, *and* Theocritus, Thomas Cooke *under* Moschus, Richard Polwhele *and* Edward Dubois *under* Theocritus, *below*.

Callimachus

Alney, John. The hymns. 1744.
Dodd, William. The hymns. 1755.
Tytler, Henry William. The works. 1793.

Chariton

The loves of Chaereas and Callirhoe. 2 vols 1764.

Demosthenes

Several orations to encourage the Athenians to oppose Philip. 1702, 1744 (rev). The translators include Samuel Garth, George Granville and Lord Peterborough.
Leland, Thomas. All the orations. 8 vols 1756–70, 1771, 1777, 2 vols 1802, 1804, 1806 etc. Includes Aeschines, De corona.
Francis, Philip. The orations. 2 vols 1757–8. *See* Thomas Dawson *and* Abraham Portal *under* Aeschines, *above*.

Dio Cassius

Manning, Francis. The history. 2 vols 1704.

Diodorus Siculus

Booth, George. The historical library, in fifteen books. 1700.

Diogenes Laertius

The lives, opinions and remarkable sayings of the most famous ancient philosophers. 2 vols 1688, 1696. The translators include T. Fetherstone, S. White, E. Smith, J. Phillips, R. Kippars and W. Baxter.

Dionysius of Halicarnassus

Spelman, Edward. The Roman antiquities. 4 vols 1758.

Epictetus

Davies, John. The life and philosophy of Epictetus. 1670.
Walker, Ellis. Epicteti Enchiridion. 1692, 1695, 1697, 1701, 1702, 1708, 1716, Dublin 1724, London 1737. Verse.
Stanhope, George. Epictetus his morals. 1694, 1700, 1721, 1741 etc.
Epictetus his morals, done from the original Greek by a Dr of Physick. 1702, 1703.
W., J. The Porch and Academy open'd or Epictetus's manual newly turn'd into English verse. 1707.
Human wisdom displayed: containing a collection of choice morals from Epictetus, by an old gentleman of Gray's Inn. 1731.
Carter, Elizabeth. All the works. 1758, Dublin 1759, 2 vols 1807 etc.

Epicurus

Digby, John. Epicurus's morals. 1712.

Euripides

[West, Richard]. The Hecuba. 1726.
Morell, Thomas. Hecuba, translated from the Greek. 1749, 1749.
West, Gilbert. Iphigenia in Taurus. In The odes of Pindar, 1749 etc.
[Lennox, Charlotte]. Hippolytus; Iphigenia in Aulis; Iphigenia in Taurus; Alcestis; Cyclops. In The Greek theatre, 3 vols 1759. From the French of Brumois.
Bannister, James. Select tragedies. 1780. Phoenissae, Iphigenia in Aulis, Troades, Orestes.
Potter, Robert. The tragedies. 2 vols 1781–3, 1807, 1808, 1814, 3 vols 1832 etc.
Wodhull, Michael. The nineteen tragedies and fragments. 4 vols 1782, 3 vols 1809.
—— Hippolytus and Iphigenia in Aulis. 1786.
Tuomy, Martin. A literal translation of Euripides's Hippolytus and Iphigenia [in Aulis]. Dublin 1790. Prose.

Heliodorus

Tate, Nahum et al. The Aethiopian history in ten books. 1686, 1687.

The adventures of Theagenes and Chariclia. 2 vols 1717.

Herodian

Herodian's History of the Roman Emperors, by a gentleman at Oxford. 1698.

Hart, J. Herodian's History of his own times. 1749.

[Graves, Richard]. The heir apparent: or the life of Commodus. 1789.

Herodotus

Littlebury, Isaac. The history. 1709, 1729, 1737 etc.

Beloe, William. The history. 4 vols 1791, 1806, 1812, 1821, 1825, 1830 etc.

Hesiod

Broome, William. The battle of the gods and Titans. In Poems on several occasions, 1727, 1739, 1750.

Cooke, Thomas. The works. 2 vols 1728, 1740, 1743.

Hippocrates

The eight sections of Hippocrates's aphorisms. 1665.

Sprengell, Sir Conrad Joachim. The aphorismes of Hippocrates and the sentences of Celsus. 1708, 1735.

Homer

Ogilby, John. Homer his Iliads. 1660, 2 vols 1669 (with Odyssey).

— Homers Odysses. 1665, 2 vols 1669 (with Iliad).

Hobbes, Thomas. Homer's Odysses. 1675.

— Homer's Iliads. 1676.

— The works. 1677, 1683, 1685, 1686.

Dryden, John. Fables ancient and modern. 1700 etc. Includes Iliad bk 1.

Parker, Samuel. Homer in a nutshell. 1700. Batrachomyomachia.

Ozell, John, [William Broome and William Oldisworth]. Iliad. 5 vols 1712, 1714–22, 1734. Prose; from Mme Dacier's French version.

Pope, Alexander. The Iliad. 6 vols 1715–20 etc.

— The Odyssey. 5 vols 1725–6 etc. With E. Fenton and W. Broome.

Tickell, Thomas. The first book of Homer's Iliad. 1715.

Parnell, Thomas. The battle of the frogs and the mice. 1717, Dublin 1717, London 1726 etc.

Wesley, Samuel. The Iliad in a nutshell. 1726. Batrachomyomachia.

Broome, William. Poems on several occasions. 1727, 1739, 1750. Includes parts of Iliad, bks x–xi in Miltonic verse.

[Price, H.] Batrachomuomachia. 1736.

Ashwick, Samuel. The eighth book of the Iliad. 1750.

Scott, Joseph Nicol. An essay towards a translation of Homer's works, in blank verse. 1755. Selections.

Langley, Samuel. Homer's Iliad translated into blank verse: book 1. 1767.

Macpherson, James. The Iliad translated into prose. 2 vols 1773.

Lucas, Robert. Homer's Hymn to Ceres. 1781.

Cowper, William. The Iliad and Odyssey. 2 vols 1791, 4 vols 1802, 1809, 1810, 1836. Includes Batrachomyomachia.

[Geddes, Alexander]. The first book of the Iliad. 1792.

Isaeus

Jones, Sir William. The speeches of Isaeus in causes concerning the law of property. 1779.

Isocrates

Advice to a young gentleman. 1696.

Digby, John. Advice to Demonicus. In Epicurus's Morals, 1712.

— Discourse to a prince; Advice to Demonicus. In The Prince's Cabala, 1715.

Brown, James. The duty of a King and his people. 1735.

Dimsdale, Joshua and W. Young. The orations and epistles. 1752.

Toulmin, Joshua. Isocrates's oration to Demonicus. In Sermons to youth, [1770].

Gillies, John. Orations out of Lysias and Isocrates. 1778. 6 speeches by Isocrates.

Josephus

The works. 1676, 1693.

The works epitomiz'd. 2 vols 1699.

L'Estrange, Sir Roger. The works. 1702, 1725.

Court, John. The works. 1733, 1755, 1770.

Jackson, Henry. A compleat collection of the genuine works. 1736.

Whiston, William. The genuine works. 1737, 4 vols 1755.

Thompson, Ebenezer and William Charles Price. The works. 2 vols 1777–8.

Neave, B. An abridgement of the History. Norwich 1785.

Maynard, George Henry. The genuine and complete works. [1785?], [1800?].

Bradshaw, Thomas. The whole works. 1792.

Longinus

P[ulteney], J[ohn]. A treatise of the loftiness or elegancy of speech. 1680. From Boileau's French version.

An essay upon sublime style. Oxford 1698.

A treatise of the sublime. In Boileau's Complete works vol 2, 1711 etc.

Welsted, Leonard. The works of Dionysius Longinus on the sublime. 1712.

Smith, William. Dionysius Longinus on the sublime. 1739, 1742, 1743, 1751, 1752, 1756, 1757, 1770, Dublin 1777.

Longus

[Craggs, James]. The pastoral amours of Daphnis and Chloe. 1720, 1733, 1764.

Lucian

Lovers of lyes. In John Wagstaffe, Question of witchcraft, 1669.

Cotton, Charles. Burlesque upon burlesque. 1675, 1687. Select dialogues.

Spence, Ferrand. Lucian's works. 5 vols 1684–5.

Lucian's Charon. [1700?].

The works of Lucian, translated by several eminent hands. 4 vols 1711, 1745. Includes Life of Lucian by Dryden, who was general editor. The 'hands' include Tom Brown, Walter Moyle, John Phillips and Sir Henry Sheers.

Moyle, Walter. Translations from Lucian. In Whole works of Walter Moyle, 1727; rptd from preceding.

West, Gilbert. The triumphs of the gout. In Odes of Pindar, 1749 etc.

Carr, John. Lucian's dialogues. 5 vols 1773–98.

Francklin, Thomas. The works. 2 vols 1780, 4 vols 1781.

Lysias

See John Gillies under Isocrates, above.

Menander

Fawkes, Francis. Original poems and translations. 1761.

Moschus

Cooke, Thomas. The Idylliums of Moschus and Bion. 1724.

See Francis Fawkes under Anacreon, above, and R. Polwhele under Theocritus, below.

Musaeus

[Hoy, Thomas]. Hero and Leander. In Two essays, 1682, and Ovid's Art of love, 1692.

[Eusden, Laurence]. Hero and Leander. In Dryden's Poetical miscellanies vol 6, 1709 etc; rptd separately Glasgow 1750.

Catcott, Alexander Stopford. The poems of Musaeus on the loves of Hero and Leander. Oxford 1715.

Theobald, Lewis. Hero and Leander. In his Grove, 1721.

Sterling, James. The loves of Hero and Leander. Dublin 1728. Includes versions from other Greek lyric poets.

Luck, Robert. The loves of Hero and Leander. In A miscellany of new poems, 1736.

Baily, George. The loves of Hero and Leander. 1747.

Slade, J. Musaeus: a poetical translation. 1753.

Graeme, James. Hero and Leander. In Poems on several occasions, Edinburgh 1773.

G[reene], E[dward] B[urnaby]. Hero and Leander. 1773.

Musaeus, translated from the Greek. 1744.

[Taylor, Edward]. Hero and Leander. Glasgow 1783.

Belford, Grosvenor Charles. The loves of Hero and Leander. 1797. With Greek.

See Francis Fawkes under Anacreon, above.

Pausanias

Price, Sir Uvedale. An account of the statues, pictures and temples in Greece. 1780.

Taylor, Thomas. The description of Greece. 3 vols 1794, 1824.

Pindar

Philips, Ambrose. Pastorals, epistles, odes. 1748, 1765. Includes trns of the first and second Olympians.

West, Gilbert. The odes. 1749, Dublin 1751, 2 vols 1753 (enlarged) 1766. A selection.

Tyrwhitt, Thomas. Translations in verse. Oxford 1752. Includes the eighth Isthmian.

Dodd, William. Four odes. In his Poems, 1767.

The first Pythian ode. 1775.

Pye, Henry James. Six Olympian odes. 1775.

Green, Edward Burnaby. The Pythian, Nemean and Isthmian odes. 1778.

Tasker, William. Select odes of Pindar and Horace. 8 vols Exeter 1780–93.

[Green, William]. A new translation of select odes of Pindar and Anacreon, and epistles of Horace. Liverpool [1783?].

Banister, James. A translation of all the Pythian, Nemean and Isthmian odes. Salisbury 1791.

Plato

Plato his Apology of Socrates and Phaedo. 1675.

The works abridg'd by several hands. 2 vols 1701, 1719–20, 1739, 1749 etc. From the French version.

Theobald, Lewis. Plato's dialogue of the immortality of the soul. 1718. Phaedo.

West, Gilbert. Menexenus. In his Odes of Pindar, 1749 etc.

Sydenham, Floyer. Dialogues. 4 vols 1759–80. 9 dialogues with separate dates and pagination.

Spens, H. The Republic. Glasgow 1768.

Phedon: or a dialogue of the immortality of the soul. [1763?]. Includes Crito.

Mills, Joseph. Plato's Apology of Socrates. Cambridge 1775.

Taylor, Thomas. The Phaedrus. 1792. Anon.

— The Republic. 1792.

— The Cratylus, Phaedo, Parmenides and Timaeus. 1793.

Plotinus

Taylor, Thomas. Concerning the beautiful. 1787. Ennead 1, bk 6.

— Five books. 1794.

Plutarch

Lloyd, David. The worthies of the world. 1665. An abridgement.

Plutarch's Lives, translated by several hands. 5 vols 1683–6, 1688, 1693, 1700, 1702–11, 1714, 1716, 1724, 8 vols 1727 etc. Life of Plutarch, Dedication and Advertisement attributed to Dryden, who was general editor.

Morgan, Matthew et al. Plutarch's Morals. 5 vols 1683–90, 1691, 1694, 1704, 1718.

Plutarch's Morals, by way of abstract. 1707.

[Gildon, Charles]. Plutarch's Lives. 1710, 1713, 1718. Abridged from the Dryden version.

Squire, Samuel. Treatise of Isis and Osiris. Cambridge 1744, 1749. With Greek.

Langhorne, John and William. Plutarch's Lives. 6 vols 1770, 1774, 1778, 1780, 1792, 1801, 1805 etc.

Northmore, Thomas. Treatise upon the distinction between a friend and a flatterer. 1793.

Polybius

S[heers], Sir H[enry]. The history. 2 vols 1693, 3 vols 1698. With a character of Polybius by Dryden.

[Spelman, Edward]. A fragment of the sixth book. 1743.

Hampton, James. The general history. Vol 1, 1756, 1761, 2 vols 1766; vol 2, 1772; vols 1–2, 4 vols 1772, 3 vols 1809.

Sappho

See George Sewell, John Addison, Francis Fawkes, Edward Burnaby Greene under Anacreon, above, and Edward Dubois under Theocritus, below.

Sophocles

[Jackson, — and Nicholas Rowe]. Ajax. 1714.

Theobald, Lewis. Electra. 1714.

— Oedipus, King of Thebes. 1715.

Sheridan, Thomas. Philoctetes. Dublin 1725.

Adams, George. The tragedies. 2 vols 1729. Prose.

[Lennox, Charlotte]. Oedipus, King of Thebes; Electra; Philoctetes. In the Greek theatre, 3 vols 1759. From the French of Brumois.

Francklin, Thomas. The tragedies. 2 vols 1759, 1766, 1788, 1806, 1809 etc.

Maurice, Thomas. A free translation of the Oedipus Tyrannus. In his Poems and miscellaneous pieces, 1797.

Potter, Robert. The tragedies. 1788, 1808, Oxford 1813.

Clarke, George Somers. Oedipus, King of Thebes. Oxford 1790. Prose.

Theocritus

Creech, Thomas. Idylliums. Oxford 1684, London 1721.

Dryden, John. Amaryllis: or the third Idyllium of Theocritus paraphras'd. In his Miscellany poems, 1684 etc.

— The Epithalamium of Helen and Menelaus [Idyllium 18]. In his Sylvae: or the second part of poetical miscellanies, 1685 etc.

— The despairing lover [Idyllium 23]. Ibid.

— Daphnis [Idyllium 27]. Ibid.

Fawkes, Francis. The Idylliums of Theocritus and Bion. 1767.

Polwhele, Richard. The Idyllia, epigrams and fragments of Theocritus, Bion and Moschus; with the elegies of Tyrtaeus. 2 vols 1786, 1789, 1792, 1810, 1811.

Dubois, Edward. The wreath. 1799. Selections from Theocritus, Sappho and Bion.

Theophrastus

The moral characters. In La Bruyère's Characters, 1698, 1700, 1702, 1709.

Budgell, Eustace. The moral characters. 1713, 1714, 1715, 1718, 1743, Edinburgh 1751.

Gally, Henry. The moral characters. 1725.

Hill, John. Theophrastus' History of stones. 1746, 1774. With Greek.

Rayner, William. The moral characters. Norwich 1797.

Thucydides

Smith, William. The history of the Peloponnesian War. 2 vols 1753, 1805 etc.

Tyrtaeus

See Richard Polwhele under Theocritus, above.

Xenophon

Newman, John. Xenophon's History of the affairs of Greece. 1685.

Digby, Francis and John Norris. Κύρου Παιδεία: or the Institution and Life of Cyrus the Great. 2 pts 1685.

M[oyle], Walter. A discourse upon improving the revenues. In his Discourses on the public revenues, 1698.

Welwood, James, The banquet. 1710, Glasgow 1750.

[Bysshe, Edward]. The memorable things of Socrates. 1712, Dublin 1758.

Hiero: or the condition of a tyrant. 1713, Glasgow 1750.

Bradley, Richard. The science of good husbandry. 1727.

Spelman, Edward. The expedition of Cyrus. 2 vols 1742, 1749 etc.

Fielding, Sarah. Xenophon's memoirs of Socrates. Bath 1762, London 1767, 1788.

[Smith, William]. Xenophon's History of the affairs of Greece. 1770, 1812 etc.

Ashley, Maurice. Xenophon's Cyropaedia. 2 vols 1770, 1803, 1811, 1816 etc.

Treatise on horsemanship. In R. Berenger, History of horsemanship vol 1, 1771.

Blane, William. Xenophon on hare hunting. In his Cynegetica: or essays on sporting, 1788.

[Graves, Richard]. Hiero: on the condition of royalty. Bath 1793.

Pye, Henry James. Xenophon's defence of the Athenian democracy. 1794.

(4) CLASSICAL LATIN LITERATURE

Unless otherwise stated trns of poetry are in verse and of prose in prose. The lists are intended to be complete for the authors included, except for paraphrases, adaptations and trns of occasional passages and short poems.

Apuleius

Lockman, John. The loves of Cupid and Psyche. Prefixed to his trn of La Fontaine, 1744.

Taylor, Thomas. The fable of Cupid and Psyche. 1795.

Gurney, Hudson. Cupid and Psyche. 1799, 1800, 1801.

Augustine

[Stanhope, George]. Pious breathings: being the meditations of St Augustine. 1701, 1704, 1714. Includes selections from St Anselm and St Bernard.

St Augustine's Confessions. 1739.

The soliloquies. Dublin 1747.

St Augustine's Confessions: or praises of God. Dublin 1770.

Boethius

Coningsby, Sir Harry. The consolation of philosophy. 1664. In verse.

[Elys, Edmund]. Summum bonum: or an explication of the divine goodness in the works of Boetius. Oxford 1674.

Preston, Richard (Viscount Preston). A.M.S. Boetius of the Consolation of philosophy. 1695, 1712.

Causton, William. A.M.T.S. Boetius his Consolation of philosophy. 1730, 1768 (in D. Bellamy, Ethic amusements).

Ridpath, Philip. Boethius's Consolation of philosophy. 1785.

Duncan, Robert. The five books on the Consolation of philosophy. Edinburgh 1789.

Caesar

Bladen, Martin. C. Julius Caesar's Commentaries. 1705, 1713, 1715, 1719, 1726, 1732, 1750.

Duncan, William. The commentaries. 1753, 2 vols 1755, 1775, 1 vol 1779.

Catullus

Translations out of Catullus, Tibullus and Propertius. In Miscellany poems and translations, Oxford 1686.

The adventures of Catullus and history of his amours with Lesbia, intermixt with translations of his choicest poems by several hands, done from the French [of Jean de la Chapelle]. 1707.

[Tooly, Thomas]. Basia: or the charms of kissing. 1719, 1719. Catullus and Secundus. With Latin.

Nott, John. The poems. 2 vols 1795. With Latin.

See also Jonas Hanway under Horace, below.

Cicero

Wase, Christopher. Cicero against Catiline. 1671.

—— The five days debate at Cicero's house in Tusculum. 1683.

L'Estrange, Sir Roger. Tully's Offices. 1680, 1681, 1684, 1688, 1699, 1720 etc.

Cicero's three books touching the nature of the gods. 1683.

The oration for M. Marcellus. 1689, 1719 (in Sir Charles Sedley's Works vol 1, 1722, where it is attributed to Sedley).

Cicero's Laelius: a discourse of friendship. 1691.

C[ockman], T[homas]. Tully's three books of offices. 1699, 1706, 1714, 1722, 1732, Dublin 1732, London 1739 etc.

P[arker], S[amuel]. Tully's five books De finibus. 1702.

—— Tully's two essays of old age and of friendship, with his stoical paradoxes and Scipio's dream. 1704, 1727.

Hicks, Robert. Tully's Laelius. 1713.

M. Tully Cicero's five books of Tusculan disputations. 1715.

Cicero on old age. Oxford 1716.

Eelbeck, Henry. A proposal for printing in English the orations of Cicero. 1720. Includes a trn of the Pro Archia.

Warburton, William. Tully's oration for Ligarius. In his Miscellaneous translations, 1724.

Francklin, Thomas. M. Tullius Cicero of the Nature of the gods. 1741, 1775.

Guthrie, William. The orations. 3 vols 1741–3, 1745–52, 1758–66, 1778.

—— M.T. Cicero de oratore. 1742, 1755.

—— The morals of Cicero: I, De finibus; II, his Academics. 1744.

—— Cicero's epistles to Atticus. 2 vols 1752.

—— M.T. Cicero his Offices. 1755, 1756. Also includes Cato Major, Laelius, moral paradoxes, Vision of Scipio, letters concerning the duties of a magistrate.

Middleton, Conyers. The epistles to M. Brutus. 1743. With Latin.

D., J. Cato Major. 1744. Also includes Laelius.

Gordon, Thomas. Four orations against Catiline. In his trn of Sallust, 1744 etc.

The oration for M. Marcellus. 1745. With Latin.

Rose, William. [Catilinarian speeches]. In his trn of Sallust, 1751 etc.

Massey, William. Tully's compendious treatise of old age. 1753.

Melmoth, William. The letters to his friends. 3 vols 1753, 1772, 1778.

—— Cato: or an essay on old age; Laelius: or an essay on friendship. 1773-7, 1785, 1807, 1820.

Duncan, William. Cicero's select orations. 1756; rev Sir Charles Whitworth 1771, 1796. With Latin.

The Tusculan disputations. 1758.

Barnes, George. Cicero, On the complete orator. 1760, 1762.

Jones, Edward. Cicero's Brutus; also his Orator. 1776.

Ellis, William. A collection of English exercises, translated from Cicero. 1782. Includes a trn of the Laelius.

White, James. Against Verres. 1787.

Sydney, George Frederic. The four [Catilinarian] orations. In his History of Catiline's conspiracy, 1795.

Claudian

Hughes, Jabez. The rape of Proserpine. 1714.

—— Two books against Rufinus. 1737, 1741. With other pieces from Claudian, Statius etc.

Warburton, William. Claudian's panegyrick on Honorius. In his Miscellaneous translations, 1724.

Polwhele, Richard. The rape of Proserpine. In his Poems by a gentleman of Devonshire, 1792.

Quintus Curtius

Codrington, Robert. The life and death of Alexander the Great. 1661, 1670, 1673, 1674.

Digby, John. History of the wars of Alexander. 2 vols 1714, 1747 (rev W. Young).

Aulus Gellius

Beloe, William. The Attic nights. 3 vols 1795.

Horace

Brome, Alexander et al. The poems, by several persons. 1666, 1671, 1680. For the contributors, see H. F. Brooks, N & Q 19 March 1938.

Dillon, Wentworth (Earl of Roscommon). Horace's Art of poetry. 1680, 1684, 1695, 1709 etc.

[Oldham, J.] Horace his Art of poetry imitated in English. In his Some new pieces never before publist, 1681.

Creech, Thomas. The odes, satyrs and epistles. 1684, 1688, 1711, 1715, 1718 (with Latin), 1720, 1730 etc.

[Harington], J[ohn]. The odes and epodes. 1684.

Dunster, Samuel. The satires and epistles. 1709, 1712 (with Ars poetica), 1729, 1739, 1743. Prose, with Latin.

[Oldisworth, William et al]. The odes, epodes and Carmen seculare, with a translation of Dr Bentley's notes; to which are added notes upon notes done in the Bentleian stile. 24 pts 1712-13, 2 vols 1714, 1719, 1725. With Latin.

The odes and satyrs, by the most eminent hands. 1715, 1715, 1717, 1721, 1730, Dublin 1730, London 1733.

Coxwell, Henry. The odes. Oxford 1718.

Ames, Henry. A new translation of Horace's Art of poetry. 1727.

Hanway, Jonas. Translations of several odes, satyrs and epistles, with some versions out of Catullus, Martial and the Italian poets. 1730.

Horace of the Art of poetry. [1730?].

Carthy, Charles. A translation of the second book of Horace's epistles. Dublin 1731. With Latin.

Ogle, George. The epistles. 1735.

Hare, Thomas. A translation of the odes and epodes. 1737.

Watson, David. The odes, epodes and Carmen seculare. 2 vols 1741-2, 1760 (as vol 1 of Works, vol 2 being Samuel Patrick's Satires); rev W. Crakelt 2 vols 1792. Prose, with Latin.

Towers, Matthew. The lyric pieces. 2 vols Dublin 1742-3, 1744 (as Odes). Poetic prose, with Latin.

Francis, Philip. The odes, epodes and Carmen seculare. 2 vols 1743, 1746. With Latin.

—— The satires. Vol 3, 1746. With Latin.

—— The epistles and Art of poetry. Vol 4, 1746. With Latin.

—— A poetical translation of the works; with the original text: the second edition. 4 vols 1747, 1749, 1750, 1753, 1756, 1760, 2 vols 1760, 4 vols 1765, 1791 etc.

Patrick, Samuel. The satires, epistles and Art of poetry. 1743, 1748, 2 vols 1760 (as vol 2 of Works, vol 1 being David Watson's Odes). Prose, with Latin.

Stirling, John. The works. 2 vols 1751-3. Prose, with Latin.

Popple, William. Horace's Art of poetry. 1753. With Latin.

Smart, Christopher. The works. 2 vols 1756, 1762, 1770, 2 vols Dublin 1772, London 1780, 1790 etc. Prose.

—— The works. 4 vols 1767. Prose and verse, with Latin.

[Duncombe, William et al]. The works in English verse, by several hands. 2 vols 1757-9, 4 vols 1767 (enlarged).

[Greene, E. B.] Lyric versions from Horace. In The works of Anacreon and Sappho, 1768.

Green, William. A new poetical translation of all the odes. Liverpool 1777, 1783.

Colman, George. Q. Horatii Flacci Epistola de arte poetica. 2 pts 1783. With Latin.

[Stedman, John?]. Horace's Epistle on the art of poetry. Edinburgh 1784.

Boscawen, William. The odes, epodes and Carmen seculare. 2 vols 1793-7. Vol 2, The satires, epistles and Art of poetry.

Wakefield, Gilbert. Odes. In his Poetical translations from the ancients, 1795.

Clubbe, William. The epistle on the art of poetry. Ipswich 1797.

The first and fourth books of the odes. 1799.

See also William Tasker and William Green under Pindar, above.

Juvenal

Holyday, Barten and William Dewey. D. J. Juvenal and A. Persius Flaccus translated. Oxford 1673. Juvenal is by Dewey.

Dryden, John et al. The satires, together with the satires of Aulus Persius Flaccus. 1693, 1697, 1702, 1711, 1713, 1726, Dublin 1732-3, London 1735 etc.

Sheridan, Thomas. The satires. 1739, 1745, Dublin 1769, Cambridge 1777. Prose, with Latin.

Stirling, John. Juvenal's satires. 1760. Prose.

Owen, Edward. The satires. 2 vols 1785, 1786. With Latin.

Madan, Martin. A new translation of Juvenal and Persius. 2 vols 1789, Oxford 1805, Dublin 1813. Prose.

Livy

[Hayes, J. et al]. The Roman history. 6 vols 1744-5, 8 vols Edinburgh 1761 etc.

Baker, George. The history of Rome. 6 vols 1797, 1822, 2 vols 1830.

Lucan

Rowe, Nicholas. Pharsalia. 1718, 2 vols 1720, 1722, 1753.

Lucretius

[Creech, Thomas]. T. Lucretius Carus his six books De natura rerum. Oxford 1682, 1683, London 1683, 1699, 1700, 2 vols 1714, 1715, 1722, 1793.

Dryden, John. Translations out of Lucretius. In his Sylvae: or the second part of poetical miscellanies, 1685 etc.

T. Lucretius Carus of the nature of things. 1743. Prose, with Latin.

Manilius

Sherburne, Sir Edward. The sphere. 1675. Bk 1 only.
C[reech], T[homas]. The five books. 1697.

Martial

Wright, James. Sales epigrammatum. 1663, 1664. With Latin.
Select epigrams. 1689.
[Killigrew, Henry]. Select epigrams. 1689, 1695
Hay, William. Martialis epigrammata selecta. 1755. With Latin.
Elphinston, James. The epigrams. 1782.
See also Jonas Hanway *under* Horace, *above.*

Origen

Bellamy, James. Origen against Celsus. [1660?].

Ovid

Wolferston, Francis. The three books De arte amandi. 1661.
[Dryden, John et al]. Ovid's epistles, translated by several hands. 1680, 1681, 1683, 1688, 1693, 1701, 1705, 1712, 1716, 1720, 1725 ('with his Amours by Dryden, Congreve etc'), 1729 etc.
[Hoy, Thomas]. Two essays. 1682 (as Ovid's Art of love). Includes De arte amandi, bk 1.
Ovid's elegies: or a translation of his choicest epistles to his lady and friends, together with three other epistles. 1683.
Ball, Thomas. Two books of elegies. 1697.
[Tate, Nahum] et al. Ovid's Metamorphoses, translated by several hands. Vol 1, 1697.
Ovid's Art of love; together with his Remedy of love, by several eminent hands [J. Dryden, W. Congreve, N. Tate]. 1709, 1712, 1719, 1725 (with the Epistles by Dryden etc), 1729, 1735, 1747, 1748, 1750 etc.
P., T. Ovid's Tristia. 1713, 1726.
Garth, Sir Samuel et al. Ovid's Metamorphoses in fifteen books, translated by the most eminent hands. 1717, 1720, 1727, 1732, 1736, 2 vols 1751 etc.
Sewell, George. Ovid's Metamorphoses, in fifteen books: a new translation by several hands. 2 vols 1717, 1724, 1733.
Stirling, John. Ovid's Tristia. 1728, 1736, 1752. With Latin.
Clarke, John. P. Ovidii Nasonis Metamorphoseon libri xv. 1735. Prose, with Latin.
[Davidson, Joseph]. The epistles. 1746, 1753, 1766. Prose, with Latin.
— A new translation of Ovid's Metamorphoses. 1748, 1753, 1759. Prose, with Latin.
Massey, William. Ovid's Fasti. 1757.
Barrett, Stephen. Ovid's epistles. 1759.
Green, William. A new translation of the second book of Ovid's Metamorphoses. Liverpool 1783.
Ewen, James. The epistles. 1787.
Bailey, Nathan. Ovid's Metamorphoses. 1797. Prose, with Latin.

Persius

Eelbeck, Henry. A prosaic translation of A. Persius Flaccus's six satyrs. 1719.
Sheridan, Thomas. The satyrs. Dublin 1728, London 1739. Prose, with Latin.
Senhouse, John. The satires. 1730. Prose, with Latin.
[Brewster, Thomas]. The satires. 5 pts 1741–2, 1 vol 1751.
Burton, Edmund. The satires. 1752. Prose, with Latin.
Greene, Edward Burnaby. The satires. 1779.
Drummond, Sir William. The satires. 1797, 1799, 1803. With Latin.
See also John Dryden *and* Martin Madan *under* Juvenal, *above.*

Pervigilium Veneris

See W. Hilton-Young, Translations of the Pervigilium Veneris into English verse, Cambridge Jnl March 1952.

Petronius

Burnaby, William et al. The satyr. 1694, 1708 (enlarged by T. Brown et al), 1710, 1713, 1714.
Addison, [John]. The Satyricon. 1736.

Plautus

Echard, Laurence. Plautus's comedies: Amphitryon, Epidicus and Rudens. 1694, 1716.
Cooke, Thomas. Mr Cooke's edition and translation of the comedys. 1746. Prose, with Latin; Amphitryo only.
Thornton, Bonnel. Comedies. 2 vols 1767, 1769. Includes the Captivi by R. Warner and the Mercator by the elder Colman; 9 plays in all.
Warner, Richard. Comedies. 3 vols 1769–74. Completes Thornton's version, above.

Pliny the Younger

Kennet, White. An address of thanks to a good Prince. 1685, 1686.
Smith, George. Pliny's panegyrick upon the Emperor Trajan. 1702, 1730.
Epistle and panegyric, by several hands. 2 vols 1724.
Toland, John. XXXV letters. 1726.
Melmoth, William. The letters. 2 vols 1747, 1748, 1757, 1770, 1777 etc.
Boyle, John (Earl of Orrery). The letters. 2 vols 1751, 1751, Dublin 1751.

Propertius

Nott, John. Propertii Μονόβιβλος: or that book of elegies entitled Cynthia. 1782. *See also under* Catullus, *above.*

Quintilian

Warr, John. The declamations. 1686.
Guthrie, William. M. Fabius Quinctilianus his Institutes of eloquence. 2 vols 1756.
Patsall, J. Quintilian's Institutes of the orator. 2 vols 1774.

Sallust

C[alle], C[aleb]. Patriae parricida. 1683. Catiline.
A new translation of all the works. 1687, 1692.
Rowe, John. Caius Crispus Sallustius made English. 1709, 1715, 1726, Dublin 1727, London 1739.
Clarke, John. C. Crispi Sallustii bellum Catilinarium et Jugurthinum. 1744. With Latin.
Mair, John. Catiline's conspiracy. Edinburgh 1741, 1793.
Gordon, Thomas. The works. Dublin 1744, Glasgow 1762.
Lee, Henry. C. Crispi Sallustii bellum Catilinarium et Jugurthinum. 1744. With Latin.
Cooke, William. The works. 1746.
Rose, William. The history of Catiline's conspiracy and the Jugurthine war. 1751, 1757.
Maffett, Hugh. The Catiline and Jugurthine wars. Dublin 1772.
Sydney, George Frederic. The history of Catiline's conspiracy. 1795.

Seneca

P[ordage], Samuel. Troades. 1660, 1679.
W[right], John. Thyestes. 1674.
L'Estrange, Sir Roger. Seneca's morals by way of abstract. 1678, 1682, 1685, 1688, 1693, 1699, 1702, 1711, 1718, 1722, 1729 etc.
Sherburne, Sir Edward. Troades: or the royal captives. 1679.
— The tragedies translated into English verse. 1700, 1702. Medea, Phaedra, Troades.

T[albot], James. L. Annaeus Seneca's Troas. 1686.
Blackmore, Sir Richard. Agamemnon. In his A collection of poems, 1718.
Select epistles on several moral subjects. 1739.
Medea. Chester 1776.
Morell, Thomas. The epistles. 2 vols 1786.

Silius Italicus

Ross, Thomas. The second Punic War. 1661, 1672.

Statius

Howard, Sir Robert. Achilleis. In his Poems, 1660.
Pope, Alexander. The first book of Statius his Thebais. In B. Lintot, Miscellaneous poems, 1712 etc.
Lewis, William Lillington. The Thebaid. 2 vols Oxford 1767, London 1773.
See also Jabez Hughes *under* Claudian, *above*.

Suetonius

The history of the twelve Caesars, by several hands. 1672. 1677, 1698, 1704.
Hughes, Jabez. The lives of the XII Caesars. 2 vols 1717.
Clarke, John. Caii Suetonii Tranquilli XII Caesares. 1732, 1739, 1761. With Latin.
Thomson, Alexander. The lives of the first twelve Caesars. 1796.

Tacitus

The annals and history, made English by several hands. 3 vols 1698, 1716. Bk 1 by Dryden.
Gordon, Thomas. The works. 2 vols 1728–31, 4 vols Dublin 1728–32, London 1737, 1753.
—— The life of Agricola. 1763.
Melmoth, William. A dialogue concerning oratory. In his Letters on several subjects vol 2, 1749.
Aikin, John. Cn Julii Agricolae vita. 1774. With Latin.
—— A treatise on Germany, and the life of Agricola. 1778.
Murphy, Arthur. The works. 4 vols 1793, 8 vols 1811, 2 vols 1813 etc.

Terence

Hoole, Charles. Publii Terentii comoediae. 1667, 1676. With Latin.
Echard, Laurence, Sir Roger L'Estrange et al. Terence's comedies. 1694, 1698, 1705, 1718, 1724, 1733, 1741.
Cooke, Thomas. P. Terentii Afri comoediae ('Terence's comedys). 3 vols 1734, 2 vols 1748–9. Prose, with Latin.
Patrick, Samuel. Terence's comedies. 2 vols 1745, 1750, 1767. Prose, with Latin.
Gordon, Thomas. The comedies. 1752. Prose.

Colman, George. The comedies translated into familiar blank verse. 1765, 2 vols Dublin 1766, 1768, London 1810 etc.
A new translation of the Adelphi. [1774]. Blank verse.
A new translation of the Heautontimorumenos, and Adelphi. Oxford 1777. Prose. Preface criticizes Colman's choice of blank verse.

Tibullus

Dart, John. The works. 1720.
Grainger, James. A poetical translation of the elegies. 2 vols 1759. With Latin.
Henley, Samuel. An essay towards a new edition of Tibullus. 1792. With Latin.
See also under Catullus, *above*.

Virgil

Dryden, John, et al. The works: containing his Pastorals, Georgics and Aeneis. 1697, 1698, 1709, 1716, 1721, 1730 etc.
Sedley, Sir Charles. The fourth book of Virgil [Georgics]. In his Miscellaneous works, ed [W.] Ayloffe 1702.
Brady, Nicholas. Virgil's Aeneis. 4 vols 1716–17.
Maitland, Richard (Earl of Lauderdale). The works. [1718], 2 vols [1730?].
Trapp, Joseph. The Aeneis translated. 2 vols 1718–20.
—— The works. 3 vols 1731.
Benson, William. Virgil's husbandry, or an essay on the Georgics: being the first book, translated into English verse. 1725.
Pitt, Christopher. An essay on Virgil's Aeneid: being a translation of the first book. 1728.
—— The Aeneid, translated. 2 vols 1740.
—— The works in Latin and English: the Aeneid translated by the Rev Mr Christopher Pitt, the Eclogues and Georgics, with notes on the whole, by the Rev Joseph Warton. 4 vols 1753, 1763, 1778, 3 vols 1790.
Strahan, Alexander. The first Aeneid. 1739.
—— The Aeneid. 2 vols 1767.
Hamilton, James. Virgil's Pastorals, as also his Georgicks. Edinburgh 1742. Prose.
[Davidson, Joseph?]. The works translated into English prose. 2 vols 1748 (2nd edn). With Latin.
Martyn, John. Publii Vergilii Maronis eclogae decem. 1749. Prose, with Latin.
Hawkins, William. The Aeneid. 1764. Bks 1–6.
Andrews, Robert. The works. Birmingham 1766.
Nevile, Thomas. The Georgics. Cambridge 1767.
Mills, William. The Georgics. 1780.
Melmoth, William Henry. The whole genuine works. [1790?].
Beresford, James. The Aeneid. 1794.   E. J. K.

B. TRANSLATIONS FROM FRENCH

Other trns from French are included under Minor Prose Fiction, col 975 above. This section is deliberately restricted to authors of literary significance.

Jean Le Rond d'Alembert

Reflections on the use and abuse of philosophy in matters that are properly relative to taste. In Alexander Gerard, An essay on taste, 1757, 1764.
Henderson, C. Miscellaneous pieces in literature, history and philosophy. 1764.
An account of the destruction of the Jesuits in France. 1766.
Eulogy of Fénelon. 1770.
Letters between d'Alembert and Frédéric II. 1789.
Life of Massillon. In Massillon, Sermons, 1797.
Aiken, J. Select eulogies of members of the French Academy. 2 vols 1799.

Arabian Nights

Arabian nights entertainments, translated into French by M. Galland and now done into English. 8 vols 1705–8, 1713–5 (4th edn) etc.

Jean Baptiste de Boyer, Marquis d'Argens

The Jewish spy. 5 vols 1739 [–40?], 1744; Jewish letters, Newcastle 1746, 4 vols Dublin 1753, 5 vols 1766.
Chinese letters. 1741, 1743; Chinese spy, 1751, 1752.
New memoirs establishing a true knowledge of mankind. 2 vols 1747.
The impartial philosopher: or the philosophy of common sense. 2 vols 1749.
Philosophical dissertations on the uncertainty of human knowledge. 2 vols 1753.
Derrick, [Samuel]. Memoirs of the Count du Beauval. 1754.

Philosophical visions. 1757.
The life and amours of Count de Turenne. 1762.

François Thomas Marie de Baculard d'Arnaud

Fanny: or the happy repentance. 1766 (*see* D. F. Bond, MP 35 1938), 1777.
The history of Sidney and Volsan. Dublin 1772.
Murdock, J. The tears of sensibility. 2 vols 1773 (including The cruel father, Rosetta, The rival friends, Sidney and Silli), 1783 (with 2 new pieces).
Lee, S. Warbeck. 2 vols 1786, Dublin 1786.
The history of count Gleichen. 1786.

Théodore Agrippa d'Aubigné

Hell illuminated. 1679; The Catholic confession of M. de Sancy, 1686.
The true history of the Duke de Guise. 1683.
[Scott, Sarah]. Life. 1772.

Marie Catherine Le Jumel de Barneville Baronne d'Aulnoy

Hickman, Spencer. The novels of Elizabeth Queen of England. 2 pts 1680-1.
The ingenious and diverting letters of the Lady —'s travels into Spain. 3 pts 1691-2, 3 vols 1692, 1697 (4th edn), 1708 (8th edn), 1717, 1735; tr T. Brown, Memoirs of the Court of Spain, 1692, 1701; and J.P., The present Court of Spain, 1693.
B., P. Memoirs of the Court of France. 1692; tr A.B. 1697.
Tales of the fairies. 1699; tr B.H., The history of the tales of the fairies, 1716, 3 vols 1728; 1717 (new trn); 1749 (new trn), 1758, 1781; Queen Mab: containing a select collection of tales of the fairies, 1782, 1799; also in The diverting works of the Countess d'Anois, 1707.
Memoirs of the Court of England. 1707, 2 pts 1708.
The diverting works of the Countess d'Anois. 1707.
Hypolitus Earl of Douglas; to which is added the Amours of Count Schlick, by Aeneas Sylvius. 2 vols 1708, 1741 etc.
Secret memoirs of the Duke and Duchess of O . . . . 1708.
The history of the Earl of Warwick. 1708.
The Prince of Carency: a novel. 1719; also as The history of John of Bourbon, Prince of Carency, 1723.
A collection of novels and tales. 2 vols 1721, 3 vols 1737-49.

Jean Louis Guez de Balzac

W., R. Aristippus: being a discourse concerning the Court. 1659, tr [T. Sheridan], Aristippus abrid'd, 1703; tr Basil Kennet, Politics in select discourses which he call'd his Aristippus, 1709.
[Sheridan, T.] A survey of princes and their favourites, in Aristippus abrid'd. 1703: tr Basil Kennet, The French favourites: or the seventh discourse of Politics, 1709.

Jean Barbeyrac

The spirit of the ecclesiastiks of all sects and ages, as to the doctrines of morality. 1722.
Carew, G. An historical and critical account of the science of morality. In S. von Pufendorf, Of the law of nature and nations, 1729 (4th edn), 1749. Barbeyrac's discourse does not appear in earlier edns.

Charles Batteux

Principles of translation. 1760.
Miller, M. A course of belles-lettres: or the principles of literature. 4 vols 1761.

Pierre Bayle

Miscellaneous reflections occasion'd by the comet [of] December 1680. 2 vols 1708.

A philosophical commentary on these words of the Gospel, Luke xiv 23: Compel them to come in. 2 vols 1708.
De La Roche et al. Dictionary. 4 vols 1709; tr P. Desmaizeaux, An historical and critical dictionary, 4 vols 1710, 5 vols 1734-8 ('revised'); tr J. P. Bernard, T. Birch et al, A general dictionary, historical and critical, 10 vols 1734-41; tr T. Brewster, The life of Persius, in his Satires of Persius, 1751.

Pierre Augustin Caron de Beaumarchais

Griffith, Elizabeth. The school for rakes. 1769 (adapted from Eugénie), 1769 (3rd edn).
Griffith, Elizabeth. The barber of Seville: or the useless precaution. 1776, 1776.
Holcroft, Thomas. The follies of a day, or the marriage of Figaro: a comedy. 1785 (performed 1784), 1785.
James, Charles. Tarare: an opera. 1787.
H., C. The two friends, or the Liverpool merchant: a drama. 1800.
Wild, James. Frailty and hypocrisy. 1804. From Mère coupable.

Nicolas Boileau-Despréaux

O., N. Le lutrin. 1682; tr John Crowne, Daeneids: an heroic poem in four cantos, 1692 (with adaptations and curtailments); tr John Ozell 1708, 1711, 1714 ('corrected'), Dublin 1730, Glasgow 1752; tr N. Rowe with A letter giving some account of Boileau and his works, 1708.
Soames, Sir William. The art of poetry. 1683, 1708; rev J. Dryden 1710, 1715, Glasgow 1755.
Dennis, John. Miscellanies in verse and prose. 1693. Contains select trns of Boileau's epistles, satires etc.
An essay upon sublime. Oxford 1698 (from a version of Longinus), 1712.
Cobb, Samuel. An ode on the taking of Namur. 1712.
Ozell, J. et al. Works. 3 vols 1712-13, 1714, 2 vols 1736.
A discourse on satires. 1730. In Walter Harte, Essay on satire. *See also* T. Ryley, A new abridgement of the rules of French prosodia, 1758 (with 4th satire).

Louis de Boissy

The Frenchman in London: a comedy. 1755, Glasgow 1758.
Conway, H. S. False appearances: a comedy altered. 1789, Dublin 1789. From Dehors trompeurs.

Charles Bonnet

The contemplation of nature. 2 vols 1766.
Boissier, J. L. Philosophical and critical inquiries concerning Christianity. 1787, 1791; tr as Interesting views of Christianity, 1787 (excerpts), Dublin 1789.
Wesley, John. Conjectures concerning the nature of future happiness. 1790, 1792.

Jacques Bénigne Bossuet

[Montague, W. A.] An exposition of the doctrine of the Catholique church. Paris 1672, 2 pts 1685, 1 vol 1686, 1735, 1790; tr J. Johnston, Paris 1685, 1686; tr J. Delusseux?, Paris 1729.
A sermon preached at the funeral of Mary Terese of Austria. 1684; tr as A sermon preached at the funeral of a person of the highest quality in France, 1696.
A conference with Mr Claude concerning the authority of the Church, 1684, 1687.
A treatise of communion under both species. 1685; tr John Davis. A treatise of communion under both kinds, 1687.
[Johnston, Joseph]. A pastoral letter to the Catholics of his diocese to keep their Easter. 1686.
A discourse on the history of the whole world. 1686; tr R. Spencer, An introduction to, or a short discourse concerning universal history, 1730 (abridged); tr J. Elphinston, A view of universal history, 2 vols 1778, 1778.

Quakerism-a-la-mode: or a history of quietism. 1698.
Maxims and reflections upon plays. 1699.
An account of the education of the Dauphine. In T. Lefèvre, A compendious way of teaching languages, 1723, 1750.
The history of the variations of the Protestant churches. 2 vols Antwerp 1728, 1742 etc.
The history of France to Charles IX. 4 vols Edinburgh 1762.
Orations pronounced at [the] interment [of] the Duchess of Orleans and Louis of Bourbon, Prince of Condé. 1799, 1800.

Dominique Bouhours

The life of the renowned Peter d'Aubusson. 1679.
Christian thoughts for every day of the month. 1680, 1683, 1685 (with Meditations upon the most important truths of the Gospel), 1692, 1700, 1705.
[Dryden, J.?] The life of St Ignatius, founder of the Society of Jesus. 1686.
Dryden, J. The life of St Francis Xavier of the Society of Jesus. 1688, Dublin 1743.
The art of criticism. 1705; tr J. Oldmixon, The arts of logick and rhetorick, 1728.
Ingenious thoughts of the fathers of the Church. 1727.

Louis Bourdaloue

C., A. Practical divinity: being a regular series of sermons. 4 vols 1776.

Gabriel de Brémond

The cheating gallant: or the false Count Brion. 1677; rptd in Modern novels vol 2, 1692.
The happy slave. 3 pts 1677, 1 vol 1686, 1699 (in A collection of novels vol 2, 1692); also in S. Croxall, A select collection of novels vol 4, 1720, 1729.
Morgan, James. The viceroy of Catalonia: or the double cuckold. 1678, [1700?].
The triumph of love over fortune. 1678; rptd in Modern novels vol 4, 1692.
The apology: or the genuine remains of Madam Maria Manchini. 1679.
B., B. Hattige: or the amours of the King of Tamaran. 1680, 1683; rptd in Modern novels vol 1, 1692; and as The beautiful Turk in S. Croxall, Select collection of novels vol 3, 1720; 1729 (new version).
S., E. The Princess of Montferrat. 1680; rptd in Modern novels vol 10, 1692.
Bellon, P. The pilgrim. 2 vols 1680-1, 1684 (pt 2 only by Bellon); rptd in A collection of pleasant modern novels, 1700.
Bellon, P. Gallant memoirs: or the adventures of a person of quality. 1681; rptd in Modern novels vol 9, 1692.
D'Urfey, T. Sir Barnaby Whigg: or no wit like a woman's. 1681. Partly from Le double cocu.
The amorous abbess: or love in a nunnery. 1684. Part of Le cercle.

Claude Buffier

Ryley, T. A new abridgement of the rules of French prosodia. 1758 (2nd edn).
First truths and the origins of our opinions explained. 1780.

George Louis Leclerc Comte de Buffon

Two memoirs: the one on preserving and repairing forests; the other on the culture of forests. In T. H. Haddington, A treatise on the manner of raising forest trees, Edinburgh 1761.
The natural history of the horse. 1762.
Kendrick, W. and J. Murdoch. The natural history of animals, vegetables and minerals. 6 vols 1775-6; tr William Smellie, Natural history, general and particular, 9 vols 1781, 1785, 1791; Natural history abridged, including the history of the elements, the earth etc,

Dublin 1791; Barr's Buffon: natural history, 10 vols 1792, 1797.
The natural history of birds. 9 vols 1793; abridged 1791, Perth 1791, 2 vols 1792; Natural history of birds, fish insects and reptiles, 5 vols 1798, 1808.

Jean Jacques Burlamaqui

Nugent, T. The principles of natural and political law. 2 vols 1748-52, 1763, Boston 1792.

Jean Calvin

The answer and judgment of Calvin concerning the English book of common prayer to Mr Knox. In An apology for English dissenters, 1707.

Denis Dominique Cardonne

A miscellany of Eastern learning, translated from Turkish, Arabian and Persian manuscripts. 2 vols 1771.

Anne Claude Philippe de Tubières Grimoard de Pestels de Levis, Comte de Caylus

Oriental tales. 2 vols [1745] etc.
The pleasures of retirement preferable to the joy of dissipation. 1774.

Jacques Cazotte (and Chavis)

Heron, Robert. Arabian nights: being a continuation of the Arabian nights entertainments. 4 vols Edinburgh 1792.
The devil in love. 1793, 1798.

Robert Challes

Aubin, P. The illustrious French lovers. 2 vols 1727. The Des Prés – Mlle de l'Epine episode also tr as The unnatural mother, 1734.

Isabelle Agnès Élisabeth van Tuyll van Serooskerken, Madame de Charrière (née van Zuylen)

Letters written from Lausanne. 2 vols 1799.

François Jean de Chastellux

An essay on public happiness. 2 vols 1774, 1790 (as Essays on historic subjects).
[Grieve, G.] Travels in North America, in 1780, 1781 and 1782. 2 vols 1787. Wrongly attributed to J. Kent.

Louis Maïeul Chaudon

Historical and critical memoirs of the life and writings of Voltaire. 1786.

François de Chavigny de la Bretonnière

The inconstant lover: an excellent romance. 1671. Trn of L'amant parjure?
The crafty lady: or the rival of himself. 1683. From L'amant artificieuse.
The gallant hermaphrodite. 1687.

Urbain Chevreau

Decoisnon, D. The mirror of fortune. 1676.
The great Scanderberg: a novel. 1690.
The history of the world, ecclesiastical and civil. 4 vols (vol 1 in 2 pts) 1703.
Remains. In Miscellaneous remains of Cardinal Perron vol 2, 1707.

Charles Nicolas Cochin and Jérôme Charles Bellicard

Observations upon the antiquities of Herculaneum. 1753 (for 1754?), 1756.

Marie Jean Antoine Nicolas de Caritat, Marquis de Condorcet

The life of Turgot. 1787.
The life of Voltaire; to which are added Memoirs of Voltaire, written by himself. 2 vols 1790.
Reflections on the French Revolution 1688 and that of 10th August 1792. In J. B. d'Aumont, Narrative of the proceedings relating to the suspension of the King of the French, 1792.
Plan of the French constitution and declaration of rights. 1793.
Outlines of an historical view of the progress of the human mind. 1795, Philadelphia 1796, Baltimore 1802.

Pierre Corneille

Rutter, J. The Cid. 1638, 1650; tr John Ozell, The Cid: or the heroick daughter, 1714. *See also* C. Cibber's adaptation, The heroick daughter: or Ximena, 1712, 1719, 1792.
Lowther, Sir W. Polyeuctes: or the martyr. 1655.
Lowther, Sir W. Horatius: a Roman tragedy. 1656; tr K. Philips, Horace, 1667 (in part) completed by Sir J. Denham 1669, 1678 etc; tr Charles Cotton, Horace: a French tragedy, 1671; adapted William Whitehead, The Roman father, 1750.
Philips, Katherine. Pompey: a tragedy. 1663, 1667 [in Poems]; tr E. Waller, C. Sedley & S. Godolphin, Pompeius called the Great, 1664; adapted C. Cibber, Caesar in Egypt, 1725.
Carlell, Lodowick. Heraclius, Emperour of the East: a tragedy. 1664 (1st performed c. 1655); adapted as Honorius: an opera, 1734 (English and Italian).
The mistaken beauty: or the lyar. [1671], 1685; adapted by Sir R. Steele, The lying lover, 1704, 1711; and S. Foote, The lyar, 1776, 1784 etc.
Dancer, John Nicomede: a tragicomedy. 1671.
[Cibber, Colley?] Cinna's conspiracy: a tragedy. 1713.
Aspinwall, S. Rodogune, or the rival brothers: a tragedy. 1765.
Melite. 1776. Prose.
Brand, Hannah. The conflict. 1798 (in her Plays and poems). From Don Sanche.

Thomas Corneille

R., T. The extravagant shepherd. 1653.
[Bulteel, J.?] The amorous Orontus: or the love in fashion. 1665. From L'amour à la mode.
The feign'd astrologer. [1668?]; adapted by J. Dryden, An evening's love: or the mock astrologer, 1671.
Ravenscroft, E. Dame Dobson: or the cunning woman. 1684. Adapted from La devineresse.
Centlivre, S. Love at a venture. 1706. Adapted from Le galand double.
Hatchett, W. The rival father: or the death of Achilles. 1730.
Young, E. The brothers. 1753. Adapted from Persée et Démétrius.
Francis, P. Constantine, 1754; tr Lady Sophia Burrell, Maximian, 1800.
Stratford, Agnes. The labyrinth: or fatal embarrassment. [1795?], Dublin [1795] (Ariane adapted). *See also* A. Murphy's adaptation, The rival sisters, 1786.

Claude Prosper Jolyot de Crébillon (Crébillon Fils)

Humphreys, S. Letters from the Marchioness de M*** to the Count de R***. 1735, 1737, 1758, 1766, Dublin 1766.
The skimmer: or the history of Tanzai and Néadarné. 2 vols 1735, 1742, 1 vol 1748. Tanzai et Néadarné, re-titled L'écumoire.
The sopha: a moral tale. 2 vols 1742, 1781.

Clancy, M. The wanderings of the heart and mind: or the memoirs of Mr de Meilcour. 1751. From Les égarements du coeur.
[Kimber, Edward]. The happy orphans. 1758, 1759, 2 vols 1770. From Les heureux orphelins, 1754, a trn of E. Haywood, The fortunate foundlings, 1744.
The secret history of Zeolsinesul, King of the Kofingns: being an authentic account of the amours of Lewis XV. 1761. From Les amours de Zeokinizul.
The night and the moment: a dialogue. 1770.
Acajou et Zuphile: a tale. nd.

Prosper Jolyot de Crébillon (Crébillon Père, the dramatist)

Murphy, A. Zenobia. 1768. From Rhadamiste et Zénobie.

Jean Pierre de Crousaz

A new treatise on the art of thinking. 2 vols 1724.
A commentary upon Mr Pope's four ethic epistles intituled an Essay on man, wherein his system is fully examined. 1738, 1740, 1742; also in Lady M. Pennyman, Miscellanies, 1740.
Tacheron, G. S. New maxims concerning the education of youth, and a discourse concerning pendantry. 2 pts 1740.

Hercule Savinien de Cyrano de Bergerac

'A person of honour'. Satyrical characters and handsome descriptions in letters. 1658.
St Serf, Sir T. (or Sydserf). Σεληναρχια [Selenarchia]: or the government of the world in the moon. 1659. Attributed to Sir R. Stapleton. From Histoire comique contenant les estats et empires de la lune. Also tr A. Lovell 1687 (with Sun, below).
Lovell, A. Comical history of the states and empires of the world of the moon and sun. 1687. From Histoire comique des estats et empires de la lune et du soleil. Also tr Samuel Derrick, A voyage to the moon with some account of the solar world, 1753.

André Dacier

Gildon, Charles. An essay upon satyr. In Miscellany poems, 1692, 1695.
Life of Marcus Aurelius. In The meditations of M. Aurelius Antoninus, 4 pts 1692 (5th edn). Also tr Jeremy Collier 1701, 1708, 1726 (in The emperour M. Antoninus; his conversations with himself).
Rowe, Nicholas. The life of Pythagoras. 1707.
The works of Plato abridg'd. 2 vols 1701, 1720, 1749 etc.
Rowe, T. The life of Hannibal. In a Supplement of Plutarch's lives, 1737.

Florent Carton Dancourt

Vanbrugh, Sir John. The confederacy. 1705. Also tr R. Estcourt, The fair example, 1706. From Les bourgeoises à la mode.
Shadwell, Charles. The humours of the army: a comedy. 1713. Adapted from Les curieux de Compiègne.
Vanbrugh, Sir John. The country house: a farce. 1715, 1719 (in A collection of plays vol 4), 1740 (as La maison rustique).

René Descartes

A discourse of a method. 1649.
The passions of the soule. 1650.
Discourses of the mechanicks. 1665 (in T. Salusbury, Mathematical collections and translations vol 2); Another trn: The use of geometrical playing-cards, as also a discourse of the mechanick powers, 1697. From Traité de la méchanique.
Molyneux, W. Six metaphysical meditations. 1680. From Meditationes (Latin), 1641; (French), 1647.

François Michel Chrétien Deschamps

Cato of Utica; a tragedy. 1716; also tr J. Ozell, Cato, 1716.

Pierre François Guyot Desfontaines

Lockman, J. The travels of Mr John Gulliver, son to Captain Lemuel Gulliver. 2 vols 1731; Le nouveau Gulliver: ou voyage de Jean Gulliver, fils du capitaine Gulliver, tr 'M.L.D.F.', 2 vols 1730 (by Desfontaines).
[The history of the revolutions of Poland. 1736, rev Desfontaines, author unknown.]
[Gunning. Memoirs of Madame de Barneveldt. 2 vols Dublin 1796. Trn of work falsely attributed to Desfontaines.]

Jean Bonaventure des Périers

Cymbalum mundi: or satyrical dialogues upon several subjects. 1712, 1723.
Walpole, Horace. The magpie and her brood: a tale [verse]. Strawberry Hill 1764.

Philippe Néricault Destouches

The married philosopher. 1732. From Le philosophe marié; also adapted by E. Inchbald, The married man, 1789.
Foote, S. The comic theatre. 3 vols 1762. Contains: The young hypocrite; the spendthrift; The triple marriage; The imaginary obstacle; The sisters; The libertine; The legacy; The generous artifice; The whimsical lovers.
Murphy, A. The citizen. 1763. Adapted from La fausse Agnès.
Murphy, A. Know your own mind. 1777. From L'irrésolu.
O'Beirne. Generous imposter. Performed 1780, from Le dissipateur.
Holcroft, Thomas. School for arrogance. Performed 1791, from Le glorieux.
[Inchbald, E.] Next-door neighbours. Performed 1791. From L'amour usé; another trn, Cross partners, 1792.

Denis Diderot

Les bijoux indiscrets: or the indiscreet toys. 1749.
An essay on blindness. [1750?] (3rd edn). From Lettre sur les aveugles.
A plan of the French Encyclopaedia. 1752. With d'Alembert.
Dorval: or the test of virtue. 1767. Another trn, The natural son, 2 vols 1799 as novel. From Le fils naturel.
Select essays from the Encyclopedy. 1772. With d'Alembert.
Hooper, W. The two friends of Bourbon. In S. Gessner, New idylls, 1776, 1797.
Tooke, William. On sculpture. In E. M. Falconet, Pieces written by Falconet and Diderot, 1777.
'A lady'. The family picture. 1781. Also tr and adapted J. Burgoyne, The heiress, 1786; T. Holcroft, Deserted daughter, 1795. From Père de famille.
James the fatalist and his master. 3 vols 1797. From Jacques le fataliste.
The nun. 2 vols 1797, Dublin 1797 etc. From La religieuse.

Claude Joseph Dorat

The fatal effect of inconstancy: or the letters of the Marchioness de Syrce. 2 vols 1774, 1774.

Jean Baptiste Dubos

The history of the league made at Cambray. 1712.
Some observations on the [masks of the Ancients]. In G. Turnbull, Three dissertations, 1740.
Nugent, T. Critical reflections on poetry, painting and music. 3 vols 1748.

Charles Pinot Duclos

A course of gallantries: or the inferiority of the tumultous joys of the passions to the serene pleasures of reason. 2 vols 1775.

Charles Alphonse du Fresnoy

De arte graphica: the art of painting; together with an original preface containing a parallel betwixt painting and poetry, by Mr Dryden. 2 pts 1695 (from Roger de Piles French trn?), 1716, 1750, 1769; also tr James Wills 1754; Thomas Birch 1765; W. Mason, The art of painting, with annotations by Sir Joshua Reynolds, York 1783, rptd in Reynolds's Works vol 3, 1798, 1801 etc.

Pierre Samuel Dupont de Nemours

Considerations upon the political situations of France, Great Britain and Spain. 1790.

Anne Louise Dumesnil-Morin, Elie de Beaumont

The history of a young lady of distinction. 2 vols 1754.
The history of the Marquis de Roselle. 2 vols 1765.
The new Clarissa. 2 vols 1768.

Louise Florence Pétronille de Tardieu d'Esclavelles, Marquise de la Live d'Epinay

The conversations of Emily. 2 vols 1787.

Jacques Esprit

See La Rochefoucauld, below.

François Eudes de Mézeray

Bulteel, J. A general chronological history of France. 3 vols 1683.

Christophe Barthélemi Fagan

Garrick, David. The guardian: a comedy. 1771, 1773 (4th edn) etc. Adapted from La pupille.

Etienne Maurice Falconet

See Diderot, above.

Charles Simon Favart

The Englishman in Bordeaux: a comedy. Dublin 1763, London 1764.
Lloyd, R. The capricious lovers: a comic opera. 1764.
The reapers, or an Englishman out of Paris: an opera. 1770.
Garrick, David. A new dramatic entertainment called a Christmas tale. 1774. From La fée urgèle.
La belle Arsène: an heroic opera. 1795.

François de Salignac de la Mothe Fénelon

The maxims of the saints explained, concerning the interior life. 1698.
Littlebury, Isaac. The adventures of Telemachus. Pt 1, 1699; Five parts complete, 1700 (2nd edn), 1700, 1703, 1705, 1707, 2 vols 1721 (tr I. Littlebury, with A. Boyer and A. Oldes), 1728, 1740, 1 vol Jena 1749, London 1766 (7th edn) etc.

Other translations
The adventures of Telemachus in English verse. Book 1, 1712.
Tr J. Ozell. The adventures of Telemachus, with the adventures of Aristonous. 2 vols 1715, 1720, 1734-5.
The adventures of Telemachus attempted in English blank verse [bks 1-2]. 1729.

The adventures of Telemachus: the translation revised by Mr Des Maizeaux, and a discourse of epic poetry [by A. M. Ramsay]. 2 vols 1742, 1767 (3rd edn), 1 vol 1779 (7th edn), Rouen 1781, 2 vols Saint-Malo 1784, Rouen 1788, London 1802.
Tr J. Kelly. The adventures of Telemachus. 2 vols 1743.
Tr Gibbon Bignall. A new translation of Telemachus in English verse. 2 vols 1756, 1 vol Hereford 1790, Dublin 1792.
Tr J. Hawkesworth, 1768, Dublin 1769, London 1784, 2 vols [1794]; rev G. Gregory 2 vols 1795, 1800 etc.
Tr W. H. Melmoth. [1770?].
Tr P. Proctor. 2 vols 1774.
Tr M. A. Meilan. The adventures of Telemachus translated into English verse. 4 vols 1776, 2 vols 1792-4.
A new translation with Ramsay's Discourse of epic poetry. 2 vols Aberdeen 1776.
Tr Tobias Smollett. The adventures of Telemachus. 2 vols 1776, 1 vol Dublin 1793, 2 vols 1795.
Tr S. Leacroft. The adventures of Telemachus in English verse [bks 1-2]. 1785.
Tr G. Canton. The adventures of Telemachus translated into blank verse [bk 1]. 1788.
Tr Isaac d'Israeli. Specimen of a new version of Telemachus [in verse]; to which is prefixed a defence of poetry. 1791 (2nd edn).
Tr 'F. Fitzgerald' (Charles Taylor). A new translation. 1792.
Tr J. Youde. The adventures of Telemachus in blank verse. 3 vols Chester [1793?].
Hickes, G. Instructions for the education of a daughter. 1707, 1713 (3rd edn), Edinburgh 1750 etc; also tr as The accomplished governess: or short instructions for the education of the fair sex, 1752.
A discourse on Christian perfection. 1711; also tr as A discourse on Christian perfection, 1711 (Works of Armand de Bourbon, ch 30 of Instructions et avis); tr as Directions for a holy life and the attaining Christian perfection, Bristol 1747 (2nd edn), London [1795?]; another trn Dublin 1759. From Entretien sur la piété.
Boyer, A. A demonstration of the existence, wisdom and omnipotence of God. 1713, Glasgow 1755; also tr S. Boyse 1749.
Ozell, J. The adventures of Aristonous. In Adventures of Telemachus, 2 vols 1715; also tr M. A. Meilan 1774 (verse); tr John Falla 1799 (verse).
Nelson, Robert. Pastoral letter concerning the love of God. 2 pts 1714-15.
Barker, Jane. The Christian pilgrimage: or a companion for the holy season of Lent. 1718.
Delacoste, J. Private thoughts upon religion, in several letters. 1719.
[Grant, W.] Two essays on the balance of Europe. 1720, 1752 (in Somers tracts vol 4).
Pious thoughts concerning the knowledge and love of God [from Œuvres spirituelles]. 1720, Glasgow 1723.
Stevenson, W. Dialogues concerning eloquence; with a letter concerning rhetoric and poetry. 1722, Glasgow 1750, 1760 etc.
[Ozell, J.] Fables and dialogues of the dead. 1723 (2nd edn), 1735; also tr G. Lyttelton 1760; A new translation, 2 vols 1776; tr Cooke [1797?].
Select letters and discourses. In Devotional tracts concerning the presence of God, 1724, 1757.
The lives and most remarkable maxims of the antient philosophers. 1726.
The adventures of Melesichton. In S. Croxall, Select collection of novels vol 2, 1729.
Bellamy, Daniel. Twenty-seven tales and fables, [with] an essay on the fable. 1729, Dublin 1736. With French.
An essay proving the immortality of the soul. 1730.
Dissertation on pure love. 1735, 1738, Dublin 1739, London 1750.
Gifford, Nathaniel. Tales and fables. 1736.

[Freoul, J. B. de]. The characters and properties of true charity. 1737.
Meditations and soliloquies on various religious subjects. 1744, Ipswich 1756. From Œuvres spirituelles.
Proper heads of self-examination for a King. 1747; also tr as Directions for the conscience of a King, 1751.
Advice and consolation for a person in distress and dejection of mind. Glasgow 1750. From Instructions et avis, ch 14-15.
A letter concerning rhetoric, poetry, history and a comparison between the antients and moderns. Glasgow 1750. *See also* Stevenson's trn of Dialogues, *above.*
Letters upon divers subjects concerning religion and metaphysics. Glasgow 1750.
An extract from a discourse on humility. Dublin [1750?].
An extract from a discourse on prayer. Dublin 1759.
Elphingston, J. Fables composed for the Duke of Burgundy. Glasgow 1760; rev Daniel Bellamy, Ethic tales and fables, [1770].
Houghton, R. Part of the spiritual works. 2 vols Dublin 1771.
[Barclay, Bishop?]. Five pieces [A discourse of Christian perfection, an extract from a discourse on humility etc]. 1779.
Clowes, J. Pious reflections for every day of the month. Manchester 1797, London [1797?], 1799, Stourport 1810. From Manuel de piété.
Kendall, J. Extracts from the writings. 1797, 1805 etc.

Claude Fleury

The history, choice and method of studies. 1695.
A historical account of the manners and behaviour of the Christians. 1698; also tr John Wesley, The manners of the antient Christians, 1749, 1795 (abridged); tr C. Cordell, The manners of the Christians, Newcastle 1786.
Discourses on ecclesiastical history. 1721, 1734.
B[eaver], J[ohn]. The history of the origine of the French laws. 1724.
An historical catechism: containing a summary of the sacred history and Christian doctrine. 2 vols 1726; also tr as An historical catechism, 1740, 1786 (Petit catéchisme only); tr as A larger historical catechism, Newcastle 1786.
[Herbert, H. and G. Adams]. The ecclesiastical history. 5 vols 1727-32; also tr W.H., A regular historical account of the first rise of the Reformation, Corke 1764 (from vols 25-7 of Ecclesiastical history).

Jean Pierre Claris de Florian

Walbeck, W. The life of Cervantes. Leeds 1785.
Robinson. Works. 2 vols 1786.
Morgan, E. The history of Numa Pompilius. 3 vols 1787; also tr as The adventures of Numa Pompilius, 2 vols 1787, Brussels 1790, London 1798 etc.
Robson, H. Look before you leap: a comedy [La bonne mère]. 1788, Dublin 1789.
The turtle-dove: a tale. Caen 1789. Verse.
Galatea: a pastoral romance, imitated from Cervantes. Dublin 1791, Boston 1798.
Morgan, E. Stella: a pastoral romance. 2 vols 1791; also tr Susannah Cummyng, Estelle with an essay upon pastoral, 2 vols 1798.
New tales.
Gonzalva of Cordova: or Granada conquered. 2 vols Dublin 1793, 3 vols 1793.
Fletcher, J. Pieces from Florian. 1795.

Bernard Le Bouyer de Fontenelle

D[ryden], J. New dialogues of the dead. 3 pts 1683, 1 vol 1684, [1685?], 1692 (in Modern novels vol 12); also tr John Hughes, Dialogues of the dead, 1708, 1730, Glasgow 1754.

D[omville], Sir W[illiam]. A discourse on the plurality of worlds. Dublin 1687; also tr Aphra Behn, The theory or system of several new inhabited worlds lately discover'd, 1688, 1690 (A discovery of new worlds), 1700, 1718 (in A. Behn, All the histories vol 2); also tr John Glanvill, A plurality of worlds, 1688, 1695, 1702, 1719; also tr W. Gardiner, Conversations on the plurality of worlds, 1715, 1728 (as A week's conversation on the plurality of worlds; to which is added Mr Addison's defence of the Newtonian philosophy), 1737, Glasgow 1749, Edinburgh 1753, London 1757, 1769 etc; also tr as Conversations on the plurality of worlds: a new translation by a gentleman of the Inner Temple, 1760; also as A conversation on the plurality of worlds, 1783.

Behn, Aphra. The history of oracles and the cheats of the pagan priest. 2 pts 1688, 1 vol 1699, Glasgow, 1753; also tr [S. Whatley], The history of oracles, 1750.

Motteux, P. Of pastorals. In W.J.'s trn of Le Bossu, Treatise of the epick poem, 1695.

Boyer, A. Letters of wit, politics and morality. 1701.

The prize of wisdom: a dialogue between Anacreon and Aristotle. In The works of Anacreon and Sappho, 1713.

Chamberlayne, J. The lives of the philosophers of the Royal Academy in Paris. 1717. Epitome of Histoire de l'Académie Royale.

The elogium of Sir Isaac Newton. 1728; also tr as An account of the life and writings of Sir Isaac Newton, 1728.

R., C. The elogium of Peter I, Czar of Muscovy. 1728.

[Price, John]. The northern worthies: or the lives of Peter the Great and of Catherine. 1728, 2 pts 1730.

Borton, William. The eloge of Professor Boerhaave; to which is added a discourse on biography in general. 1749.

Whitehead, William. The school for lovers: a comedy. 1762. Founded on Fontenelle's Testament.

Russel, George. Lettres galantes. In The works of G. Russel vol 2, Cork 1769.

Jean Henri Samuel Formey

Philosophical miscellanies on various subjects. 1759.

The logic of probabilities. [1760?].

A discourse on the death of Marshall [George] Keith. Edinburgh 1764.

A concise history of philosophy and philosophers. 1766, Glasgow 1767.

An ecclesiastical history. 2 vols 1766.

Foreman, S. Elementary principles of the belles lettres. 1766, Glasgow 1767.

François de Sales

An introduction to a devout life. [London?] 1669 ('Catholic edn'), [London?] 1675, 1686; another edn fitted for the use of Protestants, Dublin 1673, 1675; also tr W. Nicholls, An introduction to the devout life, 1701; also tr J.S., The spiritual direct[or] of devout and religious souls, [London?] 1704; also tr R. C[halloner], Philothea: or an introduction to a devout life, 1770 (2nd edn) etc.

Antoine Furetière

The city romance. 1671. Attributed wrongly to Scarron by translator.

Pierre Gassendi

Three discourses of happiness, virtue and liberty. 1699.

Stéphanie Félicité Ducrest de Saint-Aubin, Marquise de Sillery, Comtesse de Genlis

The theatre of education. 4 vols 1781 (2nd edn), Dublin 1783, 3 vols 1787 (another trn). From Le théâtre à l'usage des jeunes personnes.

Adelaide and Theodore: or letters on education. 3 vols 1783, 1784, 1 vol 1796 (4th edn). From Adèle et Théodore.

Holcroft, Thomas. Tales of the castle. 5 vols 1785, 4 vols Dublin 1785, 5 vols 1787 (3rd edn), 5 vols 1806 (8th edn) etc. From Les veillées du château.

Holcroft, Thomas. Sacred dramas. 1786, Dublin 1786.

The beauties of Genlis: being a collection of tales from Adele and Theodore; the tales of the castle; the theatre of education and sacred dramas. [Perth 1787].

Religion considered as the only basis of happiness. 2 vols Dublin 1787.

Inchbald, Elizabeth. The child of nature: a dramatic piece. 1788, 1789, Dublin 1789, Philadelphia 1790. From Zélie.

Letters of a governess to her pupils. 3 vols 1792.

Short account of the conduct of Made de Genlis since the Revolution. Perth 1796.

Beresford, James. The knights of the swan, or the Court of Charlemagne: a historical tale. 3 vols 1796. From Les chevaliers du cygne. Also abridged by C. Butler as The age of chivalry, 1799.

Hoare. Captive of Spilbury. Performed 1798. From Le souterrain.

The young exiles: or correspondence of some juvenile emigrants. 3 vols 1799.

Rash vows: a novel. 3 vols 1799, 2 vols Dublin 1799. From Les voeux téméraires.

The rival mothers: or calumny. 4 vols 1800, 2 vols Dublin 1801. From Les mères rivales.

Françoise d'Issembourg d'Happencourt de Graffigny

Letters written by a Peruvian princess. 1748, 1752, 2 vols 1771, 1 vol 1787, 1795, 1796 etc; also tr R. Roberts 1774; and F. Ashworth 2 vols 1782.

D., J. M. Cenia: or the suppos'd daughter. 1752. Play.

Jean Baptiste Louis Gresset

Cooper, J. G. Ver-Vert, or the nunnery parrot: an heroic poem. 1759; another trn in The repository: a select collection of fugitive pieces vol 1, 1790 (3rd edn).

Inchbald, Elizabeth. Young men and old women. Performed 1792. From Le méchant.

Antoine Guénée

Lefanu, P. Letters of certain Jews to Voltaire: containing an apology for their own people. 1777, 2 vols Dublin 1777.

Thomas Simon Gueullette

Macky, [Spring]. Chinese tales: or the wonderful adventures of the Mandarin Fum-Hoam. 1725; tr Thomas Stackhouse 1781.

Humphreys, Samuel. Peruvian tales, related in one thousand and one hours. 1734, 2 vols Dublin 1734, London 1735, 1764 (4th edn), 1765, 1786. Vol 3, tr Humphreys with J. Kelly 1742; vol 4 tr [Kelly]? 1745.

Mogul tales with a prefatory discourse on the usefulness of romances. 2 vols 1736, 1743.

Flloyd, T. Tartarian tales: or a thousand and one quarters of hours. 1759, Dublin 1764, London 1785.

Lavergne de Guilleragues

L'Estrange, Sir Richard. Five love letters from a nun to a cavalier. 1678; pt 2, 1681 etc; tr [J. Blankett or P. Stevens], Letters from Portugal, 1777; tr W. Bowles as M. Alcoforado, Letters from a Portuguese nun, 1808. Often attributed to Alcoforado.

Jeanne Marie Guyon

The life of Lady Guion now abridged. 2 vols Bristol 1772; also tr as The exemplary life of the pious Lady Guion, [and] a new translation of her method of prayer, Dublin 1775, Bristol 1806; tr John Wesley as An extract of the life of Madam Guion, 1776.

Brooke, T. D. A short and easy method of prayer. 1775; also tr Dublin 1775 (above); tr as The worship of God in spirit and in truth: or a short and easy method of prayer, Bristol 1775.

Antoine Hamilton

Boyer, Abel. Memoirs of the life of the Count de Grammont. 1714, 1719 (with key), 1759, 1760 etc.
Select tales. 2 vols 1760.
History of May-flower: a Circassian tale. Salisbury 1796 (2nd edn). From Fleur d'épine.

Jean Hardouin

An apology for Homer, wherein the true nature and design of the Iliad is explained. 1717.

François Hédelin, Abbé d'Aubignac

The whole art of the theatre. 1684.

Claude Adrien Helvétius

[Mudford, W.] De l'esprit: or essays on the mind. 1759.
The child of nature, improved by chance: a philosophical novel. 2 vols 1774. From De l'homme. Also tr William Hooper, A treatise on man, his intellectual faculties and his education, 2 vols 1777.
A catechism; also the picture of a King and of a priest, from the Bible. 1796.

Charles Jean François Hénault

Nugent, T. A new chronological abridgement of the history of France. 2 vols 1762.

Paul Henri Dietrich, Baron d'Holbach

See Literary Relations, col 94, above.
[Johnson, W. M.] Christianity unveiled. New York 1795. Trn attributed to Boulanger on title-page.

Marie Huber

The world unmask'd: or the philosopher the greatest cheat. 1736, 1786. Trn attributed to Defoe and Bernard Mandeville.
Letters concerning the religion essential to man. 1738, 1761. *See also* Natural and revealed religion explaining each other, in Harleian miscellany vol 6, 1744; *and* The divine instinct recommended to men, 1781.

Pierre Daniel Huet

A treatise of romances and their original. 1672; also tr S. Lewis, The history of romances, 1715. *See also* Letter to Segrais upon the original of romances, in S. Croxall, Select collection of novels vol 1, 1722.
[Gale, T.] A treatise of the situation of Paradise. 1694.
The history of the commerce and navigation of the ancients. 1717.
Memoirs of the Dutch trade. [1718?], 1722.
Diana de Castro: a novel. [1720?].
A philosophical treatise concerning the weakness of the human understanding. 1725; also tr E. Combe, An essay concerning the weakness of the human understanding; to which is added the dissertation concerning Sublimity of the style of the Holy Scriptures, translated by Mr Ozell, 1725 (2nd edn).

Pierre Jurieu

The policy of the clergy of France. 1681.
Vaughan, Walter. The last efforts of afflicted innocence. 1682.
Gilbert, Claudius. A preservative against the change of religion. 1683.
The history of the council of Trent. 1684 (abridged).

The accomplishment of the Scripture prophecies: or the approaching deliverance of the Church. 2 vols 1687, 1689; A continuation of the accomplishment of the Scripture prophecies, 1688; tr E. May, Remarkable extracts, Henley 1790; A selection of prophecies, in J. M. Dant, The illuminator [1800?].
The pastoral letter directed to the Protestants in France. 1689.
Judgement upon the question of defending our religion by arms. 1689.
Legal exceptions and lawful prejudices against Popery. 1689.
The reflections on the extasies of I. Vincent, the shepherdess of Saou. 1689.
Seasonable advice to all Protestants in Europe. 1689.
Fleetwood, W. A plain method of Christian devotion. 1692 (22nd edn), 1702, 1724 (25th edn), [1730?].
A pastoral letter written on the occasion of the death of the late Queen of England. 1695.
C., J. A critical history of the doctrines and worships of the Church. 2 vols 1705.
A prophecy of the late revolution in France. In C. Love, Strange and wonderful predictions, 1792, [1800?]. In R. Nixon, Original Cheshire prophecy, [1800?].

Laurent Angliviel de la Beaumelle

Lennox, Charlotte. Memoirs for the history of Madame de Maintenon, and of the last age. 5 vols 1757.

Etienne de la Boétie

A discourse of voluntary servitude. 1735.

Jean de la Bruyère

The characters: or manners of the age, with the characters of Theophrastus. 2 pts 1698–9, 1 vol 1700, 1702, 1708, 1709, 1713; also tr Eustace Budgell, The moral characters of Theophrastus, 1713, 1714, 1715, 1718, 1743, Edinburgh 1751; also tr N. Rowe 2 vols York 1776.
Works. 2 vols 1776.

Gautier de Costes de la Calprenède

Cotterell, Sir C. Cassandra: the fam'd romance. 1652, 1652, 1661, 1664, 1667, 1676, 1725, 1737; also tr J. Banks, The rival kings: or the loves of Oroondates and Statista, 1677; also tr N. Lee, The rival queens: or the death of Alexandra the Great, 1677; 1703 (another trn).
Loveday, R. Cleopatra: hymen's praeludia [pt 1]. 1652–5, 1668 (pts 1–6); pts 7–8, 1663; pts 9–12, 1659; other complete edns 1674, 1687, 1698; also tr N. Lee, Gloriana: or the Court of Augustus Caesar, 1676.
Davies, John. Pharamond. 4 pts 1662; also tr J. Phillips, A fam'd romance in twelve parts, 1677.

Choderlos de Laclos

Dangerous connections: or letters collected in a society by M.C**** de L**** and published for the instruction of other societies. 4 vols 1784; also adapted Thomas Holcroft, Seduction, [1787] (play).

Charles Marie de la Condamine

A succinct abridgement of a voyage [to] the inland parts of South America. 1747.
[Maty, M.] A discourse on inoculation. 1755.
Journal of a tour to Italy. 1763; also as An extract from the observations made in a tour to Italy, 1768.
An account of a savage girl caught in the woods of Champagne. [1760?]; also in M. A. Memmie Le Blanc, Account, 1768.

Jean Baptiste la Curne de Sainte-Palaye

Dobson, Susannah. Memoirs of ancient chivalry. 1784.
Dobson, Susannah. The literary history of the troubadours. 1779 (abridged).

Marie Madeleine Pioche de la Vergne, Comtesse de la Fayette

The Princess of Montpensier. 1666. Segrais lent his name to author's works.

Porter, P. Zayde: a Spanish history. 2 vols 1678, 1690; also tr S. Croxall, in Select collection of novels vol 1, 1720; 1729; also tr E. Griffith in A collection of novels vol 1, 1777; 1780.

'A person of quality'. The Princess of Cleves. 1679, 1688 etc, at least 6 edns in total by 1777; also tr S. Croxall, vol 2, 1720; 1729; tr E. Griffith, vol 2, 1777, as above.

Floyd, Ann. Fatal gallantry: or the secret history of Henrietta, Princess of England. 1722.

Jean de la Fontaine

[Mandeville, Bernard de]. Some fables after the easie and familiar method of La Fontaine. 1703, [1710?] (as Aesop dress'd). Also various trns and adaptations, including Fables and tales in French and English, 1734; Samuel Humphreys, Congreve et al, Tales and novels in verse by several hands, 2 vols 1735, 1 vol Edinburgh 1762 (from Contes et nouvelles en vers); J. Lockman, The loves of Cupid and Psyche, in verse and prose, 1744; The spectacles: a tale [in verse], 1753.

Jean François de la Harpe

Hiffernan, P. The Earl of Warwick: a tragedy. 1764, 1767; also tr T. Francklin, The Earl of Warwick, 1766, 1767 etc.

François de la Mothe le Vayer

The great prerogatives of a private life. 1678.

D['Avenant], W. Notitia historicorum selectorum: or animadversions upon the antient and famous Greek and Latin historians. Oxford 1678.

Antoine Houdart de la Motte

Samber, R. One hundred new court fables, written for the instruction of princes. 1721.

Johnson, H. Romulus: a tragedy. 1724.

François de la Rochefoucauld

D[avies], J[ohn]. Epictetus junior: or maximes of modern morality. 1670 (from unauthorized, 'pre-original' 1664 edns). Also tr Aphra Behn, Moral reflections, in Miscellany, together with reflections on morality or Seneca unmasqued, 1685 (attributed to 'Duke of Rushfaucave'); also tr Marquise de Sably, Moral maxims and reflections, 1694 (claims to be first complete trn), 1706 (2nd edn); tr W. Beauvoir, Discourse on the deceitfulness of humane virtues, to which is added the Duke de La Rochefoucauld's moral reflections, 1706; also tr 'A gentleman of Pembroke Hall in Cambridge', nd; tr Moral maxims, 1749; 1766 (another trn); tr Maxims and moral reflections, 1775; rev L.D. 1781; Edinburgh 1783, London 1784, 1788, 1791, 1795, Edinburgh 1796, Ludlow 1799; also tr as Duke de La Rochefoucault's celebrated Maxims and moral reflections [in verse], 1799.

Mlle de la Roche-Guilhem

C., E. Asteria and Tamberlain, or the distressed lovers: a novel. 1677, 1680 (as Royal lovers: or the unhappy Prince).

Almanzor and Almanzaida: a novel. 1678.

V., N. The great Scanderberg: a novel. 1690; also in Modern novels vol 11, 1692.

M., Z. Zingis: a Tartarian history. 1692; also tr D.W. Gent, Taxila: or love prefer'd before duty, 1692.

Scanderberg the great. In S. Croxall, Select collection of novels vol 5, 1722, 1729.

The history of female favourites. 1772.

Antoine de la Sale

[Decker, T. or R. Tafte]. The batchelor's banquet. 1677. First tr 1603, from Les quinze joyes de mariage, also tr The fifteen comforts of rash and inconsiderate marriage, 1681, 1682, 1683 (3rd edn with 3 new comforts), 1694; 1760 (another trn).

Jean Louis Ignace de la Serre, Sieur de Langlade

Memoirs of the life of Molière. In Works of Molière vol 1, 1739.

René le Bossu

J., W. Treatise of the epick poem. 1695, 2 vols 1719 (with Dacier's Essay upon satire and Fontenelle's Of pastorals); also as A general view of the epic poem, and of the Iliad and Odyssey, in Pope's Iliad vol 1, 1725 etc.

Jean Leclerc

See under Locke, in Literary Relations, col 108, above.

Five letters concerning the inspiration of the Holy Scriptures. 1690, 1690 (2nd edn); also in William Lowth, A vindication of divine authority, Oxford 1692; also tr as A historical vindication of The naked Gospel, 1690; also tr as Free and important disquisitions concerning the inspiration of the Holy Scriptures, 1750.

Memoirs of Emeric Count Teckely. 1693.

Brown, T. The life of the famous cardinal, Duke de Richlieu. 2 vols 1695.

Brown, T. Twelve dissertations out of Le Clerk's Genesis. 1696.

A treatise of the causes of incredulity. 1697.

Reflections upon what the world commonly calls Goodluck and Ill-luck, with regard to lotteries. 1699, 1758.

Parrhasiana: or thoughts upon several subjects, as criticism, history etc. 1700.

The lives of the primitive fathers. 1701.

Character of Mr Lock's method, with his advice about the use of common-places. 1706.

P., T. F. The life and character of Mr J. Locke. 1706, 1713, 1714, 1740.

Tindal, M. Extracts and judgement of the rights of the Christian Church asserted. 1708 (from Bibliothèque choisie vol 10); also tr as The rights of the Christian church adjusted, 1711.

O[zell], J. Account of the Earl of Clarendon's History of the civil wars. 2 pts 1710.

Against indifference in the choice of our religion. In H. de Groot, The truth of the Christian religion, 1711, 1729, 1743, 1754 etc; also tr as Concerning the choice of our opinion amongst the different sects of Christians, 1711, 1729, 1754 etc.

Extracts and judgement of the Characteristicks of men, manners, opinions, times [by Shaftesbury]. 1712.

An abstract and judgement of Dr Clark's polemical and controversial writings against the atheists, deists etc. 1713.

Judgement and censure of Dr Bentley's Horace. 1713.

A funeral oration upon the death of Mr P. Limborch. 1713.

Theobald, L. Observations upon Mr Addison's Travels through Italy. 1715.

The life of Dr Burnet, late Bishop of Sarum. 1715.

Rooke, John. History of Alexander's expedition: containing a criticism upon Quintus Curtius. 1729.

Marc Antoine le Grand

Cartouche, or the robbers: a comedy. 1722.

[Forrest, Ebenezer]. Momus turn'd fabulist: an opera. 1729. With L. Fuzelier.

Pierre Jean Baptiste le Grand d'Aussy

Tales of the twelfth and thirteenth centuries. 2 vols 1786, 1789 (as Norman tales), [1800?] (4th edn, as Tales of the minstrels).

Way, G. L. and G. Ellis. Fabliaux or tales, abridged from French manuscripts of the xii and xiii centuries. 2 vols 1796, 1800, 3 vols 1815 ('corrected').

Antoine Marin Lemierre

Starke, M. The widow of Malabar: a tragedy. 1791. Performed 1790. From Veuve du Malabar.

Anne ('Ninon') de Lenclos

Memoirs. 2 vols 1776.

Nicolas Lenglet du Fresnoy

Rawlinson, R. A new method of studying history. 2 vols 1728, 1730.

Morant, P. Geographia antiqua et nova: or a system of antient and modern geography. 1742, 1768.

[Flloyd, T.] Chronological tables of universal history to the year 1743. 2 pts 1762.

Geography for children: or a short and easy method of teaching and learning geography. 1783, 1787, 1791 (6th edn), Taunton 1804 (30th edn).

Marie Leprince de Beaumont

Letters from Emerance to Lucy. 2 vols 1766.

The young misses' magazine: containing dialogues between a governess and several young ladies. 2 vols 1767 (2nd edn), 1776, 1783, 1793, Edinburgh 1795 etc.

The virtuous widow: or memoirs of the Baroness de Batteville. Dublin 1767.

The new Clarissa: a true history. 2 vols 1768.

Moral tales. 2 vols 1775.

Dialogues for Sunday evenings. 2 vols [1797]. Tr from Magasin des pauvres.

Alain René Lesage

Turkish tales: consisting of several extraordinary adventures; with the history of the sultaness of Persia and the visiers, translator unknown. 1708; tr W. King (with Joseph Browne?), The Persian and Turkish tales compleat, translated into French [by Pétis de la Croix and Lesage] and now into English, 1714, 1809; tr Ambrose Philips, The thousand and one days: Persian tales, [1709]?, 1714, 3 vols 1722 (3rd edn), 1750 (6th edn), 1783; tr E. Button gent [1754?]. From Persian tales compiled by Seid Mocles (Moclah) and Turkish tales by Chec Zade (Shaiksadah).

Le diable boiteux: or the Devil upon two sticks. 1708 (incomplete, abridged), 1708, 1711 (2nd edn), 2 vols 1729 (full text, trn differs considerably) (6th edn), 1741 (7th edn); also tr [T. G. Smollett?], The Devil upon crutches, 2 vols [1748?], 1750; 1 vol Edinburgh 1770, 2 vols Berwick 1773 (another trn). Over 20 edns of various trns by 1800, with imitations and adaptations, notably The Devil upon crutches in England: or night scenes in London, 1756; also William Combe, The Devil upon two sticks in England: being a continuation of Le Diable boiteux of Le Sage, 6 vols 1790–1.

The history and adventures of Gil Blas de Santillane. 2 vols 1716, 3 vols 1732 (3rd edn), 4 vols 1737–42, 1 vol 1744 (5th edn), 1771. Also tr T. G. Smollett, The adventures of Gil Blas, 4 vols 1749, 1750, 1 vol [1760?], 4 vols 1766, 1 vol 1773, 1778, 1780, 1781, 1782, 1785, 1789, 1792, 1793, 1794, 1797, 1798 etc; tr Percival Proctor 2 vols 1774. Also numerous imitations, including The history and adventures of Don Alfonso Blas de Lirias, son of Gil Blas de Santillane, translated from the Spanish original, 1741; and Henri Le Maire, The French Gil Blas: or adventures of H. Lanson, 4 vols 1793.

The history of the count de Belflor and Leonora de Cespedes: the force of friendship. Both in S. Croxall, Select collection of novels vol 3, 1720; vol 2, 1729.

The comical history of Estevanille Gonzales. 1735; also tr as The history of Vanillo Gonzales, 2 vols 1797.

Lockman, [J.] The bachelor of Salamanca: or memoirs of Don Cherubin de la Ronda. 2 vols 1737–9, 1 vol 1767, Dublin 1784.

Une journée des Parques: or a day's work of the Fates. Cambridge 1745.

The adventures of Robert Chevalier, captain of a privateer in New-France. 2 vols 1745.

Garrick, D. Neck or nothing: a farce. 1766, 1774. From Crispin rival de son maître.

A continuation of the comical history of Don Quixote by Fernandez de Avellanedoc. 1784.

Louis Jean Levesque de Pouilly

The theory of agreeable sensations. 1749, 1766, 1774.

Simon Nicolas Henri Linguet

Political and philosophical speculations on the distinguishing characteristics of the present century. 1778.

Memoirs of the Bastille. 2 pts Dublin 1783.

Boardman, J. A critical analysis of all Mr Voltaire's works with occasional disquisitions on epic poetry, the drama, romance. 1790.

Gabriel Bonnot de Mably

Observations on the Romans. 1751.

Phocion's conversations. 1769. From Entretiens de Phocion.

Observations on the Greeks. In D.Y., Translations from the French, Lynn 1770, 1776; also tr Chamberland, Observations on the manners, government and policy of the Greeks, Oxford 1784.

Françoise d'Aubigné, Marquise de Maintenon

The letters of Madam de Maintenon and [others] in the age of Lewis XIV; to which are added some characters. 1753, 1754, 2 vols 1759.

Nicolas Malebranche

Taylor, T. Treatise concerning the search after truth; to which is added the author's Treatise of nature and grace. 2 vols Oxford 1694. Another edn of A treatise of nature and grace, 1695; tr Richard Sault, Search after truth: or a treatise of the nature of the humane mind, 2 vols 1694–5. From De la recherche de la vérité.

[Motteux, P. A.] Christian conferences: demonstrating the truth of the Christian religion and morality. 1695. From Conversations chrétiennes, tr J. Shipton, A treatise of morality, 2 pts 1699.

Marguerite de Valois, Reine de Navarre

Novels, tales and stories, translated by several hands. Pt 1 (all pbd), [1750?]. First trn of Heptameron by R. Codrington, 1654.

Pierre Carlet de Chamblain de Marivaux

Le paysan parvenu, or the fortunate peasant: being the memoirs of Mr —. 1735 (pts 1–4). Also freely adapted as The fortunate villager: or memoirs of Sir Andrew Thompson, 1757.

The life of Marianne. 3 vols 1736–42 (in pts); also tr and adapted to be morally improving, probably by Mary Collyer, ptd under following titles, differing considerably in content: The virtuous orphan: or the life of Marianne (between 1737–43, no known copy), [1747 (2nd edn)?]; Memoirs of the countess de Bressol, 2 vols 1743; The life and adventures of Indiana, the virtuous orphan, 1746 (abbreviated, characters renamed, pbd as original work), 1755; The virtuous orphan: or the life of Marianne Countess of *****, 4 vols 1784 (in Harrison's Novelist's Magazine). See H. S. Hughes, MP 15 1917: 'before the publication of Clarissa, at least 3 translated versions of Marianne were at hand.'

Jean François Marmontel

[Roberts, R.] Select moral tales. 1763; also tr C. Dennis and R. Lloyd, Moral tales, 3 vols 1764-6, 1767, 3 vols Edinburgh 1768, London 1781, 1781, [c. 1783], Manchester [1790?], London 1792, 2 vols 1795, 1 vol 1799, 3 vols 1800; tr as New moral tales, 1792-4, 1794; The tales of an evening followed by the honest Breton, 4 vols 1792-4 (from Nouveaux contes moraux); tr M. Pilkington, Tales selected and abridged, 1799.

[Griffith, Elizabeth]. The platonic wife. 1765. L'heureux divorce adapted.

Belisarius. 1767, 1784 (with Fragments of moral philosophy), 1786, 1794; another trn 1767, Dublin 1767, London 1768, 1794, [1796], [1800?] etc; tr F. Ashmore 1789.

Trapaud, Elisha. Aglaura: a tale taken from the moral tales. 1774. Verse.

Kelly, Hugh. The romance of an hour. 1774. From L'amitié à l'épreuve.

Zemire e Azore: a comic opera. 1779, 1781, 1783.

Burgoyne, J. Lord of the manor. 1781. Performed 1780. Opera based on Silvain.

The Peruvian: an opera. 1786.

Morton, T. Columbus. Performed 1792. From Les Incas.

The shepherdess of the Alps. 1794.

Jean Baptiste Massillon

Sermons. In various edns and trns from Trevoux 1705; also tr W. Dodd, 1769, 1776; tr H. Crabb, Discourses, in Sermons on practical subjects, 1796; tr W. Dickson 3 vols Edinburgh 1797 (with d'Alembert's life of Massillon).

An episcopal charge addressed to the Catholic clergy of Great Britain and Ireland. 1784.

Pierre Louis Moreau de Maupertuis

A dissertation of the different figures of the coelestial bodies. In J. Keill, An examination of Dr Burnet's theory of earth, Oxford 1734.

The figure of the earth, determined from observations made at the Polar circle. 1738.

A letter upon comets. In An essay towards a history of the principal comets, 1769, 1770.

Guillaume Alexandre de Méhégan

Fox, H. A view of universal modern history from the fall of the Roman Empire. 3 vols 1778.

Louis Sebastien Mercier

Memoirs of the year two thousand five hundred. 2 vols 1772, 1 vol Philadelphia 1795, London 1799, Liverpool 1802.

The distressed family: a drama. 1787. From L'indigent.

Inchbald, Elizabeth. Next door neighbours: a comedy. 1791. From Mercier, L'indigent and Néricault Destouches, Le dissipateur.

Fragments of politics and history. 2 vols 1795.

Freeman, Harriot A. Astraea's return: or the halcyon days of France in the year 2440: a dream. 1797.

New pictures of Paris. 2 vols 1800.

Kemble. Point of honour. 1800. From Le déserteur.

Honoré Gabriel de Riquetti, Comte de Mirabeau

Doubts concerning the free navigation of the Scheld claimed by the emperor. 1785. From Doutes sur la liberté de l'Escaut.

[Romilly, Sir S.] Considerations on the order of Cincinnatus. Philadelphia 1786, London [1786?].

Price, Richard. Reflections on the observations on the importance of the American revolution. Philadelphia 1786.

Enquiries concerning lettres de cachet. 2 vols 1787. From Des lettres de cachet.

The secret history of the Court of Berlin. 2 vols 1789, 1 vol Dublin 1789.

Gallery of portraits of the National Assembly. 2 vols 1790, Dublin 1790.

H., A. W. An address on the civil constitution of the clergy. [1791].

White, J. Speeches pronounced in the National Assembly. Dublin 1792.

Jean Baptiste Poquelin de Molière

Dates of first performance are given in brackets when known. Close trns have been emphasized at the expense of free adaptations and merged texts deriving from several plays. From 1714 all 31 plays were available in Ozell's trn of Works. See Literary Relations, col 120 above.

Collections

Ozell, J. The works of Monsieur de Molière. 6 vols 1714. All 31 plays.

B[aker], H[enry], [James Miller], [J.M.] Clare et al. Works. 8 vols 1732 (17 plays), 10 vols (31 plays), 1739, 1748, Glasgow 1751, London 1753, 1755.

The works of Molière. 6 vols Berwick 1771. 31 plays.

Various plays also appeared in Samuel Foote et al, The comic theatre, 5 vols 1762. Vol 4 *includes* The amorous quarrel; Les précieuses ridicules; L'étourdi: the blunderer; Le mariage forcé. Vol 4 *includes* Le médecin malgré lui; Le misanthrope; The gentleman-cit.

Etourdi: or the blunderer. nd. Further trns and adaptations by Sir G. Etherege, The comical revenge, 1664 (1664); by J. Dryden, Sir Martin Mar-All: or the feign'd innocent, 1668 (1667); S. Centlivre, The busybody, 1709; and her Marplot in Lisbon, 1710; A. Murphy, All in the wrong, 1761. L'étourdi, mingled with various other texts.

Etherege, Sir G. The comical revenge: or love in a tub. 1664 (1664) (with L'étourdi, above). Further trns and adaptations by J. Dryden, An evening's love: or the mock astrologer, 1671 (1668), 1671 (with T. Corneille, Le feint astrologue and Les précieuses ridicules); by E. Ravenscroft, Wrangling lovers, 1677 (1676); rev S. Centlivre, Wonder, a woman keeps a secret, 1714; Sir J. Vanbrugh, The mistake, 1706 (1705); rev W. Lyon, The wrangling lovers, 1745; J. Hewitt, A tutor for the beaus, 1737; and in S. Foote et al, The comic theatre vol 4, 1762. From Le dépit amoureux.

Flecknoe, R. The damoiselles à la mode. 1667 (1666) (with Ecole des femmes, Ecole des maris). Further trns and adaptations by A. Behn, False count: or a new way to play an old game, 1682; J. Crowne, Sir Courtly Nice: or it cannot be, 1685; T. Shadwell, Bury Fair, 1701 (1689); J. Miller, The man of taste, 1735; rev and abridged 1752 (anon, with Ecole des maris, Ctese d'Escarbagnas, Femmes savantes); The conceited ladies, in S. Foote, The comic theatre vol 4, 1762. From Les précieuses ridicules.

Sedley, Sir C. The mulberry garden. 1668. Further trns and adaptations by W. Wycherley, The gentleman dancing master, 1673 (1671-2); and The country wife, 1673; rev J. Lee 1765; rev D. Garrick, The country girl, 1766 (with Ecole des femmes); T. Otway, The soldier's fortune, 1681 (with Sganarelle); and The blunderer, in S. Foote et al, The comic theatre vol 4, 1762 (or L'étourdi?). From L'école des maris.

Medburne, M. Tartuffe: or the French puritan. 1670, 1707. Further trns and adaptations by Sir G. Etherege, She wou'd if she cou'd, 1668 (1668) (with other plays); J. Crowne, The English frier, 1690; C. Cibber, The non-juror, 1718 (5 edns), (1717); 1746, Dublin 1759; J.

M. Clare, 1732 (separate edn from 1732 Works); H. Fielding, The old debauchees, 1732, 1745 (2 versions); I. Bickerstaffe, The hypocrite, 1768, 1769, 1769, 1792. From Tartuffe.

Caryll, J. Sir Salomon: or the cautious coxcomb. 1671 (1669–70). Further trns and adaptations by W. Wycherley, The country wife, 1673; rev J. Lee 1765; rev D. Garrick, The country girl, 1766; E. Ravenscroft, The London cuckolds, 1682; Female innocence: or a school for a wife, [173?] (anon); I. Bickerstaffe, Love in the city, 1767; [A. Murphy], The school for guardians, 1767 (with Ecole des maris and L'étourdi); Mrs Cowley, More ways than one, 1783; Hoadley, Tatlers, 1797. From L'école des femmes.

Ravenscroft, E. Mamamouchi: or the citizen turned gentleman. 1671, [1672?], 1675 (with M. de Pourceaugnac). Further trns and adaptations by G. Farquhar, Love and a bottle, 1699; The gentleman cit, in S. Foote et al, The comic theatre vol 4, 1762 (anon); S. Foote, The commissary, 1765; R. B. Sheridan, The rivals, 1775. From Le bourgeois gentilhomme.

Lacy, J. The dumb lady: or the farrier made physician. 1672 (c. 1669) (with L'amour médecin). Further trns and adaptations by S. Centlivre, Love's contrivance, 1703, 1705 (rev), 1761 (with Le mariage forcé and Sganarelle); [H. Fielding], The mock doctor: or the dumb lady cur'd, 1732, 1732, 1734, Dublin 1735, London 1742, Dublin 1752, London 1753, Belfast 1763 etc; The faggot-binder: or the mock doctor, in S. Foote et al, The comic theatre vol 4, 1762. From Le médecin malgré lui.

Shadwell, T. The miser. 1672 (1671), 1691, 1714. Further trns and adaptations by J. Corey, The metamorphosis: or the old lover outwitted, 1704 (with Le médecin malgré lui); J. Hughes, The miser, in Monthly Amusement 1709 (periodical edn by J. Ozell, who adopted text for 1714 Works); rev J. Hughes (act 1 only) in Poems on several occasions, 1735; J. Ozell, 1732 (from Hughes trn, above); H. Fielding, The miser, 1733 (1734), Edinburgh 1733, Dublin 1733, London 1744, Glasgow 1748, London 1754, Glasgow 1755, London 1761, Dublin 1762; and M. de Boissy, The miser, 1752. From L'avare.

Howard, H. The playhouse to be let. 1673 (1663–4). Further trns and adaptations by T. Rawlins, Tom Essence: or the modish wife, 1677; T. Otway, Soldier's fortune, 1681, 1748 (rev) (with Ecole des maris); Sir J. Vanbrugh, The cuckold in conceit, 1706; [C. Molloy], The perplex'd couple: or mistake upon mistake, 1715; J. Arbuthnot, J. Gay and A. Pope, Three hours after marriage, 1717; J. Miller, The picture, 1745. From Sganarelle: ou le cocu imaginaire.

Shadwell, T. Psyche: a tragedy. 1675, 1690. Partly adapted from Psyche. Further adaptation P. Motteux, Loves of Mars and Venus, 1697.

Crowne, J. The country wit. 1675. Further adaptations by Sir R. Steele, The tender husband: or the accomplished fools, 1705; and R. B. Sheridan, The duenna, 1783, 1794 (1715). From Le Sicilien.

Shadwell, T. The libertine. 1676. Also adapted by W. Congreve, Love for love, 1695 (with Le misanthrope). From Le festin de pierre (Dom Juan); from Molière's text or T. Corneille's version?

Otway, T. The cheats of Scapin. 1677, 1701 etc; tr and adapted by E. Ravenscroft, Scaramouche a philosopher, Harlequin a schoolboy, 1677 (with Le mariage forcé, Dom Juan and Bourgeois gentilhomme) by J. Ozell [1730?] (never acted); The cure for covetousness (1733). From Les fourberies de Scapin.

Dryden, J. Amphitryon: or the two Sosies. 1690, 1691, 1694, 1706; rev J. Hawkesworth 1756. From Amphitryon.

Wright, T. The female virtuoso's. 1693; rev J. Gray, No fools like wits, 1721; also adapted C. Cibber, The refusal, 1721. From Les femmes savantes.

Love without interest: or the man too hard for the master. 1699; tr The forced marriage, 1762; An hour before marriage, 1772; D. Garrick, The Irish widow, 1772. From Le mariage forcé.

[Otway, T.] The hypochondriac. 1701. Further trns and adaptations, A. Behn, Sir Patient Fancy, 1678 (with L'amour médecin, M. de Pourceaugnac); Sir R. Steele, Funeral: or grief à la mode, 1702 (1701); J. Miller, Mother in law: or the doctor the disease, 1734, 1734; I. Bickerstaffe, Doctor Last in his chariot, 1769 (with L'amour médecin), 1773 (3rd edn), 1794; R. B. Sheridan, St Patrick's Day: or the scheming lieutenant, 1788 (pirated) (1775). From Le malade imaginaire.

Brown, T. Stage beaux toss'd in a blanket: or hypocrisy à la mode. 1704. From Critique de l'Ecole des femmes; further echoes of the Critique appeared in W. Wycherley, The plain dealer, 1677 (1674).

[Ozell, J.] Monsieur de Pourceaugnac: or Squire Trelooby. 1704 (possibly pirated from the Vanbrugh, Congreve text, below). Further trns and adaptations by E. Ravenscroft, The careless lovers, 1673; rev as Canterbury guests: or a bargain broken, 1695 (1694); Sir J. Vanbrugh, W. Congreve, W. Walsh, Squire Trelooby, (1704), (1706)(rev)(text unpbd); C. Shadwell, The plotting lovers, 1720; J. Ralph, The Cornish squire, 1734; T. Sheridan, Captain O'Blunder: or the brave Irishman, 1754, 1755, 1756, [1757], 1759, Belfast 1773; E. Parsons, Intrigues of the morning, (1792). From Monsieur de Pourceaugnac.

MacSwinney, O. The quacks: or love's the physician. 1705, 1745 (rev). Another trn, Love is the doctor, 1734 (anon); and J. Miller, Art and nature, 1738. From L'amour médecin.

Hughes, J. The misanthrope. 1709 (adapted by Ozell in 1714 Works). Further trns and adptations by W. Wycherley, The plain dealer, 1677 (3 edns) (1674?), 1678, 1681, 1686, 1691, 1694, 1700, 1709 etc; rev I. Bickerstaffe, 1766 (1765); W. Congreve, Love for love, 1695 (with Dom Juan); The way of the world, 1700; H. Fielding, Love in several masques, 1728; J. Kelly, Timon in love, 1733; The man hater, in S. Foote et al, The comic theatre vol 4, 1762. From Le misanthrope.

Johnson, C. Masquerade. 1719. From Dom Garcie.

Les fascheux: the impertinents. 1732. Separate edn from 1732 Works. Freely adapted by T. Shadwell, The sullen lovers, 1668 (1668), with Le misanthrope and Le mariage forcé. From Les fâcheux.

Miller, Baker et al. Georges Dandin. 1732 (from 1732 Works). Further trns and adaptations, Georges Dantin, (1747); No wit like a woman's, (1769); and T. Betterton, The amorous widow (c. 1670?, 1677); abridged as Barnaby Brittle, (1781); C. Dibdin, The metamorphosis, 1776 (1775) (with Le Sicilien).

Miller, J. The universal passion. 1737. From La princesse d'Elide.

Michel Eyquem de Montaigne

Cotton, C. Essays and an account of the author's life. 3 vols 1685–6, 1 vol 1693, 1700, 1711, 1738, 1743 etc. Also An abstract of the most curious and excellent thoughts, 1701.

Charles de Secondat, Baron de la Brède et de Montesquieu

Ozell, John. Persian letters. 1722, 1730, 1731, Glasgow 1751, 1760, Edinburgh 1773 (6th edn); tr G. Lyttlelton, Letters from a Persian in England, 1735; Letters from a Persian in England to his friends at Trebisond, Dublin 1756; freely adapted by O. Goldsmith, The citizen of the world, 1762; tr as The true history of the Troglodites, Chelmsford 1766 (extract).

Reflections on the causes of the grandeur and declension of the Romans. 1734, Glasgow 1751, 2 vols 1752, 1752 (3rd edn), Glasgow 1758 (4th edn), London 1759,

Edinburgh 1775 etc; tr as Reflections on the rise and fall of the Roman Empire, 1751. *See* E. Gibbon, Decline and fall of the Roman Empire, 1776–88. From Considérations sur les causes de la grandeur des Romains et de leur décadence.

Nugent, T. The spirit of the laws. 2 vols 1750; 'two chapters', Edinburgh 1750; 2 vols 1752, Aberdeen 1756, London 1758, Edinburgh 1762, 1768, 3 vols Berwick 1770, Edinburgh [1772], 2 vols Edinburgh 1773, London 1778, 1778, 1793, 2 vols Glasgow 1793 (from London 1773); tr F. Maseres, A view of the English constitution: the 6th book of L'esprit des loix, 1781.

Observations on government. Dublin 1751. From Réflexions sur la monarchie en Europe.

Gerard, A. An essay on taste. 1759, 1764. From Essai sur le goût in Encyclopédie vol 7, 1757.

Miscellaneous pieces. 1759.

The complete works. 4 vols 1777, Dublin 1777.

A sketch of an historical panegyric of the marshal of Berwick. 1779.

The temple of Gnidus, and Arsaces and Ismenia. 1797. Romances.

Louis Moréri

The great historical, geographical and poetical dictionary, especially out of Lewis Morery DD: his 6th edition corrected and enlarged by M. LeClerk. 1694.

Béat Louis de Muralt

Letters describing the character and customs of the English and French nations. 2 pts 1726. From Lettres sur les Anglois et les François et sur les voiages.

The divine instinct recommended to men. 1751, 1781.

Jacques Necker

Mortimer, T. A treatise on the administration of the finances of France. 3 vols 1785, 1 vol 1787.

Wollstonecraft, Mary. Of the importance of religious opinions. 1788, Philadelphia 1791, Boston 1796.

Reflexions submitted to the French nation on the intended process against Louis XVI. 1792.

Of the French revolution. 2 vols 1797.

Pierre Nicole

The new heresies of the Jesuits. 1662. With Arnauld.

Moral essays written by Messieurs du Port Royal. 2 vols 1677, 4 vols 1696.

Logic: or the art of thinking, in four parts. 1685, 1693, 1702 etc; or J. Ozell, Logic of the art of thinking, 1717. With Antoine Arnauld.

The constant belief of the Catholic Church in all ages, concerning the Eucharist. 1710.

Blaise Pascal

H[ammand], [Henry]. Les provinciales: or the mysterie of Jesuitisme. 1657, 1658, 1689 (for 1679), 1688; tr W. A[ndrews], Letters relating to the Jesuits, 1744.

Walker, J. Monsieur Pascall's thoughts, meditations and prayers. 1688; tr B. Kennet, Thoughts upon religion, 1704. From Pensées.

Charles Perrault

Ozell, J. Characters historical and panegyrical of the greatest men that have appeared in France during the last century. 2 vols 1704–5.

Samber, R. Tales of Mother Goose. 1729, 1736, 1764 (as Tales of passed times by Mother Goose), 2 vols 1785 (as Histories of passed times), 1795, 1796.

François Pétis de la Croix

See Lesage, *above.*

Antoine Pluche, 'Noël Pluche'

Humphreys, J. Spectacle de la nature: or nature display'd. 1733, 1736, 1739, 7 vols 1740–8, 1754; tr J. Kelly et al 4 vols 1743–4 (3rd edn).

Freval, J. B. de. The history of the heavens. 2 vols 1740, 1741. From Histoire du ciel.

The truth of the Gospel demonstrated. 2 vols 1751.

Jeanne Antoinette Poisson Lenormand d'Etioles, Marquise de Pompadour

Letters from 1753 to 1762 inclusive. 2 vols 1771, 1772.

François Poulain de la Barre

L., A. The woman as good as the man: or the equallity of both sexes. 1677. From De l'égalité des deux sexes.

Jean de Préchac

The heroin musqueteer. 1678; tr as The heroin musqueteer: or the female warrior, in A collection of pleasant novels, 1700.

The English Princess: or the Dutchess Queen. 1678.

The illustrious Parisian maid. 1680; tr Eliza Haywood, The disguis'd prince, or the beautiful Parisian: a true history, 1728, 1733.

The Princess of Fess. 1682.

[Spence, Ferrand]. The lovely Polander: a novel of gallantry. [1683].

H[ayes], T. The chaste seraglian, or Yolanda of Sicily: a novel. 1685; also in Modern novels vol 7, 1692.

The Serasquier Bassa. 1685, [1700?].

The grand vizier: or the history of the life of Cara Mustapha. 1685; tr Francis Philon, The true history of Cara Mustapha, 1685.

The amours of Count Teckeli and the Lady Aurora Veronica de Serini. 1686.

The disorders of Bassett: a novel. 1688.

Antoine François Prévost, called Prévost d'Exiles

The life and adventures of Mr Cleveland, natural son of Oliver Cromwell. 4 vols 1731, 5 vols 1734–5, 2 vols 1736, 3 vols 1741, 1750–2, 1760–80 etc. From Le philosophe anglois: ou histoire de Monsieur Cleveland.

Memoirs of a man of quality. 1738 (incomplete?), 1740, 1741, 1742, 1744, 1745; tr as Memoirs of a man of honour, 2 pts 1747; Memoirs of a man of quality, 2 vols 1770.

The Dean of Coleraine: a moral history. 3 vols 1742–3, 1752, 1780.

Erskine, [William?]. The memoirs and adventures of the marquis de Bretagne and duc d'Harcourt; to which is added the history of the chevalier des Grieux and Moll Lescaut. 3 vols 1743, 1770; tr as The history of the chevalier Des Grieux, 2 vols 1767; tr C. T. Smith, Manon Lescaut, 2 vols 1786. From Histoire du chevalier des Grieux et de Manon Lescaut, in Mémoires d'un homme de qualité vol 7.

The history of Margaret of Anjou, Queen of England. 2 vols 1755.

The history of a fair Greek, who was taken out of a seraglio at Constantinople and brought to Paris. [1755] (2nd edn).

Philippe Quinault

[Dancer, J.] Agrippa, King of Alba: or the false Tiberinus. 1675. A play.

Jean Paul Rabaut de Saint-Étienne

An address to the people of England. [1791?].

White, J. The history of the Revolution in France. 1793 (2nd edn).

François Rabelais

Urquhart, Sir T. The first book of the Works of Mr Francis Rabelais: containing five books of the lives etc of Gargantua and his sonne Pantagruel. Bks 1–2, 1653; The third book, 1693; bks 4–5, tr P. A. Motteux 1693–4; Whole works of Rabelais, tr Sir T. Urquhart, P. A. Motteux et al 2 vols 1708, rev J. Ozell 5 vols 1737, Dublin 1738, 4 vols 1748, 5 vols 1750 etc.

A faithful and full account of the surprising life and adventures of Dr Sartorius Sinegradibus. 1749.

Jean Racine

[Crowne, John]. Andromache: a tragedy. 1675 (adaptation). Further adaptation by Ambrose Philips, The distrest mother: a tragedy, 1712, Hague 1712, London 1718 (4th edn), 1731 (6th edn), 1735, 1749, 1756 etc. From Andromaque.

Dryden, J. Aureng-Zebe: or the Great Mogul. 1676. Adaptation of Mithridate.

Otway, Thomas. Titus and Berenice. 1677. Adaptation of Bérénice.

Boyer, Abel. Achilles, or Iphigenia in Aulis: a tragedy. 1700, 1714; tr Charles Johnson, The victim: or Achilles and Iphigenia in Aulis, 1714, 1717. Iphigénie.

Smith, E. Phaedra and Hippolytus. 1706, [1707?], 1711, 1719, [1720], 1745, Dublin 1751 etc. Another trn, Phedra, 1776 (anon). Phèdre, adapted.

Ozell, J. Britannicus. In Two tragedies: viz Britannicus and Alexander the Great, 1714; also adapted T. Gray, Agrippina, [c. 1747]. From Britannicus.

Ozell, J. Alexander the great. In Two tragedies: viz Britannicus and Alexander the Great, 1714. From Alexandre.

Ozell, J. The litigants. 1715. From Les plaideurs.

Brereton, T. Esther: or faith triumphant. 1715, 1719. From Esther.

Johnson, C. The sultaness. 1717. Further adaptation by W. Congreve, The mourning bride, 1697. From Bajazet.

Duncombe, W. Athaliah. 1722, 1726, 1746. From Athalie.

Robe, J. The fatal legacy. 1723. La Thébaïde, altered.

Letters to his son: containing rules and instructions for his conduct through life. 1785.

Louis Racine

Religion: a poem. 1754.

Andrew Michael Ramsay

The life of F. de Salignac de la Motte Fénelon. 1723.

A discourse upon epick poetry. In Fénelon, Adventures of Telemachus, 1728, 1735, 1749 etc.

Some few poems. Edinburgh 1728.

The travels of Cyrus; to which is annexed a discourse upon the theology and mythology of the Ancients. 2 vols 1728 (3rd edn), 1730, 1739, 1745, 1763, 2 vols Berwick 1765 etc; another trn, A new cyropaedia: or the travels of Cyrus, 1760 (with French); also The travels of Cyrus, 4 vols 1781 (English and Italian).

A plan of education for a young prince. 2 pts 1732 etc.

An essay upon civil government. 1732.

The philosophical principles of natural and revealed religion. 2 pts Glasgow 1748–9.

René Rapin

N., N. Reflections upon the eloquence of these times 1672; Reflections upon the use of eloquence of these times, Oxford 1672.

A comparison between the eloquence of Demosthenes and Cicero. Oxford 1672.

The comparison of Plato and Aristotle with the fathers. 1673.

Evelyn, John, the younger. Of gardens: four books, first written in Latin verse. 1673. Bk 2 rptd in the elder Evelyn's Sylva: or a discourse of forest-trees, 1679, 1706, 1729; tr James Gardiner the younger, Of gardens: a Latin poem in four books, [1706], [1718?], 1728.

Rymer, Thomas. Reflections on Aristotle's treatise of poesie. 1674, 1694.

L., A. Reflections upon ancient and modern philosophy. 1678, 1686.

Davies, J. Instructions for history. 1680.

Creech, T. Discourse of pastorals. In his Idylliums of Theocritus; from the Latin, 1684, 1791.

[Midgley, R.] The modest critick: or remarks upon the most eminent historians, antient and modern. 1689.

Taylor, T. The comparison of Thucydides and Livy. Oxford 1694.

Salvation every man's concern. 1699, [1700]; tr G. Stanhope 1728 (2nd edn).

[Kennet, Basil et al]. The whole critical works, newly translated. 2 vols 1706, 1716.

Bragge, Francis. Two odes, from the Latin of Rapin, imitated in English pindaricks. 1710.

Beckingham, C. Christus patiens, or the sufferings of Christ: an heroic poem. 1720.

Paul Rapin de Thoyras

Ozell, J. An historical dissertation upon Whig and Tory. 1717.

Tindal, N. The history of England. 15 vols 1725–31, 5 vols 1732–51 (with continuation by Tindal), 4 vols 1743–7, 21 vols 1757–63, 5 vols 1789; another trn, J. Kelly, The history of England [continued by T. Lediard], 3 vols 1732–7, 5 vols 1784–9; An abridged history of the history of England, 3 vols 1747, 3 pts 1751.

Guillaume Thomas François Raynal

The history of the stadtholdership from its origin to the present time. 1749. From Histoire du Stadhouderat.

The sentiments of a foreigner, on the disputes of Great Britain with America. Philadelphia 1775 (extract of Histoire des établissements et du commerce); tr J. O. A. Justamond, A philosophical and political history of the settlements and trade of the Europeans in the East and West Indies, 5 vols 1776, 1776, 2 vols Edinburgh 1776, 5 vols 1777, Edinburgh 1779, 5 vols 1783; another edn 'to which is added the Revolution of America', 6 vols Edinburgh 1782. From Histoire philosophique et politique des établissements et du commerce des Européens dans les deux Indes.

The revolution of America. 1781, Dublin 1781, Salem 1782, 6 vols Edinburgh 1782 (in A philosophical and political history etc, above), 1783. From Révolution de l'Amérique.

A letter to the National Assembly on the subject of the revolution. 1791. From Lettre de Raynal à l'Assemblée nationale.

Jean François Regnard

Centlivre, S. The gamester. 1705. From Le joueur. See Edward Moore, The gamester, 1753, which inspired B. J. Saurin, Béverlei, 1768.

Fielding, Henry, The intriguing chambermaid. 1734, 1750, 1765, [1780]. Le retour imprévu, adapted.

King, Thomas. Wit's last stake: a farce. 1769. From Le légataire universel.

Nicolas Anne Edmé Rétif de la Bretonne

Pictures of life: or a record of manners, physical and moral, on the close of the eighteenth century. 2 vols 1790.

Jean Francois Paul de Gondi, Cardinal de Retz

Davall, P. Memoirs. 4 vols 1723, Dublin 1777, 1 vol 1723 (abridged).

Luigi Riccoboni

An historical and critical account of the theatre of Europe. 1741, 1747, 1754 (as A general history of the stage), 1790 (as Declamation: or an essay on the art of speaking in public).

Marie Jeanne Laboras de Mézières, Riccoboni

[Brooke, Frances]. Letters from Juliet Lady Catesby. 1760, 1760, 1764 (4th edn), 1679, 1780.
The history of the Marquis de Cressy. 1765.
The continuation of the life of Marianne; to which is added the history of Ernestina. 1766. *See* Marivaux, *above, and in* Literary Relations, *col 141, above.*
Letters from the Countess de Sancerre to Count de Nancé, her friend. 2 vols 1767.
Maceuen. Letters from Elizabeth Sophia de Valière to her friend Louisa Hortensia de Canteleu. 2 vols 1772.
Stockdale, P. Letters from Lord Rivers to Sir Charles Cardigan. 2 vols 1778.
Select novels: containing the Blind boy, a fairy tale; Indian letters; and the Distressed orphan, or adventures of Ernestina. 1781.
The history of Christiana, Princess of Swabia, and the History of Eloisa de Livarot. 2 vols 1784.

Charles Rollin

Taste: an essay. 1732.
New thoughts concerning education. 1735; another trn as The method of teaching and studying the belles lettres, 4 vols 1737 (2nd edn), 2 vols 1742, 4 vols 1749, Edinburgh 1768, 3 vols 1769, 4 vols 1770 (7th edn) etc. From Traité des études.
The history of the arts and sciences of the antients. 4 vols 1737, 3 vols 1768.
The ancient history of the Egyptians, Carthaginians, Assyrians, Babylonians, Medes and Persians, Macedonians and Grecians. 10 vols 1734–6, 1738–40, 8 vols 1774, Durham [1780?] etc.
The Roman history from the foundation of Rome to the battle of Actium. 2 vols 1739, 16 vols 1754, 10 vols 1768.
The history of Cyrus. [1750?]. From Histoire ancienne.

Jean Baptiste Rousseau

[Miller, James]. The coffee-house. 1737.
The magic girdle: a burletta. 1770.

Jean-Jacques Rousseau

Collections

[Kenrick, W.] The miscellaneous works of Mr J. J. Rousseau. 5 vols 1767.
[Colebrooke, H.] Thoughts on different subjects. 2 vols 1768, Glasgow 1770, London 1788.
Works. 10 vols Edinburgh 1773–4 (2 edns?).
The beauties of Rousseau selected by a Lady [Eliza Roberts]. 2 vols 1788.

[Bowyer, W.] The discourse whether the reestablishment of arts and sciences has contributed to the refining of manners, by a citizen of Geneva. 1751. *See* Monthly Rev Aug 1751. Also tr R. Wynne, A discourse on this question whether the reestablishment of arts and sciences has contributed to purify our morals. 1752, [1753?], Dublin nd; another trn, 1760; tr W. Waring [1770?], [1779?]. From Discours des sciences et des arts etc. For trns in collections, *see above.*
A letter from M. Rousseau of Geneva to M. d'Alembert of Paris concerning the effects of theatrical entertainments on the manners of mankind. 1759. From Lettre à d'Alembert.
A discourse upon the origin and foundation of the in-

equality among mankind. 1762 (for 1761?), [1791?]. There is a ms trn by John Farrington, dated 1756.
A project of perpetual peace. 1761, 1767, 1795. From Extrait du projet de paix perpetuelle.
[Kenrick, W.] Eloisa: or a series of original letters. 4 vols 1761, Dublin 1761, London 1762, 4 vols 1764 (3rd edn), 1766, Dublin 1766 (4th edn); Julie: or the new Eloisa, 3 vols Edinburgh 1773 (separate edn or part of Works?); Eloisa, 4 vols 1776; Two letters on suicide (94–5) in Hume, Essays on suicide, 1783, 1789; 4 vols 1784, 1784; adapted by Reynolds, Eloisa 1786 (play); Julia: or the new Eloisa, 3 vols Edinburgh 1794; Eloisa, 3 vols 1795, 4 vols Dublin 1795. Julie ou la nouvelle Héloïse: the Dialogue between a man of letters and Rousseau on Romances, 1761, is the Préface de la nouvelle Héloïse. The spurious Letters of an Italian nun and an English gentleman tr from the French of J.-J. Rousseau, 4 vols 1781, 1784 etc are attributed to William Combe.
[Kenrick, W.] Emilius and Sophia: or a new system of education. 4 vols 1762; Emilius or an essay on education, 4 vols 1763; tr M. Nugent, Emilius or an essay on education, 2 vols 1763; Emilius and Sophia, 2 vols Dublin [1765?] (same trn); another trn, Emilius: or a treatise of education, 3 vols Edinburgh 1763, 1763; Emilius and Sophia (Kenrick text), 4 vols 1767, 1767; Emilius: or a treatise of education, 3 vols Edinburgh 1768, 1773 (Kenrick?); Emilius and Sophia, 3 vols Edinburgh 1773, 4 vols Dublin 1779, London 1783, 1783 (Kenrick text); Emilius and Sophia [with Sequel]. 1784 (Kenrick text); The gospel of reason [Profession de foi], [1795?]. From Emile ou de l'éducation: the spurious Emilius and Sophia or the solitaries, being a sequel to Emilius with additions to Eloisa, 1783, is added to some later edns. T. Day, The history of Sandford and Merton, 1783–9, is an imitation.
Various letters appeared in magazines, notably Scots Mag 1763–, and in A new collection of letters, in Confessions vol 3, 1790; and in Original letters of Rousseau, 1799.
An expostulatory letter from J.-J. Rousseau ... to Christophe de Beaumont, Archbishop of Paris. 1763. From J.-J. Rousseau citoyen de Genève à Christophe de Beaumont.
[Kenrick, W.] A treatise on the social compact: or the principles of politic law. 1764 (for 1763?), 1764, 1791; another trn, An inquiry into the nature of the social contract: or principles of political right, 1791, 1791, Dublin 1791; A treatise on the social compact, 1795.
Burney, C. The cunning man. 1766 (3 edns), Dublin 1767, London [1768], Edinburgh 1782, 1786; in Collection of the most esteemed farces vol 2, Edinburgh 1791. From Devin du village.
Sylvia's walk: a poem. In Miscellaneous works vol 2, 1767. From Allée de Sylvie.
Narcisse. 1767.
Letters written from the mountains. In Miscellaneous works vol 4, 1767. From Lettres écrites de la montagne. No separate edn.
[Waring, W.] [A complete dictionary of music. 1770], [1771]; A dictionary of music, 1779 (2nd edn), 1779; A complete dictionary of music, 1779, Dublin 1779. From Dictionnaire de musique; first pbd in sections in New Musical & Universal Mag ed J. French c. 1769–70.
Pygmalion: a poem. 1779. Performed 1777.
[Dialogues, and Rousseau juge de Jean-Jacques, not tr before 1800, but the latter first pbd Lichfield 1780.]
[Combe, W.?] The confessions of J. J. Rousseau [1–6], with the Reveries of the solitary walker. 2 vols 1783, 1790, 10 vols 1786–90 (vols 1–5); The confessions, part the second [bks 7–12], to which is added a new collection of letters, 3 vols 1790, 10 vols 1786–90 (vols 6–10), 3 vols Dublin 1791, London 1793. From Confessions and Rêveries du promeneur solitaire.
Martyn, T. Letters on the elements of botany. 1785, 1787, 1791, 1794 (with plates), 1796 (6th edn). From Lettres sur la botanique, with various separate edns of plates.

Jean Jacques Rutledge

Andrews, John. An account of the character and manners of the French, with occasional observations on the English. 2 vols 1770. From Essai sur le caractère et les moeurs des François.

The Englishman's fortnight in Paris: or the art of ruining himself there in a few days. Dublin 1777. From La quinzaine angloise à Paris.

A comparative view of the French and English nations. 1785.

Sainte-Palaye

See Jean Baptiste La Curne, above.

Charles de Marguetel de Saint-Denis, Seigneur de Saint Evremond

Judgement on Alexander and Caesar; and also on Seneca, Plutarch and Petronius. 1672.

Reflections upon tragedies. 1684; Mixt essays upon tragedies, comedies, Italian comedies, English comedies and operas, 1685, 1687; tr F. Spence, Miscellanea: or various discourses upon tragedy, comedy, the Italian and English comedy, and opera, 1686.

Brown, Thomas, James Drake, John Savage and Francis Manning. Miscellaneous essays, with a character [by Dr K. Chetwood?]. 2 vols 1692–4.

Female falsehood: or the unfortunate beau. 1697 (pt 1); 2 pts 1705–6 ('wherein is added the second part'). False attribution by translator; author P. de Villiers.

Factum for the Dutchess of Mazarin against her husband. In The arguments of Monsieur Herard, 1699.

Works with a life by Mr des Maizeaux. 2 vols 1700, 3 vols 1714, 2 vols 1728 ('corrected').

Memoirs of the life of John, Earl of Rochester. In Works of the Earls of Rochester and Roscommon, 1707, 1709, 1711 (as by 'Monsr St Evremont', but probably spurious).

Brown, T. The life of Petronius Arbiter. In Petronius' satyrical works, 1708, 1713, 1736.

Johnson, [H.?] An essay on Epicurus's morals. In John Digby, Epicurus's morals, 1712.

Jacques Henri Bernardin de Saint-Pierre

A voyage to the Island of Mauritius. 1775.

Paul and Virginie. 1788. Other trns: Paul and Virginia, 1789; tr [David Malthus], Paul and Mary: an Indian story, 2 vols 1789, Dublin 1789; also tr H. M. Williams, Paul and Virginia, [Paris?] 1795, London 1796, 1802 (6th edn); also tr C. Barett in Old tales and romances, 1795.

[Kendall, E. A.] The Indian cottage. 1791; tr as The Indian cottage: or a search after truth, 1797, 1799. From La chaumière indienne.

M., M. Voyages of Amasis. 1795.

Theory of tides. Bath 1795 (extract from Etudes de la nature). Full trn by Henry Hunter, Studies of nature, 5 vols 1796, 3 vols Worcester Mass 1797; Botanical harmony delineated: or applications of some general laws of nature, Worcester Mass 1797 (separate edn of 11th study); tr L. T. Rede, Studies of nature, carefully abridged with a copious index, 1798, Dublin 1800.

Hunter, Henry. A vindication of divine providence. Worcester Mass 1797.

Kendall, E. A. Beauties of Saint-Pierre. 1799.

Jaques Saurin

Chamberlayne, J. Dissertations on the most memorable events of the Old and New Testaments. Vol 1 (all pbd), 1723.

Robinson, R. Sermon 1: on the eternity of God. Cambridge 1770.

Wigley, B. Incredulity: a sermon. In A box-club sermon, [1782].

Robertson, R. and H. Hunter. Sermons. 6 vols 1796.

Rivers, D. The beauties of Saurin. 1797, [1800].

Horace Bénédict de Saussure

Martyn, T. A short account of an expedition to the summit of Mont Blanc. 1787.

Paul Scarron

Davies, J. Novels. [The fruitless precaution, The hypocrites, The innocent adultery]. [c. 1660], 1662 (4 novels); Novels [The judge in his own cause, The rival brothers, The invisible mistress, The chastisement of avarice], 1665, 1665 (made up edn of 7 novels), 1667, 1683 (8 novels, probably included D. Davies' trn of The unexpected choice, 1670), 1694, 1700 (4th edn). From Les nouvelles tragi-comiques. There were various separate edns of novels.

Cotton, C. Scarronides: or Virgile travestie. 1664, 1665, 1667, 1670, 1672, 1678, 1682, 1709 etc; tr R. M[onsey] 1665; tr J. Phillips 1672; tr A. Radcliffe, Ovid travestie, 1680; tr [J. Smyth] 1692; tr T. Brown, J. Savage et al in The whole comical works, 1700. From Le Virgile travesty en vers burlesques.

[Phillips, J.] Typhon: or the gyants war with the gods. 1665, 1704.

[Bulteel, J.?] Scarron's comical romance. 1665, 1676; tr O. Goldsmith, The comic romance of Monsieur Scarron, 1775, 2 vols Dublin [1780?]. Goldsmith adapted Brown's text from Works, below, and employed a ghost translator.

Davenant, Sir William. The man's the master. 1669. From the play Jodelet: ou le maître valet.

Davies, J. Letters to persons of the greatest eminency and quality. 1677.

Brown, T., J. Savage et al. The whole comical works. 3 vols 1700, 1703, 1712, 2 vols 1727, 1 vol 1741, 2 vols Dublin 1751–2, London 1759.

The innocent adultery [above]. In S. Croxall, Select collection of novels vol 4, 1720, 1729.

Georges de Scudéry

Boyle, R., Earl of Orrery. Mustapha. 1665. Play from Ibrahim: ou l'illustre Bassa.

Innes, J. Les femmes illustres: or the heroick harangues of illustrious women. Edinburgh 1681; Amaryllis to Tityrus: being the first heroic harangue of M. Scudery, 1681; another trn, The female orators: or The courage and constancy of divers famous queens and illustrious women, 1714, 1728 (3rd edn), 1678. From Les femmes illustres.

Madeleine de Scudéry

For corrections to BM catalogue attributions see G. Montgrédien, Bibliographie des oeuvres de G. et M. Scudéry, Revue d'Histoire Littéraire de la France 40 1933, 42 1935.

Cogan, H. Ibrahim: or the illustrious Bassa. 1652; tr E. Settle 1677 (play).

The history of Philoxypes and Polycrite [extract from Artamenes]. 1652. Full text as: Artamenes or the Grand Cyrus, tr F.G. 5 vols 1653–5; adapted for stage by T. Killigrew, Cecilia and Clorinda, 1664; by J. Dryden, Secret love, 1668; and by J. Banks, Cyrus the Great: or the tragedy of love, 1696. From Artamène: ou le Grand Cyrus.

[Wolley, Edward]. Curia politiae: or the apologies of several princes. 1654.

Gent, I. B. A triumphant arch erected and consecrated to the glory of the feminine sex. 1654, 1656.

[Davies, J. and G. H. Havers]. Clelia: an excellent new romance. 5 vols 1656–61, 1677–8. From Clélie: histoire romaine.

Phillips, John. Almahide, or the captive Queen: an excellent new romance. 1677, 1702, 1728. See also J. Dryden's adaptation, The conquest of Granada, 1672. J.P. Gent is suggested as translator by Montgrédien.

Spence, F. Conversations upon several subjects. 2 vols 1683.
An essay upon glory. 1708.

Michel Jean Sedaine

O'Brien, W. The duel: a play. 1772. From Le philosophe sans le savoir.
Dibdin, C. The deserter: a drama. 1773, 1776, 1789 etc. From Le déserteur.
Alina, or the Queen of Golconda: a serious opera. 1784.
MacNally, L. Richard Coeur de Lion: a comic opera. 1786; tr J. Burgoyne 1786, Dublin 1786, [1787?] etc.
[Ford, J. J.] A key to the lock: a comedy. 1788. From La gageure imprévue.

Marie de Rabutin-Chantal, Marquise de Sévigné

Letters to the Countess de Grignan. 2 vols 1727. Further edns and trns: E. Curll, Court secrets: or the lady's chronicle, extracted from the letters, 1727; Letters to her daughter the Countess de Grignan, 8 vols 1760-5, 10 vols 1764, Dublin 1768, 7 vols 1801.

Anne Louise Germaine Necker, Baronne de Staël-Holstein

Letters on the works and character of J. J. Rousseau. 1789.
A treatise on the influence of the passions. 1798.

Jean Terrasson

[Brerewood, F.] A discourse of ancient and modern learning. 1716.
[Brerewood, F.] A critical dissertation upon Homer's Iliad. 2 vols 1722-5.
Lediard, T. The life of Sethos, taken from the private memoirs of the ancient Egyptians. 2 vols 1732. Romance.

Antoine Léonard Thomas

Russell, William. Essay on the character, manners and genius of women. 2 vols 1773, Philadelphia 1774; tr Mrs Kindersley, An essay on the character, the manners and the understanding of women, 1781.

Abbé Maurice Elisabeth de Lavergne de Tressan

North, H. Mythology compared with history, together with some account of the ancient Druids. 1797.

Anne Robert Jacques Turgot

[Smith, Adam?] Reflections on the formation and distribution of wealth. 1793, 1795. From Réflexions sur la formation et la distribution des richesses.

Denis Vairasse d'Allais

The history of the Sevarites or Severambi: a nation inhabiting part of the third continent. 2 vols 1675-9, 1738; also adapted as Travels into several remote nations of the world by Capt Lemuel Gulliver, vol 3 1727. From Histoire des Sévarambes.

Pierre d'Ortigue de Vaumorière

H., G. The Grand Scipio: an excellent new romance. 1660 (2 pts only), 1661.
Agiatus, Queen of Sparta: or the civil wars of the Lacedemonians. 2 pts 1686.
The art of pleasing in conversation. 1691, 1699 (in A collection of pleasant novels vol 1), 1708. Wrongly attributed to Richelieu.
See also La Calprenède, above, whose Pharamond was completed by Vaumorière.

Vincent de Voiture

Letters written to several persons, translated from the French. 1657. Further trns and edns: Letters of affaires, love and courtship, 1657; Select letters in J. Dennis, Letters upon several occasions, 1696 (first letter tr J. Dryden); J. Dryden, T. Cheek and J. Dennis, Familiar and courtly letters, 7 pts 1700, 3 pts 1705, 2 vols 1724; Voiture's love letters, omitted in Mr Ozell's translation of his works, [1730?].
D['Urfey], T. Zelinda: an excellent new romance. 1676; in Modern novels vol 7, 1692. Not by Scudéry, but from Voiture's Alcidalis et Zélide. Also tr as The history of Alcidalis and Zélide, in A collection of select discourses, 1678.
Webster, J. Select poems. 1735.
Dryden, J., J. Dennis and J. Drake. Works. 1736. 1736 (3rd edn). Also tr J. Ozell, 2 vols 1736 (3rd edn), Dublin 1753 (4th edn?); and by J. Webster, Select poems, above, 1735.

François Marie Arouet de Voltaire

For trns of Voltaire's works in order of their first appearance in French, see under Literary Relations, *col 98, above. The following list is in order of appearance in English. Trns appearing in edns of* Voltaire's Works *from 1754 are not included here; see col 102, above.*

An essay upon the civil wars of France also upon the epick poetry of the European nations. 1727, 1728, Dublin 1728, London 1731 (4th edn; 'to which is now prefixed A discourse on tragedy'), 1745, Dublin 1760. From Essai sur les guerres civiles de France.
Essay on epick poetry. 1727. *See above.*
Ozell, John. Of the Herculean labours. 1729 (canto 1). Full trn by J. Lockman, Henriade: an epick poem, 1732 (blank verse); tr [Catherine Maria Bury, Countess of Charleville], The Henriade, 2 vols 1797 (rhyming verse). From Henriade.
The history of Charles XII, King of Sweden. Dublin 1732, London 1732 (4 edns), 1733 (5th edn), 1735, 1740, 1755, Glasgow 1754, 1762 (abridged), Edinburgh 1769, 1776, 1789; tr [Andrews Henderson?] 1734, 1739, [1750?], Glasgow 1750 (abridged); tr W. A. Dilworth 1760. From Histoire de Charles XII.
[Lockman, John]. Letters concerning the English nation. 1733, Dublin 1733, London 1739 (4th edn), Dublin 1739, London 1741 (2nd edn), Glasgow 1752 (3rd edn), 1759, London 1760, Glasgow 1766, London 1767, Glasgow 1769, London 1773, 1778. Sections of work composed in English by Voltaire. Lockman's trn appeared before first French edn. From Lettres philosophiques.
The temple of taste. 1734, Glasgow 1751, London [1766]. From Le temple du goût.
Duncombe, W. Junius Brutus. 1735, 1735, 1747. Adaptation of Brutus. Act 1 composed in English.
Hill, Aaron. The tragedy of Zara. 1736, 1736, Dublin 1737, London 1752 (3rd edn), Edinburgh 1755, London 1758 (2nd edn), 1759 (5th edn), 1760, Dublin 1762, London 1763 (2nd edn), 1776, 1777, 1778, 1791, Dublin 1791, London 1795 (in Jones's British theatre vol 2, 1795). Zaïre, adapted.
Hill, Aaron. Alzira: a tragedy. 1736, Dublin 1736, London 1737, 1744, 1745, Edinburgh 1755, London 1760, 1777, 1779, 1791. Alzire, adapted.
Hanna, J. The elements of Sir Isaac Newton's philosophy. 1738. From Eléments de la philosophie de Newton.
[Williams, D?] The prodigal son. [1738?]; in Works, ed Kenrick 14 vols 1779-81. From L'enfant prodigue.
Gordon, W. Epistles: on happiness, liberty and envy. 1738, 1738 (as Three epistles in the ethic way: happiness, freedom of will; envy). From Discours en vers sur l'homme, which appeared first as Epîtres sur le bonheur, la liberté et l'envie.

Lockman, J. An essay on the age of Lewis XIV. 1739, [1740?], 1752, Dublin 1760. From Essai sur le siècle de Louis XIV; pbd draft of later Siècle de Louis XIV.

Anti-Machiavel: or an examination of Machiavel's Prince. 1741, 1752. From Examen du Prince de Machiavel, preface by Voltaire.

Miller, James and J. Hoadley. Mahomet the imposter. 1744, 1745, Dublin 1745, Edinburgh 1755, 1759, London 1765, 1766 (4th edn), Edinburgh 1773; 1774, 1776 (5th edn), 1776, 1777, 1778, Edinburgh 1782, London 1795, 1796. From Mahomet.

Theobald, John. Merope: a tragedy. 1744; tr Aaron Hill 1749, Dublin 1749, London 1750, 1753 (3rd edn), Edinburgh 1755, London 1758, 1760, 1776, 1776, 1777, 1786, 1795. From Mérope.

Baker, D. E. The metaphysics of Sir Isaac Newton. 1747; tr as The Newtonian philosophy, Glasgow 1764. From Métaphysique de Newton.

Zadig or the book of fate: an oriental history. 1749; tr [J. Collyer?] 1754, [c. 1775]; The hermit: an oriental tale, 1779 (ch of Zadig), 1794; tr Frances Ashmore 1780; Novelist's Mag 1790, 1794; Glasgow 1796 London [1800?]. From Zadig.

The age of Lewis XIV. 2 vols 1752, Dublin 1752, 1 vol Edinburgh 1752, 2 vols Glasgow 1753, London 1753, Glasgow 1763. From Siècle de Louis XIV, first pbd under name of Francheville.

A defence of the late Lord Bolingbroke's letters on the study and use of history. 1753. From Défense de milord Bolingbroke.

Micromégas: a comic romance; together with a detail of the crusades. 1753.

Hill, Aaron. The Roman revenge: a tragedy. 1754 (2nd edn), 1760. From La mort de César.

Babouc or the world as it goes; to which are added letters; also the Force of friendship: a novel. 1754, Dublin 1754. From Le monde comme il va.

The general history and state of Europe. 6 pts 1754; The universal history and state of all nations, 3 vols Edinburgh 1758; tr T. Nugent, An essay on universal history, 4 vols 1759 (2nd edn), Dublin 1759 (3rd edn); A supplement [tr Nugent?] 2 vols 1764, Edinburgh 1777; also unidentified trns 1777, 1782. From Essai sur les moeurs.

Collyer, Joseph. Select pieces of M. de Voltaire. 1754.

Annals of the Empire. 2 vols 1755; tr D. Williams in Works, 1781. From Annales de l'Empire.

An epistle of Mr de Voltaire upon his arrival at his estate near the lake of Geneva. 1755. From Epître de Mr de V*** en arrivant dans sa terre; parallel texts.

The orphan of China: a tragedy. 1755, 1756, Edinburgh 1759; tr Arthur Murphy 1756 (2nd edn), 1756, 1759, 1759 (2nd edn), Dublin 1759, London 1761 (6th edn), Dublin 1761, London 1772 (3rd edn), 1786 (in A. Murphy, Works), 1797. From L'orphelin de la Chine.

The history of the war of seventeen hundred and forty one. 1756, 1756 (2nd edn), Dublin 1756 (2nd edn), [London?] 1756, Edinburgh 1758. From Histoire de la guerre de 1741, later developed into Précis du siècle de Louis XV.

An epistle to the King of Prussia. 1757. From Epître au Prince royal de Prusse.

The history of the voyages of Scarmentado. 1757. From Histoire des voyages de Scarmentado.

The Maid of Orleans. 2 vols 1758 (prose), 1780 (canto 1), 1782 (canto 1); as La Pucelle: or the Maid of Orleans, 2 pts 1785–6 (cantos 1–5), 1789 (2nd edn); tr [Catherine Maria Bury, Countess of Charleville?] 2 vols Dublin 1796–7 (priv ptd). From La Pucelle.

Gerard, A. An essay on taste, with three dissertations on the subject by Mr de Voltaire, Mr d'Alembert FRS, Mr de Montesquieu. Edinburgh 1759, 1764. From Essai sur le goût, and article Goût in Encyclopédie. David Hume said to have corrected essay through press.

Candid: or all for the best. 1759, 1759; another trn,

Edinburgh 1759, 1761, 1773, London 1795; tr W. Rider, Candidus, 1759; other trns and edns: Candid, Dublin 1761; Candid: or all for the best, 1771 (3rd edn); Candidus, 1773, Berwick 1795; The history of Candid, in C. Cooke, Select British novels, [1796]; nd. From Candide. Edns listed here far from complete. 'Second Part' is spurious.

The coffee-house, or fair fugitive: a comedy. 1760, Dublin 1760; adapted G. Coleman, The English merchant, 1767, Dublin 1767. From Le caffé: ou l'Ecossaise, first attributed to Hume.

Rome preserv'd. 1760. From Rome sauvée.

Semiramis. 1760, Dublin 1760, London 1776, 1794 (operatic); tr G. E. Ayscough 1776; freely adapted J. Hoole, Cyrus, 1768; and J. Murphy, Alzuma, 1773 (3 edns). From Sémiramis.

Socrates. 1760. From Socrate.

Critical essays on dramatic poetry. Glasgow 1761, 1761. From Discours sur la tragédie à mylord Bolingbroke, with Dissertation sur la tragédie ancienne et moderne, pbd with Brutus and Sémiramis respectively.

History of the Empire of Russia. Vol 1 (all pbd), Dublin 1761; tr [J. Johnson?], The history of the Russian Empire, 2 vols 1761–3, Glasgow 1764, Edinburgh 1769, Berwick [c. 1770], Aberdeen 1777, London 1778, 1780. From Histoire de l'Empire de Russie sous Pierre le Grand.

Original pieces relative to the trial of John Calas. 1762, Dublin 1763, London 1772, Edinburgh 1776. From Pièces originales concernant Calas.

No one's enemy but his own. 1764, Dublin 1764. From L'indiscret.

[Kenrick, W.] A treatise on religious toleration. 1764; another trn, A treatise upon toleration, Glasgow 1765, Edinburgh 1770. From Traité sur la tolérance.

The philosophical dictionary for the pocket, written in French by a society of men of letters [with notes critical of irreligious passages]. 1765, Glasgow 1766, London [1767?], Dublin 1793, Catskill 1796. From Dictionnaire philosophique portatif.

A letter from Mons de Voltaire to Mr Hume on his dispute with M. Rousseau. 1766. From Lettre de M. de Voltaire à M. Hume.

A letter from M. Voltaire to M. J.-J. Rousseau. 1766. From Lettre au docteur J. J. Pansophe; bilingual text.

The philosophy of history. 1766, Glasgow 1766. From La philosophie de l'histoire.

An address upon the parricides. In The ignorant philosopher, 1767, below. From Avis au public sur les parricides.

An essay on crimes and punishments. 1767, 1769, 1769, Glasgow 1769, London 1770, 1775 (4th edn), Edinburgh 1778, 1778, 1788. From Beccaria, Commentaire sur le livre des délits et des peines, ed Voltaire.

The ignorant philosopher etc. 1767, Glasgow 1767. From Le philosophe ignorant.

A defence of my uncle. 1768. From La défense de mon oncle.

The dispute between Mlle Clairon and the Fathers of the Church. 1768. From Conversation de Mr l'intendant des menus avec M. l'abbé [Grizel].

L'ingénu: or the sincere Huron. Glasgow 1768, London 1768, Dublin 1768; The pupil of nature, 1771; tr Francis Ashmore, The sincere Huron, 1786, 1786. From L'Ingénu.

Letters addressed to his Highness the Prince of *****. 1768, Glasgow 1769, London 1779. From Lettres à son altesse Monseigneur le prince de ***.

The man of forty crowns. 1768, Glasgow 1768, Dublin 1770. From L'homme aux quarante écus.

The Princess of Babylon. 1768, 1768, Glasgow 1769. From La Princesse de Babylone.

Teres, T. The civil war of Geneva, or the amours of Robert Covelle: an heroic poem. 1769. From La guerre civile de Genève.

The age of Louis XV. 2 vols 1770, Glasgow 1771, 2 vols 1774 (added to Smollett's edn of Works); tr R. Griffith, The age of Louis XIV; to which is added Louis XV, 3 vols 1779–81. From Précis du siècle de Louis XV.

Genuine letters between the archbishop of Anneci and M. de Voltaire. 1770. From Lettres de Mr l'Evêque.

[Celesia, D.] Almida. 1771, 1771. From Tancrède.

Cradock, Joseph. Zobeide: a tragedy. 1771, 1772, 1772, Dublin 1772. From Les Scythes.

Fragments relating to the late revolutions in India. 1774. Fragments sur l'Inde.

[Bentham, Jeremy]. The white bull: an oriental history. 2 vols 1774; another trn, Le taureau blanc: or the white bull, 1774 (2nd edn). From Le taureau blanc.

[Francklin, T.] Matilda: a tragedy. 1775. From Adélaïde du Guesclin.

Young James: or the sage and the atheist. 1776 (2nd edn), Dublin 1776. From Histoire de Jenni.

Francklin, T. Orestes. 1776, 1786 (as Electra). From Oreste.

A letter from M. Voltaire to the French Academy on the merits of Shakespeare. 1777. From Lettre de M. de Voltaire à l'Académie française.

Historical memoirs of the author of the Henriade. 1777. From Commentaire historique sur les oeuvres de l'auteur de la Henriade.

Memoirs of the life of Voltaire. 1784, Dublin 1784, London 1785 (3rd edn), 1790, 1792. From Mémoires de M. de Voltaire écrits par lui-même.

Macklin, Charles. The man of the world: a comedy. Dublin 1785, 1786, 1791, London 1793 (3 edns), Dublin 1793, London 1795. From Nanine.

Knight, J. The ears of Lord Chesterfield. Berne 1786. From Les oreilles du comte de Chesterfield.

Holcroft, T. Correspondence: letters between Frederick II and M. de Voltaire. In Posthumous works of Frederick II, King of Prussia vols 6–8, 1789.

Thoughts on the pernicious consequences of war. [1790?]. From Encyclopédie, article on Guerre.

S. S. B. T.

C. TRANSLATIONS FROM GERMAN

The following list is restricted to the more important works of the more important German writers. See Literary Relations with German, *col 151, above, and* B. Q Morgan, A critical bibliography of German literature in English translation 1481–1927, with supplement embracing the years 1928–55, New York 1965.

Agrippa von Nettesheim (1486–1535)
  Care, H. Female pre-eminence: or the dignity and excellency of that sex, above the male. 1670, 1688.

J. W. Archenholtz (1743–1812)
  A picture of England. 1789. Another trn 1797.

C. H. Ayrenhoff (1733–1819)
  Mackenzie, H. The set of horses. 1792.

Martin von Baumgarten (1573–1641)
  Donauer, C. Travels through Egypt, Arabia, Palestine and Syria. 1732, 1744, 1752.

Adam Beuvius
  Henrietta of Gerstenfield: a German tale. 2 vols 1787.

J. J. Bodmer (1698–1783)
  Collyer, Joseph. Noah. 1767, 1770.

Jacob Boehme (1575–1624)
  See col 160, above.

J. C. Brandes (1735–99)
  Holcroft, Thomas. The German hotel: a comedy. 1790, 1790.

G. A. Bürger (1747–94)
  Taylor, William. Ellenore. 1790, 1796. 3 other trns by H. J. Pye, 1796; by W. R. Spencer, 1796; by J. T. Stanley, 1796, 1796; by B. Beresford, 1798.
  Scott, Walter. The chase and William and Helen: two ballads. 1796.

J. H. von Campe (1746–1818)
  Robinson the younger. 1781–2. Another trn, 1788 and 1789; another trn, 1789.

K. G. Cramer (1758–1817)
  Albert de Nordenshild, or the modern Alcibiades: a novel. 2 vols 1794.

F. Dedekind (1525?–98)
  Bull, R. Grobianus, or the compleat booby: an ironical poem. 1739.

C. Ditters von Dittersdorf (1739–99)
  The doctor and the apothecary: opera. 1788.

C. H. Erndtel
  The relation of a journey into England 1706–7 by a Saxon physician. 1711.

Eulenspiegel
  The German rogue: or the life and merry adventures of Till Eulenspiegel. 1709, 1720.

Faust
  The history of Dr J. Faustus, compiled in verse, very pleasant and delightful. 1664, 1696.

The history of the damnable life and deserved death. 1696, 1700. Also various chapbooks.

'Lorenz Flammenberg' (K. F. Kahlert)
  Teuthold, Peter. The necromancer: or a tale of the Black Forest. 1794.

Fortunatus
  The history of Fortunatus. 1676, 1682, 1700, 1740 (11th edn), 1779. Also chapbooks.

Frederick II, King of Prussia (1712–86)
  Derrick, Samuel. Sylla: a dramatic entertainment presented 27th March 1753. 1753. From the French original.
  Royal matins: or Prussia's public confession. 1768. Other trns 1770, 1798. From the French.
  Holcroft, Thomas. Posthumous works. 13 vols 1789. From the French. The School of the world: a comedy. 1789.

C. F. Gellert (1717–69)
  History of the Swedish Countess of Guildenstern. 1752. N—, Rev Mr. The life of the Swedish Countess de G***. 1776. 3 other trns, 1752, 1757, 1776.

O. von Gemmingen-Hornberg (1755–1836)
  T. Holcroft. Love's frailties. 1799.

Salomon Gessner (1730–88)
  Collyer, Mary. The death of Abel. 1761, 1762, 1763 (5th edn), 1765 (7th edn), 1776 (11th edn), 1786, 1796, 1799 (20th edn).
  Pastorals. 1762. Also A. Penny, Select poems from Mr Gessner's Pastorals, 1762.
  Hooper, W. New idylles. 1776, 1798.

J. W. von Goethe (1749–1832)
  Graves, Richard. The sorrows of Werther. 1779, 1780, 1782, 1784, 1785, 1786, 1788, 1789, 1790, 1794, 1798, 1799. Also tr J. Gifford, 1789.
  Leftley, Charles. Clavidgo: a tragedy in 5 acts. 1798. Stella. 1798.
  Lawrence, Rose d'A. Gortz of Berlichingen. 1799.

K. Grosse (1761–?)
  The dagger. 1796.
  Trapp, J. The genius: or the mysterious adventures of Don Carlos de Grandez. 1796.
  Will, P. Horrid mysteries. 1796.

V. A. von Haller (1708–77)
  Usong: an eastern narrative. 1772, 1773.
  H. Barrett. The Alps: a moral and descriptive poem. 1796.
  Howorth, Mrs J. The poems of Baron Haller. 1794.

'Baron' Huffumbourghausen
  Heidegger, J. J. The congress of the beasts for negotiating a peace between the quadrupedes at war. 1748 (4 edns). Satire on the congress at Aix.

A. W. Iffland (1759–1814)
Plumptre, B. The foresters, a picture of rural manners: a comedy. 1799.
Ludger, C. The lawyers: a drama. 1799.
Lloyd, H. E. The nephews: a play. 1799.
The bachelors· a comedy in five acts. 1799.

J. G. Keyssler (1693–1743)
Travels through Germany, Bohemia etc. 4 vols 1756–7, 1758, 1760, 1778.

F. M. Klinger (1752–1831)
The modern Arria. 1795.
Travels before the flood. 1796.

F. G. Klopstock (1724–1803)
Lloyd, R. The death of Adam: a tragedy. 1763.
Collyer, J. The Messiah. 2 vols 1763, 1769 (3rd edn), 1788.

A. F. F. L. Knigge (1752–96)
The German Gil Blas: or the adventures of Peter Claus. 1793.
The history of the Amtsrath Gutmann, written by himself. 1799.

M.A. Countess of K[oenigsmarc]k (1670–1728)
Memoirs of the love and state-intrigues of the Court of H[anover]. 1743, 1744.

A. von Kotzebue (1761–1819)
The Corsicans: a drama. 1796, 1799, Dublin 1799.
The negro slaves: a dramatic-historical piece. 1796.
Thomson, A. The Indians in England. 1796.
Inchbald, Elizabeth. Lovers' vows: a play. 1798 (11 edns). Also tr S. Porter 1798, and A. Plumptre, 1798, 1798 (4th edn).
—— The wise man of the east: a drama. 1799.
Schink, A. The stranger: a comedy. 1798 (6th edn). Also tr G. Papendick, 1798.
Thompson, B. Adelaide of Wulfingen: a tragedy. 1798.
—— The happy family: a drama. 1799.
—— La Perouse: a drama. 1799.
—— The escape. 1799.
Render, W. Count Benyowsky, or the conspiracy of Kamtschatka: a tragi-comedy. 1798.
Dunlap, W. The wild goose chace. 1798.
Plumptre, A. The Count of Burgundy: a play. 1798, 1798 (3rd edn).
—— The force of calumny: a play. 1799.
—— The virgin of the sun. 1799, 1799. Also tr B. Thompson, 1799 and W. Dunlap, 1799.
—— The widow and the riding horse: a dramatic trifle. 1799.
The constant lover, or William and Jeanette: a tale. 1799.
The East Indian: a comedy. 1799.
Geisweiler, M. The noble lie: drama. 1799, 1799. Another trn 1799.
—— Poverty and nobleness of mind: a play. 1799, 1799.
Ludger, C. The peevish man: a drama. 1799.
—— The reconciliation: a comedy. 1799 (4 edns).
Sheridan, R. B. Pizarro: a drama. 1799 (20 edns), 1800 (26th edn). Also tr T. Dutton, 1799, 1799; A. Plumptre, 1799 (6th rev edn).
Hoare, P. Sighs, or the daughter: a comedy. 1799 (4 edns).
Neumann, H. Self-immolation: or the sacrifice of love. 1799. Another trn, 1799.
Will, P. The sufferings of the family of Ortenberg: a novel. 2 vols 1799.
The writing-desk, or youth in danger: a drama. 1799.

F. Kratter (1758–1830)
The maid of Marienburg. 1798.
Natalia and Menzikoff, or the conspiracy against Peter the Great: a tragedy. 1798.

A. H. J. Lafontaine (1758–1831)
Clara Duplessis and Clairant. 1797.
Saint Julien: a novel. 1798. Also another trn, 1799.
The family of Halden. 4 vols 1799.
Will, P. Romulus: a tale of ancient times. 1799.

M. S. La Roche (1731–1807)

Collyer, J. History of Lady Sophia Sternheim. 1776, 1786.
Harwood, E. The adventures of Miss Sophia Sternheim. 1776.

J. K. Lavater (1741–1801)
Will, P. Secret journal of a self-observer. 1770, 1795.
Fuseli, J. H. Aphorisms on man. 1788, 1790, 1794.

J. Leisewitz (1752–1806)
Will, P. Julius of Tarentum. 1800.

G. E. Lessing (1729–81)
Berrington. Emilia Galotti. 1794. Also tr B. Thompson, 1800.
Laocoön. 1767.
Raspe, R. E. Nathan the wise. 1781. Also tr Wm Taylor of Norwich, 1791.
Johnstone, J. The disbanded officer: or the baroness of Bruchsal. 1786. Also another trn, 1799.
Rittenhouse, D. Lucy Sampson. 1789.
The fatal elopement. 1799.

W. R. Lichtenau (1752–1820)
B-t-n, R. Confessions of the celebrated Countess of L. 1799.

J. A. von Mandelslo (1616–44)
Davies, J. The voyages and travels into the East Indies 1638–40. 1662, 1669.

G. F. Meier (1718–77)
The merry philosopher: or thoughts on jesting. 2 vols 1764.

M. Mendelssohn (1729–86)
Cullen, C. Phaedon: or the death of Socrates. 1789.

J. M. Miller (1750–1814)
L., H. Sigevart: a tale. 1799.

J. Moeser (1720–94)
Warnecke, J. A. F. Harlequin: or a defence of grotesque comic performances. 1766.

K. P. Moritz (1757–96)
Travels through various parts of England, in 1782. 1795.

K. F. H. Münchhausen (1720–97)
Raspe, R. E. Baron Munchausen's narrative of his marvellous travels. 1786, 1787, 1793, 1799 (8th edn). From G. A. Bürger's edn, with addns and a sequel.

J. K. A. Musäus (1735–87)
Beckford, W. Popular tales of the Germans. 2 vols 1791.

Christiane B. E. Naubert (1756–1819)
Booth, Miss A. E. Alf von Deulmen: or the history of the Emperor Philip and his daughters. 2 vols 1790.
Hermann of Unna: a series of adventures of the 15th century. 3 vols 1796 (3rd edn).

C. F. Nicolai (1733–1811)
Dutton, T. The life and opinions of Sebaldus Nothanker. 1798.

J. Pfeil (1732–1800)
Streit, F. W. The memoirs of the Count of P. 1767.

K. L. von Poellnitz (1692–1775)
Whatley, S. The memoirs of de Pöllnitz. 5 vols 1738, 1739, 1745, 1750.

Reynard the Fox
Shirley, J. The most delightfull history of Reynard the fox in heroic verse. 1681. Another trn, 1694, 1701; another trn, 1706, 1723, 1735. Also chapbooks.

K. U. von Salis-Marschlins (1762–1818)
Aufrere, A. Travels through various provinces of Naples in 1789. 1795.

J. C. F. von Schiller (1759–1805)
Tytler, A. F. The robbers. 1792, 1795, 1797, 1800. Also tr W. Render, 1799, and Lady Craven, 1799.
Colombine, P. (with J. J. C. Timäus?). Cabal and love: a tragedy. 1795, 1796, 1797. Also tr M. G. Lewis, 1797.
Boileau, D. The ghost-seer: or apparitionist. 1795 (abridged).
Noehden, G. H. and J. Stoddart. Fiesco: or the conspiracy of Genoa. 1796.
—— Don Carlos. 1798. Also tr Symonds, 1798.

C. O. Schönaich (1725–1807)
Arminius: or Germania freed. 1764.

J. C. F. Schultz
  Maurice: a German tale. 2 vols 1796.
C. H. Spiess (1755–99)
  Plumptre, A. The mountain cottager, or wonder upon wonder: a tale. 1798.
Baron F. Trenck (1726–94)
  Holcroft, T. The life of Baron Frederick Trenck: containing his adventures. 4 vols 1788–93, 3 vols 1795, 1800 etc.
C. Tschinck (d. 1809)
  Will, P. The victim of magical delusion. 1795.
J. C. Unzer (1747–1809)
  Andrews, J. P. and H. J. Pye. The inquisitor: a tragedy. 1798.
C. A. Vulpius (1762–1827)
  Hinckley, J. The history of Rinaldo Rinaldini. 1800.
L. Wächter ('Veit Weber') (1762–1837)

Powell, J. The black valley and the Sorcerer. 1796.
Huish, R.[?]. The sorcerer. 1795.
C. M. Wieland (1733–1813)
  Reason triumphant over fancy. 1773.
  The history of Agathon. 4 vols 1773.
  The trial of Abraham. 1764, 1777.
  Tooke, W. Private history of Peregrinus Proteus, the philosopher. 1796.
  Sotheby, W. Oberon. 1798.
  The golden mirror. 1798.
J. G. von Zimmermann (1728–95)
  Solitude considered with respect to its influence on the mind and heart. 1791, 1792, 1795, 1797, 1798, 1799 (3 edns).
J. H. D. Zschokke (1771–1848)
  Dunlap, W. Aballino, the great bandit. 1792.

J. T.

D. TRANSLATIONS FROM ITALIAN

For trns of operas, oratorios etc see A. Nicoll, A history of early eighteenth-century drama, 1929 (rev), pp. 387–400; *and his* A history of late eighteenth-century drama, 1927, pp. 348–63. *See also* R. Marshall, Italy in English literature 1755–1815, New York 1934; Literary Relations, *col 185, above.*

Leon Battista Alberti

Evelyn, John. Treatise of statues. In his A parallel of the antient architecture with the modern, 1664, 1707, 1733; in his Whole body of antient and modern architecture, 1680. From Latin.
Leoni, James. The architecture; Of painting and of statuary. 3 vols 1726, 1755. From Italian of C. Bartoli.

Francesco Algarotti

[Carter, Elizabeth]. Sir Isaac Newton's philosophy explain'd. 2 vols 1739, 1742, 1 vol Glasgow 1765. From Il newtonianismo per le dame.
An essay on painting. 1764.
An essay on the opera. 1767.
Letters from Count Algarotti to Lord Hervey and the Marquis S. Maffei: containing the state of the trade, marine, revenues and forces of the Russian Empire; to which is added A dissertation on the reigns of the Seven Kings of Rome, and another on the empire of the Incas. 2 vols 1769, Glasgow 1770.
Letters military and political. 1782.

Giovanni Battista Andreini

Hayley, William. The life of Milton. 1796. Contains passages tr from Adamo.

Lodovica Ariosto

[Huggins, William]. Orlando Furioso [first tr J. Harington 1591]. 2 vols 1755, 1757 (with Huggin's name; Ottava rima); tr John Hoole, A translation of part of the twenty-third canto of the Orlando Furioso, 1774 (decasyllabic quatrains); Orlando Furioso, 5 vols 1783 (complete), 1785, 4 vols 1789, 5 vols 1799 etc (decasyllabic couplets); The Orlando Furioso reduced to 24 books, the narrative connected and the stories disposed in a regular series, 2 vols 1791; tr Henry Boyd, A specimen of a new translation [from cantos 24, 29] of the Orlando Furioso (in A translation of Dante's Inferno vol 2, 1785) (Spenserian stanzas).
Croker, T. H. The satires. 1759. 5 of the 7 Satires tr H——n.

Francesco Barbaro

Directions for love and marriage. 1677. From Latin.

Giuseppe Marc' Antonio Baretti

See Literary Relations, *col 185, above.*

Daniello Bartoli

Salusbury, T. The learned man defended and reform'd. 1660.

Lodovico Beccadelli

Pye, B. The life of Cardinal Reginald Pole; to which is added an appendix, setting forth the plagiarisms. In T. Phillips, Life of Reginald Pole, 1766.

Cesare Bonesana Beccaria

An essay on crimes and punishments; with a commentary, attributed to Mons de Voltaire. 1767, 1769, 2 pts 1770, 1 vol 1775, 1777, Edinburgh 1778, 1778, Philadelphia 1779, Edinburgh 1788. From Dei delitti e delle pene, with Voltaire, Commentaire sur le livre des délits et des peines.
A discourse of public oeconomy and commerce. 1769. From Elementi di economica pubblica.

Giovanni Battista Beccaria

Wilson, Benjamin. A series of experiments relating to Phosphori; with a translation of two memoirs from the Bologna Acts, upon the same subject, by J. B. Beccaria. 1775, 1776.

Guido Bentivoglio

Letters of wit, politicks and morality, written originally in Italian by the famous cardinal Bentivoglio [et al], done into English by the honourable H—— H—— esq; Tho. Cheek esq; Mr Savage, Mr Boyer etc. 1701, 1753 (as A collection of letters written by the Cardinal Bentivoglio during the time that he was Nuncio in France and Flanders).

Giovanni Boccaccio

Sections of Decameron first tr William Painter *in his* Palace of pleasure, 1566; *whole text tr anon* 1620.
Dryden, John. Fables. 1700 etc (versifications of Decameron IV, i, v, i, viii). Other trns and adaptations: Il Decamerone, one hundred ingenious novels, 1702, 1712 (amended); tr William Ayre, The Saint: a tale, 1734 (Decameron, I, i); tr [C. Balguy], The Decameron: or ten days entertainment, 1741; tr Miss Sotheby, Patient Griselda: a tale, Bristol 1798, 1799 (decasyllabic couplets).

Trajano Boccalini

N., N. Advertisements from Parnassus; together with the author's politick touchstone; his secretaria, di Apollo; and an account of his life. 3 vols 1704. Secretaria di Apollo also pbd separately, 2 vols 1704. Also tr John Hughes et al, Advices from Parnassus, in two centuries, with the political touchstone; to which is added a continuation of the advices by G. Briani, 1706. From

Ragguagli di Parnaso; first tr Henry Earl of Monmouth 1656.

Girolamo Brusoni

S., T. Arnaldo, or the injur'd lover: an excellent new romance. 1660.

Ranieri de' Calsabigi

Bottarelli, G. G. Orpheus and Eurydice: an opera. 1770, 1773, 1792; another trn of Orfeo ed Euridice, 1771; tr G. F. Feuducci, Orpheus and Eurydice, Dublin 1784; tr as Orpheus and Eurydice, 1785.

[Penn, John]. A translation of his letter to Count Alfieri on tragedy. 1797.

Pietro Giovanni Capriata

Carey, Henry (Earl of Monmouth). The history of the wars of Italy from the year 1613 to 1644. 1663.

Girolamo Cardano

[Coley, H.?] The choicest aphorisms of Cardan's Seven segments. In W. Lilly, Anima astrologiae, 1676.

His three books of consolation englished. 1683.

Mensforth, G. The young student's guide in astrology: consisting of choice aphorisms from Cardan, G. Bonatus [et al]. 1785.

Giovanni della Casa

W[alker], N[athaniel]. The refin'd courtier: or a correction of several indecencies crept into civil conversation. 1663, 1679, 1686.

Stubbe, H. The arts of grandeur and submission: or a discourse concerning the behaviour of great men towards their inferiours. 1665, 1670. From De officiis inter potentiores et tenuiores amicos.

Galateo of manners: or instructions to a young gentleman how to behave himself in conversation. 1703; tr [Richard Graves], Galateo: or a treatise on politeness and delicacy of manners, addressed to a young nobleman, 1774.

Giovanni Battista Casti

Il rè Teodoro in Venezia: a new comic opera. 1787.

Baldassare Castiglione

Samber, R. The courtier: or the complete gentleman and gentlewoman. 1724, 1729; tr A. P. Castiglione, Il cortegiano: or the courtier; together with several of his celebrated pieces, as well Latin as Italian, both in prose and verse; to which is prefix'd a life of the author. 1727, 1737, 1742.

Benvenuto Cellini

Nugent, Thomas. The life of Benvenuto Cellini, a Florentine artist. 2 vols 1771, Dublin 1772.

Urbano Cerri

An account of the state of the Roman-Catholick religion throughout the world; to which is added A discourse concerning the state of religion in England, with a large dedication to the present Pope by Sir R. Steele [or Bishop Hoadly?]. 1715, 1716.

Armeno Christoforo

The travels and adventures of three princes of Sarendip, translated from Persian into French and from thence into English. 1722. From the French of de Mailly, 1719, 1772 (with Amazonta, or the politick wife: a novel).

Giovanni Battista Comazzi

Hatchett, W. The morals of princes: or an abstract of the most remarkable passages contain'd in the history of all the emperors who reigned in Rome. 1729.

Angelo Corraro

Bulteel, John. Rome exactly described: or a relation of the state of the Court of Rome, made at the late Council of Pregadi. 1664, 1668.

Dante Alighieri

See P. Toynbee, Chronological list of English translations from Dante, and his English translations of Dante in the 18th century, both in Dante studies, Oxford 1921.

Rogers, Charles. The Inferno. 1782 (blank verse); tr Henry Boyd, A translation of the Inferno, in English verse, with historical notes and the life of Dante [from Aretino], 2 vols 1785 (6-line stanzas rhyming aab ccb; also Purgatorio, xxx 115–41); tr H. C. Jennings, A translation of the fifth canto of the Inferno and of the entire scene and narrative of Hugoline (xxxII, 125–39, and xxxIII, 1–87) [1798] (blank verse).

Enrico Caterino Davila

Farneworth, E. The history of the civil wars of France. 2 vols 1758. Includes anecdotes relating to the author, chiefly from the Italian of A. Zeno.

Carlo Giovanni Maria Denina

Murdock, J. An essay on the revolutions of literature. [1771].

Langhorne, John. A dissertation, historical and political, on the ancient republics of Italy. 1773.

Lodovico Dolce

Brown, W. Aretin: a dialogue on painting. 1770.

Cesare Federici

[Chambers, W.] Voyages and travels into the East-Indies and beyond the Indies. In A short account of the Marratta State, 1787.

Odoardo Fialetti

Brown, A. The whole art of drawing, painting, limning and etching. 1660.

Gaetano Filangieri

[Kendall, W.] An analysis of the science of legislation. [1791].

Galileo

Salusbury, T. The systeme of the world in four dialogues. 1661.

Salusbury, T. Mathematical collections and translations. 5 vols 1661–2.

Venn, Thomas. The compleat gunner, to which is added the doctrine of projects by Galilaeus and Torricellio. 1672.

Weston, T. Mathematical discourses concerning two new sciences relating to mechanicks and local motions, in four dialogues. 1730.

Giovanni Battista Gelli

Brown, Thomas. Circe. 1702, 1744, 1745.

Pietro Giannone

Ogilvie, J. The civil history of the kingdom of Naples. 2 vols 1729–31.

Giovanni 'Fiorentino'

The novel from which the play of the Merchant of Venice, written by Shakespear, is taken; to which is added a translation of a novel from the Decameron of Boccaccio. 1755. Contains Giovanni's Pecorone IV, i and Decameron x, i.

Giovanni Battista Giraldi Cinthio

Parr, W. The story of the Moore of Venice. 1795. Ecatommiti, III, vii.

Carlo Goldoni

Bertoldo, Bertoldino e Cascasenno. 1755, 1762.
Pamela: a comedy. 1756. From Pamela nubile.
The father of a family. 1757. From Il padre di famiglia.
The magnet of hearts. 1763. From La calamita dei cuori.
Bottarelli, G. G. The dairy house. 1763. From La Cascina.
Bottarelli, G. G. La buona figliuola: a comic opera. 1767 (3rd edn), [1770?], 1775 (this and perhaps earlier edns as The maid of the vale), 1777; tr E. Toms, The accomplish'd maid, 1767; The accomplished maid: a comic opera, in Bell's British theatre vol 21, 1781.
Bottarelli, G. G. La buona figliuola maritata: a new comic opera. 1767.
Il signor dottore. 1767.
Storace, S. The coquet: a musical entertainment. 1771. From La cameriera spiritosa.
Dibdin, C. The wedding ring. 1773. From Il filosofo di campagna.
Bottarelli, F. Germondo: a new serious opera. 1776. From Germondo.
Bottarelli, F. Vittorina: a new comic opera. 1777. From Vittorina.
L'amor artigiano. 1778.
Fuller, H. B. The coffee-house. nd. From La bottega del caffè.

Galeazzo Gualdo-Priorato

The history of the managements of cardinal Julio Mazarine. 2 pts 1671–2, 3 pts 1691.
Carey, Henry, Earl of Monmouth. The history of France: the translation whereof, being begun by Henry, late Earl of Monmouth, was finished by W. Brent. 1676.

Giovanni Battista Guarini

Settle, Elkanah. Pastor Fido. 1677, 1689, 1694. Altered from Sir R. Fanshawe's trn of 1647. First trn by Dymock 1602. Another trn: The faithful shepherdess: a pastoral tragi-comedy, 1736; tr William Grove, The faithful shepherd, attempted in the manner of the original, 1782.

Francesco Guicciardini

The history of the Papacy which was fraudently left out of the fourth book of his history translated from the Latin. 1712.
Goddard, A. P. The history of Italy [1492–1532]. 10 vols 1753–6, 1763 (3rd edn).

Lodovico Guicciardini

Guicciardini's account of the ancient Flemish school of painting, translated from his description of the Netherlands. 1795.

Gregorio Leti

The life of Donna Olimpia Maldachini. 1666.
The loves of Charles, Duke of Mantua; and of Margaret, Countess of Rovera. 1669.
A[glionby], W. Il nipotismo di Roma: or the history of the Popes' nephews from the time of Sixtus the IV to the death of the last Pope, Alexander the VII. 2 pts 1669, 1 vol 1673.
H[avers], G. Il cardinalismo di Santa Chiesa: or the history of the cardinals of the Roman church. 1670.
The present state of Geneva, with a brief description of that city [to 1681]. 1681.
The life of Pope Sixtus the Vth. 1704; tr E. Farneworth 1754, [Dublin] 1779.

Giovanni Francesco Loredano

Bulteel, John. Accademical discourses upon severall choise and pleasant subjects. 1664.
Hare, Hugh, Baron Coleraine. The ascents of the soul: being paraphrases on the fifteen psalms of degrees. 1681.
Novels. 1682.
The history of Adam and Eve, critical and political. [17–?].
Murray, R. The life of man. 1779.

Nicolo di Bernado dei Machiavelli

Dacres, Edward. Discourses upon the first decade of T. Livius; to which is added the Prince [and the Life of Castruccio Castracani]. 1636, 2 pts 1661–3, 1 vol 1674 ('much corrected'). Dacres translated the first 3 Discourses in 1636 and the Prince in 1640.
The marriage of Belphegor. In Novels of Dom Francisco de Quevedo y Villegas, 1671; tr John Wilson, Belphegor: or the marriage of the Devil, 1691; The marriage of Belphegor, in S. Croxall, Select collection of novels vol 1, 1722, 1729; in A. Pennecuik, Collection of Scots poems, 1762 (abridged).
K., M. The Florentine history in VIII books. 8 pts 1674. Stationers' Register 20 June 1674 attributes trn to J.D. Gent.
[Nevile, Henry]. Works. 1675, 1680, 1694, 1720 ('carefully corrected'), Stationers' Register 4 Feb 1674 attributes trn to J.B.; tr E. Farneworth, Works, 2 vols 1762, 4 vols 1775 ('corrected').
The life of Castrucci Castracani. In S. Croxall, Select collection of novels vol 6, 1722, 1729.

Francesco Scipione Maffei

Rawlinson, R. A letter to the countess Canossa Tering of Seefeld: being a companion of the use of inscriptions and medals. In N. Lenglet du Fresnoy, New method of studying history vol 1, 1728.
Gordon, A. A compleat history of the ancient amphitheatres and in particular that of Verona. 1730, [1735?] (enlarged).
Ayre, W. Merope: a tragedy. 1740.

Carlo Maria Maggi

Orton, Job. Noah's faith and obedience; to which is added a prose-translation of a poem by C. M. Maggi, on the same subject. 1756.

Giovanni Paolo Marana

[Bradshaw, W.] Letters writ by a Turkish spy, who liv'd five and forty years at Paris: giving an account of the most remarkable transactions of Europe from 1637 to 1682. 8 vols 1687–93; 24 edns by 1754. From Esploratore turco.

Giovanni Ambrogio Marini

The desperadoes: an heroick history. 1733.

Giovanni Battista Marino

R., T. The slaughter of the innocents by Herod. 1675.

Agostino Mascardi

Fieschi's conspiracy. In A collection of select discourses out of the most eminent wits of France and Italy, 1678; A caveat to Britons: being the history of Fieschi's conspiracy, 1735.
Hare, Hugh. Historical relation of the conspiracy of John Lewis Fieschi. 1693.

Pietro Antonio Domenico Bonaventura Metastasio

Titus Vespasian: a tragedy. 1755; Conspiracy: a tragedy. 1796. From La clemenza di Tito.

Artaxerxes: an opera. 1734; also adapted Thomas Arne, Artaxerxes: an English opera, [1761].
Adriano in Siria. 1735.
Issipile. 1735; Hypsipile: an opera, 1735.
Didone Abbandonata. 1754.
Murphy, A. The desert island: a dramatic poem. 1760; tr Anne Williams, The uninhabited island, in Miscellanies in prose and verse, 1766. From L'isola disabitata.
Rolt, Richard. The royal shepherd. Dublin [1764?]. From Il re pastore.
Hoole, John. Works. 2 vols 1767. Contains Artaxerxes, The Olympiad, Hypsipile, Titus, Demetrius, Demophoon.
Hoole, John. Dramas and other poems. 3 vols 1800. Contains all dramas of 1767 edn, and also The dream of Scipio, Achilles in Scyros, Adrian in Syria, Dido, Aetius, The uninhabited isle, The triumph of Glory, Zenobia, Themistocles, Siroes, Regulas, Romulus and Hersilia, Discovery of Joseph and several cantatas.
Hoole, John. Timanthes. 1770. From Demofoönte.
Hamilton, Charles. The patriot. [1784], Dublin 1785. From Themistocles.
Poems. Coventry 1790.
[Le Mesurier, Thomas]. Translations chiefly from the Italian of Petrarch and Metastasio. Oxford 1795.
Olivari, T. Three dramatic pieces: The dream of Scipio; The birth of Jupiter; Astrea appeased. Dublin 1797.

Fulgentio Micanzio

The life of Father Paul [Pietro Sarpi] of the order of the Servi. In Sarpi's History of the Council of Trent, 1676.
Some letters relating to the history of Trent. 1705.

Leo Modena

Ockley, S. The history of the present Jews throughout the world. 1707, 1711.

Francesco Morosini

A journal of the Venetian Campaigne AD 1687. 1688.

Lodovico Antonio Muratori

A relation of the missions to Paraguay, done into English from the French translation. 1759.

Giovanni Battista Felice Gasparo Nani

Honywood, Sir R. The history of the affairs of Europe in this present age, but more particularly of the Republick of Venice. 1673; A complete history of Europe, 1705.

Antonio Neri

M[erret], C. The art of glass: wherein are shown the ways to make and colour glass, pastes, enamels, lakes and other curiosities. 1662.

Andrea Palladio

Richards, Godfrey. The first book of architecture: the second edition corrected and enlarged. 1668, 1676, 1708 (7th edn). Stationers' Register 31 Jan 1663. Other edns and trns: N. Du Bois, The architecture in four books; to which are added several notes and observations made by Inigo Jones, 15 pts 1715; rev G. Leoni 2 vols 1742 (3rd edn corrected); tr Isaac Ware, The four books of architecture, 1738.
Cameron, C. The baths of the Romans explained and illustrated, with the restorations of Palladio corrected and improved. 1772.

Sforza Pallavicino

The new politick light of modern Rome's church-government. 1678, 1681 (as The policy of Rome). From Pietro Sarpi, History of the Council of Trent.

Guido Panciroli

The history of many memorable things lost, which were in use among the Ancients and an account of many excellent things found, now in use among the Moderns. 2 vols 1715, 1727. From Latin.

Giuseppe Parini

A fashionable day. 1780. A free trn in prose of Il Mattino and Il Mezzogiorno.
Friendship preferred to love. In Poetry, original and selected vol 2, Glasgow [179–?].

Francesco Petrarca

See G. Watson, The English Petrarchans: a critical bibliography of the Canzoniere, 1967 (Warburg Inst).
Pope, Walter. Patient Grissel. In Select novels, 1694; tr George Ogle, Gualtherus and Griselda, Dublin 1741.
[Nott, John?]. Sonnets and odes. 1777, 1808 (rev). 30 sonnets and 3 odes.
Tytler, A. F. Essays on the life and character of Petrarch, to which are added seven of his sonnets. 1784.
Dobson, Mrs. Petrarch's view of human life. 1791, 1797. From De remediis utriusque fortunae.
[Le Mesurier, Thomas]. Translations chiefly from Petrarch and Metastasio. Oxford 1795. Contains 24 sonnets from Petrarch.

Pius II (Enea Silvio Piccolomini)

The history of the amours of Count Schlick and a young lady. 3 pts 1708, 1741 (as The art of love). Euralius and Lucretia translated.

Giovanni Battista Primi-Ammonio

An account of the reasons which induced Charles II to declare war against the States-General in 1672, as they are set down in the history of the Dutch war. 1689.
The history of the war in Holland. In A collection of State tracts vol 1, 1705.

Vincenzo Puccini

[Smith, T.] The life of St Mary Magdalene of Pazzi, a Carmelite nun. 1687.

Bernardino Ramazzini

St Clair, R. The Abyssinian philosophy confuted: or telluris theoria neither sacred nor agreeable to reason. 1697. From Latin.
Hoffmann, Friedrich. A treatise on the diseases of tradesmen. In Dissertation on endemial diseases, 1746, 1750. From Latin.

Cesare Ripa

Tempest, P. Iconologia: or moral emblems, wherein are express'd various images of virtues, vices [etc]. 1709.

Giacomo Rossi

Hill, A. Rinaldo: an opera. 1711; tr S. Humphreys 1731.
The faithful shepherd: an opera. 1712.

Bartholomaeus Sacchi (de Platina)

Rycaut, Sir Paul. The lives of the Popes from the time of our Saviour. 1685, 1688 ('corrected'). From Latin.

Pietro Sarpi (Paolo Servita)

A., E. The papacy of Paul the fourth: or the restitution of abbey lands and impropriations, an indispensable condition of reconciliation to the infallible See. 1673. From History of the Council of Trent, bk 5. Full trn by Sir Nanthaniel Brent, The history of the Council of

Trent; whereunto is added the life of the author [by F. Micanzio] and the history of the inquisition [tr R. Gentilis], 1676.

Denton, W. A treatise of matters beneficiary. 1680; tr Tobias Jenkins, A treatise of beneficiary matters: or a history of ecclesiastical benefices and revenues, 1727, Westminster 1727, London 1730, Westminster 1736 (as A treatise of ecclesiastical benefices and revenues), Dublin 1737.

Aglionby, W. The opinions of Padre Paolo in what manner the republic of Venice ought to govern themselves. 1689; The maxims of the government of Venice, in an advice to the republick how it ought to govern itself both inwardly and outwardly, 1707.

Brown, Edward. The letters of the renowned Father Paul. 1693.

Whatley, Stephen. The rights of sovereigns and subjects: to which is prefix'd the life of the author and an account of his writings. 1722, 1725.

Vincenzo Scamozzi

The mirrour of architecture: or the ground-rules of the art of building. 2 pts 1669, 1687, 1 vol 1700 (4th edn).

Alessandro Scarlatti (with Adriano Marselli)

MacSwinny, O. Pyrrhus and Demetrius. 1709. From Pirro e Demetrio.

Baptista Spagnuoli (Mantuanus)

Mantuan english'd and paraphras'd: or the character of a bad woman. [London? 1680?]. Eclogue 3, from Latin.

Lazzaro Spallanzani

[Maty, M.] An essay on animal reproduction. 1769.
Dissertations relative to the natural history of animals and vegetables. 1784, 2 vols 1789 ('corrected and enlarged'); tr J. Dalyell, Tracts on the nature of animals and vegetables, Edinburgh 1799, 2 vols Edinburgh 1803.
Travels in the two Sicilies and some parts of the Apennines. 4 vols 1798.

Famiano Strada

Musical duet, much enlarg'd in English, by the addition of several traverses between the harper and the nightingale, together with a more particular account of the contest. 1671.

Luigi Tansillo

Roscoe, W. The nurse: a poem. Liverpool 1798, 1800, Dublin 1800, New York 1800.

Torquato Tasso

Dancer, John. Aminta: the famous pastoral. 1660 (decasyllabic couplets). Other trns: John Oldmixon, Amintas, 1698 (unrhymed octosyllables); P. B. Du Bois, Tasso's Aminta: a pastoral comedy, Oxford 1726, nd; William Ayre, Amintas: a dramatick pastoral, [1737] (decasyllabic couplets); Percival Stockdale, The Amyntas, 1770 (blank verse).
Bond, William. The third book of Jerusalem delivered.

1718. Other trns: Henry Brooke, Tasso's Jerusalem: books 1–3, 1738 (decasyllabic couplets); Thomas Hooke, The Jerusalem bk i, 1738 (decasyllabic couplets); H. Layng, Tasso's xv book of Jerusalem, deliver'd; Tasso's xvi book, the recovery of Jerusalem, in Several pieces in prose and verse, 1748 (decasyllabic couplets); P. Doyne, The delivery of Jerusalem, translated into blank verse; to which is added the life of Tasso [by H. Layng], and an essay on the Gerusalemme liberata, 2 vols 1761; John Hoole, Jerusalem delivered [with a life of Tasso], 2 vols 1763, 1764, 1767, 1783 (5th edn), 1797 (decasyllabic couplets). First translated E. Fairfax 1600.

Hoole, John. Rinaldo: a poem in xii books. 1792 (decasyllabic couplets).

Pietro della Valle

Havers, George. The travels of P. della Valle [in India]. 1665.

Francesco Vanneschi

Lockman, J. Fetonte. 1747. With discourse on opera.

Giorgio Vasari

Aglionby, W. Painting illustrated in three dialogues: containing some choice observations upon the art; together with the lives of the most eminent painters, from Cimabue to Michel-Angelo. 1686, 1719. With selections from Vasari's Lives.

Alessandro Verri

The Roman nights [at the tomb of the Scipios]. 1798.

Marcus Hieronymus Vida

Silk worms: a poem in two books, with a preface giving an account of the life and writings of Vida. 1723; tr S. Pullein, The silkworm: a poem in two books, Dublin 1750. From Latin.

Pitt, Christopher. Art of poetry. 1725, 1742; tr J. Hampson, Poetics with translations from the Latin of Dr Lowth, Mr Gray and others, Sunderland 1793. From Latin.

Morell, T. Hymn to God the Father, to God the Son, to God the Holy Ghost. In Poems on divine subjects, 1732. From Hymni de rebus divinis.

Erskine, William. Scacchia ludus: or the game of chess and a translation of Vida's three pastoral eglogues, by Mr Craig. 1736; tr George Jeffreys, Chess: a poem, 1736; S. Pullein, Scacchia ludus: a poem on chess, Dublin 1750; The game of chess, Eton 1769; Oxford 1778 (another trn); tr Arthur Murphy, The game of chess, in his Works vol 7, 1786; Game of chess, first ptd from 18th-century ms in Oliver Goldsmith, Works vol 4, 1854, pp. 377–94, with erroneous attribution of trn to Goldsmith. From Latin.

Cranwell, J. The Christiad: a poem. Cambridge 1768 (with Latin); tr E. Granan, The Christiad, 1771.

Giovanni Battista Felice Zappi

[Huggins, William?] Sonetti scelti et traduti dallo traduttore dell' Ariosto. 1755 (priv ptd). Italian and English.

S. S. B. T.

V. SPORT

This section lists works of literature, including minor verse, which take sport as their subject, as well as connected treatises in English. Mere records are usually excluded, apart from some on horsemanship and cricket, and so are technical treatises, sporting prints, works expounding gambling laws, homiletic works on duelling and gaming, and religious and political pieces which treat sport as allegory. Cross-references to authors elsewhere in the volume are not included.

(1) BIBLIOGRAPHIES

Slater, J. H. Illustrated sporting books. 1899.

Nevill, R. Old English sporting books. Ed G. Holme 1924.

Wright, L. H. Sporting books in the Huntington Library. San Marino 1937.

Gee, E. R. The sportsman's library: being a descriptive list of the most important books on sport. New York 1940.

Six hundred years of sport: catalogue of an exhibition held at the Grolier Club. New York 1940.

(2) GENERAL STUDIES (INCLUDING PERIODICALS)

[Cotton, Charles]. The compleat gamester: or instructions how to play at billiards, trucks, bowls, chess, cards; to which is added the arts and mysteries of riding, racing, archery and cock-fighting. 1674, 1676, 1680, 1709, 1710, 1721, 1725.

H[owlett], R[obert]. The school of recreation: or the gentleman's tutor to the most ingenious exercises of hunting, racing, hawking, riding, cock-fighting, fowling, fishing, shooting, bowling, tennis, ringing, billiards. 1684, 1696, 1701, 1710, 1719, 1720, 1732, 1736, 1770, 1784.

[Worlidge, John]. Dictionarium rusticum et urbanicum: or a dictionary of all sorts of country affairs. 1704, 1717, 1726.

The sportsman's dictionary: or the country gentleman's companion in all rural recreations, extracted from English and French authors ancient and modern. 2 vols 1735, 1744, 1778 (as The sportsman's dictionary: or the gentleman's companion for town and country), 1782, 1785, 1786, 1792, 1800, 1807 (improved and enlarged by H. J. Pye).

The country gentleman's companion, by a country gentleman from his own experience. 2 vols 1753, 1756.

Fairfax, Thomas. The complete sportsman: or the country gentleman's recreation. 1758, [1760?], 1762, 1764, [1770?]; rev George Morgan [1770?] (as The new complete sportsman), 1795.

Strutt, Joseph. Horda Angel-cynnan: or a compleat view of the manners of the inhabitants of England from the arrival of the Saxons till the reign of Henry the Eighth. 3 vols 1775-6.

—— Glig-gamena Angel-ðeod: or the sports and pastimes of the people of England. 1801, 1810; ed J. C. Cox 1903.

Pye, Henry James. Amusement: a poetical essay. 1790.

The sporting magazine: or monthly calendar of the transactions of the turf, the chace and every other diversion interesting to the man of pleasure. 1792-1870.

Blaine, D. P. An encyclopaedia of rural sports. 1840, 1852, 1858, 1870.

The Badminton Library. Ed Duke of Beaufort 1885 etc. A series, each vol rev at intervals.

Gomme, Lady A. B. The traditional games of England, Scotland and Ireland. 2 vols 1894-9; ed D. Howard, New York 1964.

Peek, H. The poetry of sport. 1896 (Badminton Lib).

Hackwood, F. W. Old English sports. 1897, 1907.

The encyclopaedia of sport. Ed Earl of Suffolk and Berkshire 2 vols 1897-8, 4 vols 1911.

Wood, L. S. and H. L. Burrows. Sports and pastimes in English literature. 1925.

The Lonsdale Library of sports, games and pastimes. Ed E. Parker 1929 etc. A series.

Hare, C. E. The language of sport. 1939.

Kirby, C. The literary history of English field sports 1671-1850. In Studies in British history, ed C. W. de Kiewiet, Iowa City 1941.

Hole, C. English sports and pastimes. 1949.

Wymer, N. G. Sport in England. 1949.

Higginson, A. H. British and American sporting authors: their writings and biographies, with a bibliography by Sydney R. Smith. Berryville Virginia 1949, London 1951.

Brailsford, D. Sport and society: Elizabeth to Anne. 1969.

(3) INDIVIDUAL SPORTS

Horsemanship and Farriery

Hore, H. F. The history of Newmarket and the annals of the turf. 3 vols 1886.

Huth, F. H. Works on horses and equitation: a bibliographical record of hippology. 1887.

Blew, W. C. A. A history of steeplechasing. 1901.

Cook, T. A. A history of the English turf. 2 vols 1904.

Prior, C. M. Early records of the thoroughbred horse. 1924.

The Keeneland Association Library: a guide to the collection. Lexington Kentucky 1958. A catalogue of horse-racing library.

Bloodgood, L. F. and P. Santini. The horseman's dictionary: including over 3,500 words used on the turf, hunting field, in the stable or stud. 1963.

General Studies

Cheny, J. An historical list of all horse-matches run in England in 1727[-49]. 24 vols [1727-50].

Pond, J. The sporting kalendar, containing a distinct account of what plates and matches have been run for in 1751[-7]. 7 vols [1751-7].

Heber, R. An historical list of horse-matches run in Great Britain and Ireland in 1751[-68]. 18 vols 1752-69.

Walker, B. An historical list of horse-matches run in Great Britain and Ireland in 1769[-70]. 2 vols 1770-1.

Tuting, W. and T. Fawconer. The sporting calendar, containing an account of the plates, matches and sweepstakes run for in Great Britain in 1769[-75]. 8 vols 1770-6.

The racing calendar, containing an account of the plates, matches and sweepstakes run for in Great Britain and Ireland in 1773 [etc]. 1773 to the present.

An introduction to a general stud book, containing the pedigree of every horse, mare, of note that has appeared on the turf for the last fifty years. 1791.

The general stud book, from the earliest accounts to the year 1964 inclusive. 1965.

Prior, C. M. The history of the racing calendar and stud book from their inception in the eighteenth century. 1926.

§1

Cavendish, William, Duke of Newcastle. Méthode et invention nouvelle de dresser les chevaux, traduis de l'anglais de l'auteur par son commandement. Antwerp 1658, London 1737; tr as vol 1 of A general system of horsemanship in all its branches [vol 2 contains works by G. de Saunier], 2 vols 1743.

—— A new method and extraordinary invention to dress horses. 1667, 1677, Dublin 1740. Distinct from above.

The call to the races at Newmarket. [1670?], [1690?]. A ballad.

H[alfpenny], J[ohn]. The gentleman's jockey and approved

farrier, collected by J.H. esquire; T.D., N.S., R.B., J.W. and others. 1671, 1672, 1674, 1676, 1687 (8th edn).

Almond, Robert. The English horsman and complete farrier, with the humours of a Smithfield jockey. 1673.

R., E. The experienced farrier. 1678, 1691, 1720.

'Physiologus, Philotheos' (Thomas Tryon). The country-man's companion: or a new method of ordering horses and sheep. 1680, [1684?], 1700.

The horse-manship of England, most particularly relating to the breeding and training of the running-horse: a poem dedicated to the Duke of Monmouth. 1682.

Snape, Andrew. The anatomy of an horse exprest in 49 copper plates; to which is added an appendix containing two discourses, the one of the generation of animals, and the other of the motion of the chyle and the circulation of the blood. 1683, 1687, 1700.

The experienced jockey, compleat horseman or gentle-man's delight: containing plain directions in breeding and managing horses, the art of shooing. 1684.

L., G. The gentleman's new jockey: or farrier's approved guide. 1687, 1708, 1721.

The compleat jockey. 1695.

Hope, Sir William. The Parfait Mareschal or compleat farrier [tr from J. de Solleysell, Le parfait mareschal, Paris 1664]; together with a treatise how to raise and bring up a true and beautiful race of horses. Edinburgh 1696, London 1717 (as The compleat horseman); abridged 1702, 1706, 1711, 1717.

S., A., gent. The gentleman's compleat jockey, with the perfect horseman and experienc'd farrier. 1697, 1782.

Gibson, William. The farrier's new guide. 1720, 1721, 1725 (4th edn), 1727, 1729, 1731.

— The farrier's dispensatory. 1721, 1726, 1729, 1734, 1741.

— The true method of dieting horses, with a discourse of breeding. 1721, 1726, 1731.

— A new treatise on the diseases of horses. 1751, 2 vols 1754.

— A short and practical method of cure for horses. 1755.

The farrier's and horseman's dictionary: being a complete system of horsemanship. 1726.

Bambridge, Thomas. A letter to John Hawkins, late Keeper of Newgate, with a word of advice particularly on his race-horses. Dublin 1729.

Burdon, William. The gentleman's pocket farrier. 1730, 1732, 1735 (with remarks by H. Bracken), 1737, 1748, 1780, 1788.

The gentleman's farrier: containing instructions for the choice and directions in the management of horses [and] an appendix concerning dogs. 1732.

Mawer, John. Oppian's Cynegeticks [bk 1 only] translated into English verse. 1736.

Bracken, Henry. Farriery improved. 1738, 1739, 1743, 1745 (5th edn), 1749, 1756 (8th edn), 1790, York 1792.

— The traveller's pocket farrier. 1742, 1743, 1750 (5th edn).

Bridges, Jeremiah. No foot, no horse: an essay on the anatomy of the foot of that noble animal a horse. 1751, 1752, 1759.

Bartlet, John. The gentleman's farriery: or a practical treatise on the diseases of horses. 1754 (2nd edn), 1756, 1764 (5th edn), 1770 (7th edn), 1777 (9th edn), 1785 (11th edn).

— A treatise on the diseases of horses. 1758, 1764.

— Pharmacopoeia hippiatrica: or the gentleman farrier's repository, in two books. Eton 1764, [1773].

Berenger, Richard (tr). A new system of horsemanship [from Claude Bourgelat, Elémens d'hippiatrique, Lyons 1750–3]. 1754.

— The history and art of horsemanship [from Xenophon; Bourgelat, Elémens; T. Pownall, Dissertation on the ancient chariot]. 2 vols 1771.

Lafosse, Etienne Guillaume. Observations and discoveries made upon horses, with a new method of shoeing [from the French]. 1755.

Osmer, William. A dissertation on horses, wherein it is determined by matters of fact as well as from the principles of philosophy that innate qualities do not exist, and that the excellence of this animal is altogether mechanical and not in the blood. 1756, 1757.

— A treatise on the diseases and lameness of horses. 1759, 1761, 1830 (5th edn, rewritten by J. Hinds).

Reeves, John. The art of farriery both in theory and practice. 1757, 1763.

Wood, John. A compendious treatise of farriery. 1757, 1762.

Ellis, William. Every farmer his own farrier. 1759.

Wallis, Thomas. The farrier's and horseman's complete dictionary. 1759, 1764, 1775.

Roberts, James and Henry. The sportsman's pocket companion: being a striking likeness or portraiture of the most eminent race horses and stallions in this Kingdom, to which is added their pedigrees and performances. [1760?].

Wall, Richard. A dissertation on breeding of horses upon philosophical and experimental principles. [1760?].

Pembroke, Henry Herbert, 10th Earl of. A method of breaking horses and teaching soldiers to ride, designed for the use of the army. 1761, 1762, Salisbury 1778 (as Military equitation).

Thompson, Charles. Rules for bad horsemen. 1762, 1763, 1765, 1787 (5th edn), 1830 (with addns by J. Hinds).

Jackson, J. L. The art of riding: or horsemanship made easy. 1765.

Ten minutes advice to every gentleman going to purchase a horse. 1766.

Saunier, Gaspar de. A guide to the perfect knowledge of horses [tr from Jean de Saunier, La parfaite connoissance des chevaux, ed G. de S., Hague 1734]. 1769. Also pbd as vol 2 of William Cavendish, A general system of horsemanship, 1743.

Clark, James. Observations upon the shoeing of horses. Edinburgh 1770, 1775, Dublin 1777.

— A treatise on the prevention of diseases incidental to horses; to which are subjoined observations on farriery. Edinburgh 1788, 1790 (enlarged), 1805 (4th edn).

— First lines of veterinary physiology and pathology. Vol 1 (all pbd), Edinburgh 1806.

[Parsons, Philip]. Newmarket: or an essay on the turf. 2 vols 1771, 1775.

Hughes, Charles. The compleat horseman: or the art of riding made easy. [1772].

Blunt, John. Practical farriery. 1773.

Astley, Philip. The modern riding master. 1774, 1775.

— Astley's system of equestrian education. 1801, [1801] (3rd edn), [1801?] (5th edn), Dublin 1802 (7th edn).

— Astley's projects in his management of the horse: an abridgement of his Book of equestrian education. 1804.

Mills, John. A treatise on cattle, shewing the most approved methods of breeding, rearing and fitting for use, horses [etc]. 1776.

Ward, William. A new treatise on the method of breeding, breaking and training horses. Edinburgh 1776.

Consideration on the breed and management of horses: interspersed with some remarks and calculations on the exportation and importation of corn. 1778.

Maples, John. The new complete horse doctor: or horse-man's sure guide and every man his own farrier. [1778?], [1779?] (as The horseman's sure guide).

Clater, Francis. Every man his own farrier: containing the causes of the diseases of horses and dogs. Newark 1783, London 1810 (21st edn); rev E. Mayhew 1854 (30th edn), 1861.

Griffiths, William. A practical treatise on farriery. Wrexham 1784.

Watson, T. Instructions for the management of horses and dogs. 1785.

'Gambado, Geoffrey' (Henry William Bunbury). An academy for grown horsemen. 1787, 1788, 1796, 1808 (3rd edn), 1809 (illustr T. Rowlandson).

—— Annals of horsemanship. 1791, 1808. Usually bound with above and issued as one work.

Forrester, William. The gentleman's experienced farrier. 1788.

Merrick, William. The classical farrier. 1788.

Taplin, William. The gentleman's stable directory: or modern system of farriery. 1788, 2 vols 1788 (4th edn), 1 vol [1791] (11th edn), 1793. See A. G. Sinclair, 1792 below.

—— A compendium of practical and experimental farriery. Brentford 1796.

—— Taplin improved: or a compendium of farriery, by an experienced farrier. 1790, 1794, 1811.

Prosser, Thomas. A treatise on the strangles and fevers of horses. 1790.

Snape, Edward. A practical treatise on farriery. 1791.

Vial de Saint Bel, Charles. Of the proportions of Eclipse [the famous racehorse]. 1791 (in French and English), 1797.

—— Lectures on the elements of farriery. 1793.

—— The [posthumous] works. 1795. With memoir.

—— The sportsman, farrier and shoeing-smith's new guide: being the substance of the works of the late C. V. de St B., a short account of his life [and] an appendix [from other writers]. [1796?]. Compiled by John Lawrence.

Gooch, Thomas. The life and death of a racehorse; with an essay tending to excite a benevolent conduct toward the brute creation by the late Dr Hawksworth, to which is now added the Song of the race horse. 1792.

Morland, Thomas Hornby. Every man his own judge: or grandeur and utility pointed out in the formation of the horse. Ipswich 1792.

—— The genealogy of the English race horse. 1810.

Sinclair, A. G. Critical observations and remarks on A stable directory of W. Taplin; with explanations of all the diseases incident to the horse. 1792.

Stovin, Aistroppe. The law respecting horses. Hull 1794.

Chifney, Samuel. Genius genuine: why there are so few good runners or why the turf horses degenerate. [1795?], 1804.

—— The narrative or address of Samuel Chifney to the public, particularly to such of them as are connected with the turf. 1800.

The horse-race: or the pleasures of the course. Bath [1795?]. A ballad.

Hunter, James. A complete dictionary of farriery and horsemanship. Birmingham 1796.

Lawrence, John. A philosophical and practical treatise on horses. 2 vols 1796–8, 1802, 1810.

Tyndale, W. A treatise on military equitation. 1797.

Coleman, Edward. Observations on the structure, oeconomy and diseases of the foot of the horse. 2 vols 1798–1802.

—— Observation on the formation and uses of the natural frog of the horse. 1800.

Adams, John. The analysis of horsemanship. 1799, 3 vols 1805, 1812.

Blaine, Delabere Pritchett. Anatomy of the horse: accompanied with remarks, physiological, pathological, chirurgical and natural. [1799], 1802.

Moorcroft, William. Cursory account of the various methods of shoeing horses. 1800.

White, James. A compendium of the veterinary art. Canterbury 1800, 1802.

Hunting, Coursing, Hawking, Fowling, Angling etc

Kreysig, G. C. Bibliotheca scriptorum venaticorum. Altenburg 1750.

[Dansey, W.] Arrian on coursing. 1831. Xenophon's Cynegetica, tr with addn of original matter and a bibliography.

Miles, H. D. (ed). The book of field sports. [1860–3].

Lambert, O. Angling literature in England. 1881.

Catalogue of books on angling. Cambridge 1882.

Westwood, T. and F. Satchell. Bibliotheca piscatoria. 1883.

—— Supplement [with omissions and works pbd 1883–1900]. 1901. Appendix by R. B. Marston to The English catalogue of books for 1900.

Souhart, R. Bibliographie générale des ouvrages sur la chasse, la vénerie et la fauconnerie. Paris 1886.

—— Quelques additions par Paul Petit. Paris 1888.

Harting, J. E. Bibliotheca accipitraria: a catalogue of books ancient and modern relating to falconry, with notes, glossary and vocabulary. 1891, 1964.

Hore, H. F. History of the royal buckhounds. 1895.

Albee, L. R. The Bartlet collection: a list of books on angling, fishes and fish culture in Harvard College Library. Cambridge Mass 1896.

'Gerrare, W.' (W. O. Greener). A bibliography of guns and shooting. 1896.

Coaten, A. W. British hunting: a complete history. 1910.

Turrell, W. J. Ancient angling authors. 1910.

Catalogue of an exhibition of angling books 1911–12. New York [1911] (Grolier Club).

Dean, B. with C. R. Eastman, E. W. Gudger and A. W. Henn. A bibliography of fishes. 3 vols New York 1916–23, 1962.

Schwerdt, C. F. G. R. Hunting, hawking, shooting: illustrated in a catalogue of books, manuscripts, prints and drawings. 4 vols 1928–37.

Higginson, A. H. Peter Beckford, esquire, sportsman, traveller, man of letters: a biography. 1937.

Robb, James. Notable angling literature. [1947].

Riling, R. L. J. Guns and shooting: a selected chronological bibliography. New York 1951.

§ 1

Stevenson, Matthew. The twelve moneths: directions relating to husbandry as also of recreations, as hunting, hawking, fishing, fowling, coursing, cock-fighting. 1661, 1930 (selected).

Venables, Robert. The experienc'd angler: or angling improv'd. 1662, [1666] (edn destroyed in Great Fire), 1668 (enlarged), 1676, 1683, 1825 (with memoir of author); ed H. Hutchinson 1927 (with Gervase Markham, Pleasures of princes).

B[lagrave], J[oseph]. The epitome of the art of husbandry [with Brief experimental directions for the right use of the angle]. 1669, 1670, 1675, 1685.

W[orlidge], J[ohn]. Systema agriculturae: the mystery of husbandry discovered. 1669, 1675, 1681, 1687, 1697 (4th edn corrected and amended and many addns), 1716 (5th edn as A compleat system of husbandry). Includes chapter on fowling and fishing.

Barlow, Francis. Severall wayes of hunting, hawking and fishing according to the English manner, invented by F.B., etched by W. Hollar. 1671. Plates with quatrains.

Cox, Nicholas. The gentleman's recreation, in four parts: hunting, hawking, fowling, fishing. 1674, 1677, 1686 (with addn of G. Langbaine, 1685 below), 1697,1706, 1721, 1731, 4 pts [1815?]; ed E. W. D. Cuming 1928.

[Wolley, Hannah]. The accomplish'd lady's delight in preserving, physick, beautifying and cookery. 1675, 1677, 1683, 1684, 1685, 1696, 1719 (10th edn). Includes New and excellent experiments and secrets in the art of angling.

Cotton, Charles. The compleat angler, pt 2. 1676.

Gilbert, William. The angler's delight. 1676, 1682 (as The young angler's companion).

Willughby, Francis. The ornithology: to which are added discourses: 1, Of the art of fowling; 2, Of the ordering of singing birds; 3, Of falconry, by John Ray. 1678. Willughby's text first issued in Latin, 1676.

—— De historia piscium libri quatuor recognovit J. Raius. 1685–6.

[Chetham, James]. The angler's vade mecum: or a compendious yet full discourse of angling. 1681, 1689, 1700.

Nobbes, Robert. The compleat troller. 1682, other edns nd, Norwich [1800?] (in The angler's pocket-book), London 1805 (in The angler's pocket-book), 1814 (in T. Best, The art on angling).

Browne, Sir Thomas. Certain miscellany tracts. 1683, 1684. No 5 on hawks and falconry.

A treatise of oxen, sheep, hogs and dogs, with their natures, qualities and uses. 1683. Includes sporting dogs.

Smith, John. Profit and pleasure united: or the husband-man's magazine; to which is added the art of angling, hunting, hawking and the noble recreation of ringing. 1684, 1704.

[Langbaine, Gerard?]. The hunter: a discourse of horse-manship. 1685. Also incorporated in 1686 edn of N. Cox, Gentleman's recreation, above.

Blome, Richard. The gentleman's recreation, in two parts. 2 pts 1686, 3 pts 1710 (corrected and enlarged).

—— Hawking: or falconry [pt 2 of above]. Ed E. W. D. Cuming 1929.

W., R., gent. A necessary family-book for the city and country, containing directions for taking and killing all manner of vermin: as the fox, polcat. 1688, 1710.

Heyrick, Thomas. Miscellany poems. 1691. Includes 2 long poems, The chase of the fox at Welby 1677 and A pindarique ode in praise of angling.

Franck, Richard. Northern memoirs; to which is added the contemplative and practical angler. 1694; ed W. Scott 1821.

S[mith?], J[ohn?], gent. The true art of angling. 1696, 1697, 1704 (as The compleat fisher), 1716, 1725, 1740, [1750?] (6th edn), 1770.

The innocent epicure, or the art of angling: a poem. Ed Nahum Tate. 1697, 1713, 1741 (with a few new lines as Angling: a poem). With paraphrase on Horace Ep 1 10 as From J.S. to C.S.

S., A., gent. The husbandman, farmer and grasier's compleat instructor. 1697. Includes dog breeding.

S., J., gent. The experienc'd fowler: or the gentleman, citizen and countryman's pleasant and profitable recreation. 1697, 1704.

The fox chace: or the huntsman's harmony. [1700?]. A ballad.

The husbandman's jewel; to which are added the arts of angling, hawking, fowling, ringing. [1700?].

Lambert, James. The countryman's treasure; to which is added the art of hawking, hunting and the noble recreation of ringing. [1700?]. Edns of 1676 and 1683 do not include matter on field sports.

Whitney, John. The genteel recreation or the pleasure of angling: a poem, with a dialogue between Piscator and Corydon. 1700, 1820 (facs).

More, Sir J. [Sir Jonas Moore?]. England's interest: or the gentleman and farmer's friend, shewing instructions for the profitable ordering of fish-ponds and for breeding of fish. 1703 (2nd edn), 1705, 1707, 1721 (adds A guide for young anglers).

A family jewel: or the womans councellor. 1704. Pt 4, The art of angling improved.

G., C., a brother of the angle. The secrets of angling. 1705. Also included in A family jewel, 1704, above.

H[owlett], R[obert]. The angler's sure guide: or angling improved. 1706.

Mortimer, John. The whole art of husbandry. 1707, 2 pts 1708–12, 1716 (4th edn), 1721, 2 vols 1761 (rev T. Mortimer, with memoir). Includes construction of fishponds.

Ward, Edward. Wars of the elements; to which are added the Contemplative angler. 1708, 1730.

Forest harmony: or the music of the English and French horns as it is now performed in field, park, forest or chase, with the proper notes, terms and characters made use of in field hunting. [1709?].

Gay, John. Rural sports. 1713.

[North, Roger]. A discourse of fish and fish ponds. 1713, 1715, 1773, 1794 (in E. Albin, History of esculent fish).

[Curll, Edmund?]. The whole art of fishing. 1714, 1727 (as The gentleman fisher).

Stringer, Arthur. The experienced huntsman. Belfast 1714, Dublin 1780.

Tickell, Thomas. Fragment of a poem on hunting. In Tonson's poetical miscellanies, 1714.

Jacob, Giles. The country gentleman's vade-mecum. 1717.

—— The compleat sportsman. 3 pts 1718.

Markland, [George]. Pteryplegia, or the art of shooting-flying: a poem. 1717, 1727, 1727, Dublin 1727, 1735, 1767.

October: a poem inscrib'd to the fox hunters of Great Britain. 1717.

Cynegetica, or the force and pleasure of hunting: an heroi-comical poem by a gentleman of the Inner Temple. 1718.

Fishing and hunting. [1720?].

A new hunting song made on a fox chase. [1720?]. A ballad.

Bradley, Richard. A philosophical account of the works of nature. 1721, 1739 (rev). Ch 4 on fish, 15 on ponds.

—— Dictionaire oeconomique: or the family dictionary, done into English from M. Chomel with considerable alterations and improvements. 2 vols 1725. Encyclo-paedia of English country life, including sports.

—— A complete body of husbandry. 1727. Ch 15 on game preservation, 18 on horses.

—— The gentleman and farmer's guide for the increase and improvement of cattle, also the best manner of breeding and breaking horses. 1729.

King Satan or the hunting of the senator: a Newmarket tale told by an old fox hunter and address'd to all true sportsmen. 1724. Verse.

Saunders, James. The compleat fisherman. 1724, 1725 (as The compleat troller), 1778, [1800?] (as The fisherman by Guiniad Charfy esq).

The gentleman angler, by a gentleman who has made angling his diversion upwards of twenty-eight years. 1726, 1736 (with large addns), 1743, 1753, 1760 (as The angler's magazine, combined with extracts from G. Smith, The angler's magazine, 1754), 1786.

'Immerito' (Moses Browne). Piscatory eclogues. 1729; rptd in Poems on various subjects, 1739, and as Angling sports in Nine piscatory dialogues, 1773.

Keill, James. A practical treatise upon angling. Edin-burgh 1729.

The famous ballad of Badsworth hunt: or the most excellent fox chase as performed in 1730. Pontefract [1730].

'A country squire'. An essay on hunting. 1733. Incor-porated in W. Blane, Essays on hunting, 1781.

Ford, Simon and Tipping Silvester. Piscatio or angling: a poem. Oxford 1733. Ford's original Latin pbd in Musarum anglicanarum analecta, 1692; freely adapted by Silvester. Other trns in H. Travers, Miscellaneous poems, 1731 and GM April 1765.

Somervile, William. The chace: a poem. 1735.

—— Hobbinol, or the rural games: a burlesque poem. 1740.

—— Field-sports: a poem. 1742.

The complete family-piece and country gentleman and farmer's best guide. 1736, 1737, 1741 (improved), 1749. Pt 2 on hunting etc.

Green, Matthew. The spleen. 1737. Verse.

The law suit, or the farmer and the fisherman: a poem. 1739.

[Powney, Richard]. The stag chace in Windsor Forest: a poem. 1739.

Brookes, Richard. The art of angling, rock and sea fishing. 1740, 1743, 1766, 1770; ed Moses Browne? 1774 (illustr), 1781, 1785, 1789, 1790, 1795, 1801 etc.

— The natural history of fishes and serpents. 1790. Appendix with The whole art of float and fly-fishing.

Williamson, John. The British angler: or a pocket companion for gentlemen-fishers. 1740.

S., J. Angling: a poem. 1741.

Armstrong, John. The art of preserving health: a poem. 1744. Bk 3, Exercise, sport.

Griffiths, Roger. An essay to prove that the conservacy of the Thames is committed to the Lord Mayor and City of London; to which is added a brief description of those fish that are caught in the Thames, with some few observations on fish in general. 1746; ed R. Binnell 1758 (as A description of the River Thames).

[Wilkes, Wetenhall]. Hounslow-heath: a poem. 1747, 1748 (enlarged); ed W. Pinkerton 1870 (priv ptd). Angling, coursing, shooting, hunting.

Gardiner, John Smallman. The art and pleasures of hare-hunting, in six letters. 1750; rptd in W. Blane, Essays on hunting, 1781; 1807 (with laws and articles of coursing established in the reign of Queen Elizabeth).

Thoughts on the present laws for preserving the game. 1750.

Young Jockey's garland. [1750?]. Contains a hunting song.

Drake, Frank. The Nostele hunt. 1754. A broadside poem.

— A mock chase. [1760?]. A broadside poem.

Gardiner, Richard. A letter to the Honourable George Townshend, in answer to the Norfolk farmer's sentiments on a Bill for doubling the qualification of sportsmen. 1754.

— September: a rural poem humbly inscribed to all sportsmen. 1780.

S[mith], G[eorge]. The angler's magazine: or necessary and delightful store-house. 1754.

[— ?]. The angler's magazine: or complete fisherman. 1760. The above with The gentleman angler, 1726 above.

— The laboratory; or school of arts. 1799, 1810. With section on angling.

Bowlker, Richard. The art of angling improved in all its parts, especially fly-fishing. Worcester [1758?], 1766 (as The universal angler), Birmingham [1774] (2nd edn much rev as Charles Bowlker, The art of angling and compleat fly-fishing), [1785?], 1788, London [1790?], Ludlow 1806, 1826 (enlarged), 1854.

[Scott, Thomas]. The anglers: eight dialogues in verse. 1758; rptd in W. Ruddiman, Collection of scarce pieces, 1773, 1785 (as The art of angling: eight dialogues in verse).

Coote, Robert. The compleat marksman, or the true art of shooting-flying: a poem. [1760?].

Crude thoughts on the Dog-Act by a person without eyes from his birth. Norwich 1763. Against increased tax, especially on sporting dogs.

The royal sportsman's delight: being a choice collection of the newest songs. [1765], [1800?], [1812?].

The country in full cry after poachers and hunters of various denominations, in a series of letters printed in the Edinburgh Advertisers. 1766.

Page, Thomas. The art of shooting-flying. Norwich 1766, 1767, London 1770 (4th edn with addns), [1785?].

Aldington, John. A poem on the various scenes of shooting. 1767.

— A poem on the cruelty of shooting. 1769. Incorporates the preceding item, much rev.

The complete grazier: or gentleman and farmer's directory, containing particular instructions for ordering, breeding and feeding pheasants and partridges, also directions for making fish ponds. 1767, 1775, 1776.

Fawkes, Francis. Partridge-shooting: an eclogue. 1767.

Smith, Robert. The universal directory for taking alive and destroying rats and all other kinds of four-footed and winged vermin. 1768, Dublin 1772, London 1786 (3rd edn), Weybridge 1812.

— The complete rat-catcher. 1768.

Essays on the Game Laws now existing in Great Britain; also proposals for the better preservation of game, by a sportsman. 1770.

The hunter's garland, beautified with several choice new songs. [Newcastle 1770?].

The hunting of the hare's garland, containing several choice new songs. [Newcastle 1770?].

Smith, Thomas. Every man his own fisherman. [1770?].

The sportsman's garland containing five new songs. Bristol [1770?].

Goodhall, Walter. The sportsman's pocket companion. [1770?]; also as The young sportsman's pocket companion, [1770?].

Edie, George. A treatise on English shooting. 1772, 1773, 1777 (as The art of English shooting).

Taplin, William. Observations on the present state of the game in England. 1772.

— An appeal to the representatives on the part of the people respecting the present destructive state of the game, with a prefatory address by the author of the Gentleman's stable directory. 1792.

— The sporting dictionary and rural repository of general information upon every subject appertaining to the sports of the field. 2 vols 1803.

— The sportsman's cabinet: or a correct delineation of the various dogs used in the sports of the field. 2 vols 1803.

Campbell, James. A treatise of modern faulconry. Edinburgh 1773.

Fitzgerald, Gerald. The academick sportsman, or a winter's day: a poem. 1773, Dublin 1780 (with alterations and addns).

The buck's bottle companion: being a complete collection of humorous, bottle and hunting songs. 1775.

Hawking moralised. Reading 1776. Poems.

[Symonds, Rev B.] A treatise on field diversions by a gentleman of Suffolk, a staunch sportsman. Norwich 1776, Yarmouth 1824, London 1825 (as The Suffolk sportsman), Yarmouth 1828.

The complete fisherman or universal angler; to which is added the whole art of fly-fishing. [1778]; other edns nd.

[Tickell, R.] Epistle from the Honourable Charles Fox, partridge-shooting, to the Honourable John Townshend, cruising. 1779, 1780.

The angler's complete assistant: being an epitome of the whole art of angling. [1780?].

Beckford, Peter. Thoughts on hunting: in a series of familiar letters to a friend. Salisbury 1781 (anon), 1782 (with author's name and preface; hunting song at end omitted), 1784, London 1796 (as Thoughts upon hare and fox hunting, also an account of the most celebrated dog kennels in the Kingdom; illustr), 1802, 1810 (illustr John Scott), [1820] (illustr Bewick) etc; ed J. O. Paget 1899; ed E. W. D. Cuming 1911; ed C. Richardson 1923.

Blane, William. Essays on hunting. [1781] (contains A country squire's Essay on hunting, 1733, and J. S. Gardiner, Six letters, 1750, with observations on Xenophon by W.B.), [1782?] (as By a sportsman of Berkshire), 1788 (as Cynegetica: or essays on sporting, by W. Blane; with additional matter on Arrian; Somervile's Chace; and An account of the hunting excursions of Asoph Ul Doulah Nabob of Oude by Blane, 'who attended these excursions in the years 1785 and 1786').

'A barbarian'. Hunting vindicated from cruelty in a letter to the Monthly Reviewers. 1782.

Lemon, Mr. A dissertation on the errors of marksmen and a tract upon the art of shooting flying. [1782].

The dismal lamentations of a monopolist of game, sometime since mournfully sung on the banks of the Don, at present applied by Christopher Fungus esq. 1783.

Zouch, Henry. An account of the present daring practices of night-hunters and poachers. 1783.

[Pye, H. J.] Shooting: a poem. 1784. *See* The sportsman's dictionary, 1735.

Shirley, Thomas. The angler's museum: or the whole art of float and fly fishing. 1784, nd (anon), [1790?] (3rd edn, anon; To which is prefixed the sermon of St Anthony to a miraculous congregation of fishes, extracted from Addison's travels).

Kenrick, W. S. and J. Burtell. A new foxhunting song: the chase run by the Cleveland fox hounds on Saturday the 29th day of January 1785. [1785]. A broadside.

[Ustonson, O.] The angler's assistant: being an epitomy of ye whole art of angling. [1785?]. Single sheet.

The north country angler: or the art of angling as practised in the northern counties of England. 1786, 1789, 1800, 1817.

Best, Thomas. A concise treatise on the art of angling. 1787, [1790?], 1794, 1798, 1802, 1804, 1807 etc.

Greenwood, Rev William. A poem written during a shooting excursion on the moors. Bath 1787.

'Nimrod' (not C. J. Apperley). Nimrod's songs of the chace; with an animated description of a fox-chace from the Hunting Register of the Windsor Nimrod. 1788.

[Acton, John]. An essay on shooting; also the methods of training pointers and a short description of the game of this country. 1789, 1791.

Boaz, Herman. A new song called the Angler's progress, written 4 July 1789: printed for and sold by the author only. [1789], 1820 (as The angler's progress), 1836.

Dibdin, Charles [the elder]. A collection of songs selected from the works of Mr Dibdin. 2 vols [1790]. The wily fox, The high-mettled racer and various short sporting pieces, with other poems were here brought together by the author in self defence to establish their authorship.

A song on the famous fox-chase from Barber's-Cover in Holcot-Field with the Pitchley Hunt, February 8th 1790. [1790]. Signed 'E.'; a broadside.

The sportsman's delight: a choice collection of hunting songs. Tewkesbury [1790?].

The sportsman's evening brush consisting of songs of the chace; to which is added the sportsman's toast assistant. [1791].

Brooke, Henry. Poetical works. 3 vols 1792. Includes The fox chase.

City sportsmen, or the first of September: a ballad, pubd Sepr 1st 1792. 1792.

Montagu, George. The sportsman's directory: or tractate on gunpowder with some remarks on fire-arms. 1792. Includes guns for sportsmen and outlines of duelling.

Osbaldiston, William Augustus. The British sportsman: or nobleman, gentleman and farmer's dictionary of recreation and amusement. [1792].

Cole, Ralph. The young angler's pocket companion. 1795, 1813, [1816] (abridged).

[Gilpin, William]. Three dialogues on the amusements of clergymen, by the Rev Josiah Frampton. 1796, 1797, 1820 (as On the amusements etc, by Edward Stillingfleet, Lord Bishop of Worcester), Birmingham 1820 (3rd edn). Discussions on field sports.

[Scott, Sir Walter]. The chase, and William and Helen: two ballads [freely adapted] from the German of Bürger. Edinburgh 1796.

Bürger, Gottfried August. The wild huntsman's chase, from the German. 1798.

The hare: or hunting incompatible with humanity. 1799, Dublin 1800.

Frankland, Sir Thomas. Cautions to young sportsmen. 1800, 1801.

[Lowth, Robert]. Billesdon Coplow, Monday Feb 24th 1800. Melton Mowbray 1800, London 1804 (with notes), [1828], 1831 (with memoir of author) etc. Poem on a hunt.

Taylor, Samuel. Angling in all its branches, reduced to a complete science. 1800.

Archery, Fencing, Duelling and Boxing

Egan, Pierce. Boxiana: or sketches of antient and modern pugilism. 4 vols 1818–24.

Miles, H. D. Pugilistica: being one hundred and forty-four years of the history of British boxing. 3 vols [1880–1].

Thimm, C. A. A complete bibliography of the art of fence. 1891, 1896 (rev).

Castle, Egerton. Schools and masters of fence. 1892 (rev).

Longman, C. J. and H. Walrond. Archery. 1894 (Badminton Lib). With bibliography.

Pollock, W. H. et al. Fencing, boxing and sparring, wrestling. 1897 (4th edn) (Badminton Lib). With E. Castle, Bibliotheca artis dimicatoriae: a bibliography.

Magriel, P. Bibliography of boxing: a chronological check list of books in English published before 1900. BNYPL June 1948.

—— (ed). The memoirs of the life of Daniel Mendoza. 1951.

Aylward, J. D. The house of Angelo. 1953.

—— The English master of arms. 1956.

Baldick, R. The duel: a history of duelling. 1965.

§ 1

Shotterel, Robert and Thomas D'Urfey. Archerie reviv'd: an heroick poem. 1676.

C[lerk?], W[illiam?]. Archerie reviv'd: a poetical essay. 1677.

Cockburn, John. The history and examination of duels: showing their heinous nature and the necessity of suppressing them. 1677, 1720.

Wood, William. The bow-mans glory: or archery revived. 1682, 1691. A miscellany.

Hope, Sir William. The Scots fencing-master: or compleat small-sword-man. Edinburgh 1687, London 1691 (as The compleat fencing-master), 1692, 1710.

—— The sword-man's vade-mecum. Edinburgh 1691, London 1694, Edinburgh 1705.

—— The fencing-master's advice to his scholar. Edinburgh 1692.

—— A new short and easy method of fencing. Edinburgh 1707, 1714 (as Hope's new method of fencing).

—— A vindication of the true art of self-defence. Edinburgh 1724, London 1729.

—— Observations on the gladiators' stage-fighting. 1725.

Blackwell, Henry. The English fencing master, in a dialogue between master and scholar. 1702, 1705, 1730 (as The gentleman's tutor for the small-sword).

Machrie, William. An essay upon duelling. Edinburgh 1711.

Wylde, Zachary. The English master of defence: or the gentleman's Al-a-mode accomplishment, also the rules of wrestling. York 1711.

Hepburn, Robert. A discourse concerning the character of a man of genius; with a poem on the young-company of archers by Mr Boyd. Edinburgh 1715.

Poems in English and Latin on the archers and Royal Company of Archers, by several hands. Edinburgh 1726.

McBane, Donald. The expert sword-man's companion. Glasgow 1728.

Valdin, Monsieur. The art of fencing as practised by M.V. 1729. Preface signed 'Solomon Negri'.

Royal valour: a poem upon the honourable company of archers. Edinburgh 1732.

Mahon, Andrew. The art of fencing. Dublin 1734, London 1735.

Mitchell, W. A short history to the commendation of the Royal Archers. Edinburgh 1734.

Whitehead, Paul. The gymnasiad or boxing match: a very short but very curious epic poem. 1744; rptd in his Satires, 1760, and Works, 1777.

Cole, Benjamin. The soldier's pocket companion: or the manual exercise of our British Foot, to which is added a short view of the use of the small sword. [1746], 1749.

Page, T. The use of the broad sword. Norwich 1746.

Godfrey, John. A treatise upon the useful science of defence, connecting the small and back sword; with some observations upon boxing. 1747.

Memoirs of the noted Buckhorse, interspersed with remarkable anecdotes of some bloods of fortune and eminence. 2 vols 1756.

Angelo, Domenico. L'école des armes, avec des figures. 1763 (in French), 1765 (in English and French), 1767; tr T. Rowlandson and ed H. C. W. Angelo as The school of fencing, 1799.

Churchill, Charles. The duellist: a poem. 1764, 1764.

[Anstey, Christopher]. The patriot: a Pindaric address to Lord Buckhorse [the prize-fighter]. 1767, 1768, [1779].

Fergusson, Hary. A dictionary explaining the terms in the art of the small sword. 1767.

Massi, Coustard de. The history of duelling in France and England. 1770, [1880].

Lonnergan, A. The fencer's guide. 1771.

Olivier, J. Fencing familiarized. 1771, 1780. In English and French.

O'Brien, William. The duel: a comedy. 1772.

Byrom, John. Extempore verses upon a tryal of skill between the two great masters of the noble science of defence, Messrs Figg and Sutton. In his Miscellaneous poems vol 1, Manchester 1773.

Hayes, Samuel. Duelling: a poem. 1775.

McArthur, J. The army and navy gentleman's companion: or a new and complete treatise on the theory and practice of fencing. [1780], 1784 (rev).

Stanzas on duelling, inscribed to Wogden the celebrated pistol-maker. 1783.

Barrington, Daines. Observations on the practice of archery in England. 1785. Rptd from Archaeologia 7 1785.

Underwood, James. The art of fencing. Dublin 1787, 1798.

Athletic exercise: or the science of boxing displayed, containing an account of the most celebrated boxers of this country. [1788].

The complete art of boxing according to the modern method, by an amateur of eminence. 1788, 1789 (with J. Godfrey, Treatise, 1747), 1788 (corrected).

Humphries, Richard. The Odiad or battle of Humphries and Mendoza: an heroic poem; to this is added a prefatory dissertation on boxing. 1788.

Lemoine, H. Modern manhood: or the art and practice of English boxing. [1788].

Morfitt, John. Philotoxi Ardenae, the woodmen of Arden: a Latin poem with a translation [by Joseph Weston]. Birmingham 1788; rptd in Records of the woodmen of Arden, 1885.

The art of manual defence or system of boxing, by a pupil both of Humphreys and Mendoza. 1789, 1799.

Barry, Edward. A letter on the practice of boxing, addressed to the King, Lords and Commons. 1789.

Mendoza, Daniel. The art of boxing. [1789].

Fewtrell, Thomas. Boxing reviewed: or the science of manual defence comprehending a complete description of the principal pugilists to the present day. 1790.

'A Highland officer'. Anti-pugilism: or the science of defence for the practice of the broad sword and single stick. 1790.

Stanton, Samuel. The principles of duelling with rules. 1790.

Oldfield, Henry George. Anecdotes of archery ancient and modern. 1791.

Hargrove, Ely. Anecdotes of archery. 1792; rev A. E. Hargrove 1845.

Helvetic liberty, or the lass of the lakes: an opera in three acts dedicated to all the archers of Great Britain, by a Kentish bowman. 1792. A play about William Tell, to show the advantage of encouraging peasant archery.

Moseley, Walter Michael. An essay on archery. Worcester 1792.

Archery: a poem printed for the author. 1793.

The female duellist: an afterpiece with songs. 1793.

Mason, Richard Oswald. Pro aris et focis: considerations of the reasons for reviving the use of the long bow with the pike. 1798.

Pepper, W. A treatise on the new broad sword exercise. 1798 (3 edns, 2nd with addns).

[Roworth, C.] The art of defence on foot with the broad sword and sabre. 1798, 1798, 1804 (with The ten lessons of Mr John Taylor).

Cricket

Gaston, A. J. Bibliography of cricket. In Wisden's Cricketers' almanack for 1892, 1894, 1900, 1923.

—— Bibliography of cricket. 1895 (priv ptd, 25 copies).

Taylor, A. D. The catalogue of cricket literature. 1906 (priv ptd, 50 copies).

Altham, H. S. A history of cricket. 1926; subsequent edns with E. W. Swanton, 1938, 1947, 1948, 2 vols 1962.

Lewis, W. J. The language of cricket, with illustrative extracts from the literature of the game. 1934.

Goldman, J. W. Bibliography of cricket. 1937 (priv ptd).

Cricket: a catalogue of an exhibition of books, manuscripts and pictorial records presented by the National Book League with the co-operation of the Marylebone Cricket Club. 1950.

General Studies

Laws of cricket [probably first formulated in 1744]. New Universal Mag Nov 1752.

The game at cricket, as settled by the several cricket-clubs, particularly that of the Star and Garter in Pall-Mall. 1755.

The laws of cricket revised at the Star and Garter, Pall-Mall, February 25 1774. 1774.

Britcher, Samuel. A complete list of all the grand matches of cricket that has been played in the year 1792. 1792. Continued yearly to 1806 (for 1805).

Epps, W. Cricket: a collection of all the grand matches of cricket, played in England from 1771 to 1791. Rochester 1799.

Haygarth, A. Cricket scores and biographies of celebrated players. 14 vols. Vols 1–4, 1862 (pbd by John Lillywhite as Frederick Lillywhite's cricket scores); vols 5–14, 1876–95 (pbd under the auspices of the MCC). 2 preliminary pamphlets containing lists of matches and names for ultimate inclusion were issued at Greenwich 1857 and 1859. Index to vols 1–13 by A. L. Ford 1885.

—— Index to all first-class matches [in above], compiled by J. B. Payne. 1903.

Waghorn, H. T. Cricket scores, notes etc from 1730–73. 1899.

—— The dawn of cricket [1730–1800]. 1906. Both pbd by the MCC and ed Lord Harris.

'P.–T., H.' (P. F. Thomas). Old English cricket: a collection of evidences concerning the game prior to the days of Hambledon. 6 pts Nottingham 1923–9.

Cooper, F. S. A. The Hambledon cricket chronicle 1772–96. 1924.

Buckley, G. B. Fresh light on 18th-century cricket: a collection of 1000 new cricket notices from 1697 to 1800 AD arranged in chronological order. Birmingham [1935].

—— Fresh light on pre-Victorian cricket: a collection of new cricket notices from 1709 to 1837 arranged in chronological order. Birmingham [1937].

§ 1

Goldwin, William. In certamen pilae. In Musae juveniles, 1706; tr A. Perry in Etoniana, 1922.

[Love, James]. Cricket: an heroic poem illustrated with the critical observations of Scriblerus Maximus. [1744],

1745, 1770; also in Poems on several occasions, Edinburgh 1754.

Cotton, Rev Reynell. Cricket song for the Hambledon Club, Hants, 1767. Canterbury Jnl 5–12 Oct 1773; rptd in The Wiccamical chaplet, ed G. Huddesford 1804.

[Duncombe, Rev John]. Surry triumphant or the Kentishmens defeat: a new ballad, being a parody on Chevy-chase. 1773.

[Burnby, John]. The Kentish cricketers: being a reply to Surry triumphant. Canterbury 1773. Also in Burnby's Summer amusement: or miscellaneous poems, 1772.

The noble cricketers: a poetical epistle address'd to two of the idlest Lords in his Majesty's three Kingdoms. 1778.

Dancing

Sharp, C. J. and A. P. Oppé. The dance. 1924.

Beaumont, C. W. A bibliography of dancing. 1929.

Magriel, P. D. A bibliography of dancing. New York 1936. Cumulated supplements for 1936 etc, New York 1939 etc.

Fletcher, I. K. Bibliographical descriptions of forty rare books relating to the art of dancing in the collection of P. J. S. Richardson. 1954.

——, S. J. Cohen and R. Lonsdale. Famed for dance: essays on the theory and practice of theatrical dancing in England 1660–1740. New York 1960.

McConachie, Jack (ed). Scottish country dances of the eighteenth century, derived from a manuscript dated 1740 in the Bodleian Library, edited and adapted. [1960], 1963.

Franks, A. H. Social dance: a short history. 1963.

Beaumont, C. W. (ed). A bibliography of the dance collection of Doris Niles and Serge Leslie: part 1, A–K. 1966.

Derra de Moroda, F. Chorégraphie, the dance notation of the eighteenth century: Beauchamp or Feuillet? Book-Collector 16 1967. With bibliography.

§ 1

[Ward, Edward]. The dancing-school, with the adventures of the Easter holy-days. 1700.

Siris, P. The art of dancing demonstrated by characters and figures, done from the French of Monsieur [Raoul Auger] Feuillet, with many alterations. 1706.

Weaver, John. Orchesography: or the art of dancing by characters and demonstrative figures. 1706, [1722?]. From the French of R. A. Feuillet.

—— A small treatise of time and cadence in dancing. 1706.

—— An essay towards an history of dancing. 1712.

—— The loves of Mars and Venus: a dramatick entertainment of dancing attempted in imitation of the panto-mimes of the ancient Greeks and Romans, as performed at Drury-Lane. 1717.

—— The fable of Orpheus and Eurydice; with a dramatick entertainment in dancing thereupon, attempted in imitation of the ancient Greeks and Romans, as perform'd at Drury Lane. 1718.

—— Anatomical and mechanical lectures upon dancing. 1721.

—— The history of the mimes and pantomimes; with an historical account of several performers in dancing, living in the time of the Roman Emperors. 1728.

Essex, John. For the further improvement of dancing: a treatis of chorography, translated from the French of Monsr Feuillet and improv'd with many additions. 1710, [1715?].

The dancing-master, a satyr: canto 1. 1722.

'Primcock, A.' (James Ralph). Of dancing, religious and dramatical: an historical account; to which are added some reflections. In his Touchstone, 1728, 1731 (as The taste of the town).

Rameau, Pierre. The dancing-master, done from the French by J. Essex. 1728.

Brown, R. Medecina musica: or a mechanical essay on the effects of singing, musick and dancing on human bodies. 1729.

Jenyns, Soame. The art of dancing: a poem in three cantos. 1729; also in Ruddiman's Collection of scarce, curious and valuable pieces, 1773; and in Jenyns, Works vol 1, 1790.

Tomlinson, Kellom. The art of dancing explained by reading and figures. 1735, 1744.

Philpot, Stephen. A dissertation on the regulation of the art of dancing. In his Essay on the advantage of a polite education, 1747.

Dukes, Nicholas. A concise and easy method of learning the figuring part of country dances by way of characters. 1752.

Lecointe, Jean. An apology for dancing, translated into English by J. Peyton. 1752, 1752 (in French).

Gallini, Giovanni Andrea. A treatise on the art of dancing. 1762, 1772.

—— Critical observations on the art of dancing. [1770?].

Noverre, Jean Georges. The works, translated from the French. 3 vols [1783].

Gardiner, S. J. A definition of minuet-dancing, rules for behaviour in company: a dialogue. Madeley 1786.

[Nares, Robert?]. Remarks on the nature of pantomime or imitative dance, ancient and modern; with a particular account of a favourite ballet and of a very curious allegory. 1789.

Cards, Chess, Draughts and other Indoor Games

Chatto, W. A. Facts and speculations on the origin and history of playing cards. 1848.

Bohn, H. G. (ed). The hand-book of [card] games. 1850.

Marshall, J. Books on gaming. N & Q 26 April, 17 May 1884, 15–22 June, 6, 20 July, 3, 24 Aug, 14 Sept, 5 Oct, 2, 23 Nov, 21 Dec 1889, 11 Jan, 22 Feb 1890.

Jessel, F. A bibliography of works in English on playing cards and gaming. 1905.

Call, W. T. The literature of checkers. New York 1908. On draughts.

Murray, H. J. R. A history of chess. 1913.

Hargrave, C. P. A history of playing cards and a bibliography of cards and gaming. Boston 1930, London 1966.

Whitehouse, F. R. B. Table games of Georgian and Victorian days. 1951.

Murray, H. J. R. A history of board games other than chess. 1952.

Bell, R. C. Board and table games. 1960.

§ 1

The royal game of the ombre. 1665.

The nicker nicked or the cheats of gaming discovered: Leathermore's advice concerning gaming. 1669, 1711 (3rd edn, as Leathermore: or advice concerning gaming).

Instructions how to play at billiards. 1687.

Moxon, Joseph. The use of the astronomical playing-cards. 1692.

Ozanam, Jacques. Recreations mathematical and physical. 1708, Dublin 1790. On card games, from the French.

Collier, Jeremy. An essay upon gaming in a dialogue between Callimachus and Dolomedes. 1713.

Lucas, Theophilus. Memoirs of the lives, intrigues and comical adventures of the most famous gamesters, discovering all the most sharping tricks and cheats at games play'd with cards, dice, tables or otherwise. 1714, 1744 (adapted as Authentic memoirs relating to the lives and adventures of the most eminent gamesters), 1930 (with Charles Cotton, The compleat gamester, as Games and gamesters of the Restoration).

Seymour, Richard. The court-gamester: or full and easy instructions for playing the games now in vogue. 1719, 1720, 1722, 1728, 1732 (with Seymour's trn of Rizzetti); 1734 (as The compleat gamester), 1739, 1750; rev Charles Johnson 1754.

—— The knowledge of play, translated from the Latin original of John Rizzetti, with improvements by R.S. 1729.

The whole art and mystery of modern gaming fully expos'd and detected. 1726.

Thurston, Joseph. Chess. In Poems on several occasions, 1729, 1737.

A new ballad on the game of bragg as it is now sung by Mr Sullivan at the New-Gardens. [Dublin? 1730?].

Backgammon or the battle of the friars: a tragi-comic tale [in verse]; to which is added a short essay on the folly of gaming [by Daniel Bellamy the elder]. 1734.

Bertin, Joseph. The noble game of chess: containing rules and instructions. 1735.

Hoyle, Edmond. A short treatise on the game of whist. 1742.

—— A short treatise on the game of backgammon. 1743.

—— A short treatise on the game of piquet; to which are added some rules and observations for playing well at chess. 1744.

—— A short treatise on the game of quadrille; to which is added the laws of the game. 1745.

—— A short treatise on the game of brag. 1751.

—— An essay towards making the game of chess easily learned without a master. 1761.

Many rev, abridged and collected edns of Hoyle to the present day. See J. Marshall, above, for early edns.

The humours of whist: a dramatic satire as acted every day at White's and other coffee-houses. 1743, 1753 (as The polite gamester: or the humours of whist).

Docultree, Amos. The ill effects of the game of Rowlet, otherwise Rowley-Powley, and the fatal consequences attending it. 1744.

The Gamiad, by 'Candour': a poem addressed to T.W.C. esq. 1745.

Stamma, Philip. The noble game of chess. 1745; ed W. Lewis 1818, 1819.

Danican, F. A. ('Philidor'). Chess analysed: or instructions by which a perfect knowledge of this noble game may in a short time be acquired. 1750, 1762, 1777 (as Analysis of the game of chess), 2 vols 1790 (greatly enlarged), 1791 etc. First pbd in French, 1749; rev and variously rearranged by later editors.

The gamesters garland: being a choice collection of two songs. [Newcastle? 1750?].

Mumford, Erasmus. A letter to the club at White's: in which are set forth the great expediency of repealing the laws now in force against excessive gaming, and the many advantages from it. 1750. A satire.

Andro: a new game at cards invented by a young gentleman. 1752.

Payne, William. An introduction to the game of draughts. 1756.

—— Maxims for playing the game of whist. 1773, 1778, 1783, 1785, 1790.

Foubert, Thomas. The litterary cards: being a new invention to learn to read; likewise directions to play all the most usual games on the cards or dice. 1758.

The game of quadrille or ombre by four, done from the French; to which is added the game of quintille or ombre by five. [1760?].

An essay on gaming, in an epistle to a young nobleman. 1761. Verse.

A brief and necessary supplement to all former treatises on quadrille, consisting of hints, questions, explanations for the benefit of the unlearned, by no adept. 1764.

Lambe, R. The history of chess; together with short and plain instructions. 1764, 1765.

Martin, Mons. A new treatise upon real quadrille; to which is subjoined tridelle, translated from the French. 1764.

Pinto, Isaac de. On card playing. 1767, 1768. In French and English.

The academy of play, from the French of the Abbé Bellecour. Dublin 1769, London [1770?].

Coates, John. A translation of a Latin poem of Dr Cobden's on the game at draughts. In A collection of original miscellaneous poems and translations by the Rev Mr Coates, 1770.

Proctor, Henry. The sportsman's sure guide or gamester's vade-mecum: showing the exact odds at horse-racing, lotteries, raffles, cock-fighting. 1773, Dublin 1774.

Hooper, William. Rational recreations, among which are all those commonly performed with the cards. 4 vols 1774, 1782-3, 1794, 1802.

[Wilkinson, Edward]. The gamesters: a poem addressed to the Mayor of C[anterbury]. 1774 (2nd edn).

The annals of gaming, containing original treatises on games, by a connoisseur. 1775.

[Swift, Theophilus]. The gamblers: a poem. 1777.

Astley, Philip. Natural magic: or physical amusements revealed. 1785.

Rules for quadrille. [Salisbury 1785?]. Verse.

[Johnson, Anna Maria]. The gamesters: a novel. 3 vols 1786.

Painter, William. A guide to the lottery: or the laws of chance laid down; to which is added the Complete draught-player. 1787.

A new game at cards in a dialogue between a nobleman and his servant. [Edinburgh? 1790?], [Edinburgh?] 1829 (as The royal game at cards), Dublin [1830?].

[Thompson, Alexander]. Whist: a poem in twelve cantos. 1791, 1792.

Long, Robert. Short rules for playing the game of cassino. [1790?].

[Williams, John]. A treatise on the game of cribbage [edited] by Anthony Pasquin esq. 1791, 1807.

Casino: a mock-heroic poem; to which is added an appendix containing the laws of the game. [1793].

Faro and Rouge et Noir, extracted from De Moivre: to which is prefixed a history of cards. 1793.

Rules for casino: humbly inscribed to her Grace the Duchess of Marlborough. [1795?]. A facetious set of fictitious rules.

Les amusemens des Allemands: or the diversions of the Court of Vienna, in which the mystery of fortune-telling is unravelled and three pleasant games are invented. 1796.

The gamester. [1796]. A Cheap Repository tract; fiction.

Rules of reversis as played in the fashionable circles, by a gentleman. 1796.

Backgammon: rules and directions for playing the game of backgammon, illustrated with calculations. 1798, 1807 (4th edn).

The rape of the faro bank: a heroi-comical poem in eight cantos. 1797.

[Lettsom, John Coakley]. Hints addressed to card parties. 1798.

Jones, Sir William. Works. 6 vols 1799. Vol 1, On the Indian game of chess; vol 4, Caissa: or the game at chess, a poem written in 1763.

Sturges, Joshua. Guide to the game of draughts. 1800.

Other Games and Sports

Gilbey, Sir W. Sport in olden time. 1912. Chiefly cock-fighting.

Noel, E. B. and J. O. M. Clark. A history of tennis. 2 vols 1924. Pt 9, The literature of tennis.

Atkinson, H. Cock-fighting and game fowl, edited and with an introductory memoir by Game Cock. Bath 1938.

Darwin, B. et al. A history of golf in Britain. 1952.

Browning, R. A history of golf. 1955.

Scott, G. R. The history of cockfighting. [1957].

§ 1

[Wild, Robert]. A horrible narration of a cockfight at Wisbech. 1660. A local political squib, but faithfully describes cocking.

Thévenot, Melchisedech. The art of swimming. 1699, 1764, 1789. Tr from the French (1696), illustr and with addns.

Machrie, William. An essay upon the royal recreation and art of cocking. Edinburgh 1705.

H[owlett ?], R[obert]. The royal pastime of cock-fighting. 1709.

Parkyns, Sir Thomas. The inn-play: or Cornish-hugg wrestler. 1713, 1714, 1727, [1800 ?].

Hallam, Isaac. The cocker: a poem in imitation of Virgil's third Georgic. 1742.

[Mathison, T.] The goff: an heroi-comical poem. Edinburgh 1743, 1763.

Dixon, Thomas. A treatise on the nature and the foundation of breeding cocks. 1744.

The tricks of the town laid open: or a companion for country gentlemen. 1747. Originally 1699 as The

country gentleman's vade-mecum; see R. Straus's reprint, 1927. On tennis, bowls, cocking, also racing.

[Jones, Robert]. A treatise on skating, by a gentleman. 1772, [1775 ?], [1780 ?]; ed T.C.R. 1797; 1823 (as The art of skating), [1825 ?], [1855].

Jones, A. The art of playing at skittles: or the laws of nine-pins displayed. 1773.

Directions for breeding game cocks. 1780, 1818.

Macpherson, R. A dissertation on the preservative from drowning and swimmer's assistant. 1783. On a life-saving invention which could be used for teaching swimming.

Sketchley, William. The cocker, by a gentleman who has been in the habit of breeding [game cocks] these eight and twenty years. 1793, 1814 (enlarged), Burton-on-Trent 1814.

A. B.

VI. LETTERS, DIARIES, AUTOBIOGRAPHIES AND MEMOIRS

The order is chronological, based on the opening date of each entry rather than dates of pbn or composition. Cross-references for letter-writers and diarists whose works are listed elsewhere are inserted according to date of birth.

GENERAL SOURCES

Arniston memoirs 1371–1830. Ed G. W. T. Ormond, Edinburgh 1887.

Harcourt papers [15th century–1837]. Ed E. W. Harcourt 13 vols Oxford 1876–1903.

Manchester, William Montagu, Duke of (ed). Court and society from Elizabeth to Anne [Montagu family papers and letters c. 1500–1708]. 2 vols 1864.

Sitwell, Sir George (ed). Letters of the Sitwells and Sacheverells [c. 1600–c. 1800]. 2 vols Scarborough 1900–1.

Hatton correspondence [1601–1704]. Ed E. M. Thompson 1878 (Camden Soc).

Browne, Sir Thomas (1605–82). See vol 1, above.

Jackson, Charles (ed). Yorkshire diaries and autobiographies [1608–1766]. 2 vols 1877, 1886 (Surtees Soc).

Bramston, Sir John (1611–1700). Autobiography. Ed Lord Braybrooke 1845 (Camden Soc).

Herbert correspondence: the sixteenth- and seventeenth-century letters of the Herberts of Chirbury [1613–90]. Ed W. J. Smith, Cardiff 1963.

Baxter, Richard (1615–91). See vol 1, above.

Josselin, Rev Ralph. Diary and autobiography [1616–83]. Ed E. Hockliffe 1908 (Royal Historical Soc).

Ashmole, Elias (1617–92). Memoirs. 1717; ed R. T. Gunther, Oxford 1927.

Blundell, William. Cavalier: letters to his friends 1620–98. Ed M. Blundell 1933.

Evelyn, John (1620–1706). See col 1580, below.

Martindale, Adam (1623–86). Life, by himself. Ed R. Parkinson 1845 (Chetham Soc).

Culloden papers [letters 1625–1748]. Ed D. Forbes 1815; More Culloden papers [1626–1747], ed D. Warrand, Inverness 4 vols 1923–30.

Fanshawe, Lady Anne (1625–80). Memoirs. Ed N. H. Nicolas 1829; ed H. C. Fanshawe 1907.

Warwick, Mary Rich, Countess of (1625–78). Autobiography. Ed T. C. Croker 1848 (Percy Soc).

Barnes, Ambrose, sometime Alderman of Newcastle-upon-Tyne (1627–1710). Memoirs. Ed W. H. D. Longstaffe 1867 (Surtees Soc).

Lister, Joseph (1627–1709). Autobiography. Ed T. Wright 1842.

Newcome, Rev Henry (1627–95). Autobiography. Ed R. Parkinson 2 pts 1852 (Chetham Soc).

Ingram, Bruce (ed). Three sea journals of Stuart times [1628, 1659–91, 1701–5]. 1936.

Thornton, Alice. Autobiography [1629–69]. 1875 (Surtees Soc).

Heywood, Rev Oliver (1630–1702). Autobiography and diaries. Ed J. H. Turner 4 vols Brighouse 1882–5.

Wood, Anthony à. Life and times 1632–95 [diaries etc]. Ed A. Clark 5 vols 1891–1907 (Oxford Historical Soc).

Worthington, Dr John. Diary and correspondence [1632–71]. Ed J. Crossley and R. C. Christie 3 pts 1847–86 (Chetham Soc).

Pepys, Samuel (1633–1703). See col 1582, below.

Reresby, Sir John. Memoirs [1634–89]. 1734; ed J. J. Cartwright 1875; ed A. Browning 1936 (with selected letters).

Ellwood, Thomas (1639–1713). History of life. 1714; rptd 1906 etc.

Hodgson, John C. (ed). Six North Country diaries [1639–1796]. 1910 (Surtees Soc).

Thomson, Gladys. Life in a noble household 1641–1700. 1937. Letters etc of William Russell, Duke of Bedford.

Conway letters 1642–84. Ed M. H. Nicolson, New Haven 1930.

Hothams, Chronicles of the [1642–1778]. Ed A. M. W. Stirling 2 vols 1918.

Manners family correspondence [1642–1771]. Duke of Rutland mss vol 2 1889 (Historical Manuscripts Commission).

Harley papers 1643–1785 [including letters to Duchess of Portland 1735–85]. Marquis of Bath mss vol i 1904 (Historical Manuscripts Commission).

Stukeley, Rev William. Family memoirs [letters and diaries 1643–1764]. 3 vols 1882–7 (Surtees Soc).

Bohun, Edmund (1645–99). Diary and autobiography. Ed S. W. Rix, Beccles Suffolk 1853.

Verney, Lady (Frances Parthenope and Margaret). Memoirs of the Verney family [1645–96]. 4 vols 1892–9.

Ward, Rev John. Diary [1648–79]. Ed C. Severn 1839.

Fox, George. Journal [1650–75]. Ed N. Penney 2 vols Cambridge 1911. *See col 1643, below.*

Henry, Rev Philip. Diaries and letters [1650–93]. Ed M. H. Lee 1882.

Taswell, William. Autobiography and anecdotes 1651–82. Ed G. P. Elliott 1853 (Camden Soc Miscellany 2).

North, Roger (1653–1734). *See col 1698, below.*

Moore, Rev Giles. Extracts from journal and account book [1655–79]. Ed R. W. Blencowe 1847 (Sussex Archaeological Collections).

Ailesbury, Thomas Bruce, Earl of (1656–1741). Memoirs. Ed W. E. Buckley 2 vols 1890 (Roxburghe Club).

Chesterfield, Philip Stanhope, Earl of. Letters [1656–89]. 1829.

Crisp, Stephen. Correspondence 1657–92. Ed C. Fell-Smith 1892.

Haddock family correspondence 1657–1719. Ed E. M. Thompson 1881 (Camden Soc).

Rugg, Thomas. Diurnal 1659–61. Ed W. L. Sachse 1961.

Defoe, Daniel (1660–1731). *See col 880, above.*

Newton, Evelyn, Lady. Lyme letters 1660–1760. 1925.

Newcome, Rev Henry. Diary 1661–3. Ed T. Heywood 1849 (Chetham Soc).

Savile, Henry. Correspondence [1661–89]. Ed W. D. Cooper 1858 (Camden Soc).

Atterbury, Francis, Bishop of Rochester (1662–1732). *See col 1620, below.*

Bentley, Dr Richard (1662–1742). *See col 1819, below.*

Cromartie, Earls of. Correspondence [1662–1774]. Ed W. Fraser 2 vols Edinburgh 1876.

Lawrence, William. Diary 1662–81. Ed G. E. Aylmer, Beaminster Dorset 1961.

Dunlop family papers: letters and journals 1663–1889. Ed J. G. Dunlop 1953.

Graham, John M. Annals and correspondence of the Viscount and the 1st and 2nd Earls of Stair [1663–1747]. 2 vols 1875.

Lowe, Roger, of Aston-in-Makerfield Lancs. Diary 1663–74. Ed W. L. Sachse, New Haven 1938.

Giffard, Martha, Lady. Life and correspondence [1664–1722]. Ed J. G. Longe 1911.

Prior, Matthew (1664–1721). *See col 489, above.*

Lauder, Sir John. Journals [1665–76]. Ed D. Crawford, Edinburgh 1900 (Scottish Historical Soc).

Milward, John, MP for Derbyshire. Diary 1666–8. Ed C. Robbins, Cambridge 1938.

Whiston, William (1667–1752). Memoirs. 1749.

Swift, Jonathan (1667–1745). *See col 1054, above.*

Yonge, James, Plymouth surgeon. Journal [1667–1708]. Ed F. N. L. Poynter 1963.

Russell, Rachel, Lady. Letters [1670–1723]. Ed Lord John Russell 2 vols 1853.

Brockbank, Rev Thomas. Diary and letter-book 1671–1709. Ed R. T. Lomax 1930 (Chetham Soc).

Calamy, Edmund (1671–?1731). An historical account of my own life. Ed J. T. Rutt 2 vols 1829.

Cibber, Colley (1671–1757). *See col 777, above.*

Drake, Capt Peter. Amiable renegade: memoirs 1671–1753. Ed S. A. Burrell 1960.

Freke, Elizabeth. Diary [1671–1714]. Ed M. Carberry, Cork 1913.

Jolly, Rev Thomas. Notebook 1671–93. Ed H. Fishwick 1894 (Chetham Soc).

De la Pryme, Abraham. Diary [1671–1704]. Ed C. Jackson 1870 (Surtees Soc).

Addison, Joseph (1672–1719). *See col 233, above.*

Hooke, Robert. Diary 1672–80. Ed H. W. Robinson and W. Adams 1935.

Steele, Sir Richard (1672–1729). *See col 1112, above.*

Prideaux, Humphrey. Letters to John Ellis 1674–1722. Ed E. M. Thompson 1875 (Camden Soc).

Thoresby, Ralph. Diary and correspondence [1674–1724]. Ed J. Hunter 4 vols 1830–2.

Teonge, Henry, chaplain in HM's navy. Diary [1675–9]. Ed G. E. Manwaring 1927.

Clarendon, Henry Hyde, Earl of. Correspondence [1676–1705]. Ed S. W. Singer 2 vols 1828.

Jeaffreson, Christopher. A young squire of the 17th century from his papers 1676–86. Ed J. C. Jeaffreson 2 vols 1878.

Petty, Sir William. Correspondence with Sir Robert Southwell 1676–87. Ed Marquis of Lansdowne 1928.

Lake, Rev Edward. Diary [1677–8]. Ed G. P. Elliott 1847 (Camden Soc).

Bolingbroke, Henry St John, Viscount (1678–1751). *See col 1119, above.*

Hearne, Thomas (1678–1735). Remains: reliquiae Hearnianae, compiled by Dr John Bliss. 2 vols 1857; rev J. Buchanan-Brown 1966.

Pinney, John. Letters 1679–99. Ed G. F. Nuttall, Oxford 1939.

'Psalmanazar, George' (1679?–1763). Memoirs. 1764.

Sidney, Algernon. Letters to Henry Savile [1679–82]. Dublin 1742.

Romney, Henry Sidney, Earl of. Diary with letters [1679–89]. Ed R. W. Blencowe 2 vols 1843.

Warner, Rebecca (ed). Original letters from Baxter, Prior, Bolingbroke, Pope, Cheyne, Johnson and others [1679–1780]. 1817.

Newdigate, Sir Richard. Cavalier and puritan [diary 1680–1706]. Ed Lady Newdigate-Newdegate 1901.

Bristol, John Hervey, Earl of. Letter books 1681–1750. 3 vols Wells 1894.

Burrell, Timothy, barrister-at-law. Journal and account book [1683–1717]. Ed R. W. Blencowe 1850 (Sussex Archaeological Collections).

Erskine, John. Journal 1683–7. Ed W. Macleod, Edinburgh 1893 (Scottish Historical Soc).

Nicolson, William, Bishop of Carlisle. Letters [1683–1727]. Ed J. Nichols 2 vols 1809.

— Diary [1684–1725]. 1901–5, 1937, 1947 (Trans Cumberland & Westmorland Antiquarian & Archaeological Soc new ser 1–5, 35, 47).

Morris, Claver. Diary of a West Country physician 1684–1726. Ed E. Hobhouse 1934.

Woodforde papers and diaries [1684–90, 1785–6, 1792]. Ed D. H. Woodforde 1932.

Berkeley, George (1685–1753). *See col 1851, below.*

Gay, John (1685–1732). *See col 497, above.*

Marchmont papers 1685–1750. Ed G. Rose 3 vols 1831.

Prior, Matthew. Letters 1685–1721. In Marquis of Bath mss 3 1908 (Historical Manuscripts Commission).

Cartwright, Thomas, Bishop of Chester. Diary [1686–7]. 1843 (Camden Soc).

Ellis, John. Correspondence 1686–8. Ed G. J. W. Agar-Ellis 2 vols 1829.

Lapthorne, Richard. Portledge papers 1687–97 [letters to Richard Coffin]. Ed R. J. Kerr and I. C. Duncan 1928.

Bristol, John Hervey, Earl of. Diary 1688–1742. Wells 1894.

Macleod, Sgt Donald (1688–1791). Memoirs. 1791; ed J. G. Fyffe 1933.

Pope, Alexander (1688–1744). *See col 500, above.*

Spence, Joseph. Observations, anecdotes and characters of books and men [c. 1688–c. 1758]. Ed S. W. Singer 1820; ed J. M. Osborn 2 vols Oxford 1966.

Davies, Rev Rowland. Journal [1689–90]. Ed R. Caulfield 1857 (Camden Soc).

Molesworth correspondence [1689–1744]. Vol 8, 1913 (Historical Manuscripts Commission).

Montagu, Lady Mary Wortley (1689–1762). *See col 1584, below.*

Richardson, Samuel (1689–1761). *See col 917, above.*

Norris papers [c. 1690–1708]. Ed T. Heywood 1846 (Chetham Soc).

Gordon, James. Diary 1692–1710. Ed G. D. Henderson and H. H. Porter, Aberdeen 1949.

Gent, Thomas. Life of Gent, by himself [1693–1746]. Ed J. Hunter 1832.

Chesterfield, Philip Dormer Stanhope, Earl of (1694–1773). See col 1585, below.

Coke, Thomas. Correspondence [1694–1726]. In Earl Cowper manuscripts vols 2–3, 1888–9 (Historical Manuscripts Commission).

Carlisle, Charles and Henry Howard, Earls of. Letters and papers [1695–1758]. In Earl of Carlisle Manuscripts 1897 (Historical Manuscripts Commission).

Stirling, Anna. Annals of a Yorkshire house [Spencer-Stanhope family correspondence 1696–1804]. 2 vols 1911.

Verney letters [1696–1799]. Ed Margaret, Lady Verney 2 vols 1930.

Richards, John. Diary [extracts 1697–1701]. Retrospective Rev new ser 1 1853.

Pitt family correspondence [1698–1779]. In Fortescue manuscripts vol 1, 1892 (Historical Manuscripts Commission).

Cremer, Capt John (Ramblin' Jack). Journal [1700–68]. Ed R. R. Bellamy 1936.

Delany, Mary (1700–88). See col 1598, below.

Oxford, Robert and Edward Harley, Earls of. Correspondence [1700–40]. In Duke of Portland manuscripts vols 4–6, 1897–1901 (Historical Manuscripts Commission).

March, Charles Henry Gordon-Lennox, Earl of. A Duke and his friends: life and letters [1701–50] of 2nd Duke of Richmond. 2 vols 1911.

Wodrow, Rev Robert. Analecta [diary etc 1701–31]. 3 vols Edinburgh 1842–3 (Maitland Club).

Blundell, Nicholas. Diary and letter book 1702–28. Ed M. Blundell, Liverpool 1952.

Marlborough, Sarah Churchill, Duchess of. Private correspondence [1703–38]. 2 vols 1838.

Wesley, John (1703–91). See col 1631, above.

Banks family letters and papers 1704–60. Ed J. W. F. Hill 1952 (Lincoln Record Soc).

Davenant, Charles. Letters [1704–14]. Ed G. Davies and M. Scofield, HLQ 4 1941.

Isham, Sir Justinian. Diaries 1704–35. Ed H. I. Longden, Trans Royal Historical Soc 3rd ser 1 1907.

Argyll, John Campbell, Duke of (ed). Intimate society letters of the 18th century [1705–1843]. 2 vols 1910.

Cowper, William, Earl. Private diary [1705–14]. Ed E. C. Hawtrey 1833 (Roxburghe Club).

Hearne, Thomas. Collections [diary etc 1705–35]. Ed C. E. Doble, D. W. Rannie and H. E. Salter 11 vols 1885–1921 (Oxford Historical Soc).

Wentworth papers [correspondence 1705–39]. Ed J. J. Cartwright 1883.

Hanmer, Thomas, Speaker of House of Commons. Correspondence [1706–44]. Ed H. E. Bunbury 1838.

Chandos, James Brydges, Duke of. Letters to Bolingbroke [1707–30]. Ed G. Davies and M. Tinling, Huntington Lib Bull 9 1936.

Charke, Charlotte. Life, by herself [c. 1709–55]. 1755, 1927.

Johnson, Samuel (1709–84). See col 1122, above.

Lyttleton, George, Lord (1709–73). See col 555, above.

Marlborough, Sarah Churchill, Duchess of. Letters [1710–26]. 1875.

Stratford, Dr William. Letters to Edward Harley, Earl of Oxford [1710–29]. In Duke of Portland manuscripts vol 7, 1901 (Historical Manuscripts Commission).

Hume, David (1711–76). See col 1873, below.

Burnet, Thomas. Letters to George Duckett 1712–22. Ed D. N. Smith, Oxford 1914 (Roxburghe Club).

Pilkington, Laetitia (1712–50). Memoirs. 1748; ed J. Isaacs 1928.

Suffolk, Henrietta Howard, Countess of. Correspondence 1712–67. Ed J. W. Croker 2 vols 1824.

Northampton, Elizabeth Compton, Countess of. Correspondence [1713–37]. In Townshend manuscripts, 1887 (Historical Manuscripts Commission).

Sterne, Laurence (1713–68). See col 948, above.

Ailesbury, Charles Bruce, Earl of. Correspondence 1714–36 (Historical Manuscripts Commission 15th report vol 7 1898).

Cowper, Mary, Countess. Diary 1714–20. Ed S. Cowper 1865.

Marchant, Thomas. Diary [1714–28]. Ed E. Turner 1873 (Sussex Archaeological Collections).

Shenstone, William (1714–63). See col 531, above.

Sundon, Charlotte, Viscountess. Memoirs [letters 1714–36]. Ed A. T. Thomson 2 vols 1847.

Hertford, Frances Seymour, Countess of. The gentle Hertford: her life and letters [selected letters 1715–54]. Ed H. S. Hughes, New York 1940.

Ryder, Dudley. Diary [1715–16]. Ed W. Matthews 1939.

Gray, Thomas (1716–71). See col 577, above.

Ilchester, Giles Fox-Strangways, Earl of. Henry Fox, 1st Lord Holland [letters etc 1716–74]. 2 vols 1920.

Carter, Elizabeth (1717–1806). See col 1595, below.

Dodington, George Bubb. Correspondence [1717–62]. In M. Eyre-Matcham manuscripts, vol 6 1909 (Historical Manuscripts Commission).

Garrick, David (1717–79). See col 801, above.

Walpole, Horace, Earl of Orford (1717–97). See col 1588, below.

Stuart papers at Windsor [1718–49]. Ed A. and H. Tayler 1939.

Aspinall-Oglander, Cecil. Admiral's wife: life and letters of Hon Mrs Edward Boscawen 1719–61. 1940.

Montagu, Elizabeth (1720–1800). See col 1597, below.

Osborn, Sarah Byng. Political and social letters 1721–71. Ed E. F. D. Osborn 1890; ed J. McClelland, Stanford 1930.

Peake, Richard Brinsley. Memoirs of the Colman family [letters 1721–1828]. 2 vols 1841.

Smollett, Tobias (1721–71). See col 962, above.

Byrom, John. Journal [1722–44] and literary remains. Ed R. Parkinson 4 pts 1854–7 (Chetham Soc).

Carlyle, Dr Alexander (1722–1805). Autobiography. Ed J. H. Burton 1860, 1910.

Hutton, William (1723–1815). Life: autobiography finished by Catherine Hutton. 1816.

Huntingdon, Theophilus Hastings and Francis Hastings, Earls of. Correspondence 1724–86. In R. Rawdon Hastings manuscripts 3, 1934 (Historical Manuscripts Commission).

Varley, Charles (1725?–95). The unfortunate husbandman. Ed D. Clarke 1964. An autobiography.

Walkden, Rev Peter. Diary [extracts 1725, 1729, 1730]. Ed W. Dobson, Preston 1860.

Hervey, John, Lord. Lord Hervey and his friends 1726–38 [letters]. Ed Earl of Ilchester 1950.

—— Memoirs of the reign of George II [1727–37]. Ed J. W. Croker 2 vols 1848; ed R. Sedgwick 3 vols 1931.

Chapone, Hester (1727–1801). See col 1598, below.

Burke, Edmund (1729–97). See col 1184, above.

Percy, Thomas (1729–1811). See col 242, above.

Pyle, Rev Edmund. Memoirs of a royal chaplain 1729–63. Ed A. Hartshorne 1905. Letters to Samuel Kerrich.

St Clair, Rev Patrick. Country neighbourhood [letters to Ashe Windham 1729–41]. Ed R. W. Ketton-Cremer 1951.

Wyndham, Maud. Chronicles of the 18th century [Lyttleton family correspondence 1729–60]. 2 vols 1924.

Egmont, John Perceval, Earl of. Diary 1730–47. In Earl of Egmont manuscript, 3 vols 1920–3 (Historical Manuscripts Commission).

Goldsmith, Oliver (1730?–74). See col 1191, above.

Cowper, William (1731–1800). See col 595 above.

Cumberland, Richard (1732–1811). See col 814, above.

Marlborough, Sarah Churchill, Duchess of. Letters of a grandmother 1732–5. Ed G. S. Thomson 1943.

Wedlake, J. H. (ed). Eighteenth-century Quaker love-letters [1732–55]. N & Q 13 March 1937.

Priestley, Dr Joseph. Memoirs [1733–95]. 1806.

Roberts, B. Dew. Mr William Bulkeley and the pirate: a Welsh diarist of the 18th century [1734–60]. Oxford 1936.

Purefoy letters 1735–53. Ed G. Eland 2 vols 1931.

Trusler, Rev John (1735–1820). Memoirs. Bath 1806.

Somerset, Frances Seymour, Duchess of. Select letters between the Duchess of Somerset, Lady Luxborough, William Shenstone and others [1736–72]. Ed T. Hull 2 vols 1778.

Stockdale, Percival (1736–1811). Memoirs. 2 vols 1809.

Gibbon, Edward (1737–94). *See col 1721, below.*

Watson, Richard, Bishop of Llandaff (1737–1816). Anecdotes of the life. 1817.

Hertford, Frances Seymour, Countess of. Correspondence with Henrietta Louisa, Countess of Pomfret 1738–41. Ed W. Bingley 3 vols 1805.

Miller, Sanderson. An 18th-century correspondence. Ed L. Dickins and M. Stanton, New York 1910. Letters from Deane Swift, Pitt, the Lytteltons, the Grenvilles et al 1738–79.

Luxborough, Henrietta, Lady. Letters to William Shenstone [1739–56]. Ed J. Hodgetts 1775.

Wilkinson, Tate (1739–1803). Memoirs. 4 vols York 1790.

Boswell, James (1740–95). *See col 1210, above.*

Jesse, John Heneage. George Selwyn and his contemporaries [letters 1740–70]. 4 vols 1843–4.

Reynolds, Sir Joshua. Letters [1740–91]. Ed F. W. Hilles, Cambridge 1929.

Young, Edward. Letters to the Duchess of Portland [1740–65]. In Marquis of Bath manuscripts 1, 1904 (Historical Manuscripts Commission).

Somerville, Thomas. Memoirs [1741–1814]. Edinburgh 1861.

Thrale, Hester Lynch, later Piozzi (1741–1821). *See col 1596, below.*

Young, Arthur (1741–1820). Autobiography. Ed M. Betham-Edwards 1898.

Cradock, Joseph. Literary and miscellaneous memoirs [1742–c. 1800]. 4 vols 1826.

Hervey, Mary, Lady. Letters 1742–68. Ed J. W. Croker 1821.

Jones, Thomas (1742–1803). Memoirs. 1951 (Walpole Soc).

Russell, Col Charles. Correspondence 1742–54. In Frankland-Russell-Astley manuscripts 1900 (Historical Manuscripts Commission).

Brasbridge, Joseph (1743–1832). Fruits of experience. 1824.

Cappe, Catharine (1744–1821). Memoirs. 1822.

Edgeworth, Richard Lovell (1744–1817). Memoirs. 2 vols 1820. Completed by his daughter Maria.

Charlemont, James Caulfield, Earl of. Letters and memoirs 1745–99. In Charlemont manuscripts vols 1–2, 1891–4 (Historical Manuscripts Commission).

Harriott, John (1745–1817). Struggles through life. 3 vols 1815.

Holcroft, Thomas (1745–1809). *See col 837, above.*

MacDonald, John. Memoirs of an 18th-century footman [1745–79]. Ed J. Beresford 1927.

Malmesbury, James Harris, Earl of. Letters [1745–1820]. Ed 3rd Earl of Malmesbury 2 vols 1870.

More, Hannah (1745–1833). *See col 1598, below.*

Cowper, Spencer, Dean of Durham. Letters [1746–74]. Ed E. Hughes 1956 (Surtees Soc).

Hervey, Augustus. Journal of a Captain in the Royal Navy 1746–59. Ed D. Erskine 1953.

Lackington, James. Memoirs [1746–91]. 1791, 1810 (13th edn enlarged).

Coke, Lady Jane. Letters to Mrs Eyre 1747–58. Ed A. Rathborne 1899.

Hurd, Richard. Correspondence with William Mason 1747–94. Ed L. Whibley, Cambridge 1932.

Seward, Anna (1747–1809). *See col 682, above.*

Williamson letters 1748–65. Ed F. J. Manning, Streatley 1954 (Bedfordshire Historical Record Soc).

Dodington, George Bubb. Diary [1749–61]. Ed H. P. Wyndham 1784; ed J. Carswell and L. A. Dralle, Oxford 1965.

Hickey, William. Memoirs 1749–1809. Ed A. Spencer 4 vols 1913–25.

Butler, Charles (1750–1832). Reminiscences. 2 vols 1822, 1827.

Craven, Elizabeth, Baroness, later Margravine of Anspach (1750–1828). *See col 831, above.*

Norton, John and sons, merchants of London and Virginia. Papers from their counting house [letters etc 1750–95]. Ed F. N. Mason, Richmond Virginia 1937.

Baker, John. Diary [1751–79]. Ed P. C. Yorke 1931.

Knyveton, John. Diary of a surgeon 1751–2. Ed E. Gray, New York 1937.

Minto, Gilbert Elliot, Earl of. Life and letters 1751–1806. Ed Countess of Minto 3 vols 1874.

Pierce, Eliza. Letters 1751–75. Ed V. Macdonald 1927.

Sheridan, Richard Brinsley (1751–1816). *See col 816, above.*

Burney, Frances, later D'Arblay (1752–1840). *See col 970, above.*

Leinster, Emily Fitzgerald, Duchess of. Correspondence [1752–69]. Ed B. Fitzgerald, Dublin 1954 (Irish Manuscripts Commission).

Northumberland, Elizabeth Percy, Duchess of. Diaries of a Duchess [1752–74]. Ed J. Greig 1926.

Ritson, Joseph (1752–1803). *See col 1763, below.*

Shackleton, Richard and Elizabeth. Memoirs and letters [1752–92]. Ed M. Leadbeater 1822.

Benenden letters 1753–1821. Ed C. F. Hardy 1901.

Bewick, Thomas (1753–1828). Memoir by himself. Newcastle-on-Tyne 1862.

Childe-Pemberton, William S. The Earl Bishop. 2 vols 1924. Letters of Frederick Hervey, Earl of Bristol 1753–1803.

Lennox, Lord George. Letters and papers 1753–98. In Earl Bathurst manuscripts, 1923 (Historical Manuscripts Commission).

Chatham, William Pitt, Earl of. Love letters [1754]. Ed E. A. Edwards 1926.

Crabbe, Rev George (1754–1832). *See col 609, above.*

Dickinson, John. A Pennsylvania farmer at the Court of King George: London letters 1754–6. Pennsylvania Mag of History & Biography 86 1962.

Francis letters [Sir Philip Francis and others 1754–1818]. Ed B. Francis and E. Keary 2 vols 1901.

Turner, Thomas. Diary of a tradesman [1754–65]. Ed F. M. Turner 1925; ed D. K. Worcester, New Haven 1948.

Waldegrave, James, Earl. Memoirs 1754–8. 1821.

Wilkes, John. Correspondence [1754–98]. Ed J. Almon 5 vols 1805.

Bray, William. Diary [extracts 1756–1800]. Ed F. E. Bray 1938 (Surrey Archaeological Collections).

Coke, Lady Mary. Letters and journals [1756–79]. Ed J. A. Home 4 vols Edinburgh 1889–96.

Dempster, George. Letters to Sir Adam Fergusson 1756–1813. Ed J. Fergusson 1934.

Gifford, William (1756–1826). Autobiography. In J. Nichols, Illustrations of the literary history of the 18th century vol 6, 1831.

Granger, Rev James. Letters [1756–83]. Ed J. P. Malcolm 1805.

Hamilton, Mary (afterwards Mrs John Dickenson). At Court and at home [letters and diaries 1756–1816]. Ed E. and F. Anson 1925.

Knight, Cornelia (1756–1837). Autobiography. 2 vols 1861.

Knyveton, John. Surgeon's mate [diary 1756–62]. Ed E. Gray 1942.

Lewin letters: correspondence and diaries of an English family 1756–1884. Ed T. H. Lewin 2 vols 1910.

Powys, Caroline. Passages from diaries 1756–1808. Ed E. J. Climenson 1899.

Raper, Elizabeth. Receipt book [journal 1756–70]. Ed B. Grant 1924.

Blake, William (1757–1827). *See col 615, above.*

Gainsborough, Thomas. Letters [1757–88]. Ed M. Woodall, Ipswich 1963.

Romilly, Sir Samuel (1757–1818). Memoirs. 3 vols 1840.

Taylor, John (1757–1832). Records of my life. 2 vols 1832.

Telford, Thomas (1757–1834). Life, by himself. 1838.

Palmerston, Henry Temple, Viscount. Portrait of a Whig peer [letters and journals 1758–1801]. Ed B. Connell 1957.

Robinson, Mary ('Perdita') (1758–1800). Memoirs. Ed M. E. Robinson 4 vols 1801, 1 vol 1930.

Woodforde, Rev James. Diary of a country parson 1758–1802. Ed J. B. Beresford 5 vols 1924–31.

Brietzcke, Charles. Diary 1759–65. Ed E. Hailey, N & Q 28 April 1951–. Completed Nov 1964 (65 pts).

Burns, Robert (1759–96). *See col 1979, below.*

Fife, James, Lord. Lord Fife and his factor. Correspondence [1759–1809]. Ed A. and H. Tayler 1925.

Angelo, Henry C. W. [1760–1839]. Reminiscences. 2 vols 1828–30; ed H. L. Smith 2 vols 1904.

Barrington, Jonah (1760–1834). Personal sketches of his own times. 2 vols 1827, 3 vols 1830–2.

Hawkins, Laetitia M. (1760–1835). Memoirs, anecdotes, facts and opinions. 2 vols 1824.

Jenkinson papers 1760–6. Ed N. S. Jucker 1949.

Aspinall-Oglander, Cecil. Admiral's widow: life and letters of Hon Mrs Edward Boscawen 1761–1805. 1942.

Cornwallis, Sir William. Correspondence 1761–1818. In Wykeham-Martin manuscripts, 1909 (Historical Manuscripts Commission).

Lennox, Lady Sarah. Life and letters [1761–1817]. Ed Countess of Ilchester and Lord Stavordale 2 vols 1901.

Papendiek, Charlotte. Court and private life in the time of Queen Charlotte: journals [1761–92]. Ed V. D. Broughton 2 vols 1887.

Twining, Rev Thomas. Recreations and studies of a country clergyman [letters and diary 1761–1803]. Ed R. Twining 1882.

Cobbett, William (1762–1835). *See vol 3, below.*

Howard, John. Correspondence [1762–89]. Ed J. Field 1855.

Wilkes, John. Correspondence with Charles Churchill [1762–4]. Ed E. H. Weatherly, New York 1954.

Berry papers. Correspondence of Mary and Agnes Berry [1763–1852]. Ed L. Melville 1914.

Warner, Richard (1763–1857). Literary recollections. 2 vols 1830.

Gray, Almyra. Papers and diaries of a York family 1764–1839. 1927.

Mendoza, Daniel (1764–1836). Memoirs. 1816; ed P. D. Magriel 1951.

Reynolds, Frederick (1764–1841). Life and times, by himself. 2 vols 1826.

Cole, Rev William. Blecheley diary [1765–7]. Ed F. G. Stokes 1931.

Heber, Mary. Dear Miss Heber. Ed F. Bamford 1936. Letters to Miss Heber 1765–1806.

Olson, Alison G. The radical Duke: career and correspondence of Charles Lennox, 3rd Duke of Richmond [1765–1804]. 1961.

Eliot, Lady Harriot. Letters 1766–86. Ed C. Headlam, Edinburgh 1914.

Brown, James B. Memoirs of John Howard the philanthropist [diary and letters 1767–89]. 1818.

Edgeworth, Maria (1767–1849). *See vol 3, below.*

Malmesbury, James Harris, Earl of. Diaries and correspondence [1767–1809]. Ed 3rd Earl of Malmesbury 4 vols 1844.

Neville, Sylas. Diary 1767–88. Ed B. Cozens-Hardy, Oxford 1950.

The Noels and the Milbankes [letters 1767–92]. Ed M. Elwin 1967.

Selwyn, George. Letters [1767–90]. In Earl of Carlisle manuscripts, 1897 (Historical Manuscripts Commission).

— Letters [1767–90] and life. Ed E. S. Roscoe and H. Clergue 1899.

Hoare, Prince. Memoirs of Granville Sharp [letters 1769–1807]. 1820, 2 vols 1828.

Johnson, Samuel. Sir Joshua's nephew: letters by a young man to his sisters 1769–79. Ed S. M. Radcliffe 1930.

Beresford, John. Correspondence illustrative of the last 30 years of the Irish Parliament [1770–1804]. Ed W. Beresford 2 vols 1854.

Herbert, Dorothea. Retrospections [1770–89]. 2 vols 1929–30.

Cumberland, Richard Dennison and George. Letters 1771–84. Ed C. Black 1912.

Manners family correspondence [1771–87]. In Duke of Rutland manuscripts vol 3, 1894 (Historical Manuscripts Commission).

Owen, Robert (1771–1858). Life. 2 vols 1857–8; ed M. Beer 1920.

Pepys, Sir William W. A later Pepys: correspondence [1771–1825]. Ed A. C. C. Gaussen 2 vols 1904.

Sandwich, John Montagu, Earl of. Private papers 1771–82. Ed G. R. Barnes and J. H. Owen 4 vols 1932–8.

Bessborough, Henrietta Ponsonby, Countess of. Lady Bessborough and her family circle [letters 1772–1828]. Ed Earl of Bessborough and A. Aspinall 1940.

Black, Clementina. The Linleys of Bath [correspondence 1772–1830]. 1926.

Windham, William. Early life and diaries [1772–83]. Ed R. W. Ketton-Cremer 1930.

Wraxall, Sir Nathaniel. Historical and posthumous memoirs 1772–84. Ed H. B. Wheatley 5 vols 1884.

Devonshire, Georgiana Cavendish, Duchess of. Extracts from correspondence [1773–1811]. Ed Earl of Bessborough 1955.

Whalley, Dr Thomas Sedgewick. Journals and correspondence [1773–1828]. Ed H. Wickham 2 vols 1863.

Hamilton, Caroline. The Hamwood papers of the ladies of Llangollen and Caroline Hamilton [letters and diaries 1774–1831]. Ed 'Mrs G. H. Bell' (J. Travers) 1930.

Yeoman, John. Diary of visits to London [1774, 1777]. Ed M. Yearsley 1935.

Bute, John Stuart, Earl of. A Prime Minister and his son [correspondence 1775–1800]. Ed E. S. Wortley 1925.

Curwen, Samuel. Journal and letters [1775–84]. Ed G. A. Ward 1842.

Lichtenberg, Georg Christoph. Briefe aus seinem englischen Freundeskreis [letters in English 1775–99]. Ed H. Hecht, Göttingen 1925.

Pinkerton, John. Literary correspondence [1775–1815]. 2 vols 1830.

Windham papers. Life and correspondence of William Windham [1775–1810]. [Ed L. Melville] 2 vols 1913.

Drennan letters [correspondence between William Drennan and Samuel and Martha McTier 1776–1819]. Ed D. A. Chart, Belfast 1931.

Holroyd, Maria Josepha (later Lady Stanley of Alderley). Girlhood [letters 1776–96]. Ed J. H. Adeane 1896.

Knight, William A. Lord Monboddo and some of his contemporaries [letters 1776–92]. 1900.

Newdigate, Sir Roger and Lady. The Cheverels of Cheverel Manor [letters 1776–1800]. Ed Lady Newdigate-Newdegate 1898.

Devonshire, Georgiana and Elizabeth Cavendish, Duchesses of. The two Duchesses: family correspondence 1777–1859. Ed V. Foster 1898.

Elers, George (1777–1842). Memoirs. Ed Lord Monson and G. L. Gower 1903.

Jerningham, Edward, and his friends: a series of 18th-century letters [c. 1777–1801]. Ed L. Bettany 1919.

Jones, Rev William. Diary 1777–1821. Ed O. F. Christie 1929.

Stirling, Anna. Coke of Norfolk and his friends [letters 1777–1837 of Thomas William Coke, later Earl of Leicester]. 2 vols 1907, 1 vol 1912.

Barnard family letters 1778–1824. Ed A. Powell 1928.

Stuart, Lady Louisa. Gleanings from an old portfolio [correspondence 1778–1813]. Ed G. Clark, Edinburgh 3 vols 1895–8.

— Letters [1778–1834]. Ed R. B. Johnson 1926.

Twining family papers [letters and journals 1778–1844]. Ed R. Twining 1887.

Crisp, Samuel. Burford papers: letters to his sister [1779?–85]. Ed W. H. Hutton 1905.

Frampton, Mary. Journal 1779–1846. Ed H. G. Mundy 1885.

Ailesbury, Thomas Brudenell Bruce, Earl of. Letters and diary 1780–95. 1898 (Historical Manuscripts Commission 15th report vol 7).

Jerningham letters 1780–1843. Ed E. Castle 2 vols 1896.

Pembroke, Henry Herbert, Earl of. Pembroke papers: Letters and diaries 1780–94. Ed Lord Herbert 1950.

Temple, Rev William Johnston. Diaries 1780–96. Ed L. Bettany, Oxford 1929.

Dyott, William. Diary [1781–1845]. Ed R. W. Jeffrey 2 vols 1917.

Granville, Granville Leveson-Gower, Earl. Private correspondence 1781–1821. Ed Castalia, Countess Granville 2 vols 1916.

Greville, Col Robert Fulke. Diaries [1781–4]. Ed F. M. Bladon 1930.

Sinclair, John. Correspondence [c. 1781–1830]. 2 vols 1831.

Torrington, John Byng, Viscount. Diaries [1781–94]. Ed C. B. Andrews 4 vols 1934–8.

Wedgwood, Josiah. Correspondence 1781–94. Ed Lady Farrer 1906.

Auckland, William Eden, Baron. Journal and correspondence [1782–1814]. Ed G. Hogge 4 vols 1860–2.

Heber, Rev Reginald. The Heber letters 1782–1832. Ed R. H. Cholmondeley 1950.

Stuart, Dorothy M. Dearest Bess: the life and times of Lady Elizabeth Foster, afterwards Duchess of Devonshire [1782–1824]. 1955.

Wilberforce, William. Private papers [letters etc 1782–1832]. Ed A. M. Wilberforce 1897.

— Correspondence [1783–1833]. Ed R. I. and S. Wilberforce 2 vols 1840.

— Life, by his sons [letters 1783–1833]. 1838.

Berry, Mary. Journals and correspondence [1783–1852]. Ed T. Lewis 3 vols 1865.

Windham, William. Diary 1784–1810. Ed H. Baring 1866.

Nelson, Horatio, Lord. Letters to his wife and other documents 1785–1831. Ed G. P. B. Naish 1958.

Bower, Anna Catherina. Diaries and correspondence [1787–99]. 1903.

Bamford, Samuel. Early days [autobiography 1788–1815]. 1849; ed W. H. Chaloner 1967.

Fitzherbert, Mrs Maria. Letters [1788–1837]. Ed S. Leslie 1940.

Harcourt, Lady Mary. Mrs Harcourt's diary [of the Court of George III 1789–91]. 1872 (Philobiblon Soc).

More, Martha. Mendip annals [journals 1789–1800]. Ed A. Roberts 1859.

Wynne diaries 1789–1820. Ed A. Fremantle 3 vols Oxford 1935–40.

Holland, Elizabeth Fox, Lady. Journal 1791–1811. Ed Earl of Ilchester 2 vols 1908.

Stevens, Rev William Bagshaw. Journal [1792–9]. Ed E. Galbraith, Oxford 1965.

Creevey, Thomas. Creevey papers 1793–1838. Ed H. Maxwell 2 vols 1904.

Farington, Joseph. Diary [1793–1821]. Ed J. Greig 8 vols 1923–8.

Glenbervie, Douglas Sylvester, Lord. Diaries [1793–1819]. Ed F. Bickley 2 vols 1928.

— Journals [1793–1815]. Ed W. Sichel 1910.

Colchester, Charles Abbot, Lord. Diary and correspondence [1794–1829]. Ed 2nd Lord Colchester 3 vols 1861.

Dunlap, William. Memoirs of George Frederick Cooke [diaries and letters 1794–1809]. 2 vols 1813.

Paget papers [correspondence of Sir Arthur Paget 1794–1807]. Ed A. B. Paget 2 vols 1896.

Cavendish, Lady Harriet. Harry-O: letters 1796–1809. Ed G. L. Gower and I. Palmer 1940.

Wynn, Frances Williams. Diaries of a lady of quality 1797–1844. Ed A. Hayward 1864.

R. H.

JOHN EVELYN
1620–1706

The ms of the diary is in the possession of the Evelyn family. A body of unpbd mss remains, mainly at Christ Church, Oxford.

Bibliographies

Keynes, G. L. Evelyn: a study in bibliophily and a bibliography of his writings. Cambridge 1937, Oxford 1968 (with addns).

de Beer, E. S. Appendix 1. In his edn of the Diary vol 1, Oxford 1955.

Collections

The miscellaneous writings. Ed W. Upcott 1825. Besides some of Evelyn's dedications etc, this vol contains the following: Of liberty and servitude, 1649; The state of France, 1652; The golden book of St John Chrysostom (trn, 1659); A character of England (3rd edn, 1659); An apology for the royal party, 1659; The late news from Brussels unmasked, 1660; Fumifugium, 1661; Sculptura, 1662; An account of architects (from 2nd or later edn); Kalendarium hortense (from 10th edn, 1706); Public employment, 1667; The history of the three late famous impostors, 1669; Navigation and commerce, 1674; Mundus muliebris, by Mary Evelyn, 1690; Acetaria, 1699.

§ I

The state of France, by J.E. 1652.

A character of England. 1659, 1659 (both anon), 1659 (anon, as A character of England: with reflections upon Gallus castratus). Original version rptd, with omissions and alterations, as A journey to England, 1700; and complete in Somers tracts 7 1812; and in Harleian Miscellany vol 10, 1813.

An apology for the royal party. 1659 (anon); ed G. L. Keynes, Los Angeles 1951 (Augustan Reprint Soc).

The late news or message from Bruxels unmasked. 1660. Anon.

A panegyric to Charles the Second. 1661; ed G. L. Keynes with An apology, above.

A poem upon his Majestie's coronation. 1661. Anon; attribution doubtful.

Fumifugium. 1661 (2 issues), 1772 etc.

Tyrannus: or the mode. 1661 (preface signed 'J.E.'); ed J. L. Nevinson, Oxford 1951 (Luttrell Soc).

Sculptura. 1662, 1755 (with Evelyn's addns and corrections and an anon life of Evelyn) etc; ed C. F. Bell, Oxford 1906 (with unpbd 2nd part, mainly a trn of part of A. Bosse, Traicté des manieres de graver, Paris 1645).

Sylva: or a discourse of forest trees; to which is annexed Pomona, also Kalendarium hortense. 1664, 1670 (expanded). Further edns, successively expanded, and with further pieces annexed, 1679, 1706 (as Silva); the last rptd 1729. Silva (alone), ed A. Hunter, York 1776 (annotated rpt of edn of 1706 or 1729, with variations and omissions); 1786, 1801, 1812, 1825.

Kalendarium hortense. 1664 (appended to Sylva, above, 1st edn). Not issued separately. Besides the folio edns of Sylva, above, there were 9 octavo edns 1666–1706.

The English vineyard vindicated, by John Rose. 1666 (anon; for proof of authorship *see* Keynes), 1669 (with an addn by Evelyn; appended to the French gardiner, 1669), 1672, 1675, 1691.

Publick employment and an active life prefer'd to solitude. 1667.

The history of the three late famous impostors. 1669 (dedication signed 'J.E.'), 1739; tr German, 1669. For adaptations *see* Keynes.

Navigation and commerce. 1674.

A philosophical discourse of earth. 1676; rptd with Sylva, 1678, 1706 (as Terra etc).

Numismata. 1697.

Acetaria. 1699, New York 1937 (facs), 1706. Also appended to Silva, 1706, 1729.

Memoirs of John Evelyn. Ed W. Bray 2 vols 1818. An improved text, also by Bray, was pbd in 2 vols 1819. The 3rd edn, 5 vols 1827, reproduced the 2nd. The 4th edn, ed J. Forster 4 vols 1850–2, included variant passages. The 2nd, 3rd and 4th edns have been rptd several times. The only edn with important notes, before that of 1955, is by A. Dobson 3 vols 1906, rptd 1 vol 1908 (Globe edn). None of the texts before 1955 was complete or reliable.

The diary of John Evelyn. Ed E. S. de Beer 6 vols Oxford 1955. Definitive edn and full text.

The diary of John Evelyn. Ed E. S. de Beer, Oxford 1959 (OSA). Almost all the text, with a few footnotes selected from 1955 edn.

Selections from the Diary

Voyage de Lister à Paris en MDCXCVIII; on y a joint des extraits des ouvrages d'Evelyn relatifs à ses voyages en France. Ed E. de Sermizelles et al, Paris 1873 (Société des Bibliophiles François).

Evelyn in Naples 1645. Ed H. Maynard Smith, Oxford 1914.

The early life and education of Evelyn. Ed H. Maynard Smith, Oxford 1920.

Other selections, apart from Levis, below, possess no critical value.

Translations

Of liberty and servitude. 1649. Anon; dedicated to George Evelyn. From French of F. de la Mothe le Vayer.

An essay on the first book of T. Lucretius Carus De rerum natura. 1656. Text and trn with Animadversions.

The French gardiner. 1658 (dedication signed 'J.E.'), 1669 (with The English vineyard vindicated), 1672, 1675, 1691. From N. de Bonnefons.

The golden book of St John Chrysostom. 1659.

Instructions concerning erecting of a library. 1661. From French of Gabriel Naudé.

A parallel of the antient architecture with the modern, with Leon Baptista Alberti's Treatise of statues. 1664, 1707 (with expanded version of the Account of architects), 1723 (with Sir H. Wotton, The elements of architecture), 1733. Tr from French of Roland Fréart, Sieur de Chambray.

Μυστήριον τῆς ’Ανομίαις: that is another part of the Mystery of Jesuitism, together with the Imaginary heresy. 1664. Anon; tr from French of A. Arnauld and P. Nicole.

The pernicious consequences of the new heresie of the Jesuites. 1666. Anon; tr from French of P. Nicole.

An idea of the perfection of painting. 1668. Tr from French of Roland Fréart.

The compleat gard'ner. 1693. Tr from French of de la Quintinye. F. E. Budd, RES 14 1938, also ascribes to Evelyn the trn of The manner of ordering fruit-trees, 1660.

Posthumous Works

The following works were not intended for pbn:

The life of Mrs Godolphin. Ed Bishop Wilberforce 1847, 1848, 1848, 1864; ed E. W. Harcourt 1888; [ed I. Gollancz?] 1904; ed H. Sampson, Oxford 1939.

The history of religion. Ed R. M. Evanson 2 vols 1850.

[Londinium redivivum. 1666]; ed E. S. de Beer, Oxford 1938. For earlier printing *see* Keynes.

Memoires for my grand-son. Ed G. L. Keynes 1926.

Directions for the gardiner at Says-Court. Ed G. L. Keynes 1932.

A devotionarie book of John Evelyn. Ed W. Frere 1936.

Letters

A selection from his correspondence was pbd with the diary in the edns of 1818, 1819, 1827, 1850–2 and 1859. The fullest collections are in those of 1850–2 and 1859. Many of his letters are also in the various vols of Pepys's and Bentley's pbd correspondence, and elsewhere. See Keynes.

§ 2

Evelyn, H. The history of the Evelyn family. 1915.

Levis, H. C. Extracts from the diaries and correspondence of Evelyn and Pepys relating to engraving. 1915.

Squire, W. Barclay. Evelyn and music. TLS 17 Aug, 16 Oct 1924, 14 May, 10 Dec 1925, 14 Oct 1926.

Ponsonby, A. John Evelyn. 1933.

Hiscock, W. G. Evelyn and Mrs Godolphin. 1951.

—— Evelyn and his family circle. 1955. *See* de Beer's criticisms and Hiscock's reply, N & Q June–Aug, Dec 1960.

—— William Upcott and Evelyn's papers. Library 5th ser 20 1965.

Boas, G. John Evelyn, virtuoso. Essays by Divers Hands new ser 28 1956.

de Beer, E. S. John Evelyn FRS. Notes & Records of Royal Soc 15 1960.

JOHN EVELYN, son of the diarist

Of gardens. 1672, 1673. Bk 2 rptd in Silva, 3rd, 4th and 5th edns, above. Tr from Latin of Renatus Rapinus.

The history of the grand visiers. 1677. Tr from French of F. de Chassepol. For contributions to other works *see* Keynes.

MARY EVELYN, daughter of the diarist

Mundus muliebris: or the ladies dressing room unlock'd, in burlesque; together with the fop-dictionary. 1690 (anon); 1700 (as The ladies dressing-room unlock'd); rptd in Evelyn's Miscellaneous writings; the prefaces probably, and perhaps the fop-dictionary, are by him.

R. C. L.

SAMUEL PEPYS
1633–1703

The ms of the diary etc is in the Pepys Library, Magdalene College Cambridge.

Bibliographies etc

A descriptive catalogue of the naval manuscripts in the Pepysian Library. Ed J. R. Tanner 4 vols 1903–23 (Navy Records Soc).

Historical Manuscripts Commission. Report on the Pepys mss preserved at Magdalene College Cambridge. Ed E. K. Purnell 1911.

Bibliotheca Pepysiana: a descriptive catalogue of the library. Pt 1, 'Sea' mss, ed J. R. Tanner 1914; pt 2, Early printed books to 1558, ed E. Gordon Duff 1914; pt 3, Mediaeval mss, ed M. R. James 1923; pt 4, Shorthand books, ed W. J. Carlton 1940.

Chappell, E. Bibliographia Pepysiana. 1933 (priv ptd).

Charrington, J. A catalogue of the engraved portraits in the library of Pepys. Cambridge 1936.

Wilson, E. M. Pepys's Spanish chap-books. Trans Cambridge Bibl Soc 2 1955–7.

Emslie, M. Pepys's songs and songbooks in the diary period. Library 5th ser 12 1957.

§ 1

Memoires relating to the state of the Royal Navy for ten years, determin'd December 1688. 1690; ed J. R. Tanner, Oxford 1906 (as Pepys' Memoires of the Royal Navy 1679–1688).

Mr Pepys upon the state of Christ-Hospital. 1698–9; ed R. Kirk, Philadelphia 1935.

An account of the preservation of King Charles II after the battle of Worcester. Ed Sir D. Dalrymple 1766; ed W. Matthews 1966 (as Charles II's escape from Worcester); ed R. Ollard 1966 (as The escape of Charles II after the battle of Worcester). Dictated by the King to Pepys in 1680; often rptd.

The following list does not include abridgements or selections from the diary. For the general reader, the abridgement by O. F. Morshead, 1926, is the best; for the student of history, that by J. P. Kenyon, 1963.

Memoirs 1659 [1660] to 1669, and a selection from his private correspondence. Ed Richard Lord Braybrooke 2 vols 1825, 1828, 5 vols 1828, 1848–9 (as Diary, 'considerably enlarged') 1851, 4 vols 1854 ('revised and corrected'), 1854, 1858 etc. From a transcription of the original ms, mostly in shorthand, by John Smith. About one-quarter of Diary was ptd in 1825; two-fifths in 1848–9 etc.

Diary and correspondence. Ed Mynors Bright 6 vols 1875–9. From Bright's transcription, about four-fifths of Diary.

Diary. Ed H. B. Wheatley 10 vols 1893–9. From Bright's transcription, above, with alterations; about nine-tenths of ms.

Naval minutes. Ed J. R. Tanner 1926 (Navy Records Soc).

The Tangier papers of Pepys [1683–4]. Ed E. Chappell 1935 (Navy Records Soc). The best edn; text collated with transcription by W. Matthews; includes the miscellaneous papers. Other edns by Smith as Life, journals and correspondence, and by Howarth as Letters and the second diary; *see* below.

Letters

Selections from Pepys's correspondence are included in edns of Diary by Braybrooke and Bright, above, and in edn by Dalrymple of An account of the preservation of King Charles II. *For summaries of some of his official and other correspondence, see* Calendars of state papers domestic, ed M. A. Everett Green et al, 1660–79, 1684–7; Catalogi codicum manuscriptorum bibliothecae Bodleianae, pt 5 fascicules 1–2, Rawlinson mss, ed W. D. Macray 1862, 1878; A descriptive catalogue of the naval manuscripts in the Pepysian Library, ed J. R. Tanner 4 vols 1903–23 (Navy Records Soc); *and the following Reports of the Historical Mss Commission:* 8th (*Appendix 1 section 1, Trinity House mss*), 1881; 11th (*Appendix pt 5, Dartmouth mss*), 1887; 15th (*Appendix pt 1, Dartmouth mss vol 3*), 1896; 15th (*Appendix pt 2, J. Eliot Hodgkin mss*) 1897; *Downshire mss vol 1, 1924; Hastings mss vol 2, 1930.*

Smith, John. The life, journals and correspondence. 2 vols 1841.

Marshall, J. Unpublished letters. Athenaeum 31 May 1890.

Private correspondence 1679–1703. Ed J. R. Tanner 2 vols 1929; Further correspondence 1662–79, ed Tanner 1929.

Letters and the second diary. Ed R. G. Howarth 1932.

Shorthand letters. Ed E. Chappell, Cambridge 1933.

Letters of Pepys and his family circle. Ed H. T. Heath, Oxford 1955.

The Pepys Library

A Pepysian garland. Ed H. E. Rollins, Cambridge 1922. Black-letter broadside ballads 1595–1639, chiefly from Pepys's collection.

The Pepys ballads. Ed H. E. Rollins 8 vols Cambridge Mass 1929–32. With A Pepysian garland, above, reproduces about one-third of Pepys's collection 1534–1703. About another third is in Roxburghe ballads, ed W.

Chappell and J. W. Ebsworth, Hertford 1883–95, and in Bagford ballads, ed Ebsworth, Hertford 1876–8. *See* L. M. Goldstein, The Pepys ballads, Library 5th ser 21 1966.

§ 2

Plain truth: or a private discourse betwixt P. and H. [1679].

A hue and cry after P. and H. [1679].

[Scott, Sir W.] Pepys's Memoirs. Quart Rev 33 1826.

Wheatley, H. B. Pepys and the world he lived in. 1880.

Stevenson, R. L. In his Familiar studies, [1882].

Pepys, W. C. Genealogy of the Pepys family. 1887, 1952 (with addns).

Tanner, J. R. Pepys and the Popish Plot. EHR 3 1892.

—— Pepys and the Royal Navy. Cambridge 1920.

—— Mr Pepys. 1925.

—— Pepys and the Trinity House. EHR 44 1929.

Firth, C. H. The early life of Pepys. Macmillan's Mag Nov 1893.

Bridge, F. Pepys, lover of musique. 1903.

Lubbock, P. Samuel Pepys. 1909.

McAfee, H. Pepys on the Restoration stage. New Haven 1916.

Occasional Papers of the Pepys Club. 2 vols 1917–25.

Dubreton (afterwards Lucas-Dubreton), J. La petite vie de Pepys. Paris 1923; tr 1924.

Abbott, W. C. The serious Pepys. In his Conflicts with oblivion, New Haven 1924.

Bradford, G. The soul of Pepys. Boston 1924.

Whitear, W. H. More Pepysiana. 1927.

Ponsonby, A. Samuel Pepys. 1928 (EML).

Chappell, E. Eight generations of the Pepys family 1500–1800. 1936.

Bryant, A. Pepys: the man in the making. Cambridge 1933; The years of peril, Cambridge 1935; The saviour of the navy, Cambridge 1938.

Ehrman, J. P. W. The official papers transferred by Pepys to the Admiralty by 12 July 1689. Mariner's Mirror 34 1948.

—— Pepys's organization and the naval mobilization of 1688. Mariner's Mirror 35 1949.

Ranft, B. M. The significance of the political career of Pepys. Jnl of Modern History 24 1942.

Matthews, A. G. Mr Pepys and Nonconformity. 1954.

Hunt, P. Pepys in the diary. Pittsburgh 1959.

Wilson, J. H. The private life of Mr Pepys. 1960.

Andrade, E. N. Da C. Pepys and the Royal Society. Notes & Records of Royal Soc 18 1963.

Pool, B. Pepys and navy contracts. History Today 13 1963.

Emden, C. S. Pepys himself. Oxford 1963.

Nicolson, M. H. Pepys' diary and the new science. Charlottesville 1965.

R. C. L.

LADY MARY WORTLEY MONTAGU, née PIERREPOINT
1689–1762

§ 1

Court poems. 1716. 3 town eclogues, misdated 1706.

Verses address'd to the imitator of Horace. 1733. On Pope.

An elegy to a young lady in the manner of Ovid [by James Hammond] with an answer, by a lady, author of the Verses to the imitator of Horace. 1733.

The Dean's provocation for writing the lady's dressing-room. 1734. On Swift.

The nonsense of common-sense 1737–8; ed R. Halsband, Evanston 1947. 9 periodical essays.

Six town eclogues with some other poems. 1747.

Letters of Rt Hon Lady M—y W—y M—e written during her travels. 3 vols 1763 etc.

An additional volume to the letters. 1767. Spurious

except for one letter to the Abbé Conti published 1719, 2 prose pieces and some verse.

Poetical works. [Ed I. Reed] 1768.

Works, including her correspondence, poems and essays. Ed J. Dallaway 5 vols 1803, 1805 (5th edn) (with letters to Mrs Hewet).

Original letters to Sir James and Lady Frances Steuart. [Ed J. Dunlop], Greenock 1818.

Letters and works. Ed Lord Wharncliffe 3 vols 1837 (with Introductory anecdotes by Lady Louisa Stuart); ed W. M. Thomas 2 vols 1861 (3rd edn), 1893, 1887 (rev).

Letters. Ed R. B. Johnson 1906 (EL).

Complete letters. Ed R. Halsband 3 vols Oxford 1965-7.

Selected letters. Ed R. Halsband 1970.

§ 2

Hunt, Leigh. Lady Mary Wortley Montagu. Westminster Rev 27 1837; rptd in his Men, women and books 2 vols 1847.

Dilke, C. W. Lady Mary Wortley Montagu. In his Papers of a critic, 2 vols 1875.

'Paston, George' (E. M. Symonds). Lady Mary Wortley Montagu and her times. 1907.

Strachey, L. Lady Mary Wortley Montagu. Albany Rev new ser 1 1907; rptd in his Characters and commentaries, 1933.

More, P. E. Lady Mary Wortley Montagu. Atlantic Monthly 1908; rptd in his With the wits: Shelburne essays 10th ser, Boston 1919.

Bradford, G. In his Portraits of women, Boston 1916.

'Melville, Lewis' (L. S. Benjamin). Life and letters of Lady Mary Wortley Montagu. 1925.

Barry, I. Portrait of Lady Mary. 1928.

Tillotson, G. Lady Mary Wortley Montagu and Pope's Elegy to the memory of an unfortunate lady. RES 12 1936.

'Gibbs, Lewis' (J. W. Cove). The admirable Lady Mary. 1949.

Halsband, R. Addison's Cato and Lady Mary Wortley Montagu. PMLA 65 1950.

— An imitation of Perrault in England: Carabosse. Comparative Lit 3 1951.

— Pope, Lady Mary and the Court poems 1716. PMLA 68 1953.

— New light on Lady Mary Wortley Montagu's contribution to smallpox inoculation. Jnl History of Medicine 8 1953.

— Lady Mary Wortley Montagu as a friend of continental writers. John Rylands Lib Bull 39 1956.

— Life of Lady Mary Wortley Montagu. Oxford 1956, New York 1960 (corrected).

— Editing the letters of letter-writers. SB 11 1958.

— Lady Mary Wortley Montagu as letter-writer. PMLA 80 1965; rptd in The familiar letter in the 18th century, ed H. Anderson, P. Daghlian and I. Ehrenpreis, Lawrence Kansas 1966.

— Algarotti as Apollo. In Friendship's garland: essays presented to Mario Praz, 2 vols Rome 1966.

— Lady Mary Wortley Montagu and 18th-century fiction. PQ 45 1966.

— Lady Mary Wortley Montagu: her place in the 18th century. History Today 16 1966.

— Walpole versus Lady Mary. In Horace Walpole: writer, politician and connoisseur, ed W. H. Smith, New Haven 1967.

R. H.

PHILIP DORMER STANHOPE, 4th EARL OF CHESTERFIELD

1694-1773

Bibliographies

Gulick, S. L. A Chesterfield bibliography to 1800. PBSA 29 1935.

Todd, W. B. The number, order and authorship of the Hanover pamphlets attributed to Chesterfield. PBSA 44 1950.

§ 1

The first and most recent edns are cited, with significant intervening edns.

The art of pleasing: in a series of letters to Master Stanhope [later 5th Earl of Chesterfield]. Edinburgh Mag 1-2 1774. 14 letters; rptd in several periodicals, in some edns of Letters to his son, in Miscellaneous works vol 3, and separately 1783, Dublin 1783.

Letters to his son Philip Stanhope, together with several other pieces on various subjects, published by Mrs Eugenia Stanhope. 2 vols 1774, Dublin 1774, 4 vols 1774, Dublin 1776 (adds The art of pleasing), London 1787 (incorporates letters from Supplement), Paris 1789, London 1800 (11th edn), 6 vols Vienna 1800; ed C. Strachey and A. Calthrop 2 vols 1901.

Miscellaneous works: consisting of letters to his friends, never before printed, and various other articles; to which are prefixed Memoirs of his life, by M. Maty. Ed J. O. Justamond 2 vols 1777, 1778 (with 'appendix, containing sixteen characters of great personages' and the letters to Faulkner etc), 3 vols Dublin 1777 (adds letters to Faulkner etc, but not the characters), 4 vols 1779.

Letters to Alderman George Faulkner, Dr Madden, Mr Sexton, Mr Derrick and the Earl of Arran. 1777.

Characters of eminent personages of his own time. 1777 (7 characters), 1778 (16 characters and letters to Faulkner etc).

Miscellaneous works: consisting of letters, political tracts and poems: volume 3 completing edition begun by M. Maty, collected by B. W[ay]. 1778.

Letters from a celebrated nobleman to his heir [later 5th Earl of Chesterfield]. 1783. 14 letters, previously ptd as The art of pleasing, not included.

Supplement to the Letters to his son. 1787, Dublin 1787.

Letters to Arthur Charles Stanhope relative to the education of his Lordship's godson. 1817 (44 letters); rptd as appendix to Chesterfield's letters to his godson, ed Lord Carnarvon 1890.

Letters. Ed Lord Mahon 5 vols 1845-53. Vols 1-2, Letters on education and characters; vols 3-4, Political and miscellaneous letters; vol 5, Miscellanies.

The wit and wisdom of Chesterfield. Ed W. Ernst-Browning 1875. A selection, including poems.

Letters to his godson and successor. Ed Earl of Carnarvon, Oxford 1890, 1890 (adding the 44 letters to A. C. Stanhope). From ms.

Chesterfield's worldly wisdom. Ed G. B. Hill, Oxford 1891. A selection.

Letters. Ed J. Bradshaw 3 vols 1892.,

Letters to Lord Huntingdon (46). Ed A. F. Steuart 1923 (from ms).

Letters to his son and others. Ed R. K. Root 1929 (EL).

Letters. Selected by P. M. Jones, Oxford 1929 (WC).

Private correspondence of Chesterfield and Newcastle 1744-6. Ed R. Lodge 1930 (Camden Soc). 40 letters by Chesterfield.

Letters. Ed B. Dobrée 6 vols 1932 (most complete edn).

Letters and other pieces. Ed R. P. Bond, New York 1935. A selection.

Chesterfield and Dowdeswell: letters. Ed F. W. Cock, N & Q 26 Sept 1936.

Unpublished letters of Chesterfield. Ed S. L. Gulick, Berkeley 1937. 25 to his godson and one to Deyverdun.

Five unpublished letters [to the Earl of Bute]. Ed C. Price, Life & Letters 59 1948.

For minor works (speeches, political pamphlets etc) by or attributed to Chesterfield, and early selections, adaptations, burlesques and criticism of the letters to his son, see S. L. Gulick's bibliography, above.

§2

Gordon, A. The contrast: or an antidote against the pernicious principles disseminated in the letters of the late Earl of Chesterfield. 2 vols 1791.

Hayward, A. Lord Chesterfield. Edinburgh Rev 82 1845; rptd in his Biographical and critical essays, 2 vols 1858.

Cramp, W. Junius and his works compared with the character and writings of Chesterfield. 1850.

Sainte-Beuve, C. A. Lettres de Lord Chesterfield à son fils. In his Causeries du lundi vol 2, Paris 1850.

Tuckerman, H. T. Lord Chesterfield: the man of the world. In his Biographical essays, Boston 1857.

Ernst-Browning, W. Memoirs of the life of Chesterfield. 1893.

Collins, J. C. Lord Chesterfield's letters. In his Essays and studies, 1895.

Tovey, D. C. Chesterfield's letters. In his Reviews and essays in English literature, 1897.

Craig, W. H. Life of Chesterfield. 1907.

More, P. E. Chesterfield (1908). In his Selected Shelburne essays, Oxford 1935 (WC).

Schumann, K. Die pädagogischen Ansichten des Grafen Chesterfield. Langensalza 1917.

Allen, E. S. Chesterfield's objection to laughter. MLN 38 1923.

Whibley, C. Lord Chesterfield. Criterion 2 1924.

Coxon, R. Chesterfield and his critics. 1925.

Yvon, P. Chesterfield et les Français. Revue Anglo-américaine 5 1927.

Heltzel, V. G. Chesterfield and the anti-laughter tradition. MP 26 1928.

Scott, T. Lord Chesterfield and his letters to his sons. Indianapolis 1929 (priv ptd).

Baker, H. A. Chesterfield and Johnson. Contemporary Rev March 1930.

La Force, Auguste de Caumont, Duc de. Un Anglais de chez nous éducateur et humoriste: Lord Chesterfield. Revue de France Feb 1930; rptd in Comédies sanglantes, drames intimes, Paris 1930.

Jaeger, M. The man of the world. In her Experimental lives from Cato to George Sand, 1932.

Strachey, L. Lady Mary Wortley Montagu and Lord Chesterfield. In his Characters and commentaries, 1933.

Abbott, W. C. Lord Chesterfield: aristocrat. In his Adventures in reputation, Cambridge Mass 1935.

Shellabarger, S. Lord Chesterfield. 1935, Boston 1951 (rev as Lord Chesterfield and his world).

Gulick, S. L. The publication of Chesterfield's letters to his son. PMLA 51 1936.

— Johnson, Chesterfield and Boswell. In The age of Johnson: essays presented to C. B. Tinker, New Haven 1949.

O'Conor, C. George Faulkner and Chesterfield. Studies 25 1936.

Gardner, J. Chesterfield and Voltaire. Cornhill Mag Jan 1937.

Holsapple, C. Some early verses by Chesterfield. MLN 52 1937.

Radice, S. Lord Chesterfield. TLS 24–31 July 1937.

Connely, W. Chesterfield's son and grandsons. TLS 11 Nov 1939.

— The true Chesterfield. 1939.

Hare, K. Lord Chesterfield and Dr Johnson. Quart Rev 274 1940.

Blanchard, R. Steele and Chesterfield. RES 20 1944.

Bryant, D. C. Chesterfield's advice on speaking. Quart Jnl of Speech 31 1945.

De Quincey, T. Dr Johnson and Lord Chesterfield. New York 1945 (priv ptd).

Neumann, J. H. Chesterfield and the standard of usage in English. MLQ 7 1946.

Watson, M. R. Chesterfield and 'decorum'. MLN 62 1947.

Dobrée, B. Chesterfield and France. Eng Miscellany (Rome) 2 1951.

Price, C. The Edinburgh edition of Chesterfield's letters to his son. Library 5th ser 5 1951.

— Some new light on Chesterfield. Neuphilologische Mitteilungen 54 1953.

— Further Chesterfield gleanings. Neuphilologische Mitteilungen 56 1955.

Boyce, B. Johnson and Chesterfield once more. PQ 32 1953.

Voisine, J. Les Anglais en Provence au 18e siècle. Revue de Littérature Comparée 30 1956.

Brown, T. J. English literary autographs 28: Lord Chesterfield. Book Collector 7 1958.

Lucas, F. L. In his Search for good sense: four 18th-century characters, Johnson, Chesterfield, Boswell, Goldsmith, 1958.

Nelick, F. C. Lord Chesterfield's adoption of Philip Stanhope. PQ 38 1959.

Brewer, S. M. Design for a gentleman: the education of Philip Stanhope. 1963.

Cappon, A. P. The Earl of Chesterfield as educator: yesterday and today. Univ Rev 31 1965.

R. H.

HORACE WALPOLE
1717–97

The most important collection of mss is in the W. S. Lewis Library at Farmington, Conn.

Bibliographies

Hazen, A. T. Bibliography of the Strawberry Hill Press. New Haven 1942. Earlier bibliographies include Martin, 1834, Bohn's suppl to Lowndes, 1864, and P. Toynbee in A. Dobson, Horace Walpole, 1927.

— Bibliography of Walpole. New Haven 1948.

— Catalogue of Walpole's library. 3 vols New Haven 1969.

Journal of the printing office. Ed P. Toynbee 1923, Boston 1923 (with facs).

Collections

Fugitive pieces in verse and prose. Strawberry Hill 1758.

Fugitive pieces in verse and prose. 2 vols Strawberry Hill 1770. A partial collection, ptd but not pbd.

Works. Ed Mary Berry under the name of her father Robert Berry 5 vols 1798. Vol 6, Letters to Montagu and Cole, ed John Martin 1818; vol 7–8, Memoires of the last ten years of the reign of George II, ed Lord Holland 2 vols 1822; vol 9, Letters to Lord Hertford, ed J. W. Croker 1825. Rptd 9 vols in 11, Hildesheim 1971.

Historische, litterarische und unterhaltende Schriften. Tr A. W. Schlegel, Leipzig 1800. Miscellaneous pieces tr from vols 2 and 4 of Works, above.

Walpole's fugitive verses. Ed W. S. Lewis, New York 1931.

§1

Many items, especially the earlier pieces, rptd in his Fugitive pieces, 1758, as well as in miscellanie slike Dodsley's Collection and the Foundling Hospital for Wit. For late pbns of certain mss, see also under §2, below.

The lesson for the day. 1742. At least 5 edns; also imitations.

The beauties. 1746.

Epilogue to Tamerlane. 1746.

Aedes Walpolianae. 1747, 1752, 1767.

A letter to the Whigs. 1747, 1748.

A second and third letter to the Whigs. 1748.

Three letters to the Whigs. 1748.

The original speech of Sir William Stanhope. 1748, Dublin 1748.

The speech of Richard White-Liver. 1748.

A letter from Xo Ho. [1757] (5 numbered edns).

A catalogue of the royal and noble authors of England. 2 vols Strawberry Hill 1758, London 1759, Dublin 1759, Edinburgh 1792, 1 vol London (also Edinburgh) 1796; ed T. Park 5 vols 1806, New York 1967.

A dialogue between two great ladies. 1760.

Catalogue of pictures and drawings in the Holbein Chamber. Strawberry Hill 1760.

Catalogues of the pictures of the Duke of Devonshire etc. Strawberry Hill 1760.

Anecdotes of painting in England (and A catalogue of engravers). 4 vols Strawberry Hill 1762–3, 1765; vol 4 of Anecdotes, Strawberry Hill 1771 but pbd 1780; 5 vols 1782, 1786; Catalogue of engravers, 1794; ed J. Dallaway 5 vols 1826–8; ed R. N. Wornum 3 vols 1849, 1862, 1876, 1879, 1888. Vol 5 of Anecdotes, compiled from Walpole's Books of materials by F. W. Hilles and P. B. Daghlian, New Haven 1937.

The opposition to the late Minister vindicated. 1763. Probably by Walpole.

A counter-address to the public. 1764 (4 edns).

The magpie and her brood. Strawberry Hill 1764.

The castle of Otranto. 1765, 1765, Dublin 1765, 1765, London 1766, 1782, 1786, 1791, Parma 1791, London 1793, 1793, Berlin 1794, London 1796, 1800; ed W. Scott 1811 etc; ed M. Summers 1924; ed O. Doughty 1929; ed W. S. Lewis, Oxford 1964; tr French, 1767, 1797, 1943; Italian, 1795.

An account of the giants lately discovered. 1766.

Historic doubts on Richard III. 1768, 1768, Dublin 1768, London 1822; tr French, 1800; ed P. M. Kendall, New York 1965 (with More's History).

The mysterious mother. Strawberry Hill 1768, London 1781, Dublin 1791, London 1791, 1796.

Reply to Dean Milles. Strawberry Hill [1770]. 6 copies ptd.

A description of the villa of Horace Walpole. Strawberry Hill 1774, 1784, London 1842, 1965.

A letter to the editor of the Miscellanies of Thomas Chatterton. Strawberry Hill 1779.

Essay on modern gardening [in English and French]. Strawberry Hill 1785, Paris? [c. 1790]; rptd L. Buddy, Canton Pa 1904; ed W. S. Lewis, New York 1931; rptd in I. W. U. Chase, Walpole gardenist, Princeton 1943. First ptd by Walpole in vol 4 of Anecdotes, above.

Hieroglyphic tales. Strawberry Hill 1785 (7 copies ptd), Newcastle 1822, London 1926.

Postscript to the royal and noble authors. Strawberry Hill 1786.

Notes to the portraits at Woburn Abbey. 1800.

Occasional Verses, Prefaces etc

Some other occasional verses, ptd at Strawberry Hill, are recorded in Hazen, Bibliography of the Strawberry Hill Press, above. Other occasional pieces, pbd after Walpole's death, are recorded in Hazen, Bibliography of Walpole, above.

Latin verses in Gratulatio Academiae Cantabrigiensis. 1736.

Pretended advertisement of the She-witch from Lapland. Daily Advertiser 28 Dec 1741.

Essays contributed to Old England. 19 essays 1743–9. First 4 rptd as Four letters publish'd in Old England, 1743.

A narrative of the last illness of the Earl of Orford, by John Ranby. 1745, 1745. The journal for 3–17 Feb apparently by Walpole.

Two essays in Dodsley's Museum. 1746.

Verses occasion'd by a late will. London Evening Post 26 June 1746.

An epistle from Florence. In Dodsley's Collection, 1748.

Remembrancer 1748–9. 4 essays.

Gray's Elegy. 1751. Pbn arranged by Walpole, and Advertisement by him.

Designs by Bentley for six poems by Gray. 1753. Pbn arranged by Walpole, and Explanation of the prints by him.

World 1753–7. 9 essays.

Protester 1753. One essay.

Strawberry-Hill: a ballad. GM April 1756; rptd (altered) in London Chron 10 Aug 1758.

Queries [on Admiral Byng]. London Chron 10 Feb 1757.

Verses to General Conway. Public Advertiser 28 Nov 1757.

A journey into England by Paul Hentzner. Strawberry Hill 1757. Advertisement by Walpole.

Vertue's Catalogue of pictures of Charles I's collection 1757. Advertisement by Walpole.

Vertue's Catalogue of pictures belonging to James II. 1758. Advertisement by Walpole.

Vertue's Catalogue of pictures of Duke of Buckingham. 1758. Advertisement by Walpole.

Lord Cornbury's The mistakes. 1758. Advertisement by Walpole.

Whitworth's Account of Russia. Strawberry Hill 1758. Advertisement by Walpole.

R. Bentley's Reflections on cruelty. 1759. Dedication by Walpole.

A letter sent by the Corporation of Thetford to Gen. Conway. London Chron 5 May 1764; rptd GM May 1764.

The life of Edward Lord Herbert of Cherbury. Strawberry Hill 1764. Advertisement by Walpole.

Poems by Countess Temple. Strawberry Hill 1764. Prefatory verses by Walpole.

Letter from the King of Prussia to Rousseau. St James's Chron 3 April 1766.

Letter to the Mayor of Lynn. St James's Chron 28 May 1767.

Public Advertiser 28 Aug, 2 Sept 1767. 2 letters.

Verses to Miss Mendez. In Mendez's Collection of poetry, 1767.

Poems by the Rev Mr Hoyland. Strawberry Hill 1769. Advertisement by Walpole.

Epilogue spoken by Mrs Clive. Public Advertiser 24 April 1769.

Lines on the Duchess of Queensberry. GM March 1772.

Memoires du Comte de Grammont. Strawberry Hill 1772. Ed Walpole with notes; rptd 1783; ed D. Hughes 1965.

Copies of seven letters from Edward VI. Strawberry Hill 1772. Advertisement by Walpole.

Miscellaneous antiquities. 2 nos Strawberry Hill 1772. Advertisement by Walpole.

Verses for the monument to Queen Catherine. Public Advertiser 19 Oct 1773.

Jephson's Braganza. 1775. Epilogue by Walpole.

The sleep-walker: a comedy, translated by Lady Craven. Strawberry Hill 1778. Prefatory verses to Lady Craven by Walpole.

The times: a comedy by Mrs Griffith. 1780. Prologue and epilogue by Walpole.

Character of Lady Hertford. London Courant 18 Nov 1782.

Lord Harcourt's Account of Nuneham. 1783 (priv ptd). The catalogue of pictures prepared by Walpole and Reynolds.

The three Vernons. St James's Chron 17 Nov 1787.

Epitaph on Mrs Clive's monument. London Evening Post 22 Sept 1791.

Character of Lady Ravensworth. Times 16 June 1794; rptd GM 1794.

To Edward Jerningham. European Mag 28 1795.

Letters, Diaries etc

Letters to George Montagu. 1818, 1819, 1834 (reissue). Also issued with Works, above.

Letters to William Cole. 1818, 1824 (reissue). Also issued with Works, above.

Private correspondence. 4 vols 1820, 3 vols 1837.

Letters to the Earl of Hertford. 1825. Also issued with Works.

Letters to Sir Horace Mann. Ed Lord Dover 3 vols 1833, 1833, 2 vols New York 1833; Concluding ser, 4 vols 1843–4, 2 vols Philadelphia 1844.

Letters. Ed J. Wright 6 vols 1840, Philadelphia 1842, London 1846.

Short notes of the life of Horace Walpole. Ptd with his letters to Mann, 1844; rptd by Cunningham and Mrs Toynbee, and (from original ms) in the Yale edn vol 13, below.

Letters to the Countess of Ossory. Ed R. Vernon Smith 2 vols 1848, 1848, 3 vols 1903.

Correspondence with Mason. Ed J. Mitford 2 vols 1851.

Letters. Ed P. Cunningham 9 vols 1857 etc.

Some unpublished letters. Ed S. Walpole 1902.

Letters. Ed Mrs P. Toynbee 16 vols Oxford 1903–5; Supplementary vols ed P. Toynbee 3 vols 1918–25.

Correspondence of Gray, Walpole, West and Ashton. Ed P. Toynbee 2 vols Oxford 1915.

The Yale ed of Walpole's correspondence. Ed W. S. Lewis et al 31 vols New Haven 1937–67. 50 or more vols projected.

A selection of the letters. Ed W. S. Lewis 2 vols New York 1926. Many other selections have been made, including a new one-vol selection by W. S. Lewis 1951.

Reminiscences written for Mary and Agnes Berry. 1805 (priv ptd), 1818, 1819, 1819, Boston 1820, London 1830; ed P. Toynbee, Oxford 1924; tr French, 1826.

Memoires of the last ten years of the reign of George II. Ed Lord Holland 2 vols 1822 (also issued as vols 7–8 of Works), 3 vols 1846, 1847; rptd New York 1968; tr French, 2 vols 1823; German, 1846.

Memoirs of George III. Ed D. Le Marchant 4 vols 1845, Philadelphia 1845, London 1851; ed G. F. R. Barker 1894; rptd New York 1968; tr German, 1847.

Journal of George III. Ed J. Doran 2 vols 1859; rptd as Last journals, 1910.

Memoirs and portraits. Ed M. J. C. Hodgart 1963, New York 1963 (rev).

§2

Walpoliana. Ed J. Pinkerton 2 vols [1799], 1800, [1806?], Dublin 1800, London 1819, Boston 1820, London 1830.

Letters of the Marquise du Deffand to Walpole. Ed Mary Berry 4 vols 1810, Paris 1811, 1812, 1824; ed Mrs P. Toynbee 3 vols 1912.

The works of Sir C. H. Williams, with notes by Walpole. 3 vols 1822.

Macaulay, T. B. Horace Walpole. Edinburgh Rev 1833.

A catalogue of the classic contents of Strawberry Hill. April 1842. Numerous rev issues: see A. T. Hazen, N & Q 25 Jan 1947.

A catalogue of engraved portraits. June 1842.

Aedes Strawberrianae: names of purchasers and prices at the two sales. 1842.

Sainte-Beuve, C. A. Lettres de la Marquise du Deffand. In his Causeries du lundi, Paris 1850.

Warburton, E. (ed). Memoirs of Walpole and his contemporaries. 2 vols 1851. Actually ed R. F. Williams.

Rémusat, C. de. In his L'Angleterre au dix-huitième siècle, 2 vols Paris 1856.

Lewis, Lady T. (ed). Extracts of the journal and correspondence of Miss Berry. 3 vols 1865, 1866, New York 1967.

Stephen, L. Horace Walpole. Cornhill Mag June 1872.

Doran, J. 'Mann' and manners at the Court of Florence. 2 vols 1876.

[Hayward, A.] A description of the villa of Mr Horace Walpole at Strawberry Hill. Quart Rev 142 1876.

Seeley, L. B. Walpole and his world. 2 vols 1884, 1895.

Dobson, A. Walpole: a memoir. New York 1890, London 1893; ed P. Toynbee 1927.

—— A day at Strawberry Hill. In his Eighteenth-century vignettes ser 1, 1892.

—— The Officina Arbuteana. In his Eighteenth-century vignettes ser 3, 1896.

Toynbee, Mrs P. Walpole and 'St Hannah'. Temple Bar March 1897.

Raphael, H. H. Walpole: a descriptive catalogue of illustrations for the extension of Walpole's letters. Bristol 1909.

Becker, C. Walpole's memoirs. Amer Historical Rev 16 1911.

Greenwood, A. D. Walpole's world. 1913.

Edge, J. H. Walpole the great letter-writer. Dublin 1913 (priv ptd).

Cust, L. Vertue's note-books. Walpole Soc 3 1914. The note-books rptd in Walpole Soc 18, 20, 22, 24, 26, 29–30 1930–55; rptd 1969.

Saintsbury, G. In his Peace of the Augustans, 1916.

Finch, M. B. and E. A. Peers. Walpole's relations with Voltaire. MP 18 1920.

Robertson, W. G. Walpole's correspondence. In his Neglected English classics, Aberdeen 1920.

Strachey, L. Walpole and Mme du Deffand. In his Books and characters, 1922.

—— In his Characters and commentaries, 1933.

Yvon, P. La vie d'un dilettante: Walpole. Paris 1924.

—— Walpole as a poet. Paris 1924.

Ker, W. P. In his Collected essays, 1925.

Pottle, F. A. The part played by Walpole and Boswell in the quarrel between Rousseau and Hume. PQ 4 1925.

Roe, F. C. Le voyage de Gray et de Walpole en Italie. Revue de Littérature Comparée 6 1926.

Toynbee, P. (ed). Satirical poems by Mason, with notes by Walpole. Oxford 1926.

—— Strawberry Hill accounts. Oxford 1927.

—— Journals of visits to country seats. Walpole Soc 16 1928.

—— Delenda est Oxonia, written in 1749. EHR 42 1927.

—— Walpoliana. Blackwood's Mag April 1927. Selections from Walpole's Books of materials and his Paris journals.

—— Walpole's memoir of the poet Gray. MLR 27 1932.

'Maurois, André' (E. S. W. Herzog). Etudes anglaises: Dickens, Walpole, Ruskin et Wilde. Paris 1927.

Stuart, D. M. Horace Walpole. 1927 (EML).

Lewis, W. S. (ed). A commonplace book of Walpole's. 1927 (priv ptd).

—— Anecdotes told me by Lady Denbigh. 1932 (priv ptd).

—— Walpole's letter from Mme de Sévigné. 1933 (priv ptd).

—— Memoranda Walpoliana. 1937 (priv ptd).

—— Select observations assembled by Walpole. 1937 (priv ptd).

—— Notes by Walpole on several characters of Shakespeare. 1940 (priv ptd).

Whibley, L. The foreign tour of Gray and Walpole. Blackwood's Mag June 1930.

Round, J. H. The origin of the Walpoles. In his Family origins, 1930.

Meyerstein, E. H. W. In his Life of Chatterton, 1930.

'Melville, Lewis' (L. S. Benjamin). Horace Walpole. [1930].

Lewis, W. S. The forlorn printer: T. Kirgate. 1931 (priv ptd).

—— The Duchess of Portland's museum. 1936 (priv ptd).

—— Bentley's designs for Walpole's Fugitive pieces. 1936 (priv ptd).

—— The genesis of Strawberry Hill. Metropolitan Museum Stud 5 1934.

—— Three tours through London. New Haven 1941.

—— Walpole's library. Library 5th ser 2 1947.

—— Collector's progress. New York 1951.

—— Horace Walpole, antiquary. In Essays presented to Sir L. Namier, 1956.

—— Walpole's library. Cambridge 1958.

—— Horace Walpole. New York [1960].

—— Editing private correspondence. Proc Amer Philosophical Soc 107 1963.

Gwynn, S. The life of Walpole. 1932.

Hutchison, R. Medicine in Walpole's letters. Annals of Medical History 6 1934.

Mehrotra, K. K. Walpole and the English novel. Oxford 1934.

Stein, J. M. Walpole and the English novel. SP 31 1934.

Smith, W. H. Architecture in English fiction. New Haven 1934.

— Strawbery Hill and Otranto. TLS 23 May 1936.

— Walpole and two Frenchwomen. In The age of Johnson: essays presented to C. B. Tinker, New Haven 1949.

— Cipher and code in Walpole correspondence. Yale Lib Gazette 25 1951.

Perkinson, R. H. Walpole and a Dublin pirate. PQ 15 1936.

— Walpole and the Biographia dramatica. RES 15 1939.

Wasserman, E. R. The Walpole-Chatterton controversy. MLN 54 1939.

Wecter, D. Walpole and Burke. MLN 54 1939.

Woolf, V. Two antiquaries: Walpole and Cole. Yale Rev 28 1939; rptd in her Death of the moth, 1942.

Notes on the artists' exhibitions. Ed H. Gatty, Walpole Soc 27 1939.

Clarke, A. H. T. Strawbery Hill. TLS 25 May 1940.

Ketton-Cremer, R. W. Walpole: a biography. 1940, 1946 (rev).

— Advice for Richard West. TLS 29 March 1947.

— Horace Walpole. Yale Rev 58 1968.

Kilby, C. S. Walpole on Shakespeare. SP 38 1941.

Rowse, A. L. Walpole and George Montagu. In his English spirit, 1944.

Walpole. TLS 24 May 1947.

Ilchester, Lord. Mme du Deffand to Walpole. TLS 19 June 1948.

— Some pages torn from the Last journals. In Studies for Belle da Costa Greene, Princeton 1954.

Brandenburg, A. S. The theme of the Mysterious mother. MLQ 10 1949.

Boulton, J. T. Burke and Walpole. TLS 20 April 1951.

Rohde, H. P. Strawbery Hill. Odense 1957. An illustrated narrative of Walpole's career.

Shipley, J. B. Walpole: some mistaken identifications. N & Q Nov 1957.

Honour, H. Horace Walpole. 1958 (Br Council pamphlet).

Lucas, F. L. The art of living: four eighteenth-century minds. 1959.

Judd, G. P. Walpole's memoirs. New York 1960.

Dobrée, B. In Restoration and eighteenth-century literature: essays in honor of A. D. McKillop, Chicago 1963.

Rose, E. J. 'The Queenly personality'; Walpole, Melville and mother. Lit & Psychology 15 1965.

Blunden, E. Walpole's young poet. In Renaissance and modern essays presented to V. de Sola Pinto, 1966.

Coley, W. B. Henry Fielding and the two Walpoles. PQ 45 1966.

Free, W. N. Walpole's letters: the art of being graceful. In The familiar letter in the eighteenth century, ed H. Anderson et al, Lawrence Kansas 1966.

Walpole: writer, politician and connoisseur. Ed W. H. Smith, New Haven 1967.

Johnson, J. W. Walpole and W. S. Lewis. Jnl of Br Stud 6 1967.

— Walpole against Burke. Stud in Burke 10 1968.

Kallich, M. Walpole against Burke: a study in antagonism. Stud in Burke 9 1968.

— Houghton Hall: the house of the Walpoles. Papers on Lang & Lit 4 1968.

A. T. H.

GILBERT WHITE
1720–93
Bibliographies

Newton, A. The published writings of White. N & Q 31 March–28 April, 16 June 1877, 23 Feb 1878.

Martin, E. A. A bibliography of White; with a biography and a descriptive account of the village of Selborne. [1897], 1934 (rev.)

Prance, C. A. Some uncollected authors xliii: White. Book Collector 17 1968.

Collections

Writings. Ed H. J. Massingham 2 vols 1938 (Nonesuch Press). Incomplete; includes Natural history, Antiquities (selected), parts of A naturalist's calendar, the poems and selected private letters.

§ I

The natural history and antiquities of Selborne, in the county of Southampton; with engravings and an appendix. 1789; ed J. W[hite] 2 vols 1802 (with next item, as The works in natural history of the late Gilbert White); ed J.W[hite] 1813 (adds poems and notes by John Mitford); ed W. Jardine, Edinburgh 1829; ed J. Rennie 1833; ed T. Brown, Edinburgh 1833; ed E. Blyth 1836; ed E. T. Bennett 1837, 1875 (rev J. E. Harting); ed W. Jardine and E. Jesse 1851; ed F. Buckland 2 vols 1876; ed T. Bell 2 vols 1877; ed C. G. Davies [1879]; ed L. C. Miall and W. W. Fowler 1901; ed R. Kearton 1902; ed G. Allen 1902; Oxford 1902 (WC); ed B. C. A. Windle [1906] (EL). Some edns omit Antiquities.

A naturalist's calendar with observations in various branches of natural history. Ed J. Aikin 1795. Rptd, in whole or part, in most edns of Natural history, above.

The antiquities of Selborne. Ed W. S. Scott 1950. With bibliography.

Letters, Diaries etc

Correspondence of Robert Marsham and Gilbert White. Ed T. Southwell, Trans Norfolk & Norwich Naturalists' Soc 2 1876. 10 letters by White.

The life and letters of White. Ed R. Holt-White 2 vols 1901.

Journals. Ed W. Johnson 1931.

§ 2

Shelley, H. C. White and Selborne. 1909.

Markland, R. Links between Dr Samuel Johnson and the Rev Gilbert White. Lytham 1925.

Johnson, W. White: pioneer, poet and stylist. 1928.

Hammond, L. V. White, poetizer of the commonplace. In The age of Johnson: essays presented to C. B. Tinker, New Haven 1949.

Hardy, E. Selborne revisited. Quart Rev 287 1949.

Scott, W. S. White of Selborne. 1950.

Lockley, R. M. Gilbert White. 1954.

Emden, C. S. White in his village. 1956.

Stillinger, J. White to Thomas Pennant: 2 original letters at Harvard. Harvard Lib Bull 11 1957.

Brown, T. J. English literary autographs 29: White. Book Collector 8 1959.

R. H.

THE BLUESTOCKINGS

Hawkins, L. M. Anecdotes, biographical sketches and memoirs. Vol 1 (all pbd), 1822.
—— Memoirs, Anecdotes, facts and opinions. 2 vols 1824.
Elwood, A. K. Memoirs of the literary ladies of England from the commencement of the last century. 2 vols 1843.
Gaussen, A. C. C. A later Pepys: the correspondence of Sir W. W. Pepys 1758–1825, with Mrs Chapone, Mrs Hartley, Mrs Montagu, Hannah More, William Franks, Sir James Macdonald, Major Rennell, Sir N. Wraxall and others. 2 vols 1904.
Wheeler, E. R. Famous blue-stockings (Mrs Montagu, Mrs Delany, Mrs Thrale, Mrs Vesey, Mrs Chapone, Fanny Burney, Elizabeth Carter, Hannah More). 1910.
Tinker, C. B. The salon and English letters. 1915.
Reynolds, M. The learned lady in England 1650–1760. Boston 1920.
Anson, E. and F. Mary Hamilton at Court and at home, from letters and diaries 1756 to 1816. 1925. Contains letters from Mrs Boscawen, Fanny Burney, Elizabeth Carter, Mrs Delany, Hannah More, Mrs Montagu, Mrs Vesey.
Johnson, R. B. Bluestocking letters. 1926. A selection.
Tenbury letters. Ed E. H. Fellowes and E. Pine 1943. A selection.
Aspinall-Oglander, C. Admiral's wife. 1941. On Mrs Boscawen.
—— Admiral's widow. 1943.
MacCarthy, B. G. Women writers: their contribution to the English novel 1621–1818. 2 vols Cork 1944–7.
Scott, W. S. The bluestocking ladies. 1947.
Bradbrook, M. C. The elegant eccentrics. MLR 44 1949. On Lady Eleanor Butler and Miss Sarah Ponsonby of Llangollen.
Halsband, R. Ladies of letters in the eighteenth century. Los Angeles 1969.

ELIZABETH CARTER
1717–1806
§1

Poems upon particular occasions. 1738.
An examination of Mr Pope's Essay on man, translated from the French of M. Crousaz. 1739.
Sir Isaac Newton's Philosophy explain'd for the use of ladies, translated from the Italian of Sig Algarotti. 2 vols 1739 etc.
All the works of Epictetus, which are now extant: consisting of his Discourses preserved by Arrian in 4 books, the Enchiridion and Fragments, translated from the original Greek. 1758 etc; ed W. H. D. Rouse 1910.
Poems on several occasions. 1762 etc.
A series of letters between Mrs Elizabeth Carter and Miss Catherine Talbot 1741–70; to which are added letters from Mrs Elizabeth Carter to Mrs Vesey 1763–87. Ed M. Pennington 4 vols 1809.
Letters from Mrs Elizabeth Carter to Mrs Montagu 1755–1800. Ed M. Pennington 3 vols 1817.

§2

Pennington, M. Memoirs of the life of Mrs Elizabeth Carter, with a new edition of her Poems; to which are added some miscellaneous essays in prose, together with her notes on the Bible and answers to objections concerning the Christian religion. 2 vols 1807 etc.
Gaussen, A. C. C. A woman of wit and wisdom: a memoir of Elizabeth Carter. 1906. With a genealogical note by R. B. Carter.

Dobson, A. The learned Mrs Carter. In his Later essays, 1921.
Ruhe, E. Birch, Johnson and Elizabeth Carter: an episode of 1738–9. PMLA 73 1958.

HESTER LYNCH THRALE, later PIOZZI, née SALUSBURY
1741–1821
§1

The three warnings. In Anna Williams, Miscellanies in prose and verse, 1766; Kidderminster 1792 (separately); Lady's Poetical Mag 1 1781.
Florence miscellany. Florence 1785. Preface and 9 poems by Mrs Piozzi.
Anecdotes of the late Samuel Johnson LlD in the last 20 years of his life. 1786; ed G. B. Hill (in Johnsonian miscellanies vol 1, 1897); ed S. C. Roberts, Cambridge 1925.
Letters to and from Samuel Johnson; to which are added some poems never before printed. 2 vols 1788.
Observations and reflections made in the course of a journey through France, Italy and Germany. 2 vols 1789; ed H. Barrows, Ann Arbor 1967.
British synonymy: or an attempt at regulating the choice of words in familiar conversation. 2 vols 1794.
Three warnings to John Bull. 1798.
Retrospection: or a review of the most striking and important events, characters, situations and their consequences which the last 1800 years have presented to the view of mankind. 2 vols 1801.
Three dialogues. Ed M. Zamick, Bull John Rylands Lib 16 1932.

Letters, Diaries etc

Love letters of Mrs Piozzi, written when she was 80, to W. A. Conway. 1843. But see P. Merritt under §2, below.
Autobiography, letters and literary remains of Mrs Piozzi. Ed A. Hayward 2 vols 1861, 1861 (enlarged); ed J. H. Lobban 1910 (as Dr Johnson's Mrs Thrale).
Dr Johnson and Mrs Thrale, including Mrs Thrale's unpublished Journal of the Welsh tour in 1774: correspondence of the Streatham coterie, with introductory essay by T. Seccombe. Ed A. M. Broadley 1910.
Intimate letters of Hester Lynch Piozzi and Penelope Pennington 1788–1821. Ed O. G. Knapp 1914.
Unpublished manuscripts, papers and letters of Dr Johnson, Mrs Thrale and their friends, in the John Rylands library. Ed M. Tyson, Bull John Rylands Lib 15 1931. Extracts from letters and journals.
French journals of Mrs Thrale and Dr Johnson. Ed M. Tyson and H. Guppy, Manchester 1932.
Johnson and Queeney: letters from Dr Johnson to Queeney Thrale. Ed Marquis of Lansdowne 1932.
Queeney letters to Hester Maria Thrale by Dr Johnson, Fanny Burney and Mrs Thrale-Piozzi. Ed Marquis of Lansdowne 1934.
Thraliana: the diary of Mrs Thrale 1776–1809. Ed K. C. Balderston 2 vols Oxford 1942, 1951 (corrected).
Letters of Samuel Johnson, with Mrs Thrale's genuine letters to him. Ed R. W. Chapman 3 vols Oxford 1952.
For marginalia see under §2, below.

§2

[Mangin, E.] Piozziana: or recollections of Mrs Piozzi, by a friend. 1833.
Seeley, L. B. Mrs Thrale, afterwards Mrs Piozzi. 1891.
Newton, A. E. A light-blue stocking. In his Amenities of book-collecting, Boston 1918.

Merritt, P. Piozzi marginalia: comprising extracts from mss and annotations. Cambridge Mass 1925.
— The true story of the so-called love-letters of Mrs Piozzi. Cambridge Mass 1927.
Piozzi on Boswell and Johnson. Harvard Lib Notes 17 1926. Marginalia.
Lyell, J. P. R. Mrs Piozzi and Isaac Watts. 1934. Marginalia.
Scott, S. H. Dr Johnson and Mrs Thrale. Nineteenth Century Sept 1934.
Clifford, J. L. The printing of Mrs Piozzi's Anecdotes of Dr Johnson. Bull John Rylands Lib 20 1936.
— Hester Lynch Piozzi. Oxford 1941, 1952 (corrected), 1968 (with bibliography).
— Mrs Piozzi's letters. In Essays on the eighteenth century presented to David Nichol Smith, Oxford 1945.
Nicolson, M. H. Thomas Paine, Edward Nares and Mrs Piozzi's marginalia. Huntington Lib Bull 10 1936.
Vulliamy, C. E. Mrs Thrale of Streatham. 1936.
Boswell's Life of Johnson with marginal comments from 2 copies annotated by Hester Piozzi. Ed E. G. Fletcher 3 vols 1938.
Pottle, F. A. and C. H. Bennett. Boswell and Mrs Piozzi. MP 39 1942.
Ewing, M. Mrs Piozzi peruses Dr Thomas Browne. PQ 22 1943. Marginalia.
Chapman, R. W. Mrs Piozzi's omissions from Johnson's letters to Thrales. RES 22 1946.
— Mrs Thrale's letters to Johnson published by Mrs Piozzi in 1788. RES 24 1948.
Esdaile, A. Hester Thrale. Quart Rev 284 1946.
Balderston, K. C. Johnson's vile melancholy. In The age of Johnson: essays presented to C. B. Tinker, New Haven 1949.
Quennell, P. C. In his Singular preference, 1952.
Fletcher, E. G. Mrs Piozzi on Boswell and Johnson's tour. SE 32 1953. Marginalia.
Allison, J. Mrs Thrale's marginalia in Joseph Warton's Essay. HLQ 19 1956.
Hargreaves-Mawdsley, W. N. The English Della Cruscans and their time 1783-1828. Hague 1967.

ELIZABETH MONTAGU, née ROBINSON
1720–1800
§ 1

An essay on the writings and genius of Shakespear. 1769 etc, 1777 (including the 3 Dialogues 26–8, which Mrs Montagu contributed to Lyttelton's Dialogues of the dead, 1760).
Letters of Mrs Elizabeth Montagu, with some of the letters of her correspondents. Ed M. Montagu 4 vols 1809–13.
Letters to the Duchess of Portland [1740–80]. In Marquis of Bath mss 1–2, 1904, 1907 (Historical Manuscripts Commission).
Climenson, E. J. Elizabeth Montagu, the Queen of the Blue-stockings: her correspondence from 1720 [1732]–1761. 2 vols 1906.
Blunt, R. Mrs Montagu, 'Queen of the Blues': her letters and friendships from 1762–1800. 2 vols 1923.

§ 2

Doran, J. A lady of the last century, illustrated in her unpublished letters, with a chapter on blue-stockings. 1873.
Huchon, R. Mrs Montagu. 1906.
Beatty, J. M. Mrs Montagu, Churchill and Miss Cheere. MLN 41 1926.

Busse, J. Mrs Montagu, Queen of the Blues. 1928.
Jones, C. E. Johnson and Mrs Montagu: 2 letters. N & Q 7 Sept 1946.
Hornbeak, K. G. New light on Mrs Montagu. In The age of Johnson: essays presented to C. B. Tinker, New Haven 1949.
Phillips, G. L. Mrs Montagu and the climbing-boys. RES 25 1949.
Jones, W. P. The romantic bluestocking: Elizabeth Montagu. HLQ 12 1949.
Ross, I. A bluestocking over the border: Mrs Montagu's aesthetic adventures in Scotland 1766. HLQ 28 1965.

CATHERINE TALBOT
1721–70

The works of the late Mrs Catherine Talbot. 1772, 1809 (7th edn, 'with additional papers, together with notes and illustrations, and some account of her life by M. Pennington'), 1819 (9th edn).
Reflections on the seven days of the week. 1770 etc.
Essays on various subjects. 2 vols 1772.
For letters see Elizabeth Carter, above.

HESTER CHAPONE, née MULSO
1727–1801
§ 1

Letters on the improvement of the mind, addressed to a young lady. 2 vols 1773 etc, 1 vol 1806 ('with the life of the author').
Miscellanies in prose and verse [including The story of Fidelia, Adventurer 77–9]. 1775 etc.
A letter to a new-married lady. 1777 etc.
Works. 2 vols Dublin 1786, 4 vols 1807.
Posthumous works: containing her corespondence with Mr Richardson; a series of letters to Mrs Elizabeth Carter; and some fugitive pieces never before published; together with an account of her life and character, drawn up by her own family. 2 vols 1807, 1808.

§ 2

Cole, J. Memoirs of Mrs Chapone, from various authentic sources. 1839.

MARY DELANY, née GRANVILLE
1700–88
§ 1

Letters to Mrs Frances Hamilton 1779–88. 1820.
Autobiography and correspondence of Mary Granville, Mrs Delany. Ed Lady Llanover 6 vols 1861–2.
'Paston, George' (E. M. Symonds). Mrs Delany: a memoir. 1900. Abridged from above, with new material.

§ 2

Dobson, A. Dear Mrs Delany. In his Side-walk studies, 1902.

HANNAH MORE
1745–1833
Bibliographies

De Morgan, A. Cheap repository tracts. N & Q 24 Sept 1864. Replies 8 and 29 Oct 1864.

Green, E. Bibliotheca Somersetensis. 3 vols Taunton 1902.

Collections

Works. 8 vols 1801, 19 vols 1818–19, 11 vols 1830 (rev), 6 vols 1833–4.
Poems. 1816, 1829. With prose pieces Village politics and The white slave trade.

§ 1

A search after happiness: a pastoral drama by a young lady. Bristol [1766?], 1773, London 1796 (11th edn, with alterations). At end of 1st edn are Prologue to Hamlet, 1765, and Prologue to King Lear, not included in collections.
The inflexible captive: a tragedy. Bristol 1774, 1777.
Sir Eldred of the bower and the Bleeding rock: two legendary tales. 1776, 1778.
Essays on various subjects, principally designed for young ladies. 1777, 1791 (5th edn).
Ode to Dragon, Mr Garrick's house-dog at Hampton. 1777, 1778.
Percy: a tragedy. 1778 etc (prologue and epilogue by Garrick).
The fatal falsehood: a tragedy. 1779, 1780.
Sacred dramas, chiefly intended for young persons; to which is added Sensibility: a poem. 1782 etc.
Florio, a tale for fine gentlemen and fine ladies; and the Bas bleu, or conversation: two poems. 1786, 1787.
Slavery: a poem. 1788.
Thoughts on the importance of the manners of the great to general society. 1788, 1788 (with postscript), 1792 (8th edn).
Bishop Bonner's ghost. Strawberry Hill 1789.
An estimate of the religion of the fashionable world. 1791, 1793 (5th edn).
Remarks on the speech of M. Dupont, made in the National Convention of France, on the subjects of religion and education. 1793.
Village politics, by Will Chip. 1793.
Questions and answers for the Mendip and Sunday schools. 1795.
Cheap repository tracts. 1795–8. See Stories, below.
Strictures on the modern system of female education. 2 vols 1799 etc.
Hints towards forming the character of a young princess. 2 vols 1805.
Coelebs in search of a wife. 2 vols 1808 etc.
Practical piety. 2 vols 1811 etc.
Christian morals. 2 vols 1813 etc.
An essay on the character and practical writings of St Paul. 2 vols 1815 etc.
Stories for the middle ranks of society, and tales for the common people. 2 vols 1818. Rptd from Cheap repository tracts, above.
Moral sketches of prevailing opinions and manners. 1819, 1819 (rev), 1820 (6th edn with new preface).
The twelfth of August: or the feast of freedom. 1819, 1827 (as The feast of freedom: or the abolition of domestic slavery in Ceylon).

Bible rhymes on the names of all the books of the old and new testaments. 1821, 1822 (with addns).
The spirit of prayer, selected from published volumes. 1825 etc.

Letters, Diaries etc

Letters to Zachary Macaulay, containing notices of Lord Macaulay's youth. Ed A. Roberts 1860.
Letters, selected. Ed R. B. Johnson 1925.

§ 2

Bere, T. The controversy between Mrs Hannah More and the curate of Blagdon. 1801.
Elton, A. A letter to the Rev Thomas Bere, occasioned by his attack on Mrs Hannah More. 1801.
Roberts, W. Memoirs of the life and correspondence of Mrs Hannah More. 4 vols 1834. Includes letters from Mrs Montagu, Mrs Boscawen and Mrs Vesey.
Thompson, H. Life of Hannah More, with notices of her sisters. 1838.
Roberts, A. (ed). Mendip annals, or a narrative of the charitable labours of Hannah More and Martha More: being the journal of Martha More. 1859.
Knight, H. C. Hannah More: or life in hall and cottage. New York 1862.
Pitt, J. Hannah More and the Blagdon controversy. N & Q 26 Aug 1865.
Yonge, C. M. Hannah More. Boston 1888.
'Harland, Marion' (M. V. Hawes). Hannah More. New York 1900.
Meakin, A. M. B. Hannah More. 1911.
May, G. L. Hannah More. In his Some 18th-century churchmen, 1920.
Forster, E. M. Mrs Hannah More. Nation (London) 2 Jan 1926.
Knox, E. V. Percy: the tale of a dramatic success. London Mercury March 1926.
Tabor, M. E. In her Pioneer women: 2nd series, 1927.
Courtney, L. W. Hannah More's interest in education and government. Waco Texas 1929.
Aikin-Sneath, B. Hannah More. London Mercury Oct 1933.
Child, P. Portrait of a woman of affairs—old style. UTQ 3 1933.
Malin, M. C. Hannah More. Contemporary Rev Sept 1933.
Lownsbery, E. Saints and rebels. New York 1937.
Weiss, H. B. Hannah More's cheap repository tracts in America. BNYPL July–Aug 1946.
Hopkins, M. A. Hannah More and her circle. New York 1947.
Aldridge, A. O. Madame de Staël and Hannah More on society. Romanic Rev 38 1947.
Shaver, C. L. The publication of Hannah More's first play. MLN 62 1947.
Jones, M. G. Hannah More. Cambridge 1952.
Bennett, C. H. The text of Horace Walpole's correspondence with Hannah More. RES new ser 3 1952.

R. H.

VII. RELIGION

A. THE RESTORATION DIVINES 1660–1700

Most of the writers included in this section were born between 1620 and 1660. The older divines, many of whom survived the Restoration, are listed in vol 1, above, and the younger, including several whose writings begin in the 17th century, follow below. Scottish divines, col 2031, below, have normally been excluded.

GENERAL STUDIES

Baxter, Richard. Reliquiae Baxterianae: or Mr Richard Baxter's narrative of the most memorable passages of his life and times. 1696.

Calamy, Edmund. An abridgment of Mr Baxter's History of his life and times; with an account of many ministers who were ejected at the Restoration. 1702, 2 vols 1713–27; rev S. Palmer 2 vols 1775, 1778, 3 vols 1802–3.

Nelson, Robert. Works. 2 pts 1715.

Neal, D. The history of the Puritans. 4 vols 1732–8, 5 vols Bath 1793–7 (rev).

Lathbury, T. History of the nonjurors. 1845.

Stephen, J. Essays in ecclesiastical biography. 2 vols 1849.

Secretan, C. F. Memoirs of the life and times of the pious Robert Nelson. 1860.

Pattison, M. Tendencies of religious thought in England. In Essays and reviews, 1860, and in his Essays vol 2, Oxford 1889.

Hunt, J. Religious thought in England to the end of the 18th century. 3 vols 1870–3.

Tulloch, J. Rational theology and Christian philosophy in England in the 17th century. 2 vols Edinburgh 1872.

Masters of English theology. Ed A. Barry 1877.

The classic preachers of the English Church. Ed J. E. Kempe 2 sers 1877–8. On Barrow, South, Beveridge, Wilson, Butler, Tillotson et al.

Perry, G. G. The student's English Church history. Vols 2–3, 1878–87.

Overton, J. H. Life in the English Church 1680–1714. 1885.

—— The nonjurors: their lives, principles and writings. 1902.

Stephen, J. F. Horae sabbaticae. Ser 1, 1892.

Stoughton, J. H. History of religion in England. 6 vols 1901 (rev).

Hutton, W. H. The English Church from the accession of Charles I to the death of Queen Anne. 1903. With bibliographies.

Legg, J. W. English church-life from the Restoration to the Tractarian movement. 1914.

Powicke, F. J. A life of Richard Baxter. 1924.

—— The Cambridge Platonists. 1926.

—— The Rev Richard Baxter: under the cross 1662–91. 1927.

Fenn, P. Th., jr. The Latitudinarians and toleration. Washington Univ Stud (Humanistic ser) 13 1925.

Tawney, R. H. Religion and the rise of capitalism. 1926.

Richardson, C. F. English preachers and preaching 1640–70. 1928.

Nicolson, M. Christ's College and the latitude-men. MP 27 1929.

Jones, R. F. The attack on pulpit eloquence in the Restoration. JEGP 30 1931; rptd in his Seventeenth century, Stanford 1951.

Mitchell, W. F. English pulpit oratory from Andrewes to Tillotson. 1932. With select bibliography.

More, P. E. and F. L. Cross. Anglicanism: the thought and practice of the Church of England, illustrated from the religious literature of the 17th century. 1935.

Griffiths, O. M. Religion and learning: a study in English Presbyterian thought [1660–1700]. Cambridge 1935.

Sullivan, P. Church and religion in England 1660–1800. Church Quart Rev 120 1935.

Grose, C. L. The religion of Restoration England. Church History 6 1937.

—— Trends towards religious integration on the eve of 1660. Church History 10 1941.

Mullett, C. F. Some seventeenth-century manuscript sermon memoranda. HLQ 2 1939.

—— Toleration and persecution in England 1660–89. Church History 18 1949.

Douglas, D. C. English scholars 1660–1730. 1939, 1951 (rev).

Smyth, C. H. E. The art of preaching 747–1939. 1940.

Schlatter, R. B. The social ideas of religious leaders 1660–88. Oxford 1940.

Addleshaw, G. W. O. The High Church tradition: a study in the liturgical thought of the seventeenth century. 1941.

Plum, H. G. The English religious restoration 1660–5. PQ 20 1941; rptd in Renaissance studies in honor of Hardin Craig, Stanford 1941.

—— Restoration Puritanism: a study of the growth of English liberty. Chapel Hill 1943.

Steffan, T. G. The social argument against enthusiasm 1650–60. SE 1941.

Randall, H. W. The rise and fall of a martyrology: sermons on Charles I. HLQ 10 1947.

Sykes, N. The Church of England and non-episcopal churches in the 16th and 17th centuries. 1948.

—— The English religious tradition. 1953.

—— Old priest and new presbyter. Cambridge 1956.

—— From Sheldon to Secker: aspects of English Church history. Cambridge 1959.

McAdoo, H. R. The structure of Caroline moral theology. 1949.

—— The spirit of Anglicanism: a survey of Anglican theological method in the 17th century. New York 1965.

Bullett, G. The Cambridge Platonists. In his English mystics, 1950.

Cragg, G. R. From Puritanism to the age of reason: a study of changes in religious thought within the Church of England 1660–1700. Cambridge 1950, 1966.

—— The Church and the age of reason 1648–1789. 1960 (Pelican).

Bosher, R. S. The making of the Restoration settlement: the influence of the Laudians 1649–62. 1951.

Trevor-Roper, H. R. The restoration of the Church 1660. History Today 2 1952.

Cassirer, E. The Platonic renaissance in England. Edinburgh 1953.

Every, G. The High-Church party 1688–1718. 1956.

Huntley, F. L. Heads for an essay on the seventeenth-century funeral sermon in England. Anglican Theological Rev 38 1956.

Cuming, G. J. The Prayer-Book in Convocation, November 1661. Jnl of Ecclesiastical History 8 1957.

Davies, G. Tory Churchmen and James II. In his Essays on the later Stuarts, San Marino 1958.

Grisbrooke, W. J. Anglican liturgies of the seventeenth and eighteenth century. 1958.

Peck, A. L. Anglicanism and episcopacy. 1958.

Westfall, R. S. Science and religion in seventeenth-century England. New Haven 1958.

Hiscock, W. G. Henry Aldrich of Christ Church 1648–1710. Oxford 1960.

Henderson-Howat, A. M. D. Robert Nelson 1656–1714. Church Quart Rev 161 1960.

Wakefield, G. S. Arminianism in the 17th and 18th century. London Quart 185 1960.

Borinski, L. Puritanische und anglikanische Lebensideale im Zeitalter der englischen Revolution. In Theodor Spira Festschrift, ed H. Viebrock and W. Erzgräber, Heidelberg 1961.

Morgan, D. 1662 and all that: commemorating the third centenary of the Book of Common Prayer. 1961.

Stranks, C. J. Anglican devotion: studies in the spiritual life of the Church of England. 1961.

Thomas, R. The seven bishops and their petition. Jnl of Ecclesiastical History 12 1961.

Wand, J. W. C. Anglicanism in history and today. 1961.

Straka, G. M. Anglican reaction to the revolution of 1688. Madison 1962.

—— The final phase of divine right theory in England 1688–1702. EHR 1962.

Baumer, F. L. Religion and the rise of scepticism. New
York 1960.
Simon, W. G. Comprehension in the age of Charles II.
Church History 31 1962.
Surman, C. E. The Act of Uniformity 1662. London
Quart 187 1962.
Wilkinson, J. T. The Savoy Conference. Ibid.
Bridenbaugh, C. Mitre and sceptre. 1962.
Daniel-Rops, H. L'Eglise des temps classiques. Paris
1963; tr 1964.
Gaquère, Fr. Vers l'unité chrétienne: James Drummond
et Bossuet, leur correspondance 1685–1704. Paris 1963.
Marshall, J. S. Freedom and authority in classical
Anglicanism. Anglican Theological Rev 45 1963.
Boyer, R. F. English declarations of indulgence of 1687
and 1688. Catholic Historical Rev 50 1964.
Horwitz, H. Protestant reconciliation in the exclusion
crisis. Jnl of Ecclesiastical History 15 1964.
—— Comprehension in the later 17th century. Church
History 34 1965.
Kearney, H. F. Puritanism, capitalism and the scientific
revolution. Past & Present 28 1964.
Bullock, F. W. B. Evangelical conversion in Great-Britain
1516–1695. St Leonard's 1966.
Simon, I. Three Restoration divines: Barrow, South and
Tillotson, selected sermons. Vol 1, Paris 1967.

JOSEPH ALLEINE
1634–68
§ 1

A call to Archippus: or an humble and earnest petition to
some ejected ministers. 1664.
An alarme to unconverted sinners. 2 pts 1672, 1673 (with
prefaces by R. Baxter and R. Alleine), 1678, 1695,
1703 etc, 1879.
A sure guide to heaven [i.e. Pt 1 of An alarme to unconverted sinners, above]. 1675, 1688, 1689, 1691,
1700 etc.
Remaines. [Ed R. Alleine] 1674.

§ 2

Alleine, Theodosia. The life and death of Alleine [with
introd by R. Baxter]. 1672, 1673, 1677, 1822, 1832,
1838.
Stanford, C. Alleine: his companions and times. [1861].

RICHARD ALLEINE
1611–81

Godly fear. 1664, 1674. Sermons.
The world conquered. 1668. Sermons.
A rebuke to backsliders and a spur for loiterers. 1677,
1684. Sermons.
Vindiciae pietatis: or a vindication of godliness. 1663,
1664, 3 pts 1663–6.
The godly man's portion [pt 2 of Vindiciae pietatis]. 1663,
1671.
Heaven opened [pt 3 of Vindiciae pietatis]. 1665, 1666.

RICHARD ALLESTREE
1619–81
Collections
Eighteen sermons. 1669.
Forty sermons whereof twenty-one are now first published.
2 pts Oxford 1684. With biographical sketch by John
Fell.

§ 1
A paraphrase and annotations upon the epistles of St Paul
[with A. Woodhead and O. Walker as co-authors].
1675, 1702, 1708.
The whole duty of man. 1658, 2 pts 1659, 1660, 1664,
1668, 1670 etc; tr French, 1672. Anon; many anon
continuations.

§ 2
Jaggard, W. Literary secrets: authorship of the Whole
duty of man and cognate writings 1658–84. Bookman
(London) Oct 1931.
Elmen, P. Richard Allestree and the Whole duty of man.
Library 5th ser 6 1951.

THOMAS BARLOW
1607–91
Exercitationes aliquot metaphysicae de Deo. 1658.
Popery: or the principles and positions approved by the
Church of Rome very dangerous to all. 1678, 1679, 1679.
A letter concerning invocation of saints and adoration of
the Cross. 1679.
A discourse of the peerage and jurisdiction of the Lords
Spiritual in Parliament. 1679.
Brutum fulmen: or the bull of Pope Pius V concerning the
damnation of Queen Elizabeth. 1681, 1681.
A few plain reasons why a Protestant of the Church of
England should not turn Roman Catholic. 1688.
Several miscellaneous and weighty cases of conscience
resolved. 6 pts 1692.
Remains. [Ed Peter Pelt] 1693.
Two letters concerning justification by faith only. [Ed
R. Mayo] 1701.
De historicis anglicanis commentatio. 1742.

ISAAC BARROW
1630–77
Collections
Works. Ed J. Tillotson, with memoir by Abraham Hill 4
vols 1683–7, 3 vols 1700 (English works only), 1716,
1722, 1741, 6 vols 1751, Oxford 1818, 5 vols 1820–1,
8 vols Oxford 1830, 7 vols 1830–1, 3 vols Edinburgh
1841–2 (with life by J. Hamilton).
Theological works. Ed A. Napier 9 vols Cambridge 1859.
Life by W. Whewell prefixed to vol 9.
Sermons preached upon several occasions. [Ed J. Tillot-
son] 1678, 1679, 1680.
Several sermons against evil speaking. [Ed J. Tillotson]
1678, 1678, 1682.
Of the love of God and our neighbour in several sermons.
[Ed J. Tillotson] 1680.
Of contentment, patience and resignation to the will of
God. [Ed J. Tillotson] 1685. Sermons.
Practical discourses upon the consideration of our latter
end. [Ed J. Tillotson] 1694.
Sermons selected from the works of Barrow. 2 vols
Oxford 1798–1810.
[Twenty-one sermons]. Ed Ch. Wordsworth in Christian
institutes vol 2, 1837.
[Selected sermons]. Ed J. Brogden in Illustrations of the
liturgy and ritual vol 2, 1842.
[Selected sermons]. Ed I. Simon in Three Restoration
divines: Barrow, South and Tillotson vol 1, Paris 1967.

§ 1
The duty and reward of bounty to the poor. 1671, 1677,
1680. A sermon.
A sermon upon the Passion. 1677, 1678, 1682.

A treatise of the Pope's supremacy, to which is added A discourse concerning the unity of the Church. Ed J. Tillotson 1680.

A brief exposition of the Lord's prayer and the decalogue; with the doctrine of the sacraments. Ed J. Tillotson 1681.

A brief exposition on the Creed, the Lord's prayer and Ten Commandments, with the doctrine of the sacraments. 1697.

A defence of the Trinity. 1697. A sermon.

For Barrow's mathematical works see col 1902, below.

§ 2

Wace, H. Barrow, the exhaustive preacher. In J. E. Kempe, The classic preachers of the English Church ser 1, 1877.

Osmond, P. H. Barrow: his life and times. 1944.

Simon, I. Tillotson's Barrow. E Studies 45 1964.

—— In her Three Restoration divines: Barrow, South and Tillotson, Paris 1967.

WILLIAM BATES
1625–99

Collections

Works. 1700, 1723, 4 vols 1815.

Sermons upon death and eternal judgment. 1683.

The danger of prosperity. 1685. Sermons.

Sermons preached on several occasions. 1693.

Sermons on forgiveness. 1696.

§ 1

The harmony of divine attributes. 1674, 1697 (4th edn).

Considerations on the existence of God and of the immortality of the soul. 1676, 2 vols 1677.

The four last things. 1691, 1691.

Spiritual perfection. 1699.

WILLIAM BEVERIDGE
1637–1708

Collections

Works, containing all his sermons [ed T. Gregory] with an account of his life and writings [by J. Kimber]. 2 vols 1720, 1729, 6 vols Oxford 1817–18.

Works, with a memoir and a critical examination of the writings. Ed T. H. Horne 9 vols 1824.

Theological works. [Ed J. Bliss] 12 vols Oxford 1842–8 (Lib of Anglo-Catholic Theology vols 11–12).

§ 1

Codex canonum ecclesiae primitivae vindicatus ac illustratus. 1678.

The great necessity and advantage of publick prayers and frequent communion. 1708, 1750 (9th edn).

Private thoughts upon religion digested into twelve articles. 1709, 1720 (10th edn).

§ 2

Whitby, D. A short view of Dr Beveridge's writings. 1711.

GEORGE BULL
1634–1710

Collections

G. Bulli opera omnia. Ed J. E. Grabe 6 pts 1703, 1 vol 1721 (enlarged); tr 2 vols 1725, 3 vols Oxford 1851–5.

Works, collected and revised by E. Burton. 7 vols Oxford 1827, 6 vols 1846. Includes Nelson's Life.

Some important points of primitive Christianity maintained in several sermons. Ed R. Bull, with life by R. Nelson 4 vols 1713, 1714, 3 vols Oxford 1816.

§ 1

Harmonia apostolica. 1669–70; tr T. Wilkinson 1801 (abridged), Oxford 1842, London 1844.

Examen censurae [of Harmonia apostolica]. 1676; tr Oxford 1843.

Apologia pro harmonica. 1676.

Defensio fidei Nicaenae. Oxford 1685, 1688; tr 2 vols Oxford 1851–2.

Judicium ecclesiae catholicae [de divinitate Christi]. Oxford 1694, Amsterdam 1696; tr T. Rankin 1719, 1825.

A vindication of the Church of England. 1719.

§ 2

Nelson, R. The life of Bull, with the history of those controversies in which he was engaged. 1714.

Teale, W. H. Lives of English divines: George Bull. 1846.

Warburton, W. P. Bishop Bull, the primitive preacher. In J. E. Kempe, The classic preachers of the English Church ser 2, 1878.

GILBERT BURNET
1643–1715

See col 1685, below.

HENRY COMPTON
1632–1713

§ 1

The Bishop of London's letter to his clergy, 25th April 1679. 1679. On the two sacraments and catechizing.

The Bishop of London's second letter to his clergy 1680. 1680. 'Desiring their opinions on Holy Communion, prayers in an unknown tongue and those to saints.'

Episcopalia: or letters to the clergy of his diocese. 1686, 1706; ed S. W. Cornish, Oxford 1842 (with memoir).

An exact account of the whole proceedings against Henry Lord Bishop of London before the Lord Chancellor and the other ecclesiastical commissioners [9 Aug 1686]. 1688.

The Bishop of London's seventh letter, of the conference with his clergy 1686, upon the King's letter 1685, with directions concerning preachers. 1690.

The Bishop of London's charge to the clergy of his diocese at his visitation 1693–4. 1696.

The Bishop of London's ninth conference with his clergy upon the fifth and tenth injunctions given by the King February 15th 1694/5, held in 1695–6. 1699.

The Bishop of London's tenth conference with his clergy 1697–8 upon the King's directions for preserving unity in the Church and the purity of the Christian faith concerning the Holy Trinity. 1701.

The Bishop of London's eleventh conference with his clergy 1699–1700 upon the King's proclamation for preventing immorality and profaneness. 1704.

A letter concerning allegiance written to a clergyman in Essex presently after the Revolution; to which are added queries [by B. Hoadly]. 1710; rptd in A collection of papers, 1718; in Somers tracts vol 3, 1748, vol 12, 1814.

§ 2

Cockburn, J. The blessedness of Christians after death, with the character of the Rt Hon Henry Compton, late Lord Bishop of London. 1713.

[Salmon, N.?] Life. 1715.
Brown, L. L. Compton, Bishop of London 1675–1713, pioneer leader in the expansion of the Anglican communion. Historical Mag of Protestant Episcopal Church 25 1956.
Carpenter, E. The Protestant Bishop: being the life of Compton. 1956.

HERBERT CROFT
1603–91

The naked truth, or the true state of the primitive Church. 1675, 1680.
A letter to a friend concerning Popish idolatrie. 1674, 1679. Anon.
The legacy to his diocese: or a short determination of all the controversies we have with the Papists. 1679, 1679.
A short discourse concerning His Majesties late declaration in the churches. 1688.

RICHARD CUMBERLAND
1631–1718
See col 1845, below.

HENRY DODWELL the elder
1641–1711
§1

Some considerations of present concernment: how far the Romanists may be trusted by princes of another persuasion. 1675.
Two discourses against the Papists. 1676, 1688 (with a preface relating to [Bossuet]).
Separation of Churches from episcopal government proved schismatical. 1679.
Dissertationes Cyprianae. 1682, Oxford 1684, London 1691.
De jure laicorum sacerdotali. 1685.
The doctrine of the Church of England reconciled with our oath of supremacy. 1697.
An invitation to gentlemen to acquaint themselves with ancient history. 1698.
Occasional communion fundamentally destructive. 1705.
An admonitory discourse concerning the late English schism. 1704.
An epistolary discourse proving that the soul is naturally mortal, but immortalized actually by the pleasure of God. 1706, 1707 (with addns).
A preliminary defence of the Epistolary discourse. 1707.
The natural mortality of human souls demonstrated. 1708.
For Dodwell's writings on classical topics see col 1825, below.

§2

Brokesby, F. Life of Mr Dodwell with an account of his works. 1715.

JOHN EACHARD
1636?–97
Collections
Works. Ed with a life by F. Davies 3 vols 1774–3.

§1

The grounds and occasions of the contempt of the clergy and religion enquired into. 1670 (anon, at least 3 edns),

3 pts 1672 (8th edn, adds Some observations on the answer thereto, 6th edn, and Mr Hobbs's state of nature considered, 4th edn), 1685, 1698–6, 1705 (as Dr Eachard's works), 1712 (with Five letters), 2 vols 1772 (rev); ed E. Arber in An English garner vol 7, 1903.
Some observations upon the answer [by John Bramhall] to An enquiry into the grounds and occasions of contempt of the clergy. 1671 (anon, 3 edns), 1672, 1705 (7th edn).
Mr Hobbs's state of nature considered; to which are added Five letters. 1672 (anon, 3 edns), 1685, 1696; ed P. Ure, Liverpool 1958.
Some opinions of Mr Hobbs considered in a second dialogue. 1673. Anon.
A free and impartial inquiry into the causes of that esteem and honour that the nonconforming preachers are generally held in with their followers. 1673. Anon.

JOHN FELL
1625–86
§1

The interest of England stated. 1659; ed F. Maseres in Select tracts pt 2, 1815.
Life of Dr Allestree. Prefixed to Forty sermons, Oxford 1684.
Life of Dr Henry Hammond. 1661, 1662 etc; ed C. Wordsworth in Ecclesiastical biography vol 5, 1818.
Seasonable advice to Protestants, shewing the necessity of maintaining the established religion in opposition to Popery. 1688.
S. Cypriani opera. Oxford 1682, 1691. Ed Fell.
For The whole duty of man *see under Allestree, above.*

§2

Mayor, J. E. B. John Fell, Bishop of Oxford. N & Q 23 Sept 1876.

EDWARD FOWLER
1632–1714

The principles and practices of certain moderate divines called latitudinarians. 1670 (anon), 1671, 1679.
The design of Christianity. 1671, 1676, 1699 etc.
Dirt wip't off: or a manifest discovery of the gross ignorance of one John Bunyan. 1672.
Libertas evangelica: a further persuance of the argument of the Design of Christianity. 1680.
The resolution of this case of conscience, whether the Church of England's symbolizing with the Church of Rome makes it unlawful to hold communion with the Church of England. 1683.
A defence of the Resolution of this case. 1684.
An examination of Cardinal Bellarmine's 4th note on the Church. 1687, 1689.
The texts which Papists cite for the proof of the obscurity of the Holy Scripture. 1687, 1688, 1689.
Twenty-eight propositions by which the doctrine of the Trinity is endeavoured to be explained. 1693. Anon.
A discourse of the descent of the man Christ Jesus from heaven. 1706.
Rejections upon the late examination [by William Sherlock] of the Discourse. 1706.
[14 separate sermons]. 1681–1707.
A charge to the clergy of his diocese. 1707.
[Another] charge to the clergy of his diocese. 1710.

JOSEPH GLANVILL
1636–80
See col 1845, below.

THOMAS GOUGE
1609–81
Collections

Works. 1706. With an account of his life by J. Tillotson.

§ I

Christian directions. 1664, 1673, 1675 etc; tr Welsh, 1675.
The principles of Christian religion explained to the capacity of the meanest. 1675, 1679, 1684; tr Welsh, 1676.
A word to sinners and a word to saints. 1668, 1672, 1684.
The young man's guide through the wilderness of this world to the heavenly Canaan. 1672, 1684.
The surest and safest way of thriving. 1673, 1676.

§ 2

Clarke, S. In his Lives of sundry eminent persons, 1683.

GEORGE HICKES
1636–80
Collections

Sermons on various subjects. 2 vols 1713.
Posthumous discourses. Ed N. Spinckes 1726.
Thirteen sermons on practical subjects. Ed N. Spinckes 1741.

§ I

An apologetical vindication of the Church of England. 1687 (anon), 1706 (rev).
The harmony of divinity and law [on non-resistance]. 1684.
Institutiones grammaticae Anglo-Saxonicae et Mœso-Gothicae. 3 pts Oxford 1689–88, 1 vol 1703.
The doctrine of passive obedience and jure divino disproved. 1689.
An apology for the new separation. 1691.
Linguarum vett. septentrionalium thesaurus grammatico-criticus et archaeologicus. 2 vols Oxford 1703–5.
The constitution of the Catholick Church and the nature and consequences of schism. 1716.
Two treatises on the Christian priesthood. 1707, 2 vols 1711 (3rd edn enlarged), 1715 (with suppl); ed J. Barrow 3 vols Oxford 1847–8 (Lib of Anglo-Catholic Theology).
See also col 1791, below.

§ 2

Gardner, W. B. Hickes and the origin of the Bangorian controversy. SP 39 1942.
—— Hickes and his Thesaurus. N & Q May 1955.

HUMPHREY HODY
1659–1707

The unreasonableness of separation from the new bishops. 1691; tr Latin, Oxford 1691 (as Anglicani novi schismatis redargutio).
The case of sees vacant by an unjust or uncanonical deprivation stated. 1693.
The resurrection of the body asserted. 1694.
Animadversions on two pamphlets lately published by Mr Collier. 1696.
Some thoughts on a Convocation and the notion of its divine right. 1699.
A history of English councils and convocations, and of the clergy's sitting in Parliament. 1701.
De bibliorum textibus originalibus. Oxford 1705.

ANTHONY HORNECK
1641–97
Collections

Several sermons upon the 5th of St Matthew; with a life by R. [Kidder]. 2 vols 1698, 1706.

§ I

The great law of consideration. 1676, 1678 ('corrected and enlarged') etc, 1729 (11th edn).
A letter from a Protestant gentleman to a lady revolted to the Church of Rome. 1678.
Delight and judgment. 1683, 1705 (3rd edn 'corrected and enlarged').
The fire of the altar. 1683, 1718 (13th edn).
The first fruits of reason. 1686.
The crucified Jesus. 1686, 1727 (7th edn).
Questions and answers concerning the two religions, viz that of the Church of England and the other of the Church of Rome. 1688; tr French, 1723.

§ 2

Bibliotheca Horneckiana: a catalogue of Horneck's library. 1697.
A summary account of Horneck's life; to which is added a catalogue of his works. 1697.
[Kidder, R.] Life of the Rev Horneck. 1698; rptd 1840 (Lib of Christian Biography vol 12).
Hone, R. B. In his Lives of eminent Christians vol 2, 1834.

JOHN HOWE
1630–1705
Collections

Works, with memoirs of [his] life, collected by Edmund Calamy. 2 vols 1724; ed J. Hunt 8 vols 1810–22; ed J. P. Hewlett 3 vols 1848; ed H. Rogers 6 vols 1862–3.
Sermons on several occasions. Ed E. Fletcher 2 vols 1744.

§ I

The blessedness of the righteous. 1668, 2 pts 1673. With prefatory address by R. Baxter.
The case of the Protestant dissenters. 1689.
The carnality of religious contention. 1693. 2 sermons.
A calm and sober enquiry concerning the possibility of a Trinity in the Godhead. 1694.
Some considerations of a preface to an Enquiry concerning the occasional conformity of dissenters [by D. Defoe]. 1701.

§ 2

Calamy, E. Memoirs. 1724; 1832 (abridged); rptd in T. Jackson, Library of Christian Biography vol 11, 1837.
Rogers, H. The life and character of Howe, with an analysis of his writings. 1836, 1879.
Urwick, W. Life of Howe. 1853.
Grosart, A. B. Howe: intellectual sanctity. In his Representative nonconformists vol 1, 1879.
Scott, W. M. Life of Howe. 1911.

SAMUEL JOHNSON
1649–1703

See col 1846, below.

THOMAS KEN
1637–1711
Collections

[Poetical] works, published from original manuscripts. Ed W. Hawkins 4 vols 1721.
Poems, devotional and didactic. Ed J.R. 1835.
Prose works, with some of his letters and his life by W. Hawkins. Ed J. T. Round 1838.
Prose works, now first collected and edited with a biographical notice by W. Benham. 1889.

§ 1

A manual of prayers for the use of scholars of Winchester College. 1674, 1736 (25th edn).
The practice of divine love. 1685.
An exposition of the Church catechism. 1685, 1686, 1696, 1703.
Occasional prayers; A paraphrase on the Creed; A paraphrase on the Lord's prayer. 1708.
A crown of glory, the reward of the righteous: being meditations upon the vicissitude of all sublunary enjoyments. 1725.

§ 2

Hawkins, W. Life of Ken. 1713; rptd in Ken, Prose works, 1838.
Bowles, W. L. Life of Ken. 2 vols 1830.
Anderdon, J. L. Life of Ken. 1851.
Plumptre, E. H. Life of Ken. 2 vols 1888, 1890 (rev).
Marston, E. Ken and Izaak Walton. 1908.
Cropper, M. B. Flame touches flame. 1949.
Rice, H. A. L. Ken, Bishop and non-juror. 1958.
Cowley, P. Ken, Bishop of Bath and Wells 1685–91. 1961.
Maddocks, M. H. St J. Bishop Ken. Church Quart Rev 164 1963.

JOHN KETTLEWELL
1653–95
Collections

A compleat collection of the works; with the life of the author [by Francis Lee]: compiled from the collections of G. Hickes and R. Nelson. 2 vols 1719.

§ 1

The measures of Christian obedience. 1681, 1684, 1696, 1700, 1709, 1714.
A help and exhortation to worthy communicating. 1683, 1737 (10th edn).
The practical believer. 1688, 2 pts 1703, 1712–13 (3rd edn enlarged and with preface by R. Nelson).
Christianity: a doctrine of the cross or passive obedience. 1691 (anon), 1695.
The duty of allegiance settled upon its true grounds. 1691.
A companion for the persecuted. 1693.
A companion for the penitent. 1694, 1696.
Death made comfortable. 1695, 1702, 1722.

§ 2

Carter, J. F. M. The life and times of John Kettlewell, with details of the history of the non-jurors. Ed T. T. Carter 1895.

WILLIAM LLOYD
1627–1717
§ 1

A seasonable discourse shewing the necessity of maintaining the established religion in opposition to Popery. 1673 (4 edns, anon).
Papists no catholicks and Popery no Christianity. 1677 (anon), 1679.
Considerations touching the true way to suppress Popery. 1677. Anon.
An historical account of Church government in Great-Britain and Ireland. 1684, 1684.

§ 2

Hart, A. T. William Lloyd. 1952.

THOMAS MANTON
1620–77
Collections

Sermons. Ed W. Bates 1678.
Eighteen sermons. Ed R. Baxter 1679.
One hundred and ninety sermons on the 119th Psalm. 5 vols 1681–1701 (with memoirs by W. Harris and prefaces by W. Bates, J. Howe et al), 1725, 3 vols 1842.

§ 1

A practical commentary on the epistle of James. 1651.
A practical commentary on the epistle of Jude. 1657.
A practical exposition of the Lord's prayer. 1684.

§ 2

Harris, W. Some memoirs of the life of Manton. 1725.

WILLIAM NICOLSON
1655–1727

The English historical library. 3 pts 1696–9, 1714 (corrected and augmented).
The Scottish historical library. 1702.
The Irish historical library. 1714, Dublin 1724.
The English, Scottish and Irish historical libraries. 3 pts 1736, 1776.
Leges Marchiarum: or border-laws. 1705, 1747.
A true state of controversy between the present Bishop and Dean of Carlisle touching the royal supremacy. 1704, 2 pts 1705.

JOHN NORRIS
1657–1711
See col 1848, below.

SAMUEL PARKER
1640–88

A free and impartial censure of the Platonick philosophy. Oxford 1666, 1667.
An account of the nature and extent of the divine dominion of goodness. Oxford 1666.
Tentamina physico-theologica de Deo. 1665.
A discourse of ecclesiastical politie. 1670.
A defence and continuation of the ecclesiastical politie. 1671.

Disputationes de Deo et providentia divina. 1678, 1714.

A demonstration of the divine authority of the law of nature and of the Christian religion. 2 pts 1681.

The case of the Church of England. 1681.

An account of the government of the Church for the first six hundred years. 1683.

Religion and loyalty. 2 pts 1684–5.

Reasons for abrogating the tests imposed upon all members of Parliament. 1688, 1688, Edinburgh 1688; tr Dutch, 1688.

A discourse sent to the late King James to persuade him to embrace the Protestant religion. 1690.

Reverendi Patris, S. Parker, de rebus sui temporis commentariorum libri quatuor. 1726; tr T. Newlin as History of his own time, 1727, 1728 ('with remarks upon each book, and an impartial account of Parker's life and his conversion from Presbytery to Popery'), 1730 (as Bishop Parker's History: or the Tories chronicle from the restauration of King Charles II to the year 1680).

SIMON PATRICK
1626–1707
Collections

Works, including his autobiography. Ed A. Taylor 9 vols Oxford 1858.

Fifteen sermons upon contentment and resignation to the will of God; with a catalogue of his works. 1719.

§ 1

A sermon at the burial of John Smith [the Platonist]. 1652; rptd in Smith, Select discourses, ed J. Worthington 1660, 1673 etc.

A brief account of the new sect of latitude-men. 1662 (anon); ed T. A. Birrell, Los Angeles 1963 (Augustan Reprint Soc).

The parable of the pilgrim. 1664, 1687 (6th edn).

A friendly debate between a conformist and a nonconformist. 1669 (5 edns).

A continuation of the friendly debate. 1669.

A further continuation and defence of the friendly debate. 1669.

An appendix to the third part of the friendly debate. 1670.

A letter to Samuel Parker [on A friendly debate]. 1671.

Advice to a friend. 1673, 1696 (6th edn).

Search the Scriptures. 1685, 1693.

A full view of the doctrines and practices of the ancient Church relating to the Eucharist. 1688.

The texts examined which Papists cite to prove the supremacy of the Pope. 1688.

Autobiography. Ed T. Chamberlayne, Oxford 1839.

Also paraphrases and commentaries on the books of the Bible from Genesis to the Song of Solomon in 14 vols 1679–1706. For his other writings see DNB.

JOHN SHARP
1645–1714
§ 1

Works. 7 vols 1754.

Theological works. 5 vols Oxford 1829.

Sermons. 1700, 1701, 1709, 7 vols 1734–8.

§ 2

Sharp, T. The life of Sharp. Ed T. Newcome 2 vols 1825.

Solloway, J. Archbishop Sharp. 1927.

Hart, A. T. The life and times of Sharp. 1949.

WILLIAM SHERLOCK
1641?–1707
Collections

Sermons. 2 vols 1719, 1755 (4th edn).

§ 1

A discourse concerning the knowledge of Jesus Christ. 1674, 1674.

A discourse about Church unity: being a defence of Dr Stillingfleet. 1681 (anon); Continuation, 1682 (anon).

The case of resistance to the supreme powers. 1684, 1690.

A short summary of the principal controversies between the Church of England and the Church of Rome. 1687.

A preservative against Popery. 1688 (5 edns).

A letter to a member of the Convention. 1688.

A vindication of some Protestant principles of Church-unity from the charge of agreement with the Church of Rome. 1688, 1688.

A practical discourse concerning death. 1689, 1735 (22nd edn).

Proposals of terms of union between the Church and dissenters. 1689.

A vindication of the doctrine of the Trinity. 1690, 1694 (3rd edn).

A practical discourse concerning a future judgment. 1692, 1692, 1739 (11th edn).

The present state of the Socinian controversy. 1698.

For Sherlock's writings on the Socinian argument see DNB.

§ 2

Dodds, W. M. T. Robert South and Sherlock: some unpublished letters. MLR 39 1944.

Mullett, C. F. A case of allegiance: Sherlock and the revolution of 1688. HLQ 10 1946.

ROBERT SOUTH
1634–1716
Collections

[Five] sermons preached upon several occasions. Oxford 1679.

Twelve sermons. [Vol 1], 1692; vol 2, 1694; vols 1–2, 1697; vol 3, 1698; vols 1–3, 1704; vols 1–4, 1715, 1718, 1722; vols 5–6, 1717; vols 1–6, 1727, 1737.

Five additional volumes of sermons first printed from the author's manuscripts. 1744.

Sermons preached upon several occasions. 7 vols Oxford 1823, 5 vols Oxford 1842, 4 vols 1843, 2 vols 1840–65.

§ 1

Musica incantans. Oxford 1655, 1667; tr 1700. A Latin poem.

Interest deposed and truth restored, in two sermons. Oxford 1660, 1668.

Posthumous works [including Memoirs]. 1717, 1721 (as Memoirs of Dr South).

Opera posthuma latina. 1717.

Animadversions upon Dr Sherlock's Vindication of the doctrine of the Trinity. 1693. Anon.

Tritheism charged upon Dr Sherlock's new notion of the Trinity. 1695. Anon.

A short history of Valentinus Gentilis the tritheist, translated into English for the use of Dr Sherlock. 1696. Anon.

Decreti oxoniensis vindicatio. 1696. Anon.

§ 2

Memoirs of the life of Dr South. 1717 (in Posthumous works), 1721.

Lake, W. C. South the rhetorician. In J. E. Kempe, The classic preachers of the English Church ser 1, 1877.

Mattis, N. Robert South. Quart Jnl of Speech 15 1929.

Roberts, D. A. A speech by South. TLS 2 Nov 1933.

Spiker, S. Figures of speech in the sermons of South. RES 16 1940.

Dodds, W. M. T. South and William Sherlock: some unpublished letters. MLR 39 1944.

Wright, G. W. Westminster School in 1652 [a Latin poem by South]. N & Q May 1954. *See* J. B. Whitmore, Aug 1954; G. W. Wright, Oct 1954.

Sutherland, J. R. Robert South. REL 1 1960.

Alkon, P. K. South, William Law and Samuel Johnson. Stud in Eng Lit 1500–1900 6 1966.

Simon, I. In her Three Restoration divines: Barrow, South and Tillotson, Paris 1967.

RICHARD STEELE
1629–92

The husbandmans calling. 1668, 1672. 12 sermons on agriculture.

The tradesmans calling. 1684.

An antidote against distraction. 1667, 1695 (4th edn).

EDWARD STILLINGFLEET
1635–99
Collections

Works, with his life [by R. Bentley]. 6 vols 1707–10.

Sermons preached on several occasions. 4 vols 1696–1701.

Sermons preached on several occasions. 1673.

Six sermons. 1669.

Miscellaneous discourses on several occasions. Ed J. Stillingfleet 1735.

§ 1

Irenicum. 1659, 1661, 1662, 1662, 1681.

Origines sacrae: or a rational account of the grounds of the Christian faith. 1662, 1663, 1666, 1675, 1702 (7th edn).

A rational account of the grounds of the Protestant religion: being a vindication of Archbishop Laud's relation of a conference between himself and J. Fisher, a Jesuit. 1664, 1665, 1681.

A letter to a deist. 1677.

Several conferences between a Romish priest, a fanatic chaplain and a divine of the Church of England. 1679.

The mischief of separation. 1680 (4 edns).

The unreasonableness of separation. 1681, 1682.

Origines britannicae: or the antiquities of the British Church. 1685; ed T. P. Pantin 2 vols Oxford 1842.

The doctrines and practices of the Church of Rome truly represented. 1686 (3 edns).

The doctrine of the Trinity and transubstantiation compared. 2 pts 1687.

A discourse concerning the doctrine of Christ's satisfaction. 2 pts 1696–1700, 3 pts 1697–1700.

A discourse in vindication of the doctrine of the Trinity. 1696, 1697.

The Bishop of Worcester's answer to Mr Locke's letter. 1697.

The Bishop of Worcester's answer to Mr Locke's second letter. 1698.

A discourse concerning the unreasonableness of a new separation on account of the oaths. 1705.

§ 2

Nankivell, J. W. H. Stillingfleet, Bishop of Worcester. Worcester 1946.

THOMAS TENISON
1636–1715
§ 1

The creed of Mr Hobbes examined. 1670, 1671.

Baconiana. 1678.

A discourse of idolatry. 1678.

A discourse concerning a guide in matters of faith. 1683. Anon.

A true account of the conference held about religion between Andrew Pulton and Thomas Tenison. 1687 (4 edns).

Difference betwixt the Protestant and Socinian methods. 1687.

Notes of the Church as laid down by Cardinal Bellarmine examined and confuted. 1688.

A discourse concerning the ecclesiastical commission opened in the Jerusalem chamber. 1689.

§ 2

Memoirs of the life and times of Tenison, late Archbishop of Canterbury. [1715] (3 edns).

Carpenter, E. Tenison: his life and times. 1948.

Horton-Smith, L. G. H. An ardent educationalist, Tenison. N & Q 19 March 1949.

JOHN TILLOTSON
1630–94
Collections

Works, containing fifty-four sermons and the Rule of faith. 1696, 1735 (10th edn).

[Two hundred sermons]. Ed R. Barker 14 vols 1695–1704, 2 vols 1712, 1735 (5th edn). From 1717 the Works include 254 sermons and the Rule of faith.

Works. Ed T. Birch 3 vols 1752, 10 vols 1820. Includes a life, also issued separately, and 255 sermons.

Sermons preached upon several occasions. 1671, 1673, 1678; vol 2, 1678; vols 1–2, 1679, 1685, 1688, 1694.

Sermons and discourses [vol 3]. 1686, 1687, 1691, 1694.

Sermons concerning the divinity and incarnation of our Saviour. 1693.

Sermons preached upon several occasions, vol 4. 1694.

Six sermons. 1694.

[Selected] sermons. Ed G. W. Weldon 1886.

The golden book of Tillotson. Ed J. Moffat 1926. Extracts.

§ 1

About 30 sermons pbd separately by himself; many more after his death.

The morning exercise at Cripplegate. In Samuel Annesley, The morning exercise at Cripplegate, 1661. Anon.

The wisdom of being religious. 1664.

The rule of faith. 1666, 1676, 1688.

§ 2

Bibliotheca Tillotsoniana: or auction catalogue of the library. 1695.

H[utchinson], F. The life of Tillotson compiled from the minutes of [Edward] Young. 1717.

Birch, Thomas. Life. 1752.

G., E. Archbishop Tillotson and Lady Russell. More Books 20 1945. A letter.

Locke, L. G. Tillotson: a study in seventeenth-century literature. Copenhagen 1954.

Sykes, N. The sermons of Archbishop Tillotson. Theology 58 1955.

Brown, D. D. The text of Tillotson's sermons. Library 5th ser 13 1958.

—— The Dean's dilemma: a further note on a Tillotson passage. Library 5th ser 14 1959.
—— Voltaire, Archbishop Tillotson and the invention of God. Revue de Littérature Comparée 34 1960.
—— Dryden's Religio laici and the 'judicious and learned friend'. MLR 56 1961.
—— Tillotson's revisions and Dryden's 'talent for English prose'. RES new ser 12 1961.
King, B. Dryden, Tillotson and tyrannic love. RES new ser 16 1965.
Simon, I. In her Three Restoration divines: Barrow, South and Tillotson, Paris 1967.

WILLIAM WAKE
1657–1737
See col 1850, below.

HENRY WHARTON
1664–95
Collections
One and twenty sermons preached in the years 1689, 1690. 1698, 2 vols 1728. Includes Fourteen sermons preached in Lambeth Chapel in 1688 and 1689, with an account of the author's life, 1697, 1700.

§ 1
Anglia sacra. 2 vols 1691.

A defence of pluralities. 1692. Anon.
A specimen of some errors and defects in [G. Burnet's] History of the Reformation. 1693. By 'Anthony Harmer'.
A list of the suffragan bishops of England. In Bibliotheca topographica britannica, ed J. Nichols vol 6, 1790.

DANIEL WILLIAMS
1643?–1716
Collections
Practical discourses on several important subjects. [Ed W. Harris, with a life] 5 vols 1738–50.
Select sermons and tracts. 2 vols 1832.

§ 1
Gospel truth stated and vindicated. 1692, 1692.
A defence of Gospel truth. 1693.
Man made righteous. 1694.

§ 2
[Defoe, D.] Memoirs. 1718.
Papers relating to Dr Williams and the trust established by his will. 1816. Life by T. Morgan, oration by J. Lindsay.
Jones, S. K. Dr Williams and his library. 1947.
Heinemann, F. H. John Toland, France, Holland and Dr Williams. RES 25 1949.

B. THE EIGHTEENTH-CENTURY DIVINES

The writers included in this section were all born between 1660 and 1760. Divines of the Church of England born shortly before 1660 are listed col 1603, above; those born after 1760 in vol 3; and Scottish divines col 2031, below.

GENERAL STUDIES

See also under A. The Restoration Divines, above.
Nichols, J. Literary anecdotes of the eighteenth century. 9 vols 1812–15.
The lives of Dr Edward Pocock, Bishop Z. Pearce (by himself), Bishop T. Newton (by himself) and the Rev Philip Skelton. Ed L. Twells 2 vols 1816.
Watson, R. Anecdotes of the life of Bishop Richard Watson. 1817, 2 vols 1818 (rev).
Sharp, T. Life of John Sharp, Archbishop of York. Ed T. Newcome 2 vols 1825.
Thoresby, R. Diary. 2 vols 1830.
—— Letters of eminent men to Ralph Thoresby. 2 vols 1832.
Southey, R. The life of Wesley, with notes by S. T. Coleridge. 2 vols 1846.
Lathbury, T. The history of the Convocation. 1842.
Wedgwood, J. John Wesley and the evangelical reaction of the eighteenth century. 1870.
Stephen, L. History of English thought in the 18th century. 2 vols 1876, 1927 (rev).
Overton, J. H. and C. J. Abbey. The English Church in the 18th century. 2 vols 1878.
Seeley, M. The later evangelical fathers. 1879.
Lecky, W. E. H. A history of England in the eighteenth century. Vols 1–2, 1883–7 (rev).
Craven, J. B. The journals and episcopal visitations of Bishop Robert Forbes. 1886.
Abbey, C. J. The English Church and its bishops 1700–1800. 2 vols 1887.
Carter, T. T. Undercurrents of Church life in the 18th century. 1899.
Millar, J. H. The mid eighteenth century. Edinburgh 1902.
Pyle, E. Memoirs of a royal chaplain. Ed A. Hartshorne 1905.

Overton, J. H. and F. Relton. The English Church from the accession of George I to the end of the 18th century. 1906.
Rowden, A. W. The Primates of the four Georges. 1916.
Laski, H. J. Political thought in England from Locke to Bentham. 1919.
Broxap, H. The later non-jurors. Cambridge 1925.
Woodforde, J. The diary of a country parson. Ed J. Beresford 5 vols 1924–31, 2 vols 1968.
Sykes, N. Edmund Gibson, Bishop of London. Oxford 1926.
—— Church and State in England in the 18th century. Cambridge 1934.
—— Archbishop Wake and the Whig party 1716–23. Cambridge Historical Jnl 3 1945.
—— D. E. Jablonski and the Church of England. 1950.
Dimond, S. G. The psychology of the Methodist revival. Oxford 1926.
Piette, M. La réaction wesléyenne dans l'évolution protestante. Brussels 1925; tr 1937.
Hawkins, L. M. Allegiance in Church and State. 1928.
Warner, W. J. The Wesleyan movement in the industrial revolution. 1930.
Torrey, N. L. Voltaire and the English deists. New Haven 1930.
Lee, U. The historical backgrounds of early Methodist enthusiasm. New York 1931.
Evans, A. W. Warburton and the Warburtonians. Oxford 1932.
Goodman, F. R. The pretenders from the pulpit. Cambridge 1933.
Creed, J. M. and J. S. Boys Smith. Religious thought in the 18th century, illustrated from writers of the period. Cambridge 1934.

Crane, R. S. Anglican apologetics and the idea of progress 1699–1745. MP 31 1934; rptd in his Idea of the humanities and other essays vol 2, Chicago 1967.
Harvey, F. B. Methodism and the romantic movement. London Quart 159 1934.
Tayler, E. R. Methodism and politics. 1935.
Carpenter, E. Thomas Sherlock. 1936.
Mossner, E. C. Bishop Butler and the age of reason. 1936.
Bett, H. The spirit of Methodism. 1937.
—— The hymns of Methodism. 1913, 1945.
Gill, F. C. The romantic movement and Methodism. 1937, 1954.
Bready, J. W. England before and after Wesley: the evangelical revival and social reform. 1938.
Crawford, B. F. Theological trends in methodist hymnody. Carnegie Pa 1939.
Bolton, G. The dome of devotion. 1939. On St Paul's.
Shepherd, T. B. Methodism and the literature of the 18th century. 1940.
Smyth, C. Simeon and Church order: the origins of the evangelical revival in Cambridge. Cambridge 1940.
Whitaker, W. B. The eighteenth-century Sunday. 1940.
Whiting, C. E. Nathaniel Lord Crew, Bishop of Durham (1674–1721) and his diocese. 1940.
Hartford, R. R. An eighteenth-century sermon. Hermathena 56 1940.
McConnell, F. J. Evangelicals, revolutionists and idealists. Nashville 1942.
Brown-Serman, S. The Evangelicals and the Bible. Historical Mag of Protestant Episcopal Church 12 1943.
Davis, J. L. Mystical versus enthusiastic sensibility. JHI 4 1943.
Zabriskie, A. C. (ed). Anglican Evangelicalism. Philadelphia 1943.
Sampson, G. The century of divine songs. Proc Br Acad 29 1943.
Clarke, W. K. L. Eighteenth-century piety. 1944.
Wearmouth, R. F. The first Methodist conference, June 25–30 1744. London Quart 169 1944.
—— Methodism and the common people of the 18th century. 1945.
Baker, F. Methodism and the '45 rebellion. London Quart 172 1947.
—— The relations between the Society of Friends and early Methodism. London Quart 173–4 1948–9.
McCloy, S. T. Rationality and religion in the 18th century. South Atlantic Quart 46 1947.
Church, L. F. The early Methodist people. 1949.
—— More about early Methodist people. 1950.
Baur, J. E. English Protestant attempts at reunion 1689–1710. Historical Mag of Protestant Episcopal Church 18 1949.
Hart, A. T. The life and times of John Sharp, Archbishop of York. 1949.
Brown, W. E. M. The polished shaft: studies in the purpose and influence of the Christian writer in the 18th century. 1950.
Knox, R. A. Enthusiasm. Oxford 1950.
Coomer, D. The influence of Puritanism and dissent on Methodism. London Quart 175 1950.
Loane, M. L. Oxford and the evangelical succession. 1950.
Cassirer, E. The philosophy of the Enlightenment. Princeton 1951.
Poole-Connor, E. J. Evangelicalism in England. 1951.
Wand, J. W. C. The high-church schism: four lectures on the non-jurors. 1951.
King-Hall, M. The edifying Bishop: the story of Frederick Hervey, Earl of Bristol and Bishop of Derry. 1951.
Davey, C. G. The march of Methodism. 1951.
Davies, G. C. B. The early Cornish Evangelicals 1735–60. 1951.
—— The early Evangelicals. Church Quart Rev 155 1954.
Humphrey, R. H. Literature and religion in 18th-century England. Jnl of Ecclesiasical History 3 1952.

Reynolds, J. S. The Evangelicals at Oxford 1735–1871. Oxford 1953.
Elliott-Binns, L. E. The early Evangelicals. 1953.
Raven, C. E. Natural religion and Christian theology. 2 vols Cambridge 1953.
Stromberg, R. L. Religious liberalism in 18th-century England. Oxford 1954.
Cameron, R. M. The rise of Methodism: a source book. New York 1954.
van den Berg, J. Constrained by Jesus' love: an inquiry into the motives of the missionary awakening in Great Britain between 1698 and 1815. Kampen Netherlands 1956.
Towlson, C. W. Moravian and Methodist: relationships and influences in the eighteenth century. 1957.
Hobsbawm, E. J. Methodism and the threat of revolution in Britain. History Today 7 1957.
Pilkington, E. Methodism and episcopacy. Contemporary Rev June 1958.
Tate, W. E. The charity sermons 1704–32 as a source for the history of education. Jnl of Ecclesiastical History 9 1958.
Walsh, J. D. The Magdalene Evangelicals. Church Quart Rev 159 1958.
Carpenter, S. C. Eighteenth-century Church and people. 1959.
Dodwell, C. R. (ed). The English Church and the Continent. 1959.
Norwood, F. A. Methodist historical studies 1930–59. Church History 27 1959.
Lewis, A. J. Count Zinzendorf: the apostle of Christian unity. London Quart 185 1960.
Lyles, A. M. Methodism mocked; the satiric reaction to Methodism in the 18th century. 1960.
Barlow, R. B. Anti-subscription and the clerical petition movement in the Church of England 1766–72. Historical Mag of Protestant Episcopal Church 30 1961.
Davies, H. Worship and theology in England from Watts and Wesley to Maurice 1690–1850. 1961.
Henderson-Howat, A. M. D. Christian literature in the 18th century. Historical Mag of Protestant Episcopal Church 30 1961.
Macdonald, A. Enthusiasm resurgent. Dalhousie Rev 42 1962.
Benson, L. F. The English hymn: its development and use in worship. Richmond Va 1962.
Clark, B. F. L. The building of the eighteenth-century Church. 1963.
Davies, R. E. Methodism. 1963 (Pelican).
Sangster, P. Pity my simplicity: the evangelical revival and the religious education of children 1783–1800. 1964.
Bultmann, W. A. and P. W. The roots of Anglican humanitarianism: a study of the membership of the SPCK 1699–1720. Historical Mag of Protestant Episcopal Church 33 1964.
Best, G. F. A. Temporal pillars: Queen Anne's bounty, the Ecclesiastical Commissioners and the Church of England. Cambridge 1964.
Meacham, S. Henry Thornton of Clapham 1760–1815. Cambridge Mass 1964.
Davies, R. and G. Rupp (ed). A history of the Methodist Church in Great Britain. Vol 1, 1965.
Curtis, L. P. Anglican moods of the eighteenth century. Hamden Conn 1966.
Dearing, T. Wesleyan and tractarian worship. 1966.
Tice, F. The history of Methodism in Cambridge. 1966.

FRANCIS ATTERBURY
1662–1732
Collections

The epistolary correspondence, visitation charges, speeches and miscellanies, with historical notes. Ed J. Nichols 5 vols 1783–90, 1789–98 (as Miscellaneous works).

Fourteen sermons preached on several occasions; together with a large vindication of the doctrine contained in the sermon preached at the funeral of Thomas Burnet. 1708.

Sermons and discourses on several subjects and occasions. Vols 1–2, 1723, 1726, 1730; vols 3–4, ed T. Moore 1734; 4 vols 1735, 1737, 1740.

§ 1

A letter to a Convocation man concerning the rights, powers and privileges of that body. 1697.

A discourse occasioned by the death of Lady Cutts. 1698.

The rights, powers and privileges of an English Convocation stated and vindicated. 1700, 1701.

The power of the Lower House of Convocation to adjourn itself vindicated. 1701.

A letter [A second, A third letter] to a clergyman in the country concerning the choice of members for Convocation. 3 vols 1701–2.

The case of the schedule stated. 1702.

The parliamentary original and rights of the Lower House of Convocation cleared. 1702.

A faithful account of some transactions in the last three sessions of the present Convocation. 4 pts 1702–5.

The mitre and the crown: or a real distinction between them. 1711.

English advice, to the freeholders of England. 1714.

Letters

Letters of Pope to Atterbury when in the Tower of London. Ed J. Nichols 1859.

Williams, R. F. Memoirs and correspondence of Fr Atterbury. 2 vols 1869.

Letters of Canon W. Stratford. In Portland mss vol 7, 1901 (Historical Mss Commission).

§ 2

Beeching, H. C. Francis Atterbury. 1909.

JOSEPH BINGHAM
1668–1723
Collections

Works. 2 vols 1726; ed R. Bingham 9 vols 1821–9 (as Origines ecclesiasticae and other works, with Memoir); ed J. R. Pitman 9 vols 1838–40, 1843–5; ed R. Bingham 10 vols Oxford 1855; 2 vols 1856.

Opera. 11 vols Halle 1751–81.

§ 1

Three sermons on the Trinity. 3 vols 1695–7.

The French Churches apology for the Church of England. 1706.

Origines ecclesiae: or the antiquities of the Christian Church. 10 vols 1708–22; abridged by A. Blackmore as Ecclesiae primitivae notitia, 2 vols 1722; tr Latin, 10 vols Halle 1724–9, Magdeburg 1751–81.

The scholastical history of lay baptism. 2 vols 1712–14.

A discourse concerning the mercy of God. 1720.

THOMAS BRETT
1667–1744

An account of Church-government and governors. 1707.

A sermon on remission of sins. 1711, 1712, 1715.

The doctrine of remission of sins. 1712.

A sermon of the honour of the Christian priesthood. 1712.

An inquiry into the judgment and practice of the primitive Church in relation to lay baptism. 1713.

A further inquiry into the practice of the primitive Church in relation to lay baptism. 1714.

The independency of the Church upon the State. 1717.

The divine right of episcopacy. 1718.

Tradition necessary to interpret the Holy Scriptures. 1718.

A farther proof of the necessity of tradition. 1720.

A collection of the principal liturgies of the Christian Church. 1720.

Discourses concerning the Trinity. 1720.

The necessity of discerning Christ's body in the Holy Communion. 1720.

A chronological essay on the sacred history from the creation of the world to the birth of Christ. 1728, 1748.

A general history of the world, from the creation of the world to the destruction of Jerusalem by Nebuchadnezzar. 1732.

A true scripture account of the nature and benefits of the Holy Eucharist [in answer to B. Hoadly]. 1736.

Four letters on the necessity of episcopal communion. 1743.

JOSEPH BUTLER
1692–1752
See col 1852, below.

EDWARD CHANDLER
1668?–1750

A defence of Christianity from the prophecies. 1725.

A vindication of the defence of Christianity. 1728.

SAMUEL CLARKE
1675–1729
Collections

Works. 4 vols 1738. With Life by B. Hoadly.

Sermons. Ed J. Clarke, with life by B. Hoadly 10 vols 1730, 2 vols Dublin 1734, 11 vols 1749 (7th edn), 8 vols 1756.

Six sermons. 1718.

Seventeen sermons. 1724.

Eighteen sermons. 1734.

Forty sermons. Ed S. Clapham 1806.

§ 1

Three practical essays on baptism, confirmation and repentance. 1699.

A paraphrase on the four Evangelists. 2 vols 1701–2, 1 vol 1714 etc.

A discourse concerning the being and attributes of God, the obligations of natural religion and the truth of the Christian revelation [Boyle lectures, 1704 and 1705]. 2 vols 1705–6, 1 vol 1739 (8th edn); tr French, 1717; abridged by G. Burnet in A defence of natural and revealed religion vol 2, 1737.

A discourse concerning the unchangeable obligations of natural religion and the truth of the Christian revelation [8 sermons]. 1706; rptd in A collection of theological tracts vol 4, 1785, 1791.

The scripture doctrine of the Trinity. 1712, 1732 (3rd edn).

An exposition of the Church catechism. 1729, 1730.

For Clarke's philosophical works see col 1824, below.

THOMAS DEACON
1697–1753
Collections

The writings of Deacon and J. Owen. Ed C. W. Sutton, Manchester 1879.

§ I

The doctrine of the Church of Rome concerning purgatory contrary to catholic tradition. 1718.
A commission office [for non-jurors]. 1718.
A compleat collection of devotions. 1734.
A full, true and comprehensive view of Christianity. 1747, 1748.

§ 2

Broxap, H. A biography of Thomas Deacon, the Manchester non-juror. Manchester 1911.
—— The later non-jurors. 1924.
—— Jacobites and non-jurors. In The social and political ideas of some English thinkers of the Augustan age, ed F. J. C. Hearnshaw 1928.

JOHN WILLIAM FLETCHER, or
JEAN GUILLAUME DE LA FLÉCHÈRE
1729–85

Collections

Works. 9 vols 1803–4, 6 vols New York 1809, 7 vols 1826 (8th edn).

§ I

A first, [second, third, last] check to antinomianism. 4 vols 1771–5.
An appeal to matter of fact and common sense: or a rational demonstration of man's corrupt and last estate. Bristol 1772, 1773, 1774, 1785 etc.
An essay on truth: or a rational vindication of the doctrine of salvation by faith. 1773.
A first part of an equal check to pharisaism and antinomianism. 1774.
Zelotes and Honestus reconciled: or an equal check to pharisaism and antinomianism continued. Shrewsbury 1774, 1775.
A polemical essay on the twin doctrines of Christian imperfection and a death purgatory. 1775.
A vindication of Mr Wesley's Calm address to our American colonies. 1776.
American patriotism farther confronted with reason, Scripture and the Constitution: being observations on the dangerous politics taught by the Rev Mr Evans and the Rev Dr Price. Shrewsbury 1776, 1777.
Bible Arminianism and Bible Calvinism. 1777.
Letters on the spiritual manifestations of the Son of God. 1829.

§ 2

Benson, J. The life of J. W. de la Fléchère. 1805.
Wesley, J. The life of the Rev J. W. Fletcher. 1786; rptd in his Christian biography, 1832.
Ruffet, L. J. G. de la Fléchère: esquisse. Toulouse 1862.
Marrat, J. The vicar of Madeley, John Fletcher. 1902.
Seed, T. A. John and Mary Fletcher. 1906.
Baker, F. John Fletcher, Methodist clergyman. London Quart 185 1960.
Lawton, G. W. Shropshire saint: a study in the ministry and spirituality of Fletcher of Madeley. 1960.
Thompson, C. H. John Fletcher, first theologian of Methodism. Emory Univ Quart 16 1960.
Maycock, J. The Fletcher-Toplady controversy. London Quart 191 1966.

EDMUND GIBSON
1669–1748

§ I

A short state of some present questions in Convocation. 1700.

The right of the Archbishop of Canterbury to prorogue the whole of Convocation. 1701.
Synodus anglicana: or the constitutional proceedings of an English Convocation. 1672 (for 1702).
The pretended independence of the Lower House of Convocation. 1703.
Family devotions. 1705, 1750 (18th edn).
Three charges to the clergy of his diocese. 3 vols 1717–42.
Three pastoral letters occasioned by some late writings in favour of infidelity. 3 vols 1728–31, 1732, 1735 (7th edn).
A preservative against Popery, in several discourses. 1738.
Pastoral letter against lukewarmness on the one hand and enthusiasm on the other. 1739, 1741, 1748.
Observations upon the conduct and behaviour of a certain sect usually distinguished by the name of Methodists. 1740, 1744.
Pastoral letter occasioned by the present dangers and exciting to serious reformation of life and manners. 1745.
For Gibson's historical works see col 1715, below.

§ 2

Sykes, N. Edmund Gibson, Bishop of London: a study in politics and religion in the eighteenth century. Oxford 1926.

THOMAS HERRING
1693–1757

§ I

Seven sermons on public occasions. 1763.
Archbishop Herring's visitation returns 1743. Ed S. L. Ollard and P. C. Walker 5 vols Leeds 1928–31.

Letters

Letters to William Duncombe from 1728 to 1757. Ed J. Duncombe 1777.

§ 2

Yorke, P. C. The life of Chancellor Hardwicke. 3 vols 1913.
Rowden, A. W. In his Primates of the four Georges, 1916.

JAMES HERVEY
1714–58

See col 1861, below.

BENJAMIN HOADLY
1676–1761

Collections

Works. Ed J. Hoadly 3 vols 1773. With a life and a list of the tracts relating to the Bangorian controversy.
Sixteen sermons. 1754.
Twenty sermons. 1755.

§ I

A letter to Mr Fleetwood occasioned by his Essay on miracles. 1702.
A letter to a clergyman concerning the votes of the Bishops. 1703.
The reasonableness of conforming to the Church of England. 1703, 1712.
A persuasive to lay-conformity: or the reasonableness of constant communion with the Church of England. 1704.
A defence of the reasonableness of conformity. 1705.

The measures of submission to the civil magistrate considered. 1706, 1708, 1710, 1718.

A defence of episcopal ordinations. 1707.

The happiness of the present establishment and the unhappiness of absolute monarchy: a sermon. 1708.

The original and institution of civil government discussed. 1710.

The thoughts of an honest Tory upon the present proceedings of that party. 1710.

A serious enquiry into the present state of the Church of England: or the danger to the Church from the rashness of the clergy. 1711.

Several discourses concerning the terms of acceptance with God. 1711.

A preservative against the principles and practices of the non-jurors both in Church and State. 1716.

The nature of the Kingdom or Church of Christ. 1717. A sermon.

The common rights of subjects defended, and the nature of the sacramental test considered. 1718, 1719.

An answer to the representation drawn up by the committee of the Lower House of Convocation. 1718.

A plain account of the nature and end of the sacrament of the Lord's Supper. 1735, 1751, 1761, 1767, 1772. Anon.

Letters

The correspondence of J. Hughes and Hoadly. 1773.

§ 2

Sykes, N. Benjamin Hoadly, Bishop of Bangor. In The social and political ideas of some English thinkers of the Augustan age, ed F. J. C. Hearnshaw 1928.

Bingham, E. R. The political apprenticeship of Hoadly. Church History 16 1947.

RICHARD HURD
1720–1808

Collections

Works. 8 vols 1811.

Moral and political dialogues. 1759, 1760; 3 vols 1765, 1771, 1776, 1788 (with Letters on chivalry).

Sermons preached at Lincoln's Inn between 1765 and 1776. 3 vols 1776–80, 1785.

§ 1

The mischiefs of enthusiasm and bigotry. 1752. A sermon.

An introduction to the study of the prophecies concerning the Christian Church. 1772, 1772, 1773, 1776, 1788; ed E. Bickersteth 1839. 12 sermons.

A charge to the clergy of Lichfield and Coventry. 1776.

For Hurd's literary criticism see col 235, above.

Letters

The correspondence of Hurd and William Mason; and Letters of Hurd to Thomas Gray. Ed E. H. Pearce and L. Whibley, Cambridge 1932.

Nankivell, J. Extracts from the destroyed letters of Hurd to William Mason. MLR 45 1950.

§ 2

Kilvert, F. Memoirs of the life and writings of Bishop Hurd. 1860.

Pearce, E. H. Hartlebury Castle. 1926.

Evans, A. W. Warburton and the Warburtonians. Oxford 1932.

JOHN JOHNSON
1662–1725

Collections

Sermons. 2 vols 1728.

§ 1

The clergyman's vademecum. 2 pts 1708–9, 1714, 1715, 1723, 1731.

The propitiatory oblation in the Holy Eucharist. 1710.

The unbloody sacrifice and altar unvailed and supported. 2 pts 1714–17, 1 vol 1724.

§ 2

Brett, T. The life of the late John Johnson. 1748.

WHITE KENNETT
1660–1728

§ 1

A dialogue between two friends [a Jacobite and a Williamite], occasioned by the late Revolution. 1689.

An occasional letter on the subject of English convocations. 1701.

Ecclesiastical synods and parliamentary convocations in the Church of England. 1701.

The present state of Convocation. 1702.

The case of impropriations and of the augmentation of vicarages and other insufficient cures. 1704.

The Christian scholar. 1708, 1710 (5th edn).

A vindication of the Church and clergy of England. 1709.

A true answer to Dr Sacheverell's sermon. 1709.

Bibliothecae americanae primordia. 1713.

Monitions and advices delivered to the clergy of the diocese of Peterborough at the primary visitation. 2 pts 1720.

An historical account of the discipline and jurisdiction of the Church of England. 1730 (2nd edn).

§ 2

[Sharpe, J.] Short remarks on some passages in the life of Dr Kennett. 1730.

[Newton, W.] The life of White Kennett, with some original letters. 1730.

Bennett, G. V. White Kennett, Bishop of Peterborough: a study in the political and ecclesiastical history of the early eighteenth century. 1957.

JOHN NEWTON
1725–1807

Collections

Works. 6 vols 1808, 12 vols 1821, Edinburgh 1827 (with a memoir by R. Cecil), 1830, 1834, 1836, London 1839 (with a life by R. Cecil), Edinburgh 1840.

Sermons preached in the parish church of Olney. 1767.

Letters, sermons and a review of ecclesiastical history. Edinburgh 1780, 1787.

§ 1

An authentic narrative of some particulars in the life of [Newton] in a series of letters to Mr Haweis. 1764, 1765, 1775, 1792, 1799.

A review of ecclesiastical history. 1770.

Apologia: four letters to a minister of an independent Church. 1784.

Messiah: fifty discourses on the scriptural passages which form the subject of the Oratorio. 2 vols 1786.

See also under William Cowper, col 595, above.

Letters

Cardiphonia. 1781. A selection from his religious correspondence.

Letters to a wife. 2 vols 1793.

Forty-one letters on religious subjects. 1807, 1813, 1825, 1830, 1831.

Sixty-eight letters to a clergyman and his family [1791–1801]. 1845.

One hundred and twenty-nine letters from Newton to the Rev William Bull [1773–1805]. 1847.

Letters. 1960.

§2

Sargent, G. E. The white slave. 1848.

Newton of Olney and St Mary Woolnoth: an autobiography compiled by J. Bull. 1868.

Seeley, M. In his Later evangelical fathers, 1879.

Callis, J. Newton: sailor, preacher, pastor and poet. 1908.

Thomson, R. W. Newton and his Baptist friends. Baptist Quart 9 1939.

Martin, B. The ancient mariner and the authentic narrative. 1949.

—— Newton: a biography. 1950.

—— Newton and the slave trade. 1961.

Dalton, L. H. Singing slaves. 1952. A biography of Newton.

WILLIAM ROMAINE
1714–95
Collections

Works, with a life by W. B. Cadogan. 8 vols 1796, 1809, 6 vols 1813, 1837.

Treatises on the life, walk and triumph of faith, with introductory essay by T. Chalmers. 2 vols Glasgow 1824, 1 vol 1856, 1882, 1892.

§1

The life of faith. 1763.

The walk of faith. 1771.

The triumph of faith. 1795.

Letters

Letters to a friend. Ed T. Wiles 1795.

§2

Haweis, T. The life of Romaine. 1797.

Cadogan, W. B. The life of the Rev Romaine. 1796, 1827, 1832.

Fox, G. T. The life and doctrine of Romaine, vicar of St Nicholas. Durham 1876.

THOMAS SCOTT
1747–1821
Collections

Theological works. 5 vols 1805–8, 1834.

Works. Ed J. Scott 10 vols 1823–5. With a life.

Sermons. Ed J. Scott 1835.

§1

The force of truth: an authentic narrative. 1779, 1794, 1798, 1801, 1808, 1816, 1817, 1821 etc.

The Holy Bible, with notes. 4 vols 1788–92, 1809, 5 vols 1810, 6 vols 1812.

Essays on the most important subjects in religion. 1793, 1794, 1798, 1800, 1814, 1822 etc.

A treatise on growth in grace. 1795, 1797.

Sermons on select subjects. 1797.

Tracts. Ed T. Chalmers, Glasgow 1826.

Letters

Letters and papers. Ed J. Scott 1824, 1826.

§2

Scott, J. Life of Scott. 1822.

Downer, A. C. Scott the commentator. 1909.

Loane, M. L. In his Oxford and the evangelical succession, 1950.

THOMAS SECKER
1693–1768
Collections

Works. Ed B. Porteus and G. Stinton 6 vols Dublin 1775, 4 vols 1792, 6 vols 1825.

§1

Fourteen sermons on several occasions. 1766, 1771.

Lectures on the catechism of the Church of England. 2 vols 1769, 1771, 1777, 1791, 1799, 1814, 1824 etc.

Sermons on severals ubjects. Ed B. Porteus and G. Stinton 7 vols 1770–71. With a life.

Eight charges to the clergy of Oxford and Canterbury. Ed B. Porteus and G. Stinton 1769.

§2

Porteus, B. A review of the life and character of Archbishop Secker. 1773.

Yorke, P. C. In his Life of Chancellor Hardwicke, 3 vols 1913.

Sykes, N. In his From Sheldon to Secker, Cambridge 1959.

THOMAS SHERLOCK
1678–1761
Collections

Works. Ed T. S. Hughes 5 vols 1830. With a life.

Discourses preached at the Temple church. 4 vols 1754–8, 1755, 1755–8, 1756–64, Edinburgh 1770, 5 vols 1772–5 (with a life), 1797.

§1

Remarks upon the late Bishop of Bangor's [B. Hoadly's] treatment of the clergy and Convocations. 1717. Anon.

A vindication of the Corporation and Test Acts. 1718.

The proceedings of the Vice-Chancellor and University of Cambridge against Dr Bentley, stated and vindicated. 1719.

The use and intent of prophecy in the several ages of the world. 1725. Sermons.

The trial of the witnesses of the resurrection of Jesus. 1729 etc, 1800 (16th edn).

A letter to the clergy and people of London and Westminster on occasion of the late earthquakes. 1750.

§2

Wayland, D. T. A biographical sketch. Derby [1823].

Carpenter, E. Thomas Sherlock. 1936.

GEORGE SMALRIDGE
1663–1719
Collections

Sixty sermons. Oxford 1724, London 1727, Oxford 1824, 2 vols Oxford 1832, 1853, London 1862.

§ I

The thoughts of a country gentleman upon reading Dr Sacheverell's trial. 1710.
Miscellanies. 1714.
Twelve sermons. Oxford 1717.

AUGUSTUS MONTAGUE TOPLADY
1740–78
Collections

Sermons and essays. 1793.
Works, with a memoir by W. Row. 1794, 6 vols 1825, 1828, 1841, 1853.
Hymns and sacred poems. 1860. With a life.

§ I

Poems on sacred subjects. 1759.
A letter to Mr Wesley. 1770.
More work for Mr Wesley. 1772.
Historic proof of the doctrinal Calvinism of the Church of England. 2 vols 1774.
The Church of England vindicated from the charge of Arminianism. 1779.
The scheme of Christian and philosophical necessity asserted, in opposition to Mr Wesley's tract. 1775.
Psalms and hymns for public and private worship. 1776 etc.
The Rev Mr Toplady's dying avowal of his religious sentiments. 1778.

§ 2

Memoirs of the Rev Mr Toplady. 1778, 1794.
Wright, T. Augustus M. Toplady. 1912.
Wilkins, H. J. An enquiry concerning Toplady and his hymn Rock of ages. Bristol 1938.
Fasham, E. J. Rock of ages. Baptist Quart 10 1940.
Carter, C. S. Toplady: a world-famous divine. Evangelical Quart 21 1949.
Howell, A. C. Toplady and Quarles' Emblems. SP 57 1960.
Maycock, J. The Fletcher-Toplady controversy. London Quart 161 1966.

HENRY VENN
1725–97

§ I

Sermons. 1759.
The compleat duty of man. 1763, 1807 (9th edn).
Examination of Dr Priestley's Free addresses on the Lord's Supper. 1769.
A token of respect to the memory of the Rev George Whitefield. 1770. A funeral sermon.
Mistakes in religion exposed. 1774, 1807.
Memoirs of Sir John Barnard. 1776, 1807, 1825.

§ 2

Venn, J. and H. The life and a selection from the letters of the Rev Henry Venn. 1834, 1835, 1836.
Loane, M. L. Henry Venn, Fellow of Queen's College. In his Cambridge and the evangelical succession, 1952.

WILLIAM WARBURTON
1698–1779
See cols 1775, 1869, below.

DANIEL WATERLAND
1683–1740
Collections

Works, with a life by W. Van Mildert. 11 vols Oxford 1823–8.
Sermons. Ed J. Clarke 2 vols 1742, 1776.

§ I

A vindication of Christ's divinity. Cambridge 1719.
Eight sermons in defense of the divinity of our Lord Jesus Christ. Cambridge 1720.
A critical history of the Athanasian creed. Cambridge 1723, 1728, 1850; ed J. R. King, Oxford 1870.
The nature, obligation and efficacy of the Christian sacraments. Westminster 1730.
The importance of the doctrine of the Trinity asserted. 1734.
Scripture vindicated. 2 vols Cambridge 1730–2.
A review of the doctrine of the Eucharist. Cambridge 1737; rptd Oxford 1868, 1896 (with list of Waterland's main works).

Letters

Fourteen letters from D. Waterland to Z. Pearce. Ed E. Churton 1868.

§ 2

Holtby, R. T. Waterland: a study in eighteenth-century orthodoxy. Carlisle 1966.

CHARLES WESLEY
1707–88
Collections

Hymns and sacred poems. 2 vols Bristol 1749.
Sermons, with a memoir. Ed S. Wesley 1816.
Representative verse. Ed F. Baker 1962.

§ I

An epistle to the Rev Mr John Wesley. 1755.
An epistle to the Rev Mr George Whitefield. 1755.
An elegy on the late Rev George Whitefield. 1771.
Journal. Ed T. Jackson 2 vols 1849.
The early journal 1736–9. Ed J. Telford 1909.

§ 2

Jackson, T. Life and correspondence of Charles Wesley. 2 vols 1841.
—— Memoirs of the Rev Charles Wesley. 1848.
Adams, C. The poet preacher. New York 1859.
Telford, J. Life of Charles Wesley. 1887, 1900.
Jones, D. M. Charles Wesley. 1919.
Wiseman, F. L. Charles Wesley, evangelist and poet. New York 1932, 1933.
—— Charles Wesley and his hymns. 1938.
Bett, H. Some latinisms in the Wesleys' hymns. London Quart 163 1938.
Manning, B. L. The recall to religion in the hymns of Charles Wesley. Ibid.
Shepherd, T. B. The children's verse of Dr Watts and Charles Wesley. London Quart 164 1939.
Rattenbury, J. E. The evangelical doctrines of Charles Wesley's hymns. 1941.
Beckerlegge, O. A. An attempt at a classification of Charles Wesley's metres: a contribution to the study of English prosody. London Quart 169 1944.
Lloyd, A. K. Charles Wesley's debt to Matthew Henry. London Quart 171 1946.

Ker, R. E. On mending Charles Wesley. London Quart 172 1947.

Colquhoun, F. Charles Wesley. 1947.

Baker, F. Charles Wesley as revealed in his letters. 1948.

— Charles Wesley's verse. 1964.

Findlay, G. H. First and last words: a study of some Wesley metres. London Quart 177 1952.

— A study in Wesley's six-eights. London Quart 180 1955.

— Christ's standard bearer: a study in the hymns of Charles Wesley. 1956.

Flew, R. N. The hymns of Charles Wesley: a study of their structure. 1953.

Flint, Ch. Charles Wesley and his colleagues. Washington 1957.

Freeman, C. B. Charles Wesley, the poet and the editors. Theology 61 1958.

Mayer, E. Charles Wesleys Hymnen. Tübingen 1957.

Haddal, I. Nattverden i Charles Wesleys salmer. Kirke og Kultur 63 1958.

Ellingworth, P. 'I' and 'we' in Charles Wesley's hymns. London Quart 188 1963.

Gill, F. C. Charles Wesley the first Methodist. 1964.

Myers, E. Singer of a thousand songs: a life of Charles Wesley. New York 1965.

See also under John Wesley, below.

JOHN WESLEY
1703–91
Bibliographies etc

Green, R. Bibliography of the works of John and Charles Wesley. 1896, 1906.

Decanver, H. C. Catalogue of works in refutation of Methodism and of the political pamphlets relating to Wesley's Calm address to our American colonies. 1868.

Skewes, J. H. A complete classified index of the Journals. 1872.

Collections

Works. 32 vols Bristol 1771–4; ed T. Jackson 14 vols 1829–31; 15 vols 1856–62 (with a life by J. Beecham) (11th edn); 14 vols 1872, rptd Grand Rapids Michigan 1958–9.

[44] Sermons on several occasions. 4 vols Bristol 1746–60, 1 vol 1944.

Sermons on several occasions. 9 vols 1788–1800; ed T. Jackson 2 vols 1825.

Standard sermons. Ed E. H. Sugden 1921.

A collection of psalms and hymns. Charlestown 1737. For later collections of hymns issued by John and Charles Wesley, *see* J. Julian, Dictionary of hymnology, 1907 (2nd edn).

The poetical works of John and Charles Wesley. 13 vols 1868–72.

§1

For the sermons, many of which were pbd singly, see Collections, *above.*

A dialogue between a predestinarian and his friend. Bristol 1742 (3rd edn).

An earnest appeal to men of reason and religion. Bristol 1743 (2nd edn).

A farther appeal. 1745.

Advice to the people called Methodists. 1745.

A second dialogue between an antinomian and his friend. 1745.

The principles of a Methodist. Bristol 1746.

Primitive physick: or an easy and natural method of curing most diseases. Bristol 1747, Nottingham 1805 (26th edn); ed W. H. Paynter, Plymouth 1958.

The character of a Methodist. Bristol 1747, 1802 (13th edn), 1950.

A letter to a person lately joined with the people called Quakers. 1748.

A plain account of the people called Methodists. Bristol 1749, 1795 (9th edn), 1951.

A short address to the inhabitants of Ireland. Dublin 1749.

The nature, design and general rules of the United Societies. 1750 (6th edn).

Serious thoughts upon the perseverance of saints. 1751.

Popery calmly considered. 1752, 1814 (9th edn).

Serious thoughts occasioned by the late earthquake at Lisbon. Bristol 1755 (2nd edn).

Queries humbly proposed to Count Zinzendorff. 1755.

An address to the clergy. 1756.

The doctrine of original sin. Bristol 1757.

A preservative against unsettled notions in religion. Bristol 1758.

A blow at the root: or Christ stabbed in the house of his friends. 1762.

Thoughts on the imputed righteousness of Christ. Dublin 1762.

A survey of the wisdom of God in the Creation. 2 vols Bristol 1763.

The complete English dictionary. Bristol 1764.

Explanatory notes upon the Old Testament. Bristol 1765.

The witness of the Spirit. Bristol 1767.

A plain account of Christian perfection as believed and taught by John Wesley from 1725 to 1765. Bristol 1770 (3rd edn), 1797 (8th edn).

Free thoughts on the present state of public affairs. 1770. Anon.

Minutes of several conversations between the Rev Messieurs John and Charles Wesley, and others. 1770 etc.

Thoughts upon slavery. 1774.

A calm address to our American colonies. Bristol 1775 etc.

A concise history of England. 4 vols 1776.

Some observations on liberty. Edinburgh 1776.

A serious address to the people of England. 1778.

Reflections on the rise and progress of the American rebellion. 1780.

A concise ecclesiastical history. 4 vols 1781. Anon.

A short account of the life and death of the Rev J. Fletcher. 1786.

Serious considerations concerning the doctrine of election and reprobation. 1790.

The Scripture doctrine concerning predestination. 1797.

Prayers. Ed F. C. Gill 1951; ed C. E. Vulliamy 1954; ed J. A. Kay 1958.

Letters, Diaries etc

Journal. 21 pts [1739]–91, 4 vols 1827; ed F. W. Macdonald 1906; ed N. Curnock 8 vols 1909–16; 4 vols 1922–30; abridged by P. L. Parker 2 vols 1902; by N. Ratcliffe 1940; by N. Curnock 1943. Selection ed H. Martin 1955.

Letters. Ed J. Telford 1931, 1956; Selections, ed F. C. Gill 1956.

§2

The pious life and heavenly death of the late Rev John Wesley. [1791?]. Anon.

Hampson, J. Memoirs of John Wesley. 3 vols Sunderland 1791.

Coke, T. and H. Moore. Life of John Wesley. 1792, 2 vols 1824–5.

Whitehead, J. Life of John and Charles Wesley. 2 vols 1793–6.

Burkhard, J. G. Vollständige Geschichte der Methodisten in England, nebst den Lebensbeschreibungen ihrer Stifter Johann Wesley und George Whitefield. 2 pts Nuremberg 1795.

Myles, W. Chronological history of the people called Methodists. Liverpool 1799.

Nightingale, J. Portraiture of Methodism. 1807.

Southey, R. Life of Wesley. 2 vols 1820, 1846 with) Coleridge's notes).

Watson, R. Observations on Southey's Life of Wesley 1820.

—— The life of the Rev John Wesley. 1831.

Creamer, D. Methodist hymnology, with notices on the poetical works of J. and Ch. Wesley. New York 1848.

Curnock, N. The father of Methodism. 1849.

Taylor, I. Wesley and Methodism. 1851.

Holmes, D. The Wesley offering: or Wesley and his times. Auburn 1852.

Hall, S. R. Illustrative records of John Wesley and early Methodism. 1856.

[Seeley, R. B.] The life of John Wesley. 1856.

Smith, G. History of Wesleyan Methodism. 3 vols 1857–61.

Hunt, J. Wesley and Wesleyanism. 1858.

Stevens, A. A history of Methodism. 3 vols 1860–70, 1863–5 (rev).

Hoole, E. Byrom and the Wesleys. 1864.

Lelièvre, M. John Wesley: his life and his work. 1868, 1871, 1900.

Rigg, J. H. The relations of John Wesley and Wesleyan Methodism to the Church of England. 1868.

—— The living Wesley. 1875.

Wakeley, J. B. Anecdotes of the Wesleys. 1869.

Stevenson, S. J. Memorials of the Wesley family. 1869.

—— The Methodist hymn book and its associations. 1870, 1883.

Urlin, R. D. John Wesley's place in church history. 1870.

Tyerman, L. The life and times of Wesley. 3 vols 1870–1.

Keyes, E. R. Wesley and Swedenborg. Philadelphia 1872.

Kirton, J. W. Methodism and the temperance reformation. 1873.

Christie, T. W. Methodism a part of the great Christian apostacy. 1881.

Green, R. John Wesley. 1881.

—— John Wesley: evangelist. 1905.

—— The conversion of John Wesley. 1909, 1937.

Telford, J. Life of Wesley. 1886, 1899 etc, Kansas City 1936.

Overton, J. H. John Wesley. 1891.

Hatfield, J. T. John Wesley's translations of German hymns. Baltimore 1896.

Kirlew, M. The story of John Wesley. 1896.

Gounelle, E. Wesley et ses rapports avec les Français. Nyons 1898.

Thompson, D. D. John Wesley as social reformer. New York 1898.

Banfield, F. John Wesley. 1900.

Snell, F. J. Wesley and Methodism. Edinburgh 1900.

Pike, G. H. Wesley and his preachers. 1903.

—— John Wesley: the man and his mission. 1904.

Fitchett, W. H. Wesley and his century. 1906.

Winchester, C. T. Life of John Wesley. New York 1906.

Faulkner, J. A. The Socialism of John Wesley. 1908.

—— Wesley as sociologist, theologian and churchman. New York 1918.

Léger, J. A. L'Angleterre religieuse et les origines du Méthodisme au 18e siècle: la jeunesse de Wesley. Paris 1910.

Bennetts, G. A. John Wesley versus Methodism. 1913.

Hughes, H. M. Wesley and Whitefield. 6 vols 1911–13.

—— Wesley's standards in the light of today. 1921.

Findlater, J. Perfect love: a study of Wesley's view of the ideal Christian life. Leith 1914.

Carter, H. The Methodist: a survey of the Christian way in two centuries. 1914, 1938 (enlarged).

Cadman, S. P. The three religious leaders of Oxford and their movements. New York 1916.

Griffiths, D. B. Wesley the Anglican. 1919.

Morton, H. C. Messages that made the revival. 1920.

Chapman, J. A. John Wesley's quest. 1921.

George, D. L. Tribute to Wesley and Methodism. 1922.

Gifford, W. A. John Wesley, patriot and statesman. Toronto 1922.

Barber, F. L. The philosophy of John Wesley. Toronto 1923.

Holmes, J. H. John Wesley and the methodist revolt. Toronto 1923.

Simon, J. S. John Wesley and the methodist societies. 1923.

—— John Wesley and the advance of Methodism. 1925.

—— John Wesley, the master builder. 1927.

—— Wesley: the last phase. 1934.

Henderson, B. W. John Wesley's last university sermon. Cornhill Mag Jan 1925.

Eayrs, G. John Wesley, Christian philosopher and Church founder. 1926.

Prince, J. W. Wesley on religious education. 1926.

Hutton, W. H. John Wesley. 1927.

Ellis, J. J. John Wesley: the man who revolutionised Britain. 1928.

Rattenbury, J. E. Wesley's legacy to the world. 1928.

—— The conversion of the Wesleys. 1938.

—— The eucharistic hymns of John and Charles Wesley; to which is appended Wesley's Preface extracted from Brevint's Christian sacrament and sacrifice, together with Hymns on the Lord's Supper. 1948.

Lunn, A. John Wesley. 1929.

Sommer, J. W. E. John Wesley und die soziale Frage. Bremen 1930.

Turner, E. E. John Wesley and mysticism. Methodist Rev 113 1930.

Wade, J. D. John Wesley. New York 1930.

Warner, W. J. The Wesleyan movement in the industrial revolution. 1930.

Wright, L. B. John Wesley: scholar and critic. South Atlantic Quart 29 1930.

Freeman, D. John Wesley's Journal. Nat Rev July 1931.

Vulliamy, C. E. Wesley. 1931, 1954 (3rd edn).

Laver, J. Wesley. 1932.

Dobrée, B. Wesley. 1933.

Edwards, M. L. Wesley and the eighteenth century. 1933, 1955.

—— After Wesley: a study of the influence of Methodism in the middle period 1791–1849. 1943.

—— Family circle: a study of the Epworth household in relation to John and Charles Wesley. 1949.

—— The astonishing youth. 1959.

—— Sons to Samuel. 1961.

Bell, H. I. New letters of John Wesley. BM Quart 8 1934.

Eicken, E. von. Rechtfertigung und Heiligung bei Wesley. Heidelberg 1934.

Simpson, W. J. S. Wesley and the Church of England. 1934.

Cell, G. C. The rediscovery of Wesley. New York 1935.

—— (ed). John Wesley's New Testament compared with the A.V. Philadelphia 1938.

Jackson, G. John Wesley as a bookman. London Quart 160 1935.

Body, A. H. Wesley and education. 1936.

Hutchinson, F. E. John Wesley and George Herbert. London Quart 161 1936.

Greeves, F. John Wesley and divine guidance. London Quart 162 1936.

Lee, U. Wesley and modern religion. Nashville 1936.

—— The Lord's horseman: John Wesley, the man. 1956.

McArthur, K. W. The economic ethics of Wesley. New York 1936.

Bowen, M. Wrestling Jacob: the life of Wesley and some members of his family. 1937, 1948.

Harrison, G. E. Son to Susanna: the private life of Wesley. 1937, New York 1944.

Ingram, W. G. John Wesley's books. TLS 14 Aug, 18 Sept 1937.

Piette, M. Wesley in the evolution of Protestantism. Tr J. B. Howard 1937. First pbd 1925.

Schmidt, M. John Wesleys Bekehrung. Bremen 1937.

—— Die Bedeutung Luthers für Wesleys Bekehrung. Luther Jahrbuch 20 1938.

Schimdt, M. John Wesley. Vol 1, 1703–38. Zürich 1953, London 1962.
— The young Wesley, missionary and theologian of missions. 1958.
— Wesley als Organisator der methodischen Bewegung. In Für Kirche und Recht: Festschrift J. Heckel, Zürich 1961.
Shepherd, T. B. John Wesley and Matthew Prior. London Quart 163 1937.
Birrell, A. John Wesley. 1938.
Brailsford, M. R. Susanna Wesley, mother of Methodism. 1938.
— A tale of two brothers. 1954.
Bready, J. W. England before and after Wesley. 1938.
Church, L. F. Knight of the burning heart. 1938.
Clark, E. J. (ed). What happened at Aldersgate. Nashville 1938.
Crook, W. The ancestry of the Wesleys. 1938.
Daw, A. R. John Wesley in Scotland: the bicentenary of Methodism. Scots Mag 29 1938.
Frost, S. B. Die Autoritätslehre in den Werken John Wesleys. Munich 1938.
Joy, J. R. John Wesley's awakening. 1938.
La Gorce, A. de. John Wesley, réformateur de l'Angleterre. Revue des Deux Mondes April 1938.
— Le réformateur Wesley et la monarchie anglaise. Revue Universelle 78 1939.
— Wesley: maître d'un peuple. Paris 1940.
Nottingham, E. K. The making of an evangelist. New York 1938.
Nuelsen, J. L. John Wesley und das deutsche Kirchenlied. Bremen 1938.
Pyke, R. John Wesley came this way. 1938.
Smith, N. G. The literary taste of John Wesley. Queen's Quart 45 1938.
The conversion of John Wesley: a date in English history. TLS 21 May 1938.
The 'conversion' of John Wesley: the significance of May 24 1738. London Quart 164 1938.
Turnell, W. J. John Wesley, physician and electrotherapist. Oxford 1938.
Alnwick, A. B. Wesley and ourselves. Baptist Quart 9 1939.
Baker, F. Wesley's printers and booksellers. Proc of Wesley Historical Soc 22 1939–40.
— John Wesley and the Imitatio Christi. London Quart 167 1941.
— A study of John Wesley's readings. London Quart 169 1943.
— John Wesley and John Bousell. Jnl of Friends' Historical Soc 40 1948.
— Jonathan Swift and the Wesleys. London Quart 179 1954.
— John Wesley's churchmanship. London Quart 185 1960.
— Wesley's puritan ancestry. London Quart 187 1962.
Harrison, F. M. Two Johns: Bunyan–Wesley. London Quart 165 1939.
Henderson, G. D. A Scottish teacher of the Wesleys. Ibid.
Hunter, F. The origins of Wesley's covenant service. Ibid.
Kamm, O. John Wesley und die englische Romantik. Marburg 1939.
McConnell, F. J. Wesley. 1939.
— New interest in John Wesley. Jnl of Religion 20 1940.
— Evangelicals, revolutionists and idealists. Nashville 1942.
McNeill, J. T. Luther at Aldersgate. London Quart 165 1939.
— Books of faith and power. New York 1947.
Beckerlegge, O. H. John Wesley and the German hymns. London Quart 166 1940.
Bett, H. John Wesley's translations of German hymns in reference to metre and rhyme. Ibid.

C., T. C. A John Wesley find. N & Q 6 July 1940. See V., 27 July 1940.
Hall, A. F. An unpublished sermon of John Wesley London Quart 166 1940.
Herbert, T. W. Wesley as editor and author. Princeton 1940.
Manning, B. L. Wesley's hymns reconsidered. London Quart 166 1940.
— The hymns of Wesley and Watts. 1942.
Belshaw, H. The influence of John Wesley on Dr Johnson's religion. London Quart 169 1943.
Davis, S. A centenary appreciation of Southey's Life of John Wesley. Ibid.
Sangster, W. E. The path to perfection: an examination of John Wesley's doctrine of Christian perfection. 1943.
— Wesley and sanctification. London Quart 172 1946.
Dilks, T. B. The Wesleys and others: letters found in salvage. TLS 11 Dec 1943. See 8 Jan 1944.
Doughty, W. L. John Wesley: his conferences and his preachers. 1944.
— John Wesley: preacher. 1955.
N., G. John Wesley's Complete English dictionary. N & Q 26 Aug 1944. See T. Murgatroyd 7 Oct, and H. L. Davis 18 Nov 1944.
Rights, D. L. A Moravian's report on John Wesley 1737. South Atlantic Quart 43 1944.
Green, J. B. Wesley and William Law. 1945.
Taylor, A. E. St John of the Cross and John Wesley. Jnl of Theological Stud 46 1945.
Barber, F. L. John Wesley edits a novel [Henry Brooke, The fool of quality]. London Quart 172 1946.
Brett, H. Wesley and Luther. Ibid.
Cannon, W. R. The theology of Wesley, with special reference to the doctrine of justification. Nashville 1946.
Havens, R. D. Southey's revisions of his Life of Wesley. RES 22 1946.
Lawson, J. Notes on Wesley's Fourty-four sermons. 1946.
Lindström, H. Wesley and sanctification. Stockholm 1946.
Pollard, C. A Wesley legacy. London Quart 172 1946.
Harding, F. A. J. The social impact of the evangelical revival. 1947.
Hunter, F. Manchester non-jurors and Wesley's High Churchism. London Quart 173 1947.
Leatham, W. H. John Wesley 1703–91. 1947.
Powell, J. John Wesley. 1947.
Baker, E. W. A herald of the evangelical revival: a critical enquiry into the relation of William Law to John Wesley. 1948.
Evans, C. The ancestry of the Wesleys. N & Q 12 June 1948.
Haire, R. Wesley's one-and-twenty visits to Ireland. 1948.
Church, L. F. Port Royal and John Wesley. London Quart 174 1949.
— A letter from John Wesley. London Quart 176 1951.
— The pastor in the 18th century. London Quart 181 1956.
Hughes, H. T. Jeremy Taylor and John Wesley. London Quart 174 1949.
Bebb, E. D. Wesley: a man with a concern. 1950.
Stevenson, R. John Wesley's first hymnbook. Rev of Religion 14 1950.
Hildebrandt, F. From Luther to Wesley. 1951.
— Christianity according to the Wesleys. 1956.
Mitton, C. L. A clue to Wesley's sermons. 1951.
Senior, M. M. John Wesley. 1951.
Sherwin, O. Milton for the masses: John Wesley's edition of Paradise Lost. MLQ 12 1951.
Yates, A. S. The doctrine of assurance, with special reference to John Wesley. 1952.
Bolster, G. R. Wesley's doctrine of justification. Evangelical Quart 24 1953.
Bowmer, J. C. John Wesley and Ireland. London Quart 178 1953.
— John Wesley's philosophy of suffering. London Quart 84 1959.

Leach, E. A. John Wesley's use of George Herbert. HLQ 16 1953.

Pilkington, F. An annotation to Wesley's Journal. London Quart 178 1953.

Schofield, R. E. John Wesley and science in 18th-century England. Isis 44 1953.

Kepler, T. S. (ed). Christian perfection as believed and taught by John Wesley. New York 1954.

Keylnack, W. S. John Wesley's six formative years. London Quart 179 1954.

Davey, C. J. John Wesley. 1955.

Doughty, W. L. Thomas Fuller and the Wesleys. London Quart 180 1955.

The prayers of Susanna Wesley. Ed W. L. Doughty 1956.

Thompson, E. W. Episcopacy: John Wesley's view. London Quart 181 1956.

—— John Wesley, superintendent. London Quart 181 1956.

—— Wesley, apostolic man. 1957.

Todd, J. H. John Wesley's legacy. Commonweal 10 1956.

de Pauly, W. C. A study in Christian perfection. Hermathena 39 1937.

Hindley, J. C. The philosophy of enthusiasm: a study in the origins of experimental theology. London Quart 182 1957.

Kingdon, R. M. Laissez-faire or government control: a problem for John Wesley. Church History 26 1957.

Maser, F. E. Problem in preaching: an analysis of the preaching power of John Wesley. London Quart 182 1957.

Hill, A. W. John Wesley among the physicians. 1958.

Swift, W. F. John Wesley's lectionary with notes on some later methodist lectionaries. London Quart 183 1958.

Todd, J. M. John Wesley and the Catholic Church. 1958.

Strawson, W. Wesley's doctrine of the last things. London Quart 184 1959.

White, H. W. Wesley's death through the eyes of the press. Ibid.

Henry, G. C. John Wesley's doctrine of free will. London Quart 185 1960.

Lofthouse, W. F. John Wesley's letters to his brother. Ibid.

Pask, A. H. The influence of Arminius on John Wesley. Ibid.

Williams, C. W. John Wesley's theology today. New York 1960.

Deschner, J. Wesley's Christology. 1961.

Golden, J. L. John Wesley on rhetoric and belles-lettres. Speech Monographs 28 1961.

Green, V. H. H. The young Mr Wesley. 1961, 1964.

Haddal, I. John Wesley. Tr 1961.

Kissack, R. Wesley's concept of his own ecclesiastical position. London Quart 186 1961.

Sherwin, O. John Wesley, friend of the people. New York 1961.

Gill, F. C. In the steps of John Wesley. 1962.

Harper, K. Law and Wesley. Church Quart Rev 163 1962.

Lawton, G. John Wesley's English: a study of his literary style. 1962.

Beecham, H. A. Samuel Wesley senior: new biographical evidence. Renaissance & Modern Stud 7 1963.

Lawson, A. B. John Wesley and the Christian ministry. 1963.

Parris, J. R. John Wesley's doctrine of the sacraments. 1963.

Cox, L. G. John Wesley's concept of perfection. Kansas City 1964.

England, M. W. The first Wesley hymn book 1737. BNYPL April 1964.

Outler, A. C. John Wesley. Oxford 1964.

Sparrow, J. George Herbert and John Donne among the Moravians. BNYPL Dec 1964.

Dorr, D. J. Wesley's teaching on the nature of holiness. London Quart 190 1965.

Malekin, P. William Law and John Wesley. Studia Neophilologica 37 1965.

Marshall, D. John Wesley. Oxford 1965.

Monk, R. C. John Wesley: his Puritan heritage. 1966.

Sanders, P. S. Wesley's eucharistic faith and practice. Anglican Theological Rev 48 1966.

WILLIAM WHISTON
1667–1752

The accomplishment of Scripture prophecies. Cambridge 1708. 8 Boyle lectures.

Sermons and essays upon several subjects. 1709.

An essay upon the epistles of Ignatius. 1710.

Historical preface to Primitive Christianity revived; with an account of the author's prosecution at, and banishment from, the University of Cambridge. 2 pts 1711.

Primitive Christianity revived. 5 vols 1711–12.

Primitive infant-baptism revived. 1712.

A collection of ancient monuments relating to the Trinity and Incarnation. 1713.

The eternity of Hell torments considered: a collection of liturgy of the Church of England reduced nearer to the primitive standard. 1713.

Three essays. 1713.

Scripture politics: or an impartial account of the origin and measures of government ecclesiastical and civil. 1717.

The true origin of the Sabellian and Athanasian doctrines of the Trinity. 1720.

An essay towards restoring the true text of the Old Testament. 1722; Supplement, 1723.

The literal accomplishment of Scripture prophecies. 1724.

The primitive Eucharist revived. 1736.

Texts of Scripture and testimonies of the three first centuries relating to them. 1740.

Three tracts. 1742.

Friendly address to the baptists. Stamford 1748.

Memoirs of the life and writings of William Whiston, written by himself. 3 pts 1749–50, 3 vols 1753.

See also col 1871, below.

GEORGE WHITEFIELD
1714–70
Bibliographies

Austin, R. Bibliography of the works of Whitefield. Burnley [1916].

Collections

Works. Ed J. Gillies 6 vols 1771–2.

Select works. Ed G.B. 1829.

Hymns for social worship. 1753 etc, 1794 (35th edn), 1799 (rev and enlarged), 1821 (9th edn); ed W. Chapman 1836 etc.

The Christian's companion: or sermons on several subjects. 10 pts 1738.

Discourses on [several] subjects. 21 pts 1739.

Nine sermons. 1742; Five sermons, 1747; Six sermons, 1750; Ten sermons, 1760; Twelve sermons, 1771 (2nd edn); Twenty-three sermons, 1770.

Sermons on important subjects. Ed J. Smith 1828.

Selected sermons. Ed A. R. Buckland 1904.

§1

A short account of God's dealings with George Whitefield. 1740; A full account, 1747; A further account, 1747.

A letter to John Wesley in answer to his sermon on free grace. 1740.

Three letters [1–2 concerning Archbishop Tillotson; 3 to the inhabitants of Maryland]. Philadelphia 1740.

Observations on some fatal mistakes in [William Warburton's] The doctrine of grace. 1743.

A letter to the remaining disconsolate inhabitants of Lisbon. 1755.

Letters, Diaries etc

A journal of a voyage from London to Savannah. 2 pts 1738, 1740.

A continuation of the Rev Mr Whitefield's journal. 1739, 1741.

A further continuation. 1741.

Journals. Ed W. Wale 1905; ed I. Murray 1960, 1962 (complete).

A select collection of letters. 3 vols 1772.

§2

Burkhard, J. G. Vollständige Geschichte der Methodisten in England; nebst den Lebensbeschreibungen ihrer Stifter Johann Wesley und George Whitefield. 2 pts Nuremberg 1795.

W.R. An authentic memoir. 1803.

Philip, R. Life and times of George Whitefield. 1837.

Newell, D. Life of George Whitefield. New York [1846].

Ryle, J. C. George Whitefield: the Bishop, the pastor, the preacher. 1852.

Quick, H. The results of Whitefield's labours. 1854.

Smith, G. T. The times and character of Whitefield. 1854.

Stoughton, J. The pen, the palm and the pulpit. 1858.

Andrews, J. R. Whitefield: a light rising in obscurity. 1864, 1930 (7th edn).

Harsha, D. A. Life of Whitefield. Albany NY 1866.

Wakeley, J. B. The prince of pulpit orators. New York 1871.

Gledstone, J. P. Life and travels of Whitefield. 1871.

— George Whitefield, field-preacher. 1900.

Tyerman, L. Life of Whitefield. 2 vols 1876-7. With bibliography.

Macaulay, J. Whitefield anecdotes. [1886].

Butler, D. John Wesley and Whitefield in Scotland. 1898.

Hughes, H. M. Wesley and Whitefield. 5 vols 1911-13.

Belden, A. D. Whitefield the awakener. 1930.

King, C. H. Whitefield, dramatic evangelist. Quart Jnl of Speech 19 1933.

Hardy, E. N. Whitefield, the matchless soulwinner. New York 1938.

Watson, C. E. George Whitefield and Gloucestershire Congregationalism: dates. Trans of Congregational Historical Soc 13 1939.

McConnell, F. J. Evangelicals, revolutionists and idealists. Nashville 1942.

A., E. L. Whitefield's Three letters from Savannah. More Books 18 1943.

King, C. H. Whitefield: God's commoner. Quart Jnl of Speech 29 1943.

— God's dramatist. In Studies in honor of A. M. Drummond, Ithaca 1944.

Lam, G. L. and W. H. Smith. Two rival editions of Whitefield's Journal, London 1738. SP 41 1944.

Loane, M. Oxford and the evangelical succession. 1950.

Henry, S. C. Whitefield, wayfaring witness. New York 1957.

Evans, R. W. The relations of Whitefield and Howell Harris, fathers of calvinistic Methodism. Church History 30 1961.

THOMAS WILSON
1663-1755

Collections

Works, with a life. Ed C. Cruttwell 2 vols Bath 1781, 8 vols Bath 1782-89, 1797-1808, 3 vols 1785; ed J. Keble 7 vols Oxford 1847-63 (Lib of Anglo-Catholic Theology).

Sermons. 1791, 4 vols 1795-6.

Thirty-three sermons. 2 vols 1823, 1825-7 etc.

§1

The principles and duties of Christianity in English and Manks. 1707, 1738 (6th edn).

The many advantages of a good language to any nation. 1724.

A short and plain instruction for the better understanding of the Lord's Supper. 1733 etc, 1819 (38th edn). The same work, in English and Manx, Whitehaven 1777.

The knowledge and practice of Christianity made easy: or an essay towards an instruction for the Indians. 1740, 1802 (17th edn).

The sacra privata: or private meditations and prayers. Ed C. Cruttwell, Bath 1781 etc.

Parochialia. Bath 1788 etc.

Diaries

Diaries 1731-7 and 1750. Ed C. L. S. Linnell 1964.

§2

Stowell, H. The life of Wilson. 1819.

Teale, W. H. In his Lives of English divines, 1846.

Rosser, J. The history of Wesleyan Methodism in the Isle of Man. Douglas 1849.

Hone, R. B. In his Lives of eminent Christians vol 1, 1851.

Keble, J. The life of Wilson. In Works vol 1, 1863, above.

Farrar, F. W. The saintly preacher. In J. E. Kempe, The classic preachers of the English Church ser 1, 1877.

Grove, P. B. Dr Johnson and the works of the Bishop of Sodor and Man. RES 16 1940.

C. THE EARLY QUAKERS

The library of the Friends House, London, contains the most comprehensive collection of Quaker books and mss, notably the Swarthmore mss, mainly unpbd. Joseph Smith, Descriptive catalogue of Friends' books, 3 vols with supplement (pbd 1867, but kept up to date) may be consulted there. See also his Bibliotheca antiquakeriana, 1873. The unpbd Swarthmore mss form a collection of about 1,400 original seventeenth-century letters, papers etc. For a bibliography of the letters in this collection see G. F. Nuttall, Early Quaker letters from the Swarthmore mss to 1660, calendared, indexed and annotated, 1952 (unpbd but available at Friends House and in a few American libraries). See also the Swarthmore College monographs on Quaker history, Swarthmore 1933-, and generally Jnl of Friends Historical Soc 1903- and Bull of Friends Historical Assoc of America (Haverford) 1906-.

General Studies

Penn, William. A brief account of the rise and progress of the people called Quakers. 1694. Introd to Fox's Journal, but also pbd separately.

Croese, G. The general history of the Quakers. 1696.

Sewel, William. The history of the Quakers. 1722. *See* W. I. Hull, William Sewel of Amsterdam 1653-1720:

the first Quaker historian of Quakerism. Swarthmore 1933.

Besse, J. A collection of the sufferings of the people called Quakers from 1650 to 1689. 1753.

Gough, J. A history of the people called Quakers. 4 vols Dublin 1789-90.

Clarkson, T. A portraiture of Quakerism. 3 vols 1806.

Barclay, J. Letters of early Friends. Illustrative of the history of the Society from its origin to George Fox's decease. 1841.

—— A select series: production of the early Friends. 8 vols 1835–45.

Hancock, T. The peculium: an endeavour to throw light on some of the causes of the decline of the Society of Friends. 1859.

Rowntree, J. S. Quakerism past and present. 1859.

—— An inquiry into the truthfulness of Lord Macaulay's portraiture of George Fox. York 1861.

Janney, S. M. History of the religious society of Friends, from its rise to the year 1828. 4 vols Philadelphia 1861–70.

Webb, M. The Fells of Swarthmore Hall and their friends. 1865.

—— The Penns and Peningtons of the 17th century. 1867.

Barclay, R. The inner life of the religious societies of the Commonwealth. 1876.

Beck, W. The Friends: who they are, what they have done. 1893.

Combe, C. La révélation intérieure immédiate d'après l'Apologie de Robert Barclay. Montauban 1894.

Gummere, A. M. The Quaker: a study in costume. Philadelphia 1901.

—— The Quaker in the forum. Philadelphia 1910.

Thomas, A. C. and R. H. A history of the Friends in America. Philadelphia 1905.

Harvey, T. E. The rise of the Quakers. 1905.

Penney, N. The first publishers of truth: early records of the introduction of Quakerism into the counties of England and Wales. 1907.

—— Extracts from State Papers relating to Friends 1654–72. 1910–11.

—— The household account-book of Sarah Fell. 1920.

Emmott, E. B. The story of Quakerism. 1908.

Grubb, E. Authority and the light within. 1908.

Burr, A. R. The autobiography: a critical and comparative study. Boston 1909.

Jones, R. M. Studies in mystical religion. 1904.

—— The Quakers in the American colonies. 1911.

—— Spiritual reformers in the 16th and 17th centuries. 1914.

—— The later periods of Quakerism 1725–1900. 2 vols 1921.

Locker-Lampson, S. F. A Quaker postbag 1693–1742. 1910.

Braithwaite, W. C. The beginnings of Quakerism 1647–1660. 1912. Drawn from original and to a large extent contemporary sources. This and the succeeding vols by Braithwaite and R. M. Jones form the most accurate history of Quakerism; rev H. J. Cadbury, Cambridge 1955.

—— The second period of Quakerism 1660–1725. 1919; rev H. J. Cadbury, Cambridge 1961.

Graham, J. W. The faith of a Quaker. Cambridge 1920. Bk 2 on theological writings of Fox, Barclay, Penington and Penn.

Nightingale, B. Early stages of the Quaker movement in Lancashire. 1921.

Brayshaw, A. N. The Quakers: their story and message. Harrogate 1921, 1938 (rev).

Christian life, faith and thought in the Society of Friends. 1922. Anthology of Quaker writers.

Knowles, G. H. Friends: some Quaker peace documents 1654–1920. 1927 (Grotius Soc), 1939.

—— Quakers and peace. 1927.

Grubb, I. Quakerism and industry before 1800. 1930.

Wright, L. M. The literary life of the early Friends 1650–1725. 1932.

—— Literature and education in early Quakerism. Univ of Iowa Stud (Humanistic ser 5) 2 1933.

Kirby, E. W. The Quakers' efforts to secure civil and religious liberty 1660–96. Jnl of Modern History 7 1935.

Binton, H. H. (ed). Children of light: in honor of R. M. Jones. New York 1938. Essays on Penn, Byllynge et al.

Hughes, W. R. Captain May's passengers. Blackwood's Mag 243 1938.

Dalglish, D. N. People called Quakers. Oxford 1938.

Nuttall, G. F. The Quakers and the Puritans. Congregational Quart 16 1938.

Gloel, E. Die Frau bei den Quäkern des 17 Jhts in England. Halle 1939.

Cadbury, H. J. (ed). The Swarthmore documents in America. 1940. 28 early Quaker letters now in USA.

—— Quakerism and early Christianity. 1957.

Russell, E. A history of Quakerism. New York 1942.

Tolles, F. B. Quietism versus enthusiasm: the Philadelphia Quakers and the Great Awakening. Pennsylvania Mag of History & Biography 69 1945.

—— 'Of the best sort but plain': the Quaker esthetic. Amer Quart 11 1959.

—— Quakers and the Atlantic culture. New York 1960.

Baker, F. The relations between the Society of Friends and early Methodism. London Quart 173–4 1948–9.

Bowmer, J. C. The relations between the Society of Friends and early Methodism. London Quart 175 1950.

Lloyd, A. Quaker social history 1669–1738. 1950.

Maclear, J. F. Quakerism and the end of the interregnum. Church History 19 1950.

Canter, B., (ed). The Quaker bedside book. 1952. Anthology of Quaker writings.

Vipont, E. The story of Quakerism 1652–1952. 1954.

Towlson, C. W. Moravian and Methodist: relationships and influences in the eighteenth century. 1957.

Sykes, N. The Quakers: a new look at their place in society. 1958.

Barbour, H. The Quakers in Puritan England. New Haven 1964.

GEORGE FOX
1624–91

Bibliographies

[Swanner, M.?] Annual catalogue of Fox's papers, compiled in 1694–7. Ed H. J. Cadbury, Philadelphia 1939 (with omissions and addns).
See also Journal, ed J. L. Nickalls, *below*.

Collections

Gospel truth demonstrated in a collection of doctrinal books given forth by Fox. 1706.
Works. Philadelphia 1831.

§ I

A declaration against all Popery. 1655.
The great misery of the great whore unfolded. 1659.
A battle-door for teachers and professors to learn singular and plural: you to many, and thou to one. 1660. By Fox, John Stubbs, Benjamin Furly.
Truth's triumph in the eternal power over the dark inventions of fallen man. 1661.
An answer to the arguments of the Jews. 1661.
The ancient simplicity as it was once witnessed unto. 1661.
Christ's light the only antidote to overcome and expel the poison of Satan's greatest temptations. 1662.
Three general epistles to be read in all the congregations of the righteous. 1664.
The arraignment of Popery. 1667.
Some principles of the elect people of God, scornfully called Quakers. 1671.
A looking-glass for the Jews. 1674.
Christian liberty commended. 1675.
Cain against Abel, representing New England's hierarchy. 1675.

The Christian judges so-called. 1676.
Concerning revelation, prophecy, measures and rule, and the inspiration and sufficiency of the spirit. 1676.
Concerning the true baptism and the false. 1676.
The beginning of tythes in the Law, and ending of tythes in the Gospel. 1676.
Concerning Christ, the spiritual and holy head over his holy Church. 1677.
Christ's parable of Dives and Lazarus. 1677.
What election and reprobation is clearly discovered. 1679.
Concerning the living God of truth. 1680.
The devil was and is the old informer against the righteous. 1682.
An encouragement for all to trust in the Lord. 1682.
Selection from the epistles. Ed S. Tuke 1825, 1848.
Fox's teaching of the indwelling presence of Christ. Selly Oak 1935. Quotations from Journal, below.
A day-book of counsel and comfort from the epistles of Fox. Ed L. V. Hodgkin 1937.
Fox's Book of miracles. Ed H. J. Cadbury, Cambridge 1948.

Letters, Diaries etc

A journal: or historical account of the life, travels, sufferings, Christian experiences and labours of love in the work of the ministry of Fox. 1694. Rev Thomas Ellwood; preface by William Penn. Called vol 1 of Journal.
A collection of epistles, letters and testimonials. 1698. Preface by George Whitehead. Called vol 2 of Journal.
A journal [i.e. vols 1–2]. 1709, 1765 etc; ed from mss N. Penney 2 vols 1901–2; ed Penney, introd by T. E. Harvey 2 vols 1911; abridged Penney, introd by R. M. Jones 1924; ed J. L. Nickalls, introd by G. F. Nuttall, epilogue by H. J. Cadbury, Cambridge 1952 (with full collection and bibliography of mss and edns).
Autobiography, from the Journal. Ed H. S. Newman 1886; ed R. M. Jones, Philadelphia 1903.
A short journal and itinerary journal of Fox, now first published. Ed N. Penney, Cambridge 1925.

§2

Tuke, H. In his Biographical notices of members of the Society of Friends vol 1, York 1813.
Evans, W. and T. Memoirs of the life of Fox. 1837 (Friends' Lib vol 1).
Marsh, J. A popular life of Fox, the first of the Quakers. 1847.
Janney, S. M. Life of Fox. Philadelphia 1853.
N., W. Fox and his friends as leaders in the peace cause. 1859.
Watson, J. S. Life of Fox. 1860.
Brown, W. Man's restoration by reconciliation with God, through Christ; with special reference to the teaching of Fox. 1860.
Rowntree, J. S. An inquiry into the truthfulness of Lord Macaulay's portraiture of Fox. 1861.
— The life and character of Fox. Oxford 1894.
Webb, M. The Fells of Swarthmoor Hall and their friends. 1865.
Spurgeon, C. F. George Fox. 1866.
Tallack, W. Fox, the Friends and the early Baptists. 1868.
Knox, W. The life and times of Fox. Bristol [1870].
A[sh], E. Fox: his character, doctrine and work. 1873.
Barclay, R. Inner life of the religious societies of the Commonwealth. 1876.
Beck, W. Six lectures on Fox and his times. 1877.
R[ailton], G. S. Fox: his life, travels, sufferings and death. 1881.
Bickley, H. C. Fox and the early Quakers. 1884.
Budge, J. Glimpses of Fox. [1888].
Douglas, E. Fox, the red-hot Quaker. 1894.
Deacon, H. Fox and the Quaker testimony. 1896.

Pickard, E. and F. Tregelles. Fox and his latest biographer. Falmouth 1896.
Budge, F. A. The story of Fox. 1899.
Jones, R. M. Fox: an autobiography. 2 vols Philadelphia 1903–4.
— George Fox. 1930.
Lewis, G. K. George Fox. 1903.
Swainson, W. P. Christian mystics no 3. [1903].
Stähelin, M. Fox: Aufzeichnungen und Briefe des ersten Quakers. Tübingen 1908.
Wood, H. G. George Fox. [1912].
Butler, D. Fox in Scotland. 1913.
Crosfield, H. G. Margaret Fox of Swarthmore Hall. 1913.
Danchin, F. C. Fox, névropathe. 1913.
Brayshaw, A. N. The personality of Fox. 1918, 1933.
Knight, R. The founder of Quakerism: a psychological study of the mysticism of Fox. 1922.
Etten, H. van. Fox, fondateur de la Société des amis. Paris 1923.
Newman, G. Fox, the founder of Quakerism. 1924.
Diamond, A. Fox and his teaching. 1928.
Hoyland, J. S. (ed). The man of fire and steel. 1932.
Cadbury, H. J. Richardson mss: further unpublished writings of Fox. Jnl of Friends' Historical Soc 32 1935.
— The horizon of Fox's early visions. Bull of Friends' Historical Assoc 47 1958.
A. R. Barclay mss. Jnl of Friends' Historical Soc 33 1936, 35 1938, 48 1958. Letters to Fox.
King, R. H. Fox and the light within 1650–60. Philadelphia 1940.
Pritchett, V. S. The steeple house spires. In his In my good books, 1942.
Nuttall, G. F. Fox and the rise of Quakerism in the Bishoprick. Durham Univ Jnl 5 1944.
Held, P. Der Quäker Fox. Basle 1949.
Ross, I. Margaret Fell, mother of Quakerism. 1949.
Bullett, G. In his English mystics, 1950.
Wragge, J. P. George Fox. 1950.
Noble, V. The man in leather breeches: the life and times of Fox. 1953.
Jannelle, P. A propos de l'enthousiasme. Etudes Anglaises 8 1955.

WILLIAM PENN

1644–1718

Bibliographies

'Philalethes' (Henry Portsmouth). An index to Penn's works. 1730.

Collections

A collection of the works of Penn; to which is prefixed a Journal of his life, with many original letters. Ed J. Besse 2 vols 1726.
Select works; to which is prefixed a Journal. Ed J. Fathergill 1771, 5 vols 1782, 3 vols 1825.
The peace of Europe; The fruits of solitude and other writings. Ed J. V. Cheney 1906.
Selections from the works. Ed I. Sharpless 1909.

§1

Sandy foundation shaken. 1668.
Innocency with her open face. 1669.
No cross, no crown. 1669 etc; ed J. D. Hilton 1902; ed N. Penney 1930.
The great case of liberty of conscience. 1670.
The people's ancient and just liberties asserted. 1670 etc.
A seasonable caveat against Popery. 1670.
A serious apology for the principles and practices of the people called Quakers. 1671. With G. Whitehead.
The spirit of truth vindicated. 1672.
The new witnesses proved old heretics. 1672. Against Muggleton.

The Christian Quaker and his divine testimony vindicated. 2 pts 1674–3, 1699. Pt 1 by Penn, pt 2 by G. White-head.

The continued cry of the oppressed for justice. 1675.

A treatise of oaths. 1675. With R. Richardson.

An address to Protestants upon the present conjunction. 1679, 1692.

A brief account of the province of Pennsylvania. 1681. Facs in Mass Historical Soc, Americana ser 115 1924.

A brief examination and state of liberty spiritual. 1681.

The frame of Government of the province of Pennsylvania. 1682; ed M. G. Brumbaugh and J. S. Walton, Philadelphia 1898.

A brief description of Pennsylvania. 1683.

A further account of the province of Pennsylvania and its improvements. 1685.

A persuasive to moderation to Church dissenters. 1686; in California State Library, Suto Branch, occasional papers, English ser 6 pt 4 1940.

A letter upon the subject of penal laws and tests. 1687; A second letter, 1687; A third letter, 1687.

Good advice to the Church of England, Roman Catholic and Protestant dissenter. 1687. Against penal laws and tests.

The reasonableness of toleration. 1687.

The speech of William Penn to his Majesty upon the delivering the Quakers' address [after the declaration of indulgence]. 1687.

The great and popular objection against the repeal of the penal laws and tests. 1688.

Three letters on the abolishment of the penal laws and tests. 1688.

A key to discern the difference between the Quakers and their adversaries. 1693.

Some fruits of solitude. 1693 etc; ed E. Gosse 1900; ed J. Clifford 1905; ed J. V. Cheney 1906.

An account of [his] travels in Holland and Germany anno 1677. 1694 etc; ed J. Barclay 1835.

A brief account of the rise and progress and the people called Quakers. 1694. First pbd as Preface to Fox's Journal, 1694.

A call to Christendom. 1695 (2nd edn).

Primitive Christianity revived. 1696, Dublin 1702, 1779 (5th edn).

Fruits of a father's love: being advice to his children. 1726, 1780 (8th edn).

The harmony of divine and heavenly doctrines. 1723 (2nd edn). By Penn, G. Whitehead et al.

An essay towards the present and future peace of Europe. Ed J. B. Braithwaite, Gloucester 1915.

Letters, Journal

My Irish journal 1669–70. Ed I. Grub 1952.

Letters from Penn to Charles II. Philadelphia 1826 (Historical Soc of Pennsylvania, Memoirs vol 1 pt 2).

Inedited letters. Philadelphia 1826 (Memoirs vol 2 pt 2).

Correspondence between Penn and J. Logan and others. Ed E. Armstrong, Philadelphia 1826 (Memoirs vols 9–10).

§2

Besse, J. A confutation of the charge of Deism, wherein the sentiments of William Penn are cleared. 1734.

Rack, E. The life and character of Penn. In Caspipinas letters, 2 vols 1777.

Marsillac, J. La vie de Penn. Paris 1791.

Proud, R. The history of Pennsylvania, with the life of Penn. Philadelphia 1797.

Clarkson, T. Memoirs of Penn. 2 vols 1813.

Robson, M. Life of Penn. Philadelphia 1828.

Draper, B. H. The life of Penn, with his reflections and maxims. [1834?].

Fisher, J. F. A discourse on the private life and habits of Penn. Philadelphia 1836.

Weems, M. L. Life of Penn, the settler of Pennsylvania. Philadelphia 1836.

Sparks, J. Lives of eminent individuals celebrated in American history. 3 vols Boston 1836.

Alcott, W. A. Sketches of Penn. Boston 1839.

Ellis, G. E. Life of Penn. 1844.

Barker, J. Life of Penn. 1847.

Fairbairn, H. A defence of Penn from the charges in the History of England by T. B. Macaulay. Philadelphia 1849.

Foster, W. E. Memoirs of the life of Penn, with a preface in reply to the charges made by Macaulay in his History of England. 1849.

Dixon, W. H. Penn: an historical biography. 1851.

Janney, S. M. Life of Penn. Philadelphia 1852.

Jeffrey, F. Contributions to the Edinburgh Review. 3 vols 1853. Contains reviews of T. Clarkson, Portraiture of Quakerism, 1807; Memoirs of Penn, 1813.

Lewis, E. Memoirs of the life of Penn. Philadelphia 1857.

Paget, J. An inquiry into the evidence relating to the charges brought by Lord Macaulay against Penn. Edinburgh 1858; rptd as The new examen, 1861; ed W. S. Churchill, Halifax 1934.

Correspondence relating to Penn communicated by the Earl of Ellesmere. Bibl & Historical Miscellanies 6 1860.

Kingston, W. H. G. A true hero: or the story of Penn. [1872].

Vincens, C. William Penn. Paris 1877.

Harrison, G. L. The remains of Penn. Philadelphia 1882.

Stoughton, J. Penn, the founder of Pennsylvania. 1882.

Budge, J. William Penn. [1885].

Buck, W. J. Penn in America. Philadelphia 1888.

Thomas, A. C. Penn, the founder of Pennsylvania and his holy experiment. 1895.

Jenkins, H. M. The family of Penn. Philadelphia 1899.

Cooke, F. E. The story of Penn. 1899.

Sharpless, I. A history of Quaker government in Pennsylvania. 2 vols Philadelphia 1900.

Fischer, S. G. The true Penn. Philadelphia 1900.

Pennsylvania, colonial and federal. Ed H. M. Jenkins 3 vols Philadelphia 1903.

Buell, A. C. Penn as the founder of two commonwealths. New York 1904.

Sessions, F. Penn, soldier of the cross and empire builder. 1905.

Colquhoun-Grant, Mrs. Quaker and courtier: the life and work of Penn. 1907.

Holland, R. S. William Penn. New York 1915.

Graham, J. W. Penn, founder of Pennsylvania. 1917.

Riddell, W. R. Penn and witchcraft. Jnl of Amer Inst of Criminal Law & Criminology 18 1927.

Sellick, G. G. Penn, Quaker and colonist. 1929.

Brailsford, M. R. The making of Penn. 1930.

— Penn, founder of Pennsylvania. 1944, 1948.

Smyth, C. Penn, courtier and founder of colonies. New York 1931.

Dobrée, B. Penn, Quaker and pioneer. 1932.

Pound, A. The Penns of Pennsylvania. 1932.

Umbendstock, R. Penn et les précurseurs de Genève de 1500 à 1815. Saint Dizier 1932.

Vulliamy, C. E. William Penn. 1933.

Fogelkou, E. M. William Penn. Stockholm 1935; tr German, 1948.

Hull, W. I. Penn and the Dutch Quaker migration to Pennsylvania. Swarthmore 1935.

— (ed). Eight first biographies of Penn. Swarthmore 1936.

— Penn: a topical biography. 1937.

Mood, F. Penn and English politics in 1680–1: new light on the granting of the Pennsylvania Charter. Jnl of Friends' Historical Soc 32 1935.

Konkle, B. A. A new view of Penn. Pennsylvania History 4 1937.

Beatty, E. C. O. Penn as social philosopher. New York 1939.

— Penn, pragmatist. Bull of Friends' Historical Assoc 19 1940.

Goldman, I. Deviation toward ideas of natural ethics in the thought of Penn. PQ 18 1939.

Pitt, A. S. Franklin and Penn's No cross, no crown. MLN 54 1939.

Wright, L. M. Penn and the Royal Society. Bull of Friends' Historical Assoc 30 1941.

Hess, M. W. Penn and Isaac Penington. Commonweal 2 June 1943.

Comfort, W. W. William Penn. Philadelphia 1944.

— Penn and our liberties. Philadelphia 1947.

Wood, W. G. William Penn. 1944.

Hodgkin, L. V. Gulielma, wife of Penn. 1947.

Perry, J. W. I will not budge: an account of the formative years in the life of Penn. 1948.

Cadbury, H. J. More Penn correspondence, Ireland 1660–70. Pennsylvania Mag of History & Biography 73 1949.

— Hannah Callowhill and Penn's second marriage. Pennsylvania Mag of History & Biography 81 1957.

Oakley, V. The holy experiment: our heritage from Penn. Philadelphia 1951.

Langston, B. Penn and Chaucer. N & Q Feb 1954.

M., R. S. Penn and his printer. Jnl of Friends' Historical Soc 46 1954.

Pearce, C. O. Penn: a biography. Philadelphia 1957, 1960.

Tolles, F. B. and E. G. Alderfer (ed). The witness of Penn. New York 1957.

Maples, M. Penn, classical republican. Pennsylvania Mag of History & Biography 81 1957.

Roger, T. Letters of Penn and Richard Baxter. Jnl of Friends' Historical Soc 48 1958.

Buranelli, V. Penn and the Socinians. Pennsylvania Mag of History & Biography 83 1959.

— Penn and James II. Proc of Amer Philosophical Soc 104 1960.

— The King and the Quaker: Penn and James II. Philadelphia 1962.

Goodbody, O. C. and M. Pollard. The first edition of Penn's Great Case of liberty of conscience 1670. Library 5th ser 16 1961.

Olson, G. Penn, Parliament and the proprietary government. William & Mary Quart 3rd ser 18 1961.

Bronner, E. B. Penn's Holy experiment: the founding of Pennsylvania 1681–1701. New York 1962.

Dunn, M. M. Penn: politics and conscience. Princeton 1967.

ISAAC PENINGTON
1616–79
Collections

The works of the long-mournful and sorely distressed Isaac Penington. 2 pts 1680–1, 2 vols 1761, 4 vols 1784, New York 1861–3.

Selections from the works. Ed J. Barclay 1837.

The life hid with Christ in God: selections from the works. Ed C. J. Westlake 1876.

Selections from the works. Ed H. B. Binns 1909.

The inward journey: an abbreviation of Penington's Works (2nd edn 1761). Ed R. J. Leach 1944.

The hidden life: extracts from the writings of Penington. Ed R. Davis 1951.

§1

A touchstone or trial of faith. 1648.

The great and soule troubler of the times: or a glimpse of the heart of man. 1649.

The fundamental right, safety and liberty of the people. 1651.

The life of a Christian. 1653.

Divine essays. 1654.

The scattered sheep sought after. 1659, 1665.

The new covenant of the gospel distinguished from the old covenant of the law. 1660.

The great question concerning the lawfulness or unlawfulness of swearing. 1661.

Concerning the sum and substance of our religion, who are called Quakers. 1667.

Of the Church in its first and pure state, in its declining state, in its declined state and in its recovery. 1668.

The holy truth and people defended. 1672.

Naked truth. 1674.

The flesh and blood of Christ, with a brief account concerning the people called Quakers. 1675.

Letters

Letters to his relations and friends. Ed J. Kendall 1796.

Letters, the greater part not published before. Ed J. Barclay 1828, 1844 (3rd edn).

§2

Bevan, J. G. Memoirs of the life of Penington. 1807.

Budge, F. A. The shield of faith: a sketch of Isaac and Mary Penington. 1878.

Hess, M. W. The name is living: the life and teachings of Penington. Chicago 1936.

— William Penn and Penington. Commonweal 2 June 1943.

ROBERT BARCLAY
1648–90
Collections

Truth triumphant through the spiritual warfare: Christian labours and writings of Barclay. 1692. Collected works, with preface by William Penn.

§1

A catechism and confession of faith. 1673, 1803 (8th edn).

Theses theologicae. Ed B. Furly 2 pts Rotterdam 1674, 1675; tr 1711.

Theologiae verae Christianae apologia. Amsterdam 1676; tr as An apology for the true Christian divinity, Aberdeen 1678 etc; ed W. Allen 1837 (selections).

Quakerism confirmed: or a vindication of the chief doctrines and principles of the people called Quakers. 1676. With George Keith.

The anarchy of the Ranters and other libertines. 1676.

Universal love considered and established upon its right foundation. 1677.

Apology vindicated. 1679.

Barclay in brief: a condensation of Apology for the true Christian divinity. Ed E. P. Mather, Pendle Hill Pa 1941.

Letters

Reliquiae Barclaianae. Ed D. Barclay 1870.

§2

Barclay, R. (the younger). A genealogical account of the Barclays of Urie, with memoirs of Robert Barclay. 1740; ed H. Mill 1812.

Bevan, J. G. A short account of the life and writings of Barclay. 1802.

Eaton, J. Barclay and Penn self-vindicated. 1836.

Armistead, W. Memoir. 1850.

Budge, F. A. The Barclays of Ury. 1881.

Rhodes, B. Three apostles of Quakerism: Fox, Penn and Barclay. 1885.

Cadbury, M. C. Barclay: his life and work. 1912.

— The story of Barclay. New York 1926.

Wragge, J. P. The faith of Barclay. 1948. Selections with short biography.

THOMAS ELLWOOD
1639–1713
Collections

A collection of poems on various subjects. [1730?].

§1

A seasonable dissuasive from persecution. 1683.
Rogero-mastix: a rod for William Rogers. 1685. Verse.
Sacred history: or the historical part of the Holy Scriptures. 1705–9, 1794 (5th edn).
The glorious brightness of the gospel day. 1707.
Davideis: a sacred poem. 1712 etc; ed W. Fischer, Heidelberg 1936.
The history of the life of Ellwood written by his own hand. Ed J. W[yeth] 1714, 1791 (4th edn); ed C. G. Crump 1900; ed S. Graveson 1906.

§2

The lives of Lord Herbert of Cherbury and Thomas Ellwood, with essays by W. D. Howells. Boston 1877.
Budge, F. A. Ellwood and other worthies. 1891.
Brown, A. K. Ellwood, the friend of Milton. 1910.
Fischer, W. Zur Textgeschichte von Ellwoods Davideis 1712–96. Anglia 45 1931.
Snell, B. S. Thomas Ellwood. 1934, 1949.
—— The making of Ellwood. Jnl of Friends' Historical Soc 36 1939.
Brink, A and H. Ellwood's Davideis: a newly discovered version. Jnl of Friends' Historical Soc 49 1959.
See also col 473, above.

OTHER WRITERS

For Scottish Quakers, and anti-Quakers, see col 2031, below.
Bellers, John (1654–1725). Proposals for raising a college of industry. 1695, 1696.
—— Supplement to the proposal for a college of industry. 1696; ed W. H. Dunham and S. Pargellis in Complaint and reform in England 1436–1714, New York 1938.
—— Essays about the poor, manufactures, trade, plantations and immorality, and of the excellency and divinity of inward light. 1699.
—— Watch unto prayer. 1703.
—— Some reasons for a European state. 1710.
—— An essay for employing the poor to profit. 1723.
—— An abstract of George Fox's Advice and warning to the magistrates of London concerning the poor. 1724.
—— To the criminals in prison. 1725.
Seipp, C. John Bellers: ein Vertreter des frühen Quäkertums. Nuremberg 1933.
Fry, A. R. John Bellers 1654–1725, Quaker, economist and social reformer: his writings reprinted, with a memoir. 1935.
Burnyeat, John. The truth exalted in the writings of that eminent and faithful servant of Christ John Burnyeat. 1691. With preface by William Penn.
—— Journal of the life and gospel labours of William Caton and Burnyeat. Ed W. and T. Evans, Philadelphia 1837; ed A. R. Barclay 1839.
Burrough, Edward (1634–63). The memorable works of a son of thunder and consolation, with a testimony concerning Burrough's life by Francis Howgill. Ed E. Hooker 1672.
—— This is for the people called Quakers. 1675. Selections ed John Pennyman.
—— Three early Quaker writings [A declaration of the sad and great persecution and martyrdom of the people of God called Quakers, 1660; To the rulers and to such as are in authority, 1695; A vindication of the people of God called Quakers, 1660]. San Francisco 1939.

Evans, W. and T. A memoir of the life and religious labours of Burrough. Philadelphia 1850.
Taylor, E. E. Burrough: son of thunder and consolation. 1931.
Brockbank, E. Burrough: a wrestler for truth. 1949.
Caton, William (1636–65). Truths caracter of professors and their teachers. 1660.
—— The testimony of a cloud of witnesses against persecution about matters of religion. 1662.
—— A journal of the life of Caton. Ed G. Fox 1689. *See* also under Burnyeat, above.
—— Journal and letters. Ed W. and T. Evans, Philadelphia 1837.
Davies, Richard (1635–1708). An account of the convincement, exercises, services and travels of that ancient servant of the Lord, Richard Davies; with some relation of ancient friends and the spreading of truth in North Wales. 1710 etc.
Dewsbury, William (1621–88). The faithful testimony of that ancient servant of the Lord and minister of the everlasting gospel, William Dewsbury. 1689.
—— Several letters written to the saints of the most high. 1654.
—— Letters to William Dewsbury and others. Ed H. J. Cadbury 1948.
—— The discovery of man's return to his first estate by the operation of the power of God in the great work of regeneration. 1654.
—— The discovery of the great enmity of the serpent against the seed of woman. 1655.
—— Christ exalted, and alone worthy to open the seals of the book. 1656.
Smith, E. The life of William Dewsbury. 1836.
Edmundson, William (1627–1712). A journal of the life, travels, sufferings and labours of love in the ministry of Edmundson. 1715 etc.
Fisher, Samuel (1605–65). Rusticus ad academicos: the rustick's alarm to the rabbies, or the country correcting the university and the clergy. 6 pts 1660.
—— The testimony of truth exalted, by the collected labours of Fisher etc, Επισκοτος Αποσκοπος. 2 pts 1679.
Furly, Benjamin (1636–1714). Bibliotheca Furliana: sive catalogus librorum docti viri Benjamin Furly. Rotterdam 1714.
Hull, W. I. Furly and Quakerism in Rotterdam. Swarthmore 1941.
Gratton, John (1641–1712). A journal of the life of that ancient servant of Christ, John Gratton; with a collection of his books and mss. Ed J. Whiting 1720 etc; ed W. and J. Evans, Philadelphia 1837.
—— A treatise concerning baptism and the Lord's Supper. 1695.
Howgill, Francis (1618–69). The common salvation contended for. 1654.
—— The inheritance of Jacob discovered after his return out of Aegypt. 1656; tr Dutch, 1660.
—— Some of the mysteries of Gods Kingdom declared, as they have been revealed by the spirit through faith. 1658.
—— The glory of the true Church discovered. 1661, 1662, 1663; tr Dutch, 1670.
—— A general epistle to all who have believed in the light of the Lord Jesus. 1665.
—— Testimony concerning the life of Edward Burrough. *See* under Burrough, above.
—— The dawnings of the gospel day and its light and glory discovered. 1676.
—— Memoirs, with extracts from his writings. Ed J. Backhouse, York 1828.
Lurting, Thomas (1629–1713). The fighting soldier turned peaceable Christian, with a short relation of many great dangers and wonderful deliverances. 1710 etc; rptd in C. Vipont's novel, Blow the man down, Oxford 1939.
Narrative of Thomas Lurting. 1821.

Thomas Lurting, naval man who became non-fighting Quaker. 1917.

Mollineux, Mary. *See col 478, above.*

Nayler, James (1617–60). A collection of sundry books, epistles and papers written by Nayler, with an impartial relation of the most remarkable transactions relating to his life. 9 pts 1716.

— A lamentation over the ruins of this oppressed nation. York 1653.

— A salutation to the seeds of God. 1655 etc.

— Love to the lost. 1656.

— The lambs war against the man of sin. 1657.

— What the possession of the living faith is, and the fruits thereof. 1659.

Nayler, James and Richard Hubberthorn. An account from the children of light: why we have kept from joining to those forms of worship that have been imposed upon us against our consciences. 1660.

Memoirs of the life of Nayler. 1719.

Hughson, D. The life of Nayler [1814]. In M. Aiken, Memoirs of religious impostors, 1821.

Brailsford, M. R. A Quaker from Cromwell's army: James Nayler. 1927.

Fogelkou, E. Nayler, the rebel saint. Tr 1931.

Nuttall, G. F. Nayler: a fresh approach. 1954.

Parnell, James (1637?–56). A collection of the several writings given forth from the spirit of the Lord through James Parnell. Ed S. Crisp 1675.

— A trial of faith. 1654; tr French, 1660; Dutch, 1675; German, 1681.

— The lamb's defence against lies, and A true testimony concerning the sufferings and death of James Parnell. 1656.

Smith, C. F. James Parnell. 1906.

Wright, L. M. John Bunyan and Steven Crisp. Jnl of Religion 19 1939.

Penington, Mary. Some account of her exercises from childhood. [1680].

— Her testimony concerning her dear husband. In Isaac Penington, Works, 1681 etc.

Roberts, John (1623?–84). Some memoirs of the life of John Roberts, by his son Daniel. Exeter 1746 etc (abridged); ed J. Thompson 1859; ed J. Bellows (as The life of John Roberts, a Gloucestershire farmer of the time of Charles II, by his son), Gloucester 1891; ed E. T. Lawrence 1898 (complete, as A Quaker of the olden time).

Story, Thomas (1670?–1742). Discourse delivered in the public assemblies of the people called Quakers by T.S. 1738. From shorthand notes.

— Journal. Ed J. and J. Wilson, Newcastle 1747; ed W. and T. Evans, Philadelphia 1837.

— Selections from the Journal. Manchester 1830.

— Sermons preached by Story and J. Gurney. 1785.

M., M. A collection of some writings of the most noted of the people called Quakers. 1767.

Kendall, J. Life of Story. 2 vols York 1832.

Dalglish, D. N. People called Quakers. Oxford 1938. Includes studies of Story, John Woolman and Thomas Wilkinson.

Moore, E. E. Travelling with Story: the life and travels of an 18th-century Quaker. Letchworth 1947.

Whitehead, George (1636?–1723). A serious account why the people of God called Quakers cannot go to worship at those places called churches and chapels. 1661.

— The light and life of Christ within. 1668.

— The divinity of Christ and unity of the three that bear record in heaven. 2 pts 1669.

— The Quakers' plainness detecting fallacy. 1674.

— Piety promoted by faithfulness. 1686.

— The divine light in man. 1692.

— An evangelical epistle to the people of God. 1704.

— Sermons. In Sermons preached by several of the people called Quakers, 1775.

— Christian progress. Ed J. Besse 1725; ed S. Tuke 2 vols York 1830 (as Memoirs of Whitehead). An autobiography.

— Whitehead: his work and service as a minister for sixty-eight years in the Society of Friends, compiled from his autobiography by William Beck. 1901.

Barlow, J. H. Whitehead, the last of the early Friends. 1908.

D. THE MYSTICS

GENERAL STUDIES

The earlier part of this section is abbreviated and rearranged from the bibliography by Caroline Spurgeon, CHEL vol 9 pp. 510–23, which supplies much supplementary information, especially on the continental background. See also under B. Eighteenth-Century Divines, above.

Fox, George. A journal: or historical account of the life, travels and sufferings of George Fox. 1694; ed N. Penney and T. E. Harvey 2 vols 1911; ed. J. L. Nickalls, Cambridge 1952.

Baxter, Richard. Reliquiae Baxterianae: or Mr Richard Baxter's narrative of the most memorable passages of his life and times. 1696.

Woodward, J. An account of the rise and progress of the religious societies. 1701 (3rd edn).

Gichtel, J. G. Theosophia practica. Leyden 1722 (3rd edn).

Sewel, W. The history of the rise, increase and progress of the Quakers. 1722.

Southey, R. The life of Wesley, with notes by S. T. Coleridge. 2 vols 1846.

Marsden, J. B. History of Christian Churches and sects. 2 vols 1856.

Pattison, M. Tendencies of religious thought in England. In Essays and reviews, 1860, and Essays by Mark Pattison vol 2, Oxford 1889.

Wedgwood, J. John Wesley and the evangelical reaction of the 18th century. 1870.

Blunt, J. H. Dictionary of sects, heresies, ecclesiastical parties and schools of religious thought. 1874.

Barclay, R. The inner life of the religious societies of the Commonwealth. 1876.

Stephen, L. History of English thought in the 18th century. 2 vols 1876, 1927 (rev).

Overton, J. H. and C. J. Abbey. The English Church in the 18th century. 2 vols 1878.

Perry, G. G. The student's English Church history. Vols 2–3, 1878–87.

Vaughan, R. A. Hours with the mystics. 2 vols 1880.

Lecky, W. E. H. A history of England in the 18th century. Vols 1–2, 1883–7 (rev).

Abbey, C. J. The English Church and its Bishops 1700–1800. 2 vols 1887.

Julian, J. A dictionary of hymnology 1892, 1907 (rev).

Skeats, H. S. A history of the Free Churches of England. 1894.

Récejac, E. Essai sur les fondements de la connaissance mystique. Paris 1897; tr 1899.

Inge, W. R. Christian mysticism. 1899.

— Studies of English mystics. 1906.

De la Croix, H. Études d'histoire et de psychologie du mysticisme. Paris 1908.

Jones, R. M. Studies in mystical religion. 1909.

Underhill, E. Mysticism. 1911, 1930 (rev).
— The mystics of the Church. [1925].
Silberer, H. Problems of mysticism and its symbolism. New York 1917.
Davis, J. L. Mystical versus enthusiastic sensibility. JHI 4 1943.
Thune, N. The Behmenists and the Philadelphians. Upsala 1948.
Bullett, G. The English mystics. 1950.
Langton, E. History of the Moravian Church. 1956.
— N. L. Zinzendorf: the Count who became a Bishop. London Quart 182 1957.
Armytage, W. H. G. The Moravian communities in Britain. Church Quart Rev 158 1957.
— The Behmenists. Church Quart Rev 160 1959.
Towlson, C. W. Moravian and Methodist: relationships and influences in the 18th century. 1957.
Lewis, A. J. Count Zinzendorf: the apostle of Christian unity. 1960.

WILLIAM LAW
1686–1761

Collections
Works. 9 vols 1753–76; ed G. B. Morgan 9 vols Brockenhurst 1892–3 (priv ptd) (with memoir).
Liberal and mystical writings. Ed W. S. Palmer and W. P. Du Bosc 1908.
Selected mystical writings. Ed with twenty-four essays in the mystical theology of William Law and Jacob Boehme by S. Hobhouse 1938, 1948 (rev).
The pocket William Law. Ed A. W. Hopkinson 1950. Abridged edn of Christian perfection, An appeal to all that doubt, and The spirit of prayer.

§I
A sermon preached at Hazelingfield 7 July 1713. 1713. Not collected.
The Bishop of Bangor's late sermon and his letter to Dr Snape in defence of it, answered. 1717 etc, 1721 (8th edn).
A second letter to the Bishop of Bangor. 1717.
A reply to the Bishop of Bangor's answer to the representation of the committee of Convocation. 1719.
Three letters to the Bishop of Bangor 1717–19. 1753; ed J. O. Nash and C. Gore as Law's Defence of Church principles, 1893.
Remarks upon the Fable of the bees. 1724, 1725, 1726 etc; ed F. D. Maurice, Cambridge 1844.
The absolute unlawfulness of the stage-entertainments fully demonstrated. 1726 etc, 1759 (4th edn).
A practical treatise of Christian perfection. 1726 etc; ed L. H. M. Soulsby 1901; ed J. J. Trebeck 1902; abridged by J. Wesley as The nature and design of Christianity, 1740 etc.
A serious call to a devout and holy life. 1728 etc, 1772 (10th edn); ed J. H. Overton 1898; ed C. Bigg 1899, 1906; ed N. Sykes 1955. Many selections.
The case of reason: or natural religion fairly stated in answer to [M. Tindal's] Christianity as old as the creation. 1731, 1755, 1757.
A demonstration of the errors of [Bishop Hoadly's] A plain account of the nature and end of the sacrament of the Lord's Supper. 1737 etc, 1757 (4th edn).
The grounds and reasons of Christian regeneration. 1739, 1750 (3rd edn).
An answer to Dr Trapp's Discourse of the folly, sin and danger of being righteous overmuch. 1740.
An appeal to all that doubt or disbelieve the truths of the gospel; to which are added Some animadversions upon Dr Trapp's late reply. 1740, 1742.
The spirit of prayer: or the soul rising out of the vanity of time into the riches of eternity. 2 pts 1749–50.

The way to divine knowledge. 1752.
The spirit of love: being an appendix to the Spirit of prayer. 2 pts 1752–4.
Reflections on a favourite amusement [i.e. the theatre]. 1756.
A short but sufficient confutation of Dr Warburton's Projected defence (as he calls it) of Christianity in his Divine legation of Moses. 1757.
Of justification by faith and works: a dialogue between a Methodist and a Churchman. 1760.
A humble, earnest and affectionate address to the clergy. 1761.

Letters
A collection of letters. Ed T. Law and G.W. 1760. Includes a tract called Christian piety freed from the many delusions of modern enthusiasts, by Philalethes, 1756 (2nd edn).
Letters to a lady inclined to enter into the communion of the Church of Rome. 1779. Written 1731–2 to Miss Dodwell, daughter of Henry Dodwell the nonjuror.
The divine indwelling: selection from the letters of Law. Ed A. Murray 1897.
The spirit in life: a selection from the letters of Law. Ed M. M. Schofield 1917.

§2
A letter to Mr Law, occasioned by reading his treatise on Christian perfection, by a lover of mankind. 1728.
Hutcheson, E. A short account of the two charitable foundations at King's Cliffe. Stamford 1755.
Wesley, John. A letter to Mr Law, occasioned by some of his late writings. 1756.
[Langcake, Thomas]. A serious and affectionate address to all orders of men, in which are recommended the works of Law. Bath 1781. Includes 3 letters written by Law in 1749, 1750 and 1753.
GM Nov 1800. 4 letters on Law and his works by W. H. Reid, Z. Cozens, 'Ouranius' and 'Theophilus'.
Tighe, R. A short account of the life and writings of Law. 1813.
Mayow, R. W. Observations on Mr Law. In his Plain preaching, Ormskirk 1816 (2nd edn).
Behmen, Law and other mystics on the present, past and future. 1847.
Byrom, John. Private journals and literary remains. Ed R. Parkinson 2 vols Manchester 1854–7.
Walton, C. Notes and materials for an adequate biography of Law. 1854.
— An introduction to theosophy: or the science of the mystery of Christ. Vol 1, 1855.
Stephen, L. William Law. 3 vols 1877–81.
Overton, J. H. Law: nonjuror and mystic. 1881.
— The nonjurors: their lives, principles and writings. 1902.
[Moreton, G.] Memorials of the birthplace and residence of Law. Guildford 1895.
Gem, S. H. Law on Christian practice and on Christian mysticism. Oxford 1905.
— The mysticism of Law. 1914.
Hobhouse, S. Law and eighteenth-century Quakerism, including some unpublished letters and fragments of Law and John Byrom. 1927.
— Fides et ratio: the book which introduced Jacob Boehme to Law. Jnl of Theological Stud 37 1936.
Minker, K. Die Stufenfolge des mystischen Erlebnisses bei Law. Munich 1939.
Wormhoudt, A. Law and Jacob Boehme. Univ of Iowa Programs 1944.
— A note on Law's The absolute unlawfulness of stage entertainments. MLN 64 1949.
— Newton's natural philosophy in the Behmenistic works of Law. JHI 10 1949.
Green, J. B. John Wesley and Law. 1945.
McNeill, J. T. Books of faith and power. New York 1947.

Baker, E. W. A herald of the evangelical revival: a critical enquiry into the relation of Law to John Wesley and the beginnings of Methodism. 1948.
—— William Law. London Quart 186 1961.
Hopkinson, A. W. About Law: a running commentary on his works. 1948.
Talon, H. Law: a study in literary craftsmanship. 1948.
Grainger, M. Law and the life of the spirit. 1950.
Bullett, G. In his English mystics, 1950.
Clarke, W. K. L. Law and Henry Newman. Theology 56 1953.
Bielby, M. R. Works of devotion as literature. London Quart 180 1955.
Cropper, M. B. Sparks among the stubble. 1955.
de Pauley, W. C. A study in Christian perfection. Hermathena 39 1957.
Thomas, C. W. Law as an ethical religionist. Jnl of Religious Thought 12 1955.

Malekin, P. Law: a disciple of Boehme. Aryan Path Aug 1957.
—— Jacob Boehme's influence on Law. Studia Neophilologica 36 1964.
—— Law and John Wesley. Studia Neophilologica 37 1965.
—— The character-sketches in the Serious call. Studia Neophilologica 38 1966.
—— Law's career 1711–23. N & Q Nov 1967.
Armytage, W. H. G. The Behmenists. Church Quart Rev 160 1959.
Banting, M. Law, nonjuror, writer and mystic. Theology 64 1961.
Harper, K. Law and Wesley. Church Quart Rev 163 1962.
Alkon, P. K. Robert South, Law and Samuel Johnson. Stud in Eng Lit 1500–1900 6 1966.

OTHER ENGLISH MYSTICS AND FOLLOWERS OF BOEHME

THOMAS BROMLEY
d. 1691

The way to the Sabbath of rest: or the soul's progress in the work of the new birth. [c. 1678?], 1692 (2nd edn).
The way to the Sabbath of rest; The journeys of the children of Israel; A treatise of extraordinary divine dispensations. 1710 etc.
An account of the various ways of God manifesting himself to man. 1710.
See A catalogue of Bromley's library, 1691.

HENRY BROOKE
1703?–83
See col 785, above.

JOHN BYROM
1692–1763

Collections

Miscellaneous poems. 2 vols Manchester 1773; ed J. Nichols, Leeds 1814 (with a life).
Poems. Ed A. W. Ward 3 vols Manchester 1894–5, 1912 (Chetham Soc).

§1

A pastoral. Spectator 6 Oct 1714.
A review of the proceedings against Dr Bentley. 1719.
An epistle to a gentleman of the Temple. 1749.
Enthusiasm: a poetical essay. 1751.
Letter to Mr Comberbach in defence of rhyme. 1755.
Seasonably alarming and humiliating truths in a metrical version of some passages from the works of William Law. 1774. Collected by F. Okely.

Letters

Private journals and literary remains. Ed R. Parkinson 4 vols Manchester 1854–7 (Chetham Soc).
Journal, letters etc 1730–1. Manchester 1882.
Selections from his journals and papers. Ed H. Talon 1950. Contains Memoir and select bibliography.

§2

A catalogue of the library of the late John Byrom. 1848. Contains a valuable list of contemporary and earlier mystical and theological books, tracts and pamphlets.
Hoole, E. Byrom and the Wesleys. 1864.
Stephen, L. In his Studies of a biographer vol 1, 1898.

Hobhouse, S. William Law and eighteenth-century Quakerism, including some letters and fragments of William Law and Byrom. 1927.
Thomson, W. H. Christians awake written by John Byrom. Manchester [1948].
—— Previously unpublished Byromania relating to Byrom. Manchester 1954.
—— Byrom's birthplace, Manchester. Manchester 1955.
—— Byrom deeds and wills in the possession of W. H. Thomson BA; with notes on omissions and duplicates. Manchester 1956.
—— The Thomson-Byrom collection. Bull John Rylands Lib 46 1963.
Firby, N. K. John Byrom. Manchester Rev 10 1963.

GEORGE CHEYNE
1671–1743

§1

Philosophical principles of natural religion. 3 pts 1705.
Philosophical principles of religion, natural and revealed. 2 pts 1715 etc. Pt 1 containing The elements of natural philosophy and the proofs of natural religion, 2nd edn corrected and enlarged; Pt 2 containing the nature and kinds of infinities, the philosophic principles of revealed religion.

Letters

Letters to the Countess of Huntingdon. Ed C. F. Mullett, San Marino 1940.
Letters to Samuel Richardson 1733–43. Ed C. F. Mullett, Columbia Missouri 1943.

§2

Dr Cheyne's account of himself and his writings. 1743.
Greenhill, W. A. Life of Cheyne. 1846.
Viets, H. R. George Cheyne. Bull History of Medicine 23 1949.

JANE LEAD
1623–1704

§1

The heavenly cloud now breaking: the Lord Christ's ascension ladder sent down. 1681, Glasgow 1885.
The revelation of revelations, in an essay towards the unsealing, opening and discovering the seven seals, the seven thunders and the New Jerusalem state. 1683, Glasgow 1884.
The Enochian walks with God, found out by a spiritual traveller. 1694, Glasgow 1891.

The laws of paradise given forth by wisdom to a translated
spirit. 1695, Glasgow 1903.
The wonders of God's creation manifested in the variety
of eight worlds. 1695, Glasgow 1887.
The tree of faith. 1696.
The ark of faith: being a supplement to the Tree of faith.
1696.
A message to the Philadelphian Society. 1696; A second
message, 1697; A third message, 1698; Airdrie 1895.
A revelation of the everlasting gospel message. 1697,
Airdrie 1895.
The ascent of the mount of vision. [1698].
The signs of the times: forerunning the Kingdom of
Christ. 1699, Glasgow 1891.
The wars of David and the peaceable reign of Solomon
symbolizing the times of warfare and refreshment of the
saints. 1700, 1816, Glasgow 1886.
A fountain of gardens watered by the rivers of divine
pleasure and springing up into a paradise. 3 vols 1696–
1701.
A living funeral testimony, or death overcome and
drowned in the life of Christ. 1702.
The first resurrection in Christ. 1702.
For other works, see DNB and Br Quart Rev 58 1873.

§2

Jaeger, J. W. Dissertatio historico-theologica de Johannae
Leadae vita, visionibus ac doctrina. Tübingen 1716.
Offenbarungen und Biographie der Jane Lead. Stras-
bourg 1807.
Hochhuth, C. W. H. Jane Lead und die philadelphische
Gemeinde in England. Zeitschrift für Historische
Theologie 1865.

FRANCIS LEE
1661–1719

ΑΠΟΛΕΙΠΟΜΕΝΑ: or dissertations theological, mathe-
matical and physical. 2 vols 1752. With biographical note
by his daughter. A paraphrase or enlargement of
Boehme's Supersensual life, ptd in 'Law's' edn of
Boehme vol 4, 1781. The ms in Lee's hand is in Dr
Williams's Library.
The last hours of Jane Lead, by an eye and ear witness.
No English edn of this is to be found, although a
German trn was ptd at Amsterdam. A ms re-trn into
English is in Dr Williams's Library.
Three epistles addressed by Francis Lee to Peter Poiret
in Holland, 1701, 1702, 1703, tr R. C. Jenkins; ms in
Dr Williams's Library.
*The mystical poems in Jane Lead's works are almost certainly
by Lee; see N & Q 15 Nov 1873. For many other anon
books by Lee, see DNB.*

MORGAN LLWYD
1619–59

Collections

Poems, tales, odes, sonnets, translated from the British.
2 vols Chester 1804.
The poetical works of the bard of Snowdon. 1837.

§1

Llyfr y tri aderyn [The book of the three birds]. 1653; ed
O. Jones, Liverpool 1889, 1900; tr L. J. Parry, Trans
Nat Eisteddfod of Wales (Llandudno) 1896.
Lazarus and his sisters discoursing of paradise. 1655. A
ms copy in Francis Lee's hand was found among Law's
papers and is now in Dr Williams's Library.
Yr ymroddiad; Y idscybl ai Athraw Cyfarwuddid ir
Cymru; Gwyddor uchod. 1657. Verse.

Gair O'r gair. 1656; tr as A discourse of God the Word,
composed at first in Welsh, turned into English by G.
Rudd, 1730.

§2

A winding sheet for Mr Baxter's dead [defending Llwyd
from Baxter's attacks]. 1685.
Palmer, A. N. A history of the older nonconformity of
Wrexham and its neighbourhood. Wrexham 1888.
Gweithiau Morgan Llwyd, o wynedd. Vol 1 ed T. E.
Ellis, Bangor 1899; vol 2 ed J. H. Davies, Bangor 1908
(with Welsh trn of 2 works of Boehme).
Evans, E. L. Morgan Llwyd. Liverpool 1930.
—— Llwyd and Jacob Boehme. Boehme Soc Quart 1 1953.
—— Llwyd and the early Friends. Friends' Quart 8
1954.

PHILADELPHIAN SOCIETY
1697–1703

Propositions extracted from the reasons for the foundation
of a Philadelphian society. 1697.
Theosophical transactions by the Philadelphian Society.
Nos 1–5, 1697. By Francis Lee and Richard Roach.
Philadelphus (Francis Lee). The state of the Philadelphian
Society. 1697.
The declaration of the Philadelphian Society of England.
1699. Also ms in Bodley, The protestation of the Phila-
delphian Society.
See Dawn (London) Dec 1862; N. Thune, The Behmenists
and the Philadelphians, Upsala 1948.

RICHARD ROACH
1662–1730

The great crisis, or the mystery of the times and seasons
unfolded. 1725. On the contemporary mystics, the
Philadelphian Society etc.
The imperial standard of Messiah triumphant. 1727.
See mss of his Miscellaneous papers in Bodley.

THOMAS TRYON
1634–1703

The way to health, long life and happiness. 1683, 1691,
1697.
Pythagoras his mystic philosophy revived: or the mystery
of dreams unfolded; A discourse of the causes and cures
of phrensy, madness and distraction. 1691, 1700.
A treatise of dreams and visions; A discourse of the causes
and cures of phrensy, madness and distraction. 1695.
Tryon's letters, occasionally distributed in subjects, viz
philosophical, theological and moral. 1700.
The knowledge of man's self the surest guide to the true
worship of God and good government of the mind and
body. 2 pts 1703–4.
Some memoirs of the life of Mr Thomas Tryon [mostly]
by himself. 1705.
Gordon, A. A Pythagorean of the seventeenth century.
Liverpool 1871.

JACOB BOEHME
1575–1624

*Though Boehme wrote some 32 works, only one small volume,
Weg zu Christo, 13–15 below, was pbd during his lifetime.
His works, which must have circulated in ms, were tr into
English by John Sparrow, John Ellistone, Humphrey Blunden
and Charles and Durand Hotham, and pbd in London 1645–
62. Some of his books have long titles and are not always*

called by the same name, nor are the same treatises always pbd together. Below is a complete list of his works, in the order in which he wrote them; see W. Buddecke, Die Jakob Böhme-Ausgaben: ein beschreibendes Verzeichnis vol 1, Göttingen 1937.

(1) 1612, The aurora [unfinished], with notes added by his own hand in 1620; (2) 1619, The three principles of the divine essence, with an appendix concerning the Three-fold life of man; (3) 1620, The threefold life of man; (4) 1620, Answers to forty questions concerning the soul, proposed by Dr Balthasar Walter; with an appendix concerning the soul and its image, and of the turba; (5) 1620, The treatise of the incarnation in 3 parts: (i) Of the incarnation of Jesus Christ, (ii) Of the suffering, dying, death and resurrection of Christ, (iii) Of the tree of faith; (6) 1620, A book of the great six points; also a small book of other six points; (7) 1620, Of the earthly and of the heavenly mystery; (8) 1620, Of the last times [2 epistles to P[aul] K[eym], included in (32)i]; (9) 1621, De signatura rerum; (10) 1621, Of the four complexions; (11) 1621, Two apologies to Balthasar Tylcken: (i) for The aurora, (ii) for Predestination and the incarnation; (12) 1621, Considerations upon Esaiah Stiefel's book concerning the Threefold state of man and the new birth; (13) 1622, A book of true repentance; (14) 1622, A book of true resignation; (15) 1622, A book of re-generation; (16) 1622, The apology in answer to Esaiah Stiefel concerning perfection: (17) 1623, A book of predestination and election; (18) 1623, A short com-pendium of repentance; (19) 1623, Mysterious magnum; (20) 1623, A table of the divine manifestation: or an exposition of the threefold world; (21) 1624, The super-sensual [or super-rational] life; (22) 1624, Of divine contemplation or vision [unfinished]; (23) 1624, Of Christ's testaments viz: baptism and the Supper; (24) 1624, A dialogue between an enlightened and unenlight-ened soul [or Discourse of illumination]; (25) 1624, An apology in answer to Gregory Richter [for the Books of true repentance and true resignation]; (26) 1624, 177 Theosophic questions, with answers to 13 of them [un-finished]; (27) 1624, An epitome of the mysterium magnum; (28) 1624, The holy week or a prayer book [unfinished]; (29) 1624, A table of the three principles; (30) 1624, A book of the Last Judgment [lost]; (31) 1624, The clavis; (32) 1618–24, Sixty-two theosophic epistles: (i) 35 epistles, (ii) 25 epistles, (iii) 2 other epistles (nos 7 and 20 in German edn), one prefixed to The super-sensual life (21), the other as preface to the second Apology to B. Tylcken (11).

English Collections

There is no complete English edn of Boehme's works, although the various trns pbd 1644–62 make up a complete edn, with several works duplicated. The 4 vols of 1764–81, generally called Law's edn, contain only 17 of Boehme's 32 works. It was not ed Law but by his friends George Ward and Thomas Langcake, who pbd it after Law's death at the cost of Mrs Hutcheson.

Several treatises of Jacob Behmen: 1, A book of the great six points, as also a small book of other six points; 2, The 177 theosophic questions, the first thirteen answered; 3, Of the earthly and the heavenly mystery; 4, The holy week; or a prayer book; 5, Of divine vision; to which are annexed the exposition of the three principles; also an epistle of the knowledge of God and of all things. Tr Sparrow 8 pts 1661.

The remainder of books written by Jacob Behmen: 1, The first apology to Balthazar Tylcken; 11, The second apology to B.T.; 111, The four complexions; 1v, The considerations upon Esaiah Stiefel's book concerning the Threefold state of man and the new birth; v, The apology in answer to Esaiah Stiefel concerning perfec-tion; v1, The apology in answer to Gregory Richter for the Way to Christ; v11, Twenty-five epistles more than

the 35 formerly printed in English, with 2 which make 62 in all, also one epistle more of his own handwriting and one of Dr Charles Weisners [Cornelius Weissner] relating much to Jacob Behmen's life. Tr John Sparrow 1662.

The works of Jacob Behmen, the Teutonic theosopher: volume 1 containing 1, The aurora; 11 The three principles; to which is prefixed the life of the author, with figures, illustrating his principles, left by the Reverend William Law MA. Ed G. Ward and T. Langcake 4 vols 1764–81. On pp. v–vi of vol 1 there is A dialogue between Zelotes, Alphabetus, Rusticus and Theophilus, almost certainly by Law. Altogether, the following works are printed in this edn: vol 1 (1–2); vol 2 (3–5, 31); vol 3 (19–20); vol 4, (9, 17, 13–15, 21, 24, 10, 23). Weg zu Christo is the trn from the 1775 edn; the others are those by J. Sparrow, J. Ellistone and H. Blunden, with occasional alterations.

Works. Ed F.F. Glasgow 1886. Only vol 1, Epistles; *see below.*

Works. Ed C. J. Barker 5 vols 1909–24. Incomplete; *see below.*

§1

Separate English Translations

Two theosophical epistles, wherein the life of a true Christian is described; whereunto is added a dialogue between an enlightened and a distressed soul. 1645, 1653. Epistles 1 and 10 of (32)i and (24).

XL questions concerning the soul, propounded by Dr Balthasar Walter and answered by Jacob Behmen. 1647, 1665, (slightly altered). Tr J. Sparrow. (4).

Clavis, or key: or an exposition of some principal matters and words in the writing of Jacob Behmen. 1647. Tr J. Sparrow. (31).

The second book: concerning the three principles of the divine essence; [with] an appendix or description of the threefold life in man. 1648. Tr J. Sparrow, with his preface. (2).

The way to Christ discovered. 1648, 1654. (13–15). Epistle 1 of (32)iii, (21), (24), (18), ch 15 of (3) and Epistle 32 of (32)i, are all included here. Tr H. Blunden.

The fourth epistle: a letter to Paul Keym, being an answer to him concerning Our last times; The fifth epistle: another letter to Paul Keym. 1649. Tr J. Sparrow, Epistles 4–5 in (32)i.

The epistles of Jacob Behmen. 1649. 35 epistles tr J. Ellistone. (32)i.

Mercurius Teutonicus: or Christian information concern-ing the last times. 1649, 1656, 1795.

The third book: being the high and deep searching out of the threefold life of man through [or according to] the three principles. 1650. Tr J. Sparrow. (3).

Signatura rerum. 1651. Tr J. Ellistone. (9).

177 Theosophic questions. 1651. Tr J. Ellistone. (9).

Of Christ's testaments, baptism and the Supper. 1652, 1656. Tr J. Sparrow. (23).

A consideration upon the book of Esaiah Stiefel of the threefold state of man and his new birth. 1653. (12).

Mysterium magnum: or an exposition of the first book of Moses called Genesis. 1654. Tr J. Ellistone and J. Sparrow, with a life by D. Hotham. (19) and (27).

Four tables of divine revelation. 1654. Tr H. Blunden; the first of these Tables is (20), 2nd–4th are (29). In D. Hotham, The life of Jacob Behmen, 1654.

The tree of Christian faith. 1654? Tr J. Sparrow? iii of (5).

A consolatory treatise of the four complexions. 1654. Tr C. Hotham. (10).

Concerning the election of grace; [with an] appendix, being the key to the understanding of the divine hidden mysteries concerning repentance. 1655. Preface by J. Sparrow. (20).

Table of divine manifestation: or an exposition of the threefold world. 1655. Tr J. Sparrow. (20).

Aurora, that is The day-spring that is the root or mother of philosophy, astrology and theology. 1656. Tr J. Sparrow. (1).

The fifth book, in three parts: the first, of the incarnation of Jesus Christ. 1659. Tr J. Sparrow, (5)i.

The four complexions: or a treatise of consolatory instruction. 1730. Tr J. Sparrow, Preface from Hotham's 1654 trn.

The way to Christ discovered. Manchester 1752. Rptd by Byrom from Blunden's edn 1648, with slight alterations.

Treatises: Of the mixed world; Dialogue between an enlightened and an unenlightened soul; A compendium of repentance; Of true resignation. 1769. 1648 trn of Way to Christ.

The way to Christ, also the Four complexions. Bath 1775 (with preface; a difference trn from H. Blunden's, 1648); rptd 1911.

The way to Christ, with illustrated memoir by G. Moreton. Canterbury 1894. The supersensual life is the 1648 trn; the other trns are from the 1764–81 Works.

The way to Christ. Tr J. J. Stoudt, New York 1947.

The epistle of Jacob Boehme. Tr J. Ellistone, ed F.F. In Works vol 1, Glasgow 1886.

Dialogues of the supersensual life. 'Law's trn' in the 1764–81 Works. Abridged as The higher Christian life, Wakefield 1870; ed B. Holland 1901, 1908.

Selections. Ed C. A. Rainy, preface by H. Black. 1908.

The third book: being the searching out of the threefold life of man. Tr J. Sparrow, ed C. J. Barker, introd by G. W. Allen. 1909.

Concerning the three principles of the divine essence. Tr J. Sparrow, ed C. J. Barker, introd by P. Deussen 1910.

The forty questions of the soul and the Clavis. Tr J. Sparrow, ed C. J. Barker 1911.

The signature of all things, with other writings [Of the supersensual life; The way from darkness to true illumination]. Tr J. Ellistone, ed C. Bax 1912.

Aurora. Tr J. Sparrow, ed C. J. Barker and H. S. Henner 1914.

Six theosophic points and other writings [Six mystical points; On the earthly and heavenly mystery; On the divine intuition]. Tr J. R. Earle 1919.

The confessions of Jacob Boehme. Compiled by W. S. Palmer, introd by E. Underhill 1920, 1954.

Mysterium magnum [tr J. Ellistone and J. Sparrow] and the Four tables of revelation [tr H. Blunden]. Ed C. J. Barker 2 vols 1924.

De electione gratiae and questiones theosophicae. Tr J. R. Earle 1930.

The fifth book in three parts: part 1 Of the incarnation of Jesus Christ. Tr J. R. Earle, ed S. R. Webster 1934.

§2

See the mss of D. A. Freher in BM and in Dr Williams's Library.

The life of one Jacob Behmen, who although he were a very mean man, yet wrote the most wonderful deep knowledge in natural and divine things that any has been known to do since the Apostles' times; [with] a perfect catalogue of his works. 1644.

Hotham, Charles. Ad philosophiam teutonicam manuductio. 1648; tr 1650. Hotham later translated Four complexions, 1654.

Mercurius teutonicus: being divers prophetical passages gathered out of the mystical writings of Behmen. 1649, 1656, 1795.

Hotham, Durand. The life of Behmen. 1654.

Anderson, J. One blow at Babel in those of the people called Behmenites. 1662.

More, Henry. Philosophiae teutonicae censura. 1670.

Pordage, John. A treatise of eternal nature with her seven essential forms. 1681. On Boehme's philosophy. The treatise is bound up with Theologia mystica by J.P. MD 1683.

Taylor, E. Behmen's theosophic philosophy unfolded; also the principal treatises of the said author abridged and a short account of his life. 1691.

Law, William. The way to divine knowledge: being several dialogues preparatory to a new edition of the works of Jacob Behmen and the right use of them. 1752.

Theological and practical divinity, with extracts of several treatises written by Behmen, by a gentleman retired from business. 1769.

A compendious view of the grounds of the teutonic philosophy, with considerations by way of enquiry into the writings of Jacob Behmen, by a gentleman retired from business. In John Pordage, A treatise of eternal nature, 3 pts 1770.

An attestation to divine truth opened in the Teutonic philosopher. 1771.

Memoirs of the life, death, burial and wonderful writings of Behmen [i.e. life by A. von Frankenberg, with the narrative of C. Weissner]. Tr by F. Okely, Northampton 1780.

Bailey, M. L. Milton and Boehme. New York 1914.

Hartmann, F. Personal Christianity a science: the doctrine of Boehme, the God-taught philosopher. New York 1919.

Barker, C. J. Pre-requisites for the study of Jacob Boehme. 1920.

Closs, K. Böhmes Aufnahme in England 1644–1761. Archiv 148 1925.

Koyré, A. La philosophie de Boehme. Paris 1929.

Whitwell, R. Words from the mystics: 1, Boehme. Bosham 1931.

Brinton, H. H. The mystic will: based on a study of the philosophy of Boehme. 1931.

Alleman, G. M. A critique of some philosophical aspects of the mysticism of Boehme. Philadelphia 1932.

Hobhouse, S. Fides et ratio: the book which introduced Boehme to William Law. Jnl of Theological Stud 37 1936.

—— (ed). Selected mystical writings of William Law. Ed with notes and twenty-four essays in the mystical theology of Law and Boehme, and an enquiry into the influence of Boehme on Isaac Newton 1938, 1948 (rev).

Struck, W. Der Einfluss Boehmes auf die englische Literatur des 17 Jhts. Berlin 1936.

Baden, H. J. Das religiöse Problem der Gegenwart bei Boehme. Leipzig 1939.

Martensen, H. L. Boehme: studies in his life and teaching. 1885; tr T. R. Evans, ed S. Hobhouse 1949.

Muses, C. A. Illumination on Boehme: the works of Dionysius Andreas Freher. New York 1951.

Hutin, S. Les disciples anglais de Boehme. Paris 1960.

Malekin, P. Boehme's influence on William Law. Studia Neophilologica 36 1964.

E. DISSENT

Congregational, Baptist, Presbyterian and Unitarian writers. For the Quakers see above. For Restoration Nonconformists see also under A. Restoration Divines, above.

General Studies

Neal, D. The history of the Puritans 1517–1688. 4 vols 1732–8, 5 vols Bath 1793–7.

Bogue, D. and J. Bennett. History of Dissenters 1688–1808. 4 vols 1808–12.

Brook, B. The lives of the Puritans. 3 vols 1813.

— The history of religious liberty to the death of George III. 2 vols 1820.

Toulmin, J. Historical view of the state of Dissenters in England. Bath 1814.

Skeats, H. S. A history of the Free Churches of England. 1868, 1894.

Schaff, P. The progress of religious freedom as shown in the history of Toleration Acts. New York 1889.

Stoughton, J. History of religion in England 1640–1850. 6 vols 1901 (rev).

Burrage, C. Fifth-monarchy insurrections. 1910.

Brown, L. F. The political activities of the Baptists and Fifth-monarchy men in England during the Interregnum. Washington 1912.

Clark, H. W. History of English Non-conformity. 2 vols 1911–13.

McLachlan, H. English education under the Test Acts: being the history of the non-conformist academies 1662–1820. Manchester 1931.

Whiting, C. E. Studies in English Puritanism from the Restoration to the Revolution. 1931.

Price, S. J. Dissenting academies 1662–1820. Baptist Quart 6 1933.

Bebb, E. D. Nonconformity and social economic life. 1935.

Walker, J. Dissent and republicanism after the Restoration. Baptist Quart 8 1937.

Lincoln, A. Some political and social ideas of English dissent 1763–1800. Cambridge 1938.

Jewson, C. B. St Mary's Norwich: persecution and toleration 1667–1742. Baptist Quart 10 1940.

McArthur, K. W. Theological education among the Dissenters. Jnl of Religion 21 1941.

Plum, H. G. Restoration Puritanism. Chapel Hill 1943.

Payne, E. A. The Free Church tradition in the life of England. 1944.

Addison, W. G. Religious equality in modern England 1714–1914. 1944.

Micklewright, F. H. A. Some prolegomena to the history of Protestant dissent in England. N & Q 9 Sept 1944.

Mineka, F. E. The dissidence of dissent. Chapel Hill 1944.

Coomer, D. English dissent under the early Hanoverians. 1947.

— The influence of Puritanism and dissent on Methodism. London Quart 175 1950.

Schenk, V. W. D. The concern for social justice in the Puritan revolution. 1948.

Beckett, J. C. Protestant dissent in Ireland 1687–1788. 1948.

Koller, K. The Puritan preacher's contribution to fiction. HLQ 11 1948.

Watters, A. C. History of the British Churches of Christ. Indianapolis 1948.

Mullett, C. F. Protestant dissent as crime 1660–1828. Rev of Religion 13 1949.

Brauer, J. C. Puritan mysticism and the development of liberalism. Church History 19 1950.

Knox, R. A. Enthusiasm. Oxford 1950.

Huehns, G. Antinomianism in English history. 1951.

Davies, H. The English Free Churches. Oxford 1952.

Manning, B. L. The Protestant dissenting deputies. Ed O. Greenwood, Cambridge 1952.

Michaelson, R. S. Changes in the Puritan concept of calling or vocation. New England Quart 26 1953.

Thomas, R. The non-subscription controversy among Dissenters in 1719: the Salters' Hall debate. Jnl of Ecclesiastical History 4 1953.

Martin, H. Puritanism and Richard Baxter. 1954.

Dr Williams's Library: catalogue of accessions 1900–50. 1955.

Simpson, A. Puritanism in Old and New England. Chicago 1955.

Marlowe, J. The Puritan tradition in English life. 1956.

Cragg, G. R. Puritanism in the period of the great persecution 1660–88. Cambridge 1957.

Wakefield, G. S. Puritan devotion: its place in the development of Christian piety. 1957.

Braund, E. Mrs Hutchinson and her teaching. Evangelical Quart 31 1959.

Nuttall, G. F. (ed). The beginnings of nonconformity 1660–5: a check-list. 1960.

— Dissenting Churches in Kent before 1700. Jnl of Ecclesiastical History 14 1963.

Mosse, G. L. Puritan radicalism and the enlightenment. Church History 29 1960.

Routley, E. English religious dissent. 1960.

Loane, M. L. Makers of religious freedom in the 17th century. 1960.

Solt, L. F. The fifth-monarchy men: politics and the millenium. Church History 30 1961.

Goldhawk, N. P. Nonconformity in the age of Wesley. London Quart 187 1962.

Lloyd-Jones, D. M. 1662–1962: from Puritanism to Nonconformity. 1962.

Robinson, W. G. The Toleration Act of 1689. London Quart 187 1962.

Barlow, R. B. Citizenship and conscience: a study in the theory and practice of religious toleration in England during the 18th century. Philadelphia 1962.

Benson, L. F. The English hymn: its development and use in worship. Richmond Va 1962.

Wilkinson, J. T. 1662 and after: three centuries of English Non-conformity. 1962.

Caplan, N. The numerical strength of Non-conformity 1669–76. Trans of Unitarian Historical Soc 13 1963.

Goring, J. Some neglected aspects of the great ejection of 1662. Ibid.

Wood, A. H. Church unity without uniformity: a study of seventeenth-century movements and of Richard Baxter's proposal for a comprehensive Church. 1963.

Rogers, P. G. The fifth-monarchy men. Oxford 1966.

Erikson, K. T. Wayward Puritans. New York 1966.

Congregational

Calamy, Edmund. Account of ministers ejected in 1660. 1713. Continuation of Account, 2 vols 1727. Both abridged with new lives by S. Palmer in The nonconformist's memorial, 2 vols 1775, 3 vols 1802–3. Calamy revised, ed A. G. Matthews, Oxford 1934.

Hanbury, B. Historical memorials relating to the Independents. 3 vols 1839–44.

Fletcher, J. History of the revival of Independency in England. 4 vols 1847–9.

Waddington, J. Congregational history. 5 vols 1869–80.

Dexter, H. M. Congregationalism of the last three hundred years. 1879.

Dale, R. W. History of English Congregationalism. 1907.

Peel, A. First Congregational Churches. Cambridge 1920.

Selbie, W. B. Congregationalism. 1927.

Poppers, H. L. Die Entstehung des Kongregationalismus aus der puritanischen Bewegung. Berlin 1936.

Surman, C. E. A directory of Congregational biography. Trans of Congregational Historical Soc 13 1938.

Jenkins, D. T. Congregationalism. 1954.

Nuttall, G. F. Visible saints: the Congregational way 1640–60. Oxford 1957.

Jones, R. T. Congregationalism in England 1662–1962. 1962.

Morgan, E. S. Visible saints: the history of a puritan idea. New York 1963.

Baptist

Crosby, T. History of the English Baptists. 4 vols 1738–40.

Thomas, J. History of the Baptist Association in Wales. 1795.

Ivimey, J. History of the English Baptists. 4 vols 1811–30.

Benedict, D. General history of the Baptist denomination. 2 vols Boston 1813.

Taylor, T. History of the English general Baptists. 2 vols 1818.

Fuller, J. G. Brief history of the Western Association. 1843.

— Rise and progress of dissent in Bristol. 1840.

Douglas, D. History of the Baptist Churches in the North of England. 1846.

Armitage, T. History of the Baptists. New York 1888.

Whitley, W. T. A history of British Baptists. 1923.

— The Baptists of London 1612–1928. 1928.

— Seventh-day Baptists in England. Baptist Quart 12 1947.

Robinson, H. W. The life and faith of the Baptists. 1927.

Heriot, D. B. Anabaptism in England during the 17th century. Trans of Congregational Historical Soc 13 1937.

Bonner, C. Some Baptist hymnists. Baptist Quart 8 1937.

Langley, A. S. Birmingham Baptists, past and present. 1939.

Starr, E. C. A Baptist bibliography: printed material by and about Baptists, including works written against Baptists, section A. Philadelphia 1947.

Underwood, A. C. A history of the English Baptists. 1947.

Jackman, D. Baptists in the West Country. Bridgwater 1953.

Barnes, A. H. J. The preface to the orthodox confession of 1679. Baptist Quart 15 1953.

— The signatories of the orthodox confession of 1679. Baptist Quart 17 1957.

Ross, J. M. The theology of Baptism in Baptist history. Baptist Quart 15 1953.

Hamlin, G. Two Baptist pamphlets. Baptist Quart 16 1956.

Westin, G. and W. S. Hudson. Who were the Baptists? Baptist Quart 17 1957.

Winter, E. P. The Lord's Supper: admission and exclusion among the Baptists of the 17th century. Baptist Quart 17 1958.

— The administration of the Lord's Supper among the Baptists of the 17th century. Baptist Quart 18 1960.

Jewson, C. B. Norfolk Baptists up to 1700. Baptist Quart 18 1960.

Sparkes, D. C. The Portsmouth disputation of 1699. Baptist Quart 19 1961.

Brockett, A., (ed). The Exeter Assembly: the minutes of the assemblies of the United Brethren of Cornwall and Devon 1691–1717. Devon & Cornwall Record Soc new ser 6 1963.

Sellers, I. Baptists in Liverpool in the 17th century. Baptist Quart 20 1964.

Walker, M. J. Baptist theology of infancy in the seventeenth century. Baptist Quart 21 1966.

Presbyterian

Murch, J. History of the Presbyterian and General Baptist Churches in the West of England. 1835.

Wilson, J. Historical inquiry concerning the principles of the English Presbyterians from the Restoration to the death of Queen Anne. 1835.

History and principles of the Presbyterian Church in England. 1850.

McCree, T. Annals of English Presbyterianism. 1872.

Drysdale, A. H. History of the Presbyterians in England. 1889.

Griffiths, O. M. Religion and learning: a study in English Presbyterian thought from the Bartholomew ejections (1662) to the foundation of the Unitarian movement. Cambridge 1935.

Weir, J. L. Presbyterian dissent: its fundamental causes. N & Q 23 April 1938.

Spalding, J. C. The demise of English Presbyterianism 1660–1760. Church History 28 1959.

Sparkes, D. C. The Portsmouth disputation of 1699. Baptist Quart 19 1961.

Bolam, C. G. The ejection of 1662 and its consequences for the Presbyterians in England. Hibbert Jnl 60 1962.

Gerrard, L. A. The tercentenary of the great ejection. Hibbert Jnl 60 1962.

Thomas, R. Presbyterians in transition. Ibid.

Abernathy, G. R. The English Presbyterians and the Stuart revolution 1648–63. Trans of Amer Philosophical Soc new ser 55 1965.

Short, H. L. The later history of the English Presbyterians. Hibbert Jnl 64–5 1966.

Unitarian

[Nye, Stephen]. Brief history of the Unitarians also called Socinians. 1687, 1691.

Lindsey, Th. Historical view of the state of Unitarian doctrine and worship. 1783.

Hebard, J. Historical sketch of Unitarianism. 1834.

Tayler, J. J. Retrospect of the religious life of England. 1845, 1876 (with ch on recent developments by J. Martineau).

Wallace, R. Anti-Trinitarian biography. 3 vols 1850. With historical introd for 1690–1700.

New, H. Unitarian and free Christian Churches in England. 1833.

Lloyd, W. Story of Protestant dissent and English Unitarianism. 1899.

McLachlan, H. J. The Unitarian movement in the religious life of England: its contributions to thought and learning 1700–1900. 1934.

— Essays and addresses. Manchester 1950.

— Socinianism in seventeenth-century England. Oxford 1951.

Holt, R. V. The Unitarian contribution to social progress in England. 1938.

Mullett, C. F. The early letters and career of Theophilus Lindsey. N & Q 6, 20 June, 18 July 1942.

Wilbur, E. M. A history of Unitarianism, Socinianism and its antecedents. Cambridge Mass 1946.

— A history of Unitarianism in Transylvania, England and America. Cambridge Mass 1952.

Wigmore-Beddoes, D. G. How the Unitarian movement paid its debt to Anglicanism. Trans of Unitarian Historical Soc 13 1964.

THE PRINCIPAL DISSENTING WRITERS

CONGREGATIONAL

DANIEL DEFOE
1660–1731

§ I

An enquiry into the occasional conformity of Dissenters, in cases of preferment. 1697 etc.
The shortest way with the Dissenters. 1702.
For other works by Defoe see col 880, above.

§ 2

Howe, John. Some consideration of a preface to an Enquiry. 1700.

PHILIP DODDRIDGE
1702–51

Collections

Works. Ed E. Williams and E. Parsons, with memoirs of the life, character and writings of Doddridge, by J. Orton. 10 vols Leeds 1802–25, 5 vols 1803–4.
Hymns founded on various texts in the Holy Scripture. Ed J. Orton, Shrewsbury 1755, 1793 (7th edn); ed J. Humphreys 1839 (as Scriptural hymns) (with addns).
A course of lectures on pneumatology, ethics and divinity. Ed S. Clark 1763, 1776, 1794.
Sermons on various subjects. Ed J. D. Humphreys 4 vols 1826.
Ten sermons on the power and grace of Christ. 1736.
Sermons to young persons. 1737 (2nd edn).
Practical discourses on regeneration. 2 pts 1741–2 etc, 1799 (6th edn).
Three sermons on the evidence of the Gospel. 1752.

§ I

Free thoughts on the most probable means of reviving the dissenting interest. 1730.
The absurdity and iniquity of persecutions for conscience sake. 1736.
An answer to Christianity not founded on argument etc. In Three letters to the author [H. Dodwell], 3 pts 1743.
Of the evidences of Christianity. 1743.
The rise and progress of religion in the soul. 1745 etc, 1807 (15th edn).

Letters and Diaries

Correspondence and diary. Ed J. D. Humphreys 5 vols 1829–31.
Devotional letters and sacramental mediations, with lectures on preaching. 1832.

§ 2

Orton, J. Memoirs of the life, character and writings of Doddridge. Shrewsbury 1766.
Stoughton, J. Doddridge: his life and labours. 1851.
Harsha, D. A. The life of Doddridge, with notices of some of his contemporaries and specimens of his style. Albany 1864.
Stanford, C. Philip Doddridge DD. 1880.
Gibson, J. W. Dr Doddridge's nonconformist academy and education by shorthand. [place?] 1886.
Gordon, A. Doddridge and the catholicity of the old Dissent. In his Addresses, biographical and historical, 1922; 1951 (separately).

Garland, H. J. The life and hymns of Doddridge. Stirling 1951.
Nuttall, G. F. (ed). Doddridge: his contribution to English religion. 1951.
—— Richard Baxter and Doddridge. 1951.
—— Richard Baxter and Doddridge: a study in a tradition. Oxford 1952.
Church, L. F. Doddridge: poet, preacher and pedagogue. London Quart 176 1951.
Hope, E. P. Philip Doddridge. Congregational Quart 29 1951.
Kelynack, W. S. Philip Doddridge. London Quart 176 1951.
Secret, A. G. Doddridge and the evangelical revival of the eighteenth century. Evangelical Quart 23 1951.
Kissack, R. Doddridge makes a sermon. London Quart 177 1952.

JEREMIAH JONES
1693–1724

A vindication of the former part of St Matthew's Gospel from Mr Whiston's charge of dislocation. 1719.
A new and full method of settling the canonical authority of the New Testament. 2 vols 1726, 3 vols 1798 (includes A vindication).

ISAAC WATTS
1674–1748

Bibliographies

Rogal, S. J. A checklist of works by and about Watts. BNYPL April 1967.

Collections

Works. Ed D. Jennings and P. Doddridge 6 vols 1753; ed E. Parson 7 vols Leeds 1800; ed G. Burder 6 vols 1810–11, 9 vols Leeds 1812–13.
Sermons on various subjects. 3 vols 1721–7 etc, 1772 (9th edn).

§ I

An essay against uncharitableness. 1707.
A guide to prayer. 1715, 1753 (10th edn).
The art of reading and writing English. 1721.
The Christian doctrine of the Trinity. 1722.
Death and heaven: or the last enemy conquered and separate spirits made perfect. 1722 etc, 1822 (15th edn).
Three dissertations relating to the Christian doctrine of the Trinity. 1724.
Logic. 1725.
The knowledge of the heavens and the earth made easy: or the first principles of astronomy and geography. 1726.
A defense against the temptation of self-murder. 1726.
An essay towards the encouragement of charity schools. 1728.
A caveat against infidelity. 1729.
Catechisms: or instructions in the principles of the Christian religion and the history of Scripture for children and youth. 1730.
Philosophical essays on various subjects; with some remarks on Mr Locke's Essay concerning human understanding. 1733.
Reliquiae juveniles: miscellaneous thoughts in prose and verse. 1734, 1766 (5th edn).
The redeemer and the sanctifier. 1736.
Humility represented in the character of St Paul. 1737.

A new essay on civil power in things sacred. 1739.

The doctrine of the passions explained and improved. 1739 (3rd edn).

Faith and practice represented in 54 sermons preached in 1733 by Isaac Watts, D. Neal, J. Guyse, S. Price, D. Jennings and J. Hubbard. 2 vols 1739 (2nd edn).

The improvement of the mind: or a supplement to the art of logic. 1741.

The world to come: or discourses on the joys and sorrows of departed souls. 2 vols 1745.

Useful and important questions concerning Jesus, the Son of God. 1746.

The glory of Christ as God-man displayed in three discourses. 1746.

Evangelical discourses on several subjects. 1747.

The rational foundation of a Christian Church, and the terms of Christian communion. 1747.

Discourses on the love of God and its influence on all passions. 1760 (4th edn).

A treatise on the education of children and youth. 1769 (2nd edn).

§2

Davis, A. P. Watts: his life and works, with a bibliography. New York 1943.

See also col 572, above.

GEORGE WHITEFIELD

See col 1638, above.

BAPTIST

Whitley, W. T. A Baptist bibliography. 2 vols 1916.

The humble petition of the Anabaptists. 1660.

JOHN BUNYAN

See col 1875, above.

JOHN GALE
1660–1721

Inquisitio philosophica inauguralis de lapide solis. Leyden 1699.

Reflections on Mr Wall's History of infant baptism. 1711.

Sermons; to which is prefixed an account of his life. 4 vols 1724.

JOHN GILL
1697–1771

Collections

A collection of sermons and tracts, [with a memoir]. 2 vols 1773.

§1

The doctrine of justification by the righteousness of Christ. 1730

The doctrine of the Trinity. 1731.

The cause of God and truth. 4 vols 1735.

An exposition of the New Testament. 3 vols 1746–8. An exposition of the Old Testament, 6 vols 1763–6.

The divine right of infant baptism examined and disproved. 1749.

The argument from apostolic tradition in favour of infant baptism considered. 1751.

The doctrine of predestination stated and set in the scripture light, in opposition to Mr Wesley's Predestination calmly considered. 1752.

Infant baptism a part and pillar of Popery. 1766.

A body of doctrinal divinity [1767]; A body of practical divinity [1770]. 3 vols 1769–70.

§2

Rippon, J. Gill: a brief memoir. 1838.

BENJAMIN KEACH
1640–1704

§1

War with the Devil: or the young man's conflict with the powers of darkness. 1673 etc.

ΤΡΟΠΟΛΟΓΙΑ: a key to open scripture metaphors. 3 pts 1682.

The progress of sin: or the travels of ungodliness. 1684.

Antichrist stormed. 1689.

The breach repaired in God's worship: or singing of psalms, hymns and spiritual songs proved to be an ordinance of Jesus Christ. 1691.

The marrow of true justification: or justification without works. 1692.

The axe laid to the root: or one blow more at the foundation of infant baptism and Church-membership. 1693.

A golden mine opened, or the glory of God's rich grace displayed in the mediator to believers: containing the substance of near 40 sermons. 1694.

The glory of a true Church and its discipline displayed. 1697.

The display of glorious grace: or the covenant of peace opened in fourteen sermons. 1698.

Laying on of hands upon baptized believers. 1698.

The Jewish sabbath abrogated. 1700.

Gospel mysteries unveiled: or an exposition of all the parables and many similitudes spoken by Jesus Christ. 4 pts 1701.

For other prose works see DNB; for poems see col 477, above.

§2

Reid, A. A. Benjamin Keach. Baptist Quart 10 1940.

ROBERT ROBINSON
1735–90

Collections

Seventeen discourses, to which are added Six morning exercises. Cambridge 1796.

Sermons on particular occasions. 1804.

Posthumous works. [Ed B. Flower], Harlow 1792, 1812.

Miscellaneous works of Robert Robinson; to which are prefixed brief memoirs of his life and writings [by the editor]. Ed B. F[lower] 4 vols Harlow 1807.

Selections from Robinson's works, with a biographical notice. In J. Sparks, A collection of essays and tracts vol 3, Boston 1823.

§1

Hymns for the fast day. 1757. Issued by Whitefield.

Arcana: or the principles of the late petitioners to Parliament. 1774.

A plea for the divinity of our Lord Jesus Christ. Cambridge 1776.

The history and the mystery of Good-Friday. 1778.

A plan of lectures on the principles of Nonconformity. Cambridge 1778.
The general doctrine of toleration applied to the particular case of free communion. Cambridge 1781.
The history of baptism. [Ed G. Dyer] 1790.

§2

Dyer, G. Memoirs of the life and writings of Robinson. 1796.
Hughes, G. W. With freedom fired: the story of Robinson, Cambridge Nonconformist. 1955.

JOHN COLLETT RYLAND
1723–92

The life and actions of Jesus Christ, by way of question and answer, in verse. 1767.
The scheme of infidelity ruined for ever: or the deistical and Socinian schemes demonstrated to be insufficient. 1770.
A contemplation on the existence and perfection of God. 1774.
A contemplation on the insufficiency of reason and the necessity of divine revelation to enable us to attain eternal happiness. 1775.
Contemplation on the nature and evidences of divine inspiration. Northampton 1776.

ANNE STEELE
1717–78

§1

Poems on subjects chiefly devotional. 2 vols 1760, 3 vols Bristol 1780.
Works, comprehending poems and miscellaneous pieces. 2 vols Boston 1808.
Hymns, psalms, and poems; with a memoir by J. Sheppard. Ed D. Sedgwick 1863.

§2

Thomson, R. W. Anne Steele. Baptist Quart 21 1966.

JOSEPH STENNETT
1663–1713

Works. 4 vols 1731–2. Hymns, originally pbd 1697–1713, in vol 4.

JOHN STURGION
fl. 1661

A short discovery of the Lord Protector's intentions touching the Anabaptists in the army. 1655.
A plea for toleration of opinion and persuasions in matters of religion differing from the Church of England. 1661.
Sion's groans for her distressed. 1661.

PRESBYTERIAN

Excluding the Scottish Presbyterians, col 2031, below.

EDMUND CALAMY
1671–1732

An abridgement of Mr Baxter's History of his life and times. 1702, 2 vols 1713 (with continuation till 1711).
An account of the ministers, lecturers etc ejected in 1660 [ch 9 of Abridgement]. 1713.
A continuation of the account. 2 vols 1727.
The Nonconformists' memorial [Abridgement and Continuation of the account, above, condensed by S. Palmer]. 2 vols 1775, 3 vols 1802–3.
A defence of moderate nonconformity. 3 vols 1703–5.
Sermons on the inspiration of the holy writings. 1710.
Thirteen sermons concerning the doctrine of the Trinity, with four sermons on John v 7. 1719.
Memoirs of the life of John Howe. 1724.
A letter to a divine in Germany: giving a brief account of the Protestant Dissenters in England. 1736.
A historical account of my own life, with some reflections on the times I have lived in 1671–1731. Ed J. J. Rutt 2 vols 1829.

SAMUEL CHANDLER
1693–1766

Sermons on [several] subjects; with a Life by Th. Amory. 4 vols 1768.
A vindication of the Christian religion. 1725, 1728.
Reflections on the conduct of modern Deists in their late writings against Christianity. 1727.
Plain reasons for being a Christian. 1730.
A vindication of the history of the Old Testament. 2 pts 1741–3.
The witnesses of the resurrection of Jesus Christ re-examined and their testimony proved entirely consistent 1744.

JAMES DUCHAL
1697–1761

Sermons. 3 vols Dublin 1762–4.
On the presumptive arguments for the truth and divine authority of the Christian religion. 1753. 10 sermons.

MATTHEW HENRY
1662–1714

Collections

Works. 1726. With a life by W. Tong.
Select sermons. Ed S. Palmer 1782.
The beauties of Henry. Ed J. Evans et al, with a life by J. Geard 3 vols 1797–1803.

§1

A brief inquiry into the nature of schism. 1689.
The communicant's companion. 1704.
An exposition of the 5 poetical books of the Old Testament. 1708.
An exposition of all the books of the Old and New Testament. 5 vols 1710.
A method for prayer. 1710 etc.

§2

Tong, W. An account of the life and death of M. Henry. 1716.
Williams, J. B. Memoirs. 1828.
Hamilton, J. Lives of Bunyan, Henry and Hall. 2 vols 1853.
Chapman, C. Henry: his life and times. 1859.
Grosart, A. B. In his Representative Nonconformists, 1879.
Roberts, H. D. Henry and his chapel. Liverpool 1901.
Williams, P. O. Matthew Henry. Manchester [1926].

PETER KING
1669–1734

An enquiry into the constitution of the primitive Church. 1691 etc.

The history of the apostles' creed. 1703.

JOHN LELAND
1691–1766

Discourses on several subjects. 4 vols 1768–9.

An answer to [M. Tindal's] Christianity as old as the creation. 2 pts 1733.

The divine authority of the Old and New Testament asserted. 2 vols 1739–40.

Remarks on [H. Dodwell's] Christianity not founded on argument. 2 pts 1744.

A defence of Christianity. 1740, 1753.

Reflections on the late Lord Bolingbroke's Letters on the use of history. 1753 etc.

A view of the principal deistical writers that have appeared in England in the last and present century. 3 vols 1754–6.

The advantage and necessity of the Christian revelation. 2 vols 1764.

MOSES LOWMAN
1680–1752

The case of the acts against the Protestant Dissenters. 1717.

A defence of the Protestant Dissenters, in answer to the misrepresentations of Dr Sherlock. 1718.

The principles of an occasional conformist stated and defended. 1718.

Remarks on Dr Sherlock's Answer to the Bishop of Bangor. 1719.

The argument from prophecy. 1733.

A dissertation on the civil government of the Hebrews. 1740.

An appendix to A dissertation on the civil government of the Hebrews. 1741.

JAMES PIERCE
1674?–1726

Vindiciae fratrum dissentium in Anglia. 3 pts 1710; tr 1717.

Presbyterian ordination proved regular. 1716. A sermon.

A defence of the dissenting presbytery and Presbyterian ordination. 2 pts 1717.

The case of the ministers ejected at Exon. Exeter 1719 (4 edns).

The Western inquisition: or a relation of the controversy among the Dissenters in the West of England. 1720.

Dissertations on six texts of Scripture. 1727.

Fifteen sermons on various occasions. Ed B. Avery 1728.

JOHN PINNEY

Letters 1679–99. Ed G. F. Nuttall, Oxford 1939.

UNITARIANS

The distinction between Unitarians and Presbyterians and (at times) Independents is not always certain in this period. Names appear in this list of writers who were either Presbyterian or Independent before the Salters' Hall Conference of Feb 1719. Their works are chiefly concerned with the Trinitarian and Deistic controversies.

BENJAMIN BENNET
1674–1726

Occasional hymns. Newcastle 1722.

Irenicum: or a review of some late controversies about the Trinity, private judgment, Church authority etc. 1722.

The Christian oratory: or the devotion of the closet displayed. 2 vols 1726–8.

GEORGE BENSON
1699–1762

History of the first planting of the Christian religion. 3 vols 1738.

Paraphrases of St Paul's epistles. 1731–4; Paraphrases of the catholic epistles, 1738–49.

The reasonableness of the Christian religion. 1743.

A collection of tracts. 1748.

A supplement to some tracts formerly published. 1748.

Sermons. 1748.

Second thoughts concerning the sufferings and death of Christ. 1748.

A summary view of the evidences of Christ's resurrection. 1754.

The history of the life of Jesus Christ, taken from the New Testament [with memoirs of the life and writings of G. Benson by T. Amory]. 1764.

SIMON BROWNE
1680–1732

Hymns and spiritual songs. 1720.

A defence of Scripture as the only standard of faith. 1721.

Sermons on several subjects. 1722.

A fit rebuke to a ludicrous infidel. 1732.

A defence of the religion of nature and the Christian revelation [in answer to M. Tindal's Christianity as old as the creation]. 1732.

THOMAS EMLYN
1663–1741

Works, with memoirs. [Ed S. Emlyn] 3 vols 1746.

A humble inquiry into the Scripture account of Jesus Christ. 1702 (anon).

A vindication of the worship of the Lord Jesus Christ on the Unitarian principles. 1706 (anon).

A collection of tracts stating some important points relating to the deity, worship and satisfaction of the Lord Jesus Christ. 9 pts 1702–12.

CALEB FLEMING
1698–1779

Animadversions upon Mr Thomas Chubb's Discourse on miracles. 1741.

Truth and modern Deism at variance. 1746.

True Deism the basis of Christianity: or observations on Mr Thomas Chubb's Posthumous works. 1749.

A survey of the search after souls. 1758.

The reason, design and end of the sufferings of Christ. 1760.

JAMES FOSTER
1697–1750

An essay on fundamentals, with a particular regard to the doctrine of the ever-blessed Trinity. 1720.
A letter to a Deist. 1729.
The usefulness, truth and excellency of the Christian revelation defended [against M. Tindal, Christianity as old as the creation]. 1731.
Discourses on all the principal branches of natural religion and social virtue. 2 vols 1749–52.
Sermons. 4 vols 1744–55.

JOSEPH HALLETT
1691–1744

The belief of subordination of the son of God to his father no characteristic of an Arian. 1719.
The reconciler: or an essay to show that Christians are much more agreed in their notions concerning the Holy Trinity than has been commonly represented. 1727.
A free and impartial study of the Holy Scriptures recommended. 3 vols 1729–36.
An essay on the nature and use of miracles. 1730.
The immorality of the Moral philosopher. 1737. An answer to Thomas Morgan, The moral philosopher.
The consistent Christian: being a confutation of the errors advanced in Mr Chubb's True Gospel of Jesus Christ asserted. 1738.

WILLIAM HARRIS
1675–1740

Practical discourses on the principal representations of the Messiah throughout the Old Testament. 1724.
The reasonableness of believing in Christ and the un-reasonableness of infidelity. In Two sermons; with an appendix relating to Mr Woolaston's fifth discourse on miracles, 1729.
The nature of the Lord's Supper. In Four discourses at Salters' Hall, 1736.

NATHANIEL LARDNER
1684–1768

Works. Ed B. Cole [with a life by A. Kippis] 11 vols 1788, 5 vols 1815, 10 vols 1829, 1835, 1838.
The credibility of the Gospel history. Pt 1, 2 vols 1727, 1730; pt 2, 2 vols 1735–55.
A vindication of three of our Saviour's miracles, in answer to Wollaston. 1729.
Sermons upon various subjects. 2 vols 1751–60.
An essay on the Mosaic account of the creation and fall of man. 1753.
A large collection of ancient Jewish and heathen testimonies to the truth of the Christian religion. 4 vols 1764–7.
Memoirs of the life and writings of Nathaniel Lardner [by J. Jennings], with eight sermons. 1769.

THOMAS MORGAN
d. 1743

The absurdity of opposing faith to reason: or a defence of Christianity against the power of enthusiasm. 1722.
Enthusiasm in distress. 1722.
A defence of natural and revealed religion. 1728.
The moral philosopher, in a dialogue between a Christian Deist and a Christian Jew. 1737, 3 vols 1738–40.
Physico-theology: or a philosophico-moral disquisition concerning human nature. 1741.
A brief examination of William Warburton's Divine legation of Moses. 1742.

I. S.

VIII. HISTORY

A. RESTORATION HISTORIANS 1660–1700

SIR WILLIAM DUGDALE
1605–86

Bibliographies

Hamper, W. In his Life, diary and correspondence, 1827; Index, 1826 (priv ptd). Account of pbd works and index to mss collections.
Maddison, F. et al. Dugdale 1605–86: a list of his printed works. Warwick 1953. Includes mss.

§ 1

A full relation of the passages concerning the late treaty begun at Uxbridge 1644. Oxford 1645 (anon); rptd in A short view of the late troubles, 1681. See [R. Stafford], Considerations touching the late treaty for a peace held at Uxbridge; with some reflections upon the principall occasions and causes of the frustration thereof, extracted out of the late printed full relation of the passages concerning it, Oxford 1645.
Monasticon anglicanum. 3 vols 1655–73. Vols 1–2 bear names of Dodsworth and Dugdale, vol 3 that of Dugdale alone. Vol 1, 1682 (rev). Tr J. Caley, H. Ellis, B. Bandinel 6 vols in 8 1817–30 (much enlarged), 1846. Tr and abridged by J. W[right] 1693, [J. Stevens] 1718; 2-vol continuation to Stevens's abridgement as The history of the antient abbeys, monasteries, hospitals, cathedral and collegiate churches, 1722; The appendix, containing charters, grants and other original writings, 1723.
The antiquities of Warwickshire illustrated. 1656; ed W. Thomas 2 vols 1730 (enlarged), Coventry 1765, (abridged) 1817, [c. 1830]. Index of places to 1730 edn by Sir Thomas Phillipps, Middle Hill 1844?
The history of St Paul's Cathedral. 1658; ed E. Maynard 1716 (enlarged); H. Ellis 1818 (enlarged); rptd in Stowe's Survey of London, 1753.
The history of imbanking and drayning of divers fenns and marshes. 1662; rev C. N. Cole 1772.
Origines juridiciales: or historical memorials of the English laws, courts of justice, forms of tryall etc, with a chronologie of the Lord Chancellors and Keepers of the Great Seal etc. 1666, 1671 (enlarged), 1680 (enlarged); abridged by E. Cooke as Chronica juridicialia, 1685, 1739.

The baronage of England: or an historical account of our English nobility. 3 vols in 2 1675–6. *See* [C. Hornby], Three letters containing remarks on errors and defects in Dugdale's baronage, 1738.

A short view of the late troubles in England. Oxford 1681, 1681 (both anon); rptd in The good old cause: the English revolution of 1640–60, ed C. Hill and E. Dell 1949 (extracts). *See* A letter upon A short view of the late troubles in England, wherein in the viiith chapter the occasion of the execrable Irish rebellion xli is egregiously mistaken, 1681 (anon).

The antient usage in bearing of such ensigns of honour as are commonly call'd arms; with a catalogue of the present nobility. Oxford 1682, 1682; ed T. C. Banks 1811.

A perfect copy of all summons of the nobility to the great councils and parliaments of this realm. 1685.

The life of Sir William Dugdale. 1713. Also in Biographia collectanea 1713, and found with separate pagination in some copies of Miscellanies on several curious subjects [ed R. Rawlinson] 1714; rptd with The history of St Paul's, 1716, 1818; in Dallaway's Inquiries into the origin and progress of the science of heraldry in England, 1793; in his Heraldic miscellanies, [1793?]; in Hamper, under Letters, below, and in W. West, The history, topography and directory of Warwickshire, Birmingham 1830.

Some account of Wolverhampton. In S. Erdeswicke, A survey of Staffordshire, [ed R. Rawlinson?] 1717.

Directions for the search of records and making use of them, in order to an historical discourse of the antiquities of Staffordshire. In J. Ives, Select papers chiefly relating to English antiquities, 1773.

Visitations. Lancashire, 1851 (fragment) (Chetham Soc 24), ed F. R. Raines 1872–3 (Chetham Soc 84–5, 88); Derbyshire, ed J. Rogers, Middle Hill 1854, 1879 (index priv ptd F. A. Crisp 1887); Staffordshire, ed J. Rogers, Middle Hill 1854, ed H. S. Grazebrook 1885 (William Salt Archaeological Soc vol 5 pt 2), on which is based Staffordshire pedigrees ed G. J. Armytage and W. H. Rylands 1912 (Pbns Harleian Soc 62); Yorkshire, ed R. D[avies] 1859 (Pbns Surtees Soc 36) (index priv ptd G. J. Armytage 1872), ed with addns J. W. Clay in Genealogist new ser 9–33 1893–1917, and in 3 vols Exeter 1899–1917 (*see* Yorks Archaeological & Topographical Assoc Record Ser 9 1890); Durham, ed J. Foster 1887 (priv ptd), on which is based Durham monuments, Newcastle 1925 (Pbns Newcastle Records Committee 5); Cumberland and Westmorland, ed J. Foster, Carlisle [1891]; Northumberland, ed Foster, Newcastle [1891], 1924 (reshaped as Northumberland monuments). (Pbns Newcastle Records Committee 4); Cheshire, ed A. Adams 1941 (Pbns Harleian Soc 93).

Notes of the Warwickshire inquisitions 1512, 1518, 1549. In The domesday of inclosures 1517–18, ed I. S. Leadam vol 2, 1897 (Royal Historical Soc).

Dugdale also edited and contributed to vol 2 of H. Spelman, Concilia, decreta, leges etc in re ecclesiarum orbis britannici, 1664, *and edited* Spelman, Glossarium archaiologicum, 1664. *Collaboration with W. Somner in his* Dictionarium saxonico-latino-anglicum, 1659, *has also been suggested (see Maddison, above, no 27).* A. Collins, Proceedings, precedents and arguments concerning baronies by writ, 1734 *is based in part on Dugdale's collections.*

Letters and Diaries

The life, diary and correspondence. Ed W. Hamper 1827; The diary for 1656, ed F. Madan, Athenaeum 3 Nov 1888. *See also* Maddison, *above*, pp. 63–7.

§2

Brabrook, E. Sir William Dugdale. Archaeological Jnl 62 1905.

Dugdale, W. F. S. In his Memorials of old Warwickshire, 1908.

Lawrence, H. The heraldry of Dugdale's visitation of Derbyshire 1662–3. Jnl Derby Archaeological & Natural History Soc 42 1920.

Jenkins, H. M. Dr Thomas's edition of Dugdale's Antiquities of Warwickshire. Oxford 1931 (Dugdale Soc Occasional Papers 3).

Denholm-Young, N. and H. H. E. Craster. Roger Dodsworth 1585–1654 and his circle. Bodleian Quart Record 7 1934; rptd with addns Yorks Archaeological & Topographical Jnl 32 1934–6.

Douglas, D. C. Dugdale: the grand plagiary. History Dec 1935; rev as The grand plagiary in his English scholars 1660–1730, 1939, 1951 (rev).

Scroggs, E. S. Dugdale. Jnl Br Archaeological Assoc ser 3 1937.

Ewing, M. A note on the Sir Thomas Browne-Dugdale letters. PQ 21 1942.

Kirby, H. T. A note on Hollar's illustrations to Dugdale's Warwickshire. Apollo July 1943.

Styles, P. In his Sir Simon Archer 1581–1662, Oxford 1946 (Dugdale Soc Occasional Papers 6).

—— A letter of Dugdale [to William Booth]. Univ of Birmingham Historical Jnl 5 1956.

Stenton, D. M. In Sir Christopher Hatton's book of seals, Oxford 1950 (Pbns Northants Record Soc 15). Introd.

Wagner, A. R. In his Records and collections of the College of Arms, 1952.

Cronne, H. A. The study and use of charters by English scholars in the seventeenth century: Sir Henry Spelman and Dugdale. In English historical scholarship in the sixteenth and seventeenth centuries, ed L. Fox, Oxford 1956 (Dugdale Soc).

Gale, R. C. Index to armorial glass in the Inns of Court illustrated in [1680 edn of] Origines juridiciales. [1961].

EDWARD HYDE,
1st EARL OF CLARENDON
1609–74

Collections

An appendix to the History of the grand rebellion: consisting of some valuable pieces written by Clarendon. 1724. Contains A full answer; The difference and disparity; extracts from parliamentary speeches 1660–2; The petition and address; Two letters to the Duke and Duchess of York; with a life. Rptd as vol 1 of A collection of several valuable pieces of Clarendon, 2 vols 1727 (vol 2 reprints the History of the rebellion in Ireland).

A collection of several tracts of the Earl of Clarendon. 1727. Contains A discourse by way of vindication of my self from the charge of high-treason; Reflections upon several Christian duties, divine and moral, by way of essays. Rptd as A compleat collection of tracts, 1747, and as Miscellaneous works of Clarendon, 1751 (2nd edn). The essays rptd as Essays moral and entertaining, [ed J. S. Clarke] 2 vols 1815, and with omissions in British prose writers vol 1, 1819. An essay on active and contemplative life separately rptd Glasgow 1765.

Characters of eminent men in the reigns of Charles I and II from the works of Clarendon. Ed E. T[urner] 1793.

Characters and episodes of the great rebellion, selected from the History and Autobiography. Ed G. D. Boyle, Oxford 1889.

War-pictures from Clarendon: selections from the History of the great rebellion. Ed R. J. Mackenzie, Oxford 1912.

Selections from the History of the rebellion and the Life by himself. Ed G. Huehns, Oxford 1955 (WC).

The history of the great rebellion. Ed R. Lockyer 1967. Selection from bks 6–11.

§1

Mr Hides argument before the Lords [against the Council of the North]. 1641; rptd in Historical collections, ed J. Rushworth vol 4, 1721.

Mr Hyde's speech at a conference betweene both Houses, July 6 1641, at the impeachments against Lord Davenport etc. 1641; rptd in Historical collections, ed J. Rushworth vol 4, 1721; in Somers tracts, ed W. Scott vol 4, 1810.

Two speeches made in the House of Peers on Munday 19 Dec [1642] for and against accommodation, by the Earl of Pembroke [and] Lord Brooke. 1642, 1642; rptd in Somers tracts, ed W. Scott vol 6, 1811. Owned by Clarendon in his Life.

Transcendent and multiplied rebellion and treason discovered by the laws of the land. 1645. Anon.

An answer to a pamphlet entit'led A declaration of the Commons of England expressing their reasons and grounds of passing the late resolutions touching no further addresse to be made to the King. 1648, 1648 (both anon); enlarged as A full answer to an infamous and trayterous pamphlet entituled [etc], 1648; rptd in An appendix to the history of the grand rebellion, 1724; and in A collection of several valuable pieces, 1727; tr Latin, 1649.

The difference and disparity between the estates and conditions of George Duke of Buckingham and Robert Earl of Essex. In H. Wootton, Reliquiae Wottonianae, 1651. Ascribed to Clarendon in 1672 and 1685 edns of Reliquiae, pbd separately as The characters of Robert Earl of Essex and George Duke of Buckingham, 1706; rptd in An appendix to the History of the grand rebellion, 1724; and in A collection of several valuable pieces vol 1, 1727.

A letter from a true and lawfull Member of Parliament [i.e. Clarendon] to one of his Highness councell upon occasion of the last declaration 31 Oct 1655. 1656. Anon.

A collection of orders used in Chancery. 1661.

His Majesties speech, together with the Lord Chancellors [i.e. Clarendon's to Parliament] 13 Sept 1660. 1660. Other official parliamentary speeches dated 29 Dec 1660, 8, 10 May 1661, 19 May 1662 (rptd in Somers tracts, ed W. Scott vol 7, 1812), 10 Oct 1665, pbd with similar titles in year of delivery, that of 10 Oct 1665 at Oxford.

Second thoughts: or the case of a limited toleration, stated according to the present exigence of affairs in Church and State. [1671] (anon), [1689?].

Animadversions upon a book intituled Fanaticism fanatically imputed to the catholick church, by Dr Stillingfleet, and the imputation refuted by S. C[ressy]. 1673 (anon), 1674, 1685. See S. Cressy, An epistle apologetical to a person of honour [i.e. Clarendon] touching his vindication of Dr Stillingfleet, 1674.

A brief view and survey of the dangerous and pernicious errors to Church and State in Mr Hobbes's book entitled Leviathan. [Oxford] 1676, 1676.

Two letters: one to the Duke of York, the other to the Dutchess, occasioned by her embracing the Roman Catholick religion. [1680?]; rptd in State tracts, 1689, 1693; An appendix to the History of the grand rebellion, 1724; in A collection of several valuable pieces vol 1, 1727; in Harleian miscellany, ed T. Park vol 3, 1809.

To the Right Honourable the Lords Spiritual and Temporal in Parliament assembled: the humble petition and address of Clarendon. [1667?]; rptd as News from Dunkirk-house: or Clarendon's farewell to England Dec 3 1667, [1667?]; rptd in State tracts, 1693; separately as The petition and address to the House of Lords in answer to the charge of the House of Commons against his Lordship, 1715; in An appendix to the History of the grand rebellion, 1724; in A collection of several valuable pieces vol 1, 1727; in Harleian miscellany, ed T. Park vol 5, 1810; in Somers tracts, ed W. Scott vol 8, 1812; tr Dutch, [1667?].

The history of the rebellion and civil wars in England, begun in the year 1641. 3 vols Oxford 1702–4 (folio), 1705–6 (8°), 1707, 1707 (folio), 1712 (8°), 1717, Dublin 1719 (folio), Oxford 1720–1 (8°), 1731–2, 1 vol 1732 (folio), 12 vols Basle 1798 (8°), 3 vols Oxford 1807, 1816 (4°), 1819 (8°), 8 vols 1826, (8°), 6 vols Boston 1827, 7 vols Oxford 1839 (12°), 1 vol 1839 (8°), 1843, 7 vols 1849; ed W. D. Macray 6 vols Oxford 1888; tr French, 6 vols 1704–9. The edns of 1816, 1826, 1849 contain The history of the rebellion in Ireland; 1826, 1827, 1849 contain Warburton's notes; 1843 contains Clarendon's autobiography. The Lord Clarendon's history of the grand rebellion compleated, 1717 (2nd edn), Dublin 1720 contains portraits, maps and other illustrative material.

The history of the rebellion and civil wars in Ireland. Dublin 1719–20, 1720, 1721; rptd as A collection of several valuable pieces of Clarendon vol 2, 1727, and in 1816, 1826, 1849 edns of The history of the rebellion in England, above.

An appendix to the history of the grand rebellion. 1724. See Collections, above.

A collection of several valuable pieces. 2 vols 1727. See Collections, An appendix etc, above.

The life of Clarendon written by himself. Oxford 1759, 3 vols Oxford 1759, Dublin 1759, 2 vols Oxford 1760, 3 vols Oxford 1761, 2 vols Oxford 1817, 3 vols Oxford 1827, 2 vols Oxford 1857; rptd in 1843 edn of The history of the rebellion in England, above; tr French, 1823–4, rptd 1827. Contains life to 1660, continuation to 1667. The history of the reign of King Charles the Second to 1667, 2 vols [1757?] is a surreptitious edn by J. Shebbeare of pt 2 of Clarendon's life; The secret history of the Court and reign of Charles the Second [ed C. MacCormick], 2 vols 1792 is a modernized and altered version of pt 2.

Religion and policy and the countenance and assistance each should give to the other. 2 vols Oxford 1811.

Clarendon also wrote a tract on behalf of the royalists who assassinated Anthony Ascham, the agent for Parliament in Madrid, pbd in Spanish as Consideraciones dignas de atencion, y peso, sobre el caso de los cavalleros ingleses, al presente presos y detenidos en la carcel real desta corte, [Madrid 1650]. *See* Calendar of the Clarendon state papers vol 2, ed W. D. Macray, Oxford 1869 no 329.

Letters

Barwick, P. The life of Dr John Barwick. 1724.

Evelyn, J. Memoirs, to which is subjoined correspondence between Clarendon and Sir Richard Browne. Ed W. Bray vol 5, 1827.

Lister, T. H. Life and administration of Clarendon vol 3. 1837.

Notes which passed at meetings of the Privy Council between Charles II and Clarendon 1660–7, together with a few letters. Ed W. D. Macray 1896 (Roxburghe Club).

§2

L'Estrange, R. To the Right Honourable Edward, Earl of Clarendon, the humble apology of Roger L'Estrange. 1661.

A hue and crie after the Earl of Clarendon. 1667. In verse.

Articles of treason exhibited in parliament against Clarendon [14 Nov 1667]. [1667].

Vox et lacrimae Anglorum. 1668. An attack on Clarendon, in verse.

F[rench], N. A narrative of Clarendon's settlement and sale of Ireland. Louvain 1668; tr French, 1696.

The proceedings in the House of Commons touching the impeachment of Clarendon 1667. 1700.

An antidote against rebellion: or the principles of the modern politician examin'd and compar'd with the description of the last age by Clarendon [in his History of the rebellion]. 1704.

The lives of the Lords Chancellors but more at large of Clarendon and Bulstrode, Lord Whitlock. 2 vols 1708.

Le Clerc, J. Mr Le Clerc's account of Clarendon's History of the civil wars translated from the French by J. O[zell]. 1710.

Bibliotheca Clarendoniana: a catalogue of the library of Clarendon to be sold Aug 26 1756. [1756].

Auction catalogue of manuscripts of Clarendon. 1764.

State papers collected by Clarendon containing the material from which his History of the rebellion was composed. 3 vols Oxford 1767–86. Vols 1–2 ed R. Scrope, vol 3 ed T. Monkhouse.

Life. In Select biography vol 8, 1821.

Ellis, G. J. W. A. Historical inquiries respecting the character of Clarendon. 1827.

Ashburnham, J. A narrative of his attendance on Charles I [with] a vindication of his character and conduct from the misrepresentations of Clarendon [by George, Earl of Ashburnham]. 2 vols 1830.

Lister, T. H. Life and administration of Clarendon. 3 vols 1837–8. Reviewed [J. W. Croker], Quart Rev 62 1838. Reply by Lister as An answer to the misrepresentations contained in an article on the life of Clarendon in no cxxiv of the Quarterly Review, 1839.

Buff, A. Die Politik Karls des ersten in den ersten Wochen nach seiner Flucht von London, und Lord Clarendons Darstellung dieser Zeit. Giessen 1868.

Calendar of the Clarendon state papers. 4 vols Oxford 1872–1932. Vol 1 ed O. Ogle and W. H. Bliss, vols 2–3 W. D. Macray, vol 4 ed F. J. Routledge.

Ranke, L. von. In his History of England in the seventeenth century vol 6, tr Oxford 1875.

Chassant, A. A. L. Lord Clarendon. Evreux 1891. Account of his attempted murder at Evreux 1668.

Stephen, J. F. Clarendon's History of the rebellion. In his Horae sabbaticae ser 1, 1892.

Draft by Hyde of a declaration on the murder of Charles I, to be issued by Charles II in 1649, with a note by S. R. Gardiner. EHR 8 1893.

Firth, C. H. Clarendon's History of the rebellion: 1, the original History; 2, the life of himself; 3, the history of the rebellion. EHR 19 1904.

— Clarendon as statesman, historian and Chancellor of the University. Oxford 1909.

Kaye, P. L. English colonial administration under Clarendon 1660–7. Baltimore 1905.

Macleane, D. Clarendon the historian. In Memorials of old Wiltshire, ed A. Dryden 1906.

M., E. Clarendon: a striking figure in the legal history of England. Amer Law Rev 40 1906.

Craik, H. Life of Clarendon. 2 vols 1911.

Carlyle, E. I. Clarendon and the Privy Council 1660–7. EHR 27 1912.

Whibley, C. In his Political portraits [1st ser], 1917.

Davies, G. The date of Clarendon's first marriage [1631]. EHR 32 1917.

Bigham, C. C. Church and state: Clarendon and Danby. In his Chief ministers of England 920–1720, 1923.

Routledge, F. J. A letter from Sir Edward Hyde to John Nicholas 28 August 1658. Bodleian Quart Record 4 1926.

Bradford, G. Great English portrait-painter [i.e. Clarendon]. In his Naturalist of souls, New York 1926.

Theobald, J. A. Clarendon and Machiavelli. TLS 30 June 1927.

Feiling, K. A letter of Clarendon during the elections of 1661. EHR 42 1927.

— Clarendon and the act of uniformity 1662–3. EHR 44 1929.

Every, G. Clarendon and the popular front. Criterion 16 1937. On his attitude towards the Long Parliament and its successors.

Rowse, A. L. English historical literature: Clarendon's History of the rebellion and his autobiography. New Statesman 12 Feb 1944.

— Clarendon's Life. In his English spirit, 1944.

Wormald, B. H. G. How Hyde became a royalist. Cambridge Historical Jnl 8 1945.

— Clarendon: politics, history and religion 1640–60. Cambridge 1951.

Lamborn, E. A. G. Clarendon's grandparents. N & Q 15 Dec 1945.

Knights, L. C. Reflections on Clarendon's History of the rebellion. Scrutiny 15 1948; rptd in his Further explorations, 1965.

Trevor-Roper, H. R. The copyright in Clarendon's works. TLS 17 Feb 1950. See 3–10 March, 7 July 1950.

— Clarendon and the great rebellion. In his Historical essays, 1957.

— Three historians: 1, Clarendon. Listener 30 Sept 1965.

— Clarendon and the practice of history. In Milton and Clarendon, Los Angeles 1965.

Hill, C. Clarendon and the civil war. History Today Oct 1953; rptd in his Puritanism and revolution, 1958.

Wedgwood, C. V. Some contemporary accounts of the civil war. Trans Royal Soc of Lit 26 1953. On Clarendon's methods of portraiture.

Tillyard, E. M. W. In his English epic and its background, 1954.

Vale, V. Clarendon, Coventry and the sale of naval offices 1660–8. Cambridge Historical Jnl 12 1956.

Greenslade, B. D. Clarendon's and Hobbes's Element of law. N & Q April 1957.

Roberts, C. The impeachment of Clarendon. Cambridge Historical Jnl 13 1957.

Hardacre, P. H. Portrait of a bibliophile 1: Clarendon. Book Collector 7 1958.

— Clarendon and the university of Oxford 1660–7. Br Jnl of Educational Stud 9 1961.

Taylor, D. Clarendon and Ben Jonson as witnesses for the Earl of Pembroke's character. In Studies in the English Renaissance drama, ed J. W. Bennett et al, New York 1959.

Abernathy, G. R. Clarendon and the declaration of indulgence. Jnl Ecclesiastical History 11 1960.

Coltman, I. In her Private men and public causes: philosophy and politics in the civil war, 1962.

Bevan, B. The downfall of Clarendon. Contemporary Rev Oct 1967.

JOHN AUBREY
1626–97

Bibliographies

[Bligh, E.] In Brief lives, ed O. L. Dick 1949.

Selections

The scandal and credulities of Aubrey. Ed J. Collier 1931. Selections from Brief lives.

Brief lives and other selected writings. Ed A. Powell 1949.

Brief lives. Ed O. L. Dick 1949, 1950, 1958 (rev).

§1

Queries in order to the description of Britannia. [1673].

Proposals for printing Monumenta britannica. [1693].

Miscellanies: i, Day-fatality; ii, Local-fatality; iii, Ostenta; iv, Omens; v, Dreams etc, collected by Aubrey. 1696, 1721 (best edn, enlarged, with a life). 1784, 1857, 1890. Section xxi (Second-sighted persons) rptd in Miscellanea scotica vol 3, Glasgow [1820].

The natural history and antiquities of the county of Surrey. [Ed R. Rawlinson] 5 vols 1718–19.

Lives of eminent men. [Ed P. Bliss] in Letters written by eminent persons in the seventeenth and eighteenth centuries, [ed J. Walker] vol 2, 1813; Brief lives, ed A. Clark 2 vols Oxford 1898 (bowdlerized, but fullest edn). See under Selections, above.

The natural history of Wiltshire. Ed J. Britton 1847 (Wiltshire Topographical Soc). A fragment, Memoires of natural remarques in the county of Wilts, to which are annexed observable of the same kind in the county of Surrey and Flyntshire, Middle Hill 1838, was abandoned soon after printing began.

Wiltshire: the topographical collections of Aubrey. Ed J. E. Jackson 1862 (Wiltshire Archaeological & Natural History Soc). The part relating to North Wilts priv ptd in 2 pts by Sir Thomas Phillipps as Aubrey's collections for Wilts, 1821, Middle Hill 1838. The introd originally ptd in Miscellanies on several curious subjects, [ed R. Rawlinson] 1714, 1718 (2nd edn, as Introduction towards a natural history of Wiltshire, with other curious miscellanies).

Remaines of gentilisme and Judaisme. Ed J. Britten 1881 (Pbns Folk-lore Soc 4).

Letters

Memoir of Aubrey. Ed J. Britton 1845 (Wilts Topographical Soc). Extracts.

§2

Life. In Oxoniana, [ed J. Walker] vol 3, [1807?].

Masson, D. Aubrey. Br Quart Rev 24 1856.

Jackson, J. E. Memoir. In Kington St Michael, Wilts Archaeological & Natural History Mag 4 1858.

— Lost volume of Aubrey's mss. Wilts Archaeological & Natural History Mag 7 1862.

Chambers, E. K. A jotting by Aubrey. Malone Soc Collections 1 pts 4–5 1911. A possible reference to Shakespeare.

[Hutton, W. H.] Aubrey and Shakespeare. Cornhill Mag April 1916.

— Some additions to Aubrey. Cornhill Mag Dec 1921– Jan 1922.

— Additions to Aubrey: some notes of 1685. Cornhill Mag Dec 1926.

Thomas, E. In his Literary pilgrim in England, 1917.

Aubrey. TLS 11 March 1926.

Strachey, L. In his Portraits in miniature, 1931.

Gunther, R. T. The library of Aubrey. Bodleian Quart Record 6 1931.

Walters, H. B. In his English antiquaries of the sixteenth, seventeenth and eighteenth centuries, 1934.

— In Some English antiquaries, Trans Royal Soc of Lit new ser 13 1934.

[Powell, A.]. In Cameo: a bedside book no 5, [1939].

— Aubrey and his friends. 1948, 1963 (rev).

— Mr Uniades. TLS 17 Aug 1951. See N & Q April 1954; TLS 11 June, 2–9 July, 31 Dec 1954; 19 Aug, 2 Sept 1955.

Hollaender, A. Canon [J. E.] Jackson's copy of Aubrey's Wiltshire collections. Wilts Archaeological & Natural History Mag 49 1942.

Dick, O. L. Scholarship and small-talk. Listener 20 Nov 1947.

— The life and times of Aubrey. Introd to his edn of Brief lives, 1949.

Aubrey's books. TLS 13–20 Jan 1950.

Turnbull, G. H. Samuel Hartlib's acquaintance with Aubrey. N & Q 21 Jan 1950.

Young, G. M. The man who noticed. In his Last essays, 1950.

Cranston, M. John Locke and Aubrey. N & Q 23 Dec 1950, 30 Aug 1952.

Hughes, P. The vogue for Aubrey. Month Jan 1951.

Elsley, R. Aubrey's lives. TLS 5 Oct 1951.

Enright, B. Richard Rawlinson and the publication of Aubrey's Natural history and antiquities of Surrey. Surrey Archaeological Collections 54 1956.

Auden, W. H. New Yorker 15 Feb 1958. Review of Brief lives, ed Dick.

Keynes, G. L. Harvey through Aubrey's eyes. Lancet 25 Oct 1958.

Battersby, W. J. Aubrey's Idea of education. Br Jnl Educational Stud 7 1959.

ANTHONY à WOOD
1632–95
Bibliographies

Huddesford, W. Catalogus librorum manuscriptorum Antonii a Wood: a catalogue of the manuscript collections in the Ashmolean Museum. Oxford 1761; rptd by Sir Thomas Phillipps, Middle Hill 1824. See introd to Life and times, ed A. Clark vol 1, Oxford 1861.

§1

Historia et antiquitates universitatis oxoniensis [tr Latin by R. Peers and R. Reeve]. 2 vols Oxford 1674. The original English version first pbd in pts by J. Gutch 1786–96: The history and antiquities of the colleges and halls in the University of Oxford, with a continuation to the present time, Oxford 1786, 1790 (with Fasti oxonienses, separate title-page and pagination, as an appendix); The history and antiquities of the University of Oxford, 2 vols in 3 Oxford 1792–6.

Athenae oxonienses: an exact history of all the writers and Bishops who have had their education in the University of Oxford from 1500 to 1690; to which are added the Fasti or annals of the University. 2 vols 1691–2 (anon), 1721 (rev and enlarged); ed P. Bliss 5 vols 1813–20 (enlarged with continuation). Of a new edn planned by Ecclesiastical History Soc only one vol was issued, containing Wood's autobiography, ed P. Bliss 1848. See The libel issu'd out of the Chancellor's Court of the University of Oxford against Mr Anthony à Wood, by the Earl of Clarendon, with Mr Wood's answer, and the sentence given after the tryal, begun March 3 1692/3 finish'd July 29 1693, [Oxford 1693?] (anon), rptd in Miscellanies on several curious subjects, [ed R. Rawlinson] 1714.

Life 1632–72 written by himself. In Thomae Caii vindiciae antiquitatis academiae Oxoniensis, ed T. Hearne vol 2, Oxford 1730. Continued to his death in The lives of John Leland, Thomas Hearne and Anthony à Wood, ed W. Huddesford vol 2, Oxford 1772, rptd in Athenae, ed Bliss vol 1, 1813, and in vol 1 of projected edn of Athenae, 1848. Fullest edn as The life and times of Anthony Wood 1632–95, ed A. Clark 5 vols Oxford 1891–1900 (Pbns Oxford Historical Soc 19, 21, 26, 30, 40); abridged L. Powys 1932, Oxford 1961 (WC). Huddesford's edn and both of Bliss's contain additional material from Wood's ms collections; Clark's edn integrates the autobiography with all other relevant material in a single chronological sequence.

Modius salium: a collection of such pieces of humour as prevail'd at Oxford in the time of Mr Anthony à Wood. Oxford 1751.

Survey of the antiquities of the city of Oxford. Ed A. Clark 3 vols Oxford 1889–99 (Pbns Oxford Historical Soc 15, 17, 37). Extracts pbd as Some notes relating to the history of Oxford in Liber niger scaccarii, ed T. Hearne vol 2, Oxford 1728, 1771. An inaccurate edn as The ancient and present state of the city of Oxford, ed J. Peshall 1773 (with addns).

Parochial collections [of Wood and R. Rawlinson]. Ed F. N. Davis 3 vols Oxford 1920–9 (Oxfordshire Record Soc).

Wood also edited Γνωστὸν τοῦ Θεοῦ, καὶ Γνωστὸν τοῦ Χριστοῦ by [his brother] Edward Wood, Oxford 1656, 1674.

§2

[Wood, Thomas]. A vindication of the historiographer of the University of Oxford from the reproaches of the Bishop of Salisbury etc, by E.D. 1693.

[Rawlinson, R]. The life of Anthony à Wood. [1711].

Charlett, A. Letter to Archbishop Tenison concerning the death of Mr Anthony à Wood. In Johannis Glastoniensis Chronicon, ed T. Hearne vol 2, 1726.

Memoir. In Oxoniana, [ed J. Walker] vol 3, [1807?].

Wood and Oxford. Christian Remembrancer March, June 1843.

Clay, T. L. Anthony à Wood. GM July 1888.

Gibson, S. and M. A. An index to Rawlinson's collections c. 1700–50 for a new edition of Wood's Athenae oxonienses. Proc Oxford Bibl Soc 1 1925.

Richards, T. The indiscretion of Wood [in quoting Judge Jenkins's charge against Clarendon in Athenae]. Y Cymmrodor 36 1926.

Powys, L. Anthony à Wood. Saturday Rev of Lit 7 April 1928.

—— Merton Wood's luncheon. In his Earth memories, 1934.

Anthony Wood. TLS 6 Oct 1932.

Jones, I. D. Anthony Wood, the Oxford antiquary. Listener 28 Dec 1932.

Shaw, H. W. Extracts from Wood's Notes on the lives of musicians, hitherto unpublished. Music & Letters 15 1934.

Maslen, B. J. Celebrities and music: Wood. Musical Opinion Sept 1934. Reply by P. A. Scholes, Dec 1934.

Walters, H. B. In his English antiquaries of the sixteenth, seventeenth and eighteenth centuries, 1934.

—— Some English antiquaries. Trans Royal Soc of Lit new ser 13 1934.

W[right], S. G. A critic of Wood. Bodleian Quart Record 7 1934. On James Wright 1643–1713, antiquary.

Primrose, J. B. The first review of Athenae oxonienses. Bodleian Quart Record 8 1938.

Benham, A. R. The so-called anonymous or earliest life of Milton. ELH 6 1939. Reply by E. S. Parsons with rejoinder by Benham 9 1942. See TLS 13 Sept, 11 Oct, 27 Dec 1957; W. R. Parker, Wood's life of Milton: its sources and significance, PBSA 52 1958.

Bühler, C. F. A letter of Wood to Bishop William Lloyd. Historical Mag of Protestant Episcopal Church 22 1954.

French, J. M. The reliability of Wood and Milton's Oxford MA. PMLA 75 1960.

Manuel, M. The life of Milton in the history of kingkillers. N & Q Nov 1960. A scurrilous adaptation of Wood's life.

Sommerlad, M. J. The continuation of Wood's Athenae oxonienses. Bodleian Lib Record 7 1962–7.

GILBERT BURNET
1643–1715

Bibliographies

F[lexman], R. A chronological and distinct account of the works of Burnet. Appendix to his edn of Burnet's History of his own time, 1753; rptd in edns of 1823, 1833.

Foxcroft, H. C. Appendix II to T. E. S. Clarke and Foxcroft, A life of Burnet, Cambridge 1907. See W. R. Mogg, Some reflections on the bibliography of Burnet, Library 5th ser 4 1949. See also R. J. Dobell, and D. I. Masson 5th ser 5 1950; J. H. P. Pafford 6 1952.

Collections

The collections of 1685, 1689 (A second collection) and 1703 are apparently reissues of remainders bound up together. The following is a selective list. For full details see Clarke and Foxcroft's Life pp. 553–4.

A collection of several tracts and discourses written in the years 1677–85. 1685. Contains A vindication of the ordinations of the Church of England; A letter written upon the discovery of the late plot; The unreasonableness and impiety of Popery; A relation of the barbarous and bloody massacre in 1572; A decree made at Rome the second of March 1679 etc. Reissued as vol 1 of Collection, 3 vols 1704, below.

Dr Burnet's tracts. 2 vols 1689. Vol 1 contains Animadversions on Reflections upon travels; Three letters concerning the present state of Italy; vol 2 contains Burnet's trn of A relation of the death of the primitive persecutors by Lactantius; Answers to Varillas (Reflections on Mr Varillas's History, A defence of the Reflections, A continuation of Reflections etc).

A second collection of several tracts and discourses written in the years 1686–9. 1689. Contains A letter containing some remarks on two papers writ by Charles II; Reasons against repealing the acts of Parliament concerning the test; Some reflections on his Majesty's proclamation for a toleration in Scotland; A letter containing some reflections on his Majesty's declaration for liberty of conscience etc. Reissued as vol 2 Collection, 3 vols 1704, below.

A third collection of several tracts and discourses written in the years 1690 to 1703. 1703. Contains Injunctions for the archdeacons of the diocese of Sarum; A sermon preached before the Queen at Whitehall 16 July 1690; A sermon preached at the funeral of Anne Lady Brooke 19 February 1690/1 etc. Reissued as vol 3 of Collection, 3 vols 1704, below.

A collection of several tracts and discourses written in the years 1677 to 1704. 3 vols 1704. Remainders of Collections of 1685, 1689, 1703 reissued.

A collection of speeches, prefaces, letters etc, with a description of Geneva and Holland. 1713. Contains Accounts of Geneva and Holland; Extract on revision of liturgy from visitation charge 1704; Character of Tillotson etc.

§ I

Burnet pbd many sermons and many polemical and apologetic works, generally omitted in the following list. For full details see Foxcroft's Appendix, above.

A discourse on the memory of Sir Robert Fletcher of Saltoun. Edinburgh 1665. Anon.

The memoires of the lives and actions of James and William, Dukes of Hamilton; in which an account is given of the rise and progress of the civil wars of Scotland. 1677, Oxford 1852. Originally pbd as vol 2 of Spottiswoode's History of the Church and State of Scotland, 1677.

The history of the reformation of the Church of England. 3 vols 1679, 1681, 1715. Other edns: vol 1, 1681; vols 1–2 1683; tr French, 1683–5; Latin, 1689; vol 3, 1715, 1715, 1753; 3 vols Dublin 1730–3 (complete); 6 vols in 3 Oxford 1816, 1820, 1825, 4 vols Oxford 1829; ed N. Pocock 7 vols Oxford 1865 (best edn); tr German, 1764–9. Abridgements of vols 1–2 1682; of vol 3 (issued with 5th edn of abridgement of vols 1–2 1719) 1719; 1728 (6th edn of abridgement of vols 1–2, 2nd edn of abridgement of vol 3), Oxford 1808.

Reflections on Mr Varillas's History of the revolutions that have happened in Europe in matters of religion, and more particularly in his ninth book that relates to England. 'Amsterdam' (London?) 1686, rptd 1689 separately and in Tracts vol 2; tr French, 1686. See A. Varillas, Réponse à la critique de Mr Burnet sur les deux premiers tomes de l'histoire des révolutions etc, Paris 1687.

A defence of the Reflections on Mr Varillas's History of heresies: being a reply to his answer. Amsterdam 1687; rptd in Tracts vol 2, 1689.

A continuation of Reflections on Mr Varillas's History of heresies, particularly his third and fourth tomes. Amsterdam 1687; rptd in Tracts vol 2, 1689.

Reflections on the relation of the English reformation [by Obadiah Walker], lately printed at Oxford: part I. Amsterdam 1688; Reflections on the Oxford Theses relating to the English Reformation, part II, Amsterdam 1688 (anon); rptd together, 1689; reissued in A second collection of tracts, 1689.

A letter to Mr Thevenot containing a censure of M. le Grand's History of K. Henry the eighth's divorce. 1688, 1688 (with addns); rptd in Tracts vol 2, 1689; reissued in A second collection of tracts, 1689; tr French, 1688. Burnet's reply to J. Le Grand, Histoire du divorce de Henry VIII, avec la réfutation des deux premiers livres de l'Histoire de Burnet, Paris 1688.

A censure of M. de Meaux [i.e. Bossuet's] History of the variations of the Protestant churches; together with some further reflections on M le Grand. [Amsterdam?] 1688; pbd with A letter to Thevenot, 1689; rptd in Tracts vol 2, 1689; reissued in A second collection of tracts, 1689; tr French, 1689.

A letter writ by the Bishop of Salisbury to the Bishop of Coventry and Litchfield concerning a book by Anthony Harmer [i.e. Henry Wharton]. 1693; reissued in A third collection of tracts, 1703. Burnet's reply to [H. Wharton's] A specimen of some errors in The history of the Reformation by Anthony Harmer, 1693.

Some passages of the life and death of John [Wilmot] Earl of Rochester. 1680, Dublin 1681, London 1692, 1700-1, 1724, Glasgow 1752 etc; tr German, 1698; French, 1716. Abridged as The libertine overthrown: or a mirror for atheists, [1690?]; as A mirror for atheists, 1693.

The life and death of Sir Matthew Hale. 1682 (3 edns), 1700; tr French, 1688.

The history of the rights of princes in the disposing of ecclesiastical benefices and church-lands. 1682.

An answer to the animadversions on the History of the rights of princes. 1682; reissued in A collection of several tracts etc, 1685. Burnet's reply to [T. Comber's] Animadversions on Burnet's History of the rights of princes etc, 1682.

Utopia written in Latin by Sir Thomas More, translated into English. 1684. Anon.

The life of William Bedell, Bishop of Kilmore. 1685 (anon), 1692; tr French, 1687.

A letter written to Dr Burnet, giving an account of Cardinal Pool's secret powers. 1685 (anon); reissued in A collection of several tracts etc, 1685; rptd in Harleian miscellany, et T. Park vol 7, 1811.

Some letters containing an account of what seemed most remarkable in Switzerland, Italy etc, written to T.H.R.B. [i.e. The Honourable Robert Boyle]. Amsterdam 1686, 1687 (6 edns) etc; tr German, 1688 (with addns); French, 1690.

A relation of the death of the primitive persecutors, written originally in Latin by L. C. F. Lactantius, english'd by G. Burnet; to which he hath made a large preface concerning persecution. Amsterdam 1687; rptd in Tracts vol 2, 1689, rptd as God's judgements upon tyrants, 1715 (2nd edn). Part of Burnet's preface, with anti-Catholicism removed, pbd as The case of compulsion in matters of religion, 1688, the full preface as The Bishop of Salisbury's new preface to his pastoral care considered, [1713?] (2nd edn).

Supplement to Dr Burnet's letters written by a nobleman of Italy and communicated to the author. Rotterdam 1687, 1689.

Three letters concerning the present state of Italy: a supplement to Dr Burnet's letters. 1688, 1688 (both anon); rptd in Tracts vol 1, 1689; tr French, 1688; German, 1693.

Animadversions upon the Reflections upon Dr Burnet's travels. [Amsterdam?] 1688; rptd in Tracts vol 1, 1689.

A discourse of the pastoral care. 1692, 1692, 1713 (with addns), 1713.

An essay on the memory of the late Queen. 1695, Edinburgh 1695, Dublin 1695, 1696; tr French, 1695; Dutch, 1695.

An introduction to the third volume of the History of the reformation of the Church of England. 1713, 1714. See [J. Swift], A preface to the B[isho]p of S[a]r[u]m's Introduction to the third volume of The history of the reformation of the Church of England by Gregory Misosarum, 1713.

A character of Gilbert, Bishop of Sarum with a true copy of his last will and testament: containing 1, his profession of faith; 2, his charitable benefactions; 3, an account of the History of his life and times, with directions for the publication of that and other manuscripts etc. 1715 (3 edns), 1717 (omitting the Character), 1728 (in Lives and last wills of eminent persons).

Bishop Burnet's history of his own times. Vol 1, 1724, Dublin 1724, 3 vols Hague 1725, 1725; tr Dutch, 1725; French, 1725; abridged T. Stackhouse 1724; vol 2, 1734, 3 vols Hague 1734, Dublin 1734, 3 vols 1734; ed R. Flexman 4 vols 1753 (complete), 1766; ed M. J. Routh 7 vols Oxford 1823, 6 vols Oxford 1833 (enlarged); ed O. Airy, Oxford 1897 (vols 1-2); tr French, 1735; abridged 1874, 1906 (EL). See R. Elliott, A specimen of the Bishop of Sarum's posthumous History of the affairs of the Church and State of Great Britain during his life, 1715; T. Salmon, An impartial examination of Burnet's History of his own times, 2 vols 1724; M. Earbery, Impartial reflections upon Dr Burnet's posthumous History, 1724; H. Tootel, Remarks on Bishop Burnet's History of his own time, 1724; J. Cockburn, A specimen of some free and impartial remarks on publick affairs and particular persons, occasion'd by Dr Burnet's History of his own times, [1724]; [J. Oldmixon], The critical history of England, wherein particular notice is taken of the History of the grand rebellion; to which are added remarks on some objections made to Bishop Burnet's History of his times vol 1, 1724; L. Braddon, Bishop Burnet's late History charg'd with partiality and misrepresentation, 1725; B. Higgons, Historical and critical remarks on Bishop Burnet's History of his own time, 1725.

A supplement to Burnet's History of my own times, derived from his memoirs etc. Ed H. C. Foxcroft, Oxford 1902.

Certain papers of Robert Burnet [and] Burnet. Ed H. C. Foxcroft, Edinburgh 1904 (Pbns Scottish History Soc).

Thoughts on education. 1761; ed J. Clarke, Aberdeen 1914.

Letters

For a list of extant letters see Appendix III to Clarke and Foxcroft's Life, below.

Some unpublished letters of Burnet [to George Savile, Lord Halifax]. 1907 (Camden Soc 3rd ser 13). See D. L. Poole, Some unpublished letters of George Savile, Lord Halifax, to Burnet, EHR 26 1911; J. J. MacMannon, Some problems regarding a series of letters between Francis Hutcheson and Burnet, Stud in Scottish Lit 3 1965.

§2

Le Clerc, J. The life of Dr Burnet, with his character, and an account of his writings. Tr 1715.

Sewell, G. An essay towards a true account of the life and character of the late Bishop of Salisbury, in remarks upon, and collections from his own writings. 1715.

[Burnet, T.]. A character of the right reverend father in God, Gilbert Lord Bishop of Sarum. 1715 (2nd edn).

Bibliotheca Burnetiana: or a catalogue of the library of Burnet which will begin to be sold by auction 19 March 1715/16. 1716.

Extracts from the acts and proceedings of the presbytery of Haddington, relating to Dr Burnet, and the library of the kirk of Salton 1664-9. Edinburgh 1855 (Bannatyne Miscellany 3).

Macaulay and Burnet. Amer Church Rev 13 1861.

Conder, G. W. Bishop Burnet and the times of the English revolution and Protestant settlement. 1863.

Bishop Burnet and his publications. Christian Remembrancer 47 1864.

Ranke, L. von. In his History of England in the seventeenth century vol 6, tr Oxford 1875.

Davis, H. W. C. In Typical English churchmen from Parker to Maurice, ed W. E. Collins 1902 (Church Historical Soc Pbns).

Barnett, J. Macmillan's Mag Oct 1907.

Dewar, R. Burnet on the Scottish troubles. Scottish Historical Rev 4 1907.

Clarke, T. E. S. and H. C. Foxcroft. A life of Burnet. Cambridge 1907.

Foxcroft, H. C. An early revision of Burnet's Memoirs of the Dukes of Hamilton. EHR 24 1909.

Whibley, C. In his Political portraits [1st ser], 1917.

Shaw, W. A. Burnet and the 'characters' in John Macky's Memoirs. TLS 14–21 June 1928. *See* 28 June, 5 July 1928.

Muddiman, J. G. Burnet and Charles II and the murder of Sir William Estcourt. N & Q 23 Jan 1932.

Firth, C. H. Burnet as an historian. First pbd as introd to Clarke and Foxcroft, Life, 1907, above; rptd in his Essays historical and literary, Oxford 1938.

Jackson, F. J. F. Burnet's History of the Reformation and of his own times. In his A history of church history, Cambridge 1939.

Spence, L. The Scots bishop of Sarum. Scots Mag Sept 1943.

Gooch, G. P. Burnet and the Stuart kings; Burnet and William III. In his Courts and cabinets, 1944.

Kirchberger, C. Elizabeth Burnet 1661–1709. Church Quart Rev 148 1949. Memoir of Burnet's third wife.

Coleridge, S. T. In Coleridge on the seventeenth century, ed R. F. Brinkley, Durham NC 1955. On the Life of Bedell.

Clark, G. N. Aberdeen Univ Rev 37 1957.

MINOR HISTORICAL WRITERS 1660–1700

Historians

SIR PAUL RYCAUT or RICAUT
1628–1700

§I

The capitulations and articles of peace betweene the King of England and the Sultan of the Ottoman Empire, as now lately in the city of Adrianople in 1661 amplifyed. Constantinople 1663.

The present state of the Ottoman Empire. 1667, 1668, 1670 (3rd edn), 1675, 1682 (5th edn, enlarged), 1686; rptd in Knolles, Turkish history vol 2, 1687 (6th edn); abridged J. Savage in Turkish history vol 2, 1701; tr French, 1670 (3 edns), 1678, 1696; Italian, 1672; Polish, 1678; German, 1694.

The present state of the Greek and Armenian churches. 1679.

The history of the Turkish Empire from 1623 to 1677. 1680; rptd in Knolles, Turkish history vol 2, 1687 (6th edn); abridged J. Savage in Turkish history vol 2, 1701. A continuation of Knolles.

The lives of the Popes [tr from Latin of B. Planta], continued from 1471 to present time. 1685, 1688.

The history of the Turks, beginning with 1679 until the end of 1698, 1699. 1700; abridged J. Savage in Turkish history vol 2, 1701.

Rycaut's diplomatic letters from Hamburgh 1692. Middle Hill [1841 ?] (priv ptd by Sir Thomas Phillipps).

§2

Fixler, M. A note on John Evelyn's History of the three late famous imposters. Library 5th ser 9 1954. Account of Sabbatai Zevi depends upon Rycaut's.

GEORGE MACKENZIE, VISCOUNT TARBAT, EARL OF CROMARTY
1630–1714

A memorial for his Highness the Prince of Orange in relation to the affairs of Scotland. 1689. With Sir George Mackenzie. Anon.

A vindication of Robert III, King of Scotland, from the imputation of bastardy. Edinburgh 1695, 1713.

Several proposals conducing to a further union of Britain. 1711. Anon.

An historical account of the conspiracies by the Earls of Gowry and Robert Logan of Restalrig against James VI. Edinburgh 1713.

A vindication of the Historical account of the conspiracies against James VI. Edinburgh 1714.

A vindication of the reformation of the Church of Scotland, with some account of the records. Scots Mag 64 1802.

The genealogie of the Mackenzies, preceeding the year mdclxi, wreattin in the year mdclxix. [Ed J. W. Mackenzie], Edinburgh 1829. Anon.

History of the family of Mackenzie. In W. Fraser, Earls of Cromartie vol 2, 1876.

SIR GEORGE MACKENZIE
1636–91

Bibliographies

Ferguson, F. S. A bibliography of the works of Mackenzie. Trans Edinburgh Bibl Soc 1 1938.

Collections

Essays upon several moral subjects. 1713. With a life.

Works. [Ed with a life by T. Ruddiman] 2 vols Edinburgh 1716–22.

§I

Aretina: or the serious romance. Edinburgh 1660, London 1661, [1661]. Anon.

Religio stoici. Edinburgh 1663, 1663, London 1663, Edinburgh 1665, 1665 (anon); as The religious stoic, Edinburgh 1685, London 1693.

A moral essay, preferring solitude to publick employment. Edinburgh [1665] (anon), 1666, London 1685, 1693.

Moral gallantry; [and] A moral paradox. Edinburgh 1667, London 1669, 1669, 1685, 1821.

Pleadings in some remarkable cases before the supreme courts of Scotland since the year 1661. Edinburgh 1672, 1673 (anon), 1704.

Observations against dispositions made in defraud of creditors. Edinburgh 1675, 1698; rptd in The laws and customes of Scotland in matters criminal, 1699 below.

The laws and customes of Scotland in matters criminal. Edinburgh 1678, 1699.

Observations upon the laws and customs of nations as to precedency; [and] The science of herauldry treated as a part of the civil law. Edinburgh 1680; Observations rptd in J. Guillim, Display of heraldry, 1724 (6th edn).

Idea eloquentiae forensis hodiernae. Edinburgh 1681; tr 1711.

A vindication of his Majesties government and judicatures in Scotland. Edinburgh 1683, London 1683. Anon.

The institutions of the law of Scotland. Edinburgh 1684, 1688 (enlarged), London 1694, Edinburgh 1699, 1706, 1719, 1723, 1730, 1758.

Jus regium: or the just and solid foundations of monarchy; [and] That the lawful successor cannot be debarr'd from succeeding to the crown. Edinburgh 1684, 1684, London 1684, 1684.

A defence of the antiquity of the royal line of Scotland. Edinburgh 1685, London 1685, 1685; tr Latin, 1689.

The antiquity of the royal line of Scotland farther cleared and defended. 1686.

Observations on the Acts of Parliament made by James I [and his successors]. Edinburgh 1686, 1687.

A letter from the nobility, barons and Commons of Scotland in 1320 directed to Pope Iohn. Edinburgh 1689, 1700, 1703, 1745; rptd in Harleian miscellany vol 1, ed T. Park 1808; in Somers tracts vol 11, ed W. Scott 1814; in Miscellanea scotica vol 3, Glasgow [1820].

Oratio inauguralis. 1689; rptd in Catalogus librorum [of Advocates' Library], Edinburgh 1692.

A memorial for his Highness the Prince of Orange in relation to the affairs of Scotland. 1689. Anon. With George Mackenzie, Viscount Tarbat and Earl of Cromarty.

Reason: an essay. 1690, 1695; tr Latin, 1690, 1691, 1700.

The moral history of frugality. 1691, Edinburgh 1691.

A vindication of the government in Scotland during the reign of Charles II. 1691, Edinburgh 1712. See A vindication of the Presbyterians of Scotland from the malicious aspersions cast upon them in a late pamphlet written by Mackenzie, 1692.

Caelia's country-house and closet: a poem. In A choice collection of comic and serious Scots poems pt 2, ed J. Watson, Edinburgh 1709, Glasgow 1869; rptd separately [1715?].

Memoirs of the affairs of Scotland from the restoration of King Charles II. Edinburgh 1821 (priv ptd).

§2

Watt, F. In his Terrors of the law: three portraits of three lawyers, 1902.

Mackenzie, W. C. Bluidy Mackenzie: the man and the myth. GM Aug 1905.

Lang, A. Mackenzie: his life and times. 1909.

Soutar, G. The culture of Bluidy Mackenzie. Scots Mag March 1936.

de Beer, E. S. The letters from Mackenzie to Evelyn. N & Q 5 June 1937.

Loudon, J. H. Mackenzie's speech at the formal opening of the Advocates' Library Edinburgh, 15 March 1689. Trans Edinburgh Bibl Soc 2 1945.

Learney, Innis of. Mackenzie on armorial succession. N & Q 5 July 1941.

ROBERT KNOX
1641?–1720

Selections

Robert Knox in the Kandyan Kingdom. Ed E. F. C. Ludowyk, Oxford 1948.

§1

An historical relation of Ceylon. 1681; rptd J. Harris in Navigantium bibliotheca vol 2, 1705; rptd [R. Fellowes] as appendix to History of Ceylon by Philalethes, 1817, 1818; ed E. Arber in An English garner vol 1, 1877; ed J. Ryan, Glasgow 1911 (enlarged); tr Dutch, 1692; French, 1693; German, 1747.

§2

Moore, J. R. Defoe's sources for Robert Drury's Journal. Bloomington [1943]. Ch 3 on Defoe's use of Knox.

Boxer, C. R. Ceylon through puritan eyes: Knox in the Kingdom of Kandy 1660–79. History Today Oct 1954.

Williams, H. With Knox in Ceylon. 1964.

JAMES WELLWOOD or WELWOOD
1652–1727

§1

A vindication of the present great revolution in England. 1689.

An answer to the late King James's declaration. 1689, 1693; rptd in A collection of state tracts vol 2, 1706.

Memoirs of the most material transactions in England for the last hundred years preceding the Revolution in 1688. 1700 (2nd–3rd edns), 1710; ed F. Maseres 1820.

§2

Imbert-Terry, H. M. Some memorialists of the period of the Restoration. Trans Royal Soc of Lit new ser 2 1922.

ROBERT MOLESWORTH, VISCOUNT MOLESWORTH
1656–1725

§1

An account of Denmark as it was in the year 1692. 1694; tr Dutch, 1694; French, 1695, [1790?].

§2

Realey, C. B. The London Journal and its authors 1720–3. Lawrence Kansas 1935. On Molesworth et al.

Allen, R. J. Steele and the Molesworth family. RES 12 1936.

Biographers and Autobiographers

SAMUEL CLARKE
1599–1683

§1

The marrow of ecclesiastical historie, contained in the lives of the Fathers and other learned men and famous divines. 1650, 1654, 1675 (both enlarged).

A generall martyrologie from the creation to our present times. 1651, 1657, 1660, 1677 (3rd edn, with Lives of thirty-two English divines, below).

A martyrologie: containing all the persecutions which have befallen the Church of England to the end of Queen Maries reign, with the lives of ten English divines. 1652, 1677; rptd in A generall martyrologie, 1677 (3rd edn enlarged).

England's remembrancer: containing a true and full narrative of those two never to be forgotten deliverances, the one from the Spanish invasion, the other from the hellish Powder plot. 1657, 1671 (as A true and full narrative), 1676, 1677, 1679. Other edns as pt 2 of Historians guide, below.

The lives of two and twenty English divines. 1660, 1662.

A collection of the lives of ten eminent divines. 1662.

The lives of thirty-two English divines. 1677.

The historians guide: 1, A chronology of the world from the Creation; 2, England's remembrancer. 1676 (anon), 1679, 1688, 1690, 1701.

The history of the glorious life, reign and death of the illustrious Queen Elizabeth. 1682, 1683.

The lives of sundry eminent persons in this later age: 1, Divines; 2, Nobility and gentry; to which is added his own life. 1683.

LORD DENZIL HOLLES
1599–1680

§1

The grand question concerning the judicature of the House of Peers. 1669. Anon.

A true relation of the unjust accusation of certain French gentlemen. 1671.

The case stated concerning the judicature of the House of Peers in the point of appeals. 1675. Anon.

The case stated of the jurisdiction of the House of Lords in the point of appeals. 1675. Anon.

The case stated of the jurisdiction of the House of Lords in the point of impositions. 1676. Anon.

The Lord Holles his vindication of himself. 1676.

A letter of a gentleman to his friend, shewing that the Bishops are not to be judges in Parliament in cases capital. 1679 (anon), 1679.

Lord Hollis his remains: being a second letter to a friend, concerning the judicature of the Bishops in Parliament. 1682.

Memoirs from 1641 to 1648. 1699; rptd in Select tracts, ed F. Maseres 1815.

§2

Grant, W. L. A Puritan at the Court of Louis XIV. Kingston Ontario 1913.

Wood, A. C. The Holles family. Trans Royal Historical Soc 4th ser 19 1936.

Holles, G. Memorials of the Holles family 1493–1656. Ed A. C. Wood 1937 (Camden Soc).

THOMAS FAIRFAX,
1st BARON FAIRFAX
1612–71

§1

A short memorial of the northern actions in which I was engaged; Short memorials of some things to be cleared during my command. [Ed B. Fairfax] 1699, Leeds 1776; rptd in Antiquarian repertory vol 3, ed E. Lodge 1808; in Somers tracts vol 5, ed W. Scott 1811; in Select tracts, ed F. Maseres 1815; in An English garner vol 8, ed E. Arber 1896; in Stuart tracts, ed C. H. Firth 1903.

Letters

Epistolary curiosities: unpublished letters illustrative of the Herbert family from Fairfax. Pt 1, ed R. W[arner], Bath 1818.

The Fairfax correspondence: memoirs of the reign of Charles I. Ed G. W. Johnson 2 vols 1848; in Memorials of the Civil War: the correspondence of the Fairfax family, ed R. Bell 2 vols 1849.

§2

Markham, C. R. Life of Fairfax. 1870.

Huntley, L. The Fairfaxes of Denton and Nun Appleton. York 1906.

Thornton, W. H. Notes on some traditions concerning the brief visit of Cromwell and Fairfax to Bovey Tracey and its neighbourhood in 1646. Trans of Devonshire Assoc for Advancement of Science, Literature & Art 39 1907.

Fletcher, J. S. In his Yorkshiremen of the Restoration, 1921.

Woledge, G. Saint Amand, Fairfax and Marvell. MLR 25 1930.

Heseltine, G. C. A soldier [Fairfax]. In his Great Yorkshiremen, 1932.

Warner, O. Black Tom [Fairfax]. Cornhill Mag July 1936.

Gibb, M. A. The Lord General: a life of Fairfax. 1938.

Body, O. G. The new model army under Fairfax, 1645 to 1650. Jnl of Royal Artillery 65 1939.

The besieger of Colchester: a contemporary portrait. Essex Rev Oct 1940.

Mars and Euterpe. Blackwood's Mag Dec 1941. On Fairfax's patronage of Marvell.

Duncan-Jones, E. E. Marvell and the Cinque ports. TLS 11 Nov 1955. On Fairfax in Appleton House.

WILLIAM BEDELL
1613–70

A true relation of the life and death of William Bedell [1571–1642], Lord Bishop of Kilmore. Ed T. W. Jones 1872 (Camden Soc); in Cambridge in the seventeenth century, ed J. E. B. Mayor, Cambridge 1871; in Two biographies of Bedell, ed E. S. Shuckburgh, Cambridge 1902.

ALEXANDER CLOGIE or CLOGY
1614–98

Memoir of the life and episcopate of William Bedell [1571–1642], Lord Bishop of Kilmore. [Ed W. W. Wilkins] 1862; in Two biographies of Bedell, ed E. S. Shuckburgh, Cambridge 1902.

EDMUND LUDLOW
1617?–92

§1

Memoirs. 3 vols Vivay [London?] 1698–9, London 1721–0, Edinburgh 1751, 1 vol 1751, 1771; ed C. H. Firth 2 vols Oxford 1894 (with letters); tr French, 1699–1707.

§2

Ward, A. W. Memoirs of Ludlow. In his Collected papers vol 1, Cambridge 1921.

Whiting, G. W. The authorship of the Ludlow pamphlets. N & Q 16 Dec 1933.

Whitley, W. T. Ludlow's Baptist comrades. Baptist Quart new ser 11 1945.

de Beer, E. S. Ludlow in exile. N & Q June 1962.

GEORGE SIKES

The life and death of Sir Henry Vane. 1662. Anon.

LUCY HUTCHINSON
b. 1620

§1

Memoirs of the life of Colonel Hutchinson; to which is prefixed the life of Mrs Hutchinson, written by herself. Ed J. Hutchinson 1806, 1808, 2 vols 1810; ed C. H. Firth 2 vols 1885 (with Hutchinson's letters), 1906 (rev); ed H. Child 1904; [1908], 1965 (EL); tr French, 1823.

§2

Upham, A. H. Lucy Hutchinson and the Duchess of Newcastle. Anglia 36 1912.

Race, S. The British Museum ms of the life of Colonel Hutchinson, and its relation to the published memoirs. Trans Thoroton Soc 1914.

— Notes on Mrs Hutchinson's manuscripts. N & Q 7–14 July, 1 Sept 1923.

— Colonel Hutchinson, governor of Nottingham Castle and regicide. N & Q 15 Jan 1938. *See also* 19 Jan 1952, April–May 1954.

Ward, A. W. Colonel Hutchinson and his wife. In his Collected papers vol 1, Cambridge 1921.

Warburg, I. Lucy Hutchinson: das Bild einer Puritanerin. Hamburg 1937.

MacCarthy, B. G. Biography [on Lucy Hutchinson]. In her Women writers: their contribution to the English novel 1621–1744, Cork 1944.

Meynell, A. C. Seventeenth century. In her Essays, ed F. Meynell 1947.

Hobman, D. A. A Puritan lady. Contemporary Rev Aug 1949.

Weiss, S. A. Dating Mrs Hutchinson's translation of Lucretius. N & Q March 1955.

Braund, E. Mrs Hutchinson and her teaching [in Puritan theology]. Evangelical Quart 31 1959.

DAVID LLOYD
1635–92

§1

Modern policy compleated: or the publick actions and councels of General Monck, 1639 to 1660. 1660.

ΕΙΚΟΝ ΒΑΣΙΛΙΚΗ: or the true pourtraiture of his sacred Majestie Charls II. 1660 (anon), 1660; tr Dutch, 1661.

The states-men and favourites of England since the Reformation. 1665, 1670 (enlarged as State worthies), 1679; ed C. Whitworth 2 vols 1766 (enlarged).

Memoires of the lives of those personages that suffered for the Protestant religion, and allegiance to their soveraign from 1637 to 1660, continued to 1666. 1668, 1677.

§2

Jones, T. L. Studies in Welsh book-land iv: the Rev David Lloyd, Trawsfynydd, biographer. Jnl of Welsh Bibl Soc 5 1942.

Antiquaries

ELIAS ASHMOLE
1617–92

§1

The institution, laws and ceremonies of the Order of the Garter. 1672, 1693, 1715 (abridged with continuation by T. Walker as The history of the Order of the Garter).

Memoirs drawn up by himself by way of a diary. 1717 (with letters); [ed T. Davies] 1774 (with William Lilly, History of his life and times, an autobiography); ed R. T. Gunther, Oxford 1927; in Autobiographical and historical notes etc, ed C. H. Josten 5 vols Oxford 1966. Josten's edn integrates all autobiographical material, from whatever source, in a chronological sequence.

The antiquities of Berkshire. 3 vols 1719, 1723, 1 vol Reading 1736.

Letters

Autobiographical and historical notes, his correspondence etc. Ed C. H. Josten 5 vols Oxford 1966. *See above.*

§2

Rawlinson, R. Some memoirs of the life of Ashmole. In the Antiquities of Berkshire vol 1, 1719.

Tuckett, J. E. S. Dr Richard Rawlinson and the masonic entries in Ashmole's diary. Ars Quatuor Coronatorum 25 1912 (Trans of [Masonic] Lodge Quatuor Coronati no 2076 London).

Lambert, C. Ashmole. Trans of Authors' [Masonic] Lodge no 3456 1 1915.

Gunther, R. T. Ashmole: founder of the first public museum of natural history. Nature 17 May 1917.

— The Ashmole printed books. Bodleian Quart Record 6 1932.

Wood, W. A. Tercentenary of Ashmole; with a note on behalf of Ashmole by F. Madan. Lichfield 1917.

Lhuyd, E. Account of Ashmole. Bodleian Quart Record 2 1920.

Rylands, J. P. Impressions of armorial seals of Cheshire gentry made by Ashmole in 1663. Trans of Historic Soc of Lancashire & Cheshire 71 1920.

M[adan], F. Ashmole and the Ashmolean. Bodleian Quart Record 3 1923.

Wright, D. Ashmole. [1924].

Humphreys, A. L. Ashmole. Berks, Bucks & Oxon Archaeological Jnl 28 1924; Reading 1925.

Millican, C. B. The first English translation of the Prophecies of Merlin. SP 28 1931. By Ashmole.

Bowers, R. H. Lydgate's The churl and the bird, ms Harley 2407, and Ashmole. MLN 49 1934.

Viner, G. H. An unknown bookplate of Ashmole. Apollo Feb 1935.

Lamborn, E. A. G. The arms of Ashmole. N & Q 2 June 1945.

Hone, R. E. The period of Edward Phillips's work for Ashmole. N & Q April 1956.

Josten, C. H. In his edn of Autobiographical and historical notes vol 1, 1966. Biographical introd.

WILLIAM PETYT
1641?–1707

Miscellanea parliamentaria: containing presidents 1, of freedom from arrests; 2, of censures. 1680, 1681.

The antient right of the Commons of England asserted. 1680.

Britannia Languens: or a discourse of trade. 1680, 1689. Anon.

The pillars of Parliament. 1681.

Jus parliamentarium: or the ancient power of Parliament revived and asserted. 1739.

ROBERT THOROTON
1623–78

§1

The antiquities of Nottinghamshire. 1677; ed J. Throsby 3 vols 1790 (as A history of Nottinghamshire), 1797.

§2

Godfrey, J. T. Thoroton: physician and antiquary. [Nottingham?] 1890.

Blagg, T. M. Car-Colston: Dr Thoroton's headstone. Trans of Thoroton Soc 5 1901.

— Thoroton. Trans of Thoroton Soc 12 1908.

Stevenson, W. The descendants of Thoroton. Trans of Thoroton Soc 12 1908.

Schlatter, R. B. A letter from Thoroton to Archbishop Sheldon. Trans of Thoroton Soc 42 1938.

Pitman, C. F. Two reputed portraits of Thoroton. Trans of Thoroton Soc 43 1939. *See* T. M. Blagg 44 1940.

Wood, A. C. In his History of Nottinghamshire, Nottingham 1947.

Hildyard, M. T. H. The Thorotons of Thoroton etc. Trans of Thoroton Soc 58 1954.

— Thoroton. Trans of Thoroton Soc 61 1957.

JAMES WRIGHT
1643–1713

§1

The history and antiquities of the county of Rutland. 1684; addns 1687 (12 pp.), 1714, 1788 (36 pp. ed W. Harrod).

A compendious view of the late tumults and troubles in this Kingdom, by way of annals for seven years [1678–84]. 1685. Anon.

Country conversations: discourses on divers subjects—Of the modern comedies, Of drinking, Of translated verse, Of painting and painters, Of poets and poetry. 1694 (anon), 1927.

Historia histrionica: an historical account of the English-stage. 1699 (anon); rptd in A collection of old plays vol 11, ed R. Dodsley 1744 (preface); in Old English drama vol 1, ed T. White 1830; in E. W. Ashbee, Occasional fac-simile reprints, 1872 (no 28).

Wright also tr and abridged Dugdale's Monasticon, 1693.

§2

W[right], S. G. A critic of Anthony Wood. Bodleian Quart Record 7 1934.

B. EARLY EIGHTEENTH-CENTURY HISTORIANS 1700–50

JOHN STRYPE
1643–1737

Bibliographies
Wire, A. P. In his Strype, Leyton [1902].

Collections
Historical and biographical works. 19 vols Oxford 1812–24; Index [by R. F. Laurence], 2 vols Oxford 1828.

§1

Memorials of Thomas Cranmer. 1694, 2 vols Oxford 1812 (enlarged), 3 vols 1848–54 (Ecclesiastical History Soc); ed P. E. Barnes 2 vols 1853.

The life of the learned Sir Thomas Smith, principal Secretary of State to King Edward the Sixth and Queen Elizabeth. 1698, Oxford 1820.

Historical collections of the life and acts of John Aylmer, Bishop of London. 1701, Oxford 1821.

The life of the learned Sir John Cheke, Secretary of State to Edward VI. 1705, Oxford 1821.

Annals of the Reformation and establishment of religion, and other occurrences in the Church of England, during the first twelve years of Queen Elizabeth's reign. 1709 (vol 1 only), 4 vols 1725–31 (much enlarged), 1735–7, Oxford 1824.

The history of the life and acts of Edmund Grindal, Bishop of London and Archbishop of York and Canterbury in the reign of Q. Elizabeth. 1710, Oxford 1821.

The life and acts of Matthew Parker, Archbishop of Canterbury in the reign of Queen Elizabeth. 1711, 3 vols Oxford 1821.

The life and acts of John Whitgift, Archbishop of Canterbury in the reign of Queen Elizabeth. 1718, 3 vols Oxford 1822.

Ecclesiastical memorials, relating chiefly to religion and the Reformation of it under Henry VIII, Edward VI and Mary. 3 vols 1721, 1733 (with new vol 1), Oxford 1822 (enlarged).

Strype also edited and extended J. Stow, Survey of the cities of London and Westminster, *with a life of* Stow, 2 vols 1720, 1754–5 (*much enlarged*).

§2

Maitland, S. R. Remarks on the first volume of Strype's Life of Archbishop Cranmer recently published by the Ecclesiastical History Society. 1848.

Wire, A. P. Strype. Leyton [1902].

Smith, H. Strype. Essex Rev 38 1929.

Bren, R. Strype memorial slab in Leyton parish church: account of the discovery. Essex Rev 41 1932.

Strype. TLS 6 Nov 1943. *See* 13–20 Nov 1943.

ROGER NORTH
1653–1734

Collections
The lives of the Norths. Ed H. Roscoe 3 vols 1826 (Francis, Dudley and John); ed A. Jessopp 3 vols 1890 (with R. North's autobiography and [letters). *See below.*

North on music: a selection of his essays written c. 1695–1728. Ed J. Wilson 1959.

§1

A discourse on fish and fish-ponds. 1713 (anon), 1714, 1715.

Examen: or an enquiry into the credit and veracity of a pretended complete history; together with some memoirs, all tending to vindicate Charles II. [Ed M. North] 1740; pp. 329–41 rptd as A discourse on the English constitution in The scholar armed vol 1, 1795, 1800 (slightly amended).

The life of Francis North, Baron Guildford. [Ed M. North] 1742, 2 vols 1808, 1 vol [1939] (abridged). *See* Collections, *above.*

The life of Sir Dudley North and of Dr John North. 1744. *See* Collections, *above.*

A discourse of the poor. [Ed M. North] 1753.

A discourse on the study of the laws. 1824.

Memoirs of musick. Ed E. F. Rimbault 1846.

Autobiography. Ed A. Jessopp 1887 (priv ptd). *See* Collections, above.

The musicall gramarian. Ed H. Andrews, Oxford [1925].

Letters
Lives of the Norths vol 3. Ed A. Jessop 1890.

§2

Birrell, A. North's autobiography. In his Collected essays and addresses 1880–1920 vol 1, 1922.

Gore, F. C. A seventeenth-century barrister. Quart Rev 260 1933.

Carver, G. North and his brothers. In his Alms for oblivion, Milwaukee 1946.

Birrell, T. A. North and political morality in the later Stuart period. Scrutiny 17 1950.

Letwin, W. The authorship of Sir Dudley North's Discourses on trade. Economica new ser 18 1951. Ascribed to North.

Colvin, H. M. North and Sir Christopher Wren. Architectural Rev Oct 1951.

Mackerness, E. D. A speculative dilettante. Music & Letters July 1953. North's comments on musical theory and fashions in Restoration England.

Morgan, F. C. Musical history. TLS 4 Sept 1953. On ms of Musicall gramarian 1728.

Somerset, H. V. F. North on music in education. Monthly Musical Record Nov 1953. On ch 7 of North's autobiography.

Schwoerer, L. G. The chronology of North's major works. History of Ideas News Letter 3 1957.

— North and his notes on legal education. HLQ 22 1959.

Burton, M. C. Mr Prencourt and North on teaching music. Musical Quart 44 1958.

Ketton-Cremer, R. W. North. E & S new ser 12 1959.

Clifford, J. L. North and the art of biography. In Restoration and eighteenth-century literature: essays in honour of A. D. McKillop, Chicago 1963.

Morris, J. N. North: a brother's life. In his Versions of the self: studies in English autobiography from Bunyan to Mill, New York 1966.

Starr, G. A. North and the arguments and materials for a register of estates. BM Quart 31 1967.

THOMAS MADOX
1666–1727

§1

Formulare anglicanum: or a collection of ancient charters and instruments of divers kinds, from the Norman Conquest to the end of the reign of Henry VIII. 1702.

The history and antiquities of the Exchequer of the kings of England, from the Norman Conquest to the end of the reign of Edward II. 1711, 2 vols 1769 (with index).

Firma burgi: or an historical essay concerning the cities towns and buroughs of England. 1726.

Baronia anglica: an history of land-honors and baronies, and of tenure in rapite. 1736 (with index to the History of the Exchequer), 1741.

§2

Hazeltine, H. D. Madox as constitutional and legal historian. Law Quart Rev 32 1916.

Douglas, D. C. Rymer and Madox. In his English scholars 1660–1730, 1939, 1951 (rev).

Sims, C. S. An unpublished fragment of Madox, History of the Exchequer. HLQ 23 1960.

THOMAS HEARNE
1678–1735
Bibliographies

Operum nostrorum hactenus impressorum catalogus. In Hearne's edn of Benedictus abbas Petroburgensis, de vita et gestis Henrici II et Ricardi I vol 2, Oxford 1735.

Catalogus operum. In Lives of John Leland, Hearne and Anthony à Wood [ed W. Huddesford] vol 1 pt 2, Oxford 1772.

Dibdin, T. F. In E. Brydges, The British bibliographer vols 1–2, 1810–12. An attempt at a catalogue raisonné.

Hardy, T. D. In his Catalogue of materials, history of Great Britain and Ireland, to the end of the reign of Henry VII vol 1, 1862 (Rolls Ser).

Collections

Works. 4 vols 1810. Contains chronicles of Robert of Gloucester (vols 1–2) and Peter Langtoft (vols 3–4). See below.

§1

Reliquiae Bodleianae: or some genuine remains of Sir Thomas Bodley. 1703.

C. Plinii Caecilli secundi epistolae et panegyricus. Oxford 1703.

Eutropii breviarum historiae romanae. Oxford 1703, Leyden 1729, 1762, 1793.

Ductor historicus: or a short system of universal history, and an introduction to the study of it. 2 vols 1705-4 (vol 2 written, vol 1 ed Hearne); Hearne had no hand in the edns of 1714, 1723, 1724.

M. Juniani Justini historiarum ex Trogo Pompeio libri xliv. Oxford 1705.

T. Livii Patavini historiarum ab urbe condita libri qui supersunt. 6 vols Oxford 1708.

A letter containing an account of some antiquities between Windsor and Oxford. Monthly Miscellany Nov 1708–Jan 1709 (pirated); rptd 1725.

The life of Aelfred the Great by Sir John Spelman. Oxford 1709 (enlarged).

The itinerary of John Leland the antiquary. 9 vols Oxford 1710–12, 1744–5, 1768–9.

Henrici Dodwelli de Parma equestri Woodwardiana dissertatio. Oxford 1713. Includes Collegiorum scholarumque publicarum academiae oxoniensis topographica delineatio, per T. Nelum, which is rptd in Elizabethan Oxford, ed C. Plummer, Oxford 1887 (Pbns Oxford Historical Soc).

Joannis Lelandi antiquarii de rebus britannicis collectanea. 6 vols Oxford [1715], London 1770, 1774.

Acta apostolorum graeco-latine, litteris majusculis, e codice Laudiano. Oxford 1715.

Joannis Rossi antiquarii Warwicensis historia regum Angliae. Oxford 1716, 1745.

Titi Livii Foro-Juliensis vita Henrici quinti, regis Angliae. Oxford 1716.

Aluredi Beverlacensis annales. Oxford 1716.

Guilielmi Roperi vita D. Thomae Mori lingua anglicana contexta. [Oxford] 1716.

Guilielmi Camdeni annales rerum anglicarum et hibernicarum regnante Elizabetha. 3 vols [Oxford] 1717.

Guilielmi Neubrigensis historia sive chronica rerum anglicarum. 3 vols Oxford 1719.

Thomae Sprotti chronica. Oxford 1719.

A collection of curious discourses written by eminent antiquaries upon several heads in our English antiquities. Oxford 1720, 2 vols 1771 (enlarged).

Textus Roffensis. Oxford 1720.

Roberti de Avesbury historia de mirabilibus gestis Edvardi III. Oxford 1720.

Johannis de Fordun Scotichronicon. 5 vols Oxford 1722.

The history and antiquities of Glastonbury [by R. Rawlinson]. Oxford 1722.

Hemingi chartularium ecclesiae Wigorniensis. 2 vols Oxford 1723.

Robert of Gloucester's chronicle. 2 vols Oxford 1724, 1810.

Peter Langtoft's chronicle, improv'd by Robert of Brunne. 2 vols Oxford 1725, 1810.

Joannis Glastoniensis chronica: sive historia de rebus glastoniensibus. 2 vols Oxford 1726.

Adami de Domerham historia de rebus gestis glastoniensibus. 2 vols Oxford 1727.

Thomae de Elmham vita et gesta Henrici quinti. Oxford 1727.

Liber niger scaccarii. 2 vols Oxford 1728, 1771.

Historia vitae et regni Ricardi II, a monacho quodam de Evesham consignata. Oxford 1729.

Johannis de Trokelow annales Edvardi II. Oxford 1729.

Thomae Caii vindiciae antiquitatis academiae oxoniensis. 2 vols Oxford 1730.

Walteri Hemingford historia de rebus gestis Edvardi I, Edvardi II et Edvardi III. 2 vols Oxford 1731.

A vindication of those who take the oath of allegiance to his present Majestie. 1731. Unauthorized by Hearne.
Duo rerum anglicarum scriptores veteres: viz Thomas Otterbourne et Johannes Whethamstede. 2 vols Oxford 1732
Chronicon: sive annales prioratus de Dunstaple. 2 vols Oxford 1733.
Benedictus abbas Petroburgensis de vita et gestis Henrici II et Ricardi I. 2 vols Oxford 1735.
Autobiography. In Lives of John Leland, Hearne and Anthony à Wood, [ed W. Huddesford] 2 vols Oxford 1772 (enlarged).

Letters and Diaries

An account of my journey to Whaddon-hall in Bucks 1716; An account of Hearne's journey to Reading and Silchester 1714. In Letters written by eminent persons in the seventeenth and eighteenth centuries [ed J. Walker] vol 2, 1813. Extracts.
Reliquiae Hearnianae: the remains of Hearne. Ed P. Bliss 2 vols Oxford 1857, 3 vols 1869 (enlarged); rev J. Buchanan-Brown 1966. Selections.
Remarks and collections of Hearne. Ed C. E. Doble et al 11 vols Oxford 1885–1921 (Pbns Oxford Historical Soc). Fullest and best edn.

§2

Impartial memorials of the life and writings of Hearne. Ed E. Curll 1736. Partial.
A catalogue of the valuable library of Hearne. [1736].
Bibliotheca Hearneiana. [Ed B. Botfield] 1848 (priv ptd); ed P. Bliss in Reliquiae Hearnianae vol 3, 1869 (2nd edn).
Crothers, W. E. Hearne: the Oxford antiquary. Temple Bar Jan 1904.
Bodleian Quart Record 1 1916.
Darwin, F. In his Springtime and other essays, 1920.
Hutton, W. H. Hearne and the nonjurors. Edinburgh Rev 235 1922.
Emden, A. B. Hearne's rooms in St Edmund Hall. Bodleian Quart Record 3 1922.
Walters, H. B. In Some English antiquaries, Trans Royal Soc of Lit new ser 13 1934.
Hearne and Richard Gough. TLS 14 Feb 1935.
TLS 6 June 1935.
Bulloch, J. M. Hearne's first master, the Rev Patrick Gordon. N & Q 16 Nov 1935.
Askew, H. A friend of Hearne. N & Q 4 Jan 1936. On Thomas Baker.
Douglas, D. C. Portrait of Hearne. In his English scholars 1660–1730, 1939, 1951 (rev).
Philip, I. G. Hearne as a publisher. Bodleian Lib Record 3 1951.
—— The genesis of Hearne's Ductor historicus. Bodleian Lib Record 7 1967.
Johnston, A. Fielding, Hearne and Merry-Andrews. N & Q Aug 1960.

RICHARD RAWLINSON
1690–1755

§1

The life of Mr Anthony à Wood. [1711]. Anon.
Miscellanies on several curious subjects. [Ed Rawlinson] 1714.
A full and impartial account of the Oxford-riots in a letter from a member of the University [signed Philoxon]. 1715.
The history and antiquities of the cathedral church of Rochester. 1717. Anon.
The history and antiquities of the city and cathedral-church of Hereford. 1717. Anon.

A survey of Staffordshire, by S. Erdeswicke. 1717. Ed Rawlinson?
Petri Abaelardi et Heloissae epistolae. 1718.
Some memoirs of the life of Elias Ashmole. In Ashmole, Antiquities of Berkshire vol 1, 1719.
The natural history and antiquities of the county of Surrey, by John Aubrey. 5 vols 1719. Ed Rawlinson.
The history and antiquities of the cathedral-church of Salisbury, and the abbey-church of Bath. 1719 (anon), 1723.
The English topographer: or an historical account of all the pieces relating to the antiquities, natural history or topographical description of any part of England. 1720. Anon.
The history and antiquities of Glastonbury. Ed T. Hearne, Oxford 1722.
A new method of studying history, originally written in French by M. Langlet du Fresnoy. 2 vols 1728. Tr Rawlinson.
The history of Sir John Perrott, Lord Lieutenant of Ireland. 1728. Ed Rawlinson.
The deed of trust and will of R. Rawlinson of St John Baptist College, Oxford; containing his endowment of an Anglo-Saxon lecture to the College and University. 1755.
Monmouthshire, a small specimen of the many mistakes in Dugdale's Baronage: reprint of a scarce and curious pamphlet addressed to Hearne. Ed C. Heath, Monmouth 1801.
A short historical account of the life and designs of Thomas Bray DD. In T. Bray: his life and selected works, ed B. C. Steiner, Baltimore 1901 (Pbns Maryland Historical Soc).
Parochial collections [of Wood and Rawlinson]. Ed F. N. Davis 3 vols Oxford 1920–9 (Oxfordshire Record Soc).

§2

Fletcher, W. Y. The Rawlinsons and their collections. Trans of Bibl Soc 5 1899.
Tuckett, J. E. S. Rawlinson and the masonic entries in Elias Ashmole's diary. Ars Quatuor Coronatorum 25 1912 (Trans of [Masonic] Lodge Quatuor Coronati).
Gibson, S. and M. A. An index to Rawlinson's collections (c. 1700–50) for a new edition of Wood's Athenae oxonienses. Proc Oxford Bibl Soc 1 1924.
Enright, B. J. Rawlinson and the chandlers. Bodleian Lib Record 4 1953.
—— Rawlinson's proposed History of Oxfordshire. Oxoniensia 16 1953.
—— Edmund Curll and the 'cursed blunders' in Fresnoy's New method of studying history 1728. Library 5th ser 9 1954. Rawlinson assisted by Curll.
—— Rawlinson and the publication of Aubrey's Natural history and antiquities of Surrey. Surrey Archaeological Collections 54 1955.
—— Rawlinson's proposed History of Middlesex 1717–20. Trans of London & Middlesex Archaeological Soc 19 1958.

THOMAS BIRCH
1705–66

§1

A general dictionary historical and critical, in which a new and accurate translation of that of Mr Bayle is included, by John Peter Bernard, Birch etc. 10 vols 1734–41. Ed Birch, who also wrote the 615 new biographies signed T and H.
An historical and critical account of the life and writings of Mr John Milton. In A complete collection of the historical, political and miscellaneous works of John Milton, 2 vols 1738, 1 vol 1753.

The life of Mr William Chillingworth. In Works of William Chillingworth, 3 vols Oxford 1738 (9th edn), London 1742 (10th edn).

The complete works of Francis Bacon; to which is prefixed a new life of the author. 4 vols 1740. Ed Birch.

A collection of the state papers of John Thurloe, to which is prefixed the life of Thurloe. 7 vols 1742. Ed Birch.

An account of the life and writings of Ralph Cudworth. In Cudworth, The true intellectual system of the universe, 1743 (2nd edn), rptd in Cudworth's Works vol 1, 1829.

Lives and characters. In J. Houbraken and G. Vertue, Heads of illustrious persons of Great Britain, 2 vols 1743–51, 1747–52, 1 vol 1756, 1813.

The life of the Hon Robert Boyle. 1744; in Boyle's Works vol 1, 1744, 1772.

An inquiry into the share which Charles I had in the transactions of the Earl of Glamorgan for bringing over a body of Irish rebels to assist that King in 1645 and 1646. 1747 (anon), 1756 (enlarged). See [J. Boswell], The case of the royal martyr: an answer to some libels vol 2, 1758.

An historical view of the negociations between the Courts of England, France and Brussels 1592–1617; to which is added A relation of the state of France drawn up by Sir George Carew in 1609. 1749.

The life of Mrs Catharine Cockburn. In her Works, 2 vols 1751.

The life of Mr Edmund Spenser. In The Faerie Queene, 3 vols 1751.

The life of Sir Walter Ralegh. In Ralegh's Works, 2 vols 1751; rptd in Ralegh's Works vol 1, Oxford 1829.

The life of John Tillotson, Archbishop of Canterbury. 1752, 1753 (enlarged); in Tillotson's Works vol 1, 1752, 1820. See [G. Smith], Remarks upon the Life of Tillotson, 1753, 1754, 1755 (enlarged).

Memoirs of the reign of Queen Elizabeth from 1581 till her death. 2 vols 1754.

The life of Dufresnoy. In [J.] Wills, De arte graphica: or the art of painting, translated from the Latin of C. A. Dufresnoy, 1754.

The history of the Royal Society of London. 4 vols 1756–7.

The life of Henry Prince of Wales, eldest son of James I. 1760, Dublin 1760.

Letters between Colonel R. Hammond and the Committee of Lords and Commons at Derby House relating to Charles I while he was confined in Carisbrooke Castle. 1764.

An account of the life of John Ward, Professor of Rhetoric in Gresham College. 1766.

The Court and times of James the First, illustrated by authentic and confidential letters. 2 vols 1848. Transcribed by Birch, ed R. F. Williams.

The Court and times of Charles the First, including memoirs of the mission in England of the Capuchin friars in the service of Queen Henrietta Maria. 2 vols 1848. Transcribed by Birch, ed R. F. Williams.

§2

Babcock, R. W. Birch as transcriber of [Samuel] Johnson. PQ 16 1937.

Osborn, J. M. Birch and the General Dictionary 1734–41. MP 36 1939.

Ruhe, E. L. Pope's hand in Birch's account of Gay. RES new ser 5 1954.

— Birch, Johnson and Elizabeth Carter: an episode of 1738–9. PMLA 73 1958.

Hennig, J. Goethe's extracts from Birch's History of the Royal Society. MLR 52 1957.

Knapp, L. M. Comments on Smollett by Birch. N & Q June 1965.

MINOR HISTORICAL WRITERS 1700-1750

Historians

THOMAS RYMER

1641–1713

Bibliographies

Zimansky, C. A. The canon of Rymer's works. Appendix to Critical works of Rymer, New Haven 1956.

Collections

Critical works. Ed C. A. Zimansky, New Haven 1956.

§1

Reflections on Aristotle's treatise of poesie, by R. Rapin. 1674 (anon), 1694; in Whole critical works of Monsieur Rapin vol 2, 1706, 1716, 1731; in Critical works of Rymer, ed C. A. Zimansky, New Haven 1956. Tr Rymer, with a preface.

The tragedies of the last age. 1678 (for 1677), 1692; in Critical works, ed C. A. Zimansky, New Haven 1956.

Edgar, or the English monarch: an heroick tragedy. 1678, 1691, 1693.

A general draught and prospect of government in Europe, shewing the antiquity, power, decay of parliaments. 1681 (anon), 1689, 1714, 1714, 1715, 1715; rptd (with misattribution to Algernon Sydney) as A general view of government in Europe, in J. Ralph, Of the use and abuse of parliaments vol 1, 1744, and in Sidney's Works, ed J. Robertson 1772.

Historia ecclesiastica carmine elegiaco concinnata, authore Thoma Hobbio Malmesburiensi. 1688 (anon); tr as A true ecclesiastical history, from Moses to the time of Martin Luther, 1722. Preface by Rymer.

Poems on several occasions; with Valentinian: a tragedy, written by John late Earl of Rochester. 1691 (anon), 1696, 1705, 1710, 1714, 1732; in Critical works, ed C. A. Zimansky, New Haven 1956. Preface by Rymer.

A short view of tragedy. 1692; in Critical works, ed C. A. Zimansky, New Haven 1956. See J. Dennis, The impartial critick: or some observations upon A short view of tragedy, 1693.

Letters to the Bishop of Carlisle, occasioned by some passages in his late book of the Scotch Library: letter 1. 1702 (anon); letter 11, [1703?] (anon); letter 111, 1706 (anon).

Foedera, conventiones, literae et cujuscunque generis acta publica, inter reges Angliae etc. 17 vols 1704–1617 (for 1717) (vols 16–17 by R. Sanderson), on period 1101–1625; ed G. Holmes 20 vols 1727–35 (enlarged) (vols 15–20 by Sanderson); 10 vols Hague 1739–45 (enlarged); ed A. Clarke, J. Caley, F. Holbrooke 4 vols 1816–69 (incomplete). Syllabus of the Foedera by T. D. Hardy, 3 vols 1869–85. Calendar in English, with index in vol 3. See C. P. Cooper, Appendices to a report on Rymer's Foedera, 3 vols [1869?].

§2

Hardy, T. D. In his Syllabus of Rymer's Foedera vol 1, 1869. Preface.

Hofherr, A. Rymers dramatische Kritik. Heidelberg 1908.

Dutton, G. B. The French Aristotelian formalists and Rymer. PMLA 29 1914.

Stoll, E. E. Oedipus and Othello: Corneille, Rymer and Voltaire. Revue Anglo-américaine 12 1935; rptd in Shakespeare and other masters, Cambridge Mass 1940.

Walcott, F. G. John Dryden's answer to Rymer's The tragedies of the last age. PQ 15 1936.

Douglas, D. C. Rymer and Madox. In his English scholars 1660–1730, 1939, 1951 (rev).

Zimansky, C. A. The literary career of Thomas Ross. PQ 21 1942. Questions ascription of Cicero's Prince 1668 to Rymer.

—— Chaucer and the school of Provence: a problem in eighteenth-century literary history. PQ 25 1946.

—— A manuscript poem to Rymer. PQ 30 1951.

Atkins, J. W. H. New French influences [Rymer and others]. In his English literary criticism: the 17th and 18th centuries, 1951.

Leech, C. Rymer on Othello. In his Shakespeare's tragedies and other studies in seventeenth-century drama, 1950.

Watson, G. In his Literary critics, 1962 (Pelican), 1964 (rev).

—— Dryden's first answer to Rymer. RES new ser 14 1963.

HUMPHREY PRIDEAUX
1648–1724

§1

The true nature of imposture fully display'd in the life of Mahomet. 1697, 1697, 1708 (4th edn), 1723 (8th edn), Dublin 1730; tr French, 1698.

The Old and New Testament connected in the history of the Jews. 2 vols 1716–18, 1749 (11th edn), 4 vols 1808, 1815 (17th edn), 2 vols 1839, 1845; ed J. T. Wheeler 1858; tr French, 1725; German, 1726.

Letters

The life of Prideaux with several tracts and letters. 1748.

Letters to John Ellis 1674–1722. Ed E. M. Thompson 1875 (Camden Soc).

§2

The life of Prideaux with several tracts and letters. 1748.

Ketton-Cremer, R. W. In his Norfolk assembly, 1957.

JEREMY COLLIER
1650–1726

Collier's attacks upon the theatre and the literature and scholarship arising from them are not included here; see col 721 above.

§1

Miscellanies. 1694–5 (pts 1–2); 1697 (enlarged as Essays upon several moral subjects); 1705–9 (pts 3–4).

The great historical, geographical, genealogical and poetical dictionary, collected from historians, especially L. Morery. 2 vols 1701 (2nd edn, enlarged to 1688); Supplement, 1705 (continuation to 1705); Appendix, 1721.

An ecclesiastical history of Great Britain, chiefly of England, with a brief account of the affairs of religion in Ireland. 2 vols 1708–14; ed F. Barham 9 vols 1840–1; ed T. Lathbury 9 vols 1852.

§2

Bradley, L. J. H. Collier's Marcus Aurelius. TLS 19 Jan 1928. *See* 26 Jan 1928.

Freeman, E. L. Collier and Francis Bacon. PQ 7 1928.

Ressler, K. Collier's essays. In Seventeenth-century studies: second series, ed R. Shafer, Princeton 1937.

Hooker, H. M. Father John Constable on Collier. PQ 23 1944.

Wimsatt, W. K. Further comment on Constable and Collier. PQ 24 1945.

Lamb, G. F. A short view of Collier. English 7 1949.

Williamson, G. In his Senecan amble, 1951.

WHITE KENNETT
1660–1728

§1

The life of Mr Somner. In W. Somner, A treatise of the Roman ports and forts in Kent, Oxford 1693; rptd in W. Somner, A treatise of gavelkind, 1726 (2nd edn).

Parochial antiquities attempted in the history of Ambrosden, Burcester and other adjacent parts in the counties of Oxford and Bucks. Oxford 1695; ed B. Bandinel 2 vols 1818 (much enlarged).

Ecclesiastical synods and parliamentary convocations in the Church of England historically stated, and justly vindicated from the misrepresentations of Mr Atterbury. 1701.

The case of impropriations and of the augmentation of vicarages and other insufficient cures, stated by history and law, with an appendix of records and memorials. 1704.

The history of England from the commencement of the reign of Charles I to the end of the reign of William III. In A complete history of England; with the lives of all the Kings and Queens thereof to the death of William III vol 3, 1706, 1719.

Memoirs of the family of Cavendish. 1708, Dublin 1737 (enlarged); ed J. Nichols 1797 (enlarged).

A memorial to Protestants on the fifth of November; containing a more full discovery of some particulars relating to the happy deliverance of James I anno 1605. 1713.

A register and chronicle ecclesiastical and civil, from the restauration of Charles II. Vol 1, 1728 (all pbd).

An historical account of the discipline and jurisdiction of the Church of England. 1730 (2nd edn).

§2

[Newton, W.] The life of Kennett. 1730. With letters.

Kennett to Benjamin Colman. Proc Massachusetts Historical Soc 53 1920. Letters.

Liddell, M. F. Kennetts Fortsetzung der Danielschen Chronik. In his Der Stil der englischen Geschichtsschreibung im 18 Jahrhundert, Anglica 2 1925.

Hudson, H. H. Current English translations of the Praise of folly. PQ 20 1941; also in Renaissance studies in honor of Hardin Craig, [Stanford 1941]. On Kennett's 2 trns Witt against wisdom, 1683, 2nd edn as Moriae encomium: or a panegyrick upon folly, 1709.

Bennett, G. V. Kennett: a study in the political and ecclesiastical history of the early eighteenth century. 1957.

PAUL DE RAPIN DE THOYRAS
1661–1725

Histoire d'Angleterre. 13 vols Hague 1724–36 (continuation by D. Durand); tr N. Tindal 15 vols 1725–31, 4 vols 1743–7 (with continuation) etc.

JAMES ANDERSON
1662–1728

An historical essay, shewing that the crown and kingdom of Scotland is imperial and independent. Edinburgh 1705. *See* W. Atwood, The superiority and direct dominion of the imperial crown of England over the crown and kingdom of Scotland, 1704, and Atwood, The superiority re-asserted, 1705.

Collections relating to the history of Mary Queen of Scotland. 4 vols Edinburgh 1727–8.
Selectus diplomatum et numismatum Scotiae thesaurus. Edinburgh 1739.

ABEL BOYER
1667–1729

§1

A geographical and historical description of those parts of Europe which are the seat of war, particularly from 1648 to the present time. 1696, 1702.
The English Theophrastus: or the manners of the age. 1702; ed W. E. Britton, Ann Arbor 1947 (excerpts) (Augustan Reprint Soc). Attributed to Boyer.
The history of William III. 3 vols 1702–3.
The history of the reign of Queen Anne digested into annals. 11 vols 1703–13.
The political state of Great Britain. 60 vols 1711–40. 1711–29 by Boyer. Vols 1–8 rptd as Quadriennium Annae postremum, and Quadriennium Georgii, 1718–20.
Memoirs of the life and negotiations of Sir William Temple. 1714, 1715.
A compleat and impartial history of the impeachments of the last ministry. 1716 (2nd edn).
An impartial history of the occasional conformity and schism bills. 1717.
The history of the life and reign of Queen Anne. 1722, 1735.
The great theater of honour and nobility. 1729. French and English.

§2

Tillier, L. Un Huguenot français à Londres: Boyer. La France Libre Nov 1941.

LAURENCE ECHARD
1670?–1730

An exact description of Ireland. 1691.
A most compleat compendium of geography. 1691, 1691, 1693, 1697, 1713 (8th edn).
The gazetteer's or newsman's interpreter: being a geographical index of all the considerable cities etc in Europe. 1692, 1693, 1695, 1744 (16th edn); tr French, 1749; Spanish, 1750; Italian, 1761.
The Roman history, from the building of the city to the perfect settlement of the Empire by Augustus. 1695, 1696, 1697, 1699; vol 2, from Augustus to Constantine, 1698, 1699; 2 vols 1699 (4th edn).
A general ecclesiastical history from the nativity of Constantine. 1702, 2 vols 1712 (3rd edn), 1 vol 1719 (5th edn), 2 vols 1729 (7th edn).
The history of England, from the first entrance of Julius Caesar to the end of the reign of James the First. 1707. Vols 2–3, To the establishment of William and Mary, 1718; complete work 2 vols 1720 (enlarged); Appendix, 1720 (addns etc). See The conduct of the Earl of Nottingham: being a continuation by several hands of Echard's History of England etc, ed W. A. Aiken, New Haven 1941.
The history of the Revolution and the establishment of England in 1688. 1725, Dublin 1725.

GEORGE CRAWFURD
d. 1748

§1

A genealogical history of the Stewarts from 1034 to 1710, [with] a general description of the shire of Renfrew.

Edinburgh 1710, Paisley 1782 (as The history of the shire of Renfrew; containing a genealogical history etc, continued by W. Semple); continued by G. Robertson, 1818.
The peerage of Scotland: containing an historical and genealogical account of the nobility of that Kingdom. Edinburgh 1716.
The lives and characters of the officers of the Crown, and of the state in Scotland, from David I to the Union. Vol 1, Edinburgh 1726 (all pbd), 1736.
Life of Henry Guthrie. In Memoirs of Henry Guthry, late Bishop of Dunkeld, Glasgow 1748.

§2

Letters from Simon Lord Fraser of Lovat to Crawford 1728–30. In Spottiswoode miscellany vol 1, Edinburgh 1844.

JOHN KER
1673–1726

§1

Memoirs, with an account of the rise and progress of the Ostend Company. 4 pts 1726–7; tr French, 1726–8.

§2

Lang, A. Ker of Kersland: Cameronian, Jacobite and spy. Blackwood's Mag Dec 1897.

GEORGE LOCKHART
1673–1731

Memoirs concerning the affairs of Scotland from Queen Anne's accession to the commencement of the Union. 1714, 1714 (enlarged), 1714.
The Lockhart papers: containing memoirs and commentaries upon the affairs of Scotland from 1701–15 etc. 2 vols 1817.

JOHN OLDMIXON
1673–1742

§1

Poems on several occasions, written in imitation of the manner of Anacreon etc. 1696.
An idyll on the peace. 1697. Anon.
Thyrsis: a pastoral. In P. A. Motteux, The novelty, 1697.
Amintas: a pastoral, made English out of Italian from the Aminta of Tasso. 1698.
A poem humbly addresst to the Earl of Portland on his Lordships return from his embassy in France. 1698.
Reflections on the stage and Mr Collyer's Defence of the Short view. 1699.
The grove, or love's paradice: an opera. 1700.
A funerall idyll, sacred to the glorious memory of K. William III. 1702.
The governour of Cyprus: a tragedy. 1703.
Amores britannici: espistles historical and gallant, in English heroic verse. 2 vols 1703.
A pastoral poem on the victories at Schellenburgh and Blenheim, with a large preface shewing the antiquity and dignity of pastoral poetry. 1704.
Life of Blake. In Lives English and foreign including the history of England and other nations of Europe from 1550 to 1690 vol 2, 1704.
Iberia liberata: a poem occasion'd by the success of her Majesties arms in Catalonia, Valencia etc. 1706.
A complete history of England, with the lives of all the kings and queens thereof to the death of William III. 3 vols 1706, 1719. Ed Oldmixon, who also added new lives in vol 1.

The Muses Mercury: or the monthly miscellany. Jan 1707–Jan 1708. Ed and partly written by Oldmixon.

The British Empire in America. 2 vols 1708, 1741; tr Dutch, 1721; German, 1776–84. The history of the isle of Providence, ed R. Kent [1949], is a ch rptd from 1741 edn.

The history of addresses. 2 vols 1709–11; vol 1, 1710 (2nd edn). Anon.

The medley. 5 Oct 1710–6 August 1711; 1711 (collected). A weekly periodical, ed and largely written by Old-mixon.

A letter to the seven Lords of the committee appointed to examine Gregg. 1711 (anon); rptd in Prose works of Swift vol 3, ed H. Davis et al, Oxford 1950.

Remarks upon remarks: or the barrister-treaty and the succession vindicated. 1711. Anon.

Letters and negotiations of the Count D'Estrades trans-lated by several hands. 3 vols 1711. Partly tr Oldmixon.

The history of Dr Sacheverell faithfully transcribed from the Paris-gazette with remarks comical and political. 1711. Anon.

Reflections on Dr Swift's letter to the Earl of Oxford about the English tongue. [1712] (anon); ed L. A. Landa, Ann Arbor 1948 (Augustan Reprint Soc).

The Dutch barrier our's: or the interest of England and Holland inseparable. 1712, 1712. Anon.

A defence of Mr Maccartney, by a friend. 1712. Anon.

Dejanira to Hercules. In Ovid's espistles, translated by several hands, 1712 (8th edn), 1716, 1720, 1725, 1729, 1736, 1748, 1761, 1768, 1775, 1795.

The secret history of Europe. 4 vols 1712–15. Anon.

The life and history of Belisarius and a parallel between him and a modern heroe [Marlborough]. 1713. Anon.

Poems and translations by several hands; to which is added the Hospital of fools: a dialogue by the late William Walsh. 1714, 1714 (as Original poems and translations). Ed Oldmixon.

The dedication for the Latin edition of Lucretius, written in the year 1711 by Dr Garth, now made English by Mr Oldmixon. 1714.

Arcana gallica: or the secret history of France for the last century. 1714. Anon.

The false steps of the ministry after the revolution, with some reflections on the license of the pulpit and press. 1714. Anon.

The Court of Atalantis: containing a four years history of that famous island, intermixt with fables and epistles, by several hands. 1714, 1717 (for 1716) (as Court tales: or a history of the amours of the present nobility), 1720, 1732 (for 1731). Ed Oldmixon.

Memoirs of North-Britain, in which it is proved that the Scots nation have always been zealous in the defence of the Protestant religion and liberty. 1715. Anon.

Memoirs of the life of the most noble Thomas late Marquis of Wharton. 1715. Anon.

The life and posthumous works of Arthur Maynwaring. 1715. Anon.

Nixon's Cheshire prophecy at large, 1715?, 1719 (6th edn), 1740 (7th edn), 1744 (13th edn). Anon.

The Catholick poet [Pope], or Protestant Barnaby's [Lintott] sorrowful lamentation: an excellent new ballad. 1716. Anon.

Memoirs of the life of John Lord Somers, with a large introduction in vindication of the modern biography. 1716. Anon.

Memoirs of Ireland from the Restoration to the present times. 1716. Anon.

The critical history of England, ecclesiastical and civil, wherein the errors of the monkish writers, and others before the Reformation are expos'd and corrected, as are also the deficiency and partiality of later historians; and particular notice is taken of the History of the Grand Rebellion and Echard's History of England to which are added remarks on some objections made to Bishop Burnet's History of his times. Vol 1, 1724, 1725, 1726, 1728, 1730 (all with addns); vol 2, Containing an examen of Mr Echard's History of the reigns of Henry VIII etc, 1726, 1730. Anon.

A review of Dr Zachary Grey's Defence of our ancient and modern historians. 1725; reissued with subsequent edns of the Critical history vol 1, above. Anon.

Clarendon and Whitlock compar'd; to which is added a comparison between the History of the Rebellion and other histories of the Civil War. 1727, 1737. Anon.

An essay on criticism, as it regards design, thought and expression. 1728; issued with the Critical history vol 1, above, 1728, 1730; ed R. J. Madden, Los Angeles 1964 (Augustan Reprint Soc).

The arts of logick and rhetorick. 1728. Anon.

The history of England, during the reigns of the royal house of Stuart, wherein the errors of late histories are discover'd and corrected. 1730 (for 1729). Anon.

Mr Oldmixon's reply to the late Bishop Atterbury's Vindi-cation of Bishop Smallridge, Dr Aldrich and himself. 1732.

The history of England during the reigns of William and Mary, Anne, George I: being the sequel of the reigns of the Stuarts. 1735.

The history of England during the reigns of Henry VIII, Edward VI, Mary, Elizabeth. 1739.

The history and life of Robert Blake. [1741]. Anon.

Memoirs of the press, historical and political from 1710 to 1740. 1742.

§2

Liddell, M. F. Der Stil der englischen Geschichtsschrei-bung im 18 Jahrhundert. Anglica 2 1925.

Kraus, N. The first half of the eighteenth century. In his A history of American history, New York 1937.

Rogers, P. Oldmixon, Francis Gwynn and the Prideaux family. N & Q for Somerset & Dorset 29 1969.

—— The printing of Oldmixon's histories. Library 5th ser 24 1969.

DANIEL NEAL
1678–1743

§1

The history of New-England to 1700. 2 vols 1720, 1747.

The history of the Puritans or Protestant Non-conformists from the Reformation to 1689. 4 vols 1732–8, 2 vols 1754; ed J. Toulmin 5 vols Bath 1793–7 (with a life of Neal), London 1822; abridged E. Parsons 2 vols [1811].

A review of the principal facts objected to the first volume of the History of the Puritans by the author of the Vindication etc. See [Z. Grey], A vindication of the government, doctrine and worship of the Church of England, against Mr Neale in his late History of the Puritans, 1733; Z. Grey, An impartial examination of the second volume of Mr Neals' History, 1736; of vol 3, 1737; of vol 4, 1739; A review of Neal's History, 1744.

§2

Henson, H. Warburton's notes on Neal's History of the Puritans. Trans Royal Soc of Lit 2nd ser 34 1916.

Kraus, M. The first half of the eighteenth century. In his A history of American history, New York 1937.

SIMON OCKLEY
1678–1720

§1

The conquest of Syria, Persia and Aegypt, by the Saracens [The history of the Saracens]. Vol 1, 1708, vol 2, 1718; 2 vols 1718 (as The history of the Saracens), Cambridge 1757 (enlarged), 1 vol 1847, 1848 (enlarged, with a memoir of Ockley).

§2

Moore, J. R. [John] Hughes's source for the Siege of Damascus. HLQ 21 1958. On unreliability of History of the Saracens 1708.

CONYERS MIDDLETON
1683–1750
Collections

Miscellaneous works. 4 vols 1752, 5 vols 1755.

§1

A dissertation concerning the origin of printing in England. Cambridge 1735; rptd in W. Bowyer and J. Nichols, The origin of printing, 1776–81 (2nd edn); tr French, 1775.
The history of the life of Cicero. 2 vols 1741, 3 vols 1741, 2 vols Dublin 1741, 3 vols 1755 (5th edn); tr French, 1763; Spanish, 1790.
The epistles of Cicero to Brutus, and of Brutus to Cicero, with English notes [and a] prefatory dissertation. 1743.
A treatise on the Roman Senate. 1747; ed T. Knowles 1778; tr German, 1748.
A free inquiry into miraculous powers in the Christian Church. 1749.

Letters

Stuart, D. M. Some unpublished letters of John, Lord Hervey and Middleton. English 2 1938.
Horace Walpole's correspondence with Sir David Dalrymple, Middleton et al. Ed W. S. Lewis et al, New Haven 1952 (vol 15 of Yale edn of Walpole's correspondence).

§2

Middleton. Westminster Rev July 1894.
Stephen, L. In his History of English thought in the eighteenth century vol 1, 1902 (3rd edn).

THOMAS LEDIARD
1685–1743

The naval history of England in all its branches, from 1066 to 1734. 2 vols 1735.
The life of John, Duke of Marlborough. 3 vols 1736, 2 vols 1743.
The history of the reigns of William III and Mary and Anne. In continuation of Rapin de Thoyras, History of England vol 3, 1737.

ARCHIBALD BOWER
1686–1766

The history of the Popes from the foundation of the See of Rome to the present time. 7 vols 1748–66, Dublin 1749–68, London 1750–66 (3rd edn of vols 1–2 only); ed and continued by S. H. Cox 3 vols Philadelphia 1844–5. 'A summary view' of the controversy between Bower and his critics is in vol 5, 1761.

EUSTACE BUDGELL
1686–1737

§1

The moral characters of Theophrastus. 1714, 1718, 1743, 1751. Tr Budgell.
Memoirs of the life and character of the late Earl of Orrery and of the family of the Boyles. 1732, 1732,

1737 (as Memoirs of the lives and characters of the illustrious family of the Boyles, with appendix).
The bee: or the universal weekly pamphlet. 3 Feb 1733–14 June 1735, 9 vols 1733–[5]. Nos 14–16 pbd as The bee: or weekly pamphlet revived; nos 17–118 as The bee revived: or the universal weekly pamphlet.
A short history of Prime Ministers in Great Britain. 1733. Anon.

§2

Riffe, N. L. Budgell's Bee 1733–4. N & Q Feb 1964.

THOMAS CARTE
1686–1754

§1

The Irish massacre set in a clear light, wherein Mr Baxter's account of it in the history of his own life, and the abridgment thereof by Dr Calamy are fully consider'd. [1714], 1715 (enlarged); rptd in Somers tracts vol 5, ed W. Scott 1811.
An history of the life of James Duke of Ormonde; to which is added a very valuable collection of letters. 3 vols 1736–5, 6 vols Oxford 1851 (rev).
A general account of the necessary materials for an history of England. [1738].
A collection of original letters and papers concerning the affairs of England 1641 to 1660. 2 vols 1739.
The history of the revolutions of Portugal to 1667, with letters of Sir Robert Southwell. 1740. Anon.
A collection of the several papers published in relation to his History of England. 1744.
A general history of England to 1654. 4 vols 1747–55.

§2

N & Q 8 May 1926.

ARTHUR COLLINS
1690–1760

§1

The baronettage of England: an historical and genealogical account of baronets. 2 vols 1720, 4 vols 1741 (enlarged as The English baronetage).
The English baronage. 1727.
The life of William Cecil, Lord Burghley, from the original manuscript, with memoirs of the family of Cecil. 1732.
Proceedings, precedents and arguments on claims and controversies concerning baronies by writ. 1734.
The peerage of England. 3 vols 1735, 4 vols 1741 (enlarged); Supplement, 2 vols 1750; 5 vols 1756 (complete and enlarged), 7 vols 1768; ed B. Longmate 8 vols 1779, Supplement by Longmate, 1784; ed E. Brydges 9 vols 1812 (much enlarged).
The life and glorious actions of Edward Prince of Wales [the Black Prince, with] the History of John of Gaunt. 1740.
Memoirs of the family of Sackville. 1741. Rptd from Peerage, 1741 (2nd edn), with separate title-page.
Letters and memorials of state in the reigns of Mary, Elizabeth, James, Charles the First, part of the reign of Charles the Second, and Oliver's usurpation, from the originals at Penshurst Place and from his Majesty's office of papers and records [with] genealogical and historical observations. 2 vols 1746. Usually called the Sydney Papers.
An history of the family of the Percys. 1750.
Historical collections of the noble families of Cavendishe, Holles, Vere, Harley and Ogle. 1752.

Historical collections of the noble family of Windsor.
1754.
A history of the noble family of Carteret. 1756.

§2

M[orris], R. B. Collins. Devon & Cornwall N & Q July
1916. *See* Oct 1916.

JOHN, 2nd BARON HERVEY
1696–1743
Collections

The laurel: poetical works of Collins, Dr Johnson, Pom-
fret, Hammond and Hervey. [1808].
Poetical works of Hammond and Hervey. Ed G.D. 1818.
With biographical sketch.
Memoirs. Ed R. Sedgwick 1952, 1963 (rev).

§1

Observations on the writings of the Craftsman [Boling-
broke's letters on English history]. 1730 (anon); sequel,
1730 (anon).
Farther observations on the writings of the Craftsman.
1730 (anon). Reply to An answer to a late pamphlet
entitled Observations on the writings of the Craftsman,
1731.
Remarks on the Craftsman's vindication of his two honble
patrons [Bolingbroke and W. Pulteney] in his paper of
May 22, 1731. 1731 (7 edns). Anon. Sometimes
ascribed to William Arnall; *see* DNB.
An epistle from a nobleman [Hervey] to a Doctor of
Divinity. 1733 (anon); ed W. P. Jones, Los Angeles
1960 (Augustan Reprint Soc).
Letters between Hervey and Dr Middleton concerning
the Roman Senate. Ed T. Knowles 1778.
Memoirs of the reign of George the Second. Ed J. W.
Croker 2 vols 1848, 3 vols 1884 (with a life of Hervey);
ed R. Sedgwick 3 vols 1931 (as Some materials towards
memoirs of the reign of George II).

Letters

Stuart, D. M. Some unpublished letters of Hervey and
Dr Conyers Middleton. English 2 1938.
Hervey and his friends 1726–38. Ed Earl of Ilchester
1950. Extracts. *See* TLS 15 Dec 1950, 19–26 Jan, 2
Feb 1951.

§2

King, W. Hervey's Memoirs. London Mercury Jan
1927.
Woods, C. B. Captain B[oden]'s play. Harvard Stud 15
1933. On the Modish couple 1732, attributed to
C. Boden, perhaps by Hervey.
Shafer, R. Hervey's Memoirs. Amer Rev Dec 1933.
Gerig, H. Die Memoiren des Hervey als historische
Quelle. Freiburg 1936.
Namier, L. B. The Memoirs of Hervey. In his In the
margin of history, 1939; rptd in Crossroads of power:
collected essays vol 2, 1962.
Gooch, G. P. Hervey and Queen Caroline; Hervey and
George II. In his Courts and cabinets, 1944.
Quennell, P. C. In his Singular preference, 1952.
Connolly, C. In his Previous convictions, 1963.

NATHANIEL HOOKE
d. 1763

The Roman history from the building of Rome to the ruin
of the Commonwealth. 4 vols 1738–71; vol 1, 1751
(rev); 11 vols 1766–71; ed J. R. Pitman 6 vols 1821.

An account of the conduct of the Dowager Duchess of
Marlborough to 1710, in a letter from herself. 1742
(anon); ed W. King 1930 (as Memoirs of Sarah, Duchess
of Marlborough).

JOHN CAMPBELL
1708–75

§1

The military history of Prince Eugene and of John Duke
of Marlborough. 2 vols 1736–7. Anon.
A concise history of the Spanish America. 1741 (anon),
1741 (as A complete history etc), 1747 (as The Spanish
Empire in America).
The polite correspondence: or rational amusement. 1741
(anon), 1754.
A letter to a friend in the country on the publication of
Thurloe's State papers. 1742, 1742. Anon.
Lives of the admirals and other eminent British seamen.
4 vols 1742–4, 1750 (enlarged), 1761 (enlarged);
abridged 1849.
Navigantium atque itinerantium bibliotheca: or a com-
pleat collection of voyages and travels. 2 vols 1744–8,
1764. Begun by J. Harris, ed and continued by Camp-
bell.
The present state of Europe. 1750 (anon), 1759 (5th edn).
Rptd from Dodsley's Museum 1746–7.
A political survey of Britain. 2 vols 1774.
Campbell on Hume's views of Queens Elizabeth and Mary
1761. BNYPL June 1905. Ptd from original ms in New
York Public Library.
Campbell also contributed extensively to An universal
history, 23 vols 1736–65, 64 vols 1747–66, *and to the
first 4 vols of* Biographia britannica, 6 vols 1747–66.

§2

Seitz, R. W. Goldsmith and the Literary Magazine. RES
5 1929. On Goldsmith's use of Campbell's Present
state of Europe for his Political view.
Wellek, R. In his Rise of English literary history, Chapel
Hill 1941. On Campbell's contribution to literary history
in his Polite correspondence.

Antiquaries and Local Historians

SIR ROBERT ATKYNS
1647–1711

§1

The ancient and present state of Glostershire. 1712, 1768.
See T. D. Fosbroke, Abstracts of records and manuscripts respecting the county of Gloucester supplying
numerous deficiencies in Atkins etc, 2 vols Gloucester
1807.

§2

A catalogue of the library of Atkyns. [1717].
Austin, R. Some account of Atkyns the younger and other
members of the Atkyns family. Trans Bristol & Gloster
Archaeological Soc 35 1912; Bristol [1913].
—— Atkyns the younger. Trans Bristol & Gloster Archaeo-
logical Soc 60 1938.

RALPH THORESBY
1658–1725
Bibliographies

Jones, H. W. A checklist of the correspondence of
Thoresby. Leeds 1959 (Pbns of Thoresby Soc).

§1

Ducatus Leodiensis: the topography of the town and parish of Leedes and parts adjacent. 1715; ed T. D. Whitaker, Leeds 1816.

Vicaria Leodiensis: the history of the church of Leedes. 1724.

Letters and Diaries

Diary 1677–1724. Ed J. Hunter 2 vols 1830.

Letters of eminent men addressed to Thoresby. 2 vols 1832.

The wayfarings of Thoresby in the north of England. Newcastle 1847 (Reprints of Rare Tracts at the press of M. A. Richardson).

Tours in Scotland 1677 and 1681: [T. Kirk and] Thoresby. Ed P. H. Brown, Edinburgh 1892.

Letters addressed to Thoresby. Ed W. T. Lancaster, Leeds 1912 (Pbns of Thoresby Soc).

Some hitherto unpublished letters of Thoresby. Ed E. Hargrave, Leeds 1922 (Pbns of Thoresby Soc).

§2

Musaeum Thoresbyanum: a catalogue of the collection of Thoresby. [1725]; ed T. D. Whitaker in Ducatus Leodiensis, Leeds 1816 (2nd edn).

Atkinson, D. H. Thoresby: his town and times. 2 vols Leeds 1885–7.

Jenkins, R. Paper and publishing at the beginning of the eighteenth century [with particular reference to the printing of Thoresby's Ducatus Leodiensis 1715]. Lib Assoc Record June 1912.

L[umb], G. D. Mss written or possessed by Thoresby. Leeds 1927 (Pbns of Thoresby Soc).

Greene, G. To all topographers. Spectator 12 Aug 1938.

Scholes, T. W. A forgotten diarist [Thoresby]. London Quart 166 1941.

Humphreys, A. L. Horsemen on the Great North Road. N & Q 24 May 1941.

Page, R. I. Thoresby's runic coins. Br Numismatic Jnl 34 1965.

JOHN BRIDGES
1666–1724

§1

The history and antiquities of Northamptonshire. Ed P. Whalley 2 vols Oxford 1791. Thomas Dash's extra-illustrated copy, 5 vols, in BM Add mss 32, 118–22.

§2

Bibliothecae Bridgesianae catalogus. 1725.

EDMUND GIBSON
1669–1748

§1

Chronicon saxonicum, ex mss codicibus nunc primum integrum edidit. Oxford 1692.

Camden's Britannia newly translated into English, with large additions and improvements. 1695, 2 vols 1722, 1753, 1772.

Reliquiae Spelmannianae: posthumous works of Sir Henry Spelman. Oxford 1698; rptd in Spelman, English works, 1723, below. Ed Gibson.

Synodus anglicana: or an English convocation, shown from the acts and registers thereof, to be agreeable to an episcopal church. 1672 (for 1702), 1730 (as A compleat history of convocations from 1356 to 1689); ed E. Cardwell, Oxford 1854.

Codex juris ecclesiastici anglicani: or the statutes, constitutions, canons, rubricks and articles of the Church of England, methodically digested under their proper heads. 2 vols 1713, Oxford 1761.

The English works of Sir H. Spelman, together with his posthumous works. 1723, 1727. Ed Gibson.

Letters

Original letters of eminent literary men. Ed H. Ellis 1843 (Camden Soc).

Griffiths, G. M. Eight letters from Gibson to Bishop [Humphrey] Humphreys 1707–9. Jnl of Nat Lib of Wales 10 1958.

§2

Allen, F. In his A charge to the clergy belonging to the Archdeaconry of Middlesex, 1749.

Sykes, N. Gibson, Bishop of London: a study in politics and religion in the eighteenth century. Oxford 1926.

— Gibson and Sir Robert Walpole. EHR 44 1929.

Barry, J. G. H. An eighteenth-century prelate. New Amer Church Monthly Dec 1927.

Birrell, A. Dr Codex. In his Et cetera, 1930.

JOHN LEWIS
1675–1747

§1

The history of the life and sufferings of John Wicliffe. 1720, Oxford 1820 (enlarged).

The history and antiquities of the Isle of Tenet in Kent. 1723, 1736.

The history and antiquities of the abbey and church of Favresham in Kent. 1727.

The New Testament translated by Wiclif; to which is praefixt a history of translations of the Bible into English, and of the most remarkable editions of them since the invention of printing. 1731. History enlarged and rptd separately as A complete history, 1739, 1818.

The life of Mayster Wyllyam Caxton: in which is given an account of the rise and progress of the art of pryntyng in England till 1493. 1737.

A dissertation on the antiquity and use of seals in England. 1740. Anon.

The life of Reynold Pecock, Bishop of St Asaph and Chichester. 1744, Oxford 1820.

A little dissertation on the antiquities of Richborough and Sandwich. 1851.

The life of John Fisher, Bishop of Rochester. Ed T. H. Turner 2 vols 1855.

§2

Shirley, J. Lewis of Margate. Archaeologia Cantiana 64 1952.

NATHANIEL SALMON
1675–1742

§1

Roman stations in Britain. 1726.

A survey of the Roman antiquities in some Midland counties of England. 1726.

The history of Hertfordshire: describing the county and its antient monuments, particularly the Roman. 1728.

A new survey of England, wherein the defects of Camden are supplied, the Roman military ways traced and the stations settled. 11 pts 1728–9.

The lives of the English Bishops from the Restauration to the Revolution. 3 pts [1731]–3. Anon.

Antiquities of Surrey, with some account of the present state and natural history of the county. 1736.

The history and antiquities of Essex. 1740. Unfinished.

A short view of the families of the present English nobility.
1751, 1758, 1761.
A short view of the families of the Scottish nobility.
1759.
A short view of the families of the present Irish nobility.
1759.

§2

Gerish, W. B. Salmon: the Hertfordshire historian. [1911].
Aubin, R. A. Salmon on Milton 1728. MLN 56 1941.

THOMAS COX
d. 1734

Magna Britannia et Hibernia, antiqua et nova: or a new
survey of Great Britain. 6 vols 1720–31. On English
counties only.

BROWNE WILLIS
1682–1760

§1

Notitia parliamentaria: or an history of the counties, cities
and boroughs in England and Wales. 3 vols 1715–50;
vol 1, 1730 (enlarged).
A survey of the cathedral church of St David's. 1717.
An history of the mitred parliamentary abbies and con-
ventual cathedral churches. 2 vols 1718–19.
A survey of the cathedral-church of Landaff. 1719.
A survey of the cathedral-church of St Asaph. 1720; ed E.
Edwards 2 vols Wrexham 1801 (enlarged and extended).
A survey of the Cathedral Church of Bangor. 1721.
A survey of the cathedrals, with an exact account of all the
churches and chapels in every diocese. 3 vols 1727–30.
Parochiale anglicanum: or the names of all the churches
and chapels within the dioceses of Canterbury, Roch-
ester, London etc with an account of most of their
dedications, their patrons etc. 1733.
The history and antiquities of the town, hundred and
deanry of Buckingham. 1755.

§2

Ducarel, A. C. Some account of Willis. [1760].
Walters, H. B. Some English antiquaries. Trans Royal
Soc of Lit new ser 13 1934.
Richardson, A. E. The Gothic revival in the early 18th
century. Jnl of Royal Inst of Br Architects 3rd ser 45
1938.
Milne, J. G. The coin collections of Willis. Bodleian
Quart Record 8 1938.
Jenkins, J. G. The dragon of Whaddon: the life and work
of Willis. High Wycombe 1953.

JOHN HORSLEY
1685–1732

§1

Britannia romana: or the Roman antiquities of Britain.
1732.

§2

Hodgson, J. In his Memoirs of the lives of T. Gibson, J.
Harle, J. Horsley, W. Turner, Newcastle 1831.
Tate, G. Life of Horsley; with some notices of his writings.
Alnwick [1865?].
Hodgson, J. C. Remains of Horsley the historian.
Archaeologia Aeliana 3rd ser 15 1918.
Duff, J. W. Horsley. Proc Soc of Antiquaries of Newcastle
upon Tyne 4th ser 5 1931–2.

Macdonald, G. Horsley. Jnl of Roman Stud 22 1932.
—— Horsley: scholar and gentleman. Archaeologia
Aeliana 4th ser 10 1933.
R[obson], R. S. The Horsley bi-centenary 1732–1932.
Jnl of Presbyterian Historical Soc of England 5
1932–5.
Bosanquet, R. C. Horsley and his times. Archaeologia
Aeliana 4th ser 10 1933.
Collingwood, R. G. Horsley and Hadrian's wall. Archaeo-
logia Aeliana 4th ser 15 1938.
Steer, K. A. Horsley and the Antonine wall. Archaeologia
Aeliana 4th ser 42 1964.

WILLIAM STUKELEY
1687–1765

§1

An account of a Roman temple near Graham's Dike in
Scotland. [1720].
Of the Roman amphitheater at Dorchester. [1723]; ed
A. M. Broadley, Weymouth [1913] (priv ptd), 1925.
See Trans of Dorset Masters' [Masonic] Lodge no 3, 366,
5 1914.
Itinerarium curiosum: or an account of the antiquitys and
remarkable curiositys in nature or art, observed in
travels thro Great Britain. 1724 (Centuria 1); 2 vols
1776 (complete and much enlarged).
Palaeographia sacra: or discourses on monuments of
antiquity that relate to sacred history. 1736.
Stonehenge: a temple restor'd to the British druids.
1740.
Abury: a temple of the British druids, with some others,
described. 1743.
Palaeographia britannica: or discourses on antiquities in
Britain. 1743–52 (nos 1–3), Cambridge 1795.
An account of Richard of Cirencester, with his antient
map of Roman Brittain and the itinerary thereof. 1757.
The medallic history of Carausius, Emperor in Brittain.
2 vols 1757–9.
Memoirs of Isaac Newton's life 1752. Ed A. H. White
1936.

Letters and Diaries

The family memoirs of Stukeley, and the antiquarian and
other correspondence of Stukeley, R. and S. Gale etc.
[Ed W. C. Lukis] 3 vols Newcastle 1882–7 (Pbns of
Surtees Soc). Autobiography, diary, letters etc.

§2

Walters, H. B. Some English antiquaries. Trans of Royal
Soc of Lit new ser 13 1934.
Piggott, S. Stukeley, Avebury and the druids. Antiquity
9 1935.
—— Prehistory and the Romantic Movement. Antiquity
11 1937. On importance of antiquaries in romantic
thought.
—— Stukeley: an eighteenth-century antiquary. Oxford
1950.
Summers, W. G. A Lincolnshire worthy. Lincolnshire
N & Q 23 1936.
Wilson, P. M. Stukeley. Local Historian July 1941
(Lindsey Local History Soc).
Cragg, W. A. More about Stukeley. Local Historian
April–July 1942 (Lindsey Local History Soc).
Richmond, I. A. Stukeley's lamp, the badge of the Society
of Antiquaries. Antiquaries Jnl 30 1950.
Long, P. The Keiller collection of Stukeley papers.
Bodleian Lib Record 5 1956.
Sloane, W. Chaucer, Milton and Stukeley. N & Q June
1960.
Wright, C. E. Four Stukeley notebooks. BM Quart 27
1964.

JOSEPH AMES
1689–1759

§1

A catalogue of English heads: an account of two thousand prints, describing what is peculiar on each. 1748.

Typographical antiquities: an historical account of printing in England to the year 1600, with an appendix concerning printing in Scotland and Ireland. 1749; rev W. Herbert 3 vols 1785–90; rev T. F. Dibdin 4 vols 1810–19 (unfinished); Index, 1899 (Bibl Soc).

A list of various editions of the Bible in English from 1526 to 1776. [1777], 1778 (enlarged). Compiled by Ames, improved by A. C. Ducarel.

§2

A catalogue of the printed books and manuscripts of Ames, which will be sold by auction etc. [1760].

Mozley, G. Ames and the Blake portrait. N & Q 1 May 1937. On the Pelly portrait of Admiral Robert Blake.

Morris, C. Ames. Printing Rev 50 1949.

WILLIAM MAITLAND
1693?–1757

The history of London from its foundation by the Romans to the present time. 1739, 2 vols 1756, 1760, 1769; ed J. Entick 3 vols 1772, 2 vols 1775.

The history of Edinburgh from its foundation to the present time. Edinburgh 1753.

The history and antiquities of Scotland to 1437 [continued by another hand to 1603]. 2 vols 1757.

FRANCIS BLOMEFIELD
1705–52

§1

The history of the ancient city and burgh of Thetford. Fersfield 1739.

An essay towards a topographical history of the county of Norfolk. 5 vols Fersfield, Norwich and Lynn 1739–75 (continued from p. 678 of vol 3 by C. Parkin), 11 vols 1805–10. Dawson Turner's extra-illustrated copy of Blomefield's History, 56 vols, in BM Additional Mss 23013–67.

Collectanea cantabrigiensia: or collections relating to Cambridge. Norwich 1750.

§2

Rix, S. W. Cursory notices of Blomefield, from his parish register-book and from his correspondence 1733–7. Norfolk Archaeology 2 1849; [Ipswich 1849?].

Stephen, G. A. Blomefield's queries in preparation for his History of Norfolk. Norfolk Archaeology 20 1917.

Ketton-Cremer, R. W. A drawing for Blomefield's Norfolk. Norfolk Archaeology 25 1934.

— The rector of Fersfield: a bicentenary tribute. Norfolk Archaeology 30 1952.

Johnson, F. Blomefield's birthplace. Norfolk Archaeology 28 1944.

Blomefield, historian and topographer: exhibition catalogue. Norwich [1952].

Hepworth, P. Supplementing Blomefield. Norfolk Archaeology 31 1957.

HARLEIAN MISCELLANY

The Harleian miscellany: a collection of scarce, curious and entertaining pamphlets and tracts in the late Earl of Oxford's library. [Ed W. Oldys] 8 vols 1744–6; ed T. Park, index by T. H. Horne, 10 vols 1808–13.

SOMERS TRACTS

A collection of scarce and valuable tracts, selected from an infinite number in the Royal, Cotton, Sion and other publick as well as private libraries, particularly that of the late Lord Sommers. 4 vols 1748; Second collection, 4 vols 1750; Third collection, 4 vols 1751; Fourth, 4 vols 1751–2; ed W. Scott 13 vols 1809–15.

C. LATE EIGHTEENTH-CENTURY HISTORIANS 1750–1800

WILLIAM ROBERTSON
1721–93

Collections

Historical works, with an account of his life and writings by G. Gleig. 6 vols Edinburgh 1813.

Works, to which is prefixed an account of his life and writings by Dugald Stewart. 12 vols 1817, 1822; tr French, 1817–21.

Works, with a sketch of his life and writings by R. A. Davenport. 11 vols Chiswick 1824, 8 vols Oxford 1825.

§1

The situation of the world at the time of Christ's appearance, and its connexion with the success of his religion, considered: a sermon. Edinburgh 1755, London 1759, 1775 (5th edn), Edinburgh 1791, 1818.

The history of Scotland during the reigns of Queen Mary and of King James VI till his accession to the Crown of England, with a review of the Scotch history previous to that period and an appendix containing original papers. 2 vols 1759, 1759, 1760, 1761, 1762, 1769, 1771, Dublin 1772, London 1776, 1787 (11th edn 'corrected'), 1791, Edinburgh 1791, London 1794 (14th edn, 'with the author's last emendations and additions'), 3 vols 1797,

Glasgow 1800, London 1802 (16th edn, with account of the life and writings of the author by Dugald Stewart), 1806, 1809, 1812, 1817, 1821; tr French, 1764.

Memorial relating to the University of Edinburgh. 1768. Anon.

The history of the reign of the Emperor Charles V, with a view of the progress of society in Europe from the subversion of the Roman Empire to the beginning of the sixteenth century. 3 vols 1769, Dublin 1769, Philadelphia 1770, 4 vols 1774, 1777 ('new edition, with corrections'), 1782, 1787, 1792 (7th edn), 1796, 1798, 1802, Edinburgh 1805, London 1806, 1809, 1812, Philadelphia 1812, Glasgow 1817, New York 1840, 2 vols 1857 ('with an account of the Emperor's life after his abdication by W. H. Prescott'); tr German, 1770–1; French, 1771; Russian, 1775–8; Italian, 1835; Spanish 1846.

A new geographical and historical grammar by Thomas Salmon, with great amendments and improvements by Mr Robertson. 1772.

The history of America. 2 vols 1777, Dublin 1777, London 1778, 1780, 1783, 1787, Vienna 1787, London 1788 (5th edn 'with corrections'), Basle 1790, London 1792, 1796, 1796 (bks 9–10 containing the History of Virginia to the year 1688 and the History of New England to the year 1652, ed W. Robertson the younger), 3 vols 1800–1, 4 vols 1800 (9th edn 'in which is included the posthumous volume, containing the History of Virginia and of New England'), 1803, 1808, Alston 1809, London 1812, Philadelphia 1812, London 1817, Philadelphia 1821, London 1822; tr French, 1777; German, 1777; Italian, 1777–8; Greek 1792–3.

An historical disquisition concerning the knowledge which the ancients had of India. 1791, Basle 1792, Philadelphia 1792, London 1794 (2nd edn, 'with the author's last corrections and additions'), 1799, 1802, 1804, 1809, 1812, Philadelphia 1812, Calcutta 1904; tr French, 1792; Italian, 1832.

Letters

Horace Walpole's correspondence with Robertson. Ed W. S. Lewis, C. H. Bennett and A. G. Hoover, New Haven 1952 (vol 15 of Yale edn of Walpole's correspondence).

§2

Stuart, J., 1st Earl of Moray. An historical enquiry into the evidence produced against Mary Queen of Scots, with an examination of Dr Robertson's dissertation. 1760.

Henderson, A. A dissertation on the Royal Line of Scotland in which the opinion of Doctor Robertson that the ancient Britons were indebted to the Romans for the art of writing is considered. 1771.

Hume, D. Critical observations concerning the Scottish historians Hume, Stuart and Robertson. 1782.

Toup, J. A catalogue of the library of the late J. Toup, to which are added the Spanish books collected by Dr Robertson when he was engaged in writing his History of America. 1786.

Tytler, W. An inquiry into the evidence against Mary Queen of Scots, and an examination of the histories of Robertson and Hume with respect to that evidence. 1790.

Stewart, D. Account of the life and writings of Robertson. Edinburgh 1801, 1802. Rptd with various edns of Robertson's works.

—— Biographical memoirs of Adam Smith, of Robertson and of T. Reid. Edinburgh 1811.

Gleig, G. Some account of the life and writings of Robertson. [Edinburgh 1812].

Brougham, H. Lives of men of letters and science, who flourished in the time of George III. 2 vols 1845–6.

Robertson, F. L. Principal Robertson. 1883.

Black, J. B. The art of history: a study of four great historians of the eighteenth century. 1926.

Gray, W. F. Horace Walpole and Robertson. TLS 14 March 1942. Reply by C. Carswell 25 April 1942.

Humphreys, R. A. Robertson and his History of America: a lecture delivered at Canning House on 11 June 1954. 1954.

Meikle, H. W. Voltaire and Scotland. Etudes Anglaises 11 1958. Discusses Voltaire, Lord Kames, Hume, Robertson and Adam Smith.

Cuevas Cancino, F. Robertson y su visión de América. Mexico City 1958.

EDWARD GIBBON
1737–94

Bibliographies etc

Keynes, G. L. The library of Gibbon: a catalogue of his books. 1940.

Norton, J. E. A bibliography of the works of Gibbon. Oxford 1940.

Cordasco, F. Gibbon: a handlist of critical notices and studies [1878–1950]. New York 1950.

§1

Essai sur l'étude de la littérature. 1761, Paris 1761, 1762, Geneva? 1762 (with indexes), Dublin 1777; tr 1764

('presumably not written by Becket (publisher) himself but by some professional translator') (Norton). Miscellaneous works, 1837, contains what is said to be an entirely new version; rptd in The life of Edward Gibbon, Paris 1840; tr German, 1792.

Mémoires littéraires de la Grande Bretagne, pour l'an 1767. 1768, Leyden 1768 (the London edn with cancel title-page); Pour l'an 1768, 1769 (vol 2). Written by Gibbon and Deyverdun; Gibbon in later life professed to be unable to separate his work from Deyverdun's. 2 articles from vol 2, Doutes historiques par Mr Horace Walpole and Réflexions sur les Doutes historiques par Mr D. Hume, and rptd in Miscellaneous works vol 3, 1814.

Critical observations on the sixth book of the Aeneid. 1770 (anon), 1794.

The history of the decline and fall of the Roman Empire.

4°: Vol 1, chs 1–16, 1776 (17 Feb), 1776 (3 June), 1777 (May 'revised'; see Bury's edn, vol 1, pp. 506–9, for Gibbon's alterations), 1781, 1782; vols 2, chs 17–26; 3, chs 27–38; 1781 (with portrait after Reynolds and 2 maps (parts of Europe and Asia adjacent to Constantinople; eastern part of the Empire) in vol 2, and map of western part of the Empire in vol 3), 1781 (without portrait; new title-pages), 1787; vols 1–3, 3 vols 1789; vols 4, chs 39–47; 5, chs 48–57; 6, chs 58–71, 1788 (8 May).

8°: 6 vols 1783 (reprint of vols 1–3 4°), 1788; 6 vols 1790 (reprint of vols 4–6 4°); 12 vols 1791–2, 1797, 1802. London copyright edns. Dublin edns: 2 vols 1776 (reprint of vol 1 4°), 1777, 6 vols 1781 (reprint of vols 1–3 4°), 1788 (reprint of vols 4–6 4°), 1789 (reprint of vols 1–3 4°). Basle edns: 13 vols 1787–9 (reprint of vols 1–6 4°), 7 vols 1789 (reprint of vols 1–3 4°).

Later reprints and edns

8 vols Philadelphia 1804–5, 12 vols London and Edinburgh 1806, London 1807, 1807, 9 vols 1807–9, 12 vols Edinburgh 1811, London 1812, 1813, 71 pts or 14 nos 1814–15, 12 vols London and Edinburgh 1815, London 1816, 6 vols Philadelphia 1816, 12 vols 1817, 1818, 1818, 1819, 1820 (3 edns, the 3rd pbd London and Edinburgh), 1821, 8 vols 1821, 12 vols Leipzig 1821, 8 vols 1822, 6 vols New York 1822, 8 vols 1823, 12 vols 1823, 8 vols 1825, 4 vols 1825, 1826, 6 vols New York 1826, 12 vols 1827, 1827, 11 vols 1827, 4 vols 1828, 8 vols 1828, 12 vols Edinburgh 1828, 4 vols New York 1829, 12 vols Leipzig 1829, 1 vol London and Liverpool 1830, 4 vols Philadelphia 1830, London 1831 (in pts), 12 vols Edinburgh 1831, 1832, 4 vols New York 1833, 1 vol 1834, 4 vols New York 1836, 1 vol 1837, 8 vols 1838, 1 vol Oxford Ohio 1838.

Ed H. H. Milman (with maps and notes by F. P. G. Guizot from the French trn of 1812) 12 vols 1838–9, 6 vols 1846, 8 vols 1854–5 (with additional notes by William Smith and 14 maps); ed H. G. Bohn (with notes by Guizot, F. A. W. Wenck, C. G. Schreiter and G. H. Hugo) 7 vols 1853–5 etc; ed J. B. Bury (with introd, notes, appendices and maps) 7 vols 1896–1900, 1909–14 (illustr O. M. Dalton and with bibliography of edns, trns and selections from the Decline and fall by H. M. Beatty, vol 7, pp. 348–64; for corrections of text see TLS 24–31 July 1924), 7 vols 1903–4 (WC), 6 vols [1910] (EL), 7 vols 1926–9 (rev text and with 'important additions to Gibbon's notes with a view to bringing the information up to the level of modern historical scholarship').

Abridgements

2 vols 1789; ed Bowdler 5 vols 1826; ed M. K. Graham 1940 (priv ptd); ed D. M. Low 1960; ed J. Sloan 2 vols New York 1962; ed M. Hadas 1962; ed H. R. Trevor-Roper 1963 (with other selected writings); ed R. Price 1967.

Translations

French (all Paris): chs 1–7 1 vol 1776, chs 1–16 4 vols 1777, 1786, 18 vols 1788–95, 12 vols 1790–2, 13 vols 1812, 1819, 1827, 2 vols 1837.

Italian: chs 1–16? 3 vols Lausanne [Florence?] 1779, chs 1–41 10 vols Pisa 1779–92, 1789–94, 13 vols Milan 1820–4.

German: 11 vols (numbered 1–8, 13–15) Leipzig 1779–93 (unfinished), 14 vols Magdeburg 1788–92, 13 vols Frankfurt and Leipzig 1800–3, 19 vols Leipzig 1805–6, 1 vol Leipzig 1820, 12 vols Leipzig 1837, 1 vol Leipzig 1837.

Swedish: 8 vols Orebro 1820–34.

Spanish: 8 vols Barcelona 1842–7.

Russian: 7 vols Moscow 1883–6.

A vindication of some passages in the fifteenth and sixteenth chapters of the History of the decline and fall of the Roman Empire. 1779, 1779 (rev), Dublin 1779; rptd in Gibbon's Miscellaneous works vol 2 1796, vol 4 1814, vol 5 Basle 1796–7; tr German, 1792 (also in Geschichte der Abnahme und des Falls des Römischen Reiches, tr C. W. von Riemberg, vol 14 Vienna 1792, 1800 (also in Gibbons Vermischte Werke vol 2, Leipzig 1800).

Mémoire justificatif pour servir de réponse à l'exposé etc de la cour de France. 1779 (anon), 1779 (with the Exposé des motifs de la conduite du roi de France); tr 1779. A French and English version of Mémoire justificatif and Exposé pbd 1780. Mémoire rptd in S. N. H. Linguet, Annales politiques, civiles et littéraires vol 7, 1779; and in Gibbon, Miscellaneous works vol 2, 1796, vol 4 Basle 1796–7, vol 5 London 1814.

Copy of the answer transmitted to the Marquis d'Almovodar by the Lord Viscount Weymouth, July 13 1779. French version rev Gibbon.

Miscellaneous works of Edward Gibbon esquire, with memoirs of his life and writings composed by himself; illustrated from his letters with occasional notes and narrative by John [Holroyd] Lord Sheffield. 2 vols 1796, 3 vols Dublin 1796 (with notice of Mme de Sévery), 7 vols Basle 1796–7, 5 vols 1814 ('with considerable additions'), 1815 (with additional matter of 1814 edn, rptd to be uniform as vol 3 with 1796 edn), 1837 (with new trn of Essai sur l'étude de la littérature), New York 1837; tr French, 1797 (Memoirs and selections from Miscellaneous works); German, Brunswick 1796–7 (Memoirs), Leipzig 1797 (Vermischte Werke); Italian, Milan 1825 (Memoirs).

The Antiquities of the House of Brunswick *was pbd separately in one vol in 1814; there were also separate edns of the Memoirs, below.*

Memoirs. 2 vols 1827, 1830, 1 vol [1831]?; ed H. Milman 1839, Paris 1840; ed J. Murray 1896 ('printed verbatim from hitherto unpublished mss, with an introduction by the Earl of Sheffield'). This vol contains the 6 drafts of Gibbon's autobiography from which the first Lord Sheffield contructed his texts of the memoirs for his edns of Miscellaneous works, 1796 and 1814. Ed O. F. Emerson, Boston 1898; ed G. Birkbeck Hill 1900 (a conflation of 1796 and 1814 edns, with preface, notes, 68 excursuses and index); ed J. B. Bury, Oxford (WC) 1907; ed O. Smeaton 1911 (EL); ed G. A. Bonnard 1966 (from ms, as Memoirs of my life).

Letters and Journals

Private letters of Edward Gibbon 1753–94. Ed R. E. Prothero 2 vols 1896.

Historic studies in Vaud, Berne and Savoy by General Meredith Read. 2 vols 1897. Contains letters tr into English, except part of one, portraits of Gibbon and Deyverdun and photographs of Lausanne.

La vie de société dans le Pays de Vaud à la fin du dix-huitième siècle par M. et Mme William de Sévery. 2 vols Lausanne 1911–12. Vol 2, chs 1–2, devoted to Gibbon's later years at Lausanne. A number of letters are given in the original French, some of which Meredith Read ptd in trn.

Gibbon's journal to January 28th 1763; My journal I, II and III, and Ephemerides with introductory essays by D. M. Low. 1929.

Le journal de Gibbon à Lausanne 17 août 1763–19 avril 1764. Ed G. A. Bonnard, Lausanne 1945.

Miscellanea Gibboniana. Ed G. R. de Beer, G. A. Bonnard and L. Junod, Lausanne 1952. Includes: Journal de mon voyage dans quelques endroits de la Suisse, 1755; Le séjour de Gibbon à Paris du 28 janvier au 9 mai 1763; trois morceaux en fin du quatrième cahier de son Journal; and La lettre de Gibbon sur le gouvernement de Berne.

Letters. Ed J. E. Norton 3 vols 1956.

Gibbon's journey from Geneva to Rome: his journal from 20 April to 2 October 1764. Ed G. A. Bonnard 1961.

§2

Attacks on Gibbon

See also J. E. Norton, A bibliography of the works of Gibbon, Oxford 1940, pp. 233–47; S. T. McCloy, Gibbon's antagonism to Christianity, 1933, pp. 371–7.

Salisbury, W. In J. B. Bullet, The history of the establishment of Christianity, translated from the French by W. Salisbury, with notes and some strictures on Mr Gibbon's account of Christianity, 1776.

Chelsum, J. Remarks on the two last chapters of Mr Gibbon's history. 1776, Oxford 1778 (enlarged, with help of T. Randolph).

—— A reply to Mr Gibbon's Vindication. Winchester 1785.

Watson, R. An apology for Christianity, in a series of letters addressed to Edward Gibbon esq. Cambridge 1776.

Loftus, S. A reply to the reasonings of Mr Gibbons in his history of the decline and fall of the Roman Empire. Dublin 1777, London 1778.

Randolph, T. The proof of the truth of the Christian religion in two sermons, lately preached before the university of Oxford. 1777.

Apthorp, E. Letters on the prevalence of Christianity, with observations on a late history of the decline of the Roman Empire. 1778.

Burgh, W. An inquiry into the belief of the Christians of the first three centuries. York 1778.

[Dalrymple, D. (Lord Hailes)]. Remains of Christian antiquity, with explanatory notes. Vols 2–3, Edinburgh 1778–80.

—— Octavius: a dialogue by Marcus Minucius Felix. Edinburgh 1781. Notes by Dalrymple, including a long critical note on Gibbon on pp. 146–56.

—— Of the manner in which the persecutors died, by L. C. F. Lactantius. Edinburgh 1782. Notes by Dalrymple contain criticisms of passages in Decline and fall.

—— Disquisitions concerning the antiquities of the Christian Church. Glasgow 1783.

—— An inquiry into the secondary causes which Mr Gibbon has assigned for the rapid growth of Christianity. Edinburgh 1786, 1808 ('to which is prefixed a brief memoir of the author'). Memoir contains remarks about Gibbon and list of Dalrymple's works, with special mention of the references to Gibbon.

—— The address of Q. Sept. Tertullian to Scapula Tertullus. Edinburgh 1790.

Davis, H. E. An examination of the fifteenth and sixteenth chapters of Mr Gibbon's history. 1778.

—— A reply to Mr Gibbon's Vindication, wherein the charges brought against him in the examination are confirmed. 1779.

[Eyre, F.] A few remarks on the History of the decline and fall of the Roman Empire. 1778.
— A short appeal to the public, by the gentleman who is particularly addressed in the postscript of the Vindication. 1779.
Hayley, W. An essay on history, in three epistles to Edward Gibbon esq. 1780, 1785 (in Hayley's Poems and plays, vol 2).
Laughton, G. The progress and establishment of Christianity, in reply to the fifteenth chapter of the Decline and fall of the Roman Empire. 1780, 1786.
Lindsey, T. The catechist. 1781, 1792. Attack on Gibbon in the preface.
Milner, J. Gibbon's account of Christianity considered. York 1781.
Taylor, H. Thoughts on the nature of the grand apostasy, with reflections on the xvth chapter of Mr Gibbon's history. 1781.
— Farther thoughts on the nature of the grand apostasy. 1783.
Newton, T. Works. 3 vols 1782. The reference to Gibbon, which is the subject of a long entry in Gibbon's Commonplace book, quoted by Lord Sheffield in Miscellaneous works vol 1, pp. 241–2, is on pp. 129–30 of the Life in vol 1.
Priestley, J. An history of the corruptions of Christianity. Birmingham 1782. The challenge to Gibbon is in pt 1 of the General conclusion.
— Letters to a philosophical unbeliever. Birmingham 1787.
— Discourses on the evidence of revealed religion. 1794.
Mably, G. B. De la manière d'écrire l'histoire. Paris 1783, 1784 (with the Supplément à la manière d'écrire l'histoire by Gudin de la Brennellerie); rptd in the Collection complète des oeuvres de Mably, Paris 1794–5.
Ogilvie, J. An inquiry into the causes of the infidelity and scepticism of the times. 1783.
Howes, T. On the abuse of the talent of disputation in religion. Norwich 1784; rptd in his Critical observations on books ancient and modern vol 3, no 9.
Spedalieri, N. Confutazione dell' esame del cristianesimo fatto dal sig Eduardo Gibbon. 2 vols Rome 1784.
Travis, G. Letters to Edward Gibbon esq in defence of the authenticity of the seventh verse of the fifth chapter of the first epistle of St John. Chester 1784, London 1785 (corrected and enlarged), 1794 (enlarged). The letters were originally pbd in the Gentleman's Magazine during 1782; additional material was added for pbn in book form. See Richard Porson, Letters to Mr Archdeacon Travis in answer to his defence of the Three heavenly witnesses, GM 1788–9, rptd 1790 and in Porson's Tracts and miscellaneous criticisms, ed T. Kidd 1815.
White, J. Sermons preached before the university of Oxford. Oxford 1784. References to Gibbon: Sermon 3, pp. 137–45, and in notes, pp. lxxii–v.
[Cumberland, R.] The observer. 1785. Article 16, p. 143, deals with Gibbon.
'Heron, R.' (John Pinkerton). Letters of literature. 1785. References to Gibbon on pp. 68, 338–40, 358.
Paley, W. The principles of moral and political philosophy. 1785. References to Gibbon (not by name), bk 6, ch 9.
'Simplex' (John Young). Letters addressed to Soame Jenyns. 1786, 1791.
[Jesse, W.] Lectures supposed to have been delivered by the author of A view of the internal evidence of the Christian religion, dedicated to Edward Gibbon esq. 1787, New York 1791.
Observations on the three last volumes of the Roman history by Edward Gibbon esq. 1788. By Henry James Pye?
Luderwald, J. B. Die Ausbreitung der christlichen Religion nach ihrer Beweiskraft. Helmstedt 1788.

Disney, W. A sermon preached before the university of Cambridge, with some strictures on the licentious notions in the three last volumes of Mr Gibbon's history. Cambridge 1789.
Edwards, T. The Jewish and heathen rejection of the Christian miracles. Cambridge 1790.
— The predictions of the Apostles, concerning the end of the world. Bury 1790.
Hamilton, J. E. Strictures upon primitive Christianity. 2 vols 1790–2.
Porson, R. Letters to Mr Archdeacon Travis. 1790.
Kett, H. Sermons preached before the university of Oxford. Oxford 1791.
— History the interpreter of prophecy. 3 vols Oxford 1799.
Whitaker, J. Gibbon's history reviewed. 1791. Rptd from Eng Rev 12–13 1788–9.
Milner, J. An historical and critical inquiry into the existence of St George. 1792.
Nisbett, N. The scripture doctrine concerning the coming of Christ unfolded. Canterbury 1792, 1800 (as The coming of the Messiah).
— The triumphs of Christianity over infidelity displayed. 1802.
— A concise and interesting view of the objection of Gibbon that our Lord foretold his second coming. Chatham 1805.
— Letters illustrative of the Gospel history in reply to Mr Gibbon. Faversham 1812.
Thomas, G. A. The predictions of Christ and the Apostles concerning the end of the world. 1793.
Whitaker, E. W. A general and connected view of the prophecies relating to the times of the Gentiles. Egham 1795.
— A commentary on the Revelation of St John. 1802.
A letter to the Rt Hon John Lord Sheffield on the publication of the Memoirs and letters of the late Edward Gibbon esq. Shrewsbury 1796.
Evans, J. An attempt to account for the infidelity of the late Edward Gibbon esq. 1797.
Finch, W. The objections of infidel historians and other writers against Christianity considered. Oxford 1797.
Skinner, J. Primitive truth and order vindicated from modern misrepresentation. Aberdeen 1803.
[Young, P.] An antidote to infidelity insinuated in the works of E. Gibbon esq. [1805?].
[Bernard, T.] An historical view of Christianity, with a commentary by the late Edward Gibbon esq. 1806. Described by Norton as not a new work by Gibbon: it 'consists of garbled extracts from the Decline and fall designed to confound him out of his own mouth' (p. 245).
Cockburn, W. The credibility of the Jewish exodus defended against some remarks of Edward Gibbon esq. 1809. Defence of Sir Thomas Bernard's book against criticism in Edinburgh Rev 8 1806.
An analysis of the sixth chapter of the Revelation of St John, illustrated by extracts from Gibbon's history. 1815.
[Burgess, T.] An introduction to the controversy on the disputed verse of St John, as revived by Mr Gibbon. Salisbury 1835.
Guillon, M-N-S. Examen critique des doctrines de Gibbon, du Dr Strauss et de M. Salvador sur Jesus Christ. 2 vols Paris 1841.
Blunt, J. J. On the right use of the early Fathers. 1857, 1858.
Hennell, S. S. The early Christian anticipation of an approaching end of the world, including an examination of the argument of the fifteenth chapter of Gibbon. 1860.
Farrar, A. S. In his A critical history of free thought. 1862.
Macdonald, J. M. Irony in history: or the true position of Gibbon in respect to Christianity. Andover Mass 1868. Originally pbd in Bibliotheca Sacra July 1868.

Braund, J. H. History and revelation, from Gibbon, Mézéray, Mosheim, d'Aubigné and other eminent historians. 2 vols 1870.
A number of attacks in contemporary periodicals are given in J. E. Norton's bibliography.

Sainte-Beuve, C.-A. In his Causeries du lundi vol 8, Paris 1855.
Bagehot, W. In his Estimates of some Englishmen and Scotchmen, 1858.
Morrison, J. C. Gibbon. 1878 (EML).
Birrell, A. In his Res judicatae, 1892.
Proceedings of the Gibbon commemoration 1794–1894. 1895 (Royal Historical Soc). Contains introductory speech by Sir M. G. Duff, an address by Frederic Harrison, and catalogue of the exhibition at the BM of autograph mss of the Memoirs, journals, and note books, correspondence, relics and portraits.
Rae, W. F. Gibbon's library. Athenaeum 5 June 1897.
Cecil, A. In his Six Oxford thinkers, 1909.
Clarke, A. H. T. Nineteenth Century Sept–Nov 1910. 3 articles on Gibbon, and on his life, the other 2 on the ecclesiastical chs of Decline and fall.
Clodd, E. Gibbon and Christianity. 1916.
Beaunier, A. Trois amis de Mme de Staël. Revue des Deux Mondes Feb 1917.
Gunther, R. T. Some unedited accounts of Gibbon. N & Q 25 Aug–8 Sept 1923.
Robertson, J. M. Gibbon. 1924.
Black, J. B. The art of history: a study of the four great historians of the eighteenth century. 1926.
Russell, C. Johnson, Gibbon and Boswell. Fortnightly Rev May 1926.
Strachey, L. In his Portraits in miniature, 1931.
Helming, V. P. Gibbon and Georges Deyverdun. PMLA 47 1932.
Hutton, E. The conversion of Gibbon. Nineteenth Century March 1932.
Young, G. M. Gibbon. 1932, 1948 (with introd).
McCloy, S. T. Gibbon's antagonism to Christianity. 1933.
Dawson, C. Edward Gibbon. Proc Br Acad 20 1934.
Hawks, C. P. In his Authors-at-arms, 1934.
Blunden, E. Gibbon and his age. Bristol 1935.
Frazer, J. G. Gibbon at Lausanne. In his Creation and evolution in primitive cosmogonies, 1935.
Mowat, R. B. Gibbon. 1936.
Low, D. M. Edward Gibbon. 1937.
— Gibbon and the Johnsonian circle. New Rambler June 1960.
— and F. J. B. Watson. The young Gibbon. TLS 29 Jan 1960.
Thompson, J. W. The library of Gibbon the historian. Lib Quart 7 1937.
Hill, M. C. The Sheffield edition of Gibbon's Autobiography. RES 14 1938.
Powell, L. F. Friedrich von Matthisson on Gibbon. In German studies presented to H. G. Fiedler, Oxford 1938.
Machin, I. W. J. Gibbon's debt to contemporary scholarship. RES 15 1939.
Saunders, J. J. Gibbon and the Decline and fall. History 23 1939.
Toynbee, A. J. Gibbon's choice of linguistic vehicle. In his A study of history vol 5, Oxford 1939.
Baldensperger, F. A neglected letter of Gibbon (Lausanne, 1792). Modern Lang Forum 27 1942.
Pritchett, V. S. Gibbon and the Home Guard. In his In my good books, 1942.
Cochrane, D. N. The mind of Gibbon. UTQ 12 1943.
Bonnard, G. A. L'importance du deuxième séjour de Gibbon à Lausanne. In Mélanges d'histoire et de littérature offerts à Charles Gilliard, Lausanne 1944.
— Essai sur l'étude de la littérature as judged by con-temporary reviews and Gibbon himself. E Studies 32 1951.
— Le journal de Gibbon à Lausanne. Paris 1955.
Quennell, P. C. In his Four portraits, 1945.
Thompson, A. H. Gibbon. 1946 (Historical Assoc).
Boyce, G. K. The cost of publishing Gibbon's Vindication. PBSA 43 1949.
de Beer, G. R. Travellers in Switzerland. Oxford 1949. For addns on Gibbon, see his English visitors in Switzerland, N & Q 14, 28 May 1949.
— The malady of Gibbon FRS. Notes & Records of Royal Soc 7 1949.
— Gibbon and his world. 1968.
Curtis, L. P. Gibbon's Paradise lost. In The age of Johnson: essays presented to C. B. Tinker, New Haven 1949.
Offler, H. S. Gibbon and the making of his Swiss history. Durham Univ Jnl 41 1949.
Greene, D. J. Gibbon cites Johnson. N & Q 31 March 1951.
Maxwell, J. C. Gibbon, Hume and Julian the apostate. N & Q 10 Nov 1951.
Rea, R. R. Some notes on Gibbon's Mémoire justificatif. SB 5 1953.
Joyce, M. Gibbon. 1953.
Barnes, S. B. Gibbon's Utopia. Classical Jnl 49 1953.
Dwyer, J. J. TLS 19 June 1953.
Fuglum, P. Gibbon: his view of life and conception of history. Oslo 1953.
Fulton, J. F. Gibbon, the 'unprofitable undergraduate'. In his Books and the man vol 2, 1953.
Giarrizzo, G. Gibbon e la cultura europea del Settecento. Naples 1954.
Hudson, G. F. Toynbee versus Gibbon. Twentieth Century Nov 1954.
Kronenberger, L. Edward Gibbon. Atlantic Monthly Nov 1954.
Steer, F. W. Correspondence of Gibbon and John Charles Brooke. N & Q Nov 1954.
Wedgwood, C. V. Edward Gibbon. 1955.
— In her Truth and opinion, 1960.
Brown, R. D. Suetonius, Symonds and Gibbon in the Picture of Dorian Gray. MLN 71 1956.
Keast, W. R. The element of art in Gibbon's History. ELH 23 1956.
King, R. W. A note on Shelley, Gibbon, Voltaire and Southey. MLR 51 1956.
Norton, J. E. Gregory, Sheffield and Gibbon. TLS 22 June 1956.
Dyson, A. E. A note on dismissive irony. English 2 1957; rptd in his Crazy fabric, 1965.
Sarton, G. The missing factor in Gibbon's concept of history. Harvard Lib Bull 2 1957.
Carswell, J. 'A linen draper bold'. TLS 24 Jan 1958. Reply by J. E. Norton 31 Jan 1958.
Oliver, E. J. Gibbon and Rome. 1958.
Cordasco, F. Gibbon and the authorship of Junius. N & Q Nov 1959.
Watson, F. J. B. An unknown portrait of the young Gibbon. TLS 25 Dec 1959.
Spencer, T. J. B. From Gibbon to Darwin. 1959.
Bond, H. L. The literary art of Gibbon. Oxford 1960.
Gruman, G. J. 'Balance' and 'excess' as Gibbon's explanation of the Decline and fall. History & Theory 1 1960.
Pascal, R. Design and truth in autobiography. 1960. On Franklin, Gibbon, Rousseau et al.
Baridon, M. Gibbon en Italie. Etudes Anglaises 15 1962.
Syme, R. Three English historians: Gibbon, Macaulay, Toynbee. Emory Univ Quart 18 1962.
Winks, R. W. Hume and Gibbon: a view from a vantage. Dalhousie Rev 41 1962.
Africa, T. W. Gibbon and the Golden Age. Centennial Rev of Arts & Science 7 1963.
Barker, N. A note on the bibliography of Gibbon 1776–1802. Library 5th ser 18 1963.

Doggart, J. H. Gibbon's eyesight. Trans Cambridge Bibl Soc 3 1963.

Saunders, J. J. The debate on the fall of Rome. History 48 1963.

—— Gibbon in Rome 1764. History Today Sept 1964.

Danchin, P. Gibbon's journey from Geneva to Rome. E Studies 45 1964.

MacRobert, T. M. Gibbon's autobiography. REL 5 1964.

Morris, J. N. Gibbon's fortunes. Modern Age 8 1964.

Nickerson, C. C. Gibbon's copy of Steele's Dramatick works. Book Collector 13 1964.

Trevor-Roper, H. R. Gibbon after 200 years. Listener 22–9 Oct 1964.

de Beer, E. S. A reading of Gibbon. Landfall Dec 1965.

England's greatest historian commemorated. Commemorative Art 31 1964.

Swain, J. W. Gibbon the historian. 1966.

White, L. T. (ed). The transformation of the Roman world: Gibbon's problem after two centuries. 1966.

Craddock, P. B. Gibbon's revision of the Decline and fall. SB 21 1968.

JOHN NICHOLS
1745–1826

Nichols was primarily an editor and compiler. There are typescript copies of a bibliography by A. H. Smith in London and Leicester Univ libraries.

§1

Verses on the coronation of their late Majesties King George II and Queen Caroline. 1761. By W. Bowyer and Nichols.

The buds of Parnassus: a collection of original poems. 1763, 1764?

Islington: a poem. 1763.

The laurel-wreath: being a collection of original miscellaneous poems by W. P[erfect]. 1766. Nichols contributed to this collection.

The amours of Lais: or the misfortunes of love. 1766. Conclusion by Nichols.

The origin of printing, in two essays: I, The substance of Dr Middleton's dissertation on the origin of printing in England; II, Mr Meerman's account of the first invention of the art. 1774, 1776 ('with improvements'); suppl 1781. Ed Bowyer and Nichols.

The works of Jonathan Swift. Vol 9 (4°), vol 17 (large 8°), vol 18 (12°), 1775. Includes index to previous vols of this edn by Hawkesworth.

A supplement to Dr Swift's works: being a collection of miscellanies in prose and verse, by the Dean, Dr Delany, Dr Sheridan and others, with explanatory notes. Vols 24–5 (large 8°), 1776–9, vols 25–7 (small 8°), vol 14 (4°), vols 25–7 (12°), 1779.

The original works of William King, with historical notes, and memoirs of the author. 3 vols 1776.

Anecdotes, biographical and literary, of the late Mr William Bowyer, printer. 1778 (anon; priv ptd), 1782 (greatly enlarged as Biographical and literary anecdotes of William Bowyer); tr German, 1786–7. *See* Literary anecdotes of the eighteenth century, below.

A dissertation upon English typographical founders and founderies by E. R. Mores. 1778 (for 1779); ed D. B. Updike, New York 1924 (Grolier Club); ed H. Carter and C. Ricks, Oxford 1961. With appendix signed J.N.

The gentleman's magazine. 1778–92 (jointly with D. Henry), 1792–1826.

Six old plays on which Shakespeare founded his Measure for measure etc. 2 vols 1779. Comedy of Errors, Shrew, King John, Henry IV, Henry V, Lear.

The history of the royal abbey of Bec by J. Bourget, translated from the French. 1779. Ed A. C. Ducarel assisted by Nichols.

Some account of the alien priories. 2 vols 1779, 1786. By A. C. Ducarel and J. Warburton; ed Ducarel, R. Gough, Nichols et al.

Anecdotes of Mr Hogarth. [1780?] (priv ptd), 1781 (enlarged as Biographical anecdotes of William Hogarth) 1782, 1785, 3 vols 1808–17 (enlarged as The genuine works of William Hogarth by John Nichols and George Steevens), 1822 (as The works of William Hogarth, from the original plates restored by James Heath, to which is prefixed a biographical essay on the genius and productions of Hogarth, and explanations of the subjects of the plates by John Nichols), 2 vols 1833; tr German, 1783. Contributions by G. Steevens, I. Reed, S. Ireland et al, in 1781 etc.

Bibliotheca topographica britannica. 8 vols 1780–90. Ed Nichols; contributions by Nichols listed separately under date below.

A collection of all the wills of the Kings and Queens of England. 1780.

A select collection of poems. 8 vols 1780–4.

Biographical memoirs of William Ged, including a particular account of his progress in the art of block-printing. 1781, Newcastle 1819.

The history and antiquities of Hinckley, in the county of Leicester. Bibliotheca topographica britannica no 7, 1782 (in vol 7 1790), 1813 (from The history and antiquities of the county of Leicester).

Critical conjectures and observations on the New Testament by W. Bowyer. 1782 (3rd edn), 1812 (4th edn).

The epistolary correspondence of Francis Atterbury, with historical notes. 4 vols 1783–7, 5 vols 1789–98 (as Miscellaneous works).

Novum testamentum graecum [ed W. Bowyer]; editio secunda cura Johannis Nichols [assisted by H. Owen]. 1783.

The principal additions and corrections in the third edition of Dr Johnson's Lives of the poets, collected to complete the second edition. [1783]. Compiled by Nichols.

A new and general biographical dictionary. 12 vols 1784 ('a new edition, greatly enlarged and improved'). With R. Heathcote.

Miscellaneous tracts by the late William Bowyer and several of his learned friends, collected and illustrated with occasional notes. 1785.

The plays of William Shakespeare, accurately printed from the text of Mr Malone's edition, with select explanatory notes. 7 vols 1786–90.

The Tatler: the lucubrations of Isaac Bickerstaff, with notes. 6 vols 1786. Ed J. Calder and Nichols from notes of T. Percy.

The epistolary correspondence of Sir Richard Steele, with literary and historical anecdotes. 2 vols 1787, 1809.

The history and antiquities of Aston Flamvile and Burbach, with an appendix to the history of Hinckley. Bibliotheca topographica britannica no 43, 1787 (in vol 7 1790).

The works of Leonard Welsted, with historical notes and biographical memoirs of the author. 1787.

The history and antiquities of Canonbury-House at Islington. Bibliotheca topographica britannica no 49, 1788 (in vol 2 1790).

The progresses, and public processions of Queen Elizabeth. 3 vols and pt 1 of vol 4 1788–1821, 3 vols 1823. With R. Gough.

The Lover, by Marmaduke Myrtle gent, to which is added the Reader; with notes and illustrations. 1789.

The Lover and Reader: to which are prefixed the Whig-Examiner and a selection from the Medley. 1789.

The Town talk, the Fish pool, the Plebeian, the Old Whig, the Spinster etc, with notes and illustrations. 1789, 1790.

Collections towards the history and antiquities of the town and county of Leicester. 2 pts Bibliotheca topographica britannica nos 50–1, 1790 (in vols 7–8 1790).

The antiquaries museum by Jacob Schnebbelie. 1791. Ed Nichols and R. Gough.

Miscellaneous antiquities (in continuation of the Bibliotheca topographica britannica). Nos 1–6, 1791–7.

The Theatre by Sir R. Steele; to which are added the Anti-Theatre etc, illustrated with literary and historical anecdotes. 1791.

The history and antiquities of the county of Leicester. 4 vols in 8 1795–1815.

Illustrations of the manners and expences of antient times in England, with explanatory notes. 1797.

The plays of William Shakespeare, accurately printed from the text of Mr Steevens's last edition, with a selection of the most important notes. 8 vols 1797.

A sermon preached at the funeral of William Duke of Devonshire, with some memoirs of the family of Cavendish, by White Kennett. 1797 ('the second edition, with additions by the author, and by the editor').

A list of the members of the Society of Antiquaries of London, from 1717 to 1796, arranged in chronological and alphabetical order. 1798. Anon. Compiled by R. Gough and Nichols.

A comment upon part of the fifth journey of Antoninus through Britain. 1800, 1819.

An historical account of Beauchief Abbey by S. Pegge. 1801.

The works of Jonathan Swift. 19 vols 1801, 24 vols 1803, 19 vols 1808. Sheridan's edn, 'corrected and revised' by Nichols. Malone assisted Nichols with the 1808 edn.

Anecdotes of the English language by S. Pegge. 1803, 1814.

Brief memoirs of John Nichols. 1804.

Curialia: or an historical account of the Royal Household etc etc, pts 4 and 5 by Samuel Pegge. 1806.

Anonymiana, compiled by [S. Pegge], published from the ms. 1809, 1818.

Biographical memoirs of Richard Gough. GM March–April 1809; rptd 1809.

Letters on various subjects to and from William Nicolson. 2 vols 1809.

Biographical anecdotes of Richard Gough. 1810. Extracted from Literary anecdotes of the eighteenth century.

A catalogue of the library of Richard Gough. [1810]. With a biographical preface by Nichols.

The history of the worthies of England by T. Fuller, with a few explanatory notes. 2 vols 1811.

Literary anecdotes of the eighteenth century: comprising memoirs of William Bowyer and many of his learned friends. 9 vols 1812–16. Vol 7: pt 1, 1813, index to vols 1–6; pt 2, 1816, index to vols 8–9.

The battle of Bosworth Field by W. Hutton. 1813 (2nd edn, with addns).

Some account of the Abbey Church of St Alban. 1813. With Gough.

Illustrations of the literary history of the eighteenth century. 8 vols 1817–58. J. B. Nichols continued this work after Nichols's death.

Curialia miscellanea: or anecdotes of old times by Samuel Pegge. 1818.

The miscellaneous works of George Hardinge. 3 vols 1818.

Poems, Latin, Greek and English, by George Hardinge. 1818.

Two music speeches at Cambridge by Roger Long and John Taylor, [with] memoirs. 1819.

A prefatory introduction, descriptive of the rise and progress of the [Gentleman's] Magazine, with anecdotes of the projector. In general index to GM 1787–1818, vol 3 1821; rptd as The rise and progress of the Gentleman's Magazine, 1821.

Four sermons: 1, by John Taylor, 1745; 2, by Dr Taylor, 1757; 3, by Bishop Lowth, 1758; 4, by Bishop Hayter, 1750. 1822.

The progresses, processions, and magnificent festivities, of King James the First. 3 vols in 4 1828.

Birth-day odes, and other domestic poems. 1827.

§2

Nichols, J. Brief memoirs of John Nichols. 1804.
—— In his Literary anecdotes of the eighteenth century, 9 vols 1812–16. Especially vol 6, pp. 626–37.
—— In his Illustrations of the literary history of the eighteenth century, 8 vols 1817–58.
Dobson, A. A literary printer. In his Rosalba's journal, 1915.
Hart, E. Some new sources of Johnson's Lives. PMLA 65 1950.
—— The contributions of Nichols to Boswell's Life of Johnson. PMLA 67 1952.
—— An ingenious editor: John Nichols and the Gentleman's Magazine. Bucknell Rev 10 1962.
Schick, G. B. 'Kind hints' to John Nichols by Joseph Warton and others. N & Q Feb 1956.
Smith, A. H. Nichols and Hutchins's History and antiquities of Dorset. Library 5th ser 15 1960.
—— Nichols: printer and publisher. Library 5th ser 18 1963.

MINOR HISTORICAL WRITERS 1750–1800

WILLIAM BORLASE
1695–1772

Observations on the antiquities historical and monumental of the county of Cornwall. Oxford 1754, 1769 (with addns).

Observations on the ancient and present state of the islands of Scilly. Oxford 1756.

The natural history of Cornwall. Oxford 1758.

JOHN BRAND
1744–1806

§1

Observations on popular antiquities, including the whole of Mr [H.] Bourne's Antiquitates vulgares, with addenda to every chapter. 1777; ed H. Ellis 2 vols 1813 etc; ed W. C. Hazlitt 3 vols 1870 (for 1869), 2 vols 1905.

The history and antiquities of Newcastle upon Tyne. 2 vols 1789; index by W. Dodd 1881 (Soc of Antiquaries of Newcastle).

Brand also contributed many papers to Archaeologia.

§2

Bibliotheca Brandiana: a catalogue of the library of the late Rev Brand. 1807.

GEORGE CHALMERS
1742–1825

Political annals of the present united colonies, from their settlement to the peace of 1763: book 1. 1780.

An introduction to the history of the revolt of the colonies. Vol 1 ptd and cancelled, [1782]; rptd 2 vols Boston 1845.

An estimate of the comparative strength of Britain during the present and four preceding reigns, and of the losses of her trade from every war since the Revolution. 1782, 1786, 1794 (corrected and improved); tr French, 1789.

Many later edns, including An historical view of the domestic economy of G. Britain and Ireland, Edinburgh 1812.

Opinions on interesting subjects of public law and commercial policy; arising from American independence. 1784, 1785 ('corrected').

The life of Daniel De Foe. 1785 (anon), 1790. Several reprints with portions of Defoe's works.

Historical tracts by Sir John Davies, [with] a new life of the author. 1786.

A collection of treaties between Great Britain and other powers. 2 vols 1790.

Life of Thomas Pain, by Francis Oldys AM of the University of Pennsylvania [Chalmers]. 1791 (3 edns), 1792 (5th edn 'enlarged'), 1793 (10th edn).

The life of Thomas Ruddiman. 1794.

Parliamentary portraits; to which is prefixed A review of the present administration. 2 vols 1795.

A vindication of the privilege of the people in respect of the constitutional right of free discussion. 1796. Anon.

Life of Sir David Lyndsay. In Chalmers's edn of Lindsay's poetical works, 3 vols 1806.

Caledonia: or an account of North Britain. 3 vols 1807–24, 8 vols Paisley 1887–1902.

Opinions of eminent lawyers on various points of English jurisprudence, chiefly concerning the colonies, fisheries and commerce of Great Britain, collected and digested from the originals in the Board of Trade and other depositories. 1814.

Comparative views of the state of Great Britain and Ireland before the war; as it is since the peace. 1817.

The life of Mary, Queen of Scots. 2 vols 1818; tr German, 1824. See John Whitaker, below.

The poetic remains of some of the Scotish kings. 1824. Ed Chalmers.

A detection of the love-letters attributed in Hugh Campbell's work to Mary Queen of Scots, wherein his plagiarisms are proved and his fictions fixed. 1825. Anon.

Chalmers also pbd a number of pamphlets.

JOHN CHARNOCK
1756–1807

Biographia navalis: or impartial memoirs of the lives and characters of officers of the Navy from 1660. 6 vols 1794–8.

An history of marine architecture, including an enlarged view of the nautical regulations and naval history, both civil and military, of all nations, especially of Great Britain. 3 vols 1800–2.

Biographical memoirs of Nelson. 1806.

JOHN COLLINSON
1757?–93

The beauties of British antiquity, selected from the writings of esteemed antiquaries. 1779.

The history and antiquities of the county of Somerset. 3 vols Bath 1791. Index by Edwin Pearce, ed F. W. Weaver and E. H. Bates, Taunton 1898.

SIR DAVID DALRYMPLE, LORD HAILES
1726–92

§ 1

Memorials and letters relating to the history of Britain in the reign of James I. Glasgow 1762, 1766 ('corrected').

Memorials and letters relating to the history of Britain in the reign of Charles I. Glasgow 1766.

The secret correspondence of Sir R. Cecil with James VI. Edinburgh 1766. Ed Dalrymple.

Remarks on the History of Scotland. Edinburgh 1773.

Annals of Scotland, from Malcolm Canmore to Robert I. Edinburgh 1776, 1779 ('continued to the accession of the House of Stuart'), 3 vols Edinburgh 1797 ('to which are added several texts relative to the history'), 1819 (3rd edn).

Letters

Horace Walpole's correspondence with Dalrymple. Ed W. S. Lewis, C. H. Bennett and A. G. Hoover, New Haven 1952 (vol 15 of Yale edn of Walpole's correspondence).

The correspondence of Thomas Percy and Dalrymple. Ed A. F. Falconer, Baton Rouge 1954.

A letter from Lord Hailes to James Boswell in Holland. Ed. R. H. Carnie, N & Q Feb 1954. Prints the text of a letter of 27 June 1764, now in the Laing mss, University of Edinburgh.

§ 2

Carnie, R. H. Lord Hailes's notes on Johnson's Lives of the poets. N & Q Feb–April, Aug, Nov 1956. From ms in Hyde collection.

—— Lord Hailes's contributions to contemporary magazines. SB 9 1957.

SIR JOHN DALRYMPLE
1726–1810

§ 1

An essay towards a general history of feudal property in Great Britain. 1757, 1759 (4th edn, 'corrected and enlarged').

Memoirs of Great Britain and Ireland, from the dissolution of the last Parliament of Charles II until the sea-battle off La Hogue. 2 pts Edinburgh 1771, Dublin 1771, London 1771; vol 2 (appendixes to vol 1), 3 pts 1773, 1773; vol 1 (for 3) ('From the battle off La Hogue till the capture of the French and Spanish fleets at Vigo'), 2 pts Edinburgh 1788; [complete work], 3 vols 1790.

§ 2

Russell, R. Letters, with an introduction vindicating the character of Lord Russell against Dalrymple. 1773.

A discourse on the bookland and folkland of the Saxons, wherein the nature of those kinds of estates is explained; and the notion of them advanced by Dalrymple confuted. Cambridge 1775.

O'Halloran, S. Observations on the Memoirs of Dalrymple 1772. Appendix 2 of O'Halloran, An introduction to the study of the history and antiquities of Ireland, 1772.

Russell, J. In his Life of William Lord Russell. 1819. Includes criticism of Memoirs of Great Britain and Ireland.

JEAN LOUIS DE LOLME
1740?–1807

§ 1

A parallel between the English constitution and the former government of Sweden, containing some observations on the late revolution in that Kingdom. 1772.

The constitution of England: or an account of the English government, in which it is compared with the republican form of government. 1775, 1784 (4th edn, enlarged), 1789 ('corrected'), 1807 ('with supplemental notes and a preface biographical and critical by C. Coote'), 1853 (with life and notes by J. Macgregor); tr German, 1776; Spanish, 1812. Originally pbd in French, Amsterdam 1771.

The history of the Flagellants, or the advantages of discipline: being a paraphrase and commentary on the Historia flagellantium of the Abbé Boileau. 1777, 1784 (as Memorials of human superstition).

The British Empire in Europe, part the first: containing an account of the connection between England and Ireland previous to the year 1780. 1787.

§2

Ruff, E. Jean Louis de Lolme und sein Werk über die Verfassung Englands. Berlin 1934.

ANDREW COLTEE DUCAREL
1713–85

A tour through Normandy, described in a letter to a friend. 1754 (anon), 2 pts 1767 (much enlarged as Anglo-Norman antiquities considered, in a tour through part of Normandy); tr French, 1823.

A series of above two hundred Anglo-Gallic or Norman and Aquitain coins of the antient kings of England. 2 pts 1757.

Some account of Browne Willis esq LID. 1760.

A repertory of the endowments of vicarages in the diocese of Canterbury. 1763, 1782 (including those in the diocese of Rochester).

Some account of the alien priories, and of such lands as they possessed in England and Wales. 2 vols 1779 (anon), 1786. With John Warburton.

The history of the Royal Hospital and collegiate church of St Katharine, near the Tower of London. In Bibliotheca topographica britannica, ed J. Nichols no 5, 1782 (in vol 2, 1790).

Some account of the town, church and archiepiscopal palace of Croydon. In Bibliotheca topographica britannica, ed J. Nichols no 12, 1783 (in vol 2, 1790).

The history and antiquities of the archiepiscopal palace of Lambeth. In Bibliotheca topographica britannica, ed J. Nichols no 27, 1785 (in vol 2, 1790).

WALTER GOODALL or GOODAL
1706?–66

An examination of the letters, said to be written by Mary Queen of Scots to James Earl of Bothwell, shewing that they are forgeries. 2 vols Edinburgh 1754.

Preface concerning the first planting of Christianity in Scotland. In R. Keith, A large new catalogue of the bishops of Scotland, Edinburgh 1755, 1824.

Joannis de Fordun Scotichronicon. 2 vols Edinburgh 1759. Ed Goodall.

An introduction to the history and antiquities of Scotland, translated from the original Latin. 1769.

RICHARD GOUGH
1735–1809

§1

The history of Carausius: or an examination of what has been advanced on that subject by Genebrier and Stukeley. 1762. Anon.

Anecdotes of British topography: or an historical account of what has been done for illustrating the topographical antiquities of Great Britain and Ireland. 1768 (anon), 2 vols 1780 (as British topography).

Archaeologia 1. 1770. Anon introd containing an historical account of the origin and establishment of Society of Antiquaries.

Description des royaulmes d'Angleterre et d'Escosse, composé par Estienne Perlin (Paris 1558); Histoire de l'entrée de La Reine Mère dans la Grande Bretagne, par De la Serre, Paris 1639; illustrated with cuts and English notes. 1775.

A catalogue of the coins of Canute, King of Denmark and England. 1777. Anon.

The history of the town of Thetford, in the counties of Norfolk and Suffolk. 1779. Ed Gough from collections of T. Martin.

Observations on the round towers in Ireland and Scotland. 1779.

Catalogue of Sarum and York Missals. [1780]. Anon.

Bibliotheca topographica britannica. Ed J. Nichols 8 vols 1780–90. Gough's contributions include memoir of the author in no 1 (Edward Rowe Mores's History of Tunstall); nos 2, 20, Reliquiae Galeanae: account of the Gentlemen's Society at Spalding; no 3, Preface to William Orem's Description of the Chanonry in old Aberdeen (anon); nos 4, 19, Memoirs of Sir John Hawkwood (anon); nos 11, 22, The history of Croyland; no 31, A short genealogical view of the family of Oliver Cromwell (preface signed R.G.).

A comparative view of the antient monuments of India, particularly those in the island of Salset near Bombay. 1785. Preface signed R.G.

Sepulchral monuments in Great Britain applied to illustrate the history of families, manners, habits and arts, at the different periods from the Norman Conquest to the seventeenth century. 2 vols 1786–96.

Britannia by William Camden, translated and enlarged by the latest discoveries. 3 vols 1789, 4 vols 1806.

The life of Sir John Falstolff by W. Oldys. [1793]. Ed Gough.

An account of a missal executed for John Duke of Bedford. 1794. Dedication signed R.G.

The history and antiquities of Dorset by John Hutchins. 4 vols 1796–1815 (2nd edn). Ed Gough and J.B. Nichols.

The parochial history of Castor and its dependencies, [with] an account of Marham and several other places. In Kennet Gibson, A comment upon part of the fifth journey of Antoninus through Britain, 1800, 1819 ('corrected and enlarged').

The history and antiquities of Pleshy in the county of Essex. 1803. Preface signed R.G.

Coins of the Seleucidae, Kings of Syria. 1803. Anon.

Description of the Beauchamp Chapel, adjoining to the church of St Mary at Warwick. 1804 (anon), 1809.

Some account of the Abbey church of St Alban. 1813.

§2

Nichols, J. Biographical memoirs of Gough, extracted from the Gentleman's Magazine for March and April 1809. [1809].

—— Biographical anecdotes of Gough, extracted from Literary anecdotes of the eighteenth century. 1810.

A catalogue of the entire and valuable library (with the exception of the department of British topography, bequeathed to the Bodleian library) of Gough, which will be sold by auction. [1810]. Biographical preface signed J[ohn] N[ichols].

Museum Goughianum: a catalogue of the collection of prints, drawings, coins, medals, seals, painted glass etc. 1810.

A catalogue of the books relating to British topography, bequeathed to the Bodleian library in 1799 by Gough. Oxford 1814.

JAMES GRANGER
1723–76

A biographical history of England, from Egbert the Great to the Revolution. 2 vols (4 pts) and suppl 1769–74, 4 vols 1775, 1779, 1804, 3 vols 1806 (continued by M. Noble), 6 vols 1824 (with addns).

Letters

Letters between the Rev James Granger and many of the more eminent literary men of his time. Ed J. P. Malcolm 1805.
Granger also pbd sermons. See Boswell's Johnson, ed L. F. Powell vol 3, Oxford 1934, pp. 484–5.

FRANCIS GROSE
1731?–91

The antiquities of England and Wales (with supplement). 6 vols 1773–87, 8 vols [1783]–97.
A treatise on ancient armour and weapons. 3 pts 1786–9.
Military antiquities respecting A history of the English army, from the Conquest to the present time. 2 vols 1786–8, 1801, 1812.
A provincial glossary; with a collection of local proverbs and popular superstitions. 2 pts 1787, 3 pts 1790, 1 vol 1811.
The antiquities of Scotland. 2 vols 1789–91, 1 vol 1797.
The antiquities of Ireland. 2 vols 1791. The date of vol 2 varies.
Antiquities of the county of Meath; to which is prefixed a brief view of the annals and records of the county by John D'Alton. Dublin 1833.
Grose also pbd a number of miscellaneous works.

WILLIAM GUTHRIE
1708–70
§ 1

A general history of England, from the invasion of Julius Caesar to the revolution in 1688. 4 vols 1744–51.
An essay on English tragedy. [1757].
A complete history of English peerage. 2 vols 1763.
A general history of the world. 12 vols and index 1764–7; tr German, 1765–1808. With others.
A general history of Scotland, from the earliest accounts to the present time. 10 vols 1767–8.
Guthrie also pbd geographical and grammatical works.

§ 2

Lam, G. L. Note on Guthrie's History of England. N & Q 1 Aug 1942.

EDWARD HASTED
1732–1812

The history and topographical survey of the county of Kent. 4 vols Canterbury 1778–99, 12 vols Canterbury 1797–1801 ('corrected and continued to the present time').
The history of the city of Canterbury. Canterbury 1799, 2 vols Canterbury 1801 ('improved and continued to the present time').

ROBERT HENRY
1718–90

The history of Great Britain, from the first invasion of it by the Romans, written on a new plan. 5 vols 1771–85; vol 6 (posthumous), ed M. Laing 1793; 12 vols 1788–95, 1823 (6th edn); tr French, 1789–96.

JOHN HUTCHINS
1698–1773
§ 1

The history and antiquities of the county of Dorset. 2 vols 1774; ed R. Gough and J. B. Nichols 4 vols 1796–1815; ed W. Shipp and J. W. Hodson 4 vols 1861–73.

§ 2

Smith, A. H. John Nichols and Hutchins's History and antiquities of Dorset. Library 5th ser 15 1960.

WILLIAM HUTCHINSON
1732–1814

A view of Northumberland. 2 vols Newcastle-on-Tyne 1778.
The history and antiquities of the county palatine of Durham. 3 vols Newcastle-on-Tyne 1785–94, Durham 1823.
The history of the county of Cumberland. 2 vols Carlisle 1794.

THOMAS LELAND
1722–85

The history of the life and reign of Philip, King of Macedon. 2 vols 1758, 1761, 1775, 1806 ('corrected').
The history of Ireland from the invasion of Henry II, with a preliminary discourse on the antient state of that Kingdom. 3 vols 1773, Dublin 1774 (3rd edn, 'corrected'); tr French, 1779.
Leland also pbd sermons and trns from Greek.

CATHERINE MACAULAY,
afterwards CATHERINE GRAHAM
1731–91

The history of England from the accession of James I to that of the Brunswick Line. 8 vols 1763–83; tr French, 1791–2. In vol 3 and onwards, and in the 2nd edn of vols 1–2, as: To the elevation of the house of Hanover and from vol 5 as: To the Revolution. Vol 8 ends at 1688.

JAMES MACPHERSON
1736–96
§ 1

An introduction to the history of Great Britain and Ireland. Dublin 1771, London 1772 (enlarged), 1773, 1781.
The history of Great Britain from the Restoration to the accession of the House of Hanover. 2 vols 1775, 1776.
Original papers: containing the secret history of Great Britain, [1660–1714]; to which are prefixed extracts from the life of James II, as written by himself. 2 vols 1775, 1776. *See* L. von Ranke, History of England vol 6, tr Oxford 1875, pp. 35 f.
For Macpherson's Ossianic and other writings, see col 603 above.

§ 2

O'Halloran, S. Animadversions on An introduction to the history of G. Britain and Ireland, by J. Macpherson. 1772. Appendix 2 of O'Halloran, An introduction to the study of the history and antiquities of Ireland.
McDougall, D. J. Some recent books in British history. Canadian Historical Rev 38 1957.
MacLochlainn, A. Charles O'Connor and Macpherson. Irish Book 1 1960.

WILLIAM MITFORD
1744–1827

§1

The history of Greece. 5 vols 1784–1818, 10 vols 1818–20; rev W. King 10 vols 1822–1 (with life of author by his brother Lord Redesdale).

§2

Macaulay, T. B. On Mitford's History of Greece. Knight's Quart Mag 3 1824; rptd rev in Miscellaneous writings vol 1, 1860, pp. 154–180.

PHILIP MORANT
1700–70

The history and antiquities of Colchester. 3 pts 1748.
The history and antiquities of the county of Essex. 2 vols 1768.

ROBERT ORME
1728–1801

A history of the military transactions of the British nation in Indostan from 1745. 2 vols (3 pts) 1763–78, 3 vols 1803 (4th edn 'revised by author').
Historical fragments of the Mogul Empire, of the Morattoes, and of the English concerns, in British Indostan, from 1659. 1782, 1805 ('with memoir of author').

JOHN PINKERTON
1758–1826

An essay on medals. 1784 (anon), 2 vols 1789, 1808.
A dissertation on the origin and progress of the Scythians or Goths. 1787.
Vitae antiquae sanctorum qui habitaverunt in Scotia. 1789; rev and enlarged by W. M. Metcalfe 2 vols Paisley 1889.
An enquiry into the history of Scotland preceding the reign of Malcolm III or the year 1056. 2 vols 1789, Edinburgh 1814.
The medallic history of England to the Revolution. 1790 (anon), 1802.
Iconographia scotica: or portraits of illustrious persons of Scotland with biographical notices. 1797.
The history of Scotland from the accession of the House of Stuart to that of Mary. 2 vols 1797.
The Scotish gallery: or portraits of eminent persons of Scotland, with brief accounts of the characters represented. 1799.
A general collection of voyages and travels. 17 vols 1808–14. Ed Pinkerton.
For Pinkerton's other writings, see cols 237, 246, above.

WILLIAM RUSSELL
1741–93

The history of America, from its discovery by Columbus to the conclusion of the late war. 2 vols 1778.
The history of modern Europe to the peace of Paris in 1763, in a series of letters from a nobleman to his son. 5 vols 1779–84, 7 vols 1818 (continued by C. Coote et al), 6 vols 1827, 4 vols 1850.
The history of ancient Europe, with a view of the revolutions in Asia and Africa, in a series of letters. 2 vols 1793.
Russell also pbd poems.

STEBBING SHAW
1762–1802

Tour in 1787, from London to the Western Highlands of Scotland. [1788]. Anon.
Tour to the West of England in 1788. 1789.
The history and antiquities of Staffordshire. Vols 1–2 (pt 1), 1798–1801. All pbd.

THOMAS SOMERVILLE
1741–1830

The history of political transactions and of parties, from the Restoration to the death of King William. 1792.
The effects of the French Revolution, with respect to the interests of humanity, liberty, religion and morality. Edinburgh 1793.
Observations on the constitutional and present state of Britain. Edinburgh 1793.
The history of Great Britain during the reign of Queen Anne. 1798.
My own life and times 1741–1814. Ed W. L[ee], Edinburgh 1861.
Somerville also pbd sermons.

JOSEPH STRUTT
1749–1802

The regal and ecclesiastical antiquities of England, containing the representations of all the English monarchs, together with many great persons, collected from ancient illuminated manuscripts. 1773, 1793–2 (with suppl); ed J. R. Planché 1842.
Horda Angel-cynnan: or a compleat view of the manners, customs, arms, habits etc of the inhabitants of England, from the arrival of the Saxons till the reign of Henry VIII. 3 vols 1775–6; tr French, 1789.
The chronicle of England, from the arrival of Julius Caesar to the Norman Conquest. 2 vols 1777–8, 1779.
A biographical dictionary, containing an historical account of all the engravers. 2 vols 1785.
A complete view of the dress and habits of the people of England etc. 2 vols 1796–9; ed J. R. Planché 2 vols 1842; tr French, 1797 (vol 1 only).
Glig-Gamena Angel-theod: or the sports and pastimes of the people of England. 1801, 1810; ed W. Hone 1830, 1833, 1834, 1838, 1841, 1875.

GILBERT STUART
1742–86

An historical dissertation concerning the antiquity of the English constitution. Edinburgh 1768, 1770 ('corrected').
Lectures on the constitution and laws of England by F. S. Ferguson: the second edition; to which authorities are added, and a discourse is prefixed, concerning the laws and government of England, by G.S. [Gilbert Stuart]. 1776.
A view of society in Europe, in its progress from rudeness to refinement. Edinburgh 1778, London 1782, 1783, Edinburgh 1792; tr French, 1789.
Observations concerning the public law and the constitutional history of Scotland; with occasional remarks concerning English antiquity. Edinburgh 1779.
The history of the establishment of the reformation of religion in Scotland. 1780, Edinburgh 1805.
The history of Scotland from the establishment of the reformation till the death of Queen Mary. 2 vols 1782, 1783–4 (To which are added Observations concerning the public law and the constitution of Scotland, originally pbd separately 1779).
Stuart edited Edinburgh Mag & Review 1773–6.

WILLIAM TYTLER
1711–92

An historical and critical enquiry into the evidence produced by the Earls of Murray and Morton against Mary Queen of Scots. 1760, 1772 (3rd edn as Inquiry historical and critical into the evidence against Mary Queen of Scots, and an examination of the histories of Robertson and Hume, with respect to that evidence), 2 vols 1790 (4th edn, with additional chs); tr French, 1772.

ROBERT WATSON
1730?–81

The history of the reign of Philip the second, King of Spain. 2 vols 1777, 1839 (7th edn); tr French, 1778.
The history of the reign of Philip the third, King of Spain. [Eda nd completed by W. Thomson] 1783, 2 vols 1808 (3rd edn enlarged); tr French, 1809.

PETER WHALLEY
1722–91

An essay on the manner of writing history. 1746. Anon.
An enquiry into the learning of Shakespeare. 1748.
The works of Ben Jonson. 7 vols 1756. Ed Whalley.
The history and antiquities of Northamptonshire, compiled from the manuscript collections of John Bridges. 2 vols Oxford 1791.
Whalley also pbd sermons.

JOHN WHITAKER
1735–1808
§1

The history of Manchester, in four books: bk 1 (Roman and Roman-British period). 1771; Additional vol of principal corrections and 2nd edn of vol 1 in 2 vols 1773; bk 2 (Saxon period, to foundation of Heptarchy and descent upon it of the Danes), 1775. No more pbd.
The genuine history of the Britons asserted, in a refutation of Mr Macpherson's Introduction to the history of Great Britain and Ireland. 1772.
Mary Queen of Scots vindicated. 3 vols 1787. Vol of addns and 2nd edn 3 vols 1790. Whitaker's ms Private life of Mary, unfinished, was used by G. Chalmers as the basis of his Life, 1818.
The origin of Arianism disclosed. 1791.
The course of Hannibal over the Alps ascertained. 2 vols 1794.
The real origin of government. 1795.
The ancient cathedral of Cornwall historically surveyed. 2 vols 1804.
The life of Saint Neot. 1809.
Whitaker also pbd sermons.

§2

Tytler, A. F. (Lord Woodhouselee). A critical examination of Whitaker's The course of Hannibal over the Alps ascertained. 1795.
Hudson, W. M. Whitaker's attack on Johnson's etymologies. HLQ 14 1951.

PHILIP YORKE, 2nd EARL OF HARDWICKE
1720–90

Letters from and to Sir Dudley Carleton, Knt (Viscount Dorchester), during his embassy in Holland, 1616 [and] 1620. 1757, 1775, 1780. Ed with historical preface.
Miscellaneous state papers from 1501 to 1726 (the Hardwicke papers). 2 vols 1778. Anon.

A. H. S.

IX. LITERARY STUDIES

GENERAL STUDIES: Major Scholars; Minor Scholars.

SPECIAL DEPARTMENTS: Old English; Biographical Dictionaries and Collections; Dictionaries and Glossaries; Grammars.

The following sections complete the view of English scholarship of the period: Prosody and Prose Rhythm (vol 1); Literary Theory (col 23, above); Medieval Influences (col 231, above); Drama: Introduction (col 701, above); Historians, Biographers and Antiquaries (col 1675, above). No attempt has been made to duplicate these sections here.

(1) GENERAL STUDIES

Morgan, J. A. Some Shakespearean commentators. Cincinnati 1882.
Walder, E. Shakespearean criticism, textual and literary, from Dryden to the end of the 18th century. Bradford 1895.
— The text of Shakespeare. CHEL 5 1910.
Farley, F. E. Scandinavian influences on the English romantic movement. Cambridge Mass 1903. With bibliography.
Aldis, H. G. Antiquaries. CHEL 9 1912.
Ker, W. P. The literary influence of the Middle Ages. CHEL 10 1913.
Hustved, S. B. Ballad criticism in Scandinavia and Great Britain during the 18th century. New York 1916.
Crane, R. S. The vogue of Guy of Warwick from the close of the Middle Ages to the romantic revival. PMLA 30 1915.
Snyder, E. D. The Celtic revival in English literature 1760–1800. Cambridge Mass 1923.
O'Leary, J. G. English literary history and bibliography. 1928.
Nichol Smith, D. Eighteenth-century essays on Shakespeare. Glasgow 1903, Oxford 1963 (rev).
— Shakespeare in the 18th century. Oxford 1928.
— Warton's History of English poetry. Proc Br Acad 15 1929.
Oras, A. Milton's editors from Patrick Hume to H. J. Todd 1695–1801. Tartu 1929, 1931.
Babcock, R. W. The genesis of Shakespeare idolatry 1766–99. Chapel Hill 1931.

Brinkley, R. F. Arthurian legend in the 17th century. Baltimore 1932.

McKillop, A. D. A critic of 1741 on early poetry. SP 30 1933.

McKerrow, R. B. The treatment of Shakespeare's text by his earlier editors 1709–68. Proc Br Acad 19 1933; rptd in Studies in Shakespeare, ed P. Alexander, Oxford 1964.

Ford, H. L. Shakespeare 1700–40. Oxford 1935.

Noyes, R. Drayton's literary vogue since 1631. Indiana Univ Stud 22 1935.

Wurtsbaugh, J. Two centuries of Spenserian scholarship 1609–1805. Baltimore 1936.

Bennett, J. A. W. The beginnings of Norse studies in England. Saga-book 12 1937.

Wasserman, E. R. The scholarly origin of the Elizabethan revival. ELH 4 1937.

—— Elizabethan poetry in the eighteenth century. Urbana 1947.

Black, M. W. and M. A. Shaaber. Shakespeare's seventeenth-century editors 1632–85. New York 1937.

Lefranc, A. La question Shakespearienne au dix-huitième siècle. Revue Bleue 76 1938.

Williams, R. D. Antiquarian interest in Elizabethan drama before Lamb. PMLA 53 1938.

Read, A. W. Suggestions for an academy in England in the latter half of the eighteenth century. MP 36 1938.

Tuve, R. Ancients, moderns and Saxons. ELH 6 1939.

Brown, I and G. Fearon. Amazing monument: a short history of the Shakespeare industry. 1939.

Douglas, D. C. English scholars 1660–1730. 1939, 1951 (rev).

Wellek, R. The rise of English literary history. Chapel Hill 1941.

Jones, E. Geoffrey of Monmouth 1640–1800. Berkeley 1944.

Weisinger, H. The study of the revival of learning in England from Bacon to Hallam. PQ 25 1946.

—— The Middle Ages and the late eighteenth-century historians. PQ 27 1948.

Zimansky, C. A. Chaucer and the school of Provence: a problem in 18th-century literary history. PQ 25 1946.

Conklin, P. S. A history of Hamlet criticism 1601–1821. New York 1947.

Bell, C. C. A history of Fairfax criticism. PMLA 62 1947.

Neff, E. E. The poetry of history: the contribution of literature and literary scholarship to the writing of history since Voltaire. New York 1947.

Willard, R. Layamon in the seventeenth and eighteenth centuries. SE 27 1948.

Wagner, B. M. (ed). The appreciation of Shakespeare: a collection of criticism of the eighteenth, nineteenth and twentieth centuries. Washington 1949.

Kliger, S. The neo-classical view of Old English poetry. JEGP 49 1950.

—— The Goths in England. Cambridge Mass 1952.

Judson, A. C. The eighteenth-century lives of Edmund Spenser. HLQ 16 1953.

Friedman, A. B. The ballad revival: studies in the influence of popular on sophisticated poetry. Chicago 1961.

Johnston, A. Enchanted ground: the study of medieval romance in the eighteenth century. 1964.

(2) MAJOR SCHOLARS

GERARD LANGBAINE the younger
1656–92

§ 1

An exact catalogue of all the comedies that were ever printed or published, till this present year 1680. Oxford 1680.

The hunter: a discourse of horsemanship. Oxford 1686, 1697.

Momus triumphans: or the plagiaries of the English stage expos'd in a catalogue of all the comedies, tragi-comedies [etc]. 1688, 1688 (as A new catalogue of English plays).

An account of the English dramatick poets. Oxford 1691. Essay on Dryden rptd in Critical essays of the seventeenth century vol 3, ed J. E. Spingarn, Oxford 1909.

The lives and characters of the English dramatick poets; also an account of all the plays ever yet printed in the English tongue, [first] begun by Langbaine, improv'd and continued [by Charles Gildon]. 1698. Also issued nd and 1699.

§ 2

Watkin-Jones, A. Langbaine's account of the English dramatic poets 1691. E & S 21 1936.

ZACHARY GREY
1688–1766

§ 1

[Butler, Samuel]. Hudibras, in three parts; with large annotations and a preface. 2 vols Cambridge 1744 (vol 2 London), 3 vols Glasgow 1753, 2 vols 1764, 3 vols Edinburgh 1770, London 1770, Edinburgh 1779 etc.

An answer to certain passages in Mr W[arburton]'s preface

to his edition of Shakespear, together with some remarks on the many errors and false criticisms in the work itself. 1748. Anon. Perhaps by Grey.

Remarks upon a late edition of Shakespeare [Warburton's], with a defence of Sir Thomas Hanmer. [1747?], 1752 (as Examination of a late edition etc).

Critical, historical and explanatory notes upon Hudibras, by way of supplement to the two editions published in the years 1744 and 1745; [with] a dissertation on burlesque poetry by M. Bacon and a translation of part of the first canto of the first book into Latin doggerel. 1752.

Critical, historical, and explanatory notes on Shakespeare; with emendations of the text and metre. 2 vols 1754.

Miscellaneous Works

A defence of our antient and modern historians against the frivolous cavils of a late pretender to critical history [John Oldmixon]; in two parts. 1725.

In answer to J. Oldmixon, A review of Grey's defence of our ancient and modern historians. 1725.

Moss, R. Sermons and discourses on practical subjects, with a preface giving some account of the author. 8 vols 1732–8. Sermons ed A. Snape; Moss's life by Grey.

An attempt towards the character of the royall martyr King Charles I. 1738.

A review of Mr Daniel Neal's history of the puritans. Cambridge 1744, 1745.

A word or two of advice to William Warburton. 1746.

A free and familiar letter to that great refiner of Pope and Shakespeare, William Warburton. 1750.

A chronological and historical account of the most memorable earthquakes from the beginning of the Christian period to the present year 1750. 2 pts Cambridge 1750, 1756.

Fragmentum est pars rei fractae. 1751. On disputes at Cambridge University.

Masters, R. Memoirs of the life and writings of Thomas Baker BD, from the papers of Grey. Cambridge 1784.

Grey contributed at least 15 tracts to theological controversies as well as assisting Peter Whalley in his edn of Ben Jonson, and Francis Peck in Desiderata curiosa.

§2

Sale catalogue of the library of Grey. 1768.
D'Israeli, I. The miseries of the first English commentator. In his Calamities of authors, 1812.
Nichols, J. In his Anecdotes vol 2, 1812.
—— In his Illustrations vol 4, 1822.

LEWIS THEOBALD
1688–1744

For Theobald's dramatic writings see col 800, above.

§1

A Pindarick ode on the Union. 1707.
The mausoleum: a poem sacred to the memory of Queen Anne. 1714.
The cave of poverty: a poem, written in imitation of Shakespeare. [1714?].
A complete key to the last new farce, the what d'ye call it [by Gay]; to which is prefix'd a hypercritical preface on the nature of burlesque. 1715. Anon. Attributed by Pope to Theobald and Benjamin Griffin.
The censor. 1717. A collection of 96 papers by Theobald et al which appeared 3 times per week, 11 April–17 June 1715, 1 Jan–1 June 1717.
Memoirs of Sir Walter Raleigh. 1719 (3 edns).
The grove: or a collection of original poems. 1721, 1732 (as A miscellany of original poems). Contains: To Clio upon her retreat at Fulham, pp. 159–61; Prologue spoken by Mr Keene before his Royal Highness the Prince of Wales pp. 217–19; Prologue occasion'd by the death of Mr Keene, pp. 263–5. *See also below.*
Miscellaneous observations upon authors, ancient and modern. 2 vols 1731–2. By John Jortin, with the following papers by Theobald: on Eustathius, Athenaeus and Suidas, vol 1 pp. 144–50; on Strabo, Anacreon and Suidas, pp. 193–202; on Aeschylus and his Scholiast, p. 266; Shakespeare, vol 2 pp. 242–50.
An epistle humbly addressed to the Rt Hon John, Earl of Orrery. [1732]. In appendix to Eustace Budgell, Memoirs of the late Earl of Orrery, 1732, 1732, 1737.

Translations

The life and character of Marcus Portius Cato collected from Plutarch, Lucan, Sallust, Lucius Florus and other authors, designed for the readers of Cato: a tragedy. 1713, 1713 (2nd edn enlarged).
Plato's dialogue of the immortality of the soul [Phaedo], translated. 1713.
Electra: a tragedy, translated from Sophocles, with notes. 1714; rptd in Bell's British theatre vol 16, 1777.
Ajax of Sophocles, translated from the Greek, with notes. 1714. Theobald may have assisted with the notes.
Plutus, or the world's idol: a comedy, translated from the Greek of Aristophanes. 1715.
The clouds: a comedy, translated from the Greek of Aristophanes. 1715.
Monsieur [Jean] Le Clerc's observations upon Mr Addison's travels through Italy, done from the French. 1715.
Oedipus, King of Thebes: a tragedy, translated from Sophocles, with notes. 1715.
A translation of book 1 of the Odyssey, with notes. 1716.
The history of the loves of Antiochus and Stratonice, in which are interspers'd some accounts relating to Greece and Syria. 1717.
The grove: or a collection of original poems. 1721.

Contains Hero and Leander of Musaeus translated, to which is prefix'd a short essay on the original, and its author, pp. 1–32; Description of the plague of Thebes, from a chorus of Sophocles, pp. 62–6; The siege, from a chorus of Aeschylus, pp. 315–21; The fishermen: a tale, imitated from the 21st Idyllium of Theocritus, pp. 325–32.

Scholarly Works

Shakespeare restored: or a specimen of the many errors as well committed as unamended by Mr Pope, in his late edition of this poet. 1726, 1740.
The posthumous works of William Wycherley, in prose and verse, faithfully publish'd from his original manuscripts by Mr Theobald; to which are prefixed, some memoirs of Wycherley's life by Major Pack. 1728. Pope pbd a vol 2 in 1729.
A miscellany on taste. 1732. Reprints Theobald's letter to the Daily Jnl 17 April 1729, Mr Pope's taste of Shakespeare.
The works of Shakespeare, collated with the oldest copies, and corrected, with notes, explanatory and critical. 7 vols 1734, Dublin 1739, 8 vols 1740, 1752, 1757, 1762, 1767, 12 vols 1772, 8 vols 1773, 12 vols [1777?]. Preface rptd in Eighteenth-century essays on Shakespeare, ed D. Nichol Smith, Glasgow 1903, and ed H. G. Dick, Los Angeles 1949 (Augustan Reprint Soc).
The works of Beaumont and Fletcher, with notes critical and explanatory by Messrs Theobald, Seward and Sympson. 10 vols 1750. Theobald was responsible for vol 1 and parts of vols 2–3.

§2

Nichols, J. In his Literary illustrations vol 2, 1817.
Collins, J. C. Theobald: the Porson of Shakespearean criticism. Quart Rev 175 1892; rptd in his Essays and studies, 1895.
Lounsbury, T. R. The first editors of Shakespeare (Pope and Theobald). 1906.
Schevill, R. Theobald's double falsehood. MP 9 1911.
Graham, W. The Cardenio double falsehood problem. MP 14 1916.
Jones, R. F. Theobald: his contribution to English scholarship, with some unpublished letters. New York 1919.
Oliphant, E. H. C. Shakespeare, Fletcher and Theobald. N & Q Feb 1919.
Mertz, W. Die Shakespeare-Ausgabe von Theobald 1733. Giessen 1925.
Castle, E. Double falsehood und die History of Cardenio von Fletcher und Shakespeare. Archiv 169 1936.
Cadwalader, J. Theobald's alleged Shakespeare manuscript. MLN 55 1940.
Joseph, B. L. Theobald and Webster. Comparative Lit Stud 17–18 1945.
Woods, C. B. Fielding's epilogue for Theobald. PQ 28 1949.
Dearing, V. A. Pope, Theobald and Wycherley's posthumous works. PMLA 68 1953.
Muir, K. Cardenio. Etudes Anglaises 11 1958.

WILLIAM OLDYS
1696–1761

§1

A vindication of the Lord Chancellor Bacon, from the aspersion of injustice cast upon him by Mr Wraynham. 1725. Pbd by Oldys from anon ms.
A collection of epigrams; to which is prefix'd a critical dissertation on this species of poetry. 1727, 1735, 2 vols 1736 (enlarged). The dissertation is said to be by Oldys.

A dissertation upon pamphlets and the undertaking of Phoenix britannicus to revive the most excellent among them. 1731; rptd in J. Morgan, Phoenix britannicus, 1732 and in J. Nichols, Literary anecdotes vol 4, 1812.

A short view of the long life and raigne of Henry the Third, King of England, presented to King James by Sir Robt Cotton, but not printed till 1627. In Phoenix britannicus, 1732.

The polite correspondence, or rational amusement: being a series of letters, philosophical, poetical, historical, critical, amorous, moral and satyrical. [c. 1735]. By Thomas Campbell. Bk 5 attributed to Oldys.

Life of Sir Walter Raleigh. Prefixed to W. Raleigh, History of the world, 2 vols 1736; Life rptd 1740; prefixed to Works of Raleigh, 8 vols Oxford 1829.

The British librarian, exhibiting a compendious review or abstract of our most scarce, useful and valuable books. 1737, 1738.

Life of Sir John Fastolff. In Birch's General dictionary vol 5, 1737. Oldys also wrote several other lives for this compilation, but they cannot be identified.

The Muses library. 1737, 1738 (some copies as The historical and poetical medley), 1741. By Elizabeth Cooper assisted by Oldys.

The British Muse: or a collection of thoughts moral, natural and sublime of our English poets who flourished in the 16 and 17 centuries. 3 vols 1738, 1740 (as The quintessence of English poetry). By Thomas Hayward. Preface and dedication by Oldys.

Memoirs of Mrs Anne Oldfield. 1741. Attributed to Oldys.

Catalogus bibliothecae Harleianae. 5 vols 1743. By Samuel Johnson, M. Maittaire and Oldys.

The Harleian miscellany: or a collection of scarce, curious and entertaining tracts and pamphlets found in the late Earl of Oxford's library, interspersed with historical, political and critical notes. 8 vols 1744-6. Ed Oldys. Rptd 10 vols 1808-13 ed Thomas Park.

A complete and exact catalogue of pamphlets in the Harleian miscellany. 1746. At end of Harleian miscellany. Rptd in vol 10 of Park's edn, 1813.

A short view of the life and writings of Dr Thomas Moffet. Prefixed to Moffet, Health's improvement, 1746.

Biographia britannica. Vol 1, 1747. Lives signed G: George Abbot, Robert Abbot, Thomas Adams, William Alexander, (Earl of Stirling), Charles Aleyn, Edward Alleyn, William Ames, John Atherton, Peter Bates.

An historical essay on the life and writings of Michael Drayton. Prefixed to The works of Michael Drayton, now first collected into one volume, 1748, 4 vols 1753.

Biographia britannica. Vol 2, 1748. John Bradford, William Bulleyn, William Caxton.

Biographia britannica. Vol 3, 1750. Michael Drayton, Sir George Etherege, George Farquhar, Sir John Fastolff, Thomas Fuller, Sir William Gascoigne.

Biographia britannica. Vol 4, 1752. Fulke Greville (Lord Brooke), Richard Hakluyt, Wenceslaus Hollar.

Observations on the cure of William Taylor, the blind boy of Ightham, in Kent. In A specimen of some cures performed by John Taylor, 2 pts 1753.

Biographia britannica. Vol 5, 1760. Life of Thomas May.

Some account of the life and writings of Charles Cotton esq, in a letter to the editor of the Complete angler. In Sir John Hawkins' edn, 1760.

The life of Dr George Abbot, Lord Archbishop of Canterbury. Guildford 1777. Rptd from Biographia britannica vol 1, 1747.

Oldys also contributed papers to Universal Spectator 1728-31. *He left many notes in ms which were used for the second edn of* Biographia britannica. *Anecdotes of Shakespeare from Oldys' mss were pbd by Steevens in his 1778 edn, and frequently rptd.*

§2

Davies, T. A catalogue of the library of the late William Oldys. April 12 [1762].

The general biographical dictionary. Ed Alexander Chalmers. Vol 23, 1815, pp. 334-9; material not in later accounts.

Corney, B. Facts relative to Oldys: an attempt to vindicate him from the vindication published by I. D'Israeli. 1837; rptd in Corney, The curiosities of literature illustrated, Greenwich nd, 1838. D'Israeli's account of Oldys is in Curiosities of literature vol 6, 1834.

[Yeowell, J.] Memoirs of Oldys; together with his diary, notes from his adversaria and an account of the London libraries. 1862. Rptd from N & Q 1861.

JOHN JORTIN
1698-1770

§1

Miscellaneous observations upon authors, ancient and modern. 2 vols 1731-2. Ed Jortin. Tr Latin as vols 1-4 of Miscellaneae observationes, Amsterdam 1732-4.

Remarks on Spenser's poems. 1734.

Letter concerning the music of the Ancients. In Charles Avison, An essay on musical expression, 1753 (2nd edn), 1775.

The life of Erasmus. 2 vols 1758-60, 3 vols 1808.

Tracts, philological, critical and miscellaneous. 2 vols 1790. Ed Rogers Jortin, with memoir. Includes Remarks on Spenser, remarks on Milton, critical remarks on modern authors (Pope, Swift etc).

Jortin also pbd sermons. For his works on ecclesiastical history see DNB.

§2

[Heathcote, Ralph]. In his A new and general biographical dictionary, 1784. Account of Jortin rptd as An account of the life and writings of John Jortin, nd.

Disney, J. Memoirs of the life and writings of Jortin DD. 1792.

Nichols, J. In his Literary anecdotes vol 2, 1812.

JOSEPH SPENCE
1699-1768

§1

An essay on Pope's Odyssey, in which some particular beauties and blemishes of that work are considered. 2 pts Oxford 1726-7, 1737, 1747.

A full and authentick account of Stephen Duck, the Wiltshire poet, in a letter to a Member of Parliament. 1731; rptd with Duck's Poems on several occasions, 1736, 1737, 1738, and with The beautiful works of Stephen Duck, 1753, and abridged in GM June 1736.

Some account of the Lord Buckhurst [Thomas Sackville]. The tragedy of Gorboduc, written by Thomas Sackville, 1736.

Polymetis: or an enquiry concerning the agreement between the works of the Roman poets and the remains of the antient artists, in ten books. 1747, 1755, 1774; tr German, 1773-6. Abridged by Nicholas Tindal, 1764.

An apology for the late Mr Pope. 1749. Attributed by Wright, under §2, below.

Crito: or a dialogue on beauty, by Sir Harry Beaumont [Spence]. 1752, 1752; rptd in Dodsley's Fugitive pieces vol 1, 1761, 1762, 1765, 1771.

A particular account of the Emperor of China's gardens near Pekin, in a letter from J. D. Attiret, translated from the French by Sir Harry Beaumont. 1752; rptd in Dodsley's Fugitive pieces vol 1, 1761, 1762, 1765, 1771.

The works of Virgil in Latin and English, with several new observations by Mr Holdsworth, Mr Spence and others. 4 vols 1753, 1 vol 1763 (English only), 4 vols 1778 (Latin and English).

Moralities: or essays, letters, fables and translations, by Sir Harry Beaumont. 1753.

An account of the life, character and poems of Mr Blacklock, student of philosophy in the University of Edinburgh. 1754, 1756 (rev and prefixed to 2nd edn of Blacklock's poems).

Extract of a letter of the Reverend Mr Joseph Spence, Professor of Modern History of Oxford, to Dr Mead FRS. Philosophical Trans 48 1755. On antiquities at Herculaneum.

A parallel, in the manner of Plutarch, between a most celebrated man of Florence, and one, scarce ever heard of, in England. Strawberry Hill 1758, 1759; rptd in Dodsley's Fugitive pieces vol 2, 1761, 1765, 1771.

Remarks and dissertations on Virgil, with some other classical observations, by the late Mr [Edward] Holdsworth, published, with several notes and additional remarks, by Mr Spence. 1768.

The first three stanzas of the twenty-fourth canto of Dante's Inferno, made into a song, in imitation of the Earl of Surrey's stile. Museum 1746; rptd in Nichols's Select collection vol 8, 1782.

Observations, anecdotes and characters of books and men, arranged with notes by the late Edmond Malone. 1820; ed J. M. Osborn 2 vols Oxford 1966.

Anecdotes, observations and characters of books and men, with notes and a life of the author, by Samuel Weller Singer. 1820, 1858; ed J. Underhill 1890 (selection); ed B. Dobrée 1964. Malone and Singer reviewed together by W. Hazlitt, Edinburgh Rev 33 1820 and by I. D'Israeli, Quart Rev 23 1820.

Quelques remarques hist sur les poètes anglois. Ed J. M. Osborn. In his First history of English poetry, in Pope and his contemporaries: essays presented to George Sherburn, Oxford 1949.

A catalogue of the entire libraries of J. Spence, W. Duncombe etc. [1769].

§2

Ridley, J. Tales of the genii. 2 vols 1764 etc. Spence portrayed as Phesoi Ecreps.

Nichols, J. In his A select collection of poems vol 8, 1782.

—— In his Literary anecdotes vol 2, 1812.

Dobson, A. Spence's anecdotes. In his Eighteenth-century vignettes ser 1, 1892.

Beale, C. H. In his Catherine Hutton and her friends, Birmingham 1895.

Wright, A. The Charliad: an unpublished mock epic by Joseph Spence. PMLA 46 1931.

——Spence as defender of Pope's reputation. MP 36 1938.

—— The beginning of Pope's friendship with Spence. MLN 54 1939.

—— The veracity of Spence's Anecdotes. PMLA 62 1947.

—— Spence: a critical biography. Chicago 1950.

Case, A. E. Pope, Addison and the Atticus lines. MP 33 1936.

Mundy, P. D. Extracts from letters from Spence 1739-62. N & Q 16, 30 June 1945.

Wiley, M. L. A Spence letter. In English studies in honor of J. S. Wilson, Charlottesville 1951.

THOMAS BIRCH
1705-66
§1

A general dictionary historical and critical, in which a new and accurate translation of that of Mr Bayle is included, by John Peter Bernard, Tho. Birch, John Lockman and other hands. 10 vols 1734-41. Ed Birch, who also wrote the 618 new biographies signed T. and H.

A complete collection of the historical, political and miscellaneous works of Milton, with an historical and critical account of the life and writings of the author. 2 vols 1738, 1 vol 1753.

The complete works of Francis Bacon, with several additional pieces never before printed; to which is prefixed a new life of the author by Mr [David] Mallet. 4 vols 1740. Ed Birch.

The heads of illustrious persons of Great Britain, engraven by Houbraken and Vertue, with their lives and characters. 2 vols 1743-51, 1747-52, 1 vol 1756, 1813.

The Faerie Queene, by Edmund Spenser, with an exact collation of the two original editions; to which are now added a new life of the author, and also a glossary. 3 vols 1751.

The works of Sir Walter Raleigh Kt, political, commercial and philosophical, together with his letters and poems; to which is prefix'd a new account of his life by Thomas Birch. 2 vols 1751. Life rptd with Ralegh's Works, Oxford 1829.

Letters, speeches, charges, advices etc of Francis Bacon, now first published by Thomas Birch. 1763.

§2

Wurstbaugh, J. Thomas Edwards and the editorship of the Faerie Queene. MLN 50 1935.

Babcock, R. W. Birch as transcriber of Johnson. PQ 16 1937.

Osborn, J. M. Birch and the general dictionary 1734-41. MP 36 1939.

Ruhe, E. L. Pope's hand in Birch's account of Gay. RES new ser 5 1954.

—— Birch, Johnson and Elizabeth Carter: an episode of 1738-9. PMLA 73 1958.

Hennig, J. Goethe's extracts from Birch's History of the Royal Society. MLR 52 1957.

For Birch's historical work see col 1702, above.

JOHN UPTON
1707-60
§1

Miscellaneous observations upon authors, ancient and modern. 2 vols 1731-2. By Jortin. Vol 2 contains the following papers by Upton: On Hesychius; on Theocritus.

Epicteti quae supersunt dissertationes ab Arriano collectae, recensuit notisque illustravit Joannes Uptonus. 1739, 2 vols 1741, 1744. Upton's notes were incorporated in full by Schweighäuser in his edn of Epictetus 1799-1800. Upton's text of the Enchiridion was rptd Glasgow 1748, 1751, 1758, Oxford 1759, Aberdeen 1760, Glasgow 1765.

Critical observations on Shakespeare. 1746, Dublin 1747, 1748 (rev with preface on Warburton's edn).

A new canto of Spenser's Fairy Queen. 1747.

A letter concerning a new edition of Spenser's Faerie Queene, to Gilbert West. [1751].

Spenser's Faerie Queene: a new edition with a glossary, and notes explanatory and critical. 2 vols 1758.

Remarks on the action and history of the Faerie Queene. In H. J. Todd's edn of Spenser vol 2, 1805.

§2

An impartial estimate of the Rev Mr Upton's notes on the Fairy Queen. 1759. Anon.

Auction catalogue for his library. 1784.

SAMUEL JOHNSON
1709–84

§ 1

Miscellaneous observations on the tragedy of Macbeth, with remarks on Sir T[homas] H[anmer]'s edition of Shakespear; to which is affix'd proposals for a new edition of Shakespear, with a specimen. 1745.

Life of the Earl of Roscommon [with notes]. GM May 1748. Enlarged, with the notes incorporated in the text, in Lives of the poets, below.

Christian morals, with a life of the author by Johnson. 1756, 1761; ed S. C. Roberts, Cambridge 1927. By Sir Thomas Browne. Johnson added notes to those of John Jeffery.

Proposals for printing, by subscription, the dramatick works of William Shakespeare, corrected and illustrated by Johnson. 1756 etc.

The English works of Roger Ascham, with notes and observations [by James Bennet], and the author's life. 1761, 1765. The dedication and the life of Ascham and many of the notes are by Johnson; the life was rptd in T. Davies, Miscellaneous and fugitive pieces vol 1, 1772 and in 1815 with the English works of Ascham.

The plays of William Shakespeare, with the corrections and illustrations of various commentators, to which are added notes by Johnson. 8 vols 1765, 10 vols Dublin 1766, 8 vols 1768. For later edns see under George Steevens, below.

Prefaces, biographical and critical, to the works of the English poets. 10 vols 1779–81, 3 vols Dublin 1779–81 (without poems, as Lives of the English poets), 4 vols 1781 (rev as Lives of the most eminent English poets), 1783, 6 vols 1790–1 (with additional lives by Isaac Reed), 4 vols 1794, 8 vols Dublin 1795, 1 vol 1797 (abridged), 4 vols Montrose 1800 etc.

Annotations by Johnson and George Steevens and various commentators upon the Merchant of Venice written by Will Shakespeare. 1787.

Annotations by Sam Johnson and Geo Steevens, and the various commentators, upon King Henry V, written by Will Shakspere. 1787.

Johnson's prefaces and dedications. Ed A. T. Hazen, New Haven 1937.

Johnson on Shakespeare Ed A. Sherbo 2 vols New Haven 1968.

§ 2

Kenrick, W. A review of Dr Johnson's new edition of Shakespeare. 1765.

—— A defence of Mr Kenrick's review of Dr Johnson's Shakespeare, by a friend. 1766.

[Barclay, J.] An examination of Mr Kenrick's review. 1766.

Young, K. Johnson on Shakespeare. Madison 1923.

Hooker, E. N. Johnson's understanding of Chaucer's metrics. MLN 48 1933.

Osborn, J. M. Johnson on the sanctity of an author's text. PMLA 50 1935.

Watkins, W. B. C. Johnson and English poetry before 1660. Princeton 1936.

Hart, C. W. Johnson's 1745 Shakespeare proposals. MLN 53 1938.

Hazen, A. T. Johnson's Shakespeare: a study in cancellation. TLS 24 Dec 1938.

Eastman, A. M. Johnson's Shakespearean labors in 1765. MLN 63 1948.

—— Johnson's Shakespeare and the laity: a textual study. PMLA 65 1950.

—— The texts from which Johnson printed his Shakespeare. JEGP 49 1950.

—— In defense of Dr Johnson. Shakespeare Quart 8 1957.

Evans, G. B. The text of Johnson's Shakespeare. PQ 28 1949.

Hart, E. Some new sources of Johnson's lives. PMLA 65 1950. On John Nichols.

Monaghan, T. J. Johnson's additions to his Shakespeare for the edition of 1773. RES new ser 4 1953.

Sherbo, A. Dr Johnson on Macbeth: 1745 and 1765. RES new ser 2 1951.

—— The proof sheets of Dr Johnson's preface to Shakespeare. Bull John Rylands Lib 35 1952.

—— Dr Johnson's dictionary and Warburton's Shakespeare. PQ 33 1954.

—— Johnson, editor of Shakespeare. Urbana 1956.

—— Sanguine expectations: Dr Johnson's Shakespeare. Shakespeare Quart 9 1958.

Monaghan, T. J. Johnson's additions to his Shakespeare for the edition of 1773. RES new ser 4 1953.

Kolb, G. J. A note on the publication of Johnson's proposals for printing the Harleian miscellany. PBSA 48 1954.

Carnie, R. H. Lord Hailes's notes on Johnson's Lives of the poets. N & Q Feb–April, Aug, Nov 1956.

Wagley, M. F. and P. F. Comments on Johnson's biography of Sir Thomas Browne. Bull of History of Medicine 31 1957.

Greene, D. J. Johnson and the Harleian miscellany. N & Q July 1958.

Tucker, S. I. Dr Johnson, medievalist. N & Q Jan 1958.

Adler, J. H. Johnson's 'He that imagines this'. Shakespeare Quart 11 1960.

Crossett, J. Did Johnson mean 'paraphysical'? Boston Univ Stud in Eng 4 1960.

Gray, J. Dr Johnson and the 'intellectual gladiators'. Dalhousie Rev 40 1960.

Leicester, J. H. Dr Johnson and William Shenstone. New Rambler 1960.

Lucas, F. L. Johnson's bête grise. Ibid.

Scholes, R. E. Dr Johnson and the bibliographical criticism of Shakespeare. Shakespeare Quart 11 1960.

Eddy, D. D. Johnson's editions of Shakespeare 1765. PBSA 56 1962.

Keast, W. R. Johnson and 'Cibber's' Lives of the poets 1753. In Restoration and 18th-century literature, ed C. Camden, Chicago 1963.

Nagashima, D. Johnson's dictionary reconsidered. Stud in Eng Lit (Tokyo) 41 1964.

EDWARD CAPELL
1713–81

§ 1

[List of old quartos of Shakespeare, pbd as an advertisement for their purchase by Capell. c. 1746].

Antony and Cleopatra: an historical play, fitted for the stage by abridging only. 1758. By Capell and David Garrick.

Prolusions: or select pieces of antient poetry, offer'd as specimens of the integrity that should be found in the editions of worthy authors. 1760. Anon.

Mr William Shakespeare his comedies, histories and tragedies, set out by himself in quarto, or by the players his fellows in folio. 10 vols [1767–8].

The works of Shakespear adorned with sculptures. Oxford 6 vols 1770–1. Sir Thomas Hanmer's second edn, with various readings of Theobald and Capell.

The plays of Shakespeare, from the text of Dr Samuel Johnson, with the prefaces, notes etc of Rowe, Pope, Theobald, Hanmer, Warburton, Johnson, and select notes from many other critics; also the introduction of the last editor, Mr Capell, and a table shewing his various readings. 7 vols Dublin 1771.

Notes and various readings to Shakespeare: part 1; with a general glossary. [1774].

Catalogue of Mr Capell's Shakespeariana, presented by him to Trinity College Cambridge. 1779 (priv ptd); ed W. W. Greg, Cambridge 1903. Transcribed and ptd by George Steevens.

Notes and various readings to Shakespeare. 3 vols 1779–83. Contains glossary; The school of Shakespeare: or authentic extracts from divers English books that were in print in that author's time, evidently shewing whence his several fables were taken, with a preface and index of books extracted; notitia dramatica: or tables of ancient plays etc. Ed John Collins. Reviewed by George Colman, Monthly Rev Dec 1783, Jan 1784; see also Monthly Rev Nov 1775–6.

The poems of William Shakespeare, with Mr Capell's history of the origin of Shakespeare's fables, to which is added a glossary. [1798].

§2

Nichols, J. Biography of Edward Capell. Selector 1818.

Halliwell-Phillipps, J. O. A few words in defence of the memory of Capell, occasioned by a criticism in the Times, 26th Dec 1860. 1861 (priv ptd).

Greg, W. W. Editors at work and play. RES 2 1926.

Taylor, G. C. Date of Capell's notes and various readings to Shakespeare, vol 2. RES 5 1929.

Wade, E. L. Capell at Hastings. Sussex County Mag Jan 1930.

Sen, S. K. Capell and Malone and modern critical bibliography. Calcutta 1960.

Walker, A. Capell and his edition of Shakespeare. Proc Br Acad 46 1960; rptd in Studies in Shakespeare, ed P. Alexander, Oxford 1964.

SIR JOHN HAWKINS
1719–89

§1

The complete angler: or contemplative man's recreation, in two parts, by Izaac Walton and Charles Cotton; to which are now prefixed the lives of the authors. 1760, 1775, 1784, 1792, 1797, 1808, 1815, 1822, 1825, 1826; ed J. E. Harting 2 vols 1893. Ed Hawkins; the life of Cotton is by William Oldys.

The life of Samuel Johnson. 1787, 1787, Dublin 1787, London 1797 (as vol 1 of Hawkins' edn of Works of Johnson). Extracts rptd in Johnsonian miscellanies, ed G. B. Hill vol 2 Oxford 1897; abridged and ed B. H. Davis 1961.

The works of Samuel Johnson, together with his life, and notes on his lives of the poets. 15 vols 1787–9. Notes frequently rptd in part.

Annotations illustrative of the plays of Shakespeare. 2 vols 1819. Some by Hawkins.

The life of Samuel Johnson [by Boswell]; to which are added anecdotes by Hawkins. 5 vols 1835.

Miscellaneous Works

Observations on the state of the highways, and on the laws for amending and keeping them in repair, with a draught of a bill. 1763.

A charge to the grand jury of Middlesex delivered the eighth of January 1770. 1770.

Principles and power of harmony. 1771.

A general history of the science and practice of music. 5 vols 1776, 3 vols 1853 ('with the author's posthumous notes'). See also A dictionary of musicians: comprising the most important contents of the works of Sir John Hawkins, 1827 (anon).

Of the practice of bidding prayers, with an ancient form of such bidding, as also a form of cursing, communicated July 1779 [to Soc of Antiquaries]. [1779].

A charge to the grand jury of Middlesex delivered the eleventh of September 1780. 1780.

A dissertation on the armorial ensigns of the county of Middlesex and of the abbey and city of Westminster. 1780.

§2

Probationary odes for the Laureatship, with a preliminary discourse by Sir John Hawkins. 1785 (3 edns), 1787 (anon). Satire on Hawkins.

More last words of Dr Johnson: consisting of anecdotes, and a letter from a medical gentleman; to which are added several facts relative to his biographical executor, by Francis Barber. 1787. Attack on Hawkins.

A catalogue of a collection of manuscripts from the libraries of the late Sir John Hawkins [et al] offered by Thomas Thorpe. 1843.

Boyle, E. Johnson and Sir John Hawkins. Nat Rev March 1926.

— The trial of Midas the second: an account of Burney's unpublished satire on Hawkins' history of music. Bull John Rylands Lib 17 1933.

—In Biographical essays 1790–1890, Oxford 1936.

George, M. D. Hawkins as a Justice of the Peace. Nat Rev Nov 1926.

Pottle, F. A. The dark hints of Hawkins and Boswell. MLN 56 1941.

Stevenson, R. 'The rivals': Hawkins, Burney and Boswell. Musical Quart 36 1950.

Scholes, P. A. The life and activities of Hawkins. Oxford 1953.

Davis, B. H. Johnson before Boswell: a study of Hawkins' life of Samuel Johnson. New Haven 1960.

JOHN MONCK MASON
1726–1809

Dramatick works of Philip Massinger, with notes. 4 vols 1779. Contains George Colman, Critical reflections on the Old English dramatic writers, and Thomas Davies' account of the life and writings of Massinger.

Comments on the last edition of Shakespeare's plays. 1785. On Isaac Reed's edn of Steevens' Shakespeare 1785.

Comments on the plays of Beaumont and Fletcher, with an appendix containing some further observations on Shakespeare. 2 pts 1797, 1798.

Comments on the several editions of Shakespeare's plays, extended to those of Malone and Steevens. Dublin 1807.

THOMAS WARTON the younger
1728–90

For Warton's other works see col 690, above.

§1

The Union: or select Scots and English poems. Edinburgh 1753, 1753, London 1759, Dublin 1761, London 1766, Oxford 1796. Ed Warton.

Observations on the Faerie Queene of Spenser. 1754, 2 vols 1762, 1807.

The life and literary remains of Ralph Bathurst MD, Dean of Wells. 1761.

The Oxford sausage: or select poetical pieces, written by the most celebrated wits of the University of Oxford. 1764, Dublin 1766, Oxford 1772, 1777, 1804, London 1814, 1815 etc. Ed Warton.

The life of Sir Thomas Pope, founder of Trinity College. 1772, 1780, 1784.

The history of English poetry, from the close of the eleventh to the commencement of the eighteenth century; to which are prefixed two dissertations: 1, on the origin of romantic fiction in Europe; 2, on the introduction of learning into England. Vol 1, 1774; vol 2, 1778; vol 3 (containing a dissertation on the Gesta Romanorum), 1778. 2nd edn of vol 1, 1775; new edn of vol 3, 1781; vol 4 (unfinished; only 88 pages) nd; ed R. Price 4 vols 1824 (complete); ed R. Taylor 3 vols 1840; ed W. C. Hazlitt 4 vols 1872; rptd (from edns of '1778 and 1781') 1870, 1872, 1875. An index by T. Fillingham, 1806.

Milton, John. Poems upon several occasions, English, Italian and Latin, with translations; with notes and illustrations by Warton. 1785, 1791 (rev and enlarged; appendix, containing remarks on the Greek verses of Milton, by Charles Burney jr).

A history of English poetry: an unpublished continuation by Warton. Ed R. M. Baine, Los Angeles 1953 (Augustan Reprint Soc).

An enquiry into the authenticity of the poems attributed to T. Rowley [i.e. Chatterton]. 1782, 1782.

Correspondence of Thomas Percy and Warton. Ed M. G. Robinson and L. Dennis, Baton Rouge 1951.

§2

[Huggins, W.] The observer observ'd: or remarks on Observations on the Faerie Queen of Spenser by Thomas Warton. 1756. L. F. Powell, William Huggins and Tobias Smollett, MP 34 1936, proves Huggins' authorship.

[Dampier, H.] Remarks upon the eighth section of the second volume of Mr Warton's history of English poetry. [1779].

[Ritson, J.] Observations on the three first volumes of the history of English poetry, in a letter to the author. 1782.

A letter to Warton on his late edition of Milton's juvenile poems. 1785.

Rinaker, C. Warton and the historical method in literary criticism. PMLA 30 1915.

—— Warton: a biographical and critical study. Urbana 1916.

Ker, W. P. Thomas Warton. Proc Br Acad 4 1909–10 rptd in his Collected essays, 1925.

Nichol Smith, D. Warton's history of English poetry. Proc Br Acad 15 1929.

Wellek, R. In his Rise of English literary history, Chapel Hill 1941.

Blakeston, J. M. G. A Dublin reprint of Warton's history of English poetry. Library 5th ser 1 1946.

Kinghorn, A. M. Warton's history and early English poetry. E Studies 44 1963.

Johnston, A. In his Enchanted ground, 1964.

THOMAS PERCY
1729–1811
See col 242, above.

THOMAS TYRWHITT
1730–86

§1

Proceedings and debates in the House of Commons in 1620, 1621. 2 vols Oxford 1766.

Observations and conjectures upon some passages of Shakespeare. Oxford 1766.

Elsynge, Henry, The manner of holding parliaments in England, corrected and enlarged from the author's original manuscript. 1768. Ed Tyrwhitt.

The Canterbury tales of Chaucer; to which are added an essay upon his language and versification: an introductory discourse, and notes. 5 vols 1775–8, 2 vols Oxford 1798, 5 vols 1822, 1830 etc.

Poems, supposed to have been written at Bristol, by Thomas Rowley and others in the 15th century, now first published; to which are added a preface, an introductory account of the pieces and a glossary. 1777, 1777, 1778 (with an appendix containing some observations upon the language of these poems, tending to prove that they were written by Thomas Chatterton), 1782, 1794 (without appendix, ed J. Miller); ed M. E. Hare, Oxford 1911. Reviewed by John Langhorne, Monthly Rev April–June 1777.

A vindication of the appendix to the poems called Rowley's. 1782. For the literature of the Rowley controversy, *see* col 607, above.

Tyrwhitt also contributed to Steevens' Shakespeare 1778, *and to* Reed's Steevens' Shakespeare 1785.

Miscellaneous Works

An epistle to Florio, at Oxford. 1749; rptd in Crypt Dec 1829; GM Dec 1835.

The eighth Isthmian of Pindar [translated into] English [by Tyrwhitt]. In Translations in verse, Oxford 1752.

Musgrave, S., Exercitationum in Euripidem libri duo. Leyden 1762. Tyrwhitt gave Musgrave notes.

Observations on the inscriptions upon three ancient marbles said to have been brought from Smyrna, and now in the British Museum, in a letter from Tyrwhitt to Matthew Duane, read at the Society of Antiquaries July 9 1772. Archaeologia 3 1772.

Fragmenta duo Plutarchi from Harley 5612. 1773. Ed Tyrwhitt.

Dissertatio de Babrio, fabularum Aesopearum scriptore, inseruntur fabulae quaedam Aesopeae; accedunt Babrii fragmenta. 1776, 1781, Erlangen 1785 (with addns and a preface by T. C. Harles), Erlangen 1810.

Musgrave, S., Euripidis quae extant omnia, graece, latine; varias lectiones insigniores, notasque perpetuas adjecit, interpretationem latinam secundum probatissimas lectiones reformavit Sam Musgrave; accedunt scholia in septem priores tragoedias. 4 vols Oxford 1778. Tyrwhitt assisted with this.

Notae in Orpheum de lapidibus. 1781, Leipzig 1805.

Dawes, R., Miscellanea critica. Ed T. Burgess 1781. Pp. 344–491 for Tyrwhitt's contributions.

Musgrave, S., Two dissertations: 1, On the Grecian mythology; 2, An examination of Sir Isaac Newton's objections to the chronology of the Olympiads. 1782. Ed Tyrwhitt.

Conjecturae in Strabonem. 1783; ed T. C. Harles, Erlangen 1788.

Cleaver, W., De rhythmo Graecorum liber singularis, in usum juventutis coll. aen. nas. olim conscriptus, et nunc demum in lucem editus. Oxford 1789. Contains Tyrwhitt's observations and corrections.

Toup, J., Emendationes in Suidam et Hesychium et alios lexicographos. 4 vols Oxford 1790. Ed Richard Porson. Contains Notae breves in Toupii emendationes in Suidam; authore T. Tyrwhitt.

Aristotelis De poetica liber, gr et lat; lectionem constituit, animaduersionibus illustravit Tyrwhitt. Oxford 1794, 1806, 1817, 1827.

Brunck, R. F. P., Tragoediae septem [of Sophocles] ex editione R. F. P. Brunck. 2 vols Oxford 1808. Brunck used notes by Tyrwhitt.

Conjecturae in Aeschylum, Euripidem et Aristophanem; accedunt epistolae diversorum ad Tyrwhittum. Oxford 1822.

Monk, J. H., Euripides Alcestis, cum delectis adnotationibus, potissimum J. H. Monkii, accedunt emendationes G. Hermanii. Leipzig 1824. With notes from Tyrwhitt.

§2

Nichols, J. In his Literary anecdotes vol 3, 1812.

Powell, L. F. Tyrwhitt and the Rowley poems. RES 7 1931.

RICHARD FARMER
1735–97

§1

An essay on the learning of Shakespeare. Cambridge 1767, 1767, 1789, 1821. Also included in edns of Shakespeare by Steevens, Reed, Malone and James Boswell jr. Rptd in Eighteenth-century essays on Shakespeare, ed D. Nichol Smith, Glasgow 1903.
The correspondence of Thomas Percy and Farmer. Ed C. Brooks, Baton Rouge 1946.

§2

The battle between Dr Farmer and P. Musgrave, the Cambridge taylor, in Hudibrastic verse, with a number of pleasant quotations and admirable epigrams. 1792.
Biographical anecdotes of Farmer. GM Sept–Oct, Dec 1797.
Bibliotheca Farmeriana: an auction catalogue of Dr Farmer's library. 1798. See also GM June, Aug 1798.
Reed, I. In William Seward's Biographiana, 1799. Biographical sketch.
Nichols, J. In his Literary anecdotes vol 2, 1812.
Turner, B. N. Description of the visit of Dr Johnson at Cambridge with Dr Farmer in 1765. New Monthly Mag Dec 1818.
Shuckburgh, E. S. In Laurence Chaderton DD (first Master of Emmanuel), translated from a Latin memoir of Dr Dillingham, with notes and illustrations, Cambridge 1884.
Owst, G. R. Iconomania in eighteenth-century Cambridge: notes on a newly acquired miniature of Farmer and his interest in historical portraiture. Proc Cambridge Antiquarian Soc 42 1949.
Roberts, S. C. Richard Farmer. 1961 (Lib Assoc).

GEORGE STEEVENS
1736–1800

§1

Twenty of the plays of Shakespeare collated with different copies and publish'd from the originals. 4 vols 1766.
The plays of William Shakespeare, with notes by Samuel Johnson and George Steevens. 10 vols 1773, 1778; ed I. Reed 10 vols 1785, 15 vols 1793, 21 vols 1803, 21 vols 1813. Detached pieces of criticism appended to the Johnson-Steevens edns of Shakespeare, 1778, 1785, 1793.
Six old plays on which Shakespeare founded his Measure for measure, Comedy of errors, The taming of the shrew, King John, King Henry 4 and King Henry 5, King Lear. 2 vols 1779. Selected by Steevens; John Nichols prepared them for the press.
Catalogue of Mr Capell's Shakesperiana, presented by him to Trinity College Cambridge. 1779 (priv ptd). Transcribed and ptd by Steevens.
Annotations by Sam Johnson and Geo Steevens, and the various commentators, upon King Henry 5, written by Will Shakspere. 1787.
Annotations by Samuel Johnson and George Steevens and various commentators upon the Merchant of Venice, written by Will Shakespeare. 1787.
Shakspeare. 1794. Account by Steevens, under the assumed signature of William Richardson, printseller, of a pretended portrait of Shakespeare, proposals for engraving a print from it, and an eulogy upon it.

Miscellaneous Works

Biographical anecdotes of Hogarth. 1781. With John Nichols.

Johnsoniana. European Mag Jan 1785; rptd in Johnsonian miscellanies vol 2, ed G. B. Hill, Oxford 1897.
Fenn, Sir John. Original letters written during the reigns of Henry 6, Edward 4, Edward 5, Richard 3 and Henry 7, with notes. Vols 1–2, 1787, 1787. Contains contributions by Steevens.
Howard, Henry, Earl of Surrey. Songs and sonnettes. 2 vols [1795]–[1807]. Ed Thomas Percy and Steevens, but see C. Brooks, below.
Genuine works of William Hogarth, illustrated with biographical anecdotes, a chronological catalogue and commentary, by John Nichols and George Steevens. 3 vols 1808–17. Steevens also contributed to Johnson's Lives of the poets, Dodsley's Annual register, Reed's Biographia dramatica, Sayer's Caricatures, Critical Rev, St James's Chron, Public Advertiser, Morning Post, General Evening Post, GM etc.

§2

Jennens, C. The tragedy of King Lear, as lately published, vindicated from the abuse of the critical reviewers. 1772.
[Collins, J.] A letter to George Hardinge, on the subject of a passage in Mr Steevens's preface to his impression of Shakespeare. 1777.
The etymologist. 1785. A comedy satirizing reviewers and commentators, especially Steevens.
Mason, J. M. Comments on the last edition of Shakespeare's plays. Dublin 1785. On Reed's 1785 edn of Steevens's Shakespeare.
Bibliotheca Steevensiana: a catalogue of the curious and valuable library of Steevens. 1800.
Poole, J. Hamlet travestie: in three acts, with burlesque annotations, after the manner of Dr Johnson and George Steevens, and the various commentators. 1810, 1811, 1811, 1817.
D'Israeli, I. On Puck the commentator. In his Curiosities of literature vol 3, 1817.
Abrahams, A. 'Upper Heath', Hampstead. N & Q 5 Aug 1922. On his residence 1770–1800.
Greg, W. W. Editors at work and play. RES 2 1926.
Powell, L. F. Steevens and Isaac Reed's Biographia dramatica. RES 6–7 1929–30. On cancelled articles by Steevens.
Brooks, C. The history of Percy's edition of Surrey's poems. E Studien 68 1937. Many remarks on Steevens, showing he was not an editor of this edn.
Horne, C. J. Malone and Steevens in relation to Boswell's Life. N & Q 4 Feb 1950.
Macmillan, D. Steevens's contribution to Biographia dramatica. In Restoration and eighteenth-century literature: essays in honor of A. D. McKillop, Chicago 1963.

EDMOND MALONE
1741–1812

§1

Ode on the royal nuptials. In Gratulationes juventutis academiae Dubliniensis in sereniss Regis et Reginae nuptias, Dublin 1761.
Goldsmith, Oliver, Poems and plays; [with] the life of the author. 2 vols Dublin 1777, London 1780 (as Poetical and dramatic works of Goldsmith, now first collected, with an account of the life and writings of the author).
An attempt to ascertain the order in which the plays attributed to Shakespeare were written. In Steevens's edn of Shakespeare vol 1, 1778; subsequently in the variorum Shakespeares.
The tragicall hystory of Romeus and Juliet. 1780. Tr Arthur Brooke from Matteo Bandello; ed Malone from 1562 edn.

A supplement to the edition of Shakespeare published in 1778 by Johnson and Steevens: containing additional observations, with the genuine poems of the same author and seven plays which have been ascribed to him, with notes by the editor and others. 2 vols 1780.

Epilogue. In R. Jephson, The Count of Narbonne, 1781.

Remarks on two new publications on Rowley's poems. GM Dec 1781. Concluded in suppl for the year 1781; expanded and rptd as Cursory observations on the poems attributed to Thomas Rowley, 1782, 1782; ed J. M. Kuist, Los Angeles 1966 (Augustan Reprint Soc).

Baker, D. E., Biographia dramatica. 2 vols 1782. Ed I. Reed, but most of the 'additions and corrections' were supplied by Malone.

A second appendix to Mr Malone's supplement to the last edition of the plays of Shakespeare. 1783 (priv ptd).

The journal of a tour to the Hebrides with Samuel Johnson LlD by James Boswell esq. 1785. Malone revised first edn and supervised 2nd.

A dissertation on the three parts of King Henry 6. 1787; rptd in his edns of Shakespeare, 1790, 1794, 1821.

Prologue. In R. Jephson, Julia, 1787, 1787; rptd in Annual Register 1787.

Jephson, Robert, The Count of Narbonne. 1787 (2nd edn corrected). Ed Malone.

The plays and poems of William Shakespeare. 10 vols in 11 1790, 16 vols Dublin 1794. Contains: An essay on the chronological order of Shakespeare's plays; An essay relative to Shakespeare and Jonson; A dissertation on the 3 parts of King Henry 6; An historical account of the English stage; The tragical hystory of Romeo and Juliet.

The plays of William Shakespeare, accurately printed from the text of Mr Malone's edition; with select explanatory notes [by John Nichols]. 7 vols 1790.

Caveat against the booksellers respecting an edition of Shakespeare, attributed to Malone. 1790?

Prospectus of a new edition of Shakespeare's plays and poems. 1792.

A letter to Dr Richard Farmer, relative to the edition of Shakespeare published in 1790, and some late criticisms [by Joseph Ritson] on that work. 1792, 1792.

Roman portraits: a poem by Robert Jephson. 1794. Ed Malone.

The biographical mirrour. 3 vols 1795-8. Engravings by Silvester Harding; 25 lives by Malone and all corrected by him.

Proposals [for a new edition of Shakespeare]. 1795.

An inquiry into the authenticity of certain papers attributed to Shakespeare, Queen Elizabeth and Henry, Earl of Southampton. 1796.

Works of Sir Joshua Reynolds, with an account of his life and writings. 2 vols 1797, 3 vols 1798, 1809, 1819.

Boswell, James, The life of Samuel Johnson. Malone greatly assisted Boswell in preparation of the first edn; also edited and contributed notes to the 3rd edn, 4 vols 1799, 4th 1804, 5th 1807, 6th 1811.

The critical and miscellaneous prose works of John Dryden, with notes and illustrations, and an account of the life and writings of the author. 3 vols in 4 1800.

Hamilton, W. G., Parliamentary logick; to which are subjoined two speeches, delivered in the House of Commons of Ireland, and other pieces, with an appendix containing considerations on the corn laws by Samuel Johnson. 1808. Ed with a memoir of Hamilton by Malone.

An account of the incidents from which the title and part of the story of Shakespeare's Tempest were derived, and its true date ascertained. 1808 (priv ptd).

A biographical memoir of William Windham. GM June 1810; rptd with enlargements 1810.

Spence, Joseph, Observations, anecdotes and characters of books and men, arranged with notes by the late Edmond Malone esq. 1820.

[Boswell, J., jr.], The plays and poems of William Shakespeare, with a life of the poet and an enlarged history of the stage, by the late Edmond Malone, with a new glossarial index. 21 vols 1821.

Correspondence of Thomas Percy and Malone. Ed A. Tillotson, Baton Rouge 1944.

§2

[Badcock, S.] Monthly Rev Oct 1780. Review of Supplement to the edition of Shakespeare's plays pbd in 1778.

[Greene, E. B.] Strictures upon a pamphlet intitled Cursory observations on the poems attributed to Rowley. 1782.

Ode addressed to Edmond Malone esq on his presuming to examine the learned and unanswerable arguments urged by Jacob Bryant esq and the Rev Dr Milles in support of the authenticity of Rowley's poems. GM Aug 1782.

Critical Rev Dec 1791 1790. Edn of Shakespeare reviewed unfavourably. Malone was defended by Boswell, GM Jan 1792.

[Ritson, J.] Cursory criticisms on the edition of Shakespeare published by Malone. 1792.

Hurdis, J. Cursory remarks upon the arrangement of the plays of Shakspeare, occasioned by reading Mr Malone's essay on the chronological order of those celebrated pieces. 1792.

[Pearne, T.] Monthly Rev Sept 1793–March 1794. Review of Malone's edn of Shakespeare.

Ireland, S. Mr Ireland's vindication of his conduct, respecting the publication of the supposed Shakespeare mss: being a preface or introduction to a reply to the critical labours of Mr Malone in his Enquiry into the authenticity of certain papers etc. 1796.

—— An investigation of Mr Malone's claim to the character of scholar, or critic: being an examination of his inquiry into the authenticity of the Shakespeare manuscript. [1798]. By Thomas Caldecott.

[Caulfield, J.] An enquiry into the conduct of Malone concerning the manuscript papers of John Aubrey in the Ashmolean Museum Oxford. 1797.

Chalmers, G. An apology for the believers in the Shakespeare-papers which were exhibited in Norfolk-Street. 1797. Anon. Against Malone.

—— A supplemental apology for the believers in the Shakespeare-papers. 1799.

—— Another account of the incidents from which the title and part of the story of Shakespeare's Tempest were derived, and the true era of it ascertained. 1815 (priv ptd). Written to controvert Malone's pamphlet.

Sill, R. ('Charles Dirrell'). Remarks on Shakespeare's Tempest; containing an investigation of Mr Malone's attempt to ascertain the date of that play. Cambridge 1797.

Mason, J. M. Comments on the plays of Beaumont and Fletcher, with an appendix containing some further observations on Shakespeare, extended to the late editions of Malone and Steevens. 1798, 1809.

—— Comments on the several editions of Shakespeare's plays, extended to those of Malone and Steevens. Dublin 1807.

[Hardinge, G.] The essence of Malone: or the 'beauties' of that fascinating writer, extracted from his immortal work entitled Some account of the life and writings of John Dryden. 1800, 1800.

—— Another essence of Malone, or the 'beauties' of Shakspeare's editor: second part. 1801.

Howe, J. Notes upon some of the obscure passages in Shakespeare's plays, with remarks upon the editions of 1785, 1790, 1793. 1805.

Gilchrist, O. An examination of the charges maintained by Messrs Malone, Chalmers and others, of Ben Jonson's enmity etc towards Shakespeare. 1808.

Boswell, J., jr. Memoirs and character of Edmond Malone esq. GM June 1813; rptd priv 1814; prefixed to Boswell's edn of Malone's Shakespeare, 1821; prefixed to catalogue of early English poetry etc, below, 1836.

Auction catalogue of the greater portion of the library of Edmond Malone esq. 1818.

Catalogue of early English poetry and works illustrating the British drama collected by Malone and now preserved in the Bodleian Library. Oxford 1836. With Boswell's memoir of Malone.

Prior, J. Life of Malone, editor of Shakespeare; with selections from his ms anecdotes. 1860.

Halliwell[-Phillipps], J. O. A hand-list of the early English literature preserved in the Malone collection in the Bodleian Library, selected from the printed catalogue of that collection. 1860.

Original letters from Malone, the editor of Shakespeare, to John Jordan, the poet. Ed J. O. Halliwell[-Phillipps] 1864 (priv ptd).

The correspondence of Malone with J. Davenport, Vicar of Stratford-on-Avon [on Shakespeare's family]. Ed J. O. Halliwell [-Phillipps] 1864 (priv ptd).

Greg, W. W. Editors at work and play. RES 2 1926.

Powell, L. F. George Steevens and Isaac Reed's Biographia dramatica. RES 6-7 1930-1. Malone's report of cancelled passages.

Osborn, J. M. Dr Johnson on the sanctity of an author's text. PMLA 50 1935. As reported by Malone.

—— Malone and the Dryden almanac story. PQ 17 1938.

—— Malone and Baratariana. N & Q 27 Jan 1945.

—— Malone: scholar-collector. Library 5th ser 19 1964.

—— Malone and Dr Johnson. In Boswell, Johnson and their circle, ed M. Lascelles, Oxford 1965.

Read, A. W. The contemporary quotations in Johnson's dictionary. ELH 2 1935. Includes notes by Malone.

Nichol Smith, D. Malone. HLQ 3 1940.

Hogan, J. J. The bicentenary of Malone. Studies 30 1941.

Malone: scholar and antiquary. TLS 4 Oct 1941.

Chapman, R. W. Cancels in Malone's Dryden. Library 4th ser 23 1943.

Horne, C. J. Malone and Steevens in relation to Boswell's Life. N & Q 4 Feb 1950.

Wilson, J. D. Malone and the upstart crow. Shakespeare Survey 4 1951.

Landry, H. Malone as editor of Shakespeare's sonnets. BNYPL Sept 1963.

ISAAC REED
1742-1807

§1

Poetical works of the Right Hon Lady M[ar]y W[ortle]y M[ontagu]. 1768. Ed Reed.

Musae Seatonianae: a complete collection of the Cambridge prize poems, from the first institution of that premium by Thomas Seaton, in 1750, to the present time. 1772. Ed Reed.

[Nichols, J.], The original works of William King LlD. 3 vols 1776. Reed assisted Nichols.

Historical memoirs of the life and writings of the late W. Dodd LlD. 1777, 1777.

The repository: a select collection of fugitive pieces of wit and humour, in verse and prose, by the most eminent writers. 4 vols 1777-83, 1790. Ed Reed.

Middleton, Thomas, A tragi-comodie called the Witch. 1778. Rptd by Reed.

Young, Edward, The works of the author of the Night thoughts; to which is prefixed an account of the life of the author. 6 vols 1778-9. Reed edited vol 6.

Nichols, J., A supplement to Dr Swift's works. 3 vols 1779. Reed assisted Nichols.

Dodsley, R., A select collection of old plays: second edition, corrected, with notes [by Reed]. 12 vols 1780.

J. Payne Collier's edn 12 vols 1825-7, rptd Reed's notes with addns from his mss.

Dodd, W., Thoughts in prison. 1781. Ed Reed.

Nichols, J., Biographical and literary anecdotes of William Bowyer, and of his learned friends: containing an incidental view of the progress of literature in this Kingdom from the beginning of the present century to 1777. 1782. Reed assisted Nichols.

Dodsley, R., A collection of poems by several hands, with notes [by Reed]. 6 vols 1782.

Baker, D. E., Biographia dramatica, or a companion to the playhouse: a new edition [by Reed]. 2 vols 1782; ed S. Jones 1812.

Pearch, G., A collection of poems, by several hands. 4 vols 1783. Reed wrote biographical notices for this edn.

The plays of William Shakespeare, with the corrections and illustrations of various commentators; to which are added notes by S. Johnson and G. Steevens: the third edition. 10 vols 1785.

The plays of William Shakespeare. 15 vols 1793, 23 vols Basle 1779-1802, 21 vols 1803, 1813.

Johnson, Samuel, The works of the English poets, with prefaces biographical and critical. 75 vols 1790. For this edn Reed wrote biographical notices of John Armstrong, James Cawthorn, Charles Churchill, John Cunningham, William Falconer, Oliver Goldsmith, Matthew Green, Soame Jenyns, Dr Johnson, John Langhorne, Edward Moore, Paul Whitehead and William Whitehead. The life of Goldsmith was rptd in Poems by Goldsmith and Parnell, 1795.

Seward, W., Biographiana. 2 vols 1799. Reed wrote Life of Dr Farmer, pp. 578-98.

The Reed diaries 1762-1804. Ed C. E. Jones, Berkeley 1946.

Reed also contributed to Westminster Mag, European Mag and GM, and to the various pbns of John Nichols.

§2

[Pearne, T.] Monthly Rev Aug-Sept 1786. Review of Reed's 1785 edn of Shakespeare.

[Ritson, J.] The quip modest. 1788 (2 issues, first cancelled). Attack on Steevens and Reed, concerning the 1785 edn of Shakespeare.

Bibliotheca Reediana: a catalogue of the library of the late Isaac Reed. 1807.

[Nichols, J.] Biographical memoirs of the late Isaac Reed esq. GM Jan 1807.

[Bindley, J.?] Memoir of Reed. European Mag Feb 1807.

Dowden, E. Some old Shakespeareans. In his Essays modern and Elizabethan, 1910.

Powell, L. F. George Steevens and Reed's Biographia dramatica. RES 6 1929. Cancelled articles by Steevens.

Wilson, R. H. Reed and Warton on the Old wives tale. PMLA 55 1940.

Metzdorf, R. F. Reed and the unfortunate Dr Dodd. Harvard Lib Bull 6 1952.

Jones, C. E. Reed's theatrical obituary. N & Q Sept 1957.

JOHN NICHOLS
1745-1826

§1

For a full bibliography of Nichols see col 1729, above.

The works of Jonathan Swift. Vol 9 (4°), and vol 17 (8°), 1775. Ed Nichols.

The original works of William King LlD. 3 vols 1776. With Isaac Reed.

Six old plays, on which Shakespeare founded his Measure for measure, Comedy of errors, The taming of the shrew, King John, King Henry 4 and King Henry 5, King Lear. 2 vols 1779. Selected by George Steevens and prepared for the press by Nichols.

Supplement to Dr Swift's works, with explanatory notes. 1 vol (vol 14 of 4°) and 3 vols (vols 25-7 of 8°) 1779.

A select collection of poems; with notes biographical and historical. 8 vols 1780-2. With Joseph Warton, Thomas Percy and Robert Lowth.

A new and general biographical dictionary. 12 vols 1784 (2nd edn). Nichols assisted Ralph Heathcote in this edn and later Alexander Chalmers in enlarged edn of 1812-17.

The tatler, with notes [by Nichols, Thomas Percy, John Calder et al]. 6 vols 1786, 4 vols 1789.

The epistolary correspondence of Sir Richard Steele; with literary and historical anecdotes by John Nichols. 2 vols 1787, 1809 (with fragments of plays supposed to be by Addison and Steele).

The works in verse and prose of Leonard Welsted, now first collected, with historical notes and memoirs of the author by John Nichols. 1787.

The guardian. 2 vols 1789. Ed Nichols.

The Lover, written in imitation of the Tatler, by Marmaduke Myrtle gent; to which is added the Reader, both by the author of the Tatler and Spectator: a new edition with notes and illustrations. 1789.

The Town talk, the Fish pool, the Plebeian, the Old Whig, the Spinster etc, by the authors of the Tatler, Spectator and Guardian, now first collected, with notes and illustrations. 1790, Dublin 1790.

The works of Shakespeare, accurately printed from the text of Mr Malone's edition; with select explanatory notes [by Nichols]. 7 vols 1790.

The Theatre, by Sir Richard Steele; to which are added, The Anti-Theatre etc, illustrated with literary and historical anecdotes. 1791.

The works of Jonathan Swift, arranged with notes by Thomas Sheridan: new edition corrected and revised by John Nichols. 19 vols 1801, 24 vols 1803, 19 vols 1808.

Fuller, Thomas, The history of the Worthies of England, with a few explanatory notes by Nichols. 2 vols 1811.

§2

Bond, D. Friendship strikingly exhibited in a new light. 1781.

Hart, E. Some new sources of Johnson's lives. PMLA 65 1950.

— The contributions of Nichols to Boswell's Life of Johnson. PMLA 67 1952.

— An ingenious editor: Nichols and the Gentleman's Magazine. Bucknell Rev 10 1963.

Old papers. TLS 2 Nov 1951. On the sale of Nichols' family papers.

Schick, G. B. 'Kind hints' to Nichols by Joseph Warton and others. N & Q Feb 1956.

Smith, A. H. Nichols' anecdotes of Hogarth. N & Q Aug 1957.

— Nichols, printer and publisher. Library, 5th ser 18 1963.

JOSEPH RITSON
1752-1803

For a bibliography see Burd and Bronson under §2, below.

§1

Observations on the three first volumes of the history of English poetry [by Thomas Warton] in a letter to the author. 1782.

Fabularum romanensium bibliotheca: a general catalogue of old romances, French, Italian, Spanish and English. 1782. Specimen; only 2 sheets ptd. The ms, BM 10, 283-5, contains 3000 entries.

Remarks, critical and illustrative, on the text and notes of the last edition of Shakespeare. 1783. Contains, at end, proposals for publishing Shakespeare's plays in 8 vols. Reviewed by Charles Burney, Monthly Rev May 1784.

A select collection of English songs. 3 vols 1783; ed T. Park 3 vols 1813. Contains an historical essay on national song.

The bishoprick garland, or Durham minstrel: being a choice collection of excellent songs relating to the above county. Stockton 1784, Newcastle 1792.

Gammer Gurton's garland, or the nursery parnassus: a choice collection of pretty songs and verses, for the amusement of all little good children who can neither read nor run. Stockton [1784], London 1809, 1810, Glasgow 1866, Stockton nd, nd.

'Anti-Scot'. [Critique on Pinkerton's Scottish ballads]. GM May 1784.

The Spartan manual, or tablet of morality: being a genuine collection of the apophthegms, maxims and precepts of the philosophers and other celebrated characters of antiquity. 1785.

The Comedy of errors, with notes. 1787. Only 2 sheets ptd; specimen of an intended edn of Shakespeare.

The quip modest: or a few words by way of supplement to remarks, critical and illustrative, on the text and notes of the last edition of Shakespeare [i.e. Johnson's and Steevens's, 1778], occasioned by the republication of that edition by [Isaac Reed]. 1788 (cancelled), 1788.

The Yorkshire garland: being a curious collection of old and new songs concerning that famous county. Pt 1 (all pbd), York 1788.

Ancient songs, from the time of King Henry the 3rd to the Revolution. 1790, 3 vols 1829; ed W. C. Hazlitt 1877. Contains observations on the ancient English minstrels: a dissertation on the songs and music of the ancient English.

Pieces of ancient popular poetry, 1791, 1833; ed E. Goldsmid, Edinburgh 1884.

The North-country chorister: an unparalleled variety of excellent songs collected and published together, for general amusement, by a bishoprick ballad singer. Durham 1792, 1802.

Cursory criticisms on the edition of Shakespeare published by Edmond Malone. 1792.

The Northumberland garland, or Newcastle nightingale: a matchless collection of famous songs. Newcastle 1793. Ed Ritson; first edn of Northumberland garland was in 1768.

The English anthology. 3 vols 1793-4.

Scotish song. 2 vols 1794, 1866. A collection of Scotch songs, with the airs, and an historical essay.

Poems on interesting events in the reign of Edward 3 written in the year 1352 by Laurence Minot, with a preface, dissertation, notes and a glossary. 1795, 1825.

Robin Hood: a collection of all the ancient poems, songs and ballads now extant relative to that outlaw; to which are prefixed historical anecdotes of his life. 2 vols 1795, 1 vol 1820, 1832, 1853, 1862, 1884, 1885.

Ancient English metrical romances. 3 vols 1802.

Bibliographia poetica: a catalogue of English poets, of the 12th, 13th, 14th, 15th and 16th centurys, with a short account of their works. 1802. Joseph Haslewood made collections for a new edn. Addns and alterations were pbd in Sir Egerton Brydges, Censura literaria, 1805.

Dido: a tragedy as it was performed at the Theatre Royal in Drury-Lane, with universal applause, by Joseph Reed. 1808. Ptd in 1792; Ritson contributed notes and supervised the printing.

Northern garlands. 1810, Edinburgh 1887-8. The Bishoprick garland, the Yorkshire garland, the Northumberland garland and the north-country chorister, rptd by Joseph Haslewood.

The Caledonian Muse: a chronological selection of Scotish poetry from the earliest times. 1821. Ptd 1785.

Warton, Thomas, The history of English poetry: new edition carefully revised, with numerous additional notes by the late Mr Ritson [et al]. 4 vols 1824, 3 vols 1840.

The life of King Arthur. Ed J. Frank 1825.

Fairy tales, now first collected; to which are prefixed 2 dissertations: 1, On pygmies; 2, on fairies. 1831, 1875 (preface by W. C. Hazlitt).

Miscellaneous Works

Verses addressed to the ladies of Stockton. In the Newcastle miscellany, 1772; rptd Newcastle nd and in Haslewood, Account of Ritson, 1824.

The office of a Lord High Steward of England. 1776.

Tables, shewing the descent of the crown of England. 1778 (priv ptd), 1783.

The Stockton jubilee: or Shakespeare in all his glory. Newcastle 1781.

A digest of the proceedings of the Court Leet of the manor and liberty of the Savoy. 1789, 1809, 1816.

The jurisdiction of the Court Leet. 1791, 1809, 1816.

The office of Constable. 1791, 1815.

Law tracts. 1794. Reprints first edns of A digest of the proceedings of the Court Leet of the Manor and liberty of the Savoy; The jurisdiction of the Court Leet; and The office of constable.

An essay on abstinence from animal food as a moral duty. 1802.

Practical points: or maxims in conveyancing, drawn from the daily experience of a late eminent conveyancer [R. Bradley]; to which are added, critical observations on the various and essential parts of a deed, by the late Joseph Ritson. 1804, 1820, 1825.

Original memoirs written during the great war; being the life of Sir H. Slingsby, and memoirs of Captain Hodgson; with notes by Sir W. Scott. Edinburgh 1806. The advertisement to Hodgson's memoirs was written by Ritson.

The office of bailiff of a liberty. Ed J. Frank 1811.

Memoirs of the Celts or Gauls. Ed J. Frank 1827.

Annals of the Caledonians, Picts and Scots; and of Strathclyde, Cumberland, Galloway, and Murray. Ed J. Frank 2 vols Edinburgh 1828.

The letters of Ritson, edited chiefly from originals in the possession of his nephew [Joseph Frank]; to which is prefixed a memoir of the author by Sir H. Nicolas. Ed J. Frank 2 vols 1833.

§2

A familiar address to the curious in English poetry, more particularly to the readers of Shakespeare, by Thersites Literarius. 1784. Attacks Ritson.

Malone, E. A letter to Dr Farmer, relative to the edition of Shakespeare published in 1790, and some later criticisms [by Ritson] on that work. 1792, 1792.

Auction catalogue of the library of Ritson. 1803. See Nichols, Anecdotes vol 8, 1814.

Nichols, J. In his Literary anecdotes vol 8, 1814.

Haslewood, J. Some account of the life and publications of Ritson. 1824. Appendix contains verses addressed to the ladies of Stockton, first ptd in the Newcastle miscellany, 1772.

Letters to Mr George Paton [from Ritson], to which is added a Critique by John Pinkerton upon Ritson's Scottish songs. Edinburgh 1829. Pinkerton's critique rptd from Critical Rev Jan 1795.

MacCunn, F. A. In her Sir Walter Scott's friends, Edinburgh 1909.

Jones, H. S. V. Ritson, romantic antiquarian. Sewanee Rev 22 1914.

Burd, H. A. Ritson: a critical biography. Urbana 1916. Appendix C is a bibliography of the pbd and unpbd works of Ritson.

—— Eight unedited letters of Ritson. Trans Wisconsin Acad 19 1918.

Oxberry, J. Ritson of Stockton. Proc Soc Antiquaries of Newcastle 10 1922.

Ker, W. P. Ritson. 1922 (Modern Humanities Research Assoc); rptd in his Collected essays, 1925.

Hopkins, A. B. Ritson's Life of King Arthur. PMLA 43 1928.

Bronson, B. H. Ritson's Bibliographia scotia. PMLA 52 1937.

—— Ritson, scholar-at-arms. 2 vols Berkeley 1938. With bibliography.

—— The Caledonian Muse. PMLA 46 1931.

Dennis, L. Blandamour in the Percy-Ritson controversy. MP 29 1931.

Moreland, C. C. Ritson's Life of Robin Hood. PMLA 50 1935.

Osborn, J. M. Ritson, scholar at odds. MP 37 1940.

Pearsall, R. B. Scott and Ritson on Allan Ramsay. MLN 66 1951.

Todd, W. B. Ritson's Observations on the history of English poetry. Book Collector 6 1957.

Johnston, A. In his Enchanted ground, 1964.

JOHN PINKERTON
1758–1826

§1

Craigmillar castle: an elegy. Edinburgh 1776.

Rimes. 1781, 1782.

Scottish tragic ballads. 1781, 1783 (enlarged as vol 1 of Select Scotish ballads). Contains Dissertations, On the oral tradition in poetry, and On the tragic ballad.

Two dithyrambic odes. 1782.

Tales, in verse. 1782.

Other juvenile poems, by the author of Rimes. [London?] nd. Contains the Two dithyrambic odes.

Select Scotish ballads. 2 vols 1783. Vol 1, Ballads in the tragic style, 2nd edn enlarged; vol 2, Ballads of the comic kind.

Letters of literature, by R. Heron. 1785.

The treasury of wit: being a methodical selection of about twelve hundred of the best apophthegms and jests, by H. Bennet. 2 vols 1786.

Ancient Scotish poems never before in print, but now published from the ms collections of Sir R. Maitland: comprising pieces written from about 1420 till 1586, with large notes and a glossary; prefixed are an Essay on the origin of Scotish poetry, a list of all the Scotish poets; [and] an appendix is added containing an account of the contents of the Maitland and Bannatyne mss. 2 vols 1786.

A new tale of a tub. 1790.

Barbour, James, The Bruce: or the history of Robert I King of Scotland; in Scottish verse: the first genuine edition, published from a ms dated 1489, with notes and a glossary. 3 vols 1790.

Scotish poems, reprinted from scarce editions. 3 vols 1792.

Walpoliana. 2 vols [1799]. Rptd from Monthly Mag.

Miscellaneous Works

An essay on medals. 1784, 1789, 1808.

A dissertation on the origin and progress of the Scythians or Goths. 1787.

[A series of 12] letters to the people of Great Britain, on the cultivation of their national history. GM Feb (suppl) 1788.

An enquiry into the history of Scotland, preceding the year 1056. 2 vols 1789, 1795, 1814.

Vitae antiquae sanctorum qui habitaverunt in ea parte Britanniae nunc vocata Scotia, cum variis lectionibus et notis. 1789, 2 vols Paisley 1889 (rev and enlarged by W. M. Metcalfe).

The medallic history of England to the Revolution. 1790, 1802.

Iconographia scotica: or portraits of illustrious persons of Scotland, with short biographical notices. 1797.

The history of Scotland from the accession of the House of Stuart to that of Mary. 2 vols 1797.

The Scotish gallery: or portraits of eminent persons of Scotland, with brief accounts of the characters represented, and an introduction on the rise and progress of painting in Scotland. 1799.

An historical dissertation on the Gowrie conspiracy. In Malcolm Laing, History of Scotland, 2 vols 1800, 4 vols 1804.

Modern geography. 2 vols 1802, 3 vols 1807, 2 vols 1817; abridged 1803, 1806; tr French, 1811.

Critique on the Complaynt of Scotland. Critical Rev May 1802; rptd in Critiques by David Herd and others on the new edition of the Complaynt of Scotland, Edinburgh 1829.

Esquisse d'une nouvelle classification de minéralogie etc, traduit de l'anglais par H. J. Jansen. Paris 1803.

Recollections of Paris in the years 1802–5. 2 vols 1806.

A general collection of voyages and travels in all parts of the world. 17 vols 1807–14. Early Australian voyages rptd from Pinkerton in Cassell's Nat Lib, 1886.

Petralogy: a treatise on rocks. 2 vols 1811.

§2

[Ritson, J.] GM Nov 1784. Review of Scotish tragic ballads, exposing Pinkerton's forgeries.

Answer to an attack made by Pinkerton in his history of Scotland upon Mr W. Anderson: containing an account of the records of Scotland and many strange letters by Pinkerton. Edinburgh 1797.

A vindication of the Celts, with observations on Pinkerton's hypothesis concerning the origin of the European nations, in his modern geography, and dissertation on the Scythians. 1803.

Auction catalogue of his collection of books on geography, voyages, travels and belles-lettres etc also his valuable maps and charts. 1813.

Nichols, J. In his Literary illustrations vol 5, 1828.

Turner, D. The literary correspondence of Pinkerton, now first printed from the originals. 2 vols 1830.

Walpole's correspondence with Chatterton, Lort, Pinkerton [etc]. Ed W. S. Lewis, A. D. Wallace and R. M. Williams, New Haven 1952 (vol 16 of Yale edn of Walpole's correspondence).

ISAAC D'ISRAELI
1766–1848

§1

Works pbd before 1800 only. For later works see vol 3, below.

Specimens of a new version of Telemachus: to which is prefixed a defence of poetry. 1790, 1791.

Curiosities of literature: consisting of anecdotes, characters, sketches and observations, literary, critical and historical. 2 vols 1791–3 (2nd edn of vol 1, 1792), 1793, 1798. A 3rd vol was added in 1817, and a 2nd series appeared 3 vols 1823.

A dissertation on anecdotes. 1793; rptd with his Literary miscellanies, 1801.

Domestic anecdotes of the French nation, during the last thirty years, indicative of the French Revolution. 1794, 1800.

An essay on the manners and genius of the literary character. 1795.

Miscellanies: or literary recreations. 1796, 1801 (as Literary miscellanies, including a dissertation on anecdotes).

Vaurien: or sketches of the times. 2 vols 1797.

Film flams: or the life of my uncle. 1797.

Mejnoun and Leila: the Arabian Petrarch and Laura. 1797.

Romances. 1799, 1801, 1807.

§2

Samuel, W. S. D'Israeli: first published writings. N & Q 30 April 1949.

(3) MINOR SCHOLARS

Restricted to works of scholarship written before 1800. Cross-references have not been included to other sections, where fuller lists of the writings of many of these scholars will be found; see Index.

EDWARD BERNARD
1638–96

Etymologicon britannicum. Appended to G. Hickes, Institutiones grammaticae. Oxford 1689.

Catalogi librorum manuscriptorum Angliae et Hiberniae in unum collecti, cum indice alphabetico. Oxford 1697.

PATRICK HUME

§1

Annotations on Milton's Paradise lost. 1695.

§2

Oras, A. Milton's editors and commentators from Patrick Hume to H. J. Todd 1695–1801. 1931.

THOMAS RYMER
1641–1713

§1

The tragedies of the last age. 1678, 1692. For Dryden's replies, *see col 448, above.*

A short view of tragedy, its original, excellency and corruption, with some reflections on Shakespeare, and other practitioners for the stage. 1692. Selection rptd in Critical essays of the 17th century vol 2, ed J. E. Spingarn, Oxford 1908.

Critical works. Ed C. A. Zimansky, New Haven 1956.

§2

Walcott, F. G. Dryden's answer to Rymer's The tragedies of the last age. PQ 15 1936.

Stoll, E. E. Oedipus and Othello: Corneille, Rymer and Voltaire. Revue Anglo-américaine 12 1945.

Watson, G. Dryden's first answer to Rymer. RES new ser 14 1963. Reply by R. D. Hume 19 1968.

SIR THOMAS POPE BLOUNT
1649–97

Censura celebriorum authorum. 1690.

De re poetica: or remarks upon poetry, with characters and censures of the most considerable poets whether ancient or modern. 1694.

RICHARD BENTLEY
1662–1742

§ 1

Milton's Paradise lost: a new edition. 1732.
Milton restor'd and Bentley depos'd: containing i, Some observations on Dr Bentley's preface; ii, his various readings and notes on Paradise lost etc. 1732.
A review of the text of Milton's Paradise lost, in which the chief of Dr Bentley's emendations are consider'd etc. 1732, 1733.
A friendly letter to Dr Bentley, occasion'd by his new edition of Paradise lost etc. 1732, 1732.

§ 2

Pearce, Z. A review of the text of Paradise lost. 1733.
Jebb, R. C. Bentley. 1882 (EML).
Mackail, J. W. Bentley's Milton. Proc Br Acad 11 1924; rptd in his Studies in humanism, 1938.
Empson, W. Milton and Bentley. In his Some versions of pastoral, 1935.
Ricks, C. In his Milton's grand style, Oxford 1963.
Proc Leeds Philosophical & Literary Soc 10 1963. 3 commemorative lectures.
White, R. J. Dr Bentley: a study in academic scarlet. 1965.

JOHN DOWNES
1662–1710

Roscius Anglicanus: or an historical review of the stage. 1708; ed F. G. Waldron, with addns by Thomas Davies 1789, 1792 (in F. G. Waldron, Literary museum); ed J. Knight 1886 (facs); ed M. Summers 1928.

MYLES DAVIES
1662–1720

Athenae britannicae: or a critical history of the Oxford and Cambridge writers and writings, with other authors and worthies, both domestic and foreign, both ancient and modern. 6 vols 1716–19. Selections from vol 4, ed R. G. Thomas, Los Angeles 1962 (Augustan Reprint Soc).

CHARLES GILDON
1665–1724

§ 1

The lives and characters of the English dramatick poets; also an account of all the plays that were ever yet printed in the English tongue, first begun by Mr Langbaine, improv'd and continued. 1699. Anon.

§ 2

Maxwell, J. C. Gildon and the quarrel of the ancients and moderns. RES new ser 1 1950.

JONATHAN RICHARDSON the elder
1665–1745
and
JONATHAN RICHARDSON the younger
1694–1771

Explanatory notes and remarks on Milton's Paradise lost, by Jonathan Richardson father and son; with a life of the author and a discourse on the poem by Jonathan Richardson senior. 1734.

ROBERT STEPHENS
1665–1732

Bacon, Francis, Letters written during the reign of James I, now collected and augmented with several letters and memoires never before published, the whole being illustrated by an historical introduction and some observations. 2 vols 1702–34, 1736 (vol 1).

JOHN URRY
1666–1715
and
TIMOTHY THOMAS
1697–1757

§ 1

The works of Chaucer, compared with the former editions, and many valuable mss, out of which three tales are added which were never before printed, together with a glossary; to the whole is prefixed the author's life, newly written and a preface, giving an account of this edition. 1721. The glossary was by Thomas; the life by John Dart was corrected and enlarged by William Thomas, who also prepared the whole for the press; the life was rptd in 1741 in edn by George Ogle.

§ 2

Duncan, D. The Christ Church edition of Chaucer. In his Thomas Ruddiman, Edinburgh 1965, appendix 2.
Shugrue, M. The Urry Chaucer 1721 and the London uprising of 1384. JEGP 65 1966.

JOHN HARE
1668–1720

The posthumous works of Sir Thomas Browne; to which is prefix'd his life. 1712, 1723.

EDMUND GIBSON
1669–1748

§ 1

Polemo-middinia: carmen macaronicum, autore Gulielmo Drummundo; accedit Jacobi quinti, regis Scotorum, Cantilena rustica vulgo inscripta Crists Kirk on the Green. Oxford 1691. Signed E.G.

§ 2

Sykes, N. Gibson, Bishop of London: a study in politics and religion in the eighteenth century. Oxford 1926.

PIERRE DESMAIZEAUX
1673?–1745

An historical and critical account of the life and writings of Mr John Hales: being a specimen of an historical and critical English dictionary. 1719.
A collection of several pieces of Mr John Locke, never before printed, or not extant in his works. 1720, 1739.
An historical and critical account of the life and writings of William Chillingworth. 1725.
A collection of several pieces by John Toland, with some memoirs of his life and writings. 2 vols 1726, 1747.
Life of Pierre Bayle. 1734. In vol 1 of the trn of Bayle's Dictionary, 5 vols 1734–8.

Desmaizeaux was also a frequent contributor to French pbns, and pbd several trans as well as some works on the classics. Anecdotes about him appear in GM suppl 1774, and in I. D'Israeli, Curiosities of literature vol 3, 1817.

JAMES UPTON
1670–1749

Ascham, Roger, The schoolmaster: or a plain and perfect way of teaching children to understand, write and speak the Latin tongue, corrected and revis'd with an addition of explanatory notes. 1711, 1743, 1761 (in James Bennet's edn of Ascham's English works).
Remarks on three plays of Benjamin Jonson, viz Volpone, Epicoene and the Alchemist. 1749.

WILLIAM ELSTOB
1673–1715

Rogeri Aschami epistolarum libri quattuor; accedunt Jo Sturmii aliorumque ad Aschamum Anglosque alios eruditos epistolarum liber unus: editio novissima, prioribus auctior, Oxford 1703. Contains a life of Ascham by Edward Grant.

NICHOLAS ROWE
1674–1718
§1

The works of Mr William Shakespear, revis'd and corrected, with an account of the life and writings of the author. 6 vols 1709 (a 7th vol including the poems and critical essays, by Charles Gildon, followed in 1710, rptd in 1714 edn), 1710, 9 vols 1714. Life of Shakespeare rptd in Pope's version in most 18th-century edns of Shakespeare; the original version rptd in 18th-century essays on Shakespeare, ed D. Nichol Smith, Glasgow 1903; in Materials for the life of Shakespeare, ed P. Butler, Chapel Hill 1930, and ed S. H. Monk, Los Angeles 1948 (Augustan Reprint Soc).

§2

Jackson, A. Rowe's edition of Shakespeare. Library 3rd ser 10 1930.
Wagenknecht, E. The first editor of Shakespeare. Colophon 8 1931.
Summers, M. The first illustrated Shakespeare. Connoisseur 102 1938.

THOMAS RUDDIMAN
1674–1757
§1

Virgil's Aeneis, translated into Scottish verse by the famous Gawin Douglas Bishop of Dunkeld. Edinburgh 1710. Ed Ruddiman, who compiled the glossary; contains a Life of Douglas by Bishop John Sage.
The works of William Drummond of Hawthornden: consisting of those which were formerly printed, and those which were design'd for the press, now published from the author's original copies. Edinburgh 1711. Ed Ruddiman, with an introd and life of Drummond by Bishop Sage.
Buchanan, George, Opera omnia, curante Thoma Ruddimanno. 2 vols Edinburgh 1715, Leyden 1725 (cum indicibus rerum memorabilium, et praefatione Petri Burmanni).
—— Paraphrasis Psalmorum Davidis poetica, ex optimis

codicibus summo studio recognita et castigata a Thoma Ruddimanno; praemissa est accuratior quam antehac carminum explicatio; accessere duae ejusdem Geo Buchanini tragoediae Jephthes et Baptistes. Edinburgh 1716. *See also col 2068, below.*

§2

Chalmers, G. Life of Ruddiman. 1794.
Duncan, D. Thomas Ruddiman. Edinburgh 1965.

JOHN LEWIS
1675–1747

The history of the life and sufferings of John Wicliffe, with a collection of papers relating to the said history, never before printed. 1720, 1723.
The life and death of Sir Thomas Moore by William Roper; to which are added from Sir Thomas's English works some letters of his etc. 1729, 1731.
The life of Mayster Wyllyam Caxton, of the Weald of Kent. 1737; rptd in part in T. F. Dibdin's edn of Joseph Ames, Typographical antiquities vol 1, 1810.
A complete history of the several translations of the Bible. Prefixed to 1731 edn of Wyclif's trn of the New Testament; 1739 (separately).

GEORGE SEWELL
1690?–1726

Poems of Henry Howard, the Earl of Surrey, with the poems of Sir Thomas Wiat, and others his famous contemporaries; to which are added some memoirs of his life and writings. 1717.
Venus and Adonis, Tarquin and Lucrece, Miscellany poems, Essay on the stage, glossary and remarks on the plays. In Pope's edn of Shakespeare vol 7, 1725, vol 8, Dublin 1726, vol 10, 1728.

SIR THOMAS HANMER
1677–1746
§1

Some remarks on the tragedy of Hamlet, Prince of Denmark, written by Mr William Shakespeare. 1736; ed C. D. Thorpe, Los Angeles 1947 (Augustan Reprint Soc). Evidence against attributing this to Hanmer is provided by C. D. Thorpe, MLN 49 1934.
The works of Shakespear, carefully revised and corrected. Oxford 6 vols 1743–4, 1744–6, London 1745, 9 vols 1747, 1748, 1750–1, 1760; ed T. Hawkins 6 vols Oxford 1770–1.

§2

Remarks upon a late edition of Shakespeare, to which is prefixed a defence of Hanmer. [1747].
[Nichols, P.] The castrated letter of Hanmer in the 6th vol of Biographia britannica. 1763. Exposes Warburton's treatment of Hanmer.
Bunbury, H. Correspondence of Hanmer, with a memoir. 1838.
Dawson, G. E. Warburton, Hanmer and the 1745 edition of Shakespeare. SB 2 1950.

JOHN HUGHES
1677–1720
§1

The works of Spenser, to which is prefixed the life of the author and an essay on allegorical poetry; also remarks

on the Faerie Queene, the Shepherd's Calendar and the other writings of Spenser. 6 vols 1715, 1750. With glossary.
Shakespeare, William, Hamlet. 1718, 1723. Ed Hughes. *See* H. N. Paul, MLN 49 1934.

§2

Heffner, R. The printing of Hughes edition of Spenser 1715. MLN 50 1935. *See also col 552, above.*

THOMAS HEARNE
1678–1735

§1

Robert of Gloucester's Chronicle. 2 vols Oxford 1724. With a glossary and some remarks on Chaucer and his writings, vol 2 pp. 596–606.
Peter Langtoft's Chronicle (as illustrated and improv'd by Robert of Brunne) from the death of Cadwalader to the end of K. Edward the First's reign, transcribed and now first publish'd, from a ms in the Inner-Temple Library. 2 vols Oxford 1725, 1810. Vol 2 has a ME glossary.

§2

Douglas, D. C. In his English scholars 1660–1730, 1939, 1951 (rev).
Philip, I. G. Hearne as publisher. Bodleian Lib Record 3 1951. *See also col 1699, above.*

JOHN DART
d. 1730

See John Urry, above.

JOHN BLACKBOURNE
1683–1741

Bale, John. A brefe chronycle concerning Syr John Oldecastell. 1729. Ed Blackbourne.
Bacon, Francis, Opera omnia. 4 vols 1730.

ELIJAH FENTON
1683–1730

§1

Paradise lost: a poem written in twelve books by John Milton, 12th edn; to which is prefix'd an account of his life, 1725. With note on Milton's verse, and full index, with occasional textual notes; Fenton's life was frequently rptd.
Waller, Edmund, Works in verse and prose, published by Mr Fenton. 1729, 1730, 1744, 1752, 1772. With 88 pp. of Observations.

§2

Lloyd, W. W. Fenton: his poetry and friends. 1894. *See also col 548, above.*

ALEXANDER POPE
1688–1744

§1

The works of Shakespeare, collated and corrected. 6 vols 1725 (7th vol of poems ed George Sewell, above, 1725), 8 vols Dublin 1726, 10 vols Dublin 1728, 9 vols 1728 (vol 9 contains Pericles and the spurious plays), 10 vols 1728 (vol 10 Poems), 9 vols 1731 (plays only), 8 vols 1734–6 (plays only), 9 vols 1635 (for 1735), 16 vols Glasgow 1752–7, 8 vols Glasgow 1766, 9 vols Birmingham 1768.
Shakespeare, William, The tempest, collated and corrected by the former editions by Mr Pope. Dublin 1725.
Scheme for a history of English poetry. In O. Ruffhead, Life of Pope, 1769.

§2

Theobald, L. Shakespeare restored. 1726, 1740.
[Roberts, J.] An answer to Mr Pope's preface [to his edn of Shakespeare]. 1729.
Lounsbury, R. T. The first editors of Shakespeare (Pope and Theobald). 1906.
Schmidt, H. Die Shakespeare-Ausgabe von Pope. Giessen 1912.
Butt, J. Pope's taste in Shakespeare. Oxford 1936.
Dixon, P. Pope's Shakespeare. JEGP 63 1964.
— Edward Bysshe and Pope's Shakespear. N & Q Aug 1964.

THOMAS COXETER
1689–1747

§1

Bayly, T., The life and death of John Fisher, Bishop of Rochester, 1739. The real author was Richard Hall; ed Coxeter.
A verbal index to Milton's Paradise lost, adapted to every edition but the first, which was publish'd in ten books only. 1741.
The dramatic works of Philip Massinger, revised by Thomas Coxeter, with notes critical and explanatory, of various authors; to which are prefixed critical reflections on the old English dramatic writers [by George Colman the elder]. 4 vols 1761.
Coxeter's mss were used by Shiels in preparing the lives of the poets 1753; by David Erskine Baker in his companion to the Playhouse, 1764, and by Thomas Warton for his History of English poetry.

§2

A catalogue of the libraries of several gentlemen [including] Coxeter to be sold at T. Osborne's in Gray's Inn. 1748.
Nichols, J. In his Literary anecdotes vol 2, 1812.

ZACHARY PEARCE
1690–1774

A review of the text of the 12 books of Milton's Paradise lost, in which the chief of Dr Bentley's emendations are considered, and several other emendations and observations are offer'd to the public. 1732, 1733.

WILLIAM MASSEY
1691–1764?

Remarks upon Milton's Paradise lost, historical, geographical, critical and explanatory. 1761.

FRANCIS PECK
1692–1743

New memoirs of the life and poetical works of John Milton, with an examination of Milton's stile and explanatory and critical notes on divers passages of Milton and Shakespeare. 1740.

JOHN LOCKER
1693–1760

Letters and remains of the Lord Chancellor Bacon, collected by Robert Stephens. 1734. Vol 2 of Stephens' collection, above.

PETER SHAW
1694–1763

The philosophical works of Francis Bacon, methodized and made English from the originals with occasional notes. 3 vols 1733, 1737.

RICHARD MEADOWCOURT
1695–1760

A critique on Milton's Paradise regained. 1732.
An essay upon Milton's imitations of the ancients in his Paradise lost, with some observations on the Paradise regained. 1741, 1748 (as A critical dissertation, with notes, on Milton's Paradise regain'd: second edition corrected).

DAVID CASLEY
d. 1755

Mandeville, Sir John, Voyages and travels, published entire from an original ms in the Cotton Library. 1725, 1727. Ed Casley.
A catalogue of the manuscripts of the King's Library, an appendix to the catalogue of the Cottonian library; together with an account of books burnt or damaged by a late fire: one hundred and fifty specimens of the manner of writing in different ages, from the third to the fifteenth century, in copper-plates, and some observations upon mss in a preface. 1734.
A catalogue of the Harleian collection of manuscripts. 2 vols 1759 (preface dated 24 Dec 1762), 4 vols 1808–12. Casley catalogued nos 2408–5797 (erroneously given as '2408–5709' in editors' preface to 1808–12 edn).

TIMOTHY THOMAS
1697–1757
See John Urry, above.

WILLIAM WARBURTON
1698–1779

§1

The works of Shakespear: the genuine text (collated with all the former editions and then corrected and emended), with a comment and notes, by Pope and Warburton. 8 vols 1747, Dublin 1747 (plays only).
Warburton also contributed notes to Theobald's edn of Shakespeare and Zachary Grey's edn of Hudibras, and a dissertation on the origin of books of chivalry to C. Jervas' trn of Don Quixote, 2 vols 1742.

§2

Grey, Z. Remarks upon a late edition of Shakespeare. [1747].
Edwards, T. Supplement to Warburton's edition of Shakespeare: being the canons of criticism. 1747 etc.
Cooper, J. G. Cursory remarks on Warburton's edition of Pope's works. 1751.
Evans, A. W. Warburton and the Warburtonians. Oxford 1932.

Dawson, G. E. Warburton, Hanmer and the 1745 edition of Shakespeare. SB 2 1950.
Sherbo, A. Warburton and the 1745 Shakespeare. JEGP 51 1952.
—— Dr Johnson's Dictionary and Warburton's Shakespeare. PQ 33 1954.

THOMAS EDWARDS
1699–1757

§1

A supplement to Mr Warburton's edition of Shakespear: being the Canons of criticism and glossary. 1747, 1747, 1748, 1750, 1750, 1753 (rev by Edwards and Richard Roderick as The canons of criticism), 1753, 1758 (with Roderick's Remarks on Shakespeare), 1765.

§2

Wurstbaugh, J. Edwards and the editorship of the Faerie Queene. MLN 50 1935.

CHARLES JENNENS
1700–73

King Lear: a tragedy, collated with the old and modern editions. 1770.
The tragedy of King Lear as lately published, vindicated from the abuse of the critical reviewers [especially Steevens]. 1772.
Macbeth: a tragedy, collated with the old and modern editions. 1773.
Hamlet, Prince of Denmark: a tragedy, collated with the old and modern editions. 1773.
Othello, the moor of Venice: a tragedy, collated with the old and modern editions. 1773.
Julius Caesar: a tragedy, collated with the old and modern editions. 1774.

THOMAS COOKE
1703–56

The works of Andrew Marvell, to which is prefixed an account of the life and writings of the author by Mr Cooke. 2 vols 1726, 1772.

ROBERT DODSLEY
1703–64

§1

A select collection of old plays. 12 vols 1744; ed I. Reed 12 vols 1780; ed J. P. Collier 12 vols 1825–7; ed W. C. Hazlitt 15 vols 1874–6.

§2

Straus, R. Dodsley: poet, publisher and playwright. 1910.

JOHN ENTICK
1703?–73

Proposals for printing by subscription the works of Chaucer with notes [etc]. [1736].

RICHARD RODERICK
d. 1756

Remarks on Shakespear. In Thomas Edwards, Canons of criticism, 1758, 1765.

JOHN HAWKEY
1703–59

Paradise lost, edited by Hawkey. Dublin 1747.
Paradise regained, with the other poetical works, revised by Hawkey. Dublin 1752.

THOMAS MORELL
1703–84

Chaucer, Geoffrey, Canterbury Tales in the original, from the most authentic manuscripts, and as they are turn'd into modern language by Dryden, Pope and other hands. 1737.
Notes and annotations on Locke on the human understanding, written by order of the Queen, corresponding in section and page with the edition of 1793. 1794.

FERDINANDO WARNER
1703–68

Memoirs of the life of Sir Thomas More; to which is added his history of Utopia, translated into English, with notes historical and explanatory. 1758.

THOMAS BROUGHTON
1704–74

Original poems and translations by Dryden, now first collected and published together. 2 vols 1743. Ed Broughton.
Broughton wrote the lives marked 'T.' in Biographia britannica vols 1–3, 1747–50.

MOSES BROWNE
1704–87
§1

The compleat angler: or contemplative man's recreation, in two parts by Izaac Walton and Charles Cotton, published with notes by Moses Browne. 1750, 1759, 1772.

§2

Wasserman, E. R. Browne and the 1783 edition of Giles and Phineas Fletcher. MLN 56 1941.

BENJAMIN HEATH
1704–66

A revisal of Shakespeare's text, wherein the alterations introduced into it by the more modern editors and critics are particularly considered. 1765.

THOMAS NEWTON
1704–82

Paradise lost: new edition, with notes of various authors. 2 vols 1749, 1750, 1754, 1 vol Birmingham 1758 (text only), 1758, 1759, 2 vols 1760, 1763, 1770, 1777 (with Fenton's life of Milton), 1778, 1790, 3 vols 1795, 2 vols 1796 (with Johnson's criticism).
Paradise regain'd, to which is added Samson Agonistes and poems upon several occasions: new edition with notes. 2 vols 1752, 1753, 1760, 1766, 1 vol 1773, 1777, 2 vols 1785.

FRANCIS BLACKBURNE
1705–87

Remarks on Johnson's life of Milton; to which are added Milton's Tractate of education and Areopagitica. 1780.

DAVID MALLET,
originally MALLOCH
1705?–65
§1

The life of Francis Bacon, Lord Chancellor of England. 1740 (separately, and with Birch's edn of Bacon's works), 1740 etc.

§2

Boys, R. C. Malloch and the Edinburgh miscellany. MLN 54 1939.

JAMES PATERSON

A complete commentary, with etymological, explanatory, critical and classical notes on Milton's Paradise lost; explaining all the Hebrew, Arabic, Saxon, Norman, American and Miltonian words. 1744. Notes included in edn of Paradise lost, 2 vols 1751, 1752.

GEORGE SMITH GREEN
d. 1762

The state of innocence and fall of man [i.e. Paradise lost, in prose] with notes, from [N. F. Dupré] de St Maur. 1745, 1755, 1767, 1770, Aberdeen 1770.

JOHN HOLT

An attempte to rescue that aunciente English poet and playwrighte maister Williaume Shakespere from the maney errours faulsely charged on him by certaine new-fangled wittes. 1749, 1750 (as Remarks on the Tempest).

ROBERT THYER
1709–81

The genuine remains of Samuel Butler, author of Hudibras, published from the original mss with notes. 2 vols 1759.

EDWARD JACOB
1710–88

The lamentable and true tragedy of M. Arden of Feversham, in Kent, with a preface, in which some reasons are offered, in favour of its being the earliest dramatic work of Shakespear now remaining. Faversham 1770.

DAVID HUME
1711–76
§1

History of Great Britain. Edinburgh 1754. Ch 6 on the reign of James I has a section (pp. 136–41) on learning and the arts.

§2

Mossner, E. C. An historical essay on chivalry and modern honour (by Hume). MP 45 1947.
Brunius, T. Hume on criticism. Stockholm 1952. *See also col 1873, below.*

THOMAS HAYWARD
d. 1779?

The British Muse: or a collection of thoughts of our
English poets who flourished in the 16th and 17th
centuries. 3 vols 1738, 1740 (as The quintessence of
English poetry). Preface and dedication by William
Oldys.

WILLIAM TYTLER
1711–92

Poetical remains of James the First, King of Scotland.
Edinburgh 1783. With notes, a dissertation on the life
and writings of James I and a dissertation on Scottish
music.

THOMAS DAVIES
1712?–85

The works of William Browne, with the life of the author
(and a glossary). 3 vols 1772.
Lives of Elias Ashmole and William Lilly, written by
themselves. 1774. Ed Davies.
Works of John Eachard, with a life of the author.
1774.
A short essay on the life and writings of Philip Massinger.
1779 (in J. M. Mason's edn of Massinger's Dramatic
works), 1789.
Dramatic miscellanies: consisting of critical observations
on several plays of Shakespeare. 3 vols 1783–4, Dublin
1784, London 1785.

JOHN GILLIES
1712–96

Milton's Paradise lost illustrated with texts of scripture,
by John Gillies. 1788, 1793 (with addns), 1804.

RICHARD WARNER
1713–75

A letter to David Garrick esq concerning a glossary to the
plays of Shakespeare, with a specimen. 1768.

JOSEPH GROVE
d. 1764

The life of Henry 8 by Shakespeare, in which are interspersed historical notes never before published. 1758.

RICHARD BARRON
d. 1766

Milton, John, Eikonoclastes, now first published from the
second edition, printed in 1650; with many enlargements, with a preface and an original letter to Milton,
never before published. 1756, 1770, 1806. Barron also
assisted Thomas Birch in his 2nd edn of Milton's prose
works, 1753.

WILLIAM RUFUS CHETWOOD
d. 1766

A general history of the stage. 1749.
Memoirs of the life and writings of Ben Jonson, with an
abstract of the lives of Somerset and Buckingham; to
which are added two comedies the Widow and Eastward
Hoe. Dublin 1756.

THOMAS GRAY
1716–71

§1

Copy of an original letter from Gray to T. Warton on the
History of English poetry, communicated by a gentleman of Oxford. GM Feb 1783. Outlining Gray's own
scheme.
Matthias, T. J. Works of Gray. 2 vols 1814. Prints
extracts from Gray's commonplace book.
Martin, R. Chronologie de la vie et de l'oeuvre de Gray.
Toulouse 1931. Prints extracts from Gray's common-
place book.

§2

Kittredge, G. L. Gray's knowledge of Old Norse. In
Selections from Gray, ed W. P. Phelps, Boston 1894.
Snyder, E. D. Gray's interest in Celtic. MP 11 1914.
—— In his Celtic revival in English literature 1760–1800,
Cambridge Mass 1923.
Toynbee, P. Gray on the origin and date of Amadis de
Gaul. MLR 27 1932.
Jones, W. P. Books owned by Gray. TLS 1 June 1933.
—— Gray, scholar. Cambridge Mass 1937.
—— Gray's library. MP 35 1938.

HUGH BLAIR
1718–1800

§1

The works of Shakespear, in which the beauties observed
by Pope, Warburton and Dodd are pointed out. 8 vols
Edinburgh 1753, London 1753, Edinburgh 1761, 1769,
1769, 1771, London [1771?] (plays only).
A critical dissertation on the poems of Ossian. 1763, 1765,
etc.

§2

Chapman, R. W. Blair on Ossian. RES 7 1931.
Scott, W. R. A manuscript criticism of the wealth
of nations in 1776 by Blair. Economic History 3
1938.
Mays, M. J. Johnson and Blair on Addison's prose style.
SP 39 1942.
Schmitz, R. M. Hugh Blair. New York 1948.
Golden, J. L. Blair, Minister of St Giles. Quart Jnl of
Speech 38 1952.

FRANCIS FAWKES
1720–77

Douglas, Gavin, A description of May. 1752 (3 edns).
With a modern version, some account of the author and
a glossary.
A description of winter [modernized] from Douglas by
Fawkes. 1754. With original.

RICHARD HURD
1720–1808

§1

Letters on chivalry and romance. 1762; rptd and expanded
in Moral and political dialogues, 3 vols 1765; ed E. J.
Morley 1911; ed H. Trowbridge, Los Angeles 1963
(Augustan Reprint Soc). Letters 8–12 rptd in vol 2 of
Todd's edn of Spenser 1805.
Moral and political dialogues. 1759, 1760, 3 vols 1765,
1771, 1776, 1788.

Select works of Cowley. 2 vols 1772, 1772, 1777.
Hurd left material for the annotated edn of Addison 6 vols 1811.

§2

Kilvert, F. Memoirs of Hurd. 1860.
Peace, E. H. and L. Whibley. Correspondence of Hurd and William Mason and letters of Hurd to Thomas Gray. Cambridge 1932.
Correspondence between Thomas Warton and Hurd. Bodleian Quart Record 6 1932.
Hamm, V. M. A 17th-century French source for Hurd's letters on chivalry and romance. PMLA 52 1937.
Smith, A. L. Hurd's letters on chivalry and romance. ELH 6 1939.
Montague, E. Hurd's association with Thomas Warton. Stanford Stud in Lang & Lit 1941.
Trowbridge, H. Hurd: a reinterpretation. PMLA 58 1943.
Nankivell, J. Extracts from the destroyed letters of Hurd to William Mason. MLR 45 1950.
Johnston, A. In his Enchanted ground, 1964.

CHARLOTTE LENNOX
1720–1804

§1

Shakespear illustrated: or the novels and histories on which the plays of Shakespear are founded, corrected and translated from the original authors, with critical remarks. 3 vols 1753–4. With Dr Johnson.

§2

Small, R. Charlotte Ramsay Lennox. New Haven 1935.

ROBERT MORISON
1722–91

Douglas, Gavin, Select works: containing memoirs of the author, the palice of honour, prologues to the Aeneid and a glossary of obsolete words; to which is added an old poem, author unknown. Perth 1787. Ed Morison?

JAMES BENNET

§1

The English works of Ascham, with notes, observations and the author's life. 1761, 1767. The life etc are by Dr Johnson; James Upton's notes to Schoolmaster are rptd from the 2nd edn; Life rptd 1815 with Ascham's works.

§2

C[hapman], R. W. Bennet's Ascham. RES 5 1929.

JOSEPH WARTON
1722–1800

§1

The adventurer. Nos 93, 97, 113, 116, 122. 2 vols 1752–4. Remarks on Tempest and King Lear.
Sidney, Sir Philip, Defense of poesie. 1787.
The works of Pope. 9 vols 1797. Warton also contributed to John Nichols, Select collection of poems, 8 vols 1780–2 and notes to Nichols' edn of Swift, as well as to the 1811 edn of Dryden ed Todd.

§2

Wooll, J. Biographical memoir of Joseph Warton. 1806.
MacClintock, W. D. Joseph Warton's essay on Pope: a history of the five editions. Chapel Hill 1933.
Scheffer, J. D. A note on Joseph Warton and Voltaire. Bull of Citadel 7 1940.
Kinsley, J. A note on the publication of Warton's essay on Pope. MLR 44 1949.
Allison, J. Warton's reply to Dr Johnson's lives. JEGP 51 1952.
Schick, G. B. Warton's critical essays in his Virgil. N & Q July 1961.

PETER WHALLEY
1722–91

An enquiry into the learning of Shakespeare, with remarks on several passages of his plays. 1748.
The works of Ben Jonson, collated with all the former editions, with notes by Whalley. 7 vols 1756. Dramatic works rptd 1811 with Beaumont and Fletcher.

SAMUEL DERRICK
1724–69

The miscellaneous works of Dryden: containing all his original poems, tales and translations, with notes and observations; also an account of his life and writings, 4 vols 1760, 1767 (omitting the life and most of the notes).

JOHN BOWLE
1725–88

Miscellaneous pieces of antient English poesie: viz The troublesome raigne of King John, written by Shakespeare, extant in no edition of his writings; The metamorphosis of Pigmalion's image and certain satyres by John Marston; The scourge of villanie by the same, all printed before the year 1600. 1764. Anon.
Reflections on originality in authors. 1766. Anon.

TREADWAY RUSSELL NASH
1725–1811

Butler, Samuel, Hudibras. 3 vols 1793, 2 vols 1835–40, 1847. With notes by Nash.

JOHN WOOD

Milton, John, Paradise lost: a new edition; to which is added historical, philosophical and explanatory notes, translated from the French of Raymond de St Maur, with critical remarks and observations from Addison, Warburton etc. 2 vols Edinburgh 1765. Ed Wood and preceded by Fenton's life of Milton.

SIR DAVID DALRYMPLE,
LORD HAILES
1726–92

§1

Ancient Scottish poems, published from the ms of George Bannatyne 1568. Edinburgh 1770, London 1770. Ed Dalrymple.
Sketch of the life of John Barclay, author of Argenis. [Edinburgh 1786].
Horace Walpole's correspondence with Dalrymple. Ed W. S. Lewis et al, New Haven 1952.
Correspondence of Thomas Percy and Dalrymple. Ed A. F. Falconer, Baton Rouge 1954.

Campbell, J. J. Dalrymple's ballad work. PQ 29 1950.

THOMAS WILKES
d. 1786

Letters to and from Swift 1703–43, with notes by Thomas
 Birch, John Hawkesworth and Wilkes. 3 vols 1767.
 Vols 14–16 of the works of Swift, Dublin 1738–67.
Life of George Farquhar. In Works of Farquhar, 3 vols
 Dublin 1775.

WILLIAM DODD
1729–77

The beauties of Shakespear, regularly selected from each
 play, by William Dodd, illustrated with explanatory
 notes, and similar passages from antient and modern
 authors. 1752, 2 vols 1757 (with addns), Dublin 1773,
 3 vols 1780.
A familiar explanation of the works of Milton. 1762.

THOMAS HAWKINS
1729–72

The origin of the English drama, illustrated in its various
 species by specimens from our earliest writers, with
 notes by Hawkins. 3 vols Oxford 1773.
Hawkins also edited the 2nd edn of Hanmer's Shakespeare,
 6 vols Oxford 1770–1.

GEORGE COLMAN the elder
1732–94

§1

Critical reflections on the old English dramatick writers,
 intended as a preface to the works of Massinger,
 addressed to David Garrick. 1761; rptd in J. M.
 Mason's edn of Massinger, 1779.
The dramatic works of Beaumont and Fletcher, collated
 with all the former editions and corrected; with notes
 critical and explanatory by various commentators. 10
 vols 1778; rptd 1811, with Jonson's dramatic works from
 Whalley's edn.

§2

Page, E. R. George Colman the elder. New York 1935.

JAMES BUCHANAN

The first six books of Paradise lost, rendered into grammatical construction. Edinburgh 1773.

JOHN NEWTON
1725–1807

Bunyan, John, The pilgrim's progress. 1776, 1782, 1789,
 1797. With a preface and notes by Newton et al.

RALPH CHURCH
1708–87

§1

Spenser, Edmund, The Faerie Queene: new edition with
 notes critical and explanatory by Ralph Church. 4 vols
 1758–9. With a glossary and some account of the life
 and writings of Spenser.

Wurstbaugh, J. The 1758 editions of the Faerie Queene.
 MLN 48 1933.

JOHN CALLANDER
d. 1789

Milton's Paradise lost. Glasgow 1750. Bk 1 with com-
 mentary by Callander.
Two ancient Scottish poems; the Gaberlunzieman and
 Christ's Kirk on the green, with notes and observations
 by Callander. Edinburgh 1782.
Letters from T. Percy, J. Callander etc to G. Paton.
 Edinburgh 1830.

WILLIAM MASON (of Rotherhithe)

Bunyan, John, The pilgrim's progress; to which are now
 added notes. 1778, [1790?], 1799.
—— The holy war; with notes. 1782, 1795 (with notes
 attributed to S. Adams).

JOSEPH RANN
1733–1811

The dramatic works of Shakespeare with notes by Rann.
 6 vols Oxford 1786–91 and nd (vols 1–4 pbd by Clarendon Press, vols 5–6 'published at Oxford: sold by J.
 Cooke', nd).

JAMES BEATTIE
1735–1803

§1

Dissertations moral and critical [on fable and romance,
 pp. 501–74, is an historical sketch of fiction]. 1783,
 2 vols Dublin 1783, London 1786.
Beattie's London diary 1773. Ed R. S. Walker, Aberdeen
 1946.
Beattie's day book 1773–98. Ed R. S. Walker, Aberdeen
 1948.

§2

Forbes, W. Life and writings of Beattie. 1807, 1824.
Forbes, M. Beattie and his friends. 1904.
Mossner, E. C. Beattie's The Castle of scepticism: an
 unpublished allegory against Hume, Voltaire and Hobbes.
 SE 27 1948.
Tave, S. M. Some essays by Beattie in the London Maga-
 zine 1771. N & Q 6 Dec 1952.

GEORGE MASON
1735–1806

§1

Hoccleve, Thomas, Poems selected from a ms in the
 possession of Mason, with a preface, notes and glossary.
 1796. Ed Mason.

§2

Nichols, J. In his Illustrations vol 4, 1822. Correspondence with William Herbert and Samuel Pegge.

PERCIVAL STOCKDALE
1736–1811

The poems of Edmund Waller, to which is prefixed the life
 of the author by Stockdale. 1772.

Thomson, James, The seasons, with life, glossary and notes by P.S. 1793, 1794.

ALEXANDER DALRYMPLE
1737–1808

Extracts from juvenilia: or poems by George Withers. 1785.

THOMAS ZOUCH
1737–1815

Walton, Izaak, Love and truth, in two modest and peaceable letters concerning the distempers of the present times; written from a quiet and conformable citizen of London to two busie and factious shopkeepers in Coventry: a new edition, with notes and a preface. York 1795. Also added to Zouch's edn of Walton's Lives, 1817.
—The lives of Dr John Donne; Sir Henry Wotton; Mr Richard Hooker; Mr George Herbert; and Dr Robert Sanderson, with notes and the life of the author. York 1796, 2 vols Oxford 1805, York 1807, 1817 (contains Zouch's edn of Walton's Love and truth), New York 1846–8, Boston 1860. Life of Walton separately pbd 1823, 1825.
Memoir of Sir Philip Sidney. York 1808, 1809.

EDWARD THOMPSON
1736–86

The compositions in prose and verse of John Oldham, to which are added memoirs of his life and explanatory notes upon some obscure passages of his writings. 3 vols 1770.
The works of Marvell, with a new life of the author. 3 vols 1776. See GM Aug-Sept, Dec 1776, Feb 1777.

GEORGE CHALMERS
1742–1825

§ 1

Life of Defoe. 1785, 1786, 1790.
Life of Thomas Ruddiman. 1794.
An apology for the believers in the Shakspear-papers which were exhibited in Norfolk-street. 1797.
A supplemental apology for the believers in the Shakspeare-papers. 1799. Contains section on the chronology of Shakspeare's dramas.
Ramsay, Allan, Poems, with a life. 1800, 1851.
Lyndsay, David, Poetical works, with a life. 1806.
Another account of the incidents from which the title and part of the story of Shakspeare's Tempest was derived. 1815. A reply to Malone.
Henryson, Robert, Robene and Makyne and the Testament of Cresseid. 1824. Ed Chalmers.

§ 2

Cockroft, G. A. The public life of Chalmers, with bibliography. New York 1939.

FRANCIS GODOLPHIN WALDRON
1744–1818

Jonson, Ben, The sad shepherd, or a tale of Robin Hood: a fragment; with a continuation, notes and an appendix. 1783 (with notes of P. Walley); ed W. W. Greg 1905.

Downes, John, Roscius Anglicanus, with additions by Thomas Davies. 1789. Ed Waldron; rptd in his Literary museum, 1792.
The literary museum: comprising scarce and curious tracts. 1792.
Harding, Silvester, The biographical mirrour. 3 vols 1795–8. Engravings by Harding; many lives said to be by Waldron.
Free reflections on miscellaneous papers and legal instruments under the hand and seal of Shakspeare in the possession of Sam Ireland; to which are added extracts from an unpublished ms play called the Virgin queen, written by or in imitation of Shakspeare. 1796.
Chaucer, Geoffrey, The loves of Troilus and Creseid, with a commentary by Sir Francis Kinaston. 1796. Specimen extracts from Kynaston's edn; ed Waldron.
A compendious history of the English stage. 1800. Ed Waldron.
The Shakespearian miscellany: a collection of rare tracts. 1802.
L. T. Rosalynde; Euphues golden legacie, edited with notes. 1802.
An account of Waldron appears in GM March 1818.

ROBERT ALVES
1745–94

Sketches of a history of literature. Edinburgh 1794.

SAMUEL AYSCOUGH
1745–1804

Index of the remarkable passages and words made use of by Shakespeare. 1790, Dublin 1791, London 1827.
Ayscough compiled a catalogue of mss in BM, 2 vols 1782, and with P. H. Maty and S. Harper a catalogue of books in BM, 1787.

CHARLES DIBDIN the elder
1745–1814

A complete history of the English stage. 5 vols [1800].

WILLIAM HAYLEY
1745–1820

§ 1

The poetical works of Milton, with a life of the author. 3 vols 1794–7.
The life of Milton in three parts; to which are added conjectures on the origin of Paradise lost. 1796, Dublin 1797, Basle 1799, 1810. Appendix contains extracts from the Adamo of Andreini etc.

§ 2

Le Viness, W. T. The life and works of Hayley. Santa Fé, New Mexico 1945.
Bishop, E. M. Blake's Hayley. 1951.

JOHN JORDAN
1746–1809

Original collections on Shakespeare and Stratford. Ed J. O. Halliwell [-Phillipps] 1864. Written c. 1780.
Original memoirs and historical accounts of the families of Shakespeare and Hart. Ed J. O. Halliwell [-Phillipps] 1865.
A pedigree of the family of Shakespeare. 1796.
Original letters (on Shakespeare) from E. Malone to JJ. 1864.

ANDREW BECKET

A concordance to Shakespeare. 1787.
Shakespeare's himself again: an examen of the readings of
several editors. 2 vols 1815.

SAMUEL FELTON

Imperfect hints toward a new edition of Shakespeare. 2
pts 1787–8.

THOMAS SCOTT
1747–1821

Bunyan, John, The pilgrim's progress, with notes and the
life of the author by Thomas Scott. 1795, 1801, 1811
etc.

ALEXANDER FRASER TYTLER, LORD WOODHOUSELEE
1747–1813

Fletcher, Phineas, Piscatory eclogues, with other poetical
miscellanies, illustrated with notes. Edinburgh 1771.
—— The purple island, or the isle of man: an allegorical
poem; to which is added Christ's victory and triumph
by Giles Fletcher: new edition, corrected, with additional notes by the editor. 1783. Ed Tytler?

PHILIP NEVE

Cursory remarks on some of the ancient English poets,
particularly Milton. 1789 (priv ptd).

JOHN BRADFORD
1750–1805

Bunyan, John, The pilgrim's progress, with notes. 1792.

CHARLES DUNSTER
1750–1816

Philips, John, Cyder: a poem with notes provincial,
historical and classical. 1791.
Milton, John, Paradise regained: a new edition, with notes
of various authors. 1795, 1800.
Considerations on Milton's early reading and the Prima
Stamina of his Paradise lost. 1800.
*Dunster assisted H. J. Todd with his edn of Milton, 1801;
notes from his edn of Paradise regained are rptd in*
Poetical works of Milton, 1824.

CAPEL LOFFT
1751–1824

Milton, John, Paradise lost, printed from the first and
second editions collated; the original system of orthography restored, the punctuation corrected and extended,
with various readings and notes, chiefly rhythmical.
Bury St Edmunds 1792. Bk 1 only.

GEORGE BURDER
1752–1832

Bunyan, John, The pilgrim's progress: a new edition; to
which are added notes, together with the life of the
author. Coventry 1786, 1791, 1797 etc.
—— The holy war, with notes. 1803, 1821, 1824.

GEORGE ELLIS
1753–1815

§1

Specimens of the early English poets, 1790, 3 vols 1801
('to which is prefixed an historical sketch of the rise and
progress of the English poetry and language'), 1803,
1811, 1845, 1851.
Fabliaux or tales, selected and translated in English verse
[by G. L. Way]. Vol 1, 1796, 1800; vol 2, 1800; 3 vols
1815. Introd and notes by Ellis.
Specimens of early English metrical romances. 3 vols
1805, Edinburgh 1811, 1847.
Diary of William Windham 1749–1810. Ed Mrs H.
Baring 1866. Preface by Ellis.
Ellis also contributed to the Rolliad *and the* Anti-Jacobin,
and to Edinburgh Rev *and* Quart Rev.

§2

Festing, G. In his J. H. Frere and his friends, 1899.
MacCunn, F. In her Sir Walter Scott's friends, 1909.
Bagot, J. In his Canning and his friends, 1909.
Johnston, A. In his Enchanted ground, 1964.

HENRY HARINGTON
1755–91

Nugae antiquae: being a miscellaneous collection of
original papers by Sir John Harington and others, with
an original plate of the Princess Elizabeth. 2 vols 1769–
75, 3 vols 1779 (enlarged), 1792; ed T. Park 2 vols 1804.

FRANCIS DOUCE
1757–1834

§1

The dance of death, painted by J. Holbein and engraved
by W. Hollar: contains the daunce of Machabree,
wherein is lively expressed the State of Manne, made by
Dan John Lydgate, monke of St Edmunds Bury; the
whole edited by Douce. 1794, 1804, 1833, 1849.
Dissertation on the life and writings of Mary, an Anglo-
Norman poetess of the 13th century, by M. de la Rue,
communicated by Douce. [1797]. Rptd from Archaeo-
logia 13 1800, read 12 Jan 1797.
Illustrations of Shakespeare and of ancient manners. 2
vols 1807.
Judicium, a pageant, with introduction and glossary by
F.D. 1822.
The metrical life of St Robert. 1824. Introd by Douce.
*Douce assisted in the revision of the catalogue of Harley mss
1808–12 and in the catalogue of Lansdowne mss 1819.
His notes were incorporated in other men's works, especially*
Price's edn of Warton's History of English poetry, 4
vols 1824.

§2

[Singer, S. W.] GM Aug 1834. Obituary. *See also* Sept –
Oct 1834, N & Q 25 March 1905.
Symonds, H. and A. Brown. Catalogue of the printed
books and manuscripts bequeathed by Douce to the
Bodleian Library. Oxford 1840.
H., O. E. Sir Walter Scott and Douce, and amenities of
the Douce correspondence. Bodleian Quart Record 7
1934.
Mann, J. G. et al. Douce centenary. Ibid.

WALTER WHITER
1758–1832

A specimen of a commentary on Shakespeare: containing i, Notes on As you like it; ii, An attempt to explain and illustrate various passages, on a new principle of criticism, derived from Mr Locke's doctrine of the association of ideas. 1794; ed R. Over and M. Bell 1967.

AMBROSE ECCLES
d. 1809

The plays of Lear and Cymbeline, by Shakespeare, with notes and illustrations of various commentators; to which are added remarks by the editor. 2 vols Dublin 1798. Separate edns of Cymbeline, 1793, Lear, 1793, and Merchant of Venice, 1805.

CHARLES PHILPOT

An introduction to the literary history of the 14th and 15th centuries. 1798.

JOHN WALTERS the younger
1759–89

Ascham, Roger, Toxophilus, the schole or partitions of shooting; with a preface by Walters. Wrexham 1788, 1821.

WOLSTENHOLME PARR
1762–1845

The story of the Moor of Venice, translated from the Italian; with two essays on Shakespeare and preliminary observations. 1795.

HENRY JOHN TODD
1763–1845

Milton, John, Comus: a mask, with notes by various commentators. Canterbury 1798.
—— Poetical works, with the principal notes of various commentators. 6 vols 1801, 1809, 1826.
Spenser, Edmund, Works, with the notes of various commentators. 8 vols 1805.
Illustrations of the lives and writings of Gower and Chaucer. 1810.

ALEXANDER CAMPBELL
1764–1824

Introduction to the history of poetry in Scotland from the beginning of the 13th century down to the present time; together with a conversation on Scotish song. Edinburgh 1798–9.

HENRY HEADLEY
1765–88

§1

Select beauties of ancient English poetry, with remarks. 2 vols 1787, 1810 (with memoir of Headley by Henry Kett).
Fletcher, Phineas, The purple island, with critical remarks. 1816.

§2

Wasserman, E. R. Headley and the Elizabethan revival. SP 36 1939.

JAMES PLUMPTRE
1770–1832

Observations on Hamlet, and on the motives which most probably induced Shakespeare to fix upon the story of Amleth: being an attempt to prove that he designed it as an indirect censure on Mary Queen of Scots. Cambridge 1796; An appendix, Cambridge 1797.

ANONYMOUS WORKS

The following works are scholarly in intention, but the editors have not been identified.

Butler, Samuel, Hudibras, with additions and annotations. 1732.
Bunyan, John, The pilgrim's progress: a new edition; to which is now first added, practical and explanatory notes. 1775.
Mother Hubberd's tale of the fox and ape, selected from the works of Spenser with the obsolete words explained. 1784.

A. J.

(4) OLD ENGLISH SCHOLARSHIP

General Works

Turner, Sharon. History of the Anglo-Saxons. 4 vols 1799–1805, 2 vols 1807, 3 vols 1839 (as vols 1–3 of Turner's History of England, 12 vols 1839), 1852. Bk 9 is on OE literature.
Ingram, James. An inaugural lecture on the utility of Anglo-Saxon literature. Oxford 1807.
Bosworth, Joseph. The elements of Anglo-Saxon grammar. 1823. Preface contains list of previous grammars.
Michel, Francisque. Bibliothèque anglo-saxonne. Paris 1837. Prefatory letter from J. M. Kemble giving an account of the progress of OE studies in England.
Petheram, John. An historical sketch of the progress and present state of Anglo-Saxon literature. 1840.
Jefferson, T. An essay towards facilitating instruction in the Anglo-Saxon and modern dialects of the English language. New York 1851. Written for the University of Virginia, 1798.

Hunt, T. W. The study of Anglo-Saxon. Princeton Rev 57 1881.
Wülker, R. Grundriss zur Geschichte der angelsächsischen Litteratur, mit einer Übersicht der angelsächsischen Sprachwissenschaft. Leipzig 1885. A review of OE studies in English during this period, pp. 19–30.
Brooke, C. F. T. The renascence of Germanic studies in England 1559–1689. PMLA 29 1914.
Adams, E. N. Old English scholarship in England from 1566–1800. New Haven 1917.
Kennedy, A. G. A bibliography of writings on the English language. Cambridge Mass 1927.
Walters, H. B. The English antiquaries of the sixteenth, seventeenth and eighteenth centuries. 1934.
Seaton, E. Literary relations of England and Scandinavia. Oxford 1935.
Tuve, R. Ancients, Moderns and Saxons. ELH 6 1939.
Douglas, D. C. English scholars 1660–1730. 1939, 1951 (rev).

Butt, J. Facilities for antiquarian studies. E & S 24 1939.

Wellek, R. The rise of English literary history. Chapel Hill 1941, New York 1966 (rev). Ch 4, The study of early literature.

Evans, J. The history of the Society of Antiquaries. 1956.

English historical scholarship in the seventeenth and eighteenth centuries. 1956 (Dugdale Soc).

Major Scholars

FRANCISCUS JUNIUS the younger
1589–1677

Caedmonis monachi paraphrasis poetica Genesios ac praecipuarum sacrae paginae historiarum. Amsterdam 1655.

Quatuor D. N. Jesu Christi Evangeliorum versiones perantiquae duae, Gothica scil. et Anglo-Saxonica. Dordrecht 1665, Amsterdam 1684. By Junius in collaboration with Thomas Marshall.

Morley, H. An old student of English. In his Clement Marot and other studies, 1871.

GEORGE HICKES
1642–1715

§1

Institutiones grammaticae anglo-saxonicae et moeso-gothicae. Oxford 1689. Contains Runolph Jonas's Icelandic grammar, a catalogue of northern books, and Edward Bernard's Etymologicon britannicum.

[A Latin version of Aelfric's Anglo-Saxon preface to the Heptateuch]. In Henry Wharton, Auctarium historiae dogmaticae Jacobi Useeri Armachani de scripturis et sacris vernaculis, 1690, pp. 377–86.

Linguarum vett. septentrionalium thesaurus grammatico-criticus et archaeologicus. 2 vols Oxford 1703–5. Various binding orders. Contents include: vol 1, (i) Institutiones grammaticae anglo-saxonicae et moeso-gothicae; (ii) Institutiones grammaticae franco-theotiscae [both by Hickes]; (iii) Grammaticae islandicae rudimenta [by Runolph Jonas, with addns and illustrations by Hickes]; (iv) Dissertatio epistolaris [by Hickes]; (v) Numismata anglo-saxonica et anglo-danica [by Sir Andrew Fountaine with Hickes's assistance]; vol 2, Wanley's Catalogue, below, with appendices supplied by John Peringskiöld et al, and index to the whole work by William Brome. The Thesaurus was seen through the press by Edward Thwaites.

Wotton, W. Linguarum vett. septentrionalium thesauri grammatico-critici et archaeologi, auctore G. Hickesio, conspectus brevis. 1708. Attributed to Wotton but planned by Hickes, who also supplied the notes. Tr Maurice Shelton 1735, 1737.

Grammatico anglo-saxonica ex Hickesiano linguarum septentrionalium thesauro excerpta [by Edward Thwaites]. Oxford 1711.

Hickes also wrote some 25 tracts (see Gardner, below) and many prefaces; there are 3 vols of his collected sermons.

§2

A compleat collection of the works of the reverend and learned John Kettlewell. 2 vols 1719. Letters and bio-graphic material in vol 1, to which Hickes contributed the introd.

'W'. George Hickes. European Mag 23 1793.

Nichols, J. In his Literary anecdotes vol 1, 1812.

Overton, J. H. In his Nonjurors, 1902.

Douglas, D. C. In his English scholars 1660–1730, 1939, 1951 (rev).

Gardner, W. B. Hickes and the origin of the Bangorian controversy. SP 39 1942. On the political works.

— Hickes and his times. N & Q May 1955.

Bennett, J. A. W. Hickes' Thesaurus: a study in Oxford book production. E & S ('English Studies') new ser 1 1948.

EDWARD THWAITES
1667–1711

§1

Heptateuchus, Liber Job et Evangelium Nicodemi, anglo-saxonice; Historiae Judith fragmentum, dano-saxonice. Oxford 1698.

Benson, T. Vocabularium anglo-saxonicum. Oxford 1701. Thwaites was responsible for much of the work.

Notae in anglo-saxonum nummos. 1708. Also appended to Wotton's Conspectus of Hickes's Thesaurus and Shelton's trn, above.

Grammatica anglo-saxonica ex Hickesiano linguarum septentrionalium thesauro excerpta. Oxford 1711.

§2

Nichols, J. In his Literary anecdotes vol 4, 1812.

Memoranda of Thwaites the Saxonist. GM Sept 1834.

HUMFREY WANLEY
1672–1726

§1

Librorum vett. septentrionalium, qui in Angliae bibliothecis extant, nec non multorum vett. codd. septentrionalium alibi extantium Catalogus historico-criticus. In Hickes's Thesaurus, 1705. Tr Latin by Edward Thwaites.

The diary of Humfrey Wanley 1715–26. Ed C. E. Wright and R. C. Wright 2 vols 1966 (Bibl Soc).

§2

Nichols, J. In his Literary anecdotes vol 1, 1812, pp. 82–105, 530–41.

Crossley, J. Wanley: autograph notices of his family. N & Q 5 Feb 1870.

Douthwaite, W. R. Wanley and his diary. Lib Chron 1 1884.

Vincent, J. A. R. Wanley's Harleian journal. Genealogist new ser 1 1884.

Barwick, G. F. Wanley and the Harleian library. Library 2nd ser 3 1902.

— The foundation of the Harleian Library: further notes. Library 3rd ser 1 1910.

Gibson, S. Wanley and the Bodleian in 1697. Bodleian Quart Record 1 1916.

Turberville, A. S. In his History of Welbeck Abbey and its owners vol 1, 1938.

Douglas, D. C. In his English scholars 1660–1730, 1939, 1951 (rev).

Wright, R. C. Letters from Wanley to Eric Benzelius and Peter the Great's librarian. Durham Univ Jnl 1 1940.

Sisam, K. In his Studies in the history of Old English literature, Oxford 1953.

Gillam, S. C. and R. W. Hunt. The Curators of the Library and Wanley. Bodleian Lib Record 5 1954.

Wright, C. E. Humfrey Wanley: Saxonist and library keeper. Proc Br Acad 46 1960.

— Edward Harley, 2nd Earl of Oxford 1689–1741. Book Collector 11 1962.

[Hanson, L.] Some observations concerning the invention and progress of printing to the year 1465. Bodleian Lib Record 6 1961.

Bennett, J. A. W. Wanley's Life of Wolsey. Bodleian Lib Record 7 1962.

Heyworth, P. L. Thomas Smith, Wanley and the Cottonian library. TLS 31 Aug 1962.

Wakeman, G. Wanley on erecting a library. Private Lib 6 1965.

Wanley also assisted Tanner in his Notitia monastica; Nicolson in his English historical library and Chamberlayne in his State of England. He supplied much of the material for Edward Bernard's Catalogi librorum mss Angliae et Hiberniae in unum collecti, Oxford 1697; and contributed to the Philosophical Transactions of the Royal Society 1705, p. 1993.

WILLIAM ELSTOB
1673–1715

Hormesta Pauli Orosii quam olim patrio sermone donavit Aelfredus Magnus. Oxford 1699. Title and 2 leaves only ptd.

Sermo lupi ad Anglos. Oxford 1701; rptd in Hickes's Thesaurus vol 2, 1705.

Of the offices of the daily and nightly hours of prayer. OE text tr Elstob as appendix to Several letters which passed between Dr Geo. Hickes and a Popish priest, 1705.

[Latin version of the OE homily on the birthday of St Gregory]. In his sister's edn of that work, 1709, below.

Offices of devotion used in the Anglo-Saxon church, with an English translation and notes. In Hickes, Controversial discourses, 1715, 1727.

Elstob also pbd theological and other writings. For secondary works, see under Elizabeth Elstob, below.

THOMAS HEARNE
1678–1735

For Hearne's miscellaneous works, see col 1699, above.

Joannis Lelandi antiquarii de rebus Britannicus collectanae. 6 vols Oxford [1715], London 1770, 1774. Vol 5 contains Saxon dictionary.

Libri saxonici qui ad manus Joannis Joscelini venerunt. In his edn of Robert of Avesbury, 1720.

Textus Roffensis. Oxford 1720.

Hemingi chartularium ecclesiae Wigorniensis. 2 vols Oxford 1723.

Johannis confratris et monachi Glastoniensis chronica: sive historia de rebus glastoniensibus. Oxford 1726. Battle of Maldon ptd as appendix.

  Douglas, D. C. In his English scholars 1660–1730, 1939, 1951 (rev).

ELIZABETH ELSTOB
1683–1756
§ I

[Transcript of OE Athanasian Creed from the Salisbury Psalter, in Wotton's Conspectus, 1708]. *See under* Hickes, *above.*

An English-Saxon homily on the birthday of St Gregory, anciently used in the English-Saxon church. 1709; rptd as An Anglo-Saxon homily, London and Leicester 1839. William Elstob also contributed material.

Some testimonies of learned men in favour of the intended edition of the Saxon homilies, concerning the learning of the author of those homilies; and the advantages to be hoped for from an edition of them. 1713.

The English-Saxon homilies of Aelfric, Arch-bishop of Canterbury. Oxford 1715. Only 2 pp. ptd.

The rudiments of grammar for the English-Saxon tongue, first given in English; with an apology for the study of northern antiquities. 1715.

An apology for the study of northern antiquities, Ed C. Peake, Los Angeles 1956 (Augustan Reprint Soc).

§ 2

Pegge, S. In Bibliotheca topographica britannica vol 25, 1784.

Nichols, J. In his Biographical and literary anecdotes of William Bowyer, 1782.

— In his Literary anecdotes vol 4, 1812, pp. 112–40; ed C. Clair, Fontwell 1967, pp. 125–31.

R[ichardson], G. B. William and Elizabeth Elstob, the learned Saxonists. In Reprints of rare tracts vol 1, Newcastle 1847.

Reynolds, M. In her Learned lady in England 1650–1760, Boston 1920.

Ashdown, M. Elizabeth Elstob, the learned Saxonist. MLR 20 1925.

Wallas, A. In her Before the Bluestockings, 1929.

The Saxon nymph. TLS 28 Sept 1933. *See also* G. S. Hinds, TLS 5 Oct 1933; H. Michell 26 Oct 1933.

B., J. The first home student. Oxford Mag 24 Nov 1938.

Murphy, M. The Elstobs: scholars of Old English and Anglican apologists. Durham Univ Jnl 58 1966.

EDWARD LYE
1694–1767
§ I

Proposals for printing by subscription Francisci Junii etymologicon anglicanum. Oxford 1736.

Francisci Junii Francisci filii Etymologicon anglicanum. Oxford 1743. With OE grammar by Lye.

Sacrorum evangeliorum versio gothica, Oxford 1750. Ed Eric Benzelius; notes and a Gothic grammar by Lye.

Specimen dictionarii anglo-saxonici-gothici-latini. nd, 1763.

Dictionarium saxonico et gothico-latinum. Accedunt fragmenta versionis Ulphilanae, necnon opuscula quaedam anglo-saxonica. 2 vols 1772. Ed Owen Manning, who prefixed to vol 1 Lye's grammars of Gothic and Anglo-Saxon.

§ 2

Dictionarium saxonico et gothico-latinum. Monthly Rev Nov 1773.

Nichols, J. In his Literary anecdotes vol 9, 1815.

'Philosaxonicus'. Lye's Dictionary. GM Sept 1832.

Minor Scholars
WILLIAM SOMNER
1598–1669

Dictionarium saxonico-latino-anglicum. Oxford 1659.

History of Gavelkind. 1660, 1726. Appendix of charters and other instruments in OE.

  Kennett, W. The life of Mr Somner. Originally pbd in Somner's Treatise of the Roman ports and forts in Kent, 1693; rptd rev and much enlarged in 2nd edn of Somner's Gavelkind, 1726; also perhaps separately.

Somner also supplied information on OE materials to Dugdale's Monasticon anglicanum, 1655–73.

Sir THOMAS BROWNE
1605–82

Of languages and particularly of the Saxon tongue. Tract 8 of Certain miscellany tracts, 1684.

OBADIAH WALKER
1616–99

[Appendix of OE pieces to] Alfredi Magni Anglorum Regis vita. Oxford 1678.
G[ibson], S. Stone's Hospital. Bodleian Quart Record 8 1938. Letters by Walker quoted.
Turnbull, J. M. The prototype of Walter Shandy's Tristopoedia. RES 2 1926.
Rawson, C. J. Two notes on Sterne. N & Q June 1957. Both Turnbull and Rawson discuss the influence of Walker's Of education, Oxford 1673, on Tristram Shandy.

AYLETT SAMMES
1636?–79?

Britannia antiqua illustrata: or the antiquities of ancient Britain, derived from the Phoenicians. 1676. Contains the OE alphabet, an extract from ms homilies and Laws of Ine.

WILLIAM NICOLSON
1655–1727

The English historical library. 3 vols 1696–9, 1714, 1736, 1776.
Nicolson contributed a preface and other materials to Wilkins' Leges anglo-saxonicae, 1721, *below, and probably furnished addns to* Hickes's Thesaurus, 1705.
James, F. G. North Country Bishop. New Haven 1956.

JOHN SMITH
1659–1715

Historiae ecclesiasticae gentis Anglorum libri quinque auctore Sancto et Venerabili Beda. Cambridge 1722. Pbd by John Smith's son George.

WILLIAM WOTTON
1666–1727

Linguarum vet. septentrionalium thesaururi grammatico-critici et archaeologici, auctore Georgio Hickesio, conspectus brevis. 1708. Tr Maurice Shelton 1735, 1737. Hickes planned the Conspectus and furnished the notes.

EDMUND GIBSON
1669–1748

Chronicon Saxonicum: seu annales rerum in Anglia praecipue gestarum a Christo nato ad annum usque MCLIV. Oxford 1692.
[Transcription of the Saxon laws of Ethelbert, Hlothere and Eadric, in Hickes's Thesaurus, 1705.]
The Saxon Chronicle. Retrospective Rev 8th ser 2 1823.

JOHN FORTESCUE-ALAND, Baron FORTESCUE
1670–1746

On the utility of the Anglo-Saxon language, and of the study of the Anglo-Saxon laws. Preface to his edn of Sir John Fortescue, The difference between an absolute and limited monarchy, 1714, 1719.

CHRISTOPHER RAWLINSON
1677–1733

An. Manl. Sever. Boethi Consolationis philosophiae libri v, anglo-saxonice redditi ab Alfredo. Oxford 1698.

THOMAS BENSON
1679–1734

Thesaurus linguae anglo-saxonicae dictionario Gul. Somneri, quoad numerum vocum auctior. Oxford 1699. Title and one page only ptd.
Vocabularium anglo-saxonicum. Oxford 1701. A compendium of Somner's work, largely carried out by Thwaites.

DAVID WILKINS
1685–1745

Leges anglo-saxonicae ecclesiaticae et civiles. 1721. With assistance from Nicolson.
Concilia Magnae Britanniae et Hiberniae. 4 vols 1737. Supervised by William Wake.
Wilkins edited Tanner's Bibliotheca britannico-hibernica, 1748, *and an edn of Selden,* 1726.

JOHN HENLEY
1692–1756

An introduction to an English grammar; a compendious way to master any language in the world; a dissertation on the Saxon, and a grammar of it: being no x of the Complete linguist. 1726. Based entirely on Hickes.
D'Israeli, I. Disappointed genius. In his Calamities of authors, 1812.

SAMUEL PEGGE senior
1704–96

[On the Elstobs]. Archaeologia 1 1770.
A copy of a deed in Latin and Saxon, of Odo, Bishop of Baieux, with observations. Archaeologia 1 1770.
An historical account of the Textus Roffensis, including memoirs of the learned Saxonists Mr William Elstob and his sister. In J. Nichols, Bibliotheca topographica britannica 25 1784.

SAMUEL JOHNSON
1709–84

History of the English language. Prefixed to his Dictionary, 1755. Contains extracts from Alfred's Boethius, ch 1 of St Luke in OE and Wyclif's version in parallel columns, a poem in Norman-Saxon, and an excerpt from the Anglo-Saxon Chronicle between 1135 and 1140.

ROBERT HENRY
1718–90

History of Great Britain. 6 vols 1771–93, 12 vols 1788–95, 6 vols Dublin 1789–94, 12 vols 1805–6. Contains versions of the Lord's Prayer in Saxon and kindred languages derived from ancient Gothic or Teutonic; and an extract from the Anglo-Saxon Chronicle, with a trn.
Mossner, E. C. Hume as literary patron: a suppressed review of Henry's History of Great Britain 1773. MP 39 1942.
Horace Walpole's correspondence with Sir David Dalrymple, [Robert Henry et al]. Ed W. S. Lewis, C. H. Bennett and A. G. Hoover, New Haven 1951.

OWEN MANNING
1721–1801

The will of King Alfred. Oxford 1788, 1828.
Manning edited Lye's Dictionnarium, 2 vols 1772.

DAINES BARRINGTON
1727–1800

The Anglo-Saxon version from the historian Orosius, by Alfred the Great, with an English translation. 1773.

EDWARD ROWE-MORES
1731–1778

Notae in Caedmonis Paraphrasin. Oxford 1751/2. 2 leaves: reprint of Junius's ms corrections to his own copy of Caedmon.
De Aelfrico Archiepiscopo Dorobernensi commentarius. Ed Grimus J. Thorkelin 1789.

JOSEPH STRUTT
1749–1802

Chronicle of England. 2 vols 1777–8. Vol 2 contains the Lord's Prayer, part of ch 1 of St John's Gospel, part of ch 1 of Genesis, the Belief, the Exordium of Caedmon's poem, all in OE with trns, and the Lord's Prayer paraphrased in Anglo-Danish.

SAMUEL HENSHALL
1764–1807

The Saxon and English tongues reciprocally illustrative of each other; the impracticality of acquiring an accurate knowledge of Saxon literature through the medium of Latin phraseology exemplified in the errors of Hickes, Wilkins, Gibson and other scholars. 1798.

(5) BIOGRAPHICAL DICTIONARIES AND COLLECTIONS

General
THOMAS FULLER
1608–61

See S. Gibson, A bibliography of Fuller, Proc Oxford Bibl Soc 4 1936.
The history of the worthies of England. 1662, 1684 (abridged, as Anglorum speculum); ed J. Nichols 2 vols 1811; ed P. A. Nuttall 3 vols 1840; ed J. Freeman 1952 (abridged).
Addison, W. Worthy Dr Fuller. 1950.
Addison, J. T. Fuller: historian and humorist. Historical Mag of Protestant Episcopalian Church 21 1952.
Roberts, S. C. In his Dr Johnson and others, Cambridge 1958.

WILLIAM WINSTANLEY
1628?–98

England's worthies: select lives of the most eminent persons from Constantine the Great to the death of Oliver Cromwell, late Protector. 1660, 1684.

EDMOND BOHUN
1645–99

The great historical, geographical and poetical dictionary: containing the lives and most remarkable actions of all those who have recommended themselves to the world, collected from the best historians, chronologers and lexicographers. 2 vols 1694.

JEREMY COLLIER
1650–1726

An appendix to the great historical, geographical and poetical dictionary. 1721, 1727 (as A supplement to the dictionary).
Lives English and foreign, including the history of England and other nations of Europe from 1550–1690, by several hands. 2 vols 1704. Life of Admiral Blake in vol 1 almost certainly by John Oldmixon.

THOMAS BIRCH
1705–66

A general dictionary historical and critical, in which a new and accurate translation of that of Mr Bayle is included, by John Peter Bernard, Tho. Birch, John Lockman and other hands. 10 vols 1734–41.
[Lives and characters in J. Houbraken and G. Vertue, Heads of illustrious persons of Great Britain, 1743, 1747; vol 2 (addns), 1751, 1756, 1813.]
Osborn, J. M. Birch and the General dictionary 1734–41. MP 36 1938.
Ruhe, E. L. Pope's hand in Birch's account of Gay. RES new ser 5 1954.

Biographica britannica: or the lives of the most eminent persons who have flourished in Great Britain and Ireland. 6 vols (in 7 pts) 1747–66, 6 vols 1778–93 (with corrections and addns by Andrew Kippis).

THOMAS MORTIMER
1730–1810

British Plutarch: containing the lives of the most eminent statesmen, patriots, divines, warriors, philosophers, poets and artists of Great Britain and Ireland, from the accession of Henry VIII to the present time; including a complete history of England from that aera. 6 vols 1762, 1776, 8 vols Edinburgh 1791, Perth 1795; ed F. Wrangham 6 vols 1816 (with addns); tr French, 1785–6.
The student's pocket dictionary, or compendium of universal history, chronology and biography, from the earliest accounts to the present, with authorities, in two parts: part i, containing a compendium of universal history; part ii, containing a compendium of biography. 1777, 1789.

THOMAS FLLOYD

Bibliotheca biographica: a synopsis of universal biography, ancient and modern. 3 vols 1760.
A new and general biographical dictionary: containing an historical and critical account of the lives and writings of the most eminent persons in every nation, particularly the British and Irish. 12 vols 1761–7, 1784 (Ralph Heathcote a chief writer in both edns), 8 vols 1795, 15 vols 1798–1810 (vols 1–5 ed William Tooke, vols 6–15 ed Robert Nares and William Below alternately); ed A. Chalmers 32 vols 1812–17.
British biography: or an account of the lives and writings of eminent persons in Great Britain and Ireland, from Wicliffe to the present time. 10 vols 1766–82, 1773–80 (vols 1–7 ed Joseph Towers).

JAMES GRANGER
1723-76

A biographical history of England from Egbert the Great to the Revolution, adapted to a catalogue of engraved British heads. 2 vols (4 pts) 1769; suppl 1774; 4 vols 1775 (with addns), 1804, 6 vols 1824 (more than 500 additional lives). Continued from Granger's mss to the reign of George I by Mark Noble, 3 vols 1806.
Powell, L. F. Granger's biographical history. TLS 23 April 1931.

JOHN NOORTHOUCK
1746?-1816

An historical and classical dictionary: containing the lives and characters of the most eminent and learned persons in every age and nation. 2 vols 1776.
The beauties of biography: containing the lives of the most illustrious persons who have flourished in Europe. 2 vols 1777.
John Noorthouck: 'the man after God's own heart'. TLS 25 August 1925.

The biographical and imperial magazine. 1789. Only one vol appeared.

STEPHEN JONES
1763-1827

A new biographical dictionary in miniature: containing a brief account of the lives and writings of the most eminent persons and remarkable characters in every age and nation. 1794, 1796, 1811 (with addns).
The biographical magazine: containing [140] portraits and characters of eminent and ingenious persons of every age and nation. 1794.

SILVESTER HARDING
1745-1809

The biographical mirror: comprising a series of ancient and modern English portraits. 3 vols 1795-[1802]. Biographical sketches mostly by F. G. Waldron; some by Edmond Malone.

WILLIAM FORDYCE MAVOR
1758-1837

The British Nepos, or youth's mirror: being select lives of illustrious Britons who have been distinguished by their virtues, talents or remarkable progress in life; with incidental and practical reflections. 1798, 1800, 1802, 1806, 1807, 1816.

LEMAN THOMAS REDE
d. 1832

Anecdotes and biography, including many modern characters in the circles of fashionable and official life, selected from the portfolios of a distinguished literary and political character lately deceased. 1799.

JOHN ADOLPHUS
1768-1845

The British cabinet: containing portraits of illustrious personages, with biographical memoirs. 2 vols 1799-1800.

JOHN AIKIN
1747-1822

General biography: or lives, critical and historical, of the most eminent persons of all ages, countries, conditions and professions, arranged according to alphabetical order. 10 vols 1799-1815. Aikin was assisted first by William Enfield, then by Thomas Morgan, William Johnson, — Nicholson, Robert Southey et al.

JOHN WATKINS
d. 1831

The universal historical and biographical dictionary. 1800, 1806, 1807.

Specialized Biographical Collections
Of Authors and Actors

EDWARD PHILLIPS
1630-96

Theatrum poetarum: or a compleat collection of the poets; with some observations and reflections upon many of them, particularly those of our own nation. 1675; ed S. E. Brydges, Canterbury 1800. Preface rptd in Critical essays of the seventeenth century vol 2, ed J. E. Spingarn, Oxford 1908.
Albrecht, W. Über das Theatrum poetarum. Leipzig 1928.
Fletcher, H. Milton's [Index poeticus]: the Theatrum poetarum. JEGP 55 1956.
Hone, R. E. The period of Phillips's work for Elias Ashmole. N & Q April 1956.
—— New light on the Milton-Phillips's family relationship. HLQ 22 1958.
Howarth, R. G. Phillips's Compendiosa enumeratio poetarum. MLR 54 1959.
Goulding, S. The sources of the Theatrum poetarum. PMLA 76 1961.

WILLIAM WINSTANLEY
1628?-98

The lives of the most famous English poets, from the time of William the Conqueror to James II. 1687; ed W. R. Parker, Gainesville 1963 (facs).
Parker, W. R. Winstanley's Lives: an appraisal. MLQ 6 1945.

SIR THOMAS POPE BLOUNT
1649-97

Censura celebriorum authorum. 1690, Geneva 1694, 1710 (later edns with anon addns).

GERARD LANGBAINE the younger
1656-92

An account of the English dramatick poets. Oxford 1691, [1698] ('improved and continued' by Charles Gildon).
Watkin-Jones, A. Langbaine's account of the English dramatic poets 1691. E & S 21 1936.
Osborn, J. M. Dryden and Langbaine. In his Dryden: facts and problems, New York 1940.
Anderson, G. L. 'A little civil correction': Langbaine revised. N & Q June 1958. On Gildon's alterations.

GILES JACOB
1686-1744

The poetical register: or the lives and characters of the English dramatick poets, with an account of their writings. 1719, 1723 (with continuation to 1722).
An historical account of the lives and writings of our most considerable English poets. 1720, 1723 (as vol 2 of The poetical register).
Jacob also wrote several law manuals and a number of polemical tracts.

ELIZABETH COOPER

The Muses library. 1737, 1738 (as The historical and poetical medley), 1741. 'With the lives and characters of the known writers [of the poems], taken from the most authentic memoirs'.
Bronson, B. H. Chattertoniana. MLQ 11 1950. On influence of Muses library on Rowley poems.

THOMAS WHINCUP
d. 1730

Scanderberg, or love and liberty: a tragedy; to which are added a list of all the dramatic authors, with some account of their lives to 1747. 1747. List believed to be chiefly by John Mottley, *col 796, above.*

THOMAS TANNER
1674-1735

Bibliotheca britannico-hibernica: sive de scriptoribus qui in Anglia, Scotia et Hibernia ad saeculi XVII initium floruerunt, literarum ordina juxta familiarum nomina dispositis commentariis. 1748. Ed David Wilkins.
Davies, W. T. Tanner and his Bibliotheca. TLS 14 Dec 1935.
Douglas, D. C. In his English scholars 1660-1730, 1939, 1951 (rev).
Hunt, R. W. Tanner's Bibliotheca britannico-hibernica. Bodleian Lib Record 2 1949.
Tanner helped to compile Bernard's catalogue of Bodley mss; see under Humfrey Wanley, above. He wrote Notitia monastica, 1695; and contributed to other antiquarian books, including William Wake, State of the Church, 1703, and Wilkins, Concilia, 1737.

WILLIAM RUFUS CHETWOOD
d. 1766

The British theatre: containing the lives of the English dramatic poets, with an account of all their plays; together with the lives of most of the principle actors, as well as poets; to which is prefixed a short view of the rise and progress of the English stage. Dublin 1750.

THEOPHILUS CIBBER
1703-58
and
ROBERT SHIELS
d. 1753

The lives of the poets of Great Britain and Ireland, to the time of Dean Swift. 5 vols 1753, Hildesheim 1968 (facs). Although Cibber's name appears on the title-page, the work is mostly by Shiels.

Keast, W. R. Johnson and Cibber's Lives of the poets 1753. In Restoration and eighteenth-century literature, ed C. Camden, Chicago 1963.

HORACE WALPOLE
1717-97

A catalogue of the royal and noble authors of England, Scotland and Ireland; with lists of their works. 2 vols Strawberry Hill 1758, 1759, Dublin 1769, Edinburgh 1792, 1796, 5 vols 1806 (with addns by T. Park).

WILLIAM RIDER
1723-85

An historical and critical account of the lives and writings of the living authors of Great-Britain, wherein their respective merits are discussed with the utmost candour and impartiality. 1762. Anon; doubtfully attributed to Rider.

DAVID ERSKINE BAKER
1730-67

The companion to the playhouse: or an historical account of all the dramatic writers of Great Britain and Ireland, from the commencement of our theatrical exhibitions down to 1764. 2 vols 1764; ed I. Reed 2 vols 1782 (as Biographia dramatica, with addns); ed S. Jones 3 vols in 4 1812 (with addns), 3 vols 1968 (facs).

JOHN ALMON
1737-1805

Letters concerning the present state of England. 1772. Anon. Letter XXVIII, The present state of the theatre; Letter XXX, A catalogue of the most celebrated writers of the present age, with remarks on their works. Attributed to Almon.
Almon was widely active as a political journalist and miscellaneous writer.

Theatrical biography: or memoirs of the principal performers of the three Theatres Royal, Drury Lane, Covent-Garden, Haymarket, with remarks on their professional merits. 2 vols 1772, Dublin 1772.

JOHN BERKENHOUT
1730?-91

Biographia literaria: or a biographical history of literature, containing the lives of English, Scotch and Irish authors, from the dawn of letters in these kingdoms to the present time, chronologically and classically arranged. 1777. Only 1 vol pbd, to end of 16th century.

SAMUEL JOHNSON
1709-84

Prefaces, biographical and critical, to the works of the English poets. 10 vols 1779-81, 3 vols Dublin 1779-81, 4 vols 1781, 1783, 6 vols 1790-1 (with addns by I. Reed), 6 vols 1794, 8 vols Dublin 1795, 1 vol 1797 (abridged), 4 vols Montrose 1800; ed G. B. Hill 3 vols Oxford 1905.

— MARSHALL

Catalogue of five hundred celebrated authors of Great Britain, now living: the whole arranged in alphabetical order; and including a complete list of their publications, with occasional strictures, and anecdotes of their lives. 1788. Anon.

JEREMIAS DAVID REUSS

Alphabetical register of all the authors actually living in Great-Britain, Ireland and in the united provinces of North America, with a catalogue of their publications [also with title-page in German]. Berlin 1791; Supplement, 2 vols Berlin 1804. English preface signed Geo. Forster.

ROBERT ANDERSON
1750–1830

The works of the British poets, with prefaces, biographical and critical. 13 vols Edinburgh 1792–5. Vol 14, 1807.

DAVID RIVERS

Literary memoirs of living authors of Great Britain: arranged according to an alphabetical catalogue of their names, and including a list of their works, with occasional opinions upon their literary character. 1798. Anon.

Of Nobility and Clergy

SAMUEL CLARKE
1599–1683

A collection of the lives of ten eminent divines; whereunto is added the life of Gustavus Ericson, King of Sweden, who first reformed religion in Sweden; and of some other eminent Christians. 1662.
The lives of sundry eminent persons in this later age; in two parts: 1, of divines; 2, of nobility and gentry of both sexes; to which is added his own life, and the lives of the Countess of Suffolk, Sir Nath. Bernardiston etc drawn up by other hands. 1683.
Clarke's earlier works of collective biography include his Marrow of ecclesiastical history, 1650, *and* A general martyrology, 1651.

DAVID LLOYD
1635–92

The states-men and favourites of England since the Reformation, their prudence and policies, successes and miscarriages, advancements and falls [etc]. 1665, 1670 (as State worthies during the reigns of Henry VIII etc); ed Charles Whitworth 2 vols 1766.
Memoires of the lives, actions and deaths of those who suffered for the Protestant religion and allegiance to their soveraigne from the year 1637 to 1666. 1668.

WILLIAM WINSTANLEY
1628?–98

The loyall martyrology: or brief catalogues and characters of the most eminent persons who suffered for their conscience during the late times of rebellion; with the catalogue and characters of the regicides. 1665.

The lives of all the Lords Chancellors, Lords Keepers and Lords Commissioners of the Great Seal [etc], but more at large of those two great opposites, Edward Earl of Clarendon and Bulstrode Lord Whitlock. 2 vols 1708, 1712 (with addns).

JOHN LE NEVE
1679–1741

Memoirs British and foreign of the lives and characters of the most illustrious persons who died in the year 1711. 1712.
The lives and characters of the most illustrious persons who died in the year 1712. 1714.
The lives and characters of all the Protestant Bishops of the Church of England since the Reformation. Vol 1 (2 pts), 1720 (all pbd).

EDMUND CALAMY
1671–1732

An abridgement of Mr Baxter's History of his life and times; with an account of many others of these worthy Ministers who were ejected after the restauration of King Charles the Second. 1702, 2 vols 1713 (with Account continued); ed S. Palmer 2 vols 1775 (as The nonconformist's memorial), 1777, 1778, 3 vols 1803; ed A. G. Matthews, Oxford 1934 (as Calamy revised).

JOHN WALKER
1674–1747

An attempt towards recovering an account of the numbers and sufferings of the clergy of the Church of England in the late times of the Grand Rebellion. 1714; ed A. G. Matthews, Oxford 1948 (as Walker revised).
Totham, G. B. Walker and the Sufferings of the clergy. Cambridge 1910.

NATHANIEL SALMON
1675–1742

The lives of the English Bishops from the Restauration to the Revolution, with an account of the most remarkable publick transactions in which they were concerned. 3 pts [1731]–3.

JOHN WILFORD

Memorials and characters, together with the lives of divers eminent and worthy persons. 1741. An anthology of memoirs of more than 235 who died 1595–1740, first pbd in weekly pts.

RICHARD CHALLONER

Memoirs of missionary priests, as well secular as regular, and of other Catholics of both sexes, that have suffered death in England, on religious grounds, from the year of our Lord 1577 to 1684. 2 vols 1741–2. Anon.

JOHN LIVINGSTONE
1603–72

Divine Providence exemplified in the lives of the most eminent divines who lived in Scotland during the first century after the Reformation. Glasgow 1754.

RICHARD ROLT
1725?–70

Lives of the principal reformers, both Englishmen and foreigners, comprehending the general history of the Reformation. 1759.
Jones, C. Christopher Smart, Rolt and the Universal Visiter. Library 4th ser 18 1937.

ERASMUS MIDDLETON
1739–1805

Biographia evangelica: or an historical account of the lives and deaths of the most eminent and evangelical authors or preachers, both British and foreign, in the several denominations of Protestants, from the beginning of the Reformation to the Present time. 4 vols 1779–86.

Of Naval Figures

Lives of illustrious British seamen. Edinburgh 1764. Drake to Byng.

JOHN CAMPBELL
1708–75

The lives of the British admirals, displaying the conduct and heroism of the naval commanders of Great Britain. 4 vols 1742–4 etc. *See col 1714, above.*

JOHN CHARNOCK
1756–1807

Biographia navalis: or impartial memoirs of lives and characters of officers of the Navy of Great Britain, from the year 1660 to the present time. 6 vols 1794–8.

Of Scottish and Irish Figures

GEORGE MACKENZIE
1669–1725

The lives and characters of the most eminent writers of the Scotch nation; with an abstract and catalogue of their works, their various editions and the judgment of the learned concerning them. 3 vols Edinburgh 1708–22.

GEORGE CRAWFURD
d. 1748

Lives and character of the Crown officers of Scotland from the reign of King David I to the Union of the two Kingdoms. Edinburgh 1726, 1736. Only vol 1 pbd.

Sir JAMES WARE
1594–1666

Complete works. Tr Walter Harris 2 vols Dublin 1764. Contains first English trn of De scriptoribus hiberniae libri duo, Dublin 1639.

JOHN HOWIE
1735–93

Biographia scotiana: or a brief historical account of the lives of the most eminent Scots worthies. Glasgow 1775, 2 pts Glasgow 1781–2, 1796.

Of Medical Figures

JOHN AIKIN
1747–1822

Biographical memoirs of medicine in Great Britain, from the revival of literature to the time of Harvey. 1780.

BENJAMIN HUTCHINSON

Biographia medica: historical and critical memoirs of the lives and writings of the most eminent medical characters that have existed from the earliest account of time to the present period; with a catalogue of their literary productions. 2 vols 1789.

Miscellaneous Collections

ANTHONY à WOOD
1632–95

Athenae oxonienses: an exact history of all the writers and bishops who have had their education in the University of Oxford, from 1500 to 1690; to which are added the Fasti or annals of the said University. 2 vols 1691–2, 1721; ed P. Bliss 4 vols 1813–20. Only vol 1, containing Wood's autobiography, of a proposed new edn pbd in 1848, ed Bliss.
Gibson, S. and M. A. An index to Rawlinson's collections (c. 1700–50) for a new edition of Wood's Athenae oxonienses. Proc Oxford Bibl Soc 1 1925.
Hunt, R. W. The cataloguing of the Ashmolean collections of books and manuscripts. Bodleian Lib Record 4 1953.
Parker, W. R. Wood's Life of Milton: its sources and significance. PBSA 52 1958.
French, J. M. The reliability of Wood and Milton's Oxford MA. PMLA 75 1960.
Sommerlad, M. J. The continuation of Wood's Athenae oxonienses. Bodleian Lib Record 7 1966.

JOHN AUBREY
1626–97

Lives of eminent men. Ed P. Bliss in vol 2 of Letters written by eminent persons, ed J. Walker 1813; ed A. Clark 2 vols Oxford 1898; ed J. Collier 1931 (abridged as The scandal and credulities of Aubrey); ed A. Powell 1949 (abridged); ed O. L. Dick 1949 (abridged), Ann Arbor 1957 (with introd by E. Wilson), 1962 (Pelican) (rev).
Powell, A. Aubrey and his friends. 1948, New York 1964 (rev).
Elsey, R. Aubrey's Lives. TLS 5 Oct 1951.
For Aubrey's other works and secondary material see col 1682, above.

THOMAS SMITH

Vitae quorundam eruditissimorum et illustrium virorum. 1707. 8 lives.

JOHN WARD
1679?–1758

The lives of the professors of Gresham College, to which is prefixed the life of the founder, Sir Thomas Gresham. 1740. *See col 1818, below.*

GEORGE BALLARD
1706–55

Memoirs of several ladies of Great Britain, who have been celebrated for their writings or skill in the learned languages, arts and sciences. Oxford 1752.

HORACE WALPOLE
1717–97

Anecdotes of painting in England, with some account of the principal artists, collected by G. Vertue and now digested and published from his original mss. 4 vols Strawberry Hill 1762–71, 1765–71, London 1782, 5 vols 1786 (with addns); ed J. Dallaway 5 vols 1826–8; 3 vols 1849, 1 vol 1879. Continued as vol 5, ed F. W. Hilles and P. B. Daghlian, New Haven 1937.

Catalogue of engravers who have been born, or resided in England, digested by Mr Horace Walpole from the mss of G. Vertue. Strawberry Hill 1763, 1765, London 1782 (as vol 5 of Anecdotes of painting), 1786, 1794, 1828 (as vol 5 of Anecdotes of the arts in general in Great Britain, by J. Dallaway).

Biographical collections: or lives and characters, from the works of Mr Baxter and Dr Bates. 1766.

Biographium faemineum: the female worthies, or memoirs of the most illustrious ladies of all ages and nations, containing (exclusive of foreigners) the lives of above fourscore British ladies. 1766.

RICHARD PULTENEY
1730–1801

Historical and biographical sketches of the progress of botany in England. 2 vols 1790.

JOSEPH STRUTT
1749–1802

A biographical dictionary, containing an historical account of all the engravers from the earliest period of the art of engraving to the present time. 2 vols 1785–6.

H. NORTON WILLIS

Biographical sketches of eminent persons whose portraits form part of the Duke of Dorset's collection at Knole. 1795.

City biography: containing anecdotes and memoirs of the rise, progress, situation and characters of the aldermen and other conspicuous personages of the Corporation and City of London. 1799, 1800.

JAMES CAULFIELD

Portraits, memoirs and characters of remarkable persons. from the reign of Edward the Third to the Revolution. 3 vols 1794–5, 1819–20.

P. R.

(6) DICTIONARIES AND GLOSSARIES

This section is selective. For a complete list, see Kennedy and Alston, below.

General Studies

Marsden, William. A catalogue of dictionaries, vocabularies, grammars and alphabets. 1796.

Worcester, J. E. Dictionary of the English language. Boston 1860. Catalogue and survey of early dictionaries.

Wheatley, H. B. Chronological notices of the dictionaries of the English language. Trans Philological Soc 1865.

Murray, J. A. H. The evolution of English lexicography. Oxford 1900.

Long, P. W. English dictionaries before Webster. PBSA 4 1910.

Vizetelly, F. H. The development of the dictionary of the English language. New York 1915.

Kennedy, A. G. A bibliography of writings on the English language. Cambridge Mass 1927, New York 1961. Especially pp. 221–46, Modern English dictionaries, and pp. 443–7, History of English lexicography. Addns and corrections by A. Gabrielson, Studia Neophilologica 2 1929.

O[nions], C. T. Catalogue of an exhibition of books held in the Bodleian Library to celebrate the completion of the Oxford English Dictionary. Oxford 1928.

Segar, M. Dictionary making in the early eighteenth century. RES 7 1931.

Matthews, M. M. A survey of English dictionaries. Oxford 1933.

Read, A. W. Projected English dictionaries 1755–1828. JEGP 36 1937.

Starnes, DeW. T. English dictionaries of the seventeenth century. SE 17 1937.

Noyes, G. E. Some interrelations of English dictionaries of the seventeenth centuries. PMLA 54 1939.

— The development of cant lexicography in England 1566–1785. SP 38 1941.

— Edward Cocker and Cocker's English dictionary. N & Q 30 May 1942. Reply by D. Salmon 27 June 1942.

— John Dunton's Ladies dictionary 1694. PQ 21 1942.

Starnes, DeW. T. and G. E. Noyes. The English dictionary from Cawdrey to Johnson 1604–1755. Chapel Hill 1946.

Sheldon, E. K. Pronouncing systems in eighteenth-century dictionaries. Language 22 1946.

— Walker's influence on the pronouncing of English. PMLA 62 1947.

Kolb, G. J. and J. H. Sledd. Johnson's Dictionary and lexicographic tradition. MP 50 1953.

Osselton, N. E. Branded works in English dictionaries before Johnson. Groningen 1958.

Simon, I. Saxonism and the hard-word dictionaries. Revue des Langues Vivantes 26 1960.

Alston, R. C. A bibliography of the English language from the invention of printing to the year 1800. Leeds 1965–6, Bradford 1967– (priv ptd). Of a projected edn in 20 vols, 7 vols have appeared, including vol 1, Grammars; vol 5, The English dictionary.

Glossaries

Vocational and Professional Vocabularies
Encyclopedias and Comprehensive Vocabularies

Coles, Elisha. An English dictionary: explaining the difficult terms that are used in divinity, husbandry, physick, philosophy, law, navigation, mathematics and other arts and sciences. 1676, 1677, 1685, 1692, 1696, 1701, 1708, 1713, 1717, 1724, 1732. Based chiefly on Edward Phillips, The new world of English words, 1658.

Cocker, Edward. Cocker's English dictionary; interpreting the most refined and difficult words in divinity, philosophy, law, physicks, mathematics, husbandry, mechanics etc. 1704, 1715, 1724. Ed John Hawkins? For discussion of authorship, see Noyes, above, and Alston vol 5.

Harris, John. Lexicon technicum: or an universal English dictionary of arts and sciences explaining not only the terms of art, but the arts themselves. 1704, 2 vols 1708–10, 1725, 1736.

Glossographia anglicana nova: or a dictionary, interpreting such hard words of whatever language, as are at present used in the English tongue, with their etymologies; also the terms of divinity, law, physick, explain'd, from the best modern authors. 1707, 1719. Derived partly from Thomas Blount, Glossographia, 1656.

Chambers, Ephraim. Cyclopedia. 1728, Dublin 1740, London 1741, Dublin 1742, London 1743, 1750, 1751, 1778–83, 1786–9.

New and complete dictionary of arts and sciences. 1766.

Croker, Henry T. Complete dictionary of arts and sciences. 1766.

Encyclopedia britannica. 1678, 1771, 1773, 1778–88.

Trade Terms

Hatton, Edward. Merchant's dictionary: explaining the terms used in trade. In Merchant's magazine; or tradesman's treasury, 1695, 1697, 1699, 1701, 1707, 1712, 1719, 1726, 1734.

Rolt, Richard. A new dictionary of trade and commerce. 1756, 1761. Preface by Samuel Johnson.

Postlethwayt, Malachy. The universal dictionary of trade and commerce translated from the French of the celebrated Monsieur [Jacques] Savary, with large additions and improvements. 2 vols 1751, 1755, 1757, 1766, 1774.

Legal Terms

Blount, Thomas. Νομο-Λεξικογ: a law-dictionary, interpreting such difficult and obscure words and terms, as are found either in our common or statute, ancient or modern lawes. 1670, 1691, 1717.

Cowell, John. Νομοθετης: the interpreter, containing the general signification of such obscure words and terms as are used either in the common or statute laws of this realm. [Re-edited] by Thomas Manley. 1672, 1684, 1701, 1708, 1709, 1727, 1737. Based on Cowell, The interpreter, Cambridge 1607.

O., F. Law–French dictionary. 1701.

Jacob, Giles. A new law dictionary: explaining the rise, progress and present state of the English law. 1729, 1732, 1739, 1744, 1756, 1762, 1772, 1782; ed T. E. Tomlins 1797.

Cunningham, Timothy. A new and complete law dictionary: or general abridgement of the law. 2 vols 1764–5, Dublin 1764, London 1771, 1783.

Burn, Richard. A new law dictionary, continued to the present time by John Burn, esq, his son. 2 vols 1792, Dublin 1792.

Marriott, William. New law dictionary. 1798.

Medical Terms

Blancard, Stephen. The physical dictionary, wherein the terms of anatomy etc are accurately described; also the names and virtues of medicinal plants. 1684, 1693, 1697, 1702, 1708, 1715, 1726.

Quincy, John. Lexicon physico-medicum: or a new medicinal dictionary. 1719; 11 edns by 1800.

James, Robert. A medicinal dictionary, including physic, surgery, anatomy, chemistry, botany. 3 vols 1743–5.

Barrow, John. Dictionarium medicum universale: or a new medicinal dictionary containing an explanation of all the terms used in physic, anatomy, physiology, surgery. 1749.

Hooper, Robert. A compendious dictionary: containing an explanation of all the terms in anatomy, physiology, surgery. 1798.

Agricultural Terms

W[orlidge], J[ohn]. Dictionarium rusticum: or the interpretations and significations of the rustick terms. In his Systema agriculturae, 1669, 1675, 1681, 1697, 1698, 1716.

—— Dictionarium rusticum et urbanicum: or a dictionary of all sorts of country affairs, handicraft, trading and merchandising. 1704, 1717 (rev), 1726, 1741, 1765.

Wallis, Thomas. The farrier's and horseman's complete dictionary. 1759, 1764, 1775.

Hunter, James. A complete dictionary of farriery and horsemanship. Birmingham 1796.

Miscellaneous

A military dictionary, explaining all difficult terms in martial discipline, fortification and gunnery: third edition improved, to which is added a sea dictionary of all the terms of navigation. 1702, 1704, 1708, 1711.

Builder's dictionary, or gentleman and architect's companion: explaining the terms of art in all the several parts of architecture. 2 vols 1734.

The sportsman's dictionary: or the country gentleman's companion. 2 vols 1735, 1744.

Hooson, William. The miner's dictionary; explaining the terms used by miners. Wrexham 1747.

Falconer, William. An universal dictionary of the marine: or a copious explanation of the technical terms and phrases employed in the construction equipment etc of a ship. 1769; ed William Burney 1815.

The sportsman's dictionary, 1778, 1782, 1785, 1792.

Martyn, Thomas. The languages of botany: being a dictionary of the terms made use of in that science, principally by Linnaeus. 1793, 1796 (rev), 1807.

Rudiments of ancient architecture. 1789, 1794. With a dictionary of terms used in architecture pp. 79–117.

Nicholson, William. A dictionary of chemistry, exhibiting the present state of the theory and practice of that science. 2 vols 1795, 1808.

Hutton, Charles. A mathematical and philosophical dictionary. 2 vols 1795–6, 1815.

Pryce, William. An explanation of the cornu-technical terms and idioms of tinners. In his Mineralogia cornubiensis, 1798.

Regional Vocabularies

Scottish

Ruddiman, Thomas. Virgil's Aeneis, translated into Scottish verse by the famous Gawin Douglas; to which is added a large glossary explaining the difficult words, which may serve for a dictionary to the old Scottish language. Edinburgh 1710.

Duncan, D. Ruddiman: a study in Scottish scholarships in the early 18th century. Edinburgh 1965.

[Hume, David]. Scotticisms. Appended to his Political discourses, Edinburgh 1752 (not in later edns); also in Scots Mag 22 1760.

Herd, David. Ancient and modern Scottish songs, heroic ballads etc. Edinburgh 1776 (2nd edn). Glossary in vol 2, pp. 241–73; not in 1st edn, 1769.

Beattie, James. Scotticisms, arranged in alphabetical order, designed to correct improprieties of speech and writing. Aberdeen 1779 (priv ptd), Edinburgh 1787, 1797, 1811.

Mitchell, Hugh. Scotticisms, vulgar Anglicisms and grammatical improprieties corrected, with reasons for the corrections; being a collection upon a new plan, alphabetically arranged. Glasgow 1799.

Dalrymple, David. A glossary of the Scottish language. [c. 1791] (priv ptd).

A number of edns of Percy's Reliques contain A glossary of the obsolete and Scottish words; as do numerous edns of of the works of Allan Ramsay and Robert Burns. See also Pinkerton, col 1813, below.

Provincial

Ray, John. A collection of English words not generally used, with their significations and original, in two alphabetical catalogues, the one of such as are proper to the northern, the other to the southern counties. 1674, 1691, 1737. Included in John Ray, Collection of English proverbs, 1742, 1768; ed W. W. Skeat 1874 (Eng Dialect Soc); Menston 1969 (facs of 1674).

Meriton, George. Yorkshire dialogue. 1683, 1697.

Kennett, White. Parochial antiquities attempted in the history of Ambrosden. Oxford 1695. With a glossary to explain the original, the acceptation and obsoleteness of words and phrases. Rptd 1816, 1818; ed W. W. Skeat 1879 (Eng Dialect Soc).

Thoresby, Ralph. Catalogue of words then (1703) to be heard in the West Riding of Yorkshire. Pp. 321–42 of Philosophical letters between the late learned Mr Ray and several of his ingenious correspondents, published by William Derham, 1718; ed W. W. Skeat 1874; rptd 1874 (Eng Dialect Soc).

Pegge, Samuel. Alphabet of Kenticisms and collection of proverbial saying used in Kent. 1735–6; ed W. W. Skeat 1874; rptd 1876 (Eng Dialect Soc).

Collier, John. A view of the Lancashire dialect, by way of a dialogue between Tummus o' Williams o' Margits o' Roalphs and Meary o' Dicks o' Tummus o' Peggy; to which is added a glossary of all the Lancashire words and phrases therein used. By T. Bobbin. Manchester [1746] etc.

Watson, John. History and antiquities of Halifax. 1775.

West, Thomas. Guide to the lakes of Cumberland. 1780.

H[utton], J[ohn]. A tour to the caves, in the environs of Ingelbrough and Settle, in the West-Riding of Yorkshire. 1780, 1781 (glossary on pp. 84–99); rptd 1873 (Eng Dialect Soc).

Grose, Francis. A provincial glossary, with a collection of local proverbs and popular superstitions. 1787, 1790 (rev), Menston 1968 (facs of 1787).

[Ritson, Isaac]. Copy of a letter wrote by a young shepherd to his friend in Borrowdale: a new edition; to which is added a glossary of the Cumberland words [by James Clarke]. Penrith 1788.

Pryce, William. Archaeologia cornu-britannica: or an essay to preserve the ancient Cornish language containing the rudiments of that language, in a Cornish grammar and Cornish-English vocabulary. Sherborne 1790.

Biblical Concordances etc

Chadwell, W. A profitable and well grounded concordance, wherein may be readily found the chiefest words contained in the scriptures; also the chiefest doctrinal heads of Scripture. 1660.

Jackson, John. Index biblicus: or an exact concordance to the Holy Bible; whereunto are added the marginal readings. Cambridge 1668.

Powel, Vavasor. A new and useful concordance to the Holy Bible, begun by Vavasor Powel and finished by N.P. and J[ohn] F[airfax]. 1671; ed E. Bagshaw and T. Hardcastle 1673, 1792.

P., B. The parish-clerks vade mecum: or an alphabetical concordance of the most material words and sentences in the book of singing-psalms, used in the parish churches, pointing out also psalms suited to all the great festivals of the Church of England and most other special occasions. 1694.

Clark, Samuel. A brief concordance to the Holy Bible, of the most usual places which one may have occasion to seek for, in a new method. 1696.

The Cambridge concordance to the Holy Scriptures. 1720 (5th edn). Rptd from Samuel Newton, Concordance, 1658.

Shaw, Ferdinando. A summary of the Bible: or the principal heads of natural and revealed religion: alphabetically disposed in the words of scripture only, adapted to the use of a scripture-dictionary. 1730.

The fort-royal of the Scriptures: or a vade-mecum concordance, containing a hundred heads of scripture, by an admirer of the Word. Edinburgh 1732 (3rd edn). By John Hart? Rptd from 1649 edn.

Cruden, Alexander. A complete concordance to the Holy Scriptures of the Old and New Testament, containing I: the appellative or common words; II: the proper

names in the scriptures; to which is added a concordance to the Apocrypha. 1738, 1761, 1769, 1785 etc.

Pilkington, Matthew. A rational concordance or an index to the Bible. Nottingham 1749.

A dictionary of the Holy Bible. 3 vols 1759.

A concordance to the Holy Scriptures, wherein any passage in the Bible may be found by the recollection of any material word in it. 1762.

Butterworth, John. A new concordance to the Holy Scriptures of the Old and New Testament. 1767, 1785.

A compendious yet compleat concordance to the Holy Scriptures, on an improved plan: containing a scripture dictionary, a synopsis of the Pentateuch, the harmony of the four evangelists and a Scripture chronology. Newcastle 1777.

Taylor, Thomas. A new concordance to the Holy Scriptures. York 1782.

Oliver, Peter. The scripture lexicon: or a dictionary of above three thousand proper names and difficult words in the Old and New Testament, accented as they ought to be pronounced. Birmingham 1784, 1787, London 1792, 1797, Oxford 1810, 1818.

Fisher, John. A concordance to the Holy Scriptures. Paisley 1796 (3rd edn), 1799, Glasgow 1799.

Brown, John. A brief concordance to the Holy Scriptures. Edinburgh 1783, Worcester Mass 1791, Edinburgh 1799 etc.

Literary Glossaries and Dictionaries

Old English

Somner, William. Dictionarium saxonico–latino–anglicum: voces, phrasesque praecipuas anglo-saxonicas e libris, sive manuscriptis, sive typis excusis, aliisque monumentis tum publicis tum privatis, magna diligentia collectas; cum latina et anglica vocum interpretatione complectens. Oxford 1659.

Benson, Thomas. Thesaurus linguae anglo-saxonicae dictionario Gul. Somneri, quoad numerum vocum auctior. Oxford 1690. Prospectus: title and one page only ptd.

— Vocabularium anglo-saxonicum. Oxford 1701. Compendium from Somner; largely carried out by Edward Thwaites.

Hearne, Thomas. Joannis Lelandi antiquarii de rebus britannicis collectanearum tomus tertius. 1715, 1770, 1774. Ex antiquiss. dictionario latino saxonico, pp. 134–6

Wilkins, David. Leges anglo-saxonicae ecclesiasticae et civiles. 1721. Contains glossary.

Lye, Edward. Francisci Junii etymologicum anglicanum. Oxford 1743. By Junius; ed Lye.

— Dictionarium saxonico et gothico-latinum. 2 vols 1772. Ed Owen Manning. A specimen of 4 pp. ptd earlier, [1768?]; proposals ptd 1768.

Middle English

Hearne, Thomas. Robert of Glocester's chronicle. 2 vols Oxford 1724. Contains ME glossary.

— Peter Langtoft's chronicle (as illustrated and improv'd by Robert of Brunne) from the death of Cadwalader to the end of K. Edward the First's reign. 2 vols Oxford 1725. Contains ME glossary different from preceding item.

Lewis, John. The New Testament, translated out of the Latin Vulgate by John Wiclif. 1731. Contains ME glossary.

Chaucer and after

Chaucer

[Thomas, Timothy]. Glossary. In John Urry's edn of Chaucer's works, 1721.

Tyrwhitt, Thomas. Glossary. In his edn of Canterbury Tales, 5 vols 1775–8.

[Anderson, Robert]. Glossary. In Works of the British poets vol 1, Edinburgh 1792.

Gavin Douglas

[Ruddiman, Thomas]. Virgil's Aeneis, translated into Scottish verse, by the famous Gawin Douglas Bishop of Dunkeld; to which is added a large glossary, explaining the difficult words; which may serve for a dictionary to the old Scottish language. Edinburgh 1710.

Fawkes, Francis. A description of May, by Gavin Douglas. 1752 (3 edns). With a glossary.

Miscellaneous early poetry

[Dalrymple, Sir David (later Lord Hailes)]. Ancient Scottish poems, published from the ms of George Bannatyne [1568]. Edinburgh 1770, 1770. Glossary, pp. 317–28.

Pinkerton, John. Ancient Scotish poems, never before in print, but now published from the ms collections of Sir R. Maitland: comprising pieces written from about 1420 till 1586, with large notes and a glossary. 2 vols 1786.

Ritson, Joseph. Ancient songs, from the time of King Henry the Third to the Revolution. 1790, 2 vols 1829; ed W. C. Hazlitt 1877. With glossary.

— Pieces of ancient popular poetry. 1791, 1833, 1884.

— Poems on interesting events in the reign of Edward III written in the year MCCCLII by Laurence Minot; with a preface, dissertations, notes and a glossary. 1795, 1825.

— Robin Hood. 1795, 1820, 1832, 1862, 1884.

Hoccleve, Thomas. Poems. 1796. Ed George Mason.

Spenser

Hughes, John. Glossary, explaining the old and obscure words. In his edn of Spenser's Works, 6 vols 1715, 1750.

[Birch, Thomas]. The Faerie Queene, by Edmund Spenser, with an exact collation of the two original editions; to which are now added a new life of the author, and also a glossary. 3 vols 1751.

Upton, John. Spenser's Faerie Queene: a new edition, with a glossary and notes explanatory and critical. 2 vols 1758.

Church, Ralph. The Faerie Queene, by Edmund Spenser: new edition, with notes critical and explanatory. 4 vols 1758–9. With a glossary.

Shakespeare

Sewell, George. Venus and Adonis, Tarquin and Lucrece, Miscellany poems, Essay on the stage, glossary and remarks on the plays. 1725. A 7th vol added to Pope's edn of Shakespeare, 1723–5; rptd 1726, 1728.

Hanmer, Sir Thomas. A glossary explaining the obsolete and difficult words in the plays of Shakespear. Vol 6 of Works of Mr William Shakespear, 6 vols Oxford 1744–6, 1745, 1747, 1748, 1760, 1771.

[Edwards, Thomas]. Essay towards a glossary. In his Canons of criticism, 1748, 1748, 1750, 1750, 1753, 1758, 1765. Originally as A supplement to Mr Warburton's edition of Shakespeare.

Warner, Richard. A letter to David Garrick esq, concerning a glossary to the plays of Shakespeare, on a more extensive plan than has hitherto appeared; to which is annexed a specimen. 1768.

[Capell, Edward]. Glossary to Shakespeare. In his Notes and various readings to Shakespeare vol 1, 1774, 1779.

[Beckett, Andrew]. A concordance to Shakespeare, suited to all the editions; in which the distinguished and parallel passages in the plays of that justly-admired writer are methodically arranged. 1787.

Ayscough, Samuel. Index to the remarkable passages and words made use of by Shakespeare, calculated to point out the different meanings to which the works are applied. 1790, Dublin 1791, London 1827.

The poems of William Shakespeare, with Mr Capell's History of the origin of Shakespeare's fables; to which is added a glossary. [1798].

Milton

[Coxeter, Thomas]. A verbal index to Milton's Paradise lost, adapted to every edition but the first, which was publish'd in ten books only. 1741.

Newton, Thomas. Paradise lost, a poem in twelve books: new edition, with notes of various authors. 2 vols 1749. With verbal index.

Paradise lost, a poem, in twelve books: the last edition; the author, John Milton. 2 vols Paris 1754. With glossary and index, French-English.

A familiar explanation of the poetical works of Milton; to which is prefixed Mr Addison's Criticism on Paradise lost. 1762. With glossary, textual notes etc.

Slang

For a fuller list, see J. C. Hotten, The bibliography of slang, cant and vulgar language, *in his* Dictionary of modern slang, cant and vulgar words 1860 (2nd edn); W. J. Burke, The literature of slang, New York 1939; *and* G. E. Noyes, SP 38 1941, *as well as Starnes and Noyes, General Studies, above.*

Head, Richard. Canting academy: or devil's cabinet opened; to which is added a compleat canting dictionary. 1674, 1674.

E., B. A new dictionary of the terms ancient and modern of the canting crew, in its several tribes of gipsies, beggars, thieves, cheats etc. 1690; ed J. S. Farmer 1899.

[Hitchen, Charles]. The regulator: or a discovery of the conduct of thieves and thief-takers. 1718. An attack on Jonathan Wild, containing an account of all the flash words now in vogue amongst the thieves. An abridged version in F. J. Lyons, Jonathan Wild: prince of robbers, 1936, pp. 221–46.

'Smith, Capt Alexander'. Compleat history of the lives and robberies of the most notorious highwaymen, foot-pads etc. 1719 (5th edn). Vol 1, Thieves' new canting dictionary, separately pbd 1719, 1720.

A new canting dictionary: comprehending all the terms, ancient and modern, used in several tribes of gypsies, beggars etc. 1725. Appeared in several edns, sometimes metamorphosised, e.g. Bacchus and Venus, 1737.

Bailey, Nathaniel. An universal etymological dictionary, volume two. 1727. *See* (3) *below.* Later edns of vol 2 contain a collection of canting words and terms.

The life and amours of Bampfylde-Moore Carew. 1745.

An apology for the life of Bampfylde-Moore Carew. 1749. Many later edns of both these works, including cant dictionaries. Both ed C. H. Wilkinson as The king of beggars, 1931.

[Grose, Francis]. A classical dictionary of the vulgar tongue. 1785, 1788, 1796, Menston 1968 (facs of 1785).

The whole art of thieving and defrauding discovered; to which is added an explanation of most of the cant terms in the thieving language. 1786.

Potter, Humphrey T. A new dictionary of all the cant and flash languages, both ancient and modern, used by gypsies, beggars etc: carefully arranged and selected from the most approved authors, and from the mss of Jonathan Wild, Baxter and others. [1790], 1797, [1800?].

Dictionaries

Skinner, Stephen. Etymologicon linguae anglicanae: seu explicatio vocum anglicarum, etymologice ex propriis fontibus, sc. ex linguis duodecim. 1671.

Gazophylacium anglicanum. 1689, 1691 (as A new English dictionary showing the etymological derivation of the English tongue, in two parts). Mainly based on Skinner, above.

K[ersey]. J[ohn]. A new English dictionary: or a compleat collection of the most proper and significant words, with a short and clear exposition of difficult words and terms of art, chiefly designed for the benefit of young scholars,

tradesman, artificers and the female sex, who would learn to spell truely. 1702, 1713, 1731, 1739, 1748, 1752, Dublin 1757, London 1759, 1772, Menston 1969 (facs of 1702).
— Dictionarium anglo-britannicum: or a general English dictionary. 1708, 1715, 1721. Abridged from Kersey's revision of Edward Phillips, New world of words, 1706, 1720; in effect the latter is a fresh work.

Bailey, Nathaniel. An universal etymological English dictionary: containing many thousand new words more than any English dictionary before extant. 1721; 28 edns by 1800; vol 2 (suppl), 1727, 1731, 1737, 1756, 1759, 1760, 1775, 1776.
— Dictionarium britannicum: or a more compleat universal etymological dictionary than any extant, revis'd and improv'd, with many thousand additions. 1730, 1736 (with addns by Thomas Lediard et al). Dr Johnson used an interleaved copy of this work as the basis of his own dictionary. It is an expanded version of vol 1 of Universal etymological dictionary, above. *See* D. McCracken, The drudgery of defining: Johnson's debt to Bailey's Dictionarium britannicum, MP 66 1969.
— A new universal etymological dictionary, containing not only explanations of the words in the English language, and the different senses in which they are used. 1755, 1764, 1772. Based on Bailey, ed Joseph Nicol Scott. Derives many details from Johnson.
On this volume *see* P. B. Gove, Notes on serialization and competitive publishing: Johnson and Bailey's Dictionaries, 1755, in Proc Oxford Bibl Soc 5 1940.

Defoe, Benjamin Norton. A new English dictionary: containing a collection of words in the English language, properly explain'd and alphabetically dispos'd. Westminster 1735. This work was variously issued as A compleat English dictionary, Westminster 1735; and with different subtitles, 1737, 1739 (attributed to J. Sparrow gent), 1741 (attributed to James Manlove). Essentially the text is the same throughout.

Dyche, Thomas and William Pardon. A new general English dictionary. 1735, 1737, 1740, 1744, 1748, 1750, 1752/3, 1754, 1758, 1759, 1760/1, 1765, 1768, 1771, 1777, 1781, 1794. *See* S. I. Tucker, Dyche and Pardon's Dictionary: a study in personal bias, English 11 1957.

Martin, Benj[amin]. Lingua britannica reformata: or a new English dictionary; to which is prefixed an introduction, containing a physico-grammatical essay on the propriety and rationale of the English tongue. 1749, 1754.

[Wesley, John]. The complete English dictionary, explaining most of those hard words which are found in the best English writers, by a lover of good English and common sense. 1753, Bristol 1764, London 1777, 1790.

A pocket dictionary: or complete English expositor, shewing readily the part of speech to which each word belongs. 1753, 1758, 1765, 1779.

Buchanan, James. Linguae britannicae vera pronunciatio, or a new English dictionary: containing a supplement of upwards of four thousand names, so distinguished, that any person, native or foreigner, who can but read, may speedily acquire an accurate pronunciation of the English language. 1757, 1769 (as A new English dictionary).

Johnson, Samuel. A dictionary of the English language, in which the words are deduced from their originals, and illustrated in their different significations, by examples from the best writers; to which are prefixed a history of the language and an English grammar. 2 vols 1755 (folio), 2 vols Dublin 1775 (4°), 2 vols 1756 (8°) etc. *See* J. H. Sledd and G. J. Kolb, Dr Johnson's Dictionary: essays in the biography of a book, Chicago 1955.

Entick, John. The new spelling-dictionary, teaching to write and pronounce the English tongue with ease and propriety. 1765; 40 edns, London or Dublin, by 1800; later rev W. Crackelt.

Johnston, William. A pronouncing and spelling dictionary, wherein by a new and sufficient method the pro-sounds of English words are exactly ascertained, and by which both his Majesty's subjects and foreigners may correct an improper, or acquire right pronunciation of the English language. 1764, Menston 1968 (facs). Appendix on the sounds of words.

Kenrick, William. A new dictionary of the English language, to which is prefixed a rhetorical grammar. 1773.

Barclay, James. A complete and universal English dictionary, on a new plan, including not only a full explanation of difficult words and technical terms, but a pronouncing dictionary. 1774, 1782, 1792, 1799.

Walker, John. A dictionary of the English language, answering at once the purposes of rhyming, spelling and pronouncing. 1775, 1807, 1819, 1824; ed J. Longmuir 1865. Words arranged according to termination.
— A critical pronouncing dictionary and expositor of the English language. 1791, Dublin 1794, London 1797, Dublin 1798, Menston 1968 (facs of 1791). *See* J. M. Osborn, Dr Johnson and the contrary converts, in New light on Dr Johnson, ed F. W. Hilles, New Haven 1959; J. H. Lamb, Walker and Joshua Steele, Speech Monographs 32 1965.

Perry, William. The royal standard English dictionary; to which is prefixed a comprehensive grammar of the English language. Edinburgh 1775; 9 British and 5 American edns by 1800.

Ash, John. The new and complete dictionary of the English language, to which is prefixed a compendious grammar. 2 vols 1775, 1795.

Sheridan, Thomas. A general dictionary of the English language, one main object of which is to establish a standard of pronunciation; to which is prefixed a rhetorical grammar. 2 vols 1780, 1 vol Dublin 1784; many subsequent edns, London, Dublin and Philadelphia; Menston 1968 (facs of 1780).

Lemon, G. W. English etymology: or a derivative dictionary of the English language. 1783.

P. R.

(7) GRAMMARS

For a more complete list, see Kennedy and Alston, below.

General References

Brown, G. A digested catalogue of English grammars and grammarians. Pp. xi-xx of his Grammar of English grammars, New York 1857 (2nd edn).

Wells, W. H. A chronological catalogue of English grammars issued prior to 1801. Pp. 3-9 of his Historical authorship of English grammar, Chicago 1878.

Aitken, G. A. Steele and some English grammars of his time. Walford's Antiquarian Mag 8 1885.

Kittredge, G. L. Some landmarks of English grammar. Boston 1906.

Kennedy, A. G. A bibliography of writings on the English language from the beginning of printing to the end of 1922. Cambridge Mass 1927, New York 1961.

Leonard, S. A. The doctrine of correctness in English usage 1700-1800. Madison 1929.

Poldauf, I. On the history of some problems in English grammar before 1800. Prague 1948.

Jones, R. F. The triumph of the English language. Stanford 1950.

Dobson, E. J. English pronunciation 1500-1700. 2 vols Oxford 1957, 1968.

Tucker, S. I. English examined. Cambridge 1961. Extracts from seventeenth- and eighteenth-century grammarians.

Alston, R. C. A bibliography of the English language from the invention of printing to the year 1800: Vol 1, English grammars written in English and English grammars written in Latin by native speakers. Leeds 1965 (priv ptd).

Wilkins, John. An essay towards a real character and a philosophical language. 1668; Abstract in his Mathematical and philosophical works, 1706; Menston 1968 (facs). See O. Funke, Zum Weltsprachen-problem in England im 17 Jahrhundert, Anglistische Forschungen 69 1929; On the sources of Wilkins' Philosophical language, E Studies 40 1959.

Cooper, Christopher. Grammatica linguae anglicanae. 1685, 1685; ed J. D. Jones, Halle 1911; Menston 1968; tr and rev as The English teacher: or the discovery of the art of teaching and learning the English tongue, fitted for the use of schools. 1687, 1698 (as Cooper's compleat English teacher), 1688; ed B. Sundby, Lund 1953.

Miege, Guy. The English grammar: or the grounds and genius of the English tongue; with a prefatory discourse concerning its original and excellency, and at the end a collection of the English monosyllables, being the radical part of the language. 1688, [1689?] (pirated edn), 1691, Menston 1968 (facs of 1688).

Aickin, Joseph. The English grammar or the English tongue reduced to grammatical rules. 1693, 1693?, Menston 1967 (facs).

Lane, A. A key to the art of letters: or English a learned language, full of art, elegancy and variety. 1700, 1705, 1706.

Dyche, Thomas. A guide to the English tongue in two parts. [1709?], 1710; 48 edns by 1774; Menston 1968 (facs of 1709?).

Greenwood, James. An essay towards a practical English grammar, describing the genius and nature of the English tongue. 1711, 1722, 1729, 1740, 1753, Menston 1968 (facs of 1711).

— The royal English grammar. 1737, 1744, 1747, 1750, 1754, 1761, 1763, 1770, 1780.

A grammar of the English tongue, with notes, giving the grounds and reasons of grammar in general. 1711, 1712 (with addns), 1712, 1714, 1721, 1728, [1735?], 1746, 1759, 1782 (as Youth's preceptor, by Sir Richard Steele), Menston 1967 (facs of 1711). Often called Steele's grammar; it is also attributed to John Brightland and Charles Gildon.

Maittaire, Michael. The English grammar: or an essay on the art of grammar, applied to and exemplified in the English tongue. 1712, Menston 1967 (facs).

Loughton, William. A practical grammar of the English tongue. 1734, 1735, 1739, 1740; York and Scarborough 1744, London 1749, 1755.

Dilworth, Thomas. A new guide to the English tongue: containing a brief but comprehensive English grammar. 1740, Menston 1967 (facs). Numerous edns, New York, Boston or Wilmington, by 1800.

[Newbery, John]. Grammar made familiar and easy to young gentle-ladies and foreigners: an easy introduction to the English language, or a compendious grammar. 1745 (1st vol of the Circle of sciences), 1748 (2nd vol), Dublin 1752, London 1755, 1759, 1769.

— Grammar and rhetoric: being the first and third volumes of the Circle of the sciences, considerably enlarged and improved. 1776.

Wesley, John. A short English grammar. Bristol 1748, 1761, London 1778.

[Fisher, Ann?]. A new grammar: being the most easy guide to speaking and writing the English language correctly. Newcastle 1750 (2nd edn); rev J. Wilson, Congleton 1792; over 30 edns by 1800; Menston 1968 (facs of 1750).

H[arris], J[ames]. Hermes: or a philosophical enquiry concerning universal language and universal grammar. 1751, 1765, 1771, 1786, 1794, 1806, 1825, Menston 1968 (facs); tr French, 1796; tr German, 1788.

Buchanan, James. The complete English scholar, in three parts: a new, short and familiar method of instructing children and perfecting grown persons in the English tongue, and of learning grammar in general without the help of Latin. 1753. Pt 3 is a grammar.

— The British grammar: or an essay towards speaking and writing the English language grammatically and inditing elegantly. 1762 (anon), 1768, 1779, Boston 1784, Menston 1968 (facs of 1762).

— A regular English syntax, wherein is exhibited the whole variety of English construction, properly exemplified; to which is added the elegant manner of arranging words and verbs of sentences. 1767, 1769, Philadelphia 1780, London 1783, 1786, 1788, 1792. See B. Emsley, Buchanan and the eighteenth-century regulation of English usage, PMLA 48 1933.

Farro, Daniel. The royal universal British grammar and vocabulary: being a digestion of the entire English language into its proper parts of speech, in a method entirely new. 1754 (3 edns); abridged [Bristol? 1776?].

Martin, Benjamin. An introduction to the English language and learning. 1754, 1756, 1766.

Johnson, Samuel. A grammar of the English tongue. Prefixed to vol 1 of his Dictionary, 1755.

Bayly, Anselm. An introduction to languages, literary and philosophical, especially to the English, Latin, Greek and Hebrew: exhibiting at one view their grammar, rationale, analogy and idiom. 1758, Menston 1968 (facs).

— The English accidence. 1771. Included in A plain and complete grammar of the English language; to which is prefixed the English accedence, with remarks and observations on [R. Lowth's] A short introduction to English grammar, 1772.

Ward, John. Four essays upon the English language: viz I, Observations on the orthography; II, Rules for the division of syllables; III, The use of articles; IV, The formation of the verbs, and their analogy with the Latin. 1758, Menston 1968 (facs).

Bradley, B. E. Ward's concept of dispositio. Speech monographs 24 1957.

— The inventio of John Ward. Speech Monographs 26 1959.

Reid, R. F. Ward's influence in America. Speech Monographs 27 1960.

Priestley, Joseph. The rudiments of English grammar adapted to the use of school, with observations on style. 1761, 1768, 1769, 1771, 1772, Dublin 1784, London 1786, 1789, 1798.

[Lowth, Robert]. A short introduction to English grammar, with critical notes. 1762 etc, Menston 1967 (facs); tr German, 1790.

Johnson, J. The new royal and universal English dictionary, to which is prefixed a grammar of the English tongue. 2 vols 1762.

Ash, John. Grammatical institutes: or an easy introduction to Dr Lowth's grammar. 1763 etc, Menston 1967 (facs); tr German, 1775. An earlier edn, Worcester 1760?, with different subtitle. See E. Vorlat, E Studies 40 1959.

— A comprehensive grammar. Prefixed to his New and complete dictionary of the English language, 1775.

Ward, William. An essay on grammar, as it may be applied to the English language, in two treatises. 1765, 1778, 1779, 1788, Menston 1968 (facs of 1765).

— A practical grammar of the English language, in two treatises: the first, containing rules for every part of its construction; the second, shewing the nature of the several parts of speech. York [1766?], 1767, Northampton 1771.

[Baker, Robert]. Reflections on the English language, in the nature of Vaugelas's reflections on the French: being a detection of many improper expressions used in conversation. 1770, Menston 1968 (facs).

Fenning, Daniel. A new grammar of the English language. 1771, 1773, 1778, 1783, 1787, [1790], 1793, 1796, Romsey 1800, Menston 1967 (facs).

Adam, Alexander. The rudiments of Latin and English grammar. 1772.

Kenrick, William. A rhetorical grammar. Prefixed to his New dictionary of the English language, 1773.

Burn, John. A practical grammar of the English language, together with rules of composition. Glasgow 1776, 1772, 1778, 1786, 1793, 1797, 1799.

Perry, W. The only sure guide to the English tongue: or new pronouncing spelling book; to which is added a comprehensive grammar of the English language. Edinburgh 1776.

Harrison, Ralph. Institutes of English grammar, with exercises of true and false construction. Manchester 1777; many edns, American edns as Rudiments of English grammar, Philadelphia 1787 etc; Menston 1967 (facs of 1777).

Shaw, John. A methodical English grammar: containing rules and directions for speaking and writing the English language. 1778, 1785, 1788, 1793.

Sheridan, Thomas. A rhetorical grammar. Prefixed to his General dictionary of the English language, 1780; Menston 1969 (facs).

[Fell, John]. An essay towards an English grammar, with a dissertation on the nature and peculiar use of certain hypothetical verbs in the English language. 1784, Menston 1968 (facs).

Webster, Noah. A grammatical institute of the English language. Hartford 1784; many American edns by 1800; Menston 1968 (facs). Pt 2 is a comprehensive grammar.

Tooke, John Horne. Ἔπεα πτερόεγτα: the diversions of Purley. 2 pts 1786-98, 1 vol Menston 1968 (facs).

[Ussher, George Neville]. The elements of English grammar methodically arranged. Gloucester 1785, 1786, London 1787, 1789, Gloucester 1793, 1799, Menston 1967 (facs of 1785).

Coote, Charles. Elements of the grammar of the English language; to which is subjoined a history of the English language. 1788.

Alexander, Caleb. A grammatical system of the English language: comprehending a plain and familiar scheme of teaching young gentlemen and ladies the art of writing and speaking correctly their native tongue. Boston 1792, 1793, 1795, 1796, 1799 etc.

Hornsey, John. A short English grammar. York 1793, Newcastle 1798.

Murray, Lindley. English grammar, adapted to the different classes of learning, with an appendix containing rules and observations for promoting perspecuity in speaking and writing. York 1795, Menston 1968 (facs). For subsequent edns (over 200 by 1850) see Alston vol 1, pp. 92-6; abridged York 1797 etc.

P. R.

X. CLASSICAL AND ORIENTAL STUDIES

RICHARD BENTLEY

1662-1742

Bibliographies

Bartholomew, A. T. Bentley: a bibliography of his works, with introduction by J. W. Clark. Cambridge 1908.

Collections

Works. Ed A. Dyce 3 vols 1836-8. Incomplete. Includes Dissertations upon the Epistles of Phalaris etc; Epistola ad J. Millium; Sermons at Boyle's Lecture and his other sermons; Remarks upon a Discourse of free-thinking; Proposals for printing the Greek Testament etc.

Richardi Bentleii et doctorum virorum epistolae. Ed C. Burney 1807, 1825.

Epistolae Bentleii, Graevii etc. Ed F. G. Kraft, Altona 1831.

Correspondence. Ed C. Wordsworth 2 vols 1842.

Pol, E. H. Some letters of Richard Bentley. Leyden 1959.

§ 1

Epistola ad Joannem Millium [on Malalas]. Appendix to Mill's edn of the Historia chronica of Malalas, Oxford 1691.

The folly of atheism. 1692 (Boyle Lecture 1).

Matter and motion cannot think. 1692 (Boyle Lecture 2).

A confutation of atheism from the structure and origin of humane bodies. 3 pts 1692 (Boyle Lectures 3-5).

A confutation of atheism from the origin and frame of the world. 3 pts 1692-3 (Boyle Lectures 6-8).

Sermons on the confutation of atheism. 1699, 1724, 1735, 1809; tr Latin, 1696; German, 1715 (Boyle Lectures 6-8).

Of Revelation and the Messias. 1696. A sermon.

Callimachi fragmenta a Richardo Bentleio collecta; R. Bentleii Animadversiones in nonnulla hymnorum Callimachi loca. In edn by J. G. Graevius, Utrecht 1697.

A proposal for building a Royal Library. 1697; rptd in A. T. Bartholomew and J. W. Clark, Bibliography of Bentley, Cambridge 1908.

Dissertation upon the Epistles of Phalaris, Themistocles, Socrates, Euripides and others; and the Fables of Aesop. Ptd with the 2nd edn of W. Wotton, Reflections upon ancient and modern learning, 1697.

A dissertation upon the Epistles of Phalaris; with an answer to the objections of the Hon C. Boyle. 1699, 1777, 1816, 1817, 1874, 1883; tr Latin, 1777; German, 1857.

Emendationes ad Ciceronis Tusculanas. Ptd in edn by J. Davies, Cambridge 1709.

Emendationes in Menandri et Philemonis reliquias ex nupera editione Joannis Clerici, auctore Phileleuthero Lipsiensi. Utrecht 1710, Cambridge 1713.

The present state of Trinity College in Cambridge, in a letter from Dr Bentley to the Bishop of Ely, published by a gentleman of the Temple. 1710, 1710. For Bentley's Trinity College controversies, see Bartholomew and Clark, above, pp. 60-74.

Q.Horatius Flaccus ex recensione et cum notis R. Bentleii. Cambridge 1711, Amsterdam 1713, 1728.

Q. Horatius Flaccus ad nuperam Richardi Bentleii editionem accurate expressus; notas addidit Thomas Bentleius. Cambridge 1713.

Remarks upon a late discourse of free-thinking [by Anthony Collins], in a letter to F[rancis] H[are] DD, by Phileleutherus Lipsiensis. 1713.

A sermon upon Popery. Cambridge 1715.

A sermon preached before King George. 1717.

Two letters to Dr Bentley concerning his intended edition of the Greek Testament; together with the doctor's answer. 1717.

Proposals for printing a new edition of the Greek Testament. [1720].

Dr Bentley's proposals for printing a new edition of the Greek Testament; with a full answer to all the remarks [of Middleton]. 1721.

A reply to a copy of verses made in imitation of Book III Ode 2 of Horace. Ptd in The Grove, 1721, and in Monk's life of Bentley vol 2, 1833.

Publii Terentii comoediae, Phaedri fabulae Aesopiae, Publii Syri et aliorum veterum sententiae, ex recensione R. Bentleii. Cambridge 1726, Amsterdam 1727.

The case of Trinity College in Cambridge; whether the Crown or the Bishop of Ely be the General Visitor. 1729.

Milton's Paradise lost: a new edition by R[ichard B[entley]. 1732.

M. Manilii astronomicon, ex recensione R. Bentleii. 1739.

M. Annaei Lucani Pharsalia cum notis Hugonis Grotii et R. Bentleii. Ed R. Cumberland, Strawberry Hill 1760.

§2

Temple, Sir William. Upon ancient and modern learning. In Miscellanea pt 2, 1690. Extols the writings of Phalaris and Aesop.

Wotton, William. Reflections upon ancient and modern learning, 1694. Answer to Temple.

Phalaridis Agrigentinorum tyranni espistolae. Rev C. B[oyle], Oxford 1695, 1718. Preface against Bentley.

Dr Bentley's Dissertations on the Epistles of Phalaris and the Fables of Aesop, examin'd by the Hon C. Boyle. 1698. Mainly by Francis Atterbury.

Middleton, Conyers. Remarks upon the proposals for printing a new edition of the Greek Testament. 1721; Some farther remarks, 1721.

Newton, Sir Isaac. Four letters [to Bentley], containing some arguments in proof of a Deity. 1756. Written 1692–3 for Bentley to use in his Boyle Lectures.

Cumberland, R. In his Memoirs, 1806.

Monk, J. H. Life of Bentley. 1830, 2 vols 1833 (enlarged).

De Quincey, Thomas. Essay on Bentley written as review of Monk's Life. Blackwood's Mag Sept–Oct 1830; rptd in Works vol 7, 1854 etc.

Maehly, J. Richard Bentley. Leipzig 1868.

Nicoll, H. J. Great scholars: Buchanan, Bentley, Porson, Parr and others. Edinburgh 1880, 1884.

Jebb, R. C. Bentley. 1882, 1902 (EML).

Sandys, J. E. In his A history of classical scholarship vol 2, Cambridge 1908.

Beeching, H. C. In his Francis Atterbury, 1909.

Mackail, J. W. Bentley's Milton. Proc Br Acad 11 1924; rptd in his Studies in humanism, 1938.

Empson, W. Milton and Bentley. In his Some versions of pastoral, 1935.

Garrod, H. W. Phalaris and Phalarism. In Seventeenth-century studies presented to Sir Herbert Grierson, Oxford 1938.

Jolliffe, H. R. Bentley versus Horace. PQ 16 1937.

Laistner, M. L. W. Bentley 1742–1942. SP 39 1942.
—— The Palatine emigration of 1709. New York History 23 1942.

Litz, F. E. Bentley on beauty, irregularity and mountains. ELH 12 1945.

Horne, C. J. The Phalaris controversy: King versus Bentley. RES 22 1946.

Darbishire, H. Milton's Paradise lost: Bryce Memorial Lecture. Oxford 1951. On Bentley and Dr Johnson in their criticisms of Milton.

Fox, A. John Mill and Bentley: a study of the textual criticism of the New Testament. Oxford 1954.

Getty, R. J. Bentley and classical scholarship in North America. Trans & Proc of Amer Philological Assoc 93 1962.

Goold, G. P. Introduction to Epistola ad Joannnem Millium, reprinted from edition of A. Dyce. Toronto 1962.
—— Bentley: a tercentenary commemoration. Harvard Stud 67 1963.

Shackleton Bailey, D. R. Bentley and Horace. Proc Leeds Philosophical Soc 10 1963.

Hunt, C. B. Contemporary references to the work of Bentley. Bodleian Quart Record 7 1963.

White, R. J. Dr Bentley: a study in academic scarlet. 1965.

RICHARD PORSON
1759–1808

Papers in the Library of Trinity College Cambridge, arranged by H. R. Luard in 1859 and bound in 4 vols, contain (1) the originals of many of the letters ptd in the correspondence; (2) transcripts of Photius; (3) transcripts of the Medea and the Phoenissæ; (4) notes on ancient authors, including a collation of the Aldine Æschylus. Also Adversaria in most of the 274 books, formerly belonging to Porson, now in the Library of Trinity College Cambridge; and unpbd letters in the libraries of Edinburgh Univ and Magdalen College Oxford.

Editions

Ξενοφωντος Κυρου 'Αναβασις βιβλια επτα, recognovit T. Hutchinson. 1786. Notes, pp. 41–59, and preface by Porson.

Toup, J. Emendationes in Suidam et Hesychium et alios lexicographos graecos. Notæ breves ad Toupii emendationes in Suidam, a[uctore] R[icardo] P[orsono] C[ollegi] S. S[anctæ] T[rinitatis] C[antabrigiensis] s[ocio]. 4 vols Oxford 1790. Ed Porson.

Publii Virgili Maronis opera varietate lectionis et perpetua adnotatione illustrata a C. G. Heyne; accedit index uberrimus: editio tertia auctior. 4 vols 1793. Preface by Porson.

Æschyli tragœdiæ septem, cum versione latina. 2 vols Glasgow, London, Oxford 1794 (ptd) and 1806 (pbd). Anon.

Αἱ του Αἰσχυλου τραγωδιαι επτα. Glasgow 1795. Pirated by the publisher, without Porson's knowledge. Illustr Flaxman.

Ευριπιδου 'Εκαβη: Euripidis Hecuba, ad fidem manuscriptorum emendata. 1797.

Ευριπιδου 'Ορεστης: Euripidis Orestes ad fidem manuscriptorum emendata et brevibus notis emendationum potissimum rationes reddentibus instructa. 1798.

Ευριπιδου Φοινισσαι: Euripidis Phœnissæ ad fidem manuscriptorum emendata et brevibus notis emendationum potissimum rationes reddentibus instructa. 1799.

Ευριπιδου Μηδεια: Euripidis Medea ad fidem manuscriptorum emendata et brevibus notis emendationum potissimum rationes reddentibus instructa. Cambridge 1801.

'Ομηρου 'Ιλιας και 'Οδυσσεια. 4 vols Oxford 1800–1. Ed T. Grenville, Porson, W. Cleaver et al, with Porson's collation of the Harleian ms of the Odyssey.

Euripidis tragœdiæ priores quatuor ['Εκαβη, 'Ορεστης, Φοινισσαι, Μηδεια] edidit R. Porson; recensuit suasque notulas subjecit J. Scholefield. Cambridge 1826.

Contributions to Periodicals

Maty's Review. 1783 (papers on Schütz's Æschylus and on Brunck's Aristophanes); 1784 (on Stephen Weston's Fragments of Hermesianax and on G. I. Huntingford's Apology for the Monostrophics).

Gentleman's Magazine. 57 Aug–Oct 1787 (anon letters to the editor constituting an ironical panegyric of Sir John Hawkins's Life of Johnson); 58–9 1788–9 (letters to Travis, rptd separately as Letters to Mr Archdeacon Travis, in answer to his defence of the three heavenly witnesses, 1 John v. 7, 1790); 64 July 1794 (letter signed 'Urbano Amicior').

Monthly Review. 79 1788, 80 1789 (The Parian Chronicle, an anon vindication of its genuineness against strictures of T. Robertson); enlarged ser 11 1793 (anon review of Plutarchi de educatione liberorum liber, ed Thomas Edwards); enlarged ser 13 1794 (anon review of Richard Payne Knight, Analytical essay on the Greek alphabet).

Morning Chronicle. 1796 (letter signed 'S. England', making fun of the W. H. Ireland Shakespeare forgeries. Included in Luard's Correspondence of Porson, pp. 60 f.); 1797 (Imitations of Horace. Political satires partly rptd in J. S. Watson, Life of Porson).

Critical Review. 1797 (review of Vincent, On the Greek verb).

Literary Remains

R. Porsoni adversaria: notae et emendationes in poetas graecos, quas ex schedis manuscriptis Porsoni apud Collegium S.S. Trinitatis Cantabrigiæ repositis deprompserunt et ordinarunt J. H. Monk, C. J. Blomfield. Cambridge 1812.

Tracts and miscellaneous criticisms, collected and arranged by Thomas Kidd. 1815.

Ricardi Porsoni notæ in Aristophanem, quibus Plutum comœdiam partim ex ejusdem recensione partim e manuscriptis emendatam et variis lectionibus instructam præmisit, et collationum appendicem adjecit Petrus Paulus Dobree. 3 pts Cambridge 1820.

Notes on Pausanias appended to T. Gaisford's Lectiones Platonicæ. 1820.

Φωτιου Λεξεων συναγωγη: e codice Galeano descripsit R. Porsonus. 2 pts Cambridge 1822.

Σουιδας: Suidæ lexicon post L. Kusterum ad codice manuscriptos recensuit T. Gaisford. 3 vols Oxford 1834. Notes on Suidas in appendix by Porson.

Correspondence. Ed H. R. Luard, Cambridge 1867. 68 letters.

§ 2

Clarke, Adam. A narrative of the last illness and death of Porson; with the facsimile of an ancient Greek inscription which was the chief subject of his last literary conversation. 1808.

A short account of the late Richard Porson, with some few particulars relative to his extraordinary talents, by an admirer of a great genius [Stephen Weston]. 1808.

[Beloe, W.] In his Sexagenarian, 2 vols 1817.

English scholarship: its rise, progress and decay (from Gataker to Dobree). Church of England Quart Rev 4–5 1838–9. 3 anon articles.

Literary anecdotes and contemporary reminiscences of Professor Porson and others, from the manuscript papers of the late E. H. Barker. 2 vols 1852.

Recollections of the table talk of Samuel Rogers; to which is added Porsoniana [by W. Maltby]. 1856.

Luard, H. R. In Cambridge essays, 1857.

Watson, J. S. The life of Porson. 1861.

Nicoll, H. J. Great scholars: Buchanan, Bentley, Porson, Parr and others. Edinburgh 1880.

Clarke, M. L. Porson: a biographical essay. Cambridge 1937.

— In his Greek studies in England 1700–1830, Cambridge 1945.

Page, D. L. Richard Porson 1759–1808. Proc Br Acad 45 1960.

OTHER CLASSICAL SCHOLARS

See also Translations from the Classics, col 1485, above.

ROBERT AINSWORTH
1660–1743

The most natural and easie way of institution: containing proposals for making a domestic education less chargeable to parents, and more easie and beneficial to children. 1698.

Thesaurus linguae latinae compendiarius: or a compendious dictionary of the Latin tongue designed principally for the use of the British nations. 1736; rev B. W. Beatson and W. Ellis 1829.

WILLIAM BATTIE
1704–76

Aristotelis De rhetorica. Cambridge 1728.

Isocratis orationes septem et epistolae. Cambridge 1729.

Isocratis orationes xiv. 1748.

Isocratis opera omnia. 1749.

WILLIAM BAXTER
1650–1723

De analogia: sive arte latinae linguae commentariolus. 1679.

Anacreontis carmina. 1695.

Q. Horatii Flacci eclogae. 1701.

Glossarium antiquitatum britannicarum. 1719, 1733.

Reliquiae Baxterianae: sive opera posthuma. Ed M. Williams 1726.

ANTHONY BLACKWALL
1674–1730

Theognidis sententiae morales. 1706.

An introduction to the classics. 1718; tr Latin, 1735.

The sacred classics defended and illustrated. 2 pts 1725–31; tr Latin, 1736.

VINCENT BOURNE
1695–1747

Carmina comitialia cantabrigiensia. 1721. Ed Bourne.

Poematia, latine partim reddita, partim scripta. 1734, 1764 (5th edn) etc.

Miscellaneous poems. 1772.

Poetical works. 2 vols Oxford 1808.

RICHARD CHANDLER
1738–1810

Elegiaca graeca. 1759.

Marmora oxoniensia. 2 pts Oxford 1763.

Ionian antiquities, published by the Society of Dilettanti. 2 vols 1769–97.

Inscriptiones antiquæ, pleræque nondum editæ; in Asia Minori et Græcia, præ sertim Athenis, collectæ, cum appendice. Oxford 1774.

Travels in Asia Minor: or an account of a tour, made at the expense of the Society of Dilettanti. Oxford 1775.

Travels in Greece: or an account of a tour, made at the expense of the Society of Dilettanti. Oxford 1776.

The history of Ilium or Troy, including the adjacent country, and the opposite coast of the Chersonesus of Thrace. 1802. Anon.

SAMUEL CLARKE
1675–1729

Caesaris quae extant. 1712 etc.

Homeri Ilias. 2 vols 1729–32 etc.

Homeri Odyssea. 2 vols 1740, 1758.
See col 1622, above.

THOMAS COOKE
1703–56

The Idylliums of Moschus and Bion translated. 1724.
The works of Hesiod translated. 2 vols 1728; rptd in
Chalmers's English poets, 1810.
Terence's comedys translated. 3 vols 1734. With Latin.
Plautus's Amphitruo translated. 1746.
See col 542, above.

THOMAS CREECH
1659–1700

T. Lucretius Carus his six books De natura rerum, done
into English verse. 1682.
The odes, satyrs and epistles of Horace, done into English.
1684.
Idylliums of Theocritus done into English. 1684.
T. Lucretii Cari de rerum natura libri vi, quibus interpretationem et notas addidit T. Creech. 1695.
The five books of M. Manilius done into English verse.
1697.

ALEXANDER CUNNINGHAM
1655?–1730

See col 2063, below.

JOHN DAVIES
1679–1732

Caesaris quae exstant. Cambridge 1706.
Ciceronis Tusculanae. Cambridge 1709.
Ciceronis De natura deorum. Cambridge 1718.
Ciceronis De divinatione et de fato. Cambridge 1721.
Ciceronis Academica. Cambridge 1725.
Ciceronis De legibus. Cambridge 1727.
Ciceronis De finibus. Cambridge 1728.

RICHARD DAWES
1708–68

Miscellanea critica. Cambridge 1745.

HENRY DODWELL the elder
1641–1711

De veteribus graecorum romanorumque cyclis. Oxford
1692, 1701.
Exercitationes duae: prima, de aetate Phalaridis; secunda,
de aetate Pythagorae philosophi. 1704.
See col 1607, above.

JOHN FELL
1625–86

Sancti C. Cypriani opera, recognita et illustrata per
Ioannem [Fell] oxoniensem. Oxford 1682, 1691.
See col 1608, above.

JOHN FOSTER
1731–74

An essay on the different nature of accent and quantity.
Eton 1762.

HENRY GALLY
1696–1769

The moral characters of Theocritus translated from the
Greek. 1725.
A dissertation against pronouncing the Greek language
according to accents. 1754.
A second dissertation. 1763.

EDWARD HARWOOD
1729–94

A view of the various editions of the Greek and Roman
classics, with remarks. 1775.
Biographica classica: the lives and characters of the Greek
and Roman classics. 2 vols 1778.

THOMAS HEARNE
1678–1735

See col 1699, above.

JOHN HUDSON
1662–1719

Thucydidis Historia. Oxford 1696.
Geographiae veteris scriptores Graeci minores. 4 vols
Oxford 1698–1712.
The works of Flavius Josephus. Tr Sir R. L'Estrange
1702. Notes by Hudson.
Dionysii Halicarnasseos opera omnia. 2 vols Oxford
1704.
Longinus De sublimitate. Oxford 1710.
Velleius Paterculus. Oxford 1711.
Moeris atticista de vocibus atticis et hellenicis. Oxford
1712.
Flavii Josephi opera omnia. 2 vols Oxford 1720.

JOHN KING
1696–1728

Euripidis Hecuba, Orestes et Phoenissae. Cambridge
1726, 1748,

RICHARD PAYNE KNIGHT
1750–1824

An analytical essay on the Greek alphabet. 1791.
Carmina homerica a rapsodorum interpolationibus repur-
gata et in pristinam formam redacta. 1808, 1820.
An inquiry into the symbolical language of ancient art and
mythology. 1818.

ADAM LITTLETON
1627–94

Linguae latinae liber dictionarius quadripartitus: a Latine
dictionary in four parts. 1673, 1678, 1685, 1695, 1723,
1735.

WILLIAM LLOYD
1627–1717

§1

Chronological account of the life of Pythagoras. 1699.

§2

Hart, A. T. William Lloyd. 1952.

JEREMIAH MARKLAND
1693–1776

P. Papinii Statii Silvarum libri quinque. 1728.
Remarks on the epistles of Cicero to Brutus and of Brutus to Cicero. 1745.
Euripidis Supplices. 1763.
Euripidis Iphigenia in Aulide. 1771.
Euripidis Iphigenia in Tauris. 1771.
All 3 edns rptd by T. Gaisford, Oxford 1811.

CONYERS MIDDLETON
1683–1750

Miscellaneous works. 4 vols 1752, 5 vols 1755.
For Middleton's separate pbns see col 1711, above.

THOMAS MORELL
1703–84

Euripidis Hecuba, Orestes et Phoenissae. 1748.
Hecuba translated from the Greek. 1749.
Thesaurus Graecae Poeseωs. 2 vols Eton 1762; ed E. Maltby, Cambridge 1815.
Hederich, B. Graecum lexicon manuale. 1766 etc. Ed Morell.
Aeschyli Prometheus vinctus. 1767, 1773.
Ainsworth, R., Dictionary, Latin and English. 2 vols 1773. Ed Morell.
Gradus ad Parnassum. 1773. Ed Morell.
Sophoclis Philoctetes. 1777.
Ainsworth, R. Thesaurus linguae latinae compendiarius. 1783. Ed Morell.
The epistles of Seneca. 2 vols 1786. Ed Morell.
Index ad Sophoclem. 1787.
Studies in history containing the history of Greece from its earliest period to its final subjugation by the Romans. St Neots 1813.

SAMUEL MUSGRAVE
1732–80

Euripidis Hippolytus, with notes by J. Markland. Oxford 1756.
Exercitationum in Euripidem libri ii. Leyden 1762.
Euripidis quae extant. 4 vols Oxford 1778.
Two dissertations: 1, On the Graecian mythology; 2, An examination of Sir I. Newton's objections to the chronology of the Olympiads. Ed T. Tyrwhitt 1782.
Sophoclis tragoediae. Oxford 1800.

SAMUEL PARR
1747–1825
Collections

Works, with memoirs of his life and writings, and a selection from his correspondence, by J. Johnstone. 8 vols 1828.

§1

A discourse on education and on the plans pursued in charity schools, for the charity schools in Norwich. 1786.
G. Bellendeni de statu libri tres: editio secunda longe emendatior [by S. Parr]. 2 pts 1787–8.
A spital sermon preached upon Easter Tuesday, April 15 1800; to which are added notes. 1801.
Characters of the late Charles James Fox, selected and in part written by Philopatris Varvicensis. 2 vols 1809.

A letter to Dr Milner, occasioned by some passages contained in his book entitled The end of religious controversy. Ed J. Lynes 1825.

§2

Field, W. Memoirs of the life, writings and opinions of Parr. 2 vols 1828.
Barker, E. H. Parriana: or notices of the Rev S. Parr, collected from various sources, printed and manuscript, and in part written by E. H. Barker. 2 vols 1828–9.
Blunt, J. J. Essays contributed to the Quarterly Review. 1860.
Nicoll, H. J. Great scholars: Buchanan, Bentley, Porson, Parr and others. Edinburgh 1880.
De Quincey, T. Whiggism in its relations to literature. In Works, ed D. Masson, vol 9, 1890.
Colson, P. Their ruling passions. [1949].
Derry, W. Dr Parr: a portrait of the Whig Dr Johnson. Oxford 1966.

ZACHARY PEARCE
1690–1774

Cicero, Dialogi tres de oratore. Cambridge 1716, 1732.
Longini de sublimitate commentarius. 1724. Greek and Latin.
Cicero, De officiis libri tres. 1745.

JOHN POTTER
1674?–1747

Archaeologiæ Graecæ. 2 vols Oxford 1697–9.
Lycophron, Alexandra. Oxford 1697.
Clementis Alexandrini quae extant. Oxford 1715.

THOMAS ROBINSON
1701?–61

Hesiodi Ascraei quae supersunt, gr et lat cum notis variorum. Oxford 1737.

SIR HENRY SHEERES
d. 1710

The history of Polybius translated. 2 vols 1693.
The works of Lucian translated. 1711. With others.

JOSEPH SPENCE
1699–1768

Polymetis: or an enquiry concerning the agreement between the works of the Roman poets and the remains of the antient artists. 1747.
See col 1748, above.

JAMES STUART 1713–88
NICHOLAS REVETT 1720–1804

The antiquities of Athens. 4 vols 1762–1816; tr German, 1829–33.

JOHN TAYLOR
1704–66

Lysiae orationes. 1739.
Demosthenis et Aeschinis opera. 2 vols Cambridge 1748–57.

ANDREW TOOKE
1673–1732

The Pantheon: representing the fabulous histories of the heathen gods and most illustrious heroes [trn of Fr. -A. Pomey, Pantheum mythicum, 1659]. 1698, 1717 etc.
Ovidi Fasti. 1720.

JOHN HORNE TOOKE
1736–1812

Ἔπεα Πτεροεντα: or the diversions of Purley. 2 vols 1786. *See col 1893, below.*

JONATHAN TOUP
1713–85

Emendationes in Suidam: in quibus plurima loca veterum graecorum, Sophoclis et Aristophanis imprimis, cum explicantur, tum emaculantur. 3 pts 1760–6.
Epistola critica [on Suidas] ad Gulielmum [Warburton], Episcopum Glocestriensem. 1767.
Curæ novissimæ sive appendicula notarum et emendationum in Suidam in quibus plurima veterum graecorum Sophoclis et Aristophanis imprimis, cum explicantur, tum emaculantur. 1775.
Dionysii Longini quæ supersunt, græce et latine [Latin version by Z. Pearce], recensuit notasque suas atque animadversiones adjecit J. Toupius; accedunt emendationes D. Ruhnkenii (dissertatio philologica de vita et scriptis Longini, auctore P. J. Schardam [or rather D. Ruhnken]). Oxford 1778.
Emendationes in Suidam et Hesychium et alios lexicographos græcos. [Ed R. Porson] 4 vols Oxford 1790.

THOMAS TWINING
1735–1804

Aristotle's treatise on poetry, translated with notes and two dissertations. 1789; ed H. Hamilton, Dublin 1851.
Recreations and studies of a country clergyman of the eighteenth century: being selections from the correspondence of Twining. 1882.

THOMAS TYRWHITT
1730–86

Περι λιθων: poema Orpheo a quibusdam adscriptum, græce et latine, ex editione J. M. Gesneri; recensuit notasque adjecit T. Tyrwhitt; simul prodit auctarium Dissertationis de Babrio [with the Dissertation, both by Tyrwhitt]. 2 pts 1776–81.
Conjecturæ in Strabonem, edit Amstel 1707. [1783].
Isaei oratio de Meneclis hereditate. 1785.
Aristotelis De poetica liber: textum recensuit, versionem refinxit et animadversionibus illustravit T. Tyrwhitt. Oxford 1794. Only 30 copies ptd. Greek and Latin.
Conjecturae in Aeschylum, Euripidem, et Aristophanem. Oxford 1822.
For Tyrwhitt's other writings see col 1755, above.

WILLIAM VINCENT
1739–1815

The voyage of Nearchus from the Indus to the Euphrates, collected from the original journal preserved by Arrian, and illustrated by authorities; to which are added three dissertations: two on the Acronychal rising of the Pleiades, by S. Horsley and W. Wales; and one by Mr De la Rochette on the first meridian of Ptolemy. 1797.

The periplus of the Erythrean Sea, containing an account of the navigation of the Ancients. 2 pts 1800–5.
The commerce and navigation of the Ancients in the Indian Ocean. 2 vols 1807.

GILBERT WAKEFIELD
1756–1801

Silva critica: sive in auctores sacros profanosque commentarius philologus (accedunt tres hymni Orphici e codicibus mss nunc primum in lucem dati). 5 vols Cambridge 1789–95.
Memoirs, written by himself. 1792; [ed J. T. Rutt and A. Wainewright] 2 vols 1804.
Q. Horatii Flacci quæ supersunt, recensuit et notulis instruxit G. Wakefield. 2 vols 1794.
Tragœdiarum delectus: Hercules furens, Alcestis, Euripideae, Philoctetes, Sophoclea: et Eumenides, Æschylea) in scholarum usum edidit et illustravit G. Wakefield. 2 vols 1794.
Animadversiones ad Æschyli tres priores tragœdias. Jena 1794–9.
Βιωνος και Μοσχου τα λειψανα: illustrabat et emendabat G. Wakefield. 1795.
T. Lucretii Cari de rerum natura libros sex, ad exemplarium mss fidem recensitos, longe emendatiores reddidit, commentariis perpetuis illustravit, indicibus instruxit; et cum animadversionibus R. Bentleii non ante vulgatis, aliorum subinde miscuit G. Wakefield. 3 vols 1796–7, 4 vols Glasgow 1813.
Publii Virgilii Maronis opera: emendabat et notulis illustrabat G. Wakefield. 1796.
In Euripidis Hecubam, Londini nuper publicatum [by R. Porson] diatribe extemporalis. 1797.
Select essays of Dion Chrysostom translated into English from the Greek; with notes, critical and illustrative. 1800.
Noctes Carcerariae: sive de legibus metricis poetarum graecorum qui versibus hexametris scripserunt, disputatio. 1801.
Correspondence with C. J. Fox, chiefly on subjects of classical literature. 1813.

JOHN WALKER
1692 ?–1741

M. T. Ciceronis, De natura deorum libri tres. Ed J. Davisius [i.e. John Davies]; accedunt emendationes J. W[alkeri], Cambridge 1718.

JOSEPH WASSE
1672–1738

Sallustii quæ extant. Cambridge 1710.
Thucydidis De bello peloponnesiaco. Amsterdam 1731.

DAVID WATSON
1710–56

The odes, epodes and Carmen seculare of Horace, translated into English prose. 1741. With Latin.
A clear and compendious history of the gods and goddesses, and their contemporaries. 1752.

ROBERT WOOD
1717 ?–71

The ruins of Palmyra. 1753; tr French, 1753.
The ruins of Balbec. 1757; tr French, 1757.
An essay on the original genius of Homer. 1767, 1769; tr German, 1773; French, 1777.

ORIENTAL AND OTHER SCHOLARS

HENRY ALDRICH
1647–1710

Artis logicae compendium. Oxford 1691; ed H. L. Mansel, Oxford 1852.

ARTHUR BEDFORD
1668–1745

Animadversions on Sir I. Newton's Chronology of ancient kingdoms amended. 1728.
Scripture chronology demonstrated by astronomical considerations. 1741.

WILLIAM BEVERIDGE
1637–1708

De linguarum orientalium, praesertim hebraicae, chaldaicae, syriacae, arabicae et samaritanae praestantia, necessitate et utilitate quam et theologis praestant et philosophis. 1658
Grammatica linguae domini nostri Jesu Christi: sive grammatica syriaca tribus libris tradita. 1658.
Institutionum chronologicarum libri duo. 1669.
Συνοδικόν: sive pandectae canonum SS. apostolorum, et conciliorum ab ecclesia graeca receptorum. Oxford 1672.
Codex canonum ecclesiae primitivae vindicatus ac illustratus. 1678.
Private thoughts upon religion. 1709.
Theological works. [Ed J. Bliss] 12 vols Oxford 1842–8.

THOMAS HYDE
1636–1703

Historia religionis veterum Persarum. Oxford 1700.
Syntagma dissertationum. Ed G. Sharpe 2 vols Oxford 1767.

MICHAEL MAITTAIRE
1668–1747

Graecae linguae dialecti. 1706.
Stephanorum historia, vitas ipsorum ac libros complectens. 2 vols 1709.
Historia typographorum aliquot parisiensium, vitas et libros complectens. 2 vols 1717.
Annales typographici. 3 vols Hague and Amsterdam 1719–26.
Senilia sive poetica aliquot in argumentis varii generis tentamina. 1742.
Over 30 edns of classical authors 1713–41.

SIR JOHN MARSHAM
1602–85

Diatriba chronologica. 1649.
Chronicus canon aegyptiacus, ebraicus, graecus et disquisitiones. 1672.

EDWARD POCOCKE the elder
1604–91

Specimen historiae arabum: sive de origine et moribus arabum succincta narratio. Oxford 1650.

Porta Mosis: sive dissertationes aliquot arabice et latine edita. 1655.
Theological works. Ed L. Twells 2 vols 1740.

EDWARD POCOCKE the younger
1648–1727

§1

Philosophus autodidactus: sive epistola Abi Jaafar Ebn Tophail ex arabica in linguam latinam versa. Oxford 1671; tr 1674.

§2

Mercier, R. Un précurseur arabe de la philosophie du xviii° siècle. Revue de Littérature Comparée 23 1949. On influence of Philosophus autodidactus.

GEORGE SALE
1697?–1736

The Koran translated into English immediately from the original Arabic; to which is prefixed a preliminary discourse. 1734.
Sale also wrote the articles relating to oriental history in Bayle, A general dictionary, ed T. Birch 1734–41.

THOMAS SMITH
1638–1710

Diatriba de chaldaicis paraphrastis, eorumque versionibus, ex utraque Talmude ac scriptis rabbinorum concinnata. Oxford 1662.
Syntagma de druidum moribus ac institutis. 1664.
Remarks upon the manners, religion and government of the Turks; together with a survey of the seven churches of Asia, and a brief description of Constantinople. 1678. First pbd in Latin 1672–4.
Catalogus librorum manuscriptorum bibliothecae Cottonianae. Oxford 1696.
Vitae quorundam eruditissimorum et illustrium virorum [J. Ussher, J. Cosin, H. Briggs, J. Bainbridge, J. Greaves, Sir Peter Young, Patrick Young, J. Dee]. 1707.

JOHN WARD
1679?–1758

De Asse et partibus ejus commentarius. 1719.
The lives of the professors of Gresham College, to which is prefixed the life of the founder, Sir Thomas Gresham. 1740.

WILLIAM WOTTON
1666–1727

Reflections upon ancient and modern learning. 1694.
The history of Rome from the death of Antoninus Pius to the death of Severus Alexander. 1701.
Miscellaneous discourses relating to the traditions and usages of the Scribes and Pharisees. 2 vols 1710.
A discourse concerning the confusion of languages at Babel. 1730.

E. J. K.

XI. PHILOSOPHY

GENERAL STUDIES

Leland, J. A view of the principal Deistical writers. 3 vols 1754–6.

Lechler, G. V. Geschichte des englischen Deismus. Stuttgart 1841.

Janet, P. Histoire de la science politique. Vol 2, Paris 1858, 1913 (4th edn, rev).

Pattison, M. Tendencies of religious thought in England 1688–1750. In Essays and reviews, 1860; rptd in Pattison, Essays vol 2, Oxford 1889.

Farrar, A. S. Critical history of free thought. 1862.

Hunt, J. Religious thought in England from the Reformation to the end of the last century. 3 vols 1870–3.

Tulloch, J. Rational theology and Christian philosophy in England in the seventeenth century. 2 vols Edinburgh 1872.

McCosh, J. The Scottish philosophy. 1875.

Rémusat, C. de. Histoire de la philosophie en Angleterre depuis Bacon jusqu'à Locke. Paris 1875.

Stephen, L. A history of English thought in the eighteenth century. 2 vols 1876.

—— The English Utilitarians. 3 vols 1900.

Green, T. H. In his Works, ed R. L. Nettleship vols 1–2, 1885–6. On Hume, Locke, Berkeley et al.

Pringle-Pattison, A. S. Scottish philosophy. Edinburgh 1885.

Lyon, G. L'idéalisme en Angleterre au xviiie siècle. Paris 1888.

Bonar, J. In his Philosophy and political economy, 1893.

Selby-Bigge, L. A. British moralists: being selections from writers, principally of the eighteenth-century period. 2 vols Oxford 1897.

Elton, O. The Augustan ages. Edinburgh 1899.

Graham, W. English political philosophy from Hobbes to Maine. 1899.

Robertson, J. M. A short history of free thought. 1899, 2 vols 1906 (rev and enlarged).

Höffding, H. In his A history of modern philosophy, 2 vols 1900.

Halévy, E. La formation du radicalisme philosophique. 3 vols Paris 1901–4; tr 1928, 1952.

Albee, E. History of English Utilitarianism. 1902.

Millar, J. A. The mid-eighteenth century. Edinburgh 1902.

Adamson, R. The development of modern philosophy. 2 vols Edinburgh 1903.

Forsyth, T. M. English philosophy. 1910.

Seaton, A. A. The theory of toleration under the later Stuarts. Cambridge 1911.

Seth, J. English philosophers and schools of philosophy. 1912.

Sorley, W. R. CHEL vols 8–10, Cambridge 1912–13. John Locke; Berkeley and contemporary philosophy; Hume, Adam Smith et al.

—— A history of English philosophy. Cambridge 1920, 1965 (as A history of British philosophy to 1900).

Stock, St G. English thought for English thinkers. 1912.

Burtt, E. A. The metaphysical foundations of modern physical science. 1925.

Vaughan, C. E. Studies in the history of political philosophy before and after Rousseau. Vol 1, Manchester 1925.

Powicke, F. J. The Cambridge Platonists. 1926.

Hearnshaw, F. J. C. The social and political ideas of some English thinkers of the Augustan age. 1928.

Bréhier, E. Le dix-septième siècle. In his Histoire de la philosophie vol 2 pt 1, Paris 1929; tr Chicago 1966; Le dix-huitième siècle, vol 2 pt 2, Paris 1930.

Lalande, A. Les théories de l'induction et de l'expérimentation. Paris 1929.

Torrey, N. L. Voltaire and the English Deists. New Haven 1930.

Brunet, P. L'introduction des théories de Newton en France au xviiie siècle. Vol 1, Paris 1931.

Morris, C. R. Locke, Berkeley, Hume. Oxford 1931.

Muirhead, J. H. The Platonic tradition in Anglo-Saxon philosophy. 1931.

Wellek, R. Immanuel Kant in England 1793–1838. Princeton 1931.

Becker, C. L. The heavenly city of the eighteenth-century philosophers. New Haven 1932.

Cassirer, E. Die Philosophie der Aufklärung. Tübingen 1932; tr Princeton 1951.

—— Die Platonische Renaissance in England und die Schule von Cambridge. Leipzig 1932; tr Edinburgh 1953.

Creed, J. M. and J. S. Boys Smith. Religious thought in the eighteenth century illustrated from writers of the period. Cambridge 1934.

Gierke, O. Natural law and the theory of society 1500–1800. Tr E. Barker 2 vols Cambridge 1934.

—— The development of political theory. Tr B. Freyd 1939.

Mayo, T. F. Epicurus in England 1650–1725. Dallas 1934.

Willey, B. The seventeenth-century background. 1934.

—— The eighteenth-century background. 1940.

—— In his English moralists, 1964.

Hazard, P. La crise de la conscience européenne 1680–1715. 3 vols Paris 1935; tr 1953 as The European mind 1680–1715.

—— La pensée européenne au xviiie siècle. 3 vols Paris 1946; tr 1954 as European thought in the eighteenth century.

Cook, T. I. History of political philosophy from Plato to Burke. New York 1936.

Gough, J. W. The social contract. Oxford 1936, 1957 (rev).

Laski, H. J. The rise of European Liberalism. 1936.

Lovejoy, A. O. In his Great chain of being, Cambridge Mass 1936.

De Pauley, W. C. The candle of the Lord: studies in the Cambridge Platonists. 1937.

Roberts, M. In his Modern mind, 1937.

Sabine, G. H. In his A history of political theory, 1937.

Fuller, B. A. G. In his A history of modern philosophy, New York 1938.

Maxey, C. C. In his Political philosophies, New York 1938.

From Descartes to Kant: readings in the philosophy of the Renaissance and Enlightenment. Ed T. V. Smith and M. Grene, Chicago 1940.

Bryson, G. Man and society: the Scottish enquiry of the eighteenth century. Princeton 1945.

Russell, B. In his A history of Western philosophy, 1946.

Bowle, J. In his Western political thought, 1947.

Fitzgerald, M. M. First follow nature: primitivism in English poetry 1725–50. New York 1947.

Jones, W. T. Mandeville to Bentham. In Masters of political thought, ed E. M. Sait vol 2, 1947.

Raphael, D. D. In his Moral sense, 1947.

Tuveson, E. L. Millenium and Utopia: a study in the background of the idea of progress. Berkeley 1949.

Catlin, G. In his A history of the political philosophers, 1950.

Cragg, G. R. From Puritanism to the Age of Reason. Cambridge 1950.

—— Reason and authority in the eighteenth century. Cambridge 1964.

Bethell, S. L. The cultural revolution of the seventeenth century. 1951.

Jones, R. F. et al. The seventeenth century: studies in the history of English thought and literature from Bacon to Pope. Stanford 1951.

British empirical philosophers: Locke, Berkeley, Hume, Reid and J. S. Mill. Ed A. J. Ayer and R. Winch 1952.

Kliger, S. The Goths in England: a study in seventeenth- and eighteenth-century thought. Cambridge 1952.

Paul, L. In his English philosophers, 1953.

Strauss, L. Natural right and history. Chicago 1953.

Røstvig, M. S. The happy man: studies in the metamorphoses of a classical ideal 1600–1760. 2 vols Oslo 1954–8.

Howell, W. S. Logic and rhetoric in England 1500–1700. Princeton 1956.

Sampson, R. V. Progress in the Age of Reason. 1956.

Colie, R. L. Light and enlightenment: a study of the Cambridge Platonists and the Dutch Arminians. Cambridge 1957.

Koyré, A. From the closed world to the infinite universe. Baltimore 1957.

Macklem, M. The anatomy of the world: relations between natural and moral law from Donne to Pope. Minneapolis 1958.

Copleston, F. C. A history of philosophy. Vols 5–6, 1959–60.

Simon, I. 'Pride of reason' in the Restoration and earlier eighteenth century. Brussels 1959.

Bronowski, J. and B. Mazlish. The Western intellectual tradition from Leonardo to Hegel. 1960.

Cobban, A. In search of humanity: the role of the Enlightenment in modern history. 1960.

Bredvold, L. I. The brave new world of the Enlightenment. Ann Arbor 1961.

Chevalier, J. Histoire de la pensée. Vol 1, Paris 1961.

Essential articles for the study of English Augustan backgrounds. Ed B. N. Schilling, Hamden Conn 1961.

Hanzo, T. A. Latitude and Restoration criticism. Copenhagen 1961.

Macpherson, C. B. The political theory of possessive individualism, Hobbes to Locke. Oxford 1962.

Randall, J. H. The career of philosophy. 2 vols New York 1962–5.

Reason and the imagination: studies in the history of ideas 1600–1800. Ed J. A. Mazzeo, New York 1962.

Transactions of the First International Congress on the Enlightenment. 4 vols Geneva 1963.

Van Leeuwen, H. The problem of certainty in English thought 1630–90. Hague 1963.

The English mind: studies in the English moralists presented to Basil Willey. Ed H. S. Davies and G. Watson, Cambridge 1964.

Mandelbaum, M. Philosophy, science, and sense perception: historical and critical studies. Baltimore 1964.

Walker, D. P. Decline of hell: seventeenth-century discussions of eternal torment. 1964.

The Enlightenment. Ed F. E. Manuel, Englewood Cliffs NJ 1965.

Harrison, W. Conflict and compromise: history of British political thought 1593–1900. New York 1965.

— Sources in British political thought 1593–1900. New York 1965.

Schmidt, H. Seinserkenntnis und Staatsdenken: der Subjekts- und Erkenntnisbegriff von Hobbes, Locke und Rousseau als Grundlage des Rechtes und der Geschichte. Tübingen 1965.

Gay, P. The Enlightenment: an interpretation. 2 vols New York 1966–9.

Lively, J. The Enlightenment. 1966.

A. LOCKE AND HIS CONTEMPORARIES

JOHN LOCKE
1632–1704
Bibliographies etc

Christophersen, H. O. A bibliographical introduction to the study of Locke. Oslo 1930.

Hughes, H. C. Locke's library. Book-Collector's Quart 12 1933.

Ware, C. S. The influence of Descartes on Locke: a bibliographical study. Revue Internationale de Philosophie 4 1950.

Lough, J. Locke's list of books banned in France in 1679. French Stud 5 1951.

— Locke's reading during his stay in France. Library 5th ser 8 1953.

Hampton, J. Les traductions françaises de Locke au xviiie siècle. Revue de Littérature Comparée 29 1955.

Brown, T. J. English literary autographs 22: Locke. Book Collector 6 1957.

Long, P. A summary catalogue of the Lovelace Collection of the papers of Locke in the Bodleian Library. Oxford 1959.

— The Mellon donation of additional manuscripts from the Lovelace Collection. Bodleian Lib Record 7 1964.

Laslett, P. Locke's books and papers for his own University. TLS 11 March 1960.

Harrison, J. and P. Laslett. The library of Locke. Oxford 1965.

Keynes, G. L. A note on Locke's library. Trans Cambridge Bibl Soc 4 1967.

Ashcraft, R. Locke's library: portrait of an intellectual. Trans Cambridge Bibl Soc 5 1969.

Collections

Posthumous works. 1706.

Remains. 1714.

Works. 3 vols 1714, 1722, 1727, 1740, 1751, 1759, 4 vols 1768; ed Bishop Law 1777; 9 vols 1794, 10 vols 1801, 1812, 1823, Aachen 1963 (facs of 1823).

A collection of several pieces of Mr Locke, published by P. Des Maizeaux under the direction of Mr Anthony Collins. 1720, 1739.

Oeuvres philosophiques. Tr P. Coste 7 vols Paris 1821–5.

Philosophical works. Ed J. A. St John 1843, 1854.

Educational writings. Ed J. W. Adamson, Cambridge 1912, 1922 (rev); ed J. L. Axtell, Cambridge 1968.

Treatise of civil government and A letter concerning toleration. Ed C. L. Sherman, New York 1937.

The second treatise of civil government and A letter concerning toleration. Ed J. W. Gough, Oxford 1946, 1956, 1966 (both rev).

Locke. Ed A. Carlini, Milan 1949.

The reasonableness of Christianity with A discourse of miracles and part of A third letter concerning toleration. Ed I. T. Ramsey 1958.

Locke and liberty: selections from the works. Ed M. Salvadori 1960.

Locke on politics, religion and education. Ed M. Cranston, New York 1965.

Deuxième traité du gouvernement civil, Constitutions fondamentales de la Caroline. Ed B. Gilson, Paris 1967.

§I

A poem in Latin and in English dedicated to Cromwell. In Musarum oxoniensium ἐλαιοφορία, Oxford 1654.

On the marriage of King Charles II with the Infanta of Portugal. In Domiduca oxoniensis: sive musae academicae, Oxford 1662. A poem.

In Tractatum de febribus D. D. Sydenham, praxin

medicam apud Londinenses mira solertia æque ac fælicitate exercentis. In T. Sydenham, Methodus curandi febres, 1668 (2nd edn). A poem.

Méthode nouvelle de dresser des recueils. Bibliothèque Universelle et Historique July 1686; tr 1706.

Essai philosophique concernant l'entendement. Bibliothèque Universelle et Historique Jan 1688.

An essay concerning humane understanding. 1690, 1694 (with large addns), 1695, 1700, 1706, 2 vols 1716, 1729; ed A. C. Fraser 2 vols Oxford 1894, New York 1959; ed A. S. Pringle-Pattison, Oxford 1924 (abridged); ed A. J. Ayer and R. Winch in their British empirical philosophers, 1952 (abridged); tr French, 1700; Latin, 1701; Italian, 1701; Dutch, 1736; German, 1757.

An essay concerning the understanding, knowledge, opinion and assent. Ed B. Rand, Cambridge Mass 1931.

An early draft of Locke's Essay, together with excerpts from his journals. Ed R. I. Aaron and J. Gibb, Oxford 1936.

A letter to the Right Reverend Edward Ld Bishop of Worcester, concerning some passages relating to Mr Locke's Essay of humane understanding. 1697.

Mr Locke's reply to the Right Reverend the Lord Bishop of Worcester's Answer to his Letter, concerning some passages relating to Mr Locke's Essay. 1697.

Mr Locke's reply to the Right Reverend the Lord Bishop of Worcester's Answer to his second letter. 1699.

Epistola de tolerantia ad clarissimum virum TARPTOLA. Gouda 1689; tr W. Popple 1689, 1690; ed H. Morley 1889; ed M. Montuori, Hague 1963 (Latin and English); ed R. Klibansky, tr J. W. Gough, Oxford 1968 (Latin and English); ed R. Klibansky, tr R. Polin, Paris 1964 (Latin and French); tr French, 1710; German, 1710; ed J. Ebbinghaus, Hamburg 1957 (English and German); Italian, 1961; Polish, 1963.

A second letter concerning toleration. 1690.

A third letter for toleration. 1692. Part of a Fourth letter for toleration appeared in Posthumous works, 1706, above.

Scritti editi e inediti sulla tolleranza. Ed C. A. Viano, Turin 1961.

Two treatises of government. 1690, 1694, 1698; ed H. Morley 1884; ed W. F. Carpenter 1924 (EL); ed P. Laslett, Cambridge 1960, 1967 (rev); tr French, 1691; German, 1718; Swedish, 1726; Italian, 1773, ed L. Pareyson 1960; Spanish, 1821; Russian, 1902; Norwegian, 1947; Czech, 1965.

Social contract: essays by Locke, Hume and Rousseau. Ed E. Barker 1947. Second treatise of government.

Some considerations of the consequences of the lowering of interest and raising the value of money. 1692, 1696.

Further considerations concerning raising the value of money. 1695.

Short observations on a printed paper, intituled For encouraging the coinage of silver money in England, and after for keeping it there. 1695.

Several papers relating to money, interest and trade &c. 1696.

Some thoughts concerning education. 1693, 1695 (3rd enlarged edn), 1699, 1705; ed R. H. Quick, Cambridge 1880; ed P. Gay, New York 1964; ed F. W. Garforth 1964 (abridged); tr French, 1695, 1966; German, 1729; Italian, 1782; Polish, 1959.

The reasonableness of Christianity as delivered in the Scriptures. 1695, 1696; tr French, 1696; Dutch, 1729; German, 1733.

A vindication of the Reasonableness of Christianity etc, from Mr Edwards's Reflections. 1695.

A second vindication of the Reasonableness of Christianity etc. 1697.

A paraphrase and notes on the Epistle of St Paul to the Galatians. 1705.

Some thoughts on the conduct of the understanding in the search of truth. 1762; ed T. Fowler, Oxford 1881, 1901 (rev).

Essays on the law of nature: the Latin text with a translation. Ed W. von Leyden, Oxford 1954.

Two tracts on government. Ed P. Abrams, Cambridge 1967. Written 1660.

For Locke's marginalia see N. Porter, Marginalia Lockeiana, New Englander & Yale Rev 47 1887; J. W. Yolton, Locke's unpublished marginal replies to John Sergeant, JHI 12 1951.

Letters, Diaries etc

Some familiar letters between Mr Locke and several of his friends. 1708.

Original letters of Locke, Algernon Sidney and Lord Shaftesbury. Ed T. Forster 1830.

Ollion, H. Notes sur la correspondance de Locke, suivies de trente-deux lettres inédites de Locke à Thoynard 1678–81. Paris 1908.

Lettres inédites de Locke à ses amis N. Thoynard, P. van Limborch et E. Clarke. Ed H. Ollion, Hague 1912.

The correspondence of Locke and Edward Clarke. Ed B. Rand, Oxford 1927.

Locke's travels in France 1675–9, as related in his journals, correspondence and other papers. Ed J. Lough, Cambridge 1953.

Le Clerc, J. Lettres inédites à Locke. Ed G. Bonno, Berkeley 1959.

§2

Coste, P. Lettre à l'occasion de la mort de M. Locke. Nouvelles de la République des Lettres Feb 1705.

Le Clerc, J. Eloge du feu Mr Locke. Bibliothèque Choisie 6 1705; tr 1706 as The life and character of Mr John Locke, 1713 (rev as An account of the life and writings of Mr John Locke).

Leibnitz, G. W. von. Nouveaux essais sur l'entendement humain. In his Œuvres philosophiques, ed R. E. Raspe, Amsterdam 1765.

Cousin, V. La philosophie de Locke. Paris 1819.

King, P. The life of Locke. 1829, 2 vols 1830, 1 vol 1858 (Bohn's Lib) (as The life and letters of Locke).

Tagart, E. Locke's writings and philosophy historically considered and vindicated. 1855.

Webb, T. E. The intellectualism of Locke. Dublin 1857.

Brown, J. Locke and Sydenham. In his Horae subsecivae, Edinburgh 1858.

Fox-Bourne, H. R. The life of Locke. 2 vols 1876.

Marion, H. Locke: sa vie et son œuvre. Paris 1878.

Fowler, T. Locke. 1880 (EML).

Curtis, M. M. An outline of Locke's ethical philosophy. Leipzig 1890.

Fraser, A. C. Locke. 1890.

—— Locke as a factor in modern thought. Proc Br Acad 1 1904.

Hertling G. von. Locke und die Schule von Cambridge. Freiburg 1892.

Stephen, J. F. In his Horae sabbaticae ser 2, 1892. Includes 4 essays on Locke.

Fechtner, E. Locke: ein Bild aus den geistigen Kämpfen Englands im 17 Jahrhundert. Stuttgart 1898.

Thilly, F. Locke's relation to Descartes. Philosophical Rev 9 1900.

Osler, W. An address on Locke as a physician. 1901.

Pollock, F. Locke's theory of the state. Proc Br Acad 1 1904; rptd in his Essays in law, 1922.

Bastide, C. Locke: ses théories politiques et leur influence en Angleterre. Paris 1907.

Alexander, S. Locke. 1908.

Ollion, H. La philosophie générale de Locke. Paris 1908.

Krakowski, E. Les sources médiévales de la philosophie de Locke. Paris 1915.

Gibson, J. Locke's theory of knowledge and its historical relations. Cambridge 1917.

—— **Locke.** Proc Br Acad 19 1933.

Picavet, F. The mediaeval doctrines in the works of Donne and Locke. Mind 26 1917.

Hefelbower, S. G. The relation of Locke to English Deism. Chicago 1918.

Lamprecht, S. P. The moral and political philosophy of Locke. New York 1918.

— Locke and his Essay. Columbia Univ Quart 25 1933.

Rusk, R. R. In his Doctrines of the great educators, 1918, 1965 (rev).

Carlini, A. La filosofia di Locke. 2 vols Florence 1920.

Reininger, R. In his Locke, Berkeley, Hume, Munich 1922.

Tellkamp, A. Das Verhältnis Lockes zur Scholastik. Münster 1927.

Zobel, A. Darstellung und kritische Würdigung der Sprachphilosophie Lockes. Anglia 52 1928.

Jackson, R. Locke's distinction between primary and secondary qualities. Mind 38 1929.

— Locke's version of the doctrine of representative perception. Mind 39 1930.

Larkin, P. Property in the eighteenth century, with special reference to England and Locke. Cork 1930.

Morris, C. R. In his Locke, Berkeley, Hume, Oxford 1931.

Broad, C. D. John Locke. Hibbert Jnl 31 1933.

Gibson, A. G. The physician's art: an attempt to expand Locke's fragment De arte medica. Oxford 1933.

Ryle, G. Locke on the human understanding. Oxford 1933.

— John Locke. Critica 1 1967.

Smith, N. K. John Locke. Manchester 1933.

Stocks, J. L. Locke's contribution to political theory. Oxford 1933.

Greaves, H. R. G. Locke and the separation of power. Politica 1 1934.

Thompson, S. M. A study of Locke's theory of ideas. Monmouth Ill 1934.

Hofstadter, A. Locke and scepticism. New York 1935.

MacLean, K. Locke and English literature of the eighteenth century. New Haven 1936.

Aaron, R. I. John Locke. Oxford 1937, 1955 (rev).

— The character of Locke's conceptualism. In his Theory of universals, 1952.

— and P. Walters. Locke and the intuitionist theory of number. Philosophy 40 1965.

Buchler, J. Act and object in Locke. Philosophical Rev 46 1937.

Clapp, J. G. Locke's conception of the mind. New York 1937.

Curti, M. The great Mr Locke: America's philosopher 1783–1861. Huntington Lib Bull 11 1937.

Ewing, A. C. Some points in the philosophy of Locke. Philosophy 12 1937.

Petzäll, A. Ethics and epistemology in Locke's Essay concerning human understanding. Gothenburg 1937.

Tinivella, G. La dottrina di Locke e i suoi sviluppi. Giornale Critico della Filosofia Italiana 19 1938.

— Locke e i pensieri sull' educazione. Milan 1938.

— Bacone e Locke: dottrina e critica. Milan 1939.

Zwierlein, F. J. Bellarmine, Jesuits and Popery. Thought 13 1938. On Two treatises of government.

Czajkowski, C. J. The theory of private property in Locke's political philosophy. Notre Dame Indiana 1941.

Kendall, W. Locke and the doctrine of majority-rule. Urbana 1941.

— Locke revisited. Intercollegiate Rev 2 1966.

McLachlan, H. The religious opinions of Milton, Locke and Newton. Manchester 1941.

Ogden, H. V. S. The state of nature and the decline of Lockian political theory in England 1760–1800. Amer Historical Rev 46 1941.

Reicyn, N. La pédagogie de Locke. Paris 1941.

Bianchi, G. F. Locke. Brescia 1943.

Brinkley, R. F. Coleridge on John Petvin and Locke. HLQ 8 1945.

— Coleridge on Locke. SP 46 1949.

Kallich, M. The association of ideas and critical theory: Hobbes, Locke and Addison. ELH 12 1945.

Smock, G. E. Locke and the Augustan Age of literature. Philosophical Rev 55 1946.

Bonno, G. The diffusion and influence of Locke's Essay concerning human understanding in France before Voltaire's Lettres philosophiques. Proc Amer Philosophical Soc 91 1947.

— L'Abbé du Bos et Locke. Revue de Littérature Comparée 24 1950.

— Les relations intellectuelles de Locke avec la France. Berkeley 1955.

— Locke et son traducteur français Pierre Coste. Revue de Littérature Comparée 33 1959.

Maclean, A. H. George Lawson and Locke. Cambridge Historical Jnl 9 1947.

Marchi, E. de. Considerazioni intorno alla divisione dei poteri nel Locke. Occidente 4 1948.

— Le origini dell'idea della tolleranza religiosa nel Locke. Occidente 9 1953.

— Locke's Atlantis. Political Stud 3 1955.

von Leyden, W. Locke and Nicole: their proofs of the existence of God and their attitude towards Descartes. Sophia 16 1948.

— Locke's unpublished papers. Sophia 17 1949.

— Notes concerning papers of Locke in the Lovelace Collection. Philosophical Quart 2 1952.

— Locke and natural law. Philosophy 31 1956.

Brown, F. A. Locke and the religious Aufklärung. Rev of Religion 13 1949.

— Locke's Essay and Bodmer and Breitinger. MLQ 10 1949.

— German interest in Locke's Essay 1688–1800. JEGP 50 1951.

— On education: Locke, Christian Wolff and the 'moral weeklies'. California Univ Pbns in Modern Philology 36 1952.

James, D. G. The life of reason: Hobbes, Locke and Bolingbroke. 1949.

Aspelin, G. John Locke. Lund 1950.

Cranston, M. Locke and John Aubrey. N & Q Dec 1950, Aug 1952.

— Locke's correspondence with Esther Masham. Newberry Lib Bull 2 1950.

— The politics of Locke. History Today 2 1952.

— Locke the exile. Listener 4 Nov 1954.

— Men and ideas: Locke. Encounter Dec 1956.

— Locke: a biography. 1957.

— Locke. 1961 (Br Council pamphlet).

— The politics of a philosopher. Listener 5 Jan 1961. On Two treatises of government.

Gough, J. W. Locke's political studies: eight studies. Oxford 1950.

— Locke's Herbarium. Bodleian Lib Record 7 1962.

Miller, P. Edwards, Locke and the rhetoric of sensation. In Perspectives of criticism, ed H. Levin, Cambridge Mass 1950.

Pahl, G. G. Locke as literary critic and Biblical interpreter. In Essays critical and historical dedicated to L. B. Campbell, Berkeley 1950.

Pucelle, J. Du nouveau sur Locke. Revue Philosophique 140 1950.

Flew, A. G. N. Locke and the problem of personal identity. Philosophy 26 1951.

Macpherson, C. B. Locke on capitalist appropriation. Western Political Quart 4 1951.

— The social bearing of Locke's political theory. Western Political Quart 7 1954.

Neilson, F. Locke's essays on property and natural law. Amer Jnl of Economics 10 1951.

Simon, W. M. Locke: philosophy and political theory. Amer Political Science Rev 45 1951.

Yost, R. M. Locke's rejection of hypotheses about sub-microscopic events. JHI 12 1951.

Klemmt, A. Locke: theoretische Philosophie. Meisenheim 1952.

O'Connor, D. J. John Locke. 1952 (Penguin).

Strauss, L. On Locke's doctrine of natural right. Philosophical Rev 61 1952.

— Locke's doctrine of natural law. Amer Political Science Rev 52 1958.

Laslett, P. Locke and the first Earl of Shaftesbury. Mind 61 1952.

— The 1690 edition of Locke's Two treatises of government: two states. Trans Cambridge Bibl Soc 1 1953.

— F. T. Bowers and J. Gerritsen. Further observations on Locke's Two treatises of government. Trans Cambridge Bibl Soc 2 1954.

— Locke as founder of the Board of Trade. Listener 18 Nov 1954.

— The English Revolution and Locke's Two treatises of government. Cambridge Historical Jnl 12 1956.

— Locke, the great recoinage and the origins of the Board of Trade 1695–8. William & Mary Quart 14 1957.

Tuveson, E. L. Locke and the 'dissolution of the ego'. MP 52 1955.

— 'An essay on man' and 'the way of ideas'. ELH 26 1959.

— The imagination as a means of grace: Locke and the aesthetics of romanticism. Berkeley 1960.

Yolton, J. W. Locke and the seventeenth-century logic of ideas. JHI 16 1955.

— Locke and the way of ideas. Oxford 1956.

— Locke on the law of nature. Philosophical Rev 67 1958.

— The concept of experience in Locke and Hume. Jnl of Historical Philosophy 1 1963.

Doney, W. Locke's abstract ideas. Philosophy & Phenomenological Research 16 1956.

Linnell, J. Locke's abstract ideas. Ibid.

Giganti, M. A. Locke e i limiti della scienza. Padua 1957.

Dewhurst, K. Locke and Sydenham on the teaching of anatomy. Medical History 2 1958.

— Sydenham's original treatise on smallpox, with a preface and dedication to the Earl of Shaftesbury by Locke. Medical History 3 1959.

— Locke's Essay on respiration. Bull History of Medicine 34 1960.

— Locke's medical notes during his residence in Holland 1683–9. Janus 50 1962.

— A review of Locke's research in social and preventive medicine. Bull History of Medicine 36 1962.

— Locke, physician and philosopher: a medical biography. 1963.

Johnston, C. Locke's 'Examination' of Malebranche and John Norris. JHI 19 1958.

Monson, C. H. Locke and his interpreters. Political Stud 6 1958.

Rauche, G. A. Die praktischen Aspekte von Lockes Philosophie. Pretoria 1958.

Romanell, P. Locke and Sydenham: a fragment on smallpox 1670. Bull History of Medicine 32 1958. Reply by D. L. Cowen 33 1959.

— Locke's aphorisms on education and health. JHI 22 1961.

— Some medico-philosophical excerpts from the Mellon Collection of Locke papers. JHI 25 1964.

Viano, C. A. I rapporti tra Locke e Shaftesbury e le teorie economiche di Locke. Rivista di Filosofia 49 1958.

— Locke: dal razionalismo all'illuminismo. Turin 1960.

— L'abbozzo originario e gli stadi di composizione di An essay concerning toleration e la nascita delle teorie politico-religiose di Locke. Rivista di Filosofia 52 1961.

Waldman, M. A note on Locke's concept of consent. Ethics 68 1958.

Brogan, A. P. Locke and Utilitarianism. Ethics 69 1959.

Singh, R. Locke and the idea of sovereignty. Indian Jnl of Political Science 20 1959.

— Locke and the theory of natural law. Political Stud 9 1961.

Colie, R. L. Locke in the Republic of Letters. In Britain and the Netherlands, ed J. S. Bromley and E. H. Kossmann 1960.

— The social language of Locke. Jnl of Br Stud 4 1965.

— Locke and the publication of the private. PQ 45 1966.

Cox, R. H. Locke on war and peace. Oxford 1960.

— Justice as the basis of political order in Locke. Nomos 6 1963.

Polin, R. La politique morale de Locke. Paris 1960.

— Justice in Locke's philosophy. Nomos 6 1963.

Arénilla, L. The notion of civil disobedience according to Locke. Diogenes 35 1961.

Buchdahl, G. The image of Newton and Locke in the Age of Reason. 1961.

Mason, M. G. How Locke wrote Some thoughts concerning education. Pædagogica Historica 1 1961.

— The literary sources of Locke's educational thoughts. Pædagogica Historica 5 1965.

Moulds, H. Locke's four freedoms seen in a new light. Ethics 71 1961.

— Locke and rugged individualism. Amer Jnl of Economics 24 1965.

Reese, W. L. The 'experimentum crucis' in Locke's doctrine of abstraction. Philosophy & Phenomenological Research 21 1961.

Ricci Garotti, L. Locke e i suoi problemi. Urbino 1961.

Wolfe, D. E. Sydenham and Locke on the limits of anatomy. Bull History of Medicine 35 1961.

Givner, D. A. Scientific preconceptions in Locke's philosophy of language. JHI 23 1962.

Thompson, C. Locke and New England transcendentalism. New England Quart 35 1962.

Byrne, J. W. The notion of obligation in Locke's philosophy. Personalist 44 1963.

— Locke's philosophy of religious toleration. Personalist 46 1965.

Davidson, E. H. From Locke to Edwards. JHI 24 1963.

Goldwin, R. A. In History of political philosophy, ed L. Strauss and J. Cropsey, Chicago 1963.

Seliger, M. Locke's natural law and the foundation of politics. JHI 24 1963.

— Locke's theory of revolutionary action. Western Political Quart 16 1963.

— The liberal politics of Locke. 1968.

Stannard, J. Materia medica in the Locke-Clarke correspondence. Bull History of Medicine 37 1963.

Stolnitz, J. Locke and the categories of value in eighteenth-century British aesthetic theory. Philosophy 38 1963.

Aarsleff, H. Leibniz on Locke on language. Amer Philosophical Quart 1 1964.

Berlin, I. Hobbes, Locke and Professor Macpherson. Political Quart 35 1964.

Leroy, A. L. Locke: sa vie, son œuvre, avec un exposé de sa philosophie. Paris 1964.

Obertello, L. Locke e Port-Royal: il problema della probabilità. Trieste 1964.

Parry, G. Individuality, politics and the critique of paternalism in Locke. Political Stud 12 1964.

Armstrong, R. L. Locke's 'doctrine of signs': a new metaphysics. JHI 26 1965.

Axtell, J. L. Locke, Newton and the elements of natural philosophy. Pædagogica Europæa 1 1965.

— Locke's review of the Principia. Notes & Records of Royal Soc 20 1965.

Bobbio, N. Studi lockiani. Rivista Storica Italiana 77 1965.

Crane, R. S. Notes on the organization of Locke's Essay. In All these to teach: essays in honor of C. A. Robertson, ed R. A. Bryan et al, Gainesville 1965; rptd in his Idea of the humanities and other essays vol 1, Chicago 1967.

Odegard, D. Locke as an empiricist. Philosophy 40 1965.
—— Locke's epistemology and the value of experience. JHI 26 1965.
Rusk, R. R. In his Doctrines of the great educators, 1965 (rev).
Ryan, A. Locke and the dictatorship of the bourgeoisie. Political Stud 13 1965.
Allison, H. E. Locke's theory of personal identity. JHI 27 1966.
Day, J. P. Locke on property. Philosophical Quart 16 1966.
Euchner, W. Locke zwischen Hobbes und Hooker: zu neuen Interpretationen der politischen Philosophie Lockes. Archives Européennes de Sociologie 7 1966.
Jones, C. E. Locke and masonry: a document. Neuphilologische Mitteilungen 67 1966.
Rogers, G. A. J. Boyle, Locke and reason. JHI 27 1966.
Schlegelmilch, W. Locke's Thoughts concerning education zur Kontinuität pädagogischer Theorien. Die Neueren Sprachen 65 1966.
Alkon, P. K. In his Samuel Johnson and moral discipline, Evanston 1967.
de Beer, E. S. Locke: the appointment offered to him in 1698. Bull Inst of Historical Research 40 1967.
Dunn, J. Consent in the political theory of Locke. Historical Jnl 10 1967.
—— Justice and the interpretation of Locke's political theory. Political Stud 16 1968.
—— The political thought of Locke. Cambridge 1969.
Howell, W. S. Locke and the new rhetoric. Quart Jnl of Speech 53 1967.
Jeffreys, M. V. C. Locke: prophet of common sense. 1967.
Jenkins, J. J. Locke and natural rights. Philosophy 42 1967.
Laudan, L. The nature and sources of Locke's views on hypotheses. JHI 28 1967.
Smith, W. Locke in the Great Unitarian controversy. In Freedom and reform: essays in honor of H. S. Commager, New York 1967.
Thijssen Schoute, C. L. De Nederlandse vriendenkring van Locke. In his Uit de republiek der letteren, Hague 1967.
Ashcraft, R. Locke's state of nature: historical fact or moral fiction? Amer Political Science Rev 62 1968.
Kretzmann, N. The main thesis of Locke's semantic theory. Philosophical Rev 77 1968.
Locke and Berkeley: a collection of critical essays. Ed C. B. Martin and D. M. Armstrong 1968.
Margolis, J. Locke and scientific realism. Rev of Metaphysics 22 1968.
Kelly, P. A note on Locke's pamphlets on money. Trans Cambridge Bibl Soc 5 1969.
Locke, problems and perspectives: a collection of new essays. Ed J. W. Yolton, Cambridge 1969.
See also under Bold, Broughton, Burnet, Carroll, Edwards, Hampton, King, Lee, Lowde, Milner, Norris, Proast, Sergeant, Temple, Wynne, *below*; Sherlock *and* Stillingfleet, *col 1614–15, above; and* Cockburn *and* Perronet, *cols 2047, 1865 below.*

Other Philosophical Writers 1660–1700

VINCENT ALSOP
d. 1703

Anti-sozzo: sive Sherlocismus enervatus. 1675.
Duty and interest united in prayer and praise for kings. 1695.
God in the Mount: a sermon. 1696.
A confutation of some of the errors of Mr Daniel Williams. 1698.

CHARLES BLOUNT
1654–93

§1

Anima mundi. 1679.
Great is Diana of the Ephesians. 1690.
The two first books of Philostratus concerning the life of Apollonius Tyaneus. 1680.
Miscellaneous works. 1695. Preface by C. Gildon.

§2

Gilmour, J. S. L. Some uncollected authors 17: Blount. Book Collector 7 1958.

SAMUEL BOLD
1649–1737

A short discourse of the true knowledge of Christ Jesus. 1697.
A collection of tracts publish'd in vindication of Mr Lock's Reasonableness of Christianity. 5 pts 1697–1706.
Some considerations of the principal objections to the Essay on the human understanding. 1699.

JOHN BROUGHTON

Psychologia: or an account of the nature of the rational soul. 1703.

THOMAS BURNET
1635?–1715

§1

Telluris theoria sacra. 2 vols 1681–9.
The theory of the earth. 2 vols 1684–90; ed B. Willey 1965. An enlarged and rev version of above.
Remarks upon an Essay concerning humane understanding. 1697; Second remarks, 1697; Third remarks, 1699.

§2

Haller, E. Die barocken Stilmerkmale in der englischen, lateinischen und deutschen Fassung von Burnets Theory of the earth. Berne 1940.
Ogden, H. V. S. Burnet's Telluris theoria sacra and mountain scenery. ELH 14 1947.
Tuveson, E. L. The origins of the 'moral sense'. HLQ 11 1948.

RICHARD BURTHOGGE
1638?–94?

§1

Τἀγαθὸν: or divine goodness explicated and vindicated. 1672.
Causa Dei: or an apology for God. 1675.
Organum vetus et novum: or a discourse of reason and truth. 1678.
An essay upon reason and the nature of spirits. 1694.
Of the soul of the world, and of particular souls. 1699.

§2

Lyon, G. In his L'idéalisme en Angleterre au xviiie siècle, Paris 1888.
Cassirer, E. In his Das Erkenntnisproblem vol 1, Berlin 1906.

WILLIAM CARROLL

A dissertation upon the tenth chapter of the fourth book of Mr Locke's Essay concerning humane understanding, wherein that author's endeavours to establish Spinoza's atheistical hypothesis are discover'd and confuted. 1706.

SIR JOSIAH CHILD
1630–99
§ 1

A new discourse of trade. 1693, 1694, 1718.

§ 2

Scroggs, E. S. Bibliography of Child. Bull of Br Lib of Political Science 14 1921.
Bowyer, T. H. The published forms of Child's A new discourse of trade. Library 5th ser 11 1956.

RICHARD CUMBERLAND the elder
1632–1718
§ 1

De legibus naturae. 1672; tr 1692 (abridged), 1727 (complete), 1750; tr French, 1744.

§ 2

Sharp, F. C. The ethical system of Cumberland. Mind 21 1912.

CHARLES DAVENANT
1656–1714
See col 1897, below.

HENRY DODWELL the elder
1641–1711
See col 1825, above.

JOHN EDWARDS
1637–1716

Some thoughts concerning the several causes and occasions of atheism, with some brief reflections on Socinianism and on a late book entituled the Reasonableness of Christianity. 1695.
A demonstration of the existence and providence of God. 1696.
Socinianism unmasked. 1696.
A brief vindication of the fundamental articles of the Christian faith from Mr Lock's Reflections. 1697.
The Socinian creed. 1697.

JOSEPH GLANVILL
1636–80
§ 1

The vanity of dogmatizing. 1661, 1665 (rev as Scepsis scientifica); ed J. Owen 1885; ed M. E. Prior, New York 1931 (facs).
Lux orientalis. 1662, 1665, 1687 (with George Rust, Defence of truth).
Plus ultra: or the progress and advancement of knowledge since the days of Aristotle. 1668; ed J. I. Cope, Gainesville 1958 (facs).
Λόγου θρησκεία: or a seasonable recommendation and defence of reason in the affairs of religion against infidelity. 1670.

Philosophia pia: or a discourse of the religious temper of the experimental philosophy which is profest by the Royal Society. 1671.
Essays on several important subjects. 1676.
An essay concerning preaching, written for the direction of a young divine. 1678, 1703.
A seasonable defence of preaching, and the plain way of it. 1678.
Saducismus triumphatus. 1681, 1682, 1689, 1726 ('with some account of Mr Glanvill's life and writings'); ed C. O. Parsons, Gainesville 1966 (facs).
Some discourses, sermons and remains. 1681. Preface by A. Horneck.

§ 2

Pyrrhonism of Glanvill. Retrospective Rev 1 1853.
Greenslet, F. Joseph Glanvill. New York 1900.
Redgrove, H. S. and I. M. L. Glanvill and psychical research in the seventeenth century. 1921.
Prior, M. E. Glanvill, witchcraft and seventeenth-century science. MP 30 1932.
Stimson, D. Ballad of Gresham Colledge. Isis 18 1932. Attributed to Glanvill.
Habicht, H. Glanvill: ein spekulativer Denker im England des xvii Jahrhunderts. Zürich 1936.
Mullett, C. F. A letter by Glanvill on the future state. HLQ 1 1938.
Cope, J. I. The Cupri-Cosmits: Glanvill on Latitudinarian anti-enthusiasm. HLQ 17 1951.
— Glanvill: Anglican apologist. St Louis 1956.
Weiss, S. A. Glanvill and 'the character of a coffee-house'. N & Q May, Aug 1952.
Wiley, M. L. In her Subtle knot, 1952.
Popkin, R. H. Glanvill: a precursor of Hume. JHI 14 1953.
Krook, D. Two Baconians: Robert Boyle and Glanvill. HLQ 18 1955.
Edelen, G. Glanvill, Henry More and the Phantom Drummer of Tedworth. Harvard Lib Bull 10 1956.

FRANCIS GLISSON
1597–1677
§ 1

Tractatus de natura substantiae energetica: seu de vita naturae ejusque tribus primis facultatibus. 1672.

§ 2

Pagel, W. Harvey and Glisson on irritability. Bull Historical Medicine 41 1967.

JOHN GRAUNT
1620–74
See col 1897, below.

BENJAMIN HAMPTON

The existence of human soul after death, proved from Scripture, reason and philosophy; wherein Mr Lock's notion that understanding may be given to matter, and all other such books and opinions, are confuted. 1711.

SAMUEL JOHNSON
1649–1703

Julian the Apostate. 1682.
An humble and hearty address to all the English Protestants in the present army. 1686.
Julian's arts to undermine and extirpate Christianity. 1689.

An argument proving that the abrogation of King James from the regal throne was according to the Constitution. 1692.
Works. 1710, 1713.

JOHN KEILL
1671–1721

Examination of Dr Burnet's Theory of the earth. Oxford 1698.
Introductio ad veram physicam. Oxford 1702.

WILLIAM KING
1650–1729

§1

Dr origine mali. Dublin 1702; tr Edmund Law 1731.
A key to divinity: or a philosophical essay on free will. 1715.

§2

Beckett, J. C. King's administration of the diocese of Derry 1691–1703. Irish Historical Stud 4 1944.

HENRY LEE

Anti-scepticism: or notes upon each chapter of Lock's Essay. 1702.

CHARLES LESLIE
1650–1722

§1

The snake in the grass. 1696.
A short and easie method with the Deists. 1698.
Theological works. 2 vols 1721, 7 vols Oxford 1832.

§2

Leslie, R. J. Life and writings of Leslie. 1885.
Joost, N. Two American editions of Leslie's Short and easie method. N & Q 10 Nov 1951.

JAMES LOWDE

A discourse concerning the nature of man. 1694.
Moral essays wherein some of Mr Lock's and M. Malbranch's opinions are briefly examin'd. York 1699.

WILLIAM LOWNDES
1652–1724

A report containing an essay for the amendment of the silver coins. 1695.
A further essay for the amendment of the gold and silver coins. 1695.

JOHN MILNER
1628–1702

An account of Mr Lock's religion, out of his own writings and in his own words. 1700.

WILLIAM MOLYNEUX
1656–98

§1

Dioptrica nova. 1692.

§2

Molyneux, C. A memorial of the life of W. Molyneux: an autobiography. In his An account of the family and descendants of Sir T. Molyneux, Evesham 1820.

JOHN NORRIS
1657–1711

§1

A collection of miscellanies. Oxford 1687, 1692, 1699, 1706.
The theory and regulation of love: a moral essay, to which are added Letters philosophical and moral between the author and Dr Henry More. 1688, 1694.
Christian blessedness; to which is added Reflections upon a late Essay concerning the human understanding. 1690, 1692.
Cursory reflections upon a book call'd An essay concerning human understanding. 1690; ed G. D. McEwen, Los Angeles 1961 (Augustan Reprint Soc) (facs).
Practical discourses upon several divine subjects. 4 vols 1691–8.
Letters concerning the love of God. 1695.
An account of reason and faith in relation to the mysteries of Christianity. 1697.
An essay towards the theory of the ideal or intelligible world, desig'd for two parts. 2 vols 1701–4.
A philosophical discourse concerning the natural immortality of the soul. 1708.

§2

Lyon, G. In his L'idéalisme en Angleterre au xviiie siècle, Paris 1888.
Powicke, F. J. A dissertation on Norris. 1894.
MacKinnon, F. I. The philosophy of Norris of Bemerton. Baltimore 1910.
Muirhead, J. H. In his Platonic tradition in Anglo-Saxon philosophy, 1931.
Ryan, J. K. Norris: a seventeenth-century English Thomist. New Scholasticism 14 1940.
Walton, G. In his Metaphysical to Augustan, 1955.
Wasserman, G. R. Norris and the Veal-Bargrave story. MLN 75 1960.
For Norris's poems see col 479, above.

SIR DUDLEY NORTH
1641–91

Discourses upon trade. 1691, Edinburgh 1822; ed J. R. McCulloch 1856, Cambridge 1954.
Considerations upon the East India trade. 1701; ed J. R. McCulloch 1856, Cambridge 1954.

SAMUEL PARKER
1640–88

See col 1612, above.

SIMON PATRICK
1626–1707

See col 1613, above.

SIR WILLIAM PETTY
1632–87

§1

Reflections upon some persons and things in Ireland. 1660.
A treatise of taxes and contributions. 1662, 1667, 1679, 1685.

The discourse made concerning the use of duplicate pro-
portion. 1674.
An essay concerning the multiplication of mankind. 1682,
1686.
Another essay in political arithmetick. 1683.
The fourth part of the present state of England. 1683.
Observations upon the Dublin-bills of morality. 1683.
Deux essays d'arithmétique politique. 1686.
Two essays in political arithmetick. 1687.
Cinq essays sur l'arithmétique politique. 1687.
Five essays in political arithmetick. 1687; tr German 1693
(1st, 2nd, 4th, 5th Essays).
Political arithmetick. 1690, 1691.
The political anatomy of Ireland; to which is added
Verbum sapienti. 1691.
Sir William Petty's quantulumcunque concerning money.
1695.
Several essays in political arithmetick. 1699.
Economic writings. Ed C. H. Hull 2 vols Cambridge
1899.

§ 2

Bevan, W. L. Sir William Petty. Baltimore 1894.
Fitzmaurice, E. Life of Petty. 1895.
Pasquier, M. Sir William Petty. Paris 1903.
Powell, L. F. Petty and Graunt. TLS 20 Oct 1932.
Mullett, C. F. Petty on the plague. Isis 28 1938.
Havens, G. R. Rousseau, Melon and Petty. MLN 55 1940.
Strauss, E. Petty: portrait of a genius. 1954.
Masson, I. and A. J. Youngson. Sir William Petty FRS.
Notes & Records of Royal Soc 15 1960.
Hahn, R. Petty's mechanical philosophy. Isis 56 1965.
Hoppen, K. T. Petty, polymath. History Today 15 1965.
Groenewegen, P. D. Authorship of the Natural and poli-
tical observations upon the Bills of Mortality. JHI 28
1967.

JONAS PROAST

The argument of the Letter concerning toleration consider'd and answer'd. Oxford 1690.
A third letter concerning toleration. Oxford 1691.

JOHN RAY
1627–1705
See col 1908, below.

GEORGE RUST
d. 1676

A letter of resolution concerning Origen. 1661; ed M. H.
Nicolson, New York 1933 (facs).
Sermon preached at Newton at the funeral of Hugh, Earl
of Mount Alexander. Dublin 1664.
Sermon at the funeral of Jeremy Taylor. Dublin 1667.
A discourse of truth. 1677; ed J. Glanvill 1682.
Discourse of the use of reason in matters of religion. 1683.
Remains. Ed H. Hallywell 1686.

JOHN SERGEANT
1622–1707
§ I

The method to science. 1696.
Solid philosophy asserted against the fancies of the
Ideists, with reflexions on Mr Locke's Essay concerning
human understanding. 1697.
Transnatural philosophy or metaphysicks. 1700.

§ 2

Bradish, N. C. Sergeant: a forgotten critic of Descartes
and Locke. Monist 39 1929.

WILLIAM SHERLOCK
1641–1707
See col 1614, above.

EDWARD STILLINGFLEET
1635–99
See col 1615, above.

THOMAS TAYLOR

The two covenants of God with mankind: or the divine
justice and mercy explained and vindicated in an essay
design'd to shew the use and advantages of some of Mr
Malebranch's principles. 1704.

SIR RICHARD TEMPLE
1634–97
§ I

An essay upon taxes, calculated for the present juncture of
affairs in England. 1693.
Some short remarks upon Mr Lock's book, in answer to
Mr Lounds. 1696.

§ 2

Davies, G. The political career of Temple and Buckingham politics. HLQ 4 1940.
Gay, E. F. Temple: the Debt Settlement and estate litigation 1653–75. HLQ 6 1943.
Roberts, C. Temple's Discourse on the Parliament of
1667–8. HLQ 20 1957.

WILLIAM WAKE
1657–1737
§ I

Sermons. 1690.
The genuine epistles of the Apostolic Fathers, translated
with discussions. 1693.
Principles of the Christian religion. 1699.
The state of the Church and clergy of England. 1703.

§ 2

Sykes, N. Archbishop Wake and the Whig Party 1716–23.
Cambridge Historical Jnl 8 1945.
— The election and inthronization of Wake as Archbishop of Canterbury. Jnl of Ecclesiastical History 1
1950.
— Bishop Wake's primary visitation of the Diocese
of Lincoln 1706. Jnl of Ecclesiastical History 2
1951.
— Wake, Archbishop of Canterbury. 2 vols Cambridge
1957.

JOHN WILKINS
1614–72
See vol 1, above.

JOHN WYNNE
1667–1743

An abridgement of Locke's Essay concerning humane
understanding. 1696.

J. R. H.

B. BERKELEY AND HIS CONTEMPORARIES

GEORGE BERKELEY
1685–1753

Bibliographies

Mead, H. R. A. A bibliography of Berkeley. Berkeley 1910.

Jessop, T. E. A bibliography of Berkeley, with an inventory of Berkeley's manuscript remains by A. A. Luce. Oxford 1934.

—— A select bibliography. In New studies in Berkeley's philosophy, ed W. E. Steinkraus, New York 1966.

Lameere, J. et al. Revue Internationale de Philosophie 7 1953. Suppl to Jessop 1934–53.

Trinity College Library, Dublin. Catalogue of manuscripts, books and Berkeleiana exhibited on the occasion of the bicentenary of the death of Berkeley. Dublin 1953.

Turbayne, C. M. and R. Ware. A bibliography of Berkeley 1933–62. Jnl of Philosophy 60 1963.

Collections

Works, to which is added a life and several letters to T. Prior, Dean Gervais and Mr Pope. [Ed T. Stock] 2 vols Dublin 1784, 3 vols 1820, 1837.

Works. Ed G. N. Wright 2 vols 1843. Includes trns of the Latin works.

Works, including many of his writings hitherto unpublished, with prefaces, annotations, his life and letters, and an account of his philosophy. Ed A. C. Fraser 4 vols Oxford 1871, 1901 (rev).

Works. Ed G. Sampson 3 vols 1897–8.

Works. Ed A. A. Luce and T. E. Jessop 9 vols Edinburgh 1948–57. Includes all Berkeley's known letters.

Philosophical writings, selected. Ed T. E. Jessop 1952.

The principles of human knowledge, with three dialogues between Hylas and Philonous [abridged]. Ed A. J. Ayer and R. Winch 1952.

§1

Arithmetica absque algebra aut Euclide demonstrata. Dublin 1707.

Miscellanea mathematica. Dublin 1707 (in Arithmetica, above).

An essay towards a new theory of vision. Dublin 1709, London 1709 (adds appendix); tr Italian, 1732. Rptd with rev text but without appendix in Alciphron vol 2, 1732, below.

A treatise concerning the principles of human knowledge. Pt 1 (all pbd), Dublin 1710, London 1734 (rev text with Three dialogues, below); ed P. Wheelwright, New York 1935; ed T. E. Jessop 1937 (1710 texts with variants of 1734); ed C. M. Turbayne, New York 1957; ed G. J. Warnock 1962 (with Three dialogues).

Passive obedience: or the Christian doctrine of not resisting the Supreme Power, proved and vindicated upon the principles of the law of nature. 1712, 1712, 1713 (rev).

Three dialogues between Hylas and Philonous. 1713, 1725, 1734 (with Principles of human knowledge); ed C. M. Turbayne, New York 1954; ed G. J. Warnock 1962; tr French, 1750; German, 1756.

Advice to the Tories who have taken the oaths. 1715.

De motu: sive de motu principio et natura, et de causa communicationis motum. 1721; rptd in A miscellany, 1752, below.

An essay towards preventing the ruin of Great Britain. 1721; rptd in A miscellany, 1752, below.

A proposal for the better supplying of churches in our foreign plantations, and for converting the savage Americans to Christianity, by a college to be erected in the Summer Islands, otherwise called the Isles of Bermudas. 1725, 1731; rptd in A miscellany, 1752, below.

A sermon preached before the incorporated Society for the Propagation of the Gospel in foreign parts. 1732; rptd in A miscellany, 1752, below.

Alciphron: or the minute philosopher, in seven dialogues. 2 vols 1732, 1732, Dublin 1732, London 1752 (omits Theory of vision, below), 1752 (rev, omitting Theory of vision), 1767; tr French, 1734; German, 1737.

The theory of vision: or visual language, shewing the immediate presence and providence of a Deity, vindicated and explained. 1733.

The analyst: or a discourse addressed to an infidel mathematician. 1734, Dublin 1734, 1754.

A defence of free-thinking in mathematics. 1735, Dublin 1735.

Reasons for not replying to Mr Walton's Full answer in a letter to PTP. Dublin 1735.

The querist: containing several queries proposed to the consideration of the public. 3 pts Dublin 1735–7, London 1735–7, 1750 (rev, adding A word to the wise), Glasgow 1751; rptd in A miscellany, 1752, below; ed J. M. Hone, Dublin 1936.

A letter on the project of a national bank. 1737.

A discourse addressed to magistrates and men in authority. Dublin 1732, London 1736, 1738, Dublin 1738.

A chain of philosophical reflexions and inquiries concerning the virtues of tar water. 1744, 1744 (rev as Siris: a chain etc), Dublin 1744, London 1744, 1744, 1746, 1747, 1748; tr French, 1745; Spanish, 1786.

A letter to T[homas] P[rior] esq, containing some farther remarks on the virtues of tar-water. Dublin 1744, London 1744.

Two letters, the one to Thomas Prior esq concerning the usefulness of tar-water in the plague; the other to the Rev Dr Hales, on the benefit of tar-water in fevers. Dublin 1747, London 1747.

A word to the wise: or an exhortation to the Roman Catholic clergy of Ireland. Dublin 1749, Boston 1750, 1752; rptd in The querist, 1750, Glasgow 1751, and in A miscellany, 1752, below.

Maxims concerning patriotism, by a lady. Dublin 1750; rptd in A miscellany, 1752, below.

A miscellany, containing several tracts on various subjects. 1752, Dublin 1752. Includes, in addition to works already ptd, Farther thoughts on tar water, and Verses on the prospect of planting arts and learning in America.

The Irish patriot: or queries upon queries. Ed J. M. Hone, TLS 13 March, 3 April 1930.

Commonplace book. First pbd in Works, ed A. C. Fraser vol 4, 1871; ed G. A. Johnson 1930; ed A. A. Luce as Philosophical commentaries, Edinburgh 1944 (rev).

An unpublished sermon. Ed J. Wild, Philosophical Rev 40 1931.

Letters

See above, Works, ed A. A. Luce and T. E. Jessop.

Luce, A. A. Some unpublished Berkeley letters with some new Berkeleiana. Proc Royal Irish Acad 41 1932. See Hermathena 48 1933.

—— The philosophical correspondence between Berkeley and Johnson. Hermathena 56 1940.

§2

Norton, J. N. Life of Bishop Berkeley. 1861.

Fraser, A. C. Berkeley. 1881.

—— Berkeley and spiritual realism. 1908.

Balfour, A. J. In his Essays and addresses, 1893. The essay on Berkeley is also prefixed to Works, ed G. Sampson vol 1, 1897.

Tyler, M. C. In his Three men of letters, New York 1895.

Moulton, C. W. In his Library of literary criticism vol 3, New York 1902.

Rand, B. Berkeley and Percival. Cambridge 1914.

— Berkeley's American sojourn. Cambridge Mass 1932.

Johnston, G. A. The derivation of Berkeley's ethical theory. Philosophical Rev 24 1915.

— The development of Berkeley's philosophy. 1923.

Pfannenberg, I. Berkeley und die englische Romantik. Freiburg 1930.

Hone, J. M. and M. M. Rossi. Bishop Berkeley: his life, writings and philosophy. 1934.

Aaron, R. I. A catalogue of Berkeley's library. Mind 41 1932.

Hicks, G. D. Berkeley. 1933.

Luce, A. A. Berkeley and Malebranche. Oxford 1934.

— The unity of Berkeley's philosophy. Mind 46 1937.

— Developments within Berkeley's commonplace book. Mind 49 1940.

— Berkeley's existence in the mind. Mind 50 1941.

— Alleged developments of Berkeley's philosophy. Mind 52 1943.

— Berkeley's essays in the Guardian. Ibid.

— Berkeley's immaterialism. Edinburgh 1946.

— The life of Berkeley, Bishop of Cloyne. Edinburgh 1949.

— Berkeley's Philosophical commentaries. Mind 59 1950.

— The Berkeleian idea of sense. Proc Aristotelian Soc Suppl 27 1953.

— Berkeley's search for truth. Hermathena 82 1953.

— Berkeleian action and passion. Revue Internationale de Philosophie 7 1953.

— Berkeleian studies in America and France. Hermathena 94 1960.

— The dialectic of immaterialism: an account of the making of Berkeley's Principles. 1963.

Oertel, H. J. Berkeley und die englische Literatur. Halle 1934.

Wild, J. George Berkeley. Cambridge Mass 1936.

del Boca, S. L'unità del pensiero di Berkeley. Florence 1937.

Jessop, T. E. Berkeley. Philosophy 12 1937.

— Malebranche and Berkeley. Revue Internationale de Philosophie 1 1938.

— Berkeley and the contemporary physics. Revue Internationale de Philosophie 7 1953.

— L'esse est percipi de Berkeley. Revue Philosophique 143 1953.

— George Berkeley. Hermathena 82 1953.

— George Berkeley. 1959.

Broad, C. D. Berkeley's argument about material substance. 1942.

Testa, A. La filosofia di Berkeley. Urbino 1943.

Baladi, N. La pensée religieuse de Berkeley et l'unité de sa philosophie. Cairo 1945.

Bender, F. Berkeley's philosophy re-examined. Amsterdam 1946.

Leyburn, E. D. Berkeleian elements in Wordsworth's thought. JEGP 47 1948.

Brayton, A. Berkeley in Apulia. Boston 1949.

— Berkeley in Newport. Boston 1954.

Laky, J. J. A study of Berkeley's philosophy in the light of the philosophy of St Thomas Aquinas. Washington 1950.

Davie, D. A. Berkeley's style in Siris. Cambridge Jnl April 1951.

— Irony and conciseness in Berkeley and in Swift. Dublin Mag 27 1952.

— Berkeley and 'philosophic words'. Studies 44 1955.

— Berkeley and the style of dialogue. In The English mind, ed H. S. Davies and G. Watson, Cambridge 1964.

Gelber, S. Universal language and the sciences of man in Berkeley's philosophy. JHI 13 1952.

Cadbury, H. J. Berkeley's gifts to the Harvard Library. Harvard Lib Bull 7 1953.

Day, J. P. de C. George Berkeley. Rev of Metaphysics 6 1953.

Dobrée, B. Berkeley as a man of letters. Hermathena 82 1953.

Greene, D. J. Smart, Berkeley, the scientists and the poets: a note on eighteenth-century anti-Newtonianism. JHI 14 1953.

Lehec, C. Trente années d'études Berkeleyennes. Revue Philosophique 143 1953.

Leroy, A.-L. Influence de la philosophie Berkeleyenne sur la pensée continentale. Hermathena 82 1953.

— George Berkeley. Paris 1959.

Popkin, R. H. Berkeley's influence on American philosophy. Hermathena 82 1953.

Warnock, G. J. Berkeley. 1953 (Pelican).

Wisdom, J. O. The unconscious origin of Berkeley's philosophy. 1953.

Ritchie, A. D. Berkeley's Siris: the philosophy of the great chain of being and the alchemical theory. Proc Brit Acad 40 1954.

— Berkeley's Siris. 1955.

White, A. R. The ambiguity of Berkeley's 'without the mind'. Hermathena 83 1954.

Prior, A. N. Berkeley in logical form. Theoria 21 1955.

Sillem, E. A. Berkeley and the proofs of the existence of God. 1957.

Papajewski, H. Swift and Berkeley. Anglia 77 1959.

Wiener, P. Did Hume read Berkeley? Jnl of Philosophy 56 1959. Replies by R. H. Popkin, E. Mossner and A. Flew, ibid; by P. Wiener 58 1961; by R. H. Popkin 61 1964.

Armstrong, D. M. Berkeley's theory of vision. Melbourne 1960.

Carr, H. Wildon. Berkeley and Dr Johnson: an imaginary dialogue. Personalist 41 1960.

Linnell, J. Berkeley's Siris. Ibid.

Rauter, H. The veil of words: Sprachauffassung und Dialogform bei Berkeley. Anglia 79 1962.

Bennett, J. Berkeley and God. Philosophy 40 1965.

Davie, G. E. Berkeley's impact on Scottish philosophers. Philosophy 40 1965.

Furlong, E. J. Berkeley and the tree in the quad. Philosophy 41 1966.

Steinkrauss, W. E. (ed). New studies in Berkeley's philosophy. New York 1966.

Other Philosophical Writers 1700–50

PETER ANNET
1693–1769

§1

Judging for ourselves: or free-thinking the great duty of religion, with a poem to the Rev Mr Whitefield. 1739. Anon.

The resurrection of Jesus considered in answer to the tryal of the witnesses, by a moral philosopher. [1743?], 1744. Anon.

The conception of Jesus consider'd as the foundation of the Christian religion, by a moral philosopher. 1744. Anon.

Annet's short-hand. [1745?], [1770?].

Deism fairly stated, and fully vindicated from the gross imputations and groundless calumnies of modern believers, in a letter to a friend, by a moral philosopher. 1746. Anon.

A collection of the tracts of a certain free enquirer noted by his sufferings for his opinions. [1750?]. First tract signed P.A.

The history and character of St Paul, examined in a letter to Gilbert West esq; with a preface by way of post-script, by M.P. [1750?]. Anon.

Expeditious penmanship, or short hand, by P. Annet: this being his former short hand, greatly altered etc. [1750?].

Lectures by the late Mr Peter Annet. [1768?], 1822.

§ 2

Silvester, T. The evidence of the resurrection of Jesus vindicated, against the cavils of a moral philosopher. 1744.

West, G. Observations on the history and evidence of the resurrection of Jesus Christ. 1747.

Hervey, T. The writer's time redeemed: or Annet's short hand perfected. 1779.

Torrey, N. L. Voltaire and Peter Annet's Life of David. PMLA 43 1928.

Twynam, E. Peter Annet. 1938.

John Noorhouk: 'the man after God's own heart' 1761. TLS 25 Aug 1945.

JOHN BALGUY
1686–1748

§ 1

A letter to a Deist, concerning the beauty and excellence of moral virtue. 1726, 1730, 1732.

The foundations of moral goodness: or a further inquiry into the original of our idea of virtue. 1728, 1731, 1733.

The second part of the foundation of moral goodness. 1729.

Divine rectitude: or a brief inquiry concerning the moral perfections of the Deity. 1730.

A second letter to a Deist, concerning a late book entitled Christianity as old as the Creation. 1731.

The law of truth: or the obligations of reason essential to all religion. 1733.

An essay on redemption: being the second part of Divine rectitude. 1741, 1785.

Twenty sermons on the duty and advantage of studying the works of nature. 1750, 1790.

Separate sermons rptd in The English preacher, ed W. Enfield 1773–4; The practical preacher vol 1, 1762; *and in* Family lectures: or domestic divinity, ed V. Knox vol 1, 1791.

§ 2

Silvester, T. Moral and Christian benevolence: containing some reflections upon Mr Balguy's essay on moral goodness. 1734.

ANDREW BAXTER
1686–1750

§ 1

An enquiry into the nature of the human soul, wherein the immateriality of the soul is evinced from the principles of reason and philosophy. 1733, 2 vols 1737, 1745; An appendix, 2 vols 1750.

Matho: sive cosmotheoria puerilis, dialogus; in quo prima principia de mundi ordine et ornatu proponuntur. Edinburgh 1738, 1746; tr 2 vols 1740, 1745, Dublin 1754, London 1765 (rev).

A letter from Mr Baxter, author of An enquiry, to John Wilkes esq. 1753.

The evidence of reason in proof of the immortality of the soul, independent on the more abstruse inquiry into the nature of matter and spirit: collected from the mss of Mr Baxter. 1779.

§ 2

Jackson, J. A dissertation on matter and spirit; with some remarks on a book entitled An enquiry into the nature of the human soul. 1735.

Perronet, V. A second vindication of Mr Locke, wherein the various objections rais'd by the learned author of An enquiry into the nature of the human soul are consider'd. 1738.

[Wimpey, J.] Remarks on a book intitled An enquiry into the nature of the human soul. 1741.

Bracken, H. M. Baxter: critic of Berkeley. JHI 18 1957.

—— The early reception of Berkeley's immaterialism 1710–33. Hague 1959, 1965 (rev).

Davie, G. E. Berkeley's impact on Scottish philosophers. Philosophy 40 1965.

RICHARD BENTLEY
1662–1742

The folly and unreasonableness of atheism, in eight sermons [Boyle lectures 1692]. 1693, 1699, Cambridge 1724, 1735 [adds 3 sermons], Oxford 1809; tr Latin, 1696; German, 1715. Ptd in parts as The folly of atheism, 1692; Matter and motion cannot think, 1692; A confutation of atheism from the structure of humane bodies, 1692; A confutation of atheism from the origin and frame of the world, 1692–3.

Remarks upon a late Discourse of free-thinking [by A. Collins], by Phileleutherus Lipsiensis. 1713; tr French, 1738.

See col 1819, above.

PETER BROWNE
d. 1735

§ 1

A letter in answer to a book entitled Christianity not mysterious. 1697.

Of drinking to the memory of the dead. Dublin 1713, 1713, 1715.

An answer to a Right Reverend Prelate's defence of eating and drinking in remembrance of the dead. Dublin 1715.

The doctrine of parts and circumstances in religion laid open. 1716.

The procedure, extent and limits of human understanding. 1728, 1729, 1737.

Things divine and supernatural conceived by analogy with things natural and human. 1733.

§ 2

Perronet, V. A vindication of Mr Locke. 1736.

Hindley, J. C. The philosophy of enthusiasm. London Quart 182 1957.

JOSEPH BUTLER
1692–1752
Collections

Works. Ed S. Halifax 2 vols Edinburgh 1804, Oxford 1807, 1836, 1844, 1849–50.

Works. Ed W. E. Gladstone 2 vols Oxford 1896.

Works. Ed J. H. Bernard 2 vols 1900.

§ 1

Fifteen sermons preached at the Chapel of the Rolls Court. 1726, 1729 (with Preface), 1736, 1749 (adds Six sermons preached on public occasions), 1765, 2 vols Glasgow 1769 etc; ed W. R. Matthews 1914 (adds Dissertation on virtue from Analogy, below).

The analogy of religion, natural and revealed, to the constitution and course of nature. 1736, 1736 (corrected), 1740, Glasgow 1754, 1765, Aberdeen 1775; ed S. Halifax 1788; ed H. Morley 1884; ed R. Bayne 1906; ed W. E. Gladstone, Oxford 1907 (WC).

Six sermons preached upon public occasions. 1739, 1740, 1741, 1747, 1748.

A charge delivered to the clergy at the visitation of Durham. 1871.

§2

Mackintosh, J. On the progress of ethical philosophy chiefly during the seventeenth and eighteenth centuries. 1830, 1872 (rev).

Bartlett, T. Memoirs of the life, character and writings of Butler. 1839.

Steere, E. Some remains (hitherto unpublished) of Bishop Butler. 1853.

Napier, J. Lectures on Butler's Analogy. 1864.

Maurice, J. F. D. The conscience. 1872.

Eaton, J. R. J. Bishop Butler and his critics. 1877.

Egglestone, W. M. Stanhope memorials of Bishop Butler. 1878.

Huckin, H. R. Dialogues founded upon Butler's Analogy of religion. 1878.

Collins, W. L. Butler. 1881.

Gladstone, W. E. Studies subsidiary to the works of Bishop Butler. Oxford 1896.

Spooner, W. A. Bishop Butler. 1901.

Baker, A. E. Bishop Butler. 1923.

Taylor, A. E. Some features of Butler's ethics. Mind 35 1926.

Townsend, H. G. The synthetic principle in Butler's ethics. International Jnl of Ethics 37 1926.

Broad, C. D. In his Five types of ethical theory, 1930.

Gavin, E. L'etica di Butler. Giornale Critica della Filosofia Italiana 13 1932.

Mossner, E. C. Bishop Butler and the Age of Reason. New York 1936.

Stedman, R. E. Bishop Butler and his Analogy of religion. Nineteenth Century May 1936.

Tristram, H. Bishop Butler's Analogy. Dublin Rev 100 1936.

Sykes, N. Bishop Butler and the primacy. Jnl of Historic Christianity 33 1936.

—— Bishop Butler and the Church of his age. Durham Univ Jnl 43 1950.

—— Bishop Butler and the primacy. Theology 61 1958.

Beck, L. W. A neglected aspect of Butler's ethics. Sophia 5 1937.

Leslie, A. H. Butler's Analogy. London Quart 162 1937.

Norton, W. J. Bishop Butler, moralist and divine. New Brunswick NJ 1940.

Harris, W. G. Teleology in the philosophy of Butler and Abraham Tucker. Philadelphia 1941.

Hammond, T. C. Age-long questions: an examination of certain problems in the philosophy of religion. 1942. On Analogy.

Blackburn, W. Bishop Butler and the design of Arnold's Literature and dogma. MLQ 9 1948.

McPherson, T. H. The development of Bishop Butler's ethics. Philosophy 23–4 1948–9.

Raphael, D. D. Bishop Butler's view of conscience. Philosophy 24 1949.

Barnes, W. H. F. Butler: moralist. Durham Univ Jnl 43 1951.

Duncan-Jones, A. Butler's moral philosophy. 1952.

Freed, L. The good nature of Bishop Butler. Twentieth Century July 1952.

Grave, S. A. Butler's Analogy. Cambridge Jnl Dec 1952.

Matthews, W. R. Great preachers—16: Butler. Theology 55 1952.

Watson, J. H. Bishop Butler as a philosopher–theologian. Evangelical Quart 24 1952.

White, A. R. Conscience and self-love in Butler's sermons. Philosophy 27 1952.

Walsh, J. M. Benevolence and self-love in Butler's moral philosophy. Culture 19–20 1958–9.

Riddle, G. K. The place of benevolence in Butler's ethics. Philosophical Quart 9 1959.

Carlsson, P. A. Butler's ethics. Hague 1964.

Watson, G. In The English mind, ed H. S. Davies and Watson, Cambridge 1964.

Timko, M. Browning upon Butler: or natural theology in the English isle. Criticism 7 1965.

Jeffner, A. Butler and Hume on religion. Stockholm 1966. Tr from Swedish.

THOMAS CHUBB
1679–1747

§1

The supremacy of the Father asserted: or eight arguments from Scripture, to prove that the Son is a being inferior and subordinate to the Father. 1715, 1718.

The previous question with regard to religion etc. 1725, 1725, 1728.

A supplement to the previous question with regard to religion. 1725.

An examination of Mr Barclay's Principles, with regard to man's natural ability since the Fall. 1726.

A vindication of God's moral character. 1726.

Human nature vindicated. 1726.

Scripture evidence consider'd, in a view of the controversy betwixt the author and Mr Barklay's defenders. 1728.

Some short reflections on the ground and extent of authority and liberty, with respect to civil government. 1728.

The comparative excellence and obligation of moral and positive duties, fully stated and considered. 1730.

A discourse concerning reason, with regard to religion and divine revelation. 1731.

The equity and reasonableness of the divine conduct. 1737.

The true gospel of Jesus Christ asserted. 1738.

An enquiry concerning the ground and foundation of religion. 1740.

A discourse on miracles. 1741.

The ground and foundation of morality considered. 1745.

Four dissertations. 1746.

Posthumous works. 1748.

§2

Bliss, A. Observations on Mr Chubb's Discourse concerning reason. 1731.

Phelps, J. A vindication of revealed religion, in answer to Mr Chubb's Enquiry. 1740.

Fleming, C. Truth and modern-deism at variance. 1746.

JOHN CLARKE
1687–1734

An essay upon the education of youth in grammar-schools. 1720, 1730 (rev), 1740.

An examination of the notion of moral good and evil, advanced in a late book [by W. Wollaston] entitled The religion of nature delineated. 1725.

The foundation of morality in theory and practice considered. York [1726].

An examination of the sketch or plan of an Answer [by Conyers Middleton] to the book [by Matthew Tindal] entitled Christianity as old as the Creation. 1733.

JOHN CLARKE
1682–1757

An enquiry into the cause and origin of evil. 1720, 1739. Boyle lecture.

A demonstration of some of the principal sections of Sir Isaac Newton's Principles of natural philosophy. 1730.

JOSEPH CLARKE
d. 1749

A treatise of space. 1733.
A further examination of Dr Clarke's notions of space. 1734.
Waterland's sermons on several important subjects of religion and morality. Ed J. Clarke 2 vols 1742, 1776.
A full and particular reply to Mr Chandler's case of subscription to explanatory articles of faith. 1749.

SAMUEL CLARKE
1675-1729
Collections

Works, with a preface giving some account of the life, writings and character of the author, by Benjamin Hoadley. 4 vols 1738.
Sermons. Ed John Clarke 10 vols 1730-1.
Oeuvres philosophiques: édition nouvelle, précédée d'une introduction par Amédée Jacques. Paris 1843.

§ 1

Some reflections on that part of a book [by J. Toland] called Amyntor: or a defence of Milton's life, which relates to the writings of the primitive Fathers and the canon of the New Testament. 1699.
Three practical essays upon baptism, confirmation and repentance. 1699.
A paraphrase on the four Evangelists. 1701.
A demonstration of the being and attributes of God, more particularly in answer to Mr Hobbs, Spinoza and their followers. 2 vols 1705-6 (Boyle lectures for 1704-5), 1716 (adds correspondence with Joseph Butler), 1719, 1725 (adds Discourse concerning prophecies), 1732, 1739; tr French, 1717.
A letter to Mr Dodwell, wherein all the arguments in his Epistolary discourse are particularly answered. 1706.
The Scripture-doctrine of the Trinity. 1712.
A collection of papers which passed between the late learned Mr Leibnitz and Dr Clarke (to which are added remarks upon a book [by Anthony Collins] entitled A philosophical enquiry concerning human liberty). 1717; ed H. G. Alexander, Manchester 1956; tr French, 1720, 1740.
Jacobi Rohaulti physica, latine vertit, recensuit et uberioribus jam annotationibus, ex illustrissimi Isaaci Newtoni philosophia maximam partem hastis, amplificavit et ornavit S. Clarke. 1718; tr 2 vols 1735.
A discourse concerning the connexion of the prophecies in the Old Testament, and the application of them to Christ. 1725, 1725.
A letter to Benjamin Hoadly FRS occasioned by the controversy relating to the proportion of velocity and force in bodies in motion. 1728.

§ 2

Wiston, W. Historical memoirs of the life of Dr Clarke. 1741 (3rd edn). Includes The elogium of Clarke by A. A. Sykes, first pbd in Present state of the republic of letters, July 1729; and T. Emlyn, Memoirs of the life of Dr Clarke.
Le Rossignol, J. E. Ethical philosophy of Clarke. Leipzig 1892.
Leroy, G. von. Die philosophischen Probleme in dem Briefwechsel zwischen Leibnitz und Clarke. Giessen 1893.

Albee, E. Clarke's ethical philosophy. Philosophical Rev 37 1928.
Teeter, L. M. Albrecht von Haller and Clarke. JEGP 27 1928.
Towers, A. R. Fielding and Dr Clarke. MLN 70 1955.

CATHARINE COCKBURN, née Trotter
1679-1749
Collections

The works of Mrs Catharine Cockburn, with an account of the life of the author by T. Birch. 2 vols 1751.

§ 1

A defence of the Essay of human understanding [by Locke]. 1702.
A discourse concerning a guide in controversies, in two letters. 1707, 1728.
A letter to Dr Holdsworth. 1726.
Remarks upon some writers in the controversy concerning the foundations of moral duty. 1743.
Remarks upon the principles and reasonings of Dr Rutherforth's Essay on the nature and obligations of virtue, in vindication of the late Dr Samuel Clarke. 1747.
For the plays see col 802, above.

§ 2

Gosse, E. W. Catharine Trotter: the precursor of the blue stockings. 1916.

ARTHUR COLLIER
1680-1732

§ 1

Clavis universalis, or a new inquiry after truth: being a demonstration of the non-existence or impossibility of an external world. 1713, Edinburgh 1836 (with letters to Samuel Clarke), 1837 (in S. Parr, Metaphysical tracts); ed E. Bowman, Chicago 1909.
Of justification by faith, as in opposition to justification by works, in a sermon upon Romans 1 verse 17. 1716.
A specimen of true philosophy, in a discourse on Genesis, the first chapter and the first verse. Salisbury 1730, 1837 (in S. Parr, Metaphysical tracts).
Logology: or a treatise on the logos or word of God, in seven sermons on John 1, 1, 2, 3, 14. 1732.

§ 2

Benson, R. Memoirs of the life and writings of the Rev Collier. 1837.

ANTHONY COLLINS
1676-1729

§ 1

An essay concerning the use of reason in propositions, the evidence whereof depends upon human testimony. 1707, 1707.
An answer to Mr Clark's Third defence of his Letter to Mr Dodwell. 1708, 1711, 1731.
A letter to the learned Mr Henry Dodwell: containing some remarks on a—pretended—demonstration of the immateriality and natural immortality of the soul. 1709, 1731; tr French, 1769.
A vindication of the divine attributes. 1710.
Priestcraft in perfection. 1710, 1710, 1748.

A discourse of free-thinking, occasion'd by the rise and growth of a sect call'd Free-thinkers. 1713, 1713; tr French, 1714, 1766.
A philosophical inquiry concerning human liberty. 1717, 1717; ed J. Priestley 1790.
An historical and critical essay on the Thirty-Nine Articles of the Church of England. 1724.
The scheme of literal prophecy considered. 1726, 1727.
A letter to the Reverend Dr Rogers, concerning the necessity of divine revelation. 1727, 1727.
A discourse concerning ridicule and irony in writing, in a letter to the Reverend Dr Nathanael Marshall. 1729.
A dissertation on liberty and necessity: wherein the process of ideas, from their first entrance into the soul, until their production of action, is delineated. 1729.
A discourse of the grounds and reasons of the Christian religion; to which is prefix'd an apology for free debate and liberty of writing. 1734, 1737 (rev), 1741; tr French, 1768.

§ 2

Bentley, R. Remarks on a late Discourse of free-thinking. 1713.
Chandler, S. A defence of Christianity. 1725.
Sykes, A. An essay upon the truth of the Christian religion. 1725.
Broome, J. H. Une collaboration: Collins et Desmaizeaux. Revue de Littérature Comparée 30 1956.

WILLIAM DERHAM
1657–1735

§ 1

The artificial clock-maker: a treatise of watch and clock-work, by W.D. 1696, 1700 (enlarged with suppl), 1734 (rev), 1759; tr German, 1708.
Physico-theology: or a demonstration of the being and attributes of God, from his works of creation [Boyle lectures 1711–12]. 1713, 1714, 1714, 1716, 1720, 1723, 1727, 1732, 1737, etc; tr Dutch, 1728; French, 1732; Swedish, 1736; German, 1750.
Astro-theology: or a demonstration of the being and attributes of God. 1715, 1715, 1719, 1721 (corrected), 1726, 1741, Glasgow 1755; tr German, 1732.
Christo-theology: or a demonstration of the divine authority of the Christian religion. 1730.
A defence of the Church's right in leasehold estates. 1731.
The life of Mr [John] Ray. In Ray, Select remains, 1760; ed E. Lankester in Memorials of John Ray, 1846.

§ 2

Lynskey, W. Pluce and Derham: new sources of Goldsmith. PMLA 57 1942.

HENRY DODWELL the younger
d. 1784

Christianity not founded on argument. 1741, 1743, 1746.

JAMES HERVEY
1714–58
Collections

The works of the late Reverend James Hervey, with a particular account of the life of the author. 6 vols Edinburgh 1769, Newcastle 1789, 1792, 7 vols 1797, 6 vols Pontefract 1805, Edinburgh 1834.
Sermons and miscellaneous tracts. 1764, 1784–92, Glasgow 1790.

§ 1

Meditations among the tombs, in a letter to a lady. 1746.
Meditations and contemplations [vol 1 contains Meditations among the tombs]. 2 vols 1748, 1748; 26 edns to 1792; tr Dutch, 1754, 1775; French, 1770, 1775; Spanish, 1805.
Remarks on Lord Bolingbroke's Letters on the study and use of history. 1752, Dublin 1752.
Theron and Aspasio: or a series of dialogues and letters upon the most important and interesting subjects. 3 vols 1755, 1755, 1767, 2 vols 1772, 3 vols 1789.
Dialogues between Theron and Aspasio, by J.H.; together with his Letters to Mr John Wesley in vindication thereof. Ed W. Hervey 3 vols Pontefract 1805, 2 vols 1808.

Letters

A collection of the letters of J.H., to which is prefixed an account of his life and death. 2 vols 1760, Dublin 1760, London 1784.
The life of J.H.; to which is added a collection of his letters. Berwick 1770, 1772.
Letters illustrative of the author's character, never before published, by J.H. [Ed J. Burgess] 1811.

§ 2

Bellamy, J. Letters and dialogues, with remarks on the sentiments of Hervey. 1761.
Scott, A. Imputed righteousness investigated, and the arguments in favour of that doctrine in Theron and Aspasio refuted. 1822.
McKillop, A. D. Nature and science in the works of Hervey. SE 28 1949.
Baker, F. Hervey, Methodist prose poet. London Quart 182 1957.
Porter, L. E. Hervey: a bicentenary appreciation. Evangelical Quart 31 1959.
Corder, J. Limitations of nature in the landscapes of Hervey. N & Q Jan 1965.

FRANCIS HUTCHESON
1695–1747
Bibliographies

Jessop, T. E. In his A bibliography of David Hume and of Scottish philosophy from Francis Hutcheson to Lord Balfour, 1938.

§ 1

An inquiry into the original of our ideas of beauty and virtue, in two treatises. 1725 (anon), 1726 (rev), 1726, 1729, Glasgow 1738, 1753; tr French, 1749.
An essay on the nature and conduct of the passions and affections, with illustrations on the moral sense. 1728, Dublin 1728, London 1730, 1742, Dublin 1751, 1756, Glasgow 1769, 1772; tr French, 1749; German, 1762.
De naturali hominum socialitate oratio inauguralis. Glasgow 1730, 1756.
Considerations on patronages. 1735, Glasgow 1774.
Letters between the late Mr Gilbert Burnet and Mr Hutchinson concerning the true foundation of virtue or moral goodness. 1735, Glasgow 1772. First ptd in London Jnl 1728 as Letters between 'Philanthropus' and 'Philaretus'. With the title Letters concerning the true goodness between Mr Gilbert Burnet and Mr Francis Hutcheson and including 6 articles in Dublin Jnl 1725–6, later ptd in Reflections upon laughter, 1750, below.
Metaphysicae synopsis: ontologiam et pneumatologiam complecteus. Glasgow 1742, 1744, 1749, 1756, Strasbourg 1772. Anon.

Philosophiae moralis institutio compendiaria. Glasgow 1742, Rotterdam 1745, Glasgow 1745, 1755, Dublin 1787; tr Glasgow 1747, 1753.

The meditations of M. Aurelius Antoninus. Glasgow 1742, 1749, 1752, 1764. Anon.

Reflections upon laughter, and remarks upon the Fable of the bees. Glasgow 1750; rptd as Thoughts on laughter and observations on bees, Glasgow 1758. First ptd as 6 articles in Dublin Jnl 1725–6, signed 'Philomeides' and 'P.M.'.

A system of moral philosophy, in three books, to which is prefixed some account of the life, writings and character of the author. 2 vols Glasgow and London 1755; tr German, 1756; French, 1770.

Logicae compendium. Glasgow 1759, 1764, 1778, 1787.

§2

Vindication of Mr Hutcheson from the calumnious aspersions of a late pamphlet. Glasgow 1738. Anon.

Reid, T. An essay on quantity. 1748.

Price, R. Review of the principal questions and difficulties in morals. 1758.

Taylor, J. An examination of the scheme of morality advanced by Dr Hutcheson. 1759.

Arthur, A. Discourses on theological and literary subjects. Glasgow 1803.

Fowler, T. Shaftesbury and Hutcheson. 1882.

Scott, W. R. Francis Hutcheson. Cambridge 1900.

Jones, H. Hutcheson: a discourse delivered in the University of Glasgow. Glasgow 1906.

Bonar, J. Moral sense. 1930.

Thorpe, C. de W. Addison and Hutcheson on the imagination. ELH 2 1935.

Sypher, W. Hutcheson and the classical theory of slavery. Jnl of Negro History 24 1939.

Swabey, W. C. Benevolence and virtue. Philosophical Rev 3 1943.

Bryson, G. Man and society: the Scottish inquiry of the eighteenth century. Princeton 1945.

Aldridge, A. O. A preview of Hutcheson's ethics. MLN 61 1946.

—— A French critic of Hutcheson's aesthetics. MP 45 1948.

—— Edwards and Hutcheson. Harvard Theological Rev 44 1951.

—— The meaning of incest from Hutcheson to Gibbon. Ethics 61 1951.

Kallich, M. The associationist criticism of Hutcheson and Hume. SP 43 1946.

Frankena, W. Hutcheson's moral sense theory. JHI 16 1955.

Dickie, G. An examination of Hutcheson's alleged emotivism. Research Stud of State College of Washington 26 1958.

Blackstone, W. T. Hutcheson and contemporary ethical theory. Atlanta 1965.

McMannon, J. F. Some problems regarding a series of letters between Hutcheson and Gilbert Burnet. Stud in Scottish Lit 3 1965.

JOHN JACKSON
1686–1763

The existence and unity of God proved from his nature and attributes. 1734. A defence of Samuel Clarke.

NATHANIEL LARDNER
1684–1768

Collections

Works. 11 vols 1788, 5 vols 1815, 4 vols 1817, 10 vols 1838. Vol 1 includes Life by A. Kippis.

§1

The credibility of the Gospel history. 17 vols 1727–57; tr Dutch, 1730; Latin, 1733; German, 1750–1.

A vindication of three of our blessed Saviour's miracles, in answer to Woolston. 1729; tr German, 1750.

Counsels of prudence for the use of young people. 1735, 1743, 1762, 1806, 1813.

A caution against conformity to this world. 1739.

The circumstances of the Jewish people: an argument for the Christian religion. 1743; tr German, 1754.

The case of the daemoniacks. 1748; tr German, 1760.

Sermons upon various subjects. 2 vols 1750–60.

An essay on the Mosaic account of the creation and fall of man. 1753.

A letter concerning the Logos. 1759, 1788, 1793, 1833.

A large collection of ancient Jewish and heathen testimonies to the truth of the Christian revelation. 4 vols 1764–7.

EDMUND LAW
1703–87

§1

An essay on the origin of evil. 1731, 1732, 1739, 1758, 1781. Tr with notes of Archbishop King, De origine mali.

An enquiry into the ideas of space, time, immensity and eternity. Cambridge 1734.

Considerations on the state of the world with regard to the theory of religion. Cambridge 1745, 1749 (adds a Discourse upon the life of Christ), 1765, 1774, Carlisle 1784, London 1820; tr German, 1771.

Considerations on the propriety of requiring subscription to the articles of faith. 1774.

The works of John Locke. 4 vols 1777, 1794, 1801. Ed Law, with Life of Locke.

WILLIAM LAW
1686–1761

Remarks upon a late book [by B. Mandeville] entituled The fable of the bees. 1724, 1725, 1726.

The case of reason, or natural religion, fairly and fully stated. 1731, 1755, Dublin 1757.

See col 1653, above.

JOHN LELAND
1691–1766

An answer to a late book [by M. Tindal] entitled Christianity as old as the Creation. 2 pts Dublin 1733.

The divine authority of the Old and New Testament asserted. 2 vols 1739–40; tr German, 1756.

A defence of Christianity. 1740, 1753.

Remarks on [H. Dodwell's] Christianity not founded on argument. 2 pts 1744.

A view of the principal deistical writers. 3 vols 1754–6, 2 vols 1757, 1764, 1766; ed C. R. Edmonds 1837.

The advantage and necessity of the Christian revelation. 2 vols 1764, 1768, Glasgow 1819.

Discourses on various subjects, with a preface giving some account of the life, character and writings of the author [by I. Weld]. 4 vols 1768–9.

JOHN MILL
1645–1707

§1

Novum testamentum cum lectionibus variantibus J. Millii. 1707, Amsterdam 1710, Rotterdam 1710, Leipzig 1723, Amsterdam 1746.

§2

Fox, A. Mill and Richard Bentley: a study of the textual criticism of the New Testament. Oxford 1954.

THOMAS MORGAN
d. 1743

Philosophical principles of medicine. 1725, 1730 (rev).
The nature and consequences of enthusiasm considered. 1720. Followed by 2 'Defences', 1720, 1722.
The absurdity of opposing faith to reason. 1722.
The grounds and principles of Christian communion. 1720.
A collection of tracts occasioned by the late Trinitarian controversy. 1726.
A letter to Mr Thomas Chubb occasioned by his Vindication of human nature. 1727.
The mechanical practice of physick. 1735.
The moral philosopher, in a dialogue between Philalethes a Christian Deist, and Theophanes a Christian Jew. 1737, 1738; vol 2, Being a farther vindication of moral truth and reason, 1739; vol 3, Superstition and tyranny inconsistent with theocracy, 1740; vol 4, Physicotheology, 1741.
A letter to Dr Cheyne in defence of the Mechanical practice. 1738.
A vindication of the Moral philosopher against S. Chandler. 1741.
The history of Joseph considered by Philalethes. 1744.

VINCENT PERRONET
1693–1785

A vindication of Mr Locke. 1736.
A second vindication of Mr Locke. 1738.
Some enquiries relating to spiritual beings, in which the opinions of Mr Hobbes are taken notice of. 1740.
An affectionate address to the people called Quakers. 1747.
A defence of infant-baptism. 1749.
An earnest exhortation to the strict practice of Christianity. 1750.
Some reflections on original sin. 1776.

ANTHONY ASHLEY COOPER, 3rd EARL OF SHAFTESBURY
1671–1713

§1

Select sermons of Dr [Benjamin] Whichot. 1698. Ed Shaftesbury, with preface.
An inquiry concerning virtue in two discourses. 1699 (unauthorized), 1711 (rev).
A letter concerning enthusiasm. 1708; ed A.-L. Leroy, Paris 1930. With Fr trn.
Sensus communis: an essay on the freedom of wit and humour. 1709.
Soliloquy: or advice to an author. 1710.
Characteristicks of men, manners, opinions, times. 3 vols 1711, 1711, 1714 (rev), 1723, 1727, 1732, 1733, 1737, 1743, 4 vols Glasgow 1758; ed W. M. Hatch 1870; ed J. M. Robertson 2 vols 1900, New York 1964 (with new introd by S. Grean).
A notion of the historical draught: or tablature of the judgment of Hercules. 1712 (Fr trn), 1713. Included in 1714 edn of Characteristicks, above.
Second characters: or the language of forms. Ed B. Rand, Cambridge 1914. Contains the Judgment of Hercules and A letter concerning design (ptd in 1732 edn of Characteristicks, above), which Shaftesbury intended as part of a separate work, together with The picture of Cebes and Plastics.

Letters

Several letters written by a noble Lord to a young man at the university. 1716.
Letters from the Right Honourable the late Earl of Shaftesbury to Robert Molesworth esq. Ed J. Toland 1721.
Original letters of Locke, Algernon Sidney and Shaftesbury. Ed T. Forster 1830.
The life, unpublished letters and philosophical regimen of Shaftesbury. Ed B. Rand 1900.

§2

[Day, R.] Free thoughts in defence of a future state, with occasional remarks on An inquiry concerning vertue. 1700.
[Fowler, E.] Remarks upon the Letter concerning enthusiasm. 1708.
Reflections upon a letter concerning enthusiasm. 1709. Anon; often attributed to Bishop Edward Fowler.
Journal des Scavans 25 March 1709. Review of Letter concerning enthusiasm; 31 March 1710, 21 April 1710, review of An essay on the freedom of wit and humour.
Le Clerc, J. M. Le Clerc's extract and judgment of the Characteristics. 1712.
Brown, J. Essays on the Characteristics. 1751, 1752, Dublin 1752, 1764.
Bulkley, C. A vindication of my Lord Shaftesbury. 1751.
Leland, J. A view of the principal Deistical writers. 1754.
Ogilvie, J. Inquiry into the causes of infidelity [and] observations on the writings of Shaftesbury. 1783.
Schlosser, J. G. Ueber Shaftesbury von der Tugend. Basle 1785.
Spicker, G. Die Philosophie des Grafen von Shaftesbury. Freiburg 1872.
Fowler, T. Shaftesbury and Hutcheson. 1882.
Albee, E. Shaftesbury's relations to Utilitarianism. Mind 8 1896.
— The relation of Shaftesbury and Hutcheson to Utilitarianism. Philosophical Rev 5 1896.
Kohler, M. F. Shaftesbury: ein Brief über den Enthusiasmus. Leipzig 1909.
Moore, C. A. Shaftesbury and the ethical poets in England 1700–60. PMLA 31 1916.
— The return to nature in English poetry of the eighteenth-century. SP 14 1917.
Weiser, C. F. Shaftesbury und das deutsche Geistesleben. Leipzig 1916.
Folkierski, W. L'esthétique de Shaftesbury. Cracow 1920.
Tiffany, E. Shaftesbury as Stoic. PMLA 38 1923.
Alderman, W. E. The significance of Shaftesbury in English speculation. PMLA 38 1923.
— The style of Shaftesbury. MLN 38 1923.
— Bibliographical evidence of the vogue of Shaftesbury in the eighteenth century. Trans Wisconsin Acad 21 1926.
— Shaftesbury and the doctrine of benevolence in the eighteenth century. Trans Wisconsin Acad 26 1931.
— Shaftesbury and the doctrine of moral sense in the eighteenth century. PMLA 46 1931.
— Shaftesbury and the doctrine of optimism. Trans Wisconsin Acad 28 1933.
Croce, B. Shaftesbury in Italia. Bari 1927.
Bandini, L. Shaftesbury: etica e religione, la morale del sentimento. Bari 1930.
Bonar, J. Moral sense. 1930.
Casati, E. Quelques correspondants français de Shaftesbury. Revue de Littérature Comparée 11 1931.
— Hérauts et commentateurs de Shaftesbury en France. Revue de Littérature Comparée 14 1934.
— Un carnet de Shaftesbury 1711–13. Revue de Littérature Comparée 16 1936.

Cassirer, E. Shaftesbury und die Renaissance des Platonismus in England. In Vorträge Bibliothek Warburg 1930–1, Leipzig 1932; tr Edinburgh 1953.

Crane, R. S. Suggestions towards a genealogy of the man of feeling. ELH 1 1934.

Lempicki, S. von. Shaftesbury und der Irrationalismus. Studia Philosophica 2 1937.

Leroy, A.-L. Le Virtuoso de Shaftesbury. In Deuxième congrès international d'esthétique, Paris 1937.

Brett, R. L. The third Earl of Shaftesbury as a literary critic. MLR 37 1942.

—— The third Earl of Shaftesbury. 1951.

Aldridge, A. O. Lord Shaftesbury's literary theories. PQ 24 1945.

—— Shaftesbury and the test of truth. PMLA 60 1945.

—— Shaftesbury's earliest critic. MP 44 1946. On Robert Day, Free thoughts in defence of a future state, 1700.

—— Henry Needler's knowledge of Shaftesbury. MLN 63 1947.

—— Shaftesbury, Christianity and friendship. Anglican Theological Rev 32 1950.

—— Two versions of Shaftesbury's Inquiry concerning virtue. HLQ 13 1950.

—— Shaftesbury and the Deist manifesto. Trans Amer Philosophical Soc new ser 61 1951.

—— Shaftesbury and Bolingbroke. PQ 31 1952.

Tuveson, E. L. The origins of the moral sense. HLQ 11 1947.

—— The importance of Shaftesbury. ELH 20 1953.

—— Shaftesbury on the not so simple plan of human nature. Stud in Eng Lit 1500–1900 5 1965.

Whitaker, S. F. Pierre Coste et Shaftesbury. Revue de Littérature Comparée 25 1951.

—— The first edition of Shaftesbury's Moralists. Library 4th ser 7 1952.

Heinemann, F. H. The philosopher of enthusiasm, with material hitherto unpublished. Revue Internationale de Philosophie 6 1952.

Willey, B. In his Eighteenth-century background, 1953.

—— In his English moralists, 1964.

Zani, L. L'etica di Lord Shaftesbury. Milan 1954.

Schlegel, D. B. Shaftesbury and the French Deists. Chapel Hill 1956.

Peach, B. A. Shaftesbury's moral Arithmeticks. Personalist 39 1958.

Marsh, R. Shaftesbury's theory of poetry. ELH 28 1961.

Stolnitz, J. On the origins of 'aesthetic disinterestedness'. Jnl of Aesthetics 20 1961.

—— On the significance of Lord Shaftesbury in modern aesthetic theory. Philosophical Quart 11 1961.

Broadbent, J. B. Shaftesbury's horses of instruction. In The English mind, ed H. S. Davies and G. Watson, Cambridge 1964.

Grean, S. Self-interest and public interest in Shaftesbury's philosophy. Jnl History of Philosophy 2 1964.

—— Shaftesbury's philosophy of religion and ethics. Athens Georgia 1967.

MATTHEW TINDAL
1657–1733
§1

An essay concerning the law of nations and the rights of sovereigns. 1693, 1694 (with An account of what was said at the Council-board).

Essay concerning obedience to the supreme powers. 1694.

A letter to the clergy of both universities concerning the Trinity. 1694.

An essay concerning the power of the magistrates and the rights of mankind in matters of religion. 1697.

The liberty of the press. 1698.

Reasons against restraining the press. 1704.

The rights of the Christian Church asserted against the Romish and all other priests who claim an independent power over it, with a preface. 1706, 1706, 1707.

A defence of the rights of the Christian Church. 1707, 1709; A second defence, 1708.

Four discourses on obedience, laws of nations, power of the magistrate and liberty of the press. 1709.

New High Church turned old Presbyterian. 1709, 1710.

High-Church catechism. 1710.

The merciful judgements of the High Church triumphant. 1710.

The Jacobitism, perjury and Popery of High-Church priests. 1710.

The nation vindicated from the aspersions cast on it. 1711.

The defection considered, and the designs of those who divided the friends of government set in a true light. 1717 (4 edns), 1718.

Destruction a certain consequence of division. 1717.

The judgement of Dr Prideaux concerning the murder of Julius Caesar. 1721.

A defence of our present happy establishment. 1722.

Enquiry into the causes of our present disaffection. 1722.

An address to the inhabitants of London and Westminster. 1729, 1730 (rev); A second address, 1730, 1730.

Christianity as old as the Creation: or the Gospel a republication of the religion of nature. 1730, 1730, 1731; tr German, 1741.

§2

Curll, E. Memoirs of the life and writings of Tindal. 1733.

Motzo Dentice di Accadia, C. La supremazia dello stato, 1: Tindal. Giornale Critico della Filosofia Italiana 17 1936.

JOHN TOLAND
1670–1722
Bibliographies

Heinemann, F. H. Prolegomena to a Toland bibliography. N & Q Sept 1943.

Collections

A collection of several pieces. 2 vols 1726 (with Life by Des Maizeaux), 1747, 1 vol 1814.

§1

The danger of mercenary parliaments. [1695], 1722, 1810 (in Harleian Miscellany vol 9); ed W. H. Dunham and S. Pargellis in Complaint and reform in England 1436–1714, New York 1938.

Christianity not mysterious. 1696, 1696, 1702 (with Apology for Mr Toland).

The life of John Milton. 1698, 1699.

Amyntor: or a defence of Milton's Life. 1699.

Memoirs of Denzil, Lord Holles. 1699. Ed with a preface by Toland.

Clito: a poem on the force of eloquence. 1700.

The Oceana of James Harrington with his Life prefix'd, by J. Toland. 1700, 1737, 1758.

The art of governing by parties. 1701.

Propositions for uniting the two East India companies. 1701.

Anglia libera. 1701.

Paradoxes of state. 1702.

Vindicius liberius: or Mr Toland's defence of himself against Convocation. 1702.

Letters to Serena. 1704; tr French, 1768.

An account of the courts of Prussia and Hanover. 1705, 1706; tr German, 1706.

The memorial of the state of England. 1705.

Adeisidæmon and Origines judaicae. Hague 1709.

Lettre d'un Anglois à un Hollandois au sujet du Docteur Sacheverell. 1710.

The description of Epsom. 1711.

A letter against Popery. 1712.

Her Majesty's reasons for creating the electoral Prince of Hanover a Peer of the Realm. 1712.

An appeal to honest people against wicked priests. [1710], 1712.

Cicero illustratus: dissertatio philologico-critica. 1712.

Dunkirk, or Dover: or the Queen's honour. 1713, 1713.

The art of restoring: or the piety and probity of General Monk. 1714.

Reasons for naturalising the Jews in Great Britain and Ireland. 1713, 1714.

The grand mystery laid open. 1714.

The state anatomy of Great Britain. 1717 (8 edns).

The second part of the state anatomy. 1717, 1717, 1718.

Nazarenus: or Jewish, Gentile and Mahometan Christianity. 1718.

The destiny of Rome. 1718.

Pantheisticon: sive formula celebrandæ sodalitatis Socraticæ. 1720; tr 1751; French, 1927.

Tetradymus. 1720.

A critical history of the Celtic religion and learning. [1740], 1814.

Hypatia: or the history of a most learned lady. 1753.

§2

Berthold, G. Toland und der Monismus der Gegenwart. Heidelberg 1876.

Lantoine, A. Un précurseur de la franc-maçonnerie: Toland. Paris 1927.

Heinemann, F. H. Toland and the age of enlightenment. RES 20 1944.

— Toland and Leibniz. Philosophical Rev 54 1945.

— Toland and the Age of Reason (with hitherto unpublished material). Archiv für Philosophie 4 1950.

Cragg, G. R. Toland and the rise of Deism. In his From Puritanism to the Age of Reason, Cambridge 1950.

Crocker, L. G. Toland et le matérialisme de Diderot. Revue d'Histoire Littéraire de la France 53 1953.

Mautner, F. H. Noch ein Wort zu 'Amintor'. Deutsche Vierteljahrsschrift 32 1958.

Nicholl, H. F. Toland: religion without mystery. Hermathena 100 1965.

WILLIAM WARBURTON
1698–1779

Bibliographies

Evans, A. W. In his Warburton and the Warburtonians, Oxford 1932.

Collections

Works. Ed R. Hurd 7 vols 1788, 12 vols 1811.

§1

Miscellaneous translations, in prose and verse from Roman poets, orators and historians. 1724; rptd in Tracts by Warburton and a Warburtonian, 1789, below.

A critical and philosophical inquiry into the causes of prodigies and miracles, as related by historians, in two parts. 1727; rptd in Tracts by Warburton and a Warburtonian, 1789, below.

An apology for Sir Robert Sutton. 1733.

The alliance between Church and State: or the necessity and equity of an established religion and a test-law demonstrated, from the essence and end of civil society, upon the fundamental principles of the law of nature and nations, in three parts. 1736, 1741, 1748, 1766 etc.

The divine legation of Moses demonstrated on the principles of a religious Deist, in six books. 2 vols 1738–41, 1742, 1755, 1765 (first complete edn of 6 bks).

A vindication of the author of the divine legation of Moses. 1738.

Faith's working by charity to Christian edification: a sermon preach'd in the diocese of Lincoln. 1738.

A vindication of Mr Pope's Essay on man, from the misrepresentations of Mr de Crousaz, professor of philosophy and mathematicks in the university of Lausanne, in six letters. 1740; A seventh letter, which finishes the vindication of Mr Pope's Essay on man, from Lausanne, 1740. See Commentary, below.

The nature, extent and right improvement of Christian liberty: a sermon preached at Maidston. 1741.

A critical and philosophical commentary on Mr Pope's Essay on man, in which is contain'd A vindication of the said Essay from the misrepresentations of Mr De Resnel, the French translator, and of Mr De Crousaz, professor of philosophy and mathematics in the Academy of Lausanne, the commentator. 1742. Rev and enlarged version of Vindication, above.

A sermon preached at the Abbey-Church at Bath. 1742.

Remarks on several occasional reflections, in answer to the Rev Dr Middleton, Dr Pococke, the Master of the Charter House, Dr Richard Grey and others. 1744.

Remarks on several occasional reflections, in answer to the Reverend Doctors Stebbing and Sykes. 1745.

A faithful portrait of Popery: a sermon preached at St James's church, Westminster. 1745.

A sermon occasioned by the present unnatural rebellion, preached in Mr Allen's chapel at Prior-Park, near Bath. 1745.

The nature of national offences truly stated: a sermon preached on the general Fast day. 1746.

An apological dedication to the Reverend Dr Henry Stebbing in answer to his censure and misrepresentations of the sermon preached on the general Fast day. 1746.

The works of Shakespear in eight volumes, with a comment and notes, critical and explanatory, by Mr Pope and Mr Warburton. 8 vols 1747.

A sermon preach'd on the Thanksgiving appointed to be observed the ninth of October. 1746.

A letter from an author to a Member of Parliament concerning literary property. 1748.

A letter to the editor of the Letters on the spirit of patriotism, the idea of a patriot-king and the state of the parties. 1749.

Julian: or a discourse concerning the earthquake and fiery eruption which defeated that emperor's attempt to rebuild the Temple at Jerusalem. 1750, 1751.

The works of Alexander Pope esq, in nine volumes complete, together with the commentaries and notes of Mr Warburton. 9 vols 1751.

The principles of natural and revealed religion occasionally opened and explained. 2 vols 1753–4.

A view of Lord Bolingbroke's philosophy in four letters to a friend. 3 vols 1754–5.

A sermon preached before his Grace Charles Duke of Marlborough at the parish-church of St Andrew, Holborn. [1755].

Natural and civil events the instruments of God's moral government: a sermon preached at Lincoln's-Inn chapel. 1756.

Remarks on Mr David Hume's Essay on the natural history of religion. 1757.

A sermon preached in the Abbey Church, Westminster. 1760.

A rational account of the nature and end of the sacrament of the Lord's Supper. 1761.

The doctrine of grace: or the office and operations of the Holy Spirit vindicated from the insults of infidelity and the abuses of fanaticism. 2 vols 1763 (3 edns).

A sermon preached before the incorporated Society for the Propagation of the Gospel in foreign parts. 1766.

A sermon preached at St Lawrence Jewry. 1767.

Sermons and discourses on various subjects and occasions. 1767.

Tracts by Warburton and a Warburtonian not admitted into the collections of their respective works. [Ed S. Parr] 1789.

A selection from the unpublished papers. Ed F. Kilvert 1841.

Letters

Letters of a late eminent prelate to one of his friends. Ed R. Hurd, Kidderminster [1808].

Letters from the Reverend Dr Warburton, Bishop of Gloucester to the Hon Charles Yorke, from 1752 to 1770. 1812 (priv ptd by Lord Hardwicke).

§ 2

[Webster, W.] Remarks on the Divine legation of Moses. [1739].

—— A letter to a Bishop concerning the Divine legation of Moses. [1741].

Tillard, J. A reply to Mr Warburton's Appendix. 1742.

[Morgan, T.] A brief examination of the Rev Dr Warburton's Divine legation of Moses. 1742.

Bott, T. An answer to the Reverend Mr Warburton's Divine legation of Moses. 1743.

Grey, R. An answer to Mr Warburton's Remarks on several occasional reflections. 1744.

Sykes, A. A. An examination of Mr Warburton's account of the conduct of the antient legislators. 1744.

—— A defence of the examination of Mr Warburton's account of the theocracy of the Jews. 1746.

Cooper, J. G. Cursory remarks on Mr Warburton's new edition of Mr Pope's works. 1751.

Law, W. A short but sufficient confutation of the Rev Dr Warburton's projected defence of Christianity in his Divine legation of Moses. 1757.

[Lowth, R.] A letter to the Right Reverend author of the Divine legation of Moses. 1765.

Figgis, J. N. In Typical English churchmen, ed W. E. Collins 1902.

Evans, A. W. Warburton and the Warburtonians. Oxford 1932.

Griffith, R. H. Early Warburton? or late Warburton? SE 1940.

Rogers, R. W. Notes on Pope's collaboration with Warburton in preparing a final edition of the Essay on man. PQ 26 1947.

Dawson, G. E. Warburton, Hanmer and the 1745 edition of Shakespeare. SB 2 1950.

Sherbo, A. Warburton and the 1745 Shakespeare. JEGP 51 1952.

—— Dr Johnson's Dictionary and Warburton's Shakespeare. PQ 33 1954.

Templeman, W. D. Warburton and Brown continue the battle over ridicule. HLQ 17 1953.

Gilbert, V. M. The Warburton-Edwards controversy. N & Q June 1954.

Cherpack, C. Warburton and the Encyclopédie. Comparative Lit 7 1955.

—— Warburton and some aspects of the search for the primitive in eighteenth-century France. PQ 36 1957.

Steadman, J. M. Areopagitica and A critical and philosophical enquiry: a Milton-Warburton parallel. N & Q Oct 1959.

WILLIAM WHISTON

1667–1752

A new theory of the earth. 1696, Cambridge 1708, 1714, 1722, 1725, 1736 (with appendix), 1755; tr German, 1713.

A short view of the chronology of the Old Testament. Cambridge 1702.

An essay on the Revelation of St John. 1706.

The accomplishment of Scripture prophecies. Cambridge 1708, 1739. Boyle lectures.

Sermons and essays upon several subjects. 1709.

An essay upon the teaching of St Ignatius. 1710.

Primitive Christianity revived. 5 vols 1711–12.

Athanasius convicted of forgery. 1712.

Primitive infant baptism revived. 1712, 1712.

Reflexions on an anonymous pamphlet [A. Collins, Discourse of free-thinking]. 1712, 1713, 1713.

An address to the princes of Europe for the admission of the Christian religion to their dominions. 1716.

A letter to the Earl of Nottingham concerning the eternity of the Son of God. 1719, 1721 (6 edns).

The true origin of the Sabellian and Athanasian doctrines of the Trinity. 1720.

An essay towards restoring the true text of the Old Testament. 1722; A supplement, 1723.

The literal accomplishment of Scripture prophecies. 1724.

Of the thundering legion. 1725.

Historical memoirs of the life and writings of Sr Samuel Clarke. 1730, 1730, 1748.

A paraphrase on the Book of Job. 1732.

An account of the dæmoniacks. 1737.

The genuine works of Flavius Josephus, in English. 1737, 1806, 1812, 1815, 1825, 1840, 1841, 1846 etc.

The eternity of Hell torments considered. 1740.

The primitive New Testament in English. 1745.

Memoirs of the life and writings of Mr William Whiston, containing several of his friends also, and written by himself. 3 vols 1749–50, 2 vols 1753.

WILLIAM WOLLASTON

1660–1724

§ 1

The religion of nature delineated. 1722, 1724, 1725, 1726, 1731, 1738, 1750; tr French, 1726, 1756.

§ 2

Clarke, J. An examination of the notion of moral good and evil advanced in a late book entitled The religion of nature delineated. 1725.

Thompson, C. G. The ethics of Wollaston. 1922.

Stedman, R. E. The ethics of Wollaston. Nineteenth Century Aug 1935.

THOMAS WOOLSTON

1670–1733

§ 1

The old apology for the truth of the Christian religion revived. Cambridge 1705.

Dissertatio de Pontii ad Tiberium epistola. 1720; Epistola secunda, 1720.

A letter upon this question: whether Quakers do not the nearest resemble the primitive Christians. 1720; A second letter, 1721.

A free-gift to the clergy. 1722.

The exact fitness of the time in which Christ was manifested. 1722; A second free-gift to the clergy, 1723; A third free-gift, 1724; A fourth free-gift, 1724.

The ministry of the letter vindicated. 1724.

The moderator between an infidel and an apostate. 1725, 1729, 1732.

A defence of the miracle of the thundering legion. 1726.

A discourse on the miracles of our Saviour. 1727; Second discourse, 1727; Third discourse, 1728; Fourth discourse, 1728; Fifth discourse, 1728; Sixth discourse, 1729; tr French, [1780].

§ 2

[Stackhouse, T.] The life of Mr Woolston, with an impartial account of his writings. 1733.

R. L. B.

C. HUME, ADAM SMITH, BENTHAM AND THEIR CONTEMPORARIES

DAVID HUME
1711–76

The principal collection of mss is in the Royal Society, Edinburgh; for details see E. C. Mossner, Life of Hume, Edinburgh 1954, 1972 (rev).

Bibliographies

Metz, R. Bibliographie der Hume-Literatur. Literarische Berichte aus dem Gebiete der Philosophie 15–16 1928.

Jessop, T. E. In his A bibliography of Hume and of Scottish philosophy from Hutcheson to Lord Balfour, 1938, 1972 (rev).

[Lameere, J.] Notes bibliographiques. Revue Internationale de Philosophie 6 1952. Lists writings on Hume since 1938.

Todd, W. B. A bibliography of Hume. 1972.

Collections

Vermischte Schriften. Tr H. A. Pistorius et al 4 vols Hamburg and Leipzig 1754–6.

Oeuvres philosophiques. Tr J.-B. Mérian and B.-B.-R. Robinet 5 vols Amsterdam 1758–60, 2 vols Amsterdam 1759, 5 vols Amsterdam 1759–64, 6 vols 1764, 7 vols 'London' [Paris ?] 1788. Vol 7, adding 7 Political discourses, tr Mlle de la Cuaux.

Pensées de Hume. 'London' (Paris ?) 1767.

Le temple du bonheur. Tr J.-B. Mérian, Bouillon 1769. Contains 4 essays.

Recueil philosophique. 1770. Contains 2 essays.

Le génie de Hume. 'London' (Paris ?) 1770; tr German, 1774.

The philosophical works, including all the Essays. 4 vols 1825, 1836, Boston 1854.

Philosophical works. Ed T. H. Green and T. H. Grose 4 vols 1874–5.

The philosophy of Hume, selected. Ed H. A. Aikins 1893.

Oeuvres philosophiques choisies. Tr M. David 2 vols Paris 1912.

Selections. Ed C. W. Hendel 1927.

Theory of knowledge: containing the Enquiry concerning human understanding, the Abstract and selected passages from Book 1 of A treatise of human nature. Ed D. C. Yalden-Thomson 1951.

Theory of politics: containing A treatise of human nature, book III parts i and ii, and thirteen of the Essays. Ed F. Watkins 1951.

A treatise of human nature, book 1 [abridged], with extracts from An enquiry concerning human understanding. Ed A. J. Ayer and R. Winch. In their British empirical philosophers, 1952.

Political essays. Ed C. W. Hendel, New York [1953].

Writings on economics. Ed E. Rotwein 1955.

An inquiry concerning the principles of morals, with A dialogue. Ed C. W. Hendel, New York 1955.

Essential works. Ed R. Cohen, New York 1965.

Hume: philosophical historian. Ed D. F. Norton and R. H. Popkin, Indianapolis 1965.

Hume's ethical writings. Ed A. MacIntyre, New York 1965.

§1

A treatise of human nature: book 1, Of the understanding; book II, Of the passions. 2 vols 1739; Book III, Of morals, with an appendix, 1740; [bks 1–3] 2 vols 1817; ed L. A. Selby-Bigge 1888; tr German, 1790–2.

An abstract of a Treatise of human nature 1740. Ed J. M. Keynes and P. Sraffa, Cambridge 1938; tr French, G. Beaulavon, Revue d e Métaphysique 46 1939.

Essays moral and political. Edinburgh 1741, 1742; vol II, Edinburgh 1742; 1743 (both vols), 1748 (with Three essays, below, thereafter in Essays and treatises, below); tr French, 1764; Italian, 1764.

Essays moral and political; Of the original contract. Ed E. Barker in his Social contract, Oxford [1946] (WC).

A letter from a gentleman to his friend containing some observations on religion and morality. Edinburgh 1745 (anon). Unique copy in Nat Lib of Scotland ed E. C. Mossner and J. V. Price, Edinburgh 1967.

Three essays moral and political, never before published. 1748.

Philosophical essays concerning human understanding. 1748, 1750, 1751; rptd in Essays and treatises, below; tr French, 1758, 1761; German, 1755, 1793.

A true account of the behaviour and conduct of Archibald Stewart. 1748 (anon); rptd in J. V. Price, The ironic Hume, Austin 1965.

An enquiry concerning the principles of morals. 1751; rptd in Essays and treatises, below.

The petition of the Bellmen. [1751] (anon); rptd in A Scotch haggis, Edinburgh 1822. Copy of 1751 in Bodley.

Political discourses. Edinburgh 1752, 1752, 1754; rptd in Essays and treatises, below; tr French, 1754, 1755, 1767; German, 1754; Italian, 1767, 1774.

Scotticisms. [1752]. Anon. Often included in edns of the Essays, below.

Essays and treatises on several subjects. 4 vols 1753–6. Vol 1, Essays moral and political, 1753 (4th edn); vol 2, Philosophical essays, 1756 (3rd edn); vol 3, Enquiry concerning morals, 1753 (2nd edn); vol 4, Political discourses, 1754 (3rd edn), 1758 (order changed, and Philosophical essays concerning human understanding now called Enquiry concerning human understanding), 4 vols 1760 (with material from Four dissertations), 2 vols 1764, 1767, 1768, 4 vols 1770, 2 vols 1772, 1777 (with author's last corrections); ed L. A. Selby-Bigge 1894, 1902 (with Comparative table for treatise and enquiries).

An inquiry concerning human understanding. Ed C. W. Hendel, New York 1955; ed R. Kirk, Chicago 1956; ed E. C. Mossner, New York 1963 (with other essays).

History of Great Britain. Vol 1 ('containing the Reigns of James I and Charles I'), Edinburgh 1754; tr French, 1760.

Vol II ('containing the Commonwealth, and the Reigns of Charles II and James II'), 1757 (for 1756); tr French, 1760.

History of England under the house of Tudor. 2 vols 1759; tr French, 1763.

History of England from the invasion of Julius Caesar to the accession of Henry VII. 2 vols 1762; tr French, 1765.

History of England. Vols 5–6, 1762. A new edn of the Stuarts, with title-pages altered to bring them into line with other vols.

History of England from the invasion of Julius Caesar to the Revolution in 1688. 8 vols 1763, 1767, 1770, 1773, 1778 (with author's last corrections, My own life and Adam Smith's letter to Strahan); tr French, 1763 (in part), 1769; German, 1762–3 (the Stuarts). Later edns occasionally supplied with continuation by T. Smollett or others.

Four dissertations. 1757; rptd in Essays and treatises, 1760 etc; tr German, 1759. The natural history of religion, Of the passions, Of tragedy, Of the standard of taste.

The natural history of religion. Ed H. E. Root 1956.

Exposé succinct de la contestation entre Hume et Rousseau. Tr and ed J.-B. A. Suard 1766 (3 edns); tr 1766; Italian, 1767.

Two essays [Of suicide, Of the immortality of the soul]. 1777 (anon), 1783. These essays, at first intended for Four dissertations, were withdrawn in proof.

Dialogues concerning natural religion. 1779, 1779; ed N. K. Smith, Oxford 1935; tr French, 1779; German, 1781. Also rptd in many edns of Essays and treatises.

Hume as literary patron: a suppressed review of Robert Henry's History of Great Britain 1773. Ed E. C. Mossner, MP 39 1942.

An historical essay on chivalry and modern honour. Ed E. C. Mossner, MP 45 1947. First complete text of Hume's earliest extant essay.

Early memoranda 1729-40: the complete text. Ed E. C. Mossner, JHI 9 1948.

Letters

Letters. Ed J. Y. T. Greig 2 vols Oxford 1932.

New letters. Ed R. Klibansky and E. C. Mossner, Oxford 1954.

Hume at La Flèche 1735: an unpublished letter. Ed E. C. Mossner, SE 37 1958.

A fragment of a new letter by Hume in defense of his History of England. Ed J. C. Weston, N & Q Nov 1958.

Hume: some unpublished letters. Ed G. Hunter, Texas Stud in Lit & Lang 2 1960.

New Hume letters to Lord Elibank 1748-76. Ed E. C. Mossner, Texas Stud in Lit & Lang 4 1962.

Lettres inédites de Diderot et de Hume écrites de 1755 à 1763 au président de Brosses. Ed H. David, Revue Philosophique 156 1966.

§ 2

[Home, H. (Lord Kames)]. Principles of morality and natural religion. Edinburgh 1751. An attempt to refute Hume's theory of causation.

[— and H. Blair]. Observations upon a pamphlet entitled An analysis. Edinburgh 1755.

[Warburton, W. and R. Hurd]. Remarks on Hume's essay on the Natural history of religion. 1757.

Tytler, W. An historical and critical enquiry into the evidence against Mary, Queen of Scots, with an examination of Hume's History. Edinburgh 1759.

Hurd, R. Moral and political dialogues. 1759. Postscript criticizes Hume's treatment of the Tudor period.

Campbell, G. A dissertation on miracles. 1762.

Beattie, J. An essay on truth. 1770.

[Horne, G.] A letter to Adam Smith on the life, death and philosophy of his friend Hume, by one of the people called Christians. Oxford 1777.

Hume, D. The life, written by himself, and letter from Adam Smith to Wm Strahan. 1777, 1777; tr French, 1777, 1777. Included in most edns of the Essays and History after 1778.

[Pratt, S. J.] An apology for the life and writings of Hume, to which is added an address to one of the people called Christians. 1777; Supplement, 1777.

Priestley, J. Letters to a philosophical unbeliever. Bath 1787, Birmingham 1787.

Smellie, W. Literary and characteristical lives of Hume [et al]. Edinburgh 1800.

Ritchie, T. E. An account of the life and writings of Hume. 1807.

Burton, J. H. Life and correspondence of Hume. 2 vols 1846.

Knight, W. Hume. 1886.

Calderwood, H. Hume. 1898.

Orr, J. Hume and his influence on philosophy and theology. 1903.

Francken, C. J. W. Hume. Haarlem 1907.

Thomsen, A. Hume hans liv og hans filosofi. Copenhagen 1911; tr German, 1912.

Hendel, C. W. Studies in the philosophy of Hume. 1925, 1963 (rev).

Taylor, A. E. Hume and the miraculous. 1927.

Peoples, M. H. La querelle Rousseau-Hume. Annales de la Société Jean-Jacques Rousseau 1928. With bibliography.

Metz, R. Hume: Leben und Philosophie. Stuttgart 1929.

Leroy, A. La critique et la religion chez Hume. Paris 1930.

Greig, J. Y. T. Hume. 1931.

Kuypers, M. S. Studies in the eighteenth-century background of Hume's empiricism. Minneapolis 1930.

Laird, J. Hume's philosophy of human nature. 1933.

— Hume's account of sensitive belief. Mind 48 1939.

Laporte, J. Le scepticisme de Hume. Revue Philosophique 115 1933.

Church, R. W. Hume's theory of the understanding. 1935.

— Hume's theory of philosophical relations. Philosophical Rev 50 1941.

Doering, J. F. Hume and the theory of tragedy. PMLA 52 1937.

Ebert, H. Rousseau und Hume. Würzburg 1936.

Mossner, E. C. The enigma of Hume. Mind 45 1936.

— Was Hume a Tory historian? JHI 2 1941.

— An apology for Hume, historian. PMLA 56 1941.

— The forgotten Hume: le bon David. New York 1943.

— The continental reception of Hume's Treatise 1739-41. Mind 56 1947.

— Hume and the ancient-modern controversy 1725-52. SE 28 1949.

— A ms fragment of Hume's Treatise 1740. N & Q 26 Nov 1949.

— Hume's Four dissertations. MP 48 1950.

— Philosophy and biography: the case of Hume. Philosophical Rev 59 1950.

— and H. Ransom. Hume and the 'Conspiracy of the Booksellers': the publication and early fortunes of the History of England. SE 29 1950.

— The first answer to Hume's Treatise: an unnoticed item of 1740. JHI 12 1951.

— Hume and the French men of letters. Revue Internationale de Philosophie 6 1952.

— The life of Hume. Edinburgh 1954, 1972 (rev).

— Ferguson's dialogue on a Highland jaunt with Robert Adam, William Cleghorn, Hume and William Wilkie. In Restoration and eighteenth-century literature, ed C. Camden, Chicago 1963.

— The enlightenment of Hume. In Introduction to modernity, ed R. Mollenauer, Austin 1965.

— Hume's Of criticism. In Studies in criticism and aesthetics 1660-1800, ed H. P. Anderson and J. S. Shea, Minneapolis 1967.

Bayley, F. C. The causes and evidence of beliefs: an examination of Hume's procedure. Mt Hermon Mass 1936.

Maund, C. Hume's theory of knowledge. 1937.

— On the nature and significance of Hume's scepticism. Revue Internationale de Philosophie 6 1952.

Brown, S. G. Observations on Hume's theory of taste. E Studies 20 1938.

Roddier, H. La querelle Rousseau-Hume. Revue de Littérature Comparée 18 1938.

— A propos de la querelle Rousseau-Hume: précisions chronologiques. Revue d'Histoire Littéraire de la France 46 1939.

Hume and present-day problems. 1939 (Aristotelian Soc suppl vol 18).

Kruse, V. Hume's philosophy in his principal work A treatise of human nature and in his Essays. Tr P. T. Federspiel, Oxford 1939.

Maidment, H. J. In defence of Hume on miracles. Philosophy 14 1939.

Price, H. H. Hume's theory of the external world. Oxford 1940.

— The permanent significance of Hume's philosophy. Philosophy 15 1940.

Smith, N. K. The philosophy of Hume. 1941, 1960.

Guillemin, H. 'Cette affaire infernale': l'affaire Rousseau-Hume. Paris 1942.

Grene, M. Hume: sceptic and Tory? JHI 4 1943.

Clough, W. O. Reason and genius: an eighteenth-century dilemma. PQ 23 1944.

Kallich, M. The associationist criticism of Francis Hutcheson and Hume. SP 43 1946.

Kydd, R. M. Reason and conduct in Hume's Treatise. Oxford 1946.

dal Pra, M. D. Hume. Milan 1949.

— Hume's analysis of generality. Philosophical Rev 59 1950.

— Hume e Dewey. Revue Internationale de Philosophie 6 1952.

Elliott, R. C. Hume's Character of Sir Robert Walpole: some unnoticed additions. JEGP 48 1949.

Price, K. B. Does Hume's theory of knowledge determine his ethical theory? Jnl of Philosophy 47 1950.

Glathe, A. B. Hume's Theory of the passions and Of morals: a study of books II and III of the Treatise. Berkeley 1950.

Sternfield, R. The unity of Hume's Enquiry concerning human understanding. Rev of Metaphysics 3 1950.

Weinberg, J. The idea of causal efficacy. Jnl of Philosophy 47 1950.

Levett, M. J. The scepticism of Hume. Philosopher 3 1951.

MacNabb, D. G. C. Hume: his theory of knowledge and morality. 1951.

— Hume on induction. Revue Internationale de Philosophie 6 1952.

McRae, R. Hume as a political philosopher. JHI 12 1951

Meyer, P. J. Voltaire and Hume's Descent on the coast of Brittany. MLN 56 1951.

— The manuscript of Hume's account of his dispute with Rousseau. Comparative Lit 4 1952.

— Voltaire and Hume as historians. PMLA 73 1958.

Popkin, R. H. Hume and Kierkegaard. Rev of Religion 31 1951.

— Hume: his pyrrhonism and his critique of Pyrrhonism. Philosophical Quart 1 1951.

— Did Hume ever read Berkeley? Jnl of Philosophy 56 1959.

— So, Hume did read Berkeley. Jnl of Philosophy 61 1964.

Todd, W. B. The first printing of Hume's Life 1777. Library 5th ser 6 1951.

— Hume, Exposé succinct. Book Collector 7 1958.

Acton, H. B. Prejudice. Revue Internationale de Philosophie 6 1952.

Brunius, T. Hume on criticism. Stockholm [1952].

Cresson, A. and G. Deleuze. Hume: sa vie, son oeuvre, sa philosophie. Paris 1952.

Davie, G. E. Hume and the origins of the Common Sense School. Revue Internationale de Philosophie 6 1952.

Fen, S. Has James answered Hume? Jnl of Philosophy 49 1952.

Jessop, T. E. Some misunderstandings of Hume. Revue Internationale de Philosophie 6 1952.

— Reflexions sur la philosophie de Hume. Revue Philosophique 150 1960.

Lafleur, L. J. A footnote on Descartes and Hume. Jnl of Philosophy 49 1952.

McLendon, H. J. Has Russell answered Hume? Ibid.

Leroy, A.-L. Statut de l'objet extérieur dans la philosophie de Hume. Revue Internationale de Philosophie 6 1952.

— Hume. Paris 1953.

Oliver, W. D. A re-examination of the problem of induction. Jnl of Philosophy 49 1952.

Passmore, J. A. Hume's intentions. Cambridge 1952.

Shouse, J. B. Hume and William James: a comparison. JHI 13 1952.

Drever, J. A note on Hume's Pyrrhonism. Philosophical Quart 3 1953.

Marshall, G. Hume and political scepticism. Philosophical Quart 4 1954.

Wolin, S. S. Hume and Conservatism. Amer Political Science Rev 48 1954.

Mathur, G. B. Hume and Kant in their relation to the pragmatic movement. JHI 16 1955.

Penelhum, T. Hume on personal identity. Philosophical Rev 44 1955.

Vlachos, G. Essai sur la politique de Hume. Athens and Paris 1955.

Wand, B. A note on sympathy in Hume's moral theory. Philosophical Rev 44 1955.

— Hume's account of obligation. Philosophical Quart 6 1956.

Hipple, W. J. The logic of Hume's essay Of tragedy. Philosophical Quart 6 1956.

Hurlbutt, R. H. Hume and scientific theism. JHI 17 1956.

— Hume, Newton and the design argument. Lincoln 1965.

Johnstone, H. W. Hume's arguments concerning causal necessity. Philosophy & Phenomenological Research 16 1956.

Adair, D. That politics may be reduced to a science. HLQ 20 1957.

Hallie, P. P. Hume, Biran and the Méditatifs intérieurs. JHI 18 1957.

Sugg, R. S. Hume's search for the key with the leathern thong. Jnl of Aesthetics 16 1957.

von Leyden, W. Hume and imperfect identity. Philosophical Quart 7 1957.

Basson, A. H. Hume. 1958 (Pelican).

Bongie, L. L. Hume and the official censorship of the Ancien Régime. French Stud 12 1958.

— Hume: 'philosophe' and philosopher in eighteenth-century France. French Stud 15 1961.

— The eighteenth-century Marian controversy and an unpublished letter by Hume. Stud in Scottish Lit 1 1964.

— Hume: prophet of the counter-revolution. Oxford 1965.

Cohen, R. Hume's experimental method and the theory of taste. ELH 25 1958.

— The transformation of passion: a study of Hume's theories of tragedy. PQ 41 1962.

Lenz, J. W. Hume's defense of causal inference. JHI 19 1958.

Butcharov, P. The self and perceptions: a study in Humean philosophy. Philosophical Quart 9 1959.

Butts, R. E. Hume's scepticism. JHI 20 1959.

— Husserl's critique of Hume's notion of distinctions of reason. Philosophy & Phenomenological Research 20 1959.

Clive, G. Hume's Dialogues reconsidered. Jnl of Religion 39 1959.

Estall, H. M. Hume's 'ruling passion'. Queen's Quart 66 1959.

Flew, A. Hume's check. Philosophical Quart 9 1959. On Of miracles.

— Did Hume ever read Berkeley? Jnl of Philosophy 58 1961.

— Hume's philosophy of belief: a study of his first inquiry. 1961.

Jacobson, N. P. The uses of reason in religion: a note on Hume. Jnl of Religion 39 1959.

MacIntyre, A. C. Hume on is and ought. Philosophical Rev 68 1959.

Tranoy, R. E. Hume on morals, animals and men. Jnl of Philosophy 56 1959.

Davies, G. Hume's history of the reign of James I. Elizabethan & Jacobean Stud 21 1960.

Gossman, K. Berkeley, Hume and Maupertuis. French Stud 14 1960.

Noyes, C. E. Hume's 'Umbrage to the godly' in his History of England. Univ of Mississippi Stud in Eng 1 1960.

— Samuel Johnson: student of Hume. Univ of Mississippi Stud in Eng 3 1962.

Smith, J. W. Concerning Hume's intentions. Philosophical Rev 69 1960. On Hume's purpose in bk 1 of Treatise.

Wolff, R. P. Hume's theory of mental activity. Ibid.

Aschenbrenner, K. Psychologism in Hume. Philosophical Quart 11 1961.

Broad, C. D. Hume's doctrine of space. Proc Br Acad 47 1961.

Grimsley, R. D'Alembert et Hume. Revue de Littérature Comparée 35 1961.

— Concerning an unpublished note from Morellet to Hume. MLR 57 1962.

Hartshorne, C. Hume's metaphysics and its present-day influence. New Scholasticism 35 1961.

Noxon, J. Hume's opinion of critics. Jnl of Aesthetics 20 1961.

Tsugawa, A. Hume and Lord Kames on personal identity. JHI 22 1961.

Zabeeh, F. Hume, precursor of modern empiricism. Amsterdam 1961.

Courtney, C. P. Hume et l'Abbé Raynal. Revue de Littérature Comparée 36 1962.

Dean, E. Hume on religious language. Jnl of Religion 42 1962.

MacDiarmid, H. The man of (almost) independent mind. Edinburgh 1962.

Winks, R. W. Hume and Gibbon: a view from a vantage. Dalhousie Rev 41 1962.

Forbes, D. Politics and history in Hume. Historical Jnl 6 1963.

Hume: a symposium by Stuart Hampshire and others. Ed D. F. Pears 1963.

Nethery, W. Hume's manuscript corrections in a copy of A treatise of human nature. PBSA 57 1963.

Schaefer, A. Hume: Philosophie und Politik. Meisenheim 1963.

Price, J. V. Empirical theists in Cicero and Hume. Texas Stud in Lit & Lang 5 1963.

— The ironic Hume. Austin 1965.

— Hume's concept of liberty and the History of England. Stud in Romanticism 5 1966.

Stewart, J. B. The moral and political philosophy of Hume. New York 1963.

Broiles, R. D. The moral philosophy of Hume. Hague 1964.

Gaskin, J. C. A. Hume and the eighteenth-century interest in miracles. Hermathena 109 1964.

Williams, R. Hume: reasoning and experience. In The English mind: studies in the English moralists presented to Basil Willey, Cambridge 1964.

Belgion, M. Hume. 1965 (Br Council pamphlet).

Cain, R. E. Hume and Adam Smith as sources of the concept of sympathy in Hazlitt. Papers in Eng Lang & Lit 1 1965.

Day, J. Hume on justice and allegiance. Philosophy 40 1965.

Human understanding: studies in the philosophy of Hume. Ed A. Sesonske and N. Fleming, Belmont Cal 1965.

Letwin, S. R. The pursuit of certainty: Hume, Bentham, Mill, Beatrice Webb. Cambridge 1965.

Poumier, H. Hume et le problème de la liberté. Etudes Philosophiques 20 1965.

Richards, T. J. Hume's two definitions of 'cause'. Philosophical Quart 15 1965.

Stove, D. Hume, probability and induction. Philosophical Rev 74 1965.

Benn, T. V. Les Political discourses de Hume et un conte de Diderot. French Lit 70 1966.

Engel, C.-E. 1766—un duel à la mort: Rousseau et Hume. Nouvelles Littéraires 4 Aug 1966.

Santucci, A. Hume e i 'philosophes'. Rivista di Filosofia 1966.

Beitzinger, A. J. Hume's aristocratic preference. Rev of Politics 28 1966.

Capaldi, N. Hume's rejection of 'ought' as a moral category. Jnl of Philosophy 63 1966.

— Some misconceptions about Hume's moral theory. Ethics 76 1966.

Capitan, W. H. Part x of Hume's Dialogues. Amer Philosophical Quart 3 1966.

Ducasse, D. J. Critique of Hume's conception of causality. Jnl of Philosophy 63 1966.

Jacobson, N. P. Gotama Buddha et Hume. Revue Philosophique 156 1966.

Jeffner, A. Butler and Hume on religion. Tr K. Bradfield, Acta Universitatis Upsaliensis 7 1966.

Des Jardins, G. Terms of De officiis in Hume and Kant. JHI 28 1967.

Mall, R. A. Hume's concept of man. New York 1967.

Cook, T. I. Reflections on the moral and political philosophy of Hume. Stud in Burke 9 1968.

ADAM SMITH
1723–90

Bibliographies etc

Bonar, J. A catalogue of the library of Smith. 1894, 1932. See C. Jones, Smith's library: some additions, Economic History 4 1940; H. Mizuta, Smith's library: a supplement to Bonar's catalogue, 1967.

Jessop, T. E. In his A bibliography of Hume and Scottish philosophy, 1938, 1972 (rev).

Bullock, C. J. The Vanderblue Memorial Collection of Smithiana and a catalogue of the collection. Boston 1939.

Franklin, B. and F. Cordasco. Smith: a bibliographical checklist of critical writings 1876–1950. New York 1950.

Collections

Works. 5 vols 1811–12.

Smith's moral and political philosophy. Ed H. W. Schneider, New York 1948. Abridged edn of Theory of moral sentiments, with selections from Wealth of nations and Lectures on justice.

Early writings. Ed J. R. Lindgren, New York 1967.

§1

The theory of moral sentiments. 1759, 1761, 1767 (adds a Dissertation on the origin of languages), 1774, 1781, 1790; tr French, 1774, [1798]; German, 1770, 1791–5.

An inquiry into the nature and causes of the wealth of nations. 2 vols 1776, 1778, 3 vols 1784, 1786, 1789, 1791; ed J. R. McCulloch 1828; ed J. E. T. Rogers 1869; ed J. S. Nicholson 1884; ed E. Cannan 1904, 1920; tr French, 1843; German, 1812; Spanish, 1794. Additions and corrections to the first and second editions. [1778?].

Essays on philosophical subjects; to which is prefixed an account of the life and writings of the author, by Dugald Stewart. 1795; tr French, [1797].

Lectures on justice, police, revenue and arms reported by a student in 1763. Ed E. Cannan, Oxford 1896.

Lectures on rhetoric and belles lettres reported by a student in 1762–3. Ed J. M. Lothian 1963.

§2

Stewart, D. Biographical memoir of Smith. Trans Royal Soc of Edinburgh 1793; rptd separately with memoirs by William Robertson and Thomas Reid, 1811, and in Stewart's Works vol 10, 1858.

Joersson, S. A. Smith and Thomas Paine. 1796.

Oncken, A. Smith in der Culturgeschichte. Vienna 1874.
—— Smith und Immanuel Kant. Leipzig 1877.
Leslie, T. E. C. In his Essays in political and moral philosophy, 1879.
Bagehot, W. In his Economic studies, 1880.
—— In his Biographical studies, 1881.
Farrer, J. A. Adam Smith. 1881.
Haldane, R. B. Life of Smith. 1887.
Hasbach, W. Die allgemeinen philosophischen Grundlagen der von Quesnay und Smith begründeten politischen Ökonomie. Leipzig 1890.
—— Untersuchungen über Smith. Leipzig 1891.
Schubert, J. Smiths Moralphilosophie. Leipzig 1891.
Feilbogen, S. Smith und Turgot. Vienna 1892.
Bonar, J. In his Philosophy and political economy, 1893.
—— The theory of moral sentiments. Jnl of Philosophical Stud 1 1926.
Rae, J. Life of Smith. 1895. See Guide to Rae's life, ed J. Viner, New York 1965.
Macpherson, H. C. Adam Smith. 1899.
Cunningham, W. Richard Cobden and Smith. 1904.
Hirst, F. W. Adam Smith. 1904 (EML).
Small, A. W. Smith and modern sociology. 1907.
Morrow, G. The ethical and economic theories of Smith. 1923.
—— The significance of the doctrine of sympathy in Smith. Philosophical Rev 32 1923.
Scott, W. R. Adam Smith. Proc Br Acad 10 1923.
—— Smith as student and professor; with unpublished documents. Glasgow 1937.
—— A manuscript criticism of the Wealth of nations in 1776 by Hugh Blair. Economic History 3 1938.
—— Studies relating to Smith during the last fifty years. Proc Br Acad 26 1940.
Hasek, C. W. The introduction of Smith's doctrines into Germany. 1925.
Laird, J. Social philosophy in Smith's Wealth of nations. Jnl of Philosophical Stud 2 1927.
Cooke, C. A. Smith and jurisprudence. Law Quart Rev 51 1935.
Ginzberg, E. The house of Smith. New York 1935.
Bladen, V. W. Smith on value. In Essays in political economy in honour of E. J. Urwick, Toronto 1938.
—— Some reflections on the classical literature of political economy. Studia Varia 17 1959.
Jones, R. F. A conjecture about Smith. Dalhousie Rev 18 1938.
Bittermann, H. J. Smith's empiricism and the law of nature. Jnl of Political Economy 48 1940.
La Nauze, J. A. A manuscript attributed to Smith. Economic Jnl 55 1945. Meditations on Seneca's Epistles.
Grampp, W. D. Smith and the economic man. Jnl of Political Economy 56 1948.
Bagolini, L. La simpatia nella morale e nel diritto: aspetti del pensiero di Smith. Bologna 1952.
Diamond, S. Bunker Hill, Tory propaganda and Smith. New England Quart 25 1952.
Forbes, D. Scientific Whiggism: Smith and John Millar. Cambridge Jnl Aug 1954.
Fay, C. R. Burke and Smith. Belfast 1956.
—— Smith and the Scotland of his day. Cambridge 1956.
Powers, R. H. Smith: practical realist. Southwestern Social Science Rev 37 1956.
Cropsey, J. Polity and economy: an interpretation of the principles of Smith. Hague 1957.
Koebner, R. Smith and the Industrial Revolution. Economic History Rev 2nd ser 11 1959.
Raphael, D. D. Sympathy and imagination. Listener 5 March 1959.
Singh, V. B. Smith's theory of economic development. Science & Soc 23 1959.
Prybyla, J. S. The world of the Wealth of nations. UTQ 30 1960.

Dankert, C. E. Smith: man of letters. Texas Stud in Lit & Lang 3 1961.
—— Smith and James Boswell. Queen's Quart 68 1961.
Erämetsä, E. 'Art' and 'industry' in Smith's The wealth of nations. Mercurialia (Helsinki) 1961.
—— Smith als Mittler englisch-deutscher Spracheinflüsse: the Wealth of nations. Helsinki 1961.
—— Smith als Mittler englisch-niederländischer Spracheinflüsse. Neuphilologische Mitteilungen 64 1963.
Coats, A. W. Smith: the modern re-appraisal. Nottingham Renaissance & Modern Stud 6 1962.
Currie, A. W. Literary views of Smith. N & Q July 1962.
Dankert, C. E. Two eighteenth-century celebrities. Dalhousie Rev 42 1962.
Giuliani, A. Le Lectures on rhetoric and belles lettres di Smith. Revista della Storia della Filosophie 17 1962.
Fulton, R. B. Smith speaks to our times: a study of his ethical ideas. Boston 1963.
Lundberg, I. C. Turgot's unknown translator: the Reflections and Smith. Hague 1964.
Bevilacqua, V. M. Smith's Lectures on rhetoric and belles lettres. Stud in Scottish Lit 3 1965.
—— Smith and some philosophical origins of eighteenth-century rhetorical literature. MLR 63 1968.
Cain, R. E. Hume and Smith as sources of the concept of sympathy in Hazlitt. Papers in Eng Lang & Lit 1 1965.
Lothian, J. M. Smith as a critic of Shakespeare. In Papers mainly Shakespearian, ed G. I. Duthie 1966.
Zall, P. M. Smith as literary critic? BNYPL April 1966.
Macfie, A. L. The individual in society: papers on Smith. 1967.

JEREMY BENTHAM
1748–1832

Bentham's mss, largely unpbd, are deposited in University College, London (catalogue by T. Whittaker, 1892) and in BM.

Bibliographies

Everett, C. W. In E. Halévy, The growth of philosophical radicalism, 1928.
Muirhead, A. A Bentham collection. Library 5th ser 1 1946.

Collections

Works. Ed J. Bowring 11 vols 1838–43. Vols 10–11 contain a life of Bentham and an index to his works.
Benthamiana: or select extracts from the works of Bentham. Ed J. H. Burton, Edinburgh 1843.
A fragment on government: an introduction to the principles of morals and legislation. Ed W. Harrison, Oxford 1948.
Economic writings: critical edition based on his printed works and unprinted manuscripts. Ed W. Stark 3 vols 1952–4.
Collected works. Ed J. H. Burns et al 1968–.

§1

A fragment on government: being an examination of what is delivered on the subject of government in William Blackstone's Commentaries, with a preface. 1776, 1822 (3rd edn); ed F. C. Montague 1891.
View of the Hard Labour Bill. 1778.
Defence of usury. 1787, 1790, 1816.
An introduction to the principles of morals and legislation. 1789, 1823, Oxford 1879.
The limits of jurisprudence defined: being part two of An introduction. Ed C. W. Everett, New York 1945.
The panopticon: or inspection house. 1791. Written 1787.
A protest against law taxes. 1795.
Poor laws and pauper management. In Arthur Young's Annals, Sept 1797 and later.
The panopticon versus New South Wales. 1802.

Traités de législation civile et pénale. Tr E. Dumont 3 vols 1802, 1820; tr 1864, 1876, ed C. K. Ogden 1931; tr German, 1830.

A plea for the constitution. 1803.

Scotch reform, with a summary view of a plan for a judicatory. 1808, 1811.

Théorie des peines et des récompenses. Tr E. Dumont 2 vols 1811, Paris 1818, 1825; part 2 tr 1825, part 1 1830. Written c. 1775.

A table of the springs of action, printed 1815. [Ed James Mill] 1817.

Chrestomathia. 1816.

Swear not at all. 1817. Written 1813.

Tactique des assemblées délibérantes et traité des sophismes politiques. Tr E. Dumont 1816.

Catechism of parliamentary reform. Pamphleteer Jan 1817. Written 1809.

Papers upon codification and public instruction. 1817. Written 1811–15.

Church of Englandism and its catechism examined. 1818.

Radical reform bill, with explanations. Pamphleteer Dec 1819.

Elements of the art of packing as applied to special juries. 1821. Written 1809.

Three tracts relating to Spanish and Portuguese affairs. 1821.

On the liberty of the press. 1821. Addressed to Spain.

The analysis of the influence of natural religion upon the temporal happiness of mankind, by Philip Beauchamp. [Ed G. Grote] 1822.

Traité des preuves judiciaire et de la codification. Tr E. Dumont 1823.

Traité des preuves judiciaires. Tr E. Dumont 1823; tr 1825.

De l'organisation judiciaire et de la codification. Tr E. Dumont 1823.

Not Paul but Jesus, by Gamaliel Smith. 1823.

Codification proposals. 1823.

Book of fallacies. [Ed P. Bingham] 1824; ed H. A. Larrabee, Baltimore 1952.

The rationale of evidence. [Ed J. S. Mill] 5 vols 1827.

Constitutional code for the use of all nations and all governments professing liberal opinions. Vol 1 (all pbd separately), 1830.

Official aptitude maximised—expense minimised. 1831. A collection of papers written in 1810 and after.

Deontology or science of morality. [Ed J. Bowring] 2 vols 1834.

§ 2

Mill, J. S. London & Westminster Rev Aug 1838; rptd in his Dissertations and discussions vol 1, 1859, and in Mill on Bentham and Coleridge, ed F. R. Leavis 1950.

Sidgwick, H. Fortnightly Rev May 1877; rptd in his Miscellaneous essays and addresses, 1904.

Kenny, C. W. Law Quart Rev 11 1895.

Halévy, E. In his La formation du radicalisme philosophique en Angleterre, 3 vols Paris 1901–4; tr 1928.

Nys, E. Etudes de droit international. 1901.

Atkinson, C. M. Bentham. 1905.

Dicey, A. V. In his Law and public opinion in England, 1905.

Pringle-Pattison, A. S. In his Philosophical Radicals and other essays, 1907.

Everett, C. W. The education of Bentham. New York 1931.

Ogden, C. K. Bentham's theory of fictions. 1932.

Holdsworth, W. Bentham's place in English legal history. California Law Rev 28 1940.

Palmer, P. A. Benthamism in England and America. Amer Political Science Rev 35 1941.

Stark, W. Bentham as an economist. Economic Jnl 51 1941, 56 1946.

Baumgardt, D. Bentham's 'censorial' method. JHI 6 1945.

—— Bentham and the ethics of today, with Bentham manuscripts hitherto unpublished. Princeton 1952.

Jones, W. T. In his Machiavelli to Bentham, vol 2 of Masters of political thought, ed E. M. Sait 1947.

Bentham and the law: a symposium. Ed G. W. Keeton and G. Schwartzenberger 1948.

Hall, E. W. The 'proof' of utility in Bentham and Mill. Ethics 60 1949.

Stone, J. In his Province and function of law, Sydney 1950.

Peardon, P. T. Bentham's ideal republic. Canadian Jnl of Economics 17 1951.

Letwin, S. R. Utilitarianism: a system of political tolerance. Cambridge Jnl March 1953.

—— Men and ideas: Bentham. Encounter April 1958.

—— The pursuit of certainty: Hume, Bentham, Mill, Beatrice Webb. Cambridge 1965.

Williamson, C. Bentham looks at America. Political Science Quart 70 1955.

Brockriede, W. E. Bentham's philosophy of rhetoric. Speech Monographs 23 1956.

Hart, H. L. A. Bentham. Proc Br Acad 48 1962.

Mack, M. P. Bentham: an odyssey of ideas. New York 1963.

Robson, J. M. John Stuart Mill and Bentham, with some observations on James Mill. Essays in Eng Lit from Renaissance to Victorian Age 20 1964.

Robbins, L. C. Bentham in the twentieth century. 1965.

Burns, J. H. Bentham and the French Revolution. Trans Royal Historical Soc 5th ser 16 1966.

Other Philosophical Writers 1750–1800

JAMES BEATTIE
1735–1803

See col 1784, above.

SIR WILLIAM BLACKSTONE
1723–80

See col 1911, below.

GEORGE CAMPBELL
1719–96

Bibliographies

Jessop, T. E. In his A bibliography of Hume and of Scottish philosophy, 1938, 1972 (rev).

§ 1

A dissertation on miracles. Edinburgh 1762, 1766, 1796; ed L. F. Bitzer, Carbondale 1963.

The philosophy of rhetoric. 2 vols 1776, Edinburgh 1808 (rev), 1816.

§ 2

Bevilacqua, V. M. Philosophical origins of Campbell's Philosophy of rhetoric. Speech Monographs 32 1965.

For Campbell's other works, see col 2062, below.

MICHEL GUILLAUME JEAN DE CRÈVECOEUR
1731–1813

§ 1

Letters from an American farmer. 1782, 1783, Philadelphia 1793; ed W. B. Black 1912, 1926 (EL); ed W. B. Blake, New York 1957; tr Dutch, 1784; French, 1784; German, 1784.

Crèvecoeur's eighteenth-century travels in Pennsylvania and New York. Tr and ed P. G. Adams, Lexington Kentucky 1961.

§2

Rice, H. C. Le cultivateur américain: étude sur l'oeuvre de Saint John de Crèvecoeur. Paris 1933.
Bewley, M. The cage and the prairie: two notes on symbolism. Hudson Rev 10 1957. On Crèvecoeur's Letters and J. F. Cooper, Natty Bumppo.
Crèvecoeur's Hartford diploma. Connecticut Historical Soc Bull 26 1961.
Plotkin, N. A. Crèvecoeur rediscovered: critic or panegyrist? French Historical Stud 3 1964.

ERASMUS DARWIN
1731–1802
See col 650, above.

JOHN DOUGLAS
1721–1807

Criterion of miracles. 1752.

ADAM FERGUSON
1723–1816

Bibliographies
Jessop, T. E. In his A bibliography of Hume and of Scottish philosophy, 1938, 1972 (rev).

§1

Of natural philosophy. [Edinburgh c. 1760].
Analysis of pneumatics and moral philosophy. Edinburgh 1766.
An essay on the history of civil society. Edinburgh 1767, 1768, 1769, 1773 (rev), 1782, 1793, 1814; ed D. Forbes, Edinburgh 1966.
The history of the progress and termination of the Roman Republic. 3 vols 1783.
Institutes of moral philosophy. Edinburgh 1769, 1773, 1785.
Remarks on a pamphlet by [Richard] Price. 1776.
Principles of moral and political science. 2 vols Edinburgh 1792.

§2

Huth, H. Soziale und individualistische Auffassung, vornehmlich bei Adam Smith und Ferguson. Leipzig 1907.
Lehmann, W. C. Ferguson and the beginnings of modern sociology. New York 1930.
Bresky, D. Schiller's debt to Montesquieu and Ferguson. Comparative Lit 13 1961.
Mossner, E. C. Ferguson's dialogue on a Highland jaunt with Robert Adam, William Cleghorn, David Hume and William Wilkie. In Restoration and eighteenth-century literature, ed C. Camden, Chicago 1963.
Kettler, D. The social and political thought of Ferguson. Columbus 1965.
— The political vision of Ferguson. Stud in Burke 8 1967.
Walker, I. C. Scottish verse in the Weekly Mag. Stud in Scottish Lit 5 1967.

ROBERT HALL
1764–1831

Collections
Works. Ed O. Gregory 6 vols 1832–8.

§1

Christianity consistent with the love of freedom. 1791.
Apology for the freedom of the press; with remarks on Horsley's sermon 30 Jan 1793. 1793.
Modern infidelity considered in respect to its influence on society. 1800.

JAMES HARRIS
1709–80

§1

Hermes: or a philosophical inquiry concerning universal grammar. 1751, 1765, 1771, 1794; tr French, [1796].
Philosophical arrangements. 1775.
Philological inquiries in three parts. 2 vols 1780–1, 1802; tr French, 1789.

§2

Szarota, E. M. Harris: die Bedeutung seiner Three treatises. Wissenschaftliche Zeitschrift der Ernst Moritz Arndt-Universität Greifswald 7 1963.
Marsh, R. Four dialectical theories of poetry: an aspect of English neoclassical criticism. Chicago 1965. On Shaftesbury, Akenside, David Hartley and Harris.

DAVID HARTLEY
1705–57

§1

Conjecturae quaedam de sensu motu et idearum generatione. 1746; tr R. E. A. Palmer, Los Angeles 1959.
Observations on man, his frame, his duty and his expectations. 2 vols 1749, 1791 (with a sketch of the author's life, and notes and additions translated from the German of H. A. Pistorius), 3 vols 1801 (with addns by Joseph Priestley).

§2

Hartley's theory of the human mind, on the principle of the association of ideas; with essays by J. Priestley. 1775.
Bower, G. S. Hartley and James Mill. 1881.
Fairchild, H. N. Hartley, Pistorius and Coleridge. PMLA 57 1947.
Moore, N. Hartley. Hibbert Jnl 48 1949.
Haven, R. Coleridge, Hartley and the mystics. JHI 20 1959.
Marsh, R. The second part of Hartley's system. Ibid.
— Mechanism and prescription in Hartley's theory of poetry. Jnl of Aesthetics 17 1959.
— Four dialectical theories of poetry: an aspect of English neoclassical criticism. Chicago 1965. On Shaftesbury, Akenside, Hartley and James Harris.
Deen, L. W. Coleridge and the sources of pantisocracy: Godwin, the Bible and Hartley. Boston Univ Stud in Eng 5 1960.

SAMUEL HORSLEY
1733–1806

Tracts in controversy with Priestley. 1789.
Sermon before the House of Lords. 1793.
Sermons. [Ed H. Horsley] 2 vols Dundee 1810.
Speeches in Parliament. Dundee 1813.
Charges. Dundee 1813.

HENRY HOME, LORD KAMES
1696–1782
Bibliographies
Jessop, T. E. In his A bibliography of Hume and of Scottish philosophy, 1938, 1972 (rev).

§ 1
Essays on the principles of morality and natural religion. Edinburgh 1751, London 1758, 1779; tr German, 1768, 1772.
Objections against the Essays on morality and natural religion examined. Edinburgh 1756.
Introduction to the art of thinking. Edinburgh 1761, 1764, 1775.
Elements of criticism. 3 vols Edinburgh 1762, 1763 (enlarged), 2 vols Edinburgh 1769, 1785 (rev and enlarged), 1788, 1796 etc; tr German, 3 vols 1763–6.
Sketches of the history of man. 2 vols Edinburgh 1774.

§ 2
Tytler, A. F. Memoirs of the life and writings of Home. 2 vols Edinburgh 1807.
McKenzie, G. Kames and the mechanist tradition. California Univ Pbns in Eng 14 1943.
Randall, H. W. The critical theory of Kames. Northampton Mass 1944.
Bundy, M. W. Kames and the maggots in amber. JEGP 45 1946.
Shaw, L. R. Home: precursor of Herder. Germanic Rev 35 1960.
Tsugawa, A. Hume and Kames on personal identity. JHI 22 1961.
Bevilacqua, V. M. Kames's theory of rhetoric. Speech Monographs 30 1963.
Horn, A. Kames and the anthropological approach to criticism. PQ 44 1965.
Ross, I. Scots law and Scots criticism: the case of Lord Kames. PQ 45 1965.
— Quaffing the mixture of wormwood and aloes: a consideration of Kames's Historical law-traits. Texas Stud in Lit & Lang 8 1967.
Unpublished letters of Thomas Reid to Lord Kames 1762–82. Ed I. Ross, Texas Stud in Lit & Lang 7 1965.
McGuinness, A. E. Lord Kames on the Ossian poems. Texas Stud in Lit & Lang 10 1968.

JAMES BURNETT, LORD MONBODDO
1714–99
Bibliographies
Jessop, T. E. In his A bibliography of Hume and of Scottish philosophy, 1938, 1972 (rev).

§ 1
Of the origin and progress of language. 6 vols Edinburgh 1773–92.
Antient metaphysics: or the science of universals. 6 vols Edinburgh 1779–99.

§ 2
Knight, W. Lord Monboddo and some of his contemporaries. 1900.
Lovejoy, A. O. Monboddo and Rousseau. MP 30 1933; rptd in his Essays in the history of ideas, Baltimore 1948.
Sherwin, O. A man with a tail: Monboddo. Jnl History of Medicine 13 1958.

JAMES OSWALD
1715–69
An appeal to common sense in behalf of religion. Edinburgh 1766.

THOMAS PAINE
1737–1809
Bibliographies
Gimbel, R. Paine: a bibliographical check list of Common sense, with an account of its publication. New Haven 1956.

Collections
Works. 1792.
Political works. 2 vols 1817.
Writings. Ed M. D. Conway 4 vols New York 1894–6.
Paine's political writings during the American and French Revolutions. Ed H. B. Bonner 1909.
Selections from the works. Ed A. W. Peach, New York 1928.
Representative selections. Ed H. H. Clark, New York [1945].
Complete writings. Ed P. S. Foner 2 vols New York 1945.

§ 1
Common sense. 1776 (5 edns), 1791, Philadelphia 1791, London 1792; tr French, 1791, 1793.
Letter addressed to the Abbé Raynal on the affairs of North America. 1782, Boston 1782, London 1795; tr French, 1783, 1783.
Rights of man: being an answer to Burke's attack on the French Revolution. 2 pts 1791–2 (at least 9 edns); ed H. B. Bonner 1907; ed G. J. Holyoake 1915 (EL); tr French, 1791–2; German, 1793.
The age of reason: being an investigation of true and fabulous theology. 2 pts Paris 1794–London 1795 etc; ed M. D. Conway, New York 1896; ed J. M. Robertson 1905; tr French, 1794 (pt 1 only); pt 3, New York 1807, 1811.
Dissertation on the first-principles of government. 1795 (4 edns); tr French, [1795]; Spanish, 1819.

Letters
Miscellaneous letters and essays. 1819.
Six new letters of Paine. Ed H. H. Clark, Madison 1939. From Providence Gazette 1782–3.
Wecter, D. Paine and the Franklins. Amer Lit 12 1940. With 2 unpbd letters by Paine.
Landlin, H. W. Some letters of Paine and William Short on the Nootka Sound crisis. Jnl of Modern History 13 1941.
Aldridge, A. O. Some writings of Paine in Pennsylvania newspapers. Amer Historical Rev 56 1951.
Boulton, J. T. An unpublished letter from Paine to Burke. Durham Univ Jnl 43 1951.

§ 2
Conway, M. D. The life of Paine. 2 vols New York 1892.
Blunck, R. Paine: ein Leben für Amerika. Berlin 1936.
Nicolson, M. H. Paine, Edward Nares and Mrs Piozzi's Marginalia. Huntington Lib Bull 10 1936.
Pearson, H. Paine. New York 1936.
Berthold, S. M. Paine: America's first liberal. Boston 1938.
Dorfman, J. The economic philosophy of Paine. Political Science Quart 53 1938.
Smith, F. Paine, liberator. New York 1938.
McConnell, F. J. Evangelicals, revolutionists and idealists. Nashville 1942.
Penniman, H. Paine: democrat. Amer Political Science Rev 37 1943.

Smith, T. V. Paine: voice of democratic revolution. In The philosophy of American democracy, ed C. M. Perry, Chicago 1943.

Woodward, W. E. Paine: America's godfather. New York 1945.

Meng, J. J. The constitutional theories of Paine. Rev of Politics 8 1946.

Copeland, T. W. Burke, Paine and Jefferson. In his Our eminent friend Edmund Burke, New Haven 1949.

Kenyon, C. Where Paine went wrong. Amer Political Science Rev 45 1951.

Adams, T. R. The authorship and printing of Plain truth by Candidus. PBSA 49 1955. An answer to Common sense.

Aldridge, A. O. The poetry of Paine. Pennsylvania Mag of History & Biography 79 1955.

—— La signification historique, diplomatique et littéraire de la Lettre adressée à l'Abbé Raynal de Paine. Etudes Anglaises 8 1955.

—— Paine's Plan for a descent on England. William & Mary Quart 14 1957.

—— Condorcet et Paine: leurs rapports intellectuels. Revue de Littérature Comparée 32 1958.

—— Man of reason: the life of Paine. Philadelphia 1959.

—— The influence of Paine in the United States, England, France, Germany and South America. Comparative Lit 2 1960.

—— Paine and Comus. Proc Massachussetts Historical Soc 85 1961.

—— The Rights of man de Paine, symbole de siècle des lumières et leur influence en France. In Utopie et institutions au xviiie siècle: le pragmatisme des lumières, ed P. Francastel, Paris 1963.

Gabrieli, V. Paine fra l'America e l'Europa. Studi Americani 1 1955.

Meserole, H. T. W. T. Sherwin: a little-known Paine biographer. PBSA 49 1955.

Gimbel, R. New political writings by Paine. Yale Univ Lib Gazette 30 1956.

—— The first appearance of Paine's The age of reason. Yale Univ Lib Gazette 31 1956.

—— The resurgence of Paine. Proc Amer Antiquarian Soc 69 1959.

—— Paine fights for freedom in three worlds: the new, the old, the next. Proc Amer Antiquarian Soc 70 1961.

—— Paine an Albany mason. Amer N & Q 3 1964. See C. F. Gosnell, below.

Brown, T. M. Greenough, Paine, Emerson and the organic aesthetic. Jnl of Aesthetics 14 1956.

Downs, R. B. In his Books that changed the world, Chicago 1956.

Gallagher, B. G. Paine in Great American liberals. Boston 1956.

Rea, R. R. William Henry Graves: gentleman scholar [1833–1931]. Alabama Historical Quart 17 1956. On earliest exponent of the claims of Paine to the authorship of Junius letters.

Sizer, T. Paine's portrait. Yale Univ Lib Gazette 30 1956.

Bressler, L. A. Peter Porcupine and the bones of Paine. Pennsylvania Mag of History & Biography 82 1958.

The death of Paine. Ed D. Connolly, Records Amer Catholic History Soc of Philadelphia 69 1958.

Arnold, H. Die Aufnahme von Paines Schriften in Deutschland. PMLA 74 1959.

Halliday, E. M. The ghost of Paine. New Republic 15 June 1959.

Boulton, J. T. Paine and the vulgar style. EC 12 1962.

Hodgart, M. J. C. Politics and prose style in the late eighteenth century: the radicals. BNYPL Sept 1962; rev in The English mind: studies on the English novelists presented to Basil Willey, Cambridge 1964.

Kistler, M. O. German-American liberalism and Paine. Amer Quart 14 1962.

Lasser, M. K. Paine and Robert Treat Paine: a case of mistaken identity. Jnl of Rutgers Univ Lib 25 1962.

The Burke-Paine controversy: texts and criticism. Ed R. B. Browne, New York 1963.

Fennessy, R. R. Burke, Paine and the rights of man: a difference of political opinion. Hague 1963.

Gosnell, C. F. Paine an Albany mason? Amer N & Q 2 1963.

Thompson, I. M. The religious beliefs of Paine. New York 1965.

WILLIAM PALEY
1743–1805
Collections

Works. 7 vols 1825.

§ 1

The principles of moral and political philosophy. 1785; ed R. Whateley 1859; ed A. Bain nd (Moral philosophy only).

Horae Paulinae: or the truth of the scripture history of St Paul evinced. 1790.

A view of the evidences of Christianity. 1794.

Natural theology: or evidences of the existence and attributes of the Deity collected from the appearances of nature. 1802; ed Lord Brougham and C. Bell 1836.

§ 2

Wainwright, L. A vindication of Paley's theory of morals etc. 1830.

Gundry, D. W. The Paleyan argument from design. Church Quart Rev 151 1951.

RICHARD PRICE
1723–91

§ 1

A review of the principal questions and difficulties in morals. 1758, 1769, 1787; ed D. D. Raphael, Oxford 1948.

Observations on reversionary payments. 1771, 1783 (4th edn).

An appeal to the public on the subject of the national debt. 1772.

Observations on the nature of civil liberty, the principles of government and the justice and policy of the war with America. 1776; Additional observations, 1777.

The general introduction and supplement to the two tracts on civil liberty. 1778.

A free discussion of the doctrines of materialism and philosophical necessity. 1778–80.

An essay on the population of England. 1780.

A discourse on the love of our country. 1789.

§ 2

Lincoln, A. In his Some political and social ideas of English dissent 1763–1800, Cambridge 1938.

Barnes, W. H. F. Price: a neglected eighteenth-century moralist. Philosophy 17 1942.

Lough, J. Condorcet et Price. Revue de Littérature Comparée 24 1950.

Cone, C. B. Torchbearer of freedom: the influence of Price on eighteenth-century thought. Lexington Kentucky 1952.

JOSEPH PRIESTLEY
1733–1804
Bibliographies

Fulton, J. F. and C. H. Peters. Introduction to a bibliography of the educational and scientific works of Priestley. PBSA 30 1936.

Crook, R. E. A bibliography of Priestley 1733–1804. 1966.

Collections

Theological and miscellaneous works. Ed J. T. Rutt 25 vols 1817–32.

Selections. Ed I. U. Brown, University Park Pa 1962.

Writings on philosophy, science and politics. Ed J. A. Passmore, New York 1965.

§ 1

The history and present state of electricity. 1767.

An essay on the first principles of government. 1768, 1771.

A free address to protestant dissenters as such. 1769.

Institutes of natural and revealed theology. 3 vols 1772–4.

Experiments and observations on different kinds of air. 6 vols 1774–86.

An examination of Reid's Inquiry, Beattie's Essay and Oswald's Appeal to common sense. 1774.

Hartley's Theory of the human mind on the principle of the association of ideas. 1775.

Disquisitions relating to matter and spirit. 1777, 1782.

A course of lectures on oratory and criticism 1777; ed V. M. Bevilacqua and K. Murphy, Carbondale 1965.

The doctrine of philosophical necessity illustrated. 1777.

A free discussion on the doctrines of materialism etc. 1778.

Observations on the importance of the American Revolution. 1784.

§ 2

Holt, A. Life of Priestley. Oxford 1931.

Lincoln, A. In his Some political and social ideas of English dissent 1763–1800, Cambridge 1938.

Riese, T. Priestley und das 18 Jahrhundert. E Studien 74 1940.

Hartog, P. J. The newer views of Priestley and Lavoisier. Annals of Science 5 1941.

Bronk, D. W. Priestley and the early history of the American Philosophical Society. Proc Amer Philosophical Soc 86 1942.

Park, M. C. Priestley and the problem of pantisocracy. Philadelphia 1947.

Conklin, E. G. Priestley and the American Philosophical Society: his experiments on spontaneous generation. Proc Amer Philosophical Soc 94 1950.

Gillam, J. G. The crucible: the story of Priestley. 1954.

McKie, D. An unpublished letter from Priestley to John Parker. Archives Internationale d'Histoire des Sciences 9 1956.

Brown, I. T. The religion of Priestley. Pennsylvania History 24 1957.

Guerlac, H. Priestley's first papers on gases and their reception in France. Jnl History of Medicine 12 1957.

Schofield, R. E. The scientific background of Priestley. Annals of Science 13 1957.

Toulmin, S. E. Crucial experiments: Priestley and Lavoisier. JHI 18 1957.

Chaloner, W. H. Priestley, John Wilkinson and the French Revolution. Trans Royal Historical Soc 5th ser 8 1958.

Piper, H. The pantheistic sources of Coleridge's early poetry. JHI 20 1959.

Robbins, C. Honest heretic: Priestley in America 1794–1804. Proc Amer Philosophical Soc 106 1962.

Gibbs, F. W. Priestley: adventures in science and champion of truth. 1965.

Parish, C. In his History of the Birmingham library, 1966.

Gibbs, F. W. Priestley: revolutions of the eighteenth century. Garden City NY 1967.

Priestley's likeness. Hibbert Jnl 65 1967. On portraits by J. Millar and J. Opie.

THOMAS REID
1710–96

Bibliographies

Jessop, T. E. In his A bibliography of Hume and of Scottish philosophy, 1938, 1972 (rev).

Collections

Works. Ed G. N. Wright 2 vols 1843.

Works. Ed W. Hamilton 2 vols Edinburgh 1846, 1852, 1854, 1858, 1863 (with addns).

§ 1

An essay on quantity. Philosophical Trans of Royal Soc 1748.

An inquiry into the human mind on the principles of common sense. Edinburgh 1763, 1765, 1785; tr French 1768.

A brief account of Aristotle's logic. In Lord Kames, Sketches of the history of man vol 2, 1774.

Essays on the intellectual powers of man. Edinburgh 1785; ed A. D. Woozley 1941 (abridged); ed A. J. Ayer and R. Winch in British empirical philosophers, 1952 (excerpts).

Essays on the active powers of man. Edinburgh 1785.

Philosophical orations delivered at graduation ceremonies in King's College, Aberdeen 1753, 1756, 1759, 1762. Ed W. R. Humphries, Aberdeen 1937.

Unpublished letters of Reid to Lord Kames 1762–82. Ed I. Ross, Texas Stud in Lit & Lang 7 1965.

§ 2

Priestley, Joseph. An examination of Reid's Inquiry into the human mind, Beattie's Essay on truth and Oswald's Appeal to common sense. 1774.

Stewart, Dugald. Biographical memoirs of Adam Smith, William Robertson and Reid. Edinburgh 1811; rptd in his Works vol 10, 1858, and in Reid's Works, ed W. Hamilton vol 1, 1846.

Pringle-Pattison, A. S. In his Scottish philosophy, 1885.

Fraser, A. C. Thomas Reid. 1898.

Robins, E. P., J. Seth and J. C. Gregory. Philosophical Rev 7 1898, 30 1921.

Faurot, J. H. The development of Reid's theory of knowledge. UTQ 21 1952.

Winch, P. G. The notion of 'suggestion' in Reid's theory of perception. Philosophical Quart 3 1953.

Chastaign, M. Reid, la philosophie du sens commun et le problème de la connaissance d'autrui. Revue Philosophique 144 1954.

Caldwell, R. L. Another look at Reid. JHI 23 1962.

SIR JAMES STEUART
1712–80

§ 1

An inquiry into the principles of political economy: being an essay on the science of domestic policy in free nations. 2 vols 1767.

§ 2

Hasbach, W. In his Untersuchungen über Adam Smith, Leipzig 1891.

Grossman, H. The evolutionist revolt against classical economics: Steuart, Richard Jones, Marx. Jnl of Political Economy 51 1943.

Stettner, W. F. Steuart on the public debt. Quart Jnl of Economics 59 1945.

DUGALD STEWART
1753–1828

Bibliographies
Jessop, T. E. In his A bibliography of Hume and of Scottish philosophy, 1938, 1972 (rev).

Collections
Works. 7 vols Cambridge 1829.
Collected works. Ed W. Hamilton 11 vols Edinburgh 1854–8.

§ 1
Elements of the philosophy of the human mind. 3 vols 1792–1827, 1842.
Outlines of moral philosophy. Edinburgh 1793 etc.
Philosophical essays. Edinburgh 1810.
Biographical memoirs of Adam Smith, of W. Robertson and of T. Reid. Edinburgh 1811; rptd in his Works vol 10, 1858 and in Reid's Works vol 1, ed W. Hamilton 1846. Collected with notes from separate edns of 1794, 1801, 1802.
Some account of a boy born blind. Edinburgh [1815].
A general view of the progress of metaphysical, ethical and political philosophy. In Encyclopaedia britannica supplementary dissertation, 2 pts 1816–21.
The philosophy of the active and moral powers. Edinburgh 1828.

§ 2
Hipple, W. J. The aesthetics of Stewart: culmination of a tradition. Jnl of Aesthetics 14 1955.

JOHN HORNE TOOKE
1736–1812
Ἔπεα πτερόεντα: or the diversions of Purley. 2 vols 1786–1805; ed R. Taylor 2 vols 1829.
Review of the constitution. 1791.
Proceedings on trial of Tooke for high treason. 2 vols 1795.
See C. Laird, Diversions of the Diversions of Purley in the New World, Rendezvous 1 1966.

JOSEPH TOWNSEND
1739–1816
A dissertation on the poor laws. 1785.
Observations on various plans for the relief of the poor. 1788.
Journey through Spain. 1791, 1814 (3rd edn).

ABRAHAM TUCKER
1705–74
§ 1
Free will, free knowledge and fate: a fragment. 1763.
The light of nature pursued. 7 vols 1768–78. Vols 5–7 pbd posthumously by his daughter.

§ 2
Hazlitt, W. Preface to an abridgment of Tucker's work. In his Works, ed A. R. Waller and A. Glover vol 4, 1902.
Harris, W. G. Teleology in the philosophy of Joseph Butler and Tucker. Philadelphia 1941.
Carré, M. H. Tucker and the joint stock universe. Cambridge Jnl Aug 1951.

RICHARD WATSON
1737–1816
Apology for Christianity, in a series of letters to E. Gibbon. 1776.
Apology for the Bible, in answer to Thomas Paine. 1796.
Address to the people of Great Britain. 1798.
Miscellaneous tracts. 3 vols 1815.

ARTHUR YOUNG
1741–1820
§ 1
On the war in North America. 1758.
Reflections on the present state of affairs at home and abroad. 1759.
A farmer's letters to the people of England. 2 vols 1768.
A six weeks' tour through the southern counties of England and Wales. 1768, 1769 (enlarged), 1772.
A six months' tour through the north of England. 4 vols 1771.
The farmer's tour through the east of England. 4 vols 1770–1.
A course of experimental agriculture. 1770.
The farmer's calendar. 1771.
Political arithmetic. 1774.
Tour in Ireland. 2 vols 1780.
Travels during the years 1787, 1788, 1789, and 1790 undertaken with a view of ascertaining the cultivation, wealth, resources and national prosperity of the Kingdom of France. 2 vols Bury St Edmunds 1792–4; ed M. Betham-Edwards 1889 (3rd edn); ed C. Maxwell, Cambridge 1929; tr French, 1793–4.
The example of France a warning to England. 1793 etc.
Autobiography. Ed M. Betham-Edwards 1898.

§ 2
Haslam, C. S. The biography of Young until 1787. Rugby 1930.
Defries, A. Sheep and turnips: the life and times of Young. 1938.
Gazley, J. G. Young and the society of arts. Jnl of Economic History 1 1941.
— Young, agriculturalist and traveller 1741–1820: some bibliographical sources. Bull John Rylands Lib 37 1955.
Some manuscripts concerning Young. Bull John Rylands Lib 35 1953.

W. B. T.

D. ECONOMIC THEORY

Bibliographies
McCulloch, J. R. The literature of political economy. 1845, 1938.
Wagner, H. R. Irish economics 1700–83: a bibliography with notes. 1907 (priv ptd), 1969.
Scott, W. R. Scottish economic literature to 1800. Glasgow and Edinburgh 1911, New York 1967.

Williams, J. B. Guide to the printed materials for English social and economic history 1750–1850. 2 vols New York 1926, 1966, 1968.
Higgs, H. Bibliography of economics 1751–75. Cambridge 1935.
Bibliography of the collection of books and tracts on commerce, currency and poor law (1557 to 1763) formed by Joseph Massie. Ed W. A. Shaw 1937.

Hollander, J. H. The economic library of Jacob H. Hollander, compiled by E. A. G. Marsh. Baltimore 1937 (priv ptd).

Pargellis, S. M. and D. J. Medley. Bibliography of British history: the eighteenth century 1714–89. Oxford 1951, New York 1968.

The Kress Library of Business and Economics catalogue vol 1: material published through 1776. Boston 1940; Supplement, Boston 1956; vol 2: 1777–1817, Boston 1957; Supplement 1473–1848, Boston 1967.

Hanson, L. W. Contemporary printed sources for British and Irish economic history 1701–50. Cambridge 1963.

A list of pbns on the economic history of Gt Britain and Ireland appears annually in Economic History Review.

General Studies

Cunningham, W. The growth of English industry and commerce. Vols 2–3, 1882, 1912 (5th edn), 1968.

Bonar, J. Philosophy and political economy in some of their historical relations. 1893, 1922 (3rd edn), 1966.

— Theories of population from Raleigh to Arthur Young. 1931, New York 1966.

Cannan, E. A history of the theories of production and distribution in English political economy from 1776 to 1848. 1894, 1917 (3rd edn), New York 1967.

— A review of economic theory. 1929; ed B. A. Corry 1964.

Dubois, A. Précis de l'histoire des doctrines économiques. Vol 1, Paris 1903 (all pbd).

Mantoux, P. La révolution industrielle au xviii° siècle. Paris 1906; tr 1928, 1961 (12th rev edn).

Kennedy, W. English taxation 1640–1799. 1913, New York 1966.

Furniss, E. S. Position of the laborer in a system of nationalism. New York 1920, New York 1965.

Monroe, A. E. Monetary theory before Adam Smith. Cambridge Mass 1923, New York 1966.

Suviranta, B. The theory of the balance of trade in England. Helsinki 1923, New York 1967.

Hargreaves, E. L. The national debt. 1930, 1966.

Lipson, E. The economic history of England. Vols 2–3, 1931, 1943 (3rd rev edn).

Heckscher, E. F. Merkantilismen. 2 vols Stockholm 1931; tr 1935, 1955 (rev).

Viner, J. Studies in the theory of international trade. New York 1937, 1966.

Rist, C. Histoire des doctrines relatives au crédit et à la monnaie depuis John Law jusqu'à nos jours. Paris 1938; tr 1940, New York 1966.

Roll, E. A history of economic thought. 1938, 1954 (rev).

Johnson, E. A. J. Predecessors of Adam Smith: the growth of British economic thought. 1937, New York 1965.

Wermel, M. T. The evolution of the classical wage theory. New York 1939.

Clapham, J. H. The Bank of England. Vol 1, 1694–1797, Cambridge 1944, 1966.

— and W. H. B. Court. A concise economic history of Britain. Cambridge 1956.

Ashton, T. S. The Industrial Revolution 1760–1830. 1948, 1964 (rev).

— An economic history of England: the 18th century. 1955, 1961.

— Economic fluctuations in England 1700–1800. Oxford 1959.

Robbins, L. C. The theory of economic policy in English classical political economy. 1952.

Schumpeter, J. A. A history of economic analysis. New York 1954.

Vickers, D. Studies in the theory of money 1690–1776. Philadelphia 1959.

Tucker, G. S. L. Progress and profits in economic thought. 1960.

Horsefield, J. K. British monetary experiments 1650–1710. Cambridge Mass 1960.

Deane, P. M. and W. A. Cole. British economic growth 1688–1959. Cambridge 1962.

Letwin, W. The origins of scientific economics: English economic thought 1660–1776. 1963.

Taylor, W. L. Francis Hutcheson and David Hume as predecessors of Adam Smith. Durham NC 1965.

Deane, P. M. The first Industrial Revolution. Cambridge 1965.

Wilson, C. England's apprenticeship 1603–1763. 1965.

Flinn, M. W. The origins of the Industrial Revolution. 1966.

Mitchell, W. C. Types of economic theory from mercantilism to institutionalism. Vol 1, ed J. Dorfman, New York 1967.

Dickson, P. G. M. The financial revolution in England: a study in the development of public credit 1688–1756. 1967.

Contemporary Writings

Fuller bibliographies of some of these writers appear elsewhere in the volume: see index.

Anderson, Adam. An historical and chronological deduction of trade and commerce. 2 vols 1762, 1764 (2nd, augmented edn, as Deduction of the origin of commerce).

Anderson, James. Observations on the means of exciting a spirit of national industry in Scotland. Edinburgh 1778, New York 1968.

Asgill, John. Several assertations proved. 1696; ed J. H. Hollander, Baltimore 1906.

B[arbon], N[icholas]. A discourse of trade. 1690; ed J. H. Hollander, Baltimore 1905.

— A discourse concerning coining the new money lighter. 1696.

Bellers, John. Essays about the poor, manufactures, trade, plantations and immorality. 1699.

— Writings. Ed A. R. Fry 1935.

Bentham, Jeremy. A defense of usury. 1787.

— Economic writings. Ed W. Stark 3 vols New York 1952–4.

Berkeley, George. The querist. Dublin 1735–7; rptd in Works vol 6, ed A. A. Luce and T. E. Jessop 1953.

[Bindon, David]. A letter from a merchant who has left off trade. 1738.

[Bluett (Blewitt), George]. An inquiry whether a general practice of virtue tends to the wealth or poverty, benefit or disadvantage of a people? 1725.

Brewster, Sir Francis. Essays on trade. 1695.

Briscoe, John. A discourse of money. 1696.

[Browne, Sir John]. An essay on trade in general, and on that of Ireland in particular. Dublin 1728.

Cantillon, Richard. Essai sur la nature du commerce en général. 'Londres' (for Paris) 1755; ed and tr H. Higgs 1931, New York 1964. Written c. 1730.

Cary, John. An essay on the state of England, in relation to its trade. Bristol 1695.

— An essay, on the coyn and credit of England. Bristol 1696.

Chamberlen (Chamberlain), Hugh. A collection of some papers writ upon several occasions, concerning clipt and counterfeit money, and trade. 1696.

Child, Sir Josiah. Brief observations concerning trade and interest of money. 1668; rptd in W. Letwin, Sir Josiah Child, Boston 1959

— A discourse about trade. 1690, 1693 (rev as A new discourse of trade).

[Clement, Simon]. A discourse of the general notions of money, trade and exchanges. 1695.

Coke, Roger. A discourse of trade. 1670.

— A treatise wherein is demonstrated that the Church and State of England are in equal danger with the trade of it. 1671.

Considerations on the East-India trade. 1701; rptd in J. R. McCulloch, Select tracts on commerce, 1856, Cambridge 1954, New York 1966.

Considerations relating to the laying any additional duty on sugar. 1747.

Considerations relating to the late order of the two banks established at Edinburgh. Scots Mag 24 1762.

Culpeper, Sir Thomas. A discourse shewing the many advantages which will accrue to this Kingdom by the abatement of usury. 1668.

Davenant, Charles. An essay upon ways and means of supplying the war. 1695.

— An essay on the East-India trade. 1696.

— Discourses on the publick revenues, and on the trade of England. 1698.

— An essay upon the probable methods of making a people gainers in the ballance of trade. 1699.

— The political and commercial works. Ed C. Whitworth 5 vols 1771.

— Two manuscripts: A memorial concerning the coyn of England; A memorial concerning credit. Ed A. P. Usher, Baltimore 1942.

Decker, Sir Matthew. Serious considerations on the several high duties, 1743.

— An essay on the causes of the decline of the foreign trade. 1744.

Defoe, Daniel. An essay upon projects. 1697.

— Giving alms no charity. 1704.

— An essay upon loans. 1710.

— A general history of trade. 4 pts 1713.

— A tour thro' the whole island of Great Britain. 3 vols 1724–7; ed G. D. H. Cole 2 vols 1927.

— The complete English tradesman. 1726 (for 1725), New York 1967.

— A plan of the English commerce. 1728, 1730 (rev), 1967.

Eden, Sir Frederick. The state of the poor. 1797, 1966.

Ferguson, Adam. An essay on the history of civil society. Edinburgh 1767; ed D. Forbes, Edinburgh 1966.

— Institutes of moral philosophy. Edinburgh 1769.

Fielding, Henry. A proposal for making an effectual provision for the poor. 1753.

[Forster, Nathaniel]. An enquiry into the cause of the present high price of provisions. 1767.

Fortrey, Samuel. England's interest and improvement. Cambridge 1663; ed J. H. Hollander, Baltimore 1907; rptd in J. R. McCulloch, Select tracts on commerce, 1856, Cambridge 1954, New York 1966.

Gale, Samuel. Essays on the nature and principles of public credit. 4 pts 1784–7.

Gee, Joshua. The trade and navigation of Great Britain considered. 1729.

— An impartial enquiry into the importance and present state of the woollen manufactories of Great-Britain. Lincoln 1742.

Gervaise, Isaac. The system or theory of the trade of the world. 1720; ed J. M. Letiche, Baltimore 1954 (foreword by J. Viner).

Godwin, William. An enquiry concerning political justice. 2 vols 1793; ed F. E. L. Priestley 3 vols Toronto 1946.

Graunt, John. Natural and political observations made upon the bills of mortality. 1662; ed W. F. Willcox, Baltimore 1939.

Hanway, Jonas. Letters on the importance of the rising generation of the laboring part of our fellow-subjects. 2 vols 1767.

Harris, Joseph. An essay upon money and coins. 2 pts 1757–8; rptd in J. R. McCulloch, Select tracts on money, 1856, 1933.

[Hay, William]. Remarks on the laws relating to the poor. [1735], 1751.

Houghton, John. England's great happiness. 1677.

— A collection of letters for the improvement of husbandry and trade. 2 vols 1681–3.

Hume, David. Political discourses. Edinburgh 1752.

— Writings on economics. Ed A. Rotwein, Edinburgh 1955.

Hutcheson, Francis. A system of moral philosophy. 2 vols Glasgow 1755, New York 1968.

[Jenyns, Soame]. Thoughts on the causes and consequences of the present high price of provisions. 1767.

Samuel, Johnson. Considerations on the corn laws. Appendix to Parliamentary logick by William Gerard Hamilton, ed E. Malone 1808. Written 1766.

Kames, Lord (Henry Home). Sketches of the history of man. 2 vols Edinburgh 1774.

King, Gregory. Natural and political observations and conclusions upon the state and condition of England. Extracts ptd in Davenant, Essay upon the ballance of trade, 1699; ptd in full in 1802 edn of G. Chalmers, An estimate of the comparative strength of Britain, 1782; ed J. H. Hollander, Baltimore 1936. Written 1696.

[Law, John]. Money and trade considered. Edinburgh 1705, New York 1966.

— Oeuvres complètes. Ed P. Harsin 3 vols Paris 1934.

Lind[e]say, Patrick. Interest of Scotland considered. Edinburgh 1733.

[Lloyd, Henry]. An essay on the theory of money. 1771.

Locke, John. Two treatises of government. 1690; ed P. Laslett, Cambridge 1960.

— Some considerations of the consequences of the lowering of interest. 1692 (for 1691).

— Further considerations concerning raising the value of money. 1695.

— Several papers relating to money, interest, trade. 1696, New York 1968.

[Lowndes, William]. Report containing an essay for the amendment of the silver coins. 1695; rptd in J. R. McCulloch, Select tracts on money, 1856, 1933.

M[agens], N[icholas]. Further explanations of some particular subjects relating to trade, coin and exchanges, contained in the Universal Merchant. 1756.

Malthus, Thomas Robert. An essay on the principle of population. 1798, New York 1965.

Mandeville, Bernard. The fable of the bees. 1714; ed F. B. Kaye 2 vols Oxford 1924.

— A letter to Dion. 1732; ed J. Viner, Los Angeles 1953; ed B. Dobrée, Liverpool 1954.

Manley, Thomas. Usury at six per cent examined. 1669.

Massie, Joseph. An essay on the governing causes of the natural rate of interest. 1750; ed J. H. Hollander, Baltimore 1912.

— A representation concerning the knowledge of commerce as a national concern. 1760.

Mercator: or commerce retrieved. 26 May 1713–20 July 1714. A periodical, ed Defoe.

[Mildmay, Sir William]. The laws and policy of England, relating to trade. 1763.

Mun, Thomas. England's treasure by forraign trade. 1664, 1949, New York 1965.

[Murray, Patrick (Lord Elibank)]. Essays: I, on the publick debt; II, on paper money, banking etc; III, on frugality. 1755.

— Thoughts on money, circulation and paper currency. Edinburgh 1758; rptd in J. R. McCulloch, Select tracts on paper currency, 1857.

[North, Sir Dudley]. Discourses upon trade. 1691; ed J. H. Hollander, Baltimore 1907.

Ogilvy, William. Essay on the right of property in land. 1782; ed D. C. Macdonald 1891 (as Birthright in land).

Petty, Sir William. A treatise of taxes and contributions. 1662.

— Quantulumcunque concerning money. 1682.

— Political arithmetic. 1690.

— The political anatomy of Ireland, to which is added Verbum sapienti. 1691.

— Economic writings. Ed C. H. Hull 2 vols Cambridge 1899, New York 1963–4.

[Petyt, William]. Britannia languens: or a discourse of trade. 1680; rptd in J. R. McCulloch, Select tracts on commerce, 1856, Cambridge 1954, New York 1966.

Pollexfen, John. England and East-India inconsistent in their manufactures. 1697.

— A discourse of trade, coyn and paper credit. 1697.

— A vindication of some assertations relating to coin and trade. 1699.

Postlethwayt, Malachy. Britain's commercial interest explained and improved. 2 vols 1757, New York 1968.

— Great Britain's true system. 1757, New York 1967.

— The universal dictionary of trade and commerce. 2 vols 1751–5.

Pownall, Thomas. A letter to Adam Smith. 1776.

Price, Richard. An essay on the population of England. 1780.

Smith, Adam. The theory of moral sentiments. 1759, New York 1966.

— The wealth of nations. 2 vols 1776, New York 1966; ed E. Cannan 1904, 1950 (6th edn).

— Lectures on justice, police, revenue and arms, reported by a student in 1763. Ed E. Cannan, Oxford 1896, New York 1964.

Steuart, Sir James. Principles of political oeconomy. 2 vols 1767.

— Works. Ed Sir J. Steuart 6 vols 1805, New York 1967.

[Temple, William]. A vindication of commerce and the arts. 1758; rptd in J. R. McCulloch, Select tracts on commerce, 1859.

Tucker, Josiah. A brief essay on the advantages and disadvantages, which respectively attend France and Great Britain, with regard to trade. 1749.

— Reflections on the expediency of a law for the naturalization of foreign Protestants. 2 pts 1751–2.

— The elements of commerce, and theory of taxes. Bristol 1755 (priv ptd).

— Instructions for travellers. 1757 (priv ptd), Dublin 1758.

— Four tracts on political and commercial subjects. 2 pts Gloucester 1774.

— A selection from his economic and political writings. Ed R. L. Schuyler, New York 1931.

The use and abuses of money, and the improvements of it. 1671.

Vanderlint, Jacob. Money answers all things. 1734; ed J. H. Hollander, Baltimore 1914.

Vaughan, Rice. A discourse of coin and coinage. 1675; rptd in J. R. McCulloch, Select tracts on money, 1856, 1933.

Wakefield, Daniel. An essay upon political oeconomy. 1799.

[Wallace, Robert]. Characteristics of the present political state of Great Britain. 1758.

— Various prospects of mankind, nature and providence. 1761.

[Whatley, George]. Reflections upon the principle of trade in general. 1769.

[Whately, Thomas]. Considerations on the trade and finances of this Kingdom. 1769.

Wood, William. A survey of trade. 1718.

Yarranton, Andrew. England's improvement by sea and land. 2 pts 1677–81.

Young, Arthur. The expediency of a free exportation of corn. 1769.

— Political arithmetic. 1774, New York 1968.

J. H. M.

XII. SCIENCE

Facs edns usually contain critical apparatus : microprint edns are excluded. General histories of scientific writings are listed in the Renaissance section in vol 1, with further material on the origins of the Royal Society. Polemical tracts by physicians who were early Fellows of the Royal Society are listed in Part 1, other medical works in Part 3.

(1) THE ROYAL SOCIETY AND ITS CONTROVERSIES

§ I

Webster, John (1610–82). Academiarum examen. 1654. *See Part 3, below.*

Ward, Seth (1617–89). Vindiciae academiarum. 1654. *See Part 3, below.*

Charleton, Walter (1619–1707). The immortality of the human soul. 1657. *See Part 3, below.*

Hobbes, Thomas (1588–1679). Examinatio et emendatio mathematicae hodiernae in libris Johannis Wallisii. 1660.

— Dialogus physicus: sive de natura aëris. 1661.

— Opera philosophica. 1668.

— Quadratura circuli, cubatio sphaerae, duplicatio cubi. 1669. *See Robert Boyle, below.*

Glanvill, Joseph (1636–80). The vanity of dogmatising. 1661; ed M. E. Prior, New York 1932 (facs); 1664 (rev).

— Plus ultra: or the advancement of knowledge since Aristotle. 1668; ed J. I. Cope, Gainesville 1958 (facs).

— Philosophia pia: or the experimental philosophy profest by the Royal Society. 1671.

— Essays on philosophy and religion. 1676.

Cowley, Abraham (1618–67). A proposition for the advancement of experimental philosophy. 1661.

Owen, John (1616–83). Animadversions upon Fiat lux [by John Canes, 1661]. 1662. Anon.

Wallis, John (1616–1703). Hobbius heauton-timorumenos. Oxford 1662. *See Part 3, below.*

White, Thomas (1593–1676). Sciri: sive scepticorum a cura disputationis exclusio. 1663, 1665 (rewritten as An exclusion of sceptics).

Evelyn, John (1620–1706). Sylva: or a discourse of forest trees. 1664. First book ptd by Royal Society; *see* M. Denny, *below.*

Keynes, G. L. Evelyn: a bibliography. Cambridge 1937, Oxford 1968 (with addns).

Philosophical transactions of the Royal Society. 1665–. In progress.

Sprat, Thomas (1635–1713). Observations on Monsieur de Sorbier's voyage into England. 1665, 1668, 1672, 1709.

— The history of the Royal Society. 1667; ed J. I. Cope and H. W. Jones, St Louis 1958 (facs); London 1702, 1722, 1734.

Monconys, Balthasar de (1611–65). Voyages. 3 pts Lyons 1665–6, Paris 1677, 1695. In French.

Patrick, Simon (1626–1707). A friendly debate. 1669.

Wilkins, John (1614–72). An essay towards a real character and a philosophical language. 1668. *See Part 2, below.*

Casaubon, Meric (1599–1671). A letter concerning natural experimental philosophy. Cambridge 1669.

Stubbe, Henry (1632–76). Campanella revived. 1670. Attack on Sprat's History of the Royal Society, above.

— A censure upon certain passages in [Sprat's] History of the Royal Society. Oxford 1670.

—— Legends no histories: or animadversions upon [Sprat's] History of the Royal Society. 1670.
—— The plus ultra [of Glanvill] reduced to a non plus. 1670.
Merret(t), Christopher (1614–95). Self-conviction. 1670.
—— The accomplished physician. 1670.
Thom(p)son, George (fl. 1648–79). Μισοχυμίας Ἔλεγχος: or a check to Henry Stubbe, with an assertion of experimental philosophy. 1671.
Hale, Sir Matthew (1609–76). An essay touching the gravitation of fluid bodies. 1673.
—— Difficiles nugae: or observations touching the Torricellian experiment. 1674.
—— Observations touching the principles of natural motions. 1677.
More, Henry (1614–87). Remarks upon two late ingenious discourses [of Sir Matthew Hale, above]. 1676.
Wallis, John (1616–1703). A defence of the Royal Society. 1678. Anon.
King, William (1633–1712). The transactioneer. 1700. Anon. Satire on Sir Hans Sloane and the Royal Society.
Ward, John (1679?–1758). Lives of the professors of Gresham College. 1740.
Hill, John, self-styled Sir John (1716?–75). A review of the works of the Royal Society. 1751.

§ 2

Birch, T. The history of the Royal Society. 4 vols 1756–7.
Thomson, T. The history of the Royal Society. 1812.
Early days of the Royal Society. Chambers's Jnl 8 1847.
Weld, C. R. A history of the Royal Society. 2 vols 1848.
Worthington, John (1618–71). Diary and correspondence [1636–71]. Ed J. Crossley and R. C. Christie, 2 vols in 3 Manchester 1847–86.

Wheatley, H. B. Early history of the Royal Society. Hertford 1905.
Huggins, W. The Royal Society. 1906.
Pearson, N. The virtuosi. Nineteenth Century Nov 1909.
Monroe, B. S. An English academy. MP 8 1911.
Gunther, R. W. T. (ed). Early science in Oxford. 14 vols Oxford 1923–45, 1967, London 1967– (facs). Especially on Hooke, Lhuyd, Lower, Robert Plot.
Lloyd, C. Shadwell and the Virtuosi. PLMA 44 1929.
—— The Royal Society and John Dryden. PMLA 45 1930.
—— Edmund Waller as a member of the Royal Society. PMLA 43 1928.
Young, R. F. Comenius in England [and] the origins of the Royal Society. 1932.
Jones, R. F. Ancients and moderns: the background of [Swift's] The battle of the books. St Louis 1936, Los Angeles 1965.
Clark, G. N. Science and social welfare in the age of Newton. Oxford 1937, 1949 (rev).
Ornstein, M. The role of scientific societies in the seventeenth century. Chicago 1938, Hamden Conn 1963.
Denny, M. The early program of the Royal Society and John Evelyn. MLQ 1 1940.
Brown, H. Voltaire and the Royal Society. UTQ 13 1943.
Lyons, H. The Royal Society 1660–1940. Cambridge 1944.
Stimson, D. Scientists and amateurs: a history of the Royal Society. New York 1949.
Hartley, H. (ed). The Royal Society. 1960.
Andrade, E. N. da C. A brief history of the Royal Society. 1960.
Purver, M. and E. J. Bowen. The beginning of the Royal Society. Oxford 1960.
Purver, M. The Royal Society. 1967.

(2) LANGUAGE AND BIOGRAPHY

Duncan, C. S. The new science and English literature in the classical period. Menasha 1913.
Nicolson, M. H. Newton demands the Muse: Newton's Opticks and the eighteenth-century poets. Princeton 1946.
—— The breaking of the circle; the effect of the New Science on seventeenth-century poetry. Evanston 1950.
Miles, J. The primary language of poetry in the 1740s and 1840s. Berkeley 1950.

Pinto, V. de S. English biography in the seventeenth century. 1951. With texts of Abraham Hill's life of Barrow and Aubrey's lives of Boyle and Hobbes.
Davy, N. (ed). British scientific literature in the seventeenth century. 1953. Short extracts, arranged under subjects, from many writers above.
Davie, D. The language of science and the language of literature 1700–40. 1963.

(3) THE LITERATURE OF SCIENCE
(in alphabetical order)

Some works in the fields of popular science, pseudo-science, physico-theology and anti-science satire are listed, with a few on natural science as relating to technology, trades and manufactures at large; but works on specific trades, on military science (gunnery and explosives), on civil engineering and on architecture are excluded: these subjects may be explored through the dictionaries noted below. Somewhat fuller bibliographies of several writers will be found in the section on Philosophy, col 1833, above; cross-references to that section have not normally been given.

Adams, George (1750–95). Essays on the microscope. 1787.
Akenside, Mark (1721–70). De dysenteria. 1764. *See col 637, above.*
Arbuthnot, John (1667–1735). *See col 1050, above, and* J. Woodward, *below.*
Armstrong, John (1709–79). The art of preserving health. 1744. *See col 535, above.*
Ashmole, Elias (1617–92). Theatrum chemicum britannicum. 1652 (English text); ed A. G. Debus, New York 1967 (facs).

Josten, C. H. Ashmole: his autobiographical notes, his correspondence and other contemporary sources. 5 vols Oxford 1966.
Baker, Sir George (1722–1809). An inquiry into a method of inoculating the small-pox. 1766.
Baker, Henry (1698–1774). Employment for the microscope. 1753.
Banks, Sir Joseph (1743–1820). Letters. Ed W. R. Dawson 1958.
—— The Endeavour journal. Ed J. C. Beaglehole, Sydney 1962.
Dryander, J. Catalogus bibliothecae historiconaturalis Josephi Banks. 5 vols 1798–1800, 1 vol New York 1966 (facs).
Barlow, alias Booth, Edward (1639–1719). Meteorological essays. 1715.
Barrow, Isaac (1630–77). Mathematical works. 4 vols 1683–7 (with life by Abraham Hill); ed W. Whewell, Cambridge 1860 (Latin text).
Bate, George (1608–69). Pharmacopoeia Bateana: or Bate's dispensatory. 1694. Tr from Latin edn of 1688.

Battie, William (1704–76). A treatise on madness. 1758.

Beddoes, Thomas (1760–1808). Considerations on the use of factitious airs: part I by Thomas Beddoes; part II by James Watt [the engineer]. 1794, 1795.

—— Preface. In C. W. Scheele, Chemical essays, 1786.

—— Contributions to physical and medical knowledge. Bristol 1799. Contains Sir Humphry Davy's first pbd work, on heat and light.

Bell, John (1763–1820). Discourses on the nature and cure of wounds. Edinburgh 1795.

Bentley, Richard (1662–1742). Eight sermons. 1693.

—— Four letters [from] Sir Isaac Newton. 1756.

Berkeley, George (1685–1753). Essay towards a new theory of vision. Dublin 1709.

—— Three dialogues between Hylas and Philonous. 1713.

—— Alciphron: or the minute philosopher. 1732, 1752.

—— The analyst: or a discourse addressed to an infidel mathematician [Edmond Halley]. 1734.

—— Works. Ed A. A. Luce and T. E. Jessop 9 vols 1948–57.

Black, Joseph (1728–99). The supposed effect of boiling on water. Philosophical Trans of Royal Soc 65 1775.

—— Experiments upon magnesia alba, quicklime and other alcaline substances. 1777, Edinburgh 1898.

—— Lectures on the elements of chemistry. Edinburgh 1803.

—— Life and letters. Ed W. Ramsay 1918. See A. Smith, below.

Blackmore, Sir Richard (d. 1729). Essays upon several subjects. 1716, 2 vols 1717. See col 469, above.

—— A treatise on the spleen. 1725.

—— Discourses on the gout, rheumatism and the King's Evil. 1726.

Boyle, Hon Robert (1627–91). New experiments physico-mechanical touching the spring of the air. 1660, 1662 (Whereunto is added a defence of the authors explication against Francis Linus and Thomas Hobbes). The Defence contains Boyle's Law.

—— The sceptical chymist. 1661, 1965 (facs), 1680 (enlarged).

—— Some considerations touching the usefulnesse of experimental natural philosophy. 1663, 1671.

—— Experiments and considerations touching colours. 1664; ed M. B. Hall, New York 1964 (facs).

—— New experiments and observations touching cold. 1665.

—— The origine of formes and qualities, according to the corpuscular philosophy. 1666, 1667.

—— Experiments and notes about the mechanical origin of electricity. 1676, Oxford 1927. See J. T. Desaguliers, below.

—— The Christian virtuoso. 1690.

—— Philosophical works abridged, methodized and disposed by Peter Shaw. 3 vols 1725.

—— Works. Ed T. Birch 5 vols 1744, 6 vols 1772.

Fulton, J. F. A bibliography of Boyle. Oxford 1932, 1961.

Bracken, Henry (1697–1764). Farriery improv'd. 2 vols 1738. Veterinary data.

Bradley, James (1693–1762). Miscellaneous works and correspondence. Oxford 1832. On astronomy.

Burnet, Thomas (1635?–1715). Telluris theoria sacra. 2 vols 1681–9; tr as The theory of the earth, 2 vols 1684–90, Carbondale 1965 (facs).

Butler, Samuel (1613–80). Hudibras. 3 pts 1663–78.

—— Genuine remains in verse and prose. 1759. See col 435, above.

Carlisle, Sir Anthony (1768–1840). See William Nicholson, below.

Cavendish, Henry (1731–1810). Experiments on air. Philosophical Trans of Royal Soc 74 1784–5, Edinburgh 1899.

—— Electrical researches. 1879, 1967 (facs).

—— Scientific papers. Ed J. C. Maxwell 2 vols Cambridge 1921.

Berry, A. J. Henry Cavendish. 1960.

Cavendish, Margaret, Duchess of Newcastle (1624?–1674). Observations upon natural philosophy. 1666.

Chambers, Ephraim (d. 1740). Cyclopaedia: or an universal dictionary of arts and sciences. 2 vols 1728, 1738 (with addns), 1739.

Charleton, Walter (1619–1707). Physiologia Epicuro-Gassendo-Charltoniana, or science natural upon the hypothesis of atoms. 1654; ed R. H. Kargon, New York 1966 (facs).

—— The harmony of divine laws. 1682. See Part 1, above.

Clarke, Samuel (1675–1729). A collection of papers which passed between Dr Clarke and Mr Leibnitz. 1717; ed H. G. Alexander, Manchester 1956 (as The Leibniz-Clarke correspondence).

Collectanea chemica: being select treatises on alchemy and Hermetic medicine. 1893, 1963.

Cook, James (1728–79). A voyage towards the South Pole and round the world. 2 vols 1777.

—— A voyage to the Pacific Ocean. 3 vols 1784.

—— Journals. 4 vols Cambridge 1955–61.

Cotes, Roger (1682–1716). Hydrostatical and pneumatical lectures. Ed R. Smith 1738. See Sir Isaac Newton, below.

Croone or Croune, William (1633–84). De ratione motus musculorum. 1664.

—— A discourse on the conformation of a chick in the egg. Philosophical Trans of Royal Soc 28 1672.

Cudworth, Ralph (1617–88). The true intellectual system of the universe. 1678; ed J. Harrison 3 vols 1845 (with his trn of notes by J. L. Mosheim).

Cullen, William (1710–90). A treatise of the materia medica. 2 vols 1771, 1773 (vol 1 unauthorized), Edinburgh 1789.

—— Works. 2 vols Edinburgh 1827.

Thomson, J. An account of the life, lectures and writings of Cullen. Edinburgh 1832, 2 vols Edinburgh 1855.

Dalton, John (1766–1844). Meteorological observations. London and Kendal 1793.

Smyth, A. L. Dalton: a bibliography of works by and about him. Manchester 1966.

Darwin, Erasmus (1731–1802). The botanic garden. 1792.

—— Zoonomia: or the laws of organic life. 2 vols 1794–6.

—— Phytologia: or the philosophy of agriculture and gardening. 1799.

Davy, Sir Humphry (1778–1829). See T. Beddoes, above.

de Moivre, Abraham (1667–1754). The doctrine of chances. 1718, 1967 (facs). See Edmond Halley, below.

Derham, William (1657–1735). Physico-theology. 1713, 1716, 1720, 1723, 1727, 1732, etc.

—— Astro-theology. 1715, 1719, 1721, 1726 etc.

Desaguliers, Jean Théophile (1683–1744). A course of experimental philosophy. 2 vols 1733–44.

—— A dissertation concerning electricity. 1742. The first major work in English on the subject; see Robert Boyle, above.

Diaper, William (1686?–1717). See col 544, above.

Dossie, Robert (fl. 1760). Institutes of experimental chemistry. 1759.

—— Theory and practice of chirurgical pharmacy. 1761.

Dryden, John (1631–1700). An evening's love: or the mock astrologer. 1671. See col 441, above.

Ellis, John (1710?–76). An essay towards the natural history of the corallines. 1755.

Emerson, William (1701–82). The principles of mechanics. 1758.

Ent, Sir George (1604–89). Apologia pro circuitione sanguinis. 1641, 1683.

Farish, William (1759–1837). A plan of a course of lectures on arts and manufactures. Cambridge 1796, 1803, 1821.

Flamsteed, John (1646–1719). Historia coelestis britannica. 3 vols 1725.

Franklin, Benjamin (1706–90). Experiments and observations on electricity. 1751.
— New experiments and observations on electricity. 1754.
— Autobiography. 1793 (tr from French), 1817, 1868.
Freind, John (1675–1728). Praelectiones chymicae. 1709; tr 1729.
— The history of physick. 2 vols 1725–6.
Garth, Samuel (1661–1719). See col 474, above.
Glisson, Francis (1597–1677). Anatomia hepatis. 1654.
— Tractatus de ventriculo et intestinis. 1677.
Goldsmith, Oliver (1730?–74). An history of the earth and animated nature. 1774. See col 1200, above.
Graunt, John (1620–74). Upon the Bills of Mortality. 1662.
Gray, Stephen (FRS 1732). Experiments in electricity. Philosophical Trans of Royal Soc 37–9 1732–5.
Green, Matthew (1696–1737). The spleen. 1737. See col 550, above.
Gregory, David (1661–1708). Catoptricae et dioptricae sphericae elementa. Oxford 1695; tr 1715, 1735. See Edmond Halley, below.
Gregory, James (1638–75). Optica promota. 1663.
Grew, Nehemiah (1641–1712). The anatomy of vegetables begun. 1672.
— The comparative anatomy of the stomach and guts. 1681.
— The anatomy of plants. 1682; ed C. Zirkle, New York 1965 (facs).
— Cosmologia sacra. 1701.
Hales, Stephen (1677–1761). Vegetable staticks. 1727; ed M. A. Hoskin 1961.
— Haemostaticks. 1733.
— Philosophical experiments. 1739.
— A description of ventilators. 1743; Part second, 1758.
— Some considerations on the causes of earthquakes. 1750.
Halley, Edmond (1656–1742). Astronomiae cometicae synopsis. 1705.
— (ed). Miscellanea curiosa. 3 vols 1705–7, 1723–7 (3rd edn). Contributions by De Moivre, David Gregory, Halley, Hooke, Newton, Wallis et al.
— Tabulae astronomicae. 1749; tr 1752.
— Correspondence and papers. Ed E. F. MacPike, Oxford 1932.
   Armitage, A. Edmond Halley. 1966.
   See George Berkeley, above.
Harris, John (1667?–1719). Lexicon technicum: or a universal English dictionary of arts and sciences. 1704, 2 vols 1708–10, 1 vol New York 1966 (facs).
Harris, Moses (fl. 1766–85). The Aurelian: or natural history of English insects. 1766, 1778.
Harrison, John (1693–1776). An account of the proceedings in order to the discovery of the longitude. 1763 (anon), 1765.
   Quill, H. John Harrison. 1966.
Hauksbee, Francis (d. 1713?). Physico-mechanical experiments. 1709.
Helsham, Richard (1682?–1738). A course of lectures in natural philosophy. 1739.
Henry, William (1774–1836). A general view of chemistry and of its application to arts and manufactures. Manchester 1799.
Herschel or Herschell, Sir William (1738–1822). The rotation of the planets. Philosophical Trans of Royal Soc 71, 115, 1781.
Higgins, Bryan (1737?–1820). A syllabus of chemical and philosophical enquiries. [1775].
— Experiments and observations [on] the art of preparing quicklime. 1780.
Higgins, William (1763–1825). A comparative view of the phlogistic and antiphlogistic theories. 1789.
— The atomic theory and electrical phenomena. Dublin 1814.
   Wheeler, T. S. and J. R. Partington. The life and work of Higgins. 1960.

Hill, Abraham (1635–1721). Familiar letters [addressed to Hill]. 1767. See V. de S. Pinto, above.
Hoadly, Benjamin (1706–57) and Benjamin Wilson (1721–88). Observations on a series of electrical experiments. 1756.
Holder, William (1616–98). Elements of speech, with an appendix concerning persons deaf and dumb. 1669.
Hooke, Robert (1635–1703). Micrographia. 1665, New York 1961 (facs), Brussels 1966 (facs); [selection], Edinburgh 1902.
— Lectiones Cutlerianae: or [English] lectures physical, mechanical, geographical and astronomical. 1679, Oxford 1931.
— Posthumous works. 1705. With life by Richard Waller.
— Philosophical experiments and observations. 1726, 1967 (facs).
— Diary. Ed H. W. Robinson 1936.
   'Espinasse, M. M. W. Robert Hooke. 1956.
   Keynes, G. L. A bibliography of Hooke. 1960. See R. W. Gunther, above.
Horsley, Samuel (1733–1806). The power of God deduced from the solar system. 1767.
Hunter, John (1728–93). Treatise on the human teeth. 2 vols 1771, 1778.
— On the venereal disease. 1786.
— Observations on certain parts of the animal œconomy. 1786.
— Treatise on the blood, inflammation and gunshot wounds. 1794.
Hunter, William (1718–83). Anatomia uteri humani gravidi. Birmingham 1774; tr 1794.
Hurlock, Joseph (d. 1793). A practical discourse upon dentition. 1742, 1966 (facs).
Hutton, Charles (1737–1823). A mathematical and philosophical dictionary. 2 vols 1795–6.
Hutton, James (1726–97). Theory of the earth. 2 vols Edinburgh 1785, Weinheim 1959 (facs).
   Playfair, J. Illustrations of the Huttonian theory of the earth. Edinburgh 1802. See A. Smith, below.
James, Robert (1705–76). A medicinal dictionary. 3 vols 1743–5. Dedication to Richard Mead by Samuel Johnson.
Jenner, Edward (1749–1823). An inquiry into the cause and effects of the variolae vaccinae. 1798, 1966 (facs).
Jones, William (of Nayland) (1726–1800). An essay on the first principles of natural philosophy, [with reference to Newton]. Oxford 1762.
Kirwan, Richard (1733–1812). An essay on phlogiston. 1787, 1789.
— Geological essays. 1799.
Lee, James (1715–95). An introduction to botany [as regards the Linnaean system]. 1760, 1788.
Lhuyd or Llwyd, Edward (1660–1709). Lithophylacii britannici ichnographia: sive fossilium distributio. 1699. See R. W. Gunther, above.
Lind, James (1716–94). A treatise of the scurvy. Edinburgh 1753, 1953.
Lister, Martin (1638?–1712). Letters and divers other mixt discourses in natural philosophy. York 1683.
Locke, John (1632–1704). An essay concerning humane understanding. 1690. See col 1837, above.
Lovett, Richard (1692–1780). The subtil medium (the ether) prov'd. 1756. On iatro-electricity.
Lower, Richard (1631–91). Tractatus de corde. 1669.
— Dissertatio de origine catarrhi. 1672; ed R. Hunter and I. Macalpine 1963 (facs). See R. W. Gunther, above.
Maclaurin, Colin (1698–1746). A treatise of fluxions. 2 vols Edinburgh 1742. See Sir Isaac Newton, below.
Malthus, Thomas Robert (1766–1834). An essay on the principle of population. 1798 (anon), 1803 (enlarged), 1926 etc.
Martin, Benjamin (1704–82). Miscellaneous correspondence. General Mag of Arts & Sciences 1759–64.

Mayow, Mayouwe or Mayo, John (1640–79). Tractatus duo. Oxford 1668, 1671.
— Tractatus quinque medico-physici. Oxford 1674; tr Edinburgh 1907, 1957.
Mead, Richard (1673–1754). A mechanical account of poisons. 1702.
— A short discourse concerning pestilential contagion. 1720.
Merret or Merrett, Christopher (1614–95). Frauds and abuses committed by apothecaries. 1669. *See Part 1, above.*
Michell, John (1724–93). A treatise of artificial magnets. Cambridge 1750.
Milner, Isaac (1750–1820). A plan of a course of chemical lectures. Cambridge 1784, 1788 (rev).
Miscellanea curiosa. *See* Edmond Halley, *above.*
Moivre, Abraham de. *See* de Moivre, *above.*
More, Henry (1614–87). Observations upon [the] Anthroposophia theomagica [of Thomas Vaughan]. 1650. *See Part 1, above, and* T. Vaughan, *below.*
Morland, Sir Samuel (1625–95). Tuba stentorophonica. 1671.
— The description and use of two arithmetick instruments [to perform the four basic arithmetical processes]. 1673.
— Hydrostaticks: or instructions concerning waterworks. Ed S. Morland 1697.
Mortimer, Cromwell (d. 1752). An address [concerning] certain chemical remedies. 1745.
Morton, John (1671?–1726). The natural history of Northamptonshire. 1712. Includes palaeontology.
Moxon, Joseph (1627–1700). A tutor to astronomy and geography. 1665.
Needham, John Turberville (1713–81). An account of some new microscopical discoveries. 1745.
— Observations upon the general composition and decomposition of animal and vegetable substances. 1749.
Newcastle, Duchess of. *See* M. Cavendish, *above.*
Newton, Sir Isaac (1642–1727). Opera quae extant omnia. Ed Samuel Horsley 5 vols 1779–85.
— Philosophiae naturalis principia mathematica. 1687, 1960 (facs); ed R. Cotes 1713.
— The mathematical principles of natural philosophy translated by Andrew Motte. 1729; rev F. Cajori, Chicago 1955, 2 vols Berkeley 1962 (with Opticks, below).
— Opticks. 1704.
— Arithmetica universalis. 1707.
— Commercium epistolicum D. Johannis Collins et aliorum de analysi. 1712.
— Correspondence. Ed H. W. Turnbull and J. F. Scott 4 vols Cambridge 1959–. In progress.
— Unpublished scientific papers. Ed A. R. and M. B. Hall, Cambridge 1962.
Voltaire, F. M. A. de. Eléments de la philosophie de Newton. Amsterdam 1738; tr 1738, 1967.
Maclaurin, C. An account of Newton's philosophical discoveries. 1748.
Stukeley, W. Memoirs of Newton's life. 1752; ed A. H. White 1936.
Brewster, D. Memoirs of the life, writings and discoveries of Newton. 2 vols 1855; ed R. S. Westfall, New York 1965 (facs).
Gray, G. J. Bibliography of Newton. Cambridge 1888, 1907, 1966 (facs).
Isaac Newton: a memorial volume by several hands. 1927. With bibliography.
More, L. T. Isaac Newton. New York 1934.
Metzger, H. Attraction universelle et religion naturelle chez quelques commentateurs anglais de Newton. Paris 1938.
McLachlan, H. Newton: theological manuscripts. Liverpool 1950.
Thayer, H. S. Newton's philosophy of nature. New York 1953. Selections.

Cohen, I. B. Newton's papers and letters on natural philosophy. Cambridge Mass 1958.
Manuel, F. Newton, historian. Cambridge 1963.
Koyré, A. Newtonian studies. New Haven 1965.
See R. Bentley, E. Halley, W. Jones, M. H. Nicolson, *above.*
Nicholson, William (1753–1815). An essay on phlogiston [tr from Lavoisier and Berthollet], to which are added notes [by Nicholson]. 1789.
— Account of the new electrical apparatus and experiments performed with the same [by Nicholson and Carlisle]. Jnl of Natural Philosophy, Chemistry & Arts 4 1801.
Nugent, Christopher (d. 1775). An essay on the hydrophobia. 1753.
Oldenburg, Henry (1615?–77). Correspondence. Ed A. R. and M. B. Hall, Madison 1965–. In progress.
Paley, William (1743–1805). A view of the evidences of Christianity. 1794.
— Natural theology. 1802.
Papin, Denis (1647–1712?). A new digester or engine for softening bones. 1681, 1966 (facs), 1687 (enlarged).
Parkes, Samuel (1761–1825). A chemical catechism. 1806 etc.
Penrose, Francis (1718–98). Letters philosophical and astronomical. Plymouth 1789.
Petty, Sir William (1623–87). Political arithmetick. 1690.
— Economic writings. Ed C. H. Hull 2 vols Cambridge 1899, New York 1963–4.
Pike, Samuel (1717?–73). The principles of natural philosophy extracted from divine revelation. 1753.
Pope, Walter (d. 1714). The life of Seth Ward. 1697. Also on Isaac Barrow and John Wilkins.
Power, Henry (1623–68). Experimental philosophy. 1664; ed M. B. Hall, New York 1967 (facs).
Priestley, Joseph (1733–1804). The history and present state of electricity. 1767, 1775, New York 1966 (facs).
— The history and present state of discoveries relating to vision, light and colours. 1772.
— Experiments and observations on different kinds of air. Vol 1, 1774, 1775, 1785; vol 2, 1775, Edinburgh 1901 (selections), London 1784; vol 3, 1777, ed R. E. Schofield, New York 1966 (facs); vol 4, 1779; vol 5, 1780; vol 6, 1786. Vols 4–6 rev and issued as Experiments and observations relating to natural philosophy, 3 vols Birmingham 1790.
Schofield, R. E. The Lunar Society of Birmingham. Oxford 1963.
— A scientific autobiography of Priestley. Cambridge Mass 1966.
Gibbs, F. W. Joseph Priestley. 1965.
Crook, R. E. Bibliography of Priestley. 1966.
Quincy, John (fl. 1722). Pharmacopoeia officinalis: or a complete English dispensatory. 1718.
Ramsay, Andrew Michael (1686–1743). Natural religion unfolded in a geometrical order. 2 pts Glasgow 1748–9.
Ravenscroft, Edward (fl. 1671–97). The anatomist. 1697. *See col 771, above.*
Ray or Wray, John (1627–1705). Historia generalis plantarum. 3 vols 1686–1704.
— The wisdom of God manifested in the Creation. 1691.
— Synopsis methodica animalium. 1693.
— Philosophical letters. 1718.
Lankester, E. Memorials of Ray. 1846. With bibliography.
Raven, C. E. Ray, naturalist. Cambridge 1942.
Keynes, G. L. Ray: a bibliography. Oxford 1951.
See F. Willughby, *below.*
Richardson, Richard (1663–1741). Literary and scientific correspondence. Gt Yarmouth 1835.
Rigaud, S. P. Correspondence of scientific men of the seventeenth century. 2 vols Oxford 1841, 1862.
Robertson, John (1712–76). The elements of navigation. 1754, 1772.

Robins, Benjamin (1707–51). Mathematical tracts in two volumes. 1761.

Robison, John (1739–1805). Mechanical philosophy. Edinburgh 1797.

Rumford, Count. *See* Benjamin Thompson, *below*.

Russell, Richard (FRS 1681). The works of Geber. 1678. Tr Russell.

Salusbury, Thomas (fl. 1660). Mathematical collections and translations [from Archimedes, Descartes, Galileo, Roberval and Tartaglia]. 2 vols 1661, 1665; ed S. Drake 1967 (facs).

Savery, Thomas (1650–1715). Navigation improv'd. 1698.

— The miner's friend: or an engine to raise water by fire. 1702.

Shadwell, Thomas (1642?–92). The virtuoso. 1676. *See col 744 and Part 1, above.*

Sharp, Abraham (1651–1742).
Cudworth, W. The life and correspondence of Sharp. 1889.

Shaw, Peter (1694–1763). Chemical lectures for the improvement of arts, trades and natural philosophy. [1734].

Simson, Robert (1687–1768). Opera quaedam [mathematica] reliqua. Glasgow 1776.

Sloane, Sir Hans (1660–1753). A voyage to Madera, Barbadoes and Jamaica, with the natural history of the last. Vol 1, 1707; vol 2, 1725. *See* William King, *above*.

Smellie, William (1740–95). The philosophy of natural history. Vol 1, Edinburgh 1790; vol 2, (ed his son), 1799.

Smith, Adam (1723–90). Essays on philosophical subjects. 1795.

Smith, Robert (1689–1768). Compleat system of opticks. 2 vols Cambridge 1738.

Somerset, Edward, Marquis of Worcester (1601–67). A century of such inventions as I have perfected. 1663 etc.

Swift, Jonathan (1667–1745). Travels into several remote nations of the world, by Lemuel Gulliver. 1726. *See col 1061, above.*

Sydenham, Thomas (1624–89). Observationes medicae. 1676.

Thompson, Sir Benjamin, Count Rumford (1753–1814). An inquiry concerning the heat excited by friction. Philosophical Trans of Royal Soc 88 1798.

— Proposals for a public institution of useful mechanical inventions (the Royal Institution). 1799.

— Complete works, with memoir. 5 vols Boston 1875–6.
Sparrow, W. J. Knight of the White Eagle: a biography of Rumford. 1964.

Thoresby, Ralph (1658–1725). Letters of eminent men addressed to Ralph Thoresby. Ed J. Hunter 2 vols 1832.

— [Further] letters to Thoresby. Ed W. T. Lancaster, Leeds 1921.

— Diary. Ed J. Hunter 2 vols 1832.

Tull, Jethro (1674–1741). The horse-hoing husbandry. 1733–40.

Tyson, Edward (1650–1708). Orang-outang. 1699; ed A. Montagu 1966 (facs).

Vaughan, Thomas (1622–66). The man-mouse [Henry More] tortured for gnawing the margins of Eugenius Philalethes [Vaughan]. 1650.

— The chemist's key to the doctrine of corruption and generation. 1657.

Vince, Samuel (1749–1821). A complete system of astronomy. 3 vols Cambridge 1797–1808, London 1814–23 (enlarged).

Vossius, Isaac (1618–1689). De motu marium et ventorum. Hague 1663, London 1677.

Waller, Richard (fl. 1680). Essayes of natural experiments made in the Accademia del Cimento. 1684; ed A. R. Hall, New York 1964 (facs). Tr Waller. *See* Robert Hooke, *above*.

Wallis, John (1616–1703). A discourse of gravity. Oxford 1674.

— Opera mathematica. 3 vols Oxford 1685–9.
See Edmond Halley and Thomas Hobbes, *above*.

Ward, Seth (1617–89). *See* Walter Pope *and Part 1, above*.

Watson, Richard (1737–1816). An essay on the subjects of chemistry. Cambridge 1771.

— A plan of chemical lectures. Cambridge 1771.

Watson, Sir William (1715–87). An account of the experiments to discover whether the electrical power would be sensible at great distances. 1748.

— An account of experiments [on] inoculating the small-pox. 1768.

Watt, James (1736–1819). *See* Thomas Beddoes, *above*.

Watts, Isaac (1674–1748). The knowledge of the heavens and thee arth made easy. 1726, 1728, 1736. *See cols 572, 1668, above.*

Webster, John (1610–82). Metallographia: or an history of metals. 1661, 1671. *See Part 1, above.*

Wesley, John (1703–91). The desideratum: or electricity made plain and useful. 1759, 1871. *See col 1630, above.*

— A survey of the wisdom of God in the creation: or a compendium of natural philosophy. 3 vols Bristol 1763, 1770.

Whiston, William (1667–1752). A new theory of the earth. 1696.

— Memoirs written by himself. 1753.

White, Gilbert (1720–93). The natural history of Selborne. 1789.
Martin, E. A. A bibliography of White. 1897, 1934.

Whitehurst, John (1713–88). An inquiry into the original state and formation of the earth. 1778, 1786 (enlarged).

Wilkins, John (1614–72). Mathematical and philosophical works. 2 vols 1802. *See Part 1 and* W. Pope, *above*.

Willis, Benjamin. *See* Benjamin Hoadly, *above*.

Willis, Thomas (1621–75). Cerebri anatome. 1664; ed W. Feindel, Montreal 1966.

— Pharmaceutice rationalis. 2 pts 1673–5.

Willughby or Willoughby, Francis (1635–72). Ornithologiae libri tres. 1676; ed J. Ray 1678 (trn).

— Historia piscium. Ed J. Ray, Oxford 1686.

Wollaston, Francis John Hyde (1762–1823). A plan of a course of chemical lectures. Cambridge 1794, 1805.

Woodward, John (1665–1728). An essay towards a natural history of the earth. 1695, 1702, 1723.

— An attempt towards a natural history of the fossils of England. 2 vols 1728–9.
Arbuthnot, John. An examination of Dr Woodward's account of the deluge. 1697.

Worcester, Marquis of. *See* Edward Somerset.

Wotton, William (1666–1727). Reflections upon ancient and modern learning. 1694, 1697.

Wren, Sir Christopher (1632–1723). Parentalia: or the lives of the Wrens. Ed his son 1740.
Jones, H. W. Wren and natural philosophy. Notes & Records of Royal Soc 13 1958. With list of Wren's works.

Wright, Thomas (of Durham) (1711–86). Clavis coelestis. 1742; ed M. A. Hoskin 1967 (facs).

— An original theory of new hypothesis of the universe. 1750.

Young, Thomas (1773–1829). Outlines of experiments respecting sound and light. Philosophical Trans of Royal Soc 90 1800.

H. W. J.

XIII. LAW

For lists of general authorities on the history of English law and bibliographies of English legal history, see vol I.

Aston, R. Placita latinè rediviva: a book of entries. 1660, 1661, 1673.

Atkyns, Sir Robert. An enquiry into the power of dispensing with penal statutes. 1689, 1689.

—— The power, jurisdiction and priviledge of Parliament; also a discourse concerning the ecclesiastical jurisdiction in the realm of England. 1689. His writings were collected as Parliamentary and political tracts, 1734.

Ayliffe, John. Parergon juris canonici anglicani: a commentary to the canons and constitutions of the Church of England. 1726, 1734.

Bacon, Matthew. A new abridgment of the law. 5 vols 1736–66, 8 vols 1832 (7th edn).

Barrington, Daines. Observations on the statutes, chiefly the more ancient from Magna Charta to the twenty-first of James I. 1766, Dublin 1767, 1769, London 1775, 1796.

Bathurst, Henry, 2nd Earl. Introduction to the law relative to trials at Nisi Prius. 1767, Dublin 1768. Various edns continued by Sir F. Buller to 1817.

Bayley, Sir John. A short treatise on the law of bills of exchange. 1789, 1797, 1849 (6th edn).

Blackstone, Sir William. Magna Charta and Charta de Foresta. Oxford 1759.

—— Law tracts [containing Essay on collateral consanguinity, Considerations on copyholders, Law of descents, Great Charter etc]. 2 vols Oxford 1762, 1 vol Dublin 1767, 1 vol Oxford 1771.

—— Commentaries on the laws of England. 4 vols Oxford 1765–9, London 1783 (rev). Numerous edns to 1876.

Blount, Thomas. Fragmenta antiquitatis: antient tenures of land and jocular customs of some mannors. 1679, York 1784, London 1815, 1874 (with addn by W. C. Hazlitt and suppl), 1909 (priv ptd).

—— A law dictionary, interpreting difficult and obscure words and terms in common or statute, ancient or modern lawes. 1670, 1691, 1717.

Bohun, William. A collection of debates, reports, orders and resolutions of the House of Commons, touching the right of electing members to serve in Parliament. [1702].

—— Privilegia Londini: or the laws, customs and priviledges of the City of London. 1702, 1716, 1723.

—— Institutio legalis: or an introduction to the study and practice of the laws of England. 2 vols 1708–9, 1 vol 1713, 1724, 1732.

—— Cursus cancellariae: or the course of proceedings in the High Court of Chancery. 1715, 1723.

—— The practising attorney or lawyer's office, containing the business of an attorney. 1724, 1726, 2 vols 1732, 1737.

—— Law of tithes. 1730, 1731, 1744, 1760.

—— Declarations and pleadings in the Court of King's Bench and Common Pleas. 1733, 1743.

Bond, John. A complete guide for justices of peace. 1685, 1687, 1696, 1699 (2nd edn rev), 1706–7.

Boote, Richard. An historical treatise of an action or suit at law. 1766, 1781, 1795, 1839 (7th edn).

—— Solicitor's practice in the High Court of Chancery. 1767, 1775 (4th edn).

Booth, George. The nature and practice of real actions in their writs and processes. 1701, 1704, New York 1808, London 1911 (with the notes of George Hill).

Bott, Edmund. A collection of decisions of the Court of King's Bench upon the poor's laws. 1771, 1773 2 vols 1793, 3 vols 1800, 3 vols 1807; suppls, 1815–33.

Bridgman, Sir Orlando. Conveyances: being select precedents of deeds and instruments concerning the most considerable estates in England. 1682, 2 vols in 1 1725 (5th edn).

Browne, Arthur. Compendious view of the ecclesiastical law of Ireland; to which is added a sketch of the practice of the Ecclesiastical Courts. 2 vols Dublin 1797–99, 1 vol Dublin 1803.

Browne, William. Formulae benè placitandi: a book of entries. 2 pts 1671–3, 2 vols 1674–5.

—— Modus intrandi placita generalia: the entring clerk's introduction, being precedents of declarations and other pleadings. 2 pts 1674, 1687, 1702–3.

—— Compendious and accurate treatise of recoveries and fines. 1678, 1684, 1693, 1704, 2 vols 1718–19, 1 vol 1725.

—— Praxis almae Curiae Cancellariae: a collection of precedents. 2 vols 1694–5, 1704–5, 1714, 1725.

—— Practice of the Courts of King's Bench and Common Pleas. 1696, 1696, 1700 (2nd edn).

—— Methodus novissima intrandi placita generalia: or a new, compleat and exact method of drawing and entring declarations, pleas [etc]. 1699.

Brydall, John. Jus sigilli: or the law of England touching his Majestie's four principal seales. 1673.

—— Speculum juris anglicani: or a view of the laws of England. 1673.

—— Jus imaginis apud Anglos: or the law of England relating to the nobility and gentry. 1675.

—— Jura coronae: his Majesties royal rights and prerogatives asserted. 1680. Sometimes wrongly credited to Matthew Hale, below, as Sacra Coronae.

—— Ars transferendi dominium: or a sure law guide to the conveyancer. 2 vols 1697, 1 vol 1699, 1701, 1702.

Burn, Richard. The Justice of the Peace and parish officer. 2 vols 1755, 1756, 1 vol 1756, 3 vols 1757, 1 vol 1758, 3 vols 1758, 1763, 2 vols 1764, 3 vols 1765, 4 vols 1766, 1769–70, 1772, 1774 (with suppl), 1776, 1780, 1785 (16th edn, last ed Burn). 15 further edns pbd at various dates to 5 vols 1869.

—— Ecclesiastical law. 1760, 2 vols 1763, 1765 (with addn), 4 vols 1767 (2nd edn), 1775, 1781, 1788, 1797; ed Robert Phillimore 1842.

Chitty, Joseph. A treatise on the law of bills of exchange. 1799, 1878 (11th edn).

Craig, Sir Thomas. Jus feudale, tribus libris comprehensum, quibus non solum consuetudines Feudales et Praediorum Jura. Edinburgh 1655, 1665; ed Menckenius, Leipzig 1716 (with addns); 1732; ed J. Baillie 1752.

—— Scotland's soveraignty asserted: a dispute concerning homage against those who maintain Scotland is a fee-liege of England. 1695.

Cruise, William. An essay on the nature and operation of fines. 1783, 2 vols 1786, 1794.

—— Essay on uses. 1795, Dublin 1796.

Dalrymple, Sir James Viscount Stair. The institutions of the laws of Scotland. Edinburgh 1681, 1693, 1759, 2 vols 1826–31, 1832.

—— Modus litigandi: or form of process delivered before the Lords of Council and Session. Edinburgh 1681.

Dalton, Michael. The countrey justice: conteyning the practice of the justices of the peace. 1618, 1619 (rev) etc, 1746 (with large addns).

—— Officium vicecomitum: the office and authority of sherifs. 1623, 1662 (rev), 1670, 2 pts 168[1]–2, 1700. The standard authority.

Dawson, George. Origo legum: or a treatise of the origin of laws and their obliging power. 1694.

Degge, Sir Simon. The parson's counsellor, with the law of tithes. 1676, 1677, 1681, 1695, 1703, 1820.

Dutton, Matthew. Law of landlords and tenants in Ireland. 2 vols Dublin 1726.

— Office and authority of a justice of the peace for Ireland. Dublin 1709 (2nd edn), 1718, 1726, 1727.

Eden, William Baron Auckland. Principles of penal law. 1771, 1771, Dublin 1772, London 1775 (3rd edn).

Elsynge, Henry. Ancient method and manner of holding of parliaments in England. 1660, 1662, 1663, 1675 (3rd edn), 1679, 1768 (5th and most accurate edn).

Erskine, John. Principles of the law of Scotland. 2 vols in 1 Edinburgh 1754, 1757, 1 vol 1764, 1769, 1777, 1783, 1791, 1911 (21st edn).

— Institute of the laws of Scotland. 2 vols Edinburgh 1773, 1785, 1793, 1805, 1812, 1824–8, 1838, 1871.

Euer, Sampson. Doctrina placitandi: ou l'art & science de bon pleading, by S.E. 1677, 1677. Euer's system of pleading, 1771, contains trn.

— Tryals per pais: or the law concerning juries by Nisi Prius. 1665, 1666, 1682, 2 pts 1695–1700, 1702, 1718, 1725, 1739, 2 vols 1766, Dublin 1793. Edns from 1682 by G. Duncombe.

Fearne, Charles. Essay on the learning of contingent remainders and executory devises. 1772 etc, 2 vols Dublin 1844 (10th edn).

Foster, Sir Michael. Report of some proceedings of the Commission of Oyer and Terminer and gaol delivery for trial of the rebels in 1746; to which are added discourses upon Crown law. Oxford 1762, Dublin 1763, 1767, London 1776 (2nd edn), Dublin 1791, London 1792, 1809.

Gibson, Edmund. Synodus anglicana: or the constitution and proceedings of an English convocation. 1702; ed E. Cardwell, Oxford 1854. The authoritative work.

— Codex juris ecclesiastici anglicani. 1713, 2 vols Oxford 1761.

Gilbert, Sir Geoffrey. The law of tenures including theory and practice of copyholds. 1730, 1738, 1757, Dublin 1758, London 1796 (4th edn), 1824.

— The law and uses of trusts. 1734, 1741; ed E. B. Sugden 1811.

— The history and practice of the Court of Common Pleas. 1737, 1761, 1779, Dublin 1792.

— Historical view of the Court of Exchequer. 1738. A first instalment of the Treatise on the Exchequer, 1758.

— The law and practice of ejectments. 1734, 1741. Rewritten by C. Runnington as Action of Ejectment, 1781.

— The law of devises, revocations and last wills. 1756, 1773 (3rd edn), Dublin 1792.

— Treatise on the Court of Exchequer. 1758.

— The law of distresses and replevins. 1775, 1780, Dublin 1792, London 1794, 1823 (4th edn).

Godolphin, John. The orphan's legacy: or a testamentary abridgement. 1674, 1677, 1685, 1701.

— Repertorium canonicum: or the abridgement of the ecclesiastical laws of this Realm. 1678, 1680, 1687.

— A view of the Admiralty jurisdiction whereunto is added an extract of the ancient laws of Oleron. 1681, 1685.

Hale, Sir Matthew. Summary of the pleas of the Crown. 1678, 1678, 1682, 1685, 1694, 1707, 5 pts 1716, 3 pts 1716, 1759, 1773.

— History and analysis of the common law of England. 1713, 1716, 1739, Dublin 1792, 2 vols 1794, 1820.

— The analysis of the law of England. 1713, 1716, 1739, [1779], Dublin [1792] (4th edn), London 1794, 1820.

— Historia placitorum coronae: or history of the pleas of the Crown. 2 vols 1736, Dublin 1778, London 1800.

— Jurisdiction of the Lords House of Parliament. 1796.

Hargrave, Francis. Juridical arguments and collections. 2 vols 1797–9.

Hawkins, William. Pleas of the Crown. 2 pts 1716–21, 1724–6, 1 vol 1739, 1762, 1771, 2 pts 1777–87, 4 vols 1795, 2 vols 1824.

Heywood, Samuel. A digest of the law respecting county elections. 1790, 1812.

A digest of the law respecting borough elections. 1797.

Highmore, Anthony. History of mortmain, the statutes relative to charitable uses and exposition of the Mortmain Act. 1787, 1793, 1809.

Hobbes, Thomas. Dialogue between a philosopher and a student of the common laws of England. 1681.

Home, Henry Lord Kames. Statute law of Scotland abridged. Edinburgh 1757, 1767, 1769.

— Historical law tracts. 2 vols Edinburgh 1758, 1761, 1776, 1792.

— Principles of equity. Edinburgh 1760, 1767, 2 vols 1778, 1 vol 1800, 1825.

Hope, Sir Thomas. Minor practicks or treatise of the Scottish law [with] a Discourse on the rise and progress of the law of Scotland [by Alexander Bayne]. Edinburgh 1726.

Hughes, W. The grand abridgment of the law. 3 vols 1660–2.

Hume, David. Commentaries on the law of Scotland respecting the description and punishment of crimes. 2 vols 1797, 1819, 1829 (with suppl by B. R. Bell), 1844.

Jacob, Giles. Compleat court keeper: or land-steward's assistant. 1713, 1715, 1724, 1740, 1741, 1752, 1764, 1781, 1819.

— The accomplish'd conveyancer: containing deeds and instruments used in conveyancing. 3 vols 1714–15, 1736, 1 vol 1750.

— Lex mercatoria: or the merchant's companion. 1718, 1729.

— Lex constituonis: being a complete treatise of all the laws and statutes relating to the King and prerogative of the Crown, Nobility, House of Lords, Commons etc. 1719, 1737.

— Law dictionary. 1729. Numerous edns to 1809. Enlarged by T. E. Tomlins, 1797, and issued thereafter in 2 vols.

Kyd, Stewart. Treatise on the law of bills of exchange and promissory notes. 1790, Dublin 1791, London 1795.

— A treatise on the law of awards. Dublin 1791, London 1795, 1799 (2nd edn).

— A treatise on the law of corporations. 2 vols 1793–4.

Lilly, John. Continuation of the practical register [by William Style, below]. 2 vols 1710.

— Practical conveyancer. 1719, 1732, 1742.

— Practical register: or a general abridgment of the law. 2 vols 1719, 1735, 1745 (with suppl).

— Modern entries: being a collection of select pleadings in Courts of King's Bench, Common Pleas and Exchequer. 1723, 1741, 1741, 1758, 1771, 2 vols 1791, Dublin 1792.

Lucas, Charles. Great Charter of the liberties of Dublin. Dublin 1749.

MacDouall, Andrew Lord Bankton. Institutes of the laws of Scotland in civil rights. 3 vols Edinburgh 1751–3.

Mackenzie, Sir George. Laws and customs of Scotland in matters criminal. Edinburgh 1678, 1699.

— Institutions of the laws of Scotland. Edinburgh 1684, 1688, London 1694, Edinburgh 1699, 1706, 1723, 1725, 1730, 1758.

— On the modern eloquence of the Bar. Edinburgh 1704, 1707, 1711.

Mackenzie, James. Origin and progress of fees: or constitution and transmission of heritable rights. Edinburgh 1734, 1739, 1761, 1782 (with suppls to J. Spotiswood, Introduction, below).

Mallory, John. Modern entries in English: being a select collection of pleadings and also of writs. 2 vols 1734–5, 1741, 1791.

— Quare impedit. 1737. Vol 3 of J. Mallory, Modern entries.

Maseres, Francis. An enquiry into the extent of the power of juries on trials of indictment. 1785, 1792.

Meriton, George. The touchstone of wills, testaments and administrations. 1668, 1671, 1674.

— The parson's monitor: consisting of such causes and matters as concern the clergy. 1681.

Molloy, Charles. De jure maritimo et navali: or a treatise of affaires maritime and of commerce. 1676, 1677, 1682, 1688, 1690 (4th edn), 1701, 1707, 1722, 1744, 2 vols 1769, 1778.

Molyneux, William. Case of Ireland's being bound by Acts of Parliament made in England. Dublin 1697, 1698, 1719, 1720, 1725, London 1740, 1742, 1770, Belfast 1776, Dublin 1782.

Nelson, William. Office and authority of a justice of the peace. 1704, 1707, 1710, 1714, 1715, 1718, 1721, 1724, 1726, 1729, 1736, 2 vols 1745.

— Lex testamentaria: or a compendious system of all the laws of England, concerning last wills and testaments. 1714, 1724, 1728, 1733.

— Lex maneriorum: or the laws and customs of England relating to manors. 1726, 1728, 1733, 1735.

— The laws of England concerning the game: of hunting, hawking, fishing and fowling. 1727, 1732, 1736, 1751, 1753, 1762.

Newnam, William [et al]. The complete conveyancer. 3 vols 1781–[5?], Dublin 1785–6, London 1788, 6 vols 1800.

Oughton, Thomas. Ordo judiciorum: sive methodus procedendi in negotiis et litibus in foro ecclesiastico-civili britannico et hibernico. 2 vols 1728–38, 1738 (vol 2 a duplicate of 1st edn).

Park, Sir James. A system of the law of marine insurances. 1787, Dublin 1792, London 1796, 1800, 1802, 2 vols 1809, 1817, 1 vol 1842.

Pearce, Thomas. Complete Justice of the Peace and parish officer. 1756.

Richardson, Robert. The attorney's practice in the Court of King's Bench. 2 vols 1739, 1743, 1750, 1759, 1769, 1776, 1789 (8th edn), Dublin 1792.

— The attorney's practice in the Court of Common Pleas. 1741, 2 vols 1746, 1758, 1769, [1778], Dublin 1792 (7th edn).

— Law of testaments and last wills. 1744, 1769.

Robinson, Thomas. The common law of Kent: or the customs of gavelkind. 1741, 1788, 1822, 1858, 1897.

Rolle, Henry. Abridgment des plusieurs cases et resolutions del common ley; with preface by Sir Matthew Hale. 2 vols 1668.

Ryley, William. Placita parliamentaria: pleadings in Parliament, with the judgements thereon in the reigns of Edward I and Edward II. 1661.

Sayer, Joseph. The law of costs. 1768, 1777, Dublin 1792.

— The law of damages. 1770, Dublin 1792.

Scobell, Henry. Modus tenendi Parliamenta et consilia in Hibernia. Dublin [1692], 1772.

Scroggs, Sir William. The practice of Courts Leet and Courts Baron. 1701, 1702, 1714 (with addns), 1728, 1774.

Sheppard, William. Office of a Justice of the Peace. 2 pts in 1 vol 1661–2.

— Practical counsellor in the law: touching fines, common recoveries, judgements and the execution thereof. 1670, 1671.

Somers, Baron John. Jura populi anglicani: or the subject's right of petitioning set forth. 1701.

— Guide to the knowledge of the rights and priveleges of Englishmen. 1757, 1771.

Spelman, Sir Henry. Of the law terms. 1684. Written in 1614, according to Dugdale.

Spotiswood, John. Introduction to the knowledge of the style of writs. Edinburgh 1708, 1715, 1727, 1752.

Style, William. Regestum practicale: or the practical register, concerning the common-laws and the practice thereon. 1657, 1670, 1671, 1694, 1707. Continued by J. Lilly, above.

Tidd, William. Practice of the Court of King's Bench in personal actions. 2 vols 1790–4, 1799, 1803, 1817 (6th edn), 1821, 1824, 1828 (9th edn).

— Law of costs in civil actions. 1792, 1793, Dublin 1793.

— Practical forms: an appendix to the Practice of the Court of King's Bench in personal actions. 1799, 1840 (8th edn).

Townesend, George. Preparative to pleading: for the instruction of clerks of the Court of Common Pleas. 1675, 1685, 1713, 1721.

Waterhous, Edward. Fortescutus illustratus: or a commentary on that nervous treatise De laudibus legum Angliae by Sir John Fortescue. 1663.

Wentworth, John. A complete system of pleading. 10 vols 1797–9.

Williams, Thomas. The excellency and praeheminence of the law of England. 1680.

Winch, Sir Humphrey. Le beau-pledeur: a book of entries containing declarations, informations and other select pleadings. 1680. Compiled before 1625.

Wiseman, Sir Robert. The law of laws: or excellency of the civil law above all other human laws. 2 pts 1657–64, 1685–6.

Yorke, Philip 1st Earl of Hardwicke. A discourse of the judicial authority belonging to the office of Master of the Rolls in the High Court of Chancery. 1727, 1728.

Zouch, Richard. The jurisdiction of the Admiralty of England asserted. 1663, 1683, 1685.

W. W. S. B.

XIV. EDUCATION

A. CONTEMPORARY TREATISES

(1) GENERAL WORKS
(in alphabetical order)

An account of the general nursery or colledg of infants. 1686.

Addison, Joseph. A discourse on ancient and modern learning. 1739.

Ainsworth, Robert. The most natural and easie way of institution: containing proposals for making a domestic education less chargeable to parents, and more easie and beneficial to children. 1698, 1736.

Ash, J. Sentiments of education. 2 vols 1777.

Barclay, James. Treatise on education: or an easy method of acquiring language and teaching youth such moral precepts as are necessary to the conduct of life. Edinburgh 1743, 1749.

Barnes, Thomas. A brief comparison of arguments in favour of public and private education. Memoirs of Literary & Philosophical Soc, Manchester 2 1785.

— A plan for the improvement and extension of liberal education in Manchester. Ibid.

— A discourse delivered at the commencement of the Manchester Academy. Warrington [1786].

Baxter, Richard. The catechizing of families. 1683.

— Compassionate counsel to all young men. 1682.

The bear-leaders: or modern travelling stated in a proper light. 1758.

Beattie, James. Essays. Edinburgh 1778. Includes essay on the utility of classical learning, 1769.

Bell, Andrew. An experiment in education made at the Male Asylum in Madras, suggesting a system by which a school or family may teach itself under the superintendence of the master or parent. 1797, 1805.

Bettesworth, J. Observations on education in general, but particularly on naval education. 1782.

B[rokesby], F[rancis]. Of education with respect to grammar schools and the universities, concluding with directions to young students in the universities. 1701, 1751.

Brown, John. Essays on the characteristics of the Earl of Shaftesbury. 1751.

— Sermons on various subjects. 1764. 3 on 'the first principles of education'.

— Thoughts on civil liberty, on licentiousness and faction. Newcastle 1765.

Budgell, Eustace. Spectator nos 307, 313, 337, 353 1711.

Burgh, James. Thoughts on education. 1747.

Burnet, Gilbert. Thoughts on education. 1761, Aberdeen 1900. Written c. 1668.

Butler, Joseph. The London Charity Schools: a sermon. 1745. In Works, ed J. H. Bernard vol 1, 1900.

Caraccioli, Marquis of. The true mentor: or an essay on the education of young people of fashion translated from the French. 1760.

Chapman, George. A treatise on education. Edinburgh 1773, 1790 (4th and best edn).

The charter of King Charles II, impowering Erasmus Smith esq to erect grammar schools in the Kingdom of Ireland, and to endow the same with convenient maintenance for schoolmasters, and to make further provision for education of children at the university, and for several other charitable uses; together with an act of Parliament, for the further application of the said charity. Dublin 1724.

Chesterfield, Philip Dormer Stanhope, Earl of. Letters to his son Philip Stanhope. Ed E. Stanhope 2 vols 1774; Supplement, 1787; ed A. Calthrop, with introd by C. Strachey, 1901; Letters, ed B. Dobrée 6 vols 1932.

— The art of pleasing: or instructions for youth in a series of letters to his nephew; and Lord Burleigh's advice to his son. 1783.

— Letters to his godson and successor, [with appendix, letters to A. C. Stanhope]. Ed Earl of Carnarvon, Oxford 1890.

Clarke, John (Master of Hull Grammar School). An essay upon the education of youth in grammar schools. 1720, 1730 (2nd edn with large addns).

— An essay upon study: wherein directions are given for the due conduct thereof, and the collection of a library proper for the purpose. 1731.

Coke, William. A poetical essay on the early part of education; to which is prefixed an enquiry into the discipline of the ancients, with some observations on that of our public schools. Oxford 1785.

Colman, G. and B. Langton. The modern method of education. Connoisseur no 22 1754.

The common errors in the education of children and their consequences, with the methods to remedy them. 1744.

Cornish, Joseph. An attempt to display the importance of classical learning, with some candid remarks on Mr Knox's liberal education. 1783.

The country-mans care and the citizens feare, in bringing up their children in good education. 1641.

Craig, William (Lord Craig). Education for leisure. Mirror no 106 1780.

Croft, George (Master of Beverley Grammar School). General observations concerning education applied to the author's method in particular. Hull 1775.

— A plan of education delineated and vindicated, to which are added a letter to a young gentleman designed for the university and for holy orders, and a short dissertation upon the stated provision and reasonable expectations of publick teachers. Wolverhampton 1784.

— A short commentary on moral writings of Dr Paley and Mr Gisborne: observations on the duties of trustees and conductors of grammar schools. Birmingham 1797.

Cumberland, Richard. Public school education. Observer nos 36–7 [1785].

Dodsley, Robert. The preceptor: first principles of polite learning. 2 vols 1748, 1754, 1763, 1783 (7th edn).

Edgeworth, Maria and Richard Lovell. Practical education. 2 vols 1798, 3 vols 1801.

Of education. 1734, 1774.

Education of children and young students in all its branches, with a short catalogue of the best books in polite learning and the sciences: the second edition. 1752.

Elphinston, James. Education: a poem. 1762.

An essay on education, showing how Latin, Greek and other languages may be learn'd more easily, quickly and perfectly than they commonly are. 1711.

Foot, William. An essay on education: intended principally to make the business of grammar schools of real service to youth, as are not designed for the university. Bristol [1750?].

[Fordyce, David]. Dialogues concerning education. 2 vols 1745–8, 1768.

Franck, Augustus Hermann. Pietas Hallensis. 1705.

Freke, W. Select essays tending to the universal reformation of learning: concluded with the art of war. 1693.

Genlis, Comtesse de. Adelaide and Theodore, or letters on education: containing all the principles relative to three different plans of education to that of Princes and to those of young persons of both sexes, translated from the French. 3 vols [1781], 1788 (3rd edn).

'A gentleman' (Thomas Baker, St John's College, Cambridge). Reflections upon learning: wherein is shewn the insufficiency thereof in its several particulars in order to evince the usefulness and necessity of revelation. 1699, 1714 (5th edn).

'A gentleman of Bristol' (S. Butler). An essay upon education intended to show that the common method is defective, with a plan of a new method more extensive and of more general use. nd.

[Gerard, Alexander]. Plan of education in the Marischal college and university of Aberdeen. Aberdeen 1755.

Girrard, J. Practical lectures on education. Exon 1756.

Godwin, William. Enquiry concerning political justice. 2 vols 1793. Bk 6, especially ch 8 on national education.

— The enquirer: reflections on education, manners and literature. 1797. Especially pt 1.

Goldsmith, Oliver. An enquiry into the present state of polite learning in Europe. 1759, 1774 (rev).

[Gordon, J.] Occasional thoughts on the study and character of classical authors, on the course of literature, and the present plan of a learned education. 1762.

Graham, Catherine Macaulay. Letters on education. 1790.

Gray, Thomas. Alliance of education and government: a fragment with commentary. 1775. Written 1748.

— Works. Ed E. Gosse 4 vols 1884. Vol 1, pp. 113f; vol 2, p. 187.

Guardian nos 62, 72, 94, 105, 155 1713.

Hartley, David. Observations on man. 2 vols 1749. On association of ideas.

Helvétius, Claude Adrien. A treatise on man, his intellectual faculties and his education. Tr W. Hooper 2 vols 1777.

Hirst, William. The necessity and advantages of education. 1728.

Home, Henry (Lord Kames). Loose hints upon education, chiefly concerning the culture of the heart. Edinburgh 1781.

Huarte, Juan. Examen de ingenios: or the tryal of wits, made English by Mr Bellamy. 1698.

— A treatise of education and learning. 1734.

Hume, David. Essays and treatises on several subjects: new edition. 1758. Essays 16 and 26, both pbd in 1742.

Hutcheson, Francis. Inquiry into ideas of beauty and virtue and of moral good and evil. 1725, 1753 (5th edn). On Utilitarianism.

—— A system of moral philosophy. 2 vols 1755.

Kippis, Andrew. A sermon on occasion of a new academical institution among Protestant dissenters for the education of their ministers and youth. 1786.

Knox, Vicesimus. Works, with biographical preface. 7 vols 1824.

—— Essays, moral and literary. 2 vols 1778–9, 3 vols 1823.

—— Liberal education: or a practical treatise on acquiring useful and polite learning. 1781. See Joseph Cornish, above, and Percival Stockdale, below.

—— Letter to Lord North, Chancellor of the University of Oxford. 1789. In Liberal education, 10th edn.

—— Personal nobility: or letters to a young nobleman on the conduct of his studies. 1793.

Kruger, John Gottlob. An essay on the education of children (from the German). 1765.

Law, William. A serious call to a devout and holy life, adapted to the state and condition of all orders of Christians. [1728]. Chs 18–19 on education of boys and girls respectively.

Letters containing a plan of education for rural academies. 1773.

Locke, John. Some thoughts concerning education. 1693, 1705 (5th edn).

—— Educational writings. Ed J. W. Adamson, Cambridge 1922.

—— Educational writings: a critical edition. Ed J. L. Axtell, Cambridge 1968. This reprints 5th edn, 1705.

Villey, P. L'influence de Montaigne sur les idées pédagogiques de Locke et de Rousseau. Paris 1911.

Taglialatela, E. Locke, educatore: studio critico. Rome 1920.

Thiele, E. A. Montaigne und Locke: ihre Stellung zur Erziehung zur Selbsttätigkeit. Leipzig 1920.

Macnab, H. G. A plan of reform in the mode of instruction. Glasgow 1786.

Malcolm, Daniel. A collection of letters in which the imperfection of learning and a remedy are hinted. Edinburgh 1739.

Molesworth, Robert, Viscount. An account of Denmark etc. 1694. Long preface criticizing contemporary practice. See reply by J. Crull, Denmark vindicated, 1694.

Monro, George. An essay upon Christian education. 1712.

More, Hannah. Thoughts on the importance of the manners of the great to general society. 1788, 1809 (new edn).

A letter to the author of Thoughts on the manners of the great. 1788.

—— Remarks on the speech of M. Dupont in the national convention on religion and public education. 1793.

See also entries under Education of Women and Girls, below.

Nelson, James. An essay on the government of children. 1753, 1763 (3rd edn).

Newton, John. The English academy: or a brief introduction to the seven liberal arts. 1677, 1693.

Northmore, Thomas. Of education founded upon principles: part the first [all pbd]. 1800.

Mr Orde's plan for an improved system of education in Ireland. Dublin 1777.

Paine, Thomas. The rights of man. 2 pts 1791–2.

Paley, William. The principles of moral and political philosophy. 1785. On Utilitarianism.

Parr, Samuel. A discourse on education and on the plans pursued in charity schools. [1786].

Parsons, John Weddell. Essays on education. 1796.

P[etty], W[illiam]. The advice to Mr Samuel Hartlib for the advancement of some particular parts of learning. 1647, 1648.

Philpot, Stephen. An essay on the advantage of a polite education joined with a learned one. 1747.

The pleasing instructor, with new thoughts on education. 1770.

Price, Richard. The evidence for a future improvement in the state of mankind with the means and duty of promoting it: a discourse to the supporters of a new academical institution among Protestant dissenters. 1787.

Priestley, Joseph. An essay on a course of liberal education for civil and active life. 1765, 1768, 1778, 1793.

—— An essay on the first principles of government. 1768, 1771. Especially pt 2, section 2.

—— Miscellaneous observations relating to education more especially as it respects the conduct of the mind; to which is added an essay on a course of liberal education. 1778, 1788, 1796.

—— The proper objects of education. 1791.

—— A particular attention to the instruction of the young recommended in a discourse. 1791.

Proposals for an amendment of school instruction. 1772.

[Pugh, John]. The tutor's advice to parents concerning the education of their children. 1718.

Ramsay, A. A plan of education for a young Prince. 1732. Observations on a new plan of the education of a young prince by the Chevalier Ramsay, in a letter to the author. 1732. Signed A.B.

Reney, J. Proposals for erecting an academy on a new and extensive plan. 1772.

Rollin, C. New thoughts concerning education. 1735.

Rousseau, J. J. An expostulatory letter from J. J. Rousseau, citizen of Geneva, to Christopher de Beaumont, Archbishop of Paris; to which is prefixed the mandate of the said prelate, and also the proceedings of the parliament of Paris relative to the new treatise on education intituled Emilius. 1763.

—— Emilius and Sophia: or a new system of education translated [by W. Kenrick]. 4 vols 1762, 1767, 1783.

—— Emilius: or an essay on education, translated from the French. 3 vols Edinburgh 1763, 1768. A different trn.

—— Emilius: or an essay on education, translated from the French by Mr Nugent. 2 vols 1763, Dublin 1765.

Gerdil, Giacinto, Cardinal. Reflections on education, relative both to theory and practice in which some of the principles attempted to be established by Mr Rousseau in his Emilius are occasionally examined and refuted. 2 vols 1765. Tr from French.

[Shaftesbury, Earl of]. Several letters written by a noble lord to a young man at the university. 1716.

[Shaw, Peter]. The reflector: representing human affairs as they are, and may be improved. 1750, 1762 (as The tablet). In 4 sections: 1, Of literature and education; 3 has sub-section Of meliorating the universities of Europe.

Sheridan, Thomas. British education, in three parts. 1756, Dublin 1756, 1757, London 1769 (rev).

—— A general view of the scheme for the improvement of education. [Dublin 1758].

—— A plan of education for the young nobility and gentry of Great Britain. Dublin 1769, London 1769.

A letter to a school-master in the country, from his friend in town, relative to Mr Sheridan's scheme of education. Dublin 1758.

An enquiry into the plan and pretensions of Mr Sheridan. Dublin 1758.

A true history of the scheme for creating a new seminary. Dublin 1769.

A short address to the public. 1783.

An examen of Mr Sheridan's plan. 1784.

Smith, Adam. An inquiry into the nature and causes of the wealth of nations. 1776. Bk 5, articles 2–3, pt 3, Of the expense of the institutions for the education of youth.

Steele, Sir Richard. Tatler nos 63, 173, 234, 252 1709–10.

—— Spectator nos 157, 168, 230, 294, 330, 430 1712–13.

—— Guardian nos 72, 94 1713.

Stockdale, Percival. An examination whether education at a great school or by private tuition is preferable, with remarks on Mr Knox's liberal education. 1782.

Swift, Jonathan. Works. Ed Walter Scott 19 vols 1814. Vol 9, An essay on modern education: of the education of ladies.

Talbott, James. The Christian school master: or the duty of those who are employ'd in the publick instruction of children, especially in charity schools. 1707, 1811.

Tatler nos 63, 173, 197, 234, 252–3 1709–10.

Tillotson, John. Six sermons. 1694. 3–5, Of education of children.

Tryon, T. A new method of educating children. 1695.

Todd, J. Schoolboy and young gentleman's assistant: a plan of education. Edinburgh 1748.

Turnbull, George. Observations upon liberal education in all its branches designed for the assistance of young gentlemen desirous of making improvements in their studies. 1742.

Vincent, William (headmaster, Westminster School, 1788–1803). A defence of public education. 1801, 1802 (3rd edn).

[Walker, Obadiah]. Of education especially of young gentlemen, in two parts. Oxford 1673, 1699 (6th edn).

Walker, William. Some improvements in the art of teaching: a short way to bring a scholar to variety and elegancy in writing Latin. 1669 (2nd edn), 1700 (7th edn), 1730 (9th edn).

Wase, Christopher. Considerations concerning free-schools, as settled in England. Oxford 1678.

Watts, Isaac. A treatise on the education of children and youth. 1769 (2nd edn). First pbd in Posthumous works, 1754.

West, Gilbert. Education: a poem. 1751.

Whitchurch, James Wadham. An essay upon education. 1772.

Williams, David (founder of Literary Fund). A treatise upon education. 1774.

— Lectures on education. 3 vols 1789.

Wilson, Thomas. The true Christian method of educating the children both of the poor and rich. 1724.

[Witherspoon, John]. A series of letters on education. New York 1797, Bristol 1798.

Wotton, Henry. An essay on the education of children in the first rudiments of learning, together with a narrative of what knowledge William Wotton, a child six years of age, had attained unto upon the improvement of those rudiments in the Latin, Greek and Hebrew tongues. 1753. Written 1672.

Wynne, Richard. Essays on education by Milton, Locke and the authors of the Spectator. 1761.

(2) CURRICULUM

Arnold, Robert. A speech, setting forth the utility and excellencies of the mathematicks, made by Robert Arnold to several gentlemen and others belonging to his mathematical lecture. 1710.

Bellers, John. Proposals for raising a colledge of industry of all useful trades and husbandry with profit for the rich, a plentiful living for the poor and a good education for youth, which will be advantage to the government by an increase of the people and their riches. 1696.

Bentley, Richard. A dissertation upon the epistles of Phalaris. 1697.

Boswell, John. A method of study: or an useful library. 2 vols 1738–43.

B[oyle], C[harles]. Phalaridis epistolae, ex mss recensuit C.B. Oxford 1695.

— Dr Bentley's dissertations on the epistles of Phalaris etc, examin'd. 1698.

Bolingbroke, Henry St John, Viscount. Letters on the study and use of history. 2 vols 1752, 1770.

Cowley, Abraham. A proposition for the advancement of experimental philosophy. 1661. In Essays and other prose writings of Cowley, ed A. B. Gough, Oxford 1915.

D.F. [Daniel Defoe]. An essay upon projects. 1697.

Elphinston, James. The plan of education at Mr Elphinston's academy, Kensington. [c. 1760].

Enfield, William (1741–97). An essay on the cultivation of taste as a proper object of attention in the education of youth. Newcastle 1818.

Fleury, Claude. The history, choice and method of studies [from the French]. 1695.

Fontenelle, Bernard Le Bovier de. Une digression sur les anciens et les modernes. 1688.

General description of all trades. 1747.

[Godwin, William]. Account of a seminary at Epsom in Surrey for the instruction of twelve pupils in the Greek, Latin, French and English languages. 1783.

Hamilton, Sir William. Discussions on philosophy and literature, education and university reform. 1852.

Home, J. A classical contrasted with a fashionable education. Mirror no 15 1779.

Johnson, Samuel. Scheme for the [three] classes of a grammar school.

— A course of reading preparatory to a university course. Both in Boswell's Life, ch 2.

[Keith, William]. An essay on the education of a young British nobleman after he leaves the schools. 1730.

Knox, Vicesimus. Essays, moral and literary. 3 vols 1782, 2 vols 1795 (14th edn). Includes Classical learning vindicated; On the propriety of extending classical studies to natural and experimental philosophy; On Latin verse as an exercise at schools.

Mackenzie, Henry. Modern education superior to ancient. Lounger no 67 1786.

Maidwell, Lewis. An essay upon the necessity and excellency of education, with an account of erecting the Royal Mathematical Schole recommended by his Royal Highness, Lord High Admiral of England etc, upon a report from the Navy Board, declaring amongst other advantages to the nation the particular services of such a foundation to the Royal Navy of England, in its several capacitys. 1705.

Neglect of the study of English. Connoisseur no 42 1754. See A. Chalmers, British essayists vol 30, 1817.

Perrault, Charles. Parallèle des anciens et des modernes en ce qui regarde les arts et les sciences: dialogues. Paris 1688, 4 vols 1692–6.

[Petvin, J.] A letter concerning the use and method of studying history, by the author of Letters concerning mind. 1753.

Postlethwayt, Malachy. The merchant's public counting-house: or new mercantile institution; wherein is shewn the necessity of young merchants being bred to trade with greater advantages than they usually are, with a practicable plan for that purpose; also some remarks on the benefit of this instruction to the young nobility and gentry and such who are intended for the study of the law. 1751.

Swift, Jonathan. A tale of a tub, written for the universal improvement of mankind; to which is added an account of a battle between the antient and modern books in St James's Library. 1704, 1710 (5th and best edn).

— A proposal for correcting, improving and ascertaining the English tongue. 1712.

Temple, Sir William. Miscellanea. Pt 2, 1690. Contains essay on ancient and modern learning.

— Essays on ancient and modern learning and poetry. Ed J. E. Spingarn, Oxford 1909.

Tilley, A. The decline of the age of Louis XIV. Cambridge 1929. On ancient-and-modern controversy.

Trimmer, Sarah. Reflections upon the education of children in charity schools with outlines of appropriate instruction for the children of the poor. 1792.

Ward, Seth. Vindiciae academiarum; some briefe animadversions upon Mr Webster's book. 1654.

[Waterland, Daniel]. Advice to a young student, with a method of study for the first four years. 1730. With book lists.

Watts, Thomas. An essay on the proper method for forming the man of business in a letter. 1722.

Webster, John. Academiarum examen. 1654.

Wotton, William. Reflections upon ancient and modern learning. 1694, 1696 (adds Bentley's dissertation upon the epistles of Phalaris).

— A defense of the reflections upon ancient and modern learning, with observations upon the tale of a tub. 1705.

(3) HISTORICAL WORKS, MEMOIRS AND LETTERS

See also Education 1500–1660, vol 1, above.

Act of Uniformity, Documents relating to the settlement of the Church of England, by the Act of Uniformity of 1662. 1862.

Allen, W. O. and E. McClure. Two hundred years: the history of the Society for Promoting Christian Knowledge. 1898.

Aubrey, J. Letters written by eminent persons in the seventeenth and eighteenth centuries. 2 vols (vol 2 in 2 pts) 1813.

Bell, Andrew. Life of Rev Andrew Bell comprising the history of the rise and progress of mutual tuition, by Robert Southey and C. C. Southey. 3 vols 1844.

Bentham, Jeremy. Education of Bentham, by C. W. Everett. New York 1932.

Mack, M. P. Bentham: an Odyssey of ideas 1748–92. 1962.

Bentley, Richard
Monk, J. H. The life of Bentley. 2 vols 1833 (2nd edn).
White, R. J. Dr Bentley. 1965.

Bernard, Sir Thomas. Life, by James Baker. 1819.

Boultwood, M. E. A. Robert Raikes. Univ of Leeds Inst of Education Researches & Stud no 4 May 1951.

Fox Bourne, H. R. The life of John Locke. 2 vols 1876.

Brockbank, Thomas. The diary and letter-book of the Rev Thomas Brockbank 1671–1709. Ed R. Trappes-Lomax 1930 (Chetham Soc). On Oxford 1687–95.

Cairnes, W. T. John Newton: a vindication. In his Religion of Dr Johnson and other essays, Oxford 1946.

Calamy, Edmund. An abridgment of Mr Baxter's history of his life and times. 1702.

— An historical account of my own life. Ed J. T. Rutt 2 vols 1829.

Carlyle, Alexander ('Jupiter Carlyle'). Autobiography. Ed J. H. Burton, Edinburgh 1860 (2nd edn). On Edinburgh and Glasgow universities 1735–45.

Clarke, M. L. Greek studies in England 1700–1830. Cambridge 1945.

Cowie, L. W. The conflict of political, religious and social ideals in English education 1660–1714. Bull Inst of Historical Research 22 1949.

Crawford, B. U. Teaching by dialogue. PQ 3 1924.

— Questions and objections. PMLA 41 1926. Historical note on the catechetical method.

Cumberland, Richard. Memoirs of Richard Cumberland, written by himself. 2 vols 1806–7.

— The Cumberland letters: being the correspondence of Richard Denison Cumberland and George Cumberland 1771–84. Ed Clementina Black 1912. On Cambridge 1772 etc.

Curtis, S. J. History of education in Great Britain. 1948, 1953 (rev). Chs 4 and 14.

— The endowed school of Rear-Admiral Long at Burnt Yates, Ripley, Yorks. Univ of Leeds Inst of Education Researches & Stud no 2 May 1950.

Dale, R. W. and A. W. W. Dale. History of English congregationalism. 1907. Bk 5, ch 4: dissenting academies; bk 6, ch 2: national education.

Day, Thomas (author of Sandford and Merton)
Blackman, J. Life and writings of Day. 1862.
An account of the life and writings of Day. 1791.
Sadler, M. E. Day: an English disciple of Rousseau. Cambridge 1928.

Giguilliat, G. W. The author of Sandford and Merton. New York 1932.

Scott, S. H. The exemplary Mr Day 1748–89. 1935.

Dibdin, T. F. Reminiscences of a literary life. 2 vols 1836. On private schools 1784 onwards; St John's College, Oxford.

Dobbs, A. E. Education and social movements 1700–1800. 1919.

Eden, F. M. The state of the poor: or a history of the labouring classes in England from the conquest to the present period. 3 vols 1797. Documented for 2nd half of 18th century.

Edgeworth, R. L. Memoirs. 2 vols 1820. *See* Alice Paterson, *below*.

Eldon, John Scott, Earl
Twiss, H. The public and private life of Lord Chancellor Eldon, with selections from his correspondence. 1844. On Newcastle Grammar School; Oxford University.

Evelyn, John. Diary and correspondence. Ed E. S. de Beer 6 vols Oxford 1955.

Firth, C. H. Modern languages at Oxford 1724–1929. Oxford 1929.

Fries, C. C. The rules of common school grammars. PMLA 42 1927.

Gaussen, A. C. C. A later Pepys. 2 vols 1904. On Blue Stockings.

Gibbon, Edward. The memoirs of the life of Gibbon, with various observations and excursions by himself. Ed G. A. Bonnard 1966. First pbd 1796.

Giles, E. L. John Newton on education. N & Q July 1938.

Gresham College. An account of the rise, foundation, progress and present state of Gresham College in London, with the life of the founder as also some late endeavours for obtaining the revival and restitution of the lectures there. 1707. *See also* John Ward, *below*.

Hans, N. New trends in education in the eighteenth century. 1951.

Hartlib, Samuel
Dircks, H. A biographical memoir of Samuel Hartlib with bibliographical notices. [1865].
Turnbull, G. H. A sketch of his life and his relation to J. A. Comenius. Cambridge 1920.
— Hartlib, Dury and Comenius: gleanings from Hartlib's papers. Liverpool 1947.

Heal, Ambrose. The English writing-masters and their copy-books 1570–1800: a biographical dictionary and bibliography; with an historical introduction on the development of English hand-writing by Stanley Morison. Cambridge 1931.

Hearne, Thomas. Reliquiae Hearnianae, the remains of Hearne MA of Edmund Hall: being extracts from his ms diaries, collected with a few notes by Philip Bliss. 3 vols 1869.

— Peter Langtoft's chronicle transcribed by Thomas Hearne. 2 vols Oxford 1725. On the 'Arminian nunnery' at Little Gidding, Hunts. John Wallis's account of his own education and of the 'Men of Gresham'.

Horton-Smith, L. G. H. An ardent educationalist: Thomas Tenison, Archbishop of Canterbury. N & Q March 1939.

Howell, Wilbur Samuel. Logic and rhetoric in England 1500–1700. Princeton 1950.

Hunt, J. H. Leigh. Autobiography. 3 vols 1850; ed R. Ingpen 2 vols 1903. On Christ's Hospital 1791–9.

Jarman, T. L. Landmarks in the history of education. 1951.

Kelly, T. Griffith Jones: a pioneer in adult education. Cardiff 1950.

Kendal, G. Robert Raikes: a critical study. 1939.

Kerr, J. Scottish education: school and university from early times to 1909. 1910.

Kettlewell, John. Compleat works; to which is prefix'd the life of the author, with an appendix of several original papers. 2 vols 1719.

Knox, H. M. Joseph Priestley's contribution to educational thought. Univ College of Hull Stud in Education 3 1949.

Lackington, James. Memoirs of the first 45 years of the life of James Lackington, the present book-seller in Moorfields, London, written by himself. [1791].

Lambley, Kathleen. The teaching and cultivation of the French language in England during Tudor and Stuart times, with introductory chapter on the preceding period. Manchester 1920.

Laughlin, T. A. Four great headmasters. Univ College of Hull Stud in Education 2 1948.

Legg, J. Wickham. English church life from the restoration to the Tractarian movement. 1914.

Manchester Literary and Philosophical Society: memoirs. Warrington 1785. For origin ('instituted June 6 1783') and objects of the Society, see vol 2, p. 16.

— Improvement of liberal education. Memoirs vol 2, above, vols 1–2 1789 (2nd edn).

Mason, M. G. The development of educational institutes in the county of Northumberland and a survey of educational provision in 1736. Univ of Durham Research Rev 4 1953.

Montmorency, J. E. G. de. State intervention in English education: a short history from the earliest times down to 1833. 1902.

More, Hannah
Roberts, W. Memoirs of the life and correspondence of Mrs More. 4 vols 1835 (3rd edn).

Muir, J. John Anderson: pioneer of technical education and the college he founded. Glasgow 1950.

Muirhead, A. The English at school: an exhibition. 1949 (Nat Book League).

Newton, Evelyn, Lady. The Lyme letters 1660–1760. 1925. On Education of boys and girls.

Parr, Samuel
Field, W. Memoirs of the life, writings and opinions of Parr; with biographical notices of his friends, pupils etc. 2 vols 1828. On Harrow 1752–61, 1767–71; Cambridge 1765–6; Stanmore School 1771.

Johnstone, J. Works, with memoir of his life and writings and a selection from his correspondence. 2 vols 1828.

Parriana: notices of Parr. 2 vols 1828.

Derry, W. Dr Parr: a portrait of the Whig Dr Johnson. 1966.

Paterson, Alice. The Edgeworths: a study of later 18th-century education. 1914.

Priestley, Joseph. Memoirs to 1795 written by himself; continuation by his son. 1805.

Holt, A. A life of Joseph Priestley. Oxford 1931.

Quintana, Ricardo. Notes on English educational opinion during the seventeenth century. SP 27 1930.

Radcliffe, R. Letters of Richard Radcliffe and John James of Queen's College, Oxford 1753–83. Ed M. Evens, Oxford 1888 (Oxford Historical Soc).

Radcliffe, Susan M. Sir Joshua's nephew: being letters written 1769–78 by a young man to his sisters. 1930. On private school 1770; Oxford 1776.

Smith, Frank. A history of English elementary education 1760–1902. 1931.

Stewart, W. A. C. Quakers and education as seen in their schools in England. 1953.

Tuer, A. W. History of the horn-book. 2 vols 1896.

Wakefield, Gilbert. Memoirs of his life, written by himself. 1792.

Ward, John. Lives of the professors of Gresham College, the life of the founder Sir Thomas Gresham; with an appendix, orations, lectures and letters by the professors. 1740.

Watson, Foster. The beginnings of the teaching of modern subjects in England. 1909. Fully documented.

— The education of the early nonconformists. GM Sept 1901.

— Unlicensed nonconformist schoolmasters 1662 and onwards. GM Sept 1902.

— Schoolmaster followers of Bacon and Comenius. GM Nov 1903.

— List of research and literary work in the subject of education. [1913].

Wilberforce, William
Harford, J. S. Recollections of Wilberforce with notices of his friends and contemporaries. 1864. An expensive Yorkshire school; St John's College, Cambridge.

Wood, Anthony à. Athenae oxonienses: an exact history of all writers and bishops who have had their education in the University of Oxford. Ed P. Bliss 4 vols 1813.

— The history and antiquities of the University of Oxford. Ed J. Gutch 4 vols in 5 Oxford 1786–92.

— Life and times of Anthony Wood, described by himself. Ed A. Clark 5 pts Oxford 1891–1900 (Oxford Historical Soc).

Wordsworth, Christopher. Social life at the English universities in the eighteenth century. Cambridge 1874.

— Scholae academicae: some account of the studies at the English universities in the eighteenth century. Cambridge 1877.

Young, R. F. Comenius in England. Oxford 1932.

(4) ILLUSTRATIVE MATERIAL

The Academy keeper. 1770. A satire on the private school.

Apprenticeship: the covenants of an indenture familiarly explained and enforced by Scripture for the use of the apprentices of the city of London. 1736.

Bayne-Powell, R. The English child in the eighteenth century. 1939.

[Bristow, W.] The genuine account of the life and writings of Eugene Aram; to which are added the remarkable defence he made on his trial, his plan for a lexicon, some pieces of poetry. [1759].

Brown, John (vicar of Newcastle). An estimate of the manners and principles of the times. 2 vols 1757–8.

— An explanatory defence of the estimate. 1758.

L., St C. The real character of the age in a letter to Dr Brown. 1757.

Swing, S. Letters to the estimator. 1758.

Some doubts occasioned by the second volume of an estimate. 1758.

A letter to the author of the estimate on the universities. 1758.

— Thoughts on civil liberty, on licentiousness and faction. 1765.

Cashmore, N. M. On Birmingham book-sellers of the 18th century, in contradiction to Boswell and Macaulay. TLS 1 Jan 1931.

'Chip, Will' (Hannah More). Village politics. 1793.

— Modern politicians. 1848.

Colquhoun, Patrick. Treatise on the police of the metropolis. 1796 (2nd edn).

[Coventry, Francis]. The history of Pompey the Little: or the life and adventures of a lap-dog. 1751.

Craig, William (Lord Craig). The hardships of private tutor. Mirror no 88 1780.

Dean, I. F. Scottish spinning schools. 1930.

Desaguliers, J. T. A course of experimental philosophy. 2 vols 1734–44. Contains an historical account of 'popular' science teaching in London in early 18th century.

[Duncombe, John]. An evening contemplation in a college, by another gentleman of Cambridge. 1753. A parody of Gray's Elegy.

Ellis, Aytoun. The penny universities: a history of the coffee-houses. 1956.

Gray, Mrs Edwin (Almira Gray). Papers and diaries of a Yorkshire family 1764–1839. 1927.

Hailes, David Dalrymple, Lord Hailes. Master Flint's education under a private tutor. Mirror nos 97–8 1780.

Kendall, John. Remarks on attending stage entertainments, reading romances etc. 1796.

Knox, Vicesimus. Winter evenings: or lucubrations on life and letters. 3 vols 1788, 1790, 1795.

Mason, William. Isis: an elegy. 7149. *See* Thomas Warton, *below*.

[Maurice, Thomas]. The school-boy: a poem. 1775.

Moritz, C. P. Travels, chiefly on foot, through several parts of England, translated into English. 1795; rptd in John Pinkerton, A general collection of the best and most interesting voyages and travels in all parts of the world vol 2, 1808.

Newbery, John
Welsh, C. A bookseller of the last century: being some account of the life of John Newbery and of the books he published. 1885.

Paley, William. Reasons for contentment addressed to the labouring part of the British public. Carlisle 1792.

Portus, G. V. Caritas anglicana: inquiries into religious and philanthropic societies in England. 1912.

Reports of the Society for bettering the condition and increasing the comforts of the poor. 2 vols 1798–9.

Shenstone, William. The school-mistress: a poem in imitation of Spenser. 1742.

Smith, Gyles. Serious reflections on the dangerous tendency of the common practice of card-playing; especially of the game of All-Fours, as it hath been publicly play'd at Oxford in this present year of our Lord, in a letter to his friend Abraham Nixon esq of the Inner Temple. 1754.

'Surrebutter, John' (John Anstey). The pleader's guide. 1796.

Tate, W. E. The parish chest. Cambridge 1946, 1951 (rev).

Warton, Thomas. The progress of discontent. 1746; in Poetical works, ed R. Mant 2 vols Oxford 1802.

— The triumph of Isis: a poem occasioned by Isis, an elegy. [1749].

Woodforde, James. The diary of a country parson. Ed J. Beresford 5 vols 1924–31. Vol 1, Oxford University 1759–63 and 1773.

[Woodward, Josiah, DD]. An account of the societies for the reformation of manners in London and Westminster, with a persuasive against prophaneness and debauchery. 1699.

B. UNIVERSITIES

(1) GENERAL STUDIES

Armytage, W. H. G. Prejudice and promise 1600–60; some aspects of the civic university tradition in England and Wales. Universities Rev 23 1951.

Berkenhout, John. A volume of letters to his son at the university. 1790.

Davies, Richard. Epistle to the Revd Dr Hales on the general state of education in the universities with a particular view to the philosophic and medical education. Bath 1759. Modern reforms and rehabilitation of professorial teaching.

Observations on the present state of the English universities occasion'd by Dr Davies's account of the general education in them. 1759. On a collegial or a professorial university.

Fenton, Elijah (ed). Oxford and Cambridge miscellany poems. [1708].

Letter of advice to a young gentleman at the university; to which are subjoined directions for young students. 1751. Extracted from a small treatise Of education, first pbd 1701.

'Corderius'. A letter to a young gentleman upon his admission into the university. 1753.

Letter to the author of the Estimate [John Brown, vicar of Newcastle], on that part of his explanatory defence which relates to the universities. 1758.

Letters concerning education addressed to a gentleman entering at the university, by Philander. 1785.

Mansbridge, A. The older universities of England, Oxford and Cambridge. 1923.

[Poole, Matthew]. A model for the maintaining of students of choice abilities at the university. 1658.

Shadwell, L. L. Enactments in Parliament specially concerning the universities of Oxford and Cambridge and the colleges of Winchester, Eton and Westminster. 2 pts Oxford 1912 (Oxford Historical Soc).

The student: or the Oxford and Cambridge monthly miscellany. Ed B. Thornton and G. Colman 2 vols Oxford 1750–1.

Tanner, J. R. Private correspondence and miscellaneous papers of Samuel Pepys 1679–1703. 2 vols 1926.

[Warton, Thomas]. Journal of a Fellow of a College. Idler no 33 1758.

(2) SUBSCRIPTION TO THE XXXIX ARTICLES

An account of the origin of subscriptions to the Thirty-Nine Articles of the Thirty-Sixth Canon in the university of Oxford. nd.

A collection of papers designed to explain and vindicate the present mode of subscription required by the University of Oxford from all young persons at their matriculation. Oxford 1772.

Reflections on the impropriety and inexpediency of lay-subscription to the Thirty-Nine Articles in the University of Oxford. Oxford [1772]. With a legal opinion on

the University's power to alter its statutes, signed by John Morton and R. Wilbraham, 2 June 1759.

[Randolph, Thomas]. An answer to the pamphlet entitled Reflections on the impropriety. Oxford [1772].

[Sturges, John]. A letter to a Bishop occasioned by petitions for relief in the matter of subscription. 1772.

Jebb, John. Works. Ed J. Disney 3 vols 1787. On the subscription question at Cambridge, *see* vol 1 pp. 182–222.

Frend, William. Thoughts on subscription to religious tests, particularly that required by the University of Cambridge of candidates for the degree of BA in a letter to the Rev H. W. Coulthurst. St Ives 1788–9 (with appendix).

An account of the proceedings against William Frend, Fellow of Jesus College, Cambridge. 1792. *See also* Robert Robinson *and* Thomas Turton *under* Dissenting Academies, *below*.

(3) INDIVIDUAL UNIVERSITIES

Cambridge

On studies at Cambridge. Connoisseur no 107 1756.

Barrow, Isaac. Theological works. Ed A. Napier 9 vols Cambridge 1859. Vol 9 contains Barrow's life and academic times by William Whewell.

Bentley, Richard
Bartholomew, A. T. Richard Bentley DD: a bibliography of his works and of all the literature called forth by his acts or his writings. 1908. *See also under* A (*3*), *above*.

Beverley, John. Account of the ceremonies observed in the Senate House. Cambridge 1788.

Bowes, Robert. Catalogue of books printed at or relative to the university, town and county of Cambridge 1521–1893. Cambridge 1894. With index by E. Worman, 1894.

Cantabrigia depicta. Cambridge 1763.

Carter, Edmund. The history of the University of Cambridge from its original. 1753. Particular accounts of each college and hall to 1753.

[Chapman, Thomas]. An inquiry into the right of appeal from the Chancellor or Vice-Chancellor of the university of Cambridge in matters of discipline. 1751; A further inquiry, 1752. *See* replies by Richard Hurd and John Smith, 1751–2.

Colman, G. and B. Thornton. Newmarket as a supplement to the University of Cambridge. Connoisseur no 41 [1754].

Farish, William. A plan of a course of lectures on arts and manufactures, more particularly such as relate to chemistry. Cambridge 1796.

Free thoughts upon university education. Pt 1 (Cambridge), 1751.

'A gentleman of Oxford'. Letter to the University of Cambridge on a late resignation. 1756. On resignation of Newcastle as Prime Minister.

Gray, Thomas. Correspondence. Ed P. Toynbee and L. Whibley 3 vols Oxford 1935.
Tovey, D. C. Gray and his friends: letters and relics. Cambridge 1890.

Green, John. The academic: or a disputation on the state of the University of Cambridge and the propriety of the regulations made in it on the 11th of May and the 26th day of June 1750. 1750.
Considerations on the expediency of making and the manner of conducting the late regulations at Cambridge. 1751. By John Chapman.
An inquiry into the right of appeal from the Chancellor or Vice Chancellor of the University of Cambridge in matters of discipline, addressed to a Fellow of a College, 1751. *See* Winstanley *below :* The opinion of an eminent lawyer, by a Fellow of a College, 1751 (3rd edn).
Remarks on the academic. 1751. On retrenchment of expense, reformation of manners.
A further inquiry into the right of appeal in which the objections of a late pamphlet [The opinion] are fully obviated. 1752.
A letter to the author of a further inquiry. 1752.
Authentic narrative of the late extraordinary proceedings at Cambridge against the W[estminste]r Club. 1751.
Free thoughts upon university education occasioned by the present debates at Cambridge. 1751.

Gunning, Henry. Reminiscences of the University, town and county of Cambridge from 1780. 2 vols 1855 (2nd edn).

[Heberden, William]. Strictures upon the discipline of the University of Cambridge addressed to the Senate. 1792.

Ingram, R. A. The necessity of introducing divinity into the regular course of academical studies considered and other regulations suggested for the improvement of the present mode of education at the University of Cambridge. Colchester 1792.

Jebb, John. Remarks upon the present mode of education in the University of Cambridge. 1773.

Jones, W. H. S. The story of St Catharine's College, Cambridge. Cambridge 1951.

Mayor, J. E. B. Cambridge in the seventeenth century. Pt 1, Nicholas Ferrar, Cambridge 1855; pt 2, Matthew Robinson, Cambridge 1856.
Life of Ambrose Bonwicke by his father 1729. Cambridge 1870.
Life of Ambrose Bonwicke [the elder]. Cambridge 1870.
Cambridge under Queen Anne, illustrated by memoirs of Ambrose Bonwicke 1729 and diaries of Francis Burman 1710 and Z. C. von Uffenbach 1712. Ed M. R. James, Cambridge 1911.

Miller, Edmond. An account of the University of Cambridge and the colleges: a plain relation of many of their oaths, statutes and charters, by which will appear the necessity of endeavouring to obtain such alterations as may render 'em practical and more suitable to the present times. 1717 (2nd edn).

More, Henry
Life of More by Richard Ward. 1710; ed M. F. Howard 1911.

Mullinger, J. B. Cambridge characteristics in the seventeenth century: or the studies of the University and their influence. 1867.

Pitt, William, Earl of Chatham. Letters to his nephew, Thomas Pitt, afterwards Lord Camelford. 1804. On Cambridge in 1751–7.

Porson, Richard
A vindication of the literary character of the late Professor Porson by Crito Cantabrigiensis [Thomas Turton]. 1827.
Barker, E. H. Literary anecdotes and contemporary reminiscences of professor Porson and others. 2 vols 1852.

Powicke, F. J. The Cambridge Platonists. 1926.

Rud, Edward. The diary 1709–20 of Edward Rud, sometime Fellow of Trinity College; to which are added several unpublished letters of Dr Bentley. 1860 (Cambridge Antiquarian Soc).

Sinker, Robert. Biographical notes on the librarians of Trinity College on Sir E. Stanhope's foundation. 1897 (Cambridge Antiquarian Soc).

'A late undergraduate'. A plain and friendly address to the undergraduates of the University of Cambridge, particularly those of Trinity College. Bodley ms Gough Camb 65.

Vincent, William. A letter to the Rev Dr Richard Watson, King's Professor of Divinity, University of Cambridge. 1780.

Watson, Richard. Anecdotes of the life of Bishop Watson by himself. 2 vols 1818 (2nd edn).
—— A letter to the publisher of the Quarterly Review, with remarks on the want of candour and truth in the comments therein made on the life of Richard Watson, Bishop of Llandaff, by Philalethes Cantabrigiensis. 1819.

Whiston, W. Historical preface to primitive Christianity; with an account of his banishment from the University. 1711.

Winstanley, D. A. The University of Cambridge in the eighteenth century. Cambridge 1922.

— Unreformed Cambridge. Cambridge 1935.

Dublin

Dixon, W. M. Trinity College, Dublin. 1902.

Mahaffy, J. P. et al. The book of Trinity College, Dublin 1591–1891. Belfast 1892.

Mahaffy, J. P. An epoch in Irish history: Trinity College. Dublin 1591–1660. 1903.

Stubbs, J. W. History of the University of Dublin, Dublin 1889.

Swift, Thomas. Animadversions on the Fellows of Trinity College. Dublin 1794.

Edinburgh

Bower, A. History of the University of Edinburgh. 2 vols Edinburgh 1817.

Glasgow

Renwick, R. and G. Eyre-Todd. History of Glasgow. 3 vols Glasgow 1921–34. Chs on the University 1451–1800. For 'Anderson's University' see vol 3, ch 42.

Oxford

Amhurst, Nicholas. Poems on several occasions. 1720.

— Oculus Britanniae: an heroi-panegyrical poem on the University of Oxford, illustrated with divers beautiful similes and useful digressions. 1724.

— Terrae filius: or the secret history of the University of Oxford; [with] remarks upon a late book entitled University education, by R. Newton DD, Principal of Hart Hall. 1726.

Ayliffe, J. The case of Dr Ayliffe at Oxford. 1716.

Baker, Thomas. An act at Oxford: a comedy. 1704.

Bentham, Edward (Fellow of Oriel College). A letter to a young gentleman of Oxford. Oxford 1748. An anti-Jacobite.

— A letter to a Fellow of a College: being the sequel of a letter to a young gentleman of Oxford. 1749.

— Advices to a young man of quality upon his coming to the university. 1760.

— Sketch of an academical institution. 1761.

Beresford, J. An undergraduate account-book 1789–93. Oxford 1937.

Blacow, Richard. A letter to William King, Principal of St Mary Hall, concerning a particular account of a treasonable riot at Oxford, February 1747 [1748]. 1755. See C. E. Mallet, A history of the University of Oxford, vol 3, pp. 52 f.

An answer to Mr B—s's apology as it respects his King, his country, his conscience and his God by a student of Oxford. 1755.

Chalmers, Alexander. History of the colleges, halls and public buildings attached to the University of Oxford, including lives of the founders. 2 vols Oxford 1810.

[Cooper, Anthony Ashley, Earl of Shaftesbury]. Several letters written by a noble lord to a young man at the University. 1716. 10 letters written 1707–10, most of them subscribed 'Sxxxxxx'.

D'Anvers, Alicia. Academia or the honours of the University of Oxford, in burlesque verse. 1691, 1716.

— The Oxford act: a poem. 1693. Anon.

[Fulman, William]. Academiae oxoniensis notitia. Oxford 1665, 1675.

Godley, A. D. Oxford in the eighteenth century. 1908.

Gunther, R. W. T. Early science in Oxford. 1923–45 (Oxford Historical Soc). Pt 4, Philosophical Soc Trans 1683–90; pts 6–8, Life, work and lectures of Robert Hooke.

Hearne, Thomas. Remarks and collections. Ed C. E.

Doble, D. W. Rannie et al 11 vols 1885–1921 (Oxford Historical Soc).

Impartial memorials of the life and writings of Hearne, by several hands. 1736. An abusive attack.

Letters addressed to Hearne. Ed F. Ouvry 1874.

Hone, C. R. The life of Dr John Radcliffe 1652–1714: benefactor of the University of Oxford. 1950.

King, William. Oratio in Theatro Sheldoniano habita: de dedicationis bibliothecae Radclivianae. 1749, 1750.

Oxford honesty: or a case of conscience whether one may take the oaths to King George and yet may do all one can in favour of the Pretender, occasioned by the Oxford speech [by King] and behaviour at the opening of Radcliffe's library, April 13 1749. [1749] (3 edns).

A satire upon physicians or an English paraphrase, with notes and references, of Dr King's most memorable oration delivered at the dedication of the Radclivian library; to which is added a curious petition to an hon House in favour of Dr King. 1755.

— Elogium famae inserviens Jacci Etonensis, sive Gigantes: or the praises of Jack of Eton. Oxford 1750.

A defence of the Rector and Fellows of Exeter College from the accusations brought against them by Dr Huddesford in his speech Oct 8 1754, on account of the conduct of the said college. 1754.

— The last blow: or an unanswerable vindication of the society of Exeter College. 1755.

— Doctor King's apology: or vindication of himself from the several matters charged on him by the society of informers. Oxford 1755 (3 edns).

A letter to Dr King occasioned by his late apology, and in particular by such parts as are meant to defame Mr Kennicott. 1755.

The principles of the University of Oxford, as far as relates to affection to the Government, stated. 1755.

— Political and literary anecdotes of his own times. 1818.

Williams, H. The old trumpeter of Liberty Hall. Book-Collectors' Quart no 4 1931.

Knox, Vicesimus. Essays moral and literary, on some parts of the discipline in our English universities. 2 vols 1779. Formal exercises for the degree at Oxford. See A. Chalmers, British essayists vol 36, 1817.

A letter to the Rev V. Knox on his animadversions on the University. Oxford 1790.

Madan, Falconer. Oxford books: a bibliography of printed works relating to the University and city. 3 vols Oxford 1895, 1912, 1931.

Madgalen College and King James II 1686–8: a series of documents collected and edited with additions. Ed J. R. Bloxam 1886 (Oxford Historical Soc).

Legality of the court held by HM Commissioners defended: their proceedings no argument against taking off the penal laws and tests, by Henry Care, anti-Romanist. 1688.

Magrath, J. R. The Flemings in Oxford. 3 vols 1904–24 (Oxford Historical Soc). On an Oxford family 1650–1700.

[Napleton, John]. Considerations on the public exercises for the first and second degrees in the University of Oxford. Oxford 1772.

— Considerations on the residence usually required for degrees in the University. Oxford 1772.

Newton, Richard (1676–1753). Rules and statutes for the government of Hertford College, in the University of Oxford, with observations on particular parts of them, shewing the reasonableness thereof. 1714.

— University education. 1726. On advice to a parent.

— The expence of university education reduced. 1727 (anon), 1741 (4th edn).

Ollard, S. L. The six students of St Edmund Hall expelled in 1768. 1911. With bibliography.

A vindication of the proceedings against six members of E. Hall, Oxford, by a gentleman of the University. 1769 (2nd edn).

The Oxford magazine: or university museum for general instruction and amusement on a plan entirely new, by members of the University of Oxford. 1768–9.

Petter, H. M. (ed). The Oxford almanack 1674–1946. Oxford 1947.

Pointer, J. Oxoniensis academia: or the antiquities and customs of the University of Oxford. 1749.

'Servitour of Oxford University'. The servitour: a poem. 1709.

Shadwell, C. L. and H. E. Salter. Oriel College records. 1926 (Oxford Historical Soc).

Tyerman, Luke. The Oxford Methodists. 1873.

[Law, William]. The Oxford Methodists: being some account of a society of young gentlemen in that city, so denominated, setting forth their rise, views and designs. 1733.

U[sher], C. A letter to a member of the convocation of the University of Oxford. 1699.

[Warton, Thomas]. A companion to the guide and a guide to the companion: being a complete supplement to all the accounts of Oxford hitherto published. [1762?] (2nd edn).

—— The Oxford sausage: or select poetical pieces written by the most celebrated wits of the University of Oxford. 1764 etc.

C. DISSENTING ACADEMIES

Barnes, T. See Ralph Harrison, below.

Calamy, E. The nonconformist's memorial: an account of ministers ejected. 1666, 2 vols 1775; rev S. Palmer 3 vols 1802.

Matthews, A. G. Calamy revised. Oxford 1934.

Chester, Bishop of. Bishop of Chester's case with relation to the wardenship of Manchester, in which is shewn that no other degrees but such as are taken in the university can be deemed legal qualifications for any ecclesiastical preferment in England. Oxford 1721.

D[efoe], D[aniel]. More short ways with the dissenters. 1704.

Gibson, J. W. Dr Doddridge's academy. Phonetic Jnl 3 April 1886.

Gordon, Alexander. Early non-conformity and education: an address. Manchester 1902.

—— Freedom after ejection 1690–2: a review of presbyterian and congregational nonconformity. 1917.

Harrison, Ralph. A sermon preached at Manchester on the occasion of the establishment of an academy, together with a discourse delivered at the public commencement of the academy by T. Barnes. Warrington [1786].

Kippis, Andrew. See col 1919, above.

McLachlan, H. English education under the Test Acts: non-conformist academies 1662–1820. 1931.

Needham (or Nedham), Marchamont. A discourse concerning schools and school-masters offered to public consideration. 1663.

[Owen, James, of Shrewsbury]. Moderation still a virtue, in answer to several bitter pamphlets with a defence of the private academies against Mr Sacheverell's misrepresentations of 'em. 1704.

[Palmer, Samuel]. A defence of the dissenters' education in their private academies in answer to Mr W—y's disingenuous and un-Christian reflections upon 'em. 1703.

—— A vindication of the learning, loyalty, morals and most Christian behaviour of the dissenters towards the Church of England, in answer to Mr Wesley's defence of his letter concerning the dissenters' education in their private academies, and to Mr Sacheverel's injurious reflections upon them. 1705.

Parker, Irene. Dissenting academies in England. Cambridge 1914.

Price, Richard. See col 1920, above.

Price, S. J. Dissenting academies 1662–1820. Baptist Quart 6 1933.

Rees, A. The advantages of knowledge recommended to the supporters of a new academical institution among Protestant dissenters. 1788.

Robinson, Robert (Baptist minister). Memoirs of his life and writings, by George Dyer. 1796. Proposal for a dissenters' college at Cambridge; on subscription to 39 Articles.

Sacheverell, Henry. The nature and mischief of prejudice and partiality stated in a sermon preach'd at St Mary's in Oxford at the assizes held there, March 9th 1704. Oxford 1704 (2nd edn).

Turner, G. Lyon. Original records of nonconformity under persecution and indulgence. 3 vols 1914.

Turton, Thomas. A review of the principal dissenting colleges in England during the last century. Cambridge 1835 (2nd edn). Also as Thoughts on the admission of persons, without regard to their religious opinions, to certain degrees in the universities of England.

Tyerman, L. Life and times of the Reverend Samuel Wesley MA, Rector of Epworth. 2 vols 1866.

Watson, Foster. Unlicensed nonconformist schoolmasters. GM Sept 1902.

—— Religious refugees and English education. Proc Huguenot Soc of London 1911.

[Wesley, Samuel, the elder]. A letter from a country divine to his friend in London concerning the education of dissenters in their private academies, in several parts of this nation. 1703. Written 1693.

—— A defence of a letter concerning the education of dissenters in their private academies; with a more full and satisfactory account of the same, and of their morals and behaviour towards the Church of England: being an answer to the defence of dissenters' education. 1704.

—— A reply to Mr Palmer's vindication of the learning, loyalty, morals and most Christian behaviour of the dissenters towards the Church of England. 1707.

Whiting, C. E. Studies in English puritanism 1660–88. 1931 (Church History Soc). Ch 10, Dissenting academies and schoolmasters.

D. 'COURTESY' BOOKS

See G. E. Noyes, Bibliography of courtesy and conduct books in seventeenth-century England, New Haven 1937; V. B. Heltzel, A check list of courtesy books in the Newberry Library, Chicago 1942.

A., D., gent. The whole art of converse: containing necessary instructions for all persons, of what quality and condition soever. 1683.

A., P., gent. (Philip Ayres). Vox clamantis: or an essay for the honour, happiness and prosperity of the English gentry. 1684.

An address to the hopeful young gentry of England. 1669.

Advice from a lady of quality to her children. Tr from French by S. Glasse 2 vols Gloucester 1778.

The advice of a father or counsel to a child. 1664, 1716 (4th edn).

Aikin, John. Letters from a father to his son, on various topics, relative to literature and the conduct of life, written in the years 1792 and 1793. 2 vols 1793–1800.

Allestree, Richard. The gentleman's calling. 1660, 1696 (16th edn).

Argyle, Marquis of. Instructions to a son. 1661, 1689.

Astell, Mary. Some reflections upon marriage. 1700.

B., H. Schola urbanitas: sive de elegantia morum et civili conversatione inter homines. 1652.

B., I., gent. Heroick education or choice maximes and instructions for the most sure and facile training up of youth. 1657.

[Barnard, Sir John]. A present for an apprentice: or a sure guide to gain both esteem and an estate, with rules for his conduct to his master. 1740.

Bellegarde, J. B. M. de. Reflexions upon ridicule. 2 vols 1706. Vol 2, Politeness of manners and behaviour.

— Models of conversation for persons of polite education. 1765. First pbd in French in 1697.

Blackett, M. D. The monitress: or the oeconomy of female life. [1791].

Blome, William. An essay to heraldry. 1684.

— The gentleman's recreation. 1686.

[Bolton, Edmund]. The cities great concern, in the case of honour and arms, whether apprentiship extinguisheth gentry. 1674. First pbd as The cities advocate, 1629.

[Boyer, Abel]. The English Theophrastus: or the manners of the age. 1702.

— Characters of the virtues and vices of the age. 1695.

Britaine, William de. Humane prudence. 1680, 1697 (7th edn).

B[rokesby], F. Of education, with a letter of advice to a young gentleman. 1701.

[Bromley, William]. Remarks in the grande tour lately performed by a person of quality. 1692.

Browne, Simon. A caveat against evil company. 1716.

[C., S.] The art of complaisance: or the means to oblige in conversation. 1673. Largely an adaptation of Eustache Du Refuge, Traité de la cour; see Du Refuge, 1694, below.

[Callière, Jacques de]. The courtier's calling: shewing the ways of making a fortune and the art of living at Court. 1675.

Callières, Francois de. The knowledge of the world, and the attainments useful in the conduct of life, translated from the French of [1717]: a new edition revised and corrected. Dublin 1774.

Care, Henry. The female secretary. 1671.

Casa, Giovanni della. The refin'd courtier. 1663, 1679, 1686. A paraphrase of the Galateo by Nathaniel Walker.

— J. Casa his Galateus: or a treatise of manners. 1701.

— Galateo of manners: or instructions to a young gentleman how to behave himself in conversation. 1703.

— Galateo: or a treatise on politeness and delicacy of manners. 1774. A paraphrase by Richard Graves. See also Dare and Gracian Dantisco, below.

Castiglione, Baldassare. Il cortigiano: or the courtier, a new version of the same into English; to which is prefix'd the life of the author, by A. P. Castiglione. 1727.

— The courtier: or the complete gentleman and gentlewoman. [Tr Robert Samber] 1729.

Chesterfield, Philip Dormer Stanhope, Earl of. Letters to his son [written 1737–68]. 2 vols 1774.

— Letters to his godson [written 1761–70?]. 1890. See also Trusler, below, and Young gentleman's parental monitor, below.

The children's petition: or modest remonstrance of that intolerable grievance our youth lie under, in the accustomed severities of the school-discipline in this nation. 1669.

Cicero. Tully's offices, in three books, turned out of Latin into English by Sr Ro. L'Estrange. 1680.

— Tully's three books of offices. Tr Thomas Cockman 1699, 1722 (4th edn).

[Codrington, Robert]. The second part of youths behaviour: or decency in conversation amongst women. 1664, 1672. See Hawkins, below.

The conversation of gentlemen considered in six dialogues. 1738.

Costeker, John Lyttleton. The fine gentleman: or the compleat education of a young nobleman. 1732.

Cotton, Charles. The compleat gamester. 1674.

[Courtin, Antoine de]. The rules of civility: or certain ways of deportment observed in France. 1671, 1678 (with addns). Another trn, 1703.

Crossman, Samuel. The young man's monitor. 1664.

Cox, Nicholas. The gentleman's recreation. 1674, 1697 (4th edn).

Dare, Josiah. Councellor Manners his last legacy to his son. 1673, 1698 (3rd edn). Della Casa's Galateo made over.

[Darrell, William]. A gentleman instructed in the conduct of a virtuous and happy life. 1704; A supplement, with a word to the ladies, 1707; 1732 (10th edn).

Dedekind, Friedrich. Grobianus: or the compleat booby, done into English by R. Bull. 1739; tr R. F. Gent as The schoole of slovenrie, 1605.

Defoe, Daniel. The compleat English gentleman. Ed K. Bulbring 1890. Written c. 1729.

A discourse concerning the character of a gentleman. Edinburgh 1716.

Dodsley, Robert. The oeconomy of human life. 1751.

[Dorrington, Theophilus]. The excellent woman described. 1692, 2 vols 1695 (rev).

[Drake, Judith; formerly attributed to Mary Astell]. An essay in defence of the female sex. 1696, 1721 (4th edn).

Du Bosq. The accomplish'd woman. 2 vols 1753.

[Du Moulin, Peter]. Directions for the education of a young prince, till seven years of age, translated out of the French. 1673.

[Du Refuge, Eustache]. Arcana Aulica: or Walsingham's manual. [1652], 1694. See also H.W., The accomplish'd courtier, 1658, another version—both trns of pt 2 of Du Refuge, Traité de la cour, [1616?], pts 1–2 of which were pbd as Treatise of the court, tr John Reynolds 1622; also pbd as Walsingham's manual of prudential maxims in instructions for youth, 1722; see S.C., The art of complaisance, 1673.

Dykes, Oswald. Good manners for schools. 1700. Verse.

Ellis, Clement. The gentile sinner. 1660, 1690 (7th edn).

Erskine, John, Earl of Mar. The Earl of Mar's legacies to Scotland and to his son Lord Erskine 1722–7. Edinburgh 1896.

Essays relating to the conduct of life. 1717.

Evelyn, John. Memoirs for my grand-son. Ed G. L. Keynes, Oxford 1926. Written 1704.

[Fairfax, Thomas, Baron Fairfax?]. Advice to a young lord, written by his father, under these following heads: viz religion, study and exercises, travel, marriage, housekeeping and hospitality. 1691.

Fénelon, François de Salignac de la Mothe. Instructions for the education of a daughter; to which is added a small tract of instructions for the conduct of young ladies of the highest rank [Trotti de La Chetardie's instructions for a young Princess], done into English by Dr George Hickes. 1707.

Fielding, Henry. Essay on conversation. In his Miscellanies, 1743. Written 1737?

Fielding, Sir John. The universal mentor. 1763.

Fordyce, James. Addresses to young men. 2 vols 1777, 1816 (5th edn).

— The character and conduct of the female sex. 1776.

— Sermons to young women. 2 vols 1765, 1814 (14th edn).

[Forrester, James]. The polite philosopher: or an essay on that art which makes a man happy in himself, and agreeable to others. 1734.

F[ox], G[eorge]. A warning to all teachers of children and to parents. 1657.

[Foxton, T.] Serino: or the character of a fine gentleman. [1721].

Fuller, Thomas, MD. Directions, counsels and cautions tending to prudent management of affairs in common life. 1725, 1726 (enlarged).

Gailhard, Jean. The compleat gentleman: or directions for the education of youth as to their breeding at home and travelling abroad. 2 pts 1678.

— Two discourses: the first concerning a private settlement at home after travel; the second concerning the statesman, or him who is in public employments. 1682 (second discourse dated 1681).

The gentleman's library: containing rules for conduct in all part of life. 1715.

The gentleman's new-years gift: or serious advice to a nephew. 1731.

Gerbier, Sir Balthazar. Subsidium perigrinantibus. 1665.

Gisborne, Thomas. An enquiry into the duties of men in the higher and middle classes. 1794, 2 vols 1811 (6th edn).

— An enquiry into the duties of the female sex. 1797, 1836 (8th edn).

Goussault, Abbot. Advice to young gentlemen in their several conditions of life. 1698.

Gracian, Baltazar. The courtier's manual oracle. 1685.

— The art of prudence: or a companion for a man of sense. 1702.

Gracian Dantisco, Lucas. Narcissus, or the young man's entertaining mirror: containing a humorous descant on manners, taken from the Spanish Galateo by Charles Wiseman. 1778. Tr 1640 as Galateo Espagnol, an imitation of Della Casa's Galateo.

Gracian y Morales, Baltazar. The compleat gentleman: or a description of the several qualifications that are necessary to form a great man. Tr T. Saldkeld 1730.

[Graham, Richard, Viscount Preston]. Angliae speculum morale: the moral state of England. 1670.

Graile, John. Youth's grand concern. 1708, 1711.

— An essay of particular advice to the young gentry. 1711.

de Gravines. The lady's friend. 1766.

[Gough, John]. The academy of complements. 1640, 1650 etc.

Grimaldus Goslicius, Laurentius. The accomplished Senator done into English by Mr Oldisworth. 1733. Tr as The counsellor, 1598.

Gregory, John. A father's legacy for his daughters. 1774 etc.

Grove, Henry. The regulation of diversions. 1708.

Guazzo, Stephen. The art of conversation, in three parts. 1738. Tr 1581–6 as The civile conversation of M. Stephen Guazzo.

Hale, Sir Matthew. A letter of advice to his grandchildren now first published. 1816. Written c. 1673.

Hartcliffe, John. A treatise of moral and intellectual virtues. 1691.

Hawkins, Francis. Youth's behaviour: or decency in conversation amongst men. 1636, 1663 (8th edn). Enlarged from edn to edn. See also Codrington, above.

[Heydon, John]. Advice to a daughter in opposition to the advice to a sonne. 1658. See Francis Osborne, below.

Higford, William. The institution of a gentleman. 1660. First pbd 1658 as Institutions: or advice to his grandson.

Hope, Sir William. The compleat fencing master. 1691.

Hurd, Richard (ed). Dialogues on the uses of foreign travel between Lord Shaftesbury and Mr Locke. 1764.

Instructions for youth, gentlemen and noblemen, by Sir Walter Raleigh, Lord Treasurer Burleigh, Cardinal Sermonetta and Mr Walsingham. 1722, 1728 (as Walsingham's manual: or prudential maxims for statesmen and courtiers).

James I. Basilikon doron: or King James's instructions to his dearest sonne, Henry the Prince, now reprinted by his Majesties command. 1682.

The late King James [II] his advice to his son. 1703.

Jermin, Michael. The father's instruction of his childe. 1658.

The ladies library, written by a lady [Mary Wray?], published by Mr [Richard] Steele. 3 vols 1714.

Lambert, Anne Thérèse de. Advice from a mother to her son and daughter. 1729. Other trns, 1737, 1749.

La Rochefoucauld, François, Duc de. Moral maxims and reflections. 1694, 1706, 1726. A trn.

The laws of honour. 1685.

Le Noble de Tenelière, Eustache. The art of prudent behaviour, in a father's advice to his son, arriv'd to the years of manhood, english'd by Mr [Abel] Boyer. 1701.

L[ingard], R[ichard]. A letter of advice to a young gentleman leaving the University, concerning his behaviour and conversation in the world. Dublin 1670.

Mackenzie, Sir George. Moral gallantry: a discourse wherein the author endeavours to prove, that point of honor obliges men to be virtuous. Edinburgh 1667.

The man of manners: or plebeïan polish'd, being plain and familiar rules for a modest and genteel behaviour. [1735?].

Marriott, Thomas. Female conduct being an essay on the art of pleasing, to be practised by the fair sex. 1759. Verse.

Mason, John. Self-knowledge. 1745 etc.

The matrimonial preceptor. 1755, 1759.

Mavor, William. The British Nepos: or youth's mirror. 1798.

Milns, William. The well-bred scholar. 1794.

Neale, Thomas. A treatise and direction, how to travel safely. 1643, 1664.

[Nicole, Pierre]. Of the education of a prince. 1678. A trn.

[d'Ortigue, Pierre, Sieur de Vaumorière]. The art of pleasing in conversation. 1691. Wrongly attributed to Richelieu and to Bellegarde; another trn by John Ozell, 1736.

Osborne, Francis. Advice to a son: or directions for your better conduct, through the various and most important encounters of this life. 2 pts Oxford 1656–8. Also in Works, 1673 (7th edn). See Heydon, above.

'Overcome, S.' (Sam Vincent). The young gallant's academy: or directions how he should behave himself in all places and company. 1674. A version of Dekker, Guls horne-booke.

Panton, Edward. Speculum juventutis: or a true mirror. 1671.

Peacham, Henry. The compleat gentleman, fashioning him absolute in the most necessary and commendable qualities required in a person of honour; to which is added the gentlemen's exercise or an exquisite practice as well for drawing all manner of beasts as for making colours to be used in painting: third [actually 4th or 5th] edition much enlarged, especially in the art of blazonry. 1661.

Penn, William. Fruits of a father's love: being the advice of William Penn to his children, relating to their civil and religious conduct. 1726.

[Penton, Stephen]. The guardian's instruction. 1688.

— New instructions to the guardian. 1694.

Percival, Thomas. A father's instructions to his children. 2 pts 1776, 1777, 1806 (10th edn, with 3rd pt).

[Petrie, Adam]. Rules of good deportment: or of good breeding. Edinburgh 1720, 1835. A satire.

The polite academy. 1762.

The polite gentleman. 1700.

The polite lady: or a course of female education, in a series of letters, from a mother to her daughter. 1760, 1785 (4th edn).

The polite student. 1748.

Pompadour, Mme de. Advice to a female friend. 1750. A trn.

[Puckle, James]. The club: or a grey cap for a green head, containing maxims, advice and cautions. 1711.

Ralegh, Sir Walter. Instructions to his sonne, and to posterity. 1632.

[Ramesey, William]. The gentlemans companion: or a character of true nobility, and gentility. 1672, 1676.

Ramsay, Chevalier. A plan of education for a young prince. 1732.

Reflections on our common failings. 1701.

[Richardson, Samuel]. Letters written to and for particular friends, on the most important occasions. 1741, 1928.

Savile, George, Marquis of Halifax. The ladies new-years gift: or advice to a daughter. 1688, 1696 (6th edn).

Steele, Sir Richard. The Christian hero. 1701.

[Swift, Jonathan]. A complete collection of genteel and ingenious conversation, according to the most polite mode and method now used at Court, and in the best companies of England, by Simon Wagstaff esq. 1738. Written 1708–9.

— Directions to servants. 1745.

Towle, Matthew. The young gentlemen and lady's private tutor in three parts. 1770. No 3, Behaviour in the dancing school.

Trenchfield, Caleb. A cap of gray hairs, for a green head: or the father's counsel to his son an apprentice in London. 1671, 1691 (5th edn).

[Trotti de La Chetardie, Joachim]. Instructions for a young nobleman: or the idea of a person of honour, done out of French [by Ferrand Spence?]. 1683.

The true conduct of persons of quality, translated out of French. 1694.

Trusler, John. The honours of the table: or rules for behaviour during meals. 1791 (2nd edn).

— Principles of politeness and of knowing the world, necessary to complete the gentleman and man of fashion and young ladies. 1775. A methodized abridgment of Chesterfield's letters to his son.

Vane, Lyonell. Letters to a gentleman of fortune, relating to his conduct of life. 1753.

Vaughan, Thomas. Advice to young gentlemen concerning the conduct of life. [1711].

Waite, Joseph. The parents primer and mothers' looking-glass. 1681.

[Walker, Obadiah]. Of education, especially of young gentlemen. 1673, 1699 (6th edn).

Wandesforde, Sir Christopher. A book of instructions to his son and heir in order to the regulating the conduct of his whole life. 2 vols Cambridge 1777.

Waterhouse, Edward. A discourse and defence of arms. 1660.

— The gentleman's monitor. 1665.

[Wicksteed, Edward]. The young gentleman and lady instructed in such principles of politeness, prudence and virtue. 2 vols 1747.

The young gentleman's parental monitor: containing 1, Lord Chesterfield's advice to his son on men and manners; on the principles of politeness; and on the art of acquiring a knowledge of the world; 2, Marchioness De Lambert's advice to her son; 3, Lord Burghley's ten precepts to his son. Hartford 1792.

The young scholar's delight. 1770.

Mason, J. E. Gentlefolk in the making: studies in the history of English courtesy literature and related topics from 1531 to 1774. Philadelphia 1935. A bibliographical note discusses other studies.

E. SCHOOLS

See also Education 1500–1660, vol 1, above, and Education of Women and Girls, below.

Ackermann, Rudolph. The history of the colleges of Winchester, Eton and Westminster, with the Charter-House, the schools of St Paul's, Merchant Taylors', Harrow and Rugby, and the free-school of Christ's Hospital. 1816.

Shadwell, L. L. Enactments in Parliament specially concerning the universities of Oxford and Cambridge and the colleges of Winchester, Eton and Westminster. 2 pts 1912 (Oxford Historical Soc).

W., C. The shameful discipline of schools expos'd: or whipping an improper punishment for youth, by an enemy to the infamous practice of flogging. 1741.

The advertiser: or the moral and literary tribunal. Vol 1, 1803 (2nd edn). On Winchester 'rebellion', 1793.

Winchester College Archaeological Society. Winchester College: its history and customs. 1926.

Austen-Leigh, R. A. Eton College register 1698–1790. 2 vols 1921–7.

— Eton under Barnard 1754–65. Eton 1904.

Bell, Robert. Life of the Rt Hon George Canning. 1846.

Gray, Thomas. Ode on a distant prospect of Eton college. 1747.

'Gregory Griffin' (George Canning and others). The microcosm: a periodical work by Gregory Griffin of Eton College. 40 weekly nos 1786–7.

Harcourt, L. V. An Eton bibliography. 1898, 1902.

Macdonald, Violet. The letters of Eliza Pierce 1751–75, with letters from her son. 1927. On Eton 'rebellion', 1768, described from within.

Mullett, C. F. George Granville and Eton in the 1760's. HLQ 5 1942.

'A school-boy at Eton'. The old lady in her tantarums: or mother Oxford ranting at her eldest son K—ng, being a translation of part of an epistle lately published by J.B., Fellow of Eton College. Eton 1750.

Bagshawe, E. A true and perfect narrative of the differences between Mr Busby and Mr Bagshawe. 1659.

Barker, G. F. R. Memoir of Richard Busby 1606–95, with some account of Westminster School in the seventeenth century. 1895.

Cowper, William. Tirocinium. 1784. On Westminster School 1741–9.

Reply to objections to public schools with particular reference to Tyrocinium. 1814.

The London medley, containing exercises spoken at the annual meeting of the Westminster scholars. [1731].

The trifler: a new periodical miscellany by Timothy Touchstone of St Peter's College, Westminster. 1788 (2nd edn).

Butler, E. M. Sheridan: a ghost story. 1931. On Harrow 1762–8.

Howard, Robert Mowbray. Records and letters of the family of Longville, Jamaica and Hampton Lodge, Surrey. 2 vols 1925. On Harrow; Trinity Hall 1780.

Jones, Sir William

    Memoirs of life, writings and correspondence, by J. Shore, Baron Teignmouth. 2 vols 1806. On Harrow, 1753–63; Oxford.

Mack, E. C. Public schools and British opinion 1780–1860. New York 1938.

Ollard, S. L. and P. C. Walker (ed). Archbishop Herring's visitation returns 1743. Yorks Archaeological Soc Record Ser 71–9 1928–31.

Parr, Samuel. Life. In Works, ed J. Johnstone 8 vols 1828.

— Life, writings and opinions, by William Field. 2 vols 1828. On Harrow, 1752–61, 1767–71; Cambridge.

Derry, W. Dr Parr: the Whig Dr Johnson. 1967.

Forster, John. Walter Savage Landor: a biography. 2 vols 1869. On Rugby 1788–94.

Michell, A. T. Rugby School register. Vol 1, 1675–1842; vol 2, 1842–74; vol 3, 1874–94; Rugby 1901–4.

'Nimrod' (Charles James Apperley). Life and times. Fraser's Mag Aug–Sept 1842. On Rugby 1778–94.

Christ's Hospital. The present state and list of the children of Charles II his new foundation in Christ's Hospital presented to their Majesties. 1691. On the Mathematical School of Christ's Hospital.

Coleridge, S. T. Biographia literaria: sketches of my literary life and opinions. 2 vols 1817. On Christ's Hospital 1782–90.

The late Mr Thomas Firmin, by one of his most intimate acquaintances. In Tracts printed by the Unitarian

Society for Promoting Christian Knowledge vol 5, 1791. Governor, Christ's Hospital 1674 etc. Initiated the school at Hertford.

Heal, Ambrose. The English writing-masters and their copy-books 1570–1800. Cambridge 1931. Appendix 1A, Christ's Hospital writing school.

Lamb, Charles. Recollections of Christ's Hospital [1782–9]. 1813.

— Essays of Elia. Ser 1, 1823. Includes Christ's Hospital five and thirty years ago; The old and the new schoolmaster.

Tanner, J. R. Mr Pepys: introduction to the diary with sketch of his later life. 1925. References to Pepysian ms no 2612, a collection relating to Christ's Hospital.

Shrewsbury school. Register 1734–1898. Oswestry 1909; 1636–1734, Shrewsbury 1917.

Victoria county history. Notices of grammar schools 1660–1800 are contained in the 2nd vols of Bucks, Derbyshire, Essex, Hants, Lancashire, Notts, Somerset, Suffolk, Surrey, and in the first vol of Yorkshire.

Lester, D. N. R. The history of Batley grammar school 1612–1962. nd.

Sargeaunt, J. and E. Hockliffe. A history of Bedford school. 1925.

Carter, W. F. The records of King Edward's school, Birmingham. Vol 1, 1924.

D'Auvergne, E. Sermon at Bishop Stortford on the occasion of the school feast of that town. 1705.

Hill, C. P. The history of Bristol grammar school. 1951.

Duncan, L. L. The history of Colfe's grammar school 1652–1952. 1952.

An account of the Revd Mr Gilpin of Vicar's Hill. 1801. In Memoirs of Dr Richard Gilpin, ed W. Jackson 1879. On the boarding school at Cheam 1752.

Faulkner, Thomas. An historical and descriptive account of the Royal Hospital and the Royal Military Asylum at Chelsea; to which is prefixed an account of King James's College at Chelsea. 1805.

Steven, W. The history of the high school of Edinburgh. 1849.

Craze, M. A history of Felsted school 1564–1947. 1955.

Nichols, R. H. and F. A. C. Wray. The history of the Foundling Hospital. 1935.

Waugh, W. T. History of Fulneck school. 1909.

Douglas, M. A. and C. R. Ash. The Godolphin school 1726–1926. 1928.

Garside, B. History of Hampton school from 1556 to 1700. Cambridge 1931.

Dowling, P. J. The hedge schools of Ireland. 1935.

Holmes, John. The history of England: a compendium adapted to youth at school, with declamations performed by the gentlemen of the grammar school at Holt at their Christmas breaking-up 1735. 1737.

Porteus, T. C. Lancashire school founders. Coppull 1929.

Stanier, R. S. Magdalen School: a history of Magdalen College School Oxford. 1940.

Smith, J. F. Admission register of the Manchester school with some notices of the more distinguished scholars 1730–1807. 2 vols 1866–74.

[Brooke, Henry]. The Quack-doctor: a poem, as originally spoken at the free grammar school in Manchester; to which is added a declamation spoke upon the breaking up of the school for Christmas, December 13 1744. 1745.

Christ Church, Manchester. The Charters of the collegiate church, the free grammar school. 1791.

Draper, F. W. Four centuries of Merchant Taylors' school 1561–1961. 1962.

Sturge, H. W. and T. Clark. The Mount school, York 1785–1814 and 1831–91. 1931.

Day, E. S. An old Westminster endowment: the Grey Coat hospital. 1902.

Some account of Parmiter's foundation 1668–1703. 1887. On Bethnal Green; the school dates from 1722.

Peacock, M. H. History of Wakefield grammar school. 1892.

Griffith, G. Free schools of Worcestershire and their fulfilment. 1852.

— Free schools of Staffordshire and their fulfilment. 1860.

— Free schools of Birmingham and their fulfilment. 1861.

Allen, W. O. B. and E. McClure. Two hundred years: history of the Society for Promoting Christian Knowledge 1698–1898. 1898.

Barnes, W. G. Charity and charity schools defended. Norwich 1727.

Chandler, W. Doing good recommended, and an answer to essay on charity schools. 1728.

An account of charity schools lately erected in England, Wales and Ireland. 1704. Continued yearly as suppl to the anniversary sermon, with valuable statistics.

An account of the charity mathematical school in Hatton Garden, founded anno domini 1715. 1749, 1771.

Hammond, J. L. and B. The village labourer 1760–1832. 1912. On workhouse schools.

Hendley, W. A defence of the charity schools wherein the many false, scandalous and malicious objections of those advocates for ignorance and irreligion, the authors of the fable of the bees, and Cato's letter in the British Journal, June 15 1723, are fully and distinctly answer'd. 1725.

Ingram, R. A. Sermon preached in Colchester for the benefit of the charity school. Colchester 1788.

Jones, M. G. The charity school movement: a study of eighteenth-century Puritanism in action. Cambridge 1938.

A letter from a clergyman to his friend: being a short account of the charity schools lately erected. [1708].

Mandeville, Bernard. The fables of the bees. 2 pts 1714–29. With an essay on charity and charity schools in 2nd edn, 1723.

Reports. Society for bettering the condition and improving the comforts of the poor. See Of the education of the poor: being a digest of the reports of the society, 1809. On schools of industry.

Strype, John (ed). John Stow, A survey of the cities of London and Westminster. 2 vols 1720. Bk 5, ch 3.

Watts, Isaac. Essay towards the encouragement of charity schools. 1728.

Wilson, Thomas. See col 1922, above.

[Hanway, Jonas]. A letter from a member of the marine society shewing the generosity and utility of their design. 1757.

— An account of the marine society. 1759.

— A comprehensive view of Sunday schools. 1786.

— Proposal for county naval free-schools, to be built on waste lands, giving such effectual instructions to poor boys as may nurse them for the sea service, teaching also to cultivate the earth, and to spin, knit, weave etc. 1783.

— Rules and regulations of the maritime school. 1781, 1794 (4th edn).

Hutchins, J. H. Jonas Hanway 1712–86. 1940.

Lucas, R. Three sermons on Sunday schools. 1787.

Parsons, Philip. Six letters to a friend on the establishment of Sunday schools. 1786.

Pitt, William Morton. A plan for the extension and regulation of Sunday schools. 1789.

Porteous, Beilby (Bishop of Chester). A letter to the clergy of the diocese concerning Sunday schools (and charity schools). 1786.

Trimmer, Sarah. The oeconomy of charity: or the address to ladies concerning Sunday schools; the establishment of schools of industry under female inspection, and the distribution of voluntary benefactions; an appendix [on] the Sunday schools in Old Brentford. 1787, 2 vols 1801 (enlarged). See also col 1923, above.

F. SCHOOL- AND TEXT-BOOKS

Arithmetic

See A. De Morgan, Arithmetical books from the invention of printing to the present time, 1847; A. Heal, The English writing-masters and their copy-books 1570–1800, Cambridge 1931.

Ayres, Daniel. Arithmetick made easier. 1723.

Butler, William. Introduction to arithmetic designed for the use of young ladies. Ashby 1788.

Cocker, Edward and John Hawkins. The young clerk's tutor enlarged by Edward Cocker. [1660], 1664 (3rd edn).

—— Cocker's arithmetic: a plain and familiar method suitable to the meanest capacity. 1678, 1741 (60th edn).

—— Cocker's decimal arithmetic. 1685, 1729 (6th edn).

On the authorship of these very popular books, see De Morgan, pp. 56 f, *and* Heal, pp. 33 f., 58 f. *Cocker's great reputation as a writing-master seems to have been used as a stalking-horse for the arithmetical books of John Hawkins. De Morgan attributes the disappearance of abstract, theoretical arithmetic in favour of applied commercial summing to Cocker's arithmetic, 1678. But he overlooked the Italian, French and German arithmetic books of the 16th century. See* D. E. Smith, Rara arithmetica, Boston 1908.

Fenning, Daniel. The British youth's instructor: a guide to practical arithmetic, necessary to the knowledge of business; and a compendious method of book-keeping. 1754, 1777 (9th edn).

—— The schoolmaster's most uesful companion and scholar's best instructor. 1775. Arithmetic, book-keeping.

Fisher, George. Arithmetic in the plainest and most concise methods hitherto extant. 1737 (5th edn).

—— The instructor: or young man's best companion. 1740 (5th edn), 1798 (28th edn).

Morland, Sir S. The description and use of two arithmetic instruments; with a short treatise of arithmetick. 1673. On calculating machines.

[Newton, Sir Isaac]. Arithmetica universalis. Cambridge 1707.

Partridge, Seth. Description and use of an instrument called the double scale of proportion, all questions in arithmetic, dialling. 1671. On the slide rule.

Walkingame, Francis. Tutor's assistant. 1751, 1826 (67th edn). Key to Walkingame's tutor's assistant, containing the solutions of the questions and some useful rules, 1797, by T. Crosby. 'Walkingame' superseded 'Cocker'.

Wells, Edward. The young gentleman's arithmetick and geometry. 1713.

Wigan, Eleazar. Practical arithmetick: an introduction to the whole art, the most necessary rules fairly described in the usuall hands, adorn'd with great variety of flourishes perform'd by command of hand, for the more speedy fitting of youth for merchandize or trade. 1695.

Wingate, E. Mr Wingate's arithmetick: a plain and familiar method for attaining the knowledge and practice of common arithmetick, inlarged by John Kersey, with a new supplement of easie contraction in the necessary parts of arithmetick by George Shelley, writing-master of Christ's Hospital. 1630, 1704 (11th edn). *See* Kersey, *col 1948, below.*

The young man's companion or arithmetick made easy. 1752.

English

Ash, John. Grammatical institutes: or an easy introduction to Dr Lowth's English grammar. 1763, 1766, 1768, 1779, 1789, 1794.

—— New and complete dictionary of the English language with a comprehensive grammar. 2 vols 1775.

Bailey, Nathan. English and Latin exercises for school-boys. 1706, 1744 (11th edn).

—— An universal etymological English dictionary. 1721 etc.

Campbell, George. The philosophy of rhetoric. 2 vols 1776.

Coles, Elisha. The complete English school-master: or the most natural and easie method of spelling English according to the present proper pronunciation in Oxford and London. 1674, 1692.

—— An English dictionary explaining difficult terms. 1676 (11 edns by 1732).

Cooper, C. (Bishop Stortford Grammar School). The English teacher: or the discovery of the art of teaching and learning the English tongue, to read, write or speak our tongue with ease and understanding. 1688.

Coote, E. The English school-master. 1596, 1641 (19th edn), 1696 (48th edn).

Dilworth, Thomas. A new guide to the English tongue for the use of schools. 1740.

Dyche, Thomas. A guide to the English tongue. 1709, 1774 (6th edn).

Elstob, Elizabeth. Rudiments of grammar for the English-Saxon tongue. 1715. *See* The Saxon nymph, TLS 28 Sept 1933.

Enfield, William (1741–97). The speaker or miscellaneous pieces, selected from the best English writers with a view to facilitate the improvement of youth in reading and speaking; to which is prefixed an essay on elocution. 1774. Often rptd until 1850.

—— An essay on the cultivation of taste as a proper object in education. 1818.

Fenning, Daniel. New and complete spelling dictionary and sure guide to the English language. 1767.

—— A new grammar of the English language: or an easy introduction to speaking and writing English with propriety and correctness. 1771.

—— The universal spelling book. 1756, 1770 (13th edn).

Fisher, Anne. A practical new grammar. 1750, 1782 (21st edn).

Garretson, John. English exercises for school-boys. 1716 (14th edn).

General view of English pronunciation. Edinburgh 1784.

Hickes, George. Linguarum veterum septentrionalium thesaurus, grammatico-criticus et archaeologicus. 2 pts Oxford 1703–5.

Home, Henry (Lord Kames). Elements of criticism. 3 vols Edinburgh 1762, 1817 (9th edn).

Hornbooks and ABC's, by W. E. A. Axon, with an appendix on Nuremberg alphabetical tokens by W. S. Churchill. Manchester 1903.

[Tickell, Thomas]. A poem in praise of the horn book, written by a gentleman in England under a fit of the gout. Dublin 1728.

See also A. W. Tuer, *col 1926, above.*

Hunt, Thomas, Libellus orthographicus: or the diligent school-boy's directory. 1661.

Johnson, C. The art of writing letters: designed not only to finish the education of youth in general, but for every person that wishes to write letters well; and a grammar of the English language. 1770.

Johnson, Samuel. The plan of a dictionary of the English language. 1747.

—— A dictionary of the English language. 2 vols 1755.

Jones, John. The new art of spelling. 1704.

Lawson, John. Lectures concerning oratory. Dublin 1758.

Lowe, Solomon. English grammar reformed into a small and easy method for the readier learning of English by way of introduction to other languages. 1737.

[Lowth, Robert]. A short introduction to English grammar. 1762 etc.

Markham, William. Introduction to spelling and reading English. Gainsborough 1790.

Murray, Lindley. English grammar adapted to different classes of learners. York 1795, 1846 (54th edn).

Nares, R. Elements of orthoepy. 1784.

Newton, John. School pastime for young children: the rudiments of grammar. [1669].

— An introduction to the art of rhetorick for the benefit of young scholars and others. 1671.

Priestley, Joseph. The rudiments of English grammar, adapted to the use of schools. 1761. 7 edns before 1800.

— A course of lectures on the theory of language and universal grammar. 1762.

— A course of lectures on oratory and criticism. 1777.

Rollin, Charles. The method of teaching and studying the belles lettres. 4 vols 1734, 1810 (11th edn). From French.

[Sergeant, John]. The mysterie of rhetorick unveiled. 1657, 1688 (6th edn).

Sheridan, Thomas. A course of lectures on elocution. 1762.

— A dissertation on the causes of the difficulties in learning the English tongue. 1762.

— Lectures on the art of reading. 2 pts 1775.

— A general dictionary of the English language to establish a plain and permanent standard of pronunciation; to which is prefixed a rhetorical grammar. 2 vols 1780.

[Swift, Jonathan]. A proposal for correcting, improving and ascertaining the English tongue in a letter to the Lord High Treasurer. 1712.

Trimmer, Sarah. The charity school spelling book. 3 pts 1798–9.

French

Boyer, Abel. The compleat French-master for ladies and gentlemen: a method to learn with ease and delight the French tongue as it is now spoken in the court of France. 3 pts 1694, 1699.

Chenau. The true French master. 1752.

Chambaud, Lewis. The treasure of the French and English languages: vocabulary, common forms of speech, proverbs. 1762 (2nd edn).

Deletanville, Thomas. New set of exercises upon the various parts of French speech for the use of such as are desirous of making French without grammar or dictionary. 1796.

Drelincourt, Laurent. Sonnets choisis à l'usage des pensionnaires des dames Crisp à Stoke Newington. 1783.

Duval, J. An introduction to the French tongue or the new and compleat French spelling-book. 2 pts Dublin 1767.

Gerbier, Balthazar. The interpreter of the acadamie for foreign languages. 1648.

Mauger, Claudius. French grammar enriched with an exact pronunciation and many new dialogues. 1656 (2nd edn), 1694 (16th edn).
See also Kathleen Lambley, *col 1925, above.*

Porny, Marc Antoine. The practical French grammar (used at Eton). 1783 (4th edn).

Geography

Geography for youth: or a plain and easy introduction to the science for young gentlemen and ladies. 1782.

Echard, L. A most compleat compendium of geography describing all the empires, kingdoms and dominions of the whole world, with maps. 1691.

Fenning, Daniel. A new and easy guide to the use of the globes and the rudiments of geography. 1760 (2nd edn).

Guthrie, William. A new geographical, historical and commercial grammar, and present state of the several kingdoms of the world. 1770.

Greek

[Busby, Richard]. Graecae grammatices rudimenta in usum scholae Westmonasteriensis. 1647 etc.

— Rudimentum grammaticae graeco-latinae metricum in usum nobilium puerorum in schola regia Westmonasterii. 1702. Busby was headmaster of Westminster from 1638 till his death.

[Camden, William]. Institutio graecae grammatices compendiaria in usum regiae scholae Westmonasteriensis. 1643 etc.

Dugard, William (headmaster, Merchant Taylor's 1644–61). Rudimenta graecae linguae. 1656.

— Lexicon graeci testamenti. 1660.

Graeca grammatica. 1654.

Graecae grammaticae rudimenta in usum regiae scholae Etonensis. Eton 1772.

Nugent, Thomas. New method of learning with facility the Greek tongue, with variety of solid remarks for understanding the Greek writers, from the French of MM. de Port Royal. 1777 (3rd edn).

Italian

Altieri, F. A new grammar, Italian-English and English-Italian. 1728.

Baretti, Joseph. A grammar of the Italian languages. 1762, 1778, 1784.

— Easy phraseology for the use of young ladies who intend to learn the colloquial part of the Italian tongue. 1775.

Cori, A. M. A new method for the Italian tongue. 1723.

Palermo, Evangelista. A grammar of the Italian language in two parts. 1755, 1768, 1777.

Veneroni, John. The new Italian grammar: or the easiest and best method for attaining that language. 1711.

Latin

Ainsworth, Robert. Thesaurus linguae latinae compendiarius. 1736; ed W. Ellis 1840 (enlarged).

Ascham, Roger. The scholemaster [1570], corrected with notes by James Upton [assistant master at Eton]. 1711, 1743.

B., F. (Francis Brokesby?). Clavis grammatica: or the ready way to the Latin tongue. 1678.

Busby, Richard. An English introduction to the Latin tongue. 1659.

Catonis disticha de moribus: dicta insignia septum sapientium, with English translations by Charles Hoole. 1641 (at least 10 edns by 1700).

Cato's distichs with numerical clavis and construing and parsing index, in a method so easy that learners of the meanest attainment may be enabled to construe and parse with ease to themselves and without trouble to the teacher, by N. Bailey. 1724 (2nd edn).

Catonis disticha moralia et Lilii monita paedagogica: or Cato's moral distichs and Lily's paedagogical admonitions, with improvements, by John Stirling. 1783 (3rd edn).

Clarke, John. A new grammar of the Latin tongue comprising all in the art necessary for grammar schools; to which is annex'd a dissertation on language. 1733.

— An introduction to the making of Latin. 1740, 1742 (13th edn). This book, which condemned verse-making, attained a 36th edn. There was a French trn, Geneva 1745, from the 6th.
Clarke, master of Hull Grammar School, later of Gloucester, was a prolific writer of school books.

Clements, Henry. Synopsis communium locorum praecipue ad mores spectantium ex poetis latinis tum antiquioribus tum recentioribus collecta. Oxford 1700.

Cocker, Edward. Cocker's morals, or the Muses springgarden: sententious distichs and poems fitted for all publick and private grammar and writing-schools, for the scholars of the first to turn into Latin, and for those of the other to transcribe into all their various and curious hands. 1675.

Coleridge, J. Critical Latin grammar. 1772.

Coles, Elisha. Syncrisis: or the most natural and easie method of learning Latin; together with the holy history of the scripture war: or the sacred art militarie. 1675.

— Nolens volens: or you shall make Latin whether you will or no. 1675.

Comenius, Johann Amos. Orbis sensualium pictus: John Amos Comenius's visible world. Tr Charles Hoole 1658, 1777 (12th and best edn).

— Janua linguarum trilinguis, novissime ab ipso authore recognita, aucta, emendata. 1662, 1665, 1670, 1685. English, Latin, Greek.

Cordier, Maturin. Maturinus Corderius's school-colloquies, English and Latine: the children by the help of their mother tongue may the better learn to speak Latine in ordinary discourse, by Charles Hoole. 1657.

— Corderii colloquiorum centuria selecta: or a select century of Cordery's colloquies, with an English translation as literal as possible, designed for the use of beginners, by John Clarke. 1718.

Dugard, William. The English rudiments of the Latin tongue. 1656.

— Rhetorices elementa. 1648.

E., J. Grammaticus analyticus: or the analytical grammarian teaching three things necessary to the acquiring the Latine tongue, for the use of the free-school in East-Smith-Field near London. 2 vols in 1 1670.

Erasmus. Colloquiorum formulae alias colloquia. Basle 1516, 1523.

Twenty-two select colloquies. Tr Sir Roger L'Estrange 1680; ed C. Whibley [1923].

All the familiar colloquies of Desiderius Erasmus of Roterdam concerning men, manners and things, translated into English by N. Bailey. 1725.

Erasmi Colloquia selecta: or the select colloquies of Erasmus with an English translation as literal as possible designed for the use of beginners, by John Clarke. 1720.

An English essay on the syntax of the Latin tongue. 1772. An English-Latin grammar instead of the Latin-Latin grammar in general use.

Familiar forms of speaking compos'd for the use of schools. 1678 (2nd edn), 1708 (17th edn).

Greenwood, James (sub-master in St Paul's school 1721–37). The London vocabulary, English and Latin, put into a new method, adorned with 26 pictures for the use of schools. 1713 (3rd edn), 1797 (21st edn).

Hampton, B. Prosodia construed: an addition to Lily's rules. 1672.

Harblib, Samuel. The true and readie way to learne the Latine tongue. 1654.

Holyoake, Thomas. A large dictionary, in three parts: the English before the Latin, the Latin before the English, proper names of persons. 1677.

Hoole, Charles. Terminationes et exempla declinationum et conjugationum in usum grammaticastrorum. 1650 (many edns to 1780 and later).

Hunt, Thomas. Abecedarium scholasticum: or the grammar scholars abecedary. 1671.

[Huish, Anthony]. Priscianus nascens: or a key to the grammar school, to the no small ease of the master in teaching and the scholar in learning, with several copies to learn to write by. 2 pts in 1 1663.

Jasz-Berenyi Pal. Fax nova linguae latinae: a new torch to the Latine tongue. 1664.

Johnson, Richard (Free school Nottingham 1707–18). Noctes Nottinghamicae: or cursory objections against the syntax of the common grammar in order to obtain a better. Nottingham 1718.

— Grammatical commentaries: being an apparatus to a new national grammar by way of animadversion upon the falsities, obscurities, redundancies and defects of Lilly's system now in use. 1706.

Langston, J. Lusus poeticus latino-anglicanus: for that ancient exercise, capping of verses. 1675, 1688 (3rd edn).

Lily, William. Brevis institutio: or short introduction to grammar. 2 pts 1549. Continued as main class-book of the 17th and 18th century schools. 70 known separate edns before 1700. It was rev John Ward in 1734, rptd at least till 1808.

Littleton, Adam. Linguae latinae liber dictionarius quadripartitus: I, English-Latin; II, Latin classical; III, Latin proper; IV, Latin barbarous, improved from the several works of Stephens, Cooper, Holyoke and a large ms of John Milton's. 1693.

Love, John. Two grammatical treatises, viz: I, Animadversions on the Latin grammar lately published by Mr Robert Trotter, schoolmaster at Dumfries; II, A dissertation upon the way of teaching that language, the vulgar practice of teaching Latin by a grammar writ in the same language is justified and defended. 1733.

Lowe, Solomon. A critique on the etymology of the Westminster grammar. 1723.

— The occasional critique: on education. 1728.

— Mnemonics delineated. 1737.

Mair, John. The tyro's dictionary Latin and English. 1760.

Parkyns, Sir Thomas. A practical and grammatical introduction to the Latin tongue. 1716 (2nd edn).

[Port Royal]. A general and rational grammar with the reasons of the general agreement and the particular differences of languages, translated from the French of Messrs de Port Royal. 1753.

Robertson, William. Phraseologia generalis. 1681, 1693.

Robinson, H. The Latine phrases of Winchester school. 1658 (2nd edn), 1685 (11th edn).

[Shaw, Samuel]. Minerva's triumph: or grammar and rhetorick in all the parts of them personated by youths in dramatick scenes in a country school, presented to the view of all that love learning, but especially recommended to the use of schools at their breakings up. 1680.

Walker, William (master of Lough school and later of the Free school, Grantham). A treatise of English particles. 1655, 1720 (15th edn).

— Phraseologia anglo-latina; to which is added Paroemiologia anglo-latina: or a collection of English and Latin proverbs for the use of schools. 1672.

Wase, Christopher. An essay of a practical grammar: or an enquiry after a more easie and certain help to the construing and parsing of authors, and to the making and speaking of Latin. 1682.

Willymot, William. English particles exemplify'd in sentences design'd for Latin exercises. 1703, 1771 (8th edn).

Mathematics

See A. Heal, The English writing-masters and their copy-books, Cambridge 1931; and Arithmetic, above.

[Emerson, W.] Cylcomathesis: or an easy introduction to the several branches of the mathematics designed principally for young students before the more abstruse and difficult parts. 1763.

Kersey, John. Elements of that mathematical art commonly called algebra: in two books, with lectures read in the school of geometry in Oxford by Dr Edmund Halley. 1725.

See Wingate, col 1943, above.

Leadbetter, Charles. The young mathematician's companion: a compleat tutor to the mathematicks, containing geometry, trigonometry, astronomy, dyalling to form the minds of youth. 1748.

[Leybourn], W[illiam]. The art of numbering by speaking rods, vulgarly termed nepeirs bones, by which the most difficult parts of arithmetick are performed with incredible celerity, published by W.L. 1667; John Napier, Rabdologiae: seu numerationis per virgulas libri II, 1615. On a primitive calculating machine.

Maclaurin, Colin. A treatise of algebra. 1748.

Mole, John. Elements of algebra, to which is prefixed a choice collection of arithmetical questions with their solutions. 1788.

Morland, Samuel. A new and most useful instrument for addition and subtraction of pounds, shillings, pence and farthings without charging the memory, disturbing the mind or exposing the operator to any uncertainty, which no method hitherto published can justly pretend to, invented and presented to Charles I. 1666. Plates.

Seller, John (fl. 1700). A pocket-book containing severall choice collections in arithmetick, astronomy, geometry, surveying, dialling, navigation, astrology, geography, measuring, gageing. [1685]. Plates and maps.

Ward, John. The young mathematician's guide. 1713, 1724 (4th edn).

Writing and Shorthand

Bickham, George. Universal penman. 1733.

Byrom, J. The universal English shorthand. Manchester 1767.

Carlton, W. J. Samuel Pepys and his shorthand books. Library 4th ser 14 1933.

Cocker, Edward. The guide to penmanship. 1673.

The excellency of the pen and pencil, exemplifying the use of them in drawing, etching, engraving, limning. 1668.

First script system of shorthand; with an account of all the script or sloping-hand systems of shorthand in England. 1890.

Macaulay, Aulay. Polygraphy: or short-hand made easy to the meanest capacity. 1747.

Massey, William. Origin and progress of letters. 2 pts in 1 vol (i, Formation of alphabets; ii, Calligraphy and account of the most celebrated English penman) 1763.

Rich, Jeremiah. The penn's dexterity. 1659, 1680 (5th edn).

Shelton, T. Tachygraphy. Cambridge 1641 etc.

Weston, James. Stenography compleated or the art of short-hand brought to perfection. 4 pts 1727. Plates.

Miscellaneous

Abercromby, D. Academia scientiarum: introduction to the liberal arts, in English and Latine. 1687.

Artificial versifying, or the school-boy's recreation: a new way to make Latin verses, whereby anyone of ordinary capacity (though he understands not one word of Latin or what a verse means) may be plainly taught how to make hundreds of hexameter verses, which shall be true Latin, true verse and good sense, never before publish'd. 1677.

Baxter, A. Matho: or the cosmotheoria puerilis. 2 vols 1740, 1745.

[Bodenham, John?]. Politeuphuia: wits common-wealth, or a treasure of divine, historical and political admonitions, similes and sentences for the use of schools. 1699. Planned originally in 1597 in conjunction with John Bodenham.

Busby, Richard. Hebraicae grammatices rudimenta. 1717.

Clare, M. Youth's introduction to trade and business. 1751.

[Clarke, Samuel]. The historian's guide: or England's remembrancer. 1676.

Cooke, T. Universal letter writer. 1798.

Evangelia: sive excerpta quaedam ex Novo Testamento, secundum Latinum Sebast. Castellionis versionem in usum classium inferiorum scholae Etonensis. Eton 1789.

Fenning, Daniel. The young man's book of knowledge. 1764. An elementary encyclopaedia in the medieval manner, including theology, natural philosophy, geography, geometry, astronomy, navigation and plainsailing, 'music and vibration'.

Ferguson, James. An easy introduction to astronomy for young gentlemen and ladies. 1769 (2nd edn).

Grey, Richard. Memoria technica. 1730, Oxford 1824 (with Solomon Lowe's Mnemonics), 1861, 1865.

Hill, John. The young secretary's guide. 1696 (7th edn), 1764 (27th edn).

Holmes, John. The art of rhetoric made easy. 1739 (2nd edn).

Martin, Benjamin. Bibliotheca technologia. 1737.

The new art of letter writing. 1762 (2nd edn).

Moxon, Joseph. Tutor to astronomy and geography: an easie way to know the use of the globes, coelestial and terrestrial. 1659, 1699 (5th edn).

[Nowell, Alexander]. Christianae pietatis prima institutio ad usum scholarum graece et latine scripta. 1670.

Phillips, Jenkin Thomas. A compendious way of teaching ancient and modern languages successfully executed in London. 1723.

Salzman, C. G. Gymnastics for youth. 1800.

Shaw, John and Simon Wastel. The divine art of memory: or the sum of the holy scripture delivered in ackrostick verses, written originally in Latine by John Shaw and made English by Simon Wastel. 1623, 1683.

Smith, William, MD. The student's vade mecum: containing an account of knowledge, history, philosophy, institution of the society and government, heathen idolatry, different systems of philosophy, mathematics, with account of the proper books. 1770.

Watson, Richard. A plan of a course of chemistry. Cambridge 1771.

Whitby, Daniel. Ethices compendium in usum academicae juventutis. Oxford 1684.

'Juvenile' Books

See Children's books, col 1013, above.

G. EDUCATION OF WOMEN AND GIRLS

See also Courtesy Books, above.

Aldis, Mrs H. G. The bluestockings. CHEL vol 11 ch 15 1914.

[Allestree, Richard]. The ladies calling, by the author of the Whole duty of man. 1673, 1700 (7th edn).

Ballard, George. Memoirs of several ladies of Great Britain who have been celebrated for their writings or skill in the learned languages, arts and sciences. Oxford 1752.

Barbauld, Anna Laetitia

    Barbauld, A. L. le B. Memoirs of Mrs Barbauld, including letters and notices of her family and friends. 1874.

    Rodgers, B. Georgian chronicle: Mrs Barbauld and her family. 1958.

Barksdale, Clement. Whether a learned maid may be a scholar. 1659. A trn of Anna Maria Schumann, De ingenii muliebris ad doctrinam et meliores litteras aptitudine, 1641.

Beattie, James

    Forbes, W. Life and writings. 2 vols Edinburgh 1806. On Scots education and the Bluestockings.

Bellamy, Daniel (the elder). The young ladies miscellany: or youth's innocent and rational amusement; to which is prefixed a short essay on the art of pronunciation. 1723.

Bennett, John. Strictures on female education, chiefly as it relates to the culture of the heart. [1788].

Brown, John (vicar of Newcastle). On the female character and education: a sermon at the anniversary of the guardians of the asylum for deserted female orphans; with an appendix relative to a proposed code of education. 1765. On undenominational religious teaching.

Burgess, M. A. A. A history of Burlington School. 1938.

Burton, J. Lectures on female education and manners. 2 vols 1793.

Cappe, C. An account of two charity schools for girls. York 1800.

Carlisle, Countess of. Thoughts in the form of maxims addressed to young ladies, on their first establishment in the world. 1789.

Carter, Elizabeth. Letters to Mrs [Elizabeth] Montagu. Ed M. Pennington 3 vols 1817.

—— A series of letters between Mrs Elizabeth Carter and Miss Catherine Talbot from 1741 to 1770; to which are added letters from Mrs Elizabeth Carter to Mrs Vesey between 1763 and 1787. Ed M. Pennington 2 vols 1808.

—— Memoirs of the life of Mrs Elizabeth Carter. Ed M. Pennington 2 vols 1808 (2nd edn).

Cartwright, Mrs H. Letters on female education addressed to a married lady. 1777.

Chapone, Hester. The works of Mrs Chapone: containing letters on the improvement of the mind, addressed to a young lady, letters to Miss Carter, an account of her life and character. 4 vols 1773, 1807 etc.

Darwin, Erasmus. A plan for the conduct of female education in boarding schools. Derby 1797.

Defoe, Daniel. The education of women. In his Essay upon projects, 1697.

Douglas, M. A. and C. R. Ash. The Godolphin school. 1928.

Elwood, Anne Katharine. Memoirs of the literary ladies of England from the commencement of the last century. 2 vols 1843.

'Emilia'. On female accomplishments. Mirror no 89 1780.

Essex, John. The young ladies conduct: or rules for education, with instructions upon dress and advice to young wives. 1722.

Evelyn, John. Diary. Ed E. S. de Beer 6 vols Oxford 1955. A girl's private education, 10 Feb 1685.

[Fielding, Sarah]. The governess, or little female academy: the history of Mrs Teachum and her nine girls, for the entertainment and instruction of young ladies, by the author of David Simple. 1749 etc.

Gardiner, Dorothy. English girlhood at school. Oxford 1929.

Gregory, John. A father's legacy to his daughters. 1774. Many edns up to 1877. It frequently appeared, accompanied by such writings as Mrs Chapone's letters of a similar purport; Bishop George Horne, A picture of the female character as it ought to appear when formed; and Mr Tyrold's advice to his daughter, from Fanny Burney, Camilla. A London edn (1822) added to the Legacy Mrs Chapone's letter to a new married lady and Education: a fairy tale, by Miss Talbot, in order to make 'a volume of it'. The Legacy attained the popularity of a chap-book.

Hickes, George. Instruction for the education of a daughter, to which is added Instructions for the conduct of young ladies of the highest rank. 1707. Trn of Fénelon, Traité de l'éducation des filles, 1687.

Howard, Sarah. Thoughts on female education; with advice to young ladies. 1783.

Knox, Vicesimus. On the literary education of women. In his Liberal education, section 27, 1781.

—— On the ostentatious affectation of the character of a learned lady. In his Essays moral and literary no 86.

—— On the insensibility of the men to the charms of the female mind cultivated with polite and solid literature. In his Essays no 142.

The lady's preceptor: or a letter to a young lady of distinction upon politeness, taken from the French of the Abbé d'Ancourt, and adapted to the religion, customs and manners of the English nation, by a gentleman of Cambridge. 1743.

Le Fevre. The governess, from the French. 1779.

Letter to a daughter. The value of a child: or motives to a good education of children in a letter. 1752.

Lounger (Edinburgh) nos 13 (B. McLeod, 16 (W. Tytler), 52 (W. Craig) 1785–6.

'Lover of her sex' (Mary Astell). A serious proposal to the ladies for the advancement of their true and great interest. 1694, 1697 (4th edn with an added 2nd pt).

Macaulay, Catherine. Letters on education. 1790.

Mackenzie, Henry. Girls' education. Mirror nos 89, 96 1780.

[Makin, Bathsua?]. An essay to revive the antient education of gentlewomen in religion, manners, arts and tongues, with an answer to the objections against this way of education. 1673.

Moir, John. Female tuition: or an address to mothers, on the education of daughters. 1784.

Montagu, Elizabeth. Letters, with some of the letters of her correspondents, published by Matthew Montagu. 2 pts 1809–13.

—— A lady of the last century in her unpublished letters, collected with a biographical sketch and a chapter on blue stockings, by John Doran. 1873.

Montagu, Lady Mary Wortley. Letters and works. Ed Lord Wharncliffe and W. M. Thomas 2 vols 1887.

—— Complete letters. Ed R. Halsband 3 vols Oxford 1967.

More, Hannah. Essays on various subjects principally designed for young ladies. 1777.

—— Strictures on the modern system of female education with a view of the principles and conduct prevalent among women of rank and fortune. 2 vols 1799, 1811 (11th edn).

—— Remarks on the present mode of educating females: being a copious abridgement of Miss Hannah More's strictures. 1799.

—— Hints towards forming the character of a young princess. 2 vols 1805.

Jones, M. G. Hannah More. Cambridge 1952.

The new polite tutoress. [c. 1785].

A parent. An enquiry into the present state of boarding-schools for young ladies. 1776.

Pennington, Lady Sarah. An unfortunate mother's advice to her absent daughters in a letter to Miss Pennington. 1761 etc.

Percival, A. C. The English miss to-day and yesterday. 1939.

Phillips, M. and W. S. Tomkinson. English women in life and letters. 1927.

Piozzi, Hester and Penelope Pennington. The intimate letters of Hester Piozzi and Penelope Pennington 1788–1821. Ed O. G. Knapp 1914.

Pope, Alexander. Of the characters of women: an epistle to a lady. 1735.

Reeve, Clara. Plans of education. 1792.

Rice, J. A lecture rendering the English language a peculiar branch of female education. 1773.

Rice, J. A plan of female education. 1779.

Savile, George, Marquis of Halifax. The lady's new-year's-gift: or advice to a daughter. 1688; rptd in Complete works, ed W. Raleigh, Oxford 1912. The Advice 'ran through some 25 edns and held the field for almost a century, to be superseded at last by Dr Gregory's Father's legacy and Mrs Chapone's letters on the improvement of the mind', Raleigh p. xx.

Seymour, Juliana S. On the management and education of children. 1754.

Stenton, M. The English woman in history. 1957.

Thomas, D. H. A short history of St Martin-in-the-Fields high school for girls. 1929.

Trimmer, Mrs Sarah. The oeconomy of charity: or an address to ladies concerning Sunday-schools; the establishment of schools of industry under female inspection. 1787, 2 vols 1801 (enlarged).

W., W. A letter to a lady in praise of female learning. Dublin 1739.

Wakefield, Priscilla. Reflections upon the present condition of the female sex, with suggestions. 1798.

Wallas, Ada. Before the bluestockings. 1929. On Hannah Woolley, Lady Masham, Mary Astell, Elizabeth Elstob.

Wollstonecraft, Mary. A vindication of the rights of woman; with strictures on political and moral subjects. 1792.

—— Thoughts on the education of daughters; with reflections on female conduct. 1787.

Linford, M. Mary Wollstonecraft 1756–97. 1924.

James, H. R. Mary Wollstonecraft. Oxford 1932.

Wraxall, N. W. History and posthumous memoirs 1772–84. Ed H. B. Wheatley 5 vols 1884 (with notes and addns from unpbd mss). Vol I, the Bluestockings.

—— Posthumous memoirs of his own time. 3 vols 1836.

H. MANUSCRIPT MATERIAL

There is a great quantity of ms concerning English education in this period—universities, colleges, schools, educational reform etc—much of it yet unworked. Particulars must be sought in the calendars and catalogues of the collections stored in the great libraries. The following are merely illustrative instances.

Christ's Hospital. *See* Tanner, *col 1941, above.*

Cole mss. Index to the contents of the Cole manuscripts in the British Museum, by G. J. Gray. Cambridge 1912. On Cambridge; colleges, schools.

Harleian mss. A catalogue of the Harleian manuscripts in the British Museum ,with indexes of persons, places and matters, by H. Wanley, R. Nares and T. H. Horne. 4 vols 1808–12.

Madan, F. Rough list of ms materials relating to the history of Oxford contained in the printed catalogues of the Bodleian and college libraries. Oxford 1887.

—— Notes on Bodleian manuscripts relating to Cambridge: pt I, Town and University. Cambridge 1931.

Sloane mss, British Museum. Index by E. J. L. Scott. 1904.

Archbishop Secker's diary. In ms collections of the Archbishop's library, at Lambeth. On dissenting academies; Oxford; Leyden.

Thomas Baker's mss, Cambridge University Library: Harleian collection, British Museum. In BM, letters to Prof Ward on Gresham College 1733–9; ref 6209 f, 2–52.

A. M.

6. SCOTTISH LITERATURE

I. GENERAL INTRODUCTION

BIBLIOGRAPHIES

M'Kie, J. Title pages and imprints of the books in the private library of M'Kie. Kilmarnock 1867.

McBain, J. M. Bibliography of Arbroath periodical literature and political broadsides. Arbroath 1889.

Cameron, J. A bibliography of Scottish theatrical literature. Pbns of Edinburgh Bibl Soc 1 1896 (with suppl).

Aldis, H. G. A list of books printed in Scotland before 1700, including those printed furth of the realm for Scottish booksellers, with brief notes on the printers and stationers. Pbns of Edinburgh Bibl Soc 6 1904.

Terry, C. S. A catalogue of the publications of Scottish historical and kindred clubs and societies, and of the volumes relative to Scottish history issued by his Majesty's Stationery Office 1780–1908. Glasgow 1909; continuation by C. Matheson, 1908–27, Aberdeen 1928.

Black, G. F. List of works relating to Scotland. BNYPL 1914; New York 1916 (expanded).

Fasti ecclesiae scoticanae. [Ed, with biographical sketch of Hew Scott (editor of first edn) by W. S. Crockett and F. Grant] 7 vols Edinburgh 1915–28.

Maclean, D. Typographia scoto-gadelica: books in the Gaelic of Scotland 1567–1914. Edinburgh 1915. Based on J. Reid, Bibliotheca scoto-celtica, Glasgow 1832.

Anderson, A. R. A short bibliography of Scottish history and literature. Glasgow 1922.

Crane, R. S. and F. B. Kaye. A census of British newspapers and periodicals 1620–1800. Chapel Hill 1927.

Johnstone, J. F. K. and A. W. Robertson. Bibliographica aberdoniensis 1472–1640, 1641–1700. 2 vols Aberdeen 1929–30 (Third Spalding Club).

Ewing, J. C. Brash and Reid, booksellers in Glasgow, and their collection of Poetry original and selected. Records of Glasgow Bibl Soc 12 1936; also separately.

Jessop, T. E. A bibliography of David Hume and of Scottish philosophy from Francis Hutcheson to Lord Balfour. 1938.

MacPike, E. F. English, Scottish and Irish diaries, journals, common-place books 1550–1900. Bull of Bibliography 17 1943.

Dougan, R. O. Catalogue of an exhibition of 18th-century books at the Signet Library. Cambridge 1951.

Woolley, J. S. Bibliography for Scottish linguistic studies. Edinburgh 1954.

Ferguson, J. P. S. Scottish newspapers held in Scottish libraries. Edinburgh 1956.

Hancock, P. D. A bibliography of works relating to Scotland 1916–50. 2 vols Edinburgh 1960.

Scottish books: a brief bibliography. Edinburgh [1963] (Saltire Soc).

Gaskell, P. A bibliography of the Foulis Press. 1964.

Catalogue of the Lauriston Castle chapbooks. Boston 1964 (Nat Lib of Scotland). 3,700 chapbooks, mostly Scottish.

Ratcliffe, F. W. Chapbooks with Scottish imprints in the Robert White Collection, the University Library, Newcastle-upon-Tyne. Bibliotheck 4 1966. Mostly 19th century.

Montgomerie, W. A bibliography of the Scottish ballad mss 1730–1825. Stud in Scottish Lit 4– 1967–.

[Lloyd, D. M.] Reader's guide to Scotland: a bibliography. 1968.

Smith, C. and R. S. Walker. Library resources in Scotland. Glasgow 1968.

See also:

Scottish antiquary: or northern notes and queries. 17 vols 1886–1903.

Scottish notes and queries. 1st ser, 1887–99; 2nd ser, 1899–1907; as Aberdeen journal, notes and queries, 1907–22; 3rd ser, 1922–35.

Publications of the Edinburgh Bibliographical Society. 15 vols 1890–1935; [succeeded by] Transactions 1935–.

Records of the Glasgow Bibliography Society. 13 vols 1914–39.

The bibliotheck: a journal of bibliographical notes and queries mainly of Scottish interest. 1956–.

Studies in Scottish literature. 1963–.

It will also be useful to consult the following library catalogues: Aberdeen Public, Aberdeen Univ, Advocates, Edinburgh Univ, Mitchell (for lists of acquisitions), New College, Signet.

DICTIONARIES

Jamieson, J. An etymological dictionary of the Scottish tongue. 5 vols Paisley 1875–87.

MacBain, A. Etymological dictionary of the Gaelic language. Stirling 1911.

MacLennan, M. A pronouncing and etymological dictionary of the Gaelic language: Gaelic-English, English-Gaelic. Edinburgh 1925.

Jarvie, J. N. Lallans. [1947].

Dwelly, E. The illustrated Gaelic-English dictionary. Glasgow 1949.

Warrack, A. Chambers' Scots dictionary. Edinburgh 1952 (new edn).

Craigie, W. A. and A. J. Aitken. A dictionary of the older Scottish tongue from the twelfth century to the end of the seventeenth. Chicago 1931–. Incomplete.

Grant, W. and D. D. Murison. The Scottish national dictionary. Edinburgh 1931–. 'Containing all the Scottish words known to be in use or to have been in use since ca. 1700'; incomplete.

LITERARY HISTORIES

Irving, D. Lives of Scotish writers. 2 vols Edinburgh 1839, 1850.

Murray, T. The literary history of Galloway. Edinburgh 1823.

Campbell, D. A. A treatise on the language, poetry and music of the Highland clans. Edinburgh 1862.

Fraser, J. The humorous chapbooks of Scotland. 2 vols New York 1873–[4].

Blackie, J. S. The language and literature of the Scottish Highlands. Edinburgh 1876.

Macneill, N. The literature of the Highlanders: race, language, literature, poetry and music. Inverness 1892, London 1898; ed J. M. Campbell, Stirling 1929 (enlarged).

Walker, H. Three centuries of Scottish literature. 2 vols Glasgow 1893.

Williams, A. M. The Scottish school of rhetoric. Glasgow 1897.

Henderson, T. F. Scottish vernacular literature. Edinburgh 1898, 1900 (rev), 1910, Detroit 1969.

Graham, H. G. Scottish men of letters in the eighteenth century. 1901, 1908.

Maclean, M. The literature of the Celts. 1902, 1926.

— The literature of the Highlands. 1903, 1925.

Harvey, W. Scottish chapbook literature. Paisley 1903.

Millar, J. H. A literary history of Scotland. 1903.

— Scottish prose of the seventeenth and eighteenth centuries. Glasgow 1912.

Holmes, D. T. Lectures on Scottish literature. Paisley 1904.

Maclean, D. The literature of the Scottish Gael. Edinburgh 1912.

Smith, J. C. Some characteristics of Scots literature. 1912.

Smith, G. G. Scottish literature, character and influence. 1919.

Moffatt, J. The Bible in Scots literature. [1924].

Mackenzie, A. M. An historical survey of Scottish literature to 1714. 1933.

Power, W. Literature and oatmeal. 1935.

Speirs, J. The Scots literary tradition. 1940, 1962 (enlarged).

Foerster, D. Mid-eighteenth-century Scotch criticism of Homer. SP 40 1943.

Smith, S. G. A short introduction to Scottish literature. Edinburgh 1951.

Wittig, K. The Scottish tradition in literature. Edinburgh 1958.

Witte, W. Scottish influence on Schiller. In his Schiller and Burns and other essays, Oxford 1959.

Craig, D. Scottish literature and the Scottish people 1680–1830. 1961.

Kinghorn, A. M. Literary aesthetics and the sympathetic emotion: a main trend in eighteenth-century Scottish criticism. Stud in Scottish Lit 1 1964.

Price, J. V. Concepts of enlightenment in eighteenth-century Scottish literature. Texas Stud in Lit & Lang 9 1967.

MISCELLANEOUS STUDIES

Biographia presbyteriana. Edinburgh 1827.

Bower, A. History of the University of Edinburgh. 3 vols Edinburgh 1830.

The newspaper press of Scotland. Fraser's Mag May 1838.

[Alexander, W.] Notes and sketches illustrative of northern rural life in the eighteenth century. Edinburgh 1877.

Rogers, C. Social life in Scotland from early times to recent times. 3 vols Edinburgh 1884–6.

Ramsay, J. Scotland and Scotsmen in the eighteenth century, from the mss of John Ramsay of Ochtertyre. Ed A. Allardyce 2 vols Edinburgh 1888.

Bulloch, J. M. A history of the University of Aberdeen. 1895.

Rait, R. B. The University of Aberdeen. Aberdeen 1895.

Gibb, J. S. James Watson, printer: notes on his life and work, with a hand-list of books printed by him 1697–1722. Pbns of Edinburgh Bibl Soc 1 1896.

Graham, H. G. The social life of Scotland in the eighteenth century. 2 vols 1899, 1900 (rev), 1 vol 1901 (2 issues, rev), 1906, 1928.

Newbigging, T. The Scottish Jacobites and their songs and music. 1899, 1907.

Fraser, G. M. Historical Aberdeen. Aberdeen 1905.

Sinclair, G. A. Periodical literature of the eighteenth century [Scottish]. Scottish Historical Rev 2 1905.

Anderson, P. J. (ed). Studies in the history and development of the University of Aberdeen. 1906. Bibliography, including theses and disputations.

— Notes on academic theses. Aberdeen 1912.

Neilson, G. (ed). Glasgow quatercentenary studies. Glasgow 1907.

Watson, J. The Scot in the eighteenth century: his religion and his life. 1907, nd.

Couper, W. J. The Edinburgh periodical press 1642–1800. 2 vols Stirling 1908.

— James Watson, King's printer. Scottish Historical Rev 7 1910.

— The rebel press at Perth in 1715. Records of Glasgow Bibl Soc 8 1930.

— The Glasgow periodical press in the eighteenth century. Ibid.

Coutts, J. History of the University of Glasgow. Glasgow 1909.

Mathieson, W. L. The awakening of Scotland: a history from 1747 to 1797. Glasgow 1910.

Leabhar a' clachain: home life of the Highlanders 1400–1746. Glasgow 1911 (Highland Village Assoc).

Votiva tabella: a memorial vol of St Andrews University. Glasgow 1911.

Grant, W. The pronunciation of English in Scotland. Cambridge 1913.

Murray, D. Robert and Andrew Foulis and the Glasgow press. Records of Glasgow Bibl Soc 2 1913.

M'Lean, H. A. Robert Urie: printer in Glasgow. Records of Glasgow Bibl Soc 3 1914. With list of pbns.

Renwick, R. and J. Lindsay (vol 1) and G. Eyre-Todd (vols 2–3). History of Glasgow. 3 vols Glasgow 1921–34.

M'Culloch, W. E. Viri illustres Universitatum Abredonensium. Aberdeen 1923.

Craigie, W. A. et al. The Scottish tongue. 1924.

Grant, I. F. Everyday life on an old Highland farm 1769–82. 1924.

Wilson, J. The dialects of central Scotland. 1926.

Collins, A. S. Authorship in the days of Johnson 1726–80. 1927.

— The profession of letters 1780–1832. 1928.

Fyfe, J. G. (ed). Scottish diaries and memoirs 1550–1746. Stirling [1927].

— Scottish diaries and memoirs 1746–1843. Stirling 1942.

Bain, M. Les voyageurs français en Ecosse 1770–1830 et leurs curiosités intellectuelles. Paris 1931.

Craig, Mary E. The Scottish periodical press 1750–89. Edinburgh 1931.

MacLehose, J. The Glasgow University Press 1638–1931, with some notes on Scottish printing in the last three hundred years. Glasgow 1931.

Dieth, E. A grammar of the Buchan dialect. 2 vols Cambridge 1932.

Morton, R. The literature of dissent in Glasgow in the latter half of the eighteenth century. Records of Glasgow Bibl Soc 11 1933.

Dale, C. The Scottish periodical press in the eighteenth century. Scottish N & Q 13 1935.

Anderson, D. The Bible in seventeenth-century Scottish life and literature. 1936.

Menary, G. The life and letters of Duncan Forbes of Culloden. 1936.

Black, G. F. A calendar of cases of witchcraft in Scotland 1510–1727. BNYPL Nov 1937– Jan 1938.

Donaldson, J. E. Caithness in the eighteenth century. Edinburgh 1938.

Nolan, J. B. Benjamin Franklin in Scotland and Ireland, 1759 and 1771. Philadelphia 1938.

Bryson, G. Some eighteenth-century conceptions of society. Sociological Rev 31 1939.

— Man and society: the Scottish enquiry of the eighteenth century. Princeton 1945.

Etzrodt, H. Schottlandreisen im XVIII Jht: wie der Engländer die Hochlande sah. Berlin 1939.

Imrie, D. S. M. The story of the Scots Magazine. Scots Mag 30–1 1939.

Henderson, G. D. The work of a Scottish mystic: James Garden's comparative theology 1679. Church Quart Rev 129 1940.

— Puritanism in eighteenth-century Scotland. Evangelical Quart 19 1947.

Mackenzie, A. M. Scotland in modern times 1720–1939. 1941.

—(ed). Scottish pageant 1625–1707, 1707–1802. Edinburgh 1949, 1950. 2 pts of a 4-vol anthology of prose and poetry.

Gray, W. F. Allan Ramsay the younger: publicist, scholar and littérateur. Quart Rev 282 1944.

— A seventeenth-century Scottish library. TLS 5 June 1948.

Pearce, R. H. The eighteenth-century Scottish primitivists. ELH 12 1945.

Scott-Moncrieff, G. Edinburgh. 1947.

Finlay, I. Art in Scotland. 1948.

Farmer, H. G. A history of music in Scotland. [1948].

Lochhead, M. The Scots household in the eighteenth century. Edinburgh 1948.

— Scots law and letters. Quart Rev 292 1954.

MacNeill, D. H. The Scottish realm. Glasgow 1948.

Meikle, H. W. Some aspects of later seventeenth-century Scotland. Glasgow 1948.

— Voltaire and Scotland. Etudes Anglaises 11 1958.

Plant, Marjorie. Clothes and the eighteenth-century Scot. Scottish Historical Rev 27 1948.

— The domestic life of Scotland in the 18th century. Edinburgh 1952.

Elliott, R. C. The early Scots Magazine. MLQ 11 1950.

Foerster, D. Scottish primitivism and the historical approach. PQ 29 1950.

Fussell, G. E. and H. Fyrth. Eighteenth-century Scottish agricultural writings. History 35 1950.

McLaren, M. The capital of Scotland. Edinburgh 1950.

Patrick, M. Four centuries of Scottish psalmody. Oxford 1950.

Joyce, M. Edinburgh: the golden age 1769–1832. 1951.

Foster, J. Scottish evangelicals of the eighteenth century. London Quart 177 1952.

Gaskell, P. The early works of the Foulis Press and the Wilson foundry. Library 5th ser 8 1952.

MacInnes, J. The evangelical movement in the Highlands of Scotland 1688–1800. Aberdeen 1952.

Handley, J. E. Scottish farming in the eighteenth century. 1953.

Macleod, R. D. The Scottish publishing houses. Glasgow 1953.

Roe, F. C. La découverte de l'Ecosse entre 1760 et 1830. Revue de Littérature Comparée 27 1953.

Kinghorn, A. M. Scots literature and Scottish antiquarians. SE 33 1954.

'Stampoy, Pappity'. A collection of Scotch proverbs 1663. Ed A. Taylor, Los Angeles 1955 (Augustan Reprint Soc).

Pryde, G. S. The Scottish universities and the colleges of colonial America. Glasgow 1957.

Carnie, R. H. Publishing in Perth before 1807. Abertay Historical Soc 6 1960. With list of pbns 1770–1807.

— Scottish printers and booksellers 1668–1775: a study of source-material. Biblioteck 4 1966.

Mechie, S. The Church and Scottish social development 1780–1870. 1960.

Murchison, T. M. Highland life as reflected in Gaelic literature. Trans of Gaelic Soc of Inverness 38 1937–41. Pbd 1962; analysis of 20 17th- and 18th-century texts.

Daiches, D. The paradox of Scottish culture: the eighteenth-century experience. Oxford 1964.

Law, A. Education in Edinburgh in the eighteenth century. 1965.

Duncan, D. Thomas Ruddiman: a study in Scottish scholarship of the early eighteenth century. Edinburgh 1965.

Youngson, A. J. The making of classical Edinburgh 1750–1840. Edinburgh 1966.

Brumfitt, J. H. Scotland and the French Enlightenment. In W. H. Barber et al (ed), The age of Enlightenment, Edinburgh 1967.

Cameron, J. K. The Church of Scotland in the Age of Reason. Stud on Voltaire & Eighteenth Century 58 1967.

Cant, R. G. The Scottish universities and Scottish society in the eighteenth century. Ibid.

Edinburgh in the Age of Reason. Edinburgh 1967.

Hook, A. D. Scottish contributions to the American Enlightenment. Texas Stud in Lit & Lang 8 1967.

Horn, D. B. A short history of the University of Edinburgh 1556–1889. Edinburgh 1967.

Kaufman, P. Leadhills: library of Diggers. Libri 17 1967.

Trevor-Roper, H. R. The Scottish Enlightenment. Stud in Voltaire & Eighteenth Century 58 1967.

Young, D. Scotland and Edinburgh in the eighteenth century. Ibid.

Thornton, R. D. The University of Edinburgh and the Scottish Enlightenment. Texas Stud in Lit & Lang 10 1968.

II. POETRY AND DRAMA

A. COLLECTIONS

[Watson, J.] A choice collection of comic and serious Scots poems both ancient and modern. 3 pts Edinburgh 1706–11, 1711, 1 vol Glasgow 1869.

Ramsay, A. The tea-table miscellany. 4 vols Edinburgh 1723–37. For subsequent edns see under Ramsay, below.

— The ever green: being a collection of Scots poems wrote by the ingenious before 1600. 2 vols Edinburgh 1724. For subsequent edns see under Ramsay, below.

Thomson, W. Orpheus caledonius: or a collection of the best Scotch songs. [1725], 2 vols 1733, 1733 (as A collection of Scots songs), 2 vols in 1 Hatboro Pa 1962.

Lauder, W. Poetarum scotorum musae sacrae. Edinburgh 1739.

[Blacklock, T.] A collection of original poems by the Rev Mr Blacklock and other Scotch gentlemen. 2 vols Edinburgh 1760–2. A contemplated 3rd vol was never pbd.

[Herd, D.] The ancient and modern Scots songs, heroic ballads etc, now first collected. Edinburgh 1769, 2 vols

1776 (enlarged), Glasgow 1869; ed S. Gilpin 2 vols Edinburgh 1870.

Johnson, J. The Scots musical museum. 6 vols Edinburgh 1787–1803; ed W. Stenhouse, D. Laing and C. K. Sharpe 6 vols Edinburgh 1838 (with copious notes), 4 vols Edinburgh 1853 (with new addns), 2 vols Hatboro Pa 1962.

[Sisne, D.?] The Edinburgh musical miscellany. Edinburgh 1792, 1808.

Thomson, G. A select collection of original Scotish airs, also suitable English verses in addition to such of the songs as are written in the Scottish dialect. 6 vols 1793–1825. Title varies, usually including Robert Burns's name; many re-issues with variations in contents. See J. W. Egerer, Bibliography of Burns, Edinburgh 1964.

[Ritson, J.] Scotish songs. 2 vols 1794 (with lengthy Historical essay on Scotish song), 1 vol 1866 (without essay), 2 vols Glasgow 1869 (with essay).

—— The Caledonian Muse: a chronological selection of Scotish poetry from the earliest times. 1821 (ptd in 1785).

Poetry: original and selected. 99 nos Glasgow [1795?–8]. Chap-books.

The polyhymnia. 20 nos Glasgow [1799]. Chap-books.

[Leyden, J.] Scotish descriptive poems. Edinburgh 1803.

The Caledonian musical repository. 3 vols: vol 1, 1806; vols 2–3, Edinburgh 1809–11.

The cabinet of the Scottish Muses. Edinburgh 1808.

Burns, R. (son of poet). The Caledonian musical museum. 3 vols 1809–11.

Cromek, R. H. Remains of Nithsdale and Galloway song. 1810, Paisley 1880.

—— Select Scottish songs, ancient and modern. 2 vols 1810.

Campbell, A. Albyn's anthology. 2 vols Edinburgh 1816–18.

[Motherwell, W.] The harp of Renfrewshire. Paisley 1819, Glasgow 1820, 1821, Paisley 1872; 2nd ser, Paisley 1873 (not compiled by Motherwell).

—— Minstrelsy ancient and modern. Glasgow 1827, Paisley 1873, Detroit 1968.

Hogg, J. The Jacobite relics of Scotland. 2 vols Edinburgh 1819–21, Paisley 1874.

The beauties of the Scottish poets, ancient and modern, with biographical sketches. Glasgow 1823.

National songs of Scotland. 1823.

Jacobite melodies: a collection of the most popular legends, ballads and songs of the adherents to the House of Stuart 1640–1746. Glasgow 1825.

Cunningham, A. The songs of Scotland. 4 vols 1825.

[Laing, D.] Various pieces of fugitive Scotish poetry. 2 vols Edinburgh 1825–53. Type facs of 90 Scottish poems pbd 1600–1707.

Chambers, R. The popular rhymes of Scotland, with illustrations chiefly collected from oral sources. Edinburgh 1826.

—— The Scottish songs. 2 vols Edinburgh 1829–32.

—— Songs of Scotland prior to Burns. Edinburgh 1862, 1890.

The songs of England and Scotland. 2 vols 1835. Vol 2, Songs of Scotland.

[Maidment, J.] The Court of Session garland. 2 pts Edinburgh 1839; Supplement, Edinburgh 1839; Appendix, Edinburgh 1839; The Court of Session garland, Edinburgh 1871 (with supplements), London 1888 (signed).

—— Scotish elegiac verses 1629–1729. Edinburgh 1842.

—— A book of Scotish pasquils 1568–1715. Edinburgh 1868.

The ballads and songs of Ayrshire, illustrated with sketches

historical, traditional, narrative and biographical. 1st ser, Ayr 1846; 2nd ser, Edinburgh 1847.

Scotia's bards. New York 1854, 1856.

Mackay, C. The Jacobite songs and ballads of Scotland from 1688 to 1746, with an appendix of modern Jacobite songs. 1861.

—— Allan Ramsay and the Scottish poets before Burns. [1866], 2 vols [1870].

—— The illustrated book of Scottish songs from the 16th to the 19th century. 1867.

Aitken, Mary C. Scottish song: a selection of the choicest lyrics of Scotland. 1874.

Wilson, J. G. The poets and poetry of Scotland from the earliest to the present time. 2 vols New York 1876, London 1876–7.

Ross, J. The book of Scottish poems, ancient and modern. Edinburgh 1884.

Harper, M. M. The bards of Galloway: a collection of poems, songs, ballads etc. Dalbeattie 1889.

Brown, R. Paisley poets, with brief memoirs of them and selections from their poetry. 2 vols Paisley 1889–90.

Douglas, G. Poems of the Scottish minor poets. 1891.

—— The book of Scottish poetry. 1911, New York nd.

Kaye, W. J. The leading poets of Scotland from early times. [c. 1891].

Geddes, W. D. and W. K. Leask. Musa latina aberdonensis. 3 vols Aberdeen 1892–1910 (New Spalding Club).

Crocket, W. S. Minstrelsy of the Merse: the poets and poetry of Berwickshire. Paisley 1893.

Ford, R. The harp of Perthshire. Paisley 1893.

—— Vagabond songs of Scotland. 2 vols Paisley 1899–1901, 1 vol 1904.

Greig, J. Scots minstrelsie: a national monument of Scottish song. 6 vols Edinburgh 1893.

Eyre-Todd, G. Scottish poetry of the seventeenth century. Glasgow 1895, nd (Abbotsford ser of Scottish poets).

—— Scottish poetry of the eighteenth century. 2 vols Glasgow 1896, nd (Abbotsford ser).

—— The Glasgow poets. Glasgow 1903, 1906.

Reid, A. The bards of Angus and the Mearns. Paisley 1897.

Carmichael, A. (ed and translated). Carmina gadelica: hymns and incantations. 2 vols Edinburgh 1900; ed E. C. Watson and A. Matheson 5 vols Edinburgh 1928–54; [excerpts] as The sun dances, ed A. Bittleston [1960]; [selection] as Poems of the western Highlands, ed G. R. D. McLean 1961.

Hecht, H. Songs from David Herd's manuscripts. Edinburgh 1904.

Dixon, W. M. The Edinburgh book of Scottish verse. Edinburgh 1910.

MacIntosh, J. The poets of Ayrshire. Dumfries [1910].

Mitchell, D. The book of Highland verse: an (English) anthology consisting of translations from Gaelic [and] English verse relating to the Highlands. Paisley 1912.

Buchan, J. The Northern Muse. 1924.

Brougham, E. M. News out of Scotland. 1926.

Ramsay, A. A. W. The wee Apollo: twelve pre-Burnsian Scottish songs. Warlingham 1931.

'MacDiarmid, Hugh' (C. M. Grieve). The golden treasury of Scottish poetry. 1940, 1941, 1946, 1948.

Fergusson, J. The green garden: a new collection of Scottish poetry. Edinburgh 1946. To Burns.

Oliver, J. W. and J. C. Smith. A Scots anthology. Edinburgh 1949.

MacQueen, J. and T. Scott. The Oxford book of Scottish verse. Oxford 1966.

Graham, G. F. The songs of Scotland adapted to their appropriate melodies, illustrated with historical, biographical and critical notices. 3 vols Edinburgh nd.

Macquoid, G. S. Jacobite songs and ballads. nd.

B. GENERAL STUDIES

Campbell, A. An introduction to the history of poetry in Scotland. Edinburgh 1798.

Irving, D. The lives of the Scottish poets, with dissertations on the literary history of Scotland. 2 vols Edinburgh 1804, 1810, London 1810.

—— The history of Scottish poetry. Ed J. A. Carlyle, Edinburgh 1861.

[Robertson, J.] Lives of Scottish poets. 3 vols 1821–2.

Dauncey, W. Ancient Scottish melodies. Edinburgh 1838 (Bannatyne Club).

Stenhouse, W., D. Laing and C. K. Sharpe. Illustrations of the lyric poetry and music of Scotland. In J. Johnson, Scots musical museum, 6 vols Edinburgh 1838, 4 vols Edinburgh 1853 (with addns), Hatboro Pa 1962.

'Tytler, S.' and J. L Watson. The songstresses of Scotland. 2 vols 1871.

Borthwick, J. D. History of Scottish song. Montreal 1874.

Veitch, J. The history and poetry of the Scottish Border: their main features and relations. Glasgow 1878, 2 vols Edinburgh 1893.

—— The feeling for nature in Scottish poetry. 2 vols Edinburgh 1887.

Walker, W. The bards of Bon-Accord 1375–1860. Aberdeen 1887.

Blackie, J. S. Scottish song: its wealth, wisdom and significance. Edinburgh 1889.

Maclagan, D. J. Scottish paraphrases. [Edinburgh] 1889.

Borland, R. Yarrow, its poets and poetry. Dalbeattie 1890, Galashiels 1908 (rev).

Glen, J. Early Scottish melodies. 1900.

Burns, R. Notes on Scottish song. Ed J. C. Dick 1908; rptd in Dick, Songs of Burns, Hatboro Pa 1962.

Miller, F. The poets of Dumfriesshire. Glasgow 1910.

Douglas, G. Scottish poetry: Drummond of Hawthornden to Fergusson. Glasgow 1911.

Watt, L. M. Scottish life and poetry. 1912.

Kinsley, J. (ed). Scottish poetry: a critical survey. 1955.

McKenzie, J. School and university drama in Scotland 1650–1760. Scottish Historical Rev 34 1955.

Crawford, T. Scottish popular ballads and lyrics of the eighteenth and nineteenth centuries: some preliminary conclusions. Studies in Scottish Lit 1 1964.

MacLaine, A. The 'Christis Kirk' tradition: its evolution in Scots poetry to Burns. Stud in Scottish Lit 2 1965.

Walker, I. C. Scottish verse in the Weekly Magazine. Stud in Scottish Lit 5 1968.

C. INDIVIDUAL WRITERS 1660–1770

WILLIAM CLARK, advocate

Marciano, or the discovery: a tragi-comedy. Edinburgh 1663 (anon); ed W. H. Logan 1871.

The grand tryal: or poetical exercitations upon the Book of Job. Edinburgh 1685.

WILLIAM CLELAND
1661?–89

Collections

A collection of several poems and verses. [Edinburgh] 1697.

§ I

Disputatio juridica de probationibus. [Edinburgh?] 1684.

A ballad to the tune of Hey boyes up go wee. [Edinburgh?] 1685 (anon); rptd in D. Laing, Various pieces of fugitive Scotish poetry, Edinburgh 1825.

SAMUEL COLVIL

The grand impostor discovered: or an historical dispute of the Papacy and Popish religion. Edinburgh 1673, St Andrews 1796.

Mock poem: or Whiggs supplication. 2 pts 1681, Edinburgh 1687, London 1692, Edinburgh 1695, London 1710, Edinburgh 1711, Belfast 1741, Glasgow 1751, St Andrews 1796, Perth 1797 (variously as Whiggs supplication or The Scotch Hudibras). Work pbd anon, but author's apology signed S.C. or Sam Colvil.

Mr Samuel Colvil's prophecy anent the Union, as contained in his Scots Hudibras. 1707. A broadside.

MICHAEL LIVINGSTONE
fl. 1680

Albion's congratulatory: or a poem upon Prince James Duke of Albany and York, his return into Scotland. [Edinburgh?] 1680. Anon broadside.

Albion's elegie: or a poem upon James, Duke of Albany and York, his departure from Scotland. Edinburgh 1680; Albion's farewel: or a poem by the same hand, Edinburgh 1680.

Augustis ac praepotentibus heroibus Jacobo & Mariae, Albaniae & Eboraci Ducibus. [Edinburgh? 1680] (Latin and English); rptd in D. Laing, Various pieces of fugitive Scotish poetry 2nd ser, Edinburgh 1853.

Celsissimo principi Gulielmo Hamiltoniae Duci, poematûm bellaria. [Edinburgh? 1680]. A broadside in Latin and English.

Illustrissimo heroi Limnuchi comiti. [Edinburgh? 1680?].

Patronus redux, or our protectour is return'd safe again: an historicall poem. Edinburgh 1682.

Illustrissimo heroi Georgio Limnuchi comiti. [Edinburgh?] nd. A verse broadside.

Most works are signed M.L.

NINIAN PATERSON
fl. 1678–96

Epigrammatum libri octo; cum aliquot Psalmorum Davidis paraphrasi poetica. Edinburgh 1678.

On the death of Major William Cockburn. [Edinburgh? 1683]. A broadside.

The fanatick indulgence granted, anno 1679. Edinburgh 1683. Poem.

Obsequies to the memory of Alexander, Late Lord Bishop of Rosse. [Edinburgh] 1683. A broadside.

A poem on the test. Edinburgh 1683.

On the death of General Dalziel of Binns. [Edinburgh? 1685]. A broadside.

On George Monteith, merchant of Edinburgh. [Edinburgh? 1685]. A broadside.

On the death of the Lady Lee, younger. [Edinburgh? 1686]. A broadside.

To the memory of Thomas Lord Napier. [Edinburgh 1686]. A broadside.

To the memory of Thomas Robertson, bailie and builder in Edinburgh. Edinburgh [1686]. A broadside.

Moristonus martyr: to the memory of Andrew Ker of Moristoun. [Edinburgh?] 1687.

On the happy conjunction of the families of Adiston. Edinburgh 1687. A broadside.

To the memory of Adam Hepburn. Edinburgh 1687. A broadside.

To the memory of Patrick Lord Elibank. Edinburgh 1687. A broadside.

D. Ioan. Wedderburni a Gosford, On the death of the phoenix of this age, the incomparable Gosford. [Edinburgh? 1688]. A broadside.

An encomiastick character of the pleasant art of taylorie. Edinburgh 1688. A broadside.

To the memory of the Rt Hon Margaret Countess of Weems. [Edinburgh?] 1688. A broadside.

To the memory of the Right Honourable Sir John Nisbet. [Edinburgh? 1688].

To the memory of Sir Andrew Ramsay of Abbots-Hall, Provost of Edinburgh. [Edinburgh? 1688]. A broadside.

Upon the birth of the Prince and Stewart of Scotland. [Edinburgh? 1688]; rptd in D. Laing, Various pieces of fugitive Scotish poetry, Edinburgh 1825. A broadside in Latin and English.

Octulpa: hoc est paraphrases poeticae psalmi civ authoribus totidem scotis, viz Georgio Buchanano, Niniano Paterson. Edinburgh 1696.

ALEXANDER PENNECUIK, MD
1652–1722
Collections

The works, [with] memoir [by R. Brown]. Leith 1815.

§ 1

To his Highness the Prince of Orange; the humble address of the inhabitants of Lintoun. [Edinburgh? 1689] (broadside); Lintoun address revised, to his Highness the then Prince of Orange, now Monarch, [Edinburgh? c. 1690] (broadside), also in James Watson, A choice collection of comic and serious Scots poems pt 1, Edinburgh 1706, 1714 (broadside, ptd by Watson).

Caledonia triumphans: a panegyrick to the King. Edinburgh 1699, nd (broadside); rptd in D. Laing, Various

pieces of fugitive Scotish poetry, Edinburgh 1825 (not included in his collection of 1715).

The tragedy of Gray-beard. Edinburgh 1700 (3 edns); ed D. Laing [1850?].

An address to his Majesty King George, by the author of the Lintoun-Address. Edinburgh 1714. A verse broadside.

A geographical, historical description of the shire of Tweeddale; with a miscelany and curious collection of select Scotish poems. Edinburgh 1715.

A collection of curious Scots poems. Edinburgh 1762.

The interlocutor: a comedy, of one act in verse, ascribed to Alexander Pennecuik MD. Edinburgh 1803.

Comic poems of the years 1685, and 1793, on rustic scenes in Scotland. Edinburgh 1817. Contains Lintoun Green and Carlop Green and A panegyrick upon the Royal army in Scotland 1685.

Lintoun Green, or the third market-day of June 1685: a poem in nine cantos ascribed to Alexander Pennecuik. Edinburgh nd (from 2nd edn). Not same as broadside, above.

Some confusion exists about the authorship of works by Alexander Pennecuik MD and his nephew Alexander Pennecuik, merchant. The name has been variously spelled Pennycuik and Pennecuik.

§ 2

Brown, W. Writings of A. Pennecuik MD and A. Pennecuik, merchant. Pbns Edinburgh Bibl Soc 6 1906.

WALTER SCOT of Satchells
1614?–94?

A true history of several honourable families of the name of Scot in the shires of Roxburgh and Selkirk [and] Satchell's Post'ral, humbly presented to his friends of the names of Scot and Elliot [in verse]. 2 pts Edinburgh 1688, 1776, 3 pts Hawick 1786 (with notes and appendix); ed J. G. Winning 1894.

Metrical history of the honourable families of the name of Scot and Elliot in the shires of Roxburgh and Selkirk. 2 pts Edinburgh 1892 (Scottish Literary Club).

D. ALLAN RAMSAY AND HIS CONTEMPORARIES

ALLAN RAMSAY
1686–1758

Vols 4–5 of the STS edn, ed A. M. Kinghorn and A. Law, will contain supplementary bibliographical information, locations of mss and a biography.

Bibliographies

Gibson, A. New light on Ramsay. Edinburgh 1927.

Martin, B. Bibliography of the writings of Ramsay. Records of Glasgow Bibl Soc 10 1931. Also pbd separately.

Collections

Poems. Edinburgh 1720 (made up of various pamphlets, some reprints, previously issued separately by Ramsay; contents of individual copies varies considerably, and pagination is not always continuous; no copy of postulated first issue is known; of the 7 known issues 5 probably appeared in 1720, one in 1721, one in 1722), 1723 (2 issues, one issued in 1724), 1727 ('4th edn', 3 issues, one, though dated 1727, is actually of 1728, one of 1732; no copy of 1727 issue known); vol 2, Edinburgh 1729 (designed as a companion vol for 1727 edn).

Poems. Edinburgh 1721. Subscribers' edn, ptd by Ruddiman.

Miscellaneous works of that celebrated Scotch poet Allan Ramsay. Dublin 1724. Contains the Tea-Table miscellany.

Poems. 2 vols Edinburgh 1728 (vol 1 a re-issue of the 1721 edn), 2 vols 1731, 1 vol Dublin 1733, 2 vols 1751, 1 vol [London?] 1760, 2 vols 1761, 1 vol Glasgow 1770, 2 vols 1772, 1 vol Dublin 1773, 2 vols Aberdeen 1776, Edinburgh 1780, Berwick 1793, Perth 1794, 1 vol Edinburgh 1794, 1802.

Poems: a new edition corrected and enlarged. Ed with life by G. Chalmers and remarks on his poems by Lord Woodhouselee 2 vols 1800, 1 vol 1805, 2 vols Leith 1814, Paisley 1877, 3 vols 1848 (with addns), 1851, 1852, 1853, [1855?].

Poems, with an account of his life and writings. 2 vols Glasgow 1797, 1797, 3 vols Edinburgh [1808?] (as Works), 1818 (as Poetical works with a collection of Scottish proverbs), 1819.

Poems, with the life of the author and his collection of Scots proverbs. 2 vols Philadelphia 1813.

Poems, with a life by Wm Tennant. Edinburgh 1819.

Select Scottish poets, 1st series: the complete poetical works of Robert Tannahill, Hector M'Neill and Allan Ramsay. Belfast 1844.

Poetical works, with selections from the Scottish poets before Burns. Ed C. Mackay [1866–8 in pts], 2 vols [1870].

Burns, Ramsay and the earlier poets of Scotland to which is added Ancient ballads and songs. Ed A. Cunningham and C. Mackay 2 vols [1878–9]. Based on edn of 1866–8.

Works. Ed B. Martin, J. W. Oliver et al, 5 vols Edinburgh 1951–.

Selections

Scots songs. Edinburgh 1718 (7 songs), 1719 (10 songs), 1720 (13 songs), [1720?] (2nd collection with 9 new songs). For music see below.

Miscellaneous works of that celebrated Scotch poet Allan Ramsay. Dublin 1724. First Irish edn, reprints Tea-table miscellany.

The Caledonian miscellany: consisting of select and much approved pastorals, choice fables and tales, by Ramsay and other eminent northern bards. [1740?], Newcastle 1762. Almost all the poems are by Ramsay.

A compleat collection of all the poems [of] A. Pennecuik, to which is annexed some curious poems by other worthy hands. 3 pts Edinburgh [1750?], 1769, Glasgow 1787. Title varies contains several anon poems by Ramsay.

Thirty Scots songs adapted for a voice and harpsichord [by R. Bremner]. Edinburgh [1757], London nd (signed by Bremner).

A second set of Scots songs, adapted by R. Bremner. [c. 1762].

The ancient and modern Scots songs, heroic ballads etc. [Ed D. Herd], Edinburgh 1769, 2 vols 1776 (considerably enlarged). Contains numerous songs by Ramsay.

Poems on several occasions. 2 vols Aberdeen 1776, Edinburgh 1780, Berwick 1793, Edinburgh 1794.

[Six poems by Ramsay]. In Brash and Reid ser of chapbooks, 4 vols Glasgow [1795?–8].

The beauties of Allan Ramsay. Philadelphia 1815.

Select poetical works. [Ed Chambers], Edinburgh 1838, 1849, 1859, 1870, 1880.

Poems by Allan Ramsay, selected and arranged by J. L. Robertson. 1887.

Poems: epistles, fables, satires, elegies and lyrics, from the edition [of] 1721–8. Ed H. H. Wood, Edinburgh 1940.

§ I

A poem to the memory of the famous Archibald Pitcairn MD. Edinburgh [1713]. Anon; no known copy.

On this great eclipse: a poem by A.R. Edinburgh 1715. Single sheet.

The battel, or morning interview: an heroi-comical poem. Edinburgh 1716 (anon), 1719 (signed, as The morning interview), 1720, 1721, 1724, 1731.

Christ's kirk on the green in two cantos. Edinburgh 1718, [Edinburgh 1718?] (2 signed broadsides), 1718 (in three cantos), 1720, 1722; and A collection of other humorous poems in the Scottish dialect, Edinburgh 1763; [Christ's Kirk only], Glasgow 1768, 1786, 1794, 1799, 1806, Stirling 1805, Falkirk 1821, Glasgow [c. 1800], Stirling [c. 1812–20]; tr Latin, 1813. Canto 1 by James I of Scotland (supposititious), cantos 2–3 by Ramsay. For earlier edns of canto 1 see vol 1, above.

Edinburgh's address to the country. [Edinburgh 1718?] (anon); rptd with The morning interview, 1719 etc, above.

Elegies on Maggy Johnston, John Cowper and Lucky Wood. Edinburgh 1718 (2nd edn 'corrected and amended'); with Lucky Spence's last advice [Edinburgh 1719?], [Edinburgh 1720?]. No known copy of first edn.

Elegy on Lucky Wood. [Edinburgh 1718?]. Anon broadside.

Lucky Spence's last advice. [Edinburgh 1718?] (anon), [Glasgow?] nd (as Elegy on the death of an auld bawd or bawdy-house keeper), [Edinburgh?] nd (broadside).

The scriblers lash'd. Edinburgh 1718 (anon), 1718 (signed), 1720, 1721, 1723, 1728.

Tartana or the plaid. Edinburgh 1718, 1719, 1720 (Scottish version of 1719 edn), 1721, 1724, 1732, [Edinburgh 1720?] (as To the most beautiful Scots ladies, this poem on the plaid is humbly dedicated).

Content: a poem. Edinburgh 1719, 1719, London 1720, Edinburgh 1721, 1723, 1728.

An epistle to W— H— [William Hamilton] on the receiving the compliment of a barrel of Loch-fyne herrings from him. [Edinburgh 1720?]. Anon.

Familiar epistles between W— H— and A— R—. [Edinburgh 1719] (3 anon edns), [1720?].

Richy and Sandy: a pastoral on the death of Mr Joseph Addison. [Edinburgh 1719?] (2 edns); also in Pope, Eloisa to Abelard, 1720 (2nd edn).

Bessy Bell and Mary Gray. [Edinburgh 1720?] (anon, single sheet), [Edinburgh?] nd (as a broadside with The young laird and Edinburgh Katie).

Edinburgh's salutation to the most Honourable My Lord Marquess of Carnarvon. [Edinburgh 1720].

Grubstreet nae satyre, in answer to Bagpipes no musick. [Edinburgh c. 1720?]. Anon broadside.

To Mr Law. Edinburgh 1720, [Oxford 1924] (facs).

An ode with a pastoral recitative on the marriage of the Rt Hon James Earl of Wemyss and Mrs Janet Charteris. [Edinburgh 1720].

Patie and Roger: a pastoral inscribed to Josiah Burchet esq, Secretary of the Admiralty. [Edinburgh 1720] (anon), London 1720 (signed).

A poem on the South Sea by Mr Alexander Ramsay, to which is prefixed a familiar epistle to Anthony Hammond. 1720, 1720 (as Wealth, or the woody, with Ramsay's name correct), [Edinburgh 1720?], [Edinburgh 1720?] (without the epistle to Hammond), London 1720.

Prologue spoke by one of the young gentlemen who, for their improvement and diversion, acted the Orphan, and Cheats of Scapin, the last night of the year 1719. [Edinburgh 1720]. Single sheet; anon.

The prospect of plenty: a poem on the North-Sea fishery. 1720, [Edinburgh 1720] (2 edns) (as To the Royal Burrows of Scotland).

The young laird and Edinburgh Katie. [Edinburgh 1720?] (2 poems signed A.R.), [Edinburgh?] nd (as a broadside with Bessy Bell and Mary Gray).

An elegy on Patie Birnie. [Edinburgh 1721]. Broadside signed A.R.

The rise and fall of stocks 1720: an epistle to the Right Honourable My Lord Ramsay; [with] the satyr's comick project. Edinburgh 1721. Anon.

Robert, Richy and Sandy: a pastoral on the death of Matthew Prior esq. 1721.

Fables and tales. Edinburgh 1722 (15 pieces), 1722 (18 pieces, 2 edns), Edinburgh 1730 (as Collection of thirty fables).

Fy gar rub her o're wi strae: an Italian canzone (of seven hundred years standing) imitated in braid Scots. [Edinburgh? c. 1722]. A broadside, 2 issues, one unsigned, one signed A.R. Part of this poem appeared as To the Ph—: an ode, 1721. The poem was rptd in the Tea-table miscellany.

A tale of three bonnets. [Edinburgh?] 1722 (anon), Glasgow 1785, 1787, 1791, 1792, 1795, 1807, Stirling nd (2 edns), Edinburgh 1793 (as The ancient history of three bonnets), Falkirk 1820 (as Duniwhistle's testament: or a diverting tale of three bonnets).

Translation of the Aeneid x 693–6. Br Jnl 9 March 1723.

The fair assembly: a poem. Edinburgh 1723.

Jenny and Meggy, a pastoral: being a sequel to Patie and Roger. Edinburgh 1723.

The nuptials: a masque on the marriage of his Grace James Duke of Hamilton and Lady Anne Cochran. Edinburgh 1723, London 1723.

Health: a poem. Edinburgh 1724 (3 edns containing 22, 48 and 80 pp. respectively), 1730 (with addns).

The monk and the miller's wife: or all parties pleas'd. [Edinburgh 1724], Glasgow 1779, [Glasgow 1796], Edinburgh 1808, [Falkirk?] 1813, Glasgow [1840?], Kilmarnock nd, Penrith nd, [Falkirk?] nd, [Glasgow? 1800?] [no place] nd, 1771 (with William Forbes, The dominie depos'd), Ayr 1802 (in Four funny tales), Brechin 1833 (in The humorist); tr Latin 1802, 1813.

Mouldy-Mowdiwart: or the last speech of a wretched miser. [Edinburgh 1724].

An ode sacred to the memory of her Grace Anne Dutchess of Hamilton. Br Jnl 14 Nov 1724. In a letter from Ramsay denying the accuracy of an earlier version twice pbd in the same journal—3 Oct 1724, 24 Oct 1724. The spurious version contains 9 stanzas; Ramsay's contains 16.

The poetick sermon: to R— Y— [Robert Yarde] esq. [Edinburgh 1724].

On pride: an epistle to —. [Edinburgh 1724].

On the Royal Company of Archers marching under the command of his Grace Duke of Hamilton Aug 4 1724. [Edinburgh 1724]; also in Poems in English and Latin, 1726, below.

On seeing the archers diverting themselves at the butts and rovers. [Edinburgh 1724]; also in Poems in English and Latin 1726, below.

The gentle shepherd: a Scots pastoral comedy. Edinburgh 1725, 1726, Dublin 1727, Edinburgh 1729, London 1730 (copy in Nat Lib of Scotland), Edinburgh 1734, Glasgow 1743, 1745, 1747, Belfast 1748, Glasgow 1750, [New York 1750? – no known copy], Glasgow 1752, London 1752, Edinburgh 1753, Aberdeen 1754, Belfast 1755, Edinburgh 1755, 1758 (no known copy), Glasgow 1758, London 1758, Dublin 1759, Newcastle 1760, Edinburgh 1761, 1763, London 1763, Newcastle 1763, Edinburgh 1768, 1768, Newcastle 1768, Edinburgh 1769, [Philadelphia 1771 – no known copy]; Glasgow 1772 (to which is added Christ's kirk on the green), London 1772 (without Christ's kirk), Dublin 1773, Edinburgh 1773, 1774, London 1775, Edinburgh 1776, 1776, Aberdeen 1776, London 1777 (Bell's British Theatre vol 9), 1779, Edinburgh 1780, London 1780 (Bell's British Theatre), Perth 1780, Edinburgh 1781, Perth 1781, Falkirk 1782, Edinburgh 1783, Glasgow 1783, Kilmarnock 1784 (only known copy the contributor's), London 1786 (copy in Edinburgh Public Lib), Perth 1786, 1786, Glasgow 1788, Perth 1788, Edinburgh 1790, Falkirk 1790; Glasgow 1792 (with Familiar epistles between Lt Wm Hamilton and the author), 1795, 1808; Falkirk 1794, Philadelphia 1795, Glasgow 1796, London 1796 (2 edns—one vol 25 of Bell's British Theatre), Glasgow 1797 (with a life), London 1797 (copy in Edinburgh Public Lib), Berwick 1798 (copy in Nat Lib of Scotland), Edinburgh 1798, Glasgow, 1798, Philadelphia 1798, Edinburgh 1802, Newcastle 1802, Edinburgh 1804, Carlisle Pa 1805, [London 1805?], Edinburgh 1807, 1808, 2 vols 1808, Edinburgh 1812, Glasgow 1812, Pittsburgh 1812, Philadelphia 1813, 2 vols Edinburgh 1814, 1817, 1820, Haddington 1821 (2 issues, each known in only one copy: one in Nat Lib of Scotland, one the contributor's), Glasgow 1822, New York 1822 (in Works of the British poets vol 26, ed R. Walsh), Edinburgh 1823, Belfast 1826, Glasgow 1828 Alnwick 1836, Dumfries 1839, 1848, Edinburgh 1851, 1856, 1857, 1859, 1865, 1867 (with 2nd preface), 1871, London 1899; New York 1852, 1853, Edinburgh 1854, Glasgow 1856, Edinburgh 1865, [1871], Glasgow 1871, Edinburgh 1875, 1880, Glasgow [1891], Edinburgh 1895, [c. 1802], [c. 1808] (2 edns), Falkirk nd (2 edns), Glasgow nd (5 edns) [one c. 1820, one c. 1883], Newcastle nd (3 edns, one c. 1772, one 1853–71), South Shields [c. 1780] (only known copy the contributor's), [Newcastle?] nd.

Songs from Gentle shepherd

All the songs, with their tunes, in the Scots pastoral comedy of the Gentle shepherd. Dublin 1759 (without music).

The songs in the Gentle shepherd adapted for the guitar by Robert Bremner. Edinburgh [1759].

Select songs of the Gentle shepherd as it is performed at the Theatre-Royal, Drury Lane. 1781, 1784 (no known copy). These selections from Tickell's English adaptation, below.

Gentle shepherd — English versions

Cibber, T. Patie and Peggy, or the fair foundling: a Scotch ballad opera in one act and in verse. 1730, 1731. An adaptation of Gentle shepherd.

Vanderstop, C. The gentle shepherd: a dramatic poem done into English. 1777.

Tickell, R. The gentle shepherd. An adaptation performed at Drury Lane Oct 1781, apparently not pbd; but see Songs above.

Ward, W. A translation of the Scots pastoral comedy the Gentle shepherd into English. [1785?].

Shirrefs, A. Jamie and Bess, or the laird in disguise: a Scots pastoral comedy in imitation of the Gentle shepherd. Aberdeen 1787; also in Poems chiefly in the Scottish dialect. Edinburgh 1790.

Turner, Margaret. The gentle shepherd: a Scotch pastoral attempted in English. 1790. Parallel texts.

Allan, A. New gentle shepherd, reduced to English. [1798]. Copy in Library of Congress.

Maclaren, A. Spite and malice, or a laughable accident: a dramatic sketch; to which is added a humble attempt to convert the Gentle shepherd into English prose, in two acts. 1811. Maclaren also pbd Bessy Bell and Mary Gray, or love in the Highlands: a musical drama, 1808.

Bethune, G. The gentle shepherd translated into English. 1817. In 3 acts.

A poem on the Royal Company of Archers. Caledonian Mercury 12 July 1726. Anon.

Poems in English and Latin on the Archers and Royal Company of Archers by several hands. Edinburgh 1726. Contains Ramsay's On the Royal Company of Archers shooting for the bowl July 6th 1724; On his Grace the Duke of Hamilton's shooting an arrow through the neck of an eel, 4 July 1724; The poet's thanks to the Archers on being admitted into their Royal Company; and The Archers march; as well as the 2 poems noted above, 1724.

A Scots ode to the British antiquarians. [Edinburgh 1726].

Some few hints in defence of dramatic entertainments. [Edinburgh 1727?]. Anon. Prose; see George Anderson for answers.

Epilogue to the Gentle shepherd: Life's but a farce at best. Echo or Edinburgh Weekly Jnl 29 Jan 1729.

Verses by the celebrated Allan Ramsay to his son on his drawing a fine gentleman's picture. Scarborough Miscellany 1732, 1734.

[Sixteen songs by Ramsay] in Sir Ashton Cokain's The devil of a Duke, Edinburgh 1733. These songs are not in London 1732 edn. See TLS 18 July, 14 Nov 1929.

An address of thanks from the Society of Rakes. Edinburgh 1735. Anon.

Leith races. Caledonian Mercury 2 Aug 1736 (anon), London Mag Aug 1736 (signed).

Prologue for the opening of the New Theatre in Carrubber's Close 8 Nov 1736. Caledonian Mercury 8 Nov 1736. This was Ramsay's theatre.

To the Honourable Duncan Forbes of Culloden, Lord President of the Session and all our other good judges. [Edinburgh 1737]; GM Aug 1737. Ramsay's protest against the closing of his theatre.

An epistle [of farewell to James Oswald]. Scots Mag 3 Oct 1741.

The vision compylit in Latin be a most lernit clerk, in time of our hairship and oppression, anno 1300, and translatit in 1524. [Edinburgh] 1748 (anon); Scots Mag Aug 1748. First pbd pseudonymously in Ever-green 1724.

The eagle and robin red-breast. In The Union: or select Scots and English poems, Edinburgh 1753, London 1759, 1766, Oxford 1796. First pbd in Ever-green 1724. Attributed in both works to A. R. Scot, a name used elsewhere by Ramsay. Boswell claims it was written by William Guthrie.

The dominie depos'd, by William Forbes; to which is added I: Lucky Spence's last advice; II: An elegy on Maggy Johnston. Glasgow 1780, 1787 (with the Elegy on Maggy Johnston only), 1794 (both poems), 1800, Falkirk 1814, Kilmarnock 1817, Edinburgh [1820?], [Glasgow?] 1823, Aberdeen nd, Glasgow nd (2 edns).

To Mr James Home, writer to the Signet. In Blackwood's Mag Jan 1818.

The thimble. [Edinburgh? c. 1820]. Attributed to Ramsay.

Epitaph on Robert Mylne. In Nugae scoticae, ed James Maidment, Edinburgh 1829.

To Dr Robinson when at Edinburgh July 30th 1734. N & Q 6 May 1865.

Curiosities of a Scots charta chest 1600–1800. Ed Mrs Atholl Forbes, Edinburgh 1897. Previously unpbd poems and letters.

Verses by Allan Ramsay. Ed W. D. H[ogg], Trans Rymour Club 3 1924. Contains 4 unpbd poems.

To his Grace John, Duke of Roxburgh (April 20 1722). Weekly Scotsman 29 June 1929.

A new song: tune of Lochaber no more. [Edinburgh?] nd. A broadside.

Some few of the contents [of Ever green]. [Edinburgh?] nd (broadside); rptd in Poems, 1800 and in Memorials of George Bannatyne 1545–1608, ed D. Laing, Edinburgh 1829. Laing is responsible for the statement that the work first appeared in broadside form.

Letters

Letter of May 10 1736 to John Smibert. GM Sept 1784.

Letter of July 13 1732 to Andrew Miller [the London publisher of the Tea-table miscellany about this work]. GM April 1853; rptd Littell's Living Age 28 May 1853.

Letters to Lord Provost Lindsay and Patrick Lindsay. Historical Mss Commission, 8th report, appendix pt 1, 1881.

Letter to the Earl of Oxford. Historical Mss Commission, mss of the Duke of Portland vol 6, 1901.

Works edited by Ramsay

Tea-table miscellany

This collection was issued one vol at a time, and individual vols were rptd as the need arose in order to make complete sets available for sale. This procedure was followed through 1735, and probably until vol 4 was issued in 1737. There are no known copies of several of these early edns.

The tea-table miscellany [vol 1]. Edinburgh 1723 (not noted by Martin, only known copy in Yale Lib), 1724 (only known copy in Huntington Lib), 1727 (not noted by Martin), 1732 (6th edn, not noted by Martin, only known copy in Yale Lib).

Vol 2. Edinburgh 1726 (Nat Lib of Scotland has microfilm of presumed unique copy), 1735 (not noted by Martin, only known copy in Yale Lib).

Vols 1–2 as A new miscellany of Scots sangs. 1727. Anon, pirated.

Vol 3. Edinburgh 1727.

3 vols Dublin 1729 (pagination continues throughout vols), [Edinburgh 1729] (no known copy).

1 vol 1730. Includes contents of vols 1–3.

3 vols 1733, Dublin 1733 (not noted by Martin), Dublin 1734 (3 vols in one).

Vol 4. [Edinburgh 1737] (no known copy).

4 vols 1740 (pagination continues), 1750 (pagination continues), Glasgow 1753 (not noted by Martin, copy in Mitchell Lib), Edinburgh 1760, 1762, London 1763, Glasgow 1765, Edinburgh 1768, 2 vols Glasgow 1768, 1 vol Dublin 1769, 4 vols 1772 (no known copy), 2 vols Edinburgh 1775 (several variants), 1 vol Glasgow 1782, 4 vols Aberdeen 1783, 2 vols Kilmarnock 1788, 4 vols Berwick 1793, 2 vols Edinburgh 1793, 1 vol Dublin 1794, 2 vols Glasgow 1871, rptd 1875, 1876.

Ever green

Musick for Allan Ramsay's Collection of Scots songs, set by Alexr Stuart. 6 pts [Edinburgh 1724]. Contains music only to 69 songs.

See H. G. Farmer, The music to Ramsay's songs, Bibliothek 2 1959.

The ever green: being a collection of Scots poems wrote by the ingenious before sixteen hundred. 2 vols Edinburgh 1724, 1761, Glasgow 1824, 1874, 1875, 1876.

Scots proverbs

A collection of Scots proverbs, more complete and correct than any heretofore published. Edinburgh 1737 (2,522 proverbs), 1750, 1797 (to which are added A tale of three bonnets and Verses on the Bannatyne manuscript.)

A collection of above nine hundred Scots proverbs. Glasgow 1781.

A collection of Scots proverbs. Glasgow 1785, Edinburgh 1807, Glasgow [1807], Edinburgh [1809], Falkirk 1813, 1815, Glasgow 1820, Kilmarnock 1820, Glasgow 1821, Falkirk 1823, Glasgow 1824, Stirling 1827, Kilmarnock 1829, Brechin 1834, Edinburgh nd, Falkirk nd, Glasgow nd (3 edns), Paisley nd, Stirling nd (2 edns).

Proverbial sayings: or a collection of the best English proverbs by John Ray, Scots proverbs by Allan Ramsay, Italian proverbs [by] Orlando Pescetti, Spanish proverbs by Ferdinand Munez, with the wise sayings and maxims of the Ancients. [no place] 1800.

Aphorisms of wisdom: or a complete collection of the most celebrated proverbs in the English, Scotch, French, Spanish, Italian and other languages, ancient and modern, collected and digested by Thomas Fuller; to which is added Ramsay's collection of Scottish proverbs, new edition. Glasgow 1814, London 1819 (as Gnomologia).

§ 2

A block for Allan Ramsay's wigs: or the famous poet fall'n in a sleep [Edinburgh? c. 1720]. A broadside.

A satyr upon Allan Ramsay, occasioned upon a report of his translating Horace. [Edinburgh? c. 1720]. A broadside.

An habbyac on the death of Allan Ramsay. [Edinburgh? c. 1720–5]. A mock elegy.

[Essay on fortune]. Weekly Jnl or Saturday's Post 14 Sept 1723.

[Letter on Scottish dialect]. Plain Dealer 2 Nov 1724.

Starrat, W. A pastoral in praise of Allan Ramsay. [Dublin] 1726. A broadside.

Allan Ramsay metamorphosed into a heather-bloter poet in a pastoral between Aegon and Melibae. [Edinburgh c. 1735].

The flight of religious piety from Scotland upon the account of Ramsay's lewd books. [Edinburgh? c. 1735]. Sometimes attributed, probably incorrectly, to Alexander Pennecuik.

A looking glass for Allan Ramsay, wherein he may see himself and his actions delineated to the life, and likewise how far he has been instrumental in the snearing of others. [Edinburgh c. 1735].

The whores of Edinburgh's lament for want of Luckie Spence. [Edinburgh? c. 1736?]. A broadside.

To the memory of Mr Allan Ramsay. Scots Mag 20 Feb 1758.

An elegy on the much lamented death of Allen Ramsey. [Dublin? 1758]. A broadside.

Dumming, R. Essay delivered in the Pantheon on Thursday April 14 1791 on the question: Whether have the exertions of Allan Ramsay or Robert Fergusson done most honour to Scottish poetry. Edinburgh 1791. A poem.

Learmont, J. An encomium on Allan Ramsay and Robert Fergusson. In his Poems, Edinburgh 1791.

Picken, E. and A. Wilson. The laurel disputed: or the merits of Allan Ramsay and Robert Fergusson contrasted. Edinburgh 1791; rptd Glasgow 1816 (Wilson's poem only).

'Philo-scoticus'. Memoirs of the life of Allan Ramsay. Scots Mag Feb 1797.

Memoirs, critical remarks and observations on the scenery. Prefixed to Poems, Glasgow 1797.

Campbell, A. An introduction to the history of poetry in Scotland. Edinburgh 1798.

[Chalmers, G.] Life of the author [Ramsay] from authentic documents and remarks on his poems, from a large view of their merits. Prefixed to Poems, 2 vols 1800.

Irving, D. In his Lives of the Scotish poets vol 2, Edinburgh 1804, 1810.

A new biographical memoir of the author [Ramsay] and a critique on his writings. Prefixed to Gentle shepherd, Edinburgh 1808.

[Brown, R.?]. An authentic life of Allan Ramsay and an inquiry into the origin of pastoral poetry, the propriety of the rules prescribed for it and the practice of Ramsay. Prefixed to Gentle shepherd, 2 vols Edinburgh 1808.

[Robertson, J.] In his Lives of Scottish poets vol 1, 1821.

Revival and progress of national literature. Hogg's Weekly Instructor 5 Dec 1846.

Tomilson, J. Ramsay and pastoral poetry. People's Jnl 11 Jan 1849.

Scottish poets: Ramsay and Fergusson. West of Scotland Mag & Rev 2 Oct 1857.

Robertson, J. C. Bi-centennial of Ramsay. Macmillan's Mag Nov 1886.

Tulloch, W. W. Allan Ramsay and the Gentle shepherd. Good Words Oct 1886.

Veitch, J. In his Feeling for nature in Scottish poetry vol 2, Edinburgh 1887.

Holmes, D. T. In his Lectures on Scottish literature, Paisley 1904.

Smeaton, W. H. O. Allan Ramsay. Edinburgh [1896] (Famous Scots ser).

— Allan Ramsay and the Gentle shepherd. [c. 1905].

Mackail, J. W. Allan Ramsay and the Romantic revival. E & S 10 1924.

Chapman, R. W. Allan Ramsay's Poems 1720. RES 3 1927.

Gibson, A. New light on Ramsay. Edinburgh 1927.

Martin, B. Allan Ramsay. Cambridge Mass 1931.

Weir, J. L. Ramsay and the Scottish Archers. N & Q 19 June 1937.

Pearsall, R. B. Scott and Ritson on Ramsay. MLN 66 1951.

Gillis, W. Ramsay's Nanny-O. N & Q June 1958. Reply by J. A. Lavin, July 1961.

MacLaine, A. H. The Christis Kirk tradition: its evolution in Scots poetry to Burns. Stud in Scottish Lit 2 1965.

Yeo, E. The manuscript of Ramsay's Gentle shepherd. Stud in Scottish Lit 4 1967.

MINOR WRITERS 1700-50

JOHN ARMSTRONG
1709-79
See col 534, above.

ROBERT BLAIR
1699-1746
See col 537, above.

FRANCIS DOUGLAS
1710?-90?

§ 1

The history of the Rebellion in 1745 and 1746. Aberdeen 1755. By F.D.

A pastoral elegy to the memory of Miss Mary Urquhart. Aberdeen 1758.

Rural love: a tale in the Scotish dialect, to which is added a glossary. Aberdeen 1750, 1759 (anon), Edinburgh 1804, [Edinburgh?] nd.

The Earl of Douglas: a dramatick essay. 1760.

The life of [the admirable] James Crichton. [1760?]; rptd in T. Pennant, Tour in Scotland, Warrington 1774 (3rd edn) etc. Anon.

Reflections on celibacy and marriage. 1771. By F.D.

The birth-day, with a few strictures on the times: a poem in three cantos, by a farmer. Glasgow 1782, Aberdeen 1826. Anon.

A general description of the east coast of Scotland from Edinburgh to Cullen, including a brief account of the Universities of St Andrews and Aberdeen. Paisley 1782.

Letters

Familiar letters from Lady Hariet Morley and others. 1773. Anon.

§ 2

Watkins, W. K. The life and ancestry of Douglas. Boston 1903.

FORBES OF DISBLAIR
fl. 1704-34

Although sometimes listed as William, there is no evidence for the name.

An essay upon marriage in a letter adress'd to a friend [verse]. [Edinburgh? 1704]. Reply by [Allan], A satyre on F–s of D–r by way of return on his essay on marriage, [1704] (broadside).

The renegado whip't: a satyre in answer to A–n's libel [verse]. [Edinburgh] 1704. Reply by Allan, A curb for a coxcomb: or an answer to the renegado whip'd, Edinburgh 1704. Reply by Forbes, Mack-faux, the mock moralist: a satyre on A–n, the renegado, [London] 1705.

The true Scots genius reviving: a poem. [Edinburgh?] 1704; rptd in D. Laing, Various pieces of fugitive Scotish poetry, Edinburgh 1825.

An Englishman's grace over his pock-pudding. [Edinburgh? 1705].

A New Year's gift for the renegado. 1705.

A pill for pork-eaters: or a Scots lancet for an English swelling. Edinburgh 1705, 1705, [Edinburgh?] 1705; rptd in D. Laing, Various pieces of fugitive Scotish poetry, Edinburgh 1825. Anon. Sometimes ascribed to Alexander Pennecuik, merchant, and included in his posthumous Compleat collection of all the poems, Edinburgh [1750?].

The rattle-snake: or a bastonado for a whig. 1712-13.

The farthingale reviv'd. [Edinburgh? 1720?].

Edinburgh cuckolds. Edinburgh 1722.

Xantippe: or the scolding wife. Edinburgh 1724.

Some remarks on a piece call'd Schema sacrum [by Thomas Blackwell]; with a comical dialogue betwixt Ned Wilmot and Dr Mar-text. [Edinburgh?] 1728. Prose.

The patriots: a satyre. 1734.

Bang the broker: a new song. [Edinburgh?] nd. Single sheet.

A. Ramsay metamorphosed. [Edinburgh?] nd.

WILLIAM HAMILTON OF BANGOUR
1704-54
Collections

Poetical works to which is prefixed the life of the author. In A complete edition of the poets of Great Britain vol 9, ed R. Anderson, Edinburgh 1793, London 1795.

Poetical works. Ed T. Park 2 vols 1805, 1808 (in Works of the British poets vol 28-9).

Poems. In Works of the English poets vol 15, ed A. Chalmers 1810.

Poems. In British poets vol 57, Chiswick 1822 (with life by D. A. Davenport).

Poems and songs with notes and an account of the life of the author. Ed J. Paterson, Edinburgh 1850.

§ 1

The faithful few: an ode inscribed to all lovers of their country. Edinburgh 1734.

Eighteenth epistle of the second book of Horace imitated. [Edinburgh?] 1737.

Three odes. Edinburgh 1739

Contemplation: or the triumph of love. Edinburgh 1747.

Poems on several occasions. Glasgow 1748, 1749 (anon), 1758, 1758, Edinburgh 1760 (signed).

§ 2

A Jacobite laureate. Macmillan's Mag March 1893.

Bushnell, N. S. The Jacobitism of Hamilton of Bangour. SP 35 1938.

—— Hamilton of Bangour: poet and Jacobite. Aberdeen 1957. With chronology of poems and bibliography of the writings.

WILLIAM HAMILTON OF GILBERTFIELD
1665?-1751

§ 1

Life and heroick actions of Sir William Wallace [title varies]. Glasgow 1722, Edinburgh 1770, Aberdeen 1774, Crieff 1774, Falkirk 1785, New York 1820, Edinburgh [1857?].

The history of the life of Sir William Wallace; to which is annexed the life of Robert Bruce by John Harvey. [Title varies. In some instances the 2 works were separately paged, and each had its own title-page, but they were issued bound up together. In most instances the title-page mentions both works]. Dundee 1770, Air [c. 1790], 1793, 1799, 1799, 1802, Edinburgh 1807, Glasgow 1811, Edinburgh 1812, 1816, 1818, 1819, 1821, Glasgow 1822, London 1823, Aberdeen 1842, Jedburgh 1854, Edinburgh 1859.

Hamilton also contributed to James Watson's Choice collection, 3 vols 1706-11 *and* Ramsay's Tea-table miscellany, 4 vols 1723-37; Familiar epistles between Lieut W. Hamilton and A. Ramsay, [1719?] *frequently rptd in Ramsay's works.*

§ 2

Miller, J. F. Blind Harry's 'Wallace'. Records of Glasgow Bibl Soc 3 1914, 6 1920.

JOHN HARVEY
fl. 1729
Collections

A collection of miscellany poems and letters, comical and serious. Edinburgh 1726.

§ 1

The life of Robert Bruce, King of Scots: a poem. [Title varies. Only edns pbd separately are here included; for other edns, *see* Wm Hamilton of Gilbertfield, The Wallace]. Edinburgh 1729, 1768, Perth 1776, Aberdeen 1786, London 1769 (anon, as The Bruciad: an epic poem).

§ 2

M'Kinlay, R. Barbour's Brace. Records of Glasgow Bibl Soc 6 1920.

JOHN MacCODRUM
1693?-1779

The songs of John MacCodrum, bard to Sir James Mac-Donald of Sleat. Ed Wm Matheson 1938 (Scottish Gaelic Texts Soc). Gaelic texts and trns.

DAVID MALLET
1705?-65

See col 556, above.

WILLIAM MESTON
1688?-1745
Collections

Poetical works (with life). Edinburgh 1767 (6th edn), Aberdeen 1802. No earlier edn appears to have survived, though the first edn is listed as London 1737. The Edinburgh edn may be the first.

§ 1

A jeu d'esprit in verse. In J. Alexander, Tituli fontium abredonensium, [Aberdeen? 1707]. Anon.

In memory of the Right Honourable John Earl of Strath-more kill'd at the battle of Sheriffmuir, November the 13th, 1715. [1715? or 1716?]. Anon; verse.

Phaethon: or the first fable of the second book of Ovid's Metamorphoses burlesqu'd. Edinburgh 1720. Anon.

A tale of a man and his mare. [Edinburgh?] 1721 (2nd edn with addns), nd. Anon.

'Quidam'. The knight. [Edinburgh] 1723, 1723, London 1728 (as The knight of the kirk: or the ecclesiastical adventures of Sir John Presbyter).

Viri humani, salsi et faceti Gulielmi Sutherlandi. [Edinburgh? 1726]. Anon. Sometimes attributed to John Arbuthnot. *See also* The wife of Auchtermuchty, below.

Mob contra mob: or the rabblers rabbled. Edinburgh [1731?], 1738, [Edinburgh] 1769, Edinburgh nd. Anon.

Old Mother Grim's tales, found in an old manuscript, dated 1527, never before published. Decade 1, 1737 (only 3 tales); Decade 1, 1737 (10 tales). Anon.

Decadem alteram subjunxit Jodocus Grimmus. 1738. Anon.

The wife of Auchtermuchty: an ancient Scottish poem with a translation into Latin rhyme. Edinburgh 1803. Anon. Contains also Viri humani.

Unpbd verse in Scottish N & Q 3-4 Dec 1889, Jan 1890, June 1890.

§ 2

Campbell, A. Introduction to the history of poetry in Scotland. Edinburgh 1798.

[Robertson, J.]. Aberdonian worthies: II, Wm Meston. Aberdeen Mag 1 1831.

Anderson, P. J. Meston: the imitator of 'Hudibras' N & Q 12 July 1890.

Findlay, J. T. The ingenious and learned Wm Meston. Trans of Buchan Field Club 7 1902–3; Peterhead 1903 (with bibliography).

ALEXANDER NICOL

Nature without art. Edinburgh 1739.
Nature's progress in poetry. Edinburgh 1739.
The rural Muse: or a collection of miscellany poems, both comical and serious. Edinburgh 1753.
Poems on several subjects, both comical and serious, to which are added the Experienced gentleman and the She anchoret, by the Duchess of Newcastle. Edinburgh 1766.

ALEXANDER PENNECUIK, merchant
d. 1730
Collections

A collection of poet Pennecuike's satires on kirkmen. [Edinburgh?] 1744.
A collection of Scots poems on several occasions. Edinburgh 1756, 1769, Glasgow 1787.
A compleat collection of all the poems; to which is annexed some curious poems by other worthy hands. 3 pts Edinburgh [1750?], 1769, Glasgow 1787. This collection mistakenly includes Forbes of Disblair's Pill for pork-eaters, 1705.

§ 1

Pastoral poem to the memory of Lord Basil Hamiltoun. Edinburgh 1701. Signed A.P. By Pennecuik?
A pill for pork-eaters: or a Scots lancet for an English swelling. *See* Forbes of Disblair, *above*.
Britannia triumphans, in four parts. Edinburgh 1718.
Streams from Helicon: or poems on various subjects. Edinburgh 1720, London 1720 (2 issues, but actually Edinburgh? 1721?), Edinburgh 1721.
Elegy on the death of Nicol Muschet of Boghall. [Edinburgh? 1721]. An anon broadside.
Elegy on the deplorable death of the Right Honourable John Lord Belhaven, Nov 1721. [Edinburgh 1721]. A broadside.
A gentleman's letter to the Laird of Boghall the day before his execution. [Edinburgh] 1721. A broadside in prose.
An ancient prophecy concerning stock-jobbing. Edinburgh 1721. Verse.
An historical account of the Blue Blanket: or crafts-men's banner. Edinburgh 1722, 1756, 1780 (enlarged), 1832; also in An historical sketch of the municipal constitution of the city of Edinburgh, Edinburgh 1826. Prose.
Corydon and Cochrania: a pastoral. Edinburgh 1723.
An Habbiack elegy on the untimely and deplorable death of Robert F[orbe]s 1724. [Edinburgh? 1724]. An anon broadside.
The shepherds tears: a pastoral sacred to the memory of William Nisbet of Dirleton who died 1724. [Edinburgh? 1724]. An anon broadside.
A panegyrick on Philip King of Spain. [Edinburgh? 1724?]. A verse broadside.
Rome's legacy to the Kirk of Scotland. [Edinburgh?] 1724 (2nd edn with addns), [Edinburgh? 1730?], 1790, nd. Anon.
Dialogue betwixt a Glasgow malt-man and an English excise-man. [Edinburgh? 1725]. A broadside.
Groans from the grave. Edinburgh [1725].
A huy and cry after Sir John Barlycorn. [Edinburgh? 1725]. An anon broadside.
The faithful shepherd: a funeral poem (for Thomas Paterson). [Edinburgh?] 1726. An anon broadside.
A lecture to the ladies. [Edinburgh ? 1726]. An anon broadside.
The criminal Stirling imprisoned for the crime of high treason. [Edinburgh?] nd. An anon broadside.

Old-Reekie's loud and joyful acclamation for Sir John Barleycorn his restoration. [Edinburhg?] nd. A broadside.
On Rob Roy's pardon and preferment. [Edinburgh?] nd. A verse broadside.
Speech and dying words of John Dalgleish, hang-man of Edinburgh [title varies]. Edinburgh nd, [Edinburgh?] nd. A verse broadside.

§ 2

Brown, Wm. Writings of A. Pennecuik MD and A. Pennecuik, merchant. Pbns of Edinburgh Bibl Soc 6 1906.
Gillis, W. A. Pennecuik: two manuscripts. N & Q July 1957.

ALEXANDER ROSS,
schoolmaster at Lochlee
1699–1784
Bibliographies

Lawrence, R. M. Helenore: a Scottish vernacular classic. Aberdeen Book-lover 6 Nov 1928, May 1929.

Collections

Scottish works. Ed M. Wattie 1938 (STS).

§ 1

The fortunate shepherdess: a pastoral tale in three cantos, in the Scottish dialect, [with] songs. Aberdeen 1768, 1778, 1789, 1791, 1793, 1796, 1804, Edinburgh 1804, Aberdeen 1811, Dundee 1812 (2 edns, with life), Aberdeen 1826, 1839, 1842, Brechin 1851, Aberdeen 1856, 1860, Edinburgh 1866 (with life by J. Longmuir), Glasgow 1868, Aberdeen 1873, nd. Several edns are entitled Helenore: or the fortunate shepherdess; some also contain work by other poets.

§ 2

Gibb, J. S. Helenore or the fortunate shepherdess. Scottish Historical Rev 9 1912.

JAMES THOMSON
1700–48
See col 527, above.

LADY ELIZABETH WARDLAW
1677–1727

§ 1

Hardyknute: a fragment of an old heroick ballad. [Edinburgh c. 1710] (26 stanzas), Edinburgh 1719 (29 stanzas); in Allan Ramsay, Ever green vol 2, Edinburgh 1724 etc (42 stanzas); in Allan Ramsay, Tea-table miscellany vol 2, [Edinburgh 1726?] etc (no known copy) etc. Additional stanzas in Ever green are by Ramsay.
Hardyknute, a fragment: being the first canto of an epick poem, with general remarks and notes [by John Moncrief]. 1740, Glasgow 1745 (text only), 1748.
Chevy-chace: to which is subjoined Hardyknute: a fragment. Aberdeen 1754, [London?] 1783.
In 1781 John Pinkerton included in his Select Scotish ballads [tragic] (re-issued 1783) a 2nd pt, anon, consisting of 54 stanzas, but admitted in his Ancient Scotish poems 1786 that he was the author of these stanzas, claiming that Sir John Bruce was the author of the first pt.

§ 2

Clyne, N. The romantic Scottish ballads and the Lady Wardlaw heresy. Aberdeen 1859.

E. BURNS AND HIS CONTEMPORARIES

ROBERT BURNS
1759–96
Bibliographies

Chambers, R. In Poetical works, Edinburgh 1838.
— In Life and works vol 4, Edinburgh 1852; extended in Life and works vol 4, Edinburgh 1857.
[Bigmore, E. C.] Descriptive list of a collection of original manuscript poems by Burns. 1861.
[M'Kie, J.] Bibliotheca Burnsiana: life and works of Burns, title pages and imprints of the various edns in the private library of J. M'kie. Kilmarnock 1866. Includes works not in M'Kie's library.
— The Burns calendar: a manual of Burnsiana. Kilmarnock 1874.
[Gibson, J.] The bibliography of Burns. Kilmarnock 1881. Includes edns of Burns and Burnsiana, with information about authors and compilers not found in any other bibliography.
Anderson, J. P. In J. S. Blackie, Life of Burns, 1888. Also separately.
Muir, J. [et al]. Bibliography of Burns. Burns Chron 1–5, 7, 9, 10 1892–1901. Supplements M'Kie, above, and includes works about Burns as well as edns of his works.
Catalogue of the Burns exhibition, Royal Glasgow Institute of the Fine Arts. Glasgow 1896; rptd as Memorial catalogue of the Burns exhibition, Glasgow 1898 (a superior edn with plates, facsimiles etc).
[Duncan, J. and A. Balharrie]. Catalogue of the Burns, Scott and Shakespeare exhibition, from the collection of A. C. Lamb. Dundee [1896].
Wallace, W. Chief editions of life and writings of Burns. In R. Chambers, Life and works of Burns vol 4, rev Wallace, Edinburgh 1896.
Angus, W. C. The printed works of Burns: a bibliography in outline. Glasgow 1899.
Ewing, J. C. A selected list of editions of the works of Burns, and of books upon his life and writings. 1899.
— Bibliography of Burns. Pbns of Edinburgh Bibl Soc 9 1913 (for 1909); Edinburgh 1909.
— Burns's letters addressed to Clarinda. Pbns of Edinburgh Bibl Soc 11 1921; Edinburgh 1921.
— Burns's literary correspondents 1786–96. Burns Chron 2nd ser 8 1933; Ayr 1938 (with new notes). A list prepared for Dr Currie c. 1796, with précis of contents.
Wilson, J. G. American editions of Burns's poems. New York 1900.
Dick, J. C. In Songs of R. Burns, 1903. Especially useful for the sections on songs and song literature prior to Burns.
Sneddon, D. Catalogue of the M'Kie Burnsiana library, holograph mss, paintings, etchings, engravings, photographs and relics. Kilmarnock 1909. Belonging to the Kilmarnock Corporation, a major collection. An earlier edn, Kilmarnock 1883, lists only about half as many items.
The Burns Cottage catalogue of manuscripts, portraits and other relics in cottage and museum. Ayr 1923. Frequently rptd with addns. The collection is one of the largest of mss.
MacIntosh, W. Bibliography of the poetical works of Burns and of works on Burns published in Germany. Scottish N & Q 3rd ser 4 1926; rptd in Burns in Germany, Scoto-German studies, Aberdeen 1928.
Cook, D. Burns manuscripts in the Honresfield collection of Sir A. J. Law. Glasgow 1928.
Painter, A. M. American editions of the Poems of Burns before 1800. Library 4th ser 12 1932.
Namba, T. Burns bibliography in Japan. Ninon Hikaku Bungakai Kaiho [Comparative Lit Soc of Japan] 13–19, 26 1944–61.

Egerer, J. W. Burns: some early editions of his works. Hanover NH 1946.
— A bibliography of Burns. Edinburgh 1964. With bibliographical description of all edns to 1802, thereafter a list of edns which claim to be complete; excludes selections and single poems.
Rosenbach Company. Burns: a collection of original manuscripts, autograph letters, first editions and association copies. Philadelphia 1948.
Campbell, N. The Murison Burns collection. Dunfermline 1953.
Emslie, G. C. Burns in other languages. Burns Chron 3rd ser 5 1956.
[Hepburn, A. G., A. Hunter and D. R. Younger]. Catalogue of Burns collection in the Mitchell Library. Glasgow 1959. The most important collection of ptd material by and about Burns; over 3,500 entries.
Roy, G. R. Robert Burns. Columbia SC 1966. Supplements Egerer, 1964, above.

Reference Material

Cuthbertson, J. Complete glossary to the poetry and prose of Burns. Paisley 1886.
Reid, J. H. A complete word and phrase concordance to the poems and songs of Burns. Glasgow 1889, New York 1967.
Annual Burns Chronicle and Club Directory [title varies]. Kilmarnock 1st ser 34 vols 1892–1925; 2nd ser 25 vols 1926–50; as Scots Chronicle [not numbered in series] 1951; 3rd ser 1952–; Index to 1st series, 1935; index to 2nd series vols 1–20, 1945. See J. McVie, Burns Federation: a bi-centenary review, Kilmarnock 1959.
Ross, J. D. (ed). Burnsiana. 6 vols Paisley 1892–7.
Lindsay, M. The Burns encyclopaedia. 1959.

Collections

The works, with an account of his life and a criticism on his writings. [Ed J. Currie] 4 vols Liverpool 1800, London 1801, 1802, 1803, 1806, 1809, 1813, 1814; to which are added some further particulars of the author's life, new notes and many other additions by Gilbert Burns, 4 vols 1820, reissued as Stothard's illustr edn 1820 (for 1823). This edn formed the basis of many listed below.
Poems. 2 vols Edinburgh 1801 (4 variants).
The works, with an account of his life and a criticism of his writings. 4 vols Philadelphia 1801 (almost verbatim from Currie, above).
Poems, with his life and character. Dundee 1802.
Poems, with his life and character. Edinburgh 1802.
Stewart's edition of Burns's poems, with his life and character. Glasgow 1802 (4 variants).
Crerar's edition of Burns's poems, with his life and character. 2 vols Kirkcaldy 1802.
Poetical works, with an account of his life. Newcastle 1802.
Poetical works. [Ed A. Chalmers] 3 vols 1804.
Poetical works. 2 vols Philadelphia 1804.
Works. 3 vols Philadelphia 1804.
Works. 4 vols Belfast 1805 ('5th edn'). Actually first edn, but taken from the 4th of Currie, above; with Clarinda's letters added, Belfast 1806.
Works. Edinburgh 1805.
Poems. Edinburgh 1806, 1807, 1809, [1813], 1814, 1816.
Works. 4 vols Belfast 1807.
Works. Edinburgh 1807.
Poetical works. Ed T. Park 2 vols 1807, 1808, 1813 (Sharpe's British Poets 61–2).
Poetical works. Philadelphia 1807.

Poetical works. 2 vols Alnwick 1808, 1808, 1810, [1811], [1812], [1813], [1815], nd. With woodcuts by Bewick.

Works. 4 vols Belfast 1808.

Poems. Musselburgh 1808.

Poetical works. 2 vols 1810.

Poems, with an account of his life and miscellaneous remarks on his writings. [Ed J. Morison] 2 vols Edinburgh 1811.

Poetical works. 2 vols 1811, 1 vol Newcastle 1811, Philadelphia 1811, 1815, 2 vols 1812, 1 vol Alexandria [Virginia] 1813, Edinburgh 1813 (with account of life), 1813, 1814, London 1813 (with life by A. Chalmers?), 1816, 1817, 1822, Newcastle 1814.

Works. 4 vols Baltimore 1815.

Poems. Belfast 1815.

Life and works, to which is prefixed a review of the life of Burns and of various criticisms on his character and writings by A. Peterkin. 4 vols Edinburgh 1815, nd, New York 1824.

Poetical works. Edinburgh 1815, 2 vols 1817.

Poetical works, with his songs and fragments. Edinburgh 1815, 1819.

Works. 4 vols 1815.

Poetical works. 2 vols Salem NY 1815.

Works. Baltimore 1816.

Poetical works. Belfast 1816.

Findlay's edition of Burns's poems. Dublin 1816, Belfast [1816?].

Poetical works. Glasgow 1816 (separate nos), 1816, 1819.

Poetical works. 2 vols 1816.

Works. 4 vols Montrose 1816.

Poems. Kirkcaldy 1817.

Poems. Belfast 1818, Dublin 1819.

Works, with an account of his life, criticism on his writings, as edited by J. Currie. 4 vols Edinburgh 1818 (several issues).

Poetical works. Newcastle 1818 (1st issued in pts), 1821, 1826.

Poetical works, with an account of his life and his correspondence with Mr Thomson. 2 vols Philadelphia 1818.

Poems and songs with a life of the author: containing a variety of particulars, drawn from sources inaccessible by former biographers. Ed H. Paul, Ayr 1819.

Poetical works, to which is prefixed the author's life. Edinburgh 1819.

Works, with an account of his life and criticism of his writings. 2 vols Edinburgh 1819, Montrose 1819.

Works, with an account of his life, criticism of his writings. 4 vols Edinburgh 1819, London 1819.

Poetical works. 1819, 2 vols 1819.

Works. 3 vols 1819, Edinburgh 1820, London 1840.

Poetical works. Montrose 1819, Edinburgh 1820.

Works, with an account of his life. 4 vols Edinburgh 1820.

Works. 4 vols Edinburgh 1820.

Poetical works. 2 vols Chiswick 1821, London 1821, 1 vol Edinburgh 1821, Glasgow 1821, London 1821 (with life), 2 vols 1821 (with life).

Works, including his letters to Clarinda and the whole of his suppressed poems, with an essay on his life, genius and character. 4 vols 1821. An important edn, probably issued as a result of dissatisfaction with Gilbert Burns's 1820 edn of Currie.

Works. 2 vols New York 1821.

Burns. In Works of the British poets, with lives of the authors vols 38–9, ed R. Walsh, Boston 1822. Also pbd Philadelphia and New York; the 2nd vol also contains poems by Hector MacNeill.

Poetical works. Ed W. Roscoe 1822.

Poetical works, including the pieces published in his correspondence and reliques, with his songs and fragments, to which are prefixed a history of the poems. 2 vols 1822.

Poetical works. 2 vols Philadelphia 1822, 1 vol Edinburgh 1823, 1823.

Poetical works, including several pieces not inserted in Dr Currie's edition. 2 vols 1823.

Poetical works, including the pieces published in his correspondence and reliques, with his songs and fragments. 3 vols 1823.

Poetical works. 2 vols 1823, 1824, 1825, 1826, 1827, 1828, 1829, 1832, 1833, 1837.

Works. 2 vols Montrose 1823, 1824.

Poetical works. Philadelphia 1823 (an Amer edn of the 1820 Currie).

Poetical works. Edinburgh 1824.

Poetical works, including certain pieces not inserted in Dr Currie's edition. 2 vols in one 1824, 1825, 1828, 1830, 1833, 1834, 1835, nd.

Poetical works. 2 vols 1824–5, 1827, 1833.

Works. 2 vols 1824.

Works. 1824.

Works. 4 vols New York 1824.

Works. Edinburgh 1825 (3 issues), 1828, 1830.

Works. [4 vols in 1] 1825.

Poetical works. 1826 (Dove's English Classics).

Life of Burns with his correspondence and fragments. 1826.

Works. 2 vols New York 1826, Philadelphia 1828, 1829, 1831, 1832, 1832, 1833, 1834.

Poems and songs. Alnwick 1828, nd.

Poetical works, with his songs and fragments. [2 vols in 1] Glasgow 1828.

Poetical works. 2 vols Chiswick 1829, London 1829, 1830, 1837, 1830, 1839 (enlarged) (Aldine edn, ed H. Nicholas), 3 vols 1866 (further enlarged), 1870, 1875.

Works. [4 vols in 1] New York 1830.

Poetical works. 2 vols Edinburgh 1831, 1834, 1835, 1837.

Works. Edinburgh 1831, 1835, 1837, 1838.

Works, including his letters to Clarinda and the whole of his suppressed poems. 1831, 1843.

Works. 1831.

Complete works. 4 vols in 1 New York 1831.

Poetical works. Edinburgh 1832, 1834, 1836, 1837, 1838.

Works, containing his life by John Lockhart [and] poetry and correspondence [from] Dr Currie's edition. New York 1832, 1835, Hartford Conn 1836, 1837, New York 1849, 1852, 1853, 1857.

Works, with an account of his life. New York 1832.

Entire works, with an account of his life. 4 vols in 1 Edinburgh 1833, 1833, London 1835, 1836 (5th edn), 1838, 1841, 1842, Manchester 1844, 1845, 1847, 1848, 1850, nd, Edinburgh 1851. The Diamond ser; the last 3 Manchester edns are all called the 10th.

Poetical works. 2 vols Boston 1834.

Poetical works. Dunbar 1834.

Poetical works. 2 vols Dundee 1834.

Works. Ed Ettrick Shepherd [James Hogg] and William Motherwell 5 vols Glasgow 1834–6. Single vols rptd at various times, and mixed sets sold. The following dates have been recorded for one or more vols: 1835, 1836, 1837, 1838, 1840, 1841, 1848, 1851, 1852, 1853, nd, 4 vols Boston 1834–5.

Works, with his life by Allan Cunningham. 8 vols 1834, 1835. The first issue announced as 6 vols though extended to 8. The edn is unreliable, but remains essential.

Complete works: containing his poems, songs and correspondence. Ed A. Cunningham 2 vols Glasgow 1835.

Works, with selected notes of A. Cunningham, a biographical and critical introduction and a comparative etymological glossary to the poet by A. Wagner. Leipzig 1835.

Works, with an account of his life. Philadelphia 1835.

Works, including his letters to Clarinda. Glasgow 1836, 1845.

Poetical works. Halifax 1836, 1837, 1838.

Poetical works: comprising an entire collection of his poems. 1836.

Poetical works, with a memoir of the author's life. 1836, 1836.

Poetical works, with his life, glossary etc. 1836.

Poetical works. 2 vols in 1 New York 1836, nd.

Poetical works. Belfast 1837, 1838, [1850], London 1851, nd.

Poetical works, to which are now added notes illustrating historical, personal and local allusions. [Ed R. Chambers], Edinburgh 1838.

Poetical works. Edinburgh 1838.

Poetical works. 1838, 1839, 1841.

Poetical works. 1838 (Standard Lib edn).

Poetical works, with a memoir of the author's life. 1838.

Poetical works. 1839, 1848, 1857, 1858, 1859, 1868.

Poetical works, with a memoir of the author's life. 1839.

Works. New York 1839.

Poetical works. Halifax 1840, 1843, 1845, 1846, 1850, 1851, 1852, 1853, 1854, 1856, 1858, 1859, 1860, 1862, 1866, nd, London nd.

Poetical works. 1840.

Works, with life by A. Cunningham, and notes by Gilbert Burns. 1840, 1842, 1844, 1845, 1845, 1847, 1847, 1850, 1854, 1858, 1860, 1862.

Poetical works. Newcastle 1841, 1842.

Complete works. Halifax 1842, 1844, 1845, 1846, 1847, 1848, 1850, 1851, 1852, 1854, 1855, 1857, 1859, 1863, 1865, 1866, London 1867, 1875, nd.

Poetical works. 1842, 1842, Derby 1843, 1844, 1845, 1847, nd, Dublin nd, London nd.

Works, with Dr Currie's memoir of the poet and an essay on his genius and character by Professor Wilson. 2 vols Glasgow 1843-4, 1846, 1847, 1850, 1853, 1854, 1857, 1859, 1861, 1863, 1865, 1866, 1868, 1870, 1874, 1877, 1878, nd. Issued by the publisher Blackie, who used Glasgow and London interchangeably as place of pbn.

Poetical works. 1843.

Complete poetical works. New York 1843 (2nd edn), 1844, 1846, 1847, 1849, 1851.

Poetical works. 2 vols New York 1843.

Poetical works, with a life of the author. Nuremberg 1843, nd.

Works. Philadelphia 1843, 1844, 1846, 1849, London 1844, 1845, Glasgow 1845.

Works and correspondence. Glasgow 1845, 1846, nd.

Poetical works. Leipzig 1845 (vol 90 of Collection of Br Authors).

Poetical works. 1845, 1847, Belfast 1846, 1847.

Poetical works, including several pieces not inserted in Dr Currie's edition, exhibited under a new plan of arrangement. 2 vols Boston 1846, 1847, 1848, 1849, nd. From 2 vols London edn of 1819, above.

Works. Boston 1846, 1847, 1848, nd.

Poetical works. Glasgow 1846, London 1846, 1850.

Works. Philadelphia 1846.

Works. Cincinnati 1847, 1849, 1853, 1857, 1858.

Poetical works. Edinburgh 1847.

Complete works. Aberdeen 1848.

Poetical works. 2 vols New York 1849, 1852, 1855, 1858, 1 vol Boston 1850, 1852, 1853, 1854, 1855, 1856, 1857, 1859, 1866, London 1850.

Life and works. Ed R. Chambers 4 vols Edinburgh 1851, New York 1852, Edinburgh 1853, Philadelphia 1854.

Complete works. Philadelphia 1851.

Works. Philadelphia 1851.

Poetical works. Glasgow 1852, 2 vols 1855 (enlarged) (vol 2 contains songs and ballads), 1856, 1857, 1859, 1865, London 1883.

Complete poetical works. New York 1852, 1853, 1855, 1856, 1857.

Complete works. Boston 1853, 1854, 1858.

Poetical and prose works. Hartford 1855.

Poetical works. New York 1855.

Life and works. Ed R. Chambers 4 vols Edinburgh 1856-7 (enlarged from 1851, above), 1859, London 1859-60, Edinburgh 1860, London 1860, Edinburgh 1891, nd.

Poetical works, with memoir, critical dissertation and explanatory notes by G. Gilfillan. 2 vols Edinburgh 1856, 2 vols in 1 New York 1857.

Poetical works. Ed R. A. Willmott 1856, 1856, 1857, 1858, 1859, 1859, 1860, 1862, 1863, 1865, 1866, 1867, 1869, Boston 1872, 1873, 1873, 1875, 1877, London 1878, Boston 1880, London nd (several variants).

Poetical works, with life, notes and glossary by A. Cunningham. Philadelphia 1856, 1857.

Poetical works. [c. 1857].

Poems and songs. 1858, New York 1858, Glasgow nd (enlarged, several variants).

Poetical works. Philadelphia 1858; ed J. and A. Macpherson, Glasgow 1859, London nd (2 edns).

Complete poetical and prose works. New York 1859.

Poetical works. Philadelphia 1859.

Complete works, with a new life of the poet and notices, critical and biographical by A. Cunningham. Boston 1860, New York nd.

Poems and songs. 1860, 1861.

Poetical works. Philadelphia 1860, Boston 1861, 1863, 1864, 3 vols Boston 1863, 1865, 1871, 1877, 1878, 3 vols in 1 1879.

Poems. 1863, 1864, 1865, 1868, 1882. From Aldine edn of 1830, above.

Works. 2 vols Edinburgh 1864.

Poetical works. Ed C. C. Clarke 2 vols Edinburgh 1864 (with notes by G. Gilfillan) (vols 33-4 of Nichol's Library Edn of Br Poets), 2 vols in 1 Edinburgh 1866, 1868.

Poetical works. Philadelphia 1864, 1868.

Complete poetical works. Ed J. S. Roberts, memoir by W. Gunyon, Edinburgh [1865], New York 1866, Edinburgh 1873, 1874, 1876, 1877, 1877, 1878, 1880, 1881, 1883, 1884, 1887, 1888 (3 edns, title varies), 1890, 1891, 1892, 1893, 1895, nd (2 or more issues).

Complete works, with a memoir by W. Gunyon. Edinburgh 1865, 1866, 1867, Philadelphia 1867, Edinburgh 1869, 1874, Philadelphia 1875, Edinburgh 1877, London 1884, Edinburgh 1885, 1886, 1888, 1892, nd, Philadelphia nd (for Complete prose works see Selections, below, 1865).

Poetical works and letters (expurgated). Edinburgh 1865, 1869, nd.

Works, with life and notes by A. Cunningham. 2 vols Edinburgh [1865], nd.

Poetical works. Ed A. Smith 2 vols 1865 (with glossary and a biographical memoir), 1879, 1883, 1887, Chicago nd, New York nd (several edns).

Complete poetical works. New York 1865, 1869.

Poems. 2 vols Boston 1866 (vol 2 contains songs).

Works and correspondence. Glasgow 1866, nd (several issues), London nd.

Complete poetical works of Burns and Sir Walter Scott: new edition. London 1866, 1867, nd.

Poetical works. Ed R. A. Willmott 1866.

Complete works. New York 1866.

Complete works: including his correspondence, and the poetical works of Sir Walter Scott. 2 vols Glasgow 1867, 1870.

Life and works by P. H. Waddell. 2 vols Glasgow 1867, 1870, 1878, 1881. Although later edns are claimed to be 'revised with additions', they are merely reprints.

Poetical works. 2 vols New York 1867.

Poems and songs. Edinburgh 1868, 1875, 1882, 1888, London nd.

Poetical works. Halifax 1868.

Poems, songs and letters: being the complete works. Ed A. Smith 1868, Philadelphia 1868, London 1869, 1870, 1871, 1873, 1875, 1879, 1884, 1891, 1893, 1900, 1904, 1906, 1910, 1914, 1921, 1924, 1932 (Globe edn), New York nd (several edns).

Poetical works. 1868, 1870, 1871, nd.

Complete poetical and prose works. New York 1869, 1881, 1882,

Complete works. Glasgow 1870.

Poetical works. Glasgow 1870.

Poetical works. Glasgow 1870 (Universal Lib).

Works, poetical and prose. Ed 'Gertrude' (Jane C. Simpson) 2 vols Glasgow 1870, 1874.

Complete poetical works, arranged in order of their earliest publication [with] annotations, introductory notices etc by W. Scott Douglas. 2 vols Kilmarnock 1871, 1876, 1886, Edinburgh 1890, London 1890, Toronto 1890, Edinburgh 1891, 1893, 1896, 1903, 1923, Glasgow 1935, 1938 (Kilmarnock edn).

Poetical works. Ed W. M. Rossetti 1871, [1879], [1881], 1911, nd (several edns).

Works. Ed W. Scott Douglas 6 vols Edinburgh 1877-9, 1883, London 1891, Edinburgh 1895; first 3 vols only, containing all the poetry, Edinburgh 1886, London 1892, Edinburgh 1896, nd, London nd. A major edn.

Complete poetical works. Glasgow 1877.

Works. New York 1877.

Poetical works. 1878, nd.

Poetical works, [with] notes and correspondence by A. Cunningham. Ed C. Kent 1878, 1883, New York 1883, 1884, London 1885, 1890, 1893, 1895, 1896, nd (several variants).

Complete works. Edinburgh 1880.

Poems. 2 vols 1881.

Poetical works. New York 1881.

Poetical works. Boston 1882.

Complete works. New York 1882.

Poetical works. Boston 1883.

Poetical works, with the correspondence, and notes by A. Cunningham. Chicago 1884.

Poetical works. 6 vols Glasgow 1884, 1894, 1 vol Glasgow 1907, 6 vols nd.

Poetical works. Chicago 1885.

Poetical works. Ed J. Skipsey 1885 (sometimes issued in 2 vols as Poems or Songs), 1887, nd.

Complete works (self-interpreting). 6 vols Philadelphia [1886], 1898, 1905, 1909, New York 1909. Based almost entirely on W. Scott Douglas's edn of 1877.

Poetical works. Glasgow 1887.

Works. Ed C. Annandale 5 vols [1887], 1888, 1890.

Poetical works. New York 1887, 1887.

Complete works. Ed A Smith, Troy NY 1887.

Poetical works. Glasgow 1888, London 1888, 1889, 1891, 1892, 1893, 1894, 1895, 1896, nd (variants), Newcastle 1889, Halifax 1890, London 1890, 3 vols 1892, Edinburgh 1893, 1896.

Poetical works. Ed G. A. Aitken 3 vols 1893 (with memoir).

Poetical works. Oxford 1893.

Life and works. Ed R. Chambers, rev W. Wallace 4 vols Edinburgh 1896. The Chambers edn of 1856 completely re-edited, with additional material.

Poetical works. Edinburgh 1896.

Poetry. Ed W. E. Henley and T. F. Henderson 4 vols Edinburgh 1896-7, 1901, New York 1905, London nd. Until the Kinsley edn of 1968 the standard text for the poetry, and still essential for Henderson's notes.

People's edition of the poetical works. Edinburgh 1896.

Poetical works. Glasgow 1896, London 1896.

Poems and songs. Ed A. Lang 1896, New York 1896, 1899.

Poetical works. Ed J. Fawside 1896, New York 1896, London [1897], 1901, nd.

Poems, epistles, songs, epigrams and epitaphs. Ed J. Manson 2 vols 1896, 1901.

Complete poetical works. Ed J. L. Robertson 3 vols Oxford 1896 (Oxford Miniature edn), 1 vol 1904, 1906, 1908, 1910, 1912, 1913, 1916, 1917, 1921, 1923, 1926, 1928, 1936, 1939, 1942, 1945, 1948, 1951, 1958, 1960 (OSA).

Complete poetical works. Boston 1897. Based on the Henley and Henderson edn of 1896, above.

Poetical works. Ed A. Smith, New York 1897.

Poetical works. New York 1897.

Poems. 2 vols 1898.

Complete poetical works. Ed N. H. Dole, New York 1900 (with biographical sketch), 2 vols 1900.

Poems. 1901 (New Oxford Lib).

Poetical works. New York 1901.

Complete poetical works. Edinburgh 1902.

Poetical works; life and notes by W. Wallace. Edinburgh 1902, 1948, 1958.

Poetical works. Glasgow 1902.

Complete poetical works. 1902, 1904, 1923, 1927, nd (2 issues, one contains additionally Remarks on Scottish songs and ballads, ancient and modern, with anecdotes of their authors by Burns).

Poems. 1902 (Temple Classics).

Poems and songs. 1902.

Poetical works. 1902, nd.

People's edition of the poetical works, revised D. M'Naught. Edinburgh 1903.

Poetical works. 1903.

Poetical works. Oxford 1903, 1906, 1911, 1915, 1919.

Poetical works. Edinburgh 1904.

Poetical works. 1904.

Poems and songs. Ed J. Douglas 1905, [1906], 1909, 1910, 1913, nd; introd by J. Kinsley 1958, 1963 (EL).

Poems and songs. [Ed T. F. Henderson, introd by A. Lang] [1906].

Poems and songs. 1907, 1908 (People's Lib).

Poetical works. Ed C. Annandale, music harmonized by H. C. Miller 4 vols 1909.

Songs and poems, with appreciation [of 1896] by the Earl of Rosebery. 1912, 1913, 1914. Also issued in 2 vols.

Poems. Ed J. L. Hughes, New York 1920.

Complete poems, with essay on Burns's life, genius and achievement by W. E. Henley, and introduction by J. Buchan. 10 vols Boston 1926, London 1927. Vols 1-6 contain the poems, based on the Henley and Henderson text, vols 7-10 containing the letters and the first common-place book, ed F. H. Allen.

Poems, epistles, songs, epigrams and epitaphs. Ed C. S. Dougall 1927.

Complete works and letters. Introd by W. Harvey, oration by the Earl of Rosebery, life by R. Ford, introd to letters by R. W. MacKenna, Glasgow [1928], nd (several issues).

Poetry and prose, with essays by Mackenzie, Jeffrey, Carlyle and others. Ed R. Dewar, Oxford 1929.

Poems and songs. Ed J. Barke 1955.

Poems and selected letters. Ed A. Hepburn 1959.

Poems and songs. Ed J. Kinsley 3 vols Oxford 1968. Includes music for songs; vol 3 a commentary.

Poetical works. Aberdeen nd.

Poems and songs. Alnwick nd.

Poems. Boston nd.

Poetical works. Boston nd (4 edns).

Poetical works. Brooklyn nd.

Poetical works. 2 vols Chiswick [c. 1824].

Poetical works. Dublin [c. 1829].

Poems. Dundee nd.

Complete works. Edinburgh nd, 4 vols Edinburgh nd.

Entire works. 4 vols in 1 Edinburgh [c. 1865] (2 edns).

Poems. Edinburgh nd.

Poems and songs. Edinburgh nd (2 edns).

Poetical works and letters. Edinburgh [c. 1859-81] (several issues).

Poetical works. Edinburgh nd (3 edns).

Poetical works. Ed J. Fawside, Edinburgh nd.

Works. Edinburgh nd, 2 vols Edinburgh nd.

Complete poetical works. Ed W. Gunnyon, Glasgow nd.

Complete works. 2 vols Glasgow nd.

Poetical works. Glasgow nd (5 edns). One edn had 4 issues, one of c. 1876.

Poetical works. Ed W. M. Rossetti, Glasgow nd.
Complete works. [c. 1872] (3 edns).
Complete works. 3 vols [c. 1840].
Complete poetical works. nd (2 edns).
Complete works and letters. nd.
Complete works of Burns and Sir Walter Scott. nd.
Complete poetical works of Burns and Sir Walter Scott.
nd (3 edns).
National edition of the works. Ed W. Wallace 2 vols nd.
Poems and songs. nd.
Poems, letters and land of Burns, with a new memoir of the
poet, and notices, critical and biographical, of his works,
by A. Cunningham. 2 vols [1838]; reissued several
times as The complete works: containing his poems,
songs and correspondence, nd.
Poetical works. nd (at least 21 edns), 2 vols nd (2 edns).
Poetical works. Ed W. M. Rossetti, nd (5 edns).
Poetical works. Ed C. C. Clarke 2 vols nd.
Poetical works. Ed A. Cunningham, nd.
Poetical works. Ed C. Kent, nd (2 edns).
Poetical works. Ed J. R. Tutin, nd.
Poetical and prose works. [c. 1838] (2 edns).
Poetical works of Geoffrey Chaucer and Burns. [c. 1855].
Works. nd.
Poetical works. Newcastle nd.
Complete works, with a biographical memoir by A. Smith,
New York nd.
Complete poetical works. New York nd.
Complete poetical and prose works. New York nd.
Illustrated family Burns. New York nd.
Poetical works. New York nd (10 edns), 2 vols New York
nd (3 edns).
Poetical works. Ed A. Cunningham, New York nd (2 edns).
Poetical works. [Ed A. Smith], New York nd.
Works. New York nd (4 edns).
Poetical works. Philadelphia nd, 3 vols Philadelphia nd.
Poetical works. Wakefield nd.

Selections

Poetical miscellany: containing posthumous poems, songs,
epitaphs and epigrams. Glasgow 1800. Copy in
Mitchell Lib.
Burns's songster. Newcastle [c. 1800].
Beauties of Burns. Ayr 1802, London 1803.
For a' that, and a' that [and other songs by Burns].
Stirling [1805?].
Twenty songs. Glasgow [1805?]; Seventeen songs,
Glasgow 1809 (2nd edn); Seventeen favourite songs by
Burns and Tannahill, Glasgow [1815?].
Burns' celebrated songs. Edinburgh 1805.
The beauties of Burns. Falkirk 1809, 1819.
The Caledonian musical museum, edited by his son
[Robert]. 3 vols 1809–11. Contains 'upwards of two
hundred songs' by Burns.
Select poems. 1809.
Select Scotish songs. Ed R. H. Cromek 2 vols 1810.
Quotes Burns's comments on songs in Johnson's Scots
musical museum.
The Northumbrian minstrel. 3 pts Alnwick 1811. A large
number of songs by Burns.
A collection of songs in the Scotch dialect. Newcastle
1812.
The bony lass, Whistle and I'll come to you my lad [and
other songs]. Falkirk 1814.
Highland Mary [and other songs]. Glasgow [1815?].
The Scottish minstrel: being a complete collection of
Burns's songs, together with his correspondence with
Thomson. Philadelphia 1818.
Complete collection of the songs of Burns. Edinburgh 1819.
The lyric muse of Burns: containing all his songs including
the Jolly beggars. Montrose 1819.
The songs of Burns, with a preliminary discourse in which
his ideas of love are compared with those of Solomon,

Anacreon and Sappho. 1819. Copy at Kilmarnock
Burns Monument.
The miniature melodist: being a selection of the most
approved songs from the Little warbler. Glasgow [c.
1820].
Select works. 2 vols New York 1820–1.
Songs of Burns accurately copied from the originals:
improved edition. Liverpool 1822, [c. 1834.]
The songs and ballads, including ten never before pub-
lished, with preliminary discourse and illustrative
prefaces. [Ed J. Barwick?] 1823.
Songs, chiefly in the Scottish dialect. 1824.
Songs. 1824.
The British anthology or poetical library vol 8: Burns.
1825.
Songs, chiefly Scottish. 1825.
Beauties of Burns: consisting of selections from his poems
and letters. Ed A. Howard [c. 1826].
The cotter's Saturday night and other poems. Philadelphia
1826.
The cabinet of British poetry; [with Burns's] Songs
chiefly Scottish. 1830. Includes Pope, Thomson and
Armstrong.
Songs, with biographical notice and critical remarks. 1831.
Reprints the discourse on love from the edn of 1819.
Songs, with his life. Glasgow 1831.
Choice of Burns's poems. Ansbach 1832, 1834.
Selection from the Scottish poems of Burns. Edinburgh
1834.
Songs, with a biographical preface, notes and glossary.
1834.
Beauties of Byron and Burns: being a collection of poems
by the above authors. Hull 1837.
Whole songs. [c. 1840].
Select poems and songs chiefly in the Scottish dialect.
Berlin 1841.
Songs, alphabetically arranged. 1844.
Songs. Dumfries [1848?].
Burns's songster. Newcastle [1850?].
The kirk's alarm, or a present for the priest-ridden: being
a collection of the clerical satires by Burns. Edinburgh
1852. Copy in Kilmarnock Burns Museum.
The Scottish keepsake: or the songs of the Ayrshire bard.
Mauchline [1855?], 1857.
Songs and ballads: new edition. Glasgow 1857.
Select songs and ballads. Glasgow 1858, 1859.
Songs, with music. Glasgow 1859, [1859] (separate
works).
Illustrated songs. [Edinburgh] 1861.
Popular songs, words and music. Glasgow 1861.
Beauties of Burns. Glasgow 1862.
Songs. 1863, 1864, 1866, 1868.
Ballads and songs, with a lecture on his character and
genius by Carlyle. 1864.
Select songs of the Ayrshire bard. Glasgow 1865.
Songs and ballads: new edition. Glasgow 1865.
Songs and ballads. Glasgow 1867, nd.
Poems chiefly in the Scottish dialect [as in early Edinburgh
edns]. Kilmarnock 1869.
Poems chiefly in the Scottish dialect ['posthumous',
poems]. Kilmarnock 1869.
Songs, chiefly in the Scottish dialect. Kilmarnock 1869.
The above were issued as a 4-vol set including also a
facs of the Kilmarnock 1786 vol.
Tam O'Shanter, and Lament of Mary Queen of Scots.
Ed M. Thomas [1870].
Select songs of Burns and Tannahill, chronologically
arranged, with memoirs. Glasgow 1871, [1875].
Popular songs, with words and music. Glasgow [1874].
Select poems. New York 1874.
The power of poetry by M. Arnold, The cotter's Saturday
night, The banks o' Doon, Bonnie Leslie. New York 1875.
Poems selected from the works of Burns. Ed with life,
notes and glossary by A. M. Bell 1876.

Memorials of Burns and of some of his contemporaries and their descendants [by P. F. Aiken] with a numerous selection of his best poems and songs. 1876.

Favourite poems. Boston 1877.

Caledonia described by Scott, Burns and Ramsay. 1878.

Select songs, first published in a London edition of his poems in 1823, from which they are reprinted. 1878.

Burns, Ramsay and the earlier poets of Scotland. Ed A. Cunningham and C. Mackay 2 vols [1878-9].

The cotter's Saturday night and the Twa dogs [also Auld lang syne] with life, introduction and notes. [1883].

Select songs of Burns and Tannahill. In A strange life: or the life of a literary vagrant, 5 pts Glasgow [1883].

Selections. Louisville 1883.

Songs. Ed J. Skipsey [1885].

Choice selection of Burns's poems. Glasgow 1887.

Holograph manuscripts in the Kilmarnock Monument Museum. Ed D. Sneddon, Kilmarnock 1889.

Selected poems. Ed J. L. Robertson, Oxford 1889, [1904].

Songs of bonnie Scotland: containing all the finest Scotch songs by Burns and other well-known writers. [1890].

Selected poems. Ed A. Lang 1891, 1896, 1902, 1905.

[Selected poems]. In Scottish poetry of the eighteenth century vol 2, ed G. Eyre-Todd 1891, nd (Abbotsford ser of Scottish poets).

Love songs of Burns. Ed G. Douglas 1892.

Selected poems, with biographical sketch and notes by N. H. Dole. New York [1892].

The cotter's Saturday night and other poems, with biographical sketch and notes. Boston [1895].

The lyric poems. Ed E. Rhys 1895.

Selected poems and songs. 1895.

In memory of Burns; selected poems and songs. Ed R. Le Gallienne 1896.

Select poems. Ed A. J. George, Boston 1896, London 1897.

Songs, with symphonies and accompaniments by J. K. Lees, introduction and notes by H. C. Shelley. 1896 (2 issues, one Glasgow).

Auld lang syne and other songs. New York [1897].

Representative poems, with Carlyle's essay. Ed C. L. Hanson, Boston [c. 1897], 1899, [1930].

Selections. Ed J. G. Dow, Boston 1898.

Selections from the poems. Ed W. H. Venable, New York 1898.

Songs. Ed W. A. Craigie 1898.

Love poems. [Ed F. Chapman] 1901, 1902.

Songs. Edinburgh 1901, London 1901.

Songs, now first ptd with the melodies for which they were written. Ed J. C. Dick 1903, Hatboro Pa 1962.

Poems: a selection. Ed N. Munro 1904.

Poems and songs. [1904].

The people's penny Burns. Dundee [1904].

Beauties of Burns: extracts from the poems and ballads, also some of his letters, and the poet's narrative of his life. [Ed W. Whyte] [1905], [1906].

Selected poems and songs. 1905 (Penny poets no 5).

Songs. Dundee [1905].

Beauties of Burns. Ed J. Aitken, Kilmarnock [1906].

Poems. Ed T. F. Henderson, Heidelberg 1906.

Poems. Ed N. Munro, Glasgow [1906].

The cotter's Saturday night and other poems. Ed W. T. Field, San Francisco [1907].

Love songs and other poems. [Ed A. S. Cody], Chicago [1907].

Selected works. Ed R. Sutherland, Paisley 1907.

Songs, with a memoir. Glasgow [1907].

Songs, with biographical introduction by H. Bennett. 1907.

Auld lang syne and other poems. [1908]. By Burns and others.

Tam O'Shanter and other poems. [1908].

Poems: selections. New York [1910].

Moments with Burns. [1911].

Selected poems. [1911].

Songs. [1911].

Songs and lyrics. Ed W. Macdonald 1911, 1920.

Tam O'Shanter and other poems. Edinburgh [1911].

Select poems, arranged in kindred groups. Glasgow 1919.

Poems. Edinburgh [1920?], [1932] (Thistle Lib).

Songs. Edinburgh [1920?], [1932] (Thistle Lib).

Selected poems. Ed G. L. Marsh, Chicago 1920.

Selections. Ed J. H. Craig [1920].

Songs and ballads. [1923].

Scottish poems of Burns in his native dialect. Ed J. Wilson, Oxford 1925. Phonetic transcription and trns.

Songs. Ed A. E. Coppard, Waltham St Lawrence 1925 (Golden Cockerel Press).

Poems and songs. Ed C. M. Grieve 1926.

Burns [selections]. Ed M. F. Dee [1926].

Selected poems. Ed J. DeL. Ferguson, New York 1926, 1937.

Burns: a selection from his poetry. Ed W. Schallas 2 pts Brunswick [1927].

Selected poems. Ed G.D.H. and M. I. Cole 1928.

Poems. Ed G. Ogilvie, Edinburgh [1932].

Songs. Ed P. J. Dolland, Glasgow [1940].

Sprigs o' heather, songs and poems. Christchurch NZ [1942].

Songs of liberty by Burns. Ed P. J. Dollan 1943, 1944.

Burns: the inspired peasant [selected poems, ed J. C. Milne]. Stirling 1944.

Poems and songs. Ed A. Gray, Edinburgh 1945, 1946.

Songs and poems. Mount Vernon NY [1945].

Poems. Ed H. W. Meikle and W. Beattie 1946, 1947, 1953, 1958 (Penguin).

Selected songs. Glasgow 1947, 1949.

Poems. Ed 'Hugh MacDiarmid' (C. M. Grieve) 1949.

Poems. Ed L. Brander, Oxford 1950, 1957.

Some poems, songs and epistles. Ed J. McVie, Edinburgh 1951.

Little known songs of Burns, arranged by C. Prentice. [1956].

The tuneful flame: songs of R. Burns as he sang them. Ed R. D. Thornton, Lawrence Kansas 1957.

Songs and poems, with Burns's autobiographical letters. Ed R. Knight, accompaniments by P. Nordoff, New York 1959.

Selected poems. Ed G. S. Fraser 1960.

Love songs. Ed 'Hugh MacDiarmid' (C. M. Grieve) 1962.

Poems. Ed J. DeL. Ferguson, New York 1965.

A choice of Burns's poems and songs. Ed S. G. Smith 1966.

Selected poetry and prose. Ed R. D. Thornton, Boston 1966.

Poems. Ed L. Frankenberg, New York 1967.

Selections. Ed J. C. Weston, Indianapolis 1967.

Poems, selected by J. Irvine. Belfast nd.

Scottish songs. Belfast nd.

Auld lang syne and other songs. Glasgow nd.

Beauties of Burns: a selection of his most pooular songs. Glasgow nd.

Lyrics and love songs. Glasgow nd.

Select songs of the Ayrshire bard. Glasgow nd.

Songs and ballads. Glasgow nd.

Songs of Scotland's bard. Glasgow nd.

Beauties of Burns. Ed A. Howard [1822?].

Selected poems and songs. nd (Stead's Poets).

Songs. Montrose nd.

Popular songs. Paisley nd.

§ 1

Poems chiefly in the Scottish dialect. Kilmarnock 1786.

Poems chiefly in the Scottish dialect. Edinburgh 1787 (enlarged; 2 issues with many textual differences, known as the 'skinking' (earlier) and 'stinking' edn, the text of the earlier being the more accurate), London 1787, Belfast 1787, Dublin 1787.

The calf, The unco calf's answer, Virtue—to a mountain bard, and The de'il's answer to his vera worthy frien' R. Burns. [Scotland 1787]. Chap-book; only the first poem by Burns.

The Scots musical museum. Ed James Johnson 6 vols Edinburgh [1787, 1788, 1790, 1792, 1796, 1803]; vols 1–5 re-issued with vol 6; with notes by W. Stenhouse [completed by C. K. Sharpe and D. Laing] 6 vols Edinburgh 1838, 4 vols 1853; ed H. G. Farmer 2 vols Hatboro Pa 1962. Burns was the virtual editor of vols 2–5 and contributed 177 of the 600 songs, as well as collecting many others. The notes by Stenhouse were also issued separately as Illustrations of the lyric poetry and music of Scotland, Edinburgh 1853.

Here Stewarts once in triumph reign'd. In J. Maxwell, Animadversions on some poets and poetasters of the present age especially R—t B—s and J—n L—k, Paisley 1788. Copy in Mitchell Lib.

Poems chiefly in the Scottish dialect. Philadelphia 1788; to which are added Scots poems from R. Ferguson, New York 1788, Belfast 1789, Dublin 1789.

To the author ('Auld nibor, I'm three times, doubly, o'er'). In D. Sillar, Poems, Kilmarnock 1789.

The Ayrshire garland: an excellent new song. [Dumfries 1789?]. Broadside first appearance of 13 stanzas of Kirk's alarm.

The prayer of Holy Willie, a canting, hypocritical, Kirk elder. [Scotland?] 1789. First pbn of this poem; copy in Birthplace Museum, Alloway.

Poems chiefly in the Scottish dialect. Belfast 1790, Dublin 1790.

The kirk's alarm [2 new stanzas]. In A. Tait, Poems and songs. [Paisley?] 1790 (with 3 scurrilous poems on Burns).

Tam O'Shanter. In F. Grose, The antiquities of Scotland vol 2, 1791. First book pbn of this poem, which was written for the work.

The whistle: a poem. [Dumfries? 1791?]. Chapbook; first pbn of this poem.

Address to the shade of Thomson. In D. S. Erskine (Earl of Buchan), Essays on the lives and writings of Fletcher of Saltoun and the poet Thomson, 1792. Burns sent the poem on declining an invitation to attend a ceremony in honour of Thomson.

Poems chiefly in the Scottish dialect. 2 vols Edinburgh 1793 (enlarged), Belfast 1793, Edinburgh 1794.

A select collection of original Scotish airs. Ed G. Thomson 5 vols 1793–1818; various combinations re-issued 1801, 1804, 1809?, 1811?, 1815, 1817, 1822–3, 1825, 1826, 1828, 1831, 1838. First pbn of 59 songs written or altered by Burns for this work; also reprints several songs by Burns. A 6th vol without songs by Burns was pbd 1825.

O my love's like a red, red rose. In A selection of Scots songs harmonized by P. Urbani vol 2, Edinburgh [1794]. First pbn.

An address to the deil, with the answer by J. Lauderdale. Near Wigton 1795. Chapbook; Burns poem rptd from 1786 vol.

Address to the people of Scotland respecting Francis Grose, the British antiquarian; to which are added verses on seeing the ruins of an ancient magnificent structure. [Glasgow? c. 1795]. Only the first poem is by Burns.

Fy, let us a' to K[irkcudbright]. [Scotland c. 1795–6] (broadside); rptd [c. 1820].

Wha will buy my troggin? [Scotland c. 1795–6]. A broadside; copy in Birthplace Museum, Alloway.

Wham will we send to London Town. [Scotland c. 1795–6]. A broadside.

[Twas in the seventeen hunder' year]. [c. 1795–6?]. A broadside?; no copy recorded.

Poetry: original and selected. 4 vols Glasgow [1795?–8].

Pbd by Brash & Reid in 99 penny nos before being gathered into vols, contains 21 poems by Burns. Individual nos were re-issued, and odd vols made up at least till 1805.

An unco' mornfu tale; to which is added the Antiquarian ['Hear land o' cakes']. Glasgow 1796 (Stewart & Meikle chapbook).

Poems chiefly in the Scottish dialect. 2 vols Edinburgh 1797, 1798, 2 vols in 1 Philadelphia 1798.

Elegy on the year eighty-eight. Edinburgh 1799. Chapbook, also includes Burns's Written at Dalcardoch ('When death's dark stream'), and Written on a window of the Inn at Carron ('We can na here'). Copy in Nat Lib of Scotland.

Sonnets from the Robbers, by A. Thomson, the Pretender's soliloquy, Bruce's address and the Lass of Ballochmyle, by Burns. Edinburgh 1799. Contributor's is the only recorded copy.

The bonny lass of Ballochmyle. In Polyhumnia no 18, Glasgow [1799]. A ser of 20 chapbooks issued 1798–9.

The jolly-beggars: a cantata. Glasgow [1799] (Stewart & Meikle chapbooks).

The kirk's alarm: a satire; A letter to a taylor, The deil's awa' wi' the exciseman and An unco' mournfu' tale. Glasgow [1799] (Stewart & Meikle chapbook).

Holy Willie's prayer, Letter to John Goudie and six favourite songs by Burns. Glasgow [1799] (Stewart & Meikle chapbook).

Extempore verses on dining with Lord Daer, accompanied with a prose letter to a friend. Glasgow [1799] (Stewart & Meikle chapbook).

The inventory. Glasgow [1799] (Stewart & Meikle chapbook).

The henpeck'd husband, Address to his illegitimate child, An epigram and On a bank of flowers. Glasgow [1799] (Stewart & Meikle chapbook).

[7 poems by Burns]. In the passage of Mount St Gothard, by the Duchess of Devonshire, Glasgow [1799] (Stewart & Meikle chapbook). Another poem, Shelah O'Neil, is here incorrectly attributed to Burns. Rptd as The poetical miscellany: containing posthumous poems, songs, epitaphs and epigrams, by Burns, Glasgow 1800 (copy in Nat Lib of Scotland).

Poems chiefly in the Scottish dialect; to which are added Scots poems selected from the works of R. Ferguson. New York 1799. The sheets of the New York 1788 edn with new title-page.

Poems chiefly in the Scottish dialect. 2 vols Belfast 1800, Edinburgh 1800, Berwick 1801 (4 issues), Edinburgh 1801, 1 vol Glasgow 1801 (ptd by T. Duncan), Glasgow 1801 (ptd by Chapman & Lang, 5 issues), Montrose 1801.

The answer ('Guidwife: I mind it weel'). In Elizabeth Scot, Alonzo and Cora, with other original poems. 1801. First printing of poem.

Poems ascribed to Burns, the Ayrshire bard, not contained in any edition of his works hitherto published. Glasgow 1801 (several variants) rptd in part in Miscellanea Perthensis, Perth 1801, London 1802 (as The picnic).

Holy Willie's prayer and epitaph. Edinburgh 1801.

Poems chifley in the Scottish dialect. 2 vols Paisley 1801–2.

The merry diversions of Halloween. Stirling 1802.

Poems chiefly in the Scottish dialect. 2 vols Edinburgh 1802, Belfast 1803, Dublin 1803 (2 edns, one with Heron's Life), 1 vol 1803 (3 issues), 2 vols Cork 1804, 1 vol Edinburgh 1804, Glasgow 1804, Wilmington 1804, Edinburgh 1805 (2 edns, each with variants), London 1806, Edinburgh 1807 (2 edns, each with variants), 1808, Glasgow 1808.

Reliques of Burns: consisting chiefly of original letters, poems and critical observations on Scottish songs. Ed R. H. Cromek 1808 (nearly all copies have cancelled leaves (AA6–8), Wellesley College Lib has copy with original leaves), Philadelphia 1809, London 1813, 1814, 1817.

Poems, letters etc ascribed to Burns. 1809. Includes

Poems ascribed to Burns, 1801 and Letters addressed to Clarinda, 1802. Frontispiece by Isaac Cruikshant, one figure probably the earliest work in print by his son George.

Poems chiefly in the Scottish dialect. Baltimore 1812.

Poems chiefly Scottish. 2 vols Perth 1813 (vol 1 was also issued separately).

Poems chiefly in the Scottish dialect. Baltimore 1815, Edinburgh [1816] (also issued with Belfast and Dublin imprints), London 1824, 1824.

Songs chiefly in the Scottish dialect. 1824.

Poems chiefly in the Scottish dialect. Ed W. Scott Douglas, Kilmarnock 1877.

Facsimiles

Poems chiefly in the Scottish dialect [first edn, Kilmarnock 1786]. Kilmarnock 1867, 1867, 1868, 1870 (6 issues), 1886, Glasgow [1895] (miniature), re-issued nd, Kilmarnock 1909, London 1911 (type facs), re-issued Oxford 1913, Glasgow 1919, 1927, London 1927, [Edinburgh 1913].

Facsimiles of 11 letters from Burns to Peter Hill 1788–96; notes by G. Wilson. 2 pts 1890.

The Glenriddell manuscripts of Burns. 2 vols Philadelphia 1914 (150 copies). This collection of poems and letters prepared by Burns for Robert Riddell was given to the Scottish nation by J. Gribbel and is housed in the Nat Lib of Scotland.

Poems and letters in the handwriting of Burns. Ed W. B. Stevens, St Louis 1908. Mss from the collections of W. K. Bixby and F. W. Lehmann.

Autograph poems and letters of Burns in the collection of R. B. Adam. Buffalo 1922.

Single Poems
Cotter's Saturday night

In Roach's beauties of the poets, 1795, Belfast 1797, nd, London [1800?], Glasgow [1801], Edinburgh 1803, Newcastle 1807, Lancaster [1810?], Saturday Night 1821 (first issue of periodical), London 1822, 1823, Kilmarnock 1826, Glasgow nd, 1829; rendered intelligible to those unacquainted with the Scottish phrases of the original, for the use of the poorer classes in England, Frome 1831; London 1831, Irvine 1840 (facs), [Edinburgh] 1853, Edinburgh 1856, Portsea 1859 (English versification by W. Austin), New York 1867, Philadelphia 1872, nd, London 1879 and nd, Edinburgh 1884, 1893, London 1888 and nd, London [c. 1890], Belfast [1892] (introd by J. Hall), London [1892], [1893], New York [189?], Boston [1895], London 1905, Glasgow 1907, London [1908] (illustr A. Rackham), 1909, [1910], Boston 1915 (Bibliophile Soc, engraved throughout), London [1943], Chicago nd, Glasgow nd, London nd (6 edns, one also includes Tam O'Shanter, another includes Twa dogs, with life and notes).

Tr German, 1802; Russian, 1829; Italian, 1871; Dutch, nd; Japanese, 1892, nd.

Jolly beggars

Glasgow [1799], [1800]; in The poetical miscellany, Glasgow 1800; Newcastle 1804, Edinburgh 1808, 1818, Glasgow 1823 (facs), Edinburgh 1829, [Edinburgh? 1830]; as performed at the private concerts of the Leith Philharmonic Society, Leith 1832; Glasgow 1838, nd (facs, preface signed W. W[eir]), 1862; set to music by G. Linley 1862; [1907]; ed W. M. Reedy, Portland Maine 1914; ed J. C. Weston, Northampton Mass 1963; [Glasgow] nd, nd (3 edns).

Tr Italian, 1925.

Tam O'Shanter

In F. Grose, The antiquities of Scotland vol 2, 1791 (first book pbn; Burns wrote the poem for Grose), Glasgow [1795 or 1796] (in Brash & Reid chap-books, at least 6 issues), [1801], Ayr 1802 (in Four funny tales), Stirling 1802, Edinburgh 1808, Paisley 1808, [1808?], Ayr 1817; also an account of laying the foundation stone of the monument, Ayr [1820], Glasgow [1820?]; Paisley 1822, London 1824, Paisley 1825, [1829]; to which are added observations on the statues of Tam O'Shanter and Souter Johnny, [1829] (4 or more issues), 1830; 1830 (2 edns, one illustr T. Landseer); Sculpture: Tam O'Shanter, Souter Johnny, the Landlord and landlady, executed by J. Thom [with text of Tam O'Shanter], 1830, Glasgow 1830, 1830; A musical farce in two acts, as performed at the Theatre Royal, by H. R. Addison, 1834; '3rd edn', Glasgow 1837, Ayr [1851], [Edinburgh] 1855, Paisley 1855, London 1856; with Address to the de'il, [c. 1865], New York 1868; with Lament of Mary Queen of Scots, ed H. R. Sharman [1869] (facs); 1870, 1884 (illustr G. Cruikshank), [1888], Edinburgh [1892], Kirkcaldy [c. 1895], Glasgow [1899?] (facs, with English rendering by Isabella K. Gough), 1902, London 1902 (Essex House Press, ptd on vellum), Ayr [1904], Edinburgh [1906], London [1906], Perth [1924], Eugene Oregon 1934, Warlingham [1934], Dumfries [1959], Milngavie 1959, Ayr nd (3 edns, one also Glasgow [1820?]); or Harlequin and the witches, Edinburgh nd (Queen's Theatre, Edinburgh), Faversham nd, Glasgow nd (2 edns, one a broadside), Liverpool nd, London nd (2 issues, one as part of a collection in Murray's Railway Readings, also separately), New York nd, nd (4 edns); with Address to the de'il, nd.

Tr from the Scotch dialect by Clara E. Powell, St Catharines Ontario 1947; tr Gaelic, 1840 (with other poems), 1899, nd; tr Welsh, 1931; Phonetische Transkription nach A. J. Ellis, nd.

Many of Burns's Poems and songs were included in the numerous chap-books and song books of the early and mid nineteenth century.

Merry Muses

The title The merry muses was used indiscriminately in connection with Burns's name, although much of the material pbd was not by him. The only reliable text is that of 1959 and re-issues. For contents of various vols, see bibliography by G. Legman in 1965 facs of 1799 edn.

The merry Muses of Caledonia: a collection of favourite Scots songs, ancient and modern, selected for the use of the Crochallan Fencibles. 1799. There are 2 known copies of this work, one with the date torn from title-page. This date was only established with the discovery in 1965 of a 2nd copy, the contributor's. There is no mention of Burns's name in the book. Ed G. Legman, New Hyde Park NY 1965 (type facs, with bibliography from Cunningham ms etc).

The giblet pye: being the heads, tails, legs and wings of the anacreontic songs of the celebrated R. Burns, G. A. Stevens, Rochester, T. L[it]tle [Thomas Moore]. Shamborough: ptd for John Nox [spurious imprint] [1806]. Only known copy W. N. H. Harding, Chicago.

The fornicator's court, by R. Burns. [1823], [c. 1890], Metuchen NJ 1928, nd; as The court of equity: an episode in the life of Burns, ed D.R., Edinburgh 1910, 1916.

The merry Muses: a choice collection of favourite songs. Dublin [c. 1825].

The merry Muses: a choice collection of favourite songs. Glasgow [c. 1830], Dublin [c. 1830]. These edns are not the same as the earlier Dublin edn.

The merry Muses: a choice collection of favourite songs. Dublin 1832. Copy in Hornell Collection, Kirkcudbright County Lib.

The merry Muses: a choice collection of favourite songs. [c. 1840]. Copy in Hornell Collection.

The merry Muses: a choice collection of favourite songs. 1843, 1843 (for c. 1880).

The merry Muses: a choice collection of favourite songs gathered from many sources, by Burns. 1827 (actually London? ptd by J. C. Hotten? 1872?); other edns (all dated 1827) with supposititious dates 1880, 1881 (3 variants), 1903, 1903, 1905, 1905, 1910, 1920, 1930 (dated); 'verbatim reprint of the 1827 edn', [c. 1925].

Burns' Merry Muses: a choice collection of the favourite Scots songs selected for the use of the Crohallan Fencibles. Edinburgh 1884. Spurious imprint?

Forbidden fruit: a collection of popular tales by popular authors [including Burns]; also the expurgated poems of Burns known as Burns' Merry Muses. [c. 1890]. Copy in Murison Collection, Dunfermline Lib.

Merry songs and ballads prior to the year 1800. Ed J. S. Farmer 5 vols [1895]–7; ed G. Legman, New York 1964 (with selections from Merry Muses).

The merry Muses of Caledonia (original edn): a vindication of Burns in connection with the above publication. [Ed D. McNaught], [Kilmarnock] 1911 (text, inaccurate, of the 1799 edn; limited to 100 copies), [Philadelphia c. 1927].

The merry Muses of Caledonia. Ed J. Barke and S. G. Smith, with prefatory note by J. DeL. Ferguson, Edinburgh 1959, New York 1964, London 1965, 1966, New York [1967].

The merry Muses: a selection of favourite songs. San Francisco 1962, 1962.

The merry Muses and other Burnsian frolics. Ed E. L. Randall 1966.

The merry Muses. Tonawanda NY [c. 1900?].

The merry Muses. [probably 1890–1920]. Copy in Murison Collection, Dunfermline Lib.

The merry Muses of Burns, made in fac-simile of original edn. [USA c. 1907], [c. 1910?]. Edns can be distinguished by the claim on title-page of the earlier that it was ptd for members of the Caledonian Soc, whereas later edn bears no such claim. Neither edn is a facs of any previous edn. Both claim that 'the original manuscript of these poems was sold at Christie's, London, England, in 1907 for £1,800'. This is pure fantasy.

Burns in Fiction and Drama

S., C. The birth of Burns: a dramatic scrap. In Arliss's literary scraps, [1825].

Addison, H. R. Tam O'Shanter: a musical farce in two acts as performed at Drury Lane. 1834.

Miller, H. Recollections of Burns. In Tales and sketches, Edinburgh 1863 etc. A tale.

Stirling, J. H. Burns in drama. Edinburgh 1878. A play.

Duncan, J. F. Lights and shadows: or episodes in the life of Burns. Dundee 1879. A dramatic sketch.

Burns' Highland Mary. Glasgow 1896. A novel.

[Templeton, J.] The romance of Burns: a pastoral of the present and drama of days lang syne. New York 1899. A novel.

'McAulay, A.' (Charlotte Stewart). The rhymer. New York 1900. A novel.

Lane, Elinor M. Nancy Stair. New York 1904, 1905, London 1933. A novel.

Legge, C. M. Highland Mary: the romance of a poet. Boston 1906. A novel.

Wotherspoon, J. Kirk life and kirk folk: an interpretation of the clerical satires of Burns. Edinburgh 1909. Sketches.

Munro, N. Ayrshire idylls. 1912, Edinburgh 1931, 1933. Sketches.

Painton, Edith F. A. U. A Burns rebellion: a conference of the best-known character creations of Burns. Chicago 1913. A play.

Gilliam, E. W. Burns: a drama in four acts. Boston 1914.

Eyre-Todd, G. The angel of Burns: a play in four scenes showing the poet as he lived. Glasgow [1916], nd.

Drinkwater, J. Robert Burns. 1925. A play.

Housman, L. The cutty stool. Cornhill Mag Jan 1926; rptd in his Cornered poets: a book of dramatic dialogues, 1929.

Lee, H. F. Robert Burns, 1926. A play.

Steuart, J. A. The immortal lover: a Burns romance. Philadelphia 1929. A novel.

Wallace, S. A. Scenes in the life of Burns. Education 50 1930. A play.

Corrie, J. The rake o' Mauchline. Glasgow [1938]. A play.
—— Robert Burns. Glasgow [1943]. A play.

Schmitt, Gladys. 'A man's a man for a' that': a play for radio broadcasting. Scholastic 12 Feb 1938.

Burns, Annie and J. A. Conway. Burns: an historical play in six episodes. Boston 1939.

Burnett, W. and J. Pen. Immortal bachelor. Story Nov–Dec 1942. A short story.

Barke, J. The wind that shakes the barley. 1946.
—— The song in the green thorn tree. 1947.
—— The wonder of all the gay world. 1949.
—— The crest of the broken wave. 1953.
—— The well of the silent harp. 1954.
—— Bonnie Jean. 1959. A series of novels on Burns's life. Also pbd New York and Toronto, some vols rptd.

Crozier, E. J. Rab the rhymer: a play in three acts on the life and songs of Burns. 1953.

Sterling, L. M. Scotland's sons. Burns Chron 3rd ser 5 1956. A play.

Kemp, R. The other dear charmer: a comedy in three acts. 1957.

Linklater, E. The merry Muse. 1959. Novel.

Smith, S. G. The vision of the prodigal son. Edinburgh 1960. A verse play.

Stevenson, Yvonne H. Burns and his Bonnie Jean. Sidney BC 1967. A novel.

Letters and Diaries

Letters addressed to Clarinda [Agnes M'Lehose]. Glasgow 1802, 1802 (25 letters from Burns to Clarinda, 3 other letters by Burns), Belfast 1806 (5 issues), Philadelphia 1809, 1812, Belfast 1814, 1816, Dublin 1816, 1816, Washington 1818, [Edinburgh 1820], Glasgow 1820, 1822, 1825, 1826, Edinburgh 1828; ed M. Y. Bankart [1907].

Letters addressed to Clarinda and others. 1812.

Prose works. Newcastle 1816.

Letters and correspondence. 2 vols 1817.

Letters. 2 vols 1819 (3 issues).

Prose works. Newcastle 1819.

Letters. 2 vols in 1 Boston 1820.

Select works, prose [letters] vol 1. New York 1820.

Letters, chronologically arranged. Glasgow 1828.

Prose works. [Ed R. Chambers], Edinburgh 1839.

Remarks on Scottish songs and ballads. 1841 (first pbd in Cunningham in 1834); ed J. C. Dick 1908 (as Notes on Scottish song by Burns written in an interleaved copy of the Scots musical museum, with additions by Robert Riddel and others); rptd with J. C. Dick, The songs of Burns now first printed with the melodies for which they were written: a study in tone-poetry, Hatboro Pa 1962.

The correspondence between Burns and Clarinda, with a memoir of Mrs M'Lehose, arranged and edited by her grandson W. C. M'Lehose. Edinburgh 1843, New York 1843 (with many letters by Burns not in 1802 vol, above, and Clarinda's answers); ed A. J. Burr, New York 1917; rptd in R. L. Brown, Clarinda, Dewsbury 1968.

Complete prose works. Edinburgh [c. 1867], 1871, 1873, 1876, 1876, 1878, nd.

Burns's common place book [1783–5]. Edinburgh 1872; ed J. C. Ewing and D. Cook, Glasgow 1938 (facs); ed D. Daiches 1965. A fragment had been pbd in Currie, 1800, and a fuller version in Cromek, 1808.

Letters, selected and arranged by J. L. Robertson. 1887.

Burns and Mrs Dunlop correspondence, now published in full for the first time, with elucidations by W. Wallace. 1898, 2 vols New York 1898 (fuller text).

Journal of a tour in the Highlands made in 1787. Ed J. C. Ewing 1927 (facs).

Letters. Ed R. B. Johnson 1928. A selection.

Letters of the poet. Ed R. W. MacKenna, Glasgow [1928].

Letters. Ed J. DeL. Ferguson 2 vols Oxford 1931 (standard text, to be rev G. R. Roy).

Journal of the Border tour. Ed DeL. Ferguson in Burns, his associates and contemporaries, ed R. T. Fitzhugh, Chapel Hill 1943. First pbd, inaccurately, by A. Cunningham in 1834.

Selected letters. Ed J. DeL. Ferguson, Oxford 1953 (WC).

Correspondence, with his notes on Scottish songs and ballads, the Border and Highland tours, and assignment of his poems. nd.

Translations

Arranged alphabetically by language, with the exception of the languages of the USSR, which are grouped under Russian. See W. Jacks, Burns in other tongues: a critical review of the translations of the songs and poems, Glasgow 1896 (a survey with numerous trns quoted from 18 languages).

Albanian

Poems and ballads. Tr L. Poradeci, Tirana 1962.

Bulgarian

Songs and poems. Tr V. Svintila, Sofia 1957.

Chinese

Selected poems. Trans Fêng Chia Ch'in, Taipei 1961.

Czech

Selection of songs and ballads. Tr J. V. Sládek, Prague [1892].

Selected poems and songs. Tr J. Valja, Prague 1963.

Danish

[8 poems]. Caralis's digte og sange, Copenhagen 1867.

[Several songs]. In Caralis's hundrede digte, Copenhagen 1867.

Selected poems. Tr M. N. Hansen, Odense 1951 (24 poems and a life of Burns).

English

Burns in English: select poems, translated from the Scottish dialect by A. Corbett. Boston 1892, Glasgow 1892.

Burns into English: renderings of select dialect poems. Tr W. K. Seymour 1954, New York 1954.

Esperanto

[18 poems]. In M. C. Butler, Kantaro esperanta, 1926.

Faroese

Poems. Tr C. Matras, Keypmannahavn 1945.

[Trns of Holy Willie's prayer, Tam O'Shanter, John Anderson and My luv is like a red, red rose] in P. F. Joensen, Millum heims og heljar, Torshavn 1947.

Flemish

The most beautiful songs of Burns. Tr F. de Cort, Brussels 1852. 50 songs.

French

[7 poems]. In F. A. Loève-Veimars, Ballades, légendes et chants populaires de l'Angleterre, de l'Ecosse et de l'Irlande. Paris 1825.

Selected pieces from Burns. Tr J. Aytoun and J. B. Mesnard, Paris 1826.

[5 songs]. In A. Johnston, Lays, lucubrations and leaves from my log-book, Edinburgh 1833.

Complete poetry of Burns. Tr with introd by L. de Wailly, Paris 1843, 1843, 1853, 1857.

Poems imitated from Burns by L. Demouceaux. Paris 1865. Rimed trns.

Burns translated from the Scottish. Tr with preface by R. de la Madelaine, [Rouen] 1874.

[8 poems]. In A. Buisson de Berger, Poètes anglais contemporains, Paris 1890.

Angellier, A. Burns: la vie, les oeuvres. 2 vols Paris 1893. Many poems tr in text.

Gaelic

Tam O'Shanter with nine other poems. Tr R. Mac-Dougall, Glasgow 1840.

[Songs]. In T. D. MacDonald, Poems, Stirling 1903.

Songs and poems of Burns. Tr C. Macphater, Glasgow [1910].

German

Poems of Burns. Tr P. Kaufmann, Stuttgart 1839.

Burns's poems, translated with life and notes by W. Gerhard. Leipzig 1840.

Songs and ballads of Burns, translated with short life and notes by H. J. Heintze. Brunswick 1840, 1846.

Ten Scottish poems by Burns and others. Edinburgh 1854 (German and Scottish texts).

Burns's poems, translated with notes H. J. Heintze. Leipzig 1859.

Songs of Burns, translated G. Pertz, with biographical sketch by A. Traeger. Leipzig 1859.

Songs and ballads of Burns. Tr A. von Winterfeld, Berlin 1860.

Songs and ballads of Burns. Tr A. Laun, Berlin 1869, 1877, Oldenburg nd.

Songs of Burns, translated into Swiss German by A. Corrodi. Winterthur 1870, 1949.

Burns's songs and ballads for German readers: free translation by L. G. Silbergleit. Leipzig [1872?], [1878], [1889].

Burns's songs and ballads. Tr K. Bartsch, Leipzig [c. 1886], [1895], [1896].

Selection of Burns's poems. Tr G. Legerlotz, Leipzig 1889, 1893,

Poems of Burns. Tr E. Ruete, Bremen 1890.

Songs and ballads of Burns, with a selection of poems. Tr W. Prinzhorn, Halle [1896].

Burns in low German. Tr E. Hobein et al, ed F. Schult, Hamburg [1937].

Burns's works vol 1: Songs and ballads. Ed and tr O. Baisch, Stuttgart nd.

Greek

The banks o' Doon and other poems [with short biographical note] in R. Boumi and N. Pappos, Pancosmios anthologia vol 2, Athens 1953.

Hebrew

[9 poems and short biography]. In Hebrew anthology of English verse, ed R. Avinoam, Tel-Aviv 1956.

Hungarian

Burns poems. Tr J. Lévay, Budapest 1892 (over 270 poems and songs).

Selected verses. Ed K. Laszlo and K. Istvan, Budapest 1952.

Selected poems. Tr J. Arany and L. Aprily et al, Budapest 1956, 1959 (enlarged).

Icelandic

[6 poems]. In S. Thorsteinsson, Ljodatydingar, Reykjavik 1924.

Italian

Selections from Longfellow, Hemans, Cook, Burns etc. Tr R. Cardamone, Turin 1878, 1908. In verse.

Poetry of Burns. Tr U. Ortensi, with preface by J. Muir, Modena 1893 (pt 1, all pbd).

Selected poems. Ed D. H. Cornish, Florence 1908.

Poems and songs. Tr with preface U. Ortensi, Lanciano 1913.

Poems and songs. Ed A. Biagi, Florence 1953. Text in English and Italian.

Japanese

Selected poems. Tr M. Ohara, Tokyo 1906.

Selected poems. Tr Y. Okakura, Tokyo 1923, [1935].

Poetical works. Tr T. Nakamura, Tokyo 1934, 1959 (text in English and Japanese).

Poems of Burns. Tr with notes by T. Namba, Tokyo [1959] (text in English and Japanese).

The lyric poetry of Burns. Tr with notes by T. Namba, Tokyo 1960 (text in English and Japanese).

The gem of Burns. Tr with notes by T. Namba, Tokyo [1963] (text in English and Japanese).

Korean

Collected poems. Trans Chang Man-Yeong, Seoul 1961.

Latin

'To a mouse'. In J. G[rahame], Poems in English, Scotch and Latin, Paisley 1794.

The principal songs of Burns, translated into mediaeval Latin verse by A. Leighton. Edinburgh 1862.

[10 poems]. In Sabrinae corolla, 1890 (4th edn).

[6 songs]. In Cantica scotica e vulgari sermone in latinum conversa, tr A. Whamond, Hamilton 1892.

'Scots wha hae'. Tr Greek and Latin by R. Y. Tyrrell and W. Wallace, Dublin 1896, nd (Latin version only).

[4 poems]. In Florilegium latinum, ed F. St J. Thackeray and E. D. Stone 1899.

Norwegian

Poems of Burns. Tr O. Nygard, Oslo 1923.

Selected poems. Tr H. Kiran, Oslo 1959, 1966.

Polish

Burns Scottish verse. Tr Z. Kierszys, S. Kryński and L. Marhańska, Warsaw 1956.

Rumanian

Burns, peasant poets, poetry. Tr with biographical note by P. Grimm, Cluj 1925 (11 poems).

Poems. Tr M. Gheorghiu, Bucharest 1960.

Russian

[11 poems and biographical note]. In N. V. Gerbel, English poets in biographies and examples, St Petersburg 1875.

Poems. Moscow 1897.

[Selection]. In Foreign poets, 4 vols in 1 Moscow 1901.

Selected lyrics. Tr T. A. Shschepkinoy-Kupernick, ed S. Babukha, Moscow 1936.

Selections. Tr S. Marshak, Moscow 1947, 1950, 1952, 1954, 1957, 1959; with introd by Rita Wright-Kovaleva 2 vols 1963 (title varies, contents expanded); [in Cyrillic characters] 1959; also a considerable selection of trns in vol 2 of Marshak's Poems, tales, translations, Moscow 1952.

Works. Tr J. Semjažonov, Minsk 1958 (Belorussian).

Poems and songs. Tr V. Fedotov, Archangel 1959.

Poetry. Trans I. P. Simonenko, Kiev 1959 (Ukranian).

Selected works. Tr M. Lukasha and V. Mysyka, Kiev 1959, 1964, 1965 (Ukranian).

Poetical works. Tr R. Parve, Tallin 1959 (Estonian).

Poems. Tr T. Éristavi, Tbilisi 1959, 1964 (Georgian).

Songs and poems. Tr H. Bikqolov, Ufa 1960 (Baskin).

Songs and poems. Tr V. Fedotov, Moscow 1963.

Poems and songs. Tr I. Krecu, Kisinev 1966 (Moldavian).

Spanish

Poems. Tr with preface by R. Sangenis, Barcelona 1954.

Swedish

Songs and ballads. Helsinki 1854.

Some poems by Burns. Stockholm 1872.

[Trn of poems]. In E. Kruuse, Vin och kvinnor, Stockholm 1933.

[7 poems]. In E. Blomberg, Engelska dikter fran medeltiden till vara dagar, Stockholm 1942.

Songs and epigrams. Stockholm 1966.

§2

[Mackenzie, H.] Lounger 9 Dec 1786. Notice of the first edn of Burns's poems; frequently rptd.

Burns's calf turn'd a bull: or some remarks on his mean and unprovoked attack on Mr [James] S[teven] when preaching. [Scotland] 1787. Verse; copy in Mitchell Lib.

The calf; the unco calf's answer; virtue—to a mountain bard; and the de'il's answer to his vera worthy frien' Robert Burns. [Scotland 1787]. Verse; copy in Nat Lib of Scotland.

Lapraik, J. Epistle to R—t B—s, and the Devil's answer to the poet's address. In Poems on several occasions, Kilmarnock 1788.

[Marshall?]. Catalogue of five hundred celebrated authors of Great Britain, now living. 1788. Earliest biographical notice of Burns.

Maxwell, J. Animadversions on some poets and poetasters of the present age especially R—t B—s and J—n L—k. Paisley 1788. Verse.

Turnbull, G. The bard: a poem in the manner of Spencer inscribed to Mr R*** B***. Glasgow 1788.

Sillar, D. Epistle to Burns, and verses occasioned by a reply to Burns's Calf, by an unco calf. In his Poems, Kilmarnock 1789.

Tait, A. B—rns in his infancy; B—rns in Lochly; B—rns's hen. In his Poems and songs, [Paisley?] 1790 (only known copy in Mitchell Lib); rptd (above 3 poems only) [c. 1920] (10 copies).

Learmont, J. Man was not made to mourn: answer to the Deil's reply to Mr Burns. In his Poems pastoral, satirical, tragic and comic, Edinburgh 1791.

—— The kirk's alarm, a poem: or an answer to the late pastoral admonition. Edinburgh 1799 (2nd edn). Contributor's is only known copy; Nat Lib of Scotland has imperfect copy (first edn?), lacking title-page.

Little, Janet. On a visit to Mr Burns; An epistle to Mr Robert Burns. In her Poetical works, Ayr 1792.

[Riddell, Maria]. [Sketch of Burns]. Dumfries Weekly Jnl [probably 9 Aug 1796; no known copy]; rptd Courier & Evening Gazette (London) 18–19 Aug 1796; Edinburgh Evening Courant 22 Aug 1796; European Mag 30 Oct 1796; Aberdeen Mag 1 Nov 1796; as Memoir respecting Burns, by a lady, in Works of Burns vol 1, [ed J. Currie], Liverpool 1800, 1801 (rev).

Heron, R. A memoir of the life of the late Robert Burns. Edinburgh 1797; rptd in H. Hecht, Burns: the man and his work, Glasgow 1936 (not included in original German edn, 1919).

[Reid, W.] Character of Burns, with observations on his writings. In Poetry original and selected vol 2, Glasgow [1797]. A Brash & Reid chapbook, with several poems in memory of Burns.

Campbell, A. An introduction to the history of poetry in Scotland, together with a conversation on Scotish song. Edinburgh 1798. Early mention of Burns.

[Currie, J.] Life of Burns. Vol 1 of Works of Burns, 4 vols Liverpool 1800; 1826 (separately), Edinburgh 1838 (extended by R. Chambers) (rptd in all subsequent edns of Currie, and the basis of all later biographies).

D., D. Observations on the character and writings of Burns. Edinburgh Mag new ser 16 1800.

General remarks on the life and character of Burns. Scots Mag 64 1802.

Grant, Mrs Anne. Remarks on the character of Burns. In her Poems on various subjects, 1803.

Forsyth, R. In The beauties of Scotland vol 2, Edinburgh 1805.

Storer, J. and J. Greig. Views in North Britain illustrative of the works of Burns, accompanied with descriptions, and a sketch of the poet's life. 1805, 1805, 1811.

[Jeffrey, F.] Edinburgh Rev 13 1809. Review of R. H. Cromek's Reliques of Burns, rptd in Jeffrey's Essays, 1844, Jeffrey's Literary criticism, ed D. N. Smith 1910 etc.

[Mudford, W.] Conversation on Burns and his poetry. In his Nubia in search of a husband, including sketches of modern society and interspersed with moral and literary disquisitions 1809 (3rd edn). Severely critical of George Thomson.

[Scott, W.] Quart Rev 1 1809. Review of R. H. Cromek's Reliques of Burns, frequently rptd.

Skinner, J. Amusements of leisure hours: or poetical pieces. Edinburgh 1809. Includes letters to and from Burns.

— Miscellaneous collection of fugitive pieces of poetry. Ed J. Skinner (the author's son), Edinburgh 1809. This forms vol 3 of Skinner's Works, although not so indicated. In addn to the material from his Amusements, Skinner's son adds a description of the poet.

[Peebles, W.] Burnomania: the celebrity of Burns considered in a discourse addressed to all real Christians. Edinburgh 1811.

Spence, Elizabeth. In her Sketches of the present manners, customs and scenery of Scotland, 2 vols 1811.

[Walker, J.] An account of the life and character of Burns. In Poems by Burns, 2 vols Edinburgh 1811; also separately.

[Gleig, G.] A critique on the poems of Burns. Edinburgh 1812.

Mangin, E. In A view of the pleasures arising from a love of books, 1814.

Brydges, S. E. Traits of the character of Burns, with extracts from his letters and a comparison of his genius with that of Cowper. In his Censura literaria vol 8, 1815.

[MacLaren, W.] Address delivered at the celebration of the birth of Burns at the meeting of Paisley Burns Anniversary Society. In his Life of the Renfrewshire bard Robert Tannahill, Paisley 1815.

Peterkin, A. A review of the life of Burns and of various criticisms on his character and writings. In Life and works of Burns, 4 vols Edinburgh 1815; also separately; Calcutta 1827.

Wordsworth, W. Letter to a friend of Burns [James Gray] occasioned by an intended republication of the account of the life of Burns by Dr Currie. 1816 etc.

D. of Dumfries. Letter occasioned by N's vindication of Mr Wordsworth. Blackwood's Mag Nov 1817.

Hazlitt, W. On Burns and the old English ballads (lecture 7). In his Lectures on the English poets, 1818 etc.

Failure of Burns as a tragic poet. New Bon Ton Mag 3 1819.

Campbell, T. In Specimens of the British poets, with biographical and critical notices vol 7, 1819.

[Lockhart, J. G.] Burns's dinner; Edinburgh Review on Burns. In his Peter's letters to his kinsfolk vol 1, 1819.

— Life of Burns. Edinburgh 1828, 1828, 1830 (3rd edn corrected), New York 1831, London 1838, 1847, [1871]; with additional notes by W. S. Douglas 1846, 1892, 1905, 2 vols Liverpool 1914 (to which is added an essay by W. Raleigh); ed J. H. Ingram 1889, 1890; ed J. M. Sloan 1904; ed E. Rhys [1907], 1933, 1959 (EL).

[Wilson, J.] ('Christopher North'). Blackwood's Mag May 1828. Review of Lockhart's Life of Burns.

[—?] A comparative view of the genius of Burns and Ettrick Shepherd. Blackwood's Mag Feb 1819.

— On the genius and character of Burns. In D. O. Hill et al, The land of Burns, 2 vols Glasgow 1840. Frequently rptd in edns of Burns's works etc.

[Robertson, J.] In his Lives of Scottish poets pt 1, 1821.

[Ainslie, H.] Pilgrimage to the land of Burns. Deptford 1822; ed T. C. Latto, Paisley 1892 (with memoir).

[Barwick, J.] Preliminary discourse, in which the amatory ideas of Burns are compared with those of Solomon, Anacreon and Sappho. In Songs and ballads of Burns, 1823; rev 1831 (in Songs of Burns).

Letter to the Rev Thomas Brown, Dalkeith, occasioned by some remarks on the life and writings of Burns appended to his late publication of family devotion. Perth 1825.

Life of Burns. Edinburgh 1828. A chap-book.

Carlyle, T. Edinburgh Rev 48 1828; 1854 etc. Review of J. G. Lockhart, Life of Burns.

— On heroes and hero-worship, and the heroic in history: lecture 5, The hero as man of letters: Johnson, Rousseau, Burns. 1841 etc. See J. Muir, 1895, below.

— The life of Burns mostly by T. Carlyle. New York 1859.

'Ignotus'. Comparison between Horace and Burns. Friends' Monthly Mag May–June 1830.

Macminn, H. Speeches on celebrating Burns' birthday. In Speeches on various public occasions, 1831.

Montgomery, J. On the poetical character, the themes and influences of poetry. In Lectures on poetry and general literature, 1833.

Burns and Crabbe. Dublin Univ Mag 3 1834.

Cunningham, A. Life of Burns. In Works of Burns, 8 vols 1834, 1834 etc.

— Life and land of Burns. New York 1841.

Cox, R. An essay on the character and cerebral development of Burns. Phrenological Jnl & Miscellany 9 1834; Edinburgh 1859.

Hogg, J. and W. Motherwell. Memoir of Burns. In Works of Burns vol 5, Glasgow 1836.

Otis, J. F. On the poetry of Burns. Southern Literary Messenger March 1836.

De Quincey, T. Autobiography of an English opium-eater, literary connexions or acquaintances [on Currie and Burns]. Tait's Mag Feb 1837; as A Manchester Swedenborgian and a Liverpool literary coterie, in Collected writings vol 2, 1889.

[Senkovskii, O. I. ?] Robert Burns. Biblioteka Dlia Chteniia: Zhurnal Slovesnosti, Nauk i Politiki 24 1837.

[Neaves, C.] Song writing: Burns. Blackwood's Mag Aug 1839.

Hill, D. O. et al. The land of Burns: a series of landscapes and portraits. 2 vols Glasgow 1840. Includes Wilson's essay.

[Paterson, J.] The contemporaries of Burns. Edinburgh 1840.

Elliott, E. A lecture on Cowper and Burns: the two earliest great poets of the modern school. Tait's Mag June 1842.

Burns and Byron. Tait's Mag Oct 1844; rptd in Eclectic Mag Nov 1844.

McKay, A. Extract from an essay on the moral character of Burns. In his Recreations of leisure hours, 1844.

— Burns and his Kilmarnock friends. Kilmarnock 1874.

[Ferguson, S.] Burns. Dublin Univ Mag 25 1845.

Fox, W. J. Burns: the first poet of the poor. In his Lectures addressed chiefly to the working classes vol 3, 1846.

M'Conochie, J. R. A boy's recollections of Burns. In his Leisure hours, Louisville 1846.

[Marshall, J.] A winter with Burns. Edinburgh 1846.

Scottish poets: Fergusson and Burns. Renfrewshire Mag 1 1847.

Tyler, S. Burns as a poet and as a man. New York 1848, Dublin 1849.

[Kingsley, C.] Burns and his school. North Br Rev 16 1851; rptd in Littell's Living Age 20 Dec 1851 and Eclectic Mag 25 1852; also in his Miscellanies vol 1, 1859.

Remarks on Burns [chiefly his relationship to Fergusson]. New Paisley Repository pt 3 Dec 1852.

Livingston, P. Poems and songs with lecture on the genius and work of Burns. Dundee 1852 (8th edn), 1858 (10th edn), 1862, Edinburgh 1870, 1871, 1878.

Burns. Knickerbocker Mag 41 1853.

Stenhouse, W. Illustrations of the lyric poetry and music of Scotland, with additional notes and illustrations by D. Laing and C. K. Sharpe, Scots Musical Museum vol 4, Edinburgh 1853, also separately; rptd with Scots Musical Museum 2 vols Hatboro Pa 1962 (facs).

Gilfillan, G. Life of Burns vol 1; The genius and poetry of Burns vol 2. In Poetical works of Burns, ed Gilfillan 2 vols Edinburgh 1856.

—— The influence of Burns on Scottish poetry and song. In The modern Scottish minstrel vol 4, ed C. Rogers, Edinburgh 1857. See also H. Macdonald, Rev George Gilfillan versus Burns, in J. Adams, Deity or dirt? a review of an old controversy on Burns, [Kilmarnock 1895]; rptd Burns Chron 4 1895.

Porteous, M. The real Souter Johnny: a poem with explanatory notes and appendix. Glasgow [1858] (2nd edn), Ayr [1858]. Claims to identify the originals of the characters in Tam O'Shanter.

Adams, F. The writings of Burns: a discourse. Aberdeen 1859.

Alexander, W. L. The idolatry of genius: a discourse. Edinburgh 1859 (3rd edn).

Anderson, G. and J. Finlay (ed). The Burns centenary poems. Glasgow 1859.

Ballantyne, J. (ed). Chronicle of the hundredth birthday of Burns. Edinburgh 1859.

[Chisholm, H.] Burns: the representative of his era. Glasgow 1859.

Drummond, R. B. The religion of Burns. Edinburgh 1859.

Emerson, R. W. In Celebration to the hundredth anniversary of the birth of Burns by the Boston Burns Club, Boston 1859 etc. A speech, with poems by Oliver Wendell Holmes, James Russell Lowell and John Greenleaf Whittier, and a speech by Joseph Howe.

'Ben Trovato' (S. Lover) (ed). Rival rhymes in honour of Burns. 1859.

White, J. Burns: a memoir. 1859.

[Hawthorne, N.] Some of the haunts of Burns, by a tourist without imagination or enthusiasm. Atlantic Monthly Oct 1860.

Burns as man and poet. York Star 1 1861.

[Blaze de Bury, Marie]. Peasants and poets of Upper Austria and Scotland, Burns and Stelzhammer. North Br Rev Feb 1862; tr Revue Britannique July 1865 (signed E.V.).

Miller, H. Recollections of Burns. In his Tales and sketches, Edinburgh 1863 etc. Glasgow 1886.

[Hannay, J.] Three lyrists: Burns, Horace and Béranger. Cornhill Mag Feb 1868; rptd in Littell's Living Age 4 April 1868.

Ferguson, F. A manual: containing a discourse against the Christian commemoration of the birthday of Burns. Jedburgh [1869].

—— Should Christians commemorate the birthday of Burns? a discourse. Edinburgh 1869.

Turnbull, W. R. The heritage of Burns. Haddington 1869.

McDowall, W. Burns in Dumfriesshire: a sketch of the last eight years of the poet's life. Edinburgh 1870, 1881, Dumfries [1882].

Thomson, J. B. Burns and Walter Scott: a contrast and a parallel. 1871.

Burns: an essay for the working classes of Scotland, pt 1: his influence as a moral teacher and social reformer, by a member of the Literary Institute. Edinburgh 1872.

Corrodi, A. Burns und J. P. Hebel: eine literar-historische Parallele. Berlin 1873.

Bright, H. A. Some account of the Glenriddell mss of Burns's poems. Liverpool 1874.

Brooke, S. A. In his Theology in the English poets, 1874 etc. Lectures 14–16.

—— In his Naturalism in English poetry, 1920.

Bayfield, T. J. Poetry and the poet Burns. Newcastle 1875.

Burns, W. A manual of religious belief. Kilmarnock 1875. By the poet's father, from ms.

Aiken, P. F. Memorial of Burns. 1876.

Burns. Dublin Univ Mag 89 1877.

Lawson, W. The genius and poetry of Burns. Stockport [1877].

Macrae, David (stonemason). In his Poets of labour and other sketches, 1877.

[Nichol, J.] Burns: a summary of his career and genius vol 1. In Works of Burns, ed W. S. Douglas, Edinburgh 1877, 1896 (rev), 1882, nd.

Rogers, C. Geneological memoirs of the family of Burns. Edinburgh 1877.

—— The book of Burns. 3 vols Edinburgh 1889.

Scott, C. Burns: an address. Edinburgh 1877.

Ballinghall, W. Burns the ploughman-poet: a memorial tribute. [1878].

Cappelli, R. I poeti delle classi operaie gli operai poeti. Nuova Antologia 15 Jan 1878.

Jamieson, R. Burns in his youth, and how he grew to be a poet; Burns in his maturity, and how he spent it. Belfast 1878.

Jack, W. Note on Burns's common-place book. Macmillan's Mag Nov 1879.

Shairp, J. C. Burns and Scotch song before him. Atlantic Monthly Oct 1879; rptd in his Aspects of poetry, Oxford 1881.

—— Robert Burns. 1879 (EML).

[Stevenson, R. L.] Some aspects of Burns. Cornhill Mag Oct 1879; rptd in Appleton's Jnl 7 1879, and in his Familiar studies of men and books, 1882 etc.

Mackay, C. Burns and Béranger. Nineteenth Century March 1880.

Shanks, H. R. Burns as a man and a poet. Bathgate 1880; rptd in his Peasant poets of Scotland, Bathgate 1881.

Stuart-Glennie, J. S. MacPherson, Burns and Scott in their relation to the modern revolution. Fraser's Mag April 1880.

A., S. I. The life of Burns, the poet of the people, the representative of the genius of his country who held the dignity of manhood superior to the privileges of rank. In his Worthies of the world pt 6, [1881].

Elder, W. Burns as freethinker, poet and democrat. Paisley 1881.

Jolly, W. Burns at Mossgiel, with reminiscences of the poet by his herd-boy. Paisley 1881.

Little, J. An address on the characteristics of Burns. Manchester, 1881.

Hierthes, L. (ed). Wörterbuch des schottischen Dialekts in den Werken von Walter Scott und Burns. Augsburg 1882, Wiesbaden 1967.

'Aliquanto Latior' (J. Gairdner and A. T. Innes). Burns and the Ayrshire moderates. [Edinburgh] 1883. A correspondence rptd from Scotsman, with remarks.

Grant, R. Burns vindicated. Halifax Nova Scotia 1883.

Bryant, W. C. In Prose writings vol 2, New York 1884, London 1964.

Chiarini, G. Roberto Burns. Nuova Antologia 16 March–1 April 1886.

[Gairdner, M. S.] Burns: an inquiry into certain aspects of his life and character and the moral influence of his poetry, by a Scotchwoman. 1886, 1887 (with addns).

Lang, A. To Burns. In his Letters to dead authors, 1886 etc.

—— Address on Burns. In Burnsiana vol 2, 1893 (rptd from Scotsman); also in The memory of Burns, ed J. D. Ross, Glasgow 1899.

Macrae, David (minister). Burns: three lectures. Dundee 1886; rptd in his Sunday lectures, Edinburgh nd.

Mauchlen, J. Burns' sympathy with the lower creations. In his Some occasional papers read at Richmond Athenaeum, 1886.

Whitman, W. Burns as poet and person. North Amer Rev Nov 1886; rptd in his November boughs, Philadelphia 1888 etc.

Hutchinson, T. An essay on the life and genius of Burns. Kilmarnock 1887.

'Hugh Haliburton' (J. L. Robertson). The birth of Burns at Kilmarnock. In his For puir auld Scotland's sake, Edinburgh 1887.

—— In his In Scottish fields, 1890. 7 essays.

—— The prose of Burns: its biographical value. Burnsiana 1 1892. Rptd from Scotsman.

—— In his Furth in field, 1894. 8 essays.

Blackie, J. S. Life of Burns. 1888. With bibliography by J. B. Anderson.

Hay, J. Wissenschaftliche Beilage Burns. Basle 1888.

Smart, W. S. Burns: an address. Albany [1888].

Webster, A. Burns and the Kirk: a review of what the poet did for the religious and social regeneration of the Scottish people. Aberdeen 1888, 1889.

—— The ideals of Burns compared with present-day Scottish orthodoxy. 3 pts 1897 (McQuaker Trust Lectures), 1897 (enlarged).

Laun, A. In his Dichtercharaktere, Norden 1889 (2nd edn).

Minto, W. Burns in his historical relationships. Art & Lit 1 1889.

—— The metres of Burns. Scots Observer 23 March 1889.

—— Burns and Tennyson. Burnsiana 3 1894. From Aberdeen Free Press Oct 1892.

—— Scottish poetry in the eighteenth century: the historical relationships of Burns. In his Literature of the Georgian era, 1894.

Hewison, J. K. Burns and the Buchanites. Scots Mag Sept 1890.

Uemura, M. The peasant poet Burns. Japan Rev Nov 1890. In Japanese.

Buchanan, R. The carnival of Burns. In his Coming terror and other essays and letters, 1891.

Cooper, C. A. Burns: his censors, his commendators. 1891.

Bruce, W. The influence of Burns on American literature. Burns Chron 1 1892.

—— In his Here's a hand, Edinburgh 1893. 5 essays.

—— Address on Burns. In The memory of Burns, ed J. D. Ross, Glasgow 1899.

Ross, J. D. (ed). Round Burns' grave: the paeans and dirges of many bards. Paisley 1891, 1892 (enlarged).

—— (ed). Burnsiana. 6 vols Paisley 1892–7.

—— (ed). Burns scrap book. New York 1893.

—— (ed). Highland Mary. Paisley 1894.

—— (ed). Burns' Clarinda. Edinburgh 1897.

—— (ed). Burns' Bonnie Jean. New York 1898.

—— (ed). The memory of Burns: brief addresses commemorating the genius of Scotland's illustrious bard. Glasgow 1899.

—— (ed). All about Tam O'Shanter. New York 1900.

—— (ed). Early critical reviews on Burns. Glasgow 1900. Includes essays by Henry Mackenzie, Currie, D. Irving, Lord Jeffrey, Scott, J. Walker, A. Peterkin, J. Wilson and Carlyle.

—— (ed). Henley and Burns: or the critic censured. Stirling 1901.

—— (ed). Burns's 'Blue-eyed lassie'. Paisley 1924. Jeanie Jeffrey.

—— (ed). Little book of Burns lore. Stirling 1926.

—— Who's who in Burns. Stirling 1927.

—— (ed). Burns and his rhyming friends. Stirling 1928.

—— A Burns handbook. Stirling 1931.

—— The story of the Kilmarnock Burns. Stirling 1933.

Colville, J. The rural economy of Scotland in the time of Burns. Philosophical Soc of Glasgow Proc 23 1892.

—— The literary art of Burns. Philosophical Soc of Glasgow Proc 28 1897; rptd in Burns Chron 3rd ser 7 1958.

Fröding, G. Burns folk-poet. Stockholm 1892, 1909.

Hadden, J. C. Burns from a musical point of view. Burns Chron 1 1892.

—— George Thomson: the friend of Burns. 1898.

Officer, W. Burns poet-laureate of Cannongate Kilwinning a myth. Edinburgh 1892.

Rosebery, A. P. Primrose (Earl of). The poet Burns. In Burnsiana vol 1, 1892. Address on unveiling a statue of Burns in London in 1884.

—— Burns: two addresses delivered at Dumfries and Glasgow on the centenary of the poet's death. Edinburgh 1896. Sometimes rptd as Wallace, Burns, Stevenson: appreciations; with a third delivered at Paisley 26 Sept 1896, 1896 (priv ptd).

Adams, J. Burns's Chloris: a reminiscence. Glasgow 1893, 1901. Jean Lorimer.

Angellier, A. Burns: la vie, l'oeuvre. 2 vols Paris 1893.

Angus, C. Notes on the first and early editions [of Burns]. Burns Chron 2 1893.

—— Francis Jeffrey on Burns. Burns Chron 2nd ser 16 1941.

—— Burns and the circulating library. Burns Chron 2nd ser 18 1943.

—— Margaret ('Peggy') Chalmers, one of the most accomplished of women. Burns Chron 2nd ser 19 1944.

—— Burns and Mrs Cockburn. Burns Chron 2nd ser 21 1943.

—— R. L. Stevenson on Burns. Burns Chron 2nd ser 22 1947.

—— Burns's 'First cleric character I ever saw', Bishop John Geddes. Burns Chron 2nd ser 23 1948.

Higgins, J. C. Life of Burns. Edinburgh 1893, Kilmarnock 1928.

Ingersoll, R. G. R. Burns. [Chicago 1893]; rptd in Memory of Burns, ed J. D. Ross, Glasgow 1899, and in Ingersoll's works.

Ingram, J. (ed). Interesting and characteristic anecdotes of Burns. Glasgow 1893.

McNaught, D. The Edinburgh forgeries. Burns Chron 2 1893.

—— The merry Muses of Caledonia. Burns Chron 3 1894, 20 1911. McNaught also edited an edn of Burns's Merry Muses, 1911.

—— The Earnock manuscripts: new light on Currie's biography. Burns Chron 8–9 1898–9.

—— The raucle tongue of Burns. Burns Chron 10 1901; rptd 3rd ser 4 1955.

—— Kirkpatrick Sharpe on Burns. Burns Chron 12 1903, 15 1906.

—— Currie's life annotated by John Syme. Burns Chron 13 1904.

—— Some Burns fictions. Burns Chron 23 1914.

—— Highland Mary: chronology of the episode. Burns Chron 24 1915.

—— Henley on Highland Mary. Burns Chron 25 1916.

—— Mrs Dunlop: Burns's candid friend. Burns Chron 26 1917.

—— Burns's marriage in the light of up-to-date evidence. Burns Chron 27 1918.

—— Dr Currie and his biography of Burns. Burns Chron 28 1919.

—— Some addenda to the Cromek correspondence. Ibid.

—— The truth about Burns. Glasgow 1921.

—— The politics of Burns. Burns Chron 34 1925.

McNaught was editor of the Burns Chronicle from 1893 to 1925, and wrote many short items not listed above.

Muir, J. Burns in French. Scots Mag Oct 1893.

—— Burns in German. Scots Mag Feb 1894.

—— Carlyle on Burns. Caledonia Feb 1895; rptd Glasgow 1898.

—— Burns at Galston and Ecclefechan. Glasgow 1896, 1896.

—— Alexander Reid, Gallovidian Laird and miniaturist of Burns. Trans of Dumfriesshire & Galloway Natural History & Antiquarian Soc 17 1932; rptd Burns Chron 27 1918 (title varies).

—— Notes on the election ballads of Burns. Ibid.

—— Burns and Roxburghshire. [Hawick 1918].

—— Notes on Burns's library. Kilmarnock Standard March 1924–Jan 1925.

—— Burns: his French library. Scotsman 27 May 1931.

Brown, D. K. Burns and Fergusson. Burnsiana 3 1894.

Holme, G. The ploughman poet: Burns, his brief unhappy life and its many passages of romance. Munsey's Mag Nov 1894.

McIver, L. [Address on Burns]. Burnsiana 3 1894; rptd in The memory of Burns, ed J. D. Ross, Glasgow 1899. First pbd in Scotsman.

Owada, T. In his lives of literary men, Tokyo 1894. In Japanese.

Peacock, H. C. Burns, poet-laureate of Lodge Cannongate Kilwinning: facts substantiating his election and inauguration on 1st March 1787. 2 pts Edinburgh 1894.

Zenker, R. Heines achtes Traumbild und Burns Jolly Beggars. Zeitschrift für Vergleichende Literaturgeschichte 7 1894.

Holmes, D. T. Address on Burns. Burnsiana 5 1895.

—— In his Lectures on Scottish literature, Paisley 1904.

Murdoch, J. B. The second edition of Burns. Burns Chron 4 1895.

—— Burns and 'Tullochgorum'. Burns Chron 21 1912.

Sinton, J. Burns excise officer and poet: a vindication. Carlisle [1895], 1897 (4th edn enlarged).

[Brown, G. D.] Burns. Blackwood's Mag Aug 1896; rptd in Burns Chron 3rd ser 2 1953.

Craigie, W. A primer of Burns. 1896.

Hendry, H. Robin redivivus. Blackwood's Mag July 1896.

'Setoun, Gabriel' (T. N. Hepburn). Robert Burns. Edinburgh [1896].

Jacks, W. Burns in other tongues: a critical review of the translations. Glasgow 1896.

Kunikita, T. The failure of Burns. Kokumin No Tomo 19 Sept 1896. In Japanese.

M., J. Reid portrait of Burns. Athenaeum 25 July 1896. Reply by J. L. Caw 8 Aug 1896.

Munro, A. The story of Burns and Highland Mary. Paisley 1896.

Quiller-Couch, A. T. Scott and Burns. In his Adventures in criticism, 1896.

Robertson, J. M. Stevenson on Burns. Free Rev Dec 1896.

—— The art of Burns [and] Stevenson on Burns. In his New essays towards a critical method, 1897.

Schipper, J. Gedenkrede auf Burns. Vienna 1896; rptd in his Beiträge und Studien zur englischen Kultur und Literaturgeschichte, Vienna 1908.

Shelley, H. C. Burns Scotland's national poet. Glasgow [1896].

—— The Ayrshire homes and haunts of Burns. New York 1897.

—— Burns in Ayrshire. In his Literary by-paths, 1909.

Sulley, P. Burns and Dumfries. Dumfries 1896.

Tolev, I. Robert Burns. Bylgarski Pregled 7–8 1896.

Will, W. Homes and haunts of Burns's ancestors. Aberdeen 1896.

—— Burns as a volunteer. Glasgow 1919, 1927; rptd in Burns Chron 29 1920.

—— John Murdoch tutor of Burns. Glasgow 1929; rptd in Burns Chron 2nd ser 4 1929.

Cross, A. W. The religion of Burns's poems. Arena 17 1897.

Davidson, J. New light on Burns. Scottish Rev 29 1897; rptd in Littell's Living Age 31 July 1897.

[Gifford, W.] A hundred years later: Burns under the light of the higher criticism. Edinburgh 1897.

Henley, W. E. Burns, life, genius, achievement. In Centenary Burns vol 4, ed W. E. Henley and T. F. Henderson, 1897 etc; Edinburgh 1898; and in Works vol 3, 1908.

Lockhart, R. M. A study in Highland Mariology. Westminster Rev Feb 1897.

—— Mr Henley and Highland Mary. Westminster Rev March 1898.

Mitchell, J. O. Burns and his times as gathered from his poems. Glasgow 1897.

Steel, J. Burns religious reformer and political revolutionary. Hawick [1897].

Balfour, A. J. Robert Burns. Burns Chron 7 1898; rptd in A. J. Balfour as philosopher and thinker, ed W. M. Short 1912.

Findlay, W. Burns and the medical profession. Paisley 1898.

—— Lockhart on Crabbe and Burns. Burns Chron 27 1918.

McKillop, J. Burns: two speeches. In his Thoughts for the people, 1898.

Crichton, A. 'The land o' the Leal': who wrote it—Lady Nairne or Burns? Glasgow 1899, Dunedin 1903, Peterhead 1919 (enlarged) (title varies).

Harvey, W. Burns in Stirlingshire. Stirling 1899.

—— Burns as a freemason. Dundee 1921, 1944.

Hayman, H. The higher criticism applied to a modern instance. Sunday Mag 28 1899; rptd in Littell's Living Age 13 May 1899.

Japp, A. H. Burns and W. E. Henley's heavy weight on him. 1899.

McIlwraith, W. W. E. Henley as Burns critic. Burns Chron 8 1899.

—— Robert Heron: Burns's first biographer. Burns Chron 22 1913.

Meyerfeld, M. Burns: Studien zu seiner dichterischen Entwicklung. Berlin 1899.

Molenaar, H. Burns' Beziehungen zur Literatur. Erlangen 1899.

Diack, W. Burns as a social reformer. Westminster Rev Dec 1900.

Foerster, M. Burns und Würzburg. Anglia 11 1900.

[Hamilton, W. S.] Tam O'Shanter analysed. Irvine 1900.

Leatham, J. Burns: an appreciation. Peterhead 1900, 1902 (title varies).

—— Burns, Scotland's man. Peterhead [c. 1900] (2 edns).

Letham, E. H. Burns and Tarbolton. Kilmarnock 1900.

Black, G. In defence of Burns. Sydney 1901.

Ritter, O. Quellenstudien zu Burns 1773–91. Berlin 1901.

—— Neuen Quellenfunde zu Burns. Halle 1903.

—— Burnsiana. E Studien 32 1903.

—— Burnsiana. Anglia 32 1909.

Gordon, J. Stevenson on Burns. Burns Chron 11 1902.

Muir, P. M. Burns: his genius and influence. Glasgow [1902].

Murray, D. C. Burns as an English poet. Contemporary Rev Nov 1902; rptd in Littell's Living Age 13 Dec 1902.

Burns: a critical symposium. Booklovers Mag 1 1903.

Baildon, H. B. Burns and Dunbar. Scottish Art & Letters 2 1903.

Butchart, S. F. Sind die Gedichte Poem on pastoral poetry und Verses on the destruction of Drumlanrig Woods von Burns? Marburg 1903.

Dick, J. C. The songs of Burns now first printed with the melodies for which they were written: a study in tone-poetry. 1903; rptd with Notes on Scottish song, ed J. C. Dick, and Annotations of Scottish songs by Burns, by D. Cook, Hatboro Pa 1962.

—— The interleaved Scots Musical Museum manuscript: a new light on Cromek. Burns Chron 14 1905.

Nicoll, W. R. Mr Henley on Burns the rake: a letter to the British Weekly. Burns Chron 12 1903.

Thomson, J. ('B.V.'). A few words about Burns. In his Poems, essays and fragments, 1903. Written in 1859.

Wihan, J. Franz Stelzhammer und Burns. Euphorion 10 1903.

Dougall, C. S. The Burns country. 1904, 1911, 1925.

Douglas, G. and W. S. Crockett. Robert Burns. 1904.

Henderson, H. F. Robert Burns. 1904.

—— The auld Ayrshire of Burns. 1906.

—— 'Charlie he's my darling' and other Burns originals. Scottish Historical Rev 3 1906.

Lowe, D. Burns's passionate pilgrimage: or Tait's indictment of the poet. Glasgow 1904.

Ewing, J. C. George Thomson, John Wilson and Gilbert Burns's Appendix no v. Burns Chron 14 1905.

—— The Nasmyth-Raeburn portrait of Burns. Burns Chron 18 1909.

—— Prospectus of the Kilmarnock edition. Burns Chron 27 1918.

—— Authorship of the Verses on the destruction of the woods near Drumlanrig. Burns Chron 28 1919.

—— Maria Riddell's letters to Dr James Currie 1796–1805. Burns Chron 29–30, 32–33 1920–4.

—— Letters from Dr Robert Anderson to Dr James Currie 1799–1801. Burns Chron 34 1925.

—— Burns's Poems: reviews of the first edition. Burns Chron 2nd ser 2 1927.

—— with A. M'Callum. Robert Graham (12th) of Fintry. Burns Chron 2nd ser 6 1931.

—— Burns's literary correspondents 1786–96. Burns Chron 2nd ser 8 1933.

—— With A. M'Callum. Alexander Cunningham: Burns's principal Edinburgh friend. Ibid.

—— Correspondence with John Syme and Alexander Cunningham 1789–1811. Burns Chron 2nd ser 9–11, 13–15, 17–18 1934–43.

—— The letters of 'Clarinda' to 'Sylvander'. Burns Chron 2nd ser 9 1934.

—— Burns's 'Esopus to Maria'. Burns Chron 2nd ser 10 1935.

—— Louisa Fontenelle, actress. Ibid.

—— Letters of John Murdoch. Burns Chron 2nd ser 12 1937.

—— Burns's tour of Galloway in 1793 and the fable of the composition of 'Scots wha hae'. Burns Chron 2nd ser 12–13, 1937–8.

—— The Earl of Glencairn and Burns: the poet's thanks to his patron. Burns Chron 2nd ser 13 1938.

—— The Eglintons' patronage of Burns 1786–7. Burns Chron 2nd ser 14 1939.

—— Alleged commonplace books of Burns: not the poet's composition or holograph. Burns Chron 2nd ser 15 1940.

—— The last of Burns's heroines, Jessy Lewars and her story. Ibid.

—— Prototype of 'Doctor Hornbook' John Wilson 1751–1839. Burns Chron 2nd ser 16 1941.

—— Burns's visits to Glasgow, fiction and fact. Burns Chron 2nd ser 17 1942.

—— Pietro Urbani: composer, singer, teacher and publisher of Scots music. Ibid.

—— Burns and the Edinburgh Gazetteer, the poet's correspondence with Captain Johnston. Burns Chron 2nd ser 19 1944.

—— Burns's first visit to Edinburgh, Rev Archibald Lawrie's reminiscences. Burns Chron 2nd ser 20 1945.

—— Some missing Burns manuscripts: the auction sales of 1861–2. Ibid.

Ewing edited Burns Chronicle 1926–48, compiled the index to 2nd ser 1–22, and pbd several letters from and concerning Burns in the pages of this journal.

Kelly, J. K. Burns; his admirers, his inspiration, his genius, his mission. Edinburgh [1905].

Myers, W. L. The influence of Ferguson on Burns. Sewanee Rev 13 1905.

Ford, R. The heroines of Burns. Paisley 1906.

Macintosh, J. The life of Burns. Paisley 1906.

Williams, A. M. Two French critics of Burns [Taine and Angellier]. Univ Rev June 1906.

—— Burns and his predecessors. Burns Chron 2nd ser 3 1928.

Macpherson, H. Burns and the revolution spirit. In his A century of intellectual development, 1907.

Sloan, J. M. Burns and Charles Dickens. Fortnightly Rev Aug 1907; rptd in Littell's Living Age 5 Oct 1907.

Bayne, T. Andrew Lang and Burns. Nat Rev 52 1909.

MacColl, D. S. Burns the singer. Saturday Rev 30 Jan 1909; rptd in Littell's Living Age 13 March 1909.

Mabie, H. W. Burns: the poet of democracy. North Amer Rev March 1909.

Wotherspoon, J. Kirk life and kirk folk; an interpretation of the clerical satires of Burns. Edinburgh 1909.

Duncan, R. The story of the Edinburgh Burns relics. Edinburgh 1910.

—— Blacklock and Burns. Burns Chron 23 1914.

McCallum, A. Burns interpreted in the light of his own times. Burns Chron 19 1910; rptd 3rd ser 1964.

—— Burns and Renfrewshire: myth, conjecture and fact. Burns Chron 2nd ser 25 1950.

Stewart, W. Burns and the common people. Glasgow 1910, London 1925, 1927.

White, A. C. (ed). Foreign tributes to Burns. Burns Chron 19 1910.

Beaumont, F. Ferguson and Burns: the shaping of a poet. Royal Philosophical Soc of Glasgow Proc 42 1911; rptd Burns Chron 22 1913.

Goodwillie, E. (ed). The world's memorials of Burns. Detroit 1911.

St Louis Burns Club. Burns nights in St Louis. Ed W. B. Stevens, St Louis [1911]. 6 other vols till 1955, with varying titles, each containing addresses given before the club.

Streissle, A. Personifikation und poetische Beseelung bei Scott und Burns. Heidelberg 1911.

Hecht, H. Die Merry Muses of Caledonia und Burns Court of equity. Archiv für das Studium der Neueren Sprachen 129–30 1912–13.

—— Burns: Leben und Wirken des schottischen Volksdichters. Heidelberg 1919, tr 1926 (enlarged), 1950.

—— The reception of Burns in German literature: pt 1. Weimar and Berlin. Burns Chron 2nd ser 14 1939 (all pbd).

Kellow, H. A. Burns and his poetry. 1912.

Pennington, E. The politics of Burns. Burns Chron 21 1912.

S., H. J. Burns and Boswell. Ibid.

Daa, T. Burns in Denmark. Burns Chron 22 1913.

—— Burns as a song-mender. Burns Chron 24 1915.

Neilson, W. A. Burns in English. In Anniversary Papers by colleagues and pupils of George Lyman Kittredge, Boston 1913.

—— Robert Burns. Indianapolis 1917.

Steffen, R. Notes on Burns in Sweden. Burns Chron 22 1913.

Watt, L. M. Burns. Glasgow [1913].

—— Burns biography. Burns Chron 2nd ser 7 1932.

—— Highland Mary's grave: who was the child who shared it? Scots Mag Dec 1932.

—— Highland Mary. Burns Chron 2nd ser 8 1933.

Duncan, R. Blacklock and Burns. Burns Chron 23 1914.

Raleigh, W. Essay on Burns. In J. G. Lockhart, Life of Burns, ed W. D. Scott 1914; rptd in his Some authors, Oxford 1923.

Aakjär, J. Robert Burns. Burns Chron 24 1915.

Colum, P. Robert Burns. New Republic 23 Jan 1915.

—— Burns and the poetic inheritance. In Half-day's ride: or estates in Corcisa, New York 1932.

[Cameron, J.] (ed). 200 stories and incidents about Burns. Glasgow 1916.

Fulton, E. S. (ed). Gleanings from many authors in memory of Burns. Paisley 1916.

Cook, D. Burns and Stothard. Bookman (London) Sept 1917; abridged in Burns Chron 27 1918.

— The young poet. Bookman (London) Feb 1918.

— Burns and Peter Pindar. Bookman (London) Oct 1918.

— Burns mystery solved. Bookman (London) April 1919. Burns did not write 'Strait is the spot and green the sod'.

— Gallovidianus identified. Bookman (London) Aug 1920. Authorship of 'Strait is the spot'.

— Elegy on Stella. Burns Chron 30 1921. An abridged combination of the above 2 articles.

— Misdates in Burns literature. Burns Chron 28 1919.

— Burns and Aberdeen. Bookman (London) March 1920.

— Annotations of Scottish songs by Burns: an essential supplement to Cromek and Dick. Burns Chron 31 1922; Dumfries 1922; rptd in J. C. Dick, Songs of Burns, Hatboro Pa 1962.

— 'The wee, wee German lairdie': elusive Jacobite original discovered. Weekly Scotsman 24 May 1924.

— Burns's Highland laddie: an old song-book discovery. Weekly Scotsman 20 Dec 1924.

— Burns's old bacchanal found at last. Bookman (London) Jan 1925.

— Pitfalls in Burns-lore: Drinkwater and minor charges. Forward 28 Nov 1925.

— Burns and Urbani. Weekly Scotsman 10 Dec 1927.

— Burns's old song books. TLS 8 Nov 1928.

— Burns's 'Oswald': the Caledonian pocket companion. Scots Mag Aug 1933.

— Burns and 'The thorn'. Weekly Scotsman 14 Oct 1933.

— Watlen's 'Scots songs'. Scots Mag Nov 1933.

— 'The red, red rose' and its tunes. Burns Chron 2nd ser 9 1934.

— The fame of Burns. TLS 30 April 1938.

— Unknown Burns broadsides printed by William Chambers in Leith Walk. Weekly Scotsman 10 June 1939.

Ker, W. P. The politics of Burns. Scottish Historical Rev 14 Oct 1917; rptd in his Two essays, Glasgow 1918, and in his Collected essays vol 1, ed C. Whibley 1925.

Lawson, W. R. Burns as a Freemason. Edinburgh 1917.

Martin, G. C. In his Poets of democracy, 1917.

Snyder, F. B. Notes on Burns and the popular ballads. JEGP 17 1918.

— Notes on Burns's first volume. MP 16 1919; rptd in The story of the Kilmarnock Burns, ed J. D. Ross, Stirling 1933.

— Notes on Burns and Thomson. JEPG 19 1920.

— Notes on Burns and England. MLN 37 1922.

— Burns and his biographers. SP 25 1928; rptd Burns Chron 2nd ser 7 1932.

— A note on Burns's language. MLN 43 1928.

— Burns's last years. SP 26 1929; rev in Burns Chron 2nd ser 10 1935.

— The life of Burns. New York 1932, Hamden Conn 1968. See H. W. Meikle, 1934, below.

— Burns: his personality, his reputation and his art. Toronto 1936 (Alexander Lectures).

Will, W. Burns as a volunteer. Glasgow 1919, Aberdeen 1927; rptd in Burns Chron 29 1920.

— John Murdoch, tutor of Burns. Burns Chron 2nd ser 4 1929; also separately. Replies by J. M. Bulloch, N & Q 16 Feb 1929; H. Askew 30 March 1929.

Wright, D. R. Burns and Freemasonry. Paisley 1921.

Barr, J. Burns: a lecture. New Zealand Scotsman 20 Sept 1922.

Hughes, J. L. The real Burns. New York 1922.

Keith, A. Burns and folk song. Aberdeen 1922.

Wood, J. M. Burns and the Riddell family. Dumfries 1922.

Carlyle and Burns. Saturday Rev 27 Jan 1923.

Brandl, A. Zur Psychologie des Dichtens bei Burns. Berlin 1923.

Dakers, A. Burns: his life and genius. 1923.

Findlay, J. P. Footprints of Burns. Paisley 1923.

Kennedy, H. A. Burns in the twentieth century: an address. New York 1923.

Lowe, C. Burns, poet: can English people understand him? Nineteenth Century June 1923.

Marsh, G. L. The text of Burns. In J. M. Manly anniversary studies, Chicago 1923.

Meyerstein, E. H. W. Burns and the Merry beggars. TLS 13 Dec 1923.

Muir, E. Robert Burns. Freeman 9 May 1923; rptd in Latitudes, [1924], [1927].

— Burns and popular poetry. In his Essays on literature and society, 1949, Cambridge Mass 1965.

Munro, N. In his Ayrshire idylls, Edinburgh 1923.

Thomson, J. Burns and Paisley. Burns Chron 32 1923; also separately.

Wilson, J. The dialect of Burns as spoken in central Ayrshire. Oxford 1923.

Drinkwater, J. Burns: an address. Edinburgh 1924; rptd in his Muse in council, 1925.

Mackenzie, J. A new life and vindication of Burns. Edinburgh 1924.

McKnight, A. G. America's appreciation of Burns. [Duluth] 1924.

— Burns: the poet of liberalism. [St Paul] 1929.

— Burns and the modern world. [Duluth?] 1939.

— Abraham Lincoln, Burns. [Duluth?] nd; rptd in Burns Chron 2nd ser 18 1943. First pbd in Fiery Cross Jan–Feb 1942.

— Lincoln and Burns. Duluth [1943].

Clarke, J. S. Burns and his politics. Glasgow 1925.

— Burns and the Edinburgh Gazeteer: Cato's prose essay on reform. Burns Chron 2nd ser 21 1946.

Davison, E. Burns: a reconsideration. London Mercury Dec 1925; rptd in his Some modern poets and other critical essays, New York 1928.

Heller, O. Burns: a revaluation. Washington Univ Stud 12 1925.

Junior, A. Burns in Scottish scene and song. Dundee 1925.

Martin, J. S. Burns's debt to Fergusson. Scots Mag July 1925.

Praz, M. In his Poeti inglesi dell'ottocento, Florence 1925. Includes a bibliography of Burns and a rimed version of the Jolly beggars.

Barr, J. The religious teaching of Burns. Scottish N & Q 3rd ser 4 1926.

Buchan, J. In his Homilies and recreations, 1926.

Crichton-Browne, J. Burns from a new point of view. [1926], 1927 (enlarged).

— Burns and the drama, his unwritten masterpieces, life-long interest in the theatre. [1935]. First pbd as 2 articles in Glasgow Herald 24–5 Jan 1935.

Fisher, W. D. (ed). Burns and the Bible: a series of parallels. Glasgow 1926, 1927 (enlarged).

Miller, F. The original of Burns's song the Battle of Sherra-Moor. Scottish Historical Rev 23 1926.

Power, W. Burns and other essays and sketches. Edinburgh 1926.

Raithel, H. Robert Burns. Westermanns Monatshefte 70 1926.

Saintsbury, G. This fuss about Burns—and its justification. Country Life 6 Feb 1926.

Steel, J. H. The style of Burns. Burns Chron 2nd ser 1 1926.

Kent, F. Burns epigrammatist. Burns Chron 2nd ser 2 1927.

— Burns epigrams garnered by John Syme. Burns Chron 2nd ser 7 1932.

Leclercq, R. Angellier, biographe de Burns. Cahier Angellier 4 1927.

McVie, J. Burns and Stair. Kilmarnock 1927.
—— The Burns country. Edinburgh 1962.
—— Burns and Edinburgh. Burns Chron 3rd ser 13–15 1964–6.
Anderson, H. B. Burns: his medical friends, attendants and biographer. Annals of Medical History 10 1928.
Benedetti, A. Taluni espetti della poesia di Burns. Nuova Antologia 1 Dec 1928.
Ferguson, J. DeL. Cancelled passages in the letters of Burns to George Thomson. PMLA 43 1928; rptd in Burns Chron 2nd ser 4 1929.
—— Burns and the Indies in 1788. MLN 44 1929; rptd in Burns Chron 2nd ser 5 1930.
—— New light on the Burns-Dunlop estrangement. PMLA 44 1929; rptd in Burns Chron 2nd ser 5 1930.
—— Burns and Hugh Blair. MLN 45 1930; rptd in Burns Chron 2nd ser 7 1932.
—— In defense of R. H. Cromek. PQ 9 1930.
—— Burns and Maria Riddell. MP 28 1930.
—— Some notes on Burns's reading. MLN 45 1930.
—— The text of Burns's 'Passion's cry'. MLN 45 1930.
—— 'Against two things I am as fixed as fate'. MLN 46 1931.
—— The Reid miniature of Burns. Colophon 6 [1931].
—— Some aspects of the Burns legend. PQ 11 1932.
—— The suppressed poems of Burns. MP 30 1932.
—— 'Antique' Smith and his forgeries of Burns. Colophon 13 [1933].
—— Burns and the drama. Scots Mag 21 1934.
—— Burns's journal of his Border tour. PMLA 49 1934.
—— The earliest obituary of Burns: its authorship and influence. MP 32 1934.
—— Maria Riddell's sketch of Burns. PQ 13 1934.
—— The immortal memory. Amer Scholar 5 1936.
—— Pride and passion: Burns. New York 1939, 1964.
—— They censured Burns. Scotland's Mag Jan 1955.
Gemmill, J. F. Natural history of the poetry of Burns. Glasgow 1928.
MacIntosh, W. Burns in Germany: Scoto-German studies. Aberdeen 1928.
Schroeder, J. H. E. Burns and Rudel. TLS 19 April 1928. See 31 May, 7 June, 6, 27 Sept 1928.
Spence, L. Burns: anthropological study. Scotsman 26 Jan 1928.
—— Burns as a satirist. SMT Mag Jan 1950.
Thorogood, A. J. Shenstone and Burns. London Mercury May 1928.
Auld, R. C. M. The Burns we love. New York 1929.
Dobbie, J. Burns as a social force. Burns Chron 2nd ser 4 1929.
—— Burns and Dickens—the men and their mission. Dickensian 26 1930; rptd in Burns Chron 2nd ser 6 1931.
—— Burns and Scottish nationalism. Burns Chron 2nd ser 5 1930.
—— Burns as letter-writer. John O'London's Weekly 14 Nov 1931.
Finger, C. J. A man for a' that. Boston 1929.
Jefferson, B. L. 'The rural lass' and 'Tam Glen'. TLS 5 Dec 1929.
M'Lehose, A. The poems of Clarinda. Ed J. D. Ross, Stirling 1929.
Muir, J. Burns till his seventeenth (Kirkoswald) year. Kilmarnock 1929.
R., V. Scott and Burns: their only meeting. N & Q 30 March 1929.
Shearer, T. Burns as a critic of his age. Burns Chron 2nd ser 4 1929.
Watson, W. T. Burns and Walter Scott: notes of an address. Burns Chron 2nd ser 4 1929.
Wright, W. Burns and his masonic circle. 1929.
Burns in French: the first translation. Scotsman 25 Jan 1930.
Baldwin of Bewdley, S., 1st Earl. Burns. Burns Chron 2nd ser 5 1930.

Carswell, C. The life of Burns. 1930, 1951.
—— Robert Burns. 1933.
—— Burns and Scotch drink: an inquiry and a defence. Scottish Outlook 1 1936.
—— In From Anne to Victoria, ed B. Dobrée 1937.
Main, A. Burns the man. Burns Chron 2nd ser 5 1930.
Peddie, J. R. Burns as a craftsman of letters. Ibid.
Robertson, J. K. Robert Burns. Aberdeen Univ Rev 18 1930.
Craigie, J. The humanity of Burns. Wellington 1931.
Jamieson, A. B. Burns and religion. Cambridge 1931.
Lawrance, R. M. Burns's school reading-book. Aberdeen Book-Lover Nov 1931; also separately.
Thomson, A. A. The Burns we love. [1931], [1931].
Carus, G. Burns and the American Revolution. Open Court 46 1932.
Dedinszky, G. Petofi és Burns. Budapest 1932.
Roy, J. A. Burns: a refocusing. Queen's Quart 39 1932.
Carnegie, A. Burns and the modern spirit, genius illustrated from Burns [2 essays]. In Miscellaneous writings vol 1, ed B. J. Hendrick, New York 1933.
Driesch, M. Wagner and Burns. Poetry Rev 24 1933.
Hill, J. C. The life and work of Burns in Irvine. 1933.
—— The love songs and heroines of Burns. 1961.
Lehmann, E. Die französischen Lehn-und Fremdwörter in den Werken von Burns. Breslau 1933.
Mackenna, R. W. The letters of Burns. In his As shadows lengthen: later essays, New York 1933.
Murdoch, J. M. Familiar links with Burns. Ed M. M. Murdoch, Ayr 1933.
Bliss, D. P. (ed). The Devil in Scotland. 1934.
Brown, E. S. The political ideas of Burns. Papers of Michigan Acad 19 1934: rptd in Burns Chron 2nd ser 11–12 1936–7.
Fraser-Harris, D. F. Burns as a writer of prose. Dalhousie Rev 14 1934.
Gray, W. F. The discoverer of Burns. Cornhill Mag Jan 1934.
'Hugh MacDiarmid' (C. M. Grieve). The Burns cult. In his At the sign of the thistle: a collection of essays, [1934].
—— How other poets have paid tribute to Burns. Scottish Jnl 12 1954.
—— Burns today and tomorrow. Edinburgh 1959.
—— A note on some foreign translations of Burns. Burns Chron 3rd ser 8 1959.
Meikle, H. W. Burns and the capture of the Rosamond. Burns Chron 2nd ser 9 1934. Amplified from article first pbd in Glasgow Herald 11 Nov 1932. Corrects F. B. Snyder. Reply by Snyder, Burns and the smuggler Rosamond, PMLA 50 1935.
Walker, L. J. Caledonia's bard. Education 54 1934.
Fitzhugh, R. T. The paradox of Burns's character. SP 32 1935.
—— The composition of 'Scots wha hae'. MLN 51 1936.
—— Burns's Highland Mary. PMLA 52 1937.
—— Burns at Ellisland. MLN 53 1938.
—— Burns's later years: some candid notes by his friend John Syme. SP 37 1940.
—— (ed). Burns: his associates and contemporaries, the Train, Grierson, Young and Hope manuscripts; with the Journal of the Border tour. Ed DeL. Ferguson, Chapel Hill 1943.
Burns: his life and work. SMT Mag Jan 1936.
Besterman, T. Burns documents. TLS 7 March 1936.
Grierson, H. J. C. Reactions of poets to Burns. SMT Mag Jan 1936.
Leftwich, B. R. Burns and the Excise: an account of the surviving records in official custody. Burns Chron 2nd ser 11 1936.
Mitchell, W. F. Eliza Burnett of Monboddo. Ibid.
Morison, J. L. Burns and Scottish nationalism. Ibid.
Murray, J. Poetry stoops to conquer: Burns and Crabbe as poets of working-class life. In his Essays in literature, Edinburgh 1936.

Orr, C. Burns in drama. SMT Mag Jan 1936.

Selkirk, J. H. Scotland's bard Burns. [1936].

Smith, G. F. O. (ed). Robert Burns. Toronto 1936.

—— The man Burns. Toronto 1940.

Alexander Wood surgeon and friend of Burns. Annals of Medical History 9 1937.

Calder, G. Note on Burns's influence on Ross. In Gaelic songs by William Ross, ed G. Calder, Edinburgh 1937.

Jeffery, S. W. Roscoe and Burns. TLS 2 Oct 1937.

Smith, D. N. Thomson-Burns. In his Some observations on eighteenth-century poetry, Oxford 1937 (Alexander Lectures).

Henderson, K. Burns—by himself. 1938.

Howarth, R. G. Scott on Burns. N & Q 15 Oct 1938.

Mason, J. E. Robert Burns. 1938.

'Lindsey, John' (J. St C. Muriel). The ranting dog: the life of Burns. 1938, New York 1938 (as Immortal memory: the real Burns).

Paterson, A. Two of a kind [Dickens and Burns]. Dickensian 35 1938.

Delattre, F. Auguste Angellier et le génie poétique de Burns. Etudes Anglaises 4 1939.

Levenson, A. Z. Burns and Shevchenko. Trans of State Pedagogical Inst of Foreign Languages in Kharkov 1 1939. In Russian.

Orlov, S. A. Burns in Russian translations. Uchenye Zapiski (Academic Notes) 26 1939. In Russian.

Parker, W. M. Burns, Scott and Turgenev: a remarkable linkage. N & Q 29 April 1939.

Arnott, R. J. Thomas White: a friend of Burns. Burns Chron 2nd ser 15 1940.

Ewing, Elizabeth. The last of Burns's heroines: Jessy Lewars and her story. Ibid.

—— Burns's visits to Glasgow: fiction and fact. Burns Chron 2nd ser 17 1942.

—— Burns's first visit to Edinburgh: Rev Archibald Lawrie's reminiscences. Burns Chron 2nd ser 20 1945.

'Hippoclides'. Tam O'Shanter. N & Q 6 July 1940. Reply by H.G.L.K. 17 Aug 1940.

Macartney, W. N. Burns and the Buchanites. Scottish Field Jan 1940.

Shannon, G. Burns: that immortal memory. Dublin Rev 206 1940.

Spiers, J. In his Scots literary tradition, 1940, 1962 (enlarged with 2 additional essays on Burns).

Weir, J. L. An early Burns celebration. N & Q 17 Feb 1940.

Croce, B. Burns: tre canti. In Poesia antica e moderna, Bari 1941.

Goldberg, M. H. Jeffrey: mutilator of Carlyle's Burns? PMLA 56 1941.

Reynolds, P. E. An Irish imitation of Burns [John H. Kenney]. Burns Chron 2nd ser 17 1942.

Russev, R. Robert Burns. Bulgarska Misul 17 1942.

Birrell, J. H. Sir Walter Scott's debt to Burns. Burns Chron 2nd ser 18 1943.

Dollan, P. J. Burns as a world influence. Burns Chron 2nd ser 19 1944.

—— The Communists and Burns. Burns Chron 2nd ser 24 1949.

Gray, A. Burns: man and poet. Edinburgh [1944].

Harasowski, A. Burns and Mickiewicz: two national poets. Burns Chron 2nd ser 19 1944.

Noyes, R. Wordsworth and Burns. PMLA 59 1944.

Dewar, R. In Essays on the eighteenth century presented to David Nichol Smith in honour of his seventieth birthday, Oxford 1945.

—— Burns and the Burns tradition. In Scottish poetry: a critical survey, ed J. Kinsley 1955.

Robertson, J. M. Burns and Byron: a comparison. Burns Chron 2nd ser 21 1946.

Gow, P. F. Medical history of Burns: recent research and opinion. Burns Chron 2nd ser 22 1947.

Halliday, R. T. Burns and Freemasonry in Edinburgh. Ibid.

Linklater, E. In his Art of adventure, 1947.

Montgomerie, W. (ed). Burns: essays by six contemporary writers. Glasgow 1947.

—— Folk poetry and Burns. Burns Chron 2nd ser 25 1950.

—— Burns: folk-song editor. Saltire Rev 6 1959.

—— Two songs by Burns as first printed. Burns Chron 3rd ser 11 1962.

Wolf, E. 'Skinking' or 'stinking'?: a bibliographical study of the 1787 Edinburgh edition of Burns's Poems. Univ of Pennsylvania Lib Chron 14 1947.

Burns and the Scots Musical Museum. New Colophon 1 [1948].

Porter, K. Burns and Peggy Chalmers. MLN 63 1948.

Brown, H. There was a lad: an essay on Burns. 1949.

—— Burns and the Scottish milkmaid [Janet Little]. Burns Chron 2nd ser 25 1950.

Butcher, P. Burns and the democratic spirit. Phylon 10 1949.

Egerer, J. W. Burns and Guid black prent. In The age of Johnson: essays presented to Chauncey Brewster Tinker, New Haven 1949.

—— (ed). Annotated list of subscribers, first Edinburgh edition 1787. Burns Chron 3rd ser 8, 1959, 10–12 1961–3. Includes names A—F only. Suppl by A. G. Hepburn, 12 1963 (A—D).

—— Thomas Stewart, Burns and the law. PBSA 56 1962.

Fairchild, H. N. In his Religious trends in English poetry vol 3: 1780–1830, New York 1949.

Keith, C. Burns from the back o' Ben More. Queen's Quart 55 1949.

[——] Burns in his letters. Queen's Quart 57 1951; rptd in Burns Chron 3rd ser 1 1952.

—— The jolly beggars. Burns Chron 3rd ser 2 1953.

—— The russet coat: a critical study of Burns's poetry and of its background. 1956.

McGloin, J. R. Burns and the Popish Bishop. Burns Chron 2nd ser 24 1949. Rptd from Tablet.

Sells, A. L. Leconte de Lisle and Burns. In Studies in French language, literature and history presented to R.L. Graeme Ritchie, Cambridge 1949.

Daiches, D. Robert Burns. New York 1950, London 1950, 1952, 1966 (rev).

—— Robert Burns. 1957 (Br Council pamphlet).

—— Burns after 200 years. Listener 29 Jan 1959. Reply by W. Montgomerie 5 Feb; answer by Daiches 12 Feb 1959.

—— The identity of Burns. In Restoration and eighteenth-century literature: essays in honor of A. D. McKillop, Chicago 1963; rptd in his More literary essays, 1968.

Murison, D. The language of Burns. Burns Chron 2nd ser 25 1950.

—— The speech of Ayrshire in the time of Burns. Collections of Ayrshire Archaeological & Natural History Soc 5 1960.

Thornton, R. D. Burnsiana. Burns Chron 2nd ser 25 1950.

—— Robert Riddell, antiquary. Burns Chron 3rd ser 2 1953.

—— Twentieth-century scholarship on the songs of Burns. Univ of Colorado Stud in Lang & Lit 4 1953.

—— James Currie, the entire stranger, and Burns. Edinburgh 1963.

—— James Currie, editor. Burns Chron 3rd ser 14 1965.

—— Burns and the Scottish Enlightenment. Stud on Voltaire & the Eighteenth Century 58 1967.

Buchan, A. M. Word and word-tunes in Burns. SP 48 1951; rptd in Burns Chron 3rd ser 6 1957 and in Anniversary addresses presented before the Burns Club of St Louis 1945–55, [St Louis 1955].

—— Justice to Dr Currie. Burns Chron 3rd ser 12 1963.

McCourt, T. M. The forgotten songs of Burns. Etude Music Mag 69 1951.

Rundle, J. U. Burns's Holy Willie's Prayer and Browning's Soliloquy of the Spanish cloister. N & Q 9 June 1951.

Donaldson, A. M. Burns's final settlement with Creech. Burns Chron 3rd ser 1 1952.
—— Topham's letters from Edinburgh: an intimate description of the capital in the time of Burns. Burns Chron 3rd ser 3 1954.
—— Burns and the writings of Dougal Graham, the 'Skellat' bellman of Glasgow. Burns Chron 3rd ser 10 1961.
MacLaine, A. H. A source for Burns's Death and Doctor Hornbook. N & Q 12 April 1952; rptd in Burns Chron 3rd ser 3 1954.
—— New light on the genesis of the Burns stanza. N & Q Aug 1953; rptd in Burns Chron 3rd ser 3 1954.
—— Burns's Jolly beggars: a mistaken interpretation. N & Q Nov 1953.
—— Burns's use of parody in Tam O'Shanter. Criticism 1 1959.
—— Some echoes of Robert Fergusson in Burns's A Mauchline wedding. N & Q July 1961.
—— The 'Christis Kirk' tradition: its evolution in Scots poetry to Burns. Stud in Scottish Lit 2 1965.
Campbell, W. B. A Burns companion: being everybody's key to Burns's poems. Aberdeen 1953.
Craig, H. Burns and the Lowland Scotch. In his Written word and other essays, Chapel Hill 1953.
—— Burns and the English speaking world. In Anniversary addresses presented before the Burns Club of St Louis 1945–55, [St Louis 1955]; rptd in Burns Chron 3rd ser 6 1957.
Snoddy, T. G. Burns: the relation of his intellect and poetry. Burns Chron 3rd ser 2 1953.
Kinghorn, A. M. Burns and his early critics. Burns Chron 3rd ser 3 1954.
—— The place of Burns's 'Scottish dialect'. Burns Chron 3rd ser 4 1955.
—— Literary and historical origins of the Burns myth. Dalhousie Rev 39 1959.
—— Burns and Jamaica. REL 8 1967.
Lindsay, M. Burns: the man, his work, the legend. 1954, 1968.
Ostrovski, A. N. In Selected articles and translations, ed M. M. Morozov, Moscow 1954.
Smith, S. G. Burns and the Merry Muses of Caledonia. Hudson Rev 7 1954.
Wright-Kovaleva, R. Robert Burns. Sovietskaia Zhenshchina 7 1954.
—— Burns—by himself. Novyi Mir 6 1954.
—— Robert Burns. Moscow 1961.
Craig, D. Burns and Scottish culture. Voice of Scotland 7–8 1956–7.
Elistratova, A. A. Robert Burns. Moscow 1957. Extensive synopsis in Stud in Scottish Lit 2 1965.
Keir, W. Burns and the Devil. Scotland's Mag Jan 1957.
Namba, T. A study of Tam O'Shanter. Bull of Setagaya College of Liberal Arts (Nihon Univ) 6 1957.
—— Burns's poetry and the flavour of Haiku. Bull of Setagaya College of Liberal Arts 7 1961.
—— Burns in Japan. Stud in Scottish Lit 1 1964.
Brown, W. Burns and New Zealand. Burns Chron 3rd ser 7 1958.
Pearl, C. Bawdy Burns the Christian rebel. 1958.
Witte, W. Schiller and Burns and other essays. Oxford 1958.
Burroughs, J. Burns the glorious sinner. Boston Public Lib Quart 11 1959; rptd in Burns Chron 3rd ser 10 1961. An unpbd article of 1872.
Hillyer, R. In Anniversary lectures, Washington 1959 (Lib of Congress).
Kenyeres, Z. One theme, two poems: Burns's The cotter's Saturday night and Arany's Family circle. Filológiai Közlöny 5 1959.
Kéry, L. Burns in Petőfi's country. Nagyvilág 4 1959.
Lara, J. G. M. de. Vida amorosa del poeta de Alloway. Insula 14 1959.

MacCaig, N. (ed). Honour'd shade: an anthology of new Scottish poetry to mark the bicentenary of the birth of Burns. Edinburgh 1959.
Mackie, A. Burns and Fergusson. Saltire Rev 6 1959.
Marshak, S. I. Burns: for the 200th anniversary of his birth. Znanie 6 1959.
Pósa, P. Burns and some problems of English romantic poetry. Acta Universitatis Szegediensis, Sectio Litteraria 1959; 1960 (separately).
[Renwick, W. L.] (ed). Burns as others saw him. Edinburgh 1959.
—— Notes on a poem of Burns [Epistle to Major Logan]. In Of books and human kind: essays and poems presented to Bonamy Dobrée, ed J. Butt 1964.
Rudnyckyj, J. B. Burns and Shevchenko. Winnipeg 1959. In Ukranian.
Strawhorn, J. (ed). Ayrshire at the time of Burns. Glasgow 1959.
Whitley, H. C. The religion of Burns. [Edinburgh] 1959 (Thomas Green Lectures, Carlyle Soc).
Crawford, T. Burns: a study of the poems and songs. Edinburgh 1960, 1965.
—— Jean Armour's Double and adieu. Scottish Stud 7 1963.
Gillies, A. Emilie von Berlepsch and Burns. MLR 55 1960.
Kinsley, J. The rustic inhabitants of the hamlet. REL 1 1960.
—— The music of the heart. Renaissance & Modern Stud 8 1964.
—— Burns and the Merry Muses. Renaissance & Modern Stud 9 1965.
—— A note on Tam O'Shanter. English 16 1967.
McKillop, A. D. The living Burns. Rice Inst Pamphlet 47 1960.
'Rae, Elsie S.' (Elsie R. S. Wilson). Poet's pilgrimage: the story of the life and times of Burns. Glasgow 1960.
Reitemeier, R. Das Bild Burns: Tradition und Wandel. Die Neueren Sprachen 9 1960.
Weston, J. C. The text of Burns's The jolly beggars. SB 13 1960.
—— An example of Burns's contribution to the Scottish vernacular tradition. SP 57 1960.
—— The narrator of Tam O'Shanter. Stud in Eng Lit 1500–1900 8 1968.
—— The text of Maria Riddell's sketch of Burns. Stud in Scottish Lit 5 1968.
Hunter, C. Let Burns speak: an edited autobiography of Burns. Paisley 1961.
Itsuno, N. The poet Burns. Tokyo 1961.
Maxwell, J. C. Burns: an echo of Tristram Shandy. N & Q Aug 1961.
Morton, R. Narrative irony in Burns's Tam O'Shanter. MLQ 22 1961.
Werkmeister, L. Some account of Burns and the London newspapers, with special reference to the spurious Star 1789. BNYPL Oct 1961.
—— An early version of Burns's song Their groves of sweet myrtle. N & Q Dec 1962.
—— Burns and the London daily press. MP 63 1966.
Yamato, Y (ed). Essays on Burns. Tokyo 1961. In Japanese.
Cairns, D. Burns and the religious movements in the Scotland of his day. [Edinburgh] 1962 (Thomas Green Lectures, Carlyle Soc).
Képes, G. Burns and Shevchenko. Acta Litteraria Academiae Scientiarum Hungaricae 5 1962. In Russian.
Michie, J. A. Wordsworth and Burns. Burns Chron 3rd ser 11 1962.
Norton, A. S. Burns and the 'Forty-Five'. Burns Chron 3rd ser 12 1963.
Roy, G. R. French translations of Burns to 1893. Revue de Littérature Comparée 37 1963; rptd in Burns Chron 3rd ser 14–15 1965–6.

—— French critics of Burns to 1893. Revue de Littérature Comparée 38 1964.

—— Burns in France. Revue de Littérature Comparée 39 1965. An unpbd letter by Alfred de Vigny about Burns.

—— The merry Muses of Caledonia. Stud in Scottish Lit 2 1965. On only known complete copy.

—— Some notes on the facsimile of the Kilmarnock Burns. Bibliotheck 4 1965.

—— Wordsworth on Burns. Stud in Scottish Lit 3 1966.

—— Burns and the Aberdeen Magazine. Bibliotheck 5 1968.

Skinner, B. C. Burns: authentic likenesses. Edinburgh 1963.

Beaty, F. L. 'Ae spark o' nature's fire'. English Lang Notes 7 1964.

—— Burns's comedy of romantic love. PMLA 83 1968.

Bentman, R. The romantic poets and critics on Burns. Texas Stud in Lit & Lang 6 1964.

—— Burns's use of Scottish diction. In From sensibility to romanticism: essays presented to F. A. Pottle, ed F. W. Hilles and H. Bloom, New York 1965.

Soviet critics and literary specialists on Burns. In Garland for Burns, Moscow 1964.

Legman, G. The hornbook: studies in erotic folklore and bibliography. New York 1964. Contains a section on the history of Merry Muses of Caledonia.

Mackenzie, M. L. A new dimension for Tam O'Shanter. Stud in Scottish Lit 1 1963.

Souffrin, E. Burns en France: ou l'image du poète laboureur. In Connaissance de l'étranger: mélanges offerts à la mémoire de Jean-Marie Carré, Paris 1964.

Tuttleton, J. W. The Devil and John Barleycorn: comic diablerie in Scott and Burns. Stud in Scottish Lit 1 1964.

Nimmo, I. Burns: his life and tradition in words and sound. 1965.

Sinclaire, R. A. On some Hungarian Burns translations. Nagyvilág 10 1965. 7 trns of O my luve's like a red, red rose.

Dent, A. Burns in his time. 1966.

Parks, S. Justice to William Creech. PBSA 60 1966. Reply by G. R. Roy 61 1967.

Granger, B. H. Folklore in Burns's Tam O'Shanter. In Folklore international: essays in traditional literature, belief and custom in honor of W. D. Hand, ed D. K. Wilgus, Hatboro Pa 1967.

Kolesnikob, B. I. Burns: sketch of his life and works. Moscow 1967.

Morozov, M. M. In his Shakespeare, Burns, Shaw, Moscow 1967. Rptd from Marshak's trns of Burns's works, Moscow 1950.

Brown, R. L. Clarinda: the intimate story of Burns and Agnes M'Lehose. Dewsbury 1968.

Gower, H. Burns in Limbo. Stud in Scottish Lit 5 1968. Oral anecdotes.

Stamm, R. Is there for honest poverty; Thou ling'ring star. In A. T. Riese and D. Riesner (ed), Versdichtung der englischen Romantik: Interpretationen, Berlin 1968.

Troutner, J. Tam O'Shanter's paths of glory: tone in Burns's narrative. Massachussetts Stud in Eng 1 1968.

An interesting history of Burns, the Ayrshire bard. Glasgow nd. A chapbook.

Anderson, T. R. Burns: the man and his songs. Glasgow nd.

Hewat, K. Burns and the parish. In A little Scottish world, as revealed in the annals of an ancient Ayrshire parish, Kilmarnock nd.

McGown, G. W. T. A primer of Burns. Paisley nd.

McMichael, A. C. In his Reflections by the way, Ayr nd.

Simonenko, I. P. Burns: Scottish poet. Kiev nd.

OTHER WRITERS 1750–1800

JOANNA BAILLIE
1762–1851
See vol 3, below.

LADY ANNE BARNARD
1750–1825
See Lady Anne Lindsay, below.

JAMES BEATTIE
1735–1803
See col 640, above.

THOMAS BLACKLOCK
1721–91

Bibliographies
Miller, F. A bibliography of the parish of Annan. Dumfries 1925.

Collections
Poems [with life by Henry Mackenzie]. Edinburgh 1793.

Complete edition of the poets of Great Britain vol 11. Ed R. Anderson, Edinburgh 1793.

The works of the English poets vol 18. Ed A. Chambers 1810.

Selections
The cabinet of poetry vol 6. [Ed J. Pratt] 1808.

The works of the British poets: supplementary vol 5 1808. Ed T. Park.

The works of the British poets vol 35. Ed R. Walsh [continuing after E. Sanford], Philadelphia 1822.

§ 1

Poems on several occasions. Glasgow 1746, Edinburgh 1754, London 1756 (with life by J. Spence) (3 edns), 1761. Title varies.

Advice to the ladies: a satyr. [Scotland] 1754.

An essay on universal etymology or the analysis of a sentence. Edinburgh 1756. Verse.

A collection of original poems by the Rev Mr Blacklock and other Scotch gentlemen. Edinburgh 1760, 1761. Vol 2 Edinburgh 1762 omits Blacklock's name and it is doubtful if he contributed to it; a contemplated 3rd vol was never issued.

Paraclesis: or consolations deduced from natural and revealed religion. Edinburgh 1767. Includes trn of Consolatio.

A poem occasioned by the death of Lady Cunynghame of Livingstone. Edinburgh 1772.

Panegyric on Great Britain: a poem. Edinburgh 1773.

The Graham: an heroic ballad, in four cantos. Edinburgh 1774, London 1774.

Remarks on the nature and extent of liberty, as compatible with the genius of civil societies by Valerius Corvinu. Edinburgh 1776. Anon. In answer to Richard Price, Observations on the nature of civil liberty.

A discourse on national music. Scots Mag Oct 1779.

A letter from Thomas Blacklock to the author respecting Burns. In Elizabeth Scot, Alonzo and Cora, 1801. Verse.

Blacklock also issued sermons separately and contributed songs to The Scots musical museum.

§ 2

Spence, J. An account of the life, character and poems of Mr Blacklock. 1754.

Miller, F. An unpublished topical poem by Dr Blacklock. Scottish Historical Rev 4 1907; also separately as Pistapolis, Glasgow 1907.
—— Dr Blacklock's manuscripts [in Annan Public Lib]. Scottish Historical Rev 10 1913.
Duncan, R. Blacklock and Burns. Burns Chron 23 1914.

MICHAEL BRUCE
1746–67
Collections

Poetical works, with a life. In Complete edition of the poets of Great Britain vol 11, ed R. Anderson 1795.
Poetical works. In Works of the British poets vol 41, ed T. Park 1808.
Works with a memoir and notes by A. B. Grosart. Edinburgh 1865, 1865.
Poetical works with a life by W. Stephen. Paisley 1895.
Life and complete works. Ed J. Mackenzie, Edinburgh 1914.
Life and complete works. Ed J. G. Barnet 1927, nd.
Life and works. Ed E. Vernon, Perth 1951.

Selections

Lochleven (and a selection of other poems). In British poets vol 60, Chiswick 1822 (life by R. A. Davenport).
Poems [a selection with poems by Beattie and Blair]. Edinburgh 1823.
Lochleven and other poems, with a life. Ed W. Macklevie, Edinburgh 1837.
Miscellaneous poems, with a memoir. Belfast 1854.

§ 1

Poems on several occasions. Ed J. Logan, Edinburgh 1770, Stirling 1782, Edinburgh 1796 (containing additional poems from the author's ms supplied by his mother, with Lord Craig's essay), 1807.
The Buchanshire tragedy: or Sir James the Ross [title varies, frequently using the name Rose]. [Edinburgh?] 1776, Glasgow [1796], Falkirk 1804, Edinburgh [1805?], Penrith [1805?], Greenock [1810?], Paisley 1814, Falkirk 1815, London 1818, Edinburgh [1820?] (3 issues), Falkirk [1820?], Stirling [1820?], Belfast 1823, Glasgow [1825?], Stirling [1825?], Glasgow 1828, [1828?], Liverpool [1830?], Brechin 1832, Glasgow [1835?], Aberdeen 1861, Glasgow 1869 (broadside), Dunfermline nd, nd. Most of the above were chap-books; probably many more were pbd. Sir James the Rose's garland [Newcastle 1775?] containing Sir James the Rose ('Did you hear of Sir James the Rose') is not by Bruce.
In 1781 Logan pbd a vol of poems purporting to be his own, but which contains Michael Bruce's Ode to the cuckoo and nine hymns. The hymns were adopted by the Church of Scotland.

§ 2

[Craig, W. (Lord)]. [Essay on Bruce signed P.]. Mirror 36 1779.
[Laing, D.] Ode to the cuckoo with remarks on its authorship. Edinburgh 1873.
Shairp, J. C. Bruce and the Ode to the cuckoo. Good Words 14 1873.
Small, J. Bruce and the authorship of the Ode to the cuckoo. Edinburgh 1877.
Matson, W. T. A complete vindication of the Rev J. Logan from the charge of stealing the hymns of Bruce. 1892.
'Inquirer'. The Bruce-Logan controversy. Scots Mag new ser 22 1898. In defence of Logan.
Mackenzie, J. Life of Bruce, poet of Loch Leven. 1905, Kinnesswood 1908, Edinburgh 1914 (rev in Life and complete works).

Young, R. S. Concerning the gentle poet of Loch Leven. Kinross [1930].
—— Further concerning the gentle poet of Loch Leven. Kinross 1942.
Smellie, P. Bruce and his evil genius John Logan. [Perth] 1933.
Vernon, E. T. The wronging of Bruce. Kinross 1943.
Snoddy, T. G. Bruce: shepherd poet of the Lomond Braes. Edinburgh [1947].
Bouslog, C. S. Coleridge, Bruce and the Ode to the west wind. N & Q Oct 1954.

ROBERT COLVILL
d. 1788
Collections

Poetical works. 2 vols 1789.

§ 1

Britain: a poem. Edinburgh 1757.
Eidyllia: or miscellaneous poems, with a hint to the British poets. Edinburgh 1757.
On the winter-solstice: a descriptive poem. Edinburgh 1765.
The field of Flowdon: a descriptive poem. 1768.
The fate of Julia: an epic poem, in two cantos, sacred to the memory of L–dy J–n D—g—s [Lady Jane Douglas]. Edinburgh 1769, London 1769 (3rd edn, title varies).
The merry wives of Douglas: or the Douglas garland, by a young gentleman. Edinburgh 1769.
The Caledonian heroine: or the invasion and fall of Sueno the Dane. Edinburgh 1771, 1771 (enlarged).
Occasional poems. Edinburgh 1771, London 1771 (2nd edn). Collection of separately ptd works.
The Albion princess: a pindaric ode. 1772.
The Cyrnean hero: a poem. Edinburgh 1772 (2nd edn). Contains notes on Boswell's account of Corsica.
Epithalamium on the marriage of Viscount Stormont with Louisa Cathcart. 1776 (2nd edn).
Atalanta [with other poems]. 1777, [Edinburgh 1779].
The Caledonians: a poem. Edinburgh 1779, 1779.
Savannah: a poem to the memory of Col John Maitland. 1780 (2nd edn).
The downfall of the Roman confederacy, or the ever memorable 12th of April 1782: a heroic poem in three cantos. Edinburgh 1788.

ROBERT FERGUSSON
1750–74
Bibliographies

Fairley, J. A. Records of Glasgow Bibl Soc 3 1915.

Collections

Poems. Edinburgh 1773.
Poems on various subjects. Edinburgh 1779 (pt 2 of 1773, above), 1782 (with poetry from 1773 and 1779), 1785, 1785, Perth 1788, 1789, Paisley 1796, 1799, Edinburgh 1799, St Andrews 1800.
Poetical works. Ed D. Irving, Glasgow 1800, Edinburgh 1805 (with a short life, unsigned), 1806; [ed A. Peterkin] 1807, 1807, Greenock 1810; ed J. Bannington 1809; 2 vols Alnwick [1812], 1812, 1813, 1816, [c. 1825] (2 issues, with woodcuts by T. Bewick), Philadelphia 1815; ed J. Gray, Edinburgh 1821, Glasgow 1821, 1821, Edinburgh 1821, Paisley 1825, Edinburgh 1840, 1871, Belfast 1845; ed A. B. Grosart 1851, 1857, 1862, 1879; ed R. Aitken, Edinburgh 1895, [1905], [1916?]; ed R. Ford, Paisley 1905, [1917]; ed M. P. McDiarmid 2 vols Edinburgh 1954–6 (STS).

Selections

Scots poems [added to] Robert Burns, Poems chiefly in the Scottish dialect. New York 1788.

Scots poems. Edinburgh 1898, London [1911], [1913]; ed B. Dickins, Edinburgh 1925; ed J. Telfer 1948.

The farmer's ingle and other poems. Ed J. Leatham, Peterhead 1898, 1898.

Selected poems. Ed A. Law, Edinburgh 1947.

§ 1

No repose can I discover. In G. F. Tenducci's adaptation of G. Rush's opera The royal shepherd, 1769. Probably Fergusson's first appearance in print.

By Heaven's displeasure the wretch thus is thrown; What doubts oppress my wounded heart; O where shall I wander my lover to find. In Artaxerxes: an English opera as it is performed at the Theatre-Royal Edinburgh, with music composed by T. A. Arne; with the addition of three favourite Scots airs, the words by Mr R. Fergusson, Edinburgh 1769. Libretto tr from Metastasio's Artaserse.

To Andrew Gray. Perth Mag of Knowledge & Pleasure 2 July 1773. In answer to a poem by Gray 11 June 1773. Gray answered 17 Sept. With 3 poems from Weekly Mag.

Auld Reekie. Edinburgh 1773.

Poem to the memory of John Cunningham. Edinburgh 1773.

Verses on visiting Dumfries. Dumfries Weekly Mag 26 Sept 1773.

The Edinburgh buck. A burlesque pbd as an epilogue to Garrick's Bucks have at ye all, Edinburgh [1783?].

On night. In Arthur Masson, A collection of prose and verse, Perth 1792.

The ghaists: a kail-yard eclogue. Paisley 1796. First pbd in Ruddiman's Weekly Mag.

The farmer's ingle. Glasgow [1798?]. 3 24 Brash & Reid chap-books.

The daft days: The King's birth-day in Edinburgh; and Braid claith. Edinburgh 1808.

Cape song. In Songs from David Herd's manuscripts, ed H. Hecht, Edinburgh 1904.

Unpublished poems. Ed W. E. Gillis, Edinburgh 1955. *62 of Fergusson's poems were first pbd in Ruddiman's Weekly Mag 1771–3.*

§ 2

Cumming, R. Essay delivered in the Pantheon, on Thursday, April 14 1791, on the question 'Whether have the exertions of Allan Ramsay or Robert Fergusson done most honour to Scottish poetry'. Edinburgh 1791. A poem.

Picken, E. and A. Wilson. The laurel disputed: or the merits of Allan Ramsay and Robert Ferguson disputed. Edinburgh 1791. Poems; Wilson's reissued Glasgow 1816.

Campbell, A. An introduction to the history of poetry in Scotland. Edinburgh 1798. Misdates Fergusson's birth 1751.

Irving, D. The life of Fergusson. Glasgow 1799; enlarged in Lives of Scotish authors: viz Fergusson, Falconer and Russell, Edinburgh 1801.

—— In his Lives of the Scottish poets vol 2, Edinburgh 1804, 1810.

Sommers, T. Life of Fergusson. Edinburgh 1803.

[Robertson, J.] In his Lives of Scottish poets pt 4, 1822.

Scottish poets: Fergusson and Burns. Renfrewshire Mag 1 1847.

Remarks on Burns [chiefly his relationship to Fergusson]. New Paisley Repository pt 3 Dec 1852.

Scottish poets: Ramsay and Fergusson. West of Scotland Mag & Rev 2 Nov 1857.

Miller, H. Recollections of Fergusson. In his Tales and sketches, Edinburgh 1863 etc.

'Haliburton, Hugh' (J. L. Robertson). In his For puir old Scotland's sake, Edinburgh 1887.

Macarthur, H. In his Realism and romance and other essays, Edinburgh 1897.

Grosart, A. B. Robert Fergusson. Edinburgh [1898].

Ritter, O. Quellenstudien zu Robert Burns 1773–91. Berlin 1901. On Fergusson's influence on Burns.

Holmes, D. T. Fergusson: son oeuvre et son influence. In his French essays on British poets, Glasgow 1902.

Beaumont, F. Fergusson and Burns: the shaping of the poet. Proc Royal Philosophical Soc of Glasgow 42 1911 and separately; rptd in Burns Chron 22 1913.

Douglas, G. In his Scottish poetry, Drummond of Hawthornden to Fergusson, Glasgow 1911.

Bennett, A. Fergusson: an eighteenth-century St Andrews student. St Andrews [1914].

Roughhead, W. A note on Fergusson. In his Riddle of the Ruthvens, Edinburgh 1919.

Green, F. C. Fergussons Anteil an der Literatur Schottlands. Heidelberg 1923.

Fairley, J. A. Fergusson: the published portraits. Aberdeen 1932.

Roy, J. A. Fergusson and eighteenth-century Scotland. UTQ 17 1948.

Paxton, K. Fergusson and Burns. Burns Chron 2nd ser 24 1949.

Smith, S. G. (ed). Fergusson: essays by various hands to commemorate the bicentenary of his birth. Edinburgh 1952.

Gillis, W. Fergusson's first printed work. N & Q Oct 1954.

—— An authentic Fergusson portrait. Stud in Scottish Lit 1 1964.

Law, A. Inscribed copies of the first edition (1773) of the poems of Fergusson. Trans Edinburgh Bibl Soc 3 1954.

MacLaine, A. H. Fergusson's The sow of feeling and Buckingham's The rehearsal. N & Q Nov 1957.

—— Fergusson's Auld Reekie and the poetry of city life. Stud in Scottish Lit 1 1964.

—— Robert Fergusson. New York 1965.

Mackie, A. Burns and Fergusson. Saltire Rev 6 1959.

ROBERT FORBES, gent

Ajax his speech to the Grecian Knabbs; to which is added a journal to Portsmouth, and a shopbill with a key. Glasgow 1755, Edinburgh 1765, [Edinburgh?] 1768, Aberdeen 1793, 1869. From Ovid, Metamorphoses bk 13.

Ovid in the Aberdeenshire dialect. Aberdeen 1848. Latin and trn of Ajax's speech to the Grecian knabbs, and Ulysses' answer to Ajax's speech.

WILLIAM FORBES

The dominie depos'd. Edinburgh 1765.

The dominie depos'd, with the sequel. [Edinburgh?] 1771, Edinburgh 1773 (14th edn), Glasgow [1799], [Glasgow?] 1829 (with Maggy Johnston's Elegy), Glasgow nd.

RICHARD GALL
1776–1801
Collections

Poems and songs with memoir of the author. Edinburgh 1819.

Songs with memoir. In Charles Rogers, The modern Scottish minstrel vol 2, Edinburgh 1855.

§ 1

The tint-quey: or thrawart Maggy. Edinburgh 1796. Anon.

DOUGAL GRAHAM
1724–79

Bibliographies

Fairley, J. A. Bibliography of the chapbooks attributed to Dougal Graham. Records of Glasgow Bibl Soc 1 1914.

Collections

Collected writings. Ed G. MacGregor 2 vols Glasgow 1883. With biography and critical introd.

§ 1

The battle of Drummossie-Muir. [Edinburgh?] 1746.
A full, particular and true account of the Rebellion in the years 1745–6. Glasgow 1746, 1752, 1774, 1787, 1796, 1803, 1808, Falkirk 1812, Aberdeen 1850. Title varies; verse.
A dialogue of courtship between Jockey and Maggy. [Glasgow?] 1775, Glasgow 1779, 1783, [Glasgow?] 1793, Glasgow 1801, Stirling 1802, 1807, [no place] 1812, Stirling 1814, Paisley 1815, [Paisley 1823], [no place] 1823, Glasgow 1839, Falkirk nd, Glasgow nd (3 edns), Newcastle nd (4 edns), Stirling nd (2 edns), [no place] nd (2 edns). Title varies.
The history and comical transactions of Lothian Tom. [Glasgow?] 1775, 1793, Stirling 1801, Glasgow 1807, Edinburgh 1816, Glasgow 1820, Kilmarnock 1820, Stirling 1822, 1822, Paisley 1823, 1828, Glasgow 1828, Edinburgh nd (3 edns), Falkirk nd (2 edns), Glasgow nd (3 edns), Stirling nd (2 edns). Title varies.
The witty exploits of George Buchanan, commonly called the King's fool. [no place] 1780, Edinburgh 1787, Dublin 1788, Glasgow 1795, Stirling 1795, 1799, Falkirk 1799, 1799, Edinburgh 1809, Paisley 1815, Edinburgh 1818, Kilmarnock 1821, Stirling 1828, Glasgow 1829, Aberdeen nd (2 edns), Dumfries nd, Edinburgh nd (2 edns), Elgin nd, Falkirk nd (2 edns), Glasgow nd (5 edns), Newcastle nd (12 edns), Penrith nd, Stirling nd (4 edns), Whitehaven nd, York nd. Title varies.
The young coal-man's courtship to a creel-wife's daughter. Glasgow 1782, [no place] 1820, Edinburgh nd (4 edns), Falkirk nd, Glasgow nd (3 edns), Stirling nd (4 edns), [no place] nd (2 edns). Title varies.
Also several other chap-books which enjoyed wide popularity.

§ 2

Fairley, J. A. Graham: Skellat bellman of Glasgow and his chap-books. Hawick 1908.
Harvey, W. D. Graham and his History of the Rebellion of 1745. Stirling 1924.

Rev JAMES GRAHAME
1765–1811

Collections

Poems. 2 vols 1807.
The poems of James Grahame, John Logan and William Falconer [with lives of the authors]. Edinburgh 1823.
Poetical works [with H. K. White]. Ed G. Gilfillan, Edinburgh 1856.
Poetical works of H. K. White and James Grahame. Ed C. C. Clarke [1878]. With life and notes.

§ 1

Poems in English, Scotch and Latin. Paisley 1794. Anon.
Rural calender. Paisley 1797.
Wallace: a tragedy. Edinburgh 1799. Anon.
Mary Stewart, Queen of Scots: an historical drama. Edinburgh 1801. Anon; blank verse.

The Sabbath. Edinburgh 1804 (anon), 1805 (anon, adds Sabbath walks), 1805, 1806 (signed), 1808, 1812, 1817, 1821, 1827, London 1825, Paisley 1831, Edinburgh 1839, London 1851 (in Cabinet edition of the British poets vol 3), 1857, [1863] (with G. Crabbe).
Biblical pictures. Edinburgh 1806.
The birds of Scotland, with other poems. Edinburgh 1806, Philadelphia 1807 (omits Biblical pictures).
Thoughts on trial by jury in civil causes. Edinburgh 1806. Anon.
The siege of Copenhagen: a poem. 1808, Edinburgh 1808, 1808, 1840.
Africa delivered: or the slave trade abolished. In J. Montgomery, Poems on the abolition of the slave trade, 1809.
British Georgics. Edinburgh 1809, 1812, 1821 (as Rural poems or British Georgics).

§ 2

[Wilson, J.]. Lines sacred to the memory of the Rev J. Grahame. Glasgow 1811.

ANNE GRANT of Laggan
1755–1838

§ 1

Poems on various subjects. Edinburgh 1803.
The Highlanders and other poems. 1808 (2nd edn), Edinburgh 1810.
Essays on the superstitions of the Highlanders of Scotland; to which are added translations from the Gaelic, and letters connected with those formerly published, by the author of Letters from the mountains. 2 vols 1811.
Eighteen hundred and thirteen: a poem in 2 parts. Edinburgh 1814.
Blue bell of Scotland [by Anne Grant], The watchman, [and] I won't be a nun. Boston [1835?]. Anon.
The touchstone: or the claims and privileges of true religion briefly considered. 1842.

Letters and Memoirs

Letters from the mountains: being the real correspondence of a lady between 1773 and 1807. 3 vols 1807 (3 edns), 2 vols Boston 1809 (1st Amer edn from 3rd London edn), 3 vols 1809, 1813; ed J. P. Grant 2 vols 1845.
Memoirs of an American lady (Catalina Schuyler); with sketches of manners and scenery in America, as they existed to the Revolution, by the author of Letters from the mountains. 2 vols 1808, 1809, 1817, New York 1846, 1901 (with unpbd letters and a memoir by J. G. Wilson).
Memoir and correspondence of Mrs Grant. Ed J. P. Grant 3 vols 1844.
Letters concerning Highland affairs in the 18th century [with Diary of Sir Archibald Johnston, Lord Wariston, 1639 et al; an important body of Jacobite source material]. Pbns of Scottish Historical Soc 26 1896.

§ 2

'Paston, George' (E. M. Symonds). Mrs Grant of Laggan. In her Little memoirs of the eighteenth century, 1901.

ANNE HOME, later HUNTER
1742–1821

Selections

Songs. In C. Rogers, The modern Scottish minstrel vol 1, Edinburgh 1855 (with memoir).

§I

Poems. 1802, 1803.
A new ballad, entitled and call'd the Times, by A.H. [1804?].
The sports of the genii. 1804.

JOHN HOME
1722–1808

See col 840, above.

CHARLES KEITH
d. 1807

The farmer's ha': a Scots poem, by a student of Marischal College. Aberdeen 1776, Edinburgh 1804 (signed), 1808, nd.
The har'st rig, and the Farmer's ha': two poems in the Scottish dialect. Edinburgh 1801 (2nd edn). Anon.
Monody to the memory of the Rev Dr Charles Nisbet. Edinburgh 1805. Anon.

LADY ANNE LINDSAY,
afterwards BARNARD
1750–1825

§I

The history of Old Robin Gray: an ancient Scotch tale. [Edinburgh?] 1783; ed W. Scott, Edinburgh 1825 (Bannatyne Club).
Lays of the Lindsays. [Ed W. Scott], Edinburgh 1824.

Letters and Diaries

Extracts from the journal of a residence at the Cape of Good Hope. In A. W. C. Lindsay, Lives of the Lindsays, 4 vols Wigan 1840, London 1849, 1858.
South Africa a century ago: letters written from the Cape of Good Hope 1797–1801. Ed W. H. Wilkins 1901 (with memoir), [1925]; ed H. J. Anderson 2 pts Cape Town [1924].

§2

Tytler, S. and J. L. Watson. In their Songstresses of Scotland vol 2, 1871.
Fairbridge, D. Lady A. Barnard at the Cape of Good Hope. Oxford 1924.
Masson, M. Lady A. Barnard. 1948.

JOHN LOGAN
1748–88

See col 668, above.

JOHN LOWE
1750–98

Remains of Nithsdale and Galloway song. 1810.

HECTOR MacNEILL
1746–1818
Collections

Poetical works. 2 vols 1801, New York 1802, Edinburgh 1806 (corrected and enlarged), 1812, Philadelphia 1815, Edinburgh 1856.
The works of the British poets, with lives vol 39 (Burns and MacNeill). Ed E. Sanford, Philadelphia 1822.
Select Scottish poets, 1st series: the complete practical works of Robert Tannahill, Hector McNeill and Allan Ramsay. Belfast 1844.

Selections

The Scottish melodist containing choice songs from Burns, Ramsay, MacNeill etc. Edinburgh [1813].
Songs. In C. Rogers, The modern Scottish minstrel vol 1, Edinburgh 1855 (with memoir).
The poetical works of Allan Ramsay, with selections from the Scottish poets before Burns. Ed C. Mackay 2 vols [1866–8].
Burns, Ramsay and the earlier poets of Scotland. Ed A. Cunningham and C. Mackay 2 vols [1878–9].

§I

The harp: a legendary tale in two parts. Edinburgh 1789.
The links o' Forth: or a parting peep at the Carse of Stirling. Edinburgh 1795, 1799.
Scotland's skaith: or the history o' Will and Jean. Edinburgh 1795, 1795, Stirling 1795 (8th edn), Workington 1797 ('8th edn'), Edinburgh 1800, Jedburgh [1800?], Edinburgh 1808, Stirling 1816, Brechin [1836], Newcastle nd (10th edn).
The waes o' war: or the upshot o' the history o' Will and Jean. Edinburgh 1796, 1804, 1804, [Glasgow 1820?], nd (also pbd with Scotland's skaith, above).
Politics, or the history of Will and Jane: a tale for the times. 1796.
An advice from an old lover to a young wife. Glasgow [1798], [1799].
Come under my plaidie. [no place] 1798, Stirling [1800?], Edinburgh 1819, [1825?] The songs which accompany this work vary from edn to edn.
Memoirs of the life and travels of the late Charles Macpherson. Edinburgh 1800. Prose.
Observations on the treatment of the negroes in the Island of Jamaica. [London 1800?].
The pastoral or lyric Muse of Scotland in three cantos. Edinburgh 1808, London 1808, Philadelphia 1813.
Town fashions: or modern manners delineated; with James and Mary: a rural tale. Edinburgh 1810.
Bygane times and late come changes. Edinburgh 1811, 1811.
The Scottish adventures: or the way to rise, an historic tale. 2 vols Edinburgh 1812, New York 1812 (prose); abridged in Chambers miscellany vol 8, Edinburgh 1846.
Many of the above edns were pbd anon. 7 poems appear in the Brash & Reid chapbooks, Glasgow [1795?–9]. MacNeill has also been credited with the authorship of Watty and Meg; see Alexander Wilson, below.

JAMES MACPHERSON
1736–96

See col 603, above.

JOHN MAYNE
1759–1836
Selections

Songs. In C. Rogers, The modern Scottish minstrel vol 1, Edinburgh 1855 (with memoir).

§I

The siller gun. Dumfries 1777, 1779 (extended to 2 cantos), 1780 (3 cantos), Glasgow 1783, Gloucester 1803 (4 cantos), 1808, London 1836 (5 cantos), Edinburgh [1958].
English, Scots and Irishmen. [London] 1803. An address on the threatened invasion. Single sheet, verse.
Glasgow: a poem. 1803, Gloucester 1803.

CAROLINE OLIPHANT, BARONESS NAIRNE
1766–1845

Collections

Life and songs of the Baroness Nairne. Ed C. Rogers 1869, 1869, Edinburgh 1872, 1896, 1905 (with a memoir and poems of Caroline Oliphant the younger).
Songs. Edinburgh 1902.
The songs of Lady Nairne. 1911, 1912.
Songs of the Baroness Nairne: calendar for the year 1911. Edinburgh nd.
Lady Carolina Nairne and her songs, arranged A. Reid. [c. 1900].
Lays from Strathearn, arranged with symphonies and accompaniments for the pianoforte. nd.

Selections

Wha'll be King but Charlie? Boston [1835?]. A broadside.
Songs. In C. Rogers, The modern Scottish minstrel vol 1, Edinburgh 1855 (with memoir).
Charlie is my darling: Jacobite songs of Lady Nairne. [Edinburgh] nd.

§ 2

Tytler, S. and J. L. Watson. In their Songstresses of Scotland vol 2, 1871.
Simpson, M. S. The Scottish songstress Caroline Baroness Nairne. Edinburgh 1894.
Henderson, G. Lady Nairne and her songs. Paisley [1900], [1901], [1905], [1906], [1908] (each issue enlarged).
Crichton, A. The land o' the leal: who wrote it, Lady Nairne or Burns? Dunedin 1903, Peterhead 1919 (3rd edn). Title varies; the poem is usually attributed to Lady Nairne.
Montgomerie, W. Two songs by Lady Nairne. Scottish Stud 2 1957. The Laird o' Cockpen and Kitty Reid's house.
— The land o' the leal. Scottish Stud 3 1959.

Rev JOHN SKINNER
1721–1807

Collections

Theological works, to which is prefixed a biographical memoir of the author. 2 vols Aberdeen 1809; vol 3, Miscellaneous collection of fugitive pieces of poetry [Latin and English], Edinburgh 1809.

Selections

John of Badenyon's garland: containing several excellent new songs. [Newcastle 1785?].
Amusements of leisure hours or poetical pieces, chiefly in the Scottish dialect (with a life). [Ed J. Skinner, the author's son], Edinburgh 1809. Identical, except for the omission of 2 poems, to the English poetry in vol 3 of Works, above.
Songs. In C. Rogers, The modern Scottish minstrel vol 1, Edinburgh 1855 (with memoir).
Songs and poems. Ed H. G. Reid, Peterhead 1859.
Poems and songs. Ed J. Leatham, Peterhead 1900.

§ 1

A dissertation on Jacob's prophecy. 1757. Anon.
The old Scots poem of Chryste-Kirk on the green, attempted in Latin heroic verses [with the text of the original]. [Aberdeen] 1772 (anon), Edinburgh 1813 (anon). Title varies.

John o' Badenyon. [Edinburgh?] 1776, Falkirk [1795?], [no place 1800?], 1801, Falkirk 1813, 1814. Title varies.
Tullochgorum. [Edinburgh?] 1776, Stirling [1820?], Glasgow nd.
An ecclesiastical history of Scotland. 2 vols 1788.
Widow Greylocks. [Ed W. Walker, Aberdeen 1913].
A garland from the vernacular and other verses. Aberdeen 1921.
Most of these were chap-books and the songs varied from issue to issue. Several other early chap-books include songs by Skinner. 7 lyrics, including John o' Badenyon and Tullochgorum, were pbd in the Brash & Reid chapbooks, Glasgow [1795?–9].

§ 2

Walker, W. The life and times of Skinner. 1883, 1883, Aberdeen 1887.
Murdoch, J. B. Burns and 'Tullochgorum.' Burns Chron 21 1912.
Keith, A. A Skinner ms. Aberdeen Univ Rev 27 1940.

ALEXANDER WILSON
1766–1813

Collections

Poetical works; also miscellaneous prose, with a life. Belfast 1844, 1853, nd, Paisley 1857.
Poems and literary prose. Ed A. B. Grosart 2 vols Paisley 1876.

Selections

Poems. Paisley 1790.
Poems: humorous, satirical and serious. Edinburgh 1791 (2nd edn, from Paisley 1790, above).
Poems chiefly in the Scottish dialect. 1816, Glasgow 1830.
Poems, with a life. Paisley 1816.

§ 1

The Hollander, or light weight: a poem. Paisley [1790], [Paisley?] nd.
The laurel disputed: or the merits of Allan Ramsay and Robert Ferguson contrasted in two poetical essays. Edinburgh 1791, Glasgow 1816 (Wilson's poem only). One of the poems was by Ebenezer Picken.
The shark, or Lang Mills detected: a poem. [Paisley] 1792, 1832, Glasgow 1876. Title varies.
The tears of Britain: a poem. [Paisley? 1793?].
The loss o' the pack: a true tale. Glasgow [1796], [Glasgow? 1850?] (with The pack's answer), [Scotland?] nd.
Rab and Ringan: a tale in verse. Glasgow [1796], Paisley 1827, [Scotland?] nd.
Watty and Meg: or the wife reformed. [Scotland?] 1795 (copy Mitchell Lib], Glasgow [1796], 1801, Cupar 1801, Newcastle 1801, Falkirk 1802, Philadelphia 1805, Edinburgh 1808, Stirling [1810?], Glasgow 1816, Falkirk [1820?], Glasgow [1820?], Paisley 1826, Glasgow 1828, Kilmarnock [1840?], Newcastle [1840] (with poems by Hogg and Thomas Campbell), Glasgow 1858, Paisley [1860?], Glasgow 1861, nd, Newcastle nd, [Scotland?] nd. Anderson's new group of the parting scene of Watty and Meg, [Scotland? 1845]. Title varies; frequently includes other poems. This work has also been attributed to Hector MacNeil and James Wilson of Paisley.
Oration on the power and value of national liberty. Philadelphia 1801, 1818.
A rural walk. Literary Mag & Amer Register 2 Aug 1804 (signed A.W.); rptd Port folio.
The solitary tutor. Literary Mag & Amer Register 2 Oct 1804; [Paisley 1809], Paisley 1817 (to which is added the Hummingbird).
Poetical hints to a certain character (Johnny M—r). [Paisley 1809].

The foresters: a poem descriptive of a pedestrian journey to the falls of Niagara in the autumn of 1803, by the author of American ornithology. [Philadelphia 1809–10], Newton Pa 1818 (with date corrected to 1804), Paisley 1825, West Chester Pa 1838.

The spouter: a true tale. Belfast 1847. Verse.

New way of raising the wind: or Habbie Simpson and his wife [and] the Loss of the pack. Glasgow [1868].

Wilson was the noted ornithologist who emigrated to the United States in 1794. Only his literary productions are here listed. The first edn of Watty and Meg was probably pbd in 1792, and was so highly thought of that is was popularly ascribed to Burns. There were many chap-books containing poems by Wilson.

§ 2

Ord, G. Biographical sketch of Wilson. In Wilson's American ornithology vol 9, Philadelphia 1814.

—— Sketch of the life of Wilson, author of the American ornithology. Philadelphia 1828. Enlarged from 1814, above.

'Senex' (T. Crichton). Biographical sketches of the late Wilson. Weaver's Mag 2 Aug 1819.

Memoir of Wilson. Philadelphia 1831.

Dickson, J. B. The life, labours and genius of Wilson: a lecture. Paisley 1856.

Brightwell, C. L. Difficulties overcome: scenes in the life of Wilson. 1861.

Wilson, J. S. Wilson: poet-naturalist. New York 1906. With selection of Wilson's poems.

Cantwell, R. Wilson: naturalist and pioneer. Philadelphia [1961].

Plate, R. Wilson: wanderer in the wilderness. New York 1966.

Hunter, C. Wilson: poet and ornithologist. Burns Chron 3rd ser 16 1967.

JAMES WILSON
d. 1787

The last speech and dying words of the Cross of Edinburgh. [Edinburgh 1756].

The serious advice and exhortation of the Royal Exchange to the Bloody Cross of Edinburgh, immediately before its execution. [Edinburgh 1756?].

Poems on sundry occasions. [Edinburgh] 1758.

The vindication of a right honourable gentleman. [Edinburgh? 1760?]. A satire.

Poems on several occasions. Edinburgh 1762.

The last speech, confession and dying words of the Nether-bow Porch of Edinburgh. [Edinburgh 1764?]. Prose.

Miscellanies in prose and verse on several occasions. Edinburgh 1766; 2nd pt, 1767; 1771 (4th edn with addns).

A caution against mobing, with a petition to the King. [Edinburgh 1770?].

Ars Catchpolaria: or the art of destroying mankind. Edinburgh 1775.

All of Wilson's works were pbd under the pseudonym Claudero.

JOHN WILSON
1720–89

The Earl of Douglas: a dramatick essay. 1760.

Earl Douglas, or generosity betray'd: a tragedy; Clyde: a poem. Glasgow 1764. A more developed version of preceding.

Clyde: a poem. In Scottish descriptive poems, ed J. Leyden, Edinburgh 1803, London 1850, nd (separately, with life).

III. PROSE

A. THEOLOGY AND RELIGIOUS CONTROVERSY
(a) 1660–1707

General Works

Smith, J. A descriptive catalogue of Friends' books. 2 vols 1867; suppl 1893.

Smith, J. Bibliotheca anti-Quakeriana: or a catalogue of books adverse to the Society of Friends. 1873.

MacGregor, M. B. The sources and literature of Scottish church history. Glasgow 1934. MacGregor is the authority for certain unlocated edns.

Burnet, G. B. The story of Quakerism in Scotland 1650–1850. 1952.

WILLIAM ANNAND
1633–89

A funeral elegie upon the death of George Sonds. 1655. A broadside.

Fides Catholica: or the doctrine of the Catholic Church. 1661.

Panem quotidianum; with defence of the Book of common prayer. 1661, 1661.

Pater noster, our Father: or the Lord's Prayer explained. 1670, Edinburgh 1670.

Mysterium pietatis: or the mysterie of godlinesse. 1671, Edinburgh 1671.

Doxologia. 1672.

Dualitas, or a twofold subject displayed: the honour of magistracy and the agreement of magistracy and ministry. Edinburgh 1674.

ROBERT BARCLAY
1648–90

See col 1648, above.

THOMAS BELL,
Regent of Edinburgh University
fl. 1665

Roma restituta: sive antiquitatum romanarum compendium absolutum. Glasgow 1672, 1673, 1674, London 1677, Amsterdam 1700.

Grapes in the wilderness: or the solid grounds of sweet consolation. [Edinburgh?] 1680, Edinburgh 1692, 1785, Glasgow 1785, 1795. Title varies.

Nehemiah the Tirshatha: or the character of a good commissioner; to which is added Grapes in the wilderness [2 sermons ed L. R. Bell]. Edinburgh 1692.

Romanorum antiquitates. Amsterdam 1716.

JOHN BROWN,
Minister of the Gospel at Wamphray
1610?–79

§ 1

An apologicall relation of the particular sufferings of the faithful ministers and professours of the Church of Scotland since August 1660. [no place] 1665, Edinburgh 1844, 1845.

Libri duo: in priori, Wolzogium in libellis duobus de interprete Scripturarum. Amsterdam 1670.

Quakerism the pathway to paganism: or a view of the Quakers religion. Edinburgh 1671, 1678 (ptd Holland?).

Christ, the way and the truth and the life. Rotterdam 1677, Glasgow 1678, 1737, Edinburgh 1740, 1790, 1839. Also in J. Wesley, A Christian library vol 21.

The history of the indulgence; together with a demonstration of the unlawfulness thereof. [Edinburgh?] 1678, 1695. Also in J. Howie (ed), Faithful witness-bearing exemplified, Kilmarnock 1783.

The life of faith in time of trial. [Edinburgh] 1679, Edinburgh 1716, 1726, Paisley 1824. A 2nd pt was issued as Swan song, [no place] 1680.

Christ in believers the hope of glory. Edinburgh 1694, Glasgow 1719, 1736, 1763, London 1832, 1834, 1837, 1863.

The life of justification opened. [Utrecht?] 1695.

A pious and elaborate treatise concerning prayer. Glasgow 1745, 1822 (3rd edn with life of author).

A mirror or looking-glass for saint and sinner. Glasgow 1793.

Also other religious tracts.

§ 2

Lockerby, T. A sketch of the life of Brown, minister in Wamphray. Edinburgh 1839.

JAMES CLARK, Presbyterian Minister
d. 1724

Bibliographies

Couper, W. J. The writings and controversies of Clark. Records of Glasgow Bibl Soc 11 1933.

§ 1

Memento mori: or a word in season to the healthful, sick and dying. Edinburgh 1699, 1718.

Presbyterial government in the Church of Scotland, methodically described. Edinburgh 1701, 1703, [Edinburgh?] 1717.

The spiritual merchant: or the art of merchandizing spiritualized. Glasgow 1703.

A plea against pamphlets. Edinburgh 1703. A broadside.

The picture of the present generation. Edinburgh [1704]; reissued without dedication as The debauchery and vices of the present age, Edinburgh 1707.

A paper concerning Daniel DeFoe. Edinburgh 1708.

A just reprimand to Daniel de Foe. Edinburgh [1709?]. Anon reply, A reproof to Mr Clark and a brief vindication of Mr De Foe, Edinburgh 1710.

An advertisement from Scotland to England. [Edinburgh] 1710.

The practical atheist. Edinburgh 1721. Anon; sometimes attributed to James Porterfield.

Clark's other works include several separate sermons.

THOMAS FORRESTER, Principal of St
Mary's College, University of St Andrews
1635?–1706

The hierarchical Bishop's claim to a divine right tried at the Scripture-bar. Edinburgh 1699.

Also other controversial tracts.

WILLIAM GEDDES, Minister of Wick
1600?–94

The saint's recreation: third part, upon the estate of grace. Edinburgh 1683 (in verse, the only portion pbd), Glasgow 1753, 1758 (with Supplement of fifteen select poems on divine subjects from other approven authors).

WILLIAM GUTHRIE
1620–65

§ 1

A short treatise of the Christian's great interest. Edinburgh 1659 etc. Title varies.

Two sermons preached at Finnick, the 17 day of August 1662. [Edinburgh?] 1680.

Crumbs of comfort: or grace in its various degrees. [Edinburgh?] 1681.

Memoir and letters. Ed W. Muir, Edinburgh 1827.

§ 2

Watson, J. L. The lives and times of the two Guthries: or sketches of the Covenants. Glasgow 1877.

ANDREW HONYMAN, Bishop of Orkney
d. 1676

§ 1

The seasonable case of submission to the Church-government, as now re-established by law, briefly stated and determined. Edinburgh 1662.

A survey of the insolent and infamous libel entitled Naphtali. [Edinburgh] 1668; Part II, Edinburgh 1669.

§ 2

[Stewart, Sir J.] Jus populi vindicatum, or the people's right to defend themselves: a reply to the first part of the Survey. [London?] 1669.

WILLIAM JAMESON, Professor of History,
University of Glasgow

Verus Patroclus: or the weapons of Quakerism the weakness of Quakerism. Edinburgh 1689.

Mr John Davidson's catechism; also containing several things useful for determining of the Episcopal controversy. [no place] 1708.

The summ of the episcopal controversy, as it is pleaded from the holy Scriptures. Edinburgh 1712, Glasgow 1713 (enlarged), 1714.

Spicilegia antiquitatum Aegypti, atque ei vicinarum gentium. Glasgow 1720.

Also other anti-episcopalian tracts.

GEORGE KEITH, Rector of Edburton
1638–1716

§ 1

Help in time of need from the God of help. [London? or Amsterdam? 1665?].

Immediate revelation. [London? or Amsterdam?] 1668, [London] 1675 (with appendix), 1676.

An account of the oriental philosophy: shewing the wisdom of some renowned men of the East, and particularly the profound wisdom of Hai Ebn Yokhdan. [London?] 1674.

The deism of William Penn and his brethren exposed. 1699. Reply by E. Elys, A vindication of the doctrine concerning the light-within, against the objections of G. Keith, 1699.

A serious call to the Quakers, inviting them to return to Christianity. 1700, [1700?], [London] 1700, 1702 (3rd edn), [London] 1706, 1709.

The standard of the Quakers examined: or an answer to the Apology of Robert Barclay. 1702.

A journal of travels from New Hampshire to Caratuck, on the continent of North America. 1706; rptd in Protestant Episcopal Historical Soc Collections vol 1, 1851.

The magic of Quakerism: or the chief mysteries of Quakerism laid open. 1707.

Also many other Quaker treatises.

§ 2

Whitehead, G. The power of Christ vindicated against the magic of apostacy, in answer to Keith's book. 1708.

—— Light and truth triumphant: or Keith's imagined magic of Quakerism confirmed. 1711.

Nicolson, M. H. Keith and the Cambridge Platonists. Philosophical Rev 39 1930.

Kirby, E. W. George Keith. New York 1942. With bibliography.

ROBERT LEIGHTON
1611–84

See vol 1, above.

JOHN LIVINGSTONE
1603–72

A letter written by Livingstone unto his parishioners of Ancrum in Scotland, dated Rotterdam, October 7 1671. [no place] 1710 (2nd edn).

A brief historical relation of Mr John Livingston, minister of the Gospel, written by himself in Holland during his banishment. [no place] 1727, Glasgow 1754, 1773; ed T. Houston, Edinburgh 1848.

John Livingstone's views of a believer's duty, when the Church is invaded by the civil power. Edinburgh 1841, [1842?].

ROBERT McWARD
1633?–87

Collections

A collection of tracts. Dalry 1805.

§ 1

The case of the accommodation lately proposed by the bishop of Dunblane. [no place] 1671.

The true non-conformist. [no place] 1671.

The English ballance weighing the reasons of England's present conjunction with France, against the Dutch. [no place] 1672.

The poor man's cup of cold water. [no place] 1678, 1681, Edinburgh 1709; rptd with The banders disbanded, below, in A collection of tracts, Dalry 1805.

The banders disbanded. [no place] 1681.

ΕΠΑΓΩΝΙΣΜΟΙ: or earnest contendings for the faith. [Edinburgh?] 1723.

ALEXANDER MONRO DD
d. 1715?

Presbyterian inquisition. 1691. Anon.

A letter to a friend, giving an account of all the treatises that have been publish'd, with relation to the present persecution against the Church of Scotland. 1692. Anon.

An apology for the clergy of Scotland. 1693. Anon.

A collection of all the acts of Parliament relating to the clergy and ecclesiastical affairs within the Kingdom of Scotland since the Revolution. 1693. Anon.

Sermons preached upon several occasions. 1693.

An enquiry into the new opinions, chiefly propagated by the Presbyterians of Scotland. 1696.

Account of the Reformation. Edinburgh 1719.

Also other works.

ALEXANDER PEDEN
1626?–86

§ 1

The Lord's trumpet sounding an alarm against Scotland. [Glasgow?] 1682, [Glasgow? 1720?], Glasgow 1739, 1779, Newburyport Mass 1798.

A most strange and wonderful prophecy in the year 1684. [Edinburgh? before 1715].

Some remarkable passages of the life and death of Mr A. Peden [extracted from his life by P. Walker]. [Edinburgh] 1724, Glasgow 1738, Philadelphia 1758, Glasgow 1760, London 1774, Glasgow 1781, Falkirk 1815, Ayr 1817; ed J. Duncan 1774 (abridged). Title varies.

The life of Peden. [Edinburgh? 1788], Blackley 1791.

The life and prophecies of Peden [collected by P. Walker]. Edinburgh 1799, Falkirk 1810, Paisley 1814, Stirling [1820?], Falkirk 1821, Glasgow [1835?], 1838, [1850?], 1868, Dumfries nd, Edinburgh nd; to which is added his letter to the prisoners of Dunnotar Castle, July 1685, Glasgow, 1868 1872, Newton-Stewart nd, Stirling nd.

Most of these edns were chap-books; probably many more were issued.

§ 2

Walker, P. Life. In his Biographia presbyteriana, ed J. Stevenson, 2 vols Edinburgh 1827; also in Six saints of the Covenant, ed D. H. Fleming 2 vols 1901.

Brown, A. M. Peden the prophet: a tale of the Covenanters founded on fact. 1859.

Watson, J. L. Life and times of Peden. Glasgow 1881.

Johnston, J. C. Peden the prophet of the Covenant. Glasgow 1902.

Bigger, F. J. Peden the prophet. Ulster Jnl of Archaeology new ser 10 1903.

Cameron, T. Peden the prophet. [1938].

ALEXANDER REID, Scottish Covenanter
1640–1706

Life of a Scottish covenanter by himself. Ed A. Prentice, Manchester 1822.

A short account of the Lord's gracious, merciful and remarkable providences, both in spiritual and in temporal things to Alexander Reid 1660–93. Edinburgh 1825.

GILBERT RULE, Principal of University of Edinburgh

1629?–1701

§ I

A rational defence of non-conformity. 1689.
True representation of Presbyterian government. Edinburgh 1690.
A vindication of the Church of Scotland. 1691, 1691, Edinburgh 1691.
A second vindication of the Church of Scotland. Edinburgh 1691, London 1691.
A just and modest reproof of a pamphlet [by Gilbert Crokatt and John Monroe] called the Scotch Presbyterian eloquence. Edinburgh 1693.
Defence of the Vindication of the Church of Scotland. Edinburgh 1694.
A discourse of suppressing immorality and promoting godliness. Edinburgh 1701.
Also other theological works.

§ 2

'Curate, J.' (G. Crokatt and J. Monroe). The Scotch Presbyterian eloquence: or the foolishness of their teaching discovered from their books. 1692 etc. Other pamphlets by various authors followed.
On the death of Mr Gilbert Rule, Principal of the College of Edinburgh. [Edinburgh?] 1701. A broadside.

JOHN SAGE, Bishop of Episcopalian Church in Scotland

1652–1711

Collections

Works, with memoir and notes. Ed C. F. Shand 3 vols Edinburgh 1844–6 (Spottiswoode Soc).

§ I

The case of the present afflicted [episcopal] clergy in Scotland truly represented. 1690.
An account of the late establishment of Presbyterian government by the Parliament of Scotland anno 1690. 1692, 1693.
The fundamental charter of presbytery, as it hath been lately established in the Kingdom of Scotland, examin'd and disprov'd. 1695, 1697.
The principles of the Cyprianic age, with regard to episcopal power and jurisdiction asserted. 1695, Savoy 1695, London 1717.
A vindication of a discourse entitled the Principles of the Cyprianic age. 1701.
The reasonableness of a toleration to those of the episcopal persuasion. Edinburgh 1704, London 1705.
An account of the present persecution of the [Episcopal] Church in Scotland. 1792.
Also other controversial tracts on Episcopacy in Scotland.

§ 2

Gillan, J. The life of Sage. 1714.

HENRY SCOUGAL, Professor in King's College, Aberdeen

1650–78

Collections

Works. 2 vols Aberdeen 1759, 1 vol 1765, London 1818, Glasgow 1830.

§ I

The life of God in the soul of man: or the nature and excellency of the Christian religion. 1677, 1691, 1707 etc.
Private reflections and occasional meditations, together with some essays, moral and divine; to which is prefix'd a particular account of the author's life. 1740, Aberdeen 1765.
Notes upon and illustrations of the treatise the Life of God in the soul of man. Edinburgh 1744.
Discourses on important subjects. Glasgow 1751. 9 sermons.

§ 2

Menzies, J. Positiones aliquot theologicae de objecto cultus religiosi, quas in Academia regia Aberdonensi propugnabit Scougall. [Aberdeen] 1674.
Butler, D. Scougal and the Oxford Methodists. 1899.

ALEXANDER SHIELDS

1660?–1700

§ I

A hind let loose: or an historical representation of the testimony of the Church of Scotland for the interest of Christ. [Edinburgh?] 1687 (anon), Edinburgh 1744, Glasgow 1797.
An elegie upon the death of that famous minister Mr James Renwick. [Edinburgh] 1688, 1723.
A short memorial of the sufferings and grievances of the Presbyterians called by nickname Cameronians. [Edinburgh?] 1690.
The history of Scotch presbytery: being an epitome of the Hind let loose. 1692.
A true and faithful relation of the sufferings of Mr Alexander Shields written with his own hand. [no place] 1715.
The life and death of Mr James Renwick. Edinburgh 1724, Glasgow 1806; rptd in Biographia presbyteriana vol 2, Edinburgh 1827.
The Scots inquisition. Edinburgh 1745.
Biographia presbyteriana, by Patrick Walker and Shields. Edinburgh 1827.
A collection of letters by the Rev James Renwick and Shields. Ed J. M'Millan, Edinburgh 1764.
Also many other pamphlets. Shields was sent out in 1699 as minister to the Darien Expedition and died in Jamaica on his return voyage.

§ 2

MacPherson, H. The Cameronian philosopher Shields. Edinburgh 1932.

SIR JAMES STEWART of Goodtrees

d. 1713

§ I

Naphthali: or the wrestlings of the Church of Scotland for the kingdom of Christ. [Edinburgh?] 1667, [Edinburgh] 1680, [no place] 1693, Glasgow 1721, Edinburgh 1761, Glasgow 1803, Perth 1845. With James Stirling. For a reply *see* A. Honyman, *above.*
Jus populi vindicatum: or the people's right to defend themselves and their covenanted religion, vindicated. [London? Holland?] 1669.
An account of Scotland's grievances by reason of the Duke of Lauderdale's ministry. [London? 1674?] (2 edns). Also in State Tracts 1689, 1693.
The oath of abjuration, set in its true light. Edinburgh 1712.

§ 2

To the memory of Sir J. Stewart, elder. [no place 1713]. A verse broadside.

A second elegy upon the death of Stewart. [no place 1713?]. A broadside.

JAMES WEBSTER, Minister of Tolbooth Church, Edinburgh

1658?–1720

§ 1

A discourse demonstrating that the government of the Church, which is of divine right, is fixed and not ambulatory. Edinburgh [1703], 1704.

An essay upon toleration. [Edinburgh?] 1703. Anon.

Sacramental sermons and discourses at the Lord's table. Edinburgh 1705.

Three poems: Mahanaim, Peniel and the Triumph consummat. [no place] 1706. Signed J. W.

Lawful prejudices against an incorporating union with England: or some modest considerations on the sinfulness of this union, and the danger flowing from it to the Church of Scotland. Edinburgh 1707. Reply by Defoe, Dissenters in England, vindicated from some reflections in a late pamphlet entitled Lawful prejudices, 1707.

The author of the Lawful prejudices against an incorporating union with England, defended, in answer to a pamphlet entitled the Dissenters in England vindicated [by Defoe]. Edinburgh 1707.

The author of the Lawful prejudices against the union defended against the attack of DF. [no place 1707].

The author of the Lawful prejudices defended. Edinburgh 1707. Anon.

A second defence of the Lawful prejudices. [no place 1707]. Several other pamphlets by divers authors for and against Webster followed.

Webster is also author of numerous pbd sermons and pamphlets.

§ 2

Threnodia: a funeral poem to the memory of Webster. Edinburgh 1720. A collection of 4 poems on Webster.

(b) 1707–1800

General Works

Mechie, S. The Church and Scottish social development 1780–1870. 1960.

Riley, P. J. W. The English ministers and Scotland 1707–27. 1964.

GEORGE ANDERSON, Minister of the Tron Church, Edinburgh

1676?–1756

§ 1

The entertainment of the stage: a corrupt and sinful entertainment. Edinburgh 1727. Anon. In answer to Allan Ramsay, Some few hints in defence of dramatic entertainment, [Edinburgh c. 1727]. There must have been an earlier work, as Anderson here writes of 'having shown elsewhere . . .'.

The use and abuse of diversions: a sermon, with an appendix shewing that the stage in particular is an unchristian diversion. Edinburgh 1733, 1733. Anon reply, Some remarks upon the Rev Anderson's positions concerning the unlawfulness of stage plays, Edinburgh 1733.

A reinforcement of the reasons proving that the stage is an unchristian diversion: or a vindication of the appendix to the Use and abuse of diversions. Edinburgh 1733.

An estimate of the profit and loss of religion, personally and publicly stated, illustrated with references to Essays on morality and natural religion [by H. Home, Lord Kames]. Edinburgh 1753.

An analysis of the moral and religious sentiments contained in the writings of Sopho [Lord Kames] and David Hume. Edinburgh 1755.

The complaint made to the Presbytery of Edinburgh (relative to Lord Kames's Essays on morality and natural religion) verified. Edinburgh 1756.

A remonstrance against Lord Viscount Bolingbroke's philosophical religion. Edinburgh 1756.

THOMAS BLACKWELL the elder, Principal of the Marischal College

1660?–1728

Ratio sacra: or an appeal unto the rational world about the reasonableness of revealed religion. Edinburgh 1710.

Schema sacrum: or a sacred scheme of natural and revealed religion. Edinburgh 1710, Boston 1774, Glasgow 1777, 1781, Paisley [1786?], 1800, Aberdeen 1841. Title varies; reply [by Forbes of Disblair?], Some remarks on a piece called Schema scarum, [Edinburgh?] 1728.

Methodus evangelica: or a modest essay upon the true scriptural-rational way of preaching the Gospel. 1712.

Also other sermons and essays. For Blackwell's son Thomas, see col 2051, below.

THOMAS BOSTON the elder

1676–1732

Collections

Works; with the Marrow of modern divinity [by Edward Fisher] with notes [by Boston]. Ed A. Colden, Edinburgh 1767, Dundee 1773.

Works. Ed S. McMillan 12 vols Aberdeen 1848–52, London 1853.

Selections

A collection of sermons. Edinburgh 1772, London 1785.

Selected sermons. Tr Gaelic, Paisley 1830.

Beauties of Thomas Boston. Aberdeen 1831.

Select works. Edinburgh 1844.

§ 1

Human nature in its fourfold state. Edinburgh 1720, 1752, Glasgow 1761 etc; tr Gaelic, Edinburgh 1811, 1825; tr Welsh, 1821.

The sovereignty and wisdom of God displayed in the afflictions of man. Ed A. Colden et al, Edinburgh 1737 etc; also pbd as The crook in the lot; tr Welsh, 1769; Gaelic, 1837.

Sermons and discourses. Ed T. Boston the younger 2 vols Edinburgh 1753, 1756 (a different collection).

A view of the Covenant of Grace from the sacred records. Ed T. Boston younger, Edinburgh 1761, 1772, 1775, Hawick 1787, Berwick 1790; tr Welsh, 1823.

An illustration of the doctrines of the Christian religion. 3 vols Edinburgh 1773.

The Christian life delineated. 2 vols Edinburgh 1775.

Memoirs

Memoirs, written by himself and addressed to his children. Edinburgh 1776, Berwick 1805, London 1805, Edinburgh 1813, 1899; abridged 1811, Edinburgh 1827.

A general account of my life. Ed G. D. Low 1908.
Also many sermons and religious tracts.

§ 2

Watson, J. L. The pastor of Ettrick: Boston. Edinburgh 1883.
Scrymgeour, W. Thomas Boston. Edinburgh 1884.
Thomson, A. Boston of Ettrick: his life and times. 1895.
Addison, W. The life and writings of Boston. Edinburgh 1936.
Loane, M. L. Sons of the Covenant. Sydney 1963.

JOHN BROWN, Minister of the Gospel at Haddington
1722–87
Collections

Works of the late Rev John Brown: a new edition. Edinburgh 1800.

Selections

Select remains. Ed his sons John and Ebenezer 1789, 1792.

§ 1

An help for the ignorant: being an essay towards an easy explication of the Westminster Confession of faith and catechism. [Edinburgh?] 1758.
The Christian journal. Edinburgh 1765, 1782 (4th edn).
An historical account of the rise and progress of the Secession. [Edinburgh?] 1766, Edinburgh 1791 (6th edn), 1793 etc.
Sacred tropology: or a brief view of the figures, and explication of the metaphors contained in Scripture. Edinburgh 1768, 1782, Berwick 1791, London 1802, Edinburgh 1803 (new edn), London 1813.
A dictionary of the Holy Bible. 2 vols Edinburgh 1769, 1778, 1807 (5th edn with life), 1 vol Berwick 1810, 2 vols 1813, Glasgow 1839 (with Brown's concordance), Edinburgh 1866 (rev his son) etc.
A general history of the Christian Church. 2 vols Edinburgh 1771.
The self-interpreting Bible, with explanatory contents, parallel Scriptures, large notes and practical observations. 2 vols Edinburgh 1778 etc.
A concordance to the Holy Scriptures. Edinburgh 1783 etc.
Practical piety exemplified in the lives of thirteen eminent Christians. Glasgow 1783.
A compendious history of the Church of England, and of the Protestant churches in Ireland and America [including Scotland—title varies]. 2 vols Glasgow 1784, Edinburgh 1823.
Posthumous works. Perth 1797, London 1798.
Psalms in meter allowed by the General Assembly of the Church of Scotland: notes. 1831.

Letters

A compend of the letters of the Rev John Brown. Ed W. Fletcher, Stirling 1797, Glasgow 1848.
Also other works.

§ 2

Parry, J. A biography of Brown. Chester 1806.
Brown, J. C. Centenary memorial of Rev J. Brown. Edinburgh 1887.
Mackenzie, R. Brown of Haddington. 1918, 1964.

ROBERT CALDER
1658–1723

Schola sepulchri: the school of the grave. Aberdeen 1701.

Reasons for a toleration to the episcopal clergy. Edinburgh 1703.
The divine right of episcopacy. [no place] 1705.
A letter to a non-conformist minister of the kirk, showing the nullity of the presbyterian mission or authority to preach the Gospel. 1705.
The lawfulness and expediency of set forms of prayer, maintained. [no place] 1706, Leith 1766.
An answer to Mr James Hog at Carnock his Letter to a gentleman. Edinburgh 1710.
The nail struck to the head, against Mr John Anderson. [Edinburgh 1712].
The true difference between the principles and practices of the Kirk and the Church of Scotland. 1712; ed T. Stephen 1841.
Miscellany numbers relating to the controversies about the Book of common prayer, episcopal government, the power of the church in ordaining rites and ceremonies. Edinburgh 1713.
The spirit of slander exemplified in a scandalous pamphlet called the Jacobite curse [by W. Wright]. Edinburgh 1714.
The priesthood of the Old and New Testament by succession. Edinburgh 1716–17, [1720?].
Also numerous pamphlets concerning Episcopacy.
Scotch presbyterian eloquence displayed, signed Jacob Curate, 1693, is often attributed to Calder. This is probably erroneous; the authors are thought to be Gilbert Crokatt and John Monroe.

ARCHIBALD CAMPBELL DD
1691–1756

§ 1

An enquiry into the original or moral virtue, wherein it is shewn (against the author of the Fable of the bees etc) that virtue is founded in the nature of things, with some reflections on a late book [by F. Hutcheson] entitled An enquiry into the original of our ideas of beauty and virtue. Westminster 1728, Edinburgh 1733, London 1733, 1734, 1739.
The necessity of revelation: or an enquiry into the extent of human powers with respect to matters of religion. 1739.
The authenticity of the Gospel history justified. 2 vols Edinburgh 1759.
Also other tracts.

§ 2

Church of Scotland. Remarks upon some passages in books published by Campbell with his explanations on them. Edinburgh 1735; Report of the Committee for Purity of Doctrine, with Campbell's remarks upon it, Edinburgh 1736; Professor Campbell's further explications, Edinburgh 1736.

WILLIAM CROOKSHANK
1712?–69

The history of the state and sufferings of the Church of Scotland, from the Restoration to the Revolution. 2 vols 1749, Edinburgh 1751, 1762, Glasgow 1787, Edinburgh 1812, Perth 1846; tr Dutch, 1850 (abridged).

ALEXANDER CRUDEN
1701–70

§ 1

A complete concordance to the Holy Scriptures. 1737, 1738 etc (including abridgements).

The adventures of Alexander the Corrector, wherein is given an account of his being unjustly sent to Chelsea [subtitles vary]. Pts 1–2, 1754; pt 3, 1755 etc.
Also many other pamphlets.

§ 2

Olivier, E. The eccentric life of Cruden. 1934.
Shirley, R. Cruden's concordance 1737–1937. Cornhill Mag Dec 1937.

EBENEZER ERSKINE
1680–1754
Collections

Sermons and discourses. 4 vols Glasgow 1762; vol 5, Edinburgh 1765, 2 vols 1777.
Whole works. Ed J. Fisher 4 vols Edinburgh 1761, Falkirk 1761, Glasgow 1785, 2 vols Falkirk 1791; ed D. Fraser 3 vols Edinburgh 1798, London 1799, 1810, 2 vols 1826 (with enlarged memoir); abridged 1829, 3 vols Edinburgh 1871.

§ 1

A collection of sermons on several subjects. 1738.
The Assembly's shorter catechism explained by way of question and answer by some ministers of the Gospel [E. Erskine, James Fisher and Ralph Erskine]. 2 pts Glasgow 1753–60 etc.

§ 2

The vision of the two brothers Ebenezer and Ralph. Glasgow 1737. A satire, in verse, on the conduct of E. and R. Erskine in relation to the Act for bringing to justice the murderers of J. Porteous.
'Philalethes, Euzelus'. A letter to the valiant champion of our broken covenants Erskine. 1738.
Mitchel, W. The Tinclarian doctor's dream concerning those locusts who have come up out of the smoke of the pit; likewise an answer to a book against Mr Erskine. Edinburgh 1739.
Fraser, D. The life and diary of the Rev E. Erskine, father of the Secession church. Edinburgh 1831.
Harper, J., J. Eadie and W. Lindsay. Life of Erskine et al. Edinburgh 1849.
Ker, J. and J. L. Watson. The Erskines: Ebenezer and Ralph. Edinburgh 1880.
Watson, J. L. Life of Erskine. Edinburgh 1881.
MacEwen, A. R. The Erskines (Ebenezer and Ralph). Edinburgh [1900].

RALPH ERSKINE
1685–1752
Collections

Poetical works. Falkirk 1797.

§ 1

Gospel canticles: or spiritual songs, in 5 parts, by a minister of the Gospel in the Church of Scotland. Edinburgh 1720, 1726 (corrected as Gospel sonnets) etc.
A paraphrase or large explicatory poem upon the Song of Solomon. Dunfermline 1736 etc.
Faith no fancy: or a treatise of mental images. Edinburgh 1745.
Fancy no faith: or a seasonable admonition and information to seceders against the sinful constitution of some brethren into a pretended judicatory. Glasgow 1747.
Scripture songs selected from the Old and New Testament. Glasgow 1754.

The sermons and other practical works besides his poetical pieces [with life by J. Fisher]. Ed J. Newlands 2 vols Glasgow 1764–5, 10 vols Glasgow 1777–8, London 1821, 7 vols 1863.

§ 2

See Ebenezer Erskine, *above.*

JOHN GLAS
1695–1773
Collections

Works. 4 vols Edinburgh 1761–2, 5 vols Perth 1782–3.

§ 1

The testimony of the King of Martyrs concerning his Kingdom. Edinburgh 1725, 1727, 1728, 1729, 1813 (with account of the life and character) etc.
A narrative of the rise and progress of the controversy about the national covenants and of the ways that have been taken about it on both sides. Edinburgh 1728.
A continuation of Mr Glass's narrative: containing a true state of the process against him, as it is in the extracts to be laid before the Assembly in May 1729. Edinburgh 1729.
A further continuation of Mr Glass's narrative: containing his remarks on a late print [by John Willison] entitled A defence of national churches. [Edinburgh?] nd.
Christian songs. Dundee 1775 etc.

§ 2

An account of the life and character of Mr J. Glas, late minister of the Gospel at Tealing; to which is added a short account of the proceedings of the Church in his case. Edinburgh 1813.

JAMES HADOW
1670?–1764

A survey of the case of the episcopal clergy, and of those of the episcopal persuasion. Edinburgh 1703.
The antinomianism of the Marrow of modern divinity detected. Edinburgh 1721. Reply by James Hog, below.

JAMES HOG
1658?–1734

A letter to a gentleman, in which the unlawfulness of imposing forms of prayer, and other acts of worship, is plainly demonstrated. Edinburgh 1710. Reply by Robert Calder, above.
The controversy concerning the Marrow of modern divinity considered in several familiar dialogues. 2 pts [Edinburgh] 1721–2.
The scope and substance of the Marrow of modern divinity explained and vindicated. Edinburgh 1722. Written to confute James Hadow, Antinomianism, above.
A letter, wherein the scriptural grounds and warrants for the reformation of churches by way of covenant, are succinctly considered and cleared. Edinburgh 1727.
Memoirs of the public life of James Hogg, written by himself. Ed A. Bruce, Edinburgh 1798.
Hog, who was leader of the 'Marrow men' in the Church of Scotland, pbd a number of other works, chiefly controversial.

JOHN HOWIE, farmer of Lochgoin, Ayrshire
1735–93

Biographia scotiana: or a brief historical account of the lives, characters and memorable transactions of the most eminent Scots worthies. Glasgow 1775, 2 pts Glasgow 1781–2 (enlarged) etc; also pbd as Scots worthies.

An alarm unto a secure generation: or a short historical relation of some of the most strange and remarkable appearances of comets, fiery meteors, bloody signs, that have been seen through different ages, particularly those lately observed in the parishes of Fenwick, Eaglesham and Kilmarnock. Glasgow 1780, Kilmarnock 1809.

Memoirs. Glasgow 1796.

Howie also edited articles and sermons by various hands.

JOHN MacLAURIN, Minister of the North West Church, Glasgow
1693–1754
Collections

Works. Ed Rev J. Brown, Glasgow 1824, 1830; ed W. H. Goold 2 vols Edinburgh 1860.

§ 1

Sermons and essays. Ed J. Gillies, Glasgow 1755, London 1772, 1802 (with life), 1815.

MICHAEL SHIELDS
fl. 1699

Faithful contendings displayed: being an historical relation of the state and actings of the suffering remnant in the Church of Scotland; collected and kept in record by M. Shields; to which is added Ten considerations on the danger of apostacy; also A collection of sermons, collected and transcribed by J. Howie. Glasgow 1780.

PATRICK WALKER the Covenanter
d. 1745

Some remarkable passages of the life and death of Mr Alexander Peden. [Edinburgh] 1724 etc. Title varies.

Some remarkable passages of the life and death of Mr John Semple, Mr John Welwood, Mr Richard Cameron. Edinburgh 1727 etc.

Some remarkable passages in the life and death of Mr Daniel Cargill. Edinburgh 1732 etc.

Biographia presbyteriana. Ed J. Stevenson 2 vols Edinburgh 1827. Contains Walker's biographies of Peden, Semple, Welwood, Cameron, Cargill, Smith.

Six saints of the Covenant. Ed D. H. Fleming 2 vols 1901. Biographies by Walker.

JOHN WILLISON
1680–1750
Collections

Whole works. Aberdeen 1769 etc.

Practical works. Ed W. M. Hetherington, Glasgow [1846] (with essay on life and times).

§ 1

A treatise concerning the sanctifying of the Lord's day. Edinburgh 1716 etc.

An apology for the Church of Scotland, against the accusations of prelatists and Jacobites. Edinburgh 1719.

A defence of national churches and particularly of the national constitution of the Church of Scotland. Edinburgh 1729.

The mother's catechism for the young child. Edinburgh [1731], 1758 (in Gaelic and English) etc.

The afflicted man's companion. Edinburgh 1755 etc.

JOHN WITHERSPOON, President of Princeton College
1723–94
Collections

Works of the Rev John Witherspoon, late president of the College at Princeton, New Jersey. 3 vols Philadelphia 1800, 4 vols Philadelphia 1802, 9 vols Edinburgh 1804–5, 1815.

Selections

Select works. 2 vols 1804.

§ 1

Ecclesiastical characteristics: or the arcana of church policy. Glasgow 1753 etc.

Essay on the connection between the doctrine of justification by the imputed righteousness of Christ and holiness of life. Glasgow 1756.

A serious enquiry into the nature and effects of the stage. Glasgow 1757, New York 1812, Edinburgh 1876. Called forth by the production of Home's Douglas at Edinburgh in the previous year.

Seasonable advice to young persons. Glasgow 1762.

The history of a corporation of servants, discovered a few years ago in the interior parts of South America: a satire. Glasgow 1765.

The dominion of providence over the passions of men. Philadelphia 1776, Glasgow 1777, 1777, Belfast 1777, London 1778 (without the Address to the natives of Scotland).

An address to the natives of Scotland residing in America. 1778. First pbd in Dominion of providence over the passions of men, above.

Lectures on moral philosophy. Philadelphia 1810; ed V. L. Collins, Princeton 1912.

Also other sermons and pamphlets.

§ 2

[Arnot, Hugo?]. The xlv chapter of the prophecies of Thomas the Rhymer in verse, dedicated to Dr Silverspoon, preacher of sedition in America. Edinburgh 1776.

McCosh, J. Witherspoon and his times. Philadelphia [1890].

Woods, D. W. John Witherspoon. New York [1906].

Collins, V. L. President Witherspoon: a biography. 2 vols Princeton 1925.

Butterfield, L. H. Witherspoon comes to America. Princeton 1953.

B. HISTORY AND ANTIQUITIES

(a) 1660–1707

ALEXANDER BRODIE
1617–80

§ 1

The diary of Alexander Brodie of Brodie esq, who was one of the senators of the College of Justice, taken from his own manuscript. Edinburgh 1740. Covers the period April 1652 to Feb 1654 only.

The diary of Alexander Brodie of Brodie 1652–80, and of his son James Brodie of Brodie 1680–5: consisting of extracts from the existing manuscripts, and a republication of the volume printed at Edinburgh in the year 1740. Ed D. Laing, Aberdeen 1863 (Spalding Club).

§ 2

Bain, G. Lord Brodie: his life and times. Nairn 1904.

GILBERT BURNET
1643–1715

See col 1685, above.

JOHN COCKBURN DD
1652–1729

§ 1

Jacob's vow: or man's felicity and duty. 2 pts Edinburgh 1686, 1696.

An historical relation of the General Assembly held at Edinburgh in 1690. 1691 (3 edns); A continuation, 1691.

A short history of the Revolution in Scotland. 1712, 1712; rptd with C. Lindsay, An account of the affairs of Scotland, Edinburgh 1754.

The history and examination of duds: shewing their heinous nature and the necessity of suppressing them. 1720, 2 vols Edinburgh 1888.

A specimen of some free and impartial remarks on publick affairs and particular persons, especially relating to Scotland, occasioned by Dr Burnet's History of his own times. [1724?].

A defence of Dr Cockburn against the calumnies and aspersions of a libel entitled A vindication of the late Bishop Burnet. nd.

Also anti-Bourignianism works and other sermons and pamphlets.

§ 2

The downfall of C's meeting-house. [no place] nd. Song, broadside.

DAVID CRAWFURD
1665–1708

§ 1

Courtship à-la-mode: a comedy. Ed W. Pinkethman [1700].

Several letters: containing the amours of 1, The unfortunate duchess; 2, Love after enjoyment; 3, The unhappy mistake, written by Mr D. Cr—rd, gent. 2 pts 1700.

Ovidius britannicus: or love epistles in imitation of Ovid. 1703.

Love at first sight: a comedy. [1704].

Memoirs of the affairs of Scotland; containing a full and impartial account of the revolution in that Kingdom begun in 1567, faithfully published from an authentick ms 1706; corrected, with the Earl of Morton's confession. Ed W. Goodall, Edinburgh 1753, 1767.

§ 2

Epitaph on the death of Crawfurd. [Edinburgh?] 1708. A verse broadside.

Macaree, D. Three early 18th-century prose romances. Book Collector 11 1962.

—— Crawfurd: a forgotten man of Scottish letters. Stud in Scottish Lit 5 1968.

Roy, G. R. Crawfurd: an unrecorded broadside. Stud in Scottish Lit 6 1969.

SIR JAMES DALRYMPLE of Borthwick
fl. 1714

§ 1

A second edition of Camden's Description of Scotland: containing a supplement [by Dalrymple]. Edinburgh 1595 (for 1695). Ed Dalrymple.

Collections concerning the Scottish history preceding the death of King David the First in the year 1153. Edinburgh 1705.

A vindication of the ecclesiastical part of Sir J. Dalrymple's historical collections. Edinburgh 1714.

Some authentick writes and records from 1567 to 1572, for establishing King James the Sixth his authority. [Edinburgh?] nd.

§ 2

Gillan, J. Some remarks upon Dalrymple's Historical collections, with an answer to the Vindication. Edinburgh 1714.

HENRY GUTHRY
1600?–76

See vol 1, above.

CHRISTOPHER IRVINE, Physician
fl. 1638–85

Bellum grammaticale. Edinburgh 1652, 1658, 1698. A tragi-comedy in 5 acts in verse.

Medicina magnetica: or the rare and wonderful art of curing by sympathy. 1656, Edinburgh 1656.

Historiae scoticae nomenclatura latino-vernacula. Edinburgh 1684, 1697; [ed J. Watt], Glasgow 1817, 1819.

ALEXANDER JAFFRAY, Provost of Aberdeen
1614–73

§ 1

Diary. 1833, 1834, Aberdeen 1856. With life by J. Barclay.

§ 2

E., M. A man of plain speech: being some account of the youth and adventures of Jaffray. 1897.

Wyness, J. F. A Scottish Quaker of the 17th century: Jaffray. Leominster [1941]. Rptd from Friends Quart Examiner 75 1941.

JAMES KIRKTON
1620?–99

§ 1

The history of John Welsh, minister of the Gospel at Aire. Edinburgh 1703. Anon.
The secret and true history of the Church of Scotland from the restoration to the year 1678. Ed C. K. Sharpe, Edinburgh 1817.

§ 2

Long Kirkton's address. [no place] nd. A verse satire.

JOHN LAMONT of Newton, Fife
fl. 1649–71

The chronicle of Fife: being the diary of Lamont of Newton 1649–72. Ed A. Constable, Edinburgh 1810.
The diary of Mr John Lamont of Newton from 1649 to 1671. Ed G. R. Kinloch, Glasgow 1830 (Maitland Club).
The Newton estate was acquired in 1695 by John Lamont, nephew to the above, thus leading to the mistaken epithet.

ROBERT LAW, Minister of East Kilpatrick
d. 1690?

Memorialls: or the memorable things that fell out within this island of Brittain from 1638 to 1684. Ed C. K. Sharpe, Edinburgh 1818.

SIR GEORGE MACKENZIE
of Rosehaugh, Lord Advocate
1636–91

Bibliographies
Ferguson, F. S. A bibliography of the works of Mackenzie. Trans Edinburgh Bibl Soc 1 1938.

Collections
Works. 2 vols Edinburgh 1716–22.

§ 1

Aretina: or the serious romance. Edinburgh 1660, London 1661, [1661]. Anon.
Religio stoici; with a friendly address to the phanatics of all sects. Edinburgh 1663, 1663, London 1663, Edinburgh [London?] 1665, 1665, London 1685, 1685, 1693, 1698. Titles varies.
A moral essay, preferring solitude to publick employment. Edinburgh 1665, [1665], 1666, London 1685, 1693. Reply by J. Evelyn, Publick employment and an active life preferred to solitude and all its appanages, in reply to a late essay of a contrary title, 1667, 1667.
Moral gallantry: a discourse wherein the author endeavours to prove that point of honour obliges men to be virtuous. [Also issued as A moral paradox: maintaining that it is much easier to be virtuous than vicious]. Edinburgh 1667, London 1669, 1669, 1685, 1821.
The laws and customes of Scotland [with ch on witchcraft]. Edinburgh 1678 (3 edns), 1699.
Observations upon the laws and customs of nations as to precedency [with] the science of herauldry. Edinburgh 1680.
A vindication of his Majestie's government in Scotland. Edinburgh 1683, London 1683.
Jus regium? or the just and solid foundations of monarchy. Edinburgh 1684, 1684, London 1684, 1684.

A defence of the antiquities of the royal line of Scotland. 1685, 1685, Edinburgh 1685, London 1686 (title varies); tr Latin, 1689.
Reason. 1690, 1695; tr Latin, 1690, 1691, 1700.
The moral history of frugality with its opposite vices. Edinburgh 1691, London 1691.
A vindication of the government in Scotland during the reign of Charles II. 1691, Edinburgh 1712. Reply by 'W. Laick' (George Ridpath), A continuation of the answer to the Scots Presbyterian eloquence; as also Reflections on Sir G. Mackenzie's Defence of Charles the Second's government in Scotland, 1693.
Catalogus librorum bibliothecae juris utriusque tam civilis quam canonici publici quam privati. Edinburgh 1692. First pbd catalogue of the Advocates Library, ed Mackenzie.
A vindication of the Presbyterians in Scotland by a lover of truth. 1692.
Essays upon several moral subjects; to which is prefixed some account of [Mackenzie's] life and writings. 1713.
Caelia's country-house and closet: a poem. [1715?].
Memoirs of the affairs of Scotland from the restoration of King Charles II. Edinburgh 1821 (priv ptd).
Also works on law.

§ 2

[Symson, A.?]. Mackenzie's arguments against an incorporating Union. Edinburgh 1706.
Logan, G. A treatise on government, against Mackenzie. Edinburgh 1746.
O'Flaherty, R. The Ogygia vindicated against the objections of Mackenzie; to which is annexed an epistle from J. Lynch to M. Boileau on the subject of Scotish antiquities. Dublin 1775.
Watt, F. In his Terrors of the law, 1902.
Lang, A. Mackenzie, King's Advocate. 1909.
de Beer, E. S. The letters from Mackenzie to Evelyn. N & Q 5 June 1937.

JOHN NICOLL
c. 1590–c. 1667

A diary of public transactions and other occurrences chiefly in Scotland from January 1650 to June 1667. Ed D. Laing, Edinburgh 1836 (Bannatyne Club).

SIR ROBERT SIBBALD
1641–1722

Bibliographies
Bibliotheca Sibbaldiana, or a catalogue of curious and valuable books: being the library of Sibbald. Edinburgh 1722.

Collections
A collection of several treatises in folio concerning Scotland, as it was of old and also in later times. Edinburgh 1739.

§ 1

An account of the Scottish atlas or the description of Scotland ancient and modern. Edinburgh 1683; tr Latin, 1683.
Memoria Balfouriana: sive historia rerum pro literis promovendis gestarum a clarissimis fratribus Balfouriis D.D. Jacabo et D.D. Andrea. Edinburgh 1699.
The liberty and independency of the Kingdom and Church of Scotland, asserted from ancient records. Edinburgh 1702, 1703, 1704.
Historical enquiries: concerning the Roman monuments and antiquities in the north part of Britain called Scotland. Edinburgh 1707.

An account of the writers ancient and modern which treat of the description of North Britain called Scotland. Edinburgh 1710.

The history ancient and modern of the sheriffdoms of Linlithgow and Stirling. Edinburgh 1710.

Miscellanea quaedam eruditae antiquitatis, quae ad borealem Britanniae. Edinburgh 1710.

The history ancient and modern of the sheriffdoms of Fife and Kinross. Edinburgh 1710, Cupar 1803. Also in Miscellanea pictica, Edinburgh 1818; and in Miscellanea scotica vol 1, Glasgow 1818.

History and description of Stirling-shire ancient and modern 1707. Stirling 1892. Compiled from various works by Sibbald pbd 1707–10.

Letters and Memoirs

Autobiography to which is prefixed some account of his

mss. [Ed J. Maidment], Edinburgh 1833; rptd in Analecta scotica 1st ser, 1834.

Remains of Sibbald: containing his autobiography and portions of his literary correspondence. Edinburgh 1837.

Memoirs. Ed F. P. Hett, Oxford 1932. Introd denies Sibbald forged Ben Jonson's Conversations.

Also other works on Scottish antiquities. A selection of Sibbald's topographical works was pbd in W. Macfarlane, Geographical collections, Pbns Scottish Historical Soc 52 1907.

§ 2

Stainer, C. L. Jonson and Drummond, their conversations: a few remarks on an 18th-century forgery. Oxford 1925. Charges that Sibbald forged Ben Jonson's Conversations with William Drummond in a ms of 1711.

(b) 1707–1800

PATRICK ABERCROMBY
1656–1716?

§ 1

The advantages of the Act of Security, compar'd with these of the intended union, founded on the Revolution principles publish'd by Mr D. DeFoe. [Edinburgh?] 1706.

The martial achievements of the Scots nation: being an account of such Scotsmen as have signaliz'd themselves by the sword. 2 vols Edinburgh 1711–15, 4 vols 1762, 2 vols Glasgow 1804–8.

§ 2

Gordon, T. C. In his Four notable Scots, Stirling 1960.

JAMES ANDERSON
1662–1728
See col 1706, above.

THOMAS BLACKWELL the younger
Principal of the Marischal College
1701–57

§ 1

An enquiry into the life and writings of Homer. 1735, 1736, Glasgow 1761 (4th edn); tr French, 1799–1800.

Proofs of the enquiry translated into English. 1747, 1748. A trn of the passages quoted in notes to Enquiry, above.

Memoirs of the Court of Augustus. 2 vols Edinburgh 1753–5, London 1760, 1764; vol 3 continued and completed by John Mills, 1763; tr French, 2 vols 1754–9, 3 vols 1768, 1781.

Letters

Letters concerning mythology. 1748, 1757; tr French, 1771.

§ 2

Costa, G. La critica omerica di Blackwell 1701–57. Rome 1959.

GEORGE CHALMERS
1742–1825
See col 1732, above.

SIR JOHN CLERK, Bart
1676–1755

Memoirs extracted by himself from his own journals. Ed J. M. Gray, Pbns Scottish Historical Soc 13 1892.

Memoirs. 2 pts 1895 (Roxburghe Club).

Observations on the present state of Scotland 1730. Ed T. C. Smout, Pbns Scottish Historical Soc 4th ser 2 1965.

Clerk also wrote political pamphlets.

GEORGE CRAWFURD
d. 1748
See col 1707, above.

SIR DAVID DALRYMPLE,
LORD HAILES
1726–92

§ 1

Sacred poems: or a collection of translations or paraphrases from the Holy Scriptures, by various authors. Edinburgh 1751. Ed Dalrymple.

Edom of Gordon: an ancient Scottish poem. Glasgow 1755. Ed Dalrymple.

British songs sacred to love and virtue. Edinburgh 1756. Ed Dalrymple.

John Smith, Select discourses. Edinburgh 1756. Ed Dalrymple.

Memorials and letters relating to the history of Britain in the reign of James the First: published from the originals. Glasgow 1762, 1766 (corrected and enlarged).

A specimen of a book entitled Ane compendious booke of godly and spiritual sangs. Edinburgh 1765. A selection from John Wedderburn, Ane compendious booke of godly and spirituall songs, Edinburgh 1621, commonly called The gude and godlie ballatis. Ed Dalrymple.

Memorials and letters relating to the history of Britain in the reign of Charles the First, published from the originals. Glasgow 1766.

An examination of some of the arguments for the high antiquity of Regiam majestatem, and an enquiry into the authenticity of Leges Malcolmi. Edinburgh 1769.

Historical memorials concerning the provincial councils of the Scottish clergy. Edinburgh 1769.

Ancient Scottish poems published from the ms of George Bannatyne MDLXVIII. Edinburgh 1770, London 1770 (for 1815). Ed Dalrymple.

Remarks on the history of Scotland. Edinburgh 1773.

Annals of Scotland (from Malcolm III to the accession of the House of Stewart). 2 vols Edinburgh 1776–9, 3 vols 1797 (enlarged), 1819.
Miscellaneous remarks on the Enquiry into the evidence against Mary Queen of Scots. 1784. On work by William Tytler.
Sketch of the life of John Barclay, author of Argenis. [Edinburgh 1786 ?].
Davidis Humei, Scoti, summi apud suos philosophi, de vita sua acta, liber singularis. [Edinburgh] 1787.
Sketch of the life of Mark Alexander Boyd. [Edinburgh 1787].
Sketch of the life of Sir James Ramsay, a general officer in the armies of Gustavus Adolphus King of Sweden. [Edinburgh 1787].
The little freeholder: a dramatic entertainment in two acts. 1790. Anon.
Tracts relative to the history and antiquities of Scotland. Edinburgh 1800. Reissue of 5 tracts.
Of the eminent heathen writers, from Seneca to Marcus Antonius. In John Brown, Theological tracts, 3 vols Edinburgh 1853.

Letters

Correspondence of Thomas Percy and Dalrymple. Ed A. F. Falconer, Baton Rouge 1954 (vol 4 of Percy letters).
Dalrymple also edited and translated historical and legal works.

§ 2

[Murray, P.]. A letter to Lord Hailes on his Remarks on the history of Scotland. Edinburgh 1773.
Watkin-Jones, A. Bishop Percy and the Scottish ballads. E & S 18 1932. On Percy-Dalrymple correspondence.
Campbell, J. J. Dalrymple's ballad work. PQ 29 1950.
Carnie, R. H. A letter from Lord Hailes to James Boswell in Holland. N & Q Feb 1954.
—— Lord Hailes's notes on Johnson's Lives of the poets. N & Q Feb–April, Aug, Nov 1956.
—— Lord Hailes's contributions to contemporary magazines. SB 9 1957.
—— Macpherson's Fragment of ancient poetry and Lord Hailes. E Studies 41 1960.

SIR JOHN DALRYMPLE
1726–1810
See col 1734, above.

WALTER GOODALL
1706?–66
See col 1735, above.

WILLIAM GORDON of Old Aberdeen
fl. 1726

The history of the family of Gordon; together with the history of the most remarkable transactions in Scotland to the year 1690. 2 vols Edinburgh 1726–7.
Gordon also pbd religious tracts.

WILLIAM GUTHRIE
1708–70
See col 1737, above.

DAVID HUME
1711–76
See col 1873, above.

THOMAS INNES, Vice Principal of the Scots College in Paris
1662–1744

§ 1

A critical essay on the ancient inhabitants of Scotland. 2 vols 1729; rptd in The historians of Scotland vol 8, Edinburgh 1871–80.
Papers by Thomas Innes, Principal of the Scots College at Paris, and documents connected with his family. Aberdeen 1842 (Spalding Club). Documents covering 1729–87, including letters from the Old Chevalier.
The civil and ecclesiastical history of Scotland AD 80–1318. Ed G. Grub, Aberdeen 1853 (Spalding Club).

§ 2

Taitt, A. The Roman account of Britain and Ireland, in answer to Father Innes. Edinburgh 1741, 1826, 1836.
[Waddell, G.] Remarks on Mr Inne's critical essay on the ancient inhabitants of Scotland. Edinburgh 1733.

SIR WILLIAM KEITH
1680–1749
Collections
A collection of papers and other tracts. 1740, 1749.

§ 1

An essay on the education of a young British nobleman [and] Observations on the office of an ambassador. 1730, 1731.
A history of the British plantations in America: part 1, Virginia. 1738 (all pbd).
The citizen: or the weekly conversation of a society of London merchants on trade and other public affairs. 25 nos 9 Feb–27 July 1739; rptd 1740.
Keith, as Governor of Pennsylvania, was author of official pbns and also pbd political works.

JOHN KER
1673–1726
See col 1708, above.

SIR JOHN LAUDER, LORD FOUNTAINHALL
1646–1722

Chronological notes on Scottish affairs from 1680 till 1701. Ed W. Scott, Edinburgh 1822.
Historical observes of memorable occurents in Church and State from October 1680 to April 1686. Ed D. Laing and A. Urquhart, Edinburgh 1840 (Bannatyne Club).
Historical notices of Scotish affairs selected from the manuscripts of Sir John Lauder 1661–88. Ed D. Laing 2 vols Edinburgh 1848 (Bannatyne Club).
Journals, with observations on public affairs and other memoranda 1665–76. Ed D. Crawford, Pbns Scottish Historical Soc 36 1900; tr French, 1935.

GEORGE LOCKHART
1673–1731
See col 1708, above.

GEORGE MACKENZIE MD
1669–1725

Lives and characters of the most eminent writers of the Scots nation. 3 vols Edinburgh 1708–22.

DONALD MACLEOD

Memoirs of the life and gallant exploits of the old Highlander, Sergeant Donald Macleod. Ed W. Thomson 1791; ed J. G. Fyfe 1933.

JOHN MACPHERSON, Minister of Sleat
1710–65

Critical dissertations on the origin, antiquities, language of the ancient Caledonians, their posterity the Picts and the British and Irish Scots. 1768, Dublin 1768.

JOHN MILLAR, Professor of Law, University of Glasgow
1735–1801

§ 1

Observations concerning the distinction of ranks in society. 1771, Dublin 1771, London 1773 (2nd edn enlarged), 1779 (title varies), Edinburgh 1806 (corrected with life of author by J. Craig); tr German, 1772.

An historical view of the English government from the settlement of the Saxons in Britain to the accession of the House of Stewart. 1787, Dublin 1789, London 1790 (2nd edn).

An historical view of the English government from the settlement of the Saxons in Britain to the Revolution in 1688; to which are subjoined some dissertations connected with the history of the government from the Revolution to the present time. 4 vols 1803, 1812.

§ 2

Lehmann, W. C. Millar: his life and thought and his contributions to sociological analysis. Cambridge 1960.

JOHN PINKERTON
1758–1826

See col 1766, above.

GEORGE RIDPATH, Minister of Stitchel
1717?–72

§ 1

The Border history of England and Scotland. 1776, 1810, Berwick 1848.

Diary of George Ridpath, Minister of Stitchell 1755–61. Ed J. B. Paul, Pbns Scottish Historical Soc 3rd ser 2 1922.

§ 2

Paul, J. B. Life in a Border manse 160 years ago: Ridpath, Border historian. Pbns Hawick Archaeological Soc 55 1923.

WILLIAM ROBERTSON
1721–93

See col 1719, above.

GILBERT STUART
1742–86

See col 1740, above.

WILLIAM TYTLER
1711–92

See cols 1741, 1779, above.

ROBERT WATSON
1730?–81

See col 1741, above.

ROBERT WODROW, Minister of Eastwood
1679–1734
Selections

Selections from Wodrow's biographical collections: divines of the North-East of Scotland. Ed R. Lippe, Aberdeen 1890 (New Spalding Club).

§ 1

The history of the sufferings of the Church of Scotland from the Restauration to the Revolution. 2 vols Edinburgh 1721–2; with original memoir of the author by Rev Robert Burns. 4 vols Glasgow 1829–30.

Collections upon the lives of the reformers and most eminent ministers of the Church of Scotland. Ed W. J. Duncan and M. Leishman 2 vols Glasgow 1834–48 (Maitland Club).

Analecta: or materials for a history of remarkable providences, mostly relating to Scotch ministers and Christians. Ed M.L. [Matthew Leishman] 4 vols Edinburgh 1842–3.

Extracts from the manuscript collections of the Rev Robert Wodrow MDCV–MDCXCVII. In Miscellany of the Spalding Club vol 2, Aberdeen 1842.

Letters

Private letters now first printed from the original mss 1694–1732. Ed J. Maidment, Edinburgh 1829.

Correspondence between George Ridpath [pamphleteer] and the Rev Robert Wodrow. In Miscellany of the Abbotsford Club vol 1, ed J. Maidment, Edinburgh 1837.

Correspondence. Ed T. M'Crie 3 vols Edinburgh 1842–3 (Wodrow Soc Pbns).

Early letters of Robert Wodrow 1698–1709. Ed L. W. Sharp, Pbns Scottish Historical Soc 3rd ser 24 1937.

§ 2

'Philanax'. The Scottish behemoth dissected, in a letter to Mr Robert Woddrow concerning the publishing of a history of the sufferings of the Church of Scotland. Edinburgh 1722.

Walker, Patrick. Some remarkable passages of the life and death of Mr John Semple, Mr John Welwood, Mr Richard Cameron; with remarks upon twenty eight gross misrepresentations and groundless and scandalous reflections in Mr Wodrow's History. Edinburgh 1727.

Couper, W. J. Robert Wodrow. Scottish Church History Soc Records 3 1928.

Caplan, N. Calamy's visit to Scotland in 1717. Trans Congregational History Soc of England 19 1964. Unpbd letter from David Erskine to Wodrow.

Colman, B. Some unpublished letters of Benjamin Colman 1717–25 [to Wodrow]. Ed N. Caplan, Proc Massachusetts Historical Soc 77 1965.

Evans, J. Letters of a young Presbyterian minister 1722–8 [John Evans to Wodrow]. Ed N. Caplan, Jnl Presbyterian History Soc of England 13 1965.

In 1841 the Wodrow Society was founded 'for the publication of the works of the fathers and early writers of the Reformed Church of Scotland'; its first pbn was issued in 1842 and its last in 1850.

C. MISCELLANEOUS WRITINGS

(a) 1660–1707

General Works

A. Ponsonby (ed). Scottish and Irish diaries from the 16th to the 19th century. 1927.

J. G. Fyfe (ed). Scottish diaries and memoirs 1550–1746. Stirling 1928.

ANDREW BALFOUR
1630–94
Bibliographies

Bibliotheca Balfouriana: sive catalogus librorum. Edinburgh 1695.

§ 1

Letters written to a friend: containing excellent directions and advices for travelling thro' France and Italy. Edinburgh 1700, 1700.

§ 2

Sibbald, R. Memoria Balfouriana: sive historia rerum, pro literis promovendis gestarum a clarissimis fratribus Balfouriis. Edinburgh 1699.

ANDREW BROWN
fl. 1690–1706

The character of the true publick spirit, especially with relation to the ill condition of a nation, thro' the prevalency of the private spirit, selfish and sinister designs. [Edinburgh] 1702, Edinburgh 1711.

Some very weighty and seasonable considerations tending to dispose, excite and qualify the nation for the more effectual treating with England in relation to a union. [Edinburgh] 1703.

A scheme, proposing a true touch-stone for the due trial of a proper union betwixt Scotland and England. Edinburgh 1706; rptd in Three essays, Edinburgh 1711.

Also medical and political tracts.

JAMES DALRYMPLE, VISCOUNT STAIR
1619–95

§ 1

The institutions of the law of Scotland. Edinburgh 1681, 1693 (rev and enlarged), 1759 (3rd edn, with notes by J. Gordon and W. Johnstone), 2 vols 1826 (with suppl by G. Brodie), 1828 (with notes by J. S. More), 1832.

Physiologia nova experimentalis, in qua generales notiones Aristotelis, Epicuri et Cartesii supplentur, errores deteguntur et emendatur. Leyden 1686.

An apology by himself. Edinburgh 1690; ed W. Blair 1825 (Bannatyne Club).

A vindication of the divine perfections, illustrating the glory of God in them by reason and revelation. 1695.

Letters

Annals and correspondence of the Viscount and first and second Earls of Stair. Ed J. M. Graham 2 vols Edinburgh 1875.

Also other legal works. In 1934 the Stair Society was formed in Edinburgh and has issued works of Scottish legal interest since 1936.

§ 2

Grant, P. Annotations on Lord Stair's Institutions. Edinburgh 1824.

Shaw, P. Principles of the law of Scotland contained in Lord Stair's Institutions. Edinburgh 1863.

Mackay, A. J. G. Memoir of Sir J. Dalrymple: a study in the history of Scotland and Scotch law during the seventeenth century. Edinburgh 1873.

Campbell, A. H. The structure of Stair's Institutions. Glasgow 1954.

JAMES DONALDSON

§ 1

Elegie on the death of William Earl of Crawoord [Edinburgh? 1698?]. Anon broadside.

Elegie on the much to be lamented death of the Right Honourable Alexander Lord Reath. [Edinburgh 1698]. Anon broadside.

A pick-tooth for swearers: or a looking-glass for atheists and prophane persons. Edinburgh 1698. Verse.

A letter from Mr Reason, to the high and mighty Prince the Mob. 1706. On the Union.

A panegyric upon the art of malting and brewing. Edinburgh 1712. Verse.

A panegyric upon the art of weaving. Edinburgh 1712. Verse.

A panegyric upon the art of wrightcraft. Edinburgh 1713. Verse.

Also other pamphlets.

§ 2

An epithalamium on the nuptials of J. Donaldson with Lady Mrs Jean Reid, alias Mrs Scot. [Edinburgh] nd. Satire.

ROBERT KIRK, Minister at Balquidder
1641?–92

§ 1

Psalma dhaibhidh a nMeadrachd: do reir an phriomhchanamain. Edinburgh 1684. The first complete trn of Scottish metrical Psalms into Gaelic. For information on this and other trns of the Psalms *see* D. C. MacTavish, Introduction to the Gaelic Psalms 1694, Lochgilphead 1934.

Secret commonwealth: or a treatise displaying the chief curiosities as they are in use among diverse of the people of Scotland to this day, with an appendix: extracts from a treatise on the second sight, dreams, apparitions etc by Theophilus Insulanus, first published Edinburgh 1763. [Ed R. Jamieson, with foreword by W. Scott] Edinburgh 1815 (from 1691 ms); rptd with comment by A. Lang in Bibliothèque de Carabas vol 8, 1893; ed R. B. Cunningham Graham, Stirling 1933.

Kirk's note-book. Ed D. B. Smith, Scottish Historical Rev 18 1921.

§ 2

Rossi, M. M. Text-criticism of Kirk's Secret common-wealth. Trans Edinburgh Bibl Soc 3 1957.

ARCHIBALD PITCAIRNE
1652–1713
Collections

Whole works. Tr G. Sewell and J. T. Desaguliers 1715, 1727, 1740. Only medical works.
Opera omnia medica. 2 vols Hague 1722, 1 vol Leyden 1737.

§ 1

Roberto Graio Scoto Londini medicinam profitenti, Archibaldus Pitcairnius Scotus. [no place 1690?]. Verse broadside.
Poemata selecta. 9 a b 5 c 2 d 8 e g 2 h 14 i 3 18 m 1 o n 5 o 4 p 7 r 6 s 7 t 6 v. [London? 1710?]. Anon.
Good news from Scotland: or the abjuration and the Kirk of Scotland reconciled. 1712. Ascribed to A. Pitcairne; prose.
The assembly: a comedy by a Scots gentleman. 1722, [Edinburgh?] 1752, London 1766, Edinburgh 1766, 1817. Later edns have the sub-title Scotch reformation. Edn of 1766 reads 'done from the original ms written in the year 1692'.
Selecta poemata Archibaldi Pitcarnii et aliorum. Edinburgh 1727, London 1729.
Lines addressed to Gilbert Burnet, Bishop of Sarum. [Edinburgh 1825]. Broadside.
Babell: a satirical poem on the proceedings of the General Assembly in the year 1692. Ed G. R. Kinloch, Glasgow 1830 (Maitland Club).
Also numerous medical pbns in Latin and psalms tr into Latin verse under pseudonym 'Walter Denniston'. Also under this pseudonym a Latin poem with trn into English verse (1700?) to the Bailies of Musselburgh.

§ 2

Eyzat, Dr E.] Apollo mathematicus: or the art of curing diseases by the mathematicks, according to the principles of Dr Pitcairne. 2 pts [Edinburgh] 1695. A satire on Pitcairne's works, the title inspired by his Apollo staticus: the art of curing fever by statics, Edinburgh 1695. A controversy followed in which Dr Andrew Brown, Dr George Cheyne, Dr Charles Oliphant and Dr Charles Webster took part.
Moncrief, J. The poor man's physician; to which is added the method of curing the small pox and scurvy by Pitcairne. Edinburgh 1712, 1731 (3rd edn).
Kinkaid, T. In Archibaldi Pitcarnii medici dissertationes & poemata. [Edinburgh? 1713?]. Verse.
[Ramsay, A.] A poem to the memory of the famous A. Pitcairn. Edinburgh [1713].

General Works

J. G. Fyfe (ed). Scottish diaries and memoirs 1746–1843. Stirling 1942.

JAMES ANDERSON of Monk's-Hill
1739–1808
§ 1

Essays relating to agriculture and rural affairs. 2 vols Edinburgh 1775, 1777 (with addns), 1784, 3 vols 1800 (5th edn).

Wilson, J. To Dr David Dickson lamenting the death of his learned friend Dr Archibald Pitcairn. [Edinburgh 1713?]. Broadside.
Webster, C., MD. An account of the life and writings of Pitcairne. Edinburgh 1781.
Jolley, L. J. A. Pitcairne. Edinburgh Medical Jnl 60 1953.
Lindeboom, G. A. Pitcairne's Leiden interlude described from the documents. Annals of Science 19 1963.
— Pitcairne in Leiden. Rptd from Nederlands Tijdschrift voor Geneeskunde 110 1966.

GEORGE RIDPATH, pamphleteer
d. 1726

'Laick, Will'. An answer to the Scotch Presbyterian eloquence. 1693, 1694, A continuance of the answer to the Scots Presbyterian eloquence. 1693. 1789.
— The Scots Episcopal innocence: or the juggling of that party, with the late King, his present Majesty, the Church of England and the Church of Scotland, demonstrated. 1694.
The queries and protestation of the Scots episcopal clergy against the authority of the Presbyterian General Assemblies. Anon, 1694.
The stage condemn'd, and the encouragement given to the immoralities and profaneness of the theatre, by the English schools, universities and pulpits, censur'd. 1698, 1706.
An enquiry into the causes of the miscarriage of the Scots colony at Darien by Phil-Scot. Glasgow 1700. By Ridpath?
Scotland's grievances relating to Darien. [Edinburgh?] 1700. Anon.
A discourse upon the union of Scotland and England. [Edinburgh?] 1702. Anon.
The reducing of Scotland by arms, and annexing it to England as a province, considered. 1705. Anon.
Considerations upon the union of the two kingdoms. [Edinburgh?] 1706. Anon.
The Scots nation and union vindicated. 1714. Anon.

Letters

Correspondence between Ridpath and the Rev R. Wodrow. Ed J. Maidment, Edinburgh 1837.
Also other pamphlets.

GEORGE SINCLAIR
d. 1696

Satan's invisible world discovered: or a choice collection of modern relations, proving evidently that there are devils, witches and apparitions. Edinburgh 1685, 1746, 1769, 1780, 1789, 1808, 1871.
Also works on natural philosophy and mathematics.

(b) 1707–1800

The interest of Great Britain with regard to her American colonies considered. 1782.
The bee: or literary weekly intelligencer. 18 vols Edinburgh 1790–4. Ed Anderson.
Recreations in agriculture, natural history, arts and miscellaneous literature. 6 vols 1799–1802.
Other works include studies in agriculture and economics.

§ 2

Mullett, C. F. The bee: a tour of Crotchet Castle. South Atlantic Quart 66 1967.

HUGH BLAIR
1718–1800

Bibliographies

Catalogue of Dr Blair's library. Edinburgh 1816.

Collections

Lectures on rhetoric and belles lettres. 2 vols 1783, 3 vols Dublin 1783, 1 vol Philadelphia 1784, 3 vols 1785 (rev), 1787, 2 vols Paris 1788 (in English), 3 vols 1790, 1793, 2 vols Dublin 1793, New York 1793, Philadelphia 1793, 3 vols 1796, 1798, 1801 etc; ed H. F. Harding 2 vols Carbondale 1965; tr French, 1797, 1808; tr Spanish, 1798–1801, 1816–17, 1819; tr Italian, 1801, 1811, 1815, 1846, 1847 etc; tr Dutch, 1804; tr Russian, 1837–8.

Essays on rhetoric. 1784 (2nd edn), Dublin 1784, London 1785, 1787, Boston 1793, Philadelphia 1793 etc. Abridgements of lectures.

Sermons. Vols pbd separately as follows: 1, Edinburgh 1777 (20 other edns before 1801); 2, 1780 (17 other edns before 1801); 3, 1790 (9 other edns before 1801); 4, 1794 (5 other edns before 1801); 5, with a life by J. Finlayson, 1801 (available separately, or with vols 1–4 as first collected edn; frequently rptd). Single sermons were also frequently pbd in anthologies and separately. Amer edns, New York 1790, Philadelphia 1791, Baltimore 1792, Boston 1792, New York 1792, Baltimore 1793, Philadelphia 1794, 1794; tr Dutch, 1778; tr French, 3 vols 1784–6, 5 vols 1807–8, 1823–4; German, 1791–1802; Gaelic, 1812.

§ 1

A poem sacred to the memory of the Rev Mr James Smith. Edinburgh 1736.

Dissertatio philosophica inauguralis, de fundamentis & obligatione legis naturae. Edinburgh 1739.

The wrath of man praising God: a sermon. Edinburgh 1746.

The importance of religious knowledge to the happiness of mankind: a sermon. Edinburgh 1750; rptd in The Scotch preacher vol 1, Edinburgh [1775], 1789.

Observations upon a pamphlet entitled An analysis on the moral and religious sentiments contained in the writings of Sapho [Henry Home] and David Hume. Edinburgh 1755. Anon.

Objections against the essays on morality and natural religion [by Henry Home, Lord Kames] examined. Edinburgh 1756. By Blair, assisted by George Wishart, Robert Hamilton and Robert Wallace.

A critical dissertation on the poems of Ossian. 1763 (limited to a discussion of Fingal), 1765 (enlarged to include Temora), Dublin 1765, Hanover 1765. Anon; frequently rptd in edns of Ossian.

Heads of the lectures on rhetoric and belles lettres. Edinburgh 1767, 1771, 1777.

The compassion and beneficence of the deity: a sermon. Edinburgh 1796.

§ 2

Campbell, G. A dissertation on miracles with a correspondence on the subject by Mr Hume, Dr Campbell and Dr Blair. 2 vols Edinburgh 1797, 1812, 1 vol Edinburgh 1823, London 1824, 1827, 1834. The 1797 edn is the first to include Blair; for earlier edns of Dissertation see Campbell.

Finlayson, J. Life. In Sermons vol 5, Edinburgh 1801 etc.

Hill, J. An account of the life and writings of Blair. Edinburgh 1807, 1808, Philadelphia 1808.

Williams, A. M. The Scottish school of rhetoric. Glasgow 1897.

Cowling, G. H. The English teaching of Blair. Anglica 2 1925.

Ferguson, J. D. Burns and Blair. MLN 45 1930; rptd in Burns Chron 2nd ser 7 1932.

Chapman, R. W. Blair on Ossian. RES 7 1931.

Jiriczek, O. L. Zur Bibliographie und Textgeschichte von Blairs Critical dissertation on the poems of Ossian. E Studies 70 1935.

Mays, M. J. Johnson and Blair on Addison's prose style. SP 39 1942.

Schmitz, R. M. Dr Johnson and Blair's sermons. MLN 60 1945.

—— Hugh Blair. New York 1948. Contains a list of edns, adaptations and trns.

Golden, J. L. Blair, Minister of St Giles. Quart Jnl of Speech 38 1952.

Corbett, E. P. J. Blair's three (?) critical dissertations [on Ossian]. N & Q Nov 1954.

—— Blair as an analyser of English prose style. College Composition & Communication 9 1958.

Edney, C. W. Blair's theory of dispositio. Speech Monographs 23 1956.

Cohen, H. Blair's theory of taste. Quart Jnl of Speech 44 1958.

Little, G. L. A note on Wordsworth and Blair. N & Q July 1960.

Bowers, J. W. A comparative criticism of Blair's essay on taste. Quart Jnl of Speech 47 1961.

Grimsley, R. Jean-Jacques Rousseau jugé par un pasteur écossais. Revue de Littérature Comparée 36 1962.

Ehninger, D. Campbell, Blair and Whately. Southern Speech Jnl 28 1963.

Bevilacqua, V. Philosophical assumptions underlying Blair's Lectures on rhetoric and belles lettres. Western Speech 31 1967.

JAMES BOSWELL
1740–95
See col 1210, above.

JAMES BURNETT,
LORD MONBODDO
1714–99
See col 1887, above.

JOHN CALLANDER of Craigforth
d. 1789

Hymn to the power of harmony. Edinburgh 1763.

Memorial on the general culture of lands in our American colonies. Edinburgh 1766.

Two ancient Scottish poems: the Gaberlunzie-man and Christ's kirk on the green, with notes and observations. Edinburgh 1782.

A critical review of the works of Dr Samuel Johnson. 1783. Anon.

Letters to Mr George Paton. In T. Percy, Letters from Thomas Percy, John Callender and others, Edinburgh 1830.

GEORGE CAMPBELL,
Principal of Marischal College
1719–96

Collections

Works. 6 vols 1840.

§ 1

A dissertation on miracles: containing an examination of the principles advanced by David Hume. Edinburgh 1762, 1766 (enlarged), 1796, 2 vols 1797 (with a correspondence on the subject by Mr Hume, Dr Campbell and Dr Blair), 1 vol 1812, 1823, London 1824, 1827, 1834; ed L. F. Bitzer, Carbondale 1963.

The philosophy of rhetoric. 2 vols 1776, 1801, Edinburgh 1808 (rev), 1816, 1819, London 1823 (abridged), Edinburgh 1841, 1850, New York 1911 (condensed); ed L. F. Bitzer, Carbondale 1963.

Address to the people of Scotland upon the alarms that have been raised in regard to Popery. Aberdeen 1779.

Lectures on ecclesiastical history, with some account of the life and writings of the author. Ed G. S. Keith 2 vols 1800, Aberdeen 1815, 1 vol 1824.

Other works include theological studies and a trn of the 4 Gospels. On 12 Dec 1776, Campbell preached a sermon at Aberdeen on the duty of allegiance in connection with the American Revolution, Aberdeen 1777, 1778.

§ 2

Bryan, W. F. A late 18th-century purist. SP 23 1926.

Bitzer, L. F. A re-evaluation of Campbell's doctrine of evidence [in Philosophy of rhetoric 1776]. Quart Jnl of Speech 46 1960.

Ehninger, D. Campbell, Blair and Whately. Southern Speech Jnl 28 1963.

Cronkhite, G. Intuition: Campbell's escape from scepticism. Western Speech 31 1967.

Cohen, H. William Leechman in anticipation of Campbell. Western Speech 32 1968.

Dolph, P. Taste and the Philosophy of rhetoric. Ibid.

La Russo, D. A. Root or branch? a re-examination of Campbell's rhetoric. Ibid.

Mohrmann, G. P. Campbell: the psychological background. Ibid.

ALEXANDER CARLYLE,
Minister of Inveresk
1722–1805

§ 1

A full and true history of the bloody tragedy of Douglas [by John Home] as it is now to be seen acting at the theatre in the Canongate. [Edinburgh? 1757]. A broadside.

An argument to prove that the tragedy of Douglas ought to be publicly burnt by the hands of the hangman. Edinburgh 1757. A satirical tract in defence of Home's Douglas.

'O.M. Haberdasher'. Plain reasons for removing a certain great man [Pitt] from his M—y's presence and councils for ever. 1759.

A sermon on the death of Sir David Dalrymple. Edinburgh 1792.

The usefulness and necessity of a liberal education for clergymen: a sermon. Edinburgh 1793.

Autobiography. Ed J. H. Burton, Edinburgh 1860, London 1910 (enlarged).

§ 2

Carver, P. L. Collins and Carlyle. RES 15 1939.

Meikle, H. W. New Smollett letters. TLS 24 July 1943. 7 letters to Carlyle.

ALEXANDER CUNNINGHAM
1655?–1730

§ 1

Animadversiones in R. Bentleii notas et emendationes ad Q. Horatium Flaccum. 1721, Hague 1721.

Q. Horatii Flacci poemata: ex antiquis codd. et certis observationibus emendavit. 1721.

Horatius denuo castigatus: sive loci CCLXX in Horatio ex fidissimis observationibus emendati ab a Cuningamio. 1722.

Oeuvres d'Horace en Latin et en français par M Dacier: cinquième édition augmentée de notes de MM Bentlei et Cuningham. Hamburg 1733.

P. Virgilii moronis bucolica, Georgica et Aeneis, ex recensione Alexandri Cuningamii. Edinburgh 1743.

Phaedri Augusti liberti fabularum Aesopiarum libri quinque, ex recensione Alexandri Cuningamii. Edinburgh 1757.

§ 2

Bibliotheca Cuningamia. Leyden [1730].

SYLVESTER DOUGLAS,
BARON GLENBERVIE
1743–1823

An account of the life of James Mercer. In Preface to Mercer's Lyric poems, 1806.

Introduction concerning the principal romantic, burlesque and mock-heroic poets. In trn of N. Forteguerri's Ricciardetto, 1821. Anon.

The Glenbervie journals. Ed W. Sichel 1910.

Diaries. Ed F. Bickley 2 vols 1928.

JAMES DUFF, 2nd EARL OF FIFE
1729–1809

Lord Fife and his factor: being the correspondence of James, second Lord Fife. Ed A. and H. Tayler 1925.

WILLIAM DUFF, Minister of Foveran
1732–1815

An essay on original genius and its various modes of exertion in philosophy and the fine arts, particularly in poetry. 1767.

Critical observations on the writings of the most celebrated original geniuses in poetry: being a sequel to the essay on original genius. 1770.

The history of Rhedi, the hermit of Mount Ararat: an oriental tale. 1773.

Letters on the intellectual and moral character of women. Aberdeen 1807.

ADAM FERGUSON LlD
1723–1816

§ 1

The morality of stage-plays seriously considered. Edinburgh 1757. Anon. Reply by Rev Harper, Some serious remarks on a late pamphlet entitled The morality of stage-plays seriously considered, Edinburgh 1757.

The history of the proceedings in the case of Margaret, commonly called Peg, only lawful sister to John Bull esq. 1761, 1761. An anon tract on the militia question.

Essay on the history of civil society. Edinburgh 1767, Dublin 1767, London 1768, 1773 (rev), Basle 1789 etc; ed D. Forbes, Edinburgh 1966; tr German 1768, 1904, 1923; tr French, 1783, 1796.

Institutes of moral philosophy. Edinburgh 1769, 1772, 1773, Jena 1773 etc; tr German, 1772, 1779, 1787; tr French, 1775.

The history of the progress and termination of the Roman republic. 3 vols 1783, 5 vols Edinburgh 1799 (rev) etc; tr French, 7 vols 1784–91, 1810–11; tr German, 1784–6.

Principles of moral and political science. 2 vols Edinburgh 1792; tr German, 1795; French, 1821.

Also sermons including one in Gaelic to the First Highland Regiment of Foot, preached Dec 1745, tr Ferguson and pbd 1746.

§ 2

Small, J. Biographical sketch of Ferguson (from the Transactions of the Royal Society of Edinburgh). Edinburgh 1864.

Huth, H. Soziale und individualistische Auffassung im 18 Jahrhundert, vornehmlich bei Adam Smith und Ferguson. Leipzig 1907. With bibliography.

Lehmann, W. C. Ferguson and the beginnings of modern sociology. New York 1930.

Dempster, G. Letters of George Dempster to Ferguson 1756–1813. Ed J. Ferguson 1934.

Muir, J. Ferguson: a gay philosopher. Scots Mag 29 1938.

Jogland, H. H. Ursprünge und Grundlagen der Soziologie bei Ferguson. Berlin 1959. With bibliography.

Mossner, E. C. Ferguson's Dialogue on a Highland jaunt with Robert Adam, William Cleghorn, David Hume and William Wilkie. In C. Camden (ed), Restoration and eighteenth-century literature, Chicago 1963.

Kettler, D. The social and political thought of Ferguson. Columbus 1965.

—— The political vision of Ferguson. Stud in Burke 9 1967.

ALEXANDER GERARD DD
1728–95

§ 1

Plan of education in the Marischal College and University of Aberdeen. Aberdeen 1755.

An essay on taste. 1759, Edinburgh 1764 (rev), 1780; tr French, 1766. An essay on taste (1759), together with observations concerning the imitative nature of poetry, ed W. J. Hipple jr, Gainesville 1963 (facs of 1780).

Dissertations on subjects relating to the genius and the evidences of Christianity. Edinburgh 1766.

An essay on genius. 1774; ed B. Fabian, Munich 1966.

Sermons. 2 vols 1780–2.

The pastoral care. 1799.

A compendious view of the evidences of natural and revealed religion, by A. and [continued by] G. Gerard. 1828.

Also pbd single sermons separately.

§ 2

Wiley, M. L. Gerard and the Scots societies. SE 20 1940.

Grene, M. Gerard's Essay on taste. MP 41 1943.

Cohen, R. Association of ideas and poetic unity. PQ 36 1957.

Bevilacqua, V. The authorship of Gerard's Lectures on logic and rhetoric. Eng Lang Notes 5 1967.

—— Gerard's Lectures on rhetoric: Edinburgh Univ Library MS Dc 5. 61. Speech Monographs 34 1967. These notes are from James Beattie's lectures.

HENRY HOME, LORD KAMES
1696–1782

Collections

Memoirs of the life and writings of Home. Ed A. F. Tytler 2 vols Edinburgh 1807; suppl 1809; 3 vols 1814.

§ 1

Essays upon several subjects concerning British antiquities. Edinburgh 1747, London 1749, Edinburgh 1763 (with addns), 1797.

Essays on the principles of morality and natural religion. Edinburgh 1751, London 1758; tr German, 1768, 1772.

Introduction to the art of thinking. Edinburgh 1761, 1764, 1775, 1789, 1810, New York 1818. Anon.

Elements of criticism. 3 vols Edinburgh 1762, 1763, 2 vols Edinburgh 1765, 1769, Dublin 1772, Edinburgh 1774, 1785 (with last corrections and addns), 1788, 3 vols Basle 1795, 2 vols Boston 1796, London 1805, 1807 (subsequent edns based on this edn, one of 2 called 8th edn), Philadelphia 1816, Edinburgh 1817, New York 1819, 1823, 1 vol 1824, New York 1829, 1830, London 1839, [also 1840?]; abridged A. Jamieson 1823; abridged J. Frost, Philadelphia 1831, 1833, 1839; abridged A. Mills, New York 1833, 1838, 1839, 1841, 1844, 1853, 1854, 1855, 1857, 1860; rev J. R. Boyd, New York 1855, 1859, 1869, 1876, 1883; tr German, 3 vols 1763–6, 2 vols 1772.

Sketches of the history of man. 2 vols Edinburgh 1774, Dublin 1775, 4 vols Edinburgh 1778, 1788, Basle 1796, Glasgow 1802, 3 vols Edinburgh 1807, 1813, Glasgow 1817, 1819; tr German, 2 vols 1774, 1776.

Critical observations on the poems of Ossian. In The poems of Ossian, 2 vols Edinburgh 1797.

§ 2

An analysis of the moral and religious sentiments contained in the writings of Sopho [Home] and David Hume. Edinburgh 1755 (anon). Reply as Observations upon a pamphlet entitled An analysis of the moral and religious sentiments contained in the writings of Sopho, and David Hume, Edinburgh 1755. Anon.

Elphinston, J. Animadversions upon Elements of criticism with an appendix on Scoticism. 1771.

Doig, D. Two letters on the savage state addressed to the late Lord Kames [on Sketches on the history of man]. 1792.

Smellie, W. Literary and characteristical lives of J. Gregory, Kames, David Hume and Adam Smith. Edinburgh 1800.

Joseph, M. Die Psychologie Homes. Halle 1911.

McKenzie, G. Lord Kames and the mechanist tradition. Univ of California Pbns in Eng 14 1943.

Randall, H. W. The critical theory of Lord Kames. Northampton Mass 1944.

Bundy, M. W. Lord Kames and the maggots in amber. JEGP 45 1946.

Cohen, R. Association of ideas and poetic unity. PQ 36 1957.

Shaw, L. R. Home of Kames: precursor of Herder. Germanic Rev 35 1960.

Bevilacqua, V. M. Rhetoric and human nature in Kames's Elements of criticism. Quart Jnl of Speech 48 1962.

—— Lord Kames's Theory of rhetoric. Speech Monographs 30 1963.

Horn, A. Kames and the anthropological approach to criticism. PQ 44 1965.

Mohrmann, G. P. Kames and elocution. Speech Monographs 32 1965.

Reid, T. Unpublished letters of Thomas Reid to Lord Kames 1762–82. Ed I. Ross, Texas Stud in Lit & Lang 7 1965.

Ross, I. Scots law and Scots criticism: the case of Lord Kames. PQ 45 1966.

—— Quaffing the 'Mixture of wormwood & aloes': a consideration of Lord Kames's Historical law tracts. Texas Stud in Lit & Lang 8 1967.

McGuinness, A. E. Lord Kames on the Ossian poems: anthropology and criticism. Texas Stud in Lit & Lang 10 1968.

DAVID HUME
1711–76

See col 1873, above.

GEORGE LOGAN, Minister of Trinity College Church Edinburgh
1678–1755

A treatise on government: shewing that the right of the Kings of Scotland to the Crown was not strictly and absolutely hereditary; against the Earl of Cromarty, Sir George Mackenzie, Mr John Sage and Mr Thomas Ruddiman. Edinburgh 1746. Reply by T. Ruddiman, A letter to the Rev G. Logan, Edinburgh 1747 (anon); An answer to the Rev G. Logan's late treatise on government in which the ancient constitution of the Crown and Kingdom of Scotland and the hereditary succession of its monarchy are asserted and vindicated, Edinburgh 1747.

A second treatise on government showing that the right to the Crown of Scotland was not hereditary in the sense of Jacobites. Edinburgh 1747. Reply by T. Ruddiman, A dissertation concerning the competition for the crown of Scotland, betwixt Lord Robert Bruce and Lord John Baliol, in the year 1291, Edinburgh 1748 (another answer to Logan et al).

The finishing stroke: or Mr Ruddiman self-condemned. Edinburgh 1748.

The doctrine of the jure-divino-ship of hereditary monarchy exploded in a letter to Mr T. Ruddiman. Edinburgh 1749.

A second letter to Mr T. Ruddiman. Edinburgh 1749.

JOHN MACDONALD of Inverness-shire

Travels in various parts of Europe, Asia and Africa. 1790; rptd as Memoirs of an eighteenth-century footman, ed J. Beresford 1927.

HENRY MACKENZIE
1745–1831
See col 1003 f., above.

JOHN MITCHELL, Minister of Wellington St Church, Glasgow
1768–1844

Memories of Ayrshire about 1780. Ed W. K. Dickson, Pbns of Scottish Historical Soc 3rd ser 33 1939.

JAMES MOOR LlD
1712–79

Essays read to a literary society at their weekly meetings within the College at Glasgow. Glasgow 1759.

On the end of tragedy according to Aristotle. Glasgow 1763, 1794.

On the praepositions of the Greek language. Glasgow 1766.

Vindication of Virgil. Glasgow 1766.

Bibliotheca Mooriana. Edinburgh 1779.

Moor edited Homer and Archimedes in Greek and wrote Elementa linguae Graecae, Glasgow 1766 etc, as well as works on Greek syntax.

[JOHN?] PEASE
1774–1807

Journal of a traveller in Scotland 1795-6. Ed P. Barber, Scottish Historical Rev 36 1957.

THOMAS RUDDIMAN
1674–1757

§ 1

In obitum A. Pitcarnii. [Edinburgh? 1713?]. A broadside elegy.

Rudiments of the Latin tongue. Edinburgh 1714 etc.

G. Buchani opera omnia nunc primum in unum collecta. 2 vols Edinburgh 1715, Leyden 1725. Ed Ruddiman.

Grammaticae latinae institutiones. 2 vols Edinburgh 1725-31 etc.

G. Buchanan, Paraphrasis psalmorum Davidis poetica. Ed J. Love and R. Hunter, Edinburgh 1737. Ptd by Ruddiman. Replies by W. Benson, A prefatory discourse to a new edition of the Psalms of David, translated into Latin verse by Dr Arthur Johnston; to which is added a supplement containing a comparison betwixt Johnston and Buchanan, 3 pts 1741; A vindication of Mr George Buchanan's paraphrase of the Book of Psalms from the objections raised by W. Benson. Edinburgh 1745 (anon); Animadversions on a late pamphlet entitled A vindication of Mr George Buchanan, wherein the arguments brought by its author for clearing Buchanan from the two great faults he is charged with are impartially examined and confuted, Edinburgh 1749 (anon); [J. Man], A censure and examination of Mr Ruddiman's notes on the works of the great Buchanan, Aberdeen 1753; Anticrisis: or a discussion of a scurrilous and malicious libel published by one Mr James Man, of Aberdeen, entitled A censure and examination, Edinburgh 1754 (anon); Audi alteram partem: or a further vindication of Mr T. Ruddiman's edition of the great Buchanan's works, Edinburgh 1756, London 1756 (anon).

Bibliotheca romana. Edinburgh 1757.

A collection of scarce curious and valuable pieces, both in verse and prose. Edinburgh 1773, 1785.

Also other pamphlets. Ruddiman preferred Johnston's trns of the Psalms to that of Buchanan, but wrote his Vindication (1745) because he felt that Benson's attack on Buchanan was unjust. Proof of Ruddiman's enthusiasm for Johnston may be seen in the fact that he edited an edn of the Cantici Solomonis paraphrasis poetica, 1709. *Among other works edited or ptd by Ruddiman are Gavin Douglas's trn of Virgil's Aeneid, 1710; Drummond of Hawthornden's Works, 1711; Ramsay's Poems, Tea-Table Miscellany, Ever-Green and the first edn of Gentle shepherd. For works in the Ruddiman-Logan controversy, see Logan, above.*

§ 2

Chalmers, G. The life of Ruddiman. 1794.

Duncan, D. Ruddiman: a study in Scottish scholarship of the early 18th century. Edinburgh 1965. With list of pbns of Ruddiman Press.

WILLIAM SMELLIE
1740–95

§ 1

Streetum Edinese: carmen macaronicum. English proem. [Edinburgh c. 1780]. By Smellie?

Natural history, general and particular. 9 vols Edinburgh 1781, 1785, 1791. Tr and ed Smellie from Buffon, Histoire naturelle générale et particulière.

An account of the institution and progress of the Society of Antiquaries of Scotland. 2 vols Edinburgh 1782-4.

Address to the people of Scotland on juries, by a juryman. Edinburgh 1784.

The philosophy of natural history. 2 vols Edinburgh 1790-9 (vol 2 ed his son Alexander), Dublin 1790, 1 vol Philadelphia 1791, Dover NH 1808; cd J. Ware, Boston 1824, 1834, 1835, London 1837, Boston 1838, 1846, 1854, 1860, 1863, Halifax 1844; tr German, 1791; tr Danish, 1796. An embossed edn was prepared by S. G. Howe for the blind, Boston 1845.

Literary and characteristical lives of J. Gregory, Henry Home, Lord Kames, David Hume and Adam Smith; to which are added a dissertation on public spirit and three essays. Edinburgh 1800.

Smellie was editor of, and major contributor to, first edn of Encyclopaedia britannica, 1771. Also editor of Scots Mag 1759-65 and founding editor, with Gilbert Stuart, of Edinburgh Mag & Rev 1773-6. Also numerous contributions to periodicals.

§ 2

Kerr, R. Memoirs of the life, writings and correspondence. 2 vols Edinburgh 1811.

Moule, J. Memoir of Smellie. In W. Jardine, Naturalist's library vol 25, Edinburgh 1833-43 etc; rptd in Jardine, Birds of Great Britain, 4 vols 1876; and in Lives of eminent naturalists, Edinburgh 1846.

ADAM SMITH
1723-90

See col 1880, above.

TOBIAS GEORGE SMOLLETT
1721-71

See col 962, above.

DUGALD STEWART
1753-1828

See col 1893, above.

ROBERT WALLACE
1697-1771

See col 1900, above.

PETER WILLIAMSON
1730-99

See col 1465, above.

JACOBITE LITERATURE
Poetry

The Jacobite movement called forth many broadsides, chapbooks and poems inserted in newspapers, magazines and books of verse, many of them anon. The following is a chronological listing with emphasis on contemporary single poems and collections, and on later anthologies. For bibliographies see under Prose, below.

Collections

London lampoon'd; formerly in the Jacobites songs, and at present in a scandalous paper Heraclitus Ridens, with reflections upon both. 1703. Heraclitus Ridens by Thomas Flatman consists of 82 numbers from 1 Feb 1681 to 22 Aug 1682.

The state bell-man's collection of verses for the year 1711. Edinburgh 1711 ('rptd from London edn').

Collection of state songs etc that have been publish'd since the Rebellion and sung in the several mug-houses, to be publish'd annually. 1716.

A full collection of all poems upon Charles Prince of Wales published since his arrival in Edinburgh. [Edinburgh] 1745. 11 poems.

A collection of loyal songs, for the use of the Revolution Club. Edinburgh 1748.

Collection of loyal songs, poems etc. [no place] 1750.

The true loyalist, or Chevalier's favourite: being a collection of songs never before printed; also several loyal compositions wrote by eminent hands. [no place] 1779.

Hogg, James (ed). The Jacobite relics of Scotland: being the songs, airs and legends, of the adherents to the House of Stuart. 2 vols Edinburgh 1819-21.

Jacobite melodies: a collection of the most popular legends, ballads and songs 1640 to 1746. Edinburgh 1823, Glasgow 1825.

[Malcolm, R. (ed)]. Jacobite minstrelsy with notes 1640-1784. Glasgow 1829. Almost the same contents as Jacobite melodies 1823, above.

MacKenzie, J. (ed). An T-Aosdàna: or a selection of popular Gaelic Jacobite songs. Edinburgh 1844.

Thornbury, G. W. (ed). Songs of the Cavaliers and Roundheads: Jacobite ballads etc. 1857.

Mackay, C. (ed). Jacobite songs and ballads of Scotland 1688-1746. 1861.

Jacobite song book. Glasgow [1863].

[Ross, P. (ed)]. Jacobite songs of Scotland chronologically arranged. Glasgow 1871.

Grosart, A. B. (ed). English Jacobite ballads from mss at Towneley Hall. 1877.

MacQuoid, G. S. (ed). Jacobite songs and ballads. 1887, 1888, nd.

Firth, C. H. (ed). Jacobite songs. Scottish Historical Rev 8 1911.

— Two ballads on Viscount Dundee. Ibid.

— A contemporary ballad of Culloden. Jnl of Soc of Army Historical Research 1 1922.

Boulton, H. (ed). Prince Charlie in song. 1933.

§ 1

The Jacobites Hudibras: containing the late King's declaration [of 20 April 1692] in travesty. [1692].

The Jacobites invitation to the French. 1692. A broadside satire.

A scourge for the Jacobites. 1692. A satire.

[Ames, Richard]. The Jacobite conventicle: a poem. 1692.

The religious turncoat: or a late Jacobite divine turned Williamite. 1693. A broadside ballad.

The religious turncoat. 1694, [London 1695?]. Satirical verses on W. Sherlock.

The Jacobites lamentation and confession. 1696. A broadside ballad.

The generous Muse: a funeral poem in memory of his late Majesty K. James the II. 1701.

An historical poem upon his late Majesty King James II. 1701.

The King at St Germains: a poem in burlesque. 1701.

An ode on the death of the late King James, written originally in French at St Germains and dedicated to his son the Prince, and now translated into English. 1701.

L., Father. A consolatory poem in praise of retirement, spoke to the late King James at his arrival at St Germain's in the year 1688. 1701.

The British Muse: or tyranny exposed, occasioned by all the fulsom and lying poems and elegies on the death of King James. 1702.

The seven wise men. 1704. Satire on the 7 Lords appointed to look into the Scottish Plot.

[Blackmore, Sir Richard?] The flight of the Pretender, with advice to the poets: a poem in the Arthurical-Jobical-Elizabethecal style and phrase of the sublime poet Maurus. 1708, nd.

The dream of the Solan goose, with advice to Robin Red-Breast, sent in a packet from Leith. 1709.

The Jacobite's hopes: or Perkin rideing in triumph. [no place] [1709]. A print of the Pretender with accompanying verses.

The black-bird's tale: a poem. 1710.

— Tale of the Robin-red-breast: a poem, by the author of the Black bird's tale. 1710.

The fair question, or who deserves an impeachment now?: a poem. 1710.

The Jacobites' coat of arms. [1710?]. Woodcut with verses.

The ballad of the King shall enjoy his own again; with a learned comment thereupon, at the request of Capt Silk, by the author of Tom Thumb. 1711.

Political merriment: or truths told to some tune, by a lover of his country. 1714 [Anti-Jacobite songs and ballads], 1715 (2nd pt, not indicated as such).

[Wright, William]. The Jacobite curse: or excommunication of King George and his subjects; to which is added a poem on the Protestant succession, by a lover of the protestant religion. Glasgow 1714.

The blackbird's song. 1715.

— Tale of the raven and the blackbird, by the author of the Blackbird's song. 2nd edn 1715.

Four Hudibrastick cantos: being poems on four of the greatest heroes that liv'd in any age since Nero's, Don Juan Howlet, Hudibras, Dicko-Banes and Bonniface. 1715.

To the memory of Sir William Wallace. [no place 1715]. Broadside.

Brereton. George: a poem, humbly inscribed to the Earl of Warrington. 1715.

Settle, Elkanah. Rebellion display'd, or our present distractions set forth in their true light: an heroick poem. 1715.

Steddy, John. A trip to Bar-le-Duc: a poem. Edinburgh 1715.

An epistle to Sir Samuel Garth, occasion'd by the landing of the Pretender and the report of HRH the Prince of Wales's going to Scotland. 1716.

The fate of traytors: a poem upon the Rebellion. 1716.

The Pretender's declaration explained in verse. 1716.

To his Grace the Duke of Argyle upon his arrival at Court, after the defeat of the northern rebellion, Mar[ch] 6 1715. 1716.

Der trost-lose Jacobit über den weinenden Prätendenten in Schottland, aus dem Holländischen übersetzet. [no place] 1716.

B., H. The Pretender's declaration explained in verse. 1716.

The garland of merriment: 1, A game of cards for a Kingdom: or Mar routed; 2, A comical Scotch dialogue; 3, A copy of verses on the death of my Lord Derwentwater; 4, On the wonderful sight that was seen in the air on 6th Mar[ch] last, Nottingham [1717].

Rebellious fame: a poem occasion'd by the many lies dispersed against the Government since the late Rebellion. 1717.

The Chevalier de St George: an heroi-comic poem. 1718. In 6 cantos.

The garland of victory at Glenshiel. [no place 1718]. A broadside.

A mock epithalamium upon the fictitious marriage of the Pretender with the Princess Sobieskie. 1718.

Protestant popery, or the convocation: a poem. 1718.

The plotters: a satire containing a true description of all the statesmen belonging to the Chevalier's court. 1722.

H—, B—. The oracle of Avignon: or a new and true account of all the great actions and occurrences of the life of the Pretender, being a comico-prosaico-poetical essay, by B—H—, his poet-laureate, in French and English, pt 1: to be continued. 1723 (all pbd).

Welsted, Leonard. Ode to the Hon Major-General Wade, on the occasion on his disarming the Highlands, imitated from Horace; to which is added the Fourth Ode translated from the same author. 1726.

His Grace the Duke of Argyle's welcome to Edinburgh, June 16 1738. [no place 1738]. A broadside.

Melancholly sonnets: being Fergusia's complaint upon Heptarchus. Elguze (for Elgouae?) 1741.

Butler, Jemmy. The strolling hero, or Rome's knight-errant: a hudibrastick poem on the young Chevalier's expedition. 1744.

The alarm: a poem addressed to all lovers of our constitution in Church and State. 1745 (2nd edn enlarged).

Bishop Ridley's ghost: a poem occasioned by the present unnatural rebellion in favour of a popish Pretender. 1745.

Britain's lamentation and hopes of triumph. [no place c. 1745]. A chapbook.

An elegy on the memory of Col James Gardner, who was cruelly murdered near Tranent, Sept 21 1745. [no place c. 1745]; rptd in Scottish Historical Rev 6 1909.

England's danger and duty, represented in a copy of verses on the present Rebellion in Scotland. 1745.

The heroes: a new ballad. 1745.

The highland invasion: a new ballad in which is humourously described the romantic views of the Pretender. 1745.

La maison du roi: ode. [Paris] 1745.

A new ballad to the tune Highland ladie, bonnie ladie. [no place c. 1745]. Single sheet.

Ode au prince conquérant d'Ecosse. Edinburgh 1745.

An ode compos'd in the year MDCCXX on the birth of a great Prince. [no place c. 1745?].

Ode sur l'enterprise du Prince de Galles. [no place c. 1745].

An ode to his Royal Highness Charles, after the Battle of Gladsmuir. [no place] 1745.

Place-book for the year seventeen-hundred, forty-five: a new ballad. 1744-5.

Religious ode occasioned by the present Rebellion, written 11th Oct 1745, by a clergyman. 1745.

Slavery in miniature: a fable apply'd to the most factious people of Great Britain. [no place] 1745. A broadside.

Verses occasion'd by the present rebellion. 1745.

The warming-pan: a loyal song. [1745]. A broadside.

Cibber, Theophilus. The association, or liberty and loyalty: verses occasion'd by the present unnatural rebellion. 1745.

Gibbons, Thomas. Britannia's alarm: a poem occasioned by the present rebellion. 1745.

H—, J—. The national alarm, occasion'd by the rumour of a fresh invasion by their Gallic neighbours. 1745.

'Kattolikus'. Den grooten Raad van Romen. [no place 1745?]. Print with accompanying verses.

'Pelagius, Porcupinus'. The processionade, in panegyric-satiri-serio-comi-baladical versicles. 1745.

A son altesse royale Monseigneur le Prince de Galles. [no place c. 1746].

Arms and the man I sing: a ballad. 1746.

The compliment, addressed to HRH the Duke of Cumberland, by the author of the Two lurchers. 3 pts Eton 1746.

The contrast. [no place c. 1746].

An elegy, inscribed to the Duke of Cumberland. Edinburgh 1746.

Ἐωσφόρος, or the morning star: a poem inscribed to HRH the Duke of Cumberland. 1746.

Harlequin incendiary, or Colombine Cameron: a musical pantomime. 1746.

Liberty: an ode occasion'd by the happy victory obtained by HRH the Duke of Cumberland. 1746.

The northern monster, or Scotland's nurseling: a short poem occasion'd by the flight of the rebels out of England from HRH the Duke of Cumberland. 1746.

On the Battle of Culloden. [no place c. 1746]. A single sheet.

On the death of the Hon Col James Gardiner, who was slain in the Battle at Preston-Pans: a poem. 1746.

One thousand seven hundred and forty-five: a satiric-epistle after the manner of Mr Pope. 1746.

The plaid-hunting: a ballad by no Puff. [no place c. 1746].

A poem: French and English. [no place c. 1746]. Parallel texts.

Prince William's garland; to which is added Up and war them a' Willie. [no place] 1746.

The progress of glory: an irregular ode addressed to his Majesty on the happy suppression of the rebellion. 1746.

The sacred lion conquers every foe. [no place 1746]. Verses accompanying an anti-Jacobite print representing the victory at Culloden.

The sweet William. [no place c. 1746].

Two excellent new songs: I, A muzzle for the Jacobites; II, An elegy on Charles the Chevalier. [no place] 1746.

Chapman, T. The winter campaign: a poem. 1746.

Free, John. The guardian: an imitation of Horace, ode V, book IV, addressed to HRH the Duke of Cumberland upon his defeat of the royal army in Scotland. 1746.

Graham, Dougal. The battle of Drummossie-Muir. [Edinburgh?] 1746. On Culloden.

—— A full, particular and true account of the rebellion in the years 1745–6. Glasgow 1746. Title varies in the several other edns of this chap-book. *For complete list see col 2025, above.*

Lockman, J. An ode on the crushing of the rebellion. 1746.

Macdonald, Donald. The saddle put on the right horse, or thoughts on the present time: a poem in the style of Allan Ramsay. 1746.

Newcomb, Rev Thomas. Ode presented to HRH the Duke of Cumberland on his return from Scotland. 1746.

[Nihell, J.] La bataille de Preston: poème. [no place] 1746.

'Rossendaliensis, Philonactos'. A poem on the late rebellion. Manchester [1746].

Smollett, Tobias G. The tears of Scotland. [1746?] (unique copy Harvard); also in The Union: or select Scots and English poems, Edinburgh 1753, London 1759, 1766, Oxford 1796; and The beauties of English poesy, ed O. Goldsmith, 1767. Frequently rptd. There may have been a first issue entitled The groans of Scotland.

Teakel, John. An excellent new song to the excellent old tune of God prosper long our noble King. Edinburgh 1746.

Williams, Sir Charles Hanbury. An ode to the Right Honourable Stephen Poyntz esq. 1746.

[——]. The unembarrassed countenance: a new ballad. 1746.

Britain's consolation, in triumph after lamentation. [no place] 1747.

Fortune's tricks in forty-six: an allegorical satire. 1747.

Lord Lovet's reception by the spectators as he passed through the City, March 19 1747. [no place 1747]; rptd in Scottish Historical Rev 6 1909.

Lovat's ghost, or the courtier's warning-piece: a ballad. 1747.

Table-talk, September 1745. 1747.

To Mr S— M— on his turning evidence. 1747. Against Sir John Murray.

'Philibert'. A poem composed November 1747 the day the Hon Archibald Stuart [for Stewart] was assoilzied from his second trial. [no place c. 1747].

'Puerulus'. The glory of his Royal Highness the Duke of Cumberland in the Battle of Culloden. [no place] 1747.

Schomberg, Ralph, MD. An ode on the present rebellion, dedicated to her Royal Highness the Princess of Orange. Edinburgh 1747, 'Reprint of Rotterdam 1746 edn'.

'Fénelon, François de S. de la M.' The accomplish'd hero: or the Caledonian songsters from the French of Fénelon. 1748.

Manlius, or the brave adventurer: a poetical novel. Edinburgh 1749.

A new song for Thursday the 17th of May 1750. [no place 1750].

Poems on several occasions. [no place] 1750.

Robertson, Alexander, of Struan. Poems on various subjects and occasions. Edinburgh [1750?].

British worthies or characters of the age; to which is prefixed an address to the shade of the late Lord Bolingbroke. 1758.

Remarkable satires. 1760.

Galloway, Robert. Poems, epistles and songs, chiefly in the Scottish dialect; to which are added a brief account of the Revolution in 1688 and a narrative of the rebellion in 1745–6, to the death of Prince Charles 1788. Glasgow 1788.

Elegy on the death of the heroic Charles Edward Stewart. [no place 1789]. A broadside.

[Watson, A.] The anti-Jacobin: a Hudibrastic poem. Edinburgh 1794.

The Battle of Prestonpans. Stirling 1825, Dunbar nd. A chapbook.

Laing, David (ed). Killycrankie; An answer to Killychrankie. In Various pieces of fugitive Scotish poetry, principally of the seventeenth century, Edinburgh 1825. Laing's text taken from a broadside ptd about 1689. Killiechrankie was often rptd in collections of Jacobite songs, but the Answer was probably rptd for the first time by Laing.

Nairne, Caroline Baroness. Wha'll be King but Charlie [and other songs]. Boston [1835?].

[Adams, John]. Prince Charles Edward after the Battle of Culloden. Oxford 1847. A prize poem.

Philip, James. The Grameid: an heroic poem descriptive of the campaign of Viscount Dundee in 1689, and other pieces 1691 [all in Latin]. Ed A. D. Murdoch, 1888 (Scottish Historical Soc).

Julian, Charles. The last of the Stuarts: a dramatic poem. Denver 1905.

Taylor, G. The story of Glencoe and other poems. New York 1909.

The birthday ode. [no place] nd.

The contras [and] An epitaph in imitation of Dr Arbuthnot. [Scotland?] nd. On William Augustus Duke of Cumberland.

Epitaph upon an old woman's gravestone at Dunholm. [Scotland?] nd. A broadside.

Jacobite epigram, 1748. [Scotland?] nd (after 1748). A single sheet.

The little warbler vol 5: Jacobite songs. Edinburgh nd.

L'ombre de Jacques II, ou le songe de George Roi d'Angleterre: poème. [France?] nd.

'Antigallicus, Titus'. An ode for the thanksgiving-day. [London?] nd.

§ 2

Reid, A. Prince Charlie and the '45: popular reading with Jacobite songs. Paisley [1886?].

Clyne, N. The Scottish Jacobites and their poetry. Aberdeen 1887; also anon [Aberdeen? c. 1890].

Caie, N. M. Jacobite songs and Jacobite politics. Scots Mag 23 1899.

Newbigging, T. The Scottish Jacobites: their songs and music, with a succinct account of their battles. 1899, 1907.

Prose

The following is a small selection from the enormous quantity of pbd material on the risings of 1715 and 1745, mostly anon and often libellous, fictitious or inaccurate. The more fanciful fictitious material has been included in Fiction and Drama, below.

Bibliographies

Terry, C. S. The rising of 1745, with a bibliography of Jacobite history 1689–1788. 1900, 1903 (rev).

Guthrie, D. A. and C. L. Grose. Forty years of Jacobite bibliography [1895–1938]. Jnl of Modern History 11 1939.

Allardyce, M. D. Aberdeen University Library MacBean Collection: a catalogue of books, pamphlets, broadsides, portraits in the Stuart and Jacobite collection. Aberdeen 1949.

National Library of Sootland shelf-catalogue of the Blaikie collection of Jacobite pamphlets, broadsides and proclamations. Boston 1964.

§ I

Leslie, Charles. Galienus redivivus: or murther will out etc: being a true account of the De-Witting of Glencoe, Gaffney etc. Edinburgh 1695.

An account of the late Scotch invasion, with true copies of authentick papers. 1709.

Memoirs of the Lord Viscount of Dundee, the Highland clans and the massacre of Glenco; with an account of Dundee's officers after they went to France, by an officer of the army. 1711.

Memoirs of the Chevalier de St George. 1712; tr French, 1713.

The secret history of the Chevalier de St George: being an impartial account of his birth and pretences to the Crown of England. 1714.

Memoirs of John Duke of Melfort: being an account of the secret intrigues of the Chevalier de S. George, particularly relating to the present times. 1714.

Compleat history of the late rebellion. 1716.

Journal of the Earl of Marr's proceedings. 1716, nd (2nd edn).

A true account of the proceedings at Perth; the debates in the secret council there; with the reasons and causes of the suddain breaking up of the Rebellion, written by a rebel. 1716.

Patten, Robert. The history of the late rebellion. 1717.

'Philalethes' (Whitelocke Bulstrode). A letter touching the late rebellion and what means led to it; and of the Pretender's title. 1717.

A faithful register of the late rebellion: or an impartial account of the impeachments, trials, speeches etc of all who have suffered for the cause of the Pretender in Great Britain. 1718.

Rae, Peter. A history of the late rebellion. Dumfries 1718.

[Fielding, Henry]. The history of the present rebellion in Scotland. 1745.

[Gibbons, Thomas]. Miscellaneous pieces relating to the present Rebellion, collected out of the publick papers. 1745.

Macpherson, James. The history of the present rebellion in Scotland, taken from the relation of Mr James Macpherson. 1745, Belfast 1745.

'Philalethes' (Robert Forbes, Bishop of Leith). A plain authentic and faithful narrative of the several passages of the young Chevalier from the Battle of Culloden to his embarkation for France. 1745 (3rd edn); to which are added poems etc wrote on that occasion, 1765, 1765; postscript, 1750.

A serious address to the people of Great Britain, in which certain consequences of the present rebellion are fully demonstrated. 1745.

A full collection of all the proclamations and orders published by the authority of Charles Prince of Wales since his arrival in Edinburgh. 2 pts Glasgow 1745–6.

[Fielding, Henry]. The true patriot. 34 nos 5 Nov 1745–23 July 1748. Usually listed as 32 pts only.

Comparison of the spirit of the Whigs and Jacobites: being the substance of a discourse delivered in Edinburgh, Dec 24 1745. Edinburgh 1746.

An enquiry into the causes of the late rebellion and the proper methods for preventing the like misfortune for the future. 1746.

Genuine memoirs of the life of Lord Fraser of Lovat. 1746.

Indication de la prophétie de Nostradamus sur la révolution présente d'Angleterre. 1746.

Memoirs of the life of Lord Lovat. 1746.

Memoirs of the lives and families of the Lords Kilmarnock, Cromartie and Balmerino. 1746, Dublin 1746.

Spirit and principles of the Whigs and Jacobites compared: being the substance of a discourse delivered at Edinburgh, Dec 22 1745. Edinburgh 1746.

[Henderson, Andrew]. The young Chevalier: or a genuine narrative of all that befell that unfortunate adventurer from his fatal defeat to his final escape. [c. 1746].

—— The history of the rebellion, 1745 and 1746. Edinburgh 1748, 1753. Practically a new work.

Hughes, Michael. A plain narrative or journal of the late rebellion till the full and glorious defeat at Culloden. 1746.

Marchant, John. The history of the present Rebellion. 1746.

An account of the behaviour of Simon Lord Lovat. 1747.

Doddridge, Philip. Some remarkable passages in the life of the honourable Col James Gardiner. Edinburgh 1747.

Genuine memoirs of John Murray, late secretary to the Young Pretender. 1747.

History of the conspiracies, trials and dying speeches of all those who have suffered on account of the House of Stuart from the Revolution down to the commencement of the last rebellion. 1747.

The history of the Rebellion in Scotland in 1745. 1747.

'Trott-Plaid, John' (Henry Fielding). The Jacobite's journal. 49 nos 5 Dec 1747–5 Nov 1748.

A true account of the behaviour and conduct of Archibald Stewart esq, late Lord Provost of Edinburgh. 1748. Ascribed to David Hume.

Boyse, Samuel. An impartial history of the late rebellion in 1745. Reading 1748.

[Burton, John]. A genuine and true journal of the most miraculous escape of the young Chevalier from the battle of Culloden to his landing in France, by an Englishman. 1749.

[Murray, Lord George]. A particular account of the Battle of Culloden, April 16 1746, in a letter from an officer of the Highland army to his friend at London. 1749.

Ray, James. A complete history of the Rebellion. York 1749.

Report of the proceedings and opinions of the board of general officers in their examination into the conduct of Sir John Cope. 1749.

Douglas, Francis (ed). The Aberdeen intelligencer. 3 Oct 1752–22 Feb 1757. A Jacobite journal later incorporated into Aberdeen Jnl 1757.

Cameron, Archibald. An historical account of the life, actions and conduct of Dr Archibald Cameron. 1753.

Douglas, Francis. The history of the rebellion in 1745 and 1746, extracted from the Scots Magazine. Aberdeen 1755.

Istoria di il principe Carlo Odoardo Stuart di Galles. Milan 1760.

The secret history of Colonel Hoocke's negociations in Scotland in 1707. Edinburgh 1760.

Particulars of the secret history of Murray of Broughton. 1766.

Memoirs of the life of Simon Fraser, Lord Lovat. Edinburgh 1767.

A short and true narrative of the Rebellion in the year 1745. Edinburgh 1779.

Home, John. The history of the Rebellion in the year 1745. 1802.

Johnstone, James, Chevalier de. Memoirs of the Rebellion in 1745 and 1746, translated from a French ms. 1820, 1821, 1822, 3 vols Aberdeen 1870–1.

Pichot, Amédée. Histoire de Charles Edouard. 2 vols Paris 1830, 1833, 2 vols Paris 1845–6 (4th edn); tr Spanish, 1831.

Forbes, Robert. Jacobite memoirs of the rebellion of 1745. Ed R. Chambers, Edinburgh 1834. Extract

—— Journals. Ed J. B. Craven 1886. Complete.

Gordon, John. The correspondence of Sir John Gordon in 1745. Edinburgh 1835.

Jacobite correspondence of the Atholl family. Ed J. H. Burton and D. Laing, Edinburgh 1840 (Abbotsford Club).

Bisset, John. Extracts from the diary of the Rev John Bisset, Minister at Aberdeen 1745–6. In Miscellany of the Spalding Club vol 1, Aberdeen 1841.

Gordon, Lewis. Letters from Lord Lewis Gordon and others to the Laird of Stonywood 1745–6. Ibid.

Klose, C. L. Leben des Prinzen Carl, aus dem Hause Stuart. Leipsig 1842; tr 2 vols 1845, 1846.

Keith, J. F. E. Fragments of a memoir of Keith written by himself 1714–34. Edinburgh 1843 (Spalding Club).

Roy, J. J. E. Le dernier des Stuarts. Tours 1855, 1885 (11th edn).

Sinclair, John. Memoirs of the insurrection in Scotland in 1715, with notes by Walter Scott. Edinburgh 1858 (Abbotsford Club).

Extracts from the Council Register of the Burgh of Aberdeen 1643–1747. Edinburgh 1872.

O'Neil, F. A narrative of the wanderings of Prince Charles after Culloden. Ed W.M. 1873 (priv ptd). Incorrect version in Robert Forbes, Jacobite memoirs, ed R. Chambers 1834.

Dixon, Willmott. The Jacobite episode in Scottish history and its relative literature: an essay. Edinburgh 1874.

The rebellion of 1715, gathering clouds: being a contemporary account. 1884 (Clarendon Historical Soc).

Forbes, Robert. The Lyon in mourning: or a collection of speeches, letters, journals etc relative to Prince Charles Edward Stuart 1746–75. Ed H. Paton 1895–6 (Scottish Historical Soc).

Historical papers relating to the Jacobite period 1699–1750. Ed J. Allardyce 2 vols Aberdeen 1895–6 (New Spalding Club).

The Highlands of Scotland in 1750. Ed A. Lang, Edinburgh 1898.

Memorials of John Murray of Broughton sect to Prince Charles Edward 1740–7. Ed R. F. Bell 1898 (Scottish Historical Soc).

Lang, Andrew. Prince Charles Edward. Edinburgh 1900.

Terry, C. S. The rising of 1745, with a bibliography of Jacobite history 1689–1788. 1900, 1903 (enlarged).

—— The young Pretender. 1905.

The Chevalier de St George and the Jacobite movements in his favour 1701–20. Ed C. S. Terry 1901, 1915.

Letters of the Chevalier de St George. Ed C. S. Terry, EHR 16 1901.

The Albemarle papers: being the correspondence of William Anne, second Earl of Albemarle, Commander-in-chief in Scotland 1746–7. Ed C. S. Terry 2 vols Aberdeen 1902 (New Spalding Club).

Wemyss, David, Lord Elcho. A short account of the affairs of Scotland. Ed E. Charteris, Edinburgh 1907.

Origins of the '45 and other papers relating to that rising. Ed W. B. Blaikie 1916 (Scottish Historical Soc).

The Forty-Five: a narrative of the last Jacobite rising, by several contemporary hands. Ed C. S. Terry, Cambridge 1922.

The Jacobites and the Union: a narrative of the movements of 1708, 1715, 1719, by contemporary hands. Ed C. S. Terry, Cambridge 1922.

More Culloden papers [1625–1748]. Ed D. Warrand 5 vols Inverness 1923–30. Earlier edn as Culloden papers, [ed H. R. Duff] 1815.

Jacobites of Aberdeenshire and Banffshire in the Forty-five. Ed A. and H. Tayler 1928.

Jacobite letters to Lord Pitsligo 1745–6. Ed A. and H. Tayler 1930.

Petrie, Sir Charles. The Jacobite movement. 1932; expanded as The Jacobite movement: the first phase 1688–1716, 1948; The last phase 1716–1807, 1950.

—— The Stuart pretenders: a history of the Jacobite movement 1688–1807. 1933.

Wilkinson, Clennell. Bonnie Prince Charlie. 1932.

Tayler, A. and S. 1715: The story of the rising. 1936.

Yeaman, W. Edinburgh before the 'Fifteen. Juridical Rev 49 1937. Based on letters of Charles Cockburn.

Duke, W. Prince Charles Edward and the Forty-Five. 1938.

Mason, John. Conditions in the Highlands after the 'Forty-five. Scottish Historical Rev 26 1947.

Cherry, G. L. The legal and philosophical position of the Jacobites 1688–9. Jnl of Modern History 22 1950.

Insh, George Pratt. The Scottish Jacobite movement: a study in economic and social forces. Edinburgh 1952.

Tomasson, Katherine. The Jacobite General. Edinburgh 1958. A biography of Lord George Murray.

Gibson, J. S. Ships of the '45: the rescue of the Young Pretender. 1967.

The chronicle of Charles the young man. nd.

Fiction and Drama

No attempt has been made to include all works for juvenile readers, which abound; first edns only have been noted.

Retour de Jacques II à Paris: comédie. Cologne 1696.

'Philips, John' (George Sewell?). The Earl of Mar marr'd, with the humours of Jockey the Highlander: a tragi-comical farce. 1715.

—— The Pretender's flight, or a mock coronation, with the humours of the facetious Harry Saint John: a tragi-comical farce, being the sequel of the Earl of Mar marr'd. 1716.

The usurper detected, or right will prevail: a comick-tragical farce of two acts in verse and prose. 1718.

Prologue spoken Dec 9 1745 at the Theatre Royal in Drury Lane. [London? 1745]. Single sheet.

The life of Miss Jenny Cameron, the reputed mistress of the deputy Pretender. 1746.

'Arbuthnot, Archibald'. Memoirs of the remarkable life and surprising adventures of Miss Jenny Cameron. 1746.

—— The life, adventures and many and great vicissitudes of fortune of Simon Lord Lovat. 1746.

[Griffiths, Ralph?]. Ascanius: or the young adventurer. 1746; tr French, 1747; Spanish, [1750?]. Edn suppressed and author imprisoned; of many subsequent edns all lack first pt—*see* Wanderer, 1747, *below*.

[Macdonald, Donald]. Alexis: or the young adventurer. 1746. Novel with a key; rptd as Interesting and faithful narrative of the wanderings of Prince Charles Stuart and Miss Flora Macdonald after the Battle of Culloden. With Jacobite poems, ed P. Buchan, Glasgow 1839.

The female rebels: being some remarkable incidents of the lives of the titular Duke and Duchess of Perth, the Lord and Lady Ogilvie and of Miss Florence McDonald. Edinburgh 1747.

Fortune's tricks in forty-six: an allegorical satire. 1747. Drama.

The wanderer: or suprising escape, with some remarks on a romance called Ascanius. 1747, Glasgow 1752. Romance.

Young Juba: or the history of the young Chevalier, translated from the original Italian publication by M. Michell. 1748. Romance. Michael Vezazi was the Prince's valet, but not the author of this book.

Aeneas and his two sons: a true portrait. [c. 1746–50]. Romance.

Kotzebue, August F. F. von. Eduard in Schottland, oder die Nacht eines Flüchtlings: ein historisches Drama. Augsburg 1788; tr Italian, 1796; French, 1830, tr

English by J. W. Underwood 1836. For adaptation *see* Charles Kemble, *below*.

Jacobitism unmasked: or the learned speakers, as performed at the County Hall in Coventry. [1790?]. A farce.

Helme, Elizabeth. Duncan and Peggy. 2 vols 1794.

[Burges, Mary Ann]. The progress of the Pilgrim Good-Intent in Jacobinical times. 1800. A novel.

Kemble, Charles. The wanderer: or the rights of hospitality, altered from the German of A. von Kotzebue. 1808.

Scott, Sir Walter. Waverley. 3 vols Edinburgh 1814.
—— Rob Roy. 3 vols Edinburgh 1818.
—— Redgauntlet: a tale of the eighteenth century. 3 vols Edinburgh 1824.
    Also dramas founded on these 3 novels.
—— The Highland widow. In Chronicles of the Canongate: first series, Edinburgh 1827.

Stafford, J. J. The pretender, or the rose of Alvey: a petite comedy in two acts. [1834?], [1888].

[Talfourd, T. N.] Glencoe, or the fate of the Macdonalds: a tragedy in 5 acts. 1840.

Grant, J. The adventures of Rob Roy. 1848. Mostly anecdotes and traditions rather than fiction.
—— The Scottish cavalier. 3 vols 1850. A novel.
—— The white cockade. [1870].

Fillam, A. D. Stories, traditionary and romantic, of the two rebellions in Scotland in 1715 and 1745. 1849.

'1745': a tale. 1859.

Steffens, F. James II und sein Fall: historischer Roman. 3 vols Berlin 1859.

Coppée, F. Les Jacobites: drame en cinq actes en vers. Paris 1885.

Stevenson, R. L. Kidnapped. 1886.
—— The Master of Ballantrae. 1889.
—— Catriona. 1892.

Whamond, A. Delburn House, parish and people: a humorous tale of the '45. Edinburgh 1888.

Dod, S. B. A Highland chronicle. [1892].

Allardyce, A. Balmoral. Edinburgh 1893.

'Fife, M. B.' (Margaret M. Black). The ghost of Gairn. 1894.

Smith, H. B. Rob Roy, or the thistle and the rose: an opera in three acts. 1894.

'Tytler, Sarah' (Henrietta Keddie). The Macdonald lass: a study from the last century. 1895.
—— Favours from France. 1904.

Snaith, J. C. Fierceheart the soldier: a romance of 1745. New York 1897.
—— Lady Barbarity. New York 1899.

Balfour, A. To arms! Boston 1898.

'Donovan, D.' (Joyce E. P. Muddock). The lost laird. 1898.
—— For the white cockade. 1905.

'Lindsay, H.' (H. L. Hudson). The Jacobite: a romance of the conspiracy of the Forty. 1898.

McLellan, W. Spanish John. 1898.

Sutcliffe, H. Ricroft of Withens. 1898.
—— Willowdene Will. 1901.
—— The lone adventurer. 1911.

Buchan, J. A lost lady of old years. 1899.

Watson, W. L. Sir Sergeant, adventures that ensued upon the '45. Edinburgh 1899.

Findlay, J. T. A deal with the King. 1901.

McIlwraith, Jean N. The curious career of Roderick Campbell. 1901.

Mason, A. E. W. Clementina. 1901.

Munro, N. Doom castle. Edinburgh 1901.
—— The shoes of fortune. 1901.

Robertson, W. The stone of Dunalter. Paisley 1901.

'M'Aulay, A.' (Charlotte Stewart). Poor sons of a day. 1902.

Stephens, R. N. The flight of Georgiana. 1905.

Eccott, W. J. The hearth of Hutton. Edinburgh 1906.

Maclean, N. Hills of home. 1906.

'Barnett, J.' (J. R. Stagg). The Prince's valet. 1907.

Watt, L. M. Edragil 1745. 1907.

'Montgomery, K. L.' (Kathleen and Letitia Montgomery). Colonel Kate. 1908.

Peck, Theodora. The sword of Dundee: a tale of Bonnie Prince Charlie. New York 1908.

Tarbet, W. G. A loyal maid. 1908.

Dill, Bessie. The silver glen: a story of the Rebellion of 1715. 1909.

Fergusson, R. M. The silver shoe-buckle: a tale of the '15. 1909.

Brandane, J. My lady of Aros. 1910.

Jacob, Violet. Flemington. 1911.

McCarthy, J. H. The King over the water: or the marriage of Mr Melancholy. 1911.

Foster, J. The bright eyes of danger: being a chronicle of the troubled years of 1745 and 1746. Philadelphia 1916.

Milne, J. The black Colonel. 1921.

MacInnes, M. The 'Forty-five: a dramatised account of the Jacobite rising of 1745. Paisley 1923.

Broster, Dorothy K. The flight of the heron. 1925.
—— The gleam in the north. 1927.
—— Dark Mile. 1929.
—— Almond, wild almond. 1933.

Duke, Winifred. Scotland's heir. [1925], New York 1926 (as Heir to kings).
—— King of the Highland hearts. 1929.
—— The drove road. [1930].
—— Out of the north. [1939].
—— Blind geese. 1946.
—— Lost cause. 1953.
—— Ship of fools. 1956.

Lang, A. Tartan tales. Ed B. L. Gunterman 1928.

McLellan, D. T. H. The laird of Balfrie. 1931.

Cuthbertson, G. and J. Bundle and go. Edinburgh 1933.

Mackenzie, E. M. C. The lost cause: a Jacobite play. Edinburgh 1933.

Goudge, Elizabeth. The middle window. 1935.

Boileau, Ethel M. The fair Prince. [1936].

Murray, D. L. Commander of the mists. New York 1938.

Lock, N. K. Flourish for coronation. 1939.

Niven, F. J. Under which King. 1943.

Lane, J. His fight is ours. 1946.

Macarthur, D. W. Young Chevalier. [1946].

Cross, J. K. The man in moonlight. 1947.

Styles, F. S. Rising of the lark. 1948.

Whitelaw, D. Garments of repentance. 1948.

Kennaway, C. Gentleman adventurer. 1951.

Roberts, B. D. The Charlie tree. 1951.

Lewis, Josephine. As the rowans go gay. Glasgow 1952.

Wilkins, W. V. Crown without sceptre. 1952.

Campbell, Grace M. Torbeg. New York 1953.

Milne, W. P. Eppie Elrick. Peterhead 1955.

D'Oyley, Elizabeth. Play me far. 1956.

Fletcher, I. The Scotswoman. 1956.

Bawn, Mary P. Scarlett for tartan. 1958.
—— Lady Jean's feather. 1960.

Tranter, N. G. The clansman. 1959.
—— Gold for Prince Charlie. 1962.

Seton, A. Devil water. Boston 1962.

Anthony, E. Clandara. 1963.

'Oliver, Jane' (Helen Rees). Candleshine no more. 1967.

DARIEN SCHEME

The hopes and failure of this scheme called forth a considerable literature. Only the verse and 4 novels are here listed.

Reference

Laing Various pieces of fugitive Scotish poetry. Ed D. Laing 2 sers Edinburgh 1825–53.

Bibliographies

Scott, John, rev George P. Johnston. A bibliography of printed documents and books relating to the Darien Company. Pbns of Edinburgh Bibl Soc 7 1904.

Catalogue of a collection of books and manuscripts relating to the Darien Scheme. Glasgow 1932. The Glasgow Univ Spencer Collection.

§ I

A poem upon the undertaking of the Royal Company of Scotland, trading to Africa and the Indies. Edinburgh 1697; rptd Laing 2.

An congratulatory poem on the safe arrival of the Scots African and Indian fleet in Caledonia. [no place 1699?]. A broadside.

The golden island: or the Darian song in commendation of all concerned in that noble enterprize of valiant Scots, by a lady of honour. Edinburgh 1699; rptd Laing 1.

An health to Caledonia. [no place 1699?]. A broadside.

An ode made on the welcome news of the safe arrival and kind reception of the Scottish collony at Darien in America. Edinburgh 1699; rptd Laing 2.

The recruits for Caledonia of the rysing-sun their farewell to old Scotland. [no place] 1699; rptd Laing 2. Signed A volunteer in this Expedition. In the Kyles of Bute, 13 Sept 1699.

Trade's release: or courage to the Scotch-Indian Company. [no place 1699]; rptd Laing 2.

[Pennecuik, Alexander, MD]. Caledonia triumphans: a panegyrick to the King, by a lover of Caledonia and the Muses. Edinburgh 1699, 1699; rptd Laing 1. A broadside.

Symson, Matthew. Ad florentissimam Scotiae societatem ad Indus & Afros negotiantem; Isthmum olim Darienum, nunc Caledoniam, foeliciter occupantem: carmen congratulatorium. Edinburgh 1699. A broadside.

Caledonia, or the pedlar turn'd merchant: a tragi-comedy as it was acted by his Majesty's subjects of Scotland, in the King of Spain's province of Darien. 1700. A poetic satire.

Caledonia's complaint and resolution, with the Answer to the Complaint. [no place c. 1700]; rptd Laing 2. A broadside.

The causes of Scotland's miseries: a poem in imitation of the VI Ode of the Third Book of Horace. Edinburgh 1700; rptd Laing 1.

The emblem of our King and of the Scots and English Parliaments: a poem by a well wisher to King and Parliament. Edinburgh 1700; rptd Laing 1.

Scotland's lament for their misfortunes. [no place 1700?]. A broadside.

[Denneston, Gualterus?]. Ad amplissimos simul & consultissimos viros, societatis Scoticanae ad Afros & Indos. [Edinburgh? 1700].

A collection of Pindarick odes, heroick stanzas, funeral elegies, pastorals and epitaphs on the untimely death of Lord Basil Hamilton. Edinburgh 1701.

Elegie on the universally lamented death of the Right Honourable Lord Basil Hamilton. [no place 1701?]. A broadside.

The mournful Muse: or a poem upon the death of Lord Basil Hamilton. Edinburgh 1701. A broadside.

Porterfield, James. God's judgements against sin. Edinburgh 1702.

Aesop in Scotland, exposed in ten select fables relating to the times. 1704. Fable 6, The merchant and soldiers, concerns the Darien Expedition.

Captain Green's last conference with Captain Madder, his first mate, in the Tolbooth, Edinburgh. Edinburgh 1705; rptd Laing 1.

An elegy on the much lamented death of Captain Thomas Green. 1705. A broadside.

An English ointment for the Scotch mange: or a short memorandum of the Scots cruelty to Captain Thomas Green. [1705].

The horrid murther committed by Captain Green. [London? 1705]. A broadside.

The merities of piracie: or a new song on Captain Green and his bloody crue. [London? 1705]. A broadside.

A trip lately to Scotland, with a true character of the country and people to which are added several remarks on the late barbarous execution of Captain Green, Mr Madder, Mr Simpson and several others. 1705.

[Forbes of Disblair]. A pill for pork-eaters: or a Scots lancet for an English swelling. Edinburgh 1705, 1705, [Edinburgh?] 1705; rptd Laing 1. Also attributed to Alexander Pennecuik, merchant.

Borland, Francis. Memoirs of Darien. Glasgow 1715.

—— The history of Darien. Glasgow 1779. In both these works Borland, who was one of the ministers of the expedition, includes a short poem showing the disaster to have been caused by 'God's wrath against us, for our great trespasses'.

Warburton, Eliot. Darien, or the merchant prince: a historical romance. 3 vols 1852.

Burton, J. E. B. A gentleman-adventurer. [1895], [1908], [1930].

Govan, A. High adventure in Darien. 1936.

'Terry, C. V.' (F. G. Slaughter). Darien venture. 1955.

G. R. R.

INDEX

to volume 2, containing the names of primary authors together with certain headings. Numerals refer to columns. Volume 5 will eventually provide a more detailed index to the whole of New CBEL.